Microsoft Excel Inside Out

(Office 2021 and Microsoft 365)

Bill Jelen
MrExcel

Microsoft Excel Inside Out (Office 2021 and Microsoft 365)
Published with the authorization of Microsoft Corporation by:
Pearson Education, Inc.

ISBN-13: 978-0-13-755953-4
ISBN-10: 0-13-755953-4

Library of Congress Control Number: 2021948291

2 2021

Editor-in-Chief: Brett Bartow
Executive Editor: Loretta Yates
Assistant Sponsoring Editor: Charvi Arora
Development Editor: Rick Kughen
Managing Editor: Sandra Schroeder
Project Editor: Charlotte Kughen
Copy Editor: Rick Kughen
Indexer: Ken Johnson
Proofreader: Sarah Kearns
Technical Editor: Bob Umlas
Editorial Assistant: Cindy Teeters
Cover Designer: Twist Creative, Seattle
Compositor: Bronkella Publishing, LLC

Pearson's Commitment to Diversity, Equity, and Inclusion

Pearson is dedicated to creating bias-free content that reflects the diversity of all learners. We embrace the many dimensions of diversity, including but not limited to race, ethnicity, gender, socioeconomic status, ability, age, sexual orientation, and religious or political beliefs.

Education is a powerful force for equity and change in our world. It has the potential to deliver opportunities that improve lives and enable economic mobility. As we work with authors to create content for every product and service, we acknowledge our responsibility to demonstrate inclusivity and incorporate diverse scholarship so that everyone can achieve their potential through learning. As the world's leading learning company, we have a duty to help drive change and live up to our purpose to help more people create a better life for themselves and to create a better world.

Our ambition is to purposefully contribute to a world where:

- Everyone has an equitable and lifelong opportunity to succeed through learning.
- Our educational products and services are inclusive and represent the rich diversity of learners.
- Our educational content accurately reflects the histories and experiences of the learners we serve.
- Our educational content prompts deeper discussions with learners and motivates them to expand their own learning (and worldview).

While we work hard to present unbiased content, we want to hear from you about any concerns or needs with this Pearson product so that we can investigate and address them.

- Please contact us with concerns about any potential bias at https://www.pearson.com/report-bias.html.

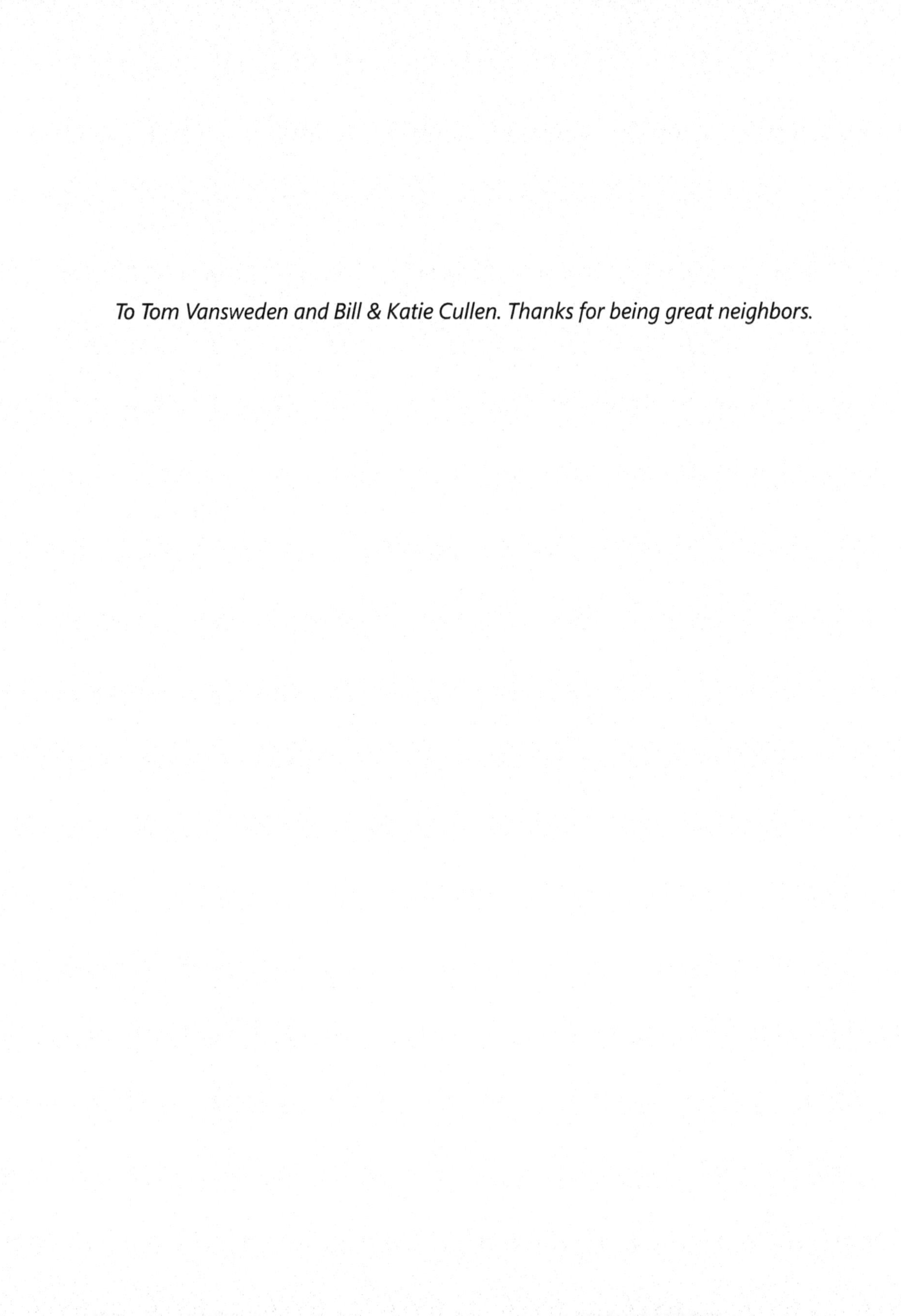

To Tom Vansweden and Bill & Katie Cullen. Thanks for being great neighbors.

Contents at a Glance

Table of Contents

Part III Data analysis with Excel

Part V Appendixes

About the author

Bill Jelen, Excel MVP and the host of MrExcel.com, has been using spreadsheets since 1985, and he launched the MrExcel.com website in 1998. He has produced more than 2,400 episodes of his daily video podcast, *Learn Excel from MrExcel*. He is the author of 64 books about Microsoft Excel and writes the monthly Excel column for *Strategic Finance* magazine. Before founding MrExcel.com, Bill Jelen spent 12 years in the trenches—working as a financial analyst for finance, marketing, accounting, and operations departments of a $500 million public company. When he is not geeking out about Excel, you will find him kayaking Sykes Creek or photographing rocket launches from Cape Canaveral. Check out his photography at WeReportSpace.com. He lives in Merritt Island, Florida, with his wife, Mary Ellen.

Inside OUT

You can find my favorite tricks in the Inside Out sidebars throughout this book.

If you have a favorite Excel trick or technique that is not in this book, consider sending it via email to *InsideTips@MrExcel.com*. Anyone sending in a tip that is new to me will win bragging rights and a collectible Excel Guru patch, designed by the same people who design the NASA mission patches.

Introduction

Microsoft 365 Excel is now the dominant way to purchase Excel. Microsoft did a good job of offering more value to Microsoft 365. They are reluctantly releasing a perpetual edition of Excel 2021, but they say that it is only for specific scenarios where people do not have access to the Internet.

Those people without the Internet will be paying quite a premium for an obsolete version of Excel without any of the connected features. The price for the perpetual version of Office increased by 10% to $440 per device for Office 2021. In contrast, you can license Microsoft 365 for five devices for $99 per year.

The Excel team has been responsive to items requested through the Excel.UserVoice.com website, and many small features and improvements have happened since the last edition of this book.

- You can now unhide multiple worksheets at once.
- The Conditional Formatting Rules Manager dialog box is now resizable.
- Scroll horizontally with Ctrl+Shift+Wheel.
- Increased the 218-character file limit.
- When copying a worksheet, added a Yes To All option for dealing with Name conflicts.
- The Excel team added a new padlock icon to the sheet tabs to indicate if a sheet was protected. When this was met with a chorus of complaints, the lock icon was promptly removed.
- The `SINGLE` function, used to trigger implicit intersection, was replaced with the `@` operator.
- You can insert new icons and cut-out people in Excel.
- Images can easily be set to semi-transparent so you can see the data behind an image.
- Right-click any object and choose Save As Image to create an image of a chart, SmartArt, shape, and so on.
- You can "write" data using the Action Pen.
- Multiple task panes now collapse into a single strip at the right side of Excel.
- There is a new Accessibility Checker tab in the ribbon.
- Several performance improvements make Excel faster.

There are also several large changes made to Excel:

- Co-authoring continues to improve. You can now @Mention people in comments and create tasks. Excel will allow each person to have their own version of the data with filters and sorting that only they can see. The new Show Changes feature lets you see changes made to your worksheet in the last 60 days. Read more in Chapter 28, "Collaborating in Excel."
- A new XLOOKUP function is designed to improve on VLOOKUP and INDEX/MATCH functions. Excel also offers XMATCH. See Chapter 9, "Using powerful functions: logical, lookup, and database functions."
- New LET and LAMBDA functions let you store logic in a formula. See Chapter 10, "Using names, LET, LAMBDA, and Data Types in Excel."
- There are new features in Power Query (found in the Get & Transform group on the Data tab). You can now import from PDF files. You can also define your own custom data types. Read about Power Query in Chapter 13, "Transforming data with Power Query."
- Data types improve with the ability to return photos and arrays. There are several new categories from Wolfram including weather history for all cities. See Chapter 10, "Using names, LET, LAMBDA, and Data Types in Excel."
- The artificial-intelligence Ideas feature is re-branded as "Analyze Data." The new version will create dynamic array formulas and allow you to ask a question about your data. Excel analyzes up to 250,000 cells of data and uses artificial intelligence to provide more than 30 charts. For now, this feature is exclusive to Office 365. See Chapter 15, "Using pivot tables to analyze data."
- Although this book covers VBA as the macro language, there is one new interesting feature in programmability: A new TypeScript macro language is available for Excel Online.

The Excel team continues to innovate, with several new features planned for the upcoming years.

Who this book is for

This book is for anyone who uses Excel twenty hours a week or more. Whether you use Excel for organizing your to-do list or to analyze 5 million rows of call center data every day, this book includes the information you need to solve problems quickly and easily.

Assumptions about you

I like to believe most of my readers use Excel 40 hours a week, and those are the weeks you are on vacation. At the very least, I'm assuming you regularly use Excel for your job. You are comfortable using Excel formulas beyond AutoSum. You likely know and use VLOOKUP and Pivot Tables regularly. You are looking for the fastest and most efficient ways to finish tasks in Excel.

How this book is organized

This book gives you a comprehensive look at the various features you will use. This book is structured in a logical approach to all aspects of using the Windows-based versions of Excel, with some mentions of Excel Online when there is important functionality available only in Excel Online.

Part I, "The Excel interface," covers the ribbon, customizing Excel, and keyboard shortcuts.

Part II, "Calculating with Excel," covers all Excel calculation functions.

Part III, "Data analysis with Excel," covers Power Query, pivot tables, and other features that help you perform data analysis.

Part IV, "Excel visuals," covers charting, 3D Map, and collaborating in Excel.

About the companion content

I have included the Excel workbooks I used to create the screenshots in this book to enrich your learning experience. You can download this book's companion content from the following page:

MicrosoftPressStore.com/Excel365insideout/downloads

The companion content includes the following:

- Workbooks used to create the examples in the workbook
- Sample data that you can use to practice the concepts in the book
- VBA macros from Chapter 19

Acknowledgments

Thanks to all the Excel project managers who were happy to take the time to discuss the how or why behind a feature. At various times, Sonia Atchinson, Andrew Becker, Darcy Cain, Elisabetta Caldesi, Howie Dickerman, Mar Gines, Sharon Grimshaw, Chris Gross, Urmi Gupta, Curt Hagenlocher, Guy Hunkin, Brian Jones, Aimee Leong, Vashisht Mahana, Michelle Maislen, Joe McDaid, David Monroy, Micah Myerscough, Meenakshi Naren, Jeet Mukeshkumar Patel, Eric Patterson, Cuong Pham, Sudhi Ramamurthy, Prash Shirolkar, Rochelle Sonnenberg, Allie Wieczorek, and Bill Wu pitched in to help with a particular issue. Thanks to Tracy Syrstad, Barb Jelen, Mary Ellen Jelen, Zeke Jelen, and Suat Ozgur for making up the MrExcel.com team.

Other Excel MVPs often offered their take on potential bugs. I could send a group email over a weekend, and someone like Ken Puls, Roger Govier, Liam Bastick, Jon Peltier, Jan-Karel Pieterse, Charles Williams, Brad Yundt, Nabil Mourad, Wyn Hopkins, David Benaim, Oz du Soleil, or Ingeborg Hawighorst would usually respond. I particularly loved launching a missive just after the Microsoft crew in Building 36 went home on Friday evening, knowing they would return on Monday morning with 40 or 50 responses to the conversation. Without any Excel project managers to temper the discussion, we would often have designed massive improvements that we would have liked to have implemented in Excel. Someone would show up on Monday and tell us why that could never be done.

Thanks to the people who frequently leave constructive comments at my MrExcel.com YouTube channel: Mike Girvin, Rico S, Wayne Edmonson, Darryl Morgan, ExcelLambda, Matt Schoular, Patrick Schardt, John Borg, Oz du Soleil, Nader Mounir, Prakash Ravikumar, Paul Sparrow, Chris M, Bradford Myers, Oakley Turvey, DRSteele, Celia Alves, TSSC, Brian Spiller, Jonathan, and Jeff Davis. Several Excel problems have been solved by suggestions from this group.

Bob Umlas is the smartest Excel guy that I know, and I was thrilled to have him as the technical editor for this book.

Putting together a book requires careful coordination with editors, proofreaders, and compositors. My sincere thanks to Charlotte and Rick Kughen for guiding this book to completion. Thanks to Sarah Kearns for having the attention to detail in proofreading and to Tricia Bronkella for her awesome compositor skills.

I've been writing books for Loretta Yates since 2004. If my spreadsheet is correct, this is our 30th project. Thanks for 17 years of trusting me with your books.

At the MrExcel website, Suat Ozgur manages the database of more than 1 million Excel posts and makes sure that Google likes our content.

I wrote this book at the Kola Mi Writing Camp. The staff there was fantastic.

Mary Ellen Jelen did a great job of keeping me on track with this book.

Support and feedback

The following sections provide information on errata, book support, feedback, and contact information.

Errata, updates, and book support

We've made every effort to ensure the accuracy of this book and its companion content. You can access updates to this book—in the form of a list of submitted errata and their related corrections—at:

MicrosoftPressStore.com/Excel365insideout/errata

If you discover an error that is not already listed, please submit it to us at the same page.

For additional book support and information, please visit *MicrosoftPressStore.com/Support*.

Please note that product support for Microsoft software and hardware is not offered through the previous addresses. For help with Microsoft software or hardware, go to *http://support.microsoft.com*.

Stay in touch

Let's keep the conversation going! We're on Twitter:

http://twitter.com/MicrosoftPress

http://twitter.com/MrExcel

PART I

The Excel interface

CHAPTER 1

What's new in Microsoft 365 Excel

This chapter explains the new features introduced in Excel since the previous edition of this book. These features are too new to have made it into the rest of the book.

Excel opens faster

Microsoft introduced a new look for Office in the summer of 2021. While the rounded edges may not seem exciting, the fact is that Excel is loading much faster now than before. The new splash screen is present for just a second or two and then the grid appears.

Unhide multiple worksheets

It was always possible to hide many sheets in one command. But then unhiding sheets had to be done one at a time. A new Unhide dialog box introduced in 2021 allows you to use Ctrl or Shift to select multiple worksheets and unhide them all at once (see Figure 1.1).

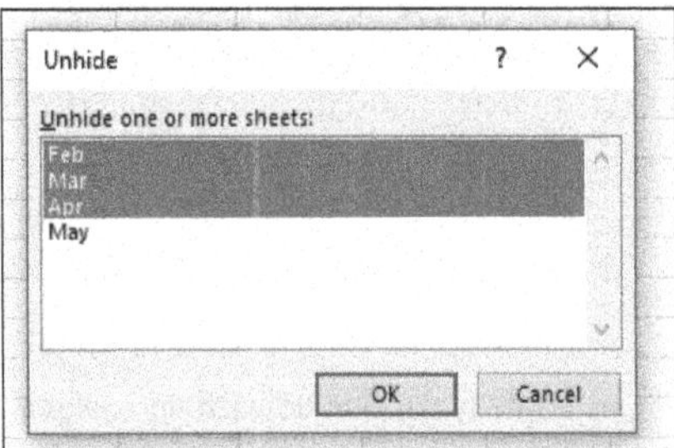

Figure 1.1 Finally, unhide multiple worksheets in a single command.

Performance improvements

A series of performance improvements rolled out to Microsoft 365 customers late in 2020:

- **Indexing for SUMIFS and similar functions:** Say you have 10,000 rows with a similar `SUMIFS` formula. While Excel is calculating the result for the first row, it is building an index that can be re-used for the remaining 9,999 rows. This improvement affects all the conditional aggregation functions: `COUNTIFS`, `AVERAGEIFS`, `MAXIFS`, `MINIFS`, `COUNTIF`, `AVERAGEIF`, and `SUMIF`.
- **Faster opening of workbooks with user-defined functions (UDFs):** The linear scan that searched for UDFs upon the opening of a workbook has been improved.
- **Improvements to pasting from the clipboard:** If you're pasting large sections of HTML or images from outside Excel, there were bottlenecks in getting that data into Excel. Microsoft made improvements to the underlying streaming data structure to make that happen faster.
- **Inserting columns in filtered data:** This was a problem, particularly when the hidden rows contained thick borders. Calculating border thickness is a time-consuming process, and there's no need to do it for the hidden rows in the data.
- **Deleting ranges that contain merged cells:** Excel was iterating through the rows multiple times before performing the delete. This has been improved.
- **Check for errors:** In the past, using Check For Errors on 10,000 rows of data with some empty cells would take minutes or hours. Most people assumed that Excel had frozen and would kill the task. The command now builds an efficient data structure and should return the results in seconds instead of minutes.
- **Faster international text comparisons:** The code to perform comparisons of text that contain international characters has been improved.

Inside Out

While Microsoft was trying to reduce bottlenecks, they discovered one problem that is within your control.

If you have a workbook that uses VBA User Defined Functions, you can speed up calculation by closing the VBA Editor. When you are creating VBA macros, it is possible to run a macro from the VBA Editor. The title bar of the VBA Editor changes to include the word "Running" while the macro is running and then changes back to the original title bar when the macro finishes.

A User Defined Function is nothing more than a VBA macro that returns the results to a cell. If you have 1,000 cells that call the same VBA macro, Excel is updating the title bar of the VBA Editor as each cell starts calculating and then updates it again as the cell finishes calculating. This happens even if the VBA editor is open in the background.

By switching to the VBA Editor and using the red X in the top-right corner to close the VBA Editor, Excel can calculate the UDF cells without having to update the title bar twice for each cell.

Stock data automatic refresh every five minutes

Excel has two ways to retrieve stock data; historical information via the `STOCKHISTORY` function and current stock price using the Stock Data Types found on the Data tab.

Since each update of a data type cell requires a call to the Internet, Microsoft decided not to update these cells at each calculation. Previously, you had to use Data, Refresh All to force an update of all cells or refresh a range at a time by right-clicking Data Type, Refresh.

A new option is introduced in 2021. Right-click any data type cell and choose Data Type, Refresh Settings. (See Figure 1.2.)

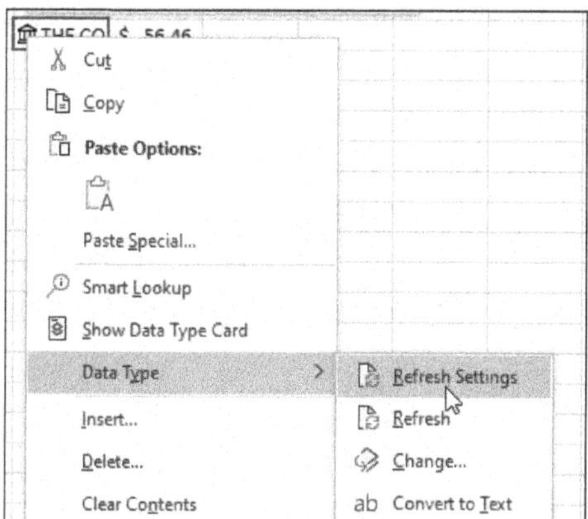

Figure 1.2 Access the new Refresh Settings for a data type cell.

A new Data Types Refresh Settings task pane will list each kind of data type in the workbook. Expand the Stocks section. You can now choose Automatically Every 5 Minutes, On File Open, or Manual. (See Figure 1.3.)

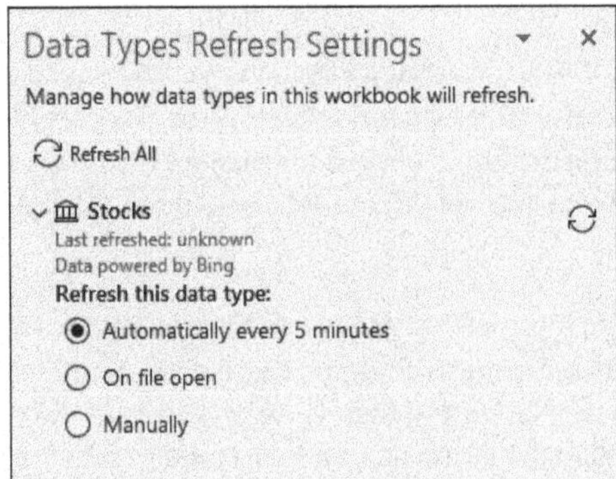

Figure 1.3 You can control if the data type cells update frequently or only on File Open.

Show changes from last 60 days

In the summer of 2021, the Show Changes feature debuted in Office Online. As soon as you save a workbook to OneDrive or SharePoint Online, Excel starts tracking every change made to a worksheet.

These changes are available for 60 days. This provides a great audit trail to see who changed a cell, when they changed it, and the new value.

To see the changes, open the workbook in Excel Online.

> NOTE
>
> **Many people have never opened Excel Online. Using any browser, search for Excel Online. In late 2021, the URL is *https://www.office.com/launch/excel*, but it could change before you read this. You will have to sign in using the same account that you use in Windows Excel, under File, Accounts.**

On the Review tab, choose Show Changes.

Here is an important distinction: Let's say that B2 contains a forecast for January. The next 11 cells use a formula to calculate the forecast for the remaining months. If someone types a new value in B2, the formulas in C2:M2 will update. Show Changes is only tracking the data entry in B2, not the changes as a result of a formula.

However, if someone edits one of the formulas, such as changing the calculation for June, that formula change will be logged.

Figure 1.4 shows an example of the Changes task pane.

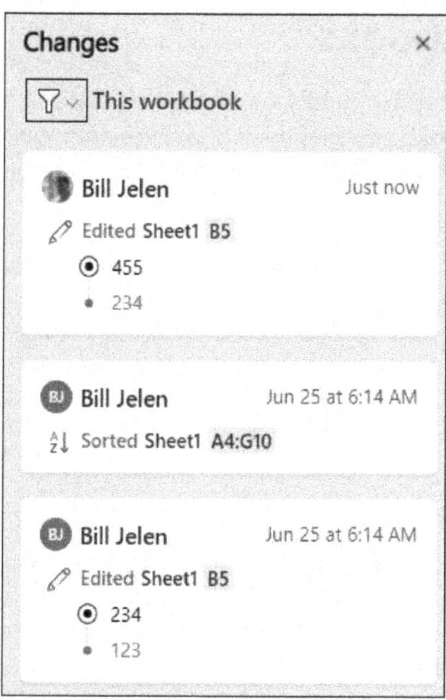

Figure 1.4 Changes to individual cells are logged with date, time, and person.

Browse during Save As

When you are performing a Save As command, the backstage view now has a folder path shown at the top of the center section. This folder is clickable and quickly opens the File Explorer.

I've always preferred navigating to a new folder using the File Explorer window instead of Excel's backstage view. Clicking this item at the top gets you to the File Explorer quicker. (See Figure 1.5.)

Yes—this is the same as clicking the Browse icon at the bottom of the left panel. But you will find that clicking the path at the top of the screen is easier and more efficient than finding Browse at the bottom of a long list of file locations.

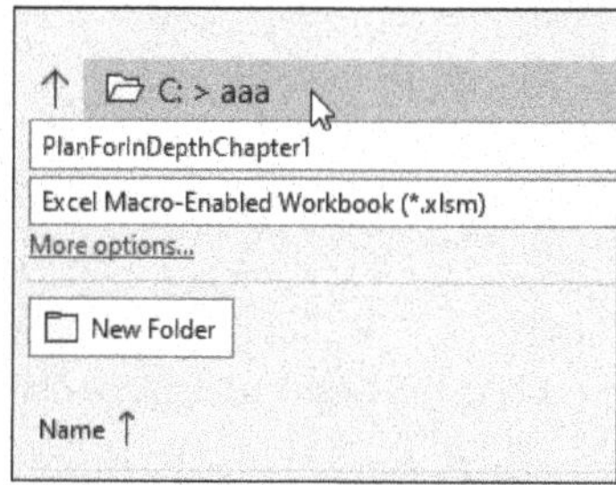

Figure 1.5 Click this folder path to abandon the backstage view and get to File Explorer to locate where to save your workbook.

Searching while opening workbooks

When you select File, Open to open a workbook, Excel shows workbooks that you have pinned to the list and then the last 10 to 50 workbooks. I frequently find that the workbook that I want to open is not in the list. It might be a workbook that I use every other week, but on days when I open dozens of files, those workbooks get pushed out of the list.

The new Search box at the top of the screen works very well. Type a word of two from the workbook name, and if you've opened the workbook recently, Excel will offer it as shown in Figure 1.6.

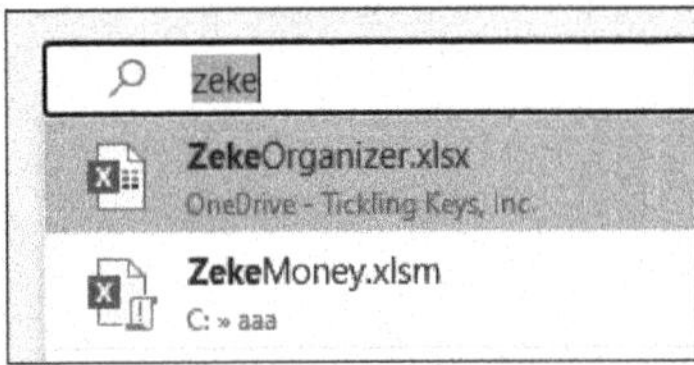

Figure 1.6 The Search box reveals all recent workbooks with the name Zeke in the file name, whether they are in the 10 most recent or not.

Find dialog box shows all options on open

Press Ctrl+F or Ctrl+H and Excel opens the dialog box shown in Figure 1.7. Previously, Excel would start at a simpler form of the dialog box, hiding the settings for Match Case and Match Entire Cell Contents. That lead to problems because the dialog box used the settings from the previous Find. So, a macro might have done a search a few hours ago and used "Match Entire Cell Contents". That setting would be remembered but was not visible in the dialog.

Today, this dialog opens to the expanded view every time. You can still collapse it to the simpler form by clicking Options<<, but it seems unlikely that you would need to do this.

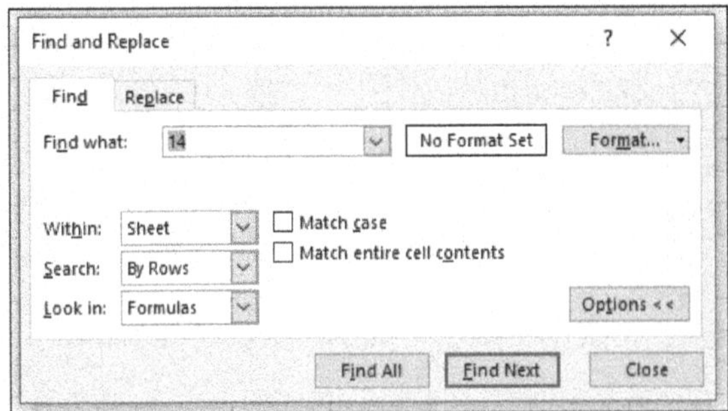

Figure 1.7 The bottom five options are now initially visible in the Find And Replace dialog box.

Another change in this dialog: the Look In drop-down menu now offers Formulas, Values, Notes, and Comments. Previously, you could only search Notes, not Threaded Comments.

Smooth scrolling for tall or wide cells

A single cell in Excel can hold over 32 thousand characters. Some people will store paragraphs in a cell. It is possible to increase the row height to 409.5 and the column width to 254.9.

Imagine that you have a worksheet with 50 rows of paragraphs that have a height of 400. When you grab the wheel mouse and scroll, Excel would scroll three rows at a time when only 1 or 2 rows are visible on the screen.

The people storing this much data in a cell have been clamoring for a way to scroll slowly. An improvement in August 2021 allows you to scroll one line at a time within a cell. If you use Ctrl+Shift+Wheel Mouse, you can scroll one character left or right at a time.

Figure 1.8 shows a large cell with several lines of text.

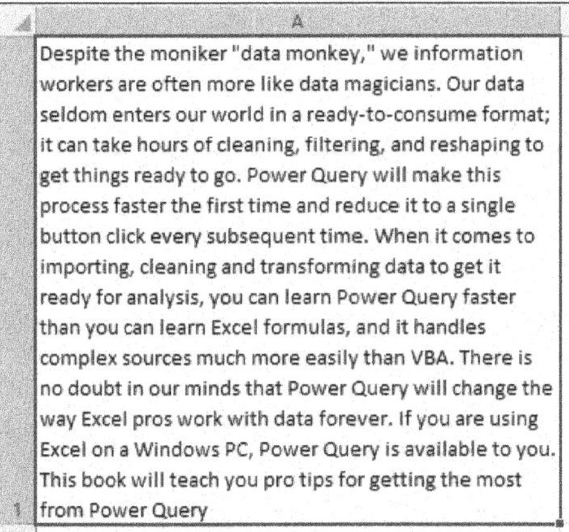

Figure 1.8 A single cell with many lines of text.

The other somewhat amazing improvement is that when you let go of the scroll wheel or the scroll bar, Excel will stay "parked" in the current view, even if it is halfway through the cell. Previously, if you scrolled part way through a cell, Excel would re-draw the screen, so the window started either at the top of that cell or the top of the next cell.

Figure 1.9 shows the same cell from Figure 1-8 with the first three lines scrolled out of view and the first seven characters scrolled out of view to the left.

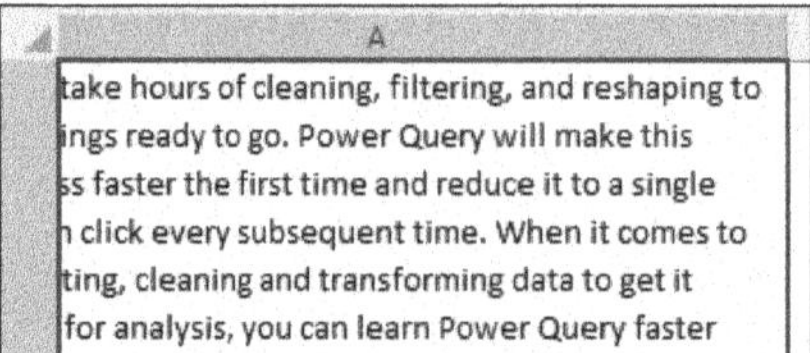
A
take hours of cleaning, filtering, and reshaping to
ings ready to go. Power Query will make this
ss faster the first time and reduce it to a single
n click every subsequent time. When it comes to
ting, cleaning and transforming data to get it
for analysis, you can learn Power Query faster

Figure 1.9 You can scroll part way through a cell and leave the cell parked in that location.

Arrange All in Windows 11

At the top of each window are three icons for Minimize, Restore, and Close. A cool trick just arrived in Windows 11 with rumors saying that it will also come to Windows 10. If you have multiple Excel windows open and right-click the Restore icon, Excel will offer to arrange your workbooks in a variety of layouts.

Once you choose a layout, the active workbook becomes the first tile in the layout. Windows then shifts focus to the next tile and waits for you to choose which workbook should be in that tile.

It takes some getting used to, but it is a useful technique.

Collapsible tasks panes now support pivot tables

It is possible to be working in Excel and have two task panes open at the same time. If you really tried, you could even get three or four task panes open. On a 1080p monitor, those four task panes might take up most of the screen real estate and you are left seeing only Columns A and B on the left side of the screen.

Microsoft introduced a dock for task panes. Any time that you opened multiple task panes, one would stay visible, and all the task panes would appear as tiny icons on a dock on the right side of the screen. It was a nice improvement. On the day it was released, it did not support the PivotTable Fields task pane, but by mid-2021, it worked with all task panes.

Figure 1.10 shows the PivotTable Fields pane. To the right are small icons for the other open task panes.

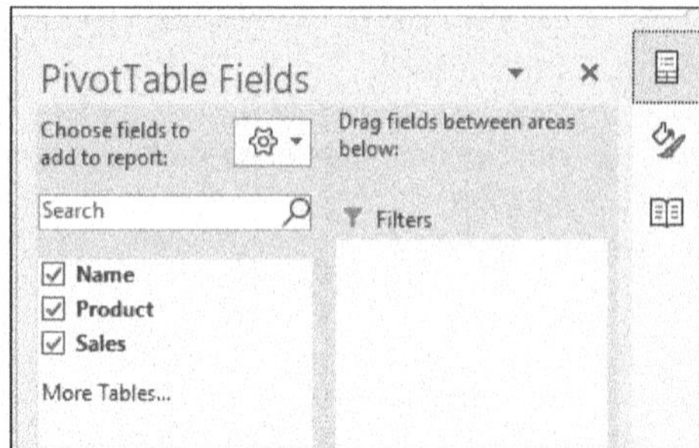
PivotTable Fields
Choose fields to add to report:
Drag fields between areas below:
Search
Filters
Name
Product
Sales
More Tables...

Figure 1.10 Two other task panes are collapsed into the dock.

TIP

What if you want to display multiple open task panes at one time? You can undock a task pane by clicking the title and dragging it to the grid. To re-dock, you can drag the title completely off the right or left side of the screen. If you dock task panes on the left side of the screen, they will never collapse.

Accessibility tab in ribbon and the navigation pane

Excel includes an Accessibility Checker and displays "Check Accessibility" prominently on the left side of the Status Bar. When you start the Accessibility Checker, a new Accessibility tab appears in the ribbon. The tab offers a collection of features that might be used to correct problems found in the Accessibility pane. (See Figure 1.11.)

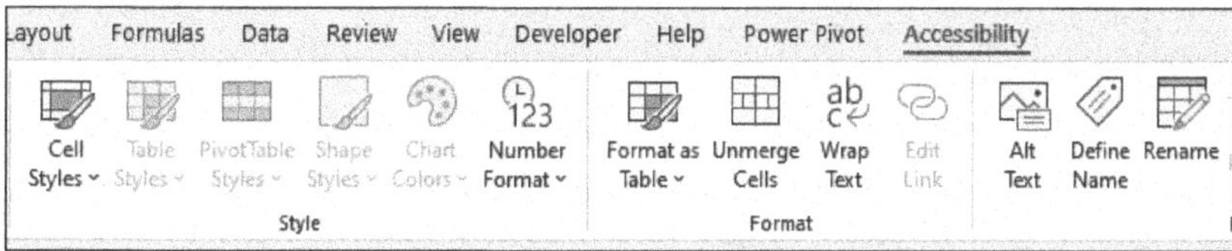

Figure 1.11 Tools for making a workbook more accessible are collected on this new tab.

Imagine having to navigate a workbook with limited vision. Microsoft talked to people who were using a screen reader with Excel and found it is difficult to get your bearings to figure out where the data and pivot tables are located.

In the summer of 2021, Microsoft added the Navigation pane to Excel. The pane will display worksheets, named ranges, charts, contiguous ranges of data, and pivot tables. To open the Navigation pane, choose View, Show, Navigation. The idea is that the person using a screen reader can use the navigation pane to find major elements of the workbook and navigate to the correct one. (See Figure 1.12.)

You can improve the navigation pane by naming your worksheets, adding range names, and so on.

CHAPTER 1

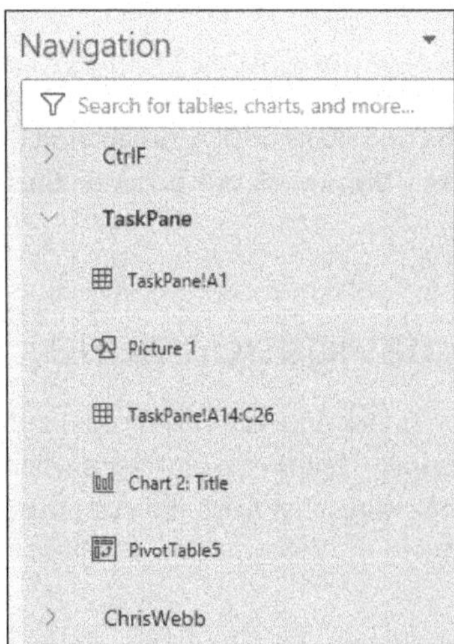

Figure 1.12 The Navigation task pane helps someone using a screen reader to find their way around a workbook.

New Lambda helper functions

LAMBDA functions debuted in beta in late 2020. By August, as they were rolling out to more people, Microsoft realized that they needed a series of helper functions to make Lambda functions easier to use.

LAMDA functions are covered in Chapter 10. But these brand-new helper functions are documented only here. It will likely be 2022 before they make it to the general Microsoft 365 audience.

Each of these new functions will iterate over a range and pass each cell or row or column to a LAMBDA function written as the last argument in the helper function.

Figure 1.13 shows a simple example. Your goal is to make a rectangular array that is 12 rows by 5 columns. The formula starts with `=MAKEARRAY(12,5,LAMBDA(...))`. The LAMBDA function has three arguments in this case:

- The first argument is a variable to hold the row number of each item in the array.
- The second argument is a variable to hold the column number of each item in the array.
- The third argument is formula logic that transforms the row and column into the value for that element in the array.

B5 =MAKEARRAY(B2,B3,LAMBDA(r,c,2*r/c))

	A	B	C	D	E	F	G
1	=MAKEARRAY(rows,columns,function)						
2	Rows:	12					
3	Columns	5					
4							
5		2	1	0.666667	0.5	0.4	
6		4	2	1.333333	1	0.8	
7		6	3	2	1.5	1.2	
8		8	4	2.666667	2	1.6	
9		10	5	3.333333	2.5	2	
10		12	6	4	3	2.4	
11		14	7	4.666667	3.5	2.8	
12		16	8	5.333333	4	3.2	
13		18	9	6	4.5	3.6	
14		20	10	6.666667	5	4	
15		22	11	7.333333	5.5	4.4	
16		24	12	8	6	4.8	
17							

Figure 1.13 Use MAKEARRAY to generate a rectangular array.

The other functions in this group are:

- **MAP:** Pass a range or an array and a LAMBDA to the MAP function. Excel will use the LAMBDA function on each element in the incoming range and produce an array that is the same size as the incoming array.

- **REDUCE:** Pass a range or an array and a LAMBDA to the MAP function. The LAMBDA needs an accumulator variable to hold the final result, the incoming array, and then the logic. The logic is applied to each element in the incoming data, and the results are added to the accumulator. For example, the logic might count how many elements are between 3 and 9. REDUCE always produces a single answer.

- SCAN is similar to REDUCE, but it returns an array of all of the intermediate answers. If the incoming array is 4 rows by 3 columns, REDUCE returns a single value. SCAN will return 4 rows and 3 columns and shows the intermediate results after each step.

- BYROW and BYCOL apply a LAMBDA to each row or each column of an incoming array. If you want to find the MAX value in each row of a rectangular array, BYROW is perfect.

Note that these functions are in a very early beta, and there is a good chance the names and arguments will change before they reach general availability. Find an example of each in "Using Lambda helper functions" in Chapter 10.

CHAPTER 1

LAMBDA functions now support optional arguments

The definition for a LAMBDA function now allows you to mark arguments as optional by placing them in square brackets. Later, in the logic for the LAMBDA, you can test to see if an argument is omitted by using the ISOMITTED function.

The ribbon has rounded edges

There was a lot of social media excitement when Microsoft announced that a new look was coming for the ribbon and then rolled it out to no one for a week. Everyone clamoring to see the new ribbon was trying to update their Microsoft 365 hourly to see the new ribbon.

When it finally arrived, all the fuss was over rounded edges. Instead of squared-off tab names, everything now has a round curve to the edge (see Figure 1.14).

You will see that Undo and Redo moved from the Quick Access Toolbar to the left side of the Home tab. This means you shouldn't have any issues if you are using the Insert, Draw, Page Layout, or other tabs. I am hoping this decision gets reversed in the final release.

If you move the Quick Access Toolbar below the ribbon, you have an option to show the name of each icon. This is actually very useful. However, it means that Microsoft renamed all 2,500+ icons so they would look better in the Quick Access Toolbar. That makes it tougher for someone trying to customize the ribbon or the Quick Access Toolbar. It used to be that all five Speak Cells commands were located together in the "S" section. Now they are spread throughout the list.

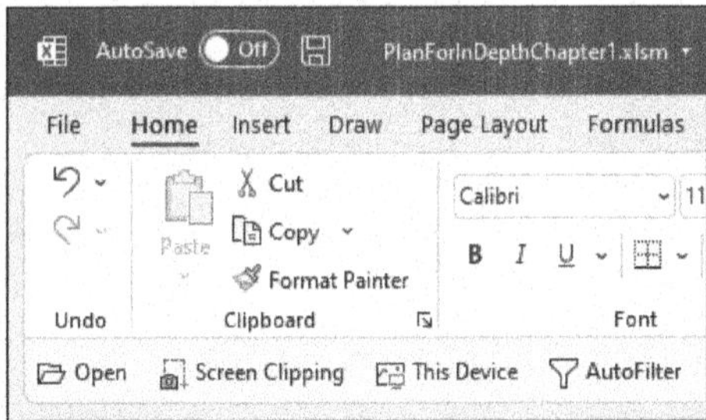

Figure 1.14 Rounded corners in the ribbon, formula bar, and sheet tabs are the big redesign for the new look for Office.

Cut-out people

Open the Icons command on the Insert tab. There are many new icons, plus stickers and a large series of cut-out people. Excel offers 20-30 poses each for 40 stock people. As the name suggests, they have a transparent background, so you can have the people next to or on top of your data.

Studies at YouTube have found that YouTube title cards that feature the face of a person get more views than title cards without, so it makes sense that adding a person to your report might make someone stop and read the report.

You can search the Cutout People by emotion or characteristic, such as Smiling, Happy, Angry, Pointing, Holding A Sign, and so on (see Figure 1.15).

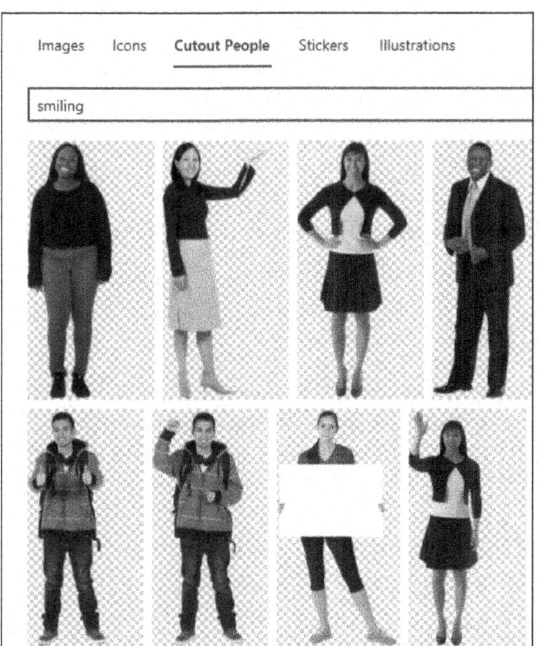

Figure 1.15 You can insert any of these smiling people in your worksheet.

Image transparency

Images in Excel are shown on a drawing layer that is above the grid. This means that any image will hide the data underneath. A new Transparency icon appears on the Picture Format tab in the ribbon. Make the image more transparent so you can see the data behind the picture (see Figure 1.16).

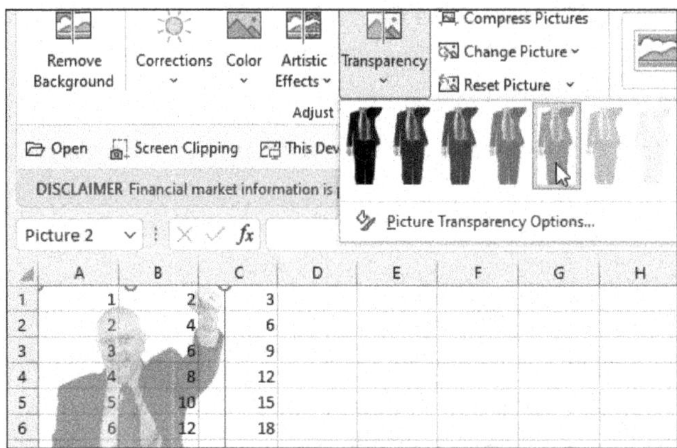

Figure 1.16 Increase transparency of any object to be able to see the data underneath the object.

Save any object as picture

Right-click any object in Excel and you can now choose Save As Picture. This might save you from using the Screen Clipping tools in Office. Note that it works with charts, Smart Art, images, and Word Art, but it does not work with cells unless you copy the cells and paste a linked picture of the cells.

Unless you need to save a lot of charts, you might find it is just as easy to keep using SnagIt or the screen snipping tools instead of the new Save As Picture feature.

Write data using the Action Pen

This is one of the bizarre features in Excel. Sometimes, Excel gets a new feature because the PowerPoint engineers designed something, and it was easy to port to Word and Excel. The Action Pen seems like it fits in that category.

First, there is a Drawing tab in the ribbon. They made a big deal a few years ago about adding new pens to the Drawing tab—glitter pens...all sorts of pens. In 2020, they added an Action Pen.

When you use an Action Pen, you can handwrite your data using a mouse or a touchscreen. A few seconds later, the handwriting is converted to data as if you had typed it.

Figure 1.17 shows the numbers "123" written using a mouse.

A few seconds later, Excel converts the handwritten text to data, as shown in Figure 1.18.

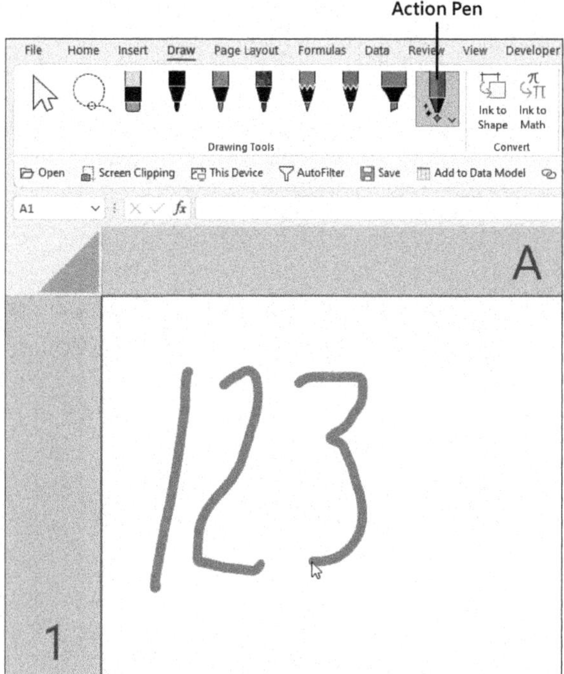

Figure 1.17 Using the touchscreen or a mouse to write some data.

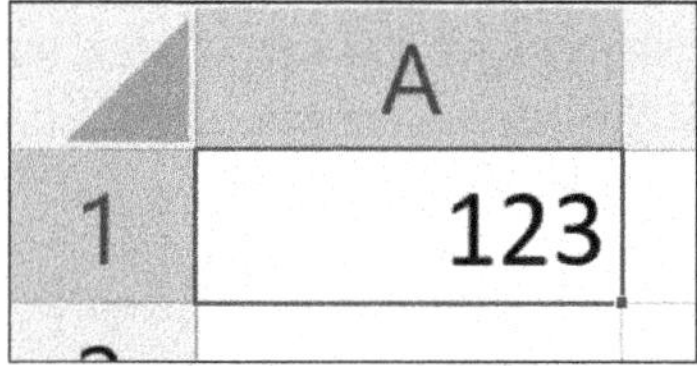

Figure 1.18 Excel recognizes your handwriting and converts it to data.

New features introduced tomorrow

Twenty years ago, it was easy to write about Excel. Changes were made every three years with a 120-day beta before things went live. Today, changes can happen any day of the year.

For the past few editions of this book, I always write Chapter 1 last and include the latest features in this chapter. Inevitably, a few days after we go to print, Microsoft will introduce a new feature, and I can't help thinking, I wish that was in the book.

In this case, I know that there are some new functions coming. I've seen them in action. I would love for them to be in this book. But I am bound by an NDA agreement that says I can't talk about them until they come out in beta.

Between this edition of this book and the next edition, subscribe to my MrExcel.com channel on YouTube. I strive to document any new features with a day or two of them reaching beta.

Other new features

In August 2021, Microsoft added the ability for shapes to look like they were hand-drawn. A new Sketch Style drop-down menu is available in the Format Shape task pane, as shown in Figure 1.19.

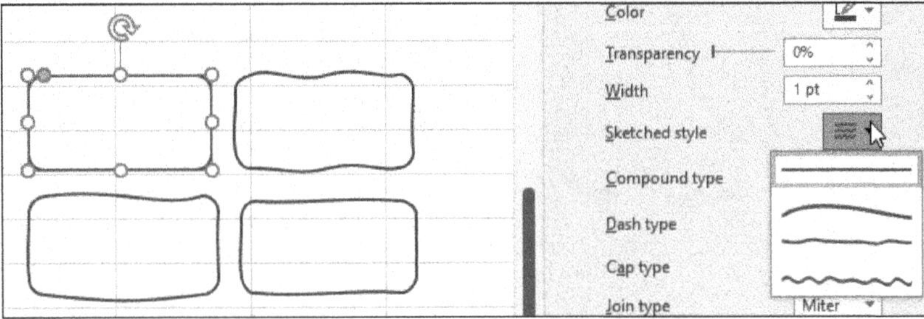

Figure 1.19 New in the summer of 2021, you can make any shape look like it is hand-drawn.

In November 2021, the Excel team added 10 new functions that are used for text manipulation and array shaping. To learn about TEXTSPLIT, TEXTBEFORE, TEXTAFTER, VSTACK, HSTACK, CHOOSEROWS, CHOOSECOLS, TOCOL, TOROW, and VECTORWRAP, see "Introducing TEXTSPLIT and other text manipulation functions" at the end of Chapter 8.

In case you are upgrading from Excel 2016, these new features debuted in the previous edition of this book and are now covered in their respective chapters:

- Unselecting a cell with Ctrl+Click is in Chapter 2, "Using the Excel interface."
- How Excel does not nag you about CSV files is covered in Chapter 2, "Using the Excel interface."
- A formula can now spill to adjacent cells. This is covered in Chapter 5, "Understanding formulas."
- A new @ operator is used for implicit intersection. See Chapter 6, "Controlling formulas."
- The ARRAYTOTEXT function is covered in Chapter 8, "Using everyday functions: math, date and time, and text functions."

- `XLOOKUP` and `XMATCH` are covered in Chapter 9, "Using powerful functions: logical, lookup, and database functions."
- New functions like `LET`, `LAMBDA`, and `STOCKHISTORY` as well as new data types are covered in Chapter 10, "Using names, `LET`, `LAMBDA`, and Data Types in Excel."
- Dynamic Array formulas are covered in Chapter 12, "Dynamic array formulas and names in Excel."
- Topics about co-authoring such as Sheet View, threaded comments, and Show Changes are covered in Chapter 28, "Collaborating in Excel."

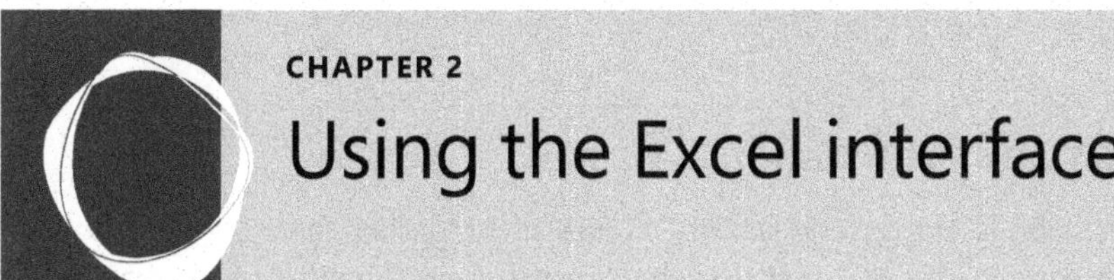

CHAPTER 2

Using the Excel interface

Using the ribbon

The ribbon is Excel's main user interface. It is comprised of tabs: Home, Insert, and so on. Each tab has several groups with a variety of icons, drop-down menus, and galleries.

After a very unpopular introduction in 2007, the ribbon is now a part of our lives, and the concept has even been embraced by other software such as Techsmith's SnagIt.

After Excel 2019, Microsoft refreshed the ribbon for Microsoft 365 customers. Old two-line contextual ribbon names such as "Chart Tools Design" is shortened to "Chart Design" on a single line. The selected ribbon is shown with a single thick line underneath, as shown on the Page Layout tab in Figure 2.1. In the summer of 2021, they added rounded corners for the formula bar and the ribbon, as well as labels for the Quick Access Toolbar when it is displayed below the ribbon.

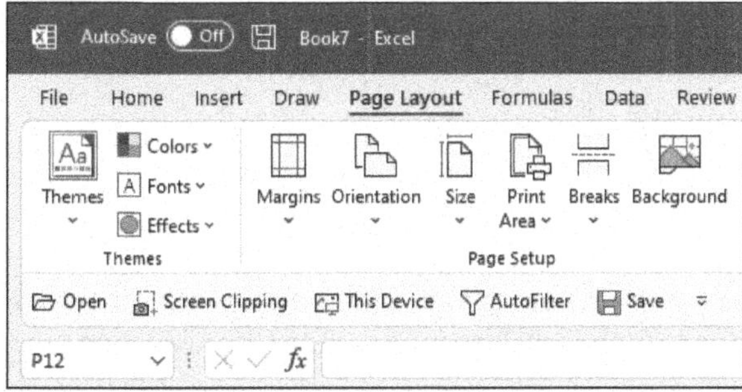

Figure 2.1 In the summer of 2021, the Office 365 ribbon switched to this style.

Using flyout menus and galleries

One element in the ribbon is the gallery control. Galleries are used when there are dozens of options from which you can choose. The gallery shows you a visual thumbnail of each choice. A gallery starts out showing a row or two of choices in the ribbon. (For an example, look at the Data Types gallery on the Excel Data tab.) The right side of the gallery offers icons for Up, Down, and Open. If you click Up or Down, you scroll one row at a time through the choices.

If you click the Open control at the bottom-right side of the gallery, the gallery opens to reveal all choices at once.

Rolling through the ribbon tabs

With Excel as the active application, move the mouse anywhere over the ribbon and roll the scroll wheel on top of the mouse. Excel quickly flips from tab to tab on the ribbon. Scroll away from you to roll toward the Home tab on the left. Scroll toward you to move to the right.

Revealing more commands using dialog box launchers, task panes, and "More" commands

The ribbon holds perhaps 20 percent of the available commands. The set of commands and options available in the ribbon will be enough 80 percent of the time, but you will sometimes have to go beyond the commands in the ribbon. You can do this with dialog box launchers, More commands, and the task pane.

A *dialog box launcher* is a special symbol in the lower-right corner of many ribbon groups. Click the dialog box launcher to open a related dialog box with many more choices than those offered in the ribbon.

Figure 2.2 shows details of the Alignment group of the Home tab. In the lower-right corner of the group is the dialog box launcher. It looks like the top-left corner of a dialog box, with an arrow pointing downward and to the right.

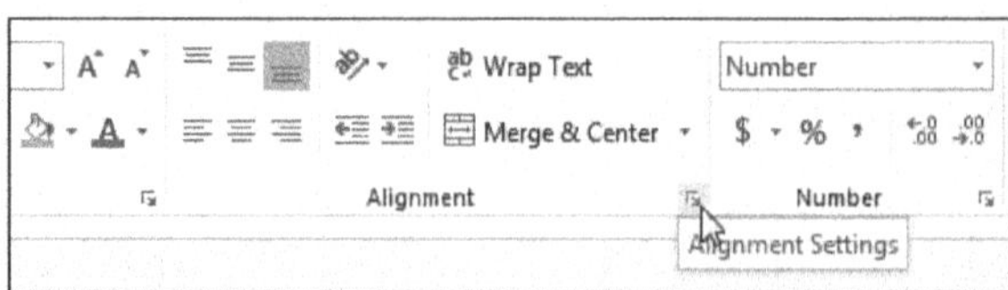

Figure 2.2 The dialog box launcher takes you to additional options.

When you click the dialog box launcher, you go to a dialog box that often offers many more choices than those available in the ribbon. In Figure 2.3, you see the Alignment tab of the Format Cells dialog box.

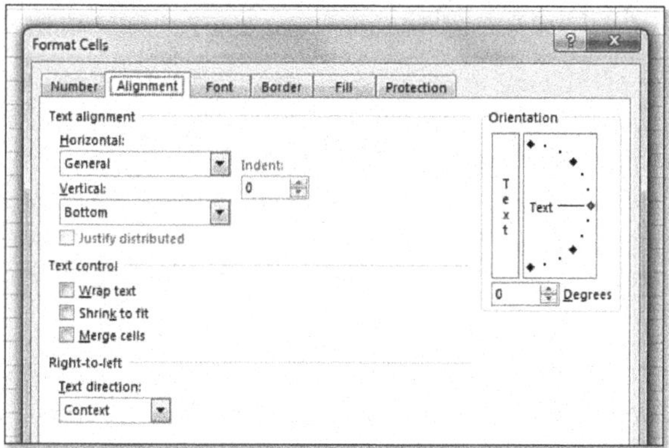

Figure 2.3 After clicking the dialog box launcher, you get access to many more choices.

Many menus in the ribbon end with an entry for finding more rules and option; these entries end with an ellipsis (...). Clicking a More item takes you to a dialog box or task pane with more choices than those available in the ribbon.

Using collapsing task panes

Many newer elements in Excel are formatted using a task pane that appears on the right side of the Excel screen. In the past, you would sometimes have two, three, or four task panes open at one time. Today, Excel collapses the task panes so you only see one task pane. The other task panes are collapsed to a small strip on the right side of Excel, as shown in Figure 2.4.

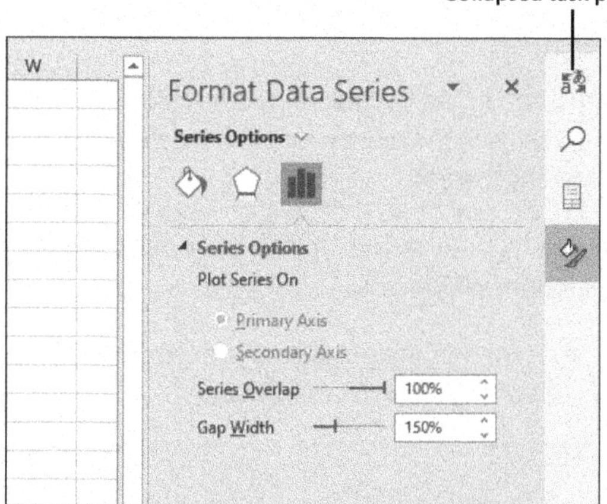

Figure 2.4 When Excel has two task panes open, the extra task panes are collapsed to a strip on the right side of the Excel screen.

You can switch between task panes by clicking any of the icons in the collapsed task pane strip.

What if you liked seeing all of the task panes? Click the title of the task pane and drag it off the left side of the screen. When you dock task panes on the left side of the screen, they will not collapse.

Resizing Excel changes the ribbon

The ribbon modifies as the size of the Excel application window changes. You should be aware of this when you are coaching a coworker over the phone. You might be looking at your screen and telling them to "look for the big Insert drop-down menu to the right of the orange word 'Calculation.'" Although this makes perfect sense on your widescreen monitor, it might not make sense on their monitor. Figure 2.5 shows some detail of the Home tab on a widescreen monitor. The Cell Styles gallery shows ten thumbnails, and Insert, Delete, and Format appear side-by-side.

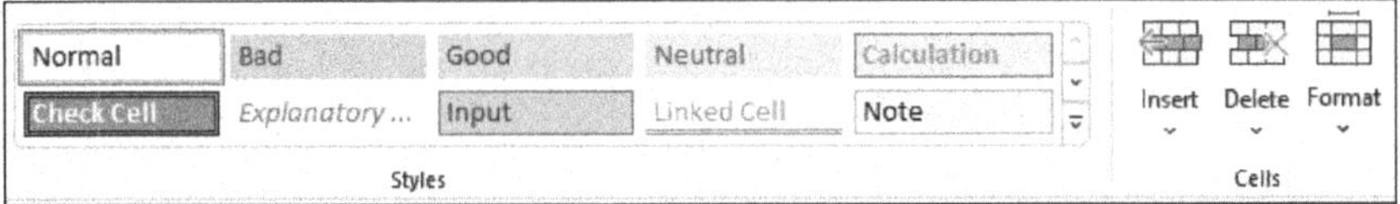

Figure 2.5 On a widescreen monitor, you see ten choices in the Cell Styles gallery.

Figure 2.6 shows the typical view on a laptop. The Cell Styles gallery is collapsed to a single drop-down menu. The Insert, Delete, and Format icons are now arranged vertically.

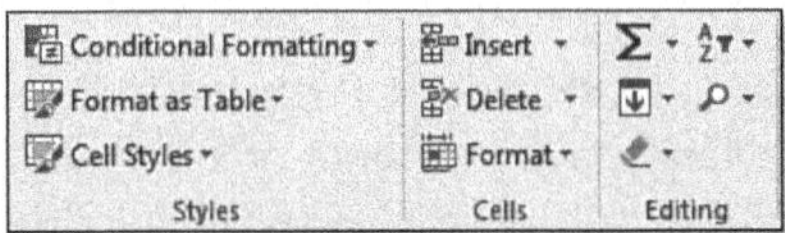

Figure 2.6 On a normal monitor, the Cell Styles gallery is collapsed.

Activating the Developer tab

If you regularly record or write macros, you might be looking for the VBA tools in the ribbon. They are all located on the Developer tab, which is hidden by default. However, it is easy to make the Developer tab visible. Follow these steps:

1. Right-click the ribbon and choose Customize The Ribbon. Excel displays the Customize Ribbon category of the Excel Options dialog box.
2. A long list box of ribbon tabs is shown on the right side of the screen. Every one of them is checked except for Developer. Check the box next to Developer.
3. Click OK. The Developer tab displays.

Activating contextual ribbon tabs

The ribbon tabs you see all the time are called the *main tabs*. Another 23 tabs come and go, depending on what is selected in Excel. In Figure 2.7, you can see two contextual tabs that appear only when a chart is selected.

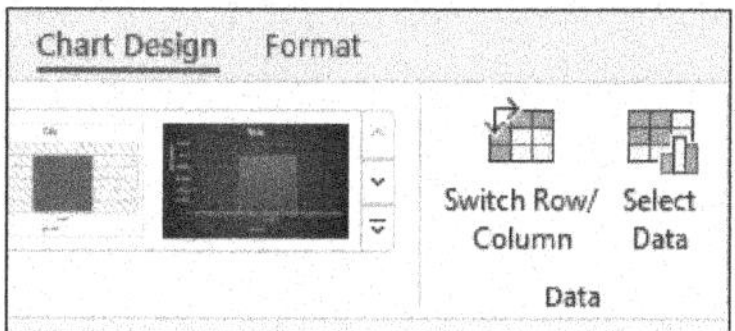

Figure 2.7 Two chart tools tabs appear temporarily while a chart is selected.

TROUBLESHOOTING

Your worksheet often has a pivot table or a chart, yet you cannot see the contextual tabs in the ribbon.

When you insert a new pivot table using the default settings, the pivot table will be the only data on a newly inserted worksheet. I've suggested to the Excel team that if the person using Excel is looking at a new worksheet that only contains a pivot table, then clearly, the customer is looking at the pivot table. However, if you accidentally click outside of the pivot table, both of the pivot table contextual tabs are deleted. To get them back, click any cell inside the pivot table.

Here is the frustrating thing: As soon as you click outside of the object (that is, the chart, or the pivot table), it is no longer selected, and the contextual tabs disappear.

If you need to format an object and you cannot find the icons for formatting it, try clicking the object to see if the contextual tabs appear.

Two other tabs occasionally appear, although Excel classifies them as main tabs instead of contextual tabs. If you add the Print Preview Full Screen icon to the interface, you arrive at a Print Preview tab. Also, from the Picture Format tab, you can click Remove Background to end up at the Background Removal tab.

Finding lost commands on the ribbon

Often, the command you need is front and center on the Home tab, and everything is fine. However, there are times when you cannot find an obscure command that you know is somewhere in Excel.

Microsoft offers a Microsoft Search box above the ribbon. The search is designed to find commands in Excel.

Type **Validation** in the box. The results are shown in Figure 2.8. They offer the Data Validation command. There is a fly-out menu with other validation choices. They offer to search for the word "validation" in the workbook. And, they offer recently opened files that have validation in the title.

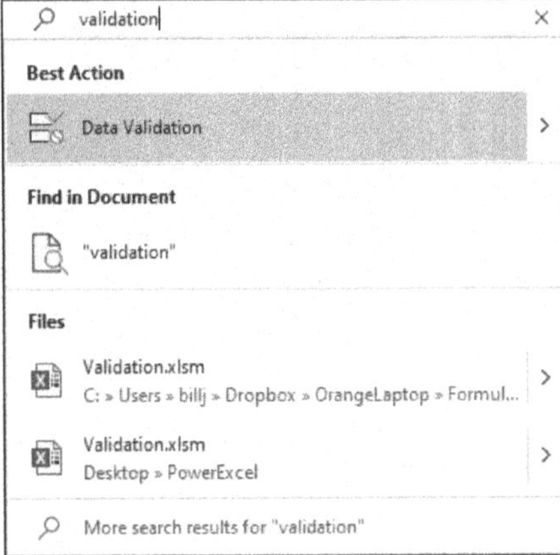

Figure 2.8 The new Search box works great.

Search for "Select from a list" and the results do not find Data Validation. They offer Select Objects, Lasso Select, Save As, Select Element, Show Field List, Get Help On Select From A List, and Smart Lookup On "Select From A List."

Shrinking the ribbon

The ribbon takes up four vertical rows of space. This won't be an issue on a big monitor, but it could be an issue on a tiny laptop.

To shrink the ribbon, you can right-click it and choose Collapse The Ribbon. Or, use the carat (^) icon on the far-right side of the ribbon. The ribbon collapses to show only the ribbon tabs. When you click a tab, the ribbon temporarily expands. To close the ribbon, choose a command or press Esc.

> TIP
>
> **The ribbon often stays open after certain commands. For example, I frequently click the Increase Decimal icon three times in a row. When the ribbon is minimized, you can click Home and then click Increase Decimal three times without having the ribbon close.**

To permanently bring the ribbon back to full size, right-click a ribbon tab and uncheck Collapse The Ribbon. Or, click any tab and then click the pushpin icon in the lower-right corner of the ribbon. You can also toggle between minimized and full size by double-clicking any ribbon tab.

Using the Quick Access Toolbar

A problem with the ribbon is that only one-tenth of the commands are visible at any given time. You will find yourself moving from one tab to another. The alternative is to use the Quick Access Toolbar (QAT) to store your favorite commands.

The QAT starts out as a tiny toolbar with AutoSave, Save, Undo, and Redo. It is initially located above the File tab in the ribbon.

If you start using the QAT frequently, you can right-click the toolbar and choose Show Quick Access Toolbar Below The Ribbon to move the QAT closer to the grid.

Adding icons to the QAT

The drop-down menu at the right side of the QAT, shown on the right side in Figure 2.9, offers 12 popular commands you might choose to add to the Quick Access Toolbar. Choose a command from this list to add it to the QAT.

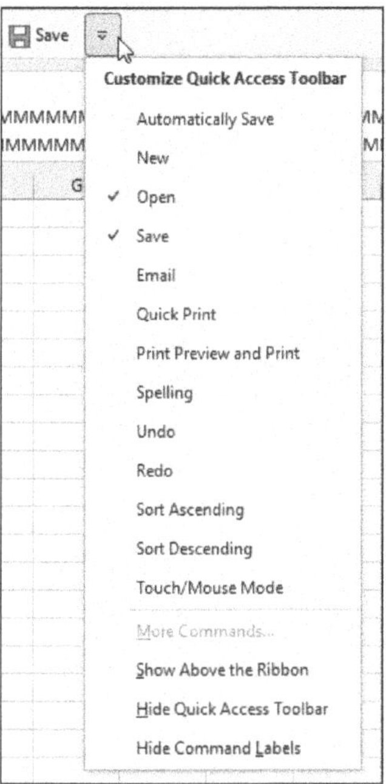

Figure 2.9 Use the drop-down menu at the right side of the QAT to add 13 popular commands.

When you find a command in the ribbon you are likely to use often, you can easily add the command to the QAT. To do so, right-click any command in the ribbon and select Add To Quick Access Toolbar. Items added to the Quick Access Toolbar using the right-click method are added to the right side of the QAT.

The right-click method works for many commands, but not with individual items within commands. For example, you can put the Font Size drop-down menu on the QAT, but you cannot specifically put size 16 font in the QAT.

Removing commands from the QAT

You can remove an icon from the QAT by right-clicking the icon and selecting Remove From Quick Access Toolbar.

Customizing the QAT

You can make minor changes to the QAT by using the context menus, but you can have far more control over the QAT if you use the Customize command. Right-click the QAT and select Customize Quick Access Toolbar to display the Quick Access Toolbar section of the Excel Options dialog box, as shown in Figure 2.10.

Note that the dialog starts out with a small list of Popular Commands. Open the top-left drop-down and choose All Commmands for more choices.

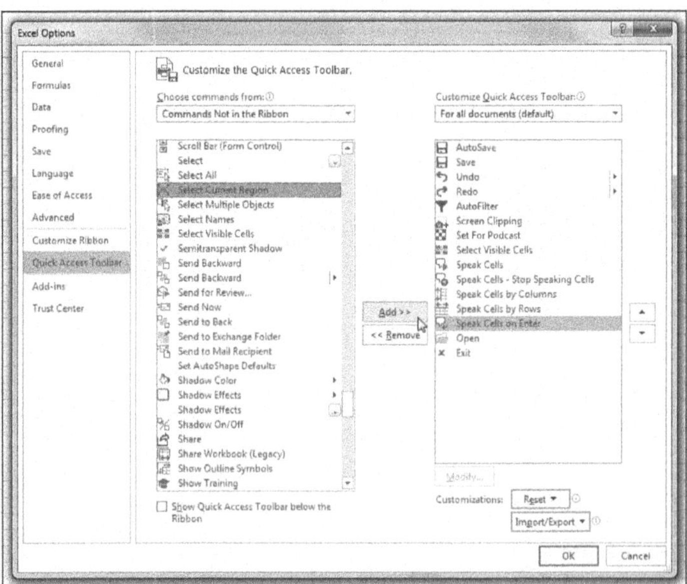

Figure 2.10 The supersript and subscript icons add functionality to Excel that is only available through these icons.

The Excel Options dialog box offers many features for customizing the Quick Access Toolbar:

1. You can choose to customize the QAT for all documents on your computer or just for the current workbook by using the top-right drop-down menu.

2. You can add separators between icons to group the icons logically. A separator icon is available at the top of the left menu. Click the separator icon in the left list box and then click the Add icon in the center of the screen.

3. You can resequence the order of the icons on the toolbar. Select an icon in the right list box, and then click the up/down arrow icons on the right side of the dialog box.

4. You can access 2,000+ commands, including the commands from every tab and commands that are not available in the ribbon. Although the dialog box starts with just 53 popular commands in the left list box, use the left drop-down menu to choose All Commands or Commands Not In The Ribbon. When you find a command in the left list box, select the command and then click Add in the center of the dialog box to add that command to the QAT.

5. You can reset the QAT to its original default state using the Reset button in the lower right.

6. You can export your custom QAT icons from your computer and import it on another computer.

7. You can move the QAT to appear above or below the ribbon using the check box in the lower left.

8. When the QAT is below the ribbon, you can choose to Show Command Labels. This feature is currently in beta and there is some hope that Microsoft will add Command Labels when the QAT is above the ribbon as well.

Formatting superscripts and subscripts

It was previously possible to format characters in a cell as superscript or subscript, but it required a trip to the Format Cells dialog box while you were in Edit mode. You can now format superscripts and subscripts by adding two buttons to the QAT.

To actually format a character in a cell, you can do it while you are typing in the cell. In Figure 2.11, type **You should drink H**. Click the Subscript icon to toggle to Subscript mode. Type a **2**. Click the Subscript icon again to leave Subscript mode. Type **O per day**. Click the Superscript icon. Type **citation needed**. When you press Enter to accept the cell, you automatically exit Superscript mode.

What if you need to format part of an existing cell? Select those characters in the formula bar, and then click either the Subscript or Superscript icon. You will not see the results in the formula bar, but they will appear in the cell.

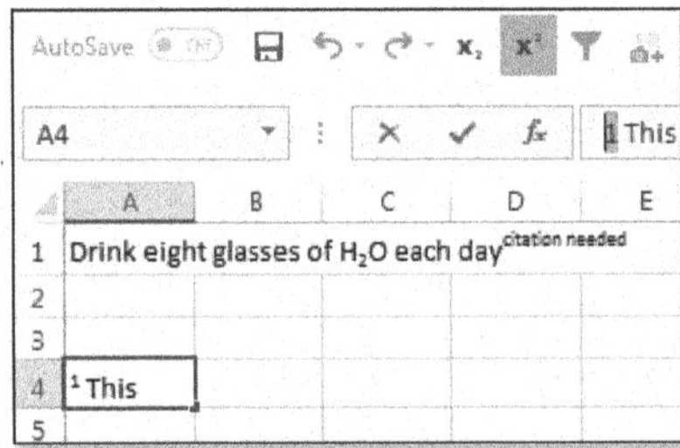

Figure 2.11 Add Superscript and Subscript icons to the Quick Access Toolbar to apply the formatting as you type.

Using the full-screen File menu

Open the File menu to see the Backstage view. Here is the logic: When you are working on most ribbon tabs, you are working *in* your document. When you are about to change the font or something like that, you want to see the results of the change *in* your document. Hence, Microsoft calls those the "in" commands. However, the Excel team thinks that after you move to the File menu, you are done working **in** your document, and you are about to do something with the whole document, such as send the workbook, print the workbook, export to PDF, and so on. Microsoft calls these the "out" commands. The theory is that you don't need to see the worksheet for the "out" commands, so Microsoft fills the entire screen with the File menu.

To open the Backstage view, click the File menu. The Backstage view fills the screen, as shown in Figure 2.12. Backstage is split into three sections: the narrow left navigation panel and two wider sections that provide information.

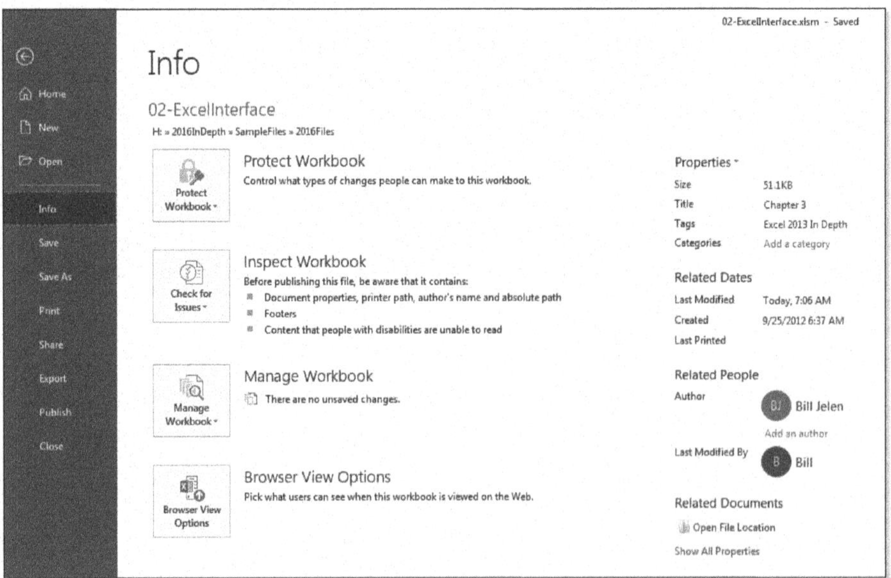

Figure 2.12 The Backstage view fills the entire screen.

The left navigation panel includes these commands:

- **Home:** A recent addition to the File menu, Home combines elements of New and Open. At the top, you can see tutorials from Microsoft and popular templates. In the middle, recent, pinned files, and files that others have shared with you. Both sections have a link to "Find More In New" or "Find More In Open."
- **Info:** Provides information about the current workbook. This is discussed later in the "Getting Information About the Current Workbook" section.
- **New:** Used to create a new workbook or start from a template.
- **Open:** Used to access a file stored on your computer or the OneDrive. See Chapter 1.
- **Save:** Saves the file in the same folder as it was previously stored. Note that Save is a command instead of a panel in Backstage.
- **Save As:** Stores the file on your computer or in OneDrive. See Chapter 1.
- **Print:** Used to choose print settings and print. Includes Print Preview. See Chapter 27, "Printing."
- **Share:** Now the entry point for sharing a workbook with your coworkers. See Chapter 28.
- **Export:** Used to create a PDF or change the file type.
- **Publish:** Used to upload your workbook to Power BI.
- **Close:** Closes the current workbook. Like Save, this entry is a pure command.
- **Account:** Sign in to Office. Choose a color theme and a background. See if updates are available. Learn your version of Excel. This and the next two items have been moved to the bottom left of the screen, below the area shown shown in Figure 2.13.
- **Feedback:** Send a smile or send a frown to the Excel team. Also contains a link to the Excel.UserVoice.com website where you can suggest new ideas for Excel.
- **Options:** Contains pages of Excel settings. See Chapter 3, "Customizing Excel," for details.
- **Recent File List:** This list appears only if you've changed a default setting in Excel Options. Visit File, Options, Advanced Display and choose Quickly Access This Number Of Recent Workbooks.

Pressing the Esc key to close Backstage view

To get out of Backstage and return to your worksheet, you can either press the Esc key or click the back arrow in the top-left corner of Backstage.

Using the new Home screen

A new Home screen appears when you start Excel or open the File menu. The first three commands in the left navigation bar are Home, New, and Open. Without clicking anything, you will be on the Home screen of the File menu. The Home screen combines a few elements from both the New screen and the Open screen.

At the top of the Home screen, you will notice a message that reads, "Good Morning," "Good Afternoon," or "Good Evening."

Below that message are tiles normally shown when you select New. The first tile is Blank Workbook. Next are a few tiles offering Excel tutorials and then some tiles of popular templates. A hyperlink at the far right offers more templates in the New screen.

The next section is Recommended For You. This will be six large tiles of files you have recently edited or files that others shared with you or files where someone mentioned you in a comment.

Next, three tabs offer Recent Files, Pinned, and Shared With Me. This is a subset of the options on the Open screen. Note that if you recently opened a pinned file, it will be in both the Recent and Pinned tabs. If you scroll all the way to the bottom of this section, a hyperlink for "Find More In Open" appears (although it would be easier to click Open in the left navigation bar).

Recovering unsaved workbooks

As in previous versions of Excel, the AutoRecover feature can create copies of your workbook every *n* minutes. If you close the workbook without saving, you might be able to get the file back, provided it was open long enough to go through an AutoRecover.

If the workbook was new and never saved, scroll to the bottom of the Recent Workbooks List and choose Recover Unsaved Workbooks.

If the workbook had previously been saved, open the last saved version of the workbook. Go to the File menu, and the last AutoSave version from before you closed the file will be available.

Clearing the Recent Workbooks list

If you need to clear out the Recent Workbooks list, you should visit File, Options, Advanced, Display. Set the Show This Number Of Recent Documents list to zero. You can then set it back to a positive number, such as 10.

Getting information about the current workbook

When a workbook is open, and you go to the File, Info, you see the Info gallery for that workbook. The Info pane lists all sorts of information about the current workbook:

1. The workbook path is shown at the top of the center panel.
2. You can see the file size.
3. You can see when the document was last modified and who modified it.
4. If any special states exist, these will be reported at the top of the middle pane. Special states might include the following:
   - Macros Not Enabled
   - Links Not Updated
   - Checked Out From SharePoint
5. You can see if the file has been AutoRecovered and recover those versions.
6. You can mark the document as final, which will cause others opening the file to initially have a read-only version of the file.
7. You can edit links to other documents.
8. You can add tags or categories to the file.
9. Using the Check For Issues drop-down menu, you can run a compatibility checker to see if the workbook is compatible with legacy versions of Excel. You can run an accessibility checker to see if any parts of the document will be difficult for people with disabilities. You can run a Document Inspector to see if any private information is hidden in the file.

Marking a workbook as final to prevent editing

Open the Protect Workbook icon in the Info gallery to access a setting called Mark As Final. This marks the workbook as read-only. It prevents someone else from making changes to your final workbook.

However, if the other person visits the Info gallery, that person can re-enable editing. This feature is designed to warn the other people that you've marked it as final and no further changes should happen.

If you can convince everyone in your workgroup to sign up for a Windows Live ID, you can use the Restrict Permission By People setting. This layer of security enables you to define who can read, edit, and/or print the document.

Finding hidden content using the Document Inspector

The Document Inspector can find a lot of hidden content, but it is not perfect. Still, finding 95 percent of the types of hidden content can protect you a lot of the time.

CAUTION

The Document Inspector is not foolproof. Do you frequently hide settings by changing the font color to white or by using the ;;; custom number format? These types of things won't be found by the Document Inspector. The Document Inspector also won't note that you scrolled over outside the print area and jotted your after-work grocery list in column X.

To run the Document Inspector, select File, Info, Check For Issues, Inspect Document, and click OK. The results of the Document Inspector show that the document has personal information stored in the file properties (author's name) and perhaps a hidden worksheet.

Avoiding nagging about CSV files

Using Comma Separated Values (CSV) is a very common way to move data between systems. Excel natively opens CSV files. CSV files are great for storing values and text, but they don't handle storing formulas or formatting or charts or pivot tables.

If you open a CSV file, the Excel team is afraid you might add some formulas and formatting and then forget to save as an Excel file. When you save as CSV, Excel would routinely nag you that you were about to lose formulas and formatting. Even if you acknowledged that warning and that you want to save as CSV, Excel would nag you again when you closed the file.

One passionate request at Excel.UserVoice.Com was from someone who had to deal with CSV files all day. This person pointed out that she understood CSV files don't support formulas, but her job was to produce CSV files all day, every day, and she did not appreciate the constant nagging. There were 1,196 votes for this idea. Excel now makes nagging optional.

The first time you try to save as a CSV file, this message appears in the information bar above the formula bar:

POSSIBLE DATA LOSS: Some features might be lost if you save this workbook in the comma-delimited (*.csv) format. To preserve these features, save it in an Excel file format.

Because the message appears in the information bar instead of a dialog box, you can simply ignore it. The information bar still offers the Save As button, but it also offers the Don't Show Again button, which when clicked, means you will never be nagged about CSV files again.

If you choose Don't Show Again and decide that you would like to be reminded about CSV files, choose File, Options, Save, and select Show Data Loss Warning When Editing Comma Delimited Files (*.csv).

Adding whitespace around icons using Touch mode

If you are trying to use Excel on a tablet or a touchscreen, you want to try Touch mode. Follow these steps:

1. Go to the right side of the QAT and open the drop-down menu that appears there.
2. The twelfth command is called Touch/Mouse Mode. The icon is a blue dot with a ring of whitespace and then dashed lines around the whitespace. Choose this command to add it to the QAT.
3. Click the icon on the QAT. You see whitespace added around all the icons.

Using the new Sheet icon to add worksheets

The Insert Worksheet icon is a circle with a plus sign that appears to the right of the last sheet tab.

When you click this icon, a new worksheet is added to the right of the active sheet. This is better than Excel 2010, where the new worksheet was added as the last worksheet in the workbook and then had to be dragged to the correct position.

Navigating through many worksheets using the controls in the lower left

Older versions of Excel had four controls for moving through the list of worksheet tabs. The worksheet navigation icons are now a left and right arrowhead in the lower left.

The controls are active only when you have more tabs than are visible across the bottom of the Excel window. Click the left or right icon to scroll the tabs one at a time. Ctrl+click either arrow to scroll to the first or last tab. Note that scrolling the tabs does not change the active sheet. It just brings more tabs into view, so you can then click the selected tab.

Just as in prior versions of Excel, you can right-click the worksheet navigation arrows to see a complete list of worksheets. Click any item in the list to move to that worksheet. Pressing Shift-click will scroll the tabs one "page" of tabs at a time.

In certain circumstances, an ellipsis (...) icon appears to the left of the worksheet navigation arrows. This icon selects the worksheet to the left of the active sheet.

Using the mini toolbar to format selected text

When you select some text in a chart title or within a cell, the mini toolbar appears above the selected text. If you move away from the mini toolbar, it fades away. However, if you move the mouse toward the mini toolbar, you see several text formatting options.

To use the mini toolbar, follow these steps:

1. Select some text. If you select text in a cell, you must select a portion of the text in the cell by using Cell Edit mode. In a chart, SmartArt diagram, or text box, you can select any text. As soon as you release the mouse button, the mini toolbar appears above and to the right of the selection.
2. Move the mouse pointer toward the mini toolbar. The mini toolbar stays visible if your mouse is above it. If you move the mouse away from the mini toolbar, it fades away.
3. Make changes in the mini toolbar to affect the text you selected in step 1.
4. When you are done formatting the selected text, you can move the mouse away from the mini toolbar to dismiss it.

Expanding the formula bar

Formulas range from very simple to very complex. As people started writing longer and longer formulas in Excel, an annoying problem began to appear: If the formula for a selected cell was longer than the formula bar, the formula bar would wrap and extend over the worksheet. In many cases, the formula would obscure the first few rows of the worksheet. This was frustrating, especially if the selected cell was in the top few rows of the spreadsheet.

Excel now includes a formula bar that prevents the formula from obscuring the spreadsheet. For example, in Figure 2.13, cell F1 contains a formula that is longer than the formula bar. Notice the down-arrow icon at the right end of the formula bar. This icon expands the formula bar.

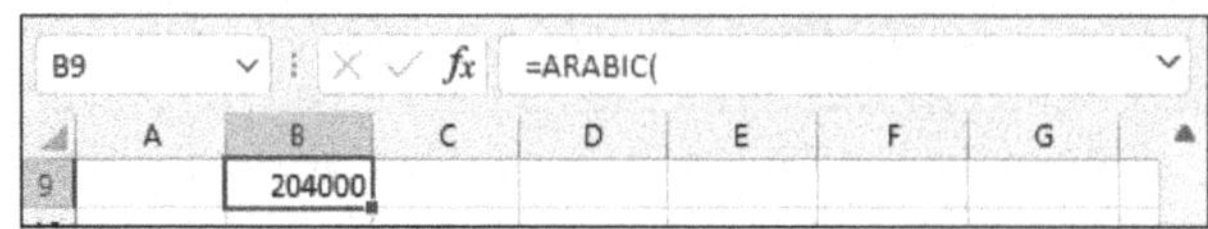

Figure 2.13 Initially, Excel shows only the first row of the formula.

Press Ctrl+Shift+U or click the down-arrow icon at the right side of the formula bar to expand the formula bar. The formula bar expands to the last manually resized height, and the entire worksheet moves down to accommodate the larger formula bar.

The formula in this example is too long for the default larger formula bar. You must hover your mouse near the bottom of the formula bar until you see the up/down white arrow cursor. Click and drag down until you can see the entire formula (see Figure 2.14).

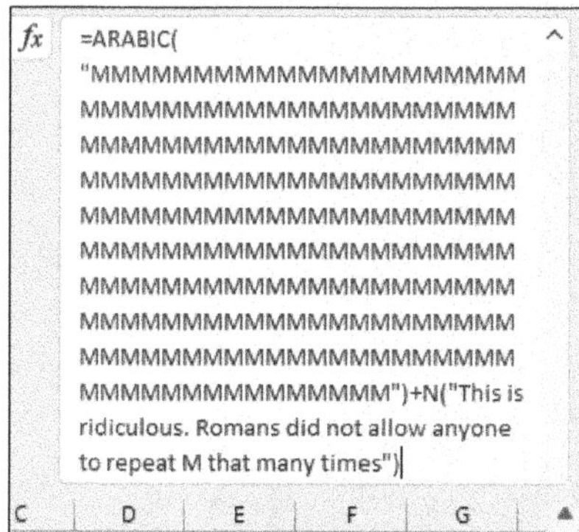

Figure 2.14 The worksheet moves down to accommodate the formula.

> NOTE
>
> **Excel guru Bob Umlas keeps suggesting that the formula bar should change color when you are not seeing the entire formula. That is a great suggestion that perhaps the Excel team will one day add to Excel.**

Zooming in and out on a worksheet

In the lower-right corner of the Excel window, a zoom slider enables you to zoom from 400 percent to 10 percent with lightning speed. You simply drag the slider to the right to zoom in and to the left to zoom out. The Zoom Out and Zoom In buttons on either end of the slider enable you to adjust the zoom in 10 percent increments.

Clicking the % indicator to the right of the zoom slider opens the legacy Zoom dialog box.

Inside OUT

If you decrease the zoom below 40%, Microsoft assumes that you are looking for an overview of the entire spreadsheet.

An interesting feature appears when you decrease the zoom to 39% or less. Any regions that have been assigned a name will appear as boxes with the name super-imposed. This is great for getting an overview of the named ranges created by someone else. Names reflecting only one cell will not show the name of that cell.

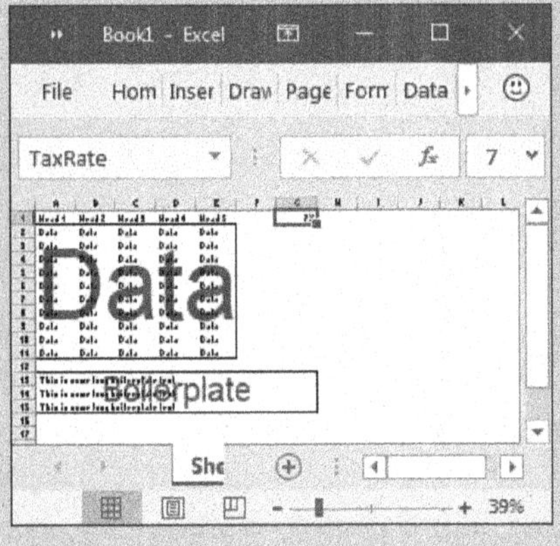

Using the status bar to add numbers

If you select several cells that contain numeric data and then look at the status bar, at the bottom of the Excel window, you can see that the status bar reports the average, count, and sum of the selected cells (see Figure 2.15).

270	229	242	236
294	228	247	224
282	263	232	266
278	226	235	289
222	221	262	267
280	258	254	224
241	295	247	269
291	261	260	265
258	280	302	267

Average: 257.3611111 Count: 36 Max: 302 Sum: 9265

Figure 2.15 The status bar shows the sum, average, and count of the selected cells.

If you need to quickly add the contents of several cells, you can select the cells and look for the total in the status bar. This feature has been in Excel for a decade, yet very few people realized it was there. In legacy versions of Excel, only the sum would appear, but you could right-click the sum to see other values, such as the average, count, minimum, and maximum.

You can customize which statistics are shown in the status bar. Right-click the status bar and choose any or all of Min, Max, Numerical Count, Count, Sum, and Average.

Switching between Normal view, Page Break preview, and Page Layout view modes

Three shortcut icons to the left of the zoom slider enable you to quickly switch between three view modes:

1. **Normal view:** This mode shows worksheet cells as normal.
2. **Page Break preview :** This mode draws the page breaks in blue. You can actually drag the page breaks to new locations in Page Break preview. This mode has been available in several versions of Excel.
3. **Page Layout view:** This view was introduced in Excel 2007. It combines the best of Page Break preview and Print Preview modes.

In Page Layout view mode, each page is shown, along with the margins, header, and footer. A ruler appears above the pages and to the left of the pages. You can make changes in this mode in the following ways:

1. To change the margins, drag the gray boxes in the ruler.
2. To change column widths, drag the borders of the column headers.
3. To add a header, select Click To Add Header.

Unselecting a cell with Ctrl+click

You can select multiple ranges in Excel by using the Ctrl key. In Figure 2,16, click and drag the mouse to select the first six cells. Hold the Ctrl key while dragging the mouse to select the eight Yes cells in columns C and D. In real life, you might have many more regions to select, and if you accidentally selected an extra cell, such as the "No" cell, there was no way to remove one cell from the selection in Excel 2016.

To remove the cell from the selection, you had to start all over again, carefully selecting one region at a time.

An improvement in Excel allows you to Ctrl+click a cell to remove it from the selection. This feature is new since Excel 2016, thanks to 327 votes at Excel.UserVoice.com.

	A	B	C	D
1				
2		Select	Select	
3		Select	Select	
4		Select	Select	
5				
6			Yes	Yes
7			Yes	Yes
8			Yes	Yes
9			Yes	Yes
10				
11		Yes	No	

Figure 2.16 Ctrl+click the No in column C to remove it from the selection.

Cleaning data with Flash Fill

Suppose that you have data with first names in column A and last names in column B. The names are in uppercase. You would like to reshape the data, so you have the full names in proper case.

Add a heading in column C. Type the first and last name from A2 and B2 in cell C2. As soon as you type the first letter in the second cell, Excel springs into action and offers to fill the rest of the column for you (see Figure 2.17). Provided the preview looks right or even close, press Enter.

	A	B	C
1	FIRST	LAST	Name
2	LARRY	VANCE	Larry Vance
3	WILL	RILEY	Will Riley
4	JEREMY	BARTZ	Jeremy Ba
5	YESENIA	GARCIA	Yesenia G
6	UTE	SIMON	Ute Simor
7	SABINE	HANSCHITZ	Sabine Ha
8	GREG	HEYMAN	Greg Heyr
9	JON	HIGBED	Jon Higbe
10	RUSSELL	WEBSTER	
11	ARLY	HANSEN	
12	JONATHAN	WERNICK	
13	ALEX	WATERTON	
14	CECELIA	RIEB	
15			

Figure 2.17 Type **W** in C3 and Excel offers to fill in the rest of the column.

In addition to filling the column, Excel provides two pieces of feedback. First, the status bar in the lower-left corner of the screen indicates that Flash Fill changed a certain number of cells.

Second, a tiny on-grid Flash Fill drop-down menu icon appears next to the first changed cell. The drop-down menu offers choices such as Undo and Accept. You can also choose to select all changed cells or all unchanged cells.

Coaching Flash Fill with a second example

After Flash Fill operates, look for any cells that don't fit the pattern. You might have a person with two first names (Mary Ellen Walton) or no last name (Pele). Type a new value in column C, and Flash Fill looks for other cells that match that pattern, correcting as it goes.

Flash Fill will not automatically fill in numbers

With only 10 digits (in contrast to 26 letters), it is too likely that Excel could detect other patterns that are not the pattern you are intending. When Flash Fill sees a potential pattern, it temporarily "grays in" the suggestion but then removes the suggestion. Press Ctrl+E or click the Flash Fill icon on the Data tab to allow Flash Fill to work.

Flash Fill does not understand mathematical transformations. If the original number is 477 and you type **479** (add 2 to each cell) or **500** (round to the nearest hundred), Excel does not know how to Flash Fill the remaining cells.

Using formatting with dates

Dates are particularly troublesome. Suppose that you have a date of birth in column E with the format of YYYYMMDD. If you type **3/5/1970** in G2 and then press the Flash Fill icon, Excel does not correctly recognize the pattern. You get 3/5/ and the first four digits from E in each row, which is an interesting result. You can sort of understand how Excel was tricked into seeing the wrong pattern.

You can solve the date problem by formatting the column to show MM/DD/YYYY first.

Troubleshooting Flash Fill

The following are some tips for making Flash Fill work correctly:

1. There can be no blank columns. It is not necessary to be in the column immediately to the right of the data, but you can't have any completely blank columns between where you want to Flash Fill and the source data.

2. For the automatic Flash Fill to work, you should type the first value and then immediately type the second value. Do not perform any other commands between the first and second values. Don't type **G2**, go to Sheet 3, and then come back and type **G3**. By then, Flash Fill has stopped watching for patterns. The only exception is sorting. You could type **G2**, sort, type **G3**, and Flash Fill will work.

3. Type a heading in the column that you are filling to prevent Flash Fill from filling your heading. Also, you could use bold for the other headings. Flash Fill follows the same rules that the Sort dialog box and the Ctrl+T Table dialog box use to detect whether there are headings. If Ctrl+T opens with the My Data Has Headings box checked, then Flash Fill does not overwrite your headings. This matters more than you might think because the headings don't usually follow the pattern of the data and they confuse Flash Fill if it is trying to find a pattern.

4. Pressing Esc makes the Flash Fill preview go away. More than once, I've pressed Esc by mistake and lost the Flash Fill. Don't worry. Type the first one or two cells and then use Ctrl+E or click the Flash Fill icon on the Data tab to force Excel to run Flash Fill again.

5. Flash Fill looks only for patterns. Flash Fill does not understand that AZ is the abbreviation for Arizona. It does not understand that Jan 23 is another way to write 1-23. Flash Fill doesn't have any opinions. Typing **Awesome** next to Bruce Springsteen does not cue Flash Fill that you are trying to classify musical acts.

Flash Fill provides an easy way to solve many data problems. Even in the cases where an Excel pro knows a formula that can solve the problem, it is still easier to use Flash Fill.

TROUBLESHOOTING

Flash Fill can be fooled by ambiguous examples. It has an uncanny ability to see ambiguity where you could not detect it.

In the following example, you might type **Brian Alberts** in D2 and invoke Flash Fill from D3. Most rational human beings would assume that you wanted first name, a space, and last name.

Flash Fill, however, assumes that you want the first name from column A, the middle initial from column B, and then everything after the first letter of column C.

This leads to Flash Fill changing David Bradley to David Mradley. Always carefully examine the Flash Fill results to see if they make sense.

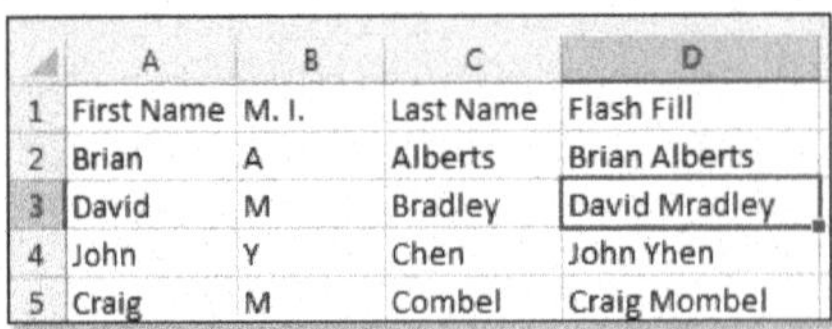

	A	B	C	D
1	First Name	M. I.	Last Name	Flash Fill
2	Brian	A	Alberts	Brian Alberts
3	David	M	Bradley	David Mradley
4	John	Y	Chen	John Yhen
5	Craig	M	Combel	Craig Mombel

Sorting data

Sorting in Excel is handled in the Sort dialog box or by using the AZ and ZA buttons on the Data tab. In all, there are six entry points for sorting:

1. Select the Home tab and then select Editing, Sort & Filter, Custom Sort.
2. Right-click any cell and choose Sort.
3. Select Sort from any filter drop-down menu.
4. Select the Data tab and then select Sort & Filter, AZ or Sort & Filter, ZA.
5. Open the Sort dialog box by going to the Data tab and selecting Sort & Filter, Sort.

The Sort dialog box in Excel offers up to 64 different sorting levels. If you get into sorting by color, you often have to specify several rules for one column, so the theoretical number of columns you can sort by is probably fewer than 64.

Sorting by color or icon

Excel can sort data by fill color, font color, or icon set. This also works with color applied through conditional formatting or color that you applied by using the cell format icons.

Because color is subjective, there is not a default color sequence. If one column contains 17 colors, you need to set up 17 rules in the Sort dialog box just to sort by that one column.

To sort by color, follow these steps:

1. Select a cell within your data.
2. Select the Sort icon on the Data tab. The Sort dialog box appears.
3. Select the desired field from the Sort By drop-down menu.
4. Change the Sort On drop-down menu to Cell Color.
5. In the Order drop-down menu, choose the color that should appear first.
6. In the final drop-down menu, select On Top.
7. To specify the next color, click the Copy Level button at the top of the Sort dialog box.
8. Choose the next color in the Order drop-down menu for the copied rule.
9. Repeat steps 7 and 8 for each additional color.

10. If you want to specify that values in another column should be used to break ties in the color column, select the Add Level button and specify the additional columns.

11. Click OK to sort the data.

Factoring case into a sort

Typically, an Excel sort ignores the case of the text. Values that are lowercase, uppercase, or any combination of the two are treated equally in a sort.

You can instead use a case-sensitive sort in Excel to sort lowercase values before uppercase values. For example, **abc** sorts before **ABC**. Similarly, **ABc** sorts before **ABC**.

If you want Excel to consider case when sorting, follow these steps:

1. Select a cell within your data.
2. Select the Sort icon on the Data tab. The Sort dialog box appears.
3. Choose the column from the Sort By drop-down menu.
4. Click the Options button. The Sort Options dialog box appears.
5. Select the Case Sensitive check box.
6. Click OK to close the Sort Options dialog box.
7. Click OK to sort.

Reordering columns with a left-to-right sort

If you receive a data set from a colleague and the columns are in the wrong sequence, you could cut and paste them into the right sequence, or you could fix them all in one pass by using a left-to-right sort. To do this, follow these steps:

1. Insert a new blank row above the headings.
2. In the new row, type numbers corresponding to the correct sequence of the columns.
3. Make sure that one cell in the range is selected.
4. Select the Sort icon on the Data tab. The Sort dialog box appears.
5. Click the Options button. The Sort Options dialog box appears.
6. Select Sort Left to Right. Click OK to close the Sort Options dialog box.
7. The Sort By drop-down menu now contains a list of row numbers. Choose the first row.

8. The remaining drop-down menus should already include Values and Smallest To Largest.

9. Click OK to perform the sort.

10. Delete your temporary extra row at the top of the data set. The columns are then resequenced into the desired order.

TIP

Excel does not change the original column widths. Select all cells with Ctrl+A and then use Home, Format, AutoFit Column Width to resize all the columns.

Sorting into a unique sequence by using custom lists

Sometimes company tradition dictates that regions or products should be presented in an order that is not alphabetic. For example, the sequence East, Central, West makes more sense geographically than the alphabetic sequence Central, East, West.

It is possible to set up a custom list to tell Excel that the region sequence is East, Central, West. You can then sort your data based on this sequence. You need to set up the custom list only once per computer. Follow these steps to do so:

1. Go to a blank section of any worksheet. Type the correct sequence for the values in a column.

2. Select this range.

3. Select File, Options. The Options dialog box appears.

4. Click the Advanced Group. Scroll down to the General section and then select Edit Custom Lists. The Custom Lists dialog box appears.

5. In the Custom Lists dialog box, the bottom section shows the range of cells you selected in step 2. If it is correct, click the Import button. Your new list, with the correct sequence, is added to the default custom lists.

6. Click OK to close the Custom Lists dialog box. Click OK to close the Options dialog box.

7. Clear your temporary data range from step 1.

To use the list with custom sorting, follow these steps:

1. Select one cell in your data.

2. Select the Sort icon on the Data tab. The Sort dialog box appears.

3. In the Sort By drop-down menu, choose the region with the custom sort sequence.

4. From the Order drop-down menu, select Custom List. You should now be back in the Custom Lists dialog box.

5. Click your custom list and then click OK. The Sort dialog box shows that the order is based on your custom list.

6. Click OK to sort into the custom sequence.

One-click sorting

All the examples discussed so far in this chapter have used the Sort dialog box, which is required for left-to-right sorting, custom sorting, and case-sensitive sorting. It also makes color sorting easier. You can accomplish all other sorts by using the AZ buttons on the various tabs.

It is important to select a single cell in the column to be sorted. When you select a single cell, Excel extends the selection to encompass the entire current region. If you select two cells or even the whole column, Excel warns you that it is about to sort part of your data and ignore the adjacent data. This is rarely what you want.

You can find the one-click sorting options on the Home and Data tabs. On the Home tab, they are buried in the Sort & Filter drop-down menu. On the Data tab, they are clearly visible as AZ and ZA buttons.

You can also find sorting options by right-clicking a cell in the column you want to sort and selecting Sort. Options in this menu enable you to sort in ascending or descending order. You can also put the cell color, font color, or icon on top.

Additional quick-sorting options are located in the Filter drop-down menus. You can use these options to sort in ascending order, in descending order, and by color.

Fixing sort problems

If it appears that a sort did not work correctly, check this list of troubleshooting tips:

1. If the headers were sorted into the data, it usually means that one or more columns had a blank heading. Every column should have a nonblank heading. If you want the heading to appear blank, use an underscore in a white font to fool Excel. If you cannot insert a heading, you will have to use the Sort dialog box.

2. Unhide rows and columns before sorting. Hidden rows are not resequenced in a sort.

3. Use only one row for headings. If you need the headings to appear as if they are taking up several rows, put the headings in one row and wrap the text. To have control over where the text wraps, type the first line, press Alt+Enter, and then type the second line.

4. Data in a column should be a similar type. For example, if you have a column of ZIP Codes, you might have numeric cells for ZIP Codes of 10001 through 99999 and text cells for ZIP Codes of 00001 through 09999. This is one common way to keep leading zeroes. Because text cells are sorted sequentially after numeric cells, sorting the ZIP Codes, in this case, will appear not to work. To fix this problem, convert the entire column to one data type to achieve the expected results.

5. If your data has volatile formulas or formulas that point to cells outside the sort range, Excel calculates the range after sorting. If your sort sequence is based on this column, Excel accurately sorts the data, based on the information before the recalculation. If the values change after calculation, it will appear that the sort did not work.

6. If your data must have blank columns or rows, be sure to select the entire sort range before starting the sort process.

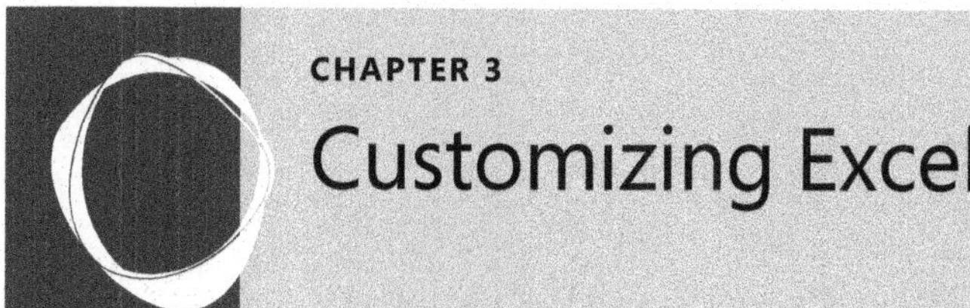

CHAPTER 3

Customizing Excel

The Excel Options dialog box offers hundreds of changes you can make in Excel. This chapter walks you through examples of customizing the ribbon and discusses some of the important option settings available in Excel.

Performing a simple ribbon modification

Suppose that you generally like the ribbon, but there is one icon that seems to be missing. You can add icons to the ribbon to make it customized to your preference. If you feel the Data tab would be perfect with the addition of a pivot table icon, you can add it (see Figure 3.1).

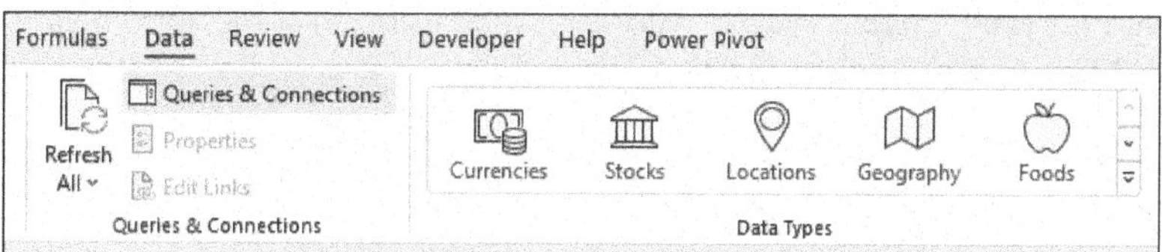

Figure 3.1 Decide where the new command should go on the ribbon.

To add the pivot table command to the Data tab, follow these steps:

1. Right-click the ribbon and select Customize The Ribbon.
2. In the right list box, expand the Data tab by clicking the + sign next to Data.
3. Click the Sort & Filter entry in the right list box. The new group will go after this entry.
4. Click the New Group button at the bottom of the right list box. A New Group (Custom) item appears after Sort & Filter, as shown in Figure 3.2.

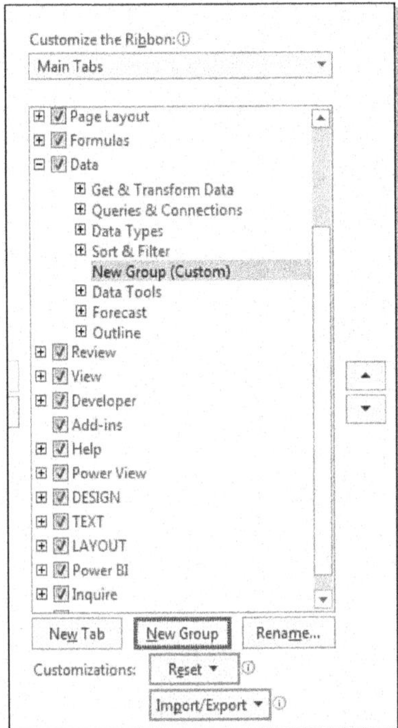

Figure 3.2 Commands must be added to a new group.

5. While the New Group is selected, click the Rename button at the bottom of the list box. The Rename dialog box appears.

6. The Rename dialog box offers to let you choose an icon and specify a name for the group. The icon is shown only when the Excel window is too small to display the whole group. Choose any icon and type a display name of `Pivot`. Click OK.

7. The left list box shows the popular commands. You could change Popular Commands to All Commands and scroll through 2,400 commands. However, in this case, the commands you want are on the Insert tab. Choose All Tabs from the top-left drop-down menu.

8. Expand the Insert tab, and then expand Tables. Click PivotTable in the left list box.

9. Click the Add button in the center of the dialog box to add PivotTable to the new custom Pivot group on the ribbon. Excel automatically advances to the next icon of Recommended PivotTables. Click Add again.

10. In the drop-down menu above the left list box, select All Commands. The left list box changes to show an alphabetical list of all commands.

11. Scroll through the left list box until you find PivotTable And PivotChart Wizard. This is the obscure entry point to create Multiple Consolidation Range pivot tables. Select that item in the left list box. Click Add. At this point, the right side of the dialog box should look like Figure 3.3.

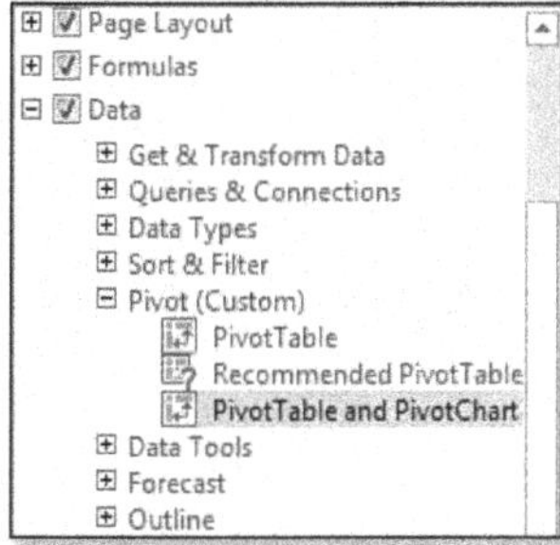

Figure 3.3 Three new icons have been added to a new custom group on the Data tab.

12. Click OK.

Figure 3.4 shows the new group in the Data tab of the ribbon.

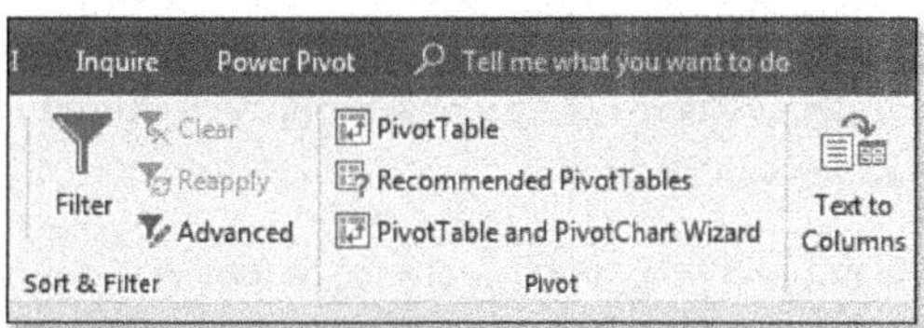

Figure 3.4 The results appear in the ribbon.

Adding a new ribbon tab

To add a new ribbon tab, follow these basic steps:

1. Right-click the ribbon and select Customize The Ribbon.
2. Click New Tab and rename the tab.
3. Add New Group(s) to the new tab.
4. Add commands to the new groups.

As you go through the steps to add a new ribbon tab, you will discover how absolutely limiting the ribbon customizations are. You have no control over which items appear with large icons and which appear with small icons. This applies even to galleries. If you add the Cell Styles gallery to a group on the ribbon, it always appears as an icon instead of a gallery, even if it is the only thing on the entire ribbon tab (see the left icon in Figure 3.5). The workaround is to add an entire built-in group to the tab. On the right of Figure 3.5, the entire Styles group was added. The Cell Styles gallery is now allowed to appear as a gallery.

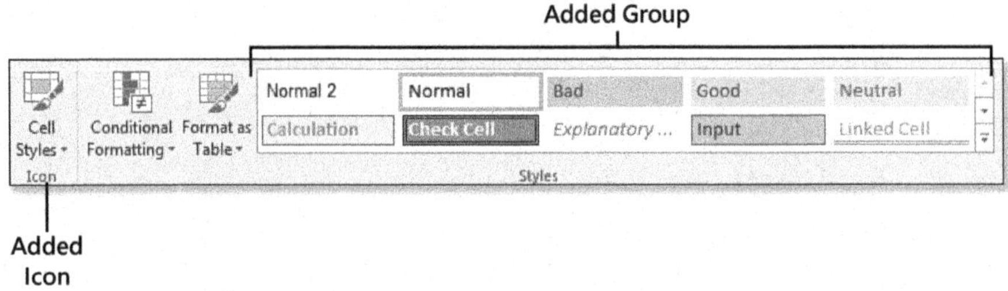

Figure 3.5 When added to a custom group, a gallery is reduced to a single icon with a drop-down menu.

CHAPTER 3

TROUBLESHOOTING

When customizing the ribbon using this interface, you cannot control which icons appear large and which appear small in the ribbon.

The Excel ribbon contains a logical mix of large icons for important features and small icons for minor features. If you would like to create a new group, you cannot control which icons will be small and which will be large.

You can either learn RibbonML or use a third-party tool such as Ribbon Commander to create custom ribbon tabs. Try a free trial of Ribbon Commander at *https://mrx.cl/ribboncommander*.

Sharing customizations with others

If you have developed the perfect ribbon customization and you want everyone in your department to have the same customization, you can export all the ribbon customizations.

To export the changes, follow these steps:

1. Right-click the ribbon and select Customize The Ribbon.
2. Below the right list box, select Import/Export, Export All Customizations.
3. Browse to a folder and provide a name for the customization file. The file type will be .exportedUI. Click OK.
4. In Windows Explorer, find the .exportedUI file. Copy it to a coworker's computer.

5. On the coworker's computer, repeat step 1. In step 2, select Import Customization File. Find the file and click OK.

   NOTE

   This is an all-or-nothing proposition. You cannot export your changes to one custom tab without exporting your changes to the Data and Home tabs.

Questions about ribbon customization

Can the customizations apply only to a certain workbook?

No. The Customize the Ribbon command in Excel applies to all workbooks.

Can I reset my customizations and go back to the original ribbon?

Right-click the ribbon and select Customize The Ribbon. Below the right list box, select Reset > Reset All Customizations.

How can I get complete control over the ribbon?

Learn RibbonX and write some VBA to build your own ribbon.

➤ **For more information on building your own ribbon, see *RibbonX: Customizing the Office 2007 Ribbon*, by Robert Martin, Ken Puls, and Teresa Hennig (Wiley, ISBN 0470191112).**

These ribbon customizations are really lacking. Is there another option that doesn't require me to write a program?

Yes, some third-party ribbon customization programs are available. For example, check out a free one from Excel MVP Andy Pope at *https://andypope.info/vba/ribboneditor_2010.htm*.

Using the Excel Options dialog box

Open the File menu and select Options from the left navigation pane to open the Excel Options dialog box. The dialog box has categories for General, Formulas, Data, Proofing, Save, Language, Ease Of Access, Advanced, Customize Ribbon, Quick Access Toolbar, Add-Ins, and Trust Center. The Trust Center leads to another 13 categories.

To the Excel team's credit, they tried to move the top options to the General category. Beyond those 19 settings, though, are hundreds of settings spread throughout 24 categories in the Excel Options and Trust Center. Table 3.1 gives you a top-level view of where to start looking for settings.

CHAPTER 3

Table 3.1 Excel Options dialog box settings

Category	Types of Settings
General	The most commonly used settings, such as user interface settings, the default font for new workbooks, number of sheets in a new workbook, customer name, and Start screen.
Formulas	All options for controlling calculation, error-checking rules, and formula settings. Note that options for multithreaded calculations are currently considered obscure enough to be on the Advanced tab rather than on the Formulas Tab.
Data	The data category is new in 2017. It offers the new Edit Default Layout for pivot tables, several other pivot table options, and then a series of checkboxes to bring back the legacy Get Data categories. When Power Query replaced Get Data on the Data tab of the ribbon, the old legacy icons were removed.
Proofing	Spell-check options and a link to the AutoCorrect dialog box.
Save	The default method for saving, AutoRecovery settings, legacy colors, and web server options.
Language	Choose the editing language, ToolTip language, and Help language.
Ease of Access	Options available are Provide Feedback With Sound, Provide Feedback With Animation, Screen Tip Style, and the default document font size.
Advanced	All options that Microsoft considers advanced, spread among 15 headings.
Customize Ribbon	Icons to customize the ribbon.
Quick Access Toolbar	Icons to customize the Quick Access Toolbar (QAT).
Add-Ins	A list of available and installed add-ins. New add-ins can be installed from the button at the bottom of this category.
Trust Center	Links to the Microsoft Trust Center, with 13 additional categories.

Getting help with a setting

Many settings appear with a small *i* icon. If you hover the mouse near this icon, Excel displays a super ToolTip for the setting. The ToolTip explains what happens when you choose the setting. It also provides some tips about what you need to be aware of when you turn on the setting. For example, the ToolTip in Figure 3.6 shows information about the calculation settings. It also explains that you should use the F9 key to invoke a manual calculation.

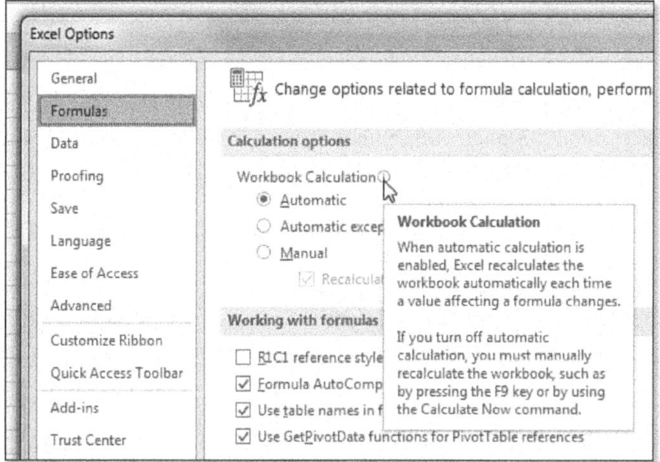

Figure 3.6 The i button explains many settings.

Inside OUT

The Excel team is actively listening to ideas suggested by their customers. Several of the settings in the following section were suggested by customers.

If you have a great idea that would make Excel easier, post your idea to Excel.UserVoice .com. Create a good title and use a slightly humorous tone when writing up how your idea would make the work life of millions of people easier.

After posting your idea, others can vote for your idea. As others browsing *https://msfeedbackprod.powerappsportals.com/feedback/* read your idea, they can vote. If you get above the 200-vote level, it is likely that your idea will be added to a future release of Office 365.

Recent new options in Excel

Excel today offers several new settings:

1. When Using Multiple Displays is found in the General category. Excel now supports newer High DPI displays, but many people might have two-monitor setups with one High DPI display and one older display. If you have problems when moving Excel between displays, choose Optimize For Compatibility from this setting.

2. Excel introduced data types for stocks, currency, geography, and more. In an effort to make the feature discoverable, if you enter city names into a few cells, Excel can offer to convert those cells to a Geography Data Type. This is great at first, but if it becomes

bothersome, unselect Show Convert To Data Types When Typing from the General category.

3. Excel offers a Search box in the title bar. This is designed for finding commands when you can't find them on the ribbon. If you think the Search box is taking up too much space, select Collapse The Microsoft Search Box By Default. It is found in the General category.

4. Microsoft added a dark mode to Excel. Use the Office Theme drop-down menu in the General category.

5. Near the bottom of the General category, you can assign which file extensions will open in Excel and ask Excel to notify you if it is not the default program for .XLSX and .XLSM files.

6. With the introduction of Dynamic Arrays, the Implicit Intersection behavior is different. If you attempt to write a formula with @ in the wrong places, Excel can warn you that the formula is not compatible with older versions of Excel. It offers to change the formula so it is backward compatible, as shown in Figure 3.7. To check any random formula, enter `=@(the formula)` and see if Excel shows a dialog box. To turn off this behavior, on the Formulas category, unselect Suggest Formula Variations That Are Supported By Older Versions of Excel.

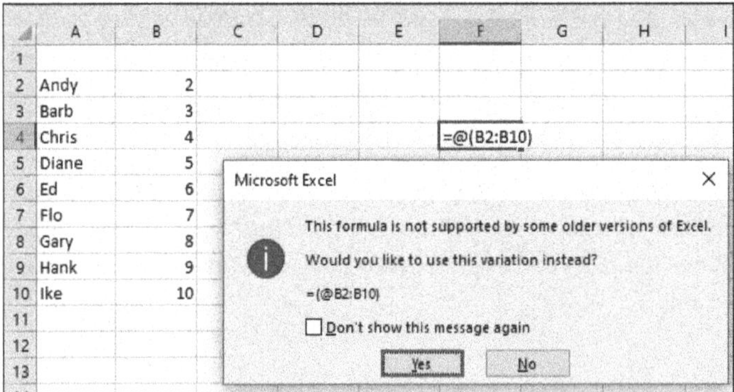

Figure 3.7 The @ will make sure that a formula designed to return a single value won't return an array in earlier versions of Excel.

7. There are two new error-checking options in the Formulas category. A warning about a Misleading Number Format appears if your formula points to a numeric cell, but the formula is formatted as a date, as shown in Figure 3.8. By choosing Update Format, the number format from the source cell will be copied to the formula cell. Another new error-checking option is Cells Containing Data Types That Couldn't Refresh. This alerts you if the linked data type cell could not be refreshed.

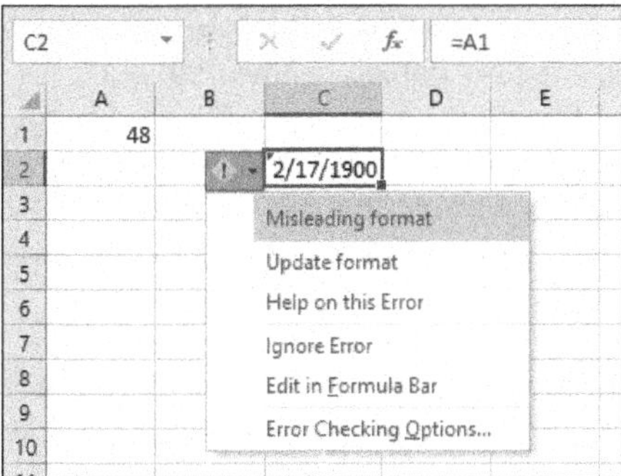

Figure 3.8 If a cell formatted as a date is pointing to cells formatted as a number, the Misleading Number Format warning displays.

8. Default PivotTable Layout is found in the new Data category. Change the default layout for all future pivot tables. Several items in the new Data category were moved to the Data category from the Advanced category.

9. Show Legacy Data Import Wizards is a series of seven choices in the new Data category. The Power Query tools debuted in Excel 2016 on the Data tab of the ribbon. These tools became so popular, Microsoft decided to remove the old Get External Data group from the ribbon, but some people had specific reasons why they liked the old icons. You can now add those old icons back by choosing From Access, From Web, From Text, From SQL Server, From OData Data Feed, From XML Data Import, or From Data Connection. If you choose something from this area, it will appear hidden on the ribbon. Look in Data, Get Data, Legacy Wizards.

10. Show Data Loss Warning when Editing Comma Delimited Files (*.csv) is found in the Save category. Excel used to nag you whenever you opened a file in CSV format. If you did not save the file as XLSX, it would warn you that you are about to lose formulas and formatting. A lot of people were tired of the nagging, and Microsoft turned off the nagging by default. If you need to be nagged, you can turn it back on here.

11. A new Cache Settings in the Save category controls how many days to keep files in the Office document cache and lets you empty the cache.

12. The Ease Of Access category is new in Excel 2019. You can choose to Provide Feedback With Sound and choose a Modern or Classic sound scheme. The new part is the Modern sound scheme. The annoying Classic Sound Scheme was previously the only choice in the Advanced category. You can turn off Animations. The choice to control whether Screen Tips are shown is repeated here from the General category. You can set the Default Font Size used in the document, and you can choose to turn off the calculation Function Screen Tips.

13. Use Pen To Select and Interact By Default is new in the Advanced category. If you prefer using a touchscreen, you can change the default behavior of touch.

14. Hyperlinks to Excel files stored in the cloud might open in Excel Online. If you prefer them to open in the desktop version of Excel, there is a new setting. The Link Handling subcategory is the third subcategory in the Advanced category. Choose Open Supported Hyperlinks To Office Files In Desktop Apps.

15. Excel lets you control how many recent files appear when you choose File > Open. The new Find Show This Number Of Recent Unpinned settings controls how many recent folders will be shown.

Using AutoRecover options

For many versions, Excel periodically saves a copy of your work every 10 minutes. If your computer crashes, the recovery pane offers to let you open the last AutoRecovered version of the file. This feature is sure to save you from retyping data that might have otherwise been lost.

Another painful situation occurs when you do not save changes and then close Excel. Yes, Excel asks if you want to save changes for each open document, but this question usually pops up at 5:00 p.m. when you are in a hurry to get out of the office. If you are thinking about what you need to do after work and not paying attention to which files are still open, you might click No to the first document and then click No again and again without noticing that the fifth open document was one that should have been saved.

Another scenario involves leaving an Excel file open overnight only to discover that Windows Update decided to restart the computer at 3 AM. After being burned a dozen times, you can change the behavior of Windows Update to stop doing this. However, if Windows Update closed Excel without saving your documents, you can lose those AutoRecovered documents.

A setting introduced in Excel 2010 has Excel save the last AutoRecovered version of each open file when you close without saving. This setting is on the Save category of Excel Options and is called Keep The Last AutoRecovered Version If I Close Without Saving.

Controlling image sizes

An Image Size & Quality section appears in the Advanced category. Most people add a photo to dress up the cover page of a document. However, you probably don't need an 8-megapixel image being saved in the workbook. By default, Excel compresses the image before saving the file. You can control the target output size using the drop-down menu in Excel options. Choices include 96ppi, 150ppi, and 220ppi. The 96ppi setting will look fine on your display. Use 220ppi for images you will print. If you want to keep your images at the original size, you can select the Do Not Compress Images In File setting.

You should also understand the Discard Editing Data check box. Suppose that you insert an image in your workbook and then crop out part of the photograph. If you do not enable Discard Editing Data, someone else can come along and uncrop your photo. This can be an embarrassing situation—just ask the former TechTV co-host who discovered certain bits of photographs were still hanging around after she cropped them out.

Working with protected view for files originating from the Internet

Starting in Excel 2010, files from the Internet or Outlook initially open in protected mode. This mode gives you a chance to look at the workbook and formulas without having anything malicious happen. Unfortunately, you cannot view the macro code while the workbook is in protected view.

If you only want to view or print the workbook, protected mode works great. One statistic says that 40% of the time, people simply open a document and never make changes to it.

After you click Enable Editing, Excel will skip protected mode the next time you open the file.

Working with Trusted Document settings

By default, Excel warns you about all sorts of things. If you open a workbook with macros, links, external data connections, or even the new `WEBSERVICE` function, a message bar appears above the worksheet to let you know that Excel disabled those "threats."

If you declare a folder on your hard drive to be a trusted folder, you can open those documents without Excel warning you about the items. Visit File, Options, Trust Center, Trust Center Settings, Trusted Locations to set up a trusted folder.

Starting in Excel 2010, if you open a file from your hard drive and enable the content, Excel automatically enables that content the next time. The inherent problem here is that if you open a file and discover the macros are bad, you will not want those macros to open the next time automatically. There is no way to untrust a single document other than deleting, renaming, or moving it. Instead, you have to go to the Trusted Documents category of the Trust Center where you can choose to clear the entire list of trusted documents.

Options to consider

Although hundreds of Excel options exist, this section provides a quick review of options that might be helpful to you:

1. Save Files In This Format in the Save category. If you regularly create macros, choose the Excel Macro-Enabled Workbook as the default format type.
2. Update your Default Local File Location on the Save tab. Excel always wants to save new documents in your My Documents folder. However, if you always work in the C:\AccountingFiles\ folder, update the default folder to match your preferred location.

3. Show This Number Of Recent Workbooks has been enhanced dramatically since Excel 2003. Whereas legacy versions of Excel showed up to nine recent workbooks at the bottom of the File menu, Excel allows you to see up to 50 recent workbooks in the Open category of the File menu. You can change this setting by visiting the Display section of the Advanced category.

4. Edit Custom Lists has been moved to the General section of the Advanced category. Custom lists add functionality to the fill handle, allow custom sort orders, and control how fields are displayed in the label area of a pivot table. Type a list in the correct sequence in a worksheet. Edit Custom Lists and click Import. Excel can now automatically extend items from that list, the same as it can extend January into February, March, and so on.

5. Make Excel look less like Excel by hiding interface elements in the three Display sections of the Advanced category. You can turn off the formula bar, scrollbars, sheet tabs, row and column headers, and gridlines. You can customize the ribbon to remove all main tabs except the File menu. The point is that if you design a model to be used by someone who never uses Excel, the person can open the model, plug in a few numbers, and get the result without having to see the entire Excel interface.

6. Show A Zero In Cells That Have Zero Value is in the Display Options For This Worksheet section of the Advanced category. Occasionally people want zeros to be displayed as blanks. Although a custom number format of `0;-0;;` will do this, you can change the setting globally by clearing this option.

7. Group Dates in the AutoFilter Menu is in the Display Options For This Workbook section of the Advanced category. Starting with Excel 2007, date columns show a hierarchical view of years, months, and days in the AutoFilter drop-down menu. If you like the old behavior of showing each date, turn off this setting.

8. Add a folder on your local hard drive as a trusted location. Files stored in a trusted location automatically have macros enabled and external links updated. If you can trust that you will not write malicious code, then define a folder on your hard drive as a trusted location. From Excel Options, select the Trust Center category and then Trust Center Settings. In the Trust Center, select Trusted Locations, Add New Location.

Five Excel oddities

You might rarely need any of the features presented in this section. However, in the right circumstance, they can be time-savers.

1. Adjust the gridline color in the Display section of the Advanced category. If you are tired of gray gridlines, you can get a new outlook with bright red gridlines. I've met people who have changed the gridline color and can attest that nothing annoys an old accountant more than seeing bright red gridlines.

2. Allow negative time by switching to the 1904 date system in the General section of the Advanced category. Excel never allows a time to return a negative time. However, if you are tracking comp time and you allow people to borrow against future comp time, it might be nice to allow negative time. In this case, switch to the 1904 date system to have up to four years of negative time. Use caution when changing this setting. All existing dates in the workbook will shift by approximately four years.

3. Put an end to the green triangles on your account numbers stored as text. Most of the green triangle indicators are useful. However, if you have a column of text account numbers in which most values are numbers, seeing thousands of green triangles can be annoying. Also, the green triangles can hide other, more serious problems. Clear the Numbers Formatted As Text or Preceded By An Apostrophe in the Error Checking Rules check box in the Formulas category.

4. Automatically Insert A Decimal Point replicates the antique adding machines that were office fixtures in the 1970s. When working with a manual adding machine, it was frustrating to type decimal points. You could type `123456`, and the adding machine would interpret the entry as `1,234.56`. If you find that you are doing massive data entry of numbers in dollars and cents, you can have Excel replicate the old adding machine functionality. After enabling this setting, you can indicate how many digits of the number should be interpreted as being after the decimal point. The only hassle is that you need to enter $5 as `500`. The old adding machines actually had a 00 key, but those are long since gone.

5. Change `Dwight` to `Diapers` using AutoCorrect Options. If you were a fan of the NBC sitcom *The Office*, you might remember the 2007 episode in which Jim allegedly put a macro on Dwight's computer that automatically changed the typed word `Dwight` to `Diapers`. However, this doesn't require a macro. From Excel Options, choose the Proofing Category and then click the AutoCorrect Options button. On the AutoCorrect tab, you can type new correction pairs. In this example, you would type `Dwight` into the Replace box and `Diapers` into the With box. The next time someone types `Dwight` and then a space, the word will automatically change to `Diapers`. You can also remove correction pairs by selecting the pairs and then pressing Delete. For example, if you hate that Microsoft converts (c) to ©, you can delete that entry from the list.

CHAPTER 4

Keyboard shortcuts

If you do a lot of typing, being able to access commands from the keyboard is faster than moving your hand to the mouse. Excel still uses many of the old Alt keyboard shortcuts from Excel 2003. All the old Ctrl shortcut keys are still functional. For instance, Ctrl+C still copies a selection, Ctrl+X cuts a selection, and Ctrl+V pastes a selection.

This chapter points out which of the old Excel 2003 keyboard shortcuts still work, shows you some new shortcuts, and introduces you to the keyboard accelerators.

Learning the right ten shortcuts from this chapter can make you twice as fast in Excel.

Using keyboard accelerators

The goal of the Excel keyboard accelerators is to enable you to access every command by using only the keyboard. In legacy versions of Excel, many popular commands had keyboard accelerators, but other commands did not. Today, Excel tries to ensure that every command can be invoked from the keyboard.

To access the new accelerators, press and release the Alt key or a forward slash (/). Notice that Excel places a KeyTip above each command. Also, numeric KeyTips appear over each icon in the Quick Access Toolbar (QAT; see Figure 4.1). Press the F10 key to display or hide the KeyTips.

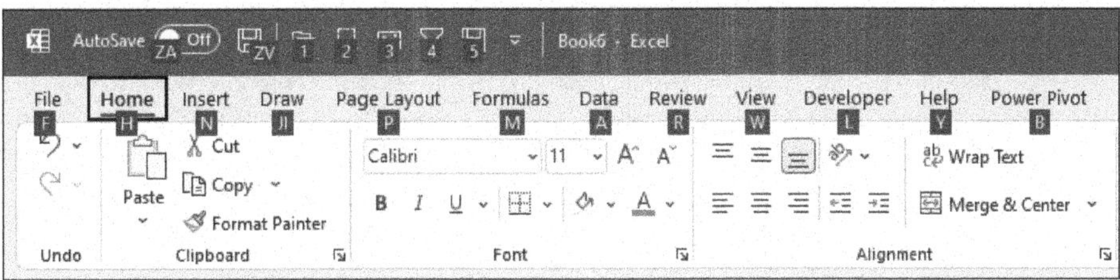

Figure 4.1 Type the letters in the KeyTips along the top to open various tabs.

It is possible to memorize the KeyTips for the ribbon tabs. Pressing Alt+F accesses the File menu in all Office applications. Alt+H accesses the Home tab in all Office applications. Alt+Q puts the cursor inside the Tell Me What You Want To Do box. The accelerator definitions for each tab remain constant even if new ribbon tabs are displayed. When you activate a pivot table, the original KeyTip letters remain, and two new KeyTips appear for the contextual tabs: JT for PivotTable Analyze and JY for Design (see Figure 4.2).

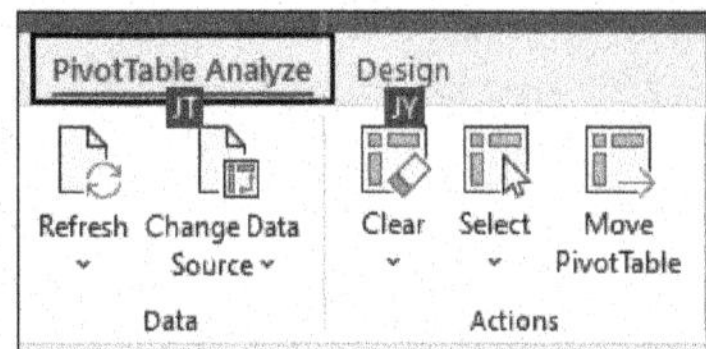

Figure 4.2 New ribbon tabs have new letters, so the old letters remain constant.

Unfortunately, the KeyTips for the Quick Access Toolbar change every time you add new buttons or rearrange buttons on the Quick Access Toolbar. If you want to memorize those KeyTips, you need to make sure you do not add a new Quick Access Toolbar icon at the beginning of the list.

Selecting icons on the ribbon

After you press the Alt key, you can press one of the KeyTip letters to bring up the appropriate tab. You now see that every icon on the ribbon has a KeyTip.

When you choose a Ribbon tab, the KeyTips on the Quick Access Toolbar disappear, so Microsoft is free to use the letters A through Z and the numbers 0 through 9.

On very busy ribbon tabs, some commands require two keystrokes: for example, A+C for Align Center in the Alignments group of the Home tab, as shown in Figure 4.3. Note that after you press Alt to display the accelerators in the ToolTips, you do not have to continue holding down the Alt key.

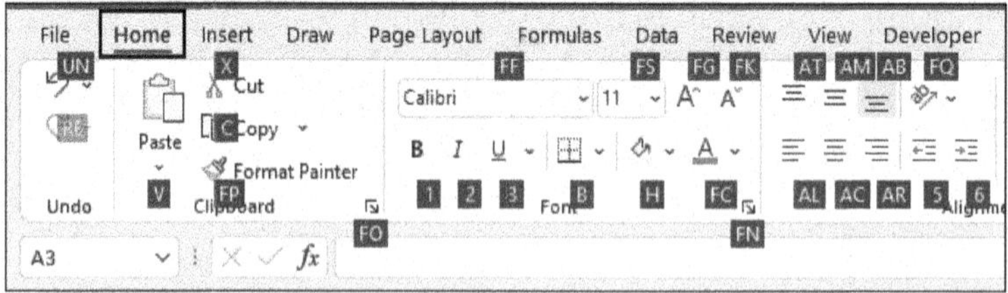

Figure 4.3 After pressing the letter to switch to the ribbon, type the letter or letters to invoke a particular command.

Some shortcut keys seem to make sense: AT for Align Top, AM for Align Middle, AB for Align Bottom, and AL for Align Left. Other shortcut keys seem to be assigned at random. Some take a little pondering: FN for the dialog box launcher in Figure 4.3 makes sense because it opens the legacy Format dialog box and moves to the Number tab. Others have a historical precedent. In Excel 2003, F was used for File, so O was used for Format.

Similarly, in the Home tab, O now opens the Format drop-down menu. However, because Microsoft no longer underlines the accelerator key in the menu name, O will never make sense to someone new to Excel. There might be some arcane, logical reason why 5 and 6 are used for increase and decrease indent, but it is unknown by most people.

Selecting options from a gallery

Figure 4.4 shows the results of pressing Alt+H+J, which is the equivalent of selecting Home, Cell Styles. This opens the gallery of cell styles. As you can see in Figure 4.4, you can invoke the New Cell Style and Merge Styles commands at the bottom of the gallery by pressing N and M, respectively. However, there are no letters on the table style choices in the gallery.

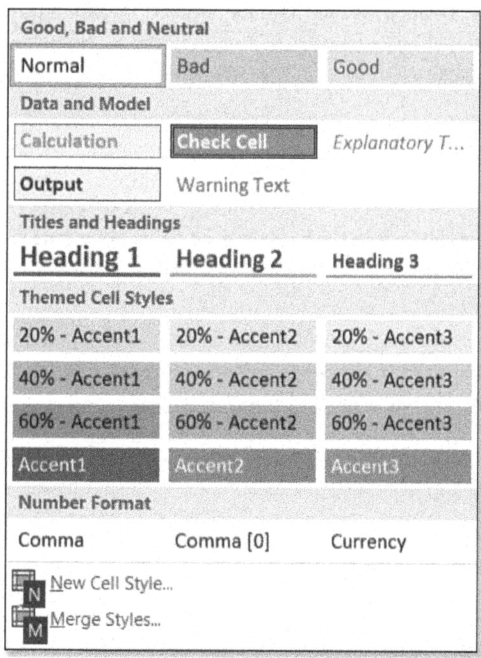

Figure 4.4 After opening a gallery, you use the arrow keys to navigate through the gallery and press Enter to select a style.

Navigating within drop-down menu lists

If you press Alt+H+F+S, which is the equivalent of selecting Home, Font Size, the font size in the drop-down menu is selected. You can either type a font size and press Enter or press the down-arrow key to open the drop-down menu. You can then use the down arrow, up arrow, Page Down, Page Up, Home, and End keys to navigate to a choice in the list. When you have the desired item highlighted, press Enter to select that item.

Backing up one level through a menu

Suppose you press Alt+H to access the Home tab and then realize you are in the wrong tab. You can press the Esc key to move back to display the ToolTips for the main menu choices. If you want to clear the ToolTips completely, press Alt again.

Dealing with keyboard accelerator confusion

If you want to select something on the Home tab (previously shown in Figure 4.2), you might be frustrated because you can see the menu choices but no ToolTips appear for most commands. For icons in the top of the ribbon, it appears that the main KeyTips apply to the menu items. For example, you might think that the H KeyTip applies to Cut. Even though you are already on the Home tab, you need to press the H key to force Excel to show the ToolTips for the individual menu items on the Home tab.

TROUBLESHOOTING

There are some parts of the Excel window that seem impossible to access using keyboard shortcuts. For example, how can you jump to a task pane without using the mouse?

It is extremely subtle, but there is something called the F6 Loop. When you press F6, the focus will move from the worksheet to the sheet tabs. Press F6 again to jump to any task pane, then to the zoom controls, and then back to the worksheet.

Once you use F6 to activate an area, you can use Tab or arrow keys to activate different controls within that area.

Inside OUT

It seems particularly tricky to use keyboard shortcuts to access a slicer.

A slicer is a visual filter that is used with pivot tables and tables formatted with Ctrl+T. They are shown in the following figure—the names below the Rep caption and the fruit below the Product caption.

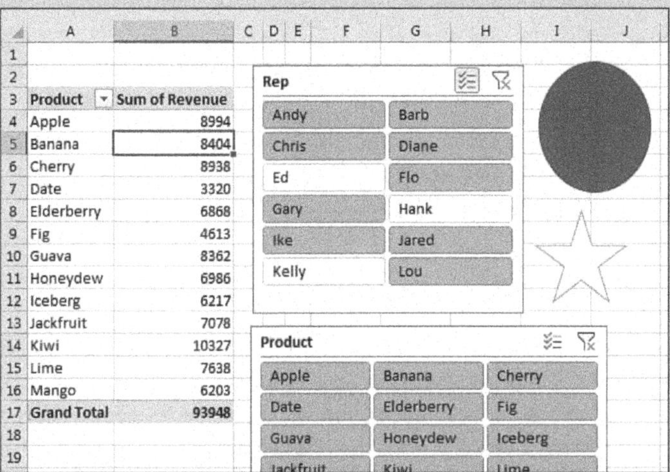

Product	Sum of Revenue
Apple	8994
Banana	8404
Cherry	8938
Date	3320
Elderberry	6868
Fig	4613
Guava	8362
Honeydew	6986
Iceberg	6217
Jackfruit	7078
Kiwi	10327
Lime	7638
Mango	6203
Grand Total	93948

The solution is not perfect, but you can select all objects using Alt, H, FD, O. Once you have selected all objects, you can cycle between the slicers, although the indicators are very subtle.

Refer to the preceding figure while reading these keyboard steps:

1. Starting from cell B5, press Alt, H, FD, O to begin Select Objects mode.
2. Press Tab once to activate the Rep slicer. At this point, you can use the arrow keys to reposition the slicer.
3. Press Tab a second time to move to the Multi-Select icon inside the Rep slicer. Press Spacebar to toggle multi-select on or off.
4. Press Tab again to move to the Clear Filter icon. Press Spacebar to clear the filter.
5. Press Tab again to move into the slicer items. This step is really subtle because exactly one slicer will have a dotted line. A black dotted line on a field of dark blue is really hard to see. Plus, while you would think that the selected slicer tile would always be Andy, it is not. Excel remembers your last selected slicer and starts there. Perhaps using arrows to move to the next slicer tile will allow your eye to see what is changing. Spacebar will toggle the slicer tile on or off if Multi-Select is enabled. If Multi-Select is off, then pressing Spacebar on one slicer tile will turn all the others off and turn that tile on. By the way, you can use Shift+Tab to move back to the Clear Filter and then Shift+Tab again to move back to Multi-Select.
6. Pressing Tab from the Slicer Items of the Rep slicer will move to the next object in the worksheet, the Oval.

7. **Press Tab again to move to the Star.**
8. **Press Tab again to move to the Product slicer. At this point, you are essentially at Step 2 for the next slicer.**
9. **When you are done accessing the slicers, use the Escape key to exit Select Objects mode and return to cell B5.**

Selecting from legacy dialog boxes

Some commands lead to legacy dialog boxes like the ones in previous editions of Excel. These dialog boxes do not display the Excel KeyTips. However, most of the dialog boxes do use the convention of having one letter of each command underlined, which is called a *hotkey* in Microsoft parlance. In this case, you can press the underlined letter to select the command.

For example, press Alt+H+V+S instead of selecting Home, Paste, Paste Special. You are then presented with the Paste Special dialog box, as shown in Figure 4.5. To select Values and Transpose in this dialog box, press V for Values and E for Transpose, because those are the letters underlined in the dialog box. You can then press Enter instead of clicking the default OK button.

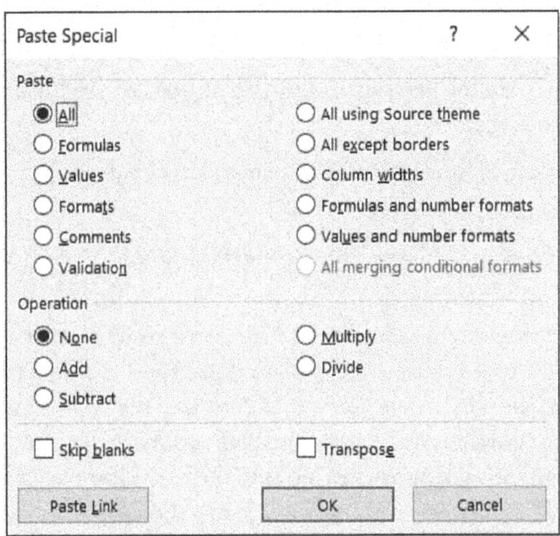

Figure 4.5 In a legacy dialog box, type the underlined letters to select options.

Using the shortcut keys

The following five tables provide what I believe to be a comprehensive list of shortcut keys. I have collected these over the many versions of Excel. For some reason, Excel Help no longer lists all the shortcut keys. I count 75 shortcut keys in the following tables that are no longer documented in Excel Help. I realize this is a mind-numbingly long list, but I want to include it here because the Excel team no longer provides a complete list.

If you decide to learn and start using one new shortcut key every week, you will quickly become very fast at using Excel. After Table 4.5, I identify my favorite shortcut keys from this list.

Table 4.1 lists the common Windows Ctrl shortcut keys.

Table 4.1 Windows shortcut keys

Key combination	Action
Ctrl+C	Copy.
Ctrl+X	Cut.
Ctrl+V	Paste.
Ctrl+Alt+V	Paste Special.
Ctrl+Z	Undo.
Ctrl+Y or F4	Redo.
Ctrl+A or Ctrl+Shift+spacebar	Select All. If the active cell contains data and is adjacent to other cells with data, Ctrl+A initially selects the current region. Pressing Ctrl+A again selects all.
Ctrl+S or Shift+F12 or Alt+Shift+F2	Save.
Alt+2 or F12	Save As.
Ctrl+O or Ctrl+F12	Open.
Ctrl+W or Ctrl+F4	Close workbook window.
Ctrl+N	New workbook.
Ctrl+P or Ctrl+F2 or Ctrl+Shift+F12	Display Print tab in File menu.
Ctrl+B	Bold.
Ctrl+U	Underline.
Ctrl+I	Italic.
Ctrl+F	Find.
Ctrl+H	Replace.
Ctrl+Shift+F or Ctrl+Shift+P	Font tab of Format Cells dialog box.
Ctrl+G or F5	Go To dialog.
Ctrl+T or Ctrl+L	Format As Table.
Ctrl+E	Flash Fill.
Ctrl+Q	Quick Analysis options.

Table 4.2 illustrates the shortcut keys you use to navigate in Excel.

Table 4.2 Shortcut keys for navigation

Shortcut key	Action
Ctrl+Home	Moves to cell A1 or the top-left unhidden cell in the worksheet. If the panes are frozen, it takes you to the top-left cell in the unfrozen section of the worksheet.
Ctrl+End	Moves to the last cell in the used range of the worksheet. If the cursor is in the formula bar, it moves to the end of the formula text.
Page Down	Moves one screen down in the worksheet.
Page Up	Moves one screen up in the worksheet.
Alt+Page Down	Moves one screen right in the worksheet.
Alt+Page Up	Moves one screen left in the worksheet.
Ctrl+Page Up	Moves to the previous worksheet.
Ctrl+Page Down	Moves to the next worksheet.
Ctrl+Shift+F6	Moves to the previous window.
Shift+F11	Inserts a new worksheet.
Ctrl+F11	Inserts an Excel 4 macro sheet.
Alt+Tab	Switches to the next program.
Alt+Shift+Tab	Switches to the previous program.
Ctrl+Esc	Displays the Windows Start menu.
Ctrl+F5	Restores the window size of the current workbook.
F6	Switches between the worksheet, ribbon, task pane, and zoom controls. If the workbook has been split, this also switches between panes.
Ctrl+F6	Switches to the next open workbook window when more than one workbook is open.
Ctrl+Shift+F6	Switches to the previous workbook window.
Ctrl+F9	Minimizes the window.
Ctrl+F10	Maximizes the window.
End	Toggles into End mode. Displays End mode in the status bar. When in End mode, press an arrow key to move to the edge of the current region. If the active cell is already at the edge of a current region or is a blank cell, this jumps to the next nonblank cell or to the edge of the worksheet.
End Home	Moves to the last-used range in the worksheet. Similar to Ctrl+End.
Ctrl+arrow key or End followed by an arrow key	Moves to the edge of the current region. If the active cell is at the edge of a current region or is a blank cell, this jumps to the next nonblank cell or to the edge of the worksheet.

Home	Moves to the beginning of the row.
Ctrl+backspace	Scrolls to display the active cell.
F5	Displays the Go To dialog box.
Shift+F5	Displays the Find dialog box.
Shift+F4	Find Next.
Ctrl+. (period)	Moves to the next corner of the selected range. For a rectangular range, the move direction is clockwise.

Table 4.3 shows the shortcut keys you use to select data and cells.

Table 4.3 Shortcut keys for selecting data and cells

<table>
<tr><th>Shortcut key</th><th>Action</th></tr>
<tr><td>Ctrl+spacebar</td><td>When an object is selected, this selects all objects on the worksheet.</td></tr>
<tr><td>Ctrl+spacebar</td><td>If used outside a table, this selects the entire column. If used inside a table, it toggles between selecting the data, the data and headers, and the entire column.</td></tr>
<tr><td>Shift+spacebar</td><td>Selects the entire row. If inside a table, this toggles between selecting the table row and the entire row.</td></tr>
<tr><td>Ctrl+Shift+spacebar or Ctrl+A</td><td>Selects the entire worksheet, unless the active cell is a region of two or more nonblank cells, in which case it selects the current region. Repeat the keystroke to select the entire worksheet. When the active cell is in a table, the first press selects the data rows of the table. The second press expands to include the headings and total row. The third press selects the entire worksheet.</td></tr>
<tr><td>Shift+backspace</td><td>With multiple cells selected, this reverts the selection to only the active cell.</td></tr>
<tr><td>Ctrl+ *</td><td>Selects the current region. In a pivot table, this selects the entire table.</td></tr>
<tr><td>Ctrl+/</td><td>Selects the array containing the active cell.</td></tr>
<tr><td>Ctrl+Shift+O (letter O)</td><td>Selects all cells that contain comments.</td></tr>
<tr><td>Ctrl+\</td><td>In a selected row, this selects the cells that do not match the formula in the active cell.</td></tr>
<tr><td>Ctrl+Shift+|</td><td>In a selected column, this selects the cells that do not match the formula in the active cell.</td></tr>
<tr><td>Ctrl+[(opening square bracket)</td><td>Selects all cells directly referenced by formulas in the selection.</td></tr>
<tr><td>Ctrl+Shift+{ (opening brace)</td><td>Selects all cells directly or indirectly referenced by formulas in the selection.</td></tr>
</table>

Ctrl+] (closing square bracket)	Selects cells that contain formulas that directly reference the active cell.
Ctrl+Shift+} (closing brace)	Selects cells that contain formulas that directly or indirectly reference the active cell.
Alt+; (semicolon)	Selects the visible cells in the current selection.
Ctrl+Shift+Page Down	Adds the next worksheet to the selected sheets and makes the next worksheet the active sheet. This puts the workbook in group mode if it is not already in group mode. Pressing Ctrl+Shift+Page Down three times puts the current sheet and the next three sheets in group mode. Any changes made to the visible sheet are also made to all sheets in group mode. To exit group mode, right-click a sheet tab and choose Ungroup Sheets.
Ctrl+Shift+Page Up	Adds the previous worksheet to the selected sheets. This puts the workbook in group mode if it was not already in group mode.

Table 4.4 shows the shortcut keys you use to extend a selection. In extend mode, clicking any cell selects from the active cell to the clicked cell.

Table 4.4 Shortcut keys for extending selections

Shortcut key	Action
F8	Turns extend mode on or off. In extend mode, EXT appears in the status line, and the arrow keys extend the selection.
Shift+F8	Adds another range of cells to the selection. You can use the arrow keys to move to the start of the range you want to add. Then press F8 and the arrow keys to select the next range.
Shift+arrow key	Extends the selection by one cell.
Ctrl+Shift+arrow key	Extends the selection to the last nonblank cell in the same column or row as the active cell.
Shift+Home	Extends the selection to the beginning of the row.
Ctrl+Shift+Home	Extends the selection to the beginning of the worksheet.
Ctrl+Shift+End	Extends the selection to the last-used cell on the worksheet in the lower-right corner. If the cursor is in the formula bar, this selects to the end of the formula.
Shift+Page Down	Extends the selection down one screen.
Shift+Page Up	Extends the selection up one screen.
End Shift+arrow key	Extends the selection to the last nonblank cell in the same column or row as the active cell.
End+Shift+Home	Extends the selection to the last-used cell on the worksheet in the lower-right corner.
End+Shift+Enter	Extends the selection to the last cell in the current row.

Scroll Lock+Shift+Home	Extends the selection to the cell in the upper-left corner of the window.
Scroll Lock+Shift+End	Extends the selection to the cell in the lower-right corner of the window.

Table 4.5 shows the shortcut keys you use for entering, editing, formatting, and calculating data.

Table 4.5 Shortcut keys for data entry, formatting, and calculating data

Shortcut	Key action
Enter	Completes a cell entry and selects the next cell. Often moves down one cell, but you can override this with File, Options, Advanced. In a data form, this moves to the first field in the next record. In a dialog box, this performs the action for the default button (often OK). After F10 is used to activate the menu bar, Enter selects the chosen menu item.
Alt+Enter	Starts a new line in the same cell.
Ctrl+Enter	After editing a cell, Ctrl+Enter fills the selected cell range with the current entry.
Shift+Enter	Completes a cell entry and selects the previous cell. Often the cell above, but you can override with File, Options, Advanced. If the Move Selection Direction is set to the right, then pressing Shift+Enter will move to the left.
Tab	Completes a cell entry and selects the next cell to the right. Moves between unlocked cells in a protected worksheet. Moves to the next option in a dialog box. In a multicell selection, selects the next cell.
Shift+Tab	Completes a cell entry and selects the previous cell to the left. In a dialog box, this moves to the previous option.
Esc	Cancels a cell entry. Closes Full-Screen mode. Closes an open menu dialog box or message window.
Arrow keys	Moves one cell up, down, left, or right. If in edit mode, this moves one character up, down, left, or right.
Home	Moves to the beginning of the line. Moves to the cell in the upper-left corner of the window when Scroll Lock is turned on. Selects the first command on the menu when a menu is visible.
F4 or Ctrl+Y	Repeats the last action. When a cell reference is selected in a formula, F4 toggles between the various combinations of relative and absolute references.
Ctrl+Alt+L	Reapplies the Filter and re-sorts the data if you used any sort commands in the filter drop-down menus. Use when you are filtering a column of formulas whose value might have changed.

Ctrl+Shift+F3	Displays the Create Names from Selection dialog box to enable you to create names from row and column labels.
Ctrl+D	Fills down.
Ctrl+R	Fills to the right.
Ctrl+F3	Displays the Name Manager.
Ctrl+K	Inserts a hyperlink or enables you to edit the selected hyperlink.
Ctrl+; (semicolon)	Enters the date.
Ctrl+Shift+: (colon)	Enters the time.
Alt+down arrow	When a drop-down menu is selected, this opens the drop-down menu. Otherwise, it displays a drop-down menu of the values in the current column of a range to enable you to select a cell value from the menu.
Ctrl+Z or Alt+backspace	Undoes the last action.
= (equal sign)	Starts a formula.
Backspace	In the formula bar or while you're editing a cell, this deletes one character to the left. When you're not in edit mode, this clears the contents of the current cell and puts the cell in edit mode.
Enter	Completes a cell entry from the cell or formula bar.
Ctrl+Shift+Enter	When typing a formula, Ctrl+Shift+Enter marks the formula as an old style array formula. Since the introduction of Dynamic Arrays, Ctrl+Shift+Enter is not necessary unless you are trying to return just a portion of the array. For example, selecting J1:J3 and typing **=SORT(A:A)** followed by pressing Ctrl+Shift+Enter will limit the result to the first three sorted values.
Shift+F3	In a formula, this displays the Insert Function dialog box.
Ctrl+A	When the insertion point is to the right of a function name in a formula, this displays the Function Arguments dialog box. See also Select All in Table 4.1.
Ctrl+Shift+A	When the insertion point is to the right of a function name in a formula, this inserts the argument names and parentheses.
F3	Pastes a defined name into a formula.
Alt+= (equal sign)	Inserts an AutoSum formula with the SUM function.
Ctrl+Shift+" (quotation mark)	Copies the value from the cell above the active cell into the cell or the formula bar.
Ctrl+' (apostrophe)	Copies a formula from the cell above the active cell into the cell or the formula bar and places the cell in edit mode. Note that the formula is an exact copy; any references are not moved down by a row.
Ctrl+` (backtick)	Alternates between displaying cell values and displaying formulas.

F9	Calculates all worksheets in all open workbooks. When a portion of a formula is selected, calculate the selected portion and then press Enter or Ctrl+Shift+Enter (for array formulas) to replace the selected portion with the calculated value.
Shift+F9	Calculates the active worksheet.
Ctrl+Alt+F9	Calculates all worksheets in all open workbooks, regardless of whether they have changed since the last calculation.
Ctrl+Alt+Shift+F9	Rechecks dependent formulas and then calculates all cells in all open workbooks, including cells not marked as needing to be calculated.
F1	Displays Help.
F2	Edits the active cell and positions the insertion point at the end of the cell contents. If in-cell editing is turned off, this moves the insertion point to the formula bar. When you're editing a formula or a reference in a dialog box, F2 toggles between Point and Enter modes. If pressing backspace starts inserting cell references instead of moving back a character, press F2 and try again.
Delete	Removes cell contents (data and formulas) from selected cells without affecting cell formats or comments. In editing mode, this deletes the character to the right of the insertion point or deletes the selection.
Ctrl+Delete	Deletes text to the end of the line.
F7	Displays the Spelling dialog box.
Shift+F2	Adds or edits a cell note.
Ctrl+– (minus sign)	Displays the Delete dialog box.
Ctrl+Shift++ (plus sign)	Displays the Insert dialog box to insert blank cells.
Alt+' (apostrophe)	Displays the Style dialog box.
Ctrl+1	Displays the Format Cells dialog box when cells are selected. When a chart element or object is selected, this displays the Format task pane for that object.
Ctrl+2 or Ctrl+B	Toggles bold formatting.
Ctrl+3 or Ctrl+I	Toggles italic formatting.
Ctrl+4 or Ctrl+U	Toggles underline formatting.
Ctrl+Shift+~	Applies the General number format.
Ctrl+Shift+$	Applies the Currency format with two decimal places (negative numbers in parentheses).
Ctrl+Shift+%	Applies the Percentage format with no decimal places.
Ctrl+Shift+^	Applies the Scientific number format with two decimal places.
Ctrl+Shift+#	Applies the Date format with the day, month, and year.
Ctrl+Shift+@	Applies the Time format with the hour and minute as well as AM or PM.

Ctrl+Shift+!	Applies the Number format with two decimal places, thousands separator, and a minus sign (–) for negative values.
Ctrl+5	Applies or removes strikethrough.
Ctrl+9	Hides the selected rows.
Ctrl+Shift+((opening parenthesis)	Unhides any hidden rows within the selection.
Ctrl+0 (zero)	Hides the selected columns.
Ctrl+Shift+) (closing parenthesis)	Unhides any hidden columns within the selection. Although this shortcut key is shown as a ToolTip in the Home tab, it has not worked since Excel 2010, and the Excel team has no immediate plans to fix it.
Ctrl+Shift+&	Applies the outline border to the selected cells.
Ctrl+Shift+_ (underscore)	Removes the outline border from the selected cells.
Ctrl+U	Toggles the formula bar between collapsed and expanded.
Ctrl+6	Toggles between hiding and displaying objects.
Ctrl+8	In group and outline mode, this toggles the display of outline symbols.
Ctrl+F1	Collapses or expands the ribbon.
Alt or F10 or forward slash	Displays KeyTips.
Shift+F10	Opens the right-click menu for the selection.
Alt+Shift+F10	Displays the menu or message for an Error Checking button.
Alt+F11	Opens the Visual Basic for Applications Editor.
Alt+F8	Opens the Macros dialog box.
Spacebar	In a dialog box, this selects or clears a check box or performs the action for a selected button.
Ctrl+Tab	In a dialog box, this switches to the next tab.
Ctrl+Shift+Tab	In a dialog box, this switches to the previous tab.
Arrow keys	In a dialog box or open menu, this moves between options in an open drop-down menu or between options in a group of options.
End	When a menu is open, this selects the last item in the menu.
Alt+Shift+F1	Inserts a new worksheet to the left of the current worksheet.
F11	Creates a chart of the data in the current range in a new chart sheet.
Alt+F1	Creates a chart of the data in the current range in the current worksheet.
Alt+spacebar	Opens the Control menu for the Excel window. The Control menu is attached to the XL logo in the top left of the window.
Ctrl+F4	Closes the selected workbook window.
Alt+F4	Closes Excel.

Ctrl+F10	Maximizes or restores the selected workbook window.
Ctrl+F7	When a workbook is not maximized, this moves the entire workbook window. Press Ctrl+F7. Use the arrow keys to move the window. Press Enter when you're finished or Esc to cancel.
Ctrl+F8	Performs the Size command when a workbook is not maximized. Using the left or right arrow key expands the width of the window by moving the right edge of the window. Using the up or down arrow key moves the bottom edge of the window to shrink or stretch the window.
Shift+F6	Moves focus between the worksheet, ribbon, status bar, and task pane. For example, when the focus is on the status bar, you can use the arrows to move between the Record Macro, Normal, Page Layout, Page Break Preview, and Zoom icons.
Ctrl+F6	Moves between windows of a workbook. This would apply only if you used View, New Window.

Using my favorite shortcut keys

The problem with a list of hundreds of shortcut keys is that it is overwhelming. You cannot possibly absorb 238 new shortcut keys and start using them. The following sections cover some of my favorite shortcuts. Try to incorporate one new shortcut key every week into your Excel routine.

Quickly move between worksheets

Ctrl+Page Down jumps to the next worksheet. Ctrl+Page Up jumps to the previous worksheet. Suppose that you have 12 worksheets named Jan, Feb, Mar, ..., Dec. If you are currently on the Jan worksheet, hold down Ctrl and press Page Down five times to move to Jun.

Jumping to the bottom of data with Ctrl+arrow

Provided there are no blank cells in your data, press Ctrl+down arrow to move to the last row in the data set. Use Ctrl+up arrow to move to the first row in the data set.

Add the Shift key to select from the current cell to the bottom. If you have data in A2:J987654 and are in A2, you can hold down Ctrl+Shift while pressing the down arrow and then the right arrow to select all the data rows but exclude the headings in row 1.

Selecting the current region with Ctrl+*

Press Ctrl+* to select the current range. The current range is the whole data set, in all directions from the current cell until Excel hits the edge of the worksheet or a completely blank row and column. On a desktop computer, pressing Ctrl and the asterisk on the numeric keypad does the trick.

Jumping to the next corner of a selection

You've just selected A2:J987654, but you are staring at the bottom-right corner of your data. Press Ctrl+period to move to the next corner of your data. Because you are at the bottom-right corner, it takes two presses of Ctrl+period to move to the top-left corner. Although this moves the active cell, it does not undo your selection.

Inside OUT

You might frequently run into a situation where the active cell is no longer in view.

This can happen when you use the scrollbars or if you select A2:J10000 by using Ctrl+Shift+Down Arrow and Ctrl+Shift+Right Arrow.

To bring the active cell back in to view, press Ctrl+Backspace.

Pop open the right-click menu using Shift+F10

When I do my seminars, people always ask why I don't use the right-click menus. I don't use them because my hand is not on the mouse! Pressing Shift+F10 opens the right-click menu. Use the up/down arrow keys to move to various menu choices and the right-arrow key to open a fly-out menu. When you get to the item you want, press Enter to select it.

Crossing tasks off your list with Ctrl+5

I love to make lists, and I love to cross stuff off my list. It makes me feel like I've gotten stuff done. Select a cell and press Ctrl+5 to apply strikethrough to the cell.

Date stamp or time stamp using Ctrl+; or Ctrl+:

Here is an easy way to remember this shortcut. What time is it right now? It is 11:21 here. There is a colon in the time. Press Ctrl+colon to enter the current time in the active cell.

Need the current date? Same keystroke, minus the Shift key. Pressing Ctrl+semicolon enters the current time.

Note that this is not the same as using `=NOW()` or `=TODAY()`. Those functions change over time. These shortcuts mark the time or date that you pressed the key, and the value does not change.

Repeating the last task with F4

Suppose that you just selected a cell and did Home, Delete, Delete Cells, Delete Entire Row, OK. You need to delete 24 more rows in various spots throughout your data set.

Select a cell in the next row to delete and press F4, which repeats the last command but on the currently selected cell.

Select a cell in the next row to delete and press F4. Before you know it, all 24 rows are deleted without your having to click Home, Delete, Delete Cells, Delete Entire Row, OK 24 times.

The F4 key works with 92 percent of the commands you will use. Try it. You'll love it. It'll be obvious when you try to use one of the unusual commands that cannot be redone with F4.

Adding dollar signs to a reference with F4

That's right—two of my favorites in a row use F4. When you are entering a formula, and you need to change A1 to $A$1, click F4 while the insertion point is touching A1. You can press F4 again to freeze only the row with A$1. Press F4 again to freeze the column with $A1. Press again to toggle back to A1.

Choosing items from a slicer

It is somewhat bizarre, but you can now use shortcut keys to jump into a slicer. Using the new Multi-Select icon, you can then select or deselect items in the slicer. To get to the slicer, use Ctrl+G to display the Go To dialog box. Press S to open Go To Special. Type **B** for Objects and press Enter to select the first object on the worksheet. You might have to press Tab to get to the slicer, but then you can navigate through the slicer using the arrow keys. Pressing Enter or the spacebar on an item toggles that item. To exit the slicer, use Ctrl+G, type a cell address such as A1, and press Enter.

Finding the one thing that takes you too much time

The shortcuts in this section are the ones I learned over the course of 20 years. They were all for tasks that I had to do repeatedly. In your job, watch for any tasks you are doing over and over, especially things that take several mouse clicks. When you identify one, try to find a shortcut key that will save you time.

TIP

When you perform commands with the mouse, do all the steps except the last one. Hover over the command until the ToolTip appears. Many times, the ToolTip tells you of the keyboard shortcut.

Using Excel 2003 keyboard accelerators

In legacy versions of Excel, most menu items included one underlined letter. In those versions, you could hold down the Alt key while pressing the underlined letter to invoke the menu item. In the Excel 2003 screen shown in Figure 4.6, you can display the Edit menu by pressing Alt+E, and you can select Edit, Fill, Justify by pressing Alt+E+I+J.

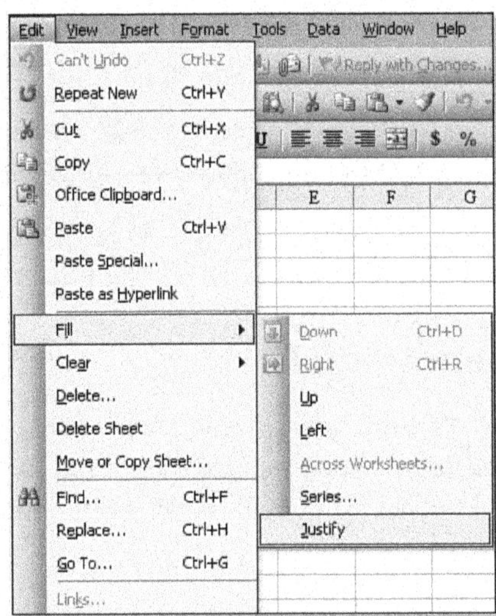

Figure 4.6 Pressing Alt+E+I+J performs Edit, Fill, Justify.

Instead of pressing Alt+E+I+J all at once, when the Edit menu is displayed, you can display the Fill fly-out menu by pressing the I key. Then you can perform the Justify command by pressing J.

If you have advanced Excel skills, you probably have a few of these commands memorized, such as Alt+E+I+J for Edit, Fill, Justify; Alt+E+S+V for Edit, Paste Special, Values; and Alt+D+L for Data Validation. If you have some of these commands memorized, when you hear that the ribbon has replaced the legacy menu, you might be worried that you have to relearn all the shortcut keys. However, there is good news for the power Excel gurus who have favorite Alt shortcut keys burned into their minds—most of them still work as they did in Excel 2003.

If you regularly use the Excel 2003 keyboard accelerators but have to look at the screen to use them, you should start using the new keyboard accelerators discussed at the beginning of this chapter.

Invoking an Excel 2003 Alt shortcut

In Excel 2003, the main menus are File, Edit, View, Insert, Format, Tools, Data, Window, and Help. The keyboard accelerator commands in Excel 2003 are Alt+F, Alt+E, Alt+V, Alt+I, Alt+O, Alt+T, Alt+D, Alt+W, and Alt+H.

If you are moving from Excel 2003 to Excel for Microsoft 365, you will have the best success when trying to access commands on the Edit, View, Insert, Format, Tools, and Data menus. None of the keyboard accelerators associated with Window or Help work in Excel today. Alt+H takes you to the Home tab instead of the few commands on the Help menu, and Alt+W takes you to the View tab.

Some of the keyboard shortcuts associated with the File menu in Excel 2003 continue to work in Excel today. Pressing Alt+F opens the File menu. In Excel 2003, pressing Alt+F+O performs File, Open. It happens that O is the shortcut on the File menu for Open, so pressing Alt+F+O in Excel also performs File, Open.

TIP

You will have to train yourself to pause briefly after typing the first letter in the legacy shortcut key sequence. For example, press Alt+E, pause for a brief moment to allow Excel to display the Office Access Key window, and then press S, V for Edit, Paste Special, Values. If you do not pause, the second letter is lost because Excel displays the pop-up Office Key Sequence window.

For the shortcut keys Alt+E, Alt+V, Alt+I, Alt+O, Alt+T, and Alt+D, Excel switches into Office 2003 Access Key mode. In this mode, a ToolTip appears over the ribbon, indicating which letters you have typed so far (see Figure 4.7). When you have entered enough letters, the command is invoked. If you have forgotten the sequence, you can press Esc to exit the Excel 2003 Access Key mode.

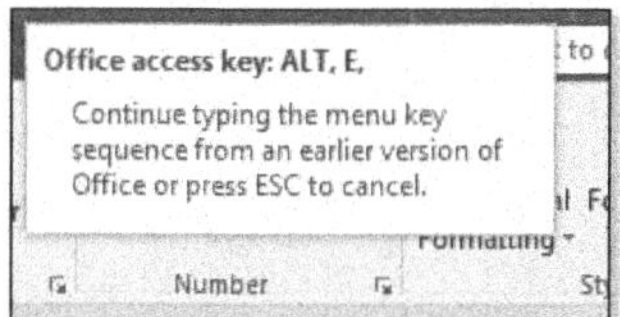

Figure 4.7 The Office 2003 access key ToolTip shows which keys you have used so far while entering a legacy shortcut.

Determining which commands work in legacy mode

If you try a command that no longer works in Excel, nothing happens. Several commands don't make sense in the framework of Excel, so they have been deprecated.

Table 4.6 lists the legacy keyboard commands and indicates which of them continue to work in Excel for Microsoft 365.

Table 4.6 Excel legacy keyboard commands

Legacy shortcut	Excel?	Command
Alt+F+N	Yes	File, New
Alt+F+O	Yes	File, Open
Alt+F+C	Yes	File, Close
Alt+F+S	Yes	File, Save

Alt+F+A	Yes	File, Save As
Alt+F+G	No	File, Save As Web Page
Alt+F+W	No	File, Save Workspace
Alt+F+H	No	File, File Search
Alt+F+M	No	File, Permission
Alt+F+E	No	File, Check Out or Check In (toggle)
Alt+F+R	No	File, Version History
Alt+F+B	No	File, Web Page Preview
Alt+F+U	No	File, Page Setup
Alt+F+T+S	No	File, Print Area, Set Print Area
Alt+F+T+C	No	File, Print Area, Clear Print Area
Alt+F+V	No	File, Print Preview
Alt+F+P	Yes as Alt+F+P+P	File, Print
Alt+F+D+M	No	File, Send To, Mail Recipient
Alt+F+D+S	No	File, Send To, Original Sender
Alt+F+D+C	No	File, Send To, Mail Recipient (For Review)
Alt+F+D+A	No	File, Send To, Mail Recipient (As Attachment)
Alt+F+D+R	No	File, Send To, Routing Recipient
Alt+F+D+E	No	File, Send To, Exchange Folder
Alt+F+D+O	No	File, Send To, Online Meeting Participant
Alt+F+D+X	No	File, Send To, Recipient Using Internet Fax Service
Alt+F+I	No	File, Properties
Alt+F+1	Yes	File, 1
Alt+F+2	Yes	File, 2
Alt+F+3	Yes	File, 3
Alt+F+4	Yes	File, 4
Alt+F+5	Yes	File, 5
Alt+F+6	Yes	File, 6
Alt+F+7	Yes	File, 7
Alt+F+8	Yes	File, 8
Alt+F+9	Yes	File, 9
Alt+F+T	No	File, Options

Alt+F+X	Yes	File, Exit
Alt+E+U	Yes	Edit, Undo
Alt+E+R	Yes	Edit, Repeat
Alt+E+T	Yes	Edit, Cut
Alt+E+C	Yes	Edit, Copy
Alt+E+B	Yes	Edit, Office Clipboard
Alt+E+P	Yes	Edit, Paste
Alt+E+S	Yes	Edit, Paste Special
Alt+E+H	No	Edit, Paste As Hyperlink
Alt+E+I+D	Yes	Edit, Fill, Down
Alt+E+I+R	Yes	Edit, Fill, Right
Alt+E+I+U	Yes	Edit, Fill, Up
Alt+E+I+L	Yes	Edit, Fill, Left
Alt+E+I+A	Yes	Edit, Fill, Across Worksheets
Alt+E+I+S	Yes	Edit, Fill, Series
Alt+E+I+J	Yes	Edit, Fill, Justify
Alt+E+A+A	Yes	Edit, Clear, All
Alt+E+A+F	Yes	Edit, Clear, Formats
Alt+E+A+C	Yes	Edit, Clear, Contents
Alt+E+A+M	Yes	Edit, Clear, Comments
Alt+E+D	Yes	Edit, Delete
Alt+E+L	Yes	Edit, Delete Sheet
Alt+E+M	Yes	Edit, Move Or Copy Sheet
Alt+E+F	Yes	Edit, Find
Alt+E+E	Yes	Edit, Replace
Alt+E+G	Yes	Edit, Go To
Alt+E+K	Yes	Edit, Links
Alt+E+O	No	Edit, Object
Alt+E+O+V	No	Edit, Object, Convert
Alt+V+N	Yes	View, Normal
Alt+V+P	Yes	View, Page Break Preview
Alt+V+K	No	View, Task Pane

Alt+V+T+C	No	View, Toolbars, Customize
Alt+V+F	Yes	View, Formula Bar
Alt+V+S	No	View, Status Bar
Alt+V+H	Yes	View, Header And Footer
Alt+V+C	Yes	View, Comments
Alt+V+V	Yes	View, Custom Views
Alt+V+U	Yes	View, Full Screen (Caution: Use the maximize button to return.)
Alt+V+Z	Yes	View, Zoom
Alt+I+E	Yes	Insert, Cells
Alt+I+R	Yes	Insert, Rows
Alt+I+C	Yes	Insert, Columns
Alt+I+W	Yes	Insert, Worksheet
Alt+I+H	Yes	Insert, Chart
Alt+I+S	Yes	Insert, Symbol
Alt+I+B	Yes	Insert, Page Break
Alt+I+A	Yes	Insert, Reset All Page Breaks
Alt+I+F	Yes	Insert, Function
Alt+I+N+D	Yes	Insert, Name, Define
Alt+I+N+P	Yes	Insert, Name, Paste
Alt+I+N+C	Yes	Insert, Name, Create
Alt+I+N+A	Yes	Insert, Name, Apply
Alt+I+N+L	Yes	Insert, Name, Label
Alt+I+M	Yes	Insert, Comment (Legacy)
Alt+I+A	Yes	Insert, Ink Annotations
Alt+I+P+C	Yes	Insert, Picture, Clip Art
Alt+I+P+F	Yes	Insert, Picture, From File
Alt+I+P+S	Yes	Insert, Picture, From Scanner Or Camera
Alt+I+P+D	Yes	Insert, Picture, Ink Drawing And Writing
Alt+I+P+A	No	Insert, Picture, AutoShapes
Alt+I+P+W	No	Insert, Picture, WordArt
Alt+I+P+O	No	Insert, Picture, Organization Chart
Alt+I+G	No	Insert, Diagram

Alt+I+O	Yes	Insert, Object
Alt+I+I	Yes	Insert, Hyperlink
Alt+O+E	Yes	Format, Cells
Alt+O+R+E	Yes	Format, Row, Height
Alt+O+R+A	Yes	Format, Row, AutoFit
Alt+O+R+H	Yes	Format, Row, Hide
Alt+O+R+U	Yes	Format, Row, Unhide
Alt+O+C+W	Yes	Format, Column, Width
Alt+O+C+A	Yes	Format, Column, AutoFit Selection
Alt+O+C+H	Yes	Format, Column, Hide
Alt+O+C+U	Yes	Format, Column, Unhide
Alt+O+C+S	Yes	Format, Column, Standard Width
Alt+O+H+R	Yes	Format, Sheet, Rename
Alt+O+H+H	Yes	Format, Sheet, Hide
Alt+O+H+U	Yes	Format, Sheet, Unhide
Alt+O+H+B	Yes	Format, Sheet, Background
Alt+O+H+T	Yes	Format, Sheet, Tab Color
Alt+O+A	No	Format, AutoFormat
Alt+O+D	Yes	Format, Conditional Formatting
Alt+O+S	Yes	Format, Style
Alt+T+S	Yes	Tools, Spelling
Alt+T+R	Yes	Tools, Research
Alt+T+K	Yes	Tools, Error Checking
Alt+T+H+H	No	Tools, Speech, Speech Recognition
Alt+T+H+T	No	Tools, Speech, Show Text To Speech Toolbar
Alt+T+D	Yes	Tools, Shared Workspace
Alt+T+B	Yes	Tools, Share Workbook
Alt+T+T+H	Yes	Tools, Track Changes, Highlight Changes
Alt+T+T+A	Yes	Tools, Track Changes, Accept Or Reject Changes
Alt+T+W	Yes	Tools, Compare And Merge Workbooks
Alt+T+P+P	Yes	Tools, Protection, Protect Sheet
Alt+T+P+A	Yes	Tools, Protection, Allow Users To Edit Ranges

Alt+T+P+W	Yes	Tools, Protection, Protect Workbook
Alt+T+P+S	Yes	Tools, Protection, Protect And Share Workbook
Alt+T+N+M	Yes	Tools, Online Collaboration, Meet Now
Alt+T+N+S	Yes	Tools, Online Collaboration, Schedule Meeting
Alt+T+N+W	Yes	Tools, Online Collaboration, Web Discussions
Alt+T+N+N	Yes	Tools, Online Collaboration, End Review
Alt+T+G	Yes	Tools, Goal Seek
Alt+T+E	Yes	Tools, Scenarios
Alt+T+U+T	Yes	Tools, Formula Auditing, Trace Precedents
Alt+T+U+D	Yes	Tools, Formula Auditing, Trace Dependents
Alt+T+U+E	Yes	Tools, Formula Auditing, Trace Error
Alt+T+U+A	Yes	Tools, Formula Auditing, Remove All Arrows
Alt+T+U+F	Yes	Tools, Formula Auditing, Evaluate Formula
Alt+T+U+W	Yes	Tools, Formula Auditing, Show Watch Window
Alt+T+U+M	Yes	Tools, Formula Auditing, Formula Auditing Mode
Alt+T+U+S	No	Tools, Formula Auditing, Show Formula Auditing Toolbar
Alt+T+V	Yes	Tools, Solver
Alt+T+M+M	Yes	Tools, Macro, Macros
Alt+T+M+R	Yes	Tools, Macro, Record New Macro
Alt+T+M+S	Yes	Tools, Macro, Security
Alt+T+M+V	Yes	Tools, Macro, Visual Basic Editor
Alt+T+M+E	No	Tools, Macro, Microsoft Script Editor
Alt+T+I	Yes	Tools, Add-Ins
Alt+T+C	No	Tools, COM Add-Ins
Alt+T+A	Yes	Tools, AutoCorrect Options
Alt+T+C	No	Tools, Customize
Alt+T+O	No	Tools, Options
Alt+T+D	No	Tools, Data Analysis
Alt+D+S	Yes	Data, Sort
Alt+D+F+F	Yes	Data, Filter, AutoFilter
Alt+D+F+S	Yes	Data, Filter, Show All
Alt+D+F+A	Yes	Data, Filter, Advanced Filter

Alt+D+O	Yes	Data, Form
Alt+D+B	Yes	Data, Subtotals
Alt+D+L	Yes	Data, Validation
Alt+D+T	Yes	Data, Table
Alt+D+E	Yes	Data, Text To Columns
Alt+D+N	Yes	Data, Consolidate
Alt+D+G+H	Yes	Data, Group And Outline, Hide Detail
Alt+D+G+S	Yes	Data, Group And Outline, Show Detail
Alt+D+G+G	Yes	Data, Group And Outline, Group
Alt+D+G+U	Yes	Data, Group And Outline, Ungroup
Alt+D+G+A	Yes	Data, Group And Outline, Auto Outline
Alt+D+G+C	Yes	Data, Group And Outline, Clear Outline
Alt+D+G+E	Yes	Data, Group And Outline, Settings
Alt+D+P	Yes	Data, PivotTable And PivotChart Report
Alt+D+D+D	Yes	Data, Import External Data, Import Data
Alt+D+D+W	Yes	Data, Import External Data, New Web Query
Alt+D+D+N	Yes	Data, Import External Data, New Database Query
Alt+D+D+E	Yes	Data, Import External Data, List
Alt+D+I+D	No	Data, List, Discard Changes And Refresh
Alt+D+I+B	No	Data, List, Hide Border Of Inactive Lists
Alt+D+X+I	Yes	Data, XML, Import
Alt+D+X+E	Yes	Data, XML, Export
Alt+D+X+R	Yes	Data, XML, Refresh XML Data
Alt+D+X+X	Yes	Data, XML, XML Source
Alt+D+X+P	Yes	Data, XML, XML Map Properties
Alt+D+X+Q	Yes	Data, XML, Edit Query
Alt+D+X+A	Yes	Data, XML, XML Expansion Packs Edit Query
Alt+D+D+A	Yes	Data, Import External Data, Data Range Properties
Alt+D+D+M	Yes	Data, Import External Data, Parameters
Alt+D+I+C	Yes	Data, List, Create List
Alt+D+I+R	Yes	Data, List, Resize List
Alt+D+I+T	Yes	Data, List, Total Row

Alt+D+I+V	Yes	Data, List, Convert To Range
Alt+D+I+P	Yes	Data, List, Publish List
Alt+D+I+L	No	Data, List, View List On Server
Alt+D+I+U	No	Data, List, Unlink List
Alt+D+I+Y	No	Data, List, Synchronize
Alt+D+R	Yes	Data, Refresh Data
Alt+W+N	No	Window, New Window
Alt+W+A	No	Window, Arrange
Alt+W+B	No	Window, Compare Side By Side With Filename
Alt+W+H	No	Window, Hide
Alt+W+U	No	Window, Unhide
Alt+W+S	No	Window, Split
Alt+W+F	No	Window, Freeze Panes
Alt+W+1	No	Window, 1
Alt+W+2	No	Window, 2
Alt+W+3	No	Window, 3
Alt+W+4	No	Window, 4
Alt+W+5	No	Window, 5
Alt+W+6	No	Window, 6
Alt+W+7	No	Window, 7
Alt+W+8	No	Window, 8
Alt+W+9	No	Window, 9
Alt+W+M	No	Window, More Windows
Alt+H+H	No	Help, Microsoft Excel Help
Alt+H+O	No	Help, Show The Office Assistant
Alt+H+M	No	Help, Microsoft Office Online
Alt+H+C	No	Help, Contact Us
Alt+H+L	No	Help, Lotus 1-2-3 Help
Alt+H+K	No	Help, Check For Updates
Alt+H+R	No	Help, Detect And Repair
Alt+H+V	No	Help, Activate Product
Alt+H+F	No	Help, Customer Feedback Options
Alt+H+A	No	Help, About Microsoft Office Excel

Some people like using Alt+F+T+S in Excel 2003 for File, Print Area, Set Print Area. If you are one of those people, you will be unhappy to hear that your favorite shortcut key is not supported in Excel. Instead, use Alt+P+R+S. However, most of the powerful and common shortcut keys are still available, so there is a good chance that your knowledge of past shortcut keys will help when you are using Excel today.

PART II

Calculating with Excel

CHAPTER 5

Understanding formulas

Excel's forté is performing calculations. When you use Excel, you typically use a combination of cells with numbers and cells with formulas. After you design a spreadsheet to calculate something, you can change the numbers used in the assumption cells and then watch Excel instantly calculate new results.

Getting the most from this chapter

Even if you think you know about formulas, you should review these points:

- Everyone should read the "Double-Click the Fill Handle to Copy a Formula" section. Somehow, most people have learned to drag the fill handle to copy a formula. This leads to horrible frustration on long data sets, as they go flying past the end of the data. This simple but powerful trick is the one that universally amazes attendees of my seminar.
- Honestly answer this question: Do you really understand the difference between cell H1 and cell $H$1? If you think the latter has anything to do with currency, you need to review the "Overriding Relative Behavior: Absolute Cell References" section thoroughly. This isn't a trick, but one of the fundamental building blocks to creating Excel worksheets. Roughly 5 percent of the people in a Power Excel seminar do not understand this concept, and about 70 percent of the people in a community computer club presentation do not understand it. If you don't know when and why to use the dollar signs, you are in good company with 20 million other people using Excel. It is worth taking time to learn this essential technique.
- There are three ways to enter formulas, and I believe my preferred way is the best. I probably will not convince you to change, but when you understand my way, you can enter formulas far faster than by using the other two ways. To get a good understanding of the alternatives, read the "Three methods of entering formulas" section later in this chapter.
- The new Dynamic Array formulas introduced in late 2019 mean that a single formula can return answers to many cells, without having to press Ctrl+Shift+Enter.

Introduction to formulas

This chapter and Chapter 6, "Controlling formulas," deal with formula basics. The chapters Chapter 7, "Understanding functions," and Chapter 9, "Using powerful functions: logical, lookup, and database functions," introduce adding functions to your formulas. Chapter 10 covers new concepts including LET, LAMBDA, and Data Types. Chapter 11, "Connecting worksheets and workbooks," introduces formulas that calculate data found on other worksheets or in other workbooks. Chapter 12, "Dynamic array formulas and names in Excel," provides interesting examples such as 3D formulas and the all-powerful array formulas.

Because of the record-oriented nature of spreadsheets, you can generally build a formula once and then copy that formula to hundreds or thousands of cells without changing anything in the formula.

Formulas versus values

When looking at an Excel grid, you cannot tell the difference between a cell with a formula and one that contains numbers. To see if a cell contains a number or a formula, select the cell. Look in the formula bar. If the formula bar contains a number, as shown in Figure 5.1, you know that it is a static value. If the formula bar contains a formula, you know that the number shown in the grid is the result of a formula calculation (see Figure 5.2). Keep in mind that formulas start with an equal sign.

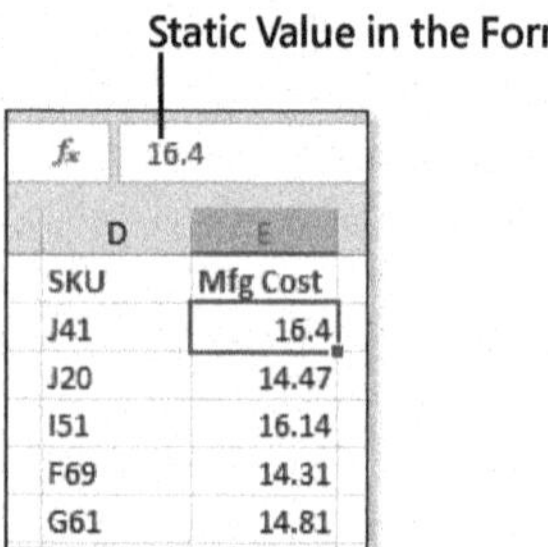

Figure 5.1 The formula bar reveals whether a value is a static number or a calculation. In this case, cell E2 contains a static number.

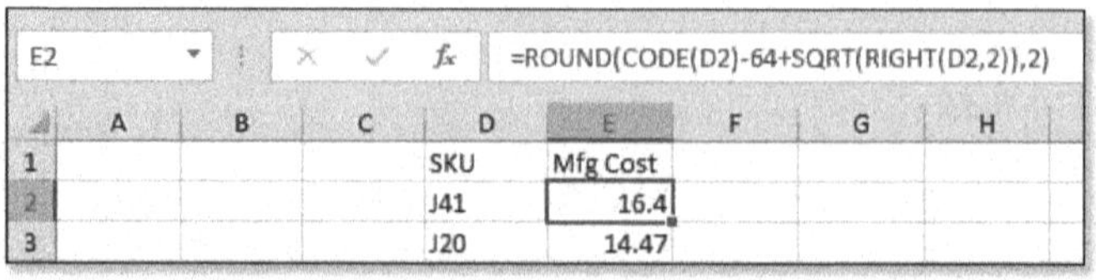

E2 =ROUND(CODE(D2)-64+SQRT(RIGHT(D2,2)),2)

	A	B	C	D	E	F	G	H
1				SKU	Mfg Cost			
2				J41	16.4			
3				J20	14.47			

Figure 5.2 In this case, cell E2 contains the result of a formula calculation. A formula starts with an equal sign.

Entering your first formula

Your first formula was probably a `SUM` function, entered with the AutoSum button. However, this discussion is talking about a pure mathematical formula that uses a value in a cell that's added, subtracted, divided, or multiplied by a number or another cell.

> **TROUBLESHOOTING**
>
> **Although your first formula was likely a `SUM` function, many people mistakenly believe that every formula must include the `SUM` function.**
>
> **If you need to multiply A2 by B2 and subtract C2, the formula should simply be `=A2*B2-C2`. There is no need to wrap this formula in the `SUM` function like this: `=SUM(A2*B2-C2)`.**

Billions of variations of formulas can be used. Everyday life throws situations at you that can be solved with a formula. Keep these important points in mind as you start tinkering with your own formulas:

- Every formula starts with an equal sign.
- Entering formulas is just like typing an equation in a calculator with one exception (see the next point).
- If one of the terms in your formula is already stored in a cell in Excel, you can point to that cell's address instead of typing the number into that cell. Using this method enables you to change the value in one cell and then watch all the formulas recalculate.

To illustrate these points, see the steps to building a basic formula included in the following example.

Building a formula

You want to enter a formula to calculate a target sales price, as shown in Figure 5.3. Cell D2 shows the product cost. In column E, you want to calculate the list price as two times the cost plus $3.

E2 | fx =2*D2+3

	A	B	C	D	E
1			SKU	Mfg Cost	List Price
2			J41	16.4	35.8
3			J20	14.47	

Figure 5.3 The formula in cell E2 recalculates if the value in cell D2 changes.

To enter a formula, follow these steps:

1. Select cell E2.

2. Type an equal sign. The equal sign tells Excel that you are starting a formula.

3. Type 2*D2 to indicate that you want to multiply two times the value in cell D2.

4. Type +3 to add three to the result. If your formula reads =2*D2+3, proceed to step 5. Otherwise, use the backspace key to correct the formula.

5. Press Enter. Excel calculates the formula in cell E2.

By default, Excel usually moves the cell pointer down or to the right after you finish entering a formula. You should move the cell pointer back to cell E2 to inspect the formula, as shown in Figure 5.3. Note that Excel shows a number in the grid, but the formula bar reveals the formula behind the number.

The relative nature of formulas

The formula =2*D2+3 really says, "multiply two by the cell immediately to the left of me and then add three." If you need to put this formula in cells E3 to E999, you do not need to re-enter the formula 997 times. Instead, copy the formula and paste it to all the cells. When you do, Excel copies the essence of the formula: "Multiply two by the cell to the left of me and add three." As you copy the formula to cell E3, the formula becomes =2*D3+3. Excel handles all this automatically. Figure 5.4 shows the formula after it is copied.

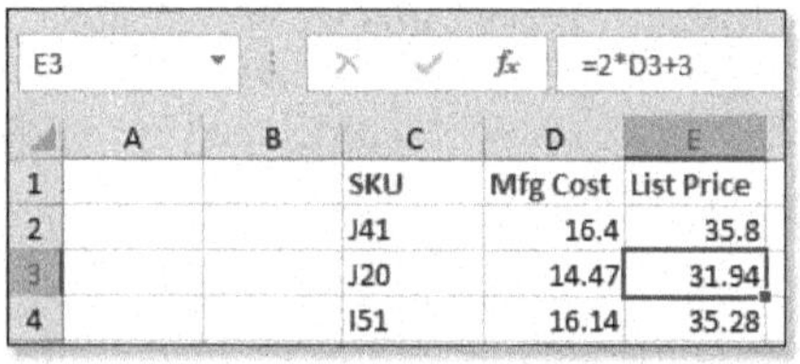

E3 =2*D3+3

	A	B	C	D	E
1			SKU	Mfg Cost	List Price
2			J41	16.4	35.8
3			J20	14.47	31.94
4			I51	16.14	35.28

Figure 5.4 After you paste the formula, Excel automatically updates the cell reference to point to the current row.

Excel's capability to change D2 to D3 in the formula is called *relative referencing*. This is the default behavior of a reference. Sometimes, you do not want Excel to change a reference as the formula is copied, as explained in the next section.

Overriding relative behavior: absolute cell references

Relative referencing, which is Excel's ability to change a formula as it is copied, is what makes spreadsheets so useful. At times, however, you need part of a formula to always point at one particular cell. This happens a lot when you have a setting at the top of the worksheet, such as a growth rate or a tax rate. It would be nice to change this cell once and have all the formulas use the new rate.

The following example sets up a sample worksheet that exhibits this problem and shows how to use an arcane notation style to solve the problem. When you see a reference with two dollar signs, such as $G$1, this indicates an absolute reference to G1. An *absolute reference* is a cell or range address in which the row numbers and the column letters are locked and do not change during copying. Absolute references have a dollar sign before each column letter and each row number. Examples include $G$1 and $T$2:$W$99.

Suppose that you have a sales tax factor in a single cell at the top of a worksheet. After you enter the formula =C2*G1, it accurately calculates the tax in cell D2, as shown in Figure 5.5.

D2 =C2*G1

	A	B	C	D	E	F	G
1	SKU	Mfg Cost	List Price	Sales Tax		Tax Factor	6.25%
2	J41	16.4	35.8	2.24			
3	J20	14.47	31.94				
4	I51	16.14	35.28				

Figure 5.5 This formula works fine in row 2.

However, when you copy the same formula to cell D3, you get a zero as the result. As you can see in Figure 5.6, Excel correctly changed cell C2 to C3 in the copied formula. However, Excel also changed G1 to G2. Because there is nothing in G2, the formula calculates a zero.

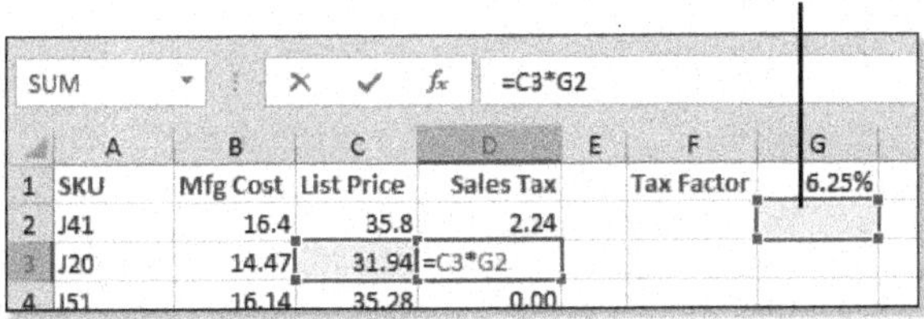

The formula now points to empty cell G2.
SUM
=C3*G2
A B C D E F G
1 SKU Mfg Cost List Price Sales Tax Tax Factor 6.25%
2 J41 16.4 35.8 2.24
3 J20 14.47 31.94 =C3*G2
4 I51 16.14 35.28 0.00

Figure 5.6 This formula fails in row 3.

Because the sales tax factor is only in G1, you want Excel to always point to G1. To make this happen, you need to build the original formula as =C2*$G$1. The two dollar signs tell Excel that you do not want to have the reference change as the formula is copied. The $ before the G freezes the reference to always point to column G. The $ before the 1 freezes the reference to always point to row 1. Now, when you copy this formula from cell D2 to other cells in column D, Excel changes the formula to =C3*$G$1, as shown in Figure 5.7.

D3 =C3*$G$1

	A	B	C	D	E	F	G	H
1	SKU	Mfg Cost	List Price	Sales Tax		Tax Factor	6.25%	
2	J41	16.4	35.8	2.24				
3	J20	14.47	31.94	2.00				
4	I51	16.14	35.28	2.21				
5	F69	14.31	31.62	1.98				

Figure 5.7 The dollar signs in the formula make sure that the copied formula always points to cell G1.

To recap, a reference with two dollars signs is called an *absolute reference*.

If you are never going to copy the formula to the left or right, you can safely use =C2*G$1. This formula freezes only the row number. Given the shape of the current data, it is likely that using a single dollar sign will be valid.

Using mixed references to combine features of relative and absolute references

In some situations, you might want to build a reference that has only one dollar sign. For example, in Figure 5.8, you want to use the monthly bonus rate in row 3, but you want to allow the column to change. In this case, the formula for cell B13 would be =B6*B$3.

B13 =B6*B$3

	A	B	C	D	E	F	G
1	Widget Sales Bonus Calculation						
2							
3	Bonus	3%	2%	0%	2%	3%	1%
4							
5	$ Sold	Jan	Feb	Mar	Apr	May	Jun
6	Rob	6237	9009	5247	9207	7029	6435
7	Matt	7722	5544	6138	5445	9603	5544
8	Ken	8712	7524	6237	6336	8415	7623
9	Miguel	5148	7524	9603	5049	5643	5445
10	Kasper	5841	6534	8118	8910	9009	9405
11							
12	Bonus	Jan	Feb	Mar	Apr	May	Jun
13	Rob	187.11	180.18	0.00	184.14	210.87	64.35
14	Matt	231.66	110.88	0.00	108.90	288.09	55.44
15	Ken	261.36	150.48	0.00	126.72	252.45	76.23
16	Miguel	154.44	150.48	0.00	100.98	169.29	54.45
17	Kasper	175.23	130.68	0.00	178.20	270.27	94.05

Figure 5.8 By having the dollar sign before the 3 in B$3, you lock the reference to row 3 but allow the formula to point to columns D, E, and so on as you copy the formula.

When you copy this formula, it always points to the bonus amount in row 3, but the remaining elements of the formula are relative. For example, the formula in E15 is =E8*E$3, which multiplies Ken's April sales by the April bonus rate.

There are two kinds of mixed references. One mixed reference freezes the row number and allows the column letter to change, as in A$1. The other mixed reference freezes the column letter but allows the row number to change, as in $A1. No one has thought up clever names to distinguish between these references, so they are simply called *mixed references*.

To illustrate the other kind of mixed reference, as shown in Figure 5.9, suppose you want a single formula to multiply the daily rate from column A by the number of days in row 4. This formula requires both kinds of mixed references.

SUM | =$A6*C$5

	A	B	C	D	E	F	G
1		XYZ Tool Rental					
2		Price List					
3							
4			------- Number of Hours ---->				
5	Per Hour	Item	4	8	24	48	72
6	13.50	Aerator TA-17D Split Drive	=$A6*C$5				
7	18.00	Aerator TA-25D Split Drive					
8	10.75	Aerator Tow Behind 36" w/weight canisters					
9	10.00	Auger One Man					

Figure 5.9 You can create a formula by using a combination of dollar signs to allow cell C6 to be copied to all cells in the table.

In this case, you want the cell A6 reference to always point to column A, even when the formula is copied to the right. Therefore, the A6 portion of the formula should be entered as $A6. You also want the C5 portion of the formula to always point to row 5, even when the formula is copied down the rows. Therefore, the C5 portion of the formula should be entered as C$5.

Using the F4 key to simplify dollar sign entry

In the preceding section, you entered quite a few dollar signs in formulas. The good news is that you do not have to type the dollar signs! Instead, immediately after entering a reference, while the cell is still in edit mode, press the F4 key to toggle the reference from a relative reference to an absolute reference, which automatically has the dollar signs before the row and column. If you press F4 again, the reference toggles to a mixed reference with a dollar sign before the row number. When you press F4 once again, the reference toggles to a mixed reference with a dollar sign before the column letter. Pressing F4 one more time returns the reference to a relative reference. You might find it easier to choose the right reference by looking at the various reference options offered by the F4 key.

The following sequence shows how the F4 key works while you are entering a formula. This particular example was included because it requires two types of mixed references.

The important concept is that you start pressing F4 after typing a cell reference but before you type a mathematical operator:

1. Type =**A6**.
2. Before typing the asterisk to indicate multiplication, press the F4 key. On the first press of F4, the reference changes to =$A$6.
3. Press the F4 key again. The reference changes to A$6 to freeze the reference to row 6. This still isn't right because freezing the reference to row 6 will not help.
4. Press F4 one more time. Excel locks just the column, changing the reference to =$A6. This is the version of the reference you want. As you copy the formula across, the formula always points back to column A. As you copy the formula down, the row number in this reference is allowed to change to point to other rows.
5. To continue the formula, type an asterisk to indicate multiplication and then click cell C5 with the mouse. Press F4 twice to change C5 to a reference that locks only the row (that is, C$5).
6. Press Enter to accept the formula.
7. When you copy the formula from cell C6 to the range C6:G28, the formula automatically multiplies the rate in column A by the number of days in row 5. Figure 5.10 shows the copied formula in cell E9. The formula correctly multiplies the 10-dollar rate in cell A9 by the 24 hours figure in cell E5.

SUM | =$A9*E$5

	A	B	C	D	E	F	G
1		XYZ Tool Rental					
2		Price List					
3							
4			------- Number of Hours ---->				
5	Per Hour	Item	4	8	24	48	72
6	13.50	Aerator TA-17D Split Drive	$54.00	$108.00	$324.00	$648.00	$972.00
7	18.00	Aerator TA-25D Split Drive	$72.00	$144.00	$432.00	$864.00	$1,296.00
8	10.75	Aerator Tow Behind 36" w/weight canisters	$43.00	$86.00	$258.00	$516.00	$774.00
9	10.00	Auger One Man	$40.00	$80.00	=$A9*E$5	$480.00	$720.00

Figure 5.10 By using the correct combination of row and column mixed references, you can enter this formula once and successfully copy it to the entire rectangular range.

Using F4 after a formula is entered

The F4 trick described in the preceding section works immediately after you enter a reference. If you try to change cell A6 after you type the asterisk, pressing the F4 key has no effect.

However, you can still use F4 by clicking somewhere in the formula bar adjacent to the characters A6. Pressing F4 now adds dollar signs to that reference.

> NOTE
>
> **After you press F4 again, Excel returns the reference to the relative state A6. As you continue to press F4, Excel toggles between the four modes. It is fine to toggle between them all and then choose the correct one. If you accidentally toggle past the $A6 version, just keep pressing F4 until the correct mode comes up again.**

Using F4 on a rectangular range

Some functions allow you to specify a rectangular range. For example, in Figure 5.11, you would like to enter a formula to calculate year-to-date sales. Although `=SUM(B2:B13)` works for cell C13, you cannot copy this formula to the other cells in the column. To copy this formula, you need to change the formula to `=SUM(B$2:B13)`.

SUM | =SUM(B2:B13

	A	B	C	D	E
1	Date	Sales	YTD Sales		
2	Jan	41610			
3	Feb	58680			
4	Mar	53670			
5	Apr	36240			
6	May	32880			
7	Jun	56070			
8	Jul	36150			
9	Aug	55740			
10	Sep	36960			
11	Oct	55770			
12	Nov	30420			
13	Dec	48240	=SUM(B2:B13		
14			SUM(**number1**, [number2], ...)		

Figure 5.11 Using F4 at this point never produces the desired result of B$2:B13.

At this point in the figure, you might be tempted to press the F4 key. This does not work. If you select B2:B13 with the mouse or arrow keys, pressing F4 now converts the reference to the fully absolute range $B$2:$B$13. Continuing to press F4 toggles to B$2:B$13, then $B2:$B13, and then B2:B13. Excel does not even attempt to go through the other 12 possible combinations of dollar signs to offer B$2:B13 eventually. If you typed B2:B13, pressing F4 adjusts only the B13 reference.

In this case, you need to click the insertion point just before, just after, or in the middle of the characters B2 in the formula. If you then press F4, toggle through the various dollar sign combinations on the B2 reference. Pressing F4 twice results in the proper combination, as shown in Figure 5.12.

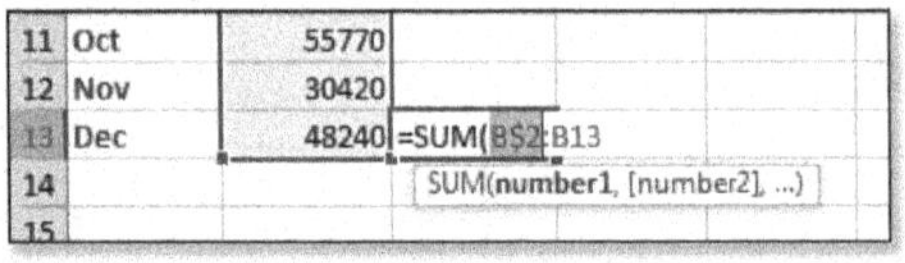

11	Oct	55770	
12	Nov	30420	
13	Dec	48240	=SUM(B$2:B13
14			SUM(number1, [number2], ...)
15			

Figure 5.12 Using F4 is tricky when your reference is a rectangular range—you must click into the formula.

TROUBLESHOOTING

Avoid referring to many cells when you need to refer to a single cell.

In the screenshot below, a formula of =B$2:B$9 brings the value from B4 to the formula in D4. While the formula works, it is taking advantage of an arcane concept called Implicit Intersection. Instead, simply enter =B2 in cell E2 and copy down.

With the introduction of Dynamic Array formulas in Office 365, the bad habit of entering =B2:B9 when you really need only B4 will lead to Excel spilling the formula into adjacent cells.

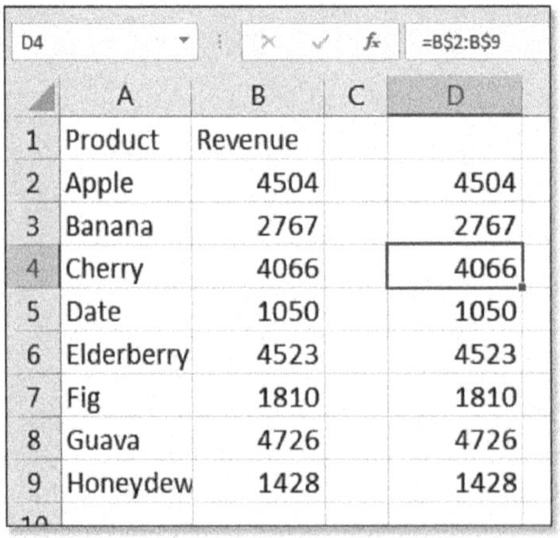

D4 =B$2:B$9

	A	B	C	D
1	Product	Revenue		
2	Apple	4504		4504
3	Banana	2767		2767
4	Cherry	4066		4066
5	Date	1050		1050
6	Elderberry	4523		4523
7	Fig	1810		1810
8	Guava	4726		4726
9	Honeydew	1428		1428
10				

Revenue numbers appear in B2:B9. The revenue for B4 is 4066. In column D, a formula of =B$2:B$9 is mysteriously returning 4066 in cell D4. The formula clearly points to eight cells. Why is the result using only one of the cells? This is because of implicit intersection.

Three methods of entering formulas

In the examples in the previous sections, you entered a formula by typing it. You generally need to start a formula by typing the equal sign (or the plus sign); after that point, you have three options:

- Type the complete formula as described in the previous sections.
- Type the operator keys, but use the mouse to touch cell references. In this book, this is referred to as the *mouse method*.
- Type the operator keys and then use the arrow keys to specify the cell references by navigating to the cells. In this book, this method is referred to as the *arrow key method*.

Assume you would like to multiply the merchandise total in cell B2 by the sales tax rate in cell F1, as shown in Figure 5.13.

XLOOKUP | fx =

	A	B	C	D	E	F
1	Invoice	Merch $	Tax		Rate	6.25%
2	1701	116.7	=			
3	1702	134.71				
4	1703	129.56				

Figure 5.13 You can use three methods to enter the formula =B2*$F$1.

Enter formulas using the mouse method

If you started using computers since 1993, it is likely that you use the mouse method for entering formulas. This method is intuitive, but it requires you to move your hand between the keyboard and the mouse several times, as in this example:

1. Type = or +.
2. Click in cell B2.
3. Type *.
4. Click in cell F1.
5. Press F4 to add the dollar signs.
6. Press Enter. This usually moves the cell pointer to cell C3.

This method requires only four keystrokes, but it requires you to move to the mouse twice. Moving the mouse is the slowest part of entering formulas, but this method is easier than typing the entire formula if you are not a touch typist.

TIP

If you have a desktop keyboard, you can use the asterisk key on the numeric keypad to avoid pressing the Shift key.

TIP

If you use the mouse method to enter formulas, customize the Quick Access Toolbar (QAT) to add icons for Equal Sign, Plus Sign, Minus Sign, Multiplication Sign, Division Sign, Exponentiation Sign, and Dollar Sign. You can then enter most formulas without reaching back to the keyboard. There isn't a QAT icon for the Enter key—use the green check mark to the left of the formula bar for Enter.

Entering formulas using the arrow key method

The arrow key method is popular with people who started using spreadsheets in the days of Lotus 1-2-3 release 2.2. It is worthwhile to learn this method because it is incredibly fast. Almost all formula entry can be accomplished using keys on the right side of the keyboard. Here's how it works:

1. In cell C2, type + using the numeric keypad if you have one. If you do not have a numeric keypad, then press the equal sign on your keyboard.

2. Press the left-arrow key to move the flashing cell border to cell B2. Note that the active cell, which is the one with a green solid border, is still cell C2. The flashing border is like a second cell pointer that you can use to point to the correct cell for the formula. As shown in Figure 5.14, the temporary formula in the formula bar reads +B2.

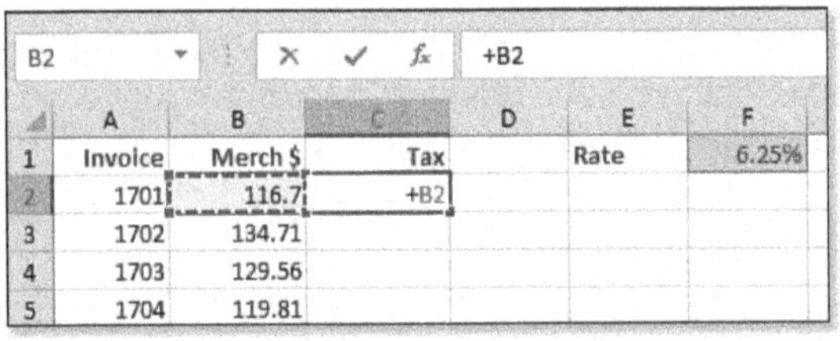

B2 | +B2

	A	B	C	D	E	F
1	Invoice	Merch $	Tax		Rate	6.25%
2	1701	116.7	+B2			
3	1702	134.71				
4	1703	129.56				
5	1704	119.81				

Figure 5.14 By using the arrow keys during formula entry, you create a flashing border that can be used to navigate to a cell reference.

3. To accept cell B2 as the correct reference in the formula, press either an operator key (for example, * or +), a parenthesis, or the Enter key. In this case, type *.

4. Note that the dashed cell pointer disappears, and the focus is now back to the original cell, C2.

5. Press the right-arrow key three times. The flashing cell border moves to D2, E2, and then F2. With the first two key presses, the temporary formula in the formula bar shows an incorrect formula (+B2*D2 and +B2*E2). Figure 5.15 shows what the screen looks like after you press the right-arrow key three times.

NOTE

As you are moving the flashing cell border with the mouse, ignore the formula bar and watch just the flashing cell border.

F2 | × ✓ *fx* | +B2*F2

	A	B	C	D	E	F
1	Invoice	Merch $	Tax		Rate	6.25%
2	1701	116.7	+B2*F2			
3	1702	134.71				
4	1703	129.56				
5	1704	119.81				

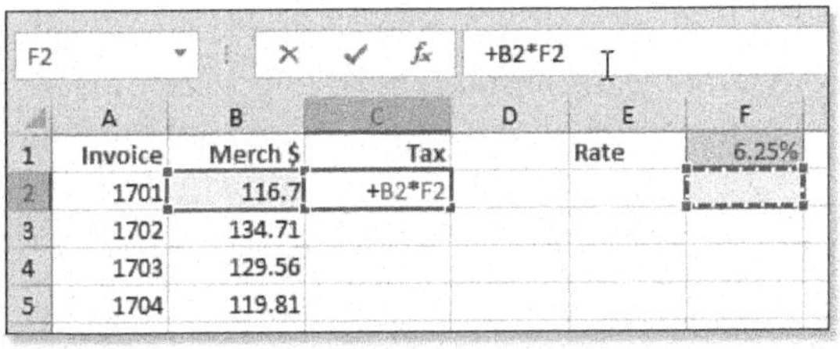

Figure 5.15 After step 4, the focus moves to the original cell. Thus, you only have to press the right arrow key three times instead of four times to arrive at cell F2.

6. Press the up-arrow key to move the flashing cell border to the correct location, cell F1. The temporary formula in the formula bar now shows +B2*F1.
7. Press the F4 key to add dollar signs to the F1 reference.
8. Press Ctrl+Enter to accept the formula and keep the cell pointer in cell C2.

Using this method requires ten keystrokes, with no trips to the mouse. You can enter formulas that have no absolute references, mixed references, parentheses, or exponents by using just the arrow keys and the keys on the numeric keypad.

TIP

Even if you are mouse-centric, you should try this method for half a day. When you get a feel for navigating by using the arrow keys, you can enter formulas much faster by using this method.

Inside Out

You can quickly enter formulas using just the arrow keys and the number keypad. However, you might drive your co-workers mad with formulas that start with =+.

Officially, every formula must start with an equal sign. However, to make former Lotus 1-2-3 customers comfortable, Excel allows you to start a formula with a plus sign. Power Excel customers have discovered that using a plus sign enables them to start a formula by typing on the numeric keypad. Because I routinely start formulas with the plus sign, I am often asked why I start with =+ instead of just =. Even though the formulas appear that way onscreen, I don't actually enter the equal sign. When a formula starts with a plus sign, Excel adds an equal sign and does not remove the plus sign, so you end up with a formula that looks like =+B2*$F$1. I tell people that I am not going to work more slowly in Excel just to allay their irrational fears of =+.

Entering the same formula in many cells

So far in this chapter, you have entered a formula in one cell and then copied and pasted to get the formula in many cells. To enter the same formula in many cells, you can use three alternatives:

- Preselect the entire range where the formulas need to go. Enter the formula for the first cell and press Ctrl+Enter to enter the formula in the entire selection simultaneously.
- Enter the formula in the first cell and then use the fill handle to copy the formula.
- Beginning with Excel 2007, the method is to define the range as a table. When you use this method, the new formulas are copied down a column automatically.

Copying a formula by using Ctrl+Enter

This strategy works when you are entering formulas for one or more screens that are full of data:

1. If you have just a few cells, select them before entering the formula.
2. Click in the first cell and drag down to the last cell. Notice from the name box that the active cell is the first cell.
3. Enter the formula by using any of the three methods described earlier in this chapter. Even if you use the arrow key method, Excel keeps the entire range selected. Figure 5.16 shows a formula after you press F4 to convert the F1 reference to $F$1.

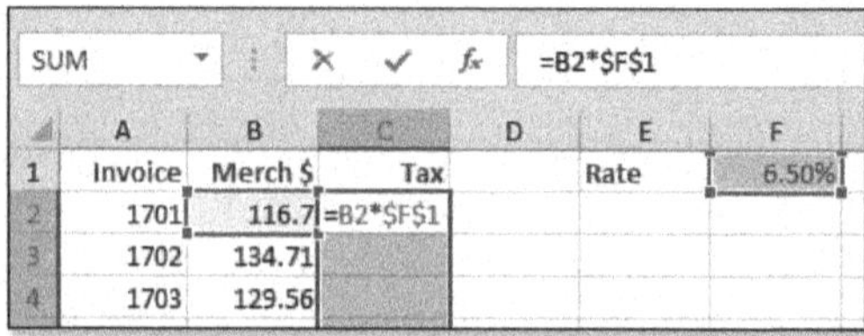

Figure 5.16 Even with a large range selected, the formula is built only in the active cell.

4. At this point, you would normally press Enter to complete the formula. Instead, press Ctrl+Enter to enter this formula in the entire selected range. Note that Excel does not enter =B2*$F$1 in each cell. Instead, it converts the formula as if it were copied to each cell.

Copying a formula by dragging the fill handle

If you want to enter a formula in one cell and then copy it to the other cells in a range, you can use the fill handle, which is the square dot in the lower-right corner of the cell pointer. There are two ways to use the fill handle:

- Drag the fill handle.
- Double-click the fill handle.

The dragging method works fine when you have less than one screen full of data:

1. Enter the formula in cell C2.
2. Press Ctrl+Enter to accept the formula and keep the cell pointer in cell C2.
3. Click the fill handle. You know that you are above the fill handle when the mouse pointer changes to a thick plus sign, as shown in Figure 5.17. Drag the mouse down to the last row of data.

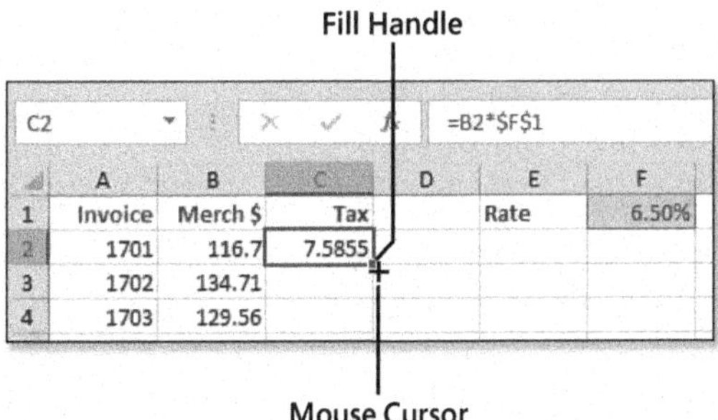

Figure 5.17 You can copy a formula by double-clicking or dragging the fill handle.

4. When you release the mouse button, the original cell is copied to all the cells in the selected range.

This method is fine for copying a formula to a few cells. However, if you have thousands or hundreds of thousands of cells, it is annoying to drag to the last row. You invariably end up flying past the last row. Note that Excel automatically slows down and briefly pauses at the last row. However, it is far easier to copy a formula by double-clicking the fill handle.

Double-click the fill handle to copy a formula

In most data sets, double-clicking the fill handle is the fastest way to copy the formula.

Instead of dragging the fill handle, double-click the fill handle. Provided one of the cells to the left, right, or below the active cell is nonblank, Excel fills to the bottom of the current region.

CHAPTER 5

Before Excel 2010, using this method would fail if there were a few blank cells in the column to the left. Starting in Excel 2010, the logic was improved, and the technique almost always finds the correct number of rows based on the adjacent data.

Use the Table tool to copy a formula

When you define your current data set as a table, Excel automatically copies new formulas down to the rest of the cells in the table.

Figure 5.18 shows an Excel worksheet that has headings at the top and many rows of data below the headings.

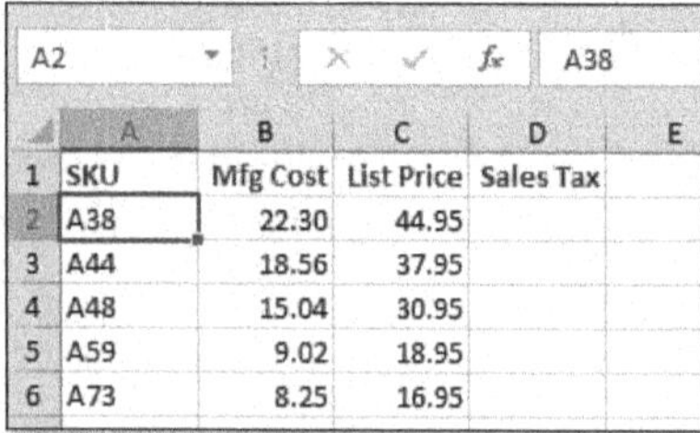
A2 | fx A38

	A	B	C	D	E
1	SKU	Mfg Cost	List Price	Sales Tax	
2	A38	22.30	44.95		
3	A44	18.56	37.95		
4	A48	15.04	30.95		
5	A59	9.02	18.95		
6	A73	8.25	16.95		

Figure 5.18 This is a typical worksheet in Excel.

To define a range as a table, select a cell within the data set and press Ctrl+T. Excel uses its IntelliSense to guess the edges of the table. If its guess is correct, click OK in the Create Table dialog box, as shown in Figure 5.19.

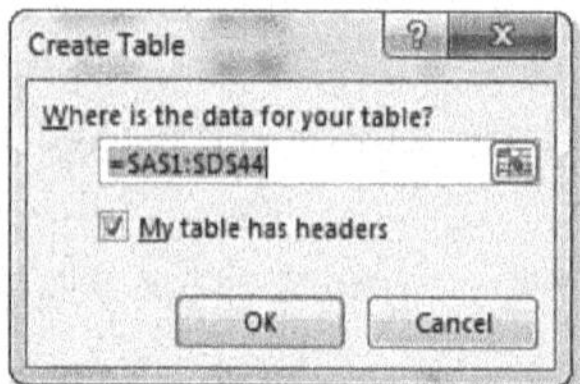

Figure 5.19 The Create Table dialog box.

Ctrl+T is one of four entry points for creating a table. You can still use the Excel 2003 shortcut of Ctrl+L (because the feature was called a List in Excel 2003). You can choose Format as Table on the Home tab. You can choose the Table icon from the Insert tab.

As shown in Figure 5.20, after Excel recognizes the range as a table, several changes occur:

- The table is formatted with the default formatting. Depending on your preferences, this might include banded rows or columns.
- AutoFilter drop-down menus are added to the headings.
- Any formulas you enter by using the mouse or arrow keys use the headings to refer to cells within the table.

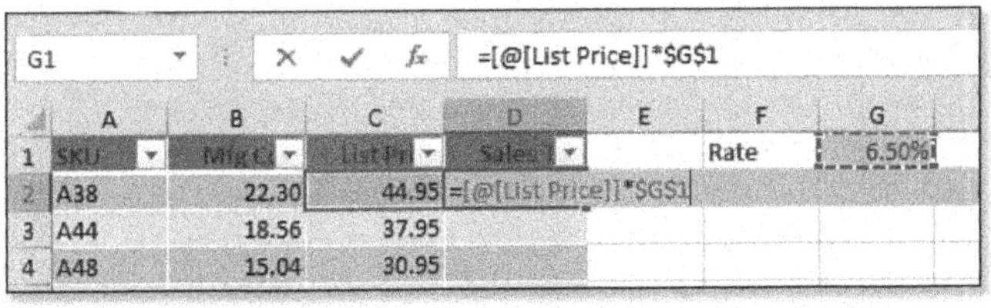

Figure 5.20 Defining a range as a table provides formatting and powerful features such as Auto-filters and natural language formulas.

Now when you enter a formula in the table, Excel automatically copies that formula down to all rows of the table.

NOTE

As shown in Figure 5.21, a lightning bolt drop-down menu appears to the right of cell D3. This drop-down menu offers you the opportunity to stop Excel from automatically copying the formula down.

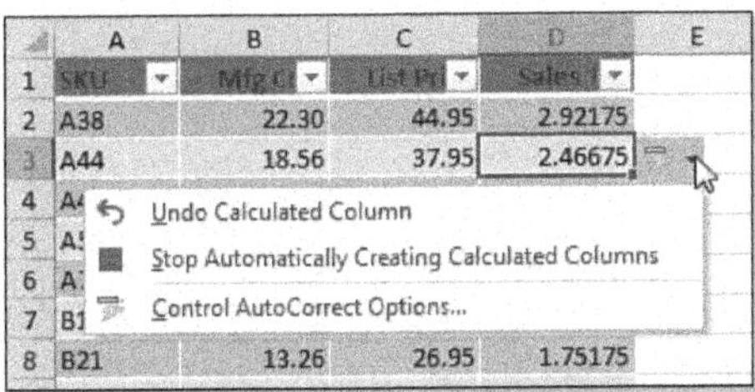

Figure 5.21 Thanks to the Table tool in Excel, a new formula entered anywhere in column D is copied automatically to all the cells in column D.

Entering one formula and spilling many results

Take a look at Figure 5.22. A formula of **=A2:A9** is typed in cell C5. Excel spills the answers into C5:C12. If you select any cell in C5:C12, the formula appears in the formula bar, and a blue outline appears around the results range. Think of the blue outline as indicating that this one formula is returning all of the answers inside the outline.

Here is an important distinction: The formula only exists in one cell: C5. When you select C6 or C7 or C12, the formula appears in the formula bar in a light gray font. But you can only edit the formula if you select C5. A formula of `=FORMULATEXT(C5)` will work. A formula of `=FORMULATEXT(C6)` will fail.

If A1:A9 happens to be a table and you add new rows to the table, the results from this one formula will automatically expand. Or if you delete row 4, the results will contract.

C6 =A2:A9

	A	B	C	D	E
1	**Product**				
2	Watermelon				
3	Orange				
4	Apple				
5	Nectarine		Watermelon		
6	Lime		Orange		
7	Lemon		Apple		
8	Zucchini		Nectarine		
9	Star fruit		Lime		
10			Lemon		
11			Zucchini		
12			Star fruit		
13					

Figure 5.22 A single formula returns many results.

The first time that this happens to you in Excel, you will see a message shown in Figure 5.23. Once you click Got It, they won't bother you again.

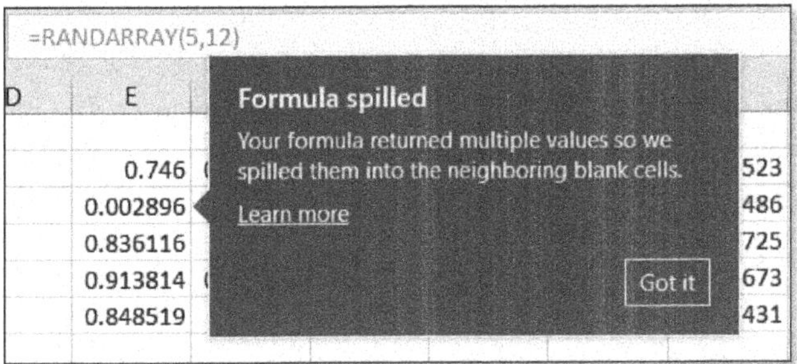

Figure 5.23 Excel tries to explain this new spill feature.

Understanding the #SPILL! error

If you use Excel a lot, you realize two problems with this new functionality. The first problem: What happens if C6 through C12 are not blank? If Excel cannot return all the answers, then you get none of the answers. A brand new `#SPILL` error will appear, and the on-grid drop-down menu explains "Spill Range Isn't Blank" (see Figure 5.24).

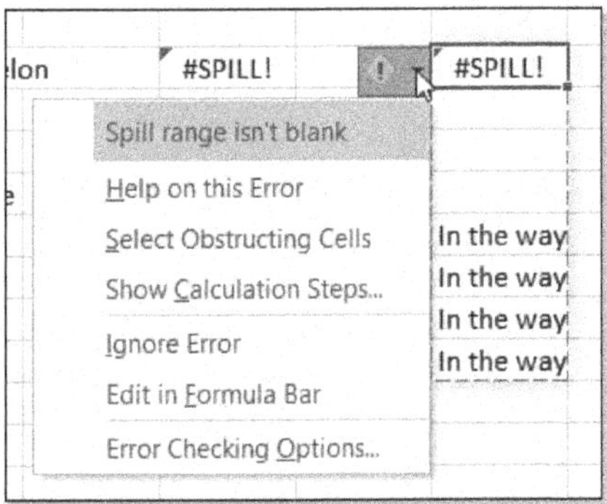

Figure 5.24 If there is not room for the results, a #SPILL error appears.

Using implicit intersection is more complicated than before

The second problem will only be apparent to hard-core Excellers. There is a concept called *implicit intersection*. In all versions of Excel up until September 2019, if you enter **=A2:A9** anywhere in rows 2 through 9, Excel will only return the value from A2:A9 that intersects the formula. In other words, `=A2:A9` in C5 will return `Nectarine` from A5. Enter that same formula in C7, and you will get `Lemon`.

CHAPTER 5

This is a bizarre trick that I've never used in real life. The only time that I've ever used implicit intersection is when trying to win a bar bet. However, someone out there is using it. Some modeler is taking advantage of this trick. Microsoft can't take this feature away, so if you want to do what implicit intersection used to do, use the @ operator. If you enter `=@$A$2:$A$9` when in rows 2 through 9, the value from that row will be returned (see Figure 5.25).

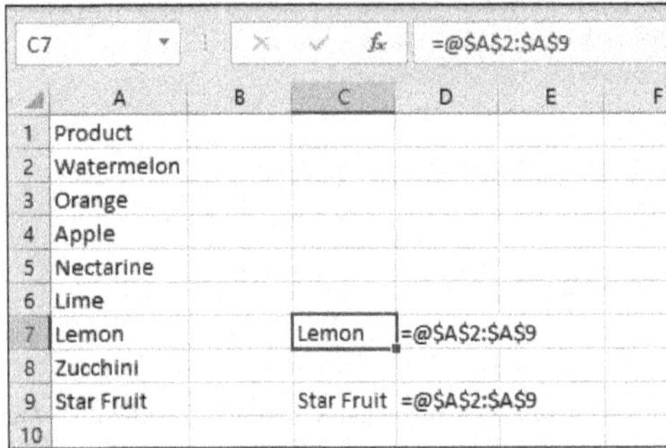

Figure 5.25 The new @ operator must be used when someone needs to do implicit intersection.

Text appears in A2:A9, and cell A7 contains `Lemon`. A formula of `=@$A$2:$A$9` entered anywhere in row 7 will return `Lemon`. Copy that formula to row 9, and it will return `Star fruit` because A9 contains Star Fruit.

Note that implicit intersection and @ also work for columns. If you had values in B1:J1 and enter `=@B1:J1` anywhere in column C, the formula will return just the value from C1.

The Excel team did a great job with backward compatibility on this feature: If you have an old workbook that is already doing implicit intersection, Excel will wrap that formula in the @ operator for you. If you create a formula using @ and send it to someone who does not have dynamic arrays, Excel will rewrite the formula as implicit intersection.

Referring to an entire array with the # operator

The hash symbol (#) is a new operator in Excel callled the Spilled Range Operator. Place a # after a reference to indicate that you want to refer to all of the cells returned by the formula in the reference.

For example, in Figure 5.26, a formula in A2 returns the numbers 2, 6, 10, 14, 18, and 22. If you simply refer to A2, you will be pointing at the 2 in A2. But if you refer to A2#, you will refer to all six numbers. =SUM(A2#) will return 72.

If the formula in A2 would change and start returning a smaller or larger array, the A2# reference will continue to point to all results of the array.

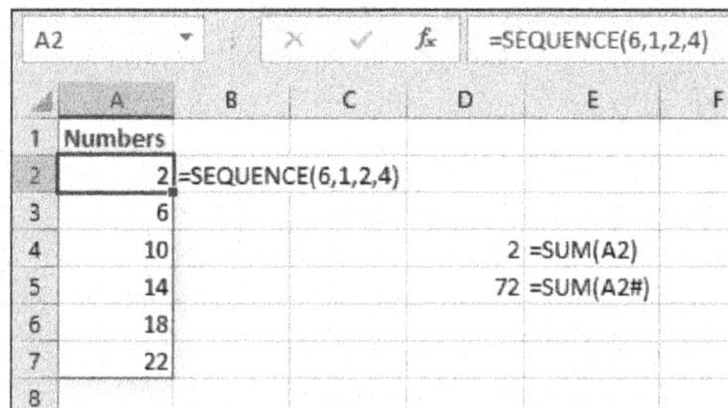

Figure 5.26 The new # operator tells Excel to refer to all of the answers from the formula in A2.

For more about the new SORT, SORTBY, SEQUENCE, FILTER, UNIQUE, and RANDARRAY functions released at the same time as Dynamic Arrays, read Chapter 12.

CHAPTER 6

Controlling formulas

Although you can go a long way with simple formulas, it is also possible to build extremely powerful formulas. The topics in this chapter explain the finer points of formula operators, date math, and how Excel distinguishes between cutting and copying cells referenced in formulas.

Formula operators

Excel offers the mathematical operators shown in Table 6.1.

Table 6.1 Mathematical operators

Operator	Description
+	Addition
-	Subtraction
*	Multiplication
/	Division or fractions
^	Exponents
()	Overriding the order of operations
-	Unary minus (for negative numbers)
&	Joining text (concatenation)
>	Greater than
<	Less than
>=	Greater than or equal to
<=	Less than or equal to
<>	Not equal to
=	Equal to
,	Union operator, as in SUM(A1,B2)

:	Range operator, as in SUM(A1:B2)
<space>	Intersection operator, as in SUM(A:J 2:4)
#	Formula Spill operator, as in =AVERAGE(E1#)
@	Implicit Intersection operator

Order of operations

When a formula contains many calculations, Excel evaluates the formula in a certain order. Rather than calculating from left to right as a calculator might, Excel performs certain types of calculations, such as multiplication, before calculations such as addition.

You can override the default order of operations with parentheses. If you do not use parentheses, Excel uses the following order of operations:

NOTE

To see how Excel calculates the formulas you enter, first, enter a formula in a cell. Next, from the Formulas tab, select Formulas, Formula Auditing, Evaluate Formula to open the Evaluate Formula dialog box. Repeatedly click the Evaluate button and watch the formula calculate in slow motion:

1. **Unary minus is evaluated first.**
2. **Exponents are evaluated next.**
3. **Multiplication and division are handled next, in a left-to-right manner.**
4. **Addition and subtraction are handled next, in a left-to-right manner.**

The following sections provide some examples of order of operations.

Unary minus example

The unary minus is always evaluated first. Think about when you use exponents to raise a number to a power. If you raise –2 to the second power, Excel calculates (–2) × (–2), which is +4. Therefore, the formula =-2^2 evaluates to 4.

If you raise –2 to the third power, Excel calculates (–2) × (–2) × (–2). Multiplying –2 by –2 results in +4, and multiplying +4 by –2 results in –8. Therefore, the simple formula =-2^3 generates –8.

You need to understand a subtle but important distinction. When Excel encounters the formula =-2^3, it evaluates the unary minus first. If you want the exponent to happen first and then have the unary minus applied, you have to write the formula as `=-(2^3)`. However, in a formula such as =100-2^3, the minus sign is considered to be a subtraction operator and not a unary minus sign. In this case, 2^3 is evaluated as 8, and then 8 is subtracted from 100. To indicate a unary minus, use `=100-(-2^3)`.

Addition and multiplication example

The order of operations is important when you are mixing addition/subtraction with multiplication/division. For example, if you want to add 20 to 30 and then multiply by 1.06 to calculate a total with tax, the following formula leads to the wrong result:

```
=20+30*1.06
```

The result you are looking for is 53. However, the Evaluate Formula dialog box shows that Excel calculates the formula =20+30*1.06 like so (see Figure 6.1):

```
1.06 × 30 = 31.8

31.8 + 20 = 51.8
```

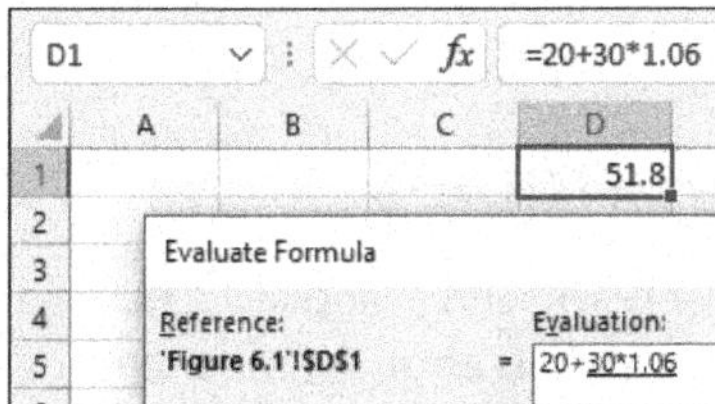

Figure 6.1 The underline indicates that Excel does the multiplication first.

Excel's answer is 1.20 less than expected because the formula is not written with the default order of operations in mind.

To force Excel to do the addition first, you need to enclose the addition in parentheses:

```
=(20+30)*1.06
```

The addition in parentheses is done first, and then 50 is multiplied by 1.06 to get the correct answer of 3.

Stacking multiple parentheses

If you need to use multiple sets of parentheses when doing math by hand, you might write math formulas with square brackets and curly braces, like this:

```
{3-[6*4*3-(3-6)+2]/27}*14
```

In Excel, you use multiple sets of parentheses, as follows:

```
=(3-(6*4*3-(3-6)+2)/27)*14
```

Formulas with multiple parentheses in Excel are confusing. Excel does two things to try to improve this situation:

- As you type a formula, Excel colors the parentheses in a set order: black, red, purple, green, violet, topaz, aquamarine, blue. The colors then repeat starting with red. By far, the most common problem is having one too few or one too many parentheses. By using red as the second color, the last parenthesis in most unbalanced equations is red. Excel uses black only for the first parenthesis and for the closing match to that parenthesis. This means if your last parenthesis in the formula is not black, you have the wrong number of parentheses.
- When you type a closing parenthesis, Excel shows the opening parenthesis in bold for a fraction of a second. This would be more helpful if Excel kept the opening parenthesis in bold for 5 seconds or 20 seconds.

Understanding error messages in formulas

Don't be frustrated when a formula returns an error result. This eventually happens to everyone. The key is to understand the difference between the various error values so that you can begin to troubleshoot the problem.

As you enter formulas, you might encounter some errors, including those listed next:

- **#VALUE!:** This error indicates that you are trying to do math with nonnumeric data. For example, the formula =4+"apple" returns a #VALUE! error. This error also occurs if you try to enter an array formula but fail to use Ctrl+Shift+Enter, as described in Chapter 12, "Dynamic array formulas and names in Excel."
- **#DIV/0!:** This error occurs when a number is divided by zero: that is, when a fraction's denominator evaluates to zero.
- **#REF!:** This error occurs when a cell reference is not valid. For example, this error can occur if one of the cells referenced in the formula has been deleted. It can also occur if you cut and paste another cell over a cell referenced in this formula. You may also get this error if you are using Dynamic Data Exchange (DDE) formulas to link to external systems and those systems are not running.

- **#N/A!:** This error occurs when a value is not available to a function or a formula. #N/A! errors most often occur because of key values not being found during lookup functions. They can occur as a result of HLOOKUP, LOOKUP, MATCH, or VLOOKUP. They can also result when an array formula has one argument that is not the same dimension as the other arguments or when a function omits one or more required arguments. Interestingly, when an #N/A! error enters a range, all subsequent calculations that refer to the range have a value of #N/A!.

- **#NULL!:** This error usually indicates that two cell references by a formula are separated by a space instead of a colon or comma. The space operator is the intersection operator. If there are no cells in common between the two references, a #NULL! error appears.

- **#SPILL!:** This error is new in Office 365 after the summer of 2018. If you use one of the new =A1:A100 formulas in cell C1 and some non-blank cells appear in the 100 cells needed for the response, you will see a #SPILL! error in the cell with the formula. Other causes of the #SPILL! error include the formula spilling beyond the edge of the worksheet or running out of memory.

- **#FIELD!:** This error is new in 2018 and indicates a problem with a Linked Data Type. The error occurs if the referenced field is not available in a linked data type or if the formula is referencing a cell that does not contain a linked data type. Here is an example: Type **Florida** in cell A1 and use the Data Types gallery on the Data tab to mark that cell as geography. You can use **=A1.Population** to retrieve the population. However, if you change cell **A1** to **Apple**, the #FIELD! error will appear because Excel does not have a geography definition for Apple.

- **#CALC:** Your formula is returning an empty array. The calculation engine can't resolve the formula yet, but the syntax might be supported in the future. The Excel team has plans for a series of new functions that will roll out over several releases, and the #CALC error is needed if they plan on rolling out part of a two-function solution.

- **######:** This is not really an error. Instead, it means that the result is too wide to display in the current column width, so you need to make the column wider to see the actual result. Although ###### usually means the column is not wide enough, it can also appear if you are subtracting one date or time from another and end up with a negative amount. Excel does not allow negative dates or times unless you switch to the 1904 Date System.

In Figure 6.2, cell E17 is a simple SUM function. It is returning an #N/A error because cell E11 contains the same error. Cell E11 contains the formula =D11*C11. The root cause of the problem is the VLOOKUP function in cell D11. Because Fig cannot be found in the product table in $G$7:$H$9, the VLOOKUP function returns #N/A.

E17 | fx =SUM(E8:E16)

	A	B	C	D	E	F	G	H
1	Apple	4	#VALUE!	=A1+B1				
2	4	0	#DIV/0!	=A2/B2				
3	4	3	#REF!	=#REF!*A3				
4		Dill	#N/A	=VLOOKUP(B4,$G$7:$H$9,2,FALSE)				
5								
6								
7	Invoice	Item	Qty	Price	Total		Apple	1
8	101	Apple	11	1	11		Banana	2
9	102	Cherry	11	4	44		Cherry	4
10	103	Banana	9	2	18			
11	104	Dill	10	#N/A	#N/A			
12	105	Apple	9	1	9			
13	106	Cherry	10	4	40			
14	107	Banana	8	2	16			
15	108	Cherry	11	4	44			
16	109	Banana	9	2	18			
17	GRAND TOTAL				#N/A			
18								

Figure 6.2 The error in E17 is actually caused by an error two calculations earlier.

Figure 6.2 shows only a small table, so it is relatively easy to find the earlier #N/A errors. However, when you're totaling 100,000 rows, it can be difficult to find the one offending cell. To track down errors, follow these steps:

1. Select the cell that shows the final error. To the left of that cell, you should see an exclamation point in a yellow diamond.
2. Hover the cursor over the yellow diamond to reveal a drop-down menu arrow.
3. From the drop-down menu, select Trace Error. Excel draws in red arrows pointing back to the source of the error, as shown in Figure 6.3. For example, from the original #N/A! error in cell D11, blue arrows demonstrate what cells were causing the error. To remove the arrows, use the Remove Arrows command on the Formulas tab.

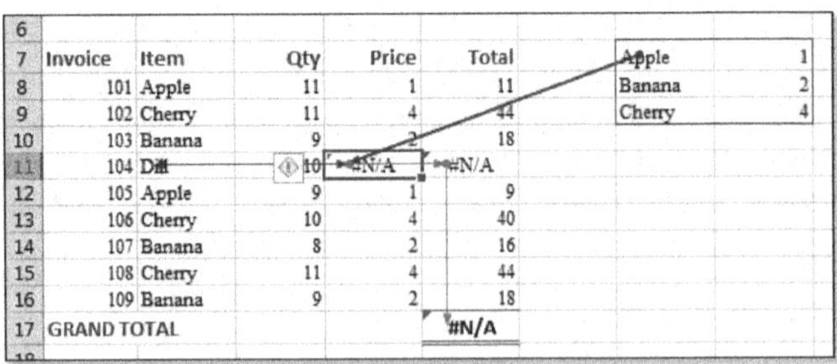

6								
7	Invoice	Item	Qty	Price	Total		Apple	1
8	101	Apple	11	1	11		Banana	2
9	102	Cherry	11	4	44		Cherry	4
10	103	Banana	9	2	18			
11	104	Dill	10	#N/A	#N/A			
12	105	Apple	9	1	9			
13	106	Cherry	10	4	40			
14	107	Banana	8	2	16			
15	108	Cherry	11	4	44			
16	109	Banana	9	2	18			
17	GRAND TOTAL				#N/A			

Figure 6.3 Selecting Trace Error reveals the cells leading to the error.

Using formulas to join text

You use the ampersand (&) operator when you need to join text. In Excel, the & operator is known as the concatenation operator.

When using the & operator, you often need to include a space between the two items that are combined to improve the appearance of the output. For example, if the cells contain first name and last name, you want to have a space between the names. To include a space between cells, you follow the & with a space enclosed in quotes, as in &" ". As shown in Figure 6.4, the formula =A2&" "&B2 joins the first name and last name with a space in between.

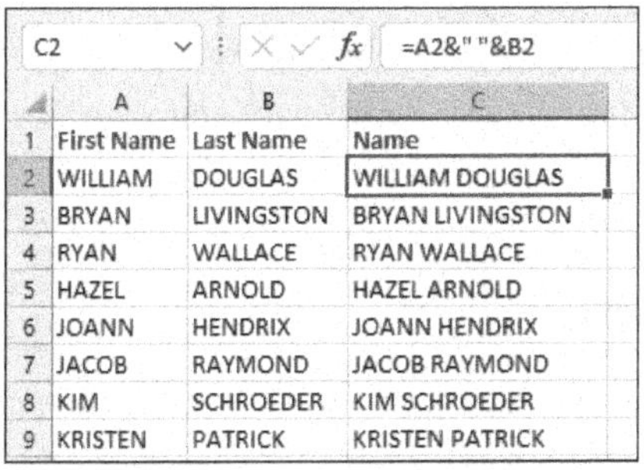

C2 | fx =A2&" "&B2

	A	B	C
1	First Name	Last Name	Name
2	WILLIAM	DOUGLAS	WILLIAM DOUGLAS
3	BRYAN	LIVINGSTON	BRYAN LIVINGSTON
4	RYAN	WALLACE	RYAN WALLACE
5	HAZEL	ARNOLD	HAZEL ARNOLD
6	JOANN	HENDRIX	JOANN HENDRIX
7	JACOB	RAYMOND	JACOB RAYMOND
8	KIM	SCHROEDER	KIM SCHROEDER
9	KRISTEN	PATRICK	KRISTEN PATRICK

Figure 6.4 You can join cells with any text in quotation marks.

NOTE

Excel includes a `TEXTJOIN` function. There are cases where `TEXTJOIN` will be easier than using the & operator. To read more about `TEXTJOIN`, see "Joining text with TEXTJOIN" in Chapter 8.

Joining text and a number

In many cases, you can use the & operator to join text with a number or a date. In Figure 6.5, the formula in cell E2 joins the words "`The price is $`" with the result of the calculation in cell D2. Although D2 is formatted to show only two decimal places, the underlying answer has more decimal places. The regular concatenation formula in E2 shows the extra decimal places. To fix the problem, use the `TEXT()` function around D2 in the formula. Specify any valid numeric formatting code in quotes as the second argument. The corrected formula in E6 uses `TEXT(D6,"#,##0.00")`.

When you join text to a date or time, you see the serial number that Excel stores behind the scenes instead of the date. Cell E3 in Figure 6.5 shows the result of joining text with a date. Use the `TEXT()` function around the date to format it as shown in cell E7. The formula in E7 is `="His birthday is "&TEXT(D7,"DDDD, MMMM D, YYYY")`.

CHAPTER 6

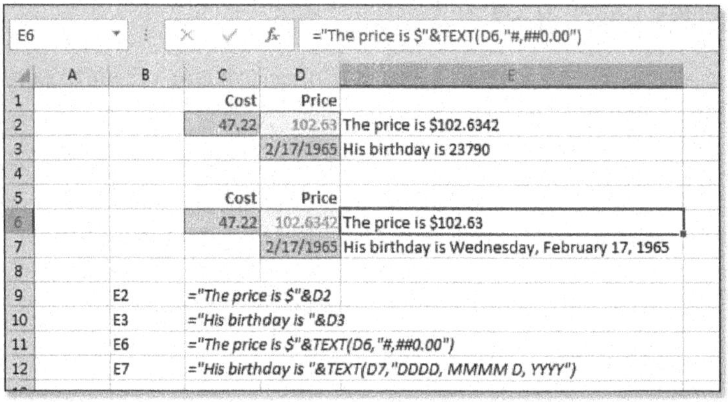

E6 ="The price is $"&TEXT(D6,"#,##0.00")

	A	B	C	D	E
1			Cost	Price	
2			47.22	102.63	The price is $102.6342
3				2/17/1965	His birthday is 23790
4					
5			Cost	Price	
6			47.22	102.6342	The price is $102.63
7				2/17/1965	His birthday is Wednesday, February 17, 1965
8					
9		E2	="The price is $"&D2		
10		E3	="His birthday is "&D3		
11		E6	="The price is $"&TEXT(D6,"#,##0.00")		
12		E7	="His birthday is "&TEXT(D7,"DDDD, MMMM D, YYYY")		

Figure 6.5 When joining numbers or dates, use the TEXT() function to control the format of the number.

Copying versus cutting a formula

In Figure 6.6, the formula in cell C4 references A4+B4. Because there are no dollar signs within the formula, those are relative references.

NOTE

For a review of relative and absolute references, see "The relative nature of formulas" in Chapter 5.

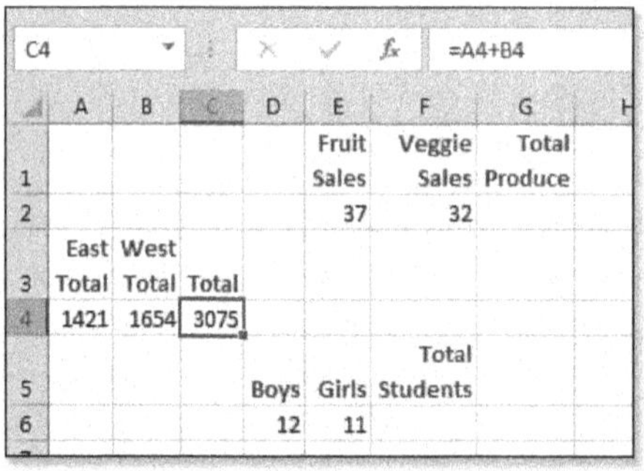

C4 =A4+B4

	A	B	C	D	E	F	G
1					Fruit Sales	Veggie Sales	Total Produce
2					37	32	
3	East Total	West Total	Total				
4	1421	1654	3075				
5				Boys	Girls	Total Students	
6				12	11		

Figure 6.6 The formula in cell C4 adds the two numbers to the left of the formula.

If you *copy* cell C4 and paste it to cell G2, the formula works perfectly, adding the two numbers to the left of G2. However, if you *cut* C4 and paste to F6, the formula continues to point to cells A4+B4, as shown in Figure 6.7. Whereas cutting and copying are relatively similar in applications such as Word, they are very different in Excel. It is important to understand the effect of cutting a formula in Excel in contrast to copying the formula. When you cut a formula, the formula continues to point to the original precedents, no matter where you paste it.

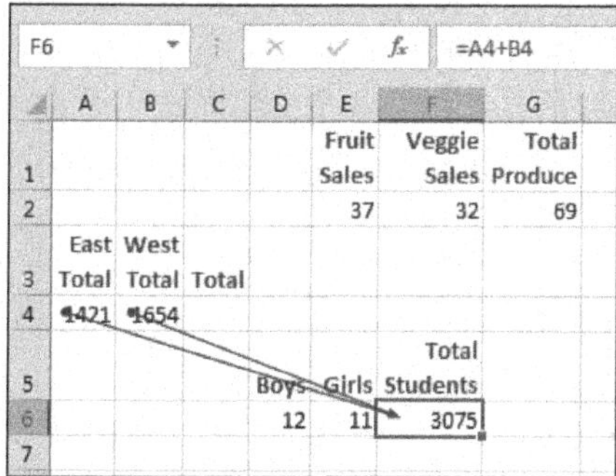

Figure 6.7 Copying C4 to G2 works. Cutting C4 to F6 fails.

A similar rule applies to the references mentioned in a formula. For example, in Figure 6.6, the formula in cell C4 points to A4 and B4. As long as you copy cell A4, you can paste it anywhere without changing the formula in C4. But if you would cut A4 and paste it elsewhere, the formula in C4 would update to reflect the new location.

Inside OUT

Sometimes you need to do a combination of a cut and a copy. You need the formulas to keep pointing to the original cells, but you need to copy the formulas to a new spot.

The common approach is to convert the formulas to text, copy and paste, and then convert from text back to formulas. Follow these steps:

1. **Select the range of formulas to cut/copy.**
2. **Press Ctrl+H to display the Replace dialog.**
3. **Replace each = with ^=.**
4. **Copy the cells.**
5. **Paste to a new place.**
6. **Use Replace to change each ^= to =.**

NOTE

There is nothing special about ^= in the example above. You could have used x= or |= or any character that won't be seen as valid at the start of a formula.

Automatically formatting formula cells

The rules for formatting the result of a formula seem to be inconsistent. Suppose that you have `$1.23` in cell A1. All cells in the worksheet have the general format except cell A1.

If you enter **=A1+3** in another cell with general format, the result automatically inherits the currency format of cell A1.

When you are referring to multiple cells in a formula, the resulting automatic format does not appear to follow a pattern. When you start the formula with an equal sign, either the format is copied from the first or the last cell referenced. When you use a plus sign, the format sometimes comes from the second, first, or last reference, and sometimes the format is a mix of two references.

If your formula is going to refer to multiple cells with different formatting, start the formula with an equal sign. Refer to the cell with the desired cell format first, but accept that you might have to explicitly format the resulting cell.

Specifying implicit intersection using the @ operator

Excel used to automatically support implicit intersection. If you were to refer to A2:A10 in any cell in rows 2 through 10, Excel would only return the cell that intersected with the formula.

In order to implement Dynamic Arrays in Excel, a formula such as `=$A$2:$A$10` will now spill and return the values from all nine cells. To force Excel to use implicit intersection, you have to precede the cell reference with an `@` sign. In Figure 6.8, a formula of `=$A$2:$A$10` in cell D4 spills to nine cells. By adding an `@` before the reference, you get only Chris from A4 in cell C4. When you copy C4 to C8, the answer "`Chris`" changes to "`Gary`" because C8 intersects with the A8 from the reference.

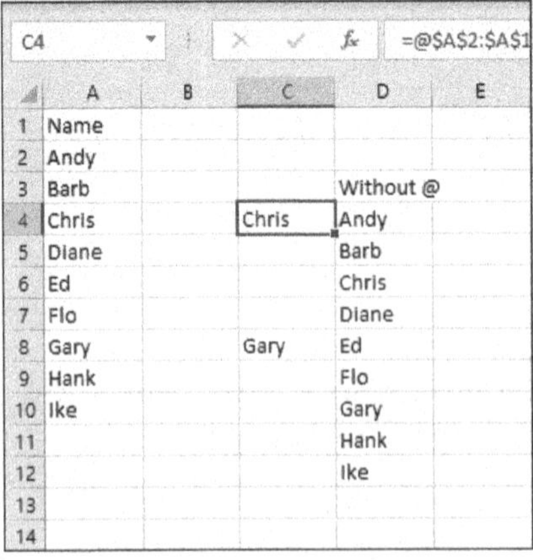

Figure 6.8 To use implicit intersection, you must add an @ Operator.

Using date math

Dates in Excel are stored as the number of days since January 1, 1900. For example, Excel stores the date Feb-17-2021 as 44244. In Figure 6.9, cell E1 contains the date. Cell E2 contains the formula =E1 and has been formatted to show a number.

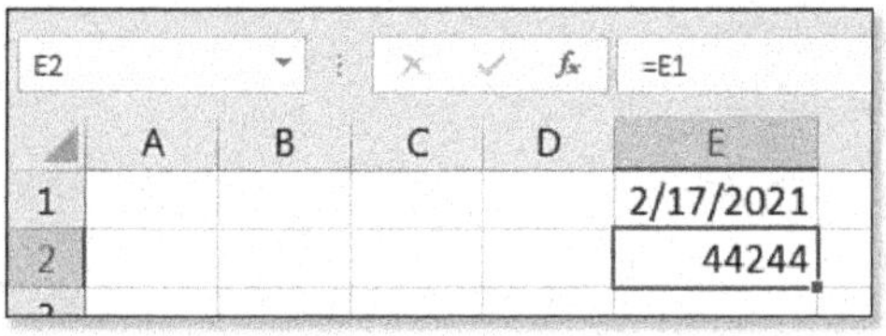

E2 =E1

	A	B	C	D	E
1					2/17/2021
2					44244

Figure 6.9 Although cell E1 is formatted as a date, Excel stores the date as the number of days since January 1, 1900.

This convenient system enables you to do some pretty simple math. For example, Figure 6.10 shows a range of invoice dates in column B. The payment terms for the invoice are in column D. You can calculate the due date by adding cells B2 and D2. Here is what actually happens in Excel's calculation engine:

1. The date in cell B2—2/1/2018—is stored as 43132.
2. Excel adds 10 to that number to get the answer 43142.
3. Excel formats this number as a date, to yield 2/11/2018.

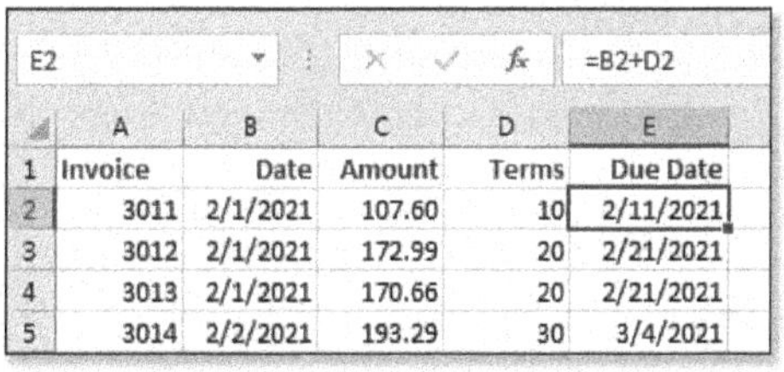

E2 =B2+D2

	A	B	C	D	E
1	Invoice	Date	Amount	Terms	Due Date
2	3011	2/1/2021	107.60	10	2/11/2021
3	3012	2/1/2021	172.99	20	2/21/2021
4	3013	2/1/2021	170.66	20	2/21/2021
5	3014	2/2/2021	193.29	30	3/4/2021

Figure 6.10 When the answer is formatted correctly, Excel's date math is very cool.

However, a frustrating problem can occur if the cell containing the formula has the wrong numeric format. For example, in Figure 6.11, the `WORKDAY` function in column D did not automatically convert the result to a date. It is important to recognize that dates in 2019–2021 fall in the range of 43,466 to 44,561. So, if you are expecting a date answer as the result of a formula and get a number in this range, the answer probably needs to have a date format applied.

To apply a date format, on the Home tab, use the Number drop-down menu to choose the Date format. The answer in column D now appears correctly.

In general, most formulas that refer to a date cell are automatically formatted as a date. Most formulas that contain functions from the Date category are formatted as a date. (The `WORKDAY` function is one annoying exception.)

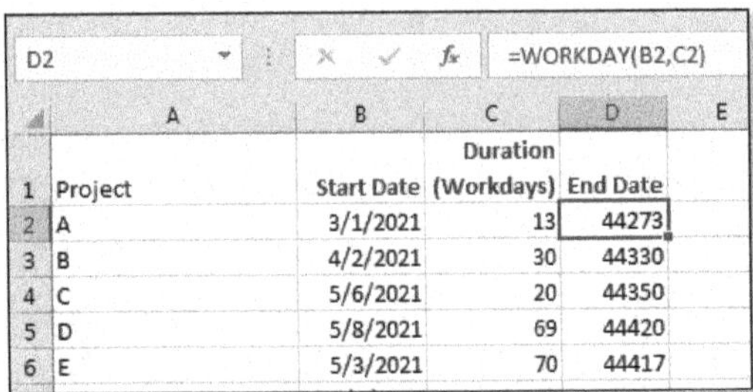

D2 =WORKDAY(B2,C2)

	A	B	C	D	E
1	Project	Start Date	Duration (Workdays)	End Date	
2	A	3/1/2021	13	44273	
3	B	4/2/2021	30	44330	
4	C	5/6/2021	20	44350	
5	D	5/8/2021	69	44420	
6	E	5/3/2021	70	44417	

Figure 6.11 The formula appears to give the wrong answer. However, this is a formatting problem.

Troubleshooting formulas

It is difficult to figure out worksheets that were set up by other people. When you receive a worksheet from a co-worker, use the information in the following sections to find and examine the formulas.

Seeing all formulas

For a long time, Excel has given customers the capability to see all the formulas in a worksheet. The mode that provides this functionality is called *Show Formulas mode.*

To toggle into Show Formulas mode for a worksheet, select the Formulas tab, and then choose the Show Formulas icon in the Formula Auditing group. Alternatively, you can press Ctrl+` (the grave accent) to toggle into this mode. On U.S. keyboards, the grave accent is usually just below the Esc key, on the same key with the tilde (~).

To hide the formulas and return to normal mode, choose the Show Formulas icon again.

Highlighting all formula cells

These steps apply a cell color to all formula cells in the worksheet:

1. Ensure that you have a single cell selected.
2. Select Home, Find & Select, Formulas.
3. Use the Paint Bucket icon in the Home tab to apply a color to all the formula cells.

Editing a single formula to show direct precedents

It is helpful to identify cells that are used to calculate a formula. These cells are called the *precedents* of the cell.

A cell can have several levels of precedents. In a formula such as =D5+D7, there are two direct precedents: D5 and D7. However, all the direct precedents of D5 and D7 are second-level precedents of the original formula.

If you are interested in visually examining the direct precedents of a cell, follow these steps:

1. Select a cell that has a formula.
2. Press F2 to put the cell in Edit mode. In this mode, each reference of the formula is displayed in a different color. For example, the formula in cell H5 in Figure 6.12 refers to three cells. The characters F5 in the formula appear in blue and correspond to the blue box around cell F5.
3. Visually check the formula to ensure that it is correct.

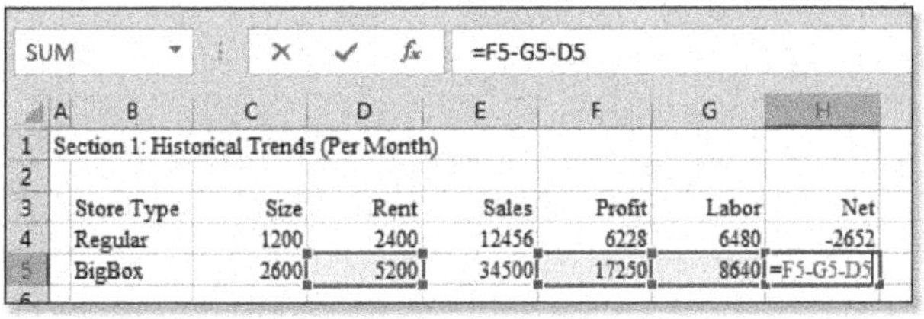

SUM | =F5-G5-D5

	A	B	C	D	E	F	G	H
1	Section 1: Historical Trends (Per Month)							
2								
3		Store Type	Size	Rent	Sales	Profit	Labor	Net
4		Regular	1200	2400	12456	6228	6480	-2652
5		BigBox	2600	5200	34500	17250	8640	=F5-G5-D5

Figure 6.12 Editing a single formula lights up the direct precedent cells.

Using formula auditing arrows

If you have a complicated formula, you might want to identify direct precedents and then possibly second- or third-level precedents. You can have Excel draw arrows from the current cells to all cells that make up the precedents for the current cell. To have Excel draw arrows, follow these steps:

1. From the Formula Auditing group on the Formulas tab, click Trace Precedents. Excel draws arrows from the current cell to all the cells that are directly referenced in the formula. For example, in Figure 6.13, an arrow is drawn to a worksheet icon near cell B30. This indicates that at least one of the precedents for this cell is on another worksheet.
2. Click Trace Precedents again. Excel draws arrows from the precedent cells to the precedents of those cells. These are the second-level precedents of the original cell. Continue clicking Trace Precedents to see additional levels. In this case, practically every cell on the worksheet is a precedent of cell D32.
3. To remove the arrows, use the Remove Arrows icon in the Formula Auditing group.

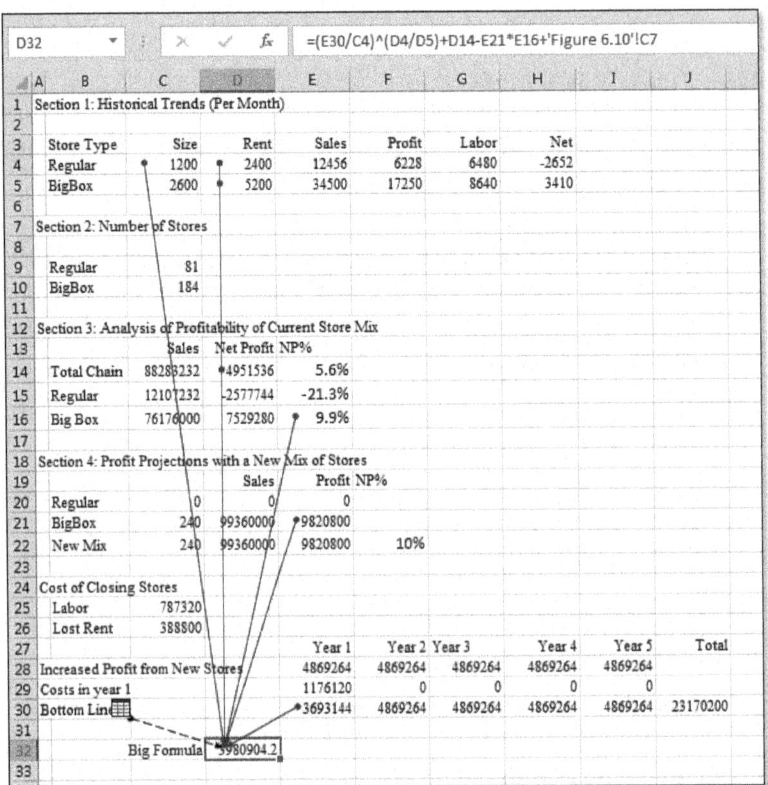

Figure 6.13 The results of Trace Precedents for cell D32.

Tracing dependents

The Formula Auditing section provides another interesting option besides the ones discussed so far in this chapter. You can use the Formula Auditing section to trace dependents, so you can find all the cells on the current worksheet that depend on the active cell. Before deleting a cell, consider clicking Trace Dependents to determine whether any cells on the current sheet refer to this cell. This prevents many #REF! errors from occurring.

CAUTION

Even if tracing dependents does not show any cells that are dependent on the current cell, other cells on other worksheets or on other workbooks might rely on this cell.

Using the Watch Window

If you have a large spreadsheet, you might want to watch the results of some distant cells. You can use the Watch Window icon in the Formula Auditing section of the Formulas tab to open a floating box called the Watch Window screen. To use the Watch Window screen, follow these steps:

1. Click the Add Watch icon. The Add Watch dialog box appears.

2. In the Add Watch dialog box, specify a cell to watch, as shown in Figure 6.14. After you add several cells, the Watch Window screen floats above your worksheet, showing the current value of each cell that was added to it. The Watch Window screen identifies the current value and the current formula of each watched cell.

In theory, this feature can be used to watch a value in a far-off section of the worksheet.

TIP

To jump to a watched cell quickly, you can double-click the cell in the Watch Window screen. You can resize the watch window and resize the columns as necessary.

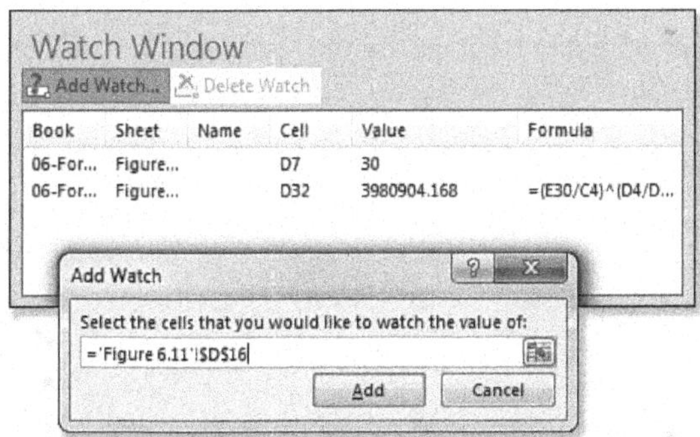

Figure 6.14 Adding a watch to the Watch Window screen.

Evaluate a formula in slow motion

Most of the time, Excel calculates formulas in an instant. It can help your understanding of the formula to watch it being calculated in slow motion. If you need to see exactly how a formula is being calculated, follow these steps:

1. Select the cell that contains the formula in which you are interested.

2. On the Formulas tab, in the Formula Auditing group, select Evaluate Formula. The Evaluate Formula dialog box appears, showing the formula. The following component of the formula is highlighted: It is the next section of the formula to be calculated.

3. If desired, click Evaluate to calculate the highlighted portion of the formula.

4. Click Step In to begin a new Evaluate section for the cell references in the underlined portion of the formula. Figure 6.15 shows the Evaluate Formula dialog box after stepping in to the E30 portion of the formula.

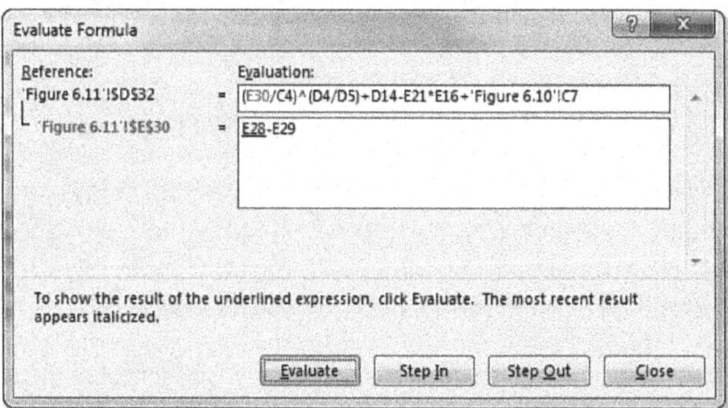

Figure 6.15 The Evaluate Formula dialog box enables you to calculate a formula in slow motion.

Evaluating part of a formula

When you do not need to evaluate an entire formula, use the F9 feature. Follow these steps to evaluate part of a formula:

1. Use the mouse to select just the desired portion of the formula in the formula bar, as shown in Figure 6.16.

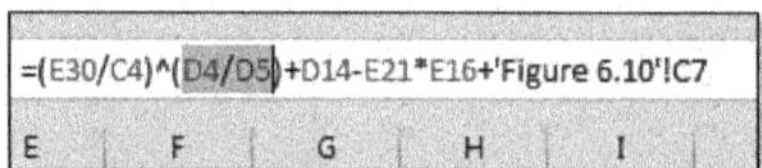

Figure 6.16 You can select a portion of the formula in the formula bar.

2. Press F9. Excel calculates just the highlighted portion of the formula, as shown in Figure 6.17.

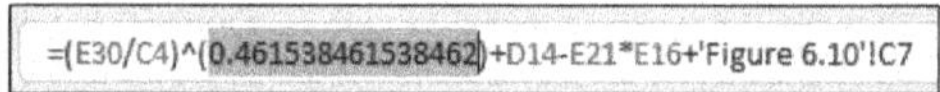

Figure 6.17 Press F9 to calculate just the highlighted portion of the formula.

Be sure to press the Esc key to exit the formula after you use this method. If you press Enter instead to accept the formula, that portion of the formula permanently stays in its calculated form, such as 0.407407. Instead of pressing the Esc key, you could press Ctrl+z to step backward in case you pressed F9 multiple times.

TROUBLESHOOTING

You might need to use Excel as a calculator without overwriting any cells.

If you must do a calculation without entering the result in a cell, follow these steps:

1. Choose any cell (regardless of whether it contains data).
2. Type an equal sign and the calculation, such as **=14215469*5**. Do not press Enter. Instead, press F9.
3. The answer, 71077345, appears in both the formula bar and in the cell. The characters are already selected, so you can easily press Ctrl+C to copy the answer to the Clipboard.
4. Press Esc to clear the temporary calculation and go back to the original cell contents.

CHAPTER 7

Understanding functions

Excel is used on 750 million desktops around the world. People in all career types use Excel, as do many home users who take advantage of Excel's powerful features to track their finances, investments, and more. Part of Excel's versatility is its wide range of built-in functions.

Excel offers 502 built-in calculation functions. This number grows with each new release. Recent additions to Excel include XLOOKUP, XMATCH, LET, LAMBDA, ARRAYTOTEXT, TEXTTOARRAY, MAP, REDUCE, SCAN, BYROW, BYCOL, and ISOMITTED.

Working with functions

To use functions successfully in a worksheet, you need to follow the function syntax. Keep in mind that a formula that makes use of a function needs to start with an equal sign. You type the function name, an opening parenthesis, function arguments (separated by commas), and the closing parenthesis.

The general syntax of a function looks like this:

```
=FunctionName(Argument1,Argument2,Argument3)
```

Parentheses are needed with every function, including functions that require no arguments. For example, these functions still require the parentheses:

```
=NOW()
```

```
=DATE()
```

```
=TODAY()
```

```
=PI()
```

The arguments for a function should be entered in the correct order, as specified in this book or Excel Help. For example, the PMT() function expects the arguments to have the interest rate first, followed by the number of periods, followed by the present value. If you attempt to enter the arguments in the wrong order, Excel happily calculates the wrong result.

In many cases, you can enter arguments as numbers or as cell references. For example, all these formulas are valid:

```
=SUM(1,2,3^2,4/5,6*7)
=SUM(A1:A9,C1,D2,Sheet2!E3:M10)
=SUM(A1:A9,100,200,B3*5)
```

NOTE

Chapters 8, "Using everyday functions: math, date and time, and text functions," and 9, "Using powerful functions: logical, lookup, and database functions," cover many interesting functions. This chapter covers a number of the most commonly used functions.

NOTE

Excel functions can return errors. This happens most frequently when one of the arguments passed to the function is outside the range of what the function expects. When you receive a `#NUM!`, `#VALUE!`, or `#N/A` error, you should look in Excel Help for the function. The Remarks section usually indicates exactly what problems can cause each type of error.

The Formulas tab in Excel

One way to find functions in Excel is on the Formulas tab. This tab offers the following icons: Insert Function, AutoSum, Recently Used, Financial, Logical, Text, Date & Time, Lookup & Reference, Math & Trig, and More Functions. As shown in Figure 7.1, when you click the More Functions icon, a drop-down menu with six additional function groups—Statistical, Engineering, Cube, Information, Compatibility, and Web—appears.

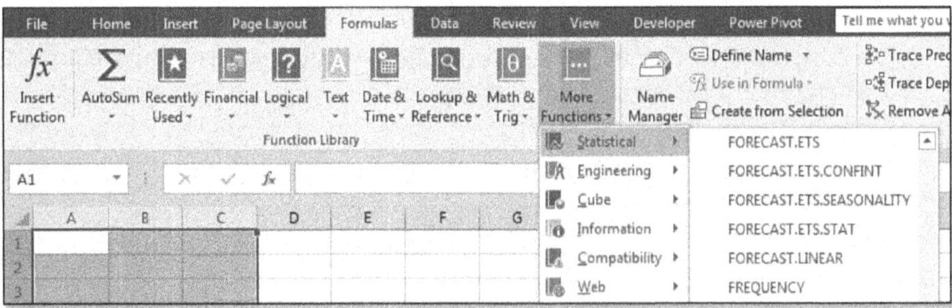

Figure 7.1 The Formulas tab contains icons for finding functions.

The Formulas tab is designed to make it easier to find the right function. You select an icon from the ribbon, and an alphabetical list of functions in that group appears. If you hover your mouse over a function in the list, Excel displays a description of what the function does, as shown in Figure 7.2.

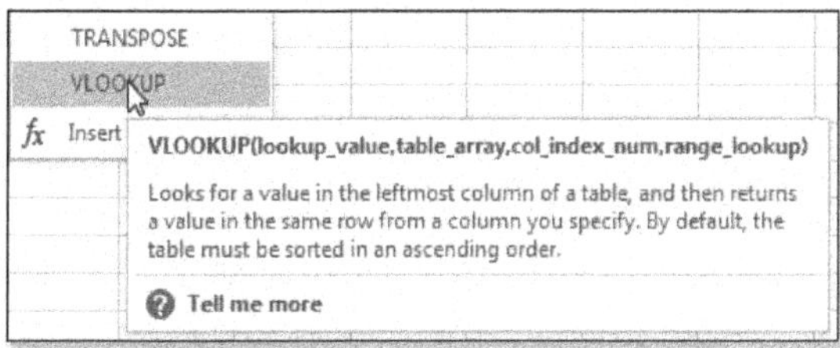

Figure 7.2 Hover over a function, and Excel displays a tip explaining what the function does.

Finding the function you need

The inherent problem with the Formulas tab is that you often have to guess where your desired function might be hiding. The function categories have been established in Excel for a decade, and in some cases, functions are tucked away in strange places.

For example, the `SUM()` function is a Math & Trig function. This makes sense because adding numbers is clearly a mathematical process. However, the `AVERAGE()` function is not available in the Math & Trig icon. (It is under More Functions, Statistical.) The `COUNT()` function could be math, reference, or information, but it is found under More Functions, Statistical.

By dividing the list of functions into categories, Microsoft has made it rather difficult to find certain functions. Fortunately, as described in the following sections, you can use some tricks to make this process simpler.

Using Tab to AutoComplete functions

One feature in Excel is Formula AutoComplete. Sometimes you might remember part of the function name but not the name. For example, if you type **=LOOK**, Excel will offer `LOOKUP`, `HLOOKUP`, `VLOOKUP`, and `XLOOKUP`. Rather than trying to figure out which category on the Formulas tab contains your function, you can just start typing =LOOK into a cell. Excel displays a pop-up window with all the functions that contain LOOK, as shown in Figure 7.3. This feature has been changed since Excel 2016. Previously, typing **=LOO** would not have returned `XLOOKUP`, `VLOOKUP`, or `HLOOKUP` because the AutoComplete only matched from the beginning of a word.

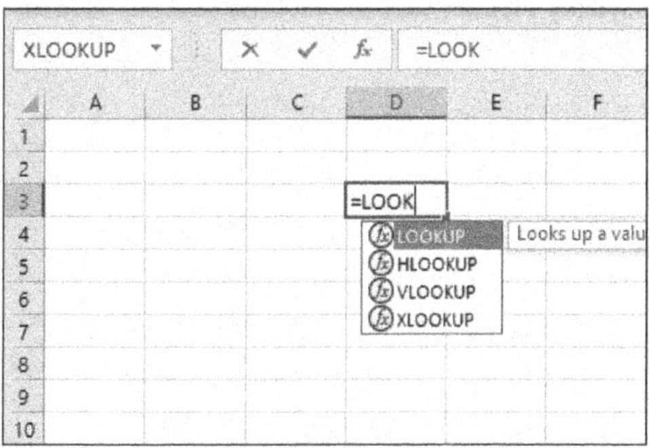

Figure 7.3 Rather than use the icons on the Formulas tab, you can type =LOOK to display a list of the Lookup functions.

To accept a function name from the list, you can either double-click the function name or select the name and press Tab.

Using the Insert Function dialog box to find functions

A large Insert Function icon appears on the Formula tab of the ribbon. This command is repeated at the bottom of every function category. These 14 new entry points for Insert Function were added in Excel 2007, but it is easier to use the fx icon located to the left of the formula bar. Click the fx, and the Insert Function dialog box appears.

Use the Search For A Function box to locate the function. For example, if you typed `loan payment` and then clicked Go, Excel would suggest `PMT` (the correct function) as well as `PPMT`, `ISPMT`, `RATE`, and others.

When you choose a function in the Insert Function dialog box, the dialog box displays the syntax for the function, as well as a one-sentence description of the function, as shown in Figure 7.4. If you need more details, you can click the Help On This Function hyperlink in the lower-left corner of the Insert Function dialog box.

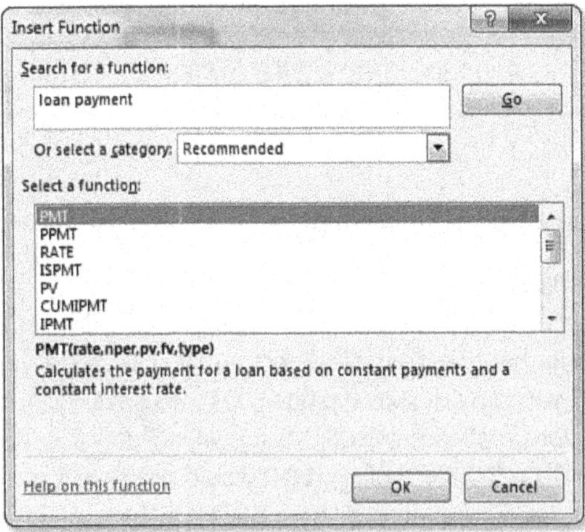

Figure 7.4 The Insert Function dialog box enables you to browse the syntax and descriptions. The Help On This Function hyperlink leads to more help.

Getting help with Excel functions

Every Excel function has three levels of help:

- On-grid ToolTip
- Function Arguments dialog box
- Excel Help

TIP

If you type =FunctionName(**in a cell, you can press Ctrl+A anytime after the opening parenthesis to display the Function Arguments dialog box. For example, type** =XLOOKUP(**followed by Ctrl+A or type** =REDUCE(**followed by Ctrl+A.**

The following sections discuss these levels of help. However, you are sure to find the Function Arguments dialog box to be one of the best ways to get help.

Using on-grid ToolTips

In any cell, you can type an equal sign, a function name, and the opening parenthesis. Excel displays a ToolTip that shows the expected arguments. In many cases, this ToolTip is enough to guide you through the function. For example, I can usually remember that the function for figuring out a car loan payment is =PMT(), but I can never remember the order of the arguments. The ToolTip, as shown in Figure 7.5, is enough to remind me that rate comes first, followed by the number of periods, and then the principal amount or present value. Any function arguments displayed in square brackets are optional, so in the example shown in Figure 7.5, you know that you might not have to enter anything for fv or type.

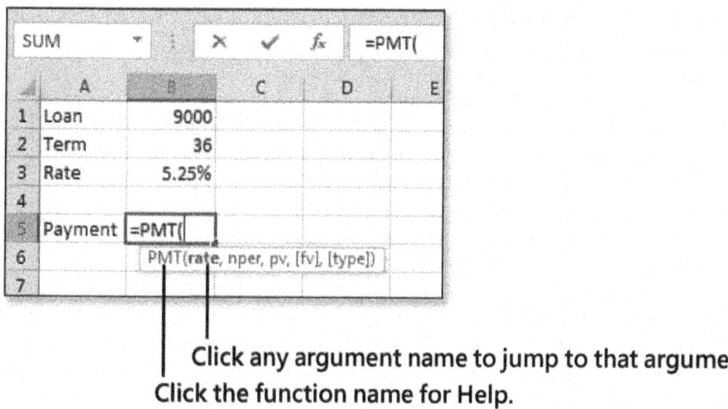

Figure 7.5 The ToolTip assists you in remembering the proper order for the arguments.

As you type each comma in the function, the next argument in the ToolTip lights up in boldface. This way, you always know which argument you are entering.

TIP

By the way, you can click the formula ToolTip and drag it to a new location on the worksheet. This can be useful if the ToolTip is covering cells that you need to click when building the function.

If you click the function name in the ToolTip, Excel opens Help for that function.

Using the Function Arguments dialog box

When you access a function through the Function Wizard or a drop-down menu, Excel displays the Function Arguments dialog box. This dialog box is one of the best features in Excel. If you've started to type the function and typed the opening parenthesis, then pressing Ctrl+A or clicking the fx icon to the left of the formula bar displays the Function Arguments dialog box.

As shown in Figure 7.6, the Function Arguments dialog box has many elements:

- The one-sentence description of the function appears in the center of the dialog box.
- As you tab into the text box for each argument, the description of the argument is shown in the dialog box. This description guides you as to what Excel is expecting. For example, in the dialog box shown in Figure 7.6, Excel reminds you that the interest rate needs to be divided by four for quarterly payments. This reminds you to divide the rate in cell B3 by 12 for monthly payments.
- To the right of each argument in the dialog box is a reference button. You can click this button to collapse the dialog box so you can point to the cells for that argument.
- To the right of each text box is a label that shows the result of the entry for that argument.
- Any arguments in bold are required. Arguments not in bold are optional.
- After you enter the required arguments, the dialog box shows the preliminary result of the formula. This is on the right side, just below the last argument text box. It appears again in the lower-left corner, just above the Help On This Function hyperlink.
- A Help On This Function hyperlink to the Help topic for the function appears in the lower-left corner of the dialog box.

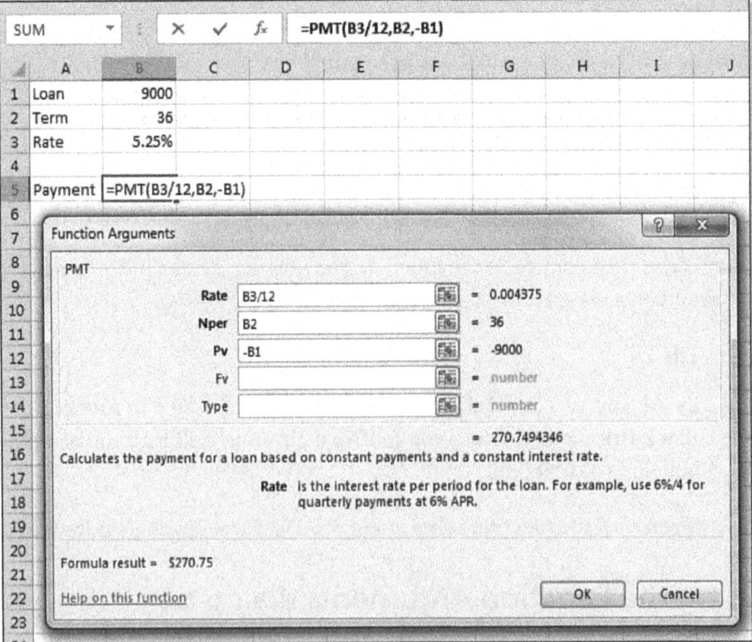

Figure 7.6 The Function Arguments dialog box helps you build a function, one step at a time.

TROUBLESHOOTING

How can you use the Function Arguments dialog when you have a nested function? For example, if you are using MATCH inside of INDEX.

Start by typing the =`INDEX(` function and press Ctrl+A to display the Function Arguments.

In the second Row_Num box of the Function Arguments dialog box, type MATCH(.

Using your mouse, reach up to the formula bar and click inside of the word `MATCH`. The Function Arguments dialog will switch to display the arguments for `MATCH`. When you complete the `MATCH` function and you want to return to the `INDEX` version of the Function Arguments dialog box, use the mouse to click INDEX in the formula bar.

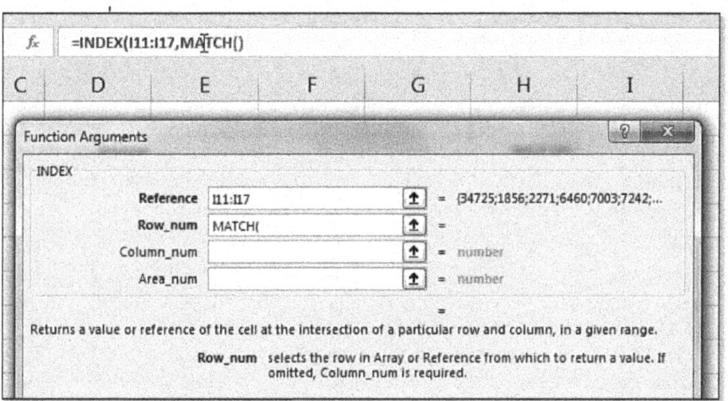

Using Excel Help

The Excel Help topics for the functions are incredibly complete. Each function's Help topic includes the following sections:

- The function syntax appears at the top of the topic. This includes a description of each function that might be more complete than the description in the Function Arguments dialog box.
- The Remarks section helps you troubleshoot possible problems with the function. It discusses specific limits for each argument and describes the meaning of each possible error that could be returned from the function.
- Each function has an example section composed of an embedded Excel Web App worksheet. You can click the XL icon in the footer of the example to download the example to your computer.

- The See Also section at the bottom of a Help topic enables you to discover related functions. The logical groupings suggested by See Also are far more useful than the category groupings in the Formulas tab.

Using AutoSum

Microsoft realizes that the most common function is the `SUM()` function. It is so popular that Excel provides one-click access to the AutoSum feature.

The AutoSum icon is the large Greek letter sigma that is the second icon on the Formulas tab or a small icon on the right side of the Home tab. You can click this icon to use AutoSum, or you can use the drop-down menu at the bottom of the icon to access AutoSum versions of Average, Count Numbers, Max, and Min, as shown in Figure 7.7.

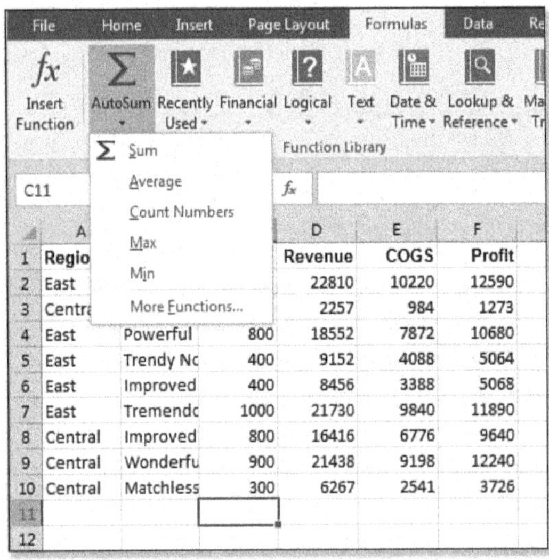

Figure 7.7 The AutoSum drop-down menu offers the capability to average and more.

> TIP
>
> **Pressing Alt+= is equivalent to clicking the AutoSum icon.**

When you click the AutoSum button, Excel seeks to add up the numbers that are above or to the left of the current cell. In general, when you click the AutoSum icon, Excel guesses which cells you are trying to sum. Excel automatically types the `SUM()` formula. You should review Excel's guess to make sure that Excel chose the correct range to sum. In Figure 7.8, for example, Excel correctly guesses that you want to sum the column of quantities above the cell.

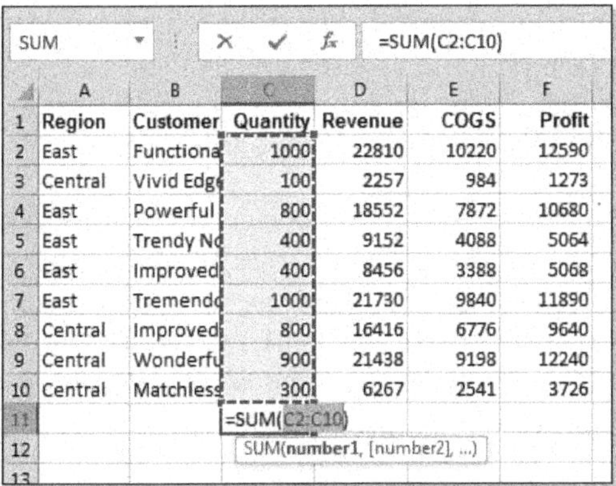

SUM | =SUM(C2:C10)

	A	B	C	D	E	F
1	Region	Customer	Quantity	Revenue	COGS	Profit
2	East	Functiona	1000	22810	10220	12590
3	Central	Vivid Edg	100	2257	984	1273
4	East	Powerful	800	18552	7872	10680
5	East	Trendy N	400	9152	4088	5064
6	East	Improved	400	8456	3388	5068
7	East	Tremend	1000	21730	9840	11890
8	Central	Improved	800	16416	6776	9640
9	Central	Wonderfu	900	21438	9198	12240
10	Central	Matchles	300	6267	2541	3726
11			=SUM(C2:C10)			
12			SUM(number1, [number2], ...)			

Figure 7.8 The AutoSum feature is proposing a formula to sum C2:C10.

Potential problems with AutoSum

Although you should always check the range proposed by the AutoSum feature, in some cases, you should be especially wary. If the headings above the data are numeric, for example, this will fool AutoSum. In Figure 7.9, the 2019 heading in B1 is numeric. This causes Excel to include the heading incorrectly in the total for column B.

SWITCH | =SUM(B1:B10)

	A	B	C	D	E	F
1	Customer	2019	2020	2021	2022	Total
2	Functional Eggbeater Co	84093	91661	101744	113953	391451
3	Vivid Edger Co	64853	68096	70820	71528	275297
4	Powerful Edger Supply	61312	63151	70098	78510	273071
5	Trendy Notebook Corp	52486	56160	62338	63585	234569
6	Improved Vegetable Inc.	66694	69362	70749	73579	280384
7	Tremendous Thermostat Partners	69840	77522	84499	92949	324810
8	Improved Vegetable Inc.	61326	62553	66306	70284	260469
9	Wonderful Kettle Corp	73658	77341	81208	90141	322348
10	Matchless Hardware Traders	72129	77178	81809	87536	318652
11	Total	=SUM(B1:B10)				
12		SUM(number1, [number2], ...)				

Figure 7.9 Numeric headings confuse AutoSum.

When Excel proposes the wrong range for a sum, use your mouse to highlight the correct range before pressing Enter.

Excel avoids including other `SUM()` functions in an AutoSum range. If a range contains a `SUM()` function that references other cells, Excel prematurely stops just before the `SUM()` function. This problem happens only when the `SUM()` function references other cells. If the cell contained `=7000+1878` or `=H3+H4` or `=SUM(7000,1878)`, AutoSum would include the cell.

Excel prefers to sum a column of numbers instead of a row of numbers. Figure 7.10 shows a strange anomaly. If you place the cell pointer in cell F2 and click AutoSum, Excel correctly guesses that you want to total B2:E2. Cell F3 works fine. However, when you get to cell F4, Excel has a choice. There are two numbers above F4 and four numbers to the left of F4. Because there are two numbers directly above, Excel tries to total those two numbers. This problem happens starting in the third row of the data set and continues to the bottom.

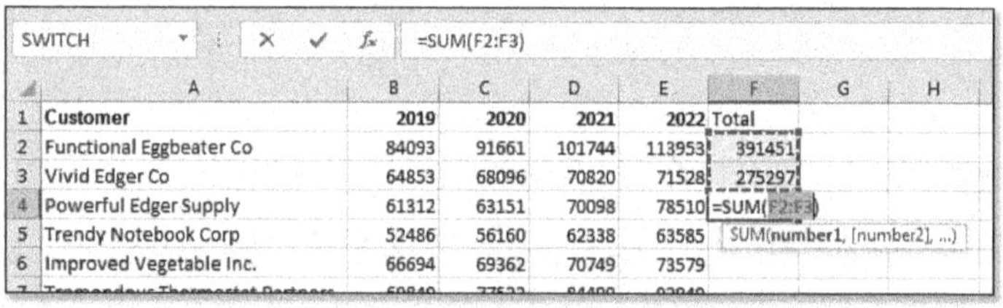

SWITCH =SUM(F2:F3)

	A	B	C	D	E	F	G	H
1	Customer	2019	2020	2021	2022	Total		
2	Functional Eggbeater Co	84093	91661	101744	113953	391451		
3	Vivid Edger Co	64853	68096	70820	71528	275297		
4	Powerful Edger Supply	61312	63151	70098	78510	=SUM(F2:F3)		
5	Trendy Notebook Corp	52486	56160	62338	63585	SUM(number1, [number2], ...)		
6	Improved Vegetable Inc.	66694	69362	70749	73579			

Figure 7.10 Excel can choose between summing two numbers above or four numbers to the left. Excel chooses incorrectly.

Special tricks with AutoSum

There is an amazing trick you can use with AutoSum. If you select a range of cells before clicking the AutoSum button, Excel does a much better job of predicting what to sum.

In Figure 7.10, for example, you could select B11:E11 before clicking the AutoSum button, and Excel would know to sum each column. Be careful, though, because Excel does not preview its guess before entering the formula. You should always check a formula after using AutoSum to make sure the correct range was selected.

If your selection contains a mix of blank cells and nonblank cells, Excel adds the AutoSum to only the blank cells. In Figure 7.11, for example, you select the range B2:F11 before clicking the AutoSum button.

After clicking the AutoSum button, Excel correctly fills in totals for all the rows and columns, as shown in Figure 7.12.

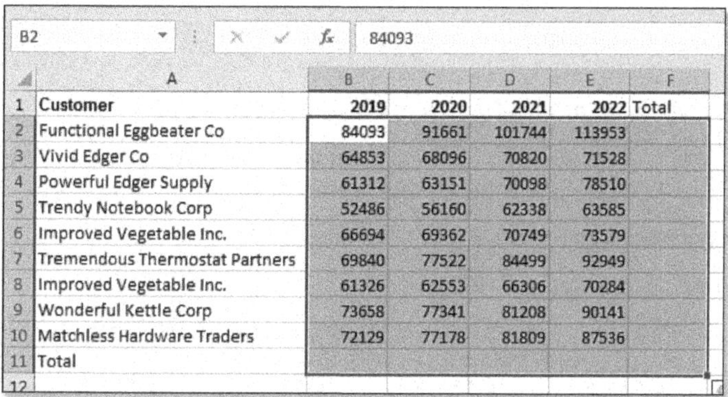

B2 | 84093

	A	B	C	D	E	F
1	Customer	2019	2020	2021	2022	Total
2	Functional Eggbeater Co	84093	91661	101744	113953	
3	Vivid Edger Co	64853	68096	70820	71528	
4	Powerful Edger Supply	61312	63151	70098	78510	
5	Trendy Notebook Corp	52486	56160	62338	63585	
6	Improved Vegetable Inc.	66694	69362	70749	73579	
7	Tremendous Thermostat Partners	69840	77522	84499	92949	
8	Improved Vegetable Inc.	61326	62553	66306	70284	
9	Wonderful Kettle Corp	73658	77341	81208	90141	
10	Matchless Hardware Traders	72129	77178	81809	87536	
11	Total					

Figure 7.11 If your selection contains a mix of blank and nonblank cells, AutoSum writes only to the blank cells.

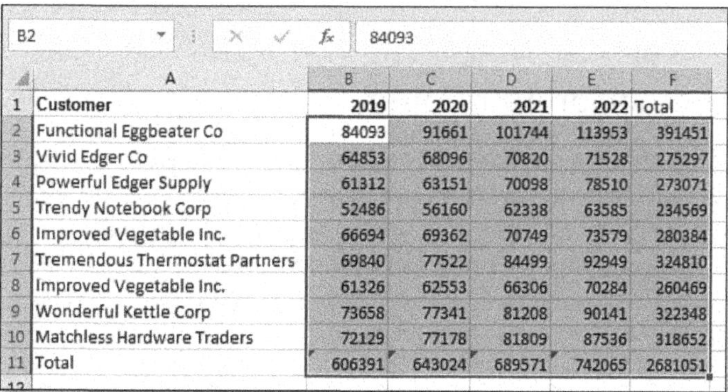

B2 | 84093

	A	B	C	D	E	F
1	Customer	2019	2020	2021	2022	Total
2	Functional Eggbeater Co	84093	91661	101744	113953	391451
3	Vivid Edger Co	64853	68096	70820	71528	275297
4	Powerful Edger Supply	61312	63151	70098	78510	273071
5	Trendy Notebook Corp	52486	56160	62338	63585	234569
6	Improved Vegetable Inc.	66694	69362	70749	73579	280384
7	Tremendous Thermostat Partners	69840	77522	84499	92949	324810
8	Improved Vegetable Inc.	61326	62553	66306	70284	260469
9	Wonderful Kettle Corp	73658	77341	81208	90141	322348
10	Matchless Hardware Traders	72129	77178	81809	87536	318652
11	Total	606391	643024	689571	742065	2681051

Figure 7.12 By using AutoSum, you can add 14 `SUM()` formulas with one click.

CAUTION

You should not try the technique shown in Figure 7.12 with AVERAGE. The formula in F11 would produce an average of the averages, which will not match the results of =AVERAGE(B2:E10). The same problem would happen with using COUNT from the AutoSum drop-down menu.

> **Inside OUT**
>
> ***Can you AutoSum from the top of a column of numbers?***
>
> There is no secret way to make the AutoSum add the numbers below the active cell. However, if you must do this frequently, follow these steps:
>
> 1. Select the blank cell above a column of numbers.
> 2. Press Alt+= to start the AutoSum.
> 3. If Excel filled in any cell reference as the beginning formula, press the Delete key.
> 4. Press the down arrow once to move to the first number in the range.
> 5. Press Ctrl+Shift+Down Arrow to select to the end of the range.
> 6. Press Enter.

Using AutoAverage or AutoCount

The AutoSum button includes a drop-down menu arrow with choices for Average, Count, Max, and Min. If you find yourself frequently using the choices in this drop-down menu, you can add an icon to the Quick Access Toolbar that will AutoAverage, AutoCount, and so on. Open the AutoSum drop-down menu. Right-click Average and choose Add To Quick Access Toolbar to have one-click access to an icon that works similar to AutoSum but uses the AVERAGE calculation instead (see Figure 7.13).

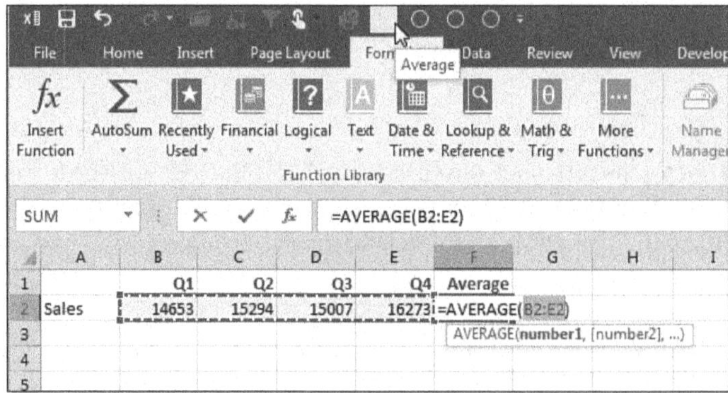

Figure 7.13 Add icons to the Quick Access Toolbar to get one-click access to AutoAverage, AutoMin, AutoMax, and AutoCount.

CAUTION

Microsoft uses the same green circle icon to represent `Average`, `Count`, `Max`, and `Min`. If you are going to add all four icons to the Quick Access Toolbar, add them in alphabetical order to help you remember the sequence in which they appear.

Function reference chapters

Appendix A contains a complete reference to all functions in Excel. Chapters 8 through 10 provide examples of some of the more popular functions.

Function coverage is broken out as follows:

- Chapter 8 describes functions that many people encounter in their everyday lives: some of the math functions, date functions, and text functions.
- Chapter 9 describes functions that are a bit more difficult, but that should be a part of your everyday arsenal. These include a series of functions for making decisions in a formula. They include the `IF` function and are known collectively as the *logical functions*. Chapter 9 also describes the information, lookup, and database functions.
- Chapter 10 provides a look at the new LET, `LAMBDA`, and data type functions.

CHAPTER 8

Using everyday functions: math, date and time, and text functions

Excel offers many functions for dealing with basic math, dates and times, and text. This chapter describes the functions that you can access with the Formulas tab using the Text icon, the Date & Time icon, and the Math portion of the Math & Trig icon.

Examples of math functions

The most common formula in Excel is a formula to add a column of numbers. In addition to SUM, Excel offers a variety of mathematical functions.

Using SUM to add numbers

The SUM function is by far the most commonly used function in Excel. This function can add numbers from one or more ranges of data.

Syntax:

```
=SUM(number1,number2,...)
```

The SUM function adds all the numbers in a range of cells. The arguments number1, number2,... are 1 to 255 arguments for which you want the total value or sum.

A typical use of this function is =SUM(B4:B12). It is also possible to use =SUM(1,2,3). In the latter example, you cannot specify more than 255 individual values. In the former example, you can specify up to 255 ranges, each of which can include thousands or millions of cells.

In Figure 8.1, cell B25 contains a formula to sum three individual cells: =SUM(B17,B19,B23).

	A	B	C	D	E	F	G	H	I
1	**XYZ Company**								
2				**6**	=SUM(1,2,"3")				
3		**Sales**							
4	Excellent Sandal Company	141		1					
5	Astonishing Raft Inc.	539		2					
6	Fabulous Shoe Corporation	446		3					
7	Powerful Vise Company	243		**3**	=SUM(D4:D6)				
8	Mouthwatering Hardware Supply	209							
9	Stunning Door Corporation	885							
10	Rare Barometer Company	329							
11	Paramount Umbrella Corporation	452				Jan	Feb	Mar	
12					A	1	2	4	
13	Total	**3244**	=SUM(B4:B12)		B	8	16	32	
14					C	64	128	256	
15	Product A - East Region	10			D	512	1024	2048	
16	Product A - West Region	20							
17	Product A Total	**30**			144	=SUM(F13:H14 G12:G15)			
18									
19	Product B - Government Sales	15							
20									
21	Product C - East Region	10							
22	Product C - West Region	20							
23	Product C Total	**30**							
24									
25	Total	**75**	=SUM(B17,B19,B23)						
26									

Figure 8.1 A variety of SUM formulas.

It is unlikely that you will need more than 255 arguments in this function, but if you do, you can group arguments in parentheses. For example, =SUM((A10,A12),(A14,A16)) would count as only two of the 255 allowed arguments.

If a text value that looks like a number is included in a range, the text value is not included in the result of the sum. Strangely enough, if you specify the text value directly as an argument in the function, Excel adds it to the result. For example, =SUM(1,2,"3") is 6, yet =SUM(D4:D6) in cell D7 of Figure 8.1 results in 3.

The comma is treated as a union operator. If you replace the comma with a space, Excel finds the cells that fall in the intersection of the selected ranges. In cell E17, the formula of =SUM(F13:H14 G12:G15) adds up the two cells that are in common between the two ranges.

If one cell in a referenced range contains an error, the result of the SUM function is an error. To add numbers while ignoring error cells, use the AGGREGATE function.

It is valid to create a spearing formula. This type of formula adds the identical cell from many worksheets. For example, =SUM(Jan:Dec!B20) adds cell B20 on all 12 sheets between Jan and Dec. If the sheet names contain spaces or other nonalphabetic characters, surround the sheet names with apostrophes: =SUM('Jan 2025:Dec 2025'!B20).

Using AGGREGATE to ignore error cells or filtered rows

Added in Excel 2010, the AGGREGATE function lets you perform 17 functions on a range of data while selectively ignoring error cells or rows hidden by a filter.

Syntax:

```
=AGGREGATE(function_num, options, array, [k])
```

The `options` argument is the interesting feature of the function. You can choose to ignore any, all, or none of these categories:

- Error values
- Hidden rows
- Other SUBTOTAL and AGGREGATE functions

The capability to ignore filtered rows and other AGGREGATE functions is similar to the SUBTOTAL function. The capability of AGGREGATE to ignore error values solves a common Excel problem. For most Excel functions, a single #N/A error cell in a range causes most functions to return an #N/A error. The options in AGGREGATE enable you to ignore any error cells in the range.

The `options` argument controls which values are ignored. This is a simple binary system, as follows:

- To ignore other subtotals, add 0. To include subtotals, add 4.
- To ignore hidden rows, add 1.
- To ignore error values, add 2.
- Thus, to ignore other subtotals, hidden rows, and error values, you specify `3 (0+1+2)` as the `options` argument.
- To ignore error values but include other SUBTOTAL values, you specify `5 (1+4)` as the argument.

This calculation works out as shown in Table 8.1.

Table 8.1 Arguments for the AGGREGATE function

Option	Meaning
0	Ignore other subtotals
1	Ignore hidden rows and subtotals
2	Ignore error cells and subtotals

3	Ignore all three
4	Ignore nothing
5	Ignore hidden rows
6	Ignore error cells
7	Ignore hidden rows and error cells

In Figure 8.2, the `#N/A` error in cell F13 causes the `SUM` function in F18 to also return an `#N/A`. If you use a 2, 3, 5, or 7 as the second argument of AGGREGATE, you can easily sum all the other numbers as in cell F1. You can also use other function numbers to calculate `MIN`, `MAX`, `COUNT`, `MEDIAN`, `MODE`, `PERCENTILE`, and `QUARTILE` values.

You can also use the function to ignore cells hidden by a filter. Whereas the old `SUBTOTAL` function enabled you to do this for 11 calculation functions, the AGGREGATE function adds eight new functions to the list.

B20 fx =AGGREGATE(14,6,(D9:D16)/((B9:B16="East")*(C9:C16="R1")),2)

	A	B	C	D	E	F	G	H	I	J
1	SUM Ignoring Errors:			255000		4530	=AGGREGATE(9,2,F9:F16)			
2	MIN Ignoring Errors:			1000		10	=AGGREGATE(5,2,F9:F16)			
3	3rd Smallest Ignoring Errors:			4000		80	=AGGREGATE(15,3,F9:F16,3)			
4	Value at 30th Percentile.exc:			4400		72	=AGGREGATE(16,3,F9:F16,0.3)			
5	Value at 30th Percentile.inc:			3400		56	=AGGREGATE(18,3,F9:F16,0.3)			
6	Value at 3rd Quartile:			40000		880	=AGGREGATE(17,3,F9:F16,3)			
7										
8	Customer	Region	Rep	Sales	Rate	Bonus				
9	Astonishing Raft Inc.	West	R3	16000	3%	480				
10	Excellent Sandal Company	East	R1	1000	1%	10				
11	Fabulous Shoe Corporation	East	R2	2000	2%	40				
12	Mouthwatering Hardware Supply	West	R4	64000	4%	2560				
13	Paramount Umbrella Corporation	West	R5	128000	#N/A	#N/A				
14	Powerful Vise Company	West	R4	32000	4%	1280				
15	Rare Barometer Company	East	R1	8000	1%	80				
16	Stunning Door Corporation	East	R2	4000	2%	80				
17										
18	SUM			255000		#N/A	=SUM(F9:F17)			
19										
20	2nd largest East R1 sale:	1000	=AGGREGATE(14,6,(D9:D16)/((B9:B16="East")*(C9:C16="R1")),2)							
21										

Figure 8.2 Using a 2 or 3 as the `options` argument for AGGREGATE allows the function to ignore error cells in a range.

Table 8.2 shows the 19 functions available in the AGGREGATE function. This list mirrors the 11 functions available in `SUBTOTAL` (arranged alphabetically to match those in the `SUBTOTAL` function) and then eight new functions arranged in order of popularity.

CHAPTER 8

Table 8.2 Functions available in AGGREGATE

Fx #	Function
1	AVERAGE
2	COUNT
3	COUNTA
4	MAX
5	MIN
6	PRODUCT
7	STDDEV.S
8	STDDEV.P
9	SUM
10	VAR.S
11	VAR.P
12	MEDIAN
13	MODE.SNGL
14	LARGE
15	SMALL
16	PERCENTILE.INC
17	QUARTILE.INC
18	PERCENTILE.EXC
19	QUARTILE.EXC

The last six functions in this list require you to specify a value for k as the fourth argument. LARGE and SMALL typically return the kth largest or smallest value from a list. Use the fourth argument in AGGREGATE to specify the value for k. The last six functions allow for a calculated array instead of a range of cells. Customers using Office 365 will be able to specify arrays for all 19 functions within AGGREGATE. Excel 2019 and earlier will allow arrays only for the last six functions.

In cell F3 of Figure 8.2, the final argument of 3 specifies that you want the third-smallest number in the array. For LARGE, SMALL, and QUARTILE, you should specify an integer for k. For PERCENTILE, specify a decimal between 0 and 1.

When you are trying to return results from the visible rows of a filtered data set, you can use either SUBTOTAL or AGGREGATE. In Figure 8.3, the SUM function in D1 returns the sum of the visible and hidden rows. The SUBTOTAL function in D2 returns the sum of the visible rows, the same as the AGGREGATE function in D3. The advantage of AGGREGATE is that it can return MEDIAN, LARGE, SMALL, PERCENTILE, and QUARTILE on the visible rows as well.

D3 =AGGREGATE(9,1,D8:D15)

	A	B	C	D	E	F	G
1	Total Using SUM			255000	=SUM(D8:D15)		
2	Total Using SUBTOTAL			15000	=SUBTOTAL(9,D$8:D$15)		
3	Total Using AGGREGATE			15000	=AGGREGATE(9,1,D8:D15)		
4	Median Using MEDIAN			12000	=MEDIAN(D8:D15)		
5	Median using AGGREGATE			3000	=AGGREGATE(12,1,D8:D15)		
6							
7	Customer	Regio	R(	Sal			
9	Excellent Sandal Company	East	R1	1000			
10	Fabulous Shoe Corporation	East	R2	2000			
14	Rare Barometer Company	East	R1	8000			
15	Stunning Door Corporation	East	R2	4000			
16							

Figure 8.3 AGGREGATE performs calculations on the visible items of a filtered data set.

Choosing between COUNT and COUNTA

The key to choosing between COUNT and COUNTA is to analyze the data you want to count. In Figure 8.4, someone has used the letter X in column B to indicate that training has been started. In this case, you would use COUNTA to get an accurate count. Column C contains dates (which are treated as numeric). In column C, either COUNT or COUNTA returns the correct result. Column D has a mix of text and numeric entries. If you want to count how many people took the test, use COUNTA. If you want to count how many people received a numeric score, use COUNT.

D18 =COUNTA(D2:D15)

	A	B	C	D
1	NAME	Training Started	Training Completed	Test Score
2	TERRY LEBLANC			
3	LUIS CHRISTENSEN	X	2/28/2018	97
4	JENNIFER GALLOWAY	X		
5	ROSEMARY ATKINS	X	3/14/2014	85
6	GLORIA DUNLAP	X		
7	PATSY WARD			
8	CLAIRE RUSH	X	3/6/2018	Incomplete
9	MARIE HOFFMAN	X		
10	JEANNE CLEMONS			
11	MARJORIE LOPEZ	X	3/4/2018	92
12	JACOB INGRAM	X		
13	EDWARD HOOD			
14	MARTIN HAYES	X	3/8/2018	45
15	CHARLENE BURKE	X		
16				
17	COUNT:	0	5	4
18	COUNTA:	10	5	5
19				

Figure 8.4 Whether you use COUNT or COUNTA depends on whether your data is numeric. COUNT counts only dates and numeric entries. COUNTA counts anything that is nonblank.

Rounding numbers

You can use a variety of functions—including ROUND, ROUNDDOWN, ROUNDUP, INT, TRUNC, FLOOR, FLOOR.MATH, CEILING, CEILING.MATH, EVEN, ODD, and MROUND—to round a result or to remove decimals from a result. The most common function is ROUND.

- `ROUND(number, num_digits)` rounds the number. To round to the nearest dollar, use 0 as the second argument. To round to the nearest penny, use 2 as the second argument. To round to the nearest thousand dollars, use –3 as the third argument. If the digit after the last significant digit is exactly 5, Excel will round away from zero. For example, `=ROUND(4.5,0)` will round to 5 and `=ROUND(-4.5,0)` will round to –5. See the note about ASTM E-29 rounding after Figure 8.5.

- `ROUNDUP(number, num_digits)` always rounds away from zero. Although this usually makes the number larger, the behavior for negative numbers is unusual. `=ROUNDUP(-1.1,0)` rounds away from zero to –2. If you want that to round to –1, use `TRUNC(number)` instead.

- `ROUNDDOWN(number, num_digits)` always rounds toward zero. Although this makes sense for positive numbers, the result for negative numbers might not make sense. `=ROUNDDOWN(-3.1,0)` rounds toward zero and produces –3. If you expect this to produce –4, use `=INT(-3.1)` instead.

- `MROUND(number, multiple)` rounds to the nearest multiple. Use for rounding to the nearest 5 or 25. `=MROUND(115,25)` rounds to 125. There are some unusual variants. `=EVEN(number)` always rounds up to an even number for the unusual situation in which items are packed two to a case. `=ODD(number)` rounds up to an odd integer.

Figure 8.5 illustrates several rounding options.

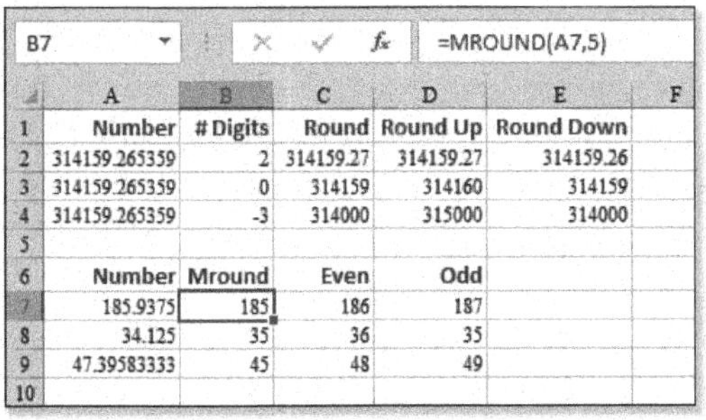

B7 =MROUND(A7,5)

	A	B	C	D	E	F
1	Number	# Digits	Round	Round Up	Round Down	
2	314159.265359	2	314159.27	314159.27	314159.26	
3	314159.265359	0	314159	314160	314159	
4	314159.265359	-3	314000	315000	314000	
5						
6	Number	Mround	Even	Odd		
7	185.9375	185	186	187		
8	34.125	35	36	35		
9	47.39583333	45	48	49		
10						

Figure 8.5 Rounding is easy in Excel using these functions.

NOTE

Note that the ASTM has published their E29 standard for rounding that differs from Excel's ROUND function. In the E29 standard, values in which the digits being removed are exactly 5, the ASTM suggests rounding toward the even number. For example, 3.5 rounds to 4 and 6.5 rounds to 6. This prevents a slight upwards skew to the numbers. While the Excel `ROUND` function does not behave this way, both the `VBA ROUND` function and the `Number.Round` function in Power Query both round toward even. To perform ASTM E-29 rounding with an Excel formula, use `=IF(MOD(A2,1)=0.5,MROUND(A2,2), ROUND(A2,0))`.

The last four functions in this group—`CEILING`, `CEILING.MATH`, `FLOOR`, and `FLOOR.MATH`—round a number in a certain direction to a certain number of digits. They require you to enter the number and the number of decimals to which to round. The behavior of the functions when a number was negative caused complaints from the mathematics community, so the Excel team reversed the behavior with the `.MATH` versions of the functions.

For example, `=CEILING(5.1,1)` rounds the 5.1 up to 6. Originally, Excel would always round away from zero: `=CEILING(-5.1,-1)` would round to –6. Mathematicians pointed out that –6 is actually lower than 5.1 and the correct answer should be –5. Thus, `CEILING.MATH(-5.1,1)` rounds up to –5.

The older CEILING function required the second argument to have the same sign as the first argument. The `.MATH` versions can deal with a negative number and a positive significance. Microsoft added an optional third Mode argument that allows `CEILING.MATH` to round away from zero. Figure 8.6 illustrates `CEILING`.

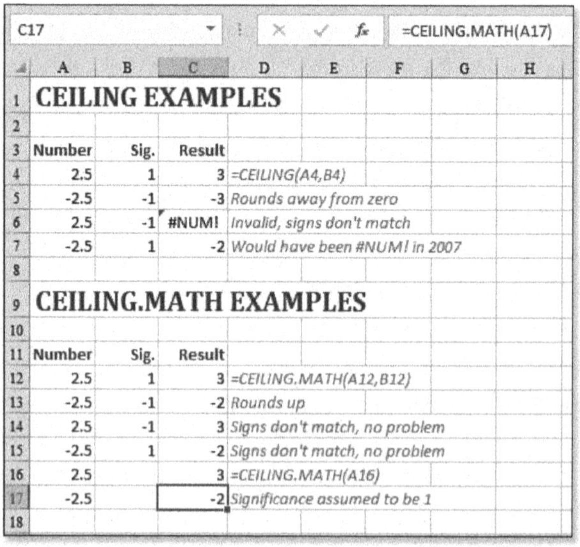

C17 | =CEILING.MATH(A17)

	A	B	C	D
1	**CEILING EXAMPLES**			
2				
3	**Number**	**Sig.**	**Result**	
4	2.5	1	3	*=CEILING(A4,B4)*
5	-2.5	-1	-3	*Rounds away from zero*
6	2.5	-1	#NUM!	*Invalid, signs don't match*
7	-2.5	1	-2	*Would have been #NUM! in 2007*
8				
9	**CEILING.MATH EXAMPLES**			
10				
11	**Number**	**Sig.**	**Result**	
12	2.5	1	3	*=CEILING.MATH(A12,B12)*
13	-2.5	-1	-2	*Rounds up*
14	2.5	-1	3	*Signs don't match, no problem*
15	-2.5	1	-2	*Signs don't match, no problem*
16	2.5		3	*=CEILING.MATH(A16)*
17	-2.5		-2	*Significance assumed to be 1*
18				

Figure 8.6 For negative numbers, `CEILING.MATH` rounds toward zero.

Using SUBTOTAL instead of SUM with multiple levels of totals

Consider the data set shown in Figure 8.7. This report shows a list of invoices for each customer. Someone has manually inserted rows and used the SUM function to total each customer. Cells C70 and C75 contain a SUM function.

E77 =SUBTOTAL(9,E2:E75)

	A	B	C	D	E	F	G	H
1	Customer	Invoice	Revenue	Revenue	Revenue			
67	Supreme Washer S	1133	562.94	562.94	562.94			
68	Supreme Washer S	1126	629.79	629.79	629.79			
69	Supreme Washer S	1148	341.13	341.13	341.13			
70	**Supreme Washer**	**Total**	**1533.86**	**1533.86**	**1533.86**			
71								
72	Well-Suited Utensi	1120	709.41	709.41	709.41			
73	Well-Suited Utensi	1153	224.07	224.07	224.07			
74	Well-Suited Utensi	1122	690.03	690.03	690.03			
75	**Well-Suited Utens**	**Total**	**1623.51**	**1623.51**	**1623.51**			
76								
77	**GRAND TOTAL**		**20598.01**	**20598.01**	**20598.01**			
78								
79	Row 70 formulas:							
80	Column C	=SUM(C67:C69)						
81	Column D	=SUM(D67:D69)						
82	Column E	=SUBTOTAL(9,E67:E69)						
83								
84	Row 77 formulas:							
85	Column C	=C5+C10+C15+C20+C25+C30+C35+C40+C45+C50+C55+C60+C65+C70+C75						
86	Column D	=SUM(D2:D75)/2						
87	Column E	=SUBTOTAL(9,E2:E75)						
88								

Figure 8.7 When you use SUBTOTAL instead of SUM for the customer totals, the problem of creating a grand total becomes simple.

It becomes incredibly difficult to total the data when it has intermediate SUM functions. The original formula in C77 must point to each subtotal cell.

Many accountants can teach you the old accounting trick whereby you total the entire column and divide by two to get the grand total. This is based on the assumption that every dollar is in the column twice: once in the detail row and once in the summary row. The formula in D77 is far shorter than the formula in C77 and produces the same answer. This trick does work, but it is hard to explain to your manager why it works.

A better solution is to use the SUBTOTAL function. Instead of `=SUM(D2:D75)`, use `=SUBTOTAL(9,D2:D75)`. The function totals all numbers in D2:D75 but ignores other subtotal functions.

While you are summing in this case, the SUBTOTAL function offers 11 arguments, numbered from 1 to 11: AVERAGE, COUNT, COUNTA, MAX, MIN, PRODUCT, STDEV, STDEVP, SUM, VAR, and VARP. It just happens that SUM is the ninth item in this list when these functions are arranged alphabetically in the English language, so 9 became the function number for SUM.

Totaling visible cells using SUBTOTAL

If you are using a filter to query a data set, you can use the SUBTOTAL function instead of the SUM function to show the total of the visible rows. In Figure 8.8, cell E1 contains a SUM function, which totals rows whether they are visible or not. Cell E2 contains a SUBTOTAL function. As you use the Filter drop-down menus to show just rows for sales of J730 by Jamie, the SUBTOTAL function updates to reflect the total of the visible rows. This makes the SUBTOTAL function a great tool for ad-hoc reporting.

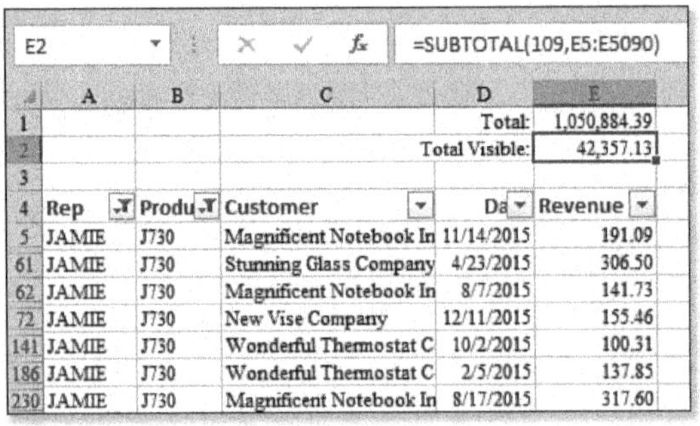

E2 =SUBTOTAL(109,E5:E5090)

	A	B	C	D	E
1				Total:	1,050,884.39
2				Total Visible:	42,357.13
3					
4	Rep	Produ	Customer	Da	Revenue
5	JAMIE	J730	Magnificent Notebook In	11/14/2015	191.09
61	JAMIE	J730	Stunning Glass Company	4/23/2015	306.50
62	JAMIE	J730	Magnificent Notebook In	8/7/2015	141.73
72	JAMIE	J730	New Vise Company	12/11/2015	155.46
141	JAMIE	J730	Wonderful Thermostat C	10/2/2015	100.31
186	JAMIE	J730	Wonderful Thermostat C	2/5/2015	137.85
230	JAMIE	J730	Magnificent Notebook In	8/17/2015	317.60

Figure 8.8 The SUBTOTAL function in cell E2 ignores rows hidden as the result of a filter.

NOTE

Although the function in Figure 8.8 uses the function number 109, the `Subtotal` command always ignores rows hidden as the result of a filter. =SUBTOTAL(9,E5:E5090) would return an identical result when the rows are hidden through a filter, as it is in this case. If you have rows hidden by the Hide command, you should use 109 to ignore the manually hidden rows.

Using RAND, RANDARRAY, and RANDBETWEEN to generate random numbers and data

In some situations, you might want to generate random numbers. Excel offers three functions to assist with this process: RAND, RANDARRAY, and RANDBETWEEN.

The RAND function returns an evenly distributed random number greater than or equal to 0 and less than 1. A new random number is returned every time the worksheet is calculated.

=RAND() generates a random decimal between 0 and 0.999999999999999. Whether you are a teacher trying to randomly assign the order for book report presentations or the commissioner of a fantasy football league trying to figure out the draft sequence, =RAND() can help.

The RANDBETWEEN function returns a random integer between the numbers you specify. A new random number is returned every time the worksheet is calculated. This function takes the following arguments:

- bottom: This is the smallest integer RANDBETWEEN can return.
- top: This is the largest integer RANDBETWEEN can return.

To generate random numbers between 50 and 59, inclusive, you use =RANDBETWEEN(50,59). RANDBETWEEN is easier to use than =RAND to achieve random integers; with =RAND, you would have to use =INT(RAND()*10)+50 to generate this same range of data.

Even though RANDBETWEEN generates integers, you can use it to generate sales prices or even letters. =RANDBETWEEN(5000,9900)/100 generates random prices between $50.00 and $99.00, including prices with cents, such as $87.65.

The capital letter A is also known as character 65 in the ASCII character set. B is 66, C is 67, and so on up through Z, which is character 90. You can use =CHAR(RANDBETWEEN(65,90)) to generate random capital letters.

Office 365 or Excel 2021 customers can use the new RANDARRAY([Rows],[Columns],[Min],[Max],[Integer]) to generate an array of results similar to RAND() or RANDBETWEEN(). To generate a column of ten random numbers, use =RANDARRAY(10). To generate 5 rows and 4 columns of integers between 11 and 19, use =RANDARRAY(5,4,11,19,True).

Sorting data randomly

Say that you have a list of eight names in D2:D9. To rearrange those into a random sequence, use a formula of =SORTBY(D2:D9,RANDARRAY(8)), as shown in Figure 8.9. Every time you press the F9 key, the formula generates a new random sequence. You might want to agree up front with the draft participants that you will press F9 three times to randomize the list and then convert the formulas to values.

fx =SORTBY(D2:D9,RANDARRAY(8))

C	D	E	F	G
	Name		**Random Order**	
	Francis		Lee	
	Glenda		Kristina	
	Jackie		Glenda	
	Kristina		Sheila	
	Lee		Jackie	
	Matt		Francis	
	Nina		Matt	
	Sheila		Nina	

Figure 8.9 Lee gets to draft first in this season's fantasy football league, thanks to the RANDARRAY function.

Choosing a random item from a list

In Figure 8.10, you want to randomly assign employees to certain projects. The list of projects is in column A. The list of employees is in E2:E6. As shown in Figure 8.10, the function for B2:B11 is `=INDEX($E$2:$E$6,RANDBETWEEN(1,5))`.

B2 =INDEX($E$2:$E$6,RANDBETWEEN(1,5))

	A	B	C	D	E	F
1	Project	Assigned To			Employees	
2	Project 101	YVETTE			WAYNE	
3	Project 102	WAYNE			ALMA	
4	Project 103	YVETTE			YVETTE	
5	Project 104	ALMA			RUBY	
6	Project 105	RUBY			SARA	
7	Project 106	WAYNE				
8	Project 107	ALMA				
9	Project 108	WAYNE				
10	Project 109	WAYNE				
11	Project 110	YVETTE				
12						

Figure 8.10 I wonder whether Dilbert's pointy-haired boss assigns projects this way?

Using =ROMAN to finish movie credits and =ARABIC to convert back to digits

Excel can convert numbers to Roman numerals. If you stay in the theater after a movie until the end of movie credits, you see that the copyright date is always expressed in Roman numerals. If you are the next J.J. Abrams, you can use `=ROMAN(2022)` or `=ROMAN(YEAR(Now()))` to generate such a numeral.

> NOTE
>
> **Romans did have a way to represent 5,000 and 10,000, but the format cannot be typed on a modern keyboard; hence, the programmers behind `ARABIC` are apparently allowing nonsensical numbers like MMMMMIV.**

The `=ARABIC()` function can convert a Roman numeral back to a regular number. Whereas `=ROMAN()`works only with the numbers 1 through 3,999, the `ARABIC` function deals with invalid Roman numerals from –255,000 through 255,000. Leviculus!

CHAPTER 8

Using ABS to figure out the magnitude of error

Suppose that you work for a local TV station, and you want to prove that your forecaster is more accurate than those at the other stations in town. The forecaster at the rival station in town is horrible—some days he misses high, and other days he misses low. The rival station uses Figure 8.11 to say that his average forecast is 99 percent accurate. All those negative and positive errors cancel each other out in the average.

I4 =ABS(G4-H4)

	A	B	C	D	E	F	G	H	I
1	Weather Forecast Accuracy - Action News					Weather Forecast Accuracy Using ABS()			
2									
3	Date	Forecast	Actual	Error		Date	Forecast	Actual	Error
4	6/1/2025	87	67	20		6/1/2025	87	67	20
5	6/2/2025	52	72	-20		6/2/2025	52	72	20
6	6/3/2025	93	73	20		6/3/2025	93	73	20
7	6/4/2025	55	75	-20		6/4/2025	55	75	20
8	6/5/2025	94	74	20		6/5/2025	94	74	20
9	6/6/2025	54	74	-20		6/6/2025	54	74	20
10	6/7/2025	89	69	20		6/7/2025	89	69	20
11	6/8/2025	49	69	-20		6/8/2025	49	69	20
12	6/9/2025	93	73	20		6/9/2025	93	73	20
13	6/10/2025	48	68	-20		6/10/2025	48	68	20
14	6/11/2025	88	68	20		6/11/2025	88	68	20
15	6/12/2025	53	73	-20		6/12/2025	53	73	20
16	6/13/2025	98	78	20		6/13/2025	98	78	20
17	6/14/2025	56	76	-20		6/14/2025	56	76	20
18	6/15/2025	100	80	20		6/15/2025	100	80	20
19	6/16/2025	62	82	-20		6/16/2025	62	82	20
20	TOTAL	1171	1171	0		TOTAL	1171	1171	320
21							=I20/G20		27.3%
22	*Claim: Our forecast is 100% accurate!*					*Reality: The forecast averages 27% wrong*			

Figure 8.11 ABS measures the size of an error, ignoring the sign.

The ABS function measures the size of the error. Positive errors are reported as positive, and negative errors are reported as positive as well. You can use `=ABS(A2-B2)` to demonstrate that the other station's forecaster is off by 20 degrees on average.

Using GCD and LCM to perform seventh-grade math

My seventh-grade math teacher, Mr. Irwin, taught me about greatest common denominators and least common multiples. For example, the least common multiple of 24 and 36 is 72. The greatest common denominator of 24 and 36 is 12. I have to admit that I never saw these concepts again until my son Josh was in seventh grade. This must be permanently part of the seventh-grade curriculum.

If you are in seventh grade or you are assisting a seventh grader with his or her math lesson, you will be happy to know that Excel can calculate these values for you.

Syntax:

```
=GCD(number1,number2,...)
```

The `GCD` function returns the greatest common divisor of two or more integers. The greatest common divisor is the largest integer that divides both `number1` and `number2`, and so on, without a remainder.

The arguments `number1, number2,...` are 1 to 255 values. If any value is not an integer, it is truncated. If any argument is nonnumeric, `GCD` returns a `#VALUE!` error. If any argument is less than zero, `GCD` returns a `#NUM!` error. The number 1 divides any value evenly. A prime number has only itself and 1 as even divisors.

Syntax:

```
=LCM(number1,number2,...)
```

The `LCM` function returns the least common multiple of integers. The least common multiple is the smallest positive integer that is a multiple of all integer arguments—`number1`, `number2`, and so on. You use `LCM` to add fractions with different denominators.

The arguments `number1, number2,...` are one to 255 values for which you want the least common multiple. If the value is not an integer, it is truncated. If any argument is nonnumeric, `LCM` returns a `#VALUE!` error. If any argument is less than 1, `LCM` returns a `#NUM!` error.

Using `MOD` to find the remainder portion of a division problem

The `MOD` function is one of the obscure math functions that I find myself using quite frequently. Have you ever been in a group activity in which everyone in the group was to count off by sixes? This is a great way to break up a group into six subgroups. It makes sure that friends who were sitting together get put into disparate groups.

Using the `MOD` function is a great way to perform this concept with records in a database. Perhaps for auditing, you need to check every eighth invoice. Or you need to break up a list of employees into four groups. You can solve these types of problems by using the `MOD` function.

Think back to when you were first learning division. If you had to divide 43 by 4, you would have written that the answer was 10 with a remainder of 3. If you divide 40 by 4, the answer is 10 with a remainder of 0.

The MOD function divides one number by another and reports back just the remainder portion of the result. You end up with an even distribution of remainders. If you convert the formulas into values and sort, your data is broken into similar-sized groups.

The MOD function returns the remainder after `number` is divided by `divisor`. The result has the same sign as `divisor`. This function takes the following arguments:

- `number`: This is the number for which you want to find the remainder.
- `divisor`: This is the number by which you want to divide `number`. If `divisor` is 0, MOD returns a #DIV/0! error.

> **NOTE**
>
> **MOD is short for modulo, the mathematical term for this operation. You would normally say that 17 modulo 3 is 2.**

The MOD function is good for classifying records that follow a certain order. For example, the SmartArt gallery contains 84 icons arranged with 4 icons per row. To find the column for the 38th icon, use `=MOD(38,4)`.

The example in Figure 8.12 assigns all employees to one of four groups.

B2 =MOD(ROW(),4)

	A	B	C	D	E	F
1	NAME	MOD 4			NAME	MOD 4
2	DELORES REYNOLDS	2			MAXINE HILL	0
3	ALLISON CAREY	3			SANDY DILLARD	0
4	MAXINE HILL	0			VINCENT CANNON	0
5	THERESA VAUGHN	1			MAXINE ROMAN	0
6	EUNICE GILLIAM	2			RALPH FRANKLIN	0
7	CLAIRE SOLOMON	3			MISTY HUFF	0
8	SANDY DILLARD	0	Paste Values and Sort		RANDY DECKER	0
9	ERIC DANIEL	1			BARBARA ACOSTA	0
10	NORA OCHOA	2			ANN MEJIA	0
11	LORI WILEY	3			DELORES HINES	0
12	VINCENT CANNON	0			CATHERINE CASEY	0
13	TINA KINNEY	1			MARIE MASSEY	0
14	CARLOS HOLMAN	2			CANDICE VASQUEZ	0
15	BRANDI ACOSTA	3			KEVIN DELGADO	0
16	MAXINE ROMAN	0			LYNN JIMENEZ	0
17	SAMUEL ROJAS	1			HARRIET CLARKE	0
18	DANNY HINTON	2			THERESA VAUGHN	1
19	JEREMY HESTER	3			ERIC DANIEL	1
20	RALPH FRANKLIN	0			TINA KINNEY	1

Figure 8.12 To organize these employees into four groups, use `=MOD(ROW(),4)`. Then paste the values and sort by the remainders.

Inside OUT

The MOD function can be used to create green bar formatting.

Back in the 1980s, many computer reports were printed on green bar paper. Two rows would have a white background followed by two rows with a green background. This allowed your eye to follow the data across the row easily.

Green bar effects are available when you format a range as a table using Ctrl+T. However, many people don't like tables because they eliminate the ability for custom views and subtotals.

A workaround is to apply conditional formatting to a range. Specify a formula, such as =MOD(ROW(),4)<=1, for a light green background. The MOD function, in this case, returns 0, 1, 2, or 3. Anything with a MOD of 0 or 1 will be formatted in green.

Using `SQRT` and `POWER` to calculate square roots and exponents

Most calculators offer a square root button, so it seems natural that Excel would offer a `SQRT` function to do the same thing. To square a number, you multiply the number by itself, ending up with a square. For example, 5×5 = 25.

A square root is a number that, when multiplied by itself, leads to a square. For example, the square root of 25 is 5, and the square root of 49 is 7. Some square roots are more difficult to calculate. The square root of 8 is a number between 2 and 3—somewhere close to 2.828. You can calculate the number with `=SQRT(8)`.

A related function is the `POWER` function. If you want to write the shorthand for 6×6×6×6×6, you would say "six to the fifth power," or `6^5`. Excel can calculate this with `=POWER(6,5)`.

> NOTE
>
> **`SQRTPI` is a specialized version of `SQRT`. This function is handy for converting square shapes to equivalent-sized round shapes.**

Figuring Out Other Roots and Powers

The `SQRT` function is provided because some math people expect it to be there. There are no equivalent functions to figure out other roots.

If you multiply 5×5×5 to get 125, then the third root of 125 is 5. The fourth root of 625 is 5. Even a $30 calculator offers a key to generate various roots beyond a square root. Excel does not offer a cube root function. In reality, even the POWER and the SQRT functions are not necessary.

- =6^3 is 6 raised to the third power, which is 6×6×6, or 216.
- =2^8 is 2 to the eighth power, which is 2×2×2×2×2×2×2×2, or 256.

For roots, you can raise a number to a fractional power:

- =256^(1/8) is the eighth root of 256. This is 2.
- =125^(1/3) is the third root of 125. This is 5.

Thus, instead of using =SQRT(25), you could just as easily use =25^(1/2). However, people reading your worksheets are more likely to understand =SQRT(25) than =25^(1/2).

Using SUMIFS, AVERAGEIFS, COUNTIFS, MAXIFS, and MINIFS to conditionally calculate

The COUNTIF and SUMIF functions debuted in Excel 97. They would let you sum or count records that met a single condition. Microsoft dramatically improved those functions with updated functions SUMIFS, COUNTIFS, and AVERAGEIFS. The plural version of the functions can handle up to 127 conditions.

In February 2017, Microsoft added MAXIFS and MINIFS to find the smallest or largest value for records that meet one or more conditions.

Figure 8.13 shows a database. You want to examine all of the Central region sales where the product is Widget. If column B is Widget and column C is Central, you want to perform calculations on the revenue in column D. In this figure, the text values Widget and Central are stored in F1 and G1 respectively.

The SUMIFS function starts with a reference to the revenue amounts in D2:D16. After that first argument, you will provide anywhere from 1 to 127 pairs of arguments. In each pair, the first argument is the range to examine. The second argument is the value to match. For example, to find records in the Central region, you could specify C2:C16,F1. To find records where the product is Widget, you would use B2:B16,G1.

Thus, for a formula to test two conditions, you will have five arguments. The SUMIFS, AVERAGEIFS, MINIFS, and MAXIFS all follow the same syntax. The difference is the COUNTIFS function, which omits the initial argument to specify the numeric column.

	A	B	C	D	E	F	G	H	I	J
1	Customer	Product	Region	Revenue		Central	Widget			
2	Wonderful I	Widget	East	76,906						
3	Forceful Fla	Widget	East	32,297		277,591	Total			
4	Best Paint I	Gadget	East	59,761		=SUMIFS(D2:D16,C2:C16,F1,B2:B16,G1)				
5	Guarded Ra	Widget	East	66,858						
6	Rare Quilt I	Widget	Central	99,613		69,398	AVERAGE			
7	Rare Juicer (	Widget	Central	47,138		=AVERAGEIFS(D2:D16,C2:C16,F1,B2:B16,G1)				
8	Improved R	Gadget	Central	61,763						
9	Different Tu	Widget	Central	47,363		47,138	Smallest			
10	Best Paint I	Widget	Central	83,477		=MINIFS(D2:D16,C2:C16,F1,B2:B16,G1)				
11	Fascinating	Widget	West	73,950						
12	Crisp Eggbe	Gadget	West	46,113		99,613	Largest			
13	Different Ac	Widget	West	22,334		=MAXIFS(D2:D16,C2:C16,F1,B2:B16,G1)				
14	Rare Vise In	Widget	West	70,064						
15	Rare Oven (	Gadget	West	63,138		4	Count			
16	Effortless Cl	Widget	West	55,642		=COUNTIFS(C2:C16,F1,B2:B16,G1)				

Figure 8.13 SUMIFS, AVERAGEIFS, MINIFS, MAXIFS, and COUNTIFS calculate only the records that fall in the Central region for product Widget.

Syntax:

```
SUMIFS(sum_range,criteria_range1,criteria1[,criteria_range2, criteria2...])
```

The `SUMIFS()` function adds the cells in a range that meet multiple criteria.

Note the following in this syntax:

- `sum_range` is the range to sum.
- `criteria_range1, criteria_range2, ...` are one or more ranges in which to evaluate the associated criteria.
- `criteria1, criteria2, ...` are one or more criteria in the form of a number, an expression, a cell reference, or text that define which cells will be added. For example, they can be expressed as 32, "32", ">32", "apples", or B4.
- Each cell in `sum_range` is summed only if all the corresponding criteria specified are true for that cell.
- You can use the wildcard characters question mark (?) and asterisk (*) in `criteria`. A question mark matches any single character; an asterisk matches any sequence of characters. If you want to find an actual question mark or asterisk, you need to type a tilde (~) before the character.
- Unlike the range and criteria arguments in `SUMIF`, the size and shape of each `criteria_range` and `sum_range` must be the same.

In Figure 8.14, you want to build a table that shows the total by region and product. `sum_range` is the revenue in H11:H5011. The first criteria pair consists of the regions in $C$11:$C$5011 being compared to the word East in B$1. The second criteria pair consists of the divisions in

CHAPTER 8

$B$11:$B$5011 being compared to G854 in $A2. The formula in B2 is `=SUMIFS($H$11:$H$5011, $C$11:$C$5011,B$1,$B$11:$B$5011,$A2)`. You can copy this formula to B2:D6.

B2 | =SUMIFS($H$11:$H$5011,$C$11:$C$5011,B$1,$B$11:$B$5011,$A2)

	A	B	C	D	E	F	G	H	I
1		East	Central	West					
2	G854	18,931K	17,327K	13,339K					
3	A105	18,440K	21,199K	12,636K					
4	V937	17,574K	18,157K	13,660K					
5	I543	19,488K	21,257K	13,246K					
6	H833	19,065K	19,484K	12,843K					
7		=SUMIFS($H$11:$H$5011,$C$11:$C$5011,B$1,$B$11:$B$5011,$A2)							
8									
9									
10	Customer	Product	Region	District	Rep	Date	Qty	Revenue	Profit
11	Wonderful Faucet C	V937	East	Southeast	ADAM DU	2/3/14	730	76,906	41,529
12	Forceful Flagpole Cc	H833	East	Southeast	ADAM DU	12/19/14	804	32,297	16,794

Figure 8.14 The `SUMIFS()` function is used to create this summary by region and product.

Dates and times in Excel

Date calculations can drive people crazy in Excel. If you gain a certain confidence with dates in Excel, you will be able to quickly resolve formatting issues that come up.

Here is why dates are a problem. First, Excel stores dates as the number of days since January 1, 1900. For example, June 30, 2025, is 45,838 days since 1/1/1900. When you enter 6/30/2025 in a cell, Excel secretly converts this entry to 45,838 and formats the cell to display a date instead of the value. So far, so good. The problem arises when you try to calculate something based on the date.

When you try to perform a calculation on two cells when the first cell is formatted as currency and the second cell is formatted as fixed numeric with three decimals, Excel has to decide if the new cell inherits the currency format or the fixed with three decimals format. These rules are hard to figure out. In any given instance, you might get the currency format or the fixed with three decimals format, or you might get the format previously assigned to the cell with the new formula. With numbers, a result of $80.52 or 80.521 looks about the same. You can probably understand either format.

However, imagine that one of the cells is formatted as a date. Another cell contains the number 30. If you add the 30 to the date, which format does Excel use? If the cell containing the new formula happened to be previously assigned a numeric format, the answer suddenly switches from a date format to the numeric equivalent. This is frustrating and confusing. You start with June 30, 2025, add 30 days, and get an answer of 45,868. This makes no sense to an Excel novice. It forces many people to give up on dates and start storing dates as text that looks like dates. This is unfortunate because you can't easily do calculations on text cells that look like dates.

Here is a general guideline to remember: If you work with dates in the range of the years 2017 to 2028, those numeric equivalents are from 42,736 through 47,118. If you do some date math and get a strange answer in the 40,000–50,000 range, Excel probably has the right answer, but the numeric format of the answer cell is wrong. You need to select Short Date from the Number drop-down menu on the Home tab to correct the format.

The Excel method for storing dates is simple when you understand it. If you have a date cell and need to add 15 days to it, you add the number 15 to the cell. Every day is equivalent to the number 1, and every week is equivalent to the number 7. This is very simple to understand.

When you see 45,838 instead of June 30, 2025, Excel calls the 48,838 a serial number. Some of the Excel functions discussed here convert from a serial number to text that looks like a date, or vice versa.

For time, Excel adds a decimal to the serial number. There are 24 hours in a day. The serial number for 6:00 a.m. is 0.25. The serial number for noon is 0.5. The serial number for 6:00 p.m. is 0.75. The serial number for 3:00 p.m. on June 30, 2025 is 45,838.625. To see how this works, try this out:

1. Create a blank Excel workbook.
2. In any cell, enter a number in the range of 40,000 to 45,000.
3. Add a decimal point and any random digits after the decimal.
4. Select that cell.
5. From the Home tab, select the dialog box launcher in the lower-right corner of the Number group or press Ctrll+1.
6. In the Date category, scroll down and select the format 3/14/01 1:30 PM. Excel displays your random number as a date and time. If the decimal portion of your number is greater than 0.5, the result is in the p.m. portion of the day.
7. Go to another cell and enter the date you were born, using a four-digit year.
8. Again, select the cell and format it as a number. Excel converts it to show how many days after the start of the last century you were born. This is great trivia but not necessarily useful.

CAUTION

Although most Excel date issues can be resolved with formatting, you should be aware of some real date problems:

- **On a Macintosh, Excel dates are stored since January 1, 1904. If you are using a Mac, your serial number for a date in 2025 will be different from that on a Windows PC. Excel handles this conversion when files are moved from one platform to another.**
- **Excel cannot handle dates in the 1800s or before. This really hacks off all my friends who do genealogy. If your Great-Great-Great Uncle Felix was born on February 17, 1895, you are going to have to store that as text.**

- Around Y2K, someone decided that 1930 is the dividing line for two-digit years. If you enter a date with a two-digit year, the result is in the range of 1930 through 2029. If you enter 12/31/29, this will be interpreted as 2029. If you enter 1/1/30, it will be interpreted as 1930. If you need to enter a mortgage ending date of 2040, for example, be sure to use the four-digit year, 6/15/2040. If you are regularly entering dates in the 2030–2040 range, you can change the dividing line for two-digit years. Go to Region And Language settings in the Control Panel. Click Additional Settings. Click the Date tab. The When A Two Digit Year Is Entered setting allows you to change the dividing line.

The point is that Excel dates are nothing to be afraid of. You need to understand that behind the scenes, Excel is storing your dates as serial numbers and your times as decimal serial numbers. Occasionally, circumstances cause a date to be displayed as a serial number. Although this freaks some people out, it is easy to fix using the Format Cells dialog box. Other times, when you want the serial number (for example, to calculate elapsed days between two dates), Excel converts the serial number to a date, indicating, for example, that an invoice is past due by "February 15, 1900" days. When you get these types of nonsequiturs, you can visit the Format Cells dialog box. Or press the shortcut key—Ctrl+Shift+tilde—to format the cell as General.

TROUBLESHOOTING

For compatibility with ancient spreadsheet programs, Excel includes the date of February 29, 1900—a date that does not exist.

Leap day is not added to the years 1700, 1800, 1900, 2100, 2200, 2300, and 2500. Lotus 1-2-3 erroneously included February 29, 1900. To allow Lotus files to convert to Excel, Microsoft repeated the error. The result is that any weekdays from January 1, 1900, to February 28, 1900, are off by one day.

Saturday, March 03, 1900	Saturday is correct
Friday, March 02, 1900	Friday is correct
Thursday, March 01, 1900	Thursday is correct
Wednesday, February 29, 1900	No such day!
Tuesday, February 28, 1900	Really Wednesday
Monday, February 27, 1900	Really Tuesday
Sunday, February 26, 1900	Really Monday
Saturday, February 25, 1900	Really Sunday
Sunday, January 01, 1900	Really Monday

A table of dates formatted as a long date spans from March 3, 1900, back to February 25, 1900. Excel shows that March 1, 1900, is a Thursday, and this is correct. However, Microsoft says the Wednesday before this day is February 29, 1900—a day that does not exist. This causes all weekdays from January 1, 1900, to February 28, 1900, to be wrong in Excel. When Excel says that February 28, 1900, was on a Tuesday, that is incorrect; February 28, 1900, really was a Wednesday.

Understanding Excel date and time formats

It is worthwhile to learn the various Excel custom codes for date and time formats. Figure 8.15 shows a table of how March 5, 2025, would be displayed in various numeric formats. The codes in A4:A17 are the possible codes for displaying just date, month, or year. Most people know the classic `mm/dd/yyyy` format, but far more formats are available. You can cause Excel to spell out the month and weekday by using codes such as `dddd, mmmm d, yyyy`. Here are the possibilities:

- **mm**: Displays the month with two digits. Months before October are displayed with a leading zero (for example, January is 01).
- **m**: Displays the month with one or two digits, as necessary.
- **mmm**: Displays a three-letter abbreviation for the month (for example, Jan, Feb).
- **mmmm**: Spells out the month (for example, January, February).
- **mmmmm**: First letter of the month, useful for creating "JFMAMJJASOND" chart labels.
- **dd**: Displays the day of the month with two digits. Dates earlier than the 10th of the month are displayed with a leading zero (for example, the 1st is 01).
- **d**: Displays the day of the month with one or two digits, as needed.
- **ddd**: Displays a three-letter abbreviation for the name of the weekday (for example, Mon, Tue).
- **dddd**: Spells out the name of the weekday (for example, Monday, Tuesday).
- **yy or y**: Uses two digits for the year (for example, 15).
- **yyyy or yyy**: Uses four digits for the year (for example, 2025).

You are allowed to string together any combination of these codes with a space, comma, slash, or dash. It is valid to repeat a portion of the date format. For example, the format `dddd, mmmm d, yyyy` shows the day portion twice in the date and would display as Thursday, March 5, 2018.

Although the date formats are mostly intuitive, several difficulties exist in the time formats. The first problem is the `M` code. Excel has already used `M` to mean month. In a time format, you cannot use `M` alone to mean minutes. The `M` code must either be preceded or followed by a colon.

K22			
	A	B	C
1	3/5/2025		
2			
3	**FORMAT**	**DISPLAYS AS**	**NOTE**
4	m	3	*1 or 2 digit month as needed*
5	mm	03	*Always 2 digits for month*
6	mmm	Mar	*3 letter month abbreviation*
7	mmmm	March	*Spell out the month*
8	mmmmm	M	*1st text - for JFMAMJJASOND*
9	d	5	*1 or 2 digit day as needed*
10	dd	05	*Always 2 digits for day*
11	ddd	Wed	*3 letter day abbreviation*
12	dddd	Wednesday	*Spell out the weekday*
13	yy	25	*2 digits for year*
14	yyyy	2025	*4 digits for year*
15	mm/dd/yyyy	03/05/2025	
16	mmm d, yy	Mar 5, 25	
17	d-mmmm-yyyy	5-March-2025	
18			

Figure 8.15 Any of these custom date format codes can be typed in the Custom Numeric Format box.

Appreciating Excel's flexibility in showing part of a date

There is another difficulty: When you are dealing with years, months, and days, it is often perfectly valid to mention only one of the portions of the date without the other two. It is common to hear any of these statements:

- "I was born in 1965."
- "I am going on vacation in July."
- "I will be back on the 27th."

If you have a date such as March 5, 2018, and use the proper formatting code, Excel happily tells you that this date is March or 2018 or the 5th. Technically, Excel is leaving out some really important information—the 5th of what? As humans, we can often figure out that this probably means the 5th of the next month. Thus, we aren't shocked that Excel is leaving off the fact that it is March 2018.

TIP

Custom number formats are entered in the Format Cells dialog box. There are three ways to display this dialog:

- Press Ctrl+1.
- **From the Home tab, in the Number group, select the drop-down menu and select More Number Formats from the bottom of the drop-down menu.**
- **Click the dialog launcher in the lower-right corner of the Number group on the Home tab.**

When the Format Cells dialog box is displayed, you select the Number tab. In the Category list, you select Custom. In the Type box, you enter your custom format. The Sample box displays the active cell with the format applied.

Imagine how strange it would be if Excel did this with regular numbers. Suppose you have the number 352. Would Excel ever offer a numeric format that would display just the tens portion of the number? If you put 352 in a cell, would Excel display 5 or 50? It would make no sense.

Regretting why that same date flexibility makes weekly time sheets so difficult

Excel treats time as an extension of dates and is happy to show you only a portion of the time. This can cause great confusion. To Excel, 40 hours really means 1 day and 16 hours. If you create a timesheet in Excel and format the total hours for the week as `H:MM`, Excel thinks that you are purposefully leaving off the day portion of the format! Excel presents 45 hours as just 21 hours because it assumes you can figure out there is 1 day from the context. But our brains don't work that way; 21 hours means 21 hours, not 1 day and 21 hours.

To overcome this problem in Excel, you use square brackets. Surrounding any time element with square brackets tells Excel to include all greater time/date elements in that one element, as in the following examples:

- 5 days and 10 hours in `[H]` format would be 130.
- 5 days and 10 hours in `[M]` format would be 7800, to represent that many minutes.
- 5 days and 10 hours in `[S]` format would be 468000, to represent that many seconds.

As shown in Figure 8.16, the time formatting codes include various combinations of `h`, `hh`, `s`, `ss`, `:mm`, and `mm:`, all of which can be modified with square brackets.

To display date and time, you enter the custom date format code, a space, and then the time format code.

B4	=TEXT($A$1,A4)			
	A	B	C	D	E

	A	B	C	D	E
1	20:05:07				
2					
3	FORMAT	DISPLAYS AS	NOTE		
4	h	20	*1 or 2 digit hour as needed*		
5	hh	20	*Always 2 digits for hour*		
6	h:mm	20:05	*1 or 2 digit hour as needed*		
7	hh:mm	20:05	*Always 2 digits for hour*		
8	h:mm:ss	20:05:07	*Hours, minutes, seconds in military time*		
9	h:m:s	20:5:7	*Strange looking, but a valid code*		
10	s	7	*Seconds, using 1 or 2 digits*		
11	ss	07	*Seconds, using 2 digits*		
12	h:mm AM/PM	8:05 PM	*Hours and minutes with AM or PM*		
13	[h]:mm	44:05	*Include any full days as hours*		
14	[m]	2645	*Include any hours or days as minutes*		
15	[s]	158707	*Include any days, hours or minutes as seconds*		
16	mm.ss.00	05.07.00	*Show decimal portions of seconds*		

Figure 8.16 Custom time format codes.

Examples of date and time functions

In all the examples in the following sections, you should use care to ensure that the resulting cell is formatted using the proper format, as discussed in the preceding section.

Using `NOW` and `TODAY` to calculate the current date and time or current date

There are a couple of keyboard shortcuts for entering date and time. Pressing Ctrl+; enters the current date in a cell. Pressing Ctrl+: enters the current time in a cell. However, both of these hotkeys create a static value; that is, the date or time reflects the instant that you typed the hotkey, and it never changes in the future.

Excel offers two functions for calculating the current date: `NOW` and `TODAY`. These functions are excellent for figuring out the number of days until a deadline or how late an open receivable might be.

CAUTION

It would be nice if NOW() would function like a real-time clock, constantly updating in Excel. However, the result is calculated when the file is opened, with each press of the F9 key, and when an entry is made elsewhere in the worksheet.

Syntax:

```
=NOW()

=TODAY()
```

NOW returns the serial number of the current date and time. TODAY returns the serial number of the current date. The TODAY function returns today's date, without a time attached. The NOW function returns the current date and time.

Both of these functions can be made to display the current date, but there is an important distinction when you are performing calculations with the functions. In Figure 8.17, column A contains NOW functions, and column C contains TODAY functions. Row 2 is formatted as a date and time. Row 3 is formatted as a date. Row 4 is formatted as numeric. Cell A3 and C3 look the same. If you need to display the date without using it in a calculation, NOW or TODAY work fine.

	A	B	C	D
1	**NOW()**		**TODAY()**	**Comment**
2	5/21/21 7:22 AM		5/21/21 12:00 AM	*Formatted as Date/Time*
3	5/21/21		5/21/21	*Formatted as Date*
4	44337.3076		44337.0000	*Formatted as Serial Number*
5				
6				
7	8/13/2021		8/13/2021	*Deadline*
8	83.6924		84.0000	*Days Until Deadline*

Figure 8.17 NOW and TODAY can be made to look alike, but you need to choose the proper one if you are going to be using the result in a later calculation.

Row 8 calculates the number of days until a deadline approaches. Although most people would say that tomorrow is one day away, the formula in A8 would tend to say that the deadline is 83.6924 days away. This can be deceiving. If you are going to use the result of NOW or TODAY in a date calculation, you should use TODAY to prevent Excel from reporting fractional days. The formula in A8 is =A7-A3, formatted as numeric instead of a date.

Using YEAR, MONTH, DAY, HOUR, MINUTE, and SECOND to break a date/time apart

If you have a column of dates from the month of July 2025, you can easily make them all look the same by using the MMM-YY format. However, the dates in the actual cells are still different. The July 2025 records are not sorted as if they were a tie. Excel offers six functions that you can use to extract a single portion of the date: YEAR, MONTH, DAY, HOUR, MINUTE, and SECOND.

In Figure 8.18, cell A1 contains a date and time. Functions in A3 through A8 break out the date into components:

- `=YEAR(date)` returns the year portion as a four-digit year.
- `=MONTH(date)` returns the month number, from 1 through 12.
- `=DAY(date)` returns the day of the month, from 1 through 31.
- `=HOUR(date)` returns the hour, from 0 to 23.
- `=MINUTE(date)` returns the minute, from 0 to 59.
- `=SECOND(date)` returns the second, from 0 to 59.

	A	B
1	7/14/21 7:18:29 PM	
2		
3	2021	=YEAR(A1)
4	7	=MONTH(A1)
5	14	=DAY(A1)
6	19	=HOUR(A1)
7	18	=MINUTE(A1)
8	29	=SECOND(A1)

Figure 8.18 These six functions allow you to isolate any portion of a date or time.

In each case, `date` must contain a valid Excel serial number for a date. The cell containing the date serial number may be formatted as a date or as a number.

Using DATE to calculate a date from year, month, and day

The DATE function is one of the most amazing functions in Excel. Microsoft's implementation of this function is excellent, allowing you to do amazing date calculations.

Syntax:

`=DATE(year,month,day)`

The DATE function returns the serial number that represents a particular date. This function takes the following arguments:

- `year`: This argument can be one to four digits. If `year` is between 0 and 1899 (inclusive), Excel adds that value to 1900 to calculate the year. For example, `=DATE(100,1,2)` returns January 2, 2000 (1900+100). If `year` is between 1900 and 9999 (inclusive), Excel uses that value as the year. For example, `=DATE(2000,1,2)` returns January 2, 2000. If `year` is less than 0 or is 10,000 or greater, Excel returns a `#NUM!` error.
- `month`: This is a number representing the month of the year. If `month` is greater than 12, `month` adds that number of months to the first month in the year specified. For example, `=DATE(1998,14,2)` returns the serial number representing February 2, 1999. If zero, it represents December of the previous year. If negative, returns prior months, although –1 represents November, –2 is October, and so on.
- `day`: This is a number representing the day of the month. If `day` is greater than the number of days in the month specified, it adds that number of days to the first day in the month. For example, `=DATE(2018,1,35)` returns the serial number representing February 4, 2018. Zero represents the last day of the previous month. Negative numbers return days earlier, just as with month. In a trivial example, `=DATE(2018,3,5)` returns March 5, 2018.

The true power in the DATE function occurs when one or more of the year, month, or day are calculated values. Here are some examples:

- If cell A2 contains an invoice date and you want to calculate the day one month later, you use `=DATE(Year(A2),Month(A2)+1,Day(A2))`.
- To calculate the beginning of the month, you use `=DATE(Year(A2),Month(A2),1)`.
- To calculate the end of the month, you use `=DATE(Year(A2),Month(A2)+1,1)-1 or =DATE(YEAR(A2),MONTH(A2)+1,0)`.

The DATE function is amazing because it enables Excel to deal perfectly with invalid dates. If your calculations for Month cause it to exceed 12, this is no problem. For example, if you ask Excel to calculate `=DATE(2025,16,45)`, Excel considers the 16th month of 2025 to be April 2026. To find the 45th day of April 2026, Excel moves ahead to May 15, 2026.

Figure 8.19 shows various results of the DATE and TIME functions.

CHAPTER 8

	A	B	C	D	E	F
1	Year	Month	Day	DATE		
2	2021	16	45	5/15/2022	=DATE(A2,B2,C2)	
3	2022	1	60	3/1/2022	=DATE(A3,B3,C3)	
4	2021	1	60	3/1/2021	=DATE(A4,B4,C4)	
5	2021	3	5	3/5/2021	=DATE(A5,B5,C5)	
6						
7						
8	Hour	Minute	Second	TIME		
9	1	12	23	1:12:23 AM	=TIME(A9,B9,C9)	
10	13	12	23	1:12:23 PM	=TIME(A10,B10,C10)	
11	12	72	23	1:12:23 PM	=TIME(A11,B11,C11)	
12	37	12	23	1:12:23 PM	=TIME(A12,B12,C12)	
13						

Figure 8.19 The formulas in column D use DATE or TIME functions to calculate an Excel serial number from three arguments.

Using TIME to calculate a time

The TIME function is similar to the DATE function. It calculates a time serial number given a specific hour, minute, and second.

Syntax:

```
=TIME(hour,minute,second)
```

The TIME function returns the decimal number for a particular time. The decimal number returned by TIME is a value ranging from 0 to 0. 999988425925926, representing the times from 0:00:00 (12:00:00 a.m.) to 23:59:59 (11:59:59 p.m.). This function takes the following arguments:

- hour: This is a number from 0 to 23, representing the hour.
- minute: This is a number from 0 to 59, representing the minute.
- second: This is a number from 0 to 59, representing the second.

As with the DATE function, Excel can handle situations in which the minute or second argument calculates to more than 60. For example, =TIME(12,72,120) evaluates to 1:14 p.m.

Additional examples of TIME are shown in the bottom half of Figure 8.19.

Using DATEVALUE to convert text dates to real dates

It is easy to end up with a worksheet full of text dates. Sometimes this is due to importing data from another system. Sometimes it is caused by someone not understanding how dates work.

If your dates are in many conceivable formats, you can use the DATEVALUE function to convert the text dates to serial numbers, which can then be formatted as dates.

Syntax:

`=DATEVALUE(date_text)`

The DATEVALUE function returns the serial number of the date represented by `date_text`. You use DATEVALUE to convert a date represented by text to a serial number. The argument `date_text` is text that represents a date in an Excel date format. For example, "3/5/2018" and "05-Mar-2018" are text strings within quotation marks that represent dates. Using the default date system in Excel for Windows, `date_text` must represent a date from January 1, 1900, to December 31, 9999. DATEVALUE returns a #VALUE! error if `date_text` is out of this range. If the year portion of `date_text` is omitted, DATEVALUE uses the current year from your computer's built-in clock. Time information in `date_text` is ignored.

Any of the text values in column A of Figure 8.20 are successfully translated to a date serial number. In this instance, Excel should have been smart enough to automatically format the resulting cells as dates. By default, the cells are formatted as numeric. This leads many people to believe that DATEVALUE doesn't work. You have to apply a date format to achieve the desired result.

> CAUTION
>
> **The** DATEVALUE **function must be used with text dates. If you have a column of values in which some values are text, and some are actual dates, using** DATEVALUE **on the actual dates causes a** #VALUE **error. You could use** `=IF(ISNUMBER(A1),A1,DATEVALUE(A1))`**. Also consider the** `=DAYS(end,start)` **function, which deals with either text dates or real dates.**

> CAUTION
>
> **There are a few examples of text that** DATEVALUE **cannot recognize. One common example is when there is no space after the comma. For example, "January 21,2011" returns an error. To solve this particular problem, use** SUBSTITUTE **to change a comma to a comma space:** `=DATEVALUE(SUBSTITUTE(A2,",",", "))`.

	A	B
1	TEXT	DATEVALUE
2	3/5/2021	44260
3	03/05/2021	44260
4	3/5/2021	44260
5	5-Mar-21	44260
6	Mar 5, 2021	44260
7	March 05, 2021	44260
8	03-05-2021	44260
9	3-5-2021	44260

Figure 8.20 The formulas in column B use DATEVALUE to convert the text entries in column A to date serial numbers.

Using TIMEVALUE to convert text times to real times

It is easy to end up with a column of text values that look like times. Similar to using DATEVALUE, you can use the TIMEVALUE function to convert these to real times.

Syntax:

```
=TIMEVALUE(time_text)
```

The TIMEVALUE function returns the decimal number of the time represented by a text string. The decimal number is a value ranging from 0 to 0.999988425925926, representing the times from 0:00:00 (12:00:00 a.m.) to 23:59:59 (11:59:59 p.m.). The argument `time_text` is a text string that represents a time in any one of the Microsoft Excel time formats. For example, `"6:45 PM"` and `"18:45"` are text strings within quotation marks that represent time. Date information in `time_text` is ignored.

The TIMEVALUE function is difficult to use because it is easy for a person to enter the wrong formats. In Figure 8.21, many people would interpret cell A8 as meaning 45 minutes and 30 seconds. Excel, however, treats this as 45 hours and 30 minutes. This misinterpretation makes TIMEVALUE almost useless for a column of cells that contain a text representation of minute and seconds.

CAUTION

There are a few examples of text that TIMEVALUE cannot recognize. One common example is when there is no space before the AM or PM. For example, "11:00PM" returns an error. To solve this particular problem, use SUBSTITUTE to change "PM" to " PM" and to change "AM" to " AM." This is an involved formula:

```
=SUBSTITUTE(SUBSTITUTE(A2,"PM"," PM"),"AM"," AM")*1
```

You need the `*1` at the end to ensure it is numeric. Also, the result should be formatted as time because the SUBSTITUTE function returns a string. This function works for time formats with or without the space before the A or P!

B2 =TIMEVALUE(A2)

	A	B	C
1	TEXT	TIMEVALUE	FORMATTED
2	1:10	0.048611111	1:10:00 AM
3	1:10 AM	0.048611111	1:10:00 AM
4	1:10 PM	0.548611111	1:10:00 PM
5	13:10	0.548611111	1:10:00 PM
6	1:10:30	0.048958333	1:10:30 AM
7	1:45:30	0.073263889	1:45:30 AM
8	45:30	0.895833333	9:30:00 PM
9	0:45:30	0.031597222	12:45:30 AM
10			

Figure 8.21 The formulas in column B use `TIMEVALUE` to convert the text entries in column A to times. If there is no leading zero before entries with minutes and seconds, the formula produces an unexpected result.

Frustratingly, Excel does not automatically format the results of this function as a time. Column B shows the result as Excel presents it. Column C shows the same result after a time format has been applied.

Using `WEEKDAY` to group dates by day of the week

The `WEEKDAY` function would not be so intimidating if people could just agree how to number the days. This one function can give eight different results, just for Monday.

Syntax:

```
=WEEKDAY(serial_number,return_type)
```

The `WEEKDAY` function returns the day of the week corresponding to a date. The day is given as an integer, ranging from 1 (Sunday) to 7 (Saturday), by default. This function takes the following arguments:

- `serial_number` is a sequential number that represents the date of the day you are trying to find. Dates may be entered as text strings within quotation marks (for example, `"1/30/2018"`, `"2018/01/30"`), as serial numbers (for example, 43130, which represents January 30, 2018), or as results of other formulas or functions (for example, `DATEVALUE("1/30/2018")`).
- `return_type` is a number that determines the type of return value:

- If `return_type` is 1 or omitted, `WEEKDAY` works like the calendar on your wall. Typically, calendars are printed with Sunday on the left and Saturday on the right. The default version of `WEEKDAY` numbers these columns from 1 through 7.
- If `return_type` is 2, you are using the biblical version of `WEEKDAY`. In the biblical version, Sunday is the seventh day. Working backward, Monday must occupy the 1 position.
- If `return_type` is 3, you are using the accounting version of `WEEKDAY`. In this version, Monday is assigned a value of 0, followed by 1 for Tuesday, and so on. This version makes it very easy to group records by week. If cell A2 contains a date, then `A2-WEEKDAY(A2,3)` converts the date to the Monday that starts the week.
- `return_types` of 11 through 17 were added in Excel 2010. 11 returns Monday as 1 and Sunday as 7 (the same as using 2). 12 returns Tuesday as 1, 13 returns Wednesday as 1, and so on, up to 17 returning Sunday as 1.

Figure 8.22 shows the results of `WEEKDAY` for all 10 return types.

	A	B	C	D	E	F	G	H	I	J	K
1	WEEKDAY()	*Return_Type ----->*									
3	**Date**	**1**	**2**	**3**	**11**	**12**	**13**	**14**	**15**	**16**	**17**
4	**Sunday, April 04, 2021**	1	7	6	7	6	5	4	3	2	1
5	**Monday, April 05, 2021**	2	1	0	1	7	6	5	4	3	2
6	**Tuesday, April 06, 2021**	3	2	1	2	1	7	6	5	4	3
7	**Wednesday, April 07, 2021**	4	3	2	3	2	1	7	6	5	4
8	**Thursday, April 08, 2021**	5	4	3	4	3	2	1	7	6	5
9	**Friday, April 09, 2021**	6	5	4	5	4	3	2	1	7	6
10	**Saturday, April 10, 2021**	7	6	5	6	5	4	3	2	1	7
11	**Sunday, April 11, 2021**	1	7	6	7	6	5	4	3	2	1

Figure 8.22 Columns B:K compare the `WEEKDAY` function for the ten different `return_type` values shown in row 3.

Using `WEEKNUM` or `ISOWEEKNUM` to group dates into weeks

For many versions, Excel did not calculate weeks to match the ANSI standard. The `return_type` of 21 or the `ISOWEEKNUM` function returns the week number to match the ANSI standard. In this system, weeks always start on Monday. The first week of the year must have four days that fall into this year. Another way to say this is that the week containing the first Thursday of the month is numbered as Week 1.

In the ANSI system, you might have Week 1 actually starting as early as December 29 or as late as January 4. The last week of the year is numbered 52 in most years but is 53 every fourth year.

This system ensures that a year is made up of whole seven-day weeks. This is better than the old results of WEEKNUM.

In the old system with WEEKNUM, the week containing the first of the year was always labeled as Week 1. If the first fell on a Sunday, and your weeks started on Monday, then Sunday, January 1 is Week 1 and Monday, January 2 is Week 2. The possibility of having weeks that last for one day made it difficult to compare one week to the next. Nonetheless, the Excel team added new return_types for this system as well. In the past, 1 meant weeks started on Sunday, and 2 meant weeks started on Monday. Now, you can specify weeks should start on Monday (11), Tuesday (12), and so on, up to Sunday (17).

Syntax:

```
=WEEKNUM(serial_num,[return_type])
```

The WEEKNUM function returns a number that indicates where the week falls numerically within a year. This function takes the following arguments:

- serial_num: This is a date within the week.
- return_type: This is a number that determines on what day the week begins. The default is 1. If return_type is 1 or omitted, the week begins on Sunday. If return_type is 2, the week begins on Monday. return_types of 11 through 17 were added to Excel 2013 and specify that the week should start on Monday (11) through Sunday (17). The new return_type of 21 ensures that every week has exactly seven days. Weeks always start on Monday, but the first Thursday of the year is the middle of Week 1.

Calculating elapsed time

If you work in a human resources department, you might be concerned with years of service to calculate a certain benefit. Excel provides one function, YEARFRAC, that can calculate decimal years of service in five ways. An old function, DATEDIF (pronounced Date Dif), has been hanging around since Lotus 1-2-3; it can calculate the difference between two dates in complete years, months, or days. Excel 2013 added the DAYS function, which can calculate elapsed days even if one or both of the values are text dates.

Syntax:

```
=DATEDIF(start_date,end_date,unit)
```

The DATEDIF function calculates complete years, months, or days. This function calculates the number of days, months, or years between two dates. It is provided for compatibility with Lotus 1-2-3. This function takes the following arguments:

- start_date: This is a date that represents the first, or starting, date of the period.
- end_date: This is a date that represents the last, or ending, date of the period.

- `unit`: This is the type of information you want returned. The various values for `unit` are shown in Table 8.3.

Table 8.3 Unit values used by the `DATEDIF` function

Unit value	Description
Y	The number of complete years in the period. A complete year is earned on the anniversary date of the employee's start date.
M	The number of complete months in the period. This number is incremented on the anniversary date. If the employee was hired on January 18, that person has earned 1 month of service on the 18th of February. If an employee is hired on January 31, then she earns credit for the month when she shows up for work on the 1st after any month with fewer than 31 days.
D	The number of days in the period. This could be figured out by simply subtracting the two dates.
MD	The number of days, ignoring months and years. You could use a combination of two DATEDIF functions—one using M and one using MD—to calculate days.
YM	The number of months, ignoring years. You could use a combination of two DATEDIF functions—one using Y and one using YM—to calculate months.
YD	The number of days, ignoring complete years.

Figure 8.23 compares the six unit values of `DATEDIF`. Each cell uses $A$1 as the start date and that row's column A as the end date.

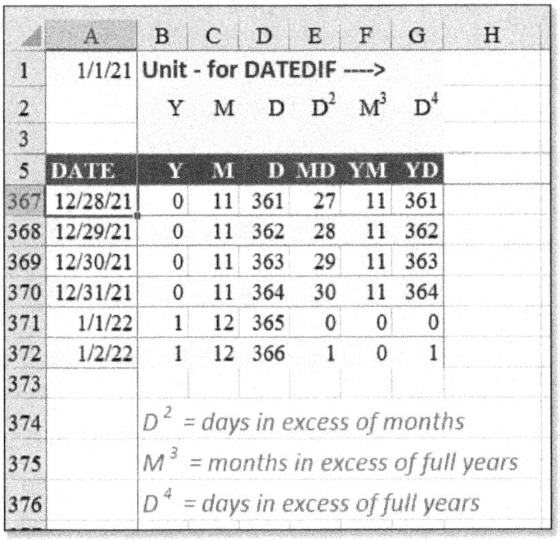

	A	B	C	D	E	F	G	H
1	1/1/21	**Unit - for DATEDIF ---->**						
2		Y	M	D	D^2	M^3	D^4	
3								
5	DATE	Y	M	D	MD	YM	YD	
367	12/28/21	0	11	361	27	11	361	
368	12/29/21	0	11	362	28	11	362	
369	12/30/21	0	11	363	29	11	363	
370	12/31/21	0	11	364	30	11	364	
371	1/1/22	1	12	365	0	0	0	
372	1/2/22	1	12	366	1	0	1	
373								
374		*D^2 = days in excess of months*						
375		*M^3 = months in excess of full years*						
376		*D^4 = days in excess of full years*						

Figure 8.23 `DATEDIF` is great for calculating elapsed years, months, and days.

CAUTION

DATEDIF has been in Excel forever, but it was only documented in Excel 2000. Why doesn't Microsoft reveal DATEDIF in Help? Probably because of the strange anomaly when you try to calculate the gap from the 31st of January to the 1st of March in a non-leap year.

- The "D" version of DATEDIF reports this as 29 days. This is correct.
- The "M" version of DATEDIF reports this as one full month. This must be correct because the dates span the entire month of February.
- The "MD" version of DATEDIF reports this as a negative two days more than a full month. See cell D7 in Figure 8.24. This is the downside of trying to express a measurement in months when the length of a month is not constant. Negative values for this version of DATEDIF happen only when the end date is March 1 or March 2.

Despite this problem, for 363 days a year, DATEDIF remains an effective way to express a date delta as a certain number of years, months, and days.

	A	B	C	D	E	F
1	**Anomaly with DATEDIF...**					
3	Start Date	1/31/2021			End Date	3/1/2021
5	Y		Years:	0	*Years (Y)*	
6	YM		Months:	1	*Months in Excess of Years (YM)*	
7	MD		Days:	-2	*Days in Excess of Months (MD)*	
8	D		Days:	29	*Days (D)*	
9						
10	**...but it is still a cool function**					
11						
12			Start Date	2/17/1965		
13			End Date	6/30/2021		
14			Difference	56 years, 4 months, 13 days		
15	*=DATEDIF(D12,D13,"Y")&" years, "&DATEDIF(D12,D13,"YM")&" months, "&DATEDIF(D12,D13,"MD")&" days"*					
16						
17	**DAYS() handles text or dates**					
18						
19	Start	End	Formats	DAYS		
20	1/1/2021	3/17/2021	Date/Date	75	*=DAYS(B20,A20)*	
21	3/1/2021	3/1/2022	Text/Test	365	*=DAYS(B21,A21)*	
22	4/1/2022	5/15/2022	Date/Text	44	*=DAYS(B22,A22)*	
23	5/15/2022	4/1/2022	Text/Date	-44	*=DAYS(B23,A23)*	

Figure 8.24 In rare cases, DATEDIF will report 1 month and –2 days.

Syntax:

```
=DAYS(end_date, start_date,)
```

The DAYS function always calculates elapsed days between two dates. Introduced in Excel 2013, the function offers one new trick: It works with text dates as well as real dates. This function takes the following arguments:

- `end_date, start_date`: The two dates between which you want to know the number of days. If either argument is text, that argument is passed through DATEVALUE() to return a date.

Using EOMONTH to calculate the end of the month

Syntax:

```
=EOMONTH(start_date,months)
```

The EOMONTH function returns the serial number for the last day of the month that is the indicated number of months before or after `start_date`. You use EOMONTH to calculate maturity dates or due dates that fall on the last day of the month. This function takes the following arguments:

- `start_date`: This is a date that represents the starting date.
- `months`: This is the number of months before or after `start_date`. A positive value for `months` yields a future date; a negative value yields a past date. If `months` is not an integer, it is truncated.
- =EOMONTH(A2,0) converts any date to the end of the month.

  CAUTION

  You must format the result of the EOMONTH formula to be a date to see the expected results.

Using WORKDAY or NETWORKDAYS or their international equivalents to calculate workdays

The functions WORKDAY and NETWORKDAYS are pretty cool. They calculate days by excluding weekends and holidays. Weekends can be any two-day period, such as Saturday/Sunday or Thursday/Friday, or any one day, such as only Sunday. As of Excel 2013, you can specify odd work weeks such as Monday, Thursday, Friday, Saturday.

These functions are great for calculating shipping days when you ship with FedEx or UPS. They are also great for making sure your result doesn't fall on a bank holiday. Here's how you do it:

1. In an out-of-the-way section of a spreadsheet, enter any holidays that will fall during the workweek. This might be federal holidays, floating holidays, company holidays, and so on. The list of holidays can either be entered down a column or across a row. In the top portion of Figure 8.25, the holidays are in E2:E11.

	A	B	C	D	E
1	Start Date:	Thursday, April 17, 2025			Holidays
2	# Work Days	65			1/1/2025
3	End Date:	Tuesday, July 22, 2025			1/20/2025
4		=WORKDAY(B1,B2,E2:E12)			2/17/2025
5					5/26/2025
6	Start Date:	Monday, April 14, 2025			6/19/2025
7	End Date:	Tuesday, June 17, 2025			7/4/2025
8	# Work Days	46			9/1/2025
9		=NETWORKDAYS(B6,B7,E2:E12)			10/13/2025
10					11/11/2025
11					11/27/2025
12					12/25/2025

Figure 8.25 WORKDAY and NETWORKDAYS can calculate the number of Monday-through-Friday days, exclusive of a range of holidays.

2. Enter a starting date in a cell, such as B1.

3. In another cell, enter the number of workdays that the project is expected to take, such as B2.

4. Enter the ending date formula as **=WORKDAY(B1,B2,E2:E11)**.

The NETWORKDAYS function takes two dates and figures out the number of workdays between them. For example, you might have a project that is due on June 17, 2025. If today is April 14, 2025, NETWORKDAYS can calculate the number of workdays until the project is due.

Syntax:

```
=WORKDAY(start_date,days,holidays)
```

Syntax:

```
=NETWORKDAYS(start_date,end_date,holidays)
```

The NETWORKDAYS function returns the number of whole workdays between `start_date` and `end_date`. Workdays exclude weekends and any dates identified in holidays. You use

NETWORKDAYS to calculate employee benefits that accrue based on the number of days worked during a specific term. This function takes the following arguments:

- start_date: This is a date that represents the start date.
- end_date: This is a date that represents the end date.
- holidays: This is an optional range of one or more dates to exclude from the working calendar, such as state and federal holidays and floating holidays. The list can be either a range of cells that contain the dates or an array constant of the serial numbers that represent the dates. If any argument is not a valid date, NETWORKDAYS returns a #NUM! error.

Both of the functions described in this section assume that Saturday and Sunday are weekends and are not workdays. If you have any other weekend system, you can use WORKDAY.INTL or NETWORKDAYS.INTL, as described in the next section.

In Figure 8.25, the current date is entered in cell B6. The project due date is entered in cell B7. The holidays range is in E2:E11, as in the previous example. The formula in cell B8 to calculate workdays is =NETWORKDAYS(B6,B7,E2:E11).

Using international versions of WORKDAY or NETWORKDAYS

Two functions introduced in Excel 2010 expand the WORKDAY and NETWORKDAYS functions for situations in which the work week is not Monday through Friday. The most common example is a weekend on Friday and Saturday, which has become popular in Qatar, Bahrain, Kuwait, United Arab Emirates, and Algeria. It also handles the situation in which a manufacturing plant is working six days and the weekend is only Sunday. A new form of the weekday argument introduced in Excel 2013 allows for a nonstandard workweek, such as those found at farm markets or barbershops.

Syntax:

```
=WORKDAY.INTL(start_date,days,weekend,holidays)
```

Syntax:

```
=NETWORKDAYS.INTL(start_date,end_date,weekend,holidays)
```

Both functions work as their noninternational equivalents, with the addition of having the weekend specified as shown below. (Note that there are no noninternational equivalents for 8, 9, and 10.)

1—Weekend on Saturday and Sunday

2—Weekend on Sunday and Monday

3—Weekend on Monday and Tuesday

4—Weekend on Tuesday and Wednesday

5—Weekend on Wednesday and Thursday

6—Weekend on Thursday and Friday

7—Weekend on Friday and Saturday

11—Sunday only

12—Monday only

13—Tuesday only

14—Wednesday only

15—Thursday only

16—Friday only

17—Saturday only

You can specify any nonstandard workweek by using a seven-digit binary text as the weekend argument. The seven digits correspond to Monday through Sunday in order. A 1 indicates the company is closed that day (that is, it is a weekend), and a 0 indicates the company is open.

For example, the Hartville Marketplace is open Monday, Thursday, Friday, and Saturday. The weekend argument would be "0110001," as shown in Figure 8.26.

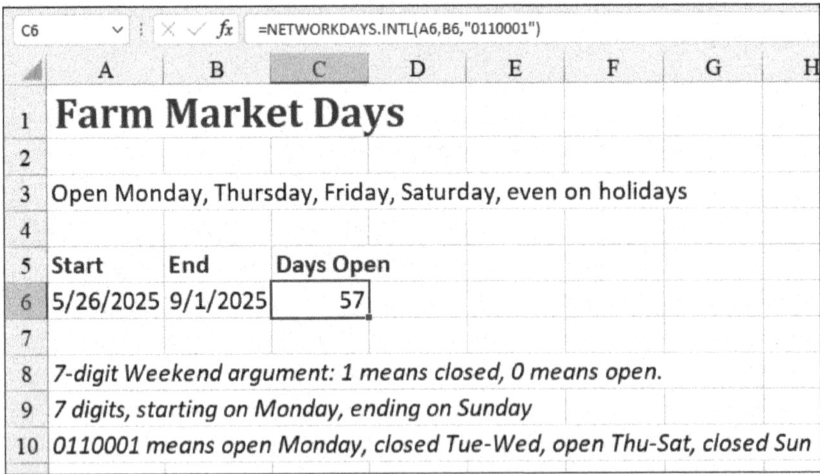

Figure 8.26 Use the seven-digit binary text as the weekday argument to handle nonstandard work weeks.

Examples of text functions

When they think of Excel, most people think of numbers. Excel is great at dealing with numbers, and it lets you write formulas to produce new numbers. Excel offers a whole cadre of formulas for dealing with text.

You might sometimes be frustrated because you receive data from other people, and the text is not in the format you need. Or the mainframe might send customer names in uppercase, or the employee in the next department might put a whole address into a single cell. Excel provides text functions to deal with all these situations and more.

Joining text with TEXTJOIN

Microsoft introduced two new functions for joining text in February 2017. The CONCAT function will join text in several cells. While CONCAT is better than the legacy CONCATENATE, it is not as flexible as the amazing TEXTJOIN function.

In Figure 8.27, CONCAT successfully joins a long list of names. However, there is no space or comma between each item. The TEXTJOIN function lets you specify a delimiter. In D6 of the figure, `=TEXTJOIN(", ",True,A2:A24)` joins all of the names, and each name is separated by a comma and a space.

Further, the third argument of TEXTJOIN can be an array or a 3-D reference. That means you can make choices about whether to include each name or not. To join only the names where column B indicates the RSVP is Yes, you could use `=TEXTJOIN(", ",True,IF(B2:B24="Yes", A2:A24,""))`.

	A	B	C	D	E	F	G	H	I
1	Name	RSVP		Join All					
2	Ellen Atkins	Yes		Ellen AtkinsErnest BullockSandra CarrollSonia DavidJason E					
3	Ernest Bullock	No		=CONCAT(A2:A24)					
4	Sandra Carroll	Yes							
5	Sonia David	Yes		Join All with Commas					
6	Jason Everett	No		Ellen Atkins, Ernest Bullock, Sandra Carroll, Sonia David, Jas					
7	Gary Hammond	Yes		=TEXTJOIN(", ",TRUE,A2:A24)					
8	Jacqueline Kemp	No							
9	Stacy King	Yes		Join only where RSVP=Yes					
10	Bradley Marks	No		Ellen Atkins, Sandra Carroll, Sonia David, Gary Hammond, S					
11	Madeline Martinez	Yes		=TEXTJOIN(", ",TRUE,IF(B2:B24="Yes",A2:A24,""))					
12	Bertha Moreno	Yes							
13	Delores Peck	No		Old Way					
14	Mattie Pierce	Yes		Ellen Atkins, Ernest Bullock, Sandra Carroll					
15	Vera Powers	No		=A2&", "&A3&", "&A4					
16	Kay Quinn	Yes							

Figure 8.27 TEXTJOIN offers new ways to a range of names.

Syntax:

```
=TEXTJOIN(delimiter,ignore_empty,text1,[text2,...])
```

The TEXTJOIN function joins a list or a range of text using a delimiter.

Before the introduction of TEXTJOIN in 2017, you would have had to use =A2&" "&A3&" "&A4& and so on. Even the legacy CONCATENATE function could not accept a range of cells. The formula would have been =CONCATENATE("A2"," ",A3," ",A4," ",…).

Using LOWER, UPPER, or PROPER to convert text case

Three functions—LOWER, UPPER, and PROPER—convert text to or from capital letters. In Figure 8.28, the products in column B were entered in a haphazard fashion. Some products used lowercase, and some products used uppercase. Column C uses =UPPER(B2) to make all the products a uniform uppercase.

F2 =PROPER(E2)

	A	B	C	D	E	F	G
1	Quantity	Product	Upper		NAME	Proper	
2	2	q754	Q754		ERIN RICHMOND	Erin Richmond	
3	1	g644	G644		JACK O'RASI	Jack O'Rasi	
4	5	G644	G644		KEITH MCCARTNEY	Keith Mccartney	
5	4	q754	Q754		ERNEST CURTIS	Ernest Curtis	
6	7	Q754	Q754		LEAH HARRISON	Leah Harrison	
7	7	d350	D350		ALLISON BRIGGS	Allison Briggs	
8	1	Q754	Q754		STEVEN CARR	Steven Carr	
9	1	g644	G644		TERRI HARDY	Terri Hardy	
10	3	G644	G644		KYLE SANCHEZ	Kyle Sanchez	
11	2	n870	N870		RYAN PITTS	Ryan Pitts	
12	3	q754	Q754				
13	4	d350	D350		MY MANAGER TYPES IN ALL CAPITALS		
14	8	q754	Q754		my manager types in all capitals		
15	5	I175	I175				
16	2	i175	I175				
17	3	i175	I175				
18							
19	C2: =UPPER(B2)						
20	E14: =LOWER(E13)						
21							

Figure 8.28 UPPER, LOWER, and PROPER can convert text to and from capital letters.

In cell E13, the text was entered by someone who never turns off Caps Lock. You can convert this uppercase to lowercase with =LOWER(E13).

In column E, you see a range of names in uppercase. You can use =PROPER(E2) to convert the name to the proper case, which capitalizes just the first letter of each word. The PROPER function is mostly fantastic, but there are a few cells that you have to manually correct. PROPER correctly capitalizes names with apostrophes, such as O'Rasi in cell F3. It does not, however, correctly capitalize the interior *c* in McCartney in cell F4. The function is also notorious for creating company names such as Ibm, 3m, and Aep.

> NOTE
>
> **If you want to keep the data only in column C, you have to convert the formulas to values before deleting columns A and B. To do this, select the data in column C and then press Ctrl+C to copy. Then select Home, Paste, Paste Values to convert the formulas to values.**

Syntax:

`=LOWER(text)`

The LOWER function converts all uppercase letters in a text string to lowercase. The argument `text` is the text you want to convert to lowercase. LOWER does not change characters in `text` that are not letters.

Syntax:

`=PROPER(text)`

The PROPER function capitalizes the first letter in a text string and any other letters in text that follow any character other than a letter. It converts all other letters to lowercase letters.

The argument `text` is text enclosed in quotation marks, a formula that returns text, or a reference to a cell containing the text you want to capitalize partially.

Syntax:

`=UPPER(text)`

The UPPER function converts text to uppercase. The argument `text` is the text you want to be converted to uppercase. `text` can be a reference or text string.

Using TRIM to remove leading and trailing spaces

If you frequently import data, you might be plagued with a couple of annoying situations. This section and the next one deal with those situations.

You may have trailing spaces at the end of text cells. Although " ABC" and "ABC " might look alike when viewed in Excel, they cause functions such as MATCH and VLOOKUP to fail. TRIM removes leading and trailing spaces. It also changes strings of more than one space to just one space. That is, =TRIM(" a   b   c ") would be "a b c".

CHAPTER 8

In Figure 8.29, you can see a simple `VLOOKUP` in column B. The formula in cell B2 is `=VLOOKUP(A2,$F$2:$G$5,2,FALSE)`. Even though you can clearly see that `M40498` is in the lookup table, `VLOOKUP` returns an `#N/A!` error, which indicates that the product ID is missing from the lookup table.

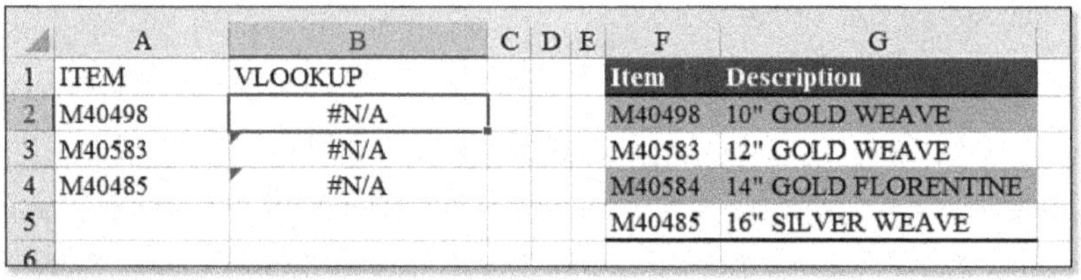

	A	B	C	D	E	F	G
1	ITEM	VLOOKUP				Item	Description
2	M40498	#N/A				M40498	10" GOLD WEAVE
3	M40583	#N/A				M40583	12" GOLD WEAVE
4	M40485	#N/A				M40584	14" GOLD FLORENTINE
5						M40485	16" SILVER WEAVE
6							

Figure 8.29 This `VLOOKUP` should work, but in this instance, it fails.

To diagnose and correct this problem, follow these steps:

1. Select one of the data cells in column F. Press the F2 key to put the cell in Edit mode. A flashing insertion character appears at the end of the cell. Check to see if the flashing cursor is immediately after the last character.

2. Select one of the data cells in column A. Press the F2 key to put the cell in Edit mode. Note whether the flashing insertion character is immediately after the last character. Figure 8.30 shows that the products in column A have several trailing spaces after them. The products in the lookup table do not have any trailing spaces.

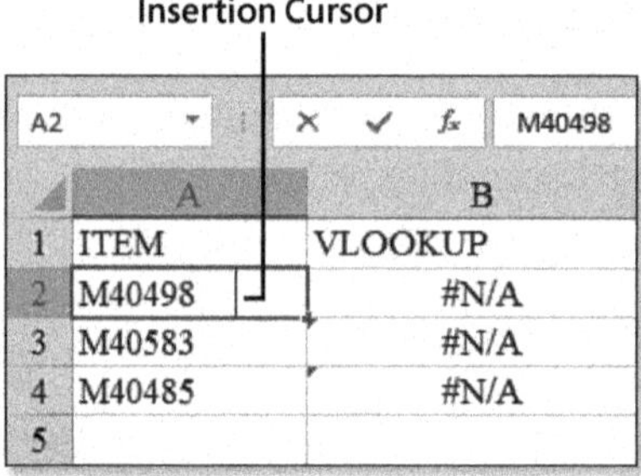

Figure 8.30 Spaces are padding the right side of the products in column A.

3. If the problem is occurring in the values being looked up, you could modify the formula in cell B2 to use the `TRIM` function. The new formula would be `=VLOOKUP(TRIM(A2),$F$2:$G$5,2,FALSE)`. Figure 8.31 shows how this solves the problem.

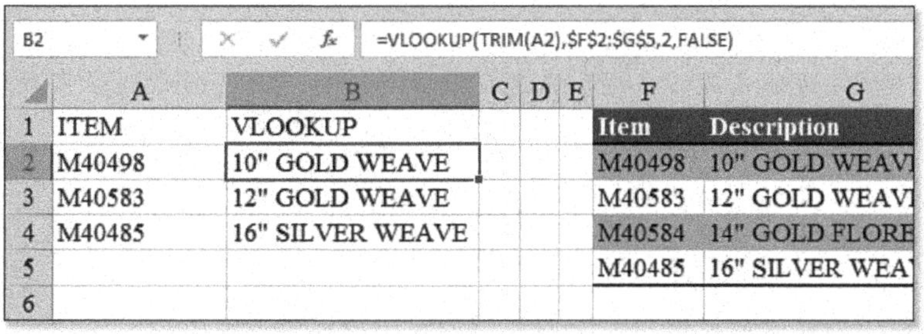

B2 =VLOOKUP(TRIM(A2),$F$2:$G$5,2,FALSE)

	A	B	C	D	E	F	G
1	ITEM	VLOOKUP				Item	Description
2	M40498	10" GOLD WEAVE				M40498	10" GOLD WEAV
3	M40583	12" GOLD WEAVE				M40583	12" GOLD WEAV
4	M40485	16" SILVER WEAVE				M40584	14" GOLD FLORE
5						M40485	16" SILVER WEA
6							

Figure 8.31 Using `TRIM` to remove leading spaces allows `VLOOKUP` to work.

4. If the problem is occurring in the first column of the lookup table, insert a new temporary column. Enter the function **`=TRIM(F2)`** in the temporary column. Copy this formula down to all rows of the lookup table. Copy the new formulas. Select cell F2. Select Home, Paste, Values to paste the new values. Although the old and new values look the same, the `TRIM` function has removed the trailing spaces, and now the products match.

NOTE

It is not necessarily efficient to calculate, but you can solve the trailing spaces in column F by using `=VLOOKUP(A2,TRIM(F$2:G$5),2,FALSE)`.

Syntax:

`=TRIM(text)`

The `TRIM` function removes all spaces from text except for single spaces between words. You use `TRIM` on text that you have received from another application that might have irregular spacing. The argument `text` is the text from which you want spaces removed.

In Figure 8.32, cell C1 contains six letters: ABC DEF. You might assume that the cell is set to be centered. However, the formula in cell C2 appends an asterisk to each end of the value in cell C1. This formula shows that there are several leading and trailing spaces in the value.

Using `=LEN(C1)` shows that the text actually contains 15 characters instead of six characters. The `TRIM(C1)` formula removes any leading spaces, any trailing spaces, and any extra interior spaces. The function still leaves one space between ABC and DEF because you want to continue to have words separated by a single space.

The formulas in cells C5 and C6 confirm that the leading and trailing spaces are removed and that the length of the new value is only seven characters.

C1 | ABC DEF

	A	B	C
1		Original Value:	ABC DEF
2		="*"&C1&"*"	* ABC DEF *
3		Length(C1)	15
4		TRIM(C1)	ABC DEF
5		="*"&C4&"*"	*ABC DEF*
6		LENGTH(C4)	7
7			

Figure 8.32 TRIM removes leading spaces and extra interior spaces.

Inside OUT

Sometimes TRIM appears to not remove spaces. This is particularly true when the data originated from a web page.

Look at your keyboard. By far, the largest key on the keyboard is the spacebar. Press that space bar, and you will type an ASCII Character 32—also known as a space. However, there at least 20 varieties of space characters, such as the Unicode 200A hair space. The problem—since the rise of the web—is that the ASCII Character 160 is a nonbreaking space.

A web browser will always render "space space space" as "space," which causes problems when people try to get words to line up or VBA code to be indented. The solution is to change the space to a   or a nonbreaking space.

TRIM was written long before the web became common, and TRIM only operates on Character 32 spaces. If you have data with nonbreaking spaces or Mongolian vowel separators, TRIM will not remove those spaces.

Use the CHAR or UNICHAR functions to discover the character code behind your spaces. Then use SUBSTITUTE to change those back to regular spaces.

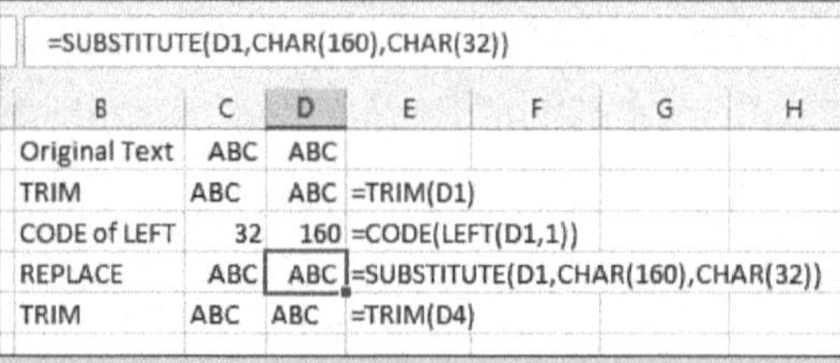

=SUBSTITUTE(D1,CHAR(160),CHAR(32))

B	C	D	E	F	G	H
Original Text	ABC	ABC				
TRIM	ABC	ABC	=TRIM(D1)			
CODE of LEFT	32	160	=CODE(LEFT(D1,1))			
REPLACE	ABC	ABC	=SUBSTITUTE(D1,CHAR(160),CHAR(32))			
TRIM	ABC	ABC	=TRIM(D4)			

> Two identical-looking cells contain two spaces followed by ABC. In the first column, the `TRIM` function correctly removes the leading spaces. However, in the second column, the spaces stay even after using `TRIM`. Formulas in the next row use the CODE from the LEFT of each original cell. In the first column, the ASCII code for the space is 32. In the second column, the ASCII code is 160. A workaround of `=SUBSTITUTE(D1,CHAR(160),CHAR(32))` is shown to change the non-breaking spaces to regular spaces. After that formula, the `TRIM` works as expected.

Using the CHAR or UNICHAR function to generate any character

Early computers used a character set of 128 ASCII characters. Any computer that you've had in your home offered at least an 8-bit processor and could easily display 255 characters. Thus, computers sold in the United States offered the original 128 ASCII characters and an extended 128 characters with accented characters needed for German, French, and some other European languages. The `CHAR()` function makes it possible to display any of these 255 characters.

Today, the Unicode character set includes more than 137,000 characters, covering most written languages used on Earth. Unicode includes glyphs used in languages from Aboriginal to Yijing. You will find glyphs from Braille, Burmese, Cherokee, Greek, Old Persian, and many languages that you have not heard of. There are also map symbols, playing card symbols, emoticons, dice, domino, music, and mahjong markings. Unfortunately, the Unicode organization officially rejected including Klingon in 2001. Also, although the Calibri font will render chess, dice, and playing card symbols, it does not support domino or mahjong.

All versions of Excel supported `CHAR()` to generate symbols 0 through 255. Excel 2013 added support for `UNICHAR()` to render the 100,000+ symbols defined by Unicode.

You might have ventured into Start, All Programs, Accessories, System Tools, Character Map to find a particular character in the Wingdings character set. Also, if you have a favorite symbol, you might have memorized that you can insert the symbol by using a hotkey. For example, if you hold down Alt, type **0169** on the numeric keypad, and then release Alt, an Office program inserts the copyright symbol (©).

> TIP
>
> **Although I know a few characters off the top of my head, I usually take a look at all characters in a set by entering `=CHAR(ROW())` in cells A1:A255. This returns character A in row 65, and so on. In Excel, you can use `=UNICHAR(ROW())` in column A1:A1048576 to browse for symbols. To find something in particular, check out *https://unicode-table.com/en/#control-character*.**

Syntax:

`=CHAR(number)`

The CHAR function returns the character specified by a number. You use CHAR to translate code page numbers you might get from files on other types of computers into characters.

The argument `number` is a number between 1 and 255 that specifies which character you want. The character is from the character set used by your computer and based on the font used in the cell.

Syntax:

`=UNICHAR(number)`

The UNICHAR function returns the Unicode character specified by a number.

Figure 8.33 shows some symbols available from CHAR and UNICHAR.

F3 =UNICHAR(E3)

	A	B	C	D	E	F	G	H	I	J	K	L	M	N	O
1	CHAR Examples				UNICHAR Examples										
2															
3	35	#			9812	♔		9810	♒		9833	♩		9856	⚀
4	36	$			9813	♕		9807	♏		9834	♪		9857	⚁
5	37	%			9814	♖		9801	♉		9835	♫		9858	⚂
6	48	0			9815	♗		9824	♠		9836	♬		9859	⚃
7	49	1			9816	♘		9825	♡		9842	♲		9860	⚄
8	57	9			9817	♙		9826	♢		9843	♳		9861	⚅
9	65	A			9818	♚		9827	♣		9844	♴		9892	⚤
10	90	Z			9819	♛		9828	♤		9845	♵		9992	✈
11	97	a			9820	♜		9829	♥		9846	♶		10042	✺
12	122	z			9821	♝		9830	♦		9847	♷		10667	⦫
13	153	™			9822	♞		9831	♧		9848	♸		13219	㎣
14	169	©			9823	♟		9832	♨		9849	♹		14615	㤗
15															

Figure 8.33 This figure shows examples of CHAR and UNICHAR results.

If you see a strange character in your data, you can learn the character number by using the `CODE` or `UNICODE` function, as described in the following section.

Using the CODE or UNICODE function to learn the character number for any character

If you can't remember that a capital A is character code 65, you can use the `CODE` function to learn the code associated with the character. The function returns the ASCII code for the first character in the text. `=CODE("A")` returns 65.

The old `CHAR` function did not work with characters beyond the first 255 characters. Starting in Excel 2013, the Excel team added the `UNICODE` function to return the Unicode character number for a character.

Syntax:

`=CODE(text)`

`=UNICODE(text)`

The `CODE` function returns a numeric code for the first character in a text string. The returned code corresponds to the character set used by your computer. The argument `text` is the text for which you want the code of the first character. This is an important distinction. `CODE` returns the code for only the first character in a cell. `=CODE("A")` and `=CODE("ABC")` return only 65 to indicate the capital letter A.

The `UNICODE` function returns the character code for the 100,000+ characters currently defined.

Using LEFT, MID, or RIGHT to split text

One of the newer rules in information processing is that each field in a database should contain exactly one piece of information. Throughout the history of computers, there have been millions of examples of people trying to cram many pieces of information into a single field. Although this works great for humans, it is pretty difficult to have Excel sort a column by everything in the second half of a cell.

Column A in Figure 8.34 contains part numbers. As you might guess, the Part Number field contains two pieces of information: a three-character vendor code, a dash, and a numeric part number.

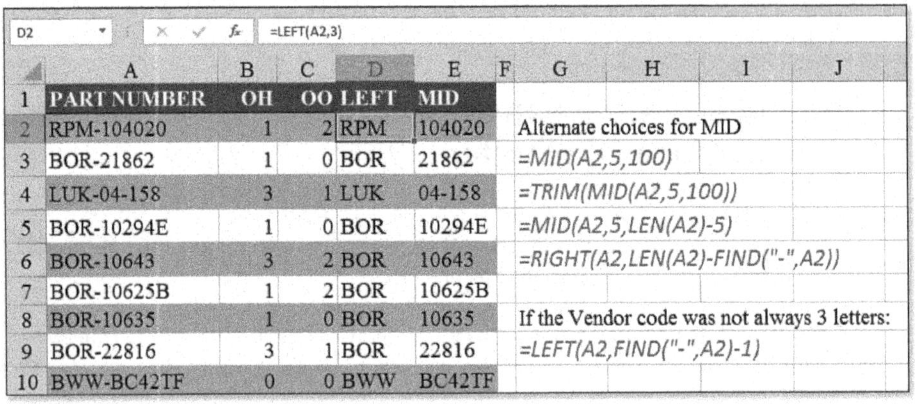

D2 =LEFT(A2,3)

	A	B	C	D	E	F	G	H	I	J
1	PART NUMBER	OH	OO	LEFT	MID					
2	RPM-104020	1	2	RPM	104020		Alternate choices for MID			
3	BOR-21862	1	0	BOR	21862		=MID(A2,5,100)			
4	LUK-04-158	3	1	LUK	04-158		=TRIM(MID(A2,5,100))			
5	BOR-10294E	1	0	BOR	10294E		=MID(A2,5,LEN(A2)-5)			
6	BOR-10643	3	2	BOR	10643		=RIGHT(A2,LEN(A2)-FIND("-",A2))			
7	BOR-10625B	1	2	BOR	10625B					
8	BOR-10635	1	0	BOR	10635		If the Vendor code was not always 3 letters:			
9	BOR-22816	3	1	BOR	22816		=LEFT(A2,FIND("-",A2)-1)			
10	BWW-BC42TF	0	0	BWW	BC42TF					

Figure 8.34 `LEFT` makes quick work of extracting the vendor code. Several varieties of `MID` or `RIGHT` extract the part number.

When a customer comes in to buy a part, he probably doesn't care about the vendor. So the real question is, "Do you have anything in stock that can fix my problem?"

Excel offers three functions—`LEFT`, `MID`, and `RIGHT`—that enable you to isolate just the first or just the last characters, or even just the middle characters, from a column.

Syntax:

```
=LEFT(text,num_chars)
```

The `LEFT` function returns the first character or characters in a text string, based on the number of characters specified. This function takes the following arguments:

- `text`: This is the text string that contains the characters you want to extract.
- `num_chars`: This specifies the number of characters you want `LEFT` to extract. `num_chars` must be greater than or equal to zero. If `num_chars` is greater than the length of the text, `LEFT` returns all the `text`. If `num_chars` is omitted, it is assumed to be `1`.

Syntax:

```
=RIGHT(text,num_chars)
```

The `RIGHT` function returns the last character or characters in a text string, based on the number of characters specified. This function takes the following arguments:

- `text`: This is the text string that contains the characters you want to extract.
- `num_chars`: This specifies the number of characters you want `RIGHT` to extract. `num_chars` must be greater than or equal to zero. If `num_chars` is greater than the length of text, `RIGHT` returns all of `text`. If `num_chars` is omitted, it is assumed to be `1`.

Syntax:

```
=MID(text,start_num,num_chars)
```

MID returns a specific number of characters from a text string, starting at the position specified, based on the number of characters specified. This function takes the following arguments:

- text: This is the text string that contains the characters you want to extract.
- start_num: This is the position of the first character you want to extract in the text. The first character in the text has start_num 1, and so on. If start_num is greater than the length of the text, MID returns "" (that is, empty text). If start_num is less than the length of the text, but start_num plus num_chars exceeds the length of the text, MID returns the characters up to the end of the text. If start_num is less than 1, MID returns a #VALUE! error.
- num_chars: This specifies the number of characters you want MID to return from the text. If num_chars is negative, MID returns a #VALUE! error.

In Figure 8.34, it is easy to extract the three-character vendor code by using =LEFT(A2,3). It is a bit more difficult to extract the part number. As you scan through the values in column A, it is clear that the vendor code is consistently three letters. With the dash in the fourth character of the text, it means that the part number starts in the fifth position. If you are using MID, you, therefore, use 5 as the start_num argument.

However, there are a few thousand part numbers in the data set. Right up front, in cell A4, is a part number that breaks the rule. LUK-04-158 contains six characters after the first dash. This might seem to be an isolated incident, but in row 10, BWW-BC42TF also contains six characters after the dash. Because this type of thing happens in real life, two errors in the first nine records are enough to warrant a little extra attention. The four possible strategies for extracting the part number are listed in G2:G6. They are as follows:

- Ask MID to start at the fifth character and return a large enough number of characters to handle any possible length (that is, =MID(A2,5,100)).
- Ask MID to start at the fifth character but use TRIM around the whole function to prevent any trailing spaces from being included (that is, =TRIM(MID(A2,5,100))).
- Ask MID to start at the fifth character, but calculate the exact number of characters by using the LEN function (that is, =MID(A2,5,LEN(A2)-4)).
- Skip MID altogether and ask RIGHT to return all the characters after the first dash. This requires you to use the FIND function to locate the first dash—that is, =RIGHT(A2,LEN(A2)-FIND("-",A2)).

Using LEN to find the number of characters in a text cell

It seems pretty obscure, but you will find the `LEN` function amazingly useful. The `LEN` function determines the length of characters in a cell, including any leading or trailing spaces.

Syntax:

```
=LEN(text)
```

The `LEN` function returns the number of characters in a text string. The argument `text` is the text whose length you want to find. Spaces count as characters.

There are instances in which you can use `LEN` along with `LEFT`, `MID`, or `RIGHT` to isolate a portion of text.

You can also use `LEN` to find records that are longer than a certain limit. Suppose you are about to order nameplates for company employees. Each nameplate can accommodate 15 characters. In Figure 8.35, you add the `LEN` function next to the names and sort by the length, in descending order. Any problem names appear at the top of the list.

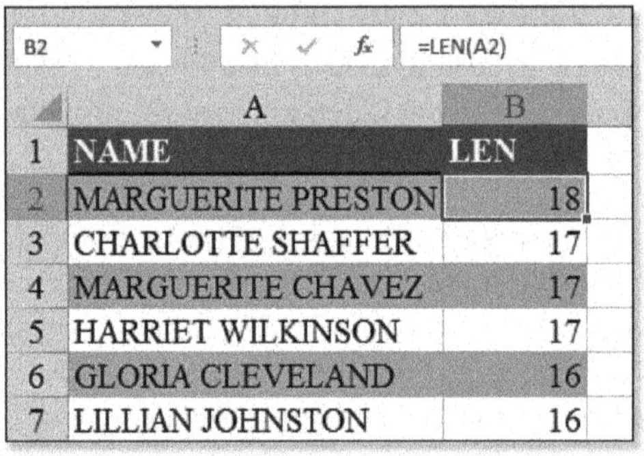

B2 =LEN(A2)

	A	B
1	NAME	LEN
2	MARGUERITE PRESTON	18
3	CHARLOTTE SHAFFER	17
4	MARGUERITE CHAVEZ	17
5	HARRIET WILKINSON	17
6	GLORIA CLEVELAND	16
7	LILLIAN JOHNSTON	16

Figure 8.35 `LEN` identifies the number of characters in a cell.

Using SEARCH or FIND to locate characters in a particular cell

Two nearly identical functions can scan through a text cell, looking for a particular character or word. Many times, you just want to know if the word appears in the text. These functions go further than telling you if the character exists in the text; they tell you at exactly which character position the character or word is found. The character position can be useful in subsequent formulas with `LEFT`, `RIGHT`, or `REPLACE`.

First, let's look at an example of using `FIND` to determine whether a word exists in another cell. Figure 8.36 shows a database of customers. The database was created by someone who doesn't know Excel and jammed every field into a single cell.

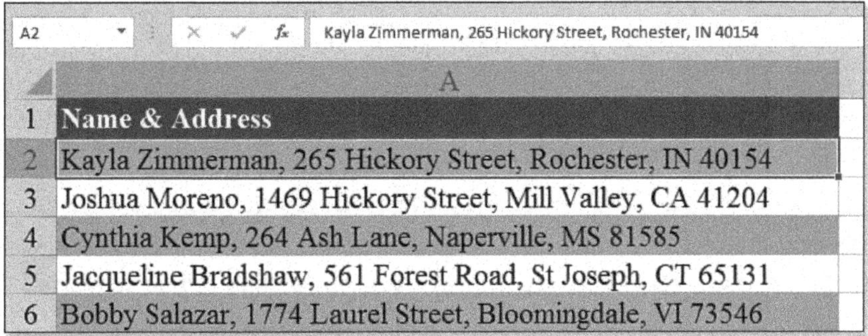

A2 | Kayla Zimmerman, 265 Hickory Street, Rochester, IN 40154

	A
1	**Name & Address**
2	Kayla Zimmerman, 265 Hickory Street, Rochester, IN 40154
3	Joshua Moreno, 1469 Hickory Street, Mill Valley, CA 41204
4	Cynthia Kemp, 264 Ash Lane, Naperville, MS 81585
5	Jacqueline Bradshaw, 561 Forest Road, St Joseph, CT 65131
6	Bobby Salazar, 1774 Laurel Street, Bloomingdale, VI 73546

Figure 8.36 When the manager asked an employee to type this in Excel, she didn't realize that the employee had never used Excel before.

Here is how to make this work properly:

1. To find all the customers in California, in cell B2, enter **`=FIND(", CA",A2)`**. When you enter the formula, you get a `#VALUE!` error. This is okay. In fact, it is useful information: It tells you that CA is not found in the first record.

2. Copy the formula down to all rows.

   NOTE

   Like all the other data sets in this book, these names and addresses are randomly generated from lists of the most popular first name, last name, street name, and city names. Don't try to send Christmas cards to these people, because none of the addresses exist. And don't think that the ZIP Codes are real; everything here is completely random.

3. Sort low to high by column B. You'll see that 98% of the records have a `#VALUE!` error and sort to the bottom of the list. The few California records have a valid result for the formula in column B and sort to the top of the list, as shown in Figure 8.37.

B2 | =FIND(", CA",A2)

	A	B
1	**Name & Address**	**California?**
2	Marilyn Atkins, 1581 Twelfth Avenue, Oak Grove, CA 69942	47
3	Joshua Moreno, 1469 Hickory Street, Mill Valley, CA 41204	48
4	Kayla Zimmerman, 265 Hickory Street, Rochester, IN 40154	#VALUE!
5	Cynthia Kemp, 264 Ash Lane, Naperville, MS 81585	#VALUE!
6	Jacqueline Bradshaw, 561 Forest Road, St Joseph, CT 65131	#VALUE!
7	Bobby Salazar, 1774 Laurel Street, Bloomingdale, VI 73546	#VALUE!

Figure 8.37 You don't care where `FIND` found the text; you simply want to divide the list into records with valid values versus errors.

FIND and SEARCH are similar to one another. The SEARCH function does not distinguish between uppercase and lowercase letters. SEARCH identifies CA, ca, Ca, and cA as matches for CA. If you need to find a cell with exactly AbCdEf, you need to use the FIND command instead of SEARCH. Also, SEARCH allows for wildcard characters in `find_text`. A question mark (?) finds a single character, and an asterisk (*) finds any number of characters.

The FIND function makes it easy to find the first instance of a particular character in a cell. However, if your text values contain two instances of a character, your task is a bit more difficult. In Figure 8.38, the part numbers in column A really contain three segments, each separated by a dash:

1. To find the first dash, enter **=FIND("-",A2)** in column B.

   CAUTION

   The trick with this application of FIND is to look for something that is likely to be found only in California records. If you had customers in Cairo, Illinois, they would have also been found by the FIND command you just used. The theory with this sort of search is that you can quickly check through the few matching records to find false positives.

C2 =FIND("-",A2,B2+1)

	A	B	C	D	E	F	G	H
1	Part Number	First Dash	Second Dash	First Part	2nd Part	3rd Part		*Formulas:*
2	37767-33-385568	6	9	37767	33	385568		B2: =FIND("-",A2)
3	632-6-43	4	6	632	6	43		C2: =FIND("-",A2,B2+1)
4	10-13-5656	3	6	10	13	5656		D2: =LEFT(A2,B2-1)
5	9-671672-119067	2	9	9	671672	119067		E2: =MID(A2,B2+1,C2-B2-1)
6	41-50555-51	3	9	41	50555	51		F2: =RIGHT(A2,LEN(A2)-C2)
7	568-536-177914	4	8	568	536	177914		

Figure 8.38 Formulaically isolating data between the first and second dashes can be done, but it helps to break each number down into small parts.

2. To find the second dash, use the optional `start_num` parameter to the FIND function. The `start_num` parameter is a character position. You want the function to start looking after the first instance of a dash. This can be calculated as the result of the first FIND in column B plus one. Thus, the formula in cell C2 is =FIND("-",A2,B2+1).

3. After you find the character positions of the dashes, isolate the various portions of the part number. In column D, for the first part of the number, enter **=LEFT(A2,B2-1)**. This basically asks for the left characters from the part number, stopping at one fewer than the first dash.

4. In column E, for the middle part of the number, enter **=MID(A2,B2+1,C2-B2-1)**. This asks Excel to start at the character position one after the first dash and then continue for a length that is one fewer than the first dash subtracted from the second dash.

5. In column F, for the final part of the number, enter **=RIGHT(A2,LEN(A2)-C2)**. This calculates the total length of the part number, subtracts the position of the second dash, and returns those right characters.

Syntax:

```
=FIND(find_text,within_text,start_num)
```

FIND finds one text string (find_text) within another text string (within_text) and returns the number of the starting position of find_text from the first character of within_text. You can also use SEARCH to find one text string within another, but unlike SEARCH, FIND is case sensitive and doesn't allow wildcard characters.

The FIND function takes the following arguments:

- find_text: This is the text you want to find. If find_text is "" (that is, empty text), FIND matches the first character in the search string (that is, the character numbered start_num or 1). find_text cannot contain wildcard characters.
- within_text: This is the text that contains the text you want to find.
- start_num: This specifies the character at which to start the search. The first character in within_text is character number 1. If you omit start_num, it is assumed to be 1.

Syntax:

```
=SEARCH(find_text,within_text,start_num)
```

SEARCH returns the number of the character at which a specific character or text string is first found, beginning with start_num. You use SEARCH to determine the location of a character or text string within another text string so that you can use the MID or REPLACE function to change the text.

The SEARCH function takes the following arguments:

- find_text: This is the text you want to find. You can use the wildcard characters question mark (?) and asterisk (*) in find_text. A question mark matches any single character; an asterisk matches any sequence of characters. If you want to find an actual question mark or asterisk, you type a tilde (~) before the character. If you want to find a tilde, you type two tildes. If find_text is not found, a #VALUE! error is returned.
- within_text: This is the text in which you want to search for find_text.

- `start_num`: This is the character number in `within_text` at which you want to start searching. If `start_num` is omitted, it is assumed to be 1. If `start_num` is not greater than zero or is greater than the length of `within_text`, a `#VALUE!` error is returned.

  CAUTION

  If `find_text` does not appear in `within_text`, `FIND` returns a `#VALUE!` error. If `start_num` is not greater than zero, `FIND` returns a `#VALUE!` error. If `start_num` is greater than the length of `within_text`, `FIND` returns a `#VALUE!` error.

Using SUBSTITUTE to replace characters

When you have the capability to find text, you might want to replace text. Excel offers two functions for this: `SUBSTITUTE` and `REPLACE`. The `SUBSTITUTE` function is easier to use and should be your first approach.

Syntax:

```
=SUBSTITUTE(text,old_text,new_text,instance_num)
```

The `SUBSTITUTE` function substitutes `new_text` for `old_text` in a text string. You use `SUBSTITUTE` when you want to replace specific text in a text string; you use `REPLACE` when you want to replace any text that occurs in a specific location in a text string.

The `SUBSTITUTE` function takes the following arguments:

- `text`: This is the text or the reference to a cell that contains text for which you want to substitute characters.
- `old_text`: This is the text you want to replace.
- `new_text`: This is the text you want to replace `old_text` with.
- `instance_num`: This specifies which occurrence of `old_text` you want to replace with `new_text`. If you specify `instance_num`, only that instance of `old_text` is replaced. Otherwise, every occurrence of `old_text` in text is changed to `new_text`. The ability of `SUBSTITUTE` to target a specific instance is often useful. For example, you might need to change the third space to a dash. Using an instance_num of 3 is one way to do this.

Using REPT to repeat text multiple times

The `REPT` function repeats a character or some text a certain number of times.

Syntax:

```
=REPT(text,number_times)
```

The REPT function repeats text a given number of times. You use REPT to fill a cell with a number of instances of a text string. This function takes the following arguments:

- `text`: This is the text you want to repeat.
- `number_times`: This is a positive number that specifies the number of times to repeat text. If `number_times` is 0, REPT returns `""` (that is, empty text). If `number_times` is not an integer, it is truncated. The result of the REPT function cannot be longer than 32,767 characters.

In Microsoft Word, it is easy to create a row of periods between text and a page number. In Excel, you have to resort to clever use of the REPT function to do this.

In Figure 8.39, column A contains a page number. Column B contains a chapter title. The goal in column C is to join enough periods between columns B and A to make all the page numbers line up.

C2 | =B2&REPT(".",45-(LEN(A2)+LEN(B2)))&A2

	A	B	C
1	Page	Title	=B2&REPT(".",45-(LEN(A2)+LEN(B2)))&A2
2	7	Chapter 1 - Backstage View	Chapter 1 - Backstage View.................7
3	23	Chapter 2 - The Ribbon	Chapter 2 - The Ribbon....................23
4	39	Chapter 3 - Other Excel Improvements	Chapter 3 - Other Excel Improvements.......39
5	47	Chapter 4 - Customizing the Ribbon	Chapter 4 - Customizing the Ribbon.........47
6	105	Chapter 5 - Keyboard Shortcuts	Chapter 5 - Keyboard Shortcuts...........105
7			
8		Hello Hello Hello	
9		=REPT("Hello ",3)	
10			

Figure 8.39 The REPT function can be used to calculate a certain number of repeated entries.

The number of periods to print is the total desired length, less the length of columns A and B. The formula for cell C2 is `=B2&REPT(".",45-(LEN(A2)+LEN(B2)))&A2`.

> **NOTE**
>
> **To make this work, you must change the font in column C to be a fixed-width font, such as Courier New.**

TIP

An alternative solution is to format column B with the custom format of "@*.". This shows the text in the cell and follows it with a series of periods, enough to fill the current width of the column. Then, copy the left-aligned numbers from column A to column C.

Using EXACT to test case

For the most part, Excel isn't concerned about the case. To Excel, ABC and abc are the same things. In Figure 8.40, cells A1 and B1 contain the same letters, but the capitalization is different.

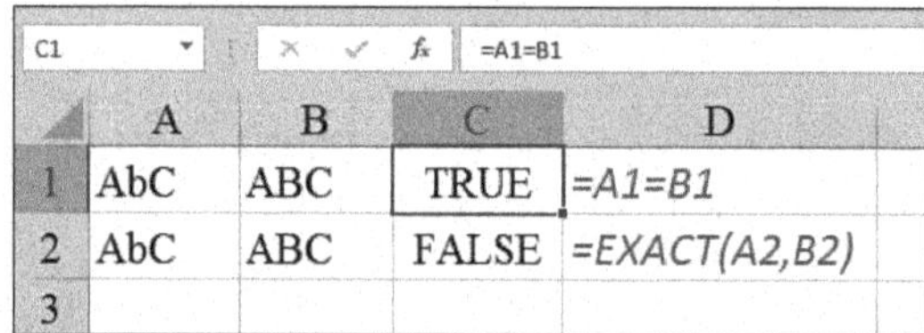

Figure 8.40 Excel usually overlooks differences in capitalization when deciding whether two values are equal. You can use EXACT to find out whether they are equal and the same case.

The formula in cell C1 tests whether these values are equal. In the rules of Excel, AbC and ABC are equivalent. The formula in cell C1 indicates that the values are equal. To some people, these two text cells might not be equivalent. If you work in a store that sells the big plastic letters that go on theater marquees, your order for 20 letter *a* figures should not be filled with 20 letter *A* figures.

Excel forces you to use the EXACT function to compare these two cells to learn that they are not the same.

Syntax:

```
=EXACT(text1,text2)
```

The EXACT function compares two text strings and returns TRUE if they are the same and FALSE otherwise. EXACT is case sensitive but ignores formatting differences. You use EXACT to test text being entered into a document. This function takes the following arguments:

- `text1`: This is the first text string.
- `text2`: This is the second text string.

Using TEXT to format a number as text

Excel is great at numbers. Put a number in a cell, and you can format it in a variety of ways. However, when you join a cell containing text with a cell containing a number or a date, Excel falls apart.

Consider Figure 8.41. Cell A11 contains a date and is formatted as a date. When you join the name in cell B11 with the date in cell A11, Excel automatically converts the date back to a numeric serial number. This is frustrating.

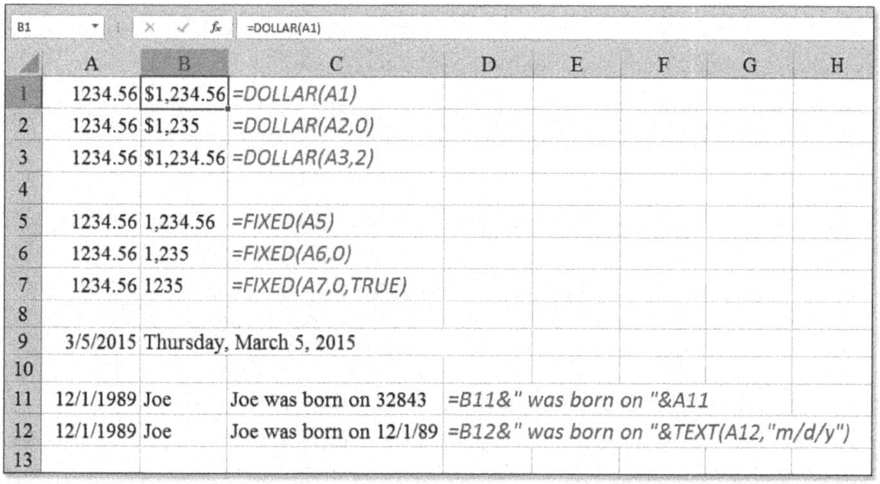

B1 =DOLLAR(A1)

	A	B	C	D	E	F	G	H
1	1234.56	$1,234.56	=DOLLAR(A1)					
2	1234.56	$1,235	=DOLLAR(A2,0)					
3	1234.56	$1,234.56	=DOLLAR(A3,2)					
4								
5	1234.56	1,234.56	=FIXED(A5)					
6	1234.56	1,235	=FIXED(A6,0)					
7	1234.56	1235	=FIXED(A7,0,TRUE)					
8								
9	3/5/2015	Thursday, March 5, 2015						
10								
11	12/1/1989	Joe	Joe was born on 32843	=B11&" was born on "&A11				
12	12/1/1989	Joe	Joe was born on 12/1/89	=B12&" was born on "&TEXT(A12,"m/d/y")				
13								

Figure 8.41 TEXT can be used to format a number as text.

Today, the TEXT function is the most versatile solution to this problem. If you understand the basics of custom numeric formatting codes, you can easily use TEXT to format a date or a number in any conceivable format. For example, the formula in cell C12 uses =TEXT(A12,"m/d/y") to force the date to display as a date.

The TEXT function gives you a lot of versatility. To learn the custom formatting codes for a cell, you can select the cell, display the Format Cells dialog box (by pressing Ctrl+1), and select the Custom category on the Number tab. Excel shows you the codes used to create that format.

If you don't care to learn the number formatting codes, you can use either the DOLLAR or FIXED function to return a number as text, with a few choices regarding the number of decimals and whether Excel should use the thousands separator. The formulas shown in C1:C7 in Figure 8.41 return the formatted text values shown in column B.

Syntax:

```
=TEXT(value,format_text)
```

The TEXT function converts a value to text in a specific number format. Formatting a cell with an option on the Number tab of the Format Cells dialog box changes only the format, not the value. Using the TEXT function converts a value to formatted text, and the result is no longer calculated as a number.

The TEXT function takes the following arguments:

- `value`: This is a numeric value, a formula that evaluates to a numeric value, or a reference to a cell that contains a numeric value.
- `format_text`: This is a number format in text form from the Category box on the Number tab in the Format Cells dialog box. `format_text` cannot contain an asterisk (*) or color codes such as `[red]`.

Inside OUT

If you are exporting data to text for importing to another system, you might need numbers to appear with leading zeroes. While a combination of* TEXT *with* LEN *or* RIGHT *has been used in the past, a hack with the new* BASE *function solves the problem.

The BASE function introduced in Excel 2013 expands upon the old DEC2OCT, DEC2BIN, and DEC2HEX functions. If you want to express 25 in binary, the formula of =BASE(25,2) will return 11001. If you need 25 in hexadecimal, use =BASE(25,16). If an alien race takes over Earth and they use a Base 5 numbering scheme, we could use Excel to communicate using =BASE(25,5).

However, no self-respecting computer would ever write 11001. Binary systems are going to want an eight-digit number of 00011001. So, the BASE function allows an optional third argument for a minimum number of digits. In cell E4 below, the 00011001 result is from =BASE(A4,B4,8).

Astute reader Mordechai Steinfeld in Toronto realized that he could hack the BASE function to take advantage of its ability to add leading zeroes to a number. Mordechai takes any number in Base 10 and converts it to Base 10 just to add the leading zeroes. See rows 11 through 16 to see several examples.

By the way, a hat tip to the awesome Debra Dalgleish of Contextures.com. Debra recognized the brilliance of Mordechai's idea and communicated it in her weekly Excel newsletter in September 2017. I definitely recommend signing up for her free newsletter for great weekly Excel tips.

	A	B	C	D	E
1	Hacking the BASE function to add leading zero				
2					
3	Number	Radix	Result	Min digits	Result
4	25	2	11001	8	00011001
5	25	8	31	4	0031
6	25	16	19	4	0019
7					
8	Show numbers with leading zeroes				
9					
10	Desired Width	Number	Result		
11	5	25	00025	=BASE(B11,10,A11)	
12	5	1234	01234	=BASE(B12,10,A12)	
13	7	25	0000025	=BASE(B13,10,A13)	
14	7	12345	0012345	=BASE(B14,10,A14)	
15	9	25	000000025	=BASE(B15,10,A15)	
16	9	12345	000012345	=BASE(B16,10,A16)	

> The binary representation of 25 is 11001. However, if you need to show that with eight digits, you would use =BASE(25,2,8) to produce 00011001. To convert a number to hexadecimal with four digits, use =BASE(25,16,4) to produce 0019. To pad a decimal number with leading zeroes, use =BASE(25,10,5) to convert 25 to 00025. Use =BASE(25,10,8) to produce 00000025.

Using the T and VALUE functions

The T and VALUE functions are left over from Lotus days.

=T("text") returns the original text. If cell B1 contains the number 123, =T(B1) will return empty text. Basically, T() returns the value in the cell only if it is text.

=VALUE() converts text that looks like a number or a date to the number or the date.

Introducing TEXTSPLIT and other text manipulation functions

The Excel team introduced 12 new functions to Microsoft 365 in November 2021. Here is an overview of the functions.

The first three functions are found in the Text category (where they belong). The remaining nine functions really belong in a new category, but for now, they are placed in the Lookup And Reference category.

- **TEXTSPLIT:** Splits the `input_text` based on a row and/or column delimiter. You can also specify whether empty elements should be suppressed. Multiple delimiters can be provided as an array. Syntax: `TEXTSPLIT(input_text, col_delimiter, [row_delimiter], [ignore_empty])`.
- **TEXTBEFORE and TEXTAFTER:** Returns the text that appears before (or after) the `find_text`. There are options to specify the `instance_num` and request a case insensitive match. If a negative number is provided for the `instance_num`, it will index from the end of the text. Syntax: `TEXTBEFORE(within_text, find_text, [instance_num], [ignore_case])` or `TEXTAFTER(within_text, find_text, [instance_num], [ignore_case])`.
- **VSTACK and HSTACK:** These functions stack multiple arrays vertically or horizontally. Syntax: `VSTACK(array1, [array2], ...)` or `HSTACK(array1, [array2], ...)`.

- **EXPAND(array,rows,[cols],[pad]):** Expands an array to the desired size. If pad is not specified, N/A is used to pad. DROP(array,row,[col]), TAKE(array,row,[col]) drops or extracts sequential rows or columns from the start or end of an array. TAKE(A1:J10,2) returns A1:J2. TAKE(A1:J10,,-3) returns H1:J10. DROP(A1:J10,1) returns A2:J10.
- **CHOOSECOLS:** Returns the requested columns from an array based on the column_num. This can be used to re-sequence the columns in an array. For example, if you have a four-column array starting in A1#, and you want to return column D, then column B, then column C, but not column A, you would use =CHOOSECOLS(A1#,4,2,3). If you specify a negative number as the column index, it will count from the right side of the array. This formula will return the first and last columns of the array in A#: =CHOOSECOLS(A#,1,-1). Syntax: CHOOSECOLS(array, [col_num1], [col_num2], ...).
- **CHOOSEROWS:** Returns the requested rows from an array based on the row_num. This can be used to resequence the rows in an array. Use negative numbers to start from the bottom. This formula would return the first and last five rows from A#: =CHOOSEROWS(A#,1,-SEQUENCE(5)). Syntax: CHOOSEROWS(array, [row_num1], [row_num2], ...).
- **TOCOL:** Converts a 2D array into a single column. The optional ignore argument can be used to ignore error values and/or blank. By default, the new column would contain all of the values in the first row, then the second row, and so on. To sequence the result with all of the values in the first column and the second column, specify TRUE for the optional scan_by_column argument. In Figure 8.42, the 4-column array of playing cards starting in B6# is arranged in a single column using =TOCOL(B6#,,TRUE). Syntax: TOCOL(array, [ignore], [scan_by_column]).
- **TOROW:** Converts a 2D array into a single row. It offers the same options as TOCOL. Syntax: TOROW(array, [ignore], [scan_by_column]).
- **VECTORWRAP:** Converts a single row or column into a 2D array by wrapping it into the number of rows specified by the wrap_count. In Figure 8.42, you want to deal 52 cards to 6 players. =VECTORWRAP(H6#,6) will deal the first six cards into K6:K11, the next six cards to L6:L11, and so on. There aren't enough cards to give everyone nine cards, so cells S10 and S11 return #N/A. To prevent the #N/A, specify a substitute value in the optional pad_with argument. Syntax: VECTORWRAP(vector, wrap_count, [pad_with]).

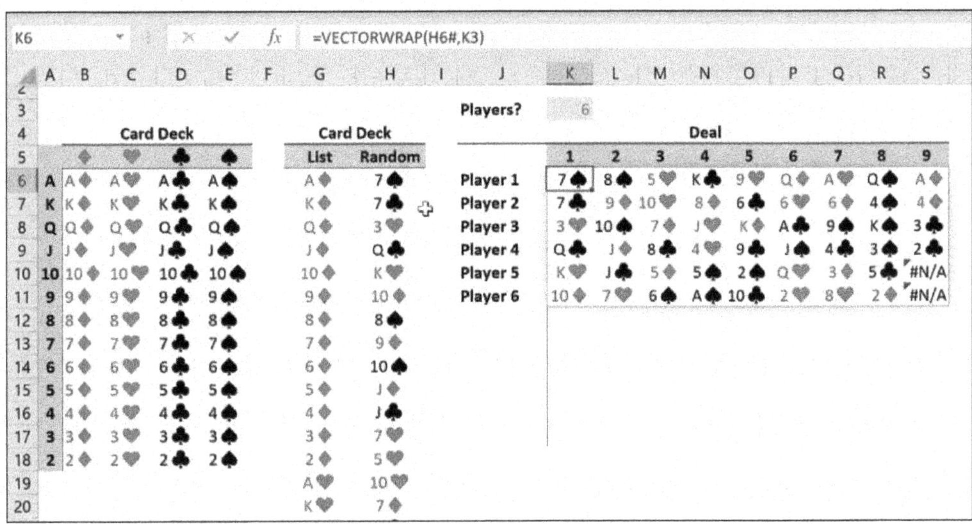

Figure 8.42 TOCOL and VECTORWRAP can be used to re-shape an array.

CHAPTER 9

Using powerful functions: logical, lookup, and database functions

This chapter covers four groups of workhorse functions. If you process spreadsheets of medium complexity, you turn to logical and lookup functions regularly.

- The logical functions, including the ubiquitous `IF` function, help make decisions.
- The information functions might be less important than they once were because Microsoft has added the `IFERROR` function, but `INFO`, `CELL`, and `TYPE` still come in handy. The lookup functions include the powerful `VLOOKUP`, `MATCH`, and `INDEX` functions as well as the new `XLOOKUP` function.. These functions are invaluable, particularly when you are doing something in Excel when it would be better to use Access.
- The database functions provide the `D` functions, such as `DSUM` and `DMIN`. Even though these functions fell out of favor with the introduction of pivot tables, they are a powerful set of functions that are worthwhile to master.

Examples of logical functions

With only eight functions, the logical function group is one of the smallest in Excel. The `IF` function is easy to understand, and it enables you to solve a variety of problems.

Using the `IF` function to make a decision

Many calculations in our lives are not straightforward. Suppose that a manager offers a bonus program if her team meets its goals. Or perhaps a commission plan offers a bonus if a certain profit goal is met. You can solve these types of calculations by using the `IF` function.

Syntax:

```
IF(logical_test,value_if_true,value_if_false)
```

There are three arguments in the `IF` function. The first argument is any logical test that results in a TRUE or FALSE. For example, you might have logical tests such as these:

A2>100

`B5="West"`

C99<=D99

All logical tests involve one of the comparison operators shown in Table 9.1.

Table 9.1 Comparison operators

Comparison operator	Meaning	Example
=	Equal to	C1=D1
>	Greater than	A1>B1
<	Less than	A1<B1
>=	Greater than or equal to	A1>=0
<=	Less than or equal to	A1<=99
<>	Not equal to	A2<>B2

The remaining two arguments are the formula or value to use if the logical test is TRUE and the formula or value to use if the logical test is FALSE.

When you read an `IF` function, you should think of the first comma as the word *then* and the second comma as the word *otherwise*. For example, `=IF(A2>10,25,0)` would be read as "If A2>10, then 25; otherwise, 0."

Figure 9.1 calculates a sales commission. The commission rate is 1.5 percent of revenue. However, if the gross profit percentage is 50 percent or higher, the commission rate is 2.5 percent of revenue.

NOTE

Mathematicians would correctly note that in both the second and third arguments of the formula =IF(H2>=50%,0.025*F2,0.015*F2), you are multiplying by F2. Therefore, you could simplify the formula by using =IF(H2>=50%,0.025,0.015)*F2.

I2 =IF(H2>=50%,0.025*F2,0.015*F2)

	D	E	F	G	H	I	J
1	Associate	Qty	Revenue	Cost	GP%	Commission	
2	GERALD	400	15456	8400	45.7%	231.84	1.5%
3	JOSEPH	700	53928	25200	53.3%	1348.2	2.5%
4	SHELLY	100	4784	2600	45.7%	71.76	1.5%
5	JOY	1000	67680	36000	46.8%	1015.2	1.5%
6	JOY	300	20088	9300	53.7%	502.2	2.5%
7	FANNIE	600	32760	15600	52.4%	819	2.5%

Figure 9.1 In rows 2, 4, and 5, the commission is 1.5%. In rows 3 and 6 through 7 the commission is 2.5 percent.

In this case, the logical test is `H2>=50%`. The formula for whether that test is true is `0.025*F2`. Otherwise, the formula is `0.015*F2`. You could build the formula as `=IF(H2>=50%,0.025*F2,0.015*F2)`.

Using the AND function to check for two or more conditions

The previous example had one simple condition: If the value in column H was greater than or equal to 50 percent, the commission rate changed.

However, in many cases, you might need to test for two or more conditions. For example, suppose that a retail store manager offers a $25 bonus for every leather jacket sold on Fridays this month. In this case, the logical test requires you to determine whether both conditions are true. You can do this with the AND function.

Syntax:

```
AND(logical1,logical2,...)
```

The arguments `logical1,logical2,...` are from one to 255 expressions that evaluate to either TRUE or FALSE. The function returns TRUE only if all arguments are TRUE.

In Figure 9.2, the function in cell F2 checks whether cell E2 is a jacket and whether the date in cell D2 falls on a Friday:

```
=AND(E2="Jacket",WEEKDAY(D2,2)=5)
```

F2 =AND(E2="Jacket",WEEKDAY(D2,2)=5)

	A	B	C	D	E	F	G	H
1	Store	Cust	Associate	Date	Item	Bonus?		
2	S18	C422	Jenny	Tue 4/17/2018	Handbag	FALSE		
3	S5	C244	Bill	Fri 4/13/2018	Jacket	TRUE		
4	S13	C668	Diana	Mon 4/30/2018	Hat	FALSE		
5	S19	C825	Bill	Tue 4/17/2018	Jacket	FALSE		
6	S15	C590	Bill	Fri 4/27/2018	Coaster	FALSE		
7	S5	C857	Bill	Fri 4/13/2018	Handbag	FALSE		

Figure 9.2 The AND function is TRUE only when every condition is met.

CHAPTER 9

Using OR to check whether one or more conditions are met

In the earlier examples, all the conditions had to be met for the IF function to be true. In other cases, you might need to identify when exactly one condition is true, or when one or more conditions are true.

For example, a sales manager may want to reward big orders and orders from new customers. The manager may offer a commission bonus if the order is more than $50,000 or if the customer is a new customer this year. The bonus is awarded if either condition is true. But only one bonus is paid; you do not give two bonuses if a customer is both new and the order is large. In this case, you would use the OR function with logical tests to check whether the customer is new or if the order is large.

To test whether a particular sale meets either condition, use the OR function. The OR function returns TRUE if any condition is TRUE and returns FALSE if none of the conditions are TRUE.

Syntax:

```
OR(logical1,logical2,...)
```

The OR function checks whether any of the arguments are TRUE. It returns a FALSE only if all the arguments are FALSE. If any argument is TRUE, the function returns TRUE.

The arguments `logical1,logical2,...` are 1 to 255 conditions that can evaluate to TRUE or FALSE.

Nesting IF functions versus IFS, SWITCH, or CHOOSE

The IF function offers only two possible values: Either the logical test is TRUE, and the first formula or value is used, or the logical test is FALSE and the second formula or value is used.

Many situations have a series of choices. For example, in a human resources department, annual merit raises might be given based on the employee's numeric rating in an annual review in which employees are ranked on a five-point scale. The rules for setting the raise are as follows:

- 5: 8 percent raise
- 4: 7 percent raise
- 3: 5 percent raise
- 2: 3 percent raise
- 1: No raise

Traditionally, you would test for five conditions by nesting four IF functions:

```
=IF(D2=5,8%,IF(D2=4,7%,IF(D2=3,5%,IF(D2=2,3%,0%))))
```

You only needed four `IF` functions to test for five conditions. After testing for the first four conditions, the fifth answer would be provided in the `Value_If_False` for the last IF function.

In February 2017, Office 365 customers were offered two alternatives:

```
=IFS(D2=5,8%,D2=4,7%,D2=3,5%,D2=2,3%,TRUE,0%)
```

```
=SWITCH(D2,5,8%,4,7%,3,5%,2,3%,0%)
```

Syntax:

```
IFS(logical_test1, value_if_true1, [logical_test2, value_if_true2…])
```

Syntax:

```
SWITCH(Expression, Value1, Result1,[Default_or_value2],[Result2]…)
```

In the `IFS` function, you can handle multiple conditions without nesting new functions. The `IFS` means that you have multiple `IF` conditions. The `IFS` formula above reads, "If D2 is 5, then return 8%. Otherwise, if D2=4, then return 7%. Otherwise, if D2=3, then return 5%. Otherwise, if D2=2, then return 3%." The last two arguments in `IFS` are a little bizarre. You essentially want to have a value to return if none of the previous conditions are true. You need to put a logical test that is always `True`. Explicitly typing **TRUE** solves the problem.

Inside OUT

The Excel team had two choices for how to handle the final* Else *in* `IFS`*. The solution is a tiny bit nerdy.

For decades, people using Excel were used to a syntax in which the final argument in an `IF` or a nested `IF` is the "value if false" or the "else" clause.

You are likely very used to the `=IF(Something is True,Do This,O That)` construct, even if you had to nest IF statements with `=IF(A2 is high,then this,IF(A2 is medium,then this,otherwise that))`. The last argument of the function outlines what to do if none of the other tests are true.

There is a guy on the Excel team who had to decide how `IFS` would work. For ease, let's refer to him as Joe. Well, Joe is facing a dilemma. The `IF` function will always have three arguments. Excel had it easy because the Else clause was always in the last position.

However, for `IFS`, the Else clause could come after 4 arguments or 6 arguments or 120 arguments. Joe does not know where to look for the Else clause.

As a long-time fan of `IF`, I would have expected that the Else clause would be the fifth, seventh, or 121st argument in the function, but that is harder to program.

> **Joe wants to know that every odd-numbered argument is a logical test, and every even-numbered argument outlines what to do if the logical test is true.**
>
> **There was a suggestion to use** `=IFS(A2>10,"*****",A2>7,"***",Else,"*")`**, but this causes language problems. Joe finally opted for having the next to last argument be** `TRUE`**. This makes it easier for Excel because there is already logic to convert True to a local language.**
>
> **So, the Else clause if the** `IFS` **function is a bit unusual, but it is not impossible to deal with. If you leave off the Else clause and if nothing else was** `True`**, then IFS will return** `FALSE`**, just like this function:** `=IF(5<4,"Miracle")`**.**

The `SWITCH` function is better, in this case, because you only specify cell D2 once. You tell the `SWITCH` function that you want to return a value based on the value of D2. If it is 5, then 8 percent. If it is 4, then 7 percent. If it is 3, then 5 percent. If it is 2, then 3 percent. For any other value, use 0 percent. Note that `SWITCH` does not require you to enter the `TRUE` argument as the second-to-last argument.

In this particular case, because the five possible scores are 1 through 5, the `CHOOSE` function will be shortest:

```
=CHOOSE(D2,0,3%,5%,7%,8%)
```

The `CHOOSE` function points to a single value and then expects the value to return if the answer is 1, 2, 3, 4, 5, and so on.

Note that Excel classifies `CHOOSE` as a Lookup and Reference function instead of a Logical function.

➤ **Read more about** `CHOOSE` **in "Examples of lookup and reference functions."**

Figure 9.3 compares the four formulas. In this case, `CHOOSE` is the shortest.

CAUTION

These `IF` **formulas are hard to read. There is a temptation to use them for situations with very long lists of conditions. Whereas Excel 2003 prevented you from nesting more than seven levels of** `IF` **functions, Excel 2007 and later allow you to nest up to 64** `IF` **statements. Before you start nesting that many** `IF` **statements, you should consider using** `VLOOKUP`**, which is explained later in this chapter.**

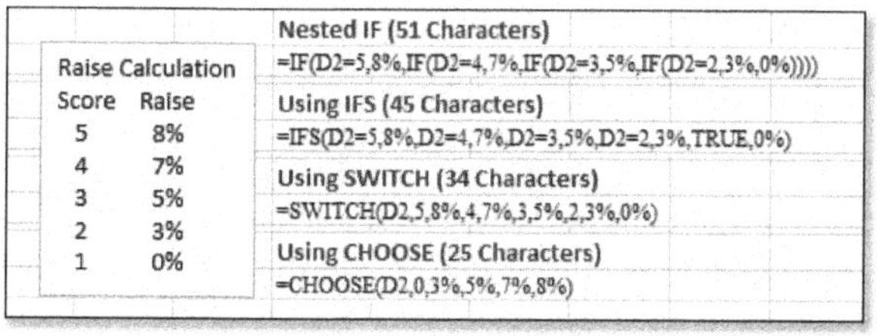

Raise Calculation	
Score	Raise
5	8%
4	7%
3	5%
2	3%
1	0%

Nested IF (51 Characters)
=IF(D2=5,8%,IF(D2=4,7%,IF(D2=3,5%,IF(D2=2,3%,0%))))

Using IFS (45 Characters)
=IFS(D2=5,8%,D2=4,7%,D2=3,5%,D2=2,3%,TRUE,0%)

Using SWITCH (34 Characters)
=SWITCH(D2,5,8%,4,7%,3,5%,2,3%,0%)

Using CHOOSE (25 Characters)
=CHOOSE(D2,0,3%,5%,7%,8%)

Figure 9.3 Four different ways to calculate the raise percentage.

CHOOSE will not always be the shortest formula. SWITCH will win if you have to look for values that are not sequential or don't have to start with 1:

```
=SWITCH(A2,30,"CURRY",35,"DURANT",23,"GREEN",11,"THOMPSON","OTHER")
```

IFS will be better if you need to look for ranges of values:

```
=IFS(A2>80,"Top Tier",A2>50,"Group 2",A2>20,"Group 3",TRUE,"Bottom Tier")
```

Nested IF will be better if there is any chance the workbook will be opened in Excel 2016, Excel 2013, Excel 2010, or an earlier version. The new IFS and SWITCH functions will return #NAME? error if opened in a prior version of Excel.

CHAPTER 9

Using the NOT function to simplify the use of AND and OR

In the language of Boolean logic, there are typically NAND, NOR, and XOR functions, which stand for Not And, Not Or, and Exclusive Or. To simplify matters, Excel offers the NOT function.

Syntax:

```
NOT(logical)
```

Quite simply, NOT reverses a logical value. TRUE becomes FALSE, and FALSE becomes TRUE when processed through a NOT function.

For example, suppose you need to find all flights landing outside Oklahoma. You can build a massive OR statement to find every airport code in the United States. Alternatively, you can build an OR function to find Tulsa and Oklahoma City and then use a NOT function to reverse the result: =NOT(OR(A2="Tulsa",A2="Oklahoma City")).

Using the IFERROR or IFNA function to simplify error checking

The IFERROR function, which was introduced in Excel 2007, was added at the request of many customers. To better understand the IFERROR function, you need to understand how error checking was performed during the 22 years before Excel 2007 was released.

Consider a typical spreadsheet that calculates a ratio of sales to hours. A formula of =B2/C2 returns the #DIV/0 error in the records when column C contains a zero. The typical workaround is to test for this error condition: `=IF(C2=0,0,B2/C2)`.

In legacy versions of Excel, it was typical to use this type of `IF` formula on thousands of rows of data. The formula is more complex and takes longer to calculate than the new `IFERROR` function. However, this particular formula is tame compared to some of the formulas needed to check for errors.

A common error occurs when you use the VLOOKUP function to retrieve a value from a lookup table. In Figure 9.4, the VLOOKUP function in cell D2 asks Excel to look for the rep number S07 from cell B2 and find the corresponding name in the lookup table of F2:G9. This works great, returning `JESSE` from the table. However, a problem arises when the sales rep is not found in the table. In row 7, rep S09 is new and has not yet been added to the table, so Excel returns the #N/A result.

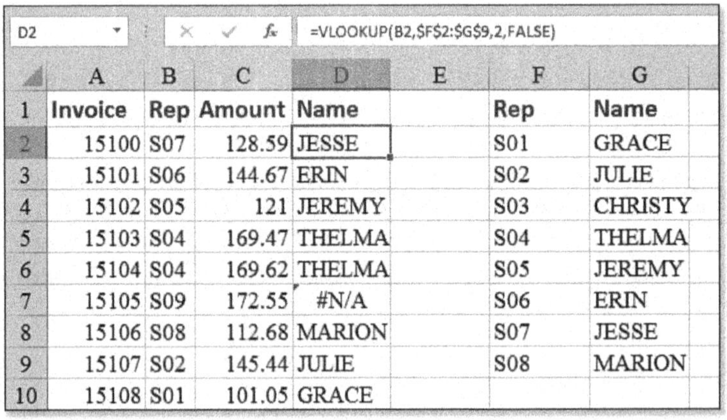

D2 =VLOOKUP(B2,$F$2:$G$9,2,FALSE)

	A	B	C	D	E	F	G
1	Invoice	Rep	Amount	Name		Rep	Name
2	15100	S07	128.59	JESSE		S01	GRACE
3	15101	S06	144.67	ERIN		S02	JULIE
4	15102	S05	121	JEREMY		S03	CHRISTY
5	15103	S04	169.47	THELMA		S04	THELMA
6	15104	S04	169.62	THELMA		S05	JEREMY
7	15105	S09	172.55	#N/A		S06	ERIN
8	15106	S08	112.68	MARION		S07	JESSE
9	15107	S02	145.44	JULIE		S08	MARION
10	15108	S01	101.05	GRACE			

Figure 9.4 An #N/A error means that the value is not in the lookup table.

If you want to avoid #N/A errors, the generally accepted workaround in legacy versions of Excel was to write this horrible formula:

```
=IF(ISNA(VLOOKUP(B7,$F$2:$G$9,2,FALSE)),"New Rep", VLOOKUP(B7,$F$2:$G$9,2,FALSE))
```

In English, this formula says the rep name in the lookup table is found first. If the rep is not found and the #N/A error is returned, then use some other text, which in this case, is the words *New Rep*. If the rep is found, then perform the lookup again and use that result.

Because VLOOKUP was one of the most time-intensive functions, it was horrible to have Excel perform every VLOOKUP twice in this formula. In a data set with 50,000 records, it could take minutes for the VLOOKUP to complete. Microsoft wisely added the new `IFERROR` function in Excel 2010 to handle all these error-checking situations.

Starting in Excel 2013, Microsoft added the IFNA function. It works just like the IFERROR function, but the second argument is used only when the first argument results in an #N/A error. You might be able to imagine a situation in which you want to replace the #N/A errors but allow other errors to appear.

Syntax:

```
IFERROR(value,value_if_error)
```

The advantage of the IFERROR function is that the calculation is evaluated only once. If the calculation results in any type of an error value, such as #N/A, #VALUE!, #REF!, #DIV/0!, #NUM!, #NAME?, #NULL!, #GETTING_DATA, #SPILL!, #CONNECT!, #BLOCKED!, #UNKNOWN, #FIELD, or #CALC, Excel returns the alternative value. If the calculation results in any other valid value, whether it is numeric, logical, or text, Excel returns the calculated value.

Syntax:

```
IFNA(value,value_if_na)
```

If the expression evaluates to a value of #N/A, then IFNA returns value_if_na instead of the expression. Added in Excel 2013, this function replaces only #N/A errors and allows other errors to appear as the result.

The formula from the preceding section can be rewritten as =IFERROR(VLOOKUP(B7, $F$2:$G$9,2,FALSE),"New Rep") or as =IFNA(VLOOKUP(B7, $F$2:$G$9,2,FALSE),"New Rep"). Although IFNA is a bit shorter than IFERROR, the new IFNA function fails for anyone using Excel 2010 or earlier. This makes IFERROR a safer function to use for the next several years. Either IFERROR or IFNA calculates much more quickly than putting two VLOOKUPs in an IF function.

Examples of information functions

Found under the More Function icon, the 20 information functions return eclectic information about any cell. Eleven of the 20 functions are called the IS functions because they test for various conditions.

Using the ISFORMULA function with conditional formatting to mark formula cells

The Excel team introduced the ISFORMULA function in Excel 2013 to identify whether a cell contains a formula. A hack had been floating around for years to mark formula cells using an old XL4 Macro Language function. Being able to use ISFORMULA is a great improvement.

Syntax:

```
ISFORMULA(reference)
```

Checks whether `reference` contains a formula. Returns TRUE or FALSE.

Figure 9.5 shows a worksheet in which all the cells have a conditional formatting formula that uses =`ISFORMULA`. Any cells that contain a formula are shown in white text on black fill.

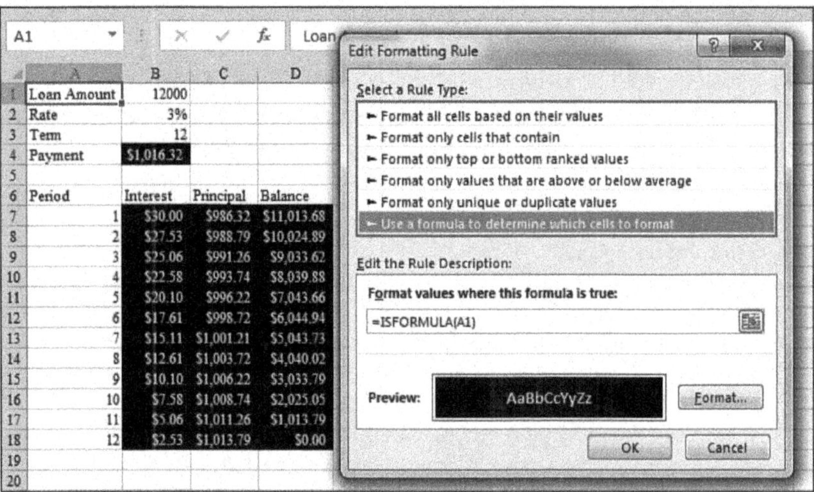

Figure 9.5 Use the `ISFORMULA` function with conditional formatting to mark all the formula cells.

Using IS functions to test for types of values

The remaining `IS` functions enable you to test whether a cell contains numbers, text, or various other data types.

Figure 9.6 shows a common solution. Column C contains a mix of text and numeric ZIP Codes. The formula in column D, `=IF(ISNONTEXT(C2),RIGHT("0000"&C2,5),C2)`, replaces numeric ZIP Codes with text ZIP Codes. If the value in column C is nontext, the program pads the left side of the ZIP Code with zeros and then takes the five rightmost digits.

CHAPTER 9

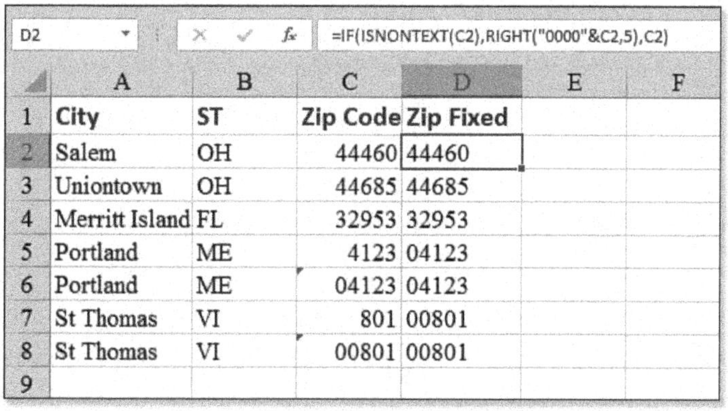

D2 =IF(ISNONTEXT(C2),RIGHT("0000"&C2,5),C2)

	A	B	C	D	E	F
1	City	ST	Zip Code	Zip Fixed		
2	Salem	OH	44460	44460		
3	Uniontown	OH	44685	44685		
4	Merritt Island	FL	32953	32953		
5	Portland	ME	4123	04123		
6	Portland	ME	04123	04123		
7	St Thomas	VI	801	00801		
8	St Thomas	VI	00801	00801		
9						

Figure 9.6 The formula in column D detects nontext ZIP Codes and converts to text with five digits.

Using the N function to add a comment to a formula

You can call Excel's N function a creative use for an obsolete function. Lotus 1-2-3 used to offer an N() function that converted True to 1 and False to 0. The N of any text is zero. Some have figured they could use this function to add a comment to a formula:

```
=VLOOKUP(A2,MyTable,2,False)+N("The False ensures an exact match. Don't omit False")
```

This technique only works when the original formula returns a numeric value.

Using the NA function to force charts to not plot missing data

Suppose that you are in charge of a school's annual fund drive. Each day, you mark the fundraising total on a worksheet by following these steps:

1. In column A, you enter the results of each day's collection through nine days of the fund drive (see Figure 9.7).

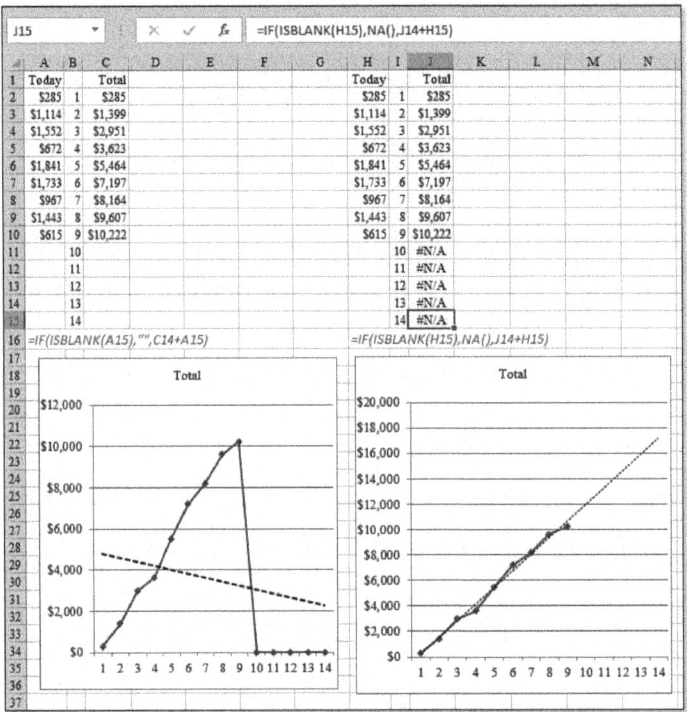

Figure 9.7 Using NA in the chart on the right allows the trendline to ignore future missing data points and project a reasonable ending result.

2. You enter a formula in column C to keep track of the total collected throughout the fund drive.

3. To avoid making it look like the fund drive collected nothing in days 10 through 14, you enter a formula in column C to check whether column A is blank. If it is, then the `IF` function inserts a null cell in column C. For example, the formula in cell C15 is `=IF(ISBLANK(A15),"",A15+C14)`.

4. You build a line chart based on B1:C15. You then add a trendline to the chart to predict future fundraising totals.

5. As shown in columns A:C of Figure 9.7, this technique fails. Even though the totals for days 10 through 14 are blank, Excel charts those days as zero. The linear trendline predicts that your fundraising will go down, with a projected total of just over $2,000.

6. You try the same chart again, but this time you use the NA function instead of `""` in the `IF` statement in step 3. The formula is shown in cell H16, and the results are in cell J15. Excel understands that NA values should not be plotted. The trendline is calculated based on only the data points available and projects a total just under $18,000.

In many cases, you are trying to avoid #N/A errors. However, in the case of charting a calculated column, you might want to have #N/A produce the correct look to the chart.

Using the CELL function to return the worksheet name

The CELL function can tell you information about a specific cell. Although the function can return many ancient bits of information (Excel 2003 color index, for example), it has one argument that allows you to put the worksheet name in a cell.

=CELL("filename",A1) returns the complete path, filename, and worksheet name. The technique is to locate the right square bracket at the end of the filename. Everything after that character is the worksheet tab name.

The longest worksheet name is 32 characters. You can use MID to find up to 32 characters after the right square bracket.

Figure 9.8 shows an example.

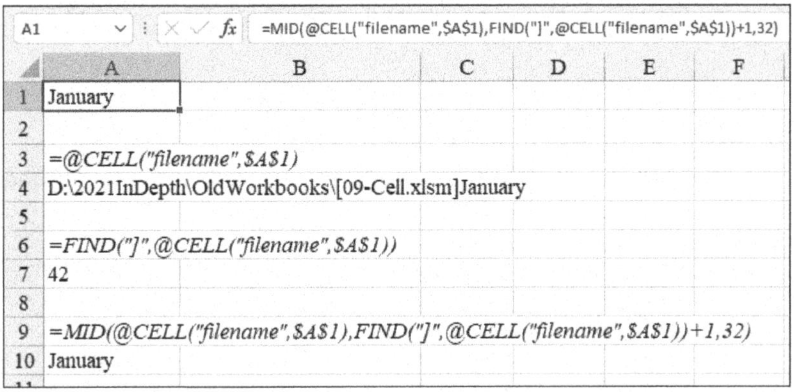

A1 | fx =MID(@CELL("filename",$A$1),FIND("]",@CELL("filename",$A$1))+1,32)

	A	B	C	D	E	F
1	January					
2						
3	=@CELL("filename",$A$1)					
4	D:\2021InDepth\OldWorkbooks\[09-Cell.xlsm]January					
5						
6	=FIND("]",@CELL("filename",$A$1))					
7	42					
8						
9	=MID(@CELL("filename",$A$1),FIND("]",@CELL("filename",$A$1))+1,32)					
10	January					

Figure 9.8 The CELL function returns the full path, filename, and tab name to a cell.

Examples of lookup and reference functions

The Lookup & Reference icon contains 35 functions. The new all-star of this group is the XLOOKUP function, which is one of the most powerful functions, offering several improvements over VLOOKUP. As database people point out, a lot of work done in Excel should probably be done in Access. The XLOOKUP function enables you to perform the equivalent of a join operation in a database.

This lookup and reference group also includes several functions that seem useless when considered alone. However, when combined, they allow for some very powerful manipulations of data.

The examples in the following sections reveal details on how to use the lookup functions and how to combine them to create powerful results.

Using the CHOOSE function for simple lookups

Most lookup functions require you to set up a lookup table in a range on the worksheet. However, the CHOOSE function enables you to specify up to 254 choices right in the syntax of the function. The formula that requires the lookup should be able to calculate an integer from 1 to 254 to use the CHOOSE function.

Syntax:

```
CHOOSE(index_num,value1,value2,...)
```

The CHOOSE function chooses a value from a list of values, based on an index number. The CHOOSE function takes the following arguments:

- `index_num`: This specifies which value argument is selected. `index_num` must be a number between 1 and 254 or a formula or reference to a cell containing a number between 1 and 254:
  - If `index_num` is 1, CHOOSE returns `value1`; if it is 2, CHOOSE returns `value2`; and so on.
  - If `index_num` is a decimal, it is rounded down to the next lowest integer before being used.
  - If `index_num` is less than 1 or greater than the number of the last value in the list, CHOOSE returns a #VALUE! error.
- `value1,value2,...`: These are 1 to 254 value arguments from which CHOOSE selects a value or an action to perform based on `index_num`. The arguments can be numbers, cell references, defined names, formulas, functions, or text.

The example in Figure 9.9 shows survey data from some respondents. Columns B:F indicate their responses on five measures of your service. Column G calculates an average that ranges from 1 to 5. Suppose that you want to add words to column H to characterize the overall rating from the respondent. The following formula is used in cell H4:

```
=CHOOSE(G4,"Strongly Disagree","Disagree","Neutral","Agree","Strongly Agree")
```

CHAPTER 9

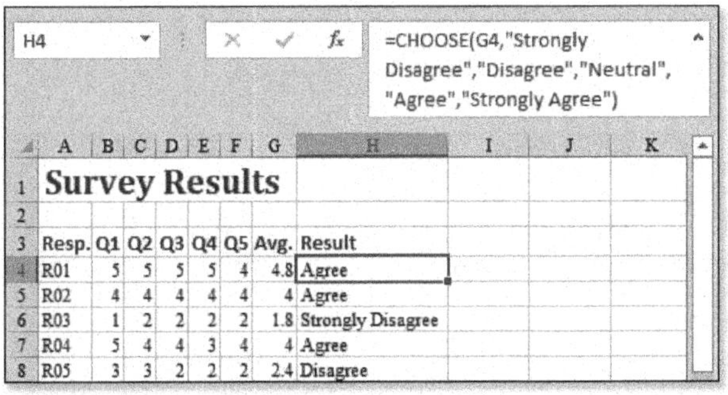

H4 =CHOOSE(G4,"Strongly Disagree","Disagree","Neutral","Agree","Strongly Agree")

	A	B	C	D	E	F	G	H
1	Survey Results							
2								
3	Resp.	Q1	Q2	Q3	Q4	Q5	Avg.	Result
4	R01	5	5	5	5	4	4.8	Agree
5	R02	4	4	4	4	4	4	Agree
6	R03	1	2	2	2	2	1.8	Strongly Disagree
7	R04	5	4	4	3	4	4	Agree
8	R05	3	3	2	2	2	2.4	Disagree

Figure 9.9 CHOOSE is great for simple choices in which the index number is between 1 and 254.

Moving from VLOOKUP to XLOOKUP

In 2019, the XLOOKUP function was introduced in Excel. It is designed to replace VLOOKUP, HLOOKUP, and INDEX/MATCH. The Excel Calc team, lead by Joe McDaid, wanted to remove many of the potential errors that happen with the old VLOOKUP and HLOOKUP scenarios.

Although XLOOKUP offers a total of six arguments, only the first three are required to perform an exact match XLOOKUP. To build an exact match XLOOKUP that returns a single value, you will specify:

- `Lookup_value`: This is exactly like you would use in HLOOKUP or VLOOKUP.
- `Lookup_Array`: This is a single column or row where the `lookup_value` should be found. Typically with a VLOOKUP, you would specify a rectangular range. When using XLOOKUP, you will specify only the first column or row of the range.
- `Return_array`: This is a range of the same shape as a `Lookup_Array`. If the `lookup_value` is found in the fifth position of the `Lookup_Array`, then XLOOKUP will return the fifth item from the `return_array`.

Consider the data in Figure 9.10. To find the sales rep name associated with the ID in A2 using VLOOKUP, you would have used this formula:

```
=VLOOKUP(A2,$H$2:$I$7,2,FALSE)
```

To perform the same task with XLOOKUP, you would use:

```
=XLOOKUP(A2,$H$2:$H$7,$I$2:$I$7)
```

Both formulas start by pointing to cell A2 as the lookup_value. While VLOOKUP points to a 2-D range of H2:I7, XLOOKUP only points to the column containing the Rep ID numbers H2:H7. While VLOOKUP specifies that the function should return the second column from lookup_table, the XLOOKUP function instead points to a return_array of I2:I7.

For exact match scenarios, VLOOKUP would end in `False` or zero. This is not required with XLOOKUP because XLOOKUP defaults to an exact match.

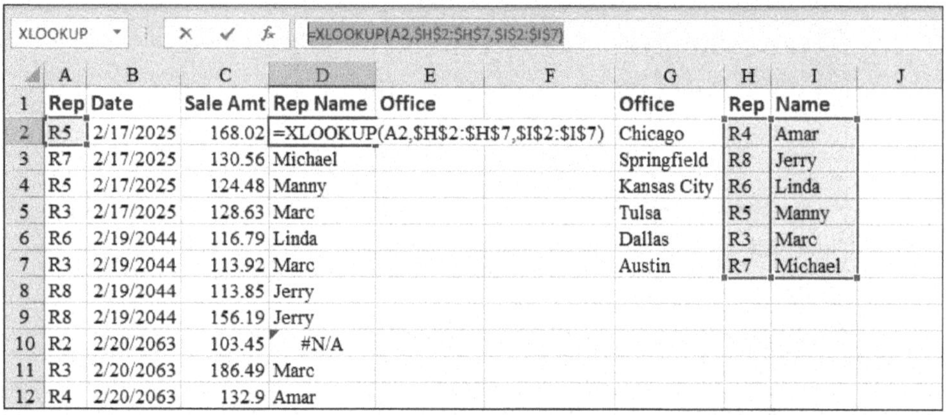

XLOOKUP | fx =XLOOKUP(A2,$H$2:$H$7,$I$2:$I$7)

	A	B	C	D	E	F	G	H	I	J
1	**Rep**	**Date**	**Sale Amt**	**Rep Name**	**Office**		**Office**	**Rep**	**Name**	
2	R5	2/17/2025	168.02	=XLOOKUP(A2,$H$2:$H$7,$I$2:$I$7)			Chicago	R4	Amar	
3	R7	2/17/2025	130.56	Michael			Springfield	R8	Jerry	
4	R5	2/17/2025	124.48	Manny			Kansas City	R6	Linda	
5	R3	2/17/2025	128.63	Marc			Tulsa	R5	Manny	
6	R6	2/19/2044	116.79	Linda			Dallas	R3	Marc	
7	R3	2/19/2044	113.92	Marc			Austin	R7	Michael	
8	R8	2/19/2044	113.85	Jerry						
9	R8	2/19/2044	156.19	Jerry						
10	R2	2/20/2063	103.45	#N/A						
11	R3	2/20/2063	186.49	Marc						
12	R4	2/20/2063	132.9	Amar						

Figure 9.10 XLOOKUP accomplishes in three arguments what would have required four arguments with VLOOKUP.

The preceding example illustrates the first three benefits of XLOOKUP over VLOOKUP:

- XLOOKUP assumes that you are doing an exact match. Most VLOOKUPs were performing exact matches. Because VLOOKUP defaulted to a range match, anyone who left off the fourth argument of VLOOKUP could potentially get the wrong results.
- XLOOKUP uses a range reference for the return_array instead of VLOOKUP using an integer-based column index number. Imagine if a coworker inserted a column between columns H and I in Figure 9.10. The VLOOKUP would break. The XLOOKUP will continue to point to the correct range.
- XLOOKUP would have no problem returning a result that is found to the left of the lookup_value. If you need to return the office from column G to cell E2, the XLOOKUP formula would be `=XLOOKUP(A2,$H$2:$H$7,$G$2:$G$7)`. This would have been extremely complicated with VLOOKUP.

Using the optional arguments in XLOOKUP

The function syntax for XLOOKUP offers three optional arguments:

```
=XLOOKUP(lookup_value,Lookup_Array,return_array,[if_not_found],[match_
mode],[search_mode])
```

Notice that the XLOOKUP in cell D10 is returning an `#N/A` error because sales rep R2 is not found in the lookup table. To avoid this error with VLOOKUP, you would wrap the VLOOKUP function in the `IFNA` or `IFERROR` function. In contrast, XLOOKUP has the `If_Not_Found` argument as an optional fourth argument. Simply specify =XLOOKUP(A2,$H$2:$H$7,$I$2:$I$7,"Not Found").

The match_mode optional argument offers four choices:

- 0—Exact match. This is the default.
- 1—Exact match or next larger item. In contrast to the old MATCH function, the lookup_range does not have to be sorted to use this option.
- -1—Exact match or next smaller item. The lookup range does not have to be sorted for this option.
- 2—Wildcard search. Many people did not realize that VLOOKUP, HLOOKUP, and MATCH treated ?, *, and ~ as wildcards. By default, XLOOKUP will treat ?, *, and ~ as text. If you specifically need to have them treated as wildcards, then specify 2 for the match_mode.

Figure 9.11 shows XLOOKUP using ranges for a grading scale. If a student scores a 92, XLOOKUP will return an A because the match_mode argument is looking for the row equal to or larger than 92.

C2 =XLOOKUP(B2,$F$2:$F$6,$E$2:$E$6,,1)

	A	B	C	D	E	F	G	H
1	Student	Score	Grade					
2	CECILIA ALBERT	100	A		A	100		
3	KRISTEN FOREMAN	90	A		B	89		
4	DOROTHY MARTINEZ	89	B		C	79		
5	LUIS FISCHER	80	B		D	69		
6	TERRY SKINNER	79	C		F	65		
7	SHELLEY OSBORN	70	C					
8	MARVIN SCHULTZ	69	D					
9	JOE TRUJILLO	65	F					
10	WILLIAM SKINNER	64	F					
11	CAROLYN CURRY	68	D					
12	CARL ZAMORA	96	A					

Figure 9.11 The XLOOKUP formula in column C finds the correct grade from the table in columns E and F.

The optional sixth argument for XLOOKUP is the search_mode. It accepts these values:

- 1—Search first to last. This is how VLOOKUP and MATCH work. It is the default for XLOOKUP.
- -1—Search last to first allows you to search from the bottom of the list. This provides a new feature that MATCH and VLOOKUP could not offer, since they always search from the top of the list.

- 2—Binary search, from the top of the list. Before 2018, binary searches were faster than regular searches. The Excel team rewrote the search logic used in VLOOKUP, MATCH, and HLOOKUP. There is no longer any advantage to using a binary search. There is one disadvantage: The binary search option requires the lookup_range to be sorted ascending.
- -2—Binary search, from the bottom of the list. This option requires the lookup_range to be sorted in descending sequence. The Excel team does not expect anyone to use the binary search options because they are not faster than using 1 or -1.

Using one XLOOKUP to return multiple values

Thanks to the new Dynamic Arrays, XLOOKUP can return multiple answers. There are two different uses for this feature.

In Figure 9.12, the formula sends 64 cells in to the lookup_value argument. The formula returns a match for each of the 64 values. A single formula of `=XLOOKUP(A2:A65,$H$2:$H$7,$G$2:$G$7,"Not Found")` in cell E2 returns the Office column in E2:E65.

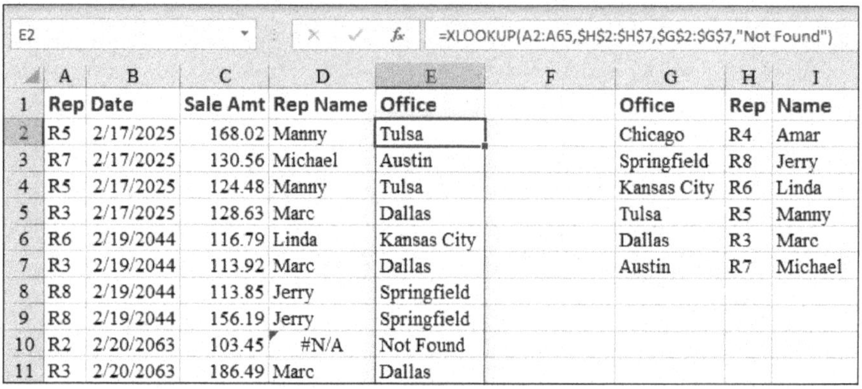

E2 =XLOOKUP(A2:A65,$H$2:$H$7,$G$2:$G$7,"Not Found")

	A	B	C	D	E	F	G	H	I
1	Rep	Date	Sale Amt	Rep Name	Office		Office	Rep	Name
2	R5	2/17/2025	168.02	Manny	Tulsa		Chicago	R4	Amar
3	R7	2/17/2025	130.56	Michael	Austin		Springfield	R8	Jerry
4	R5	2/17/2025	124.48	Manny	Tulsa		Kansas City	R6	Linda
5	R3	2/17/2025	128.63	Marc	Dallas		Tulsa	R5	Manny
6	R6	2/19/2044	116.79	Linda	Kansas City		Dallas	R3	Marc
7	R3	2/19/2044	113.92	Marc	Dallas		Austin	R7	Michael
8	R8	2/19/2044	113.85	Jerry	Springfield				
9	R8	2/19/2044	156.19	Jerry	Springfield				
10	R2	2/20/2063	103.45	#N/A	Not Found				
11	R3	2/20/2063	186.49	Marc	Dallas				

Figure 9.12 A single XLOOKUP formula in E2 returns all of the values in the Office column.

Another use for returning multiple answers is when your lookup table contains several columns of answers. In Figure 9.13, the table contains a value for each month. To return data from all 12 months, you would specify a return_array that is 12 columns wide.

In contrast to using VLOOKUP or INDEX/MATCH, the formula shown in Figure 9.13 can find the lookup_value once for each item instead of having to find the lookup_value 12 times for each item. This means XLOOKUP is faster than VLOOKUP.

C5 =XLOOKUP(B5,$A$17:$A$14056,$B$17:$M$14056)

One XLOOKUP returns all 12 columns

=XLOOKUP(B5,$A$17:$A$14056,$B$17:$M$14056)

Qty	Item	Jan	Feb	Mar	Apr	May	Jun	Jul	Aug	Sep	Oct	Nov	Dec
2	C529	0	5	0	81	96	5	5	0	2	0	4	2
10	F708	1	2	0	88	1	0	53	2	0	0	80	47
9	X291	0	80	0	0	0	50	29	33	0	87	1	4
1	E890	2	87	0	1	2	0	5	0	95	4	78	2
5	C299	0	2	4	0	48	0	2	0	89	66	0	3
4	S323	4	5	3	69	5	0	4	102	97	0	30	4
1	V600	131	48	129	1	0	1	0	105	67	117	105	4
9	P765	3	0	70	2	1	3	0	0	0	0	0	91

Inventory By Month

Item	Jan	Feb	Mar	Apr	May	Jun	Jul	Aug	Sep	Oct	Nov	Dec
G245	36	2	71	1	96	83	0	34	81	59	0	0
J535	0	3	0	0	0	85	5	137	0	32	0	5
X286	113	2	2	0	0	35	29	0	58	4	0	1
M562	4	72	0	58	5	0	110	133	0	3	0	136
V241	1	120	0	4	105	0	1	134	0	0	0	3
I238	1	0	48	0	0	5	131	40	0	132	2	0
E599	0	24	122	4	3	4	30	75	4	5	0	0
B372	0	80	0	1	100	0	0	1	4	0	5	0
M769	2	85	0	141	0	4	33	3	0	0	0	112
E187	0	56	0	131	115	0	2	1	4	130	2	0
I664	5	0	4	0	125	3	3	40	67	4	0	89
F142	0	5	5	85	5	0	0	71	90	0	0	3

Figure 9.13 A single XLOOKUP formula in C5 returns all 12 months of answers.

The techniques shown in Figures 9.12 and 9.13 are nice improvements over `VLOOKUP`. The natural next step is to combine the two techniques to look up all rows and columns in a single formula. As of June 2021, this is not supported by Excel. In Figure 9.13, a formula in C5 of `=XLOOKUP(B5:B12,A17:A14056,B17:M14056)` only returns one column of answers. Excel can extend the array in one direction or the other but not in both directions at the same time.

Using XLOOKUP to search sideways

The XLOOKUP function can also replace the old `HLOOKUP` and `LOOKUP` functions. `HLOOKUP` was used when your lookup table was arranged horizontally. In Figure 9.14, the `Lookup_Array` is B5:F5. The return _array is B6:F6.

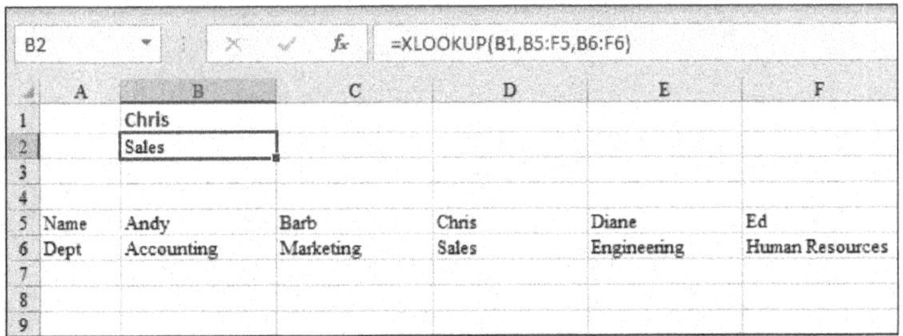

B2 =XLOOKUP(B1,B5:F5,B6:F6)

	A	B	C	D	E	F
1		Chris				
2		Sales				
3						
4						
5	Name	Andy	Barb	Chris	Diane	Ed
6	Dept	Accounting	Marketing	Sales	Engineering	Human Resources
7						
8						
9						

Figure 9.14 Search for Chris in row 5 and return the department from row 6.

The `LOOKUP` function is one of the earliest lookup functions. It would allow you to do all of the lookups in one formula. It also had the unusual ability to search a vertical array and return the answer

CHAPTER 9

from a horizontal array. This is called a *twisted XLOOKUP*, and to do it, you would have to use a TRANSPOSE function around one of the arrays: =XLOOKUP(C17,B10:B14,TRANSPOSE(C9:G9)).

Matching Two Lists Using XLOOKUP or XMATCH

If Excel is used throughout your company, you undoubtedly have many lists in Excel. People use Excel to track everything. How many times are you faced with a situation in which you have two versions of a list, and you need to match them up?

In Figure 9.15, the worksheet has two simple lists. Column A shows last week's version of who was coming to an event. Column C shows this week's version of who is coming to an event. Column D uses XLOOKUP to find who is new this week: =XLOOKUP(C6,$A$6:$A$18,$A$6:$A$18, "New this week"). In column D, having the name appear means they are in both lists. Having New this week appear means that the person was not in the previous list.

Column E uses XMATCH to find who is new: =XMATCH(C6,$A$6:$A$18). The formula is simpler. However, because XMATCH does not offer the if_not_found argument, an error value of #N/A means that the person was not in the previous list.

N31

	A	B	C	D	E	F
1	**Matching Two Lists Using XLOOKUP or XMATCH**					
2		D6	*=XLOOKUP(C6,$A$6:$A$18,$A$6:$A$18,"New this week")*			
3		D7	*=XMATCH(C6,$A$6:$A$18)*			
4						
5	**RSVP's LAST WEEK**		**RSVP's THIS WEEK**	**There?**	**There?**	
6	VERONICA HAHN		ARTHUR FLETCHER	ARTHUR FLETCHER	11	
7	ELLEN LINDSAY		BARBARA BERGER	BARBARA BERGER	7	
8	CECILIA HARMON		CANDICE GLENN	CANDICE GLENN	9	
9	DONALD TYLER		CECILIA HARMON	CECILIA HARMON	3	
10	NICOLE KELLY		CHRIS PAGE	CHRIS PAGE	8	
11	MARCIA ERICKSON		CHRISTOPHER DONOVAN	New this week	#N/A	
12	BARBARA BERGER		JOANN BROOKS	New this week	#N/A	
13	CHRIS PAGE		ELLEN LINDSAY	ELLEN LINDSAY	2	
14	CANDICE GLENN		JACOB MCINTYRE	New this week	#N/A	
15	STACY DUNLAP		JOHN GARRISON	JOHN GARRISON	13	
16	ARTHUR FLETCHER		KATHLEEN RICHARD	KATHLEEN RICHARD	12	
17	KATHLEEN RICHARD		MARCIA ERICKSON	MARCIA ERICKSON	6	
18	JOHN GARRISON		MYRTLE MOON	New this week	#N/A	
19			NICOLE KELLY	NICOLE KELLY	5	
20			STACY DUNLAP	STACY DUNLAP	10	
21			VERONICA HAHN	VERONICA HAHN	1	
22						

Figure 9.15 An #N/A error as the result of XMATCH tells you that the person is new to the list.

Performing a two-way lookup with XLOOKUP

Remember that XLOOKUP is designed to replace VLOOKUP, HLOOKUP, LOOKUP, and INDEX/MATCH. In just about every case so far, XLOOKUP or XMATCH feels like the function it is replacing. However, this example of doing a two-way lookup requires a new thought process.

In Figure 9.16, a table of inventory by month is shown in rows 14 to 22. In cell B9, a formula finds the intersection of item X286 and March using the old syntax of `INDEX` with two `MATCH` functions inside. The formula of `=INDEX(B15:G22,MATCH(A9,A15:A22,0),MATCH(B8,B14:G14,0))` uses `INDEX` to point to all of the inventory values. You then specify in which row and column the answer can be found. This formula uses one `MATCH` to find which row contains `X286` and then a second `MATCH` to find which column contains `Mar`.

The new solution using `XLOOKUP` is quite different. With the month abbreviation of `Mar` in B5, the inner formula fragment of `XLOOKUP(B4,B14:G14,B15:G22)` looks for `Mar in` B14:G14 and then returns a vertical range of answers that appear beneath the matching month. To illustrate what this formula is doing, Figure 9.16 shows the formula entered in J5. The values of `71; 0; 77; 0; 0; 48; 122; 0` represent the inventory values for March. If you would change B4 to `May`, then the formula fragment would return `96;0;0;5;105;0;3;100` instead.

The second `XLOOKUP` in the formula is finding and returning the `Results_Array` for the desired month.

The formula in B5 is `=XLOOKUP(A5,A15:A22,XLOOKUP(B4,B14:M14,B15:M22))`. This formula finds the item number from A5 in the list of item numbers in A15:A22. In this case, A15:A22 is the `Lookup_Array`. The third argument in the formula is the `Results_Array` and is generated by the second `XLOOKUP`.

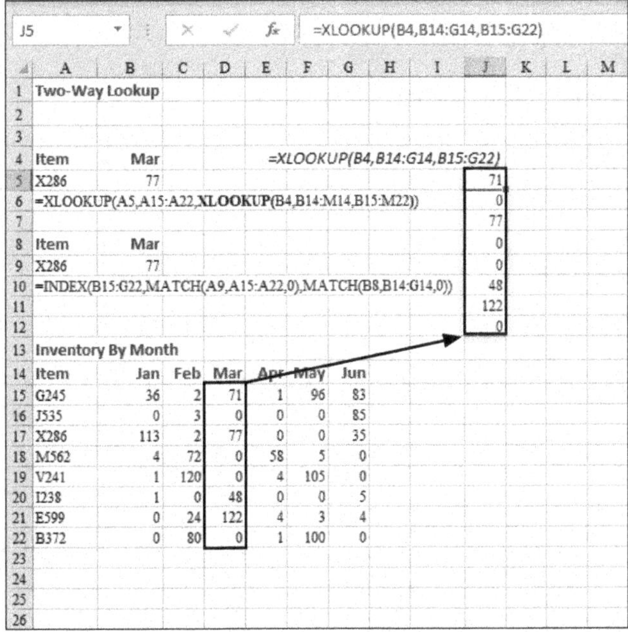

Figure 9.16 Using two XLOOKUPs to perform a two-way lookup. The inner XLOOKUP is finding the `Results_Array` for the correct month.

Returning a cell reference with XLOOKUP

XLOOKUP is the eighth function in Excel that can return a cell reference when the formula is adjacent to a colon. XLOOKUP joins CHOOSE, IF, IFS, INDEX, INDIRECT, OFFSET, and SWITCH.

In Figure 9.17, you want to sum all of the sales from March through September. With `March` in D4, a formula of `=XLOOKUP(D4,$A$2:$A$13,$B$2:$B$13)` in E4 will return March sales of `30101`. In a similar fashion, with `September` in D6, a formula of `=XLOOKUP(D6,$A$2:$A$13,$B$2:$B$13)` in E6 will return September sales of `36900`.

If you join those two formulas with a colon and wrap them in the SUM function, an amazing thing happens. At the point where the first XLOOKUP should return `30101`, it insteads returns `$B$4`. You can see this happen in the Evaluate Formula dialog box. Keep pressing Evaluate in the Evaluate Formula dialog box, and you will see the second XLOOKUP return `$B$10` instead of `36900`. Both of these are triggered by the colon between the XLOOKUPs.

Subsequently, the formula sums everything from B4 to B10, giving you the sales from the start month to the end month.

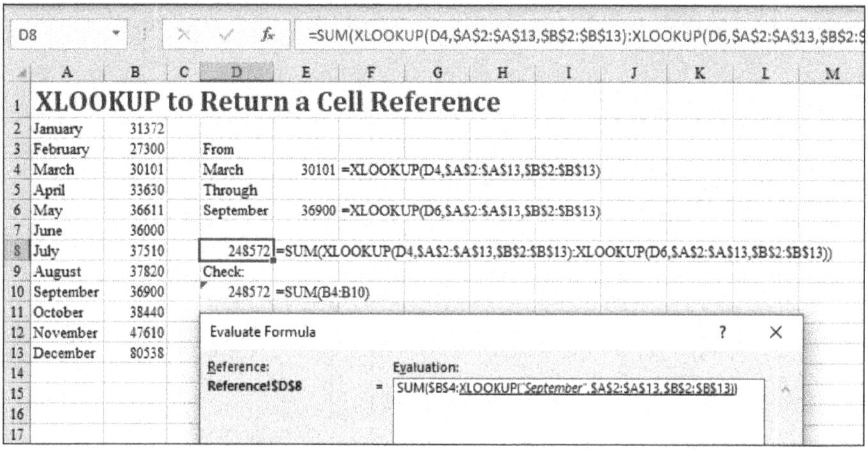

D8 =SUM(XLOOKUP(D4,$A$2:$A$13,$B$2:$B$13):XLOOKUP(D6,$A$2:$A$13,$B$2:$

	A	B	C	D	E
1	**XLOOKUP to Return a Cell Reference**				
2	January	31372			
3	February	27300		From	
4	March	30101		March	30101 =XLOOKUP(D4,$A$2:$A$13,$B$2:$B$13)
5	April	33630		Through	
6	May	36611		September	36900 =XLOOKUP(D6,$A$2:$A$13,$B$2:$B$13)
7	June	36000			
8	July	37510		248572	=SUM(XLOOKUP(D4,$A$2:$A$13,$B$2:$B$13):XLOOKUP(D6,$A$2:$A$13,$B$2:$B$13))
9	August	37820		Check:	
10	September	36900		248572	=SUM(B4:B10)
11	October	38440			
12	November	47610			
13	December	80538			

Evaluate Formula ? ×

Reference: Reference!$D$8 = Evaluation: SUM($B$4:XLOOKUP("September",$A$2:$A$13,$B$2:$B$13))

Figure 9.17 Using two XLOOKUPs with a colon in between causes each XLOOKUP to return a cell reference instead of the number found in that cell.

Using FORMULATEXT to document a worksheet

Quiz: Which Excel function is used the most in this book? It is FORMULATEXT. The FORMULATEXT function was added in Excel 2013. If you ask for the `=FORMULATEXT(A1)`, Excel shows the formula that is in cell A1 as text. All the formulas shown in this book (such as cell C1 in Figure 9.17) are generated with the FORMULATEXT function.

You can use FORMULATEXT to document the formulas used in your worksheet. Normally, you can either print your worksheet with formulas showing or with the results from the formulas. By using FORMULATEXT, you can show both the formula and the result.

If you use FORMULATEXT on a cell with an array formula, the resulting text will be wrapped in curly braces that are shown in the formula bar.

In Figure 9.18, the text of the formula shown in C3 comes from a FORMULATEXT function.

C3 | =FORMULATEXT(B3)

	A	B	C	D	E	F	G	H	I	J
1										
2		Formula	Text of the Formula							
3		15.5	=SUM(INDEX(A6:E9,0,WEEKDAY(TODAY(),2)))/MONTH(TODAY())							
4										
5										
6	69	20	11	59	59					
7	41	64	62	14	14					
8	11	98	7	63	63					
9	77	7	13	30	30					
10										
11		Formula in C3:								
12		=FORMULATEXT(B3)								
13										

Figure 9.18 A FORMULATEXT function in C3 shows the formula used in B3.

Syntax:

```
FORMULATEXT(reference)
```

This function returns a formula as text.

TROUBLESHOOTING

FORMULATEXT fails when your reference does not contain a formula.

There are people who had written their own versions of `FormulaText` as a VBA function before Excel 2013 added `FormulaText`. The version that was made popular on the Internet would return the formula as text if the cell contained a formula. Otherwise, it would return the value in the cell.

However, Excel's built-in version of FORMULATEXT returns a #N/A error if the cell does not contain a formula.

One workaround is to wrap FORMULATEXT **in** IFNA**. Instead of** =FORMULATEXT(C2), **use** =IFNA(FORMULATEXT(C2),C2)**. However, that formula will return** 0 **if B2 is an empty cell.**

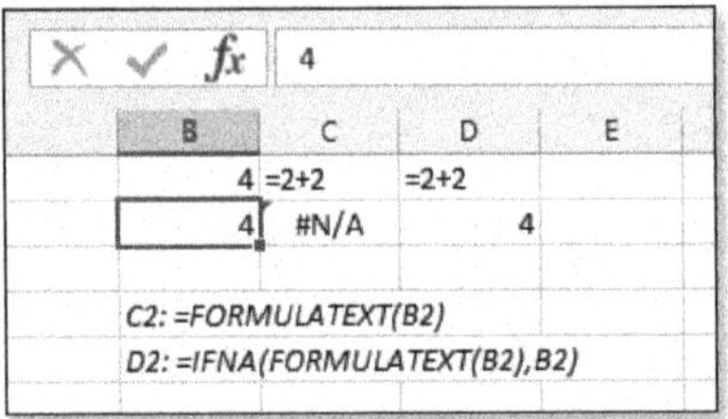

Using numbers with OFFSET to describe a range

The language of Excel is numbers. There are functions that count the number of entries in a range. There are functions that can tell you the numeric position of a looked-up value. You might know that a particular value is found in row 20, but what if you want to perform calculations on other cells in row 20?

The OFFSET function handles this very situation. You can use OFFSET to describe a range using mostly numbers. OFFSET is flexible: It can describe a single cell, or it can describe a rectangular range.

Although INDEX can return a single cell, row, or column from a rectangular range, it has limitations. If you specify C5:Z99 as the range for an INDEX function, you can select only cells below and/or to the right of C5. The OFFSET function can move up and down or left and right from the starting cell, which is C5.

Syntax:

```
OFFSET(reference,rows,cols,height,width)
```

The OFFSET function returns a reference to a range that is a given number of rows and columns from a given reference. This function takes the following arguments:

- `reference`: This is the reference from which you want to base the offset. `reference` must be a reference to a cell or range of adjacent cells; otherwise, OFFSET returns a #VALUE! error.
- `rows`: This is the number of rows, up or down, that you want the upper-left cell to refer to. Using 5 as the `rows` argument, for example, specifies that the upper-left cell in the reference is five rows below `reference`. `rows` can be positive, which means below the starting reference, or negative, which means above the starting reference.

- `cols`: This is the number of columns to the left or right that you want the upper-left cell of the result to refer to. For example, using `5` as the `cols` argument specifies that the upper-left cell in the reference is five columns to the right of `reference`. `cols` can be positive, which means to the right of the starting reference, or negative, which means to the left of the starting reference. If `rows` and `cols` offset `reference` over the edge of the worksheet, `OFFSET` returns a `#REF!` error. Figure 9.19 demonstrates various combinations of `rows` and `cols` from a starting cell of cell C5.

- `height`: This is the height, in number of rows, that you want the returned reference to be. `height` must be a positive number.

- `width`: This is the width, in number of columns, that you want the returned reference to be. `width` must be a positive number. If `height` or `width` is omitted, Excel assumes it is the same height or width as `reference`.

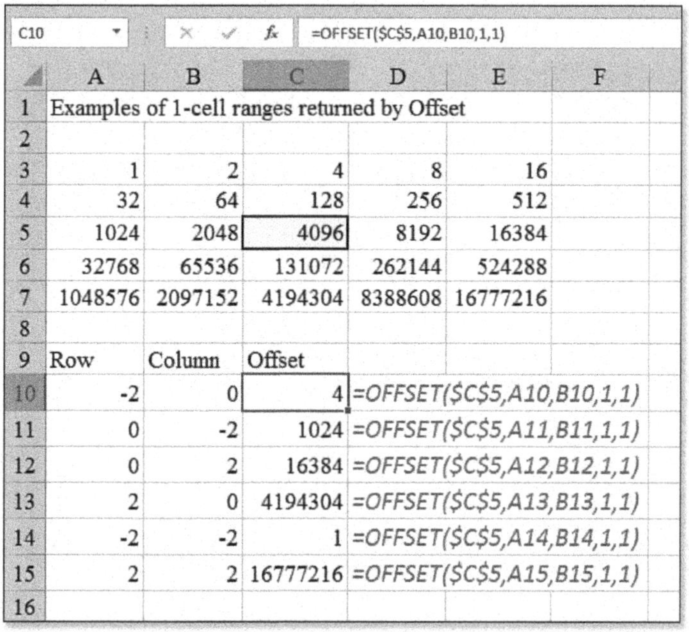

C10 =OFFSET($C$5,A10,B10,1,1)

	A	B	C	D	E	F
1	Examples of 1-cell ranges returned by Offset					
2						
3	1	2	4	8	16	
4	32	64	128	256	512	
5	1024	2048	4096	8192	16384	
6	32768	65536	131072	262144	524288	
7	1048576	2097152	4194304	8388608	16777216	
8						
9	Row	Column	Offset			
10	-2	0	4	=OFFSET($C$5,A10,B10,1,1)		
11	0	-2	1024	=OFFSET($C$5,A11,B11,1,1)		
12	0	2	16384	=OFFSET($C$5,A12,B12,1,1)		
13	2	0	4194304	=OFFSET($C$5,A13,B13,1,1)		
14	-2	-2	1	=OFFSET($C$5,A14,B14,1,1)		
15	2	2	16777216	=OFFSET($C$5,A15,B15,1,1)		
16						

Figure 9.19 These `OFFSET` functions return a single cell that is a certain number of rows and columns away from cell C5.

`OFFSET` enables you to specify a reference. It does not move a cell. It does not change the selection. It is just a numeric way to describe a reference. `OFFSET` can be used in any function that is expecting a reference argument.

Excel Help provides a trivial example of =SUM(OFFSET(C2,1,2,3,1)), which sums E3:E5. However, this example is silly because no one would ever write such a formula! If you were to write such a formula, you would just write =SUM(E3:E5) instead. The power of OFFSET comes when at least one of the four numeric arguments is calculated by the COUNT function or a lookup function.

In Figure 9.20, you can use COUNT(A5:A999) to count how many entries are in column A. If you assume that there are no blanks in the range of data, you can use the COUNT result as the height argument in OFFSET to describe the range of numbers. Here's what you do:

1. There is nothing magical about the reference, so write it as =OFFSET(A5,.
2. Do not move the starting position any rows or columns from cell A5. The starting position is A5, so you always use 0 and 0 for rows and columns. Therefore, the formula is now =OFFSET(A5,0,0,.

A3 =SUM(OFFSET(A5,0,0,COUNT(A5:A999),1))

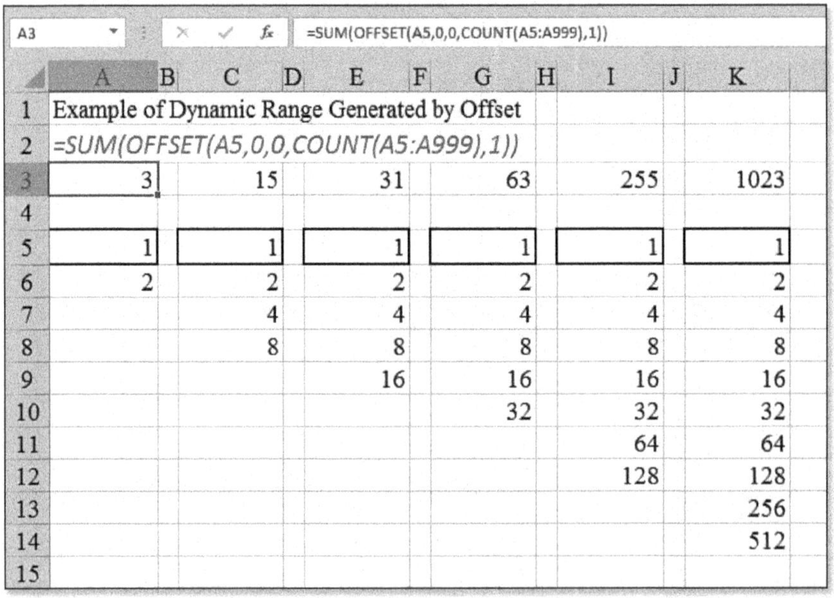

	A	B	C	D	E	F	G	H	I	J	K
1	Example of Dynamic Range Generated by Offset										
2	=SUM(OFFSET(A5,0,0,COUNT(A5:A999),1))										
3	3		15		31		63		255		1023
4											
5	1		1		1		1		1		1
6	2		2		2		2		2		2
7			4		4		4		4		4
8			8		8		8		8		8
9					16		16		16		16
10							32		32		32
11									64		64
12									128		128
13											256
14											512
15											

Figure 9.20 Every argument except height is hard-coded in these functions. The height argument comes from a COUNT function to allow the range to expand as more entries are added.

3. If you want to include only the number of entries in the list, use COUNT(A5:A999) as the height of the range. The formula is now =OFFSET(A5,0,0,COUNT(A5:A999),.
4. The width is one column, so make the function =OFFSET(A5,0,0,COUNT(A5:A999),1).

5. Use your `OFFSET` function anywhere you would normally specify a reference. You can use `=SUM(OFFSET(A5,0,0,COUNT(A5:A999),1))` or specify that formula as the series in a chart. This creates a dynamic chart that grows or shrinks as the number of entries changes.

TROUBLESHOOTING

OFFSET is a volatile function and will slow recalculation of your worksheet. Avoid OFFSET using a little-known version of INDEX.

Normally, `=INDEX(A1:A12,5)` will return the value stored in the fifth row of A1:A12. Excel guru Dan Mayoh discovered an alternate use for `INDEX`. If the `INDEX` function is placed adjacent to a colon, the `INDEX` function returns the cell address instead of the value stored in the cell. `=SUM(A1:INDEX(A1:A12,5))` will sum A1:A5.

Of course, you would not hard-code the 5 in the `INDEX` function. You might use `MONTH(TODAY())` to dynamically choose the number corresponding to the current month.

`=SUM(A1:INDEX(A1:A12,MONTH(TODAY())))` is not volatile and does the same thing as `=SUM(OFFSET(A1,0,0,MONTH(TODAY()),1))`.

Using INDIRECT to build and evaluate cell references on the fly

The `INDIRECT` function is deceivingly powerful. Consider this trivial example: In cell A1, enter the text **B2**. In cell B2, enter a number. In cell C3, enter the formula **`=INDIRECT(A1)`**. Excel returns the number that you entered in cell B2 in cell C3. The `INDIRECT` function looks in cell A1 and expects to find something that is a valid cell or range reference. It then looks in that address to return the answer for the function.

The reference text can be any text that you can string together using various text functions. This enables you to create complex references that dynamically point to other sheets or to other open workbooks.

The reference text can also be a range name. You could have a validation list box in which someone selects a value from a list. If you have predefined a named range that corresponds to each possible entry on the list, `INDIRECT` can point to the various named ranges on the fly.

When you use traditional formulas, even absolute formulas, there is a chance that someone might insert rows or columns that will move the reference. If you need a formula to always point to cell J10, no matter how someone rearranges the worksheet, you can use `=INDIRECT("J10")` to handle this.

Syntax:

`INDIRECT(ref_text,a1)`

The `INDIRECT` function returns the reference specified by a text string. This function takes the following arguments:

- `ref_text`: This is a reference to a cell that contains an A1-style reference, an R1C1-style reference, a name defined as a reference, or a reference to a cell as a text string. If `ref_text` is not a valid cell reference, `INDIRECT` returns a `#REF!` error. If `ref_text` refers to an external workbook, the other workbook must be open. If the source workbook is not open, `INDIRECT` returns a `#REF!` error.

- `a1`: This is a logical value that specifies what type of reference is contained in the cell `ref_text`. If `a1` is TRUE or omitted, `ref_text` is interpreted as an A1-style reference. If `a1` is FALSE, `ref_text` is interpreted as an R1C1-style reference.

Figure 9.21 is a monthly worksheet in a workbook that has 12 similar sheets. In each worksheet, the total for the worksheet appears in cell D2. To build a summary sheet that points to D2 on the individual worksheets, you can concatenate the month name from column A with "!D2" to build a reference.

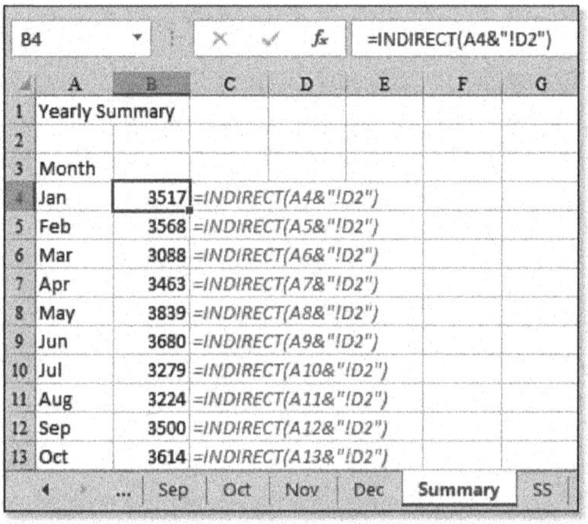

B4 =INDIRECT(A4&"!D2")

	A	B	C
1	Yearly Summary		
2			
3	Month		
4	Jan	3517	=INDIRECT(A4&"!D2")
5	Feb	3568	=INDIRECT(A5&"!D2")
6	Mar	3088	=INDIRECT(A6&"!D2")
7	Apr	3463	=INDIRECT(A7&"!D2")
8	May	3839	=INDIRECT(A8&"!D2")
9	Jun	3680	=INDIRECT(A9&"!D2")
10	Jul	3279	=INDIRECT(A10&"!D2")
11	Aug	3224	=INDIRECT(A11&"!D2")
12	Sep	3500	=INDIRECT(A12&"!D2")
13	Oct	3614	=INDIRECT(A13&"!D2")

... Sep | Oct | Nov | Dec | Summary | SS

Figure 9.21 Cell D4 dynamically builds a text formula to reference the sheet shown in A4.

Using the HYPERLINK function to add hyperlinks quickly

Excel enables you to add a hyperlink by using the Excel interface. On the Insert tab, select the Hyperlink icon. Next, you specify text to appear in the cell and the underlying address. Building links in this way is easy, but it is tedious to build them one at a time. If you have hundreds of links to add, you can add them quickly by using the HYPERLINK function.

Syntax:

```
HYPERLINK(link_location,friendly_name)
```

The HYPERLINK function creates a shortcut that opens a document stored on your hard drive, a network server, or the Internet. This function takes the following arguments:

- `link_location`—This is the URL address on the Internet. It could also be a path, filename, location in the same workbook, and location in another file. For example, you could link to `"[C:\files\Jan2018.xls]!Sheet1!A15"`. Note that `link_location` can be a text string enclosed in quotes or a cell that contains the link.
- `friendly_name`—This is the underlined text or numeric value that is displayed in the cell. `friendly_name` is displayed in blue and is underlined. If `friendly_name` is omitted, the cell displays the `link_location` value as the jump text. `friendly_name` can be a value, a text string, a name, or a cell that contains the jump text or value. If `friendly_name` returns an error (for example, `#VALUE!`), the cell displays the error instead of the jump text.

Figure 9.22 shows a list of web pages in column A. Column B contains the titles of those web pages. To quickly build a table of hyperlinks, you use `=HYPERLINK(A2,B2)` in cell C2 and copy the formula down the column. Unfortunately, you must keep columns A and B intact for the hyperlink to keep working. You can hide those columns, but there is no Paste Special option to convert the formula to values that will keep the hyperlink.

> NOTE
>
> **Note that Excel does not check whether the link location is valid at the time you created the link. If the link is not valid when someone clicks it, the person encounters an error.**

> TIP
>
> **It is difficult to select a cell that contains a HYPERLINK function. If you click the cell, Excel attempts to follow the hyperlink. Instead, click the cell and hold the mouse button until the pointer changes from a hand to a plus. Alternatively, click a nearby cell and use the arrow keys to move to the cell with the hyperlink.**

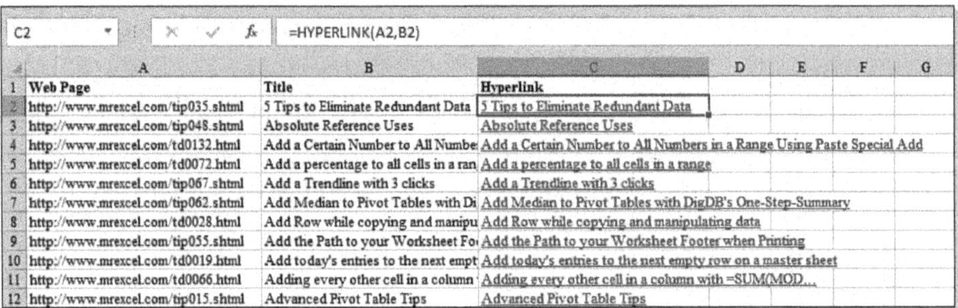

C2 =HYPERLINK(A2,B2)

	A	B	C	D	E	F	G
1	Web Page	Title	Hyperlink				
2	http://www.mrexcel.com/tip035.shtml	5 Tips to Eliminate Redundant Data	5 Tips to Eliminate Redundant Data				
3	http://www.mrexcel.com/tip048.shtml	Absolute Reference Uses	Absolute Reference Uses				
4	http://www.mrexcel.com/td0132.html	Add a Certain Number to All Numbe	Add a Certain Number to All Numbers in a Range Using Paste Special Add				
5	http://www.mrexcel.com/td0072.html	Add a percentage to all cells in a ran	Add a percentage to all cells in a range				
6	http://www.mrexcel.com/tip067.shtml	Add a Trendline with 3 clicks	Add a Trendline with 3 clicks				
7	http://www.mrexcel.com/tip062.shtml	Add Median to Pivot Tables with Di	Add Median to Pivot Tables with DigDB's One-Step-Summary				
8	http://www.mrexcel.com/td0028.html	Add Row while copying and manipu	Add Row while copying and manipulating data				
9	http://www.mrexcel.com/tip055.shtml	Add the Path to your Worksheet Fo	Add the Path to your Worksheet Footer when Printing				
10	http://www.mrexcel.com/td0019.html	Add today's entries to the next empt	Add today's entries to the next empty row on a master sheet				
11	http://www.mrexcel.com/td0066.html	Adding every other cell in a column	Adding every other cell in a column with =SUM(MOD...				
12	http://www.mrexcel.com/tip015.shtml	Advanced Pivot Table Tips	Advanced Pivot Table Tips				

Figure 9.22 The formulas in column C enable you to create hundreds of hyperlinks in seconds.

To keep only the hyperlinks, copy column C and paste to a blank Word document. Open a new workbook. Copy from Word and paste back to the new Excel document.

Alternatively, use `="#HYPERLINK("""&A2&""""&", "&""""&B2&""""&")"` in C2. Copy down and paste special values. Use Find and Replace to change # to =.

Using the TRANSPOSE function to formulaically turn data

With many people using Excel in a company, there are bound to be different usage styles from person to person. Some people build their worksheets horizontally, and other people build their worksheets vertically. For example, in Figure 9.23, the monthly totals stretch horizontally across row 80. However, for some reason, you need these figures to be arranged going vertically down from cell B84.

The typical method is to copy C80:N80 and then choose Home, Paste, Transpose. This copies a snapshot of the totals in row 80 to a column of data.

This is fine if you need only a snapshot of the totals. However, what if you want to see the totals continually updated in column B? Excel provides the `TRANSPOSE` function for such situations.

Thanks to the new dynamic array formulas, it is easier to enter the `TRANSPOSE` function. In cell B84, type `=TRANSPOSE(C80:N80)` and press Enter. The 12 results will spill from B84 to B95.

Syntax:

```
TRANSPOSE(array)
```

The `TRANSPOSE` function transposes a vertical range into a horizontal array or vice versa.

The argument `array` is an array or a range of cells on a worksheet that you want to transpose. The transposition of an array is accomplished by using the first row of the array as the first column of the new array, the second row of the array as the second column of the new array, and so on.

CHAPTER 9

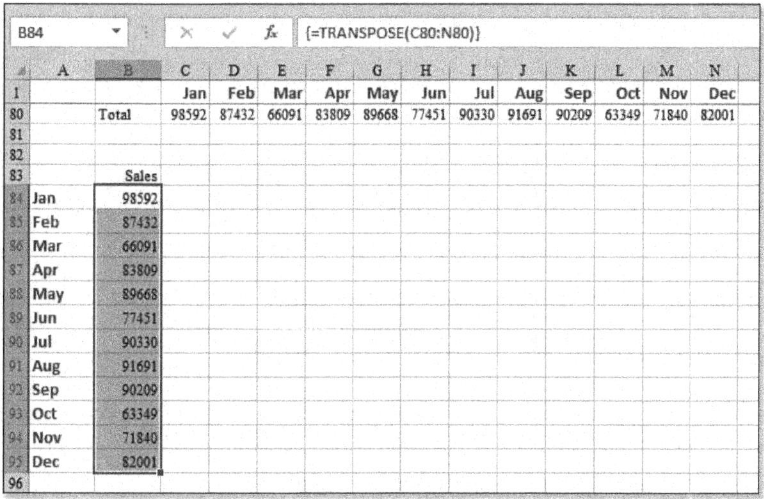

B84 {=TRANSPOSE(C80:N80)}

	A	B	C	D	E	F	G	H	I	J	K	L	M	N
1			Jan	Feb	Mar	Apr	May	Jun	Jul	Aug	Sep	Oct	Nov	Dec
80		Total	98592	87432	66091	83809	89668	77451	90330	91691	90209	63349	71840	82001
81														
82														
83		Sales												
84	Jan	98592												
85	Feb	87432												
86	Mar	66091												
87	Apr	83809												
88	May	89668												
89	Jun	77451												
90	Jul	90330												
91	Aug	91691												
92	Sep	90209												
93	Oct	63349												
94	Nov	71840												
95	Dec	82001												
96														

Figure 9.23 One TRANSPOSE function occupies 12 cells, from B84:B95.

> NOTE
>
> **You can also use** `TRANSPOSE` **to turn a vertical range into a horizontal range.**

Using GETPIVOTDATA to retrieve one cell from a pivot table

You might turn to this book to find out how to use most of the Excel functions. However, for the `GETPIVOTDATA` function, you are likely to turn to this book to find out why the function is being automatically generated for you.

Suppose that you have a pivot table on a worksheet. You should click outside the pivot table. Next, you type an equal sign and then use the mouse to click one of the cells in the data area of the pivot table. Although you might expect this to generate a formula such as =E9, instead, Excel puts in the formula =`GETPIVOTDATA("Sales",$B$5,"Customer","Astonishing Glass Company","Region","West")`, as shown in Figure 9.24.

H9 =GETPIVOTDATA("Sales",$B$5,"Customer","Astonishing Glass Company","Region","West")

	B	C	D	E	F	G	H	I
5	Sum of Sales	Region						
6	Customer	East	Central	West	Grand Total			
7	Alluring Ink Company	0	170	0	170			
8	Alluring Quilt Company	289	0	0	289			
9	Astonishing Glass Company	0	0	314	314		314	
10	Astonishing Shovel Inc.	190	0	0	190			
11	Bright Shoe Company	0	246	0	246			
12	Brilliant Luggage Inc.	0	307	0	307			
13	Different Belt Corporation	0	0	249	249			

Figure 9.24 Excel inserts this strange function in the worksheet.

This function is annoying. As you copy the formula down to more rows, the function keeps retrieving sales to Astonishing Glass in the West region. By default, Excel is generating this function instead of a simple formula such as =E9. This happens whether you use the mouse or the arrow keys to specify the cell in the formula.

To avoid this behavior, you can enter the entire formula by manually typing it on the keyboard. Typing **=E9** in a cell forces Excel to create a relative reference to cell E9. You are then free to copy the formula to other cells.

There is also a way to turn off this behavior permanently:

1. Select a cell inside an active pivot table.
2. The Pivot Table contextual tabs are displayed. Select the PivotTable Analyze tab. From the PivotTable group, select the Options drop-down menu and then select the Generate GetPivotData icon. The behavior turns off.
3. Enter formulas by using the mouse, arrow keys, or keyboard without generating the `GETPIVOTDATA` function.

Microsoft made `GETPIVOTDATA` the default behavior because the function is pretty cool. Now that you have learned how to turn off the behavior, you might want to understand exactly how it works in case you ever need to use the function.

Syntax:

`GETPIVOTDATA(data_field,pivot_table,field1,item1,field2,item2,...)`

The `GETPIVOTDATA` function returns data stored in a pivot table report. You can use `GETPIVOTDATA` to retrieve summary data from a pivot table report, provided that the summary data is visible in the report. This function takes the following arguments:

- `data_field`: This is the name, enclosed in quotation marks, for the data field that contains the data you want to retrieve.
- `pivot_table`: This is a reference to any cell, range of cells, or named range of cells in a pivot table report. This information is used to determine which pivot table report contains the data you want to retrieve.
- `field1`, `item1`, `field2`, `item2`, `...`: These are 1 to 126 pairs of field names and item names that describe the data you want to retrieve. The pairs can be in any order. Fieldnames and names for items other than dates and numbers are enclosed in quotation marks. For OLAP pivot table reports, items can contain the source name of the dimension as well as the source name of the item.

Calculated fields or items and custom calculations are included in GETPIVOTDATA calculations:

- If pivot_table is a range that includes two or more pivot table reports, data is retrieved from whichever report was created in the range most recently.
- If the field and item arguments describe a single cell, the value of that cell is returned, regardless of whether it is a string, a number, an error, and so on.
- If an item contains a date, the value must be expressed as a serial number or populated by using the DATE function so that the value is retained if the spreadsheet is opened in a different locale. For example, an item referring to the date March 5, 2025, could be entered as 45721 or DATE(2025,3,5). Times can be entered as decimal values or by using the TIME function.
- If pivot_table is not a range in which a pivot table report is found, GETPIVOTDATA returns #REF!. If the arguments do not describe a visible field, or if they include a page field that is not displayed, GETPIVOTDATA returns #REF!.

Examples of database functions

If you were a data analyst in the 1980s and the early 1990s, you would have been enamored with the database functions. I used @DSUM every hour of my work life for many years. It was one of the most powerful weapons in any spreadsheet arsenal. Combined with a data table, the DSUM, DMIN, DMAX, and DAVERAGE functions got a serious workout when people performed data analysis in a spreadsheet.

Then, in 1993, Microsoft Excel added the pivot table to the Data menu in Excel. Pivot tables changed everything. Those powerful database functions seemed tired and worn out. Since that day in 1993, I had never used DSUM again until I created the example described in the following section. As far as I knew, the database functions had been living in a cave in South Carolina.

Maybe it is like the nostalgia of finding a box of photos of an old girlfriend, but I realized that the database functions are still pretty powerful. Customers whined enough to have Microsoft add AVERAGEIF to the COUNTIF and SUMIF arsenal. This was unnecessary: Customers could have done this easily by setting up a small criteria range and using DAVERAGE.

Inside OUT

The database functions would be far more popular if they did not require headings for the criteria range.

The DSUM is ultra-powerful to return all records in which a specific criteria range appears (such as the region is East). However, in real life, your manager is going to want to see the records where the region is Central and West instead of East. When you start to copy the DSUM function for other regions, you realize that you need an additional two cells to hold each criteria range.

If you wanted 100 rows of DSUM to return the sales for 100 employees, you would need 200 cells of criteria range. Arranging those cells vertically would make it difficult to point to the correct criteria range. In the figure here, a blend of horizontal criteria ranges, OFFSET, and MATCH provide a method, but it will be slow to calculate. This is why you don't see DSUM functions everywhere.

As shown in the figure, modern functions, such as SUMIFS or FILTER, provide easier ways than DSUM to arrive at the results.

	A	B	C	D	E	F	G	H	I	J
1	Employee	Sales		Helper Cells with Many Criteria Ranges						
2	Jared	1277		Employee	Employee	Employee	Employee	Employee	Employee	Employee
3	Andy	1099		Andy	Barb	Chris	Diane	Ed	Flo	Gary
4	Jared	1356		*Use OFFSET in E7 so criteria range moves to the right as you copy down*						
5	Kelly	1830								
6	Gary	1119			DSUM	SUMIFS	FILTER			
7	Jared	1086		Andy	99621	99621	99621			
8	Barb	1444		Barb	105899	105899	105899			
9	Ike	1674		Chris	92882	92882	92882			
10	Flo	1383		Diane	89747	89747	89747			
11	Barb	1590		Ed	98890	98890	98890			
12	Gary	1567		Flo	135856	135856	135856			
13	Ed	1199		Gary	95926	95926	95926			
14	Barb	1934		Hank	96658	96658	96658			
15	Chris	1041		Ike	77656	77656	77656			
16	Flo	1684		Jared	102762	102762	102762			
17	Jared	1680		Kelly	90389	90389	90389			
18	Diane	1190		*E7: =DSUM($A$1:$B$726,"Sales",OFFSET($C$2,0,MATCH(D7,$D$3:$N$3,0),2,1))*						
19	Gary	1916		*F7: =SUMIFS($B$2:$B$726,$A$2:$A$726,D7)*						
20	Flo	1293		*G7: =SUM(FILTER($B$2:$B$726,$A$2:$A$726=D7))*						

Eleven of the 12 database functions are similar. DSUM, DAVERAGE, DCOUNT, DCOUNTA, DMAX, DMIN, DPRODUCT, DSTDEV, DSTDEVP, DVAR, and DVARP all perform the equivalent operation of their non-D equivalents, but they allow for complex criteria to include records that meet certain criteria. See examples of each of these in Figure 9.25.

CHAPTER 9

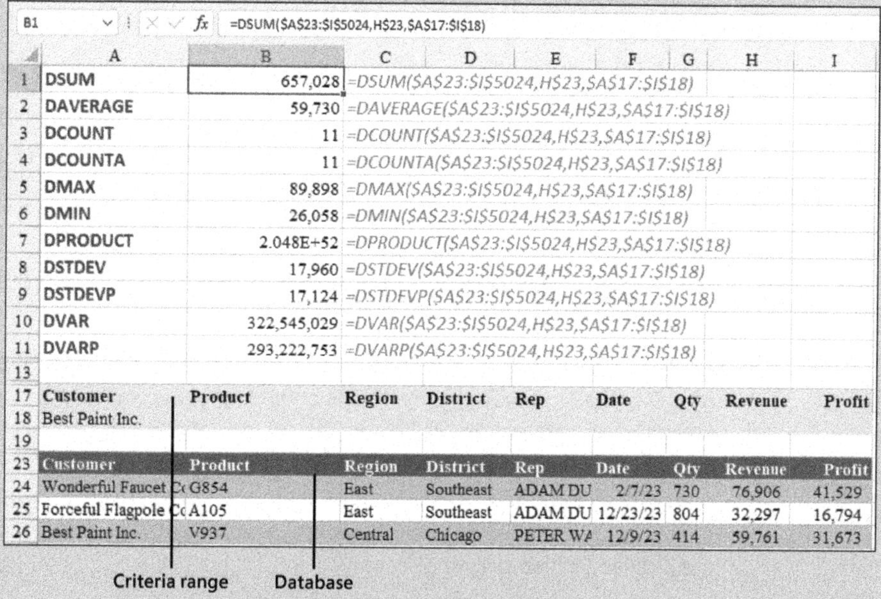

B1 =DSUM($A$23:$I$5024,H$23,$A$17:$I$18)

	A	B	C	D	E	F	G	H	I
1	DSUM	657,028	=DSUM($A$23:$I$5024,H$23,$A$17:$I$18)						
2	DAVERAGE	59,730	=DAVERAGE($A$23:$I$5024,H$23,$A$17:$I$18)						
3	DCOUNT	11	=DCOUNT($A$23:$I$5024,H$23,$A$17:$I$18)						
4	DCOUNTA	11	=DCOUNTA($A$23:$I$5024,H$23,$A$17:$I$18)						
5	DMAX	89,898	=DMAX($A$23:$I$5024,H$23,$A$17:$I$18)						
6	DMIN	26,058	=DMIN($A$23:$I$5024,H$23,$A$17:$I$18)						
7	DPRODUCT	2.048E+52	=DPRODUCT($A$23:$I$5024,H$23,$A$17:$I$18)						
8	DSTDEV	17,960	=DSTDEV($A$23:$I$5024,H$23,$A$17:$I$18)						
9	DSTDEVP	17,124	=DSTDEVP($A$23:$I$5024,H$23,$A$17:$I$18)						
10	DVAR	322,545,029	=DVAR($A$23:$I$5024,H$23,$A$17:$I$18)						
11	DVARP	293,222,753	=DVARP($A$23:$I$5024,H$23,$A$17:$I$18)						
13									
17	Customer	Product	Region	District	Rep	Date	Qty	Revenue	Profit
18	Best Paint Inc.								
19									
23	Customer	Product	Region	District	Rep	Date	Qty	Revenue	Profit
24	Wonderful Faucet C	G854	East	Southeast	ADAM DU	2/7/23	730	76,906	41,529
25	Forceful Flagpole C	A105	East	Southeast	ADAM DU	12/23/23	804	32,297	16,794
26	Best Paint Inc.	V937	Central	Chicago	PETER WA	12/9/23	414	59,761	31,673

Criteria range   Database

Figure 9.25 A simple criteria range specifies to limit DSUM to only records for Best Paint Inc. as a customer.

To save you the hassle of looking up the confusing few, DCOUNT counts numeric cells, and DCOUNTA counts nonblank cells. DSTDEV and DVAR calculate the standard deviation and variance of a sample of a population, respectively. DSTDEVP and DVARP calculate the standard deviation and variance of the entire population, respectively. The 12th database function, DGET, has the same arguments, but it acts a bit differently, as explained later in this chapter.

Using DSUM to conditionally sum records from a database

There are three arguments to every database function. It is very easy to get your first DSUM working. The `criteria` argument is the one that offers vast flexibility. The following section explains the syntax for DSUM. The syntax for the other 11 database functions is identical to this.

Syntax:

```
DSUM(database,field,criteria)
```

The DSUM function adds records from one field in a data set, provided that the records meet some criteria that you specify. The DSUM function takes the following arguments:

- `database`: This is the range of cells that make up the list or database, including the heading row. A `database` is a list of related data in which rows of related information are records, and columns of data are fields. In Figure 9.25, the database is the 5,002 rows of data located at A23:I5024.

- `field`: This indicates which column is used in the function. You have three options when specifying a field:
  - You can point to the cell with the `fieldname`, such as H23 for Revenue.
  - You can include the word `Revenue` as the `field` argument.
  - You can use the number 8 to indicate that `Revenue` is the eighth field in the database.
- `criteria`: This is the range of cells that contains the conditions specified. You can use any range for the `criteria` argument. The criteria range typically includes at least one column label and at least one cell below the column label for specifying a condition for the column. You can also use the computed criteria discussed in "Using the miracle version of a criteria range," later in this chapter. Learning how to create powerful criteria ranges enables you to unlock the powerful potential of the database functions. Several examples are provided in the following sections.

NOTE

To conserve space, the remaining examples in the following sections show only the DSUM result. You can compare the various results to the $657,028 of revenue for the current example.

Creating a simple criteria range for database functions

Although a criteria range needs only one field heading from the database, it is just as easy to copy the entire set of headings to a blank section of the worksheet. In Figure 9.25, for example, the headings in A17:I17, along with at least one additional row, create a criteria range.

In Figure 9.25, you see results of the 11 database functions for a simple criteria in which the customer is Best Paint Inc. Each formula specifies a database of $A$23:$I$5024. The field is H23, which is the heading for Revenue. The criteria range is A17:I18. In this example, the criteria range could have easily been A17:A18, but the A17:I18 form enables you to enter future criteria without specifying the criteria range again.

Using a blank criteria range to return all records

This is a trivial example, but if the second row of the criteria range is completely blank, the database function returns the total of all rows in the data set. As shown in Figure 9.26, this is $256.6 million. This is equivalent to using the `SUM` function.

B1 =DSUM($A$23:$I$5024,H$23,$A$17:$I$18)

	A	B	C	D	E	F	G	H	I
1	DSUM	256,645,202	=DSUM($A$23:$I$5024,H$23,$A$17:$I$18)						
13									
17	Customer	Product	Region	District	Rep	Date	Qty	Revenue	Profit
18									
19									
23	Customer	Product	Region	District	Rep	Date	Qty	Revenue	Profit
24	Wonderful Faucet Co	G854	East	Southeast	ADAM DU	2/7/23	730	76,906	41,529
25	Forceful Flagpole Co	A105	East	Southeast	ADAM DU	12/23/23	804	32,297	16,794
26	Best Paint Inc.	V937	Central	Chicago	PETER WA	12/9/23	414	59,761	31,673

Figure 9.26 If the second row of the criteria is blank, the result reflects all rows.

Using AND to join criteria

Many people who have used SUMIF in Excel 2003 and earlier are likely to want to know how to conditionally sum based on two conditions. This is simple to do with DSUM. If two criteria are placed on the same row of the criteria range, they are joined by an AND. In Figure 9.27, for example, the $123,275 is the sum of records in which the customer is Best Paint Inc. and the product is V937.

B1 =DSUM($A$22:$I$5023,H$22,$A$17:$I$18)

	A	B	C	D	E	F	G	H	I
1	DSUM	123,275	=DSUM($A$22:$I$5023,H$22,$A$17:$I$18)						
13									
17	Customer	Product	Region	District	Rep	Date	Qty	Revenue	Profit
18	Best Paint Inc.	V937							
19									
22	Customer	Product	Region	District	Rep	Date	Qty	Revenue	Profit
23	Wonderful Faucet Co	G854	East	Southeast	ADAM DU	2/7/23	730	76,906	41,529
24	Forceful Flagpole Co	A105	East	Southeast	ADAM DU	12/23/23	804	32,297	16,794
25	Best Paint Inc.	V937	Central	Chicago	PETER WA	12/9/23	414	59,761	31,673
26	Guarded Raft Corpor	I543	West	California	BILLY JAC	1/8/25	793	66,858	35,435

Figure 9.27 When two criteria are on the same line, they are joined by an AND function; rows must meet both criteria to be included in the DSUM.

Using OR to join criteria

When two criteria are placed on separate rows of the criteria range, they are joined by an OR function. In Figure 9.28, the $2.1 million represents records for either Improved Radio Traders or Best Paint Inc.

CHAPTER 9

B1 =DSUM($A$23:$I$5024,H$23,$A$17:$I$19)

	A	B	C	D	E	F	G	H	I
1	DSUM	2,106,524	=DSUM($A$23:$I$5024,H$23,$A$17:$I$19)						
13									
17	Customer	Product	Region	District	Rep	Date	Qty	Revenue	Profit
18	Improved Radio Traders								
19	Best Paint Inc.								
20									
23	Customer	Product	Region	District	Rep	Date	Qty	Revenue	Profit
24	Wonderful Faucet Cc	G854	East	Southeast	ADAM DU	2/3/15	730	76,906	41,529
25	Forceful Flagpole Cc	A105	East	Southeast	ADAM DU	12/19/15	804	32,297	16,794
26	Best Paint Inc.	V937	Central	Chicago	PETER WA	12/5/15	414	59,761	31,673
27	Guarded Raft Corpor	I543	West	California	BILLY JAC	1/4/17	793	66,858	35,435
28	Rare Quilt Inc.	G854	Central	Southwest	MELVIN S	3/31/17	993	104,613	47,076
29	Rare Juicer Company	H833	East	Southeast	TERRY MA	3/26/20	322	47,138	22,155
30	Improved Radio Trad	T859	West	California	BILLY JAC	12/9/16	918	61,763	33,352
31	Different Tuner Cor	C757	Central	Midwest	EVA STEV	3/7/20	821	47,363	22,734
32	Best Paint Inc.	X538	Central	Chicago	PETER WA	5/12/15	871	83,477	40,069

Figure 9.28 When two criteria are on different rows, they are joined by an OR function; rows can meet either criterion to be included in the DSUM.

You can use OR to join criteria from different fields. The criteria range in Figure 9.29 shows a `Region` value of `West` joined by an OR with a `District` value of `Texas`. This pulls a superset of all the West records plus just the Texas records, which happen to fall in the Central region.

B1 =DSUM($A$23:$I$5024,H$23,$A$17:$I$19)

	A	B	C	D	E	F	G	H	I
1	DSUM	65,724,062	=DSUM($A$23:$I$5024,H$23,$A$17:$I$19)						
13									
17	Customer	Product	Region	District	Rep	Date	Qty	Revenue	Profit
18			West						
19				Texas					
20									
23	Customer	Product	Region	District	Rep	Date	Qty	Revenue	Profit
24	Wonderful Faucet Cc	G854	East	Southeast	ADAM DU	2/7/23	730	76,906	41,529
25	Forceful Flagpole Cc	A105	East	Southeast	ADAM DU	12/23/23	804	32,297	16,794
26	Best Paint Inc.	V937	Central	Chicago	PETER WA	12/9/23	414	59,761	31,673

Figure 9.29 The criteria to be joined with OR can be in separate columns.

Using dates or numbers as criteria

The example in Figure 9.30 finds records with a date after 2024 and with revenue under $50,000. The criteria in F18 for the date could have used any of these formats:

```
>12/31/2024
```

```
>=1/1/2025
```

```
>31-Dec-2024
```

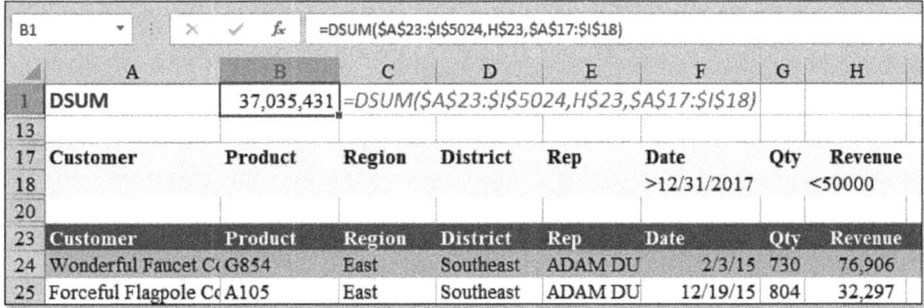

B1 =DSUM($A$23:$I$5024,H$23,$A$17:$I$18)

	A	B	C	D	E	F	G	H
1	DSUM	37,035,431	=DSUM($A$23:$I$5024,H$23,$A$17:$I$18)					
13								
17	Customer	Product	Region	District	Rep	Date	Qty	Revenue
18						>12/31/2017		<50000
20								
23	Customer	Product	Region	District	Rep	Date	Qty	Revenue
24	Wonderful Faucet C(	G854	East	Southeast	ADAM DU	2/3/15	730	76,906
25	Forceful Flagpole Cc	A105	East	Southeast	ADAM DU	12/19/15	804	32,297

Figure 9.30 Using dates or numbers in criteria.

Using the miracle version of a criteria range

Using the criteria ranges in the preceding examples, you could easily build any complex criteria with multiple AND or OR operators.

However, this could get complex. Imagine if you wanted to pull all the records for five specific customers and five specific products. You would have to build a criteria range that is 26 rows tall. Basically, the first row is the headings for customer and product. The second row indicates that you want to see records for Customer1 and Product1. The third row indicates that you want to see records for `Customer1` and `Product2`. The fourth row indicates that you want to see records for `Customer1` and `Product3`. The seventh row indicates `Customer2` and `Product1`. The 26th row indicates `Customer5` and `Product5`.

If you need to pull the records for seven customers and seven products from five districts, your criteria range would grow to 246 rows tall and would probably never finish calculating.

There is a miraculous version of the criteria range that completely avoids this problem. Here's how it works:

- The criteria range consists of a range that is two cells tall and one or more cells wide.
- Contrary to instructions in Excel Help, the top cell of the criteria range cannot contain a field heading. The top cell must be blank or contain anything that does not match the database header row. For example, you could use a heading of "Computed Criteria."
- The second row in the criteria range can contain any formula that evaluates to TRUE or FALSE. This formula must point to cells in the first data row of the database. The formula can be as complex as you want provided the formula returns TRUE or FALSE. You can combine AND, OR, VLOOKUP, NOT, MATCH, and any other functions.

For a simple example, suppose you want to find records that match one of 15 customers. You copy the customers to K24:K38. In the second row of the criteria field, write the formula **`=NOT(ISNA( MATCH(A24,$K$24:$K$38,0)))`**. This formula does a MATCH on the first customer in the database to see if it is in the list in K. The ISNA and NOT functions make sure that the criteria cell returns a TRUE when the customer is one of the 15 customers.

Very quickly and without complaint, Excel compares the 5,000 rows of your database with this complex formula, and the DSUM produces the correct value, as shown in Figure 9.31.

B1 =DSUM(A23:I5024,H23,B17:B18)

	A	B	C	D	E	F	G	H	I	J	K	L	M
1	DSUM	11,812,600	=DSUM(A23:I5024,H23,B17:B18)										
13			=NOT(ISNA(MATCH(A24,$K$24:$K$38,0)))										
17													
18		TRUE											
20													
23	Customer	Product	Region	Distric	Rep	Date	Qty	Revenue	Profit				
24	Wonderful Fau	G854	East	Southea	ADAM DU	2/7/23	730	76,906	41,529		Best Doorbell Company		
25	Forceful Flagp	A105	East	Southea	ADAM DU	12/23/23	804	32,297	16,794		Cool Shoe Corporation		
26	Best Paint Inc.	V937	Central	Chicago	PETER WA	12/9/23	414	59,761	31,673		Crisp Patio Corporation		
27	Guarded Raft (	I543	West	Califorr	BILLY JAC	1/8/25	793	66,858	35,435		Easy Banister Inc.		
28	Rare Quilt Inc.	G854	Central	Southw	MELVIN S	4/4/25	993	104,613	47,076		Enhanced Xylophone Corporation		
29	Rare Juicer Cc	H833	East	Southea	TERRY MA	3/30/28	322	47,138	22,155		Flexible Tackle Inc.		
30	Improved Radi	T859	West	Califorr	BILLY JAC	12/13/24	918	61,763	33,352		Fully Raft Corporation		
31	Different Tune	C757	Central	Midwes	EVA STEV	3/11/28	821	47,363	22,734		Fully Yardstick Corporation		
32	Best Paint Inc.	X538	Central	Chicago	PETER WA	5/16/23	871	83,477	40,069		Ideal Aquarium Supply		
33	Fascinating Wi	M489	East	Southea	ADAM DU	6/17/28	563	73,950	34,017		Leading Tripod Corporation		
34	Crisp Eggbeate	H833	East	Northea	NAOMI BA	3/8/27	315	46,113	20,751		Reliable Chopstick Corporation		
35	Different Adhe	O913	West	Califorr	JOHNNY F	2/26/25	547	22,334	10,497		Secure Electronics Corporation		
36	Rare Vise Inc.	O651	East	Midatla	BOBBIE R	11/16/26	604	70,064	32,229		Unique Bicycle Supply		
37	Rare Oven Cor	H957	Central	Southw	JENNIFER	10/7/27	437	63,138	29,675		Unique Quilt Corporation		
38	Effortless Clip	Z819	East	Northea	CAROLINE	8/7/26	703	55,642	27,821		Wonderful Faucet Corporation		

Figure 9.31 The formula version of the criteria range is rare but incredibly powerful.

Using the DGET function

The DGET function returns a single cell from a database. The problem is that this function is picky. If your criteria range matches zero records, DGET returns a #VALUE error. If your criteria range returns more than one row, DGET returns a #NUM! error.

To have DGET work, you need to write a criteria record that causes one and only one row to be evaluated as TRUE.

Syntax:

```
DGET(database,field,criteria)
```

The DGET function returns a single cell matching criteria from a data set.

Inside OUT

Microsoft Labs offer a free Fuzzy Lookup add-in for Excel.

Doing a VLOOKUP is impossible when you have names like "ABC Corp." and "ABC Incorporated" and "A B C". Back in Excel 2010, the research team at Microsoft Labs created a Fuzzy Lookup add-in for Excel. The technology was cool, but Microsoft ended up adding the functionality to SQL Server instead of to Excel.

However, the add-in still works in Excel today and is free from Microsoft Labs. Download it from *https://www.microsoft.com/en-us/download/details.aspx?id=15011*.

Set the tool to return the two best matches. In the figure below, there were two valid matches for Coca-Cola, and a human will do a better job of knowing which one is your customer.

Original Company	Matched Company	Similarity
AMAZON COM INC STK	Amazon.com Inc.	94%
MOTOROLA	Motorola Solutions, Inc.	90%
MOTOROLA	Motorola Mobility Holdings, Inc.	87%
ATT CORP	AT&T, Inc.	81%
ATT CORP	ITT Corporation	51%
BERSHIER HATHWAY	Berkshire Hathaway Inc.	91%
MICROSOFT	Microsoft Corporation	95%
COCACOLA	The Coca-Cola Company	91%
COCACOLA	Coca-Cola Enterprises Inc.	90%
DR PEPPER CORP	Dr Pepper Snapple Group, Inc.	79%
AUTO DESK INC COM STK NPV	Autodesk, Inc.	85%
MELLON BANK	The Bank of New York Mellon Corporation	87%

CHAPTER 10

Using names, LET, LAMBDA, and Data Types in Excel

Names have always played a role in Excel. You could name a range in order to create easier-to-read formulas. For instance, `=SUM(MyExpenses)` makes formulas more self-documenting than `=SUM(Sheet5!AB2:AB99)`.

But names have been chosen as the place to store a new class of powerful formulas called LAMBDA functions. You can define your own logic in a LAMBDA function, store it in the Name Manager, and then re-use that logic in the workbook.

This chapter also covers the new LET function and Data Types.

Using names in Excel

Names have a variety of uses in a workbook. A name can be applied to any cell or range. Names are also useful for the following:

- Making formulas easier to understand and write. Defined names are offered in the Formula AutoComplete drop-down menu as you start to type a formula.
- Quick navigation.
- Forcing a formula reference to remain absolute—without having to use the dollar sign.
- Doing a two-way lookup with the intersection operator.
- Storing a value that will be used repeatedly but that might occasionally need to change, such as a sales tax rate.
- Storing formulas, including the new LAMBDA functions
- Defining a dynamic range.

You have various ways to name a cell. The easiest way to define a name for a cell is to use the Name Box. To do so, select any cell in your worksheet. To the left of the Formula Bar is a box with the address of that cell. This box is known as the Name Box (see Figure 10.1). The quick way to assign a name is to click inside the Name Box and type the name, such as Revenue.

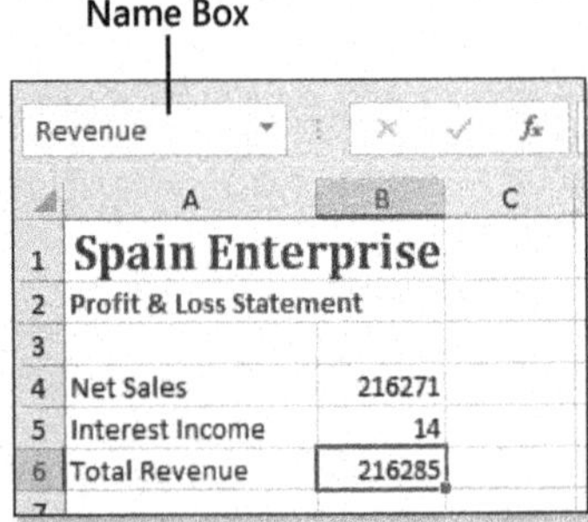

Figure 10.1 The Name Box is to the left of the Formula Bar.

When you press Enter, Excel tries to assign the name. If you get no message, the name is valid. If you get the message, "You must enter a valid reference you want to go to, or type a valid name for the selection," then the name is invalid. If you are taken to a new range, that name already exists.

> NOTE
>
> **Excel offers the Table functionality. Although the Table feature enables you to create formulas using column names, the individual column names and table names are not considered named ranges.**

The following are some basic rules for valid names:

- Names can be up to 255 characters long.
- Names can start with a letter, an underscore, or a backslash. Numbers can be used in a name, but they can't be the first character in the name.
- Names cannot contain spaces. However, you can use an underscore or a period in a name. For example, the names `Gross_Profit` and `Gross.Profit` are valid.
- Names cannot look like cell addresses. ROI2015 is already a cell address. The names R, r, C, and c cannot be used because these are the shorthand for selecting an entire row or column.
- Names cannot contain operator characters such as these:

  `+ - * / ( ) ^ & < > = %`

- Names cannot contain special characters such as these:

  `! " # $ ' , ; : @ [ ] { } ' | ~`

- Names cannot start with "c" or "r" followed by numbers and text. For example, `r82hello` or `c123test` are not valid. There is no longer a valid reason for this anomaly.

Table 10.1 provides some examples of valid and invalid names.

Table 10.1 Examples of valid and invalid names

Valid names	Invalid names (and reasons)
SalesTax	Sales Tax (includes a space)
Sales_Tax	XFD123 (valid cell address)
Sales.Tax	Tax2015 (valid cell address)
SalesTax2017	MyResults! (invalid special character)

NOTE

It is possible to have an old XLS file that might have had a name that was valid back when Excel only went to column IV—something like `TAX2025` that is now invalid because there is already a cell called `TAX2025`. If you find an old XLS file with a name like `ROI2027` and open it in Excel today, Excel will change the name to put an underscore before the name: `_TAX2025` or `_ROI2027`.

Using the Name Box for quick navigation

One advantage of using names is that you can use the drop-down menu in the Name Box to jump to any named cell or range. This includes cells that might be in distant sections of the worksheet or even on other sheets in the workbook.

If you plan to use the Name Box for navigation, assign a name to the upper-left corner of each section of your workbook. The Name Box drop-down menu then provides a mini table of contents, and people can use the Name Box to jump to any section of the workbook.

To illustrate this concept, follow these steps:

1. Click the New Sheet icon (next to the right-most sheet tab) to add a new sheet to the workbook.
2. On the new sheet, go to a distant cell. Give that cell a name, such as **SectionTwo**. Return to the original sheet in the workbook.
3. Click the Name Box's drop-down menu arrow to access a list of all names in the workbook, as shown in Figure 10.2.
4. Choose a name from the list to navigate quickly to that cell, even if it is on another worksheet.

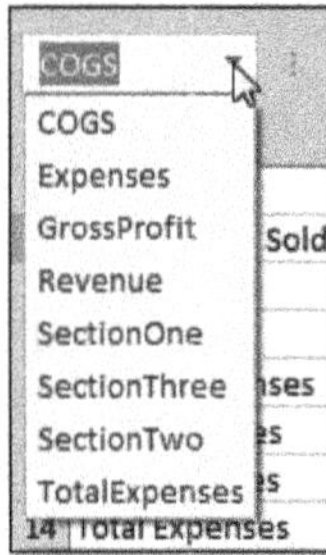

Figure 10.2 The Name Box drop-down menu contains a list of all names in the workbook.

Avoiding problems by using worksheet-level scope

Most names have a workbook-level scope. There are two specific reasons why you might want to use worksheet-level scope instead:

- You have many similar worksheets in a workbook, and you want to define the same names on each sheet. For example, you might want Revenue and COGS on each sheet from January through December. As an example, `Print_Area` and `Print_Titles` are some worksheet-level names that you've probably been using for a long time.
- You routinely copy a worksheet from one workbook, and you want to avoid having phantom names with `#REF!` errors appear in the copied sheet. Note that this problem was prevalent before Excel 2013 but has now been corrected.

Defining a worksheet-level name

To declare a name with worksheet-level scope, you can use one of these methods:

- Use Insert, Define Name. In the New Name dialog box, choose Worksheet from the Scope drop-down menu.
- Click in the Name Box and type **Jan!Rev**, as shown in Figure 10.3. If the sheet name contains a space, wrap the sheet name in apostrophes: **'Budget 2025'!Rev**.

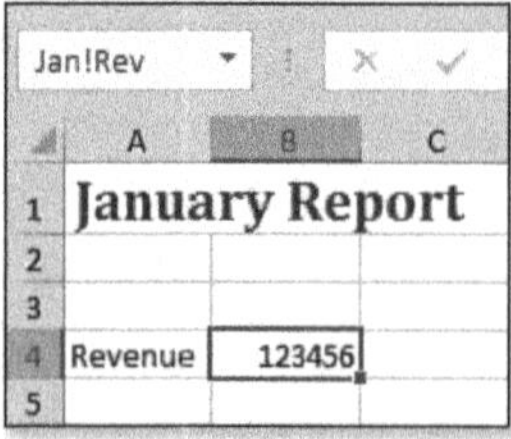

Figure 10.3 Create worksheet-level scope in the Name Box using this syntax.

- You will often inadvertently create a worksheet-level name by using a duplicate name. If you define Revenue on the January worksheet without declaring a scope, the name will have a workbook-level scope. If you then define Revenue on the February worksheet, it will automatically have a worksheet-level scope.

Referring to worksheet-level names

If you want to refer to the Rev cell on the January worksheet from anywhere else on the January worksheet, simply use `=Rev`.

If you want to refer to the Revenue cell on the January worksheet from anywhere else in the workbook, use `=Jan!Rev`.

Using named ranges to simplify formulas

As introduced at the start of this chapter, the original reason for having named ranges was to simplify formulas. In theory, it is easier to understand a formula such as `=(Revenue-COGS)/Revenue`.

Be sure to define the names before entering formulas that refer to those cells. When you create a formula using the mouse or arrow-key method, Excel automatically uses the names in the formula.

In the following example, the worksheet in Figure 10.4 has a name of `Revenue` assigned to B6 and a name of COGS assigned to B8. Rather than typing **=B6-B8** in cell B9, follow these steps to have Excel create a formula using names:

1. Select the cell where the formula should go. In this example, it is cell B9.
2. Type =.
3. Using the mouse, click the first cell in your formula. In this case, it is cell B6.
4. Type -.
5. Using the mouse, click the next cell in your formula. In this case, it is cell B8.
6. Press Enter.
7. Move the cell pointer back to the formula cell and look in the Formula Bar. You can see that Excel has built the formula `=Revenues-COGS`, as shown in Figure 10.4. This formula is self-documenting and easier to understand than `=B6-B8`.

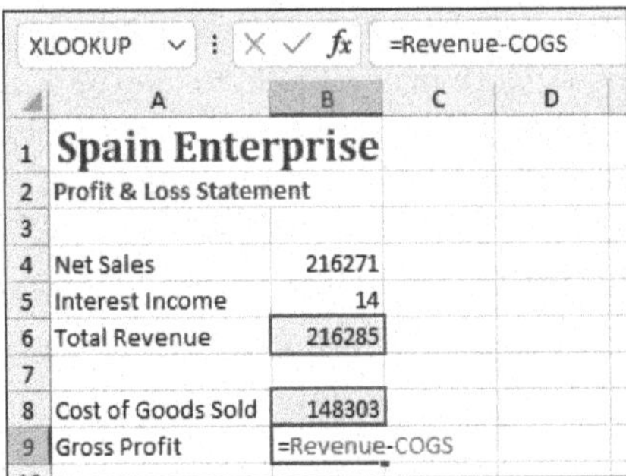

Figure 10.4 New formulas created after names have been assigned reflect the cell names in the formula.

If you prefer to type your formulas, named ranges can also be a timesaver. Say that you start to type **=R**. Excel displays a drop-down menu offering many functions that start with R, such as RADIANS, RAND, and RANDBETWEEN. Your defined name of Revenue will be in this list of 20 items.

Keep typing. After you type **E**, the list shortens to four items: RECEIVED, REPLACE, REPT, and Revenue (see Figure 10.5). As you continue typing and type **V**, the only item in the list is your defined name of Revenue. You can now press Tab to insert this named range into your formula.

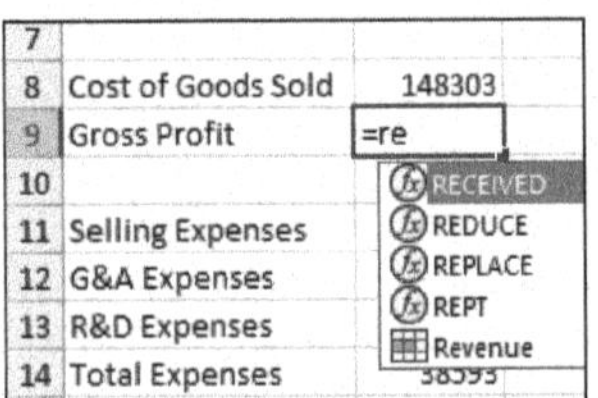

Figure 10.5 Type enough of the name to be unique, and then press Tab to insert the name in your formula.

Type the minus sign, type **COG**, and then press Tab to select COGS from the list.

Retroactively applying names to formulas

When you learn the trick that was discussed in the "Using Named Ranges to Simplify Formulas" section, you might start naming all the input cells in your workbook, hoping that all the preexisting formulas will take on the new names. Unfortunately, this does not work automatically.

To make the names become part of existing formulas, you have to use the Apply Names command. To do this, follow these steps:

1. On the Formulas tab, select the drop-down menu next to Define Name and select Apply Names. The Apply Names dialog box appears.

2. Choose as many names as you want in the Apply Names box. In this example, you should choose at least GrossProfit and TotalExpenses and then click OK. Existing formulas that point to these named cells change to include the cell names in the formula.

Adding many names at once from existing labels and headings

With Excel, you can add many names in a single command, particularly if the names exist as labels or headings adjacent to the cells.

Suppose you have a worksheet with a series of labels in column A and values in column B. One example is shown in Figure 10.6. To do a wholesale assignment of names to the cells in column B, follow these steps:

1. Select the range of labels and the cells to which they refer. In this example, that range is A4:B16.

2. Select Formulas, Defined Names, Create From Selection. Excel displays the Create Names From Selected Range dialog box.

3. Because the row labels are in the left column of the selected range, select Left Column and then click OK, as shown in Figure 10.6.

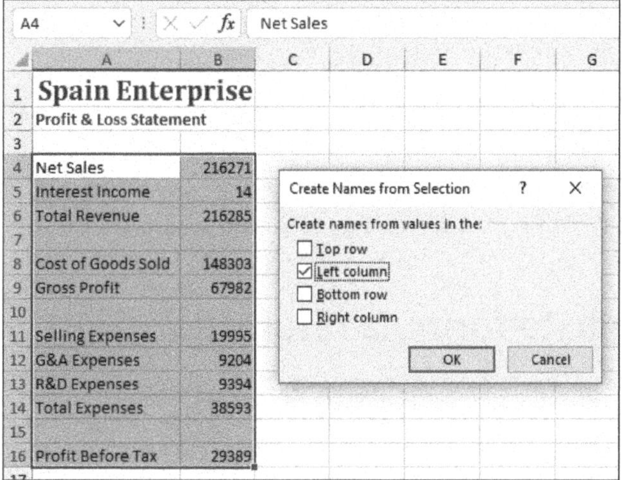

Figure 10.6 When you make this selection, Excel uses the text values in the left column to assign names to all the nonblank cells in column B of this range.

Excel does a fairly good job of assigning the names. Spaces are replaced with underscores to make the names valid. In this example, cell B4 is assigned the name Net_Sales. Cell B8 is assigned the name Cost_of_Goods_Sold. In row 12, where the label contains an ampersand (&),

Excel replaces the ampersand with an underscore, to form the name G_A_Expenses. Although this is not as meaningful as it could be if you wrote the name yourself, it is still pretty good.

Using a name to avoid an absolute reference

A common scenario is when a formula such as `VLOOKUP` is used in a data set to look up data on another worksheet. You might enter a `VLOOKUP` formula in cell B2 and copy it to hundreds of records. The formula in cell B2 might be `=VLOOKUP(A2,'Lookup Table'!A2:B25,2,FALSE)`. As you copy this formula to row 3, the reference in the second argument incorrectly changes to `'Lookup Table'!A3:B26`. When you need the reference to always point to A2:B25, you can add dollar signs to the reference: `$A$2:$B$25`.

If you will be frequently adding `VLOOKUP` formulas that will point to `'Lookup Table'!$A$2:$B$25`, it can get tedious to continually use the syntax. After all, it is a confusing mix of dollar signs, apostrophes, and exclamation points.

To simplify the `VLOOKUP` formula, give A2:B25 a name such as ItemLookup. Then, the formula simply becomes `=VLOOKUP(A2,ItemLookup,2,FALSE)`. As you copy the formula down, it continues to point to A2:B25 on the Lookup Table worksheet. Figure 10.7 compares the formula without a name in B2 and the formula with a name in B3.

B2 =VLOOKUP(A2,'Lookup Table'!$A$2:$B$25,2,FALSE)

	A	B	C	D	E	F	G
1	SKU	Title					
2	B2	Don't Fear the Spreadsheet	=VLOOKUP(A2,'Lookup Table'!$A$2:$B$25,2,FALSE)				
3	C9	VBA & Macros for Microsoft Excel 2013	=VLOOKUP(A3,ItemLookup,2,FALSE)				
4	C4	Excel Gurus Gone Wild	=VLOOKUP(A4,ItemLookup,2,FALSE)				
5	A4	Slaying Excel Dragons	=VLOOKUP(A5,ItemLookup,2,FALSE)				

Figure 10.7 The formula in B3 is easier to type because it uses a named range for the Lookup Table.

Storing intermediate formula results using LET

There are often problems in Excel where you have to calculate an intermediate result and use that intermediate result multiple times in a formula. One prior solution was to build the formula using many helper columns. With the new `LET` function, you can easily combine all of those helper formulas into a single formula without having to recalculate the intermediate results.

The syntax of `LET` starts out with pairs of arguments. In each pair, you assign a variable name and then the logic for that variable. The logic for the second variable is allowed to re-use any earlier variables.

The final argument for LET is the calculation that will be returned to the cell containing the formula.

One best practice is to write the LET function with an Alt+Enter after each pair of variables:

```
=LET(Name1,Definition_of_Name1,
Name2,Definition_of_Name2,
Name3,Definition_of_Name3,
Name4,Definition_of_Name4,
Name5,Definition_of_Name5,
Final_Calculation)
```

Here is an example of how LET can simplify a formula and make it easier to read.

I often use an example to find the last word in a cell. Here is the thought process for the formula:

- Start with a list of names in a column starting in A2.
- B2: Get rid of any extra spaces using TRIM(A2).
- C2: Get rid of all spaces by substituting spaces (" ") with "".
- D2: Find the length of B2.
- E2: Find the length of C2.
- F2: Now that you know the length of the name with spaces and the length of the name without spaces, subtract those two values. This tells you how many spaces are in the name in B2.
- G2: There is a feature of SUBSTITUTE that can change the Nth occurrence of a character. Change the Nth space in B2 to a character that won't likely be in the name, such as an exclamation point.
- H2: Find the location of the exclamation point in G2.
- I2: The last word in B2 starts one space after the character location in H2. Use MID to start at that location. For the length of the last word, use D2-H2.

Figure 10.8 shows the calculation in eight columns.

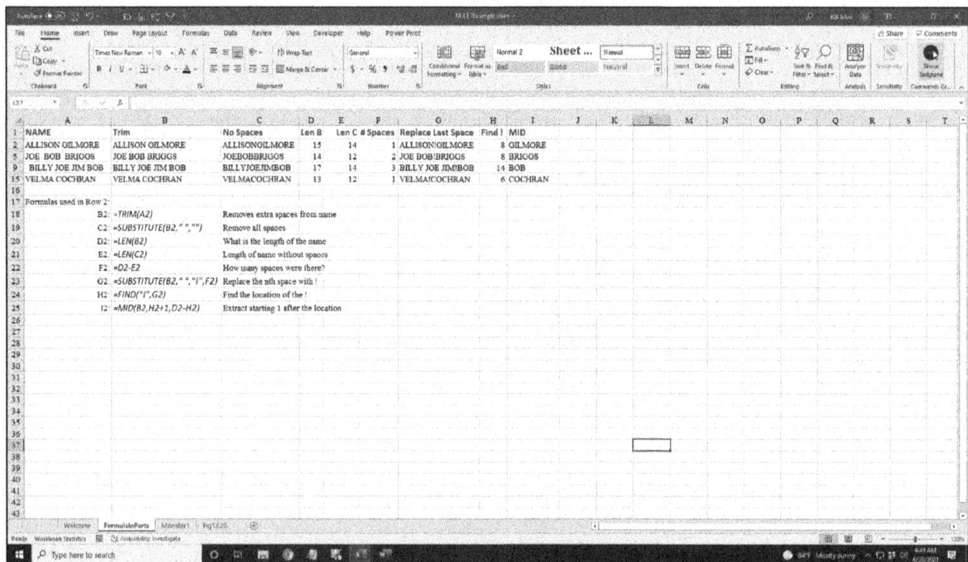

Figure 10.8 A series of eight formulas find the last word in A2.

The logic to find the last word works fine, but you eventually want to combine all of those calculations into a single formula in column B. But this ends up being harder that you would think. Quickly look through the formulas shown in B18:B25 in Figure 10.8. How many times is B2 mentioned in the subsequent formulas? A quick count shows that B2 is used four times. But it is actually used more than that. The formula in G2 refers to F2. The F2 formula refers to B2. After combining all the formulas into one formula, you end up calculating the `TRIM(A2)` a total of eight times, as shown in Figure 10.9.

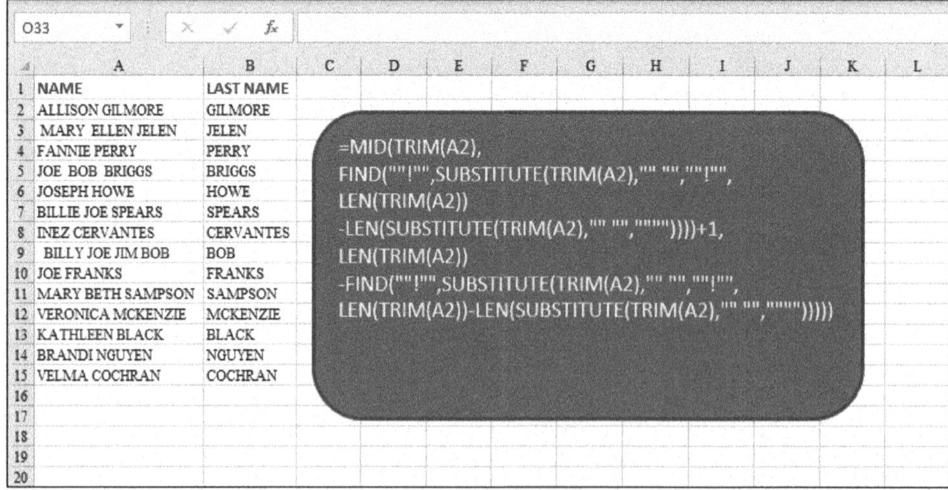

Figure 10.9 When you combine all eight formulas into a single formula, you end up referring to `TRIM(A2)` eight times.

Besides making the formula hard to read, the Excel calculation engine has to calculate `TRIM(A2)` eight times for each name instead of one time.

The `LET` function makes this simpler. Here is the logic in English:

- Have a variable called `OrigText` and store the `TRIM(A2)` in it.
- Remove the spaces from `OrigText` and store that in a variable called `NoSpaces`.
- Store the length of `OrigText` in `LengthA`.
- Store the length of `NoSpaces` in `LengthB`.
- Subtract `LengthB` from `LengthA` to find how many spaces were in the name. Store that in `SpaceCount`.
- Use `SUBSTITUTE` to change one particular space in the name to an exclamation point. Change the Nth space where `n` is stored in `SpaceCount`. This gets stored in a variable called `ReplaceLastSpace`.
- Find the location of the exclamation point. Store that location in `LastWordStart`.
- Finally, the calculation that gets returned to the cell uses `MID` to start after the last space and goes to the end of the value in A2.

Here is that logic written in the `LET` function in Figure 10.10:

```
=LET(OrigText,TRIM(A2),
NoSpaces,SUBSTITUTE(OrigText," ",""),
LengthA,LEN(OrigText),
LengthB,LEN(NoSpaces),
SpaceCount,LengthA-LengthB,
ReplaceLastSpace,SUBSTITUTE(OrigText," ","!",SpaceCount),
LastWordStart,FIND("!",ReplaceLastSpace)+1,
MID(OrigText,LastWordStart,LengthA-LastWordStart+1))
```

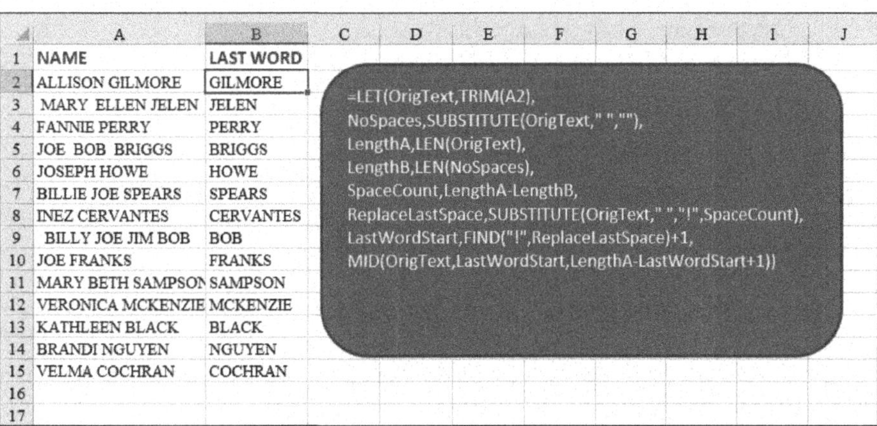

Figure 10.10 The `LET` function is long, but with meaningful variable names, it should be somewhat easier to follow.

There is nothing to say that you must use meaningful variable names and use Alt+Enter after each variable definition. The following formula includes the same logic on the previous page.

```
=LET(T,TRIM(A2),N,SUBSTITUTE(T," ",""),A,LEN(T),B,LEN(N),C,A-B,R,SUBSTITUTE(T,"
","!",C),S,FIND("!",R)+1,MID(T,S,A-S+1))
```

There are many advantages to using LET. First, rather than calculating TRIM(A2) eight different times, the TRIM can be calculated once and used repeatedly. Second, the formula is somewhat self-documenting.

I have a YouTube channel with more than 2,200 Excel videos. I get a fair number of Excel questions sent in, and about once a month, I get a question that requires one of these formulas that reuses intermediate results. The LET function can be applied to a wide variety of problems.

Storing logic in LAMBDA functions

Excel has more than 500 calculation functions. There are a few functions directed as specific industries, such as bond traders, engineers, and bankers. But every industry has specialized calculations that are not already in Excel. The LAMBDA function allows you to encapsulate the logic in a name and then re-use that name throughout your workbook.

> NOTE
>
> **There is some interesting history behind the LAMBDA name. You might have heard of the British mathemetician Alan Turing (1912-1954). In the year 1936, Turing proposed a machine that could perform any computational algorithm using an infinitely long loop of tape. This became known as a Turing Machine.**
>
> **Turing's Doctoral advisor was another mathemetician named Alonzo Church (1903-1995). Church was the inventor of a method of defining functions called Lambda Calculus, which became a foundation for modern computing. Church and Turing published the Church-Turing thesis to define what computations are calculable. A computer is said to be "Turing Complete" if it can calculate any compuation that could be solved with a Turing Machine.**

The LAMBDA functions will not be in Excel 2021. They were released to the beta channel of Office 365 in late 2020 and expanded to the Monthly channel in July of 2021.

While people rushed to embrace the LAMBDA functions and discovered how you could use a loop or branching inside of a LAMBDA, there are currently several limitations. Microsoft wants to address those before rolling the feature out widely. In particular:

- Currently, the LAMBDA definition is stored in a name in Excel. The current Define Name dialog box is tiny and not suitable for editing long formulas. With the July 2021 update, LAMBDA functions can now be used inside of several new functions: SCAN, MAKEARRAY, BYROW, BYCOL, REDUCE, and MAP.

- AutoComplete and automatic parentheses are not working for LAMBDA.
- There is a very shallow recursion limit of about 128 times that a LAMBDA can call itself. Microsoft made a big deal on their Twitter account of saying that Excel was now Turing Complete with the addition of LAMBDA. But that isn't really true. Anything that can be solved within 128 calls could have easily been solved previously using 128 rows in Excel. Excel is going to have to improve on the recursion limit.

With the July 2021 update to LAMBDA, Microsoft added support for optional arguments and introduced the ISOMITTED function so the logic inside of the LAMBDA can test whether an argument is missing.

Creating a simple LAMBDA function for the hypotenuse of a right triangle

Here is a simple example that shows how logic can be stored in a LAMBDA function and re-used. About 2,600 years ago, a Greek mathemetician named Pythagoras of Samos figured out the formula to calculate the hypotenuse of a right triangle. If the two legs of the triangle are measured as A and B, then the length of the hypotenuse C is calculated as `SQRT(A^2+B^2)`.

If you frequently had to do this calculation for the hypotenuse, it might be easier to write `=HYP(A,B)`.

In the past, you could easily do this using some VBA code and a user-defined function. But Microsoft says that VBA will never be coming to Excel Online. And Microsoft believes their fastest growing customer segment is people who use Excel Online. So, they need a way to define custom functions without VBA.

Currently, the definition for HYP using LAMBDA should be stored in the Name Manager. But for testing, you can store the LAMBDA function in a cell.

The LAMBDA function takes a series of parameters. The final argument in the LAMBDA uses those parameters to perform the calculation.

Note that you are allowed to use the LET function in the calculation portion of the LAMBDA.

Your goal is to have a HYP function that takes arguments A and B. The function should calculate the hypoteneuse of a right triangle with legs that have a length of A & B.

Start your formula with `=LAMBDA(A,B,`.

The calculation argument will be `SQRT(A^2+B^2)`.

Thus, the complete LAMBDA formula is `=LAMBDA(A,B,SQRT(A^2+B^2))`.

> NOTE
>
> **A and B are variable names. They don't have to be a single letter. You could use** `=LAMBDA(Length_Of_Side_A,Length_Of_Side_B,`.

For testing purposes, you can enter the LAMBDA function in the grid, followed by the parameters in parentheses. For example: `=LAMBDA(A,B,SQRT(A^2+B^2))(3,4)` will return 5.

Instead of hard-coding the parameters, you can point to cells, as shown in Figure 10.11.

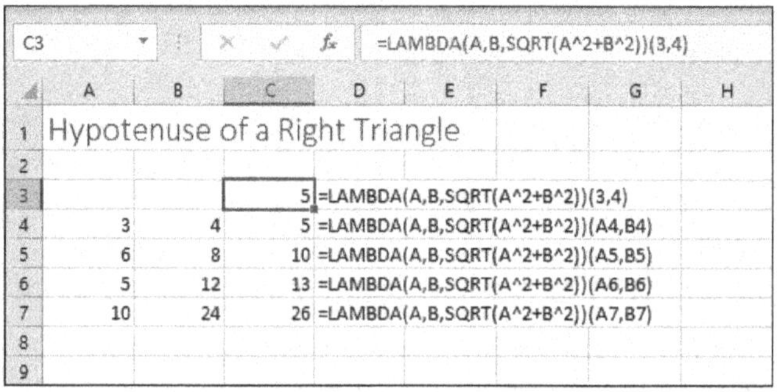

C3 =LAMBDA(A,B,SQRT(A^2+B^2))(3,4)

	A	B	C	D	E	F	G	H
1	Hypotenuse of a Right Triangle							
2								
3			5	=LAMBDA(A,B,SQRT(A^2+B^2))(3,4)				
4	3	4	5	=LAMBDA(A,B,SQRT(A^2+B^2))(A4,B4)				
5	6	8	10	=LAMBDA(A,B,SQRT(A^2+B^2))(A5,B5)				
6	5	12	13	=LAMBDA(A,B,SQRT(A^2+B^2))(A6,B6)				
7	10	24	26	=LAMBDA(A,B,SQRT(A^2+B^2))(A7,B7)				
8								
9								

Figure 10.11 During development of a LAMBDA, you can test it in the grid.

Once you are sure the LAMBDA logic is working in the grid, you can define the LAMBDA in the Name Manager:

1. The easiest way to start is to edit the formula in C3 from Figure 10.11. Copy the formula logic but not the parentheses and values.
2. On the Formulas tab, choose Define Name.
3. In the New Name dialog box, give your LAMBDA a name. In Figure 10.12, you are using HYP as the function name.
4. In the Refers To box, paste the formula that you copied in step 1.
5. Click OK to define the name.
6. In the Excel grid, you can enter **=HYP(3,4) or =HYP(A4,B4)**. The HYP function will work anywhere in this workbook.

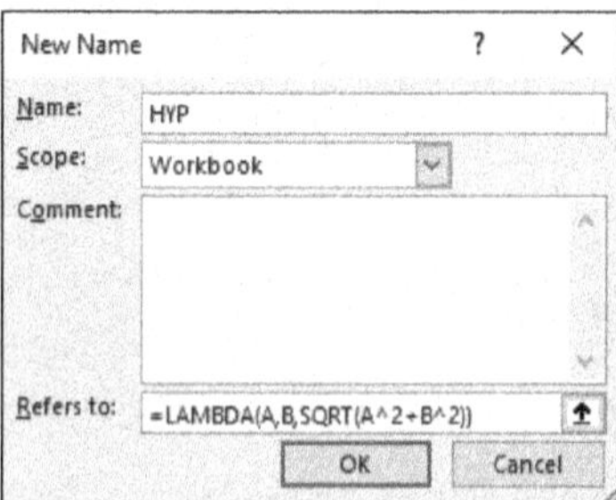

Figure 10.12 Define the LAMBDA as a name.

Figure 10.13 shows the HYP function working in the grid.

1	Hypotenuse of a Right Triangle			
2				
3			5	=HYP(3,4)
4	3	4	5	=HYP(A4,B4)
5	6	8	10	=HYP(A5,B5)
6	5	12	13	=HYP(A6,B6)
7	10	24	26	=HYP(A7,B7)
8				
9				

Figure 10.13 Once the LAMBDA is assigned to the name HYP, you can use =HYP anywhere in the workbook.

Sharing LAMBDA functions with other workbooks

Defined names will move to a new workbook if you copy a worksheet to that workbook. Say that you have developed a dozen useful LAMBDA functions and they are all stored in Workbook 1. You would like to copy those functions to Workbook 2. Follow these steps:

CHAPTER 10

1. Open Workbook 1 and Workbook 2.
2. Insert a blank worksheet in Workbook 1.
3. Right-click the Sheet tab and choose Move or Copy.
4. Choose Create A Copy. Open the To Book drop-down menu and choose Workbook 2.
5. Click OK. The blank sheet is copied to Workbook 2, but all of the defined names also are copied to the new workbook.

Inside OUT

Using a loop in a LAMBDA

One advanced technique with a LAMBDA function is to call itself recursively in order to loop through all characters in a cell.

The Slugify function is used to change an article title to a friendly URL. The title is converted to lowercase. Letters and numbers are kept, but anything is replaced with a dash. In the final answer, any consecutive dashes are converted to a single dash.

The logic inside this formula says:

- **The parameter i stores which character is being examined.**
- **Code the CODE of the LOWER of that character.**
- **If the code is between 48 to 57 or 97 to 122, keep the character. Otherwise, use a dash instead.**

You start out by calling =SLUGIFY(A2,1).

The 1 in the formula is telling the LAMBDA function that you want to start looking at character number 1.

There is a bunch of normal Excel logic to check the code of that character and to update the phrase.

The last part of the loop will call the same function again, this time with the new phrase and an i value of i+1.

The IF at the beginning of the function checks to see if i is less than the length of the phrase. When the function has checked and fixed all characters, the final logic of using SUBSTITUTE and TRIM gets rid of multiple dashes in a row.

Slugify is defined as:

```
=LAMBDA(phrase,i,
    IF(i <= LEN(phrase),
        Slugify(
            LET(
                char, LOWER(MID(phrase, i, 1)),
                charcode, CODE(char),
                LEFT(phrase, i - 1) &
                IF(OR(AND(charcode > 96, charcode < 123),
                    AND(charcode > 47, charcode < 58)), char, "-")
                    & RIGHT(phrase, LEN(phrase) - i) ),
                i + 1),
      SUBSTITUTE(TRIM(SUBSTITUTE(phrase, "-", " "))," ","-")))
```

This concept of using a loop inside of a LAMBDA function is fairly advanced, but it allows you to create more advanced logic.

Note that there is a limit in how many times one function can call itself. In the first version of LAMBDA, the limit was 127 times. Microsoft is hoping to improve this.

Note that it will be particularly difficult to debug and test loops in LAMBDA functions. The technique of entering the LAMBDA in the grid (refer back to Figure 10.11) won't work when a LAMBDA is calling itself.

The LAMBDA functionality described in this section is based on the second beta of the feature. The Excel team is working diligently to improve the experience. By the time you read this, there might be a better formula editor or a different way to store LAMBDA formulas and possibly a way to share LAMBDAs with coworkers.

Using LAMBDA helper functions

In July 2021, the Excel team released new functions to expand the usefulness of the LAMBDA function. Each of these functions uses a LAMBDA function as the final argument to the function. This avoids the awkwardness of storing the LAMBDA in the Name Manager.

Performing calculations for each row or column

The BYROW and BYCOL functions allow a LAMBDA to operate on each row or each column of a range. Each function accepts a range and then a LAMBDA function with the logic to perform.

In Figure 10.14, you have a rectangular range in A6:D10. You want to find the maximum value in each column. A single dynamic array formula in A13 performs the calculation:

```
=BYCOL(A6:D10,LAMBDA(array,MAX(array))).
```

In this formula, A6:D10 is the range to evaluate. Inside of the LAMBDA, the first argument is a variable name to refer to the range. You can call this "array" or "a," or "range" or any name. After the variable name is the logic to be performed on a column-by-column basis. In this case, MAX(array).

A slightly more complicated example appears in F6. In this case, a BYROW evaluates each row in the array and returns the second largest value using the LARGE function.

F6 =BYROW(A6:D10,LAMBDA(array,LARGE(array,2)))

	A	B	C	D	E	F
1	New LAMBDA helper functions					
2						
3	=BYCOL(array,LAMBDA(accumlator,value))					
4	=BYROW(array,LAMBDA(accumlator,value))					2nd Largest
5						each row
6	11	89	48	26		48
7	92	83	32	221		92
8	62	4	77	61		62
9	777	39	24	43		43
10	57	30	50	86		57
11						
12	Max Each Column					
13	777	89	77	221		
14	*A13: =BYCOL(A6:D10,LAMBDA(array,MAX(array)))*					
15	*F6: =BYROW(A6:D10,LAMBDA(array,LARGE(array,2)))*					

Figure 10.14 These functions allow you to perform a calculation for each row or column in a range.

Performing calculations for each item in an array

MAP, REDUCE, and SCAN are similar functions. Each repeats a LAMBDA calculation for each cell in an array. The MAP function returns an array that is the same size as the incoming array. The REDUCE function performs a calculation on each cell and accumulates the results to a single value. SCAN works like REDUCE, but shows you the intermediate results at each point in the calculation.

All three examples for MAP, REDUCE, and SCAN are calculating a mythical PRODUCTIF function. There currently is not a PRODUCTIF function, but these new helper array functions show you how to multiply all values where the name is Andy.

The MAP function can accept multiple arrays. This makes it much easier to use than SCAN or REDUCE, which can only accept a single array.

In Figure 10.15, the MAP function starts by specifying an array of names in A2:A24, then a second array of values in B2:B24.

You then add a LAMBDA as the last argument of MAP. Because this MAP function is accepting two arrays, the LAMBDA function has to start with two variable names—one for each array. The final argument in the LAMBDA is the logic to be calculated for each cell in the array.

To do a PRODUCTIF equivalent, the logic says that if column A contains Andy, then use the corresponding value from column B. Otherwise, use a 1. In Column D of the figure, you will see the results of the MAP function. In real life, you would not need to show those intermediate results; you could wrap the MAP function in the PRODUCT function as shown in F19.

One important distinction: The MAP function is accepting an array of cells, not just the values in those cells. For cell A3, you can see that the value is Andy, but you could also ask for the ROW(A) or COLUMN(A) or if column A contained a Data Type, something like A.[place of birth].

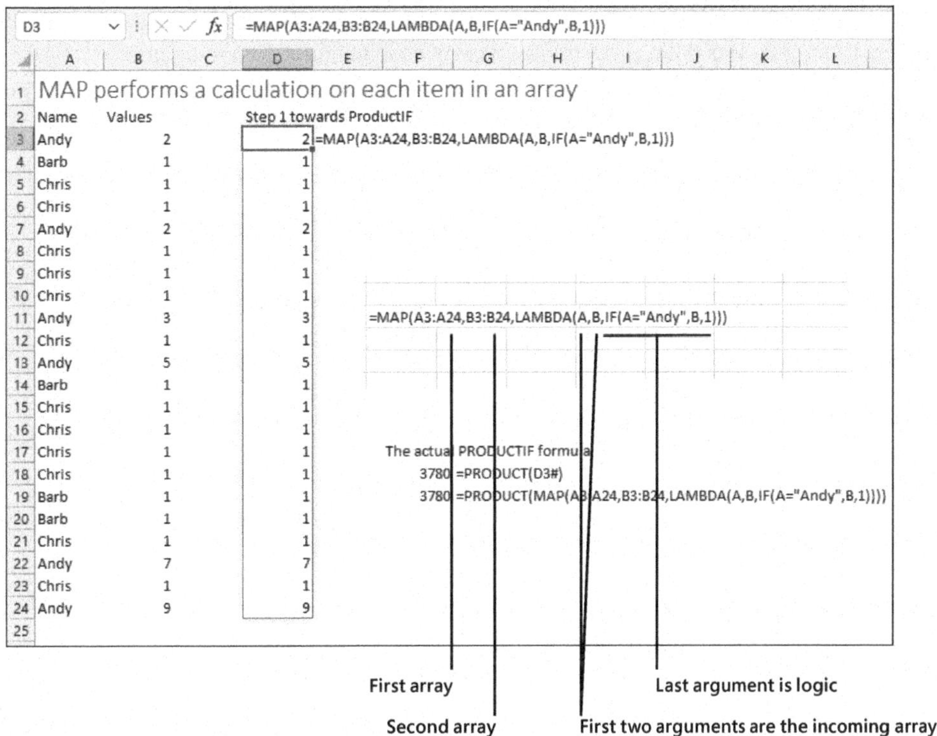

Figure 10.15 MAP performs a LAMBDA calculation for each cell in an array.

Performing calculations for each item in an array and returning a single value

Continuing the example of how to perform a mythical PRODUCTIF, you don't really need to return all 23 cells to Excel. The REDUCE function will perform a calculation for each cell and accumulate the results into a single value that is returned to the grid.

Here is the logic in English: You are going to calculate a value called Total. For each cell in A2:A24, determine whether the name is Andy. If the name is Andy, then multiply the existing Total by the value to the right of Andy. If it is not Andy, then don't change the Total.

In order for that logic to work, you need to make sure that Total starts out with a value of 1.

In Figure 10.16, the logic would start with a Total of 1. It looks at cell A4. Since A4 is Andy, then Total becomes Total times the 2 in B4. The function then looks at Barb in A5. Because this is not Andy, the current value of Total gets passed on to the next cell. The Total value does not change again until you encounter another Andy in A8. Then Total becomes Total times 2 or 4. After processing all the cells in the array, you end up with a final answer of 3780.

Again, this only works if you can initialize the Total variable to be 1 at the start of the REDUCE function. The REDUCE function starts with an initial value for the accumulator. Then you pass it a single array. It is not as cool as MAP, which can accept multiple arrays. You can only pass a single array to REDUCE.

Next is the LAMBDA, which starts with a variable to hold the accumulator and is followed by a variable for the incoming array and then the logic to apply to each cell.

Back in the previous example, you had names stored in the A variable and values stored in the B variable. With the limitation of just one array, that A variable holds the names, and then the formula uses OFFSET to get the value to the right of the name.

The formula in D6 is as follows:

```
=REDUCE(1,B4:B25,LAMBDA(Total,B,IF(OFFSET(B,0,-1,1,1)="Andy",Total*B,Total)))
```


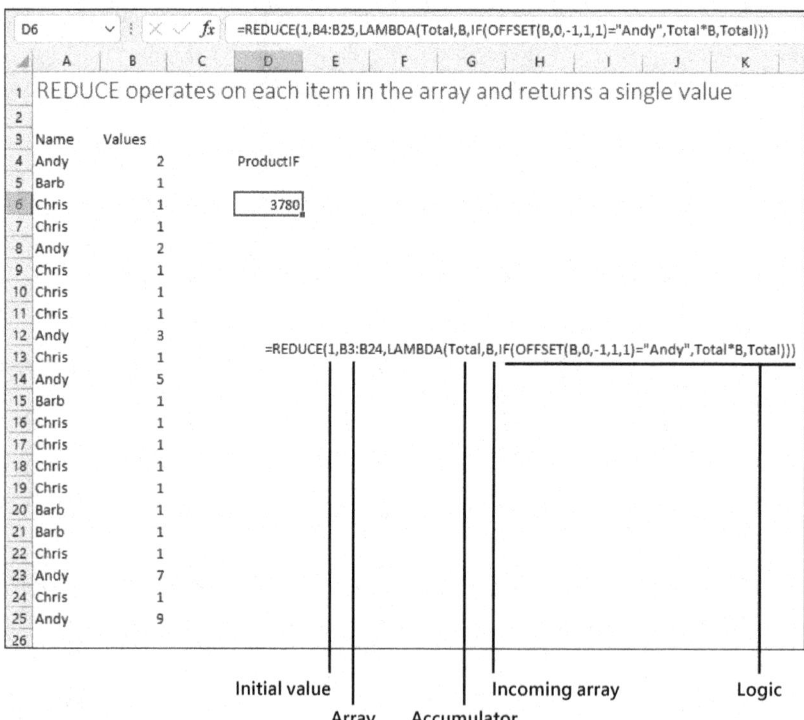

Figure 10.16 REDUCE will perform a calculation on each cell in an array and return a single accumulated value.

Performing calculations for each item in an array and returning each intermediate value

The SCAN function is identical to REDUCE, but it shows you the value of the accumulator after each step. Figure 10.17 is working toward a PRODUCTIF and eventually gets to the 3780 in cell C26, but the other cells in C5:C25 show the value of the accumulator after each step of the calculation.

A single formula in C5 is as follows:

```
=SCAN(1,A5:A26,LAMBDA(Total,A,IF(A="Andy",Total*OFFSET(A,0,1,1,1),Total)))
```

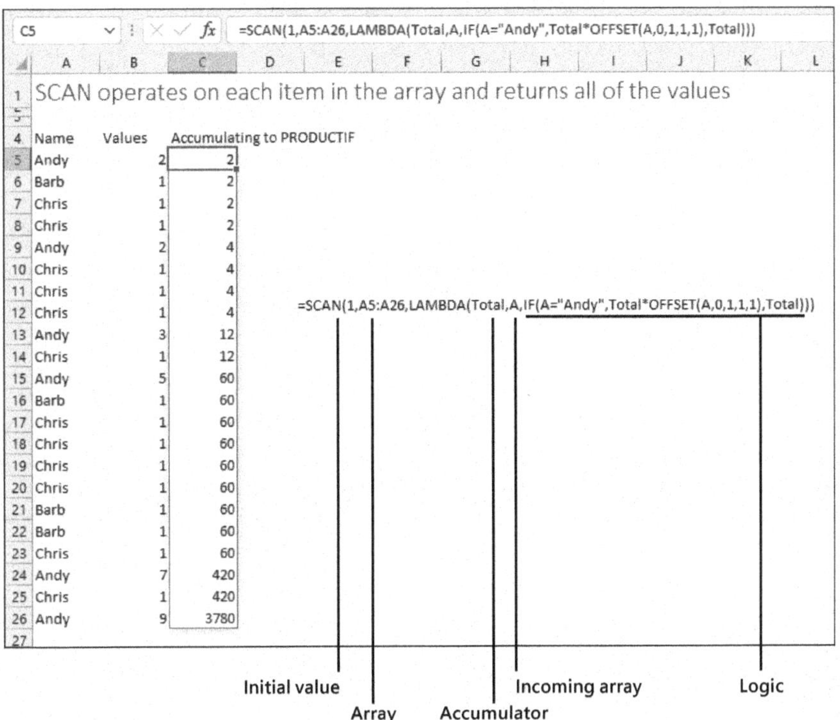

Name	Values	Accumulating to PRODUCTIF
Andy	2	2
Barb	1	2
Chris	1	2
Chris	1	2
Andy	2	4
Chris	1	4
Chris	1	4
Chris	1	4
Andy	3	12
Chris	1	12
Andy	5	60
Barb	1	60
Chris	1	60
Chris	1	60
Chris	1	60
Chris	1	60
Barb	1	60
Barb	1	60
Chris	1	60
Andy	7	420
Chris	1	420
Andy	9	3780

Figure 10.17 SCAN reveals the interim steps of the calculation.

Making an array using MAKEARRAY

You can generate an array using MAKEARRAY. The three arguments are how many rows, how many columns, and a LAMBDA for calculating each cell in the array.

The LAMBDA has three argument: a variable for which row, a variable for which column, and the logic to calculate that cell in the array.

Figure 10.18 shows a very simple example. Based on the 5 in B2 and the 4 in B3, MAKEARRAY will generate a 5-row by 4-column array. The LAMBDA inside MAKEARRAY uses the variable r for the row number and the variable c for the column number. Each cell in the resulting array is two times the row number divided by the column.

B5 =MAKEARRAY(B2,B3,LAMBDA(r,c,2*r/c))

	A	B	C	D	E	F	G
1	=MAKEARRAY(rows,columns,function)						
2	Rows:	5					
3	Columns	4					
4							
5		2	1	0.666667	0.5		
6		4	2	1.333333	1		
7		6	3	2	1.5		
8		8	4	2.666667	2		
9		10	5	3.333333	2.5		
10							

Figure 10.18 Generate an array of any size with a custom calculation for each point in the array.

Figure 10.19 shows a far more complex use of MAKEARRAY. The UNIQUE function in Excel operates on a row-by-row basis. What if you want the unique values from each cell, not from each row of the array? In this case, you need to unwind the rectangular array into a very tall, one-column-wide array.

I've covered this topic twice on my YouTube channel—once before MAKEARRAY and once after. For a complete explanation of this formula, search YouTube for "UNIQUE of Rectangular Range Using MAKEARRAY in Excel – 2416."

F3 =SORT(UNIQUE(LET(array,B3:D10,

	A	B	C	D	E	F
1	MAKEARRAY to Unwind to a Single Column To Pass to UNIQUE					
2		Jan	Feb	Mar		
3	Andy	Orange	Banana	Zucchini		Banana
4	Barb	Guava	Lime	Quince		Fig
5	Chris	Vanilla	Mango	Plum		Guava
6	Diane	Raspberry	Plum	Quince		Lime
7	Ed	Fig	Ugli fruit	Ugli fruit		Mango
8	Flo	Zucchini	Tangerine	Tangerine		Nectarine
9	Gary	Orange	Nectarine	Watermelon		Orange
10	Hank	Xigua	Vanilla	Guava		Plum
11						Quince
12						Raspberry
13						Tangerine
14						Ugli fruit
15						Vanilla
16						Watermelon
17						Xigua
18						Zucchini
19						

```
=SORT(UNIQUE(
LET(array,B3:D10,
rowcount,ROWS(array),
colcount,COLUMNS(array),
itemcount,rowcount*colcount,
MAKEARRAY(itemcount,1,
LAMBDA(r,c,
INDEX(array,
LET(a,MOD(r,rowcount),IF(a=0,rowcount,a)),
ROUNDUP(r/rowcount,0))
)))))
```

Figure 10.19 This long formula uses MAKEARRAY to generate a tall column of values found in the original rectangular range.

Testing for optional arguments using `ISOMITTED`

Starting in July 2021, a `LAMBDA` definition can allow for optional arguments. The optional arguments have to be listed last and wrapped in parentheses. In this formula, `=LAMBDA(A,B,[C],Logic...)`, the C argument is optional.

As part of the logic of the `LAMBDA`, you might need to check to see if C is present or not. Use `ISOMITTED(C)` to test whether the formula passed a value for C.

Using Data Types in Excel

Microsoft debuted linked Data Types in 2018. They first offered Stocks, Geography, and then Currency. In 2021, they added a collection of data from Wolfram that includes movies, songs, locations, structures, space, food, and more.

Enter a list of states, cities, or countries in some cells. Select those cells and choose Geography from the Data Types gallery on the Data tab. As shown in Figure 10.20, a map icon appears next to each value to tell you that the cells contain a Geography Data Type.

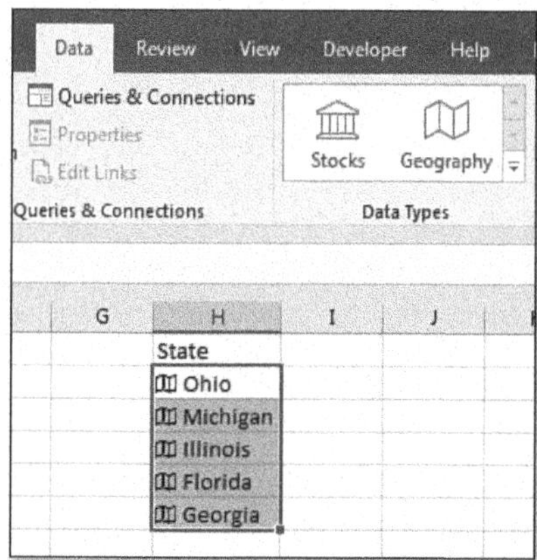

Figure 10.20 Mark cells as the Geography Data Type.

If you click the map icon for a cell, a data card appears with information from Wikipedia about the state listed in the cell.

However, the more interesting feature is the new formulas that can point to the linked cell. In this example, Ohio is in H2. Go to any cell and type **=H2** followed by a period. A list of fields appears, as shown in Figure 10.21. You can choose any of these fields to retrieve information about the geography. For example, `=H2.Capital` or `=H2.Population`. If the field name contains a space, wrap the name in square brackets: `=H2.[Building Permits]`.

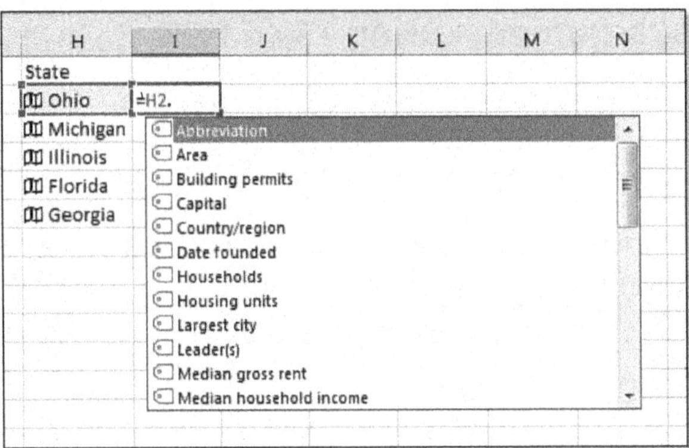

Figure 10.21 Build a formula to return a property of the state.

After entering the formula for the first state, you can copy the formula to pull similar data for each state. Figure 10.22 shows the largest city in each state. Each answer is also a Geography Data Type. You can use `=I2.Population` to get the population of Columbus, Ohio. Or, you can get the population for Columbus, Ohio by using `=H2.[Largest city].Population`.

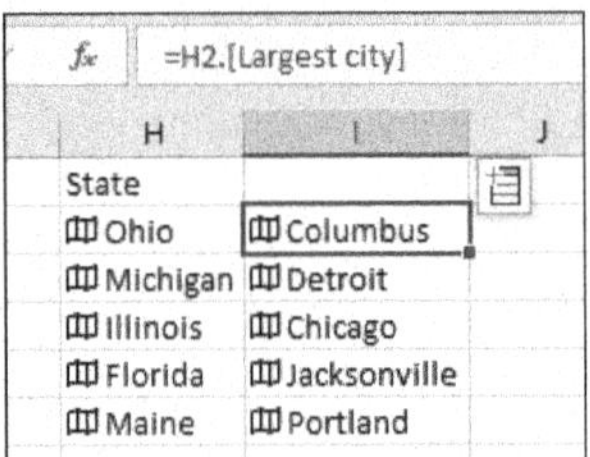

Figure 10.22 Once you've entered a formula, copy it down to other states.

If you type a different state name in a cell, the formulas will update. In Figure 10.23, Hawaii replaced Illinois. In a second or so, Chicago is replaced with Honolulu.

What if you mistype a name? You will see a brand-new error value called `#FIELD!`.

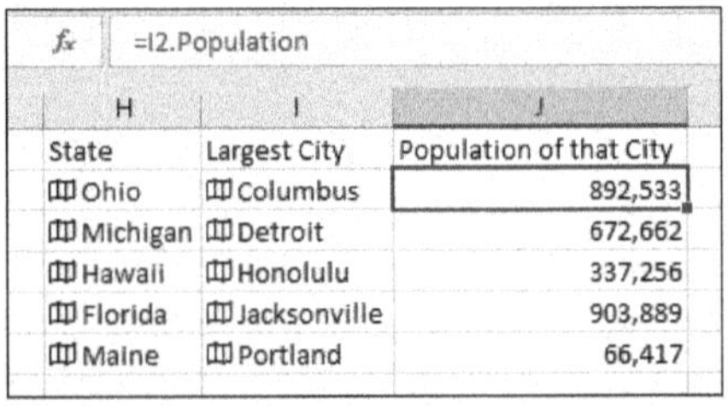

fx =I2.Population

State	Largest City	Population of that City
Ohio	Columbus	892,533
Michigan	Detroit	672,662
Hawaii	Honolulu	337,256
Florida	Jacksonville	903,889
Maine	Portland	66,417

Figure 10.23 Change a state name and the calculated fields update.

Your computer will have to be connected to the Internet to retrieve fields associated with linked Data Types.

While the Geography, Stocks, and Currency Data Types should be available to any Microsoft 365 subscriber, the Wolfram Data Types require your I.T. department to opt in. If you don't have the Wolfram Data Type, check with your I.T. department.

TROUBLESHOOTING

Data Types won't work with custom lists.

My computer always includes a custom list with the U.S. states from Alabama to Wyoming. This allows me to type **Alabama** and drag the fill handle to get the other state names. You must be careful to drag the states before marking Alabama as a Geography type. Once the cell is marked as Geography, the fill handle will not fill from custom lists.

If you try to create a new custom list that contains Data Types, Excel says that cells without simple text are ignored.

Dealing with Data Type formulas that return an array

The new Wolfram Data Types offer several fields that return an array of data. For example, if you mark some cities using the Location type, you can ask for a list of notable people born in the city.

If you want all of the answers to come back to a single cell, Excel will wrap the answers in the ARRAYTOTEXT function. This function will wrap all of the answers into a single cell with commas in between. Cells B2:B4 in Figure 10.24 use ARRAYTOTEXT.

Alternatively, if you are looking for people born in a single city, you can leave off the ARRAYTOTEXT and Excel will spill the results into a column. In Figure 10.24, cell B6 uses `=A6.[notable people born in city]`. Cell C6 gets the date of birth for all of the people using `=B6#.[date of birth]`, and cell D6 gets the occupation for all of the people using `=B6#.occupation`.

B2 | =ARRAYTOTEXT(A2.[notable people born in city])

	A	B	C	D
1	Location	Notable People Born in City		
2	Chicago	Robin Williams, Hillary Clinton, Walt Disney, Harrison Ford, C		
3	Memphis	Megan Fox, Justin Timberlake, Morgan Freeman, Michael Oh		
4	New Orleans	Lil Wayne, Peyton Manning, Reese Witherspoon, Tyler Perry,		
5				
6	Chicago	Robin Williams	7/21/1951	comedian
7		Hillary Clinton	10/26/1947	politician
8		Walt Disney	12/5/1901	businessperson
9		Harrison Ford	7/13/1942	actor
10		CM Punk	10/26/1978	wrestler

Figure 10.24 With Data Types possibly returning an array, you can choose to have the array spill or to use ARRAYTOTEXT.

Drilling down through the data card to find an array

Each cell that contains a Data Type has an icon to the left of the value. Click the icon to display a data card. With the introduction of Wolfram Data Types, the cards have been improved. You can use the three dots in the lower-right corner of a card to drag the card to a larger size.

Figure 10.25 shows a location data card for Chicago. Click the building icon to open the card. When you expand the Weather category, there is a single item called weather for Chicago. To the right is the Insert Data icon. Instead of clicking that icon, click on the weather icon to the left to drill down.

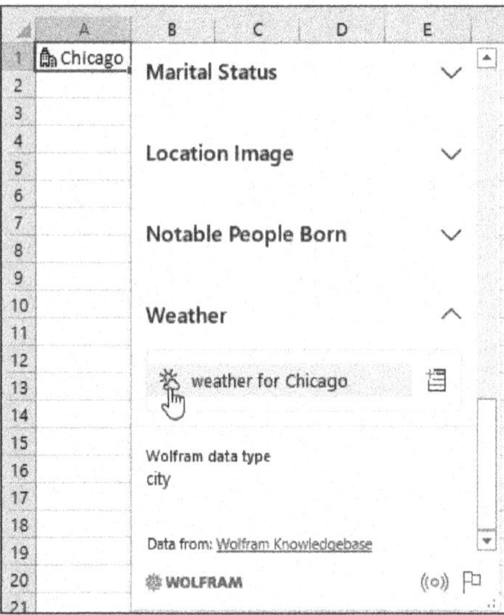

Figure 10.25 Use the icon to the left to drill down.

After clicking the icon to the left of Weather For Chicago, you are given a new card with a single item: Weather History For Chicago. Again, click the icon to the left to drill down.

After drilling down twice, you finally reveal three arrays of weather data: daily, weekly, or monthly weather history. Now you can use the Insert Data icon to the right of the table (see Figure 10.26).

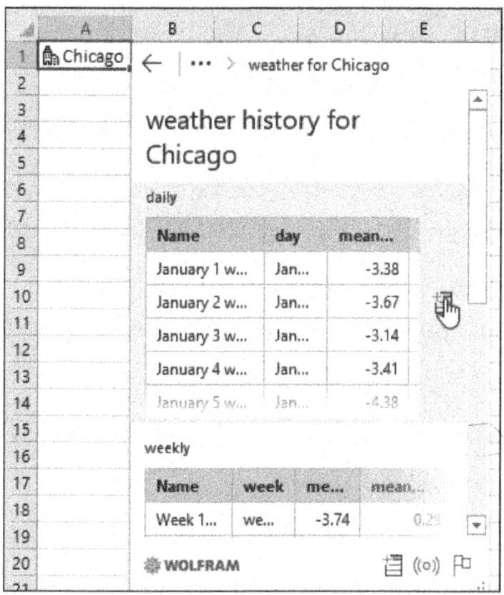

Figure 10.26 Drill down until you find the array of data; then use the Insert Data icon.

After using the Insert Data icon, a single formula in B1 spills 366 answers. =`A1.weather.history`.daily returns 366 cells that each contain a Data Type.

If you enter =`B1.[mean maximum temperature]` in C1, you will get the average high temperature for January 1 in Celsius. Make two changes to this formula. First, add a hash after B1 to return the temperature for all 366 days. =`B1#.[mean maximum temperature]`. To convert from Celsius to Fahrenheit, use =`CONVERT(B1#.[mean maximum temperature],"C","F")`, as shown in Figure 10.27.

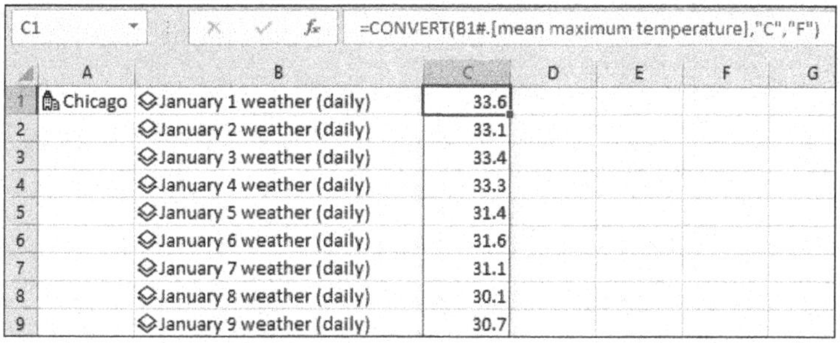

C1 =CONVERT(B1#.[mean maximum temperature],"C","F")

	A	B	C	D	E	F	G
1	Chicago	January 1 weather (daily)	33.6				
2		January 2 weather (daily)	33.1				
3		January 3 weather (daily)	33.4				
4		January 4 weather (daily)	33.3				
5		January 5 weather (daily)	31.4				
6		January 6 weather (daily)	31.6				
7		January 7 weather (daily)	31.1				
8		January 8 weather (daily)	30.1				
9		January 9 weather (daily)	30.7				

Figure 10.27 Weather history data for Chicago.

CHAPTER 10

Using stock or currency Data Types

The stock and currency Data Types return the current stock price or exchange rate. Type a stock symbol in a cell and use choose Stocks from the Data Type gallery on the Data tab.

Figure 10.28 shows some of the fields available for the Microsoft stock data. The stock data is delayed. The delay is based on the exchange. Click the Disclaimer link above the grid for the current delay information.

Note that Excel will not update the Data Type during each recalc. You have to use the Refresh All icon on the Data tab to force a refresh.

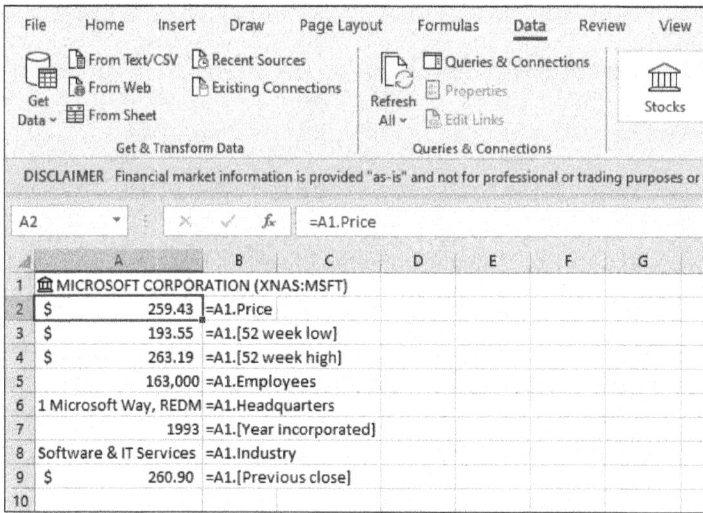

Figure 10.28 Stock prices with a 15-minute delay.

For currency exchange rates, use a code such as USD-GBP for U.S. Dollars to Great Britain Pounds. In Figure 10.29, the codes in column A were converted to Currency Data Types in column B. The price in column C is the current exchange rate.

C2 =B2.Price

	A	B	C
1	Currency Pair	Currency	Price
2	USD-GBP	USD/GBP	£ 0.72
3	USD-CAD	USD/CAD	$ 1.24
4	USD-AUD	USD/AUD	$ 1.33
5	USD-EUR	USD/EUR	€ 0.84
6	USD-BTC	USD/BTC	0.00003080
7	GBP-USD	GBP/USD	$ 1.39
8	CAD-USD	CAD/USD	$ 0.81
9	AUD-USD	AUD/USD	$ 0.75
10	EUR-USD	EUR/USD	$ 1.19
11	BTC-USD	BTC/USD	$ 32,451.01
12			

Figure 10.29 Current exchange rates.

Retrieving historical stock prices using STOCKHISTORY

When Stock Data Types debuted, the first question was how could you get historical stock quotes. Microsoft introduced the new `STOCKHISTORY` function to provide this.

Pass a stock symbol or currency pair to `STOCKHISTORY`. You can specify a start date and end date. Ask for Daily, Weekly, or Monthly data. Specify headers or no headers. You can then specify up to six fields in any order to provide Date, Close, Open, High, Low or Volume (see Figure 10.30).

	A	B	C	D	E	F	G	H
1	MSFT	=STOCKHISTORY(stock,start_date,end_date,interval,headers,properties1,...)						
2		Interval: 0=Daily, 1=Weekly, 2=Monthly						
3		Properties: 0=Date, 1=Close, 2=Open, 3=High, 4=Low, 5=Volume)						
4								
5	=STOCKHISTORY(A1,DATE(2000,1,1),TODAY(),2,1,0,1,2,3,4,5)							
6								
7	Date	Close	Open	High	Low	Volume		
8	1/1/2000	$ 48.94	$ 58.69	$ 59.31	$ 47.44	637,439,300		
9	2/1/2000	$ 44.69	$ 49.25	$ 55.00	$ 44.06	667,249,100		
10	3/1/2000	$ 53.13	$ 44.81	$ 57.50	$ 44.47	1,014,095,600		
11	4/1/2000	$ 34.88	$ 47.22	$ 48.25	$ 32.50	1,130,123,500		

Figure 10.30 Use the `STOCKHISTORY` function to return historical data for stocks or exchange rates.

CHAPTER 11

Connecting worksheets and workbooks

In Chapter 7, "Understanding functions," and Chapter 8, "Using everyday functions: math, date and time, and text functions," you find out how to set up formulas that calculate based on values within one worksheet. You can also easily connect a worksheet to several other worksheets or connect various workbooks. Excel offers easier-than-ever ways to connect a worksheet to data from the Web, data from text files, or data from databases such as Access.

In this chapter, you discover how to do the following:

- Connect two worksheets
- Connect two workbooks
- Manage links between workbooks

Connecting two worksheets

Although Excel offers 17 billion cells on every worksheet, it is fairly common to separate any model onto several worksheets. You might choose to have one worksheet for each month in a year or to have one worksheet for each functional area of a business. For example, Figure 11.1 shows a workbook with worksheets for revenue and expenses. Because different departments might be responsible for the functional areas, it makes sense to separate them into different worksheets. Eventually, though, you will want to pull information from the various worksheets into a single summary worksheet.

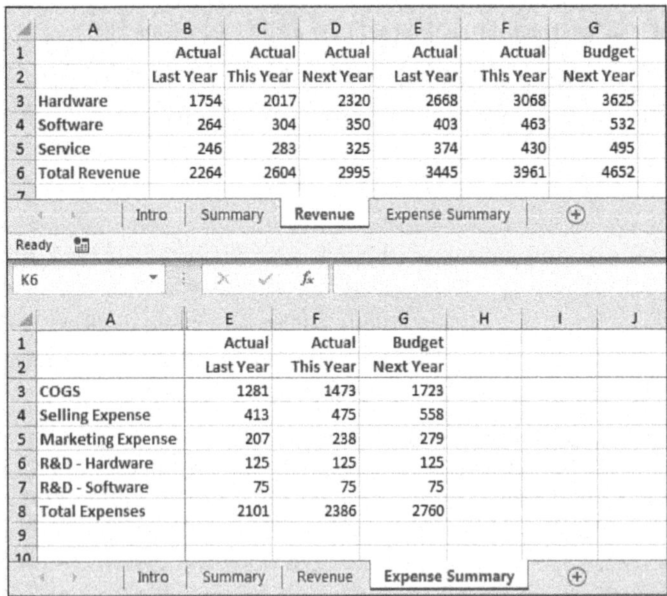

	A	B	C	D	E	F	G
1		Actual	Actual	Actual	Actual	Actual	Budget
2		Last Year	This Year	Next Year	Last Year	This Year	Next Year
3	Hardware	1754	2017	2320	2668	3068	3625
4	Software	264	304	350	403	463	532
5	Service	246	283	325	374	430	495
6	Total Revenue	2264	2604	2995	3445	3961	4652

	A	E	F	G	H	I	J
1		Actual	Actual	Budget			
2		Last Year	This Year	Next Year			
3	COGS	1281	1473	1723			
4	Selling Expense	413	475	558			
5	Marketing Expense	207	238	279			
6	R&D - Hardware	125	125	125			
7	R&D - Software	75	75	75			
8	Total Expenses	2101	2386	2760			
9							

Figure 11.1 Different functional areas need to work on budgets for revenue and expenses, so revenue and expenses are kept on separate worksheets.

Excel in practice: seeing two worksheets of the same workbook side by side

The workbook in Figure 11.1 illustrates a useful trick—seeing two worksheets of the same workbook side by side. Follow these steps to see two worksheets of the same workbook side by side:

1. Open the first worksheet that you want to view.
2. On the View tab, click New Window. If your workbook is in full-screen mode, it appears that nothing happened. However, when you look in the title bar, you see your workbook title has " - 2" after the title.
3. On the View tab, click Arrange All and then click either Vertical or Horizontal. Click the Windows Of Active Workbook check box. The arrangement in Figure 11.1 is horizontal, whereas the arrangement in Figure 11.2 is vertical.
4. In the second window, click the second worksheet tab that you want to view. You can now see both worksheets of the same workbook side by side. In Excel today, each window has its own ribbon and status bar.

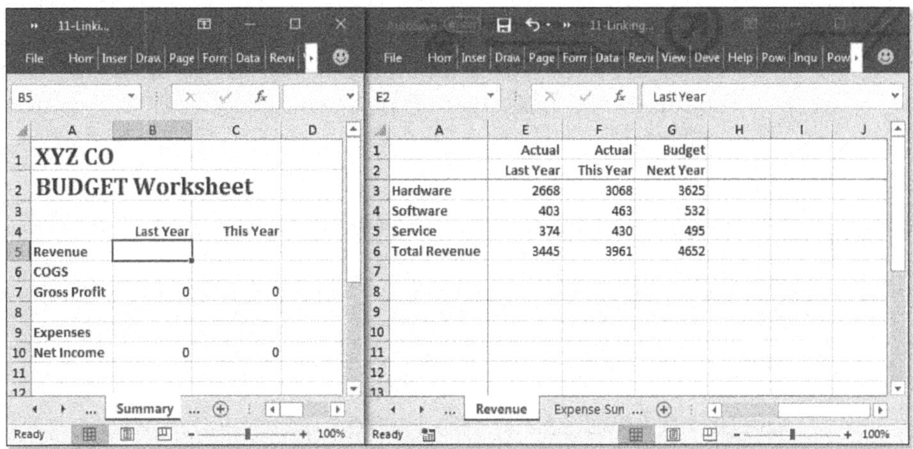

Figure 11.2 The goal is to set up a link to get information from the Revenue tab to appear on the Summary tab.

To return to a single window, click the Close Window icon, which is the X in the top-right corner of the second window.

As shown in Figure 11.2, the goal is to have the values from cells F6:G6 on the Revenue tab carry forward to cells B5:C5 on the Summary tab. There are four ways to achieve this goal:

- Type a formula, such as **=Revenue!F6**, in cell B5.
- Build the formula using the mouse. For example, type an equal sign in B5 of the Summary sheet and then using the mouse, click on cell E6 of the Revenue sheet. Then press Enter.
- Right-drag cells F6:G6 on the Revenue tab to the proper location on the Summary tab and select Link Here.
- Copy cells F6:G6 on the Revenue tab. Paste to cells B5:C5, and then use the Paste Options fly-out menu to choose Link Here. This is the newest method and is discussed in the next section.

NOTE

Note that you have not created a second workbook. Instead, you have created a second camera looking at a different section of the same workbook. Any changes you make in one window appear in the other window.

NOTE

In late 2021, a new Arrange feature appeared in the beta version of Excel if you had upgraded to the beta version of Windows 11. Read more in "Arrange All in Windows 11" in Chapter 1.

Creating links between worksheets

There are a variety of easy ways to create a link between worksheets or even between workbooks. Rather than typing the same value in multiple places, you can enter it once and have that value carry through to other worksheets and workbooks.

Creating links using the Paste Options menu

Follow these steps to set up a link using the new Paste Options fly-out menu:

1. Select the cells that have the figures you want to copy. For this example, select cells F6:G6 on the Revenue tab.
2. Press Ctrl+C to copy those cells.
3. Right-click the cell where the link should appear. For this example, right-click B5 on the Summary tab. In the menu that pops up, the sixth icon under Paste Options is Paste Link.
4. Choose Paste Link from the menu that appears (see Figure 11.3). Excel will insert formulas in B5:C5 on the Summary worksheet.

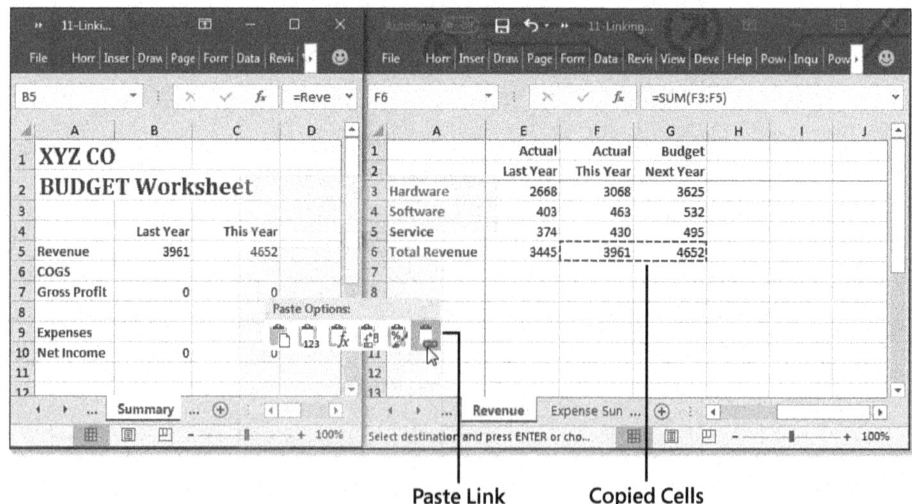

Figure 11.3 Copy the source cells to the target range.

Excel inserts a formula with the correct syntax to point to cells F6 on the Revenue tab (see Figure 11.4). Note that if data changes on the Revenue worksheet, the new results appear on the Summary worksheet.

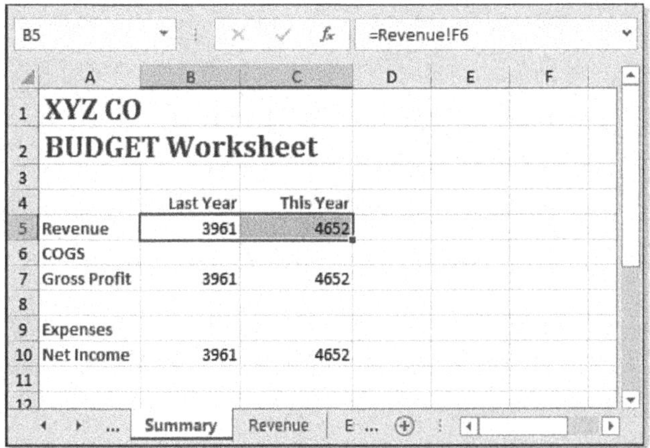

Figure 11.4 After you choose Paste Link, a formula points to the other worksheet.

Creating links using the right-drag menu

If you are adept with the mouse, there is an easier way to create links. This is particularly true if you have the two worksheets arranged side by side, which was presented previously in the "Excel in practice" section.

This method uses the Alternate Drag-And-Drop menu. This amazing menu, which has been hiding in Excel for several versions, offers a fast way to copy cells, link cells, change formulas to values, and more.

The Alternate Drag-and-Drop menu appears anytime you right-click the border of a selection, right-drag to a new location, and then release the mouse button.

In Figure 11.5, on the Expense Summary tab, select cells F3:G3. Hover over the edge of the selection rectangle until you see the four-headed arrow. Right-click and begin to drag to the other window.

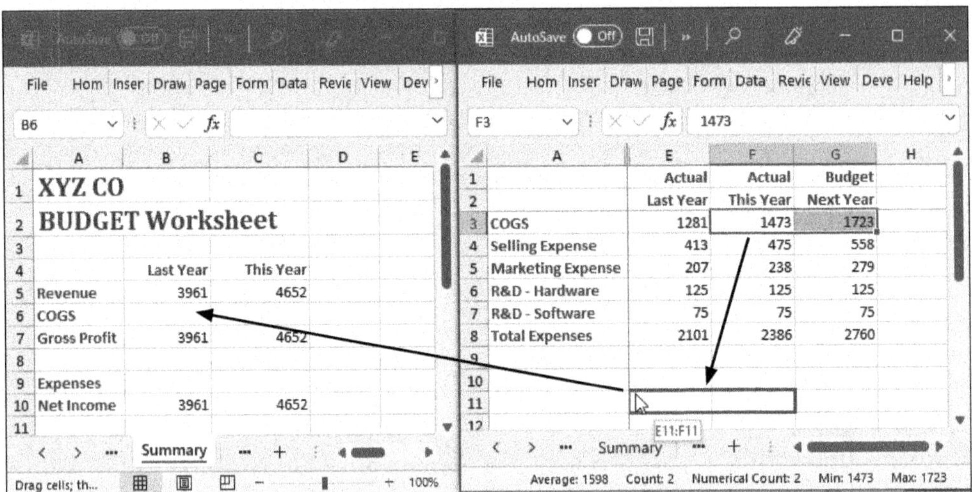

Figure 11.5 Right-click and drag the source cells.

When you have arrived at the new location, release the right mouse button and select Link Here, as shown in Figure 11.6. Excel builds a formula in the target location that has the proper syntax to link to the source cells. Note that because the worksheet name contains a space, Excel wraps the sheet name in apostrophes: `='Expense Summary'!F3` (see Figure 11.7).

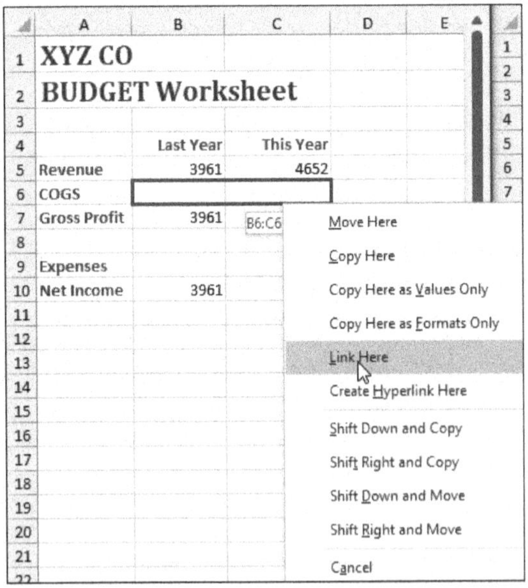

Figure 11.6 Release the mouse button to access this menu.

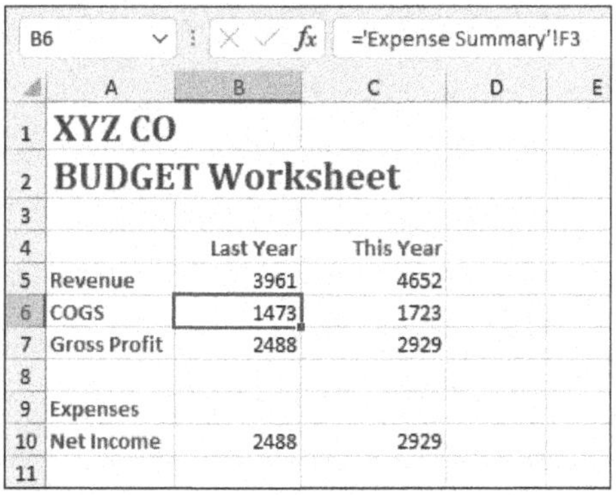

B6 | =‘Expense Summary’!F3

	A	B	C	D	E
1	XYZ CO				
2	BUDGET Worksheet				
3					
4		Last Year	This Year		
5	Revenue	3961	4652		
6	COGS	1473	1723		
7	Gross Profit	2488	2929		
8					
9	Expenses				
10	Net Income	2488	2929		
11					

Figure 11.7 Excel builds the proper formula.

Inside OUT

The menu shown in Figure 11.6 has a wide variety of uses. My favorite is converting formulas to values without doing copy and paste values.

I do about 35 live all-day Excel seminars every year. The people who come to my seminars are there to earn Continuing Education credit hours, and they are almost always accountants who use Excel 40 hours a week. I’ve learned that someone in every room has some awesome trick that I have never seen before.

I first learned about the Right-Drag menu while doing a seminar in Columbus, Indiana. A fellow named Dave in the first row showed me how to replace formulas with values: Select the range of formulas. Hold down the right mouse button while you drag the range to the right one column. Keep holding down the right mouse button while you drag back to the original location. Then choose Copy Here As Values Only.

Given that the right-drag menu is not documented in Excel Help, you wonder how Dave ever accidentally discovered this technique.

Building a link by using the mouse

Another method is to build a formula by pointing to the correct cell with the mouse. Start in a target cell, such as cell B9 on the Summary tab (see Figure 11.8).

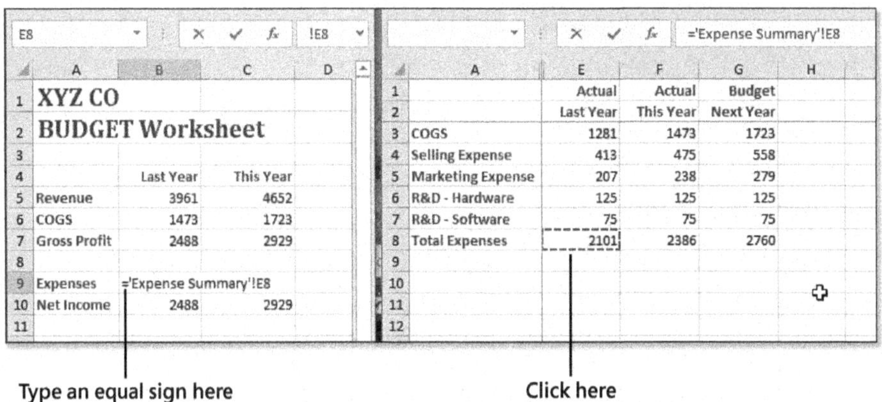

Figure 11.8 Type an equal sign and then click the source cell.

Instead of trying to remember the exact syntax, you can point to the correct cell. Type the equal sign and then click the desired worksheet tab. Using the mouse, click a cell to get the value from that cell. Excel builds the formula `='Expense Summary'!F8` in the formula bar (see Figure 11.8). Excel waits for you to either press the Enter key to accept the formula or press another operator key to add other cells to the formula.

NOTE

Because the source and target worksheet are in the same workbook, the formula that Excel builds is a relative formula. You can copy B9 to B10 to retrieve the 2018 budget.

When you press the Enter key to accept the formula, Excel jumps back to the starting worksheet. The desired figure is carried through to the worksheet.

Links to external workbooks default to absolute references

You can use any of the four methods described previously for building links to other worksheets when you want to build links to external workbooks. It is easiest if you open both workbooks.

Note that if you use any of the methods illustrated previously, Excel defaults to adding dollar signs into the external reference. The dollar signs create an absolute reference that makes it more difficult to copy.

Here is an example. When you use the mouse method described in Figure 11.8 to link to a worksheet in the same workbook, the cell reference is something like F8. If you use the same method to link to a worksheet in a different workbook, the cell reference created by Excel is automatically `$F$8`. The dollar signs make this an absolute reference, which is difficult to copy. If you need to copy this formula to other cells, you should press the F4 key three times to change from an absolute reference to a relative reference.

CHAPTER 11

Building a formula by typing

You can always build the links by typing the formula. This is the least popular method because you need to understand a variety of syntax rules. Keep in mind that these syntax rules change depending on whether the worksheet name contains a space, whether the link is external, and whether the linked workbook is open or closed.

Here are the syntax rules:

- For an internal link in which the worksheet name does not contain a space or special characters, use `=SheetName!CellAddress`. An example is `=Result!B3`.
- When the worksheet name contains a space or certain special characters, add apostrophes around the workbook name and sheet name. An example is `='Result Sheet'!B3`.
- For an external link, the name of the workbook is wrapped in square brackets and appears before the sheet name. An example is `=[LinkToMe.xlsm]Sheet1!B3`.
- If the workbook name or sheet name contains a space, add an apostrophe before the opening square bracket and after the sheet name. An example is `='[My File.xls] Income Statement'!B3`.
- When Excel refers to a file such as [RegionTotals.xlsm], you can assume that the file is currently open. When you close the linked file, Excel updates the formula in the linking workbook to include the complete pathname. An example is `=SUM('C:\[Region Totals.xlsm]Quota'!$B$2:$E$2)`.

Figure 11.9 illustrates examples of various formulas.

	A	B	C	D
1	Link Syntax			
2				
3	Type	Spaces?	Link Formula	Formula Text
4	Internal	No	5	=Result!B3
5	Internal	Yes	6	='Result Sheet'!B3
6	External	No	1	='G:\2016InDepth\SampleFiles\[16LinkToMe.xlsm]Sheet1'!$B$3
7	External	Yes	3	='[11-Link To Me.xlsm]Sheet3'!$B$4
8	External Closed	No	7	='G:\2016InDepth\SampleFiles\[16Closed.xlsm]Sheet1'!$B$3
9	External Closed	No	8	='G:\2016InDepth\SampleFiles\[16Closed.xlsm]Sheet 2'!$B$3

Figure 11.9 Syntax for various types of links.

Creating links to unsaved workbooks

You can build a formula that links to a source workbook that has not been saved. This formula might point to Book1, Book3, or the like. When you attempt to save the target workbook, Excel presents a Save <filename> With References To Unsaved Documents? dialog box. In general, you should cancel the save, switch to the unsaved source workbook, and then select File, Save As to save the file with a permanent name. Then you can come back to save the linking workbook.

Using the Links tab on the Trust Center

By default, Excel applies security settings that frustrate your attempts to pull values from closed workbooks. Consider the following scenario using two workbooks labeled Workbook A and Workbook B:

1. Establish a link from Workbook A to Workbook B.
2. Save and close Workbook A.
3. Make changes to Workbook B. Save and close Workbook B.
4. Later, open Workbook B.
5. Open Workbook A.

In this case, the new values in Workbook B automatically flow through to Workbook A.

However, if you attempt to open Workbook A before opening Workbook B later, you see the following message: Automatic Update Of Links Has Been Disabled (see Figure 11.10).

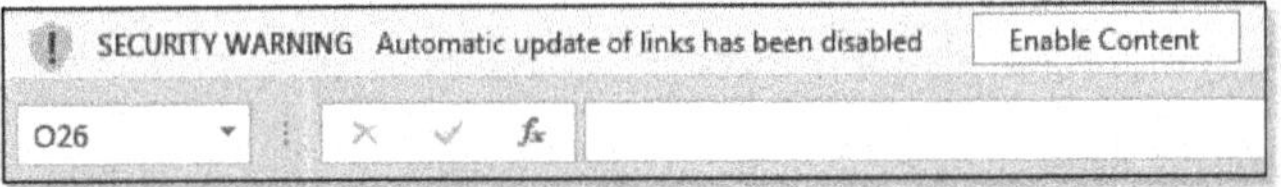

Figure 11.10 The link message initially appears in the info bar.

After you enable the content the first time, Excel marks the document as a trusted document. The next time you open the workbook, Excel displays a different cautionary message about links to external sources that could be unsafe, as shown in Figure 11.11.

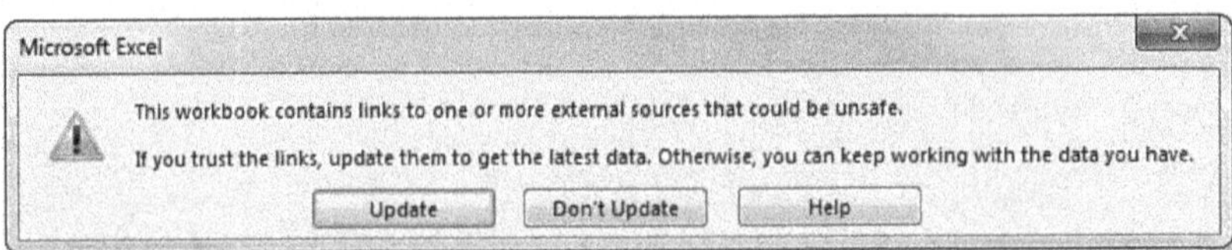

Figure 11.11 Later, the Excel 2003–style link question appears.

You might wonder what could be unsafe about a link. I do, too. When I asked someone at Microsoft about this, they painted an incredibly convoluted scenario that I have never seen happen. The links that are described in this section are safe. Feel free to click Update.

Opening workbooks with links to closed workbooks

Suppose that you have saved and closed the linking workbook. You update numbers in the linked workbook. You save and close the linked workbook. Later, when you open the linking workbook, Excel asks if you want to update the links to the other workbook. If you created both workbooks and you have possession of both workbooks, it is fine to allow the workbooks to update.

Dealing with missing linked workbooks

If you receive a linking workbook via email and you do not have access to the linked workbooks, Excel alerts you that the workbook contains links that cannot be updated right now. In this case, you should click Continue in the dialog box, as shown in Figure 11.12.

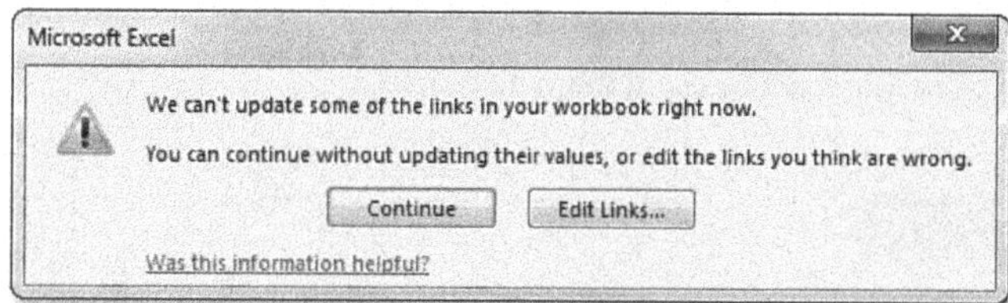

Figure 11.12 This message means that the linked workbook cannot be found. It shows up most often when someone emails you only the linking workbook.

Updating links when a workbook is renamed or moved

It is common to have the source workbook get renamed or moved. For example, if you link to `CommissionRates2025.xlsx` and a new commission plan is created for 2026, someone will use File, Save As to create a new `CommissionRates2026.xlsx` workbook. In this scenario, any workbooks linking to `CommissionRates2025.xlsx` would have to be updated to point to `CommissionRates2026.xlsx`. As you can imagine, this process happens once a year.

In an ideal scenario, you would open `CommissionRates2025.xlsx` and all the workbooks that link to `CommissionRates2025.xlsx`. With all the workbooks open, activate `CommissionRates2025.xlsx` and select File, Save As. Change the workbook name to `CommissionRates2026.xlsx`. All the links in the open workbooks that were pointing to `CommissionRates2025.xlsx` will now point to `CommissionRates2026.xlsx`.

However, the reality is that the person who maintains the Commission Rates workbook is in another office, and they will often make changes without remembering that there are other workbooks linked to his workbook.

To change all links in a workbook to point to a new workbook, select Data, Edit Links to display the Edit Links dialog box (see Figure 11.13). Then you should click the Change Source button to tell Excel that the linked workbook has a new name or location. Alternatively, you might need to click the Break Link button to change all linked formulas to their current values.

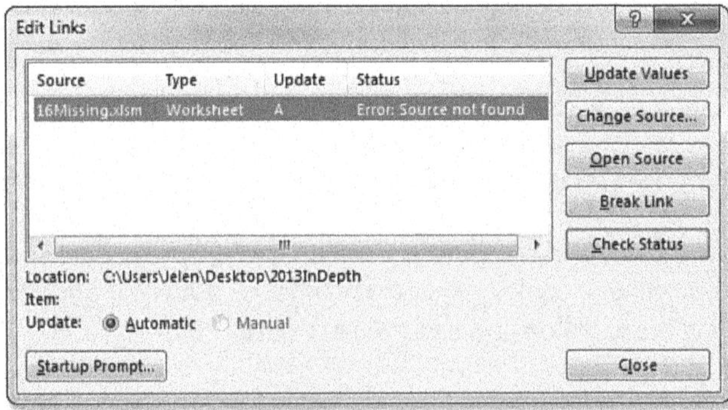

Figure 11.13 Manage or change links by using this dialog box.

TROUBLESHOOTING

Excel warns you about links when you open the workbook and offers an Edit Links button. If you skip that box and need to Edit Links later, how do you get back to the Edit Links dialog box?

Finding the Edit Links icon does not seem logical. I am old enough to remember that it used to be on the Excel 2003 Edit menu. Now, it turns out that Edit Links is in the Queries & Connections group on the Data tab of the ribbon.

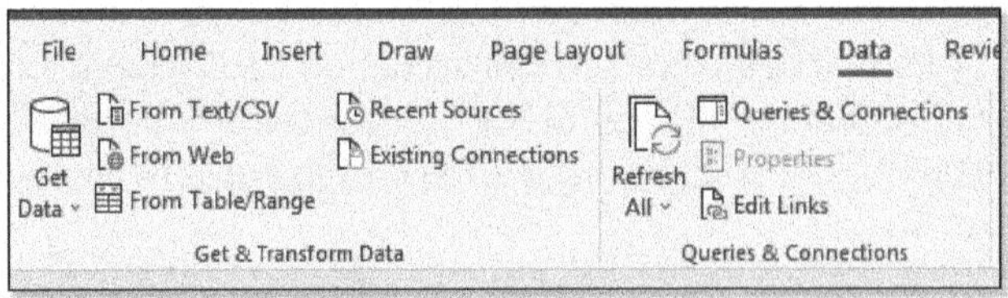

Preventing the Update Links dialog box from appearing

Suppose that you need to send a linking workbook to a co-worker. You want your co-worker to see the current values of the linking formulas without having the linked workbook. In this case, you want the co-worker to click Continue in Figure 11.12. However, some newer Excel customers think that every warning box is a disaster, so you might prefer to suppress that box for your co-worker. To do so, follow these steps:

1. On the Data tab, in the Queries & Connections group, select Edit Links.
2. In the lower-left corner of the dialog box that appears, click the Startup Prompt button. The Startup Prompt dialog box appears.
3. Select Don't Display The Alert And Don't Update Automatic Links (see Figure 11.14).

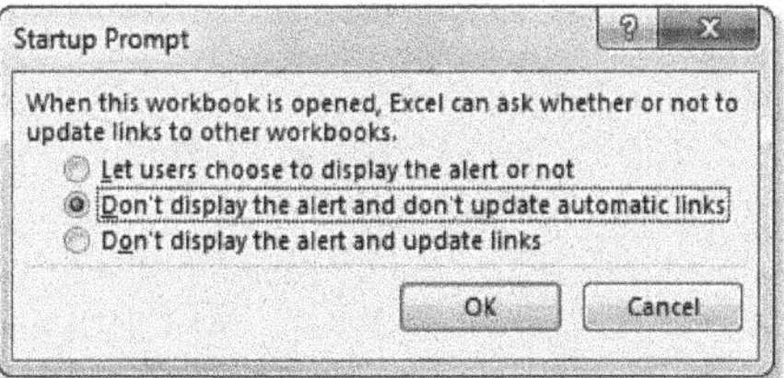

Figure 11.14 You can prevent others from seeing the Update Links message.

After emailing the workbook to your co-worker, you need to redisplay the Startup Prompt dialog box and change it back so that you will get the updated links.

CHAPTER 12

Dynamic array formulas and names in Excel

Using dynamic array functions to return many results

Excel dynamic array formulas are entered in a single cell but return a large range of answers. This is much easier than the old array formulas. You won't have to remember Ctrl+Shift+Enter anymore to use an Array formula. They debuted just after Excel 2019 shipped. People using Microsoft 365 have had access to them, but Excel 2019 did not support them.

The dynamic array functions are FILTER, RANDARRAY, SEQUENCE, SORT, SORTBY, and UNIQUE. Any functions introduced after the dynamic arrays can natively work with arrays. For example, see XLOOKUP in Chapter 9.

Inside OUT

This improvement represents new engineering to the Calculation engine in Excel. Excel now understands how to deal with a formula that spills into multiple answers.

The possible combinations of these new functions stretch far beyond the six functions. You will be able to use SEQUENCE inside just about any other Excel formula function to generate several answers where you would have previously seen just one answer.

In the following image, the rarely-used ROMAN function returns an array of answers thanks to SEQUENCE.

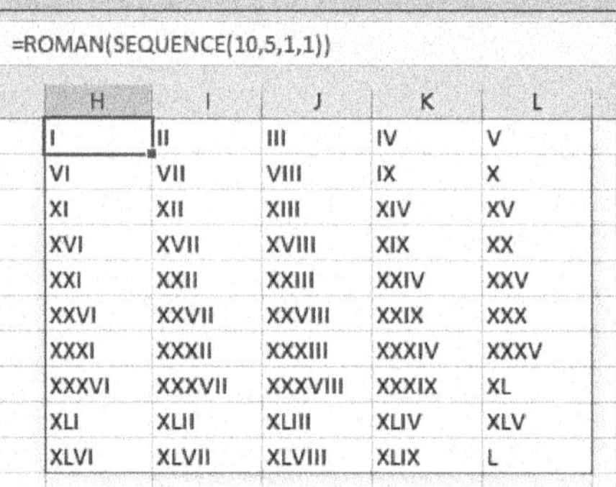

=ROMAN(SEQUENCE(10,5,1,1))

H	I	J	K	L
I	II	III	IV	V
VI	VII	VIII	IX	X
XI	XII	XIII	XIV	XV
XVI	XVII	XVIII	XIX	XX
XXI	XXII	XXIII	XXIV	XXV
XXVI	XXVII	XXVIII	XXIX	XXX
XXXI	XXXII	XXXIII	XXXIV	XXXV
XXXVI	XXXVII	XXXVIII	XXXIX	XL
XLI	XLII	XLIII	XLIV	XLV
XLVI	XLVII	XLVIII	XLIX	L

`=ROMAN(SEQUENCE(10,5,1,1))` generates 50 cells of Roman numerals from 1 to 50 (or I, II, III, IV, to XLIX, L). The new calculation engine makes almost every function potentially an array function. There are a few annoying exceptions, mostly from the functions that were originally in the Analysis ToolPak and incorporated into Excel in 2007. For example, ISEVEN and ISODD cannot work with an array.

Even without using an array function, you can simply refer to a range from a single cell. `=A1:C10` entered in E2 will return 30 cells. Because this new syntax breaks the behavior of implicit intersection, an @ operator has been added for cases where you want to use implicit intersection.

This is amazing. Take a look at Figure 12.1. A formula of `=A2:A9` is typed in cell C5. Excel spills the answers into C5:C12. If you select any cell in C5:C12, the formula appears in the formula bar, and a blue outline appears around the results range. Think of the blue outline as indicating that this one formula is returning all of the answers inside the outline.

Here is an important distinction: The formula only exists in one cell: C5. When you select C6, C7, or C12, the formula appears in the formula bar in a light-gray font. But you can only edit the formula if you select C5. A formula of `=FORMULATEXT(C5)` will work. A formula of `=FORMULATEXT(C6)` will fail.

If A1:A9 happens to be a table and you add new rows to the table, the results from this one formula will automatically expand. If you delete row 4, the results will contract.

The first time this happens to you in Excel, you will see the message shown in Figure 12.2. Once you click Got It, they won't bother you again.

If you use Excel a lot, you realize two problems with this new functionality. The first problem: What happens if C6 through C12 are not blank? If Excel cannot return all the answers, then you get none of the answers. A brand-new `#SPILL` function will appear, and the on-grid drop-down menu explains "Spill Range Isn't Blank" (see Figure 12.3).

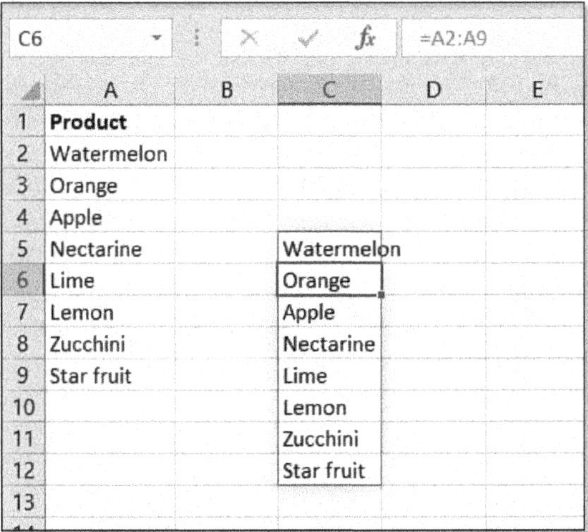

Figure 12.1 A single formula returns many results.

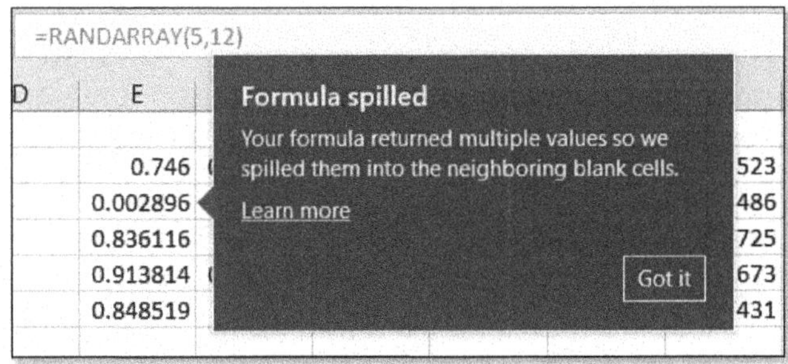

Figure 12.2 Excel tries to explain this new spill feature.

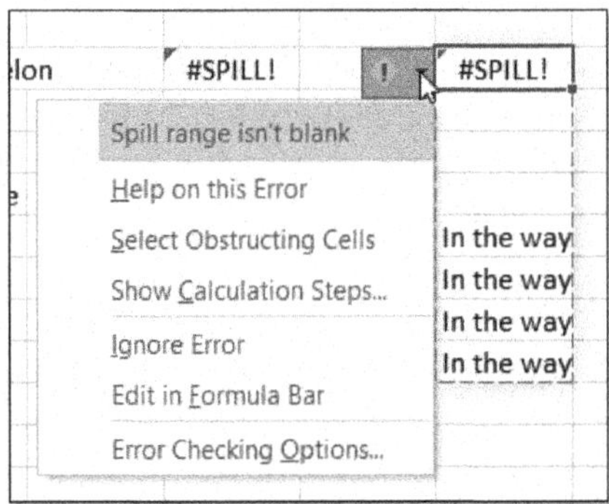

Figure 12.3 If there is no room for the results, a #SPILL error appears.

The second problem will only be apparent to hard-core Excellers. There is a concept called implicit intersection. If you enter **=A2:A9** anywhere in rows 2 through 9, earlier versions of Excel will only return the value from A2:A9 that intersects the formula. In other words, `=A2:A9` in C5 will return `Nectarine` from A5. Enter that same formula in C7, and you will get `Lemon`.

This is a bizarre trick that I've never used in real life. The only time that I've ever used implicit intersection is when trying to win a bar bet. However, someone out there is using it. Some modeler is taking advantage of this trick. Microsoft can't take this feature away, so if you want to do what implicit intersection used to do, use the @ operator. If you enter `=@A$2:A$9` when in rows 2 through 9, the value from that row will be returned (see Figure 12.4).

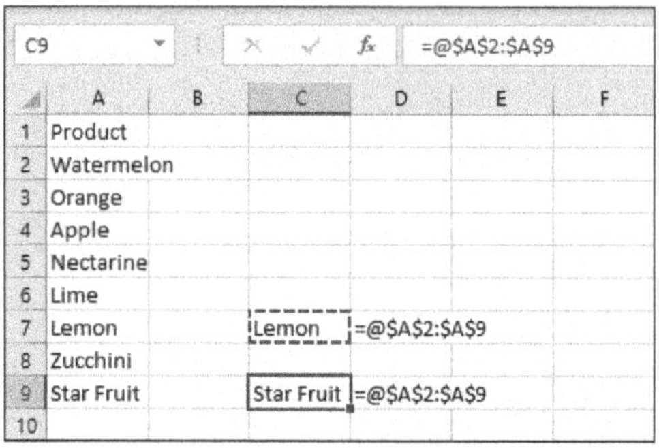

C9 =@$A$2:$A$9

	A	B	C	D	E	F
1	Product					
2	Watermelon					
3	Orange					
4	Apple					
5	Nectarine					
6	Lime					
7	Lemon		Lemon	=@$A$2:$A$9		
8	Zucchini					
9	Star Fruit		Star Fruit	=@$A$2:$A$9		
10						

Figure 12.4 The new @ operator must be used when someone needs to do implicit intersection.

Text appears in A2:A9, and cell A7 contains `Lemon`. A formula of `=@$A$2:$A$9` entered anywhere in row 7 will return `Lemon`. Copy that formula to row 9, and it will return `Star fruit` because A9 contains Star Fruit. Copy that formula to row 10 and you will get a #VALUE! error because the formula does not intersect with the range.

Note that implicit intersection and @ also work for columns. If you had values in B1:J1 and enter `=@B1:J1` anywhere in column C, the formula will return just the value from C1.

The Excel team did a great job with backward compatibility on this feature: If you have an old workbook that is already doing implicit intersection, Excel will wrap that formula in the @ operator for you. If you create a @ function and send it to someone who does not have dynamic arrays, Excel will rewrite the formula as an implicit intersection.

NOTE

You can ask Excel to warn you if you have accidentally created a formula that will require an implicit intersection. In Excel Options, select the Formulas category and then Suggest Formula Variations That Are Supported By Earlier Versions Of Excel.

Sorting with a formula

Sorting with a formula is easier thanks to the new SORT and SORTBY array functions.

In Figure 12.5, you have a two-column range of results in A4:B16. Those results are constantly changing because of formulas that sum daily sales. You would like a formula to sort the results.

Sorting might be easy for you, but you can't trust your manager's manager to click the AZ button. That is why you used to go to crazy lengths with RANK, SMALL, MATCH, and INDEX to sort with a formula. All that goes away with the introduction of SORT.

The SORT function is a dynamic array function that returns a sorted list. The syntax is:

```
SORT( Array, [Sort_Index], [Sort_Order], [By_Column])
```

In Figure 12.5, the data in A4:B16 is sorted by name. You would like the results to be sorted by score, with the highest scores at the top. To sort that data with a formula, you would follow these steps:

1. Start by selecting where you want the results to appear. In Figure 12.5, this is cell D4.
2. Begin typing a formula: **=SORT(A4:B16,**
3. If you want to sort based on the score in column B, use **2** as the Sort_index because column B is the second column of the A4:B9 range. Type **2** and a comma.
4. For the Sort_Order, use **1** for ascending or **-1** for descending. Choose **-1**.
5. The fourth argument is rarely used. There is an obscure version of sorting where you don't sort the rows, but you sort the columns. Use **True** for the fourth argument if you want to sort by columns. In most cases, you will leave this blank.
6. Type the closing parenthesis.
7. Press Enter. The results will spill into D4:E16.

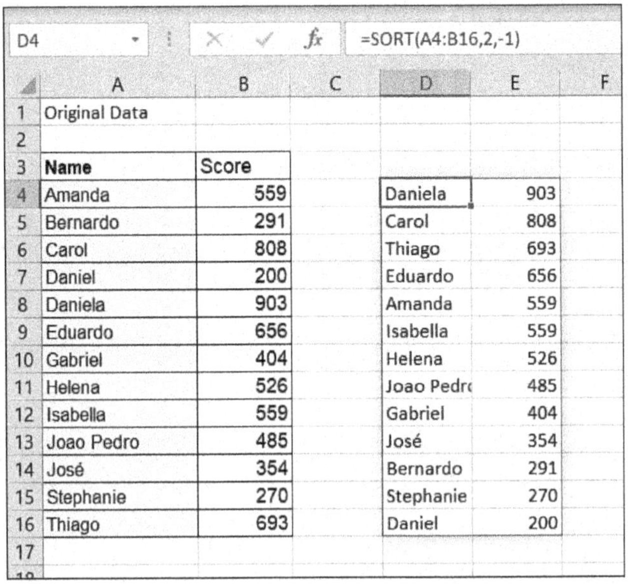

D4 =SORT(A4:B16,2,-1)

	A	B	C	D	E	F
1	Original Data					
2						
3	**Name**	Score				
4	Amanda	559		Daniela	903	
5	Bernardo	291		Carol	808	
6	Carol	808		Thiago	693	
7	Daniel	200		Eduardo	656	
8	Daniela	903		Amanda	559	
9	Eduardo	656		Isabella	559	
10	Gabriel	404		Helena	526	
11	Helena	526		Joao Pedr	485	
12	Isabella	559		Gabriel	404	
13	Joao Pedro	485		José	354	
14	José	354		Bernardo	291	
15	Stephanie	270		Stephanie	270	
16	Thiago	693		Daniel	200	
17						

Figure 12.5 A formula sorts the data from A4:B16 in a new location.

Convert the original range to a table using Ctrl+T. Type a new row at the bottom of the table with a high score. The SORT function automatically expands, and the new high score appears at the top of the results (see Figure 12.6).

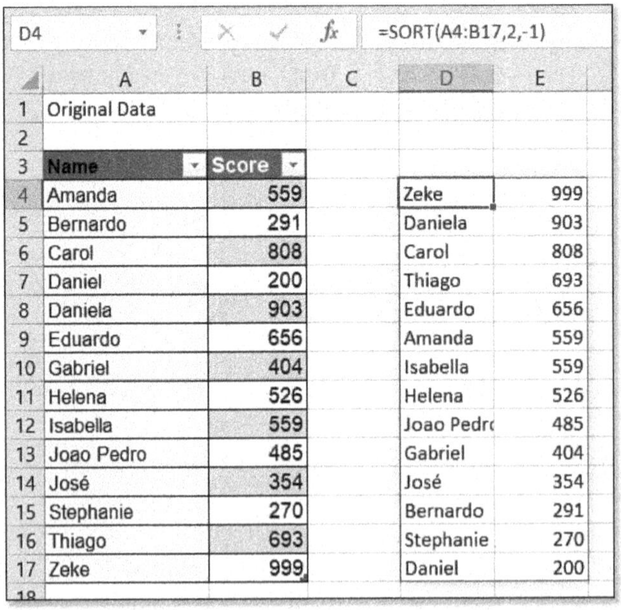

D4 =SORT(A4:B17,2,-1)

	A	B	C	D	E
1	Original Data				
2					
3	**Name**	**Score**			
4	Amanda	559		Zeke	999
5	Bernardo	291		Daniela	903
6	Carol	808		Carol	808
7	Daniel	200		Thiago	693
8	Daniela	903		Eduardo	656
9	Eduardo	656		Amanda	559
10	Gabriel	404		Isabella	559
11	Helena	526		Helena	526
12	Isabella	559		Joao Pedr	485
13	Joao Pedro	485		Gabriel	404
14	José	354		José	354
15	Stephanie	270		Bernardo	291
16	Thiago	693		Stephanie	270
17	Zeke	999		Daniel	200

Figure 12.6 Add new data to the original data set, and the SORT results expand.

Inside OUT

What if you only want the top three results and just the names, not the scores?

The SORT function is very flexible. What if you only wanted to return the top three scores and only needed to see the names? Select G3:G5. Type the SORT formula and press Ctrl+Shift+Enter. The formula wants to return all fifteen sales rows and two columns. However, because you selected three cells, you only see the first column and first three rows.

The SORT function is fine for simple situations. But sometimes, you need to do more complex sorting. In Figure 12.7, the original data in A3:C16 contains Name, Team, and Score. You want to present the results sorted by Team ascending and Score descending. You only want to show the names, not the teams or the scores. The SORTBY function offers this flexibility:

1. You want to sort the names from A4:A16. The formula in E4 starts with `=SORTBY(A4:A16,`.
2. You want to first sort by team name, so type **B4:B16,**.
3. You want the teams to sort ascending, so type **1** as the third argument.
4. SORTBY allows a multi-level sort. The second key is `C4:C16`, so type **C4:C16**, as the fourth argument.
5. The scores from `C4:C16` should be sorted descending. Type **-1** as the last argument. Close the formula with a close parenthesis and press Enter.

The results shown in `E4:E16` have `Eduardo` at the top. Just to make sure it is working, I copied the data to `G4:I16` and performed the sort using the Sort dialog. The results match.

E4 =SORTBY(A4:A16,B4:B16,1,C4:C16,-1)

	A	B	C	D	E	F	G	H	I
1									
2									
3	Name	Team	Score				Name	Team	Score
4	Amanda	Red	559		Eduardo		Eduardo	Blue	656
5	Bernardo	Blue	291		Helena		Helena	Blue	526
6	Carol	Red	808		Joao Pedro		Joao Pedr	Blue	485
7	Daniel	Blue	200		Bernardo		Bernardo	Blue	291
8	Daniela	Red	903		Stephanie		Stephanie	Blue	270
9	Eduardo	Blue	656		Daniel		Daniel	Blue	200
10	Gabriel	Red	404		Daniela		Daniela	Red	903
11	Helena	Blue	526		Carol		Carol	Red	808
12	Isabella	Red	559		Thiago		Thiago	Red	693
13	Joao Pedro	Blue	485		Amanda		Amanda	Red	559
14	José	Red	354		Isabella		Isabella	Red	559
15	Stephanie	Blue	270		Gabriel		Gabriel	Red	404
16	Thiago	Red	693		José		José	Red	354
17									

Figure 12.7 A formula performs a multi-level sort.

CHAPTER 12

TROUBLESHOOTING

There might be times when you need a multi-level SORT, but you cannot use SORTBY to refer to ranges.

In the example below, you want to sort the results of a UNIQUE function. Those results live only in memory and do not have a cell address.

In this case, you can force a multi-level sort with the SORT function by passing an array constant as the Sort_index and another array constant as the Sort_order.

If you want to sort by the second column ascending and the first column descending, use:

```
=SORT(UNIQUE(B4:C29,FALSE,FALSE),{2,1},{1,-1})
```

F5 =SORT(UNIQUE(B4:C29,FALSE,FALSE),{2,1},{1,-1})

	A	B	C	D	E	F	G
1							
2							
3	Team	Name	Product	Score		Sorted Unique Combination of Name/Product	
4	Red	Amanda	Apple	559			
5	Blue	Bernardo	Orange	291		Thiago	Apple
6	Red	Carol	Lemon	808		Isabella	Apple
7	Blue	Daniel	Lime	200		Helena	Apple
8	Red	Daniela	Apple	903		Daniela	Apple
9	Blue	Eduardo	Orange	656		Daniel	Apple
10	Red	Gabriel	Lemon	404		Amanda	Apple
11	Blue	Helena	Lime	526		Thiago	Kiwi
12	Red	Isabella	Apple	559		José	Lemon
13	Blue	Joao Pedro	Orange	485		Joao Pedr	Lemon

Inside OUT

A classic question is how to randomly sort a list of people. This is popular in Human Resources where they do random drug testing.

You can use the new RANDARRAY function as the second argument of the SORTBY function. In the following figure, use:

```
=SORT(A4:A16,RANDARRAY(13))
```

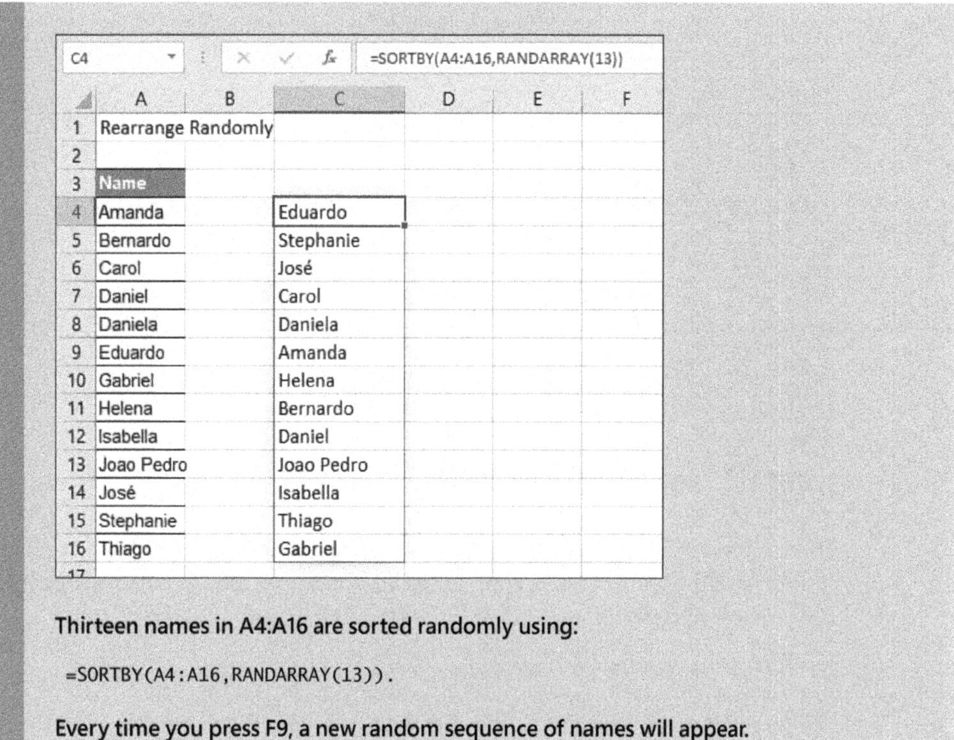

Thirteen names in A4:A16 are sorted randomly using:

`=SORTBY(A4:A16,RANDARRAY(13)).`

Every time you press F9, a new random sequence of names will appear.

Filtering with a formula

In Figure 12.8, you have a database in A3:C16. You want to use a formula to extract all records where the person is on the Red team. Use the new `FILTER` function.

The syntax is `=FILTER(array,include,[if_empty])`.

In this case, the array to filter is A4:C16. The include argument is `B4:B16="Red"`. The optional third argument will prevent an error that occurs if no one is assigned to the Red team. You could specify `"None"`, `"None Found"`, or 0 here.

Figure 12.8 shows the results of a `FILTER` function. The beauty of this single formula solution is that you don't need to know how many Red team records there will be. The old array formula solution required you to pre-plan the largest possible number of matches. This formula is so much easier.

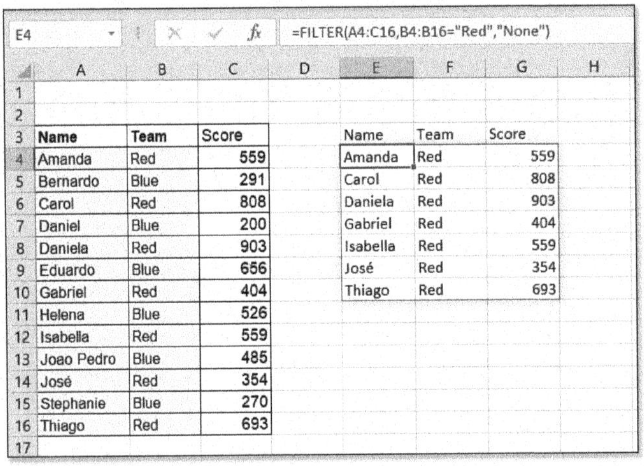

E4 =FILTER(A4:C16,B4:B16="Red","None")

	A	B	C	D	E	F	G	H
1								
2								
3	**Name**	**Team**	Score		Name	Team	Score	
4	Amanda	Red	559		Amanda	Red	559	
5	Bernardo	Blue	291		Carol	Red	808	
6	Carol	Red	808		Daniela	Red	903	
7	Daniel	Blue	200		Gabriel	Red	404	
8	Daniela	Red	903		Isabella	Red	559	
9	Eduardo	Blue	656		José	Red	354	
10	Gabriel	Red	404		Thiago	Red	693	
11	Helena	Blue	526					
12	Isabella	Red	559					
13	Joao Pedro	Blue	485					
14	José	Red	354					
15	Stephanie	Blue	270					
16	Thiago	Red	693					
17								

Figure 12.8 Extract all Red team records.

The example in Figure 12.8 has the Red team hard-coded into the formula. It is simple to change this to have the team name in another cell. In Figure 12.9, the team name is stored in cell F1. Change the formula to:

```
=FILTER(A4:C16,B4:B16=F1,"None")
```

When you change from Red to Blue, the output range returns the records for the Blue team. This may be the same number of rows, it might be more, or it might be less.

Because there are no people assigned to the Yellow team, if you type **Yellow** in F1, the result will be the word **None** in E4. This is because the last argument in the formula is `"None"`. If you leave this optional argument off, you will get an #N/A error instead.

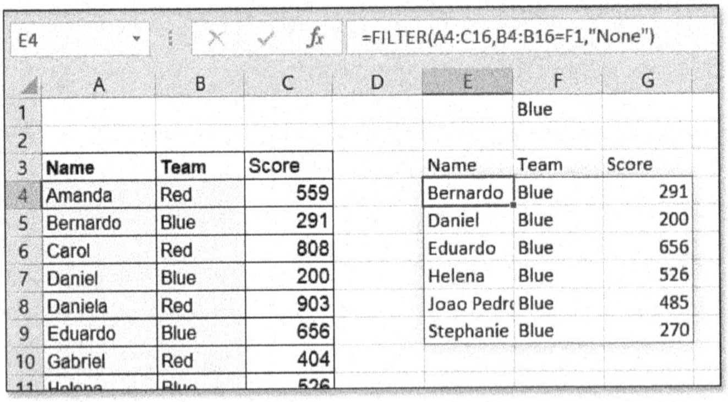

E4 =FILTER(A4:C16,B4:B16=F1,"None")

	A	B	C	D	E	F	G
1						Blue	
2							
3	**Name**	**Team**	Score		Name	Team	Score
4	Amanda	Red	559		Bernardo	Blue	291
5	Bernardo	Blue	291		Daniel	Blue	200
6	Carol	Red	808		Eduardo	Blue	656
7	Daniel	Blue	200		Helena	Blue	526
8	Daniela	Red	903		Joao Pedr	Blue	485
9	Eduardo	Blue	656		Stephanie	Blue	270
10	Gabriel	Red	404				
11	Helena	Blue	526				

Figure 12.9 Instead of hard coding Red in the formula, point to cell F1 instead.

Using FILTER to select a subset of columns

If the Include argument in filter is a one-row array, Excel will assume that you are filtering by column. In Figure 12.10, the original array in columns A:D includes Name, Team, Department, and Score. If you wanted to use a formula to extract just the Name and Department, you could use an Include argument of `{1,0,1,0}`. This argument is an array constant. The commas between the values mean "next column". If you use a `1` or `True`, the column will be returned. If you use a `0` or `False`, the column will be skipped.

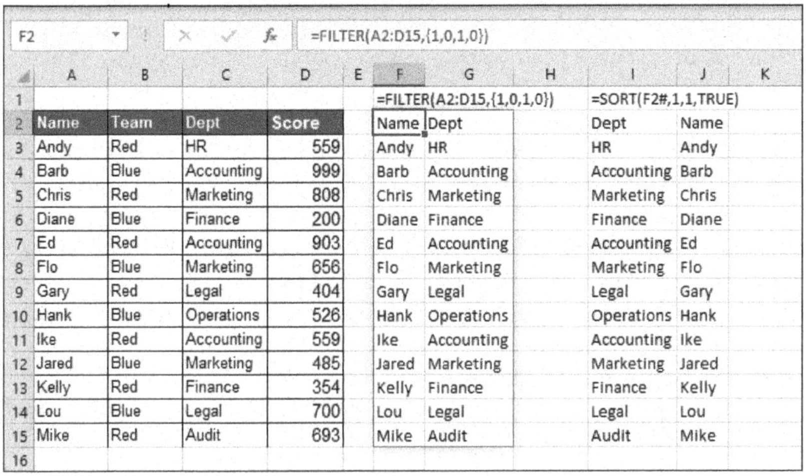

F2 =FILTER(A2:D15,{1,0,1,0})

	A	B	C	D	E	F	G	H	I	J	K
1						=FILTER(A2:D15,{1,0,1,0})			=SORT(F2#,1,1,TRUE)		
2	Name	Team	Dept	Score		Name	Dept		Dept	Name	
3	Andy	Red	HR	559		Andy	HR		HR	Andy	
4	Barb	Blue	Accounting	999		Barb	Accounting		Accounting	Barb	
5	Chris	Red	Marketing	808		Chris	Marketing		Marketing	Chris	
6	Diane	Blue	Finance	200		Diane	Finance		Finance	Diane	
7	Ed	Red	Accounting	903		Ed	Accounting		Accounting	Ed	
8	Flo	Blue	Marketing	656		Flo	Marketing		Marketing	Flo	
9	Gary	Red	Legal	404		Gary	Legal		Legal	Gary	
10	Hank	Blue	Operations	526		Hank	Operations		Operations	Hank	
11	Ike	Red	Accounting	559		Ike	Accounting		Accounting	Ike	
12	Jared	Blue	Marketing	485		Jared	Marketing		Marketing	Jared	
13	Kelly	Red	Finance	354		Kelly	Finance		Finance	Kelly	
14	Lou	Blue	Legal	700		Lou	Legal		Legal	Lou	
15	Mike	Red	Audit	693		Mike	Audit		Audit	Mike	
16											

Figure 12.10 Use an array constant as the Include argument to filter by column.

The Advanced Filter command on the Data tab would let you extract a subset of columns and change the order of those columns. Using the `FILTER` function is not as flexible. If you want to have Department appear before Name, you would have to wrap the `FILTER` function in a `SORT` function: `=SORT(FILTER(A2:D15,{1,0,1,0}),1,1,True)`.

TROUBLESHOOTING

How can you use `FILTER` to get all of the cells with a red font? Can you `SORT` by color or cell icon?

No. The `FILTER`, `SORT`, and `SORTBY` are operating on values in the cell. You cannot sort by font color, cell color, or icon.

Extracting unique values with a formula

Getting a unique list of values has always been difficult in Excel. Excel MVP Mike "Excelisfun" Girvin spends two entire chapters of his "Ctrl+Shift+Enter: Mastering Excel Array Formulas: Do the Impossible with Excel Formulas Thanks to Array Formula Magic" book explaining how you can write a formula to return a unique list of values. This becomes dramatically simpler using the UNIQUE array function. The syntax is:

```
=UNIQUE(Array, [by_col], [occurs_once])
```

The By_Col argument will usually be False. The Filter command in Excel operates on a row-by-row basis. I've occasionally heard of people who want to filter by columns, so in this case, setting this argument to True would allow you to filter sideways from normal.

The Occurs_Once choice in this argument makes me smile because to me, it proves that the Excel team's definition of "unique" is out of step with the rest of the world. Say that you have a list in A2:A5. The list is Apple, Butter, Cherry, Apple, Butter. If you used the Excel Conditional Formatting command to mark the "unique" values, Excel would only mark Cherry. Their twisted rationale is that Cherry is the only item in the list to appear exactly once. This is never what I need when I want a list of unique values. I expect to get a list of Apple, Butter, Cherry.

The default value for Occurs_Once is True when it returns the nearly useless list of items that occur only once in the list. I think most people will be choosing False for this argument for "occurs one or more times."

Consider Figure 12.11. A list of products and customers appears in A2:B116. The silly formula in D3 shows that Lemon is the only product to be ordered exactly once:

```
=UNIQUE(A2:A116,FALSE,TRUE)
```

Who would ever need to know this? The person charged with figuring out the list of one-hit wonders might be the only case.

The far more common formula shown in D7 returns a list of every product that has been ordered one or more times. Change the third argument from TRUE to FALSE to switch to the common-sense situation of any product that has been ordered one or more times. The formula is:

```
=UNIQUE(A2:A116,FALSE,FALSE)
```

Going beyond the simple example, you could ask for all unique combinations of product and customer by entering the formula in two columns and specifying an array of A2:B116. A partial list of the results appears in H7:I17 of Figure 12.11.

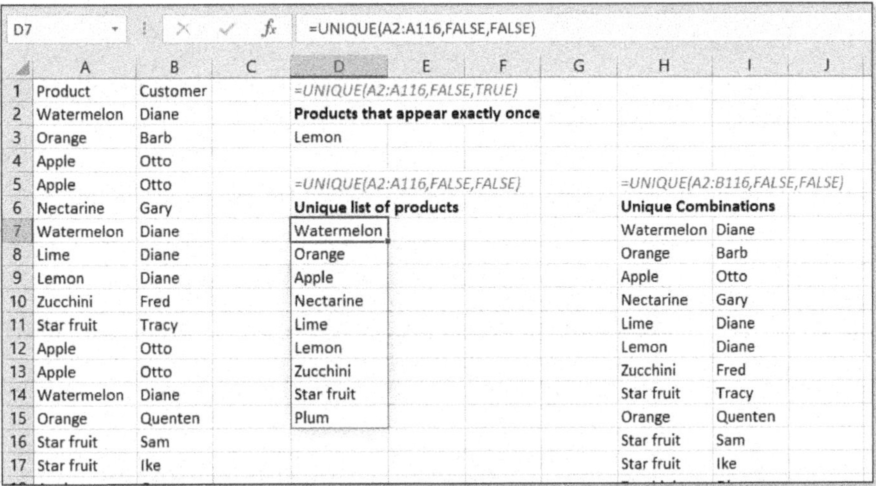

D7 =UNIQUE(A2:A116,FALSE,FALSE)

	A	B	C	D	E	F	G	H	I	J
1	Product	Customer		=UNIQUE(A2:A116,FALSE,TRUE)						
2	Watermelon	Diane		**Products that appear exactly once**						
3	Orange	Barb		Lemon						
4	Apple	Otto								
5	Apple	Otto		=UNIQUE(A2:A116,FALSE,FALSE)				=UNIQUE(A2:B116,FALSE,FALSE)		
6	Nectarine	Gary		**Unique list of products**				**Unique Combinations**		
7	Watermelon	Diane		Watermelon				Watermelon	Diane	
8	Lime	Diane		Orange				Orange	Barb	
9	Lemon	Diane		Apple				Apple	Otto	
10	Zucchini	Fred		Nectarine				Nectarine	Gary	
11	Star fruit	Tracy		Lime				Lime	Diane	
12	Apple	Otto		Lemon				Lemon	Diane	
13	Apple	Otto		Zucchini				Zucchini	Fred	
14	Watermelon	Diane		Star fruit				Star fruit	Tracy	
15	Orange	Quenten		Plum				Orange	Quenten	
16	Star fruit	Sam						Star fruit	Sam	
17	Star fruit	Ike						Star fruit	Ike	

Figure 12.11 The `UNIQUE` function dramatically simplifies returning a unique list of products.

The `UNIQUE` function does not sort the results. They appear in the same sequence they are found in the original data, just as the Advanced Filter command would do.

What if you need the results sorted? Simply wrap the `FILTER` or `UNIQUE` function inside of `SORT`. Figure 12.12 shows an example.

D3 =SORT(UNIQUE(A2:A116,FALSE,FALSE),1)

	A	B	C	D	E	F	G
1	Product	Customer		=SORT(UNIQUE(A2:A116,FALSE,FALSE),1)			
2	Watermelon	Diane		**Sorted unique list of products**			
3	Orange	Barb		Apple			
4	Apple	Otto		Lemon			
5	Apple	Otto		Lime			
6	Nectarine	Gary		Nectarine			
7	Watermelon	Diane		Orange			
8	Lime	Diane		Plum			
9	Lemon	Diane		Star fruit			
10	Zucchini	Fred		Watermelon			
11	Star fruit	Tracy		Zucchini			
12	Apple	Otto					

Figure 12.12 Combine `SORT` and `UNIQUE` to get a sorted and unique list.

TROUBLESHOOTING

The previous example used two dynamic array functions nested inside each other. The limit is 32 functions nested.

Although the dynamic array functions are more powerful than regular functions, they support the same limit of up to 32 levels of nesting.

In the following figure, `FILTER` is wrapped in `UNIQUE` and then wrapped in `SORT`. Excel has no problem dealing with these complex combinations.

Note, however, that you cannot use 3-D references in the new array functions. There will also never be support for sorting by color or icon.

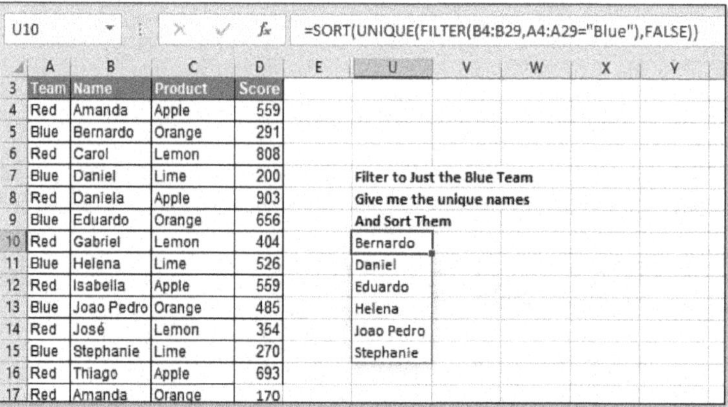

U10 =SORT(UNIQUE(FILTER(B4:B29,A4:A29="Blue"),FALSE))

	A	B	C	D	E	U
3	Team	Name	Product	Score		
4	Red	Amanda	Apple	559		
5	Blue	Bernardo	Orange	291		
6	Red	Carol	Lemon	808		
7	Blue	Daniel	Lime	200		Filter to Just the Blue Team
8	Red	Daniela	Apple	903		Give me the unique names
9	Blue	Eduardo	Orange	656		And Sort Them
10	Red	Gabriel	Lemon	404		Bernardo
11	Blue	Helena	Lime	526		Daniel
12	Red	Isabella	Apple	559		Eduardo
13	Blue	Joao Pedro	Orange	485		Helena
14	Red	José	Lemon	354		Joao Pedro
15	Blue	Stephanie	Lime	270		Stephanie
16	Red	Thiago	Apple	693		
17	Red	Amanda	Orange	170		

Generating a sequence of numbers

The new `SEQUENCE` function will generate a sequence of numbers. This function can be very simple: `=SEQUENCE(10)` entered in A1 will generate the numbers 1 through 10 in A1:A10. However, the syntax allows for a lot of flexibility:

```
=SEQUENCE([Rows],[Columns],[Start],[Stop])
```

In Figure 12.13, the formula `=SEQUENCE(10,3)` returns a 10-row by 3-column array with the numbers 1 to 30. A formula of `=SEQUENCE(10,1,7,3)` in G1 returns a 10-row by 1-column range with numbers starting with the number 7 and incrementing by 3.

C1 | fx =SEQUENCE(10,3)

	A	B	C	D	E	F	G	H
1	1		1	2	3		7	
2	2		4	5	6		10	
3	3		7	8	9		13	
4	4		10	11	12		16	
5	5		13	14	15		19	
6	6		16	17	18		22	
7	7		19	20	21		25	
8	8		22	23	24		28	
9	9		25	26	27		31	
10	10		28	29	30		34	
11	=SEQUENCE(10)		=SEQUENCE(10,3)				=SEQUENCE(10,1,7,3)	
12								

Figure 12.13 Generate a sequence of numbers.

You might be thinking that SEQUENCE is the most boring new function. I don't think Microsoft intended SEQUENCE to be used, as shown in Figure 12.13. They did not give us SEQUENCE just to save us the hassle of Ctrl+dragging the fill handle or using =A1+1.

The power of SEQUENCE is when you need to return a sequence of numbers to another formula.

My favorite examples in this realm are the IPMT and PPMT functions that are often used to calculate amortization tables for loans. These functions are discussed in Chapter 10, but you can see the power of SEQUENCE in the examples in Figure 12.14.

In Figure 12.14, you are planning on borrowing $772,000 for 30 years. A PMT function in B4 calculates the monthly payment.

But to create an amortization table, you need the IPMT and PPMT functions. A sequence of 5 numbers in A7:A11 is used to calculate the interest portion of the payment in B7:B11. As you would expect, the interest portion of the payment goes down a little bit each month. Say that you need to know the total interest paid in months 1 through 5. A SUM function in B12 calculates the total as $13,633.03. It took 11 cells to calculate that value.

Can we shorten this by using SEQUENCE as the Period Number inside of IPMT? The formula in D7 is `=IPMT($B$3/12,SEQUENCE(5),$B$2,$B$1)`. Press Enter, and Excel returns the five monthly answers. That is fine, but you want the answer in one formula.

The formula in F7 wraps the IPMT inside a SUM function. Amazingly, there is no need to press Ctrl+Shift+Enter to make this work: `=SUM(IPMT($B$3/12,SEQUENCE(5),$B$2,B$B1))` returns the same answer that required 11 cells over in B12.

CHAPTER 12

What if you want to know the total interest paid in each year of the loan for tax planning purposes? The formula in G10 uses a SEQUENCE function to return 12 consecutive numbers starting from the month number in F10. Copy this down for each row of the loan.

Couldn't you do this with CUMIPMT? Sure, but it requires an extra argument. The point of the example is that you will can insert the SEQUENCE function inside of other functions to generate array functions.

D7 =IPMT($B$3/12,SEQUENCE(5),$B$2,$B$1)

	A	B	C	D	E	F	G	H	I
1	Price	772000		B7	=IPMT($B$3/12,A7,$B$2,$B$1)				
2	Term	360		D7	=IPMT($B$3/12,SEQUENCE(5),$B$2,$B$1)				
3	Rate	4.25%		F7	=SUM(IPMT($B$3/12,SEQUENCE(5),$B$2,$B$1))				
4	Payment	($3,797.78)		G10	=SUM(IPMT($B$3/12,SEQUENCE(12,1,F10,1),$B$2,$B$1))				
5									
6	Month	Interest				Interest Months 1-5			
7	1	($2,734.17)		($2,734.17)		($13,633.03)			
8	2	($2,730.40)		-2730.3997					
9	3	($2,726.62)		-2726.6194		Interest in 12 months starting			
10	4	($2,722.83)		-2722.8257		1	($32,558.42)		
11	5	($2,719.02)		-2719.0186		13	($31,994.39)		
12		($13,633.03)				25	($31,405.91)		
13						37	($30,791.92)		
14						349	($1,032.02)		

Figure 12.14 Use SEQUENCE inside of other functions to generate new array formulas.

TROUBLESHOOTING

The format of the spill range will not be updated by the formula. The answers can spill, but the spill cells will remain unformatted.

If you know that your formula is going to return currency or dates, you should pre-format the range. In the following image, you would format B3:B12 as a date before entering =SEQUENCE(10,1,C1) in B3.

B3 =SEQUENCE(10,1,C1)

	A	B	C	D	E
1			2/17/2025		
2					
3		2/17/2025			
4		2/18/2025			
5		2/19/2025			
6		2/20/2025			
7		2/21/2025			
8		2/22/2025			
9		2/23/2025			
10		2/24/2025			
11		2/25/2025			
12		2/26/2025			

CHAPTER 12

Generating an array of random numbers with a formula

The new RANDARRAY function will return a range of any number of rows and columns of random numbers.

The syntax is = `RANDARRAY(rows,columns,min,max,integer)`.

A trivial example shown in Figure 12.15 generates five rows and three columns of random integers between 11 and 99.

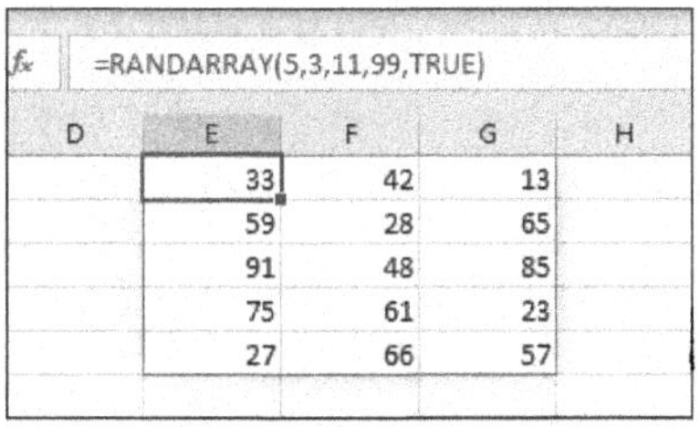

fx =RANDARRAY(5,3,11,99,TRUE)

D	E	F	G	H
	33	42	13	
	59	28	65	
	91	48	85	
	75	61	23	
	27	66	57	

Figure 12.15 Use RANDARRAY to generate an array of random numbers.

The power of RANDARRAY will be in building simulations and Monte-Carlo models where you need to multiply a range of numbers by a series of random numbers.

Refer to the entire array

To refer to the entire spilled dynamic array in another formula, use the new Spilled Range Operator. =`AVERAGE(E1#)` would average all the numbers returned by the formula in E1 in Figure 12.15.

Learning about new functions and features

The funny thing about Microsoft 365 is that any book will become just a little more obsolete on any given Tuesday as the Excel team pushes new features out to the Microsoft 365 subscribers. Once a year, Microsoft invites me to a non-disclosure session and shows me what they are working on. Some of those new features are in the product now. But there are other notes in my notebook about features that will be coming sometime in the future.

Using power formula techniques

Excel offers an amazing variety of formulas. This chapter covers some of the unorthodox formulas you can build in Excel. In this chapter, you discover the following:

- Using a formula to add the same cell across many sheets
- Using a formula to reference the previous sheet

- Editing multiple formulas into one
- Letting data determine the cell reference to use with the `INDIRECT` function
- Transposing relative column references to rows
- Using `ROW()` or `COLUMN()` to return an array of numbers
- Using one formula to return a whole range of answers

Using 3D formulas to spear through many worksheets

It is common to have a workbook composed of identical worksheets for each month or quarter of the year. Every worksheet needs to have the same arrangement of rows.

If you want to total a particular cell across all the worksheets, you might try to write a formula with one term for each sheet—for example, `=Sheet1!A1+Sheet2!A1+Sheet3!A1`.... However, Excel supports a special type of formula that spears through several worksheets to add a particular cell from each worksheet. The syntax of the formula is `=SUM(Sheet1:Sheetn!A1)`. If you use spaces in your worksheet names, add apostrophes around the pair of sheet names `=SUM('Jan 2021:Dec2021'!A1)`.

As shown in Figure 12.16, Net Revenue is in row 4 on the January worksheet and is in the same row on the February worksheet. You cannot see this in Figure 12.16, but the arrangement of rows is identical on every worksheet.

	A	B	C
1	January		
2			
3		This Year	Prior Year
4	Net Revenue	9231	8049
5	Cost of Sales	4028	3269
6			
7	**Gross Margin**	**5203**	**4780**
8			
9	R&D	1176	1186
10	Mktg, G&A	1342	1170
11			
12	**Operating Expenses**	**2518**	**2356**
13			
14	**Operating Income**	**2685**	**2424**
15			
16	Interest	127	47
17			
18	**Income Before Taxes**	**2812**	**2471**
19			
20	Provision for Taxes	716	663
21			
22	**Net Income**	**2096**	**1808**
23			

	A	B	C
1	February		
2			
3		This Year	Prior Year
4	Net Revenue	9416	8210
5	Cost of Sales	4109	3335
6			
7	**Gross Margin**	**5307**	**4875**
8			
9	R&D	1200	1210
10	Mktg, G&A	1369	1193
11			
12	**Operating Expenses**	**2569**	**2403**
13			
14	**Operating Income**	**2738**	**2472**
15			
16	Interest	130	48
17			
18	**Income Before Taxes**	**2868**	**2520**
19			
20	Provision for Taxes	730	676
21			
22	**Net Income**	**2138**	**1844**
23			

Figure 12.16 The 12 workbooks, January through December, contain an identical arrangement of rows and columns.

When creating a worksheet, you might be tempted to write a formula such as `=Jan!B4+Feb!B4+Mar!B4+Apr!B4`, but doing so would be rather tedious.

Instead, you can write a formula that totals cell B4 from each worksheet, Jan through Dec. An example of the formula is `=SUM(Jan:Dec!B4)`. After you enter this formula in cell B4, you can easily copy it to all the other relevant cells in the worksheet, as shown in Figure 12.17.

Excel offers a worksheet function called `SHEETS()`. You can use `=SHEETS(Jan:Dec!A1)` to learn that there are 12 sheets in the reference.

TIP

Sometimes you might need to sum a cell on all sheets that have a common naming convention. Perhaps you have worksheet names such as CostQ1, ExpensesQ1, CostQ2, ExpensesQ2, CostQ3, ExpensesQ3, CostQ4, and ExpensesQ4. To sum cell B4 on all the cost sheets, type `=SUM('Cost*'!B4)`. Remarkably, Excel converts this shorthand to a formula that points to each of the cost sheets:

```
=SUM(CostQ1!B4,CostQ2!B4,CostQ3!B4,CostQ4!B4)
```

I need to give a tip of the cap to Microsoft guru Bob Umlas for this cool trick. Bob cautions that if you enter this formula on a worksheet that starts with Cost, the active sheet will be left out of the equation.

B4 =SUM(Jan:Dec!B4)

	A	B	C	D	E	F
1	Total Year					
2						
3		This Year	Prior Year		# of Sheets in references	
4	Net Revenue	119727	104394		12	=SHEETS(Jan:Dec!B4)
5	Cost of Sales	49911	40508			
6						
7	**Gross Margin**	**69816**	**63886**			
8						
9	R&D	15253	15383			
10	Mktg, G&A	17406	15176			
11						
12	**Operating Expenses**	**32659**	**30559**			
13						
14	**Operating Income**	**37157**	**33327**			
15						
16	Interest	1648	610			
17						
18	**Income Before Taxes**	**38805**	**33937**			
19						
20	Provision for Taxes	9286	8599			
21						
22	**Net Income**	**29519**	**25338**			
23						

Figure 12.17 This formula spears through 12 worksheets to total cell B4 from each worksheet from January through December.

Inside OUT

The 3-D reference syntax is difficult to remember, particularly if you are not sure if you need apostrophes around the worksheet names.

There is an easy way to build these formulas using the mouse. Say that you want to total cells B5:N20 on all twelve sheets from Jan 2021 to Dec 2021. That total should appear on the Summary worksheet in cell B5. Follow these steps:

1. **Start on the Summary worksheet, in cell B5.**
2. **Start typing =SUM(.**
3. **Using the mouse, click on the sheet tab for Jan 2021. Do not select any cells on that worksheet.**
4. **Hold down the shift key and click on the sheet tab for Dec 2021. At this point, the formula in the formula bar is:**

   ```
   =SUM('Jan 2021:.m.Dec 2021'!
   ```

5. **Click on B5 and drag to N20.**
6. **Type the closing parenthesis and press Enter. You will end up with this formula:**

   ```
   =SUM('Jan 2021:Dec 2021'!B5:N20)
   ```


Referring to the previous worksheet

When you have an arrangement of several sequential worksheets, you might want to keep a running total. This total would be calculated as the total on this sheet plus the running total from the previous sheet.

It is somewhat difficult to build a formula that always points to the previous sheet. Maybe you've tried the wrong approach shown in Figure 12.18: On the Feb worksheet, a formula refers to =Jan!B4. However, if you copy the formula to Mar or Apr, the formula still points to the Jan worksheet, which is not what you want.

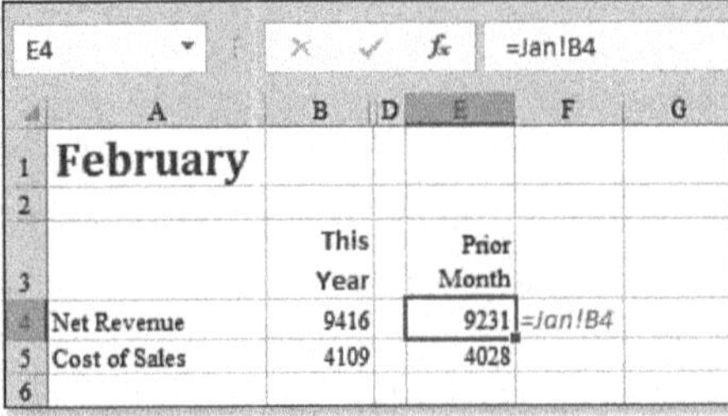

Figure 12.18 You must rewrite this formula for each of the 11 other months.

Excel offers a very cool solution to this problem. The solution requires a few lines of VBA macro code. Don't be afraid. I can get you there and back without any problems. Here's what you do:

1. Press Alt+F11 to launch the VBA Editor.
2. In the VBA Editor, select Insert, Module.
3. Type the following lines into the blank module:

```
Function PrevSheet(ByVal MyCell As Range)
 Application.Volatile
 On Error Resume Next
 PrevSheet = Sheets(MyCell.Parent.Index - 1).Range(MyCell.Address)
End Function
```

4. Select File, Close, and Return To Microsoft Excel to return to Excel.

To realize the power of this function, you can put the workbook in Group mode and enter the function in 11 worksheets at once:

1. Select the Feb worksheet.
2. Hold down the Shift key while clicking the Dec worksheet tab. This highlights all 11 worksheets. Although you see the Feb worksheet, anything you do on that worksheet is also done to all 11 selected worksheets.
3. In cell E4, enter *=PrevSheet(B4)*. Press Enter to accept the formula. The Feb worksheet picks up the value from Jan, but each additional worksheet picks up the value from the previous sheet, as shown in Figure 12.19.

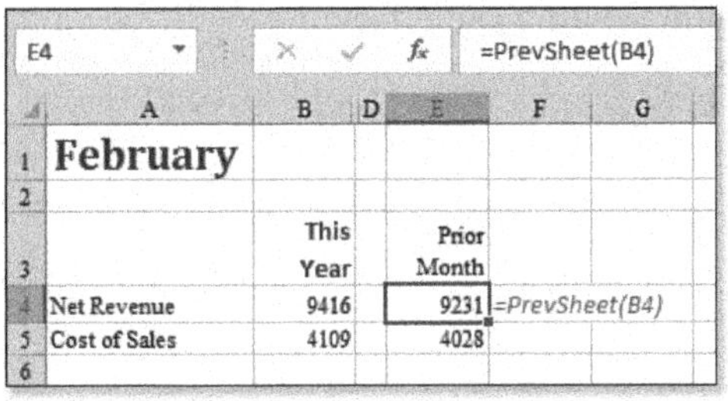

E4 =PrevSheet(B4)

	A	B	D	E	F	G
1	February					
2						
3		This Year		Prior Month		
4	Net Revenue	9416		9231	=PrevSheet(B4)	
5	Cost of Sales	4109		4028		
6						

Figure 12.19 One formula using the custom function PrevSheet solves the prior month problem seamlessly across all the worksheets.

4. With the worksheets still in Group mode, copy cell B4 from the Feb worksheet to cells B5, B7, and so on.
5. Right-click any sheet tab and select Ungroup.

PART III

Data analysis with Excel

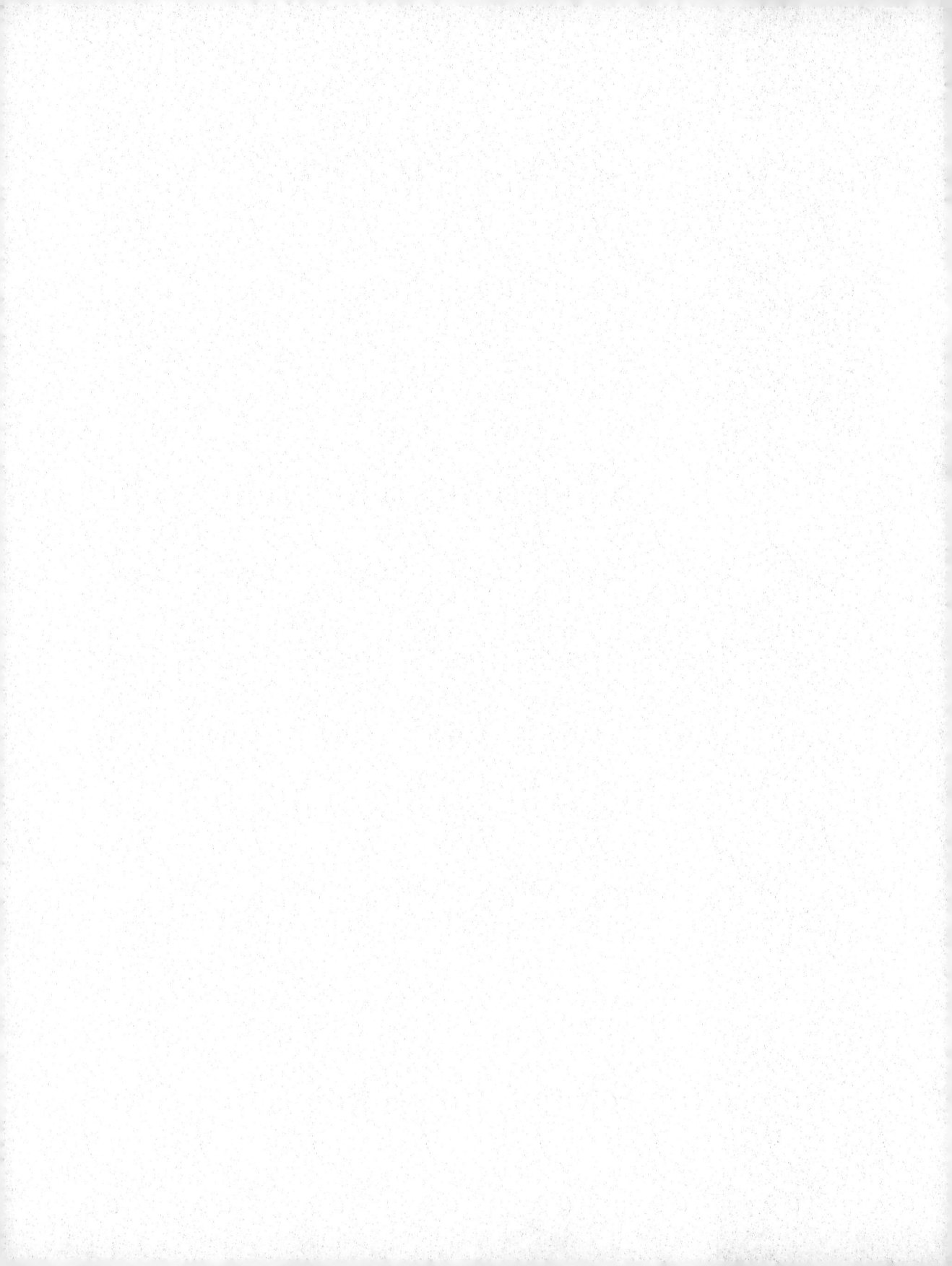

CHAPTER 13

Transforming data with Power Query

What if there was a tool that let you clean data 20 percent faster on day one? What if that tool accurately remembered all your steps so you could clean the data 99 percent faster on days 2 through 750? That tool has been hiding on the Data tab since Excel 2016.

Power Query is the best feature to arrive in Excel about which most people have never heard. After Excel 2013 was released, the Power Query add-in was released for Excel 2010 and Excel 2013. The add-in was great, but many people in corporate environments don't ever see the add-ins. By the time Excel 2016 shipped, Power Query was old news for the Excel team, and it was quietly slipped into the Data tab of the ribbon. Unfortunately, most people never realize that the icons in the Get & Transform group are as powerful as they are.

Between Excel 2016 and today, the tool continues to grow by leaps and bounds. You can now split by delimiter to rows, and you can combine a whole folder of Excel files or combine all worksheets in a workbook. Power Query is the method for adding custom data types to your workbook.

This chapter introduces some of the tools available in Power Query.

Using Power Query

The Power Query tools were created to make it easier to clean ugly data. Suppose that your IT department provides a data set every day that has some problems. Rather than wait for the IT department to rewrite the query, you can use Power Query to memorize the steps needed to clean the data. When the IT department provides a new file, you simply refresh the query and Excel repeats all the data cleansing steps.

Figure 13.1 shows an ugly data set. Two different fields are in column A, separated by a comma. The customer column is in uppercase. Columns D through O are a repeating group with various month values going across. To pivot this data, you must unpivot D:O, creating an extra date column and then 12 times as many rows.

	A	B	C	D	E	F
1	REGION, MARKET	PRODUCT	CUSTOMER	Jan-21	Feb-21	Mar-21
2	CENTRAL, CHICAGO	XYZ	SPRINGBOARD	13962	2401	13867
3	EAST, ORLANDO	DEF	EXCEL LEARNING ZONE	2358	15104	5532
4	SOUTH, HOUSTON	XYZ	RIBBON COMMANDER FRAMEWORK	7167	21456	17150
5	CENTRAL, CHICAGO	DEF	DATASOLVERZ.COM	4380	7032	21357
6	EAST, ORLANDO	ABC	NEW HOPE LAUNDRY	16784	7132	11430
7	WEST, SEATTLE	DEF	MYSPREADSHEETLAB	13853	11220	7136
8	CENTRAL, CHICAGO	XYZ	SURTEN EXCEL	5532	6714	14497
9	EAST, BALTIMORE	ABC	NETCOM COMPUTER	4948	13206	5700
10	SOUTH, HOUSTON	XYZ	MIKE'S DOG STORE, SAN ANTONIO	11550	17757	14497

Figure 13.1 There are some problems in this data set created by the IT department.

Establishing a workflow

Say that the IT department sends you this data every month. Your plan could be to save the workbook in the same folder with the same name, and you will build your query in a new workbook. This workbook will be designed to always open the file located at `C:\Foo\Ugly-DataFromIT.xlsx`.

Or, perhaps the file that they send each month must be combined with all of the previous monthly files. In that case, you should create a new folder to hold all of the workbooks from IT. Do not store anything else in this folder. A new workbook with the query would be saved in a different folder. In this case, you would choose Get Data, From File, From Folder.

Either of the above workflows will make it easier to refresh the query in the future. The "wrong" approach is to open the file from IT and then build the query in that file.

Loading data using Power Query

Power Query can load data from any of these sources:

- **Files:** Workbook, PDF, Text, CSV, XML, JSON, or from a folder
- **Database:** SQL Server, Access, Analysis Services, Oracle, IBM DB2, MySQL, PostgreSQL, Sybase, Teradata, and SAP HANA
- **Azure:** SQL Database, Synapse Analytics, HDInsight (HDFS), Blob Storage, Table Storage, and Data Lake Storage, and Data Explorer
- **Power BI:** Create a pivot table connected to your company's Power BI data
- **Online:** SharePoint, Exchange, Dynamics 365, Salesforce Objects, and Salesforce Reports
- **Other:** Table or range on a sheet, Microsoft Query, SharePoint List, OData Feed, Hadoop File, ActiveDirectory, Microsoft Exchange, ODBC, and OLEDB

All the preceding items are found in the Get Data menu. This is the first icon on the Data tab. It is found in the Get & Transform Data group. A few of those choices are repeated in the Get & Transform Data group: From Text/CSV, From Web, and From Sheet.

NOTE

You might have previously used the legacy connectors. In previous versions of Excel, the Data tab contained seven icons: From Access, From Web, From Text, From SQL Server, From OData Data Feed, From XML Data Import, and From Data Connection Wizard. While these seven commands still exist, they have been removed from the ribbon. If you need to access the old commands, go to File, Options, Data. The various checkboxes in the Show Legacy Data Import Wizards section allow you to bring the icons back. Any icons you choose here will appear under Data, Get Data, Legacy Wizards.

Loading data from a single Excel workbook

Create a new blank workbook. Save the workbook with a name such as `PowerQueryToLoadUglyData.xlsx`.

Choose Data, Get Data, From File, From Workbook, as shown in Figure 13.2.

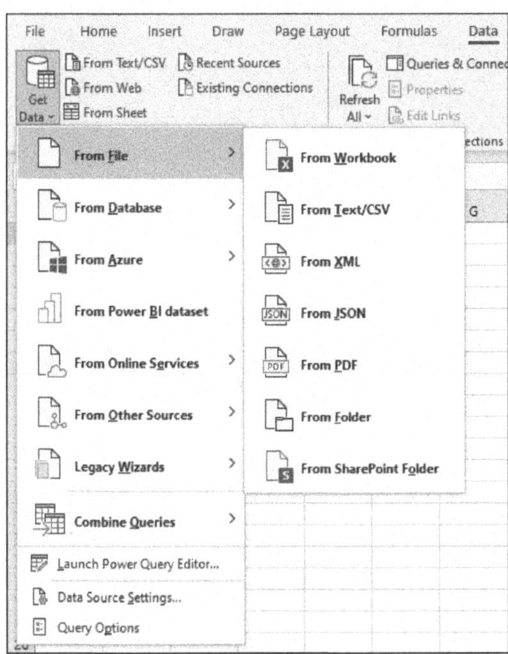

Figure 13.2 Specify the source of the data to be transformed.

Depending on the source, you will need to browse to the file, provide a connect string to the database, or provide a URL.

The Navigator dialog box will appear. Initially, nothing is shown in the Data Preview on the right. On the left side of the dialog box, click on the worksheet named Data. The Preview will appear on the right.

Below the Preview, you have choices to Load, Transform Data, or Cancel. You want to choose Transform Data so you can specify the data cleansing steps (see Figure 13.3).

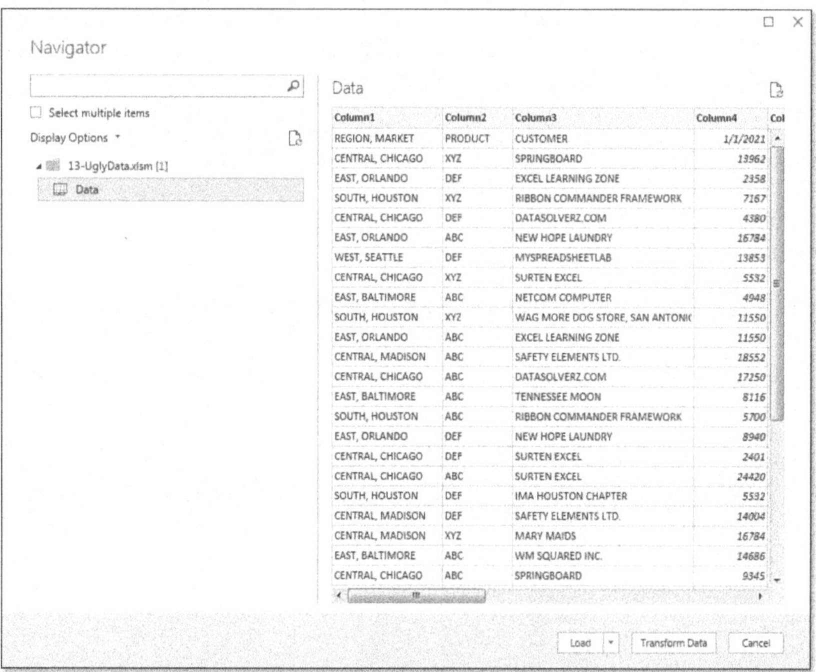

Figure 13.3 Select the worksheet in the left pane to see a preview on the right pane.

Transforming data in Power Query

The data appears in a new window called the Query Editor. Ribbon tabs appear for Home, Transform, Add Column, and View.

As shown in Figure 13.4, Power Query is treating the header row as a data row. Use Home, Use First Row As Headers to convert that row to a header row. If you ever had the opposite problem, in which Power Query assumed the first data row is headers, you could open the same drop-down menu and choose Use Headers As First Row.

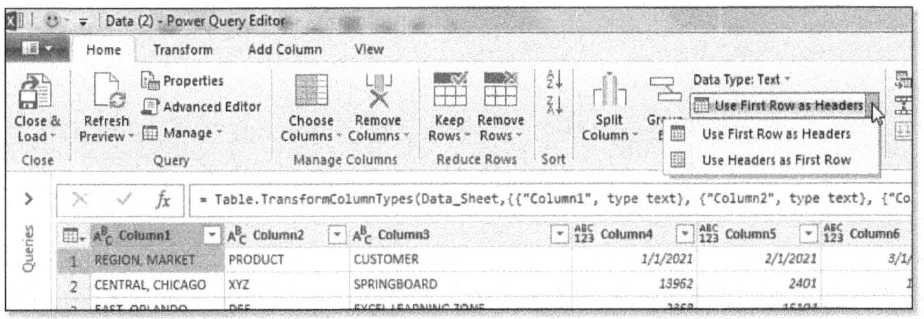

Figure 13.4 The first edit is to identify the first row as headers.

Column A has both `Region` and `Market` in a single column, separated by a comma. Select that column by clicking the `REGION, MARKET` header and choosing Home, Split Column, By Delimiter.

Take a look at the Split By Delimiter dialog box in Figure 13.5, which feels like the Text To Columns Wizard in Excel. However, this version is far superior.

First, Power Query was able to guess that your delimiter is a comma. How did it do this? It looked at every cell in the first 20 rows and noticed a comma in each one. This is not rocket science. It makes me wonder why the Excel Text To Columns Wizard can't figure it out.

Second, Power Query will let you split at every comma or only the first and last comma. For anyone who ever had "Mary Ellen Walton," "Judy Norton Taylor," or "Billy Joe Jim Bob Briggs" overwrite adjacent data after choosing Text To Columns, you will appreciate the ability to force the results into two columns.

Finally, Power Query offers the amazing ability to split each delimiter to a new row. Data in the other columns is copied down to the new rows.

After you split a column, the first column from the split will have a heading of `REGION, MARKET.1`. The second column from the split will have a heading of `REGION, MARKET.2`. Double-click each heading and type a new name such as **Region** for column A and **Market** for column B.

If you need to convert a column of uppercase words to proper case, select the column and select Transform, Format, Capitalize Each Word (see Figure 13.6).

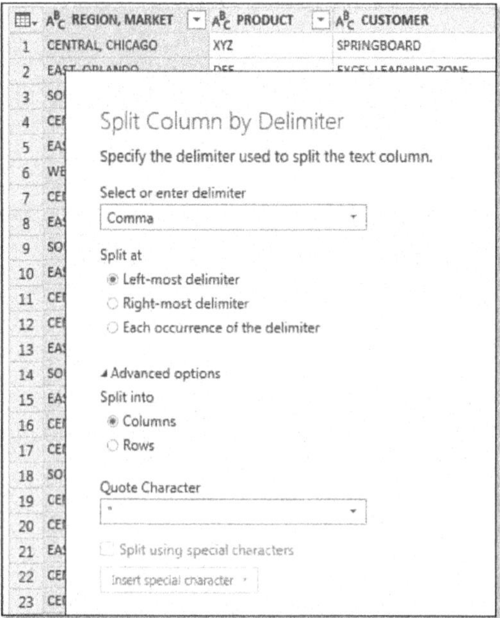

Figure 13.5 Split By Delimiter is better than Text To Columns.

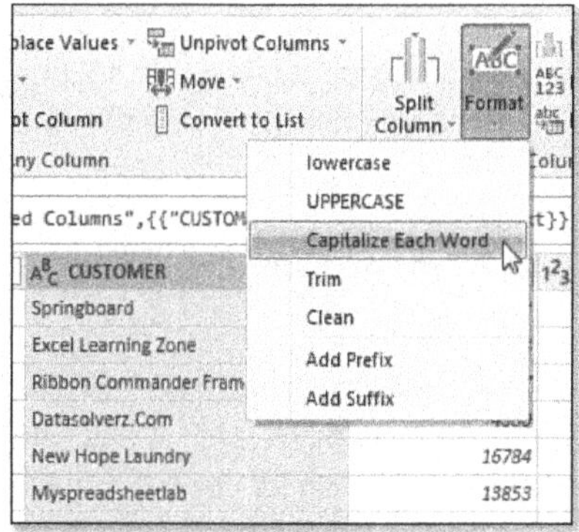

Figure 13.6 The menu options for converting to proper case, uppercase, or lowercase.

Unpivoting data in Power Query

It is very common to see data with months or years stretching across the columns. Pivot tables made from this structure are very difficult to use. In the past, fixing the data structure involved repeatedly copying and pasting, or using an obscure trick with Multiple Consolidation Ranges. Power Query makes this process amazingly simple.

In Figure 13.7, the first four columns are selected. Choose Transform, Unpivot Columns, Unpivot Other Columns.

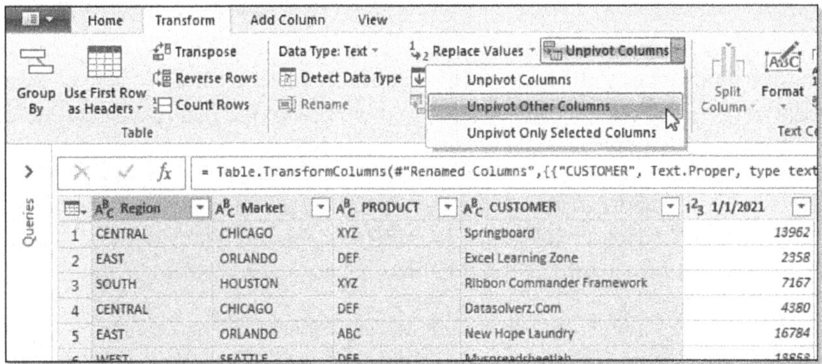

Figure 13.7 Select the label columns and choose to unpivot the other columns.

In this example, you go from 81 rows of 16 columns to 972 rows of six columns. As you can see in Figure 13.8, the fifth column is called `Attribute`, and the sixth column is called `Value`. You can use the Rename function to give these meaningful names, such as `Month` and `Value` or `Month` and `Revenue`.

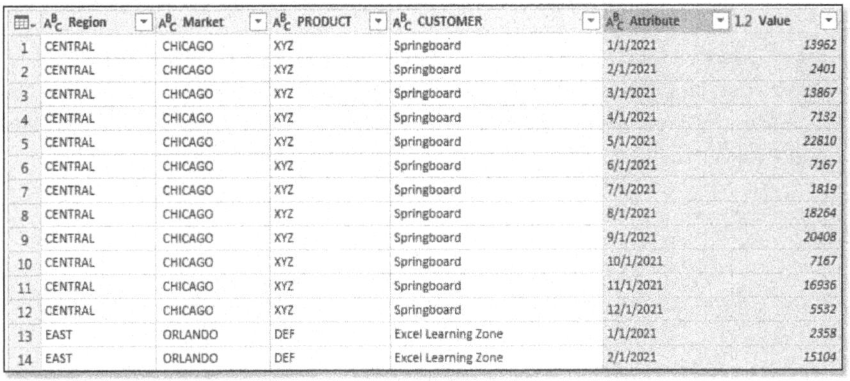

	Region	Market	PRODUCT	CUSTOMER	Attribute	Value
1	CENTRAL	CHICAGO	XYZ	Springboard	1/1/2021	13962
2	CENTRAL	CHICAGO	XYZ	Springboard	2/1/2021	2401
3	CENTRAL	CHICAGO	XYZ	Springboard	3/1/2021	13867
4	CENTRAL	CHICAGO	XYZ	Springboard	4/1/2021	7132
5	CENTRAL	CHICAGO	XYZ	Springboard	5/1/2021	22810
6	CENTRAL	CHICAGO	XYZ	Springboard	6/1/2021	7167
7	CENTRAL	CHICAGO	XYZ	Springboard	7/1/2021	1819
8	CENTRAL	CHICAGO	XYZ	Springboard	8/1/2021	18264
9	CENTRAL	CHICAGO	XYZ	Springboard	9/1/2021	20408
10	CENTRAL	CHICAGO	XYZ	Springboard	10/1/2021	7167
11	CENTRAL	CHICAGO	XYZ	Springboard	11/1/2021	16936
12	CENTRAL	CHICAGO	XYZ	Springboard	12/1/2021	5532
13	EAST	ORLANDO	DEF	Excel Learning Zone	1/1/2021	2358
14	EAST	ORLANDO	DEF	Excel Learning Zone	2/1/2021	15104

Figure 13.8 Unpivoting creates a data set that is easy to pivot.

Select the Date column. Look at the Data Type value on the Transform tab. Power Query is treating these dates like text. With the Date column selected, choose Date from the Data Type drop-down menu.

If there are customers who had no revenue in a certain month, you could open the Filter drop-down menu on the Value column and uncheck 0 values to remove those records.

Adding columns in Power Query

The new Column From Examples feature in Power Query is like Flash Fill in Excel. Column From Examples creates a formula that can be re-used later. Back in Excel 2016, you would have to write a new formula to create a column. The formula language is not like the Excel language. The formula to get a month name from a date is `Date.MonthName([Date])`. Power Query would not accept `date.monthname` or `Date.Monthname`. You had to type **Date.MonthName** with the three capital letters.

Every time that I had to create a formula in Power Query, I was always going out to the web to the Power Query Function Reference. Table B.2 in Appendix B provides a cross-reference showing the Excel formula functions and their Power Query M equivalent functions.

Today, the new Column From Examples features simplifies the process (see Figure 13.9). Follow these steps:

1. Select the Date column.
2. In Power Query, choose Add Column, Column From Examples. A new Column1 appears on the far-right side of the window.
3. Click the first cell of Column1 and type **`January`**.
4. Power Query will offer a choice of Month Name From Date. Click OK.

Power Query will add a new column called Month Name. If you do not see the formula bar above your data, choose View, Formula Bar. The formula bar shows that Month Name From Date uses the `Date.MonthName([Month])` function. This is useful if you plan on learning Power Query formulas.

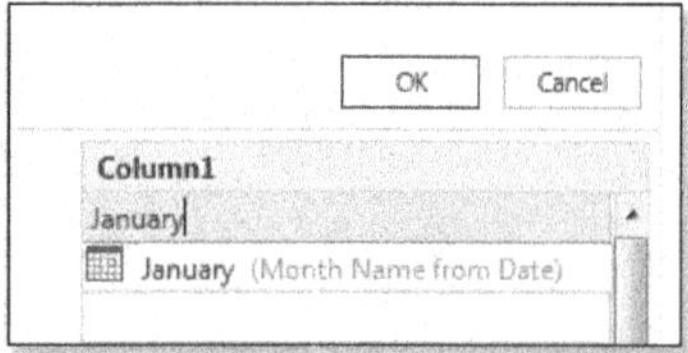

Figure 13.9 Add a new column to the query by typing an example.

Reviewing the query

As shown in Figure 13.10, the right side of the Query Editor shows all the transformation steps that you've taken so far. You can see any settings associated with a step by clicking the gear icon. You can see the data at any point in the process by clicking the step. You can delete a step by using the X icon to the left of any step.

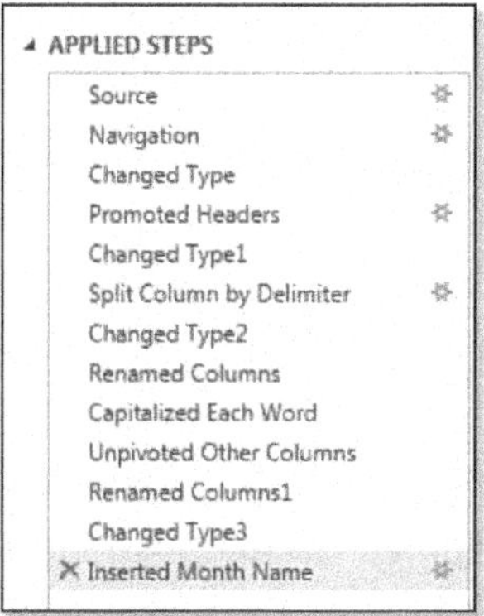

Figure 13.10 A list of transformation steps is saved with the query.

Power Query is writing an entire program in the M language behind the scenes. Go to View, Advanced Editor to see the M that was generated as you performed the data cleansing steps. Figure 13.11 shows an example.

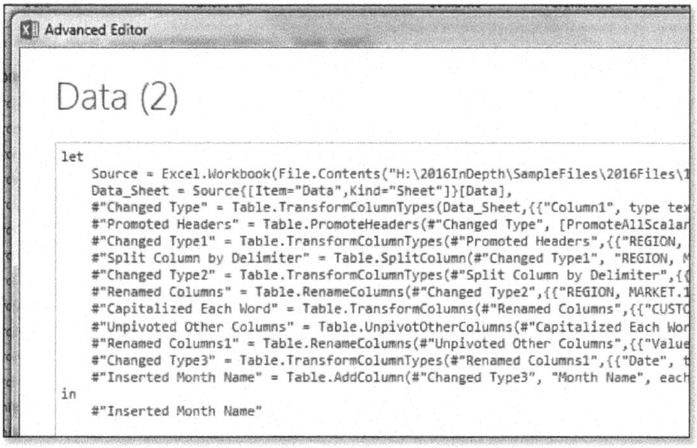

Advanced Editor

Data (2)

```
let
    Source = Excel.Workbook(File.Contents("H:\2016InDepth\SampleFiles\2016Files\1
    Data_Sheet = Source{[Item="Data",Kind="Sheet"]}[Data],
    #"Changed Type" = Table.TransformColumnTypes(Data_Sheet,{{"Column1", type tex
    #"Promoted Headers" = Table.PromoteHeaders(#"Changed Type", [PromoteAllScalar
    #"Changed Type1" = Table.TransformColumnTypes(#"Promoted Headers",{{"REGION,
    #"Split Column by Delimiter" = Table.SplitColumn(#"Changed Type1", "REGION, M
    #"Changed Type2" = Table.TransformColumnTypes(#"Split Column by Delimiter",{{
    #"Renamed Columns" = Table.RenameColumns(#"Changed Type2",{{"REGION, MARKET.1
    #"Capitalized Each Word" = Table.TransformColumns(#"Renamed Columns",{{"CUSTC
    #"Unpivoted Other Columns" = Table.UnpivotOtherColumns(#"Capitalized Each Wor
    #"Renamed Columns1" = Table.RenameColumns(#"Unpivoted Other Columns",{{"Value
    #"Changed Type3" = Table.TransformColumnTypes(#"Renamed Columns1",{{"Date", t
    #"Inserted Month Name" = Table.AddColumn(#"Changed Type3", "Month Name", each
in
    #"Inserted Month Name"
```

Figure 13.11 This M language query is written while you use the interface.

Loading and refreshing the data

After doing all the steps to clean the data, you can choose Home, Close & Load, as shown in Figure 13.12. You can either load to an Excel worksheet or directly to the Data Model. If you are loading more than 1,048,576 records, you will want to load the data to the Data Model.

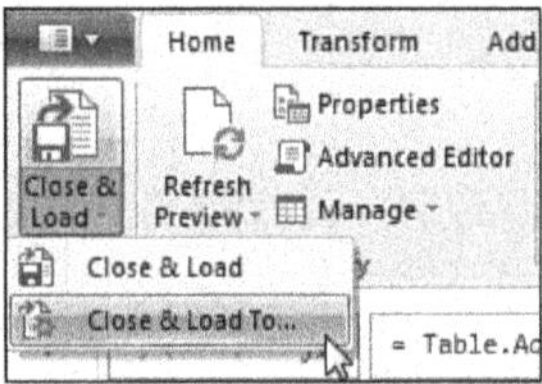

Figure 13.12 Load the query and query definition to Excel or the Data Model.

Here is the beautiful feature: After you load the data to Excel, you can use Data, Refresh All to have the query go back to the data source, load the current data, and perform all the data cleansing steps automatically.

This is one example of the transformations available in Power Query. There is more functionality, and new functions are added monthly. You can use Power Query to consolidate all worksheets from a single file or one worksheet from multiple files.

Splitting each delimiter to a new row

Look at the second row of Figure 13.13. MyOnlineTrainingHub.com ordered 637 bundles of Apple; Cherry; Iceberg. You need to split those products into three rows. The customer name and all other information should be copied to the new rows.

Select the Products column. Select Split Column, By Delimiter. Power Query displays the Split Column By Delimiter dialog box and correctly guesses the delimiter is a semicolon.

Click the Advanced Options, and you will see an option to Split Into either columns or rows; choose Rows.

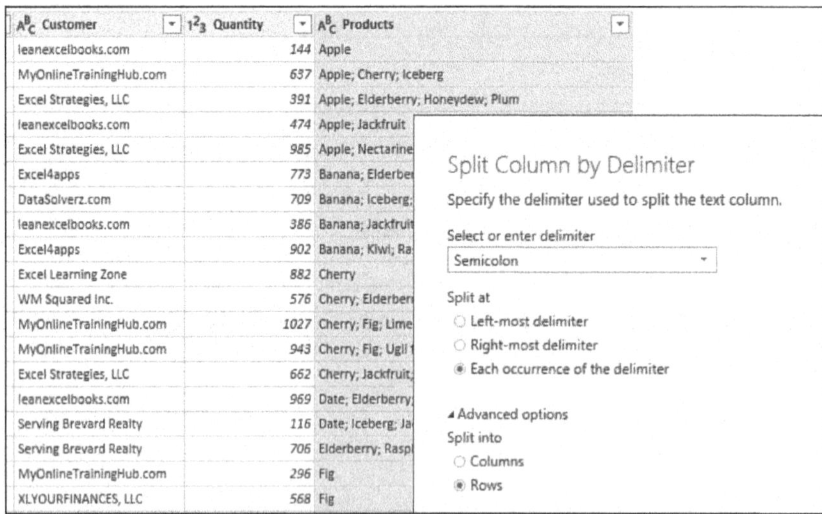

Figure 13.13 Split each semicolon to a new row.

When you click OK to complete the split, the 126 rows transform into 367 rows. Look how the 637 items for MyOnlineTrainingHub.com now appear on three separate rows in Figure 13.14.

Customer	Quantity	Products
leanexcelbooks.com	144	Apple
MyOnlineTrainingHub.com	637	Apple
MyOnlineTrainingHub.com	637	Cherry
MyOnlineTrainingHub.com	637	Iceberg
Excel Strategies, LLC	391	Apple
Excel Strategies, LLC	391	Elderberry
Excel Strategies, LLC	391	Honeydew
Excel Strategies, LLC	391	Plum

Figure 13.14 Excel splits each product to a new row and copies the other information down.

Appending one worksheet from every workbook in a folder

Power Query's best trick is to combine all of the single-sheet workbooks from a single folder.

From Excel, choose Get Data, From File, From Folder, then specify the folder. Power Query will show you a list of files in the folder. Choose Combine & Edit, as shown in Figure 13.15. In the Navigator screen, choose the correct worksheet.

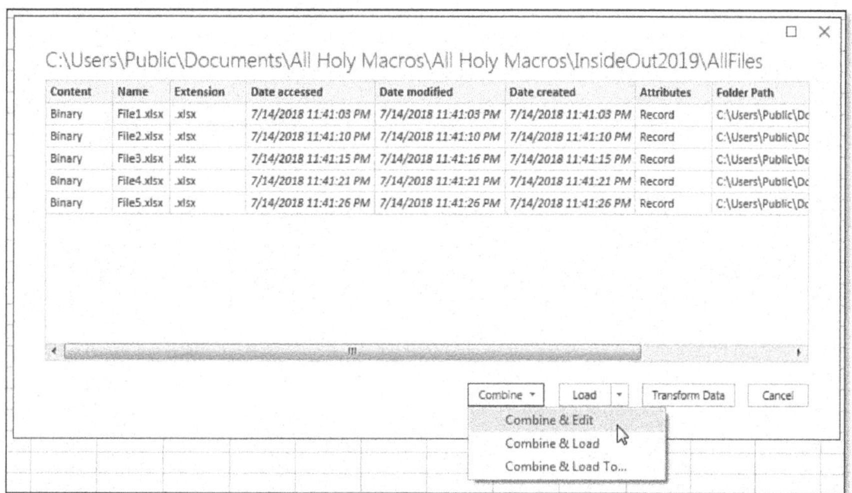

Content	Name	Extension	Date accessed	Date modified	Date created	Attributes	Folder Path
Binary	File1.xlsx	.xlsx	7/14/2018 11:41:03 PM	7/14/2018 11:41:03 PM	7/14/2018 11:41:03 PM	Record	C:\Users\Public\Dc
Binary	File2.xlsx	.xlsx	7/14/2018 11:41:10 PM	7/14/2018 11:41:10 PM	7/14/2018 11:41:10 PM	Record	C:\Users\Public\Dc
Binary	File3.xlsx	.xlsx	7/14/2018 11:41:15 PM	7/14/2018 11:41:16 PM	7/14/2018 11:41:15 PM	Record	C:\Users\Public\Dc
Binary	File4.xlsx	.xlsx	7/14/2018 11:41:21 PM	7/14/2018 11:41:21 PM	7/14/2018 11:41:21 PM	Record	C:\Users\Public\Dc
Binary	File5.xlsx	.xlsx	7/14/2018 11:41:26 PM	7/14/2018 11:41:26 PM	7/14/2018 11:41:26 PM	Record	C:\Users\Public\Dc

Figure 13.15 Choose to combine all of the workbooks in a folder.

Power Query is smart enough to promote the first row of the first file as headers. It will then discard all of the other headers in the remaining workbooks.

If you have extra columns in some files, those columns will appear in the final query, with the word "null" for the records that did not have the extra column.

Over time, if more workbooks are added to the folder, you simply have to click Refresh to have Excel reload everything from the folder.

Appending worksheets from one workbook

What if you have a workbook with several worksheets and you need to combine those records? This trick from Matt Allington works, but it is not as smart as combining workbooks. You have to make sure that all of the worksheets contain the same columns in the same order.

Follow these steps:

1. Say you have a workbook with several worksheets. There is one worksheet that does not need to be combined because it only contains boilerplate instructions. Keep the workbook closed, and start with a new blank workbook.
2. Choose, Data, Get Data, From Workbook.
3. Navigate to and select the workbook. Excel displays the Navigator dialog box.
4. At the top left of the Navigator is a folder with the workbook name and then a list of worksheets. Right-click on the folder name and choose Transform Data, as shown in Figure 13.16. This step is not obvious and is the key to combining worksheets.

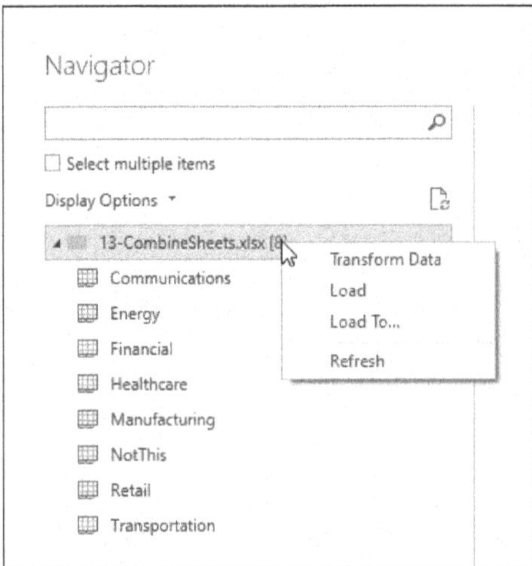

Figure 13.16 Right-click on the workbook name and choose Transform Data.

5. The Power Query Editor opens. You will see one row for each worksheet and a second set of rows with hidden names for each worksheet, as shown in Figure 13.17. Use the Filter drop-down menu in the Kind column to remove the DefinedName rows. Use the Filter drop-down menu in the Name column to remove any sheets that should not be combined.

= Excel.Workbook(File.Contents("D:\2021InDepth\NewWorkbooks\13-CombineSheets.xlsx"), null, true)

	Name	Data	Item	Kind	Hidden
1	Communications	Table	Communications	Sheet	FALSE
2	Energy	Table	Energy	Sheet	FALSE
3	Financial	Table	Financial	Sheet	FALSE
4	Healthcare	Table	Healthcare	Sheet	FALSE
5	Manufacturing	Table	Manufacturing	Sheet	FALSE
6	Retail	Table	Retail	Sheet	FALSE
7	Transportation	Table	Transportation	Sheet	FALSE
8	NotThis	Table	NotThis	Sheet	FALSE
9	_xlnm._FilterDatabase	Table	Communications!_xlnm._Filte...	DefinedName	TRUE
10	_xlnm._FilterDatabas...	Table	Energy!_xlnm._FilterDatabase	DefinedName	TRUE
11	_xlnm._FilterDatabas...	Table	Financial!_xlnm._FilterData...	DefinedName	TRUE
12	_xlnm._FilterDatabas...	Table	Healthcare!_xlnm._FilterDat...	DefinedName	TRUE
13	_xlnm._FilterDatabas...	Table	Manufacturing!_xlnm._Filter...	DefinedName	TRUE
14	_xlnm._FilterDatabas...	Table	Retail!_xlnm._FilterDatabase	DefinedName	TRUE
15	_xlnm._FilterDatabas...	Table	Transportation!_xlnm._Filte...	DefinedName	TRUE

Figure 13.17 You need to remove the rows that say DefinedName in the Kind column by using the Filter drop-down menu.

6. Right-click the Data heading and choose Remove Other Columns.

7. Click the Expand icon to the right of the Data heading. Unselect Use Original Column Name As Prefix. Click OK. The Power Query Editor combines all records from all worksheets, as shown in Figure 13.18. Note that the headings in row 1 need to be promoted. The remaining headings that appear at the top of each worksheet need to be deleted.

	Column1	Column2	Column3	Column4
1	Region	Product	Date	Sector
2	East	XYZ	1/11/2018	Communications
3	East	DEF	1/18/2018	Communications
4	West	XYZ	3/19/2018	Communications
5	Central	DEF	3/25/2018	Communications

Figure 13.18 The headings and records from each worksheet are combined.

8. On the Power Query Editor Home tab, choose Use First Row As Headers.

9. The heading for the first column in this data set is "Region." Open the filter drop-down menu for this column and deselect Region. This will remove the headings throughout the data.

10. On the Home tab, choose Close & Load. The resulting data set will contain all records from all worksheets in the other workbook.

Inside OUT

Power Query includes new data profiling features.

On the View tab in Power Query, there are three new features in the Data Preview group. Choosing Column Quality and/or Column distribution adds a small chart to the top of each column. Choosing Column Profile adds a section with column statistics when a single column is selected.

The following figure shows the column quality and column distribution statistics.

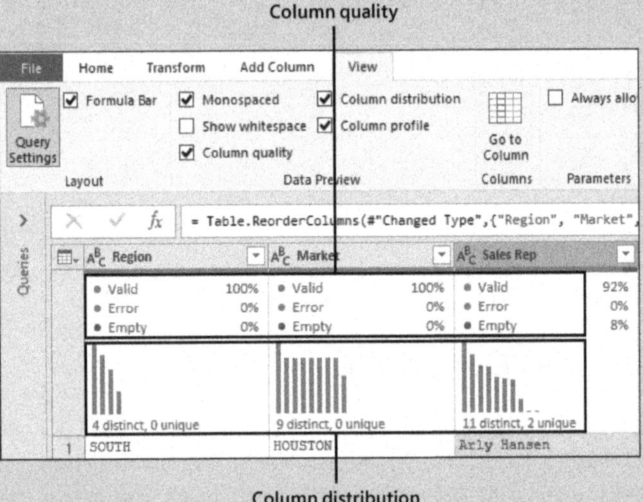

In the following figure, the column profile reveals these facts about a Sales Representative column:

- There are 972 valid values in the column.
- There are 11 distinct values.
- Two values occur exactly once in the column. Power Query calls these "Unique Values."
- A chart shows a histogram of the 11 unique values.

These statistics will give you an overview of data before you import it. For example, an invoice number column might need to have 100 percent unique values. If there are duplicates, you can see this instantly and track down the problem.

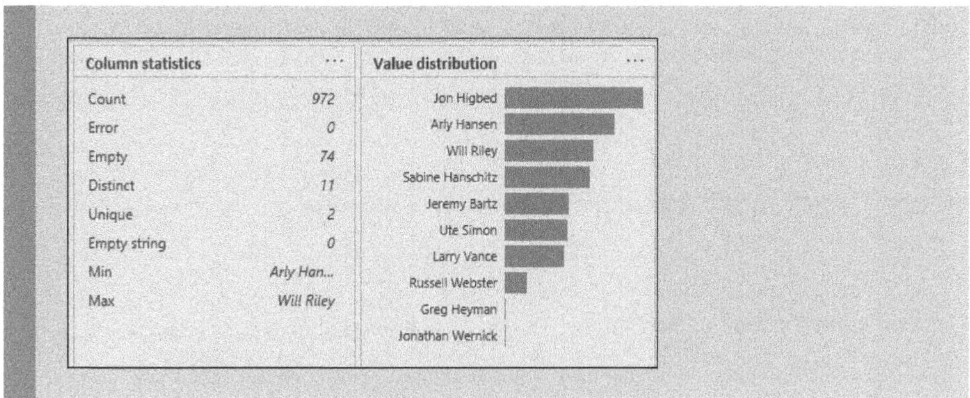

Creating a custom data type in Excel

The new data types were introduced in Chapter 10. What if you want to create your own custom data types? You will use Power Query to define these.

In Figure 13.19, you have data that you would like to make into a data type. The Name column will be displayed in the cells and the other columns will be available in the Card or through formulas. Format the data as a table with Ctrl+T.

	A	B	C	D
1	Excel YouTubers			
2				
3	Name	Channel Name	Lifetime Videos	Channel URL
4	Jon Acampora	Excel Campus - Jon	238	https://www.youtube.com/user/ExcelCampus
5	Ajay Anand	Ajay Anand	183	https://www.youtube.com/user/connectajayanand
6	Randy Austin	Excel For Freelancers	185	https://www.youtube.com/channel/UCXhiOv9VT_0XSnVXyEh4pWw
7	Sumit Bansal	TrumpExcel	358	https://www.youtube.com/c/Trumpexcel
8	David Benaim	David Benaim	154	https://www.youtube.com/channel/UClSY1Zpzy0qKZ-hcRnlxg-Q
9	Purna Duggirala	Chandoo	247	https://www.youtube.com/user/ExcelTutorials

Figure 13.19 Start with a table of data to be used in the data type.

Follow these steps to create a new data type:

1. Select one cell in your data table.
2. From the Data tab, choose From Sheet.
3. In the Power Query Editor, select all the columns. You can do this by clicking on the heading for column 1 and then shift-clicking the heading for the last column.
4. On the Transform tab, select the Create Data Type at the far-right.
5. If you want to remove any columns from the data type, click Advanced in the Create Data Type dialog box to remove a column (see Figure 13.20).

Figure 13.20 If there are columns you don't need in your data type, click Remove Column.

6. Type a name for the data type and choose which column will be displayed in Excel when the data type is shown as a single cell. In Figure 13.20, the Data Type Name is Excel YouTubers, and by default, the data type will display the Name column.

7. Click OK to close the Create Data Type dialog box. Everything except for the one column used as the Display Column is hidden in the Power Query editor.

8. Choose Home, Close And Load. A new worksheet is added to your workbook with the data type in column A.

Now that the data type is created, you can copy the results of the query to another workbook, and the data types will continue to work.

In Figure 13.21, the data is sorted by total videos using the same technique described in Chapter 10.

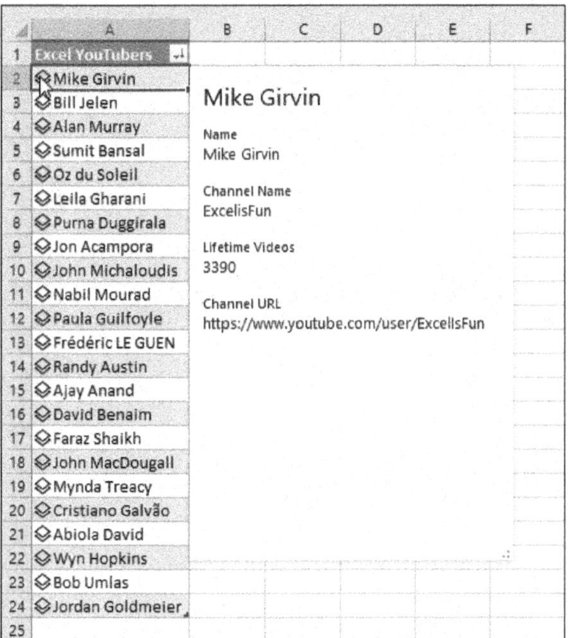

Figure 13.21 A custom data type can be created from any data.

CHAPTER 14

Summarizing data using subtotals or filter

The Subtotal command was added way back in Excel 97. Not enough people realize that the command is in Excel, and those who have tried it often don't realize how powerful the command truly is. I used to have a regular gig as the Excel guy on Leo Laporte's *Call for Help* television show. During one appearance, I showed people how to use the Subtotal command. I figured it was probably the most boring six minutes of television in the history of the world. However, that one show generated more fan email than any other. People wrote to say that they had been spending two hours every day adding subtotals manually, and now they used the trick from the show to reduce the task to a minute.

Filtering enables you to quickly wade through waves of data and see only the records needed to answer an ad-hoc query. Excel continues to improve the AutoFilter feature with hopes that you will never have to venture into the complicated Advanced Filter feature. When it's combined with the Remove Duplicates command, you might never have to use the Advanced Filter.

The elusive Filter By Selection feature enables you to invoke filters even faster than before.

Duplicate data is a common problem in Excel. Beginning with Excel 2007, Microsoft provided tools to make finding and eliminating duplicates easier.

Adding automatic subtotals

When you have a database of detailed data, you might want to add subtotals to each group of records. If your data has one field that identifies the groups, you can use the Subtotals command to add the subtotals quickly. Figure 14.1 shows a data set that is suitable for this.

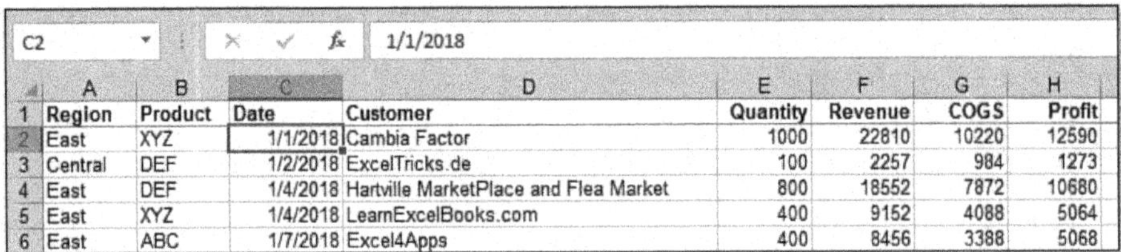

C2 | 1/1/2018

	A	B	C	D	E	F	G	H
1	Region	Product	Date	Customer	Quantity	Revenue	COGS	Profit
2	East	XYZ	1/1/2018	Cambia Factor	1000	22810	10220	12590
3	Central	DEF	1/2/2018	ExcelTricks.de	100	2257	984	1273
4	East	DEF	1/4/2018	Hartville MarketPlace and Flea Market	800	18552	7872	10680
5	East	XYZ	1/4/2018	LearnExcelBooks.com	400	9152	4088	5064
6	East	ABC	1/7/2018	Excel4Apps	400	8456	3388	5068

Figure 14.1 After sorting, you can quickly add subtotals to this data set.

Follow these steps to add subtotals to a data set:

1. Sort the data set by your group field. In this example, it's Column D, Customer. Select one cell in that column and then select Data, Sort & Filter, AZ.

2. Select one cell in your data set.

3. Select Data, Outline, Subtotal. Excel displays the Subtotal dialog box.

4. In the Subtotal dialog box, change the At Each Change In drop-down menu to reflect your group field.

5. Ensure that Use Function is set to Sum.

6. For each field you want to be totaled, select the field in the Add Subtotal To list, as shown in Figure 14.2.

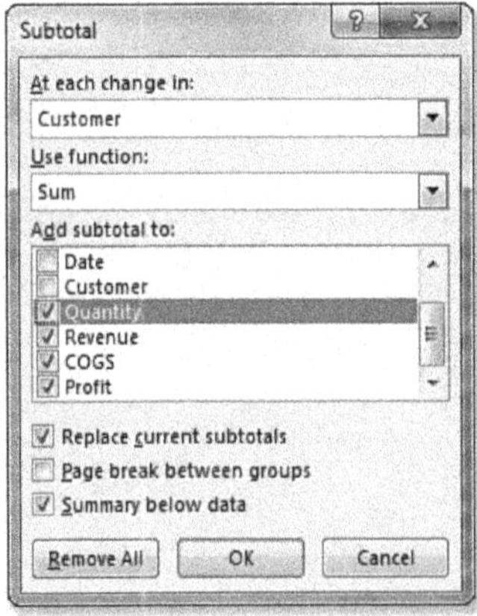

Figure 14.2 You specify the fields to be totaled in the Subtotal dialog box.

7. If you want a page break after each group, select Page Break Between Groups.

8. Click OK to add subtotals. Excel adds a subtotal between each group, as shown in Figure 14.3.

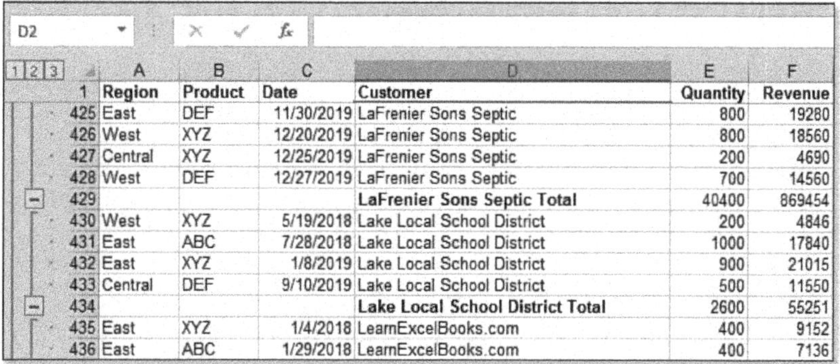

D2

	A	B	C	D	E	F
1	Region	Product	Date	Customer	Quantity	Revenue
425	East	DEF	11/30/2019	LaFrenier Sons Septic	800	19280
426	West	XYZ	12/20/2019	LaFrenier Sons Septic	800	18560
427	Central	XYZ	12/25/2019	LaFrenier Sons Septic	200	4690
428	West	DEF	12/27/2019	LaFrenier Sons Septic	700	14560
429				**LaFrenier Sons Septic Total**	40400	869454
430	West	XYZ	5/19/2018	Lake Local School District	200	4846
431	East	ABC	7/28/2018	Lake Local School District	1000	17840
432	East	XYZ	1/8/2019	Lake Local School District	900	21015
433	Central	DEF	9/10/2019	Lake Local School District	500	11550
434				**Lake Local School District Total**	2600	55251
435	East	XYZ	1/4/2018	LearnExcelBooks.com	400	9152
436	East	ABC	1/29/2018	LearnExcelBooks.com	400	7136

Figure 14.3 Excel inserts extra rows between groups and adds subtotals.

At the very bottom of the data set, Excel has added a Grand Total row. This row is smart enough to ignore all the other subtotal rows in the data set (see Figure 14.4).

E592 =SUBTOTAL(9,E2:E590)

	A	B	C	D	E	F
1	Region	Product	Date	Customer	Quantity	Revenue
580	Central	ABC	12/24/2019	Spain Enterprise	100	1968
581				**Spain Enterprise Total**	19700	427349
582	West	XYZ	8/31/2018	Vertex42	800	18072
583	East	DEF	4/14/2019	Vertex42	600	14004
584	Central	DEF	6/25/2019	Vertex42	200	4060
585	West	ABC	11/5/2019	Vertex42	800	15104
586				**Vertex42 Total**	2400	51240
587	East	DEF	6/6/2018	WM Squared Inc.	200	4282
588	Central	XYZ	7/10/2018	WM Squared Inc.	400	8876
589	West	ABC	10/11/2019	WM Squared Inc.	500	8940
590	West	XYZ	11/4/2019	WM Squared Inc.	600	12612
591				**WM Squared Inc. Total**	1700	34710
592				**Grand Total**	313900	6707812
593						

Figure 14.4 At the bottom of the data set, Excel inserted a Grand Total row.

Adding hundreds of subtotal rows is amazing in and of itself. However, the subtotals command offers so much more. You can go on to show only the subtotals, show the largest groups at the top, or copy the subtotals.

Working with the subtotals

Take a close look at the left side of the worksheet in Figure 14.3. You see three new buttons to the left of column A labeled 1, 2, and 3. Those buttons are called Group and Outline buttons and were added automatically by the Subtotals command. They are the key to further analysis of the subtotals.

Showing a one-page summary with only the subtotals

Click the #2 button that appears to the left of and just above cell A1. Excel hides all the detail rows, leaving only the customer subtotals and the Grand Total row.

After setting the print area, you would have a one-page summary of the 500+ rows of data (see Figure 14.5).

E592 | =SUBTOTAL(9,E2:E590)

	C	D	E	F	G	H
1	Date	Customer	Quantity	Revenue	COGS	Profit
6		Association for Computers & Taxation T	2800	60299	27049	33250
11		Bits of Confetti Total	2300	50030	21612	28418
68		Cambia Factor Total	28900	622794	274978	347816
73		Construction Intelligence & Analytics, In	1400	31369	13730	17639
140		CPASelfStudy.com Total	33400	704359	311381	392978
145		Data2Impact Total	3300	72680	31946	40734
150		Excel Learning Zone Total	2600	54048	23780	30268
211		Excel4Apps Total	35700	750163	334614	415549
216		Excelerator BI Total	1400	31021	13745	17276
253		ExcelTricks.de Total	18600	390978	177281	213697
258		Fintega Financial Modelling Total	2700	59881	25913	33968
307		F-Keys Ltd. Total	29100	613514	275105	338409
348		Frontline Systems Total	23100	498937	219978	278959
353		Hartville MarketPlace and Flea Market T	1900	42316	18764	23552
358		IMA Houston Chapter Total	3300	71651	32471	39180
363		Juliet Babcock-Hyde CPA, PLLC Total	2000	46717	19961	26756
429		LaFrenier Sons Septic Total	40400	869454	382170	487284
434		Lake Local School District Total	2600	55251	24632	30619
439		LearnExcelBooks.com Total	1600	34364	15576	18788
444		MyOnlineTrainingHub.com Total	3000	62744	28644	34100
449		MySpreadsheetLab Total	2700	57516	26765	30751
454		New Hope Laundry Total	2000	39250	18614	20636
483		Profology.com Total	18700	406326	178585	227741
536		Serving Brevard Realty Total	26600	568851	252522	316329
581		Spain Enterprise Total	19700	427349	189331	238018
586		Vertex42 Total	2400	51240	22824	28416
591		WM Squared Inc. Total	1700	34710	16423	18287
592		Grand Total	313900	6707812	2978394	3729418
593						

Figure 14.5 Click the #2 Group and Outline button to show a summary report.

If you click the #1 Group and Outline button, Excel hides everything except for the Grand Total. If you click the #3 button, Excel brings the detail rows back.

Sorting the collapsed subtotal view with the largest customers at top

In Figure 14.5, you have the customers in alphabetical sequence. However, your manager is probably going to want to see the largest customers at the top of the report.

Think about this request, though. In row 211, the subtotal for Excel4Apps is one of the largest customers in the group, adding up data in rows 151 through 210. If you try to sort in descending order, and the data in row 211 comes up to row 3, the formula that looks at 60 rows of data will certainly evaluate to a #REF! error.

Amazingly, though, you can easily sort data when it is in the collapsed #2 view. Follow these steps:

1. Add subtotals as described earlier in this chapter.
2. Collapse the subtotals by clicking the #2 Group and Outline button.
3. Select one single cell in your revenue column.
4. Sort in descending order by clicking the ZA button on the Data tab.

The result is shown in Figure 14.6. The total for Excel4Apps flies out near the top of the data set, but it does not come to row 3. Instead, the total comes to row 128. The total for the largest customer is in row 67.

F67 =SUBTOTAL(9,F2:F66)

	C	D	E	F	G	H
1	Date	Customer	Quantity	Revenue	COGS	Profit
67		LaFrenier Sons Septic Total	40400	869454	382170	487284
128		Excel4Apps Total	35700	750163	334614	415549
195		CPASelfStudy.com Total	33400	704359	311381	392978
252		Cambia Factor Total	28900	622794	274978	347816
301		F-Keys Ltd. Total	29100	613514	275105	338409
354		Serving Brevard Realty Total	26600	568851	252522	316329
395		Frontline Systems Total	23100	498937	219978	278959
440		Spain Enterprise Total	19700	427349	189331	238018
469		Profology.com Total	18700	406326	178585	227741

Figure 14.6 Amazingly, you can sort data when it is collapsed.

Figure 14.7 shows the #3 view of Figure 14.6. You can see that Excel sorted groups of records when the data was collapsed. All the detail rows for a customer come along with the subtotal row, but the detail rows are not sorted by revenue.

F67 =SUBTOTAL(9,F2:F66)

	C	D	E	F	G	H
1	Date	Customer	Quantity	Revenue	COGS	Profit
119	11/9/2019	Excel4Apps	700	17059	7154	9905
120	11/17/2019	Excel4Apps	600	13680	6132	7548
121	11/21/2019	Excel4Apps	500	11330	4920	6410
122	11/28/2019	Excel4Apps	500	11470	5110	6360
123	12/1/2019	Excel4Apps	900	22887	9198	13689
124	12/7/2019	Excel4Apps	1000	23690	9840	13850
125	12/10/2019	Excel4Apps	1000	17410	8470	8940
126	12/10/2019	Excel4Apps	200	4492	1968	2524
127	12/29/2019	Excel4Apps	900	15363	7623	7740
128		Excel4Apps Total	35700	750163	334614	415549

Figure 14.7 Excel brings all the collapsed detail rows along with the subtotal row during a sort.

Copying only the subtotal rows

A problem occurs when you try to copy the collapsed subtotal rows from Figure 14.6. If you select D1:H592, Copy, and then Paste the data to a new worksheet, you discover that Excel has copied all the hidden rows as well. Worse, the pasted data no longer has the group and outline symbols, so there is no way to collapse the data again.

The key to this task is to use a trick called Go To Special, Visible Cells Only. Excel still makes it hard to find this command.

Follow these steps:

1. Add subtotals to a data set as described previously.
2. Collapse to the subtotal-only view by clicking the #2 Group and Outline button.
3. Select the entire range of collapsed subtotals.
4. Open the Find and Select drop-down menu from the right side of the Home tab. Select the Go To Special command. Excel displays the Go To Special dialog box, as shown in Figure 14.8. This dialog box enables you to narrow a selection to only certain types of elements within your selection. This is a powerful dialog box.

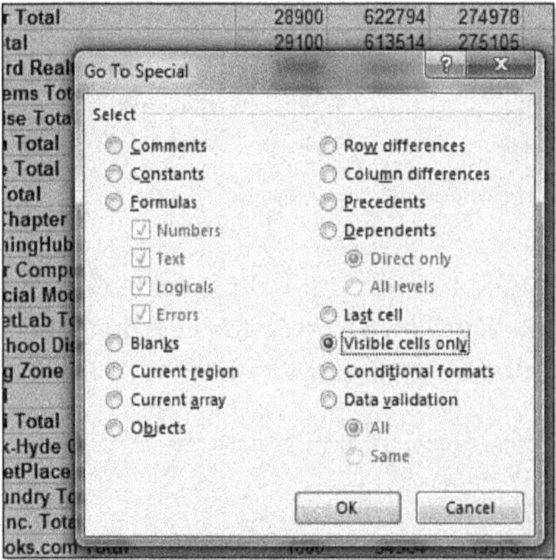

Figure 14.8 The Go To Special dialog box enables you to reduce your selection to items meeting certain criteria.

5. In the Go To Special dialog box, select Visible Cells Only. Click OK. Excel deselects all the hidden rows.

TIP

You can replace steps 4 and 5 with a single keystroke. Hold down the Alt key while pressing the semicolon key. It turns out that Alt+; is the equivalent of selecting Home, Find & Select, Go To Special, Visible Cells Only, OK. Or, if you prefer to use the mouse, customize the Quick Access Toolbar (QAT) with an icon called Select Visible Cells.

6. Click Ctrl+C to copy those rows. As you can see in Figure 14.9, Excel has selected each visible row separately.

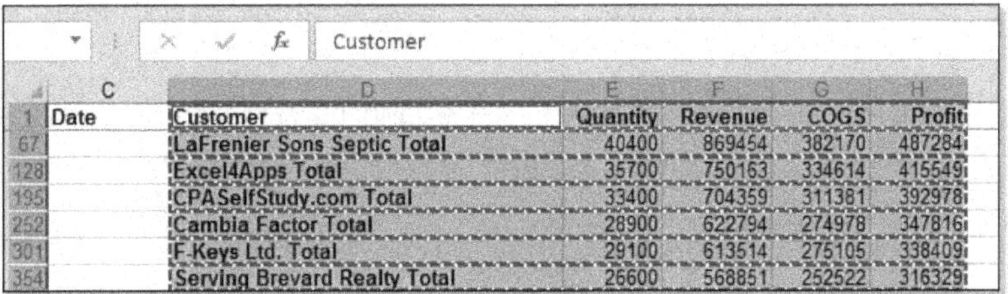

	C	D	E	F	G	H
1	Date	Customer	Quantity	Revenue	COGS	Profit
67		LaFrenier Sons Septic Total	40400	869454	382170	487284
128		Excel4Apps Total	35700	750163	334614	415549
195		CPASelfStudy.com Total	33400	704359	311381	392978
252		Cambia Factor Total	28900	622794	274978	347816
301		F-Keys Ltd. Total	29100	613514	275105	338409
354		Serving Brevard Realty Total	26600	568851	252522	316329

Figure 14.9 Excel copies only the visible rows.

7. Select a blank section of the workbook. Use Ctrl+V to paste only the subtotals. The subtotal formulas are converted to values. This is the only thing that would make sense.

Formatting the subtotal rows

When the Subtotal command adds subtotals, it inserts a new row for each subtotal. Excel copies your key field to the new row and appends the word *Total* after the key field. This text in the key field column appears in bold font. Unfortunately, Excel does not widen this column, so frequently the word *Total* appears to be truncated because it will not fit in the column.

The other subtotal columns get a formula that uses the SUBTOTAL function. Strangely, the cells containing the formulas in each subtotal row are not bold.

When I am doing my Power Excel seminars, I'm frequently asked how to bold the subtotal rows. Many people will try selecting E67:H592 in the collapsed #2 view and pressing Ctrl+B. Although this initially looks like it works, it actually fails.

The problem becomes apparent when you go back to the #3 view to see the detail rows. The detail rows up through row 66 are fine. The problem is that all the detail rows from row 68 through the end of the data set have been bolded. For some reason, Microsoft formats the rows that are hidden as a result of the Subtotal command.

At this point, many people press Undo twice and start the process of manually formatting each subtotal row. There is, of course, an easier way. Follow these steps to format the subtotal rows:

1. Add subtotals to a data set as described previously.
2. Click the #2 Group and Outline button to collapse the data set to show only the subtotals.
3. Select from the first subtotal row down to the grand total row. In the current data set, select from D67 through H592.
4. Hold down Alt and press semicolon. Excel selects only the visible rows, which in this case are only the subtotal rows.
5. Apply any desired formatting. In Figure 14.10, the cells are showing a mix of Cell Styles, Heading 4, and a light red background from the Fill drop-down menu.

D67 | LaFrenier Sons Septic Total

	C	D	E	F	G	H
1	Date	Customer	Quantity	Revenue	COGS	Profit
559	11/24/2018	Juliet Babcock-Hyde CPA, PLLC	100	2538	1022	1516
560	7/21/2019	Juliet Babcock-Hyde CPA, PLLC	1000	22840	10220	12620
561		Juliet Babcock-Hyde CPA, PLLC Total	2000	46717	19961	26756
562	1/4/2018	Hartville MarketPlace and Flea Market	800	18552	7872	10680
563	1/21/2018	Hartville MarketPlace and Flea Market	200	3552	1694	1858
564	3/24/2019	Hartville MarketPlace and Flea Market	100	2484	1022	1462
565	4/24/2019	Hartville MarketPlace and Flea Market	800	17728	8176	9552
566		Hartville MarketPlace and Flea Market T	1900	42316	18764	23552
567	11/15/2018	New Hope Laundry	1000	17250	8470	8780

Figure 14.10 Format only the subtotal rows.

6. Click the #3 Group and Outline button to show all the detail rows.

Step 4 in this process is the key step. Using Alt+; selects only the visible rows in the collapsed subtotal view.

Removing subtotals

After you add subtotals and copy those subtotal rows to another worksheet, you might want to remove the subtotals from the original data set. Follow these steps to remove the subtotals:

1. Select one cell in the subtotaled data set.
2. Go back to the Subtotals command on the Data tab of the ribbon.
3. In the lower-left corner of the Subtotals dialog box, click the button for Remove All.

The subtotal rows are removed.

Subtotaling multiple fields

Suppose you want to add subtotals by region and product. You will add the subtotals twice. In the second Subtotal command, make sure you clear the Replace Current Subtotals check box.

Make sure that your data is sorted properly. You can use the Sort dialog box to sort by region and then by product, or you can follow this set of steps, which requires only four clicks:

1. Select one cell in the Product column.
2. Click the AZ button on the Data tab.
3. Select one cell in the Region column.
4. Click the AZ button on the Data tab.

Because the sort in step 4 keeps the ties in the previous sequence, this set of steps effectively sorts by product within the region.

It is important that you add subtotals to the outer group first. Use the instructions earlier in this chapter in the "Adding automatic subtotals" section to add totals to the Region field.

Run the Subtotals command again. This time, specify Each Change In Product. Clear the Replace Current Subtotals check box.

You now have four Group and Outline buttons. If you press the #3 button, you see product totals and region totals, as shown in Figure 14.11. Note that Excel supports a maximum of eight Group and Outline buttons so that you could add up to six levels of subtotals.

A2 | 1 2 3 4

	A	B	C	D	E
1	Region	Product	Date	Customer	Quantity
76		ABC Total			40200
137		DEF Total			34900
205		XYZ Total			36200
206	Central Total				111300
277		ABC Total			36500
354		DEF Total			40300
418		XYZ Total			39600
419	East Total				116400
479		ABC Total			33300
522		DEF Total			22600
575		XYZ Total			30300
576	West Total				86200
577	Grand Total				313900
578					

Figure 14.11 Two sets of subtotals mean four Group and Outline buttons.

Subtotaling daily dates by month

Say that you have daily dates and want to apply the subtotal after each month. Sort your data by the data field. Select the data column and apply a format that shows month and year, as shown in Figure 14.12.

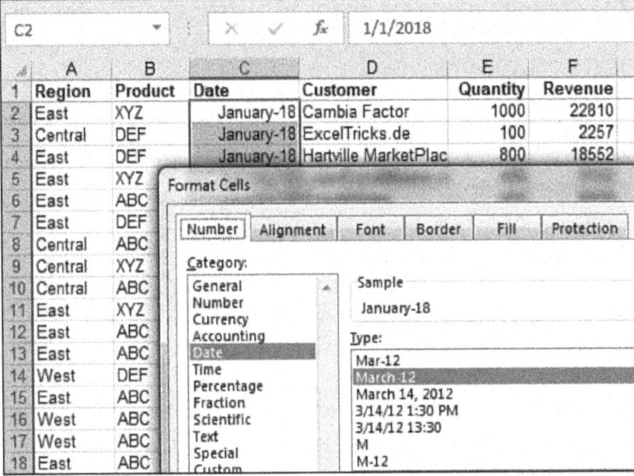

Figure 14.12 Format the date fields to show months.

Add the Subtotals for each change in Date. The subtotals will appear after each month. You can change the format for the date column back to a short date. The result, as shown in Figure 14.13, is daily dates with monthly subtotals.

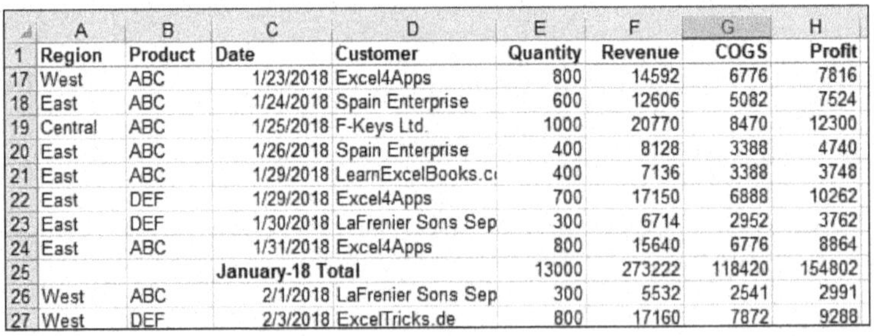

	A	B	C	D	E	F	G	H
1	Region	Product	Date	Customer	Quantity	Revenue	COGS	Profit
17	West	ABC	1/23/2018	Excel4Apps	800	14592	6776	7816
18	East	ABC	1/24/2018	Spain Enterprise	600	12606	5082	7524
19	Central	ABC	1/25/2018	F-Keys Ltd.	1000	20770	8470	12300
20	East	ABC	1/26/2018	Spain Enterprise	400	8128	3388	4740
21	East	ABC	1/29/2018	LearnExcelBooks.c	400	7136	3388	3748
22	East	DEF	1/29/2018	Excel4Apps	700	17150	6888	10262
23	East	DEF	1/30/2018	LaFrenier Sons Sep	300	6714	2952	3762
24	East	ABC	1/31/2018	Excel4Apps	800	15640	6776	8864
25			**January-18 Total**		13000	273222	118420	154802
26	West	ABC	2/1/2018	LaFrenier Sons Sep	300	5532	2541	2991
27	West	DEF	2/3/2018	ExcelTricks.de	800	17160	7872	9288

Figure 14.13 After adding subtotals, change the date format back to a short date.

Filtering records

The feature formerly known as AutoFilter is now called Filter. Along with the new name, the command has new features. Filtering works on any range of data with headings in the first row of the range. It works with ranges that have been defined as tables as well as regular ranges.

When Microsoft renamed AutoFilter to Filter, they added the following features:

- The Search box enables you to search for values that match a wildcard. You can add the search results to a previous filter. Thus, you could quickly find all records that contain "bank" or "credit union."
- Multiselection is available in the Filter drop-down menu. If you need to select two, three, or ten values from the filter, it is easy to do now. On the flip side, it is slightly more difficult to filter to a single value because you first must uncheck the (Select All) box.
- You can filter by color or icon set.
- You can filter text columns based on cells that begin with a value, end with a value, or contain a value.
- You can filter number columns based on cells that are greater than, less than, or between values. You can choose Top 10, Above Average, or Below Average.
- You can filter date values by year or month. You can filter to conceptual values such as This Month, Last Quarter, or Year To Date.
- You can filter by selection. Rather than choosing from the Filter drop-down menu, you can select any value and use Filter By Selection to filter the data to that value.

The various features work great when one column contains values of the same type. For example, Excel expects that if you have dates in a column, all the cells except the header will be dates. Excel offers special text, number, or date formats based on what it sees in the column.

Using a filter

The icon to turn on the filter drop-down menus toggles the feature on and off. To turn on the feature, click the icon once. To turn off the feature, click the icon again. You must select one cell in your data range before clicking the filter. You should have no blank rows or blank columns in the range to be filtered.

You can turn on the filter drop-down menus by using any of these methods:

- From the Data tab, select Sort & Filter, then Filter.
- From the Home tab, open the Sort & Filter drop-down menu and choose Filter.
- Apply a table format to a range.
- Right-click any cell, select Filter, and then select one of the options under Filter. In addition to performing the filter, this will turn on the Filter feature if it was not previously turned on.

- Choose any value and then select the AutoFilter icon from the QAT. The Filter By Selection feature has been in Excel since Excel 2003, but the icon has never been included in the standard user interface. Also, this icon has always been mislabeled in the Customize dialog box. See "Filtering by selection—easy way," later in this chapter, for more information.

When the filter is turned on, a drop-down menu arrow is added to each heading in the range.

Figure 14.14 shows the menu available for one drop-down menu. This particular column includes text values, so the special filter fly-out menu includes various special text filters.

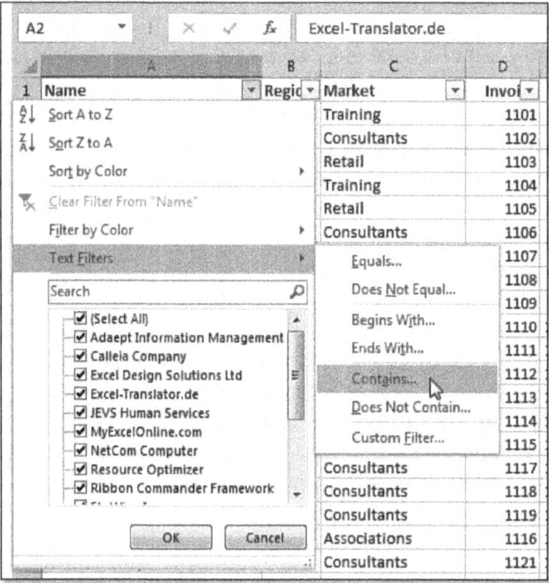

Figure 14.14 The filter drop-down menu now features a multiselect list, as well as new special filters.

Inside OUT

There is a subtle difference between filtering using the Search box and filtering using the Contains Text filter.

If you needed to find all customers with Excel in their names in Figure 4.14, it would seem like typing **Excel** in the Search box is the best way.

However, if you plan on re-applying the filter later, either with the Reapply icon or by refreshing a pivot table, you should know that the Search box is a one-time snapshot of the current data. If the underlying data changes and you re-apply, the filter will not include new customers such as Turbo Excel.

To solve the problem, choose Text Filters, Contains.... In the Contains dialog box, type **Excel.** This creates a filter that can be re-applied.

Selecting one or multiple items from the filter drop-down

In legacy versions of Excel, the filter drop-down menu included a simple list of items in the column, and you selected one of the values. The multiselect nature of filters included since Excel 2007 offers far more power, but you have to exercise special care in using the drop-down menu.

Follow these steps to select a single item:

1. When you initially select the drop-down menu, all the check boxes that appear in the column are selected, as shown in Figure 14.14.
2. To select a single value, click Select All. This clears all the items in the list, as shown in Figure 14.15.

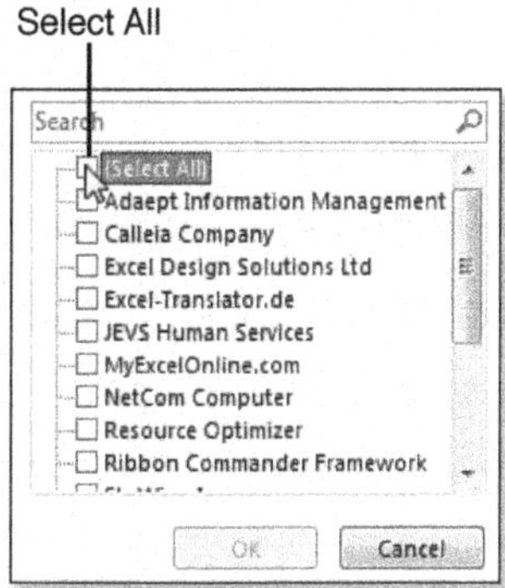

Figure 14.15 Click Select All to clear the check boxes for all items.

3. Click the value on which you want to filter, as shown in Figure 14.16.
4. Click OK at the bottom of the drop-down menu to apply the filter.

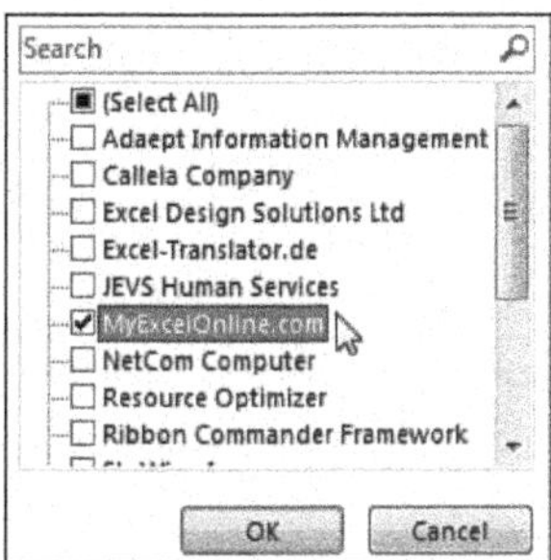

Figure 14.16 When the check boxes have been cleared, select the one value of interest and click OK.

The process you use to filter to multiple values is similar. First, click Select All to clear the check boxes for all items. You can then select the items that should be included in the filter.

> TIP
>
> **With more than 1 million rows in Excel, you have the possibility for a long list of items in the Filter list—up to 10,000 items. Using the scrollbar to navigate through a list of 10,000 items will be inexact. However, there is a fast way to jump to a certain section of the list. Click any name in the list to activate the list. Then, type the first letter of your selection. Excel instantly jumps to the first item that starts with this letter. You can then use the PgDn or PgUp keys to move quickly through the items that start with that letter.**

The multiselection capability is a vast improvement for filtering that can be completed in four clicks. Even though the old AutoFilter in legacy versions of Excel required only two clicks, the improvements are worth this hassle. For example, when you need to select everything except one certain value, you select the drop-down menu, clear the undesired value, and click OK.

Identifying which columns have filters applied

Listed here are the visual clues in Excel you can use to identify columns in which a filter has been applied to a data set:

- The row numbers in the range appear in blue to indicate that the rows have a filter applied.
- The message area of the status bar in the lower-left corner of the screen shows a message similar to "2 of 34 records found."
- The drop-down menu for the filtered column changes from a simple drop-down menu arrow to a Filter icon, as shown in Figure 14.17.

Figure 14.17 After you apply a filter to column A, the icon on the filter drop-down menu changes.

Combining filters

Filters are additive, which means that after you place a filter on a column, you can apply a filter to another column to show even fewer rows. You can apply two filters to the same column, such as when you want to select all the West region cells that are red.

Clearing filters

After you apply a filter, you have several options for clearing it:

- From the filter drop-down menu, select Clear Filter From Column. This leaves filters on in other columns.
- From the filter drop-down menu, choose a different filter.
- From the Data tab, select Clear from the Sort & Filter group. This clears selected filters from any column but leaves the drop-down menus in place, so you can continue to select other filters.
- Select the Filter icon from the Data tab or the Home tab to clear all filters and turn off the filter feature.
- Press Ctrl+Shift+L to clear all the filters and turn off the filter feature

Refreshing filters

Keep in mind that when data in a range changes, the filters do not update automatically. This can happen when you add new rows or edit data. It can also happen if your data range has formulas that point to lookup tables in other parts of the workbook. In such a case, you need to have Excel calculate the filter again. Excel calls this feature *Reapply*. There are several ways you can reapply a filter:

- On the Data tab, select the Reapply icon.
- On the Home tab, select Sort & Filter, Reapply.
- Right-click a cell and then select Filter, Reapply.

Resizing the filter drop-down

The filter drop-down menu always starts fairly small. If you have a long list of items, you might want the drop-down menu to be larger. To do this, hover your mouse over the three dots in the lower-right corner of the drop-down menu. (Refer back to Figure 14.14 to see the three dots.) When the mouse pointer changes to a two-headed diagonal arrow, click and drag down or to the right.

Filtering by selection—hard way

You can filter without using the filter drop-down menus. Microsoft Access has offered a Filter By Selection icon in the toolbar for more than a decade. Excel includes this functionality, but it is hidden where most people will never find it.

To access the Filter By Selection feature, right-click any cell and then select Filter from the context menu. You then have an opportunity to filter based on the cell's value, color, font color, or icon, as shown in Figure 14.18.

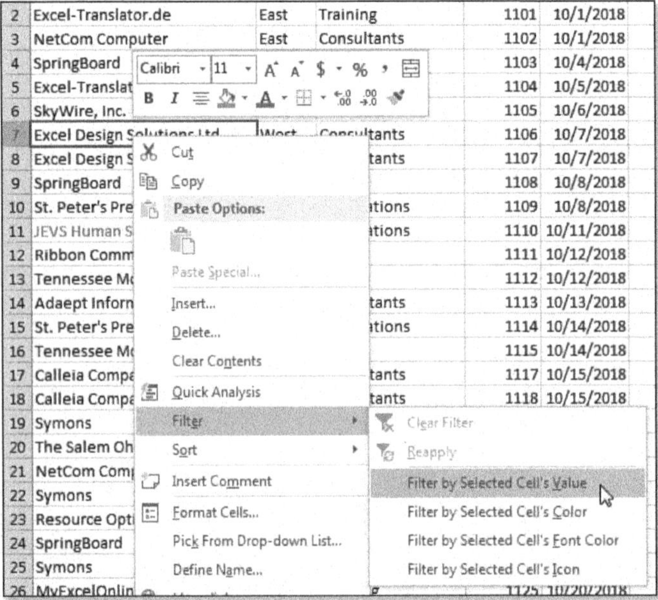

Figure 14.18 Although it is hidden, the Filter By Selection command provides a quick way to see all the other rows that match a single cell.

The Filter By Selection feature works even if the filter drop-down menus have not been activated previously. Using this feature turns on the filter drop-down menus for the data set.

It would be helpful if you could use this feature to select multiple values, such as selecting a cell that says East and then Ctrl+clicking a cell for West. You might think that filtering by selection would filter to both East and West, but that does not work.

Filtering by selection—easy way

Provided your data is in a regular range and not stored as a Ctrl+T Table, you can filter by selection quickly by adding the AutoFilter icon to the Quick Access Toolbar.

To get one-click access to Filter By Selection, follow these steps:

1. Right-click the Quick Access Toolbar and select Customize Quick Access Toolbar.

2. In the Choose Commands From drop-down menu, select Commands Not In The Ribbon.

3. In the left list box, browse to and select AutoFilter, as shown in Figure 14.19. Click the Add button.

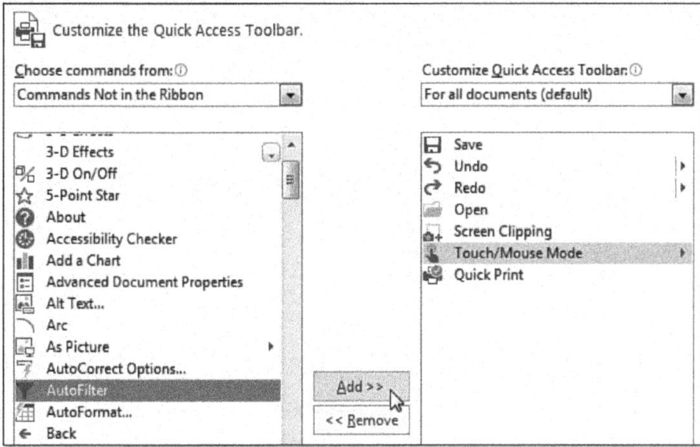

Figure 14.19 The icon labeled "AutoFilter" actually is Filter By Selection.

4. Click OK to close the Excel Options dialog box.

To use Filter By Selection, select a value in one of the data rows. Click the AutoFilter icon in the Quick Access Toolbar. If the data set did not previously have the filter drop-down menus, Excel turns on the Filter feature and filters the data set based on the value in the active cell.

Filter By Selection is additive, which means you can choose another value in another column and click the AutoFilter icon to filter the data set further.

In Figure 14.20, the data set is filtered to show Central region invoices for the Consultants market. This was accomplished in four mouse clicks:

1. Select a cell that contains Central, such as B17.
2. Click the AutoFilter icon in the Quick Access Toolbar.
3. Select Consultants in cell C17.
4. Click the AutoFilter icon.

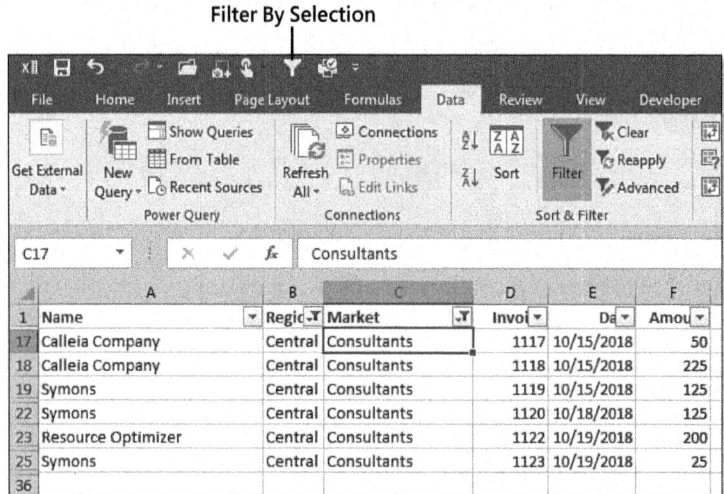

Figure 14.20 Filter By Selection is used twice to filter based on column B and then on column C.

Filtering by color or icon

The improved Conditional Formatting commands give you many ways to change the color of a cell. Filter By Color is a great way to find all of the records that match a color applied either through conditional formatting or the fill color or font color drop-down menu menus.

Imagine that you are tracking numerous projects in Excel. You manually highlight certain projects in red if you are missing key elements of the project information. You can use Filter By Color to show only the rows that have a red fill.

Filter By Color works for the cell color, font color, or the icon in the cell.

As shown in Figure 14.21, the Filter By Color fly-out menu offers to filter based on fill color or font color. Had an icon set been applied to the data, you could filter by icon as well. . Note that the sections of the fly-out menu appear only if you have used color or icons in the range. If all your cells contain black text, Filter By Font Color will not appear in the fly-out menu. If your range contains all black text on a white background, without icons, the Filter By Color menu will be disabled.

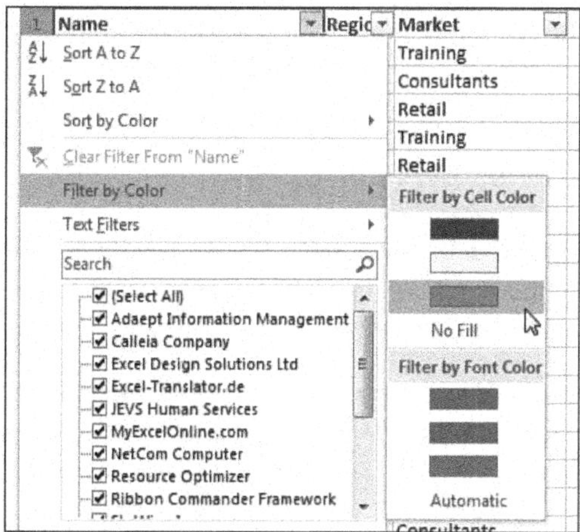

Figure 14.21 The Filter By Color fly-out menu offers to filter by icon, cell color, or font color.

CAUTION

There is no way to select two colors from one section of the Filter By Color menu. You might want to filter to everything with a cell color of red or yellow, but this is not possible.

Handling date filters

The filter drop-down menu for date columns automatically groups the dates into hierarchical groups.

In Figure 14.22, the underlying data contains daily dates. However, the default drop-down menu shows options for the years found in the data set.

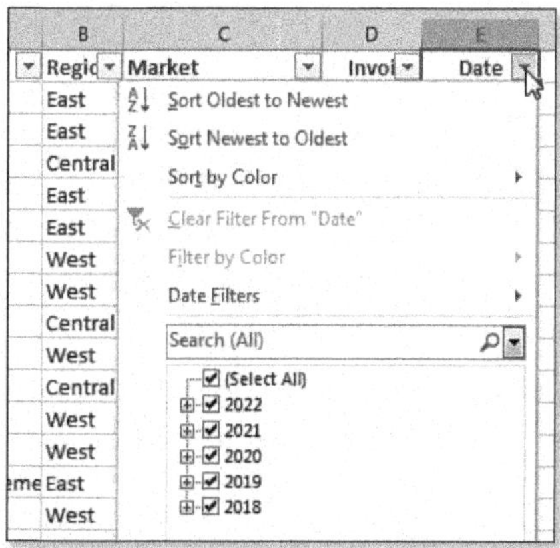

Figure 14.22 Excel automatically groups dates up to years in the filter drop-down menu.

Click the plus sign next to any year to expand the list to show months within the year, as shown in Figure 14.23. You can then click the plus sign next to a month to see the days within the month.

TROUBLESHOOTING

You might hate the grouping of dates in the Filter menu. If your data set includes only a few scattered dates, such as February 2, May 30, July 4, and September 4, wading through the grouped filters is annoying.

You can turn off the hierarchical grouping of dates in the filter drop-down menu. To do so, click the File menu and choose Options. In the Options dialog box, choose the Advanced category. Scroll down to the section for Display For This Workbook. Next, select a workbook, and then clear the check box for Group Dates in the AutoFilter menu.

Figure 14.23 Expand the hierarchical view to see months within the years.

Using special filters for dates, text, and numbers

Excel examines the data in a column to determine whether it contains mostly text, dates, or numeric values. Depending on which data type appears most often, Excel offers special filters designed for that data type.

For columns that contain mostly text, Excel offers the filters Begins With, Ends With, Contains, Does Not Contain, Equals, and Does Not Equal. You are allowed to use wildcard characters in these filters. For example, you can use an asterisk (*) for any number of characters or a question mark (?) to represent a single character. The Contains filter seems obsolete with the Search box in the Filter drop-down menu.

For columns with mostly numeric values, the special filters include Top 10, Above Average, Below Average, Between, Less Than, Greater Than, Does Not Equal, and Equals. For the Top 10 filter, you can specify the top or bottom values. You can also specify whether the results are based on the top 10 items or the top 10 percent of items. Finally, you can change the number 10 to any number. Thus, you can use this filter to show the bottom 20 percent or the top 3 items.

For columns with mostly dates, the special filters include Before, After, or Between a particular day, week, month, quarter, or year. The special filters also include Year To Date or All Dates In The Period, as shown in Figure 14.24.

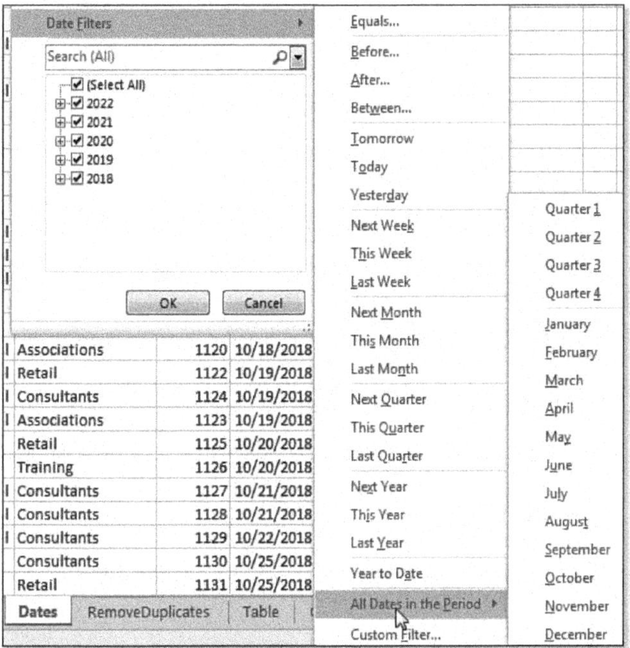

Figure 14.24 Excel offers myriad date filters.

All the special filters offer a pathway to the legacy Custom AutoFilter dialog box. This filter enables you to combine two conditions by using an AND or OR clause. This feature solves your problems some of the time, but there are still complex conditions that require you to resort to using the Advanced Filter.

The Custom AutoFilter dialog box was nominally improved in Excel 2007. For example, a calendar control was added that can be used to select dates when you are filtering a date column. You can use the dialog box shown in Figure 14.25 to select dates that are within a certain range of dates.

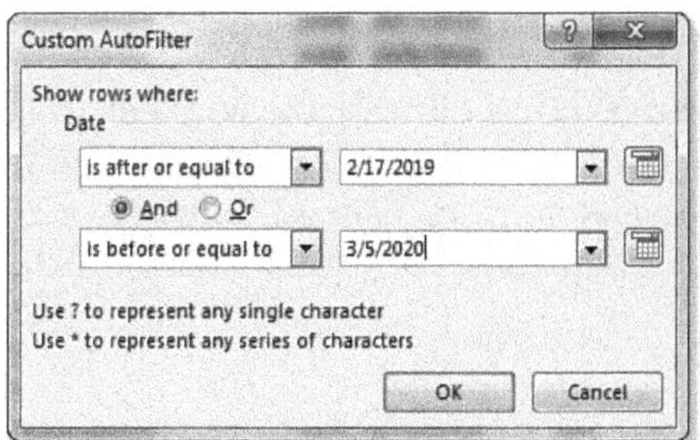

Figure 14.25 The custom filters allow you to build simple combinations of two conditions for filtering.

Totaling filtered results

After you have applied a filter, you might want to sum the visible cells in a column. This task is straightforward in Excel. Select the first visible blank cell below the column and click the AutoSum button. Instead of inserting a `SUM` function, Excel inserts a `SUBTOTAL` function. The `=SUBTOTAL(9,F2:F1874)` function sums the visible rows from a data set that has been filtered. You can edit the first argument in the `SUBTOTAL` function to find the count, average, minimum, and maximum, as well as other calculations on the visible rows.

Formatting and copying filtered results

When you apply a filter, some rows are hidden and other rows are visible. The rows hidden by the filter are different from rows hidden with the Hide Rows command. Rows that are hidden using Hide Rows are often included when you copy or format a range that contains those rows. When you have manually hidden rows, you must use Alt+; to narrow your selection to only the visible rows. It is not necessary to use Alt+; when the rows have been hidden by the Filter command. Alt+; is the shortcut for Go To Special, Visible Cells Only.

You can use this behavior to format or copy rows matching certain criteria. If you want to highlight all rows matching a criterion by changing the background color of the cell, follow these steps:

1. Select one cell in the unfiltered data set that matches the proper criterion.
2. Click the Filter By Selection icon in the Quick Access Toolbar. If you don't have this icon available, refer to Figure 14.17 and follow the instructions there.
3. Select the first visible cell below the headings.
4. Press Ctrl+Shift+Down Arrow and then Ctrl+Shift+Right Arrow to select all the cells below the heading.
5. Format the cells as desired.
6. Select Data, Filter to remove the filter and show all rows. You will find that only the rows that were visible during the filter have the new formatting.

Using the Advanced Filter command

The Advanced Filter command is still present in Excel. Microsoft should give this feature a new name because it is remarkably powerful and does much more than filtering. However, the Advanced Filter command is admittedly one of the more confusing commands in Excel. This is particularly true because you can use the Advanced Filter in eight ways, and each method requires slightly different steps.

TIP

You can only copy filtered results to the active sheet, not to a new sheet. However, if you start on a blank sheet, you can specify that you want to filter data from another sheet and pull that data to the active sheet.

The eight ways to use the Advanced Filter are derived by multiplying 2×2×2. There are three options in the Advanced Filter dialog box, and depending on your choices for those three options, you can have possible combinations:

- You can choose either Filter In Place or Copy To A New Location.
- You can choose to filter with a criteria range or without any criteria.
- You can choose to return all matching values or only the unique values.

In reality, there are more than eight ways to use Advanced Filter. If you choose to copy records to a new location, you can either copy all the input columns in order or specify a subset of columns and/or a new sequence of columns.

You can build a simple filter for one column. You can combine any number of filters for multiple columns. You can build incredibly complex filters, using any formula imaginable. Alternatively, you can use no criteria at all. Using no criteria is common when you are using Advanced Filter to extract unique values or when you want to use Advanced Filter to reorder the sequence of columns.

To use Advanced Filter on a data set, follow these steps:

1. If you are using criteria, copy one or more headings from your data set to a blank section of the worksheet. Under each heading, list the value(s) you want to be included.
2. If you are using an output range and want to reorder the columns or include a subset of the columns, copy the headings into the appropriate order in a blank section of the worksheet. If you want all the original columns in their original sequence, the output range can be any blank cell.
3. Select a cell in your data range.
4. Select Data, Sort & Filter, Advanced.
5. Verify that the list range contains your original data set.
6. If you are using criteria, enter the criteria range.
7. If you want to copy the matching records to a new location, select Copy To Another Location. This enables the reference box for Copy To. Fill in the output range.

8. If you want the output range to contain only unique values, click Unique Records Only. If your output range contains a single field, a list of the values in that field is displayed that match the criteria. If your output range contains two or more fields, every unique combination of those two or more fields is displayed.

9. Click OK to perform the filter.

Excel in practice: using formulas for Advanced Filter criteria

Sometimes you might need to filter based on criteria that are too complex for any of Excel's built-in rules. For example, suppose you want to create an Advanced Filter to find all records in which one of 30 customers bought one of 20 products. The necessary criteria range would cover 601 rows and would take hours to build.

There is one obscure syntax of Advanced Filter criteria that enables you to filter to anything for which you can build a TRUE/FALSE formula. Use the following specifics to set up a filter that contains formulas:

1. This criteria range is two cells tall by one column wide.

2. The top cell is blank or contains text not found in the data range headers.

3. The second cell contains a formula that should have relative references pointing to the first data row of the input range.

4. The formula should evaluate to TRUE or FALSE. For example, to select all the West records where the invoice is above average for the West, use this:

```
=AND(B2="West",F2>AVERAGEIF($B$2:$B$1874,"West",$F$2:$F$1874))
```

When Excel sees that the first row of the criteria range is blank, it takes the formula in the second cell and applies it to all rows in the range. Any rows that would evaluate to TRUE are returned in the filter.

Advanced Filter criteria

Even though it is not obvious from the instructions for using Advanced Filter, you can build Advanced Filter criteria that can ask for a range of values. For example, if you are using an Advanced Filter, it is unlikely you will want to filter to the customer with exactly $7,553 in sales. However, you might want to filter to invoices that are more than $5,000 in sales. To set up this criterion, type **Sales** into cell K1. In cell K2, type **>5000**. When you issue the Advanced Filter, Excel returns all invoices more than $5,000.

In Figure 14.26, the Advanced Filter operation extracts all East region sales in the Training market. Three columns from the matching records will be copied to Columns L:N.

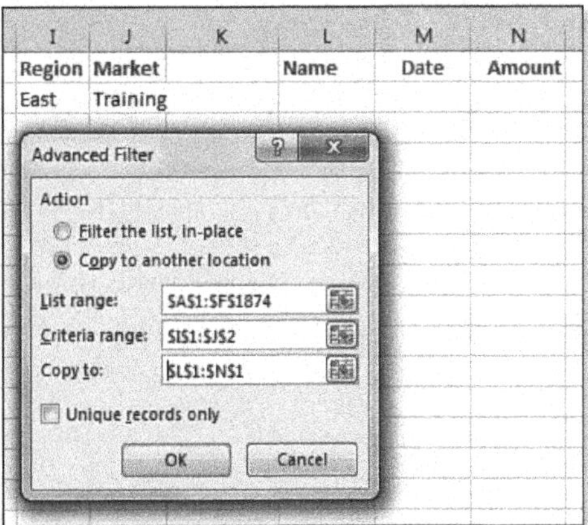

Figure 14.26 Advanced Filter is a powerful tool that can do much more than filter.

Note that criteria values that are in the same row are treated as if they were joined by AND. Because East and Training are both in row 2, a record must be from the East region and have a market of vehicles to appear in the data set. If you move Training from row 2 to row 3 and expand the criteria range to I1:J3, the two values are joined with an OR. All records that are from either the East region or the Training market appear in the results.

Replacing Advanced Filter with a dynamic array formula

One advantage of Advanced Filter is that you can control which columns are returned and the sequence of those columns. The new `FILTER` dynamic array function, discussed in Chapter 12, allows you to return all rows that match one or more criteria.

By wrapping the `FILTER` function in an `INDEX` function, you can also control which columns are returned and the sequence of those columns. Thanks to Excel MVP Purna Duggirala (also known as "Chandoo" on YouTube) for proposing this solution.

Say that you have a data set with six columns: Name, Region, Market, Invoice, Date, and Amount. You want to keep only the records where the Region is East and the Market is Training. Rather than returning all six columns, you want to return Date, Name, and Amount in that sequence.

With East in I2 and Market in J2, you could filter the data set with `=FILTER(A2:F1874,(B2:B1874=I2)*(C2:C1874=J2))`. But this formula will return all six columns in their original order.

To return Date, Name, and Amount, you want to specify that you want columns 5, 1, and 6. The `INDEX` function offers a chance to specify columns: `=INDEX(array, rows, columns)`.

In order to specify the rows argument for the `INDEX` function, you need to generate the numbers 1 to N where N is the total number of records found. Use `SEQUENCE(COUNTIFS(B2:B1874, I2,C2:C1874,J2))` to count the number of rows returned by the filter, and then `SEQUENCE` will generate that many numbers.

Finally, the columns argument is an array constant of {5,1,6} to specify which columns and the sequence of those columns.

Putting it all together, you end up with the formula shown in Figure 14.27.

```
=INDEX(
    FILTER(A2:F1874,(B2:B1874=I2)*(C2:C1874=J2)),
    SEQUENCE(COUNTIFS(B2:B1874,I2,C2:C1874,J2)),
    {5,1,6})
```



```
=INDEX(
  FILTER(A2:F1874,(B2:B1874=I2)*(C2:C1874=J2)),
  SEQUENCE(COUNTIFS(B2:B1874,I2,C2:C1874,J2)),
  {5,1,6})
```

I	J	K	L	M	N
Region	Market		Date	Name	Amount
East	Training		10/1/2018	MyExcelOnline.com	300
			10/5/2018	MyExcelOnline.com	125
			10/29/2018	MyExcelOnline.com	300
			11/2/2018	MyExcelOnline.com	125

Figure 14.27 The formulas combined FILTER, INDEX, and SEQUENCE to return three non-adjacent columns in a new sequence.

Using Remove Duplicates to find unique values

By its nature, transactional data has a lot of detail. You end up with transactional data in Excel because it is often the easiest to obtain. As you start to analyze transactional data, you often want to find the number of customers, number of products, or number of something in the data set.

For example, transactional data can tell you that there were 34 invoices issued last month, but that doesn't mean there were 34 customers. Some of those customers might have made repeat purchases. In this case, 20 customers could account for 34 invoices.

To find the number of unique customers, you need a way to eliminate the duplicate records in a data set. In legacy versions of Excel, this usually meant using Advanced Filter, some `IF` functions, or possibly a pivot table. However, in Excel today, the Remove Duplicates data tool makes it easier to remove duplicates.

The first thing to realize is that the Remove Duplicates tool is destructive because it really removes the duplicate records. If you want to keep the original transactional data intact, you should either make a copy of the customer column in a blank section of the workbook or make a backup copy of the workbook.

To find the unique values in a data set, follow these steps:

1. Copy the data set to a blank section of the worksheet. Make sure to leave a blank column between your real data and the copy of the data.
2. Select a single cell within the data set.
3. On the Data tab, in the Data Tools group, select Remove Duplicates. Excel expands the selection to include the entire range. In the Remove Duplicates dialog box, Excel predicts if your data has headers. This dialog box also shows a list of all the fields in the data set.
4. Because you are interested in a unique list of customers, click the Unselect All button to clear all check boxes, and then select the Customer field, as shown in Figure 14.28.

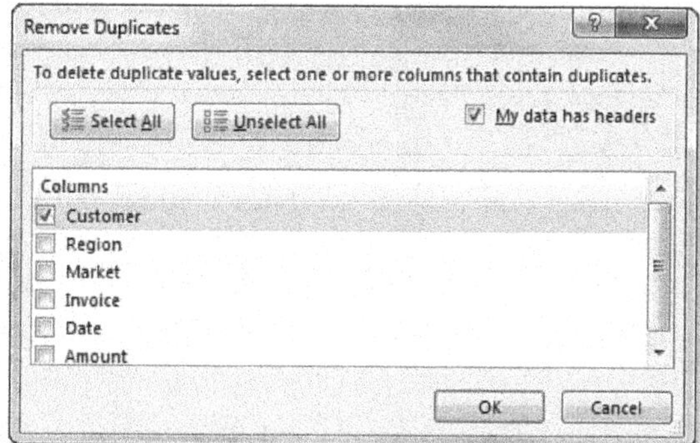

Figure 14.28 Choose which columns should be considered when analyzing duplicates.

5. Click OK to perform the action. Excel tells you how many duplicate values were found and removed. It also tells you how many unique values remain.

TIP

Remember that the Remove Duplicates command is destructive. For this reason, sometimes, you might want to find the duplicates and choose which version to remove. In that case, you Select Home, Conditional Formatting, Highlight Cell Rules, Duplicate Values.

Other times, you might want to send a copy of the unique values to a new location. In this case, use the Advanced Filter command discussed earlier in this chapter.

Finally, you might want to remove duplicates but add up the sales for all the removed records and then add them to the Customer field. Although this can be achieved with

pivot tables, it can also be achieved using the Consolidate feature, which is discussed in the next section.

Combining duplicates and adding values

In columns A:D of Figure 14.29, each customer appears one or more times in the list with sales, cost, and profit values. In addition to finding a unique list of customers, you would like to know the total sales and profit for each customer. You can use a pivot table to find the total sales for each customer. Alternatively, you can use the data tools to consolidate the table down to one record per customer.

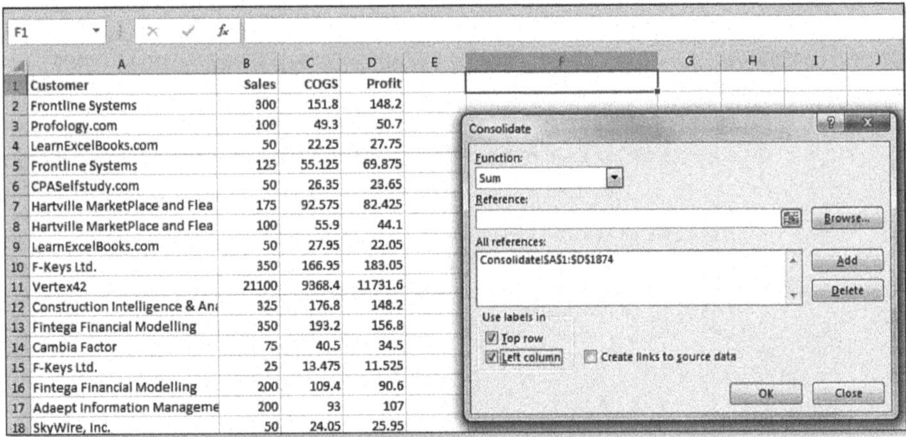

	A	B	C	D
1	Customer	Sales	COGS	Profit
2	Frontline Systems	300	151.8	148.2
3	Profology.com	100	49.3	50.7
4	LearnExcelBooks.com	50	22.25	27.75
5	Frontline Systems	125	55.125	69.875
6	CPASelfstudy.com	50	26.35	23.65
7	Hartville MarketPlace and Flea	175	92.575	82.425
8	Hartville MarketPlace and Flea	100	55.9	44.1
9	LearnExcelBooks.com	50	27.95	22.05
10	F-Keys Ltd.	350	166.95	183.05
11	Vertex42	21100	9368.4	11731.6
12	Construction Intelligence & An	325	176.8	148.2
13	Fintega Financial Modelling	350	193.2	156.8
14	Cambia Factor	75	40.5	34.5
15	F-Keys Ltd.	25	13.475	11.525
16	Fintega Financial Modelling	200	109.4	90.6
17	Adaept Information Manageme	200	93	107
18	SkyWire, Inc.	50	24.05	25.95

Figure 14.29 Start at a blank section of the workbook before invoking the Consolidate feature.

To use the Consolidate feature to total sales from all the records for that customer, follow these steps:

1. Instead of preselecting the data, move the cell pointer to a blank section of the worksheet.

2. Select Data, Data Tools, Consolidate. The Consolidate dialog box appears.

3. In the Consolidate dialog box, enter the reference to your data in the Reference box. The data will be combined based on the field in the left column of the range. If you have multiple lists of customers, you can click the Add button and enter additional ranges.

4. Make sure to select the Top Row and Left Column check boxes in the Use Labels In section.

5. Click OK.

Excel creates a new table. Each customer appears in the table just once. The sales associated with all the records of the customer appear in the new total, as shown in Figure 14.30.

F	G	H	I
	Sales	COGS	Profit
Frontline Systems	532675	263796.6	268878.4
Profology.com	946850	470308.7	476541.3
LearnExcelBooks.com	1228675	629414.6	599260.5
CPASelfstudy.com	2750	1376.4	1373.6
Hartville MarketPlace and Flea	658125	334804.7	323320.3
F-Keys Ltd.	702625	337767.2	364857.9
Vertex42	1124375	559745.1	564629.9
Construction Intelligence & Ana	17875	8945.95	8929.05
Fintega Financial Modelling	1265625	647611.6	618013.4
Cambia Factor	1233625	620172.9	613452.2
Adaept Information Manageme	620000	319127.8	300872.2
SkyWire, Inc.	609125	309001.4	300123.6
Data2Impact	648125	307050.8	341074.2
MyOnlineTrainingHub.com	755000	367083.2	387916.8
Surten Excel	33000	16735.3	16264.7
Wag More Dog Store, San Antor	17875	8984.95	8890.05

Figure 14.30 Excel consolidates all data by customer.

Two annoyances remain with this command. First, the heading for the leftmost column is never filled in. Second, the command leaves the results in the same sequence in which they originally appeared. In this example, you will probably want to add the heading above cell F2 and sort the data.

CHAPTER 15

Using pivot tables to analyze data

A pivot table enables you to summarize thousands or millions of records of data to a one-page summary in just a few clicks.

Suppose you have 400,000 records of transactional data. It is easy for some people to look at this and figure out that it represents $x million. But to learn some things about the data, you need to do some more analysis to spot trends in the data. A pivot table enables you to analyze trends in data without having to worry about formulas.

By using a pivot table, it is possible to create many views of your data, including the following:

- Breakdown of sales by product
- Sales by month, this year versus last year
- Percentage of sales by customer
- Customers who bought XYZ product in the East region
- Sales by product by month
- Top five customers with products

Of course, these are just examples. You can use pivot tables to slice and dice your data in almost any imaginable way.

Pivot tables were introduced in Excel 95 and have been evolving ever since:

- Office 365 introduced the ability to format a single cell in a pivot table and have that formatting travel with the cell. Format "East" and "Widgets" in red fill and the formatting will move as you rearrange the pivot table.

- Excel 2019 introduced Pivot Table Defaults. A huge number of default settings in pivot tables are annoying. You can now fix these settings once, and all future pivot tables will have your favorite settings.
- Office 365 in 2018 has a new artificial intelligence feature (originally called Insights, then Ideas, and now Analyze Data). Excel uses artificial intelligence to analyze your data and suggest up to 30 pivot tables or pivot charts. You can even ask a question about your data to generate a pivot table.
- You can build a pivot table on a map using 3D Maps.
- Excel 2013 added a new entry point for pivot tables called Recommended Pivot Tables. This feature shows you various thumbnails of pivot tables before you begin creating one.
- Excel 2013 added the capability to create a data model from several different tables. You can create a relationship between tables without using VLOOKUPs and base pivot tables on the model.
- Timelines are a visual date filter introduced in Excel 2013. They join slicers, the visual filter introduced in Excel 2010. The best feature of timelines and slicers is the capability for them to drive multiple pivot tables built from the same data set.
- Power Pivot is a powerful add-in for Excel that enhances pivot tables. Power Pivot enhances the ability to build multi-table models and provides key performance indicators (KPIs) and the DAX formula language.
- Excel 2010 introduced new calculations such as Rank, Percent Of Parent, and Running Percentage Of Total.
- Excel 2010 introduced the option to replace blanks in the outer row fields by repeating item labels from above.
- Excel 2007 simplified the pivot table interface and added new filters.

Creating your first pivot table

Pivot tables are best created from transactional data—that is, raw data files directly from your company's IT department.

To create the best pivot tables, make sure your data follows these rules:

- Ensure each column has a one-cell heading. Keep the headings unique; don't use the same heading for two columns. If you need your headings to appear on two rows, type the first word, press Alt+Enter, and then type the second word.

- If a column should contain numeric data, don't allow blank cells in the column. Use zeros instead of blanks.
- Do not use blank rows or blank columns.
- If totals are embedded in your report, remove them.
- The workbook should not be in Compatibility mode. Many pivot table features from Excel 2007–2019 are disabled if the workbook is in Compatibility mode.
- If you add new data to the bottom of your data set each month, you should strongly consider converting your data set to a table using Ctrl+T. Pivot tables created from tables automatically pick up new rows pasted to the bottom of the tables after a refresh.
- If your data has months spread across many columns, go back to the source software program to see if a different view of the data is available with months going down the rows.

For most of this chapter, the pivot tables shown in the figures are from the data set in Figure 15.1. This data set has two years of transactional data. There is a single text column of Customer. There is a single date column. Numeric columns include Quantity, Revenue, COGS, and Profit.

	A	B	C	D	E	F	G	H
1	Region	Product	Date	Customer	Quantity	Revenue	COGS	Profit
2	East	XYZ	1/1/2024	MyOnlineTrainingHub.com	954	22810	10213	12597
3	Central	DEF	1/2/2024	WM Squared Inc.	124	2257	998	1259
4	East	XYZ	1/4/2024	SlinkyRN Excel Instruction	425	9152	4083	5069
5	East	DEF	1/4/2024	MrExcel.com	773	18552	7883	10669
6	East	ABC	1/7/2024	DataSolverz.com	401	8456	3389	5067
7	East	DEF	1/7/2024	Excel Design Solutions Ltd	1035	21730	9839	11891

Figure 15.1 This data set follows the rules of a good pivot table source.

Using artificial intelligence for inspiration with pivot tables

Microsoft 365 subscribers have access to an artificial intelligence tool called Analyze Data. The tool will analyze up to 250,000 cells and suggest interesting pivot tables, pivot charts, or formulas to show trends in the data. (See Figure 15.2.)

Select one cell in your data. Click the Analyze Data icon (found near the right side of the Home tab). In a few seconds, Excel will show previews of a few interesting analyses. Give the tool a few more seconds, and a Show More hyperlink will appear below the last preview, which leads to 30 or more suggested pivot tables.

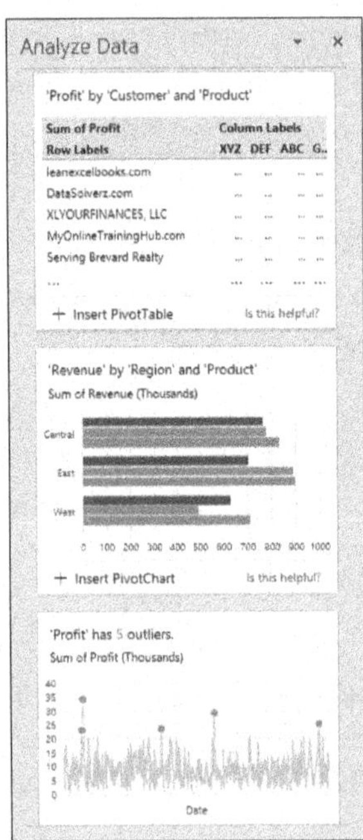

Figure 15.2 Excel uses artificial intelligence to look for interesting trends in your data.

Another interesting use for Analyze Data is that you can ask a question about your data. In Figure 15.3, Excel quickly finds the top three customers in the East region.

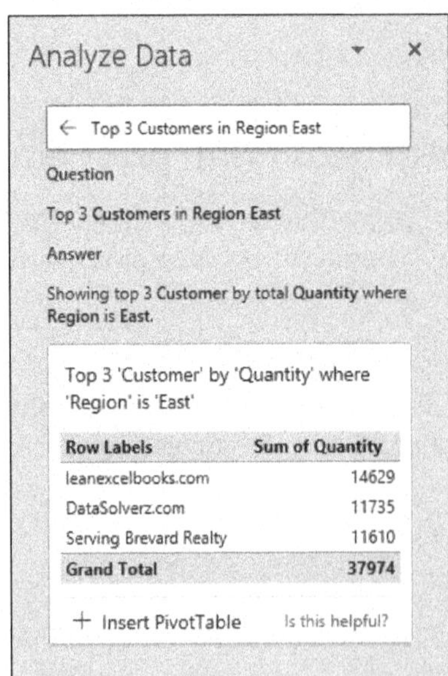

Figure 15.3 You can ask a question using natural language and Excel will create a pivot table or pivot chart to answer the question.

If you do not have Microsoft 365, then you will be forced into using the Recommended PivotTables icon on the Insert tab. This feature is limited to 10 pivot tables. As a precursor to the artificial intelligence features, it would often get you to a final pivot table in fewer clicks.

Starting with a blank pivot table

The traditional method for creating a pivot table is to create a blank one. Choose one cell in your data. Select PivotTable from the Insert tab. Excel displays the Create PivotTable dialog box, as shown in Figure 15.4.

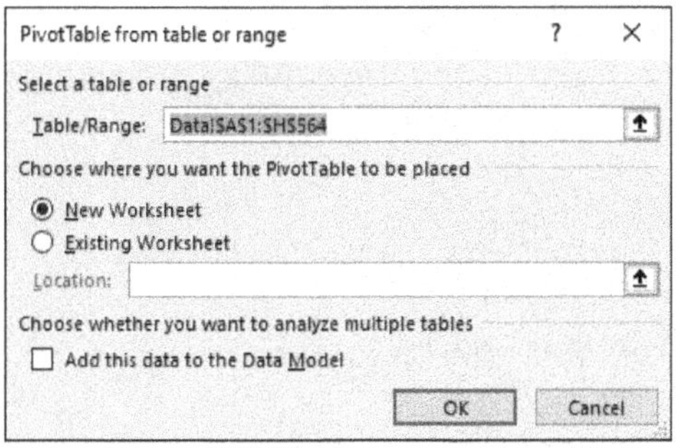

PivotTable from table or range
Select a table or range
Table/Range: Data!$A$1:$H$564
Choose where you want the PivotTable to be placed
New Worksheet
Existing Worksheet
Location:
Choose whether you want to analyze multiple tables
Add this data to the Data Model
OK Cancel

Figure 15.4 Using the Create PivotTable dialog box, you can choose where to place the pivot table.

This dialog box confirms the range of your data. Provided you have no blank rows or blank columns, Excel normally gets this right.

Using the Create PivotTable dialog box, you have the choice of creating the pivot table on a new blank worksheet or in an existing location. You might decide to put the pivot table in J2 on this worksheet or next to another existing pivot table or pivot chart if you plan on building a dashboard of several pivot tables.

You can build a pivot table from a relational model by checking the Add This Data To The Data Model check box. For details on building a pivot table from two or more tables, see Chapter 17, "Mashing up data with Power Pivot."

Adding fields to your pivot table using the field list

If you started with a blank pivot table, you see a PivotTable Fields panel that looks like Figure 15.5. The graphic shown in columns A:C is a placeholder to indicate where the pivot table will appear after you choose some fields. The PivotTable Fields area has a list of fields from your original data set at the top and four drop zones at the bottom. To build your report, you add fields to the drop zones at the bottom.

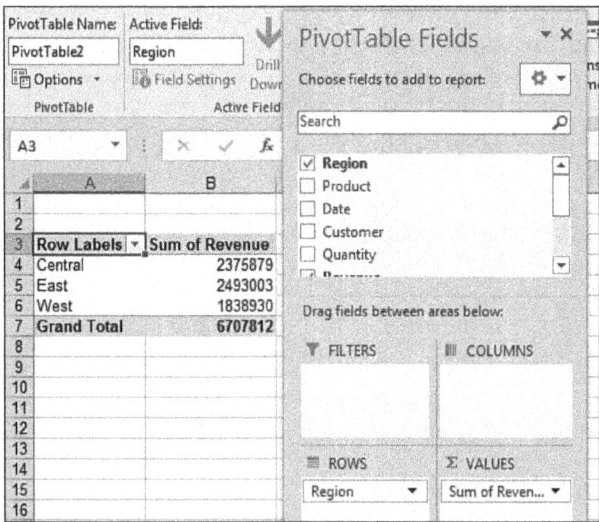

Figure 15.5 A blank pivot table and the PivotTable Fields list.

NOTE

The field list is generally docked to the right side of the Excel window. The figures in this book show the field list as undocked. To undock the field list, drag the title bar away from the edge of the window. It is hard to re-dock the field list. You must grab the left side of the title bar and drag the field list more than 50 percent off the right side of the Excel window.

Changing the pivot table report by using the field list

Check the Region, Product, and Revenue fields.

When you check a text or date field, that field automatically moves to the Rows drop zone in the PivotTable Fields list. When you check a numeric field, that field moves to the Values drop zone and is changed to Sum of *Field*.

By choosing Region, Product, and Revenue, you see Sum of Revenue by region and product, as shown in Figure 15.6.

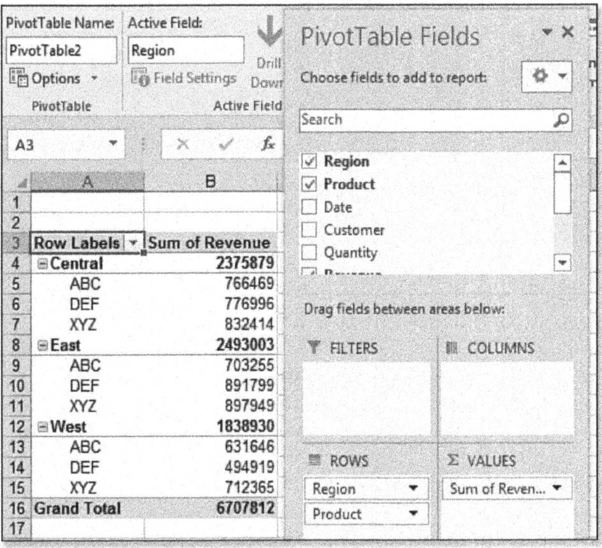

Figure 15.6 Check fields in the top of the field list to build this report.

You can further customize the pivot table by moving fields around in the drop zones. For example, drag the Region field so it is below the Product field in the Rows drop zone. The report updates to show Region within Product, as shown in Figure 15.7.

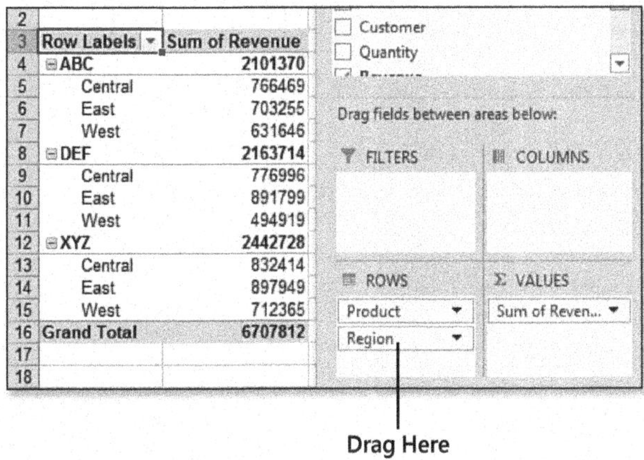

Figure 15.7 Drag the Region field to appear after the Product field in the Rows drop zone to change the report.

Drag the Product field from the Rows drop zone to the Columns drop zone, and you have a cross-tab report, as shown in Figure 15.8.

Sum of Revenue	Column Labels			
Row Labels	ABC	DEF	XYZ	Grand Total
Central	766469	776996	832414	2375879
East	703255	891799	897949	2493003
West	631646	494919	712365	1838930
Grand Total	2101370	2163714	2442728	6707812

Figure 15.8 Pivot the Product field to the columns of the report.

Dealing with the compact layout

If you've been using pivot tables for many versions of Excel, you have to wonder about the bizarre layout of the pivot table shown previously in Figure 15.6. The totals appear at the top of each group instead of at the bottom. Two fields—Region and Product—appear in column A. Collapse buttons appear next to the regions.

This is a report layout called Compact Form. Introduced in Excel 2007, it is beautiful if you plan to present your pivot table in an interactive touch-screen kiosk complete with slicers. However, if you plan to reuse the results of the pivot table, the Compact Form is horrible. Every pivot table you create in the Excel interface starts with Compact Form. Here is how to go back to the Tabular Form layout:

1. Make sure that the active cell is inside the pivot table.
2. Go to the Design tab in the ribbon. Open the Report Layout drop-down. Select Show in Tabular Form. As shown in Figure 15.9, the totals move back to the bottom of each region. Also, Product moves to column B.

Region	Product	Sum of Revenue
Central	ABC	766469
	DEF	776996
	XYZ	832414
Central Total		2375879
East	ABC	703255
	DEF	891799
	XYZ	897949
East Total		2493003
West	ABC	631646
	DEF	494919
	XYZ	712365
West Total		1838930
Grand Total		6707812

Figure 15.9 Change from Compact Form to Tabular Form to put each field in a new column.

3. Open the Report Layout drop-down and select Repeat All Item Labels. This eliminates the blanks in column A of the pivot table, as shown in Figure 15.10.

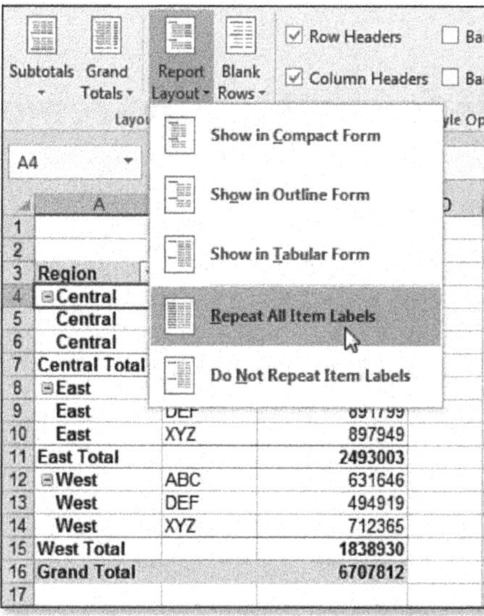

Figure 15.10 Using Repeat All Item Labels fills in blanks in the row area.

Rearranging a pivot table

The drop zone sections of the PivotTable Fields list box are as follows:

- **Filter:** You use this section to limit the report to only certain criteria. This section is virtually replaced by the slicer feature.

➤ **To learn more about filtering pivot tables, see** Chapter 16, "Using slicers and filtering a pivot table."

- **Rows:** This section is for fields that appear on the left side of the table. By default, all text fields move here when you select the check boxes in the top of the field list.
- **Columns:** This section is for fields that stretch along the top rows of columns of your table. Old database geeks refer to this as a *crosstab report.*
- **Values:** This section is for all the numeric fields that are summarized in the table. By default, most fields are automatically summed, but you can change the default calculation to an average, minimum, maximum, or other calculations.

You can add fields to a drop zone by dragging from the top of the PivotTable Fields list to a drop zone or by dragging from one drop zone to another. To remove a field from a drop zone, drag the field from the drop zone to outside of the PivotTable Fields list or uncheck it from the field list.

Finishing touches: numeric formatting and removing blanks

After you arrange your data in the report, you want to consider formatting the numeric fields. For example, the pivot table in Figure 15.11 has Customer and Product in the Rows drop zone, Region in Columns, and Revenue in Values. It would be helpful if the numbers were formatted with commas as thousands separators. Also, consider changing the words "Sum Of Revenue" to something less awkward, such as "Total Revenue" or even "Revenue."

	A	B	C	D	E	F
1						
2						
3	**Sum of Revenue**		**Region**			
4	**Customer**	**Product**	**Central**	**East**	**West**	**Grand Total**
5	**data2impact**	ABC		5532		5532
6	**data2impact**	DEF	16784			16784
7	**data2impact**	XYZ		18264	16936	35200
8	**data2impact Total**		**16784**	**23796**	**16936**	**57516**
9	**Data Solverz.com**	ABC	124738	69040	87189	280967
10	**Data Solverz.com**	DEF	47373	132844	53218	233435
11	**Data Solverz.com**	XYZ	121922	58279	55560	235761
12	**Data Solverz.com Total**		**294033**	**260163**	**195967**	**750163**
13	**Excel Design Solutions Ltd**	ABC			13853	13853
14	**Excel Design Solutions Ltd**	DEF	4754	21730		26484
15	**Excel Design Solutions Ltd**	XYZ			19544	19544

Figure 15.11 You should add numeric formatting to this pivot table.

Follow these steps to apply a numeric format to the Revenue field:

1. Select cell A3 with the Sum Of Revenue heading. Type **Revenue** followed by a space and press Enter. You can't re-use the word "Revenue," but naming the column "Revenue " (with a space after "Revenue") works.
2. Right-click any number in the pivot table and choose Number Format. The familiar Format Cells dialog box appears.
3. Select the Number category. Select 0 decimal places and add a thousands separator. Click OK to close the Format Cells dialog box. Click OK to close the Value Field Settings dialog box.
4. Right-click any cell in the pivot table and choose PivotTable Options.
5. On the Layout & Format tab of the PivotTable Options dialog box, type **0** next to For Empty Cells Show.

Figure 15.12 shows the new number format applied to the pivot table, along with the empty cells replaced with zero.

	A	B	C	D	E	F
1						
2						
3	Revenue		Region			
4	Customer	Product	East	Central	West	Grand Total
5	⊟data2impact	ABC	5,532	0	0	5,532
6	data2impact	DEF	0	16,784	0	16,784
7	data2impact	XYZ	18,264	0	16,936	35,200
8	**data2impact Total**		**23,796**	**16,784**	**16,936**	**57,516**
9	⊟Data Solverz.com	ABC	69,040	124,738	87,189	280,967
10	Data Solverz.com	DEF	132,844	47,373	53,218	233,435
11	Data Solverz.com	XYZ	58,279	121,922	55,560	235,761
12	Data Solverz.com Total		260,163	294,033	195,967	750,163

Figure 15.12 The finished pivot table has better numeric formatting.

> ## Inside OUT
>
> ***Sometimes, you might need to format a single cell in a pivot table.***
>
> For example, your manager might need the sales figures for bananas in the Central region to always be shown in blue.
>
> A new feature appeared in Office 365 during 2018. Right-click the desired cell and choose Format Cells. The formatting will be applied in a new rule for the specific cell (in this example, the cell containing Central region banana sales). This formatting is sticky; if you rearrange the pivot table, the formatting will move to the new location, meaning if you move the location for Central region banana sales, the formatting moves with it. I can't imagine the overhead required for this simple feature.
>
> In this example, you will notice if you remove "Banana" or "Central" from the pivot table via a slicer or a filter, the formatting will return when the item returns. However, if you completely remove "Region" or "Product" from the pivot table, the formatting is lost.

Three things you **must** know when using pivot tables

Pivot tables are the greatest invention in spreadsheets. However, you must understand the following three issues, presented in order of importance.

Your pivot table is in manual calculation mode until you click Refresh!

Most people are shocked to learn that changes to underlying data do not appear in a pivot table. After all, you change a cell in Excel, and all the formulas derived from the cell automatically change. You would think that the same should hold true for pivot tables, but it does not. Pivot tables are fast because the original data from the worksheet is loaded into a pivot cache in memory. Until you click the Refresh icon on the Analyze ribbon, Excel does not pick up the changes to the underlying data.

If you click outside the pivot table, all the pivot table tools disappear

If your field list disappeared and the Options and Design tabs are missing, it is likely that you clicked outside of the pivot table.

I've argued with Microsoft that because nothing is on the worksheet other than the pivot table, I am still looking at the pivot table even when I click outside of the pivot table. I continue to lose this argument, however. If the field list disappears and the tabs are gone, click back inside your pivot table.

You cannot change, move a part of, or insert cells in a pivot table

Many times, pivot tables get you very close to the final report you want, and you just want to insert a row or move one bit of the table. You cannot do this. If you try, you will be greeted with the ubiquitous message: "We can't make this change for the selected cells because it will affect a PivotTable." This is a fair limitation. After all, Excel needs to figure out how to redraw the table when you move something in the field list.

One solution is to copy the entire pivot table and then use Paste Values to convert the report to regular Excel data. You can either put this on a new worksheet or paste the entire table back over itself. If you go to a new worksheet, you can continue to modify the original pivot table. If you paste values over the original worksheet, the pivot table converts to a range, and you cannot pivot it further.

> TIP
>
> **Another way to insert a blank row in your pivot table is to make the next row twice as tall as other rows. Although you are not actually inserting a row, it will appear as though there is a blank row when it is printed.**

Calculating and roll-ups with pivot tables

Pivot tables offer many more calculation options than those shown so far in this chapter. One of the most amazing features is the capability to roll daily dates up to months, quarters, and years.

Grouping daily dates to months, quarters, and years

Good pivot tables start with good transactional data. Invariably, that transactional data is stored with daily dates instead of monthly summaries.

To produce a summary by month, quarter, and year, follow these steps:

1. Start with data that contains daily dates. Build a pivot table with daily dates going down the row field, Region in the columns, and Sum Of Revenue in the value area.
2. Select one cell that contains a date. On the PivotTable Analyze tab, choose Group Field.
3. In the Grouping dialog box, choose Months, Quarters, and Years. Click OK.
4. Figure 15.13 shows a pivot table with daily dates rolled up to months, quarters, and years.

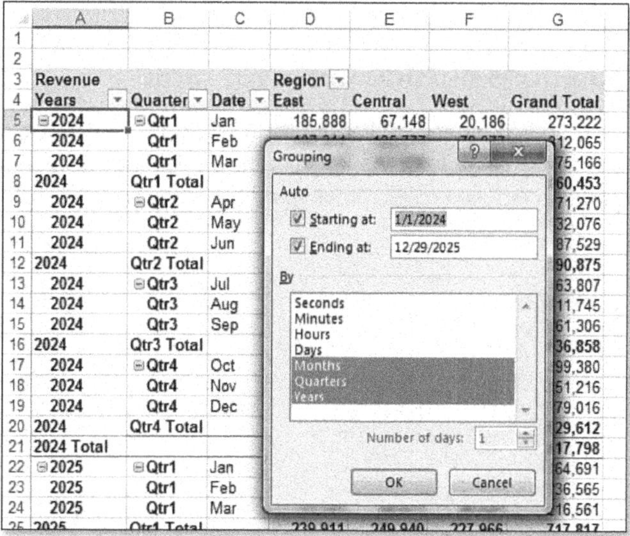

Figure 15.13 Roll your daily dates up to months, quarters, and/or years.

For an interesting alternative to the report in Figure 15.13, follow these steps:

1. Uncheck the Region and Quarter fields to remove them from the report.
2. Drag the Years field from the Rows area to the Columns area.

You now have a pivot table that provides totals by month and quarter and compares years going across the report (see Figure 15.14). Notice that your pivot table field list includes three fields related to dates: The years and quarters fields are virtual fields. The original Date field includes the months. This was a brilliant design decision on Microsoft's part because it allows years and months to be pivoted to different sections of the pivot table.

	A	B	C	D	E
1					
2					
3	**Revenue**	**Years**			
4	**Date**	**2024**	**2025**	**Grand Total**	
5	Jan	273,222	264,691	537,913	
6	Feb	312,065	236,565	548,630	
7	Mar	275,166	216,561	491,727	
8	Apr	271,270	292,003	563,273	
9	May	332,076	287,443	619,519	
10	Jun	187,529	241,883	429,412	
11	Jul	363,807	295,851	659,658	
12	Aug	311,745	286,891	598,636	
13	Sep	261,306	217,076	478,382	
14	Oct	299,380	308,986	608,366	
15	Nov	251,216	301,880	553,096	
16	Dec	279,016	340,184	619,200	
17	**Grand Total**	**3,417,798**	**3,290,014**	**6,707,812**	

Figure 15.14 Pivot years to the column area to show year over year.

Adding calculations outside the pivot table

Figure 15.15 shows % Growth instead of Grand Total in column D. However, after you group the dates in the pivot table, you are prevented from adding a calculated field inside the pivot table, so you must turn back to regular Excel to provide the % Growth column.

D5 =C5/B5-1

	A	B	C	D	E
1					
2					
3	**Revenue**	**Years**			
4	**Date**	**2024**	**2025**	% Growth	
5	Jan	273,222	264,691	-3.1%	
6	Feb	312,065	236,565	-24.2%	
7	Mar	275,166	216,561	-21.3%	
8	Apr	271,270	292,003	7.6%	
9	May	332,076	287,443	-13.4%	
10	Jun	187,529	241,883	29.0%	
11	Jul	363,807	295,851	-18.7%	
12	Aug	311,745	286,891	-8.0%	
13	Sep	261,306	217,076	-16.9%	
14	Oct	299,380	308,986	3.2%	
15	Nov	251,216	301,880	20.2%	
16	Dec	279,016	340,184	21.9%	
17	**Grand Total**	**3,417,798**	**3,290,014**	-3.7%	

Figure 15.15 The % Growth column is a regular formula outside the pivot table, formatted to look like it is part of the pivot table.

However, it is not simple for Excel to create that column. In particular, step 3 trips up most people. Follow these steps:

1. Right-click the Grand Total in D4 and choose Remove Grand Total.
2. Type a heading of % Growth in D4
3. In cell D5, type **`=C5/B5-1`**. You really have to type this formula! Do not touch the mouse or the arrow keys while you are building the formula, or you will be stung by the `GetPivotData` bug.
4. Format cell D5 as a percentage with one decimal place.
5. Double-click the fill handle in D5 to copy the formula down to all rows.

Changing the calculation of a field

By default, a numeric column will be added to the pivot table with a default calculation of Sum. Excel offers ten other calculations, such as Average, Count, Max, and Min.

For this section, the figures start with a completely new pivot table. You can follow along with these steps:

1. Delete the worksheet that contains the pivot table from the previous examples. This clears the pivot cache from memory.
2. Select one cell on the Data worksheet.
3. Choose Insert, PivotTable.
4. Add a check next to the Region, Product, and Revenue fields.
5. Drag Revenue to the Values area two more times. They will appear in the pivot table as Sum Of Revenue2 and Sum Of Revenue3.
6. On the Design tab, choose Report Layout, Show In Tabular Form.
7. On the Design tab, choose Report Layout and Repeat All Item Labels.
8. You will have the pivot table shown in Figure 15.16.

	A	B	C	D	E
1					
2					
3	Region	Product	Sum of Revenue	Sum of Revenue2	Sum of Revenue3
4	East	ABC	703255	703255	703255
5	East	DEF	891799	891799	891799
6	East	XYZ	897949	897949	897949
7	East Total		2493003	2493003	2493003
8	Central	ABC	766469	766469	766469
9	Central	DEF	776996	776996	776996
10	Central	XYZ	832414	832414	832414
11	Central Total		2375879	2375879	2375879
12	West	ABC	631646	631646	631646
13	West	DEF	494919	494919	494919
14	West	XYZ	712365	712365	712365
15	West Total		1838930	1838930	1838930
16	Grand Total		6707812	6707812	6707812

Figure 15.16 This new pivot table starts with three numeric columns that default to Sum.

In column D, you would like a count of the number of records. Follow these steps to change column D to a count of the number of records:

1. Double-click the Sum Of Revenue2 heading in D3. This opens the Value Field Settings dialog box.
2. In the Value Field Settings dialog box, choose Count instead of Sum.
3. In the Custom Name field, type **`Number of Orders`** or any other name that makes sense to you.
4. Click OK. Column D now shows a count of records instead of a sum (see Figure 15.17).

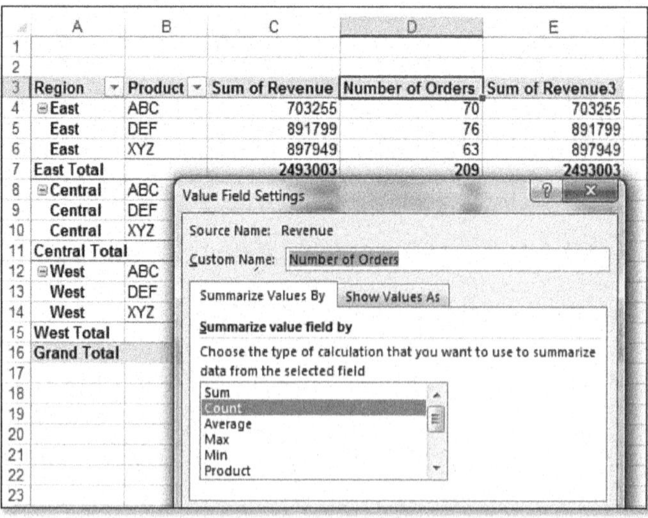

Figure 15.17 Change column C to show a count instead of a sum.

To change column E to show average revenue per order, follow these steps:

1. Double-click the Sum Of Revenue3 heading in E3. Change the calculation to Average.
2. Change the Custom Name field to "**Avg Revenue**."
3. Click the Number Format button.
4. Choose Currency with two decimal places.
5. Click OK twice to close the Format Cells and the Value Field Settings dialog boxes. Excel now shows Avg Revenue in column E.

You can use a similar method to change to any of the 11 calculations offered in the Summarize Values By tab.

That's not all—there are more ways to show the values, as discussed in the next section.

Showing percentage of total using Show Value As settings

In addition to the 11 ways to summarize values, Excel offers 14 calculation options on the second tab of the Value Field Settings dialog box. To experiment with these 14 calculations, drag the Revenue field to the Values drop zone two more times. Follow these steps:

1. Double-click the heading in F3 to open the Value Field Settings. Select the second tab in the Value Field Settings dialog box. Choose % Of Column Total from the drop-down. Change the Custom Name to % Of Total. Click OK.
2. Double-click G3 and select the second tab in the Value Field Settings dialog box. Choose % Of Parent Row Total from the drop-down. Change the Custom Name to % Of Parent and click OK.

Figure 15.18 shows the result. In row 4, the $703,255 of revenue in C4 is 10.48% of the grand total revenue. The calculation in G4 shows that the revenue in C4 is 28.21% of the East region revenue shown in C7.

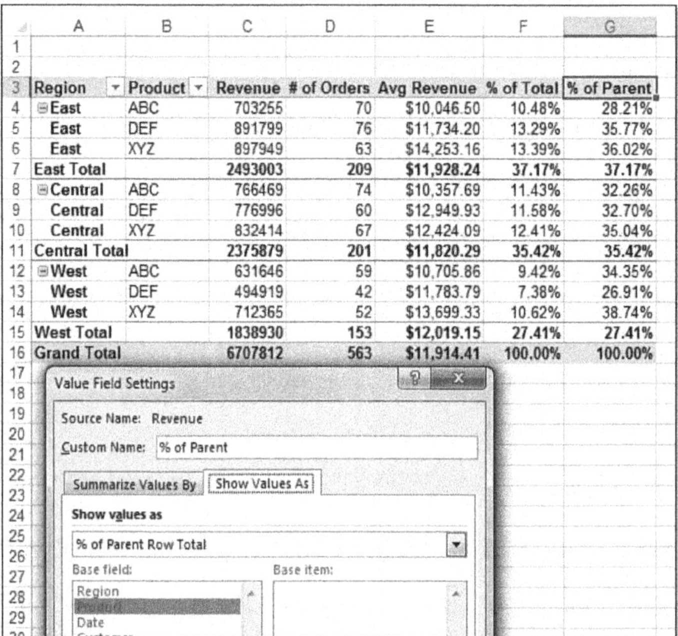

Region	Product	Revenue	# of Orders	Avg Revenue	% of Total	% of Parent
East	ABC	703255	70	$10,046.50	10.48%	28.21%
East	DEF	891799	76	$11,734.20	13.29%	35.77%
East	XYZ	897949	63	$14,253.16	13.39%	36.02%
East Total		**2493003**	**209**	**$11,928.24**	**37.17%**	**37.17%**
Central	ABC	766469	74	$10,357.69	11.43%	32.26%
Central	DEF	776996	60	$12,949.93	11.58%	32.70%
Central	XYZ	832414	67	$12,424.09	12.41%	35.04%
Central Total		**2375879**	**201**	**$11,820.29**	**35.42%**	**35.42%**
West	ABC	631646	59	$10,705.86	9.42%	34.35%
West	DEF	494919	42	$11,783.79	7.38%	26.91%
West	XYZ	712365	52	$13,699.33	10.62%	38.74%
West Total		**1838930**	**153**	**$12,019.15**	**27.41%**	**27.41%**
Grand Total		**6707812**	**563**	**$11,914.41**	**100.00%**	**100.00%**

Figure 15.18 Use Show Values As for 14 additional calculations.

Showing running totals and rank

Other options in the Show Values As drop-down include running totals and a ranking. These work best when there is only one field in the row area.

Delete the worksheet that contains the existing pivot table. Build a new pivot table with Customer in the Rows area. Drag Revenue six times to the Values area.

Initially, the customers are sorted alphabetically. Open the Row Labels drop-down in cell A3. Choose More Sort Options. In the Sort (Customer) dialog box, choose Descending (Z to A) By. In the drop-down, choose Sum Of Revenue. Click OK. The pivot table shows the largest customers at the top.

To change the calculation in each column, follow these steps:

1. Select cell B3, and type the new name, **Revenue**, with a leading or trailing space. Choose Currency with 0 decimal places. Click OK.

2. Double-click cell C3. On the Show Values As tab, choose Running Total In. In the Base Field list, choose Customer. Change the Custom Name to `Accum. Total`. Click Number Format. Choose Currency with 0 decimal places. Click OK twice.

3. Double-click cell D3. Click Field Settings. On the Show Values As tab, choose % Running Total In. In the Base Field list, choose Customer. Change the Custom Name to **Accum %**. Click Number Format. Choose Percentage with two decimal places. Click OK twice.

4. Double-click cell E3. Click Field Settings. On the Show Values As tab, choose Rank Largest To Smallest. In the Base Field list, choose Customer. Change the Custom Name to **Rank**. Click OK.

5. Double-click cell F3. Click Field Settings. On the Show Values As tab, choose % of Column Total. Change the Custom Name to **% of Total**. Click Percentage 1 Decimal Place. Click OK twice.

6. Double-click cell G3. Click Field Settings. On the Show Values As tab, choose % Of. In the Base Field list, choose Customer. In the Base Item field, you can choose (previous), (next), or a specific customer. Because the largest customer is leanexcelbooks.com, choose that customer as the Base Item setting. Change the Custom Name to **% of Top**. Choose the Number Format button. Click Percentage 1 Decimal Place. Click OK twice.

The resulting pivot table in Figure 15.19 shows examples of the 14 Show Values As options. Note that many of the options require the choice of a base field. A few also require that you select a base item.

	A	B	C	D	E	F	G
1							
2							
3	Customer	Revenue	Accum. Total	Accum. %	Rank	% of Total	% of Top
4	leanexcelbooks.com	$869,454	$869,454	12.96%	1	13.0%	100.0%
5	DataSolverz.com	$750,163	$1,619,617	24.15%	2	11.2%	86.3%
6	XLYOURFINANCES, LLC	$704,359	$2,323,976	34.65%	3	10.5%	81.0%
7	MyOnlineTrainingHub.com	$622,794	$2,946,770	43.93%	4	9.3%	71.6%
8	Serving Brevard Realty	$613,514	$3,560,284	53.08%	5	9.1%	70.6%
9	Excel4apps	$568,851	$4,129,135	61.56%	6	8.5%	65.4%
10	Mary Maids	$498,937	$4,628,072	69.00%	7	7.4%	57.4%
11	Excel Strategies, LLC	$427,349	$5,055,421	75.37%	8	6.4%	49.2%
12	MN Excel Consulting	$406,326	$5,461,747	81.42%	9	6.1%	46.7%
13	WM Squared Inc.	$390,978	$5,852,725	87.25%	10	5.8%	45.0%
14	LaFrenier Sons Septic	$72,680	$5,925,405	88.34%	11	1.1%	8.4%
15	Tennessee Moon	$71,651	$5,997,056	89.40%	12	1.1%	8.2%
16	Roto-Rooter	$62,744	$6,059,800	90.34%	13	0.9%	7.2%
17	Harvest Consulting	$60,299	$6,120,099	91.24%	14	0.9%	6.9%
18	Excel Design Solutions Ltd	$59,881	$6,179,980	92.13%	15	0.9%	6.9%
19	data2impact	$57,516	$6,237,496	92.99%	16	0.9%	6.6%
20	The Lab with Leo Crew	$55,251	$6,292,747	93.81%	17	0.8%	6.4%
21	Excel Learning Zone	$54,048	$6,346,795	94.62%	18	0.8%	6.2%
22	MAU Workforce Solutions	$51,240	$6,398,035	95.38%	19	0.8%	5.9%
23	Frontline Systems	$50,030	$6,448,065	96.13%	20	0.7%	5.8%
24	Resource Optimizer	$46,717	$6,494,782	96.82%	21	0.7%	5.4%
25	MrExcel.com	$42,316	$6,537,098	97.45%	22	0.6%	4.9%
26	Spain Enterprise	$39,250	$6,576,348	98.04%	23	0.6%	4.5%
27	University of North Carolina	$34,710	$6,611,058	98.56%	24	0.5%	4.0%
28	SlinkyRN Excel Instruction	$34,364	$6,645,422	99.07%	25	0.5%	4.0%
29	St. Peter's Prep	$31,369	$6,676,791	99.54%	26	0.5%	3.6%
30	Ribbon Commander Framework	$31,021	$6,707,812	100.00%	27	0.5%	3.6%
31	Grand Total	$6,707,812				100.0%	

Figure 15.19 Columns C:G are created using the Show Values As tab.

TROUBLESHOOTING

Excel offers many different ways of ranking ties. Pivot tables do not follow any of the existing methods and introduce a new method.

Say that you have five sales reps with sales of 1000, 800, 800, 400, and 200. The RANK.EQ **function will rank two people in second place and no one in third place. The** RANK.AVG **function will rank both reps with sales of 800 with the tie in the 2.5 place. Pivot table ranks follow neither rule. In a pivot table, people would be ranked, 1, 2, 2, 3, 4; no one would be ranked fifth.**

Using a formula to add a field to a pivot table

The previous examples took an existing field and used the Show Values As setting to change how the data is presented in the pivot table. In this example, you learn how to add a brand-new calculated field to the pivot table. Follow these steps:

1. Select one of the numeric cells in the pivot table.
2. On the PivotTable Analyze tab in the ribbon, choose Fields, Items & Sets. Choose Calculated Field from the drop-down. (If this option is not available, choose a cell in the value area of the pivot table.) Excel displays the Insert Calculated Field dialog box. The default field name of Field 1 and the default formula of =0 appear in the dialog box.
3. Type a new name, such as **GP%.**
4. The Formula field starts out as an equal sign, a space, and then a zero. You have to click in this field and press backspace to remove the zero. Alternatively, you can press Tab after typing the Name. This will select the entire text in the Formula field. Type an equal sign to replace the default formula.
5. Build the formula by double-clicking Profit, typing a slash, and then double-clicking Revenue. The dialog box should look like Figure 15.20. Click OK.

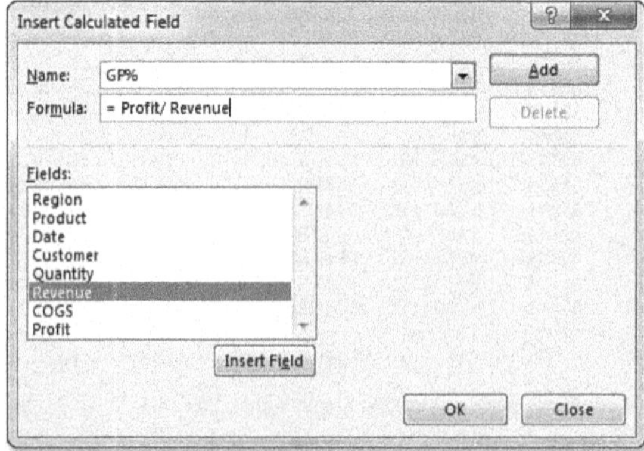

Figure 15.20 Build a calculated field.

6. The headings for calculated fields always appear strange. Select a cell in column H and choose Field Settings. Change the Custom Name from Sum Of GP% to **GP%** with a leading or trailing space. Change the Number Format to Percentage with one decimal. Click OK twice. The final pivot table is shown in Figure 15.21.

2								
3	Row Labels	Revenue	Accum. Total	Accum %	Rank	% of Total	% of Top	GP%
4	leanexcelbooks.com	$869,454	$869,454	13.0%	1	13.0%	100.0%	56.0%
5	DataSolverz.com	$750,163	$1,619,617	24.1%	2	11.2%	86.3%	55.4%
6	XLYOURFINANCES, LLC	$704,359	$2,323,976	34.6%	3	10.5%	81.0%	55.8%
7	MyOnlineTrainingHub.com	$622,794	$2,946,770	43.9%	4	9.3%	71.6%	55.8%
8	Serving Brevard Realty	$613,514	$3,560,284	53.1%	5	9.1%	70.6%	55.1%
9	Excel4apps	$568,851	$4,129,135	61.6%	6	8.5%	65.4%	55.6%
10	Mary Maids	$498,937	$4,628,072	69.0%	7	7.4%	57.4%	55.9%
11	Excel Strategies, LLC	$427,349	$5,055,421	75.4%	8	6.4%	49.2%	55.7%
12	MN Excel Consulting	$406,326	$5,461,747	81.4%	9	6.1%	46.7%	56.0%

Figure 15.21 This pivot table includes four value fields plus two calculated fields.

Formatting a pivot table

Excel offers a PivotTable Styles gallery on the Design tab. Instead, if you try to format individual cells in a pivot table, you will experience frustration. After you rearrange the pivot table, your manual formatting will be lost.

The PivotTable Styles gallery on the Design tab contains 73 built-in styles for a pivot table. The 73 styles are further modified by using the four check boxes for Banded Rows, Banded Columns, Row Headers, and Column Headers. Multiply that by the 20 color themes on the Page Layout tab, and you have 23,360 different styles. Multiply by the three report layouts, two options for blank rows, Grand Totals On or Off for Rows or Columns, Subtotals Above or Below, and you have more than a million styles available for your pivot table.

You can also build new styles. For example, if you would like the banded rows to be two rows tall, you can design a style for that.

To format a pivot table, select Banded Rows, Row Headers, and Column Headers from the Design tab of the ribbon. Then open the Styles gallery. Figure 15.22 shows some of the choices available in the gallery.

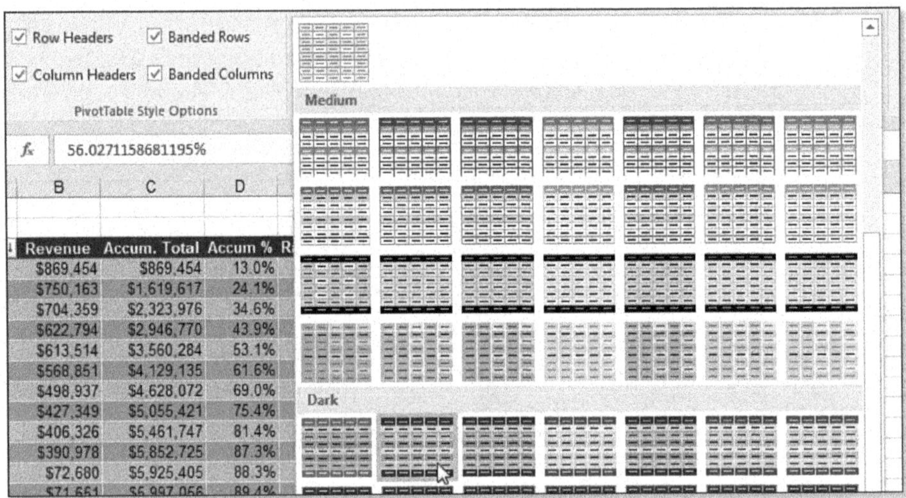

Figure 15.22 Select a style from the gallery on the Design tab.

Setting defaults for future pivot tables

Once you get some experience with pivot tables, you might find that you have favorite settings that you apply to every pivot table. Excel lets you specify the defaults for future pivot tables.

To find the feature, choose File, Options, Data. The first choice is Edit Default Layout.

My favorite choices are:

- Change the Report Layout to Show In Tabular Form.
- Choose the checkbox for Repeat All Item Labels.
- I prefer Include Filtered Items In Totals, although this only affects pivot tables based on the Data Model.

These settings are shown in Figure 15.23.

For settings not shown in the Edit Default Layout dialog box, click the PivotTable Options button in the Edit Default Layout dialog box. This can be confusing: If you click PivotTable Options from the Edit Default Layout dialog box, any changes you make to the PivotTable Options dialog box shown in Figure 15.24 will become the default pivot table. However, if you open the PivotTable Options by right-clicking a pivot table or using the Options button in the Design tab of the ribbon, you will only change the current pivot table.

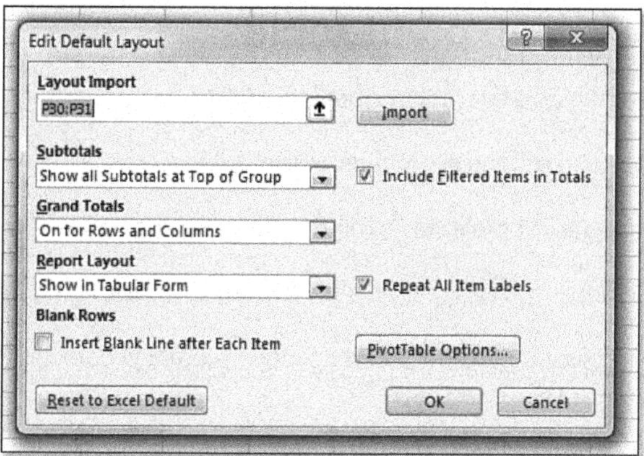

Figure 15.23 Specify your favorite pivot table settings as the default.

In Figure 15.24, I change the For Empty Cells Show setting to zero. Other people suggest using the Classic PivotTable Layout from the Display tab.

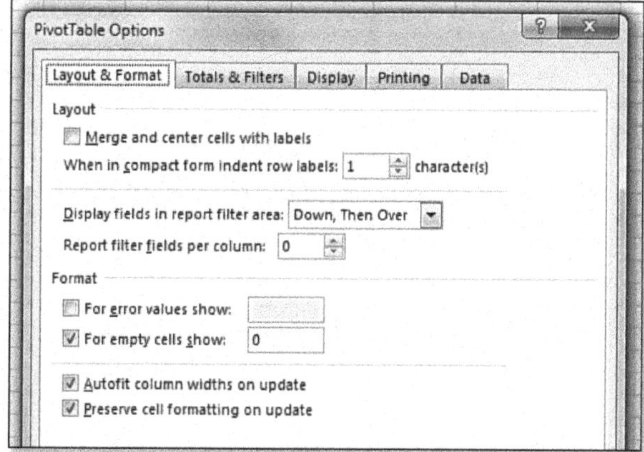

Figure 15.24 Anything beyond the settings in Figure 15.23 can be changed in this dialog box.

If you already have an existing pivot table with your favorite settings, you can import those settings as a default using the Import button in the Edit Default Layout dialog box.

Finding more information on pivot tables

More information about pivot tables is available in these locations:

- Chapter 16 covers slicers and other ways to filter a pivot table.
- Chapter 17 covers creating pivot tables from multiple tables using Power Pivot.
- Chapter 24, "Using 3D Maps," covers creating a pivot table on a map using 3D Maps.

For even more information on pivot tables, check out my upcoming new book on the subject: *Excel Pivot Table Data Crunching* (Microsoft Press).

CHAPTER 16

Using slicers and filtering a pivot table

Pivot table filters, including the visual *slicer* and date-centric *timeline,* allow you to analyze only a portion of your data.

Filtering using the row label filter

To follow along, create a new pivot table from the 16-Slicers.xlsx file. Check the Customer, Date, Quantity, Revenue, COGS, and Profit fields. On the Design tab, open the Report Layout drop-down menu. Choose Tabular form and then choose Repeat All Item Labels. Choose the Banded Rows check box on the Design tab. You will end up with the pivot table shown in Figure 16.1. Drop-down lists in cells A3 and B3 lead to the row filter menus.

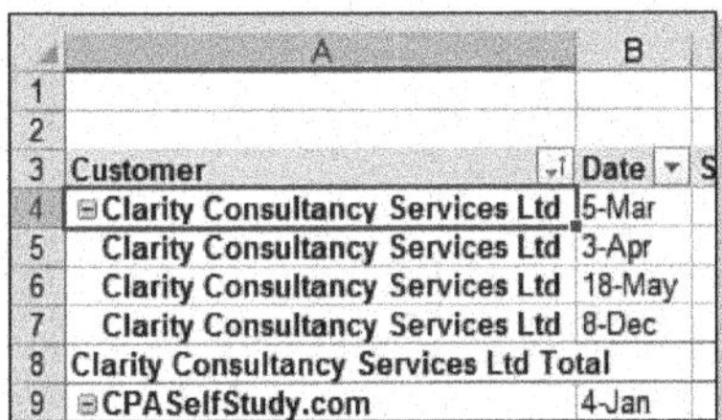

	A	B
1		
2		
3	Customer	Date
4	⊟Clarity Consultancy Services Ltd	5-Mar
5	Clarity Consultancy Services Ltd	3-Apr
6	Clarity Consultancy Services Ltd	18-May
7	Clarity Consultancy Services Ltd	8-Dec
8	Clarity Consultancy Services Ltd Total	
9	⊟CPASelfStudy.com	4-Jan

Figure 16.1 Drop-down lists in A3 and B3 lead to filters for Customer and Date.

Figure 16.2 shows the Filter menu for the Customer field. This drop-down menu contains four separate filter mechanisms:

- The Label Filters fly-out menu appears for fields that contain text values. You can use this fly-out to select customer names that contain certain words, begin with, end with, or fall between certain letters.

- The Value Filters fly-out menu enables you to filter the customers based on values elsewhere in the pivot table. If you want only orders over $20,000, or if you want to see the Top 10 customers, use the Value Filters fly-out.

- The Search box was added in Excel 2010 and is similar to using Label Filters, but faster.
- The check boxes enable you to exclude individual customers, or you can clear or select all customers by using Select All.

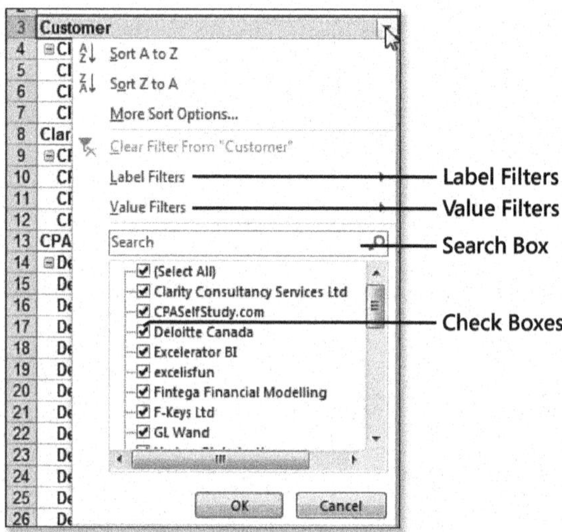

Figure 16.2 Four separate filter mechanisms exist in this drop-down menu.

Figure 16.3 shows the detail of the Value Filters fly-out.

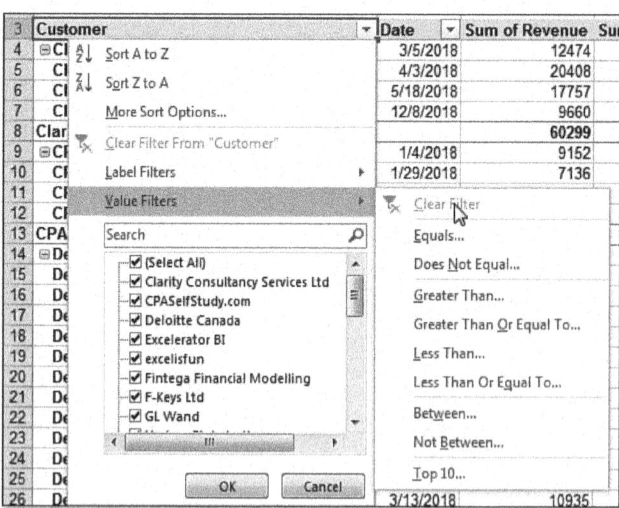

Figure 16.3 Detail of the Value Filters fly-out.

When you access the filter drop-down menu for a field that contains 100% dates, the Label Filters fly-out is replaced by a Date Filters fly-out, as shown in Figure 16.4. This fly-out offers conceptual filters, such as Yesterday, Last Month, Next Quarter, and This Year. The All Dates In The Period choice leads to a second fly-out where you can choose based on month or quarter.

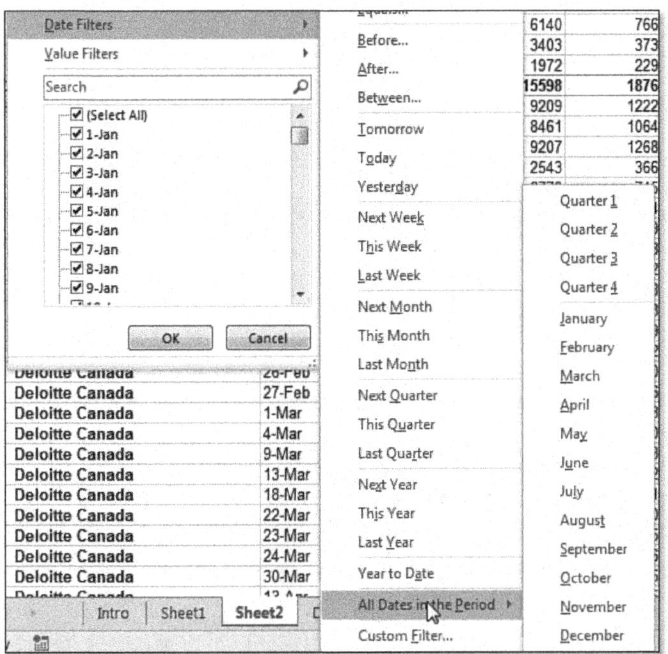

Figure 16.4 The Date Filters fly-out appears when your field contains all date values.

Clearing a filter

To clear all filters in the pivot table, use the Clear icon in the Sort & Filter group of the Data tab. To clear filters from one field in the pivot table, open the filter drop-down menu for that field and select Clear Filter from "Field."

Filtering using the check boxes

The Customer drop-down menu includes a list of all the customers in the database. If you need to exclude a few specific customers, you can clear their check boxes in the filter list.

The (Select All) item restores any cleared boxes. If all the boxes are already selected, clicking (Select All) clears all the boxes.

Because it is easier to select three customers than to clear 27, if you need to remove most of the items from the list of customers, you can follow these steps:

1. If any customers are cleared, choose Select All to reselect all customers.
2. Choose Select All to clear all customers.
3. Select the particular customers you want to view, as shown in Figure 16.5.

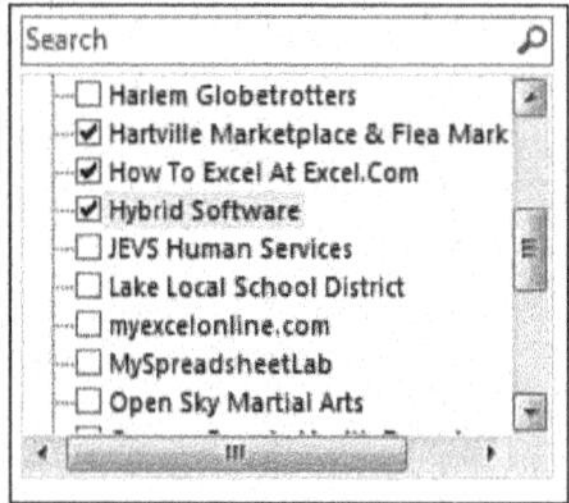

Figure 16.5 Choose Select All to clear all customers and then select the few desired customers.

TROUBLESHOOTING

The Search box above the checkboxes does not get re-applied if you refresh the pivot table.

Perhaps you need to select all the customers with "Bank" in their names. You could do this with the Search box, and it would work. However, after adding more data to the source data and refreshing the pivot table, Excel will not pick up any new customers with "Bank" in their names.

A workaround is to use the Label Filters for Contains Bank. The label filter will be re-applied after a refresh.

Filtering using the Label Filters fly-out

All the Label Filters choices shown previously in Figure 16.2 lead to the same dialog box. Suppose that you are interested in finding all customers whose name includes "Excel." Follow these steps:

1. Open the Customer filter drop-down menu.
2. Open the Label Filters fly-out.
3. Select Contains. Excel displays the Label Filter dialog box.
4. Type **Excel**. Click OK. The pivot table is filtered to customers whose name includes "Excel."

If you open the first drop-down menu in the Label Filter dialog box, you see the following choices:

- Equals
- Does Not Equal
- Is Greater Than
- Is Greater Than Or Equal To
- Is Less Than
- Less Than Or Equal To
- Begins With
- Does Not Begin With
- Ends With
- Does Not End With
- Contains
- Does Not Contain
- Is Between
- Is Not Between

You can use the wildcards * and ?, with * representing any character(s) and the ? wildcard representing a single character.

Filtering using the date filters

When a field in the original data set contains only values formatted as dates, Excel offers the Date Filters fly-out shown previously in Figure 16.4.

Many of the date filters contain conceptual filters. If you filter a pivot table to Yesterday and then refresh the data set a week later, the dates returned by the filter will change.

The list of conceptual filters feels like it was borrowed from QuickBooks, but it is not quite as complete as those from QuickBooks. It would be nice to have choices such as Last 30 Days, Month to Date, and so on.

The penultimate choice in the first fly-out is All Dates In The Period, which leads to a second fly-out. Choosing January or Quarter 1 is great when you have dates from several years, and you want to compare January from each year.

The last choice in the first fly-out is Custom Filter. As shown in Figure 16.6, you can use this filter to build a custom date range.

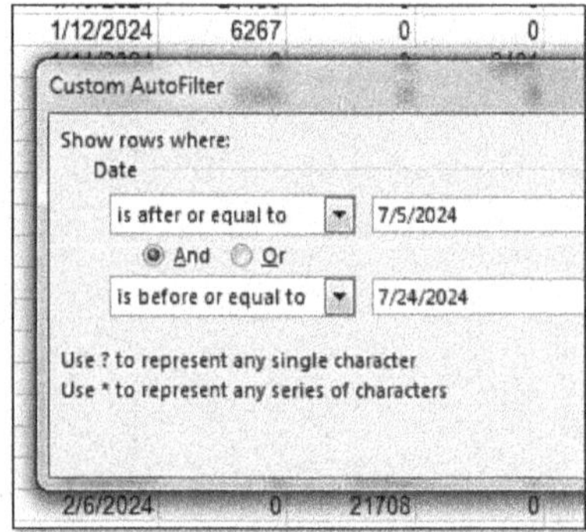

Figure 16.6 The Custom Filter for a date field offers to let you build any range of dates.

Filtering to the top 10

Pivot tables offer a feature called Top 10. Despite the name, the filter is not just for finding the top 10 values. You can use the filter to find the top or bottom items. You can specify 5, 7, 10, or any number of items.

To start the filter, open the Customer filter drop-down menu. Open the Value Filters fly-out and select Top 10. Excel displays the Top 10 Filter dialog box. In Figure 16.7, the report has been filtered to show the top five customers based on revenue.

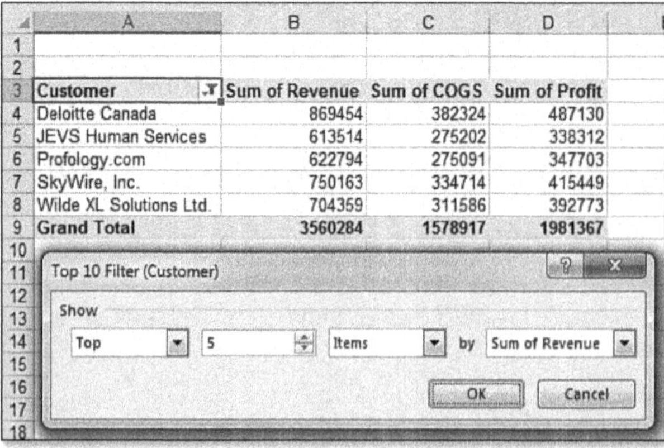

	A	B	C	D
1				
2				
3	Customer	Sum of Revenue	Sum of COGS	Sum of Profit
4	Deloitte Canada	869454	382324	487130
5	JEVS Human Services	613514	275202	338312
6	Profology.com	622794	275091	347703
7	SkyWire, Inc.	750163	334714	415449
8	Wilde XL Solutions Ltd.	704359	311586	392773
9	Grand Total	3560284	1578917	1981367

Figure 16.7 Filter to the top five customers based on revenue.

The Top 10 filter offers these options:

- The first drop-down menu in the dialog box offers a choice between Top and Bottom.
- The second field is a spin button and a text box. You can use the spin button to change from 5 to 10. If you need to get to 1,000,000, you should type that value into the text box instead of trying to hit the spin button 999,990 times.
- The next field is a drop-down menu with the choices Items, Percent, and Sum. These three choices are discussed in the next sections.
- The final drop-down menu offers all the numeric fields in the VALUES area of the pivot table.

The Items/Percent/Sum drop-down menu offers a lot of flexibility. If you select Percent, the pivot table shows you enough customers so that you see *n*% of the value field. For example, you might ask for the top 80% of profit.

If you choose Sum, you can specify a large number as the second field in the dialog box. For example, you might want to see enough customers to reach $5 million in sales.

Filtering using slicers

Slicers are visual filters that make it easy to run various ad-hoc analyses. While slicers are easier to use than the Report Filter, they offer the added benefit that a slicer can filter multiple pivot tables and pivot charts created from the same data set.

Adding slicers

To add default slicers, follow these steps:

1. Select one cell in your pivot table.
2. On the PivotTable Analyze tab, select the Insert Slicer icon. Excel shows the Insert Slicers dialog box.
3. Choose any fields that would make suitable filter fields. In Figure 16.8, Region, Product, and Years are selected. Months, Quarters, and Date would also be effective, but you see how they can be filtered using a timeline later in this chapter. Click OK.

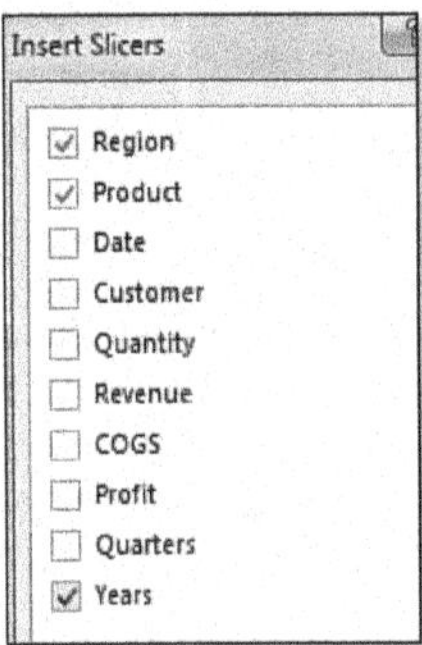

Figure 16.8 Choose all fields that are suitable for visual filters.

Excel adds default filters, tiled in the center of your screen (see Figure 16.9).

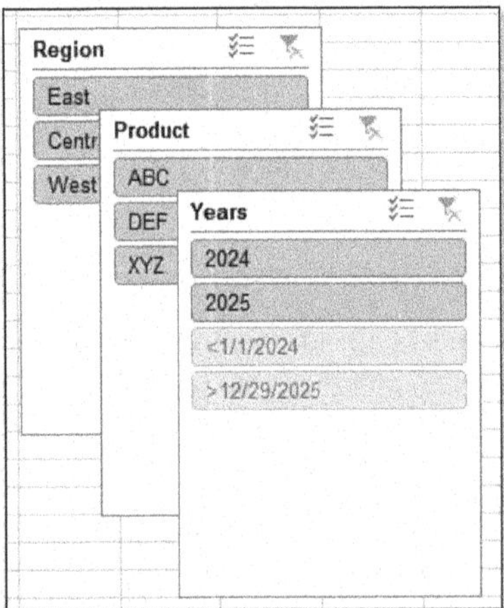

Figure 16.9 Excel tiles a bunch of one-column slicers.

Arranging the slicers

You can reposition and resize the slicers. Choose a logical arrangement for the slicers. Following are some examples.

The Region and Product slicers contain short entries. Make each slicer wider and then use the Columns setting in the Slicer Tools Options tab to increase each slicer to three columns. See Figure 16.10 for the setting.

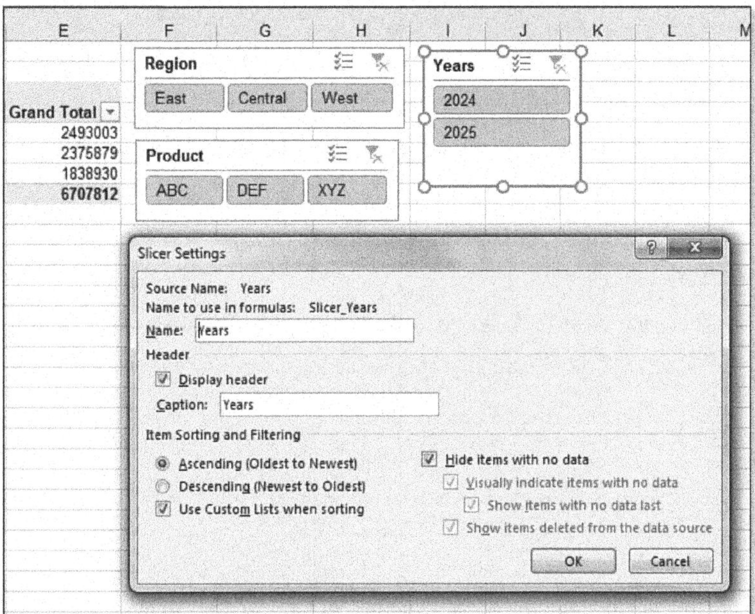

Figure 16.10 The Slicer Tools Options tab allows you to control the number of columns in a slicer. Further settings are in the Slicer Settings dialog box.

The Year slicer is wider than it needs to be. There are also two extra items (<1/1/2024 and >12/31/2025) in the slicer that are remnants of Auto Group. You can turn these off in the Slicer Settings dialog box. Select the slicer and choose Slicer Settings. Also, Hide Items With No Data is checked.

Using the slicers in Excel

To select a single item from a slicer, choose that item. To multiselect in Excel, first, choose the icon at the top of the slicer that has the three check marks. You can now click each item. You can also use the Ctrl key to select multiple nonadjacent items or drag the mouse to select adjacent items.

Selections in one slicer might cause items in other slicers to become unavailable. In this case, those items move to the end of the list. This gives you a visual indication that the item is not available based on the current filters.

To clear a filter from a slicer, click the Funnel-X icon in the top right of the slicer.

Inside OUT

Slicers can be configured to filter multiple pivot tables and pivot charts at the same time.

If both pivot tables are using the same data source, you can ensure that the slicers will affect both pivot tables.

If multiple pivot tables exist, follow these steps:

1. **Select the slicer.**
2. **From the Slicer Tools Options tab of the ribbon, choose Report Connections.**
3. **Select each pivot table that should be filtered by the slicer.**

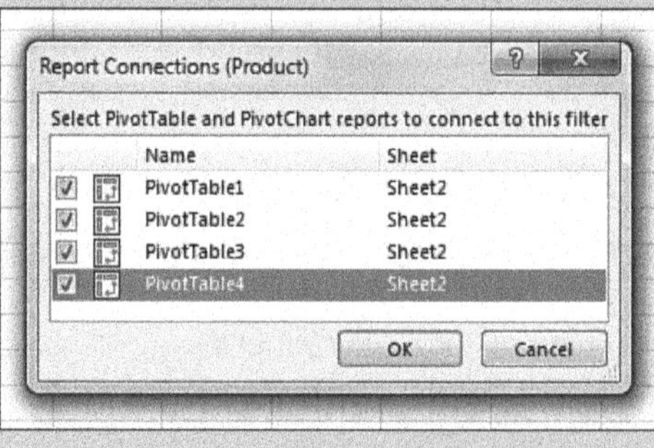

To connect two pivot tables that came from two different data sets, the process is more complex. Say that you have a Customer field in the Actuals table and in the Forecast table. The customers are similar, but each table might have a few customers who are not in the other table.

This method requires all the pivot tables to be based on the Data Model. If you have existing pivot tables, you will have to re-create them and use the selection for Add This Data To The Data Model in the Create PivotTable dialog box.

Follow these steps:

1. Make sure to format both the Actuals table and the Forecast table as a table using Ctrl+T.
2. Rename the tables as "Actuals" and "Forecast" instead of "Table1" and "Table2."
3. Copy the Customer column from both tables into a new area (you don't need the heading from the second copy).
4. Use Data, Remove Duplicates on the new single-column region table so each region appears once.

5. Format this single-column table as a table. Rename it as Customers.

6. Choose Data, Relationships. Excel displays the Manage Relationships dialog. Click the New... button to display the Create Relationship dialog.

7. As shown in Figure 16.11, define a new relationship from Customer in the Forecast table to Customer in the Customers table. Repeat to create a relationship from Customer in the Actuals table to Customer in the Customers table. Creating these relationships automatically adds the three tables to the Data Model in the workbook.

8. Select a blank cell for the first pivot table. From the Insert tab, choose PivotTable, From Data Model, as shown in Figure 16.12. Create a pivot table with Revenue from the Forecast table and Customer from the Customers table. It is important that you choose Customer from the Customers table instead of Customer from the Forecast or Actuals tables.

9. Create an Actuals pivot table following the same guidance in step 8.

10. Select one cell in the Actuals pivot table. Select Insert, Slicer. Choose the All tab at the top of the Insert Slicer dialog. Choose to create a slicer from the Customer field in the Customers table. Again, for the slicer to be able to control both pivot tables, you must choose Customer from the Customers table instead of from the Actuals or Forecast table.

11. With the new slicer selected, go to the Slicer tab in the ribbon and choose Report Connections. The Report Connections (Customer) dialog will show that the slicer is currently connected to your first pivot table. Select the unchecked box to connect the slicer to the other pivot table.

This new Customers slicer will control both pivot tables, as shown in Figure 16.13.

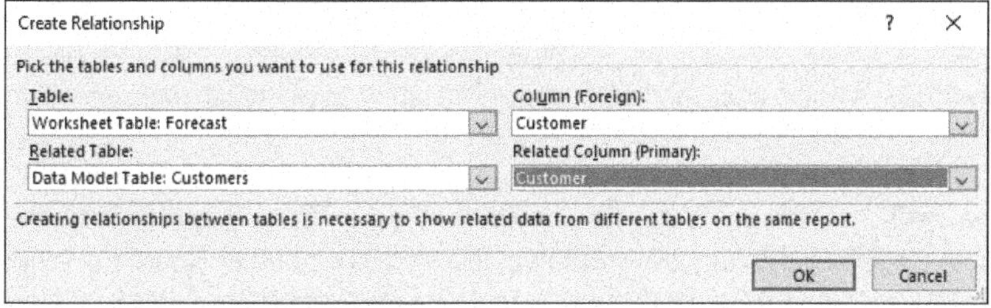

Figure 16.11 Creating a relationship in the Excel data model is similar to joining two tables in Access.

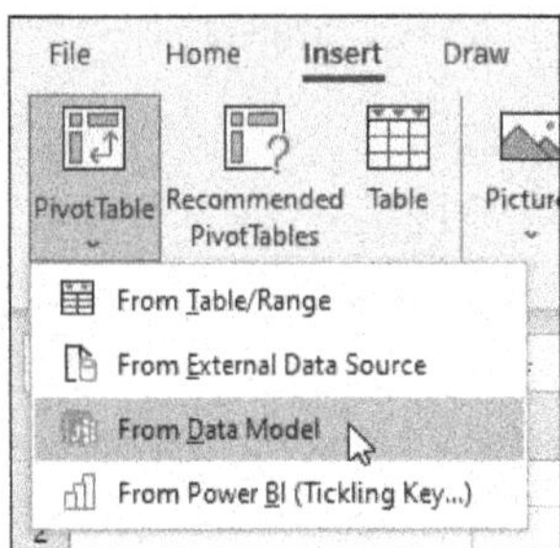

Figure 16.12 Once a relationship has been defined, a new From Data Model choice is available in the PivotTable drop-down.

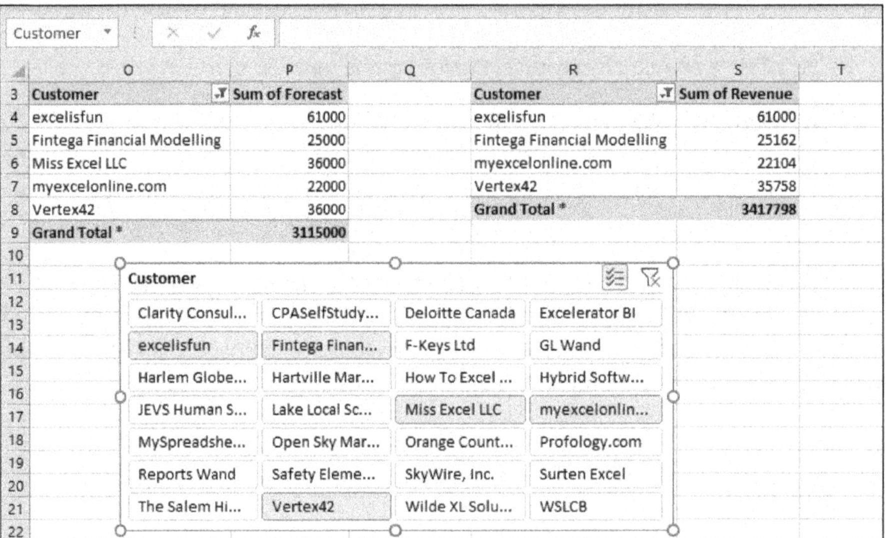

Figure 16.13 A single slicer controls multiple pivot tables, even though they came from different data sets.

In Chapter 17, "Mashing up data with Power Pivot," you will see that when using the Data Model, you can combine fields from all three tables in a single pivot table. Figure 16.14 shows a pivot table with customers from the Customers table, a forecast from the Forecast table, and revenue from the Actuals table.

Customer	Sum of Forecast	Sum of Revenue
Clarity Consultancy Services Ltd	50000	60299
CPASelfStudy.com	15000	16288
Deloitte Canada	439000	439390
Excelerator BI	320000	319553
excelisfun	61000	61000
Fintega Financial Modelling	25000	25162

Figure 16.14 Combining data from three tables in a single pivot table.

Filtering dates

Excel 2013 added a Timeline control for filtering date fields. It is difficult to use. Instead of the Timeline, you could achieve more flexibility by arranging three slicers for Year, Quarter, and Month, as shown in Figure 16.15.

Figure 16.15 shows a timeline. The timeline has been set to filter by quarter.

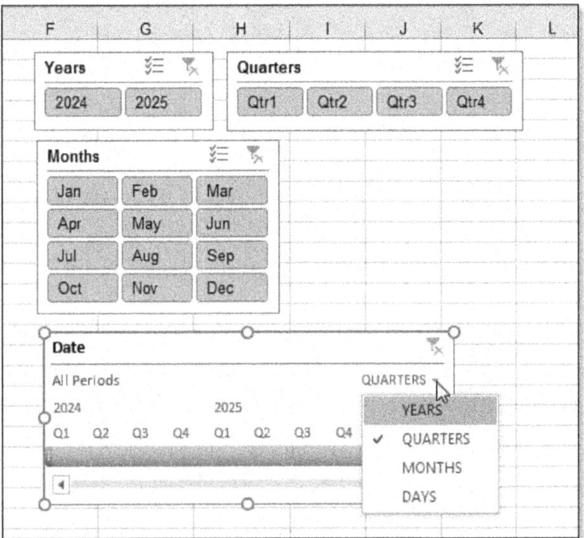

Figure 16.15 A timeline control lets you filter daily dates by month, quarter, or year without grouping.

Filtering oddities

The next sections discuss a few additional features available for filtering pivot tables.

Autofiltering a pivot table

I was doing a Power Excel seminar in Philadelphia when someone in the audience asked whether it is possible to AutoFilter a pivot table. The answer is no; the Filter field is not available when you are inside a pivot table.

There is a surprising bug, however. If you put the cell pointer to the right of the last heading of a data set and click the Filter icon, Excel turns on the AutoFilter drop-down menus. I call this cell the magic cell.

The guy at Microsoft in charge of making the AutoFilter icon unavailable when you are in a pivot table evidently forgot about that magic cell to the right of the headings. If you put the cell pointer in cell D1 in Figure 16.16, the Filter icon remains available.

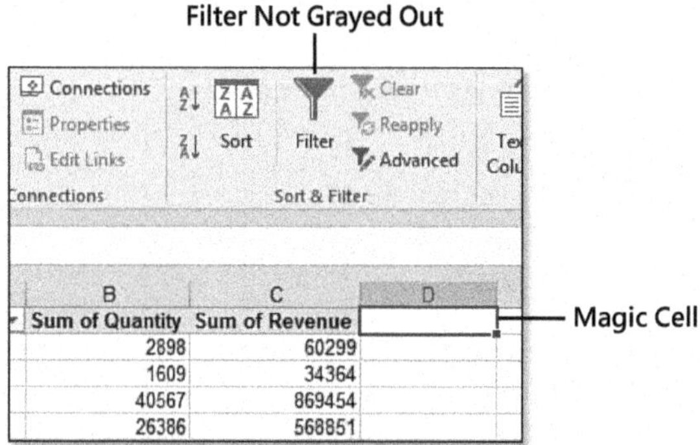

Figure 16.16 Although this works, the AutoFilters are not recalculated after a refresh.

What is the advantage of using the AutoFilters? The Top 10 AutoFilter works differently from the Top 10 PivotTable filter. In Figure 16.17, the Top 10 AutoFilter for the top six items returns the top five customers and the true grand total.

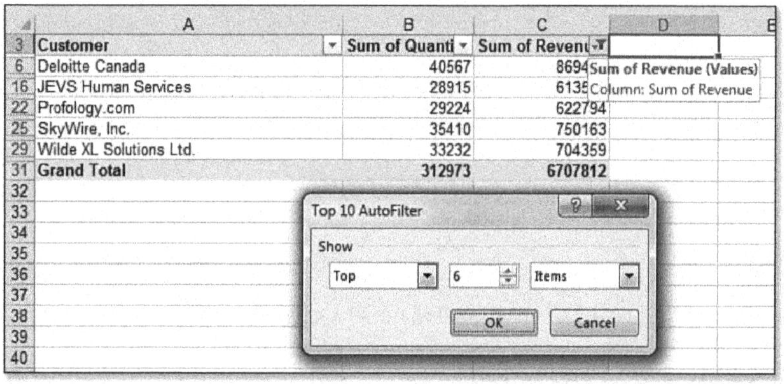

	A	B	C	D
3	Customer	Sum of Quanti	Sum of Revenu	
6	Deloitte Canada	40567	8694	Sum of Revenue (Values)
16	JEVS Human Services	28915	6135	Column: Sum of Revenue
22	Profology.com	29224	622794	
25	SkyWire, Inc.	35410	750163	
29	Wilde XL Solutions Ltd.	33232	704359	
31	Grand Total	312973	6707812	

Top 10 AutoFilter
Show
Top | 6 | Items
OK | Cancel

Figure 16.17 The AutoFilter Top 10 works differently from the pivot table filters.

If you try this method, remember that you have to go back to the magic cell to toggle off the AutoFilter. Also, if you change the underlying data and refresh the pivot table, the AutoFilter is not updated. After all, the Excel team believes that you can't AutoFilter a pivot table.

The AutoFilter lets you filter by one item along the Column field. In Figure 16.18, the report is showing the top five customers for product XYZ in column D. A regular pivot table filter would always be based on the Grand Total in column E. By using the AutoFilter drop-downs, you could filter to the top five customers in any column in the pivot table.

	A	B	C	D	E
3	Sum of Revenue	Product			
4	Customer	ABC	DEF	XYZ	Grand Total
6	CPASelfStudy.com	7136	4270	22958	34364
13	Harlem Globetrotters	13853	26484	19544	59881
14	Hartville Marketplace & Flea Market	99544	178254	149551	427349
24	Reports Wand	142412	182755	173770	498937
28	The Salem Historical Society, Salem, Ohio	15104	18064	18072	51240
32	Grand Total	3069797	3254120	383895	6707812
33					

Figure 16.18 Use the AutoFilter to filter based on sales of one item.

Replicating a pivot table for every customer

This technique makes many copies of the pivot table, with a different Report Filter value in each copy. To use the feature, you have to move the field to the FILTERS drop zone in the PivotTable Fields list. To create a report for every customer, move the Customer field to the FILTERS drop zone. Select the Options drop-down menu from the Analyze tab. Select Show Report Filter Pages from the drop-down menu, as shown in Figure 16.19. Confirm which field should be used. Excel adds worksheets to your workbook. Each worksheet contains the original pivot table, with a different value chosen for the selected filter field.

> CAUTION
>
> **Slicers are not visible on the copied pivot tables when you use this technique.**

Options
Field Settings
Down
Up
Group Field
Group
Options
Show Report Filter Pages...
Generate GetPivotData
Central

	A	B	C	D	E
1	Customer	(All)			
2					
3	Sum of Revenue	Product			
4	Region	ABC	DEF	XYZ	Grand Total
5	Central	1148804	1135935	91140	2375879
6	East	991076	1354290	147637	2493003
7	West	929917	763895	145118	1838930
8	Grand Total	3069797	3254120	383895	6707812
9					

Figure 16.19 Replicate your pivot table for every value in a Report Filter field.

Sorting a pivot table

In all the pivot tables so far in this chapter, the customers are presented in alphabetical sequence. In each case, the report would be more interesting if it were presented sorted by revenue instead of by customer name.

If you use the AZ or ZA icons on the Data tab, Excel automatically sets up rules in the Sort and More Sort Options dialog boxes.

To access these settings later, open a row field drop-down menu and choose More Sort Options. This opens the Sort (Customer) dialog box. Click the More icon to access More Sort Options (Customer).

CHAPTER 17

Mashing up data with Power Pivot

The Power Pivot add-in debuted in Excel 2010. The add-in allowed you to:

- Load 100 million records in an Excel workbook
- Join data from Sheet1 and Sheet2 in a single workbook
- Create new calculated fields using a formula language called DAX
- Use time intelligence functions to handle fiscal years not ending in December

Power Pivot was not developed by the Excel team. It was developed by the SQL Server Analysis Services team. In Excel 2010, the add-in was free and mostly separate from Excel. It proved so popular that the Excel team slowly began incorporating Power Pivot into the core Excel product.

- In Excel 2013, the Add This Data To The Data Model check box was added to the Create PivotTable dialog box. This allowed you to create pivot tables from multiple sheets.
- In Excel 2016, the Add Measure choice was added to the PivotTable Fields list. Make sure to choose Add To Data Model. Right-click any table name in the PivotTable Fields to find the Add Measure selection. This allows you to use DAX formulas.
- In Office 365, a new Relationships icon was added to the Data tab of the ribbon. This made it easier to define relationships between tables.
- In Excel 2016, the Power Query tools were added to the Data tab of the ribbon. This allows you to get more than 1,048,576 records into Excel.
- In Excel 2019, a Manage Data Model icon is added to the Data tab of the ribbon. This allows you to open the Power Pivot grid, define sort order, hide fields, define relationships using a diagram view, and more.
- With Excel, the full benefits of Power Pivot are freely available to anyone using Windows versions of Excel. This is a great improvement over Excel 2013 and 2016 when only the Pro Plus and E3 versions of Office had full access to the Power Pivot grid.

- In Microsoft 365, a From Data Model option is now available in the Insert PivotTable drop-down menu. This option is available after you create a relationship or add a table to the Data Model.

Joining multiple tables using the Data Model

When you see the term *Data Model* in Excel, it's Microsoft's way of saying you are using Power Pivot without calling it Power Pivot.

Preparing data for use in the Data Model

When you are planning to use the Data Model to join multiple tables, you should always convert your Excel ranges to tables before you begin. You theoretically do not have to convert the ranges to tables, but it is far easier if you convert the ranges to tables and give the tables a name. If you don't convert the ranges to tables first, Excel secretly does it in the background and gives your tables meaningless names such as "Range."

Choose one cell in a data set and use Ctrl+T or Home, Format As Table. In the Create Table dialog box, make sure My Table Has Headers is selected. After you create a table, Excel gives your table a basic name, such as Table1, Table2, and so on. Go to the Table Design tab of the ribbon and type a meaningful name, such as **Sales** or **Sectors**.

Figure 17.1 shows two ranges in Excel. Columns A:H contain a transactional data set named Sales. Columns J:K contain a customer lookup table called Sector. You would like to create a pivot table showing revenue by sector.

1	Customer	Quantity	Revenue	COGS	Profit
9	Wonderful Kettle Corp	901	21438	9209	12229
10	Matchless Hardware Traders	342	6267	2541	3726
11	Cool Bottle Co	91	2401	1031	1370
12	Vivid Edger Co	547	9345	4239	5106
13	Excellent Doghouse Corp	558	11628	5093	6535
14	Vivid Edger Co	100	2042	983	1059
15	Powerful Edger Supply	250	3552	1696	1856
16	Supreme Clipboard Inc.	760	14440	6790	7650
17	Improved Vegetable Inc.	810	14592	6781	7811
18	Matchless Hardware Traders	606	12606	5090	7516
19	Excellent Doghouse Corp	964	20770	8463	12307
20	Matchless Hardware Traders	365	8128	3400	4728
21	Trendy Notebook Corp	389	7136	3403	3733
22	Improved Vegetable Inc.	652	17150	6888	10262
23	Wonderful Kettle Corp	338	6714	2967	3747
24	Improved Vegetable Inc.	766	15640	6782	8858
25	Wonderful Kettle Corp	346	5532	2541	2991
26	Vivid Edger Co	817	17160	7864	9296
27	Guaranteed Paint Co	902	21708	8866	12842
28	Matchless Hardware Traders	985	19890	8467	11423
29	Excellent Doghouse Corp	116	1817	838	979

Customer	Sector
Fine Shingle Supply	Hardware
Flexible Aerobic Co	Apparel
Functional Eggbeater Co	Consumer
Guaranteed Paint Co	Chemical
Improved Vegetable Inc.	Food
Inventive Door Inc.	Hardware
Magnificent Shingle Corp	Hardware
Matchless Hardware Traders	Hardware
Mouthwatering Bicycle Corp	Consumer
New Faucet Co	Hardware
Powerful Edger Supply	Hardware
Rare Door Inc.	Hardware
Savory Opener Inc.	Hardware
Special Luggage Inc.	Consumer
Supreme Clipboard Inc.	Consumer
Sure Linen Corp	Textiles
Tremendous Thermostat Partners	Electronics
Trendy Notebook Corp	Consumer
Vivid Edger Co	Hardware
Wonderful Kettle Corp	Consumer

Figure 17.1 You want to join these two tables together in a single pivot table.

Excel gurus are thinking, "Why don't you do an XLOOKUP to join the tables?" Power Pivot lets you avoid the XLOOKUP. In this case, the tables are small and a XLOOKUP would calculate quickly. However, imagine that you have a million records in the transactional table and 10 columns in the lookup table. The XLOOKUP solution quickly becomes unwieldy. The Power Pivot engine available in the Data Model can join the tables without the overhead of XLOOKUP.

Creating a relationship between two tables in Excel

Look in the Data Tools group of the Data tab of the ribbon for the Relationships icon. Click the icon to open the Manage Relationships dialog box. Click on New... to open the Create Relationship dialog box.

Your relationship should start from the transactional data set. Open the Table drop-down menu and choose the Sales table. Open the Column (Foreign) drop-down menu and choose the Customer column. The Related Table is the Sectors table. The Related Column is also Customer. Figure 17.2 shows the completed dialog box. Click OK to create the relationship. Click Close to close the Manage Relationships dialog box.

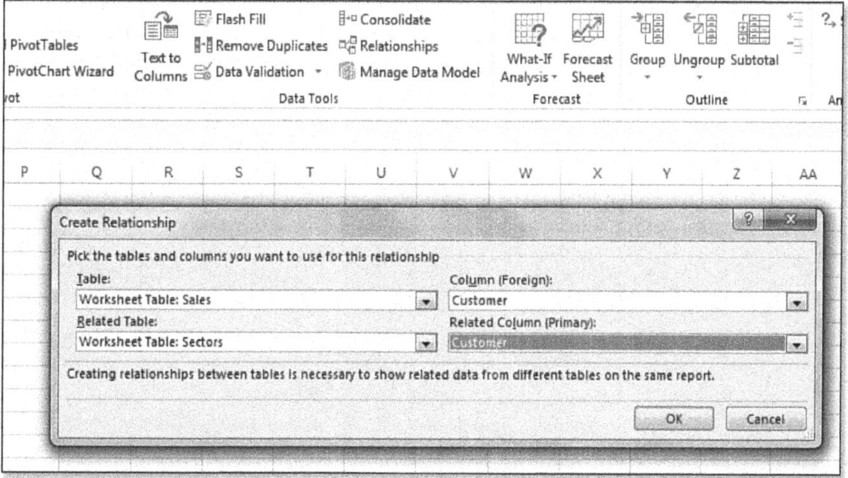

Figure 17.2 Create a relationship between two tables.

Creating a relationship automatically loads both tables to the Data Model. This is a great way to accomplish two tasks with one action.

In the past, it was common to add the first table to the model by using Add This Data To The Data Model in the Create PivotTable dialog box. This method works fine, all except for the point where the pivot table shows the wrong numbers as it displays the A Relationship May Be Needed. I always cringed at that step. By building the relationship in advance, you avoid having wrong numbers in the pivot table.

Creating a relationship using Diagram view

The Power Pivot tab in the ribbon offers a quicker way to create a relationship. If you don't see this tab, go to File, Options, Data and choose Enable Data Analysis Add-Ins: Power Pivot, Power View, 3D Maps.

Follow these steps to create a relationship:

1. Select one cell in the first table. Use Power Pivot, Add To Data Model to add the data to the Data Model.
2. Repeat step 1 for the second table.
3. Click on the Manage icon in the Power Pivot tab or the Manage Data Model icon in the Data tab. The Power Pivot grid opens.
4. On the right side of the ribbon, choose Diagram View.
5. In Diagram View, click on the Customer field in the Sales table and draw a line to the Customer field in the Sector table (see Figure 17.3).
6. Use the Switch To Workbook icon in the Power Pivot Quick Access Toolbar to return to Excel.

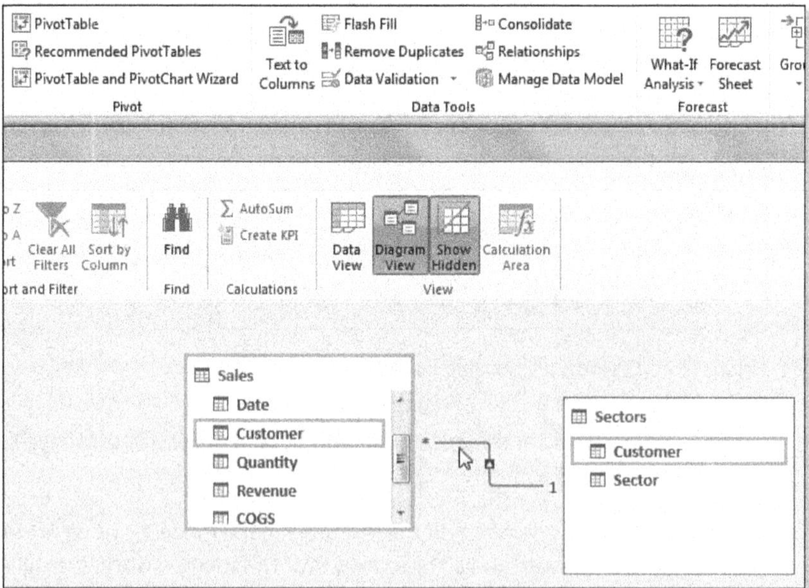

Figure 17.3 Create a relationship quickly with the Diagram view.

Building a pivot table from the Data Model

Choose a blank cell where you want your pivot table to appear. Select Insert, PivotTable, From Data Model (see Figure 17.4).

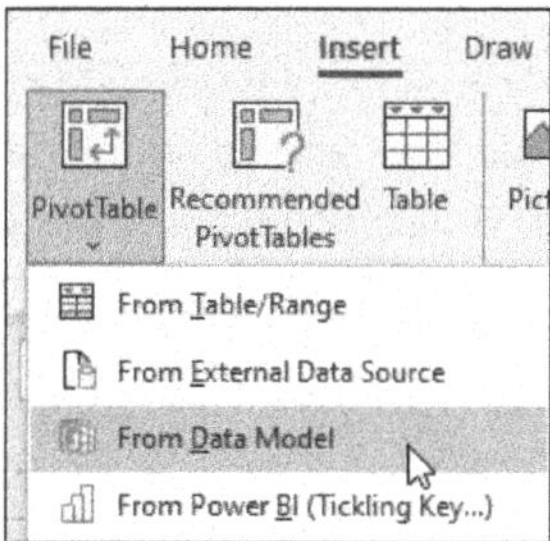

Figure 17.4 Because you've added data to the Data Model, the From Data Model choice is available for a new pivot table.

Look at the PivotTable Fields task pane. In the second line of the pane, you have a choice for Active or All. When you choose All, you will see a list of each defined table in the Excel workbook. There is an arrow icon next to each table. Click the arrow icon to expand the table. In Figure 17.5, the Sales table is not expanded and the Sector table is expanded.

Click the arrow next to Sectors to see a list of the available fields in the Sectors table. Drag the Sector field to the Rows area. Click the arrow next to Sales to expand that table. Drag Revenue to the Values area. You can click any arrow again to collapse the table.

As shown in Figure 17.5, you have successfully created a pivot table from two different data sets.

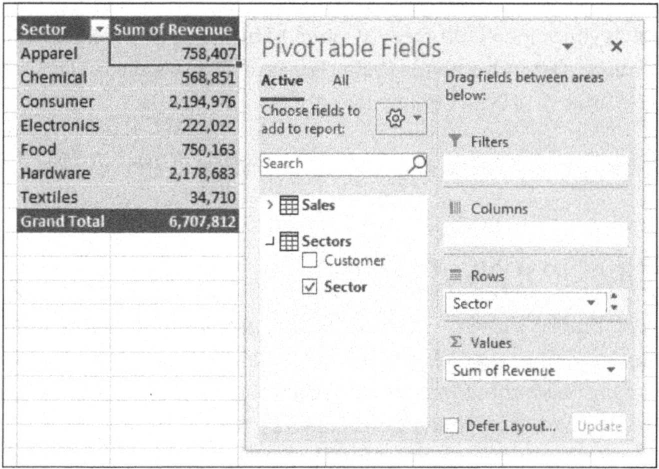

Figure 17.5 Without doing a VLOOKUP, you've successfully joined data from two tables in this report.

Unlocking hidden features with the Data Model

Creating a relationship forces Excel to build a Power Pivot Data Model. Even though the Data Model is stored inside the Excel workbook, the pivot table engine treats data in the Data Model as external data.

There are some useful features in pivot tables that are only available when you are accessing external data in the Data Model. Even if your data is a single table and you don't need a relationship, there are features that you unlock when you add your single table to the Data Model.

The simplest way to add your data to the Data Model is to choose Insert, PivotTable, From Table Or Range, and then choose Add This Data To The Data Model from the PivotTable From Table Or Range dialog box (see Figure 17.6).

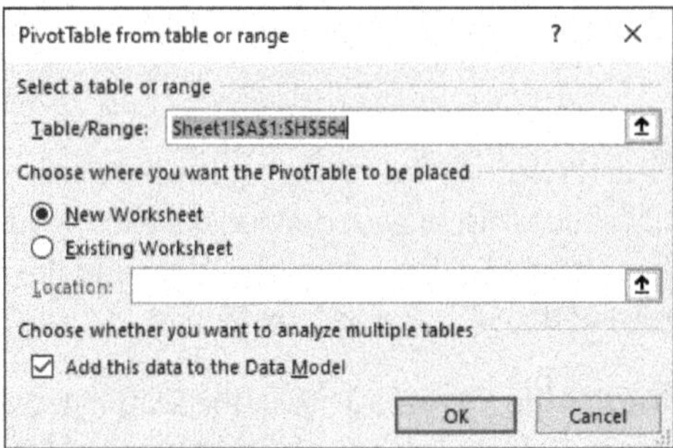

Figure 17.6 Even with a single range of data, choose Add This Data To The Data Model to unlock extra features.

> TIP
>
> **If you decide that you want all future pivot tables to be based on the Data Model, choose File, Options, Data. Choose the Prefer The Excel Data Model When Creating PivotTables, QueryTables, And Data Connections option.**

Read below for the extra capabilities available when you choose to add your data to the Data Model.

Counting distinct in a pivot table

Consider the three pivot tables shown in Figure 17.7. The question is "How many unique customers are in each sector?". The pivot table in columns A and B allow you to figure out the answer. You can mentally count that there are two customers (B4 and B5) in the Associations sector. There are six customers listed in the Consultants sector.

But how would you present the top-left pivot table to your manager? You would have to grab some paper and jot down Associations: 2, Consultants: 6, Professional: 3, and so on.

When you try to build a pivot table to answer the question, you might get the wrong results shown in D3:D10. This pivot table says it is calculating a "Count of Customer," but this is actually counting the number of invoices in each sector.

The trick to solving the problem is to add your data to the Data Model.

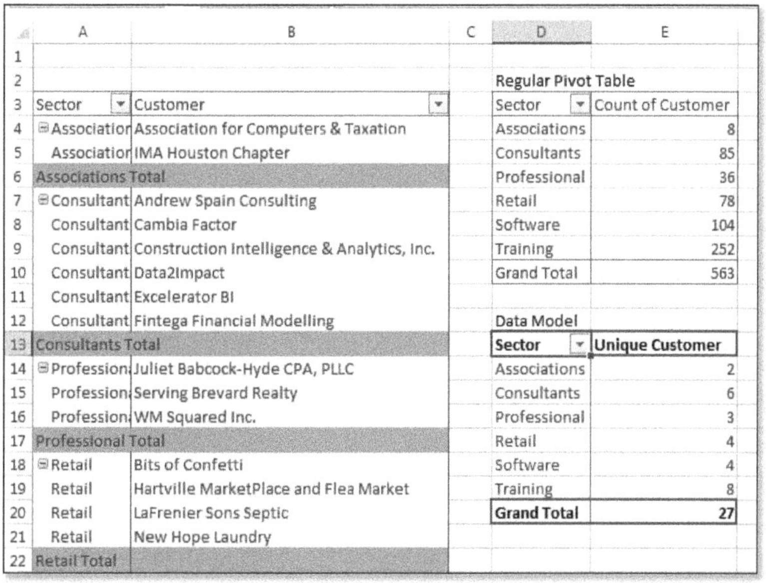

	A	B	C	D	E
1					
2				Regular Pivot Table	
3	Sector	Customer		Sector	Count of Customer
4	⊟Associatior	Association for Computers & Taxation		Associations	8
5	Associatior	IMA Houston Chapter		Consultants	85
6	Associations Total			Professional	36
7	⊟Consultant	Andrew Spain Consulting		Retail	78
8	Consultant	Cambia Factor		Software	104
9	Consultant	Construction Intelligence & Analytics, Inc.		Training	252
10	Consultant	Data2Impact		Grand Total	563
11	Consultant	Excelerator BI			
12	Consultant	Fintega Financial Modelling		Data Model	
13	Consultants Total			**Sector**	**Unique Customer**
14	⊟Profession	Juliet Babcock-Hyde CPA, PLLC		Associations	2
15	Profession	Serving Brevard Realty		Consultants	6
16	Profession	WM Squared Inc.		Professional	3
17	Professional Total			Retail	4
18	⊟Retail	Bits of Confetti		Software	4
19	Retail	Hartville MarketPlace and Flea Market		Training	8
20	Retail	LaFrenier Sons Septic		**Grand Total**	**27**
21	Retail	New Hope Laundry			
22	Retail Total				

Figure 17.7 When you try to figure out the number of customers in a sector, it does not work.

The pivot table in D13:E20 in Figure 17.7 is somehow reporting the correct number of unique customers in each sector.

A regular pivot table offers 11 calculations: `Sum`, `Count`, `Average`, `Max`, `Min`, `Product`, `Count Numbers`, `StdDev`, `StdDevP`, `Var`, and `VarP`. These calculations have not changed in 35 years.

But if you create your pivot table and choose the box for Add This Data To The Data Model, a twelfth calculation option appears at the end of the Value Field Settings dialog box: Distinct Count, as shown in Figure 17-8.

CHAPTER 17

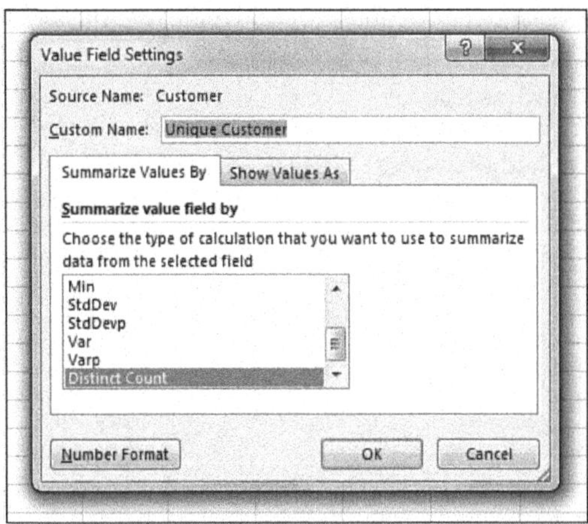

Figure 17.8 Distinct Count appears in Data Model pivot tables.

Drag customer to the Values area. Double-click the Count Of Customer heading. In the Summarize Values By tab, scroll to the bottom of the list. Choose Distinct Count. Change the title, and you have the solution shown in Figure 17.8.

One oddity: The Product calculation is missing from the Value Field Settings for the Data Model. I've never met anyone who actually used the Product calculation. But if you were a person who loved Product, then having Excel swap out Product to make room for Distinct Count will not be popular. You can add a new Measure with `=PRODUCT([Revenue])` to replicate the Product calculation. See the example about creating Median later in this chapter.

Including filtered items in totals

Excel pivot tables offer an excellent filtering feature called Top 10. This feature is very flexible: It can be Top 10 Items, Bottom 5 Items, Top 80%, or Top Records to get to $4 Million In Revenue.

Shortening a long report to show only the top five items is great for a dashboard or a summary report.

But there is an annoyance when you use any of the filters.

In Figure 17.9, the top pivot table occupies rows 3 through row 31. Revenue is shown both as Revenue and as a % of Total. The largest customer is Andrew Spain Consulting with 869,000. In the top pivot table, the Grand Total is $6.7 Million and Andrew Spain is 12.96% of that total.

In the same figure, rows 34:40 show the same pivot table with the Top 5 selected in the Top 10 filter. The Grand Total now shows only $3.56 Million. Andrew Spain is 24% of the smaller total number.

This is wrong. Andrew should be 13% of the total, not 24%.

	A	B	C
3	**Customer**	**Sum of Revenue**	**% of Total**
25	CPASelfStudy.com	568851	8.48%
26	MySpreadsheetLab	613514	9.15%
27	599CD.com	622794	9.28%
28	Hartville MarketPlace and Flea Market	704359	10.50%
29	Excel4Apps	750163	11.18%
30	Andrew Spain Consulting	869454	12.96%
31	**Grand Total**	**6707812**	**100.00%**
32			
33	**Values Filters, Top 10, Top 5 Items**		
34	**Customer**	**Sum of Revenue**	**% of Total**
35	MySpreadsheetLab	613514	17.23%
36	599CD.com	622794	17.49%
37	Hartville MarketPlace and Flea Market	704359	19.78%
38	Excel4Apps	750163	21.07%
39	Andrew Spain Consulting	869454	24.42%
40	**Grand Total**	**3560284**	**100.00%**

Figure 17.9 Using the Top 10 Filter can change the Percentage of Total calculation.

On January 30, 2007, Microsoft released Excel 2007. A new feature was added to Excel called Include Filtered Items In Totals. This feature would solve the problem in Figure 17.9. However, as you can see, the feature is not available, as shown in Figure 17.10. It has been unavailable every day since January 30, 2007. I can attest to that because I check every day to see if it is enabled.

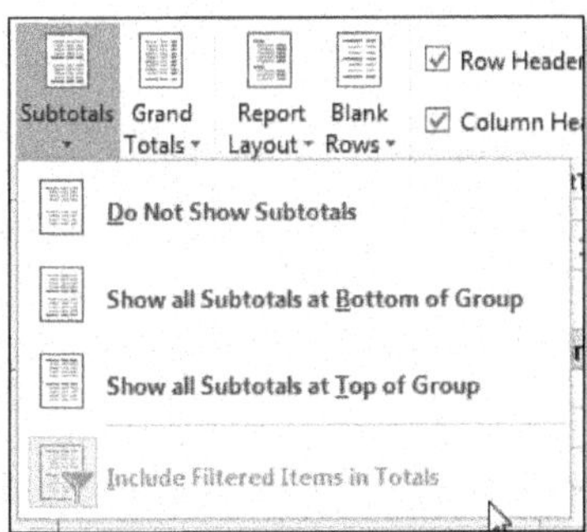

Figure 17.10 Include Filtered Items In Totals is not available.

How do you solve this problem? Choose Add This Data To The Data Model as you create the pivot table. Include Filtered Items In Totals is now enabled. The asterisk on the Grand Total in cell A49 means that there are rows hidden from the pivot table that are included in the totals.

More importantly, the % Of Column calculation is still reporting the correct 12.96% for Andrew Spain Consulting in cell C48 of Figure 17.11.

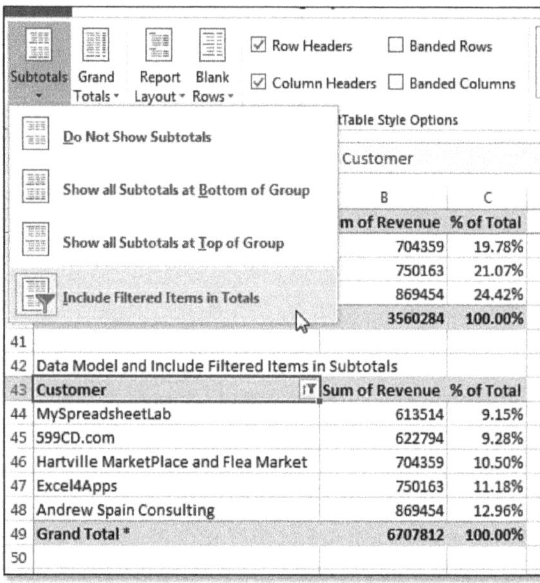

Figure 17.11 By choosing the Data Model, the calculation is correct.

Creating Median in a pivot table using DAX Measures

Pivot tables still do not support the median calculation. But when you add the data to the Data Model, you can build any calculation supported by the DAX formula language. Between Excel 2016 and Excel 2019, the DAX formula language was expanded to include a `Median` calculation.

Calculations made with DAX are called *Measures*. Figure 17.12 shows different ways to start a DAX calculation. You can right-click the table name in the PivotTable Fields list and choose Add Measure. Or, you can use the Measures drop-down menu on the Power Pivot tab in Excel. Using the Measures drop-down menu is slightly better because any new measures are automatically added to the Values area of a pivot table.

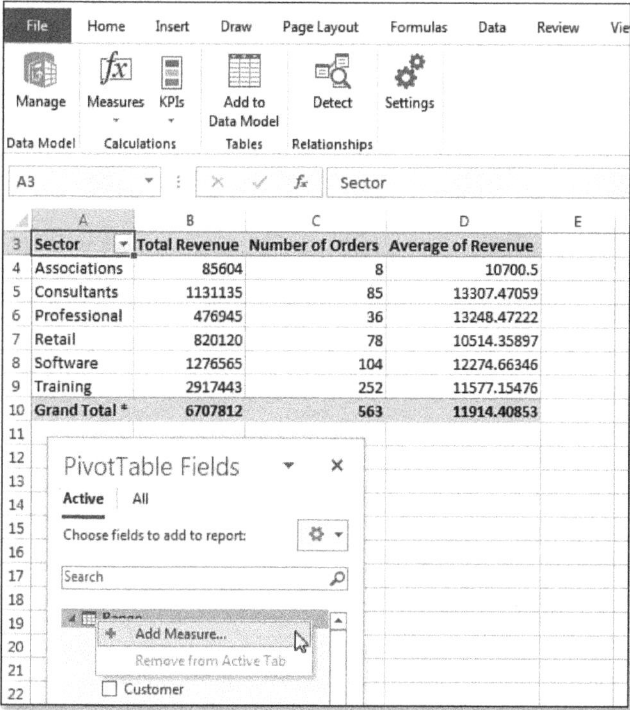

Figure 17.12 Build a pivot table using the Data Model and then add a measure.

Figure 17.13 shows the Measure dialog box. There are several fields:

- The Table Name will be filled in automatically for you.
- Type a meaningful name for the new calculation in the Measure Name box.
- You can leave the Description box empty.
- The *fx* button lets you choose a function from a list.
- The Check Formula button will look for syntax errors.
- Type `=Median(Range[Revenue])` as the formula.
- In the lower-left, choose a number format.

As you type the formula, something that feels like AutoComplete will offer tool tips on how to build the formulas. When you finish typing the formula, click the Check Formula button. You want to see the result No Errors In Formula, as shown in Figure 17.13.

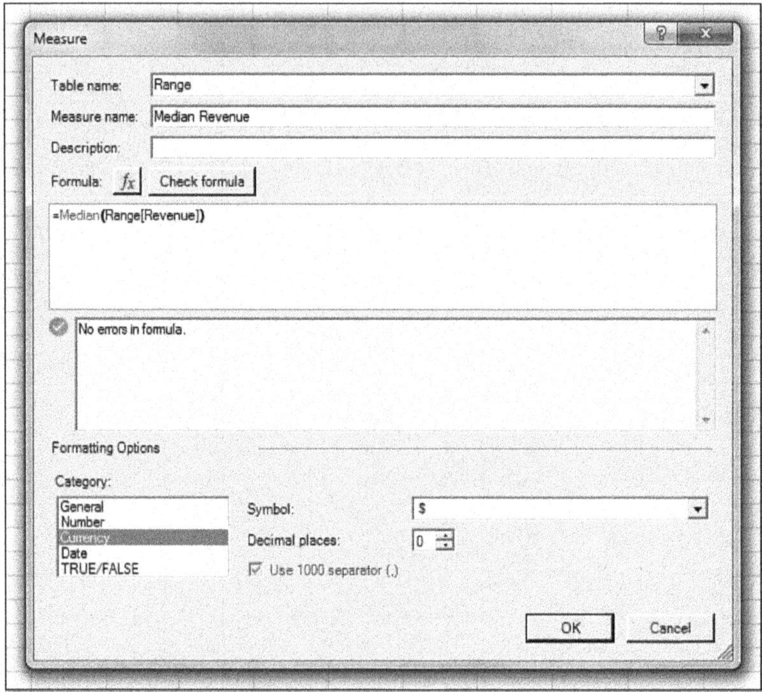

Figure 17.13 Build a measure to calculate Median.

Click OK. The Median Revenue will appear in the Fields list. Choose the field in the Fields list and it will be added to your pivot table.

Column E in Figure 17.14 shows the Median for each sector.

Preview Layout Views
Workbook Views
Show

B4 fx 85604

	A	D	E
3	Sector	Average of Revenue	Median Revenue
4	Associations	10700.5	$11,479
5	Consultants	13307.47059	$13,936
6	Professional	13248.47222	$14,048
7	Retail	10514.35897	$10,477
8	Software	12274.66346	$12,744
9	Training	11577.15476	$11,268
10	Grand Total *	11914.40853	$11,858
11			

PivotTable Fields
Active All
Choose fields to add to report:
Search
☐ Quantity
☑ Revenue
☐ Profit
☑ Sector
☐ Region
☑ fx Median Revenue

Figure 17.14 A pivot table with Medians.

TROUBLESHOOTING

The Check Formula button in the Measure dialog box does ensure the formula will calculate correctly.

Shown previously in Figure 17.13, the Check Formula button will often return a message: `No Errors in Formula`. You add the measure to your pivot table and get a `#VALUE!` error.

The `No Errors In Formula` error message means that you spelled all of the functions and field names correctly and that you are not missing any parentheses. It does not mean that the calculation will do what you want.

There have been many times when I have struggled to finally get the `No Errors In Formula` message and then been crushed to find that the formula still does not work. This is when I head to the forums to see if someone can spot the logic error in my formula.

Calculations created by Measures are easy to re-use. Change the pivot table from Figure 17.14 to show Regions in A instead of Sector. The measure is re-used and starts calculating statistics by Region (see Figure 17.15).

	A	D	E	F
3	Region	Average of Revenue	Median Revenue	
4	Midwest	12093.22222	$12,642	
5	Northeast	11301.12766	$10,624	
6	South	12333.29384	$12,360	
7	West	11972.55	$10,307	
8	Grand Total *	11914.40853	$11,858	
9				

Figure 17.15 The measure keeps working if you change the shape of the pivot table.

Time intelligence using DAX

The DAX formula language supports new functions for month-to-date, year-to-date, prior period, and so on.

Create a new `MTDSales` measure with the formula:

```
=CALCULATE([Sum of Revenue],DatesMTD(Sales[Date]))
```

The function `CALCULATE` is similar to `SUMIFS`, with one cool exception. Normally, a cell in a pivot table is filtered by the slicers, the row fields, and the column fields. In cell B21 of Figure 17.16, the row field is imposing a filter of 1/30/2018. The DAX measure is redefining the filter. By asking for all dates in `DATESMTD(Sales[Date])`, the `MTDSales` field returns all January 2018 dates up to and including the 30th of January.

	A	B	C	D
3		Date	Sum of Revenue	MTDSales
16		1/23/2018	14,592	185,078
17		1/24/2018	12,606	197,684
18		1/25/2018	20,770	218,454
19		1/26/2018	8,128	226,582
20		1/29/2018	24,286	250,868
21		1/30/2018	6,714	257,582
22		1/31/2018	15,640	273,222
23		2/1/2018	5,532	5,532
24		2/3/2018	17,160	22,692
25		2/6/2018	21,708	44,400
26		2/7/2018	19,890	64,290
27		2/8/2018	1,817	66,107
28		2/9/2018	5,157	71,264
29		2/14/2018	13,867	85,131
30		2/16/2018	16,936	102,067
31		2/17/2018	11,430	113,497

Figure 17.16 The MTD calculation accumulates until a new month starts.

CHAPTER 17

To calculate sales for the same day last year, use DATEADD to move back one year:

```
Prior Year Sales
=CALCULATE(Sales[Sum of Revenue],
ALL(Sales[Date (Year)]),
DATEADD(Sales[Date],-1,YEAR))
```

After you define a calculated field, you can use that field in future calculations:

```
Prior Year MTD Sales
=CALCULATE([PriorYearSales],
DATESMTD(Sales[Date]))
```

And then:

```
MTDChangeOverLastYear
=[MTDSales]-[PriorYearMTDSales]
```

Figure 17.17 shows the results of those calculations.

3	Date	Sum of Revenue	MTDSales	PriorYearSales	PriorYearMTDSales	MTDChangeOverLastYear
229	12/27/2018	9,460	277,825			277,825
230	12/28/2018	10,290	288,115			288,115
231	1/1/2019	10,245	10,245	22,810	22,810	-12,565
232	1/2/2019	11,240	21,485	2,257	25,067	-3,582
233	1/3/2019	9,204	30,689		25,067	5,622
234	1/4/2019	6,860	37,549	27,704	52,771	-15,222
235	1/6/2019	13,806	51,355		52,771	-1,416
236	1/8/2019	21,015	72,370		82,957	-10,587
237	1/9/2019	21,465	93,835	16,416	99,373	-5,538
238	1/11/2019	9,144	102,979		120,811	-17,832

Figure 17.17 Each formula can build on a prior formula.

Here is the beautiful thing: If your goal is to show MTD sales growth, you can remove all the intermediate calculations from the pivot table and show only the final calculated field.

The DAX formula language supports new functions for month-to-date, year-to-date, prior period, and so on.

Converting your pivot table to formulas for use on a dashboard

Pivot tables are great at summarizing data, but the formatting available in a pivot table is limited. Imagine if you could use the power of pivot tables to summarize the data but then rearrange the cells into a dashboard.

When you create a pivot table based on the Data Model, you can convert the entire pivot table to formulas. The formulas will use the cube functions to retrieve summary data from the data model.

From a pivot table that is based on the data model, select PivotTable Analyze, OLAP Tools, Convert To Formulas, as shown in Figure 17-18.

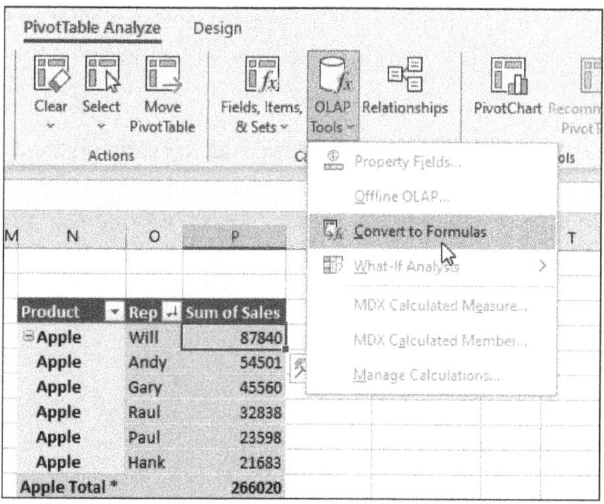

Figure 17.18 Convert the pivot table to formulas.

After converting to formulas, Excel uses a clever combination of CUBEVALUE and CUBEMEMBER formulas to retrieve each number. Referring to Figure 17.18, the 87840 in Cell P4 uses a formula of:

```
=CUBEVALUE("ThisWorkbookDataModel",$O4,P$3)
```

O4 is pointing to `Will`. The formula in that cell is

```
=CUBEMEMBER("ThisWorkbookDataModel",{"[Table3].[Product].&[Apple]","[Table3].
[Rep].&[Will]"})
```

P3 is pointing to `Sum of Sales`. The formula in P3 is

```
=CUBEMEMBER("ThisWorkbookDataModel","[Measures].[Sum of Sales]")
```

If you cut O4 and P3 and paste them outside the print range, the formula in P4 continues to return the correct answer.

Overcoming limitations of the Data Model

When you use the Data Model, you transform your regular Excel data into an OLAP model. There are annoying limitations and some benefits available to pivot tables built on OLAP models. The Excel team tried to mitigate some of the limitations for Excel 2019, but some are still present. Here are some of the limitations and the workarounds:

- **Less grouping:** You cannot use the Group feature of pivot tables to create territories or to group numeric values into bins. You will have to add calculated fields to your data with the grouping information.
- **Product is not a built-in calculation:** I've never created a pivot table where I had to multiply all the rows. That is the calculation that happens when you change Sum to Product. If you need to do this calculation, you can add a new Measure using the `PRODUCT` function in DAX.
- **Pivot tables won't automatically sort by custom lists:** It is eight annoying clicks to force a field to sort by a custom list: Open the field drop-down menu and choose More Sort Options. In the Sort Options dialog box, click More Options. In the More Sort Options dialog box, unselect Sort Automatically. Open the First Key Sort Order and choose your Custom List. Click OK to close More Sort Options dialog box. Click OK to close the Sort dialog box.

Inside OUT

The custom sorting solution mentioned previously requires eight mouse clicks. It works in the pivot table, but not in any slicers. There is possibly an easier way.

Check to see if both these things are true: Your Excel has a tab in the ribbon for Power Pivot, and you have a field with month name and another field with month number. If so, then you can try these steps:

1. Select the Manage icon in the Power Pivot tab of the Excel ribbon to open the Power Pivot grid.
2. Use the tab icons in the bottom of the Power Pivot grid to find the correct sheet that contains your month names.

3. **In the Power Pivot grid, select the column that contains the month names or month abbreviations.**
4. **In the Power Pivot ribbon, select Home, Sort By Column, as shown in the figure below.**
5. **In the resulting Sort By Column dialog box, specify that you want to sort Month By MonthNo. Click OK. From this point forward, the month name will appear correctly in both the pivot table and any slicers.**

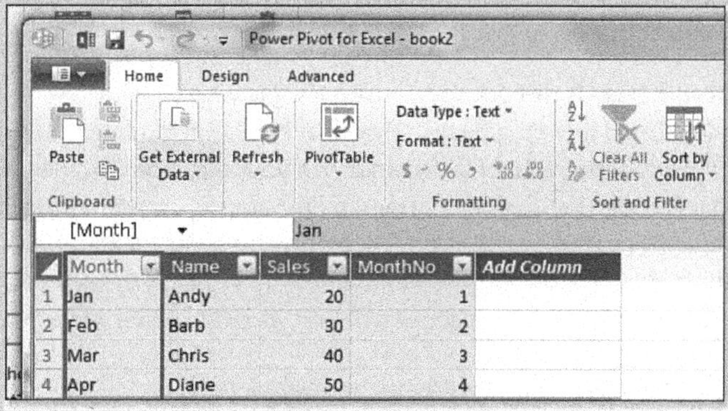

- **Strange drill-down:** Usually, you can double-click a cell in a pivot table and see the rows that make up that cell. This does work with the Data Model, but only for the first 1,000 rows.
- **No calculated fields or calculated items:** This is not a big deal, because DAX Measures run circles around calculated items.
- **Odd re-ordering items:** There is a trick in regular Excel pivot tables that you can do instead of dragging field names where you want them. Say that you go to a cell that contains the word *Friday* and type **Monday** there. When you press Enter, the Monday data moves to that new column. This does not work in Power Pivot pivot tables! You can still select Monday, hover over the edge, and drag the item to a new location.
- **No support for arrow keys in formula creation:** In the Excel interface, you might build a formula with =<LeftArrow>*<LeftArrow><LeftArrow><Enter>. This is not supported in Power Pivot. You will have to reach for the mouse to click on the columns that you want to reference.
- **Refresh will be slow:** The Refresh button on the Analyze tab forces Excel to update the data in the pivot table. Think before you do this. In the current example, this forces Excel to go out and import the 1.7 million–row data set again.

- **February 29, 1900 does not exist in Power Pivot:** There was no February 29 in 1900. Lotus 1-2-3 had a bug: The date algorithms assumed that 1900 was a leap year. As Excel was battling for market share, they had to produce the same results as Lotus, so Excel repeated the February 29, 1900 bug. The SQL Server Analysis Team refused to perpetuate this bug and does not recognize February 29, 1900. In Excel, day 1 is January 1, 1900. In Power Pivot, day 1 is December 31, 1899. None of this matters unless you have sales that happened during January 1, 1900 through February 28, 1900. In that case, the two pivot tables will be off by a day. No one has data going back that far, right? It will never be an issue, right? Well, in 2018, I met a guy who had a column of quantities. He had values like 30 and 42 and 56. But that column was accidentally imported as a date. All the quantities were off by one.

- **32-bit Excel is not enough:** I meet people who complain Excel is slow, even though they added more memory to their machine. Unfortunately, the 32-bit version of Excel can only access 3GB of the memory on your machine. To really use Power Pivot and the Data Model with millions of rows of data, you will need to install 64-bit Excel. This does not cost anything extra. It does likely involve some pleading with the IT department. Also, there are some old add-ins that do not run in 64-bit Excel. If you happen to be using that add-in, then you must choose whether you want faster performance or the old add-in.

Enjoying other benefits of Power Pivot

Nothing in the previous list is a deal-breaker. In the interest of fairness, here are several more benefits that come from using Power Pivot and the Data Model:

- You can hide or rename columns. If your Database Administrator thinks `TextSlsRepNbr` is a friendly name, you can change it to `Sales Rep Number`. Or, if your data tables are littered with useless fields, you can hide them from the PivotTable Fields list. In the Power Pivot window, right-click any column heading and choose Hide From Client Tools.

- You can assign categories to fields, such as Geography, Image URL, and Web URL. Select the column in the Power Pivot window and choose a column. On the Advanced tab, choose a Data Category.

- You can define key performance indicators or hierarchies.

Learning more

Power Pivot and Power Query are powerful tools that are completely new for most Excellers. These are my favorite books to learn more:

- I cover more about Power Pivot in *Microsoft 365 Excel Pivot Table Data Crunching* (ISBN 978-0-1375-2183-8).

- For Power Query, read *M Is for Data Monkey* by Ken Puls and Miguel Escobar (ISBN 978-1-61547-034-1).
- For DAX formulas in Power Pivot, read *Supercharge Excel* by Matt Allington (ISBN 978-1-61547-053-2).
- For Advanced Power Pivot, read *Power Pivot and Power BI* by Rob Collie and Avi Singh (ISBN 978-1-61547-039-6).

CHAPTER 18

Using What-If, Scenario Manager, Goal Seek, and Solver

When Dan Bricklin invented VisiCalc in 1979, he was trying to come up with a tool that would let him quickly recalculate his MBA school case studies. Forty years later, spreadsheets are still used for the same functionality.

Newer spreadsheet tools such as Goal Seek and an improved Solver enable you to back directly into the assumptions that lead to a solution. This chapter discusses some of Excel's features that are helpful when you are trying to find a specific answer.

CHAPTER 18

Using What-If

After you have set up a model in Excel, you can make copies of the model side by side and then change the various input variables to test their impact on the final result. Because this type of analysis answers the question of what happens if a change is made, it is known generically as *what-if analysis*.

What-if analyses are the least formal method in this chapter. You copy the input variables and formulas multiple times. You can then vary the input variables until you reach a suitable solution.

For example, Figure 18.1 shows a worksheet to calculate the monthly payment on a car purchase. Cells E1, E2, and E3 are the known values: the price, term, and interest rate. Cell E4 calculates the monthly payment using the =PMT() function.

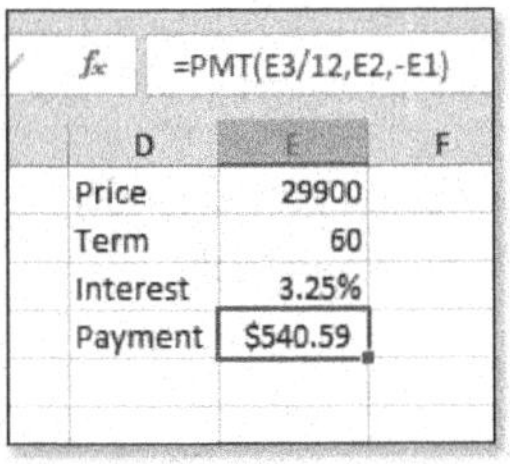

fx =PMT(E3/12,E2,-E1)

D	E	F
Price	29900	
Term	60	
Interest	3.25%	
Payment	$540.59	

Figure 18.1 You might not like the answer in cell E4, but Excel makes the answer easy to find.

Cells E1:E4 are a self-contained mini-model. You can copy these cells several times over and perform what-if analysis on the car payment model.

Figure 18.2 shows a basic what-if worksheet that you can use to plug in different numbers manually. Each column uses a different combination of price, term, and interest rate.

D	E	F	G	H	I	J	K	L	M	N	O
Price	29900	29900	29900	29900	29900	29900	27500	27500	27500	25995	25995
Term	60	66	72	60	66	72	60	66	48	60	48
Interest	3.25%	3.50%	3.75%	4.50%	4.50%	4.50%	5.00%	5.00%	5.00%	5.00%	5.00%
Payment	$541	$499	$464	$557	$512	$475	$519	$477	$633	$491	$599

Figure 18.2 By making multiple copies of the table, you can create a what-if model.

There is nothing magic about this type of what-if analysis. There are no ribbon commands involved (other than applying Conditional Formatting, Color Scale to highlight the prices). You copy the model and plug in a few numbers. This is how most Excel worksheets use what-if analyses. The remaining topics in this chapter cover the What-If commands on the ribbon.

TROUBLESHOOTING

The Excel PMT function is great for calculating loan payments, but it frequently returns negative payments.

The `PMT` function shown in the previous figures has two annoying issues to make it work correctly.

When you go to the bank to get a loan, you will pay a specific interest rate to get that loan. In this example, let's say the interest rate is 4.5%. However, you cannot enter `4.5%` as the first argument in `PMT` and get a correct answer. The Rate argument in the `PMT` function is expecting an interest rate per period for the loan. If you are making monthly payments, you will specify `4.5%/12`.

Second, let's say you are buying a car that costs $25,000. The `Present Value` of the car is $25,000. If you enter `=PMT(4.5%/12,60,25000)`, the formula will return a negative number. The logic here is that if a positive $25,000 pulls in to your garage, then a negative $466.08 will be leaving your checking account each month. However, you never write a check for -466.08. In order to get the `PMT` answer to return positive 466.08, you have to write the Present Value argument as negative: `=PMT(4.5%/12,60,-25000)`.

Because most people buy a car once every five years and a house once every ten years, the `PMT` function is particularly easy to forget between major purchases.

Creating a two-variable What-If table

The analysis in Figure 18.2 is fairly ad hoc in that it basically enables you to try various combinations until you find one that is close to your target payment. If you have two variables to manipulate, you can use Excel's fairly powerful Data Table command. To use a data table, follow these steps to build the table shown in Figure 18.3:

1. Enter a formula in the upper-left corner of the table. This formula should point to at least two variable cells.

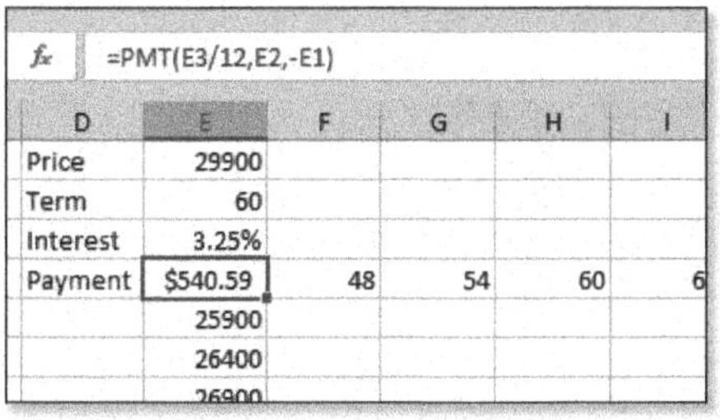

fx =PMT(E3/12,E2,-E1)

D	E	F	G	H	I
Price	29900				
Term	60				
Interest	3.25%				
Payment	$540.59	48	54	60	6
	25900				
	26400				
	26900				

Figure 18.3 Preparing for a two-variable what-if analysis.

2. Along the left column of the table, enter various values for one of the input values. These values are substituted in a cell known as the *column input cell*.
3. Along the top row of the table, enter various values for the other input variable. These values are substituted in a cell that Excel calls the *row input cell*.
4. Select the entire table.
5. From the Data tab, select Data Tools, What-If Analysis, Data Table.
6. In the Data Table dialog, enter a row input cell and a column input cell.
7. Click OK to complete the table.

You can use the Data Table command to negotiate the price and term of the loan by following these steps:

1. Use the formula in cell E4 as the formula in the top-left corner of your table.
2. From E5:E21, fill in various possible values for purchase price.
3. From F4:K4, fill in various possible values for the term of the loan.
4. Select the entire table, E4:K21, as shown in Figure 18.4.

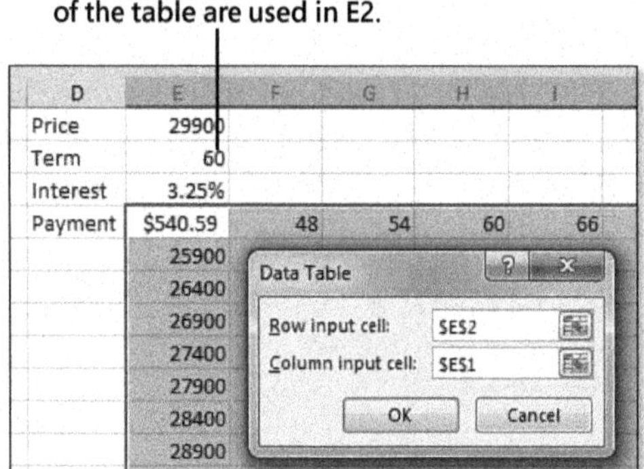

Figure 18.4 Setting up the Data Table dialog.

5. Select Data Table from the Data tab to display the Data Table dialog, as shown in Figure 18.4. The dialog asks you for a row input cell and a column input cell. The Row Input Cell field offers to take each value from the top row of the table and plug it into a particular cell.

6. Because the values in F4:K4 are loan terms, specify E2 for the row input cell.

7. Similarly, the Column Input Cell field offers to take each value from the left column and replace that value in a particular cell. Because these cells contain vehicle prices, select E1 as the column input cell.

8. Click OK. Excel fills in the intersection of each row and column with the monthly payment, based on the price in the left column combined with the loan term in the top row.

9. Select just the interior of the table. You can see that Excel represents the table with the TABLE() array function. Figure 18.5 shows the table after a color scale has been applied.

$540.59	48	54	60	66	72	78
25900	576.15	516.21	468.27	429.07	396.42	368.81
26400	587.27	526.17	477.31	437.35	404.07	375.93
26900	598.39	536.14	486.35	445.64	411.73	383.05
27400	609.51	546.10	495.39	453.92	419.38	390.17
27900	620.64	556.07	504.43	462.20	427.03	397.29

Figure 18.5 The values in the table are calculated by a single TABLE() array formula. Oddly, you cannot enter the TABLE formula by typing it. You must use the Data Table command.

NOTE

You can use the Data Table command when only a single variable is changing. Enter values for the variable down the left column and enter a single cell with 1 in the top row. In the Data Table dialog, specify any blank cell as the row input cell. Alternatively, enter the changing values across the top row, and use a blank cell as the column input cell.

Modeling a random scenario using a data table

The model shown in Figure 18.6 is known as a Random Walk Down Wall Street. In this simple model, a penny is flipped 25 times. If the penny comes up heads, you win a dollar. If the penny comes up tails, you lose $1. The model uses `=IF(RAND()>.5,1,-1)` to simulate the coin flip. The chart shows that the stock analyst running this model did well; he was always up and finished by making money (see Figure 18.6).

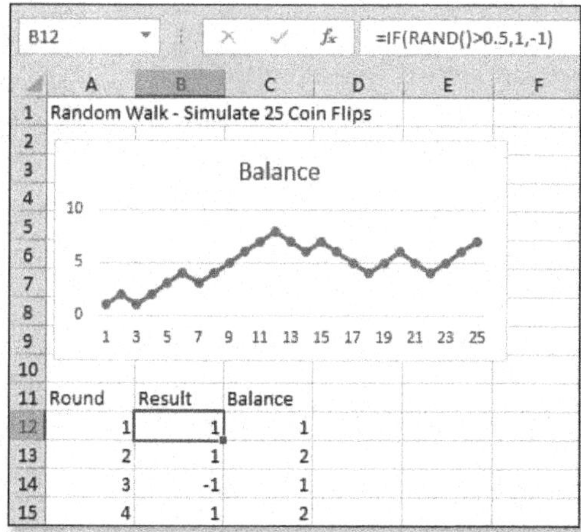

Figure 18.6 This hot-shot Wall Street analyst has been on a positive win streak.

Credit for this technique goes to Professor Simon Benninga. If you ever had a college class in financial modeling, you likely used Simon's textbook on the subject.

United States law requires financial firms to add the note that past results are not indicative of future returns. With the current model, press F9 to run the simulation again and you could see very different results. Same model. Same methods. Same guy pressing the F9 key, but the hot-shot stock analyst now loses someone's money—hopefully not yours (see Figure 18.7).

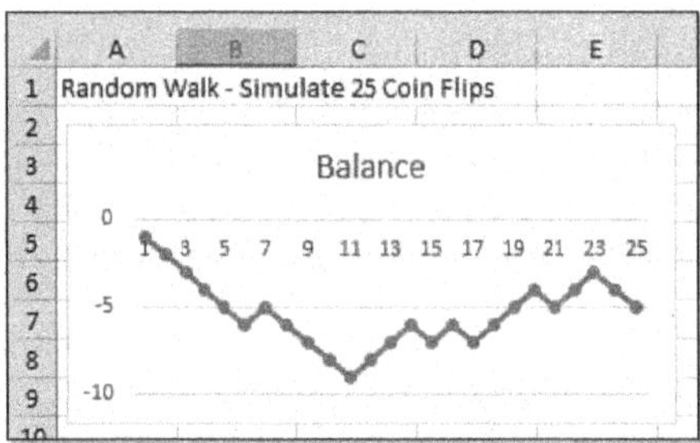

Figure 18.7 The same model loses money.

In my simple model, there are 25 coin flips. But it is possible to model 500 or 1,000 iterations with far more data points than a simple coin flip. After each run through the model, you might be interested in tracking the Max, the Min, the Standard Deviation, plus the most important statistic—did you make or lose money at the end?

In Figure 18.8, five formulas track the performance of one run of the model. It is possible to use Data, What-If Analysis, Data Table as shown in this figure. The top-left corner cell is blank. The Row Input Cell field is blank. The Column Input Cell field is pointing to a blank cell completely unrelated to the model.

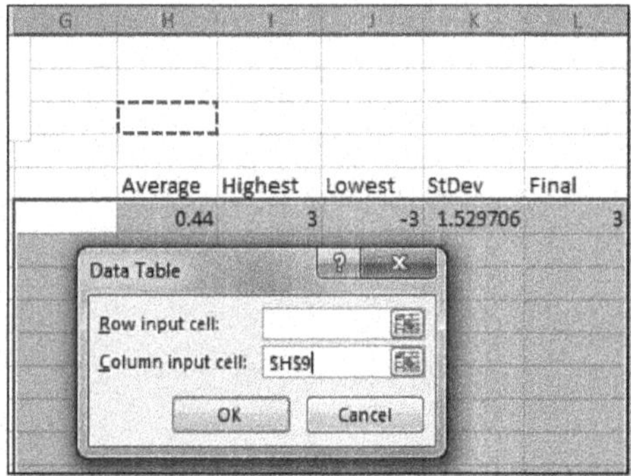

Figure 18.8 This data table runs the entire model once for every row selected.

When you click OK to run the data table, every row returns the results of flipping the coin 25 times. Imagine if you had a model with many random variables and 1,000 iterations. You can use this technique to exercise the model hundreds of times (see Figure 18.9).

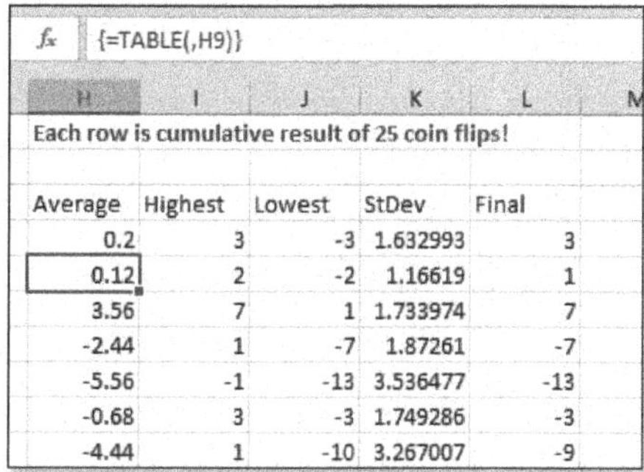

{=TABLE(,H9)}

Each row is cumulative result of 25 coin flips!

Average	Highest	Lowest	StDev	Final
0.2	3	-3	1.632993	3
0.12	2	-2	1.16619	1
3.56	7	1	1.733974	7
-2.44	1	-7	1.87261	-7
-5.56	-1	-13	3.536477	-13
-0.68	3	-3	1.749286	-3
-4.44	1	-10	3.267007	-9

Figure 18.9 Each row in the resulting data table represents the results of dozens of coin flips.

Using Scenario Manager

The Data Table command is great for models with two variables that can change. However, sometimes you have models with far more variables that can change. In such a case, you could use the Scenario Manager, which enables you to create multiple scenarios, each changing up to 32 variables. With the added flexibility, it takes longer to create each scenario.

TIP

With up to 32 variables changing, it is best to use named ranges for all the input variables before you define your first scenario. One of the results of the Scenario Manager is a summary report. Using named ranges for all the input cells makes the report easier to understand.

➤ **To learn how to use named ranges to your advantage, see "Using Named Ranges to Simplify Formulas," in Chapter 12, "Array formulas and names in Excel."**

Figure 18.10 shows a sales model. Several input cells are highlighted in gray. The Scenario Manager dialog offers various scenarios that someone manually set up. Double-click any scenario to load those values into the model.

You can compare the results of all scenarios using either a regular summary report or a pivot table summary report. Figure 18.11 shows the regular summary report.

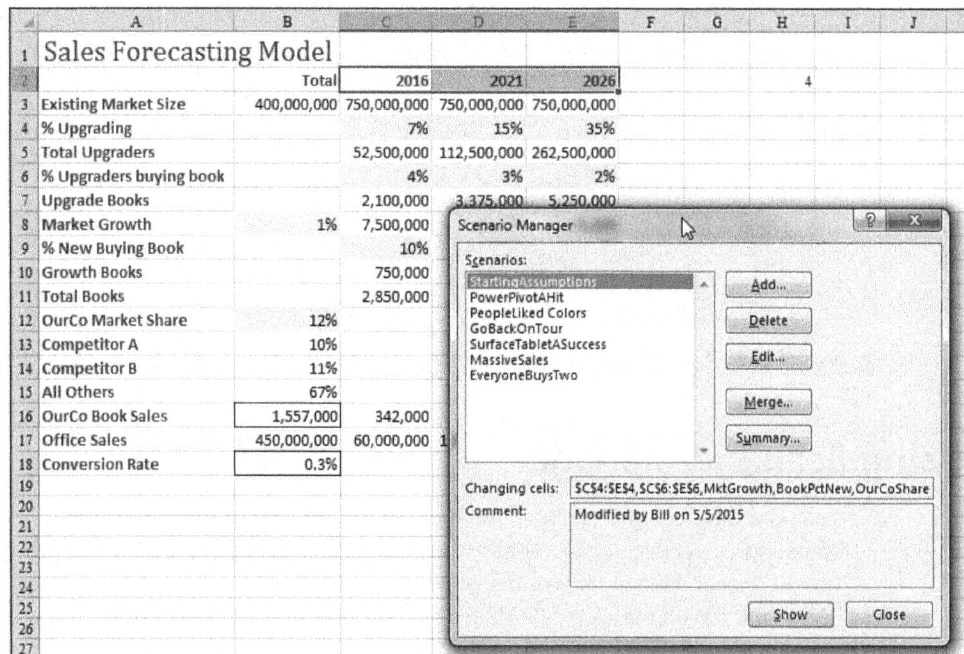

Figure 18.10 Choose any scenario to change all the input cells at once.

Scenario Summary	Current Values:	StartingAssumptions	PowerPivotAHit	PeopleLiked Colors	GoBackOnTour	SurfaceTabletASuccess
		Created by Bill Jelen	Assumes PowerPivot Drives Massive Growth	Assumes people reject office because of lack of color	Assumes World Tour in 2013-2014	Surface drives massive market growth, none buy books
Changing Cells:						
UpgradePct14	7%	7%	8%	6%	7%	7%
UpgradePct13	15%	15%	25%	4%	15%	15%
UpgradePct08	35%	35%	55%	3%	35%	35%
BookPct12	4%	4%	4%	4%	4%	4%
BookPct13	3%	3%	4%	3%	3%	3%
BookPct14	2%	2%	4%	2%	2%	2%
MktGrowth	1%	1%	2%	-1%	1%	80%
BookPctNew	10%	10%	10%	0%	10%	0%
OurCoShare	12%	12%	12%	12%	18%	12%
Result Cells:						
OurCoSalesForecast	1,557,000	1,557,000	3,708,000	378,000	2,335,500	1,503,000
OurCoConversionPct	0.3%	0.3%	0.5%	0.5%	0.5%	0.1%

Notes: Current Values column represents values of changing cells at time Scenario Summary Report was created. Changing cells for each scenario are highlighted in gray.

Figure 18.11 After you identify the Results cells, Excel summarizes all scenarios.

Unfortunately, it is a tedious process to set up each scenario. To set up a scenario, use the following steps:

CHAPTER 18

1. Select Data, Data Tools, What-If Analysis, Scenario Manager to display the Scenario Manager dialog. Initially, the Scenario Manager indicates that no scenarios are defined. Click the Add button to add a scenario. The Add Scenario dialog appears.

2. In the Add Scenario dialog, enter a name for this scenario and then choose which cells will be changing. Because the variable cells are not adjacent, select the first contiguous range and then Ctrl+click to add additional ranges (see Figure 18.12).

   NOTE

   It is best to add one scenario that represents your starting assumptions. Otherwise, those numbers will be lost.

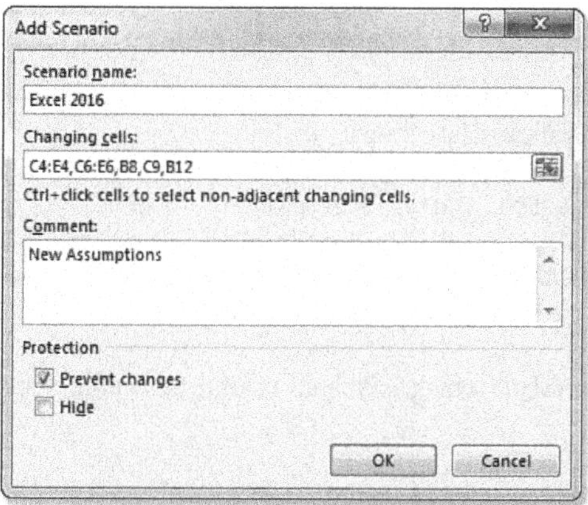

Figure 18.12 Name your new scenario.

3. The Scenario Values dialog box appears, which can be used to edit the values for each starting cell (see Figure 18.13). Note that if you had previously named your input cells, the cell names appear in this dialog instead of addresses. Type new values. If you are finished creating scenarios, click OK. If you want to return to the Add Scenario dialog box to define another scenario, click OK.

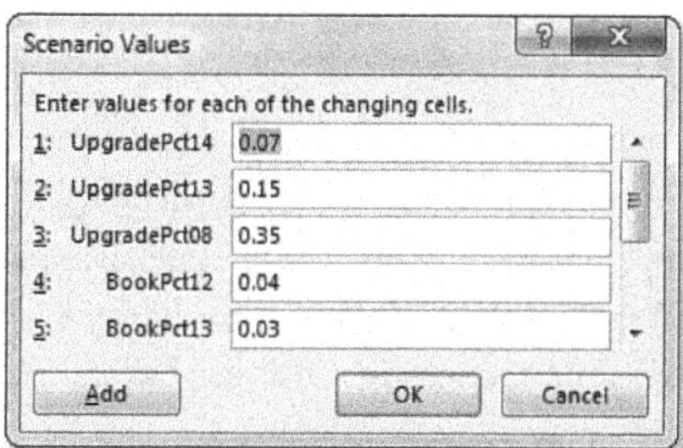

Figure 18.13 Typing the input values is the tedious part.

CHAPTER 18

Creating a Scenario Summary report

One powerful feature of Excel scenarios is the capability to create a Scenario Summary report. When you click the Summary button on the Scenario Manager dialog, Excel enables you to choose either a Scenario Summary report or a Pivot Table report. In either case, you should select one or more cells that represent the results of the model.

> CAUTION
>
> **The Scenario Summary report is a snapshot in time. If you later change scenarios or add new scenarios, you must re-create and reformat the Scenario Summary report.**

Adding multiple scenarios

You might want to share a workbook with others and have them add their own scenarios to get opinions from people in other areas of your company, such as sales, marketing, engineering, and manufacturing. To do this, follow these steps:

1. Save the workbook with just the starting scenario.
2. Route the workbook to each person. In a hidden field, Excel keeps track of who adds each scenario.
3. When you get the routed workbook back, open both the original workbook and the routed workbook.
4. Display the Scenario Manager in the original workbook.
5. Click the Merge button to display the Merge Scenarios dialog.
6. In the Book drop-down, select the name of the routed workbook.
7. Excel usually encounters identically named scenarios in the merge process. It differentiates any scenarios with identical names by adding a date or name to the incoming scenarios. If these scenarios are truly identical to the scenario that you originally sent out, delete them.

Using Goal Seek

On the television show *The Price Is Right*, one of the games is the Hi-Lo game. A contestant tries to guess the price of an item, and the host tells the player that the actual price is higher or lower. The process of honing in on a price of $1.67 might involve guesses of $2, $1, $1.50, $1.75, $1.63, $1.69, $1.66, $1.68, and finally $1.67. Using the techniques described so far in this chapter, you might play this game with Excel to try to hone in on an answer.

You might have an Excel worksheet set up that calculates a final value using several input variables. To solve the formula in reverse, you need to find input variables that generate a certain answer. There are several possible approaches:

- One difficult approach is to determine whether another Excel function reverses the calculation. For example, =ARCSIN() performs the opposite of =SIN(), and =NPER(), =RATE(), or =PV() back into a =PMT().

- Another approach is to use algebra to attempt to solve for one of the input variables.

- Most people simply play the Hi-Lo game by successively plugging in higher and lower answers to the input cell until they narrow in on an input variable that produces the desired result.

- If you play the Hi-Lo game, consider using the Goal Seek command. In effect, this command plays the Hi-Lo game at hyperspeed, arriving at an answer within a second.

Consider the car payment example at the beginning of the chapter. You want to find a price that yields a $475 monthly payment. You might find a =PV() function that can solve this. However, most people plug in successively higher or lower values for the price in cell E1 (see Figure 18.14).

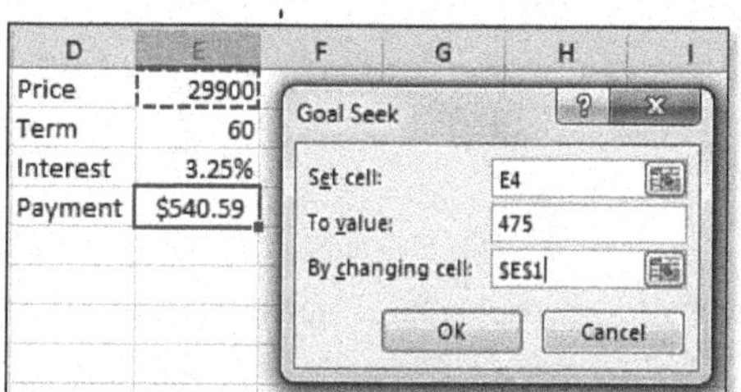

Figure 18.14 Goal Seek lets you find one value by changing one other cell.

Excel's Goal Seek option, on the other hand, enables you to hone in quickly on a value. To use Goal Seek, follow these steps:

1. Select the answer cell. In this example, it would be the payment in cell E4.

2. From the Data Tools group of the Data tab, select the What-If Analysis drop-down, and then select Goal Seek. The Goal Seek dialog appears, as shown in Figure 18.14.

3. In the Goal Seek dialog, indicate that you want to set the answer cell to a particular value by changing a particular input cell. In this example, set cell E4 to the value of 475 by changing cell E1. Excel begins trying to hone in on a value. When Excel gets to within a penny of the value, the results are presented. Behind the dialog, the worksheet shows the proposed price of 26272.12 in the worksheet.

4. Either accept this value by clicking OK or revert to the original value by clicking Cancel.

Goal Seek can be applied to other input cells. For example, in Figure 18.15, the Goal Seek in column F sought a $475 monthly payment by changing the term. If you are willing to make payments for 69 months, you can buy the desired car. However, when Goal Seek tried to get a $475 monthly payment by changing the interest rate, the result was the impossible negative interest rate.

	Original	Price	Term	Interest
Price	29900	26272.12	29900	29900
Term	60	60	69.10666	60
Interest	3.25%	3.25%	3.25%	-1.87%
Payment	$540.59	$475.00	$475.00	$475.00

Figure 18.15 Three different Goal Seek commands find how to yield a $475 payment by changing either the price, the term, or the rate.

Using Solver

It is possible to design problems that are far too complex for Goal Seek. These problems might have dozens of independent variables and various constraints. In such a case, you can use the Excel Solver add-in.

TIP

Solver was improved in Excel 2010. To get the old Solver to work, you had to have a good grasp on linear mathematics. Hence, the old Solver never worked for me. The new Solver offers advanced methodologies that find solutions to far more problems. If you had tried Solver before without success, it is time to try it again.

With Solver, you identify an output formula cell that you want to be maximized, minimized, or set to a particular value. You specify a range of cells that can be changed. You then specify a number of constraints on input cells or other formulas in the model.

The Solver add-in, which is free with Excel, was written by Dan Fylstra and Frontline Systems. History buffs might remember that Dan Fylstra was the president of VisiCorp—the world's first spreadsheet program. Frontline Systems offers more advanced versions of Solver plus an Excel Data Miner tool at www.Solver.com.

Installing Solver

To install Solver, follow these steps:

1. Press Alt+T and then press I to display the Add-Ins dialog.
2. In the Add-Ins dialog, make sure that Solver is checked.

Solving a model using Solver

To use Solver, your worksheet should contain one or more input variables. The worksheet should also contain one or more formulas that result in a solution within a single cell.

For each input variable, there might be certain constraints. For example, you might want to assume that a certain variable must be positive or that it should be in a certain range of values.

When using Solver, you identify the input range, the output cell, and the constraints. You can ask Solver to minimize or maximize the input cell. Alternatively, you can ask Solver to set the output cell to a particular value. Solver uses advanced algorithms to find input variables that meet your goal and fit within the constraints.

This might be easier to understand with a concrete example. Figure 18.16 shows a worksheet used to model the production of widgets. Cell B23 indicates that each worker in your factory can make 40 widgets per hour. Workers who work evenings, nights, or weekends are paid a shift differential. You can choose to keep your factory running for anywhere from five shifts a week (Monday through Friday, first shift) up to 21 shifts per week. You can sell as many widgets as you can produce, provided that the overall cost is less than $2 per widget. You have a skilled workforce of 100 workers available for first shift, 82 workers for second shift, and 75 workers for third shift. How many shifts should the plant be open to maximize production? Solver runs circles around Goal Seek in situations that deal with multiple constraints.

To use Solver to find the answer, use the following steps:

1. Note that cells B3 through B11 define how many shifts the factory will be open. All the remaining cells in the model calculate the total number of widgets produced and the average cost per widget. Your goal is to maximize the number of widgets produced (cell D22) while keeping the average cost per widget in F22 to less than $2.00.
2. Select Solver from the Data tab in the ribbon.
3. Enter D22 as the Objective. Choose to set this to a Max (see Figure 18.17).

	A	B	C	D	E	F
1	**Manufacturing Plant Productivity**					
2						
3	Day Shift M-F	5		Goals:		
4	Evening Shift M-F	5		*Maximize widget production*		
5	Night Shift M-F	5		*Keep cost of widgets < $2.00*		
6	Day Shift Saturday	1				
7	Evening Shift Saturday	1				
8	Night Shift Saturday	1				
9	Day Shift Sun	1				
10	Evening Shift Sun	1				
11	Night Shift Sun	1				
12	Labor Cost Per Shift		Workers Avail per Shift	Total Widgets	Total Cost	
13	Day Shift M-F	8.25	100	20000	38000	
14	Evening Shift M-F	8.75	82	16400	33700	
15	Night Shift M-F	9.25	75	15000	32750	
16	Day Shift Saturday	12.38	80	3200	8923.2	
17	Evening Shift Saturday	13.13	72	2880	8562.88	
18	Night Shift Saturday	13.88	65	2600	8217.6	
19	Day Shift Sun	16.5	50	2000	7600	
20	Evening Shift Sun	17.5	36	1440	6040	
21	Night Shift Sun	18.5	30	1200	5440	Per Widget
22	Overhead per shift	1000	Total	64720	149234	2.3058356
23	Widgets Per Worker Per Shift	40				

Figure 18.16 A worksheet to model widget production.

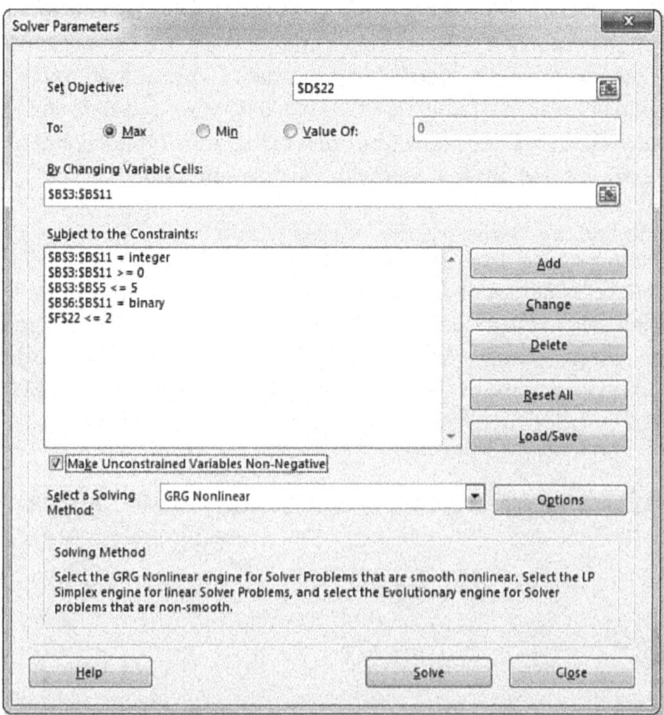

Figure 18.17 Define the model for Solver.

4. Define the input cells as B3:B11 in the By Changing Variable Cells box.

5. Use the Add button to add new constraints. One obvious constraint is that F22 must be less than a $2 cost. Cells B3:B5, which represent weekday shifts, cannot be higher than 5 per week because there are only 5 weekday shifts. There are other important constraints. You probably don't want an answer that says you work 0.329454 of a shift, so add a constraint that says B3:B11 must remain integers. Add a constraint that says those same cells cannot be negative. For the weekend shifts, the only valid values are 0 or 1. Use a constraint of Binary to allow only 0 or 1 as the input cells.

6. Three Solving Methods are available. Always start with GRG Nonlinear. If that doesn't work, try Evolutionary. If you are a math genius and have built a model with pure linearity, try Simplex LP.

7. Click the Solve button. Solver begins to iterate through possible solutions. If Solver finds a result, it reports success.

8. Click Save Scenario and give the scenario a solution such as SolverSolution. If you are going to define the solutions as a scenario, after doing this step, you can choose Restore Original Values and click OK. You can then use Data, What-If Analysis, Scenario Manager to add a scenario with your original values.

9. Select the Answer Report to have Excel provide a new worksheet that compares the original and final values.

NOTE

The GRG engine finds a solution that matches the constraints. However, it might not be the best solution. The LP Solver engine finds the best solution but only if you set up the model as a linear problem. The Evolutionary engine uses Monte Carlo to try random choices, hoping to hone in on a better solution.

In the answer report, Solver tells you that you can produce 42,400 widgets by operating five day and evening shifts and two night shifts. The remaining shifts are not cost effective to keep the cost per widget in cell F22 less than $2.

With this current solution, the cost per widget is exactly $2.

TIP

Frontline Systems offer premium versions of their Solver products that can handle more input variables than the Solver in Excel. If you find that Solver cannot solve your problem, sign up for a free trial of Premium Solver at *http://mrx.cl/solver77*.

Inside OUT

Some problems cannot be solved in a single lifetime using Solver. Say that you have a billion possible input values and that the logic inside the model is not linear. Solver will often fail to come up with the best solution.

In this case, you can switch over to Monte Carlo analysis. Set up a model where you calculate the results a thousand or five thousand times. The Monte Carlo range would start with a column of `=RANDBETWEEN(1,100000000)`. More columns in the Monte Carlo range would calculate the output of the model.

Let's say you are trying to find the largest possible output value. Add a `=MAX(B1:B1000)` off to the right of your model. Press F9 a few times and keep your eye on the result of the Max function. After a few presses of F9, you will start to notice the usual range for Max and the super-high range for Max. When you press F9 and get a large result for Max, scroll through the Monte Carlo range to find the input cell with the best output cell. Copy that row as values to a "Best Answer So Far" section (usually right near the Max result).

Now, keep pressing F9 until the Max function is larger than the Best Answer So Far. Copy that row and replace the Best Answer So Far.

After ten minutes of this process, you will usually have an answer better than Solver would have found.

CHAPTER 19

Automating repetitive functions using VBA macros

Every copy of Excel shipped since 1995 has included the powerful Visual Basic for Applications (VBA) lurking behind the grid. With VBA, you can do anything that you can do in the regular interface, and you can do it much faster. VBA shines when you have many repetitive tasks to undertake.

As of mid-2021, there are two technologies that might eat into some of VBA's solutions. First, the Power Query tools on the Get & Transform group on the Data tab can automate routine data cleaning operations. You clean the data once using Power Query and then you can refresh the query when the underlying data changes. Read more about Power Query in Chapter 13, "Transforming data with Power Query."

In May 2021, Microsoft officially released TypeScript as a language for Excel Online. This new programming language will eventually make it to Win32 versions of Excel. Microsoft has said that VBA will never be ported to Excel Online. If Microsoft's vision that Excel Online will eventually become as popular as Win32 versions of Excel, then some people will be compelled to implement solutions using TypeScript instead of VBA. The performance of TypeScript is still much slower than VBA, but this will improve over time. TypeScript is not covered in this book, but for an introduction to TypeScript in Excel, read Suat Ozgur's *Excel Custom Functions Straight to the Point.*

Learning to use macros is a good news/bad news proposition. The good news is that Microsoft Office provides a macro recorder that can write a macro as you work. The bad news is that it is not easy to record a macro that works consistently with any data set. To unleash the power of macros, you need to understand how to edit recorded macro code. You can then record a macro that is close to what you want and edit that macro to create something that runs the way you want it to work.

Checking security settings before using macros

Before you can use macros, you have to take some positive steps to affirm that you want to record or run a macro.

To enable VBA security, follow these steps:

1. Select File, Options to open the Excel Options dialog.
2. Select the Customize Ribbon category. In the right-side list box, select the Developer tab check box.
3. Click OK to exit the Excel Settings dialog. You now have a Developer tab on the ribbon.
4. On the Developer tab, click Macro Security in the Code group. The Security dialog appears.
5. In the Security dialog, change the Macro Settings option to Disable All Macros With Notification. With this setting, Excel alerts you whenever you open a workbook that has macros attached.
6. When you open a document and get the warning that the document has macros attached, if this is a document that you wrote and you expect macros to be there, click Enable Content to enable the macros. Otherwise, make sure the workbook came from someone you trust.

   NOTE

   In step 5, *with* is the operative word. You are choosing to disable macros and to display a notification to let you decide whether the macros should be enabled. Before choosing to enable macros, you can switch over to VBA and see what macros are in the workbook.

Recording a macro

Plan your macro before recording it by thinking through the steps you need to perform. If you need to fix many items in a worksheet, you might want to select the first item first. This way, the macro can perform an action on cells relative to the original selection.

To record a macro, follow these steps:

1. On the Developer tab, select Record Macro.
2. In the Record Macro dialog box, type a name for the macro. The name cannot contain spaces. For example, instead of typing **Macro Name**, you need to type **MacroName**.
3. Choose whether you want to store the macro in the current workbook, a new workbook, or a special personal macro workbook. The personal macro workbook is a special

workbook designed to hold general-purpose macros that might apply to any workbook. If you are unsure, select to store the recorded macro in the current workbook.

4. Assign a shortcut key for the macro. Ctrl+J is a safe key because nothing is currently assigned to Ctrl+J. This shortcut key enables you to run the macro again.

5. Click OK to close the Record Macro dialog.

6. Turn on relative recording by clicking the Use Relative References icon in the Code group of the Developer tab. Relative recording records the action of moving a certain number of cells from the active cell.

7. Perform the actions you want to store in the macro.

8. Click the Stop Recording button on the left side of the status bar at the bottom of the Excel window.

9. Save the workbook before testing the macro.

10. Test the macro playback by typing the shortcut key assigned in step 4.

CAUTION

The alternative is an absolute recording. This method is extremely literal. The action of moving down three cells from A1 is recorded as "Select cell A4." That action is extremely limited—it would work only when the macro is played back with the active cell in A1.

Case study: macro for formatting for a mail merge

Suppose that your coworker has some names and addresses in Excel and she needs to do a mail merge in Word. Instead of teaching her how to do a mail merge, you offer to do the mail merge for her. In theory, this should take you a couple of minutes. However, when the list of names arrives in the Excel worksheet, you realize the data is in the wrong format. In the Excel worksheet, the names are going down column A, as shown in Figure 19.1.

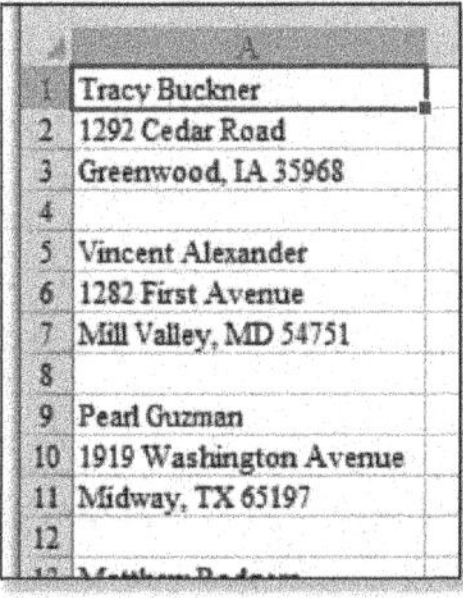

Figure 19.1 A simple task, such as doing a mail merge, is incredibly difficult when the data is in the wrong format.

To complete a mail merge successfully, the Excel worksheet should have fields for name, street address, and city+state+ZIP Code, as shown in Figure 19.2.

J26

	A	B	C	D
1	Tracy Buckner	1292 Cedar Road	Greenwood, IA 35968	
2	Vincent Alexander	1282 First Avenue	Mill Valley, MD 54751	
3	Pearl Guzman	1919 Washington Avenue	Midway, TX 65197	
4	Matthew Rodgers	1825 Jackson Blvd.	Greenwood, AZ 75420	
5	Nancy Roach	1144 Davis Lane	Riverside, NY 89224	
6	Jeannette Ross	454 Hill Highway	Centerville, WA 82020	
7	William Hester	405 Poplar Circle	Georgetown, ME 38799	
8	Tina Morrison	551 Fourteenth Highway	Mount Pleasant, VI 29331	
9	Victor Gilliam	828 Adams Highway	Akron, NE 29598	
10	Sandy Pickett	941 Spring Blvd	Rosemount, WY 17764	

Figure 19.2 The goal is to produce data with fields in columns.

Before you start recording a macro, you need to think about how to break the task into easily repeatable steps.

It would be good to record a macro that can fix one name in the list. Assume that you start with the cell pointer on a person's name at the beginning of the macro, as shown in Figure 19.1. The macro would need to perform these steps to fix one record and end up on the name of the second person in the list:

1. Press the down-arrow key to move to the address cell.
2. Press Ctrl+X to cut the address.
3. Press the up-arrow key and then the right-arrow key to move next to the name.
4. Press Ctrl+V to paste the address.
5. Press the left-arrow key once and the down-arrow key twice to move to the cell for city, state, and ZIP Code.
6. Press Ctrl+X to cut the city.
7. Press the up-arrow key twice and the right-arrow key twice to move to the right of the street cell.
8. Press Ctrl+V to paste the city.
9. Press the left-arrow key twice and the down-arrow key once to move to the now blank row just below the name.
10. Hold down the Shift key while pressing the down-arrow key twice to select the three blank rows.
11. Press Ctrl+- to invoke the Delete command. Press R and then Enter to delete the row.

When you run a macro that goes through these steps, Excel deletes the three blank rows, but the selection now contains the three cells that encompass the next record, as shown in Figure 19.3. Ideally, the macro should end with only the name selected. Press Shift+Backspace to reduce the selection to the active cell.

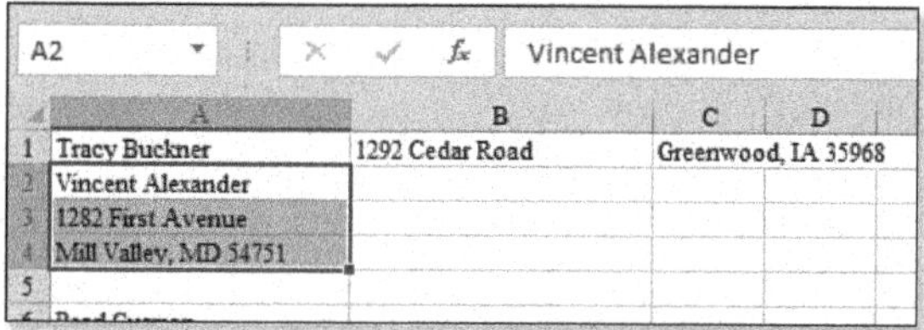

Figure 19.3 You need only one cell selected instead of three.

If the macro correctly performs all these steps, the first name and address are properly formatted. The blank rows left between the first and second names are deleted.

By making sure that the macro starts on a name and ends up on the next name, you allow the macro to be run repeatedly. If you assign this macro to the keyboard shortcut Ctrl+J, you can then hold down Ctrl+J and quickly fix records, one after the other.

How not to record a macro: the default state of the macro recorder

The default state of the macro recorder is a stupid state. If you recorded the preceding steps in the macro recorder, the macro recorder would take your actions literally. The English pseudocode for recording these steps would say this:

1. Move to cell A2.
2. Cut cell A2 and paste to cell B1.
3. Move to cell A3.
4. Cut cell A3 and paste to cell C1.
5. Delete rows 2 through 4.
6. Select cell A2.

This macro works, but it works for only one record. After you've recorded this macro, your worksheet looks like the one shown previously in Figure 19.3.

When the default macro runs, it moves the name Vincent Alexander from cell A2 and pastes it on top of the address in cell B1. It then takes the address in cell A3 and pastes it on top of the city in cell C1. After that, it deletes rows 2, 3, and 4, removing the city and state. As shown in Figure 19.4, the macro provides the wrong result.

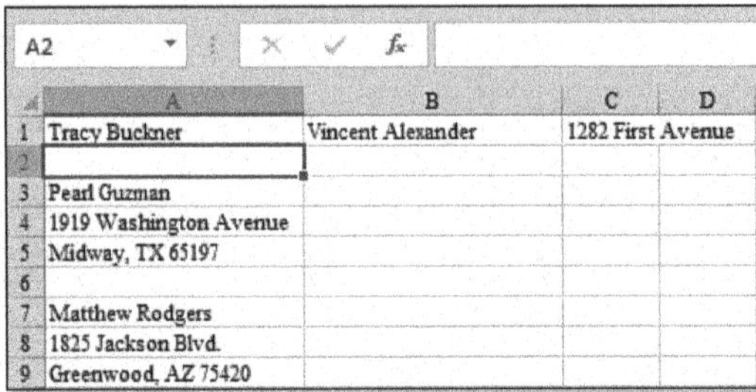

Figure 19.4 When the default macro runs, it ruins two records.

If you blindly ran this macro 100 times to convert 100 addresses, the macro would happily "eat" all 100 records, leaving you with just one record (and not even a correct record). To overcome this problem, use relative references, as discussed in the next section.

Relative references in macro recording

The key to recording a successful macro is to enable the Use Relative References setting in Excel. Had Microsoft made this the default, far more people would have success with their recorded macros. Locate the icon in the Code group on the Developer tab on the ribbon called Use Relative References. If you performed the steps described in the preceding section in relative recording mode, Excel would write code that does this:

1. Move down one cell.
2. Cut that cell.
3. Move up and over one cell and paste.
4. Move left and down two cells.
5. Cut that cell.
6. Move up and over two cells and paste.
7. Move left two cells, move down one cell, and delete three rows.
8. Move up and down one cell to select a single cell.

TIP

Ninety-eight percent of the time you are recording macros, you should have Use Relative Reference turned on.

These steps are far more generic than those recorded using the default state of the macro recorder. These steps work for any record, provided that you started the macro with the cell pointer on the first cell that contains a name.

For this example, you need to record the entire macro with relative recording turned on.

Starting the macro recorder

At this point, you have rehearsed the steps needed for a macro that puts data records into a format that is usable for a mail merge. After you make sure that the cell pointer is starting on the name in cell A1, you are ready to turn on the macro recorder.

You should not be nervous, but you need to perform the steps correctly. If you move the cell pointer in the wrong direction, the macro recorder happily records that for you and plays it back. It is annoying to watch the macro recorder play back your mistakes 100 times a day for the next 5 years. Therefore, follow these steps to create the macro correctly:

1. On the Developer tab, click the Record Macro icon from the Code group. The Record Macro dialog appears, as shown in Figure 19.5.

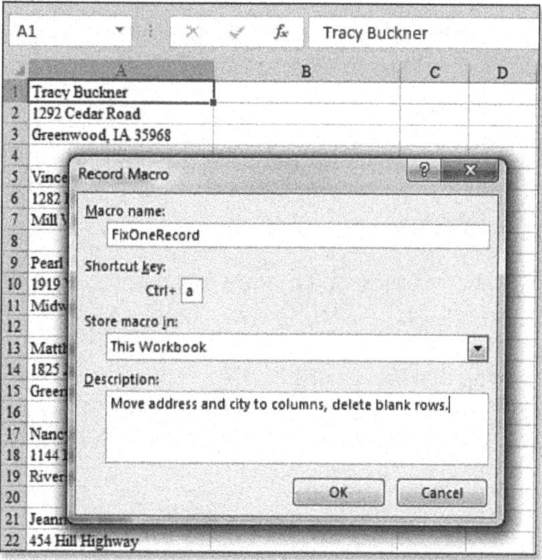

Figure 19.5 After making the needed selections, click OK to begin recording.

2. Excel suggests giving this macro the unimaginative name Macro1. Use any name you want, up to 64 characters and without spaces. For this example, name the macro **FixOneRecord**. Choose a shortcut key for the macro. The shortcut key is important. Because you have to run this macro once for each record in the present example, you might choose something like Ctrl+a, which is easy to press.

3. Make a selection from the Store Macro In drop-down. You have the option of storing the macro in this workbook, in a new workbook, or in the personal macro workbook. If this is a general-purpose macro that you will use every day on every file, it makes sense to store the macro in the personal macro workbook. However, because this macro will be used just to solve a current problem, store it in the current workbook.

4. Fill in a description if you think you will be using this macro long enough to forget what it does. When you are done making selections on the Record Macro dialog (refer to Figure 19.5), click OK. The Record Macro icon changes to a Stop Recording icon.

   NOTE

   Keep in mind that assigning a macro to Ctrl+A overwrites the usual action of that keystroke (selecting all cells). If you are writing a macro that will be used all day, every day, you should use a shortcut key that is not assigned to existing shortcuts, such as Ctrl+J. Although most of the letter keys are already assigned to a shortcut, you can always use the shifted shortcut keys. To assign a macro to Ctrl+Shift+A, press Shift+A into the shortcut field.

5. Click the Use Relative References icon in the Developer tab. The icon is highlighted.

6. Press the down-arrow key to move to the address cell.

7. Press Ctrl+X to cut the address.

8. Press the up-arrow key and then the right-arrow key to move next to the name.

9. Press Ctrl+V to paste the address.

10. Press the left-arrow key once and the down-arrow key twice to move to the cell for city, state, and ZIP Code.

11. Press Ctrl+X to cut the city.

12. Press the up-arrow key twice and the right-arrow key twice to move to the right of the street cell.

13. Press Ctrl+V to paste the city.

14. Press the left-arrow key twice and the down-arrow key once to move to the now-blank row just below the name.

15. Hold down the Shift key while pressing the down-arrow key twice to select the three blank rows.

16. Press Ctrl+- to invoke the Delete command. Press R and then Enter to delete the row.

CHAPTER 19

17. Press the up-arrow key and the down-arrow key. Moving the cell pointer up a cell and then back to the name causes only a single cell to be selected.

18. When you are done, click the Stop Recording button.

This macro successfully fixes any record in the database, provided the cell pointer is on the cell containing the name when you run the macro. Try playing back the macro by pressing Ctrl+A to fix one record. To fix all records, hold down Ctrl+A until all records are fixed.

Running a macro

To run a macro, follow these steps:

1. Click the Macros icon in the Code group of the Developer tab. The Macro dialog appears, as shown in Figure 19.6.

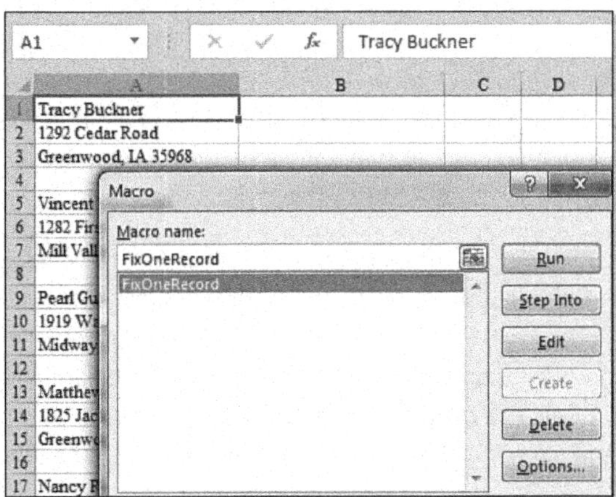

Figure 19.6 Playing back a macro by using the Macro dialog.

2. Select your macro and click the Run button. The macro fixes the first record.

3. Press Ctrl+A to run the FixOneRecord macro. The second record is fixed.

4. Hold down Ctrl+A to repeatedly run the macro. In a matter of seconds, all 100 names are in a format ready to use in a mail merge.

TIP

Displaying the Macro dialog every time you want to run a macro is not efficient. Try running the macro with a shortcut key.

CAUTION

When you run a macro, there is no undo. Therefore, you should save a file before running a new macro on it. It is easy to have accidentally recorded the macro in default mode instead of relative mode. You need to save the macro so that you can easily go back to the current state in case something does not work right.

This example represents an ideal use of a one-time macro. The process of fixing the data someone gave you involved mindless repetition. If there had just been four records, you could have mindlessly fixed them. However, because there were 100 records in this example, it made sense to record a macro and then run the macro repeatedly to solve the problem. You recorded the entire macro in relative mode, and you did not have to edit the macro. You probably run into a few situations a week in which a quick one-time-use macro would make your job easier.

Everyday-use macro example: formatting an invoice register

The macro recorder does not solve all tasks perfectly, however. Many times, you need to record a macro and then edit the recorded code to make the macro a bit more general. This example demonstrates how to do that.

In this example, a system writes out a file every day. This file contains a list of invoices generated on the previous day. The file predictably contains six columns—`NAME`, `DATE`, `INVOICE`, `REVENUE`, `SALES TAX`, and `TOTAL`—as shown in Figure 19.7. The file also looks horrible: The columns are the wrong width, there is no title, and there isn't a Total row at the bottom. You would like a macro that opens this file, makes the columns wider, adds a Total row, adds a title, makes the headings bold, and saves the file with a new name. The following sections describe how to create this macro.

A1 | NAME

	A	B	C	D	E	F
1	NAME	DATE	INVOICE	REVENUE	SALES TAX	TOTAL
2	TERRI DC	2/17/2018	10217	252.11	15.13	267.24
3	ELSIE HO	2/17/2018	10218	68.67	4.12	72.79
4	HAROLD	2/17/2018	10219	111.4	6.68	118.08
5	SHAWN (	2/17/2018	10220	151.47	9.09	160.56
6	KRISTIN.	2/17/2018	10221	131.71	7.9	139.61
7	DAVID A	2/17/2018	10222	221.62	13.3	234.92
8	ROSA PR	2/17/2018	10223	225.02	13.5	238.52
9	NORA SH	2/17/2018	10224	261.84	15.71	277.55
10	CRAIG BI	2/17/2018	10225	195.08	11.7	206.78
11	BILLIE CF	2/17/2018	10226	72.31	4.34	76.65
12	ADAM W	2/17/2018	10227	168.12	10.09	178.21
13	ANDREW	2/17/2018	10228	79.54	4.77	84.31
14	BRANDI :	2/17/2018	10229	258.73	15.52	274.25
15	LAURIE F	2/17/2018	10230	248.44	14.91	263.35
16						

Figure 19.7 Create a macro to format this file every day.

Using the Ctrl+Down-Arrow key to handle a variable number of rows

One of the inherent problems with this example is that your file will have a different number of rows every day. If you record a macro for this today to add totals in row 16, it will not work tomorrow, when you might have 22 invoices. The solution is to use the Ctrl+Down-Arrow key to navigate to the last row of your data.

You use Ctrl and any arrow key to move to the edge of a contiguous range of data. In Figure 19.7, if you press Ctrl+Down Arrow, you would move to cell A15. From cell A15, press Ctrl+Up Arrow to move back to cell A1. You can press the Ctrl+Right Arrow to move to cell F1.

You can also use the Ctrl+arrow key to jump over an abyss of empty cells. If you are currently at the edge of a range (for example, cell F1) and press Ctrl+Right Arrow, Excel jumps over all the blank cells and stops either at the next nonblank cell in row 1 or at the right edge of the worksheet, cell XFD1.

Making sure you find the last record

You might be tempted to start in cell A1, press Ctrl+Down Arrow, and then press the down-arrow key again to move to the first blank row in the data. However, that is not the safest method. This data file is coming from another system. Undoubtedly, one day a cashier will find a way to enter an order without a customer name. She will happen upon the accidental keystroke combination that causes the cash register to allow an order without a customer name. On that day, the Ctrl+Down-Arrow combination will stop at the wrong row and add totals in the middle of your data set. Thus, it is safer to use the Go To dialog to move to A1048576 and use Ctrl+Up Arrow to find the last record.

Recording the macro in a blank workbook

Open a blank workbook and save it with a filename such as **MacroToImportInvoices.xlsm**. You can record your macro in this blank workbook and save it. Then, each day, you can open the macro workbook. The macro will handle opening the data file and formatting it. Go through these steps while the macro recorder is running:

1. Open the file.
2. Press the F5 key to display the Go To dialog.
3. Go to cell A1048576 (the last cell in column A).

4. Turn on relative recording by clicking Use Relative References in the Developer tab. You use relative recording because you want to record the action of jumping to the last row, and that row will be in a different location each day.
5. Press Ctrl+Up Arrow to move to the last row that contains data.
6. Press the down-arrow key to move to the blank row below the last row for data.
7. Type the word `Total`.
8. Move right three cells.
9. Type the formula `=SUM(D$2:D15)`. Press Ctrl+Enter to stay in the current cell. Be sure to include a single dollar sign to lock the start of the range to row 2. Do not use the AutoSum icon to add this formula!
10. Drag the fill handle to the right two cells to copy the formula from D to E and F.
11. Select all cells with Ctrl+Shift+Home.
12. Select Home, Format, AutoFit Column Width to make all the columns wide.
13. Turn off relative recording by clicking the Use Relative References icon in the Developer tab. At this point, you always want to return to row 1 to format the headings. You don't want the recorder to record "Move up 15 rows." You always want to go to row 1.
14. Select row 1.
15. Open the Cell Styles gallery on the Home tab and choose Heading 4. Insert two rows using your favorite method. One method is to press Alt+I+R twice.
16. Move to cell A1.
17. Type the formula `="Invoices for "&TEXT(B4,"mmmm d, yyyy")`. Press Ctrl+Enter to accept the formula and stay in the cell.
18. Open the Cell Styles gallery and choose Title.
19. Use Save As to save the file with a new name to reflect today's date.
20. Click the Stop Recording button.

In this macro example, you use a mix of relative and absolute recording to produce a macro that handles any number of rows of data. The macro will be somewhat useful, with two annoying limitations:

- If you saved the file as 2018-Feb-17Invoices.xls, the macro will attempt to overwrite that file every day.
- The macro will always want to open the same file. This is great if your cash register system always produces a file with the same name in the same folder. However, you might want the option to browse for a different file each day.

Both changes require you to edit the recorded macro. Before editing the macro, here is a look at how to open the Visual Basic Editor and at the syntax of VBA. To see the code to finish this example, refer to "Customizing the everyday-use macro example: `GetOpenFileName` and `GetSaveAsFileName`," later in this chapter.

Editing a macro

To edit a macro, follow these steps:

1. Open the Macro dialog by pressing Alt+F8. The Macro dialog appears.
2. In the Macro dialog, select your macro and click Edit (refer to Figure 19.6). The Visual Basic Editor (VBE) is launched.

A number of panes are available in the VBE, but it is common to have three particular panes displayed, as shown in Figure 19.8:

- **Code pane:** The actual lines of the macro code are in the Code pane, which is usually on the right side of the screen.
- **Project pane:** This pane, which is in the upper left, shows every open workbook. Within the workbooks, you can see objects for each worksheet, an object for this workbook, and one or more code modules. If you cannot see the Project pane, press Ctrl+R or select View, Project Explorer to open it.
- **Properties pane:** This pane, in the lower left, is useful if you design custom dialogs. You can press F4 to display the Properties pane.

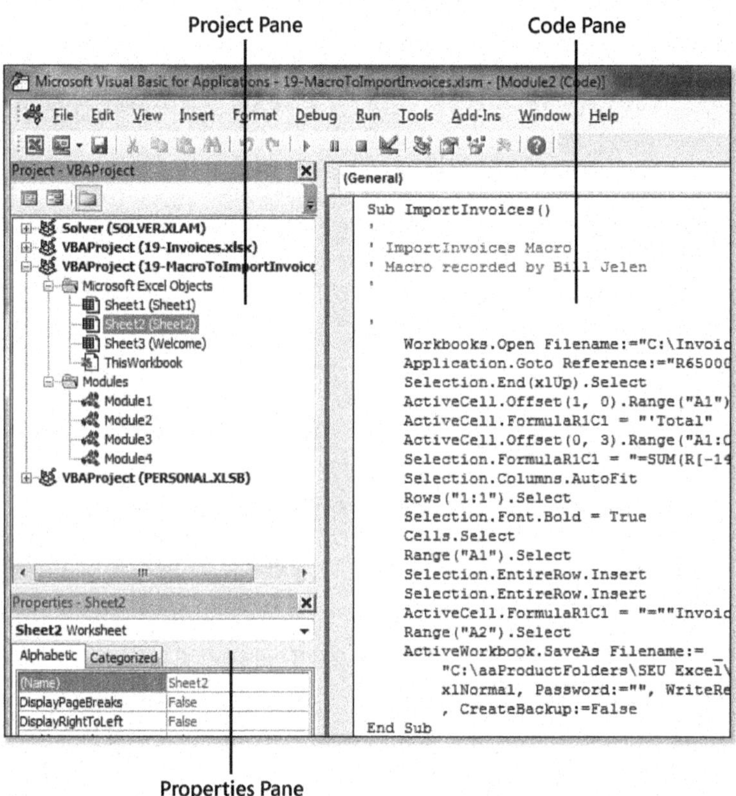

Figure 19.8 The VBE allows editing of recorded macro code.

Understanding VBA code—an analogy

In the 1980s and early 1990s, many people going through school were exposed to an introductory class in a programming language called BASIC. Although Excel macros are written in Visual Basic for Applications, the fact that both languages contain the word *basic* does not mean that BASIC and VBA are the same or even similar. BASIC is a procedural language. VBA is an object-oriented language. In VBA, the focus is on objects. This can make VBA confusing to someone who has learned to program in BASIC.

The syntax of VBA consists of objects, methods, collections, arguments, and properties. If you have never programmed in an object-oriented language, these terms, and the VBA code itself, might seem foreign to you. The following sections compare these five elements to parts of speech:

- An object is similar to a noun.
- A method is similar to a verb.

- A collection is similar to a plural noun.
- An argument is similar to an adverb.
- A property is similar to an adjective.

Each of the following sections describes the similarity between the VBA element and a part of speech. These sections also describe how to recognize the various elements when you examine VBA code.

Comparing object.method to nouns and verbs

As an object-oriented language, the objects in VBA are of primary importance. Think of an object as any noun in Excel. Examples of objects are a cell, a row, a column, a worksheet, and a workbook.

A method is any action that you can perform on an object. This is similar to a verb. You can add a worksheet. You can delete a row. You can clear a cell. In Excel VBA, words such as *Add*, *Delete*, and *Clear* are methods.

Objects and methods are joined by a period, although in VBA, people pronounce the period as *dot*. The object is first, followed by a dot, followed by the method. For example, object.method, which is pronounced "object-dot-method," indicates that the method performs on the object. This is confusing because it is backward from the way English is spoken. If everyone spoke VBA instead of English, we would use sentences such as "car.drive" and "dinner.eat." When you see a period in VBA, it usually means that the word after the period is acting upon the word to the left of the period.

Comparing collections to plural nouns

In an Excel workbook, there is not a single cell but rather a collection of many cells. Many workbooks contain several worksheets. Anytime you have multiple instances of a certain object, VBA refers to this as a *collection*.

The *s* at the end of an object may seem subtle, but it indicates you are dealing with a collection instead of a single object. Whereas ThisWorkbook refers to a single workbook, Workbooks refers to a collection of all the open workbooks. This is an important distinction to understand.

You have two main ways to refer to a single worksheet in a collection of worksheets:

- By its number, such as `Worksheets(1)`
- By its name, such as `Worksheets("Jan")`

Comparing parameters to adverbs

When you invoke a command such as the Save As command, a dialog pops up, and you have the opportunity to specify several options that change how the command is carried out. If the Save As command is a method, the options for it are parameters. Just as an adverb modifies a verb, a parameter modifies a method.

Most of the time, parameters are recorded by using this syntax:

```
ParameterName:=ParameterValue
```

One of the reasons that recorded code gets to be so long is that the macro recorder makes note of every option on the dialog, whether you select it or not.

Consider this line of code for `SaveAs`:

```
ActiveWorkbook.SaveAs Filename:="C:\Something.xlsx", _
    FileFormat:=xlOpenXMLWorkbook, CreateBackup:=False
```

In this recorded macro for `SaveAs`, the recorder noted parameter values for `Filename`, `FileFormat`, and `CreateBackup`. Figure 19.9 shows the Save As dialog. `Filename` and `FileFormat` are evident on the form. However, where is the option for Create Backup?

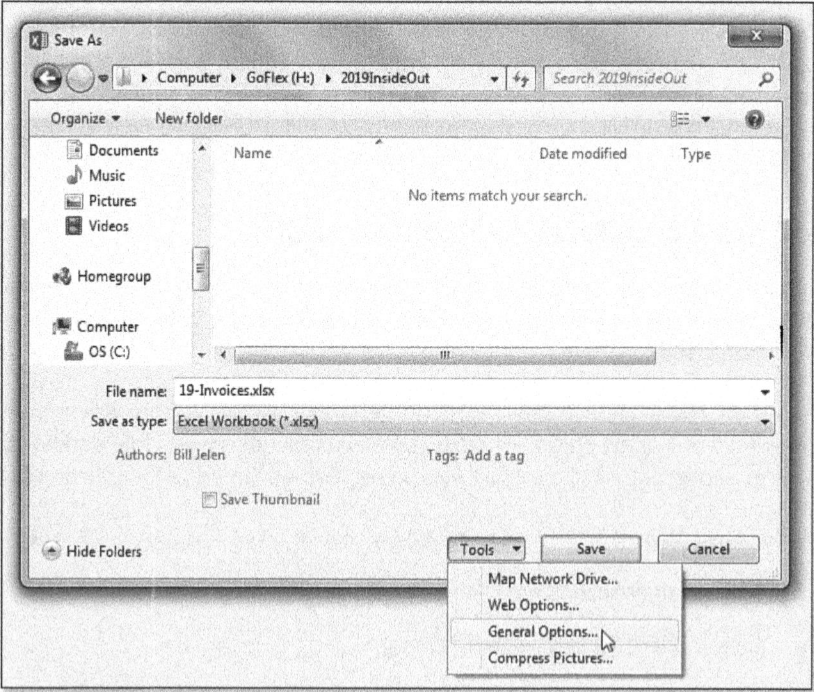

Figure 19.9 It seems like the macro recorder is making up options that are not on the dialog.

In the bottom center of the dialog is a Tools drop-down. If you select Tools, General Options, you see a dialog with four additional options, as shown in Figure 19.10. Even though you did not touch this Save Options dialog, Excel recorded the Backup value from the dialog for you.

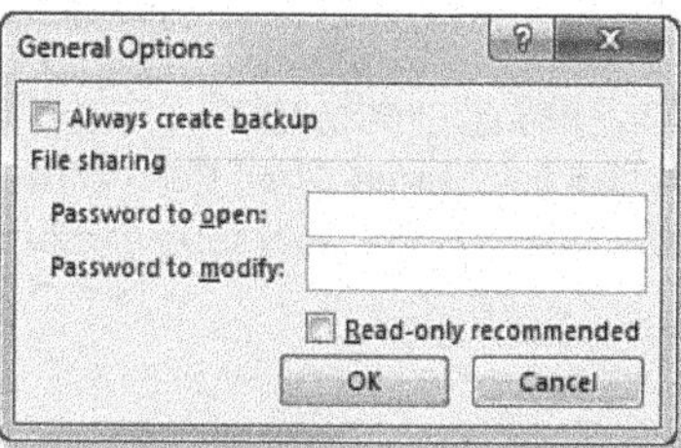

Figure 19.10 Even though you did not touch the Save Options dialog, the macro recorder recorded the values from it.

Parameters have some potentially confusing aspects. Most of the time, there is a space following the method and then a list of one or more `ParameterName:=ParameterValue` constructs, separated by a comma and a space. However, there are a few exceptions:

- If the result of the method is acted upon by another method, the list of parameters is enclosed in parentheses, and there is no space after the method name. One example is when you add a shape to a worksheet and then Excel selects the shape. The code to insert the shape uses the `AddShape` method and five named parameters:

```
ActiveSheet.Shapes.AddShape Type:=msoShapeRectangle, _
 Left:=60, Top:=120, _
 Width:=100, Height:=100
```

- The macro recorder will record the process of adding the shape and then selecting the shape. Because the `.Select` method is acting upon the result of the `.AddShape` method, you see the parameters for the `AddShape` method surrounded by parentheses:

```
ActiveSheet.Shapes.AddShape(Type:=msoShapeRectangle, _
 Left:=60, Top:=120, _
 Width:=100, Height:=100).Select
```

- When you use the parameter name, you can specify the parameters in any sequence you like. The Help topic for the method reveals the official default order for the parameters. If you specify the parameters in the exact sequence specified in Help, you are allowed to leave off the parameter names. However, this is a poor coding practice. Even if you have memorized the default order for the parameters, you cannot assume that everyone else reading your code will know the default order. The problem is that sometimes the macro recorder will record code in this style. For example, here is the actual line of code that was recorded when I added a shape to a worksheet:

```
ActiveSheet.Shapes.AddShape(msoShapeRectangle, 60, 120, 100, 100).Select
```

- It would be difficult to figure out this line of code without looking at the Help topic. To access Help, click anywhere in the method of `AddShape` and then press the F1 key. The Help topic reveals that the correct parameter order is `Type`, `Left`, `Top`, `Width`, `Height`.

NOTE

Keep in mind that parameters are like adverbs. They generally appear with a Parameter Name:=Parameter Value construct. However, there are times when the macro recorder lists the parameter values in their default order, without the parameter names or the :=.

Accessing VBA help

You can click any object, method, argument, or parameter in VBA and press the F1 key to display a complete description of the item. The Help topic lists the valid properties associated with the object and the valid methods that can be used on the object. Often, the Help topic will include an example as well. To use the code in the example, you can highlight the code, press Ctrl+C to copy, and then paste this code directly into the Code pane of the Visual Basic Editor (also known as the VBE).

Comparing adjectives to properties

The final construct in VBA is the adjective used to describe an object. In VBA, adjectives are called *properties*. Think about a cell in Excel with a formula in it. The cell has many properties. These are some of the most popular properties:

- Value (the value shown in the cell)
- Formula (the formula used to calculate the value)
- Font Name
- Font Size
- Font Color
- Cell Interior Color

In VBA, you can check on the value of a property, or you can set the property to a new value. To change several cells to be bold, for example, you would change their `Bold` property to `True`:

```
Selection.Font.Bold = True
```

You can also check to see whether a property equals a certain value:

```
If Selection.Value = 100 then Selection.Font.Bold = True
```

Properties are generally used with the dot construct, and they are almost always followed by =, as contrasted with the := used with parameters (for example, `PropertyName = value`).

Using the analogy while examining recorded code

When you understand that a period generally separates an object from a method or a property, you can start to make sense of the recorded code.

For example, the following line performs the `Open` method:

```
Workbooks.Open Filename:="C:\Invoices.xls"
```

In this example, the `Filename` parameter is shown with `:=` after the parameter name. This first line in the following example performs the `Select` method on one particular member of the Rows collection:

```
Rows("1:1").Select
Selection.Font.Bold = True
```

The second line then sets the `Bold` property of the `Font` property of the selection to `True`. Using these two lines of code is equivalent to selecting row 1 and clicking the Bold icon. You notice that one property, such as `Font`, can have subproperties, such as `Bold` and `Italic`.

> TIP
>
> **In the Excel user interface, you generally need to select a cell before you can change something in it. In a macro, there is no need to select something first. For example, you can replace the two lines in the preceding example with this single line of code: Rows("1:1").Font.Bold = True.**

Using simple variables and object variables

The macro recorder never records a variable, but you can add variables to a macro when you edit the code. Suppose that you need to do a number of operations to the row where the totals will be located. Instead of repeatedly going to the last row in the spreadsheet and pressing End+Up Arrow, you can assign the row number to a variable:

```
FinalRow = Range("A1048576").End(xlup).Row
TotalRow = FinalRow + 1
```

The words `FinalRow` and `TotalRow` are variables that each hold a single value. If you have data in rows 2 through 25 today, `FinalRow` will hold the value `25`, and `TotalRow` will hold the value `26`. This enables you to use efficient code, such as the following:

```
Range("A" & TotalRow).Value = "Total"
Range("C" & TotalRow).Formula = "=SUM(C2:C"& TotalRow & ")"
Range("D" & TotalRow).Formula = "=SUM(D2:D"& TotalRow & ")"
Range("E" & TotalRow).Formula = "=SUM(E2:E"& TotalRow & ")"
```

VBA also offers a powerful variable called an *object variable*. An object variable can be used to represent any object such as a worksheet, chart, or cell. Whereas a simple variable holds one value, an object variable holds values for every property associated with the object.

Object variables are declared using the `Dim` statement and then assigned using the `Set` statement:

```
Dim WSD as worksheet
Set WSD = ActiveWorkbook.Worksheets("Sheet1")
```

Using object variables offers the following advantages:

- It is easier to refer to `WSD` than to `ActiveWorkbook.Worksheets("Sheet1")`.
- If you define the object variable with a `DIM` statement at the beginning of the macro, as you type new lines of code, the VBE's AutoComplete feature shows a list of valid methods and properties for the object.

Using R1C1-style formulas

If you are a history buff of technology, you might know that VisiCalc was the first spreadsheet program for PCs. When Dan Bricklin and Bob Frankston invented VisiCalc, they used the A1 style for naming cells. In those early days, VisiCalc had competitors such as SuperCalc and a Microsoft program called MultiPlan. This early Microsoft spreadsheet used the notation of R1C1 to refer to cell A1. The cell that we know today as E17 would have been called R17C5, for row 17, column 5.

In 1985, Microsoft launched Excel version 1.0 for the Macintosh. Excel originally continued to use the R1C1 style of notation. During the next 10 years, Excel and Lotus 1-2-3 were locked in a bitter battle for market share. Lotus was the early leader, and it had adopted the A1 notation style familiar to VisiCalc customers. To capture more market share, Microsoft allowed Excel to use either A1-style notation or R1C1-style notation. Even today, in Excel, you can turn on R1C1-style notation by selecting File, Options, Formulas, R1C1 Reference Style. In R1C1 reference style, column letters A, B, C are replaced with column numbers 1, 2, 3. Hardly anyone uses R1C1 reference style today; however, the macro recorder always records formulas in R1C1 style.

In R1C1 notation, the reference RC refers to the current cell. You can modify RC by adding a particular row number or column number. For example, R2C refers to the cell in row 2 of the current column. RC1 refers to the cell in this row that is in column 1.

If you put a row number or column number in square brackets, it refers to a relative number of cells from the current cell. If you have a formula in cell D16 and use the reference `R[1]C[-2]`, you are referring to the cell one row below D16 and two columns to the left of D16, which would be cell B17.

You are probably wondering why the macro recorder uses this arcane notation style when recording formulas. It turns out that this style is fantastic for formulas. Whereas a column of formulas in A1 style will have a different formula in each cell, the same column of formulas in R1C1 style will be identical down the column. For example, enter a formula of =D2+E2 in cell F2. When you copy F2 to F3, Excel changes the references of E2 and D2 to be E3 and D3.

Now look at these same formulas in R1C1 style, as shown in Figure 19.11. Every formula in E2:E15 is identical. This makes sense because the formula is saying, "Add the sales tax one cell to the left of me to the merchandise amount that is two cells to the left of me." Every formula in F2:F15 is identical; even the total formulas in D16:F16 are identical.

	4	5	6
1	REVENUE	SALES TAX	TOTAL
2	252.11	=ROUND(0.06*RC[-1],2)	=RC[-1]+RC[-2]
3	68.67	=ROUND(0.06*RC[-1],2)	=RC[-1]+RC[-2]
4	111.4	=ROUND(0.06*RC[-1],2)	=RC[-1]+RC[-2]
5	151.47	=ROUND(0.06*RC[-1],2)	=RC[-1]+RC[-2]
6	131.71	=ROUND(0.06*RC[-1],2)	=RC[-1]+RC[-2]
7	221.62	=ROUND(0.06*RC[-1],2)	=RC[-1]+RC[-2]
8	225.02	=ROUND(0.06*RC[-1],2)	=RC[-1]+RC[-2]
9	261.84	=ROUND(0.06*RC[-1],2)	=RC[-1]+RC[-2]
10	195.08	=ROUND(0.06*RC[-1],2)	=RC[-1]+RC[-2]
11	72.31	=ROUND(0.06*RC[-1],2)	=RC[-1]+RC[-2]
12	168.12	=ROUND(0.06*RC[-1],2)	=RC[-1]+RC[-2]
13	79.54	=ROUND(0.06*RC[-1],2)	=RC[-1]+RC[-2]
14	258.73	=ROUND(0.06*RC[-1],2)	=RC[-1]+RC[-2]
15	248.44	=ROUND(0.06*RC[-1],2)	=RC[-1]+RC[-2]
16	=SUM(R2C:R[-1]C)	=SUM(R2C:R[-1]C)	=SUM(R2C:R[-1]C)
17			

Figure 19.11 In R1C1 style, every formula in F2:F15 is identical.

If you are forced to use A1-style formulas in a macro, you might try to enter the formula in cell F2 and then copy the formula from F2 to the remaining cells:

```
Range("F2").Formula = "=D2+E2"
Range("F2").Copy Destination:=Range("F3:F15")
```

On the other hand, you can enter all the formulas in one line of code when using R1C1-style formulas:

```
Range("F2:F15").FormulaR1C1 = "=RC[-2]+RC[-1]"
```

TIP

Although the macro recorder always records formulas in R1C1 style, you are allowed to write the macros using regular formulas. Change the FormulaR1C1 property to Formula. The following two lines of code are equivalent:

```
Range("F2:F15").FormulaR1C1 = "=RC[-2]+RC[-1]"
Range("F2:F15").Formula = "=D2-E2"
```

Entering spillable formulas in macros

When Dynamic Arrays were introduced in 2018, some people were surprised to learn that a few formulas that did not spill to adjacent cells would suddenly start spilling. If you enter a formula in Excel and see the spill, you can correct it. However, if a macro enters a formula and it suddenly spills instead of appearing in one cell, this could cause problems.

In an effort to not break existing VBA macro solutions, the existing `.Formula` property will never be used to create a spillable formula. If you want to have a formula spill, you should use the new `.Formula2` property.

For example, this code will cause only a 1 in cell A1 instead of the numbers 1 to 30 in A1:A30:

```
Range("A1").Formula = "=SEQUENCE(30)"
```

It is interesting that Excel VBA will add an `@` operator to make sure that you only get a single row: `=@SEQUENCE(30)`.

To actually get the numbers 1 to 30, you would use `.Formula2` as shown here:

```
Range("A1").Formula2 = "=SEQUENCE(30)"
```

Fixing Autosum errors in macros

Probably the most important reason to understand R1C1 formulas is to make sure that the macro recorder recorded the proper formula. This is important because the macro recorder does not do a good job of recording the intent of the AutoSum button. If your data set has numbers in D2:D15 today, pressing AutoSum from cell D16 will record the following line of macro code:

```
Selection.FormulaR1C1 = "=SUM(R[-14]C:R[-1]C)"
```

This formula adds a range from 14 rows above the selection to the cell just above the selection. This works only on days when you have exactly 14 rows of data. This is one of the most annoying bugs in a macro.

It is annoying because this type of logic error will not cause an actual error. If you run this macro on the invoice file you receive tomorrow that contains 20 invoices, the macro will happily total only the last 14 invoices instead of all 20. This means that you could distribute this report with a wrong total for several days before someone realizes that something is amiss.

However, you can correct this formula. You know that you have headings in row 1 and that the first invoice will appear in row 2. You need the macro to sum from row 2 to the row just above the current cell. Therefore, you need to change the formula to this:

```
Selection.FormulaR1C1 = "=SUM(R2C:R[-1]C)"
```

Customizing the everyday-use macro example: GetOpenFileName and GetSaveAsFileName

The everyday-use macro you recorded earlier in this chapter for formatting an invoice register is hard-coded to always open the same file and always save with the same filename. To make the macro more general, you can allow the person running the macro to browse for the file each morning and to specify a new filename during the Save As. Excel offers a straightforward way to display the File Open or File Save As dialog. Here is the code you need to use:

```
FileToOpen = Application.GetOpenFileName( _
 FileFilter:="Excel Files,*.xl*", _
 Title:="Select Today's Invoice File")
```

Note that this code displays the File Open dialog and allows a file to be selected. When you click Open, the dialog assigns the filename to the variable. It does not actually open the file. You then need to open the file specified in the variable:

```
Workbooks.Open Filename:=FileToOpen
```

When you want to ask for the filename to use in saving the file, use this code:

```
NewFileName = Application.GetSaveAsFilename( _
 Title:="Select File Name for Today")
ActiveWorkbook.SaveAs Filename:=NewFileName, _
 FileFormat:=xlOpenXMLWorkbookMacroEnabled
```

The following macro is the final macro to use each day:

```
Sub ImportInvoicesFixed()
' ImportInvoices Macro
' With Changes
 FileToOpen = Application.GetOpenFileName( _
  FileFilter:= _
  "Excel files (*.xls;*.xlsb;*.xlsx;*.xlsm)" & _
  ",*.xls;*.xlsb;*.xlsx;*.xlsm)", _
  Title:="Select Today's Invoice File")
 Workbooks.Open Filename:=FileToOpen
 Application.Goto Reference:="R1048576C1"
 Selection.End(xlUp).Select
 ActiveCell.Offset(1, 0).Range("A1").Select
 ActiveCell.FormulaR1C1 = "Total"
 ActiveCell.Offset(0, 3).Range("A1").Select
 Selection.FormulaR1C1 = "=SUM(R2C:R[-1]C)"
 Selection.AutoFill Destination:=ActiveCell.Range("A1:C1"), Type:= _
  xlFillDefault
 ActiveCell.Range("A1:C1").Select
 Range(Selection, Cells(1)).Select
 Selection.Columns.AutoFit
 Rows("1:1").Select
 Selection.Style = "Heading 4"
```

```
 Selection.Insert Shift:=xlDown
 Selection.Insert Shift:=xlDown
 Range("A1").Select
 Selection.FormulaR1C1 = "=""Invoices for ""&TEXT(R[3]C[1],""mmmm d, yyyy"")"
 Selection.Style = "Title"
 NewFileName = Application.GetSaveAsFilename( _
  Title:="Select File Name for Today")
 ActiveWorkbook.SaveAs Filename:=NewFileName, _
  FileFormat:=xlOpenXMLWorkbookMacroEnabled
End Sub
```

Of the 22 lines in the macro, you added two lines and corrected two lines. This is typical because between 10% and 20% of a recorded macro generally needs to be adjusted.

From-scratch macro example: loops, flow control, and referring to ranges

Suppose you work for a company that sells printers and scanners to commercial accounts. When you sell a piece of hardware, you also try to sell a service plan for that hardware. Customers in your state are taxed. Your accounting software provides a daily download that looks like columns A:D in Figure 19.12.

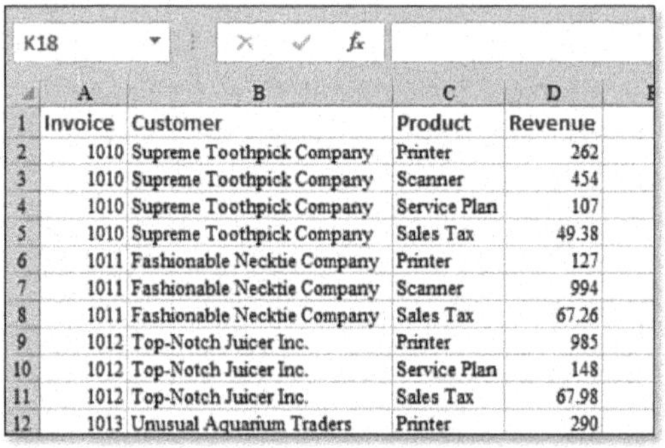

K18

	A	B	C	D
1	Invoice	Customer	Product	Revenue
2	1010	Supreme Toothpick Company	Printer	262
3	1010	Supreme Toothpick Company	Scanner	454
4	1010	Supreme Toothpick Company	Service Plan	107
5	1010	Supreme Toothpick Company	Sales Tax	49.38
6	1011	Fashionable Necktie Company	Printer	127
7	1011	Fashionable Necktie Company	Scanner	994
8	1011	Fashionable Necktie Company	Sales Tax	67.26
9	1012	Top-Notch Juicer Inc.	Printer	985
10	1012	Top-Notch Juicer Inc.	Service Plan	148
11	1012	Top-Notch Juicer Inc.	Sales Tax	67.98
12	1013	Unusual Aquarium Traders	Printer	290

Figure 19.12 Your accounting software groups all hardware, service, and tax amounts into a single column.

You want to create a macro that examines each row in the data set and carries out a different action, based on the value in column C. You will probably want to write this macro from scratch. The following sections describe how to do this.

Finding the last row with data

The recorded macro examples discussed earlier in this chapter suggested going to the last cell in column A and then pressing End followed by the up-arrow key to find the last row with data in column A.

In legacy versions of Excel, this would be accomplished with this code:

```
FinalRow = Range("A65536").End(xlUp).Row
```

This command became more complicated in Excel 2007. The last row in the worksheet is either 1048576 or 65536, depending on whether the workbook is in compatibility mode. The solution is to use `Rows.Count`, which is shorthand for `Application.Rows.Count`. This solution returns the total number of rows available in the current worksheet. Note that this property returns 65,536 in compatibility mode and 1,048,576 in regular mode.

The following line of code finds the last row in column A with a nonblank value:

```
FinalRow = Cells(Rows.Count, 1).End(xlUp).Row
```

> TIP
>
> **Use XLUP as the argument for END. The lowercase "l" used in the code is often seen as the numeral 1. Using x1Up instead of xlUp causes an error.**

Looping through all rows

The loop most commonly used in VBA is a `For-Next` loop. This is identical to the loop that you might have learned about in a BASIC class.

In this example, the loop starts with a `For` statement. You specify that on each pass through the loop, a certain variable will change from a low value to a high value. This simple macro will run through the loop 10 times. On the first pass through the loop, the variable x will be equal to 1. The two lines inside the loop will assign the value 1 to cells A1 and B1. When the macro encounters the `Next x` line, it returns to the start of the loop, increments x by 1, and runs through the loop again. The next time through the loop, the value of x is 2. Cell A2 is assigned the number 2, and cell B2 shows 4, which is the square of 2. Eventually, x will be equal to 10. At the `Next x` line, the macro will allow the loop to finish. The following is the code for this macro:

```
Sub WriteSquares()
 For x = 1 To 10
  Cells(x, 1).Value = x
  Cells(x, 2).Value = x * x
 Next x
End Sub
```

After you run this macro, you have a simple table that shows the numbers 1 through 10 and their squares, as shown in Figure 19.13.

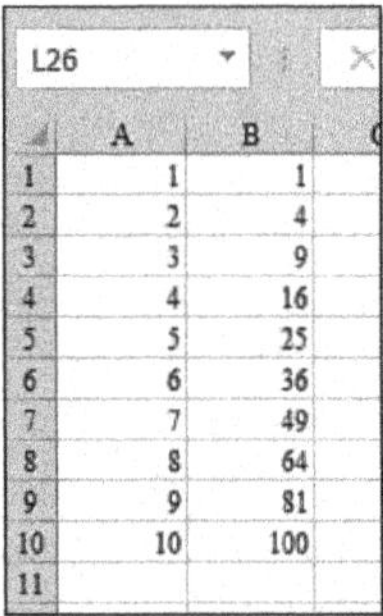

Figure 19.13 This simple loop fills in ten rows.

After a loop is written, it can be adjusted easily. For example, if you want a table showing all the squares from 1 to 100, you can adjust the `For x = 1 to 10` line to be `For x = 1 to 100`.

There is an optional clause in the `For` statement called the *step value*. If no step value is shown, the program moves through the loop by incrementing the variable by one each time through the loop. If you wanted to check only the even-numbered rows, you could change the loop to be `For x = 2 to 100 step 2`.

If you are going to be optionally deleting rows from a range of data, it is important to start at the bottom and proceed to the top of the range. You would use `-1` as the step value:

```
For x = 100 to 1 step -1
```

Referring to ranges

The macro recorder uses the `Range` property to refer to a particular range. You might see the macro recorder refer to ranges such as `Range("B3")` and `Range("W1:Z100")`.

The loop code shown in the preceding section emulates this style of referring to ranges. On the third time through the loop, this line of code would refer to cell B3:

```
Range("B" & x).value = x * x
```

However, how would you handle looping through each column? If you want to continue using the `Range` property, you need to jump through some hoops to figure out the letter associated with column 5:

```
For y = 1 to 26
 ThisCol = Chr(64+y)
 Range(ThisCol & 1).value = ThisCol
Next y
```

This method works fine if you are using 26 or fewer columns. However, if you need to loop through all the columns out to column XFD, you will spend all day trying to write the logic to assign the column label `WMJ` to column 15896.

The solution is to use the `Cells` property instead of the `Range` property. `Cells` requires you to specify a numeric row number and a numeric column number. For example, cell B3 is specified as follows:

```
Cells(3, 2)
```

If you need to refer to a rectangular range, you can use the `Resize` property. `Resize` requires you to specify the number of rows and the number of columns. For example, to refer to W1:Z100, use this:

```
Cells(1, 23).Resize(100, 4)
```

It is difficult to figure out that this refers to W1:Z100, but it enables you to loop through rows or columns.

You can use the following code to make every other column bold:

```
For y = 1 to 100 step 2
 Cells(1, y).Resize(200, 1).Font.Bold = True
Next y
```

Combining a loop with `FinalRow`

Earlier in this chapter, you learned how to use the Ctrl+Up Arrow to find the final row in a data set. After finding the final row in the data set and assigning it to a variable, you can specify that the loop should run through `FinalRow`:

```
FinalRow = Cells(Rows.Count, 1).End(xlUp).row
For x = 2 to FinalRow
 ' Perform some action
Next x
```

Making decisions by using flow control

Flow control is the capability to make decisions within a macro. The following sections describe two commonly used flow control constructs: If-End If and Select Case.

Using the `If-End If` construct

Suppose you need a macro to delete any records that say Sales Tax. You could accomplish this with a simple `If-End If` construct:

```
If Cells(x, 4).Value = "Sales Tax" Then
 Rows(x).Delete
End If
```

This construct always starts with the word `If`, followed by a logical test, followed by the word `Then`. Every line between the first line and the `End If` line is executed only if the logical test is `True`.

Now suppose that you want to enhance the macro so that any other amounts that contain service plan revenue are moved to column F. To do this, you use the `ElseIf` line to enter a second condition and block of lines to be used in that condition:

```
If Cells(x, 4).Value = "Sales Tax" Then
 Cells(x, 1).EntireRow.Delete
ElseIf Cells(x, 4).Value = "Service Plan" Then
 Cells(x, 5).Cut Destination:=Cells(x, 6)
End If
```

You could continue adding `ElseIf` statements to handle other situations. Eventually, just before the `End If`, you could add an `Else` block to handle any other condition you have not thought about.

> NOTE
>
> **When you want to delete an entire row, you can refer to one cell in the row and add** `.EntireRow.Delete`**. Alternatively, you could use** `Rows(x).Delete`**.**

Using the `Select Case` construct

If you reach a point where you have many `ElseIf` statements all testing the same value, it might make sense to switch to a `Select Case` construct. For example, suppose you want to loop through all the records to examine the product in column C. If column C contains a printer, you want to move the amount in column D to a new column E. Scanner revenue should go to a new column F. Service plans go to a new column H. Sales tax goes to a new column I. You should also handle the situation when something is sold that contains none of those products. In that case, you would move the revenue to a new column G.

The construct begins with `Select Case` and then the value to check. The construct ends with `End Select`, which is similar to `End If`.

Each subblock of code starts with the word `Case` and one or more possible values. If you needed to check for `Printer` or `Printers`, you would enclose each in quotes and separate them with a comma.

After checking for all the possible values you can think of, you might add a `Case Else` subblock to handle any other stray values that might be entered in column C.

The following code checks to see what product is in column C. Depending on the product, the program copies the revenue from column D to a specific column:

```
Select Case Cells(x, 3).Value
 Case "Printer", "Printers"
```

```
  Cells(x, 4).Copy Destination:=Cells(x, 5)
 Case "Scanner", "Scanners"
  Cells(x, 4).Copy Destination:=Cells(x, 6)
 Case "Service Plan"
  Cells(x, 4).Copy Destination:=Cells(x, 8)
 Case "Sales Tax"
  Cells(x, 4).Copy Destination:=Cells(x, 9)
 Case Else
 ' Something unexpected was sold
  Cells(x, 4).Copy Destination:=Cells(x, 7)
End Select
```

Putting together the from-scratch example: testing each record in a loop

Using the building blocks described in the preceding sections, you can now write the code for a macro that finds the last row, loops through the records, and copies the total revenue to the appropriate column. Now you need to add new headings for the additional columns.

The macro should use the `End` property to locate the final row and prefill columns E through I with zeros. Next, it should loop from row 2 down to the final row. For each record, the revenue column should be moved to one of the columns. At the end of the loop, the program alerts you that the program is complete, using a `MsgBox` command. The following is the complete code of this macro:

```
Sub MoveRevenue2()
 FinalRow = Cells(Rows.Count, 1).End(xlUp).Row
 Range("E2", Cells(FinalRow, 9)).Value = 0
 For x = 2 To FinalRow
  Select Case Cells(x, 3).Value
  Case "Printer", "Printers"
   Cells(x, 4).Copy Destination:=Cells(x, 5)
  Case "Scanner", "Scanners"
   Cells(x, 4).Copy Destination:=Cells(x, 6)
  Case "Service Plan"
   Cells(x, 4).Copy Destination:=Cells(x, 8)
  Case "Sales Tax"
   Cells(x, 4).Copy Destination:=Cells(x, 9)
  Case Else
   ' Something unexpected was sold - Accessory?
   Cells(x, 4).Copy Destination:=Cells(x, 7)
  End Select
 Next x
 MsgBox "Macro complete"
End Sub
```

CHAPTER 19

TIP

An alternative syntax of the `Range` property is to specify the top-left and bottom-right cells in the range, separated by a comma. In the macro described here, for example, you know you want to fill from cell E2 to the last row in column I. You can describe this range as follows:

```
Range("E2", Cells(FinalRow, 9))
```

This syntax is sometimes simpler than using Cells() and Resize().

After you run this macro, you see that the revenue amounts have been copied to the appropriate columns, as shown in Figure 19.14.

R27

	A	B	C	D	E	F	G	H	I
1	Invoice	Customer	Product	Revenue	Printer	Scanner	Accessory	Service	Tax
2	1010	Supreme Toothpick Company	Printer	262	262	0	0	0	0
3	1010	Supreme Toothpick Company	Scanner	454	0	454	0	0	0
4	1010	Supreme Toothpick Company	Service Plan	107	0	0	0	107	0
5	1010	Supreme Toothpick Company	Sales Tax	49.38	0	0	0	0	49.38
6	1011	Fashionable Necktie Company	Printer	127	127	0	0	0	0
7	1011	Fashionable Necktie Company	Scanner	994	0	994	0	0	0
8	1011	Fashionable Necktie Company	Sales Tax	67.26	0	0	0	0	67.26
9	1012	Top-Notch Juicer Inc.	Printer	985	985	0	0	0	0
10	1012	Top-Notch Juicer Inc.	Service Plan	148	0	0	0	148	0
11	1012	Top-Notch Juicer Inc.	Sales Tax	67.98	0	0	0	0	67.98

Figure 19.14 After running the macro, you have a breakout of revenue by product.

A special case: deleting some records

If a loop is conditionally deleting records, you will run into trouble if it is a typical `For-Next` loop. Suppose you want to delete all the sales tax records, as follows:

```
Sub ThisWontWork()
 FinalRow = Cells(Rows.Count, 1).End(xlUp).Row
 For x = 2 To FinalRow
  If Cells(x, 3).Value = "Sales Tax" Then
   Cells(x, 1).EntireRow.Delete
  Else
   Cells(x, 5).Value = "Checked"
  End If
 Next x
End Sub
```

Consider the data in Figure 19.15. The first time through the loop, x is equal to 2. Cell C2 does not contain sales tax, so cell E2 has the word "checked." A similar result occurs for rows 3 and 4. The fourth time through the loop, cell C5 contains sales tax. The macro deletes the tax in row 5.

However, Excel then moves the old row 6 up to row 5, as shown in Figure 19.16. The next time through the loop, the program inspects row 6, and the data that is now in row 5 will never be checked.

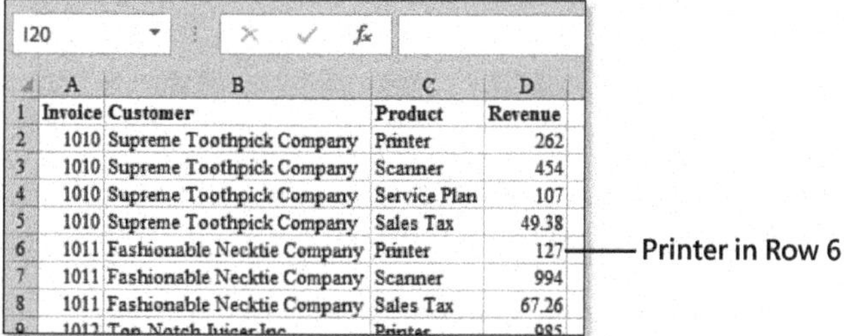
I20

	A	B	C	D
1	Invoice	Customer	Product	Revenue
2	1010	Supreme Toothpick Company	Printer	262
3	1010	Supreme Toothpick Company	Scanner	454
4	1010	Supreme Toothpick Company	Service Plan	107
5	1010	Supreme Toothpick Company	Sales Tax	49.38
6	1011	Fashionable Necktie Company	Printer	127
7	1011	Fashionable Necktie Company	Scanner	994
8	1011	Fashionable Necktie Company	Sales Tax	67.26

Figure 19.15 Before the macro deletes row 5, the Printer record is in row 6.

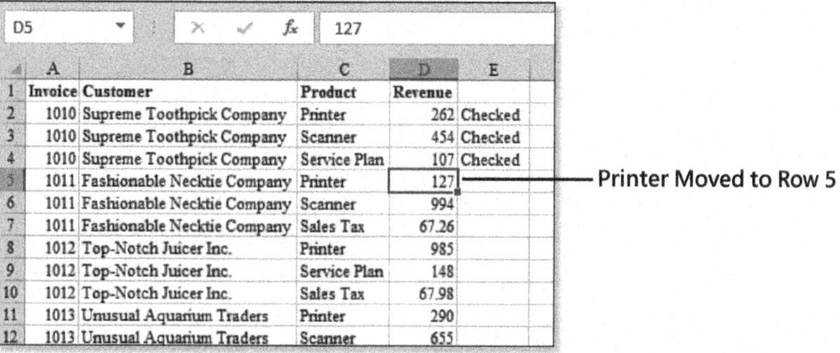
D5 127

	A	B	C	D	E
1	Invoice	Customer	Product	Revenue	
2	1010	Supreme Toothpick Company	Printer	262	Checked
3	1010	Supreme Toothpick Company	Scanner	454	Checked
4	1010	Supreme Toothpick Company	Service Plan	107	Checked
5	1011	Fashionable Necktie Company	Printer	127	
6	1011	Fashionable Necktie Company	Scanner	994	
7	1011	Fashionable Necktie Company	Sales Tax	67.26	
8	1012	Top-Notch Juicer Inc.	Printer	985	
9	1012	Top-Notch Juicer Inc.	Service Plan	148	
10	1012	Top-Notch Juicer Inc.	Sales Tax	67.98	
11	1013	Unusual Aquarium Traders	Printer	290	
12	1013	Unusual Aquarium Traders	Scanner	655	

Figure 19.16 The old row 6 data moves up to occupy the deleted row 5. However, the macro blindly moves on to check row 6 next. The printer that moved to row 5 never gets checked.

The macro succeeds in deleting tax. However, several rows were not checked, as shown in Figure 19.17. Further, several extra blank rows at the bottom were likely checked needlessly.

	A	B	C	D	E
1	Invoice	Customer	Product	Revenue	
2	1010	Supreme Toothpick Company	Printer	262	Checked
3	1010	Supreme Toothpick Company	Scanner	454	Checked
4	1010	Supreme Toothpick Company	Service Plan	107	Checked
5	1011	Fashionable Necktie Company	Printer	127	
6	1011	Fashionable Necktie Company	Scanner	994	Checked
7	1012	Top-Notch Juicer Inc.	Printer	985	
8	1012	Top-Notch Juicer Inc.	Service Plan	148	Checked
9	1013	Unusual Aquarium Traders	Printer	290	

Figure 19.17 Several rows were not checked in this loop.

The solution is to have the loop run backward. You need to start at the final row and proceed up through the sheet to row 2. When the macro deletes tax in row 31, it can then proceed to checking row 30, knowing that nothing has been destroyed (yet) in row 30 and above.

To reverse the flow of the loop, you have to tell the loop to start at the final row, but you also have to tell the loop to use a step value of -1. The start of the loop would use this line of code:

```
For x = FinalRow to 2 Step -1
```

The macro you need here represents a fairly common task: looping through all the records to do something conditionally to each record.

The following macro correctly deletes all the sales tax records:

```
Sub DeleteTaxOK()
 FinalRow = Cells(Rows.Count, 1).End(xlUp).Row
 For x = FinalRow To 2 Step -1
  If Cells(x, 3).Value = "Sales Tax" Then
   Cells(x, 1).EntireRow.Delete
  Else
   Cells(x, 5).Value = "Checked"
  End If
 Next x
End Sub
```


For the example described here, the macro recorder would be almost no help. You would have to write this simple macro from scratch. However, it is a powerful macro that can simplify tasks when you have hundreds of thousands of rows of data.

Inside OUT

Running a macro in slow motion is the key to successful debugging.

Seeing Figures 19.15 and 19.16 is the key in figuring out why your macro to delete some rows was not deleting all of the desired rows.

When you run a macro, the execution is so fast, you never can see those intermediate results. They key to getting those screenshots is to run the macro in debugging mode.

Switch to VBA. Click anywhere on any line of code in the macro that you want to debug. Press F8 to begin running the macro one line at a time. Each time you press F8, a line of code is highlighted in yellow. Press F8 to run the line of code in yellow.

Stepping through the code one line at a time allows you to see the code and the results of the code side-by-side. You can switch back and forth between Excel and VBA, or if you have two monitors, arrange the screens so VBA is on one monitor and Excel is on the

other monitor. If you have a large monitor, you can arrange the windows so Excel and the VBA Editor window are both arranged on the screen.

Keep pressing F8 to run the next line of code. If you discover the problem, you can press F5 to run the rest of the macro at normal speed or select Run, Reset from the VBA Editor to stop the macro.

TROUBLESHOOTING

Sometimes while debugging a macro, the code will work fine as you are stepping through the code. But it fails when you run the macro at full speed.

As you are stepping through the code, you are pressing F8 and then looking at the Excel screen. This might take you a few seconds between commands. Those few seconds often give Excel the time to complete the last command issued by the VBA macro.

In contrast, when you run the macro at full speed, Excel might not be done with one command before it tries to run the next command.

Consider the following pseudocode:

```
Add Error Bars to a Chart
Format the newly added Error Bars
```

If the second line tries to run before the error bars are added, then you will get an error. This never used to be a problem, but with Excel today, it happens more often.

You can add a few lines of code, as shown below, to encourage the Excel macro to slow down and allow pending events to complete. The hardest part is figuring out which lines of code need the `DoEvents` code. In the example described here, the following code might fix the problem:

```
'Add Error Bars to a Chart
Application.DoEvents
'Format the newly added Error Bars
```

Combination macro example: creating a report for each customer

Many real-life scenarios require you to use a combination of recorded code and code written from scratch. For example, Figure 19.18 shows a data set with all your invoices for the year. In this case, suppose you would like to produce a workbook for each customer that you can mail to the customer.

	A	B	C	D	E	F
1	Customer	Invoice	Date	Purchases	Paid	Open Balance
2	Hip Lawn Corporation	1001	1/4/18	8846	8846	0
3	Vivid Chopstick Traders	1002	1/4/18	1688	1688	0
4	Unusual Doorbell Company	1003	1/4/18	8415	8415	0
5	Excellent Utensil Corporatic	1004	1/4/18	2619	2619	0
6	Hip Lawn Corporation	1005	1/5/18	11476	11476	0
7	Fascinating Oven Supply	1006	1/5/18	4958	0	4958
8	Savory Glass Inc.	1007	1/5/18	11243	11243	0
9	Superior Bobsled Corporati	1008	1/5/18	4419	4419	0
10	Hip Lawn Corporation	1009	1/5/18	12562	12562	0
11	Savory Glass Inc.	1010	1/5/18	7409	7409	0

Figure 19.18 The goal is to provide a subset of this data to each customer.

One way to handle this task would be to use an advanced filter to get a list of all unique customers in column A. You would then loop through these customers, applying an AutoFilter to the data set to see only the customers that match the selected customer. After the data set is filtered, you can select the visible cells only and copy them to a new workbook. Then you can save the workbook with the name of the customer and return to the original workbook.

You can start by creating a blank procedure with comments to spell out the steps in the preceding paragraphs. Then you add code for the loop and other simple tasks, such as copying the selection to a new workbook. Whenever you encounter a step for which you have never written code, you can leave a comment with question marks. This enables you to go back and record parts of the process to finish the macro.

NOTE

It is common to indent each line of code with four spaces. Any lines of code inside an If-EndIf block or inside a For-Next loop are indented an additional four spaces. If you have typed a line of code that is indented eight spaces and then press Enter at the end of the line of code, the VBE automatically indents the next line to eight spaces. Each press of the Tab key indents by an additional four spaces. Pressing Shift+Tab removes four spaces of indentation. Although four is the default number of spaces for a tab, you can change this to any number of spaces using Tools, Options in the Visual Basic Editor.

Your first pass at a well-commented macro might look like this:

```
Sub ProduceReportForEachCustomer()
  ' Define object variables for new workbook
  ' Suffix of N means New
 Dim WBN As Workbook
 Dim WSN As Worksheet
  ' Define object variables for the current workbook
  ' Suffix of O means Old
 Dim WBO As Workbook
 Dim WSO As Worksheet
 Set WBO = ActiveWorkbook
 Set WSO = ActiveSheet
```

```
 ' Find the FinalRow in today's dataset
 FinalRow = Cells(Rows.Count, 1).End(xlUp).Row
 ' Use an Advanced filter to copy unique customers
 ' from column A to column H
 ' ???
 'Find the final customer in column H
 FinalCust = Cells(Rows.Count, 8).End(xlUp).Row
 ' Loop through each customer
 For x = 2 To FinalCust
  ' Turn on the AutoFilter for this customer
  ' ???
  ' Create a new workbook
  Set WBN = Workbooks.Add
  Set WSN = WBN.Worksheets(1)
  ' In the original workbook, select visible cells
  ' ???
  ' Copy the selection to the new workbook
  Selection.Copy Destination:=WSN.Cells(3, 1)
  ' AutoFit columns in the new workbook
  WSN.Columns.AutoFit
  ' Add a title to the new workbook
  WSN.Range("A1").Value = _
  "Recap of Purchases for " & WSN.Cells(4, 1).Value
  ' Save the new book
  WBN.SaveAs Filename:="C:\" & WSN.Cells(4, 1).Value & ".xlsx"
  WBN.Close SaveChanges:=False
  'Return to the original workbook
  WBO.Activate
  WSN.Select
 Next x
End Sub
```

CHAPTER 19

The following sections explain that to create this macro, you need to figure out how to code the advanced filter to copy a unique list of customers to column H. You then need to figure out how to apply a filter to column A. Finally, you need to figure out how to select only the visible cells from the filter.

Using the Advanced Filter for unique records

You need to figure out how to use an advanced filter to finish the following section of code:

```
' Find the FinalRow in today's dataset
FinalRow = Cells(Rows.Count, 1).End(xlUp).Row
' Use an Advanced filter to copy unique customers
' from column A to column H
' ???
```

To use an advanced filter on this section of code, follow these steps:

1. Turn on the macro recorder.
2. On the Data tab, in the Sort & Filter group, click the Advanced icon to open the Advanced Filter dialog.

3. Select the option Copy to Another Location.

4. Adjust the list range to refer only to column A. The copy-to range will be cell H1.

5. Check the Unique Records Only box.

6. When the dialog looks as shown in Figure 19.19, click OK. The result is a new range of data in column H, with each customer listed just once, as shown in Figure 19.20.

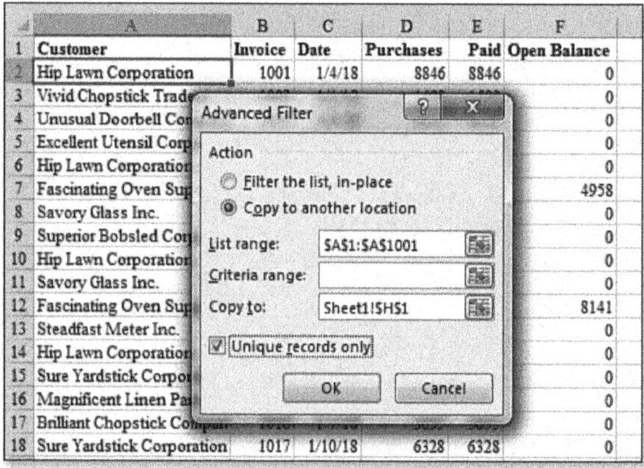

Figure 19.19 Using an advanced filter to get a unique list of customers.

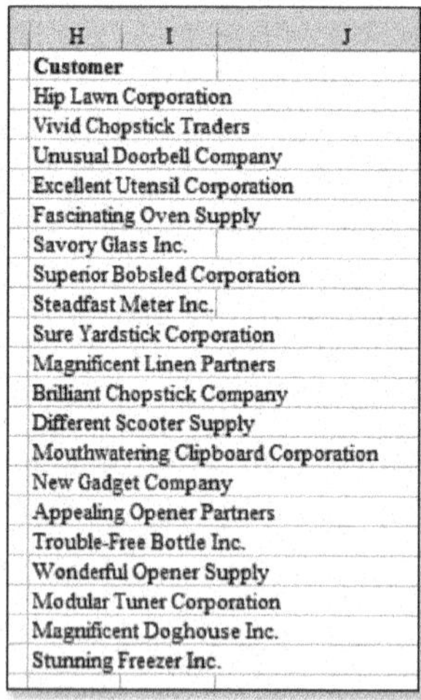

Customer
Hip Lawn Corporation
Vivid Chopstick Traders
Unusual Doorbell Company
Excellent Utensil Corporation
Fascinating Oven Supply
Savory Glass Inc.
Superior Bobsled Corporation
Steadfast Meter Inc.
Sure Yardstick Corporation
Magnificent Linen Partners
Brilliant Chopstick Company
Different Scooter Supply
Mouthwatering Clipboard Corporation
New Gadget Company
Appealing Opener Partners
Trouble-Free Bottle Inc.
Wonderful Opener Supply
Modular Tuner Corporation
Magnificent Doghouse Inc.
Stunning Freezer Inc.

Figure 19.20 The advanced filter produces a list of customers for the macro to loop through.

7. On the Developer tab, click Stop Recording.

8. Use the Macros button to select Macro1 and then select Edit.

Even though the Advanced Filter dialog is still one of the most complicated facets of Excel, the recorded macro is remarkably simple:

```
Sub Macro1()
'
' Macro1 Macro
'
'
 Range("A1:A1001").AdvancedFilter Action:=xlFilterCopy, CopyToRange:=Range( _
  "H1"), Unique:=True
 Range("H1").Select
End Sub
```

In your macro, there is no reason to select cell H1, so delete that line of code. The remaining problem is that the macro recorder hard-coded that today's data set contains 1,001 rows. You might want to generalize this to handle any number of rows. The following code reflects these changes:

```
FinalRow = Cells(Rows.Count, 1).End(xlUp).Row
Range("A1:A" & FinalRow) .AdvancedFilter Action:=xlFilterCopy, _
 CopyToRange:=Range("H1"), Unique:=True
```

Using AutoFilter

When you have a list of customers, the macro loops through each customer. The goal is to use an AutoFilter to display only the records for each particular customer. Next, finish this section of code as follows:

```
' Loop through each customer
For x = 2 To FinalCust
  ' Turn on the AutoFilter for this customer
  ' ???
```

To apply an AutoFilter to this section of code, follow these steps:

1. On the Developer tab, select Record Macro.
2. On the Home tab, select the icon Sort & Filter–Filter. Drop-down arrows are turned on for each field.
3. In the drop-down in cell A1, clear Select All and then select Hip Lawn Corporation.
4. Back on the Developer tab, stop recording the macro.
5. Use the Macros button to locate and edit Macro2 as follows:

```
Sub Macro2()
'
' Macro2 Macro
'
'
```

CHAPTER 19

```
    Range("A2").Select
    Application.CutCopyMode = False
    Selection.AutoFilter
    Selection.AutoFilter Field:=1, Criteria1:="Hip Lawn Corporation"
End Sub
```

The macro recorder always does too much selecting. You rarely have to select something before you can operate on it. You can theorize that the only line of this macro that matters is the `Selection.AutoFilter` line. Because you will always be looking at the AutoFilter drop-down in cell A1, you can replace `Selection` with `Range("A1")`. Rather than continually ask for one specific customer, you can replace the end of the line with a reference to a cell in column H:

```
Range("A1").AutoFilter Field:=1, _
Criteria1:=Cells(x,8).Value
```

TIP

Even though you have an existing Module1 with your code, Excel chooses to record the new macro into a new module. Therefore, you need to copy recorded code from Module2 and then use the Project Explorer to switch to Module1 to paste the code into your macro.

Selecting Visible Cells Only

After you use the AutoFilter in the macro, you see records for only one customer. However, the other records are still there, but they are hidden. If you copied the range to a new worksheet, all the hidden rows would come along, and you would end up with 20 copies of your entire data set.

The long way to select only visible cells is to press F5 to display the Go To dialog. In the Go To dialog, click the Special button and then click Visible Cells Only. However, the shortcut is to press Alt+;.

To learn how to select only visible cells in VBA, record the macro by following these steps:

1. Select the data in columns A through F.
2. Turn on the macro recorder and press Alt+;.
3. Stop the macro recorder. You should see that the recorded macro has just one line of code:

```
Sub Macro5()
'
' Macro5 Macro
'
'
    Selection.SpecialCells(xlCellTypeVisible).Select
End Sub
```

In your original outline of the macro, you had contemplated selecting only visible cells and then doing the copy in another statement, like this:

```
' In the original workbook, select visible cells
' ???
' Copy the selection to the new workbook
Selection.Copy Destination:=WSN.Cells(3, 1)
```

Instead, copy the visible cells in one statement:

```
' In the original workbook, select visible cells
WSO.Range("A1:F" & FinalRow).SpecialCells(xlCellTypeVisible).Copy _
 Destination:=WSN.Cells(3, 1)
```

Combination macro example: putting it all together

The following macro started as a bunch of comments and a skeleton of a loop:

```
Sub ProduceReportForEachCustomerFinished()
 ' Define object variables for new workbook
 Dim WBN As Workbook
 Dim WSN As Worksheet
 ' Define object variables for the current workbook
 Dim WBO As Workbook
 Dim WSO As Worksheet
 Set WBO = ActiveWorkbook
 Set WSO = ActiveSheet
 ' Find the FinalRow in today's dataset
 FinalRow = Cells(Rows.Count, 1).End(xlUp).Row
 ' Use an Advanced filter to copy unique customers
 ' from column A to column H
 Range("A1:A" & FinalRow).AdvancedFilter Action:=xlFilterCopy, _
 CopyToRange:=Range("H1"), Unique:=True
 'Find the final customer in column H
 FinalCust = Range("H1").End(xlDown).Row
 ' Loop through each customer
 For x = 2 To FinalCust
  ' Turn on the AutoFilter for this customer
  Range("A1").AutoFilter Field:=1, Criteria1:=Cells(x, 8).Value
  ' Create a new workbook
  Set WBN = Workbooks.Add
  Set WSN = WBN.Worksheets(1)
  ' In the original workbook, select visible cells
  WSO.Range("A1:F" & FinalRow).SpecialCells(xlCellTypeVisible).Copy _
  Destination:=WSN.Cells(3, 1)
  ' AutoFit columns in the new workbook
  WSN.Columns.AutoFit
  ' Add a title to the new workbook
  WSN.Range("A1").Value = "Recap of Purchases for " & WSN.Cells(4, 1).Value
  ' Save the new book
  WBN.SaveAs Filename:="C:\" & WSN.Cells(4, 1).Value & ".xls"
  WBN.Close SaveChanges:=False
```

```
  'Return to the original workbook
  WBO.Activate
  WSO.Select
 Next x
End Sub
```

After doing three small tests with the macro recorder, you were able to fill in the sections to copy the customer records to a new workbook. After running this macro, you should have a new workbook for each customer on your hard drive, ready to be distributed via email.

VBA macros open up a wide possibility of automation for Excel worksheets. Anytime you are faced with a daunting, mindless task, you can turn it into a challenging exercise by trying to design a macro to perform the task instead. It usually takes less time to design a macro than it does to complete the task. You should save every macro you write. Soon you will have a library of macros that handle many common tasks, and they will enable you to develop macros faster. The next time you need to perform a similar task, you can roll out the macro and perform the steps in seconds instead of hours.

CHAPTER 20

More tips and tricks for Excel

The chapters in this book are full of tips and tricks. This particular chapter is a catch-all for some of the tips that did not find a home elsewhere in the book.

Watching the results of a distant cell

Sometimes you need to keep an eye on a single result on a worksheet other than the one you're currently in. For example, you might have a workbook in which assumptions on multiple worksheets produce a final ROI. As you change the assumptions, it would be good to know the effect on ROI.

It can be time consuming to constantly switch back and forth to the results worksheet after every change. Instead, you can set up a watch to show you the current value of the distant cell(s).

To set up a watch, follow these steps:

1. Select Formulas, Watch Window to display the floating Watch Window dialog box over the worksheet.
2. Click Add Watch in the Watch Window dialog box.
3. In the Add Watch dialog box, click the RefEdit button and then click the cells you want to watch.
4. Click Add to add the cell(s) to the Watch Window dialog box.
5. Repeat steps 2 through 4, as necessary.

6. Position the Watch Window dialog box in an out-of-the-way location above your worksheet so that you can continue to work. Note that the Watch Window can be docked above the formula bar.

Every time you make a change to the worksheet, the Watch Window dialog box shows you the current value of the watched cells, as shown in Figure 20.1.

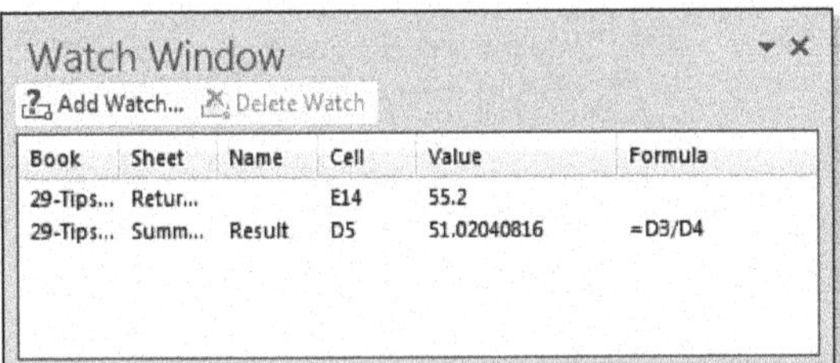

Figure 20.1 The Watch Window dialog box shows you the results of key cells that you define. These cells can be in far-off cells or on other worksheets.

When the watch is defined, you can toggle the Watch Window dialog box by using the Watch Window icon in the Formulas tab.

TIP

You can double-click any entry in the Watch Window dialog box to scroll to that cell.

Calculating a formula in slow motion

If you have a particularly complicated formula, you can watch how Excel calculates the formula in slow motion. This can help you locate any logic errors in the worksheet.

To evaluate a formula in slow motion, follow these steps:

1. Select the cell that contains the formula.
2. Select Formulas, Evaluate Formula. The Evaluate Formula dialog box appears, showing the formula. One element of the formula is underlined, indicating that this element will be calculated next.
3. To see the value of the underlined element immediately, click Evaluate.
4. If you want to see how that element is calculated, instead of clicking Evaluate, click Step In. Excel shows the formula for that element.
5. Eventually, the final level is evaluated to a number. Click Step Out to return one level up the dialog box.
6. Continue clicking Evaluate until you arrive at the answer shown in the cell.

Figure 20.2 shows an Evaluate Formula dialog box after Evaluate was clicked a few times.

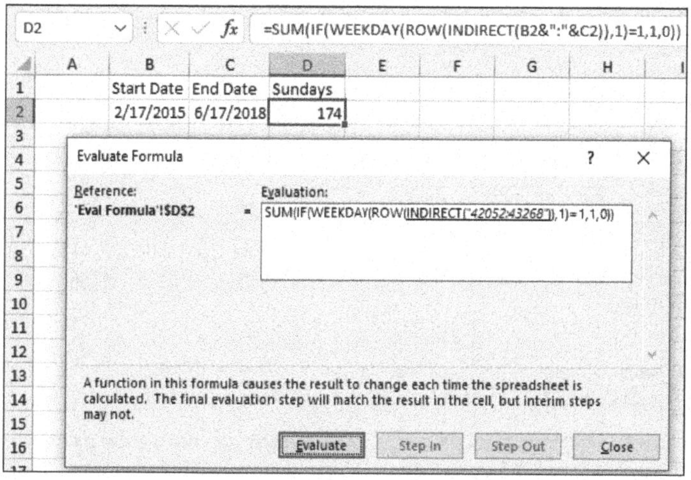

Figure 20.2 The Evaluate Formula dialog box enables you to watch the formula calculation in slow motion.

Inserting a symbol in a cell

Obscure key combinations are available to insert many symbols. However, you do not have to learn any of them. Instead, you can use the Symbol icon on the Insert tab to display the Symbol dialog box.

In the Symbol dialog box, you scroll through many subsets of the current font. When you find the desired symbol, select it and click the Insert button.

Editing an equation

The Equation drop-down menu on the Insert tab offers eight prebuilt equations. If you happen to need one of these equations, you can select it from the drop-down menu.

If you need to build some other equation, insert a shape in the worksheet first. While the shape is selected, use Insert, Equation, Insert New Equation. A blank equation is added to the shape.

It seems very touchy, but you have to be inside the equation to have the Equation Tools Design tab showing. From the ribbon, you can open the various drop-down menus to insert a mathematical symbol. In Figure 20.3, some symbols have three placeholders. These are tiny text boxes where you can type various values.

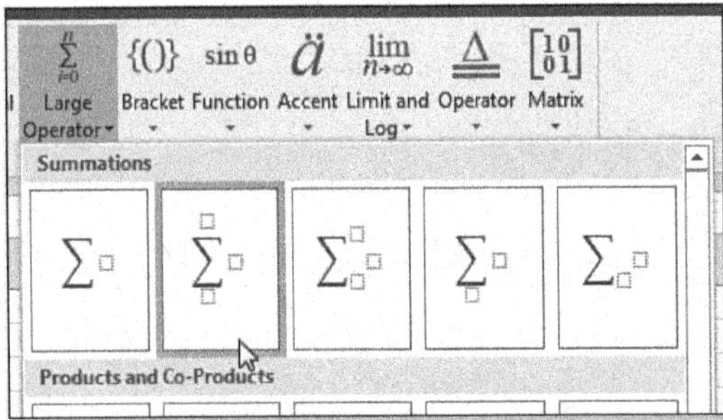

Figure 20.3 You will build most equations using the drop-down menus on the Equation Tools Design tab.

TROUBLESHOOTING

Although Excel can display equations, they are nothing more than drawing objects. You cannot have Excel solve the equations.

The Equation Editor originated in Word. I am sure the people writing for academic journals wanted a way to craft an equation in the papers, which led to the birth of the Equation Editor.

However, there is no actual mathematical ability built into the Equation Editor. There is no magic button to have Excel actually integrate from x to y based on the equation.

Protecting a worksheet

If you have many formulas in a worksheet, you might want to prevent others from changing them. In a typical scenario, your worksheet might have some input variables at the top. You might want to allow those items to be changed, but you might not want your formulas to be changed.

To protect a worksheet, follow these steps:

1. Select the input cells in your worksheet. These are the cells you want to allow someone to change.
2. Press Ctrl+1 or go to the Cells group of the Home tab and select Format, Format Cells. The Format Cells dialog box appears.
3. On the Protection tab of the Format Cells dialog box, clear the Locked check box. Click OK.
4. Select Review, Protect Sheet. The Protect Sheet dialog box appears.

5. Optionally, change what can happen in the protected workbook.

6. Click OK to apply the protection.

> Inside OUT
>
> ***A common scenario is to protect only the formula cells in a worksheet. While this is not as simple as clicking Protect Formulas, there is a buried command that can simplify the process.***
>
> **First, unlock all cells as described in steps 2 and 3 in "Protecting a Worksheet."**
>
> **Then, from any cell in your worksheet, select Home, Find & Select, Formulas. All the formula cells in the worksheet will be selected.**
>
> **With the formulas selected, repeat step 2 above, but change the Locked status to Selected. Continue with steps 4 through 6 in "Protecting a Worksheet."**

Repeat the last command with F4

Most people know that F4 is great for adding dollar signs to a reference when you are building a formula. When you are not editing a formula, the F4 key is used to repeat the previous command. Let's say that you had to change column widths of every other column to a width of 1. After you select cell B1 and press Alt+OCW1<Enter>, you can simply press the Right Arrow key twice and press F4 to repeat the Column Width command on column D. Keep pressing Right Arrow, Right Arrow, F4 until all the column widths are fixed.

Bring the active cell back into view with Ctrl+Backspace

Sometimes, you end up at the bottom of a data set while the active cell is at the top. Press Ctrl+Backspace and Excel will scroll the active cell back into view.

Separating text based on a delimiter

Depending on the source of your data, you might find that information is loaded into Excel with many fields in one cell. If the fields are separated by a character, you can separate the data into multiple columns. To do so, follow these steps:

1. Select the one-column range that contains multiple values in each cell.

2. Select Data, Data Tools, Text to Columns. Excel displays the Convert Text To Columns Wizard dialog box.

3. In step 1 of the wizard, select Delimited and click Next.

4. In step 2 of the wizard, choose your delimiter. Excel offers check boxes for Tab, Semicolon, Comma, and Space. If your delimiter is something different, select the Other box and type the delimiter. Click Next (see Figure 20.4).

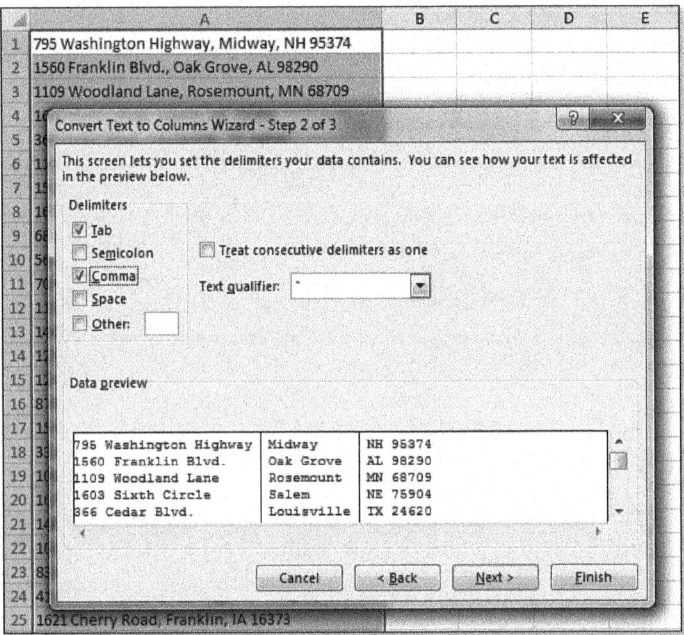

Figure 20.4 Identify the delimiter in step 2 of the wizard.

5. In step 3 of the wizard, indicate whether any of your columns are dates. Click the column in the Data Preview section and then select Date in the Column Data Format section. By default, Excel replaces the selected column and uses adjacent blank columns. To write the results to a different output area, enter a destination in step 3 of the wizard.

6. Click Finish to parse the column.

7. Excel does not automatically make the columns wide enough, so select the Cells section of the Home tab and then select Format, Autofit Column Width to make the output columns wide enough for the contents.

Auditing worksheets using Inquire

If you have Office Pro Plus or a Microsoft 356 E3 subscription or higher, you can enable the Inquire add-in. The add-in enables tools for discovering potential problems in workbooks. You can see a visual map of relationships, mark cells that contain certain potential problems, or compare two versions of the same workbook.

To enable Inquire, select File, Options, Add-Ins. At the bottom of the screen, choose Manage Com Add-Ins and click Go. Choose Inquire and click OK. A new Inquire tab appears in the ribbon.

Suppose that you have a workbook that you send to a co-worker for review. When you receive the changed version of the workbook from the co-worker, you would like to see if any changes were made to the workbook.

Rename one or both workbooks so you can tell which is the original and which is the changed version. Open both workbooks. From the Inquire tab, choose Compare Files. Specify the newer, changed version of the workbook in the Compare drop-down menu. Specify the original workbook in the To drop-down menu. This might seem backward from the way that you would think the files should be specified.

After you click Compare, the results show in the Spreadsheet Compare tool.

If you don't care about cell formatting changes, uncheck that category in the lower left of the window.

The top of the window shows a view of the two workbooks. Any changes are color coded to match the color legend shown in the lower left.

Inserting and exploring 3D models

Almost half of all manufacturing companies are using 3D printing as a tool for rapid prototyping. Forbes estimates that 3D printing is a 12-billion-dollar industry, and it is growing. Excel now allows you to import and rotate 3D printing files.

Specifically, Excel supports these file types: Filmbox (*.fbx), Object (*.obj), 3D Manufacturing Format (*.3mf), Polygon (*.ply), StereoLithography (*.stl), and Binary GL Transmission (*.glb).

On the Insert tab, choose 3D Models. There are a few sample files provided by Microsoft, or you can import any file you have. One great resource for free 3D models is NASA; browse for royalty-free models at *https://nasa3d.arc.nasa.gov/models/printable*.

Figure 20.5 shows a 3D model of the Hubble Space Telescope.

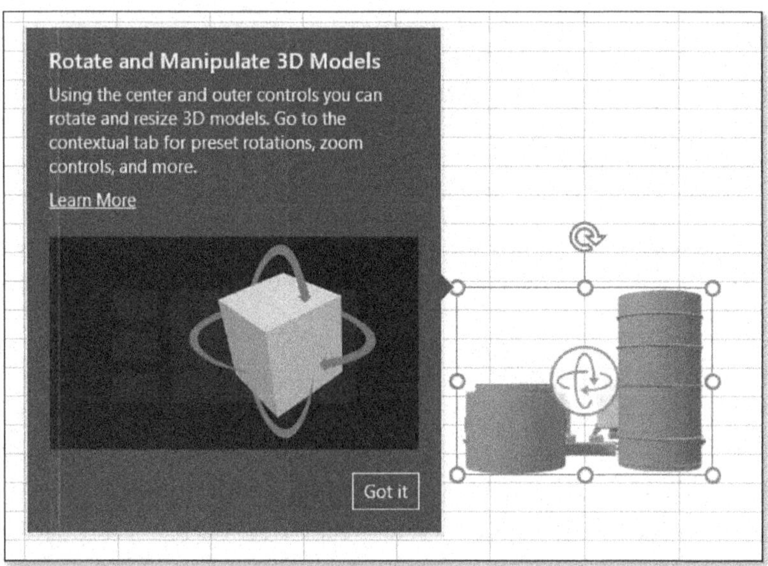

Figure 20.5 Notice the 3D rotation icon in the center of the model.

Click the center rotation icon and drag your mouse in any direction to rotate the model. Figure 20.6 reveals that the side view of Figure 20.5 is actually several pieces that you could print on a 3D printer and assemble.

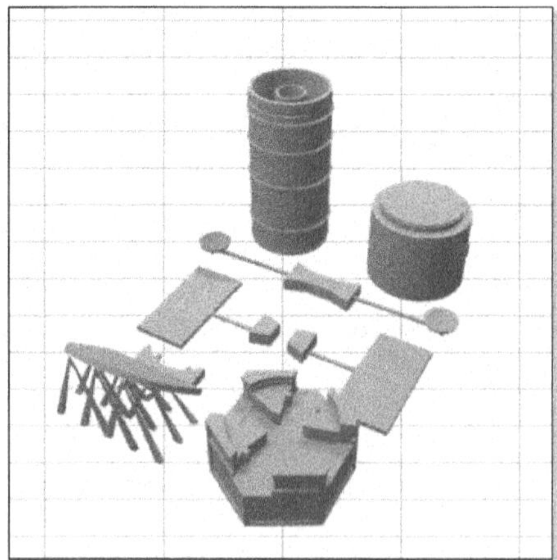

Figure 20.6 After rotating the 3D model, you can see all seven pieces.

Using the inking tools and the Action Pen

The Draw tab on the ribbon is probably a very popular feature in PowerPoint. This is a case where Word and Excel received the feature because it had already been developed for PowerPoint.

If you don't see the Draw tab in Excel, follow these steps:

1. Right-click the ribbon and choose Customize The Ribbon.
2. On the right side of the Excel Options dialog is a list of all of the built-in tabs in Excel. Find the Draw tab and choose it.
3. Click OK to close Excel Options.

In 2020, Microsoft added the Action Pen to the right side of the Drawing Tools gallery. Using the Action Pen, you can draw numbers or letters, and Excel will convert to text or numbers.

Figure 20.7 shows 1234 drawn using the mouse. After you stop drawing, Excel converts the drawing to the numbers 1234, as shown in Figure 20.8.

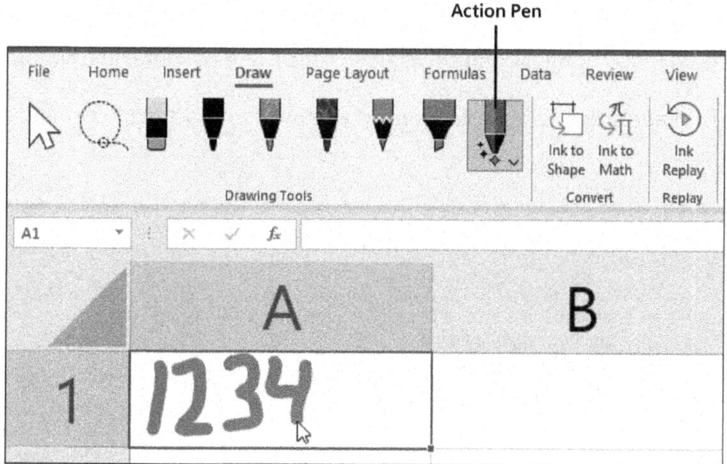

Figure 20.7 Use the Action Pen and draw some numbers or letters.

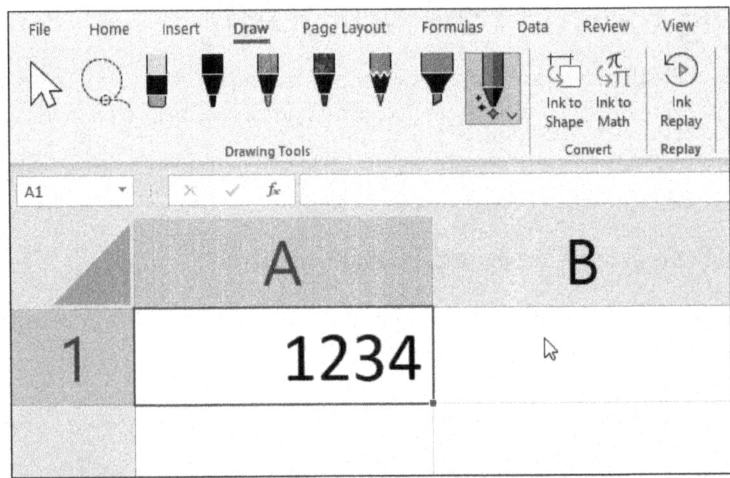

Figure 20.8 When you stop drawing, Excel converts the action pen to data.

The rest of the pens in the Drawing Tools group are markers, pencils, or highlighters. Right-click any pen and choose Modify to change the color or width. Highlighters offer the ability to snap to text. Turn this on to have the highlight fill the entire cell.

You can add new pens by right-clicking any marker, pencil, or highlighter and choosing New.

Choosing Ink To Shape or Ink To Math will convert a drawn form to a shape or math symbol, respectively.

Figure 20.9 shows a variety of lines drawn with various pens. The hand-drawn circle in C1:C2 becomes a perfect circle after using Ink To Shape.

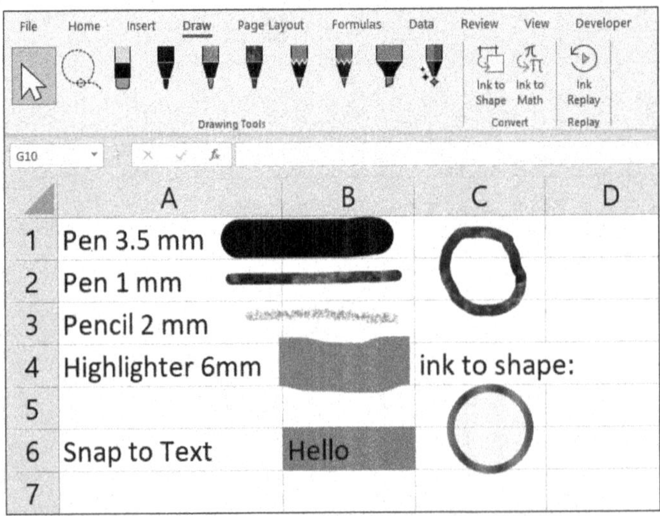

Figure 20.9 A variety of drawings with different pens and thicknesses.

One oddity is the ability to play back your drawing. If you've highlighted five cells, clicking Ink Replay will highlight those cells in an animated fashion. I have no idea when you would use this; if you could add each highlight one at a time like a PowerPoint slide, I would get it. However, this feature is like speeding through the entire PowerPoint deck in one second.

Seeing Workbooks Statistics and Smart Lookup

Two new icons will appear on the Review tab of Office 365. The Workbook Statistics icon opens a panel showing the number of cells and formulas in the workbook (see Figure 20.10).

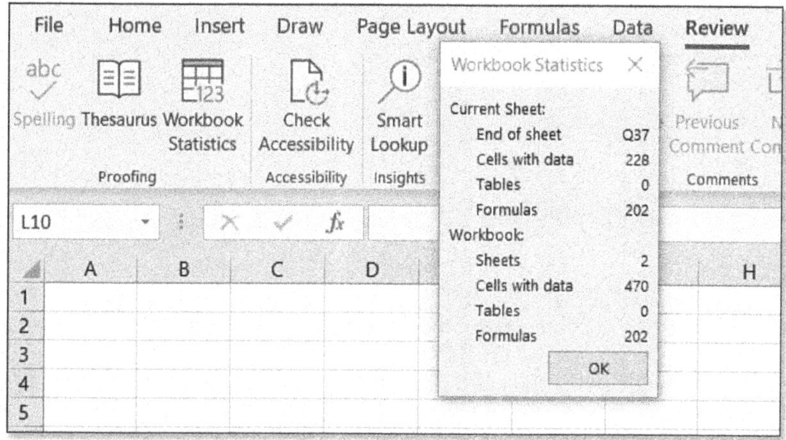

Figure 20.10 The Workbook Statistics panel identifies the number of active cells and formulas in this sheet and the entire workbook.

The Smart Lookup feature is branded as an "Insights" feature and using it requires you to opt-in to the artificial intelligence features. Click on any cell and ask for a Smart Lookup by clicking the large Smart Lookup icon in the Review tab (see Figure 20.10). In Figure 20.11, if you click Smart Lookup for the word "Hypergolic," it returns a definition and some links to pages about rockets. This does not seem like "artificial intelligence," but I guess it is just as easy as opening a browser.

Figure 20.11 The only thing new about the Smart Lookup tool is that it is branded as Insights.

PART IV

Excel visuals

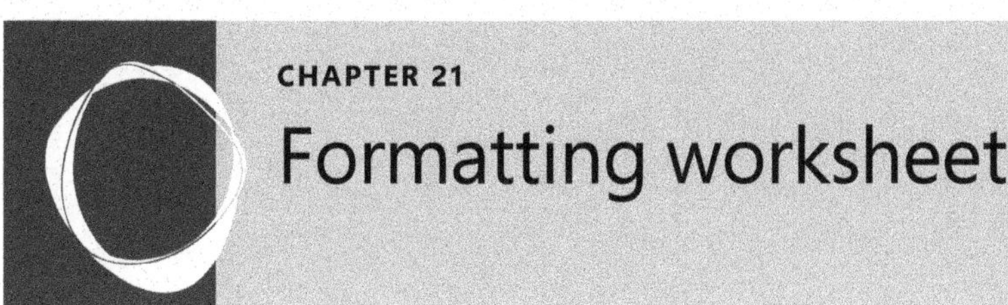

CHAPTER 21

Formatting worksheets

Formatting adds interest and readability to documents. If you have taken time to create a spreadsheet, you should also take the time to make sure that it is eye catching and readable.

You can format documents in Excel with any of these three methods:

- **Use table styles:** You can use table styles to format a table with banded rows, accents for totals, and so on.
- **Use cell styles:** You can use cell styles to identify titles, headings, and accent cells. The advantage of using cell styles is that you can quickly apply new themes to change the look and feel of a document.
- **Use formatting commands:** You can use traditional formatting commands to change the font, borders, fill, numeric formatting, column widths, and row heights. The usual formatting icons are on the Home tab as well as in the Format Cells dialog box.

Why format worksheets?

You can open a blank worksheet and fill it with data without ever touching any of Excel's formatting commands. The result is functional, but not necessarily readable or eye catching. Figure 21.1 contains an unformatted report in Excel.

	A	B	C	D	E	F	G	H
1	Astonishing Treadmill Inc.							
2	Sales Forecast							
3	2018							
4								
5	Line	Product	Jan	Feb	Mar	Q1	Apr	May
6	Consumer	A451	278	285	271	834	291	332
7		A636	357	334	387	1078	456	358
8		A686	161	144	244	549	165	225
9		B416	428	443	425	1296	448	432
10		B519	711	706	764	2181	697	789
11		D553	128	116	104	348	147	194
12		D555	376	405	378	1159	471	450
13		D801	353	352	377	1082	366	354
14		D914	296	274	279	849	394	315
15		E196	625	611	724	1960	700	651
16		E476	458	471	479	1408	484	463
17		Subtotal	4171	4141	4432	12744	4619	4563

Figure 21.1 After typing data into a spreadsheet, you have an unformatted report.

Figure 21.2 contains the same data but with formatting applied. The formatted report in Figure 21.2 is more interesting and easier to read than the unformatted one for the following reasons:

- The reader can instantly focus on the totals for each line.
- Headings are aligned with the data.
- Borders break the data into sections.
- Accent colors highlight the subtotals and totals.
- The title is prominent, in a larger font, and a headline typeface is used.
- Numeric formatting has added thousands separators.
- Quarterly totals appear in italic.
- The column widths are adjusted properly.
- A short row adds a visual break between the product lines.
- Headings for each product line are rotated, merged, and centered.

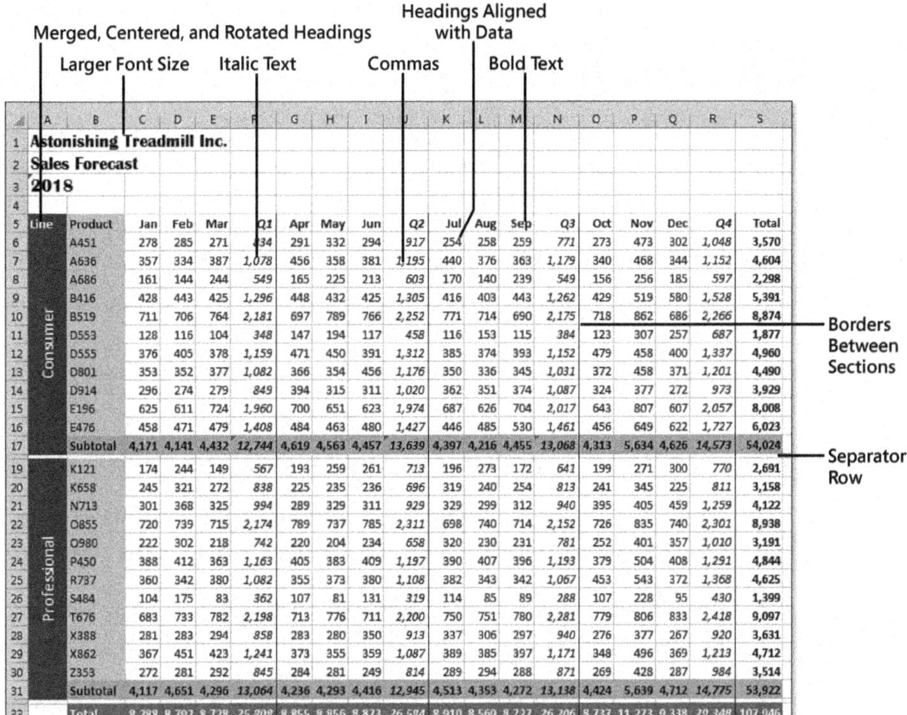

Astonishing Treadmill Inc.
Sales Forecast
2018

Line	Product	Jan	Feb	Mar	Q1	Apr	May	Jun	Q2	Jul	Aug	Sep	Q3	Oct	Nov	Dec	Q4	Total
Consumer	A451	278	285	271	*834*	291	332	294	*917*	254	258	259	*771*	273	473	302	*1,048*	**3,570**
	A636	357	334	387	*1,078*	456	358	381	*1,195*	440	376	363	*1,179*	340	468	344	*1,152*	**4,604**
	A686	161	144	244	*549*	165	225	213	*603*	170	140	239	*549*	156	256	185	*597*	**2,298**
	B416	428	443	425	*1,296*	448	432	425	*1,305*	416	403	443	*1,262*	429	519	580	*1,528*	**5,391**
	B519	711	706	764	*2,181*	697	789	766	*2,252*	771	714	690	*2,175*	718	862	686	*2,266*	**8,874**
	D553	128	116	104	*348*	147	194	117	*458*	116	153	115	*384*	123	307	257	*687*	**1,877**
	D555	376	405	378	*1,159*	471	450	391	*1,312*	385	374	393	*1,152*	479	458	400	*1,337*	**4,960**
	D801	353	352	377	*1,082*	366	354	456	*1,176*	350	336	345	*1,031*	372	458	371	*1,201*	**4,490**
	D914	296	274	279	*849*	394	315	311	*1,020*	362	351	374	*1,087*	324	377	272	*973*	**3,929**
	E196	625	611	724	*1,960*	700	651	623	*1,974*	687	626	704	*2,017*	643	807	607	*2,057*	**8,008**
	E476	458	471	479	*1,408*	484	463	480	*1,427*	446	485	530	*1,461*	456	649	622	*1,727*	**6,023**
	Subtotal	**4,171**	**4,141**	**4,432**	***12,744***	**4,619**	**4,563**	**4,457**	***13,639***	**4,397**	**4,216**	**4,455**	***13,068***	**4,313**	**5,634**	**4,626**	***14,573***	**54,024**
Professional	K121	174	244	149	*567*	193	259	261	*713*	196	273	172	*641*	199	271	300	*770*	**2,691**
	K658	245	321	272	*838*	225	235	236	*696*	319	240	254	*813*	241	345	225	*811*	**3,158**
	N713	301	368	325	*994*	289	329	311	*929*	329	299	312	*940*	395	405	459	*1,259*	**4,122**
	O855	720	739	715	*2,174*	789	737	785	*2,311*	698	740	714	*2,152*	726	835	740	*2,301*	**8,938**
	O980	222	302	218	*742*	220	204	234	*658*	320	230	231	*781*	252	401	357	*1,010*	**3,191**
	P450	388	412	363	*1,163*	405	383	409	*1,197*	390	407	396	*1,193*	379	504	408	*1,291*	**4,844**
	R737	360	342	380	*1,082*	355	373	380	*1,108*	382	343	342	*1,067*	453	543	372	*1,368*	**4,625**
	S484	104	175	83	*362*	107	81	131	*319*	114	85	89	*288*	107	228	95	*430*	**1,399**
	T676	683	733	782	*2,198*	713	776	711	*2,200*	750	751	780	*2,281*	779	806	833	*2,418*	**9,097**
	X388	281	283	294	*858*	283	280	350	*913*	337	306	297	*940*	276	377	267	*920*	**3,631**
	X862	367	451	423	*1,241*	373	355	359	*1,087*	389	385	397	*1,171*	348	496	369	*1,213*	**4,712**
	Z353	272	281	292	*845*	284	281	249	*814*	289	294	288	*871*	269	428	287	*984*	**3,514**
	Subtotal	**4,117**	**4,651**	**4,296**	***13,064***	**4,236**	**4,293**	**4,416**	***12,945***	**4,513**	**4,353**	**4,272**	***13,138***	**4,424**	**5,639**	**4,712**	***14,775***	**53,922**
	Total	**8,288**	**8,792**	**8,728**	***25,808***	**8,855**	**8,856**	**8,873**	***26,584***	**8,910**	**8,569**	**8,727**	***26,206***	**8,737**	**11,273**	**9,338**	***29,348***	**107,946**

Figure 21.2 Readability is improved after formatting the report.

The formatting applied to Figure 21.2 takes a few extra minutes, but it dramatically increases the readability of the report. Because you have taken the time to put the worksheet together, it is worth a couple of extra minutes to make the worksheet easier for the consumer to read.

Using traditional formatting

Formatting is typically carried out in the Format Cells dialog box or using the formatting icons located on the Home tab.

In Excel, the traditional formatting icons are in the Font, Alignment, and Number groups on the Home tab, as shown in Figure 21.3. Additional column- and row-formatting commands are available in the Format drop-down menu in the Cells group on the Home tab.

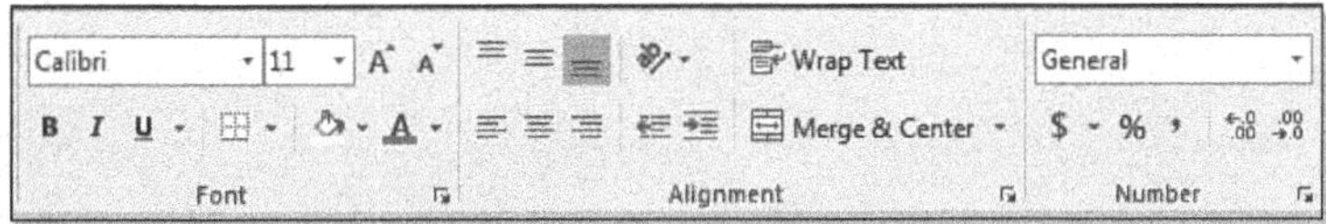

Figure 21.3 Most traditional formatting icons are in the Font, Alignment, and Number groups on the Home tab.

If your favorite setting is not on the Home tab, you can take one of the four entry paths to the Format Cells dialog box, which provides access to additional settings, such as Shrink To Fit, StrikeThrough, and more border settings:

- Press Ctrl+1, which is Ctrl and the number 1. You can press Ctrl+Shift+F to display the Font tab on the same dialog box.
- Click the dialog box launcher icons in the lower-right corner of the Font, Alignment, or Number groups. Each icon opens the dialog box, with the focus on a different tab.
- Right-click any cell and select Format Cells.
- Select Format Cells from the Format drop-down menu in the cells group on the Home tab.

As shown in Figure 21.4, the Format Cells dialog box includes the following six tabs:

- **Number:** Gives you absolute control over numeric formatting. You can choose from 96,885 built-in formats or use the Custom category to create your own.
- **Alignment:** Offers settings for horizontal alignment, vertical alignment, rotation, wrap, merge, and shrink to fit.
- **Font:** Controls font, size, style, underline, color, strikethrough, superscript, and subscript.
- **Border:** Controls line style and color for each of the four borders and the diagonals on each cell.
- **Fill:** Offers over 16 million fill colors and patterns.
- **Protection:** Used to lock or unlock cells or to hide contents from view when the sheet is protected.

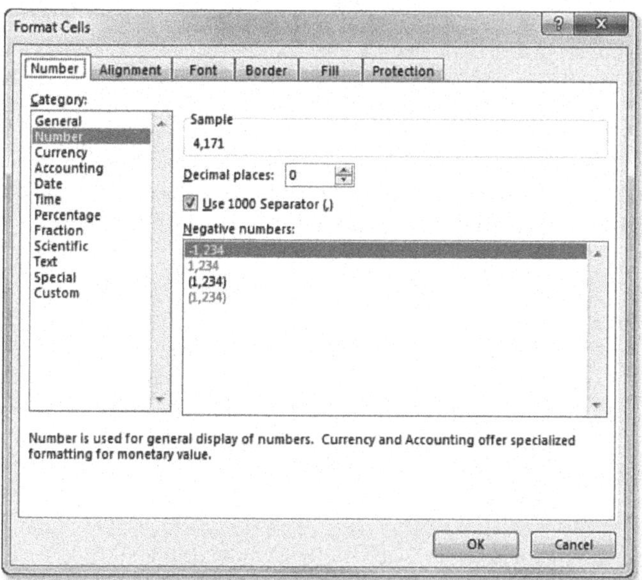

Figure 21.4 The Format Cells dialog box offers complete control over cell formatting. You can visit this dialog box when the icons on the ribbon do not provide enough detail.

Changing numeric formats by using the Home tab

If you ever shop for hardware at a general-purpose store, you have probably experienced how it can have almost what you need, but never exactly what you need. At this point, you probably curse your decision to stop at the general-purpose retailer and drive another mile down the road to Home Depot or Lowe's, where you can always find exactly what you need.

Using the Number group on the Home tab is like shopping at a general-purpose retailer. It has many settings for numeric formatting, but often they are not exactly what you need. When this happens, you end up visiting the Number tab on the Format Cells dialog box.

To start, there are three icons—for currency, percentage, and comma style. The Percentage icon is useful. Unfortunately, the Currency and Comma icons apply an Accounting style to a cell, and the Accounting style is inappropriate for everyone except accountants. Furthermore, these three icons are not toggle buttons, which means that when you use one of them, there is not an icon to go back quickly to a general style, other than Undo.

The Increase and Decrease Decimal icons are useful. Each click of one of these buttons forces Excel to show one more or one fewer decimal place. If you have numbers showing two decimal places in all cells, two clicks on the Decrease Decimal icon solves the problem.

Figure 21.5 shows the Currency, Percentage, Comma, Increase Decimal, and Decrease Decimal buttons in the Number group of the Home tab. The Currency button offers a drop-down menu with choices based on your regional settings.

TIP

Excel uses the value in the active cell for each of the formats inside the drop-down menu, and no sample if the cell is blank.

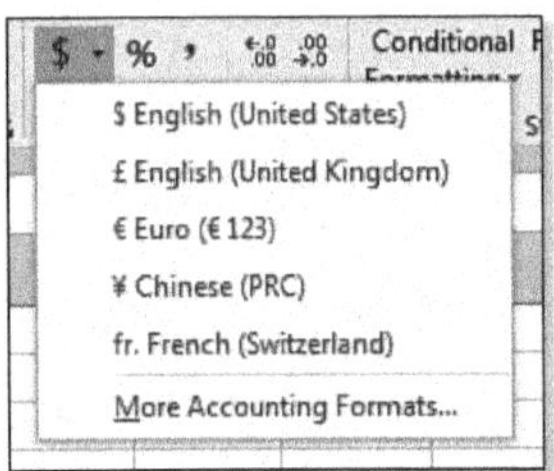

Figure 21.5 The Currency and Comma icons both use an Accounting style. This is wonderful for accountants, but others should resist using them.

Above the five buttons in the Number group is a drop-down menu that has a dozen popular number styles. Figure 21.6 shows the styles in the drop-down menu. The range A2:F12 shows these styles applied to four numbers.

B2 | 1234.567

	A	B	C	F
1				
2	General	1234.567	0.625	-1
3	Number	1234.57	0.63	-1.00
4	Currency	$1,234.57	$0.63	-$1.00
5	Accounting	$ 1,234.57	$ 0.63	$ (1.00)
6	Short Date	5/18/1903	1/0/1900	
7	Long Date	Monday, May 18, 1903	Saturday, January 00, 1900	
8	Time	1:36:29 PM	3:00:00 PM	
9	Percentage	123456.70%	62.50%	-100.00%
10	Fraction	1234 4/7	5/8	-1
11	Scientific	1.23E+03	6.25E-01	-1.00E+00
12	Text	1234.567	0.625	-1

Format	Sample
General	No specific format
Number	1234.57
Currency	$1,234.57
Accounting	$1,234.57
Short Date	5/18/1903
Long Date	Monday, May 18, 1903
Time	1:36:29 PM
Percentage	123456.70%
Fraction	1234 4/7
Scientific	1.23E+03
Text	1234.567

More Number Formats...

Figure 21.6 Excel offers 11 popular number styles in this drop-down menu.

The following list provides some comments and cautions about using the number styles from the drop-down menu in the Home tab:

- General format is a number format. Decimal places are shown if needed. No thousands separator is used. A negative number is shown with a minus sign before the number.
- Number does not use a thousands separator. It forces two decimal places, even with numbers that do not need decimal places, such as in cell F3.
- Currency is a useful format for everyone. The currency symbol is shown immediately before the number. All numbers are expressed with two decimal places. Negatives are shown with a hyphen before the number.
- Accounting is great for financial statements and annoying for everything else. Negative numbers are shown in parentheses. Currency symbols are left-aligned with the edge of the cell. Positive numbers appear one character from the right edge of the cell to allow them to line up with negative numbers.
- Percentage uses two decimal places when selected from the drop-down menu. This is one format for which it is actually better to use the icon on the ribbon than the Format Cells dialog box.
- Fraction defaults to showing a fraction with a one-digit divisor. If you have a number such as 0.925, some Excel number formats correctly show this as 15/16. Unfortunately, the Fraction setting in this drop-down menu rounds it to one-digit divisors.

Changing numeric formats by using built-in formats in the Format Cells dialog box

The Format Cells dialog box offers more number formats than the Home tab. My favorite number format can be accessed only through the Format Cells dialog box. I find that I avoid the buttons in the Number group in the Home tab and go directly to the Format Cells dialog box.

You can display the Format Cells dialog box by clicking the dialog box launcher icon in the lower-right corner of the Number group of the Home tab. When you open the Format Cells dialog box this way, the Number tab is the active tab.

Twelve categories appear on the left side of the Number tab. The General and Text categories each have a single setting. The Custom category enables you to use formatting codes to build any number format. The remaining nine categories each offer a collection of controls to customize the numeric format.

Using numeric formatting with thousands separators

Using numeric formatting with thousands separators is my favorite format. The thousands separators make the number easy to read. You can suppress the decimal places from the numbers. Microsoft does not offer buttons on the Home tab to select this format. The comma button is a perfect place for it, but instead Microsoft assigns that to the accounting format.

To format cells in numeric format, follow these steps:

1. Press Ctrl+1 to display the Format Cells dialog box.
2. Select the Number category from the Number tab.
3. Select the Use 1000 Separator check box.
4. Optionally, adjust the Decimal Places spin button to 0.
5. Optionally, select a method for displaying negative numbers.

Figure 21.7 shows the Number category of the Format Cells dialog box.

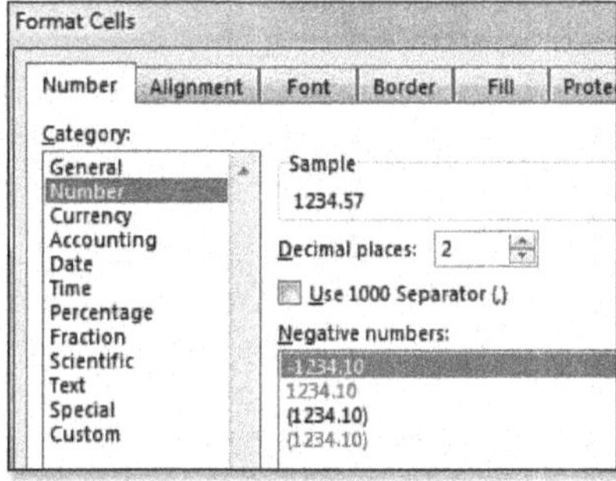

Figure 21.7 The Number category is the workhorse in Excel.

Displaying currency

Two categories are used for currency: Currency and Accounting. The Currency category is identical to the Number category shown in Figure 21.7, with the addition of a currency symbol drop-down menu. This drop-down menu offers 409 different currencies from around the world.

The second category is Accounting. With this category, the currency symbol is always left aligned in the cell. The last digit of positive numbers appears one character from the right edge of the cell so that positive and negative numbers line up. In addition, negative numbers are always shown in parentheses.

Displaying dates and times

The Date category offers 17 built-in formats for displaying dates, and the Time category offers nine built-in formats for displaying time. Each category has two formats that display both date and time.

The date formats vary from short dates such as 3/14 to long dates such as Wednesday, March 14, 2012. You should pay particular attention to the Date formats and the Sample box. Some formats show only the month and the day. Other formats show the month and the year. For example, the values in the Type box are for March 14, 2012. Other types such as March-01 display month-year. Types, such as 14-Mar, display day-month.

An interesting format near the bottom of the list is the M type. This displays month names in JFMAMJJASOND style, as shown in Figure 21.8. Readers of the *Wall Street Journal*'s financial charts will instantly recognize that each month is represented by the first letter of the month in this style. This style works great when used as the labels along the x-axis of a chart.

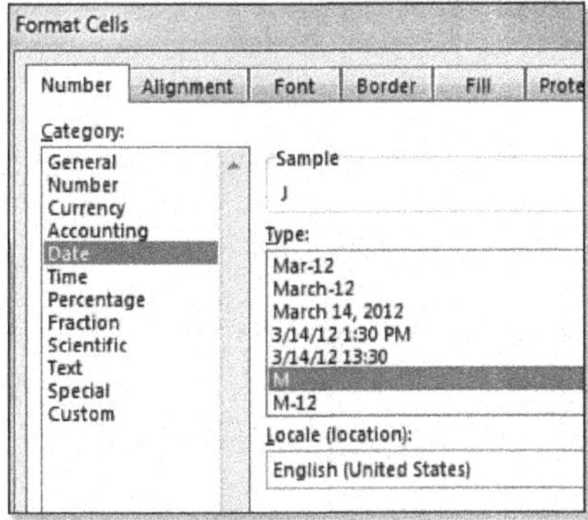

Figure 21.8 A variety of date and time formats is available.

In the Time category, pay attention to an important distinction between the 1:30 p.m., 13:30, and 37:30:55 types. The first type displays times from 12:00 a.m. through 11:59 p.m. The second type displays military time. In this system, midnight is 0:00, and 11:59 p.m. is 23:59. Neither of these types displays hours exceeding 24 hours. If you are working on a weekly timesheet or any application in which you need to display hours that total to more than 24 hours, you need to use the 37:30:55 type in the Time category. This format is one of a few that displays hours exceeding 24.

Displaying fractions

The Fractions category rounds a decimal number to the nearest fraction. Types include fractions in halves, quarters, eighths, sixteenths, tenths, and hundredths. In addition, the first three types specify that the decimal should be reduced to the nearest fraction with up to one, two, or three digits in the denominator.

Figure 21.9 shows a variety of decimals formatted with five different fractional types. In row 14, notice that this random number can appear as 1/2, 49/92, or 473/888 when using the Up To *N* Digit types. Excel rounds the number to the closest fraction.

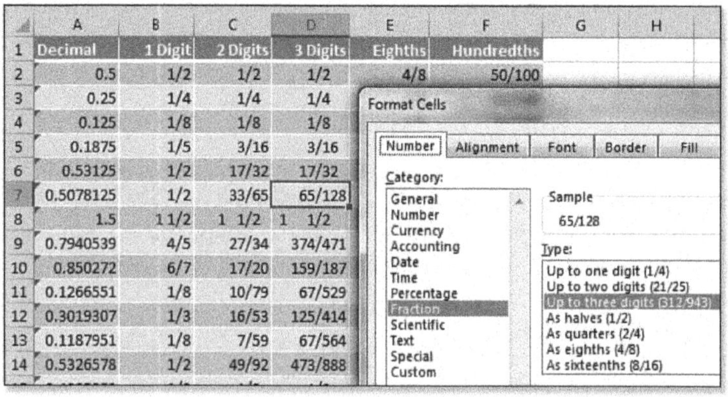
A B C D E F G H
1 Decimal 1 Digit 2 Digits 3 Digits Eighths Hundredths
2 0.5 1/2 1/2 1/2 4/8 50/100
3 0.25 1/4 1/4 1/4
4 0.125 1/8 1/8 1/8
5 0.1875 1/5 3/16 3/16
6 0.53125 1/2 17/32 17/32
7 0.5078125 1/2 33/65 65/128
8 1.5 1 1/2 1 1/2 1 1/2
9 0.7940539 4/5 27/34 374/471
10 0.850272 6/7 17/20 159/187
11 0.1266551 1/8 10/79 67/529
12 0.3019307 1/3 16/53 125/414
13 0.1187951 1/8 7/59 67/564
14 0.5326578 1/2 49/92 473/888
Format Cells
Number
Alignment
Font
Border
Fill
Category:
General
Number
Currency
Accounting
Date
Time
Percentage
Fraction
Scientific
Text
Special
Custom
Sample
65/128
Type:
Up to one digit (1/4)
Up to two digits (21/25)
Up to three digits (312/943)
As halves (1/2)
As quarters (2/4)
As eighths (4/8)
As sixteenths (8/16)

Figure 21.9 Excel can display decimals as fractions in a variety of formats.

In column E, note that if you ask Excel to show the number in eighths, Excel uses 4/8 and 2/8 instead of 1/2 or 1/4.

You probably feel as if you spent too much time in junior high math learning how to reduce fractions. The good news is that the first three fraction types of number formatting in Excel eliminate the need for manually reducing fractions.

Displaying ZIP Codes, telephone numbers, and social security numbers

Spreadsheets were invented in Cambridge, Massachusetts. However, if you enter the ZIP Code for Cambridge (02138) in a cell, Excel does not display the ZIP Code correctly. It truncates the leading zero, giving you a ZIP Code of 2138.

To combat this problem, Excel provides four special formatting types, all of which are U.S. centric:

- The Zip Code and Zip Code + 4 styles ensure that East Coast cities do not lose the leading zeros in their ZIP Codes.
- The Phone Number type formats a telephone number with parentheses around the area code and a hyphen after the exchange.

- The Social Security Number type groups the digits into groups of three, two, and four numbers that are separated by hyphens.

Figure 21.10 shows cells formatted with the four types available in the Special category.

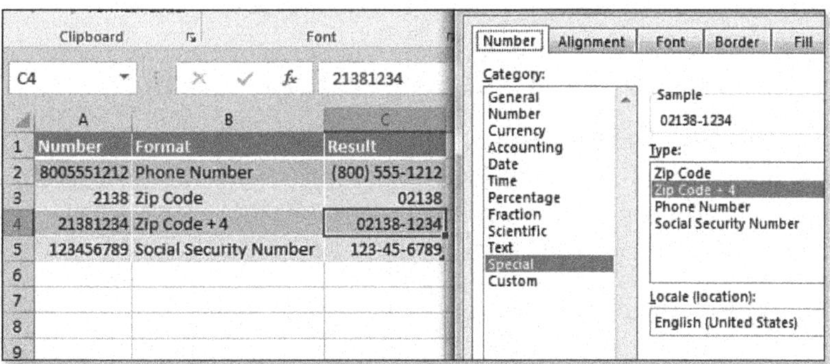

Figure 21.10 United States customers will appreciate the Special category in the Format Cells dialog box.

> NOTE
>
> **If you happen to live in one of the 195 countries in the world besides the United States, you will undoubtedly need other formatting for your postal codes, telephone numbers, or national ID numbers. You can create number formats such as the ones shown in the Special category as well as the other formats you might need by using the Custom category, as discussed in the next section.**

Changing numeric formats using custom formats

Custom number formats provide incredible power and flexibility. Although you do not need to know the complete set of rules for them, you will probably find a couple of custom number formats that work perfectly for you.

> TIP
>
> **A good way to learn custom number formatting codes is to select a format and then click Custom to see the code for the selected format. For example, click Fraction and then click As Quarters (2/4). When you click Custom, you learn that the custom number code is `# ?/4`. Using this knowledge, you could build a new custom format code to show data in 17ths: `# ?/17`.**

To use a custom number format, follow these steps:

1. Select the cells to be highlighted.
2. Display the Format Cells dialog box by pressing Ctrl+1.
3. Select the Number tab.

4. Select the Custom category.
5. Type the formatting codes into the Type box. Excel shows you a sample of the active cell with this format in the Sample box.
6. After you make sure this format looks correct, click OK to accept it.

Using the four zones of a custom number format

A custom number format can contain up to four different formats, each separated by a semicolon. The semicolons divide the format into as many as four zones. Excel allows different formatting, depending on whether a cell contains a positive number, a negative number, a zero, or text. You need to keep in mind the following:

- Separate formatting codes for zones by using semicolons.
- If you type only one number format, it applies to all numbers. A leading minus sign will be used for negative numbers.
- If you type only two formats, the first format applies to positive and zero. The second format is used for negative.
- If all four formats are used, they refer to positive, negative, zero, and text values, respectively.

CHAPTER 21

In Figure 21.11, a custom number format uses all four zones. The table in rows 11:14 shows how various numbers are displayed in this format. Notice that cell B12 appears in red type.

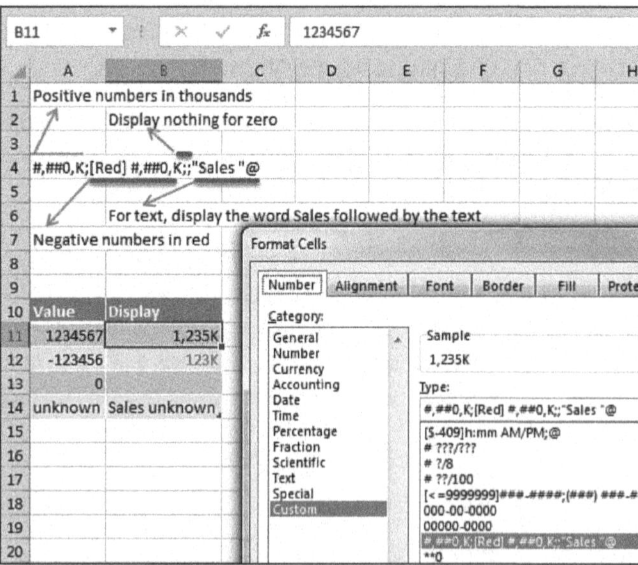

Figure 21.11 The four zones of a custom number format can cause positive, negative, zero, and text values to display differently.

Controlling text and spacing in a custom number format

You can display a mix of text and numbers in a numeric cell by including the text in double quotation marks. For example, `"The total is "$#,##0` precedes the number with the text shown in quotes.

If you need a single character, you can omit the quotation marks and precede the character with a backslash (\). For example, the code `$#,##0,,\M` displays numbers in millions and adds an M indicator after the number. The letters `BDEGHMNSY` require a backslash. The rest of the letters can be used without a backslash.

Some characters require neither a backslash nor quotation marks. These special characters are `$ - + / ( ) : ! ^ & ' ~ { } = < >` and the space character.

To add a specific amount of space to a format, you enter an underscore followed by a character. Excel then includes enough space to include that particular character. One frequent use for this is to include `_)` at the end of a positive number to leave enough space for a closing parenthesis. The positive numbers then line up with the negative numbers shown in parentheses.

To fill the space in a cell with a repeating character, use an asterisk followed by the character. For example, the format `**0` fills the leading space in a cell with asterisks. The format `0*-` fills the trailing space in a cell with hyphens.

If you are expecting numbers but think you might occasionally have text in the cell, you can use the fourth zone of the format. You use the `@` character to represent the text in the cell. For example, `0;0;0;"Unexpected entry of "@` highlights the text cells with a note. If someone types a number, she gets the number. If someone types **hello**, they get `"Unexpected entry of hello."`

Controlling decimal places in a custom number format

Use a zero as a placeholder when you want to force the place to be included. For example, `0.000` formats all numbers with three decimal places. If the number has more than three places, it is rounded to three decimal places.

Use a pound sign (#) as a placeholder to display significant digits but not insignificant zeros. For example, `0.###` displays up to three decimal places, if needed, but can display `"1."` for a whole number.

Use a question mark to replace insignificant zeros on either size of the decimal point with enough space to represent a digit in a fixed-width font. This format was designed to allow decimal points to line up, but with proportional fonts, it may not always work.

To include a thousands separator, include a comma to the left of the decimal point. For example, `#,##0` displays a thousands separator. `#,##0` also displays a millions, billions, and so on separator if the number is large enough.

To scale a number by thousands, include a comma after the numeric portion of the format. Each comma divides the number by a thousand. For example, `0,` displays numbers in thousands, and `0,,` displays numbers in millions.

Using conditions and color in a custom number format

The condition codes available in numeric formatting predate conditional formatting by a decade. You should consider the flexible conditional formatting features for any new conditions. However, in case you encounter an old worksheet with these codes, it is valid to use colors in the format: red, blue, green, yellow, cyan, black, white, magenta, Color 1, ..., Color 56. You include the color in square brackets. It should be the first element of any numeric formatting zone.

You can include a condition in square brackets after the color but before the numeric formatting. For example, `[Red][<=100];[Color 17][>100]` displays numbers under 100 in red and other numbers in blue. The United States telephone special format uses this custom condition:

```
[<=9999999]###-####;(###) ###-####
```

Using dates and times in a custom number format

Although many of these settings are arcane, I still regularly use many of the date and time formats shown in Table 21.1. The various `m` and `d` codes allow flexibility in expressing dates.

Table 21.1 Date and time formats

To display this:	Use this code:
Months as 1–12	m
Months as 01–12	mm
Months as Jan–Dec	mmm
Months as January–December	mmmm
Months as the first letter of the month	mmmmm
Days as 1–31	d
Days as 01–31	dd
Days as Sun–Sat	ddd
Days as Sunday–Saturday	dddd
Years as 00–99	yy
Years as 1900–9999	yyyy

Hours as 0–23	h
Hours as 00–23	hh
Minutes as 0–59	m
Minutes as 00–59	mm
Seconds as 0–59	s
Seconds as 00–59	ss
Hours as 4 AM	h AM/PM
Time as 4:36 PM	h:mm AM/PM
Time as 4:36:03 P	h:mm:ss A/P
Elapsed time in hours such as 25:02	[h]:mm
Elapsed time in minutes such as 63:46	[mm]:ss
Elapsed time in seconds	[ss]
Fractions of a second	h:mm:ss.00

The custom number format `m/d/yy` or `m/d/y` displays the month and day numbers as one digit if possible. For example, dates formatted with this code display as 1/9/08, 1/31/08, 9/9/09, and 12/31/08. Note that you cannot display the year as a single digit.

A custom number format of `mm/dd/yy` always uses two digits to display the month and day. Examples are 01/09/08 and 01/31/08.

The remaining date and time codes can display months as Jan, January, or J and days as 1, 01, Fri, or Friday.

NOTE

Note that the letter `m` can be used either as a month or as a minute. If the `m` is preceded by an `h` or followed by an `s`, Excel assumes you are referring to minutes. Otherwise, the month is displayed instead.

Displaying scientific notation in custom number formats

To display numbers in scientific format, you use `E-` or `E+` exponent codes in a zone.

If a format contains a zero (0) or pound sign (#) to the right of an exponent code, Excel displays the number in scientific format and inserts an `E`. The number of zeros or pound signs to the right of a code determines the number of digits in the exponent. `E-` or `e-` places a minus sign by negative exponents. `E+` or `e+` places a minus sign by negative exponents and a plus sign by positive exponents.

Take the following, for example:

- 1450 formatted with `0.00E+00` displays as 1.45E+03.
- 1450 formatted with `0.00E-00` displays as 1.45E03.
- 0.00145 formatted with either code displays as 1.45E-03.

Aligning cells

Worksheets look best when the headings above a column are aligned with the data in the column. Excel's default behavior is to left align text and right align values and dates.

In Figure 21.12, the month heading in F1 is left aligned, and the numeric values starting in row 2 are right aligned. This makes the worksheet look haphazard. To solve the problem, you can right align the headings cells.

To right align cells, select the cells and click the Right Align icon in the Alignment group of the Home tab.

> NOTE
>
> **The Alignment tab of the Format Cells dialog box offers additional alignment choices, such as justified and distributed.**

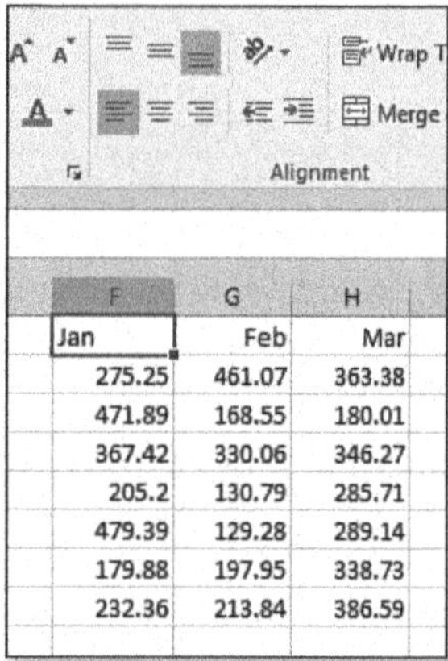

F	G	H
Jan	Feb	Mar
275.25	461.07	363.38
471.89	168.55	180.01
367.42	330.06	346.27
205.2	130.79	285.71
479.39	129.28	289.14
179.88	197.95	338.73
232.36	213.84	386.59

Figure 21.12 In column F, the left-aligned heading appears out of alignment with the numbers. Columns G and H show the headings after the Right Align icon is clicked.

Changing font size

There are three icons in the Font group of the Home tab for changing font size:

- The Increase Font Size A icon increases the font size in the selected cells to the next larger setting.
- The Decrease Font Size A icon decreases the font size in the selected cells to the next smaller setting.
- The Font Size drop-down menu offers a list of font sizes. You can hover over any font size to see the Live Preview of that size in the selected cells of the worksheet (see Figure 21.13).

NOTE

If you need a font size that is not in the drop-down menu, you can type a new value in the drop-down menu. For example, although the drop-down menu jumps from 12 to 14, you can click the value and type 13.

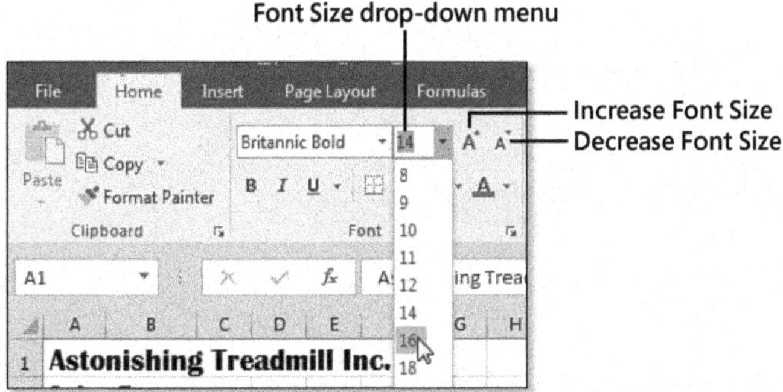

Figure 21.13 When you use the Font Size drop-down menu, Live Preview shows you the effect of an increased font size before you select the font.

Changing font typeface

Since Excel 2007, changing the font typeface has been vastly improved over earlier versions of Excel. In some legacy versions of Excel, the Font drop-down menu showed the font names in the style of each font. However, beginning with Excel 2007, Live Preview shows how the font will look as you hover over the font in the selected cells (see Figure 21.14). Notice that the Font name drop-down menu is in the Font group of the Home tab.

NOTE

By using the Font tab of the Format Cells dialog box, you can also apply strikethrough, superscript, and subscript.

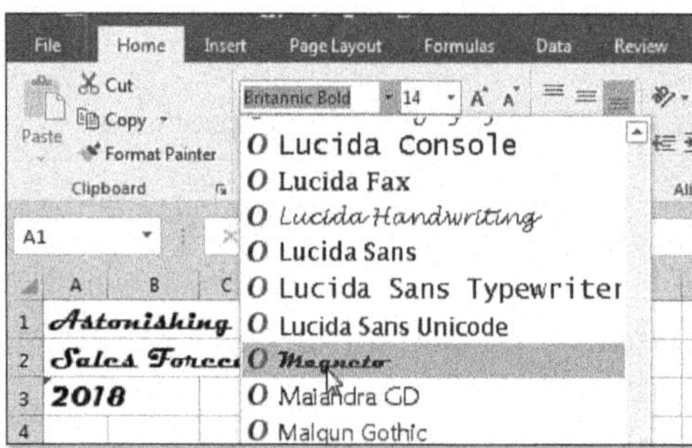

Figure 21.14 The Font drop-down menu in the Home tab shows the look of each font, and Live Preview shows how individual cells will look with the font applied.

Applying bold, italic, and underline

Three icons in the Font group in the Home tab enable you to change the font to apply bold, italic, and underline. Unlike the icons in the Number group, these icons behave properly, toggling the property on and off. The Bold icon is a bold letter *B*. The Italic icon is an italic letter *I*. The Underline icon is either an underlined *U* or a double-underlined *D*. The Underline icon is actually a drop-down menu. As shown in Figure 21.15, you can select the drop-down menu to change from Single Underline to Double Underline.

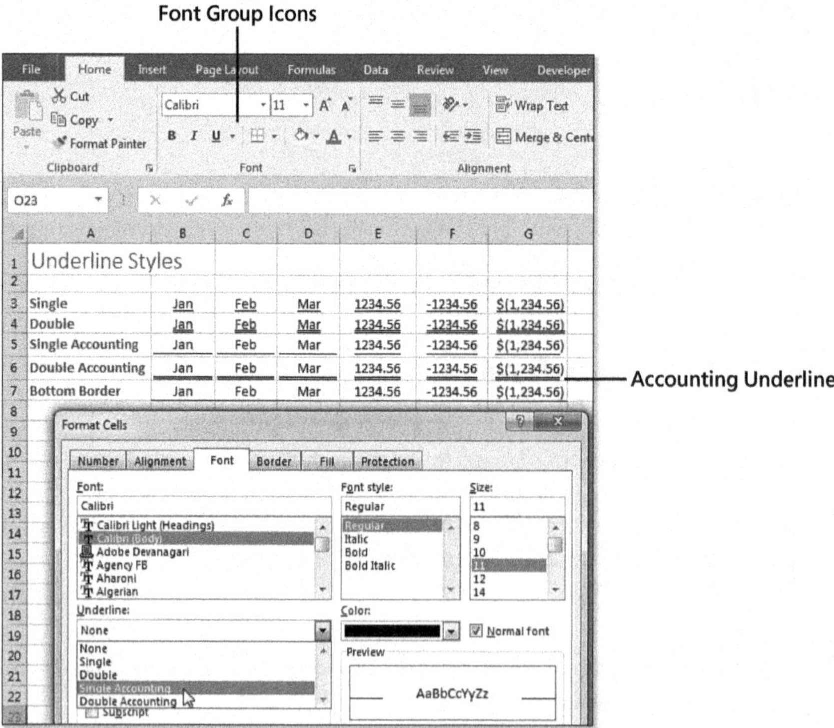

Figure 21.15 The underline drop-down menu offers single or double underlining, but the extra choices in the Format Cells dialog box solve some text underlining issues.

The underline style applies to the characters in the cell. If you have a cell that contains 123, the underline is three characters wide. If you have a cell with 1,234,567.89, the underline is 12 characters wide.

The Format Cells dialog box offers more choices. Settings for Single Accounting underline create an underline that extends nearly to the edges of the cell but leaves a gap between the underline in the next cell. This often looks better than using a bottom border across the cells.

Using borders

There are 1.7 billion unique combinations of borders for any four-cell range. The Borders drop-down menu in the Font group of the Home tab offers 13 popular border options plus five border tools. If you must draw nonstandard borders, explore the Draw Borders tool in this drop-down menu.

You must understand an important concept when applying borders to a range. Suppose you select 20 rows by 20 columns, such as cells A1:T20. If you apply a top border by using the drop-down menu, only the top row of cells A1:T1 have the border. Often, this is not what you were expecting. For example, you might have wanted a border on the top of all 400 cells.

Notice that in the Format Cells dialog box, there is a representation of a 2×2 cell range. The border style drawn in the top edge of this box affects only the top edge of the range. The border style drawn in the middle horizontal line of the box affects all the horizontal borders on the inside of the selected range.

The fastest way to select all horizontal and vertical borders in the range is to click the Outline button and then the Inside button in the Presets section of the dialog box.

Coloring cells

Excel allows you to use a gradient to fill a cell. This can provide an interesting look for a title cell. Gradient formatting is available only in the Format Cells dialog box.

The Font group on the Home tab offers a paint bucket drop-down menu and an A drop-down menu. The paint bucket is a color chooser for the background fill of the cell. The A drop-down menu is a color chooser for the font color in the cell. Both drop-down menus offer six shades of the 10 theme colors, 10 standard colors, and the More Colors option. The paint bucket drop-down menu also offers the menu choice No Fill, as shown in Figure 21.16.

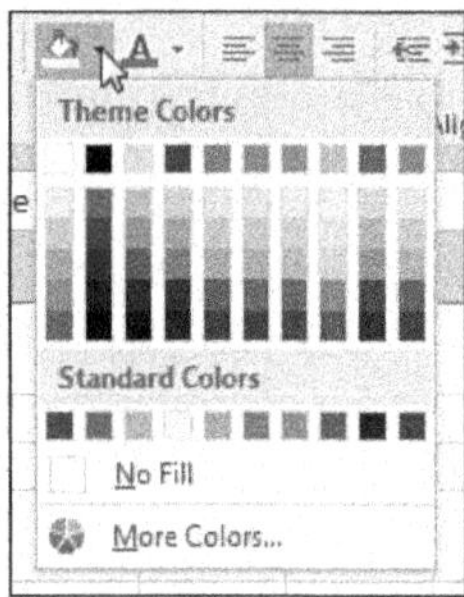

Figure 21.16 The paint bucket drop-down menu offers theme colors, 10 standard colors, and the link More Colors.

The More Colors link offers the two-tabbed Colors dialog box. You can either choose a color from the Standard tab or enter an RGB value on the Custom tab.

The ability to use a two-color gradient in a cell was a new feature beginning with Excel 2007. To activate this feature, follow these steps:

1. Select one or more cells. If you select a range of cells, Excel repeats the gradient for each cell in the range.
2. Press Ctrl+1 to display the Format Cells dialog box.
3. Select the Fill tab.
4. Click the Fill Effects button.
5. In the Color 1 and Color 2 drop-down menus, choose two colors or choose one color and white.
6. In the Shading Styles section, choose a shading style.
7. In the Variants section, choose one of the three variations. A sample is shown in the Sample box.
8. Click OK to close the Fill Effects dialog box.
9. Click OK to close the Format Cells dialog box.

Figure 21.17 shows the Fill Effects dialog box. Cell A1 contains a vertical shading, from left to right. Cell A4 shows the opposite variant of vertical shading. Cell A9 shows the from-the-center variant of the vertical shading. Cell A13 shows a diagonal-down shading style.

In all versions except Excel 2007, pattern fills are available. Use the Pattern Color and Pattern Style drop-down menus in the Fill tab of the Format Cells dialog box to add a pattern shading to a cell. A15 of Figure 21.17 shows a pattern.

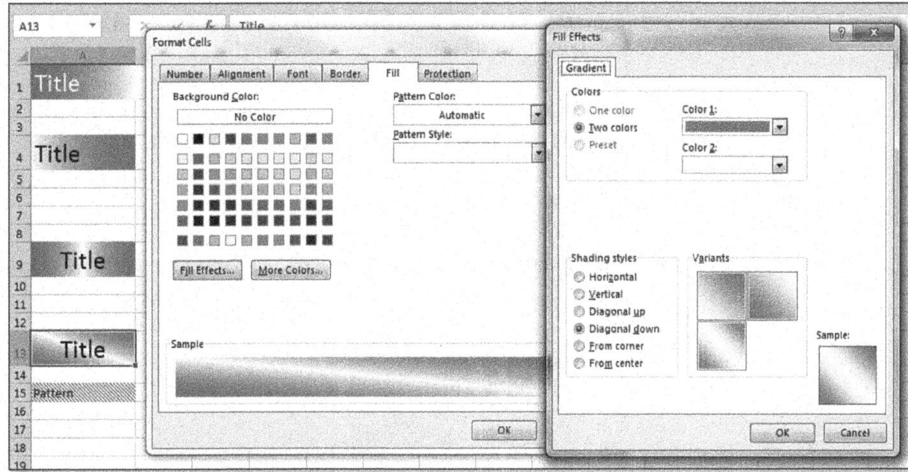

Figure 21.17 You can add gradients as the fill within cells.

Adjusting column widths and row heights

You can adjust the width of every column in a worksheet. In many cases, narrowing the columns to reduce wasted space can allow a report to fit on one page.

Most tasks in Excel can be accomplished in three or more ways. In most cases, I have a favorite method to perform any task and use that method exclusively. However, setting column widths and row heights is a task where I actively use many methods, depending on the circumstances.

You can use the following seven methods to adjust column width (each method applies equally well to adjusting row heights):

- **Click the border between the column headings:** As shown in Figure 21.18, you can drag to the left to make the column narrower. You can drag to the right to make the column wider. A ToolTip appears, showing the width in points and pixels. The advantage of this method is that you can drag until the column feels like it is the right width. The disadvantage is that this method fixes one column at a time.

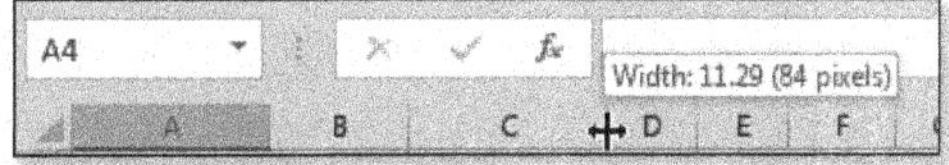

Figure 21.18 The right border between one cell letter and the next is the key to adjusting column widths.

- **Double-click the border between column headings:** Excel automatically adjusts the left column to fit the widest value in the column. The advantage of this method is that the column is exactly wide enough for the contents. The disadvantage is that a very long title in cell A1, for example, makes this method ineffective. You might have been planning to allow the title in cell A1 to spill over to B1, C1, and D1. However, the double-click method makes the column wide enough for the long title. In this case, you want to use the last method in this list.
- **Select many columns and drag the border for one column:** When you do this, the width for all columns is adjusted. The advantage of this method is that you can adjust all columns at once, and they are all a uniform width.
- **Select many columns and double-click one of the borders between column letters:** When you do this, all the columns adjust to fit their widest value.
- **Use the ribbon:** Select one or more columns. From the Cells group of the Home tab, select Format, Column Width. Then enter a width in characters and click OK.
- **Apply one column's width to other columns:** If one column is a suitable width, and you want all other columns to be the same width, you should use this method. Select the column with the correct width and then press Ctrl+C to copy. Next, select the columns to be adjusted. Select the Clipboard section of the Home tab and select Paste, Paste Special, Column Widths. Finally, click OK.
- **AutoFit a column to all the data below the title rows:** If you have a long title in the first few rows and need to AutoFit the column to all the data below the title rows, use this method. Click the first cell in the data range and then press the End key. Next, hold down the Ctrl and Shift keys while pressing the down-arrow key. This selects a contiguous range from the starting cell downward. Now select the Cells section of the Home tab and then select Format, AutoFit Selection. If you were a power user in Excel 2003 or earlier, you might remember this method as Alt+O+C+A. This legacy keyboard shortcut still works.

Using merge and center

In general, merged cells are bad. If you have a merged cell in the middle of a data table, you will be unable to sort the data. You will be unable to cut and paste data unless the same cells are merged. However, it is okay to use merged cells as a title to group several columns together.

In Figure 21.19, the Consumer and Professional headings correspond to the columns B:F and G:K, respectively. It is appropriate to center each heading above its columns.

CAUTION

Merging cells brings some negative side effects. Suppose that you had merged B100:G100. You start in cell B1, hold down the Shift key, and start pressing PgDn to select cells in column B. When you reach or pass the merged cell B100, your selection size will automatically expand to be six columns wide because this is the width of the merged cell. To prevent this problem, you might use Center Across Selection, found in the Home tab. This gives the same look as the merged cell, without the problems caused by the merge.

	A	B	C	D	E	F	G	H	I	J	K
1											
2		Consumer					Professional				
3	Month	A451	A636	A686	B416	B519	K121	K658	N713	O855	O980
4	Jan	167	198	168	139	153	145	144	198	195	168
5	Feb	166	132	135	150	183	170	198	103	195	194
6	Mar	191	103	112	190	136	124	151	108	167	182
7	Apr	125	147	175	150	190	182	154	140	173	178
8	May	121	160	147	169	170	183	147	138	196	181
9	Jun	131	166	548	179	196	165	140	177	191	177
10	Jul	182	118	144	116	172	171	158	141	149	170
11	Aug	137	129	183	163	105	188	103	116	195	102
12	Sep	130	108	124	177	170	108	168	168	142	138
13	Oct	146	197	180	177	143	180	152	177	188	123
14	Nov	154	153	180	158	129	110	118	179	151	155
15	Dec	107	162	151	145	158	178	180	159	129	188
16											

Figure 21.19 Because the row 2 categories are not part of the data table and will never need to be sorted, it is okay to merge and center those cells.

To merge and center cells, follow these steps:

1. Click in the cell that contains the value that is to be centered, and then drag to select the entire range to be merged. In this example, click in cell B2 and drag to cell F2. The result is that B2 is the active cell, and B2:F2 is selected.

2. From the Home tab, select Alignment, Merge & Center, and then select Merge & Center again, as shown in Figure 21.20.

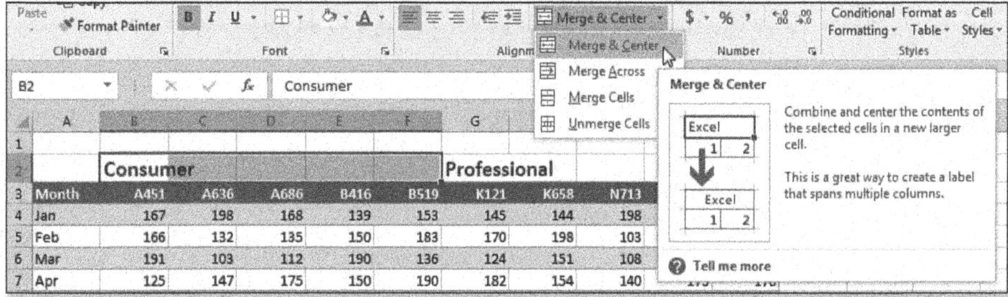

Figure 21.20 Select Merge & Center from the drop-down menu.

3. Repeat steps 1 and 2 for any other column headings.

4. Optionally, apply an outline border around the merged cells.

Note that after you merge the cells, the entire range becomes one cell. In Figure 21.21, the word *Consumer* is in an ultra-large cell B2. In this worksheet, cells C2, D2, E2, and F2 no longer exist. If you attempt to use the Go To dialog box to move to cell C2, you will be taken to cell B2 instead.

P19 fx

	A	B	C	D	E	F	G	H	I	J	K
1											
2		Consumer					Professional				
3	Month	A451	A636	A686	B416	B519	K121	K658	N713	O855	O980
4	Jan	167	198	168	139	153	145	144	198	195	168
5	Feb	166	132	135	150	183	170	198	103	195	194
6	Mar	191	103	112	190	136	124	151	108	167	182

Figure 21.21 Columns are visually grouped into product lines by the merged cells.

TROUBLESHOOTING

While selecting cells, if you touch a merged cell, your selection will instantly become as wide as the merged cell.

In the figure below, you might try selecting A1:A99 by pressing Ctrl+Shift+Up Arrow. That would usually be a great way to select the cells with data in the column.

	A	B	C	D	E
1	This title is a merged cell				
2	Product	Rep	Sales		
94	Date	Chris	940		
95	Date	Barb	950		
96	Fig	Barb	960		
97	Elderberry	Chris	970		
98	Elderberry	Andy	980		
99	Date	Andy	990		
100					

However, the merged cell in A1 causes your selection to become as wide as the merged cell. You end up selecting A1:E99 instead of A1:A99.

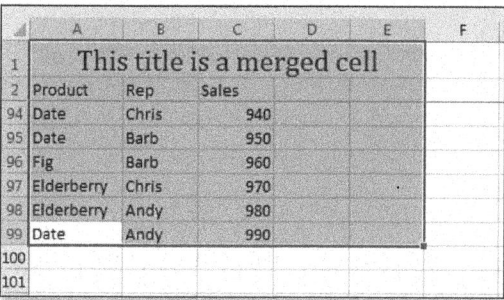

	A	B	C	D	E	F
1	This title is a merged cell					
2	Product	Rep	Sales			
94	Date	Chris	940			
95	Date	Barb	950			
96	Fig	Barb	960			
97	Elderberry	Chris	970			
98	Elderberry	Andy	980			
99	Date	Andy	990			
100						
101						

To prevent the problem, you could add a blank Row 2 to separate the merged cell from your data.

Or you could stop using merged cells. Select A1:E1 and then select, Home, Format, Format Cells, Alignment, and then open the Horizontal drop-down menu and choose Center Across Selection. This creates the same look as Merge & Center, but the selection rectangle will not widen when you touch A1.

To fix the problem shown in the figure, hold down the Shift key while you press the down arrow key. You will have A2:E99 selected. Now that the merged cell is no longer part of the selection, hold down Shift while pressing the left arrow key four times.

CHAPTER 21

Rotating text

Vertical text is difficult to read. However, at times, space considerations make it advantageous to use vertical text. In Figure 21.22, for example, the names in row 5 are much wider than the values in the rest of the table. If you use Format, AutoFit Selection, the report is too wide.

	A	B	C	D	E	F	G
5		Product	Blankenship	Cunningham	Fitzpatrick	Hamilton	Hernderson
6	Consumer	A451	339	258	293	316	252
7		A636	438	332	377	408	325
8		A686	218	166	188	203	162
9		B416	513	389	442	477	380
10		B519	844	640	727	786	626
11		D553	178	135	154	166	132
12		D555	472	358	407	439	350
13		D801	427	324	368	397	317
14		D914	374	283	322	348	277
15		E196	761	578	656	709	564
16		E476	573	434	494	533	425
17		Subtotal	5,137	3,897	4,428	4,782	3,810

Figure 21.22 The headings are much wider than the data. Vertical text can solve the problem.

In the Alignment tab of the Home group, an Orientation drop-down menu offers five variations of vertical text. Figure 21.23 compares the five available options. Although the Angle options look great, they reduce the column width by only 12%. Vertical Text reduces the column width by 75% but takes far more vertical space. The option Rotate Text Up reduces the column width by 73% and takes up less than half the vertical space of the Vertical Text option.

NOTE

After you rotate the text, select the Cells section of the Home tab and then select Format, AutoFit Selection again to narrow the columns.

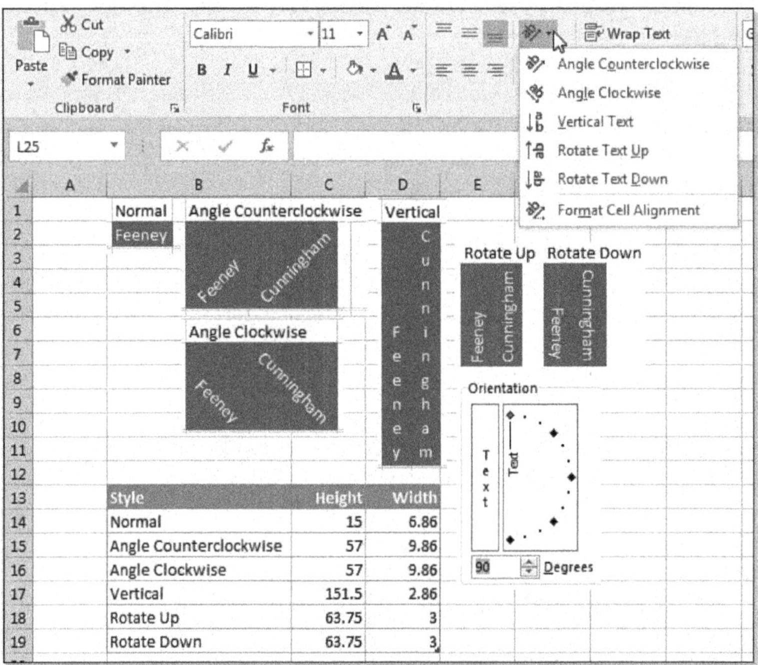

Figure 21.23 Of the five options, the Rotate Text options take up the least space.

If you need more control over the text orientation, you can select the Alignment option in the drop-down menu to display the Alignment tab of the Format Cells dialog box. This tab allows rotation from 90 degrees to –90 degrees, in 1-degree increments, as shown in the bottom right of Figure 21.23.

Formatting with styles

Instead of using the settings in the Font group of the Home tab, you can format a report by using the built-in cell styles. Cell styles have been popular in Word for more than a decade. They have been available in legacy versions of Excel, but because they were not given a spot on the Formatting toolbar, few people took advantage of them.

Figure 21.24 shows the styles available when you select Styles, Cell Styles in the Home tab.

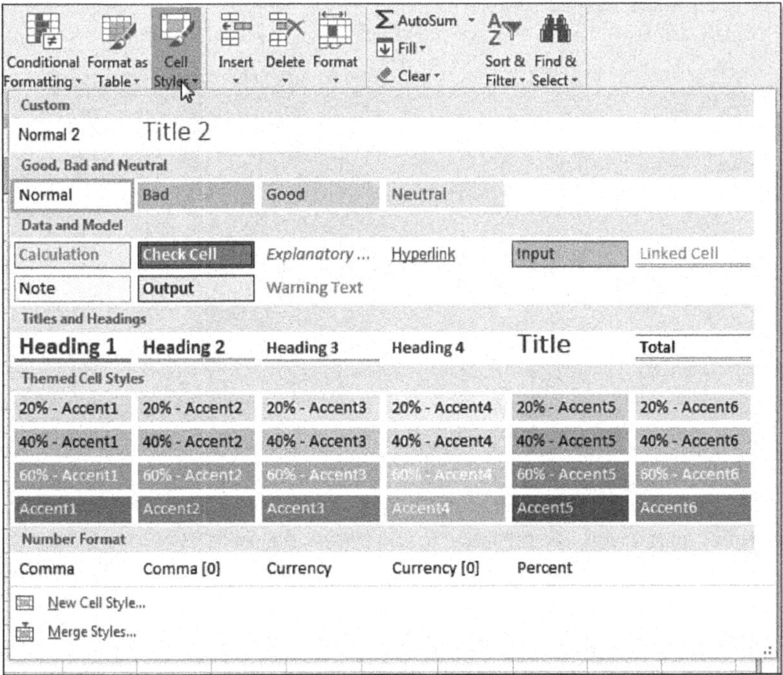

Figure 21.24 The Cell Styles gallery offers various built-in cell styles.

An advantage to using cell styles is that you can convert the look and feel of a report by choosing from the themes on the Page Layout tab. Figure 21.25 shows one of the several themes applied to the report.

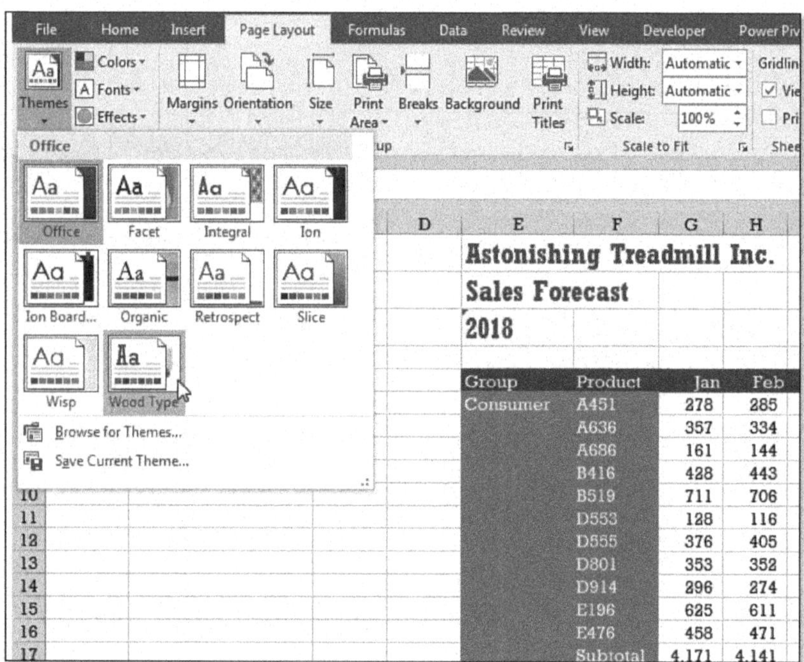

Figure 21.25 When you choose a new theme, a report formatted with cell styles takes on a new look.

The Cell Styles gallery offers a menu item to add additional styles to a workbook. Using cell styles provides an interesting alternative to the traditional method of formatting.

NOTE

You might wonder why Excel suggests that calculated cells should be in orange font or why Notes should have a yellow background. I spent the first two years of working with Excel 2007 wondering why calculated cells should be orange. However, the better question is, "Why not orange?" When I receive worksheets from others who use this convention, it is easy to understand that they are using the built-in cell styles, which makes it easier to follow the logic of the worksheet. In Figure 21.26, the forecasting model was formatted using cell styles from the Data And Model section of the Cell Styles menu. If everyone in your company used these styles, it would be easier to spot the input cells in any model.

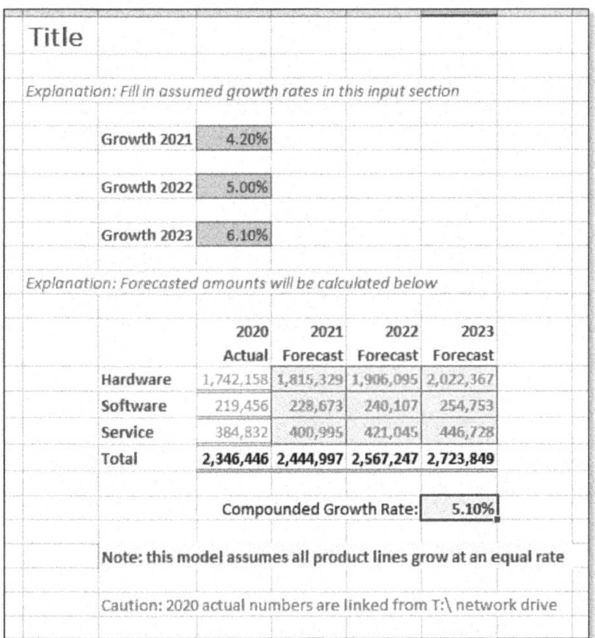

Figure 21.26 Adopt the cell styles suggestions for input cells, calculated cells, and so on to make it easier to see the logic in the model.

Understanding themes

A *theme* is a collection of colors, fonts, and effects. Office has 20 built-in themes. If you've upgraded your computer from a previous version, you can also download new themes from Office Online or design your own themes.

TIP

The Office theme is the default theme in Excel. In an effort to look modern, Microsoft changed the Office theme starting in Excel 2013. If you had previously embraced themes in Excel 2007 or Excel 2010, you might have become a fan of the old Office theme. The Title cell style in the old Office theme was better than the Title cell style in the new Office theme. Worse, if you open an old document created with Excel 2007 or Excel 2010, the old Office theme will still be available. New workbooks have the new Office theme. It is annoying that they used the same name for two different themes.

Here is how to get the old Office theme back. On the Page Layout tab, open three drop-down menus for color, font, and effects. In each drop-down menu, choose Office 2007–2010 theme. After choosing from those three drop-down menus, choose Themes, Save Current Theme. Save the theme with a name such as `OfficeReal` or `aaaOffice`. Custom themes appear at the top of the Themes drop-down menu, so it will be relatively easy to go back to the old theme, even in new workbooks.

Themes are shared in simple XML files, which means they can be propagated throughout a company. A theme has the following components:

- **Fonts:** A theme has two fonts: one for body text and one for titles. The fonts come into play more often in PowerPoint and Word than in Excel. However, styles in Excel also use fonts.
- **Colors:** There are 12 colors: four for text and backgrounds, six accent colors that are used in charts and table accents, and two for hyperlinks. One of the two colors for hyperlinks indicates followed hyperlinks, whereas the other color indicates hyperlinks that have not been followed. The colors shown here appear in the top of the Color Chooser shown previously in Figure 21.16.
- **Effects:** Each theme includes several object effects, such as bevel and line style.

Choosing a new theme

Themes are managed on the Page Layout tab. Listed next are the four drop-down menus available in the Themes group:

- **Themes:** Allows you to switch among the built-in themes.
- **Colors:** Allows you to change the color scheme to use the colors from another theme.
- **Fonts:** Allows you to use the fonts from another theme.
- **Effects:** Allows you to use the effects from another theme.

NOTE

Note that you can use only one theme per workbook. If you are changing the theme on Sheet33, the same changes are made on all the other worksheets in the workbook.

Changing a theme affects charts, tables, SmartArt diagrams, and inserted objects.

To switch to another theme, follow these steps:

1. Arrange your worksheet so that you can see any themed elements, such as tables or charts, on the right side of the screen.
2. From the Page Layout tab, select the Themes drop-down menu from the Themes group.
3. Hover over the various themes. The worksheet updates to show the new colors, fonts, and effects.
4. When you identify a theme you like, click the theme to apply it to the workbook.

If you are strictly interested in the accent colors, you can select the Colors drop-down menu from the Themes group to see the accent colors used in each theme. Note that this drop-down menu offers a grayscale option that is not available in the Themes drop-down menu.

Inside OUT

One common request is to go back to the theme used in Excel 2007 and 2010. People had six years to create documents with the bold colors introduced in Excel 2007.

The colors used in the Office theme changed in Excel 2013. When you open the Themes drop-down menu, there is nothing offering you to go back to the Office 2007–2010 colors.

However, each theme is defined by colors, fonts, and effects. If you skip the Theme drop-down menu and head directly to each of the three component drop-downs, you will find a theme called Office 2007 – 2010.

It seems just a bit rotten that Microsoft hid the old theme in the Color/Fonts/Effects drop-down menus when most people would think to look in the Themes drop-down menu.

Creating a new theme

You might want to develop a special theme, which is fairly easy to do. First, you need to select two fonts and six accent colors. For example, suppose you want to create a theme to match your company's color scheme. The hardest part is finding six colors to represent your company, because most company logos have two or three colors. Use a tool such as *https://paletton.com* to find complementary colors for your company colors.

Specifying a theme's colors

To specify new theme colors, follow these steps:

1. Select Page Layout, Themes, Colors, Create New Theme Colors. The Create New Theme Colors dialog box appears.
2. To change any accent color, select the drop-down menu next to Accent 1 through Accent 6. The Color Chooser appears. Select More Colors. Enter the color codes for Red, Green, and Blue. Repeat for the other accent colors.
3. In the Name box, give the theme a name, such as your company name.
4. Click Save to accept the theme.

Specifying a theme's fonts

To specify new theme fonts, follow these steps:

1. Select Page Layout, Themes, Fonts, Create New Theme Fonts.
2. Select a font from the Heading Font drop-down menu. If a custom font is used in your company's logo, using it might be appropriate.
3. Select a font from the Body Font drop-down menu. This should be a font that is easy to read. Avoid stylized fonts for body copy.
4. Give the theme a name. It is okay to reuse the same name from the color theme.
5. Click Save to accept the theme changes.

> TIP
>
> **In June 2009, famed font designer Erik Spiekermann released the Axel font family, which he designed specifically for showing tables of numbers in Microsoft Excel. You can purchase Axel from *https://www.fontshop.com/families/axel.***

Reusing another theme's effects

There is no dialog box to choose the effects associated with a theme. Other than editing the XML by hand, you are limited to using the effects from one of the built-in themes.

To select effects for a theme, from the Page Layout tab, select Themes, Effects. Then choose one of the existing themes.

The Effects drop-down menu is initially vexing. There are only subtle clues about the effects used in the theme. Each effects icon consists of a circle, an arrow, and a rectangle. The circle represents effects for simple shapes. The arrow represents moderate effects. The rectangle represents intense effects. These roughly correspond to rows in the Shape Styles gallery found on the Drawing Tools Format tab. Row 1 in the gallery is simple, row 4 is moderate, and row 6 is intense.

Saving a custom theme

To reuse a theme, you must save it. To save a theme, from the Page Layout tab, select Themes, Save Current Theme.

By default, themes are stored in the Document Themes folder. In Windows Vista and Windows 7, the folder is in `C:\Users\user name\AppData\Roaming\Microsoft\Templates\Document Themes`.

Be sure to give your theme a useful name and then click Save.

Using a theme on a new document

When you open a new document on the same computer, the Custom theme is in the Themes drop-down menu on the Page Layout tab. You can use this theme on all future documents.

Sharing a theme with others

If you want to share a theme with others, you need to send them the .thmx file from the theme folder.

The people you share the theme with can either copy the .thmx file to their equivalent folder or save the .thmx file to their desktop and use the Browse For Themes option, by choosing Page Layout, Themes, Browse For Themes.

Other formatting techniques

Now that you have the basics for formatting cells and worksheets, the rest of this chapter provides an overview of various formatting tips and tricks. These techniques discuss how to mix formatting within a single cell, wrap text in several cells, and use cell comments.

> TIP
>
> **After selecting characters in the cell, move the mouse pointer to the right and up to activate a shortened version of the mini toolbar. You can use icons on this floating toolbar to format the selected characters.**

Formatting individual characters

Occasionally, you might find yourself entering a short memo on a worksheet. This might occur as an introduction or as instructions to a lengthy workbook. Although Excel is not a full-featured word processor, it can do a few word processing tricks.

One trick is to highlight individual characters in a cell to add emphasis or to make them stand out. You can do this to any cell that does not contain a formula. In Figure 21.27, for example, text has been typed in column A and allowed to extend over the edge of the column into columns A:J. One word in row 4 is in a bold, underlined, red font.

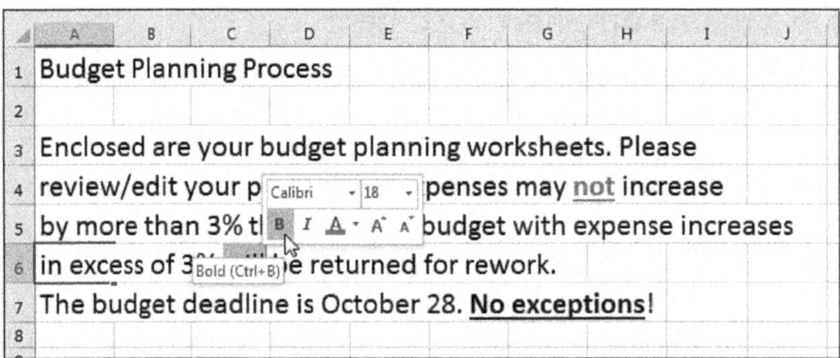

Figure 21.27 Formatting for individual characters in a cell can be changed by selecting those characters while in Edit mode.

To format individual characters, follow these steps:

1. Display the Home tab.
2. Select the cell that contains the characters to be formatted.
3. Press the F2 key to edit the cell.
4. Using the mouse, highlight the characters in the cell. Move up and to the right to display the Mini toolbar.
5. Although most of the ribbon is grayed out, the options for font size, color, underline, bold, italic, and font name are available in the Font group of the Home tab. Apply any formatting, as desired, from this group.
6. If the changes are not visible in the formula bar, press Enter to accept the changes to preview them.

Changing the default font

Excel offers a default font setting to be used for all new workbooks. With the Excel paradigm of themes, the default font for new workbooks is initially the generic value of BODY FONT. However, this is not an actual font; instead, it refers to the main font used by the current theme.

To change your default font for all new workbooks, follow these steps:

NOTE

If you like the concept of using themes to change the look and feel of a document, you should leave the default font setting as BODY FONT and change the font used in the theme.

1. The menu for changing the default font does not offer Live Preview of the fonts. Therefore, go to the Font section of the Home tab and select the Font drop-down menu to inspect the available fonts in their actual styles. Find the name of the font you want to use.

2. From the File menu, select Excel Options. The Excel Options dialog box appears.

3. Click the General category in the left margin.

4. In the second section, When Creating New Workbooks, select the Use This Font drop-down menu. Select the font name you chose in step 1.

5. Click OK to close the Excel Options dialog box.

6. Close and restart Microsoft Excel for the changes to take effect.

The default font setting has an effect only in new workbooks. It does not affect workbooks previously created.

Wrapping text in a cell

You might have one column in a table that contains long, descriptive text. If the text contains several sentences, it would be impractical to make the column wide enough to include the longest value in the column. Excel offers the capability to wrap text on a cell-by-cell basis to solve this problem.

When you wrap text, one annoying feature of Excel becomes evident. All cells in Excel are initially set to have their contents aligned with the bottom of the cell. You probably do not notice this because most cells in Excel are the same height. However, when you wrap text, the cell heights double or more. When this occurs, it becomes evident that the bottom alignment looks strange. To correct this problem, follow these steps:

> NOTE
>
> **If the rows are too tall, you will have a tendency to grab the right edge of the column and drag it outward to make the description column wider. A long-standing bug causes Excel not to resize the row heights automatically after this step. Instead, you need to select the Cells section of the Home tab and then select Format, AutoFit Row Height to resize the row height after adjusting the column width.**

1. Decide on a reasonable column width for the column that contains the descriptive text. If you try to wrap text in a column that is only 8 points wide, you will be lucky to fit one word per line. If you have the space, a width of at least 24 allows suitable results for the text wrapping.

2. From the Cells section of the Home tab, select Format, Column Width. Choose a width of 24 or greater.

3. Choose the cells in the column to be wrapped.

4. From the Home tab, select Alignment, Wrap Text.

5. Select all cells in the range.

6. From the Home tab, select Alignment, Top Align. The values in the other columns now align with the top of the descriptive text.

Figure 21.28 shows a table where the descriptions in column B have had their text wrapped and all the cells are top aligned.

	A	B	C	D	E
1	Product	Description	Jan	Feb	Mar
2	A451	Run up to six preset programs and two customizable workout programs. Other safety features include a large stop switch, starts from only .05 mph and low-profile running hood. A great value. Additional features include cooling fans and speed and incline controls on the arm rests.	278	285	271
	A636	Folding treadmill frame design originated from the demand of hotels for a treadmill as mobile as a room	357	334	387

Figure 21.28 After wrapping text in a column, you should top align all columns.

Justifying text in a range

When using Excel as a word processor to include a paragraph of explanatory body copy in a worksheet, you usually have to decide where to break each line manually. Otherwise, Excel offers a command that reflows the text in a paragraph to fit a certain number of columns.

For this reason, you should do some careful preselection work before invoking the command by following these steps:

1. Ensure that your text is composed of one column of cells that contain body copy. It is fine if the sentences extend beyond one column, but the text should be arranged so that the left column contains text, and the remaining columns are blank.

2. Ensure that the upper-left cell of your selection starts with the first line of text.

3. Ensure that the selection range is as wide as you want the finished text to be.

4. If your sentences currently extend beyond the desired width, Excel requires more rows to wrap the text. Include several extra rows in the selection rectangle. Figure 21.29 shows a suitable-sized selection range.

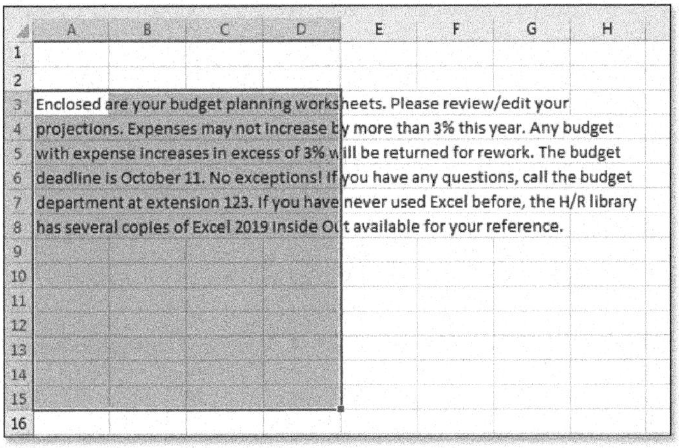

Figure 21.29 You need to select more rows than necessary. The number of columns selected determines the width of the final text.

5. From the Home tab, select Editing, Fill, Justify. Excel flows the text so that each line is shorter than the selection range. Figure 21.30 shows the result.

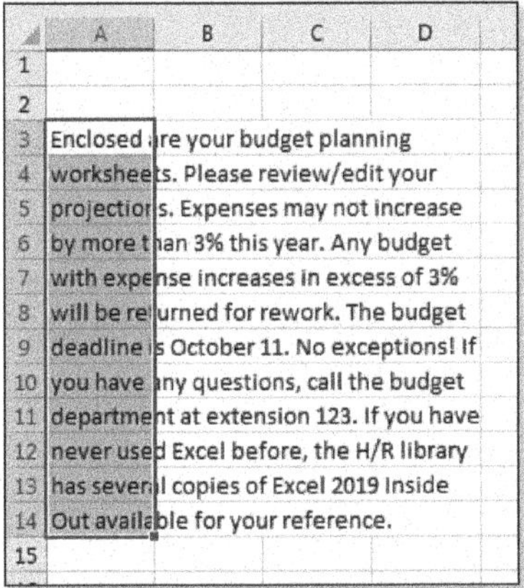

Figure 21.30 Excel flows the text to fit the width of the original selection.

Adding cell notes

Cell notes debuted in Excel 97 and were called Notes for three years. In Excel 2000, Microsoft changed the name to Comments. In 2019, Microsoft introduced new threaded comments and changed the name of this feature back to Notes. While Comments are great for collaboration, Notes offer several techniques that are useful when formatting worksheets.

Cell notes can contain a few sentences or paragraphs to explain the contents of a cell. Although the default is for all notes to use a yellow sticky-note format, you can customize notes with colors, fonts, different shapes, or even pictures.

In the default case, a note causes a red triangle to appear in a cell. If you hover over the triangle, the note appears. Alternatively, you can request that notes be displayed all the time. This creates an easy way to add instructions to a worksheet.

Follow these steps to insert a note, format it, and cause it to be displayed continuously:

1. Select a cell to which you want to add a note.
2. Select Review, Notes, New Note, or right-click the cell and select New Note or press Shift+F2.
3. The default note starts with your name in bold on line 1 and the insertion point on line 2. To remove your name from the note, backspace through your name and then press Ctrl+B to turn off the bold.
4. Type instructions to the person using the worksheet. You can make the instructions longer than the initial size of the note.

   NOTE

   Keep in mind that a note can contain more than 2,000 words of body copy.

5. After entering the text, click the resize handle in the lower-right corner of the note. Drag to allow the note to fit the text.
6. The selection border around the note can be made of either diagonal lines or dots. If your selection border is diagonal lines, click the selection border to change it to dots.
7. Right-click the selection border and select Format Note. The Format Note dialog box appears.
8. In the Format Note dialog box, change the font, alignment, colors, and so on, as desired. The Transparency setting on the Colors and Lines tab allows the underlying spreadsheet to show through the note. If you choose the Fill Color drop-down menu, you can select Fill Effects and insert a picture as the background in the note.
9. Click OK to return to the note.
10. Right-click in the cell and select Show/Hide Note. This causes the note to be permanently displayed on the worksheet.
11. To reposition the note, click the note. Drag the selection border to a new location.

Figure 21.31 shows a note that has been formatted, resized, and set to be displayed.

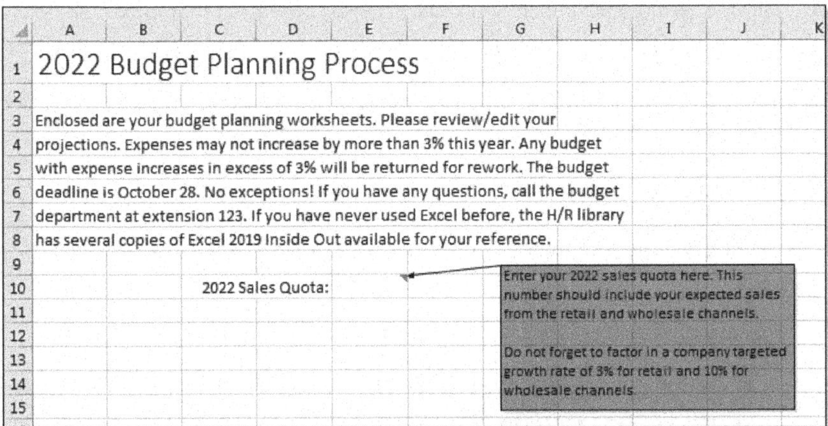

Figure 21.31 Cell notes can provide instructions or tips for people who use your spreadsheet.

To show a picture in a note, follow these steps:

1. Select the cell where you want the pop-up picture to appear.
2. Shift+F2 to add a note.
3. Backspace through the name that appears.
4. Carefully, click on the border of the comment to leave Edit mode and select the entire comment. Note that nothing changes in the Excel screen when you click properly. You will know if you clicked in the correct place during step 6.
5. Press Ctrl+1 to display the Format Note dialog box. As of the middle of 2021, Microsoft still has not updated the title bar of the Format Note dialog, so it is still appearing as Format Comment.
6. Look at the tabs across the top of the dialog. You should have eight tabs, such as Font, Alignment, Colors And Lines, and so on. If you only have a single tab for Font, then you did not click properly in step 4. Close the dialog and go back to step 4.
7. Click the Colors And Lines tab in the dialog box.
8. The top section is for Fill. Open the Color drop-down menu. The final choice is Fill Effect. Choose Fill Effects. Excel opens the Fill Effects dialog box with tabs for Gradient, Texture, Pattern, and Picture.
9. Choose the Picture tab in the Fill Effects dialog box.

10. Click the Select Picture button. Browse to and select a picture.

11. Click OK to close Fill Effects. Click OK to close the Format dialog box. The picture will appear in the note, and you should still see the selection handles around the note.

12. Resize the note, including changing the aspect ratio so the image does not look squashed.

13. Click away from the note.

At this point, any time you hover over the cell, a box will appear with the photo, as shown in Figure 21.32.

Figure 21.32 Change the fill of a note to a picture to create pop-up pictures in the grid. Photo credit: Mary Ellen Jelen / We Report Space.

Copying formats

Excel worksheets tend to have many similar sections of data. After you have taken the time to format the first section, it would be great to be able to copy the formats from one section to another section. The next sections in this chapter discuss the two methods offered in Excel for doing this: pasting formats and using the Format Painter icon.

Pasting formats

An option on the Paste Options menu allows you to paste only the formats from the Clipboard. The rules for copying and pasting formats are as follows:

- If your original selection is one cell, you can paste the formats to as many cells as you want.
- If your original selection is one row tall and multiple cells wide, you can paste the formats to multiple rows, and the final paste area will be as wide as the original copied range.
- If your original selection is one column wide and multiple cells tall, you can paste the formats to multiple columns, and the final paste area will be as tall as the original copied range.

Follow these steps to copy formats:

1. Select a formatted section of a report. This might be one cell, one row of cells, or a rectangular range of cells.
2. Press Ctrl+C to copy the selected section to the Clipboard.
3. Select an unformatted section of your worksheet. If your selection in step 1 is a rectangular range, you can select just the top-left cell of the destination range.
4. Press Ctrl+V to paste. Press Ctrl again to open the Paste Options menu. Press R to paste only the formats. The formats from the original selection are copied to the new range. Although the amounts initially changed after you pressed Ctrl+C, the original amounts are restored after you press R.
5. If you have multiple target destinations to format, repeat step 4 as needed.

The disadvantage of using the Paste Formats method is that it does not change column widths. To copy column widths without pasting values, on the Home tab, click the Paste drop-down menu and then select Paste Special, Column Widths, OK.

CAUTION

Do not attempt to use the Column Widths icon in the Paste Options menu to solve this problem. The Column Widths icon always pastes the values along with the column widths. Because you are only trying to copy formats and column widths in this example, this is not a suitable result.

Pasting conditional formats

Starting with Excel 2010, the rules changed when you paste a range with one conditional formatting onto another range with a different conditional formatting. The copied conditional format replaces the existing conditional formatting. There might be times when you want to merge the existing icon set in the source range with the existing color scale in the target range. In this case, choose All Merging Conditional Formats from the Paste Special dialog box, or the elusive icon in the second row, fourth column of the Paste Options menu. Note that this pastes formats, formulas, and borders as well as merges the conditional formats.

Using the Format Painter

The Format Painter icon appears in the Clipboard group of the Home tab. The prominent location of the icon might encourage you to attempt to use this feature. The Format Painter is still tricky to use.

To copy a format from a source range to a destination range, follow these steps:

1. Select the source range. If you want to copy column widths, the source range must include complete columns.
2. Click the Format Painter icon once in the Clipboard group of the Home tab. The mouse icon changes to a plus and a paintbrush.
3. Immediately use the mouse to click and drag to select a destination range. If the source range was five columns wide, the destination range should also be five columns wide.
4. If you accidentally click somewhere else or click the wrong size range, undo and start over.

The ToolTip for the Format Painter icon advertises a little-known feature. This feature enables you to copy a format to many ranges. To do this, follow these steps:

1. Select the source range.
2. Double-click the Format Painter icon.
3. Click a new destination range. The format is copied. Alternatively, you can drag to paint a different size range.
4. Repeat step 3 as many times as you want.
5. When you are done formatting ranges, press Esc or single-click the Format Painter icon to turn off the feature.

Copying formats to a new worksheet

You can use a straightforward way to make a copy of a worksheet. This method is better than creating a new worksheet and copying formats from the original sheet to the new sheet. Among its advantages are that column widths and row heights are copied and page setup settings are copied.

To copy a worksheet within the current workbook, follow these steps:

1. Activate the worksheet to be copied.
2. Hold down the Ctrl key. Click the worksheet tab and drag it to a new location. A new sheet is created with a strange name, such as Sheet3 (2).
3. Right-click the sheet tab and select Rename. The cursor moves to the tab, which is now editable.
4. Type a new name and press Enter. The tab has a new name.

To copy a worksheet to a new workbook, follow these steps:

1. Activate the worksheet to be copied.
2. Right-click the sheet tab. Select Move Or Copy to display the Move Or Copy dialog box.
3. In the To Book drop-down menu, select (new book).
4. Click Create A Copy.

CHAPTER 22

Using data visualizations and conditional formatting

Many people feel their eyes glaze over when they encounter a screen full of numbers. Fortunately, Microsoft offers data-visualization features to Excel that make those screens full of numbers easier to interpret.

The following are some of the possibilities in data visualization:

- Adding data bars (that is, tiny, in-cell bar charts) to cells based on the cell value. Data bars can be negative, include an axis, and have scaling options.
- Adding color scales to cells based on the cell value. This is often called a *heat map*. Whereas the old conditional formatting would allow you to apply one color if a value exceeds a certain amount, a color scale applies a range from a gradient based on how high the value is.
- Adding icon sets (think traffic lights) to cells based on the cell value.
- Adding color, bold, italic, strikethrough, number formatting, and so on to cells based on the cell values.
- Quickly identifying cells that are above average.
- Quickly identifying the top *n* or bottom *n*% of cells.
- Quickly identifying duplicate values.
- Quickly identifying dates that are today or yesterday or last week.
- Sorting by color or by icon (after you've added color or icons).

Although it is easy to set up basic conditional formatting, you need to know a few tricks, which you discover later in this chapter, for creating better conditional formatting than most people will figure out on their own.

Using data bars to create in-cell bar charts

A *data bar* is a swath of color that starts at the side of a cell and extends into the cell based on the value of the cell. Small numbers get less color. The largest numbers might be 100% filled with color. This creates a visual effect that enables you to visually pick out the larger and smaller values. Figure 22.1 shows many examples of data bars.

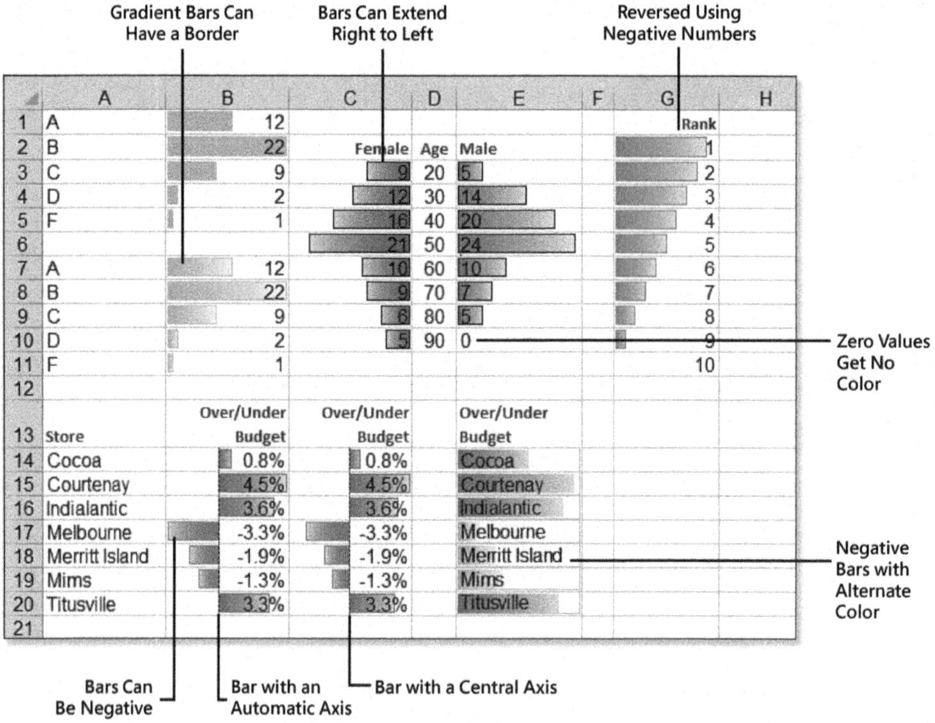

	A	B	C	D	E	F	G	H
1	A	12					Rank	
2	B	22	Female	Age	Male		1	
3	C	9	9	20	5		2	
4	D	2	12	30	14		3	
5	F	1	16	40	20		4	
6			21	50	24		5	
7	A	12	10	60	10		6	
8	B	22	9	70	7		7	
9	C	9	6	80	5		8	
10	D	2	5	90	0		9	
11	F	1					10	
12								
13	Store	Over/Under Budget	Over/Under Budget		Over/Under Budget			
14	Cocoa	0.8%	0.8%		Cocoa			
15	Courtenay	4.5%	4.5%		Courtenay			
16	Indialantic	3.6%	3.6%		Indialantic			
17	Melbourne	-3.3%	-3.3%		Melbourne			
18	Merritt Island	-1.9%	-1.9%		Merritt Island			
19	Mims	-1.3%	-1.3%		Mims			
20	Titusville	3.3%	3.3%		Titusville			
21								

Gradient Bars Can Have a Border
Bars Can Extend Right to Left
Reversed Using Negative Numbers
Zero Values Get No Color
Negative Bars with Alternate Color
Bars Can Be Negative
Bar with an Automatic Axis
Bar with a Central Axis

Figure 22.1 Examples of many of the properties in Excel 2019 data bars.

Many options are available in Excel data bars:

- Data bars can be solid or a gradient.
- Values of zero get no data bar, as shown in cell E10.
- Data bars can be negative. Negative bars are shown in a different color and usually extend to the left of a central axis. You have three choices in where to place the zero axis. In cells B14:B20, the setting is Automatic. Because the largest positive number is further from zero than the smallest negative number, the axis appears slightly to the left of center. This allows the bar for 4.5% in B15 to appear larger than the bar for –3.3% in B17. You can also force the axis to appear in the center, as in cells C14:C20. Or, in a bizarre setting,

you can force the negative bars to extend in the same direction as the positive values, but with a different color. There are two philosophical ways to show the negative bars. You can assign –3.3% the most color because it is farthest from zero, or you could assign –1.3% the most color because it is the mathematically the largest of the negative numbers (–1.3% > –3.3%). Excel uses the latter method.

- To "reverse" a data bar—to show the most color for the largest number—multiply the numbers by –1 to make them negative. Use a custom number format of "0;0;0;" to display the negative numbers as positive. Make the negative bars extend in the same direction as positive. You end up with the surprising results shown in G1:G11.
- You can control the color of the positive bar, the positive bar border, the negative bar, the negative bar border, and the axis color.
- Bars can now extend right to left, as shown in cells C3:C10. This allows comparative histograms as in C2:E10.
- You can specify the scale of the data bars. Although the scale is initially set to automatic, you can specify that the min or max is set to a certain number or to the lowest value, a percentage, a percentile, or a formula.
- You can choose to show only the data bar and to hide the number in the cell. This is how I managed to get words in cells E14:E20. The numbers are hidden by the conditional formatting dialog box, and then a linked picture of the words is pasted over the cells. Because the data bars are on a drawing layer above the regular drawing layer, this works.
- All data bars in a group have the same scale. This is unlike sparklines, where the scale is allowed to change from graphic to graphic.

NOTE

If you don't like the six basic colors Excel offers for data bars, you can choose any other color, as described in the next section.

Creating data bars

Creating data bars requires just a few clicks. Follow these steps:

CAUTION

In step 1, if you attempt to select a range that contains both units sold and revenue dollars, the size of the revenue numbers overpowers the units sold numbers, and no color appears in the units sold cells.

1. Select a range of numeric data. Do not include the total in this selection. If the data is in noncontiguous ranges, hold down the Ctrl key while selecting additional areas. This range

should be composed of numbers of similar scale. For example, you can select a column of sales data or a column of profit data.

2. From the Home tab, select Conditional Formatting, Data Bars. You see six built-in colors for the data bars: blue, green, red, orange, bright blue, and pink. The colors appear in both solid and gradient forms. Select one of them. The result is a swath of color in each cell in the selection, as shown in Figure 22.2.

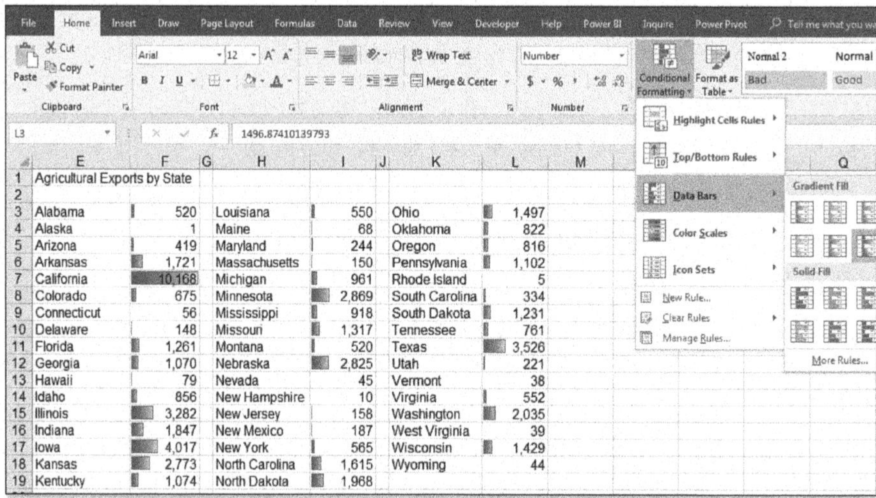

Figure 22.2 After applying a data bar, you can easily see that California is a leading exporter of agriculture products.

Customizing data bars

By default, Excel assigns the largest data bar to the cell with the largest value and the smallest data bar to the cell with the smallest value. You can customize this behavior by following these steps:

1. From the Conditional Formatting drop-down list on the Home tab, select Manage Rules.

2. From the Show Formatting Rules drop-down list, select This Worksheet. You now see a list of all rules applied to the sheet.

3. Click the Data Bar rule.

4. Click the Edit Rule button. Alternatively, you could double-click the rule in step 3. You see the Edit Formatting Rule dialog box, as shown in Figure 22.3.

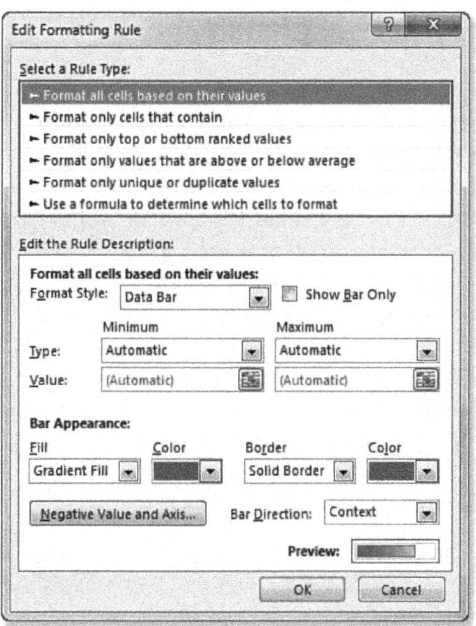

Figure 22.3 You customize data bars by using the Edit Formatting Rule dialog box.

A number of customizations are available in this dialog box:

- Select the Show Bar Only setting to hide the numbers in the cells and to show only the data bar.
- For the Minimum and Maximum values, you can choose from Automatic, Number, Percent, Percentile, Formula, and Smallest/Largest Number. If you select Automatic, Excel chooses a minimum and maximum value. You can override this by setting one value to a specific number.
- In the Bar Appearance section, you can specify gradient or solid fill for the bar. You can specify a solid border or no border. Two color chooser drop-down lists enable you to change the color of the bar and the border.
- The Bar Direction drop-down list enables you to select Context, Left to Right, or Right to Left. The default choice of Context is always left to right unless you are in an international edition of Excel in which the language reading order is right to left.

When you choose Negative Values and Axis, you have new settings to adjust the color of the bar and the border for negative bars. You can also control whether the zero axis is shown at the cell midpoint or at an automatic location based on the relative size of the negative and positive numbers. If the axis is shown, you can adjust the color as well.

Showing data bars for a subset of cells

In the data bars examples given in the previous sections, every cell in the range receives a data bar. But what if you just want some of the values (for example, the top 20% or the top 10) to have data bars? The process for making this happen isn't intuitive, but it is possible. You apply the data bar to the entire range. Then you add a new conditional format (a very plain format) to all the cells that you don't want to have data bars. For example, you might tell Excel to use a white background on all cells with values outside of the top 10.

The final important step is to manage the rules and tell Excel to stop processing more rules if the white background rule is met. This requires clever thinking. If you want to apply data bars to cells in the top 10, you first tell Excel to make all the cells in the bottom 21 look like every other cell in Excel. Turning on Stop If True (in the Conditional Formatting Rules Manager dialog box) is the key to getting Excel to not apply the data bar to cells with values outside of the top 10.

Figure 22.4 shows data bars applied to only the top 10 states.

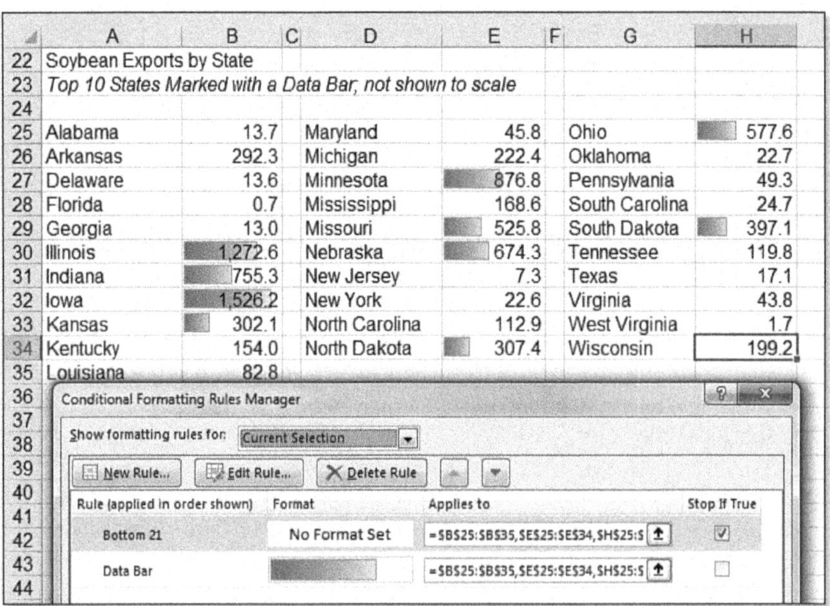

Figure 22.4 Using Stop If True after formatting the lower 21 with no special formatting allows the data bars to appear only for the top states.

Using color scales to highlight extremes

Color scales are similar to data bars. Instead of having a variable-size bar in each cell, however, color scales use gradients of two or three different colors to communicate the relative size of each cell. Here's how you apply color scales:

1. Select a range that contains numbers. Be sure not to include headings or total cells in the selection.
2. Select Conditional Formatting, Color Scales from the Home tab.
3. From the Color Scales fly-out menu, select one of the 12 styles to apply the color scale to the range. (Note that this fly-out menu offers subtle differences that you should pay attention to. The first six options are scales that use three colors. These are great onscreen or with color printers. The last six options are scales that use two colors. These are better with monochrome printers.)

In a two-color red/white color scale, the largest number is formatted with a dark red fill. The smallest number has a white fill. All the numbers in between receive a lighter or darker shade of pink based on their position within the range (see Figure 22.5).

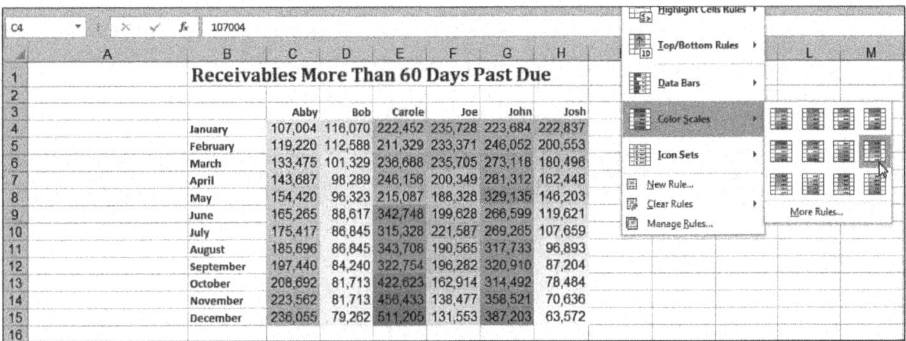
Receivables More Than 60 Days Past Due

	Abby	Bob	Carole	Joe	John	Josh
January	107,004	116,070	222,452	235,728	223,684	222,837
February	119,220	112,588	211,329	233,371	246,052	200,553
March	133,475	101,329	236,688	235,705	273,118	180,498
April	143,687	98,289	246,156	200,349	281,312	162,448
May	154,420	96,323	215,087	188,328	329,135	146,203
June	165,265	88,617	342,748	199,628	266,599	119,621
July	175,417	86,845	315,328	221,587	269,265	107,659
August	185,696	86,845	343,708	190,565	317,733	96,893
September	197,440	84,240	322,754	196,282	320,910	87,204
October	208,692	81,713	422,623	162,914	314,492	78,484
November	223,562	81,713	456,433	138,477	358,521	70,636
December	236,055	79,262	511,205	131,553	387,203	63,572

Figure 22.5 Excel provides a range of shading, depending on the value. You can see that Carole's and John's receivables have been increasing throughout the year.

You are not limited to the color scales shown in the fly-out menu. If you select Home, Conditional Formatting, Manage Rules, Edit Rule, you can choose any two or three colors for the color scale.

You also can choose where to assign the smallest, largest, and midpoint values (see Figure 22.6). Column E and the Edit Formatting Rule show how to highlight central values. Using a three-color scale, the minimum and maximum are set to white, whereas the middle numbers are assigned a color.

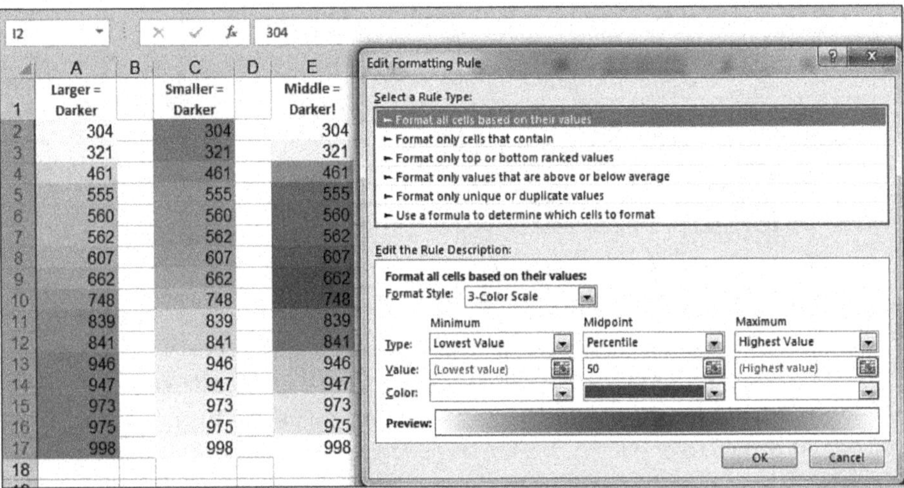

Figure 22.6 You can choose any colors to use in the color scale.

You should be aware of one strange situation: Normally, Excel lets you mix conditional formatting in the same range. You might apply both a color scale and an icon set.

If you have a three-color scale applied to some cells and choose a different three-color scale from the fly-out menu, the latter choice overwrites the first choice.

However, Excel treats two-color scales as a different visualization than three-color scales. If you have a three-color scale applied and you then try to switch it to a two-color scale using the fly-out menu, Excel creates two rules for those cells. The latter two-color scale is the only one to appear in Excel, but you might be confused when you go to the Manage Rules dialog box to see two different rules applied to the cells.

Using icon sets to segregate data

Icon sets, which were popular with expensive management reporting software in the late 1990s, have now been added to Excel. An icon set might include green, yellow, and red traffic lights or another set of icons to show positive, neutral, and negative meanings. With icon sets, Excel automatically applies an icon to a cell, based on the relative size of the value in the cell compared to other values in the range.

Excel ships with 20 icon sets that contain three, four, or five different icons. The icons are always left-aligned in the cell. Excel applies rules to add an icon to every cell in the range:

- **Three-icon sets:** For the three-icon sets, you have a choice between arrows, flags, two varieties of traffic lights, signs, stars, triangles, and two varieties of what Excel calls 3 Symbols. This last group consists of a green check mark for the good cells, a yellow exclamation point for the middle cells, and a red X for the bad cells. You can get the symbols either in a circle—that is, 3 Symbols (Circled)—or alone on a white background (that is, 3 Symbols). One version of the arrows is available in gray. All the other icon sets use red, yellow, and green.

- **Four-icon sets:** For the four-icon sets, there are two varieties of arrows: a black-to-red circle set, a set of cell phone power bars, and a set of four traffic lights. In the traffic light option, a black light indicates an option that is even worse than the red light. The power bars icons seem to work well on both color displays and monochromatic printouts.

  TIP

  After creating several reports with icon sets, I have started to favor the cell phone power bars, which look good in both color and black and white.

- **Five-icon sets:** For the five-icon sets, there are two varieties of arrows, boxes, a five-power bar set, and an interesting set called 5 Quarters. This last set is a monochromatic circle that is completely empty for the lowest values, 25% filled, 50% filled, 75% filled, and completely filled for the highest values.

Setting up an icon set

Icon sets require a bit more thought than the other data visualization offerings. Before you use icon sets, you should consider whether they will be printed in monochrome or displayed in color. Several of the 20 icon sets rely on color for differentiation and look horrible in a black-and-white report.

To set up an icon set, follow these steps:

1. Select a range of numeric data of a similar scale. Do not include the headers or total rows in this selection.

2. From the Home tab, select Conditional Formatting, Icon Sets. Select one of the 20 icon sets. Figure 22.7 shows the five-power bar set selected.

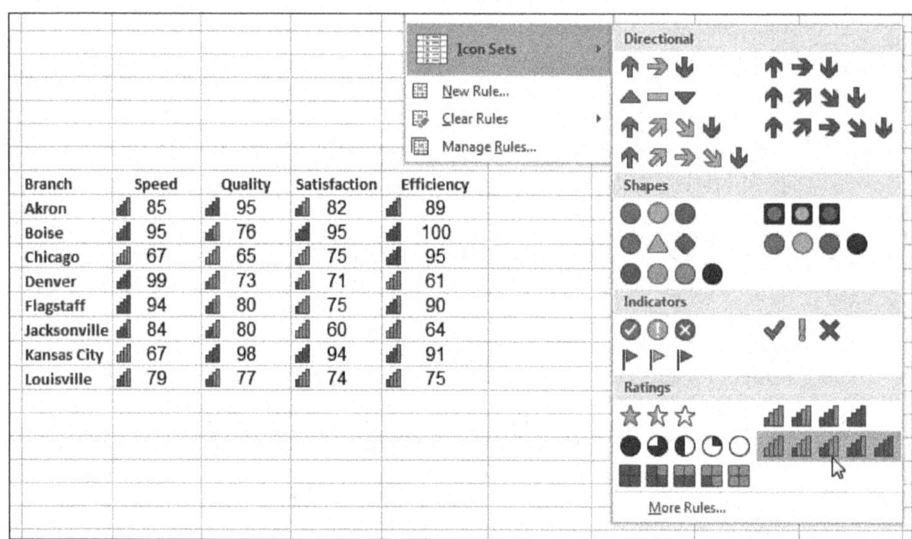

Figure 22.7 You can choose from the 20 icon sets.

Moving numbers closer to icons

In the top rows of Figure 22.8, the icon set has been applied to a rectangular range of data. The icons are always left aligned. Numbers are typically right-aligned. This can be problematic. Someone might think that the icon at the left side of cell G3 is really referring to the right-aligned number in F3, for example.

You might try centering the numbers to get the numbers closer to the icons in rows 7–9 in Figure 22.8. This drives purists crazy because the final digit of the 100 in cell H8 doesn't line up with the final digits of cells H7 and H9.

A better solution is shown in rows 12–14. Keep the numbers right aligned, and use the Increase Indent icon to move the numbers closer to the icon.

If you don't want to show numbers at all, you can edit the conditional formatting rule and select Show Icon Only. Rows 17–19 show this solution. Ironically, when the numbers are no longer displayed, you can position the icons by using the Left Align, Center Align, and Right Align icons.

The over-the-top solution in rows 22–24 involves using Show Icon Only and then pasting a linked picture of the numbers from other cells.

	D	E	F	G	H
1	**Normal**	Speed	Quality	Satisfaction	Efficiency
2	Akron	85	95	82	89
3	Boise	95	76	95	100
4	Chicago	67	65	75	95
5					
6	**Centered**	Speed	Quality	Satisfaction	Efficiency
7	Akron	85	95	82	89
8	Boise	95	76	95	100
9	Chicago	67	65	75	95
10					
11	**Indented**	Speed	Quality	Satisfaction	Efficiency
12	Akron	85	95	82	89
13	Boise	95	76	95	100
14	Chicago	67	65	75	95
15					
16	**Icon Only**	Speed	Quality	Satisfaction	Efficiency
17	Akron				
18	Boise				
19	Chicago				
20					
21	**Tricky**	Speed	Quality	Satisfaction	Efficiency
22	Akron	85	95	82	89
23	Boise	95	76	95	100
24	Chicago	67	65	75	95
25					

Figure 22.8 Changing the alignment of the numbers moves them closer to the icon.

Here are the steps to create rows 22 through 24:

1. Select one of the cells with the icon set formatting.
2. From the Home tab, select Conditional Formatting, Manage Rules.
3. In the Conditional Formatting Rules Manager dialog box, click the Icon Set rule and then click Edit Rule.
4. In the middle of the Edit Formatting Rule dialog box, select Show Icon Only. Click OK twice to close the two dialog boxes.
5. Select all the cells that contain icons and click the Align Center button on the Home tab.
6. Page down so that you are outside of the printed range. Stay in the same column. Set up a formula to point to the number in the top-left corner of the icon set range. Copy this formula down and over to be the same size as your icon set range. This gives you a range of just the numbers.
7. Format this range of numbers to be right-aligned with an indent of 1.
8. Copy this range of numbers.
9. Go back to the original set of icons and select Paste, Picture Link. A picture of the original numbers appears behind the icons.

Mixing icons or hiding icons

As of Excel 2010, it became possible to mix icons from different sets. In Figure 22.9, A2:C7 is a five-icon set with a mix of icons—gold star, green flag, yellow caution sign, and so on. You start with any five-icon set. Edit the rule and change the icon for each position.

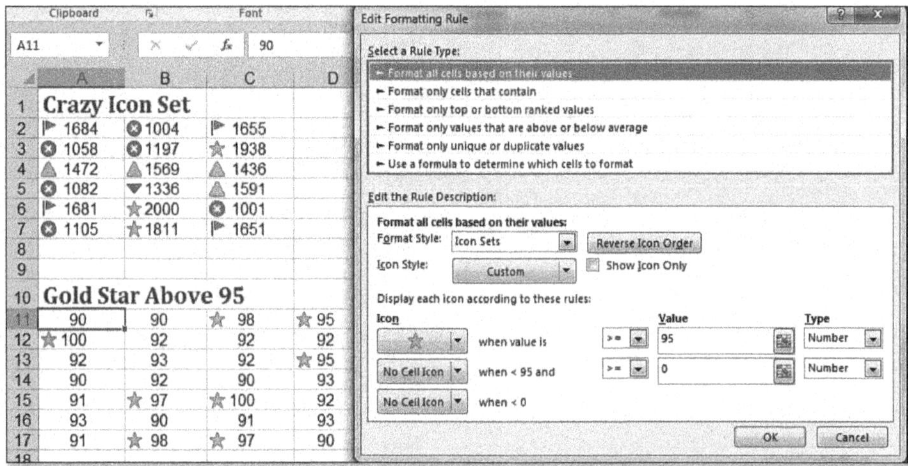

Figure 22.9 Mix icons to create unusual sets.

In A11:D17, scores of 95 and higher receive a gold star, and all other scores get no icon. The open dialog box shows how this is done; the lower two rules show No Cell Icon.

Using the top/bottom rules

The top/bottom rules are a mix of the old- and new-style conditional formatting. They are similar to the old conditional formatting because you must select one formatting scheme to apply to all the cells that meet the rule. However, they are new because rather than specifying a particular number limit, you can ask for any of these conditions:

- **Top 10 Items:** You can ask for the top 10, top 20, or any number of items.
- **Top 10%:** If 20% of your records account for 80% of your revenue, you can highlight the top 20% or any other percentage.
- **Bottom 10 Items:** To highlight the lowest-performing records, select Bottom 10.
- **Bottom 10%:** To highlight the records in the lowest 5%, select Bottom 10%.
- **Above Average:** You can highlight the records that are above the average. As with all the other rules, the average is recalculated as the numbers in the range change.
- **Below Average:** You can highlight the records that are below the average.

To set up any of these conditional formatting rules, follow these steps:

1. From the Home tab, select Conditional Formatting, Top/Bottom Rules, and then choose one of the six rule types shown in Figure 22.10.

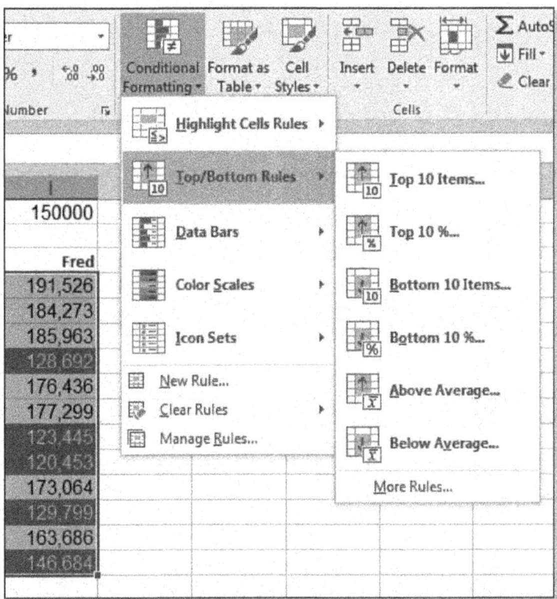

Figure 22.10 You can choose one of these six rule types.

2. The dialog box for above/below average does not require you to select a threshold value, but for the other four rule types, Excel asks you to enter the value for N. As you change the spin button, the Live Preview feature keeps updating the selection with the appropriate number of highlighted cells.

3. The drop-down list portion of the dialog box initially shows Light Red Fill with Dark Red Text. When you select the drop-down list, you have six default styles and the powerful Custom Format option. If one of the six styles is suitable, choose it. Otherwise, proceed to step 4.

4. If you choose Custom Format, you are taken to a special version of the Format Cells dialog box. This version has Number, Font, Border, and Fill tabs. You can choose settings on one or more of these tabs. Click OK to close the Format Cells dialog box.

5. Click OK to close the dialog box for your particular rule.

Excel adds the rule to the list of rules. By default, rules added most recently are applied first.

Using the highlight cells rules

The traditional conditional formatting rules appear in the Highlight Cells Rules menu item of the Conditional Formatting drop-down list, along with several new rules. The traditional rules include Greater Than, Less Than, Between, and Equal To. Note that slightly obscure rules such as Greater Than or Equal To are hidden behind the More Rules option. The following are the traditional rules:

- **Text That Contains:** This rule enables you to highlight cells that contain certain text.
- **A Date Occurring:** With this rule, you can define conceptual rules such as yesterday, today, tomorrow, last week, this week, next week, last month, this month, next month, or in the last seven days.
- **Duplicate Values:** With this rule, you can highlight both records of a duplicate or highlight all the records that are not duplicated.

TROUBLESHOOTING

Excel's definition of unique values does not match what you likely mean by unique values.

To the Excel team, a unique value is a value that occurs exactly once in the range. It does not seem helpful in most situations. Would Amazon care about the products that sold exactly one time? Outside of someone trying to find one-hit wonders from the Billboard music charts, I am not sure when finding values that occur exactly once is useful.

Instead, I would prefer that Excel highlight the cells that would be left after using Remove Duplicates. Highlight the first occurrence of each product whether it occurs once or 100 times.

To highlight the first occurrence of a value in C2:C100, use a formula-based condition where `=COUNTIF(C$1:C2,C2)=1`. Be cautious to use only one dollar sign in that formula. This formula creates an expanding range that looks from C1 down to the current row.

To create a formula-based conditional format, use Home, Conditional Formatting, New Rule, Use A Formula To Determine Which Cells To Format.

The options for Highlight Cells Rules are shown in Figure 22.11.

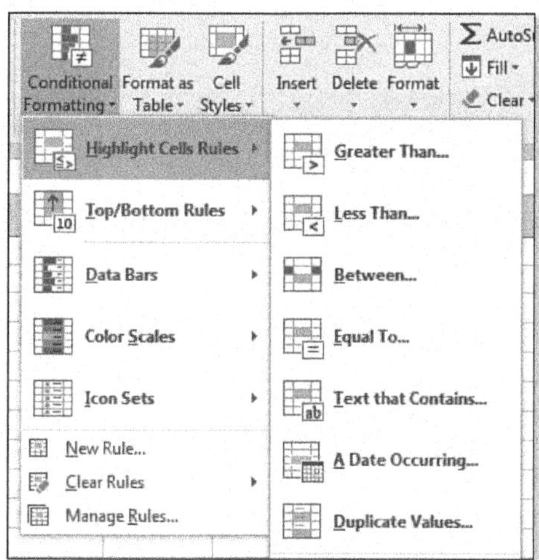

Figure 22.11 Many powerful and easy conditions are available in the Highlight Cells Rules menu.

Highlighting cells by using greater than and similar rules

You might think that Greater Than and the similar rules for Less Than, Equal To, and Not Equal To are some of the less powerful conditional formatting rules. In fact, these are the first rules described in this chapter that you can use to base the conditional format threshold on a particular cell or cells. This enables you to build some fairly complex rules without having to resort to the formula option of conditional formatting.

To set up a rule to highlight values greater than a threshold, follow these steps:

1. Select a range of data. Unlike with the other rules, you might choose to include totals in this selection.
2. Select Home, Styles, Conditional Formatting, Highlight Cell Rules, Greater Than to display the Greater Than dialog box.
3. Enter a threshold value in the Greater Than dialog box.
4. Choose one of the six formats from the With drop-down list. Or choose Custom Format from the With drop-down list to have complete control over the number format, font, borders, and fill.
5. Click OK to apply the format.

By way of example, let's look at several options for filling in the threshold value in the Greater Than dialog box. Figure 22.12 shows the conditional formatting rule for all cells greater than 200,000. This is a simple threshold value.

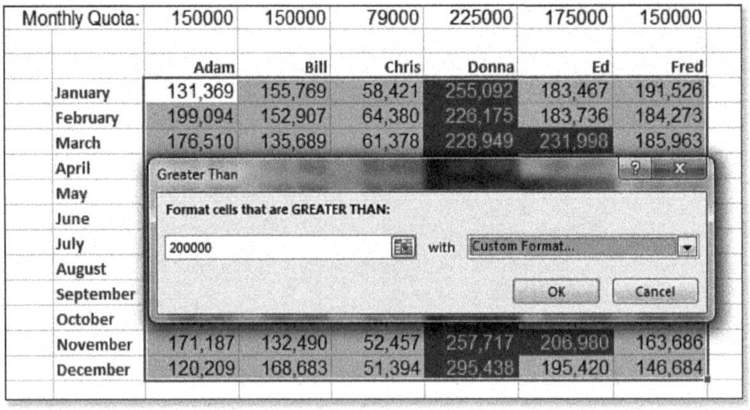

Monthly Quota:	150000	150000	79000	225000	175000	150000
	Adam	Bill	Chris	Donna	Ed	Fred
January	131,369	155,769	58,421	255,092	183,467	191,526
February	199,094	152,907	64,380	226,175	183,736	184,273
March	176,510	135,689	61,378	228,949	231,998	185,963
April						
May						
June						
July						
August						
September						
October						
November	171,187	132,490	52,457	257,717	206,980	163,686
December	120,209	168,683	51,394	295,438	195,420	146,684

Greater Than

Format cells that are GREATER THAN:

200000 with Custom Format...

OK Cancel

Figure 22.12 You can format all cells greater than a certain value, such as 200,000.

You can specify a cell as the threshold value. You can either use the reference icon at the right side of the box or type an equal sign and the cell reference. In Figure 22.13, the formula highlights any cell that does not exceed the quota in row 1 above the current cell using =D$1.

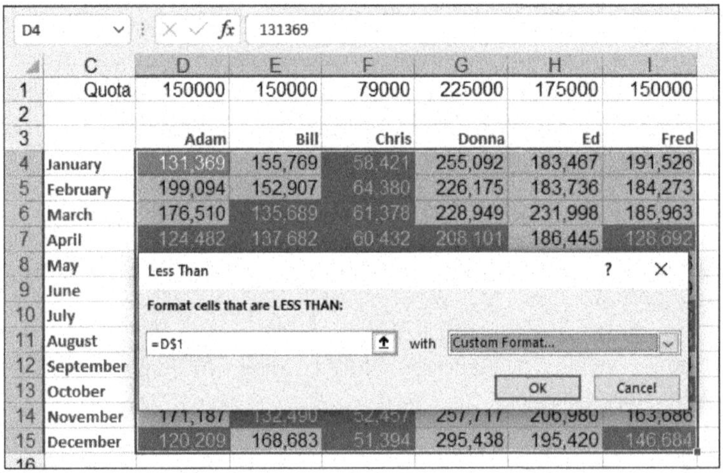

D4 fx 131369

	C	D	E	F	G	H	I
1	Quota	150000	150000	79000	225000	175000	150000
2							
3		Adam	Bill	Chris	Donna	Ed	Fred
4	January	131,369	155,769	58,421	255,092	183,467	191,526
5	February	199,094	152,907	64,380	226,175	183,736	184,273
6	March	176,510	135,689	61,378	228,949	231,998	185,963
7	April	124,482	137,682	60,432	208,101	186,445	128,692
8	May						
9	June						
10	July						
11	August						
12	September						
13	October						
14	November	171,187	132,490	52,457	257,717	206,980	163,686
15	December	120,209	168,683	51,394	295,438	195,420	146,684
16							

Less Than ? X

Format cells that are LESS THAN:

=D$1 with Custom Format...

OK Cancel

Figure 22.13 You can format all cells less than a certain cell. Prefix the cell reference with an equal sign.

The formula in Figure 22.13 has to be written for the active cell. Although D4:I15 is the selected range, the name box shows that D4 is the active cell. The formula of =D$1 is compared to the active cell of D4. The threshold cell then becomes the cell in row 1 that is in the same column as each cell in the selection.

The Greater Than concepts discussed here apply equally well to the Less Than, Equal To, and Between rules. If you need to access other rules, such as Less Than or Equal To, you can follow these steps:

1. Set up the rule by using Less Than.
2. From the Conditional Formatting icon, select Manage Rules.
3. Select the Less Than rule and click Edit Rule.
4. Use the drop-down list shown in Figure 22.14 to select Less Than or Equal To.

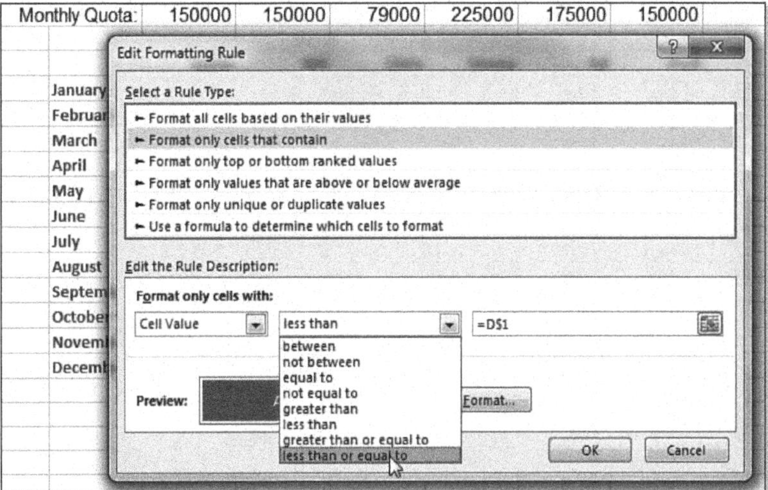

Figure 22.14 After using a quick format with Less Than, you can go to the Manage Rules option to access Less Than or Equal To.

Comparing dates by using conditional formatting

The date feature was added in Excel 2007. If you are familiar with the reporting engine in Quicken or QuickBooks, the list of available dates will seem similar. A nice feature is that Excel understands the dates conceptually. If you define a feature to highlight dates from last week, the rule automatically updates based on the system clock. If you open the workbook a month from now, new dates are formatted, based on the conditional formatting.

Some of the date selections are self-explanatory, such as Yesterday, Today, and Tomorrow. Other items need some explanation:

- A Week is defined as the seven days from Sunday through Saturday. Choosing This Week highlights all days from Sunday through Saturday, including the current date.
- In The Last 7 Days includes today and the six days before today.

- This Month corresponds to all days in this calendar month. Last Month is all days in the previous calendar month. For example, if today is May 1 or May 31, the period Last Month applies to April 1 through April 30.

Figure 22.15 shows the various formatting options, with a system date of June 22, 2018.

	A	B	C	D	E	F	G
1	Today is Friday, Jun 22, 2018						
2	This Week		Last Week		Next Week		Last 7 Days
3	Wed 6/20		Thu 6/14		Wed 6/27		Thu 6/14
4	Thu 6/21		Fri 6/15		Thu 6/28		Fri 6/15
5	Fri 6/22		Sat 6/16		Fri 6/29		Sat 6/16
6	Sat 6/23		Sun 6/17		Sat 6/30		Sun 6/17
7	Sun 6/24		Mon 6/18		Sun 7/1		Mon 6/18
8	Mon 6/25		Tue 6/19		Mon 7/2		Tue 6/19
9	Tue 6/26		Wed 6/20		Tue 7/3		Wed 6/20
10	Wed 6/27		Thu 6/21		Wed 7/4		Thu 6/21
11	Thu 6/28		Fri 6/22		Thu 7/5		Fri 6/22
12	Fri 6/29		Sat 6/23		Fri 7/6		Sat 6/23
14	Today		Yesterday		Tomorrow		
15	Wed 6/20		Wed 6/20		Wed 6/20		
16	Thu 6/21		Thu 6/21		Thu 6/21		
17	Fri 6/22		Fri 6/22		Fri 6/22		
18	Sat 6/23		Sat 6/23		Sat 6/23		
19	Sun 6/24		Sun 6/24		Sun 6/24		
21	This Month		Last Month		Next Month		
22	Sun 4/22		Sun 4/22		Sun 4/22		
23	Thu 5/31		Thu 5/31		Thu 5/31		
24	Sat 6/30		Sat 6/30		Sat 6/30		
25	Tue 7/31		Tue 7/31		Tue 7/31		
26	Fri 8/31		Fri 8/31		Fri 8/31		

Figure 22.15 Note that Last 7 Days includes today and the previous six days.

The date formatting option would be particularly good for highlighting the items in a to-do list that are due, overdue, or about to be due.

Identifying duplicate or unique values by using conditional formatting

Conditional formatting claims that it can mark either duplicate or unique values in a list of values. It seems that Microsoft missed an opportunity to include a different version of unique values than the one that it included. It would be very useful if Microsoft had included an option to mark only the first occurrence of each unique item.

In column A of Figure 22.16, Excel has marked the duplicate values. Both Adam and Bill appear twice in the list, and Excel has marked both occurrences of the values. You might be tempted to sort by color to bring the red cells to the top, but you still have to carefully go through to delete one of each pair.

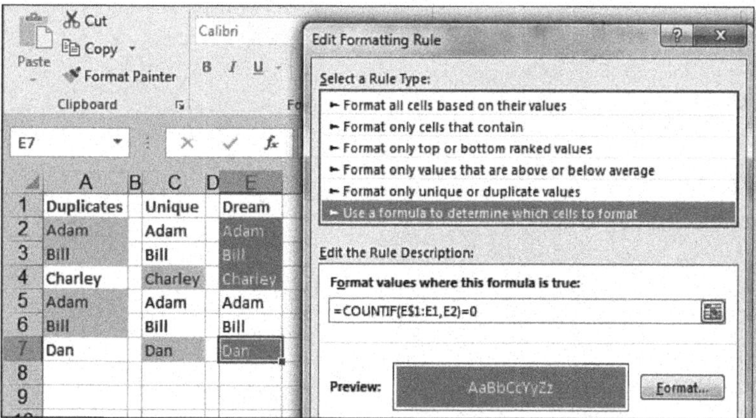

Figure 22.16 Marking duplicates or unique values with the built-in conditional formatting choices requires additional work to decide which of the duplicates to keep to produce a unique list.

In column C of Figure 22.16, Excel has applied a conditional format to the unique values in the list. In Excel parlance, this means that Excel marks the items that appear only once in a list. If you would keep just the marked cells as a list of the unique names in the list, you would effectively miss any name that was duplicated.

In a perfect world, this feature would have the logic to include one of each name in the conditional format. The conditional formatting in column E resorts to using the fairly complex formula of =`COUNTIF(E$1:E1,E2)`=0 to highlight the unique values.

➤ **To learn more about using formulas to mark cells, see "Using a formula for rules," p. 564.**

Using conditional formatting for text containing a value

The Text That Contains formatting rule is designed to search text cells for cells that contain a certain value.

Figure 22.17 contains a column of cells. Each cell in the column contains a complete address, with street, city, state, and ZIP. It would normally be fairly difficult to find all the records for a particular state. However, this is easy to do with conditional formatting. Follow these steps:

1. Select a range of cells that contains text.
2. From the Home tab, select Conditional Formatting, Highlight Cell Rules, Text That Contains.

3. In the Refers To box, enter a comma, a space, and the state you want to find. Note that this test is not case sensitive (for example, searching for ", pa" is the same as searching for ", PA").
4. Choose an appropriate color from the drop-down list.
5. Click OK to apply the format.

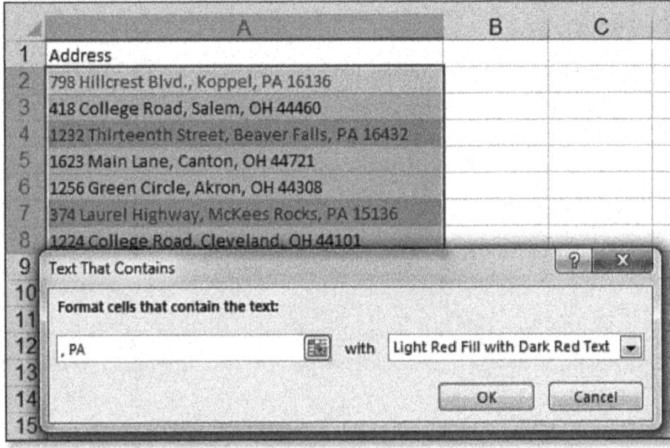

Figure 22.17 Without having to use a wildcard character, you can use the Text That Contains dialog box to mark cells based on a partial value.

As with the Find dialog box, you can use wildcard characters. You can use an asterisk (*) to indicate any number of characters and a question mark (?) to indicate a single character.

Tweaking rules with advanced formatting

All the formats available from icons on the Conditional Formatting group are referred to as *quick formatting*. According to legend, the Excel team bought and read a number of Excel books, and if the author spent a page trying to explain a convoluted way to format something using formulas in conditional formatting, then that option became a quick formatting icon.

Every quick formatting item has an option at the bottom called More Rules. When you click this option and get to the New Formatting Rule dialog box, you find options that didn't make it as quick formatting icons.

The next section of this chapter discusses using the formula option for conditional formatting. Almost anything is possible by using the formula option, but it is harder to use than the quick formatting icons. If Excel offers a built-in, advanced option, you should certainly use it instead of trying to build a formula to do the same thing.

The lists shown in Tables 22.1 and 22.2 are organized to show all the options for specific rule types. The six rule types are in the top of the New Formatting Rule dialog box. Items listed in the right column are advanced options that are available only by clicking More Rules.

Table 22.1 Options for formatting cells based on content

Option	Advanced options available using More Rules
Cell value between x and y	Cell value not between x and y
Cell value equal to x	Cell value not equal to x
Cell value greater than x	Cell value less than x
Cell value greater than or equal to x	Cell value less than or equal to x
Specific text containing x	Specific text not containing x
	Specific text beginning with x
	Specific text ending with x
Dates occurring yesterday	
Dates occurring today	
Dates occurring tomorrow	
Dates occurring in the last 7 days	
Dates occurring last week	
Dates occurring next week	
Dates occurring last month	
Dates occurring this month	
Dates occurring next month	
More Rules	Blanks
	No Blanks
	Errors
	No Errors

Table 22.2 Options for formatting values that are above or below average

Option	Advanced options available using More Rules
Above the average for the selected range	One standard deviation above the average for the selected range
	Two standard deviations above the average for the selected range
	Three standard deviations above the average for the selected range
Below the average for the selected range	One standard deviation below the average for the selected range
	Two standard deviations below the average for the selected range
	Three standard deviations below the average for the selected range

Using a formula for rules

Excel has three dozen quick conditional formatting rules and twice as many advanced conditional formatting rules. What if you need to build a conditional format that is not covered in the quick or advanced rules? As long as you can build a logical formula to describe the condition, you can build your own conditional formatting rule based on a formula.

Some basic tips can help you successfully use formulas in conditional formatting rules. When you understand these rules, you can build just about any rule you can imagine.

Starting in Excel 2007, a formula is allowed to refer to cells on another worksheet. This enables you to compare cells on one worksheet to a worksheet from a previous month or to use a VLOOKUP table on another worksheet.

Getting to the formula box

To set up a conditional format based on a rule, follow these steps:

1. Select a range of cells.
2. In the Style group of the Home tab, select Conditional Formatting, Add New Rule.
3. In the New Formatting Rule dialog box, choose the rule type Use A Formula To Determine Which Cells To Format. You now see the New Formatting Rule dialog box.

The following sections give you some tips for building a successful formula.

Working with the formula box

Following are the key concepts involved in writing a successful formula:

- The formula must start with an equal sign.
- The formula must evaluate to a logical value of TRUE or FALSE. The numeric equivalents of 1 and 0 are also acceptable results.
- When you use the mouse to select a cell or cells on a worksheet, Excel inserts an absolute reference to the cell. This is rarely what you need for a successful conditional formatting rule. You can immediately press the F4 key three times to toggle away the dollar signs in the formula.
- You probably have many cells selected before starting the conditional formatting rule. You need to look at the left of the formula bar to see which cell in the selection is the active cell. If you write a relative formula, you should write the formula that will appear in the active cell. Excel applies the formula appropriately to all cells. This is a key point.

- If the dialog box is in the way of cells you need to select, you can drag the dialog box out of the way by dragging the title bar. If you absolutely need to get the dialog box out of the way, you can use the Collapse Dialog box button at the right side of the formula box. This collapses the dialog box to a tiny area. To return it to full size, you click the Expand Dialog box button at the right side of the collapsed dialog box.
- The formula box is one of the evil sets of controls that have three possible statuses: Enter, Point, and Edit. Look in the lower-left corner of the Excel screen. The status initially says that you are in Enter mode. This means that Excel is expecting you to type characters such as the equal sign. If, instead, you use the mouse or arrow keys to select a cell, Excel changes to Point mode. In Point mode, the selected cell's address is added to the formula box.

  CAUTION

  The annoying thing about the formula box is that you always start in something called Enter mode. When you are in Enter mode, if you use any of the navigation keys (that is, Page Down, Page Up, left arrow, right arrow, down arrow, up arrow), Excel changes to Point mode and starts inserting random cell addresses at inappropriate places in your formula. Press F2 until you see Edit in the lower-left corner of the Excel window. You can now use the left and right arrows to move through the formula.

The following sections describe several useful conditional formatting rules. This list only scratches the surface of the possible rules you can build. It is designed to generate ideas of what you can accomplish by using conditional formatting.

Finding cells within three days of today

The quick formatting feature offers to highlight yesterday or today or tomorrow, but what if you need to find any cells within three days of today, either plus or minus? If the active cell is B2, use a formula of `=ABS(TODAY()-B2)<4`.

Finding cells containing data from the past 30 days

The Excel quick formatting option offers to highlight this month or last month. However, highlighting this month or last month can mean a number of vastly different things. Highlighting this month on the second of the month shows a lot of the future and only one day of the past. The same rule on the 29th of the month highlights a lot of the past and only a few days of the future. It would be more predictable to write a rule that shows the past 30 days.

You create this rule similarly to the way you created the Next Three Days rule in the preceding section. You first compare the date in the cell by using `TODAY()` to make sure the date in the cell is less than today. If the active cell is F4, you use the following formula:

```
=AND(F4<TODAY(),(TODAY()-F4)<=30)
```

To generalize this formula for other periods, such as the past 15 days or the past 45 days, you change the 30 to a different number.

Highlighting data from specific days of the week

The `WEEKDAY()` function converts a date to a number from 1 through 7. When used without additional arguments, the value of `WEEKDAY(date)` for a Sunday is 0 and for Saturday is 7.

Suppose the active cell is H4. If you needed to highlight all the Wednesdays, for example, you could check to see whether `WEEKDAY(H4)=4`. To find all the Fridays, you would check to see whether `WEEKDAY(H4)=6`. To find either date, you would use `=OR(WEEKDAY(H4)=4, WEEKDAY(H4)=6)`.

To generalize this formula, you could substitute any number from 1 through 7 to highlight Sundays, Mondays, and so on.

Highlighting an entire row

Most conditional formatting highlights a cell based on the value in that cell. In this case, you would like to highlight the entire row for the row with the largest product sale.

In Figure 22.18, cell A2 is the active cell. You need to select the entire range of A2:F14. Your goal is to write a rule for all those cells that will always look at column D, but the row will vary based on the cell being evaluated. In this case, and in any case in which you want to highlight the entire row based on one column, you use the mixed reference with a dollar sign before the column letter. You want to see whether `=$D2` is equal to the largest value in the range.

	A	B	C	D	E	F
1	Invoice	Customer	Product	Tax	S&H	Total
2	8422	Ideal Linen Corpora	181	10.86	7.95	199.81
3	8423	Effortless Luggage (	361	21.66	15.95	398.61
4	8424	Dependable Spraye	319	19.14	15.95	354.09
5	8425	Amazing Adhesive	245	14.7	11.95	271.65
6	8426	Guaranteed Thermo	275	16.5	11.95	303.45
7	8427	Unique Utensil Corp	341	20.46	15.95	377.41
8	8428	Effortless Wax Inc.	215	12.9	11.95	239.85
9	8429	Supreme Kettle Inc.	273	16.38	11.95	301.33
10	8430	Different Utensil Inc	363	21.78	15.95	400.73
11	8431	Cool Gadget Inc.	267	16.02	11.95	294.97
12	8432	Superior Linen Inc.	279	16.74	11.95	307.69
13	8433	Vivid Paint Compan	174	10.44	7.95	192.39
14	8434	Leading Chopstick I	172	10.32	7.95	190.27
15						

Figure 22.18 The combination of a mixed reference and the absolute reference enables you to highlight an entire row.

To find the largest value in column D, you use an absolute reference to D2:D14—that is, `=MAX($D$2:$D$14)`. The conditional formatting formula for this specific case is `=$D2=MAX($D$2:$D$14)`.

To change this rule to highlight the smallest value in column D, you change `MAX` to `MIN`. To base the test on another column, change D to the other column in three places in the formula.

Highlighting every other row without using a table

You might find yourself using the Format as Table feature only to add alternating bands of color to a table. If you don't need the other table features, using a conditional format can achieve the same effect.

Do you remember when you were first learning to do division? You would express the quotient as an integer and then a remainder. For example, 9 divided by 2 is 4 with a remainder of 1, sometimes written as 4R1.

The trick to formatting every other row is to check the remainder of the row number after dividing by 2. Excel has functions that make this easy. First, `=ROW()` returns the row number of the given cell. Next, `=MOD(ROW(),2)` divides the row number by 2 and tells you the remainder. The task is then simply to highlight the rows where the remainder is equal to 1 or equal to zero.

NOTE

The Excel table formatting enables you to create alternate formatting in which every other two rows are formatted. To duplicate this with conditional formatting, you have to divide the row number by 4 and examine the remainder. There are four possible remainders: 0, 1, 2, and 3. You can look for results greater than 1 or less than 2 to be formatted. To do this, you change the preceding formula to =MOD(ROW(),4)<2.

In Figure 22.19, the active cell is A2. The formula to achieve the banding effect is `=MOD(ROW(),2)=0`.

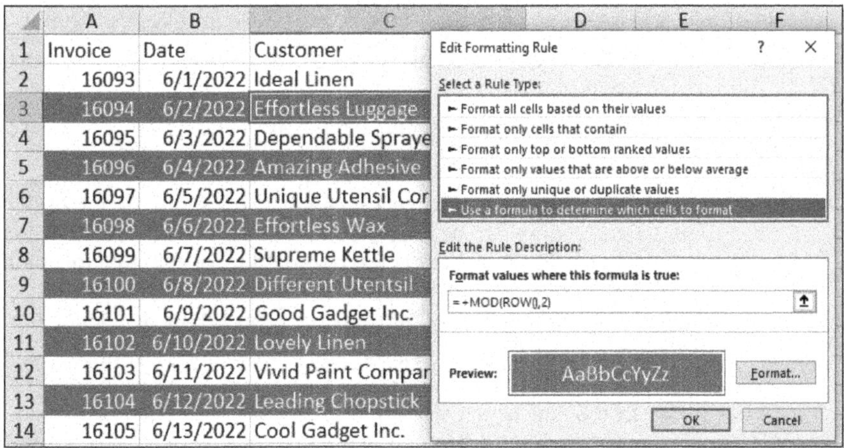

Figure 22.19 It is possible to create a row-banding effect without using the Excel table formatting.

To generalize this formula for your particular data set, you could change A2 to be the active cell's address.

Combining rules

Excel allows multiple conditions to evaluate to TRUE. In legacy versions of Excel, when a condition was met, Excel quit evaluating additional conditions. For each rule in Excel, you can decide whether Excel should stop evaluating additional rules or whether Excel can continue evaluating rules.

For example, one rule might set the font color to blue. Another rule might set the font style to bold. Cells meeting both rules can be formatted in blue bold. Cells meeting one rule can be either blue or bold. Cells meeting neither rule will be in normal font style.

If two rules attempt to create conflicting formatting, Excel uses the first rule in the list. For example, if Rule 1 turns the font red and Rule 7 turns the font blue, the font is red.

Ten types of formatting can be changed in each cell. Naturally, each type conflicts with others of the same type. Only the first rule that evaluates to TRUE can change the fill color.

Very few formatting styles conflict with each other. Only the cell fill and the color scale are mutually exclusive. Otherwise, you can have up to nine rules evaluate to TRUE for any given cell. Table 22.3 illustrates the interplay between the ten formatting styles.

Table 22.3 Cell formatting styles

Style	Effect
Font color	Changes the font color for cells meeting a condition.
Font style	Applies normal, bold, italic, or bold italic to cells meeting a condition.
Underline	Adds or removes single or double underlining for cells meeting a condition.
Strikethrough	Applies strikethrough for cells meeting a condition.
Number format	Changes the number format for cells meeting a condition.
Border	Alters the borders for cells meeting a condition. You might think that you could combine two rules that both affect the border. For example, you might want to make the top border blue for cells that meet Rule 1 and the right border red for cells that meet Rule 2. Even though this conceptually makes sense, Excel allows only the first true rule to change the borders.
Cell fill	Changes the cell background for cells meeting a condition. Amazingly, this works fine in combination with data bars. (The cell fill appears to the right of the data bar.) It also works fine with icon sets, and it works fine with all the preceding options. However, cell fill and color scales cannot coexist. Only the first true rule appears in the cell.

Color scale	Changes the cell background for all cells in the range, with the color being determined by the value of one cell in relation to the other cells in the range. This rule can coexist with everything but itself and the cell fill formatting.
Data bar	Adds an in-cell bar chart in each cell. This rule can coexist with any other type of rule.
Icon set	Adds an icon in the left side of the cell. This rule can coexist with any other type of rule.

You can use a number of ways to clear conditional formats. A few quick options are available from the ribbon:

- You can highlight the entire range with conditional formatting and then use Home, Styles, Conditional Formatting, Clear, Selected Cells. This removes all conditions from the current selection.
- To clear all the conditional formats from the current worksheet, you can use Home, Styles, Conditional Formatting, Clear, Entire Sheet. This is handy if you have only one set of rules set up on the sheet. You can delete all the rules without having to select the entire range.

  NOTE

  Deleting columns or rows deletes the rules associated with those columns or rows. Selecting Home, Editing, Clear, All or Home, Editing, Clear, Formats removes the rules.

- If you have rules assigned to a pivot table or a table, you can select one cell in the pivot table or table. This enables new options for Home, Styles, Conditional Formatting, Clear, This Table or Home, Styles, Conditional Formatting, Clear, This PivotTable.

If you have multiple rules assigned to a range and you need to delete just a portion of those rules, you can use Home, Styles, Conditional Formatting, Manage Rules. In the Conditional Formatting Rules Manager dialog box, you should use the top drop-down list to display rules in the current selection, this worksheet, or any other worksheet. You can then highlight a specific rule and click the Delete Rule button.

Extending the reach of conditional formats

In every example in this chapter, you have been advised to highlight the entire range before setting up the conditional format. It is also possible to assign a conditional format to one cell and then extend the rule to other cells. There are three ways to copy a conditional format:

- You can select a cell with the appropriate rule and then press Ctrl+C to copy it. Then you select the new range and select Home, Clipboard, Paste, Paste Special, Formats, OK to copy the conditional formatting from the one cell to the entire range.

- Select a cell with the appropriate rule. Click the Format Painter icon in the Home tab. Select a new range to paste the conditional format to the new range.
- You can select Home, Styles, Conditional Formatting, Manage Rules. Then you select a rule. In the Applies To column, you see the list of cells that have this rule. You can type a new range there or use the collapse button to make the dialog box smaller so that you can highlight the new range.

When you are using conditional formats that compare one cell to the entire range, using the second method is safer to ensure that Excel understands your intention.

Special considerations for pivot tables

This section talks about the special conditional formatting options that are available for pivot tables.

➤ **See Chapter 15, "Using pivot tables to analyze data," to review the detailed discussion of pivot tables.**

A typical pivot table might contain two or more levels of summary data. In the pivot table in Figure 22.20, for example, cells H4:J16 contain sales data. However, if you tried to create a data bar for this entire range, the subtotal values in rows 9 and 15 would make the data bars in the other rows look too small.

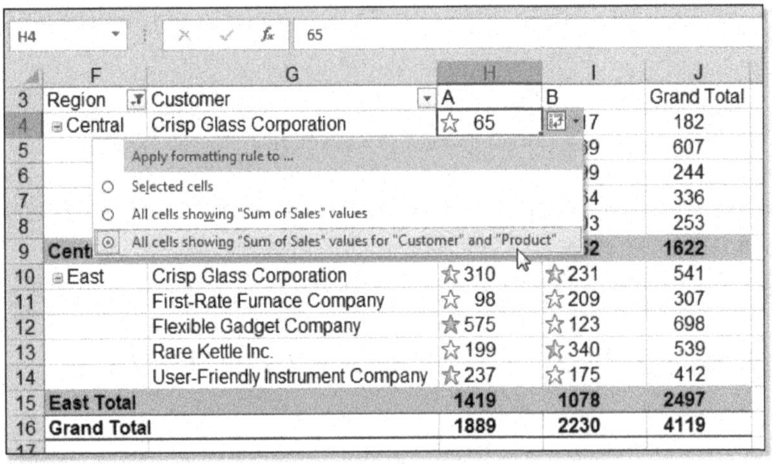

H4 | 65

	F	G	H	I	J
3	Region	Customer	A	B	Grand Total
4	Central	Crisp Glass Corporation	65	17	182
5				9	607
6				9	244
7				4	336
8				3	253
9	Cent			2	1622
10	East	Crisp Glass Corporation	310	231	541
11		First-Rate Furnace Company	98	209	307
12		Flexible Gadget Company	575	123	698
13		Rare Kettle Inc.	199	340	539
14		User-Friendly Instrument Company	237	175	412
15	East Total		1419	1078	2497
16	Grand Total		1889	2230	4119

Apply formatting rule to ...
- Selected cells
- All cells showing "Sum of Sales" values
- All cells showing "Sum of Sales" values for "Customer" and "Product"

Figure 22.20 The trick to a successful conditional format in a pivot table is to apply the format only to items at the same detail level.

CHAPTER 22

To set up a data bar for the detail items in a pivot table, follow these steps:

1. Select a detail cell in the pivot table. In Figure 22.20, a cell such as H4 will do.
2. Choose any visualization from the Conditional Formatting drop-down list. In Figure 22.20, the 3-stars icons set is shown.
3. A tiny pivot icon appears to the right of the cell. Click this drop-down list to access three conditional formatting settings for pivot tables. The choices are the following:
    a. **Selected Cells:** You can apply the rule to just the one cell. This is not what you want in this case.
    b. **All Cells Showing Sum Of Sales Values:** You can apply the rule to cells including the total column, grand total row, and all the subtotal rows. Remember that the size of the grand total causes all the detail items to have data bars that are too small.
    c. **All Cells Showing Sum Of Sales Values For "Customer" And "Product":** This is the option you use most of the time. The meaning of this option is dependent on careful selection of a detail cell in step 1. If you selected a subtotal row instead, this option would apply the data bars only to the subtotal rows.

The actual words in the second and third options vary, depending on the fields displayed in your pivot table. For successful pivot table formatting, select the third option.

Inside OUT

There is a great trick for showing data bars in two different colors. It was documented once on the Excel team blog in 2007 but has since been deleted and lost forever.

This obscure trick has been posted in the Microsoft Excel team blog. It turns out that every conditional formatting rule has a formula value that determines whether the rule is shown. Microsoft exposed this rule in the user interface for some conditional formatting rules but not for the data bars. You can, however, access it in the VBA editor!

Suppose that your goal is to add a data bar to a range of cells. If the value is 90 or greater, you would like the bars to be green. If the value is 89 or less, you would like the bars to be red. Here's how you accomplish this:

1. Select the range of cells to be formatted.
2. Use the Conditional Formatting quick options to add to the range of a data bar that is red.
3. Select Conditional Formatting, Add New Rule to add a second rule that applies a green data bar. You see only the most recent rule, so all the data bars are green.

4. In the Name box, note which cell is the active cell because you need this information in step 7.
5. Press Alt+F11 to switch to the VBA editor.
6. Press Ctrl+G to display the Immediate pane.
7. Type `Selection.FormatConditions(1).Formula = "=if(A2>89, TRUE, FALSE)"` and then press Enter. Cell A2 should be changed to the name of the active cell from step 4.
8. The result is that the green bars are visible only when the value is 90 or greater. In all other cases, the bars appear red.

CHAPTER 23

Graphing data using Excel charts

Between Excel 2016 and Excel 2019, two new charts were added to Excel: the funnel chart and the filled map chart.

Before getting to the new charts, the chapter covers general techniques for creating graphs.

After you have the chart, a paintbrush icon offers 10 to 15 ways to style the chart. Styles range from minimalist to intense. If you are a disciple of Professor Edward R. Tufte and you believe every bit of ink on the chart must have a meaning, you will prefer minimalist styles.

Choosing from recommended charts

The data in Figure 23.1 is a simple trend of monthly sales. Headings for the months appear in B1:M1. Sales appear in B2:M2. A label of "Sales" appears in A2. The label in A1 is optional. To create a chart, follow these steps:

1. Select A1:M2 or select one cell in A1:M2.
2. On the Insert tab, choose Recommended Charts. Excel displays the Insert Chart dialog box. The Recommended Charts tab shows four thumbnails on the left side and part of a fifth. Click each thumbnail to see a larger chart on the right side. A description below the chart explains why this chart is appropriate.
3. Click OK to insert the chart in the center of the visible window. Grab the border of the chart and drag to the appropriate place. (See the following Troubleshooting Tip if you have to move the chart more than a screenful of data away.)
4. Notice the three icons to the right of the chart and the two contextual ribbon tabs that appear while the chart is selected. The following sections show you how to use those tools to polish the chart.

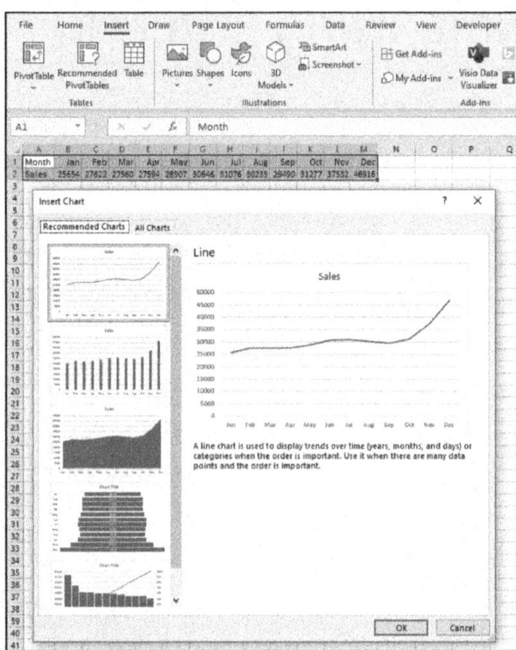

Figure 23.1 Select the data, and Excel suggests possible chart styles.

TROUBLESHOOTING

Excel plots the chart in the middle of the visible screen. By selecting your data, the visible portion of the window is often at the bottom of the worksheet instead of the top.

Suppose you have data in A1:C500 that should appear on a chart. You would probably start in A1, press Ctrl+Shift+Down Arrow, and then press Ctrl+Shift+Right Arrow. You would end up with rows 490 through 520 visible on your screen. However, if you insert a chart, it would appear at the bottom of your data instead of at the top of your data. Instead, press Ctrl+Backspace before creating the chart, which brings the active cell back into view.

Using the paintbrush icon for styles

Click the paintbrush icon to reveal a flyout menu with 12 to 15 professionally designed chart styles for the selected chart (see Figure 23.2).

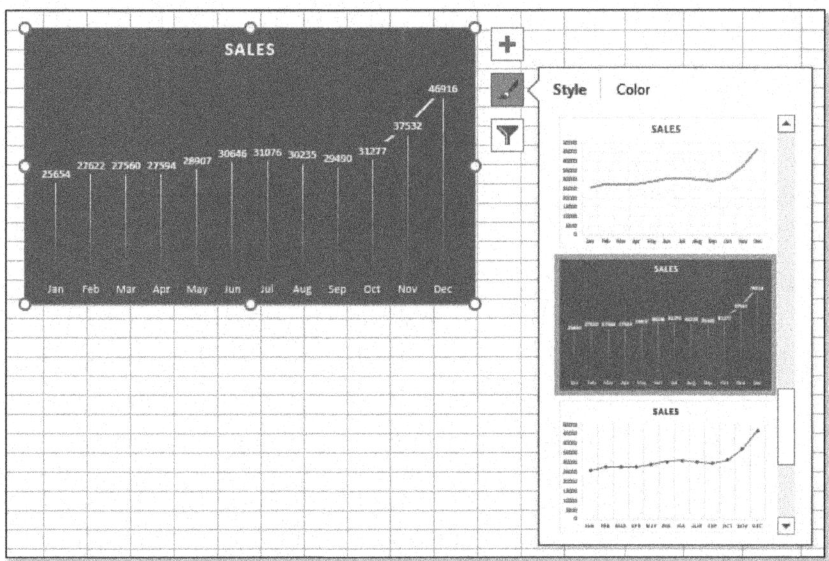

Figure 23.2 The paintbrush icon leads to these professionally designed chart styles.

The chart styles in this menu look new and stylish. Consider the style shown in Figure 23.2. You have fading drop lines extending from a data label down toward the baseline of the chart. The chart area and plot area are dark blue, and all chart elements are white. The marker is really the data label. The actual line appears only between October and December because of the jump in sales. I went back to Excel 2010 to see whether it's possible to create the identical chart. You can. It takes 26 separate steps, most of which require at least two mouse clicks. And that is 26 steps when you are trying to mimic an existing chart. If you were to try to come up with those steps without having a pattern to follow, it would be very time consuming. Excel makes it available with just a few clicks.

Deleting extraneous data using the funnel

The data in Figure 23.3 includes quarterly totals and an annual total. Accidentally including this data in the chart is a common mistake. The size of the subtotals and total columns makes all the other columns indistinguishable from each other.

Open the funnel icon. You can unselect the quarterly and annual totals.

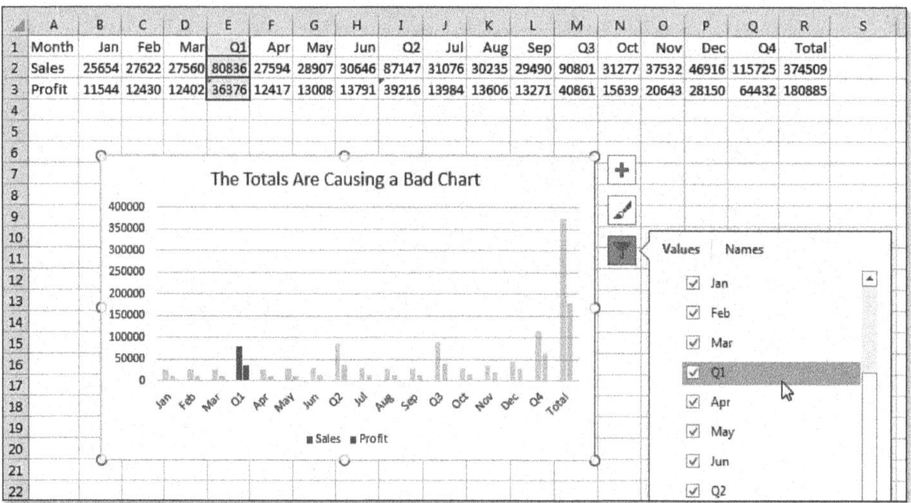

Figure 23.3 This chart is doomed because the selected data includes quarterly totals.

Changing chart options using the plus icon

Most chart elements can be formatted using a plus icon to the right of a selected chart. As shown in Figure 23.4, click the plus icon. Hover over Legend to have a flyout appear to the right with choices of Right, Top, Left, Bottom, and More Options. If you decide you don't need a legend, simply uncheck the option from the initial menu.

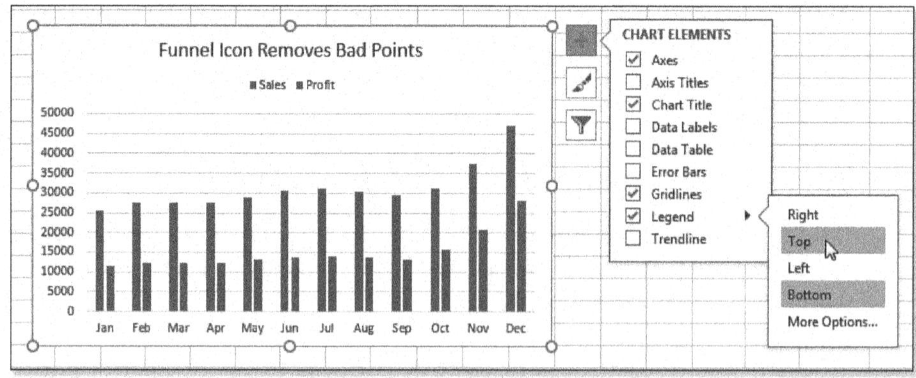

Figure 23.4 Use the plus icon to reach settings for major chart elements.

CHAPTER 23

Easy combo charts

These charts are great when you have two different orders of magnitude in the same chart. While they used to be difficult to build in legacy versions of Excel, today you have an incredibly flexible interface for creating combo charts.

Figure 23.5 shows a perfect example of data in need of a combo chart. Row 2 shows monthly sales. Row 3 shows the YTD number and accumulates all the monthly sales. The problem, again, is that the height of the December YTD number forces the monthly sales line to be too small for you to actually notice any variability. Choose Insert, Recommended Chart, All Charts, Combo. The new interface for combo charts enables you to identify which series should be plotted on the secondary axis.

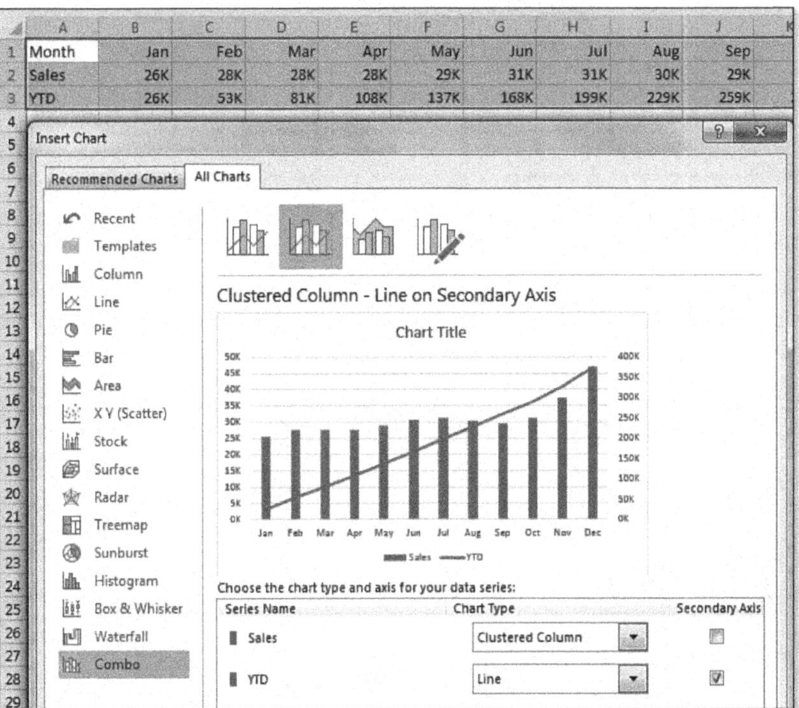

Figure 23.5 Choose a combo chart to move the line to the secondary axis.

Creating a frequency distribution with a histogram chart

Creating a frequency distribution using the FREQUENCY function is difficult and confusing. The Histogram chart in Excel makes it easy. In Figure 23.6, you want to summarize thousands of points. Select the points. Choose Insert, Recommended Chart, and choose Histogram.

Excel creates bins along the bottom of the chart. Because the chart doesn't use round numbers when establishing groups, the automatic bins will be chaotic. Double-click the bins along the bottom to display the Format Axis task pane. Choose Axis Options, then the chart icon, and specify a round number for the Bin Width. In Figure 23.6, the Bin Width is 10. Control the starting bin by using the Underflow Bin.

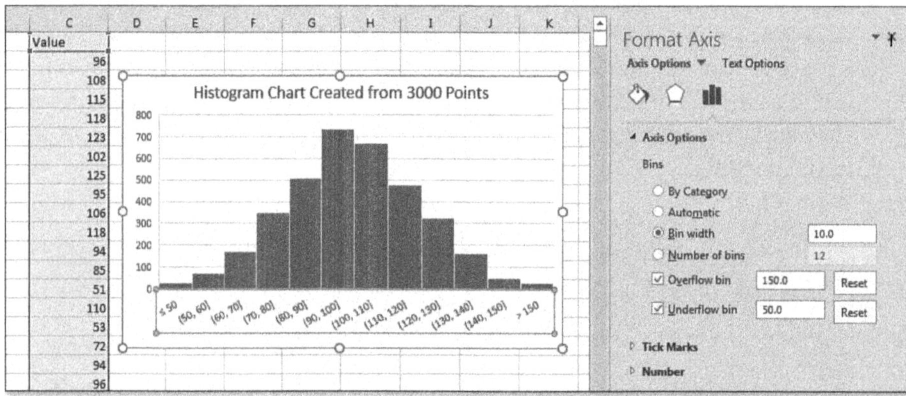

Figure 23.6 Excel easily turns thousands of data points into a histogram.

The Pareto chart rearranges the bins from the histogram so the bins with the most values appear on the left side of the chart. The Pareto line is tied to the secondary axis and shows what percentage of the population is to the left of the bin (see Figure 23.7).

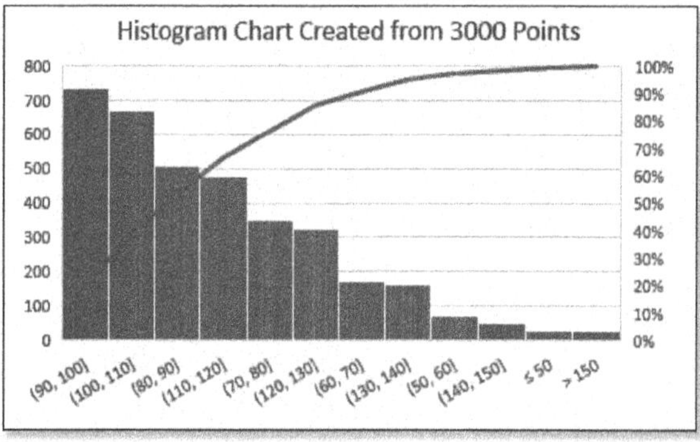

Figure 23.7 A Pareto chart shows the most popular categories on the left.

In Figure 23.7, it is difficult to get an exact reading of the Pareto line. What percentage of the data points falls within the first two columns? You must mentally draw a vertical line up the center of the second column. When it intersects the Pareto line, extend that point to the right axis. About 39 percent of the points fall in the first two columns.

Showing financial data with a waterfall chart

Figure 23.8 shows a profit waterfall chart that analyzes a pricing proposal. The total list price of the deal is $10 million. The sales team is offering two discounts to get the total revenue down to $6 million. Various cost components take the deal down to $1.2 million of gross profit. Sales commissions take the net profit to $1.1 million.

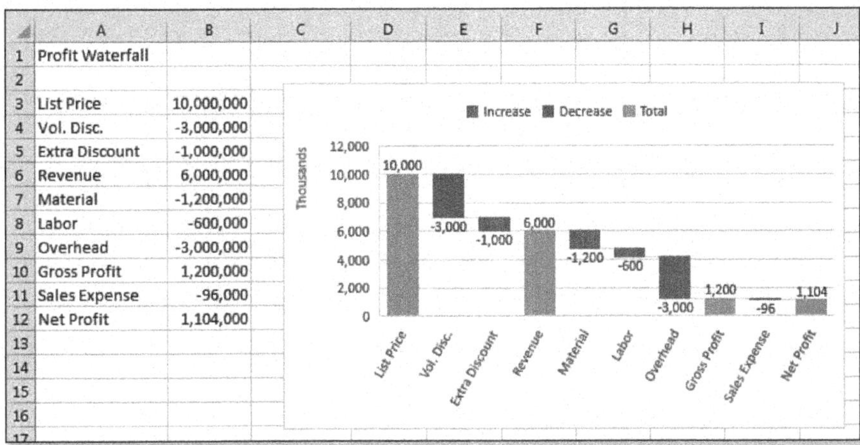

	A	B
1	Profit Waterfall	
2		
3	List Price	10,000,000
4	Vol. Disc.	-3,000,000
5	Extra Discount	-1,000,000
6	Revenue	6,000,000
7	Material	-1,200,000
8	Labor	-600,000
9	Overhead	-3,000,000
10	Gross Profit	1,200,000
11	Sales Expense	-96,000
12	Net Profit	1,104,000

Figure 23.8 Waterfall charts show increases or decreases.

In Figure 23.8, four columns are marked as totals and will touch the zero axis. The other markers are either increases or decreases from the previous value. Set up your data so that the increases are positive, and the decreases are negative.

The chart will always initially look wrong because Excel cannot tell which columns should touch the zero axis.

After creating the chart, double-click the first column that should touch the axis. Check the Set as Total box. From there, single-click the other total columns and choose the same box.

Changing the colors in the chart is particularly hidden in the Ivy charts. To change the color, follow these steps:

1. Click once on the legend to select the whole legend.
2. Click a second time on one individual legend entry to select one type of data point.
3. Right-click the legend entry and a Fill drop-down list appears, as shown in Figure 23.9.

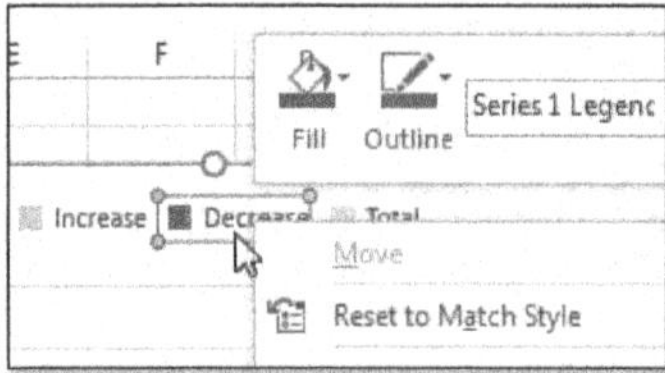

Figure 23.9 Changing the colors in a waterfall can only be done through the legend.

Mapping geographic data with a filled map chart

Excel recently added two new chart types: a funnel chart to show a sales funnel and a filled map chart. The important word here is "filled." You can color code countries, states, provinces, counties, and zip code boundaries. However, you cannot plot individual points for each city. I never quite understood why Excel downloads the shape of a county but not the shape of a city. Figure 23.10 shows a filled map chart.

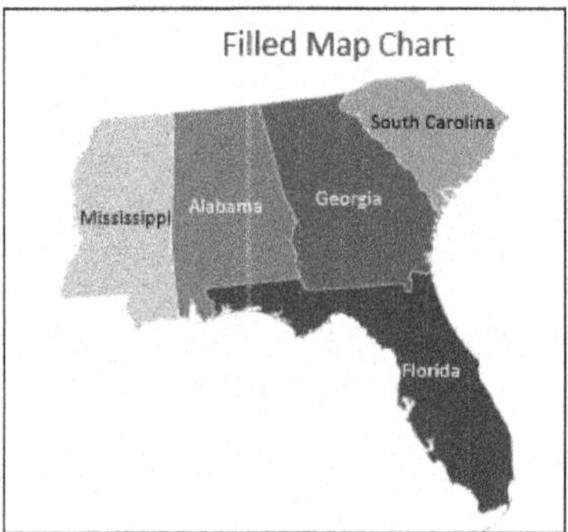

Figure 23.10 A filled map chart showing five states in the southeastern United States.

Saving time with charting tricks

Here are some charting techniques that have been in Excel for several versions.

Adding new data to a chart by pasting

Even though this next trick has existed in Excel since 1997, not many people know about it—you can add new data to a chart by pasting. Suppose you have a chart showing data for several months. You have nicely formatted and customized the chart. You now have new data available. Instead of re-creating the chart, you can paste the new data to the existing chart.

Follow these steps to expand the chart by pasting new data on it:

1. Make sure the new data has a heading consistent with the old data. Note that if you accidentally enter the heading as Text instead of Date, or vice versa, the trick has unexpected results.
2. Select the new data, including the heading.
3. Press Ctrl+C to copy the new data.
4. Select the chart.
5. Press Ctrl+V to paste the new data on the chart.

Inside OUT

Building X Y Scatter charts with two series is particularly difficult. You can create the chart using a Paste Special.

In the first image below, a scatter chart has been created from B1:C21. Follow these steps to add the second population:

1. Select the X and Y values with headings from G1:G7.
2. Copy that data to the Clipboard.
3. Click the chart to select it.
4. From the ribbon, select Home and open the Paste Options drop-down menu by clicking the bottom of the Paste icon. Do not choose the icon for Paste; instead, click Paste Special.
5. The Paste Special dialog offers to Add Cells As New Series. The Values (Y) In option is already set to Columns, and Series Names In First Row is already checked. However, you will need to choose Categories (X Values) in First Column. Leave Replace Existing Categories unchecked.
6. Click OK to add the second series to the chart.
7. Use the plus icon at the top right of the chart to add Legend and Axis Titles.

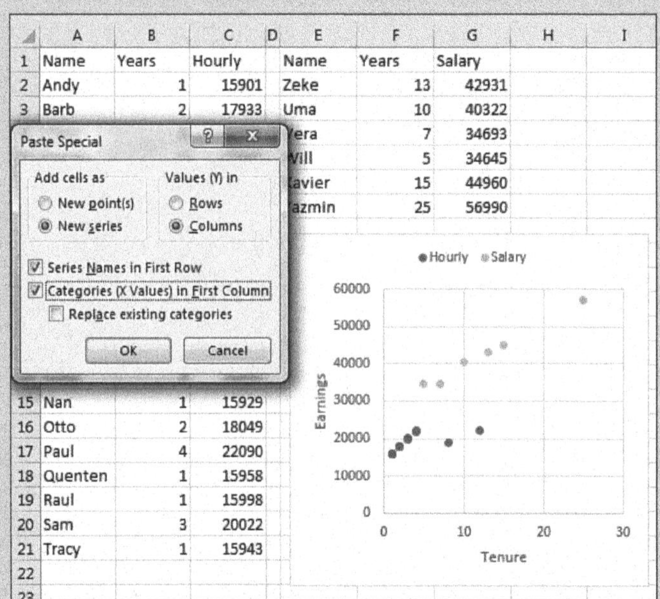

Two series appear on a scatter chart. One shows tenure earnings versus earnings for hourly workers. A second series shows the tenure earnings versus earnings for salaried workers.

Note that if you are willing to reorient your data so you have adjacent pairs of columns, you can create the chart by using the All Charts tab of the Insert Chart dialog box. Choose X Y (Scatter) category from the left navigation bar and then choose the top-right tile in the preview area. The tile does not have a name, but it will show two series of dots instead of three series.

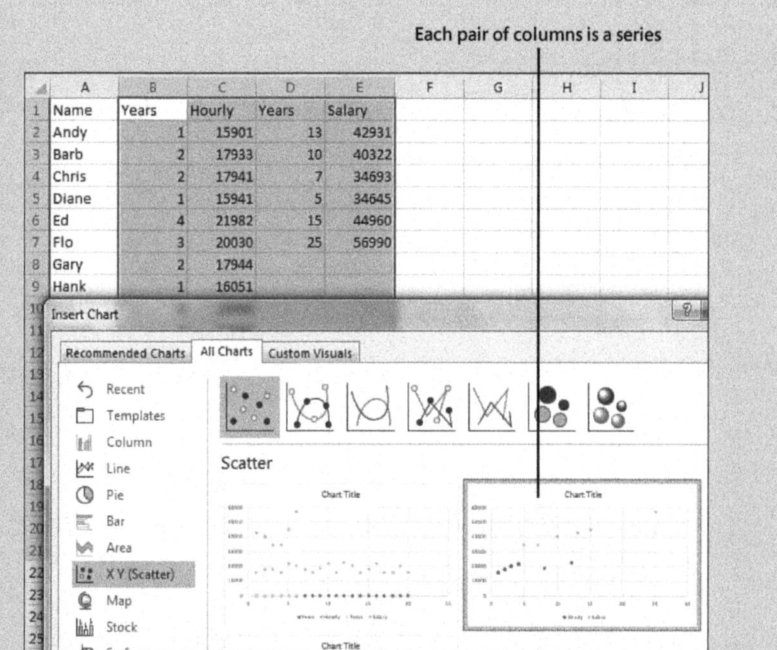

The Insert Chart dialog box offers three preview tiles for X Y (Scatter charts). Choose the top-right tile to treat each pair of columns as a series.

Dealing with small pie slices

In many data series, a few pie slices take up 80% of the pie, and many tiny slices account for the rest of the pie. Typically, the last pie slices end up at the back of the pie, where it is impossible to fit the labels, so no one can make out what they are.

When you have several small data points at the end of a pie chart series, and you need to see all the smaller segments, you can change the chart type to a special type called Bar Of Pie. In this type, the smallest few categories are exploded out and shown as a bar chart next to the pie.

To change an existing pie chart to a Bar of Pie chart, follow these steps:

1. Select the chart.

2. From the Type group of the Design tab, select Change Chart Type. The Change Chart Type dialog box appears.

3. In the Change Chart Type dialog box, select the last option for pie charts: Bar Of Pie.

4. Click OK to close the dialog box.

5. Double-click the bar chart. The Format Data Series task pane appears. Choose the chart icon.

6. In the Format Data Series task pane, you have control over the number of values in the bar chart. You can indicate to Split Series By Percentage Value and specify that any items less than 10 percent should end up in the bar portion of the chart. The result is shown in Figure 23.11.

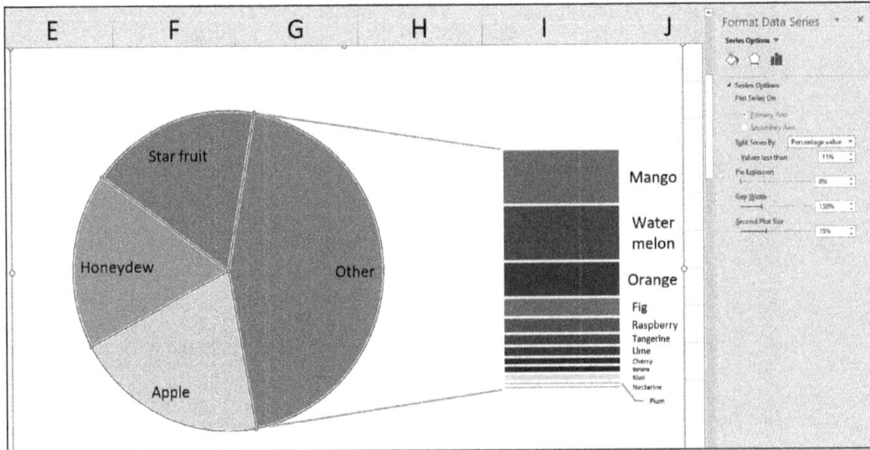

Figure 23.11 A series has been split by percentage with items less than 10% appearing in the bar portion of the chart.

Saving a favorite chart style as a template

Although Microsoft has provided great-looking built-in charts, you will likely design some great-looking charts of your own. After you have designed a chart, you can save it as a template. When you build new charts based on that template, all the settings for colors, fonts, effects, and chart elements are applied to the new data.

For all the power and glitz of Excel's built-in chart styles, the chart templates feature can save you massive amounts of time, such as if you routinely customize your charts to meet company standards.

Follow these steps to create a template:

1. Build a chart and customize it as necessary.
2. Right-click the chart. Choose Save As Template. Give the chart template a name. Excel saves the template with a .crtx file extension.

To create a chart by using your template, follow these steps:

1. Select the data you want to chart.
2. From the Insert tab, choose any of the Chart drop-down lists and then select All Chart Types. The Create Chart dialog box appears.
3. In the Create Chart dialog box, select the Templates category.
4. Click the desired template if there is more than one.
5. Click OK. Excel creates the chart with all the custom formatting from the saved template.

If you like your template so much that you want all future charts to be based on the template, follow these steps to make the template your default style:

1. Select a chart based on the desired template.
2. From the Design tab, select Change Chart Type. The Create Chart dialog box appears.
3. In the Create Chart dialog box, select the Templates category.
4. Select the desired template.
5. In the lower-left corner of the Change Chart Type dialog box, select Set As Default Chart.

In the future, you can create a chart that uses this template by following these steps:

1. Select the data you want to chart.
2. Press Alt+F1 to apply your default template.

CHAPTER 24

Using 3D Maps

You can build a pivot table and display the results on an animated map using the 3D Maps feature. This functionality debuted as the Power Map add-in for Excel 2013. The functionality was renamed 3D Maps and built in to Excel starting with Excel 2016.

Examples of 3D Maps

The first three figures represent corn acreage by state for the year 2014. Figure 24.1 shows a shaded area map. Iowa and Illinois are the leading producers of corn.

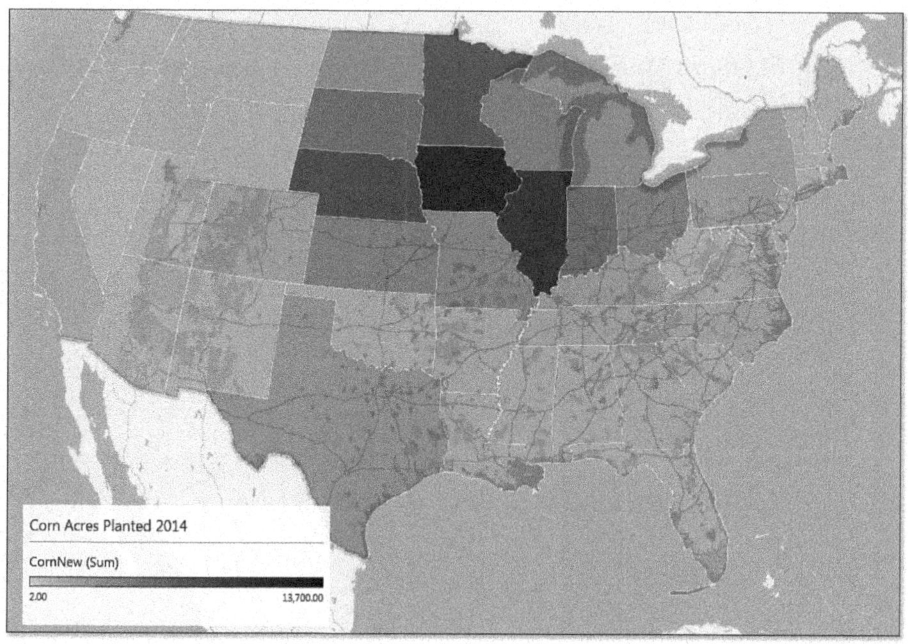

Figure 24.1 In a shaded area map, a darker color indicates a higher value.

Figure 24.2 shows a column chart. The height of each column correlates to acres of corn planted. Note that this visualization looks best when you tip the map to look at it closer to ground level.

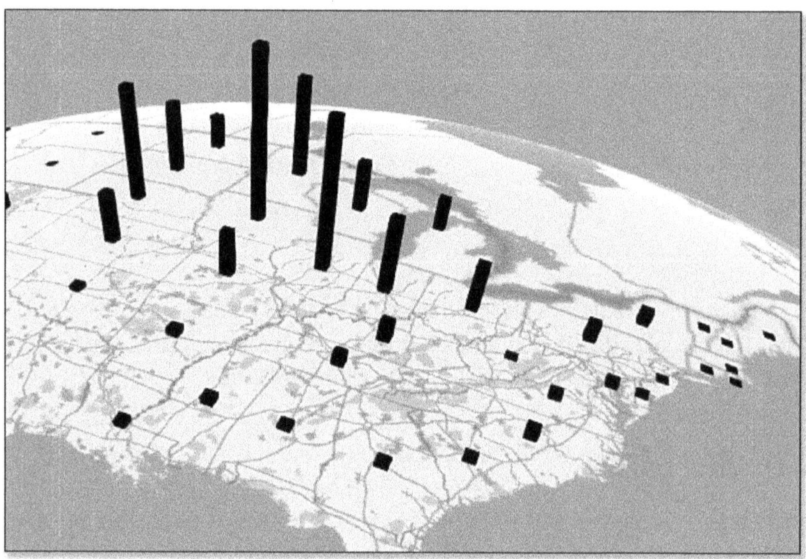

Figure 24.2 A column chart in each state indicates the amount of corn planted.

Figure 24.3 shows a heat map. The points with the highest value are shown in a red/yellow/green/blue circle, whereas smaller points might appear in just blue.

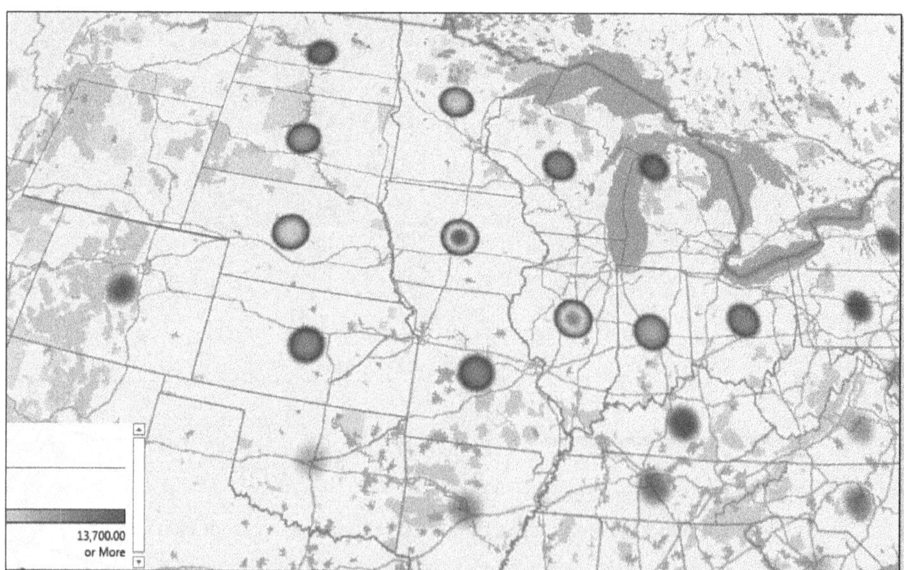

Figure 24.3 A heat map uses red and yellow to indicate the highest values.

Adding color information for categories

The next figures are based on data from FlightStats.com. Figure 24.4 shows the position and altitude of a Southwest Airlines flight from Akron, Ohio, to Orlando, Florida. By using a Category field, the columns are a different color based on whether the flight is below 10,000 feet, climbing, level, or descending.

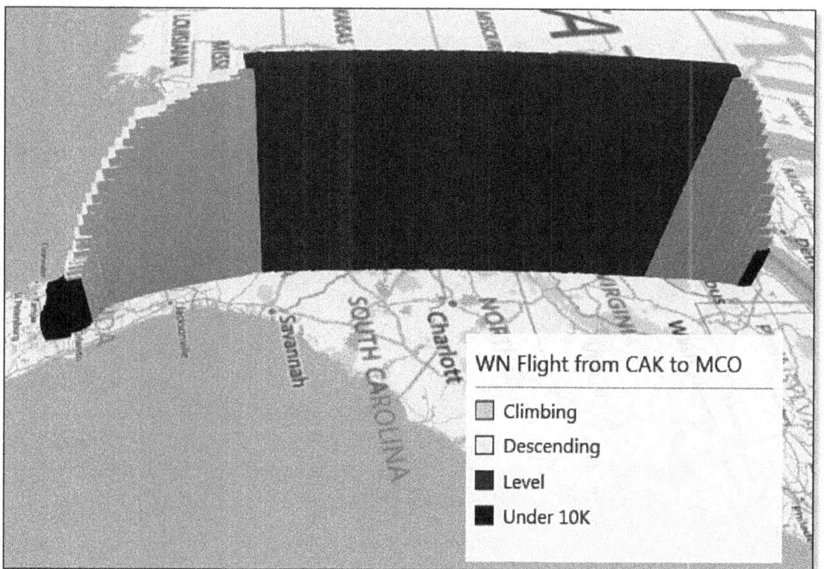

Figure 24.4 Different colors indicate different stages of this aircraft flight.

Zooming in

FlightStats provides new data every minute. Although the flight in Figure 24.4 looks like a solid line, when you zoom in, as in Figure 24.5, you can see the gaps between the columns. While landing, this flight flew west of downtown Orlando, flew four minutes south of the airport, turned, and landed four minutes later.

When you pan to the beginning of the flight as in Figure 24.6, you see the first four minutes of the flight as viewed southwest of Akron, Ohio. By changing the theme to use a satellite photograph of the ground, you can see that the plane took off to the northeast from runway 5 and began turning south three minutes into the flight.

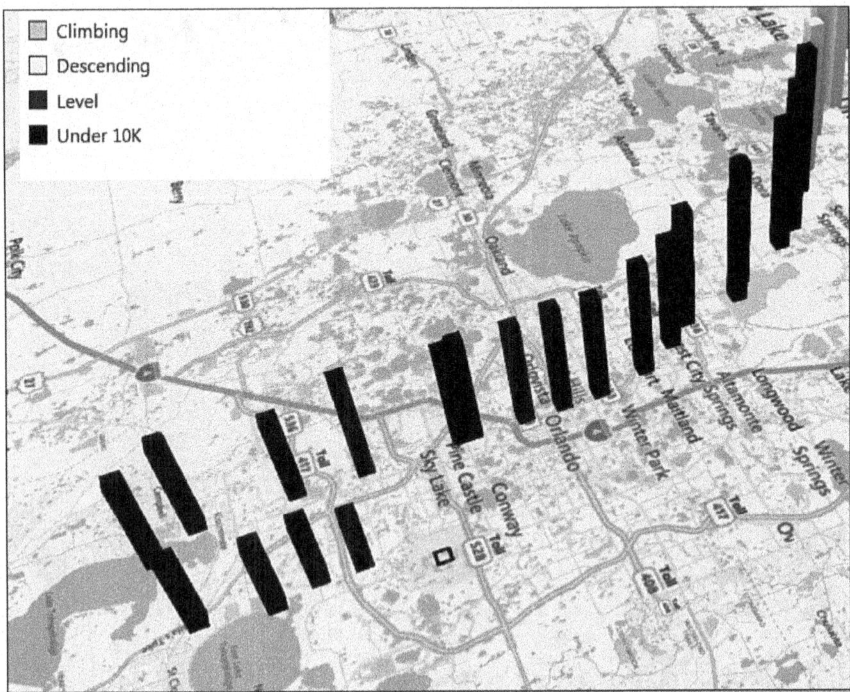

Figure 24.5 You can zoom in on any portion of the map.

Figure 24.6 Using the satellite theme, you can make out individual streets, buildings, and runways.

Animating over time

If your data set includes a date or time field, you can animate the data over time. A time scrubber appears at the bottom of the map. Click the Play button to the left of the scrubber to play the entire sequence or grab the scrubber and drag to any particular day or time.

In Figure 24.7, the flight has reached Columbus, Ohio, by 8:47 a.m. In Figure 24.8, the flight crosses through the northeast corner of Tennessee by 9:15 a.m.

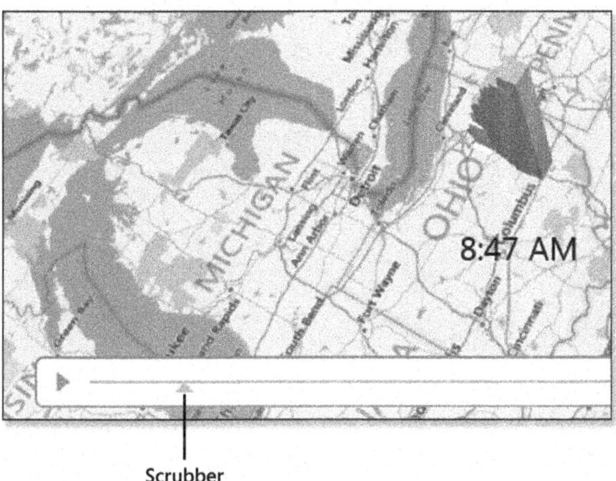

Figure 24.7 Animate the map over time to watch events unfold.

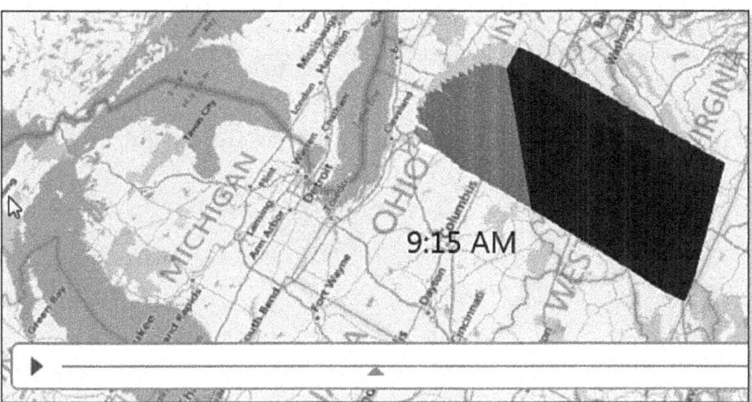

Figure 24.8 Either allow the scene to play the entire time span or drag the scrubber to a specific time.

Going ultra-local

The previous example showed a 1,000-mile journey that spanned more than two hours. This example shows a 2-mile story that spans 50 years. Figure 24.9 shows Merritt Island, Florida, in November 1967. Engineers who work at Kennedy Space Center on the Apollo program had started building houses on the canals of Merritt Island. Each tiny square is a house.

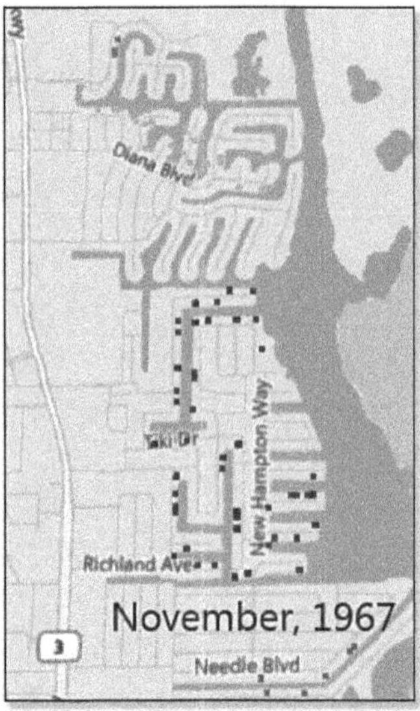

Figure 24.9 Each tiny square is a house on a canal.

Figure 24.10 shows the same area at the end of the Apollo program in 1972. More houses have been built.

Figure 24.11 shows the area as the first Shuttle mission took off in 1981.

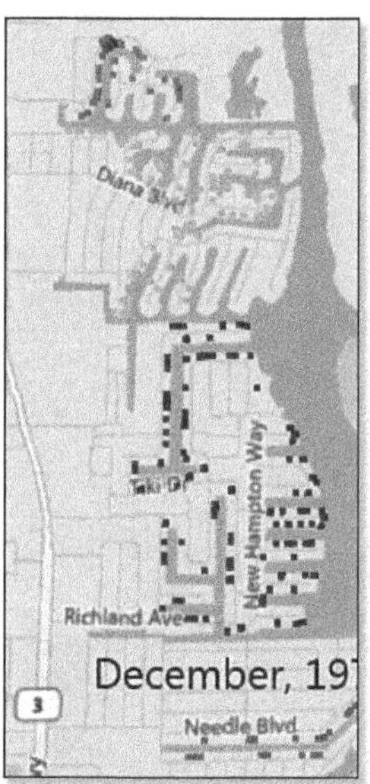

Figure 24.10 You can see which neighborhoods developed during the Apollo years.

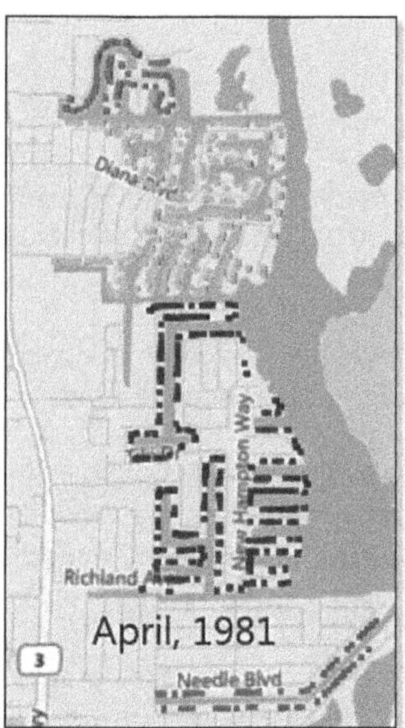

Figure 24.11 By the Space Shuttle era, more neighborhoods had filled in.

Figure 24.12 shows the detail of two neighborhoods. The height of the column is the last sale amount. When you animate this data over time, you can see the run-up of sale prices in 2009 leading up to the housing bubble.

Figure 24.12 Zoom in and change to a satellite photo to see individual houses.

Getting your data into a 3D Map

The mapping engine is always using data from the Power Pivot data model. You don't have to load your data to the data model. Just choose one cell in the data set and select Insert, 3D Map. Excel loads the data to the data model for you.

However, if your data is in multiple tables, and if you have the full version of Power Pivot, you can load your tables to Power Pivot and define relationships between the tables.

3D Maps requires one or more geographic fields, such as City, County, Country, State or Province, Street, Postal or ZIP Code, or Full Address. If you have data that already has latitude and longitude, the program can use that. If you are using a custom map, the X, Y coordinates will work. If you are using custom shapes, 3D Maps can accept .kml or .shp files.

Figure 24.13 shows a simple data set. Columns A and B provide enough geography with City and State. Column C is a Category column to provide different colors on the map. It rounds the population from column D to the nearest 25,000. Column D contains the population. This data will be plotted at the city level. For some cities, it would be possible to get by with only column A. However, without the FL qualifier in column B, it is likely that Melbourne would appear in Australia instead of Florida. When in doubt, add extra geography fields, even if every value in column B is FL.

=MROUND(D2,25000)

	B	C	D
City	State	Category	Population
Jacksonville	FL	825000	821784
Miami	FL	400000	399457
Tampa	FL	325000	335709
St. Petersburg	FL	250000	244769
Orlando	FL	250000	238300
Hialeah	FL	225000	224669
Tallahasee	FL	175000	181376
Fort Lauderdale	FL	175000	165521
Port St. Lucie	FL	175000	164603
Pembrooke Pines	FL	150000	154750
Cape Coral	FL	150000	154305
Hollywood	FL	150000	140768
Gainesville	FL	125000	124354
Miramar	FL	125000	122041
Coral Springs	FL	125000	131096
Clearwater	FL	100000	107685
Miami Gardens	FL	100000	107167

Figure 24.13 Select one cell in your data and choose Insert, 3D Map.

With one cell in your data selected, choose Insert, 3D Map. It takes several seconds for the data to be loaded to the Power Pivot data model. You are then presented with the 3D Maps window. A Field List is hovering above the map. The Location box on the right shows the fields that Excel detected as being geography. Pay particular attention that this is correct. A field that contains values such as "123 Main Street" should be classified as Street and not Address. The Address data type is reserved for values that contain a complete address, such as "30 Rockefeller Plaza, New York, NY 10112."

In Figure 24.14, the Location box has a 93% hyperlink on the right side. You can see many blue columns already appearing in Florida. The hyperlink indicates that geocoding is finished and 93% successful, but there were some places that Bing was unsure of.

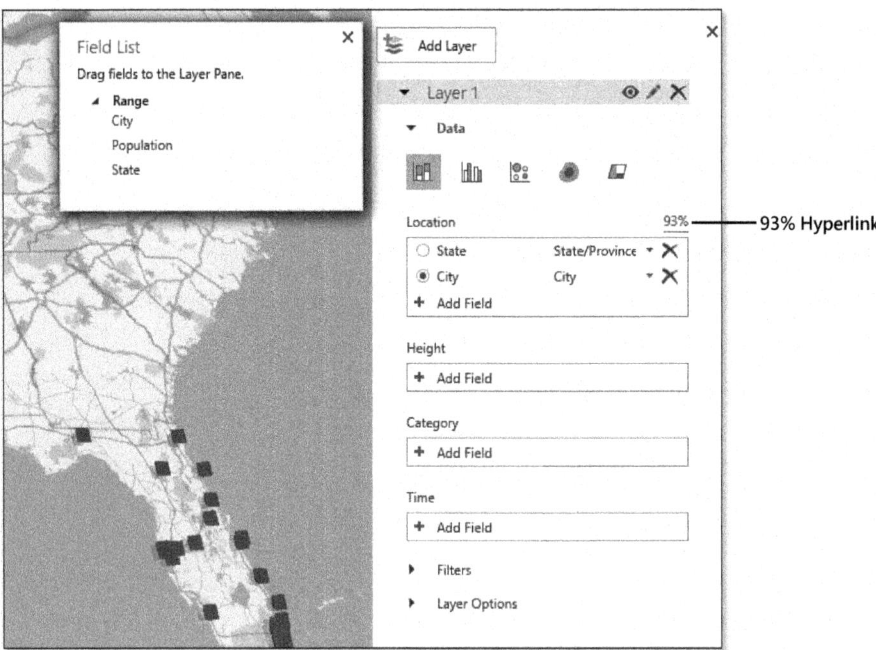

Figure 24.14 Things look good, but only 93% of points were correctly located.

Click the 93% hyperlink for a report of the places with low mapping confidence. As shown in Figure 24.15, everything is actually correct. If something was not correct, you would have to go back to the original data in Excel, add more geography, and then refresh the data in 3D Maps.

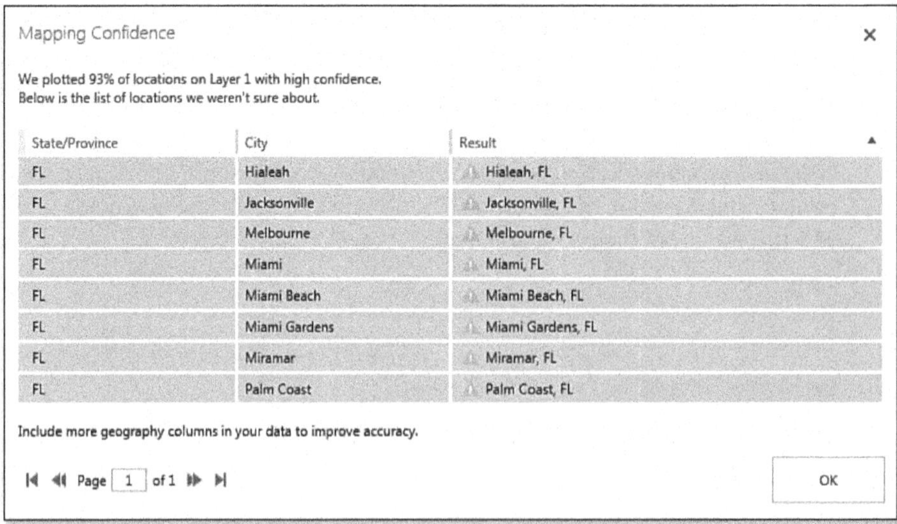

Figure 24.15 Currently, the only way to improve accuracy is to include more fields in the original data set.

TROUBLESHOOTING

When 3D Maps cannot find a location, there is no way to specifically point to it on a map.

I've seen data sets where Excel thinks Paris is in Kentucky and Melbourne is in Florida. In these cases, adding a new column named "Country" with the appropriate country can help.

Also, when assigning your fields to a geography category, understand the difference between "Street" and "Address." If your data has a column with values such as "123 Main Street," this should be classified as a street. If you have values such as "123 Main Street, New York, NY," this should be classified as an address.

If you refer to "123 Main Street" as an address, there will be many points misplaced.

After the records are assigned to the correct geography, you can move fields from the Field List to the drop zones. In Figure 24.16, the population is the height. The columns are different colors thanks to a new field added to the category area. Note that to add a new field, you would return to Excel and insert a new column in the middle of the data. Add a formula, such as `=MROUND(D2,25000)`. Return to 3D Maps and click Refresh.

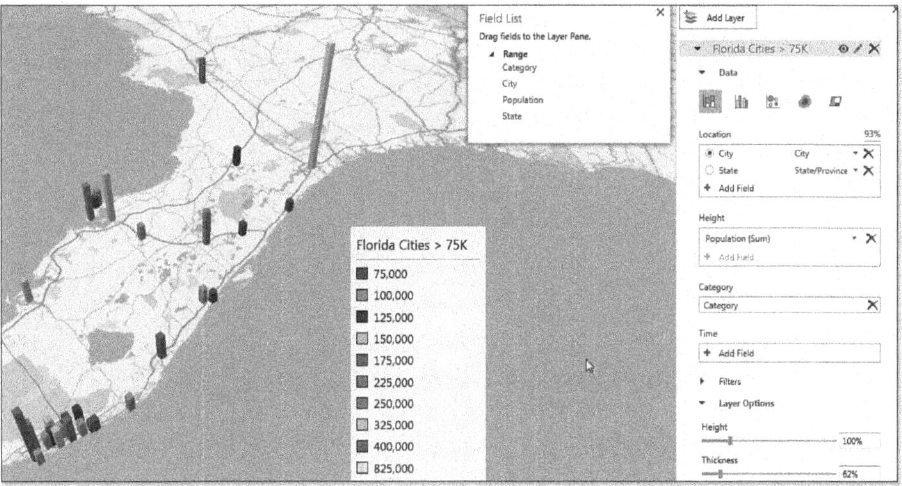

Figure 24.16 A map showing the largest cities in Florida.

Techniques when using 3D Maps

Here are some useful techniques when using 3D Map.

Tipping, rotating, and zooming the map

There are clickable navigation icons on the map. But master these mouse techniques for faster navigation:

- Hold down Alt. Left-click and drag the mouse left or right to rotate the map. In most of the Florida examples in this chapter, the map looks best when you are viewing it from the Atlantic Ocean. I made that happen by dragging the mouse left while holding down Alt.
- Hold down Alt. Left-click and drag the mouse up or down to tip the map. Dragging down gives you a view looking straight down on the map. Dragging up gives you a view from ground level.
- Hold down Ctrl. Scroll the wheel on your mouse to zoom in or out. Note that you often have to click the map once before the wheel mouse will start to work.

Adding a photo to a point

Right-click any column and choose Add Annotation. In the Description field, choose Image and browse to the location of the image. Choose a size and a placement. The image appears next to the column with an arrow (see Figure 24.17).

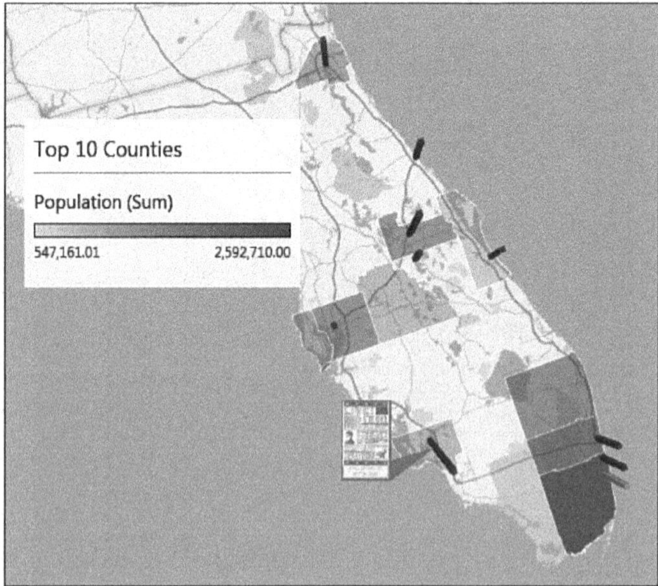

Figure 24.17 This map shows two map types on two different layers.

Combining layers

Figure 24.17 shows a map made from two different tables. This is easy if you have the Power Pivot tab displayed in your ribbon. Follow these steps:

1. Format both data sets in Excel as a table.
2. On the Power Pivot tab, choose Create Linked Table from both tables.
3. On the Insert tab, choose 3D Map.
4. Both tables appear in the field list. Drag County and State from the first table to the Location box. Choose a shaded area map. Add Population as the Value for the map.
5. Click Add Layer. You get a new Location box. Drag City and State from the second table. Build a column chart from this layer.

If you are using Excel 2016 and do not have the Power Pivot tab in the ribbon, there are two alternate ways to get the tables into the data model:

- One simple method is to create a pivot table from each data set. In the Insert PivotTable dialog box, choose the box for Add This Data To The Data Model. It does not matter what you put in the pivot table; simply creating the pivot table is enough.
- The other method is to use Power Query. From each table, choose Data, From A Table/Range. When the Power Query window opens, you will see the Close & Load icon on the left side. Open the drop-down menu below that icon and choose Close & Load To. In the Close & Load dialog box, choose Only Create A Connection and choose Add This Data To The Data Model.

The result: Figure 24.17 shows a map in which the top 10 Florida counties are highlighted. The columns indicate places where I have done my live Power Excel seminar. Any county that is shaded without a column indicates a market I have been overlooking.

Changing column size or color

The thickness of a column is more than one city block. If you want to show multiple houses on a street, you won't be able to tell one point from the others. In the right panel, choose Layer Options. Change the Thickness slider to 10% or less.

To change the colors used on the map, go to Layer Options. Use the 60 colors in the color drop-down menu or define your own color.

Resizing the various panes

Almost every legend or information pane takes up too much room. If you are working on a small laptop, your inclination will be to close all panes because they are covering up the map. If you have a large monitor, you can resize each pane. Click on the pane, and then use one of the two resize handles. To move a pane, click and drag the pane to a new location.

When you have a Time panel on the map, right-click and choose Edit. You can control the Time Format.

Adding a satellite photograph

Use the Themes drop-down menu in the ribbon. The second theme offers a satellite image. Outside of the first two themes, I rarely find anything that looks acceptable.

Showing the whole earth

What if you have data points in America and Australia? There is no way to see both halves of the globe at the same time. Use the Flat Map option in the ribbon. When you zoom out, you can see the entire world map, as shown in Figure 24.18.

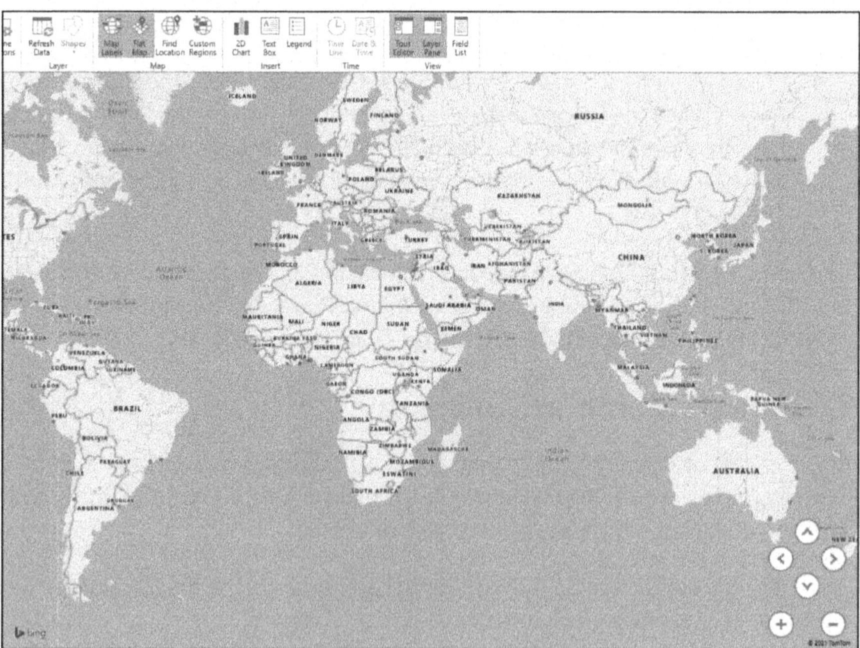

Figure 24.18 Use the Flat Map option to see both hemispheres at one time.

Understanding the time choices

When you add a field to the Time drop zone, a small clock icon appears above the right side of the field. This icon offers three choices, as shown in Figure 24.19:

- **Data Shows for an Instant:** The point appears when the scrubber reaches the date associated with that record. As the scrubber moves to the next day, the point disappears.
- **Data Accumulates Over Time:** Suppose you are showing ticket sales over time. After a ticket has been purchased, it should stay on the map. Choose Data Accumulates Over Time.
- **Data Stays Until It Is Replaced:** One map that I frequently use shows the last sale price for various houses in a neighborhood. A house might sell once every 7 years. In this case, you want the last sales price to remain until the house is sold at a different price.

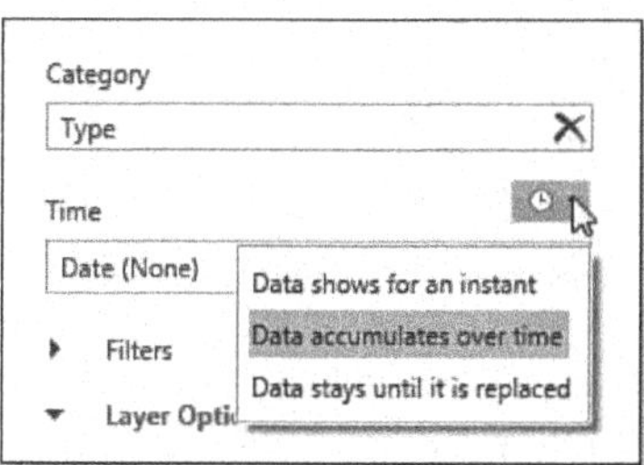

Figure 24.19 Three choices are available near the Time field.

Note that there is no good way to change a category as time progresses. You might want to show Chicago as red from 2013 to 2015 and then as green from 2019 to 2020. There currently is no good way to do this in 3D Maps.

> Inside OUT
>
> ***Is it possible to animate a line between two points in 3D Maps?***
>
> The capability to show movement along a path is not built into 3D Maps, but you can fake it. Find the latitude and longitude of both points. Build a new table in Excel with 1,000 rows. Add a date field that increments by an hour or a day in each row. For the latitude and longitude, add 1/1000 of the difference between the start and end point in each row. Set the time value that each point shows for an instant. When you press the Play button, the points will rapidly appear, then disappear, giving the illusion of a point racing from the start point to the end point.

Controlling map labels

You have only one option with map labels—either show them or do not. After you turn them on, they seem to have a mind of their own. If you zoom way out, you see large labels for each continent and map labels for some countries (see Figure 24.20).

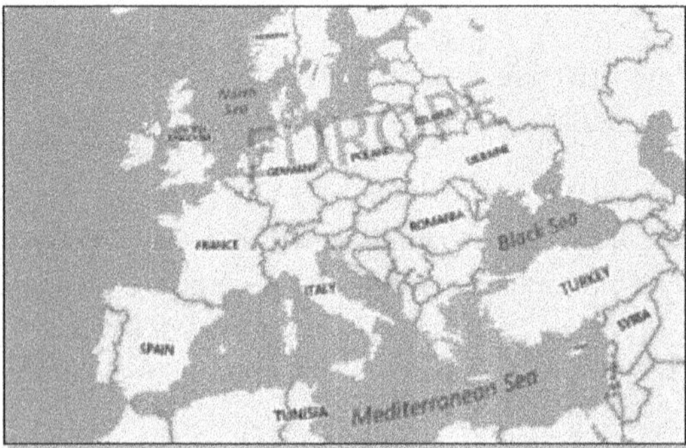

Figure 24.20 Some countries are labeled, and others are not.

As you zoom in, more countries are labeled, and some city labels appear.

Zoom in to a city, as in Figure 24.21. Some streets are labeled and others are not. What if an important street is one that is not named? You have no explicit control over which items are labeled and which are not. Your only hope is to zoom out, recenter the map slightly, and then zoom back in. Keep doing this until luck falls on your side and the particular street is labeled.

Figure 24.21 Some streets are labeled, and others are not. You have little control over which get labels.

Building a tour and creating a video

A tour is composed of multiple scenes. You can use the New Scene drop-down menu to duplicate the current scene as a new scene.

Your first scene might start out with a view of the entire country. Your next scene might zoom in on one portion of the country. Then a scene might add an annotation to one point. The next scene might fly to another part of the country. Each scene has a duration and an Effects duration. The various effects are designed to add visual interest.

CAUTION

You rarely want a Time field in more than one scene. If your first scene shows the data growing over time, and then the next scene zooms in on one portion of the map, you must remove the Time field in the second scene or you will watch the data repopulate in each scene.

After building several scenes, use the Play Tour icon to test the timing of the scenes. When you have a tour that looks good, use the Create Video icon to build a video of the tour. Note that this step can take up to an hour, so it makes sense to test the tour before building a video.

Using an alternate map

You can use 3D Maps to show data on something other than a globe. For example, a retail store might have transaction data showing sales by time and item. If you can map the item number to a location in the store map, you can plot sales by location.

Preparing the store image

First, find (or create) a map of the store. Figure out the height and width of the image in pixels. When you look at your store map, the lower-left corner has a coordinate of X=0, Y=0. As you move from left to right across the image, the X values increase. As you move from bottom to top, the Y values increase.

The process of locating each item in the store can be tedious. If you have Photoshop, open the image in Photoshop and press F8 to display a panel showing the X,Y coordinates of the mouse. Make sure to change the measurement units from inches to pixels. You can hover your mouse over a location on the store map. The X value reported by Photoshop is correct. The Y value is the distance from the top edge of the image, so you have to subtract the reported Y value from the height of the image. Or, if it is easier, key the reported Y values into Excel and then use a formula to change.

Specifying a custom map

After launching 3D Maps, move your X and Y field to the Location box. Choose X Coordinate and Y Coordinate as the field type. You see a question asking whether you want to change to a custom map (see Figure 24.22). Choose Yes.

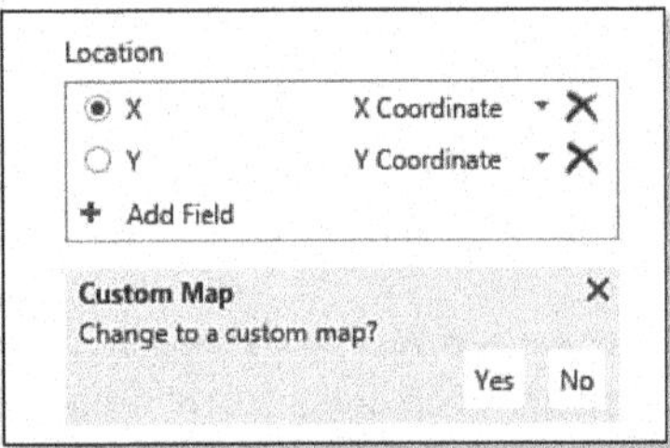

Figure 24.22 Specify X and Y as the location type.

In the Change Map Type dialog box, choose New Custom Map, as shown in Figure 24.23.

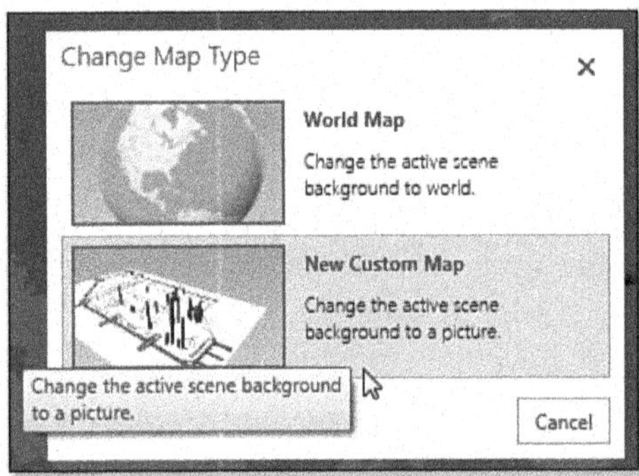

Figure 24.23 Specify a custom map.

Although I appreciate the team who built 3D Maps, the Custom Map Options dialog box always requires a lot of tweaking. Unless you managed to sell something at the X=0, Y=0 position in your store map, the default settings will always be wrong. Use the following steps to change the settings:

1. For the X Max, specify the width of the image in pixels.
2. For the Y Max, specify the height of the image in pixels.
3. Click the Picture icon and browse to the image of your store map.
4. Change from Auto Fit to Pixel Space.

Figure 24.24 shows the settings.

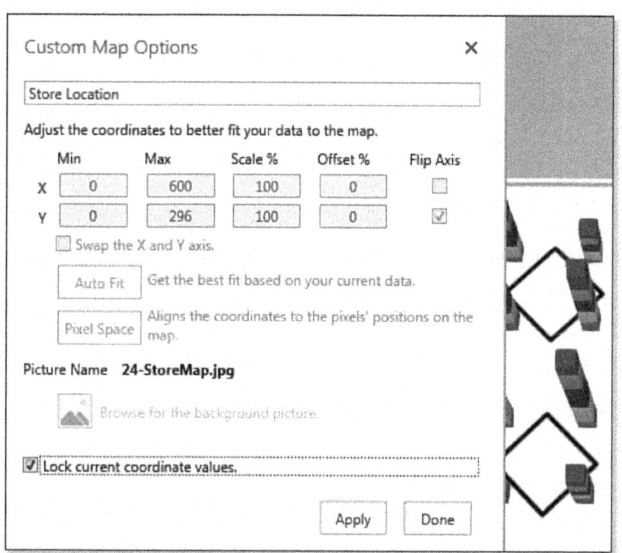

Figure 24.24 Change the settings for converting X,Y locations to a position in your image.

Your data is plotted on the store map. You can use the Alt and Ctrl navigation keys to rotate, tip, and zoom in on the map (see Figure 24.25).

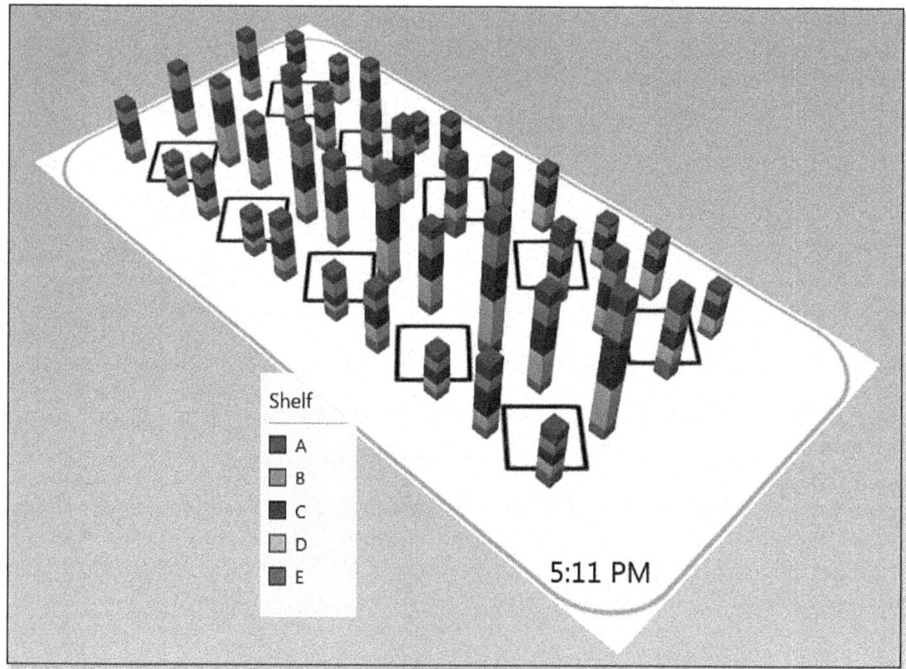

Figure 24.25 Data animates over time on a map of your retail store floor plan.

CHAPTER 25

Using sparklines

Edward Tufte wrote about small, intense, simple datawords in his 2006 book, *Beautiful Evidence*. Tufte called them *sparklines* and produced several examples where you could fit dozens of points of data in the space of a word. Tufte's concepts made it into Excel a few years later.

Fitting a chart into the size of a cell with sparklines

Excel's implementation of sparklines offers line charts, column charts, and a Win/Loss chart. Figure 25.1 shows an example of each:

- **Win/Loss:** The 1951 Pennant Race (in rows 7 and 8) shows two examples of a Win/Loss chart. Each event (in this case, a baseball game) is represented by either an upward-facing marker (to indicate a win) or a downward-facing marker (to indicate a loss). This type of chart shows winning streaks. The final three games were the playoffs between the Dodgers and the Giants, with the Giants winning two games to one.
- **Line:** The sparkline in row 12 shows 120 monthly points of the Dow Jones Industrial Index, indicating the closing price for each month in one decade.
- **Column:** Rows 16 through 21 compare monthly high temperatures for various cities using sparkcolumns. The minimum and maximum values for each city are marked in a contrasting color. Curitiba, in the southern hemisphere, has its warmest month in February.

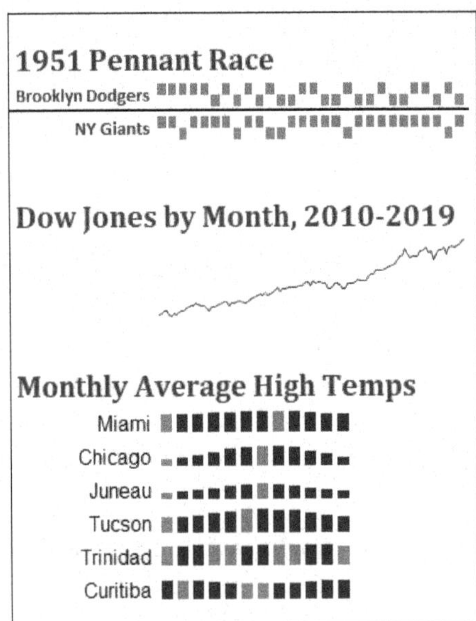

Figure 25.1 Excel offers three types of sparklines.

Sparklines can exist as a single cell (the Dow Jones example) or as a group of sparklines (the temperature example). When sparklines are created as a group, you can specify that all the sparklines should have the same scale or that they should be independent. There are times where each is appropriate.

The Sparkline feature offers the capability to mark the high point, the low point, the first point, the last point, or all negative points.

There is no built-in way to label sparklines. However, sparklines are drawn on a special drawing layer that was added to Excel 2007 to accommodate the data visualizations discussed in Chapter 22, "Using data visualizations and conditional formatting." This layer is transparent, so with some clever formatting, you can add some label information in the cell behind the sparkline.

Understanding how Excel maps data to sparklines

Contrary to most examples that you see in the Microsoft demos, sparklines do not have to be created adjacent to the original data set.

Suppose that you have the 4-row-by-12-column data set shown in Figure 25.2. This data shows four series of economic data. It can be used to create four sparklines.

	2003	2004	2005	2006	2007	2008	2009	2010	2011	2012	2013	2014	2015	2016	2017	2018	2019	2020
Unemployment	6	5.5	5.1	4.6	4.6	5.8	9.3	9.6	8.9	8.1	7.4	6.2	5.3	4.9	4.4	3.9	3.7	8.1
GDP	11458	12214	13037	13815	14452	14713	14449	14992	15543	16197	16785	17527	18238	18745	19543	20612	21433	20937
New Construction	1679	1842	1931	1979	1503	1120	794	652	585	649	764	884	968	1060	1153	1185	1255	1287
Consumer Credit	2103	2220	2321	2457	2609	2644	2555	2647	2756	2913	3090	3310	3400	3636	3831	4007	4193	4188

Figure 25.2 Four series of economic indicators over 18 years.

You can create the sparklines in a four-row-by-one-column range, as shown in D3:D6 of Figure 25.3, or in a one-row-by-four-column range, as shown in A1:D1 of the same figure. When you specify a sparkline, you specify the source data and the target range. Given a 4×12 cell source data and a 1×4 or 4×1 target range, Excel figures out that it should create four sparklines.

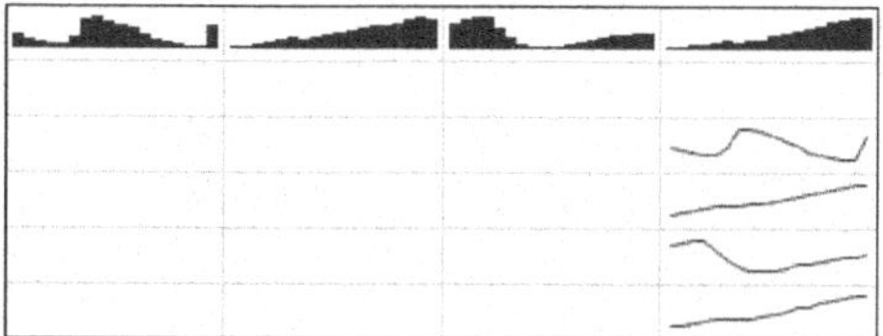

Figure 25.3 The sparklines can be plotted in a row or a column, regardless of whether the original data was in rows or columns.

What if your original data set is perfectly square? This occurs when you have four rows by four columns, as shown in Figure 25.4.

	2011	2012	2013	2014
Unemployment	8.9	8.1	7.4	6.2
GDP	15518	16163	16768	17419
New Construction	608.8	780.6	924.9	1003
Consumer Credit	2756	2924	3098	3317

Figure 25.4 The original data set has the same number of rows and columns.

You then have the chance that Excel will choose to create the sparklines along the wrong axis (see Figure 25.5).

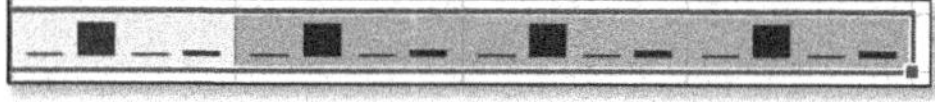

Figure 25.5 Excel might choose the wrong way to draw the sparklines.

While those sparklines are selected, go to the Sparkline Tools Design tab of the ribbon, open the Edit Data drop-down menu, and select Switch Row/Column (see Figure 25.6). The sparkline is reversed.

CHAPTER 25

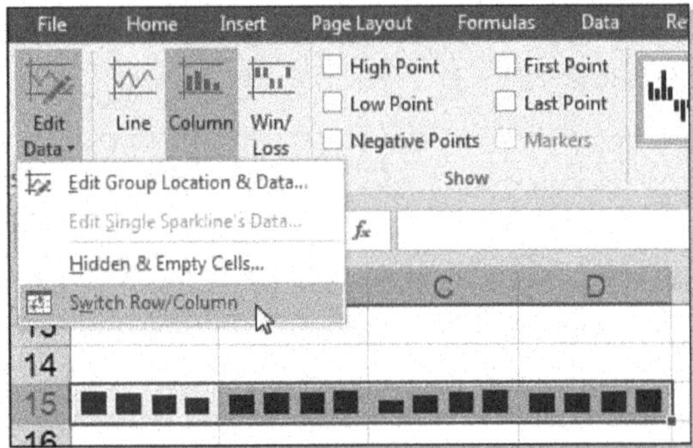

Figure 25.6 Excel offers a way to reverse the row and column.

TROUBLESHOOTING

Sparklines are scaled independently. Because there are no labels along the left axis, it is hard to see the magnitude of each line.

This is by design and allows you to see unemployment in percentages compared to GDP in trillions. There are cases where each sparkline is showing items that can be compared to each other.

In these cases, use the Axis settings in the Sparkline Tools. Change the Minimum Value and the Maximum Value to the Same For All Sparklines.

Creating a group of sparklines

The worksheet in Figure 25.7 includes almost two decades of leading economic indicators. Use the following steps to add sparklines to the table.

Economic Indicators 2003-2020				
		2003	2004	2005
Unemployment		6	5.5	5.1
GDP		11458	12214	13037
New Construction		1679	1842	1931
Consumer Credit		2103	2220	2321

Figure 25.7 Add space in your table for the sparklines.

1. Insert a column between columns A and B. This provides room for the sparklines to appear next to the labels in column A.
2. Select the data in C4:T8. Note that you should not include any headings in this selection.

3. On the Insert tab, select Column from the Sparkline group. Excel displays the Create Sparklines dialog box. This dialog box is the same for all three types of sparklines. You have to specify the location of the data and the location where you want the sparklines. Because your data is 4 rows by 12 columns, the Location Range must be a four-cell vector. You can either specify one row by four columns or four rows by one column.

   TIP

   In step 1, you might find that you don't need to print the table of numbers; just the labels and sparklines will suffice.

4. Select B5:B8 as the location range, as shown in Figure 25.8.
5. Click OK to create the default sparklines.

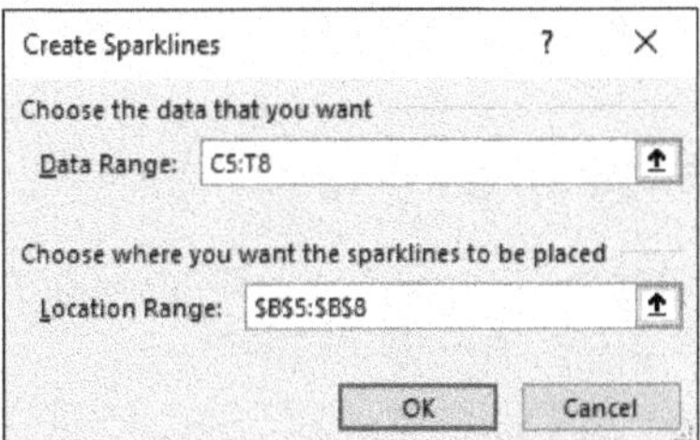

Figure 25.8 Preselect the data range and then specify the location range.

As shown in Figure 25.9, the sparklines have no markers. They are scaled independently of each other. The unemployment max of 9.6 reaches nearly to the top of cell B5, indicating the maximum for Unemployment is probably about 10. By contrast, the maximum for GDP in B6 is closer to 21,500.

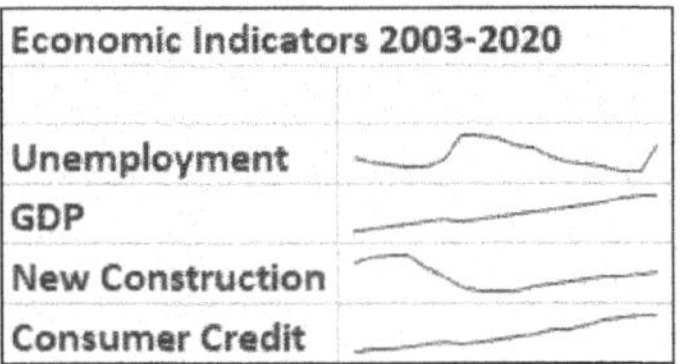

Figure 25.9 Default sparklines have no markers and are autoscaled to fit the cell.

The Show group of the Sparkline toolbar enables you to mark certain points on the line. In Figure 25.10, the high point is marked with a dot. This one change adds a lot of information to the sparklines. New Construction peaked around 2006. Unemployment peaked around 2010, and GDP and Consumer Credit both hit a new high in 2019.

CHAPTER 25

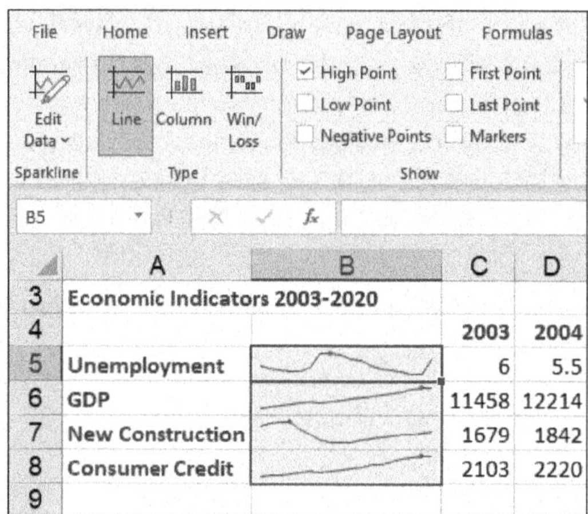

Figure 25.10 Placing a marker at the high point adds key information to the sparkline.

Built-in choices for customizing sparklines

The Sparkline Tools Design tab offers five groups of choices for customizing sparklines: Edit Data, Type, Show, Style, and Group. Each is discussed in this section.

The Edit Data drop-down menu enables you to redefine the data range for the source data and the location. If you have to add new data to existing sparklines, you can do so here. Generally, you would edit the location for the whole group, but the drop-down menu enables you to edit data for a single sparkline.

The Type group enables you to switch between Line, Column, and Win/Loss charts.

The Show group offers the second-most useful settings in the tab. The six check boxes here control which points should display markers in the sparkline:

- High Point
- Low Point
- First Point
- Last Point
- Negative Points
- All Points

Here, you can choose to highlight the high point, the low point, the first point, or the last point. Note that if there is a tie for high or low point, both points in the tie are marked. You can also choose to highlight all points and/or the negative points.

For sparklines, any item you choose in the Show group is drawn as a marker on the line. You can control the color for each of the six options using the Marker Color drop-down menu, discussed next.

For sparkcolumns, the markers are always shown for All Points, so the All Points check box is grayed out. Choosing any of the five other check boxes in the Show group causes those particular columns to be drawn in a different color.

For Win/Loss, you'll generally choose Markers and Negative. This is how the losses show in a contrasting color from the wins.

In Figure 25.11, examples of the various options are shown:

- In cell B3, the high, low, first, and last points are shown.
- In cell B5, all markers are shown in the same color.
- When you choose Markers and Negative, all points appear, but you can change the negative points to another color, as shown in cell B7.
- In cells B11 and B13, the chosen markers are shown in a contrasting color.
- Cells B9 and B15 are examples where the horizontal axis is shown. This helps to differentiate positive from negative. Note that the axis always appears at a zero location.

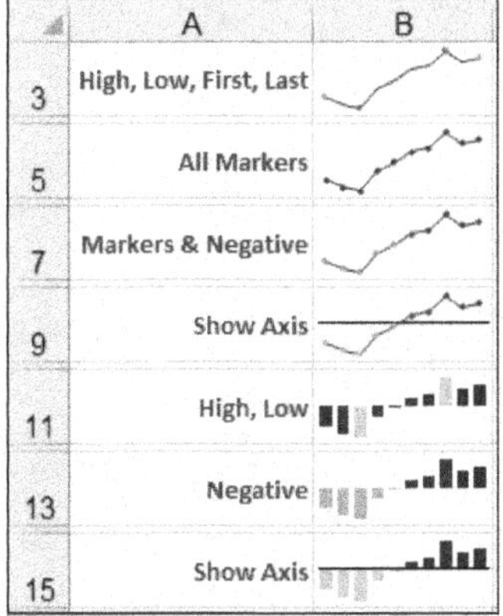

Figure 25.11 Use the Show group to highlight certain points.

The Style gallery seems to be a huge waste of real estate. In the Office theme, it offers 36 ugly alternatives for sparkline color. This group also offers the Sparkline Color drop-down menu, which is the standard Excel color chooser. The color chosen here controls the line in a sparkline. You use the Marker Color drop-down menu to control the color of the high, low, first, last, and negative points, as well as the default color for regular markers.

Any changes that you make on the Sparkline tab apply to all the sparklines in the group. This is usually a desired outcome. However, if you needed to mark the high point in one line and the low point in another line, you would ungroup the sparklines. Find the Ungroup icon on the far right side of the Sparkline tab in the ribbon.

> NOTE
>
> **For sparklines, the sparkline color controls the color of the line. For sparkcolumns or the Win/Loss chart, the sparkline color controls the color of the columns.**

You can also group sparklines or clear sparklines using icons in the Group group. The Axis drop-down menu appears in this group and contains the most important settings for sparklines. You learn how to use the Axis drop-down menu in the next example.

Controlling axis values for sparklines

Figure 25.12 presents a group of sparkcolumns showing the average high temperatures for several cities. These cities are a mix of tropical and frigid locales.

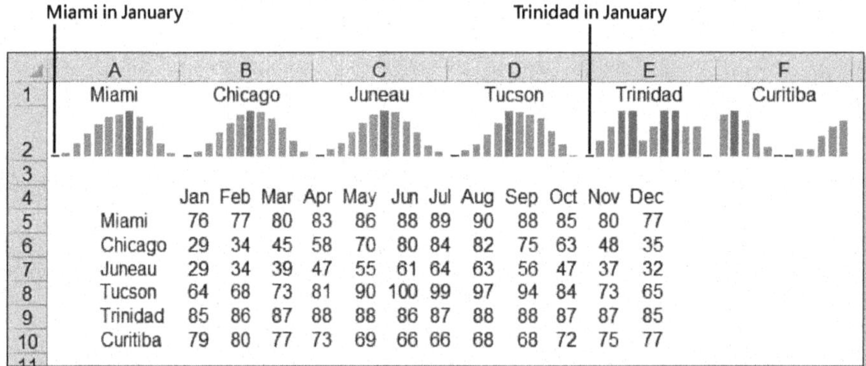

	Jan	Feb	Mar	Apr	May	Jun	Jul	Aug	Sep	Oct	Nov	Dec
Miami	76	77	80	83	86	88	89	90	88	85	80	77
Chicago	29	34	45	58	70	80	84	82	75	63	48	35
Juneau	29	34	39	47	55	61	64	63	56	47	37	32
Tucson	64	68	73	81	90	100	99	97	94	84	73	65
Trinidad	85	86	87	88	88	86	87	88	88	87	87	85
Curitiba	79	80	77	73	69	66	66	68	68	72	75	77

Figure 25.12 The automatic vertical scale assigned to each sparkline doesn't work in this example.

The default behavior is that each sparkline in the group gets its own scale. This worked for the varying economic indicators in Figure 25.10. However, it does not work here.

When the vertical axis scale is set to Automatic, you can never really know the high and low of the scale in use. If you study the data and the sparkline for Trinidad, it appears as if Excel has chosen a min point of 84.8 and a max point of 89. Without any scale, you might think that Trinidad in January is as cold as Chicago in January.

Figure 25.13 shows the options available in the Axis drop-down menu on the right end of the Sparkline Tools Design tab. The important settings here are the options for the minimum value and maximum value.

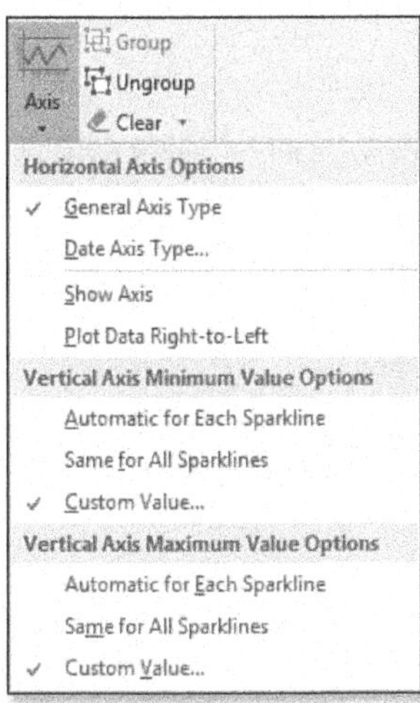

Figure 25.13 Control the vertical axis using this drop-down menu.

If you change the minimum and maximum values to the setting Same For All Sparklines, then all six sparklines in this group have the same min and max scale. The sparklines in Figure 25.14 initially look better. Juneau is never as warm as Tucson, but you still do not know the min and max values.

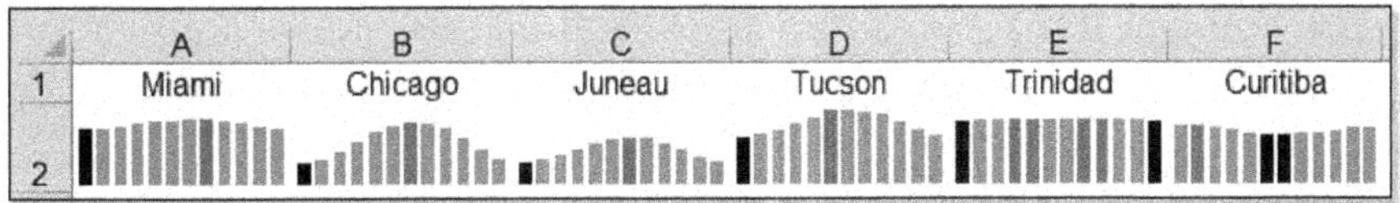

Figure 25.14 Force all sparklines to have the same vertical scale.

Take a close look at Chicago. It appears that the January high temperature is about zero, but the data table shows that the average high temperature in January is 29. You can estimate that these columns run from a minimum of 28 to a maximum of 101, based on looking through the data.

My suggestion is to always visit the Axis drop-down menu and set custom min and max values. For example, in the temperature example, you would set a minimum of 0 and a maximum of 100.

CHAPTER 25

Setting up Win/Loss sparklines

The data for a Win/Loss sparkline is simple: Put a 1 (or any positive number) for a win and put a –1 (or any negative number) for a loss. Put a zero to have no marker.

In Figure 25.15, you can see the data for a pair of Win/Loss sparklines. The 2 in cell F3 does not cause the marker to appear any taller than any of the 1s in the other cells. However, it does cause that marker to be shown as the max point.

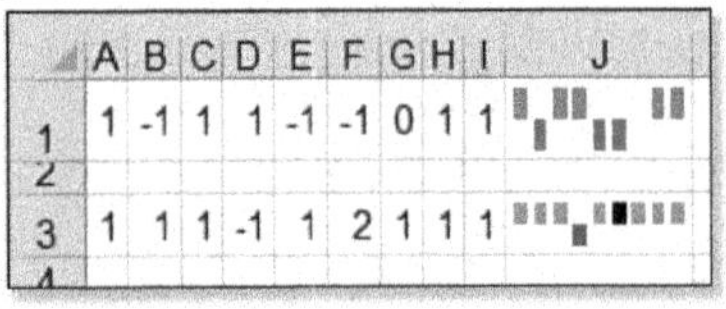

	A	B	C	D	E	F	G	H	I	J
1	1	-1	1	1	-1	-1	0	1	1	
2										
3	1	1	1	-1	1	2	1	1	1	
4										

Figure 25.15 Data sets for wins and losses are composed of 1s and –1s.

The data for the Win/Loss sparkcolumn chart does not have to be composed of 1s and –1s. Any positive and negative numbers will work.

In Figure 25.16, the data shows the closing price for the Dow for a period of a few months. Column D calculates the daily change. The Win/Loss chart in rows 4 and 5 does not show the magnitude of the change but instead focuses on how many days in a row had market gains versus market losses.

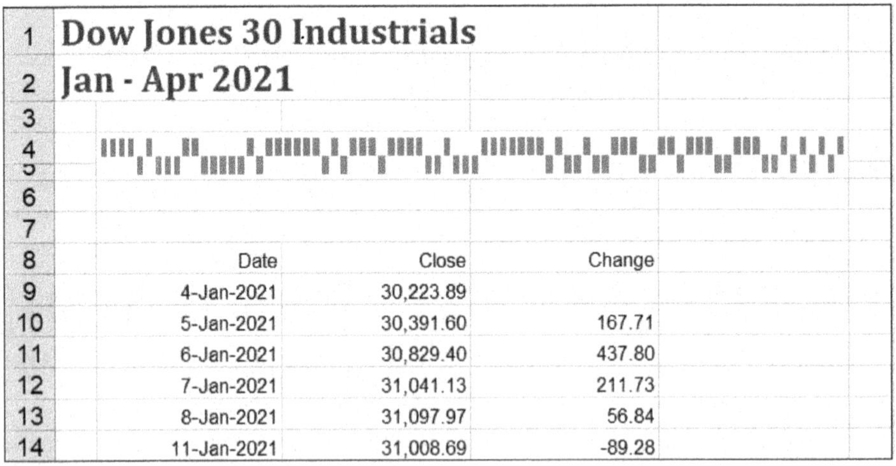

1	**Dow Jones 30 Industrials**			
2	**Jan - Apr 2021**			
3				
4				
5				
6				
7				
8		Date	Close	Change
9		4-Jan-2021	30,223.89	
10		5-Jan-2021	30,391.60	167.71
11		6-Jan-2021	30,829.40	437.80
12		7-Jan-2021	31,041.13	211.73
13		8-Jan-2021	31,097.97	56.84
14		11-Jan-2021	31,008.69	-89.28

Figure 25.16 This chart focuses on how many days in a row were gains or losses. The magnitude of the change is not factored in.

The following are some notes about the chart in Figure 25.16:

- Cells B4:E5 are merged to show a larger sparkline.
- If you stretch out a sparkcolumn or a Win/Loss chart wide enough, gaps eventually show up between the columns. This helps to quantify the number of events in a streak.

Inside OUT

Sparklines do not officially support stacked column charts, but you can create one with a little trickery.

(This method was discovered by long-time Excel MVP Ingeborg Hawighorst of Teylyn.com.)

To create a stacked column chart sparkline from two series, follow these steps:

1. Start two series, white and black.
2. Add a White+Black helper series. This sparkline will be as tall as the white and black series combined.
3. Create three column sparklines from the three series.

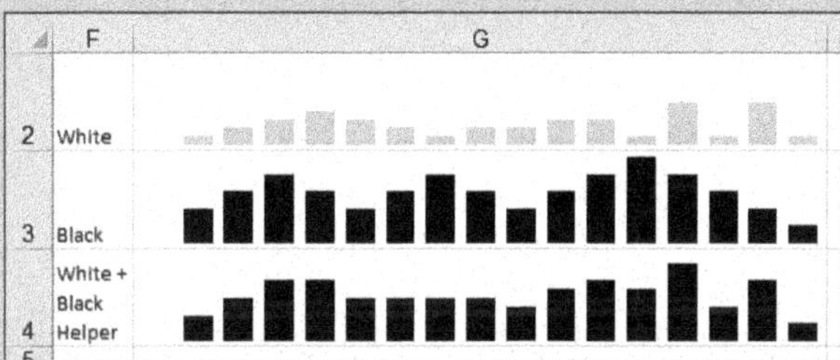

4. Click each sparkline and use the Ungroup command on the Sparkline Tools Design tab of the ribbon. From this point on, you only need to work with the White sparkline and the Helper sparkline. You can ignore the Black sparkline.
5. For each sparkline, go to Sparkline Tools, Axis. Set the Minimum Axis to zero for both sparklines. Set the Maximum Axis to the same number for both sparklines.
6. Copy the cell containing the Helper sparkline.
7. Go to a new location and click Home, select the Paste drop-down menu, and choose Linked Picture.
8. Copy the cell containing the White sparkline.
9. Paste a Linked Picture in the same vicinity of the White sparkline using the same steps. Drag the White sparkline over the Helper sparkline and nudge carefully until they line up.

Provided you pasted the Helper sparkline picture before the White sparkline picture, the White sparkline should be on top. If not, right-click the White sparkline picture and choose Bring To Front.

As shown in the image below, the White sparkline in front of the Black sparkline gives the illusion that you have a stacked column.

CHAPTER 25

Showing detail by enlarging the sparkline and adding labels

The examples of sparklines created by Tufte in *Beautiful Evidence* almost always label the final point. Some examples include min and max values or a gray box to indicate the normal range of values.

Professor Tufte's definition of sparklines includes the word *small*. If you are going to be showing sparklines on a computer screen, there is no reason they have to stay small.

When you increase the height and width of a cell, the sparkline automatically grows to fill the cell. If you merge cells, the sparkline fills the complete range of merged cells.

In Figure 25.17, the height of row 2 is set to 56.25. This height allows for five rows of 8-point Calibri text to appear in the cell. To determine the optimum height for your font, type 1 and press Alt+Enter, type 2 and press Alt+Enter, type 3 and press Alt+Enter, type 4 and press Alt+Enter, and then type 5 in a cell. Then select Home, Format, AutoFit Row Height.

	A	B	C	D	E
1	YTD Sales vs. Budget by Month, 2025				
2	17 -13		-2		1 2 3 4 5
3		J F M A M J J A S O N D			
4					
5					
6				YTD % to Budget	Budget
7			Jan	17	120K
8	Min	-13	Feb	3	120K
9	Max	17	Mar	-5	120K
10	Range	30	Apr	-13	120K
11	Final	-2	May	-10	120K
12			Jun	0	120K
13	Quintile	3	Jul	5	120K
14			Aug	4	120K

Figure 25.17 This sparkline has many labels, but they are all manually added outside the sparkline.

The sparkline in cell B2 is set to have a custom minimum and a custom maximum that match the minimum and maximum of the data set.

The label in cell A2 is right-justified 8-point Calibri font. The formula in A2 is `=B9&REPT(CHAR(10),4)&B8`. This formula concatenates the maximum value, four line feeds, and the minimum value. Ensure the Wrap Text icon is selected on the Home tab.

The labels in B3 are 10-point Calibri. Type **J F M A M J J A S O N D** in cell B3 and adjust the column width to fit the text. (Note: Be sure to place spaces between each of the letters.)

Formulas in B10 and B13 calculate the range from min to max as well as the quintile where the final value falls. The formula in C2 uses `=REPT(CHAR(10),B13-1)&B11` to put the final label at about the right height to match the final point.

In Figure 25.18, the city labels are values typed in the same cell as the sparkcolumns. The max scale is set to 120 to make sure there is room for the city name to appear. The Month abbreviations below the charts are **J F M A M J J A S O N D** in 6.5-point Courier New font.

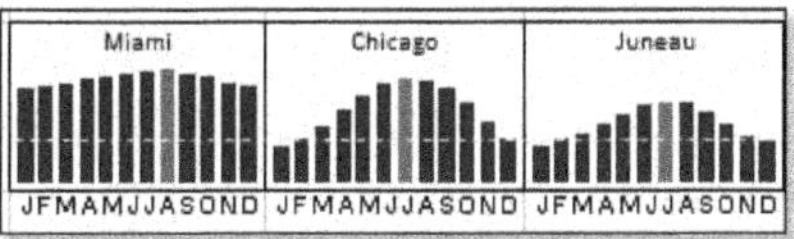

Figure 25.18 Labels are created by typing in a small font in the cell.

If you set a row height equal to 110, you can fit 10 lines of text in the cell using Alt+Enter. Even with a height of 55, you can fit five lines of text. This enables the label for the final point to get near to the final point.

In Figure 25.19, a semitransparent gray box indicates the acceptable limits for a measurement. In this case, anything outside of 95% to 105% is sent for review. These gray boxes are shapes from the Insert tab.

> TIP
>
> **After trying both 6-point and 7-point font and not having the labels line up with the bars, I ended up using 6.5-point font and adjusting the column widths until the columns lined up with the labels.**

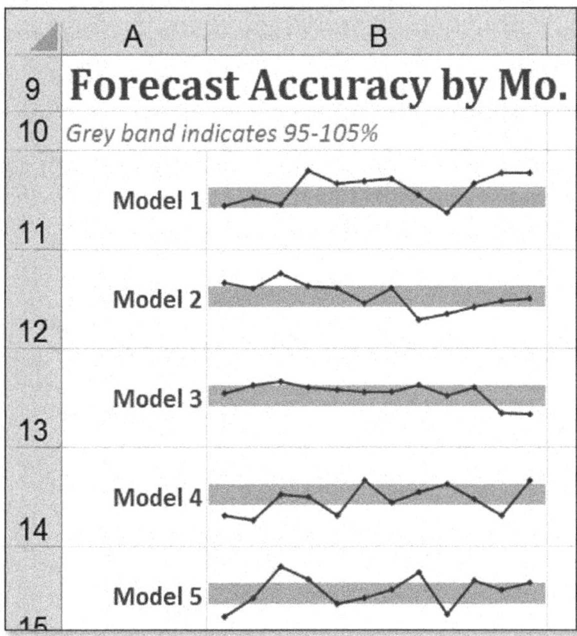

Figure 25.19 A gray box shows the acceptable range to help the reader locate items outside of this range.

Use the following tips when setting up the box:

1. Temporarily change the first two points in the first cell to be at the min and max for the box.
2. Increase the zoom to 400%.
3. Draw a rectangle in the cell.
4. Use the Drawing Tools Format tab to set the outline to None.
5. Under Shape Fill, select More Fill Colors. Choose a shade of gray. Because shapes are drawn on top of the sparkline layer, drag the transparency slider up to about 70% transparent.
6. Use the resize handles to make sure the top and bottom of the box go through the first and second points of the line.
7. After getting the box sized appropriately, reset the first two data points back to their original values.
8. Copy the cell that contains the first box. Paste onto the other sparkline cells. Because the sparklines are not copied, only the box is pasted.

TIP

It is possible to copy sparklines. You have to copy both the sparkline and the data source in a single copy. If your copy range includes both elements, the sparkline is pasted.

Other sparkline options

You can choose how to deal with gaps in the data. Select Sparkline Tools Design, Edit Data, Hidden And Empty Cells to display the Hidden And Empty Cell Settings dialog box, shown in Figure 25.20.

By default, any missing data in the source range is plotted as a gap, as shown in the top chart in Figure 25.20. Alternatively, you can choose to plot the missing values as zero (center chart) or have Excel connect the data points with a straight line (bottom chart). Also, by default, any data in hidden rows or columns is removed from the sparkline. To keep the hidden data in the chart, select the Show Data In Hidden Rows And Columns check box in Figure 25.20.

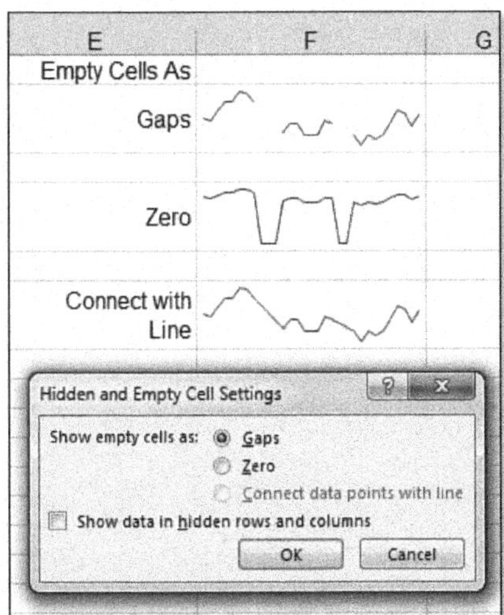

Figure 25.20 Choose how to deal with missing points.

CHAPTER 26

Formatting spreadsheets for presentation

Images and artwork provide an interesting visual break from tables of numbers in Excel. Office provides ten elements that you can use to illustrate a workbook:

- **SmartArt:** SmartArt is a collection of similar shapes, arranged to imply a process, groups, or a hierarchy. You can add new shapes, reverse the order of shapes, and change the color of shapes. SmartArt includes a text editor that allows for Level 1 and Level 2 text for each shape in a diagram. Many styles of SmartArt include the capability to add a small picture or logo to each shape.
- **Shapes:** You can add interesting shapes to a document. Shapes can contain words. In fact, shapes are the only art objects in which the words can come from a cell on the worksheet. You can add glow, bevel, and 3D effects to shapes.
- **WordArt:** WordArt enables you to present ordinary text in a stylized manner. You can use WordArt to bend, rotate, and twist the characters in text.
- **Text Boxes:** With text boxes, you can flow text in a defined area. The text box feature is excellent if you need to include paragraphs of body copy in a worksheet. Text boxes support multiple columns of text.

- **Pictures:** Excel worksheets tend to be dominated by numbers. Add a picture to liven up a spreadsheet and add interest. Excel offers an impressive number of ways to format your picture.
- **Online Pictures:** Insert a Creative Commons cartoon or image from a Bing Image Search.
- **Icons:** Insert an icon from a selection of hundreds of icons.
- **Cut-out People:** Microsoft 365 customers can insert photos of people showing a variety of emotions. These are found on the second tab of the Icons dialog box.
- **Stickers and Illustrations:** The Icons dialog box also offers images, illustrations, and stickers.
- **3D Models:** Insert a 3D model file and rotate it along all axes.

Using SmartArt

You use SmartArt to show a series of similar shapes, in which each shape represents a related step, concept, idea, or grouping. You build SmartArt by typing Level 1 text and Level 2 text in a text pane. Excel automatically updates the diagram, adding shapes as you add new entries in the text pane.

The goal of SmartArt is to enable you to create a great-looking graphic with a minimum of effort. After you define a SmartArt image, you can change to any of the other 221 layouts by choosing the desired layout from the gallery. Text is carried from one layout to the next. Figure 26.1 shows four SmartArt styles:

- **Chevron Accent Process:** In this layout, all text is typed as Level 1.
- **Pie Process:** A pie chart advances to show more and more of the process complete.
- **Hexagon Cluster:** Each shape has a corresponding accent picture. Small hexagons indicate the picture and text pair.
- **Continuous Picture List:** Used to show groups of interconnected information. Includes a round accent picture.

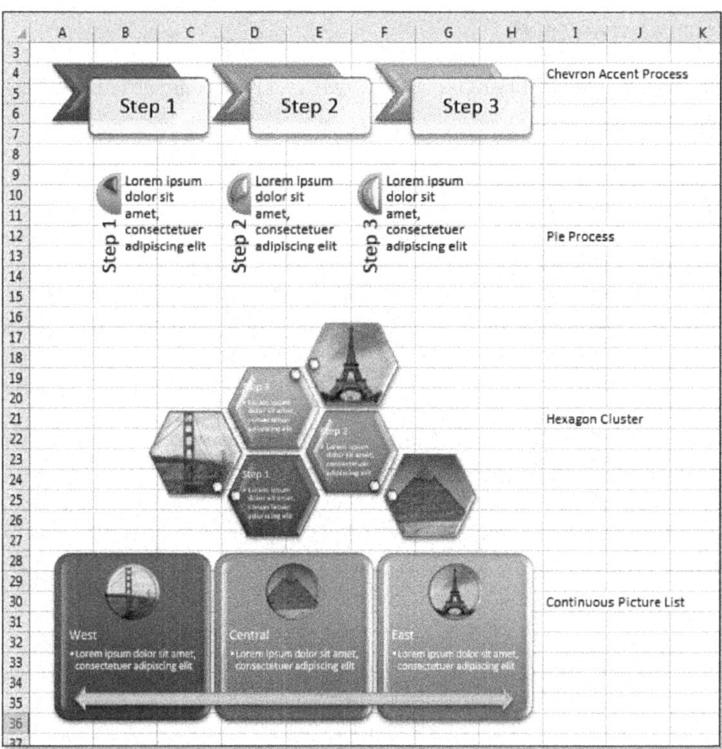

Figure 26.1 Subtle differences in four of the 195 possible SmartArt layouts give more weight to either Level 1 or Level 2 text.

Elements common in most SmartArt

A SmartArt style is a collection of two or more related shapes. In most styles, you can add additional shapes to illustrate a longer process. However, a few styles are limited to only a certain number of items.

Each shape can contain a headline (Level 1 text). Most shapes allow for body copy (Level 2 text). A few shapes allow for a picture. Some of the 199 layouts show only Level 1 text. If you switch to a style that does not display Level 2 text and then back, the shape remembers the Level 2 text it originally included. After you save and close the file, the hidden text is removed.

While you are editing SmartArt, a text pane that is slightly reminiscent of PowerPoint appears. You can type some bullet points into the text pane. If you demote a bullet point, the text changes from Level 1 text to Level 2 text. If you add a new Level 1 bullet point, Excel adds a new shape to the SmartArt.

Inserting SmartArt

Although there are 195 different layouts of SmartArt, you follow the same basic steps to insert any SmartArt layout:

1. Select a cell in a blank section of the workbook.
2. From the Insert tab, select SmartArt from the Illustrations group. The Choose A SmartArt Graphic dialog box appears.
3. Choose a category in the left side of the Choose A SmartArt Graphic dialog box.
4. Click a SmartArt type in the center of the Choose A SmartArt Graphic dialog box.
5. Read the description on the right side. This description tells you whether the layout is good for Level 1 text, Level 2 text, or both.
6. Repeat steps 4 and 5 until you find a style suitable for your content. Click OK. Figure 26.2 shows an outline of the SmartArt drawn on the worksheet. When you type text in the text pane, it is added to the selected shape.

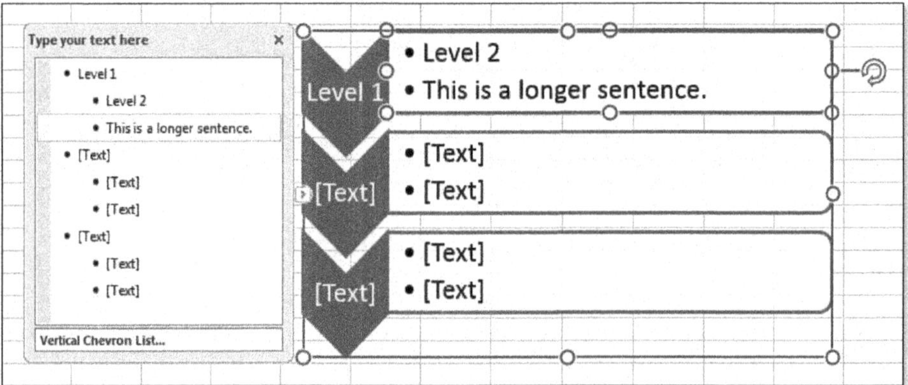

Figure 26.2 When you type in the text pane, the text is added to the selected element of the SmartArt.

7. Fill in the text pane with text for your SmartArt. You can add, delete, promote, or demote items by using icons in the SmartArt Tools Design tab. Or, use the tab key to demote an item and Shift+Tab to promote an item. The SmartArt updates as you type more text. In most cases, adding a new Level 1 item adds a new shape element to the SmartArt.
8. Add longer text to the SmartArt, and Excel shrinks the font size of all the elements to make the text fit. You can make the entire SmartArt graphic larger at any time by grabbing the resize handles in the corners of the SmartArt and dragging to a new size.

After you resize the graphic, Excel resizes the text to make it fit in the SmartArt at the largest size possible.

9. The color scheme of the SmartArt initially appears in one color. To change the color scheme, use the Change Colors drop-down menu in the SmartArt Design tab, the SmartArt Styles group. Excel offers several versions of monochrome styles and five styles of color variations for each diagram.

10. Choose a basic or 3D style from the SmartArt Styles gallery. The first three 3D styles (Polished, Inset, or Cartoon) have a suitable mix of effects but are still readable.

11. Move the SmartArt to the proper location. Position the mouse over the border of the SmartArt, avoiding the eight Resize handles. The cursor changes to a four-headed arrow. Click and drag the SmartArt to a new location. If you drag the SmartArt to the left side of the worksheet, the text pane moves to the right of the SmartArt.

12. Click outside the SmartArt. Excel embeds the SmartArt graphic in the worksheet and hides the SmartArt tabs, as shown in Figure 26.3.

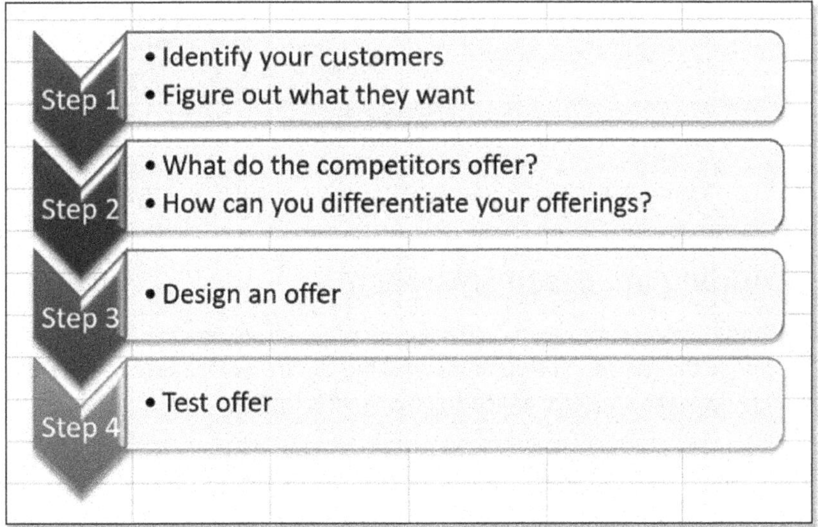

Figure 26.3 Click outside the SmartArt boundary to embed the completed SmartArt.

Changing existing SmartArt to a new style

You can change SmartArt to a new style in a couple of ways:

- Left-click the SmartArt and then select SmartArt Design, Layouts to choose a new layout. The Layouts drop-down menu initially shows only the styles that Excel thinks are a close fit to the current style. Hover over layouts to preview how the message will appear in the new layout. If you want to access the complete list of styles, you have to select More Layouts. Figure 26.4 shows the same message from Figure 26.3 in four different layouts.

- A faster way to access the complete list of styles is to right-click between two shapes in the SmartArt and select Change Layout from the context menu. This step is a little tricky because you cannot click an existing shape. Instead, you must click inside the SmartArt border, but on a portion of the SmartArt that is empty.

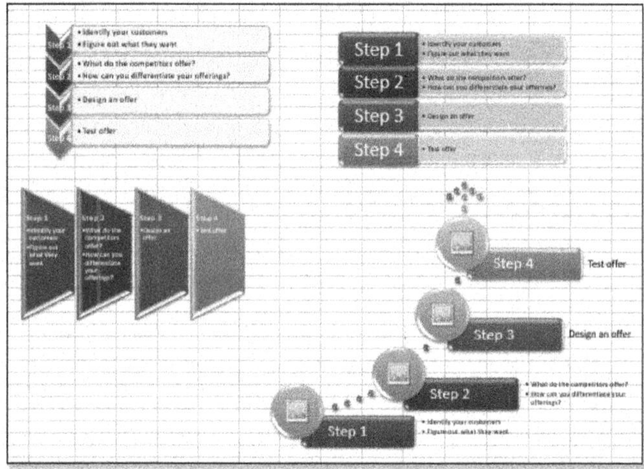

Figure 26.4 The same words are shown in four different layouts.

Adding images to SmartArt

Thirty-six SmartArt layouts in the Picture category are designed to hold small images in addition to the text. In some of these styles, the picture is emphasized. However, in other pictures, the focus is on the text, and the picture is an accent.

When you select one of these styles, you can add text using the text pane and then specify pictures by clicking the picture icon inside each Level 1 shape.

You can click a picture icon to display the Insert Picture dialog box. Then you can choose a picture and click Insert. Repeat this process to add each additional picture. The pictures are cropped automatically to fit the allotted area.

After adding pictures, you can use all the formatting tools on the Picture Tools Format tab.

Special considerations for organizational charts and hierarchical SmartArt

Hierarchical SmartArt can contain more than two text levels. As you add more levels to the SmartArt, Excel continues to intelligently add boxes and resize them to fit.

Figure 26.5 shows a diagram created in the Hierarchy layout. In this layout, each level is assigned a different color.

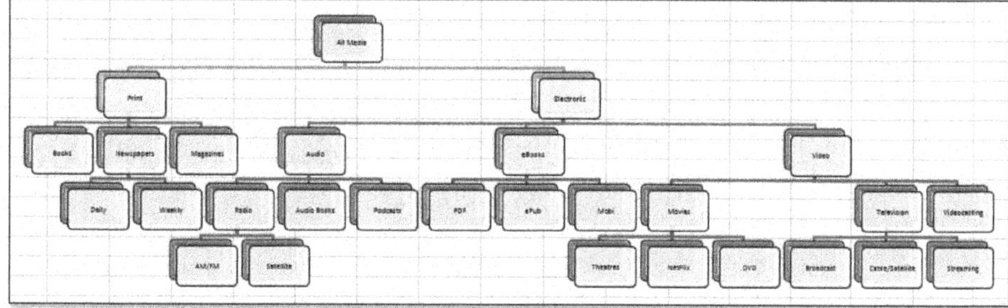

Figure 26.5 Hierarchical SmartArt can contain more than two levels.

Four styles in the Hierarchical category are organization charts. These layouts are used to describe reporting relationships in an organization. There are a few extra options in the ribbon for organization charts. For example, if you select the SmartArt Tools Design tab, the Add Shape drop-down menu includes the option Add Assistant. You can select this option to add an extra shape immediately below the selected level.

In the Create Graphic group of the SmartArt Design tab, the Org Chart drop-down menu offers four options for showing the boxes within a group. First, you select the manager for the group. Then you select the appropriate type from the drop-down menu to affect all direct reports for the manager. Figure 26.6 illustrates the four options for Org Chart:

- **VP Sales:** Shows a standard organization chart. The regions are arranged side by side.
- **VP Manufacturing:** Includes a Right Hanging group that enables departments to be arranged vertically to the right of the line.
- **VP Engineering:** Includes a Left Hanging group that enables departments to be arranged vertically to the left of the line.
- **CFO:** Includes a Both group that lists direct reports in two columns under the manager on both sides of the vertical line.

In each group, the assistant box is set off from the other boxes.

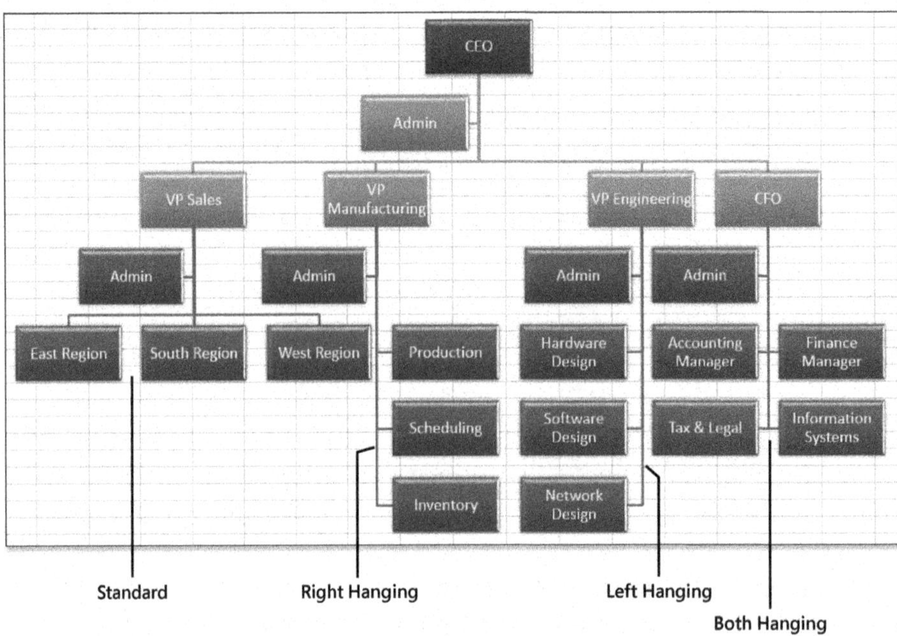

Figure 26.6 Organization charts include additional options to control the arrangement of direct reports.

Using shapes to display cell contents

In legacy versions of Excel, shapes were known as AutoShapes. Today, Excel shapes have some new formatting options, such as shadow, glow, and bevel.

Perhaps the best part of shapes is that you can tie the text on a shape to a worksheet cell. For example, in Figure 26.7, the shape is set to display the current value of cell B2. Every time the worksheet is calculated, the text on the shape is updated.

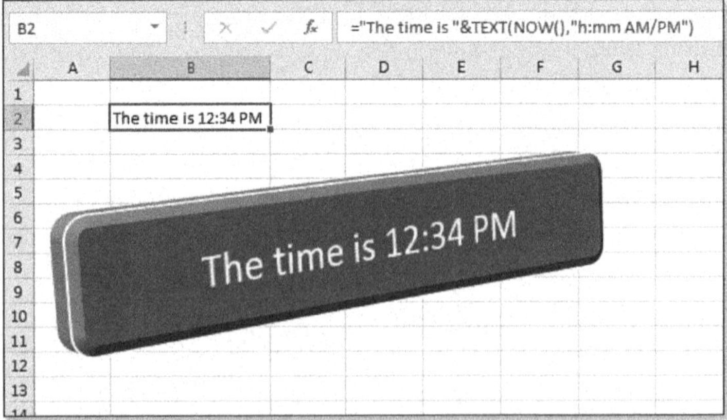

Figure 26.7 You can set shapes to display the current value of a cell.

Follow these steps to insert a shape into a worksheet:

1. Select a blank area of the worksheet.
2. From the Insert tab, open the Shapes drop-down menu.
3. Select one of the 147 basic shapes.
4. The mouse pointer changes to a small crosshair. Click and drag in the worksheet to draw the shape.
5. Choose a color scheme from the Shapes Styles drop-down menu.
6. Select Shape Effects, Preset, and select an effect.
7. Look for a yellow handle on the shape, which enables you to change the inflection point for the shape. For example, on the rounded rectangle, sliding the yellow handle controls how wide the rounded corners are.
8. Look for a gray circle on the outside of the shape. If necessary, drag this circle to rotate the shape.
9. To include static text in the shape, click in the middle of the shape and type the text. You can control the style by using the WordArt Styles drop-down menu. You can control text size and color by using the formatting buttons on the Home tab. The shape can include text from any cell, but it cannot perform a calculation.

   NOTE

   If you want the shape to include a calculated value, skip step 9 and follow steps 10 through 12.

10. If desired, add a new cell that formats a message for the shape. As shown in Figure 26.8, add the formula `="We are at "&TEXT(B13,"0%")&" of our goal with "&DOLLAR(B12)&" collected to date!"` to an empty cell to convert the calculation in cell B13 to a suitable message.

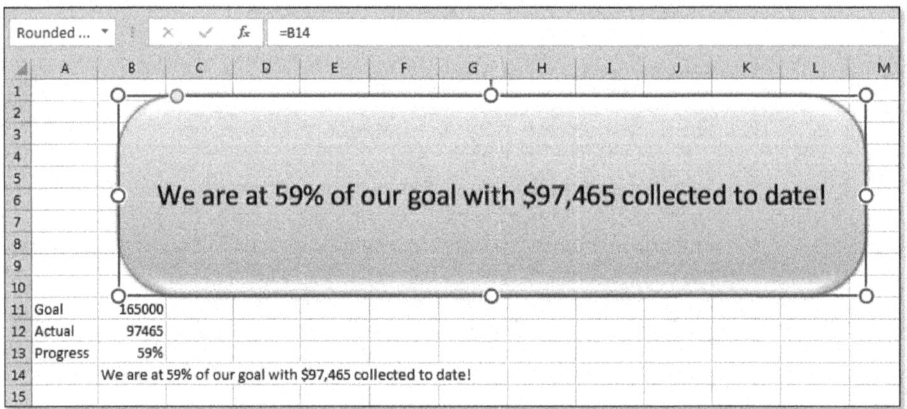

Figure 26.8 This shape picks up the formula from cell B14 to show how a message changes with the worksheet.

11. Click in the middle of the text box as you would if text was being added.

12. Click in the formula bar, type **=B14**, and then press Enter. As shown in Figure 26.8, the shape displays the results from the selected cell.

Working with shapes

The Drawing Tools section of the Format tab contains sections to change the shape style, fill, outline, effects, and WordArt effects.

In the Insert Shapes dialog box, use the Edit Shape, Change Shape command to choose another shape style.

If you right-click a shape and select Format Shape, Excel displays the Format Shape dialog box, with the fine-tuning settings Fill, Line, Line Style, Shadow, 3D Format, 3D Rotation, and Text Placement.

Using WordArt for interesting titles and headlines

Even though WordArt was redesigned in Excel 2007, it is still best to use it sparingly, such as for a headline or title at the top of a page. It is best to use it for impressive display fonts to add interest to a report. However, you would not want to create an entire 20-page document in WordArt.

To use WordArt, follow these steps:

1. Select a blank section of the worksheet.

2. From the Insert tab, in the Text group, select the WordArt drop-down menu.

3. Choose from the 20 WordArt presets in the drop-down menu. Do not worry that these presets seem less exciting than the WordArt in legacy versions of Excel. You can customize the WordArt later.

4. Excel adds the generic text "Your Text Here" in the preset WordArt you chose. Select this default text and then type your own text.

5. Select the text. Choose a new font style by using either the mini toolbar that appears or the Home tab.

6. Use the WordArt Styles group on the Drawing Tools Format tab to color the WordArt. To the right of the Styles drop-down menu are icons for text color and line color and a drop-down menu for effects. The Effects drop-down menu includes the fly-out menus Shadow, Reflection, Glow, Soft Edges, Bevel, and 3D Rotation.

7. To achieve the old-style WordArt effects, from the Format tab, select Drawing Tools, WordArt Styles, Text Effects, Transform, and then select a shape for the text. Figure 26.9 shows the WordArt with a Curve Down transformation.

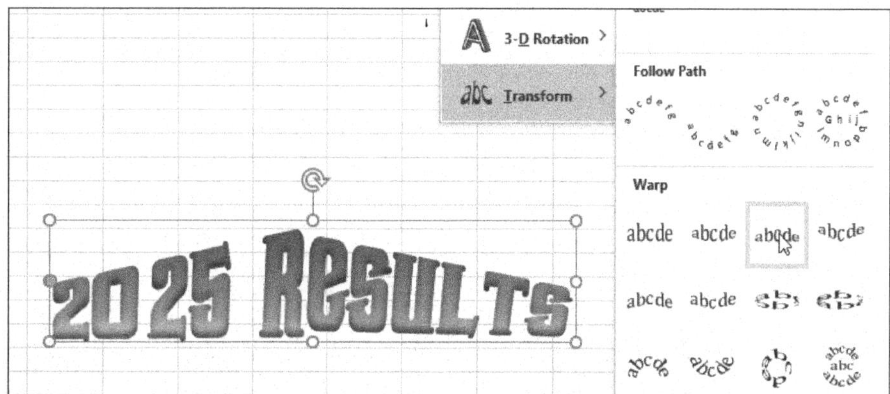

Figure 26.9 WordArt includes the Transform menu to bend and twist type.

Using text boxes to flow long text passages

WordArt is perfect for short titles. However, it is not suitable for long text passages that you want to fit in a range. Whereas the Home, Fill, Justify command works for text that is less than 256 characters, a text box allows long paragraphs of text to flow.

To use a text box object to create two columns of text, follow these steps:

1. Select a blank section of the worksheet.

2. From the Insert tab, select Text, Text Box.

3. Drag in your document to draw a large text box on the worksheet.
4. Either type your text here or switch to Word, copy the text, and then switch back to Excel and paste the text.
5. Right-click the text box and select Exit Edit Mode.
6. Use the Font group on the Home tab to adjust the font size and face.
7. Right-click the text box and select Format Shape. The Format Shape task pane appears.
8. In the headline of the task pane, choose Text Options.
9. Choose the third icon below the headline to display the Text Box options.
10. Adjust the margins and alignment, if desired.
11. Click the Columns button. The Columns dialog box appears.
12. Choose two columns with nonzero spacing between them, as shown in Figure 26.10.
13. Click the X at the top right of the task pane to close the task pane. The result is a text box that has two columns of text. As you change the size of the text, it automatically reflows to fit the desired columns.

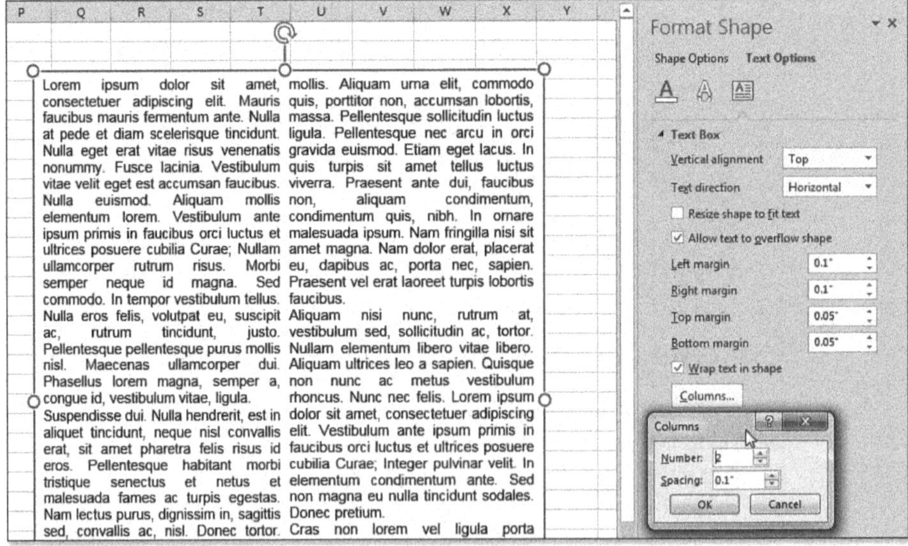

Figure 26.10 You can change the number of columns.

Using pictures and clip art

Excel offers 28 quick picture styles and the tools to create thousands of additional effects.

When the spreadsheet was invented in 1979, accountants were amazed and thrilled with the simple black-and-white, numbers-only spreadsheets. The image processing tools available in Excel elevate spreadsheets from simple tables of numbers to beautiful marketing showpieces.

Getting your picture into Excel

For reasons unknown, you cannot simply drag and drop photographs into Excel. Drag and drop works in Word, PowerPoint, and even OneNote, but not Excel. In Excel, you have to use the Insert tab and choose either Pictures or Pictures Online:

- Use the Pictures icon for pictures stored on your PC, network, or OneDrive account.
- Use stock images that Microsoft has licensed for use in Office.
- Use Online Pictures to do a Bing Image search.
- Use Screenshot to capture a picture already displayed in a browser or other application on your computer.

Inserting a picture from your computer

When you choose the Picture icon, you can browse to any folder on your computer or network. Use the Views drop-down menu to display thumbnails so you can browse by picture instead of picture name.

For photos stored in your personal OneDrive account, use Insert, Pictures, Online Pictures and then click the OneDrive button in the lower-left portion of the gallery.

Excel inserts the picture so that the top-left corner of the picture is aligned with the active cell. The picture usually extends and covers hundreds of cells.

Inserting multiple pictures at once

If you multiselect pictures using the Ctrl key while browsing, Excel inserts all the pictures, overlaps them, and selects all the pictures. If the size of the entire stack of pictures seems too large, you can resize them all by using the Height and Width settings in the ribbon. But soon, you have to rearrange the pictures so you can actually see them. Follow these steps:

1. Click outside the picture stack, on the Excel grid, to deselect the pictures.
2. Click the top photo in the stack to select that one single photo.

3. Drag the photo to a new location on the worksheet.

4. Repeat steps 2 and 3 for the remaining pictures in the stack.

Inserting a picture from stock images

When you choose the Insert, Pictures, Stock Images, you can search through hundreds of photos that Microsoft has licensed for your use in Excel.

If you can't find something appropriate there, you could use Insert, Pictures, Online Pictures to search Bing for images that Microsoft believes have a a Creative Commons license. Note that Microsoft cannot guarantee that the images in Online Images are free to use, so you should always start with stock images first.

Follow these steps to use a stock image:

1. Select a cell where you want the picture to start.

2. Choose Insert, Pictures, Stock Pictures.

3. In the Images gallery, type a search term and press Enter to search, as shown in Figure 26.11.

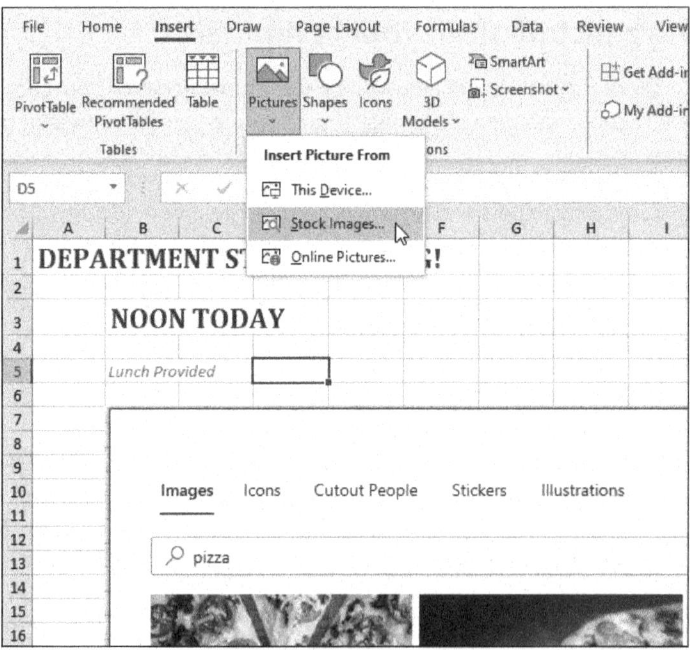

Figure 26.11 Enter a keyword to search.

4. Choose an image and click Insert. Excel pauses briefly while the image is downloaded and then inserts the image in the worksheet.

CAUTION

You can also search Bing Images. Initially, the results will show only images that Bing believes to be licensed under Creative Commons, which clearly is not a perfect system. In my first search, the first set of results included a trademarked Pizza Hut logo from some random website. Just because that site's webmaster stole the image and slapped a Creative Commons license on his website does not protect you if you use the image illegally. Therefore, use caution when distributing worksheets that contain images sourced from Bing (and even more so if you unselect the Creative Commons Only checkbox to broaden the Bing search to include copyrighted images).

TIP

Microsoft 365 introduced a setting for Picture Transparency on the Picture Tools, Format tab. If you need to see the values in cells behind the picture, you easily can adjust the transparency.

Adjusting the picture using the ribbon tab

When a picture is selected, the Picture Tools Format tab of the ribbon is available. The choices on this ribbon tab offer a number of presets that will save you time in adjusting the picture. For example, a single click in the Picture Styles gallery can replace 16 micro-adjustments in the Format Picture task pane. To save time, always try using the presets on the ribbon. If you can't quite get the right setting, you can press Ctrl+1 to display the Format Picture task pane to reach additional adjustment settings.

Resizing the picture to fit

One problem you might have when using a picture on a worksheet is that the image may be too large. As digital cameras improve, it is becoming increasingly common for digital images to be 9, 10, 11, or more megapixels. These images are very large. For example, an image from a 3-megapixel camera occupies the area from A1 through Q41. You would have to zoom out before you can even see the whole photo. Your first step is usually to reduce the picture size so it fits on your cover page or report.

If you frequently use the mouse, your first inclination would be to drag the lower-right corner of the picture up and to the left to reduce the picture size. If the picture is too large for the window, you can zoom out to 1 percent. Instead, use the spin buttons for Height and Width located in the Size group of the Picture Tools Format tab of the ribbon. Reduce the height or width, and the other setting reduces proportionally. Click and hold the "down" icon next to height until you can see the entire image in the Excel window.

When the entire picture is visible in the window, you can use the resize handle in any corner to change the picture size.

NOTE

When you use the mouse or the ribbon tools to resize a photo, Excel ensures that the picture stays proportional. If you want to change a landscape picture to portrait, you can either use the Crop tool or turn off the Lock Aspect Ratio setting. Figure 26.12 compares these methods. The original picture is too large. A proportional resize keeps everything from the original picture while changing the size. If you need the picture to be taller than wide, you can unlock the aspect ratio and change the width. This creates a funny-looking picture, such as trees that are skinny and too tall. A better choice might be using the Crop tool to remove unnecessary parts of the photograph.

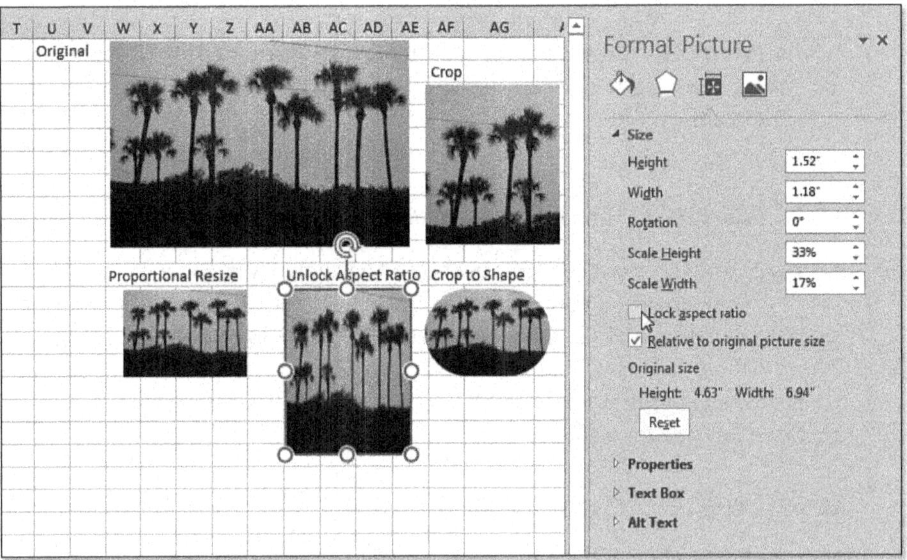

Figure 26.12 Resize proportionally or use the cropping tool to avoid distortion in the photograph.

To unlock the aspect ratio for a photograph, follow these steps:

1. Select the photograph by clicking it.
2. Press Ctrl+1 to display the Format Picture task pane.
3. Four icons appear at the top of the task pane. Click the third icon to display the Size, Properties, Text Box, and Alt Text categories.
4. Click the Size heading to open the size choices.

5. Uncheck the Lock Aspect Ratio check box. You can now stretch or compress the height or width alone.

Cropping a picture involves removing extraneous parts of the picture while in Crop mode. To crop a picture, follow these steps:

1. Select a picture.
2. Click the top half of the Crop icon in the Size group of the Picture Tools section of the Format tab. Eight crop handles appear on the edges and corners of the picture. Use the handles as follows:
   - To crop out one side of a picture, drag the center handle on that side inward toward the middle of the picture.
   - To crop both sides equally, hold down Ctrl while you drag the center handle on either side inward.
   - To crop equally on all four sides, hold down Ctrl while dragging one of the corner handles inward.
3. When the picture is cropped appropriately, click the Crop icon in the Picture Tools Format tab to exit Crop mode.

The rounded corners of the bottom-right photo in Figure 26.12 are achieved by cropping the photo to a shape. Open the Crop drop-down menu and choose Crop to Shape. You can choose from the 135 built-in shapes and then further change the shape using the yellow inflection handles on the shape.

Adjusting the brightness and contrast

You might capture a photograph in less than optimal lighting conditions. I went out one evening to capture photos of the latest rocket launch from Cape Canaveral when an osprey came flying by with his freshly caught dinner. The photograph was a cool action shot but was too dark because I did not have time to adjust the camera settings. Excel offers 201 choices each for Brightness, Contrast, and Sharpness. With 201 choices each, you have 8.1 million ways to adjust a photo, which is overwhelming.

Starting in Excel 2010, Microsoft began offering 25 thumbnails in the Corrections drop-down menu (see Figure 26.13). Select the picture, open the drop-down menu, and choose the thumbnail that gives the best light to the picture. You can also choose from the five thumbnails at the top to soften or sharpen the image. Most people will be able to tell which of these 25 thumbnails makes the picture look the best. If you are a professional photographer, you can access the Format Picture task pane to micromanage the settings.

For more adjustments, the Color drop-down menu offers Sepia, Black And White, and various other settings.

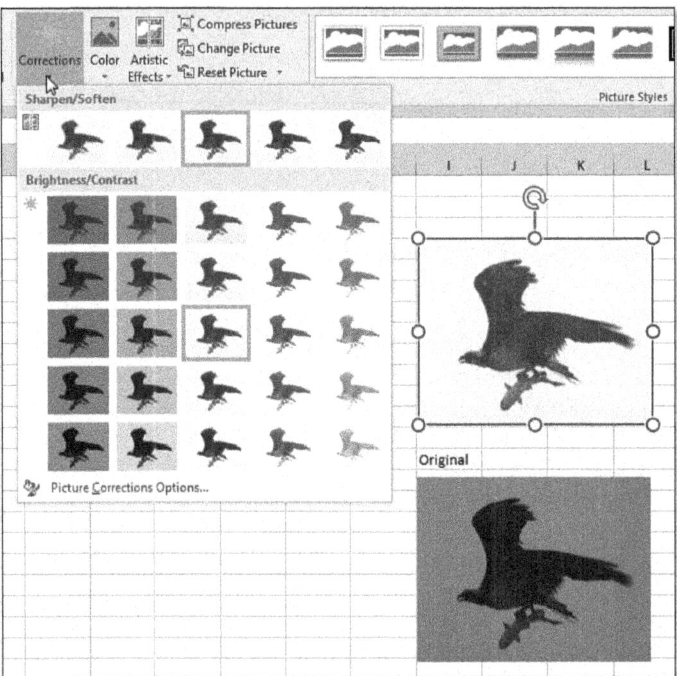

Figure 26.13 One of the presets rescued this photograph.

Adjusting picture transparency so cell values show through

Any inserted picture appears on top of the cells. If you want to see the cell values behind the picture, use the Transparency drop-down menu. This new feature debuted in Office 365 in September 2018. You can find it just to the right of the Artistic Effects drop-down menu.

Adding interesting effects using the picture styles gallery

For a quick way to make a picture look interesting, you can use one of the 28 presets in the Picture Styles gallery. These presets include various combinations of rotation, bevel, lighting, surface, shadow, frame, and shape. Here's how you use them:

1. Select a picture. The Picture Tools Format tab appears.
2. To the right of the Picture Styles icon, select the drop-down menu arrow.
3. Hover over the 28 built-in styles until you find one that is suitable.
4. To apply the style, click the style in the gallery.

Figure 26.14 shows the gallery and several varieties of built-in picture styles.

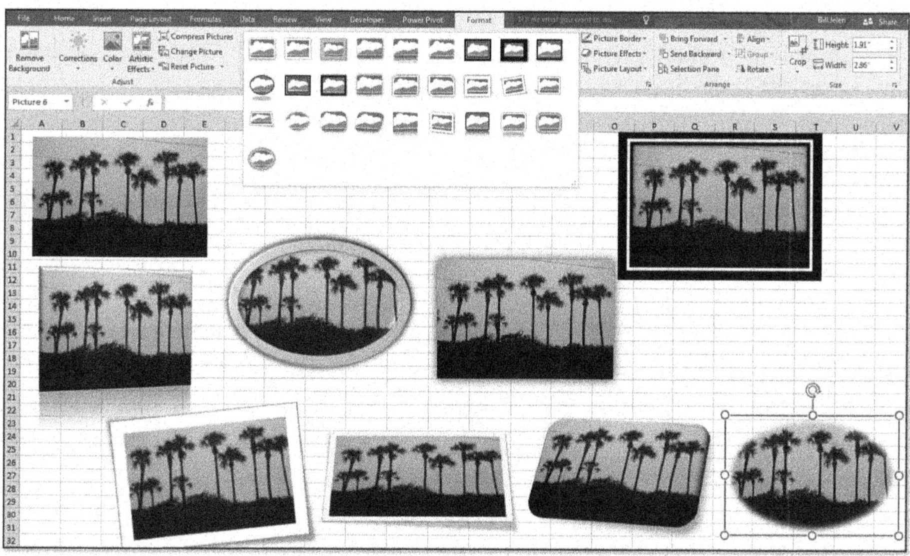

Figure 26.14 The Picture Styles gallery offers many quick alternatives for formatting pictures.

The 28 styles in the Picture Styles gallery were professionally chosen by graphic design experts. There is nothing in here that you could not do using the settings in the Format Picture task pane. However, choosing a style is much faster and requires less experimentation. To illustrate, two similar pictures appear in Figure 26.15. The top picture was formatted in two clicks using the Picture Styles gallery. The bottom picture was formatted by adjusting 16 different settings in the Format Picture task pane. The list of settings is shown in column L.

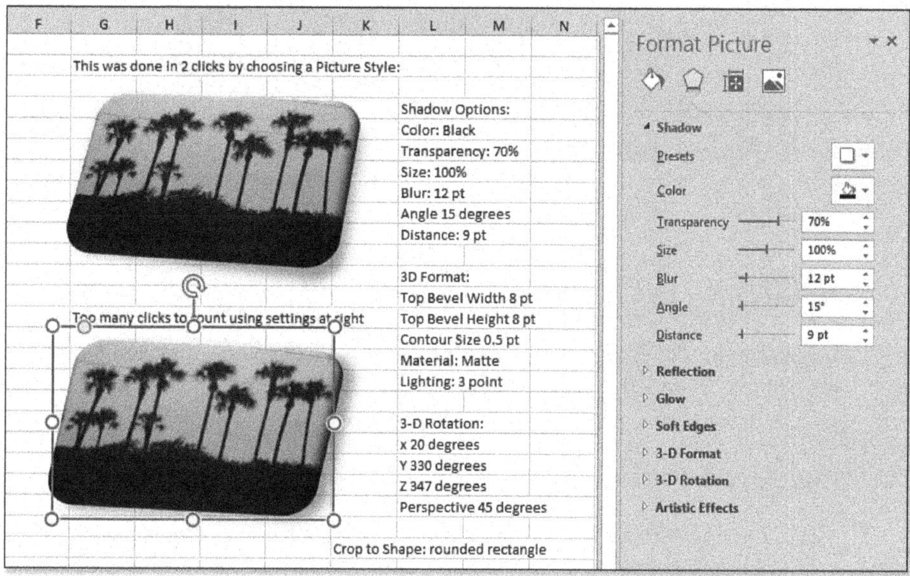

Figure 26.15 You can replicate the styles in the gallery by combining 16 different settings.

By using the Format Picture task pane, you could expand the 28 styles to millions of styles. However, it takes much longer to find the right combination of shadow, reflection, and so on when you opt to use the task pane instead of the Picture Styles gallery.

Applying artistic effects

Figure 26.16 shows the Artistic Effects fly-out menu. All these effects were new in Excel 2010. You can make your photo look like a pencil sketch, a mosaic, a photocopy, and more. Figure 26.16 shows some of the more interesting artistic effects.

The original photo is in the top left. Artistic effects make the photo look like an illustration.

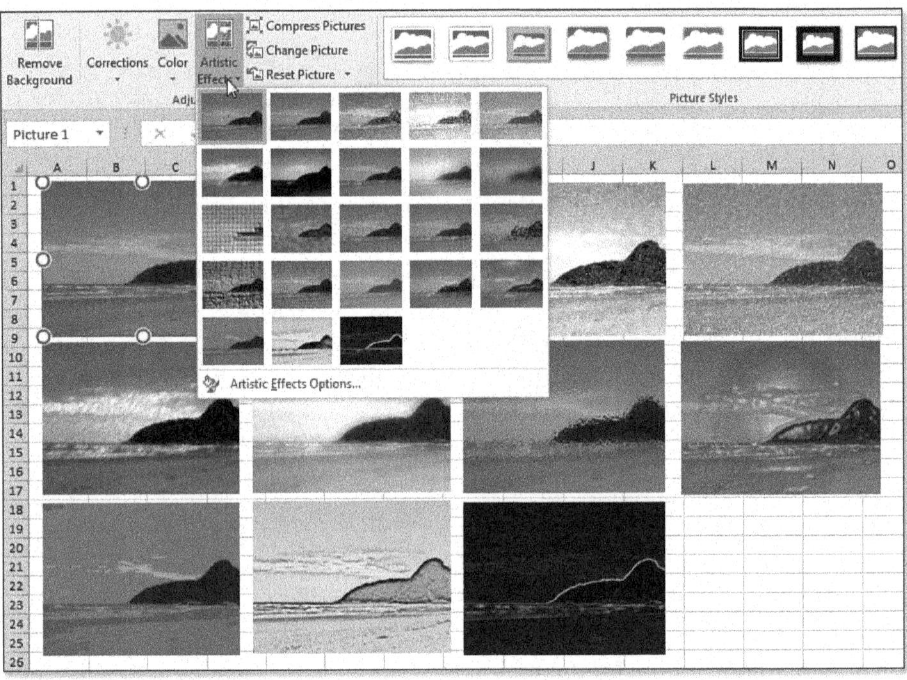

Figure 26.16 These artistic effects were added in Excel 2019.

Removing the background

Legacy versions of Excel offered a Set Transparent Color setting that would never work. However, Microsoft added impressive logic to Excel 2010 to help you remove the background from a picture. A few simple tweaks will make the tool even better. Follow these steps:

1. Select the photo.
2. Click the Remove Background icon. A new Background Removal tab appears in the ribbon. Excel also takes a first guess at which portions of the photo are background. You can improve this guess dramatically in step 3.

3. Excel draws a bounding box around the area it believes is the subject of the photograph. It often misses a corner of the subject; for example, a foot or an arm is outside of the box. When you resize the bounding box to exactly include 100 percent of the subject, Excel recalculates which portions of the photograph are background. Anything deemed to be background is shown in purple. I usually find that the first guess in step 2 is about 50 percent correct, and that the second guess after step 3 is about 95 percent correct.

4. If there are tiny areas of background to which Excel failed to apply purple shading, use the Areas To Remove icon and click those areas. If there are tiny areas of the subject that are erroneously shaded in purple, click the Mark Areas To Keep icon and click those areas (see Figure 26.17).

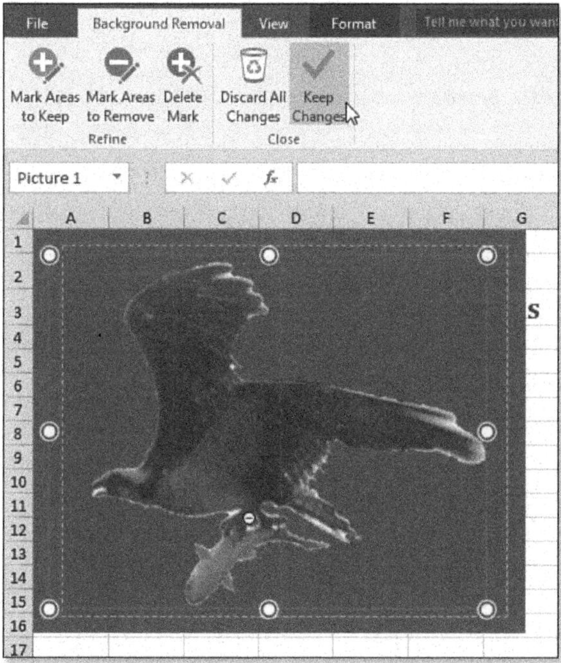

Figure 26.17 Adjust the bounding box to improve Excel's prediction of the background.

5. When the image looks correct, click Keep Changes. The grid now shows through the background of the photograph.

6. To edit cells behind the photograph, you cannot click on the cells. Click outside of the photograph and use the arrow keys to move underneath the photograph or press Ctrl+G for Go To and type an address for a cell behind the image. You can then add text or titles (see Figure 26.18).

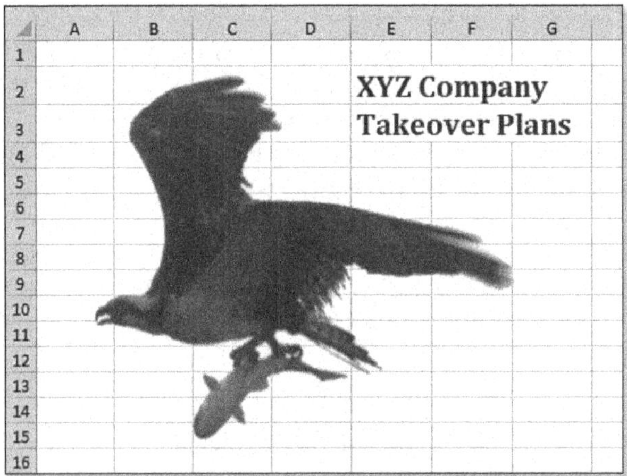

Figure 26.18 Use the arrow keys to reach cells behind the photograph.

Inside OUT

When you import pictures into a workbook, the file size of the workbook can increase dramatically.

If you plan to view the image onscreen only, you can reduce the size of the picture to reduce the size of the workbook. Here's how you do it:

1. Select the picture.
2. In the Picture Tools Format tab, select Compress Pictures from the Adjust group. Excel displays the Compress Pictures dialog box. Based on your choices here, Excel reduces the file size and removes the cropped areas of the photo.

To globally reduce the size of all images in a workbook, select File, Options, Advanced, and change the Default Resolution from 220 ppi to 96 ppi.

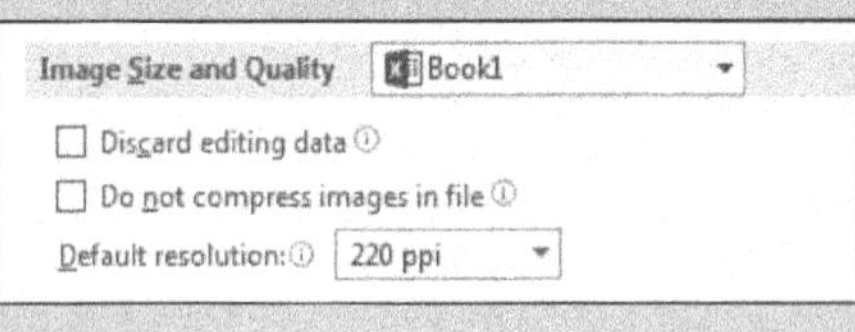

Inserting screen clippings

If you need to grab an image of a web page, a PDF file, or a PowerPoint slide, you can grab a screen capture of the entire window or a portion of the window. I use this feature frequently and find the technique for inserting a portion of a window is more useful most of the time:

1. In Excel, position the cell pointer at the point where you want to insert the screen clipping.
2. If you have two monitors, get the other application visible in the other monitor. If you have a single monitor, switch to the other application and then immediately back to Excel. The screen clipping tool is going to hide the current Excel window, revealing the previously active application. Thanks to the Single Document Interface, you can now use this trick to capture a picture of another Excel workbook.
3. Select Insert, Screenshot. You see a thumbnail of each open window. Skip all those big icons and go to the words Screen Clipping at the bottom of the menu (see Figure 26.19). The current Excel screen disappears, and the remaining window's screen stays visible but dims.

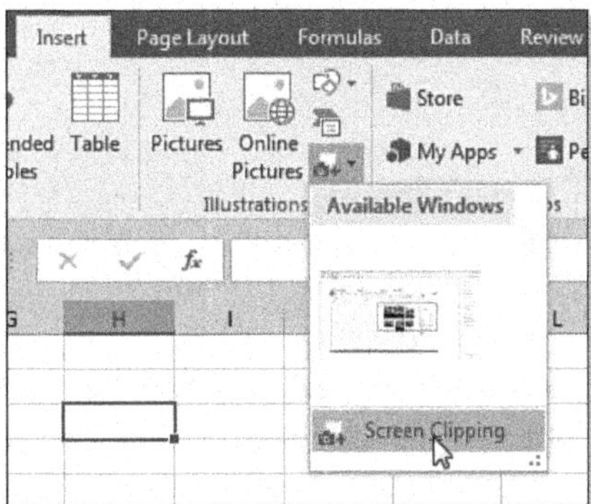

Figure 26.19 Choose Screen Clipping to copy a portion of another window.

4. Using the mouse, draw a rectangle around the portion of the application window that you want to capture. As you drag, that portion of the screen brightens.
5. Release the mouse. The original Excel window reappears, and a picture of the clipped screen is inserted in the workbook.

Selecting and arranging pictures

You will sometimes have two pictures that overlap. Excel maintains an order for the pictures. Typically, the picture inserted most recently is shown on top of earlier pictures. You can haphazardly resequence the pictures using the Send Backward or Send Forward command on the Picture Tools Format tab. Suppose that you've inserted 12 pictures. Picture 1 and Picture 12 are overlapping, and you want Picture 1 to be on top of Picture 12. You would have to choose Send Backward 11 times before they appear correctly. Next to Send Backward is a drop-down menu with a choice called Send to Back. This moves the selected picture to the back of the stack.

Even easier is the Selection pane. Use Home, Find & Select, Selection Pane to list all shapes and pictures in the sheet. You can drag a picture to a new location in the list, as shown in Figure 26.20. Pictures at the top of the list appear on top of pictures at the bottom of the list. You can also choose to hide a picture by clicking the Eye icon.

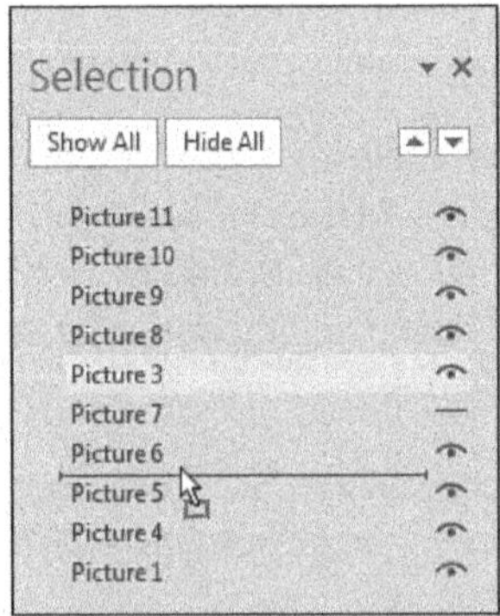

Figure 26.20 Picture 7 has been hidden, and Picture 3 is in the process of being moved within the stack.

TROUBLESHOOTING

Worksheets with an excessive number of images can slow down dramatically. Using the Hide All button allows you to quickly scroll through the workbook without the delays from rendering images.

I once received a call from someone who said his workbook had been getting progressively slower and was now running at a crawl even though it was just a simple worksheet containing 12 images.

However, I learned that the creator of the worksheet had been copying data from another workbook and pasting it into this worksheet each time he had to generate a new work order.

The person did not realize that he was pasting the same 12 images with each workorder. The images were nicely stacked right on top of each other. Although only 12 images were visible, there were more than 1,400 images in the worksheet.

If someone tried to scroll one row down the worksheet, Excel would re-draw the 1,400 images, which meant scrolling just a short distance could take more than a minute.

The fix was simple. Clicking Hide All made the worksheet responsive. Note that pressing Ctrl+6 will toggle the visibility of all objects.

If you need to select many pictures at once, choose Home, Find & Select, Select Objects. Draw a large rectangle around many objects, and they all will be selected.

The Align option enables you to make sure that several images line up. To make Picture 3 and Picture 2 line up with Picture 1, follow these steps:

1. Select Picture 3.
2. Ctrl+click Picture 2 and then Ctrl+click Picture 1.
3. Select Align, Align Left. The left edges of Picture 2 and Picture 3 move so they line up with the left edge of Picture 1.

CAUTION

After you use Select Objects, the mouse pointer remains a white arrow, and you will be unable to select cells. Press the Escape key to exit this mode.

If you select multiple images and group them together by using the Group drop-down menu, you can then move the images, and their location relative to each other remains the same.

Inserting icons, stickers, illustrations, and cut-out people

The Icons feature in Excel was refreshed during 2020 to include more icons. The same dialog box also offers stock images, illustrations, stickers, and cut-out people.

To explore what is available, choose an empty cell and select Insert, Icons. You will see tabs across the top for Images, Icons, Cutout People, Stickers, and Illustrations. Each tab offers a search box and several tiles that can be used to filter by category, as shown in Figure 26.21.

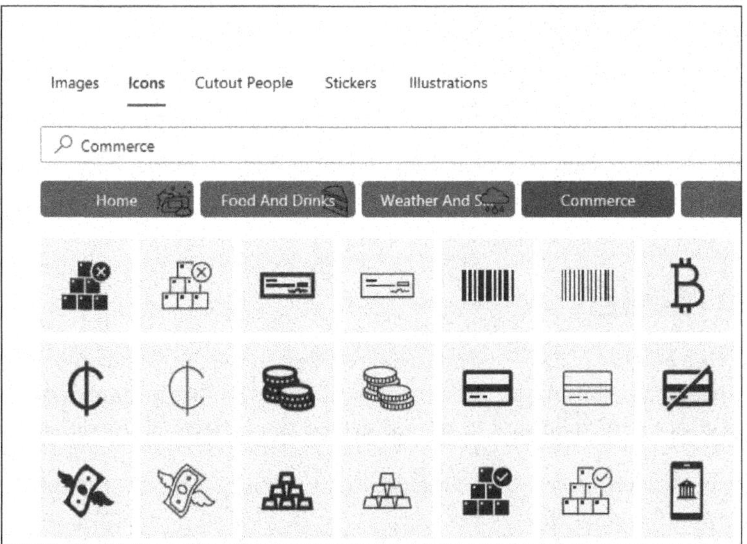

Figure 26.21 More than 200 royalty-free icons are available.

To insert an icon, select the icon and then press Insert.

CAUTION

The order of the category tiles is randomized each time you open the dialog box. In some cases, there are more categories than can be shown in the dialog box, so, you might see a category for Randy one day and not the next.

Once inserted into your worksheet, you can use the Graphic Format tab of the ribbon to change the color, outline, and bevel. Handles on the icon allow you to change the size and rotations.

In the Cutout People tab, you can search for people who are angry, happy, facing to the side, pointing, holding a sign, and more.

Figure 26.22 shows examples of a cut-out person, sticker, and an illustration.

Figure 26.22 Add interest to your worksheet using people, stickers, or illustrations.

Examining 3D models

There are a large number of 3D models available on the Internet. Excel can import files saved with any of these extensions: *.fbx, .obj, .3mf, .ply, .stl, and .glb. A large number of 3D model files are available from NASA. Point your favorite search engine at NASA 3D models to find them.

Select Insert, 3D Models, From File, and select a model. Initially, the model appears in the worksheet, as shown in Figure 26.23.

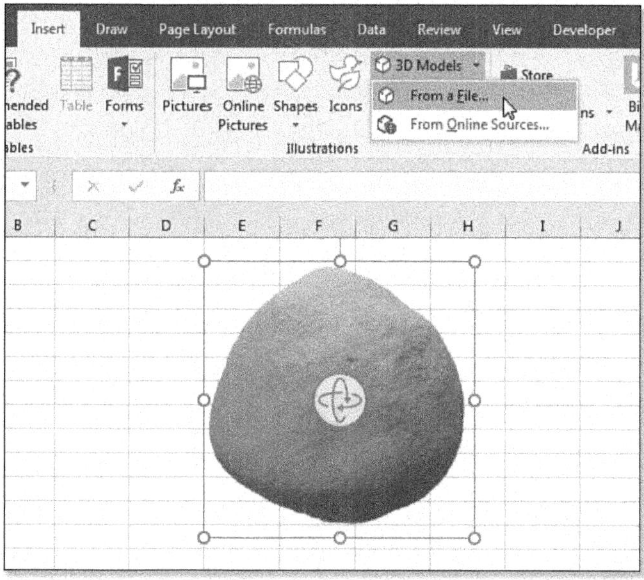

Figure 26.23 The icon in the middle of this asteroid means that you can rotate it in several dimensions.

With the object selected, click the 3D Rotation icon and drag it in any direction.

- Dragging right and left will rotate sideways.
- Dragging up and down will rotate vertically.
- Dragging diagonally will rotate diagonally.
- If you drag far enough, the object will rotate so you can see the back side of the object.

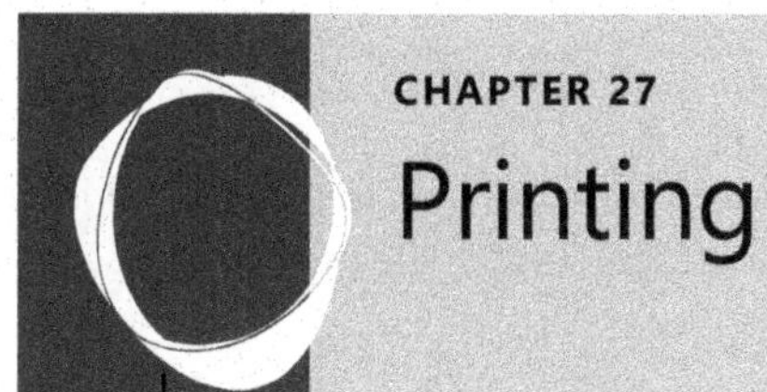

CHAPTER 27

Printing

You've finished your workbook model and now it is time to print. In reality, you are most likely going to email the workbook or export it to a PDF. But there are still some workbooks that you will print on real paper. This chapter gives you some tips to making that printout look great.

Printing in one click

If you're a keyboard enthusiast, you might be upset that in Excel, Ctrl+P takes you to the Print panel instead of performing a quick print. In a few steps, you can bring Quick Print back to Excel.

The Quick Access Toolbar (QAT) is the row of small icons that appears just above or just below the ribbon. At the right edge of this toolbar is a drop-down menu. Open the drop-down menu at the right edge of the Quick Access Toolbar to display a short list of popular commands. Choose Quick Print, as shown in Figure 27.1.

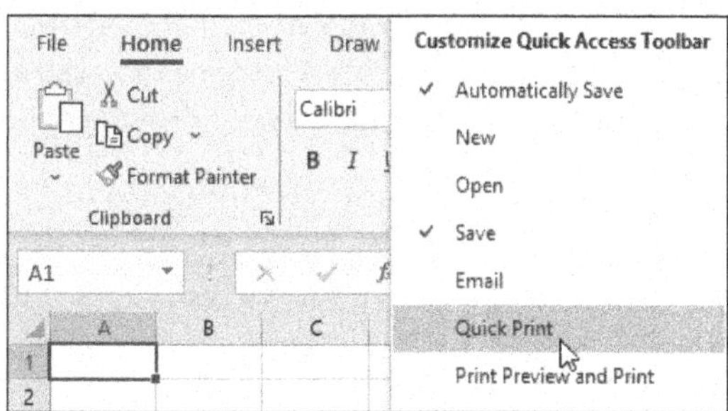

Figure 27.1 Add Quick Print to the Quick Access Toolbar.

When you click the Quick Print icon, one copy of the current worksheet is sent to the last printer you used in Excel. If you have not previously printed in this Excel session, the worksheet is sent to the default printer.

Although this brings the Quick Print back as a mouse click, it still isn't great for keyboard-centric people. If you press and release the Alt key in Excel, you see a row of shortcuts for the first nine items in the Quick Access Toolbar. Because Quick Print is the fifth icon in Figure 27.1, Alt+5 does a Quick Print.

Finding print settings

There are at least nine places in Excel where you can change the print settings or page setup. The most common tasks are found in multiple places. For example, you can change margins in five of the nine places. You can change paper size and orientation in four of the nine places.

As you move down to the obscure settings, you might be able to find them in only one or two places. Figure 27.2 shows a cross-reference. For any given task, you can locate where you might be able to change the setting.

Nine places are listed across the top of Figure 27.2. Here is where to find each place:

- **File, Print:** Open the File menu and choose Print to display the Print panel. This panel has a mix of Printer and Page Setup settings in the center and a large Print Preview on the right. Introduced in Excel 2010, it aims to be a one-stop place for getting your printout to look right.
- **Page Layout Tab of the Ribbon:** Click the Page Layout tab in the ribbon. You find three groups related to printing: Page Setup, Scale to Fit, and Sheet Options.
- **Page Setup Dialog:** Click the diagonal arrow icon in the lower-right corner of the three groups in the Page Layout ribbon tab to launch the legacy Page Setup dialog box. This dialog box contains four tabs. The superscript next to each bullet in Figure 27.2 identifies the tab: 1 for Page, 2 for Margins, 3 for Header/Footer, 4 for Sheet. You can also reach this dialog box by clicking the Print Titles icon in the Page Layout tab of the ribbon.
- **Page Layout View:** Choose Page Layout on the View tab. This icon also appears in the lower right of the Excel screen.

Task	File, Print	Page Layout Tab	Page Setup Dialog	Page Layout View	Header & Footer Tab	Page Break Preview View	Printer Properties Dialog	Excel Options	Print Preview Full Screen
Get the Report to Fit On the Page									
Set the Paper Size	•	•	•[1]				•		
Select Portrait or Landscape Orientation	•	•	•[1]				•		
Adjust the Margins on the Printed Page	•	•	•[2]	•					•
Repeat titles and headings on each printed page			•[4]						
Add a page number and other header/footer items			•[3]	•	•				
Exclude part of your worksheet from the print range		•	•[4]						
Add manual page breaks to the document		•				•			
Display page breaks	•							•	•
Hide page breaks								•	
Force more data to fit on a page	•	•	•[1]			•			
Preview the printed page	•			•	•	•			•
Print the Report									
Choose which printer to use	•								
Control settings specific to that printer	•		•[2]				•		
Print multiple worksheets at once	•								
Other Print Settings									
Center the report on the page			•[2]						
Collate multiple printed sets	•						•		
Control the first page number			•[1]						
Print the Excel gridlines		•	•[4]						
Print the A, B, C column headings and row numbers		•	•[4]						
Print comments			•[4]						
Replace error values when printing			•[4]						
Print on both sides of the page	•						•		
Control the order in which pages print			•[4]						
Adjust the print quality			•[1]						
Force the printout to greyscale			•[4]				•		
Print in draft quality			•[4]				•		

Figure 27.2 Various printing tasks are spread throughout the Excel interface. The superscript in the Page Setup Dialog column refers to the tab within the dialog box.

- **Header & Footer Tools Design Tab:** When you are in Page Layout view, click one of the three header or three footer zones on any page to have the Header & Footer Tools Design tab appear in the ribbon. Note that you have to click away from the header or footer zone to exit Page Layout view. Although this tab is the most hidden, it offers an easier way to control headers and footers (see Figure 27.3).

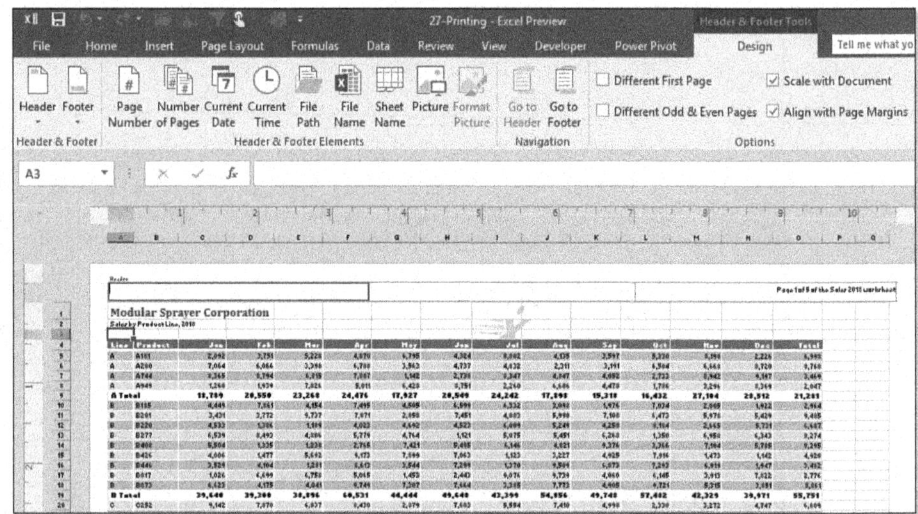

Figure 27.3 After you click into a header in Page Layout view, you can access the Header & Footer Tools tab in the ribbon.

- **Page Break Preview View:** Click Page Break Preview on the View tab. This icon also appears at the bottom right of the Excel window.
- **Printer Properties Dialog:** Use Ctrl+P to display the Print panel. A Printer Properties link appears just below the printer name.
- **Excel Options:** Open the File menu and then choose Options, Advanced. This is the only place to turn off the display of automatic page breaks after you've done a Print Preview.
- **Print Preview Full Screen:** Add this icon to the Quick Access Toolbar to reach a full-screen version of Print Preview similar to older versions of Excel.

The rest of this chapter covers most of the tasks along the left side of Figure 27.2.

Previewing the printed report

Before you start adjusting the page settings, you can take a quick look at how the worksheet currently will print.

Using the Print Preview on the print panel

One method to view the printed document is to use File, Print or Ctrl+P. For now, ignore the settings in the middle panel and look at the Print Preview pane on the right.

If your document is larger than one page, you have a vertical scrollbar to the right of the Print Preview. Use this scrollbar to move to other pages.

Four icons are available at the bottom of the Print Preview window (see Figure 27.4):

- To navigate to a new page, use the left-arrow or right-arrow icon in the lower left. You can also type a new page number in the page number text box and press Enter or Tab. The PgDn and PgUp keys still work, but only when you click the preview first.

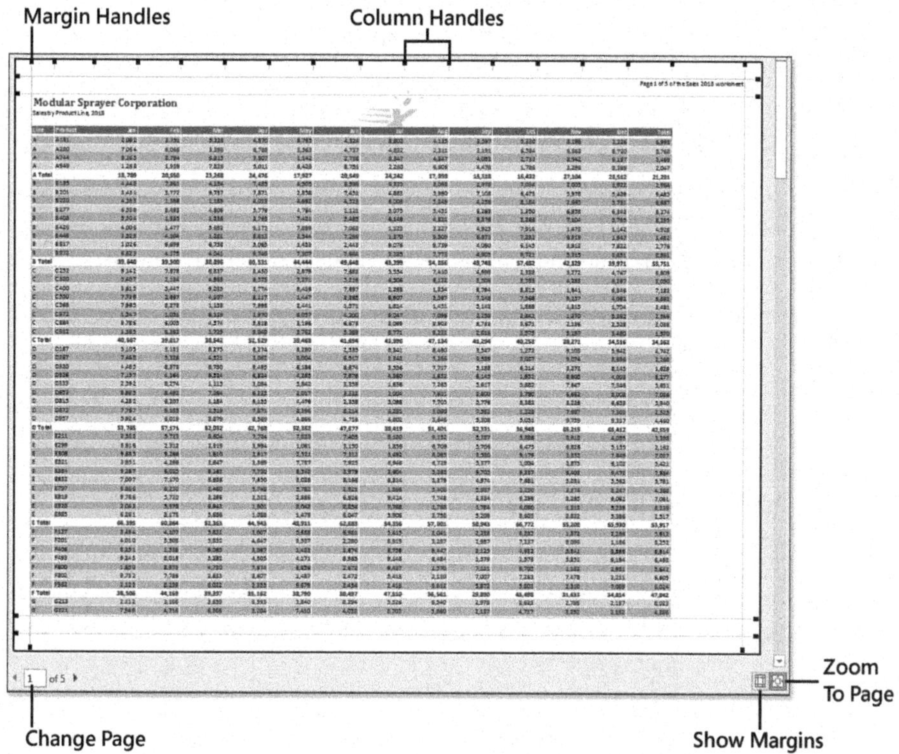

Figure 27.4 Print Preview controls.

- The Zoom check box feels like it is reversed. If you clear this check box, Excel zooms in to a smaller section of your printout.
- Select the Show Margins check box to have Excel draw draggable margins in the page. Drag any of the margin lines to change the page margins. Drag any of the column handles to resize columns.

When you first look at the Print Preview, check for these obvious problems:

- Does one column or a few rows spill over to a second page when you want everything to fit on one page? See "Repeating the headings on each page," later in this chapter.

- On a multipage report, go to page 2 of the document. Are the titles and headings appearing on pages after the first page? If not, see "Repeating the headings on each page," later in this chapter.
- Are page numbers appearing where you want them? If not, see the "Adding headers or footers to the printed report" section, later in this chapter.

To close the File menu and return to your document, click the large left-pointing arrow in the top-left corner of the File menu.

Using full-screen Print Preview

Some people develop macros in Excel where they want someone to preview a report in Print Preview. The new Print Preview on the Print panel doesn't work with these macros, so the Excel team added a command that gets you to a full-screen Print Preview.

The full-screen Print Preview works particularly well with wide reports in a landscape orientation.

You must add the Print Preview Full Screen to your ribbon or Quick Access Toolbar. For instructions, see Chapter 3, "Customizing Excel."

Making the report fit on the page

Before you print, you want to make sure your data is going to fit on the page. You can control the paper size, orientation, and margins. You can make a few heading rows print at the top of each page. You can add information such as page number, file location, date, and time in the header or footer.

TROUBLESHOOTING

Page numbers always start at 1 each time you print. This can be frustrating if you want to number a worksheet named "Sheet1" as pages 1 to 5 and a worksheet named "Sheet2" as pages 6 to 8.

The workaround is to print both worksheets in a single print command. Follow these steps:

1. Start with the first sheet selected.
2. Ctrl+click on each additional worksheet tab to be included. This puts those worksheets in group mode. Be careful not to edit any cells on the visible worksheet because similar changes will happen on all the worksheets.
3. Select File, Print. In the first drop-down menu below the Settings heading, choose Print Active Sheets. The sheets will print and use consecutive page numbers.
4. Right-click any of the selected sheets and choose Ungroup Sheets.

Setting worksheet paper size

You can choose from a variety of paper size options in the Size drop-down menu in the Page Layout tab, as shown in Figure 27.5. When you encounter a report that is too wide for a regular sheet of paper, you can switch to a larger page size, such as Legal paper. You can choose one paper size or select More Paper Sizes from the bottom of the list to specify a new size.

> TIP
>
> **Some paper sizes, such as 11"×17", are available only if your selected printer offers that size. If your default printer cannot print large-format paper, you should change the printer selection in the Print panel and then return to the Page Setup dialog box to select the larger-format paper.**

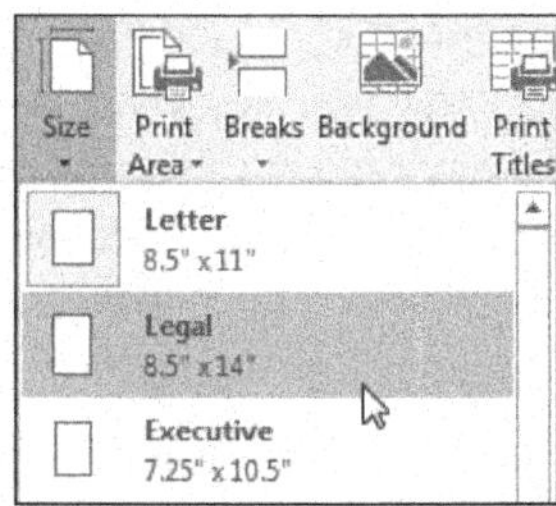

Figure 27.5 Choose a paper size.

Adjusting worksheet orientation

Changing a report to print sideways, which is also referred to as *landscape*, takes just a couple of mouse clicks. From the Page Layout tab, select Page Setup to see the Orientation drop-down menu, which offers Portrait and Landscape options.

Adjusting worksheet margins

When you are trying to squeeze an extra column into a report, you can tweak the report to have smaller margins. Figure 27.2 shows that there are five different places you can adjust the margins for your worksheet. Here are my favorite three methods:

- **Choose Page Layout, Margins:** This drop-down menu offers three settings: Normal, Wide, and Narrow. If you have previously used custom margins, another setting appears as the first choice with the last custom margins you used, called Last Custom Setting. To apply one of these standard setups, choose the setup you want to use from the Margins drop-down menu. To apply a different custom margin, select Custom Margins from the bottom of this menu. Selecting Custom Margins takes you to the Page Setup dialog box, discussed next.
- **Use the Page Setup dialog box:** When you click the dialog box launcher arrow in the bottom right of the Page Setup group, Excel displays the Page Setup dialog box. Use the

CHAPTER 27

Margins tab to adjust the margins at the top, left, right, and bottom, as well as the margins for the footer and header. This dialog box offers precise control of the six margin settings.

- **Choose View, Workbook Views, Page Layout:** When you use this option, gray margins appear on each edge of the ruler. You can drag the gray margins in or out to decrease/increase the margin.

Either version of the Print Preview window has a Show Margins setting. After you've displayed the margins in Print Preview, you can move the margins in or out, or up or down.

Repeating the headings on each page

For reports that span more than one page, you might want the headings from the report to print at the top of each page. Although the Print Titles icon was promoted to a large icon on the Page Layout tab in the ribbon, this command leads back to the somewhat confusing Page Setup dialog box, as shown in Figure 27.6. Suppose that you have a report that is two pages wide and several pages long. However, you notice that the printed page 2 of the printed report does not include title or column headings. If you want to have the titles and column headings repeat at the top of each row, you need to select 1:4 in the Rows to repeat at top option and A:B in the Columns to repeat at left option. When you return to the Page Setup dialog box later, Excel will have added dollar signs to these settings. You don't need to type the dollar signs; Excel will add them.

NOTE

To specify rows to repeat at the top, you can indicate either a single row using 1:1 or a range of rows using 1:4. Similarly, columns to repeat at left might be a single column (A:A) or a range of columns (A:B).

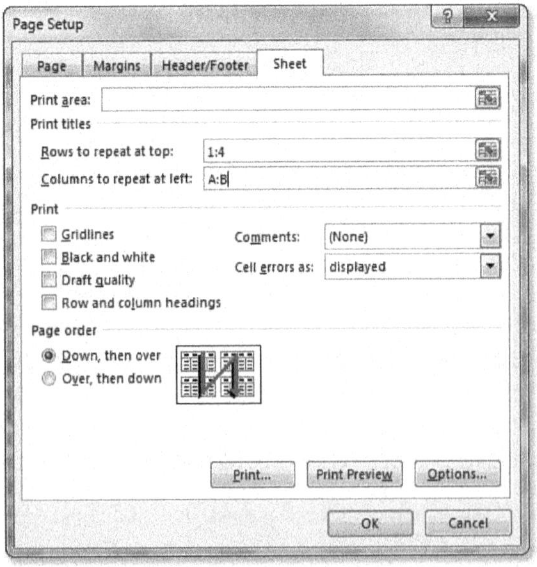

Figure 27.6 Use the Page Setup dialog box to specify print titles to repeat on each page.

Excluding part of your worksheet from the print range

By default, Excel prints all the nonblank cells on a worksheet. Sometimes, you have a nicely formatted table of data to print, but the spreadsheet also includes some work cells in an out-of-the-way location that you do not want to print. To prevent the work cells from being printed, follow these steps:

1. Select the range of cells to be included in the print range, such as cells A1:Z99. Alternatively, you can print everything in certain columns. For example, you might select columns C:X to be printed.

2. From the Page Layout tab, select Page Setup, Print Area, Set Print Area.

To clear the print area and to print everything on the worksheet, you can use the Clear Print Area option from the Set Print Area drop-down menu.

Occasionally, you will want to ignore the print areas and print everything on the worksheet. Select File, Print and then open the first drop-down menu under Settings, as shown in Figure 27.7. You can use the Ignore Print Areas setting to temporarily override the print area. Alternatively, you can print a certain range by selecting the range and then using Selection in the Print panel.

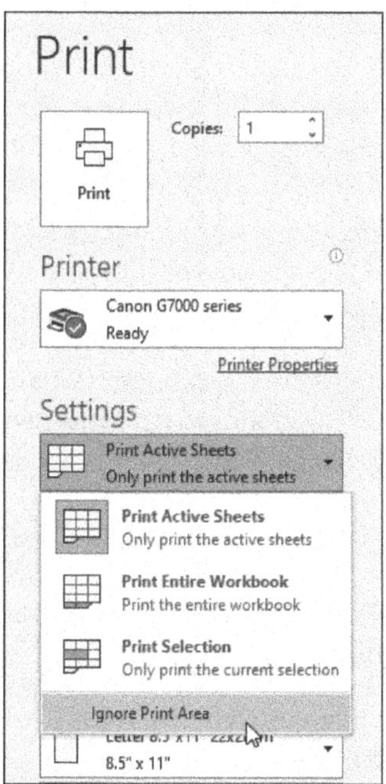

Figure 27.7 Choose to Ignore Print Area or Print Selection from the File menu.

Forcing more data to fit on a page

You will often have worksheets in Excel that are a few columns too wide or a few rows too long to fit on a page.

The Scale to Fit group on the Page Layout tab provides options for width, height, and a percentage scale. In most cases, you change the height, width, or both to achieve the desired effect.

If your worksheet is a few columns too wide, change the Width drop-down menu to specify that the worksheet should fit on one page. If you have a report that is too tall, change the Height drop-down menu to specify that the worksheet should be one page tall. When you select either of these options, the Scale option is grayed out, but it still shows the scaling percentage used to make the report fit.

Sometimes, a report cannot fit into one page and still be readable. This is when you can make intelligent decisions about the best location for page breaks.

Working with page breaks

The two varieties of page breaks are automatic and manual. An *automatic page break* occurs when Excel reaches the bottom or right margin of a physical page. These page breaks change automatically as you adjust margins, add rows, delete rows, or even change the height of certain rows on the page.

Initially, automatic page breaks are not shown in the worksheet. However, after you go to Print Preview and return to Normal view, automatic page breaks are shown using a thin dashed line in the document. Automatic page breaks are also evident in Page Layout view and Page Break Preview mode. To turn off the page breaks, use File, Options, Advanced, Display Options for This Worksheet to find a check box for Show Page Breaks. If you find yourself doing this frequently, the shortcut keys /fta followed by Alt+k will get you there.

You can manually insert page breaks at rows or columns where you want to start a new page. For example, you might want to insert a manual page break at the start of a new section in a report. A manual page break does not automatically change in response to changes in the worksheet rows.

Manually adding page breaks

To add a page break manually at a certain row, follow these steps:

1. Select an entire row by clicking the row number that should be the first row on the new page. Alternatively, select the cell in column A in that row.
2. From the Page Layout tab, select Page Setup, Breaks, Insert Page Break.

To add a page break manually at a certain column, follow these steps:

1. Select an entire column by clicking the letter above the column that should be the first column on the new page. Alternatively, select row 1 in that column.
2. From the Page Layout tab, select Page Setup, Breaks, Insert Page Break.

   CAUTION

   If you insert a page break while the cell pointer is outside row 1 or column A, Excel simultaneously inserts a row page break and a column page break. This is rarely what you want. Make sure to select a cell in column A to insert a row break or to select a cell in row 1 to insert a column break.

Manual versus automatic page breaks

In Normal view, a subtle visual difference exists between manual and automatic page breaks. The dashed line used to indicate a manual page break is more pronounced than the line used to indicate an automatic page break.

To see a better view of page breaks, you can select View, Page Break Preview to switch to Page Break Preview mode. In this mode, automatic page breaks are shown as dotted blue lines. Manual page breaks are shown as solid lines.

Using Page Break Preview to make changes

An advantage of Page Break Preview mode is that while you are in this mode, you can move a page break by dragging the line associated with the page break. If you drag an automatic page break to expand the number of rows or columns on a page, Excel automatically changes the Scale percentage for all pages.

Removing manual page breaks

To remove a manual page break for a row, follow these steps:

1. Position the cursor in the row below the page break.
2. From the Page Layout tab, select Page Setup, Breaks, Remove Page Break.

To remove a manual page break for a column, follow these steps:

1. Position the cursor in the column to the right of the page break.
2. From the Page Layout tab, select Page Setup, Breaks, Remove Page Break.

To remove all manual page breaks, from the Page Layout tab, select Page Setup, Breaks, Reset All Page Breaks. Note that clearing the page breaks also resets the scaling back to 100%.

Adding headers or footers to the printed report

Although you might describe the row of labels that appear at the top of the report as "headings," in this section "headers" are elements that are not in the cells of the worksheet but print at the top of the page. Excel offers three header areas: left, center, and right. Similarly, there are three footer areas.

You can build headers and footers using the third tab of the legacy Page Setup dialog box, but Excel now offers a graphical method for building your headers.

The only entry point for the new Header & Footer Tools Design tab of the ribbon is in Page Layout view. From the View tab, select Page Layout View. Or you can use the Page Layout View icon in the lower-right part of the screen, near the Zoom slider. Excel displays the worksheet with white space for margins.

At the top of each page, you see gray Click To Add Header text. Hover the mouse in this area, and you see that there are three header zones. Click in the Left, Center, or Right header to display the Header & Footer Tools Design tab in the ribbon.

You can either type a static header in the box or use the icons on the ribbon tab to add text that will change at print time. For example, if you insert the code for Date or Time, the printed header reflects the date or time that the report was printed. You can use the formatting tools on the Home tab to format the text in the header.

To exit Header/Footer mode, click in any cell of the worksheet.

Adding an automatic header

For a quick header or footer, you can click the Header or Footer drop-down menu in the Header & Footer Tools Design tab. The drop-down menu offers 16 different automatic headers, including various page-numbering styles, the system date, your name, your company name, the sheet name, and the file path and filename.

Some of the Header entries include values separated by commas. These entries put header values into the left, center, and right header sections.

TIP

Although you cannot add to the automatic header list, you can select an automatic header that is close to what you want and then customize it.

NOTE

The process for adding footers is to the same as the process for adding headers. Throughout the rest of this chapter, several sections include additional information about headers. Keep in mind that the identical instructions apply to footers as well.

Adding a custom header

You can type any text you want into the three header areas. One of the automatic headers reads Confidential, but you can customize this in any way dictated by your company. No matter what type of header you need, you can add it by clicking in any header area and then typing the desired text. To start a new line, press Enter.

Icons for dynamic fields are located in the Header & Footer Tools Design tab. To add an element, click in a header or footer area, position the cursor in the proper place, and click the appropriate icon in the ribbon. As long as the insertion cursor is in the header area, the screen displays the code for that field, such as &[Date] or &[Time].

TIP

To include an ampersand in the header or footer, you must use the code &&. For example, to add the header Profit & Loss, type Profit && Loss.

You can mix static text and dynamic text. For example, you could type **`Page`**, and then click the Page Number icon. Type **`of`** and then click the Number Of Pages icon. Type **`of the`**, and then click the Sheet Name icon. Type **`Worksheet`**. The resulting text shows Page &[Page] of &[Pages] of the &[Tab] Worksheet. When you print, the actual text might be Page 3 of 5 of the Sales 2018 Worksheet.

Inserting a picture or a watermark in a header

You can add a picture to a header or footer. It can be either a small picture that prints in the header area or a large picture that extends below the header area and acts as a watermark behind the worksheet.

To add a picture to a header, follow these steps:

1. Select View, Page Layout View.
2. Click in the header area of the document.
3. From the Header & Footer Tools Design tab, select Header & Footer Elements, Picture. Excel displays the Insert Online Picture dialog box.
4. Select the picture to include in the header. Select a picture and click Insert. Excel adds the text &[Picture] to the header. You cannot tell how large the picture will print at this point.

5. Click in the spreadsheet to see the size of the picture.
6. If you discover that the picture is too large, click in the header area.
7. From the Header & Footer Tools Design tab, select Header & Footer Elements, Format Picture. The Format Picture dialog box appears.

   TIP

   Keep in mind that you won't see how large the picture will be until you click outside the header.

8. In the Format Picture dialog box, use the Size section to reduce the scale of the picture.
9. If you want your picture to appear as a watermark behind the spreadsheet, you need to lighten the picture. To do so, click the Picture tab of the Format Picture dialog box. Change the Color drop-down menu to Washout.
10. None of the picture items in the header features Live Preview. To preview your picture, close the dialog box and then click outside the header. If the picture is not the way you want it, repeat steps 6 through 9 as necessary.

    NOTE

    If you use the spin button to change the height in the Scale section, the width is automatically changed as well, to keep the scale proportional.

Using different headers and footers in the same document

Excel allows the following four header and footer scenarios:

- The same header/footer on all pages
- One header/footer on page 1 and a different header/footer on all other pages
- One header/footer on all odd pages and a different header/footer on all even pages
- One header/footer on page 1, a second header/footer on even pages, and a third header/footer on all odd pages from 3 and up

Excel manages these scenarios by storing three headers for each worksheet. The first header is variously called the `odd page header` or just the `header`. As you select and clear the options' check boxes, the contents of each header remain constant, even though they might be used on different pages. Table 27.1 shows the details of each header option.

Table 27.1 Header options

Different first page	Different odd and even pages	Odd page header	Even page header	First page header
Cleared	Cleared	Called the header and used on all pages	Not used	Not used
Cleared	Selected	Called the odd page header and used for pages 1, 3, 5, and so on	Called the even page header and used for pages 2, 4, 6, and so on	Not used
Selected	Cleared	Called the header and used for pages 2, 3, 4, and so on	Not used	Called the first page header and used for page 1
Selected	Selected	Called the odd page header and used for pages 3, 5, 7, and so on	Called the even page header and used for pages 2, 4, 6, and so on	Called the first page header and used for page 1

If you add a header in Page Layout view, it is known as the `odd page header`. In the default configuration, Excel displays the odd page header on all pages of the printout.

Excel has two other sets of headers that are initially hidden. One set is called the `First Page Header`. The other set is called the `Different First Page`, which you can select from the Options group on the Header & Footer Tools Design tab. When this option is used, Excel displays the first page header above page 1 and uses the odd page header everywhere else.

TIP

To minimize confusion, it is best to select the Options section check boxes Different First Page and Different Odd & Even before entering headers.

Scaling headers and footers

Settings in the Page Layout tab allow you to force a worksheet to fit a certain number of pages. If the scaling options require a 75 percent scale on Sheet1 and a 95 percent scale on Sheet2, your headings are scaled as well. This causes your page numbers to appear at a different point size in various sections of the report.

Excel offers an option to force all headers and footers to print at 100 percent scale, regardless of the zoom for the sheet. To select this option, from the Header & Footer Tools Design tab, select Options and clear the Scale With Document check box.

Printing from the File menu

To access the Print panel, you can either select File, Print or press Ctrl+P. The panel merges settings from the Print and Page Setup dialog boxes in the middle of the screen and the Print Preview on the right side of the screen. As you update settings in the middle of the screen, the Print Preview updates, which enables you always to see the current preview (see Figure 27.8).

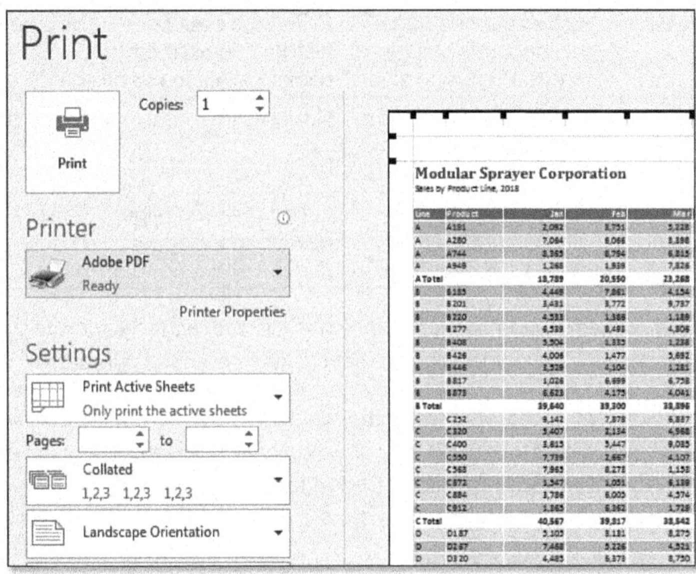

Figure 27.8 Print Preview and Print Settings are combined in a single screen.

The left side of the screen starts with a very large Print button. Click this button to print the document. The spin button next to the Print button enables you to control the number of copies to print.

The rest of the left panel contains a new kind of gallery. You can see the current choice of the gallery without opening the gallery. If the correct printer is already selected, there is no need to open the drop-down menu.

Choosing a printer

When you open the Printer drop-down menu, Excel displays all the current printers and indicates if the printer is currently online and/or available. This handy improvement enables you to detect if the department printer is in a paper jam condition so you can print to a different printer.

Choosing what to print

As shown in Figure 27.9, the Print What gallery offers Active Sheets, Entire Workbook, and Selection settings. You can further modify these settings by choosing Ignore Print Area.

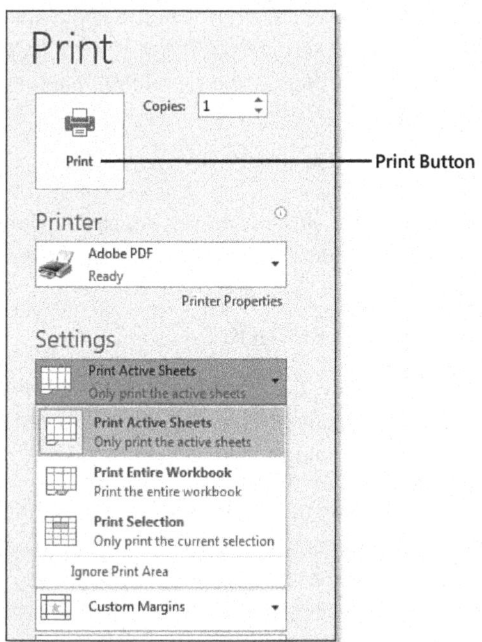

Figure 27.9 Choosing what to print.

If you choose the Active Sheets option, the currently selected sheet prints. If you have specified a print area, only that range prints; otherwise, Excel prints the entire used range of the document. However, if you select multiple sheets in Group mode, all the selected sheets print.

If you choose the Entire Workbook option, all the nonhidden worksheets in the workbook print. One advantage to this option is that the pages are numbered consecutively as the printout moves from Sheet1 to Sheet2.

Choosing the Selection option enables you to override the print area temporarily. However, if you need to print one small range of a large report, select that range and then choose the Selection option in the Print What gallery. This prevents you from having to change the Print Area twice.

The Ignore Print Area option causes Excel to ignore any print areas specified previously. This causes the entire used area of the worksheet to be printed.

You can select specific pages to print using the Pages spin buttons. To print a single page, enter that page number in both the Pages and To boxes.

Changing printer properties

After you choose a printer, the remaining galleries on the left side of the Print panel are redrawn. If you are printing to an office printer that supports collating and stapling, use the galleries to select each of these options. If you are printing to a home printer that does not have these options, Excel does not show those galleries.

> TIP
>
> **If a specific property does not appear, you can click the Printer Properties hyperlink at the bottom of the left panel to access the vendor-supplied Printer Property dialog box.**

Changing some of the Page Setup settings

Even though it might seem like they are out of place, the last settings on the left side of the Print panel are used to control portrait versus landscape, paper size, and margins. If you change a setting here, it will also change in the Page Setup dialog box.

If your initial reaction is to wonder why these settings are repeated here, you might also wonder why your favorite Page Setup settings are not also repeated. Even though it is nice to switch from portrait to landscape here, it would also be nice to be able to change the Page Scaling or Rows To Repeat At Top settings here. However, this cannot be done because those settings require you to close the Print panel and to use the Page Layout tab of the ribbon.

Using Page Layout view

When you open Excel, the default view is called Normal view. In legacy versions of Excel, your only choices were Normal view and Page Break Preview mode. However, beginning with Excel 2007, Microsoft added the Page Layout view, which works well when you are preparing a document for printing.

In Excel, the three views are available either in the View tab or on the right side of the status bar.

In Page Layout view, you have a fully functioning worksheet. For example, the formula bar works, and you can scroll around the worksheet. However, listed next are the differences between Page Layout and Normal view:

- White space appears to show the margins on each page. This is usually an advantage because you have a clear view of any page breaks between columns or rows. If you want to hide the white space, you can click the white space and choose Hide White Space.

- A ruler appears below the formula bar that you can use to change margins by dragging the gray areas of the ruler.
- Areas are marked Click To Add Header and Click To Add Footer. Whereas headers and footers are buried in legacy versions of Excel, in the Page Layout view of Excel, it is obvious that headers and footers are available.
- Areas outside the data area of a worksheet are marked with Click To Add Data. One of the problems with Page Break Preview mode is that areas outside the data area were grayed out. However, the Click To Add Data labels option invites you to continue adding pages to your worksheet.

The only disadvantage to Page Layout view is that Excel turns off your Freeze Panes settings in Page Layout view. Excel warns you that this is happening. Excel does this to emphasize that Print Titles are different from Freeze Panes.

TIP

Keep in mind that Excel does not restore the Freeze Panes settings when you return to Normal view.

Exploring other page setup options

Other page setup options are scattered throughout the various interface areas. Although some of these are fairly obscure, you might need to use them in certain situations.

Printing gridlines and headings

To print the gridlines on a worksheet, from the Page Layout tab, select Sheet Options, Gridlines, Print.

You can also print the A-B-C column headings and 1-2-3 row headings. To do this, from the Page Layout tab, select Sheet Options, Headings, Print. This option is helpful when you are printing formulas using the `FORMULATEXT` function, and you need to see the cell address of each cell.

Centering a small report on a page

Small reports can look out of place printed in the upper-left corner of a page. Rather than increasing margins, you can choose to center the report horizontally or vertically on a page.

Select Page Layout, Margins, Custom Margins to display the Page Setup dialog box. Two check boxes at the bottom of the dialog box center the report on the page.

Replacing error values when printing

Excel calculations sometimes result in various errors such as `#N/A!` or `DIV/0`. Although these error values help you determine how to fix the errors, they look out of place on a printed page. You can choose to replace any error cells with a blank or two hyphens.

Choose Page Layout, Print Titles to open the Sheet tab of the Page Setup dialog box. Open the Cell Errors As drop-down menu and choose <blank> or --.

Printing comments

Cell comments often appear as a tiny red triangle in a cell. You can print a table of all the comments at the bottom of your report. Use the Comments And Notes drop-down menu in the Sheet tab of the Page Setup dialog box and choose At End Of Sheet.

Excel prints your report and then starts a new page listing each comment/note. The new page shows the cell and the comment/note content.

The other option for printing comments and notes is to print any visible ones where they are currently displayed. To show all of them, choose Review, Notes, Show All Notes. When they are displayed, you can drag them to a new location, so they are not covering up important cells.

Controlling the first page number

You might be inserting a printed Excel worksheet in the middle of a printed Word document. If the Excel worksheet is appearing as the tenth page in the Word report, for example, you would want the Excel page numbers to start at 10 instead of 1.

From the Page Layout tab, choose the dialog box launcher at the bottom right of the Page Setup group. Excel displays the Page tab of the Page Setup dialog box. The last setting is First Page Number and is initially set to Auto. Type **10** in this box, and Excel prints the Excel worksheet using page numbers 10, 11, 12, and so on.

Inside OUT

Exporting a worksheet as a PDF is really like printing.

You can create a PDF from any workbook in Excel. Think of creating a PDF as if you are "printing" to a special printer that makes PDF files. Thus, it is important that you set the print ranges before you begin. If you want multiple worksheets in your PDF, select those worksheets in Group mode before creating the PDF. (For example, select Sheet1 and then Ctrl+click the tabs for Sheet3 and Sheet7 to put those three sheets in Group mode.)

To save a worksheet as a PDF file, select File, Export, Create PDF/XPS. You have the option to save the file in a high-resolution format suitable for printing or a low-resolution format that is suitable for viewing onscreen.

If you frequently work with PDF files, you might have noticed that some PDFs contain data that can be selected, copied, and pasted to Excel. Other PDFs contain strange formatting that causes the content pasted back to Excel to render horribly. You would think that a PDF file created by the Excel team would have the capability to paste back into Excel, but this is not the case. Try opening the PDF in Word and then copying the data from Word to Excel.

CHAPTER 28

Collaborating in Excel

Microsoft introduced the ability for multiple people to collaborate on a worksheet back in 2017. The first release of any product from Microsoft has rough edges. As I am writing this, the collaboration tools are four years old. Microsoft has improved the collaboration tools, offering better commenting, mentions, and show changes. As of 2021, collaboration is fairly stable for files of 1 MB or less and with five or fewer people working in the workbook at one time.

Microsoft is also addressing the fundamental question that every spreadsheet author asks themselves: "Do I trust my coworkers not to mess up my workbook?" With Show Changes and Version History, spreadsheet authors can roll back changes that your coworkers might make in the document.

Finally, the Excel team is trying to make it more discoverable that you can collaborate with others.

The rise of working remotely in 2020

The pandemic of 2020 changed the way that we work. Before 2020, only 15% of companies allowed their employees to work from home. By July 2020, 76% of companies allowed people to work from home. In a Microsoft survey, 88% of those companies said they expect working from home to continue after the pandemic.

Rather than walk down the hall to discuss a worksheet, you are working in the same workbook with someone else who is across town or across the country.

To successfully collaborate on a document, you should meet these criteria:

- The workbook must be stored online. Today, that means OneDrive, OneDrive for Business, or SharePoint online. In the future, this might expand to Dropbox or Box.
- You should turn AutoSave on for the workbook. This setting is found in the Quick Access toolbar.
- Everyone working in the document should be on the latest version of Microsoft 365 on Windows or Mac, or using Excel Online in a browser. In the future, this will extend to mobile platforms such as iOS and Android phones.
- The collaboration process is much simpler if everyone is working at the same company. Microsoft calls this "working under the same tenant." If everyone is signing in to Office with an email such as *Me@MyCompany.OnMicrosoft.com*, then you are all working in the same tenant. Collaboration is possible across companies, but it is not as smooth.

Storing documents in the cloud

In order to effectively collaborate, the document must be stored in the cloud. Today, that means OneDrive. In the future, it might mean Dropbox or Box.

I remember that I used to carry work home with me on a USB flash drive. At the end of my work day, I would copy the workbooks that I needed to work on to a flash drive. Often, I would leave the flash drive plugged into the computer as I left the building and drove home.

By storing your workbooks in OneDrive, they are always available. You don't have to copy them to a flash drive. You don't have to remember to put the flash drive in your pocket. If you work at home three days and work in the office two days each week, the files will always be available in either location.

They will be available with one caveat: They are available until the Internet goes down. But even in these cases, the Windows or Mac versions of Excel will let you keep working on a document. The changes that you make will be batched up and applied to the online version of the workbook when the Internet returns.

I am not sure which is more annoying: going offline for a few minutes while the Internet is down or losing all of your workbooks once every few years due to a hard drive crash. There are advantages and disadvantages to saving online and saving locally.

Here is an important distinction: I am suggesting that you store your workbooks in the cloud but that you continue to work in the desktop version of Excel.

People seem to think that because a document is stored in the cloud, then you have to work in Excel Online. This is not correct. For me, Excel Online is for emergency use only. Perhaps your manager needs something done right now, and you are visiting your grandmother who does not have Excel. In that case, you might open Excel Online in order to make the edits.

There is an exception where you might want to try out Excel Online. New features have been appearing in Excel Online first, then migrating to Windows and Mac and then finally to Excel for mobile devices. As I am writing this chapter, the awesome Show Changes feature has been added to Excel Online but is not yet visible in Windows Excel. While I might do 99% of my work in Excel for Windows, I could see opening the workbook in Excel Online if I needed to see who changed a cell.

➤ **Read about Show Changes in Chapter 1, "What's new in Microsoft 365 Excel."**

Sharing documents with others

There are at least three ways to share a document that has been stored in the cloud. In an effort to make sharing discoverable, the Excel team added the ability to share the workbook in the Save This File dialog.

Sharing during the initial save

Press Ctrl+S from a new document to display the modern Save This File dialog. Once you choose an online location, the same dialog offers the ability to optionally collaborate with others (see Figure 28.1).

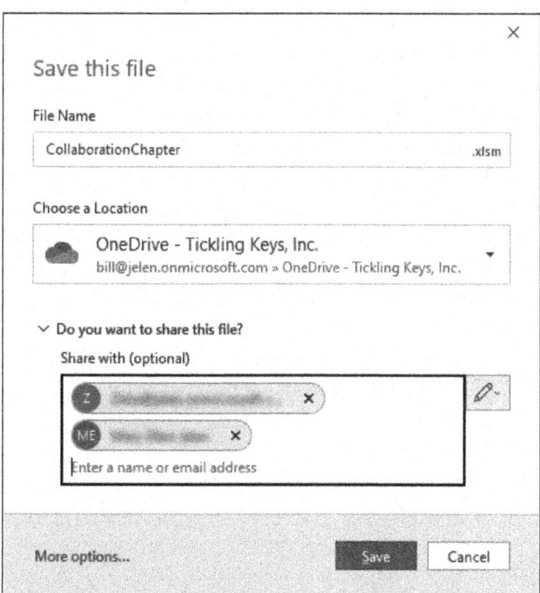

Figure 28.1 If you choose to save to an online location, the Save This File dialog offers the optional ability to share the workbook.

Sharing using the Share button

If you want to share the workbook with others later, you can use the Share button in the top right of the Excel screen. You have more choices in this dialog. You can choose to create a link. Use the Pencil icon to choose if you are giving the person access to edit or to read only. There is a popular request on UserVoice to add a "Comment Only" option to this list. By the time you are reading this, there may be a new Comment Only choice available.

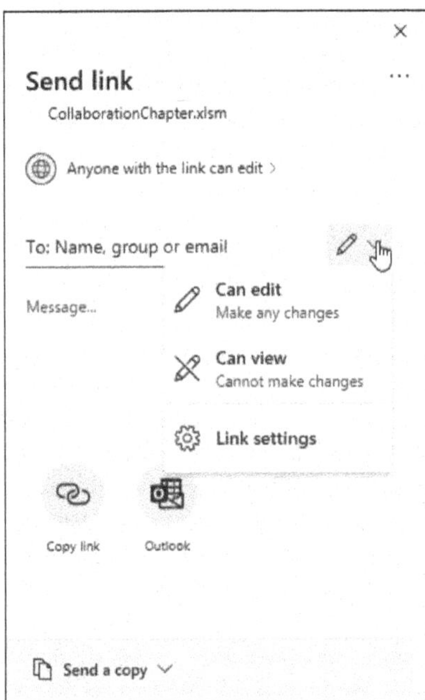

Figure 28.2 Use the Share button to create a sharing link or to invited specific people.

If you click the Link Settings icon shown in Figure 28.2, you can set an expiration date, prevent downloading the document, and more in the Link Settings dialog (see Figure 28.3). Note that Block Download is only available if you uncheck Allow Editing.

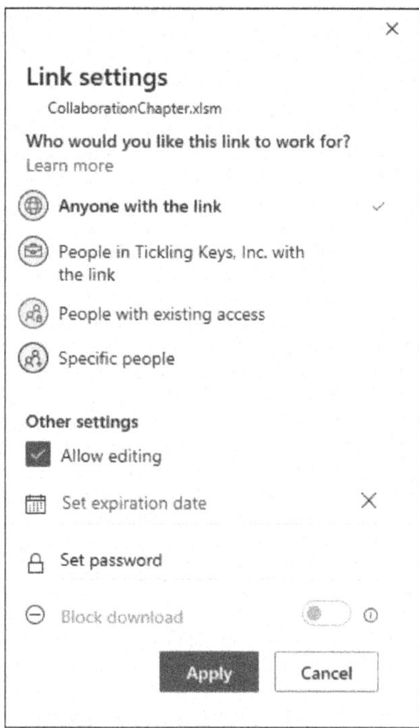

Figure 28.3 Set an expiration date, add a password, or block downloading in the Link Settings dialog.

Sharing by mentioning in a modern comment

The third way of sharing the file is to @Mention someone in a comment or to assign them a task through a comment. Read more about mentions and tasks later in this chapter.

You can easily imagine a scenario where you share a workbook with three members of your department. Someone asks a question about a cell in a comment. The person replying says, "This isn't my area. Let's ask @Joe in Finance." Even though Joe from Finance was not among the collaborators, the workbook is now shared with him so he can reply to the comment.

After a few weeks of working in the document, you might have many people who were mentioned and now have access to the document. You need a way to monitor who has access.

Seeing who has access to the workbook

Here is how to see who has access to the active workbook. Click the Share button in the top-right corner of Excel. This opens the Send Link dialog box previously shown in Figure 28.2. At the top-right of the dialog, there are three dots. Click the three dots and choose Manage Access. The Manage Access dialog box shows a list of links created and people who have access (see Figure 28.4). Use the Pencil icon to the right of each person to choose Can Edit, Can View, or Stop Sharing.

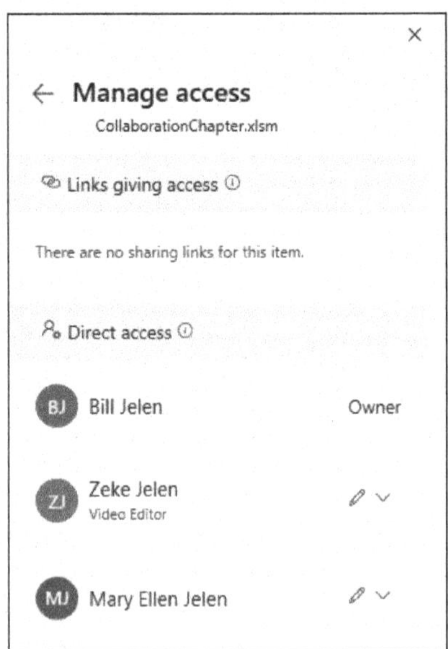

Figure 28.4 See everyone who has access and revoke that access using the Manage Access dialog.

Knowing when someone shares a workbook with you

When someone shares a workbook or @Mentions you, there are several ways for you to be notified. First, an email will be sent to you in Outlook, as shown in Figure 28.5.

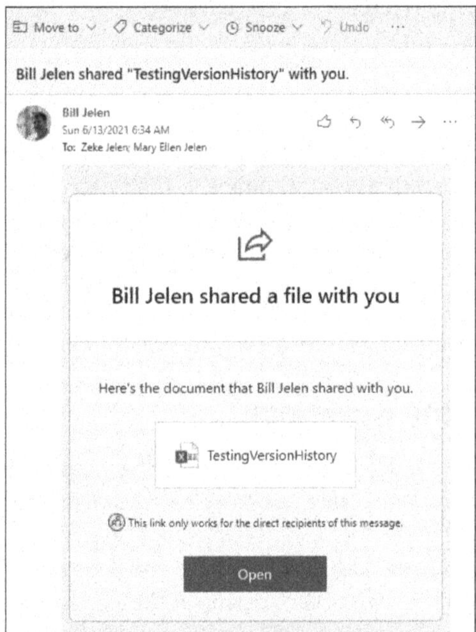

Figure 28.5 When someone shares a file or mentions you, an email is sent to you in Outlook.

CAUTION

When you click the Open button in the email, it will automatically open the workbook in Excel Online. Microsoft is aware that you need an option in the email to open the shared workbook in the desktop version of Excel.

For now, however, you will have to use the Mode Menu shown in Figure 28.6. This menu appears in Excel Online. You can open it and choose Open In Desktop App.

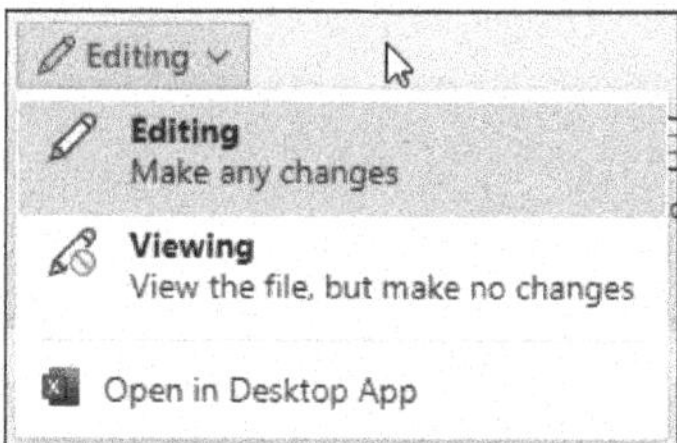

Figure 28.6 Until the Outlook notification includes a choice to open in the Desktop, you will first have to open in Excel Online and then switch to the Desktop.

Personally, I never use Outlook. If you send an email to *bill@jelen.onmicrosoft.com*, I will never see it. So, I never see the email notifications. However, I know when someone shares a workbook with me from two places on the Excel Home screen.

When you select File, Home, there is a section called Recommended For You. This will contain any workbooks where you were recently mentioned or workbooks that were recently shared with you. Below the Recommended For You section are three tabs: Recent, Pinned, and Shared With Me. Use the Shared With Me option (see Figure 28.7).

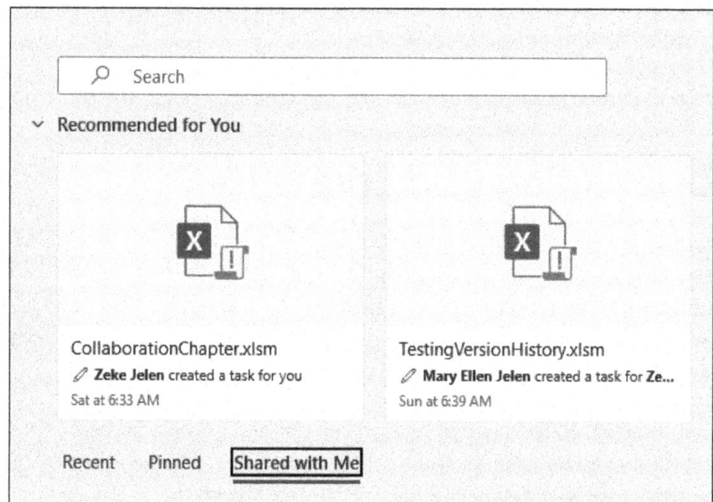

Figure 28.7 The File, Home screen in Excel offers shared workbooks.

Another place to find shared workbooks is found by choosing File, Open, Shared With Me, as shown in Figure 28.8.

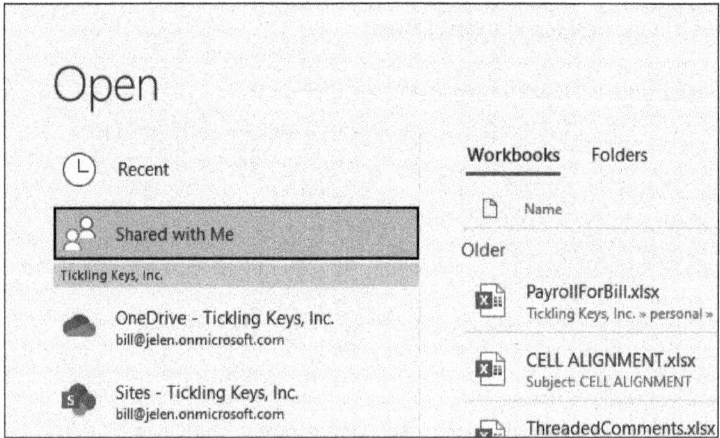

Figure 28.8 Using File, Open, Shared With Me will provide a longer list of workbooks that have been shared with you.

Editing the same workbook at the same time

When you invite someone to collaborate on a workbook, they will receive an Outlook message with the link to the workbook. The other person will also see the workbook in the Shared With Me section of the Excel Home screen and in the Recommended For Me section of the Excel Home screen.

In the past, if several people had access to the same workbook, it was a "one-at-a-time" situation. Now, you can all be editing at the same time.

The only caveat is that you should not both be editing the same cell at the same time.

Seeing who else is editing using presence

When multiple people are editing the same workbook at the same time, you will see multiple cell pointers. The active cell in your session will be green. Each other person who is editing will be assigned a different color cell pointer. Tiny circles in the top right of the Excel window indicates who is present and editing the file (see Figure 28.9). Hover over any circle to get their full name and what cell they are currently working on.

It takes some getting used to to figure out which cell pointer is yours. Some people on UserVoice are asking for the ability to hide all the presence features because it can be distracting to see the cell pointers for several coworkers moving around the screen.

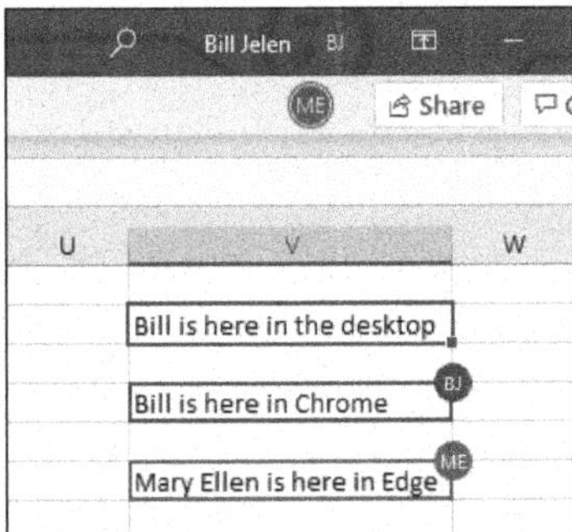

Figure 28.9 Each person editing the workbook has their own cell pointer visible.

Etiquette for editing at the same time

You won't have any trouble if you do not select any cells that other people are editing. When someone starts editing a cell on another computer, you will see an animated three dots appear by that cell. This indicates that someone else is editing that cell. In Figure 28.10, MJ is in cell A73 but not editing. You are in cell B72. Someone is in cell D72 and is currently typing.

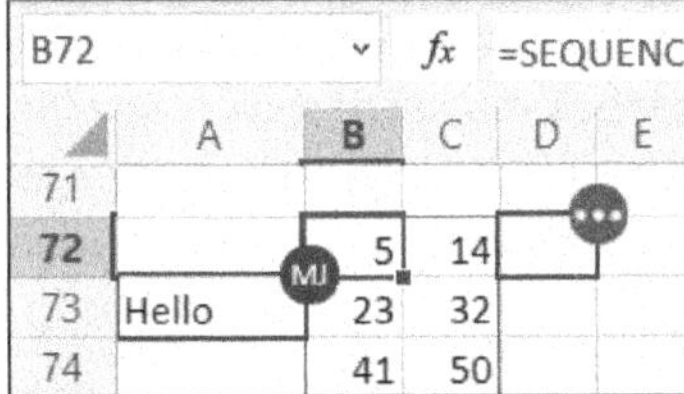

Figure 28.10 When a coworker starts editing a cell, their initials are replaced by three animated dots.

Wait until they finish editing the cell and for the cell to update. You are then free to edit the cell.

If two people edit the same cell at the same time, Excel will choose one who wins. In general, the last person to change the cell "wins," but not in all cases. Different endpoints support coauthoring in different ways. Sometimes, a person with an older version of Excel won't have full support for coauthoring, and that person will always win. You can avoid the problem by not selecting a cell that someone else is editing.

Avoiding the dreaded veto

Coauthoring can work great for several hours, but then something can go wrong and cause the dreaded "Upload Failed" or "Can't Save Your Changes" messages. Microsoft calls this situation a "veto." They are working diligently to reduce the number of veto errors. There are now 80% fewer veto errors than a few years ago.

I appreciate the progress, but getting a veto error is horrible. I was burned by a veto error in 2017 and refused to collaborate again for four years.

Here are some situations that can cause a veto:

- Someone goes offline, makes a million changes, and then comes back online. The sheer number of changes being transferred can overwhelm the system. A similar problem can happen in PowerPoint when one person tries to insert a 1 GB video in a shared workbook.
- Someone is using an old version of Microsoft 365 and makes edits. You know this guy. Up until last year, he was still using Lotus 1-2-3.
- Someone using the Desktop version of Excel tries to use a feature that is not supported in Excel Online.

In my opinion, once you get one of these messages—see Figure 28.11—you start over. Microsoft says it is not that bad. Their advice:

- If you don't have any unsaved changes, simply click Refresh.
- If you have unsaved changes that you were not particularly fond of, click Discard.
- If you have unsaved changes that you need to keep, click Save A Copy and save the file with a different name. Select and copy the changes you need to keep. Reopen the original file and paste the changes back in. To me, this option is completely unacceptable. Everyone keeps promising one version of the truth, but this solution is forking your workbook.

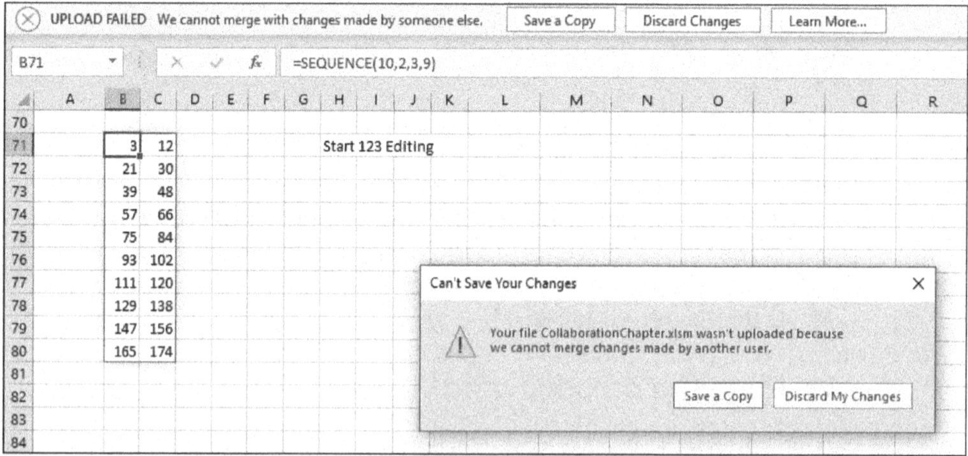

Figure 28.11 If Walter keeps trying to edit your workbook with an old version of Excel, this message will keep appearing.

Filtering and sorting with Sheet Views

Many years ago, as soon as coauthoring was introduced, I set up a department task list. My brilliant idea was that everyone could use this task list. I shared it with a few people, and almost immediately Scottie filtered the list to just his tasks. To my dismay, this meant that everyone could only see Scottie's tasks. The great experiment failed.

I emailed the Excel team and asked if each person could have the ability to filter independently from each other. The Excel Project Manager explained that it was particularly difficult because there are two Excel functions that calculate based on visible rows: `SUBTOTAL` and `AGGREGATE`.

If each person could filter independently, then how would Excel know how to calculate these formulas?

The problem was solved in 2019. See the new Sheet View group on the left side of the View tab to set up and control various views of the data.

The "real" version of the worksheet is given the name of `Default`. If someone tries to Sort or Filter, they are encouraged to have the action appear only for them. If they choose this, then a new view called `Temporary View` is created. If you like the temporary view and want to access it again, you click Keep and provide a name such as `BillView`.

Once you've made a view permanent, everyone collaborating would be able to choose that view.

Figure 28.12 shows an example with a small data set with Filter drop-down menus enabled. At the top of the image, the Sheet View shows that this unfiltered and unsorted version is called `Default`.

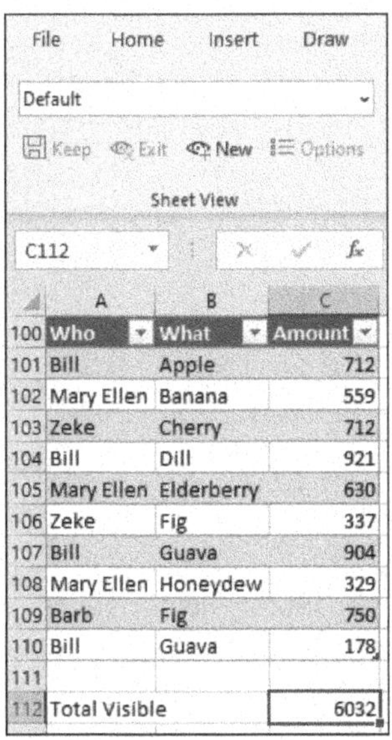

Figure 28.12 The subtotal formula at the bottom of this data shows the visible cells total 6032.

If you filter the data set to just the Bill records, the Others Are Also Making Changes dialog box appears (see Figure 28.13). It asks if you want to see sorting and filtering from others. Your choices are See Just Mine or See Everyone's. The natural choice here is to only see your filtering.

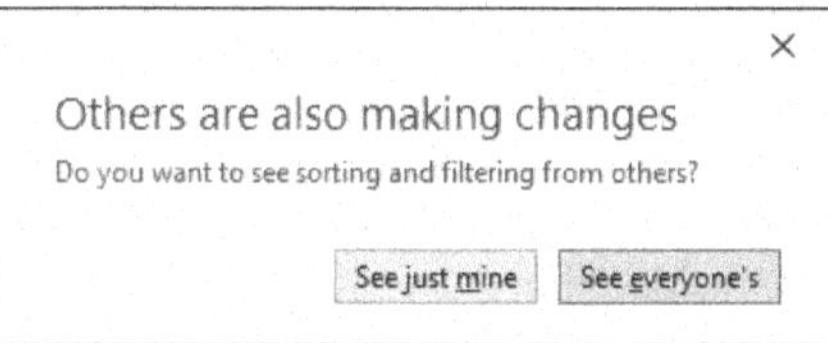

Figure 28.13 When you choose See Just Mine, you are setting up a custom Sheet View.

If you dismiss the message shown in Figure 28.13, you can create a new Sheet View using the New icon shown previously in Figure 28.12.

After choosing to See Just Mine, Excel creates a new Sheet View called Temporary View. This means that only you are seeing this view of the data.

Notice in Figure 28.14 that the Subtotal formula in C129 has changed to reflect only the records visible to you. However, any external workbooks that are linking to this workbook will be getting the Total Visible from the Default View.

Also notice that the column letters and row numbers are now on a dark background. This is your reminder that you are in a Sheet View.

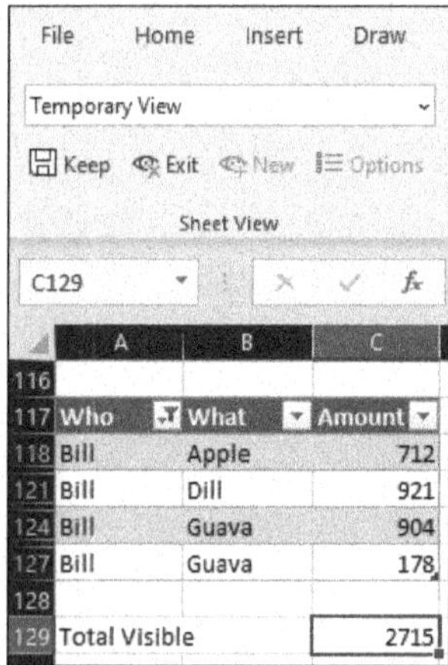

Figure 28.14 At first, a Sheet View is called Temporary View.

When you have a Temporary View, you can use the Exit icon on the View tab to return to the Default View. However, if you want to frequently return to this Sheet View, use the Keep icon and provide a name for the view. Figure 28.15 shows the Temporary View renamed as BillView.

CHAPTER 28

Note that if you create a view called BillView, then everyone collaborating will have the option to switch to the view that you created.

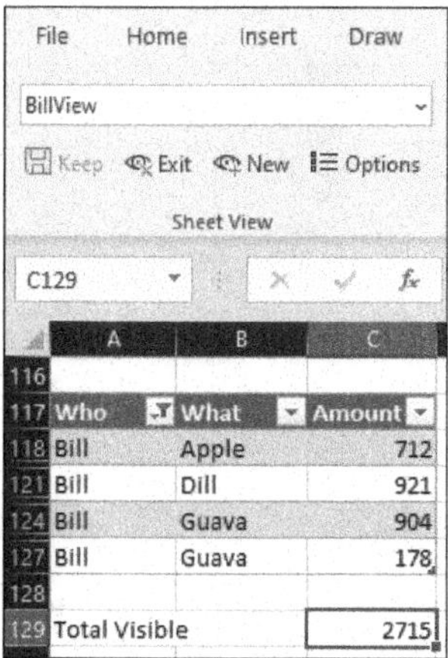

Figure 28.15 When you keep a view and give it a name, everyone collaborating can choose to switch to this view.

The Sheet View feature is awesome. Soon, everyone will be creating their own views of the data. In Figure 28.16, Mary Ellen's view has the data sorted high to low and filtered to show only Mary Ellen records. Note that the total visible formula is showing a different answer.

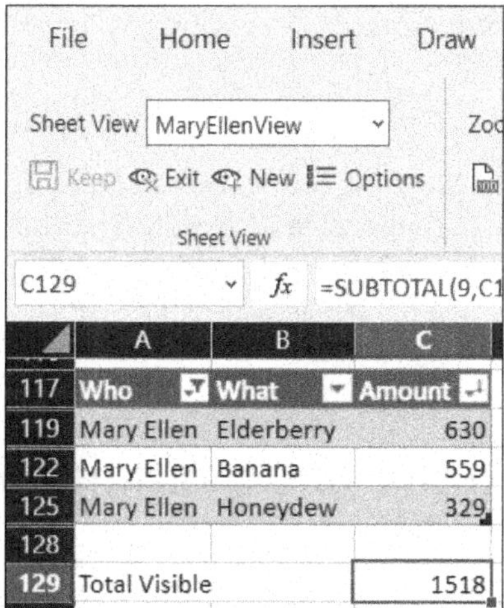

Figure 28.16 In this view, the data is sorted descending and filtered to one person.

You can easily switch to any Sheet View using the Sheet View drop-down menu on the View tab of the ribbon. For more options, click the Options icon. Here, you can rename a view, duplicate an existing view, or switch to any view (see Figure 28.17).

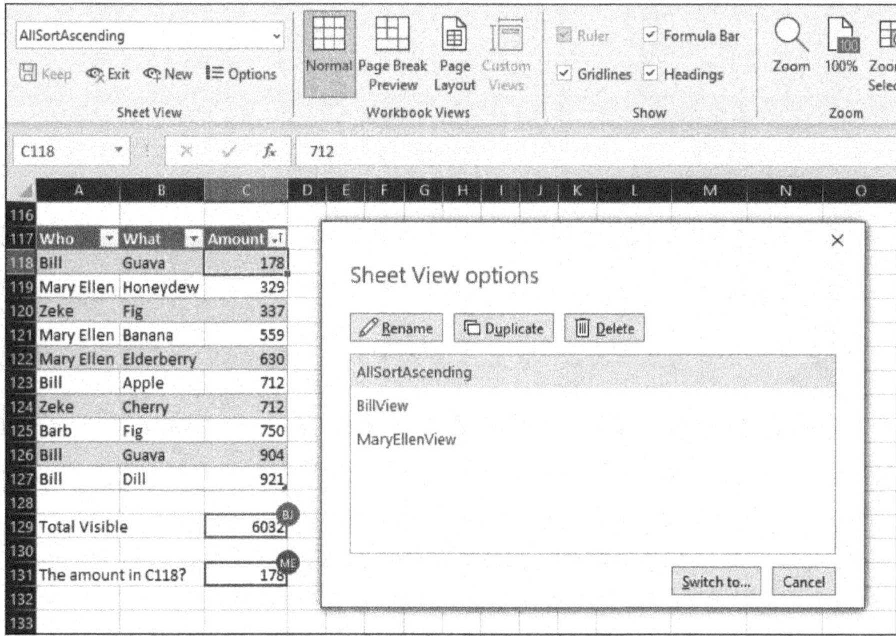

Figure 28.17 The Sheet View dialog lets you manage views.

CAUTION

While the obvious calculation problems are SUBTOTAL **and** AGGREGATE **formulas, any formula that is pointing at a specific cell in the table could potentially return different results. In Figure 28.17, a formula =C118 is showing 178 for the AllSortAscending View and 712 for the MaryEllenView. Remember that the actual value that is used for external linked workbooks is the value shown in the Default View.**

Using threaded comments, mentions, and assigning tasks

It used to be that a single cell could have only a single note. One of the improvements in a collaboration environment is the new threaded comments. To start a comment thread, select a cell and choose Review, New Comment.

As you are typing your comment, you can address the comment to a particular person by typing an @ sign immediately followed by the person's name. This is called an @Mention (pronouced "at mention").

As of 2021, the @Mention system requires the Active Directory feature of Microsoft Exchange. This means @Mentions won't work in home or consumer editions of Excel. Microsoft would love to figure out a way to make @Mentions work for home customers, so it might be working by the time you read this.

Figure 28.18 shows a comment in the process of creating an @Mention. If you type **@Mary**, the Active Directory suggests Mary Ellen. If your company has 20 people named Mary, choose one from the list. If there is only one in the list, simply press Tab to insert them in the comment.

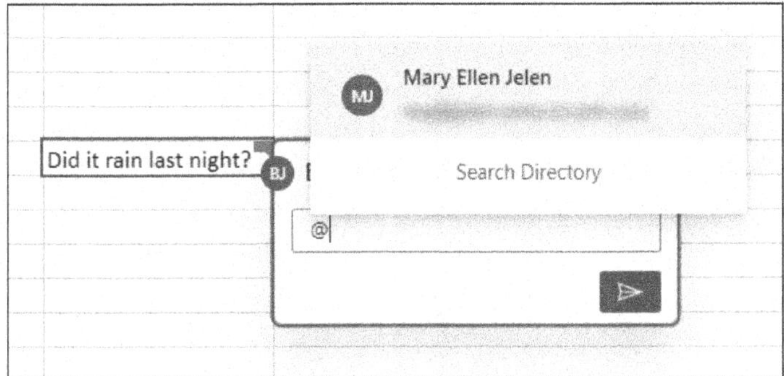

Figure 28.18 Type an @ sign and the start of someone's name to create an @Mention.

TIP

If you @Mention someone and that person has not been invited to the workbook, they are added to the list of collaborators. This can quickly cause a workbook shared with just a few people to be shared with many people. Remember to periodically check to see who has access to the workbook, as described earlier in this chapter.

New in 2021: If you @Mention someone in a comment, you can create a task for that person. After typing the @Mention, a box appears asking if you want to create a task. Currently, task creation is still rolling out as a new feature. It is working in Excel Online but needs to come to the desktop and mobile. You can expect that they will incorporate tasks with either Outlook Tasks or with Microsoft To Do.

Each new comment has a green icon in the lower left that looks like a paper airplane. Click this icon to add the comment to the cell (see Figure 28.19).

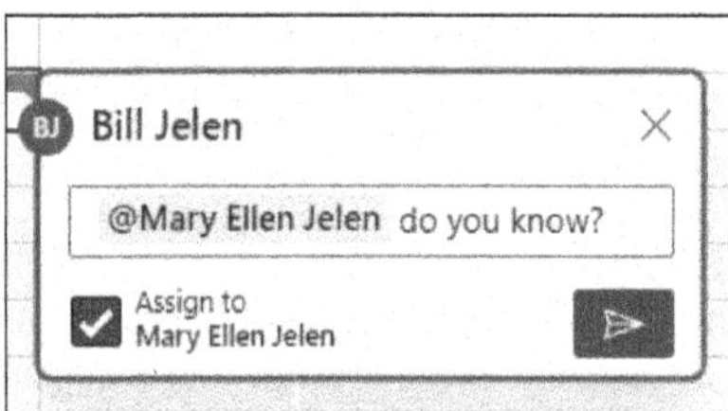

Figure 28.19 If you @Mention someone, you can create a task for that person before sending the comment.

When someone @Mentions you in a comment, you receive a notification in your email. The email notification will have a little bit of context, such as the text in the commented cell and the comment. From email, you can either follow the link to open the workbook or answer by replying in the email (see Figure 28.20).

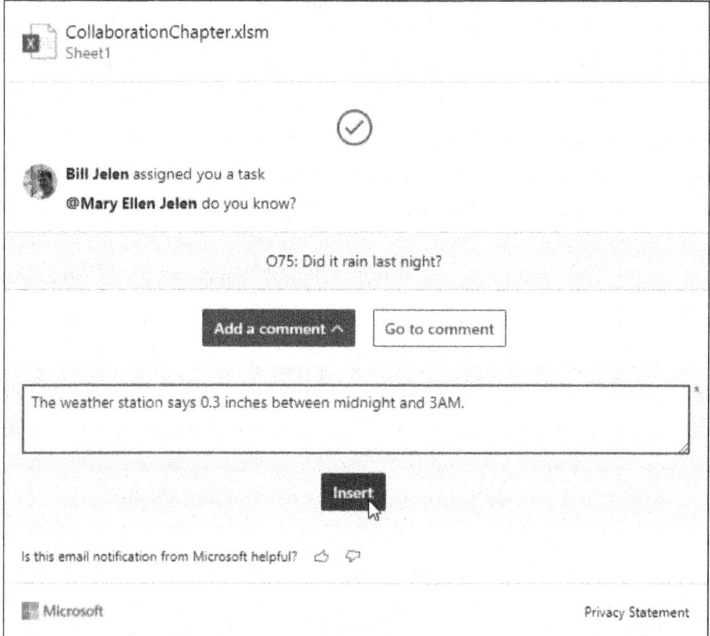

Figure 28.20 You can add a reply to the comment without ever leaving Outlook.

After inserting a reply from Outlook, the threaded comment chain in Excel is updated to show the reply. Because the Assign A Task feature is new, you can't mark the task as complete from Outlook yet. You have to go to Excel and choose Resolve Task (see Figure 28.21).

To display the comment for a cell, hover over the five-sided purple indicator in the top-right part of a cell with a comment. Alternatively, you can click the Comments button in the top-right part of Excel to display a task pane with all the comments. As commenting becomes more prevalent, Microsoft will have to invent a way to filter the comment pane to show only items that mention a particular person or only comments from your manager.

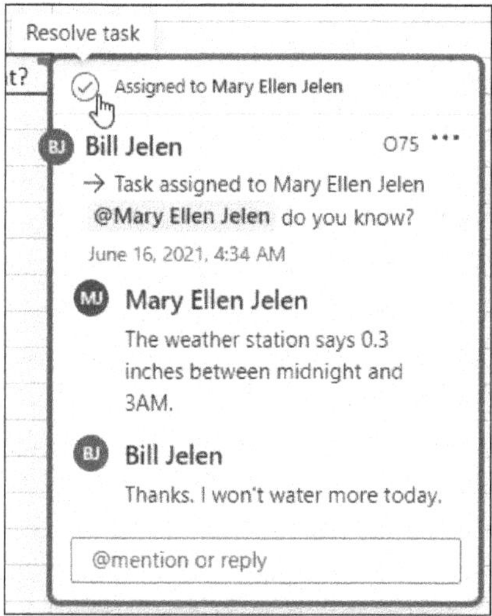

Figure 28.21 One cell can have a comment and multiple replies.

Inside OUT

Legacy Comments Are Now "Notes"

Excel tricksters have long used various cool tricks to alter the formatting of comments. For example, the late David Hawley showed how you could change the shape of a comment to a star in his 2007 book, *Excel Hacks: Tips & Tools for Streamlining Your Spreadsheets*. I remember doing a segment for Leo Laporte on TechTV where I used comments to hold a photo that would pop-up when you hovered over the comment indicator. Others will color-code comments so that pink comments are warnings and yellow icons are cautions.

If you want to continue to use any of the legacy commenting tricks to format or display comments, you need to switch to using Notes instead of Comments. The Excel team added a Notes drop-down menu next to Comments on the Review tab, and the new menu includes all the old legacy comment functionality. The legacy comments are now called Notes. Actually, if you go back to Excel 97, the first version of comments were originally called Notes, so they are simply going back to the old name.

New threaded comments and old Notes can coexist in the same worksheet. Notes will have a red triangle indicator. Comments will have a purple thought-bubble-shaped indicator.

Legacy Notes will not yet work in Excel Online.

Tracking who did what in the workbook

My biggest fear about inviting my coworkers to collaborate on a workbook is that someone will inadvertently overwrite a formula, sort part of the data, and so on. In desktop Excel, you've had the ability to protect sheets and workbooks, but as of June 2021, those proactive methods of protecting a workbook don't work in Excel Online.

Until sheet protection comes to Excel Online, Microsoft has provided tools to help you reactively undo bad changes made by others:

- The Show Changes feature will show all changes made to the workbook in the last 60 days. You can see anything typed into the cell, who did it, and when. If a cell has been changed multiple times, then Show Changes will show the complete history. You can roll back to any previous value.
- Version History shows you the last 25 versions of the workbook. In Excel Online, you can see the changes made in each version. You can restore back to an earlier version or save an earlier version as a copy.

Seeing who changed what with Show Changes

The Show Changes icon debuted in Excel Online in June of 2021. It opens a pane that shows all changes in the workbook for the last 60 days. Note that this includes changes made in Desktop Excel or mobile, even though the Show Changes icon is not yet available in those platforms.

Rather than showing all changes to all cells, you can right-click a cell or a range and choose Show Changes from the menu that appears. Although the Show Changes panel shows the history for a cell, you cannot use the panel to roll back to an earlier version. You can see that the answer used to be 42 and that Joe changed it, and you can decide to type 42 into the cell again.

Show Changes is only showing values typed into cells by a person. It does not track changes made by a VBA macro. It does not track changes to formula results. Say that you type 42 into A1 and then enter a formula of =2*A1 into C1. You then change the 42 in A1 to 17. Then change the 17 to 29. This will generate the following changes, as shown in Figure 28.22:

- Typing 42 into A1.
- Typing =2*A1 into C1.
- Typing 17 into A1.
- Typing 29 into A1.

There is no record of the fact that the formula in C1 changed from 84 to 34 to 58.

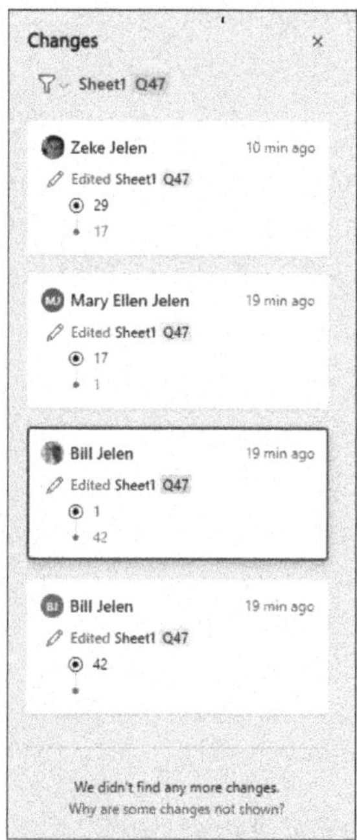

Figure 28.22 This value started as 42 and was changed to 1, 17, and 29 by various coworkers.

Show Changes also does not track changes to charts, shapes, or other objects. It does not track changes to pivot tables, formatting changes, filtering, or hidden cells.

If you delete a row or column, then Show Changes will lose all of the changes for those cells. Show Changes will show that column X was deleted, but not any of the changes that happened in column X.

CAUTION

As I write this chapter, Show Changes is in its infancy, and everyone thinks it is adorable. There are going to be problems with Show Changes revealing things that people did not want to be released. What if, in a fit of rage, you happen to type "My Manager is a Freaking Jerk!!!!" in a cell and then clear it out? For the next 59 days, this will become part of the history of the document. Currently, there is not a way to clear history. Microsoft is going to have to add that. In the meantime, you can wipe out all of the changes using either of these methods:

- **Edit the document from a perpetual version of Excel, such as Office 2019.**
- **Save A Copy will clear out all changes. You could choose Save A Copy, choose a new name, and then choose Save A Copy using the original name.**

Catching up

Excel Online offers a Catch Up button in the top right, as shown in Figure 28.23. This panel is supposed to show you all of the commenting and tasks that either @Mention you or are assigned to you. This feature is still new in 2021. It remains to be seen if it comes to Mobile and Desktop Excel and if it expands to include more information.

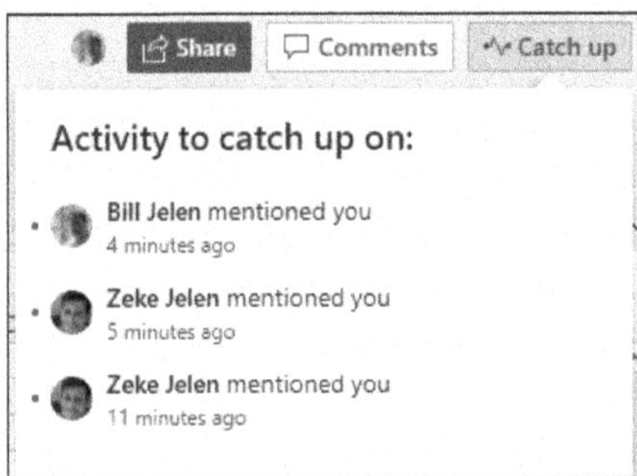

Figure 28.23 See who mentioned you while you were away from the workbook.

Rolling back using Version History

If your workbook is stored in the cloud, Microsoft keeps a version history of the workbook. Use File, Info, Version History for a list of available versions.

Excel Help says that it defaults to 25 versions, but this can be changed using your SharePoint Library Configuration.

The Version History pane is more robust in Excel Online. As shown in Figure 28.24, you can see who made edits in each version. This might be helpful if you had a rogue employee and you want to see which versions contain edits by that person.

When you select a version from the Version History pane and choose Show Changes, then you can scroll through the changes using the < and > icons. Figure 28.24 shows that 17 changes have been made in that version.

There are two choices as you are reviewing a previous version. If the current version of the workbook is simply rubbish, you can click Restore to bring this version back as the current version.

If, however, you need to rescue just a portion of this version, it is much harder. There is a Save Copy button. This will save the workbook with the same name. The only option is to choose a different folder.

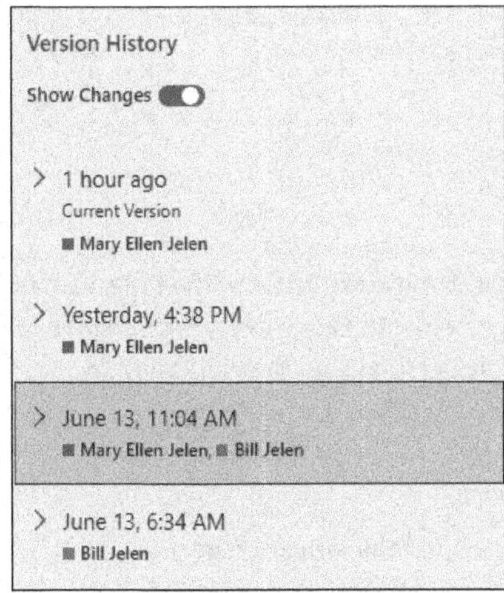

Figure 28.24 If your manager's manager completely trashed the workbook, you can roll back to a previous version.

You then will have to copy the good cells from the copy to a blank workbook. Close the copy. Open the original. Copy from the blank workbook to the original version. If there were unlimited resources on the Collaboration team at Microsoft, I would have dozens of ideas of how to streamline the task of taking one range from a previous version and bringing it forward. Ten years from now, this will all be perfect.

Figure 28.25 shows the Save A Copy and Restore buttons. Also, the outlines in the grid are used to show each change made in this version.

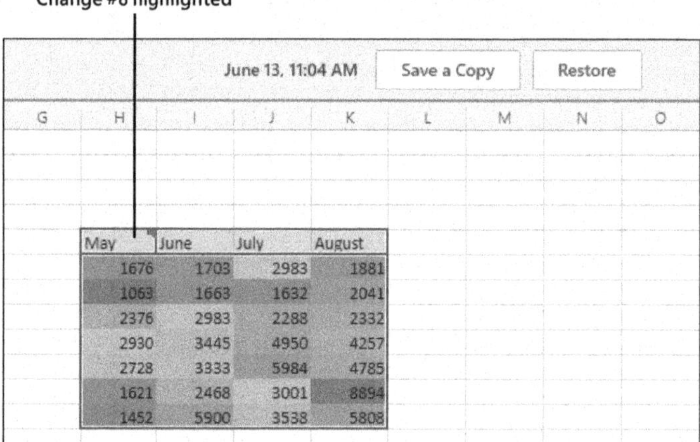

Figure 28.25 If you find a previous version without the problems introduced by your manager, you can restore that version to be the official version.

TROUBLESHOOTING

The Bad Side of AutoSave

In my work day, I very rarely need to share workbooks. Most of the time, I am not collaborating. AutoSave is great when everyone needs to see every change that you make, but AutoSave is horrible if you are the only person using the workbook.

How often do you do steps like this?

1. You need to create a February report.
2. Rather than start from nothing, you open the January report.
3. Then, you change the title.
4. You change the headings.
5. You clear out the January data.
6. Finally, you click File, Save As to save the workbook with "February" in the name.

With AutoSave, you destroy the January workbook after every step of the process.

Here's another scenario: You have a great forecast model. Your manager has a crazy idea and wants to see the impact on the profit if you do X. You know this idea will never work, but you need to give the manager the results. So, you open the forecast file, make the crazy changes, print, and then close the workbook without saving. This ability to close the workbook without saving is gone with AutoSave. Every change gets saved automatically.

In 99.5 percent of the cases, AutoSave is really bad. If you regularly save your workbooks to OneDrive, AutoSave will be enabled by default. The Excel MVPs complained loudly to the Excel team on your behalf, and we were able to get a setting added to Excel Options. Choose File, Options, Save, and unselect AutoSave OneDrive and SharePoint Online Files By Default On Excel, as shown in the following figure:

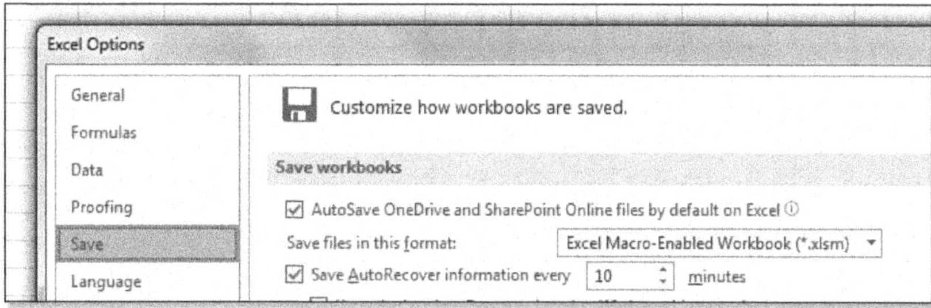

PART V

Appendixes

APPENDIX A

Excel functions

This appendix provides the argument lists and a short description of each of Excel's functions. It is presented in the same order that the function categories appear on the Formulas tab in the Ribbon.

The final table is an alphabetical cross-reference, showing where each function can be found.

> NOTE
>
> **I am frequently asked "How many functions are in Excel?" For this edition of the book, there are 510 functions documented by Microsoft. I will concede that most people won't have all 510 functions. For example, you are likely to only have `MID` or `MIDB` depending on your language. Also, a few functions documented by Microsoft require you to enable certain add-ins. Finally, almost all of the functions in the Compatibility category have an identical function in another category, and some may argue these should not be counted. However, over the years, my answer to the question includes all the functions listed here, so when asked, I will be quoting 510 functions. Until next Tuesday, when the Excel team will undoubtedly add a few more!**

Financial functions in Excel

Although the bulk of Excel's financial functions are for professional financiers and investors, a few functions are useful for anyone planning to use a loan to purchase a car or house.

Table A.1 provides an alphabetical list of the Financial functions in Excel. In this table, the `STOCKHISTORY` function is new since the previous edition of this book.

Table A.1 Alphabetical list of financial functions

Function	Description
ACCRINT(*issue, first_interest, settlement, rate, par, frequency, basis, calc method*)	Returns the accrued interest for a security settlement that pays periodic interest.
ACCRINTM(*issue, settlement, rate, par, basis*)	Returns the accrued interest for a security that pays interest at maturity.
AMORDEGRC(*cost, date_purchased, first_period, salvage, period, rate, basis*)	Returns the depreciation for each accounting period. This function is provided for the French accounting system. If an asset is purchased in the middle of the accounting period, the prorated depreciation is taken into account. The function is similar to AMORLINC, except that a depreciation coefficient is applied in the calculation, depending on the life of the assets.
AMORLINC(*cost, date_purchased, first_period, salvage, period, rate, basis*)	Returns the depreciation for each accounting period. This function is provided for the French accounting system. If an asset is purchased in the middle of the accounting period, the prorated depreciation is taken into account.
COUPDAYBS(*settlement, maturity, frequency, basis*)	Returns the number of days from the beginning of the coupon period to the settlement date.
COUPDAYS(*settlement, maturity, frequency, basis*)	Returns the number of days in the coupon period that contains the settlement date.
COUPDAYSNC(*settlement, maturity, frequency, basis*)	Returns the number of days from the settlement date to the next coupon date.
COUPNCD(*settlement, maturity, frequency, basis*)	Returns a number that represents the next coupon date after the settlement date. To view the number as a date, you select Date in the Number Format drop-down menu on the Home tab.
COUPNUM(*settlement, maturity, frequency, basis*)	Returns the number of coupons payable between the settlement date and maturity date, rounded up to the nearest whole coupon.
COUPPCD(*settlement, maturity, frequency, basis*)	Returns a number that represents the previous coupon date before the settlement date. To view the number as a date, choose a date from the Number Format drop-down menu on the home tab.
CUMIPMT(*rate, nper, pv, start_period, end_period, type*)	Returns the cumulative interest paid on a loan between *start_period* and *end_period*.
CUMPRINC(*rate, nper, pv, start_period, end_period, type*)	Returns the cumulative principal paid on a loan between *start_period* and *end_period*.

`DB(cost, salvage, life, period, month)`	Returns the depreciation of an asset for a specified period, using the fixed-declining balance method.
`DDB(cost, salvage, life, period, factor)`	Returns the depreciation of an asset for a specified period, using the double-declining-balance method or some other specified method.
`DISC(settlement, maturity, pr, redemption, basis)`	Returns the discount rate for a security.
`DOLLARDE(fractional_dollar, fraction)`	Converts a dollar price expressed as a fraction into a dollar price expressed as a decimal number. Use DOLLARDE to convert fractional dollar numbers, such as securities prices, to decimal numbers.
`DOLLARFR(decimal_dollar, fraction)`	Converts a dollar price expressed as a decimal number into a dollar price expressed as a fraction. Use DOLLARFR to convert decimal numbers to fractional dollar numbers, such as securities prices.
`DURATION(settlement, maturity, coupon yld, frequency, basis)`	Returns the Macaulay duration for an assumed par value of $100. The duration is defined as the weighted average of the present value of the cash flows and is used as a measure of a bond price's response to changes in yield.
`EFFECT(nominal_rate, npery)`	Returns the effective annual interest rate, given the nominal annual interest rate and the number of compounding periods per year.
`FV(rate, nper, pmt, pv, type)`	Returns the future value of an investment, based on periodic, constant payments and a constant interest rate.
`FVSCHEDULE(principal, schedule)`	Returns the future value of an initial principal after applying a series of compound interest rates. Use FVSCHEDULE to calculate the future value of an investment with a variable or adjustable rate.
`INTRATE(settlement, maturity, investment, redemption, basis)`	Returns the interest rate for a fully invested security.
`IPMT(rate, per, nper, pv, fv, type)`	Returns the interest payment for a given period for an investment, based on periodic, constant payments and a constant interest rate. For a more complete description of the arguments in IPMT and more information about annuity functions, see PV.
`IRR(values, guess)`	Returns the internal rate of return for a series of cash flows represented by the numbers in values. These cash flows do not have to be even, as they would be for an annuity. However, the cash flows must occur at regular intervals, such as monthly or annually. The internal rate of return is the interest rate received for an investment consisting of payments (negative values) and income (positive values) that occur at regular periods.

`ISPMT(rate, per, nper, pv)`	Calculates the interest paid during a specific period of an investment. This function is provided for compatibility with Lotus 1-2-3.
`MDURATION(settlement, maturity, coupon, yld, frequency, basis)`	Returns the modified duration for a security coupon with an assumed par value of $100.
`MIRR(values, finance_rate, reinvest_rate)`	Returns the modified internal rate of return for a series of periodic cash flows. `MIRR` considers both the cost of the investment and the interest received on reinvestment of cash.
`NOMINAL(effect_rate, npery)`	Returns the nominal annual interest rate, given the effective rate and the number of compounding periods per year.
`NPER(rate, pmt, pv, fv, type)`	Returns the number of periods for an investment, based on periodic, constant payments and a constant interest rate.
`NPV(rate, value1, value2, ...)`	Calculates the net present value of an investment by using a discount rate and a series of future payments (negative values) and income (positive values).
`ODDFPRICE(settlement, maturity, issue, first_coupon, rate, yld, redemption, frequency, basis)`	Returns the price per $100 face value of a security having an odd (short or long) first period.
`ODDFYIELD(settlement, maturity, issue, first_coupon, rate, pr, redemption, frequency, basis)`	Returns the yield of a security that has an odd (short or long) first period.
`ODDLPRICE(settlement, maturity, last_interest, rate, yld, redemption, frequency, basis)`	Returns the price per $100 face value of a security having an odd (short or long) last coupon period.
`ODDLYIELD(settlement, maturity, last_interest, rate, pr, redemption, frequency, basis)`	Returns the yield of a security that has an odd (short or long) last period.
`PDURATION(rate, pv, fv)`	Returns the number of periods required by an investment to reach a specified value.
`PMT(rate, nper, pv, fv, type)`	Calculates the payment for a loan based on constant payments and a constant interest rate.
`PPMT(rate, per, nper, pv, fv, type)`	Returns the payment on the principal for a given period for an investment based on periodic, constant payments and a constant interest rate.
`PRICE(settlement, maturity, rate, yld, redemption, frequency, basis)`	Returns the price per $100 face value of a security that pays periodic interest.

PRICEDISC(*settlement, maturity, discount, redemption, basis*)	Returns the price per $100 face value of a discounted security.
PRICEMAT(*settlement, maturity, issue, rate, yld, basis*)	Returns the price per $100 face value of an issue security that pays interest at maturity.
PV(*rate, nper, pmt, fv, type*)	Returns the present value of an investment. The present value is the total amount that a series of future payments is worth now. For example, when you borrow money, the loan amount is the present value to the lender.
RATE(*nper, pmt, pv, fv, type, guess*)	Returns the interest rate per period of an annuity. RATE is calculated by iteration and can have zero or more solutions. If the successive results of RATE do not converge to within 0.0000001 after 20 iterations, RATE returns a NUM! error.
RECEIVED(*settlement, maturity, investment, discount, basis*)	Returns the amount received at maturity for a fully invested security.
RRI(*nper, pv, fv*)	Returns an equivalent interest rate for the growth of an investment.
SLN(*cost, salvage, life*)	Returns the straight-line depreciation of an asset for one period.
STOCKHISTORY(*stock, start_date, end_date, interval, headers, properties1,...*)	Returns an array of historical quote data for a date range and symbol you specify.
SYD(*cost, salvage, life, per*)	Returns the sum-of-years'-digits depreciation of an asset for a specified period.
TBILLEQ(*settlement, maturity, discount*)	Returns the bond-equivalent yield for a Treasury bill (T-bill).
TBILLPRICE(*settlement, maturity, discount*)	Returns the price per $100 face value for a T-bill.
TBILLYIELD(*settlement, maturity, pr*)	Returns the yield for a T-bill.
VDB(*cost, salvage, life, start_period, end_period, factor, no_switch*)	Returns the depreciation of an asset for any specified period, including partial periods, using the double-declining-balance method or some other specified method. VDB stands for variable declining balance.
XIRR(*values, dates, guess*)	Returns the internal rate of return for a schedule of cash flows that is not necessarily periodic. To calculate the internal rate of return for a series of periodic cash flows, use the IRR function.

APPENDIX A

XNPV(*rate, values, dates*)	Returns the net present value for a schedule of cash flows that is not necessarily periodic. To calculate the net present value for a series of cash flows that is periodic, use the NPV function.
YIELD(*settlement, maturity, rate, pr, redemption, frequency, basis*)	Returns the yield on a security that pays periodic interest. You use YIELD to calculate bond yield.
YIELDDISC(*settlement, maturity, pr, redemption, basis*)	Returns the annual yield for a discounted security.
YIELDMAT(*settlement, maturity, issue, rate, pr, basis*)	Returns the annual yield of a security that pays interest at maturity.

Logical functions in Excel

Table A.2 provides an alphabetical list of all the logical functions in Excel. Examples of these functions are provided in Chapter 9.

Table A.2 Alphabetical list of logical functions

Function	Description
AND(*logical1, logical2,...*)	Returns TRUE if all its arguments are TRUE; returns FALSE if one or more arguments are FALSE.
FALSE()	Returns the logical value FALSE. This function is useless, considering that typing FALSE without the parentheses returns the same value.
IF(*logical_test, value_if_true, value_if_false*)	Returns one value if a condition specified evaluates to TRUE and another value if it evaluates to FALSE.
IFERROR(*value, value_if_error*)	Returns value_if_error if the expression is an error; otherwise, returns the value itself.
IFNA(*value, value_if_na*)	Returns value_if_na if the expression resolves to #N/A; otherwise, returns the result of the expression.
IFS(*logical_test1, value_if_true1, logical_test2, value_if_true2...*)	Checks whether one or more conditions are met and returns a value corresponding to the first TRUE condition.
NOT(*logical*)	Reverses the value of its argument. You use NOT when you want to make sure a value is not equal to another particular value.
OR(*logical1, logical2,...*)	Returns TRUE if any argument is TRUE; returns FALSE if all arguments are FALSE.

SWITCH(*Expression, Value1, Result1, Default_or_value2, Result2...*)	Evaluates an expression against a list of values and returns the result corresponding to the first matching value. If there is no match, an optional default value is returned.
TRUE()	Returns the logical value TRUE. Equivalent to typing **TRUE**.
XOR(*Logical1, Logical2,...*)	Returns the logical Exclusive Or of the arguments. However, to be compatible with an XOR chip frequently used in electrical engineering, this function actually measures if an odd number of arguments are TRUE. People who don't make their living designing electrical circuits will wonder why =XOR(True,True,True) is True.

Text functions

Table A.3 provides an alphabetical list of the text functions in Excel. Detailed examples of these functions are in Chapter 8.

Some of these text functions have equivalent functions for use in languages that use double-byte characters. Those are listed in Table A.4.

In this section, ARRAYTOTEXT, LAMBDA, and VALUETOTEXT are new since the previous edition.

Table A.3 Alphabetical list of text functions

Function	Description
ARRAYTOTEXT(*array, format*)	Returns a text representation of an array. Introduced to allow Wolfram data types to present an array of information in a single cell.
ASC(*text*)	Changes full-width (double-byte) English letters or katakana within a character string to half-width (single-byte) characters.
BAHTTEXT(*number*)	Converts a number to Thai text and adds the suffix Baht.
CHAR(*number*)	Returns the character specified by number. You use CHAR to translate code page numbers you might get from files on other types of computers into characters. See also UNICHAR.
CLEAN(*text*)	Removes all nonprintable characters from text. You use CLEAN on text imported from other applications that contains characters that might not print with your operating system. For example, you can use CLEAN to remove some low-level computer code that frequently appears at the beginning and end of data files and cannot be printed.

APPENDIX A

CODE(*text*)	Returns a numeric code for the first character in a text string. The returned code corresponds to the character set used by your computer. See also UNICODE.
CONCAT(*Text1, Text2...*)	Concatenates a list or range of text strings.
DOLLAR(*number, decimals*)	Converts a number to text using currency format, with the decimals rounded to the specified place. The format used is `$#,##0.00_);($#,##0.00)`.
EXACT(*text1, text2*)	Compares two text strings and returns TRUE if they are the same and FALSE otherwise. EXACT is case-sensitive but ignores formatting differences. You use EXACT to test text being entered into a document.
FIND(*find_text, within_text, start_num*)	Finds one text string (`find_text`) within another text string (`within_text`) and returns the number of the starting position of `find_text`, from the first character of `within_text`. You can also use SEARCH to find one text string within another, but unlike SEARCH, FIND is case sensitive and doesn't allow wildcard characters.
FIXED(*number, decimals, no_commas*)	Rounds a number to the specified number of decimals, formats the number in decimal format using a period and commas, and returns the result as text.
LAMBDA(*parameter_or_calculation,...*)	Creates a function value, which can be called from within formulas.
LEFT(*text, num_chars*)	Returns the first character or characters in a text string, based on the number of characters specified.
LEN(*text*)	Returns the number of characters in a text string.
LOWER(*text*)	Converts all uppercase letters in a text string to lowercase.
MID(*text, start_num, num_chars*)	Returns a specific number of characters from a text string, starting at the position specified, based on the number of characters specified.
NUMBERVALUE(*text, decimal_separator, group_separator*)	Converts text to a number, allowing for different punctuation for thousands separators and decimal separators.
PROPER(*text*)	Capitalizes the first letter in a text string and any other letters in text that follow any character other than a letter. Converts all other letters to lowercase.
REPLACE(*old_text, start_num, num_chars, new_text*)	Replaces part of a text string, based on the number of characters specified, with a different text string.
REPT(*text, number_times*)	Repeats text a given number of times. You use REPT to fill a cell with some instances of a text string.
RIGHT(*text, num_chars*)	Returns the last character or characters in a text string, based on the number of characters specified.

SEARCH(*find_text, within_text, start_num*)	Returns the number of the character at another a specific character or text string is first found, beginning with `start_num`. You use SEARCH to determine the location of a character or text string within another text string so that you can use the MID or REPLACE function to change the text.
SUBSTITUTE(*text, old_text, new_text, instance_num*)	Substitutes `new_text` for `old_text` in a text string. You use SUBSTITUTE when you want to replace specific text in a text string; you use REPLACE when you want to replace any text that occurs in a specific location in a text string.
T(*value*)	Returns the text referred to by value.
TEXT(*value, format_text*)	Converts a value to text in a specific number format.
TEXTAFTER(*within_text, find_text, instance_num, ignore_case]*)	Returns the text that appears after the `find_text`. There are options to specify the `instance_num` and request a case insensitive match. If a negative number is provided for the `instance_num`, it will index from the end of the text, which would allow you to find all text after the last comma, for example.
TEXTBEFORE(*within_text, find_text, [instance_num], [ignore_case]*)	Returns the text that appears before the `find_text`. The same options that apply to TEXTAFTER are available for TEXTBEFORE.
TEXTJOIN(*delimiter, ignore_empty, text1, text2...*)	Concatenates a list of range of text strings using a delimiter.
TEXTSPLIT(*input_text, col_delimiter, row_delimiter, ignore_empty*)	Splits the `input text` based on a row and/or column delimiter. You can also specify whether empty elements should be suppressed. Multiple delimiters can be provided as an array.
TRIM(*text*)	Removes all spaces from text except for single spaces between words. You use TRIM on text that you have received from another application that might have irregular spacing.
UNICHAR(*number*)	Returns the Unicode character references by the given number.
UNICODE(*text*)	Returns the number (code point) of the first character of the text.
UPPER(*text*)	Converts text to uppercase.
VALUE(*text*)	Converts a text string that represents a number to a number.
VALUETOTEXT(*value, format*)	Returns text from any specified value

Text functions for double-byte languages

Table A.4 provides an alphabetical list of the double-byte text functions in Excel. If you are using an English-language version of Excel, these functions will not appear in the function icon drop-down menus.

Table A.4 Alphabetical list of double-byte text functions

Function	Description
DBCS(*text*)	Changes half-width (single-byte) English letters or katakana within a character string to full-width (double-byte) characters
FINDB(*find_text*, *within_text*, *start_num*)	Finds one text string (*find_text*) within another text string (*within_text*) and returns the number of the starting position of *find_text*, based on the number of bytes each character uses, from the first character of *within_text*. You use FINDB with double-byte characters. You can also use SEARCHB to find one text string within another.
JIS(*text*)	Changes half-width (single-byte) characters within a string to full-width (double-byte) characters
LEFTB(*text*, *num_bytes*)	Returns the first character or characters in a text string, based on the number of bytes specified. You use LEFTB with double-byte characters.
LENB(*text*)	Returns the number of bytes used to represent the characters in a text string. You use LENB with double-byte characters.
MIDB(*text*, *start_num*, *num_bytes*)	Returns a specific number of characters from a text string, starting at the position specified, based on the number of bytes specified. You use MIDB with double-byte characters.
PHONETIC(*reference*)	Extracts the phonetic (furigana) characters from a text string. Furigana are a Japanese reading aid. They consist of smaller kana printed next to a kanji to indicate its pronunciation.
REPLACEB(*old_text*, *start_num*, *num_bytes*, *new_text*)	Replaces part of a text string, based on the number of bytes specified, with a different text string. You use REPLACEB with double-byte characters.
RIGHTB(*text*, *num_bytes*)	Returns the last character or characters in a text string, based on the number of bytes specified. You use RIGHTB with double-byte characters.
SEARCHB(*FIND_TEXT*, *WITHIN_TEXT*, *START_NUM*)	Finds one text string (*find_text*) within another text string (*within_text*) and returns the number of the starting position of *find_text*. The result is based on the number of bytes each character uses, beginning with *start_num*. You use SEARCHB with double-byte characters. You can also use FINDB to find one text string within another.

APPENDIX A

Date and time functions

Table A.5 provides an alphabetical list of the date and time functions in Excel. Detailed examples of these functions are provided in Chapter 8.

Table A.5 Alphabetical list of date and time functions

Function	Description
DATE(*year, month, day*)	Returns the formatted serial number that represents a particular date.
DATEDIF(*start_date, end_date, unit*)	Calculates the number of days, months, or years between two dates. This function is provided for compatibility with Lotus 1-2-3. Note that DATEDIF is not shown in the Date & Time drop-down menu.
DATEVALUE(*date_text*)	Returns the serial number of the date represented by date_text. You use DATEVALUE to convert a date represented by text to a serial number.
DAY(*serial_number*)	Returns the day of a date, represented by a serial number. The day is given as an integer ranging from 1 to 31.
DAYS(*end_date, start_date*)	Calculates the difference in days between two dates. Works even if one or both dates are stored as text instead of as a date.
DAYS360(*start_date, end_date, method*)	Returns the number of days between two dates, based on a 360-day year (that is, twelve 30-day months), which is used in some accounting calculations. You use this function to help compute payments if your accounting system is based on twelve 30-day months.
EDATE(*start_date, months*)	Returns the serial number that represents the date that is the indicated number of months before or after a specified date (that is, the *start_date*). You use EDATE to calculate maturity dates or due dates that fall on the same day of the month as the date of issue.
EOMONTH(*start_date, months*)	Returns the serial number for the last day of the month that is the indicated number of months before or after *start_date*. You use EOMONTH to calculate maturity dates or due dates that fall on the last day of the month.
HOUR(*serial_number*)	Returns the hour of a time value. The hour is given as an integer, ranging from 0 (12:00 a.m.) to 23 (11:00 p.m.).
ISOWEEKNUM(*date*)	Returns the ISO week number of the given date.
MINUTE(*serial_number*)	Returns the minutes of a time value. The minutes are given as an integer, ranging from 0 to 59.
MONTH(*serial_number*)	Returns the month of a date represented by a serial number. The month is given as an integer, ranging from 1 (for January) to 12 (for December).

NETWORKDAYS(*start_date, end_date, holidays*)	Returns the number of whole working days between *start_date* and *end_date*. Working days exclude weekends and any dates identified in holidays. You use NETWORKDAYS to calculate employee benefits that accrue based on the number of days worked during a specific term. Weekdays are defined as Saturday and Sunday. To handle other calendars, see NETWORKDAYS.INTL.
NETWORKDAYS.INTL(*start_date, end_date, weekend, holidays*)	Returns the number of whole working days between the *start_date* and the *end_date*. Added in Excel 2010 to support calendars in which the weekend is a pair of days other than Saturday and Sunday.
NOW()	Returns the serial number of the current date and time.
SECOND(*serial_number*)	Returns the seconds of a time value. The seconds are given as an integer in the range 0 to 59.
TIME(*hour, minute, second*)	Returns the decimal number for a particular time. The decimal number returned by TIME is a value ranging from 0 to 0.99999999, representing the times from 0:00:00 (12:00:00 a.m.) to 23:59:59 (11:59:59 p.m.).
TIMEVALUE(*time_text*)	Returns the decimal number of the time represented by a text string. The decimal number is a value ranging from 0 to 0.99999999, representing the times from 0:00:00 (12:00:00 a.m.) to 23:59:59 (11:59:59 p.m.).
TODAY()	Returns the serial number of the current date. The serial number is the date/time code that Microsoft Excel uses for date and time calculations.
WEEKDAY(*serial_number, return_type*)	Returns the day of the week corresponding to a date. The day is given as an integer, ranging from 1 (for Sunday) to 7 (for Saturday), by default.
WEEKNUM(*serial_num, return_type*)	Returns a number that indicates where the week falls numerically within a year. See also ISOWEEKNUM.
WORKDAY(*start_date, days, holidays*)	Returns a number that represents a date that is the indicated number of working days before or after a date (the starting date). Working days exclude weekends and any dates identified as holidays. You use WORKDAY to exclude weekends and holidays when you calculate invoice due dates, expected delivery times, or the number of days of work performed. To view the number as a date, format the cell as a date. Weekends are defined as Saturday and Sunday. For alternative calendars, see WORKDAY.INTL.
WORKDAY.INTL(*start_date, days, weekend, holidays*)	Returns a number that represents a date that is the indicated number of working days before or after a starting date. Added to Excel 2010 to accommodate calendar systems where the weekend is a pair of days other than Saturday and Sunday.

YEAR(*serial_number*)	Returns the year corresponding to a date. The year is returned as an integer in the range 1900 through 9999.
YEARFRAC(*start_date, end_date, basis*)	Calculates the fraction of the year represented by the number of whole days between two dates (*start_date* and *end_date*). You use the YEARFRAC worksheet function to identify the proportion of a whole year's benefits or obligations to assign to a specific term.

Lookup and reference functions

Table A.6 provides an alphabetical list of the lookup and reference functions in Excel. Detailed examples of these functions are provided in Chapter 9. In this table, FIELDVALUE, XLOOKUP, and XMATCH are new since the previous edition. The SINGLE function, which was in the previous edition, has been replaced with the @ operator. See the discussion of implicit intersection in Chapter 6.

Table A.6 Alphabetical list of lookup and reference functions

Function	Description
ADDRESS(*row_num, column_num, abs_num, a1, sheet_text*)	Creates a cell address as text, given specified row and column numbers.
AREAS(*reference*)	Returns the number of areas in a reference. An area is a range of contiguous cells or a single cell.
CHOOSE(*index_num, value1, value2,...*)	Uses *index_num* to return a value from the list of value arguments. You use CHOOSE to select one of up to 254 values, based on the index number. For example, if *value1* through *value7* are the days of the week, CHOOSE returns one of the days when a number between 1 and 7 is used as *index_num*.
CHOOSECOLS(*array, col_num1, col_num2, ...*)	Returns the requested columns from an array based on the column number. Use negative numbers to count from the right side of the array. For example, =CHOOSECOLS(A#,1,-1) would return the first and last columns from an array.
CHOOSEROWS(*array, row_num1, row_num2, ...*)	Returns the requested rows from an array based on the row number.
COLUMNS(*array*)	Returns the number of columns in an array or a reference.
FIELDVALUE(*value, fieldname*)	Extracts a value from a field of a given record. Used with cells that contain data types.
FILTER(*Array,Include, If_Empty*)	Filter a range or array. Office 365 exclusive.

FORMULATEXT(*reference*)	Returns a formula as a string.
GETPIVOTDATA(*data_field, pivot_table, field1, item1,...*)	Returns data stored in a pivot table report. You can use GETPIVOTDATA to retrieve summary data from a pivot table report if the summary data is visible in the report.
HSTACK(*array1, array2, ...*)	Stacks multiple arrays horizontally. Missing cells are filled with #N/A.
HLOOKUP(*lookup_value, table_array, row_index_num, range_lookup*)	Searches for a value in the top row of a table or an array of values, and then returns a value in the same column from a row you specify in the table or array. You use HLOOKUP when your comparison values are located in a row across the top of a table of data, and you want to look down a specified number of rows. You use VLOOKUP when your comparison values are located in a column to the left of the data you want to find.
HYPERLINK(*link_location, friendly_name*)	Creates a shortcut or jump that opens a document stored on a network server, an intranet, or the Internet. When you click the cell that contains the HYPERLINK function, Excel opens the file stored at *link_location*.
INDEX(*array, row_num, column_num*)	Returns the value of a specified cell or array of cells within the array.
INDEX(*reference, row_num, column_num, area_num*)	Returns a reference to a specified cell or cells within the reference.
INDIRECT(*ref_text, a1*)	Returns the reference specified by a text string. References are evaluated immediately to display their contents. You use INDIRECT when you want to change the reference to a cell within a formula without changing the formula itself.
LOOKUP(*lookup_value, lookup_vector, result_vector*)	Returns a value from either a one-row or one-column range. This vector form of LOOKUP looks in a one-row or one-column range, known as a vector, for a value and returns a value from the same position in a second one-row or one-column range. This function is included for compatibility with other worksheets. You should use VLOOKUP instead.
LOOKUP(*lookup_value, array*)	Returns a value from an array. The array form of LOOKUP looks in the first row or column of an array for the specified value and returns a value from the same position in the last row or column of the array. This function is included for compatibility with other spreadsheet programs. You should use VLOOKUP instead. However, unlike VLOOKUP, the LOOKUP function can process an array of *lookup_values*.

`MATCH(lookup_value, lookup_array, match_type)`	Returns the relative position of an item in an array that matches a specified value in a specified order. You use `MATCH` instead of one of the `LOOKUP` functions when you need the position of an item in a range instead of the item itself.
`OFFSET(reference, rows, cols, height, width)`	Returns a reference to a range that is a specified number of rows and columns away from a cell or range of cells. The reference that is returned can be a single cell or a range of cells. You can specify the number of rows and the number of columns to be returned.
`ROW(reference)`	Returns the row number of a reference.
`ROWS(array)`	Returns the number of rows in a reference or an array.
`RTD(progid, server, topic, topic2, ...)`	Retrieves real-time data from a program that supports COM automation.
`SORT(Array,Sort_index, Sort_order,By_col)`	Sorts a range or array. Office 365 exclusive.
`SORTBY(Array, by_array1, sort_order1, ...)`	Sorts a range or array based on the values in a corresponding range or array. Office 365 exclusive.
`TOCOL(array, ignore, scan_by_column)`	Converts a 2D array into a single column. The optional *ignore* argument can be used to ignore error values and/or blank. By default, the new column would contain all of the values in the first row, then second row, and so on. Set *scan_by_column* to `TRUE` in order to have the column 2 values begin below the column 1 values.
`TOROW(array, ignore, scan_by_column)`	Converts a 2D array into a single row. The same options as in `TOCOL` apply.
`TRANSPOSE(array)`	Returns a vertical range of cells as a horizontal range, or vice versa. You use `TRANSPOSE` to shift the vertical and horizontal orientation of a range on a worksheet. For example, some functions, such as `LINEST`, return horizontal arrays. `LINEST` returns a horizontal array of the slope and y-intercept for a line. Use `TRANSPOSE` to convert the `LINEST` result to a vertical array.
`UNIQUE(array, by_col, occurs_once)`	Returns the unique values from a range or array. Office 365 exclusive.
`VECTORWRAP(vector, wrap_count, pad_with)`	Converts a single row or column into a 2D array by wrapping it based on the number of rows specified in *wrap_count*.
`VLOOKUP(lookup_value, table_array, col_index_num, range_lookup)`	Searches for a value in the leftmost column of a table and then returns a value in the same row from a column you specify in the table. You use `VLOOKUP` instead of `HLOOKUP` when your comparison values are located in a column to the left of the data you want to find.

APPENDIX A

VSTACK(*array1, array2, ...*)	Stacks multiple arrays vertically. Missing cells are filled with #N/A.
XLOOKUP(*lookup_value, lookup_array, return_array, if_not_found, match_mode, search_mode*)	Searches a range or an array for a match and returns the corresponding item from a second range or array. By default, an exact match is used.
XMATCH(*lookup_value, lookup_array, match_mode, search_mode*)	Returns the relative position of an item in an array. By default, an exact match is used.

Math and trig functions

Table A.7 provides an alphabetical list of the math and trig functions in Excel This large category includes matrix functions. Detailed examples of these functions are provided in Chapter 8.

Table A.7 Alphabetical list of math and trig functions

Function	Description
ABS(*number*)	Returns the absolute value of a number. The absolute value of a number is the number without its sign.
ACOS(*number*)	Returns the arccosine of a number. The arccosine is the angle whose cosine is *number*. The returned angle is given in radians in the range 0 to π.
ACOSH(*number*)	Returns the inverse hyperbolic cosine of a *number*, which must be greater than or equal to 1. The inverse hyperbolic cosine is the value whose hyperbolic cosine is *number*, so ACOSH(COSH(number)) equals number.
ACOT(*number*)	Returns the arccotangent of a number in radians, in the range of 0 to π.
ACOTH(*number*)	Returns the inverse hyperbolic cotangent of a number.
AGGREGATE(*function, options, array, k*)	Performs one of 17 functions with the capability to ignore error values, other subtotals, or rows hidden by a filter.
ARABIC(*text*)	Converts a Roman numeral to Arabic.
ASIN(*number*)	Returns the arcsine of a number. The arcsine is the angle whose sine is *number*. The returned angle is given in radians in the range –π / 2 to π / 2.
ASINH(*number*)	Returns the inverse hyperbolic sine of a number. The inverse hyperbolic sine is the value whose hyperbolic sine is *number*, so ASINH(SINH(number)) equals *number*.
ATAN(*number*)	Returns the arctangent of a number. The arctangent is the angle whose tangent is *number*. The returned angle is given in radians in the range –π / 2 to π / 2.

APPENDIX A

ATAN2(*x_num, y_num*)	Returns the arctangent of the specified x- and y-coordinates. The arctangent is the angle from the x-axis to a line containing the origin (0, 0) and a point with coordinates (*x_num, y_num*). The angle is given in radians between –π and π, excluding –π.
ATANH(*number*)	Returns the inverse hyperbolic tangent of a number. *number* must be between –1 and 1 (excluding *–1 and 1)*. The inverse hyperbolic tangent is the value whose hyperbolic tangent is *number*, so ATANH(TANH(number)) equals number.
BASE(*number, radix, min_length*)	Converts a number into a text representation with the given radix (base).
BYCOL(*array, function)*	Applies a LAMBDA to each column and returns an array of the results.
BYROL(*array, function)*	Applies a LAMBDA to each row and returns an array of the results.
CEILING.MATH(*number, significance,mode*)	Rounds a number up to the nearest multiple of significance. (Before Excel 2013, this function was named CEILING.PRECISE.) Provides compatibility with the ISO standard for computing the ceiling of a negative number.
COMBIN(*number,number_ chosen*)	Returns the number of combinations for a given number of items. You use COMBIN to determine the total possible number of groups for a given number of items.
COMBINA(*number,number_chosen*)	Returns the number of combinations with repetitions for a given number of items.
COS(*number*)	Returns the cosine of the given angle.
COSH(*number*)	Returns the hyperbolic cosine of a number.
COT(*number*)	Returns the cotangent of an angle.
COTH(*number*)	Returns the hyperbolic cotangent of a number.
CSC(*number*)	Returns the cosecant of a number.
CSCH(*number*)	Returns the hyperbolic cosecant of a number.
DECIMAL(*number, radix*)	Converts a text representation of a number with a given base into a decimal number.
DEGREES(*angle*)	Converts radians into degrees.
EVEN(*number*)	Returns the number rounded up to the nearest even integer. You can use this function for processing items that come in twos. For example, suppose a packing crate accepts rows of one or two items. The crate is full when the number of items, rounded up to the nearest two, matches the crate's capacity.

EXP(*number*)	Returns e raised to the power of a number. The constant e equals 2.718281828459045..., the base of the natural logarithm. Note that Excel 2016 began returning a 16th digit of precision, potentially causing different answers from Excel 2013.
FACT(*number*)	Returns the factorial of a number. The factorial of a number is equal to 1x2x3x...x*number*.
FACTDOUBLE(*number*)	Returns the double factorial of a number.
FLOOR.MATH(*number*, *significance*,*mode*)	Rounds the number down to the nearest multiple of significance. (Before Excel 2013, this function was known as FLOOR.PRECISE.) Differs from FLOOR when you have negative numbers. Whereas FLOOR(-1.2,-1) rounds toward zero to produce –1, the new FLOOR.MATH(-1.2, -1) rounds to the lower number, which is –2.
GCD(*number1*,*number2*,...)	Returns the greatest common divisor of two or more integers. The greatest common divisor is the largest integer that divides each number without a remainder.
INT(*number*)	Rounds a number down to the nearest integer.
LCM(*number1*,*number2*,...)	Returns the least common multiple of integers. The least common multiple is the smallest positive integer that is a multiple of all integer arguments *number1*, *number2*, and so on. You use LCM to add fractions that have different denominators.
LET(*name1*,*name_value1*,*calculation_or_name2*,*name_value2*,...)	Assigns names to calculation results to allow storing intermediate calculations, values, or defining names inside a formula
LN(*number*)	Returns the natural logarithm of *number*. Natural logarithms are based on the constant e (2.71828182845904...).
LOG(*number*, *base*)	Returns the logarithm of *number* to the specified base.
LOG10(*number*)	Returns the base-10 logarithm of *number*.
MAKEARRAY(*rows*, *columns*, *function*)	Returns a calculated array of a specified row and column size by applying a LAMBDA.
MAP(*array1*, *[array2...]*, *function*)	Returns an array formed by mapping each value in the array(s) to a new value by applying a LAMBDA to create a new value.
MDETERM(*array*)	Returns the matrix determinant of an array.
MINVERSE(*array*)	Returns the inverse matrix for the matrix stored in an array.
MMULT(*array1*, *array2*)	Returns the matrix product of two arrays. The result is an array with the same number of rows as *array1* and the same number of columns as *array2*.

MOD(*number*,*divisor*)	Returns the remainder after a number is divided by the divisor. The result has the same sign as the divisor.
MROUND(*number*,*multiple*)	Returns a number rounded to the desired multiple.
MULTINOMIAL(*number1*, *number2*,...)	Returns the ratio of the factorial of a sum of values to the product of factorials.
MUNIT(*dimension*)	Returns the unit matrix for the specified dimension.
ODD(*number*)	Returns a number rounded up to the nearest odd integer.
PI()	Returns the number 3.14159265358979, the mathematical constant pi, accurate to 15 digits.
POWER(*number*, *power*)	Returns the result of a number raised to a power.
PRODUCT(*number1*, *number2*,...)	Multiplies all the numbers given as arguments and returns the product.
QUOTIENT(*numerator*, *denominator*)	Returns the integer portion of a division operation. You use this function when you want to discard the remainder of a division.
RADIANS(*angle*)	Converts degrees to radians.
RAND()	Returns an evenly distributed random number greater than or equal to 0 and less than 1. A new random number is returned every time the worksheet is calculated.
RANDARRAY(*rows*,*columns*,*min*,*max*,*integer*)	Returns an array of random numbers. New random numbers are returned every time the worksheet is calculated.
RANDBETWEEN(*bottom*, *top*)	Returns a random number between the numbers specified. A new random number is returned every time the worksheet is calculated.
REDUCE(*[initial value for accumulator]*, *array*, *LAMBDA(accumulator, function)*)	Reduces an array to an accumulated value by applying a *LAMBDA* to each value and returning the total value in the accumulator.
ROMAN(*number*, *form*)	Converts an Arabic numeral to Roman, as text.
ROUND(*number*, *num_ digits*)	Rounds a number to a specified number of digits.
ROUNDDOWN(*number*, *num_digits*)	Rounds a number down, toward zero.
ROUNDUP(*number*,*num_ digits*)	Rounds a number up, away from zero.
SCAN(*[initial value for accumulator]*, *array*, *LAMBDA(accumulator, function)*)	Scans an array by applying a *LAMBDA* to each value and returns an array that has each intermediate value.
SEC(*number*)	Returns the secant of an angle.
SECH(*number*)	Returns the hyperbolic secant of an angle.
SEQUENCE(*rows*,*columns*,*start*, *step*)	Returns a sequence of numbers. Office 365 exclusive.

APPENDIX A

SERIESSUM(*x, n, m, coefficients*)	Returns the sum of a power series based on the formula SERIES(x,n,m,a) $\approx a_1x^n + a_2x(n+m) + a_3x(n+2m) + \ldots + a_ix(n+(i-1)m)$.
SIGN(*number*)	Determines the sign of a number. Returns 1 if the number is positive, 0 if the number is 0, and –1 if the number is negative.
SIN(*number*)	Returns the sine of the given angle.
SINH(*number*)	Returns the hyperbolic sine of *number*.
SQRT(*number*)	Returns a positive square root.
SQRTPI(*number*)	Returns the square root of (number × pi).
SUBTOTAL(*function_num, ref1,ref2,...*)	Returns a subtotal in a list or database. It is generally easier to create a list with subtotals by using the Subtotals command (from the Data menu). After the subtotal list is created, you can modify it by editing the SUBTOTAL function.
SUM(*number1,number2,...*)	Adds all the numbers in a range of cells.
SUMIF(*range,criteria,sum_range*)	Adds the cells specified by the given criteria.
SUMIFS(*sum_range, criteria_range1, criteria1, criteria_range2, criteria2 ...*	Adds the cells specified by a given set of conditions or criteria.
SUMPRODUCT(*array1, array2, array3,...*)	Multiplies corresponding components in the given arrays and returns the sum of those products.
SUMSQ(*number1, number2, ...*)	Returns the sum of the squares of the arguments.
SUMX2MY2(*array_x, array_y*)	Returns the sum of the difference of squares of corresponding values in two arrays.
SUMX2PY2(*array_x, array_y*)	Returns the sum of the sum of squares of corresponding values in two arrays. The sum of the sum of squares is a common term in many statistical calculations.
SUMXMY2(*array_x, array_y*)	Returns the sum of squares of differences of corresponding values in two arrays.
TAN(*number*)	Returns the tangent of the given angle.
TANH(*number*)	Returns the hyperbolic tangent of *number*.
TRUNC(*number,num_digits*)	Truncates a number to an integer by removing the fractional part of the number.

Statistical functions

Table A.8 provides an alphabetical list of the statistical functions.

Table A.8 Alphabetical list of statistical functions

Function	Description
COUNT(*value1,value2,...*)	Counts the number of cells in a range that contain numbers.
COUNTA(*value1,value2,...*)	Counts the numbers of cells in a range that are not empty.
COUNTBLANK(*range*)	Counts the number of empty cells in a specified range of cells.
AVEDEV(*number1, number2, ...*)	Returns the average of the absolute deviations of data points from their mean. AVEDEV is a measure of the variability in a data set.
AVERAGE(*number1, number2, ...*)	Returns the average (arithmetic mean) of the arguments.
AVERAGEA(*value1, value2, ...*)	Calculates the average (arithmetic mean) of the values in the list of arguments. In addition to numbers, text and logical values, such as TRUE and FALSE, are included in the calculation.
AVERAGEIF(*range, criteria, average_range*)	Finds average (arithmetic mean) for the cells specified by a given condition or criteria.
AVERAGEIFS(*average_range, criteria_range1, criteria1, criteria_range2, criteria2 ...*)	Returns the average value among cells specified by a given set of conditions or criteria.
BETA.DIST(*x, alpha, beta, cumulative, A, B*)	Returns the cumulative beta probability density function. The cumulative beta probability density function is commonly used to study variation in the percentage of something across samples, such as the fraction of the day people spend watching television.
BETA.INV(*probability, alpha, beta, A, B*)	Returns the inverse of the cumulative beta probability density function. That is, if probability is equal to BETADIST(*x,...*), then BETA.INV(*probability,...*) is equal to x. You can use the cumulative beta distribution in project planning to model probable completion times, given an expected completion time and variability.
BINOM.DIST(*number_s, trials, probability_s, cumulative*)	Returns the individual term binomial distribution probability. You use BINOM.DIST in problems with a fixed number of tests or trials, when the outcomes of any trial are only success or failure, when trials are independent, and when the probability of success is constant throughout the experiment. For example, BINOM.DIST can calculate the probability that two of the next three babies born will be male.

BINOM.DIST.RANGE(*trials, probability_s, number_s, number_s2*)	Returns the probability of a trial result using a binomial distribution.
BINOM.INV(*trials, probability_s, alpha*)	Returns the smallest value for which the cumulative binomial distribution is greater than or equal to a criterion value. You use this function for quality assurance applications. For example, you can use BINOM.INV to determine the greatest number of defective parts that are allowed to come off an assembly line run without having to reject the entire lot.
CHISQ.DIST(*x, degrees_freedom, cumulative*)	Returns the left-tailed probability of the chi-squared distribution. The chi-squared distribution is associated with a chi-squared test. You use the chi-squared test to compare observed and expected values. For example, in a genetic experiment, you might hypothesize that the next generation of plants will exhibit a certain set of colors. By comparing the observed results with the expected ones, you can decide whether your original hypothesis is valid.
CHISQ.DIST.RT(*x, degrees_freedom*)	Returns the right-tailed probability of the chi-squared distribution.
CHISQ.INV(*probability, degrees_freedom*)	Returns the inverse of the left-tailed probability of the chi-squared distribution. If the probability is equal to CHISQ.DIST(*x*,...), then CHISQ.INV(*probability*,...) is x. You use this function to compare observed results with expected ones to decide whether your original hypothesis is valid.
CHISQ.INV.RT(*probability, degrees_freedom*)	Returns the inverse of the right-tailed probability of the chi-squared distribution.
CHISQ.TEST(*actual_range, expected_range*)	Returns the test for independence. CHISQ.TEST returns the value from the chi-squared distribution for the statistic and the appropriate degrees of freedom. You can use chi-squared tests to determine whether hypothesized results are verified by an experiment.
CONFIDENCE.NORM(*alpha, standard_dev, size*)	Returns the confidence interval for a population mean. The confidence interval is a range on either side of a sample mean. For example, if you order a product through the mail, you can determine, with a particular level of confidence, the earliest and latest the product will arrive. Uses standard normal distribution.
CONFIDENCE.T(*alpha, standard_dev, size*)	Returns the confidence interval based on the Student's t-distribution.

CORREL(*array1*, *array2*)	Returns the correlation coefficient of the *array1* and *array2* cell ranges. You use the correlation coefficient to determine the relationship between two properties. For example, you can examine the relationship between a location's average temperature and the use of air conditioners.
COUNTIF(*range*,*criteria*)	Counts the number of cells within a range that meet the given criteria.
COUNTIFS(*criteria_range1*, *criteria1*, *criteria_range2*,*criteria2*...)	Counts the number of cells within a range that meet the given set of conditions or criteria.
COVARIANCE.P(*array1*, *array2*)	Returns covariance, the average of the products of deviations for each data point pair. You use covariance to determine the relationship between two data sets. For example, you can examine whether greater income accompanies greater levels of education. Based on a population.
COVARIANCE.S(*array1*, *array2*)	Returns covariance, the average of the products of deviations for each data point pair. You use covariance to determine the relationship between two data sets. For example, you can examine whether greater income accompanies greater levels of education. Based on a sample.
DEVSQ(*number1*, *number2*, ...)	Returns the sum of squares of deviations of data points from their sample mean.
EXPON.DIST(*x*, *lambda*, *cumulative*)	Returns the exponential distribution. You use EXPON.DIST to model the time between events, such as how long a bank's automated teller machine takes to deliver cash. For example, you can use EXPON.DIST to determine the probability that the process takes, at most, 1 minute.
F.DIST(*x*, *degrees_freedom1*, *degrees_freedom2*, *cumulative*)	Returns the F probability distribution. You can use this function to determine whether two data sets have different degrees of diversity. For example, you can examine test scores given to men and women entering high school and determine whether the variability in the females is different from that found in the males.
F.DIST.RT(*x*, *degrees_freedom1*, *degrees_freedom2*)	Returns the right-tailed F probability distribution.
F.INV(*probability*, *degrees_freedom1*, *degrees_freedom2*)	Returns the inverse of the F probability distribution. If the probability is equal to F.DIST(*x*,...), then F.INV(*probability*,...) is equal to x.
F.INV.RT(*probability*, *degrees_freedom1*, *degrees_freedom2*)	Returns the inverse of the right-tailed F probability distribution.

`F.TEST(`*array1, array2*`)`	Returns the result of an F-test. An F-test returns the one-tailed probability that the variances in *array1* and *array2* are not significantly different. You use this function to determine whether the two samples have different variances. For example, given test scores from public and private schools, you can test whether those schools have different levels of diversity.
`FISHER(`*x*`)`	Returns the Fisher transformation at *x*. This transformation produces a function that is approximately normally distributed rather than skewed. You use this function to perform hypothesis testing on the correlation coefficient.
`FISHERINV(`*y*`)`	Returns the inverse of the Fisher transformation. You use this transformation when analyzing correlations between ranges or arrays of data. If y is equal to `FISHER(x)`, then `FISHERINV(y)` is equal to x.
`FORECAST.ETS(`*target_date, values, timeline, seasonality, data_completion, aggregation*`)`	Returns the forecasted value for a specific future target date using the exponential smoothing method.
`FORECAST.ETS.CONFINT(`*target_date, values, timeline, confidence_level, seasonality,data_completion, aggregation*`)`	Returns a confidence interval for the forecast value at the specified target date.
`FORECAST.ETS.SEASONALITY(`*values, timeline, data_completion, aggregation*`)`	Returns the length of the repetitive pattern Microsoft Excel detects for the specified time series.
`FORECAST.ETS.STAT(`*values, timeline, statistic_type, seasonality, data_completion, aggregation*`)`	Returns the requested statistic for the forecast. The eight available statistics are Alpha, Beta, Gamma, mean absolute scaled error (MASE), symmetric mean absolute percentage error (SMAPE), mean absolute percentage error (MAE), root mean squared error metric (RMSE), and step size.
`FORECAST.LINEAR(`*x, known_ys, known_xs*`)`	Calculates, or predicts, a future value by using existing values. The predicted value is a y value for a given x value. The known values are existing x values and y values, and the new value is predicted by using linear regression. You can use this function to predict future sales, inventory requirements, or consumer trends.
`FREQUENCY(`*data_array, bins_array*`)`	Calculates how often values occur within a range of values and returns a vertical array of numbers. For example, you can use FREQUENCY to count the number of test scores that fall within ranges of scores.
`GAMMA(`*x*`)`	Returns the gamma function value.

APPENDIX A

`GAMMA.DIST(`*`x, alpha, beta, cumulative`*`)`	Returns the gamma distribution. You can use this function to study variables that might have a skewed distribution. The gamma distribution is commonly used in queuing analysis.
`GAMMA.INV(`*`probability, alpha, beta`*`)`	Returns the inverse of the gamma cumulative distribution. If the *`probability`* is equal to `GAMMA.DIST(x,...)`, then `GAMMA.INV (probability,...)` is equal to `x`.
`GAMMALN(`*`x`*`)`	Returns the natural logarithm of the gamma function.
`GAMMALN.PRECISE(`*`x`*`)`	Returns the natural logarithm of the gamma function.
`GAUSS(`*`x`*`)`	Returns 0.5 less than the standard normal curve distribution.
`GEOMEAN(`*`number1, number2, ...`*`)`	Returns the geometric mean of an array or a range of positive data. For example, you can use `GEOMEAN` to calculate average growth rate given compound interest with variable rates.
`GROWTH(`*`known_ys, known_xs, new_xs, const`*`)`	Calculates predicted exponential growth by using existing data. `GROWTH` returns the y values for a series of new x values that you specify by using existing x values and y values. You can also use the `GROWTH` worksheet function to fit an exponential curve to existing x values and y values.
`HARMEAN(`*`number1, number2, ...`*`)`	Returns the harmonic mean of a data set. The harmonic mean is the reciprocal of the arithmetic mean of reciprocals.
`HYPGEOM.DIST(`*`sample_s, number_sample, population_s, number_population`*`)`	Returns the hypergeometric distribution. `HYPGEOM.DIST` returns the probability of a given number of sample successes, given the sample size, population successes, and population size. You use `HYPGEOM.DIST` for problems with a finite population, in which each observation is either a success or a failure, and each subset of a given size is chosen with equal likelihood.
`INTERCEPT(`*`known_ys, known_xs`*`)`	Calculates the point at which a line will intersect the y-axis by using existing x values and y values. The intercept point is based on a best-fit regression line plotted through the known x values and known y values. You use the intercept when you want to determine the value of the dependent variable when the independent variable is 0. For example, you can use the `INTERCEPT` function to predict a metal's electrical resistance at 0 degrees Celsius when your data points were taken at room temperature or higher.
`KURT(`*`number1, number2, ...`*`)`	Returns the kurtosis of a data set. Kurtosis characterizes the relative peakedness or flatness of a distribution compared with the normal distribution. Positive kurtosis indicates a relatively peaked distribution. Negative kurtosis indicates a relatively flat distribution.

LARGE(*array*, *k*)	Returns the *k*th largest value in a data set. You can use this function to select a value based on its relative standing. For example, you can use LARGE to return a highest, runner-up, or third-place score.
LINEST(*known_ys*, *known_xs*, *const*, *stats*)	Calculates the statistics for a line by using the least-squares method to calculate a straight line that best fits the data and returns an array that describes the line.
LOGEST(*known_ys*, *known_xs*, *const*, *stats*)	In regression analysis, calculates an exponential curve that fits the data and returns an array of values that describes the curve.
LOGNORM.DIST(*x*, *mean*, *standard_dev*, *cumulative*)	Returns the cumulative lognormal distribution of *x*, in which LN(*x*) is normally distributed with the parameters *mean* and *standard_dev*. You use this function to analyze data that has been logarithmically transformed.
LOGNORM.INV(*probability*, *mean*, *standard_dev*)	Returns the inverse of the lognormal cumulative distribution function of *x*, where LN(*x*) is normally distributed with the parameters mean and standard_dev. If the *probability* is equal to LOGNORM.DIST(*x*,...), LOGNORM.INV(*probability*,...) is equal to *x*.
MAX(*number1*, *number2*, ...)	Returns the largest value in a set of values.
MAXA(*value1*, *value2*, ...)	Returns the largest value in a list of arguments. Text and logical values such as TRUE and FALSE are compared, as are numbers.
MAXIFS(*max_range*, *criteria_range1*, *criteria1*, *criteria_range2*, *criteria2*...)	Returns the maximum value among cells specified by a given set of conditions or criteria.
MEDIAN(*number1*, *number2*, ...)	Returns the median of the given numbers. The median is the number in the middle of a set of numbers; that is, half the numbers have values that are greater than the median and half have values that are less.
MIN(*number1*, *number2*, ...)	Returns the smallest number in a set of values.
MINA(*value1*, *value2*, ...)	Returns the smallest value in a list of arguments. Text and logical values such as TRUE and FALSE are compared, as are numbers.
MINIFS(*min_range*, *criteria_range1*, *criteria1*, *criteria_range2*, *criteria2*...)	Returns the minimum value among cells specified by a given set of conditions or criteria.
MODE.MULT(*number1*, *number2*, ...)	Returns a vertical array of the most frequently occurring, or repetitive, values in an array or a range of data. MODE.MULT was new in Excel 2010 and handles the specific case when there are two or more values that are tied for the most frequently occurring value. Whereas MODE.SNGL returns only the first mode value, MODE.MULT returns all the mode values.

`MODE.SNGL(`*`number1, number2,`*` ...)`	Returns the most frequently occurring, or repetitive, value in an array or a range of data. Like `MEDIAN`, `MODE.SNGL` is a location measure. If there are two values that are tied for the most frequently occurring value, only the first one will be returned by `MODE.SNGL`. If you need to return all of the tied values, use the new `MODE.MULT`.
`NEGBINOM.DIST(`*`number_f, number_s, probability_s, cumulative`*`)`	Returns the negative binomial distribution. `NEGBINOM.DIST` returns the probability that there will be *`number_f`* failures before the *`number_s`*th success when the constant probability of a success is *`probability_s`*. This function is similar to the binomial distribution function, except that the number of successes is fixed and the number of trials is variable. As with the binomial distribution function, trials are assumed to be independent.
`NORM.DIST(`*`x, mean, standard_dev, cumulative`*`)`	Returns the normal cumulative distribution for the specified mean and standard deviation. This function has a wide range of applications in statistics, including hypothesis testing.
`NORM.INV(`*`probability, mean, standard_dev`*`)`	Returns the inverse of the normal cumulative distribution for the specified mean and standard deviation.
`NORM.S.DIST(`*`z,cumulative`*`)`	Returns the standard normal cumulative distribution function. The distribution has a mean of zero and a standard deviation of one. You use this function in place of a table of standard normal curve areas.
`NORM.S.INV(`*`probability`*`)`	Returns the inverse of the standard normal cumulative distribution. The distribution has a mean of zero and a standard deviation of one.
`PEARSON(`*`array1, array2`*`)`	Returns the Pearson product–moment correlation coefficient, r, a dimensionless index that ranges from `–1.0` to `1.0`, inclusive, and reflects the extent of a linear relationship between two data sets.
`PERCENTILE.EXC(`*`array, k`*`)`	Returns the *k*th percentile of values in a range. You can use this function to establish a threshold of acceptance. For example, you can decide to examine candidates who score above the 90th percentile. `PERCENTILE.EXC` assumes the percentile is between 0 and 1, exclusive.
`PERCENTILE.INC(`*`array, k`*`)`	Returns the *k*th percentile of values in a range. `PERCENTILE.INC` assumes the percentile is between 0 and 1, inclusive.
`PERCENTRANK.EXC(`*`array, x, significance`*`)`	Returns the rank of a value in a data set as a percentage of the data set. You can use this function to evaluate the relative standing of a value within a data set. `PERCENTRANK.EXC` is renamed from `PERCENTRANK`. It assumes the percentile is between 0 and 1, exclusive.

PERCENTRANK.INC(*array, x, significance*)	Returns the rank of a value in a data set as a percentage of the data set. You can use this function to evaluate the relative standing of a value within a data set. For example, you can use PERCENTRANK.INC to evaluate the standing of an aptitude test score among all scores for the test. PERCENTRANK.INC assumes percentiles from 0 to 1, inclusive.
PERMUT(*number, number_chosen*)	Returns the number of permutations for a given number of objects that can be selected from number objects. A permutation is any set or subset of objects or events in which internal order is significant. Permutations are different from combinations, for which the internal order is not significant. You use this function for lottery-style probability calculations.
PERMUTATIONA(*number, number_chosen*)	Returns the number of permutations for a given number of objects (with repetitions) that can be selected from the total objects.
PHI(*x*)	Returns the value of the density function for a standard normal distribution.
POISSON.DIST(*x, mean, cumulative*)	Returns the Poisson distribution. A common application of the Poisson distribution is predicting the number of events over a specific time, such as the number of cars arriving at a toll plaza in 1 minute.
PROB(*x_range, prob_range, lower_limit, upper_limit*)	Returns the probability that values in a range are between two limits. If *upper_limit* is not supplied, returns the probability that values in *x_range* are equal to *lower_limit*.
QUARTILE.EXC(*array, quart*)	Returns the quartile of a data set. Quartiles are often used in sales and survey data to divide populations into groups. For example, you can use QUARTILE.EXC to find the top 25% of incomes in a population. This function assumes percentiles run from 0 to 1, exclusive.
QUARTILE.INC(*array, quart*)	Returns the quartile of a data set. Quartiles are often used in sales and survey data to divide populations into groups. This function assumes percentiles run from 0 to 1, inclusive.
RANK.AVG(*number, ref, order*)	Returns the rank of a number in a list of numbers. The rank of a number is its size relative to other values in a list. (If you were to sort the list, the rank of the number would be its position.) When two or more items are tied, RANK.AVG averages their ranks.
RANK.EQ(*number, ref, order*)	Returns the rank of a number in a list of numbers. When two or more items are tied, RANK.EQ assigns the lower rank to all items in the tie. Renamed from RANK in Excel 2010.

`RSQ(known_ys, known_xs)`	Returns the square of the Pearson product–moment correlation coefficient through data points in known_ys and known_xs. The r-squared value can be interpreted as the proportion of the variance in y attributable to the variance in x.
`SKEW(number1, number2, ...)`	Returns the skewness of a distribution. Skewness characterizes the degree of asymmetry of a distribution around its mean. Positive skewness indicates a distribution with an asymmetric tail extending toward more positive values. Negative skewness indicates a distribution with an asymmetric tail extending toward more negative values.
`SKEW.P(number1, number2, ...)`	Returns the skewness of a distribution based on a population. Skewness characterizes the degree of asymmetry of a distribution around its mean. Positive skewness indicates a distribution with an asymmetric tail extending toward more positive values. Negative skewness indicates a distribution with an asymmetric tail extending toward more negative values.
`SLOPE(known_ys, known_xs)`	Returns the slope of the linear regression line through data points in *known_ys* and *known_xs*. The *slope* is the vertical distance divided by the horizontal distance between any two points on the line, which is the rate of change along the regression line.
`SMALL(array, k)`	Returns the *k*th smallest value in a data set. You use this function to return values with a particular relative standing in a data set.
`STANDARDIZE(x, mean, standard_dev)`	Returns a normalized value from a distribution characterized by *mean* and *standard_dev*.
`STDEV.P(number1, number2, ...)`	Calculates standard deviation based on the entire population given as arguments. The standard deviation is a measure of how widely values are dispersed from the average value (that is, the mean).
`STDEV.S(number1, number2, ...)`	Estimates standard deviation based on a sample. The standard deviation is a measure of how widely values are dispersed from the average value (that is, the mean).
`STDEVA(value1, value2, ...)`	Estimates standard deviation based on a sample. The standard deviation is a measure of how widely values are dispersed from the average value (that is, the mean). Text and logical values such as TRUE and FALSE are included in the calculation.
`STDEVPA(value1, value2, ...)`	Calculates standard deviation based on the entire population given as arguments, including text and logical values. The standard deviation is a measure of how widely values are dispersed from the average value (that is, the mean).

APPENDIX A

STEYX(*known_ys*, *known_xs*)	Returns the standard error of the predicted y value for each x in the regression. The standard error is a measure of the amount of error in the prediction of y for an individual x.
T.DIST(*x*, *degrees_freedom*, *cumulative*)	Returns the percentage points (that is, probability) for the Student's t-distribution, where a numeric value (x) is a calculated value of t for which percentage points are to be computed. The t-distribution is used in the hypothesis testing of small sample data sets. You use this function in place of a table of critical values for the t-distribution.
T.DIST.2T(*x*, *degrees_freedom*)	Returns the two-tailed probability for the Student's t-distribution.
T.DIST.RT(*x*, *degrees_freedom*)	Returns the right-tailed probability for the Student's t-distribution.
T.INV(*probability*, *degrees_freedom*)	Returns the t-value of the Student's t-distribution as a function of the probability and the degrees of freedom.
T.INV.2T(*probability*, *degrees_freedom*)	Returns the right-tailed t-value of the Student's t-distribution as a function of the probability and the degrees of freedom.
T.TEST(*array1*, *array2*, *tails*, *type*)	Returns the probability associated with a Student's t-test. You use T.TEST to determine whether two samples are likely to have come from the same two underlying populations that have the same mean.
TREND(*known_ys*, *known_xs*, *new_xs*, *const*)	Returns values along a linear trend. Fits a straight line (using the method of least squares) to the arrays *known_ys* and *known_xs*. Returns the y values along that line for the array of *new_xs* that you specify.
TRIMMEAN(*array*, *percent*)	Returns the mean of the interior of a data set. TRIMMEAN calculates the mean taken by excluding a percentage of data points from the top and bottom tails of a data set. You can use this function when you want to exclude outlying data from your analysis.
VAR.P(*number1*, *number2*, ...)	Calculates variance based on the entire population.
VAR.S(*number1*, *number2*, ...)	Estimates variance based on a sample.
VARA(*value1*, *value2*, ...)	Estimates variance based on a sample. In addition to numbers, text and logical values such as TRUE and FALSE are included in the calculation.
VARPA(*value1*, *value2*, ...)	Calculates variance based on the entire population. In addition to numbers, text and logical values such as TRUE and FALSE are included in the calculation.
WEIBULL.DIST(*x*, *alpha*, *beta*, *cumulative*)	Returns the Weibull distribution. You use this distribution in reliability analysis, such as to calculate a device's mean time to failure.

`Z.TEST(array, x, sigma)`	Returns the two-tailed p value of a `z-test`. The `z-test` generates a standard score for *x* with respect to the data set, *array*, and returns the two-tailed probability for the normal distribution. You can use this function to assess the likelihood that a particular observation is drawn from a particular population.

Engineering functions

Table A.9 provides an alphabetical list of the engineering functions in Excel.

Table A.9 Alphabetical list of engineering functions

Function	Description
`BESSELI(x, n)`	Returns the modified Bessel function, which is equivalent to the `BESSELJ` function evaluated for purely imaginary arguments.
`BESSELJ(x, n)`	Returns the `Bessel` function of the first kind.
`BESSELK(x, n)`	Returns the modified Bessel function of the second kind, which is equivalent to the BESSELY functions evaluated for purely imaginary arguments.
`BESSELY(x, n)`	Returns the Bessel function of the second kind. This is the most commonly used form of the Bessel functions. This function provides solutions of the Bessel differential equation and are infinite at x=0. This function is sometimes called the Neumann function.
`BIN2DEC(number)`	Converts a binary number to decimal.
`BIN2HEX(number, places)`	Converts a binary number to hexadecimal.
`BIN2OCT(number, places)`	Converts a binary number to octal.
`BITAND(number1, number2)`	Returns a bitwise AND of two numbers.
`BITLSHIFT(number, shift_amount)`	Returns a number shifted left by *shift_amount* bits.
`BITOR(number1, number2)`	Returns a bitwise OR of two numbers.
`BITRSHIFT(number, shift_amount)`	Returns a number shifted right by *shift_amount* bits.
`BITXOR(number1, number2)`	Returns a bitwise Exclusive OR of two numbers.
`COMPLEX(real_num, i_num, suffix)`	Converts real and imaginary coefficients into a complex number in the form `x + yi` or `x + yj`. Use *suffix* to control whether "`i`" or "`j`" is used.

CONVERT(*number*, *from_unit*, *to_unit*)	Converts a number from one measurement system to another. For example, CONVERT can translate a table of distances in miles to a table of distances in kilometers.
DEC2BIN(*number*, *places*)	Converts a decimal number to binary.
DEC2HEX(*number*, *places*)	Converts a decimal number to hexadecimal.
DEC2OCT(*number*, *places*)	Converts a decimal number to octal.
DELTA(*number1*, *number2*)	Tests whether two values are equal. Returns 1 if *number1* = *number2*; returns 0 otherwise. You use this function to filter a set of values. For example, by summing several DELTA functions, you can calculate the count of equal pairs. This function is also known as the Kronecker Delta function.
ERF(*lower_limit*, *upper_limit*)	Returns the ERROR function integrated between *lower_limit* and *upper_limit*.
ERF.PRECISE(*X*)	Returns the ERROR function integrated between *X* and infinity.
ERFC(*x*)	Returns the complementary ERF function integrated between *x* and infinity.
ERFC.PRECISE(*X*)	Returns the complementary ERF function integrated between *X* and infinity.
GESTEP(*number*, *step*)	Returns 1 if *number* is greater than or equal to *step*; otherwise, returns 0. You use this function to filter a set of values. For example, by summing several GESTEP functions, you can calculate the count of values that exceed a threshold.
HEX2BIN(*number*, *places*)	Converts a hexadecimal number to binary.
HEX2DEC(*number*)	Converts a hexadecimal number to decimal.
HEX2OCT(*number*, *places*)	Converts a hexadecimal number to octal.
IMABS(*inumber*)	Returns the absolute value (modulus) of a complex number in x + yi or x + yj text format.
IMAGINARY(*inumber*)	Returns the imaginary coefficient of a complex number in x + yi or x + yj text format.
IMARGUMENT(*inumber*)	Returns the argument θ (theta), an angle expressed in radians.
IMCONJUGATE(*inumber*)	Returns the complex conjugate of a complex number in x + yi or x + yj text format.
IMCOS(*inumber*)	Returns the cosine of a complex number in x + yi or x + yj text format.
IMCOSH(*inumber*)	Returns the hyperbolic cosine of a complex number.
IMCOT(*inumber*)	Returns the cotangent of a complex number.
IMCSC(*inumber*)	Returns the cosecant of a complex number.

`IMCSCH(inumber)`	Returns the hyperbolic cosecant of a complex number.
`IMDIV(inumber1, inumber2)`	Returns the quotient of two complex numbers in `x + yi` or `x + yj` text format.
`IMEXP(inumber)`	Returns the exponential of a complex number in `x + yi` or `x + yj` text format.
`IMLN(inumber)`	Returns the natural logarithm of a complex number in `x + yi` or `x + yj` text format.
`IMLOG10(inumber)`	Returns the common logarithm (base-10) of a complex number in `x + yi` or `x + yj` text format.
`IMLOG2(inumber)`	Returns the base-2 logarithm of a complex number in `x + yi` or `x + yj` text format.
`IMPOWER(inumber, number)`	Returns a complex number in `x + yi` or `x + yj` text format raised to a power.
`IMPRODUCT(inumber1, inumber2, ...)`	Returns the product of 2 to 255 complex numbers in `x + yi` or `x + yj` text format.
`IMREAL(inumber)`	Returns the real coefficient of a complex number in `x + yi` or `x + yj` text format.
`IMSEC(inumber)`	Returns the secant of a complex number.
`IMSECH(inumber)`	Returns the hyperbolic secant of a complex number.
`IMSIN(inumber)`	Returns the sine of a complex number in `x + yi` or `x + yj` text format.
`IMSINH(inumber)`	Returns the hyperbolic sin of a complex number.
`IMSQRT(inumber)`	Returns the square root of a complex number in `x + yi` or `x + yj` text format.
`IMSUB(inumber1, inumber2)`	Returns the difference of two complex numbers in `x + yi` or `x + yj` text format.
`IMSUM(inumber1, inumber2,...)`	Returns the sum of two or more complex numbers in `x + yi` or `x + yj` text format.
`IMTAN(inumber)`	Returns the tangent of a complex number.
`OCT2BIN(number, places)`	Converts an octal number to binary.
`OCT2DEC(number)`	Converts an octal number to decimal.
`OCT2HEX(number, places)`	Converts an octal number to hexadecimal.

Cube functions

Table A.10 provides an alphabetical list of the cube functions in Excel. If you have a pivot table based on external data, you can convert the pivot table to formulas using cube functions.

Table A.10 Alphabetical list of cube functions

Function	Description
CUBEKPIMEMBER(*connection, kpi_name, kpi_property, caption*)	Returns a key performance indicator (KPI) property and displays the KPI name in the cell. A KPI is a quantifiable measurement, such as monthly gross profit or quarterly employee turnover, that is used to monitor an organization's performance.
CUBEMEMBER(*connection, member_expression, caption*)	Returns a member or tuple from the cube. Use to validate that the member or tuple exists in the cube.
CUBEMEMBERPROPERTY(*connection, member_expression, property*)	Returns the value of a member property from the cube. Use to validate that a member name exists within the cube and to return the specified property for this member.
CUBERANKEDMEMBER(*connection, set_expression, rank, caption*)	Returns the nth, or ranked, member in a set. Use to return one or more elements in a set, such as the top sales performer or the top 10 students.
CUBESET(*connection, set_expression, caption, sort_order, sort_by*)	Defines a calculated set of members or tuples by sending a set expression to the cube on the server, which creates the set, and then returns that set to Microsoft Excel.
CUBESETCOUNT(*set*)	Returns the number of items in a set.
CUBEVALUE(*connection, member_expression1, ...*)	Returns an aggregated value from the cube.

Information functions

Table A.11 provides an alphabetical list of the information functions in Excel. Detailed examples of these functions are provided in Chapter 9.

Table A.11 Alphabetical list of information functions

Function	Description
CELL(*info_type, reference*)	Returns information about the formatting, location, or contents of the upper-left cell in a reference.
ERROR.TYPE(*error_val*)	Returns a number corresponding to one of the error values in Microsoft Excel or returns an #N/A error if no error exists. You can use ERROR.TYPE in an IF function to test for an error value and return a text string, such as a message, instead of the error value.
INFO(*type_text*)	Returns information about the current operating environment.

`ISBLANK(value)`	Returns TRUE if *value* refers to an empty cell. Note that if a cell contains "blanks" or spaces, this function will not return TRUE.
`ISERR(value)`	Returns TRUE if *value* refers to any error value except #N/A.
`ISERROR(value)`	Returns TRUE if *value* refers to any error value (that is, #CALC!, #DIV/0!, #FIELD!, #N/A, #NAME?, #NULL!, #NUM!, #REF!, #SPILL!, or #VALUE!).
`ISEVEN(number)`	Returns TRUE if *number* is even and FALSE if *number* is odd.
`ISFORMULA(reference)`	Checks whether a reference is to a cell containing a formula and returns TRUE or FALSE.
`ISLOGICAL(value)`	Returns TRUE if *value* refers to a logical value.
`ISNA(value)`	Returns TRUE if *value* refers to the #N/A (value not available) error value.
`ISNONTEXT(value)`	Returns TRUE if *value* refers to any item that is not text. (Note that this function returns TRUE if value refers to a blank cell.)
`ISNUMBER(value)`	Returns TRUE if *value* refers to a number.
`ISODD(number)`	Returns TRUE if the number is odd and FALSE if the number is even.
`ISOMITTED(argument)`	Checks whether the value in a LAMBDA is missing and returns TRUE or FALSE.
`ISREF(value)`	Returns TRUE if *value* refers to a reference.
`ISTEXT(value)`	Returns TRUE if *value* refers to text.
`N(value)`	Returns a value converted to a number.
`NA()`	Returns the error value #N/A, which means "no value is available." You use NA to mark empty cells or cells that are missing information to avoid the problem of unintentionally including empty cells in your calculations. When a formula refers to a cell containing #N/A, the formula returns the #N/A error value.
`SHEET(value)`	Returns the sheet number of the referenced sheet.
`SHEETS(reference`	Returns the number of sheets in a reference.
`TYPE(value)`	Returns the type of *value*. You use TYPE when the behavior of another function depends on the type of value in a particular cell.

Web functions

Table A.12 provides an alphabetical list of all the Web functions from Excel. Note that none of these functions will calculate in Excel online.

Table A.12 Alphabetical list of web functions

Function	Description
`ENCODEURL(text)`	Returns a URL-encoded string.
`FILTERXML(xml, xpath)`	Returns specific data from the XML content by using the `xpath`.
`WEBSERVICE(url)`	Returns data from a web service.

Inside OUT

These three functions are designed to work together, and they pre-date the new tools in Power Query.

The main function is the `WEBSERVICE` function. Provide a URL to a web service that will return the results as an ATOM feed or a JSON feed. One free example is search.twitter.com. Specify a URL with `q=vlookup` and the function will return the last ten tweets about `VLOOKUP`.

Before using `WEBSERVICE`, you might have to run the URL through `ENCODEURL()`. This function replaces all illegal characters with their &20 equivalents. For example, pivot table will become pivot&20table after using `ENCODEURL`.

You might put the Twitter search term in A2 and then URL prefix in A1. Entering `=WEBSERVICE(ENCODEURL(A1&A2))` in cell A3 will return somewhere around 20,000 characters of results to a single cell.

To select specific fields from the ATOM or JSON feed, use the `FILTERXML` function. The returned results can be described using `XPATH`. For example, if you select B1:B25 and type **=FILTERXML(A3,"//title")**, Excel will return the 15 tweets parsed out of cell A4.

TROUBLESHOOTING

Excel allows 32,768 characters in a cell but will not show you more than the first 1,000 characters.

In the `WEBSERVICE` example, the result of the `WEBSERVICE` function is more than 20,000 characters. Excel can store them, and `FILTERXML` can parse the data, but you cannot look at the data. One strategy: Copy the results in A4 and paste to Notepad. This will help you to find the various `XPATH` field names being used.

Database functions

Table A.13 provides an alphabetical list of all the database functions in Excel. Curiously, the database functions are not anywhere to be found in the drop-down menus on the Formulas tab. You can enter these using the Insert Function dialog box or by simply typing the formula in a cell. Detailed examples of these functions are provided in Chapter 9.

Table A.13 Alphabetical list of database functions

Function	Description
DAVERAGE(*database, field, criteria*)	Averages the values in a column in a list or database that match the conditions specified.
DCOUNT(*database, field, criteria*)	Counts the cells that contain numbers in a column in a list or database that match the conditions specified.
DCOUNTA(*database, field, criteria*)	Counts all the nonblank cells in a column in a list or database that match the conditions specified.
DGET(*database, field, criteria*)	Extracts a single value from a column in a list or database that matches the conditions specified. If multiple matches are found, returns #NUM! error.
DMAX(*database, field, criteria*)	Returns the largest number in a column in a list or database that matches the conditions specified.
DMIN(*database, field, criteria*)	Returns the smallest number in a column in a list or database that matches the conditions specified.
DPRODUCT(*database, field, criteria*)	Multiplies the values in a column in a list or database that match the conditions specified.
DSTDEV(*database, field, criteria*)	Estimates the standard deviation of a population based on a sample, using the numbers in a column in a list or database that match the conditions specified.
DSTDEVP(*database, field, criteria*)	Calculates the standard deviation of a population based on the entire population, using the numbers in a column in a list or database that match the conditions specified.
DSUM(*database, field, criteria*)	Adds the numbers in a column in a list or database that match the conditions specified.
DVAR(*database, field, criteria*)	Estimates the variance of a population based on a sample, using the numbers in a column in a list or database that match the conditions specified.
DVARP(*database, field, criteria*)	Calculates the variance of a population based on the entire population, using the numbers in a column in a list or database that match the conditions specified.

Add-in functions

Table A.14 provides a list of functions that are only available when an add-in is activated. These only include add-ins that are shipped as part of Excel. To activate an add-in, use Alt+T followed by I.

Table A.14 Alphabetical list of functions from Microsoft add-ins

Function name	Description
CALL(*register_id,argument1,...*)	Calls a procedure in a dynamic link library or code resource. There are two syntax forms of this function. Use syntax 1 only with a previously registered code resource, which uses arguments from the REGISTER function. Use syntax 2a or 2b to simultaneously register and call a code resource.
EUROCONVERT(*number, source, target, full_precision, triangulation_precision*)	Converts a number to euros, converts a number from euros to a euro member currency, or converts a number from one euro member currency to another by using the euro as an intermediary (triangulation). Requires activation of the Euro Currency Tools Add-in (choose File, Options, Add-Ins, Excel Add-Ins, Manage).
REGISTER.ID(*module_text, procedure, type_text*)	Returns the register ID of the specified dynamic link library (DLL) or code resource that has been previously registered. If the DLL or code resource has not been registered, this function registers the DLL or code resource and then returns the register ID. REGISTER.ID can be used on worksheets (unlike REGISTER), but you cannot specify a function name and argument names with REGISTER.ID.

Compatibility functions

Table A.15 provides a list of compatibility functions. These are functions that have been replaced in Excel 2010, 2013, 2016, or 2019. In case you open a workbook created in Excel 2007, these old function names need to continue to work.

If you have a coworker with an old version of Excel who needs to use your workbooks, you could continue to use the legacy function name. Otherwise, you should start using the new function name.

Table A.15 Alphabetical list of compatibility functions

Function name	Replaced by
BETADIST	Replaced by `BETA.DIST` in Excel 2010
BETAINV	Replaced by `BETA.INV` in Excel 2010
BINOMDIST	Replaced by `BINOM.DIST` in Excel 2010
CEILING	Replaced by `CEILING.MATH` in Excel 2013
CEILING.PRECISE	Replaced by `CEILING.MATH` in Excel 2013
CHIDIST	Replaced by `CHISQ.DIST` in Excel 2010
CHIINV	Replaced by `CHISQ.INV` in Excel 2010
CHITEST	Replaced by `CHISQ.TEST` in Excel 2010
CONCATENATE	Replaced by `CONCAT` in Excel 2019
CONFIDENCE	Replaced by `CONFIDENCE.NORM` in Excel 2010
COVAR	Replaced by `COVARIANCE.P` in Excel 2010
CRITBINOM	Replaced by `BINOM.INV` in Excel 2010
EXPONDIST	Replaced by `EXPON.DIST` in Excel 2010
FDIST	Replaced by `F.DIST` in Excel 2010
FINV	Replaced by `F.INV` in Excel 2010
FLOOR	Replaced by `FLOOR.MATH` in Excel 2013
FLOOR.PRECISE	Replaced by `FLOOR.MATH` in Excel 2013
FORECAST	Replaced by `FORECAST.LINEAR` in Excel 2016
FTEST	Replaced by `F.TEST` in Excel 2010
GAMMADIST	Replaced by `GAMMA.DIST` in Excel 2010
GAMMAINV	Replaced by `GAMMA.INV` in Excel 2010
HYPGEOMDIST	Replaced by `HYPGEOM.DIST` in Excel 2010
ISO.CEILING	Replaced by `CEILING.MATH` in Excel 2013
LOGINV	Replaced by `LOGNORM.INV` in Excel 2010
LOGNORMDIST	Replaced by `LOGNORM.DIST` in Excel 2010
MODE	Replaced by `MODE.SNGL` in Excel 2010
NEGBINOMDIST	Replaced by `NEGBINOM.DIST` in Excel 2010
NORMDIST	Replaced by `NORM.DIST` in Excel 2010
NORMINV	Replaced by `NORM.INV` in Excel 2010
NORMSDIST	Replaced by `NORM.S.DIST` in Excel 2010
NORMSINV	Replaced by `NORM.S.INV` in Excel 2010
PERCENTILE	Replaced by `PERCENTILE.INC` in Excel 2010
PERCENTRANK	Replaced by `PERCENTRANK.INC` in Excel 2010

POISSON	Replaced by `POISSON.DIST` in Excel 2010
QUARTILE	Replaced by `QUARTILE.INC` in Excel 2010
RANK	Replaced by `RANK.EQ` in Excel 2010
STDEV	Replaced by `STDEV.S` in Excel 2010
STDEVP	Replaced by `STDEV.P` in Excel 2010
TDIST	Replaced by `T.DIST` in Excel 2010
TINV	Replaced by `T.INV` in Excel 2010
TTEST	Replaced by `T.TEST` in Excel 2010
VAR	Replaced by `VAR.S` in Excel 2010
VARP	Replaced by `VAR.P` in Excel 2010
WEIBULL	Replaced by `WEIBULL.DIST` in Excel 2010
ZTEST	Replaced by `Z.TEST` in Excel 2010
BINOMDIST	Replaced by `BINOM.DIST` in Excel 2010
CHIDIST	Replaced by `CHISQ.DIST` in Excel 2010

Alphabetical cross-reference

Sometimes, the hardest part of using a function is figuring out where in Excel the Excel team has categorized each function. Table A.16 provides an alphabetical list of function names and the category where each can be found on the Formulas tab.

TABLE A.16 Alphabetical list of functions and their category

Function Name	Category
ABS	Math & Trig
ACCRINT	Financial
ACCRINTM	Financial
ACOS	Math & Trig
ACOSH	Math & Trig
ACOT	Math & Trig
ACOTH	Math & Trig
ADDRESS	Lookup & Reference
AGGREGATE	Math & Trig
AMORDEGRC	Financial
AMORLINC	Financial
AND	Logical

ARABIC	Math & Trig
AREAS	Lookup & Reference
ARRAYTOTEXT	Text
ASC	Text
ASIN	Math & Trig
ASINH	Math & Trig
ATAN	Math & Trig
ATAN2	Math & Trig
ATANH	Math & Trig
AVEDEV	More Functions, Statistical
AVERAGE	More Functions, Statistical
AVERAGEA	More Functions, Statistical
AVERAGEIF	More Functions, Statistical
AVERAGEIFS	More Functions, Statistical
BAHTTEXT	Text
BASE	Math & Trig
BESSELI	More Functions, Engineering
BESSELJ	More Functions, Engineering
BESSELK	More Functions, Engineering
BESSELY	More Functions, Engineering
BETA.DIST	More Functions, Statistical
BETA.INV	More Functions, Statistical
BETADIST	More Functions, Compatibility
BETAINV	More Functions, Compatibility
BIN2DEC	More Functions, Engineering
BIN2HEX	More Functions, Engineering
BIN2OCT	More Functions, Engineering
BINOM.DIST	More Functions, Statistical
BINOM.DIST.RANGE	More Functions, Statistical
BINOM.INV	More Functions, Statistical
BINOMDIST	More Functions, Compatibility
BINOMDIST	More Functions, Compatibility
BITAND	More Functions, Engineering
BITLSHIFT	More Functions, Engineering
BITOR	More Functions, Engineering

BITRSHIFT	More Functions, Engineering
BITXOR	More Functions, Engineering
BYCOL	Math & Trig
BYROW	Math & Trig
CALL	Use Insert Function dialog box
CEILING	More Functions, Compatibility
CEILING.MATH	Math & Trig
CEILING.PRECISE	#N/A
CELL	More Functions, Information
CHAR	Text
CHIDIST	More Functions, Compatibility
CHIDIST	More Functions, Compatibility
CHIINV	More Functions, Compatibility
CHISQ.DIST	More Functions, Statistical
CHISQ.DIST.RT	More Functions, Statistical
CHISQ.INV	More Functions, Statistical
CHISQ.INV.RT	More Functions, Statistical
CHISQ.TEST	More Functions, Statistical
CHITEST	More Functions, Compatibility
CHOOSE	Lookup & Reference
CHOOSECOLS	Lookup & Reference
CHOOSEROWS	Lookup & Reference
CLEAN	Text
CODE	Text
COLUMN	Lookup & Reference
COLUMNS	Lookup & Reference
COMBIN	Math & Trig
COMBINA	Math & Trig
COMPLEX	More Functions, Engineering
CONCAT	Text
CONCATENATE	More Functions, Compatibility
CONFIDENCE	More Functions, Compatibility
CONFIDENCE.NORM	More Functions, Statistical
CONFIDENCE.T	More Functions, Statistical
CONVERT	More Functions, Engineering

CORREL	More Functions, Statistical
COS	Math & Trig
COSH	Math & Trig
COT	Math & Trig
COTH	Math & Trig
COUNT	More Functions, Statistical
COUNTA	More Functions, Statistical
COUNTBLANK	More Functions, Statistical
COUNTIF	More Functions, Statistical
COUNTIFS	More Functions, Statistical
COUPDAYBS	Financial
COUPDAYS	Financial
COUPDAYSNC	Financial
COUPNCD	Financial
COUPNUM	Financial
COUPPCD	Financial
COVAR	More Functions, Compatibility
COVARIANCE.P	More Functions, Statistical
COVARIANCE.S	More Functions, Statistical
CRITBINOM	More Functions, Compatibility
CSC	Math & Trig
CSCH	Math & Trig
CUBEKPIMEMBER	More Functions, Cube
CUBEMEMBER	More Functions, Cube
CUBEMEMBERPROPERTY	More Functions, Cube
CUBERANKEDMEMBER	More Functions, Cube
CUBESET	More Functions, Cube
CUBESETCOUNT	More Functions, Cube
CUBEVALUE	More Functions, Cube
CUMIPMT	Financial
CUMPRINC	Financial
DATE	Date & Time
DATEDIF	#N/A
DATEVALUE	Date & Time
DAVERAGE	Use Insert Function dialog

DAY	Date & Time
DAYS	Date & Time
DAYS360	Date & Time
DB	Financial
DBCS	Text
DCOUNT	Use Insert Function dialog box
DCOUNTA	Use Insert Function dialog box
DDB	Financial
DEC2BIN	More Functions, Engineering
DEC2HEX	More Functions, Engineering
DEC2OCT	More Functions, Engineering
DECIMAL	Math & Trig
DEGREES	Math & Trig
DELTA	More Functions, Engineering
DEVSQ	More Functions, Statistical
DGET	Use Insert Function dialog box
DISC	Financial
DMAX	Use Insert Function dialog box
DMIN	Use Insert Function dialogbox
DOLLAR	Text
DOLLARDE	Financial
DOLLARFR	Financial
DPRODUCT	Use Insert Function dialog box
DSTDEV	Use Insert Function dialog box
DSTDEVP	Use Insert Function dialog box
DSUM	Use Insert Function dialog box
DURATION	Financial
DVAR	Use Insert Function dialog box
DVARP	Use Insert Function dialog box
EDATE	Date & Time
EFFECT	Financial
ENCODEURL	More Functions, Web
EOMONTH	Date & Time
ERF	More Functions, Engineering
ERF.PRECISE	More Functions, Engineering

ERFC	More Functions, Engineering
ERFC.PRECISE	More Functions, Engineering
ERROR.TYPE	More Functions, Information
EUROCONVERT	Use Insert Function dialog box
EVEN	Math & Trig
EXACT	Text
EXP	Math & Trig
EXPON.DIST	More Functions, Statistical
EXPONDIST	More Functions, Compatibility
F.DIST	More Functions, Statistical
F.DIST.RT	More Functions, Statistical
F.INV	More Functions, Statistical
F.INV.RT	More Functions, Statistical
F.TEST	More Functions, Statistical
FACT	Math & Trig
FACTDOUBLE	Math & Trig
FALSE	Logical
FDIST	More Functions, Compatibility
FIELDVALUE	Lookup & Reference
FILTER	Lookup & Reference
FILTERXML	More Functions, Web
FIND	Text
FINDB	Text
FINV	More Functions, Compatibility
FISHER	More Functions, Statistical
FISHERINV	More Functions, Statistical
FIXED	Text
FLOOR	More Functions, Compatibility
FLOOR.MATH	Math & Trig
FLOOR.PRECISE	#N/A
FORECAST	More Functions, Compatibility
FORECAST.ETS	More Functions, Statistical
FORECAST.ETS.CONFINT	More Functions, Statistical
FORECAST.ETS.SEASONALITY	More Functions, Statistical
FORECAST.ETS.STAT	More Functions, Statistical

FORECAST.LINEAR	More Functions, Statistical
FORMULATEXT	Lookup & Reference
FREQUENCY	More Functions, Statistical
FTEST	More Functions, Compatibility
FV	Financial
FVSCHEDULE	Financial
GAMMA	More Functions, Statistical
GAMMA.DIST	More Functions, Statistical
GAMMA.INV	More Functions, Statistical
GAMMADIST	More Functions, Compatibility
GAMMAINV	More Functions, Compatibility
GAMMALN	More Functions, Statistical
GAMMALN.PRECISE	More Functions, Statistical
GAUSS	More Functions, Statistical
GCD	Math & Trig
GEOMEAN	More Functions, Statistical
GESTEP	More Functions, Engineering
GETPIVOTDATA	Lookup & Reference
GROWTH	More Functions, Statistical
HARMEAN	More Functions, Statistical
HEX2BIN	More Functions, Engineering
HEX2DEC	More Functions, Engineering
HEX2OCT	More Functions, Engineering
HLOOKUP	Lookup & Reference
HOUR	Date & Time
HSTACK	Lookup & Reference
HYPERLINK	Lookup & Reference
HYPGEOM.DIST	More Functions, Statistical
HYPGEOMDIST	More Functions, Compatibility
IF	Logical
IFERROR	Logical
IFNA	Logical
IFS	Logical
IMABS	More Functions, Engineering
IMAGINARY	More Functions, Engineering

IMARGUMENT	More Functions, Engineering
IMCONJUGATE	More Functions, Engineering
IMCOS	More Functions, Engineering
IMCOSH	More Functions, Engineering
IMCOT	More Functions, Engineering
IMCSC	More Functions, Engineering
IMCSCH	More Functions, Engineering
IMDIV	More Functions, Engineering
IMEXP	More Functions, Engineering
IMLN	More Functions, Engineering
IMLOG10	More Functions, Engineering
IMLOG2	More Functions, Engineering
IMPOWER	More Functions, Engineering
IMPRODUCT	More Functions, Engineering
IMREAL	More Functions, Engineering
IMSEC	More Functions, Engineering
IMSECH	More Functions, Engineering
IMSIN	More Functions, Engineering
IMSINH	More Functions, Engineering
IMSQRT	More Functions, Engineering
IMSUB	More Functions, Engineering
IMSUM	More Functions, Engineering
IMTAN	More Functions, Engineering
INDEX	Lookup & Reference
INDEX	Lookup & Reference
INDIRECT	Lookup & Reference
INFO	More Functions, Information
INT	Math & Trig
INTERCEPT	More Functions, Statistical
INTRATE	Financial
IPMT	Financial
IRR	Financial
ISBLANK	More Functions, Information
ISERR	More Functions, Information
ISERROR	More Functions, Information

ISEVEN	More Functions, Information
ISFORMULA	More Functions, Information
ISLOGICAL	More Functions, Information
ISNA	More Functions, Information
ISNONTEXT	More Functions, Information
ISNUMBER	More Functions, Information
ISO.CEILING	#N/A
ISODD	More Functions, Information
ISOMITTED	Math & Trig
ISOWEEKNUM	Date & Time
ISPMT	Financial
ISREF	More Functions, Information
ISTEXT	More Functions, Information
JIS	Text
KURT	More Functions, Statistical
LAMBDA	Text
LARGE	More Functions, Statistical
LCM	Math & Trig
LEFT	Text
LEFTB	Text
LEN	Text
LENB	Text
LET	Math & Trig
LINEST	More Functions, Statistical
LN	Math & Trig
LOG	Math & Trig
LOG10	Math & Trig
LOGEST	More Functions, Statistical
LOGINV	More Functions, Compatibility
LOGNORM.DIST	More Functions, Statistical
LOGNORM.INV	More Functions, Statistical
LOGNORMDIST	More Functions, Compatibility
LOOKUP	Lookup & Reference
LOOKUP	Lookup & Reference
LOWER	Text

MAKEARRAY	Math & Trig
MAP	Math & Trig
MATCH	Lookup & Reference
MAX	More Functions, Statistical
MAXA	More Functions, Statistical
MAXIFS	More Functions, Statistical
MDETERM	Math & Trig
MDURATION	Financial
MEDIAN	More Functions, Statistical
MID	Text
MIDB	Text
MIN	More Functions, Statistical
MINA	More Functions, Statistical
MINIFS	More Functions, Statistical
MINUTE	Date & Time
MINVERSE	Math & Trig
MIRR	Financial
MMULT	Math & Trig
MOD	Math & Trig
MODE	More Functions, Compatibility
MODE.MULT	More Functions, Statistical
MODE.SNGL	More Functions, Statistical
MONTH	Date & Time
MROUND	Math & Trig
MULTINOMIAL	Math & Trig
MUNIT	Math & Trig
N	More Functions, Information
NA	More Functions, Information
NEGBINOM.DIST	More Functions, Statistical
NEGBINOMDIST	More Functions, Compatibility
NETWORKDAYS	Date & Time
NETWORKDAYS.INTL	Date & Time
NOMINAL	Financial
NORM.DIST	More Functions, Statistical
NORM.INV	More Functions, Statistical

NORM.S.DIST	More Functions, Statistical
NORM.S.INV	More Functions, Statistical
NORMDIST	More Functions, Compatibility
NORMINV	More Functions, Compatibility
NORMSDIST	More Functions, Compatibility
NORMSINV	More Functions, Compatibility
NOT	Logical
NOW	Date & Time
NPER	Financial
NPV	Financial
NUMBERVALUE	Text
OCT2BIN	More Functions, Engineering
OCT2DEC	More Functions, Engineering
OCT2HEX	More Functions, Engineering
ODD	Math & Trig
ODDFPRICE	Financial
ODDFYIELD	Financial
ODDLPRICE	Financial
ODDLYIELD	Financial
OFFSET	Lookup & Reference
OR	Logical
PDURATION	Financial
PEARSON	More Functions, Statistical
PERCENTILE	More Functions, Compatibility
PERCENTILE.EXC	More Functions, Statistical
PERCENTILE.INC	More Functions, Statistical
PERCENTRANK	More Functions, Compatibility
PERCENTRANK.EXC	More Functions, Statistical
PERCENTRANK.INC	More Functions, Statistical
PERMUT	More Functions, Statistical
PERMUTATIONA	More Functions, Statistical
PHI	More Functions, Statistical
PHONETIC	Text
PI	Math & Trig
PMT	Financial

POISSON	More Functions, Compatibility
POISSON.DIST	More Functions, Statistical
POWER	Math & Trig
PPMT	Financial
PRICE	Financial
PRICEDISC	Financial
PRICEMAT	Financial
PROB	More Functions, Statistical
PRODUCT	Math & Trig
PROPER	Text
PV	Financial
QUARTILE	More Functions, Compatibility
QUARTILE.EXC	More Functions, Statistical
QUARTILE.INC	More Functions, Statistical
QUOTIENT	Math & Trig
RADIANS	Math & Trig
RAND	Math & Trig
RANDARRAY	Math & Trig
RANDBETWEEN	Math & Trig
RANK	More Functions, Compatibility
RANK.AVG	More Functions, Statistical
RANK.EQ	More Functions, Statistical
RATE	Financial
RECEIVED	Financial
REDUCE	Math & Trig
REGISTER.ID	Use Insert Function dialog box
REPLACE	Text
REPLACEB	Text
REPT	Text
RIGHT	Text
RIGHTB	Text
ROMAN	Math & Trig
ROUND	Math & Trig
ROUNDDOWN	Math & Trig
ROUNDUP	Math & Trig

ROW	Lookup & Reference
ROWS	Lookup & Reference
RRI	Financial
RSQ	More Functions, Statistical
RTD	Lookup & Reference
SCAN	Math & Trig
SEARCH	Text
SEARCHB	Text
SEC	Math & Trig
SECH	Math & Trig
SECOND	Date & Time
SEQUENCE	Math & Trig
SERIESSUM	Math & Trig
SHEET	More Functions, Information
SHEETS	More Functions, Information
SIGN	Math & Trig
SIN	Math & Trig
SINH	Math & Trig
SKEW	More Functions, Statistical
SKEW.P	More Functions, Statistical
SLN	Financial
SLOPE	More Functions, Statistical
SMALL	More Functions, Statistical
SORT	Lookup & Reference
SORTBY	Lookup & Reference
SQRT	Math & Trig
SQRTPI	Math & Trig
STANDARDIZE	More Functions, Statistical
STDEV	More Functions, Compatibility
STDEV.P	More Functions, Statistical
STDEV.S	More Functions, Statistical
STDEVA	More Functions, Statistical
STDEVP	More Functions, Compatibility
STDEVPA	More Functions, Statistical
STEYX	More Functions, Statistical

STOCKHISTORY	Financial
SUBSTITUTE	Text
SUBTOTAL	Math & Trig
SUM	Math & Trig
SUMIF	Math & Trig
SUMIFS	Math & Trig
SUMPRODUCT	Math & Trig
SUMSQ	Math & Trig
SUMX2MY2	Math & Trig
SUMX2PY2	Math & Trig
SUMXMY2	Math & Trig
SWITCH	Logical
SYD	Financial
T	Text
T.DIST	More Functions, Statistical
T.DIST.2T	More Functions, Statistical
T.DIST.RT	More Functions, Statistical
T.INV	More Functions, Statistical
T.INV.2T	More Functions, Statistical
T.TEST	More Functions, Statistical
TAN	Math & Trig
TANH	Math & Trig
TBILLEQ	Financial
TBILLPRICE	Financial
TBILLYIELD	Financial
TDIST	More Functions, Compatibility
TEXT	Text
TEXTAFTER	Text
TEXTBEFORE	Text
TEXTJOIN	Text
TEXTSPLIT	Text
TIME	Date & Time
TIMEVALUE	Date & Time
TINV	More Functions, Compatibility
TOCOL	Lookup & Reference

TODAY	Date & Time
TOROW	Lookup & Reference
TRANSPOSE	Lookup & Reference
TREND	More Functions, Statistical
TRIM	Text
TRIMMEAN	More Functions, Statistical
TRUE	Logical
TRUNC	Math & Trig
TTEST	More Functions, Compatibility
TYPE	More Functions, Information
UNICHAR	Text
UNICODE	Text
UNIQUE	Lookup & Reference
UPPER	Text
VALUE	Text
VALUETOTEXT	Text
VAR	More Functions, Compatibility
VAR.P	More Functions, Statistical
VAR.S	More Functions, Statistical
VARA	More Functions, Statistical
VARP	More Functions, Compatibility
VARPA	More Functions, Statistical
VDB	Financial
VECTORWRAP	Lookup & Reference
VLOOKUP	Lookup & Reference
VSTACK	Lookup & Reference
WEBSERVICE	More Functions, Web
WEEKDAY	Date & Time
WEEKNUM	Date & Time
WEIBULL	More Functions, Compatibility
WEIBULL.DIST	More Functions, Statistical
WORKDAY	Date & Time
WORKDAY.INTL	Date & Time
XIRR	Financial
XLOOKUP	Lookup & Reference

XMATCH	Lookup & Reference
XNPV	Financial
XOR	Logical
YEAR	Date & Time
YEARFRAC	Date & Time
YIELD	Financial
YIELDDISC	Financial
YIELDMAT	Financial
Z.TEST	More Functions, Statistical
ZTEST	More Functions, Compatibility

APPENDIX B

Excel functions with DAX or Power Query equivalents

As an Excel pro, you probably have a fairly good handle on the calculation functions used in Excel. Today, you might need to dabble in the Data Analysis Expressions (DAX) formula language when creating a new measure in a pivot table or in the M function language when cleaning data with Power Query. This chapter will help you transfer your knowledge of Excel functions to either DAX or Power Query.

The first table is an alphabetical list of Excel functions and the equivalent DAX function. If the Excel function is not in Table B.1, then there is no direct DAX equivalent.

The second table is an alphabetical list of Excel functions and the equivalent Power Query function.

If you compare Table B.1 below to Table B.2, you will note that in 90 percent of the cases, the DAX function names are the same. That is likely thanks to Rob Collie, an Excel Project Manager who moved over to the Power Pivot team. In Table B.2, there are hardly any similarities between the Power Query functions and their Excel equivalents.

Excel functions and DAX equivalents

Table B.1 shows an alphabetical list of Excel functions with their DAX equivalents.

Table B.1 Excel functions with DAX equivalents

Excel function	DAX equivalent
ABS	ABS
ACOS	ACOS
ACOSH	ACOSH
AND	AND
ASIN	ASIN
ASINH	ASINH
ATAN	ATAN

ATANH	ATANH
AVERAGE	AVERAGE
AVERAGEA	AVERAGEA
BETA.DIST	BETA.DIST
BETA.INV	BETA.INV
CEILING	CEILING
CEILING.MATH	ISO.CEILING
CHISQ.INV	CHISQ.INV
CHISQ.INV.RT	CHISQ.INV.RT
CODE	CODE
COMBIN	COMBIN
COMBINA	COMBINA
CONCATENATE	CONCATENATE
CONFIDENCE.NORM	CONFIDENCE.NORM
CONFIDENCE.T	CONFIDENCE.T
COS	COS
COSH	COSH
COUNT	COUNT
COUNTA	COUNTA
COUNTBLANK	COUNTBLANK
DATE	DATE
DATEDIF	DATEDIFF
DATEVALUE	DATEVALUE
DAY	DAY
DEGREES	DEGREES
DIVIDE	DIVIDE
EDATE	EDATE
EOMONTH	EOMONTH
EVEN	EVEN
EXACT	EXACT
EXP	EXP
EXPON.DIST	EXPON.DIST

FACT	FACT
FALSE	FALSE
FILTER	FILTER
FIND	FIND
FIXED	FIXED
FLOOR.MATH	FLOOR
GCD	GCD
GEOMEAN	GEOMEAN
HOUR	HOUR
IF	IF
IFERROR	IFERROR
INT	INT
ISBLANK	ISBLANK
ISERROR	ISERROR
ISEVEN	ISEVEN
ISLOGICAL	ISLOGICAL
ISNONTEXT	ISNONTEXT
ISNUMBER	ISNUMBER
ISTEXT	ISTEXT
LCM	LCM
LEFT	LEFT
LEN	LEN
LN	LN
LOG	LOG
LOG10	LOG10
LOWER	LOWER
MAX	MAX
MAXA	MAXA
MEDIAN	MEDIAN
MID	MID
MIN	MIN
MINA	MINA

MINUTE	MINUTE
MONTH	MONTH
MROUND	MROUND
NORM.DIST	NORM.DIST
NORM.INV	NORM.INV
NORM.S.DIST	NORM.S.DIST
NORM.S.INV	NORM.S.INV
NOT	NOT
NOW	NOW
ODD	ODD
OR	OR
PERCENTILE.EXC	PERCENTILE.EXC
PERCENTILE.INC	PERCENTILE.INC
PI	PI
POISSON.DIST	POISSON.DIST
POWER	POWER
PRODUCT	PRODUCT
QUOTIENT	QUOTIENT
RADIANS	RADIANS
RAND	RAND
RANDBETWEEN	RANDBETWEEN
RANK.EQ	RANK.EQ
REPLACE	REPLACE
REPT	REPT
RIGHT	RIGHT
ROUND	ROUND
ROUNDDOWN	ROUNDDOWN
ROUNDUP	ROUNDUP
SEARCH	SEARCH
SECOND	SECOND
SIGN	SIGN
SIN	SIN

SINH	SINH
SQRT	SQRT
SQRTPI	SQRTPI
STDEV.P	STDEV.P
STDEV.S	STDEV.S
SUBSTITUTE	SUBSTITUTE
SUM	SUM
SUMIFS	CALCULATE
SWITCH	SWITCH
T.DIST	T.DIST
T.DIST.2T	T.DIST.2T
T.DIST.RT	T.DIST.RT
T.INV	T.INV
T.INV.2T	T.INV.2T
TAN	TAN
TANH	TANH
TEXT	FORMAT
TEXTJOIN	CONCATENATEX
TIME	TIME
TIMEVALUE	TIMEVALUE
TODAY	TODAY
TRIM	TRIM
TRUE	TRUE
TRUNC	TRUNC
UNICHAR	UNICHAR
UNIQUE	DISTINCT
UNIQUE	VALUES
UPPER	UPPER
VALUE	VALUE
VAR.P	VAR.P
VAR.S	VAR.S
VLOOKUP	RELATED

WEEKDAY	WEEKDAY
WEEKNUM	WEEKNUM
XIRR	XIRR
XNPV	XNPV
YEAR	YEAR
YEARFRAC	YEARFRAC

The next table is an alphabetical list of Excel functions and the equivalent Power Query M function. If the Excel function is not in Table B.2, then there is no direct Power Query M equivalent.

TROUBLESHOOTING

Power Query M functions are case sensitive.

In the Excel formula bar, you can enter `=max(` or `=Max(` or `=MAX(` or even `=MAX (`. In Power Query, you must enter the function with the exact case shown in the tables included in this appendix.

Excel functions with Power Query M equivalents

Table B.2 shows an alphabetical list of Excel functions with their Power Query M equivalents.

Table B.2 Excel functions and Power Query M equivalents

Excel function	Power Query
ABS	Number.Abs
ACOS	Number.Acos
ASIN	Number.Asin
ATAN	Number.Atan
AVERAGE	List.Average
BITAND	Number.BitwiseAnd
BITLSHIFT	Number.BitwiseShiftLeft
BITOR	Number.BitwiseOr
BITRSHIFT	Number.BitwiseShiftRight
BITXOR	Number.BitwiseXor
CEILING	Number.RoundAwayFromZero
CEILING.MATH	Number.RoundUp

CHAR	Character.FromNumber
CLEAN	Text.Clean
CODE	Character.ToNumber
COMBIN	Number.Combinations
CONCAT	Text.Combine
COS	Number.Cos
COSH	Number.Cosh
COVARIANCE.P	List.Covariance
DATEVALUE	Date.FromText
DAY	Date.Day
DEC2BIN	Text.ToBinary
ENCODEURL	Uri.EscapeDataString
EOMONTH	Date.EndOfMonth
EXP	Number.E
EXP	Number.Exp
FACT	Number.Factorial
FLOOR	Number.RoundTowardZero
FLOOR.MATH	Number.RoundDown
HOUR	Duration.Hours
HOUR	Time.Hour
ISEVEN	Number.IsEven
ISODD	Number.IsOdd
ISOWEEKNUM	Date.WeekOfYear
LEFT	Text.Start
LEN	Text.Length
LN	Number.Ln
LOG	Number.Log
LOG10	Number.Log10
LOWER	Text.Lower
MAX	List.Max
MEDIAN	List.Median
MID	Text.Middle

MIN	List.Min
MINUTE	Duration.Minutes
MINUTE	Time.Minute
MOD	Number.Mod
MONTH	Date.Month
PERMUT	Number.Permutations
PI	Number.PI
POWER	Number.Power
PRODUCT	List.Product
PRODUCT	Value.Multiply
PROPER	Text.Proper
QUOTIENT	Value.Divide
RAND	Number.Random
RANDBETWEEN	Number.RandomBetween
REPLACE	Text.Replace
REPT	Text.Repeat
RIGHT	Text.End
ROUND	Number.Round
SECOND	Duration.Seconds
SECOND	Time.Second
SIGN	Number.Sign
SIN	Number.Sin
SINH	Number.Sinh
SORT	List.Sort
SQRT	Number.Sqrt
STDEV	List.StandardDeviation
SUM	List.Sum
SUM	Value.Add
TAN	Number.Tan
TANH	Number.Tanh
TEXT	Date.ToText
TEXT	Number.FromText
TEXT	Number.ToText

TEXT	Text.From
TEXT	Time.ToText
TEXTJOIN	Combiner.CombineTextByDelimiter
TRIM	Text.Trim
UNIQUE	List.Distinct
UPPER	Text.Upper
VALUE	Number.From
VALUE	Value.FromText
WEEKDAY	Date.DayOfWeek
YEAR	Date.Year

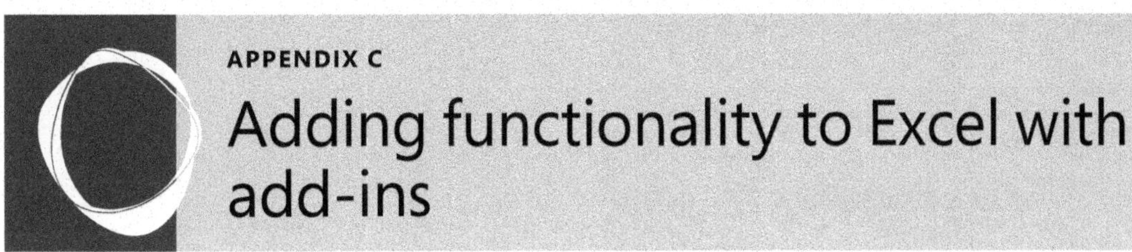

APPENDIX C

Adding functionality to Excel with add-ins

There are several free add-ins that ship with Excel but are not enabled. Each add-in takes a tiny amount of time to load, and there is no reason to lengthen the load time for Excel if you are never going to use the functionality.

This appendix will mention the add-ins that ship with Excel or are freely available in the App Store, which can be accessed from the Insert tab in Excel.

Understanding three types of add-ins and how to activate

Add-ins from different eras were written in different languages and are found in different places within Excel. Here is a quick overview on how to enable add-ins written in VBA, COM, or Javascript.

The oldest add-ins are developed in VBA. There is a quick shortcut to reach these add-ins. From Excel, press Alt+T. Excel will display the Office Access Key pane at the top of Excel. Press I. Excel will display the Add-Ins dialog box, as shown in Figure C.1.

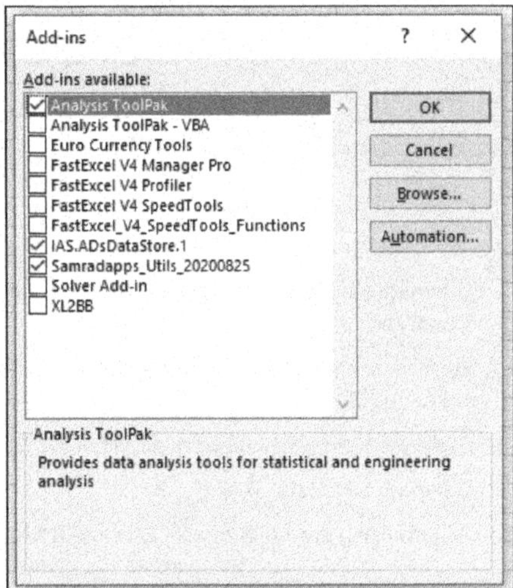

Figure C.1 A list of available add-ins.

Notice that core add-ins like Solver and the Analysis ToolPak are in this list. These add-ins are available to everyone with Excel. Choose the checkbox, click OK, and the add-in will load for use and continue to load each time you open Excel.

If you download an add-in from the Internet, you can use the Browse button on the right side of the dialog box to locate the add-in on your computer.

Later add-ins are written in COM. There are two ways to enable COM add-ins. If you have the Developer tab displayed in the ribbon, the second group is called Add-Ins. Click the COM Add-Ins icon to access the list of COM add-ins. If you don't have the Developer tab displayed, you can still get there by following these steps:

1. Go to File, Options.
2. Along the left side, choose Add-ins. A list of add-ins appears, but you cannot enable them yet. At the bottom of the dialog is a drop-down menu next to the word Manage.
3. Open the Manage drop-down menu and change Excel Add-Ins to COM Add-Ins. Click Go.
4. The COM Add-Ins dialog appears, as shown in Figure C.2. Click the checkbox next to any add-in to load that add-in.

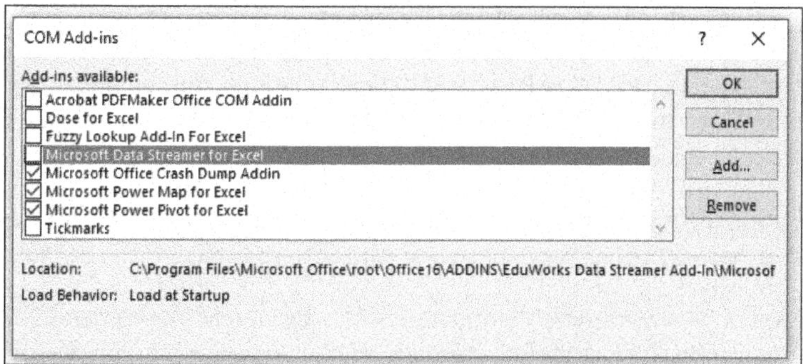

Figure C.2 Choose which COM add-ins should load at startup.

The third type of add-in uses an App Store concept. On the Insert tab, find the Add-ins group and choose Get Add-Ins. The Office Adds-In store appears where you can search for add-ins. Click the Add button to download and load an add-in (see Figure C.3).

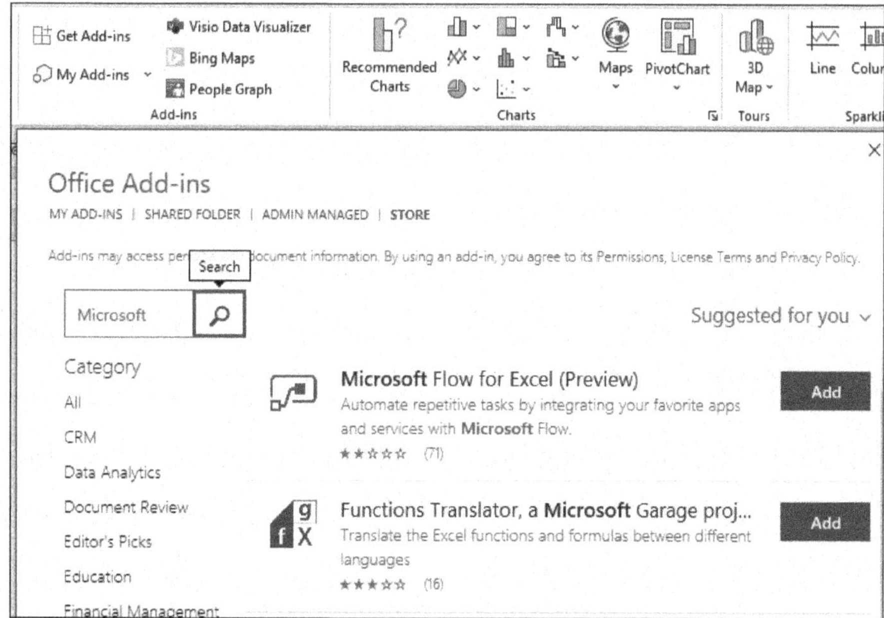

Figure C.3 Download add-ins from the Office Add-Ins store. Most of these are free.

The add-ins here don't automatically load the next time you open Excel. Use the My Add-ins icon shown in Figure C.3 to access an add-in in the future.

While there are hundreds of add-ins available, the rest of this appendix provides an overview of the Microsoft add-ins that are likely available in your copy of Excel.

Find optimal solutions with Solver

Solver will analyze a model to try to find optimal solutions. You can specify a variety of constraints and then specify which cell in your model you are trying to minimize, maximize, or set to a particular value.

Solver works great with linear problems and will usually find the optimal solution. But even problems that are not linear can be solved with Solver's evolutionary solving method.

Solver was originally written by Frontline Systems and spreadsheet legend Dan Fylstra. A copy of their Solvsamp.xls workbook is included with the downloads for this workbook. Those samples walk you through five solver scenarios.

Solver is a VBA add-in. Use Alt+T+I to enable it.

Audit workbooks with Inquire

Just before Excel 2013 was released, Microsoft bought the Prodiance company in order to get their auditing add-in. They include it for free with each enterprise copy of Excel (either at the E-3 or E-5 level). However, because Inquire requires several seconds to load, it is not enabled by default.

Inquire is a COM add-in, so use the method shown in Figure C.2 to see if it is available to you.

Once installed, you will have a new Inquire tab on the ribbon (see Figure C.4). The following tools are available in Inquire:

- **Workbook Analysis:** Searches a workbook and looks for potentially risky operations. You will get a detailed report showing 80+ situations that might cause problems. This is a great way to discover circular references, plug numbers, very hidden worksheets, and more.

- **Relationship Diagrams:** Inquire provides interactive diagrams at the workbook, worksheet, or cell level. If you inherited a large workbook, these diagrams can help you understand how the worksheets and cells are connected to each other.

- **Compare Files:** If you have two versions of a workbook, the Compare Files tool will show all changes made between the two versions.

- **Clean Excess Formatting:** If you ever received the "Too Many Formats" error, this tool will help you clean the extra unused formats.

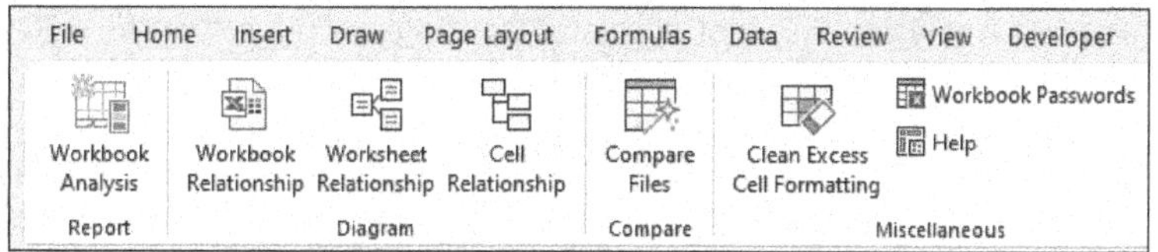

Figure C.4 Use the Inquire add-in to find potential problems in your workbook.

Get descriptive statistics with the Analysis ToolPak

Before Excel 2007, many people had the Analysis ToolPak installed because it provided 89 calculation functions. But starting with Excel 2007, those 89 functions became part of Excel. After that, the only reason to install the Analysis ToolPak was for a series of statistics reports.

Those reports are ugly. The user interface to select data for the reports looks 30 years old. It is pretty clear that no one at Microsoft is actively paying attention to this add-in.

Dan Fylstra from Frontline Solvers took it upon himself to rewrite the suite of tools. Search the Add-In Store for XLMiner Analysis ToolPak. It is free. It runs in desktop Excel and in Excel Online. The add-in runs from a new, modern task pane, as shown in Figure C.5.

The tools include:

- **Anova:** Analysis of variance (ANOVA) can be used to compare the means between two or more groups of values.
- **Correlation:** A statistical measure of the degree to which one variable is related to another.
- **Covariance:** This is another statistical tool that measures how two random variables are related to each other.
- **Descriptive Statistics:** This tool generates the Mean, Standard Error, Median, Mode, Standard Deviation, Sample Variance, Kurtosis, Skewness, Range, Minimum, Maximum, Sum, and Count for a data set.
- **Exponential Smoothing:** Data is likely to show some random variation over time. Exponential smoothing can be used to reduce the effect of these variations to reveal any underlying trends that may exist.
- **F-Test:** This tool tests the null hypothesis that two samples come from two independent populations having the equal variances.

- **Fourier Analysis** This tool calculates the discrete Fourier transform (DFT) or its inverse for a column of data.
- **Histogram** This tool creates individual and cumulative frequencies for a range of cells and a specified number of bins. A histogram uses bars of different heights to display the number of records in the population.
- **Linear Regression** This tool creates a statistical model that can be used to predict the value of a dependent variable based on the value(s) of one more independent variables.
- **Logistic Regression** This tool is used when the dependent variable represents the occurrence or nonoccurrence of some outcome event and are usually coded as 0 or 1 (success).
- **Moving Average** This is another smoothing technique that is less complex than Exponential Smoothing described previously. Each point is smoothed by averaging it with the previous two points. This should not be used if you have seasonality in your data.
- **Random Number Generation** This returns a range of random numbers drawn from one of seven distributions: Uniform, Normal, Bernoulli, Binomial, Poisson, Patterned, or Discrete.
- **Rank and Percentile** This generates an output table containing the ordinal and percentage ranking of each value in the dataset.
- **Sampling** This selects a sample of values from a population. It can be a random sample or a periodic sample, such as every 7th cell.
- **t-Test** This performs a paired two-sample Student's t-Test to ascertain if the null hypothesis (means of two populations are equal) can be accepted or rejected.
- **z-Test** This runs a two-sample z-Test means with known variances to test the null hypothesis that there is no difference between the means of two independent populations.

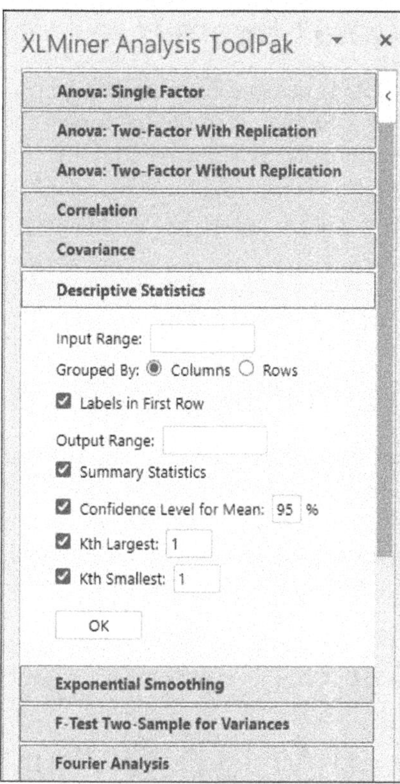

Figure C.5 The old Analysis ToolPak reports have been replaced by a free add-in from Dan Fylstra.

Find near matches with Fuzzy Lookup

Long before Power Query offered a fuzzy match join, the team at Microsoft Labs had published their Fuzzy Lookup Add-In for Excel. This tool never shipped as part of Excel, but it is a free download hosted by Microsoft. Download it from: https://www.microsoft.com/en-us/download/details.aspx?id=15011. In a fuzzy match, Excel can detect that John Smith and Smith John might be the same person. Alternatively, you can specify that Corp and Corporation are synonyms so that Alexander Corporation and Alexander Corp are the same.

Being an experimental tool, the main documentation is a ReadMe.docx and a Portfolio.xlsx that ships as part of the add-in installation package. You have to be a detective to locate the files at C:\Users\[your name]\AppData\Local\Apps\Microsoft\Fuzzy Lookup Add-In For Excel\.

Perform science projects with Data Streamer

Designed specifically for classroom use, the Data Streamer will collect data from a variety of microcontrollers. If your science classroom has a thermometer with the correct connection, it can stream data periodically into Excel so the students can build a chart from the data. It is a great tool that prevents the students from having to record values with a pencil before tranferring to a spreadsheet. The students will have to learn how to create a graph from the data streamed to Excel.

Data Streamer is a COM add-in. Enable it as shown in Figure C.2.

Perform Euro conversions with Euro Currency Tools

The Euro Currency Tools add-in activates the `EUROCONVERT` function in Excel. It can be used to convert the currencies replaced by the Euro to other currencies. As Excel geeks were waiting for the 500th Excel function, this add-in from nearly 20 years ago received new attention. Enabling the add-in enables one new calculation function: `EUROCONVERT`. The 500th function finally arrived once the `MAKETABLE`, `BYROW`, `BYCOL`, `SCAN`, `REDUCE`, and `ISOMITTED` functions arrived in summer 2021.

Find Euro Currency Tools in the Add-ins dialog box, as shown in Figure C.1.

Generate diagrams from data with Visio Data Visualizer

At first glance, this free add-in is cool. You can take data in Excel and generate some interesting diagrams right in Excel. The tool supports organization charts, flowcharts, and cross-functional flowcharts (also known as swim lane charts).

Find the add-in in the Add-In Store (refer to Figure C.3). They have robust examples that you can easily adapt and build some cool charts.

However, once you are done with the diagram, you might find that you want to do some simple formatting. Perhaps you want to change the title or resize something. Those simple changes require you to buy Visio, which adds hundreds of dollars of cost to your Microsoft 365 subscription.

Perform sentiment analysis using Azure Machine Learning

This one is free and is not trying to sell you anything. Search the Add-In store (see Figure C.3) for Azure Machine Learning. There is a silly Titanic predictor, but the real power comes from the Text Sentiment Analysis. If you have survey data with comments from your customers, the Sentiment Analysis tool will rank each comment on a scale from 0% to 100%. Low numbers are likely negative comments and high numbers are likely positive comments.

Generate a chart with people using People Graph

If you have data with statistics that represent the number of people in certain categories, the People Graph add-in can create an interesting chart of that data.

People Graph is free from Microsoft. Use the App Store as shown previously in Figure C.3.

Figure C.6 shows a typical graph generated by the add-in. You can customize the theme, colors, and even the icon that is used for to represent people.

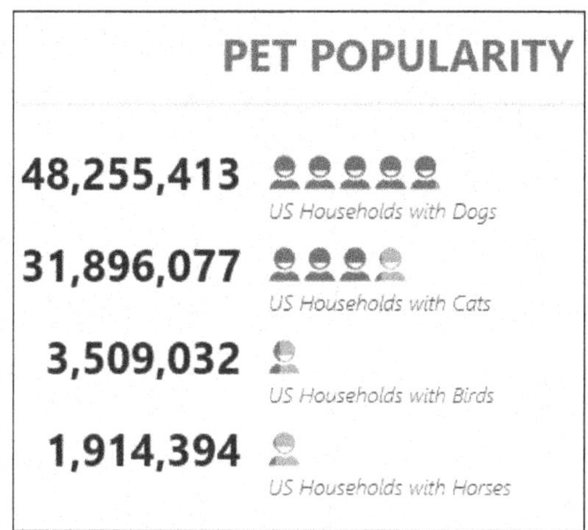

Figure C.6 Generate a graph indicating how many people fall into certain categories using the free People Graph add-in.

Generate fake data

This one is not from Microsoft the corporation, but it is some freeware from one of the veteran Excel Project Managers, Sam Radakovitz.

Download the add-in from *http://samradapps.com/fake-data*. This is one that I recommend only opening when you need to generate fake data. Sam has some event handlers in the code that can be a little annoying when you aren't generating fake data.

When the add-in is open, a lightning bolt appears to the right of the Home tab. Use the icons to generate a table of fake data or add columns with names, addresses, or dates to existing data (see Figure C.7). The data shown in rows 1-7 in Figure C.7 was generated using the Table drop-down menu in the app.

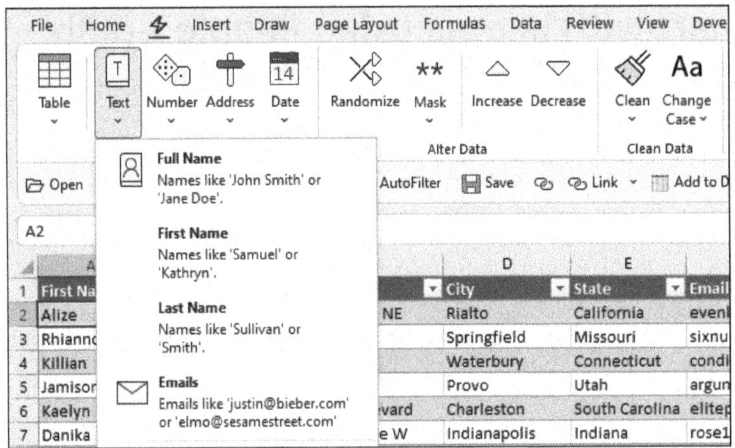

Figure C.7 Quickly generate fake data using this add-in from Sam Radakovitz.

Test brilliant new functions for Excel with Fast Excel

There are many commercial add-ins available for sale that I am not listing here—with one exception. Charles Williams is a long-time Excel MVP. He is famous for his whitepapers on improving calculation times in Excel.

He has written a library of very useful functions that should be in Excel. In fact, the Excel calc team has replicated a few of Charles' functions and added them to Excel. Compared to Charles, the Excel team moves very slowly. It can take 18 months from conception until a new function arrives in the beta version of Excel. In contrast, Charles Williams wrote all the functions shown in Figure C.8 in about three weeks.

If you buy one copy of Fast Excel V4 to author the functions, Charles will include a free run-time component that your coworkers can use, so the functions will continue to calculate when they open your workbooks. Download the 30-day trial from https://mrx.cl/speedv4, and test it out. There is a good chance you can convince your CFO that they should spend the money for a copy of the add-in in order to cut down your time developing solutions in Excel.

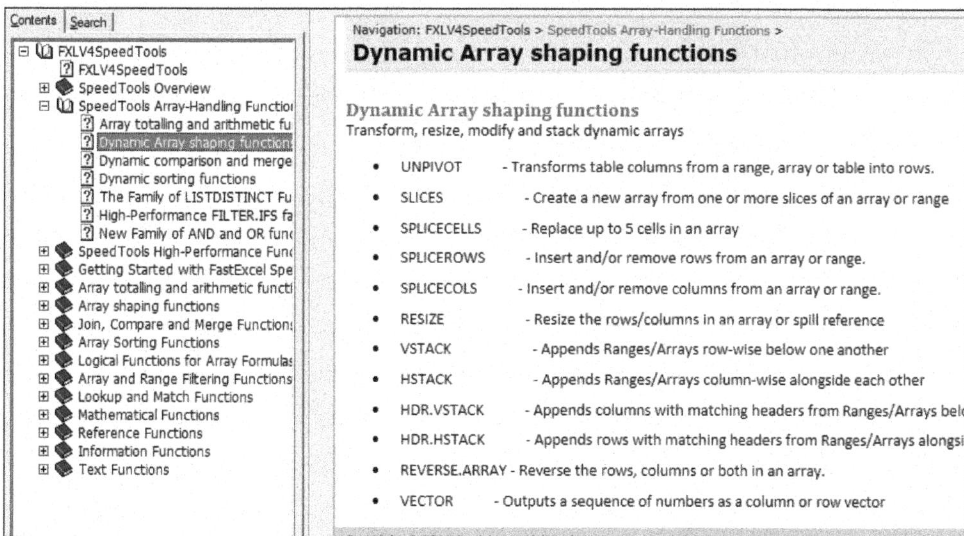

Figure C.8 Add over 60 great new calculation functions to Excel using FastExcel V4 from Charles Williams.

APPENDIX C

Index

Symbols

A

D

E

F

K

L

M

N

O

P

Q

R

S

T

U

V

X

Y

Z

G2 Entertainment

Publishers Jules Gammond and Edward Adams
First edition published in the UK in 2015
G2 Entertainment 2015

Print Edition ISBN: 978-1-7828-1167-1

DESIGN BY **FLOKK** LTD

THE PFA PREMIER

FOOTBALL LEAGUE PLAYERS' RECORDS

1946 – 2015

EDITED AND COMPILED BY BARRY J. HUGMAN

G2 Entertainment

CONTENTS

FOREWORD

'A definitive record of all professional (and a few amateur) players who have graced the Football and Premier Leagues': that's the proud achievement of the PFA and the publishers of this unique book.

Barry Hugman and his team of enthusiasts have worked tirelessly to compile a list of every footballer to have played in the Football League and Premier League since the Second World War – a thankless task you might think, but one which has been carried out and completed with all the professionalism of those contained within.

So, here then is the official list of all those who actually wore their club colours in League battle. And, of course, this book also shows the transfers, plus the career records of every single player. All of these players have been members of the Professional Footballers' Association and we at the PFA are proud to see such a magnificently produced record of the careers of so many members, past and present.

In my opinion, this book will not only give hours of pleasure to football fans throughout the country, but to ex-players who love reminiscing, love comparing records, and who love following the modern game and the fortunes of today's stars. It is a veritable 'who's who' of all the players who have brought so much pleasure to so many people over the last 70 years.

We are delighted to be involved with this publication and anticipate referring to it time and time again, and our thanks go to Barry and his team for all their dedicated hard work.

Gordon Taylor OBE
Chief Executive
Professional Footballers' Association

INTRODUCTION

BY BARRY J. HUGMAN (EDITOR & COMPILER)

Since the first edition of *(Premier &) Football League Players' Records* appeared in 1980, I have strived to improve the accuracy of this now well-established work of reference on post-war footballers' careers, not only by updating the statistics and listing new entries for players who made their Premier and Football League debuts since the last edition, but also correcting, where necessary, the details of players long since retired.

When I first started this compendium in the mid-1970s, the only source of data was the hardy football perennials – the *News of the World* and *News Chronicle* (later *Playfair*) football annuals – which listed each player's appearances and goals for the previous season. During the 1980s, a number of football statisticians began to chronicle the detailed history of their favourite clubs, match by match, with reference to Football League archives and local newspapers. Much of their research came to fruition in the shape of club histories, which included line-ups for every match played, and, at the time of going to press, many clubs are now covered. A big thank you should also be given to Tony Brown of SoccerData Publications, who continues to publish the definitive histories of clubs yet to be dealt with, and Dave Twydell of Yore Publications.

All their research has been cross-referenced with the data contained in previous editions of this book and many discrepancies in appearances and goals have been noted. In most cases the discrepancies were trivial, a question of one or two appearances or goals difference. In a few cases they were significant, usually when players with the same (or similar) surname played in the same season for the same club. If the *P&FLPR's* team are satisfied that the research has been done correctly and that the statistics continued in these books are more reliable than the figures in by-gone football annuals, we have corrected our records accordingly.

It should be noted, however, that while an appearance in a particular match is a matter of fact, goalscorers are often a matter of opinion. In a goalmouth scramble, a goal may be credited to one player by the assembled journalists sitting 100 yards from the action and reported as such by the press the following day, whilst the club, following a post-mortem, credits the goal to another of its players. In such cases we accept the opinion of the club rather than the press. However, there are other cases where the club is anxious to credit a goal to one of its own players when it is quite manifestly an own goal. For example, the misjudged back pass, the misdirected shot deflected into goal by an opposing defender, or the goalkeeper stepping over the line after safely catching a high ball. Such examples we consider as 'own goals' and not credited to any player. More recently, the Premier League has set up a panel to deal with disputed goals and it's their decision that we accept. As a result of these differences of interpretation, there are inevitably some small discrepancies between the goalscoring figures of some players in this book and those logged by other sources.

Players Names: As far as is humanly possible we have listed players' names in alphabetical order, firstly by surname and then by Christian names. However, in cases where players' are better known by their second or third Christian name, we have listed that (name) in brackets. For example Mark Hughes of Manchester United was christened 'Leslie Mark' and is shown as 'Leslie Mark (Mark)'. Other players are not recorded under the family surname. For example, the Brazilian, Mirandinha, of Newcastle United, is in fact 'Francisco da Silva', but is listed under his adopted moniker rather than his family name. In the case of double-barrelled surnames we have taken a pragmatic view, according to the name most commonly used by themselves or the media. Thus, Ian Storey-Moore and Forbes Phillipson-Masters will be found under their full names while the Martin-Chambers brothers, David and Philip, will be found under 'Chambers' and Jeffrey Thompson-Minton will be found under 'Minton'. In many cases players were known by a corruption of their Christian names or by a totally different nickname, such as the Brentford goalkeeper, 'Sonny' Feehan, christened Ignatius. In these cases, players are listed under their christened name with their familiar moniker shown in brackets afterwards. Surnames that start with Mac and Mc are listed side by side so that they are not missed by those who are not sure of the spelling, while men whose surnames start with Mack, but may not be considered to be a 'Mack' by us, are still shown in the same area of the alphabet for ease.

Birthplaces: The purpose of showing birthplaces is to indicate the area of the British Isles a player originates from. Occasionally, this is misleading. Many UK players were born overseas, either as sons of fathers serving in the armed forces stationed in West Germany, or in former British colonies in Africa or Asia. When this occurs, the birthplace does not indicate their nationality, which is conferred on them by their parentage. A player may be born in one area, but grow up in another. In such cases the place of education is more meaningful than place of birth. Some players were born while their parents were on holiday, such as the Kimble brothers, Alan and Garry, in Poole (Dorset). In their particular case, as it was known to us, the birthplace is shown as the family home of Dagenham. In most cases birthplaces are recorded from birth certificates, which may only indicate an area such as a county or a registration district with an historic (and therefore obscure) name, without stating the town or village of birth. For example, all players born in the counties of Gloucestershire and Cornwall (Truro) are registered as born in the county town when their actual birthplace was many miles distant. Those born in County Durham and Surrey are often shown by obscure registration districts entitled 'Central South-East' or 'North West' which do not specify an actual place name. In such cases we have selected the largest town in those districts unless a more precise birthplace is known to us from other sources.

With nearly all births from the 1950s onwards occurring in maternity hospitals, rather than in the family home as was the custom previously, most births are registered at, or by, the hospital often located in a different administrative area from the family home - such as Rochford (for Southend-on-Sea) and Orsett (for Grays and the Thurrock area). In some rural areas the hospital may be up to 30 miles from the family home. This often robs the villages and small market towns of their 'claim to fame' as the birthplace (or, to be more exact, the origin) of a famous footballer. In cases where the 'true' birthplace is known to the authors the original birthplace (shown in earlier editions) has been corrected. However, where the birthplace is an obscure country village, or a little-known suburb of a large city, the name of the nearest market town (or city) has been substituted. The only exception to this rule is the case of former mining villages in County Durham, Northumberland and Scotland, which, however small, produced many outstanding players. In those cases we have taken care to acknowledge their contribution to football history.

Birthdate: For recent players we have checked our data against the PFA's records, and although some discrepancies with club histories have been noted against older players, mainly in the year of birth, when we are satisfied that a transcribing error has occurred we have corrected the original birthdate.

International Appearances: Shown by country – full international appearances are displayed first, followed by Wartime; u23; u21; Semi Pro; Amateur; Youth; School where relevant. Representative levels include: (FLge) Football League; (ILge) Irish League; (LoI) League of Ireland; (NILge) Northern Ireland Regional League; (SLge) Scottish League; (WLge) Welsh League.

League Clubs: During the post-war period, although several clubs have changed their name we show their current name so not to confuse the reader. For example, Hartlepool United began 1946-47 as Hartlepools United, before becoming Hartlepool in 1968-69 and then Hartlepool United in 1977-78. However, where the club name changes dramatically such as Wimbledon to Milton Keynes Dons, any player who appeared during the transition is shown on two separate club lines.

Source (or Previous Club): This column indicates a player's origins, whether from outside the P/FL or within the ranks of the Leagues. For the latter the following code is used:-

Jnr = Junior players signed from school/college without serving an apprenticeship or trainee period.

App = Apprentice signing prior to 1986.

YT = Trainee. This term was introduced by the FA from 1984 onwards to replace 'Apprentice' and includes players sponsored by the then government Youth Training Scheme.

Sch = Scholar. From 1999 onwards trainees were gradually reclassified as 'scholars' under the newly introduced FA Academy system of youth training, of which status was granted to all Premier League and most Championship clubs immediately, and over time to nearly all Football League clubs. Thus we have shown most young players who signed professional contracts after July 2002 as former scholars who graduated through their club's youth team.

Tr = Transfers. This is used for direct transfers, players who moved to a new club after being released, and some players who signed for a new club several months later after not appearing elsewhere. It also includes players who initially went out on loan before signing on a permanent basis.

L = Loan signing, or temporary transfer, shown only when the player made an appearance.

For players who arrived from overseas clubs, the following country codes are employed against the club they signed from: Albania (ALB); Algeria (ALG); Angola (ANG); Antigua (ANT); Argentina (ARG); Armenia (ARM); Australia (AUS); Austria (AUT); Azerbaijan (AZE); Bahamas (BAH); Bahrain (BRN); Bangladesh (BAN); Barbados (BAR); Belarus (BLR); Belgium (BEL); Benin (BEN); Bermuda (BER); Bolivia (BOL); Bosnia (BOS); Brazil (BRA); Brunei (BRU); Bulgaria (BUL); Cameroon (CMR); Canada (CAN); Chile (CHL); China (CHN); Colombia (COL); Commonwealth of Independent States (CIS); Costa Rica (CRC); Croatia (CRO); Cyprus (CYP); Czechoslovakia (TCH); Czech Republic (CZE); Denmark (DEN); East Germany (GDR); Ecuador (ECU); Egypt (EGY); Estonia (EST); Finland (FIN); France (FRA); Gabon (GAB); Gambia (GAM); Georgia (GEO); Germany (GER); Ghana (GHA); Greece (GRE); Grenada (GRN); Guatemala (GUA); Guinea (GUI); Guinea-Bissau (GBS); Honduras (HON); Hong Kong (HKG); Hungary (HUN); Iceland (ICE); India (IND); Indonesia (INA); Iran (IRA); Iraq (IRQ); Israel (ISR); Italy (ITA); Ivory Coast (IVC); Jamaica (JAM); Japan (JPN); Kosovo (KOS); Kuwait (KUW); Latvia (LAT); Libya (LBA); Lithuania (LTU); Luxembourg (LUX); Macedonia (MCD); Malaysia (MLY); Malta (MLT); Mexico (MEX); Moldova (MDA); Montenegro (MNE); Morocco (MOR); Mozambique (MOZ); Namibia (NAM); Netherlands (NED); New Zealand (NZL); Nicaragua (NCA); Nigeria (NIG); Norway (NOR); Paraguay (PAR); Peru (PER); Poland (POL); Portugal (POR); Qatar (QAT); Republic of Ireland (ROI); Reunion (REU); Rhodesia (RHO); Romania (ROM); Russia (RUS); St Vincent (SVG); Saudi Arabia (SAU); Senegal (SEN); Serbia (SRB); Sierra Leone (SLE); Singapore (SIN); Slovakia (SVK); Slovenia (SVN); South Africa (RSA); South Korea (KOR); Soviet Union (URS); Spain (SPN); Suriname (SUR); Sweden (SWE); Switzerland (SUI); Tanzania (TAN); Thailand (THA); Togo (TOG); Trinidad (TRD); Tunisia (TUN); Turkey (TKY); Ukraine (UKR); United Arab Emirates (UAE); United States of America (USA); Uruguay (UGY); Venezuela (VEN); Vietnam (VIE); West Germany (FRG); Yugoslavia (YUG); Zambia (ZAM); Zimbabwe (ZIM).

Date Signed: The date given by month/year is when the player signed professional or non-contract forms. In the case of amateurs, the date of their initial signing is indicated. For players first signed on loan, before a permanent transfer was arranged, the date of signing is that of the loan transfer, except when the player returned to his former club and made further appearances in the reserves or first team.

Seasons Played: The year shown is the first year of the season played. Thus, 1997 indicates the season 1997-98, '1979-85' means that the player made his debut in 1979-80 and his last appearance in 1985-86, but does not necessarily mean that he played in every intervening season.

Appearances, Subs and Goals: The statistics shown are for Premier League and Football League matches only. Cup games and end of season play-offs are not included, nor are appearances made for clubs before they entered the League or in temporary absence (e.g. Lincoln City 1987-88 and Darlington 1989-90). Whilst other sources have aggregated full and substitute appearances into a single total, we consider it important to maintain the distinction. Most substitutions occur in the final quarter of the game and we feel that one full appearance, plus 17 substitute appearances, is not the same as 18 appearances.

Positions:

G = Goalkeeper
FB = Full Back
LB = Left Back
RB = Right Back
D = Defender
CD = Central Defender
CH = Centre Half
WH = Wing Half
LH = Left Half
RH = Right Half
M = Central Midfielder
DM = Defensive Midfielder
LM = Left-Sided Midfielder
RM = Right-Sided Midfielder
W = Winger
LW = Left Winger
RW = Right Winger
IF = Inside Forward
CF = Centre Forward
F = Forward

Few players occupy the same playing position for every game in their career. Some players may start their careers as central defenders but achieve success as goal-scoring forwards, with shot-shy forwards finally making their mark as defenders. Wingers may be converted to full back or ball-winning midfielders, whilst forwards in the latter stages of their career may lose their pace and are successfully converted to play-making midfielders. In this edition we have attempted to describe a player's position with more precision than previously. Thus, we show Left/Right Back, Left/Right Half and Left/Right Winger as well as Full Back, Wing Half and Winger. Generally speaking (LB), (LH), (LM) and (LW) indicates that the player was left footed, but given the relative scarcity of left-footed players this cannot always be assumed to be the case.

As a rule of thumb, players who occupied the same position for 70% or more of their appearances are shown by that position, but where the frequency of position is less than 70% the two most common positions are shown, such as LB/M or WH/IF. Utility players, of whom the most well-known historic example is Paul Madeley of Leeds United, who famously played in every position on the pitch (or at least played in every outfield shirt number from 2 to 11), are shown as D/M. This indicates that the player was utilised at full back, central defence and all, or some, of the midfield positions. This should not be confused with the defensive midfielder (DM), a specialist position which became fashionable with Claude Makelele of Chelsea, but had been a key component of successful teams for at least 20 years previously in the form of players such as Kevin Richardson of Everton, Arsenal and Aston Villa, and Ronnie Whelan of Liverpool. Since the defensive midfielder scores very few goals and rarely runs with the ball he is often the least glamorous member of the team, as his role is to sit deep in front of the defence in order to break up attacks with interceptions and winning tackles before transferring the ball quickly to set up counter attacks by more adventurous colleagues.

The nomenclature of playing positions has changed considerably since the last war. From 1946 to the early 1960s it was widely assumed that teams played a 2-3-5 formation with two full backs, three half backs and five forwards. In fact, after the change to the offside law in 1925 the true formation was usually 3-2-2-3, with the centre half converted to a centre back, or even 3-3-4, with one of the inside forwards withdrawn to a deeper position. Despite all the changes, the term 'full back' still persists up to the present day, whilst, until the adoption of the term 'midfielder' in the mid-1960s, 'inside forwards' could be either deep lying schemers such as Johnny Haynes (Fulham), or lethal goalscorers such as Ted Phillips (Ipswich Town). In 1958 Brazil introduced 4-2-4 to the world, when winning the World Cup in Sweden. Under this system, one wing half was converted to twin centre back, while the other wing half, plus an inside forward, patrolled the middle of the park. Although this system was copied by many English clubs, it was not entirely successful since it required two talented and hard-working players in the central positions.

After Alf Ramsey won the 1966 World Cup for England with a 4-3-3 system, with one winger withdrawn to augment the midfield, most English clubs adopted the same system, and when Ramsey dispensed with wingers altogether with a 4-4-2 system for the 1970 World Cup in Mexico the orthodox attacking winger disappeared for several years from the English game, to be replaced by workaholic midfielders. By 1970 the terms 'centre half', 'wing half', 'inside forward', 'outside right' and 'outside left' were virtually obsolescent, to be replaced by 'central defenders', 'midfielders', 'strikers' and 'wingers'. Happily, the orthodox winger returned to favour in the 1980s, with a corresponding increase in the goal rate as some clubs reverted to 4-3-3 instead of 4-4-2. In more recent times many teams have deployed three central defenders with the two full backs pushed forward into midfield as auxiliary wingers or wing backs. The result has been the emergence of a 3-5-2 formation, with overcrowded midfield areas, or a more fluid 3-4-3 system with one winger deployed as an extra forward.

From the late 1960s onwards shirt numbers became increasingly unrelated to a player's position in the team formation. The trend was started by Dick Graham, manager of Crystal Palace (1963-66), Leyton Orient (1966-68) and Colchester United (1968-72), who would swap around players shirt numbers, often from match to match, in order to confuse the opposition. Many managers followed suit, although thankfully not to the same extent as Graham. With the temporary demise of wingers the redundant No. 7 (RW) and No. 11 (LW) shirts were often allocated to auxiliary defenders, whilst at some clubs the No. 5 shirt became the 'marque' of a defensive midfielder rather than the traditional central defender. The introduction of squad numbers on players' shirts from 1993 onwards almost entirely eliminated the link between shirt number and position, although most clubs still allocate the Nos. 2 to 6 shirts to defenders and the Nos. 9 to 11 shirts to forwards.

Since the first edition we have implemented several changes, including that of listing the complete career record of all players who played in the Football League prior to the last war. This takes into account famous players like Sir Stanley Matthews, who played for eight seasons before the outbreak of war and for nearly 20 after, and also many other stars whose careers ran parallel such as Stan Cullis. These are the players who had lost the best years of their football life because of hostilities and retired early into the post-war period. Early editions showed Cullis as having played only 37 games for 'Wolves', whereas, in fact, he played 152 times between 1934-35 and 1946-47.

Prior to the last edition, we carried out further research into players whose careers were interrupted by the Second World War. The tale of the three (yes, three) Harry Toppings, all full backs, all from Lancashire, and all playing League football in the 1930s, is worth a chapter on its own. Only one of them played post-war League football and his record appears here, having been revised from what was published before. Similar stories could be told about the two James Henry Clarkes and the two goalkeepers called John Daniels. Even in the early 1960s, Stockport County had two wingers – Michael Connolly and Michael Connelly – who were originally confused. We have also introduced full Christian names, along with many additional notifications of players who have unfortunately deceased, provided by Michael Featherstone, and will continue to bring on board relevant information as and when it becomes available.

As we have stated in previous editions, one thing is for sure... if they have played in the post-war Football League and Premier League, they are included within the pages of this book and somebody, somewhere, sometime, will look them up. *Premier & Football League Players' Records* is a testament to all of the men who have donned the colours of their specific side(s) since 1946/47 and to the Professional Footballers' Association, who have magnificently supported their members throughout that period.

Finally, we have tried without success to trace birth and birthplace details for the following:- William E. Davies (Crewe), Len Davis (Southend), James Grant (Brighton), Michael Gray (Aldershot and Watford), Leslie James (Darlington), William Johnston (Barrow), Stan J. Jones (Crewe), James J. Kelly (Barrow), Michael J. Kelly (Wolves and Crewe), John Peat (Workington), Joe Riley (Darlington), Alex Shaw (Crewe), Alf Smith (Walsall), Allan Smith (Hull), George T. Smith (Walsall), John Smith (Ipswich), Tommy Teasdale (Hull), Ken Williams (Watford) and Robert Wilson (Workington). If anyone has further information the editor would like to hear from them.

ACKNOWLEDGMENTS

With *Premier & Football League Players' Records* now in its seventh edition, the editor would once again like to thank the many experts without whose help this book would not have been updated as effectively.

The assistant editor, **Alan Platt**, who by profession was a freelance transport planner working overseas, first introduced himself to me as long ago as 1981, following the release of the first edition. His help on the ever-continuing project has been invaluable, especially regarding players' biodata, such as birthplaces, source clubs, signing dates and international appearances, which he researches diligently. Since 1960 he has kept detailed records on all League clubs and their players. He has assisted me on all of my football publications since 1981, namely the six editions of this book, the two editions of *Premier League: The Players,* and *The PFA Footballers Who's Who,* which ran for 16 years. He has also assisted Jack Rollin with the updating of international data for the *Sky Sports Football Yearbook*. Now residing in Manchester, he takes a keen interest in the lower levels of football outside the Premier League and Football League from the Football Conference (now renamed the National League) down to more regional leagues.

Another important member of the production team, and also an assistant editor, is **Michael Featherstone**. Michael was a willing helper when I first conceived the idea for such a book way back in 1975. His speciality is in researching births and deaths, something he also does for the various cricketing societies and the new wave of soccer histories that have begun to be produced over the last 20 years or so. He started out by collecting both cricket and football information, often topping up with visits to the Colindale National Newspaper Library. Eventually, he joined Ray Spiller's Association of Football Statisticians after being introduced by his good friend, the late Morley Farror. He has also contributed to the *British Boxing Yearbook*, *The Olympic Games: Complete Track & Field Results 1896-1988*, *Cricket Who's Who*, *The Official Football League Yearbook*, *PFA Footballers' Who's Who*, and many other publications.

Dan Stott has been a passionate follower of football since the late 1980s and is also active in grassroots football, playing mostly as a defender in the local Saturday leagues. Professionally, he has built his career as a software engineer, and more recently has using been using his technical skills to build several football and boxing websites.

Again, I would like to place on record my thanks to all the editors of the various club histories that have been published since the first edition of *Premier & Football League Players Records*. My gratitude is also extended to all the contributors of the *PFA Footballers Who's Who*, an annual work which went much of the way in updating this edition. **Tony Brown** and **Michael Joyce**, who produce the *English National Football Archive Yearbook*, were also kind enough to allow me to audit my 2014/15 records against their excellent publication.

I am indebted to **Gordon Small**, who visited the National Football Museum in Preston to examine information relating to certain players who played both before and after the war. Another die-hard fan, **Paul Kellett,** was extremely helpfully when it came to Chesterfield players.

Once again I would like to show my appreciation for the support given by **Gordon Taylor OBE**, the Chief Executive of the Professional Footballers' Association, who has always recognised that this book is a testament to their members, both past and present.

Barry J. Hugman

League Club	Source	Date Signed	Seasons Played	Career Record Apps	Subs	Gls
AARONS Rolando						
Born: Kingston, Jamaica, 16 November, 1995						W
England: Youth						
Newcastle U	Sch	03/14	14	0	4	1
AAS Einar Jan						
Born: Moss, Norway, 12 October, 1955						CD
Norway: 35						
Nottingham F	Bayern Munich (GER)	03/81	80-81	20	1	1
ABADAKI Godwin Ebenmosi						
Born: Kwara, Nigeria, 21 October, 1993						F
Rochdale	Jnr	07/11	11	0	2	0
ABBEY Benjamin Charles (Ben)						
Born: Westminster, Central London, England, 13 May, 1977						F
Oxford U	Crawley T	09/99	99	0	10	0
Southend U	Tr	10/00	00	15	9	8
ABBEY George Peterson						
Born: Port Harcourt, Nigeria, 20 October, 1978						RB
Nigeria: 18						
Macclesfield T	Sharks (NIG)	08/99	99-03	79	21	1
Port Vale	Tr	12/04	04-06	53	9	1
Crewe Alex	Tr	07/07	07-08	24	6	0
ABBEY Nathanael (Nathan)						
Born: Islington, N London, England, 11 July, 1978						G
Luton T	YT	05/96	98-00	54	1	0
Chesterfield	Tr	06/01	01	46	0	0
Northampton T	Tr	08/02	02	4	1	0
Burnley	Ipswich T (NC)	12/03				
Boston U	Tr	07/04	04-05	61	0	0
Bristol C	Tr	02/06	05	0	1	0
Torquay U	Tr	08/06	06	24	0	0
Brentford	Tr	12/06	06	16	0	0
MK Dons	Tr	08/07	08	0	1	0
ABBEY Zema						
Born: Luton, England, 17 April, 1977						F
Cambridge U	Hitchin T	02/00	99-00	16	6	5
Norwich C	Tr	12/00	00-03	30	29	7
Boston U	L	08/04	04	3	2	1
Wycombe W	Tr	10/04	04	3	2	0
Bradford C	Tr	11/04	04	6	0	1
Torquay U	Tr	03/05	04	2	4	1
ABBIS Keith Douglas						
Born: Hatfield, Hertfordshire, England, 26 April, 1932						LH
Brighton & HA	Letchworth T	10/57	59-60	19	-	3
ABBLEY Stephen George (Steve)						
Born: Liverpool, England, 19 March, 1957						W
Swindon T	Parks	10/79	79-81	14	9	0
ABBOTT Bradley Ian						
Born: Doncaster, South Yorkshire, England, 24 December, 1994						M
Barnsley	Sch	07/13	14	4	1	0
ABBOTT Gregory Stephen (Greg)						
Born: Coventry, England, 14 December, 1963						M
Coventry C	App	01/82				
Bradford C	Tr	09/82	82-90	256	25	38
Halifax T	Tr	07/91	91	24	4	1
Hull C	Guiseley	12/92	92-95	120	4	16
ABBOTT John						
Born: Winsford, Cheshire, England, 25 May, 1943						CH
Died: South Cheshire, England, December, 2002						
Crewe Alex	Winsford U	06/61	61-64	2	-	0
ABBOTT Pawel Tadeusz Howard						
Born: York, England, 2 December, 1981						F
Poland: U21-1						
Preston NE	LKS Lodz (POL)	02/01	02-03	8	17	6
Bury	L	08/02	02	13	0	5
Bury	L	03/03	02	4	0	1
Huddersfield T	Tr	02/04	03-06	83	28	48
Swansea C	Tr	01/07	06	9	9	1
Darlington	Tr	07/07	07-08	31	11	17
Oldham Ath	Tr	07/09	09	38	1	13
Charlton Ath	Tr	08/10	10	10	7	2
ABBOTT Peter Ashley						
Born: Rotherham, South Yorkshire, England, 1 October, 1953						F
Manchester U	App	10/70				
Swansea C	Tr	02/74	73-75	35	7	3
Crewe Alex	Hartford B'ls (USA)	08/76	76	27	4	8
Southend U	Tr	07/77	77-78	26	1	4
ABBOTT Ronald Frederick (Ron)						
Born: Lambeth, S London, England, 2 August, 1953						CD
Queens Park Rgrs	App	07/71	73-78	32	14	4
ABBOTTS John						
Born: Stoke-on-Trent, England, 10 October, 1924						CH
Died: Stoke-on-Trent, England, 10 February, 2008						
Port Vale	Ravenscliffe	05/49	50	3	-	0
ABDI Almen						
Born: Priznen, Kosovo, 21 October, 1986						M
Switzerland: 6/U21-5						
Watford	Udinese (ITA)	08/12	12-14	73	10	23
ABDOU Nadjim (Jimmy)						
Born: Martigues, France, 13 July, 1984						DM
Comoros: 7						
Plymouth Arg	CS Sedan (FRA)	08/07	07	22	9	1
Millwall	Tr	07/08	08-14	225	24	6
ABDOUN Djamel						
Born: Paris, France, 14 February, 1986						RW
Algeria: 11//France: Youth						
Nottingham F	Olympiakos (GRE)	08/13	13	15	7	1
ABDULLAH Ahmed Mohamed						
Born: Jeddah, Saudi Arabia, 12 November, 1991						M
West Ham U	Sch	12/08				
Swindon T	L	08/11	11	1	5	0
Dagenham & Red	Tr	01/12	11	4	1	0
Barnet	Tr	07/12	12	4	2	0
ABE Yuki						
Born: Ichikawa, Japan, 6 September, 1981						W
Japan: 53/U23-13/Youth						
Leicester C	Urawa RD (JPN)	09/10	10-11	38	14	2
ABEID Mehdi						
Born: Paris, France, 6 August, 1992						M
Algeria: U23-4//France: Youth						
Newcastle U	RC Lens (FRA)	05/11	14	7	6	0
ABEL Graham						
Born: Runcorn, Cheshire, England, 17 September, 1960						CD
Chester C	Northwich Victoria	10/85	85-92	287	9	29
Crewe Alex	Tr	08/93	93	18	2	1
ABIDALLAH Nabil						
Born: Amsterdam, Netherlands, 5 August, 1982						M
Morocco: Youth						
Ipswich T	Ajax (NED)	07/00	00	0	2	0
Northampton T	L	01/04	03	0	1	0
ABIODUN Ayodeji Opeyemi (Yemi)						
Born: Clapton, NE London, England, 29 December, 1980						F
Southend U	YT	07/99	99	1	2	0
ABLETT Gary Ian						
Born: Liverpool, England, 19 November, 1965						CD
Died: Tarleton, Lancashire, England, 1 January, 2012						
England: B-1/U21-1						
Liverpool	App	11/83	86-91	103	6	1
Derby Co	L	01/85	84	3	3	0
Hull C	L	09/86	86	5	0	0
Everton	Tr	01/92	91-95	128	0	5
Sheffield U	L	03/96	95	12	0	0
Birmingham C	Tr	07/96	96-98	96	8	1
Wycombe W	L	12/99	99	4	0	0
Blackpool	Tr	01/00	99	9	1	1
ABORAH Stanley Opoku						
Born: Kumasi, Ghana, 23 June, 1987						M
Belgium: Youth						
Gillingham	AS Trencin (SVK)	08/10	10	0	1	0
ABOU Samassi						
Born: Gagnoa, Ivory Coast, 4 April, 1973						F
France: U21						
West Ham U	AS Cannes (FRA)	11/97	97-98	14	8	5

League Club	Source	Date Signed	Seasons Played	Career Record Apps	Subs	Gls
Ipswich T	L	12/98	98	5	0	1
Walsall	L	10/99	99	7	1	0

ABRAHAM Gareth John
Born: Aberfan, Merthyr Tydfil, Wales, 13 February, 1969 CD

League Club	Source	Date Signed	Seasons Played	Apps	Subs	Gls
Cardiff C	YT	07/87	87-91	82	5	4
Hereford U	Tr	01/93	92-93	48	1	2

ABRAHAMS Lawrence Adam Michael (Lawrie)
Born: Stepney, E London, England, 3 April, 1953 F

League Club	Source	Date Signed	Seasons Played	Apps	Subs	Gls
Charlton Ath	Barking	05/77	77	12	4	2

ABRAHAMS Paul
Born: Colchester, Essex, England, 31 October, 1973 F

League Club	Source	Date Signed	Seasons Played	Apps	Subs	Gls
Colchester U	YT	08/92	92-94	30	25	8
Brentford	Tr	03/95	94-96	26	9	8
Colchester U	L	12/95	95	8	0	2
Colchester U	Tr	10/96	96-98	56	25	16

ABREY Brian Anthony
Born: Hendon, N London, England, 25 April, 1939 CH

League Club	Source	Date Signed	Seasons Played	Apps	Subs	Gls
Chelsea	Jnr	10/56				
Colchester U	Tr	05/61	61	38	-	2

ABRUZZESE David John
Born: Aberdare, Rhondda Cynon Taff, Wales, 8 October, 1969 RB
Wales: Youth

League Club	Source	Date Signed	Seasons Played	Apps	Subs	Gls
Newport Co	App	08/86	86-87	24	1	0

ABTHORPE John
Born: Mansfield, Nottinghamshire, England, 19 January, 1933 CF
Died: Mansfield, Nottinghamshire, England, 7 July, 2005

League Club	Source	Date Signed	Seasons Played	Apps	Subs	Gls
Notts Co (Am)	Wolverhampton W (Am)	09/55	55	5	-	3

ACHAMPONG Kenneth (Kenny)
Born: Kilburn, NW London, England, 26 June, 1966 W

League Club	Source	Date Signed	Seasons Played	Apps	Subs	Gls
Fulham	App	06/84	84-87	68	13	15
Charlton Ath	Tr	08/89	89	2	8	0
Leyton Orient	Tr	08/90	90-92	64	19	7

ACHTERBERG John
Born: Utrecht, Netherlands, 8 July, 1971 G

League Club	Source	Date Signed	Seasons Played	Apps	Subs	Gls
Tranmere Rov	Eindhoven FC (NED)	09/98	98-08	253	4	0

ACIMOVIC Milenko
Born: Ljubljana, Slovenia, 15 February, 1977 M
Slovenia: 74

League Club	Source	Date Signed	Seasons Played	Apps	Subs	Gls
Tottenham H	R Star Belgrade (YUG)	05/02	02	4	13	0

ACKERLEY Ernest Nicol (Ernie)
Born: Manchester, England, 23 September, 1943 F

League Club	Source	Date Signed	Seasons Played	Apps	Subs	Gls
Manchester U	Jnr	10/60				
Blackburn Rov	Tr	03/63				
Barrow	Tr	04/63	62-63	53	-	12

ACKERLEY Stanley (Stan)
Born: Manchester, England, 12 July, 1942 LB
Australia:

League Club	Source	Date Signed	Seasons Played	Apps	Subs	Gls
Manchester U	Jnr	11/59				
Oldham Ath	Tr	06/61	61	2	-	0

ACKERMAN Alfred Arthur Eric (Alf)
Born: Pretoria, South Africa, 5 January, 1929 CF
Died: Dunottan, South Africa, 10 July, 2007

League Club	Source	Date Signed	Seasons Played	Apps	Subs	Gls
Hull C	Clyde	07/50	50	34	-	21
Norwich C	Tr	08/51	51-53	66	-	31
Hull C	Tr	10/53	53-54	58	-	28
Derby Co	Tr	03/55	54-56	36	-	21
Carlisle U	Tr	11/56	56-58	97	-	61
Millwall	Tr	01/59	58-60	81	-	35

ACKERMAN Tony Charles George
Born: Islington, N London, England, 20 February, 1948 CH

League Club	Source	Date Signed	Seasons Played	Apps	Subs	Gls
Leyton Orient	West Ham U (Am)	10/66	66-67	4	0	0

ACLAND Michael Edward (Mike)
Born: Sidcup, SE London, England, 4 June, 1935 CF

League Club	Source	Date Signed	Seasons Played	Apps	Subs	Gls
Gillingham	Harland Social	08/55	56	2	-	0

A'COURT Alan
Born: Rainhill, Merseyside, England, 30 September, 1934 LW
Died: Nantwich, Cheshire, England, 14 December, 2009
England: 5/FLge-2/U23-7

League Club	Source	Date Signed	Seasons Played	Apps	Subs	Gls
Liverpool	Prescot Cables	09/52	52-62	355	-	61
Tranmere Rov	Tr	10/64	64-65	50	0	11

ACRES Basil Derek John
Born: Brantham, Suffolk, England, 27 October, 1926 RB
Died: Ipswich, England, 23 July, 2000

League Club	Source	Date Signed	Seasons Played	Apps	Subs	Gls
Ipswich T	Brantham	09/50	51-59	217	-	6

ACTON Alec Edward
Born: Billesdon, Leicestershire, England, 12 November, 1938 LH
Died: Leicester, England, June, 1994

League Club	Source	Date Signed	Seasons Played	Apps	Subs	Gls
Stoke C	Leicester C (Am)	01/56				
Stockport Co	Brush Sports	08/58	58-59	9	-	0

ACUNA Carlos Javier (Javier)
Born: Encarnacion, Paraguay, 23 June, 1988 F
Paraguay: Youth

League Club	Source	Date Signed	Seasons Played	Apps	Subs	Gls
Watford (L)	Udinese (ITA)	07/13	13	3	6	0

ACUNA Donoso Clarence Williams (Clarence)
Born: Rancagua, Chile, 8 February, 1975 M
Chile: 60/Youth

League Club	Source	Date Signed	Seasons Played	Apps	Subs	Gls
Newcastle U	Univ de Chile (CHL)	10/00	00-02	35	11	6

ADAGGIO Marco
Born: Malaga, Spain, 6 October, 1987 F

League Club	Source	Date Signed	Seasons Played	Apps	Subs	Gls
Shrewsbury T	Jnr	03/05	04-05	0	10	0

ADAM Charles (Charlie)
Born: Glasgow, Scotland, 22 March, 1919 LW
Died: Leicester, England, 30 September, 1996

League Club	Source	Date Signed	Seasons Played	Apps	Subs	Gls
Leicester C	Strathclyde	09/38	46-50	158	-	22
Mansfield T	Tr	07/52	52-54	93	-	6

ADAM Charles Graham (Charlie)
Born: Dundee, Scotland, 10 December, 1985 M
Scotland: 25/B-3/U21-5

League Club	Source	Date Signed	Seasons Played	Apps	Subs	Gls
Blackpool	Glasgow Rangers	01/09	08-10	88	3	30
Liverpool	Tr	07/11	11	27	1	2
Stoke C	Tr	08/12	12-14	57	30	17

ADAM James (Jimmy)
Born: Blantyre, Lanarkshire, Scotland, 13 May, 1931 LW

League Club	Source	Date Signed	Seasons Played	Apps	Subs	Gls
Luton T	Spennymoor U	07/53	53-58	137	-	22
Aston Villa	Tr	08/59	59-60	24	-	3
Stoke C	Tr	07/61	61	22	-	7

ADAM James (Jimmy)
Born: Paisley, Renfrewshire, Scotland, 22 April, 1931 IF

League Club	Source	Date Signed	Seasons Played	Apps	Subs	Gls
Leeds U	Penilee U	06/51				
Mansfield T	Tr	08/54	54	39	-	10

ADAM Jamil Buba
Born: Bolton, Greater Manchester, England, 5 June, 1991 F
Republic of Ireland: Youth//Nigeria: Youth

League Club	Source	Date Signed	Seasons Played	Apps	Subs	Gls
Barnsley	Sch	07/09	07-09	0	3	0

ADAMCZUK Dariusz
Born: Szczecin, Poland, 20 October, 1969 M
Poland: 11

League Club	Source	Date Signed	Seasons Played	Apps	Subs	Gls
Wigan Ath (L)	Glasgow Rangers	08/01	01	3	0	0

ADAMS Blair Vincent
Born: South Shields, Tyne and Wear, England, 8 September, 1991 LB
England: Youth

League Club	Source	Date Signed	Seasons Played	Apps	Subs	Gls
Sunderland	Sch	07/10				
Brentford	L	09/11	11	6	1	0
Northampton T	L	01/12	11	21	1	0
Coventry C	Tr	11/12	12-13	50	2	0
Notts Co	Tr	07/14	14	31	3	1

ADAMS Brian Thomas
Born: Tottenham, N London, England, 18 May, 1947 RH

League Club	Source	Date Signed	Seasons Played	Apps	Subs	Gls
Millwall	Chelsea (App)	08/64	64-65	15	0	0

ADAMS Charles James (Charlie)
Born: Hendon, N London, England, 16 May, 1994 LB

League Club	Source	Date Signed	Seasons Played	Apps	Subs	Gls
Brentford	Sch	06/12	12-13	0	4	0
Stevenage	L	10/14	14	5	4	0

ADAMS Che Zach Everton Fred
Born: Leicester, England, 13 July, 1996 F

League Club	Source	Date Signed	Seasons Played	Apps	Subs	Gls
Sheffield U	Ilkeston	11/14	14	5	5	0

ADAMS Christopher James (Chris)
Born: Hornchurch, E London, England, 6 September, 1927 LW
Died: Brentwood, Essex, England, 24 June, 2012

League Club	Source	Date Signed	Seasons Played	Apps	Subs	Gls
Tottenham H	Leytonstone	11/48	51-52	6	-	1
Norwich C	Tr	12/52	52-53	29	-	3
Watford	Tr	03/54	53-55	75	-	5

ADAMS Craig John
Born: Northampton, England, 9 November, 1974 CD

League Club	Source	Date Signed	Seasons Played	Apps	Subs	Gls
Northampton T	YT	-	91	0	1	0

ADAMS Daniel Benjamin (Danny)
Born: Manchester, England, 3 January, 1976 LB

League Club	Source	Date Signed	Seasons Played	Apps	Subs	Gls
Macclesfield T	Altrincham	08/00	00-03	146	2	1

League Club	Source	Date Signed	Seasons Played	Apps	Subs	Gls
Stockport Co	Tr	03/04	03-04	39	0	1
Huddersfield T	Tr	03/05	04-06	68	0	0
Morecambe	Tr	01/07	07-09	96	2	0

ADAMS Darren Steven
Born: Bromley, SE London, England, 12 January, 1974 — F

League Club	Source	Date Signed	Seasons Played	Apps	Subs	Gls
Cardiff C	Danson Furness	01/94	93-95	21	13	4

ADAMS Derek Watt
Born: Aberdeen, Scotland, 25 June, 1975 — M

League Club	Source	Date Signed	Seasons Played	Apps	Subs	Gls
Burnley	Aberdeen	01/95	95	0	2	0

ADAMS Donald Frederick (Don)
Born: Northampton, England, 15 February, 1931 — CF
Died: Northampton, England, 3 January, 1993

League Club	Source	Date Signed	Seasons Played	Apps	Subs	Gls
Northampton T		05/51	51-55	23	-	7

ADAMS Ernest Robert (Ernie)
Born: Hackney, E London, England, 17 January, 1948 — G

League Club	Source	Date Signed	Seasons Played	Apps	Subs	Gls
Arsenal	App	01/65				
Colchester U	Tr	07/67	67-68	48	0	0
Crewe Alex	Tr	07/69	69-71	112	0	0
Darlington	Tr	07/72	72	25	0	0

ADAMS Ernest William (Ernie)
Born: Willesden, NW London, England, 3 April, 1922 — W
Died: Hertford, England, September, 2009

League Club	Source	Date Signed	Seasons Played	Apps	Subs	Gls
Preston NE	Army	01/45				
Fulham	Tr	03/47				
Queens Park Rgrs	Tr	09/47	47-49	5	-	0

ADAMS Francis Nicholas (Frank)
Born: Liverpool, England, 8 February, 1933 — G
Died: Huyton, Merseyside, England, 25 March, 2009

League Club	Source	Date Signed	Seasons Played	Apps	Subs	Gls
Bury	Bury Amats	01/56	56-61	169	-	0
Chester C	Tr	07/63	63	8	-	0
Tranmere Rov	Tr	02/64				

ADAMS George
Born: Falkirk, Scotland, 16 October, 1926 — WH
Died: Wandsworth, SW London, England, July, 2011

League Club	Source	Date Signed	Seasons Played	Apps	Subs	Gls
Crystal Palace	Bath C	-				
Leyton Orient	Chelmsford C	05/49	49	4	-	0

ADAMS George Robert
Born: Shoreditch, Central London, England, 28 September, 1947 — M

League Club	Source	Date Signed	Seasons Played	Apps	Subs	Gls
Chelsea	Jnr	09/65				
Peterborough U	Tr	07/66	66-67	13	3	2

ADAMS Graham Wallace
Born: Torrington, Devon, England, 1 March, 1933 — FB

League Club	Source	Date Signed	Seasons Played	Apps	Subs	Gls
Plymouth Arg	RAF	01/58	57	1	-	0

ADAMS James Arthur (Jim)
Born: Stoke-on-Trent, England, 2 August, 1937 — FB
Died: Stoke-on-Trent, England, 30 December, 2005

League Club	Source	Date Signed	Seasons Played	Apps	Subs	Gls
Port Vale		06/56	57	1	-	0
Crewe Alex	Tr	08/60				

ADAMS Kieran Charles
Born: St Ives, Cambridgeshire, England, 20 October, 1977 — M

League Club	Source	Date Signed	Seasons Played	Apps	Subs	Gls
Barnet	YT	07/96	94-97	8	11	1

ADAMS Laurence Edward (Laurie)
Born: Barnet, N London, England, 14 February, 1931 — IF

League Club	Source	Date Signed	Seasons Played	Apps	Subs	Gls
Watford	Army	01/52	51	1	-	0

ADAMS Michael Alan (Mike)
Born: Banwell, Somerset, England, 20 February, 1965 — M

League Club	Source	Date Signed	Seasons Played	Apps	Subs	Gls
Bristol Rov	App	02/83	82	0	1	0

ADAMS Michael Richard (Micky)
Born: Sheffield, England, 8 November, 1961 — LB
England: Youth

League Club	Source	Date Signed	Seasons Played	Apps	Subs	Gls
Gillingham	App	11/79	79-82	85	7	4
Coventry C	Tr	07/83	83-86	85	5	9
Leeds U	Tr	01/87	86-88	72	1	2
Southampton	Tr	03/89	88-93	141	3	7
Stoke C	Tr	03/94	93	10	0	3
Fulham	Tr	07/94	94-96	25	4	9

ADAMS Nathan Mark
Born: Lincoln, England, 6 October, 1991 — F

League Club	Source	Date Signed	Seasons Played	Apps	Subs	Gls
Lincoln C	Sch	07/10	08-09	0	4	0

ADAMS Neil James
Born: Stoke-on-Trent, England, 23 November, 1965 — W
England: U21-1

League Club	Source	Date Signed	Seasons Played	Apps	Subs	Gls
Stoke C	QM Rgrs	07/85	85	31	1	4
Everton	Tr	07/86	86-87	17	3	0
Oldham Ath	L	01/89	88	9	0	0
Oldham Ath	Tr	06/89	89-93	93	36	23
Norwich C	Tr	02/94	93-98	164	18	25
Oldham Ath	Tr	07/99	99-00	47	0	4

ADAMS Nicholas William (Nicky)
Born: Bolton, Greater Manchester, England, 16 October, 1986 — M
Wales: U21-5

League Club	Source	Date Signed	Seasons Played	Apps	Subs	Gls
Bury	Sch	06/06	05-07	61	16	14
Leicester C	Tr	07/08	08-09	5	25	0
Rochdale	L	01/09	08	12	2	1
Leyton Orient	L	01/10	09	6	0	0
Brentford	Tr	08/10	10	3	4	0
Rochdale	Tr	10/10	10-11	55	16	4
Crawley T	Tr	07/12	12-13	69	1	9
Rotherham U	Tr	01/14	13	7	8	1
Bury	Tr	05/14	14	29	9	1

ADAMS Rex Malcolm
Born: Oxford, England, 13 February, 1928 — RW
Died: Blackpool, Lancashire, England, 14 January, 2014

League Club	Source	Date Signed	Seasons Played	Apps	Subs	Gls
Blackpool	Oxford C	06/48	48-50	16	-	1
Oldham Ath	Worcester C	06/53	53	23	-	1

ADAMS Rodney Leslie
Born: Bath, England, 15 September, 1945 — M

League Club	Source	Date Signed	Seasons Played	Apps	Subs	Gls
Bournemouth	Frome T	06/66	66-68	15	2	4

ADAMS Stephen (Steve)
Born: Sheffield, England, 7 September, 1959 — RW

League Club	Source	Date Signed	Seasons Played	Apps	Subs	Gls
Scarborough	Worksop T	09/87	87-88	25	23	5
Doncaster Rov	Tr	10/89	89-90	25	10	2

ADAMS Stephen Marc (Steve)
Born: Plymouth, England, 25 September, 1980 — DM

League Club	Source	Date Signed	Seasons Played	Apps	Subs	Gls
Plymouth Arg	YT	07/99	99-04	131	26	7
Sheffield Wed	Tr	03/05	04-06	18	2	0
Swindon T	Tr	08/07	07	2	0	0
Torquay U	Tr	01/08				

ADAMS Stephen Thomas (Steve)
Born: Windsor, Berkshire, England, 18 June, 1958 — M

League Club	Source	Date Signed	Seasons Played	Apps	Subs	Gls
Queens Park Rgrs	App	07/75				
Millwall	Tr	07/77	77	1	0	0
Cambridge U	Windsor & Eton	03/78	77-78	1	2	0

ADAMS Tony Alexander
Born: Romford, E London, England, 10 October, 1966 — CD
England: 66/B-4/U21-5/Youth

League Club	Source	Date Signed	Seasons Played	Apps	Subs	Gls
Arsenal	App	01/84	83-01	500	4	32

ADAMS Vincent (Vince)
Born: Chesterfield, Derbyshire, England, 16 October, 1946 — M
England: Schools

League Club	Source	Date Signed	Seasons Played	Apps	Subs	Gls
Arsenal	App	10/63				
Chesterfield	Tr	11/65	65-66	15	2	1

ADAMS William Henry (Billy)
Born: Arlecdon, Cumbria, England, 8 January, 1919 — RB
Died: Cockermouth, Cumbria, England, 1 March, 1989

League Club	Source	Date Signed	Seasons Played	Apps	Subs	Gls
Tottenham H	Hartlepool U (Am)	05/39				
Carlisle U	Tr	06/46	46	33	-	1
Workington	Chelmsford C	08/51	51	3	-	0

ADAMS William Victor (Bill)
Born: Plymouth, England, 10 May, 1921 — FB
Died: Plymouth, England, June, 1997

League Club	Source	Date Signed	Seasons Played	Apps	Subs	Gls
Plymouth Arg	Plymouth U	04/45	46	1	-	0

ADAMSON Christopher (Chris)
Born: Ashington, Northumberland, England, 4 November, 1978 — G

League Club	Source	Date Signed	Seasons Played	Apps	Subs	Gls
West Bromwich A	YT	07/97	97-99	12	0	0
Mansfield T	L	04/99	98	2	0	0
Halifax T	L	07/99	99	7	0	0
Plymouth Arg	L	01/02	01	1	0	0
Sheffield Wed	St Patricks Ath (ROI)	01/05	04-06	9	2	0
Stockport Co	Tr	08/07				
Hereford U	Tr	07/09	09	1	0	0

ADAMSON David Henry (Dave)
Born: Chester-le-Street, County Durham, England, 7 May, 1951 — LB
England: Semi Pro-5

League Club	Source	Date Signed	Seasons Played	Apps	Subs	Gls
Doncaster Rov	Durham C	07/70	70-71	28	0	0

ADAMSON Henry (Harry)
Born: Kelty, Fife, Scotland, 27 June, 1924 — WH
Died: Dunfermline, Fife, Scotland, 23 May, 1997

League Club	Source	Date Signed	Seasons Played	Apps	Subs	Gls
Notts Co	Jeanfield Swifts	08/46	47-55	233	-	5

ADAMSON James (Jimmy)
Born: Ashington, Northumberland, England, 4 April, 1929 — WH/CH

Died: Nelson, Lancashire, England, 8 November, 2011
England: B-1/FLge-1

League Club	Source	Date Signed	Seasons Played	Apps	Subs	Gls
Burnley	Ashington	01/47	50-63	426	-	17

ADAMSON Keith Brian
Born: Houghton-le-Spring, Tyne and Wear, England, 3 July, 1945 — F

League Club	Source	Date Signed	Seasons Played	Apps	Subs	Gls
Barnsley	Tow Law T	03/66	65-66	7	0	0

ADAMSON Terence (Terry)
Born: Houghton-le-Spring, Tyne and Wear, England, 15 October, 1948 — FB

League Club	Source	Date Signed	Seasons Played	Apps	Subs	Gls
Sunderland	App	11/65				
Luton T	Tr	07/66	66	2	0	0
Hartlepool U	Tr	07/67	67	1	0	0

ADA OMGBA Patrick
Born: Yaounde, Cameroon, 14 January, 1985 — CD

League Club	Source	Date Signed	Seasons Played	Apps	Subs	Gls
Crewe Alex	Histon	05/09	09-10	55	3	1
Burton A	Kilmarnock	02/12	11	5	4	0

ADCOCK Anthony Charles (Tony)
Born: Bethnal Green, E London, England, 27 March, 1963 — F

League Club	Source	Date Signed	Seasons Played	Apps	Subs	Gls
Colchester U	App	03/81	80-86	192	18	98
Manchester C	Tr	06/87	87	12	3	5
Northampton T	Tr	01/88	87-89	72	0	30
Bradford C	Tr	10/89	89-90	33	5	6
Northampton T	Tr	01/91	90-91	34	1	10
Peterborough U	Tr	12/91	91-93	107	4	35
Luton T	Tr	08/94	94	0	2	0
Colchester U	Tr	08/95	95-98	86	22	28

ADCOCK Paul Malcolm
Born: Ilminster, Somerset, England, 2 May, 1972 — F

League Club	Source	Date Signed	Seasons Played	Apps	Subs	Gls
Plymouth Arg	YT	08/90	90-92	11	10	2
Torquay U	Bath C	08/95	96	0	1	0

ADDINALL Albert William (Bert)
Born: Paddington, Central London, England, 30 January, 1921 — CF
Died: West Surrey, England, May, 2005

League Club	Source	Date Signed	Seasons Played	Apps	Subs	Gls
Queens Park Rgrs	British Oxygen	04/45	46-52	150	-	59
Brighton & HA	Tr	01/53	52-53	60	-	31
Crystal Palace	Tr	07/54	54	12	-	2

ADDISON Colin
Born: Taunton, Somerset, England, 18 May, 1940 — M/F

League Club	Source	Date Signed	Seasons Played	Apps	Subs	Gls
York C	Jnr	05/57	57-60	87	-	28
Nottingham F	Tr	01/61	60-66	160	0	62
Arsenal	Tr	09/66	66-67	27	1	9
Sheffield U	Tr	12/67	67-70	93	1	22
Hereford U	Tr	10/71	72-73	23	0	1

ADDISON Miles Vivien Esifi
Born: Newham, E London, England, 7 January, 1989 — DM
England: U21-1

League Club	Source	Date Signed	Seasons Played	Apps	Subs	Gls
Derby Co	Sch	07/07	05-10	51	14	3
Barnsley	L	06/11	11	9	2	0
Bournemouth	Tr	02/12	11-12	34	0	1
Rotherham U	L	01/14	13	4	2	0
Scunthorpe U	L	07/14	14	3	0	0
Blackpool	L	03/15	14	6	0	0

ADDY Michael (Mike)
Born: Knottingley, West Yorkshire, England, 20 February, 1943 — WH

League Club	Source	Date Signed	Seasons Played	Apps	Subs	Gls
Leeds U	Jnr	05/62	62	2	-	0
Barnsley	Tr	06/64	64-66	50	1	5

ADEBAYOR Sheyi Emmanuel Lame (Emmanuel)
Born: Lome, Togo, 26 February, 1984 — F
Togo: 63

League Club	Source	Date Signed	Seasons Played	Apps	Subs	Gls
Arsenal	AS Monaco (FRA)	01/06	05-08	86	18	46
Manchester C	Tr	07/09	09-10	27	7	15
Tottenham H	Tr	08/11	11-14	79	13	35

ADEBOLA Bamderdele (Dele)
Born: Lagos, Nigeria, 23 June, 1975 — F

League Club	Source	Date Signed	Seasons Played	Apps	Subs	Gls
Crewe Alex	YT	06/93	92-97	98	27	39
Birmingham C	Tr	02/98	97-00	86	43	31
Oldham Ath	L	03/02	01	5	0	0
Crystal Palace	Tr	08/02	02	32	7	5
Coventry C	Tr	07/03	03-07	115	48	31
Burnley	L	03/04	03	0	3	1
Bradford C	L	08/04	04	14	1	3
Bristol C	Tr	01/08	07-08	48	8	16
Nottingham F	Tr	07/09	09-10	17	45	5
Hull C	Tr	06/11	11	2	8	0
Notts Co	L	03/12	11	3	3	1
Rochdale	Tr	08/12	12	22	4	6

ADEBOYEJO Ayomide Victor (Victor)
Born: Ibadan, Nigeria, 12 January, 1998 — F

League Club	Source	Date Signed	Seasons Played	Apps	Subs	Gls
Leyton Orient	Sch	-	14	0	1	0

ADEKOLA David Adeolu
Born: Lagos, Nigeria, 19 May, 1968 — F

League Club	Source	Date Signed	Seasons Played	Apps	Subs	Gls
Bury	AS Cannes (FRA)	01/93	92-93	21	14	12
Exeter C	L	02/94	93	1	2	1
Wigan Ath	Bournemouth (NC)	10/94	94	1	3	0
Hereford U	Tr	02/95				
Cambridge U	Bath C	08/95	95	1	4	1
Brighton & HA	Preussen Munster (GER)	10/96	96	1	0	0

ADELAKUN Hakeeb Ademola
Born: Hackney, E London, England, 11 June, 1996 — W

League Club	Source	Date Signed	Seasons Played	Apps	Subs	Gls
Scunthorpe U	Sch	01/14	12-14	15	47	8

ADEMENO Charles Adesola Oludare
Born: Milton Keynes, England, 12 December, 1988 — F

League Club	Source	Date Signed	Seasons Played	Apps	Subs	Gls
Southend U	Sch	07/07	05-08	1	3	0
AFC Wimbledon	Grimsby T	06/11	11	5	10	1

ADEMOLA Moses Oluwafemi
Born: Lewisham, SE London, England, 9 August, 1989 — F

League Club	Source	Date Signed	Seasons Played	Apps	Subs	Gls
Brentford	Croydon Ath	06/08	08	0	8	0

ADEY Arthur Lewis
Born: Glasgow, Scotland, 1 March, 1930 — CF
Died: Suffolk, England, January, 1994

League Club	Source	Date Signed	Seasons Played	Apps	Subs	Gls
Doncaster Rov	Bishop Auckland	09/50	50-53	48	-	9
Gillingham	Tr	07/54	54	7	-	1
Bradford Park Ave	Tr	10/54	54	13	-	4

ADEYEMI Thomas Oluseun (Tom)
Born: Milton Keynes, England, 24 October, 1991 — M

League Club	Source	Date Signed	Seasons Played	Apps	Subs	Gls
Norwich C	Sch	11/08	09	2	9	0
Bradford C	L	07/10	10	30	4	5
Oldham Ath	L	08/11	11	33	3	2
Brentford	L	08/12	12	21	9	2
Birmingham C	Tr	07/13	13	32	3	1
Cardiff C	Tr	08/14	14	11	9	1

ADJEI Samuel
Born: Eksjo, Sweden, 18 January, 1992 — F

League Club	Source	Date Signed	Seasons Played	Apps	Subs	Gls
Newcastle U	Jonkoping (SWE)	03/09				
Hartlepool U	L	03/12	11	0	1	0

ADJEMAN-PAMBOE Kwame
Born: Bowie, Maryland, USA, 24 October, 1987 — F

League Club	Source	Date Signed	Seasons Played	Apps	Subs	Gls
Barnet	Tampa Bay R's (USA)	02/11	10	0	1	0

ADKINS Nigel Howard
Born: Birkenhead, Wirral, England, 11 March, 1965 — G
England: Schools

League Club	Source	Date Signed	Seasons Played	Apps	Subs	Gls
Tranmere Rov	App	03/83	82-85	86	0	0
Wigan Ath	Tr	07/86	86-92	155	0	0

ADKINS Sam
Born: Birmingham, England, 3 December, 1990 — LB

League Club	Source	Date Signed	Seasons Played	Apps	Subs	Gls
Walsall	Sch	07/09	08-09	0	2	0

ADLINGTON Terence (Terry)
Born: Blackwell, Derbyshire, England, 21 November, 1935 — G
Died: 1994

League Club	Source	Date Signed	Seasons Played	Apps	Subs	Gls
Derby Co	Blackwell Colliery	12/55	56-60	36	-	0
Torquay U	Tr	06/62	62-65	148	0	0

ADOMAH Albert Danquah
Born: Lambeth, S London, England, 13 December, 1987 — RW
Ghana: 16

League Club	Source	Date Signed	Seasons Played	Apps	Subs	Gls
Barnet	Harrow Bor	01/08	07-09	104	8	19
Bristol C	Tr	07/10	10-12	113	18	17
Middlesbrough	Tr	08/13	13-14	78	7	17

[ADRIAN] SAN MIGUEL Adrian
Born: Seville, Spain, 3 January, 1987 — G

League Club	Source	Date Signed	Seasons Played	Apps	Subs	Gls
West Ham U	Real Betis (SPN)	08/13	13-14	58	0	0

[ADRYAN] OLIVEIRA Adryan
Born: Rio de Janeiro, Brazil, 8 October, 1994 — M
Brazil: Youth

League Club	Source	Date Signed	Seasons Played	Apps	Subs	Gls
Leeds U (L)	Flamengo (BRA)	08/14	14	9	3	0

ADVICE-DESRUISSEAUX Frederic
Born: Paris, France, 12 January, 1983 — M

League Club	Source	Date Signed	Seasons Played	Apps	Subs	Gls
Kidderminster Hrs	OSC Lille (FRA)	07/04	04	9	0	0

AFFOR Louis Kofi Jeffrey
Born: Accra, Ghana, 29 August, 1972 — W

League Club	Source	Date Signed	Seasons Played	Apps	Subs	Gls
Barnet	Southend U (YT)	08/93	93	0	3	0

AFFUL Leslie Samuel
Born: Liverpool, England, 4 February, 1984 — W

League Club	Source	Date Signed	Seasons Played	Apps	Subs	Gls

England: Semi Pro-2

League Club	Source	Date Signed	Seasons Played	Apps	Subs	Gls
Exeter C	Sch	08/02	01	0	2	0
Torquay U	L	01/06	05	0	5	0

AFOBE Benik Tunani (Ben)
Born: Leyton, NE London, England, 12 February, 1993 — F
England: U21-2/Youth

League Club	Source	Date Signed	Seasons Played	Apps	Subs	Gls
Arsenal	Sch	02/10				
Huddersfield T	L	11/10	10	14	14	5
Reading	L	03/12	11	1	2	0
Bolton W	L	08/12	12	5	15	2
Millwall	L	02/13	12	5	0	0
Sheffield Wed	L	01/14	13	4	8	2
MK Dons	L	08/14	14	11	11	10
Wolverhampton W	Tr	01/15	14	20	1	13

AGANA Patrick Anthony Olozinka (Tony)
Born: Bromley, SE London, England, 2 October, 1963 — F
England: Semi Pro-1

League Club	Source	Date Signed	Seasons Played	Apps	Subs	Gls
Watford	Weymouth	08/87	87	12	3	1
Sheffield U	Tr	02/88	87-91	105	13	42
Notts Co	Tr	11/91	91-96	114	31	15
Leeds U	L	02/92	91	1	1	0
Hereford U	Tr	03/97	96	3	2	2

AGAR Frederick Royston (Roy)
Born: Islington, N London, England, 1 April, 1936 — IF
England: Amateur-5

League Club	Source	Date Signed	Seasons Played	Apps	Subs	Gls
Swindon T (Am)	Barnet	12/55	55-56	12	-	0

AGARD Kieran Ricardo
Born: Newham, E London, England, 10 October, 1989 — F

League Club	Source	Date Signed	Seasons Played	Apps	Subs	Gls
Everton	Sch	10/06	09	0	1	0
Yeovil T	Tr	06/11	11	13	16	6
Rotherham U	Tr	08/12	12-14	56	22	27
Bristol C	Tr	08/14	14	34	5	13

AGATHE Fernand Didier (Didier)
Born: Saint-Pierre, Reunion, 16 August, 1975 — RB/M

League Club	Source	Date Signed	Seasons Played	Apps	Subs	Gls
Aston Villa	Glasgow Celtic	09/06	06	0	5	0

AGBONLAHOR Gabriel (Gabby)
Born: Birmingham, England, 13 October, 1986 — F
England: 3/U21-15/Youth

League Club	Source	Date Signed	Seasons Played	Apps	Subs	Gls
Aston Villa	Sch	03/05	05-14	279	28	72
Watford	L	09/05	05	1	1	0
Sheffield Wed	L	10/05	05	4	4	0

AGBOOLA Reuben Omajola Folasanje
Born: Camden, N London, England, 30 May, 1962 — LB

League Club	Source	Date Signed	Seasons Played	Apps	Subs	Gls
Southampton	App	04/80	80-84	89	1	0
Sunderland	Tr	01/85	84-91	129	11	0
Charlton Ath	L	10/86	86	1	0	0
Port Vale	L	11/90	90	9	0	0
Swansea C	Tr	11/91	91-92	26	2	0

AGDESTEIN Torbjorn (Toby)
Born: Stord, Norway, 29 November, 1991 — F
Norway: U21-1

League Club	Source	Date Signed	Seasons Played	Apps	Subs	Gls
Brighton & HA	Stord IL (NOR)	09/10	10-12	0	6	0

AGGER Daniel Munthe
Born: Copenhagen, Denmark, 12 December, 1984 — CD
Denmark: 67/U21-10/Youth

League Club	Source	Date Signed	Seasons Played	Apps	Subs	Gls
Liverpool	Brondby (NOR)	01/06	05-13	156	19	9

AGGREY James Emmanuel (Jimmy)
Born: Hammersmith, W London, England, 26 October, 1978 — CD

League Club	Source	Date Signed	Seasons Played	Apps	Subs	Gls
Fulham	Chelsea (YT)	07/97				
Torquay U	Airdrieonians	10/98	98-01	87	8	2

AGHAHOWA Julius
Born: Benin City, Nigeria, 12 February, 1982 — F
Nigeria: 32

League Club	Source	Date Signed	Seasons Played	Apps	Subs	Gls
Wigan Ath	Shakhtar Donetsk (UKR)	01/07	06-07	5	15	0

AGNEW David George
Born: Belfast, Northern Ireland, 31 March, 1925 — G
Died: Sunderland, England, September, 1966
Northern Ireland: Amateur

League Club	Source	Date Signed	Seasons Played	Apps	Subs	Gls
Sunderland	Crusaders	01/50	50	1	-	0

AGNEW David Young
Born: Kilwinning, Ayrshire, Scotland, 4 August, 1939 — LB

League Club	Source	Date Signed	Seasons Played	Apps	Subs	Gls
Leicester C	Jnr	08/58				
Scunthorpe U	Tr	06/61	61	1	-	0
Notts Co	Tr	06/62	62-66	85	0	1

AGNEW John Terence (Terry)
Born: Stockton-on-Tees, Cleveland, England, 27 June, 1935 — LW

League Club	Source	Date Signed	Seasons Played	Apps	Subs	Gls

League Club	Source	Date Signed	Seasons Played	Apps	Subs	Gls
Sheffield Wed	South Bank Jnrs	11/53				
Darlington	Tr	08/54	54-55	25	-	4

AGNEW Paul
Born: Lisburn, Belfast, Northern Ireland, 15 August, 1965 — LB
Northern Ireland: U23-1/Youth/Schools

League Club	Source	Date Signed	Seasons Played	Apps	Subs	Gls
Grimsby T	Cliftonville	02/84	83-94	219	24	3
West Bromwich A	Tr	02/95	94-96	38	1	1
Swansea C	Ilkeston T	09/97	97	7	0	0

AGNEW Stephen Mark (Steve)
Born: Shipley, West Yorkshire, England, 9 November, 1965 — M

League Club	Source	Date Signed	Seasons Played	Apps	Subs	Gls
Barnsley	App	11/83	83-90	185	9	29
Blackburn Rov	Tr	06/91	91	2	0	0
Portsmouth	L	11/92	92	3	2	0
Leicester C	Tr	02/93	92-94	52	4	4
Sunderland	Tr	01/95	94-97	56	7	9
York C	Tr	07/98	98-00	76	5	4

AGOGO Manuel (Junior)
Born: Accra, Ghana, 1 August, 1979 — F
England: Semi Pro-3//Ghana: 27

League Club	Source	Date Signed	Seasons Played	Apps	Subs	Gls
Sheffield Wed	Willesden Constantine	10/96	97-98	0	2	0
Oldham Ath	L	07/99	99	2	0	0
Chester C	L	09/99	99	10	0	6
Chesterfield	L	11/99	99	3	1	0
Lincoln C	L	12/99	99	3	0	1
Queens Park Rgrs	San Jose E'quake (USA)	03/02	01	0	2	0
Bristol Rov	Barnet	07/03	03-06	109	17	41
Nottingham F	Tr	08/06	06-07	47	17	20

AGOMBAR Harry George
Born: Stepney, E London, England, 12 July, 1992 — M

League Club	Source	Date Signed	Seasons Played	Apps	Subs	Gls
Swindon T	Floriana (MLT)	07/13	14	1	0	0

AGOSTINO Paul
Born: Adelaide, Australia, 9 June, 1975 — F
Australia: 18/U23-3/Youth

League Club	Source	Date Signed	Seasons Played	Apps	Subs	Gls
Bristol C	Young Boys Bern (SUI)	07/95	95-96	63	21	19

AGUERO Sergio Leonel
Born: Quilmes, Argentina, 2 June, 1988 — F
Argentina: 63/U23-5/Youth

League Club	Source	Date Signed	Seasons Played	Apps	Subs	Gls
Manchester C	Independiente (ARG)	07/11	11-14	103	17	78

AGUSTIEN Germain (Kemy)
Born: Willemstad, Curacao, 20 August, 1986 — M
Netherlands: U21-6

League Club	Source	Date Signed	Seasons Played	Apps	Subs	Gls
Birmingham C (L)	AZ Alkmaar (NED)	08/08	08	13	5	0
Swansea C	AZ Alkmaar (NED)	10/10	10-12	14	25	0
Crystal Palace	L	03/11	10	6	2	0
Brighton & HA	Tr	08/13	13-14	6	7	0

AGYEMANG Montel Kofi Owusu
Born: Southwark, S London, England, 22 November, 1996 — M

League Club	Source	Date Signed	Seasons Played	Apps	Subs	Gls
Leyton Orient	Sch	-	14	0	1	0

AGYEMANG Patrick
Born: Walthamstow, NE London, England, 29 September, 1980 — F
Ghana: 2

League Club	Source	Date Signed	Seasons Played	Apps	Subs	Gls
Wimbledon	YT	05/99	00-03	68	53	20
Brentford	L	10/99	99	3	9	0
Gillingham	Tr	01/04	03-04	29	4	8
Preston NE	Tr	11/04	04-07	55	67	21
Queens Park Rgrs	Tr	01/08	07-11	35	40	15
Bristol C	L	01/10	09	5	2	0
Millwall	L	10/11	11	1	1	0
Stevenage	Tr	03/12	11-12	15	12	1
Portsmouth	Tr	02/13	12-14	42	22	7
Dagenham & Red	L	11/14	14	2	2	0

AHEARNE-GRANT Karlan Laughton
Born: Greenwich, SE London, England, 18 September, 1997 — F
England: Youth

League Club	Source	Date Signed	Seasons Played	Apps	Subs	Gls
Charlton Ath	Sch	09/14	14	2	3	0

AHERNE Thomas (Tom)
Born: Limerick, Republic of Ireland, 26 January, 1919 — LB
Died: Luton, England, 30 December, 1999
Republic of Ireland: 16/LoI-4//Northern Ireland: 4/NILge-6/War-2

League Club	Source	Date Signed	Seasons Played	Apps	Subs	Gls
Luton T	Belfast Celtic	03/49	48-56	267	-	0

AHMED Adnan Farooq
Born: Burnley, Lancashire, England, 7 June, 1984 — RM
Pakistan: 26

League Club	Source	Date Signed	Seasons Played	Apps	Subs	Gls
Huddersfield T	Sch	08/03	03-06	24	17	1
Tranmere Rov	Tr	07/07	07	3	3	0
Port Vale	L	01/09	08	4	1	1

AHMED Shahed
Born: East Ham, E London, England, 13 September, 1985 — F

League Club	Source	Date Signed	Seasons Played	Apps	Subs	Gls
Wycombe W	Wimbledon (YT)	07/04	04	0	4	1

AIKEN Thomas (Tommy)
Born: Ballymena, Antrim, Northern Ireland, 18 March, 1946 — RW
Northern Ireland: Amateur

League Club	Source	Date Signed	Seasons Played	Apps	Subs	Gls
Doncaster Rov	Ballymena U	11/67	67-68	12	1	1

AIMSON Paul Edward
Born: Macclesfield, Cheshire, England, 3 August, 1943 — F
Died: Christchurch, Dorset, England, 9 January, 2008

League Club	Source	Date Signed	Seasons Played	Apps	Subs	Gls
Manchester C	Jnr	08/60	61-63	16	-	4
York C	Tr	07/64	64-65	77	0	43
Bury	Tr	03/66	65-66	30	1	11
Bradford C	Tr	09/67	67	23	0	11
Huddersfield T	Tr	03/68	67-68	34	4	13
York C	Tr	08/69	69-72	133	8	55
Bournemouth	Tr	03/73	72	7	2	2
Colchester U	Tr	08/73	73	3	1	2

AIMSON William Stewart (Will)
Born: Christchurch, Dorset, England, 1 January, 1994 — CD

League Club	Source	Date Signed	Seasons Played	Apps	Subs	Gls
Hull C	Eastleigh	07/12				
Tranmere Rov	L	11/14	14	2	0	0

AINDOW Roger Allan
Born: Bootle, Merseyside, England, 23 October, 1946 — CD

League Club	Source	Date Signed	Seasons Played	Apps	Subs	Gls
Southport	Formby	10/67	68-70	52	6	4

AINGE Ronald Percy (Ron)
Born: Pontardawe, Swansea, Wales, 5 August, 1920 — W
Died: Newport, Wales, March, 2008

League Club	Source	Date Signed	Seasons Played	Apps	Subs	Gls
Newport Co	Llanelli	10/46	46	5	-	0

AINGE Simon Christopher
Born: Shipley, West Yorkshire, England, 18 February, 1988 — CD

League Club	Source	Date Signed	Seasons Played	Apps	Subs	Gls
Bradford C	Sch	07/06	06-08	6	8	0

AINSCOUGH John (Jack)
Born: Adlington, Greater Manchester, England, 26 March, 1926 — CD
Died: Bolton, Greater Manchester, England, 16 December, 2004

League Club	Source	Date Signed	Seasons Played	Apps	Subs	Gls
Blackpool	Astley Bridge	08/49	50-53	7	-	0

AINSCOW Alan
Born: Bolton, Greater Manchester, England, 15 July, 1953 — M
England: Youth

League Club	Source	Date Signed	Seasons Played	Apps	Subs	Gls
Blackpool	App	07/71	71-77	178	14	28
Birmingham C	Tr	07/78	78-80	104	4	16
Everton	Tr	08/81	81-82	24	4	3
Barnsley	L	11/82	82	2	0	0
Wolverhampton W	Eastern AA (HKG)	08/84	84-85	56	2	5
Blackburn Rov	Tr	12/85	85-88	42	23	5
Rochdale	Tr	07/89	89	19	1	0

AINSCOW Andrew Paul (Andy)
Born: Orrell, Greater Manchester, England, 1 October, 1968 — F
England: Youth

League Club	Source	Date Signed	Seasons Played	Apps	Subs	Gls
Wigan Ath	App	10/86	87-88	14	8	4
Rotherham U	Tr	08/89	89	0	1	0

AINSLEY George Edward
Born: South Shields, Tyne and Wear, England, 15 April, 1915 — CF
Died: Leeds, England, April, 1985

League Club	Source	Date Signed	Seasons Played	Apps	Subs	Gls
Sunderland	S Shields St Andrews	04/32	32-33	4	-	0
Bolton W	Tr	08/36	36	7	-	0
Leeds U	Tr	12/36	36-47	89	-	30
Bradford Park Ave	Tr	11/47	47-48	44	-	29

AINSLEY Jack William
Born: Ipswich, England, 17 September, 1990 — D
England: Youth

League Club	Source	Date Signed	Seasons Played	Apps	Subs	Gls
Ipswich T	Sch	07/09	10-12	2	2	0

AINSLEY Jason
Born: Stockton-on-Tees, Cleveland, England, 30 July, 1970 — M

League Club	Source	Date Signed	Seasons Played	Apps	Subs	Gls
Hartlepool U	Spennymoor U	07/94	94	14	1	1

AINSWORTH Alphonso (Alf)
Born: Manchester, England, 31 July, 1913 — IF
Died: Rochdale, Greater Manchester, England, 25 April, 1975

League Club	Source	Date Signed	Seasons Played	Apps	Subs	Gls
Manchester U	Ashton Ath	02/34	33	2	-	0
New Brighton	Tr	09/35	35-38	150	-	39
Oldham Ath	Tr	09/42				
New Brighton	Tr	08/46	46-47	28	-	9

AINSWORTH David
Born: Bolton, Greater Manchester, England, 28 January, 1958 — F

League Club	Source	Date Signed	Seasons Played	Apps	Subs	Gls
Rochdale	App	01/76	75	0	2	0

AINSWORTH Gareth
Born: Blackburn, Greater Manchester, England, 10 May, 1973 — RW

League Club	Source	Date Signed	Seasons Played	Apps	Subs	Gls
Preston NE	Northwich Victoria	01/92	91	2	3	0
Cambridge U	Tr	08/92	92	1	3	1
Preston NE	Tr	12/92	92-95	76	6	14
Lincoln C	Tr	10/95	95-97	83	0	37
Port Vale	Tr	09/97	97-98	53	2	10
Wimbledon	Tr	11/98	98-02	21	15	6
Preston NE	L	03/02	01	3	2	1
Walsall	L	12/02	02	2	3	1
Cardiff C	Tr	03/03	02	9	0	0
Queens Park Rgrs	Tr	07/03	03-09	102	39	21
Wycombe W	Tr	11/09	09-12	79	35	16

AINSWORTH John (Jack)
Born: Wallasey, Wirral, England, 20 September, 1922 — CF
Died: Wallasey, Wirral, England, 26 March, 1981

League Club	Source	Date Signed	Seasons Played	Apps	Subs	Gls
New Brighton (Am)		03/47	46-47	14	-	3

AINSWORTH Lionel Glenn Robert
Born: Nottingham, England, 1 October, 1987 — RW
England: Youth

League Club	Source	Date Signed	Seasons Played	Apps	Subs	Gls
Derby Co	Sch	08/05	05	0	2	0
Bournemouth	L	08/06	06	2	5	0
Wycombe W	L	02/07	06	3	4	0
Hereford U	Tr	08/07	07	13	2	4
Watford	Tr	11/07	07-08	4	11	0
Hereford U	L	11/08	08	7	0	3
Huddersfield T	Tr	01/09	08-09	9	16	0
Brentford	L	01/10	09	1	8	0
Shrewsbury T	Tr	08/10	10-11	40	14	11
Burton A	L	03/12	11	4	3	0
Rotherham U	Tr	07/12	12	8	8	0
Aldershot T	L	01/13	12	3	4	0

AIRD John Rae (Jock)
Born: Glencraig, Fife, Scotland, 18 February, 1926 — LB
New Zealand: 2//Scotland: 4/B-2

League Club	Source	Date Signed	Seasons Played	Apps	Subs	Gls
Burnley	Jeanfield Swifts	08/48	49-54	132	-	0

AIREY Carl
Born: Wakefield, England, 6 February, 1965 — F

League Club	Source	Date Signed	Seasons Played	Apps	Subs	Gls
Barnsley	App	02/83	82-83	30	8	5
Bradford C	L	10/83	83	4	1	0
Darlington	Tr	08/84	84-85	72	3	28
Chesterfield (L)	RSC Charleroi (BEL)	12/86	86	24	2	4
Rotherham U	Tr	08/87	87	25	7	11
Torquay U	RSC Charleroi (BEL)	01/89	88-89	21	8	11

AIREY John (Jack)
Born: Bedford, England, 28 November, 1937 — W

League Club	Source	Date Signed	Seasons Played	Apps	Subs	Gls
Blackburn Rov	Blackburn Olympic	01/59	58-59	3	-	1

AISTON Samuel James (Sam)
Born: Newcastle-upon-Tyne, England, 21 November, 1976 — LW
England: Schools

League Club	Source	Date Signed	Seasons Played	Apps	Subs	Gls
Sunderland	Newcastle U (YT)	07/95	95-98	5	15	0
Chester C	L	02/97	96	14	0	0
Chester C	L	11/98	98	11	0	0
Stoke C	L	08/99	99	2	4	0
Shrewsbury T	L	12/99	99	10	0	0
Shrewsbury T	Tr	07/00	00-04	99	34	7
Tranmere Rov	Tr	07/05	05	23	13	3
Northampton T	Tr	07/06	06-07	14	8	0
Wrexham	Tr	10/07	07	13	6	0

AITCHISON Barrie George
Born: Colchester, Essex, England, 15 November, 1937 — W

League Club	Source	Date Signed	Seasons Played	Apps	Subs	Gls
Tottenham H	Colchester U (Jnr)	01/55				
Colchester U	Tr	08/64	64-65	49	1	6

AITCHISON Peter Munro
Born: Harlow, Essex, England, 19 September, 1931 — W

League Club	Source	Date Signed	Seasons Played	Apps	Subs	Gls
Colchester U	Rowhedge	10/51	51-54	18	-	2

AITKEN Andrew Fox Scott (Andy)
Born: Craigmillar, Edinburgh, Scotland, 21 August, 1934 — W
Died: Edinburgh, Scotland, 28 February, 2005

League Club	Source	Date Signed	Seasons Played	Apps	Subs	Gls
West Bromwich A	Hibernian	09/59	59-60	22	-	2

AITKEN Charles Alexander (Charlie)
Born: Edinburgh, Scotland, 1 May, 1942 — LB
Scotland: U23-3

League Club	Source	Date Signed	Seasons Played	Apps	Subs	Gls
Aston Villa	Edinburgh Thistle	08/59	60-75	559	2	14

AITKEN George Bruce
Born: Dalkeith, Midlothian, Scotland, 13 August, 1928 — CH
Died: Brighton, England, August, 2006

League Club	Source	Date Signed	Seasons Played	Apps	Subs	Gls
Middlesbrough	Edinburgh Thistle	06/46	51-52	17	-	0
Workington	Tr	07/53	53-59	262	-	3

AITKEN George Graham
Born: Lochgelly, Fife, Scotland, 28 May, 1925 — WH
Died: Sunderland, England, 22 January, 2003
Scotland: 8

League Club	Source	Date Signed	Seasons Played	Apps	Subs	Gls
Sunderland	Third Lanark	11/51	51-58	245	-	3
Gateshead	Tr	03/59	58-59	58	-	0

AITKEN Glenn Leslie
Born: Woolwich, SE London, England, 30 September, 1952 — LB/M
England: Youth

League Club	Source	Date Signed	Seasons Played	Apps	Subs	Gls
Gillingham	Chelsea (Am)	12/72	72-74	19	4	0
Wimbledon	Tr	09/74	77	11	0	1

AITKEN Peter Gerald
Born: Cardiff, Wales, 30 June, 1954 — CD

League Club	Source	Date Signed	Seasons Played	Apps	Subs	Gls
Bristol Rov	App	07/72	72-79	230	4	3
Bristol C	Tr	11/80	80-81	41	0	1
York C	Tr	02/82	81	18	0	2
Bournemouth	Forest Green Rov	11/82	82	1	0	0

AITKEN Robert Sime (Roy)
Born: Ardrossan, Ayrshire, Scotland, 24 November, 1958 — M
Scotland: 57/U21-16/Schools

League Club	Source	Date Signed	Seasons Played	Apps	Subs	Gls
Newcastle U	Glasgow Celtic	01/90	89-90	54	0	1

AITKEN William Robert Crawford (Billy)
Born: Dumfries, Scotland, 11 January, 1951 — M

League Club	Source	Date Signed	Seasons Played	Apps	Subs	Gls
Oldham Ath	App	01/68	68	1	0	0

AIZLEWOOD Mark
Born: Newport, Wales, 1 October, 1959 — M
Wales: 39/U21-2/Schools

League Club	Source	Date Signed	Seasons Played	Apps	Subs	Gls
Newport Co	App	10/77	75-77	35	3	1
Luton T	Tr	04/78	78-81	90	8	3
Charlton Ath	Tr	11/82	82-86	152	0	9
Leeds U	Tr	02/87	86-88	65	5	3
Bradford C	Tr	08/89	89	39	0	1
Bristol C	Tr	08/90	90-93	99	2	3
Cardiff C	Tr	10/93	93-94	39	0	3

AIZLEWOOD Steven (Steve)
Born: Newport, Wales, 9 October, 1952 — CD
Died: Newport, Wales, 6 August, 2013
Wales: Schools

League Club	Source	Date Signed	Seasons Played	Apps	Subs	Gls
Newport Co	Jnr	01/70	68-75	191	5	18
Swindon T	Tr	03/76	75-78	111	1	10
Portsmouth	Tr	07/79	79-83	175	0	13

AJALA Ridwan Oluwatobi (Toby)
Born: Newham, E London, England, 27 September, 1991 — RW

League Club	Source	Date Signed	Seasons Played	Apps	Subs	Gls
Bristol C	Hayes & Yeading U	08/12	12	0	2	0
AFC Wimbledon	L	11/12	12	11	1	0

AJDAREVIC Astrit
Born: Pristina, Kosovo, 17 April, 1990 — M
Sweden: U21-14/Youth

League Club	Source	Date Signed	Seasons Played	Apps	Subs	Gls
Liverpool	Falkenberg (SWE)	05/07				
Leicester C	Tr	03/09	08	0	5	0
Hereford U	L	03/10	09	0	1	0
Charlton Ath (L)	Standard Liege (BEL)	01/14	13	13	6	2

AJOSE Nicholas Olushola (Nicky)
Born: Bury, Greater Manchester, England, 7 October, 1991 — F
England: Youth

League Club	Source	Date Signed	Seasons Played	Apps	Subs	Gls
Manchester U	Sch	07/09				
Bury	L	09/10	10	22	6	13
Peterborough U	Tr	07/11	11-13	20	4	7
Scunthorpe U	L	09/11	11	2	5	0
Chesterfield	L	01/12	11	5	7	1
Crawley T	L	08/12	12	10	9	2
Bury	L	01/13	12	15	4	4
Swindon T	L	08/13	13	12	4	6
Leeds U	Tr	08/14	14	2	1	0
Crewe Alex	L	11/14	14	23	4	8

AKE Nathan Benjamin
Born: Den Haag, Netherlands, 18 February, 1995 — D
Netherlands: U21-13/Youth

League Club	Source	Date Signed	Seasons Played	Apps	Subs	Gls
Chelsea	Sch	07/12	12-14	1	4	0
Reading	L	03/15	14	5	0	0

AKERS Victor David (Vic)
Born: Islington, N London, England, 24 August, 1946 — LB

League Club	Source	Date Signed	Seasons Played	Apps	Subs	Gls
Cambridge U	Bexley U	07/71	71-74	122	7	5
Watford	Tooting & Mitcham U	07/75	75	22	0	0

AKIN Bulent
Born: Brussels, Belgium, 28 August, 1979 — M
Turkey: U21-6

League Club	Source	Date Signed	Seasons Played	Apps	Subs	Gls
Bolton W	Galatasaray (TKY)	08/02	02	0	1	0

AKINBIYI Adeola Oluwatoyin (Ade)
Born: Hackney, E London, England, 10 October, 1974 — F
Nigeria: 1

League Club	Source	Date Signed	Seasons Played	Apps	Subs	Gls
Norwich C	YT	02/93	93-96	22	27	3
Hereford U	L	01/94	93	3	1	2
Brighton & HA	L	11/94	94	7	0	4
Gillingham	Tr	01/97	96-97	63	0	28
Bristol C	Tr	05/98	98-99	47	0	21
Wolverhampton W	Tr	09/99	99	36	1	16
Leicester C	Tr	07/00	00-01	49	9	11
Crystal Palace	Tr	02/02	01-02	11	13	3
Stoke C	L	03/03	02	4	0	2
Stoke C	Tr	09/03	03-04	52	7	17
Burnley	Tr	02/05	04-05	38	1	16
Sheffield U	Tr	01/06	05-06	12	6	3
Burnley	Tr	01/07	06-08	30	40	10
Notts Co	Houston Dynamo (USA)	10/09	09	1	9	0

AKINDE John Job Ayo
Born: Camberwell, S London, England, 8 July, 1989 — F

League Club	Source	Date Signed	Seasons Played	Apps	Subs	Gls
Bristol C	Ebbsfleet U	09/08	08-10	1	15	1
Wycombe W	L	03/09	08	11	0	7
Wycombe W	L	11/09	09	4	2	1
Brentford	L	02/10	09	2	0	0
Bristol Rov	L	08/10	10	9	5	0
Dagenham & Red	L	01/11	10	8	1	2
Crawley T	Tr	05/11	11-12	7	24	1
Dagenham & Red	L	03/12	11	4	1	0
Portsmouth	Tr	02/13	12	3	8	0

AKINFENWA Saheed Adebayo (Adebayo)
Born: Islington, N London, England, 10 May, 1982 — F

League Club	Source	Date Signed	Seasons Played	Apps	Subs	Gls
Boston U	Barry T	09/03	03	2	1	0
Leyton Orient	Tr	10/03	03	0	1	0
Rushden & D	Tr	12/03				
Doncaster Rov	Tr	02/04	03	4	5	4
Torquay U	Tr	07/04	04	28	9	14
Swansea C	Tr	07/05	05-06	41	18	14
Millwall		11/07	07	1	6	0
Northampton T	Tr	01/08	07-09	78	10	37
Gillingham	Tr	08/10	10	40	4	11
Northampton T	Tr	05/11	11-12	63	17	34
Gillingham	Tr	07/13	13	17	17	10
AFC Wimbledon	Tr	06/14	14	43	2	13

AKINS Lucas-Jordan Jeremiah (Lucas)
Born: Huddersfield, West Yorkshire, England, 25 February, 1989 — RW

League Club	Source	Date Signed	Seasons Played	Apps	Subs	Gls
Huddersfield T	Sch	07/07	06-07	0	5	0
Tranmere Rov	Hamilton Academical	08/10	10-11	59	18	7
Stevenage	Tr	08/12	12-13	66	11	13
Burton A	Tr	06/14	14	32	3	10

AKINTUNDE James Ayoade
Born: Brent, NW London, England, 23 September, 1996 — F

League Club	Source	Date Signed	Seasons Played	Apps	Subs	Gls
Cambridge U	Sch	07/14	14	0	1	0

AKPA AKPRO Jean-Louis
Born: Toulouse, France, 4 January, 1985 — F

League Club	Source	Date Signed	Seasons Played	Apps	Subs	Gls
Grimsby T	FCM Brussels (BEL)	12/08	08-09	45	11	8
Rochdale	Tr	07/10	10-11	38	35	11
Tranmere Rov	Tr	07/12	12-13	48	5	10
Bury	L	01/14	13	5	5	0
Shrewsbury T	Tr	07/14	14	26	19	9

AKPAN Hope Ini
Born: Liverpool, England, 14 August, 1991 — M
Nigeria: 4

League Club	Source	Date Signed	Seasons Played	Apps	Subs	Gls
Everton	Sch	11/08				
Hull C	L	03/11	10	1	1	0
Crawley T	Tr	06/11	11-12	38	9	5
Reading	Tr	01/13	12-14	37	21	1

AKPOM Chuba Amechi
Born: Newham, E London, England, 9 October, 1995 — F
England: Youth

League Club	Source	Date Signed	Seasons Played	Apps	Subs	Gls
Arsenal	Sch	10/11	13-14	0	4	0
Brentford	L	01/14	13	0	4	0
Coventry C	L	02/14	13	5	1	0
Nottingham F	L	03/15	14	5	2	0

AKURANG Cliff
Born: Newham, E London, England, 27 February, 1981 — F

League Club	Source	Date Signed	Seasons Played	Apps	Subs	Gls
Barnet	Histon	01/08	07-08	29	16	10

ALABI James Bamidele
Born: Southwark, S London, England, 8 November, 1994 — F

League Club	Source	Date Signed	Seasons Played	Apps	Subs	Gls
Stoke C	Sch	09/12				
Scunthorpe U	L	02/13	12	0	9	1
Mansfield T	L	10/13	13	1	0	0
Scunthorpe U	L	03/14	13	0	1	0
Accrington Stan	L	08/14	14	1	1	0
ALBENTOSA Raul						
Born: Alzira, Spain, 7 September, 1988						CD
Derby Co	SD Eibar (SPN)	01/15	14	7	1	0
ALBERRY William Edward (Ted)						
Born: Doncaster, South Yorkshire, England, 21 July, 1922						CF
Died: Doncaster, South Yorkshire, England, 1978						
Leeds U	Doncaster Rov (Am)	05/46				
Hull C	Tr	04/47	46	1	-	0
ALBERT Philippe						
Born: Bouillon, Belgium, 10 August, 1967						CD
Belgium: 41/U21-4						
Newcastle U	Anderlecht (BEL)	08/94	94-98	87	9	8
Fulham	L	01/99	98	12	1	2
ALBERTI Matteo						
Born: Brescia, Italy, 4 April, 1988						RM
Queens Park Rgrs	Chievo Verona (ITA)	08/08	08	6	6	2
ALBESON Brian						
Born: Oldham, Greater Manchester, England, 14 December, 1946						CD
Died: Darlington, County Durham, England, 15 October, 2003						
England: Youth						
Bury	Jnr	05/65	65	0	1	0
Darlington	Tr	07/67	67-70	134	2	2
Southend U	Tr	07/71	71-73	109	1	9
Stockport Co	Tr	03/74	73-74	54	0	1
Hartlepool U	Tr	07/75				
ALBISTON Arthur Richard						
Born: Edinburgh, Scotland, 14 July, 1957						LB
Scotland: 14/U21-5/Schools						
Manchester U	App	07/74	74-87	364	15	6
West Bromwich A	Tr	08/88	88	43	0	2
Chesterfield (L)	Dundee	11/90	90	3	0	1
Chester C	Dundee	08/91	91	44	0	0
Chester C	Molde FK (NOR)	11/92	92	23	1	0
ALBRECHTSEN Martin						
Born: Copenhagen, Denmark, 31 March, 1980						RB
Denmark: 4/U21-14/Youth						
West Bromwich A	FC Copenhagen (DEN)	06/04	04-07	100	18	4
Derby Co	Tr	07/08	08	35	0	2
ALBRIGHTON Marc Kevin						
Born: Tamworth, Staffordshire, England, 18 November, 1989						RW
England: U21-8/Youth						
Aston Villa	Sch	07/08	09-13	48	38	7
Wigan Ath	L	10/13	13	2	2	0
Leicester C	Tr	05/14	14	10	8	2
ALBRIGHTON Mark Christopher						
Born: Nuneaton, Warwickshire, England, 6 March, 1976						CD
Doncaster Rov	Telford U	07/02	03-05	58	3	4
Chester C	L	02/06	05	9	0	0
Boston U	Tr	07/06	06	12	0	0
Darlington	L	11/06	06	3	0	0
ALBURY William Frederick (Bill)						
Born: Portsmouth, England, 10 August, 1933						IF
Portsmouth	Jnr	10/51	56-57	23	-	0
Gillingham	Tr	07/59	59	38	-	12
ALCARAZ Antolin						
Born: San Roque Gonzalez, Paraguay, 30 July, 1982						CD
Paraguay: 24						
Wigan Ath	Club Brugge (BEL)	05/10	10-12	67	2	3
Everton	Tr	07/13	13-14	11	3	0
ALCIDE Colin James						
Born: Huddersfield, West Yorkshire, England, 14 April, 1972						F
Lincoln C	Emley	12/95	95-98	105	16	26
Hull C	L	02/99	98	5	0	1
Hull C	Tr	03/99	98-99	22	2	3
York C	Tr	11/99	99-00	33	20	7
Cambridge U	Tr	06/01	01	7	1	0
Exeter C	Gainsborough Trinity	11/02	02	1	0	0
ALCOCK Craig						
Born: Truro, Cornwall, England, 8 December, 1987						RB
Yeovil T	Jnr	07/06	06-10	88	19	3
Peterborough U	Tr	07/11	11-13	87	9	0
Sheffield U	Tr	07/14	14	17	7	0

League Club	Source	Date Signed	Seasons Played	Apps	Subs	Gls
ALCOCK Daniel James (Danny)						
Born: Stafford, England, 15 February, 1984						G
Barnsley	Stoke C (YT)	10/03	03	0	1	0
ALCOCK Terence (Terry)						
Born: Hanley, Potteries, England, 9 December, 1946						CD
Port Vale	App	09/64	63-66	112	0	0
Blackpool	Tr	08/67	67-75	185	6	21
Bury	L	02/72	71	6	0	1
Blackburn Rov	L	12/76	76	3	0	1
Port Vale	Tr	02/77	76-77	4	0	0
Halifax T	Tr	09/77	77	14	0	2
ALDECOA Emilio Gomez						
Born: Bilbao, Spain, 30 November, 1922						W
Died: Spain, September, 1999						
Spain: 1						
Wolverhampton W	English Elec, Stafford	12/43				
Coventry C	Tr	12/45	46	29	-	0
ALDERSON Brian Roderick						
Born: Dundee, Scotland, 5 May, 1950						W
Died: Atlanta, USA, 23 April, 1997						
Scotland: U23-1						
Coventry C	Lochee Harp	07/70	70-74	116	11	29
Leicester C	Tr	07/75	75-77	87	3	9
ALDERSON Kevin						
Born: Shildon, County Durham, England, 21 August, 1953						W
Darlington	App	-	70	2	0	0
ALDERSON Richard						
Born: Durham, England, 27 January, 1975						RW
York C	Spennymoor U	12/97	97	0	1	0
ALDERSON Stuart						
Born: Bishop Auckland, County Durham, England, 15 August, 1948						RW
Newcastle U	Evenwood T	08/65	66	3	0	0
York C	Tr	06/67	67	17	2	5
ALDERTON James Harris (Jim)						
Born: Wingate, County Durham, England, 6 December, 1924						WH
Died: Kidderminster, Worcestershire, England, June, 1998						
Wolverhampton W	Jnr	12/41	46	11	-	0
Coventry C	Tr	10/47	47-51	62	-	0
ALDERTON Rio Kevin						
Born: Colchester, Essex, England, 12 August, 1982						M
Millwall	YT	07/01				
Southend U	Tr	03/02	01	0	2	0
ALDERWEIRELD Tobias Albertine Maurits (Toby)						
Born: Antwerp, Belgium, 2 March, 1989						CD
Belgium: 43/U21-5/Youth						
Southampton (L)	Atletico Madrid (SPN)	09/14	14	26	0	1
ALDIS Basil Peter (Peter)						
Born: Birmingham, England, 11 April, 1927						LB
Died: Chichester, West Sussex, England, 13 November, 2008						
Aston Villa	Hay Green	05/49	50-58	262	-	1
ALDOUS Stanley Elvey Reginald (Stan)						
Born: Northfleet, Kent, England, 10 February, 1923						CH
Died: Ely, Cambridgeshire, England, 17 October, 1995						
Leyton Orient	Gravesend & Northfleet	07/50	50-57	302	-	3
ALDREAD Paul						
Born: Mansfield, Nottinghamshire, England, 6 November, 1946						F
Died: Sutton-in-Ashfield, Nottinghamshire, England, 14 August, 2014						
Mansfield T	Jnr	12/63	65-66	11	1	3
ALDRED Arthur						
Born: Atherton, Greater Manchester, England, 27 August, 1919						RW
Died: Birmingham, England, 23 May, 2002						
Aston Villa	Hereford U	07/46				
Walsall	Tr	05/48	48	11	-	1
ALDRED Graeme						
Born: Ferryhill, County Durham, England, 11 September, 1966						RB
Died: Ashton-under-Lyne, Greater Manchester, England, July, 1987						
Darlington	Newcastle U (YT)	09/84	84-85	30	14	0
ALDRED Thomas Michael (Tom)						
Born: Bolton, Greater Manchester, England, 11 September, 1990						CD
Carlisle U	Sch	12/08	09	4	1	0
Watford	Tr	07/10				
Stockport Co	L	11/10	10	7	0	0
Colchester U	Tr	09/11				
Accrington Stan	Tr	01/13	12-14	83	1	3
Blackpool	Tr	01/15	14	6	0	0

ALDRIDGE John William
Born: Liverpool, England, 18 September, 1958 — F
Republic of Ireland: 69

League Club	Source	Date Signed	Seasons Played	Apps	Subs	Gls
Newport Co	South Liverpool	05/79	79-83	159	11	69
Oxford U	Tr	01/84	83-86	111	3	72
Liverpool	Tr	01/87	86-89	69	14	50
Tranmere Rov	Real Sociedad (SPN)	07/91	91-97	221	21	138

ALDRIDGE Martin James
Born: Northampton, England, 6 December, 1974 — F
Died: Oxford, England, 30 January, 2000

League Club	Source	Date Signed	Seasons Played	Apps	Subs	Gls
Northampton T	YT	08/93	91-94	50	20	17
Oxford U	Tr	12/95	95-97	46	26	19
Southend U	L	02/98	97	7	4	1
Blackpool	Tr	08/98	98-99	19	8	7
Port Vale	L	09/99	99	0	3	0

ALDRIDGE Neil Robert
Born: Manchester, England, 10 January, 1966 — LB
England: Youth/Schools

League Club	Source	Date Signed	Seasons Played	Apps	Subs	Gls
Manchester C	App	11/83				
Crewe Alex	Tr	07/84	84	12	3	0

ALDRIDGE Norman Hubert
Born: Coventry, England, 23 February, 1921 — FB
Died: Nuneaton, Warwickshire, England, 14 January, 2007

League Club	Source	Date Signed	Seasons Played	Apps	Subs	Gls
West Bromwich A	Foxford	05/46	46	1	-	0
Northampton T	Tr	06/48	48	2	-	0

ALDRIDGE Paul John
Born: Liverpool, England, 2 December, 1981 — M

League Club	Source	Date Signed	Seasons Played	Apps	Subs	Gls
Tranmere Rov	YT	03/00	99-00	0	6	0
Macclesfield T	Tr	03/02	02	0	1	0

ALDRIDGE Stephen Paul (Steve)
Born: Armthorpe, South Yorkshire, England, 2 November, 1957 — F

League Club	Source	Date Signed	Seasons Played	Apps	Subs	Gls
Sheffield U	App	12/75				
Doncaster Rov		02/81	80	1	0	0

ALEKSIC Milija Antony
Born: Newcastle-under-Lyme, Potteries, England, 14 April, 1951 — G
Died: Johannesburg, South Africa, 17 October, 2012

League Club	Source	Date Signed	Seasons Played	Apps	Subs	Gls
Plymouth Arg	Stafford Rgrs	02/73	73-75	32	0	0
Luton T	Tr	12/76	76-78	77	0	0
Tottenham H	Tr	12/78	78-81	25	0	0
Luton T	L	11/81	81	4	0	0

ALEKSIDZE Rati
Born: Tbilisi, Georgia, 6 August, 1978 — F
Georgia: 28/U21-19/Youth

League Club	Source	Date Signed	Seasons Played	Apps	Subs	Gls
Chelsea	Dynamo Tbilisi (GEO)	02/00	00	0	2	0

ALESINLOYE Martin
Born: Middlesbrough, England, 1 October, 1955 — M

League Club	Source	Date Signed	Seasons Played	Apps	Subs	Gls
Doncaster Rov	Barnsley (Am)	10/75	75	13	1	1

ALESSANDRA Lewis Peter
Born: Heywood, Greater Manchester, England, 8 February, 1989 — F

League Club	Source	Date Signed	Seasons Played	Apps	Subs	Gls
Oldham Ath	Sch	07/07	07-10	34	33	8
Morecambe	Tr	06/11	11-12	55	27	7
Plymouth Arg	Tr	07/13	13-14	82	4	18

[ALEX] DIAS DA COSTA Alex Rodrigo
Born: Rio de Janeiro, Brazil, 17 June, 1982 — CD
Brazil: 17/U23-8

League Club	Source	Date Signed	Seasons Played	Apps	Subs	Gls
Chelsea	PSV Eindhoven (NED)	06/07	07-11	72	14	7

ALEXANDER Alan
Born: Cumbernauld, Lanarkshire, Scotland, 1 November, 1941 — G

League Club	Source	Date Signed	Seasons Played	Apps	Subs	Gls
Bradford Park Ave	Glenluce Ath	07/59	61	5	-	0

ALEXANDER Alexander (Alex)
Born: Glasgow, Scotland, 28 September, 1924 — LW
Died: Bath, England, 14 May, 2005

League Club	Source	Date Signed	Seasons Played	Apps	Subs	Gls
Tranmere Rov	New Brighton (Am)	10/47	46-48	23	-	3

ALEXANDER Angus Charles (Gus)
Born: Arbroath, Angus, Scotland, 10 January, 1934 — IF
Died: Workington, Cumbria, England, 10 January, 2010

League Club	Source	Date Signed	Seasons Played	Apps	Subs	Gls
Burnley	Arbroath YC	01/51				
Southport	Tr	07/57	57	14	-	1
Workington	Tr	02/58	57-58	49	-	4
York C	Tr	06/59	59	7	-	0

ALEXANDER Anthony Alan (Tony)
Born: Reading, England, 8 February, 1935 — IF
Died: Swindon, England, 9 October, 2013

League Club	Source	Date Signed	Seasons Played	Apps	Subs	Gls
Reading	Jnr	08/52	52-55	11	-	2
Crystal Palace	Yeovil T	08/60				

ALEXANDER Dennis Leslie
Born: Nottingham, England, 19 February, 1935 — IF
Died: Bilborough, Nottinghamshire, England, 1 November, 2011

League Club	Source	Date Signed	Seasons Played	Apps	Subs	Gls
Nottingham F	Jnr	06/55	55-56	20	-	4
Brighton & HA	Tr	03/58				
Gateshead	Tr	10/58	58	17	-	1

ALEXANDER Gary George
Born: Lambeth, S London, England, 15 August, 1979 — F

League Club	Source	Date Signed	Seasons Played	Apps	Subs	Gls
West Ham U	YT	07/98				
Exeter C	L	08/99	99	37	0	16
Swindon T	Tr	08/00	00	30	7	7
Hull C	Tr	06/01	01-02	64	4	23
Leyton Orient	Tr	01/03	02-06	163	14	52
Millwall	Tr	07/07	07-09	69	17	19
Brentford	Tr	08/10	10-11	57	5	21
Crawley T	Tr	03/12	11-13	48	14	15
AFC Wimbledon	L	01/13	12	16	2	3
Burton A	Tr	01/14	13	7	4	0

ALEXANDER Graham
Born: Coventry, England, 10 October, 1971 — RB/M
Scotland: 40/B-1

League Club	Source	Date Signed	Seasons Played	Apps	Subs	Gls
Scunthorpe U	YT	03/90	90-94	149	10	18
Luton T	Tr	07/95	95-98	146	4	15
Preston NE	Tr	03/99	98-07	350	2	52
Burnley	Tr	08/07	07-10	137	17	20
Preston NE	Tr	08/11	11	17	1	2

ALEXANDER Ian
Born: Glasgow, Scotland, 26 January, 1963 — RB

League Club	Source	Date Signed	Seasons Played	Apps	Subs	Gls
Rotherham U	Leicester Juveniles	10/81	81-82	5	6	0
Bristol Rov	Pez Larnaca (CYP)	08/86	86-93	284	7	6

ALEXANDER James Neil (Neil)
Born: Edinburgh, Scotland, 10 March, 1978 — G
Scotland: 3/B-1/U21-10

League Club	Source	Date Signed	Seasons Played	Apps	Subs	Gls
Cardiff C	Livingston	08/01	01-06	212	1	0
Ipswich T	Tr	07/07	07	29	0	0
Crystal Palace	Tr	08/13				

ALEXANDER John David
Born: Middlesbrough, England, 24 September, 1985 — F

League Club	Source	Date Signed	Seasons Played	Apps	Subs	Gls
Darlington	Sch	-	02-03	0	4	0

ALEXANDER John Eric
Born: Liverpool, England, 5 October, 1955 — F

League Club	Source	Date Signed	Seasons Played	Apps	Subs	Gls
Millwall	Ulysses	07/77	76-77	10	5	2
Reading	Tr	10/78	78-80	22	3	9
Northampton T	Tr	08/81	81	21	1	4

ALEXANDER Keith
Born: Nottingham, England, 14 November, 1956 — F
Died: Lincoln, England, 3 March, 2010
Saint Lucia:

League Club	Source	Date Signed	Seasons Played	Apps	Subs	Gls
Grimsby T	Barnet	07/88	88-90	64	19	26
Stockport Co	Tr	09/90	90	9	2	0
Lincoln C	Tr	12/90	90-92	26	19	4
Mansfield T	Tr	08/94	94	0	2	0
Mansfield T	Cliftonville	01/96	95	0	1	0

ALEXANDER Philip James (Phil)
Born: Slough, Berkshire, England, 4 September, 1962 — CD
England: Schools

League Club	Source	Date Signed	Seasons Played	Apps	Subs	Gls
Norwich C	Wokingham T	08/81	82	0	1	0

ALEXANDER Rowan Samuel
Born: Ayr, Scotland, 28 January, 1961 — F

League Club	Source	Date Signed	Seasons Played	Apps	Subs	Gls
Brentford	St Mirren	09/84	84-85	41	6	6

ALEXANDER Timothy Mark (Tim)
Born: Chertsey, Surrey, England, 29 March, 1974 — CD

League Club	Source	Date Signed	Seasons Played	Apps	Subs	Gls
Barnet	Wimbledon (YT)	08/92	93-94	29	7	0

ALEXANDERSSON Niclas
Born: Halmstad, Sweden, 29 December, 1971 — RM
Sweden: 109/U23-3

League Club	Source	Date Signed	Seasons Played	Apps	Subs	Gls
Sheffield Wed	IFK Goteberg (SWE)	12/97	97-99	73	2	8
Everton	Tr	07/00	00-02	49	9	4
West Ham U	L	09/03	03	5	3	0

ALEY Zachary George (Zac)
Born: Bootle, Merseyside, England, 17 August, 1991 — W

League Club	Source	Date Signed	Seasons Played	Apps	Subs	Gls
Blackburn Rov	Southport	03/10				
Morecambe	L	03/11	10	1	1	0
Macclesfield T	L	03/12	11	1	0	0

ALFEI Daniel Mark
Born: Swansea, Wales, 23 February, 1992 — RB

Wales: U21-13/Youth

League Club	Source	Date Signed	Seasons Played	Apps	Subs	Gls
Swansea C	Sch	07/10	10	0	1	0
Portsmouth	L	01/14	13	15	0	0
Northampton T	L	07/14	14	9	2	0

ALFORD Carl Peter
Born: Denton, Greater Manchester, England, 11 February, 1972 — F

League Club	Source	Date Signed	Seasons Played	Apps	Subs	Gls
Rochdale	YT	-	88	0	4	0

ALGAR Benjamin Christopher (Ben)
Born: Dronfield, Derbyshire, England, 3 December, 1989 — LM

League Club	Source	Date Signed	Seasons Played	Apps	Subs	Gls
Chesterfield	Sch	07/08	07-08	2	3	0

AL HABSI Ali Abdullah Harib
Born: Muscat, Oman, 30 December, 1981 — G
Oman: 106

League Club	Source	Date Signed	Seasons Played	Apps	Subs	Gls
Bolton W	Lyn Oslo (NOR)	01/06	07	10	0	0
Wigan Ath	Tr	07/10	10-14	136	0	0
Brighton & HA	L	10/14	14	1	0	0

ALIADIERE Jeremie
Born: Rambouillet, France, 30 March, 1983 — F
France: U21-7/Youth

League Club	Source	Date Signed	Seasons Played	Apps	Subs	Gls
Arsenal	YT	04/00	01-06	7	22	1
West Ham U	L	08/05	05	1	6	0
Wolverhampton W	L	02/06	05	12	2	2
Middlesbrough	Tr	07/07	07-09	69	9	11

ALISON James (Jimmy)
Born: Peebles, Borders, Scotland, 11 October, 1923 — WH
Died: Bournemouth, England, February, 1998

League Club	Source	Date Signed	Seasons Played	Apps	Subs	Gls
Manchester C	Falkirk	12/49	49-50	19	-	0
Aldershot	Tr	07/52	52-56	171	-	8

AL JABER Sami Abdullah
Born: Riyadh, Saudi Arabia, 11 December, 1972 — M
Saudi Arabia: 156

League Club	Source	Date Signed	Seasons Played	Apps	Subs	Gls
Wolverhampton W (L)	Al-Hilal (SAU)	09/00	00	0	4	0

ALJOFREE Hasney
Born: Manchester, England, 11 July, 1978 — CD
England: Youth

League Club	Source	Date Signed	Seasons Played	Apps	Subs	Gls
Bolton W	YT	07/96	97-99	6	8	0
Plymouth Arg	Dundee U	08/02	02-06	109	8	3
Sheffield Wed	L	09/04	04	2	0	0
Oldham Ath	L	03/07	06	5	0	0
Swindon T	Tr	07/07	07-08	55	2	2
Oldham Ath	Tr	02/10	09	1	0	0

ALLAN Alexander Begg (Sandy)
Born: Forfar, Angus, Scotland, 29 October, 1947 — F

League Club	Source	Date Signed	Seasons Played	Apps	Subs	Gls
Cardiff C	Rhyl	03/67	67-69	8	1	1
Bristol Rov	Tr	03/70	69-72	51	6	18
Swansea C	L	03/73	72	6	1	1

ALLAN Derek Thomas
Born: Irvine, Ayrshire, Scotland, 24 December, 1974 — CD
Scotland: Youth

League Club	Source	Date Signed	Seasons Played	Apps	Subs	Gls
Southampton	Ayr U	03/93	92	0	1	0
Brighton & HA	Tr	03/96	95-98	77	3	2

ALLAN James (Jimmy)
Born: Inverness, Scotland, 10 November, 1953 — G

League Club	Source	Date Signed	Seasons Played	Apps	Subs	Gls
Swindon T	App	07/71	71-83	371	0	0

ALLAN John
Born: Stirling, Scotland, 22 March, 1931 — CF
Died: Aberdeen, Scotland, 16 June, 2003

League Club	Source	Date Signed	Seasons Played	Apps	Subs	Gls
Bradford Park Ave	Third Lanark	02/59	58-60	70	-	51
Halifax T	Tr	03/61	60	10	-	1

ALLAN John
Born: Amble, Northumberland, England, 26 September, 1931 — G
Died: Luton, England, February, 2013

League Club	Source	Date Signed	Seasons Played	Apps	Subs	Gls
Barnsley	Amble Welfare	01/49	51-52	11	-	0

ALLAN Jonathan Michael (Jonny)
Born: Carlisle, Cumbria, England, 24 May, 1983 — F

League Club	Source	Date Signed	Seasons Played	Apps	Subs	Gls
Carlisle U	YT	05/00	01	10	19	2

ALLAN Scott
Born: Glasgow, Scotland, 29 November, 1991 — M
Scotland: U21-10/Youth

League Club	Source	Date Signed	Seasons Played	Apps	Subs	Gls
West Bromwich A	Dundee U	01/12				
Portsmouth	L	02/12	11	15	0	1
MK Dons	L	09/12	12	2	2	0
Portsmouth	L	10/12	12	6	3	1
Birmingham C	L	07/13	13	2	3	0

ALLAN Thomas James (Tom)
Born: York, England, 30 October, 1994 — CD

League Club	Source	Date Signed	Seasons Played	Apps	Subs	Gls
York C	Sch	12/12	12-13	5	5	0

ALLANSON Ashley Gary
Born: Hull, England, 13 November, 1986 — M

League Club	Source	Date Signed	Seasons Played	Apps	Subs	Gls
Scunthorpe U	Hull C (Sch)	11/05	05	0	1	0

ALLANSON Gary Ernest
Born: Hull, England, 6 March, 1965 — RB

League Club	Source	Date Signed	Seasons Played	Apps	Subs	Gls
Doncaster Rov	App	03/83	81-83	11	2	0

ALLARDYCE Craig Samuel
Born: Bolton, Greater Manchester, England, 9 June, 1975 — CD

League Club	Source	Date Signed	Seasons Played	Apps	Subs	Gls
Preston NE	YT	07/93	92	0	1	0
Blackpool	Northwich Victoria	09/94	95	0	1	0
Chesterfield	Chorley	03/98	97	0	1	0
Peterborough U	Tr	08/98	98	4	0	0
Mansfield T	Welling U	12/98	98-99	7	3	0

ALLARDYCE Samuel (Sam)
Born: Dudley, West Midlands, England, 19 October, 1954 — CD

League Club	Source	Date Signed	Seasons Played	Apps	Subs	Gls
Bolton W	App	11/71	73-79	180	4	21
Sunderland	Tr	07/80	80	24	1	2
Millwall	Tr	09/81	81-82	63	0	2
Coventry C	Tampa Bay R's (USA)	09/83	83	28	0	1
Huddersfield T	Tr	07/84	84	37	0	0
Bolton W	Tr	07/85	85	14	0	0
Preston NE	Tr	08/86	86-88	88	2	2
West Bromwich A	Tr	06/89	89	0	1	0
Preston NE	Rtd	08/92	92	1	2	0

ALLATT Vernon
Born: Cannock, Staffordshire, England, 28 May, 1959 — F

League Club	Source	Date Signed	Seasons Played	Apps	Subs	Gls
Halifax T	Hednesford T	11/79	79-81	66	4	7
Bolton W	Tr	08/82				
Halifax T	Tr	11/82	82	27	1	7
Rochdale	Tr	08/83	83	40	0	8
Crewe Alex	Tr	06/84	84-85	36	3	8
Preston NE	Tr	11/85	85	17	2	3
Stockport Co	Tr	10/86	86	23	1	10
Crewe Alex	Hednesford T	12/87	87	4	1	2

ALLAWAY James Frederick (Jim)
Born: Bristol, England, 23 April, 1922 — IF
Died: Australia, 1991

League Club	Source	Date Signed	Seasons Played	Apps	Subs	Gls
Bristol Rov		12/46	46	4	-	0
Bristol C	Tr	08/47				

ALLBACK Marcus
Born: Gothenburg, Sweden, 5 July, 1973 — F
Sweden: 42

League Club	Source	Date Signed	Seasons Played	Apps	Subs	Gls
Aston Villa	Heerenveen (NED)	05/02	02-03	16	19	6

ALLCHURCH Ivor John
Born: Swansea, Wales, 16 December, 1929 — IF
Died: Swansea, Wales, 9 July, 1997
Wales: 68/WLge-4

League Club	Source	Date Signed	Seasons Played	Apps	Subs	Gls
Swansea C	Plasmarl	05/47	49-58	327	-	124
Newcastle U	Tr	10/58	58-61	143	-	46
Cardiff C	Tr	08/62	62-64	103	-	39
Swansea C	Tr	07/65	65-67	116	2	40

ALLCHURCH Leonard (Len)
Born: Swansea, Wales, 12 September, 1933 — RW
Wales: 11/Schools

League Club	Source	Date Signed	Seasons Played	Apps	Subs	Gls
Swansea C	Jnr	10/50	50-60	276	-	49
Sheffield U	Tr	03/61	60-64	123	-	32
Stockport Co	Tr	09/65	65-68	131	0	16
Swansea C	Tr	07/69	69-70	70	1	11

ALLCOCK Frank Edward
Born: Beeston, Nottinghamshire, England, 7 September, 1925 — LB
Died: Nottingham, England, June, 2005

League Club	Source	Date Signed	Seasons Played	Apps	Subs	Gls
Nottingham F	Beeston BC	03/45				
Aston Villa	Tr	08/46				
Bristol Rov	Cheltenham T	06/52	53-55	59	-	0

ALLCOCK Kenneth (Ken)
Born: Kirkby-in-Ashfield, Nottinghamshire, England, 24 April, 1921 — CF
Died: Mansfield, Nottinghamshire, England, September, 1996

League Club	Source	Date Signed	Seasons Played	Apps	Subs	Gls
Mansfield T	East Kirkby MW	04/47	47	1	-	0

ALLCOCK Terence (Terry)
Born: Leeds, England, 10 December, 1935 — IF

League Club	Source	Date Signed	Seasons Played	Apps	Subs	Gls
Bolton W	Jnr	12/52	53-57	31	-	9
Norwich C	Tr	03/58	57-68	334	5	106

ALLDER Douglas Stewart (Doug)
Born: Hammersmith, W London, England, 30 December, 1951 — LW

England: Youth

League Club	Source	Date Signed	Seasons Played	Apps	Subs	Gls
Millwall	App	10/69	69-74	191	11	10
Leyton Orient	Tr	07/75	75-76	34	7	0
Watford	Torquay U (NC)	09/77	77	1	0	0
Brentford	Tr	10/77	77-79	68	20	2

ALLDIS Gilbert John (Gillie)
Born: Birkenhead, Wirral, England, 26 January, 1920 WH
Died: Prenton, Merseyside, England, 8 January, 1998

League Club	Source	Date Signed	Seasons Played	Apps	Subs	Gls
Tranmere Rov		10/38	38-48	75	-	4
New Brighton	Tr	07/50	50	12	-	0

ALLEN Adrian
Born: Preston, Lancashire, England, 23 March, 1934 RW
Died: Sheffield, England, 12 March, 2009

League Club	Source	Date Signed	Seasons Played	Apps	Subs	Gls
Southport	Preston NE (Am)	05/54	54	6	-	0

ALLEN Albert Robert (Bob)
Born: Bow, E London, England, 11 October, 1916 W
Died: Epping Forest, Essex, England, February, 1992
England: Schools

League Club	Source	Date Signed	Seasons Played	Apps	Subs	Gls
Leyton Orient	Leytonstone (Am)	12/33	33	1	-	0
Fulham	Tr	05/34	34-36	11	-	0
Doncaster Rov	Tr	06/37	37	31	-	6
Brentford	Tr	06/38				
Northampton T	Dartford	09/45	46	5	-	0
Colchester U	Tr	08/47	50	29	-	1

ALLEN Andrew (Andy)
Born: Liverpool, England, 4 September, 1974 W

League Club	Source	Date Signed	Seasons Played	Apps	Subs	Gls
Chester C	YT	-	91	0	1	0

ALLEN Anthony (Tony)
Born: Stoke-on-Trent, England, 27 November, 1939 LB
England: 3/FLge-2/U23-3/Youth

League Club	Source	Date Signed	Seasons Played	Apps	Subs	Gls
Stoke C	Jnr	11/56	57-69	414	3	2
Bury	Tr	10/70	70-71	29	0	0

ALLEN Arthur Reginald (Reg)
Born: Marylebone, Central London, England, 3 May, 1919 G
Died: Ealing, W London, England, 3 April, 1976
England: FLge-2

League Club	Source	Date Signed	Seasons Played	Apps	Subs	Gls
Queens Park Rgrs	Corona	05/38	38-49	183	-	0
Manchester U	Tr	06/50	50-52	75	-	0

ALLEN Bradley James
Born: Harold Wood, E London, England, 13 September, 1971 F
England: U21-8/Youth

League Club	Source	Date Signed	Seasons Played	Apps	Subs	Gls
Queens Park Rgrs	Jnr	09/88	88-95	56	25	27
Charlton Ath	Tr	03/96	95-97	30	10	9
Colchester U	L	02/99	98	4	0	1
Grimsby T	Tr	07/99	99-01	46	34	15
Peterborough U	Tr	08/02	02	10	1	3
Bristol Rov	Tr	11/02	02	5	3	1

ALLEN Brynley William (Bryn)
Born: Gilfach Goch, Rhondda Cynon Taff, Wales, 23 March, 1921 IF
Died: Rhondda, Rhondda Cynon Taff, Wales, 7 July, 2005
Wales: 2

League Club	Source	Date Signed	Seasons Played	Apps	Subs	Gls
Swansea C	Gilfach Welfare	03/39				
Cardiff C	Tr	12/45	46-47	41	-	17
Newport Co	Tr	10/47	47	26	-	8
Cardiff C	Tr	08/48	48	17	-	4
Reading	Tr	05/49	49	26	-	12
Coventry C	Tr	02/50	49-52	88	-	26

ALLEN Charlie
Born: Slough, Berkshire, England, 24 March, 1992 M

League Club	Source	Date Signed	Seasons Played	Apps	Subs	Gls
Notts Co	Billericay T	06/11	11	4	5	0
Gillingham	Tr	07/12	12-13	24	13	2

ALLEN Christopher Anthony (Chris)
Born: Oxford, England, 18 November, 1972 LW
England: U21-2

League Club	Source	Date Signed	Seasons Played	Apps	Subs	Gls
Oxford U	YT	05/91	91-95	110	40	12
Nottingham F	L	02/96	95	1	2	1
Nottingham F	Tr	07/96	96-97	17	8	0
Luton T	L	11/97	97	14	0	1
Cardiff C	L	10/98	98	3	1	0
Port Vale	Tr	03/99	98	2	3	1
Stockport Co	Tr	10/99	99	10	6	0

ALLEN Christopher Martin (Chris)
Born: Devizes, Wiltshire, England, 3 January, 1989 M

League Club	Source	Date Signed	Seasons Played	Apps	Subs	Gls
Swindon T	Sch	07/07	07-08	9	3	0

ALLEN Clive Darren
Born: Stepney, E London, England, 20 May, 1961 F
England: 5/FLge/U21-3/Youth/Schools

League Club	Source	Date Signed	Seasons Played	Apps	Subs	Gls
Queens Park Rgrs	App	09/78	78-79	43	6	32
Arsenal	Tr	06/80				
Crystal Palace	Tr	08/80	80	25	0	9
Queens Park Rgrs	Tr	06/81	81-83	83	4	40
Tottenham H	Tr	08/84	84-87	97	8	60
Manchester C	Bordeaux (FRA)	08/89	89-91	31	22	16
Chelsea	Tr	12/91	91	15	1	7
West Ham U	Tr	03/92	91-93	36	2	17
Millwall	Tr	03/94	93	11	1	0
Carlisle U	Tr	09/95	95	3	0	0

ALLEN Damien Samuel
Born: Cheadle, Greater Manchester, England, 1 August, 1986 M

League Club	Source	Date Signed	Seasons Played	Apps	Subs	Gls
Stockport Co	Sch	07/04	04-06	28	22	1
Morecambe	Tr	08/07	07	16	4	0
Bury	FC Halifax T	08/09				

ALLEN Dennis James
Born: Dagenham, E London, England, 2 March, 1939 IF
Died: Reading, England, 9 July, 1995

League Club	Source	Date Signed	Seasons Played	Apps	Subs	Gls
Charlton Ath	Jnr	08/56	57-60	5	-	1
Reading	Tr	06/61	61-69	331	4	84
Bournemouth	Tr	08/70	70	17	0	3

ALLEN Derrick
Born: Wombwell, South Yorkshire, England, 14 July, 1946 M

League Club	Source	Date Signed	Seasons Played	Apps	Subs	Gls
Rotherham U	Jnr	11/65	65	1	0	0

ALLEN Derrick Sydney
Born: Luton, England, 18 April, 1930 W
Died: Luton, England, 30 November, 1978

League Club	Source	Date Signed	Seasons Played	Apps	Subs	Gls
Luton T	Alton T	01/52	54	1	-	0
Watford	Tr	06/56	56	6	-	1

ALLEN Frank
Born: Shirebrook, Derbyshire, England, 28 June, 1927 WH
Died: Chesterfield, Derbyshire, England, 2 February, 2014

League Club	Source	Date Signed	Seasons Played	Apps	Subs	Gls
Chesterfield	Langwith Imperial	03/51	51-52	3	-	0
Mansfield T	Tr	07/53	53-54	6	-	0

ALLEN Geoffrey Barry (Geoff)
Born: Newcastle-upon-Tyne, England, 10 November, 1946 LW
England: Youth

League Club	Source	Date Signed	Seasons Played	Apps	Subs	Gls
Newcastle U	Jnr	02/64	63-68	22	0	1

ALLEN George Henry
Born: Birmingham, England, 23 January, 1932 LB

League Club	Source	Date Signed	Seasons Played	Apps	Subs	Gls
Birmingham C	Coventry C (Am)	11/52	53-61	135	-	0
Torquay U	Tr	01/62	61-64	134	-	0

ALLEN Graham
Born: Bolton, Greater Manchester, England, 8 April, 1977 CD
England: Youth

League Club	Source	Date Signed	Seasons Played	Apps	Subs	Gls
Everton	YT	12/94	96-97	2	4	0
Tranmere Rov	Tr	08/98	98-03	193	7	10
Rushden & D	Tr	06/04	04-05	30	1	2
Chester C	Tr	07/06	06	2	1	0

ALLEN Graham Frederick
Born: Walsall, West Midlands, England, 30 August, 1932 IF

League Club	Source	Date Signed	Seasons Played	Apps	Subs	Gls
Walsall (Am)		04/54	53	2	-	1

ALLEN Gregory Frank (Greg)
Born: West Ham, E London, England, 18 October, 1967 M

League Club	Source	Date Signed	Seasons Played	Apps	Subs	Gls
Arsenal	App	07/85				
Cambridge U	Dagenham	08/88	88	4	0	0

ALLEN Herbert Anthony (Anthony)
Born: Beeston, Nottinghamshire, England, 27 October, 1924 FB
Died: Nottingham, England, 13 February, 2014

League Club	Source	Date Signed	Seasons Played	Apps	Subs	Gls
Nottingham F	Beeston BC	01/46	47	1	-	0
Notts Co	Tr	08/49	51-53	30	-	0

ALLEN Ifeanyi Tafari Decosta (Iffy)
Born: Lambeth, S London, England, 15 March, 1994 W

League Club	Source	Date Signed	Seasons Played	Apps	Subs	Gls
Barnet	Sch	01/13	12	0	2	0

ALLEN Jamie Paul
Born: Rochdale, Greater Manchester, England, 29 January, 1995 M

League Club	Source	Date Signed	Seasons Played	Apps	Subs	Gls
Rochdale	Sch	07/13	13-14	55	5	6

ALLEN Jamie Paul
Born: Wigan, Greater Manchester, England, 25 May, 1995 W

League Club	Source	Date Signed	Seasons Played	Apps	Subs	Gls
Fleetwood T	Jnr	07/12	12-13	2	3	1

ALLEN John
Born: Coventry, England, 24 April, 1955 F

League Club	Source	Date Signed	Seasons Played	Apps	Subs	Gls
Leicester C	Hinckley Ath	08/78				
Port Vale	Tr	06/80	80	18	0	4

ALLEN John
Born: Deeside, Flintshire, Wales, 14 November, 1964 M

Wales: Youth/Schools

League Club	Source	Date Signed	Seasons Played	Apps	Subs	Gls
Chester C	App	11/81	81-83	67	12	5
Mansfield T	Tr	08/84	84	1	1	0

ALLEN John Craig (Ian)
Born: Johnstone, Renfrewshire, Scotland, 27 January, 1932 — W

League Club	Source	Date Signed	Seasons Played	Apps	Subs	Gls
Queens Park Rgrs	Beith Jnrs	09/52	53	1	-	0
Bournemouth	Tr	07/54	54-55	52	-	11

ALLEN Joseph Michael (Joe)
Born: Carmarthen, Wales, 14 March, 1990 — M
Wales: 21/U21-14/Youth

League Club	Source	Date Signed	Seasons Played	Apps	Subs	Gls
Swansea C	Sch	08/07	06-11	93	35	7
Liverpool	Tr	08/12	12-14	52	20	2

ALLEN Keith
Born: Newport, Isle of Wight, England, 9 November, 1943 — F

League Club	Source	Date Signed	Seasons Played	Apps	Subs	Gls
Portsmouth	Ryde	12/62				
Grimsby T	Tr	05/64	64	6	-	1
Stockport Co	Tr	06/65	65-66	49	0	15
Luton T	Tr	03/67	66-69	128	9	36
Plymouth Arg	Tr	07/70	70-72	74	5	10

ALLEN Kenneth Richard (Kenny)
Born: Thornaby, Cleveland, England, 12 January, 1948 — G

League Club	Source	Date Signed	Seasons Played	Apps	Subs	Gls
Hartlepool U (Am)	Tow Law T	08/68	68	7	0	0
Burnley	Tr	11/69				
Barnsley	Tr	08/70				
West Bromwich A	Hellenic (RSA)	12/72				
Bournemouth	Bath C	08/78	78-82	152	0	0
Peterborough U	Bury (NC)	12/83				
Torquay U	Tr	03/84	83-85	58	0	0
Swindon T	Tr	09/85	85-86	45	0	0
Torquay U	Tr	12/86	86-87	74	0	0

ALLEN Kevin
Born: Ryde, Isle of Wight, England, 22 March, 1961 — FB

League Club	Source	Date Signed	Seasons Played	Apps	Subs	Gls
Bournemouth	Jnr	08/79	79	1	0	0

ALLEN Leighton Gary
Born: Brighton, England, 22 November, 1973 — F

League Club	Source	Date Signed	Seasons Played	Apps	Subs	Gls
Wimbledon	YT	07/92				
Colchester U	Tr	08/94	94	0	2	0

ALLEN Leslie William (Les)
Born: Dagenham, E London, England, 4 September, 1937 — IF
England: FLge-1/U23-1

League Club	Source	Date Signed	Seasons Played	Apps	Subs	Gls
Chelsea	Briggs Sports	09/54	56-59	44	-	11
Tottenham H	Tr	12/59	59-64	119	-	47
Queens Park Rgrs	Tr	07/65	65-68	123	5	55

ALLEN Malcolm
Born: Deiniolen, Gwynedd, Wales, 21 March, 1967 — F
Wales: 14/B/Youth

League Club	Source	Date Signed	Seasons Played	Apps	Subs	Gls
Watford	App	03/85	85-87	27	12	5
Aston Villa	L	09/87	87	4	0	0
Norwich C	Tr	08/88	88-89	24	11	8
Millwall	Tr	03/90	89-92	64	17	24
Newcastle U	Tr	08/93	93-94	9	1	5

ALLEN Mark Stephen
Born: Newcastle-upon-Tyne, England, 18 December, 1963 — F

League Club	Source	Date Signed	Seasons Played	Apps	Subs	Gls
Burnley	App	12/81	81	0	2	1
Tranmere Rov	Tr	08/83	83	6	4	0

ALLEN Martin James
Born: Reading, England, 14 August, 1965 — M
England: U21-2/Youth

League Club	Source	Date Signed	Seasons Played	Apps	Subs	Gls
Queens Park Rgrs	App	05/83	84-89	128	8	16
West Ham U	Tr	08/89	89-95	163	27	25
Portsmouth	Tr	09/95	95-97	34	11	4
Southend U	L	09/97	97	5	0	0

ALLEN Michael (Mike)
Born: South Shields, Tyne and Wear, England, 30 March, 1949 — LB/M

League Club	Source	Date Signed	Seasons Played	Apps	Subs	Gls
Middlesbrough	App	05/66	67-71	32	2	0
Brentford	Tr	10/71	71-78	223	10	11

ALLEN Oliver Thomas (Ollie)
Born: Brentwood, Essex, England, 7 September, 1986 — F

League Club	Source	Date Signed	Seasons Played	Apps	Subs	Gls
Birmingham C	West Ham U (Sch)	11/05				
Barnet	Tr	01/07	06	7	7	4

ALLEN Paul Kevin
Born: Aveley, Essex, England, 28 August, 1962 — M
England: U21-3/Youth

League Club	Source	Date Signed	Seasons Played	Apps	Subs	Gls
West Ham U	App	08/79	79-84	149	3	6
Tottenham H	Tr	06/85	85-93	276	16	23
Southampton	Tr	09/93	93-94	40	3	1
Luton T	L	12/94	94	4	0	0
Stoke C	L	01/95	94	17	0	1
Swindon T	Tr	10/95	95-96	30	7	1
Bristol C	Tr	01/97	96	13	1	0
Millwall	Tr	08/97	97	21	7	0

ALLEN Paul Michael
Born: Leeds, England, 30 July, 1967 — G

League Club	Source	Date Signed	Seasons Played	Apps	Subs	Gls
Doncaster Rov	Bradford C (YT)	10/84	84-85	4	0	0

ALLEN Paul Robert
Born: Bury, Greater Manchester, England, 13 March, 1968 — M

League Club	Source	Date Signed	Seasons Played	Apps	Subs	Gls
Bolton W	App	07/86	86	0	1	0

ALLEN Peter Charles
Born: Hove, East Sussex, England, 1 November, 1946 — M

League Club	Source	Date Signed	Seasons Played	Apps	Subs	Gls
Leyton Orient	Tottenham H (Am)	07/65	65-77	424	8	27
Millwall	Tr	03/78	77-78	16	2	0

ALLEN Peter Michael
Born: Bristol, England, 8 October, 1934 — CD

League Club	Source	Date Signed	Seasons Played	Apps	Subs	Gls
Bristol C		07/53	54	1	-	0

ALLEN River Brian Zach
Born: Plymouth, England, 7 October, 1995 — M

League Club	Source	Date Signed	Seasons Played	Apps	Subs	Gls
Plymouth Arg	Sch	05/14	14	0	3	0

ALLEN Robert (Bob)
Born: Belfast, Northern Ireland, 16 January, 1939 — WH

League Club	Source	Date Signed	Seasons Played	Apps	Subs	Gls
Wolverhampton W	Denbigh T	09/57				
Coventry C	Tr	06/59	60-61	25	-	2

ALLEN Robert Howard Allen
Born: Shepton Mallet, Somerset, England, 5 December, 1916 — FB
Died: Shepton Mallet, Somerset, England, 16 February, 2001

League Club	Source	Date Signed	Seasons Played	Apps	Subs	Gls
Notts Co	Aero Engines	02/45	46	1	-	0
Bristol C	Tr	11/46	46	1	-	0

ALLEN Ronald (Ronnie)
Born: Fenton, Potteries, England, 15 January, 1929 — CF
Died: Great Wyrley, West Midlands, England, 11 June, 2001
England: 5/B-2/FLge-1

League Club	Source	Date Signed	Seasons Played	Apps	Subs	Gls
Port Vale	Jnr	04/46	46-49	123	-	34
West Bromwich A	Tr	03/50	49-60	415	-	208
Crystal Palace	Tr	05/61	61-64	100	-	34

ALLEN Ronald Leslie (Ron)
Born: Birmingham, England, 22 April, 1935 — RB
Died: Leicester, England, August, 2006

League Club	Source	Date Signed	Seasons Played	Apps	Subs	Gls
Birmingham C	Ladywood Jnrs	05/53				
Lincoln C	Tr	07/58	58-60	60	-	1

ALLEN Rory William
Born: Beckenham, SE London, England, 17 October, 1977 — F
England: U21-3

League Club	Source	Date Signed	Seasons Played	Apps	Subs	Gls
Tottenham H	YT	03/96	96-98	10	11	2
Luton T	L	03/98	97	8	0	6
Portsmouth	Tr	07/99	99	10	5	3

ALLEN Russell Philip
Born: Smethwick, West Midlands, England, 9 January, 1954 — F

League Club	Source	Date Signed	Seasons Played	Apps	Subs	Gls
West Bromwich A	Arsenal (App)	05/71				
Tranmere Rov	Tr	07/73	73-77	137	19	42
Mansfield T	Tr	07/78	78-80	99	17	18

ALLEN William (Bill)
Born: Newburn, Tyne and Wear, England, 22 October, 1917 — WH
Died: Westerhope, Tyne and Wear, England, 21 May, 1981

League Club	Source	Date Signed	Seasons Played	Apps	Subs	Gls
Chesterfield	Throckley Welfare	11/37	38	2	-	0
York C	Tr	05/39	46-49	130	-	23
Scunthorpe U	Tr	06/50	50-51	64	-	1

ALLEYNE Andrew McArthur (Andy)
Born: Springtown, Barbados, 19 May, 1951 — FB
Died: Reading, England, June, 2012

League Club	Source	Date Signed	Seasons Played	Apps	Subs	Gls
Reading	Newbury T	11/72	72-75	46	2	2

ALLEYNE Robert Anthony
Born: Dudley, West Midlands, England, 27 September, 1968 — F

League Club	Source	Date Signed	Seasons Played	Apps	Subs	Gls
Leicester C	Jnr	01/87	86	1	2	0
Wrexham	L	10/87	87	7	3	2
Chesterfield	Tr	03/88	87-88	32	8	5

ALLI Bamidele Jermaine (Dele)
Born: Milton Keynes, England, 11 April, 1996 — M
England: Youth

League Club	Source	Date Signed	Seasons Played	Apps	Subs	Gls
MK Dons	Sch	05/13	12-14	52	10	18
Tottenham H	Tr	01/15				
MK Dons	L	02/15	14	12	0	4

ALLINSON Ian James Robert
Born: Hitchin, Hertfordshire, England, 1 October, 1957 — LW

League Club	Source	Date Signed	Seasons Played	Apps	Subs	Gls
Colchester U	App	10/75	74-82	291	17	69
Arsenal	Tr	08/83	83-86	60	23	16
Stoke C	Tr	06/87	87	6	3	0
Luton T	Tr	10/87	87-88	24	8	3
Colchester U	Tr	12/88	88-89	36	2	10
ALLINSON Jamie						
Born: Stockton-on-Tees, Cleveland, England, 15 June, 1978						CD
Hartlepool U	YT	07/96	95	3	1	0
ALLISON John (Jack)						
Born: Stannington, Northumberland, England, 31 July, 1922						LW
Died: Northumberland, England, 22 January, 1985						
Chesterfield	West Sleekburn	04/47				
Reading	Blyth Spartans	01/49	48-49	29	-	4
Walsall	Tr	06/50	50-51	47	-	1
ALLISON John Alfred						
Born: Cramlington, Northumberland, England, 9 August, 1932						CH
Died: Gateshead, Tyne and Wear, England, 15 October, 2007						
Chesterfield	Blyth Spartans	05/55	57-60	32	-	0
ALLISON John Joseph						
Born: Consett, County Durham, England, 17 November, 1913						WH
Died: Rochdale, Greater Manchester, England, 23 August, 1971						
Barnsley	Workington	05/39				
Hartlepool U	Tr	09/46	46	13	-	0
ALLISON Kenneth (Kenny)						
Born: Edinburgh, Scotland, 6 January, 1937						IF
Darlington	Cowdenbeath	07/63	63-65	74	0	40
Lincoln C	Tr	02/66	65-66	41	1	13
ALLISON Malcolm Alexander						
Born: Dartford, Kent, England, 5 September, 1927						CH
Died: Trafford, Greater Manchester, England, 15 October, 2010						
Charlton Ath	Erith & Belvedere	02/45	49	2	-	0
West Ham U	Tr	02/51	50-57	238	-	10
ALLISON Michael (Mike)						
Born: Bolton, Greater Manchester, England, 17 March, 1966						G
Chesterfield	Horwich RMI	07/89	90	16	0	0
ALLISON Neil James						
Born: Hull, England, 20 October, 1973						CD
Hull C	YT	07/92	90-96	95	11	3
Chesterfield	North Ferriby U	03/97	96	0	2	0
ALLISON Thomas (Tom)						
Born: Fencehouses, County Durham, England, 20 February, 1921						IF
Died: Hartlepool, Cleveland, England, 1 November, 2010						
Darlington	South Hetton	09/46	46	6	-	0
ALLISON Wayne Anthony						
Born: Huddersfield, West Yorkshire, England, 16 October, 1968						F
Halifax T	YT	07/87	86-88	74	10	23
Watford	Tr	07/89	89	6	1	0
Bristol C	Tr	08/90	90-94	149	46	48
Swindon T	Tr	07/95	95-97	98	3	31
Huddersfield T	Tr	11/97	97-99	71	3	15
Tranmere Rov	Tr	09/99	99-01	85	18	26
Sheffield U	Tr	07/02	02-03	29	44	7
Chesterfield	Tr	07/04	04-07	66	49	21
ALLISTER John Grandison (Jack)						
Born: Edinburgh, Scotland, 30 June, 1927						CF
Died: Edinburgh, Scotland, 11 February, 1999						
Chelsea	Tranent Jnrs	07/49	51-52	4	-	1
Chesterfield	Aberdeen	06/58				
ALLMAN George						
Born: Stockport, Greater Manchester, England, 23 July, 1930						CF
Stockport Co		05/50	50-51	7	-	1
Chester C	Holywell T	07/55	55-56	49	-	13
ALLON Joseph Ball (Joe)						
Born: Gateshead, Tyne and Wear, England, 12 November, 1966						F
England: Youth						
Newcastle U	App	11/84	84-86	9	0	2
Swansea C	Tr	08/87	87-88	27	7	12
Hartlepool U	Tr	11/88	88-90	112	0	48
Chelsea	Tr	08/91	91-92	3	11	2
Port Vale	L	02/92	91	2	4	0
Brentford	Tr	11/92	92-93	38	7	19
Southend U	L	09/93	93	2	1	0
Port Vale	Tr	03/94	93-94	13	10	9
Lincoln C	Tr	07/95	95	3	1	0
Hartlepool U	Tr	10/95	95-97	52	4	19

League Club	Source	Date Signed	Seasons Played	Apps	Subs	Gls
ALLOTT Mark Stephen						
Born: Middleton, Greater Manchester, England, 3 October, 1977						M
Oldham Ath	YT	10/95	96-01	105	49	31
Chesterfield	Tr	12/01	01-06	205	16	11
Oldham Ath	Tr	07/07	07-08	78	9	7
Chesterfield	Tr	07/09	09-12	118	7	3
ALLOU Anoh Bernard (Bernard)						
Born: Cocody, Ivory Coast, 19 June, 1975						M
France: U21-24						
Nottingham F	Grampus 8 (JPN)	03/99	98-99	1	5	1
ALLPRESS Timothy John (Tim)						
Born: Hitchin, Hertfordshire, England, 27 January, 1971						D
Luton T	YT	07/89	89	1	0	0
Preston NE	L	10/91	91	7	2	0
Colchester U	Bayer Uerdingen (GER)	08/93	93-94	24	10	0
ALLSOP Norman						
Born: West Bromwich, West Midlands, England, 1 November, 1930						IF
Died: Sandwell, West Midlands, England, 16 March, 2011						
West Bromwich A	Hednesford T	05/48				
Walsall	Worcester C	10/53	53	9	-	0
ALLSOP Ryan						
Born: Birmingham, England, 17 June, 1992						G
Millwall	West Bromwich A (Sch)	05/11				
Leyton Orient	Tr	08/12	12	20	0	0
Bournemouth	Tr	01/13	12-13	21	1	0
Coventry C	L	07/14	14	24	0	0
ALLSOP William Henry (Bill)						
Born: Ripley, Derbyshire, England, 29 January, 1912						FB
Died: Halifax, West Yorkshire, England, 2 April, 1997						
Port Vale	Bolton W (Am)	08/31	31-32	6	-	0
Halifax T	Tr	05/34	34-46	239	-	1
ALLSOPP Daniel (Danny)						
Born: Melbourne, Australia, 10 August, 1978						F
Australia: 3/U23-7/Youth						
Manchester C	Carlton (AUS)	08/98	98-00	3	26	4
Notts Co	L	11/99	99	3	0	1
Wrexham	L	02/00	99	3	0	4
Bristol Rov	L	10/00	00	4	2	0
Notts Co	Tr	11/00	00-02	97	8	42
Hull C	Tr	05/03	03-04	45	19	22
ALLUM Albert Edward (Bert)						
Born: Notting Hill, Central London, England, 15 October, 1930						W
Brentford	Hereford U	10/52				
Queens Park Rgrs	Dover	06/57	57	1	-	0
ALMEIDA Marco Antonio						
Born: Lisbon, Portugal, 4 April, 1977						CD
Portugal: U21-1						
Southampton (L)	Sporting Lisbon (POR)	07/99	99	0	1	0
ALMEIDA Mauro Alexandro						
Born: Viseu, Portugal, 29 January, 1982						CD
Accrington Stan	Vihren Sandanski (BUL)	01/07	06	5	0	0
Swindon T	Tr	08/07				
ALMOND Louis James						
Born: Blackburn, Greater Manchester, England, 5 January, 1992						F
Blackpool	Sch	02/10	13	0	1	0
Cheltenham T	L	03/10	09	2	2	0
ALMUNIA Manuel						
Born: Pamplona, Spain, 19 May, 1977						G
Arsenal	Celta Vigo (SPN)	07/04	04-10	109	0	0
West Ham U	L	09/11	11	4	0	0
Watford	Tr	07/12	12-13	76	0	0
ALNWICK Benjamin Robert (Ben)						
Born: Prudhoe, Northumberland, England, 1 January, 1987						G
England: U21-1/Youth						
Sunderland	Sch	03/04	04-06	19	0	0
Tottenham H	Tr	01/07	09	1	0	0
Luton T	L	09/07	07	4	0	0
Leicester C	L	01/08	07	8	0	0
Carlisle U	L	10/08	08	6	0	0
Norwich C	L	07/09	09	3	0	0
Leyton Orient	L	09/11	11	6	0	0
Barnsley	Tr	07/12	12	10	0	0
Charlton Ath	Tr	09/13	13	10	0	0
Leyton Orient	Tr	01/14	13	1	0	0
Peterborough U	Tr	07/14	14	41	0	0
ALNWICK Jak						
Born: Prudhoe, Northumberland, England, 17 June, 1993						G

League Club	Source	Date Signed	Seasons Played	Apps	Subs	Gls
England: Youth						
Newcastle U	Sch	07/10	14	5	1	0
Bradford C	L	03/15	14	1	0	0
ALOISI John						
Born: Adelaide, Australia, 5 February, 1976						F
Australia: 55/U23-7/Youth						
Portsmouth	Cremonese (ITA)	08/97	97-98	55	5	25
Coventry C	Tr	12/98	98-00	18	24	10
ALONSO Marcos						
Born: Madrid, Spain, 28 December, 1990						LB
Spain: Youth						
Bolton W	Real Madrid (SPN)	08/10	10-12	33	2	5
Sunderland (L)	Fiorentina (ITA)	01/14	13	16	0	0
ALONSO Mikel						
Born: Tolosa, Spain, 16 May, 1980						M
Bolton W (L)	Real Sociedad (SPN)	07/07	07	4	3	0
Charlton Ath	CD Tenerife (SPN)	06/11				
ALONSO Xabi						
Born: Tolosa, Spain, 25 November, 1981						M
Spain: 114/U21-9/Youth						
Liverpool	Real Sociedad (SPN)	08/04	04-08	121	22	15
[ALPAY] OZALAN Fehmi						
Born: Izmir, Turkey, 29 May, 1973						CD
Turkey: 84						
Aston Villa	Fenerbahce (TKY)	07/00	00-03	56	2	1
ALSAKER Paul Christian						
Born: Stord, Norway, 6 November, 1973						M
Stockport Co	Flora Tallin (EST)	08/98	98	1	0	0
ALSFORD Julian						
Born: Poole, Dorset, England, 24 December, 1972						CD
Watford	YT	04/91	92-93	9	4	1
Chester C	Tr	08/94	94-97	136	5	6
Barnet (L)	Dundee U	09/98	98	9	0	1
Chester C	Dundee U	02/99	98	9	1	1
ALSOP Gilbert Arthur						
Born: Frampton Cotterell, Avon, England, 10 September, 1908						CF
Died: Walsall, West Midlands, England, 16 April, 1992						
Coventry C	Bath C	12/29	29-30	16	-	4
Walsall	Tr	10/31	31-35	160	-	126
West Bromwich A	Tr	11/35	35	1	-	0
Ipswich T	Tr	06/37	38	9	-	2
Walsall	Tr	11/38	38-46	35	-	25
ALSOP Julian Mark						
Born: Nuneaton, Warwickshire, England, 28 May, 1973						F
Bristol Rov	Halesowen T	02/97	96-97	20	13	4
Swansea C	L	01/98	97	5	0	2
Swansea C	Tr	03/98	97-99	73	12	14
Cheltenham T	Tr	07/00	00-02	99	18	35
Oxford U	Tr	07/03	03-04	29	5	5
Northampton T	Tr	10/04	04	1	6	1
Cheltenham T	Bishops Cleeve	08/09	09	21	20	4
ALSTON Adrian						
Born: Preston, Lancashire, England, 6 February, 1949						F
Australia:						
Luton T	South Coast U (AUS)	08/74	74-75	26	3	8
Cardiff C	Tr	10/75	75-76	44	4	16
ALSTON Alexander George (Alec)						
Born: Preston, Lancashire, England, 26 February, 1937						F
Died: Blackpool, Lancashire, England, 20 January, 2009						
Preston NE	Netherfield	05/55	57-62	102	-	26
Bury	Tr	03/63	62-65	85	0	22
Barrow	Tr	09/65	65-66	46	1	13
ALTIDORE Josmer Volmy (Jozy)						
Born: New Jersey, USA, 6 November, 1989						F
USA: 80						
Hull C (L)	Villarreal (SPN)	08/09	09	16	12	1
Sunderland	AZ Alkmaar (NED)	07/13	13-14	21	21	1
ALTY Colin						
Born: Southport, Merseyside, England, 23 October, 1944						D/F
Preston NE	Jnr	10/61				
Southport	Tr	06/64	64-69	184	6	22
ALUKO Omatsone Folarin (Sone)						
Born: Birmingham, England, 19 February, 1989						LW
England: Youth//Nigeria: 7/Youth						
Birmingham C	Sch	08/06				
Blackpool	L	08/08	08	0	1	0
Hull C	Glasgow Rangers	08/12	12-14	45	20	10

League Club	Source	Date Signed	Seasons Played	Apps	Subs	Gls
ALVAREZ Luciano Jose						
Born: Buenos Aires, Argentina, 30 November, 1978						F
Yeovil T	Inter Turku (FIN)	08/05	05	4	0	1
ALVAREZ Ricardo Gabriel						
Born: Buenos Aires, Argentina, 12 April, 1988						W
Argentina: 8						
Sunderland (L)	Inter Milan (ITA)	09/14	14	5	8	0
ALVES Afonso						
Born: Belo Horizonte, Brazil, 30 January, 1981						F
Brazil: 8						
Middlesbrough	Heerenveen (NED)	01/08	07-08	31	11	10
ALVES Paulo Laurenco						
Born: Vila Real, Portugal, 10 December, 1969						F
Portugal: 14/U21-9/Youth						
West Ham U (L)	Sporting Lisbon (POR)	11/97	97	0	4	0
AMALFITANO Morgan						
Born: Nice, France, 20 March, 1985						RW
France: 1						
West Bromwich A (L)	Olymp Marseille (FRA)	09/13	13	26	2	4
West Ham U	Olymp Marseille (FRA)	09/14	14	14	10	3
AMANKWAAH Kevin Osei-Kuffour						
Born: Harrow, NW London, England, 19 May, 1982						RB
England: Youth						
Bristol C	YT	06/00	99-04	35	19	1
Torquay U	L	01/03	02	6	0	0
Cheltenham T	L	08/03	03	11	1	0
Yeovil T	Tr	02/05	04-05	48	5	1
Swansea C	Tr	08/06	06	23	6	0
Swindon T	Tr	07/08	08-10	76	10	5
Burton A	Tr	09/11	11	8	0	0
Rochdale	Tr	01/12	11	15	1	0
Exeter C	Tr	07/12	12	27	7	0
Northampton T	Tr	08/13	13	21	0	0
AMAT Jordi						
Born: Canet de Mar, Spain, 21 March, 1992						CD
Spain: U21-15/Youth						
Swansea C	RCD Espanyol (SPN)	06/13	13-14	20	7	0
AMBLER Roy						
Born: Wakefield, England, 2 December, 1937						CF
Died: Leeds, England, 5 May, 2007						
Leeds U	Outwood Stormcocks	12/54				
Shrewsbury T	Tr	01/59	58-60	29	-	8
Wrexham	Tr	05/61	61-62	21	-	13
York C	Tr	11/62	62	12	-	3
Southport	Tr	07/63	63	11	-	0
AMBROSE Anthony Leroy (Leroy)						
Born: Kingstown, St Vincent & The Grenadines, 22 June, 1960						W
Charlton Ath	Croydon	08/79	79-81	28	5	1
AMBROSE Darren Paul Francis						
Born: Harlow, Essex, England, 29 February, 1984						W
England: U21-10/Youth						
Ipswich T	YT	07/01	01-02	20	10	8
Newcastle U	Tr	03/03	02-04	18	19	5
Charlton Ath	Tr	07/05	05-08	78	34	13
Ipswich T	L	11/08	08	6	3	0
Crystal Palace	Tr	07/09	09-11	97	13	29
Birmingham C	Tr	07/12	12-13	4	3	0
Ipswich T	Tr	09/14	14	1	5	0
AMBROSETTI Gabriele						
Born: Varese, Italy, 7 August, 1973						M
Chelsea	Vicenza (ITA)	08/99	99	9	7	0
AMBROSIO Marco						
Born: Brescia, Italy, 30 May, 1973						G
Chelsea	Chievo (ITA)	07/03	03	8	0	0
AMEOBI Foluwashola (Shola)						
Born: Zaria, Nigeria, 12 October, 1981						F
England: U21-21//Nigeria: 10						
Newcastle U	YT	10/98	00-13	167	145	53
Stoke C	L	03/08	07	3	3	0
Crystal Palace	Gaziantep (TKY)	01/15	14	0	4	0
AMEOBI Oluwatomiwo (Tomi)						
Born: Newcastle-upon-Tyne, England, 16 August, 1988						F
Leeds U	Sch	08/07				
Scunthorpe U	L	10/07	07	0	9	0
Doncaster Rov	Tr	08/08	08	0	1	0
Grimsby T	L	09/08	08	2	0	0

AMEOBI Samuel Oluwaseyi (Sammy)
Born: Newcastle-upon-Tyne, England, 1 May, 1992 — LW
England: U21-5//Nigeria: Youth

League Club	Source	Date Signed	Seasons Played	Apps	Subs	Gls
Newcastle U	Sch	07/10	10-14	21	33	2
Middlesbrough	L	02/13	12	7	2	1

AMES Kenneth George (Ken)
Born: Poole, Dorset, England, 17 September, 1933 — CF
Died: Poole, Dorset, England, 12 May, 2010
England: Schools

League Club	Source	Date Signed	Seasons Played	Apps	Subs	Gls
Portsmouth	Jnr	09/50	53	2	-	0

AMES Percy Talbot
Born: Bedford, England, 13 December, 1931 — G
Died: Bedford, England, 4 December, 1998

League Club	Source	Date Signed	Seasons Played	Apps	Subs	Gls
Tottenham H	Bedford Ave	05/51				
Colchester U	Tr	05/55	55-64	397	-	0

AMES Trevor
Born: Poole, Dorset, England, 14 December, 1962 — F

League Club	Source	Date Signed	Seasons Played	Apps	Subs	Gls
Hereford U	Aston Villa (App)	10/80	80-81	5	3	0
Crystal Palace	Tr	10/81				

AMMANN Michael Anton (Mike)
Born: Orange, California, USA, 8 February, 1971 — G

League Club	Source	Date Signed	Seasons Played	Apps	Subs	Gls
Charlton Ath	E Los Angeles (USA)	07/94	94-95	28	2	0

AMOKACHI Daniel Owofen
Born: Kaduna, Nigeria, 30 December, 1972 — F
Nigeria: 44

League Club	Source	Date Signed	Seasons Played	Apps	Subs	Gls
Everton	Club Brugge (BEL)	08/94	94-95	34	9	10

AMOND Padraig
Born: Carlow, Republic of Ireland, 15 April, 1988 — F
Republic of Ireland: U21-4

League Club	Source	Date Signed	Seasons Played	Apps	Subs	Gls
Accrington Stan	Pacos Ferreira (POR)	08/11	11-12	61	17	16
Morecambe	Tr	08/13	13-14	50	32	19

AMOO David Oluwaseun Segun
Born: Southwark, S London, England, 13 April, 1991 — W

League Club	Source	Date Signed	Seasons Played	Apps	Subs	Gls
Liverpool	Sch	07/08				
MK Dons	L	01/11	10	0	3	0
Hull C	L	02/11	10	1	6	1
Bury	L	09/11	11	19	8	4
Preston NE	Tr	07/12	12	6	11	0
Tranmere Rov	Tr	01/13	12	6	5	1
Carlisle U	Tr	07/13	13-14	51	19	13

AMOO Ryan Lee
Born: Leicester, England, 11 October, 1983 — M

League Club	Source	Date Signed	Seasons Played	Apps	Subs	Gls
Aston Villa	YT	07/01				
Northampton T	Tr	03/04	03-04	2	4	0
Lincoln C	Barrow T, Leicester	07/06	06-07	45	11	3

AMOR William George (Bill)
Born: Pewsey, Wiltshire, England, 6 November, 1919 — RW
Died: Reading, England, 1 May, 1988
England: Amateur-1

League Club	Source	Date Signed	Seasons Played	Apps	Subs	Gls
Reading (Am)	Huntley & Palmers	12/47	47-51	66	-	12

AMOREBIETA Fernando Gabriel
Born: Cantaura, Venezuela, 29 March, 1985 — CD
Spain: Youth//Venezuela: 14

League Club	Source	Date Signed	Seasons Played	Apps	Subs	Gls
Fulham	Atletico Bilbao (SPN)	05/13	13-14	27	3	2
Middlesbrough	L	03/15	14	2	2	0

AMORUSO Lorenzo
Born: Bari, Italy, 28 June, 1971 — CD

League Club	Source	Date Signed	Seasons Played	Apps	Subs	Gls
Blackburn Rov	Glasgow Rangers	07/03	03-04	16	2	3

AMOS Benjamin Paul (Ben)
Born: Macclesfield, Cheshire, England, 10 April, 1990 — G
England: U21-3/Youth

League Club	Source	Date Signed	Seasons Played	Apps	Subs	Gls
Manchester U	Sch	01/08	11	1	0	0
Peterborough U	L	10/09	09	1	0	0
Oldham Ath	L	01/11	10	16	0	0
Hull C	L	07/12	12	17	0	0
Carlisle U	L	11/13	13	9	0	0
Bolton W	L	01/15	14	8	1	0

AMOS Keith James
Born: Walton-on-Thames, Surrey, England, 13 January, 1932 — G

League Club	Source	Date Signed	Seasons Played	Apps	Subs	Gls
Arsenal	Jnr	05/52				
Aldershot	Tr	08/54	55-57	77	-	0
Fulham	Tr	08/58				

AMPADU Patrick Kwame (Kwame)
Born: Bradford, England, 20 December, 1970 — M/D
Republic of Ireland: U21-4/Youth

League Club	Source	Date Signed	Seasons Played	Apps	Subs	Gls
Arsenal	YT	11/88	89	0	2	0
Plymouth Arg	L	10/90	90	6	0	1
West Bromwich A	Tr	06/91	90-93	27	22	4
Swansea C	Tr	02/94	93-97	128	19	12
Leyton Orient	Tr	07/98	98-99	69	3	1
Exeter C	Tr	07/00	00-02	80	15	0

AMPHLETT Raymond Henry (Ray)
Born: Manchester, England, 25 September, 1922 — LB
Died: Oxfordshire, England, February, 2004

League Club	Source	Date Signed	Seasons Played	Apps	Subs	Gls
Cardiff C	Guildford C	04/48				
Newport Co	Tr	04/49	49	13	-	0
Stockport Co	Tr	08/50				

AMPOFO Christopher John Kwasi (Chris)
Born: Paddington, Central London, England, 6 October, 1963 — CD

League Club	Source	Date Signed	Seasons Played	Apps	Subs	Gls
West Ham U	App	10/81				
Aldershot	Tr	08/83	83	4	0	0

AMSALEM David
Born: Lod, Israel, 4 September, 1971 — CD
Israel: 31/U21-11

League Club	Source	Date Signed	Seasons Played	Apps	Subs	Gls
Crystal Palace	Beitar Jerusalem (ISR)	08/98	98	6	4	0

ANDERS Henry (Harry)
Born: St Helens, Merseyside, England, 28 November, 1926 — RW
Died: Blackpool, Lancashire, England, October, 1994

League Club	Source	Date Signed	Seasons Played	Apps	Subs	Gls
Preston NE	St Helens	08/45	47-52	69	-	4
Manchester C	Tr	03/53	52-54	32	-	4
Port Vale	Tr	07/56	56	3	-	0
Accrington Stan	Tr	06/57	57-59	114	-	18
Workington	Tr	07/60	60	7	-	1

ANDERS James (Jimmy)
Born: St Helens, Merseyside, England, 8 March, 1928 — LW
Died: Blackburn, Greater Manchester, England, September, 2002

League Club	Source	Date Signed	Seasons Played	Apps	Subs	Gls
Preston NE	St Helens	08/45				
Brentford	Tr	09/48	49-50	12	-	0
Bradford C	Tr	06/51	51-52	51	-	11
Rochdale	Tr	07/53	53-56	123	-	28
Bradford Park Ave	Tr	09/56	56	20	-	4
Accrington Stan	Tr	01/57	56-59	129	-	29
Bradford Park Ave	Buxton	09/60	60-61	39	-	8
Tranmere Rov	Tr	11/61	61	8	-	1

ANDERS Jason Stuart
Born: Rochdale, Greater Manchester, England, 13 March, 1974 — F

League Club	Source	Date Signed	Seasons Played	Apps	Subs	Gls
Rochdale	YT	07/90	90-92	2	15	1

ANDERSEN Braastrup (Bo)
Born: Slagelse, Denmark, 26 March, 1976 — G

League Club	Source	Date Signed	Seasons Played	Apps	Subs	Gls
Bristol C	Lyngby (DEN)	12/98	98	10	0	0

ANDERSEN Leif Erik
Born: Fredrikstad, Norway, 19 April, 1971 — CD

League Club	Source	Date Signed	Seasons Played	Apps	Subs	Gls
Crystal Palace	Moss FK (NOR)	01/96	95-96	19	11	1

ANDERSEN Mikkel
Born: Copenhagen, Denmark, 17 December, 1988 — G
Denmark: U21-3/Youth

League Club	Source	Date Signed	Seasons Played	Apps	Subs	Gls
Reading	AB Copenhagen (DEN)	01/07	14	3	0	0
Brentford	L	12/08	08	1	0	0
Brighton & HA	L	03/09	08	5	0	0
Bristol Rov	L	09/09	09	39	0	0
Bristol Rov	L	08/10	10	19	0	0
Portsmouth	L	08/12	12	18	0	0

ANDERSEN Nicholas John (Nicky)
Born: Lincoln, England, 29 March, 1969 — FB

League Club	Source	Date Signed	Seasons Played	Apps	Subs	Gls
Mansfield T	YT	01/87	86-88	9	11	0
Lincoln C	Tr	08/89	89	1	0	0

ANDERSEN Soren
Born: Aarhus, Denmark, 31 January, 1970 — F
Denmark: 12/U21-7/Youth

League Club	Source	Date Signed	Seasons Played	Apps	Subs	Gls
Bristol C	Aalborg BK (DEN)	07/98	98	26	13	10

ANDERSEN Stephan Maigaard
Born: Copenhagen, Denmark, 26 November, 1981 — G
Denmark: 28/U21-21/Youth

League Club	Source	Date Signed	Seasons Played	Apps	Subs	Gls
Charlton Ath	AB Copenhagen (DEN)	05/04	04-05	17	0	0

ANDERSEN Trond
Born: Kristiansand, Norway, 6 January, 1975 — DM
Norway: 38/B-1/U21-30/Youth

League Club	Source	Date Signed	Seasons Played	Apps	Subs	Gls
Wimbledon	Molde FK (NOR)	08/99	99-02	136	10	6

ANDERSEN Vetle Gregle
Born: Kristiansand, Norway, 20 April, 1964 — CD

League Club	Source	Date Signed	Seasons Played	Apps	Subs	Gls
West Bromwich A	Lyngby (DEN)	12/89	89	0	1	0

[ANDERSON] ABREAU OLIVEIRA Anderson Luis
Born: Porto Alegre, Brazil, 13 April, 1988 — M
Brazil: 8/U23-5/Youth

League Club	Source	Date Signed	Seasons Played	Apps	Subs	Gls
Manchester U	FC Porto (POR)	07/07	07-14	70	35	5

[ANDERSON] SILVA Anderson
Born: Sao Paulo, Brazil, 28 August, 1982 — M

League Club	Source	Date Signed	Seasons Played	Apps	Subs	Gls
Everton	RC Santander (SPN)	08/05	06	0	1	0
Barnsley	Tr	08/07	07-09	78	6	5

ANDERSON Alexander (Alex)
Born: Glasgow, Scotland, 8 January, 1922 — G
Died: Southport, Merseyside, England, 10 October, 1984
Republic of Ireland: LoI-1

League Club	Source	Date Signed	Seasons Played	Apps	Subs	Gls
Rochdale	Heart of Midlothian	02/48	47	4	-	0
Southport	Dundalk (ROI)	11/49	49-50	21	-	0

ANDERSON Alexander Ferguson (Alex)
Born: Monifieth, Angus, Scotland, 15 November, 1921 — RB
Died: Monifieth, Angus, Scotland, 18 January, 1999

League Club	Source	Date Signed	Seasons Played	Apps	Subs	Gls
Southampton	Forfar Ath	11/49	49-51	20	-	0
Exeter C	Tr	06/52	52	6	-	0

ANDERSON Alexander Ogilvie Walker (Sandy)
Born: Auchtermuchty, Fife, Scotland, 20 February, 1930 — LB

League Club	Source	Date Signed	Seasons Played	Apps	Subs	Gls
Southend U	Newburgh Jnrs	04/50	50-62	452	-	8

ANDERSON Arthur Alan Duncan (Alan)
Born: Edinburgh, Scotland, 21 December, 1939 — LH

League Club	Source	Date Signed	Seasons Played	Apps	Subs	Gls
Millwall	Falkirk	09/59	60-61	74	-	0
Scunthorpe U	Tr	07/62	62	6	-	0

ANDERSON Benjamin Cummings (Ben)
Born: Aberdeen, Scotland, 18 February, 1946 — CD

League Club	Source	Date Signed	Seasons Played	Apps	Subs	Gls
Blackburn Rov	Peterlee Jnrs	03/64	64-67	21	7	7
Bury	Tr	07/68	68-69	52	2	6
Crystal Palace	Cape Town C (RSA)	11/73	73	11	0	1

ANDERSON Blair Thomas
Born: Reading, England, 1 July, 1992 — W

League Club	Source	Date Signed	Seasons Played	Apps	Subs	Gls
Crawley T	Basford U	01/15	14	0	1	0

ANDERSON Christopher (Chris)
Born: Aberdeen, Scotland, 30 August, 1925 — RH
Died: Peterculter, Aberdeenshire, Scotland, 27 May, 1986

League Club	Source	Date Signed	Seasons Played	Apps	Subs	Gls
Hartlepool U	Aberdeen	09/46	46	2	-	0

ANDERSON Christopher Shelley Inglis (Chris)
Born: East Wemyss, Fife, Scotland, 28 November, 1928 — RW
Died: Derby, England, 20 July, 1996

League Club	Source	Date Signed	Seasons Played	Apps	Subs	Gls
Blackburn Rov	Lochore Welfare	08/50	50-51	13	-	1
Stockport Co	Nelson	06/53	53	34	-	0
Southport	Tr	07/54	54	28	-	0

ANDERSON Colin Russell
Born: Newcastle-upon-Tyne, England, 26 April, 1962 — M/RB

League Club	Source	Date Signed	Seasons Played	Apps	Subs	Gls
Burnley	App	04/80	80-81	3	3	0
Torquay U	North Shields	09/82	82-84	107	2	10
West Bromwich A	Tr	03/85	85-90	131	9	10
Walsall	Tr	08/91	91	25	1	2
Hereford U	Tr	08/92	92-93	67	3	1
Exeter C	Tr	07/94	94-95	26	8	1

ANDERSON Dale
Born: Newton Aycliffe, County Durham, England, 23 August, 1970 — F

League Club	Source	Date Signed	Seasons Played	Apps	Subs	Gls
Darlington	YT	09/88	86-88	4	11	0
Middlesbrough	Tr	06/90				

ANDERSON Darren Irwin
Born: Merton, SW London, England, 6 September, 1966 — CD
England: Youth

League Club	Source	Date Signed	Seasons Played	Apps	Subs	Gls
Charlton Ath	Coventry C (App)	03/84	83-84	10	0	1
Crewe Alex	L	10/85	85	5	0	0
Aldershot	Tr	07/86	86-89	69	29	4

ANDERSON Desmond (Des)
Born: Edinburgh, Scotland, 9 January, 1938 — WH
Scotland: Schools

League Club	Source	Date Signed	Seasons Played	Apps	Subs	Gls
Millwall	Greenock Morton	06/61	61-63	46	-	1

ANDERSON Douglas Eric (Doug)
Born: Hong Kong, 29 August, 1963 — LW

League Club	Source	Date Signed	Seasons Played	Apps	Subs	Gls
Oldham Ath	Port Glasgow Rgrs	09/80	81-83	4	5	0
Tranmere Rov	Tr	08/84	84-86	125	1	15
Plymouth Arg	Tr	08/87	87	17	2	1
Cambridge U	L	09/88	88	8	0	2
Northampton T	L	12/88	88	4	1	0

ANDERSON Edward (Eddie)
Born: Glasgow, Scotland, 23 September, 1917 — FB
Died: Liverpool, England, May, 1999

League Club	Source	Date Signed	Seasons Played	Apps	Subs	Gls
Rochdale	Stirling A	03/48	47	1	-	0

ANDERSON Edward Walton (Ted)
Born: Dudley, West Midlands, England, 17 July, 1911 — FB
Died: Birkenhead, Wirral, England, 23 March, 1979

League Club	Source	Date Signed	Seasons Played	Apps	Subs	Gls
Wolverhampton W	Worksop T	12/29	30	3	-	0
Torquay U	Tr	12/31	31-32	61	-	2
West Ham U	Tr	06/33	33-34	26	-	0
Chester C	Tr	06/35	35-36	23	-	0
Tranmere Rov	Tr	07/37	37-47	73	-	0

ANDERSON Eric
Born: Manchester, England, 7 December, 1931 — IF
Died: Salford, England, March, 1990

League Club	Source	Date Signed	Seasons Played	Apps	Subs	Gls
Liverpool	Army	12/51	52-56	73	-	21
Barnsley	Tr	07/57	57	9	-	1

ANDERSON Gary Leslie
Born: Bow, E London, England, 20 October, 1955 — RB

League Club	Source	Date Signed	Seasons Played	Apps	Subs	Gls
Tottenham H	App	12/72				
Northampton T	Tr	03/75	74-75	14	0	0

ANDERSON Geoffrey Thomas (Geoff)
Born: Sheerness, Kent, England, 26 November, 1944 — RW

League Club	Source	Date Signed	Seasons Played	Apps	Subs	Gls
Birmingham C	Ramsgate Ath	12/62	63	1	-	0
Mansfield T	Tr	05/64	64-65	43	0	13
Lincoln C	Tr	07/66	66	44	0	6
Brentford	Tr	08/67				
Port Vale	Tr	11/67				

ANDERSON Harry John
Born: Slough, Berkshire, England, 9 January, 1997 — W

League Club	Source	Date Signed	Seasons Played	Apps	Subs	Gls
Peterborough U	Crawley T (Sch)	03/15	14	6	4	0

ANDERSON Iain William
Born: Glasgow, Scotland, 23 July, 1977 — LW
Scotland: U21-15

League Club	Source	Date Signed	Seasons Played	Apps	Subs	Gls
Preston NE	Toulouse (FRA)	02/00	99-02	46	36	13
Tranmere Rov	L	03/03	02	7	0	2
Grimsby T	Tr	07/03	03	24	5	5

ANDERSON Ijah Massai
Born: Hackney, E London, England, 30 December, 1975 — LB

League Club	Source	Date Signed	Seasons Played	Apps	Subs	Gls
Southend U	Tottenham H (YT)	08/94				
Brentford	Tr	07/95	95-02	196	6	4
Wycombe W	L	11/02	02	5	0	0
Bristol Rov	Tr	02/03	02-03	51	2	0
Swansea C	Tr	11/04	04-05	8	10	0

ANDERSON James (Jimmy)
Born: Gateshead, Tyne and Wear, England, 23 July, 1913 — LB

League Club	Source	Date Signed	Seasons Played	Apps	Subs	Gls
Brentford	Queen of the South	07/39				
Carlisle U	Tr	09/46	46	11	-	0

ANDERSON James McFarland (Jimmy)
Born: Glasgow, Scotland, 25 December, 1932 — LH

League Club	Source	Date Signed	Seasons Played	Apps	Subs	Gls
Bristol Rov	RAOC Hilsea	04/53	54-56	24	-	0
Chester C	Tr	06/57	57-59	62	-	0

ANDERSON Jermaine Barrington
Born: Camden, N London, England, 16 May, 1996 — M
England: Youth

League Club	Source	Date Signed	Seasons Played	Apps	Subs	Gls
Peterborough U	Sch	05/13	12-14	28	10	1

ANDERSON Joe William
Born: Stepney, E London, England, 13 October, 1989 — LB

League Club	Source	Date Signed	Seasons Played	Apps	Subs	Gls
Fulham	Sch	12/08				
Lincoln C	Tr	01/10	09-10	42	3	0

ANDERSON John (Johnny)
Born: Salford, England, 11 October, 1921 — WH
Died: Manchester, England, 8 August, 2006

League Club	Source	Date Signed	Seasons Played	Apps	Subs	Gls
Manchester U	Jnr	11/38	47-48	33	-	1
Nottingham F	Tr	10/49	49-50	40	-	1

ANDERSON John (Johnny)
Born: Barrhead, Renfrewshire, Scotland, 8 December, 1929 — G
Died: Leicester, England, 22 August, 2001
Scotland: 1/B

League Club	Source	Date Signed	Seasons Played	Apps	Subs	Gls
Leicester C	Arthurlie	12/48	48-58	261	-	0
Peterborough U	Tr	07/60				

ANDERSON John Christopher Patrick
Born: Dublin, Republic of Ireland, 7 November, 1959 — RB
Republic of Ireland: 16/U21-1/Youth

League Club	Source	Date Signed	Seasons Played	Apps	Subs	Gls
West Bromwich A	App	11/77				
Preston NE	Tr	08/79	79-81	47	4	0
Newcastle U	Tr	09/82	82-90	283	16	14

League Club	Source	Date Signed	Seasons Played	Apps	Subs	Gls
ANDERSON John Curr (Jock)						
Born: Dundee, Scotland, 8 May, 1915						CF
Died: Portsmouth, England, February, 1987						
Portsmouth	Stobswell	01/33	33-38	81	-	33
Aldershot	Tr	06/46	46	4	-	1
ANDERSON John Desmond (Des)						
Born: Downpatrick, Northern Ireland, 11 September, 1940						CD
Exeter C	Glenavon	08/62	62-65	142	2	1
Chesterfield	Tr	07/66	66-67	8	0	0
ANDERSON John Ephraim						
Born: Ridsdale, Northumberland, England, 7 June, 1931						FB
Died: North East Lincolnshire, England, May, 2003						
Grimsby T	Langold WMC	05/54	55	3	-	0
Crystal Palace	Tr	08/58				
ANDERSON John Hugh Todd						
Born: Johnstone, Renfrewshire, Scotland, 11 January, 1937						W
Stoke C	Johnstone Burgh	01/57	57-60	24	-	2
ANDERSON John Lochart (Johnny)						
Born: Glasgow, Scotland, 5 April, 1928						IF
Died: Aldershot, Hampshire, England, 6 April, 2001						
Northampton T	Partick Thistle	06/53	53	14	-	5
Exeter C	Tr	07/54	54	7	-	0
Wrexham	Dundee	06/56	56-58	98	-	27
Rochdale	Tr	07/59	59	28	-	5
Chester C	Tr	07/60	60	17	-	2
Wrexham	Tr	08/61	61	1	-	0
ANDERSON John Patton						
Born: Greenock, Inverclyde, Scotland, 2 October, 1972						CD
Hull C	Livingston	06/02	02	42	1	1
Bristol Rov	Tr	03/04	03-05	46	8	2
ANDERSON John Robert (Bob)						
Born: Prestwick, Ayrshire, Scotland, 9 November, 1924						G
Died: Bristol, England, 14 November, 1994						
Middlesbrough	Blackhall CW	11/45	47	1	-	0
Crystal Palace	Blackhall CW	10/51	51-52	38	-	0
Bristol Rov	Tr	03/53	52-53	10	-	0
Bristol C	Tr	04/54	54-58	106	-	0
ANDERSON Lee Charles						
Born: Tottington, Greater Manchester, England, 4 October, 1973						RB
Bury	YT	10/91	91-93	27	2	0
Doncaster Rov	Southport	03/97	96	6	0	0
ANDERSON Mark James						
Born: Scunthorpe, North Lincolnshire, England, 7 October, 1981						F
Scunthorpe U	YT	07/01	01	0	1	0
ANDERSON Myles						
Born: Westminster, Central London, England, 9 January, 1990						D
Blackburn Rov	Aberdeen	07/11				
Aldershot T	L	08/12	12	0	5	0
Exeter C	Tr	01/13	12	0	1	0
ANDERSON Norman Hindmarsh						
Born: Hebburn, Tyne and Wear, England, 30 November, 1930						IF
Died: S.Tyneside, Tyne and Wear, England, November, 2004						
Gateshead	Reyrolles	03/51	53-55	21	-	2
ANDERSON Paul						
Born: Leicester, England, 23 July, 1988						LW
England: Youth						
Liverpool	Hull C (Sch)	01/06				
Swansea C	L	07/07	07	22	9	7
Nottingham F	L	07/08	08	24	2	2
Nottingham F	Tr	07/09	09-11	70	20	7
Bristol C	Tr	07/12	12	18	11	3
Ipswich T	Tr	07/13	13-14	42	24	6
ANDERSON Percy Archibald						
Born: Cambridge, England, 22 September, 1930						WH
Died: Cambridge, England, 4 March, 2006						
West Bromwich A	Cambridge U	09/51				
Stockport Co	Tr	07/53	53	1	-	0
ANDERSON Peter Dennis						
Born: Devonport, Devon, England, 11 September, 1932						W
Plymouth Arg	Oak Villa	07/50	52-62	241	-	41
Torquay U	Tr	12/62	62-64	77	-	18
ANDERSON Peter Thomas						
Born: Hendon, N London, England, 31 May, 1949						RW
Luton T	Hendon	02/71	70-75	178	3	34
Sheffield U	Tampa Bay R's (USA)	09/78	78	28	2	12
Millwall	Tampa Bay R's (USA)	12/80	80-82	30	2	4

League Club	Source	Date Signed	Seasons Played	Apps	Subs	Gls
ANDERSON Philip Oswald (Phil)						
Born: Portadown, Armagh, Northern Ireland, 5 January, 1948						W
Bury	Portadown	05/66	66-68	4	3	1
ANDERSON Robert						
Born: Aberdeen, Scotland, 21 January, 1937						RW
Chesterfield	Partick Thistle	08/59	59	4	-	0
ANDERSON Robert (Bobby)						
Born: Newton Mearns, Renfrewshire, Scotland, 11 August, 1928						W
Died: Leicester, England, 29 August, 2000						
Leicester C	Mearns Amats	01/46	46-47	19	-	2
ANDERSON Robert John						
Born: Portsmouth, England, 23 February, 1936						RW
Died: Sheffield, England, November, 1996						
Mansfield T	Chesterfield Tube W'ks	09/56	56-59	40	-	4
ANDERSON Robert Lymbun (Bert)						
Born: Derry, Northern Ireland, 23 April, 1926						FB
Died: Worksop, Nottinghamshire, England, 15 October, 1986						
Doncaster Rov	Ulsterville	11/49	50-51	3	-	0
ANDERSON Ronald James (Ron)						
Born: Gateshead, Tyne and Wear, England, 3 July, 1922						IF
Died: Chatham, Kent, England, February, 1984						
Bury	Newcastle YMCA	08/39	46	2	-	0
Crystal Palace	Tr	05/47				
ANDERSON Russell						
Born: Aberdeen, Scotland, 25 October, 1978						CD
Scotland: 11/U21-15						
Sunderland	Aberdeen	07/07	07	0	1	0
Plymouth Arg	L	02/08	07	14	0	0
Burnley	L	08/08	08	4	0	0
Derby Co	Tr	01/10	09-11	18	16	1
ANDERSON Samuel (Sammy)						
Born: Manchester, England, 11 January, 1936						FB
Oldham Ath		08/54	55-56	6	-	0
ANDERSON Stanley (Stan)						
Born: Horden, County Durham, England, 27 February, 1934						RH
England: 2/B-1/U23-4/Schools						
Sunderland	Jnr	03/51	52-63	402	-	31
Newcastle U	Tr	11/63	63-65	81	0	13
Middlesbrough	Tr	11/65	65	21	0	2
ANDERSON Stuart						
Born: Banff, Aberdeenshire, Scotland, 22 April, 1986						M
Scotland: Youth						
Southampton	Sch	04/04				
Blackpool	Tr	12/04	04	1	3	0
ANDERSON Terence Keith (Terry)						
Born: Woking, Surrey, England, 11 March, 1944						W
Died: Great Yarmouth, Norfolk, England, January, 1980						
England: Youth						
Arsenal	App	08/61	62-64	25	-	6
Norwich C	Tr	02/65	64-73	218	18	16
Colchester U	L	02/74	73	4	0	0
Scunthorpe U	Baltimore Comets (USA)	09/74	74	10	0	0
Crewe Alex	Tr	11/74	74	4	0	0
Bournemouth	Tr	01/75				
Colchester U	Baltimore Comets (USA)	08/75	75	13	3	0
ANDERSON Thomas Cowan (Tommy)						
Born: Haddington, East Lothian, Scotland, 24 September, 1934						IF
Scotland: Schools						
Watford	Queen of the South	12/56	56-57	52	-	12
Bournemouth	Tr	06/58	58	5	-	1
Queens Park Rgrs	Tr	11/58	58	10	-	3
Torquay U	Tr	07/59	59	9	-	4
Stockport Co	Tr	06/60	60-61	60	-	17
Doncaster Rov	Tr	11/61	61	16	-	3
Wrexham	Tr	03/62	61-62	12	-	3
Barrow	Hellas (AUS)	12/63	63	11	-	3
Watford	Hellas (AUS)	12/64	64-65	21	0	2
Leyton Orient	George Cross (AUS)	07/67	67	8	1	0
ANDERSON Thomas Robert (Tom)						
Born: Burnley, Lancashire, England, 2 September, 1993						CD
Burnley	Sch	03/12				
Carlisle U	L	10/14	14	8	0	0
ANDERSON Trevor						
Born: Belfast, Northern Ireland, 3 March, 1951						LW
Northern Ireland: 22/NILge-1/U21-1						
Manchester U	Portadown	10/72	72-73	13	6	2
Swindon T	Tr	11/74	74-77	128	3	34
Peterborough U	Tr	12/77	77-78	49	0	6

ANDERSON Vivian Alexander (Viv)
Born: Nottingham, England, 29 August, 1956 RB
England: 30/B-7/U21-1

League Club	Source	Date Signed	Seasons Played	Apps	Subs	Gls
Nottingham F	App	08/74	74-83	323	5	15
Arsenal	Tr	07/84	84-86	120	0	9
Manchester U	Tr	05/87	87-90	50	4	2
Sheffield Wed	Tr	01/91	90-92	60	10	8
Barnsley	Tr	07/93	93	20	0	3
Middlesbrough	Tr	07/94	94	2	0	0

ANDERSON William (Bill)
Born: Lochore, Fife, Scotland, 6 November, 1926 IF
Scotland: Amateur-5

League Club	Source	Date Signed	Seasons Played	Apps	Subs	Gls
Southend U	Hibernian	05/54	54-55	16	-	1

ANDERSON William Boston (Billy)
Born: Sunderland, England, 28 March, 1935 D

League Club	Source	Date Signed	Seasons Played	Apps	Subs	Gls
Barnsley	Silksworth Jnrs	09/52	55	6	-	0
Hartlepool U	Tr	02/56	55-60	179	-	11

ANDERSON William John (Willie)
Born: Liverpool, England, 24 January, 1947 LW

League Club	Source	Date Signed	Seasons Played	Apps	Subs	Gls
Manchester U	App	02/64	63-66	7	2	0
Aston Villa	Tr	01/67	66-72	229	2	36
Cardiff C	Tr	02/73	72-76	122	4	12

ANDERSON William Ronald (Ron)
Born: Ponteland, Northumberland, England, 20 September, 1927 G
Died: Sunderland, England, August, 1995

League Club	Source	Date Signed	Seasons Played	Apps	Subs	Gls
Newcastle U	Throckley Welfare	02/47	46	1	-	0

ANDERSON William Ross
Born: Kilmarnock, Ayrshire, Scotland, 13 November, 1917 CF
Died: Ayr, Scotland, 13 August, 1981

League Club	Source	Date Signed	Seasons Played	Apps	Subs	Gls
Millwall	Dundee	07/44	46-47	32	-	6

ANDERSSON Anders Per
Born: Tomelilla, Sweden, 15 March, 1974 M
Sweden: 26

League Club	Source	Date Signed	Seasons Played	Apps	Subs	Gls
Blackburn Rov	FF Malmo (SWE)	06/97	97	1	3	0

ANDERSSON Andreas Claes
Born: Stockholm, Sweden, 10 April, 1974 F
Sweden: 43

League Club	Source	Date Signed	Seasons Played	Apps	Subs	Gls
Newcastle U	AC Milan (ITA)	01/98	97-98	21	6	4

ANDERSSON Patrik Jonas
Born: Borgeby, Sweden, 18 August, 1971 CD
Sweden: 96/U23-4

League Club	Source	Date Signed	Seasons Played	Apps	Subs	Gls
Blackburn Rov	FF Malmo (SWE)	12/92	92-93	7	5	0

ANDERTON Darren Robert
Born: Southampton, England, 3 March, 1972 M/W
England: 30/B-1/U21-12/Youth

League Club	Source	Date Signed	Seasons Played	Apps	Subs	Gls
Portsmouth	YT	02/90	90-91	53	9	7
Tottenham H	Tr	06/92	92-03	273	26	34
Birmingham C	Tr	08/04	04	9	11	3
Wolverhampton W	Tr	08/05	05	20	4	1
Bournemouth	Tr	09/06	06-08	65	1	12

ANDERTON John
Born: Skelmersdale, Lancashire, England, 7 February, 1933 LB

League Club	Source	Date Signed	Seasons Played	Apps	Subs	Gls
Everton	Jnr	03/51				
Torquay U	Tr	07/54	54-57	40	-	2

ANDERTON Steven David
Born: Lancaster, England, 2 October, 1969 M

League Club	Source	Date Signed	Seasons Played	Apps	Subs	Gls
Preston NE	YT	07/88	89	0	1	0

ANDERTON Sylvan James
Born: Reading, England, 23 November, 1934 WH

League Club	Source	Date Signed	Seasons Played	Apps	Subs	Gls
Reading	Jnr	06/52	52-58	155	-	18
Chelsea	Tr	03/59	58-61	76	-	2
Queens Park Rgrs	Tr	01/62	61	4	-	0

ANDRADE Bruno Miguel Carvalho
Born: Aveiro, Portugal, 2 October, 1993 W

League Club	Source	Date Signed	Seasons Played	Apps	Subs	Gls
Queens Park Rgrs	Sch	10/10	10-11	0	2	0
Aldershot T	L	09/11	11	0	1	0
Wycombe W	L	10/12	12	15	8	2
Stevenage	L	10/13	13	3	10	0
Stevenage	L	02/15	14	5	11	1

ANDRADE Jose Manuel
Born: Sao Vicente, Cape Verde Islands, 1 June, 1970 F

League Club	Source	Date Signed	Seasons Played	Apps	Subs	Gls
Stoke C (L)	Acad Viseu (POR)	03/95	94	2	2	1
Stoke C (L)	Acad Viseu (POR)	08/97	97	4	8	1

ANDRE Carlos Paulino de Oli
Born: Lisbon, Portugal, 28 November, 1971 M

League Club	Source	Date Signed	Seasons Played	Apps	Subs	Gls
Walsall	Vit Guimaraes (POR)	12/01	01	5	0	0

ANDRE Helio
Born: Luanda, Angola, 3 December, 1992 F

League Club	Source	Date Signed	Seasons Played	Apps	Subs	Gls
Rochdale	Sch	-	10	0	1	0

ANDRE Pierre-Yves
Born: Lannion, France, 14 May, 1974 F
France: 3/U21-9

League Club	Source	Date Signed	Seasons Played	Apps	Subs	Gls
Bolton W (L)	FC Nantes (FRA)	01/03	02	0	9	0

ANDREASEN Leon Hougaard
Born: Aarhus, Denmark, 23 April, 1983 M
Denmark: 15/U21-23/Youth

League Club	Source	Date Signed	Seasons Played	Apps	Subs	Gls
Fulham	Werder Bremen (GER)	01/08	07-08	9	10	0

ANDREASSEN Svein Are
Born: Hadsel, Norway, 3 July, 1968 M

League Club	Source	Date Signed	Seasons Played	Apps	Subs	Gls
Portsmouth (L)	Lillestrom (NOR)	12/98	98	0	2	0

ANDREASSON Marcus Yates
Born: Monrovia, Liberia, 13 July, 1978 CD

League Club	Source	Date Signed	Seasons Played	Apps	Subs	Gls
Bristol Rov	Osters IF (SWE)	07/98	98-99	5	1	0
Bristol Rov	Kalmar FF (SWE)	03/00	99-00	9	0	1

ANDRESEN Martin
Born: Oslo, Norway, 2 February, 1977 M
Norway: 43/U21-24/Youth

League Club	Source	Date Signed	Seasons Played	Apps	Subs	Gls
Wimbledon	Stabaek (NOR)	10/99	99	4	10	1
Blackburn Rov (L)	Stabaek (NOR)	01/04	03	11	0	0

ANDREU Anthony (Tony)
Born: Nice, France, 22 May, 1988 M

League Club	Source	Date Signed	Seasons Played	Apps	Subs	Gls
Norwich C	Hamilton Academical	02/15	14	0	6	0

ANDREW Calvin Hyden
Born: Luton, England, 19 December, 1986 F

League Club	Source	Date Signed	Seasons Played	Apps	Subs	Gls
Luton T	Sch	09/04	04-07	26	29	4
Grimsby T	L	08/05	05	3	5	1
Bristol C	L	01/06	05	1	2	0
Crystal Palace	Tr	07/08	08-11	17	36	1
Brighton & HA	L	01/09	08	3	6	2
Millwall	L	11/10	10	3	0	0
Swindon T	L	03/11	10	9	1	1
Leyton Orient	L	03/12	11	2	8	0
Port Vale	L	11/12	12	7	15	1
Mansfield T	Tr	08/13	13	11	4	1
York C	Tr	03/14	13	5	3	0
Rochdale	Tr	07/14	14	5	27	5

ANDREW Daniel Kenny (Danny)
Born: Holbeach, Lincolnshire, England, 23 December, 1990 LB

League Club	Source	Date Signed	Seasons Played	Apps	Subs	Gls
Peterborough U	Sch	07/09	09	2	0	0
Cheltenham T	L	01/10	09	9	1	0
Cheltenham T	Tr	07/10	10-12	53	1	4
Fleetwood T	Macclesfield T	05/14	14	6	1	0

ANDREW George
Born: Glasgow, Scotland, 24 November, 1945 CD
Died: Edinburgh, Scotland, 30 July, 1993

League Club	Source	Date Signed	Seasons Played	Apps	Subs	Gls
West Ham U	Possilpark Jnrs	09/63	66	2	0	0
Crystal Palace	Tr	07/67				

ANDREW Matthew (Matt)
Born: Johnstone, Renfrewshire, Scotland, 5 January, 1922 D
Died: Port Talbot, Wales, 19 August, 1999

League Club	Source	Date Signed	Seasons Played	Apps	Subs	Gls
Bristol C		10/47				
Swansea C	Tr	08/48	48-50	4	-	0
Workington	Tr	06/51	51	22	-	0
Queens Park Rgrs	Tr	09/52				

ANDREW Ronald Edward Harold (Ron)
Born: Bebington, Wirral, England, 5 January, 1936 CH

League Club	Source	Date Signed	Seasons Played	Apps	Subs	Gls
Stoke C	Ellesmere Port T	05/54	57-63	115	-	1
Port Vale	Tr	06/64	64	8	-	1

ANDREWS Arthur Percy (Percy)
Born: Alton, Hampshire, England, 12 June, 1922 LB
Died: Pocklington, East Riding of Yorkshire, England, 28 February, 1985

League Club	Source	Date Signed	Seasons Played	Apps	Subs	Gls
York C	Portsmouth (Am)	09/47	47-54	176	-	0

ANDREWS Benjamin Philip (Ben)
Born: Burton-on-Trent, Staffordshire, England, 18 November, 1980 FB

League Club	Source	Date Signed	Seasons Played	Apps	Subs	Gls
Brighton & HA	YT	03/98	97-98	2	2	0

ANDREWS Bradley James
Born: Bristol, England, 8 December, 1979 M

League Club	Source	Date Signed	Seasons Played	Apps	Subs	Gls
Norwich C	YT	07/98				
Bristol Rov	Tr	03/99	98	3	0	0

ANDREWS Cecil James (Archie)
Born: Alton, Hampshire, England, 1 November, 1930 WH

League Club	Source	Date Signed	Seasons Played	Apps	Subs	Gls
Died: Ealing, W London, England, July, 1986						
Portsmouth	Alton T	01/49				
Crystal Palace	Tr	06/52	52-55	104	-	12
Queens Park Rgrs	Tr	06/56	56-57	58	-	1
ANDREWS Derek						
Born: Bury, Greater Manchester, England, 14 December, 1934 — IF						
Rochdale		03/55	55	22	-	4
ANDREWS Gary Michael						
Born: Nottingham, England, 12 May, 1968 — RB/M						
Nottingham F	App	09/85				
Peterborough U	Tr	08/88	88-89	42	1	0
ANDREWS George						
Born: Dudley, West Midlands, England, 23 April, 1942 — F						
Luton T	Vono Sports	01/60				
Cardiff C	Lower Gornal Ath	10/65	65-66	43	0	21
Southport	Tr	02/67	66-69	115	2	41
Shrewsbury T	Tr	11/69	69-72	123	1	49
Walsall	Tr	01/73	72-76	156	3	38
ANDREWS Glendon (Glen)						
Born: Dudley, West Midlands, England, 11 February, 1945 — RB/F						
Manchester U	Jnr	09/63				
Wolverhampton W	Tr	07/66				
Bradford Park Ave	Tr	09/67	67-68	47	1	6
ANDREWS Ian Edmund						
Born: Nottingham, England, 1 December, 1964 — G						
England: U21-1/Youth						
Leicester C	App	12/82	83-87	126	0	0
Swindon T	L	01/84	83	1	0	0
Leeds U (L)	Glasgow Celtic	12/88	88	1	0	0
Southampton	Glasgow Celtic	12/89	89-93	10	0	0
Bournemouth	Tr	09/94	94-95	64	0	0
ANDREWS James Patrick (Jimmy)						
Born: Invergordon, Highlands, Scotland, 1 February, 1927 — LW						
Died: Bridgend, Wales, 12 September, 2012						
West Ham U	Dundee	11/51	51-55	114	-	21
Leyton Orient	Tr	06/56	56-58	36	-	8
Queens Park Rgrs	Tr	06/59	59-61	82	-	16
ANDREWS John Edward						
Born: York, England, 3 February, 1950 — G						
York C (Am)	Moor Lane YC	08/68	68	11	0	0
ANDREWS John Henry						
Born: Cork, Republic of Ireland, 27 September, 1978 — FB						
Coventry C	YT	05/97				
Mansfield T	Grantham T	10/99	99-00	34	4	1
ANDREWS Keith Joseph						
Born: Dublin, Republic of Ireland, 13 September, 1980 — M						
Republic of Ireland: 35/Youth						
Wolverhampton W	YT	09/97	99-04	41	24	0
Oxford U	L	11/00	00	4	0	1
Stoke C	L	08/03	03	16	0	0
Walsall	L	03/04	03	10	0	2
Hull C	Tr	06/05	05-06	24	5	0
MK Dons	Tr	08/06	06-08	75	1	18
Blackburn Rov	Tr	08/08	08-10	51	19	5
Ipswich T	L	08/11	11	19	1	9
West Bromwich A	Tr	01/12	11	8	6	2
Bolton W	Tr	06/12	12-13	23	3	4
Brighton & HA	L	08/13	13	28	3	1
Watford	L	07/14	14	4	5	1
MK Dons	L	02/15	14	2	3	0
ANDREWS Keri Anthony						
Born: Swansea, Wales, 28 April, 1968 — LW						
Wales: Youth						
Swansea C	App	04/86	84-87	32	9	3
ANDREWS Lee David						
Born: Carlisle, Cumbria, England, 23 April, 1983 — CD						
Carlisle U	YT	06/01	01-05	82	10	0
Rochdale	L	02/03	02	8	0	0
Torquay U	Tr	03/06	05-06	52	1	0
ANDREWS Leslie Lindon (Les)						
Born: Dudley, West Midlands, England, 29 October, 1953 — F						
Wolverhampton W	Jnr	09/72				
Scunthorpe U	L	03/74	73	7	2	1
ANDREWS Philip Donald (Phil)						
Born: Andover, Hampshire, England, 14 September, 1976 — F						
Brighton & HA	YT	05/95	93-96	2	23	1
ANDREWS Wayne Michael Hill						
Born: Paddington, Central London, England, 25 November, 1977 — F						
Watford	YT	07/96	95-97	16	12	4
Cambridge U	L	10/98	98	1	1	0
Peterborough U	L	02/99	98	8	2	5
Oldham Ath	Chesham U	05/02	02	28	9	11
Colchester U	Tr	08/03	03-04	36	10	14
Crystal Palace	Tr	09/04	04-05	5	28	1
Coventry C	Tr	07/06	06-07	0	10	1
Sheffield Wed	L	11/06	06	7	2	1
Bristol C	L	01/07	06	3	4	2
Leeds U	L	10/07	07	1	0	0
Bristol Rov	L	03/08	07	1	0	0
Luton T	Tr	10/08	08	1	6	0
ANDRUSZEWSKI Emanuel Franciszek (Manny)						
Born: Eastleigh, Hampshire, England, 4 October, 1955 — D						
Southampton	App	10/73	74-79	82	1	3
Aldershot	Tampa Bay R's (USA)	08/82	82	25	2	0
ANEKE Chukwuemeka Ademola Amachi (Chuks)						
Born: Newham, E London, England, 3 July, 1993 — M/F						
England: Youth						
Arsenal	Sch	07/10				
Stevenage	L	11/11	11	2	4	0
Preston NE	L	03/12	11	3	4	1
Crewe Alex	L	09/12	12	21	9	6
Crewe Alex	L	08/13	13	34	6	14
ANELKA Nicolas						
Born: Versailles, France, 14 March, 1979 — F						
France: 69/Youth						
Arsenal	Paris St-Germain (FRA)	03/97	96-98	50	15	23
Liverpool (L)	Paris St-Germain (FRA)	12/01	01	13	7	4
Manchester C	Paris St-Germain (FRA)	07/02	02-04	87	2	37
Bolton W	Fenerbahce (TKY)	08/06	06-07	53	0	21
Chelsea	Tr	01/08	07-11	104	21	38
West Bromwich A	Tr	07/13	13	11	1	2
ANGEL Juan Pablo						
Born: Medellin, Colombia, 24 October, 1975 — F						
Colombia: 33/Youth						
Aston Villa	River Plate (ARG)	01/01	00-06	134	41	44
ANGEL Mark						
Born: Newcastle-upon-Tyne, England, 23 August, 1975 — LW						
England: Semi Pro-3						
Sunderland	Walker Central	12/93				
Oxford U	Tr	08/95	95-97	40	33	4
West Bromwich A	Tr	07/98	98-99	4	21	1
Darlington	Tr	08/00	00	1	4	0
Boston U	Queen of the South	06/01	02-03	36	18	6
ANGELERI Marcos						
Born: La Plata, Argentina, 4 July, 1983 — D						
Argentina: 4						
Sunderland	Estudiantes (ARG)	07/10	10	0	2	0
ANGELL Brett Ashley Mark						
Born: Marlborough, Wiltshire, England, 20 August, 1968 — F						
Portsmouth	YT	08/86				
Derby Co	Cheltenham T	02/88				
Stockport Co	Tr	10/88	88-89	60	10	28
Southend U	Tr	08/90	90-93	109	6	47
Everton	L	09/93	93	0	1	0
Everton	Tr	01/94	93-94	16	3	1
Sunderland	Tr	03/95	94-95	10	0	0
Sheffield U	L	01/96	95	6	0	2
West Bromwich A	L	03/96	95	0	3	0
Stockport Co	Tr	08/96	96-99	122	4	50
Notts Co	L	12/99	99	6	0	5
Preston NE	L	02/00	99	9	6	8
Walsall	Tr	07/00	00-01	36	25	16
Rushden & D	Tr	02/02	01	3	2	2
Port Vale	Tr	08/02	02	13	2	5
Queens Park Rgrs	Tr	11/02	02	8	5	0
ANGELL Darren James						
Born: Marlborough, Wiltshire, England, 19 January, 1967 — CD						
Portsmouth	Newbury T	06/85				
Colchester U	L	12/87	87	1	0	0
ANGELL Peter Frank						
Born: Eton, Berkshire, England, 11 January, 1932 — LH						
Died: Waltham Forest, NE London, England, 18 July, 1979						
Queens Park Rgrs	Slough T	07/53	53-64	417	-	37
ANGELLA Gabriele						
Born: Florence, Italy, 28 April, 1989 — CD						

League Club	Source	Date Signed	Seasons Played	Apps	Subs	Gls
Italy: U21-3						
Watford	Udinese (ITA)	07/13	13-14	71	4	9
ANGOL Lee Anthony						
Born: Carshalton, S London, England, 4 August, 1994						F
Wycombe W	Tottenham H (Sch)	07/12	12	0	3	0
Luton T	Tr	07/14				
ANGUS John						
Born: Warkworth, Northumberland, England, 2 September, 1938						RB
England: 1/FLge-1/U23-7/Youth						
Burnley	Amble BC	09/55	56-71	438	1	4
ANGUS John (Jack)						
Born: Amble, Northumberland, England, 12 March, 1909						CH
Died: Amble, Northumberland, England, 1965						
Wolverhampton W	Amble Welfare	09/28				
Exeter C	Scunthorpe U	05/30	30-47	246	-	1
ANGUS Michael Anthony (Mike)						
Born: Middlesbrough, England, 28 October, 1960						M
Middlesbrough	Jnr	08/78	79-81	35	2	1
Scunthorpe U	L	09/82	82	20	0	2
Southend U	Tr	08/83				
Darlington	Tr	03/84	83-84	18	0	7
ANGUS Stevland Dennis (Stev)						
Born: Westminster, Central London, England, 16 September, 1980						CD
West Ham U	YT	07/99				
Bournemouth	L	08/00	00	7	2	0
Cambridge U	Tr	07/01	01-04	134	1	1
Hull C	L	12/04	04	1	1	0
Scunthorpe U	L	01/05	04	9	0	0
Torquay U	Grays Ath	07/06	06	33	3	1
Barnet	Tr	08/07	07	1	0	0
ANGUS Terence Norman (Terry)						
Born: Coventry, England, 14 January, 1966						CD
Northampton T	VS Rugby	08/90	90-92	115	1	6
Fulham	Tr	07/93	93-96	107	15	5
ANICHEBE Victor Chinedu						
Born: Lagos, Nigeria, 23 April, 1988						F
Nigeria: 11/U23-5						
Everton	Sch	04/06	05-13	58	73	17
West Bromwich A	Tr	09/13	13-14	22	23	6
ANITA Vurnon San Benito						
Born: Willemstad, Curacao, 4 April, 1989						DM
Netherlands: 3/U21-6/Youth						
Newcastle U	Ajax (NED)	08/12	12-14	62	16	1
ANKERGREN Casper						
Born: Koge, Denmark, 9 November, 1979						G
Denmark: U21-3						
Leeds U	Brondby (DEN)	01/07	06-09	117	2	0
Brighton & HA	Tr	08/10	10-13	67	1	0
ANNAN Richard Amondo						
Born: Leeds, England, 4 December, 1968						LB
Leeds U	App	12/86				
Doncaster Rov	Tr	10/87				
Crewe Alex	Guiseley	05/92	92-93	17	2	1
ANNERSON James Paul (Jamie)						
Born: Sheffield, England, 1 November, 1988						G
England: Youth						
Sheffield U	Sch	03/07				
Rotherham U	Tr	07/09	10	8	1	0
ANNON Darren Carlton						
Born: Chelsea, W London, England, 17 February, 1972						W
Brentford	Carshalton Ath	03/94	93-95	14	6	2
ANSAH Andrew Owusu (Andy)						
Born: Lewisham, SE London, England, 19 March, 1969						F/RW
Crystal Palace		09/86				
Brentford	Dorking	03/89	88-89	3	5	2
Southend U	Tr	03/90	89-95	141	16	33
Brentford	L	11/94	94	2	1	1
Brentford	L	11/95	95	6	0	1
Peterborough U	Tr	03/96	95	0	2	1
Gillingham	Tr	03/96	95	0	2	0
Leyton Orient	Tr	12/96	96	0	2	0
Brighton & HA	Heybridge Swifts	11/97	97-98	10	15	3
ANSAH Zak Andrew						
Born: Sidcup, SE London, England, 4 May, 1994						F
Arsenal	Sch	05/11				
Charlton Ath	Tr	07/14				
Plymouth Arg	L	03/15	14	2	6	1

League Club	Source	Date Signed	Seasons Played	Apps	Subs	Gls
ANSELIN Cedric						
Born: Lens, France, 24 July, 1977						M
France: Youth						
Norwich C	Bordeaux (FRA)	03/99	98-99	22	4	1
Cambridge U	Mildenhall T	11/04	04	2	0	0
ANSELL Barry						
Born: Birmingham, England, 29 September, 1947						FB
Aston Villa	Jnr	10/67	67	1	0	0
ANSELL Gary Scott						
Born: Ilford, E London, England, 8 November, 1978						M
Barnet	Barking	08/99	99	0	3	0
ANSELL William John (Jack)						
Born: Newport Pagnell, Buckinghamshire, England, 4 August, 1921						G
Died: Milton Keynes, England, 12 April, 2008						
Northampton T	Bletchley Brick Works	03/48	47-51	131	-	0
ANSLOW Stanley Thomas (Stan)						
Born: Hackney, E London, England, 5 May, 1931						LB
Millwall	Eton Manor	03/51	51-58	131	-	13
ANTENUCCI Mirco						
Born: Termoli, Italy, 8 September, 1994						F
Leeds U	Ternana (ITA)	08/14	14	24	12	10
ANTHONY Byron Joseph						
Born: Newport, Wales, 20 September, 1984						CD
Wales: U21-8/Youth						
Cardiff C	Sch	07/03				
Bristol Rov	Tr	08/06	06-11	155	8	7
Hereford U	L	02/12	11	13	2	1
Newport Co	Hereford U	11/12	13	7	0	0
ANTHONY Graham John						
Born: Jarrow, Tyne and Wear, England, 9 August, 1975						M
Sheffield U	YT	07/93	94-96	0	3	0
Scarborough	L	03/96	95	2	0	0
Swindon T	Tr	03/97	96	3	0	0
Plymouth Arg	Tr	08/97	97	5	0	0
Carlisle U	Tr	11/97	97-99	58	11	3
ANTHONY Thomas Henry (Tom)						
Born: Hounslow, SW London, England, 16 August, 1943						LB
Brentford	Jnr	12/61	62	33	-	1
Coventry C	Tr	08/65				
Millwall	Tr	11/65				
ANTHROBUS Stephen Anthony (Steve)						
Born: Lewisham, SE London, England, 10 November, 1968						F/LW
Millwall	Jnr	08/86	87-89	19	2	4
Wimbledon	Tr	02/90	89-92	27	1	0
Peterborough U	L	01/94	93	2	0	0
Chester C	L	08/94	94	7	0	0
Shrewsbury T	Tr	08/95	95-96	60	12	16
Crewe Alex	Tr	03/97	96-98	53	8	9
Oxford U	Tr	07/99	99-00	38	18	3
ANTIC Radomir (Raddy)						
Born: Zitiste, Yugoslavia, 22 November, 1949						M
Yugoslavia: 1						
Luton T	Real Zaragoza (SPN)	07/80	80-83	54	40	9
ANTOINE-CURIER Mickael						
Born: Paris, France, 5 March, 1983						F
Guadeloupe: 16						
Preston NE	AS Nancy (FRA)	11/00				
Nottingham F	Tr	06/01				
Brentford	L	03/03	02	11	0	3
Oldham Ath	Tr	08/03	03	5	3	2
Kidderminster Hrs	Tr	09/03	03	0	1	0
Rochdale	Tr	09/03	03	5	3	1
Sheffield Wed	Tr	11/03	03	0	1	0
Notts Co	Tr	02/04	03	4	0	1
Grimsby T	Tr	03/04	03	3	2	0
Burton A	Hamilton Academical	02/15	14	1	4	0
ANTONIO George Rowlands						
Born: Whitchurch, Shropshire, England, 20 October, 1914						IF
Died: Oswestry, Shropshire, England, 2 July, 1997						
Stoke C	Oswestry T	02/36	35-46	84	-	13
Derby Co	Tr	03/47	46-47	18	-	2
Doncaster Rov	Tr	10/48	48-49	34	-	7
Mansfield T	Tr	10/49	49-50	67	-	2
ANTONIO Michail Gregory						
Born: Wandsworth, SW London, England, 28 March, 1990						LW
Reading	Tooting & Mitcham U	10/08	09-11	4	24	1
Cheltenham T	L	02/09	08	7	2	0

League Club	Source	Date Signed	Seasons Played	Apps	Subs	Gls
Southampton	L	10/09	09	14	14	3
Colchester U	L	08/11	11	14	1	4
Sheffield Wed	Tr	02/12	11-13	75	3	17
Nottingham F	Tr	08/14	14	46	0	14

ANTWI Agyei William Kwabena (Will)
Born: Epsom, Surrey, England, 19 October, 1982 — CD
Ghana: 3

League Club	Source	Date Signed	Seasons Played	Apps	Subs	Gls
Crystal Palace	Sch	07/02	02	0	4	0
Wycombe W	Tr	07/05	05-08	40	2	1
Dagenham & Red	Tr	07/09	09-10	28	2	2
AFC Wimbledon	Staines T	09/12	12-13	36	5	1

ANTWI-BIRAGO Godwin
Born: Kumasi, Ghana, 7 June, 1988 — D
Spain: Youth

League Club	Source	Date Signed	Seasons Played	Apps	Subs	Gls
Liverpool	Real Zaragoza (SPN)	08/05				
Accrington Stan	L	03/07	06	9	0	0
Hartlepool U	L	07/07	07	27	0	1
Tranmere Rov	L	07/08	08	4	1	0
Hereford U	L	02/09	08	5	0	0

ANYA Ikechi
Born: Glasgow, Scotland, 3 January, 1988 — W
Scotland: 14

League Club	Source	Date Signed	Seasons Played	Apps	Subs	Gls
Wycombe W	Sch	07/05	04-06	1	17	0
Northampton T	Halesowen T	02/09	08	6	8	3
Watford	Cadiz (SPN)	08/12	12-14	74	21	8

ANYINSAH Joseph Greene (Joe)
Born: Bristol, England, 8 October, 1984 — RW

League Club	Source	Date Signed	Seasons Played	Apps	Subs	Gls
Bristol C	YT	10/01	04	2	5	0
Preston NE	Tr	07/05	05-06	0	6	0
Bury	L	02/06	05	3	0	0
Carlisle U	L	09/07	07	10	2	3
Crewe Alex	L	03/08	07	6	2	0
Brighton & HA	L	09/08	08	10	1	0
Carlisle U	Tr	01/09	08-09	36	11	13
Charlton Ath	Tr	08/10	10	14	5	3
Bristol C	Tr	07/11	11-12	47	15	8

ANYON Joseph (Joe)
Born: Poulton-le-Fylde, Lancashire, England, 29 December, 1986 — G
England: Youth

League Club	Source	Date Signed	Seasons Played	Apps	Subs	Gls
Port Vale	Sch	08/05	06-09	108	1	0
Lincoln C	Tr	07/10	10	21	0	0
Morecambe	L	03/11	10	4	0	0
Shrewsbury T	Tr	07/12	13	11	0	0
Scunthorpe U		01/15				

APPIAH Kwesi
Born: Peckham, SE London, England, 12 August, 1990 — F
Ghana: 5

League Club	Source	Date Signed	Seasons Played	Apps	Subs	Gls
Peterborough U	Ebbsfleet U	12/08				
Crystal Palace	Margate	01/12	11-12	0	6	0
Aldershot T	L	09/12	12	0	2	0
Yeovil T	L	01/13	12	1	4	0
Notts Co	L	01/14	13	1	6	0
AFC Wimbledon	L	03/14	13	6	1	3
Cambridge U	L	07/14	14	19	0	6
Reading	L	03/15	14	2	4	1

APPLEBY Andrew (Andy)
Born: Seaham, County Durham, England, 11 October, 1985 — F

League Club	Source	Date Signed	Seasons Played	Apps	Subs	Gls
Hartlepool U	Sch	07/05	04	0	15	2

APPLEBY James Park (Jim)
Born: Shotton Colliery, County Durham, England, 15 June, 1934 — CH
Died: Peterlee, County Durham, England, 6 January, 2014

League Club	Source	Date Signed	Seasons Played	Apps	Subs	Gls
Burnley	Wingate Welfare	02/53	56	1	-	0
Blackburn Rov	Tr	02/58	58-61	2	-	0
Southport	Tr	10/61	61	13	-	0
Chester C	Tr	06/62	62	1	-	0

APPLEBY Matthew Wilfred (Matty)
Born: Middlesbrough, England, 16 April, 1972 — M

League Club	Source	Date Signed	Seasons Played	Apps	Subs	Gls
Newcastle U	YT	05/90	90-93	18	2	0
Darlington	L	11/93	93	10	0	1
Darlington	Tr	06/94	94-95	77	2	7
Barnsley	Tr	07/96	96-00	131	8	7
Oldham Ath	Tr	01/02	01-04	36	10	2
Darlington	Tr	03/05	04-05	28	8	0

APPLEBY Richard Dean (Richie)
Born: Middlesbrough, England, 18 September, 1975 — M
England: Youth

League Club	Source	Date Signed	Seasons Played	Apps	Subs	Gls
Newcastle U	YT	08/93				
Ipswich T	Tr	12/95	95	0	3	0
Swansea C	Tr	08/96	96-01	90	30	11
Kidderminster Hrs	Tr	11/01	01	18	1	4
Hull C	Tr	07/02	02	6	0	0
Kidderminster Hrs	Tr	07/04	04	6	3	1

APPLEBY Robert (Bob)
Born: Warkworth, Northumberland, England, 15 January, 1940 — G

League Club	Source	Date Signed	Seasons Played	Apps	Subs	Gls
Middlesbrough	Amble Welfare	05/57	59-66	99	0	0

APPLETON Colin Harry
Born: Scarborough, North Yorkshire, England, 7 March, 1936 — LH
England: FLge-1

League Club	Source	Date Signed	Seasons Played	Apps	Subs	Gls
Leicester C	Scarborough	03/54	54-65	277	0	19
Charlton Ath	Tr	06/66	66	28	0	1
Barrow	Tr	08/67	67-68	39	4	1

APPLETON Michael Antony
Born: Salford, England, 4 December, 1975 — M

League Club	Source	Date Signed	Seasons Played	Apps	Subs	Gls
Manchester U	YT	07/94				
Lincoln C	L	09/95	95	4	0	0
Grimsby T	L	01/97	96	10	0	3
Preston NE	Tr	08/97	97-00	90	25	12
West Bromwich A	Tr	01/01	00-01	33	0	0

APPLETON Ronald (Ron)
Born: Cleator Moor, Cumbria, England, 24 September, 1932 — RW

League Club	Source	Date Signed	Seasons Played	Apps	Subs	Gls
Workington	Frizington White Star	02/53	52	3	-	0

APPLETON Stephen (Steve)
Born: Liverpool, England, 27 July, 1973 — D

League Club	Source	Date Signed	Seasons Played	Apps	Subs	Gls
Wigan Ath	YT	09/90	90-92	31	17	1

APPLETON Thomas Henry (Tom)
Born: Stanley, County Durham, England, 9 June, 1936 — WH

League Club	Source	Date Signed	Seasons Played	Apps	Subs	Gls
Burnley	Annfield Plain	08/54				
Gateshead	Tr	08/58	58	26	-	0
Accrington Stan	Tr	06/59				

AQUILANI Alberto
Born: Rome, Italy, 7 July, 1984 — M
Italy: 35/U21-20/Youth

League Club	Source	Date Signed	Seasons Played	Apps	Subs	Gls
Liverpool	AS Roma (ITA)	08/09	09	9	9	1

ARANALDE Zigor
Born: Guipuzcoa, Spain, 28 February, 1973 — LB

League Club	Source	Date Signed	Seasons Played	Apps	Subs	Gls
Walsall	CD Logrones (SPN)	08/00	00-04	183	12	5
Sheffield Wed	Tr	03/05	04	1	1	0
Carlisle U	Tr	07/05	05-07	108	1	6

ARBELOA Alvaro
Born: Salamanca, Spain, 17 January, 1983 — RB
Spain: 56/U21-1/Youth

League Club	Source	Date Signed	Seasons Played	Apps	Subs	Gls
Liverpool	Depo la Coruna (SPN)	01/07	06-08	63	3	2

ARBER Mark Andrew
Born: Johannesburg, South Africa, 9 October, 1977 — CD

League Club	Source	Date Signed	Seasons Played	Apps	Subs	Gls
Tottenham H	YT	03/96				
Barnet	Tr	09/98	98-00	123	2	15
Peterborough U	Tr	12/02	02-03	67	2	5
Oldham Ath	Tr	07/04	04	13	1	1
Peterborough U	Tr	12/04	04-06	98	3	3
Dagenham & Red	Tr	02/08	07-11	175	1	12

ARBER Robert Leonard (Bobby)
Born: Poplar, E London, England, 13 January, 1951 — FB

League Club	Source	Date Signed	Seasons Played	Apps	Subs	Gls
Arsenal	App	03/68				
Leyton Orient	Tr	11/68	71-72	31	0	0

ARBLASTER Michael Brian (Brian)
Born: Kensington, Central London, England, 6 June, 1943 — G
Died: Killamarsh, Derbyshire, England, 24 January, 2013

League Club	Source	Date Signed	Seasons Played	Apps	Subs	Gls
Sheffield U	Mosborough Trinity	07/62				
Chesterfield	Tr	12/64	64-66	55	0	0
Scunthorpe U	Tr	06/67	67	10	0	0
Barnsley	Tr	05/68	67-73	111	0	0

ARCA Julio Andres
Born: Quilmes, Argentina, 31 January, 1981 — M/LB
Argentina: Youth

League Club	Source	Date Signed	Seasons Played	Apps	Subs	Gls
Sunderland	Argentinos Jnrs (ARG)	08/00	00-05	145	12	17
Middlesbrough	Tr	08/06	06-12	131	29	7

ARCHDEACON Owen Duncan
Born: Greenock, Inverclyde, Scotland, 4 March, 1966 — LW
Scotland: U21-1/Youth

League Club	Source	Date Signed	Seasons Played	Apps	Subs	Gls
Barnsley	Glasgow Celtic	07/89	89-95	222	11	22
Carlisle U	Tr	07/96	96-97	64	0	10

ARCHELL Graham Leonard
Born: Islington, N London, England, 8 February, 1950 — LW

League Club	Source	Date Signed	Seasons Played	Apps	Subs	Gls
Leyton Orient	Jnr	11/67	67-68	5	2	0

League Club	Source	Date Signed	Seasons Played	Career Record Apps	Subs	Gls

ARCHER John
Born: Biddulph, Staffordshire, England, 18 June, 1941 M

League Club	Source	Date Signed	Seasons Played	Apps	Subs	Gls
Port Vale	Jnr	07/58	59-60	10	-	3
Bournemouth	Tr	07/61	61-65	139	0	37
Crewe Alex	Tr	09/66	66-67	59	1	16
Huddersfield T	Tr	01/68	67	7	2	0
Chesterfield	Tr	05/69	69-71	116	0	24

ARCHER John George
Born: Whitstable, Kent, England, 9 April, 1936 G
Died: Canterbury, England, 28 May, 1987

League Club	Source	Date Signed	Seasons Played	Apps	Subs	Gls
Grimsby T	Whitstable T	04/54	54	10	-	0

ARCHER Jordan Gideon
Born: Walthamstow, NE London, England, 12 April, 1993 G
Scotland: U21-13/Youth

League Club	Source	Date Signed	Seasons Played	Apps	Subs	Gls
Tottenham H	Sch	07/11				
Wycombe W	L	09/12	12	27	0	0
Northampton T	L	08/14	14	13	0	0

ARCHER Lee
Born: Bristol, England, 6 November, 1972 M

League Club	Source	Date Signed	Seasons Played	Apps	Subs	Gls
Bristol Rov	YT	07/91	91-96	104	22	15

ARCHER Philip (Phil)
Born: Rotherham, South Yorkshire, England, 25 August, 1952 D

League Club	Source	Date Signed	Seasons Played	Apps	Subs	Gls
Reading	Sheffield U (App)	09/70	71	12	5	0

ARCHER Ronald (Ron)
Born: Barnsley, South Yorkshire, England, 3 September, 1933 WH
Died: Torbay, Devon, England, 17 January, 2005
England: Schools

League Club	Source	Date Signed	Seasons Played	Apps	Subs	Gls
Barnsley	Jnr	09/50	51-55	29	-	0

ARCHER William Henry (Bill)
Born: Scunthorpe, North Lincolnshire, England, 5 February, 1914 CH
Died: Scunthorpe, North Lincolnshire, England, 17 October, 1992

League Club	Source	Date Signed	Seasons Played	Apps	Subs	Gls
Lincoln C	Grantham	06/39				
Doncaster Rov	Tr	10/45	46-47	14	-	0

ARCHIBALD John Murray (Murray)
Born: Carron, Falkirk, Scotland, 19 March, 1917 CF
Died: Falkirk, Scotland, 9 January, 2006

League Club	Source	Date Signed	Seasons Played	Apps	Subs	Gls
Wrexham	Bangor C	03/46	46	1	-	0

ARCHIBALD Steven (Steve)
Born: Glasgow, Scotland, 27 September, 1956 F
Scotland: 27/U21-5

League Club	Source	Date Signed	Seasons Played	Apps	Subs	Gls
Tottenham H	Aberdeen	05/80	80-83	128	3	58
Blackburn Rov (L)	Barcelona (SPN)	12/87	87	20	0	6
Reading	St Mirren	01/92	91	1	0	0
Fulham	Clyde	09/92	92	2	0	0

ARCHIBALD-HENVILLE Troy Patrick
Born: Newham, E London, England, 4 November, 1988 CD

League Club	Source	Date Signed	Seasons Played	Apps	Subs	Gls
Tottenham H	Sch	07/07				
Exeter C	L	01/09	08	19	0	0
Exeter C	Tr	07/09	09-11	90	6	3
Swindon T	Tr	07/12	12-13	16	3	0
Carlisle U	L	08/13	13	4	0	0
Carlisle U	Tr	07/14	14	24	0	1

ARDILES Osvaldo Cesar (Ossie)
Born: Cordoba, Argentina, 3 August, 1952 M
Argentina: 52

League Club	Source	Date Signed	Seasons Played	Apps	Subs	Gls
Tottenham H	Huracan (ARG)	07/78	78-87	221	16	16
Blackburn Rov	L	03/88	87	5	0	0
Queens Park Rgrs	Tr	08/88	88	4	4	0
Swindon T	Ft Laud'ale St's (USA)	07/89	89	0	2	0

ARDLEY Neal Christopher
Born: Epsom, Surrey, England, 1 September, 1972 RM
England: U21-10

League Club	Source	Date Signed	Seasons Played	Apps	Subs	Gls
Wimbledon	YT	07/91	90-01	212	33	18
Watford	Tr	08/02	02-04	105	6	7
Cardiff C	Tr	03/05	04-05	30	8	1
Millwall	Tr	08/06	06-07	15	6	0

ARDRON Walter (Wally)
Born: Rotherham, South Yorkshire, England, 19 September, 1918 CF
Died: Rotherham, South Yorkshire, England, February, 1978

League Club	Source	Date Signed	Seasons Played	Apps	Subs	Gls
Rotherham U	Denaby U	12/38	38	1	-	0
Rotherham U	Denaby U	12/41	46-48	122	-	98
Nottingham F	Tr	07/49	49-54	182	-	123

ARENDSE Andre Leander
Born: Cape Town, South Africa, 27 June, 1967 G
South Africa: 67

League Club	Source	Date Signed	Seasons Played	Apps	Subs	Gls
Fulham	Cape Town Spurs (RSA)	08/97	97	6	0	0
Oxford U	Tr	07/99	99	13	0	0

ARENTOFT Preben (Ben)
Born: Copenhagen, Denmark, 1 November, 1942 M
Denmark: 9

League Club	Source	Date Signed	Seasons Played	Apps	Subs	Gls
Newcastle U	Greenock Morton	03/69	68-70	46	4	2
Blackburn Rov	Tr	09/71	71-73	94	0	3

ARESTIDOU Andreas
Born: Lambeth, S London, England, 6 December, 1989 G

League Club	Source	Date Signed	Seasons Played	Apps	Subs	Gls
Blackburn Rov	Sch	07/07				
Shrewsbury T	Tr	07/09	09	2	0	0
Preston NE	Tr	07/10	11	7	0	0
Morecambe	Tr	08/12	12-14	22	2	0

ARFIELD Scott
Born: Livingston, West Lothian, Scotland, 1 November, 1988 M
Scotland: B-1/U21-17/Youth

League Club	Source	Date Signed	Seasons Played	Apps	Subs	Gls
Huddersfield T	Falkirk	07/10	10-12	66	30	7
Burnley	Tr	07/13	13-14	78	4	10

ARGUE James (Jimmy)
Born: Glasgow, Scotland, 26 November, 1911 IF
Died: Lennoxtown, Dunbartonshire, Scotland, 11 April, 1978

League Club	Source	Date Signed	Seasons Played	Apps	Subs	Gls
Birmingham C	St Roch's	12/31				
Chelsea	Tr	05/33	33-46	118	-	30

ARINS Anthony Francis (Tony)
Born: Chesterfield, Derbyshire, England, 26 October, 1958 RB/M

League Club	Source	Date Signed	Seasons Played	Apps	Subs	Gls
Burnley	App	07/76	78-79	29	0	2
Leeds U	Tr	05/80	81	0	1	0
Scunthorpe U	Tr	11/81	81	20	0	1

ARISMENDI Hugo Diego (Diego)
Born: Montevideo, Uruguay, 25 January, 1988 M
Uruguay: 2

League Club	Source	Date Signed	Seasons Played	Apps	Subs	Gls
Stoke C	Nacional (UGY)	09/09				
Brighton & HA	L	03/10	09	3	3	0
Barnsley	L	07/10	10	24	7	1
Huddersfield T	L	03/12	11	7	2	0

ARIYIBI Omogbolahan Gregory (Gboly)
Born: West Virginia, USA, 18 January, 1995 W
USA: Youth

League Club	Source	Date Signed	Seasons Played	Apps	Subs	Gls
Leeds U	Southampton (Sch)	12/13	13	0	2	0
Tranmere Rov	L	03/14	13	0	2	0
Chesterfield	Tr	08/14	14	5	12	1

ARKINS Vincent Thomas (Vinny)
Born: Dublin, Republic of Ireland, 18 September, 1970 F
Republic of Ireland: B/U21-8/Youth

League Club	Source	Date Signed	Seasons Played	Apps	Subs	Gls
Notts Co	Shelbourne (ROI)	09/95	95-96	30	8	8

ARKWRIGHT Ian
Born: Shafton, South Yorkshire, England, 18 September, 1959 M

League Club	Source	Date Signed	Seasons Played	Apps	Subs	Gls
Wolverhampton W	App	09/77	78	3	1	0
Wrexham	Tr	03/80	79-83	102	2	10
Torquay U	L	03/84	83	2	0	0

[ARMANDO SA] CORREIA DE SA Armando Miguel
Born: Maputo, Mozambique, 16 September, 1975 FB
Mozambique: 21

League Club	Source	Date Signed	Seasons Played	Apps	Subs	Gls
Leeds U (L)	Villarreal (SPN)	01/07	06	6	5	0

ARMERO Pablo Estifer
Born: Tumaco, Colombia, 2 November, 1986 LB
Colombia: 58

League Club	Source	Date Signed	Seasons Played	Apps	Subs	Gls
West Ham U (L)	Napoli (ITA)	02/14	13	3	2	0

ARMES Ivan William
Born: Lowestoft, Suffolk, England, 6 April, 1924 WH

League Club	Source	Date Signed	Seasons Played	Apps	Subs	Gls
Norwich C	Brooke Marine	11/46	46-49	61	-	1
Exeter C	Tr	12/51	51-52	14	-	2

ARMFIELD James Christopher (Jimmy)
Born: Denton, Greater Manchester, England, 21 September, 1935 RB
England: 43/FLge-12/U23-9

League Club	Source	Date Signed	Seasons Played	Apps	Subs	Gls
Blackpool	Jnr	09/54	54-70	568	0	6

ARMITAGE Andrew Mark (Andy)
Born: Leeds, England, 17 October, 1968 LB

League Club	Source	Date Signed	Seasons Played	Apps	Subs	Gls
Leeds U	YT	08/87				
Rochdale	Tr	07/88	88	33	3	0

ARMITAGE (FENTON) Kenneth James (Ken)
Born: Sheffield, England, 23 October, 1920 CH
Died: Sheffield, England, 1952

League Club	Source	Date Signed	Seasons Played	Apps	Subs	Gls
Leyton Orient	Gainsborough Trinity	04/46	46	7	-	0
Oldham Ath	Tr	07/47	47	5	-	0

ARMITAGE Louis Greaves
Born: Hull, England, 15 December, 1921 IF

League Club	Source	Date Signed	Seasons Played	Career Record Apps	Subs	Gls

Died: North East Lincolnshire, England, September, 2000

League Club	Source	Date Signed	Seasons Played	Apps	Subs	Gls
Rotherham U	Goole T	12/40	46-47	15	-	9
Grimsby T	Tr	01/48	47	8	-	2

ARMITAGE Stanley Albert (Stan)
Born: Woolwich, SE London, England, 5 June, 1919 IF
Died: Greenwich, SE London, England, 1997

League Club	Source	Date Signed	Seasons Played	Apps	Subs	Gls
Charlton Ath		05/38				
Queens Park Rgrs	Tr	06/46	46	2	-	0

ARMSTRONG Adam James
Born: Newcastle-upon-Tyne, England, 10 February, 1997 F
England: Youth

League Club	Source	Date Signed	Seasons Played	Apps	Subs	Gls
Newcastle U	Sch	02/14	13-14	1	14	0

ARMSTRONG Adam John (Johnny)
Born: Blackpool, Lancashire, England, 6 June, 1925 W
Died: Sligo, Republic of Ireland, February, 2004
Republic of Ireland: LoI-2

League Club	Source	Date Signed	Seasons Played	Apps	Subs	Gls
Chesterfield	Petershill Jnrs	09/49	49	1	-	0

ARMSTRONG Alun
Born: Gateshead, Tyne and Wear, England, 22 February, 1975 F

League Club	Source	Date Signed	Seasons Played	Apps	Subs	Gls
Newcastle U	YT	10/93				
Stockport Co	Tr	06/94	94-97	151	8	48
Middlesbrough	Tr	02/98	97-99	10	19	9
Huddersfield T	L	03/00	99	4	2	0
Ipswich T	Tr	12/00	00-03	50	29	14
Bradford C	L	12/03	03	6	0	1
Darlington	Tr	09/04	04	31	1	9
Rushden & D	Tr	10/05	05	6	3	0
Doncaster Rov	Tr	02/06	05	1	5	0
Darlington	Tr	08/06	06	16	13	2

ARMSTRONG Christopher (Chris)
Born: Newcastle-upon-Tyne, England, 5 August, 1982 M/LB
England: Youth

League Club	Source	Date Signed	Seasons Played	Apps	Subs	Gls
Bury	YT	03/01	00-01	33	0	1
Oldham Ath	Tr	10/01	01-02	64	1	1
Sheffield U	Tr	08/03	03-07	76	19	6
Blackpool	L	10/05	05	5	0	0
Reading	Tr	08/08	08-10	46	1	1

ARMSTRONG Christopher David (Chris)
Born: Ripon, North Yorkshire, England, 8 November, 1984 F

League Club	Source	Date Signed	Seasons Played	Apps	Subs	Gls
Leeds U	YT	11/01				
Stockport Co	Queen of the South	01/05	04	9	2	1

ARMSTRONG Christopher Peter (Chris)
Born: Newcastle-upon-Tyne, England, 19 June, 1971 F
England: B-1

League Club	Source	Date Signed	Seasons Played	Apps	Subs	Gls
Wrexham	Llay Welfare	03/89	89-90	40	20	13
Millwall	Tr	08/91	91-92	11	17	5
Crystal Palace	Tr	09/92	92-94	118	0	45
Tottenham H	Tr	06/95	95-00	117	24	48
Bolton W	Tr	08/02				
Wrexham	Tr	07/03	03-04	37	22	13

ARMSTRONG David
Born: Durham, England, 26 December, 1954 M
England: 3/B-2/U23-4

League Club	Source	Date Signed	Seasons Played	Apps	Subs	Gls
Middlesbrough	App	01/72	71-80	357	2	59
Southampton	Tr	08/81	81-86	222	0	59
Bournemouth	Tr	07/87	87	6	3	2

ARMSTRONG David Thomas (Dave)
Born: Mile End, E London, England, 9 November, 1942 LW

League Club	Source	Date Signed	Seasons Played	Apps	Subs	Gls
Millwall	Hornchurch	12/65	65-67	14	6	1
Brighton & HA	Tr	09/68	68-69	38	6	6

ARMSTRONG Derek James
Born: Carlisle, Cumbria, England, 16 March, 1939 IF

League Club	Source	Date Signed	Seasons Played	Apps	Subs	Gls
Blackpool		08/58	58	1	-	0
Carlisle U	Morecambe	08/61	61	1	-	0

ARMSTRONG Eric
Born: Hebburn, Tyne and Wear, England, 25 May, 1921 WH
Died: Colchester, Essex, England, 28 October, 1975

League Club	Source	Date Signed	Seasons Played	Apps	Subs	Gls
West Ham U	Cramlington Welfare	01/47	47	1	-	0

ARMSTRONG Gary Stephen
Born: West Ham, E London, England, 2 January, 1958 LB

League Club	Source	Date Signed	Seasons Played	Apps	Subs	Gls
Gillingham	Jnr	01/76	75-79	82	4	2
Wimbledon	Tr	03/80	79-81	71	0	0
Gillingham	Barnet	11/83	83	7	1	0
Crewe Alex	Tr	08/84	84	31	0	0

ARMSTRONG George
Born: Hebburn, Tyne and Wear, England, 9 August, 1944 W
Died: Hemel Hempstead, Hertfordshire, England, 31 October, 2000
England: U23-5/Youth

League Club	Source	Date Signed	Seasons Played	Apps	Subs	Gls
Arsenal	Jnr	08/61	61-76	490	10	53
Leicester C	Tr	09/77	77-78	14	1	0
Stockport Co	Tr	09/78	78	34	0	0

ARMSTRONG Gerard Joseph (Gerry)
Born: Belfast, Northern Ireland, 23 May, 1954 F
Northern Ireland: 63

League Club	Source	Date Signed	Seasons Played	Apps	Subs	Gls
Tottenham H	Bangor	11/75	76-80	65	19	10
Watford	Tr	11/80	80-82	50	26	12
West Bromwich A	RCD Mallorca (SPN)	08/85	85	7	1	0
Chesterfield	L	01/86	85	12	0	1
Brighton & HA	Tr	07/86	86-88	30	17	6
Millwall	L	01/87	86	7	0	0

ARMSTRONG Gordon Ian
Born: Newcastle-upon-Tyne, England, 15 July, 1967 M

League Club	Source	Date Signed	Seasons Played	Apps	Subs	Gls
Sunderland	App	07/85	84-95	331	18	50
Bristol C	L	08/95	95	6	0	0
Northampton T	L	01/96	95	4	0	1
Bury	Tr	07/96	96-98	49	22	4
Burnley	Tr	08/98	98-02	88	17	5

ARMSTRONG Ian
Born: Kirkby, Merseyside, England, 16 November, 1981 LW
England: Youth/Schools

League Club	Source	Date Signed	Seasons Played	Apps	Subs	Gls
Liverpool	YT	12/98				
Port Vale	Tr	07/01	01-04	50	39	14

ARMSTRONG James (Jimmy)
Born: Ulverston, Cumbria, England, 14 September, 1943 W

League Club	Source	Date Signed	Seasons Played	Apps	Subs	Gls
Barrow	App	01/61	60-62	17	-	3
Chesterfield	Tr	07/63	63	7	-	0

ARMSTRONG Joel
Born: Chesterfield, Derbyshire, England, 25 September, 1981 G

League Club	Source	Date Signed	Seasons Played	Apps	Subs	Gls
Chesterfield	YT	07/01	99-00	3	1	0

ARMSTRONG John
Born: Airdrie, Lanarkshire, Scotland, 5 September, 1936 G

League Club	Source	Date Signed	Seasons Played	Apps	Subs	Gls
Barrow	Bellshill Ath	03/58	57-58	21	-	0
Nottingham F	Tr	11/58	58-62	20	-	0
Portsmouth	Tr	02/63	62-66	79	0	0
Southport	Tr	08/67	67-70	86	0	0

ARMSTRONG John Robert (Bob)
Born: Newcastle-upon-Tyne, England, 1 November, 1938 IF

League Club	Source	Date Signed	Seasons Played	Apps	Subs	Gls
Darlington		07/59	59	1	-	0

ARMSTRONG Joseph (Joe)
Born: Brighton, England, 16 November, 1931 IF
Died: Barrow, Cumbria, England, 28 February, 1986

League Club	Source	Date Signed	Seasons Played	Apps	Subs	Gls
Southend U	Red Star, Edinburgh	11/52				
Barrow	Tr	07/53	53-57	103	-	33
Workington	Tr	03/58	57-58	25	-	10

ARMSTRONG Joseph Michael (Joe)
Born: Newcastle-upon-Tyne, England, 29 January, 1939 IF

League Club	Source	Date Signed	Seasons Played	Apps	Subs	Gls
Leeds U	Leslie BC	05/57				
Gateshead	Tr	07/59	59	22	-	9

ARMSTRONG Keith Thomas
Born: Corbridge, Northumberland, England, 11 October, 1957 W

League Club	Source	Date Signed	Seasons Played	Apps	Subs	Gls
Sunderland	Jnr	01/75	77	7	4	0
Newport Co	L	08/78	78	3	1	0
Scunthorpe U	L	10/78	78	0	1	0

ARMSTRONG Kenneth (Ken)
Born: Bradford, England, 3 June, 1924 WH
Died: New Zealand, 13 June, 1984
England: 1/B-3/FLge//New Zealand: 9

League Club	Source	Date Signed	Seasons Played	Apps	Subs	Gls
Chelsea	Bradford Rov	12/46	47-56	362	-	25

ARMSTRONG Kenneth Charles (Ken)
Born: Bridgnorth, Shropshire, England, 31 January, 1959 CD

League Club	Source	Date Signed	Seasons Played	Apps	Subs	Gls
Southampton	Kilmarnock	06/83	83	26	0	0
Notts Co	L	03/84	83	10	0	0
Birmingham C	Tr	08/84	84-85	58	0	2

ARMSTRONG Lee William
Born: Cockermouth, Cumbria, England, 19 October, 1972 RB

League Club	Source	Date Signed	Seasons Played	Apps	Subs	Gls
Carlisle U	YT	07/91	90-91	12	8	0

ARMSTRONG Paul George
Born: Dublin, Republic of Ireland, 5 October, 1978 M
Republic of Ireland: U21-2

League Club	Source	Date Signed	Seasons Played	Apps	Subs	Gls
Brighton & HA	YT	07/97	97-99	33	20	2

ARMSTRONG Stephen Mark
Born: Birkenhead, Wirral, England, 23 July, 1976 — F

League Club	Source	Date Signed	Seasons Played	Apps	Subs	Gls
Watford	Vastra Frolunda (SWE)	10/00	00	0	3	0

ARMSTRONG Steven Craig (Craig)
Born: South Shields, Tyne and Wear, England, 23 May, 1975 — M/LB

League Club	Source	Date Signed	Seasons Played	Apps	Subs	Gls
Nottingham F	YT	06/92	97-98	24	16	0
Burnley	L	12/94	94	4	0	0
Bristol Rov	L	01/96	95	4	1	0
Bristol Rov	L	03/96	95	9	0	0
Gillingham	L	10/96	96	10	0	0
Watford	L	01/97	96	3	0	0
Watford	L	03/97	96	12	0	0
Huddersfield T	Tr	02/99	98-01	101	6	5
Sheffield Wed	Tr	02/02	01-03	29	6	1
Grimsby T	L	02/04	03	9	0	1
Bradford C	Tr	01/05	04	4	3	0
Cheltenham T	Tr	07/05	05-06	70	6	2
Gillingham	Tr	07/07	07	12	1	0
Cheltenham T	Tr	01/08	07-08	16	3	0

ARMSTRONG Terence (Terry)
Born: Barnsley, South Yorkshire, England, 10 July, 1958 — M

League Club	Source	Date Signed	Seasons Played	Apps	Subs	Gls
Huddersfield T	App	07/76	76-78	36	4	2
Port Vale	Tr	02/81	80-84	113	3	12

ARMSTRONG Thomas (Tom)
Born: Carlisle, Cumbria, England, 27 February, 1920 — WH
Died: Carlisle, Cumbria, England, April, 1985

League Club	Source	Date Signed	Seasons Played	Apps	Subs	Gls
Carlisle U	Holme Head	08/46	46	4	-	0

ARNASON Kari
Born: Reykjavik, Iceland, 13 October, 1982 — M/CD
Iceland: 38

League Club	Source	Date Signed	Seasons Played	Apps	Subs	Gls
Plymouth Arg	AGF Aarhus (DEN)	07/09	09-10	71	1	3
Rotherham U	Aberdeen	07/12	12-14	115	1	5

ARNAUTOVIC Marko
Born: Vienna, Austria, 19 April, 1989 — RW
Austria: 41/U21-5/Youth

League Club	Source	Date Signed	Seasons Played	Apps	Subs	Gls
Stoke C	Werder Bremen (GER)	09/13	13-14	47	12	5

ARNDALE Neil Darren
Born: Bristol, England, 26 April, 1984 — RB
England: Youth

League Club	Source	Date Signed	Seasons Played	Apps	Subs	Gls
Bristol Rov	Sch	07/03	01-03	2	3	0

ARNELL Alan Jack
Born: Chichester, West Sussex, England, 25 November, 1933 — IF
Died: Chichester, West Sussex, England, 5 May, 2013

League Club	Source	Date Signed	Seasons Played	Apps	Subs	Gls
Liverpool	Worthing	03/54	53-60	69	-	33
Tranmere Rov	Tr	02/61	60-62	68	-	34
Halifax T	Tr	07/63	63	14	-	6

ARNISON Joseph William (Billy)
Born: Johannesburg, South Africa, 27 June, 1924 — CF
Died: South Africa, August, 1996

League Club	Source	Date Signed	Seasons Played	Apps	Subs	Gls
Luton T	Glasgow Rangers	08/48	48-50	44	-	19

ARNISON Paul Simon
Born: Hartlepool, Cleveland, England, 18 September, 1977 — RB

League Club	Source	Date Signed	Seasons Played	Apps	Subs	Gls
Newcastle U	YT	03/96				
Hartlepool U	Tr	03/00	99-03	53	24	3
Carlisle U	Tr	10/03	03-07	72	23	1
Bradford C	Tr	07/08	08	25	2	0
Darlington	Tr	08/09	09	17	1	1

ARNOLD Eric Arthur
Born: Kessingland, Suffolk, England, 13 September, 1922 — LB
Died: Great Yarmouth, Norfolk, England, April, 2002

League Club	Source	Date Signed	Seasons Played	Apps	Subs	Gls
Norwich C	Lowestoft T	09/47	47-51	13	-	0

ARNOLD Ian
Born: Durham, England, 4 July, 1972 — F
England: Semi Pro-2

League Club	Source	Date Signed	Seasons Played	Apps	Subs	Gls
Middlesbrough	YT	01/90	90-91	0	3	0
Carlisle U	Tr	08/92	92-94	34	13	11

ARNOLD James Alexander (Jim)
Born: Stafford, England, 6 August, 1950 — G
England: Semi Pro-2

League Club	Source	Date Signed	Seasons Played	Apps	Subs	Gls
Blackburn Rov	Stafford Rgrs	06/79	79-80	58	0	0
Everton	Tr	08/81	81-83	48	0	0
Preston NE	L	10/82	82	6	0	0
Port Vale	Tr	08/85	85-86	53	0	0

ARNOLD John Walter Leonard
Born: Southwark, S London, England, 6 December, 1954 — F

League Club	Source	Date Signed	Seasons Played	Apps	Subs	Gls
Charlton Ath	App	12/72	72-73	1	4	0

ARNOLD Nathan
Born: Mansfield, Nottinghamshire, England, 26 July, 1987 — LW
England: Semi Pro-1

League Club	Source	Date Signed	Seasons Played	Apps	Subs	Gls
Mansfield T	Sch	08/05	05-07	32	30	8

ARNOLD Nicholas Samuel (Nick)
Born: Tadley, Hampshire, England, 3 July, 1993 — M/RB

League Club	Source	Date Signed	Seasons Played	Apps	Subs	Gls
Reading	Sch	07/11				
Wycombe W	L	06/13	13	30	1	0

ARNOLD Roderick James (Rod)
Born: Wolverhampton, England, 3 June, 1952 — G

League Club	Source	Date Signed	Seasons Played	Apps	Subs	Gls
Wolverhampton W	App	06/70				
Mansfield T	L	02/71	70	17	0	0
Mansfield T	Tr	03/73	72-83	423	0	0

ARNOLD Stephen Frank (Steve)
Born: Crewe, Cheshire, England, 5 January, 1951 — M

League Club	Source	Date Signed	Seasons Played	Apps	Subs	Gls
Crewe Alex	App	01/69	68-70	13	2	0
Liverpool	Tr	09/70	70	1	0	0
Southport	L	01/72	71	16	0	3
Torquay U	L	09/72	72	2	1	1
Rochdale	Tr	06/73	73	37	3	1

ARNOLD Steven John William (Steve)
Born: Welham Green, Hertfordshire, England, 2 August, 1989 — G
England: Semi Pro-1

League Club	Source	Date Signed	Seasons Played	Apps	Subs	Gls
Norwich C	Sch	07/07				
Wycombe W	Eastleigh	01/10				
Stevenage	Tr	07/12	12-13	32	1	0

ARNOTT Andrew John (Andy)
Born: Chatham, Kent, England, 18 October, 1973 — M

League Club	Source	Date Signed	Seasons Played	Apps	Subs	Gls
Gillingham	YT	05/91	91-95	50	23	12
Leyton Orient	Tr	01/96	95-96	47	3	6
Fulham	Tr	06/97	97	0	1	0
Brighton & HA	Tr	10/98	98-99	27	1	2
Colchester U	Tr	09/99	99-00	5	10	0

ARNOTT George William (William)
Born: Edinburgh, Scotland, 29 May, 1935 — RH

League Club	Source	Date Signed	Seasons Played	Apps	Subs	Gls
Crewe Alex	Berwick Rgrs	12/57	57	8	-	0

ARNOTT John Henry
Born: Sydenham, S London, England, 6 September, 1932 — RH

League Club	Source	Date Signed	Seasons Played	Apps	Subs	Gls
West Ham U	Churchfield OB	07/54	53-54	6	-	2
Shrewsbury T	Tr	08/55	55	30	-	6
Bournemouth	Tr	07/56	56-61	173	-	21
Gillingham	Tr	08/62	62-67	183	2	2

ARNOTT Kevin William
Born: Gateshead, Tyne and Wear, England, 28 September, 1958 — M

League Club	Source	Date Signed	Seasons Played	Apps	Subs	Gls
Sunderland	App	09/76	76-81	132	1	16
Blackburn Rov	L	11/81	81	17	0	2
Sheffield U	Tr	06/82	82-86	120	1	11
Blackburn Rov	L	11/82	82	11	1	1
Rotherham U	L	03/83	82	9	0	2
Chesterfield	Vasalund (SWE)	11/87	87-89	67	4	4

ARPHEXAD Pegguy Michel
Born: Les Abymes, Guadeloupe, 18 May, 1973 — G

League Club	Source	Date Signed	Seasons Played	Apps	Subs	Gls
Leicester C	RC Lens (FRA)	08/97	97-99	17	4	0
Liverpool	Tr	07/00	01	1	1	0
Stockport Co	L	09/01	01	3	0	0
Coventry C	Tr	08/03	03	5	0	0
Notts Co	L	03/04	03	3	0	0

ARQUIN Yoann Axel Cyriac
Born: Le Havre, France, 15 April, 1988 — F

League Club	Source	Date Signed	Seasons Played	Apps	Subs	Gls
Hereford U	Red Star Paris (FRA)	07/11	11	16	18	8
Notts Co	Tr	07/12	12-13	31	22	10

ARRIETA Ibon Perez
Born: San Sebastian, Spain, 9 June, 1977 — F

League Club	Source	Date Signed	Seasons Played	Apps	Subs	Gls
Swindon T	Maccabi Hasliya (ISR)	08/07	07	0	4	0

ARROWSMITH Alfred William (Alf)
Born: Manchester, England, 11 December, 1942 — F
Died: Tameside, Greater Manchester, England, May, 2005

League Club	Source	Date Signed	Seasons Played	Apps	Subs	Gls
Liverpool	Ashton U	09/60	61-67	43	4	20
Bury	Tr	12/68	68-69	45	3	11
Rochdale	Tr	06/70	70-71	40	4	14

ARROWSMITH Brian William
Born: Barrow, Cumbria, England, 2 July, 1940 — CD

League Club	Source	Date Signed	Seasons Played	Apps	Subs	Gls
Barrow	Vickers Sports	10/61	61-70	376	2	3

ARSHAVIN Andrei Sergeyevich
Born: Saint Petersburg, Russia, 29 May, 1981 — M/F

Russia: 75

League Club	Source	Date Signed	Seasons Played	Apps	Subs	Gls
Arsenal	Zenit St P'burg (RUS)	02/09	08-12	70	35	23

ARTELL David John (Dave)
Born: Rotherham, South Yorkshire, England, 22 November, 1980 — CD

League Club	Source	Date Signed	Seasons Played	Apps	Subs	Gls
Rotherham U	YT	07/99	99-00	35	2	4
Shrewsbury T	L	09/02	02	27	1	1
Mansfield T	Tr	08/03	03-04	43	2	5
Chester C	Tr	07/05	05-06	76	4	3
Morecambe	Tr	07/07	07-09	102	8	13
Crewe Alex	Tr	07/10	10-11	71	1	6
Northampton T	Tr	08/12	12	10	1	3

ARTER Harry Nicholas
Born: Sidcup, SE London, England, 28 December, 1989 — M
Republic of Ireland: 1/Youth

League Club	Source	Date Signed	Seasons Played	Apps	Subs	Gls
Charlton Ath	Sch	07/07				
Bournemouth	Woking	07/10	10-14	144	19	25
Carlisle U	L	03/11	10	2	3	1

ARTETA Mikel
Born: San Sebastian, Spain, 26 March, 1982 — M
Spain: U21-12/Youth

League Club	Source	Date Signed	Seasons Played	Apps	Subs	Gls
Everton	Real Sociedad (SPN)	01/05	04-11	166	8	27
Arsenal	Tr	08/11	11-14	96	5	14

ARTHUR Adam Joseph
Born: Nottingham, England, 27 October, 1985 — M

League Club	Source	Date Signed	Seasons Played	Apps	Subs	Gls
York C	Sch	-	03	2	1	0

ARTHUR Christopher Anton (Chris)
Born: Enfield, N London, England, 25 January, 1990 — LB/M

League Club	Source	Date Signed	Seasons Played	Apps	Subs	Gls
Northampton T	Havant & Waterlooville	09/11	11	5	2	0
AFC Wimbledon	Havant & Waterlooville	05/13	13	2	24	1

ARTHUR David Robert
Born: Wolverhampton, England, 9 March, 1960 — RB

League Club	Source	Date Signed	Seasons Played	Apps	Subs	Gls
West Bromwich A	App	03/78	81	2	1	0
Walsall	Tr	08/82	82	8	1	0

ARTHUR John (Jackie)
Born: Edenfield, Lancashire, England, 14 December, 1917 — RW
Died: Bury, Greater Manchester, England, 19 November, 1986

League Club	Source	Date Signed	Seasons Played	Apps	Subs	Gls
Everton	Blackburn Rov (Am)	09/36				
Stockport Co	Tr	05/38	38	2	-	0
Chester C	Tr	05/46	46	24	-	3
Rochdale	Tr	04/47	46-53	170	-	25

ARTHUR Kenneth James (Kenny)
Born: Airdrie, Lanarkshire, Scotland, 7 December, 1978 — G

League Club	Source	Date Signed	Seasons Played	Apps	Subs	Gls
Accrington Stan	Partick Thistle	07/07	07-08	66	0	0
Rochdale	Tr	07/09	09	15	0	0

ARTHUR Koby Owusu
Born: Kumasi, Ghana, 3 January, 1996 — W

League Club	Source	Date Signed	Seasons Played	Apps	Subs	Gls
Birmingham C	Sch	03/13	12-14	7	5	0
Cheltenham T	L	07/14	14	1	6	3

ARTHURWORREY Stephen Roy
Born: Hackney, E London, England, 15 October, 1994 — CD

League Club	Source	Date Signed	Seasons Played	Apps	Subs	Gls
Fulham	Sch	10/11				
Tranmere Rov	L	01/14	13	15	2	0
Yeovil T	L	10/14	14	29	0	2

ARTUS Frankie
Born: Bristol, England, 27 September, 1988 — M

League Club	Source	Date Signed	Seasons Played	Apps	Subs	Gls
Bristol C	Sch	04/06				
Brentford	L	08/08	08	0	1	0
Cheltenham T	L	03/09	08	9	0	3
Cheltenham T	L	08/09	09	7	0	0
Chesterfield	L	01/10	09	2	1	0
Cheltenham T	Tr	07/10	10	21	8	3

ARUNDEL Frank William
Born: Plymouth, England, 20 February, 1939 — W
Died: Tavistock, Devon, England, May, 1994

League Club	Source	Date Signed	Seasons Played	Apps	Subs	Gls
Plymouth Arg	Oak Villa	08/56	56	4	-	0
Torquay U	Tr	07/59	59-60	6	-	0

ASABA Carl Edward
Born: Westminster, Central London, England, 28 January, 1973 — F

League Club	Source	Date Signed	Seasons Played	Apps	Subs	Gls
Brentford	Dulwich Hamlet	08/94	95-96	49	5	25
Colchester U	L	02/95	94	9	3	2
Reading	Tr	08/97	97-98	31	2	8
Gillingham	Tr	08/98	98-00	65	12	36
Sheffield U	Tr	03/01	00-02	52	15	23
Stoke C	Tr	08/03	03-04	40	30	9
Millwall	Tr	08/05	05	17	4	3

ASAFU-ADJAYE Edward Yaw (Ed)
Born: Bermondsey, SE London, England, 22 December, 1988 — RB

League Club	Source	Date Signed	Seasons Played	Apps	Subs	Gls
Luton T	Sch	07/07	07-08	24	2	0

ASAMOAH Derek
Born: Accra, Ghana, 1 May, 1981 — F
Ghana: 4

League Club	Source	Date Signed	Seasons Played	Apps	Subs	Gls
Northampton T	Slough T	07/01	01-03	27	86	10
Mansfield T	Tr	08/04	04	24	6	5
Lincoln C	Tr	03/05	04-05	27	8	2
Chester C	L	01/06	05	14	3	8
Shrewsbury T	Tr	08/06	06	34	5	10
Carlisle U	Daegu (KOR)	10/14	14	13	14	4

ASANOVIC Aljosa
Born: Split, Croatia, 14 December, 1965 — M
Croatia: 62//Yugoslavia: 3

League Club	Source	Date Signed	Seasons Played	Apps	Subs	Gls
Derby Co	Real Valladolid (SPN)	06/96	96-97	37	1	7

ASANTE Akwasi
Born: Amsterdam, Netherlands, 6 September, 1992 — F

League Club	Source	Date Signed	Seasons Played	Apps	Subs	Gls
Birmingham C	Sch	02/11				
Northampton T	L	01/12	11	3	1	1
Shrewsbury T	L	03/13	12	3	4	1
Shrewsbury T	L	07/13	13	1	0	0

ASANTI Kyle Emmanuel Kwabena
Born: Ingatestone, Essex, England, 13 November, 1991 — F

League Club	Source	Date Signed	Seasons Played	Apps	Subs	Gls
Southend U	Sch	06/11	10	1	8	1

ASH Mark Christian
Born: Sheffield, England, 22 January, 1968 — RB

League Club	Source	Date Signed	Seasons Played	Apps	Subs	Gls
Rotherham U	App	01/86	86-88	14	6	0
Scarborough	Tr	08/89	89-91	32	7	0

ASH Michael (Micky)
Born: Sheffield, England, 4 September, 1943 — M
Died: Sheffield, England, November, 2012
England: Youth/Schools

League Club	Source	Date Signed	Seasons Played	Apps	Subs	Gls
Sheffield U	App	11/60	63	3	-	1
Scunthorpe U	Tr	09/65	65-66	48	1	7

ASHALL George Henry
Born: Killamarsh, Derbyshire, England, 29 September, 1911 — LW
Died: Wolverhampton, England, May, 1998
England: FLge-1

League Club	Source	Date Signed	Seasons Played	Apps	Subs	Gls
Wolverhampton W	Frickley Colliery	02/36	35-37	84	-	14
Coventry C	Tr	07/38	38-47	62	-	10

ASHALL James (Jimmy)
Born: Chesterfield, Derbyshire, England, 13 December, 1933 — RB

League Club	Source	Date Signed	Seasons Played	Apps	Subs	Gls
Leeds U	Hasland OB	10/51	55-60	89	-	0

ASHBEE Ian
Born: Birmingham, England, 6 September, 1976 — DM
England: Youth

League Club	Source	Date Signed	Seasons Played	Apps	Subs	Gls
Derby Co	YT	11/94	94	1	0	0
Cambridge U	Tr	12/96	96-01	192	11	11
Hull C	Tr	07/02	02-10	243	0	10
Preston NE	Tr	01/11	10-11	22	4	0

ASHBY Barry John
Born: Harlesden, NW London, England, 2 November, 1970 — CD

League Club	Source	Date Signed	Seasons Played	Apps	Subs	Gls
Watford	YT	12/88	89-93	101	13	3
Brentford	Tr	03/94	93-96	119	2	4
Gillingham	Tr	08/97	97-04	270	3	7

ASHBY Joshua James (Josh)
Born: Oxford, England, 3 May, 1996 — M

League Club	Source	Date Signed	Seasons Played	Apps	Subs	Gls
Oxford U	Sch	02/14	14	2	0	0

ASHCROFT Charles Thomas (Charlie)
Born: Chorley, Lancashire, England, 3 July, 1926 — G
Died: Preston, Lancashire, England, 15 March, 2010
England: B-1

League Club	Source	Date Signed	Seasons Played	Apps	Subs	Gls
Liverpool	Eccleston Jnrs	05/46	46-54	87	-	0
Ipswich T	Tr	06/55	55	7	-	0
Coventry C	Tr	06/57	57	19	-	0

ASHCROFT Kane John
Born: Leeds, England, 19 March, 1986 — M

League Club	Source	Date Signed	Seasons Played	Apps	Subs	Gls
York C	Sch	-	03	1	1	0

ASHCROFT Lee
Born: Preston, Lancashire, England, 7 September, 1972 — W
England: U21-1

League Club	Source	Date Signed	Seasons Played	Apps	Subs	Gls
Preston NE	YT	07/91	90-92	78	13	13
West Bromwich A	Tr	08/93	93-96	66	24	17
Notts Co	L	03/96	95	4	2	0
Preston NE	L	09/96	96	7	0	3

League Club	Source	Date Signed	Seasons Played	Apps	Subs	Gls
Preston NE	Tr	11/96	96-97	56	1	19
Grimsby T	Tr	08/98	98-99	52	9	15
Wigan Ath	Tr	08/00	00-01	37	9	8
Port Vale	L	10/02	02	3	0	0
Huddersfield T	L	12/02	02	4	0	0

ASHCROFT Llewellyn Lloyd (Llew)
Born: Flint, Wales, 10 July, 1921 — RW
Died: Southport, Merseyside, England, 13 June, 2005

League Club	Source	Date Signed	Seasons Played	Apps	Subs	Gls
Tranmere Rov	Flint T	08/45	46	20	-	4

ASHCROFT William (Billy)
Born: Liverpool, England, 1 October, 1952 — F

League Club	Source	Date Signed	Seasons Played	Apps	Subs	Gls
Wrexham	Jnr	10/70	70-77	196	23	72
Middlesbrough	Tr	09/77	77-81	139	20	21
Tranmere Rov	Twente Enschede (NED)	08/85	85	16	7	2

ASHDJIAN John Anthony
Born: Hackney, E London, England, 13 September, 1972 — W

League Club	Source	Date Signed	Seasons Played	Apps	Subs	Gls
Scarborough	Northampton T (YT)	07/91	91-93	40	27	14

ASHDOWN Jamie Lawrence
Born: Wokingham, Berkshire, England, 30 November, 1980 — G

League Club	Source	Date Signed	Seasons Played	Apps	Subs	Gls
Reading	YT	11/99	00-03	12	1	0
Bournemouth	L	08/02	02	2	0	0
Rushden & D	L	11/03	03	19	0	0
Portsmouth	Tr	07/04	04-11	108	1	0
Norwich C	L	10/06	06	2	0	0
Leeds U	Tr	08/12				
Crawley T	Tr	08/14	14	9	0	0
Oxford U	Tr	02/15	14	5	0	0

ASHE Armour Donald
Born: Paisley, Renfrewshire, Scotland, 14 October, 1925 — RB
Died: Accrington, Lancashire, England, 15 June, 1968

League Club	Source	Date Signed	Seasons Played	Apps	Subs	Gls
Stockport Co	St Mirren	06/53	53	2	-	0
Accrington Stan	Tr	09/53	53-57	162	-	0
Gateshead	Tr	11/57	57-58	54	-	1
Southport	Tr	07/59	59	14	-	2

ASHE Norman James
Born: Bloxwich, West Midlands, England, 16 November, 1943 — RW
England: Youth/Schools

League Club	Source	Date Signed	Seasons Played	Apps	Subs	Gls
Aston Villa	App	05/61	59-61	5	-	0
Rotherham U	Tr	03/63	62	6	-	1

ASHENDEN Russell Edward
Born: South Ockendon, Essex, England, 4 February, 1961 — M

League Club	Source	Date Signed	Seasons Played	Apps	Subs	Gls
Northampton T	App	02/79	78-79	6	12	0

ASHENDEN Scott
Born: Basildon, England, 3 February, 1974 — W

League Club	Source	Date Signed	Seasons Played	Apps	Subs	Gls
Southend U	YT	07/92	92	4	1	0

ASHER Alistair Andrew
Born: Leicester, England, 14 October, 1980 — RB

League Club	Source	Date Signed	Seasons Played	Apps	Subs	Gls
Mansfield T	YT	06/99	99-01	53	20	0

ASHER Sydney James (Syd)
Born: Portsmouth, England, 24 December, 1930 — CF
Died: Portsmouth, England, 13 August, 1994

League Club	Source	Date Signed	Seasons Played	Apps	Subs	Gls
Portsmouth	Jnr	08/48				
Northampton T	Hastings U	11/56	56	21	-	11

ASHER Thomas (Tommy)
Born: Dunscroft, South Yorkshire, England, 21 December, 1936 — IF
England: Schools

League Club	Source	Date Signed	Seasons Played	Apps	Subs	Gls
Notts Co	Ilkeston T	07/54	57-58	31	-	4

ASHFIELD George Owen
Born: Manchester, England, 7 April, 1934 — FB
Died: Chester, England, March, 1985

League Club	Source	Date Signed	Seasons Played	Apps	Subs	Gls
Stockport Co	Jnr	09/51				
Aston Villa	Tr	03/54	55-57	9	-	0
Chester C	Tr	02/59	58	5	-	0

ASHFORD Ryan Marc
Born: Honiton, Devon, England, 13 October, 1981 — LB

League Club	Source	Date Signed	Seasons Played	Apps	Subs	Gls
Southampton	YT	01/01				
Torquay U	Tr	03/02	01	1	1	1

ASHIKODI Moses
Born: Lagos, Nigeria, 27 June, 1987 — F/LW
England: Youth

League Club	Source	Date Signed	Seasons Played	Apps	Subs	Gls
Millwall	Sch	-	02	0	5	0
West Ham U	Tr	08/04				
Gillingham	L	08/05	05	0	4	0
Watford	Glasgow Rangers	01/07	06	0	2	0
Bradford C	L	03/07	06	8	0	2
Swindon T	L	01/08	07	4	6	0
Hereford U	L	08/08	08	4	2	0
Shrewsbury T	Tr	02/09	08	4	4	1

ASHINGTON Ryan David
Born: Paignton, Devon, England, 28 March, 1983 — RW

League Club	Source	Date Signed	Seasons Played	Apps	Subs	Gls
Torquay U	YT	07/01	00-02	9	7	0

ASHLEY John (Joe)
Born: Clowne, Derbyshire, England, 10 June, 1931 — G
Died: Chesterfield, Derbyshire, England, 24 August, 2008

League Club	Source	Date Signed	Seasons Played	Apps	Subs	Gls
York C	Frickley Colliery	10/50	50	9	-	0

ASHLEY Kevin Mark
Born: Birmingham, England, 31 December, 1968 — RB

League Club	Source	Date Signed	Seasons Played	Apps	Subs	Gls
Birmingham C	App	01/87	86-90	56	1	1
Wolverhampton W	Tr	09/90	90-92	87	1	1
Peterborough U	Tr	08/94	94-95	36	0	0
Doncaster Rov	L	03/96	95	3	0	0

ASHMAN George Allan (Allan)
Born: Rotherham, South Yorkshire, England, 30 May, 1928 — CF
Died: Walsall, West Midlands, England, 30 November, 2002

League Club	Source	Date Signed	Seasons Played	Apps	Subs	Gls
Nottingham F	Sheffield U (Am)	04/46	48-49	13	-	3
Carlisle U	Tr	06/51	51-57	206	-	99

ASHMAN Ronald George (Ron)
Born: Whittlesey, Cambridgeshire, England, 19 May, 1926 — WH
Died: Scunthorpe, North Lincolnshire, England, 24 January, 2004

League Club	Source	Date Signed	Seasons Played	Apps	Subs	Gls
Norwich C	Whittlesey	05/44	47-63	592	-	55

ASHMORE Alfred Maxwell (Max)
Born: Sheffield, England, 11 September, 1937 — G

League Club	Source	Date Signed	Seasons Played	Apps	Subs	Gls
Sheffield U		08/57	57	1	-	0
Bradford C	Tr	07/61	61	9	-	0
Chesterfield	Tr	10/62	62	2	-	0

ASHMORE George Arthur (Arthur)
Born: Swadlincote, Derbyshire, England, 11 August, 1946 — M

League Club	Source	Date Signed	Seasons Played	Apps	Subs	Gls
Doncaster Rov	Frickley Colliery	11/66	66-67	3	0	0

ASHMORE James Charles
Born: Sheffield, England, 2 March, 1986 — M

League Club	Source	Date Signed	Seasons Played	Apps	Subs	Gls
Sheffield U	Sch	07/04				
Macclesfield T	L	01/08	07	7	1	0

ASHTON Dean
Born: Crewe, Cheshire, England, 24 November, 1983 — F
England: 1/U21-8/Youth

League Club	Source	Date Signed	Seasons Played	Apps	Subs	Gls
Crewe Alex	YT	02/01	00-04	131	28	60
Norwich C	Tr	01/05	04-05	44	0	17
West Ham U	Tr	01/06	05-06	33	13	15

ASHTON Derek
Born: Worksop, Nottinghamshire, England, 4 July, 1922 — FB
Died: Telford, England, 16 February, 1997

League Club	Source	Date Signed	Seasons Played	Apps	Subs	Gls
Wolverhampton W		09/41				
Aston Villa	Tr	05/46	46-48	8	-	0

ASHTON John
Born: Reading, England, 4 July, 1954 — F

League Club	Source	Date Signed	Seasons Played	Apps	Subs	Gls
Reading	Jnr	04/72	71-74	10	3	1

ASHTON Jonathan Frank (Jon)
Born: Plymouth, England, 4 August, 1979 — RB

League Club	Source	Date Signed	Seasons Played	Apps	Subs	Gls
Plymouth Arg	YT	07/97	98-99	27	7	0
Exeter C	Tr	07/00	00	7	6	0

ASHTON Jonathan James (Jon)
Born: Nuneaton, Warwickshire, England, 4 October, 1982 — CD
England: Semi Pro-4

League Club	Source	Date Signed	Seasons Played	Apps	Subs	Gls
Leicester C	YT	01/01	01-02	3	6	0
Notts Co	L	11/02	02	4	0	0
Oxford U	Tr	08/03	03-05	92	5	1
Stevenage	Grays Ath	05/10	10-14	142	4	2

ASHTON Kenneth James (Ken)
Born: Irlam, Greater Manchester, England, 12 December, 1936 — RB
Died: Warrington, Cheshire, England, March, 2008

League Club	Source	Date Signed	Seasons Played	Apps	Subs	Gls
Stockport Co	Bolton W (Am)	09/56	57-61	39	-	0

ASHTON Nathan Wesley
Born: Beckton, E London, England, 30 January, 1987 — LB
England: Youth

League Club	Source	Date Signed	Seasons Played	Apps	Subs	Gls
Charlton Ath	Sch	02/05				
Fulham	Tr	08/07	07	1	0	0
Crystal Palace	L	03/08	07	1	0	0
Wycombe W	Tr	07/08	08	0	11	0

ASHTON Neil John
Born: Liverpool, England, 15 January, 1985 — LB

League Club	Source	Date Signed	Seasons Played	Apps	Subs	Gls
Tranmere Rov	Sch	04/03	03	0	1	0

League Club	Source	Date Signed	Seasons Played	Career Record Apps	Subs	Gls
Shrewsbury T	L	12/04	04-08	133	24	3
Macclesfield T	L	01/08	07	19	0	1
ASHTON Roger William						
Born: Llanidloes, Powys, Wales, 16 August, 1921						G
Died: Neath, Wales, July, 1985						
Wrexham		12/45				
Cardiff C		04/48	47	1	-	0
Newport Co	Bath C	12/49	49	10	-	0
Newport Co	Merthyr Tydfil	12/50	50	1	-	0
ASHURST John (Jackie)						
Born: Coatbridge, Lanarkshire, Scotland, 12 October, 1954						CD
Sunderland	App	10/71	72-79	129	11	4
Blackpool	Tr	10/79	79-80	53	0	3
Carlisle U	Tr	08/81	81-85	194	0	2
Leeds U	Tr	07/86	86-88	88	1	1
Doncaster Rov	Tr	11/88	88-89	73	0	1
Doncaster Rov	Bridlington T	11/90	90-91	66	0	1
Rochdale	Tr	08/92	92	1	0	0
ASHURST Leonard (Len)						
Born: Liverpool, England, 10 March, 1939						LB
England: U23-1/Youth						
Sunderland	Prescot Cables	12/57	58-69	403	5	4
Hartlepool U	Tr	03/71	70-72	42	4	2
ASHWORTH Alec						
Born: Southport, Merseyside, England, 1 October, 1939						IF
Died: Southport, Merseyside, England, 20 June, 1995						
Everton	Jnr	05/57	57-59	12	-	3
Luton T	Tr	10/60	60-61	63	-	20
Northampton T	Tr	07/62	62	30	-	25
Preston NE	Tr	06/63	63-65	42	1	14
ASHWORTH Barry						
Born: Stockport, Greater Manchester, England, 18 August, 1942						M
Southend U	Bangor C	07/63	63-64	31	-	5
Hartlepool U	Tr	03/65	64-65	45	0	4
Tranmere Rov	Tr	07/66	66	21	0	3
Chester C	Tr	08/67	67-69	116	3	12
ASHWORTH Frederick (Fred)						
Born: Oldham, Greater Manchester, England, 26 January, 1928						CH
Died: Bury, Greater Manchester, England, December, 2010						
Blackburn Rov		10/48				
Shrewsbury T	Tr	11/51	51-52	56	-	1
ASHWORTH Ian						
Born: Blackburn, Greater Manchester, England, 17 December, 1958						LW
Manchester U	App	12/75				
Crewe Alex	Tr	07/79	79	7	6	0
ASHWORTH John						
Born: Nottingham, England, 4 July, 1937						CD
England: Amateur-6						
Portsmouth (Am)	Wealdstone	08/62	62	1	-	0
ASHWORTH Joseph Matthew (Joe)						
Born: Huddersfield, West Yorkshire, England, 6 January, 1943						CD
Died: Rochdale, Greater Manchester, England, 23 May, 2002						
Bradford Park Ave	Jnr	01/60	61	3	-	0
York C	Tr	05/62	62-64	57	-	0
Bournemouth	Tr	06/65	65-66	60	0	2
Southend U	Tr	07/67	67	36	0	2
Rochdale	Tr	07/68	68-71	132	0	3
Chester C	Tr	12/71	71	5	0	0
Stockport Co	Tr	06/72	72	14	0	0
ASHWORTH Luke Alexander						
Born: Bolton, Greater Manchester, England, 4 December, 1989						CD
Wigan Ath	Sch	07/08				
Leyton Orient	L	08/08	08	1	2	0
Leyton Orient	Tr	01/09	08-09	7	3	0
Rotherham U	Tr	07/10	10	3	6	0
ASHWORTH Neil						
Born: Southend-on-Sea, England, 16 January, 1968						M
Rochdale	App	07/85	84	1	0	0
ASHWORTH Philip Anthony (Phil)						
Born: Burnley, Lancashire, England, 4 April, 1953						F
Blackburn Rov	Nelson	01/75				
Bournemouth	Tr	09/75	75	30	1	2
Workington	Tr	07/76	76	38	1	7
Southport	Tr	08/77	77	22	2	9
Rochdale	Tr	07/78	78	9	2	0
Portsmouth	Tr	09/79	79	3	1	4
Scunthorpe U	Tr	07/80	80	14	9	3

League Club	Source	Date Signed	Seasons Played	Career Record Apps	Subs	Gls
ASKEW William (Billy)						
Born: Great Lumley, County Durham, England, 2 October, 1959						M
Middlesbrough	App	10/77	79-81	10	2	0
Hull C	Gateshead	09/82	82-89	247	6	19
Newcastle U	Tr	03/90	89-90	5	1	0
Shrewsbury T	L	01/91	90	5	0	0
ASKEY Colin						
Born: Stoke-on-Trent, England, 3 October, 1932						RW
Port Vale	Jnr	10/49	49-57	200	-	21
Walsall	Tr	07/58	58-61	83	-	12
Mansfield T	Tr	06/62	62-63	30	-	2
ASKEY John Colin						
Born: Stoke-on-Trent, England, 4 November, 1964						RW
England: Semi Pro-1						
Macclesfield T	Milton U	01/86	97-02	136	45	31
ASKHAM Lee Raymond						
Born: Killamarsh, Derbyshire, England, 25 February, 1990						M
Chesterfield	Sheffield U (Sch)	12/08	08	0	1	0
ASKOU Jens Berthel						
Born: Videbaek, Denmark, 19 August, 1982						CD
Norwich C	Kasimpasa (TKY)	08/09	09-10	23	4	2
Millwall	L	01/11	10	1	0	0
ASPAS Iago						
Born: Moana, Spain, 1 August, 1987						F
Liverpool	Celta Vigo (SPN)	06/13	13	5	9	0
ASPDEN John Raymond (Ray)						
Born: Horwich, Greater Manchester, England, 6 February, 1938						CH
Rochdale	Bolton W (Am)	05/55	55-65	297	0	2
ASPIN Neil						
Born: Gateshead, Tyne and Wear, England, 12 April, 1965						CD
Leeds U	App	10/82	81-88	203	4	5
Port Vale	Tr	07/89	89-98	343	5	3
Darlington	Tr	07/99	99-00	50	0	0
Hartlepool U	Tr	01/01	00	5	5	0
ASPINALL Brendan James						
Born: Johannesburg, South Africa, 22 July, 1975						CD
Mansfield T	Huddersfield T (Jnr)	07/94	94	13	7	0
ASPINALL John						
Born: Ashton-under-Lyne, Greater Manchester, England, 27 April, 1916						WH
Died: Tameside, Greater Manchester, England, September, 1996						
Oldham Ath	Stalybridge Celtic	05/36	36-38	11	-	0
Bolton W	Ashton National	09/45	46-49	14	-	0
ASPINALL John Joseph						
Born: Birkenhead, Wirral, England, 15 March, 1959						M
Tranmere Rov	Cammell Laird	10/82	82-84	100	7	25
Tranmere Rov	Bangor C	07/87	87	11	1	1
ASPINALL Warren						
Born: Wigan, Greater Manchester, England, 13 September, 1967						M
England: Youth						
Wigan Ath	App	08/85	84-85	21	12	10
Everton	Tr	02/86	85-86	0	7	0
Wigan Ath	L	02/86	85	18	0	12
Aston Villa	Tr	02/87	86-87	40	4	14
Portsmouth	Tr	08/88	88-93	97	35	21
Bournemouth	L	08/93	93	4	2	1
Swansea C	L	10/93	93	5	0	0
Bournemouth	Tr	12/93	93-94	26	1	8
Carlisle U	Tr	03/95	94-97	99	8	12
Brentford	Tr	11/97	97-98	41	2	5
Colchester U	Tr	02/99	98-99	22	0	5
Brighton & HA	Tr	09/99	99-00	19	13	3
ASPINALL Wayne						
Born: Wigan, Greater Manchester, England, 10 December, 1964						LB
Wigan Ath	Atherton Collieries	06/83	83-84	8	0	0
ASPREY William (Bill)						
Born: Wolverhampton, England, 11 September, 1936						D
Stoke C	Jnr	09/53	53-65	304	0	23
Oldham Ath	Tr	01/66	65-67	80	0	4
Port Vale	Tr	12/67	67-68	30	1	0
ASPRILLA Hinestroza Faustino Hernan (Faustino)						
Born: Cali, Colombia, 10 November, 1969						F
Colombia: 57						
Newcastle U	Parma (ITA)	02/96	95-97	36	12	9
ASQUITH Beaumont						
Born: Wakefield, England, 16 September, 1910						IF

Died: Barnsley, South Yorkshire, England, 12 April, 1977

League Club	Source	Date Signed	Seasons Played	Apps	Subs	Gls
Barnsley	Painthorpe A	07/33	34-38	105	-	40
Manchester U	Tr	05/39				
Barnsley	Tr	07/42	46-47	40	-	5
Bradford C	Tr	09/48	48-49	31	-	4

ASSAIDI Oussama
Born: Nador, Morocco, 15 August, 1988 LW
Morocco: 13

League Club	Source	Date Signed	Seasons Played	Apps	Subs	Gls
Liverpool	Heerenveen (NED)	08/12	12	0	4	0
Stoke C	L	08/13	13	12	7	4
Stoke C	L	09/14	14	1	8	0

ASSOMBALONGA Britt Curtis
Born: Kinshasa, DR Congo, 6 December, 1992 F

League Club	Source	Date Signed	Seasons Played	Apps	Subs	Gls
Watford	Jnr	07/10	11	2	2	0
Southend U	L	08/12	12	40	3	15
Peterborough U	Tr	07/13	13	41	2	23
Nottingham F	Tr	08/14	14	27	2	15

ASSOU-EKOTTO Benoit Pierre David
Born: Arras, France, 24 March, 1984 LB
Cameroon: 24

League Club	Source	Date Signed	Seasons Played	Apps	Subs	Gls
Tottenham H	RC Lens (FRA)	07/06	06-12	151	4	4
Queens Park Rgrs	L	09/13	13	30	1	0

ASSOUMANI Mansour
Born: Nice, France, 30 January, 1983 CD
Mali: 1

League Club	Source	Date Signed	Seasons Played	Apps	Subs	Gls
Leeds U	SF Siegen (GER)	12/08	08	0	1	0
Stockport Co	Wrexham	08/10	10	34	2	1

ASSULIN Gai Yigaal
Born: Nahariya, Israel, 9 April, 1991 LW
Israel: 1/U21-22

League Club	Source	Date Signed	Seasons Played	Apps	Subs	Gls
Manchester C	Barcelona Jnrs (SPN)	12/10				
Brighton & HA	L	02/12	11	2	5	0

ASTAFJEVS Vitalis
Born: Riga, Latvia, 3 April, 1971 M
Latvia: 167

League Club	Source	Date Signed	Seasons Played	Apps	Subs	Gls
Bristol Rov	Skonto Riga (LAT)	01/00	99-02	87	22	16

ASTALL Gordon
Born: Horwich, Greater Manchester, England, 22 September, 1927 RW
England: 2/B-1/FLge-1

League Club	Source	Date Signed	Seasons Played	Apps	Subs	Gls
Plymouth Arg	Southampton (Am)	11/47	47-53	188	-	42
Birmingham C	Tr	10/53	53-60	235	-	59
Torquay U	Tr	07/61	61-62	33	-	10

ASTBURY Michael John (Mike)
Born: Kippax, West Yorkshire, England, 22 January, 1964 G

League Club	Source	Date Signed	Seasons Played	Apps	Subs	Gls
York C	App	01/82	80-85	48	0	0
Peterborough U	L	01/86	85	4	0	0
Darlington	Tr	03/86	85-86	38	0	0
Chester C	Tr	07/87	87	5	0	0
Chesterfield	Tr	07/88	88	8	0	0

ASTBURY Thomas Arthur (Tommy)
Born: Buckley, Flintshire, Wales, 9 February, 1920 RH
Died: Chester, England, October, 1993
Wales: War-2

League Club	Source	Date Signed	Seasons Played	Apps	Subs	Gls
Chester C	Mold Alex	05/38	46-54	303	-	38

ASTLE Jeffrey (Jeff)
Born: Eastwood, Nottinghamshire, England, 13 May, 1942 F
Died: East Staffordshire, England, 19 January, 2002
England: 5/FLge-2

League Club	Source	Date Signed	Seasons Played	Apps	Subs	Gls
Notts Co	John Player	10/59	61-64	103	-	31
West Bromwich A	Tr	09/64	64-73	290	2	137

ASTON Alfred John (John)
Born: Newport, Wales, 29 July, 1930 LW
Died: Newport, Wales, 30 November, 1992

League Club	Source	Date Signed	Seasons Played	Apps	Subs	Gls
Newport Co	Newport YMCA	04/48	47-50	6	-	1

ASTON John
Born: Manchester, England, 28 June, 1947 LW
England: U23-1

League Club	Source	Date Signed	Seasons Played	Apps	Subs	Gls
Manchester U	App	06/63	64-71	139	16	25
Luton T	Tr	07/72	72-77	171	3	31
Mansfield T	Tr	09/77	77	24	7	4
Blackburn Rov	Tr	07/78	78-79	12	3	2

ASTON John
Born: Prestwich, Greater Manchester, England, 3 September, 1921 LB
Died: Glossop, Derbyshire, England, 31 July, 2003
England: 17/FLge-2

League Club	Source	Date Signed	Seasons Played	Apps	Subs	Gls
Manchester U	Jnr	12/39	46-53	253	-	29

ASTON Philip Thomas
Born: Measham, Leicestershire, England, 13 May, 1924 WH
England: Amateur-3

League Club	Source	Date Signed	Seasons Played	Apps	Subs	Gls
Walsall	Measham Imperial	12/51	51	10	-	0

ASTON Stanley (Stan)
Born: Nuneaton, Warwickshire, England, 10 May, 1940 CD

League Club	Source	Date Signed	Seasons Played	Apps	Subs	Gls
Hartlepool U	Burton A	12/66	66-67	20	1	0

ASTON Walter Vivian (Viv)
Born: Coseley, West Midlands, England, 16 October, 1918 FB
Died: Bury, Greater Manchester, England, March, 1999

League Club	Source	Date Signed	Seasons Played	Apps	Subs	Gls
Bournemouth	Wolverhampton W (Am)	12/35				
Bury	Tr	12/36	38-47	23	-	0
Oldham Ath	Tr	07/48	48-51	30	-	1
Chester C	Tr	01/52				

ATAJIC Bahrudin
Born: Vastervik, Sweden, 16 November, 1993 F
Bosnia & Herzegovina: U21-3

League Club	Source	Date Signed	Seasons Played	Apps	Subs	Gls
Shrewsbury T (L)	Glasgow Celtic	01/14	13	3	10	0

ATANGANA Nigel Steven Alfred
Born: Corbeil-Essonnes, France, 9 September, 1989 DM

League Club	Source	Date Signed	Seasons Played	Apps	Subs	Gls
Portsmouth	Havant & Waterlooville	06/14	14	16	14	1

ATANGANA Simon Pierre Mvondo (Mvondo)
Born: Yaounde, Cameroon, 10 July, 1979 F
Cameroon: 1

League Club	Source	Date Signed	Seasons Played	Apps	Subs	Gls
Port Vale (L)	Dundee U	01/02	01	1	1	0
Colchester U	Dundee U	11/02	02	1	5	0

ATHERSYCH Russell (Russ)
Born: Sheffield, England, 21 September, 1962 M

League Club	Source	Date Signed	Seasons Played	Apps	Subs	Gls
Chesterfield	App	09/80	81-82	11	9	0

ATHERTON Dewi Lewis
Born: Bangor, Gwynedd, Wales, 6 July, 1951 M

League Club	Source	Date Signed	Seasons Played	Apps	Subs	Gls
Blackburn Rov	Jnr	07/68	68-70	9	1	0

ATHERTON Francis Gordon (Gordon)
Born: Horwich, Greater Manchester, England, 18 June, 1934 LH

League Club	Source	Date Signed	Seasons Played	Apps	Subs	Gls
Bury	Bury Amats	09/55	55-64	327	-	14
Swindon T	Tr	12/64	64-65	31	0	0
Bury	Tr	01/66	65	7	0	0

ATHERTON James Geoffrey (Jim)
Born: Queensferry, Flintshire, Wales, 2 April, 1923 G
Died: Flint, Wales, 1 February, 2010
Wales: Amateur

League Club	Source	Date Signed	Seasons Played	Apps	Subs	Gls
Wrexham (Am)	Chester C (Am)	07/47	47-48	18	-	0

ATHERTON Peter
Born: Orrell, Greater Manchester, England, 6 April, 1970 CD
England: U21-1/Schools

League Club	Source	Date Signed	Seasons Played	Apps	Subs	Gls
Wigan Ath	YT	02/88	87-91	145	4	1
Coventry C	Tr	08/91	91-93	113	1	0
Sheffield Wed	Tr	06/94	94-99	214	0	9
Bradford C	Tr	07/00	00-04	90	4	3
Birmingham C	L	02/01	00	10	0	0

ATIENO Taiwo Leo
Born: Brixton, S London, England, 6 August, 1985 F
Kenya: 4

League Club	Source	Date Signed	Seasons Played	Apps	Subs	Gls
Walsall	Tr	07/04	04-05	1	4	0
Rochdale	L	10/04	04	6	7	2
Chester C	L	02/05	04	3	1	1
Darlington	L	03/06	05	0	3	0
Stevenage	Luton T	02/11	10	1	0	0
Torquay U	Tr	07/11	11	17	26	6
Barnet		12/12	12	1	3	0

ATKIN John Michael (Mick)
Born: Scunthorpe, North Lincolnshire, England, 14 February, 1948 CD
Died: Grimsby, North Lincolnshire, England, 15 January, 2008

League Club	Source	Date Signed	Seasons Played	Apps	Subs	Gls
Scunthorpe U		09/69	69-74	115	4	0

ATKIN Paul Anthony
Born: Nottingham, England, 3 September, 1969 CD
England: Youth/Schools

League Club	Source	Date Signed	Seasons Played	Apps	Subs	Gls
Notts Co	YT	07/87				
Bury	Tr	03/89	88-90	14	7	1
York C	Tr	07/91	91-96	131	22	3
Leyton Orient	L	03/97	96	5	0	0
Scarborough	Tr	08/97	97	26	8	1

ATKINS Alfred James Trevor (Trevor)
Born: Exeter, England, 17 August, 1941 RW

League Club	Source	Date Signed	Seasons Played	Apps	Subs	Gls
Exeter C	Jnr	08/58	57-59	3	-	3

ATKINS Arthur Walter
Born: Tokyo, Japan, 21 February, 1925 CH
Died: Sutton Coldfield, West Midlands, England, 7 January, 1988

League Club	Source	Date Signed	Seasons Played	Apps	Subs	Gls
Birmingham C	Paget Rgrs	11/48	49-53	97	-	0
Shrewsbury T	Tr	06/54	54	16	-	0

ATKINS Dennis
Born: Bradford, England, 8 November, 1938 RB

League Club	Source	Date Signed	Seasons Played	Apps	Subs	Gls
Huddersfield T	Jnr	12/55	59-66	194	0	0
Bradford C	Tr	05/68	67-70	108	0	0

ATKINS Ian Leslie
Born: Birmingham, England, 16 January, 1957 M

League Club	Source	Date Signed	Seasons Played	Apps	Subs	Gls
Shrewsbury T	App	01/75	75-81	273	5	58
Sunderland	Tr	08/82	82-83	76	1	6
Everton	Tr	11/84	84-85	6	1	1
Ipswich T	Tr	09/85	85-87	73	4	4
Birmingham C	Tr	03/88	87-89	93	0	6
Birmingham C	Colchester U	09/91	91	5	3	0
Cambridge U	Tr	12/92	92	1	1	0
Doncaster Rov	Sunderland (NC)	01/94	93	7	0	0

ATKINS Mark Nigel
Born: Doncaster, South Yorkshire, England, 14 August, 1968 DM
England: Schools

League Club	Source	Date Signed	Seasons Played	Apps	Subs	Gls
Scunthorpe U	Jnr	07/86	84-87	45	5	2
Blackburn Rov	Tr	06/88	88-95	224	33	35
Wolverhampton W	Tr	09/95	95-98	115	11	9
York C	Tr	08/99	99	10	0	2
Hull C	Doncaster Rov	03/01	00	8	0	0
Shrewsbury T	Tr	07/01	01-02	71	1	3

ATKINS Robert Gary (Bob)
Born: Leicester, England, 16 October, 1962 CD

League Club	Source	Date Signed	Seasons Played	Apps	Subs	Gls
Sheffield U	Enderby T	07/82	82-84	36	4	3
Preston NE	Tr	02/85	84-89	198	2	5

ATKINS Ross Michael
Born: Derby, England, 3 November, 1989 G

League Club	Source	Date Signed	Seasons Played	Apps	Subs	Gls
Derby Co	Sch	07/08	10	1	0	0
Burton A	L	07/11	11	45	0	0
Burton A	L	08/12	12	4	0	0

ATKINS William Mark (Bill)
Born: Solihull, West Midlands, England, 9 May, 1939 F

League Club	Source	Date Signed	Seasons Played	Apps	Subs	Gls
Aston Villa	Birmingham GPO	05/58				
Swindon T	Tr	06/59	59-64	75	-	28
Halifax T	Tr	08/65	65-66	74	0	33
Stockport Co	Tr	03/67	66-68	92	0	37
Portsmouth	Tr	04/69	68-69	11	0	2
Halifax T	Tr	11/69	69-72	123	2	37
Rochdale	Tr	12/72	72-73	25	0	7
Darlington	Tr	09/73	73-74	41	3	12

ATKINSON Arthur Ian (Ian)
Born: Carlisle, Cumbria, England, 19 December, 1932 IF
Died: Poole, Dorset, England, March, 1995

League Club	Source	Date Signed	Seasons Played	Apps	Subs	Gls
Carlisle U		06/51	52-56	123	-	54
Exeter C	Tr	07/57	57	8	-	2

ATKINSON Brian
Born: Sheffield, England, 16 November, 1934 RH

League Club	Source	Date Signed	Seasons Played	Apps	Subs	Gls
Sheffield U		06/53				
Halifax T	Tr	06/56	56-58	67	-	0

ATKINSON Brian
Born: Darlington, County Durham, England, 19 January, 1971 LM
England: U21-6

League Club	Source	Date Signed	Seasons Played	Apps	Subs	Gls
Sunderland	YT	07/89	88-95	119	22	4
Carlisle U	L	01/96	95	2	0	0
Darlington	Tr	08/96	96-01	174	19	12

ATKINSON Bryan Herbert
Born: Saffron Walden, Essex, England, 15 April, 1934 WH
Died: Hertford, England, 10 August, 1989

League Club	Source	Date Signed	Seasons Played	Apps	Subs	Gls
Watford	Bishops Stortford	06/54	55-56	20	-	0

ATKINSON Charles (Charlie)
Born: Hull, England, 17 December, 1932 WH/IF
Died: Pudsey, West Yorkshire, England, November, 2010

League Club	Source	Date Signed	Seasons Played	Apps	Subs	Gls
Hull C	Marist OB	05/50	53-55	37	-	2
Bradford Park Ave	Tr	07/56	56-63	339	-	50
Bradford C	Tr	06/64	64	16	-	1

ATKINSON Charles Brown Clayton (Charlie)
Born: Haswell, County Durham, England, 5 May, 1938 CD

League Club	Source	Date Signed	Seasons Played	Apps	Subs	Gls
Hartlepool U	Eppleton CW	12/58	59-63	47	-	0

ATKINSON Christopher Roy (Chris)
Born: Halifax, West Yorkshire, England, 13 February, 1992 M

League Club	Source	Date Signed	Seasons Played	Apps	Subs	Gls
Huddersfield T	Sch	07/10	10-12	5	5	1
Chesterfield	L	09/12	12	13	2	5
Tranmere Rov	L	07/13	13	22	0	2
Bradford C	L	01/14	13	1	3	0
Crewe Alex	Tr	07/14	14	8	11	0

ATKINSON Dalian Robert
Born: Shrewsbury, Shropshire, England, 21 March, 1968 F
England: B-1

League Club	Source	Date Signed	Seasons Played	Apps	Subs	Gls
Ipswich T	App	06/85	85-88	49	11	18
Sheffield Wed	Tr	07/89	89	38	0	10
Aston Villa	Real Sociedad (SPN)	09/91	91-94	79	8	23
Manchester C (L)	Fenerbahce (TKY)	03/97	96	7	1	2

ATKINSON David
Born: Shildon, County Durham, England, 27 April, 1993 D
England: Youth

League Club	Source	Date Signed	Seasons Played	Apps	Subs	Gls
Middlesbrough	Sch	07/10				
Carlisle U	L	03/15	14	6	1	0

ATKINSON David John
Born: Hull, England, 3 April, 1951 W

League Club	Source	Date Signed	Seasons Played	Apps	Subs	Gls
Hartlepool U	App	-	68	8	0	1
Charlton Ath	Tr	05/69				

ATKINSON Frederick James (Fred)
Born: Newcastle-upon-Tyne, England, 24 August, 1919 WH/IF
Died: Newcastle-upon-Tyne, England, July, 1991

League Club	Source	Date Signed	Seasons Played	Apps	Subs	Gls
Gateshead		12/45	46-48	32	-	6

ATKINSON Graeme
Born: Hull, England, 11 November, 1971 LW/M

League Club	Source	Date Signed	Seasons Played	Apps	Subs	Gls
Hull C	YT	05/90	89-94	129	20	23
Preston NE	Tr	10/94	94-97	63	16	6
Rochdale	L	12/97	97	5	1	0
Brighton & HA	Tr	03/98	97-98	16	0	0
Scunthorpe U	Tr	11/98	98	0	1	0
Scarborough	Tr	02/99	98	15	0	1
Rochdale	Tr	07/99	99-01	40	11	5

ATKINSON Graham James
Born: Liverpool, England, 17 May, 1943 M

League Club	Source	Date Signed	Seasons Played	Apps	Subs	Gls
Oxford U	Aston Villa (Am)	02/60	62	18	-	4
Oxford U	Cambridge U	12/64	64-73	303	4	73

ATKINSON Harold
Born: Liverpool, England, 28 July, 1925 CF
Died: Newcastle-upon-Tyne, England, 4 September, 2003

League Club	Source	Date Signed	Seasons Played	Apps	Subs	Gls
Tranmere Rov	Carlton	03/45	46-54	185	-	91
Chesterfield	Tr	07/55				

ATKINSON Hugh Anthony
Born: Dublin, Republic of Ireland, 8 November, 1960 M
Republic of Ireland: U21-1

League Club	Source	Date Signed	Seasons Played	Apps	Subs	Gls
Wolverhampton W	App	11/78	79-81	38	8	3
Exeter C	Tr	10/83	83	28	0	1
York C	Tr	07/84	84	3	4	0
Darlington	L	03/85	84	7	0	0

ATKINSON John Edward (Jack)
Born: Washington, Tyne and Wear, England, 20 December, 1913 CH
Died: Bolton, Greater Manchester, England, 1977
England: Schools

League Club	Source	Date Signed	Seasons Played	Apps	Subs	Gls
Bolton W	Washington Colliery	09/31	32-47	240	-	4
New Brighton	Tr	05/48	48-49	52	-	0

ATKINSON Jonathan David (Jon)
Born: Ashington, Northumberland, England, 18 September, 1972 F

League Club	Source	Date Signed	Seasons Played	Apps	Subs	Gls
Darlington	Morpeth T	03/97	96	2	3	0

ATKINSON Patrick Darren (Paddy)
Born: Downtown Core, Singapore, 22 May, 1970 LB

League Club	Source	Date Signed	Seasons Played	Apps	Subs	Gls
Hartlepool U	Sheffield U (YT)	08/88	88-89	9	12	3
York C	Workington	11/95	95-97	36	5	0
Scarborough	Tr	08/98	98	23	4	0

ATKINSON Paul
Born: Chester-le-Street, County Durham, England, 19 January, 1966 W
England: Youth

League Club	Source	Date Signed	Seasons Played	Apps	Subs	Gls
Sunderland	App	11/83	83-87	46	14	5
Port Vale	Tr	06/88	88	4	0	3
Hartlepool U	L	03/90	89	5	6	1

ATKINSON Paul Graham
Born: Pudsey, West Yorkshire, England, 14 August, 1961 W

League Club	Source	Date Signed	Seasons Played	Apps	Subs	Gls
Oldham Ath	App	08/79	79-82	139	4	11
Watford	Tr	07/83	83	8	3	0
Oldham Ath	Tr	08/85	85-87	29	4	1
Swansea C	L	12/86	86	6	0	1
Bolton W	L	02/87	86	2	1	0

League Club	Source	Date Signed	Seasons Played	Apps	Subs	Gls
Swansea C	L	03/87	86	12	0	2
Burnley	Tr	07/88	88-89	18	4	1

ATKINSON Peter
Born: Gainsborough, Lincolnshire, England, 14 December, 1949 — D

League Club	Source	Date Signed	Seasons Played	Apps	Subs	Gls
Rotherham U		05/69	69	3	0	0

ATKINSON Peter
Born: Middlesbrough, England, 13 September, 1924 — G
Died: Middlesbrough, England, 1972

League Club	Source	Date Signed	Seasons Played	Apps	Subs	Gls
Hull C	Billingham Synthonia	04/47	46-47	6	-	0

ATKINSON Peter Maurice Carl
Born: Spilsby, Lincolnshire, England, 20 September, 1929 — G
Died: Leatherhead, Surrey, England, 29 January, 2000

League Club	Source	Date Signed	Seasons Played	Apps	Subs	Gls
Walsall	Walsall YMCA	11/49	49-51	2	-	0

ATKINSON Robert Guy (Rob)
Born: North Ferriby, East Riding of Yorkshire, England, 29 April, 1987 — CD
England: Semi Pro-2

League Club	Source	Date Signed	Seasons Played	Apps	Subs	Gls
Barnsley	Sch	07/06	03-06	6	2	0
Rochdale	L	10/07	07	0	2	0
Grimsby T	L	11/07	07	24	0	1
Grimsby T	Tr	10/08	08-09	67	1	4
Fleetwood T	Tr	07/12	12	18	0	1
Accrington Stan	L	09/12	12	12	0	0
Accrington Stan	Tr	07/13	13-14	55	4	3

ATKINSON Ronald Frederick (Ron)
Born: Liverpool, England, 18 March, 1939 — RH

League Club	Source	Date Signed	Seasons Played	Apps	Subs	Gls
Aston Villa	BSA Tools	05/56				
Oxford U	Tr	07/59	62-71	383	1	14

ATKINSON Trevor
Born: Bishop Auckland, County Durham, England, 23 November, 1942 — CD
Died: Durham, England, 31 October, 1992

League Club	Source	Date Signed	Seasons Played	Apps	Subs	Gls
Darlington	Spennymoor U	11/63	63-68	135	4	3
Bradford Park Ave	Tr	01/69	68-69	59	1	6

ATKINSON Trevor Royal
Born: Barnsley, South Yorkshire, England, 19 November, 1928 — LW
Died: Wrexham, Wales, July, 2011

League Club	Source	Date Signed	Seasons Played	Apps	Subs	Gls
Hull C	Buckley Jnrs	05/46	46	2	-	0
Barnsley	Tr	08/48				

ATKINSON Walter
Born: Ryton-on-Tyne, Tyne and Wear, England, 31 August, 1920 — WH
Died: Newcastle-upon-Tyne, England, June, 2009

League Club	Source	Date Signed	Seasons Played	Apps	Subs	Gls
Norwich C	Hexham Hearts	01/49	51	1	-	0

ATKINSON Wesley (Wes)
Born: West Bromwich, West Midlands, United Kingdom, 13 October, 1994 — RB

League Club	Source	Date Signed	Seasons Played	Apps	Subs	Gls
West Bromwich A	Sch	07/14				
Cambridge U	L	11/14	14	0	2	0

ATKINSON William (Bill)
Born: Sunderland, England, 21 December, 1944 — RW
Died: Nuneaton, Warwickshire, England, 24 June, 2013
England: Schools

League Club	Source	Date Signed	Seasons Played	Apps	Subs	Gls
Birmingham C	App	03/62				
Torquay U	Tr	06/64	64	19	-	7

ATKINSON William Henry (Will)
Born: Beverley, East Riding of Yorkshire, England, 14 October, 1988 — W

League Club	Source	Date Signed	Seasons Played	Apps	Subs	Gls
Hull C	Sch	12/06	09-10	5	1	1
Port Vale	L	10/07	07	3	1	0
Mansfield T	L	01/08	07	10	2	0
Rochdale	L	11/09	09	15	0	3
Rotherham U	L	11/10	10	3	0	1
Rochdale	L	01/11	10	15	6	2
Plymouth Arg	L	08/11	11	20	2	4
Bradford C	Tr	01/12	11-12	32	22	2
Southend U	Tr	07/13	13-14	69	12	4

ATOUBA Thimothee Essama
Born: Douala, Cameroon, 17 February, 1982 — M/LB
Cameroon: 42

League Club	Source	Date Signed	Seasons Played	Apps	Subs	Gls
Tottenham H	FC Basel (SUI)	08/04	04	15	3	1

ATSU Christian Twasam
Born: Accra, Ghana, 10 January, 1992 — RW
Ghana: 33

League Club	Source	Date Signed	Seasons Played	Apps	Subs	Gls
Chelsea	FC Porto (POR)	09/13				
Everton	L	08/14	14	1	4	0

ATTEVELD Raymond (Ray)
Born: Amsterdam, Netherlands, 8 September, 1966 — RB/M

League Club	Source	Date Signed	Seasons Played	Apps	Subs	Gls
Everton	Haarlem (NED)	08/89	89-91	41	10	1
West Ham U	L	02/92	91	1	0	0
Bristol C	Tr	03/92	91-92	9	5	1

ATTHEY Nicholas (Nick)
Born: Tantobie, County Durham, England, 8 May, 1946 — CD

League Club	Source	Date Signed	Seasons Played	Apps	Subs	Gls
Walsall	App	07/63	63-76	429	10	17

ATTLEY Brian Robert
Born: Cardiff, Wales, 23 August, 1955 — FB/M

League Club	Source	Date Signed	Seasons Played	Apps	Subs	Gls
Cardiff C	App	08/73	74-78	73	6	1
Swansea C	Tr	02/79	78-81	83	6	6
Derby Co	Tr	02/82	81-83	54	1	1
Oxford U	L	03/83	82	5	0	0

ATTWELL Frederick Reginald (Reg)
Born: Shifnal, Shropshire, England, 23 March, 1920 — WH
Died: Burnley, Lancashire, England, 2 December, 1986
England: FLge-1

League Club	Source	Date Signed	Seasons Played	Apps	Subs	Gls
West Ham U	Denaby U	04/38	37-46	5	-	0
Burnley	Tr	10/46	46-54	244	-	9
Bradford C	Tr	10/54	54	24	-	0

ATTWELL Jamie Wayne
Born: Bristol, England, 8 June, 1982 — G

League Club	Source	Date Signed	Seasons Played	Apps	Subs	Gls
Bristol C	Tottenham H (YT)	08/01				
Torquay U	Tr	07/02	02	2	2	0

ATYEO Peter John Walter (John)
Born: Dilton, Wiltshire, England, 7 February, 1932 — CF
Died: Warminster, Wiltshire, England, 8 June, 1993
England: 6/B-3/FLge-2/U23-2/Youth

League Club	Source	Date Signed	Seasons Played	Apps	Subs	Gls
Portsmouth (Am)	Westbury U	09/50	50	1	-	0
Bristol C	Tr	06/51	51-65	596	0	315

AUBEY Lucien Yann Sherril
Born: Brazzaville, Congo, 24 May, 1984 — LB
Congo: 3//France: U21

League Club	Source	Date Signed	Seasons Played	Apps	Subs	Gls
Portsmouth (L)	RC Lens (FRA)	01/08	07	1	2	0

AUDEL Thierry Gerard
Born: Nice, France, 15 January, 1987 — D

League Club	Source	Date Signed	Seasons Played	Apps	Subs	Gls
Crewe Alex	Macclesfield T	06/13	13-14	3	1	0

AUGER Ryan Scott
Born: Cambridge, England, 9 May, 1994 — RB/M

League Club	Source	Date Signed	Seasons Played	Apps	Subs	Gls
Southend U	Sch	07/13	13	1	0	0

AUGUSTE Joseph (Joe)
Born: Port of Spain, Trinidad, 24 November, 1955 — F

League Club	Source	Date Signed	Seasons Played	Apps	Subs	Gls
Exeter C	Hounslow	09/83	83	7	3	0

AULD Robert (Bertie)
Born: Glasgow, Scotland, 23 March, 1938 — LW
Scotland: 3/SLge-2

League Club	Source	Date Signed	Seasons Played	Apps	Subs	Gls
Birmingham C	Glasgow Celtic	05/61	61-64	126	-	26

AULD Walter Bottomley
Born: Bellshill, Lanarkshire, Scotland, 9 July, 1929 — LW
Died: Newcastle-upon-Tyne, England, December, 1988

League Club	Source	Date Signed	Seasons Played	Apps	Subs	Gls
Middlesbrough	Bellshill Ath	12/50	50	2	-	1

AUNGER Geoffrey Edward Ramer (Geoff)
Born: Red Deer, Alberta, Canada, 4 February, 1968 — F
Canada:

League Club	Source	Date Signed	Seasons Played	Apps	Subs	Gls
Luton T	Vancouver 86ers (CAN)	09/93	93	5	0	1
Chester C	Tr	12/94	94	1	4	0
Stockport Co	New England Rev (USA)	12/97	97	0	1	0

AURELIO Fabio
Born: Sao Carlos, Brazil, 24 September, 1979 — LB/M
Brazil: U23-13

League Club	Source	Date Signed	Seasons Played	Apps	Subs	Gls
Liverpool	Valencia (SPN)	07/06	06-11	58	29	3

AUSTIN Charles (Charlie)
Born: Hungerford, Berkshire, England, 5 July, 1989 — F

League Club	Source	Date Signed	Seasons Played	Apps	Subs	Gls
Swindon T	Poole T	10/09	09-10	49	5	31
Burnley	Tr	01/11	10-12	69	13	41
Queens Park Rgrs	Tr	08/13	13-14	63	3	35

AUSTIN Dean Barry
Born: Hemel Hempstead, Hertfordshire, England, 26 April, 1970 — RB

League Club	Source	Date Signed	Seasons Played	Apps	Subs	Gls
Southend U	St Albans C	03/90	89-91	96	0	2
Tottenham H	Tr	06/92	92-96	117	7	0
Crystal Palace	Tr	07/98	98-02	127	15	6

AUSTIN John Frank (Frank)
Born: Stoke-on-Trent, England, 6 July, 1933 — LB
Died: Erewash, Derbyshire, England, 12 July, 2004
England: Schools

League Club	Source	Date Signed	Seasons Played	Apps	Subs	Gls
Coventry C	Toton	07/50	52-62	302	-	2
Torquay U	Tr	01/63	62-63	24	-	0

League Club	Source	Date Signed	Seasons Played	Career Record Apps	Subs	Gls
AUSTIN Karl						
Born: Stoke-on-Trent, England, 7 August, 1961						G
Port Vale	Stafford Rgrs	02/85	84	1	0	0
AUSTIN Kevin Levi						
Born: Hackney, E London, England, 12 February, 1973						CD
Trinidad & Tobago: 1						
Leyton Orient	Saffron Walden T	08/93	93-95	101	8	3
Lincoln C	Tr	07/96	96-98	128	1	2
Barnsley	Tr	07/99	99	3	0	0
Brentford	L	10/00	00	3	0	0
Cambridge U	Tr	11/01	01	4	2	0
Bristol Rov	Kettering T	07/02	02-03	52	4	0
Swansea C	Tr	07/04	04-07	107	10	0
Chesterfield	Tr	07/08	08-09	41	13	0
AUSTIN Mitchell Gregory (Mitch)						
Born: Rochdale, Greater Manchester, England, 3 April, 1991						LW
Cambridge U	Stalybridge Celtic	05/13	14	1	0	0
AUSTIN Neil Jeffrey						
Born: Barnsley, South Yorkshire, England, 26 April, 1983						RB
England: Youth						
Barnsley	YT	04/00	02-06	132	16	0
Darlington	Tr	07/07	07-08	52	10	5
Hartlepool U	Tr	07/09	09-14	217	6	10
AUSTIN Rodolph William						
Born: May Pen, Jamaica, 1 June, 1985						M
Jamaica: 71						
Leeds U	SK Brann Bergen (NOR)	08/12	12-14	90	11	8
AUSTIN Roy Leonard						
Born: Islington, N London, England, 26 March, 1960						F
Doncaster Rov	Millwall (App)	08/78	78	3	0	0
AUSTIN Ryan						
Born: Stoke-on-Trent, England, 15 November, 1984						CD
England: Semi Pro-2						
Burton A	Crewe Alex (Sch)	07/09	09-11	72	8	2
AUSTIN Samuel Joseph (Sam)						
Born: Stourbridge, West Midlands, England, 19 December, 1996						F
Burton A	Sch	05/15	14	0	1	0
AUSTIN Terence Willis (Terry)						
Born: Isleworth, W London, England, 1 February, 1954						F
Crystal Palace	Jnr	06/72				
Ipswich T	Tr	05/73	74-75	10	9	1
Plymouth Arg	Tr	10/76	76-77	58	0	18
Walsall	Tr	03/78	77-78	44	3	19
Mansfield T	Tr	03/79	78-80	84	0	31
Huddersfield T	Tr	12/80	80-82	39	3	10
Doncaster Rov	Tr	09/82	82	30	4	5
Northampton T	Tr	08/83	83	42	1	10
AVDIU Kemajl						
Born: Pristina, Kosovo, 22 December, 1976						RW
Bury	Esbjerg (DEN)	08/98	98-99	8	19	1
AVERY Roger Joseph						
Born: Cambridge, England, 17 February, 1961						F
Cambridge U	App	02/79	77	0	1	0
AVEYARD Walter						
Born: Thurnscoe, South Yorkshire, England, 11 June, 1918						CF
Died: Blackpool, Lancashire, England, 16 July, 1985						
Sheffield Wed	Denaby U	10/38	46	4	-	3
Birmingham C	Tr	04/47	47	7	-	3
Port Vale	Tr	06/48	48-51	103	-	26
Accrington Stan	Tr	03/52	51-52	24	-	4
AVINEL Cedric Mickael						
Born: Paris, France, 11 September, 1986						CD
Watford	Creteil (FRA)	02/07	06	1	0	0
AVIS Vernon Charles Sidney						
Born: Marylebone, Central London, England, 24 October, 1935						LB
Died: Northampton, England, June, 1996						
Brentford	Jnr	11/52	53-60	19	-	0
AVRAMOVIC Radojko (Raddy)						
Born: Rijeka, Croatia, 29 November, 1949						G
Yugoslavia: 1						
Notts Co	NK Rijeka (CRO)	08/79	79-82	149	0	0
Coventry C	Inter Montreal (CAN)	09/83	83	18	0	0
AWFORD Andrew Terence (Andy)						
Born: Worcester, England, 14 July, 1972						CD

League Club	Source	Date Signed	Seasons Played	Career Record Apps	Subs	Gls
England: U21-9/Youth/Schools						
Portsmouth	YT	07/89	88-00	293	20	3
AWFORD Nicholas Andrew (Nick)						
Born: Portsmouth, England, 15 April, 1995						LM
Portsmouth	Sch	07/13	12-14	1	1	0
AWUAH Jones						
Born: Accra, Ghana, 10 July, 1983						F/LW
Gillingham	Sch	07/03	02	1	3	0
AXELDAHL Jonas Michael						
Born: Holm, Sweden, 2 September, 1970						F
Sweden: U23-2						
Ipswich T	Foggia (ITA)	07/99	99	1	15	0
Cambridge U	Tr	08/00	00	12	6	2
AYALA Daniel Sanchez						
Born: Seville, Spain, 7 November, 1990						CD
Spain: U21-1						
Liverpool	Sch	02/08	09	2	3	0
Hull C	L	09/10	10	12	0	1
Derby Co	L	02/11	10	16	1	0
Norwich C	Tr	08/11	11	6	1	0
Nottingham F	L	08/12	12	12	0	1
Middlesbrough	Tr	10/13	13-14	46	3	7
AYLING Luke David						
Born: Lambeth, S London, England, 25 August, 1991						RB
Arsenal	Sch	07/09				
Yeovil T	Tr	03/10	09-13	155	11	2
Bristol C	Tr	07/14	14	46	0	4
AYLOTT Stephen John (Steve)						
Born: Ilford, E London, England, 3 September, 1951						DM
West Ham U	App	08/69				
Oxford U	Tr	04/71	71-75	143	11	8
Brentford	Tr	07/76	76-77	6	1	0
AYLOTT Trevor Keith Charles						
Born: Bermondsey, SE London, England, 26 November, 1957						F
Chelsea	App	11/75	77-79	26	3	2
Barnsley	Tr	11/79	79-81	93	3	26
Millwall	Tr	08/82	82	32	0	5
Luton T	Tr	03/83	82-83	32	0	10
Crystal Palace	Tr	07/84	84-85	50	3	12
Barnsley	L	02/86	85	9	0	0
Bournemouth	Tr	08/86	86-90	137	10	27
Birmingham C	Tr	10/90	90-91	25	2	0
Oxford U	Tr	09/91	91	35	2	6
Gillingham	Tr	07/92	92	8	2	2
AYORINDE Samuel Tayo (Sammy)						
Born: Lagos, Nigeria, 20 October, 1974						F
Nigeria: 2/U23/U21						
Leyton Orient	Sturm Graz (AUT)	04/96	95-96	7	6	2
AYRE Colin						
Born: Ashington, Northumberland, England, 14 March, 1956						W
Newcastle U	App	09/73				
Torquay U	Telstar (NED)	09/76	76	2	0	0
AYRE Robert William (Bobby)						
Born: Berwick-on-Tweed, Northumberland, England, 26 March, 1932						CF
England: U23-2						
Charlton Ath	Chippenham T	07/52	52-57	109	-	48
Reading	Tr	05/58	58-59	57	-	24
AYRE William (Billy)						
Born: Ryton-on-Tyne, Tyne and Wear, England, 7 May, 1952						CD
Died: West Lancashire, England, 17 April, 2002						
Hartlepool U	Scarborough	08/77	77-80	141	0	27
Halifax T	Tr	01/81	80-81	63	0	5
Mansfield T	Tr	08/82	82-83	67	0	7
Halifax T	Tr	07/84	84-85	32	0	2
AYRES Frederick Edward (Fred)						
Born: Stoke-on-Trent, England, 17 July, 1926						RW
Crewe Alex		11/48	48	3	-	0
AYRES Harold (Harry)						
Born: Redcar, Cleveland, England, 10 March, 1920						LH
Died: Grays, Essex, England, 5 March, 2002						
Fulham	Clapton	07/46	46-48	38	-	8
Gillingham	Tr	06/50	50-54	136	-	2
AYRES Kenneth Edward (Ken)						
Born: Oxford, England, 15 May, 1956						F
England: Schools						
Manchester U	App	06/73				
Crystal Palace	Tr	11/73	74	3	3	0

League Club	Source	Date Signed	Seasons Played	Apps	Subs	Gls
AYRES Lee Terence						
Born: Birmingham, England, 28 August, 1982						CD
Kidderminster Hrs	Evesham U	06/01	01-02	27	8	2
AYRIS John Patrick (Johnny)						
Born: Wapping, E London, England, 8 January, 1953						RW
England: Youth						
West Ham U	App	10/70	70-76	41	16	1
AYRTON Neil John						
Born: Lewisham, SE London, England, 11 February, 1962						F
Portsmouth	Maidstone U	12/79	80	1	1	0
AYTON James (Jimmy)						
Born: Barrhead, Renfrewshire, Scotland, 15 October, 1923						IF
Died: Leicester, England, 25 August, 1988						
Leicester C	Third Lanark	10/48	48-50	8	-	1
Shrewsbury T	Tr	06/51	51	25	-	1
AZEEZ Adebayo Linford (Ade)						
Born: Orpington, SE London, England, 8 January, 1994						F
England: Youth						
Charlton Ath	Sch	07/12				
Wycombe W	L	11/12	12	0	4	0
Leyton Orient	L	01/13	12	1	0	0
Torquay U	L	09/13	13	6	3	2
Dagenham & Red	L	02/14	13	10	5	3
AFC Wimbledon	Tr	06/14	14	12	31	5
AZPILICUETA Cesar						
Born: Pamplona, Spain, 28 August, 1989						FB
Spain: 10/U21-19/Youth						
Chelsea	Olymp Marseille (FRA)	08/12	12-14	79	6	0

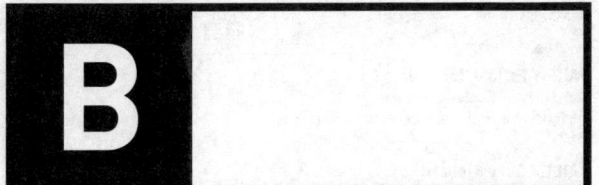

League Club	Source	Date Signed	Seasons Played	Career Record Apps	Subs	Gls
BA Demba						
Born: Paris, France, 25 May, 1985						F
Senegal: 19						
West Ham U	TSG Hoffenheim (GER)	01/11	10	10	2	7
Newcastle U	Tr	06/11	11-12	51	3	29
Chelsea	Tr	01/13	12-13	16	17	7
BA El Hadji						
Born: Paris, France, 5 March, 1993						DM
France: Youth						
Sunderland	Le Havre (FRA)	07/13	13	0	1	0
BA Georges						
Born: Abidjan, Ivory Coast, 24 January, 1979						F
Ivory Coast: 2						
Gillingham (L)	Maccabi Netanya (ISR)	03/08	07	1	3	0
BA Ibrahim						
Born: Dakar, Senegal, 12 November, 1973						M
France: 8						
Bolton W	AC Milan (ITA)	09/03	03	0	9	0
BAAH Peter Hayford						
Born: Rochdale, Greater Manchester, England, 1 May, 1973						LW
Blackburn Rov	YT	06/91	91	1	0	0
Fulham	Tr	07/92	92-93	38	11	4
BAARDSEN Per Espen (Espen)						
Born: San Rafael, USA, 7 December, 1977						G
Norway: 4/U21-31/Youth//USA: Youth						
Tottenham H	S Francisco UAB (USA)	07/96	96-98	22	1	0
Watford	Tr	08/00	00-01	41	0	0
Everton	Tr	12/02	02	1	0	0
BABAYARO Celestine Hycieth						
Born: Kaduna, Nigeria, 29 August, 1978						LB
Nigeria: 27/U23/Youth						
Chelsea	Anderlecht (NED)	06/97	97-04	118	14	5
Newcastle U	Tr	01/05	04-06	45	2	0
BABB Philip Andrew (Phil)						
Born: Lambeth, S London, England, 30 November, 1970						CD
Republic of Ireland: 35/B-1						
Millwall	YT	04/89				
Bradford C	Tr	08/90	90-91	73	7	14
Coventry C	Tr	07/92	92-94	70	7	3
Liverpool	Tr	09/94	94-98	124	4	1
Tranmere Rov	L	01/00	99	4	0	0
Sunderland	Sporting Lisbon (POR)	06/02	02-03	48	0	0
BABBEL Markus						
Born: Munich, Germany, 8 September, 1972						RB
Germany: 51/U21-12						
Liverpool	Bayern Munich (GER)	07/00	00-02	42	0	3
Blackburn Rov	L	08/03	03	23	2	3
BABEL Ryan Guno						
Born: Amsterdam, Netherlands, 19 December, 1986						W
Netherlands: 43/U21-5/Youth						
Liverpool	Ajax (NED)	07/07	07-10	31	60	12
BABER John Michael						
Born: Lambeth, S London, England, 10 October, 1947						W
Southend U	Charlton Ath (App)	08/66	66-70	72	10	18
BABES John						
Born: Lurgan, Armagh, Northern Ireland, 20 November, 1929						RB
Arsenal	Glentoran	01/48				
Scunthorpe U	Tr	09/50	50-51	9	-	0
BACCI Alfredo Giovanni (Alf)						
Born: Bedlington, Northumberland, England, 15 July, 1922						IF
Died: Bedlington, Northumberland, England, January, 1993						
Chesterfield	West Sleekburn Jnrs	08/50	50-51	6	-	2
BACKOS Desmond Patrick (Des)						
Born: Cape Town, South Africa, 13 November, 1950						F
Stoke C	Los Angeles Azt (USA)	10/77	77	1	1	0

League Club	Source	Date Signed	Seasons Played	Career Record Apps	Subs	Gls
BACON Cyril William						
Born: Hammersmith, W London, England, 9 November, 1919						RH
Leyton Orient	Hayes	06/46	46-49	118	-	3
Brentford	Tr	08/50				
BACON Daniel Stephen (Danny)						
Born: Mansfield, Nottinghamshire, England, 20 September, 1980						F
Mansfield T	YT	01/00	99-02	14	30	4
Lincoln C	Hucknall T	07/05	06	1	1	0
BACON Paul Darren						
Born: Forest Gate, E London, England, 20 December, 1970						M
Charlton Ath	YT	01/89	90-92	25	8	0
BACON Ronald Alfred Sydney (Ron)						
Born: Fakenham, Norfolk, England, 4 March, 1935						RW
Norwich C	Holt	12/55	55-57	42	-	6
Gillingham	Tr	05/58	58-60	128	-	15
BACQUE Herve						
Born: Bordeaux, France, 13 July, 1976						F
Luton T	AS Monaco (FRA)	08/98	98	2	5	0
BACUNA Leandro Jones Johan						
Born: Groningen, Netherlands, 21 August, 1991						RB/M
Netherlands: U21-10/Youth						
Aston Villa	Groningen (NED)	06/13	13-14	38	16	5
BACUZZI Guiseppe Luigi Davide (Joe)						
Born: Holborn, Central London, England, 25 September, 1916						RB
Died: Clerkenwell, Central London, England, 1 February, 1995						
England: FLge-1/War-13						
Fulham	Tufnell Park	04/36	36-55	283	-	2
BACUZZI Reno David (Dave)						
Born: Islington, N London, England, 12 October, 1940						RB
England: Youth//Republic of Ireland: LoI-2						
Arsenal	Eastbourne U	05/59	60-63	46	-	0
Manchester C	Tr	04/64	64-65	56	1	0
Reading	Tr	09/66	66-69	107	0	1
BADDELEY Kevin Stuart						
Born: Swindon, England, 12 March, 1962						LB
Bristol C	App	03/80	80	1	0	0
Swindon T	Tr	06/81	81-84	94	1	2
BADDELEY Lee Matthew						
Born: Cardiff, Wales, 12 July, 1974						CD
Wales: U21-2/Youth						
Cardiff C	YT	08/91	90-96	112	21	1
Exeter C	Tr	02/97	96-98	60	6	1
BADES Brian Lawrence						
Born: Farnworth, Greater Manchester, England, 3 July, 1939						W
Accrington Stan		02/60				
Chester C	Horwich RMI	08/63	63	15	-	1
BADGER Colin Albert (Albert)						
Born: Rotherham, South Yorkshire, England, 16 June, 1930						W
Died: Rotherham, South Yorkshire, England, September, 1985						
Rotherham U		11/50	50	2	-	0
BADGER Leonard (Len)						
Born: Sheffield, England, 8 June, 1945						RB
England: FLge-3/U23-13/Youth/Schools						
Sheffield U	App	08/62	62-75	457	1	7
Chesterfield	Tr	01/76	75-77	46	0	0
BADHAM John (Jack)						
Born: Birmingham, England, 31 January, 1919						D
Died: Bromsgrove, Worcestershire, England, 1 January, 1992						
Birmingham C	Muntz Street YC	05/46	47-56	175	-	4
BADIR Walid						
Born: Kafr Qasim, Israel, 12 March, 1974						M
Israel: 74						
Wimbledon	Hapoel PT (ISR)	08/99	99	12	9	1
BADMINTON Roger Geoffrey						
Born: Portsmouth, England, 15 September, 1947						FB
Brighton & HA	Jnr	07/66	66	1	0	0
BADOCK Stephen William (Steve)						
Born: Kensington, Central London, England, 10 September, 1958						RW
Bristol Rov	Bristol Portway	07/85	85	14	3	3
BAGAYOKO Mamadou						
Born: Paris, France, 21 May, 1979						F
Mali: 31						
Doncaster Rov	PAS Giannina (GRE)	01/12	11	2	3	2

BAGGIO Dino
Born: Camposampiero, Italy, 24 July, 1971 — DM
Italy: 60

League Club	Source	Date Signed	Seasons Played	Apps	Subs	Gls
Blackburn Rov	SS Lazio (ITA)	09/03	03	0	9	1

BAGHERI Karim
Born: Tabriz, Iran, 20 February, 1974 — M
Iran: 87

League Club	Source	Date Signed	Seasons Played	Apps	Subs	Gls
Charlton Ath	Pirouzi (IRA)	08/00	00	0	1	0

BAGNALL Reginald (Reg)
Born: Brinsworth, South Yorkshire, England, 22 November, 1926 — FB
Died: Rotherham, South Yorkshire, England, 25 April, 2012

League Club	Source	Date Signed	Seasons Played	Apps	Subs	Gls
Notts Co	Rotherham U (Am)	06/45	46-47	9	-	0

BAGSHAW Paul John
Born: Sheffield, England, 29 May, 1979 — M

League Club	Source	Date Signed	Seasons Played	Apps	Subs	Gls
Barnsley	YT	07/97	98	0	1	0
Carlisle U	L	03/99	98	5	4	0

BAIANO Francesco
Born: Naples, Italy, 24 February, 1968 — F
Italy: 2

League Club	Source	Date Signed	Seasons Played	Apps	Subs	Gls
Derby Co	Fiorentina (ITA)	08/97	97-99	52	12	16

BAIDOO Shabazz Kwame
Born: Hackney, E London, England, 13 April, 1988 — F
England: Youth

League Club	Source	Date Signed	Seasons Played	Apps	Subs	Gls
Queens Park Rgrs	Sch	06/06	04-06	10	18	3
Dagenham & Red	Tr	01/08	07	1	2	0

BAILEY Alan
Born: Macclesfield, Cheshire, England, 1 November, 1978 — F

League Club	Source	Date Signed	Seasons Played	Apps	Subs	Gls
Manchester C	YT	07/97				
Macclesfield T	L	01/99	98	5	5	1
Stockport Co	Tr	08/99	99-00	6	12	1

BAILEY Alexander Christopher (Alex)
Born: Newham, E London, England, 21 September, 1983 — RB
England: Youth

League Club	Source	Date Signed	Seasons Played	Apps	Subs	Gls
Arsenal	YT	07/01				
Chesterfield	Tr	07/04	04-06	87	6	1

BAILEY Alfred Benjamin (Alf)
Born: West Bromwich, West Midlands, England, 16 December, 1927 — CF
Died: Fleetwood, Lancashire, England, September, 1978

League Club	Source	Date Signed	Seasons Played	Apps	Subs	Gls
Walsall (Am)	Darwen	09/53	53	1	-	0

BAILEY Anthony (Tony)
Born: Winsford, Cheshire, England, 3 December, 1939 — RW

League Club	Source	Date Signed	Seasons Played	Apps	Subs	Gls
Crewe Alex (Am)		05/59	59	2	-	0

BAILEY Anthony David (Tony)
Born: Burton-on-Trent, Staffordshire, England, 23 September, 1946 — CD

League Club	Source	Date Signed	Seasons Played	Apps	Subs	Gls
Derby Co	Burton A	09/70	71	1	0	0
Oldham Ath	Tr	01/74	73-74	26	0	1
Bury	Tr	12/74	74-78	124	7	1

BAILEY Danny Stephen
Born: Leyton, NE London, England, 21 May, 1964 — M

League Club	Source	Date Signed	Seasons Played	Apps	Subs	Gls
Bournemouth	App	-	80	1	1	0
Torquay U	Walthamstow Ave	03/84	83	1	0	0
Exeter C	Wealdstone	08/89	89-90	63	1	2
Reading	Tr	12/90	90-91	49	1	2
Fulham	L	07/92	92	2	1	0
Exeter C	Tr	12/92	92-96	143	9	4

BAILEY David
Born: Worksop, Nottinghamshire, England, 11 January, 1957 — F

League Club	Source	Date Signed	Seasons Played	Apps	Subs	Gls
Chesterfield	Jnr	01/76	75	1	0	1

BAILEY Dennis
Born: Holmes Chapel, Cheshire, England, 24 September, 1935 — W

League Club	Source	Date Signed	Seasons Played	Apps	Subs	Gls
Bolton W	Jnr	09/53	56	1	-	0
Port Vale	Tr	08/58	58	1	-	0

BAILEY Dennis Lincoln
Born: Lambeth, S London, England, 13 November, 1965 — F

League Club	Source	Date Signed	Seasons Played	Apps	Subs	Gls
Fulham	Barking	11/86				
Crystal Palace	Farnborough T	12/87	87	0	5	1
Bristol Rov	L	02/89	88	17	0	9
Birmingham C	Tr	08/89	89-90	65	10	23
Bristol Rov	L	03/91	90	6	0	1
Queens Park Rgrs	Tr	07/91	91-92	32	7	10
Charlton Ath	L	10/93	93	0	4	0
Watford	L	03/94	93	2	6	4
Brentford	L	01/95	94	6	0	3
Gillingham	Tr	08/95	95-97	63	25	11
Lincoln C	Tr	03/98	97	1	4	1

BAILEY Ernest John (Jack)
Born: Bristol, England, 17 June, 1921 — LB
Died: Bristol, England, 4 December, 1986

League Club	Source	Date Signed	Seasons Played	Apps	Subs	Gls
Bristol C	BAC, Filton	05/45	46-57	347	-	0

BAILEY Gary Richard
Born: Ipswich, England, 9 August, 1958 — G
England: 2/B-2/U21-14

League Club	Source	Date Signed	Seasons Played	Apps	Subs	Gls
Manchester U	Wits Univ (RSA)	01/78	78-86	294	0	0

BAILEY George Ernest
Born: Doncaster, South Yorkshire, England, 31 October, 1958 — W
England: Schools

League Club	Source	Date Signed	Seasons Played	Apps	Subs	Gls
Manchester U	App	11/75				
Doncaster Rov	L	02/78	77	3	0	0

BAILEY Ian Craig
Born: Middlesbrough, England, 20 October, 1956 — LB

League Club	Source	Date Signed	Seasons Played	Apps	Subs	Gls
Middlesbrough	App	10/74	75-81	140	4	1
Doncaster Rov	L	11/76	76	9	0	0
Carlisle U	L	02/77	76	7	0	1
Bolton W	L	11/81	81	5	0	0
Sheffield Wed	Tr	08/82	82	35	0	0
Blackpool	L	10/84	84	3	0	0
Bolton W	Tr	03/85	84	10	0	0

BAILEY James Joseph
Born: Bollington, Cheshire, England, 18 September, 1988 — DM

League Club	Source	Date Signed	Seasons Played	Apps	Subs	Gls
Crewe Alex	Sch	05/07	07-09	44	2	0
Derby Co	Tr	06/10	10-13	49	10	1
Coventry C	L	09/12	12	29	1	2
Barnsley	Tr	07/14	14	19	6	0

BAILEY John Andrew
Born: Lambeth, S London, England, 6 May, 1969 — M

League Club	Source	Date Signed	Seasons Played	Apps	Subs	Gls
Bournemouth	Enfield	07/95	95-99	136	13	6

BAILEY John Anthony
Born: Liverpool, England, 1 April, 1957 — LB
England: B-1

League Club	Source	Date Signed	Seasons Played	Apps	Subs	Gls
Blackburn Rov	App	04/75	75-78	115	5	1
Everton	Tr	07/79	79-85	171	0	3
Newcastle U	Tr	10/85	85-87	39	1	0
Bristol C	Tr	09/88	88-90	79	1	1

BAILEY John Anthony Kenneth
Born: Manchester, England, 2 July, 1984 — LW
England: Youth

League Club	Source	Date Signed	Seasons Played	Apps	Subs	Gls
Preston NE	YT	07/01	02	0	1	0

BAILEY John Stephen
Born: Oxford, England, 30 July, 1950 — M

League Club	Source	Date Signed	Seasons Played	Apps	Subs	Gls
Swindon T	App	08/68	67	0	2	0

BAILEY Malcolm
Born: Halifax, West Yorkshire, England, 7 May, 1937 — W

League Club	Source	Date Signed	Seasons Played	Apps	Subs	Gls
Bradford Park Ave	Luddendenfoot	04/58	57-58	10	-	1
Leeds U	Tr	08/60				
Accrington Stan	Tr	10/60	60	2	-	0

BAILEY Malcolm Roy
Born: Biddulph, Staffordshire, England, 14 April, 1950 — RH

League Club	Source	Date Signed	Seasons Played	Apps	Subs	Gls
Port Vale	Jnr	05/67	68	2	0	0

BAILEY Mark
Born: Stoke-on-Trent, England, 12 August, 1976 — RB/M

League Club	Source	Date Signed	Seasons Played	Apps	Subs	Gls
Stoke C	YT	07/94				
Rochdale	Tr	10/96	96-98	49	18	1
Lincoln C	Northwich Victoria	10/01	01-03	97	1	1
Macclesfield T	Tr	07/04	04-05	25	1	2

BAILEY Matthew John (Matt)
Born: Crewe, Cheshire, England, 12 March, 1986 — CD

League Club	Source	Date Signed	Seasons Played	Apps	Subs	Gls
Stockport Co	Sch	07/03	04	0	1	0
Scunthorpe U	L	08/04	04	2	2	0
Crewe Alex	Tr	05/05	07	0	2	0

BAILEY Michael Alfred (Mike)
Born: Wisbech, Cambridgeshire, England, 27 February, 1942 — M
England: 2/FLge-3/U23-5

League Club	Source	Date Signed	Seasons Played	Apps	Subs	Gls
Charlton Ath	Jnr	03/59	60-65	151	0	20
Wolverhampton W	Tr	03/66	65-76	360	1	19
Hereford U	Minnesota Kicks (USA)	08/78	78	13	3	1

BAILEY Neil
Born: Billinge, Merseyside, England, 26 September, 1958 — M/LB

League Club	Source	Date Signed	Seasons Played	Apps	Subs	Gls
Burnley	App	07/76				
Newport Co	Ashton U	09/78	78-83	129	5	7
Wigan Ath	Tr	10/83	83-85	31	10	2
Stockport Co	Tr	07/86	86-87	50	1	0

League Club	Source	Date Signed	Seasons Played	Apps	Subs	Gls
Newport Co	L	03/87	86	7	1	1
Blackpool	Rtd	09/92	92-93	8	1	0

BAILEY Nicholas Francis (Nicky)
Born: Putney, SW London, England, 10 June, 1984 — M
England: Semi Pro-4

League Club	Source	Date Signed	Seasons Played	Apps	Subs	Gls
Barnet	Sutton U	06/04	05-06	88	1	12
Southend U	Tr	08/07	07	43	2	9
Charlton Ath	Tr	08/08	08-09	86	1	25
Middlesbrough	Tr	07/10	10-12	84	15	4
Millwall	Tr	08/13	13-14	31	5	1

BAILEY Raymond Reginald (Ray)
Born: Bedford, England, 16 May, 1944 — CD

League Club	Source	Date Signed	Seasons Played	Apps	Subs	Gls
Gillingham	Bedford T	05/66	66-70	154	6	7
Northampton T	L	10/71	71	1	0	0

BAILEY Roy Norman
Born: Epsom, Surrey, England, 26 May, 1932 — G
Died: South Africa, 9 April, 1993

League Club	Source	Date Signed	Seasons Played	Apps	Subs	Gls
Crystal Palace	Jnr	06/49	49-55	118	-	0
Ipswich T	Tr	03/56	55-64	315	-	0

BAILEY Stefan Kyon Lloyd
Born: Brent, NW London, England, 10 November, 1987 — M
England: Semi Pro-1

League Club	Source	Date Signed	Seasons Played	Apps	Subs	Gls
Queens Park Rgrs	Sch	03/06	04-07	14	4	0

BAILEY Steven John (Steve)
Born: Bristol, England, 12 March, 1964 — M

League Club	Source	Date Signed	Seasons Played	Apps	Subs	Gls
Bristol Rov	App	03/82	81	15	1	1

BAILEY Terence (Terry)
Born: Stoke-on-Trent, England, 18 December, 1947 — M

League Club	Source	Date Signed	Seasons Played	Apps	Subs	Gls
Port Vale	Stafford Rgrs	08/74	74-77	161	4	26

BAILEY Thomas Graham (Graham)
Born: Dawley, Telford & Wrekin, England, 22 March, 1920 — RB

League Club	Source	Date Signed	Seasons Played	Apps	Subs	Gls
Huddersfield T	Donnington Wood	03/37	46	33	-	0
Sheffield U	Tr	03/48	47-48	20	-	0

BAILEY William Craig (Craig)
Born: Airdrie, Lanarkshire, Scotland, 6 July, 1944 — CF

League Club	Source	Date Signed	Seasons Played	Apps	Subs	Gls
Brighton & HA	Kirkintilloch Rob Roy	12/61	62	4	-	1

BAILIE Colin James
Born: Belfast, Northern Ireland, 31 March, 1964 — FB/M

League Club	Source	Date Signed	Seasons Played	Apps	Subs	Gls
Swindon T	App	03/82	81-84	105	2	4
Reading	Tr	07/85	85-87	83	1	1
Cambridge U	Tr	08/88	88-91	104	15	3

BAILLIE Douglas (Doug)
Born: Douglas Water, Lanarkshire, Scotland, 27 January, 1937 — CH
Scotland: U23-2/Schools

League Club	Source	Date Signed	Seasons Played	Apps	Subs	Gls
Swindon T	Airdrieonians	03/56	55	1	-	0

BAILLIE James Stuart Andrew
Born: Warrington, Cheshire, England, 27 March, 1996 — RB

League Club	Source	Date Signed	Seasons Played	Apps	Subs	Gls
Crewe Alex	Sch	05/14	14	12	1	0

BAILLIE Joseph (Joe)
Born: Dumfries, Scotland, 26 February, 1929 — LB
Died: Maryhill, Glasgow, Scotland, 23 March, 1966
Scotland: B/SLge-3

League Club	Source	Date Signed	Seasons Played	Apps	Subs	Gls
Wolverhampton W	Glasgow Celtic	12/54	54	1	-	0
Bristol C	Tr	06/56	56	10	-	0
Leicester C	Tr	06/57	57-59	75	-	0
Bradford Park Ave	Tr	06/60	60	7	-	1

BAILY Edward Francis (Eddie)
Born: Clapton, NE London, England, 6 August, 1925 — IF
Died: Welwyn Garden City, England, 10 October, 2010
England: 9/B-3/FLge-6

League Club	Source	Date Signed	Seasons Played	Apps	Subs	Gls
Tottenham H	Jnr	02/46	46-55	296	-	64
Port Vale	Tr	01/56	55-56	26	-	8
Nottingham F	Tr	10/56	56-58	68	-	14
Leyton Orient	Tr	12/58	58-59	29	-	3

BAIN Alexander Edward (Alex)
Born: Edinburgh, Scotland, 22 January, 1936 — CF
Died: 7 November, 2014

League Club	Source	Date Signed	Seasons Played	Apps	Subs	Gls
Huddersfield T	Motherwell	08/57	57-58	29	-	11
Chesterfield	Tr	02/60	59	18	-	9
Bournemouth	Falkirk	08/61	61	8	-	4

BAIN James Alistair (Jimmy)
Born: Blairgowrie, Perthshire, Scotland, 14 December, 1919 — LW

League Club	Source	Date Signed	Seasons Played	Apps	Subs	Gls
Chelsea	Gillingham	05/45	46	9	-	1
Swindon T	Tr	05/47	47-53	235	-	40

BAIN John
Born: Falkirk, Scotland, 23 June, 1957 — M

League Club	Source	Date Signed	Seasons Played	Apps	Subs	Gls
Bristol C	App	07/74	76-78	5	1	0
Brentford	L	02/77	76	17	1	1

BAIN John Shanks
Born: Airdrie, Lanarkshire, Scotland, 20 July, 1946 — RB

League Club	Source	Date Signed	Seasons Played	Apps	Subs	Gls
Bury	Clarkston	07/63	64-66	9	3	0

BAIN Kevin
Born: Kirkcaldy, Fife, Scotland, 19 September, 1972 — M
Scotland: U21-4/Youth/Schools

League Club	Source	Date Signed	Seasons Played	Apps	Subs	Gls
Rotherham U (L)	Dundee	03/97	96	10	2	0

BAIN Kithson Anthony
Born: Grenada, 26 May, 1982 — F
Grenada: 25

League Club	Source	Date Signed	Seasons Played	Apps	Subs	Gls
Tranmere Rov	Ball Dogs (GRN)	09/09	09	0	10	0

BAIN William Clark (Billy)
Born: Alloa, Stirlingshire, Scotland, 16 November, 1924 — CF
Died: East Kilbride, Lanarkshire, Scotland, 7 February, 2010

League Club	Source	Date Signed	Seasons Played	Apps	Subs	Gls
Hartlepool U	Dunfermline Ath	08/50	50	2	-	0

BAINBRIDGE Kenneth Victor (Ken)
Born: Barkingside, E London, England, 15 January, 1921 — LW
Died: Waltham Forest, NE London, England, June, 2011

League Club	Source	Date Signed	Seasons Played	Apps	Subs	Gls
West Ham U	Leyton	11/44	46-49	80	-	16
Reading	Tr	06/50	50-52	89	-	32
Southend U	Tr	02/53	52-54	78	-	25

BAINBRIDGE Peter Edgar
Born: Newton-on-Ouse, North Yorkshire, England, 30 January, 1958 — CD

League Club	Source	Date Signed	Seasons Played	Apps	Subs	Gls
York C	Middlesbrough (App)	11/77	77-78	9	0	0
Darlington	Tr	08/79	79	16	0	0

BAINBRIDGE Robert Esmond
Born: York, England, 22 February, 1931 — CF

League Club	Source	Date Signed	Seasons Played	Apps	Subs	Gls
York C	Terry's	04/54	53-54	4	-	0

BAINBRIDGE Terence (Terry)
Born: Hartlepool, Cleveland, England, 23 December, 1962 — CD

League Club	Source	Date Signed	Seasons Played	Apps	Subs	Gls
Hartlepool U	Henry Smith's BC	12/81	81-83	34	3	1

BAINBRIDGE William (Bill)
Born: Gateshead, Tyne and Wear, England, 9 March, 1922 — IF

League Club	Source	Date Signed	Seasons Played	Apps	Subs	Gls
Manchester U	Ashington	12/45				
Bury	Tr	05/46	46	2	-	1
Tranmere Rov	Tr	11/48	48-53	168	-	64

BAINES Cecil Peter (Peter)
Born: Australia, 11 September, 1919 — IF
Died: Manchester, England, 6 January, 1997

League Club	Source	Date Signed	Seasons Played	Apps	Subs	Gls
Wrexham	Oldham Ath (Am)	04/43	46	6	-	2
Crewe Alex	Tr	11/46	46	8	-	0
Hartlepool U	Tr	06/47	47	9	-	1
New Brighton	Tr	10/47	47	2	-	0

BAINES John Robert
Born: Colchester, Essex, England, 25 September, 1937 — CF

League Club	Source	Date Signed	Seasons Played	Apps	Subs	Gls
Colchester U	Colchester Casuals	01/60	60-62	4	-	0

BAINES Leighton John
Born: Liverpool, England, 11 December, 1984 — LB
England: 30/U21-16

League Club	Source	Date Signed	Seasons Played	Apps	Subs	Gls
Wigan Ath	Sch	01/03	02-06	140	5	4
Everton	Tr	08/07	07-14	248	14	23

BAINES Paul
Born: Burton-on-Trent, Staffordshire, England, 15 January, 1972 — W

League Club	Source	Date Signed	Seasons Played	Apps	Subs	Gls
Stoke C	YT	07/90	90	1	1	0

BAINES Stanley Norman (Stan)
Born: Syston, Leicestershire, England, 28 July, 1920 — W
Died: Leicester, England, March, 1990

League Club	Source	Date Signed	Seasons Played	Apps	Subs	Gls
Leicester C	Coalville T	11/37	38	7	-	1
Northampton T	Tr	07/46	46	1	-	0

BAINES Stephen John (Steve)
Born: Newark, Nottinghamshire, England, 23 June, 1954 — CD

League Club	Source	Date Signed	Seasons Played	Apps	Subs	Gls
Nottingham F	App	07/72	72	2	0	0
Huddersfield T	Tr	07/75	75-77	113	1	10
Bradford C	Tr	03/78	77-79	98	1	17
Walsall	Tr	07/80	80-81	47	1	5
Bury	L	12/81	81	7	0	0
Scunthorpe U	Tr	08/82	82	37	1	1
Chesterfield	Tr	07/83	83-86	132	1	9

BAINES-PILART Adolfo
Born: Pamplona, Spain, 12 February, 1972 — G

League Club	Source	Date Signed	Seasons Played	Apps	Subs	Gls
MK Dons	CD Tenerife (SPN)	08/06	06	19	0	0

BAINS Rikki Lee
Born: Nuneaton, Warwickshire, England, 3 February, 1988 CD

League Club	Source	Date Signed	Seasons Played	Apps	Subs	Gls
Accrington Stan	Coventry C (Sch)	09/06	06	2	1	0
Macclesfield T	Corby T	01/09	08	1	1	0
Darlington	Tr	08/09	09	3	1	0

BAIRD Andrew Crawford (Andy)
Born: East Kilbride, Lanarkshire, Scotland, 18 January, 1979 F

League Club	Source	Date Signed	Seasons Played	Apps	Subs	Gls
Wycombe W	YT	03/98	97-01	55	24	13

BAIRD Christopher Patrick (Chris)
Born: Ballymoney, Antrim, Northern Ireland, 25 February, 1982 RB
Northern Ireland: 65/U21-6/Youth

League Club	Source	Date Signed	Seasons Played	Apps	Subs	Gls
Southampton	YT	01/01	02-06	62	6	3
Walsall	L	09/03	03	10	0	0
Watford	L	03/04	03	8	0	0
Fulham	Tr	07/07	07-12	101	26	4
Reading	Tr	09/13	13	9	0	0
Burnley	Tr	03/14	13	5	2	0
West Bromwich A	Tr	07/14	14	9	10	0

BAIRD Douglas Francis Hogg (Doug)
Born: Falkirk, Scotland, 26 November, 1935 RB
Died: Falkirk, Scotland, December, 2002
Scotland: SLge-1/U23-1

League Club	Source	Date Signed	Seasons Played	Apps	Subs	Gls
Nottingham F	Partick Thistle	09/60	60-62	32	-	0
Plymouth Arg	Tr	10/63	63-67	147	1	1

BAIRD Henry (Harry)
Born: Belfast, Northern Ireland, 17 August, 1913 WH
Died: Northern Ireland, 22 May, 1973
Northern Ireland: 1/NILge-2

League Club	Source	Date Signed	Seasons Played	Apps	Subs	Gls
Manchester U	Linfield	01/37	36-37	49	-	15
Huddersfield T	Tr	09/38	38	19	-	4
Ipswich T	Linfield	06/46	46-51	216	-	6

BAIRD Hugh
Born: Airdrie, Lanarkshire, Scotland, 14 March, 1930 CF
Died: Aberdeen, Scotland, 19 June, 2006
Scotland: 1

League Club	Source	Date Signed	Seasons Played	Apps	Subs	Gls
Leeds U	Airdrieonians	06/57	57-58	45	-	22

BAIRD Ian James
Born: Rotherham, South Yorkshire, England, 1 April, 1964 F
England: Schools

League Club	Source	Date Signed	Seasons Played	Apps	Subs	Gls
Southampton	App	04/82	82-84	20	2	5
Cardiff C	L	11/83	83	12	0	6
Newcastle U	L	12/84	84	4	1	1
Leeds U	Tr	03/85	84-86	84	1	33
Portsmouth	Tr	08/87	87	20	0	1
Leeds U	Tr	03/88	87-89	76	1	17
Middlesbrough	Tr	01/90	89-90	60	3	19
Bristol C	Heart of Midlothian	07/93	93-95	45	12	11
Plymouth Arg	Tr	09/95	95	24	3	5
Brighton & HA	Tr	07/96	96-97	43	1	14

BAIRD John Alfred Gordon (Gordon)
Born: Nottingham, England, 14 January, 1924 WH
Died: Westminster, Central London, England, May, 1999

League Club	Source	Date Signed	Seasons Played	Apps	Subs	Gls
Mansfield T	New Houghton	11/46	46-47	9	-	0

BAIRD Samuel (Sammy)
Born: Denny, Falkirk, Scotland, 13 May, 1930 IF
Died: Bangor, Down, Northern Ireland, 21 April, 2010
Scotland: 7/SLge-5

League Club	Source	Date Signed	Seasons Played	Apps	Subs	Gls
Preston NE	Clyde	06/54	54	15	-	2

BAIRSTOW David Leslie
Born: Bradford, England, 1 September, 1951 F
Died: Marton-cum-Grafton, North Yorkshire, England, 5 January, 1998

League Club	Source	Date Signed	Seasons Played	Apps	Subs	Gls
Bradford C	Jnr	12/71	71-72	10	7	1

BAJNER Balint Marcell
Born: Szombathely, Hungary, 18 November, 1990 F
Hungary: Youth

League Club	Source	Date Signed	Seasons Played	Apps	Subs	Gls
Ipswich T	Bor Dortmund (GER)	07/14	14	1	4	0
Notts Co	Tr	01/15	14	8	11	3

BAK Arkadiusz
Born: Szczecin, Poland, 6 January, 1974 M
Poland: 14

League Club	Source	Date Signed	Seasons Played	Apps	Subs	Gls
Birmingham C (L)	Polonia Warsaw (POL)	12/01	01	2	2	0

BAKALLI Adrian
Born: Bruges, Belgium, 22 November, 1976 F

League Club	Source	Date Signed	Seasons Played	Apps	Subs	Gls
Watford	RWD Molenbeek (BEL)	01/99	99	0	2	0
Swindon T	Tr	03/01	00	1	0	0

BAKARE Michael Adewale Oluwabunmi
Born: Hackney, E London, England, 1 December, 1986 M

League Club	Source	Date Signed	Seasons Played	Apps	Subs	Gls
Macclesfield T	Chelmsford C	01/12	11	0	9	0

BAKAYOGO Zoumana
Born: Paris, France, 11 August, 1986 LB
Ivory Coast: U23-4

League Club	Source	Date Signed	Seasons Played	Apps	Subs	Gls
Millwall	Paris St-Germain (FRA)	08/06	06-07	8	7	0
Tranmere Rov	Alfortville (FRA)	09/09	09-12	98	30	6
Leicester C	Tr	08/13				
Yeovil T	L	01/14	13	1	0	0

BAKAYOKO Amadou
Born: Freetown, Sierra Leone, 1 January, 1996 F

League Club	Source	Date Signed	Seasons Played	Apps	Subs	Gls
Walsall	Sch	12/13	13-14	0	13	0

BAKAYOKO Ibrahima
Born: Seguela, Ivory Coast, 31 December, 1976 F
Ivory Coast: 45

League Club	Source	Date Signed	Seasons Played	Apps	Subs	Gls
Everton	Montpellier (FRA)	10/98	98	17	6	4

BAKER Adam
Born: Leeds, England, 8 December, 1993 F

League Club	Source	Date Signed	Seasons Played	Apps	Subs	Gls
Bradford C	Sch	07/12	11	0	1	0

BAKER Alan Reeves
Born: Tipton, West Midlands, England, 22 June, 1944 M
England: Youth/Schools

League Club	Source	Date Signed	Seasons Played	Apps	Subs	Gls
Aston Villa	App	07/61	60-65	92	1	13
Walsall	Tr	07/66	66-70	128	9	31

BAKER Carl Paul
Born: Prescot, Merseyside, England, 26 December, 1982 RM
England: Semi Pro-2

League Club	Source	Date Signed	Seasons Played	Apps	Subs	Gls
Morecambe	Southport	07/07	07	40	2	10
Stockport Co	Tr	07/08	08-09	34	8	12
Coventry C	Tr	01/10	09-13	125	35	21
MK Dons	Tr	09/14	14	24	8	9

BAKER Charles Joseph (Charlie)
Born: Turners Hill, West Sussex, England, 6 January, 1936 G

League Club	Source	Date Signed	Seasons Played	Apps	Subs	Gls
Brighton & HA	Horsham	05/60	60-62	81	-	0
Aldershot	Tr	07/64	64-65	28	0	0

BAKER Christopher (Chris)
Born: Maltby, South Yorkshire, England, 2 February, 1952 F

League Club	Source	Date Signed	Seasons Played	Apps	Subs	Gls
Barnsley (Am)	Maltby Main	10/71	71	0	1	0

BAKER Clifford Henry (Cliff)
Born: Bristol, England, 11 January, 1924 IF
Died: Bristol, England, December, 2010

League Club	Source	Date Signed	Seasons Played	Apps	Subs	Gls
Bristol Rov	Coalpit Heath	01/47	46	5	-	2

BAKER Clive
Born: Adwick-le-Street, South Yorkshire, England, 5 July, 1934 IF
Died: Rotherham, South Yorkshire, England, 20 February, 2012

League Club	Source	Date Signed	Seasons Played	Apps	Subs	Gls
Doncaster Rov	Intake YC	08/52				
Halifax T	Tr	08/55	55-58	58	-	22
Southport	Tr	07/59				

BAKER Clive Edward
Born: North Walsham, Norfolk, England, 14 March, 1959 G

League Club	Source	Date Signed	Seasons Played	Apps	Subs	Gls
Norwich C	Jnr	07/77	77-80	14	0	0
Barnsley	Tr	08/84	84-90	291	0	0
Coventry C	Tr	08/91				
Ipswich T	Tr	08/92	92-94	47	1	0

BAKER Colin Walter
Born: Cardiff, Wales, 18 December, 1934 LH
Wales: 7/U23-1

League Club	Source	Date Signed	Seasons Played	Apps	Subs	Gls
Cardiff C	Cardiff Nomads	03/53	53-65	297	1	18

BAKER Darren Spencer
Born: Wednesbury, West Midlands, England, 28 June, 1965 M
Wales: Schools

League Club	Source	Date Signed	Seasons Played	Apps	Subs	Gls
Wrexham	Jnr	08/83	82-83	18	6	1

BAKER David Henry
Born: Penzance, Cornwall, England, 21 October, 1928 CH
Died: Nottingham, England, June, 2009

League Club	Source	Date Signed	Seasons Played	Apps	Subs	Gls
Nottingham F	Brush Sports	10/49	49	3	-	0

BAKER David Paul (Paul)
Born: Newcastle-upon-Tyne, England, 5 January, 1963 F

League Club	Source	Date Signed	Seasons Played	Apps	Subs	Gls
Southampton	Bishop Auckland	07/84				
Carlisle U	Tr	07/85	85-86	66	5	11
Hartlepool U	Tr	07/87	87-91	192	5	67
Gillingham	Motherwell	01/93	92-94	58	4	16
York C	Tr	10/94	94-95	36	12	18
Torquay U	Tr	01/96	95-96	30	0	8
Scunthorpe U	Tr	10/96	96	21	0	9
Hartlepool U	Tr	03/97	96-98	25	10	9
Carlisle U	Tr	08/99	99	12	5	2

BAKER Douglas Graham (Doug)
Born: Lewisham, SE London, England, 8 April, 1947 — F

League Club	Source	Date Signed	Seasons Played	Apps	Subs	Gls
Arsenal	App	05/64				
Millwall	Tr	06/66	66	4	1	1

BAKER Frank
Born: Stoke-on-Trent, England, 22 October, 1918 — LW
Died: Stoke-on-Trent, England, 13 November, 1989

League Club	Source	Date Signed	Seasons Played	Apps	Subs	Gls
Stoke C	Port Vale (Am)	06/36	36-49	162	-	32

BAKER Gerald (Gerry)
Born: South Hiendley, West Yorkshire, England, 22 April, 1939 — RB

League Club	Source	Date Signed	Seasons Played	Apps	Subs	Gls
Bradford Park Ave	Jnr	01/57	57-60	16	-	0

BAKER Gerard (Gerry)
Born: Wigan, Greater Manchester, England, 16 September, 1938 — RB

League Club	Source	Date Signed	Seasons Played	Apps	Subs	Gls
Nottingham F	Wigan Ath	12/59				
York C	Tr	07/63	63-68	214	0	7

BAKER Gerard Austin (Gerry)
Born: New York, USA, 11 April, 1938 — CF
Died: Wishaw, Lanarkshire, Scotland, 24 August, 2013
USA: 7

League Club	Source	Date Signed	Seasons Played	Apps	Subs	Gls
Chelsea	Larkhall Thistle	06/55				
Manchester C	St Mirren	11/60	60-61	37	-	14
Ipswich T	Hibernian	12/63	63-67	135	0	58
Coventry C	Tr	11/67	67-69	27	4	5
Brentford	L	10/69	69	8	0	2

BAKER Graham Edgar
Born: Southampton, England, 3 December, 1958 — M
England: U21-2

League Club	Source	Date Signed	Seasons Played	Apps	Subs	Gls
Southampton	App	12/76	77-81	111	2	22
Manchester C	Tr	08/82	82-86	114	3	19
Southampton	Tr	06/87	87-89	57	3	9
Aldershot	L	03/90	89	7	0	2
Fulham	Tr	07/90	90-91	8	2	1

BAKER Harry Kenneth
Born: Bexleyheath, SE London, England, 20 September, 1990 — RW

League Club	Source	Date Signed	Seasons Played	Apps	Subs	Gls
Leyton Orient	Sch	01/09	08-09	2	6	0

BAKER Joseph Henry (Joe)
Born: Liverpool, England, 17 July, 1940 — CF
Died: Lanark, Scotland, 6 October, 2003
England: 8/U23-6//Scotland: Schools

League Club	Source	Date Signed	Seasons Played	Apps	Subs	Gls
Arsenal	Torino (ITA)	08/62	62-65	144	0	93
Nottingham F	Tr	03/66	65-68	117	1	41
Sunderland	Tr	07/69	69-70	39	1	12

BAKER Joseph Philip (Joe)
Born: Kentish Town, N London, England, 19 April, 1977 — W

League Club	Source	Date Signed	Seasons Played	Apps	Subs	Gls
Leyton Orient	Charlton Ath (YT)	05/95	95-98	23	52	3

BAKER Keith
Born: Oxford, England, 15 October, 1956 — G
Died: Oxford, England, 19 December, 2013
England: Schools

League Club	Source	Date Signed	Seasons Played	Apps	Subs	Gls
Oxford U	App	11/74				
Grimsby T	L	08/75	75	1	0	0

BAKER Kieron Richard
Born: Ryde, Isle of Wight, England, 29 October, 1949 — G

League Club	Source	Date Signed	Seasons Played	Apps	Subs	Gls
Bournemouth	Fulham (Am)	07/67	69-77	217	0	0
Brentford	L	02/73	72	6	0	0

BAKER Lewis Renard
Born: Luton, England, 25 April, 1995 — M
England: Youth

League Club	Source	Date Signed	Seasons Played	Apps	Subs	Gls
Chelsea	Sch	07/12				
Sheffield Wed	L	01/15	14	2	2	0
MK Dons	L	02/15	14	8	4	3

BAKER Mark
Born: Swansea, Wales, 26 April, 1961 — F

League Club	Source	Date Signed	Seasons Played	Apps	Subs	Gls
Swansea C	Jnr	09/78	78-79	3	8	2

BAKER Matthew Christopher (Matt)
Born: Harrogate, North Yorkshire, England, 18 December, 1979 — G
England: Semi Pro-4

League Club	Source	Date Signed	Seasons Played	Apps	Subs	Gls
Hull C	YT	07/98	99	0	2	0
Wrexham	Hereford U	07/04	04	11	2	0
MK Dons	Tr	12/04	04-05	57	0	0

BAKER Nathan Luke
Born: Worcester, England, 23 April, 1991 — CD
England: U21-3/Youth

League Club	Source	Date Signed	Seasons Played	Apps	Subs	Gls
Aston Villa	Sch	09/08	10-14	72	7	0
Lincoln C	L	10/09	09	17	1	0
Millwall	L	11/11	11	6	0	0

BAKER Peter Robert
Born: West Ham, E London, England, 24 August, 1934 — RB

League Club	Source	Date Signed	Seasons Played	Apps	Subs	Gls
Sheffield Wed	Tottenham H (Am)	11/54	57	11	-	0
Queens Park Rgrs	Tr	03/61	60-62	27	-	0

BAKER Peter Russell Barker
Born: Hampstead, NW London, England, 10 December, 1931 — RB
England: Youth

League Club	Source	Date Signed	Seasons Played	Apps	Subs	Gls
Tottenham H	Enfield	10/52	52-64	299	-	3

BAKER Philip (Phil)
Born: Birkenhead, Wirral, England, 4 November, 1982 — CD

League Club	Source	Date Signed	Seasons Played	Apps	Subs	Gls
Tranmere Rov	Sch	05/02				
Exeter C	Bangor C	03/03	02	5	1	0

BAKER Richard Peter (Richie)
Born: Burnley, Lancashire, England, 29 December, 1987 — M

League Club	Source	Date Signed	Seasons Played	Apps	Subs	Gls
Bury	Preston NE (Sch)	07/06	06-09	68	39	7
Oxford U	Tr	07/10	10	0	6	0

BAKER Roy Vincent
Born: Bradford, England, 8 June, 1954 — F

League Club	Source	Date Signed	Seasons Played	Apps	Subs	Gls
Bradford C		07/72	72-74	39	7	11

BAKER Stephen (Steve)
Born: Wallsend, Tyne and Wear, England, 2 December, 1961 — RB/M

League Club	Source	Date Signed	Seasons Played	Apps	Subs	Gls
Southampton	App	12/79	80-87	61	12	0
Burnley	L	02/84	83	10	0	0
Leyton Orient	Tr	03/88	87-90	105	7	5
Bournemouth	Tr	08/91	91	5	1	0

BAKER Steven Richard (Steve)
Born: Pontefract, West Yorkshire, England, 8 September, 1978 — RB
Republic of Ireland: U21-4

League Club	Source	Date Signed	Seasons Played	Apps	Subs	Gls
Middlesbrough	YT	07/97	97-98	6	2	0
Huddersfield T	L	08/99	99	3	0	0
Darlington	L	03/00	99	4	1	0
Hartlepool U	L	09/00	00	9	0	0

BAKER Terence (Terry)
Born: Southend-on-Sea, England, 13 November, 1965 — CD

League Club	Source	Date Signed	Seasons Played	Apps	Subs	Gls
West Ham U	App	11/83				
Colchester U	Billericay T	11/85	85-87	55	0	2

BAKER Thomas (Tom)
Born: Salford, England, 28 March, 1985 — M

League Club	Source	Date Signed	Seasons Played	Apps	Subs	Gls
Barnsley	Sch	07/04	03-04	0	4	0

BAKER Thomas Arthur (Tom)
Born: Stepney, E London, England, 9 August, 1939 — IF

League Club	Source	Date Signed	Seasons Played	Apps	Subs	Gls
Bristol Rov		10/56	62	1	-	0

BAKER Thomas George (George)
Born: Maerdy, Rhondda Cynon Taff, Wales, 6 April, 1936 — CF/W
Wales: U23-2

League Club	Source	Date Signed	Seasons Played	Apps	Subs	Gls
Plymouth Arg	Maerdy	10/53	54-59	78	-	16
Shrewsbury T	Tr	06/60	60-61	52	-	5

BAKER Wayne Robert
Born: Leeds, England, 4 December, 1965 — G

League Club	Source	Date Signed	Seasons Played	Apps	Subs	Gls
Sheffield Wed	App	12/83				
Darlington	Whitby T	11/86	86	5	0	0

BAKER William George (Billy)
Born: Penrhiwceiber, Rhondda Cynon Taff, Wales, 3 October, 1920 — WH
Died: Cardiff, Wales, 6 February, 2005
Wales: 1/WLge-4/Schools

League Club	Source	Date Signed	Seasons Played	Apps	Subs	Gls
Cardiff C	Troedyrhiw	01/38	38-54	292	-	5
Ipswich T	Tr	06/55	55	20	-	0

BAKES Martin Stansfield
Born: Bradford, England, 8 February, 1937 — LW

League Club	Source	Date Signed	Seasons Played	Apps	Subs	Gls
Bradford C	Jnr	02/54	53-58	72	-	7
Scunthorpe U	Tr	06/59	59-62	77	-	5

BAKEWELL Herbert
Born: Barnsley, South Yorkshire, England, 8 March, 1921 — G
Died: Bolton, Greater Manchester, England, 6 May, 1998

League Club	Source	Date Signed	Seasons Played	Apps	Subs	Gls
Barnsley	Jnr	02/39				
Newport Co	Tr	09/46	46	8	-	0

BAKHOLT Kurt
Born: Odense, Denmark, 12 August, 1963 — M

League Club	Source	Date Signed	Seasons Played	Apps	Subs	Gls
Queens Park Rgrs	Vejle BK (DEN)	01/86	85	0	1	0

BAKKE Eirik
Born: Sogndal, Norway, 13 September, 1977 — M
Norway: 27/U21-34/Youth

League Club	Source	Date Signed	Seasons Played	Apps	Subs	Gls
Leeds U	Sogndal IF (NOR)	07/99	99-06	116	27	8
Aston Villa	L	08/05	05	8	6	0

BALABAN Bosko
Born: Rijeka, Croatia, 15 October, 1978 F
Croatia: 35

League Club	Source	Date Signed	Seasons Played	Apps	Subs	Gls
Aston Villa	Dinamo Zagreb (CRO)	08/01	01	0	8	0

BALA'C Peta John
Born: Exeter, England, 9 December, 1953 G

League Club	Source	Date Signed	Seasons Played	Apps	Subs	Gls
Plymouth Arg	App	12/71	71-72	40	0	0
Hereford U	L	08/73	73	2	0	0
Swansea C	L	09/73	73	4	0	0

BALANTA Angelo Jasiel
Born: Cali, Colombia, 1 July, 1990 F

League Club	Source	Date Signed	Seasons Played	Apps	Subs	Gls
Queens Park Rgrs	Sch	01/08	07-09	9	16	2
Wycombe W	L	11/08	08	9	2	3
MK Dons	L	07/10	10	9	2	3
MK Dons	L	03/11	10	3	4	3
MK Dons	L	07/11	11	10	10	4
MK Dons	L	10/12	12	11	1	1
Yeovil T	L	03/13	12	4	2	0

BALCOMBE Stephen William (Steve)
Born: Bangor, Gwynedd, Wales, 2 September, 1961 F
Wales: U21-1

League Club	Source	Date Signed	Seasons Played	Apps	Subs	Gls
Leeds U	App	06/79	81	1	0	1

BALDACCHINO Ryan Lee
Born: Leicester, England, 13 January, 1981 W

League Club	Source	Date Signed	Seasons Played	Apps	Subs	Gls
Blackburn Rov	YT	02/99				
Bolton W	Tr	03/01				
Carlisle U	Tr	08/02	02-03	11	12	0

BALDERSTONE John Christopher (Chris)
Born: Huddersfield, West Yorkshire, England, 16 November, 1940 M
Died: Carlisle, Cumbria, England, 6 March, 2000

League Club	Source	Date Signed	Seasons Played	Apps	Subs	Gls
Huddersfield T	Jnr	05/58	59-64	117	-	24
Carlisle U	Tr	06/65	65-74	368	7	66
Doncaster Rov	Tr	07/75	75	38	1	1

BALDIE Douglas Wilson
Born: Scone, Perthshire, Scotland, 16 April, 1921 IF
Died: Bristol, England, 10 November, 1998

League Club	Source	Date Signed	Seasons Played	Apps	Subs	Gls
Bristol Rov	Luton T (Am)	04/46	46-47	8	-	4

BALDOCK George Henry Ivor
Born: Buckingham, England, 26 January, 1993 M/RB

League Club	Source	Date Signed	Seasons Played	Apps	Subs	Gls
MK Dons	Sch	06/11	09-14	27	25	2
Northampton T	L	09/11	11	4	1	0
Oxford U	L	02/15	14	12	0	1

BALDOCK Samuel Edward (Sam)
Born: Buckingham, England, 15 March, 1989 F

League Club	Source	Date Signed	Seasons Played	Apps	Subs	Gls
MK Dons	Sch	04/06	06-11	67	33	33
West Ham U	Tr	08/11	11	10	13	5
Bristol C	Tr	08/12	12-14	71	12	34
Brighton & HA	Tr	08/14	14	19	1	3

BALDRIDGE Robert William
Born: Sunderland, England, 26 November, 1932 CF

League Club	Source	Date Signed	Seasons Played	Apps	Subs	Gls
Gateshead	Hendon Social	02/57	56-59	59	-	21

BALDRY Simon Jonathan
Born: Huddersfield, West Yorkshire, England, 12 February, 1976 RW

League Club	Source	Date Signed	Seasons Played	Apps	Subs	Gls
Huddersfield T	YT	07/94	93-02	87	59	8
Bury	L	09/98	98	0	5	0
Notts Co	Tr	08/03	03	32	3	1

BALDRY William Joseph (Bill)
Born: Luton, England, 9 July, 1956 LB

League Club	Source	Date Signed	Seasons Played	Apps	Subs	Gls
Cambridge U	Luton T (Am)	03/76	75-77	27	0	0

BALDWIN Harold (Harry)
Born: Birmingham, England, 17 July, 1920 G
Died: Northampton, England, 28 October, 2010

League Club	Source	Date Signed	Seasons Played	Apps	Subs	Gls
West Bromwich A	Sutton T	04/38	37	5	-	0
Brighton & HA	Tr	05/39	46-51	164	-	0
Walsall	Kettering T	12/53	53-54	37	-	0

BALDWIN Jack
Born: Barking, E London, England, 30 June, 1993 CD

League Club	Source	Date Signed	Seasons Played	Apps	Subs	Gls
Hartlepool U	Faversham T	07/11	11-13	70	7	4
Peterborough U	Tr	01/14	13-14	21	1	0

BALDWIN James (Jimmy)
Born: Blackburn, Greater Manchester, England, 12 January, 1922 RH
Died: Romford, E London, England, 13 July, 1985

League Club	Source	Date Signed	Seasons Played	Apps	Subs	Gls
Blackburn Rov	Mill Hill St Peter's	12/45	46-49	88	-	0
Leicester C	Tr	02/50	49-55	180	-	4

BALDWIN Joseph George (George)
Born: Islington, N London, England, 26 July, 1921 WH
Died: Romford, E London, England, 5 January, 1976

League Club	Source	Date Signed	Seasons Played	Apps	Subs	Gls
Gillingham	Gravesend & Northfleet	08/51	51	1	-	0

BALDWIN Patrick Michael (Pat)
Born: City of London, England, 12 November, 1982 CD

League Club	Source	Date Signed	Seasons Played	Apps	Subs	Gls
Colchester U	Chelsea (Sch)	08/02	02-11	182	26	1
Bristol Rov	L	11/09	09	6	0	0
Southend U	L	01/10	09	18	0	1
Southend U	Tr	01/12	11	2	0	0
Exeter C	Tr	03/12	11-14	80	2	1

BALDWIN Thomas (Tommy)
Born: Gateshead, Tyne and Wear, England, 10 June, 1945 F
England: U23-2

League Club	Source	Date Signed	Seasons Played	Apps	Subs	Gls
Arsenal	Wrekenton Jnrs	12/62	64-66	17	0	7
Chelsea	Tr	09/66	66-74	182	5	74
Millwall	L	11/74	74	6	0	1
Manchester U	L	01/75	74	2	0	0
Brentford	Gravesend & Northfleet	10/77	77	4	0	1

BALE Gareth Frank
Born: Cardiff, Wales, 16 July, 1989 LW
Wales: 50/U21-4/Youth

League Club	Source	Date Signed	Seasons Played	Apps	Subs	Gls
Southampton	Sch	07/06	05-06	40	0	5
Tottenham H	Tr	05/07	07-12	136	10	42

BALIS Igor
Born: Trnava, Slovakia, 5 January, 1970 RB
Slovakia: 41

League Club	Source	Date Signed	Seasons Played	Apps	Subs	Gls
West Bromwich A	Slov Bratislava (SVK)	12/00	00-02	60	9	4

BALKENSTEIN Pim
Born: Gouda, Netherlands, 29 April, 1987 CD

League Club	Source	Date Signed	Seasons Played	Apps	Subs	Gls
Ipswich T	Heerenveen (NED)	06/08	08-09	23	6	0
Brentford	L	11/09	09	8	0	0
Brentford	Tr	03/10	09-11	25	6	2
Rochdale	L	08/11	11	12	1	0
AFC Wimbledon	Tr	03/12	11-12	28	2	2

BALL Alan James
Born: Farnworth, Greater Manchester, England, 12 May, 1945 M
Died: Warsash, Hampshire, England, 24 April, 2007
England: 72/FLge-6/U23-8

League Club	Source	Date Signed	Seasons Played	Apps	Subs	Gls
Blackpool	App	05/62	62-65	116	0	40
Everton	Tr	08/66	66-71	208	0	66
Arsenal	Tr	12/71	71-76	177	0	45
Southampton	Tr	12/76	76-79	132	0	9
Blackpool	Vancouver W'caps (CAN)	07/80	80	30	0	5
Southampton	Tr	03/81	80-82	63	0	2
Bristol Rov	Eastern AA (HKG)	01/83	82	17	0	2

BALL Callum Reece
Born: Leicester, England, 8 October, 1992 F

League Club	Source	Date Signed	Seasons Played	Apps	Subs	Gls
Derby Co	Sch	07/10	09-11	12	17	3
Coventry C	L	07/12	12	6	9	0
Torquay U	L	07/13	13	9	0	2
Notts Co	L	11/13	13	2	4	1

BALL David Michael
Born: Whitefield, Greater Manchester, England, 14 December, 1989 F

League Club	Source	Date Signed	Seasons Played	Apps	Subs	Gls
Manchester C	Sch	09/07				
Swindon T	L	07/10	10	7	11	2
Peterborough U	Tr	01/11	10-11	13	28	9
Rochdale	L	08/11	11	7	0	3
Rochdale	L	11/11	11	5	2	2
Fleetwood T	Tr	07/12	12-14	72	24	23

BALL Dominic
Born: Welwyn Garden City, Hertfordshire, England, 2 August, 1995 DM
England: Youth//Northern Ireland: U21-2/Youth

League Club	Source	Date Signed	Seasons Played	Apps	Subs	Gls
Tottenham H	Sch	09/13				
Cambridge U	L	01/15	14	9	2	0

BALL Donald
Born: Barnard Castle, County Durham, England, 14 June, 1962 CD

League Club	Source	Date Signed	Seasons Played	Apps	Subs	Gls
Darlington	App	06/80	79-81	57	3	2

BALL Geoffrey Hudson (Geoff)
Born: Nottingham, England, 2 November, 1944 RB

League Club	Source	Date Signed	Seasons Played	Apps	Subs	Gls
Nottingham F	Ericsson's Electronic	02/63	64-65	3	0	0
Notts Co	Tr	11/67	67-71	111	1	0

BALL James Alan (Alan)
Born: Farnworth, Greater Manchester, England, 23 September, 1924 IF
Died: Nicosia, Cyprus, 2 January, 1982

League Club	Source	Date Signed	Seasons Played	Apps	Subs	Gls
Southport	Bolton Boys Federation	03/46	46	2	-	0
Birmingham C	Tr	05/47				
Southport	Tr	02/48	47-49	39	-	9
Oldham Ath	Tr	07/50	50	7	-	1
Rochdale	Tr	02/52	51	5	-	1

BALL John
Born: Wigan, Greater Manchester, England, 13 March, 1925 — RB
England: B/FLge-2

League Club	Source	Date Signed	Seasons Played	Apps	Subs	Gls
Manchester U	Wigan Ath	03/48	47-49	22	-	0
Bolton W	Tr	09/50	50-57	200	-	2

BALL John Albert (Jack)
Born: Brighton, England, 16 July, 1923 — G
Died: Brighton, England, July, 1999

League Club	Source	Date Signed	Seasons Played	Apps	Subs	Gls
Brighton & HA	Vernon Ath	02/43	46-52	113	-	0

BALL Jordan Darren
Born: Mansfield, Nottinghamshire, England, 12 September, 1993 — F

League Club	Source	Date Signed	Seasons Played	Apps	Subs	Gls
Doncaster Rov	Sch	07/12	12	0	1	0

BALL Joseph Howard (Joe)
Born: Walsall, West Midlands, England, 4 April, 1931 — W
Died: Farnham, Surrey, England, 4 December, 1974

League Club	Source	Date Signed	Seasons Played	Apps	Subs	Gls
Ipswich T	Banbury Spencer	08/51	51-52	32	-	2
Aldershot	Tr	06/54	54-55	31	-	5

BALL Keith
Born: Walsall, West Midlands, England, 26 October, 1940 — G

League Club	Source	Date Signed	Seasons Played	Apps	Subs	Gls
Walsall	Jnr	01/59	58-61	11	-	0
Walsall	Worcester C	05/65	66-67	34	0	0
Port Vale	Tr	11/68	68-71	130	0	0
Walsall	Stourbridge	11/72	72	2	0	0

BALL Kevin Anthony
Born: Hastings, East Sussex, England, 12 November, 1964 — DM

League Club	Source	Date Signed	Seasons Played	Apps	Subs	Gls
Portsmouth	Coventry C (App)	10/82	83-89	96	9	4
Sunderland	Tr	07/90	90-99	329	10	21
Fulham	Tr	12/99	99	15	3	0
Burnley	Tr	07/00	00-01	77	5	2

BALL Matthew Gerard (Matt)
Born: Welwyn Garden City, Hertfordshire, England, 26 March, 1993 — M
Northern Ireland: U21-5/Youth

League Club	Source	Date Signed	Seasons Played	Apps	Subs	Gls
Norwich C	Sch	05/11				
Stevenage	Tr	07/12	12	1	1	0

BALL Michael John
Born: Crosby, Merseyside, England, 2 October, 1979 — LB
England: 1/U21-7/Youth/Schools

League Club	Source	Date Signed	Seasons Played	Apps	Subs	Gls
Everton	YT	10/96	96-00	102	19	8
Manchester C	PSV Eindhoven (NED)	01/07	06-08	39	9	0
Leicester C	Tr	08/11				

BALL Stephen (Steve)
Born: Leeds, England, 22 November, 1973 — M

League Club	Source	Date Signed	Seasons Played	Apps	Subs	Gls
Darlington	Leeds U (YT)	08/92	92-93	30	12	3

BALL Stephen Gary (Gary)
Born: St Austell, Cornwall, England, 15 December, 1959 — M

League Club	Source	Date Signed	Seasons Played	Apps	Subs	Gls
Plymouth Arg	App	12/77	79	0	1	0
Lincoln C	Tr	10/79	79	3	0	0

BALL Steven James (Steve)
Born: Colchester, Essex, England, 2 September, 1969 — M

League Club	Source	Date Signed	Seasons Played	Apps	Subs	Gls
Arsenal	YT	09/87				
Colchester U	Tr	12/89	89	3	1	0
Norwich C	Tr	09/90	91	0	2	0
Colchester U	Cambridge U (NC)	09/92	92-95	52	12	7

BALLACK Michael
Born: Gorlitz, Germany, 26 September, 1976 — M
Germany: 98

League Club	Source	Date Signed	Seasons Played	Apps	Subs	Gls
Chelsea	Bayern Munich (GER)	07/06	06-09	87	18	17

BALLAGHER John
Born: Ashton-under-Lyne, Greater Manchester, England, 21 March, 1936 — IF

League Club	Source	Date Signed	Seasons Played	Apps	Subs	Gls
Sheffield Wed	Dukinfield T	02/57	58	3	-	0
Doncaster Rov	Tr	02/61	60-61	41	-	13
Gillingham	Tr	08/62	62-63	41	-	10

BALLANTYNE John Dixon (Dick)
Born: Newburn, Tyne and Wear, England, 16 September, 1927 — LB
Died: Newburn, Tyne and Wear, England, July, 2007

League Club	Source	Date Signed	Seasons Played	Apps	Subs	Gls
West Ham U		05/46				
Hartlepool U	Tr	07/50	50-51	13	-	0
Millwall	Tr	08/53				

BALLARD Edgar Albert (Ted)
Born: Brentford, W London, England, 16 June, 1920 — FB
Died: Hastings, East Sussex, England, 10 June, 2008

League Club	Source	Date Signed	Seasons Played	Apps	Subs	Gls
Leyton Orient	Hayes	04/46	46	26	-	1
Southampton	Tr	06/47	47-50	45	-	0
Leyton Orient	Tr	08/52				

BALMER John (Jack)
Born: Liverpool, England, 6 February, 1916 — IF
Died: Liverpool, England, 25 December, 1984
England: War-1

League Club	Source	Date Signed	Seasons Played	Apps	Subs	Gls
Liverpool	Everton (Am)	08/35	35-51	289	-	98

BALMER John Michael (Mike)
Born: Hexham, Northumberland, England, 25 May, 1946 — CF

League Club	Source	Date Signed	Seasons Played	Apps	Subs	Gls
Leicester C	App	01/64				
Halifax T	Tr	05/65	65-66	28	0	9

BALMER Stuart Murray
Born: Falkirk, Scotland, 20 September, 1969 — CD
Scotland: Youth/Schools

League Club	Source	Date Signed	Seasons Played	Apps	Subs	Gls
Charlton Ath	Glasgow Celtic	08/90	90-97	201	26	8
Wigan Ath	Tr	09/98	98-00	99	2	4
Oldham Ath	Tr	07/01	01	35	1	6
Scunthorpe U	L	10/02	02	6	0	0
Boston U	Tr	12/02	02-03	46	1	3

BALMY Jeremy
Born: Le Havre, France, 19 April, 1994 — W

League Club	Source	Date Signed	Seasons Played	Apps	Subs	Gls
Notts Co	Le Havre (FRA)	08/13	13-14	0	2	0
Oxford U	Tr	02/15				

BALOGH Bela
Born: Budapest, Hungary, 30 December, 1984 — CD
Hungary: 9

League Club	Source	Date Signed	Seasons Played	Apps	Subs	Gls
Colchester U (L)	MTK Budapest (HUN)	08/07	07	10	7	0

BALOGUN Teslim Ayinde
Born: Lagos, Nigeria, 27 March, 1931 — CF
Died: Nigeria, 30 July, 1972

League Club	Source	Date Signed	Seasons Played	Apps	Subs	Gls
Queens Park Rgrs	Skegness T	09/56	56	13	-	3

BALOTELLI Mario Barwuah
Born: Palermo, Italy, 12 August, 1990 — F
Italy: 33/U21-16

League Club	Source	Date Signed	Seasons Played	Apps	Subs	Gls
Manchester C	Inter Milan (ITA)	08/10	10-12	33	21	20
Liverpool	AC Milan (ITA)	08/14	14	10	6	1

BALSOM Clifford Gene (Cliff)
Born: Torquay, Devon, England, 25 March, 1946 — FB

League Club	Source	Date Signed	Seasons Played	Apps	Subs	Gls
Torquay U	App	03/64	63	4	-	0
Swindon T	Tr	06/64				
Torquay U	Tr	07/65				

BALSON Michael John Charles (Mike)
Born: Bridport, Dorset, England, 9 September, 1947 — CD

League Club	Source	Date Signed	Seasons Played	Apps	Subs	Gls
Exeter C	Jnr	08/65	66-73	273	3	9

BALTACHA Sergei Pavlovich
Born: Kiev, Ukraine, 17 February, 1958 — M
Soviet Union: 45

League Club	Source	Date Signed	Seasons Played	Apps	Subs	Gls
Ipswich T	Dynamo Kiev (UKR)	01/89	88-89	22	6	1

BALTACHA Sergei Sergeivich
Born: Kiev, Ukraine, 28 July, 1979 — LB
Scotland: U21-3

League Club	Source	Date Signed	Seasons Played	Apps	Subs	Gls
Millwall	St Mirren	01/03	02	1	1	0

BAMBA Souleymane (Sol)
Born: Paris, France, 13 January, 1985 — CD
Ivory Coast: 44/U23-2

League Club	Source	Date Signed	Seasons Played	Apps	Subs	Gls
Leicester C	Hibernian	01/11	10-11	48	4	3
Leeds U	US Palermo (ITA)	01/15	14	19	0	1

BAMBER John David (Dave)
Born: Prescot, Merseyside, England, 1 February, 1959 — F

League Club	Source	Date Signed	Seasons Played	Apps	Subs	Gls
Blackpool	St Helens T	09/79	79-82	81	5	29
Coventry C	Tr	06/83	83	18	1	3
Walsall	Tr	03/84	83-84	17	3	7
Portsmouth	Tr	12/84	84	4	0	1
Swindon T	Tr	11/85	85-87	103	3	31
Watford	Tr	06/88	88	16	2	3
Stoke C	Tr	12/88	88-89	43	0	8
Hull C	Tr	02/90	89-90	25	3	5
Blackpool	Tr	11/90	90-94	111	2	60

BAMBER Lee
Born: Burnley, Lancashire, England, 31 October, 1968 — G

League Club	Source	Date Signed	Seasons Played	Apps	Subs	Gls
Preston NE	Chorley	08/93	93	0	1	0

BAMBER Michael John (Mike)
Born: Preston, Lancashire, England, 1 October, 1980 — FB

League Club	Source	Date Signed	Seasons Played	Apps	Subs	Gls
Macclesfield T	Blackpool (YT)	12/99	99-00	2	4	0

BAMBRIDGE Keith Graham
Born: Rawmarsh, South Yorkshire, England, 1 September, 1935 — LW

League Club	Source	Date Signed	Seasons Played	Apps	Subs	Gls
Rotherham U	Masborough St Paul's	02/55	55-62	162	-	15
Darlington	Tr	12/64	64	6	-	0
Halifax T	Tr	03/65	64-65	8	1	1

BAMBRIDGE Stephen Martin (Steve)
Born: Marylebone, Central London, England, 27 May, 1960 — F

League Club	Source	Date Signed	Seasons Played	Apps	Subs	Gls
Aldershot	App	05/78	76	0	2	0

BAMFORD Harry Frank Ernest
Born: Kingston-on-Thames, SW London, England, 8 April, 1914 — RB
Died: Rochdale, Greater Manchester, England, 4 June, 1949

League Club	Source	Date Signed	Seasons Played	Apps	Subs	Gls
Brentford	Ealing YC	05/39				
Brighton & HA	Tr	06/46	46	8	-	0

BAMFORD Henry Charles (Harry)
Born: Bristol, England, 8 February, 1920 — RB
Died: Bristol, England, 3 October, 1958

League Club	Source	Date Signed	Seasons Played	Apps	Subs	Gls
Bristol Rov	Ipswich T (Am)	01/46	46-58	486	-	5

BAMFORD Patrick James
Born: Newark, Nottinghamshire, England, 5 September, 1993 — F
England: U21-2/Youth

League Club	Source	Date Signed	Seasons Played	Apps	Subs	Gls
Nottingham F	Sch	12/10	11	0	2	0
Chelsea	Tr	01/12				
MK Dons	L	11/12	12	11	3	4
MK Dons	L	07/13	13	22	1	14
Derby Co	L	01/14	13	14	7	8
Middlesbrough	L	08/14	14	32	6	17

BAMOGO Habib
Born: Paris, France, 8 May, 1982 — F
Burkina Faso: 7

League Club	Source	Date Signed	Seasons Played	Apps	Subs	Gls
Doncaster Rov	Panetolikos (GRE)	01/12	11	4	0	0

BAMPTON David Peter (Dave)
Born: Swindon, England, 5 May, 1985 — M

League Club	Source	Date Signed	Seasons Played	Apps	Subs	Gls
Swindon T	Sch	-	02	0	3	0

BANCE Daniel Robert (Danny)
Born: Plymouth, England, 27 September, 1982 — FB

League Club	Source	Date Signed	Seasons Played	Apps	Subs	Gls
Plymouth Arg	YT	-	00	1	0	0

BANCESSI Eusebio Gomes
Born: Bissau, Guinea-Bissau, 4 August, 1995 — W

League Club	Source	Date Signed	Seasons Played	Apps	Subs	Gls
Wolverhampton W	Benfica Jnrs (POR)	09/13				
Cheltenham T	L	10/14	14	2	2	0

BANCROFT Paul Andrew
Born: Derby, England, 10 September, 1964 — M

League Club	Source	Date Signed	Seasons Played	Apps	Subs	Gls
Derby Co	App	09/82				
Crewe Alex	L	01/83	82	21	0	3
Northampton T	Tr	07/84	84	15	1	0

BANFIELD Neil Anthony
Born: Poplar, E London, England, 20 January, 1962 — CD
England: Youth/Schools

League Club	Source	Date Signed	Seasons Played	Apps	Subs	Gls
Crystal Palace	App	08/79	80	2	1	0
Leyton Orient	Adelaide C (AUS)	12/83	83-84	30	1	0

BANGER Nicholas Lee (Nicky)
Born: Southampton, England, 25 February, 1971 — F

League Club	Source	Date Signed	Seasons Played	Apps	Subs	Gls
Southampton	YT	04/89	90-94	18	37	8
Oldham Ath	Tr	10/94	94-96	44	20	10
Oxford U	Tr	07/97	97-99	41	22	8
Scunthorpe U (L)	Dundee	11/00	00	0	1	0
Plymouth Arg	Dundee	08/01	01	3	7	2
Torquay U	Merthyr Tydfil	03/02	01	1	0	0

BANGOURA Sambegou (Sammy)
Born: Conakry, Guinea, 3 April, 1983 — F
Guinea: 22

League Club	Source	Date Signed	Seasons Played	Apps	Subs	Gls
Stoke C	Standard Liege (BEL)	08/05	05-06	24	4	9

BANGURA Alhassan (Al)
Born: Freetown, Sierra Leone, 24 January, 1988 — M
Sierra Leone: 1

League Club	Source	Date Signed	Seasons Played	Apps	Subs	Gls
Watford	Sch	06/05	04-08	27	35	1
Brighton & HA	L	03/09	08	6	0	0
Blackpool	Tr	08/09	09	2	7	0

BANHAM Roy
Born: Nottingham, England, 30 October, 1936 — CD

League Club	Source	Date Signed	Seasons Played	Apps	Subs	Gls
Nottingham F	Hyson Green BC	11/53	55-56	2	-	0
Peterborough U	Tr	07/58	60-61	16	-	0

BANJO Tunji Babajide
Born: Kennington, S London, England, 19 February, 1960 — M
Nigeria: 9

League Club	Source	Date Signed	Seasons Played	Apps	Subs	Gls
Leyton Orient	App	03/77	77-81	20	7	1

BANKOLE Ademola (Ade)
Born: Abeokuta, Nigeria, 9 September, 1969 — G

League Club	Source	Date Signed	Seasons Played	Apps	Subs	Gls
Crewe Alex	Shooting Stars (NIG)	09/96	96-97	6	0	0
Queens Park Rgrs	Tr	07/98	99	0	1	0
Crewe Alex	Tr	07/00	00-02	51	1	0
Brentford	Maidenhead U	02/05	04-05	5	0	0
MK Dons	Tr	08/06	06	5	1	0

BANKS Alan
Born: Liverpool, England, 5 October, 1938 — CF

League Club	Source	Date Signed	Seasons Played	Apps	Subs	Gls
Liverpool	Rankin Boys	05/58	58-60	8	-	6
Exeter C	Cambridge C	10/63	63-65	85	0	43
Plymouth Arg	Tr	06/66	66-67	19	0	5
Exeter C	Tr	11/67	67-72	160	13	58

BANKS Christopher Noel (Chris)
Born: Stone, Staffordshire, England, 12 November, 1965 — CD
England: Semi Pro-2

League Club	Source	Date Signed	Seasons Played	Apps	Subs	Gls
Port Vale	Jnr	12/82	84-87	50	15	1
Exeter C	Tr	06/88	88	43	2	1
Cheltenham T	Bath C	08/94	99-01	119	1	1

BANKS Eric
Born: Workington, Cumbria, England, 7 April, 1950 — RW

League Club	Source	Date Signed	Seasons Played	Apps	Subs	Gls
Workington	Jnr	09/68	67-72	26	4	1

BANKS Francis Stanley (Frank)
Born: Hull, England, 21 August, 1945 — RB

League Club	Source	Date Signed	Seasons Played	Apps	Subs	Gls
Southend U	Jnr	10/62	63-65	4	0	0
Hull C	Tr	09/66	67-75	284	4	6
Southend U	Tr	03/76	75-77	75	0	0

BANKS George Ernest
Born: Wednesbury, West Midlands, England, 28 March, 1919 — CF
Died: Sandwell, West Midlands, England, October, 1991

League Club	Source	Date Signed	Seasons Played	Apps	Subs	Gls
West Bromwich A	Brownhills Ath	06/38	38	1	-	2
Mansfield T	Tr	11/47	47-48	63	-	21

BANKS Gordon
Born: Sheffield, England, 30 December, 1937 — G
England: 73/FLge-6/U23-2

League Club	Source	Date Signed	Seasons Played	Apps	Subs	Gls
Chesterfield	Rawmarsh Welfare	09/55	58	23	-	0
Leicester C	Tr	05/59	59-66	293	0	0
Stoke C	Tr	04/67	66-72	194	0	0

BANKS Ian Frederick
Born: Mexborough, South Yorkshire, England, 9 January, 1961 — M

League Club	Source	Date Signed	Seasons Played	Apps	Subs	Gls
Barnsley	App	01/79	78-82	158	6	37
Leicester C	Tr	06/83	83-86	78	15	14
Huddersfield T	Tr	09/86	86-87	78	0	17
Bradford C	Tr	07/88	88	26	4	3
West Bromwich A	Tr	03/89	88	2	2	0
Barnsley	Tr	07/89	89-91	87	9	7
Rotherham U	Tr	07/92	92-93	76	0	8
Darlington	Tr	08/94	94	39	0	1

BANKS Jason Mark
Born: Farnworth, Greater Manchester, England, 16 November, 1968 — FB

League Club	Source	Date Signed	Seasons Played	Apps	Subs	Gls
Wigan Ath	App	11/86				
Chester C	Atherton Collieries	10/87	87	1	1	0

BANKS Kenneth (Kenny)
Born: Wigan, Greater Manchester, England, 19 October, 1923 — WH
Died: Abergele, Conwy, Wales, 9 August, 1994

League Club	Source	Date Signed	Seasons Played	Apps	Subs	Gls
Southport	Wigan BC	08/45	46-51	118	-	5

BANKS Oliver Ian (Ollie)
Born: Rotherham, South Yorkshire, England, 21 September, 1992 — M

League Club	Source	Date Signed	Seasons Played	Apps	Subs	Gls
Rotherham U	Sch	06/11	10	0	1	1
Chesterfield	FC United, Manchester	09/13	13-14	34	15	7
Northampton T	L	11/14	14	3	0	0

BANKS Ralph
Born: Farnworth, Greater Manchester, England, 28 June, 1920 — LB
Died: Bolton, Greater Manchester, England, 31 October, 1993

League Club	Source	Date Signed	Seasons Played	Apps	Subs	Gls
Bolton W	South Liverpool	12/40	46-52	104	-	0
Aldershot	Tr	01/54	53-54	44	-	1

BANKS Steven (Steve)
Born: Hillingdon, W London, England, 9 February, 1972 — G

League Club	Source	Date Signed	Seasons Played	Apps	Subs	Gls
West Ham U	YT	03/90				
Gillingham	Tr	03/93	93-94	67	0	0
Blackpool	Tr	08/95	95-98	150	0	0
Bolton W	Tr	03/99	98-01	20	1	0
Rochdale	L	12/01	01	15	0	0
Bradford C	L	08/02	02	8	1	0
Stoke C	Tr	12/02	02	14	0	0
Wimbledon	Tr	08/03	03	24	0	0
Gillingham	Tr	03/04	03-04	39	0	0

BANKS Thomas (Tommy)
Born: Farnworth, Greater Manchester, England, 10 November, 1929 — LB
England: 6/FLge-1

League Club	Source	Date Signed	Seasons Played	Apps	Subs	Gls
Bolton W	Partridges	10/47	47-60	233	-	2

BANNAN Barry Ryan
Born: Airdrie, Lanarkshire, Scotland, 1 December, 1989 M
Scotland: 20/B-1/U21-10

League Club	Source	Date Signed	Seasons Played	Apps	Subs	Gls
Aston Villa	Sch	07/08	10-12	35	29	1
Derby Co	L	03/09	08	6	4	1
Blackpool	L	11/09	09	8	12	1
Leeds U	L	03/11	10	3	4	0
Crystal Palace	Tr	08/13	13-14	15	7	1
Bolton W	L	02/15	14	15	1	0

BANNAN Thomas Neilson (Tommy)
Born: Airdrie, Lanarkshire, Scotland, 13 April, 1930 CF
Died: Manchester, England, October, 2003

League Club	Source	Date Signed	Seasons Played	Apps	Subs	Gls
Wrexham	Airdrieonians	06/51	51-54	158	-	60
Lincoln C	Tr	06/55	55-56	67	-	19
Wrexham	Tr	08/57	57-58	68	-	23
Barrow	Tr	08/59	59-60	45	-	15

BANNER Arthur
Born: Sheffield, England, 28 June, 1918 LB
Died: Thorpe Bay, Southend, Essex, England, 30 April, 1980

League Club	Source	Date Signed	Seasons Played	Apps	Subs	Gls
Doncaster Rov	Lopham Street	03/37				
West Ham U	Tr	05/38	38-47	27	-	0
Leyton Orient	Tr	02/48	47-52	164	-	1

BANNERMAN Telford Gordon
Born: Coupar Angus, Perthshire, Scotland, 17 September, 1924 W
Died: Coupar Angus, Perthshire, Scotland, 19 September, 1980

League Club	Source	Date Signed	Seasons Played	Apps	Subs	Gls
New Brighton	Blairgowrie Jnrs	01/49	48-50	35	-	3

BANNISTER Bruce Ian
Born: Bradford, England, 14 April, 1947 F
England: Schools

League Club	Source	Date Signed	Seasons Played	Apps	Subs	Gls
Bradford C	Leeds U (Jnr)	08/65	65-71	199	9	60
Bristol Rov	Tr	11/71	71-76	202	4	80
Plymouth Arg	Tr	12/76	76	24	0	7
Hull C	Tr	06/77	77-79	79	6	20

BANNISTER Edward (Eddie)
Born: Leyland, Lancashire, England, 2 June, 1920 RB
Died: Preston, Lancashire, England, October, 1991

League Club	Source	Date Signed	Seasons Played	Apps	Subs	Gls
Leeds U	Oaks Fold	05/46	46-49	44	-	1
Barnsley	Tr	07/50	50	32	-	0

BANNISTER Gary
Born: Warrington, Cheshire, England, 22 July, 1960 F
England: U21-1

League Club	Source	Date Signed	Seasons Played	Apps	Subs	Gls
Coventry C	App	05/78	78-80	17	5	3
Sheffield Wed	Tr	08/81	81-83	117	1	55
Queens Park Rgrs	Tr	08/84	84-87	136	0	56
Coventry C	Tr	03/88	87-89	39	4	11
West Bromwich A	Tr	03/90	89-91	62	10	18
Oxford U	L	03/92	91	7	3	2
Nottingham F	Tr	08/92	92	27	4	8
Stoke C	Tr	05/93	93	10	5	2
Lincoln C	Hong Kong Rgrs (HKG)	09/94	94	25	4	7
Darlington	Tr	08/95	95	39	2	10

BANNISTER Jack
Born: Chesterfield, Derbyshire, England, 26 January, 1942 LB

League Club	Source	Date Signed	Seasons Played	Apps	Subs	Gls
West Bromwich A	Jnr	08/59	59-62	9	-	0
Scunthorpe U	Tr	06/64	64	9	-	0
Crystal Palace	Tr	07/65	65-68	117	3	7
Luton T	Tr	10/68	68-70	79	4	0
Cambridge U	Tr	05/71	71-73	28	4	0

BANNISTER James Henry (Jimmy)
Born: Chesterfield, Derbyshire, England, 1 February, 1929 RB
Died: North Yorkshire, England, April, 2007

League Club	Source	Date Signed	Seasons Played	Apps	Subs	Gls
Chesterfield	New Whittington Ath	12/50				
Shrewsbury T	Tr	06/52	52-57	238	-	6
Northampton T	Tr	07/58	58	24	-	0
Aldershot	Tr	08/59	59-60	85	-	0

BANNISTER Keith
Born: Sheffield, England, 27 January, 1923 RB
Died: Rotherham, South Yorkshire, England, 13 March, 2012

League Club	Source	Date Signed	Seasons Played	Apps	Subs	Gls
Sheffield Wed	Sheffield YMCA	02/45	46-52	75	-	0
Chesterfield	Tr	06/53	53	17	-	0

BANNISTER Keith
Born: Sheffield, England, 13 November, 1930 RH
England: Youth

League Club	Source	Date Signed	Seasons Played	Apps	Subs	Gls
Sheffield U	Jnr	05/48				
Birmingham C	Tr	08/50	52-53	22	-	0
Wrexham	King's Lynn	07/55	55	14	-	0
Chesterfield	Tr	12/55	55	21	-	1
Norwich C	Tr	07/56	56	7	-	0

BANNISTER Neville
Born: Brierfield, Lancashire, England, 21 July, 1937 RW

League Club	Source	Date Signed	Seasons Played	Apps	Subs	Gls
Bolton W	Jnr	07/54	55-60	26	-	4
Lincoln C	Tr	03/61	60-63	68	-	16
Hartlepool U	Tr	08/64	64	41	-	8
Rochdale	Tr	07/65	65	18	1	2

BANNISTER Paul Francis
Born: Stoke-on-Trent, England, 11 October, 1947 F

League Club	Source	Date Signed	Seasons Played	Apps	Subs	Gls
Port Vale	Jnr	04/65	64-67	12	0	2

BANNON Eamonn John Peter
Born: Edinburgh, Scotland, 18 April, 1958 M
Scotland: 11/SLge-1/U21-7/Schools

League Club	Source	Date Signed	Seasons Played	Apps	Subs	Gls
Chelsea	Heart of Midlothian	01/79	78-79	25	0	1

BANNON Ian
Born: Bury, Greater Manchester, England, 3 September, 1959 CD

League Club	Source	Date Signed	Seasons Played	Apps	Subs	Gls
Rochdale	App	09/77	76-79	112	10	0

BANNON Paul Anthony
Born: Dublin, Republic of Ireland, 15 November, 1956 F

League Club	Source	Date Signed	Seasons Played	Apps	Subs	Gls
Nottingham F	Jnr	06/75				
Carlisle U	Everwarm, Bridgend	02/79	78-83	127	13	45
Darlington	L	10/83	83	2	0	0
Bristol Rov	Tr	01/84	83-84	27	2	8
Cardiff C	L	08/84	84	3	1	0
Plymouth Arg	L	11/84	84	0	2	0

BANOVIC Vjekoslav (Yakka)
Born: Bihac, Bosnia & Herzegovina, 12 November, 1956 G
Australia: 2

League Club	Source	Date Signed	Seasons Played	Apps	Subs	Gls
Derby Co	Heidelberg U (AUS)	09/80	81-83	35	0	0

BANTON Dale Conrad
Born: Kensington, Central London, England, 15 May, 1961 F

League Club	Source	Date Signed	Seasons Played	Apps	Subs	Gls
West Ham U	App	05/79	79-81	2	3	0
Aldershot	Tr	08/82	82-84	105	1	47
York C	Tr	11/84	84-88	129	9	49
Walsall	Tr	10/88	88	9	1	0
Grimsby T	Tr	03/89	88	3	5	1
Aldershot	Tr	08/89	89-90	29	15	3

BANTON Geoffrey (Geoff)
Born: Ashton-under-Lyne, Greater Manchester, England, 16 March, 1957 CD

League Club	Source	Date Signed	Seasons Played	Apps	Subs	Gls
Plymouth Arg	Bolton W (App)	05/75	76-77	6	1	0
Fulham	Tr	07/78	78-81	37	1	3

BANTON Jason Steven
Born: Tottenham, N London, England, 15 December, 1992 W
England: Youth

League Club	Source	Date Signed	Seasons Played	Apps	Subs	Gls
Blackburn Rov	Sch	12/09				
Liverpool	Tr	12/10				
Leicester C	Tr	07/11				
Burton A	L	09/11	11	0	1	0
Crystal Palace		10/12				
Plymouth Arg	L	01/13	12	14	0	6
MK Dons	L	07/13	13	10	1	2
Plymouth Arg	Tr	01/14	13-14	22	16	1

BANVO Anderson
Born: Paris, France, 4 February, 1994 F

League Club	Source	Date Signed	Seasons Played	Apps	Subs	Gls
Blackpool	Paris St-Germain (FRA)	08/12				
Stevenage	L	03/14	13	0	1	0

BANYA Charles (Kai)
Born: Tulse Hill, S London, England, 18 September, 1993 W

League Club	Source	Date Signed	Seasons Played	Apps	Subs	Gls
Fulham	Sch	07/11				
Crawley T	Tr	08/14	14	0	9	0

BAPTISTA Cesar Julio (Julio)
Born: Sao Paulo, Brazil, 1 October, 1981 M/F
Brazil: 47

League Club	Source	Date Signed	Seasons Played	Apps	Subs	Gls
Arsenal (L)	Real Madrid (SPN)	08/06	06	11	13	3

BAPTISTE Alexander Aaron John (Alex)
Born: Sutton-in-Ashfield, Nottinghamshire, England, 31 January, 1986 CD

League Club	Source	Date Signed	Seasons Played	Apps	Subs	Gls
Mansfield T	Sch	02/03	02-07	170	4	5
Blackpool	Tr	07/08	08-12	168	2	8
Bolton W	Tr	05/13	13	37	2	4
Blackburn Rov	L	07/14	14	29	3	3

BAPTISTE Jairzinho Rocky Alon (Rocky)
Born: Neasden, NW London, England, 8 July, 1978 F

League Club	Source	Date Signed	Seasons Played	Apps	Subs	Gls
Luton T	Hayes	10/00	00	0	3	0

BARACLOUGH Ian Robert
Born: Leicester, England, 4 December, 1970 LB/M
England: Youth

League Club	Source	Date Signed	Seasons Played	Apps	Subs	Gls
Leicester C	YT	12/88				

League Club	Source	Date Signed	Seasons Played	Apps	Subs	Gls
Wigan Ath	L	03/90	89	8	1	2
Grimsby T	L	12/90	90	1	3	0
Grimsby T	Tr	08/91	92	1	0	0
Lincoln C	Tr	08/92	92-93	68	5	10
Mansfield T	Tr	06/94	94-95	47	0	5
Notts Co	Tr	10/95	95-97	107	4	10
Queens Park Rgrs	Tr	03/98	97-00	120	5	1
Notts Co	Tr	07/01	01-03	93	8	5
Scunthorpe U	Tr	08/04	04-07	124	9	7

BARADA Taylor
Born: Charlottesville, Virginia, USA, 14 August, 1972 — G

League Club	Source	Date Signed	Seasons Played	Apps	Subs	Gls
Colchester U	Notts Co (NC)	03/94	93	1	0	0

BARADJI Sekou
Born: Paris, France, 24 April, 1984 — M

League Club	Source	Date Signed	Seasons Played	Apps	Subs	Gls
West Ham U	UC Le Mans (FRA)	08/05				
Reading	L	09/05	05	0	1	0

BARAZITE Nacer
Born: Arnhem, Netherlands, 27 May, 1990 — RM
Netherlands: U21-9/Youth

League Club	Source	Date Signed	Seasons Played	Apps	Subs	Gls
Arsenal	Sch	07/07				
Derby Co	L	08/08	08	21	9	1

BARBARA Daniel
Born: France, 12 October, 1974 — F

League Club	Source	Date Signed	Seasons Played	Apps	Subs	Gls
Darlington	FC Lourosa (POR)	12/96	96	1	5	1

BARBER David Eric (Dave)
Born: Wombwell, South Yorkshire, England, 6 December, 1939 — WH
Died: Pretoria, South Africa, June, 2006
England: Youth

League Club	Source	Date Signed	Seasons Played	Apps	Subs	Gls
Barnsley	Jnr	06/58	57-60	83	-	4
Preston NE	Tr	06/61	61-63	37	-	2

BARBER Eric
Born: Stockport, Greater Manchester, England, 25 March, 1926 — W

League Club	Source	Date Signed	Seasons Played	Apps	Subs	Gls
Sheffield U	Stockport Co (Am)	02/47				
Stockport Co	Tr	03/49				
Bolton W	Macclesfield T	03/50				
Rochdale	Tr	04/51	50-51	17	-	2

BARBER Eric
Born: Dublin, Republic of Ireland, 18 January, 1942 — IF
Died: USA, 20 August, 2014
Republic of Ireland: 2/LoI-3

League Club	Source	Date Signed	Seasons Played	Apps	Subs	Gls
Birmingham C	Shelbourne (ROI)	03/66	65-66	3	1	1

BARBER Frederick (Fred)
Born: Ferryhill, County Durham, England, 26 August, 1963 — G

League Club	Source	Date Signed	Seasons Played	Apps	Subs	Gls
Darlington	App	08/81	82-85	135	0	0
Everton	Tr	04/86				
Walsall	Tr	10/86	86-90	153	0	0
Peterborough U	L	10/89	89	6	0	0
Chester C	L	10/90	90	3	0	0
Blackpool	L	11/90	90	2	0	0
Chester C	L	03/91	90	5	0	0
Peterborough U	Tr	08/91	91-93	63	0	0
Colchester U	L	03/93	92	10	0	0
Luton T	Tr	08/94				
Peterborough U	L	12/94	94	5	0	0
Ipswich T	L	11/95	95	1	0	0
Blackpool	L	12/95	95	1	0	0
Birmingham C	Tr	01/96	95	1	0	0

BARBER John Nathaniel
Born: Lichfield, Staffordshire, England, 9 October, 1929 — LW
Died: Lichfield, Staffordshire, England, September, 2002

League Club	Source	Date Signed	Seasons Played	Apps	Subs	Gls
Swansea C	Arsenal (Am)	08/50	50	4	-	0
Walsall	Tr	07/51	51	6	-	0

BARBER Keith
Born: Luton, England, 21 September, 1947 — G

League Club	Source	Date Signed	Seasons Played	Apps	Subs	Gls
Luton T	Dunstable T	04/71	70-76	142	0	0
Swansea C	Tr	07/77	77	42	0	0
Cardiff C	L	09/78	78	2	0	0

BARBER Leonard (Len)
Born: Stoke-on-Trent, England, 3 July, 1929 — CF
Died: Stoke-on-Trent, England, February, 1988

League Club	Source	Date Signed	Seasons Played	Apps	Subs	Gls
Port Vale	Bury (Am)	06/47	49-54	47	-	12

BARBER Michael James (Mike)
Born: Kensington, Central London, England, 24 August, 1941 — LW

League Club	Source	Date Signed	Seasons Played	Apps	Subs	Gls
Queens Park Rgrs	Arsenal (Am)	12/59	60-62	63	-	11
Notts Co	Tr	07/63	63-64	33	-	3

BARBER Philip Andrew (Phil)
Born: Tring, Hertfordshire, England, 10 June, 1965 — M

League Club	Source	Date Signed	Seasons Played	Apps	Subs	Gls
Crystal Palace	Aylesbury U	02/84	83-90	207	27	35
Millwall	Tr	07/91	91-93	104	6	12
Plymouth Arg	L	12/94	94	4	0	0
Bristol C	Tr	07/95	95	3	0	0
Mansfield T	L	11/95	95	4	0	1
Fulham	L	01/96	95	13	0	1

BARBER William George (Billy)
Born: Bushey, Hertfordshire, England, 19 September, 1939 — WH

League Club	Source	Date Signed	Seasons Played	Apps	Subs	Gls
Watford	Jnr	03/57	56-59	25	-	0
Aldershot	Tr	08/62	62	1	-	0

BARCHAM Andrew (Andy)
Born: Basildon, England, 16 December, 1986 — W

League Club	Source	Date Signed	Seasons Played	Apps	Subs	Gls
Tottenham H	Sch	07/05				
Leyton Orient	L	11/07	07	15	10	1
Gillingham	Tr	09/08	08-10	87	12	19
Scunthorpe U	Tr	06/11	11-12	60	15	9
Portsmouth	Tr	07/13	13-14	24	21	4

BARCLAY Dominic Alexander
Born: Bristol, England, 5 September, 1976 — F

League Club	Source	Date Signed	Seasons Played	Apps	Subs	Gls
Bristol C	YT	07/95	93-97	2	10	0
Macclesfield T	Tr	07/98	98	3	6	1

BARCLAY John Mitchell
Born: Mid Calder, West Lothian, Scotland, 8 September, 1921 — CF
Died: Bournemouth, England, 16 September, 1996

League Club	Source	Date Signed	Seasons Played	Apps	Subs	Gls
Bournemouth	Haddington Ath	12/47	47-48	5	-	2

BARCLAY Robert Lindsay Guthrie (Bobby)
Born: Perth, Scotland, 13 November, 1922 — CF
Died: Stockport, Greater Manchester, England, April, 1991

League Club	Source	Date Signed	Seasons Played	Apps	Subs	Gls
Preston NE		10/45				
Stockport Co	Alloa Ath	08/48	48	1	-	0

BARCLAY William Wood (Willie)
Born: Larkhall, Lanarkshire, Scotland, 11 July, 1924 — LW
Died: Larkhall, Lanarkshire, Scotland, 25 December, 2005

League Club	Source	Date Signed	Seasons Played	Apps	Subs	Gls
Bury	Motherwell	03/49	48-49	17	-	1

BARDSLEY David John
Born: Manchester, England, 11 September, 1964 — RB
England: 2/Youth

League Club	Source	Date Signed	Seasons Played	Apps	Subs	Gls
Blackpool	App	11/82	81-83	45	0	0
Watford	Tr	11/83	83-87	97	3	7
Oxford U	Tr	09/87	87-89	74	0	7
Queens Park Rgrs	Tr	09/89	89-97	252	1	4
Blackpool	Tr	07/98	98-99	64	0	0

BARDSLEY Leslie (Les)
Born: Stockport, Greater Manchester, England, 18 August, 1925 — LH
Died: Bristol, England, 30 January, 2012

League Club	Source	Date Signed	Seasons Played	Apps	Subs	Gls
Manchester C	Jnr	01/45				
Bury	Linfield	04/48	47-54	200	-	2
Barrow	Tr	09/55	55	22	-	0

BARDSLEY Philip Anthony (Phil)
Born: Salford, England, 28 June, 1985 — RB
Scotland: 13

League Club	Source	Date Signed	Seasons Played	Apps	Subs	Gls
Manchester U	Sch	07/03	05	3	5	0
Burnley	L	03/06	05	6	0	0
Aston Villa	L	01/07	06	13	0	0
Sheffield U	L	10/07	07	16	0	0
Sunderland	Tr	01/08	07-13	154	20	7
Stoke C	Tr	05/14	14	24	1	0

BARFOOT Stuart John
Born: Southampton, England, 10 December, 1975 — FB

League Club	Source	Date Signed	Seasons Played	Apps	Subs	Gls
Bournemouth	YT	07/94	94	0	2	0

BARGH George Wolfenden
Born: Bilsborrow, Lancashire, England, 27 May, 1910 — IF
Died: Preston, Lancashire, England, 13 September, 1995

League Club	Source	Date Signed	Seasons Played	Apps	Subs	Gls
Preston NE	Garstang	02/28	28-34	142	-	42
Sheffield Wed	Tr	09/35	35	5	-	0
Bury	Tr	05/36	36-38	90	-	13
Chesterfield	Tr	06/39				
Bury	Tr	09/46	46	1	-	0

BARHAM Mark Francis
Born: Folkestone, Kent, England, 12 July, 1962 — RW
England: 2/Youth

League Club	Source	Date Signed	Seasons Played	Apps	Subs	Gls
Norwich C	App	04/80	79-86	169	8	23
Huddersfield T	Tr	07/87	87-88	25	2	1
Middlesbrough	Tr	11/88	88	3	1	0
West Bromwich A	Tr	09/89	89	4	0	0
Brighton & HA	Millwall (NC)	12/89	89-91	70	3	8
Shrewsbury T	Tr	09/92	92	7	1	1

BARK Robert (Bobby)
Born: Stranraer, Dumfries & Galloway, Scotland, 27 January, 1926 LW
Died: Barrow, Cumbria, England, 1 January, 2007

League Club	Source	Date Signed	Seasons Played	Apps	Subs	Gls
Barrow	Queen of the South	04/48	48	1	-	0

BARKAS Samuel (Sam)
Born: Wardley, Tyne and Wear, England, 29 December, 1909 LB
Died: Shipley, West Yorkshire, England, 8 December, 1989
England: 5/FLge-3

League Club	Source	Date Signed	Seasons Played	Apps	Subs	Gls
Bradford C	Middle Dock	08/27	27-33	202	-	8
Manchester C	Tr	04/34	33-46	175	-	1

BARKAS Thomas (Tommy)
Born: Gateshead, Tyne and Wear, England, 27 March, 1912 IF
Died: Halifax, West Yorkshire, England, June, 1991

League Club	Source	Date Signed	Seasons Played	Apps	Subs	Gls
Bradford C	Washington Colliery	09/32	32-34	16	-	2
Halifax T	Tr	12/34	34-38	169	-	35
Rochdale	Tr	09/46	46-47	44	-	17
Stockport Co	Tr	11/47	47-48	44	-	18
Carlisle U	Tr	02/49	48	14	-	5

BARKE John Lloyd (Lloyd)
Born: Nuncargate, Nottinghamshire, England, 16 December, 1912 CH
Died: Kirkby-in-Ashfield, Nottinghamshire, England, 7 March, 1976

League Club	Source	Date Signed	Seasons Played	Apps	Subs	Gls
Sheffield U	Scunthorpe U	05/33	34-36	6	-	0
Mansfield T	Tr	06/37	37-46	114	-	0

BARKE (NAYLOR) William Henry (Bill)
Born: Sheffield, England, 23 November, 1919 IF
Died: Sheffield, England, January, 1989

League Club	Source	Date Signed	Seasons Played	Apps	Subs	Gls
Crystal Palace	Hampton Sports	01/39	46	18	-	9
Brentford	Tr	02/47	46	11	-	2
Leyton Orient	Tr	06/47	47-49	64	-	14

BARKER Allan Michael (Mickey)
Born: Bishop Auckland, County Durham, England, 23 February, 1956 LB

League Club	Source	Date Signed	Seasons Played	Apps	Subs	Gls
Newcastle U	Jnr	03/73	74-78	21	2	0
Gillingham	Tr	01/79	78-79	64	0	2
Hartlepool U	Bishop Auckland	09/82	82-83	59	1	1

BARKER Christopher Andrew (Chris)
Born: Sheffield, England, 2 March, 1980 D

League Club	Source	Date Signed	Seasons Played	Apps	Subs	Gls
Barnsley	Alfreton T	08/98	99-01	110	3	3
Cardiff C	Tr	07/02	02-05	144	15	0
Stoke C	L	08/04	04	4	0	0
Colchester U	L	08/06	06	38	0	0
Queens Park Rgrs	Tr	06/07	07	25	0	0
Plymouth Arg	Tr	08/08	08-09	48	6	0
Southend U	Tr	08/10	10-12	113	4	0

BARKER Donald (Don)
Born: Long Eaton, Derbyshire, England, 17 June, 1911 IF
Died: Derby, England, 1979

League Club	Source	Date Signed	Seasons Played	Apps	Subs	Gls
Bradford Park Ave	Johnson & Barnes	01/34	33-36	55	-	15
Millwall	Tr	01/37	36-38	62	-	18
Brighton & HA	Tr	07/46	46	14	-	4

BARKER Geoffrey Arthur (Geoff)
Born: Hull, England, 7 February, 1949 CD

League Club	Source	Date Signed	Seasons Played	Apps	Subs	Gls
Hull C	Jnr	03/67	68-70	29	1	2
Southend U	L	12/70	70	25	0	0
Darlington	Tr	07/71	71-74	151	0	6
Reading	Tr	02/75	74-76	51	1	2
Grimsby T	Tr	07/77	77-78	66	0	1

BARKER George John
Born: Portsmouth, England, 26 September, 1991 F

League Club	Source	Date Signed	Seasons Played	Apps	Subs	Gls
Brighton & HA	Sch	06/10	12-13	0	4	0
Barnet	L	11/12	12	1	0	0
Newport Co	L	11/13	13	0	2	0
Swindon T	Tr	01/14	13-14	3	10	0
Tranmere Rov	L	10/14	14	4	0	0

BARKER Gordon
Born: Pudsey, West Yorkshire, England, 6 July, 1931 W
Died: Chelmsford, England, 10 February, 2006

League Club	Source	Date Signed	Seasons Played	Apps	Subs	Gls
Southend U	Bishop Auckland	12/54	54-58	57	-	9

BARKER Jeffrey (Jeff)
Born: Scunthorpe, North Lincolnshire, England, 16 October, 1915 RB
Died: Scunthorpe, North Lincolnshire, England, March, 1985

League Club	Source	Date Signed	Seasons Played	Apps	Subs	Gls
Aston Villa	Scunthorpe U	11/36	37	3	-	0
Huddersfield T	Tr	11/45	46-47	67	-	0
Scunthorpe U	Tr	08/48	50-51	73	-	1

BARKER John
Born: Huddersfield, West Yorkshire, England, 4 July, 1948 LB
Died: Scunthorpe, North Lincolnshire, England, 14 December, 2004

League Club	Source	Date Signed	Seasons Played	Apps	Subs	Gls
Scunthorpe U	App	07/66	65-74	261	2	6

BARKER Keith
Born: Stoke-on-Trent, England, 22 February, 1949 G
Died: Norwich, England, 1 January, 2008

League Club	Source	Date Signed	Seasons Played	Apps	Subs	Gls
Barnsley	Cambridge U	03/71	71	9	0	0

BARKER Keith Hubert Douglas
Born: Accrington, Lancashire, England, 21 October, 1986 F
England: Youth

League Club	Source	Date Signed	Seasons Played	Apps	Subs	Gls
Blackburn Rov	Sch	03/05				
Rochdale	L	08/06	06	11	1	0

BARKER Leonard (Len)
Born: Salford, England, 26 March, 1924 W
Died: Macclesfield, Cheshire, England, 9 September, 1991

League Club	Source	Date Signed	Seasons Played	Apps	Subs	Gls
Stockport Co	Manchester Transport	01/48	48-50	40	-	12

BARKER Richard Ian (Richie)
Born: Sheffield, England, 30 May, 1975 F
England: Youth/Schools

League Club	Source	Date Signed	Seasons Played	Apps	Subs	Gls
Sheffield Wed	Jnr	07/93				
Doncaster Rov	L	09/95	95	5	1	0
Brighton & HA	Linfield	12/97	97-98	48	12	12
Macclesfield T	Tr	07/99	99-00	58	0	23
Rotherham U	Tr	01/01	00-04	69	71	12
Mansfield T	Tr	11/04	04-06	93	2	40
Hartlepool U	Tr	01/07	06-08	49	13	23
Rotherham U	Tr	10/08	08	4	9	1

BARKER Richard Joseph (Richie)
Born: Loughborough, Leicestershire, England, 23 November, 1939 F

League Club	Source	Date Signed	Seasons Played	Apps	Subs	Gls
Derby Co	Burton A	10/67	67-68	30	8	12
Notts Co	Tr	12/68	68-71	99	12	37
Peterborough U	Tr	09/71	71	36	0	9

BARKER Robert Campbell (Bobby)
Born: Kinglassie, Fife, Scotland, 1 December, 1927 LW
Died: Poole, Dorset, England, March, 2013

League Club	Source	Date Signed	Seasons Played	Apps	Subs	Gls
West Bromwich A	Kelty Rgrs	09/45	48	14	-	2
Shrewsbury T	Tr	08/50	50	25	-	1

BARKER Shaun
Born: Trowell, Nottinghamshire, England, 19 September, 1982 CD

League Club	Source	Date Signed	Seasons Played	Apps	Subs	Gls
Rotherham U	Sch	07/02	02-05	119	4	7
Blackpool	Tr	08/06	06-08	133	1	5
Derby Co	Tr	07/09	09-11	94	4	6

BARKER Simon
Born: Farnworth, Greater Manchester, England, 4 November, 1964 M
England: U21-4

League Club	Source	Date Signed	Seasons Played	Apps	Subs	Gls
Blackburn Rov	App	11/82	83-87	180	2	35
Queens Park Rgrs	Tr	07/88	88-97	291	24	33
Port Vale	Tr	09/98	98-99	26	6	2

BARKER Thomas Haydn (Haydn)
Born: Tyldesley, Greater Manchester, England, 12 January, 1936 IF

League Club	Source	Date Signed	Seasons Played	Apps	Subs	Gls
Southport	Holy Family	12/57	57-58	35	-	4

BARKER William (Bill)
Born: Stoke-on-Trent, England, 31 May, 1924 CF
Died: Stoke-on-Trent, England, April, 2002

League Club	Source	Date Signed	Seasons Played	Apps	Subs	Gls
Stoke C		10/48	49	1	-	0

BARKHUIZEN Thomas John (Tom)
Born: Blackpool, Lancashire, England, 4 July, 1993 F

League Club	Source	Date Signed	Seasons Played	Apps	Subs	Gls
Blackpool	Sch	07/11	13-14	6	15	1
Hereford U	L	08/11	11	32	6	11
Fleetwood T	L	08/12	12	8	5	1
Morecambe	L	10/14	14	1	4	0

BARKLEY Ross
Born: Liverpool, England, 5 December, 1993 M
England: 12/U21-5/Youth

League Club	Source	Date Signed	Seasons Played	Apps	Subs	Gls
Everton	Sch	12/10	11-14	51	25	8
Sheffield Wed	L	09/12	12	12	1	4
Leeds U	L	01/13	12	3	1	0

BARKS Edwin (Eddie)
Born: Heanor, Derbyshire, England, 1 September, 1921 WH
Died: Derby, England, 26 March, 1989

League Club	Source	Date Signed	Seasons Played	Apps	Subs	Gls
Nottingham F	Heanor T	04/39	46-48	66	-	5
Mansfield T	Tr	01/49	48-54	213	-	6

BARKUS Lea Paul
Born: Reading, England, 7 December, 1974 W

League Club	Source	Date Signed	Seasons Played	Apps	Subs	Gls
Reading	YT	08/92	91-92	8	7	1
Fulham	Tr	07/95	95	3	6	1

BARLEY Charles Derek (Charlie)
Born: Highbury, N London, England, 20 March, 1932 CF

Died: Reading, England, 17 March, 1994
England: Youth

League Club	Source	Date Signed	Seasons Played	Apps	Subs	Gls
Arsenal	Maidenhead U	12/51				
Queens Park Rgrs	Tr	05/53	53	4	-	0
Aldershot	Tr	07/54	54	2	-	0

BARLEY Peter James
Born: Scunthorpe, North Lincolnshire, England, 25 April, 1936 — G
Died: Lincoln, England, June, 2011

League Club	Source	Date Signed	Seasons Played	Apps	Subs	Gls
Scunthorpe U	Leeds U (Am)	10/53	53	5	-	0

BARLOW Andrew John (Andy)
Born: Oldham, Greater Manchester, England, 24 November, 1965 — LB

League Club	Source	Date Signed	Seasons Played	Apps	Subs	Gls
Oldham Ath	Jnr	07/84	84-94	245	16	5
Bradford C	L	11/93	93	2	0	0
Blackpool	Tr	07/95	95-96	77	3	2
Rochdale	Tr	07/97	97-98	60	7	1

BARLOW Colin James
Born: Manchester, England, 14 November, 1935 — RW

League Club	Source	Date Signed	Seasons Played	Apps	Subs	Gls
Manchester C	Tarporley BC	12/56	57-62	179	-	78
Oldham Ath	Tr	08/63	63	6	-	1
Doncaster Rov	Tr	08/64	64	3	-	0

BARLOW Frank Charles
Born: Mexborough, South Yorkshire, England, 15 October, 1946 — CD
England: Schools

League Club	Source	Date Signed	Seasons Played	Apps	Subs	Gls
Sheffield U	Jnr	09/65	65-71	116	5	2
Chesterfield	Tr	08/72	72-75	140	1	3

BARLOW Harold (Harry)
Born: Manchester, England, 25 October, 1925 — LH
Died: Shropshire, England, 10 September, 2014

League Club	Source	Date Signed	Seasons Played	Apps	Subs	Gls
Crewe Alex	Manchester C (Am)	02/46	46-50	27	-	1

BARLOW Herbert (Bert)
Born: Kilnhurst, South Yorkshire, England, 22 July, 1916 — IF
Died: Colchester, Essex, England, 19 March, 2004

League Club	Source	Date Signed	Seasons Played	Apps	Subs	Gls
Barnsley	Silverwood Colliery	07/35	35-37	58	-	12
Wolverhampton W	Tr	06/38	38	3	-	1
Portsmouth	Tr	02/39	38-49	104	-	34
Leicester C	Tr	12/49	49-51	42	-	9
Colchester U	Tr	07/52	52-53	60	-	16

BARLOW Martin David
Born: Barnstaple, Devon, England, 25 June, 1971 — RW

League Club	Source	Date Signed	Seasons Played	Apps	Subs	Gls
Plymouth Arg	YT	07/89	88-00	294	35	24
Exeter C	Tr	07/01	01	26	4	0

BARLOW Matthew John (Matty)
Born: Oldham, Greater Manchester, England, 25 June, 1987 — F

League Club	Source	Date Signed	Seasons Played	Apps	Subs	Gls
Oldham Ath	Sch	-	03-04	1	9	0

BARLOW Neil Keith
Born: Bury, Greater Manchester, England, 24 March, 1978 — CD

League Club	Source	Date Signed	Seasons Played	Apps	Subs	Gls
Rochdale	YT	07/96	95	1	1	0

BARLOW Peter
Born: Portsmouth, England, 9 January, 1950 — F

League Club	Source	Date Signed	Seasons Played	Apps	Subs	Gls
Colchester U	App	01/68	66-68	18	3	4
Workington	Tr	02/69	68-69	41	1	11
Hartlepool U	Tr	07/70	70	8	3	0

BARLOW Philip Douglas (Phil)
Born: Shipley, West Yorkshire, England, 19 December, 1946 — CH

League Club	Source	Date Signed	Seasons Played	Apps	Subs	Gls
Bradford C	Guiseley	07/66	66	15	1	0
Lincoln C	Tr	08/67	67	5	0	0

BARLOW Raymond John (Ray)
Born: Swindon, England, 17 August, 1926 — LH
Died: Bridgend, Wales, 14 March, 2012
England: 1/B-2/FLge-4

League Club	Source	Date Signed	Seasons Played	Apps	Subs	Gls
West Bromwich A	Garrards	06/44	46-59	403	-	31
Birmingham C	Tr	08/60	60	5	-	0

BARLOW Stuart
Born: Liverpool, England, 16 July, 1968 — F

League Club	Source	Date Signed	Seasons Played	Apps	Subs	Gls
Everton	Sherwood Park	06/90	90-95	24	47	10
Oldham Ath	Tr	11/95	95-97	78	15	31
Wigan Ath	Tr	03/98	97-99	72	11	40
Tranmere Rov	Tr	07/00	00-02	62	32	19
Stockport Co	Tr	08/03	03-04	26	35	11
Bury	Tr	07/05	05	2	11	0

BARMBY Jack
Born: Harlow, Essex, England, 14 November, 1994 — W
England: Youth

League Club	Source	Date Signed	Seasons Played	Apps	Subs	Gls
Manchester U	Sch	07/13				
Hartlepool U	L	01/14	13	12	5	5
Leicester C	Tr	07/14	14			
Rotherham U	L	01/15	14	2	0	0

BARMBY Jeffrey (Jeff)
Born: Hull, England, 15 January, 1943 — CF

League Club	Source	Date Signed	Seasons Played	Apps	Subs	Gls
York C (Am)	Selby T	03/63	62-63	2	-	0

BARMBY Nicholas Jonathan (Nick)
Born: Hull, England, 11 February, 1974 — M
England: 23/B-2/U21-4/Youth/Schools

League Club	Source	Date Signed	Seasons Played	Apps	Subs	Gls
Tottenham H	YT	04/91	92-94	81	6	20
Middlesbrough	Tr	08/95	95-96	42	0	8
Everton	Tr	11/96	96-99	105	11	18
Liverpool	Tr	07/00	00-01	23	9	2
Leeds U	Tr	08/02	02-03	17	8	4
Nottingham F	L	02/04	03	6	0	1
Hull C	Tr	07/04	04-11	98	82	26

BARNARD Arthur
Born: Boothstown, Greater Manchester, England, 20 June, 1932 — G

League Club	Source	Date Signed	Seasons Played	Apps	Subs	Gls
Bolton W	Astley & Tyldesley	11/51	54-55	2	-	0
Stockport Co	Tr	07/56	56-58	53	-	0
Southport	Tr	09/59	59	42	-	0

BARNARD Christopher Leslie (Chris)
Born: Cardiff, Wales, 1 August, 1947 — M

League Club	Source	Date Signed	Seasons Played	Apps	Subs	Gls
Southend U	App	08/65	65	4	4	0
Ipswich T	Tr	07/66	66-70	18	3	0
Torquay U	Tr	10/70	70-71	29	3	3
Charlton Ath	Tr	01/72	71	0	1	0

BARNARD Darren Sean
Born: Rinteln, Germany, 30 November, 1971 — LB/M
England: Youth/Schools//Wales: 22

League Club	Source	Date Signed	Seasons Played	Apps	Subs	Gls
Chelsea	Wokingham T	07/90	91-93	18	11	2
Reading	L	11/94	94	3	1	0
Bristol C	Tr	10/95	95-96	77	1	15
Barnsley	Tr	08/97	97-01	151	19	28
Grimsby T	Tr	08/02	02-03	55	8	4

BARNARD Donny Gary
Born: Forest Gate, E London, England, 1 July, 1984 — RB

League Club	Source	Date Signed	Seasons Played	Apps	Subs	Gls
Leyton Orient	Sch	03/03	01-06	90	50	1

BARNARD Geoffrey (Geoff)
Born: Southend-on-Sea, England, 23 March, 1946 — G

League Club	Source	Date Signed	Seasons Played	Apps	Subs	Gls
Norwich C	Jnr	09/63	64-66	6	0	0
Scunthorpe U	Tr	07/68	68-74	265	0	0
Scunthorpe U	Scarborough	09/76	76	6	0	0

BARNARD Henry Michael (Mike)
Born: Portsmouth, England, 18 July, 1933 — IF

League Club	Source	Date Signed	Seasons Played	Apps	Subs	Gls
Portsmouth	Gosport Bor	08/51	53-58	116	-	25

BARNARD Lee James
Born: Romford, E London, England, 18 July, 1984 — F
England: Youth

League Club	Source	Date Signed	Seasons Played	Apps	Subs	Gls
Tottenham H	Sch	07/02	05	0	3	0
Exeter C	L	11/02	02	3	0	0
Leyton Orient	L	11/04	04	3	5	0
Northampton T	L	03/05	04	3	2	0
Crewe Alex	L	08/07	07	9	1	3
Southend U	Tr	01/08	07-09	60	15	35
Southampton	Tr	01/10	09-11	38	24	23
Bournemouth	L	08/12	12	15	0	4
Oldham Ath	L	01/13	12	14	0	3
Southend U	Tr	01/14	13-14	11	11	2
Stevenage	L	10/14	14	6	0	3

BARNARD Leigh Kenneth
Born: Worsley, Greater Manchester, England, 29 October, 1958 — M

League Club	Source	Date Signed	Seasons Played	Apps	Subs	Gls
Portsmouth	App	10/76	77-81	71	8	8
Peterborough U	L	03/82	81	1	3	0
Swindon T	Tr	07/82	82-89	212	5	22
Exeter C	L	02/85	84	6	0	2
Cardiff C	Tr	10/89	89-90	61	2	9

BARNARD Mark
Born: Sheffield, England, 27 November, 1975 — LB

League Club	Source	Date Signed	Seasons Played	Apps	Subs	Gls
Rotherham U	YT	07/94				
Darlington	Worksop T	09/95	95-98	131	12	4

BARNARD Raymond Scholey (Ray)
Born: Middlesbrough, England, 16 April, 1933 — RB
England: Schools

League Club	Source	Date Signed	Seasons Played	Apps	Subs	Gls
Middlesbrough	Jnr	04/50	51-59	113	-	0
Lincoln C	Tr	06/60	60-62	43	-	0

BARNES Andrew John (Andy)
Born: Croydon, S London, England, 31 March, 1967 — F

League Club	Source	Date Signed	Seasons Played	Apps	Subs	Gls
Crystal Palace	Sutton U	09/91	91	0	1	0
Carlisle U	L	12/93	93	2	0	0

BARNES Ashley Luke
Born: Bath, England, 30 October, 1989 — F

League Club	Source	Date Signed	Seasons Played	Apps	Subs	Gls
Plymouth Arg	Paulton Rov	03/07	08-09	15	7	2
Torquay U	L	02/10	09	6	0	0
Brighton & HA	Tr	03/10	09-13	114	35	46
Burnley	Tr	01/14	13-14	39	17	8

BARNES Bernard Noel Preston
Born: Plymouth, England, 25 December, 1937 — CF
Died: West Devon, England, April, 2004

League Club	Source	Date Signed	Seasons Played	Apps	Subs	Gls
Plymouth Arg	Bideford T	01/55	56-57	4	-	1

BARNES Charles Ronald (Ron)
Born: Bolton, Greater Manchester, England, 21 February, 1936 — RW
Died: Darcy Lever, Greater Manchester, England, 7 December, 1991

League Club	Source	Date Signed	Seasons Played	Apps	Subs	Gls
Blackpool	Jnr	05/54	56-58	9	-	0
Rochdale	Tr	06/59	59-60	91	-	7
Wrexham	Tr	07/61	61-63	88	-	24
Norwich C	Tr	08/63	63	21	-	1
Peterborough U	Tr	07/64	64-65	39	0	6
Torquay U	Tr	01/66	65-68	110	4	25

BARNES Colin
Born: Notting Hill, Central London, England, 28 May, 1957 — F

League Club	Source	Date Signed	Seasons Played	Apps	Subs	Gls
Torquay U	Barnet	08/83	83-84	42	1	11

BARNES Corey
Born: Sunderland, England, 1 January, 1992 — M

League Club	Source	Date Signed	Seasons Played	Apps	Subs	Gls
Darlington	Sch	-	08-09	6	3	0

BARNES David
Born: Paddington, Central London, England, 16 November, 1961 — LB
England: Youth

League Club	Source	Date Signed	Seasons Played	Apps	Subs	Gls
Coventry C	App	05/79	79-81	9	0	0
Ipswich T	Tr	05/82	82-83	16	1	0
Wolverhampton W	Tr	10/84	84-87	86	2	4
Aldershot	Tr	08/87	87-88	68	1	1
Sheffield U	Tr	07/89	89-93	82	0	1
Watford	Tr	01/94	93-95	16	0	0
Colchester U	Tr	08/96	96	11	0	0

BARNES David Oswald (Bobby)
Born: Kingston-on-Thames, SW London, England, 17 December, 1962 — RW
England: Youth

League Club	Source	Date Signed	Seasons Played	Apps	Subs	Gls
West Ham U	App	09/80	80-85	31	12	5
Scunthorpe U	L	11/85	85	6	0	0
Aldershot	Tr	03/86	85-87	49	0	26
Swindon T	Tr	10/87	87-88	43	2	13
Bournemouth	Tr	03/89	88-89	11	3	0
Northampton T	Tr	10/89	89-91	97	1	37
Peterborough U	Tr	02/92	91-93	42	7	9
Torquay U	Hong Kong Rgrs (HKG)	09/95	95	0	1	0

BARNES Eric
Born: Wythenshawe, Greater Manchester, England, 29 November, 1937 — CH
Died: Crewe, Cheshire, England, 3 January, 2014

League Club	Source	Date Signed	Seasons Played	Apps	Subs	Gls
Crewe Alex	RAF	01/58	57-69	352	2	1

BARNES Giles Gordon
Born: Barking, E London, England, 5 August, 1988 — M
England: Youth

League Club	Source	Date Signed	Seasons Played	Apps	Subs	Gls
Derby Co	Sch	08/05	05-08	61	21	10
West Bromwich A	Tr	02/10	09-10	2	21	0
Doncaster Rov	Tr	06/11	11	24	9	1

BARNES John Charles Bryan
Born: Kingston, Jamaica, 7 November, 1963 — W/F
England: 79/FLge/U21-3

League Club	Source	Date Signed	Seasons Played	Apps	Subs	Gls
Watford	Sudbury Court	07/81	81-86	232	1	65
Liverpool	Tr	06/87	87-96	310	4	84
Newcastle U	Tr	08/97	97-98	22	5	6
Charlton Ath	Tr	02/99	98	2	10	0

BARNES Kenneth Herbert (Ken)
Born: Birmingham, England, 16 March, 1929 — RH
Died: Macclesfield, Cheshire, England, 13 July, 2010

League Club	Source	Date Signed	Seasons Played	Apps	Subs	Gls
Manchester C	Stafford Rgrs	05/50	51-60	258	-	18
Wrexham	Tr	05/61	61-64	132	-	24

BARNES Kevin
Born: Fleetwood, Lancashire, England, 12 September, 1975 — F

League Club	Source	Date Signed	Seasons Played	Apps	Subs	Gls
Blackpool	Lancaster C	03/99	98	2	2	0

BARNES Michael Frederick
Born: Reading, England, 17 September, 1963 — CD

League Club	Source	Date Signed	Seasons Played	Apps	Subs	Gls
Reading	App	09/81	80-83	29	5	2
Northampton T	Tr	08/84	84	19	0	1

BARNES Michael Thomas
Born: Chorley, Lancashire, England, 24 June, 1988 — W

League Club	Source	Date Signed	Seasons Played	Apps	Subs	Gls
Manchester U	Sch	07/06				
Chesterfield	L	01/08	07	1	2	0
Shrewsbury T	L	03/08	07	2	0	0

BARNES Paul Lance
Born: Leicester, England, 16 November, 1967 — F

League Club	Source	Date Signed	Seasons Played	Apps	Subs	Gls
Notts Co	App	11/85	85-89	36	17	14
Stoke C	Tr	03/90	89-91	10	14	3
Chesterfield	L	11/90	90	1	0	0
York C	Tr	07/92	92-95	147	1	76
Birmingham C	Tr	03/96	95	15	0	7
Burnley	Tr	09/96	96-97	63	2	30
Huddersfield T	Tr	01/98	97-98	13	17	2
Bury	Tr	03/99	98-00	31	23	8
Doncaster Rov	Tr	07/01	03	2	5	0

BARNES Peter
Born: St Albans, Hertfordshire, England, 29 June, 1938 — LH
Died: Bushey, Hertfordshire, England, 7 October, 2014

League Club	Source	Date Signed	Seasons Played	Apps	Subs	Gls
Watford	Jnr	03/57	60-61	10	-	0

BARNES Peter Simon
Born: Manchester, England, 10 June, 1957 — LW
England: 22/B-1/FLge/U21-9/Youth

League Club	Source	Date Signed	Seasons Played	Apps	Subs	Gls
Manchester C	App	08/74	74-78	108	7	15
West Bromwich A	Tr	07/79	79-80	76	1	23
Leeds U	Tr	08/81	81	31	0	1
Leeds U	Real Betis (SPN)	08/83	83	25	2	4
Coventry C	Tr	10/84	84	18	0	2
Manchester U	Tr	07/85	85-86	19	1	2
Manchester C	Tr	01/87	86	8	0	0
Bolton W	L	10/87	87	2	0	0
Port Vale	L	12/87	87	3	0	0
Hull C	Tr	03/88	87	11	0	0
Bolton W	Depo Farense (POR)	11/88	88	2	1	0
Sunderland	Tr	02/89	88	1	0	0

BARNES Philip Kenneth (Phil)
Born: Sheffield, England, 2 March, 1979 — G

League Club	Source	Date Signed	Seasons Played	Apps	Subs	Gls
Rotherham U	YT	06/97	96	2	0	0
Blackpool	Tr	07/97	97-03	141	0	0
Sheffield U	Tr	07/04	04	1	0	0
Torquay U	L	02/05	04	5	0	0
Queens Park Rgrs	L	02/06	05	1	0	0
Grimsby T	Tr	07/06	06-08	120	0	0

BARNES Richard Ian
Born: Wrexham, Wales, 6 September, 1975 — FB

League Club	Source	Date Signed	Seasons Played	Apps	Subs	Gls
Wrexham	YT	05/94	94	0	1	0

BARNES Robert Alan
Born: Stoke-on-Trent, England, 26 November, 1969 — FB

League Club	Source	Date Signed	Seasons Played	Apps	Subs	Gls
Manchester C	YT	07/88				
Wrexham	Tr	06/89	89-90	8	1	0

BARNES Sam
Born: Liverpool, England, 16 October, 1991 — CD

League Club	Source	Date Signed	Seasons Played	Apps	Subs	Gls
Stockport Co	Sch	-	09	2	0	0

BARNES Steven Leslie (Steve)
Born: Harrow, NW London, England, 5 January, 1976 — LW

League Club	Source	Date Signed	Seasons Played	Apps	Subs	Gls
Birmingham C	Welling U	10/95	95	0	3	0
Brighton & HA	L	01/98	97	12	0	0
Barnet	Tr	10/98	98-99	4	11	0

BARNES Walley
Born: Brecon, Powys, Wales, 16 January, 1920 — FB
Died: Hammersmith, W London, England, 4 September, 1975
Wales: 22/War-2

League Club	Source	Date Signed	Seasons Played	Apps	Subs	Gls
Arsenal	Southampton (Am)	09/43	46-55	267	-	11

BARNES William (Billy)
Born: Dumbarton, Dunbartonshire, Scotland, 16 March, 1939 — D

League Club	Source	Date Signed	Seasons Played	Apps	Subs	Gls
Bradford C	Rutherglen Glencairn	04/58	58-60	59	-	0
Bradford Park Ave	Scarborough	09/66	66-67	53	0	0

BARNES-HOMER Matthew Brian (Matt)
Born: Dudley, West Midlands, England, 2 March, 1979 — F
England: Semi Pro-5

League Club	Source	Date Signed	Seasons Played	Apps	Subs	Gls
Wycombe W	Willenhall T	03/07	06	0	1	0
Rochdale (L)	Luton T	08/11	11	1	4	0

BARNESS Anthony
Born: Lewisham, SE London, England, 25 March, 1973 — LB

League Club	Source	Date Signed	Seasons Played	Apps	Subs	Gls
Charlton Ath	YT	03/91	91-92	21	6	1
Chelsea	Tr	09/92	92-94	12	2	0
Southend U	L	02/96	95	5	0	0
Charlton Ath	Tr	08/96	96-99	83	13	3
Bolton W	Tr	07/00	00-04	73	20	0
Plymouth Arg	Tr	07/05	05-06	34	3	0

BARNETT Benjamin James (Ben)
Born: Islington, N London, England, 18 December, 1969 — F

League Club	Source	Date Signed	Seasons Played	Apps	Subs	Gls
Barnet	Heybridge Swifts	08/93	93	0	2	0

BARNETT Charlie John
Born: Liverpool, England, 19 September, 1988 — M

League Club	Source	Date Signed	Seasons Played	Apps	Subs	Gls
Liverpool	Sch	07/06				
Tranmere Rov	Tr	08/08	08-09	26	10	4
Accrington Stan	Tr	08/10	10-12	64	32	3

BARNETT David (Dave)
Born: Lambeth, S London, England, 24 September, 1951 — CD

League Club	Source	Date Signed	Seasons Played	Apps	Subs	Gls
Southend U	App	09/69	68-72	48	9	0

BARNETT David Kwame (Dave)
Born: Birmingham, England, 16 April, 1967 — CD

League Club	Source	Date Signed	Seasons Played	Apps	Subs	Gls
Colchester U	Windsor & Eton	08/88	88	19	1	0
West Bromwich A	Edmonton Brick'n (CAN)	10/89				
Walsall	Tr	07/90	90	4	1	0
Barnet	Kidderminster Hrs	02/92	91-93	58	1	3
Birmingham C	L	12/93	93	2	1	0
Birmingham C	Tr	02/94	93-96	43	0	0
Port Vale	Dunfermline Ath	03/98	97-98	34	2	1
Lincoln C	Tr	07/99	99	20	2	3

BARNETT Gary Lloyd
Born: Stratford-on-Avon, Warwickshire, England, 11 March, 1963 — W

League Club	Source	Date Signed	Seasons Played	Apps	Subs	Gls
Coventry C	App	01/81				
Oxford U	Tr	07/82	82-85	37	8	9
Wimbledon	L	02/83	82	5	0	1
Fulham	L	12/84	84	0	2	1
Fulham	Tr	09/85	85-89	167	13	30
Huddersfield T	Tr	07/90	90-93	92	8	11
Leyton Orient	Tr	08/93	93-94	47	16	7
Kidderminster Hrs	Barry T	08/99	00	2	0	0

BARNETT Geoffrey Colin (Geoff)
Born: Northwich, Cheshire, England, 16 October, 1946 — G
England: Youth/Schools

League Club	Source	Date Signed	Seasons Played	Apps	Subs	Gls
Everton	App	05/64	65-67	10	0	0
Arsenal	Tr	10/69	69-75	39	0	0

BARNETT George Alan Samuel (Alan)
Born: Croydon, S London, England, 4 November, 1934 — G
Died: Portsmouth, England, October, 1978

League Club	Source	Date Signed	Seasons Played	Apps	Subs	Gls
Portsmouth	Croydon Amats	09/55	55-57	25	-	0
Grimsby T	Tr	12/58	58-62	116	-	0
Exeter C	Tr	07/63	63-65	57	0	0
Torquay U	Tr	06/66				

BARNETT Graham
Born: Stoke-on-Trent, England, 17 May, 1936 — IF

League Club	Source	Date Signed	Seasons Played	Apps	Subs	Gls
Port Vale	Jnr	06/56	58-59	49	-	34
Tranmere Rov	Tr	03/60	59-60	32	-	11
Halifax T	Tr	08/61	61	32	-	10

BARNETT Jason Vincent
Born: Shrewsbury, Shropshire, England, 21 April, 1976 — RB/M

League Club	Source	Date Signed	Seasons Played	Apps	Subs	Gls
Wolverhampton W	YT	07/94				
Lincoln C	Tr	10/95	95-01	189	18	6

BARNETT Leon Peter
Born: Stevenage, Hertfordshire, England, 30 November, 1985 — CD

League Club	Source	Date Signed	Seasons Played	Apps	Subs	Gls
Luton T	Sch	09/04	05-06	51	8	3
West Bromwich A	Tr	07/07	07-09	40	5	3
Coventry C	L	11/09	09	19	1	0
Norwich C	Tr	08/10	10-12	44	6	2
Cardiff C	L	03/13	12	8	0	0
Wigan Ath	Tr	07/13	13-14	55	6	4

BARNETT Moses
Born: Freetown, Sierra Leone, 3 December, 1990 — LB

League Club	Source	Date Signed	Seasons Played	Apps	Subs	Gls
Everton	Sch	05/08				
Darlington	L	10/09	09	4	0	0

BARNETT Thomas Andrew (Tommy)
Born: Muswell Hill, N London, England, 12 October, 1936 — CF

League Club	Source	Date Signed	Seasons Played	Apps	Subs	Gls
Crystal Palace	Chatham	12/58	58-60	14	-	2

BARNETT Tyrone Benjamin
Born: Stevenage, Hertfordshire, England, 28 October, 1985 — F

League Club	Source	Date Signed	Seasons Played	Apps	Subs	Gls
Macclesfield T	Hednesford T	07/10	10	45	0	13
Crawley T	Tr	06/11	11	25	1	14
Peterborough U	Tr	02/12	11-14	38	18	11
Ipswich T	L	11/12	12	2	1	0
Bristol C	L	01/14	13	7	10	1
Oxford U	L	09/14	14	11	1	4
Shrewsbury T	Tr	02/15	14	8	10	4

BARNEY Victor Charles (Vic)
Born: Stepney, E London, England, 3 April, 1922 — IF
Died: Oxford, England, 26 May, 2006

League Club	Source	Date Signed	Seasons Played	Apps	Subs	Gls
Reading	Oxford C	09/46	46-48	45	-	12
Bristol C	Tr	10/48	48	28	-	4
Grimsby T	Tr	06/49	49	7	-	0

BARNEY Victor Roy (Vic)
Born: Shipton, Gloucestershire, England, 18 November, 1947 — M

League Club	Source	Date Signed	Seasons Played	Apps	Subs	Gls
Bristol Rov	App	12/65	66-69	30	1	3

BARNHOUSE David John
Born: Swansea, Wales, 19 March, 1975 — RB
Wales: U21-3/Youth/Schools

League Club	Source	Date Signed	Seasons Played	Apps	Subs	Gls
Swansea C	YT	07/93	91-95	18	5	0

BARNSLEY Andrew (Andy)
Born: Sheffield, England, 9 June, 1962 — D

League Club	Source	Date Signed	Seasons Played	Apps	Subs	Gls
Rotherham U	Denaby U	06/85	85	28	0	0
Sheffield U	Tr	07/86	86-88	73	4	0
Rotherham U	Tr	12/88	88-90	77	6	3
Carlisle U	Tr	08/91	91-92	53	2	5

BARNSLEY Geoffrey Robert (Geoff)
Born: Bilston, West Midlands, England, 9 December, 1935 — G

League Club	Source	Date Signed	Seasons Played	Apps	Subs	Gls
West Bromwich A	Jnr	12/52	54	1	-	0
Plymouth Arg	Tr	06/57	57-60	131	-	0
Norwich C	Tr	05/61	61	8	-	0
Torquay U	Tr	12/62	63	6	-	0

BARNWELL John
Born: Newcastle-upon-Tyne, England, 24 December, 1938 — M
England: U23-1/Youth

League Club	Source	Date Signed	Seasons Played	Apps	Subs	Gls
Arsenal	Bishop Auckland	11/56	56-63	138	-	23
Nottingham F	Tr	03/64	63-69	172	8	22
Sheffield U	Tr	04/70	70	9	0	2

BARNWELL-EDINBORO Jamie
Born: Hull, England, 26 December, 1975 — F

League Club	Source	Date Signed	Seasons Played	Apps	Subs	Gls
Coventry C	YT	07/94	95	0	1	0
Swansea C	L	12/95	95	2	2	0
Wigan Ath	L	02/96	95	2	8	1
Cambridge U	Tr	03/96	95-97	53	10	12

BARON Kevin Mark Patrick
Born: Preston, Lancashire, England, 19 July, 1926 — IF
Died: Ipswich, England, 5 June, 1971

League Club	Source	Date Signed	Seasons Played	Apps	Subs	Gls
Liverpool	Preston NE (Am)	08/45	47-53	140	-	32
Southend U	Tr	05/54	54-58	138	-	45
Northampton T	Tr	09/58	58	25	-	4
Aldershot	Wisbech T	07/60	60	6	-	0

BAROS Milan
Born: Ostrava, Czech Republic, 28 October, 1981 — F
Czech Republic: 93/U21-19/Youth

League Club	Source	Date Signed	Seasons Played	Apps	Subs	Gls
Liverpool	Banik Ostrava (CZE)	12/01	02-04	45	23	19
Aston Villa	Tr	08/05	05-06	34	8	9
Portsmouth (L)	Olymp Lyonnais (FRA)	01/08	07	8	4	0

BARR Hugh Henry
Born: Ballymena, Antrim, Northern Ireland, 17 May, 1935 — IF
Northern Ireland: 3/NILge-6/Schools

League Club	Source	Date Signed	Seasons Played	Apps	Subs	Gls
Coventry C	Linfield	07/62	62-63	47	-	15

BARR John Millar
Born: Bridge of Weir, Renfrewshire, Scotland, 9 September, 1917 — CD
Died: Paisley, Renfrewshire, Scotland, 27 March, 1997

League Club	Source	Date Signed	Seasons Played	Apps	Subs	Gls
Queens Park Rgrs	Third Lanark	05/39	46	4	-	0

BARR Robert Andrew (Bobbie)
Born: Halifax, West Yorkshire, England, 5 December, 1969 — CD

League Club	Source	Date Signed	Seasons Played	Apps	Subs	Gls
Halifax T	YT	06/88	86-88	4	1	0

BARR William Joseph (Billy)
Born: Halifax, West Yorkshire, England, 21 January, 1969 — D

League Club	Source	Date Signed	Seasons Played	Apps	Subs	Gls
Halifax T	YT	07/87	87-92	178	18	13
Crewe Alex	Tr	06/94	94-96	73	12	7
Carlisle U	Tr	07/97	97-99	88	3	3

BARRAS Anthony (Tony)
Born: Billingham, Cleveland, England, 29 March, 1971 — CD

League Club	Source	Date Signed	Seasons Played	Apps	Subs	Gls
Hartlepool U	YT	07/89	88-89	9	3	0
Stockport Co	Tr	07/90	90-93	94	5	5
Rotherham U	L	02/94	93	5	0	1
York C	Tr	07/94	94-98	167	4	11
Reading	Tr	03/99	98	4	2	1
Walsall	Tr	07/99	99-02	91	14	9
Plymouth Arg	L	11/02	02	4	0	0
Notts Co	Tr	08/03	03	38	2	2
Macclesfield T	Tr	07/04	04-05	29	2	1

BARRASS Malcolm Williamson
Born: Blackpool, Lancashire, England, 15 December, 1924 CH
Died: Tottington, Greater Manchester, England, 5 August, 2013
England: 3/FLge-2/War-1

League Club	Source	Date Signed	Seasons Played	Apps	Subs	Gls
Bolton W	Ford Motors	11/44	46-56	329	-	25
Sheffield U	Tr	09/56	56	18	-	0

BARRASS Matthew Robert (Matt)
Born: Bury, Greater Manchester, England, 28 February, 1980 RB

League Club	Source	Date Signed	Seasons Played	Apps	Subs	Gls
Bury	YT	05/99	99-04	77	7	2

BARRATT Alfred George (Alf)
Born: Weldon, Northamptonshire, England, 13 April, 1920 CH
Died: Leicester, England, 3 June, 2001

League Club	Source	Date Signed	Seasons Played	Apps	Subs	Gls
Northampton T	Kettering T	07/38	38	1	-	0
Leicester C	Stewart & Lloyds	09/46	47-48	4	-	0
Grimsby T	Tr	07/50	50	23	-	0
Southport	Tr	07/51	51-55	198	-	0

BARRATT Anthony (Tony)
Born: Salford, England, 18 October, 1965 FB

League Club	Source	Date Signed	Seasons Played	Apps	Subs	Gls
Grimsby T	Billingham T	08/85	85	20	2	0
Hartlepool U	Billingham T	12/86	86-88	93	5	4
York C	Tr	03/89	88-94	116	31	10

BARRATT Harold (Harry)
Born: Headington, Oxfordshire, England, 25 December, 1918 D
Died: Coventry, England, 25 September, 1989

League Club	Source	Date Signed	Seasons Played	Apps	Subs	Gls
Coventry C	Herberts Ath	12/35	37-51	170	-	12

BARRATT Leslie Edwin (Les)
Born: Nuneaton, Warwickshire, England, 13 August, 1945 IF

League Club	Source	Date Signed	Seasons Played	Apps	Subs	Gls
Barrow	App	08/62	62-63	10	-	0
Grimsby T	Tr	07/64	64	4	-	1
Southport	Tr	07/65	65	9	1	0

BARRAU Xavier
Born: Lyon, France, 26 August, 1982 LW

League Club	Source	Date Signed	Seasons Played	Apps	Subs	Gls
Bradford C	Airdrieonians	03/07	06	1	2	2
Darlington	Tr	08/07	07	0	1	0

BARRELL Leslie Peter (Les)
Born: Colchester, Essex, England, 30 August, 1932 W

League Club	Source	Date Signed	Seasons Played	Apps	Subs	Gls
Colchester U	Lexden W	12/56	56	4	-	1

BARRERA Pablo Edison
Born: Mexico City, Mexico, 21 June, 1987 W
Mexico: 57

League Club	Source	Date Signed	Seasons Played	Apps	Subs	Gls
West Ham U	UNAM Pumas (MEX)	07/10	10-11	6	9	0

BARRETT Adam Nicholas
Born: Dagenham, E London, England, 29 November, 1979 CD

League Club	Source	Date Signed	Seasons Played	Apps	Subs	Gls
Plymouth Arg	Leyton Orient (YT)	01/99	98-00	47	5	3
Mansfield T	Tr	12/00	00-01	34	3	1
Bristol Rov	Tr	07/02	02-03	90	0	5
Southend U	Tr	07/04	04-09	244	3	26
Crystal Palace	Tr	07/10	10	5	2	0
Leyton Orient	L	03/11	10	14	0	0
Bournemouth	Tr	07/11	11	21	0	1
Gillingham	Tr	08/12	12-13	88	0	3
AFC Wimbledon	L	08/14	14	23	0	1
Southend U	Tr	01/15	14	9	1	0

BARRETT Arthur Henry
Born: Liverpool, England, 21 December, 1927 WH
Died: Cheshire, England, 10 January, 2011

League Club	Source	Date Signed	Seasons Played	Apps	Subs	Gls
Tranmere Rov	Jnr	03/45	46	1	-	0

BARRETT Charles Roger (Roger)
Born: Doncaster, South Yorkshire, England, 19 October, 1946 F

League Club	Source	Date Signed	Seasons Played	Apps	Subs	Gls
Doncaster Rov	Doncaster U	10/68	68	1	0	0

BARRETT Colin
Born: Stockport, Greater Manchester, England, 3 August, 1952 D

League Club	Source	Date Signed	Seasons Played	Apps	Subs	Gls
Manchester C	Cheadle Heath	05/70	72-75	50	3	0
Nottingham F	Tr	03/76	75-78	64	5	4
Swindon T	Tr	06/80	80	3	0	0

BARRETT Daniel Thomas (Danny)
Born: Bradford, England, 25 September, 1980 M

League Club	Source	Date Signed	Seasons Played	Apps	Subs	Gls
Chesterfield	YT	07/99	99-00	0	3	0

BARRETT Earl Delisser
Born: Rochdale, Greater Manchester, England, 28 April, 1967 D
England: 3/B-4/FLge/U21-4

League Club	Source	Date Signed	Seasons Played	Apps	Subs	Gls
Manchester C	App	04/85	85-86	2	1	0
Chester C	L	03/86	85	12	0	0
Oldham Ath	Tr	11/87	87-91	181	2	7
Aston Villa	Tr	02/92	91-94	118	1	1
Everton	Tr	01/95	94-97	73	1	0
Sheffield U	L	01/98	97	5	0	0
Sheffield Wed	Tr	02/98	97-98	10	5	0

BARRETT George Thomas (Tom)
Born: Salford, England, 16 March, 1934 CH
Died: Salford, England, 8 March, 2014

League Club	Source	Date Signed	Seasons Played	Apps	Subs	Gls
Manchester U	Jnr	08/52				
Plymouth Arg	Tr	07/57	57-58	26	-	1
Chester C	Tr	07/60	60	39	-	2

BARRETT Graham
Born: Dublin, Republic of Ireland, 6 October, 1981 F/W
Republic of Ireland: 6/U21-24/Youth/Schools

League Club	Source	Date Signed	Seasons Played	Apps	Subs	Gls
Arsenal	YT	10/98	99	0	2	0
Bristol Rov	L	12/00	00	0	1	0
Crewe Alex	L	09/01	01	2	1	0
Colchester U	L	12/01	01	19	1	4
Brighton & HA	L	08/02	02	20	10	1
Coventry C	Tr	07/03	03-04	32	23	6
Sheffield Wed	L	03/05	04	5	1	1

BARRETT James Guy (Jimmy)
Born: West Ham, E London, England, 5 November, 1930 IF
Died: Suffolk, England, 21 October, 2014

League Club	Source	Date Signed	Seasons Played	Apps	Subs	Gls
West Ham U	Jnr	02/49	49-54	85	-	24
Nottingham F	Tr	12/54	54-58	105	-	64
Birmingham C	Tr	10/59	59	10	-	4
West Ham U	Tr	08/60				

BARRETT John
Born: Birmingham, England, 26 March, 1931 WH
Died: Horsham, West Sussex, England, October, 2002
England: Youth

League Club	Source	Date Signed	Seasons Played	Apps	Subs	Gls
Aston Villa	Jnr	07/49				
Scunthorpe U	Tr	06/54	54-55	17	-	0

BARRETT Kenneth Brian (Ken)
Born: Bromsgrove, Worcestershire, England, 5 May, 1938 LW
Died: Droitwich, Worcestershire, England, 7 June, 2015

League Club	Source	Date Signed	Seasons Played	Apps	Subs	Gls
Aston Villa	Stoke Works	02/57	58	5	-	3
Lincoln C	Tr	06/59	59-62	17	-	4

BARRETT Leslie (Les)
Born: Chelsea, W London, England, 22 October, 1947 LW
England: U23-1

League Club	Source	Date Signed	Seasons Played	Apps	Subs	Gls
Fulham	Jnr	10/65	65-76	421	3	74
Millwall	Tr	10/77	77	8	0	1

BARRETT Michael John (Mike)
Born: Bristol, England, 12 September, 1959 LW
Died: Yate, Avon, England, 14 August, 1984

League Club	Source	Date Signed	Seasons Played	Apps	Subs	Gls
Bristol Rov	Bristol Portway	10/79	79-83	119	10	18

BARRETT Michael John (Mike)
Born: Exeter, England, 20 October, 1963 G

League Club	Source	Date Signed	Seasons Played	Apps	Subs	Gls
Exeter C	Liskeard Ath	12/94	94	4	0	0

BARRETT Neil William
Born: Tooting, SW London, England, 24 December, 1981 M
England: Schools

League Club	Source	Date Signed	Seasons Played	Apps	Subs	Gls
Portsmouth	Chelsea (Jnr)	07/01	01	23	3	2

BARRETT Paul David
Born: Newcastle-upon-Tyne, England, 13 April, 1978 M
England: Youth

League Club	Source	Date Signed	Seasons Played	Apps	Subs	Gls
Newcastle U	YT	06/96				
Wrexham	Tr	03/99	98-03	98	22	5

BARRETT Ronald Harold (Ron)
Born: Reading, England, 22 July, 1939 CF

League Club	Source	Date Signed	Seasons Played	Apps	Subs	Gls
Grimsby T	Maidenhead U	08/58	58	3	-	0

BARRETT Scott
Born: Ilkeston, Derbyshire, England, 2 April, 1963 G

League Club	Source	Date Signed	Seasons Played	Apps	Subs	Gls
Wolverhampton W	Ilkeston T	09/84	84-86	30	0	0
Stoke C	Tr	07/87	87-89	51	0	0
Colchester U	L	01/90	89	13	0	0
Stockport Co	L	03/90	89	10	0	0
Gillingham	Colchester U	08/92	92-94	51	0	0
Cambridge U	Tr	08/95	95-97	119	0	0
Leyton Orient	Tr	01/99	98-02	99	0	0

BARRICK Dean
Born: Hemsworth, West Yorkshire, England, 30 September, 1969 LB

League Club	Source	Date Signed	Seasons Played	Apps	Subs	Gls
Sheffield Wed	YT	05/88	88-89	11	0	2
Rotherham U	Tr	02/91	90-92	96	3	7
Cambridge U	Tr	08/93	93-95	90	1	3
Preston NE	Tr	09/95	95-97	98	11	1
Bury	Tr	07/98	98-00	37	10	1

BARRIE John
Born: Hamilton, Lanarkshire, Scotland, 17 May, 1925 — CF

League Club	Source	Date Signed	Seasons Played	Apps	Subs	Gls
Cardiff C	Thorniewood Ath	07/48				
Tranmere Rov	Tr	11/48	48-50	14	-	3

BARRITT Ronald (Ron)
Born: Huddersfield, West Yorkshire, England, 15 April, 1919 — CF
Died: Huddersfield, West Yorkshire, England, 27 June, 2004

League Club	Source	Date Signed	Seasons Played	Apps	Subs	Gls
Doncaster Rov	Wombwell	01/49	48-49	13	-	5
Leeds U	Frickley Colliery	04/51	51	6	-	1
York C	Tr	07/52	52	5	-	0

BARRON James (Jim)
Born: Tantobie, County Durham, England, 19 October, 1943 — G

League Club	Source	Date Signed	Seasons Played	Apps	Subs	Gls
Wolverhampton W	Newcastle West End	11/61	63-64	8	-	0
Chelsea	Tr	04/65	65	1	0	0
Oxford U	Tr	03/66	65-69	152	0	0
Nottingham F	Tr	07/70	70-73	155	0	0
Swindon T	Tr	08/74	74-76	79	0	0
Peterborough U	Connecticut B'ls (USA)	08/77	77-80	21	0	0

BARRON James (Jim)
Born: Burnhope, County Durham, England, 19 July, 1913 — G
Died: Newcastle-upon-Tyne, England, 15 September, 1969

League Club	Source	Date Signed	Seasons Played	Apps	Subs	Gls
Blackburn Rov	Blyth Spartans	03/35	35-38	76	-	0
Darlington	Tr	06/46	46	23	-	0

BARRON Michael James (Mike)
Born: Chester-le-Street, County Durham, England, 22 December, 1974 — CD

League Club	Source	Date Signed	Seasons Played	Apps	Subs	Gls
Middlesbrough	YT	02/93	93-95	2	1	0
Hartlepool U	L	09/96	96	16	0	0
Hartlepool U	Tr	07/97	97-06	299	10	3

BARRON Paul George
Born: Woolwich, SE London, England, 16 September, 1953 — G

League Club	Source	Date Signed	Seasons Played	Apps	Subs	Gls
Plymouth Arg	Slough T	07/76	76-77	44	0	0
Arsenal	Tr	07/78	78-79	8	0	0
Crystal Palace	Tr	08/80	80-82	90	0	0
West Bromwich A	Tr	12/82	82-84	63	0	0
Stoke C	L	01/85	84	1	0	0
Queens Park Rgrs	Tr	03/85	85-86	32	0	0
Reading	L	12/86	86	4	0	0

BARRON Roger William
Born: Northampton, England, 30 June, 1947 — G

League Club	Source	Date Signed	Seasons Played	Apps	Subs	Gls
Northampton T	App	07/65	67-68	17	0	0

BARRON Scott
Born: Preston, Lancashire, England, 2 September, 1985 — LB

League Club	Source	Date Signed	Seasons Played	Apps	Subs	Gls
Ipswich T	Sch	03/04	05	14	1	0
Wrexham	L	02/07	06	3	0	0
Millwall	Tr	07/07	07-11	79	28	2
Brentford	Tr	08/12	12-13	7	7	0

BARRON William (Bill)
Born: Houghton-le-Spring, Tyne and Wear, England, 26 October, 1917 — LB
Died: Northampton, England, 2 January, 2006

League Club	Source	Date Signed	Seasons Played	Apps	Subs	Gls
Wolverhampton W	Hartlepool U (Am)	11/36				
Charlton Ath	Annfield Plain	10/37	37	3	-	2
Northampton T	Tr	05/38	38-50	166	-	4

BARROW Graham
Born: Chorley, Lancashire, England, 13 June, 1954 — M

League Club	Source	Date Signed	Seasons Played	Apps	Subs	Gls
Wigan Ath	Altrincham	07/81	81-85	173	6	35
Chester C	Tr	07/86	86-93	244	4	17

BARROW Lee Alexander
Born: Belper, Derbyshire, England, 1 May, 1973 — CD

League Club	Source	Date Signed	Seasons Played	Apps	Subs	Gls
Notts Co	YT	07/91				
Scarborough	Tr	08/92	92	11	0	0
Torquay U	Tr	02/93	92-97	154	10	5

BARROW Modou Secka (Mo)
Born: Banjul, Gambia, 13 October, 1992 — W
Gambia: 1

League Club	Source	Date Signed	Seasons Played	Apps	Subs	Gls
Swansea C	Ostersunds (SWE)	08/14	14	1	10	0
Nottingham F	L	03/15	14	2	2	0

BARROWCLIFF Paul Joseph
Born: Hillingdon, W London, England, 15 June, 1969 — M

League Club	Source	Date Signed	Seasons Played	Apps	Subs	Gls
Brentford	Stevenage Bor	08/97	97	5	6	0

BARROWCLIFFE Geoffrey (Geoff)
Born: Ilkeston, Derbyshire, England, 18 October, 1931 — RB
Died: Ilkeston, Derbyshire, England, 26 September, 2009

League Club	Source	Date Signed	Seasons Played	Apps	Subs	Gls
Derby Co	Ilkeston T	10/50	51-65	475	0	37

BARROWCLOUGH Carl William
Born: Doncaster, South Yorkshire, England, 25 September, 1981 — W

League Club	Source	Date Signed	Seasons Played	Apps	Subs	Gls
Barnsley	YT	03/01	00-02	2	10	0

BARROWCLOUGH Stewart James
Born: Barnsley, South Yorkshire, England, 29 October, 1951 — W
England: U23-5

League Club	Source	Date Signed	Seasons Played	Apps	Subs	Gls
Barnsley	App	11/69	69	9	0	0
Newcastle U	Tr	08/70	70-77	201	18	21
Birmingham C	Tr	05/78	78	26	3	2
Bristol Rov	Tr	07/79	79-80	60	1	14
Barnsley	Tr	02/81	80-82	46	6	1
Mansfield T	Tr	08/83	83-84	50	4	10

BARROWMAN Andrew
Born: Wishaw, Lanarkshire, Scotland, 27 November, 1984 — F
Scotland: Youth

League Club	Source	Date Signed	Seasons Played	Apps	Subs	Gls
Birmingham C	YT	12/01	03	0	1	0
Crewe Alex	L	10/03	03	3	1	1
Blackpool	L	08/04	04	0	2	0
Mansfield T	L	03/05	04	1	2	0
Walsall	Tr	01/06	05	10	3	1

BARRY Anthony Jonathan
Born: Liverpool, England, 29 May, 1986 — M

League Club	Source	Date Signed	Seasons Played	Apps	Subs	Gls
Coventry C	Everton (Sch)	07/04				
Yeovil T	Accrington Stan	01/06	05-07	42	22	0
Chester C	Tr	07/08	08	38	5	1
Fleetwood T	Wrexham	01/10	12	9	3	0
Accrington Stan (L)	Forest Green Rov	10/14	14	9	4	0

BARRY Gareth
Born: Hastings, East Sussex, England, 23 February, 1981 — DM
England: 53/U21-27/Youth

League Club	Source	Date Signed	Seasons Played	Apps	Subs	Gls
Aston Villa	YT	02/98	97-08	353	12	41
Manchester C	Tr	06/09	09-12	123	9	6
Everton	Tr	09/13	13-14	65	0	3

BARRY George
Born: Islington, N London, England, 19 September, 1967 — RB

League Club	Source	Date Signed	Seasons Played	Apps	Subs	Gls
Leyton Orient	Fisher Ath	03/95	94	5	1	0

BARRY Kevin Anthony
Born: Woolwich, SE London, England, 13 September, 1930 — LW

League Club	Source	Date Signed	Seasons Played	Apps	Subs	Gls
Charlton Ath	Jnr	12/47	52	3	-	0

BARRY Kevin Thomas
Born: Newcastle-upon-Tyne, England, 9 January, 1961 — G

League Club	Source	Date Signed	Seasons Played	Apps	Subs	Gls
Darlington	Nottingham F (App)	09/79	79-80	18	0	0

BARRY Michael James (Mike)
Born: Hull, England, 22 May, 1953 — M
Wales: U23-1

League Club	Source	Date Signed	Seasons Played	Apps	Subs	Gls
Huddersfield T	App	06/70	70-72	21	5	0
Carlisle U	Tr	05/73	73-76	73	8	10
Bristol Rov	Tr	09/77	77-78	46	1	3

BARRY Patrick Percival (Pat)
Born: Southampton, England, 25 October, 1920 — LB
Died: Birmingham, England, 11 November, 1994

League Club	Source	Date Signed	Seasons Played	Apps	Subs	Gls
Southampton		02/40				
Blackburn Rov	Hyde U	05/48				
Bournemouth	Tr	05/50	50	4	-	0

BARRY Roy Alexander
Born: Edinburgh, Scotland, 19 September, 1942 — CD

League Club	Source	Date Signed	Seasons Played	Apps	Subs	Gls
Coventry C	Dunfermline Ath	10/69	69-72	82	1	2
Crystal Palace	Tr	09/73	73-74	41	1	1

BARRY-MURPHY Brian
Born: Cork, Republic of Ireland, 27 July, 1978 — DM
Republic of Ireland: U21-6/Youth

League Club	Source	Date Signed	Seasons Played	Apps	Subs	Gls
Preston NE	Cork C (ROI)	08/99	99-02	6	15	0
Southend U	L	02/02	01	8	0	1
Hartlepool U	L	10/02	02	7	0	0
Sheffield Wed	Tr	01/03	02-03	55	3	0
Bury	Tr	08/04	04-09	200	18	13
Rochdale	Tr	07/10	10-13	57	8	1

BART-WILLIAMS Christopher Gerald (Chris)
Born: Freetown, Sierra Leone, 16 June, 1974 — M
England: B-1/U21-16/Youth

League Club	Source	Date Signed	Seasons Played	Apps	Subs	Gls
Leyton Orient	YT	07/91	90-91	34	2	2
Sheffield Wed	Tr	11/91	91-94	95	29	16
Nottingham F	Tr	07/95	95-01	200	7	30
Charlton Ath	Tr	12/01	01-02	17	12	2
Ipswich T	Tr	09/03	03	23	3	2

BARTHEZ Fabien Alain
Born: Lavelanet, France, 28 June, 1971 — G
France: 87

League Club	Source	Date Signed	Seasons Played	Apps	Subs	Gls
Manchester U	AS Monaco (FRA)	06/00	00-02	92	0	0

BARTHOLOMEW Henry (Harry)
Born: Motherwell, Lanarkshire, Scotland, 18 January, 1920 — WH
Died: Exeter, England, January, 2001

League Club	Source	Date Signed	Seasons Played	Apps	Subs	Gls
Exeter C	Motherwell	05/47	47-48	66	-	6
Bournemouth	Tr	08/49				
Newport Co	Tr	06/50	50	3	-	0

BARTHRAM Jack Patrick
Born: Newham, E London, England, 13 October, 1993 — RB

League Club	Source	Date Signed	Seasons Played	Apps	Subs	Gls
Tottenham H	Sch	07/12				
Swindon T	Tr	07/13	13-14	6	10	0

BARTLETT Adam James
Born: Newcastle-upon-Tyne, England, 27 February, 1986 — G
England: Semi Pro-6

League Club	Source	Date Signed	Seasons Played	Apps	Subs	Gls
Hereford U	Kidderminster Hrs	06/09	09-11	109	1	0

BARTLETT Frank
Born: Chester-le-Street, County Durham, England, 8 November, 1930 — RH/LW
Died: Barnsley, South Yorkshire, England, 6 December, 2013

League Club	Source	Date Signed	Seasons Played	Apps	Subs	Gls
Barnsley	Blackhall CW	08/50	52-62	297	-	68
Halifax T	Tr	07/63	63	21	-	4

BARTLETT Frederick Leslie (Fred)
Born: Reading, England, 5 March, 1913 — CH
Died: Henley-on-Thames, Oxfordshire, England, 1968

League Club	Source	Date Signed	Seasons Played	Apps	Subs	Gls
Queens Park Rgrs	Great Eastern Railway	10/32	34-36	48	-	0
Leyton Orient	Tr	05/37	37-47	96	-	0

BARTLETT Gordon
Born: Chiswick, W London, England, 3 December, 1955 — F

League Club	Source	Date Signed	Seasons Played	Apps	Subs	Gls
Portsmouth	App	12/73	74	0	2	1
Brentford	Tr	09/75				

BARTLETT Kevin Francis
Born: Portsmouth, England, 12 October, 1962 — F

League Club	Source	Date Signed	Seasons Played	Apps	Subs	Gls
Portsmouth	App	10/80	80-81	0	3	0
Cardiff C	Fareham T	09/86	86-88	60	21	25
West Bromwich A	Tr	02/89	88-89	25	12	10
Notts Co	Tr	03/90	89-92	86	13	33
Port Vale	L	09/92	92	5	0	1
Cambridge U	Tr	03/93	92	3	5	1

BARTLETT Neal James
Born: Southampton, England, 7 April, 1975 — M
England: Schools

League Club	Source	Date Signed	Seasons Played	Apps	Subs	Gls
Southampton	YT	07/93	92-93	4	4	0
Hereford U	BK Hacken (SWE)	09/96	96	0	3	0

BARTLETT Paul John
Born: Grimsby, North Lincolnshire, England, 17 January, 1960 — W

League Club	Source	Date Signed	Seasons Played	Apps	Subs	Gls
Derby Co	App	12/77	77-79	7	6	0

BARTLETT Terence Richard (Terry)
Born: Cleethorpes, North Lincolnshire, England, 28 August, 1948 — W

League Club	Source	Date Signed	Seasons Played	Apps	Subs	Gls
Grimsby T (Am)	Jnr	08/67	67	1	0	0

BARTLETT Thurston Shaun (Shaun)
Born: Cape Town, South Africa, 31 October, 1972 — F
South Africa: 74

League Club	Source	Date Signed	Seasons Played	Apps	Subs	Gls
Charlton Ath	FC Zurich (SUI)	12/00	00-05	95	28	24

BARTLEY Anthony (Tony)
Born: Stalybridge, Greater Manchester, England, 8 March, 1938 — LW

League Club	Source	Date Signed	Seasons Played	Apps	Subs	Gls
Bolton W	Stalybridge Celtic	09/56				
Bury	Stalybridge Celtic	11/58	58-64	116	-	24
Oldham Ath	Tr	09/64	64-65	48	2	13
Chesterfield	Tr	07/66	66	12	0	2

BARTLEY Carl Alexander
Born: Lambeth, S London, England, 6 October, 1976 — F

League Club	Source	Date Signed	Seasons Played	Apps	Subs	Gls
Fulham	YT	07/95	94	1	0	0

BARTLEY Daniel Robert (Danny)
Born: Paulton, Somerset, England, 3 October, 1947 — LW
England: Youth

League Club	Source	Date Signed	Seasons Played	Apps	Subs	Gls
Bristol C	App	10/64	65-72	92	8	7
Swansea C	Tr	08/73	73-79	195	4	8
Hereford U	Tr	03/80	79-82	112	2	7

BARTLEY John Reginald
Born: Camberwell, S London, England, 15 September, 1958 — F

League Club	Source	Date Signed	Seasons Played	Apps	Subs	Gls
Millwall	Welling U	10/80	80-81	39	1	8

BARTLEY Kyle Louie
Born: Stockport, Greater Manchester, England, 22 May, 1991 — CD
England: Youth

League Club	Source	Date Signed	Seasons Played	Apps	Subs	Gls
Arsenal	Sch	07/08				
Sheffield U	L	02/10	09	10	4	0
Sheffield U	L	08/10	10	21	0	0
Swansea C	Tr	08/12	12-14	9	2	0
Birmingham C	L	07/13	13	14	3	3

BARTLEY Marvin Clement
Born: Reading, England, 4 July, 1986 — M

League Club	Source	Date Signed	Seasons Played	Apps	Subs	Gls
Bournemouth	Hampton & Richmond Bor	07/07	07-10	89	24	3
Burnley	Tr	01/11	10-12	36	29	3
Leyton Orient	Tr	08/13	13-14	26	21	2

BARTON Adam James
Born: Clitheroe, Lancashire, England, 7 January, 1991 — M
Republic of Ireland: U21-5//Northern Ireland: 1

League Club	Source	Date Signed	Seasons Played	Apps	Subs	Gls
Preston NE	Sch	01/09	09-11	37	13	1
Coventry C	Tr	08/12	12-14	43	20	3

BARTON Anthony Edward (Tony)
Born: Sutton, S London, England, 8 April, 1937 — RW
Died: Southampton, England, 20 August, 1993
England: Schools

League Club	Source	Date Signed	Seasons Played	Apps	Subs	Gls
Fulham	Sutton U	05/54	53-58	49	-	8
Nottingham F	Tr	12/59	59-61	22	-	1
Portsmouth	Tr	12/61	61-66	129	1	34

BARTON Charles Reginald (Reg)
Born: Chester, England, 4 March, 1942 — G

League Club	Source	Date Signed	Seasons Played	Apps	Subs	Gls
Chester C	Jnr	06/61	61-64	14	-	0

BARTON David
Born: Bishop Auckland, County Durham, England, 9 May, 1959 — CD

League Club	Source	Date Signed	Seasons Played	Apps	Subs	Gls
Newcastle U	App	05/77	77-81	101	1	5
Blackburn Rov	L	08/82	82	8	0	1
Darlington	Tr	02/83	82-83	49	0	3

BARTON David Roger (Roger)
Born: Jump, South Yorkshire, England, 25 September, 1946 — M
Died: Bawtry, South Yorkshire, England, 4 November, 2013

League Club	Source	Date Signed	Seasons Played	Apps	Subs	Gls
Wolverhampton W	App	10/63				
Lincoln C	Tr	07/64	64-65	28	0	1
Barnsley	Tr	07/66	66-68	52	3	3

BARTON Douglas Joseph (Dougie)
Born: Islington, N London, England, 31 July, 1927 — RB
Died: Chelmsford, England, 3 July, 2002

League Club	Source	Date Signed	Seasons Played	Apps	Subs	Gls
Reading	Ford Sports	02/49	50-52	10	-	0
Newport Co	Tr	01/53	52-53	23	-	0

BARTON Frank
Born: Barton-on-Humber, North Lincolnshire, England, 22 October, 1947 — M
England: Youth

League Club	Source	Date Signed	Seasons Played	Apps	Subs	Gls
Scunthorpe U	App	08/65	64-67	93	0	26
Carlisle U	Tr	01/68	67-71	161	4	22
Blackpool	Tr	07/72	72	18	0	1
Grimsby T	Tr	06/73	73-75	123	0	15
Bournemouth	Tr	06/76	76-77	66	0	13
Hereford U	Tr	01/78	77-78	22	0	3
Bournemouth	Tr	09/78	78	22	0	2

BARTON John Birchall
Born: Orrell, Greater Manchester, England, 27 April, 1942 — G
Died: Orrell, Greater Manchester, England, 21 September, 2014

League Club	Source	Date Signed	Seasons Played	Apps	Subs	Gls
Preston NE	Jnr	05/59	58-65	48	0	0
Blackburn Rov	Tr	06/66	66-71	68	0	0

BARTON John Stanley
Born: Birmingham, England, 24 October, 1953 — RB

League Club	Source	Date Signed	Seasons Played	Apps	Subs	Gls
Everton	Worcester C	12/78	78-80	18	2	0
Derby Co	Tr	03/82	81-83	68	1	1

BARTON Joseph Anthony (Joey)
Born: Huyton, Merseyside, England, 2 September, 1982 — M
England: 1/U21-2

League Club	Source	Date Signed	Seasons Played	Apps	Subs	Gls
Manchester C	YT	07/01	02-06	123	7	15
Newcastle U	Tr	07/07	07-11	68	13	7
Queens Park Rgrs	Tr	08/11	11-14	91	2	7

BARTON Kenneth Rees (Ken)
Born: Caernarfon, Gwynedd, Wales, 20 September, 1937 — FB
Died: Chester, England, 6 September, 1982
Wales: Schools

League Club	Source	Date Signed	Seasons Played	Apps	Subs	Gls
Tottenham H	Jnr	10/56	60-63	4	-	0
Millwall	Tr	09/64				
Luton T	Tr	12/64	64	11	-	0

BARTON Leslie (Les)
Born: Rochdale, Greater Manchester, England, 20 March, 1920 — FB
Died: Ipswich, England, July, 2002

League Club	Source	Date Signed	Seasons Played	Apps	Subs	Gls
Bolton W		09/46				
New Brighton	Tr	08/49	49-50	64	-	1

BARTON Michael Geoffrey
Born: Gainsborough, Lincolnshire, England, 23 September, 1973 — G

League Club	Source	Date Signed	Seasons Played	Apps	Subs	Gls
Shrewsbury T	YT	07/90	91	1	0	0

BARTON Peter
Born: Barrow, Cumbria, England, 3 April, 1951 — G

League Club	Source	Date Signed	Seasons Played	Apps	Subs	Gls
Barrow	App	04/69	68	2	0	0

BARTON Warren Dean
Born: Stoke Newington, N London, England, 19 March, 1969 — RB
England: 3/B-3

League Club	Source	Date Signed	Seasons Played	Apps	Subs	Gls
Maidstone U	Leytonstone & Ilford	07/89	89	41	1	0
Wimbledon	Tr	06/90	90-94	178	2	10
Newcastle U	Tr	06/95	95-01	142	22	4
Derby Co	Tr	02/02	01-02	53	0	0
Queens Park Rgrs	Tr	10/03	03	2	1	0
Wimbledon	Tr	02/04	03	5	0	0

BARTRAM Andreas Per (Per)
Born: Odense, Denmark, 8 January, 1944 — F
Denmark: 1

League Club	Source	Date Signed	Seasons Played	Apps	Subs	Gls
Crystal Palace	Greenock Morton	08/69	69	8	2	2

BARTRAM Samuel (Sam)
Born: Jarrow, Tyne and Wear, England, 22 January, 1914 — G
Died: Harpenden, Hertfordshire, England, 17 July, 1981
England: B/War-3

League Club	Source	Date Signed	Seasons Played	Apps	Subs	Gls
Charlton Ath	Boldon Villa	09/34	34-55	579	-	0

BARTRAM Vincent Lee (Vince)
Born: Birmingham, England, 7 August, 1968 — G

League Club	Source	Date Signed	Seasons Played	Apps	Subs	Gls
Wolverhampton W	Jnr	08/85	86-90	5	0	0
Blackpool	L	10/89	89	9	0	0
Bournemouth	Tr	07/91	91-93	132	0	0
Arsenal	Tr	08/94	94	11	0	0
Huddersfield T	L	10/97	97	12	0	0
Gillingham	Tr	03/98	97-03	186	1	0

BARWICK Terence Patrick (Terry)
Born: Sheffield, England, 11 January, 1983 — M

League Club	Source	Date Signed	Seasons Played	Apps	Subs	Gls
Scunthorpe U	Sch	07/02	99-03	35	11	1
Grimsby T	Tr	08/05	05	2	6	0

BARWOOD Daniel David (Danny)
Born: Caerphilly, Wales, 25 February, 1981 — LW
Wales: Youth

League Club	Source	Date Signed	Seasons Played	Apps	Subs	Gls
Swansea C	YT	07/99	97	1	2	1

BASEY Grant William
Born: Bromley, SE London, England, 30 January, 1988 — LB
Wales: U21-1/Youth

League Club	Source	Date Signed	Seasons Played	Apps	Subs	Gls
Charlton Ath	Sch	07/07	07-09	32	14	1
Brentford	L	07/07	07	8	0	0
Barnet	Tr	09/10	10	11	0	1
Peterborough U	Tr	01/11	10-11	7	3	1
Wycombe W	Tr	10/11	11-12	32	3	2

BASEY Philip John (Phil)
Born: Cardiff, Wales, 27 August, 1948 — LW

League Club	Source	Date Signed	Seasons Played	Apps	Subs	Gls
Brentford	Jnr	06/66	66	2	0	0

BASEYA Cedric
Born: Bretigny, France, 19 December, 1987 — F

League Club	Source	Date Signed	Seasons Played	Apps	Subs	Gls
Southampton	Sch	04/07	07	0	1	0
Crewe Alex	L	11/07	07	1	2	0
Reading	OSC Lille (FRA)	09/11				
Barnet	L	11/11	11	0	2	0

BASFORD John (Jack)
Born: Crewe, Cheshire, England, 24 July, 1925 — CF
Died: Leek, Staffordshire, England, 14 March, 1998

League Club	Source	Date Signed	Seasons Played	Apps	Subs	Gls
Crewe Alex	Wolverhampton W (Am)	04/48	47-53	144	-	58
Chester C	Tr	01/54	53	10	-	1

BASFORD Luke William
Born: Croydon, S London, England, 6 January, 1980 — LB

League Club	Source	Date Signed	Seasons Played	Apps	Subs	Gls
Bristol Rov	YT	07/98	97-98	11	5	0

BASHAM Christopher Paul (Chris)
Born: Hebburn, Tyne and Wear, England, 20 July, 1988 — M/RB

League Club	Source	Date Signed	Seasons Played	Apps	Subs	Gls
Bolton W	Sch	10/07	08-09	6	13	1
Rochdale	L	02/08	07	5	8	0
Blackpool	Tr	08/10	10-13	70	15	5
Sheffield U	Tr	06/14	14	35	2	0

BASHAM Michael (Mike)
Born: Barking, E London, England, 27 September, 1973 — CD
England: Youth/Schools

League Club	Source	Date Signed	Seasons Played	Apps	Subs	Gls
West Ham U	YT	07/92				
Colchester U	L	11/93	93	1	0	0
Swansea C	Tr	03/94	93-95	27	2	1
Peterborough U	Tr	12/95	95-96	17	2	1
Barnet	Tr	08/97	97-00	74	1	2
York C	Tr	03/01	00-01	32	4	3

BASHAM Steven Brian (Steve)
Born: Southampton, England, 2 December, 1977 — F

League Club	Source	Date Signed	Seasons Played	Apps	Subs	Gls
Southampton	YT	05/96	96-98	1	18	1
Wrexham	L	02/98	97	4	1	0
Preston NE	Tr	02/99	98-01	37	31	15
Oxford U	Tr	08/02	02-05	122	26	39
Exeter C	Tr	07/07	08	12	11	2

BASHIR Naseem
Born: Amersham, Buckinghamshire, England, 12 September, 1969 — M

League Club	Source	Date Signed	Seasons Played	Apps	Subs	Gls
Reading	Jnr	06/88	89	1	2	1

BASINAS Angelos
Born: Chalkis, Greece, 3 January, 1976 — M
Greece: 100

League Club	Source	Date Signed	Seasons Played	Apps	Subs	Gls
Portsmouth	AEK Athens (GRE)	02/09	08-09	10	5	0

BASON Brian
Born: Epsom, Surrey, England, 3 September, 1955 — M
England: Schools

League Club	Source	Date Signed	Seasons Played	Apps	Subs	Gls
Chelsea	App	09/72	72-76	18	1	1
Plymouth Arg	Tr	09/77	77-80	127	3	10
Crystal Palace	Tr	03/81	80-81	25	2	0
Portsmouth	L	01/82	81	9	0	0
Reading	Tr	08/82	82	41	0	0

BASS David
Born: Frimley, Surrey, England, 29 November, 1974 — M

League Club	Source	Date Signed	Seasons Played	Apps	Subs	Gls
Reading	YT	07/93	91-96	7	4	0
Rotherham U	Tr	07/97	97	13	5	0
Carlisle U	Tr	03/99	98	8	1	0

BASS Jonathan David (Jon)
Born: Weston-super-Mare, Somerset, England, 1 January, 1976 — RB
England: Schools

League Club	Source	Date Signed	Seasons Played	Apps	Subs	Gls
Birmingham C	Jnr	06/94	95-00	60	8	0
Carlisle U	L	10/96	96	3	0	0
Gillingham	L	03/00	99	4	3	0
Hartlepool U	Tr	07/01	01-02	21	3	1
Bristol Rov	Pahang FA (MLY)	03/05	04-05	10	2	0

BASSEDAS Christian Gustavo
Born: Buenos Aires, Argentina, 16 February, 1973 — M
Argentina: 23

League Club	Source	Date Signed	Seasons Played	Apps	Subs	Gls
Newcastle U	Velez Sarsfield (ARG)	07/00	00-01	18	6	1

BASSETT David (Dave)
Born: Hendon, N London, England, 4 September, 1944 — CD
England: Amateur-10

League Club	Source	Date Signed	Seasons Played	Apps	Subs	Gls
Wimbledon	Walton & Hersham	08/74	77	35	0	0

BASSETT George Raymond
Born: Birmingham, England, 12 May, 1943 — LW

League Club	Source	Date Signed	Seasons Played	Apps	Subs	Gls
Coventry C	Jnr	08/61	61	1	-	0

BASSETT Graham Raymond
Born: Sunderland, England, 6 October, 1964 — F

League Club	Source	Date Signed	Seasons Played	Apps	Subs	Gls
Hartlepool U	Sunderland (App)	08/83	83	4	3	0

BASSETT William Edward George (Billy)
Born: Bargoed, Caerphilly, Wales, 8 June, 1912 — CH
Died: Pwllheli, Gwynedd, Wales, 1977

League Club	Source	Date Signed	Seasons Played	Apps	Subs	Gls
Cardiff C	Aberaman Ath	08/34	34-38	154	-	2
Crystal Palace	Tr	09/42	46-48	70	-	0

BASSHAM Alan John
Born: Kensington, Central London, England, 3 October, 1933 — RB
Died: Richmond, SW London, England, 1982
England: Schools

League Club	Source	Date Signed	Seasons Played	Apps	Subs	Gls
Brentford	Jnr	10/51	53-57	43	-	0

BASSILA Christian
Born: Paris, France, 5 October, 1977 — DM
France: U21-1

League Club	Source	Date Signed	Seasons Played	Apps	Subs	Gls
West Ham U (L)	Stade Rennais (FRA)	08/00	00	0	3	0
Sunderland	Strasbourg (FRA)	08/05	05	12	1	0

BASSINDER Gavin David
Born: Mexborough, South Yorkshire, England, 24 September, 1979 — CD

League Club	Source	Date Signed	Seasons Played	Apps	Subs	Gls
Barnsley	YT	07/98				
Mansfield T	Tr	03/00	99	1	3	0

BASSO Adriano
Born: Jundiai, Brazil, 18 April, 1975 — G

League Club	Source	Date Signed	Seasons Played	Apps	Subs	Gls
Bristol C	Woking	11/05	05-09	165	0	0
Wolverhampton W	Regatas Flamenco (BRA)	01/11				
Hull C	Tr	07/11	11	12	1	0

BASSONG Sebastien Aymar
Born: Paris, France, 9 July, 1986 — CD

Cameroon: 14//France: U21-2

League Club	Source	Date Signed	Seasons Played	Apps	Subs	Gls
Newcastle U	FC Metz (FRA)	08/08	08	26	4	0
Tottenham H	Tr	08/09	09-11	33	12	2
Wolverhampton W	L	01/12	11	9	0	0
Norwich C	Tr	08/12	12-14	79	0	3
Watford	L	10/14	14	11	0	0

BASTIANINI Pablo Emanuel
Born: Zarate, Argentina, 9 November, 1982 — F

League Club	Source	Date Signed	Seasons Played	Apps	Subs	Gls
Yeovil T	FC Quilmes (ARG)	08/05	05	15	5	3

BASTIANS Felix
Born: Bochum, Germany, 9 May, 1988 — LW
Germany: U21-9/Youth

League Club	Source	Date Signed	Seasons Played	Apps	Subs	Gls
Nottingham F	Sch	05/05	05-07	2	12	0
Gillingham	L	03/07	06	5	0	1
Chesterfield	L	10/07	07	12	0	1
Notts Co	L	01/08	07	5	0	0

BASTIN Clifford Sydney (Cliff)
Born: Exeter, England, 14 March, 1912 — LW
Died: Exeter, England, 4 December, 1991
England: 21/FLge-4/Schools

League Club	Source	Date Signed	Seasons Played	Apps	Subs	Gls
Exeter C	Jnr	03/29	27-28	17	-	6
Arsenal	Tr	05/29	29-46	350	-	150

BASTOCK Paul Anthony
Born: Leamington Spa, Warwickshire, England, 19 May, 1970 — G

League Club	Source	Date Signed	Seasons Played	Apps	Subs	Gls
Cambridge U	Coventry C (YT)	03/88	87-88	12	0	0
Boston U	Kettering T	08/92	02-03	92	0	0

BASTOW Darren John
Born: Torquay, Devon, England, 22 December, 1981 — M

League Club	Source	Date Signed	Seasons Played	Apps	Subs	Gls
Plymouth Arg	YT	01/99	98-99	28	14	3

BASTOW Ian John
Born: Torquay, Devon, England, 12 August, 1971 — M

League Club	Source	Date Signed	Seasons Played	Apps	Subs	Gls
Torquay U	YT	03/89	88-89	7	4	0

BASTURK Yildiray
Born: Herne, Germany, 24 December, 1978 — M
Turkey: 49

League Club	Source	Date Signed	Seasons Played	Apps	Subs	Gls
Blackburn Rov	VfB Stuttgart (GER)	01/10	09	1	0	0

BATCH Nigel Anthony
Born: Huddersfield, West Yorkshire, England, 9 September, 1957 — G

League Club	Source	Date Signed	Seasons Played	Apps	Subs	Gls
Grimsby T	Derby Co (App)	07/76	76-86	348	0	0
Darlington	Lincoln C	09/88	88	30	0	0
Stockport Co	Tr	03/89	88	12	0	0
Scunthorpe U	Rtd	08/91	91	1	0	0

BATCHELOR Edward (Ted)
Born: Rugby, Warwickshire, England, 4 August, 1930 — WH
Died: Swindon, England, 19 November, 2006

League Club	Source	Date Signed	Seasons Played	Apps	Subs	Gls
Wolverhampton W	Jnr	10/47				
Swindon T	Tr	08/50	50-54	91	-	0

BATEMAN Albert
Born: Stocksbridge, South Yorkshire, England, 13 June, 1924 — RW

League Club	Source	Date Signed	Seasons Played	Apps	Subs	Gls
Huddersfield T	Yorkshire Iron & Steel	09/43	46-48	73	-	14

BATEMAN Arthur
Born: Audley, Staffordshire, England, 12 June, 1918 — LB
Died: Leek, Staffordshire, England, 16 October, 1984

League Club	Source	Date Signed	Seasons Played	Apps	Subs	Gls
Crewe Alex	Rolls Royce	11/42	46	4	-	0

BATEMAN Colin
Born: Hemel Hempstead, Hertfordshire, England, 22 October, 1930 — FB

League Club	Source	Date Signed	Seasons Played	Apps	Subs	Gls
Watford	Hemel Hempstead	03/53	54-57	50	-	0

BATEMAN Ernest (Ernie)
Born: Hemel Hempstead, Hertfordshire, England, 5 April, 1929 — CD

League Club	Source	Date Signed	Seasons Played	Apps	Subs	Gls
Watford	Hemel Hempstead	03/52	55-56	23	-	0

BATER Philip Thomas (Phil)
Born: Cardiff, Wales, 26 October, 1955 — D
Wales: U21-2

League Club	Source	Date Signed	Seasons Played	Apps	Subs	Gls
Bristol Rov	App	10/73	74-80	211	1	2
Wrexham	Tr	09/81	81-82	73	0	1
Bristol Rov	Tr	09/83	83-85	90	8	1
Brentford	Tr	05/86	86	19	0	2
Cardiff C	Tr	07/87	87-88	67	9	0

BATES Anthony Norman (Tony)
Born: Blidworth, Nottinghamshire, England, 6 April, 1938 — CF

League Club	Source	Date Signed	Seasons Played	Apps	Subs	Gls
Notts Co	Blidworth Welfare	07/59	58	1	-	0

BATES Brian Frederick
Born: Beeston, Nottinghamshire, England, 4 December, 1944 — W

League Club	Source	Date Signed	Seasons Played	Apps	Subs	Gls
Notts Co	Loughborough College	07/63	63-68	125	3	24
Mansfield T	Tr	07/69	69	20	0	3

BATES Donald Lawson (Don)
Born: Brighton, England, 10 May, 1933 — WH
Died: Brighton, England, 29 May, 2005

League Club	Source	Date Signed	Seasons Played	Apps	Subs	Gls
Brighton & HA	Lewes	11/50	57	21	-	1

BATES Edric Thornton (Ted)
Born: Thetford, Norfolk, England, 3 May, 1918 — IF
Died: Winchester, Hampshire, England, 26 November, 2003

League Club	Source	Date Signed	Seasons Played	Apps	Subs	Gls
Norwich C	Thetford T	09/36				
Southampton	Tr	05/37	37-52	202	-	65

BATES Ernest (Ernie)
Born: Huddersfield, West Yorkshire, England, 10 June, 1935 — LB
Died: Blackpool, Lancashire, England, February, 1995

League Club	Source	Date Signed	Seasons Played	Apps	Subs	Gls
Huddersfield T	Deighton YMCA	08/55				
Bradford Park Ave	Tr	05/57	57-58	44	-	0

BATES George Reginald
Born: Sheffield, England, 21 November, 1923 — W
Died: Sheffield, England, January, 1995

League Club	Source	Date Signed	Seasons Played	Apps	Subs	Gls
Sheffield Wed	Shardlows	03/45				
Darlington	Tr	07/46	46	3	-	0
Lincoln C	Tr	04/47				

BATES Guy Leslie
Born: Newcastle, NSW, Australia, 31 October, 1985 — F

League Club	Source	Date Signed	Seasons Played	Apps	Subs	Gls
Darlington	Newcastle Jets (AUS)	02/06	05	6	3	1

BATES James Alan (Jamie)
Born: Croydon, S London, England, 24 February, 1968 — CD

League Club	Source	Date Signed	Seasons Played	Apps	Subs	Gls
Brentford	App	08/86	86-98	399	20	18
Wycombe W	Tr	03/99	98-00	76	4	4

BATES John Wilfred
Born: Newcastle-upon-Tyne, England, 28 April, 1942 — RW
Died: Winlaton, Tyne and Wear, England, 23 June, 2009

League Club	Source	Date Signed	Seasons Played	Apps	Subs	Gls
Hartlepool U	Consett	03/66	65	11	0	0

BATES Keith
Born: Huddersfield, West Yorkshire, England, 1 September, 1933 — IF
Died: Huddersfield, West Yorkshire, England, October, 2009

League Club	Source	Date Signed	Seasons Played	Apps	Subs	Gls
Halifax T (Am)	Bradley Rgrs, Wrexham	11/56	56	1	-	0

BATES Mark
Born: Walsall, West Midlands, England, 25 April, 1965 — RB

League Club	Source	Date Signed	Seasons Played	Apps	Subs	Gls
Walsall	App	04/83	82-83	6	0	0
Shrewsbury T	Tr	07/84	84	7	1	0

BATES Matthew David
Born: Stockton-on-Tees, Cleveland, England, 10 December, 1986 — CD
England: Youth

League Club	Source	Date Signed	Seasons Played	Apps	Subs	Gls
Middlesbrough	Sch	01/05	04-11	95	9	6
Darlington	L	03/05	04	4	0	0
Ipswich T	L	11/06	06	2	0	0
Norwich C	L	01/08	07	2	1	0
Bristol C	Tr	11/12	12	12	1	0
Bradford C		10/13	13	20	2	0
Hartlepool U	Tr	06/14	14	25	0	1

BATES Michael John (Mick)
Born: Armthorpe, South Yorkshire, England, 19 September, 1947 — M

League Club	Source	Date Signed	Seasons Played	Apps	Subs	Gls
Leeds U	App	09/64	66-75	106	15	4
Walsall	Tr	06/76	76-77	84	1	4
Bradford C	Tr	06/78	78-79	54	2	1
Doncaster Rov	Tr	06/80	80	3	1	0

BATES Philip Desmond (Chic)
Born: West Bromwich, West Midlands, England, 28 November, 1949 — F

League Club	Source	Date Signed	Seasons Played	Apps	Subs	Gls
Shrewsbury T	Stourbridge	05/74	74-77	160	0	45
Swindon T	Tr	01/78	77-79	50	13	15
Bristol Rov	Tr	03/80	79-80	26	3	4
Shrewsbury T	Tr	12/80	80-85	114	20	19

BATES Thomas (Tom)
Born: Coventry, England, 31 August, 1985 — LW

League Club	Source	Date Signed	Seasons Played	Apps	Subs	Gls
Coventry C	Bedworth U	03/03	02	0	1	0
Rochdale	Leamington	03/07	06	0	2	0

BATES William Henry (Billy)
Born: Eaton Bray, Bedfordshire, England, 13 January, 1922 — W
Died: Luton, England, August, 1997

League Club	Source	Date Signed	Seasons Played	Apps	Subs	Gls
Luton T	Waterlows	09/41	46	1	-	0
Watford	Tr	07/48	48	13	-	1

BATESON Jonathan Alan (Jon)
Born: Preston, Lancashire, England, 20 September, 1989 — RB

League Club	Source	Date Signed	Seasons Played	Apps	Subs	Gls
Blackburn Rov	Sch	07/08				
Bradford C	Tr	07/09	07	14	7	0
Accrington Stan	Tr	08/10	10	12	0	0
Macclesfield T	Altrincham	06/11	11	17	4	0

League Club	Source	Date Signed	Seasons Played	Apps	Subs	Gls

BATEY Norman Robert (Bob)
Born: Greenhead, Northumberland, England, 18 October, 1912 — CH
Died: Chorley, Lancashire, England, 29 November, 1988

League Club	Source	Date Signed	Seasons Played	Apps	Subs	Gls
Carlisle U	Greenhead S Tyne Rgrs	09/32	32-33	23	-	0
Preston NE	Tr	03/34	34-38	90	-	0
Leeds U	Tr	04/46	46	8	-	0
Southport	Tr	06/47	47	29	-	0

BATHGATE Sidney (Syd)
Born: Aberdeen, Scotland, 20 December, 1919 — FB
Died: Aberdeen, Scotland, 15 February, 1963

League Club	Source	Date Signed	Seasons Played	Apps	Subs	Gls
Chelsea	Parkvale Jnrs	09/46	46-52	135	-	0

BATISTA Ricardo
Born: Setubal, Portugal, 19 November, 1986 — G

League Club	Source	Date Signed	Seasons Played	Apps	Subs	Gls
Fulham	Vitoria Setubal (POR)	01/05				
MK Dons	L	01/06	05	9	0	0
Wycombe W	L	08/06	06	29	0	0

BATSON Brendan Martin
Born: St George's, Grenada, 6 February, 1953 — RB
England: B-3

League Club	Source	Date Signed	Seasons Played	Apps	Subs	Gls
Arsenal	App	06/71	71-73	6	4	0
Cambridge U	Tr	01/74	73-77	162	1	6
West Bromwich A	Tr	02/78	77-82	172	0	1

BATT Damian Alexander Nathaniel
Born: Hoddesdon, Hertfordshire, England, 16 September, 1984 — RB

League Club	Source	Date Signed	Seasons Played	Apps	Subs	Gls
Barnet	Norwich C (Sch)	09/04	05	12	10	0
Oxford U	Grays Ath	01/09	10-12	98	7	2
Dagenham & Red	Eastleigh	06/14	14	24	4	0

BATT Shaun Anthony
Born: Harlow, Essex, England, 22 February, 1987 — W

League Club	Source	Date Signed	Seasons Played	Apps	Subs	Gls
Peterborough U	Fisher Ath	07/08	08-09	15	35	4
Millwall	Tr	01/10	09-12	14	22	4
Crawley T	L	02/12	11	2	3	0
Leyton Orient	L	01/13	12	7	4	2
Leyton Orient	Tr	06/13	13-14	12	39	5

BATT Victor Thomas (Vic)
Born: Dorking, Surrey, England, 13 March, 1943 — RW

League Club	Source	Date Signed	Seasons Played	Apps	Subs	Gls
Reading	Jnr	08/61	61-62	15	-	0

BATTERSBY Anthony (Tony)
Born: Doncaster, South Yorkshire, England, 30 August, 1975 — F

League Club	Source	Date Signed	Seasons Played	Apps	Subs	Gls
Sheffield U	YT	07/93	95	3	7	1
Southend U	L	03/95	94	6	2	1
Notts Co	Tr	01/96	95-96	20	19	8
Bury	Tr	03/97	96-97	37	11	8
Lincoln C	Tr	08/98	98-02	95	35	21
Northampton T	L	09/99	99	0	3	1
Boston U	Tr	10/02	02	7	4	1
Rushden & D	Tr	02/03	02	2	3	0

BATTH Daniel Tanveer (Danny)
Born: Brierley Hill, West Midlands, England, 21 January, 1990 — CD

League Club	Source	Date Signed	Seasons Played	Apps	Subs	Gls
Wolverhampton W	Sch	07/09	12-14	95	7	7
Colchester U	L	09/09	09	16	1	1
Sheffield U	L	11/10	10	0	1	0
Sheffield Wed	L	03/11	10	10	0	0
Sheffield Wed	L	07/11	11	44	0	2

BATTIPIEDI Agustin Emilio
Born: Buenos Aires, Argentina, 1 September, 1989 — M

League Club	Source	Date Signed	Seasons Played	Apps	Subs	Gls
Brighton & HA	Comunicaciones (ARG)	07/10	10	3	5	0

BATTOCCHIO Cristian Damian
Born: Rosario, Argentina, 10 February, 1992 — M
Italy: Youth

League Club	Source	Date Signed	Seasons Played	Apps	Subs	Gls
Watford	Udinese (ITA)	08/12	12-13	36	21	6

BATTY David
Born: Leeds, England, 2 December, 1968 — DM
England: 42/B-5/U21-7

League Club	Source	Date Signed	Seasons Played	Apps	Subs	Gls
Leeds U	YT	08/87	87-93	201	10	4
Blackburn Rov	Tr	10/93	93-95	53	1	1
Newcastle U	Tr	03/96	95-98	81	2	3
Leeds U	Tr	12/98	98-03	79	11	0

BATTY Frederick Robson (Fred)
Born: Wakefield, England, 20 December, 1934 — CH
Died: Northumberland, England, 23 June, 2007

League Club	Source	Date Signed	Seasons Played	Apps	Subs	Gls
Bradford Park Ave	Stanley U	01/56	55-58	56	-	0

BATTY Laurence William
Born: Westminster, Central London, England, 15 February, 1964 — G

League Club	Source	Date Signed	Seasons Played	Apps	Subs	Gls
Fulham	Depo Farense (POR)	08/84	85-90	9	0	0
Brentford	Tr	03/91				

BATTY Michael (Mike)
Born: Manchester, England, 10 July, 1944 — CH

League Club	Source	Date Signed	Seasons Played	Apps	Subs	Gls
Manchester C	App	07/61	62-64	13	-	0
Rochdale	Rhyl	08/66				

BATTY Paul William
Born: Edington, Wiltshire, England, 9 January, 1964 — M

League Club	Source	Date Signed	Seasons Played	Apps	Subs	Gls
Swindon T	App	01/82	82-84	102	6	7
Chesterfield	Tr	07/85	85	24	2	0
Exeter C	Tr	07/86	86-90	98	13	11

BATTY Ronald Robson (Ron)
Born: Lanchester, County Durham, England, 5 October, 1925 — LB
Died: Chester, England, 1971

League Club	Source	Date Signed	Seasons Played	Apps	Subs	Gls
Newcastle U	Quaking Houses	10/45	48-57	161	-	1
Gateshead	Tr	03/58	57-58	40	-	0

BATTY Stanley George (Stan)
Born: Tottenham, N London, England, 14 February, 1913 — WH
Died: Torbay, Devon, England, October, 1998

League Club	Source	Date Signed	Seasons Played	Apps	Subs	Gls
Aston Villa	Finchley	11/37				
Newport Co	Tr	12/45	46-47	60	-	3

BATTYE John Edward
Born: Clayton West, West Yorkshire, England, 19 May, 1926 — RH

League Club	Source	Date Signed	Seasons Played	Apps	Subs	Gls
Huddersfield T	Shepley Jnrs	12/43	49-57	71	-	1
York C	Tr	07/59	59	17	-	0

BAUDET Julien
Born: Grenoble, France, 13 January, 1979 — CD

League Club	Source	Date Signed	Seasons Played	Apps	Subs	Gls
Oldham Ath	Toulouse (FRA)	10/01	01-02	34	10	3
Rotherham U	Tr	08/03	03	8	3	0
Notts Co	Tr	07/04	04-05	80	1	11
Crewe Alex	Tr	06/06	06-08	112	0	2

BAUDRY Mathieu Marian Ghislain
Born: Le Havre, France, 24 February, 1988 — CD

League Club	Source	Date Signed	Seasons Played	Apps	Subs	Gls
Bournemouth	Troyes AC (FRA)	01/11	10-11	6	4	1
Dagenham & Red	L	03/12	11	11	0	0
Leyton Orient	Tr	07/12	12-14	88	6	6

BAUGH John Robert
Born: Kampala, Uganda, 23 February, 1956 — G

League Club	Source	Date Signed	Seasons Played	Apps	Subs	Gls
Exeter C	St Luke's College	02/77	76-77	20	0	0

BAULD Philip Spinelli (Phil)
Born: Glasgow, Scotland, 20 September, 1929 — WH
Died: Plymouth, England, April, 1994

League Club	Source	Date Signed	Seasons Played	Apps	Subs	Gls
Plymouth Arg	Clyde	06/53				
Aldershot	Tr	07/54	54	3	-	0

BAURESS Gary Joseph
Born: Liverpool, England, 19 January, 1971 — M

League Club	Source	Date Signed	Seasons Played	Apps	Subs	Gls
Tranmere Rov	YT	08/89	89	1	0	0

BAUZA Guillem
Born: Mallorca, Spain, 25 October, 1984 — F

League Club	Source	Date Signed	Seasons Played	Apps	Subs	Gls
Swansea C	RCD Espanyol B (SPN)	07/07	07-09	19	30	9
Hereford U	Tr	09/10	10	9	3	2
Northampton T	Tr	03/11	10	9	1	4
Exeter C	Tr	07/11	11-12	16	30	4

BAVERSTOCK Raymond (Ray)
Born: Southall, W London, England, 3 December, 1963 — RB

League Club	Source	Date Signed	Seasons Played	Apps	Subs	Gls
Swindon T	App	12/81	82	17	0	0

BAVIN John (Jack)
Born: South Ferriby, North Lincolnshire, England, 25 May, 1921 — FB
Died: Scunthorpe, North Lincolnshire, England, 11 March, 2001

League Club	Source	Date Signed	Seasons Played	Apps	Subs	Gls
Tranmere Rov	Leith Ath	04/49	48	2	-	0

BAWLING Alfred Bobson (Bobson)
Born: Islington, N London, England, 21 September, 1995 — M

League Club	Source	Date Signed	Seasons Played	Apps	Subs	Gls
Crawley T	Watford (Sch)	07/14	14	13	15	0

BAXENDALE James Robert
Born: Thorne, South Yorkshire, England, 16 September, 1992 — W

League Club	Source	Date Signed	Seasons Played	Apps	Subs	Gls
Doncaster Rov	Leeds U (Sch)	07/11	11	0	2	0
Hereford U	L	03/12	11	0	1	0
Walsall	Tr	08/12	12-14	65	35	7

BAXTER Darren Lee
Born: Brighton, England, 26 October, 1981 — M

League Club	Source	Date Signed	Seasons Played	Apps	Subs	Gls
Torquay U	Toronto Lynx (CAN)	01/07	06	0	1	0

BAXTER James Cunningham (Jimmy)
Born: Dunfermline, Fife, Scotland, 8 November, 1925 — IF
Died: Barnsley, South Yorkshire, England, May, 1994

League Club	Source	Date Signed	Seasons Played	Apps	Subs	Gls
Barnsley	Dunfermline Ath	08/45	46-51	222	-	54
Preston NE	Tr	07/52	52-58	245	-	65
Barnsley	Tr	07/59	59	26	-	3

League Club	Source	Date Signed	Seasons Played	Apps	Subs	Gls

BAXTER James Curran (Jim)
Born: Cowdenbeath, Fife, Scotland, 29 September, 1939 — M
Died: Glasgow, Scotland, 14 April, 2001
Scotland: 34/SLge-5/U23-1

League Club	Source	Date Signed	Seasons Played	Apps	Subs	Gls
Sunderland	Glasgow Rangers	05/65	65-67	87	0	10
Nottingham F	Tr	12/67	67-68	47	1	3

BAXTER Jose
Born: Bootle, Merseyside, England, 7 February, 1992 — F
England: Youth

League Club	Source	Date Signed	Seasons Played	Apps	Subs	Gls
Everton	Sch	03/09	08-11	1	6	0
Tranmere Rov	L	09/11	11	14	0	3
Oldham Ath	Tr	09/12	12-13	37	6	15
Sheffield U	Tr	08/13	13-14	57	12	16

BAXTER Lawrence Raymond (Larry)
Born: Leicester, England, 24 November, 1931 — RW

League Club	Source	Date Signed	Seasons Played	Apps	Subs	Gls
Northampton T		03/52	52-53	17	-	2
Norwich C	Tr	11/54	54	5	-	0
Gillingham	Tr	10/55	55-57	64	-	7
Torquay U	Tr	09/57	57-61	165	-	22

BAXTER Lee Stuart
Born: Helsingborg, Sweden, 17 July, 1976 — G

League Club	Source	Date Signed	Seasons Played	Apps	Subs	Gls
Sheffield U (L)	Malmo FF (SWE)	12/03	03	1	0	0

BAXTER Michael John (Mick)
Born: Birmingham, England, 30 December, 1956 — CD
Died: Preston, Lancashire, England, 16 January, 1989

League Club	Source	Date Signed	Seasons Played	Apps	Subs	Gls
Preston NE	App	12/74	74-80	208	1	17
Middlesbrough	Tr	08/81	81-83	122	0	7

BAXTER Paul Albert
Born: Hackney, E London, England, 22 April, 1964 — FB

League Club	Source	Date Signed	Seasons Played	Apps	Subs	Gls
Crystal Palace	Tottenham H (App)	09/81	81	1	0	0

BAXTER Robert Denholm (Bobby)
Born: Redcar, Cleveland, England, 4 February, 1937 — LB

League Club	Source	Date Signed	Seasons Played	Apps	Subs	Gls
Darlington	Bo'ness	11/59	59-60	64	-	30
Brighton & HA	Tr	06/61	61-66	195	0	6
Torquay U	Tr	07/67	67-68	58	4	6
Darlington	Tr	07/69	69	41	1	0

BAXTER Stuart William
Born: Wolverhampton, England, 16 August, 1953 — CD
Australia:

League Club	Source	Date Signed	Seasons Played	Apps	Subs	Gls
Preston NE	App	10/71	72-75	35	7	1
Stockport Co	Dundee	12/76	76	4	0	0

BAXTER William (Billy)
Born: Leven, Fife, Scotland, 21 September, 1924 — WH
Died: East Wemyss, Fife, Scotland, 9 November, 2002

League Club	Source	Date Signed	Seasons Played	Apps	Subs	Gls
Wolverhampton W	Jnr	03/45	48-53	43	-	1
Aston Villa	Tr	11/53	53-56	98	-	6

BAXTER William Alexander (Bill)
Born: Edinburgh, Scotland, 23 April, 1939 — CD
Died: Dunfermline, Fife, Scotland, 25 May, 2009

League Club	Source	Date Signed	Seasons Played	Apps	Subs	Gls
Ipswich T	Broxburn Ath	06/60	60-70	409	0	21
Hull C	Tr	03/71	70-71	20	1	0
Watford	L	10/71	71	11	0	0
Northampton T	Tr	06/72	72	41	0	4

BAXTER William Amelius (Bill)
Born: Nottingham, England, 6 September, 1917 — CH
Died: Nottingham, England, 21 February, 1992

League Club	Source	Date Signed	Seasons Played	Apps	Subs	Gls
Nottingham F	Berridge Road Inst	12/36	37-46	15	-	0
Notts Co	Tr	10/46	46-53	140	-	0

BAYES Ashley John
Born: Lincoln, England, 19 April, 1972 — G
England: Youth

League Club	Source	Date Signed	Seasons Played	Apps	Subs	Gls
Brentford	YT	07/90	89-92	4	0	0
Torquay U	Tr	08/93	93-95	97	0	0
Exeter C	Tr	07/96	96-98	127	0	0
Leyton Orient	Tr	07/99	99-01	68	1	0

BAYLEY Thomas Kenneth (Tom)
Born: Wednesbury, West Midlands, England, 25 June, 1921 — G
Died: Stafford, England, March, 1996

League Club	Source	Date Signed	Seasons Played	Apps	Subs	Gls
Wrexham	Walsall (Am)	08/47	47	6	-	0

BAYLISS David Anthony (Dave)
Born: Liverpool, England, 8 June, 1976 — CD

League Club	Source	Date Signed	Seasons Played	Apps	Subs	Gls
Rochdale	YT	06/95	94-01	169	17	9
Luton T	Tr	12/01	01-03	28	9	0
Chester C	L	12/04	04	9	0	0
Wrexham	Tr	07/05	05	21	1	0
Rochdale	L	02/06	05	4	0	0

BAYLISS Ronald (Ron)
Born: Belfast, Northern Ireland, 20 September, 1944 — D

League Club	Source	Date Signed	Seasons Played	Apps	Subs	Gls
Reading		02/65	64-67	35	2	1
Bradford C	Tr	07/68	68-69	35	4	0

BAYLY Martin Joseph
Born: Dublin, Republic of Ireland, 14 September, 1966 — M
Republic of Ireland: U21-1/Youth

League Club	Source	Date Signed	Seasons Played	Apps	Subs	Gls
Wolverhampton W	App	07/84	83-84	9	1	0

BAYLY Robert Sean
Born: Dublin, Republic of Ireland, 22 February, 1988 — M
Republic of Ireland: Youth

League Club	Source	Date Signed	Seasons Played	Apps	Subs	Gls
Leeds U	Sch	03/06	06	1	0	0

BAYNES Wesley (Wes)
Born: Chester, England, 8 June, 1976 — M/FB

League Club	Source	Date Signed	Seasons Played	Apps	Subs	Gls
Wrexham	Sch	07/07	07	10	2	2

BAYNHAM John (Johnny)
Born: Ystrad Rhondda, Rhondda Cynon Taff, Wales, 21 April, 1918 — W
Died: Hillingdon, W London, England, February, 1995

League Club	Source	Date Signed	Seasons Played	Apps	Subs	Gls
Leyton Orient	Brentford (Am)	03/46	46-47	60	-	7
Swindon T	Tr	08/48	48	4	-	1

BAYNHAM Ronald Leslie (Ron)
Born: Birmingham, England, 10 June, 1929 — G
England: 3/B-1/FLge-2

League Club	Source	Date Signed	Seasons Played	Apps	Subs	Gls
Luton T	Worcester C	11/51	52-64	388	-	0

BAZ Cristian Martin
Born: Buenos Aires, Argentina, 5 May, 1987 — M

League Club	Source	Date Signed	Seasons Played	Apps	Subs	Gls
Brighton & HA	Comunicaciones (ARG)	07/10	10	0	7	0

BAZELEY Darren Shaun
Born: Northampton, England, 5 October, 1972 — RB/M
England: U21-1

League Club	Source	Date Signed	Seasons Played	Apps	Subs	Gls
Watford	YT	05/91	89-98	187	53	21
Wolverhampton W	Tr	07/99	99-00	69	1	4
Walsall	Tr	07/02	02-04	83	6	0

BAZLEY John Alfred
Born: Runcorn, Cheshire, England, 4 October, 1936 — RW

League Club	Source	Date Signed	Seasons Played	Apps	Subs	Gls
Oldham Ath	Bangor C	10/56	56-61	130	-	19

BEACH Douglas Frederick (Doug)
Born: Watford, Hertfordshire, England, 2 February, 1920 — FB
Died: Tavistock, Devon, England, 18 August, 2006

League Club	Source	Date Signed	Seasons Played	Apps	Subs	Gls
Luton T	Sheffield Wed (Am)	08/45	46	23	-	0
Southend U	Tr	07/47	47-48	41	-	0

BEACOCK Gary Cedric
Born: Scunthorpe, North Lincolnshire, England, 22 January, 1960 — M

League Club	Source	Date Signed	Seasons Played	Apps	Subs	Gls
Grimsby T	VV Ripperda (NED)	05/80	80-82	10	7	0
Hereford U	Tr	08/83	83-85	22	5	4

BEADLE Peter Clifford William James
Born: Lambeth, S London, England, 13 May, 1972 — F

League Club	Source	Date Signed	Seasons Played	Apps	Subs	Gls
Gillingham	YT	05/90	88-91	42	25	14
Tottenham H	Tr	06/92				
Bournemouth	L	03/93	92	9	0	2
Southend U	L	03/94	93	8	0	1
Watford	Tr	09/94	94-95	12	11	1
Bristol Rov	Tr	11/95	95-97	98	11	39
Port Vale	Tr	08/98	98	18	5	6
Notts Co	Tr	02/99	98-99	14	8	3
Bristol C	Tr	10/99	99-02	51	31	14
Brentford	Tr	08/03	03	1	0	0

BEADNELL William (Bill)
Born: Sunderland, England, 25 January, 1933 — IF
Died: Stockton-on-Tees, Cleveland, England, 30 August, 2011

League Club	Source	Date Signed	Seasons Played	Apps	Subs	Gls
Chesterfield	Burnley (Am)	06/50				
Sunderland	Hylton CW	03/53				
Middlesbrough	Tr	05/53				
Southport	Tr	05/54	54-55	63	-	19

BEAGRIE Peter Sydney
Born: Middlesbrough, England, 28 November, 1965 — LW
England: B-2/U21-2

League Club	Source	Date Signed	Seasons Played	Apps	Subs	Gls
Middlesbrough	Jnr	09/83	84-85	24	9	2
Sheffield U	Tr	08/86	86-87	81	3	11
Stoke C	Tr	06/88	88-89	54	0	7
Everton	Tr	11/89	89-93	88	26	11
Sunderland	L	09/91	91	5	0	1
Manchester C	Tr	03/94	93-96	46	6	3
Bradford C	Tr	07/97	97-00	113	18	20
Everton	L	03/98	97	4	2	0
Wigan Ath	L	02/01	00	7	3	1
Scunthorpe U	Tr	07/01	01-05	153	19	34
Grimsby T	Tr	07/06	06	6	3	0

BEAL Philip (Phil)
Born: Godstone, Surrey, England, 8 January, 1945 — CD
England: Youth

League Club	Source	Date Signed	Seasons Played	Apps	Subs	Gls
Tottenham H	App	01/62	63-74	330	3	1
Brighton & HA	Tr	07/75	75-76	9	1	0
Crewe Alex	Memphis Rogues (USA)	08/79	79	4	0	0

BEALE John Michael
Born: Portsmouth, England, 16 October, 1930 — WH
Died: Droxford, Hampshire, England, September, 1995

League Club	Source	Date Signed	Seasons Played	Apps	Subs	Gls
Portsmouth	Jnr	08/48	51-52	14	-	1

BEALL Matthew John (Billy)
Born: Enfield, N London, England, 4 December, 1977 — LM

League Club	Source	Date Signed	Seasons Played	Apps	Subs	Gls
Cambridge U	YT	03/96	95-97	73	9	7
Leyton Orient	Tr	10/98	98-01	62	22	3

BEAMAN Ralph Wesley
Born: Willenhall, West Midlands, England, 14 January, 1943 — CF

League Club	Source	Date Signed	Seasons Played	Apps	Subs	Gls
Walsall	Jnr	12/60	61	1	-	0

BEAMENT Roger John
Born: Croxley Green, Hertfordshire, England, 28 September, 1937 — G
Died: Watford, Hertfordshire, England, 20 July, 2012

League Club	Source	Date Signed	Seasons Played	Apps	Subs	Gls
Watford (Am)	Croxley BC	07/56	56	1	-	0

BEAMISH Kenneth George (Ken)
Born: Bebington, Wirral, England, 25 August, 1947 — F

League Club	Source	Date Signed	Seasons Played	Apps	Subs	Gls
Tranmere Rov	Jnr	07/66	65-71	176	2	49
Brighton & HA	Tr	03/72	71-73	86	10	27
Blackburn Rov	Tr	05/74	74-76	86	0	19
Port Vale	Tr	09/76	76-78	84	1	29
Bury	Tr	09/78	78-79	49	0	20
Tranmere Rov	Tr	11/79	79-80	57	2	15
Swindon T	Tr	08/81	81	1	1	0

BEAN Alan
Born: Doncaster, South Yorkshire, England, 17 January, 1935 — CD

League Club	Source	Date Signed	Seasons Played	Apps	Subs	Gls
Blackburn Rov	Jnr	04/52	52-54	2	-	0

BEAN Alfred Samuel (Alf)
Born: Lincoln, England, 25 August, 1915 — LB
Died: Lincoln, England, 25 November, 1993

League Club	Source	Date Signed	Seasons Played	Apps	Subs	Gls
Lincoln C	Lincoln Corinthians	05/35	34-48	171	-	10

BEAN Marcus Tristam
Born: Hammersmith, W London, England, 2 November, 1984 — M
Jamaica: 1

League Club	Source	Date Signed	Seasons Played	Apps	Subs	Gls
Queens Park Rgrs	Sch	07/04	02-05	44	23	2
Swansea C	L	02/05	04	6	2	0
Swansea C	L	09/05	05	9	0	1
Blackpool	Tr	01/06	05-06	19	4	1
Rotherham U	L	08/07	07	11	1	1
Brentford	Tr	07/08	08-11	122	22	14
Colchester U	Tr	07/12	12-14	60	9	5
Portsmouth	L	11/14	14	6	0	1
Wycombe W	Tr	01/15	14	16	1	0

BEAN Ronald Eric (Ron)
Born: Crayford, SE London, England, 10 April, 1926 — G
Died: Bournemouth, England, 7 July, 1992

League Club	Source	Date Signed	Seasons Played	Apps	Subs	Gls
Gillingham	Gravesend & Northfleet	06/51	51	3	-	0

BEANEY William Ronald (Bill)
Born: Southampton, England, 29 May, 1954 — CD

League Club	Source	Date Signed	Seasons Played	Apps	Subs	Gls
Southampton	App	06/72	72-74	2	1	0

BEANLAND Anthony (Tony)
Born: Bradford, England, 11 January, 1944 — D/M

League Club	Source	Date Signed	Seasons Played	Apps	Subs	Gls
Blackpool	App	01/62				
Southport	Tr	07/62	62-65	143	0	3
Southend U	Tr	03/66	65-66	57	0	3
Wrexham	Tr	07/67	67-68	84	0	5
Bradford Park Ave	Tr	06/69	69	29	2	1

BEARD Malcolm
Born: Cannock, Staffordshire, England, 3 May, 1942 — LH
England: Youth

League Club	Source	Date Signed	Seasons Played	Apps	Subs	Gls
Birmingham C	Jnr	05/59	60-70	349	1	26
Aston Villa	Tr	07/71	71-72	5	1	0

BEARD Mark
Born: Roehampton, SW London, England, 8 October, 1974 — RB/M

League Club	Source	Date Signed	Seasons Played	Apps	Subs	Gls
Millwall	YT	03/93	93-94	32	13	2
Sheffield U	Tr	08/95	95-97	22	16	0
Southend U	L	10/97	97	6	2	0
Southend U	Tr	07/98	98-99	74	4	1
Southend U	Kingstonian	10/01	01-02	34	16	0

BEARDALL James Thomas (Jim)
Born: Manchester, England, 18 October, 1946 — F

League Club	Source	Date Signed	Seasons Played	Apps	Subs	Gls
Blackburn Rov	Bury (Am)	03/68	67-68	4	2	1
Oldham Ath	Tr	05/69	69	21	1	10

BEARDS Allan
Born: Normanton, West Yorkshire, England, 19 October, 1932 — LW

League Club	Source	Date Signed	Seasons Played	Apps	Subs	Gls
Bolton W	Whitewood Jnrs	10/50	50-53	14	-	2
Swindon T	Tr	03/54	53-54	21	-	4
Stockport Co	Tr	07/55	55	5	-	0

BEARDSHAW Ernest Colin (Colin)
Born: Crawcrook, Tyne and Wear, England, 26 November, 1912 — CH
Died: Southport, Merseyside, England, 22 August, 1977

League Club	Source	Date Signed	Seasons Played	Apps	Subs	Gls
Gateshead (Am)	South Hetton CW	02/36	35	12	-	0
Stockport Co	Tr	05/36	37	18	-	0
Bradford C	Tr	07/38	38	42	-	0
Southport	Cork U (ROI)	10/48	48-50	61	-	0

BEARDSLEY Christopher Kelan (Chris)
Born: Derby, England, 28 February, 1984 — F

League Club	Source	Date Signed	Seasons Played	Apps	Subs	Gls
Mansfield T	Sch	07/03	02-03	3	17	1
Doncaster Rov	Tr	08/04	04	1	3	0
Kidderminster Hrs	Tr	12/04	04	15	10	5
Mansfield T	Tr	08/05	05-06	5	8	0
Stevenage	Kettering T	06/09	10-11	29	25	8
Preston NE	Tr	08/12	12	12	7	2
Bristol Rov	L	11/13	13	16	8	1
Stevenage	Tr	07/14	14	23	6	4

BEARDSLEY Donald Thomas (Don)
Born: Alyth, Perthshire, Scotland, 23 October, 1946 — FB

League Club	Source	Date Signed	Seasons Played	Apps	Subs	Gls
Hull C	App	11/64	66-72	128	2	0
Doncaster Rov	L	03/72	71	10	0	0
Grimsby T	Tr	08/73	73-74	66	0	0

BEARDSLEY Jason Clive
Born: Uttoxeter, Staffordshire, England, 12 July, 1989 — RB

League Club	Source	Date Signed	Seasons Played	Apps	Subs	Gls
Derby Co	Sch	07/07				
Notts Co	L	07/08	08	11	0	0
Macclesfield T	Tampa Bay R's (USA)	08/10				

BEARDSLEY Peter Andrew
Born: Longbenton, Tyne and Wear, England, 18 January, 1961 — F
England: 59/B-2/FLge

League Club	Source	Date Signed	Seasons Played	Apps	Subs	Gls
Carlisle U	Wallsend BC	08/79	79-81	93	11	22
Manchester U	Vancouver W'caps (CAN)	09/82				
Newcastle U	Vancouver W'caps (CAN)	09/83	83-86	146	1	61
Liverpool	Tr	07/87	87-90	120	11	46
Everton	Tr	08/91	91-92	81	0	25
Newcastle U	Tr	07/93	93-96	126	3	46
Bolton W	Tr	08/97	97	14	3	2
Manchester C	L	02/98	97	5	1	0
Fulham	Tr	03/98	97-98	19	2	4
Hartlepool U	Tr	12/98	98	22	0	2

BEARDSMORE Russell Peter
Born: Wigan, Greater Manchester, England, 28 September, 1968 — M
England: U21-5

League Club	Source	Date Signed	Seasons Played	Apps	Subs	Gls
Manchester U	App	10/86	88-90	30	26	4
Blackburn Rov	L	12/91	91	1	1	0
Bournemouth	Tr	06/93	93-97	167	11	4

BEARPARK Ian Harper
Born: Dursley, Gloucestershire, England, 13 January, 1939 — G
Died: Mid Devon, England, December, 1997

League Club	Source	Date Signed	Seasons Played	Apps	Subs	Gls
Bristol Rov	Stonehouse	08/60	60	2	-	0
Exeter C	Tr	01/61				
Bristol Rov	Tr	02/61				

BEARRYMAN Henry William (Harry)
Born: Wandsworth, SW London, England, 26 September, 1924 — WH
Died: Banstead, Surrey, England, December, 1976

League Club	Source	Date Signed	Seasons Played	Apps	Subs	Gls
Chelsea	Jnr	09/41				
Colchester U	Tr	07/47	50-53	173	-	3

BEASANT David John (Dave)
Born: Willesden, NW London, England, 20 March, 1959 — G
England: 2/B-7

League Club	Source	Date Signed	Seasons Played	Apps	Subs	Gls
Wimbledon	Edgware T	08/79	79-87	340	0	0
Newcastle U	Tr	06/88	88	20	0	0
Chelsea	Tr	01/89	88-92	133	0	0
Grimsby T	L	10/92	92	6	0	0
Wolverhampton W	L	01/93	92	4	0	0
Southampton	Tr	11/93	93-96	86	2	0
Nottingham F	Tr	08/97	97-00	139	0	0
Portsmouth	Tr	08/01	01	8	0	0
Tottenham H	Tr	11/01				
Portsmouth	Tr	01/02	01	19	0	0

League Club	Source	Date Signed	Seasons Played	Apps	Subs	Gls
Bradford C	Tr	09/02				
Wigan Ath	Tr	10/02				
Brighton & HA	Tr	01/03	02	16	0	0

BEASANT Samuel James (Sam)
Born: Denham, Buckinghamshire, England, 8 April, 1988 G

League Club	Source	Date Signed	Seasons Played	Apps	Subs	Gls
Stevenage	Woking	06/14	14	8	0	0

BEASLEY Albert Edward (Pat)
Born: Stourbridge, West Midlands, England, 27 July, 1913 W
Died: Taunton, Somerset, England, 27 February, 1986
England: 1

League Club	Source	Date Signed	Seasons Played	Apps	Subs	Gls
Arsenal	Stourbridge	05/31	31-36	79	-	19
Huddersfield T	Tr	10/36	36-38	108	-	24
Fulham	Tr	12/45	46-49	152	-	13
Bristol C	Tr	08/50	50-51	66	-	5

BEASLEY Andrew (Andy)
Born: Sedgley, West Midlands, England, 15 February, 1964 G

League Club	Source	Date Signed	Seasons Played	Apps	Subs	Gls
Luton T	App	02/82				
Mansfield T	Tr	07/84	84-91	94	0	0
Peterborough U	L	07/86	86	7	0	0
Scarborough	L	03/88	87	4	0	0
Bristol Rov	L	03/93	92	1	0	0
Doncaster Rov	Tr	07/93	93	37	0	0
Chesterfield	Tr	08/94	94-95	31	1	0

BEASLEY DeMarcus Lamont
Born: Fort Wayne, Indiana, USA, 24 May, 1982 W
USA: 120/Youth

League Club	Source	Date Signed	Seasons Played	Apps	Subs	Gls
Manchester C (L)	PSV Eindhoven (NED)	08/06	06	11	7	3

BEASON Malcolm Lloyd
Born: Dulwich, S London, England, 1 December, 1955 M

League Club	Source	Date Signed	Seasons Played	Apps	Subs	Gls
Crystal Palace	App	08/73				
Leyton Orient	Tr	09/75	75	0	1	0

BEATON William (Bill)
Born: Kincardine, Fife, Scotland, 30 September, 1935 G

League Club	Source	Date Signed	Seasons Played	Apps	Subs	Gls
Aston Villa	Dunfermline Ath	10/58	58	1	-	0

BEATTIE Andrew (Andy)
Born: Kintore, Aberdeenshire, Scotland, 11 August, 1913 FB
Died: Nottingham, England, 20 September, 1983
Scotland: 7/War-5

League Club	Source	Date Signed	Seasons Played	Apps	Subs	Gls
Preston NE	Inverurie Loco	05/35	34-46	125	-	4

BEATTIE Andrew Hugh (Andy)
Born: Liverpool, England, 9 February, 1964 CD

League Club	Source	Date Signed	Seasons Played	Apps	Subs	Gls
Cambridge U	App	02/82	83-87	94	4	2

BEATTIE Bradley Steven
Born: Torquay, Devon, England, 20 August, 1957 F

League Club	Source	Date Signed	Seasons Played	Apps	Subs	Gls
Torquay U	App	-	73-74	2	2	0

BEATTIE Craig
Born: Glasgow, Scotland, 16 January, 1984 F
Scotland: 7/U21-7

League Club	Source	Date Signed	Seasons Played	Apps	Subs	Gls
West Bromwich A	Glasgow Celtic	07/07	07-09	7	24	4
Preston NE	L	03/08	07	1	1	0
Crystal Palace	L	09/08	08	15	0	5
Sheffield U	L	02/09	08	1	12	1
Swansea C	Tr	08/09	09-10	21	24	7
Watford	L	10/11	11	1	3	1
Barnet	St Johnstone	02/13	12	1	4	0

BEATTIE George
Born: Aberdeen, Scotland, 16 June, 1925 IF
Died: Newport, Wales, 10 March, 2012

League Club	Source	Date Signed	Seasons Played	Apps	Subs	Gls
Southampton	Rosslyn Rosemount	08/47	47	1	-	0
Newport Co	Gloucester C	09/50	50-52	113	-	23
Bradford Park Ave	Tr	07/53	53-54	53	-	16

BEATTIE James Scott
Born: Lancaster, England, 27 February, 1978 F
England: 5/U21-5

League Club	Source	Date Signed	Seasons Played	Apps	Subs	Gls
Blackburn Rov	YT	03/95	96-97	1	3	0
Southampton	Tr	07/98	98-04	161	43	68
Everton	Tr	01/05	04-06	51	25	13
Sheffield U	Tr	08/07	07-08	57	5	34
Stoke C	Tr	01/09	08-09	27	11	10
Blackpool (L)	Glasgow Rangers	01/11	10	5	4	0
Sheffield U	Glasgow Rangers	11/11	11	2	16	0
Accrington Stan	Rtd	11/12	12	18	7	6

BEATTIE Richard Scott (Dick)
Born: Glasgow, Scotland, 24 October, 1936 G
Died: Old Kilpatrick, Dunbartonshire, Scotland, 15 August, 1990
Scotland: SLge-1/U23-3

League Club	Source	Date Signed	Seasons Played	Apps	Subs	Gls
Portsmouth	Glasgow Celtic	08/59	59-61	122	-	0
Peterborough U	Tr	06/62	62	10	-	0

BEATTIE Robert (Bobby)
Born: Stevenston, Ayrshire, Scotland, 24 January, 1916 IF
Died: Irvine, Ayrshire, Scotland, 21 September, 2002
Scotland: 1

League Club	Source	Date Signed	Seasons Played	Apps	Subs	Gls
Preston NE	Kilmarnock	09/37	37-53	264	-	57

BEATTIE Stuart Richard
Born: Stevenston, Ayrshire, Scotland, 10 July, 1967 CD

League Club	Source	Date Signed	Seasons Played	Apps	Subs	Gls
Doncaster Rov	Glasgow Rangers	01/87	86-88	26	0	1

BEATTIE Thomas
Born: Stakeford, Northumberland, England, 12 March, 1921 IF
Died: Morpeth, Northumberland, England, 4 February, 1988

League Club	Source	Date Signed	Seasons Played	Apps	Subs	Gls
Gateshead	Morpeth T	01/47	46-47	18	-	4

BEATTIE Thomas Kevin (Kevin)
Born: Carlisle, Cumbria, England, 18 December, 1953 CD
England: 9/Youth

League Club	Source	Date Signed	Seasons Played	Apps	Subs	Gls
Ipswich T	App	07/71	72-80	225	3	24
Colchester U	Tr	07/82	82	3	1	0
Middlesbrough	Tr	11/82	82	3	1	0

BEAUCHAMP Joseph Daniel (Joey)
Born: Oxford, England, 13 March, 1971 LW

League Club	Source	Date Signed	Seasons Played	Apps	Subs	Gls
Oxford U	YT	05/89	88-93	117	7	20
Swansea C	L	10/91	91	5	0	2
West Ham U	Tr	06/94				
Swindon T	Tr	08/94	94-95	39	6	3
Oxford U	Tr	10/95	95-01	203	35	43

BEAUMONT Alan
Born: Liverpool, England, 9 January, 1927 WH
Died: Liverpool, England, July, 1999

League Club	Source	Date Signed	Seasons Played	Apps	Subs	Gls
Chester C	South Liverpool	09/48	48	5	-	0

BEAUMONT Christopher Paul (Chris)
Born: Sheffield, England, 5 December, 1965 M

League Club	Source	Date Signed	Seasons Played	Apps	Subs	Gls
Rochdale	Denaby U	07/88	88	31	3	7
Stockport Co	Tr	07/89	89-95	238	20	39
Chesterfield	Tr	07/96	96-00	132	26	6

BEAUMONT David Alan (Dave)
Born: Edinburgh, Scotland, 10 December, 1963 CD
Scotland: U21-1/Youth

League Club	Source	Date Signed	Seasons Played	Apps	Subs	Gls
Luton T	Dundee U	01/89	88-91	66	10	0

BEAUMONT Frank
Born: Hoyland, South Yorkshire, England, 22 December, 1939 IF
Died: Barnsley, South Yorkshire, England, 6 November, 2011
England: Youth

League Club	Source	Date Signed	Seasons Played	Apps	Subs	Gls
Barnsley	Jnr	12/57	57-61	107	-	37
Bury	Tr	09/61	61-63	68	-	12
Stockport Co	Tr	09/64	64-65	52	3	4

BEAUMONT James
Born: Stockton-on-Tees, Cleveland, England, 11 December, 1984 M

League Club	Source	Date Signed	Seasons Played	Apps	Subs	Gls
Newcastle U	Sch	05/02				
Nottingham F	Tr	08/03				
Darlington	L	03/06	05	0	1	0

BEAUMONT Nigel
Born: Hemsworth, West Yorkshire, England, 11 February, 1967 CD

League Club	Source	Date Signed	Seasons Played	Apps	Subs	Gls
Bradford C	App	07/85	85	2	0	0
Wrexham	Tr	07/88	88-91	112	3	4

BEAUSEJOUR Jean Andre Eman
Born: Santiago, Chile, 1 June, 1984 M/LW
Chile: 68

League Club	Source	Date Signed	Seasons Played	Apps	Subs	Gls
Birmingham C	Club America (MEX)	08/10	10-11	31	8	3
Wigan Ath	Tr	01/12	11-13	78	5	3

BEAUTYMAN Harry
Born: Newham, E London, England, 1 April, 1992 M
England: Semi Pro-2

League Club	Source	Date Signed	Seasons Played	Apps	Subs	Gls
Leyton Orient	Sch	07/10				
Peterborough U	Welling U	11/14	14	15	3	2

BEAVAN George David
Born: Erith, SE London, England, 12 January, 1990 CD

League Club	Source	Date Signed	Seasons Played	Apps	Subs	Gls
Luton T	Sch	08/08	07-08	4	2	0

BEAVEN Kenneth (Ken)
Born: Bovingdon, Hertfordshire, England, 26 December, 1949 W

League Club	Source	Date Signed	Seasons Played	Apps	Subs	Gls
Luton T	App	-	67	1	0	0

BEAVER David
Born: Kirkby-in-Ashfield, Nottinghamshire, England, 4 April, 1966 M

League Club	Source	Date Signed	Seasons Played	Apps	Subs	Gls
Notts Co	App	04/84	84	1	0	0

BEAVERS Paul Mark
Born: Blackpool, Lancashire, England, 2 October, 1978 — F

League Club	Source	Date Signed	Seasons Played	Apps	Subs	Gls
Sunderland	YT	04/97				
Shrewsbury T	L	12/98	98	2	0	0
Oldham Ath	Tr	03/99	98-99	10	1	2
Hartlepool U	L	03/00	99	2	5	0
Darlington	Tr	09/00	00	3	4	1

BEAVON Cyril
Born: Barnsley, South Yorkshire, England, 27 September, 1937 — RB
England: Youth

League Club	Source	Date Signed	Seasons Played	Apps	Subs	Gls
Wolverhampton W	Jnr	12/54				
Oxford U	Tr	01/59	62-68	271	2	7

BEAVON David George
Born: Nottingham, England, 8 December, 1961 — FB

League Club	Source	Date Signed	Seasons Played	Apps	Subs	Gls
Notts Co	App	12/79	80	5	0	0
Lincoln C	Tr	11/81	81-82	7	1	0
Northampton T	Tsuen Wan (HKG)	03/83	82	2	0	0

BEAVON Michael Stuart (Stuart)
Born: Wolverhampton, England, 30 November, 1958 — M

League Club	Source	Date Signed	Seasons Played	Apps	Subs	Gls
Tottenham H	App	07/76	78-79	3	1	0
Notts Co	L	12/79	79	6	0	0
Reading	Tr	07/80	80-89	380	16	44
Northampton T	Tr	08/90	90-92	95	3	14

BEAVON Stuart Leigh
Born: Reading, England, 5 May, 1984 — F

League Club	Source	Date Signed	Seasons Played	Apps	Subs	Gls
Wycombe W	Weymouth	02/09	09-12	88	27	28
Preston NE	Tr	08/12	12-13	49	9	9
Burton A	Tr	06/14	14	41	3	6

BEBBINGTON Peter Andrew
Born: Oswestry, Shropshire, England, 13 October, 1946 — LB/M

League Club	Source	Date Signed	Seasons Played	Apps	Subs	Gls
Leicester C	Oswestry T	10/65				
Barrow	Tr	11/67	67-68	52	1	3
Stockport Co	Tr	07/69	69	16	1	1

BEBBINGTON Richard Keith (Keith)
Born: Cuddington, Cheshire, England, 4 August, 1943 — W

League Club	Source	Date Signed	Seasons Played	Apps	Subs	Gls
Stoke C	Jnr	08/60	62-65	99	1	17
Oldham Ath	Tr	08/66	66-71	237	0	39
Rochdale	Tr	07/72	72-73	57	3	6

[BEBE] DIAS CORREIA Tiago Manuel
Born: Lisbon, Portugal, 12 July, 1990 — W
Portugal: U21-6

League Club	Source	Date Signed	Seasons Played	Apps	Subs	Gls
Manchester U	ED Amadora (POR)	08/10	10	0	2	0

BECCHIO Luciano Hector
Born: Cordoba, Argentina, 28 December, 1983 — F

League Club	Source	Date Signed	Seasons Played	Apps	Subs	Gls
Leeds U	UD Merida (SPN)	08/08	08-12	156	34	76
Norwich C	Tr	01/13	12-13	2	11	0
Rotherham U	L	09/14	14	3	2	2

BECK Daniel Gordon (Dan)
Born: Worthing, West Sussex, England, 14 November, 1983 — F

League Club	Source	Date Signed	Seasons Played	Apps	Subs	Gls
Brighton & HA	Sch	07/03	03	0	1	0

BECK John Alexander
Born: Edmonton, N London, England, 25 May, 1954 — M

League Club	Source	Date Signed	Seasons Played	Apps	Subs	Gls
Queens Park Rgrs	App	05/72	72-75	32	8	1
Coventry C	Tr	06/76	76-78	60	9	6
Fulham	Tr	10/78	78-81	113	1	12
Bournemouth	Tr	09/82	82-85	132	5	13
Cambridge U	Tr	07/86	86-89	105	7	11

BECK Mark Andrew
Born: Sunderland, England, 2 February, 1994 — F
Scotland: Youth

League Club	Source	Date Signed	Seasons Played	Apps	Subs	Gls
Carlisle U	Sch	04/12	11-14	23	43	7

BECK Mikkel Venge
Born: Aarhus, Denmark, 12 May, 1973 — F
Denmark: 19/U21-9

League Club	Source	Date Signed	Seasons Played	Apps	Subs	Gls
Middlesbrough	Fortuna Cologne (GER)	09/96	96-98	66	25	24
Derby Co	Tr	03/99	98-99	11	7	2
Nottingham F	L	11/99	99	5	0	1
Queens Park Rgrs	L	02/00	99	10	1	4

BECKERS Peter
Born: Dundee, Scotland, 3 October, 1947 — W
Died: Skegness, Lincolnshire, England, 6 June, 1996

League Club	Source	Date Signed	Seasons Played	Apps	Subs	Gls
Grimsby T	Craigmore Thistle	11/64	64	1	-	0

BECKETT Luke John
Born: Sheffield, England, 25 November, 1976 — F

League Club	Source	Date Signed	Seasons Played	Apps	Subs	Gls
Barnsley	YT	06/95				
Chester C	Tr	06/98	98-99	70	4	25
Chesterfield	Tr	07/00	00-01	58	4	22
Stockport Co	Tr	12/01	01-04	79	5	45
Sheffield U	Tr	11/04	04	1	4	0
Huddersfield T	L	01/05	04	7	0	6
Oldham Ath	L	03/05	04	9	0	6
Oldham Ath	L	07/05	05	27	7	18
Huddersfield T	Tr	07/06	06-08	57	21	23

BECKETT Roy Wilson
Born: Stoke-on-Trent, England, 20 March, 1928 — CH
Died: Poole, Dorset, England, August, 2008

League Club	Source	Date Signed	Seasons Played	Apps	Subs	Gls
Stoke C	Jnr	04/45	50-53	14	-	1

BECKETT William (Billy)
Born: Bootle, Merseyside, England, 4 July, 1915 — W
Died: Ormskirk, Lancashire, England, 5 April, 1999

League Club	Source	Date Signed	Seasons Played	Apps	Subs	Gls
New Brighton	Litherland	11/34	34-35	25	-	4
Tranmere Rov	Tr	07/36				
Blackpool	South Liverpool	04/37				
Bradford C	Tr	07/38	38	5	-	1
Watford	Tr	05/39	46	7	-	1
Northampton T	Tr	06/47				

BECKFORD Darren Richard Lorenzo
Born: Manchester, England, 12 May, 1967 — F
England: Youth/Schools

League Club	Source	Date Signed	Seasons Played	Apps	Subs	Gls
Manchester C	App	08/84	84-86	7	4	0
Bury	L	10/85	85	12	0	5
Port Vale	Tr	03/87	86-90	169	9	72
Norwich C	Tr	06/91	91-92	32	6	8
Oldham Ath	Tr	03/93	92-95	31	21	11
Preston NE	Heart of Midlothian	01/97	96	0	2	0
Walsall	Fulham (NC)	03/97	96	3	5	0

BECKFORD Jason Neil
Born: Manchester, England, 14 February, 1970 — W
England: Youth/Schools

League Club	Source	Date Signed	Seasons Played	Apps	Subs	Gls
Manchester C	YT	08/87	87-90	8	12	1
Blackburn Rov	L	03/91	90	3	1	0
Port Vale	L	09/91	91	4	1	1
Birmingham C	Tr	01/92	91-92	5	2	2
Bury	L	03/94	93	3	0	0
Stoke C	Tr	08/94	94	2	2	0
Millwall	Tr	12/94	94	6	3	0
Northampton T	Tr	05/95	95	0	1	0

BECKFORD Jermaine Paul Alexander
Born: Ealing, W London, England, 9 December, 1983 — F
Jamaica: 6

League Club	Source	Date Signed	Seasons Played	Apps	Subs	Gls
Leeds U	Wealdstone	03/06	05-09	111	15	71
Carlisle U	L	10/06	06	4	0	1
Scunthorpe U	L	01/07	06	17	1	8
Everton	Tr	06/10	10-11	15	19	8
Leicester C	Tr	08/11	11-12	35	8	9
Huddersfield T	L	09/12	12	14	7	8
Bolton W	Tr	07/13	13-14	25	21	7
Preston NE	L	11/14	14	19	4	12

BECKHAM David Robert Joseph
Born: Leytonstone, NE London, England, 2 May, 1975 — RM
England: 81/U21-9/Youth

League Club	Source	Date Signed	Seasons Played	Apps	Subs	Gls
Manchester U	YT	01/93	94-02	237	28	62
Preston NE	L	02/95	94	4	1	2

BECKWITH Dean Stuart
Born: Southwark, S London, England, 18 September, 1983 — CD

League Club	Source	Date Signed	Seasons Played	Apps	Subs	Gls
Gillingham	Sch	08/03	04	0	1	0
Hereford U	Tr	07/05	06-08	92	3	3
Northampton T	Tr	07/09	09-10	69	6	3

BECKWITH Robert (Rob)
Born: Hackney, E London, England, 12 September, 1984 — G

League Club	Source	Date Signed	Seasons Played	Apps	Subs	Gls
Luton T	Sch	07/04	02-03	17	0	0
Chesterfield	L	03/06	05	2	0	0
Barnet	Hitchin T	08/07	07-08	14	0	0

BEDDOW Ronald Malcolm (Ronnie)
Born: Walsall, West Midlands, England, 11 May, 1936 — FB

League Club	Source	Date Signed	Seasons Played	Apps	Subs	Gls
Walsall	Jnr	10/54	54	1	-	0

BEDEAU Anthony Charles Osmond (Tony)
Born: Hammersmith, W London, England, 24 March, 1979 — F/W
Grenada: 4

League Club	Source	Date Signed	Seasons Played	Apps	Subs	Gls
Torquay U	YT	07/97	95-05	233	72	58
Barnsley	L	02/02	01	0	3	0
Walsall	Tr	07/06	06	8	10	1
Bury	L	01/07	06	2	2	0

BEDFORD Kevin Edward
Born: Carshalton, S London, England, 26 December, 1968 — LB

League Club	Source	Date Signed	Seasons Played	Apps	Subs	Gls
Wimbledon	App	11/86	87	4	0	0
Aldershot	L	02/88	87	16	0	0
Colchester U	Tr	07/88	88	24	2	0

BEDFORD Noel Brian (Brian)
Born: Ferndale, Rhondda Cynon Taff, Wales, 24 December, 1933 — IF

League Club	Source	Date Signed	Seasons Played	Apps	Subs	Gls
Reading	Beddau YC	04/54	54	3	-	1
Southampton	Tr	07/55	55	5	-	2
Bournemouth	Tr	08/56	56-58	75	-	32
Queens Park Rgrs	Tr	07/59	59-64	258	-	161
Scunthorpe U	Tr	09/65	65-66	37	0	23
Brentford	Tr	09/66	66	21	0	10

BEDNAR Roman
Born: Prague, Czech Republic, 26 March, 1983 — F
Czech Republic: 3

League Club	Source	Date Signed	Seasons Played	Apps	Subs	Gls
West Bromwich A (L)	Heart of Midlothian	08/07	07	18	11	13
West Bromwich A	Tr	07/08	08-10	34	23	17
Leicester C	L	11/10	10	4	1	0
Blackpool	Tr	01/12	11	3	6	1

BEDROSSIAN Ara
Born: Nicosia, Cyprus, 2 June, 1967 — M

League Club	Source	Date Signed	Seasons Played	Apps	Subs	Gls
Fulham	Apoel Limassol (CYP)	03/93	92-94	34	8	1

BEDSON Raymond Arthur (Ray)
Born: Newcastle-under-Lyme, Potteries, England, 4 February, 1929 — WH
Died: Nantwich, Cheshire, England, 9 April, 1976

League Club	Source	Date Signed	Seasons Played	Apps	Subs	Gls
Crewe Alex		08/52	53	2	-	0

BEDWELL Leigh Andrew
Born: Wantage, Oxfordshire, England, 8 January, 1994 — G

League Club	Source	Date Signed	Seasons Played	Apps	Subs	Gls
Swindon T	Sch	07/12	12	0	1	0

BEE Francis Eric (Frank)
Born: Nottingham, England, 23 January, 1927 — IF
Died: Wollaton, Nottinghamshire, England, 26 July, 2010

League Club	Source	Date Signed	Seasons Played	Apps	Subs	Gls
Sunderland	Nottingham F (Am)	06/47	47	5	-	1
Blackburn Rov	Tr	03/49	48	4	-	0

BEEBY Oliver
Born: Whetstone, Leicestershire, England, 2 October, 1934 — LB
England: Youth

League Club	Source	Date Signed	Seasons Played	Apps	Subs	Gls
Leicester C	Whitwick Colliery	05/53	55	1	-	0
Notts Co	Tr	06/59	59	13	-	0

BEECH Christopher (Chris)
Born: Congleton, Cheshire, England, 5 November, 1975 — LB
England: Youth/Schools

League Club	Source	Date Signed	Seasons Played	Apps	Subs	Gls
Manchester C	YT	11/92				
Cardiff C	Tr	08/97	97	46	0	1
Rotherham U	Tr	06/98	98-02	40	15	1
Doncaster Rov	Tr	12/02	03-04	13	0	0

BEECH Christopher Stephen (Chris)
Born: Blackpool, Lancashire, England, 16 September, 1974 — M

League Club	Source	Date Signed	Seasons Played	Apps	Subs	Gls
Blackpool	YT	07/93	92-95	53	29	4
Hartlepool U	Tr	07/96	96-98	92	2	23
Huddersfield T	Tr	11/98	98-01	63	8	12
Rochdale	Tr	07/02	02-03	25	7	1

BEECH Cyril
Born: Tamworth, Staffordshire, England, 12 March, 1925 — LW
Died: Merthyr Tydfil, Wales, 8 May, 2001

League Club	Source	Date Signed	Seasons Played	Apps	Subs	Gls
Swansea C	Merthyr Tydfil	08/49	49-53	136	-	29
Newport Co	Worcester C	07/55	55-56	40	-	8

BEECH Gilbert
Born: Tamworth, Staffordshire, England, 9 January, 1922 — LB
Died: Swansea, Wales, March, 2009

League Club	Source	Date Signed	Seasons Played	Apps	Subs	Gls
Swansea C	Merthyr Tydfil	11/49	49-57	157	-	3

BEECH Harry William
Born: Kearsley, Greater Manchester, England, 7 January, 1946 — M

League Club	Source	Date Signed	Seasons Played	Apps	Subs	Gls
Bolton W	Jnr	06/64	65-66	14	1	0
Southport	Tr	07/67	67	2	2	0

BEECH Kenneth (Ken)
Born: Stoke-on-Trent, England, 18 March, 1958 — M

League Club	Source	Date Signed	Seasons Played	Apps	Subs	Gls
Port Vale	App	01/76	74-80	169	6	18
Walsall	Tr	08/81	81-82	78	1	5
Peterborough U	Tr	08/83	83-84	58	2	5

BEECH Thomas Philip Edward (Tom)
Born: Potton, Bedfordshire, England, 2 December, 1985 — F

League Club	Source	Date Signed	Seasons Played	Apps	Subs	Gls
Cambridge U	Sch	-	04	0	4	0

BEECHERS Billy Junior
Born: Oxford, England, 1 June, 1987 — F

League Club	Source	Date Signed	Seasons Played	Apps	Subs	Gls
Oxford U	Sch	06/06	04-05	0	4	0

BEEKS Stephen John (Steve)
Born: Ashford, Surrey, England, 10 April, 1971 — M

League Club	Source	Date Signed	Seasons Played	Apps	Subs	Gls
Aldershot	YT	07/89	89-90	0	3	0

BEEL William John Leonard (Lenny)
Born: Leominster, Herefordshire, England, 23 August, 1945 — G

League Club	Source	Date Signed	Seasons Played	Apps	Subs	Gls
Shrewsbury T	App	07/63	62-63	3	-	0
Birmingham C	Tr	01/65	64	1	-	0

BEELEY Shaun Anthony
Born: Cheadle, Greater Manchester, England, 21 November, 1988 — RB
England: Semi Pro-1

League Club	Source	Date Signed	Seasons Played	Apps	Subs	Gls
Fleetwood T	Southport	11/07	12	34	0	0
Bury	L	07/13	13	20	0	0
Morecambe	Tr	01/14	13-14	52	2	0

BEENEY Mark Raymond
Born: Tonbridge, Kent, England, 30 December, 1967 — G
England: Semi Pro

League Club	Source	Date Signed	Seasons Played	Apps	Subs	Gls
Gillingham	Jnr	08/85	86	2	0	0
Maidstone U	Tr	01/87	89-90	50	0	0
Aldershot	L	03/90	89	7	0	0
Brighton & HA	Tr	03/91	90-92	68	1	0
Leeds U	Tr	04/93	92-97	35	0	0

BEER Alan Desmond
Born: Swansea, Wales, 11 March, 1950 — F
Wales: Amateur

League Club	Source	Date Signed	Seasons Played	Apps	Subs	Gls
Swansea C	West End, Swansea	02/71	70-71	10	5	3
Exeter C	Weymouth	11/74	74-77	114	0	52

BEER Colin Edwin
Born: Exeter, England, 15 August, 1936 — W

League Club	Source	Date Signed	Seasons Played	Apps	Subs	Gls
Exeter C	Exbourne	05/56	56-57	5	-	2

BEERE Thomas Keith Robert (Tom)
Born: Southwark, S London, England, 27 January, 1995 — W

League Club	Source	Date Signed	Seasons Played	Apps	Subs	Gls
AFC Wimbledon	Sch	07/13	14	6	12	0

BEESLEY Colin
Born: Stockton-on-Tees, Cleveland, England, 6 October, 1951 — W

League Club	Source	Date Signed	Seasons Played	Apps	Subs	Gls
Sunderland	App	01/69	68	0	3	0

BEESLEY Mark Anthony
Born: Burscough, Lancashire, England, 10 November, 1981 — F

League Club	Source	Date Signed	Seasons Played	Apps	Subs	Gls
Preston NE	YT	06/99	99	0	1	0

BEESLEY Michael Albert (Mike)
Born: High Beach, Essex, England, 10 June, 1942 — M/CF

League Club	Source	Date Signed	Seasons Played	Apps	Subs	Gls
West Ham U	Jnr	10/59	60	2	-	1
Southend U	Tr	08/62	62-64	79	-	34
Peterborough U	Tr	07/65	65-66	23	2	3
Southend U	Tr	08/67	67-70	119	14	11

BEESLEY Paul
Born: Liverpool, England, 21 July, 1965 — CD

League Club	Source	Date Signed	Seasons Played	Apps	Subs	Gls
Wigan Ath	Marine	09/84	84-89	153	2	3
Leyton Orient	Tr	10/89	89	32	0	1
Sheffield U	Tr	07/90	90-94	162	6	7
Leeds U	Tr	08/95	95-96	19	3	0
Manchester C	Tr	02/97	96-97	10	3	0
Port Vale	L	12/97	97	5	0	0
West Bromwich A	L	03/98	97	8	0	0
Port Vale	Tr	08/98	98	33	2	3
Blackpool	Tr	07/99	99	15	3	0

BEESTON Carl Frederick
Born: Stoke-on-Trent, England, 30 June, 1967 — M
England: U21-1

League Club	Source	Date Signed	Seasons Played	Apps	Subs	Gls
Stoke C	App	07/85	84-96	224	12	13
Hereford U	L	01/97	96	9	0	2
Southend U	Tr	08/97	97	5	1	0

BEESTON Thomas
Born: Gateshead, Tyne and Wear, England, 26 April, 1933 — G
Died: Gateshead, Tyne and Wear, England, October, 2010

League Club	Source	Date Signed	Seasons Played	Apps	Subs	Gls
Gateshead (Am)	Heaton Stannington	09/56	56	1	-	0

BEETON Alan Matthew
Born: Watford, Hertfordshire, England, 4 October, 1978 — LB

League Club	Source	Date Signed	Seasons Played	Apps	Subs	Gls
Wycombe W	YT	07/97	97-00	39	16	0

BEEVER Anthony (Tony)
Born: Huddersfield, West Yorkshire, England, 18 September, 1974 — F

League Club	Source	Date Signed	Seasons Played	Apps	Subs	Gls
Rochdale	YT	07/93	92	0	1	0

BEEVERS Lee Jonathan
Born: Doncaster, South Yorkshire, England, 4 December, 1983 RB
Wales: U21-7/Youth

League Club	Source	Date Signed	Seasons Played	Apps	Subs	Gls
Ipswich T	YT	03/01				
Boston U	Tr	03/03	02-04	71	1	3
Lincoln C	Tr	02/05	04-08	154	12	9
Colchester U	Tr	07/09	09-10	16	7	0
Walsall	Tr	07/11	11	28	7	0
Mansfield T	Tr	07/12	13-14	57	4	2

BEEVERS Mark Geoffrey
Born: Barnsley, South Yorkshire, England, 21 November, 1989 CD
England: Youth

League Club	Source	Date Signed	Seasons Played	Apps	Subs	Gls
Sheffield Wed	Sch	11/06	06-12	126	14	2
MK Dons	L	08/11	11	14	0	1
Millwall	Tr	10/12	12-14	86	2	3

BEGG James Alexander (Jim)
Born: Dumfries, Scotland, 14 February, 1930 G
Died: Liverpool, England, 10 April, 1987

League Club	Source	Date Signed	Seasons Played	Apps	Subs	Gls
Liverpool	Auchinleck Talbot	04/52				
Bradford Park Ave	Tr	08/53	53-54	10	-	0

BEGLIN James Martin (Jim)
Born: Waterford, Republic of Ireland, 29 July, 1963 LB
Republic of Ireland: 15/B/U21-4

League Club	Source	Date Signed	Seasons Played	Apps	Subs	Gls
Liverpool	Shamrock Rov (ROI)	05/83	84-86	64	0	2
Leeds U	Tr	07/89	89	18	1	0
Plymouth Arg	L	11/89	89	5	0	0
Blackburn Rov	L	10/90	90	6	0	0

BEGOVIC Asmir
Born: Trebinje, Bosnia & Herzegovina, 20 June, 1987 G
Bosnia & Herzegovina: 41//Canada: Youth

League Club	Source	Date Signed	Seasons Played	Apps	Subs	Gls
Portsmouth	Sch	10/06	08-09	10	1	0
Macclesfield T	L	11/06	06	2	1	0
Bournemouth	L	08/07	07	8	0	0
Yeovil T	L	03/08	07	2	0	0
Yeovil T	L	08/08	08	14	0	0
Ipswich T	L	10/09	09	6	0	0
Stoke C	Tr	10/10	09-14	158	2	1

BEHAN Denis
Born: Tralee, Republic of Ireland, 2 January, 1984 F
Republic of Ireland: U23-3/U21-2

League Club	Source	Date Signed	Seasons Played	Apps	Subs	Gls
Hartlepool U	Cork C (ROI)	07/09	09-10	22	20	6

BEHARALL David Alexander (Dave)
Born: Wallsend, Tyne and Wear, England, 8 March, 1979 CD

League Club	Source	Date Signed	Seasons Played	Apps	Subs	Gls
Newcastle U	YT	07/97	98-99	4	2	0
Grimsby T	L	08/01	01	13	1	0
Oldham Ath	Tr	11/01	01-04	58	2	3
Carlisle U	Tr	02/05	05	6	0	0
Stockport Co	Tr	01/06	05	10	2	0

BEHRAMI Valon
Born: Mitrovica, Kosovo, 19 April, 1985 RB/M
Switzerland: 55

League Club	Source	Date Signed	Seasons Played	Apps	Subs	Gls
West Ham U	SS Lazio (ITA)	07/08	08-10	54	4	4

BEIGHTON Graham
Born: Sheffield, England, 1 July, 1939 G

League Club	Source	Date Signed	Seasons Played	Apps	Subs	Gls
Sheffield Wed	Firth Brown Tools	03/59				
Stockport Co	Tr	06/61	61-65	137	0	0
Wrexham	Tr	01/66	65	23	0	0

BEINLICH Stefan
Born: Berlin, Germany, 13 January, 1972 M
Germany: 5

League Club	Source	Date Signed	Seasons Played	Apps	Subs	Gls
Aston Villa	Bergmann Bosnig (GER)	10/91	91-93	7	9	1

BEIRNE Michael Andrew
Born: Manchester, England, 21 September, 1973 F

League Club	Source	Date Signed	Seasons Played	Apps	Subs	Gls
Doncaster Rov	Droylsden	02/97	96	1	0	0

BEKKER Jan Franciscus
Born: Cardiff, Wales, 24 December, 1951 F
Died: Bridgend, Wales, 26 December, 2007

League Club	Source	Date Signed	Seasons Played	Apps	Subs	Gls
Swansea C	Bridgend T	02/75	74-75	16	6	4

BELAID Tijani
Born: Paris, France, 6 September, 1987 M
Tunisia: 18

League Club	Source	Date Signed	Seasons Played	Apps	Subs	Gls
Hull C	Slavia Prague (CZE)	01/11	10	3	5	0

BELCHER James Alfred (Jimmy)
Born: Stepney, E London, England, 31 October, 1932 WH

League Club	Source	Date Signed	Seasons Played	Apps	Subs	Gls
Leyton Orient	Jnr	03/50				
West Ham U	Snowdown CW	08/52				
Crystal Palace	Tr	06/54	54-57	127	-	22
Ipswich T	Tr	05/58	58-59	27	-	0
Brentford	Tr	07/61	61	30	-	1

BELECK Leo Steve (Leo)
Born: Yaounde, Cameroon, 21 February, 1993 F

League Club	Source	Date Signed	Seasons Played	Apps	Subs	Gls
Watford (L)	Udinese (ITA)	08/12	12	0	5	0
Stevenage (L)	Udinese (ITA)	01/13	12	6	7	0

BELEZIKA Glenn
Born: Camden, N London, England, 24 December, 1993 CD

League Club	Source	Date Signed	Seasons Played	Apps	Subs	Gls
Oldham Ath	Stalybridge Celtic	08/11	11-12	3	1	0

BELFIELD Michael Robert (Mike)
Born: Wandsworth, SW London, England, 10 June, 1961 F

League Club	Source	Date Signed	Seasons Played	Apps	Subs	Gls
Wimbledon		03/80	79-82	16	8	4

BELFITT Roderick Michael (Rod)
Born: Doncaster, South Yorkshire, England, 30 October, 1945 F

League Club	Source	Date Signed	Seasons Played	Apps	Subs	Gls
Leeds U	Retford T	07/63	64-71	57	18	17
Ipswich T	Tr	11/71	71-72	40	0	13
Everton	Tr	11/72	72	14	2	2
Sunderland	Tr	10/73	73-74	36	3	4
Fulham	L	11/74	74	6	0	1
Huddersfield T	L	02/75	74	6	0	2
Huddersfield T	Tr	06/75	75	28	0	6

BELFON Frank (Frankie)
Born: Wellingborough, Northamptonshire, England, 18 February, 1965 F

League Club	Source	Date Signed	Seasons Played	Apps	Subs	Gls
Northampton T	Jnr	04/82	81-84	64	15	15

BELFORD Cameron Dale
Born: Nuneaton, Warwickshire, England, 16 October, 1988 G

League Club	Source	Date Signed	Seasons Played	Apps	Subs	Gls
Bury	Coventry C (Sch)	08/07	07-12	74	4	0
Southend U	L	03/12	11	13	0	0
Southend U	L	08/12	12	4	0	0
Accrington Stan	L	12/12	12	5	0	0
Swindon T	Rushall Olympic	03/15	14	0	1	0

BELFORD Dale
Born: Burton-on-Trent, Staffordshire, England, 11 July, 1967 G

League Club	Source	Date Signed	Seasons Played	Apps	Subs	Gls
Aston Villa	App	07/85				
Notts Co	Sutton Coldfield T	03/87	87	1	0	0

BELFORD Tyrell
Born: Nuneaton, Warwickshire, England, 6 May, 1994 G
England: Youth

League Club	Source	Date Signed	Seasons Played	Apps	Subs	Gls
Liverpool	Sch	07/11				
Swindon T	Tr	07/13	13-14	7	0	0

BELGRAVE Barrington
Born: Bedford, England, 16 September, 1980 F

League Club	Source	Date Signed	Seasons Played	Apps	Subs	Gls
Plymouth Arg	Norwich C (YT)	07/99	99	2	13	0
Southend U	Yeovil T	09/01	01-02	38	17	8

BELHADJ Nadir
Born: Saint-Claude, Jura, France, 18 June, 1982 LB
Algeria: 54

League Club	Source	Date Signed	Seasons Played	Apps	Subs	Gls
Portsmouth	RC Lens (FRA)	09/08	08-09	37	11	5

BELKALEM Essaid
Born: Mekla, Algeria, 1 January, 1989 CD
Algeria: 14/U23-4

League Club	Source	Date Signed	Seasons Played	Apps	Subs	Gls
Watford (L)	Granada (SPN)	08/13	13	5	3	0

BELL Alexander Stewart (Alex)
Born: Auchendinny, Midlothian, Scotland, 13 March, 1931 G

League Club	Source	Date Signed	Seasons Played	Apps	Subs	Gls
Exeter C	Partick Thistle	08/54	54-57	40	-	0
Grimsby T	Tr	07/58	58	8	-	0

BELL Amari'i Kyren
Born: Burton on Trent, Staffordshire, England, 5 May, 1994 LB

League Club	Source	Date Signed	Seasons Played	Apps	Subs	Gls
Birmingham C	Sch	07/12	13	1	0	0
Swindon T	L	09/14	14	7	3	0
Gillingham	L	03/15	14	6	1	0

BELL Andrew (Andy)
Born: Blackburn, Greater Manchester, England, 12 February, 1984 F
England: Youth

League Club	Source	Date Signed	Seasons Played	Apps	Subs	Gls
Blackburn Rov	YT	02/01				
Wycombe W	Tr	09/03	03	3	8	3
York C	Tr	02/04	03	3	7	1

BELL Andrew Donald (Andy)
Born: Taunton, Somerset, England, 6 May, 1956 F

League Club	Source	Date Signed	Seasons Played	Apps	Subs	Gls
Exeter C	Taunton T	07/79	79	2	1	0

BELL Anthony (Tony)
Born: North Shields, Tyne and Wear, England, 27 February, 1955 G

League Club	Source	Date Signed	Seasons Played	Apps	Subs	Gls
Newcastle U	App	03/73	74	1	0	0

League Club	Source	Date Signed	Seasons Played	Career Record Apps	Subs	Gls
BELL Arthur						
Born: Sedgefield, County Durham, England, 5 March, 1931						WH
Barrow	Castletown	08/50	50	1	-	0
BELL Barry Russell						
Born: Woolwich, SE London, England, 9 April, 1941						CF
Millwall	Jnr	10/58	58	1	-	0
BELL Charles Thomas (Charlie)						
Born: Sheffield, England, 21 March, 1945						CD
Sheffield U	Jnr	01/64	66	3	0	1
Chesterfield	Tr	06/68	68-72	148	3	11
BELL Colin						
Born: Horsley Woodhouse, Derbyshire, England, 24 March, 1926						WH
Died: Heanor, Derbyshire, England, 21 July, 2004						
Derby Co	Holbrook MW	09/46	50-54	77	-	2
BELL Colin						
Born: Hesleden, County Durham, England, 26 February, 1946						M
England: 48/FLge-4/U23-2						
Bury	Horden CW	07/63	63-65	82	0	25
Manchester C	Tr	03/66	65-78	393	1	117
BELL David (Dave)						
Born: Gorebridge, Midlothian, Scotland, 24 December, 1909						FB
Died: Whitley Bay, Tyne and Wear, England, 16 April, 1986						
Newcastle U	Wallyford Bluebell	05/30	31-33	21	-	1
Derby Co	Tr	06/34	34-38	52	-	0
Ipswich T	Tr	10/38	38-49	171	-	3
BELL David Anthony						
Born: Northampton, England, 21 April, 1984						M
Republic of Ireland: U21-2/Youth						
Rushden & D	Jnr	07/01	01-05	109	13	10
Luton T	Tr	01/06	05-07	62	13	7
Leicester C	L	03/08	07	6	0	0
Norwich C	Tr	07/08	08	12	7	0
Coventry C	Tr	01/09	08-12	69	25	5
Notts Co	Tr	07/13	13	4	6	0
BELL David John						
Born: Carlisle, Cumbria, England, 13 September, 1939						IF
Carlisle U	Jnr	03/57	58	1	-	1
BELL Derek Martin						
Born: Wyberton, Lincolnshire, England, 30 October, 1956						F
Derby Co	App	10/74				
Halifax T	Tr	05/75	75-78	104	8	21
Sheffield Wed	L	03/76	75	5	0	1
Barnsley	Tr	10/78	78-79	45	1	20
Lincoln C	Tr	11/79	79-82	69	14	33
Chesterfield	Tr	08/83	83	15	2	3
Scunthorpe U	Tr	01/84	83-84	22	0	7
BELL Derek Stewart						
Born: Newcastle-upon-Tyne, England, 19 December, 1963						M
Newcastle U	App	12/81	81-82	3	1	0
BELL Douglas (Doug)						
Born: Paisley, Renfrewshire, Scotland, 5 September, 1959						M
Scotland: U21-2						
Shrewsbury T	Hibernian	12/87	87-89	47	3	6
Hull C	L	03/89	88	4	0	0
Birmingham C	Tr	10/89	89-90	15	1	0
BELL Eric						
Born: Manchester, England, 27 November, 1929						LH
Died: Wythenshawe, Greater Manchester, England, 22 July, 2012						
England: B-2/FLge-1						
Bolton W	Manchester U (Am)	11/49	50-57	102	-	1
BELL Ernest (Ernie)						
Born: Hull, England, 22 July, 1918						IF
Died: Hull, England, 8 December, 1968						
Hull C	Blundell Street OB	03/36	36-37	22	-	4
Mansfield T	Tr	05/38	38	28	-	1
Aldershot	Tr	07/39				
Hull C	Tr	08/46	46	5	-	1
BELL Fergus Stuart						
Born: Wandsworth, SW London, England, 25 January, 1991						M
Mansfield T	Monza (ITA)	07/14	14	10	6	1
Yeovil T	Tr	01/15	14	1	1	0
BELL Gary						
Born: Stourbridge, West Midlands, England, 4 April, 1947						LB
Cardiff C	Lower Gornal Ath	02/66	66-73	222	1	10
Hereford U	L	03/74	73	8	0	0
Newport Co	Tr	08/74	74-77	126	0	5

League Club	Source	Date Signed	Seasons Played	Career Record Apps	Subs	Gls
BELL George William						
Born: South Shields, Tyne and Wear, England, 26 March, 1937						CF
Doncaster Rov	St Mary's BC	05/55	55	1	-	0
Cardiff C	Frickley Colliery	03/59				
BELL Graham Thomas						
Born: Middleton, Greater Manchester, England, 30 March, 1955						M
England: Youth						
Oldham Ath	Chadderton	12/73	74-78	166	4	9
Preston NE	Tr	03/79	78-82	140	3	9
Huddersfield T	L	11/81	81	2	0	0
Carlisle U	Tr	08/83	83	11	3	0
Bolton W	Tr	02/84	83-85	86	6	3
Tranmere Rov	Tr	08/86	86	41	1	4
BELL Harold						
Born: Liverpool, England, 22 November, 1924						CH
Died: Liverpool, England, 17 July, 1994						
Tranmere Rov	Jnr	11/41	46-59	595	-	11
BELL Henry Davey (Harry)						
Born: Sunderland, England, 14 October, 1924						WH/IF
Died: Newcastle-on-Tyne, England, 22 April, 2014						
Middlesbrough	Hylton CW	09/45	46-54	290	-	9
Darlington	Tr	09/55	55-58	126	-	19
BELL Ian Charles (Charlie)						
Born: Middlesbrough, England, 14 November, 1958						M
Middlesbrough	App	12/76	77-80	10	0	1
Mansfield T	Tr	07/81	81-82	82	2	12
BELL James (Jay)						
Born: Liverpool, England, 24 November, 1989						FB
Accrington Stan	Sch	08/08	07-08	7	1	0
BELL John Albert						
Born: Edinburgh, Scotland, 25 April, 1936						WH
Swindon T	Stirling A	07/60	60-61	29	-	2
BELL John Eric (Eric)						
Born: Bedlington, Northumberland, England, 13 February, 1922						WH
Died: Heysham, Lancashire, England, 22 October, 2004						
England: FLge-2						
Blackburn Rov	Blyth Shipyard	05/45	46-56	323	-	9
BELL John Henry						
Born: Morpeth, Northumberland, England, 29 August, 1919						FB
Died: Morpeth, Northumberland, England, 3 June, 1994						
Gateshead	Ashington	01/45	46-49	50	-	0
BELL John Russell (Jackie)						
Born: Evenwood, County Durham, England, 17 October, 1939						LH
Died: Gainford, County Durham, England, 22 April, 1991						
Newcastle U	Jnr	10/56	57-61	111	-	8
Norwich C	Tr	07/62	62-63	48	-	3
Colchester U	Tr	06/65	65	7	0	0
BELL Joseph (Joe)						
Born: Sunderland, England, 28 July, 1924						LB
Died: Sunderland, England, 14 January, 2007						
Chesterfield	Stockton	05/46	47-48	37	-	0
Coventry C	Tr	06/49	49-51	10	-	0
BELL Lee						
Born: Alsager, Cheshire, England, 26 January, 1983						DM
Crewe Alex	YT	02/01	02-05	34	20	3
Mansfield T	Burton A	08/07	07	23	0	1
Macclesfield T	Tr	07/08	08-09	74	9	3
Crewe Alex	Tr	07/10	10-11	67	8	1
Burton A	Tr	08/12	12-14	71	11	6
BELL Leon Earl						
Born: Hitchin, Hertfordshire, England, 19 December, 1980						M
England: Schools						
Barnet	YT	07/99	99-00	7	5	0
BELL Michael (Mickey)						
Born: Newcastle-upon-Tyne, England, 15 November, 1971						LB
Northampton T	YT	07/90	89-94	133	20	10
Wycombe W	Tr	10/94	94-96	117	1	5
Bristol C	Tr	07/97	97-04	276	16	34
Port Vale	Tr	08/05	05	14	1	2
Cheltenham T	Tr	01/06	05-06	12	4	0
BELL Norman						
Born: Sunderland, England, 16 November, 1955						F
Wolverhampton W	App	11/73	75-81	58	22	17
Blackburn Rov	Tr	11/81	81-83	57	4	10
BELL Nyal Aston Nathaniel						
Born: Manchester, England, 18 January, 1997						F
Rochdale	Sch	06/15	14	0	3	0

League Club	Source	Date Signed	Seasons Played	Career Record Apps	Subs	Gls

BELL Raymond Lloyd (Ray)
Born: Seaham, County Durham, England, 6 December, 1930 — G

League Club	Source	Date Signed	Seasons Played	Apps	Subs	Gls
Lincoln C	Seaham CW	01/50	50	1	-	0

BELL Robert (Bobby)
Born: Glasgow, Scotland, 20 March, 1935 — IF
Scotland: Schools

League Club	Source	Date Signed	Seasons Played	Apps	Subs	Gls
Plymouth Arg	Partick Thistle	11/55	55	2	-	1
Carlisle U	Partick Thistle	06/59	59	1	-	0

BELL Robert Charles (Bobby)
Born: Cambridge, England, 26 October, 1950 — CD

League Club	Source	Date Signed	Seasons Played	Apps	Subs	Gls
Ipswich T	Tottenham H (App)	10/68	68-71	32	0	1
Blackburn Rov	Tr	09/71	71	2	0	0
Crystal Palace	Tr	09/71	71-73	31	0	0
Norwich C	L	02/72	71	3	0	0
York C	Hellenic (RSA)	02/77	76	5	0	0

BELL Robert McDicker (Bobby)
Born: Ayr, Scotland, 16 September, 1934 — RB
Died: Bournemouth, England, March, 2007

League Club	Source	Date Signed	Seasons Played	Apps	Subs	Gls
Watford	Ayr U	05/57	57-64	268	-	2

BELL Stanley (Stan)
Born: West Ham, E London, England, 28 October, 1923 — W

League Club	Source	Date Signed	Seasons Played	Apps	Subs	Gls
Southend U		07/48	48	3	-	0

BELL Stephen (Steve)
Born: Middlesbrough, England, 13 March, 1965 — LW
Died: Middlesbrough, England, 22 April, 2001
England: Youth

League Club	Source	Date Signed	Seasons Played	Apps	Subs	Gls
Middlesbrough	App	05/82	81-84	79	6	12
Darlington	Whitby T	03/87	86-87	28	12	3

BELL Stuart
Born: Carlisle, Cumbria, England, 15 March, 1984 — M

League Club	Source	Date Signed	Seasons Played	Apps	Subs	Gls
Carlisle U	Sch	07/02	01	3	2	0

BELL Sydney Edgar (Syd)
Born: Stepney, E London, England, 8 January, 1920 — FB
Died: Havering, E London, England, January, 2007

League Club	Source	Date Signed	Seasons Played	Apps	Subs	Gls
Southend U		11/45	46-47	16	-	0

BELL Terence John (Terry)
Born: Nottingham, England, 1 August, 1944 — F
Died: Reading, England, 20 May, 2014

League Club	Source	Date Signed	Seasons Played	Apps	Subs	Gls
Nottingham F	Burton A	08/64				
Manchester C	Tr	10/64				
Portsmouth	Tr	11/64				
Hartlepool U	Nuneaton Bor	07/66	66-69	111	6	34
Reading	Tr	03/70	69-72	82	5	20
Aldershot	Tr	07/73	73-77	112	12	49

BELL Thomas Anthony Peter (Tommy)
Born: Shaw, Greater Manchester, England, 30 December, 1923 — D
Died: Oldham, Greater Manchester, England, 21 November, 1988

League Club	Source	Date Signed	Seasons Played	Apps	Subs	Gls
Oldham Ath	Mossley	12/46	46-51	170	-	0
Stockport Co	Tr	08/52	52	31	-	0
Halifax T	Tr	07/53	53-55	117	-	1

BELL Thomas Henry (Tom)
Born: Stanley, County Durham, England, 14 June, 1924 — CD
Died: Essex, England, February, 2012

League Club	Source	Date Signed	Seasons Played	Apps	Subs	Gls
Millwall (Am)	Hammersmith U	03/49	48	1	-	0

BELL William (Billy)
Born: Manchester, England, 16 June, 1953 — M

League Club	Source	Date Signed	Seasons Played	Apps	Subs	Gls
Rochdale	Hyde U	05/74	74	5	1	0

BELL William John (Willie)
Born: Johnstone, Renfrewshire, Scotland, 3 September, 1937 — LB
Scotland: 2/Amateur

League Club	Source	Date Signed	Seasons Played	Apps	Subs	Gls
Leeds U	Queen's Park	07/60	60-67	204	0	15
Leicester C	Tr	09/67	67-68	49	0	0
Brighton & HA	Tr	07/69	69	44	0	1

BELL-BAGGIE Abdulai Hindolo
Born: Freetown, Sierra Leone, 28 April, 1992 — RW
England: Youth//Sierra Leone: 4

League Club	Source	Date Signed	Seasons Played	Apps	Subs	Gls
Reading	Sch	02/10				
Rotherham U	L	03/10	09	2	9	0
Port Vale	L	08/10	10	0	3	0
Yeovil T	Tr	07/11				
Tranmere Rov	Salisbury C	08/12	12-14	32	23	4

BELLAMY Arthur
Born: Consett, County Durham, England, 5 April, 1942 — M
Died: Brierfield, Lancashire, England, 22 January, 2014

League Club	Source	Date Signed	Seasons Played	Apps	Subs	Gls
Burnley	Jnr	06/59	62-71	204	13	29
Chesterfield	Tr	07/72	72-75	133	0	12

BELLAMY Craig Douglas
Born: Cardiff, Wales, 13 July, 1979 — F
Wales: 78/U21-8/Youth/Schools

League Club	Source	Date Signed	Seasons Played	Apps	Subs	Gls
Norwich C	YT	01/97	96-00	71	13	32
Coventry C	Tr	08/00	00	33	1	6
Newcastle U	Tr	07/01	01-04	87	6	27
Blackburn Rov	Tr	07/05	05	22	5	13
Liverpool	Tr	07/06	06	23	4	7
West Ham U	Tr	07/07	07-08	20	4	7
Manchester C	Tr	01/09	08-09	33	7	13
Cardiff C	L	08/10	10	34	1	11
Liverpool	Tr	08/11	11	12	15	6
Cardiff C	Tr	08/12	12-13	41	14	5

BELLAMY Gary
Born: Worksop, Nottinghamshire, England, 4 July, 1962 — CD

League Club	Source	Date Signed	Seasons Played	Apps	Subs	Gls
Chesterfield	App	06/80	80-86	181	4	7
Wolverhampton W	Tr	07/87	87-91	133	3	9
Cardiff C	L	03/92	91	9	0	0
Leyton Orient	Tr	09/92	92-95	129	3	6

BELLAS William Joseph (Bill)
Born: Crosby, Merseyside, England, 21 May, 1925 — CH
Died: Huyton, Merseyside, England, 28 April, 1994

League Club	Source	Date Signed	Seasons Played	Apps	Subs	Gls
Notts Co	Marine	05/45				
Nottingham F	Tr	05/46				
Southport	Tr	10/48	48-50	88	-	0
Grimsby T	Tr	07/51	51	5	-	0

BELLE Cortez
Born: Newport, Wales, 27 August, 1983 — F

League Club	Source	Date Signed	Seasons Played	Apps	Subs	Gls
Chester C	Merthyr Tydfil	07/04	04	17	5	1

BELLERIN Hector
Born: Barcelona, Spain, 19 March, 1995 — RB/M
Spain: U21-1/Youth

League Club	Source	Date Signed	Seasons Played	Apps	Subs	Gls
Arsenal	Sch	07/12	14	17	3	2
Watford	L	11/13	13	6	2	0

BELLETT Walter Ronald (Wally)
Born: Stratford, E London, England, 14 November, 1933 — LB
England: Youth

League Club	Source	Date Signed	Seasons Played	Apps	Subs	Gls
Chelsea	Barking	09/54	55-58	35	-	1
Plymouth Arg	Tr	12/58	58-59	41	-	1
Leyton Orient	Chelmsford C	01/61				
Chester C	Tr	07/61	61	12	-	1
Wrexham	Tr	07/62	62	2	-	0
Tranmere Rov	Tr	07/63				

BELLETTI Juliano Haus
Born: Cascavel, Brazil, 20 June, 1976 — RB
Brazil: 23

League Club	Source	Date Signed	Seasons Played	Apps	Subs	Gls
Chelsea	Barcelona (SPN)	08/07	07-09	29	25	5

BELLION David
Born: Paris, France, 27 November, 1982 — W
France: U21-4

League Club	Source	Date Signed	Seasons Played	Apps	Subs	Gls
Sunderland	AS Cannes (FRA)	08/01	01-02	5	15	1
Manchester U	Tr	07/03	03-04	5	19	3
West Ham U	L	08/05	05	2	6	0

BELLIS Alfred (Alf)
Born: Ellesmere Port, Cheshire, England, 8 October, 1920 — LW
Died: Ramsgate, Kent, England, 28 April, 2013

League Club	Source	Date Signed	Seasons Played	Apps	Subs	Gls
Port Vale	Burnell's Ironworks	03/38	37-47	82	-	18
Bury	Tr	01/48	47-50	95	-	18
Swansea C	Tr	08/51	51-52	41	-	11
Chesterfield	Tr	08/53	53	13	-	3

BELLIS Thomas Gilbert (Gib)
Born: Mold, Flintshire, Wales, 21 April, 1919 — WH
Died: Mold, Flintshire, Wales, 1 September, 2000

League Club	Source	Date Signed	Seasons Played	Apps	Subs	Gls
Wrexham	Buckley T	05/38	38-48	95	-	1

BELLOTTI Derek Christopher
Born: East Ham, E London, England, 25 December, 1946 — G

League Club	Source	Date Signed	Seasons Played	Apps	Subs	Gls
Gillingham	Bedford T	07/66	66-69	35	0	0
Southend U	L	10/70	70	3	0	0
Charlton Ath	Tr	10/70	70-71	14	0	0
Southend U	Tr	12/71	71-73	74	0	0
Swansea C	Tr	05/74	74	19	0	0

BELLOTTI Ross Christopher
Born: Tonbridge, Kent, England, 15 May, 1978 — G

League Club	Source	Date Signed	Seasons Played	Apps	Subs	Gls
Exeter C	YT	07/96	94	1	1	0

BELLUSCI Giuseppe
Born: Trebbisacce, Italy, 21 August, 1989 — CD
Italy: U21-6

League Club	Source	Date Signed	Seasons Played	Apps	Subs	Gls
Leeds U	Catania (ITA)	08/14	14	29	1	2

BELMADI Djemal
Born: Champigny-sur-Marne, France, 27 March, 1976 W
Algeria: 20

League Club	Source	Date Signed	Seasons Played	Apps	Subs	Gls
Manchester C (L)	Olymp Marseille (FRA)	01/03	02	2	6	0
Southampton	Al Ittihad (SAU)	08/05	05-06	30	6	3

BELSON Flavien
Born: Le Havre, France, 22 February, 1987 M

League Club	Source	Date Signed	Seasons Played	Apps	Subs	Gls
MK Dons (L)	FC Metz (FRA)	08/08	08	9	4	0
Yeovil T	SU Dives (FRA)	09/11	11	1	0	0

BELSVIK Petter
Born: Lillehammer, Norway, 2 October, 1967 F

League Club	Source	Date Signed	Seasons Played	Apps	Subs	Gls
Southend U (L)	IK Start (NOR)	11/95	95	3	0	1

BEMBO-LETA Djenny
Born: Kinshasa, DR Congo, 9 November, 1991 RW

League Club	Source	Date Signed	Seasons Played	Apps	Subs	Gls
Oldham Ath	Sch	04/10	10	2	1	0

BEMROSE Frank Edward (Ted)
Born: Caistor, Lincolnshire, England, 20 October, 1935 W
Died: Caistor, Lincolnshire, England, 29 April, 2001

League Club	Source	Date Signed	Seasons Played	Apps	Subs	Gls
Grimsby T (Am)	Caistor	08/58	58-60	2	-	0

BENALI Ahmad
Born: Manchester, England, 7 February, 1992 DM
England: Youth//Libya: 2

League Club	Source	Date Signed	Seasons Played	Apps	Subs	Gls
Manchester C	Sch	03/09				
Rochdale	L	08/11	11	0	2	0

BENALI Francis Vincent
Born: Southampton, England, 30 December, 1968 LB
England: Schools

League Club	Source	Date Signed	Seasons Played	Apps	Subs	Gls
Southampton	App	01/87	88-02	271	40	1
Nottingham F	L	01/01	00	15	0	0

BENARBIA Ali
Born: Oran, Algeria, 8 October, 1968 M
Algeria: 7

League Club	Source	Date Signed	Seasons Played	Apps	Subs	Gls
Manchester C	Paris St-Germain (FRA)	09/01	01-02	59	12	11

BEN ARFA Hatem
Born: Paris, France, 7 March, 1987 W
France: 13/U21-4

League Club	Source	Date Signed	Seasons Played	Apps	Subs	Gls
Newcastle U	Olymp Marseille (FRA)	08/10	10-13	48	28	13
Hull C	L	09/14	14	5	3	0

BEN ASKAR Aziz
Born: Chateau Gontier, France, 30 March, 1976 CD

League Club	Source	Date Signed	Seasons Played	Apps	Subs	Gls
Queens Park Rgrs (L)	Stade Lavallois (FRA)	08/01	01	18	0	0

BENAYOUN Yossi Shai
Born: Beersheba, Israel, 5 May, 1980 M
Israel: 96/U21-11/Youth

League Club	Source	Date Signed	Seasons Played	Apps	Subs	Gls
West Ham U	RC Santander (SPN)	07/05	05-06	55	8	8
Liverpool	Tr	07/07	07-09	55	37	18
Chelsea	Tr	07/10	10-12	1	13	1
Arsenal	L	08/11	11	10	9	4
West Ham U	L	08/12	12	4	2	0
Queens Park Rgrs	Tr	12/13	13	10	6	3

BENBOW Ian Robert
Born: Hereford, England, 9 January, 1969 M/F

League Club	Source	Date Signed	Seasons Played	Apps	Subs	Gls
Hereford U	YT	07/87	87-90	60	23	4

BENCE Paul Ian
Born: Littlehampton, West Sussex, England, 21 December, 1948 M/RB

League Club	Source	Date Signed	Seasons Played	Apps	Subs	Gls
Brighton & HA	App	12/66	67	0	1	0
Reading	Tr	06/68	68-69	12	2	2
Brentford	Tr	07/70	70-76	238	6	6
Torquay U	L	11/76	76	5	0	0

BENCHERIF Hamza
Born: Paris, France, 9 February, 1988 M
Algeria: Youth

League Club	Source	Date Signed	Seasons Played	Apps	Subs	Gls
Nottingham F	Sch	08/06				
Lincoln C	L	10/07	07	11	1	1
Macclesfield T	Tr	07/09	09-10	55	5	16
Notts Co	Tr	06/11	11-12	15	16	2
Plymouth Arg	Tr	09/13	13	5	2	0

BENDER Thomas Joseph (Tom)
Born: Harlow, Essex, England, 19 January, 1993 LB/M
Wales: U21-4/Youth

League Club	Source	Date Signed	Seasons Played	Apps	Subs	Gls
Colchester U	Sch	01/10	09	0	1	0
Accrington Stan	L	08/11	11	0	2	0
Millwall	Tr	03/13				

BENDTNER Nicklas
Born: Copenhagen, Denmark, 16 January, 1988 F
Denmark: 68/U21-4/Youth

League Club	Source	Date Signed	Seasons Played	Apps	Subs	Gls
Arsenal	Sch	12/05	07-13	41	67	24
Birmingham C	L	08/06	06	38	4	11
Sunderland	L	08/11	11	25	3	8

BENEDICIC Zan
Born: Kranj, Slovenia, 3 October, 1995 M
Slovenia: U21-6/Youth

League Club	Source	Date Signed	Seasons Played	Apps	Subs	Gls
Leeds U (L)	AC Milan Jnrs (ITA)	08/14	14	0	1	0

BENEFIELD James Patrick (Jimmy)
Born: Torquay, Devon, England, 6 May, 1983 M

League Club	Source	Date Signed	Seasons Played	Apps	Subs	Gls
Torquay U	YT	07/01	00-03	6	26	0

BEN HAIM Tal
Born: Rishon Le Zion, Israel, 31 March, 1982 CD
Israel: 87/U21-6

League Club	Source	Date Signed	Seasons Played	Apps	Subs	Gls
Bolton W	Maccabi Tel Aviv (ISR)	07/04	04-06	81	7	1
Chelsea	Tr	07/07	07	10	3	0
Manchester C	Tr	07/08	08	8	1	0
Sunderland	L	02/09	08	5	0	0
Portsmouth	Tr	09/09	09-11	54	1	0
West Ham U	L	08/10	10	8	0	0
Queens Park Rgrs	Toronto FC (CAN)	01/13	12	2	1	0
Charlton Ath	Standard Liege (BEL)	07/14	14	37	0	0

BENITEZ Christian Rogelio
Born: Quito, Ecuador, 1 May, 1986 F
Died: Qatar, 29 July, 2013
Ecuador: 58

League Club	Source	Date Signed	Seasons Played	Apps	Subs	Gls
Birmingham C (L)	Santos Laguna (MEX)	07/09	09	21	9	3

BENJAFIELD Brian James
Born: Barton-on-Sea, Hampshire, England, 2 August, 1960 M

League Club	Source	Date Signed	Seasons Played	Apps	Subs	Gls
Bournemouth	Jnr	01/79	78	2	0	0

BENJAMIN Christopher (Chris)
Born: Sheffield, England, 5 December, 1972 F

League Club	Source	Date Signed	Seasons Played	Apps	Subs	Gls
Chesterfield	YT	07/91	90-91	5	10	1

BENJAMIN Ian Tracey
Born: Nottingham, England, 11 December, 1961 F
England: Youth

League Club	Source	Date Signed	Seasons Played	Apps	Subs	Gls
Sheffield U	App	07/79	78-79	4	1	3
West Bromwich A	Tr	08/79	80	1	1	0
Notts Co	Tr	02/82				
Peterborough U	Tr	08/82	82-83	77	3	14
Northampton T	Tr	08/84	84-87	147	3	58
Cambridge U	Tr	10/87	87	20	5	2
Chester C	Tr	07/88	88	18	4	2
Exeter C	Tr	02/89	88-89	30	2	4
Southend U	Tr	03/90	89-92	122	0	33
Luton T	Tr	11/92	92-93	7	6	2
Brentford	Tr	09/93	93-94	13	2	2
Wigan Ath	Tr	09/94	94-95	13	7	6

BENJAMIN Joseph John (Joe)
Born: Woodford, NE London, England, 8 October, 1990 F

League Club	Source	Date Signed	Seasons Played	Apps	Subs	Gls
Northampton T	Sch	01/09	08-09	2	5	0

BENJAMIN Ronayne Jentil
Born: Chiswick, W London, England, 13 November, 1984 LW

League Club	Source	Date Signed	Seasons Played	Apps	Subs	Gls
Macclesfield T	Crawley T	03/07	06	0	3	0

BENJAMIN Trevor Junior
Born: Wellingborough, Northamptonshire, England, 8 February, 1979 F
England: U21-1//Jamaica: 2

League Club	Source	Date Signed	Seasons Played	Apps	Subs	Gls
Cambridge U	YT	02/97	95-99	96	27	35
Leicester C	Tr	07/00	00-04	33	48	11
Crystal Palace	L	12/01	01	5	1	1
Norwich C	L	02/02	01	3	3	0
West Bromwich A	L	03/02	01	0	3	1
Gillingham	L	09/03	03	1	3	1
Rushden & D	L	11/03	03	5	1	1
Brighton & HA	L	01/04	03	10	0	5
Northampton T	Tr	12/04	04	5	0	2
Coventry C	Tr	02/05	04	6	6	1
Peterborough U	Tr	07/05	05-06	20	27	8
Watford	L	09/05	05	2	0	0
Swindon T	L	01/06	05	5	3	2
Boston U	L	02/07	06	2	1	0
Walsall	L	03/07	06	8	0	2
Hereford U	Tr	07/07	07	15	19	10

BENJAMIN Tristan
Born: St Kitts & Nevis, 1 April, 1957 CD

League Club	Source	Date Signed	Seasons Played	Apps	Subs	Gls
Notts Co	App	03/75	74-86	296	15	4
Chesterfield	Tr	07/87	87	32	2	0

[BENJANI] MWARUWARI Benjani
Born: Bulawayo, Zimbabwe, 13 August, 1978 — F
Zimbabwe: 33

League Club	Source	Date Signed	Seasons Played	Apps	Subs	Gls
Portsmouth	AJ Auxerre (FRA)	01/06	05-07	62	8	19
Manchester C	Tr	02/08	07-09	21	2	4
Sunderland	L	02/10	09	1	7	0
Blackburn Rov	Tr	08/10	10	6	12	3
Portsmouth	Tr	08/11	11	6	12	1

BENN Alfred (Alf)
Born: Leeds, England, 26 January, 1926 — WH
Died: Wakefield, England, July, 2014

League Club	Source	Date Signed	Seasons Played	Apps	Subs	Gls
Leeds U	East Leeds	01/47				
Southport	Tr	07/48	48	3	-	0

BENN Wayne
Born: Pontefract, West Yorkshire, England, 7 August, 1976 — D

League Club	Source	Date Signed	Seasons Played	Apps	Subs	Gls
Bradford C	YT	06/94	94	8	2	0

BENNELLICK James Arthur (Jim)
Born: Torquay, Devon, England, 9 September, 1974 — M

League Club	Source	Date Signed	Seasons Played	Apps	Subs	Gls
Torquay U	YT	-	91	0	1	0

BENNETT Alan
Born: Stoke-on-Trent, England, 5 November, 1931 — LW
Died: Stoke-on-Trent, England, 17 January, 2006
England: Youth

League Club	Source	Date Signed	Seasons Played	Apps	Subs	Gls
Port Vale	Jnr	05/49	48-56	123	-	8
Crewe Alex	Tr	09/57	57	11	-	0

BENNETT Alan John
Born: Cork, Republic of Ireland, 4 October, 1981 — CD
Republic of Ireland: 2/B-1/U21-1

League Club	Source	Date Signed	Seasons Played	Apps	Subs	Gls
Reading	Cork C (ROI)	01/07				
Southampton	L	08/07	07	10	0	0
Brentford	L	03/08	07	11	0	1
Brentford	L	08/08	08	44	0	0
Brentford	Tr	08/09	09	11	2	1
Wycombe W	L	02/10	09	5	0	0
Wycombe W	L	03/10	09	1	0	1
Wycombe W	Tr	07/10	10	16	1	0
Cheltenham T	Tr	06/11	11-12	61	0	2
AFC Wimbledon	Tr	01/13	12-14	66	0	2

BENNETT Albert
Born: Chester-le-Street, County Durham, England, 16 July, 1944 — F
England: U23-1/Youth

League Club	Source	Date Signed	Seasons Played	Apps	Subs	Gls
Rotherham U	Chester Moor Jnrs	10/61	61-64	108	-	64
Newcastle U	Tr	07/65	65-68	85	0	22
Norwich C	Tr	02/69	68-70	54	1	15

BENNETT Craig
Born: Doncaster, South Yorkshire, England, 29 August, 1973 — F

League Club	Source	Date Signed	Seasons Played	Apps	Subs	Gls
Doncaster Rov	YT	07/91	90-92	5	3	0

BENNETT Dale Owen
Born: Enfield, N London, England, 6 January, 1990 — CD

League Club	Source	Date Signed	Seasons Played	Apps	Subs	Gls
Watford	Sch	07/08	09-11	14	8	0
Brentford	L	10/11	11	5	0	1
AFC Wimbledon	L	10/12	12	5	0	0
Yeovil T	L	11/12	12	0	1	0

BENNETT Daniel Mark (Dan)
Born: Great Yarmouth, Norfolk, England, 7 January, 1978 — CD
Singapore: 128

League Club	Source	Date Signed	Seasons Played	Apps	Subs	Gls
Wrexham	Tanjong Pagar (MLY)	01/02	01	5	1	0
Wrexham	Armed Forces (SIN)	08/02	02	14	4	0

BENNETT David Anthony (Dave)
Born: Manchester, England, 11 July, 1959 — RW
England: FLge

League Club	Source	Date Signed	Seasons Played	Apps	Subs	Gls
Manchester C	Jnr	08/78	78-80	43	9	9
Cardiff C	Tr	09/81	81-82	75	2	18
Coventry C	Tr	07/83	83-88	157	15	25
Sheffield Wed	Tr	03/89	88-89	20	8	0
Swindon T	Tr	09/90	90	1	0	0
Shrewsbury T	L	11/91	91	2	0	2

BENNETT David Michael (Dave)
Born: Southampton, England, 5 March, 1939 — W
Died: Dorset, England, November, 2009
England: Schools

League Club	Source	Date Signed	Seasons Played	Apps	Subs	Gls
Arsenal	Jnr	05/56				
Portsmouth	Tr	06/58				
Southampton	Tr	08/60				
Bournemouth	Tr	12/60	60-61	12	-	2

BENNETT David Paul (Dave)
Born: Oldham, Greater Manchester, England, 26 April, 1960 — W

League Club	Source	Date Signed	Seasons Played	Apps	Subs	Gls
Norwich C	Manchester C (App)	08/78	78-83	64	7	9

BENNETT Dean Alan
Born: Wolverhampton, England, 13 December, 1977 — M
England: Semi Pro-1

League Club	Source	Date Signed	Seasons Played	Apps	Subs	Gls
West Bromwich A	Aston Villa (Jnr)	12/96	96	0	1	0
Kidderminster Hrs	Bromsgrove Rov	01/99	00-03	136	18	16
Wrexham	Tr	08/04	04-05	27	20	2
Chester C	Tr	07/06	06	27	5	1

BENNETT Desmond (Des)
Born: Doncaster, South Yorkshire, England, 30 October, 1963 — M

League Club	Source	Date Signed	Seasons Played	Apps	Subs	Gls
Doncaster Rov	App	06/80	80-81	0	2	0

BENNETT Donald (Don)
Born: Wakefield, England, 18 December, 1933 — FB
Died: Hertfordshire, England, 12 June, 2014
England: Youth

League Club	Source	Date Signed	Seasons Played	Apps	Subs	Gls
Arsenal	Jnr	08/51				
Coventry C	Tr	09/59	59-61	73	-	0

BENNETT Edgar William
Born: Stoke-on-Trent, England, 29 March, 1929 — W
Died: Luton, England, 1 September, 2008

League Club	Source	Date Signed	Seasons Played	Apps	Subs	Gls
Luton T	Vauxhall Motors	09/52	53	1	-	0

BENNETT Edward Ernest (Ted)
Born: Kilburn, NW London, England, 22 August, 1925 — G
England: Amateur-8

League Club	Source	Date Signed	Seasons Played	Apps	Subs	Gls
Queens Park Rgrs (Am)	Southall	02/49	48	2	-	0
Watford	Southall	12/53	53-55	81	-	0

BENNETT Elliott
Born: Telford, England, 18 December, 1988 — LW

League Club	Source	Date Signed	Seasons Played	Apps	Subs	Gls
Wolverhampton W	Sch	03/07				
Crewe Alex	L	10/07	07	4	5	1
Bury	L	01/08	07	18	1	1
Bury	L	07/08	08	46	0	3
Brighton & HA	Tr	08/09	09-10	88	1	13
Norwich C	Tr	06/11	11-14	35	33	2
Brighton & HA	L	11/14	14	7	0	0

BENNETT Frank (Frankie)
Born: Birmingham, England, 3 January, 1969 — W

League Club	Source	Date Signed	Seasons Played	Apps	Subs	Gls
Southampton	Halesowen T	02/93	93-95	5	14	1
Shrewsbury T	L	10/96	96	2	2	3
Bristol Rov	Tr	11/96	96-99	15	29	4
Exeter C	L	02/00	99	8	1	1

BENNETT Gary
Born: Enfield, N London, England, 13 November, 1970 — W/F

League Club	Source	Date Signed	Seasons Played	Apps	Subs	Gls
Colchester U	YT	11/88	88-93	65	22	13

BENNETT Gary Ernest
Born: Manchester, England, 4 December, 1961 — CD

League Club	Source	Date Signed	Seasons Played	Apps	Subs	Gls
Manchester C	Ashton U	09/79				
Cardiff C	Tr	09/81	81-83	85	2	11
Sunderland	Tr	07/84	84-94	362	7	23
Carlisle U	Tr	11/95	95	26	0	5
Scarborough	Tr	08/96	96-97	86	2	18
Darlington	Tr	07/98	98-99	30	4	4

BENNETT Gary Michael
Born: Kirkby, Merseyside, England, 20 September, 1962 — F

League Club	Source	Date Signed	Seasons Played	Apps	Subs	Gls
Wigan Ath	Kirkby T	10/84	84	10	10	3
Chester C	Tr	08/85	85-88	109	17	36
Southend U	Tr	11/88	88-89	36	6	6
Chester C	Tr	03/90	89-91	71	9	15
Wrexham	Tr	08/92	92-94	120	1	77
Tranmere Rov	Tr	07/95	95	26	3	9
Preston NE	Tr	03/96	95-96	15	9	4
Wrexham	Tr	02/97	96	15	0	5
Chester C	Tr	07/97	97-98	42	6	13

BENNETT George Forest
Born: South Shields, Tyne and Wear, England, 16 March, 1938 — LB

League Club	Source	Date Signed	Seasons Played	Apps	Subs	Gls
Burnley	Jnr	04/55				
Barnsley	Tr	01/60	59-60	24	-	0

BENNETT Henry Sylvester (Harry)
Born: Liverpool, England, 16 May, 1949 — CD

League Club	Source	Date Signed	Seasons Played	Apps	Subs	Gls
Everton	Jnr	03/67	67	2	0	0
Aldershot	Tr	01/71	70-72	77	12	7
Crewe Alex	Tr	07/73	73	28	2	1

BENNETT Ian Michael
Born: Worksop, Nottinghamshire, England, 10 October, 1971 — G

League Club	Source	Date Signed	Seasons Played	Apps	Subs	Gls
Newcastle U	Queens Park Rgrs (YT)	03/89				
Peterborough U	Tr	03/91	91-93	72	0	0
Birmingham C	Tr	12/93	93-03	285	2	0
Sheffield U	L	12/04	04	5	0	0

League Club	Source	Date Signed	Seasons Played	Career Record Apps	Subs	Gls
Coventry C	L	02/05	04	6	0	0
Leeds U	Tr	07/05	05	4	0	0
Sheffield U	Tr	07/06	06-09	14	2	0
Huddersfield T	Tr	07/10	10-12	57	1	0
BENNETT James Richard						
Born: Beverley, East Riding of Yorkshire, England, 4 September, 1988						M
Hull C	Sch	12/06				
Darlington	Tr	08/09	09	3	1	0
BENNETT John						
Born: Rotherham, South Yorkshire, England, 15 May, 1949						W
Rotherham U	App	-	65	1	0	0
BENNETT John Graham						
Born: Liverpool, England, 27 March, 1946						LB
Liverpool	App	04/63				
Chester C	Tr	06/66	66-68	72	4	0
BENNETT Joseph (Joe)						
Born: Rochdale, Greater Manchester, England, 28 March, 1990						LB
England: U21-3/Youth						
Middlesbrough	Sch	07/08	08-11	78	7	1
Aston Villa	Tr	08/12	12-13	24	6	0
Brighton & HA	L	08/14	14	41	0	1
BENNETT Julian Llewellyn						
Born: Nottingham, England, 17 December, 1984						LB
Walsall	Sch	07/04	03-05	47	4	3
Nottingham F	Tr	01/06	05-10	85	12	8
Crystal Palace	L	08/10	10	10	3	1
Sheffield Wed	Tr	07/11	11	16	5	2
Shrewsbury T	L	11/12	12	4	0	0
Southend U	Tr	08/13				
BENNETT Kenneth Edgar (Ken)						
Born: Wood Green, N London, England, 2 October, 1921						IF
Died: Rochford, Essex, England, December, 1994						
Tottenham H	Wood Green T	10/40				
Southend U	Tr	06/46	46-47	50	-	10
Bournemouth	Tr	06/48	48	19	-	1
Brighton & HA	Guildford C	06/50	50-52	101	-	37
Crystal Palace	Tr	07/53	53	17	-	2
BENNETT Kyle						
Born: Telford, England, 9 September, 1990						W
England: Youth						
Wolverhampton W	Sch	09/07				
Bury	Tr	08/10	10	13	19	2
Doncaster Rov	Tr	07/11	11-14	72	44	15
Crawley T	L	10/13	13	4	0	0
Bradford C	L	01/14	13	14	4	1
BENNETT Lawson Henry						
Born: Blackburn, Greater Manchester, England, 28 August, 1938						RW
Died: Blackburn, Greater Manchester, England, January, 2011						
Accrington Stan	Darwen	05/58	58-60	29	-	2
BENNETT Lee						
Born: Barnsley, South Yorkshire, England, 19 September, 1990						M
Lincoln C	Sch	-	09	0	1	0
BENNETT Leslie Donald (Les)						
Born: Wood Green, N London, England, 10 January, 1918						IF
Died: Wood Green, N London, England, 29 April, 1999						
Tottenham H	Jnr	05/39	46-54	272	-	104
West Ham U	Tr	12/54	54-55	26	-	3
BENNETT Martyn						
Born: Birmingham, England, 4 August, 1961						CD
England: Schools						
West Bromwich A	App	08/78	78-89	181	1	9
BENNETT Mason Kane						
Born: Shirebrook, Derbyshire, England, 15 July, 1996						F
England: Youth						
Derby Co	Sch	07/13	11-14	4	26	1
Chesterfield	L	03/14	13	1	4	0
Bradford C	L	08/14	14	4	7	1
BENNETT Michael (Mike)						
Born: Bolton, Greater Manchester, England, 24 December, 1962						LB
England: Youth						
Bolton W	App	01/80	79-82	62	3	1
Wolverhampton W	Tr	06/83	83	6	0	0
Cambridge U	Tr	03/84	83-85	76	0	0
Preston NE	Bradford C (NC)	09/86	86-89	85	1	1
Carlisle U	Tr	07/90	90-91	21	3	0

League Club	Source	Date Signed	Seasons Played	Career Record Apps	Subs	Gls
BENNETT Michael Richard (Mickey)						
Born: Camberwell, S London, England, 27 July, 1969						W
England: Youth						
Charlton Ath	App	04/87	86-89	24	11	2
Wimbledon	Tr	01/90	89-91	12	6	2
Brentford	Tr	07/92	92-93	40	6	4
Charlton Ath	Tr	03/94	93-94	19	5	1
Millwall	Tr	05/95	95	1	1	0
Cardiff C	Tr	08/96	96	5	9	1
Leyton Orient	Cambridge C	12/97	97	1	1	0
Brighton & HA	Tr	08/98	98	37	1	0
BENNETT Neil Robert						
Born: Dewsbury, West Yorkshire, England, 29 October, 1980						G
Sheffield Wed	YT	10/98				
Rochdale	Drogheda U (ROI)	03/03	02	1	0	0
BENNETT Paul						
Born: Liverpool, England, 30 January, 1961						M
Port Vale	Everton (App)	09/78	80-81	28	2	1
BENNETT Paul Reginald						
Born: Southampton, England, 4 February, 1952						CD
Southampton	App	11/69	71-75	116	0	1
Reading	Tr	07/76	76-78	105	0	3
Aldershot	Tr	08/79	79-81	112	1	2
BENNETT Peter Christopher						
Born: Plymouth, England, 29 November, 1939						CF
Exeter C	Plymstock	08/59	59-60	6	-	5
BENNETT Peter Leigh						
Born: Hillingdon, W London, England, 24 June, 1946						M
England: Schools						
West Ham U	App	07/63	63-70	38	4	3
Leyton Orient	Tr	10/70	70-78	195	4	13
BENNETT Rhys Gordon						
Born: Manchester, England, 1 September, 1991						D
Bolton W	Sch	07/11				
Rochdale	Tr	07/12	12-14	82	12	4
BENNETT Richard John						
Born: Northampton, England, 16 February, 1945						WH
Died: Northampton, England, September, 2007						
England: Youth						
Peterborough U	Wellingborough T	08/63	63-64	4	-	0
BENNETT Robert (Bobby)						
Born: Harrow, NW London, England, 29 December, 1951						F
Southend U	Staines T	06/72	72	1	0	0
Scunthorpe U	L	10/73	73	2	1	0
BENNETT Ronald (Ron)						
Born: Hinckley, Leicestershire, England, 8 May, 1927						LW
Died: Maidstone, Kent, England, October, 1997						
Wolverhampton W		01/45				
Portsmouth	Tr	07/48	49-51	8	-	1
Crystal Palace	Tr	01/52	51-52	27	-	5
Brighton & HA	Tr	07/53	53	3	-	0
BENNETT Ryan						
Born: Grays, Essex, England, 6 March, 1990						CD
England: U21-2/Youth						
Grimsby T	Sch	04/07	06-09	89	14	6
Peterborough U	Tr	10/09	09-11	80	4	6
Norwich C	Tr	12/11	11-14	35	11	2
Peterborough U	L	01/12	11	4	0	0
BENNETT Scot Andrew						
Born: Newquay, Cornwall, England, 30 November, 1990						D/M
Exeter C	Sch	07/08	10-14	124	8	18
BENNETT Sean						
Born: Newport, Wales, 3 September, 1970						LB
Newport Co	YT	-	87	4	1	0
BENNETT Stanley Thomas (Stan)						
Born: Birmingham, England, 18 September, 1944						CD
Walsall	App	09/62	63-74	378	8	12
BENNETT Steven						
Born: Grimethorpe, South Yorkshire, England, 21 November, 1991						F
Barnsley	Sch	07/10	10	0	4	0
BENNETT Thomas McNeill (Tom)						
Born: Falkirk, Scotland, 12 December, 1969						DM
Aston Villa	YT	12/87				
Wolverhampton W	Tr	07/88	88-94	103	12	2
Stockport Co	Tr	06/95	95-99	105	5	5

League Club	Source	Date Signed	Seasons Played	Apps	Subs	Gls
Walsall	L	12/99	99	4	0	1
Walsall	Tr	03/00	99-01	75	10	7
Boston U	Tr	08/02	02-04	75	4	1
Kidderminster Hrs	Tr	11/04	04	24	0	0

BENNETT Troy
Born: Barnsley, South Yorkshire, England, 25 December, 1975 — LW

League Club	Source	Date Signed	Seasons Played	Apps	Subs	Gls
Barnsley	YT	12/93	92	2	0	0
Scarborough	Tr	03/97	96-97	28	11	3

BENNETT Walter Henry
Born: Mexborough, South Yorkshire, England, 15 December, 1918 — CF
Died: Doncaster, South Yorkshire, England, December, 2009

League Club	Source	Date Signed	Seasons Played	Apps	Subs	Gls
Barnsley	Mexborough Olympia	04/38	46-47	38	-	23
Doncaster Rov	Tr	01/48	47-49	39	-	14
Halifax T	Tr	01/50	49	7	-	1

BENNING Malvind Singh
Born: West Bromwich, West Midlands, England, 2 November, 1993 — LB

League Club	Source	Date Signed	Seasons Played	Apps	Subs	Gls
Walsall	Sch	07/12	12-14	31	15	2
York C	L	01/15	14	9	0	0

BENNING Michael David (Micky)
Born: Watford, Hertfordshire, England, 3 February, 1938 — RW

League Club	Source	Date Signed	Seasons Played	Apps	Subs	Gls
Watford	Jnr	09/56	58-61	103	-	14

BENNING Paul Martin
Born: Watford, Hertfordshire, England, 7 June, 1963 — FB

League Club	Source	Date Signed	Seasons Played	Apps	Subs	Gls
Peterborough U	Hayes	12/87	87	2	0	0

BENNION John Raymond (Jack)
Born: Manchester, England, 2 April, 1934 — WH
Died: Beverley, East Riding of Yorkshire, England, 14 September, 2006

League Club	Source	Date Signed	Seasons Played	Apps	Subs	Gls
Burnley	Burnley Belvedere	01/52				
Hull C	Tr	06/57	57-59	35	-	1
Stockport Co	Tr	07/60	60	26	-	1
Barrow	Tr	07/61	61-62	16	-	0

BENNION Stanley (Stan)
Born: Chester, England, 9 February, 1938 — W/IF
Died: Llay, Wrexham, Wales, 5 August, 2013

League Club	Source	Date Signed	Seasons Played	Apps	Subs	Gls
Wrexham	Jnr	10/59	59-62	54	-	18
Chester C	Tr	06/63	63	20	-	3

BENNYWORTH Ian Robert
Born: Hull, England, 15 January, 1962 — CD

League Club	Source	Date Signed	Seasons Played	Apps	Subs	Gls
Hull C	App	01/80	79	1	0	0
Scarborough	Nuneaton Bor	08/86	87-89	88	1	3
Hartlepool U	Tr	12/89	89-91	81	1	3

BENSKIN Denis Walter
Born: Ruddington, Nottinghamshire, England, 28 May, 1947 — LW

League Club	Source	Date Signed	Seasons Played	Apps	Subs	Gls
Notts Co (Am)	Jnr	05/65	65	4	0	1

BENSON John Harvey
Born: Arbroath, Angus, Scotland, 23 December, 1942 — D/M
Died: Macclesfield, Cheshire, England, 30 October, 2010

League Club	Source	Date Signed	Seasons Played	Apps	Subs	Gls
Manchester C	Jnr	07/61	61-63	44	-	0
Torquay U	Tr	06/64	64-70	233	7	7
Bournemouth	Tr	10/70	70-73	85	7	0
Exeter C	L	03/73	72	4	0	0
Norwich C	Tr	12/73	73-74	29	1	1
Bournemouth	Tr	01/75	74-78	56	1	0

BENSON Joseph Robert (Joe)
Born: Misterton, Nottinghamshire, England, 7 January, 1933 — WH

League Club	Source	Date Signed	Seasons Played	Apps	Subs	Gls
Scunthorpe U		09/55	55	2	-	0

BENSON Paul Andrew
Born: Southend-on-Sea, England, 12 October, 1979 — F
England: Semi Pro-1

League Club	Source	Date Signed	Seasons Played	Apps	Subs	Gls
Dagenham & Red	White Ensign	05/05	07-10	98	5	40
Charlton Ath	Tr	08/10	10-11	28	5	10
Swindon T	Tr	01/12	11-12	26	5	12
Portsmouth	L	11/12	12	7	0	2
Cheltenham T	L	01/13	12	15	1	4
Luton T	Tr	07/14	14	16	5	1

BENSON Ronald (Ron)
Born: York, England, 26 March, 1925 — RW
Died: York, England, 6 November, 1997

League Club	Source	Date Signed	Seasons Played	Apps	Subs	Gls
York C	Holgates OB	10/47	49	20	-	3

BENSTEAD Graham Mark
Born: Aldershot, Hampshire, England, 20 August, 1963 — G
England: Youth

League Club	Source	Date Signed	Seasons Played	Apps	Subs	Gls
Queens Park Rgrs	App	07/81				
Norwich C	Tr	03/85	84-87	16	0	0
Colchester U	L	08/87	87	18	0	0
Sheffield U	Tr	03/88	87-88	47	0	0
Brentford	Tr	07/90	90-93	112	0	0
Brentford	Rushden & D	07/97	97	1	0	0

BENSTOCK Danny
Born: Hackney, E London, England, 10 July, 1970 — M

League Club	Source	Date Signed	Seasons Played	Apps	Subs	Gls
Leyton Orient	Barking	12/92	92-93	17	4	0

BENT Darren Ashley
Born: Tooting, SW London, England, 6 February, 1984 — F
England: 13/U21-14/Youth

League Club	Source	Date Signed	Seasons Played	Apps	Subs	Gls
Ipswich T	YT	07/01	01-04	103	19	49
Charlton Ath	Tr	06/05	05-06	68	0	31
Tottenham H	Tr	06/07	07-08	32	28	18
Sunderland	Tr	08/09	09-10	58	0	32
Aston Villa	Tr	01/11	10-14	45	16	21
Fulham	L	09/13	13	11	13	3
Brighton & HA	L	11/14	14	5	0	2
Derby Co	L	01/15	14	11	4	10

BENT Geoffrey (Geoff)
Born: Salford, England, 27 September, 1932 — LB
Died: Munich, Germany, 21 February, 1958

League Club	Source	Date Signed	Seasons Played	Apps	Subs	Gls
Manchester U	Jnr	04/51	54-56	12	-	0

BENT Graham William
Born: Ruabon, Wrexham, Wales, 6 October, 1945 — LW
Died: Nuneaton, Warwickshire, England, 15 May, 2002
Wales: Schools

League Club	Source	Date Signed	Seasons Played	Apps	Subs	Gls
Wrexham	Aston Villa (App)	12/63	63-64	10	-	2

BENT Jason Andrew
Born: Toronto, Canada, 8 March, 1977 — M
Canada: 32/U23-5/Youth

League Club	Source	Date Signed	Seasons Played	Apps	Subs	Gls
Plymouth Arg	Colorado Rapids (USA)	09/01	01-03	52	12	5

BENT Junior Antony
Born: Huddersfield, West Yorkshire, England, 1 March, 1970 — RW

League Club	Source	Date Signed	Seasons Played	Apps	Subs	Gls
Huddersfield T	YT	12/87	87-89	25	11	6
Burnley	L	11/89	89	7	2	3
Bristol C	Tr	03/90	89-97	142	41	20
Stoke C	L	03/92	91	1	0	0
Shrewsbury T	L	10/96	96	6	0	0
Blackpool	Tr	08/97	97-99	64	39	5

BENT Marcus Nathan
Born: Hammersmith, W London, England, 19 May, 1978 — F
England: U21-2

League Club	Source	Date Signed	Seasons Played	Apps	Subs	Gls
Brentford	YT	07/95	95-97	56	14	8
Crystal Palace	Tr	01/98	97-98	13	15	5
Port Vale	Tr	01/99	98-99	17	6	1
Sheffield U	Tr	10/99	99-00	48	0	20
Blackburn Rov	Tr	11/00	00-01	22	15	8
Ipswich T	Tr	11/01	01-03	51	10	21
Leicester C	L	09/03	03	28	5	9
Everton	Tr	07/04	04-05	38	17	7
Charlton Ath	Tr	01/06	05-07	32	14	4
Wigan Ath	L	08/07	07	25	6	7
Birmingham C	Tr	07/08	08	16	17	3
Middlesbrough	L	10/09	09	3	4	0
Queens Park Rgrs	L	02/10	09	2	1	0
Wolverhampton W	L	08/10	10	0	3	0
Sheffield U	L	01/11	10	4	7	0

BENTALEB Nabil
Born: Lille, France, 24 November, 1994 — M
Algeria: 16//France: Youth

League Club	Source	Date Signed	Seasons Played	Apps	Subs	Gls
Tottenham H	Sch	09/12	13-14	36	5	0

BENTALL Charles Edward (Edward)
Born: Helmsley, North Yorkshire, England, 28 January, 1922 — CD
Died: York, England, 10 December, 1947

League Club	Source	Date Signed	Seasons Played	Apps	Subs	Gls
York C	English Martyrs	10/45	46	1	-	0

BENTEKE Christian
Born: Kinshasa, DR Congo, 3 December, 1990 — F
Belgium: 24/U21-9/Youth

League Club	Source	Date Signed	Seasons Played	Apps	Subs	Gls
Aston Villa	KRC Genk (BEL)	08/12	12-14	82	7	42

BENTHAM Alan
Born: Liverpool, England, 12 September, 1940 — RB
England: Schools

League Club	Source	Date Signed	Seasons Played	Apps	Subs	Gls
Everton	Flint T	11/57				
Southport	Tr	06/60	60-61	25	-	1

BENTHAM Craig Martin
Born: Bingley, West Yorkshire, England, 7 March, 1985 — M

League Club	Source	Date Signed	Seasons Played	Apps	Subs	Gls
Bradford C	Sch	08/04	04-07	18	12	0

BENTHAM John James
Born: South Elmsall, West Yorkshire, England, 3 March, 1963 — LW

League Club	Source	Date Signed	Seasons Played	Apps	Subs	Gls
York C	App	03/81	81	22	1	0

BENTHAM Stanley Joseph (Stan)
Born: Leigh, Greater Manchester, England, 17 March, 1915 — WH
Died: Southport, Merseyside, England, 29 May, 2002

League Club	Source	Date Signed	Seasons Played	Apps	Subs	Gls
Everton	Wigan Ath	01/34	35-48	110	-	17

BENTLEY Aaron Stuart James
Born: Plymouth, England, 8 November, 1995 — CD

League Club	Source	Date Signed	Seasons Played	Apps	Subs	Gls
Plymouth Arg	Sch	07/14	14	3	0	0

BENTLEY Alfred (Alf)
Born: Eythorne, Kent, England, 28 October, 1931 — G
Died: Dover, Kent, England, 28 October, 1996

League Club	Source	Date Signed	Seasons Played	Apps	Subs	Gls
Coventry C	Snowdown CW	10/55	55-56	29	-	0
Gillingham	Margate	08/58	58-61	13	-	0

BENTLEY Anthony (Tony)
Born: Stoke-on-Trent, England, 20 December, 1939 — RB/W

League Club	Source	Date Signed	Seasons Played	Apps	Subs	Gls
Stoke C	Jnr	12/56	58-60	43	-	15
Southend U	Tr	05/61	61-70	379	2	14

BENTLEY Daniel Ian
Born: Wickford, Essex, England, 13 July, 1993 — G

League Club	Source	Date Signed	Seasons Played	Apps	Subs	Gls
Southend U	Sch	07/11	11-14	96	2	0

BENTLEY David Alwyn
Born: Edwinstowe, Nottinghamshire, England, 30 May, 1950 — M

League Club	Source	Date Signed	Seasons Played	Apps	Subs	Gls
Rotherham U	App	07/67	66-73	241	8	13
Mansfield T	L	09/72	72	1	3	1
Chesterfield	Tr	06/74	74-76	53	2	1
Doncaster Rov	Tr	08/77	77-79	87	2	4

BENTLEY David Michael
Born: Peterborough, England, 27 August, 1984 — RW
England: 7/B-1/U21-8/Youth

League Club	Source	Date Signed	Seasons Played	Apps	Subs	Gls
Arsenal	YT	09/01	03	1	0	0
Norwich C	L	06/04	04	22	4	2
Blackburn Rov	Tr	08/05	05-07	96	6	13
Tottenham H	Tr	07/08	08-10	32	10	3
Birmingham C	L	01/11	10	9	4	0
West Ham U	L	08/11	11	2	3	0
Blackburn Rov	L	02/13	12	4	1	0

BENTLEY James Graham (Jim)
Born: Liverpool, England, 11 June, 1976 — CD

League Club	Source	Date Signed	Seasons Played	Apps	Subs	Gls
Manchester C	YT	07/93				
Morecambe	Telford U	05/02	07-10	122	2	13

BENTLEY John (Jack)
Born: Liverpool, England, 17 February, 1942 — RW
Died: Liverpool, England, 27 May, 2007

League Club	Source	Date Signed	Seasons Played	Apps	Subs	Gls
Everton	Jnr	11/59	60	1	-	0
Stockport Co	Tr	05/61	61-62	49	-	5

BENTLEY Keith James
Born: Hull, England, 27 July, 1936 — IF
Died: Hessle, East Riding of Yorkshire, England, 15 September, 2008

League Club	Source	Date Signed	Seasons Played	Apps	Subs	Gls
Hull C		11/57	57	4	-	0

BENTLEY Mark James
Born: Hertford, England, 7 January, 1978 — M

League Club	Source	Date Signed	Seasons Played	Apps	Subs	Gls
Southend U	Dagenham & Red	01/04	03-05	70	23	12
Gillingham	Tr	07/06	06-10	156	18	11

BENTLEY Thomas Frank Roy (Roy)
Born: Shirehampton, Avon, England, 17 May, 1924 — CF/CH
England: 12/B-2/FLge-3

League Club	Source	Date Signed	Seasons Played	Apps	Subs	Gls
Bristol C	Jnr	09/41				
Newcastle U	Tr	06/46	46-47	48	-	22
Chelsea	Tr	01/48	47-56	324	-	130
Fulham	Tr	09/56	56-60	142	-	23
Queens Park Rgrs	Tr	06/61	61-62	45	-	0

BENTLEY William John (Bill)
Born: Stoke-on-Trent, England, 21 October, 1947 — LB
England: Youth/Schools

League Club	Source	Date Signed	Seasons Played	Apps	Subs	Gls
Stoke C	App	10/64	65-68	44	4	1
Blackpool	Tr	01/69	68-76	289	7	11
Port Vale	Tr	07/77	77-79	92	3	0

BENTON James
Born: Wexford, Republic of Ireland, 9 April, 1975 — M

League Club	Source	Date Signed	Seasons Played	Apps	Subs	Gls
Northampton T	YT	-	91-92	6	4	1

BENYON Elliot Paul
Born: High Wycombe, Buckinghamshire, England, 29 August, 1987 — F

League Club	Source	Date Signed	Seasons Played	Apps	Subs	Gls
Bristol C	Sch	07/06				
Torquay U	Tr	08/07	09-10	53	15	24
Swindon T	Tr	01/11	10	7	5	1
Wycombe W	L	07/11	11	2	7	0
Southend U	Tr	01/12	11-12	10	11	2
Torquay U	Tr	02/13	12-13	35	17	7

BEN YOUSSEF Syam Habib
Born: Marseille, France, 31 March, 1989 — RB
Tunisia: 5/U21-8

League Club	Source	Date Signed	Seasons Played	Apps	Subs	Gls
Leyton Orient	Esperance Tunis (TUN)	01/12	11	6	3	0

BERAHINO Saido
Born: Bujumbura, Burundi, 4 August, 1993 — F
England: U21-13/Youth

League Club	Source	Date Signed	Seasons Played	Apps	Subs	Gls
West Bromwich A	Sch	08/10	13-14	43	27	19
Northampton T	L	10/11	11	14	0	6
Brentford	L	02/12	11	5	3	4
Peterborough U	L	10/12	13	7	3	2

BERARDI Gaetano
Born: Lugano, Switzerland, 21 August, 1988 — RB
Switzerland: 1/U21-20/Youth

League Club	Source	Date Signed	Seasons Played	Apps	Subs	Gls
Leeds U	Sampdoria (ITA)	07/14	14	19	3	0

BERBATOV Dimitar Ivan
Born: Blagoevgrad, Bulgaria, 30 January, 1981 — F
Bulgaria: 78/U21-3/Youth

League Club	Source	Date Signed	Seasons Played	Apps	Subs	Gls
Tottenham H	Bayer Leverkusen (GER)	07/06	06-08	63	7	27
Manchester U	Tr	09/08	08-11	82	26	48
Fulham	Tr	08/12	12-13	50	1	19

BERCHICHE Yuri
Born: San Sebastian, Spain, 10 February, 1990 — LB
Spain: Youth

League Club	Source	Date Signed	Seasons Played	Apps	Subs	Gls
Tottenham H	Athletic Bilbao (SPN)	08/07				
Cheltenham T	L	03/09	08	7	0	0

BERESFORD David
Born: Middleton, Greater Manchester, England, 11 November, 1976 — LW
England: Youth/Schools

League Club	Source	Date Signed	Seasons Played	Apps	Subs	Gls
Oldham Ath	YT	07/94	93-96	32	32	2
Swansea C	L	08/95	95	4	2	0
Huddersfield T	Tr	03/97	96-00	24	11	3
Preston NE	L	12/99	99	1	3	0
Port Vale	L	09/00	00	4	0	0
Hull C	Tr	07/01	01	33	8	1
Plymouth Arg	Tr	07/02	02-03	6	11	0
Macclesfield T	L	10/03	03	5	0	0
Tranmere Rov	Tr	11/03	03-04	21	23	3
Macclesfield T	Tr	07/05	05	9	7	0

BERESFORD John
Born: Sheffield, England, 4 September, 1966 — LB
England: B-2/Youth/Schools

League Club	Source	Date Signed	Seasons Played	Apps	Subs	Gls
Manchester C	App	09/83				
Barnsley	Tr	08/86	86-88	79	9	5
Portsmouth	Tr	03/89	88-91	102	5	8
Newcastle U	Tr	07/92	92-97	176	3	3
Southampton	Tr	02/98	97-99	11	6	0
Birmingham C	L	10/99	99	1	0	0

BERESFORD John Turner
Born: Sunderland, England, 2 January, 1943 — WH

League Club	Source	Date Signed	Seasons Played	Apps	Subs	Gls
Hartlepool U (Am)		08/66	66	3	0	0

BERESFORD John William
Born: Sheffield, England, 25 January, 1946 — LH
Died: Chesterfield, Derbyshire, England, 24 August, 2003

League Club	Source	Date Signed	Seasons Played	Apps	Subs	Gls
Chesterfield	App	01/63	62-64	52	-	10
Notts Co	Tr	05/65	65-66	49	1	13

BERESFORD Marlon
Born: Lincoln, England, 2 September, 1969 — G

League Club	Source	Date Signed	Seasons Played	Apps	Subs	Gls
Sheffield Wed	YT	09/87				
Bury	L	08/89	89	1	0	0
Northampton T	L	09/90	90	13	0	0
Crewe Alex	L	02/91	90	3	0	0
Northampton T	L	08/91	91	15	0	0
Burnley	Tr	08/92	92-97	240	0	0
Middlesbrough	Tr	03/98	97-01	8	2	0
Sheffield Wed	L	01/00	00	4	0	0
Burnley	Tr	01/02	01	13	0	0
York C	Tr	08/02	02	6	0	0
Burnley	Tr	10/02	02	33	1	0
Bradford C	Tr	09/03	03	5	0	0
Luton T	Tr	10/03	03	11	0	0
Barnsley	Tr	01/04	03	14	0	0
Luton T	Tr	07/04	04-07	105	0	0
Oldham Ath	L	10/07	07	5	0	0

BERESFORD Philip
Born: Hollingwood, Derbyshire, England, 30 November, 1944 CF

League Club	Source	Date Signed	Seasons Played	Apps	Subs	Gls
Chesterfield		01/64	63	7	-	3

BERESFORD Reginald (Reg)
Born: Chesterfield, Derbyshire, England, 29 June, 1924 CF
Died: Nottingham, England, October, 2012

League Club	Source	Date Signed	Seasons Played	Apps	Subs	Gls
Notts Co	Hardwick Colliery	09/45	46	9	-	1

BERESFORD Reginald Harold (Reg)
Born: Walsall, West Midlands, England, 3 June, 1921 WH

League Club	Source	Date Signed	Seasons Played	Apps	Subs	Gls
Aston Villa	Jnr	10/38				
Birmingham C	Tr	09/46				
Crystal Palace	Tr	08/48	48	7	-	1

BERG Henning
Born: Eidsvoll, Norway, 1 September, 1968 D
Norway: 100/U21-15/Youth

League Club	Source	Date Signed	Seasons Played	Apps	Subs	Gls
Blackburn Rov	Lillestrom (NOR)	01/93	92-96	154	5	4
Manchester U	Tr	08/97	97-00	49	17	2
Blackburn Rov	Tr	09/00	00-02	90	1	3

BERGER Patrik
Born: Prague, Czechoslovakia, 10 November, 1973 LW/F
Czechoslovakia: 2/Youth//Czech Republic: 42/U21-1

League Club	Source	Date Signed	Seasons Played	Apps	Subs	Gls
Liverpool	Bor Dortmund (GER)	08/96	96-02	106	42	28
Portsmouth	Tr	07/03	03-04	50	2	8
Aston Villa	Tr	07/05	05-07	8	21	2
Stoke C	L	11/06	06	1	6	0

BERGERSEN Kent Roger
Born: Oslo, Norway, 8 February, 1967 M

League Club	Source	Date Signed	Seasons Played	Apps	Subs	Gls
Stockport Co	Stromgodset (NOR)	09/99	99-00	18	8	1

BERGET Jo Inge
Born: Oslo, Norway, 11 September, 1990 F
Norway: 4/U21-21

League Club	Source	Date Signed	Seasons Played	Apps	Subs	Gls
Cardiff C	Molde FK (NOR)	01/14	13	0	1	0

BERGKAMP Denis Nicolaas Maria
Born: Amsterdam, Netherlands, 18 May, 1969 F
Netherlands: 79/U21-2

League Club	Source	Date Signed	Seasons Played	Apps	Subs	Gls
Arsenal	Inter Milan (ITA)	07/95	95-05	253	62	87

BERGKAMP Roland Adrianus Martinus
Born: Amsterdam, Netherlands, 3 April, 1991 F
Netherlands: U21-1

League Club	Source	Date Signed	Seasons Played	Apps	Subs	Gls
Brighton & HA	Excelsior (NED)	07/11				
Rochdale	L	11/11	11	2	1	0

BERGQVIST Jan Douglas (Doug)
Born: Stockholm, Sweden, 29 March, 1993 D

League Club	Source	Date Signed	Seasons Played	Apps	Subs	Gls
Aldershot T	Sch	04/11	10-12	1	6	0
Exeter C	Tr	06/13				

BERGSSON Gudni
Born: Reykjavik, Iceland, 21 July, 1965 CD
Iceland: 80/U21-4/Youth

League Club	Source	Date Signed	Seasons Played	Apps	Subs	Gls
Tottenham H	Valur (ICE)	12/88	88-92	51	20	2
Bolton W	Tr	03/95	94-02	263	7	23

BERHALTER Gregg
Born: New Jersey, USA, 8 January, 1973 CD
USA: 44

League Club	Source	Date Signed	Seasons Played	Apps	Subs	Gls
Crystal Palace	Cambuur Leeuw (NED)	02/01	00-01	10	9	1

BERKLEY Austin James
Born: Dartford, Kent, England, 28 January, 1973 W

League Club	Source	Date Signed	Seasons Played	Apps	Subs	Gls
Gillingham	YT	05/91	91	0	3	0
Swindon T	Tr	05/92	94	0	1	0
Shrewsbury T	Tr	07/95	95-99	152	20	12
Barnet	Tr	07/00				
Carlisle U	L	08/01	01	2	3	0

BERKOVIC Eyal
Born: Haifa, Israel, 2 April, 1972 M
Israel: 78/U21

League Club	Source	Date Signed	Seasons Played	Apps	Subs	Gls
Southampton (L)	Maccabi Haifa (ISR)	10/96	96	26	2	4
West Ham U	Tr	07/97	97-98	62	3	10
Blackburn Rov (L)	Glasgow Celtic	02/01	00	4	7	2
Manchester C	Glasgow Celtic	08/01	01-03	48	8	7
Portsmouth	Tr	01/04	03-04	16	6	2

BERMINGHAM Alan
Born: Liverpool, England, 11 September, 1944 FB

League Club	Source	Date Signed	Seasons Played	Apps	Subs	Gls
Wrexham	Skelmersdale U	06/67	67-70	114	2	2

BERMINGHAM Karl Joseph Kevin
Born: Dublin, Republic of Ireland, 6 October, 1985 F
Republic of Ireland: U21-1/Youth

League Club	Source	Date Signed	Seasons Played	Apps	Subs	Gls
Manchester C	Sch	10/02				
Lincoln C	L	02/05	04	0	2	0
Burnley	L	08/05	05	1	3	0

BERNAL Andrew (Andy)
Born: Canberra, Australia, 16 July, 1966 D
Australia: 21

League Club	Source	Date Signed	Seasons Played	Apps	Subs	Gls
Ipswich T	Sporting Gijon (SPN)	09/87	87	4	5	0
Reading	Olympic Sharks (AUS)	07/94	94-99	179	8	2

BERNARD Michael Peter (Mike)
Born: Shrewsbury, Shropshire, England, 10 January, 1948 M
England: U23-3/Youth

League Club	Source	Date Signed	Seasons Played	Apps	Subs	Gls
Stoke C	App	01/65	65-71	124	11	6
Everton	Tr	04/72	72-76	139	8	8
Oldham Ath	Tr	07/77	77-78	6	0	0

BERNARD Narada Michael
Born: Bristol, England, 30 January, 1981 LB
Jamaica: 1

League Club	Source	Date Signed	Seasons Played	Apps	Subs	Gls
Arsenal	Tottenham H (YT)	07/99				
Bournemouth	Tr	07/00	00-02	13	16	0
Torquay U	Woking	11/03	03	0	1	0

BERNARD Olivier Clive
Born: Paris, France, 14 October, 1979 LB

League Club	Source	Date Signed	Seasons Played	Apps	Subs	Gls
Newcastle U	Olymp Lyonnais (FRA)	10/00	01-04	82	20	6
Darlington	L	03/01	00	9	1	2
Southampton	Tr	01/05	04	12	1	0
Newcastle U	Glasgow Rangers	08/06				

BERNARD Paul Robert James
Born: Edinburgh, Scotland, 30 December, 1972 M
Scotland: 2/B-1/U21-15

League Club	Source	Date Signed	Seasons Played	Apps	Subs	Gls
Oldham Ath	YT	07/91	90-95	105	7	18
Plymouth Arg	Aberdeen	12/02	02	7	3	0

BERNARDEAU Olivier
Born: Bourges, France, 19 August, 1962 W

League Club	Source	Date Signed	Seasons Played	Apps	Subs	Gls
Chesterfield	Leeds U (NC)	08/86	86	5	4	0

BERNER Bruno George
Born: Zurich, Switzerland, 21 November, 1977 LB
Switzerland: 16

League Club	Source	Date Signed	Seasons Played	Apps	Subs	Gls
Blackburn Rov	FC Basel (SUI)	01/07	06-07	3	0	0
Leicester C	Tr	09/08	08-10	70	14	8

BERNTSEN Robin
Born: Tromso, Norway, 10 July, 1970 F

League Club	Source	Date Signed	Seasons Played	Apps	Subs	Gls
Port Vale (L)	Tromso (NOR)	11/98	98	1	0	0

BERNTSEN Thomas (Tommy)
Born: Oslo, Norway, 18 December, 1973 CD
Norway: 2

League Club	Source	Date Signed	Seasons Played	Apps	Subs	Gls
Portsmouth (L)	Lillestrom (NOR)	11/99	99	1	1	0

BERRA Christophe Didier (Chris)
Born: Edinburgh, Scotland, 31 January, 1985 CD
Scotland: 30/B-1/U21-6

League Club	Source	Date Signed	Seasons Played	Apps	Subs	Gls
Wolverhampton W	Heart of Midlothian	01/09	08-12	137	4	0
Ipswich T	Tr	07/13	13-14	86	1	11

BERRETT James Trevor
Born: Halifax, West Yorkshire, England, 13 January, 1989 M
Republic of Ireland: U21-5/Youth

League Club	Source	Date Signed	Seasons Played	Apps	Subs	Gls
Huddersfield T	Sch	07/07	06-09	20	15	2
Carlisle U	Tr	07/10	10-13	168	2	23
Yeovil T	Tr	07/14	14	18	10	1

BERRY David Gilbert (Dave)
Born: Newton-le-Willows, Merseyside, England, 1 June, 1945 CD

League Club	Source	Date Signed	Seasons Played	Apps	Subs	Gls
Blackpool	Jnr	09/63				
Chester C	Tr	07/64	66	0	1	0

BERRY Durrell Joel
Born: Derby, England, 27 May, 1992 RB

League Club	Source	Date Signed	Seasons Played	Apps	Subs	Gls
Aston Villa	Sch	07/10				
Plymouth Arg	Tr	06/11	11-13	87	8	1
Cheltenham T	Torquay U	01/15	14	8	4	2

BERRY George Frederick
Born: Ammerland, Germany, 19 November, 1957 CD
Wales: 5

League Club	Source	Date Signed	Seasons Played	Apps	Subs	Gls
Wolverhampton W	App	11/75	76-81	124	0	4
Stoke C	Tr	08/82	82-89	229	8	27
Doncaster Rov	L	08/84	84	1	0	0
Peterborough U	Tr	07/90	90	28	4	6
Preston NE	Tr	08/91	91	4	0	0

BERRY Gregory John (Greg)
Born: Grays, Essex, England, 5 March, 1971 LW

League Club	Source	Date Signed	Seasons Played	Career Record Apps	Subs	Gls
Leyton Orient	East Thurrock U	07/89	89-91	68	12	14
Wimbledon	Tr	08/92	92-93	6	1	1
Millwall	Tr	03/94	93-96	23	11	1
Brighton & HA	L	08/95	95	6	0	2
Leyton Orient	L	03/96	95	4	3	0
BERRY John Andrew						
Born: Manchester, England, 27 August, 1965						FB
Torquay U		01/84	83	1	0	0
BERRY Leslie Dennis (Les)						
Born: Plumstead, SE London, England, 4 May, 1956						CD
Charlton Ath	App	03/74	75-85	352	6	11
Brighton & HA	Tr	08/86	86	22	1	0
Gillingham	Tr	03/87	86-87	26	5	0
Maidstone U	Tr	07/88	89-90	62	1	2
BERRY Luke David						
Born: Royston, Hertfordshire, England, 12 July, 1992						M
Barnsley	Cambridge U	07/14	14	25	6	1
BERRY Michael James (Mike)						
Born: Newbury, Berkshire, England, 14 February, 1955						FB
Southampton	App	02/73	74	2	0	0
BERRY Neil						
Born: Edinburgh, Scotland, 6 April, 1963						CD
Scotland: Youth						
Bolton W	App	03/81	81-84	25	7	0
BERRY Norman						
Born: Bury, Greater Manchester, England, 15 August, 1922						W
Died: Rochdale, Greater Manchester, England, 26 April, 2002						
Bury (Am)	Bury Amats	05/46	46-47	23	-	6
BERRY Paul						
Born: Chadwell St Mary, Essex, England, 15 November, 1935						CH
Chelsea	Jnr	04/53	56-57	3	-	0
BERRY Paul Alan						
Born: Oxford, England, 8 April, 1958						F
Oxford U	App	04/76	76-81	98	12	20
BERRY Paul Andrew						
Born: Warrington, Cheshire, England, 6 December, 1978						M
Chester C	Warrington T	08/99	99	0	9	1
BERRY Peter						
Born: Aldershot, Hampshire, England, 20 September, 1933						RW
Crystal Palace	Jnr	08/51	53-57	151	-	27
Ipswich T	Tr	05/58	58-59	38	-	6
BERRY Reginald John (Johnny)						
Born: Aldershot, Hampshire, England, 1 June, 1926						RW
Died: Farnham, Surrey, England, 0 September, 1994						
England: 4/B-1/FLge-1						
Birmingham C	Aldershot YMCA	12/44	47-51	104	-	6
Manchester U	Tr	08/51	51-57	247	-	37
BERRY Stephen Andrew (Steve)						
Born: Liverpool, England, 4 April, 1963						M
Portsmouth	App	01/81	81-82	26	2	2
Aldershot	L	03/84	83	5	2	0
Sunderland	Tr	07/84	84-85	32	3	2
Newport Co	Tr	12/85	85-86	60	0	6
Swindon T	Tr	03/87	86-87	4	0	0
Aldershot	Tr	10/87	87-88	48	0	6
Northampton T	Tr	10/88	88-90	95	7	7
BERRY Thomas (Tom)						
Born: Clayton-Le-Moors, Lancashire, England, 31 March, 1922						CH
Died: Clayton-Le-Moors, Lancashire, England, 14 September, 2003						
Hull C	Great Harwood	05/47	47-57	275	-	1
BERRY Trevor John						
Born: Haslemere, Surrey, England, 1 August, 1974						RW
England: Youth						
Aston Villa	Bournemouth (YT)	04/92				
Rotherham U	Tr	09/95	95-00	126	47	20
Scunthorpe U	L	02/01	00	6	0	1
BERRY Tyrone Michael						
Born: Brixton, S London, England, 20 February, 1987						RW
Crystal Palace	Sch	08/05				
Notts Co	L	09/05	05	4	1	0
Rushden & D	Tr	01/06	05	13	7	0
Gillingham	Stevenage Bor	08/08	08	2	3	0
BERRY William						
Born: Mansfield, Nottinghamshire, England, 4 April, 1934						IF
Mansfield T	Langwith MW	03/56	56	10	-	1

League Club	Source	Date Signed	Seasons Played	Career Record Apps	Subs	Gls
BERRYMAN Stephen Christopher (Steve)						
Born: Blackburn, Greater Manchester, England, 26 December, 1966						G
Hartlepool U	Leyland Motors	03/90	89	1	0	0
Exeter C	Leyland Motors	08/90				
Cambridge U	Tr	03/91	90	1	0	0
BERSON Mathieu						
Born: Vannes, France, 23 February, 1980						M
France: U21-2						
Aston Villa	FC Nantes (FRA)	08/04	04	7	4	0
BERTHE Mohamed						
Born: Conakry, Guinea, 12 September, 1972						M
West Ham U	Gazelec Ajaccio (AUT)	03/98				
Bournemouth	Tr	07/98	98	12	3	2
BERTHE Sekou						
Born: Bamoko, Mali, 7 October, 1977						CD
Mali: 4						
West Bromwich A	Troyes AC (FRA)	09/03	03	2	1	0
BERTHELIN Cedric						
Born: Lens, France, 25 December, 1976						G
Luton T	ASOA Valence (FRA)	10/02	02	9	0	0
Crystal Palace	Tr	12/02	02-03	26	0	0
BERTI Nicola						
Born: Salsomaggiore Terme, Italy, 14 April, 1967						M
Italy: 39						
Tottenham H	Inter Milan (ITA)	01/98	97-98	21	0	3
BERTIN Alexis						
Born: Le Havre, France, 13 May, 1980						M
Brighton & HA (L)	Le Havre (FRA)	01/07	06	15	1	0
BERTOLINI John (Jack)						
Born: Alloa, Stirlingshire, Scotland, 21 March, 1934						RH
Workington	Stirling A	01/53	52-57	183	-	36
Brighton & HA	Tr	07/58	58-65	258	0	12
BERTOS Leonida Christos (Leo)						
Born: Wellington, New Zealand, 20 December, 1981						M
New Zealand: 56/U23-5/Youth/Schools						
Barnsley	Wellington Oly'c (NZL)	09/00	00-02	4	8	1
Rochdale	Tr	07/03	03-04	73	9	13
Chester C	Tr	08/05	05	2	3	0
BERTRAM James Terence (Jim)						
Born: Whitehaven, Cumbria, England, 3 February, 1953						CD
Workington	Carlisle U (App)	02/72	71	0	1	0
BERTRAND Ryan Dominic						
Born: Southwark, S London, England, 5 August, 1989						LB
England: 4/U21-16/Youth						
Chelsea	Sch	08/06	10-13	21	7	0
Bournemouth	L	11/06	06	5	0	0
Oldham Ath	L	08/07	07	21	0	0
Norwich C	L	01/08	07	18	0	0
Norwich C	L	07/08	08	37	1	0
Reading	L	08/09	09	44	0	1
Nottingham F	L	08/10	10	19	0	0
Aston Villa	L	01/14	13	16	0	0
Southampton	Tr	07/14	14	34	0	2
BERTSCHIN Christian Frederick (Chris)						
Born: Kensington, Central London, England, 7 September, 1924						W
Died: Hillingdon, W London, England, 17 September, 1995						
Reading	Ilford	08/47	47-48	12	-	1
BERTSCHIN Keith Edwin						
Born: Enfield, N London, England, 25 August, 1956						F
England: U21-3/Youth						
Ipswich T	Barnet	10/73	75-76	19	13	8
Birmingham C	Tr	07/77	77-80	113	5	29
Norwich C	Tr	08/81	81-84	112	2	29
Stoke C	Tr	11/84	84-86	82	6	29
Sunderland	Tr	03/87	86-87	25	11	7
Walsall	Tr	08/88	88-89	40	15	9
Chester C	Tr	11/90	90	14	5	0
BESAGNI Remo Giovanni						
Born: Islington, N London, England, 22 April, 1935						CF
Died: Camden, N London, England, 27 May, 2011						
Crystal Palace	Jnr	10/52	52	2	-	0
BESIC Mohamed						
Born: Berlin, Germany, 10 September, 1992						DM
Bosnia & Herzegovina: 20/U21-10						
Everton	Ferencvaros (HUN)	07/14	14	15	8	0

BESSONE Federico (Fede)
Born: Cordoba, Argentina, 23 January, 1984 LB

League Club	Source	Date Signed	Seasons Played	Apps	Subs	Gls
Swansea C	RCD Espanyol (SPN)	07/08	08-09	34	2	1
Leeds U	Tr	07/10	10	6	0	0
Charlton Ath	L	01/11	10	13	0	0
Swansea C	Tr	08/11	11	0	1	0
Swindon T	Tr	08/12	12	4	1	0
Oldham Ath	Tr	03/13				
Millwall	Sport'g Kansas C (USA)	02/14	13	1	1	0

BEST Andrew Keith (Andy)
Born: Dorchester, Dorset, England, 5 January, 1959 RW

League Club	Source	Date Signed	Seasons Played	Apps	Subs	Gls
Torquay U	Teignmouth	10/84	84	15	4	2

BEST Cyril Clyde (Clyde)
Born: Somerset, Bermuda, 24 February, 1951 F

League Club	Source	Date Signed	Seasons Played	Apps	Subs	Gls
West Ham U	Somerset Trojans (BER)	03/69	69-75	178	8	47

BEST David
Born: Wareham, Dorset, England, 6 September, 1943 G

League Club	Source	Date Signed	Seasons Played	Apps	Subs	Gls
Bournemouth	Jnr	10/60	60-66	230	0	0
Oldham Ath	Tr	09/66	66-68	98	0	0
Ipswich T	Tr	10/68	68-73	168	0	0
Portsmouth	Tr	02/74	73-74	53	0	0
Bournemouth	Tr	07/75	75	2	0	0

BEST George
Born: Belfast, Northern Ireland, 22 May, 1946 F/W
Died: Kensington, Central London, England, 25 November, 2005
Northern Ireland: 37

League Club	Source	Date Signed	Seasons Played	Apps	Subs	Gls
Manchester U	Jnr	05/63	63-73	361	0	137
Stockport Co	L	11/75	75	3	0	2
Fulham	Los Angeles Azt (USA)	09/76	76-77	42	0	8
Bournemouth	Glentoran	03/83	82	5	0	0

BEST John Bowers
Born: Liverpool, England, 11 July, 1940 WH
Died: Republic of Ireland, 5 October, 2014

League Club	Source	Date Signed	Seasons Played	Apps	Subs	Gls
Liverpool	Jnr	05/58				
Tranmere Rov	Tr	08/60	60	7	-	0

BEST Leon Julian Brendan
Born: Nottingham, England, 19 September, 1986 F
Republic of Ireland: 7/U21-1/Youth

League Club	Source	Date Signed	Seasons Played	Apps	Subs	Gls
Southampton	Sch	09/04	04-06	8	7	4
Queens Park Rgrs	L	12/04	04	2	3	0
Sheffield Wed	L	08/05	05	2	0	1
Sheffield Wed	L	01/06	05	3	8	1
Bournemouth	L	08/06	06	12	3	3
Yeovil T	L	11/06	06	14	1	10
Coventry C	Tr	07/07	07-09	70	22	19
Newcastle U	Tr	01/10	09-11	31	11	10
Blackburn Rov	Tr	07/12	12-13	9	5	2
Sheffield Wed	L	02/14	13	12	3	4
Derby Co	L	08/14	14	0	15	0
Brighton & HA	L	01/15	14	6	7	0

BEST Thomas Hubert (Tommy)
Born: Milford Haven, Pembrokeshire, Wales, 23 December, 1920 CF

League Club	Source	Date Signed	Seasons Played	Apps	Subs	Gls
Chester C	Milford Haven U	07/47	47-48	40	-	14
Cardiff C	Tr	10/48	48-49	28	-	11
Queens Park Rgrs	Tr	12/49	49	13	-	3

BEST William James Blaikley (Billy)
Born: Gartcosh, Lanarkshire, Scotland, 7 September, 1943 F

League Club	Source	Date Signed	Seasons Played	Apps	Subs	Gls
Northampton T	Pollok Jnrs	07/62	63-67	40	0	11
Southend U	Tr	01/68	67-72	225	1	106
Northampton T	Tr	09/73	73-77	201	2	37

BESWETHERICK Jonathan Barry (Jon)
Born: Liverpool, England, 15 January, 1978 LB

League Club	Source	Date Signed	Seasons Played	Apps	Subs	Gls
Plymouth Arg	YT	07/96	97-01	133	13	0
Sheffield Wed	Tr	06/02	02-03	9	2	0
Swindon T	L	02/03	02	3	0	0
Macclesfield T	L	01/04	03	3	1	0
Bristol Rov	Tr	07/04				
Kidderminster Hrs	Tr	11/04	04	10	0	0

BESWICK Ivan
Born: Manchester, England, 2 January, 1936 FB
Died: St Martins, Guernsey, England, 4 June, 2012

League Club	Source	Date Signed	Seasons Played	Apps	Subs	Gls
Manchester U		10/54				
Oldham Ath	Tr	08/58	58-60	47	-	0

BESWICK Keith
Born: Cardiff, Wales, 3 February, 1943 G

League Club	Source	Date Signed	Seasons Played	Apps	Subs	Gls
Millwall	Cardiff Corinthians	01/62	62	12	-	0
Newport Co	Tr	08/64	64-66	56	0	0

[BETINHO] ALVES Alberto
Born: Aveiro, Portugal, 21 July, 1993 F
Portugal: U21-4/Youth

League Club	Source	Date Signed	Seasons Played	Apps	Subs	Gls
Brentford (L)	Sporting Lisbon (POR)	09/14	14	0	1	0

BETMEAD Harry
Born: Grimsby, North Lincolnshire, England, 11 April, 1912 CH
Died: Middlesbrough, England, 26 August, 1984
England: 1

League Club	Source	Date Signed	Seasons Played	Apps	Subs	Gls
Grimsby T	Haycroft Rov	10/30	31-46	296	-	10

BETSY Kevin Eddie Lewis
Born: Woking, Surrey, England, 20 March, 1978 M
England: Semi Pro-1//Seychelles: 7

League Club	Source	Date Signed	Seasons Played	Apps	Subs	Gls
Fulham	Woking	09/98	98-01	3	12	1
Bournemouth	L	09/99	99	1	4	0
Hull C	L	11/99	99	1	1	0
Barnsley	Tr	02/02	01-03	84	10	15
Hartlepool U	L	08/04	04	3	3	1
Oldham Ath	Tr	09/04	04	34	2	5
Wycombe W	Tr	07/05	05-06	70	1	13
Bristol C	Tr	01/07	06-07	16	2	1
Yeovil T	L	10/07	07	5	0	1
Walsall	L	01/08	07	16	0	2
Southend U	Tr	08/08	08-09	28	15	3
Wycombe W	Tr	09/09	09-11	77	10	11

BETT Frederick (Fred)
Born: Scunthorpe, North Lincolnshire, England, 5 December, 1920 IF
Died: Scunthorpe, North Lincolnshire, England, 14 April, 2005

League Club	Source	Date Signed	Seasons Played	Apps	Subs	Gls
Sunderland	Scunthorpe U	12/37	37-38	3	-	0
Coventry C	Tr	05/46	46-48	27	-	11
Lincoln C	Tr	09/48	48	14	-	2

BETTANY Colin David
Born: Leicester, England, 15 June, 1932 D

League Club	Source	Date Signed	Seasons Played	Apps	Subs	Gls
Crewe Alex	Leicester C (Am)	08/53	53-54	26	-	6
Birmingham C	Tr	06/55				
Torquay U	Tr	04/57	57-65	335	0	4

BETTANY John William
Born: Laughton, South Yorkshire, England, 16 December, 1937 M

League Club	Source	Date Signed	Seasons Played	Apps	Subs	Gls
Huddersfield T	Thurcroft Main	09/60	60-64	59	-	6
Barnsley	Tr	03/65	64-69	194	4	25
Rotherham U	Tr	06/70	70	17	0	1

BETTERIDGE Raymond Michael (Mick)
Born: Alcester, Warwickshire, England, 11 August, 1924 IF
Died: Ashbourne, Derbyshire, England, 5 April, 1999

League Club	Source	Date Signed	Seasons Played	Apps	Subs	Gls
West Bromwich A	Warslow Celtic	11/48	49-50	5	-	0
Swindon T	Tr	07/51	51-53	108	-	23
Chester C	Tr	03/54	53	8	-	1

BETTINELLI Marcus
Born: Camberwell, S London, England, 24 May, 1992 G
England: U21-1

League Club	Source	Date Signed	Seasons Played	Apps	Subs	Gls
Fulham	Sch	07/10	14	39	0	0
Accrington Stan	L	08/13	13	39	0	0

BETTNEY Christopher John (Chris)
Born: Chesterfield, Derbyshire, England, 27 October, 1977 W

League Club	Source	Date Signed	Seasons Played	Apps	Subs	Gls
Sheffield U	YT	05/96	96	0	1	0
Hull C	L	09/97	97	28	2	1
Chesterfield	Tr	07/99	99	7	6	0
Rochdale	Tr	11/99	99	12	12	0
Macclesfield T	Tr	07/00	00	0	2	0

BETTS Anthony Thomas (Tony)
Born: Derby, England, 31 October, 1953 F
England: Youth

League Club	Source	Date Signed	Seasons Played	Apps	Subs	Gls
Aston Villa	Jnr	03/72	74	1	3	0
Southport	L	12/74	74	8	0	1
Port Vale	Portland Timbers (USA)	10/75	75	1	0	0

BETTS Eric
Born: Coventry, England, 27 June, 1925 LW
Died: Rochdale, Greater Manchester, England, 16 March, 1990

League Club	Source	Date Signed	Seasons Played	Apps	Subs	Gls
Mansfield T	Mansfield Villa	02/46	46	19	-	5
Coventry C	Tr	08/47	47	1	-	0
Walsall	Nuneaton Bor	05/49	49	30	-	3
West Ham U	Tr	04/50	50	3	-	1
Rochdale	Nuneaton Bor	10/51	51-52	52	-	8
Crewe Alex	Tr	02/53	52-53	25	-	5
Wrexham	Tr	10/53	53-55	53	-	21
Oldham Ath	Tr	02/56	55-56	26	-	5

BETTS James Barrie (Barrie)
Born: Barnsley, South Yorkshire, England, 18 September, 1932 RB

League Club	Source	Date Signed	Seasons Played	Apps	Subs	Gls
Barnsley	Worsbrough DST	11/50	52-56	55	-	0

League Club	Source	Date Signed	Seasons Played	Apps	Subs	Gls
Stockport Co	Tr	11/57	57-59	112	-	3
Manchester C	Tr	06/60	60-63	101	-	5
Scunthorpe U	Tr	08/64	64	7	-	0

BETTS Michael James (Mike)
Born: Barnsley, South Yorkshire, England, 21 September, 1956 — CD

League Club	Source	Date Signed	Seasons Played	Apps	Subs	Gls
Blackpool	App	10/73	75	4	3	0
Bury	Northwich Victoria	11/80	80	1	0	0

BETTS Robert
Born: Doncaster, South Yorkshire, England, 21 December, 1981 — M

League Club	Source	Date Signed	Seasons Played	Apps	Subs	Gls
Doncaster Rov	YT	-	97	2	1	0
Coventry C	Tr	12/98	99-02	5	8	0
Plymouth Arg	L	02/01	00	3	1	0
Lincoln C	L	10/01	01	1	2	0
Rochdale	Tr	08/03	03	4	1	2
Kidderminster Hrs	Tr	09/03	03	8	1	0

BETTS Simon Richard
Born: Middlesbrough, England, 3 March, 1973 — FB

League Club	Source	Date Signed	Seasons Played	Apps	Subs	Gls
Ipswich T	YT	07/91				
Colchester U	Scarborough (NC)	12/92	92-98	182	9	11
Darlington	Yeovil T	07/01	01-02	69	0	1

BETTS Stuart
Born: Barnsley, South Yorkshire, England, 21 September, 1956 — F

League Club	Source	Date Signed	Seasons Played	Apps	Subs	Gls
Blackpool	App	10/73				
Halifax T		09/76				
Crewe Alex	Tr	08/77	77	2	0	0

BEUZELIN Guillaume Pierre
Born: Le Havre, France, 14 April, 1979 — M

League Club	Source	Date Signed	Seasons Played	Apps	Subs	Gls
Coventry C	Hibernian	07/08	08	28	7	1

BEVAN Brian Edward
Born: Bristol, England, 20 March, 1937 — LW

League Club	Source	Date Signed	Seasons Played	Apps	Subs	Gls
Bristol C	Bridgwater T	02/56	57-59	2	-	0
Carlisle U	Tr	03/60	59-60	27	-	2
Millwall	Tr	02/61	60	3	-	0

BEVAN David Michael
Born: Cork, Republic of Ireland, 24 June, 1989 — G

League Club	Source	Date Signed	Seasons Played	Apps	Subs	Gls
Aston Villa	Sch	07/07				
Walsall	Tr	07/10	10	4	0	0

BEVAN Paul Philip
Born: Shrewsbury, Shropshire, England, 20 October, 1952 — CD

League Club	Source	Date Signed	Seasons Played	Apps	Subs	Gls
Shrewsbury T	App	10/70	70-72	66	7	1
Swansea C	Tr	08/73	73-74	77	3	5
Crewe Alex	Tr	07/75	75-79	170	2	7

BEVAN Scott Anthony
Born: Southampton, England, 16 September, 1979 — G

League Club	Source	Date Signed	Seasons Played	Apps	Subs	Gls
Southampton	YT	01/98				
Huddersfield T	L	07/02	02	30	0	0
Wycombe W	L	01/04	03	5	0	0
Wimbledon	Tr	03/04	03	10	0	0
MK Dons	Wimbledon relocation	07/04	04	7	0	0
Shrewsbury T	Kidderminster Hrs	01/08	07	5	0	0
Torquay U	Tr	09/08	09-10	54	1	0
Bristol Rov	Tr	06/11	11	37	0	0

BEVANS Matthew David
Born: Enfield, N London, England, 19 September, 1993 — RB

League Club	Source	Date Signed	Seasons Played	Apps	Subs	Gls
Watford	Sch	07/12				
Oxford U	Tr	07/13	13	9	1	0

BEVANS Stanley (Stan)
Born: Kingsley, Hampshire, England, 16 April, 1934 — RW

League Club	Source	Date Signed	Seasons Played	Apps	Subs	Gls
Stoke C	Jnr	04/51	50-54	15	-	1

BEVIS David Roger (Dave)
Born: Southampton, England, 27 June, 1942 — G

League Club	Source	Date Signed	Seasons Played	Apps	Subs	Gls
Ipswich T	Jnr	08/59	63-65	6	0	0

BEVIS William Ernest (Billy)
Born: Warsash, Hampshire, England, 29 September, 1918 — RW
Died: Southampton, England, 22 August, 1994

League Club	Source	Date Signed	Seasons Played	Apps	Subs	Gls
Portsmouth	Jnr	07/36				
Southampton	Gosport Ath	06/37	37-46	82	-	16

BEWERS Jonathan Anthony (Jon)
Born: Wellingborough, Northamptonshire, England, 10 September, 1982 — FB
England: Youth/Schools

League Club	Source	Date Signed	Seasons Played	Apps	Subs	Gls
Aston Villa	YT	09/99	99	0	1	0
Notts Co	Tr	03/04	03	0	3	0
Walsall	Tr	09/04	04	1	0	0

BEWLEY David George (Dave)
Born: Bournemouth, England, 22 September, 1920 — FB
Died: Luton, England, 6 March, 2013
England: Schools

League Club	Source	Date Signed	Seasons Played	Apps	Subs	Gls
Fulham	Gravesend & Northfleet	05/45	46-48	17	-	1
Reading	Tr	03/50	49-50	11	-	1
Fulham	Tr	11/50				
Watford	Tr	05/53	53-55	113	-	1

BEYE Habib
Born: Paris, France, 19 October, 1977 — RB
Senegal: 45

League Club	Source	Date Signed	Seasons Played	Apps	Subs	Gls
Newcastle U	Olymp Marseille (FRA)	08/07	07-08	49	3	1
Aston Villa	Tr	08/09	09-10	7	2	0
Doncaster Rov	Tr	11/11	11	22	0	2

BEYNON Edgar Norman
Born: Swansea, Wales, 3 May, 1940 — IF

League Club	Source	Date Signed	Seasons Played	Apps	Subs	Gls
Wrexham	RAF Egypt	07/59	59	1	-	0

BEYNON Edwin Rees (Eddie)
Born: Aberdare, Rhondda Cynon Taff, Wales, 17 November, 1924 — IF
Died: Merthyr Tydfil, Wales, February, 2002
Wales: Schools

League Club	Source	Date Signed	Seasons Played	Apps	Subs	Gls
Wrexham	RAF	01/47	46-51	72	-	21
Shrewsbury T	Tr	10/51	51-54	91	-	6

BHASERA Onismor
Born: Mutare, Zimbabwe, 7 February, 1986 — LB
Zimbabwe: 19

League Club	Source	Date Signed	Seasons Played	Apps	Subs	Gls
Plymouth Arg	Kaizer Chiefs (RSA)	03/10	09-12	99	6	3

BHUTIA Baichung
Born: Sikkim, India, 15 June, 1976 — F
India: 107

League Club	Source	Date Signed	Seasons Played	Apps	Subs	Gls
Bury	East Bengal (IND)	09/99	99-01	20	17	3

BIAGINI Leonardo Angel
Born: Rosario, Argentina, 13 April, 1977 — F
Argentina: Youth

League Club	Source	Date Signed	Seasons Played	Apps	Subs	Gls
Portsmouth (L)	RCD Mallorca (SPN)	02/02	01	6	2	2

BIALKOWSKI Bartosz Marek
Born: Braniewo, Poland, 6 July, 1987 — G
Poland: U21-1/Youth

League Club	Source	Date Signed	Seasons Played	Apps	Subs	Gls
Southampton	Gornik Zabrze (POL)	01/06	05-11	21	1	0
Barnsley	L	09/09	09	2	0	0
Notts Co	Tr	07/12	12-13	84	0	0
Ipswich T	Tr	07/14	14	30	1	0

BIANCALANI Frederic
Born: Villerupt, France, 21 July, 1974 — M

League Club	Source	Date Signed	Seasons Played	Apps	Subs	Gls
Walsall	AS Nancy (FRA)	08/01	01	13	5	2

BIANCHI Rolando
Born: Bergamo, Italy, 15 February, 1983 — F
Italy: U21-13

League Club	Source	Date Signed	Seasons Played	Apps	Subs	Gls
Manchester C	Reggina (ITA)	07/07	07	7	12	4

BIANCHI Tomasso
Born: Piombino, Italy, 1 November, 1988 — M
Italy: U21-1/Youth

League Club	Source	Date Signed	Seasons Played	Apps	Subs	Gls
Leeds U	US Sassuolo (ITA)	07/14	14	24	0	0

BIBBO Salvatore (Sal)
Born: Basingstoke, Hampshire, England, 24 August, 1974 — G

League Club	Source	Date Signed	Seasons Played	Apps	Subs	Gls
Bournemouth	YT	08/92				
Sheffield U	Crawley T	08/93				
Chesterfield	L	02/95	94	0	1	0
Reading	Tr	08/96	96-97	7	0	0

[BICA] DI GIUSEPPE Marcos
Born: Sao Paulo, Brazil, 12 March, 1972 — F

League Club	Source	Date Signed	Seasons Played	Apps	Subs	Gls
Sunderland	SB Callao (PER)	09/99				
Walsall	Tr	10/99	99	0	1	0

BICKERSTAFFE John (Jack)
Born: St Helens, Merseyside, England, 8 November, 1918 — CH
Died: Knowsley, Merseyside, England, 5 February, 1982

League Club	Source	Date Signed	Seasons Played	Apps	Subs	Gls
Bury	Peasley Cross	05/39	46-48	27	-	0
Lincoln C	Tr	12/48	48-50	12	-	0
Halifax T	Tr	09/51	51-52	37	-	0

BICKLE Michael John (Mike)
Born: Plymouth, England, 25 January, 1944 — F

League Club	Source	Date Signed	Seasons Played	Apps	Subs	Gls
Plymouth Arg	St Austell	12/65	65-71	171	10	71
Gillingham	Tr	11/71	71-72	32	0	7

BICKLES David (Dave)
Born: West Ham, E London, England, 6 April, 1944 — CD
Died: Romford, E London, England, November, 1999
England: Youth

League Club	Source	Date Signed	Seasons Played	Apps	Subs	Gls
West Ham U	App	07/61	63-66	24	1	0

League Club	Source	Date Signed	Seasons Played	Apps	Subs	Gls
Crystal Palace	Tr	10/67				
Colchester U	Tr	09/68	68-69	67	0	3

BICKNELL Charles (Charlie)
Born: Somercotes, Derbyshire, England, 6 November, 1905 LB
Died: Bedford, England, 6 September, 1994

League Club	Source	Date Signed	Seasons Played	Apps	Subs	Gls
Chesterfield	New Tupton Ivanhoe	10/27	28-29	79	-	0
Bradford C	Tr	03/30	30-35	240	-	2
West Ham U	Tr	03/36	35-46	137	-	1

BICKNELL John (Jack)
Born: Edlington, South Yorkshire, England, 16 December, 1931 IF

League Club	Source	Date Signed	Seasons Played	Apps	Subs	Gls
Walsall	Retford T	02/54	53	3	-	0

BICKNELL Roy
Born: Doncaster, South Yorkshire, England, 19 February, 1926 CH
Died: Colchester, Essex, England, 31 January, 2005

League Club	Source	Date Signed	Seasons Played	Apps	Subs	Gls
Wolverhampton W	Jnr	09/43				
Charlton Ath	Tr	05/47	47-48	7	-	0
Bristol C	Tr	06/49	49-50	21	-	0
Colchester U	Gravesend & Northfleet	06/52	52-53	25	-	0

BICKNELL Stephen John (Steve)
Born: Southam, Warwickshire, England, 28 November, 1958 LW

League Club	Source	Date Signed	Seasons Played	Apps	Subs	Gls
Leicester C	App	12/76	76	6	1	0
Torquay U	Tr	08/78	78	0	3	0

BIDSTRUP Stefan
Born: Helsingoer, Denmark, 24 February, 1975 M

League Club	Source	Date Signed	Seasons Played	Apps	Subs	Gls
Wigan Ath	Lyngby (DEN)	11/00	00	10	5	2

BIDWELL Jake Brian
Born: Southport, Merseyside, England, 21 March, 1993 LB
England: Youth

League Club	Source	Date Signed	Seasons Played	Apps	Subs	Gls
Everton	Sch	04/10				
Brentford	L	11/11	11	24	0	0
Brentford	Tr	08/12	12-14	117	4	0

BIELBY Paul Anthony
Born: Darlington, County Durham, England, 24 November, 1956 LW
England: Youth

League Club	Source	Date Signed	Seasons Played	Apps	Subs	Gls
Manchester U	App	11/73	73	2	2	0
Hartlepool U	Tr	11/75	75-77	74	21	8
Huddersfield T	Tr	08/78	78	29	2	5

BIGGINS Brian
Born: Ellesmere Port, Cheshire, England, 19 May, 1940 G
Died: Chester, England, 13 September, 2006

League Club	Source	Date Signed	Seasons Played	Apps	Subs	Gls
Chester C	Jnr	06/57	57-58	5	-	0

BIGGINS Graham William
Born: Chapeltown, South Yorkshire, England, 10 March, 1958 G

League Club	Source	Date Signed	Seasons Played	Apps	Subs	Gls
Doncaster Rov	Rotherham U (Am)	07/77	77	2	0	0

BIGGINS Stephen James (Steve)
Born: Lichfield, Staffordshire, England, 20 June, 1954 F

League Club	Source	Date Signed	Seasons Played	Apps	Subs	Gls
Shrewsbury T	Hednesford T	12/77	77-81	140	6	41
Oxford U	Tr	07/82	82-84	44	15	22
Derby Co	Tr	10/84	84	8	2	1
Wolverhampton W	L	03/85	84	4	0	0
Port Vale	L	03/86	85	1	3	0
Exeter C	Trelleborg FF (SWE)	10/86	86	14	0	2

BIGGINS Wayne
Born: Sheffield, England, 20 November, 1961 F

League Club	Source	Date Signed	Seasons Played	Apps	Subs	Gls
Lincoln C	App	11/79	80	8	0	1
Burnley	Matlock T	02/84	83-85	78	0	29
Norwich C	Tr	10/85	85-87	66	13	16
Manchester C	Tr	07/88	88	29	3	9
Stoke C	Tr	08/89	89-92	120	2	46
Barnsley	Tr	10/92	92-93	44	3	16
Stoke C	Glasgow Celtic	03/94	93-94	18	9	6
Luton T	L	01/95	94	6	1	1
Oxford U	Tr	07/95	95	8	2	1
Wigan Ath	Tr	11/95	95-96	35	16	5

BIGGS Alfred George (Alfie)
Born: Bristol, England, 8 February, 1936 F
Died: Poole, Dorset, England, 20 April, 2012

League Club	Source	Date Signed	Seasons Played	Apps	Subs	Gls
Bristol Rov	Jnr	02/53	53-60	214	-	77
Preston NE	Tr	07/61	61-62	48	-	22
Bristol Rov	Tr	10/62	62-67	210	0	101
Walsall	Tr	03/68	67-68	23	1	9
Swansea C	Tr	11/68	68	16	0	4

BIGGS Anthony (Tony)
Born: Greenford, W London, England, 17 April, 1936 CF
England: Amateur-2

League Club	Source	Date Signed	Seasons Played	Apps	Subs	Gls
Arsenal	Hounslow T	08/56	57-58	4	-	1
Leyton Orient	Tr	12/58	58-59	4	-	1

BIGIRIMANA Gael
Born: Bujumbura, Burundi, 22 October, 1993 DM
England: Youth

League Club	Source	Date Signed	Seasons Played	Apps	Subs	Gls
Coventry C	Sch	08/11	11	16	10	0
Newcastle U	Tr	07/12	12	3	10	1

BIGNALL Nicholas Colin
Born: Reading, England, 11 July, 1990 F

League Club	Source	Date Signed	Seasons Played	Apps	Subs	Gls
Reading	Sch	07/08	09	0	1	0
Northampton T	L	11/08	08	1	4	1
Cheltenham T	L	01/09	08	8	5	1
Stockport Co	L	08/09	09	11	0	2
Southampton	L	10/10	10	0	3	0
Bournemouth	L	11/10	10	3	2	0
Brentford	L	01/11	10	1	5	0
Exeter C	L	08/11	11	3	0	0
Wycombe W	L	10/11	11	0	1	0

BIGNOT Marcus
Born: Birmingham, England, 22 August, 1974 RB
England: Semi Pro-1

League Club	Source	Date Signed	Seasons Played	Apps	Subs	Gls
Crewe Alex	Kidderminster Hrs	09/97	97-99	93	2	0
Bristol Rov	Tr	08/00	00	26	0	1
Queens Park Rgrs	Tr	03/01	00-01	49	5	1
Rushden & D	Tr	08/02	02-03	68	0	2
Queens Park Rgrs	Tr	03/04	03-07	123	5	0
Millwall	Tr	11/07	07-08	18	5	0

BIGNOT Paul Junior
Born: Birmingham, England, 14 February, 1986 RB
England: Semi Pro-1

League Club	Source	Date Signed	Seasons Played	Apps	Subs	Gls
Crewe Alex	Sch	03/05	04-06	16	5	0
Blackpool	Newport Co	07/11				
Plymouth Arg	L	11/11	11	14	0	0

BIKEY-AMOUGOU Andre Stephane
Born: Douala, Cameroon, 8 January, 1985 CD
Cameroon: 25

League Club	Source	Date Signed	Seasons Played	Apps	Subs	Gls
Reading	Lokomotiv Moscow (RUS)	08/06	06-08	44	18	6
Burnley	Tr	08/09	09-11	62	8	3
Bristol C	L	03/12	11	7	0	0
Middlesbrough	Tr	09/12	12	31	2	1
Charlton Ath	Panetolikos (GRE)	07/14	14	29	2	1

BILCLIFF Raymond (Ray)
Born: Blaydon, Tyne and Wear, England, 24 May, 1931 RB
Died: Blidworth, Nottinghamshire, England, 10 March, 2009

League Club	Source	Date Signed	Seasons Played	Apps	Subs	Gls
Middlesbrough	Spennymoor Jnrs	05/49	51-60	182	-	0
Hartlepool U	Tr	01/61	60-63	117	-	0

BILEY Alan Paul
Born: Leighton Buzzard, Bedfordshire, England, 26 February, 1957 F

League Club	Source	Date Signed	Seasons Played	Apps	Subs	Gls
Cambridge U	Luton T (App)	07/75	75-79	160	5	74
Derby Co	Tr	01/80	79-80	47	0	19
Everton	Tr	07/81	81	16	3	3
Stoke C	L	03/82	81	8	0	1
Portsmouth	Tr	08/82	82-84	101	4	50
Brighton & HA	Tr	03/85	84-85	34	1	8
Cambridge U	New York Express (USA)	11/86	86	0	3	0

BILIC Slaven
Born: Split, Croatia, 11 September, 1968 CD
Croatia: 44

League Club	Source	Date Signed	Seasons Played	Apps	Subs	Gls
West Ham U	Karlsruhe (GER)	02/96	95-96	48	0	2
Everton	Tr	07/97	97-98	26	2	0

BILL Roger James
Born: Creswell, Derbyshire, England, 17 May, 1944 RW

League Club	Source	Date Signed	Seasons Played	Apps	Subs	Gls
Reading	Chelsea (Am)	09/62	62	4	-	0

BILLING Peter Graham
Born: Liverpool, England, 24 October, 1964 CD

League Club	Source	Date Signed	Seasons Played	Apps	Subs	Gls
Everton	South Liverpool	01/86	85	1	0	0
Crewe Alex	Tr	12/86	86-88	83	5	1
Coventry C	Tr	06/89	89-92	51	7	1
Port Vale	Tr	02/93	92-94	23	3	0
Hartlepool U	Tr	08/95	95	35	1	0
Crewe Alex	Tr	08/96	96	9	6	0

BILLING Philip Anyanwu
Born: Esbjerg, Denmark, 11 June, 1996 M
Denmark: Youth

League Club	Source	Date Signed	Seasons Played	Apps	Subs	Gls
Huddersfield T	Sch	10/13	13	0	1	0

BILLINGHAM John (Jack)
Born: Daventry, Northamptonshire, England, 3 December, 1914 CF
Died: Northampton, England, 7 October, 1981

League Club	Source	Date Signed	Seasons Played	Apps	Subs	Gls
Northampton T	Stead & Simpson	09/35	35	3	-	0
Bristol C	Tr	07/37	37	7	-	0
Burnley	Tr	05/38	38-48	93	-	36

League Club	Source	Date Signed	Seasons Played	Apps	Subs	Gls
Carlisle U	Tr	09/49	49-50	65	-	17
Southport	Tr	03/51	50-54	150	-	37

BILLINGHAM Peter Arnold
Born: Brierley Hill, West Midlands, England, 8 October, 1938 — RH

League Club	Source	Date Signed	Seasons Played	Apps	Subs	Gls
Walsall	Jnr	10/55	55-59	99	-	11
West Bromwich A	Tr	05/60	60	7	-	0

BILLINGS John
Born: Doncaster, South Yorkshire, England, 30 March, 1944 — IF

League Club	Source	Date Signed	Seasons Played	Apps	Subs	Gls
Doncaster Rov	Jnr	05/61	62-64	18	-	4

BILLINGTON Brian Keith
Born: Leicester, England, 28 April, 1951 — M

League Club	Source	Date Signed	Seasons Played	Apps	Subs	Gls
Notts Co	Leicester C (Am)	10/69	69	4	3	0

BILLINGTON Charles Roy (Charlie)
Born: Chesterfield, Derbyshire, England, 8 November, 1927 — CD
Died: Chesterfield, Derbyshire, England, 19 November, 1985

League Club	Source	Date Signed	Seasons Played	Apps	Subs	Gls
Aldershot	Chesterfield (Am)	12/46	46-55	212	-	11
Norwich C	Tr	01/56	55-56	22	-	0
Watford	Tr	07/57	57	14	-	0
Mansfield T	Tr	06/58	58	1	-	0

BILLINGTON David James
Born: Oxford, England, 15 October, 1980 — FB

League Club	Source	Date Signed	Seasons Played	Apps	Subs	Gls
Peterborough U	YT	-	96	2	3	0

BILLINGTON Hugh John Richard
Born: Ampthill, Bedfordshire, England, 24 February, 1916 — CF
Died: Luton, England, 16 January, 1988

League Club	Source	Date Signed	Seasons Played	Apps	Subs	Gls
Luton T	Waterlows	05/38	38-47	86	-	63
Chelsea	Tr	03/48	47-50	82	-	28

BILLINGTON Stanley (Stan)
Born: Wallasey, Wirral, England, 23 February, 1937 — D
Died: Wirral, England, November, 2011
England: Youth

League Club	Source	Date Signed	Seasons Played	Apps	Subs	Gls
Everton	Jnr	06/55				
Tranmere Rov	Tr	07/60	60-63	93	-	0

BILLINGTON Wilfred Francis (Wilf)
Born: Blackburn, Greater Manchester, England, 28 January, 1930 — G

League Club	Source	Date Signed	Seasons Played	Apps	Subs	Gls
Blackburn Rov	Rochdale (Am)	04/48				
Workington	Tr	07/54	54-57	53	-	0

BILLIO Patrizio
Born: Treviso, Italy, 19 April, 1974 — M

League Club	Source	Date Signed	Seasons Played	Apps	Subs	Gls
Crystal Palace	Monza (ITA)	03/98	97	1	2	0

BILLY Christopher Anthony (Chris)
Born: Huddersfield, West Yorkshire, England, 2 January, 1973 — DM

League Club	Source	Date Signed	Seasons Played	Apps	Subs	Gls
Huddersfield T	YT	07/91	91-94	76	18	4
Plymouth Arg	Tr	08/95	95-97	107	11	9
Notts Co	Tr	07/98	98	3	3	0
Bury	Tr	09/98	98-02	165	13	11
Carlisle U	Tr	08/03	03-06	100	4	1

BILYALETDINOV Diniyar Rinatovich
Born: Moscow, Russia, 27 February, 1985 — LW
Russia: 46/U21-7

League Club	Source	Date Signed	Seasons Played	Apps	Subs	Gls
Everton	Lokomotiv Moscow (RUS)	08/09	09-11	33	26	8

BIMPSON James Louis (Louis)
Born: Rainford, Merseyside, England, 14 May, 1929 — CF

League Club	Source	Date Signed	Seasons Played	Apps	Subs	Gls
Liverpool	Burscough	01/53	52-59	94	-	39
Blackburn Rov	Tr	11/59	59-60	22	-	5
Bournemouth	Tr	02/61	60	11	-	1
Rochdale	Tr	08/61	61-62	54	-	16

BIMSON Stuart James
Born: Liverpool, England, 29 September, 1969 — LB

League Club	Source	Date Signed	Seasons Played	Apps	Subs	Gls
Bury	Macclesfield T	02/95	94-96	36	0	0
Lincoln C	Tr	11/96	96-02	157	18	4
Cambridge U	Tr	07/03	03-04	37	6	0

BINCH David
Born: Nottingham, England, 10 February, 1956 — F

League Club	Source	Date Signed	Seasons Played	Apps	Subs	Gls
Doncaster Rov		02/76	75-76	3	2	0

BINES Henry Melvin
Born: Cardiff, Wales, 17 May, 1930 — WH
Died: Swindon, England, 27 June, 1979

League Club	Source	Date Signed	Seasons Played	Apps	Subs	Gls
Swindon T		08/50	51-52	6	-	0

BING Douglas (Doug)
Born: Broadstairs, Kent, England, 27 October, 1928 — WH
Died: Margate, Kent, England, 5 February, 2013

League Club	Source	Date Signed	Seasons Played	Apps	Subs	Gls
West Ham U	Margate	01/51	51-54	29	-	3

BING Thomas Edward (Tommy)
Born: Broadstairs, Kent, England, 24 November, 1931 — W
Died: 18 May, 2015

League Club	Source	Date Signed	Seasons Played	Apps	Subs	Gls
Tottenham H	Margate	09/54	57	1	-	0

BINGHAM Billy Christopher
Born: Welling, SE London, England, 15 July, 1990 — M

League Club	Source	Date Signed	Seasons Played	Apps	Subs	Gls
Crystal Palace	Sch	07/08				
Dagenham & Red	Tr	02/09	09-14	88	29	8

BINGHAM John George
Born: Ilkeston, Derbyshire, England, 23 September, 1949 — LW

League Club	Source	Date Signed	Seasons Played	Apps	Subs	Gls
Manchester C	Charlton Ath (App)	10/67				
Oldham Ath	Tr	07/69	69	16	1	3
Mansfield T	Tr	08/70	70-71	18	3	0
Chester C	L	03/72	71	7	0	1
Stockport Co	Tr	07/72	72	16	4	3

BINGHAM Michael James
Born: Leyland, Lancashire, England, 21 May, 1981 — G
England: Schools

League Club	Source	Date Signed	Seasons Played	Apps	Subs	Gls
Blackburn Rov	YT	07/98				
Mansfield T	Tr	07/01	01	1	1	0

BINGHAM Rakish Philip
Born: Newham, E London, England, 25 October, 1993 — F

League Club	Source	Date Signed	Seasons Played	Apps	Subs	Gls
Wigan Ath	Sch	04/12				
Mansfield T	Tr	08/14	14	15	13	6
Hartlepool U	L	01/15	14	5	0	1

BINGHAM William Laurence (Billy)
Born: Belfast, Northern Ireland, 5 August, 1931 — RW
Northern Ireland: 56/NILge-2

League Club	Source	Date Signed	Seasons Played	Apps	Subs	Gls
Sunderland	Glentoran	11/50	50-57	206	-	45
Luton T	Tr	07/58	58-60	87	-	27
Everton	Tr	10/60	60-62	86	-	23
Port Vale	Tr	08/63	63-64	40	-	6

BINGHAM William Peter (Peter)
Born: Swindon, England, 12 July, 1922 — WH
Died: Chippenham, Wiltshire, England, 25 July, 1997

League Club	Source	Date Signed	Seasons Played	Apps	Subs	Gls
Swindon T	Swindon Victoria	08/46	46-47	20	-	0

BINGLEY Walter
Born: Sheffield, England, 17 April, 1930 — FB

League Club	Source	Date Signed	Seasons Played	Apps	Subs	Gls
Bolton W	Eccleshall MW	04/48	49-54	6	-	0
Sheffield Wed	Tr	05/55	55-57	38	-	0
Swindon T	Tr	01/58	57-59	101	-	0
York C	Tr	08/60	60-62	130	-	5
Halifax T	Tr	07/63	63-64	64	-	1

BINKS Martin John
Born: Romford, E London, England, 15 September, 1953 — CD

League Club	Source	Date Signed	Seasons Played	Apps	Subs	Gls
Colchester U	Leyton Orient (App)	05/72	72	10	0	0
Cambridge U	Tr	01/73	72	1	0	0

BINNEY Frederick Edward (Fred)
Born: Plymouth, England, 12 August, 1946 — F

League Club	Source	Date Signed	Seasons Played	Apps	Subs	Gls
Torquay U	Launceston	10/66	67-68	5	7	1
Exeter C	L	02/69	68	17	0	11
Torquay U	Tr	08/69	69	19	3	10
Exeter C	Tr	03/70	69-73	160	0	79
Brighton & HA	Tr	05/74	74-76	68	2	35
Plymouth Arg	St Louis AS (USA)	10/77	77-79	67	4	39
Hereford U	Tr	01/80	79-81	21	6	6

BINNIE Lawrence (Laurie)
Born: Falkirk, Scotland, 17 December, 1917 — WH
Died: Falkirk, Scotland, 20 February, 1991

League Club	Source	Date Signed	Seasons Played	Apps	Subs	Gls
Chesterfield	Camelon Jnrs	05/39				
Mansfield T	Tr	11/46	46	20	-	0

BINNOM-WILLIAMS Jerome Craig
Born: Croydon, S London, England, 7 March, 1995 — D
England: Youth

League Club	Source	Date Signed	Seasons Played	Apps	Subs	Gls
Crystal Palace	Sch	07/13				
Southend U	L	09/14	14	18	3	0

BINNS Eric
Born: Halifax, West Yorkshire, England, 13 August, 1924 — CH
Died: Burnley, Lancashire, England, 20 September, 2007

League Club	Source	Date Signed	Seasons Played	Apps	Subs	Gls
Halifax T	Huddersfield T (Am)	05/46	46	6	-	1
Burnley	Goole T	03/49	52-54	15	-	0
Blackburn Rov	Tr	05/55	55-56	23	-	0

BIRBECK Joseph (Joe)
Born: Stanley, County Durham, England, 15 April, 1932 — LH

League Club	Source	Date Signed	Seasons Played	Apps	Subs	Gls
Middlesbrough	Evenwood T	04/53	53-58	38	-	0
Grimsby T	Tr	07/59	59	18	-	0

BIRCH Alan
Born: West Bromwich, West Midlands, England, 12 August, 1956 — RW

League Club	Source	Date Signed	Seasons Played	Apps	Subs	Gls
Walsall	App	08/73	72-78	158	13	23

League Club	Source	Date Signed	Seasons Played	Apps	Subs	Gls
Chesterfield	Tr	07/79	79-80	90	0	35
Wolverhampton W	Tr	08/81	81	13	2	0
Barnsley	Tr	02/82	81-82	43	1	10
Chesterfield	Tr	08/83	83	30	2	5
Rotherham U	Tr	03/84	83-85	99	2	28
Scunthorpe U	Tr	06/86	86-87	19	4	2
Stockport Co	Tr	10/87	87	18	2	3

BIRCH Brian
Born: Southport, Merseyside, England, 9 April, 1938 RW
England: Youth/Schools

League Club	Source	Date Signed	Seasons Played	Apps	Subs	Gls
Bolton W	Jnr	04/55	54-63	165	-	23
Rochdale	Tr	07/64	64-65	60	1	6

BIRCH Brian
Born: Salford, England, 18 November, 1931 IF
England: Youth

League Club	Source	Date Signed	Seasons Played	Apps	Subs	Gls
Manchester U	Jnr	05/49	49-51	11	-	4
Wolverhampton W	Tr	03/52	51	3	-	1
Lincoln C	Tr	12/52	52-54	56	-	16
Barrow	Boston U	06/56	56-58	60	-	27
Exeter C	Tr	09/58	58-59	19	-	1
Oldham Ath	Tr	01/60	59-60	35	-	11
Rochdale	Tr	03/61	60-61	11	-	0

BIRCH Clifford (Cliff)
Born: Newbridge, Caerphilly, Wales, 1 September, 1928 RW
Died: Norwich, England, 28 February, 1990
Wales: WLge-2

League Club	Source	Date Signed	Seasons Played	Apps	Subs	Gls
Norwich C	Ebbw Vale	12/46	49	5	-	3
Newport Co	Tr	10/50	50-53	143	-	28
Colchester U	Tr	06/54	54	12	-	3

BIRCH Gary Stephen
Born: Birmingham, England, 8 October, 1981 F

League Club	Source	Date Signed	Seasons Played	Apps	Subs	Gls
Walsall	YT	10/98	01-04	42	26	7
Exeter C	L	03/01	00	6	3	2
Exeter C	L	08/01	01	5	10	0
Barnsley	L	03/04	03	8	0	2
Kidderminster Hrs	Tr	12/04	04	11	3	4
Lincoln C	Tr	08/05	05	23	14	8

BIRCH Harold Kelvin (Harry)
Born: Crieff, Perthshire, Scotland, 11 January, 1914 RH
Died: Barrow, Cumbria, England, July, 1985

League Club	Source	Date Signed	Seasons Played	Apps	Subs	Gls
Barrow	Bangor	09/45	46	26	-	2

BIRCH James Victor Tomlinson (Jim)
Born: Ashover, Derbyshire, England, 25 October, 1927 IF
Died: Leeds, England, May, 2012

League Club	Source	Date Signed	Seasons Played	Apps	Subs	Gls
Huddersfield T	Grenoside	05/45				
Halifax T		08/48	48	3	-	1

BIRCH James Walter (Walter)
Born: Ecclesfield, South Yorkshire, England, 5 October, 1917 CH
Died: Rochdale, Greater Manchester, England, 3 June, 1991

League Club	Source	Date Signed	Seasons Played	Apps	Subs	Gls
Huddersfield T		05/39				
Rochdale	Tr	03/46	46-52	243	-	10

BIRCH Jeffrey (Jeff)
Born: Sheffield, England, 21 October, 1927 LW
Died: Sheffield, England, June, 2005

League Club	Source	Date Signed	Seasons Played	Apps	Subs	Gls
Sheffield U	Selby T	09/47				
York C	Scarborough	10/49	49	7	-	1

BIRCH Kenneth Joseph (Ken)
Born: Birkenhead, Wirral, England, 31 December, 1933 RH
Died: 24 January, 2015

League Club	Source	Date Signed	Seasons Played	Apps	Subs	Gls
Everton	Jnr	08/51	55-57	43	-	1
Southampton	Tr	03/58	57-58	34	-	3

BIRCH Mark
Born: Stoke-on-Trent, England, 5 January, 1977 RB

League Club	Source	Date Signed	Seasons Played	Apps	Subs	Gls
Stoke C	YT	07/95				
Carlisle U	Northwich Victoria	08/00	00-03	109	3	1

BIRCH Paul
Born: West Bromwich, West Midlands, England, 20 November, 1962 M
Died: Sutton Coldfield, West Midlands, England, 2 February, 2009

League Club	Source	Date Signed	Seasons Played	Apps	Subs	Gls
Aston Villa	App	07/80	83-90	153	20	16
Wolverhampton W	Tr	02/91	90-95	128	14	15
Preston NE	L	03/96	95	11	0	2
Doncaster Rov	Tr	06/96	96	26	1	2
Exeter C	Tr	03/97	96-97	33	2	5

BIRCH Paul Anthony
Born: Reading, England, 3 December, 1968 F

League Club	Source	Date Signed	Seasons Played	Apps	Subs	Gls
Portsmouth	Arsenal (App)	01/87				
Brentford	Tr	12/87	87-88	13	5	2

BIRCH Trevor
Born: West Bromwich, West Midlands, England, 20 November, 1933 RH
Died: Staffordshire, England, May, 2013

League Club	Source	Date Signed	Seasons Played	Apps	Subs	Gls
Aston Villa	Accles & Pollock	01/52	54-59	22	-	0
Stockport Co	Tr	11/60	60-61	43	-	0

BIRCH Trevor Nigel
Born: Ormskirk, Lancashire, England, 16 February, 1958 M

League Club	Source	Date Signed	Seasons Played	Apps	Subs	Gls
Liverpool	App	12/75				
Shrewsbury T	Tr	03/79	78-79	23	2	4
Chester C	Tr	07/80	80	30	1	0

BIRCH William (Billy)
Born: Southport, Merseyside, England, 20 October, 1944 F

League Club	Source	Date Signed	Seasons Played	Apps	Subs	Gls
West Bromwich A	App	10/62				
Crystal Palace	Tr	06/63	63-64	6	-	0

BIRCHALL Adam Stephen
Born: Maidstone, Kent, England, 2 December, 1984 F
Wales: U21-12

League Club	Source	Date Signed	Seasons Played	Apps	Subs	Gls
Arsenal	Sch	07/02				
Wycombe W	L	08/04	04	11	1	4
Mansfield T	Tr	08/05	05-06	16	20	2
Barnet	Tr	11/06	06-08	77	27	19
Gillingham	Dover Ath	07/11	12-13	7	10	0

BIRCHALL Christopher (Chris)
Born: Stafford, England, 5 May, 1984 RM
Trinidad & Tobago: 43

League Club	Source	Date Signed	Seasons Played	Apps	Subs	Gls
Port Vale	Sch	05/04	01-05	53	25	7
Coventry C	Tr	08/06	06-07	18	11	2
Carlisle U	L	11/08	08	0	2	0
Brighton & HA	Tr	01/09	09	8	1	0
Port Vale	Columbus Crew (USA)	01/13	12-14	31	34	5

BIRCHALL Paul William
Born: Liverpool, England, 3 September, 1957 M

League Club	Source	Date Signed	Seasons Played	Apps	Subs	Gls
Southport	Everton (Am)	03/77	76-77	16	3	1

BIRCHAM Bernard (Barney)
Born: Newbottle, Tyne and Wear, England, 31 August, 1924 G
Died: Grimsby, North Lincolnshire, England, 17 October, 2007

League Club	Source	Date Signed	Seasons Played	Apps	Subs	Gls
Sunderland	Jnr	07/43				
Chesterfield	Tr	11/46				
Grimsby T	Tr	06/48	49	8	-	0
Colchester U	Tr	07/50	50	7	-	0

BIRCHAM Marc Stephen John
Born: Wembley, NW London, England, 11 May, 1978 M
Canada: 17/U23-1

League Club	Source	Date Signed	Seasons Played	Apps	Subs	Gls
Millwall	YT	05/96	96-01	86	18	3
Queens Park Rgrs	Tr	07/02	02-06	138	14	7
Yeovil T	Tr	07/07	07-08	12	4	0

BIRCHAM Walter Clive (Clive)
Born: Herrington, Tyne and Wear, England, 7 September, 1939 RW

League Club	Source	Date Signed	Seasons Played	Apps	Subs	Gls
Sunderland	Shiney Row Swifts	09/56	58-59	28	-	2
Hartlepool U	Tr	02/60	59-62	105	-	15

BIRCHENALL Alan John
Born: East Ham, E London, England, 22 August, 1945 M
England: U23-4

League Club	Source	Date Signed	Seasons Played	Apps	Subs	Gls
Sheffield U	Thorneywood Thistle	06/63	64-67	106	1	31
Chelsea Tr		11/67	67-69	74	1	20
Crystal Palace	Tr	06/70	70-71	41	0	11
Leicester C	Tr	09/71	71-76	156	7	12
Notts Co	L	03/76	75	5	0	0
Notts Co	San Jose E'quake (USA)	09/77	77	28	0	0
Blackburn Rov	Memphis Rogues (USA)	07/78	78	17	1	0
Luton T	Tr	03/79	78-79	9	1	0
Hereford U	Tr	10/79	79	11	0	0

BIRCUMSHAW Anthony (Tony)
Born: Mansfield, Nottinghamshire, England, 8 February, 1945 RB

League Club	Source	Date Signed	Seasons Played	Apps	Subs	Gls
Notts Co	App	02/62	60-65	148	0	1
Hartlepool U	Tr	07/66	66-70	182	3	11

BIRCUMSHAW Peter Brian
Born: Mansfield, Nottinghamshire, England, 29 August, 1938 LW

League Club	Source	Date Signed	Seasons Played	Apps	Subs	Gls
Notts Co	Jnr	07/56	56-61	72	-	40
Bradford C	Tr	06/62	62	27	-	7
Stockport Co	Tr	06/63	63	17	-	4

BIRD Adrian Lee
Born: Bristol, England, 8 July, 1969 CD

League Club	Source	Date Signed	Seasons Played	Apps	Subs	Gls
Birmingham C	YT	07/87	86-88	23	4	0

BIRD Anthony (Tony)
Born: Cardiff, Wales, 1 September, 1974 F

Wales: U21-8/Youth

League Club	Source	Date Signed	Seasons Played	Apps	Subs	Gls
Cardiff C	YT	08/93	92-95	44	31	13
Swansea C	Barry T	08/97	97-99	51	35	18
Kidderminster Hrs	Tr	07/00	00-01	30	21	3

BIRD David Alan
Born: Cinderford, Gloucestershire, England, 26 December, 1984 M/RB

League Club	Source	Date Signed	Seasons Played	Apps	Subs	Gls
Cheltenham T	Cinderford T	02/01	02-10	232	56	8

BIRD Francis John (Johnny)
Born: Cardiff, Wales, 21 November, 1940 RB
Wales: Schools

League Club	Source	Date Signed	Seasons Played	Apps	Subs	Gls
Newport Co	Jnr	11/57	57-66	277	0	4
Swansea C	Tr	07/67	67	8	0	0

BIRD John Charles
Born: Doncaster, South Yorkshire, England, 9 June, 1948 CD

League Club	Source	Date Signed	Seasons Played	Apps	Subs	Gls
Doncaster Rov	Doncaster U	03/67	67-70	48	2	3
Preston NE	Tr	03/71	70-75	166	0	9
Newcastle U	Tr	08/75	75-79	84	3	5
Hartlepool U	Tr	07/80	80-84	139	2	16

BIRD Kenneth Benjamin (Ken)
Born: Norwich, England, 25 September, 1918 G
Died: Poole, Dorset, England, October, 1987
England: Schools

League Club	Source	Date Signed	Seasons Played	Apps	Subs	Gls
Wolverhampton W	Willenhall Rov	05/37				
Bournemouth	Tr	10/38	38-52	249	-	0

BIRD Kevin
Born: Doncaster, South Yorkshire, England, 7 August, 1952 CD

League Club	Source	Date Signed	Seasons Played	Apps	Subs	Gls
Mansfield T	Doncaster Rov (Am)	07/72	72-82	372	5	55
Huddersfield T	Tr	08/83	83	1	0	0

BIRD Matthew Louis
Born: Grimsby, North Lincolnshire, England, 31 October, 1990 CD

League Club	Source	Date Signed	Seasons Played	Apps	Subs	Gls
Grimsby T	Sch	03/08	07	0	2	0

BIRD Ronald Philip (Ronnie)
Born: Birmingham, England, 27 December, 1941 LW
Died: Cardiff, Wales, 14 March, 2005
England: Youth

League Club	Source	Date Signed	Seasons Played	Apps	Subs	Gls
Birmingham C	Jnr	01/59				
Bradford Park Ave	Tr	06/61	61-65	129	0	39
Bury	Tr	10/65	65	13	0	3
Cardiff C	Tr	02/66	65-70	97	11	25
Crewe Alex	Tr	07/71	71	19	1	0

BIRD Ryan
Born: Slough, Berkshire, England, 15 November, 1987 F

League Club	Source	Date Signed	Seasons Played	Apps	Subs	Gls
Portsmouth	Burnham	07/13	13-14	5	15	3
Cambridge U	Tr	09/14	14	10	14	6
Hartlepool U	L	02/15	14	6	0	2

BIRKBECK John David
Born: Lincoln, England, 1 October, 1932 CF
Died: Australia, 29 February, 2004

League Club	Source	Date Signed	Seasons Played	Apps	Subs	Gls
Lincoln C	Spilsby	01/52	54	2	-	0

BIRKETT Clifford (Cliff)
Born: Haydock, Merseyside, England, 17 September, 1933 CF
Died: Haydock, Merseyside, England, 11 January, 1997
England: Schools

League Club	Source	Date Signed	Seasons Played	Apps	Subs	Gls
Manchester U	Jnr	10/50	50	9	-	2
Southport	Tr	06/56	56	14	-	4

BIRKETT Ronald (Ronnie)
Born: Warrington, Cheshire, England, 21 July, 1927 LW
Died: Salford, England, December, 1992

League Club	Source	Date Signed	Seasons Played	Apps	Subs	Gls
Manchester C	Crompton's Rec	01/46				
New Brighton	Tr	01/47	46-47	8	-	0
Oldham Ath	Tr	08/48	48	4	-	0
Accrington Stan	Tr	07/49	49	14	-	2

BIRKETT Wilfred (Wilf)
Born: Haydock, Merseyside, England, 26 June, 1922 G
Died: Haydock, Merseyside, England, 24 December, 1993

League Club	Source	Date Signed	Seasons Played	Apps	Subs	Gls
Everton	Haydock C&B	02/44				
Southport	Tr	11/46	46-51	162	-	0
Shrewsbury T	Tr	07/52	52	20	-	0
Southport	Tr	07/53	53	15	-	0

BIRKS Graham
Born: Sheffield, England, 25 January, 1942 LB

League Club	Source	Date Signed	Seasons Played	Apps	Subs	Gls
Sheffield Wed	Jnr	01/60	62	4	-	0
Peterborough U	Tr	05/64	64-65	34	0	0
Southend U	Tr	01/66	65-69	139	1	1
Chester C	Tr	10/69	69-71	71	2	0

BIRLEY Matthew Mark (Matt)
Born: Bromsgrove, Worcestershire, England, 26 July, 1986 M

League Club	Source	Date Signed	Seasons Played	Apps	Subs	Gls
Birmingham C	Sch	07/05	05	0	1	0
Lincoln C	L	11/06	06	3	1	0

BIRMINGHAM Charles Henry
Born: Liverpool, England, 24 August, 1922 IF
Died: Wallasey, Wirral, England, 1 January, 1993

League Club	Source	Date Signed	Seasons Played	Apps	Subs	Gls
Tranmere Rov	Everton (Am)	08/46	46	2	-	1

BIRMINGHAM David Paul
Born: Portsmouth, England, 16 April, 1981 FB

League Club	Source	Date Signed	Seasons Played	Apps	Subs	Gls
Portsmouth	Bournemouth (YT)	08/99	99	1	1	0
Bournemouth	Bognor Regis T	03/01	01	3	1	0

BIRSE Charles Duncan Valentine (Charlie)
Born: Dundee, Scotland, 26 October, 1916 WH
Died: Dundee, Scotland, 31 October, 1995

League Club	Source	Date Signed	Seasons Played	Apps	Subs	Gls
Watford	Hibernian	05/46	46	7	-	0
Northampton T	Tr	07/47				

BIRTLES Garry
Born: Nottingham, England, 27 July, 1956 F
England: 3/B-1/U21-2

League Club	Source	Date Signed	Seasons Played	Apps	Subs	Gls
Nottingham F	Long Eaton U	12/76	76-80	87	0	32
Manchester U	Tr	10/80	80-81	57	1	11
Nottingham F	Tr	09/82	82-86	122	3	38
Notts Co	Tr	06/87	87-88	62	1	9
Grimsby T	Tr	07/89	89-91	54	15	9

BISCAN Igor
Born: Zagreb, Croatia, 4 May, 1978 M
Croatia: 15/U21-15/Youth

League Club	Source	Date Signed	Seasons Played	Apps	Subs	Gls
Liverpool	Dinamo Zagreb (CRO)	12/00	00-04	50	22	2

BISCHOFF Amaury Armindo
Born: Colmar, France, 31 March, 1987 W
Portugal: U21-1

League Club	Source	Date Signed	Seasons Played	Apps	Subs	Gls
Arsenal	Werder Bremen (GER)	08/08	08	0	1	0

BISCHOFF Mikkel Rufus Mutahi
Born: Copenhagen, Denmark, 3 February, 1982 CD
Denmark: U21-4/Youth

League Club	Source	Date Signed	Seasons Played	Apps	Subs	Gls
Manchester C	AB Copenhagen (DEN)	07/02	02	1	0	0
Wolverhampton W	L	09/04	04	7	0	1
Wolverhampton W	L	03/05	04	2	2	0
Sheffield Wed	L	03/06	05	4	0	0
Coventry C	Tr	07/06	06	2	1	0

BISGAARD Morten
Born: Randers, Denmark, 25 June, 1974 M
Denmark: 8/U21-8/Youth

League Club	Source	Date Signed	Seasons Played	Apps	Subs	Gls
Derby Co	FC Copenhagen (DEN)	06/04	04-06	73	28	10

BISHOP Andrew Jamie (Andy)
Born: Cannock, Staffordshire, England, 19 October, 1982 F
England: Semi Pro-4

League Club	Source	Date Signed	Seasons Played	Apps	Subs	Gls
Walsall	Sch	08/02				
Kidderminster Hrs	L	11/02	02	22	7	5
Kidderminster Hrs	L	08/03	03	8	3	2
Rochdale	L	11/03	03	8	2	1
Yeovil T	L	02/04	03	4	1	2
Bury	York C	06/06	06-12	197	40	69

BISHOP Charles Darren (Charlie)
Born: Nottingham, England, 16 February, 1968 D

League Club	Source	Date Signed	Seasons Played	Apps	Subs	Gls
Watford	Stoke C (App)	04/86				
Bury	Tr	08/87	87-90	104	10	6
Barnsley	Tr	07/91	91-95	124	6	1
Preston NE	L	01/96	95	4	0	0
Burnley	L	03/96	95	9	0	0
Wigan Ath	Tr	06/96	96-97	27	1	0
Northampton T	Tr	12/97	97-98	11	0	0

BISHOP Colby David
Born: Nottingham, England, 4 November, 1996 F

League Club	Source	Date Signed	Seasons Played	Apps	Subs	Gls
Notts Co	Sch	11/14	14	2	1	0

BISHOP Edward James (Teddy)
Born: Cambridge, England, 15 July, 1996 M

League Club	Source	Date Signed	Seasons Played	Apps	Subs	Gls
Ipswich T	Sch	07/14	14	23	10	1

BISHOP Edward Michael (Eddie)
Born: Liverpool, England, 28 November, 1962 M

League Club	Source	Date Signed	Seasons Played	Apps	Subs	Gls
Tranmere Rov	Runcorn	03/88	87-90	46	30	19
Chester C	Tr	12/90	90-95	97	18	28
Crewe Alex	L	03/92	91	3	0	0

BISHOP Ian William
Born: Liverpool, England, 29 May, 1965 M

England: B-1

League Club	Source	Date Signed	Seasons Played	Apps	Subs	Gls
Everton	App	05/83	83	0	1	0
Crewe Alex	L	03/84	83	4	0	0
Carlisle U	Tr	10/84	84-87	131	1	14
Bournemouth	Tr	07/88	88	44	0	2
Manchester C	Tr	08/89	89	18	1	2
West Ham U	Tr	12/89	89-97	240	14	12
Manchester C	Tr	03/98	97-00	53	25	2
Rochdale	Barry T	08/02	02	5	3	0

BISHOP Neal Robert
Born: Stockton-on-Tees, Cleveland, England, 7 August, 1981 — DM
England: Semi Pro-2

League Club	Source	Date Signed	Seasons Played	Apps	Subs	Gls
Barnet	York C	07/07	07-08	80	3	3
Notts Co	Tr	07/09	09-12	162	6	11
Blackpool	Tr	08/13	13	29	6	1
Scunthorpe U	Tr	06/14	14	34	1	4

BISHOP Peter Jason
Born: Sheffield, England, 4 January, 1944 — LW
England: Youth

League Club	Source	Date Signed	Seasons Played	Apps	Subs	Gls
Sheffield U	Jnr	04/63				
Chesterfield	Tr	05/65	65-70	78	3	7

BISHOP Raymond John (Ray)
Born: Hengoed, Caerphilly, Wales, 24 November, 1955 — F

League Club	Source	Date Signed	Seasons Played	Apps	Subs	Gls
Cardiff C	Cheltenham T	01/77	77-80	92	9	26
Newport Co	Tr	02/81	80-81	8	10	2
Torquay U	Tr	08/82	82-83	33	7	8

BISHOP Sidney Harold Richard (Sid)
Born: Tooting, SW London, England, 8 April, 1934 — CH

League Club	Source	Date Signed	Seasons Played	Apps	Subs	Gls
Leyton Orient	Chase of Chertsey	06/52	53-64	296	-	4

BISHTON Dennis Roy
Born: Windsor, Berkshire, England, 22 September, 1950 — RB

League Club	Source	Date Signed	Seasons Played	Apps	Subs	Gls
Reading	App	09/68	68	2	0	0

BISSELL Steven John (Steve)
Born: Coleshill, Warwickshire, England, 8 October, 1958 — W

League Club	Source	Date Signed	Seasons Played	Apps	Subs	Gls
Nottingham F	App	10/76				
Blackpool	Tr	09/78	78	1	0	0

BISSET Thomas Alexander (Tommy)
Born: Croydon, S London, England, 21 March, 1932 — FB

League Club	Source	Date Signed	Seasons Played	Apps	Subs	Gls
Brighton & HA	Redhill	01/53	52-60	115	-	5

BISSETT Nicholas (Nicky)
Born: Fulham, W London, England, 5 April, 1964 — CD

League Club	Source	Date Signed	Seasons Played	Apps	Subs	Gls
Brighton & HA	Barnet	09/88	88-94	94	3	8

BITHELL Brian
Born: Winsford, Cheshire, England, 5 October, 1956 — D/M

League Club	Source	Date Signed	Seasons Played	Apps	Subs	Gls
Stoke C	App	10/73	76	16	1	0
Port Vale	L	09/77	77	2	0	0
Wimbledon	Tr	12/77	77	6	0	0

BITTNER James Mark
Born: Devizes, Wiltshire, England, 2 February, 1982 — G
England: Semi Pro-2

League Club	Source	Date Signed	Seasons Played	Apps	Subs	Gls
Fulham	Swindon T (YT)	07/00				
Torquay U	Exeter C	07/05				
Newport Co	Hereford U	07/13				
Plymouth Arg	Salisbury C	07/14	14	0	1	0

BJORKLUND Joachim
Born: Vaxjo, Sweden, 15 March, 1971 — CD
Sweden: 78

League Club	Source	Date Signed	Seasons Played	Apps	Subs	Gls
Sunderland	Venezia (ITA)	02/02	01-03	49	8	0
Wolverhampton W	Tr	08/04	04	2	1	0

BJORNEBYE Stig Inge
Born: Elverum, Norway, 11 December, 1969 — LB
Norway: 76/B-1/U21/Youth

League Club	Source	Date Signed	Seasons Played	Apps	Subs	Gls
Liverpool	Rosenborg (NOR)	12/92	92-98	132	7	2
Blackburn Rov	Tr	06/00	00-01	53	3	1

BJORNSSON Armann Smari
Born: Hornafjordur, Iceland, 7 January, 1981 — CD/F
Iceland: 6/U21-7/Youth

League Club	Source	Date Signed	Seasons Played	Apps	Subs	Gls
Hartlepool U	SK Brann Bergen (NOR)	09/09	09-10	13	23	3

BLACK Adam James
Born: Liverpool, England, 24 May, 1992 — F

League Club	Source	Date Signed	Seasons Played	Apps	Subs	Gls
Accrington Stan	Sch	-	09	0	1	0

BLACK Alan Douglas
Born: Alexandria, Dunbartonshire, Scotland, 4 June, 1943 — LB

League Club	Source	Date Signed	Seasons Played	Apps	Subs	Gls
Sunderland	Dumbarton	08/64	64-65	4	2	0
Norwich C	Tr	09/66	66-73	172	4	1

BLACK Andrew (Andy)
Born: Stirling, Scotland, 23 September, 1917 — IF
Died: Bannockburn, Stirlingshire, Scotland, 16 February, 1989
Scotland: 3/SLge-2/War-4

League Club	Source	Date Signed	Seasons Played	Apps	Subs	Gls
Manchester C	Heart of Midlothian	06/46	46-49	139	-	47
Stockport Co	Tr	08/50	50-52	94	-	38

BLACK Anthony Paul (Tony)
Born: Barrow, Cumbria, England, 15 July, 1969 — RW

League Club	Source	Date Signed	Seasons Played	Apps	Subs	Gls
Wigan Ath	Bamber Bridge	03/95	94-97	17	14	2

BLACK Christopher David (Chris)
Born: Ashington, Northumberland, England, 7 September, 1982 — M

League Club	Source	Date Signed	Seasons Played	Apps	Subs	Gls
Sunderland	YT	08/00	02-03	2	1	0
Doncaster Rov	Tr	03/04	03	1	0	0

BLACK Ian Henderson
Born: Aberdeen, Scotland, 27 March, 1924 — G
Died: Kingston-on-Thames, SW London, England, 13 December, 2012
Scotland: 1

League Club	Source	Date Signed	Seasons Played	Apps	Subs	Gls
Southampton	Aberdeen	12/47	47-49	97	-	0
Fulham	Tr	08/50	50-57	263	-	1

BLACK John
Born: Blackburn, Greater Manchester, England, 4 November, 1945 — G
Wales: Schools

League Club	Source	Date Signed	Seasons Played	Apps	Subs	Gls
Arsenal	App	02/63				
Swansea C	Tr	12/64	64-65	15	0	0

BLACK John
Born: Helensburgh, Argyll & Bute, Scotland, 10 November, 1957 — M

League Club	Source	Date Signed	Seasons Played	Apps	Subs	Gls
Wolverhampton W	App	12/75	77-78	5	1	0
Bradford C	L	01/80	79	6	0	4
Bradford C	Tr	11/80	80-82	44	5	9
Hereford U	Tr	08/83	83	8	1	0

BLACK Kenneth George (Kenny)
Born: Stenhousemuir, Falkirk, Scotland, 29 November, 1963 — M
Scotland: Youth/Schools

League Club	Source	Date Signed	Seasons Played	Apps	Subs	Gls
Portsmouth	Heart of Midlothian	07/89	89-90	50	12	3

BLACK Kingsley Terence
Born: Luton, England, 22 June, 1968 — LW
England: Schools//Northern Ireland: 30/B-3/U21-1

League Club	Source	Date Signed	Seasons Played	Apps	Subs	Gls
Luton T	Jnr	07/86	87-91	123	4	26
Nottingham F	Tr	09/91	91-95	80	18	14
Sheffield U	L	03/95	94	8	3	2
Millwall	L	09/95	95	1	2	1
Grimsby T	Tr	07/96	96-00	91	50	8
Lincoln C	L	10/00	00	5	0	0
Lincoln C	Tr	07/01	01-02	30	2	5

BLACK Michael James
Born: Chigwell, Essex, England, 6 October, 1976 — M
England: Schools

League Club	Source	Date Signed	Seasons Played	Apps	Subs	Gls
Arsenal	YT	07/95				
Millwall	L	10/97	97	13	0	2
Tranmere Rov	Tr	07/99	99	7	15	0
Southend U	Tr	12/00	00	10	5	1

BLACK Neville
Born: Pegswood, Northumberland, England, 19 June, 1931 — IF
Died: Northumberland, England, August, 2004

League Club	Source	Date Signed	Seasons Played	Apps	Subs	Gls
Newcastle U	Pegswood	09/49				
Exeter C	Tr	01/53	52	4	-	0
Rochdale	Tr	07/53	53-55	62	-	13

BLACK Paul Michael
Born: Middleton, Greater Manchester, England, 18 May, 1990 — LB

League Club	Source	Date Signed	Seasons Played	Apps	Subs	Gls
Oldham Ath	Sch	01/08	07-11	55	5	1
Tranmere Rov	Tr	07/12	12	2	8	0
Mansfield T	Tr	07/13				
Carlisle U	L	09/13	13	3	1	0
Cheltenham T	Tr	06/14	14	3	0	0

BLACK Russell Palmer
Born: Dumfries, Scotland, 29 July, 1960 — F

League Club	Source	Date Signed	Seasons Played	Apps	Subs	Gls
Sheffield U	Gretna	08/84	84-85	10	4	0
Halifax T	Dundee	08/86	86-87	63	9	14

BLACK Simon Anthony
Born: Marston Green, West Midlands, England, 9 November, 1975 — F

League Club	Source	Date Signed	Seasons Played	Apps	Subs	Gls
Birmingham C	YT	06/94	93	2	0	0

BLACK Thomas Robert (Tommy)
Born: Chigwell, Essex, England, 26 November, 1979 — W

League Club	Source	Date Signed	Seasons Played	Apps	Subs	Gls
Arsenal	YT	07/98	99	0	1	0
Carlisle U	L	08/99	99	5	0	1
Bristol C	L	12/99	99	4	0	0
Crystal Palace	Tr	07/00	00-05	67	60	10

League Club	Source	Date Signed	Seasons Played	Apps	Subs	Gls
Sheffield U	L	09/04	04	3	1	1
Gillingham	L	01/06	05	17	0	5
Bradford C	L	11/06	06	4	0	0
Southend U	Tr	07/07	07	29	9	2
Barnet	Stevenage Bor	01/09	08	5	0	0

BLACKADDER Frederick (Fred)
Born: Carlisle, Cumbria, England, 13 January, 1916 — CD
Died: Carlisle, Cumbria, England, November, 1992

League Club	Source	Date Signed	Seasons Played	Apps	Subs	Gls
Carlisle U (Am)	Penrith	05/37	37	2	-	0
Carlisle U (Am)	Blackhall CW	05/46	46	1	-	0

BLACKBURN Allan
Born: Pleasley, Derbyshire, England, 4 August, 1935 — CF/LW
Died: Telford, England, 14 January, 2014

League Club	Source	Date Signed	Seasons Played	Apps	Subs	Gls
West Ham U	Jnr	08/53	54-57	15	-	3
Halifax T	Tr	11/57	57-60	124	-	34

BLACKBURN Christopher Raymond (Chris)
Born: Crewe, Cheshire, England, 2 August, 1982 — CD
England: Semi Pro-4

League Club	Source	Date Signed	Seasons Played	Apps	Subs	Gls
Accrington Stan	YT	-	99	0	1	0
Swindon T	Morecambe	07/07	07	4	3	0
Aldershot T	Tr	06/08	08-09	72	6	0

BLACKBURN Colin
Born: Thirsk, North Yorkshire, England, 16 January, 1961 — W

League Club	Source	Date Signed	Seasons Played	Apps	Subs	Gls
Middlesbrough	Jnr	12/79	80	1	0	0

BLACKBURN Derrick John
Born: Ryhill, West Yorkshire, England, 5 July, 1931 — CH

League Club	Source	Date Signed	Seasons Played	Apps	Subs	Gls
Burnley		06/53				
Chesterfield	Tr	06/54				
Swansea C	Ossett T	01/57	57	2	-	0

BLACKBURN Edwin Huitson (Eddie)
Born: Houghton-le-Spring, Tyne and Wear, England, 18 April, 1957 — G

League Club	Source	Date Signed	Seasons Played	Apps	Subs	Gls
Hull C	App	09/74	74-79	68	0	0
York C	Tr	04/80	80-81	76	0	0
Hartlepool U	Tr	01/83	82-86	161	0	0

BLACKBURN Keith
Born: Manchester, England, 17 July, 1940 — IF
Died: Portsmouth, England, 4 February, 2014

League Club	Source	Date Signed	Seasons Played	Apps	Subs	Gls
Portsmouth	Bolton W (Am)	07/59	60-63	34	-	8

BLACKBURN Kenneth Alan (Ken)
Born: Wembley, NW London, England, 13 May, 1951 — F

League Club	Source	Date Signed	Seasons Played	Apps	Subs	Gls
Brighton & HA	App	05/69	68	1	0	1

BLACKBURN Lee Charles
Born: Hornchurch, E London, England, 1 October, 1985 — M

League Club	Source	Date Signed	Seasons Played	Apps	Subs	Gls
Cambridge U	Sch	02/05	04	0	3	0

BLACKER James Arthur (Jim)
Born: Leeds, England, 10 August, 1945 — CH

League Club	Source	Date Signed	Seasons Played	Apps	Subs	Gls
Bradford C	Middleton Parkside	01/63	63-64	21	-	0

BLACKETT Shane Jerome
Born: Luton, England, 26 June, 1981 — CD
England: Semi Pro-2

League Club	Source	Date Signed	Seasons Played	Apps	Subs	Gls
Peterborough U	Dagenham & Red	01/07	06-08	28	7	0

BLACKETT Tyler Nathan
Born: Manchester, England, 2 April, 1994 — CD
England: U21-1/Youth

League Club	Source	Date Signed	Seasons Played	Apps	Subs	Gls
Manchester U	Sch	07/12	14	6	5	0
Blackpool	L	10/13	13	5	0	0
Birmingham C	L	01/14	13	6	2	0

BLACKFORD Gary John
Born: Redhill, Surrey, England, 25 September, 1968 — RB

League Club	Source	Date Signed	Seasons Played	Apps	Subs	Gls
Barnet	Fisher Ath	07/91	91	2	4	0

BLACKHALL Mark Christopher
Born: Barking, E London, England, 17 November, 1960 — F

League Club	Source	Date Signed	Seasons Played	Apps	Subs	Gls
Leyton Orient	App	11/78	81-82	12	6	1

BLACKHALL Raymond (Ray)
Born: Ashington, Northumberland, England, 19 February, 1957 — RB

League Club	Source	Date Signed	Seasons Played	Apps	Subs	Gls
Newcastle U	App	08/74	74-77	25	12	0
Sheffield Wed	Tr	08/78	78-81	115	0	1
Mansfield T	IK Tord (SWE)	11/82	82	15	0	0
Carlisle U	Tr	08/84	84	1	0	0

BLACKHALL Sidney (Sid)
Born: Ashington, Northumberland, England, 25 September, 1945 — CF

League Club	Source	Date Signed	Seasons Played	Apps	Subs	Gls
Bradford Park Ave	App	10/62	63	1	-	0

BLACKLAW Adam Smith
Born: Aberdeen, Scotland, 2 September, 1937 — G
Died: Barnoldswick, Lancashire, England, 28 February, 2010
Scotland: 3/U23-2/Schools

League Club	Source	Date Signed	Seasons Played	Apps	Subs	Gls
Burnley	Jnr	10/54	56-66	318	0	0
Blackburn Rov	Tr	07/67	67-69	96	0	0
Blackpool	Tr	06/70	70	1	0	0

BLACKLER Martin John
Born: Swindon, England, 14 March, 1963 — M

League Club	Source	Date Signed	Seasons Played	Apps	Subs	Gls
Swindon T	App	03/81	82	8	1	0

BLACKLEY Arthur
Born: Carlisle, Cumbria, England, 31 January, 1939 — RW

League Club	Source	Date Signed	Seasons Played	Apps	Subs	Gls
Chelsea	Jnr	10/56				
Carlisle U	Tr	11/60	60-61	38	-	7

BLACKLEY John Henderson
Born: Falkirk, Scotland, 12 May, 1948 — CD
Scotland: 7/SLge-1/U23-4

League Club	Source	Date Signed	Seasons Played	Apps	Subs	Gls
Newcastle U	Hibernian	10/77	77-78	46	0	0
Preston NE	Tr	07/79	79-81	51	2	2

BLACKMAN Andre Alexandre George
Born: Lambeth, S London, England, 10 November, 1990 — LB

League Club	Source	Date Signed	Seasons Played	Apps	Subs	Gls
Bristol C	Portsmouth (Sch)	08/09				
Plymouth Arg	Glasgow Celtic	07/13	13	3	3	0
Blackpool	Maidenhead U	09/14	14	2	1	0

BLACKMAN Lloyd Jason
Born: Ashford, Surrey, England, 24 September, 1983 — F

League Club	Source	Date Signed	Seasons Played	Apps	Subs	Gls
Brentford	Sch	07/02	02-03	1	3	0

BLACKMAN Nicholas Alexander (Nick)
Born: Whitefield, Greater Manchester, England, 11 November, 1989 — F

League Club	Source	Date Signed	Seasons Played	Apps	Subs	Gls
Macclesfield T	Sch	02/07	06-07	1	11	1
Blackburn Rov	Tr	01/09	11	0	1	0
Blackpool	L	03/09	08	2	3	1
Oldham Ath	L	08/09	09	6	6	1
Sheffield U	Tr	08/12	12	28	0	11
Reading	Tr	01/13	12-14	28	50	7

BLACKMAN Ronald Henry (Ronnie)
Born: Portsmouth, England, 2 April, 1925 — CF

League Club	Source	Date Signed	Seasons Played	Apps	Subs	Gls
Reading	Gosport Bor	03/47	46-53	228	-	158
Nottingham F	Tr	06/54	54	11	-	3
Ipswich T	Tr	07/55	55-57	27	-	12

BLACKMORE Clayton Graham
Born: Neath, Wales, 23 September, 1964 — FB/M
Wales: 39/U21-3/Youth/Schools

League Club	Source	Date Signed	Seasons Played	Apps	Subs	Gls
Manchester U	App	09/82	83-92	150	36	19
Middlesbrough	Tr	07/94	94-97	45	8	4
Bristol C	L	11/96	96	5	0	1
Barnsley	Tr	02/99	98	4	3	0
Notts Co	Tr	07/99	99	21	0	2

BLACKSHAW William (Bill)
Born: Ashton-under-Lyne, Greater Manchester, England, 6 September, 1920 — W
Died: Ashton-under-Lyne, Greater Manchester, England, 17 June, 1994

League Club	Source	Date Signed	Seasons Played	Apps	Subs	Gls
Manchester C	Ashton National	05/38	38	3	-	0
Oldham Ath	Audenshaw U	07/46	46-48	67	-	22
Crystal Palace	Tr	07/49	49-50	32	-	5
Rochdale	Tr	02/51				

BLACKSTOCK Dexter Anthony Titus
Born: Oxford, England, 20 May, 1986 — F
Antigua & Barbuda: 4//England: U21-2/Youth

League Club	Source	Date Signed	Seasons Played	Apps	Subs	Gls
Southampton	Sch	05/04	04-05	15	13	4
Plymouth Arg	L	02/05	04	10	4	4
Derby Co	L	10/05	05	8	1	3
Queens Park Rgrs	Tr	08/06	06-08	89	21	30
Nottingham F	Tr	03/09	08-14	98	43	38
Leeds U	L	10/13	13	2	2	1

BLACKSTONE Ian Kenneth
Born: Harrogate, North Yorkshire, England, 7 August, 1964 — F

League Club	Source	Date Signed	Seasons Played	Apps	Subs	Gls
York C	Harrogate T	03/90	90-93	107	22	37
Scarborough	Tr	08/94	94	11	2	0

BLACKWELL Dean Robert
Born: Camden, N London, England, 5 December, 1969 — CD
England: U21-6

League Club	Source	Date Signed	Seasons Played	Apps	Subs	Gls
Wimbledon	YT	07/88	89-00	180	25	1
Plymouth Arg	L	03/90	89	5	2	0
Brighton & HA	Tr	10/02	02	18	3	2

BLACKWELL Kevin Patrick
Born: Luton, England, 21 December, 1958 — G

League Club	Source	Date Signed	Seasons Played	Apps	Subs	Gls
Scarborough	Barnet	11/86	87-89	44	0	0
Notts Co	Tr	11/89				
Torquay U	Tr	01/93	92	18	0	0

League Club	Source	Date Signed	Seasons Played	Apps	Subs	Gls
Huddersfield T	Tr	08/93	93-94	3	2	0
Plymouth Arg	Tr	08/95	95-96	24	0	0

BLACKWELL Paul
Born: Deeside, Flintshire, Wales, 13 January, 1963 — M

League Club	Source	Date Signed	Seasons Played	Apps	Subs	Gls
Chester C	Jnr	09/81	81-84	89	5	3

BLACKWELL Stephen Geoffrey
Born: Wolverhampton, England, 8 June, 1967 — F

League Club	Source	Date Signed	Seasons Played	Apps	Subs	Gls
Wolverhampton W	App	11/84	84	0	1	0

BLACKWELL Wilfred (Wilf)
Born: Maltby, South Yorkshire, England, 19 November, 1926 — W
Died: Sheffield, England, 1959

League Club	Source	Date Signed	Seasons Played	Apps	Subs	Gls
Portsmouth		10/47				
Mansfield T	Tr	08/48				
Aldershot	Tr	06/50	50	1	-	0

BLACKWOOD John Syme Duncan
Born: Cumnock, Ayrshire, Scotland, 25 January, 1935 — IF

League Club	Source	Date Signed	Seasons Played	Apps	Subs	Gls
Accrington Stan (Am)	Girvan Jnrs	10/58	58-59	4	-	1
York C	Tr	11/59				

BLACKWOOD Michael Andrew
Born: Birmingham, England, 30 September, 1979 — LW

League Club	Source	Date Signed	Seasons Played	Apps	Subs	Gls
Aston Villa	YT	04/98				
Chester C	L	09/99	99	9	0	2
Wrexham	Tr	07/00	00-01	24	22	2
Lincoln C	Telford U	07/04	04	5	4	0

BLACKWOOD Robert Rankin (Bobby)
Born: Edinburgh, Scotland, 20 August, 1934 — M
Died: Edinburgh, Scotland, 25 June, 1997
Scotland: SLge-1

League Club	Source	Date Signed	Seasons Played	Apps	Subs	Gls
Ipswich T	Heart of Midlothian	06/62	62-64	62	-	12
Colchester U	Tr	05/65	65-67	104	1	6

BLADES Paul Andrew
Born: Peterborough, England, 5 January, 1965 — D
England: Youth

League Club	Source	Date Signed	Seasons Played	Apps	Subs	Gls
Derby Co	App	12/82	82-89	157	9	1
Norwich C	Tr	07/90	90-91	47	0	0
Wolverhampton W	Tr	08/92	92-94	103	4	2
Rotherham U	Tr	07/95	95-96	43	0	2

BLAGG Edward Arthur (Ted)
Born: Shireoaks, Nottinghamshire, England, 9 February, 1918 — CH
Died: Sheffield, England, 28 October, 1976

League Club	Source	Date Signed	Seasons Played	Apps	Subs	Gls
Nottingham F	Woodend	02/38	46-47	54	-	0
Southport	Tr	11/48	48	11	-	0

BLAIKIE James Shearlaw (Jimmy)
Born: Staveley, Cumbria, England, 9 December, 1926 — LW
Died: Dunfermline, Fife, Scotland, 22 October, 2002

League Club	Source	Date Signed	Seasons Played	Apps	Subs	Gls
Barrow		08/50	50	9	-	1

BLAIN Colin Anthony
Born: Urmston, Greater Manchester, England, 7 March, 1970 — M

League Club	Source	Date Signed	Seasons Played	Apps	Subs	Gls
Halifax T	YT	06/88	87-88	18	5	0

BLAIN James Donald (Jimmy)
Born: Liverpool, England, 9 April, 1940 — LB/IF

League Club	Source	Date Signed	Seasons Played	Apps	Subs	Gls
Everton	Jnr	05/59				
Southport	Tr	02/60	59-62	127	-	40
Rotherham U	Tr	12/62	62-63	23	-	1
Carlisle U	Tr	04/64	64-65	41	0	7
Exeter C	Tr	10/65	65-73	310	10	14

BLAIR Andrew (Andy)
Born: Kirkcaldy, Fife, Scotland, 18 December, 1959 — M
Scotland: U21-5

League Club	Source	Date Signed	Seasons Played	Apps	Subs	Gls
Coventry C	App	10/77	78-80	90	3	6
Aston Villa	Tr	08/81	81-83	24	9	0
Wolverhampton W	L	10/83	83	10	0	0
Sheffield Wed	Tr	08/84	84-85	58	0	3
Aston Villa	Tr	03/86	85-87	19	1	1
Barnsley	L	03/88	87	6	0	0
Northampton T	Tr	10/88	88	1	2	0

BLAIR Douglas (Dougie)
Born: Ecclesfield, South Yorkshire, England, 26 June, 1921 — IF
Died: Chippenham, Wiltshire, England, July, 1998

League Club	Source	Date Signed	Seasons Played	Apps	Subs	Gls
Blackpool	Jnr	05/39				
Cardiff C	Tr	08/47	47-53	204	-	30

BLAIR James (Jim)
Born: Calderbank, Lanarkshire, Scotland, 13 January, 1947 — F
Died: Keebergen, Belgium, 6 April, 2011

League Club	Source	Date Signed	Seasons Played	Apps	Subs	Gls
Norwich C	St Mirren	09/72	72-73	3	3	0

BLAIR James Alfred (Jimmy)
Born: Partick, Glasgow, Scotland, 6 January, 1918 — IF
Died: Llanelli, Carmarthenshire, Wales, 1983
Scotland: 1

League Club	Source	Date Signed	Seasons Played	Apps	Subs	Gls
Blackpool	Cardiff C (Am)	06/35	37-46	50	-	8
Bournemouth	Tr	10/47	47-49	80	-	8
Leyton Orient	Tr	12/49	49-52	104	-	26

BLAIR Kenneth George (Kenny)
Born: Portadown, Armagh, Northern Ireland, 28 September, 1952 — M

League Club	Source	Date Signed	Seasons Played	Apps	Subs	Gls
Derby Co	Jnr	06/70				
Halifax T	Tr	10/74	74-75	42	1	4
Stockport Co	L	02/76	75	7	0	0
Southport	Tr	08/76	76	17	0	0

BLAIR Matthew James (Matty)
Born: Warwick, England, 21 June, 1989 — W
England: Semi Pro-2

League Club	Source	Date Signed	Seasons Played	Apps	Subs	Gls
York C	Kidderminster Hrs	06/11	12	35	9	6
Fleetwood T	Tr	05/13	13-14	16	16	3
Northampton T	L	01/14	13	3	0	1
Cambridge U	L	11/14	14	1	1	0
Mansfield T	Tr	01/15	14	2	1	0

BLAIR Ronald Victor (Ronnie)
Born: Coleraine, Derry, Northern Ireland, 26 September, 1949 — D/M
Northern Ireland: 5/Schools

League Club	Source	Date Signed	Seasons Played	Apps	Subs	Gls
Oldham Ath	Coleraine	10/66	66-69	74	3	1
Rochdale	Tr	03/70	69-71	65	5	3
Oldham Ath	Tr	08/72	72-80	285	10	21
Blackpool	Tr	08/81	81	35	1	3
Rochdale	Tr	08/82	82	3	0	0

BLAKE Anthony John (Tony)
Born: Cofton Hackett, Worcestershire, England, 26 February, 1927 — RB
Died: Worcester, England, November, 2014

League Club	Source	Date Signed	Seasons Played	Apps	Subs	Gls
Birmingham C	Rubery Owen	01/49	49	2	-	0
Gillingham	Tr	07/52	52	10	-	1

BLAKE Darcy James
Born: New Tredegar, Caerphilly, Wales, 13 December, 1988 — D
Wales: 14/U21-14/Youth

League Club	Source	Date Signed	Seasons Played	Apps	Subs	Gls
Cardiff C	Sch	10/06	05-11	48	42	0
Plymouth Arg	L	08/09	09	5	2	0
Crystal Palace	Tr	08/12	12	9	1	0
Newport Co	Tr	03/14	13	8	0	0

BLAKE Jack James
Born: Worksop, Nottinghamshire, England, 22 September, 1994 — M
Scotland: Youth

League Club	Source	Date Signed	Seasons Played	Apps	Subs	Gls
Nottingham F	Sch	05/12				
Mansfield T	L	10/13	13	3	0	0

BLAKE James Bernard (Jimmy)
Born: Manchester, England, 5 May, 1966 — RB

League Club	Source	Date Signed	Seasons Played	Apps	Subs	Gls
Rochdale	Jnr	09/83	83	2	0	0

BLAKE Mark Antony
Born: Nottingham, England, 16 December, 1970 — M
England: U21-9/Youth/Schools

League Club	Source	Date Signed	Seasons Played	Apps	Subs	Gls
Aston Villa	YT	07/89	89-92	26	5	2
Wolverhampton W	L	01/91	90	2	0	0
Portsmouth	Tr	08/93	93	15	0	0
Leicester C	Tr	03/94	93-95	42	7	4
Walsall	Tr	08/96	96-97	51	10	5
Mansfield T	Tr	08/99	99-00	78	6	9
Kidderminster Hrs	Tr	07/01	01	23	1	4

BLAKE Mark Christopher
Born: Portsmouth, England, 17 December, 1967 — CD
England: Youth

League Club	Source	Date Signed	Seasons Played	Apps	Subs	Gls
Southampton	App	12/85	85-88	18	0	2
Colchester U	L	09/89	89	4	0	1
Shrewsbury T	L	03/90	89	10	0	0
Shrewsbury T	Tr	07/90	90-93	132	0	3
Fulham	Tr	09/94	94-97	133	7	17

BLAKE Nathan Alexander
Born: Cardiff, Wales, 27 January, 1972 — F
Wales: 29/B-1/U21-5/Youth

League Club	Source	Date Signed	Seasons Played	Apps	Subs	Gls
Cardiff C	Chelsea (YT)	08/90	89-93	113	18	35
Sheffield U	Tr	02/94	93-95	55	14	34
Bolton W	Tr	12/95	95-98	102	5	38
Blackburn Rov	Tr	10/98	98-01	37	17	13
Wolverhampton W	Tr	09/01	01-03	70	5	24
Leicester C	Tr	08/04	04	4	10	0
Leeds U	L	12/04	04	2	0	1

BLAKE Noel Lloyd George
Born: Kingston, Jamaica, 12 January, 1962 — CD

League Club	Source	Date Signed	Seasons Played	Apps	Subs	Gls
Aston Villa	Sutton Coldfield T	08/79	79-81	4	0	0
Shrewsbury T	L	03/82	81	6	0	0
Birmingham C	Tr	09/82	82-83	76	0	5
Portsmouth	Tr	04/84	84-87	144	0	10
Leeds U	Tr	07/88	88-89	51	0	4
Stoke C	Tr	02/90	89-91	74	1	3
Bradford C	L	02/92	91	6	0	0
Bradford C	Tr	07/92	92-93	38	1	3
Exeter C	Dundee	08/95	95-00	135	12	10

BLAKE Robert James (Robbie)
Born: Middlesbrough, England, 4 March, 1976 — F

League Club	Source	Date Signed	Seasons Played	Apps	Subs	Gls
Darlington	YT	07/94	94-96	54	14	21
Bradford C	Tr	03/97	96-01	109	44	40
Nottingham F	L	08/00	00	9	2	1
Burnley	Tr	01/02	01-04	103	17	42
Birmingham C	Tr	01/05	04	2	9	2
Leeds U	Tr	07/05	05-06	58	19	19
Burnley	Tr	07/07	07-09	94	28	19
Bolton W	Tr	07/10	10-11	0	9	1
Doncaster Rov	Tr	07/12	12	0	7	0

BLAKE Russell Timothy
Born: Colchester, Essex, England, 24 July, 1935 — RW

League Club	Source	Date Signed	Seasons Played	Apps	Subs	Gls
Colchester U		04/56	55-60	58	-	8

BLAKE Ryan George
Born: Weybridge, Surrey, England, 8 December, 1991 — LB
Northern Ireland: U21-2/Youth

League Club	Source	Date Signed	Seasons Played	Apps	Subs	Gls
Brentford	Sch	08/09	09	0	1	0

BLAKEMAN Alan
Born: Oldham, Greater Manchester, England, 2 November, 1937 — CF

League Club	Source	Date Signed	Seasons Played	Apps	Subs	Gls
Rotherham U	Ashton U	05/58	58	2	-	0
Workington	Tr	01/59	58	14	-	7
Southport	Tr	07/59				

BLAKEMAN Alec George
Born: Oxford, England, 11 June, 1918 — IF
Died: Headington, Oxfordshire, England, November, 1994

League Club	Source	Date Signed	Seasons Played	Apps	Subs	Gls
Brentford	Oxford C	05/46	46-48	42	-	7
Sheffield U	Tr	11/48	48	5	-	0
Bournemouth	Tr	02/49	48-49	25	-	8

BLAKEY David (Dave)
Born: Newburn, Tyne and Wear, England, 22 August, 1929 — CH
Died: Rotherham, South Yorkshire, England, 4 April, 2014

League Club	Source	Date Signed	Seasons Played	Apps	Subs	Gls
Chesterfield	East Chevington Jnrs	05/47	48-66	617	0	20

BLAMEY Nathan George
Born: Plymouth, England, 10 June, 1977 — RB

League Club	Source	Date Signed	Seasons Played	Apps	Subs	Gls
Southampton	YT	07/95				
Shrewsbury T	Tr	02/97	96-97	15	0	1

BLAMPEY Stuart Leslie
Born: North Ferriby, East Riding of Yorkshire, England, 13 June, 1951 — D/M

League Club	Source	Date Signed	Seasons Played	Apps	Subs	Gls
Hull C	Jnr	08/68	69-74	61	11	1

BLANC Laurent Robert
Born: Ales, France, 19 November, 1965 — CD
France: 97

League Club	Source	Date Signed	Seasons Played	Apps	Subs	Gls
Manchester U	Inter Milan (ITA)	08/01	01-02	44	4	1

BLANCHARD Maxime Edouard Camille
Born: Alencon, France, 27 September, 1986 — CD

League Club	Source	Date Signed	Seasons Played	Apps	Subs	Gls
Tranmere Rov	Moulins (FRA)	08/10	10	14	6	0
Plymouth Arg		11/11	11-13	100	4	4

BLANCHETT Daniel William (Danny)
Born: Wembley, NW London, England, 6 May, 1987 — LB

League Club	Source	Date Signed	Seasons Played	Apps	Subs	Gls
Peterborough U	Cambridge C	03/07	06-08	3	4	1
Hereford U	L	09/09	09	13	0	0
Crewe Alex	Tr	07/10	10	38	1	0
Burton A	Tr	07/11	11	9	5	0
York C	Tr	07/12	12	2	2	0

BLANCHFLOWER John (Jackie)
Born: Belfast, Northern Ireland, 7 March, 1933 — IF
Died: Stalybridge, Greater Manchester, England, 2 September, 1998
Northern Ireland: 12/Schools

League Club	Source	Date Signed	Seasons Played	Apps	Subs	Gls
Manchester U	Jnr	03/50	51-57	105	-	26

BLANCHFLOWER Robert Dennis (Danny)
Born: Belfast, Northern Ireland, 10 February, 1926 — RH
Died: Belfast, Northern Ireland, 9 December, 1993
England: FLge-1//Northern Ireland: 56/NILge-6

League Club	Source	Date Signed	Seasons Played	Apps	Subs	Gls
Barnsley	Glentoran	04/49	48-50	68	-	2
Aston Villa	Tr	03/51	50-54	148	-	10
Tottenham H	Tr	12/54	54-63	337	-	15

BLANCO Sebastian Marcelo
Born: Buenos Aires, Argentina, 15 March, 1988 — W
Argentina: 2

League Club	Source	Date Signed	Seasons Played	Apps	Subs	Gls
West Bromwich A	Metalist Kharkiv (UKR)	08/14	14	0	3	0

BLANEY Steven David
Born: Thurrock, Essex, England, 24 March, 1977 — FB
England: Schools//Wales: U21-3

League Club	Source	Date Signed	Seasons Played	Apps	Subs	Gls
West Ham U	YT	07/95				
Brentford	Tr	03/98	97	4	1	0

BLANKLEY Barry Steven
Born: Farnborough, Hampshire, England, 27 October, 1964 — RB

League Club	Source	Date Signed	Seasons Played	Apps	Subs	Gls
Southampton	App	10/82				
Aldershot	Tr	12/84	84-86	90	0	0

BLANT Colin
Born: Rawtenstall, Lancashire, England, 7 October, 1946 — CD

League Club	Source	Date Signed	Seasons Played	Apps	Subs	Gls
Burnley	Rossendale U	08/64	66-69	46	7	7
Portsmouth	Tr	04/70	70-71	64	0	1
Rochdale	Tr	07/72	72-73	51	0	0
Darlington	Tr	01/74	73-75	89	0	0
Grimsby T	Tr	08/76	76	9	0	0
Workington	Tr	11/76	76	21	0	0

BLATCHFORD Patrick John (Paddy)
Born: Plymouth, England, 28 December, 1925 — LW
Died: St Germans, Cornwall, England, 1981

League Club	Source	Date Signed	Seasons Played	Apps	Subs	Gls
Plymouth Arg	Saltash U	11/48	48-50	19	-	2
Leyton Orient	Tr	08/51	51-52	60	-	8

BLATHERWICK Steven Scott (Steve)
Born: Hucknall, Nottinghamshire, England, 20 September, 1973 — CD

League Club	Source	Date Signed	Seasons Played	Apps	Subs	Gls
Nottingham F	Notts Co (YT)	08/92	93-96	10	0	0
Wycombe W	L	02/94	93	2	0	0
Hereford U	L	09/95	95	10	0	1
Reading	L	03/97	96	6	1	0
Burnley	Tr	07/97	97-98	16	8	0
Chesterfield	L	09/98	98	2	0	0
Chesterfield	Tr	12/98	98-05	213	10	10

BLATSIS Constantinos (Con)
Born: Melbourne, Australia, 6 July, 1977 — CD
Australia: 2/U23

League Club	Source	Date Signed	Seasons Played	Apps	Subs	Gls
Derby Co	South Melbourne (AUS)	08/00	00	2	0	0
Sheffield Wed	L	12/00	00	6	0	0
Colchester U	Tr	03/02	01	7	0	0

BLAYNEY Alan
Born: Belfast, Northern Ireland, 9 October, 1981 — G
Northern Ireland: 5/U23-1/U21-4

League Club	Source	Date Signed	Seasons Played	Apps	Subs	Gls
Southampton	YT	07/01	03-04	3	0	0
Stockport Co	L	10/02	02	2	0	0
Bournemouth	L	12/02	02	2	0	0
Rushden & D	L	01/05	04	4	0	0
Brighton & HA	L	03/05	04	7	0	0
Brighton & HA	L	09/05	05	8	0	0
Doncaster Rov	Tr	01/06	05-06	24	0	0
Oldham Ath	Tr	01/07	06	2	1	0

BLEANCH Norman Wesley Swan
Born: Houghton-le-Spring, Tyne and Wear, England, 19 August, 1940 — CF

League Club	Source	Date Signed	Seasons Played	Apps	Subs	Gls
West Ham U	Willington	02/60				
Southend U	Tr	07/61	61	3	-	0
Bradford Park Ave	Tr	11/61	61	9	-	3

BLEARS Brian Thomas
Born: Prestatyn, Denbighshire, Wales, 18 November, 1933 — WH
Died: Chester, England, 10 November, 2005

League Club	Source	Date Signed	Seasons Played	Apps	Subs	Gls
Chester C	Everton (Am)	07/54	54-55	2	-	0

BLEASDALE David George
Born: St Helens, Merseyside, England, 23 March, 1965 — M

League Club	Source	Date Signed	Seasons Played	Apps	Subs	Gls
Preston NE	Liverpool (App)	03/83	83	4	1	0

BLEASE Rory
Born: Bebington, Wirral, England, 16 August, 1960 — M

League Club	Source	Date Signed	Seasons Played	Apps	Subs	Gls
Chester C	Pwllheli	12/84	84	4	0	0

BLEIDELIS Imants
Born: Riga, Latvia, 16 August, 1975 — M
Latvia: 106

League Club	Source	Date Signed	Seasons Played	Apps	Subs	Gls
Southampton	Skonto Riga (LAT)	02/00	00-01	0	2	0

BLENKINSOPP Thomas William (Tommy)
Born: Blyth, Northumberland, England, 13 May, 1920 — RH
Died: Witton Park, County Durham, England, 29 January, 2004
England: FLge-2

League Club	Source	Date Signed	Seasons Played	Apps	Subs	Gls
Grimsby T	West Auckland T	03/39	46-47	74	-	10
Middlesbrough	Tr	05/48	48-52	98	-	0
Barnsley	Tr	11/52	52	8	-	0

BLEWITT Darren Lee
Born: Newham, E London, England, 3 September, 1985 CD

League Club	Source	Date Signed	Seasons Played	Apps	Subs	Gls
West Ham U	Sch	07/04				
Southend U	L	03/05	04	0	1	0

BLICK Michael Robert (Mike)
Born: Berkeley, Gloucestershire, England, 20 September, 1948 CD

League Club	Source	Date Signed	Seasons Played	Apps	Subs	Gls
Swindon T	App	09/66	67-70	6	0	0

BLINCOW Ernest (Ernie)
Born: Walsall, West Midlands, England, 9 September, 1921 LW
Died: Walsall, West Midlands, England, 19 February, 2010

League Club	Source	Date Signed	Seasons Played	Apps	Subs	Gls
Walsall	West Bromwich A (Am)	01/47	46	1	-	0

BLIND Daley
Born: Amsterdam, Netherlands, 9 March, 1990 DM
Netherlands: 29/U21-23/Youth

League Club	Source	Date Signed	Seasons Played	Apps	Subs	Gls
Manchester U	Ajax (NED)	09/14	14	25	0	2

BLINKER Reginald Waldie (Regi)
Born: Paramaribo, Suriname, 4 June, 1969 W
Netherlands: 3

League Club	Source	Date Signed	Seasons Played	Apps	Subs	Gls
Sheffield Wed	Feyenoord (NED)	03/96	95-96	24	18	3

BLINKHORN Matthew David
Born: Blackpool, Lancashire, England, 2 March, 1985 F

League Club	Source	Date Signed	Seasons Played	Apps	Subs	Gls
Blackpool	Sch	06/03	01-06	13	31	5
Luton T	L	07/04	04	0	2	0
Bury	L	11/06	06	1	9	0
Morecambe	Tr	03/07	07-08	41	11	10

BLISSETT Gary Paul
Born: Manchester, England, 29 June, 1964 F

League Club	Source	Date Signed	Seasons Played	Apps	Subs	Gls
Crewe Alex	Altrincham	08/83	83-86	112	10	38
Brentford	Tr	03/87	86-92	220	13	79
Wimbledon	Tr	07/93	93-95	10	21	3
Wycombe W	L	12/95	95	4	0	2
Crewe Alex	L	03/96	95	10	0	1

BLISSETT Luther Loide
Born: Falmouth, Jamaica, 1 February, 1958 F
England: 14/B-1/U21-4

League Club	Source	Date Signed	Seasons Played	Apps	Subs	Gls
Watford	Jnr	07/75	75-82	222	24	95
Watford	AC Milan (ITA)	08/84	84-88	113	14	44
Bournemouth	Tr	11/88	88-90	121	0	56
Watford	Tr	08/91	91	34	8	9
West Bromwich A	L	10/92	92	3	0	1
Bury	Tr	08/93	93	8	2	1
Mansfield T	L	12/93	93	4	1	1

BLIZZARD Dominic John
Born: High Wycombe, Buckinghamshire, England, 2 September, 1983 M

League Club	Source	Date Signed	Seasons Played	Apps	Subs	Gls
Watford	Sch	04/02	03-05	22	7	2
Stockport Co	L	02/07	06	7	0	0
MK Dons	L	03/07	06	8	0	0
Stockport Co	Tr	08/07	07-08	52	6	4
Bristol Rov	Tr	07/09	09-10	25	14	1
Port Vale	L	03/11	10	1	0	0
Yeovil T	Tr	07/11	11-12	39	15	4
Plymouth Arg	Tr	06/13	13-14	45	12	2

BLIZZARD Leslie William Benjamin (Les)
Born: Acton, W London, England, 13 March, 1923 CH
Died: Northampton, England, December, 1996

League Club	Source	Date Signed	Seasons Played	Apps	Subs	Gls
Queens Park Rgrs	Mosborough Trinity	07/41	46	5	-	0
Bournemouth	Tr	05/47	47	1	-	0
Leyton Orient	Yeovil T	07/50	50-56	222	-	12

BLOCHEL Jozef Edward (Joe)
Born: Chalfont St Giles, Buckinghamshire, England, 3 March, 1962 F

League Club	Source	Date Signed	Seasons Played	Apps	Subs	Gls
Southampton	App	03/80				
Wimbledon	L	01/82	81	6	0	1

BLOCK Michael John (Mike)
Born: Ipswich, England, 28 January, 1940 RW
England: Youth

League Club	Source	Date Signed	Seasons Played	Apps	Subs	Gls
Chelsea	Jnr	02/57	57-61	37	-	6
Brentford	Tr	01/62	61-65	146	0	30
Watford	Tr	10/66	66	11	2	2

BLOCKLEY Jeffrey Paul (Jeff)
Born: Leicester, England, 12 September, 1949 CD
England: 1/FLge-1/U23-10

League Club	Source	Date Signed	Seasons Played	Apps	Subs	Gls
Coventry C	App	06/67	68-72	144	2	6
Arsenal	Tr	10/72	72-74	52	0	1
Leicester C	Tr	01/75	74-77	75	1	2
Notts Co	Tr	06/78	78-79	57	2	5

BLOMQVIST Lars Jesper (Jesper)
Born: Umea, Sweden, 5 February, 1974 LM
Sweden: 30

League Club	Source	Date Signed	Seasons Played	Apps	Subs	Gls
Manchester U	Parma (ITA)	07/98	98	20	5	1
Everton	Tr	11/01	01	10	5	1
Charlton Ath	Tr	08/02	02	0	3	0

BLONDEAU Patrick
Born: Marseille, France, 27 January, 1968 RB
France: 2

League Club	Source	Date Signed	Seasons Played	Apps	Subs	Gls
Sheffield Wed	AS Monaco (FRA)	07/97	97	5	1	0
Watford	Olymp Marseille (FRA)	07/01	01	24	1	0

BLONDEL Frederick (Fred)
Born: Lancaster, England, 31 October, 1923 IF
Died: Keighley, West Yorkshire, England, February, 1989

League Club	Source	Date Signed	Seasons Played	Apps	Subs	Gls
Bury	Morecambe	07/46	46	1	-	0

BLONDEL Jonathan
Born: Ypres, Belgium, 3 April, 1984 M
Belgium: 4/U21-20/Youth

League Club	Source	Date Signed	Seasons Played	Apps	Subs	Gls
Tottenham H	RE Mouscron (BEL)	07/02	02-03	0	2	0

BLOOD John Foster (Jack)
Born: Nottingham, England, 2 October, 1914 FB
Died: Kingsteignton, Devon, England, 4 February, 1992

League Club	Source	Date Signed	Seasons Played	Apps	Subs	Gls
Notts Co	Johnson & Barnes	06/38	38	8	-	0
Exeter C	Tr	05/39	46-47	39	-	1

BLOOMER Brian McGregor
Born: Cleethorpes, North Lincolnshire, England, 3 May, 1952 F

League Club	Source	Date Signed	Seasons Played	Apps	Subs	Gls
Scunthorpe U	Brigg T	08/78	78	3	4	1

BLOOMER James (Jimmy)
Born: Rutherglen, Glasgow, Scotland, 10 April, 1926 IF
Died: Grimsby, North Lincolnshire, England, 7 December, 2011

League Club	Source	Date Signed	Seasons Played	Apps	Subs	Gls
Hull C	Strathclyde	02/48	47	4	-	2
Grimsby T	Tr	07/49	49-54	109	-	42

BLOOMER James Moore (Jimmy)
Born: Glasgow, Scotland, 22 August, 1947 RB

League Club	Source	Date Signed	Seasons Played	Apps	Subs	Gls
Grimsby T	Jnr	11/64	65-68	48	4	0

BLOOMER Matthew Brian (Matt)
Born: Grimsby, North Lincolnshire, England, 3 November, 1978 CD

League Club	Source	Date Signed	Seasons Played	Apps	Subs	Gls
Grimsby T	Jnr	07/97	98-00	3	9	0
Hull C	Tr	07/01	01	0	3	0
Lincoln C	L	03/02	01	4	1	0
Lincoln C	Tr	12/02	02-05	55	34	3
Grimsby T	L	01/06	05	3	0	0
Grimsby T	Cambridge U	01/07	06	5	4	0

BLOOMER Robert Stephen (Bob)
Born: Sheffield, England, 21 June, 1966 M

League Club	Source	Date Signed	Seasons Played	Apps	Subs	Gls
Chesterfield	Jnr	08/85	85-89	120	21	15
Bristol Rov	Tr	03/90	90-91	11	11	0
Cheltenham T	Tr	08/92	99-00	6	17	1

BLOOMFIELD Edward William Ashworth (Eddie)
Born: Wisbech, Cambridgeshire, England, 28 June, 1932 IF
Died: Southport, Merseyside, England, July, 2012

League Club	Source	Date Signed	Seasons Played	Apps	Subs	Gls
Carlisle U	Wisbech Cons	08/53	53-55	5	-	1
Southport	Tr	07/56	56	2	-	0

BLOOMFIELD James Henry (Jimmy)
Born: Kensington, Central London, England, 15 February, 1934 IF
Died: Chingford, NE London, England, 3 April, 1983
England: FLge-1/U23-2

League Club	Source	Date Signed	Seasons Played	Apps	Subs	Gls
Brentford	Walthamstow Ave	10/52	52-53	42	-	5
Arsenal	Tr	07/54	54-60	210	-	54
Birmingham C	Tr	11/60	60-63	123	-	28
Brentford	Tr	06/64	64-65	44	0	4
West Ham U	Tr	10/65	65	9	1	0
Plymouth Arg	Tr	09/66	66-67	25	0	1
Leyton Orient	Tr	03/68	67-68	43	2	3

BLOOMFIELD Mason Ozail
Born: Westminster, Central London, England, 4 November, 1996 F

League Club	Source	Date Signed	Seasons Played	Apps	Subs	Gls
Dagenham & Red	Sch	-	14	0	1	0

BLOOMFIELD Matthew (Matt)
Born: Felixstowe, Suffolk, England, 8 February, 1984 M
England: Youth

League Club	Source	Date Signed	Seasons Played	Apps	Subs	Gls
Ipswich T	YT	07/01				
Wycombe W	Tr	12/03	03-14	257	62	25

BLOOMFIELD Raymond George (Ray)
Born: Kensington, Central London, England, 15 October, 1944 W
England: Youth/Schools

League Club	Source	Date Signed	Seasons Played	Apps	Subs	Gls
Arsenal	Jnr	11/61				
Chelsea	Tr	05/64				
Aston Villa	Tr	08/64	64-65	3	0	0

BLOOMFIELD William George (Billy)
Born: Kensington, Central London, England, 25 August, 1939 IF
Died: Kensington, Central London, England, September, 2003

League Club	Source	Date Signed	Seasons Played	Apps	Subs	Gls
Brentford	Jnr	08/56	56-57	2	-	0

BLOOR Alan
Born: Stoke-on-Trent, England, 16 March, 1943 CD
England: Youth

League Club	Source	Date Signed	Seasons Played	Apps	Subs	Gls
Stoke C	Jnr	03/60	61-77	384	4	17
Port Vale	Tr	06/78	78	5	1	1

BLOOR Michael Bennett (Micky)
Born: Wrexham, Wales, 25 March, 1949 RB

League Club	Source	Date Signed	Seasons Played	Apps	Subs	Gls
Stoke C	Newport, Shropshire	04/67				
Lincoln C	Tr	05/71	71-72	71	2	0
Darlington	Tr	08/73	73	7	0	0

BLOOR Robert
Born: Stoke-on-Trent, England, 8 July, 1932 WH

League Club	Source	Date Signed	Seasons Played	Apps	Subs	Gls
Crewe Alex		01/54	53-54	26	-	1

BLORE Reginald (Reg)
Born: Wrexham, Wales, 18 March, 1942 CF/M
Wales: U23-4

League Club	Source	Date Signed	Seasons Played	Apps	Subs	Gls
Liverpool	Jnr	05/59	59	1	-	0
Southport	Tr	07/60	60-63	139	-	55
Blackburn Rov	Tr	11/63	63-65	11	0	0
Oldham Ath	Tr	12/65	65-69	182	5	20

BLOSS Philip Kenneth (Phil)
Born: Colchester, Essex, England, 16 January, 1953 M

League Club	Source	Date Signed	Seasons Played	Apps	Subs	Gls
Colchester U	App	01/71	70-72	32	2	2

BLOTT John Paul
Born: Redcar, Cleveland, England, 26 February, 1965 G

League Club	Source	Date Signed	Seasons Played	Apps	Subs	Gls
Manchester C	Jnr	09/82				
Carlisle U	Scunthorpe U (NC)	11/84	84	2	0	0
Newport Co	Mansfield T (NC)	03/87	86	1	0	0

BLOUNT Mark
Born: Derby, England, 5 January, 1974 CD

League Club	Source	Date Signed	Seasons Played	Apps	Subs	Gls
Sheffield U	Gresley Rov	02/94	94-95	11	2	0
Peterborough U	Tr	03/96	95	4	1	0

BLOWMAN Peter
Born: Thornaby, Cleveland, England, 12 December, 1949 F

League Club	Source	Date Signed	Seasons Played	Apps	Subs	Gls
Hartlepool U	Billingham Synthonia	11/67	67-69	57	9	15

BLOXHAM James Alexander (Alec)
Born: Pleasley, Derbyshire, England, 2 July, 1920 RW
Died: Swindon, England, 1982

League Club	Source	Date Signed	Seasons Played	Apps	Subs	Gls
Hull C	Ollerton Colliery	10/47	47-49	33	-	2

BLUCK David Albert (Dave)
Born: India, 31 January, 1930 WH
Died: Bristol, England, January, 2012

League Club	Source	Date Signed	Seasons Played	Apps	Subs	Gls
Aldershot (Am)	Aldershot Garrison	08/51	51	1	-	0

BLUE Archibald (Archie)
Born: Glasgow, Scotland, 8 April, 1940 CF

League Club	Source	Date Signed	Seasons Played	Apps	Subs	Gls
Exeter C	Heart of Midlothian	07/61	61	34	-	6
Carlisle U	Tr	07/62	62	2	-	1

BLUNDELL Alan
Born: Birkenhead, Wirral, England, 18 August, 1947 RB/M

League Club	Source	Date Signed	Seasons Played	Apps	Subs	Gls
Tranmere Rov	App	08/65	65-66	3	0	0

BLUNDELL Christopher Kenneth (Chris)
Born: Billinge, Merseyside, England, 7 December, 1969 CD

League Club	Source	Date Signed	Seasons Played	Apps	Subs	Gls
Oldham Ath	YT	07/88	87-88	2	1	0
Rochdale	Tr	09/90	90	10	4	0

BLUNDELL Gregg Steven
Born: Liverpool, England, 3 October, 1977 F
England: Semi Pro-1

League Club	Source	Date Signed	Seasons Played	Apps	Subs	Gls
Tranmere Rov	YT	07/96				
Doncaster Rov	Northwich Victoria	03/03	03-04	74	11	27
Chester C	Tr	07/05	05-06	44	13	13
Darlington	Tr	01/07	06-08	33	38	11
Accrington Stan	L	11/08	08	2	0	0

BLUNSTONE Frank
Born: Crewe, Cheshire, England, 17 October, 1934 LW
England: 5/FLge-2/U23-5/Youth

League Club	Source	Date Signed	Seasons Played	Apps	Subs	Gls
Crewe Alex	Jnr	01/52	51-52	47	-	12
Chelsea	Tr	03/53	52-63	317	-	47

BLUNT David
Born: Goldthorpe, South Yorkshire, England, 29 April, 1949 F

League Club	Source	Date Signed	Seasons Played	Apps	Subs	Gls
Bradford Park Ave (Am)		03/68	67	2	0	0
Chester C	Tr	06/68				

BLUNT Edwin (Eddie)
Born: Tunstall, Potteries, England, 21 May, 1918 WH
Died: Stoke-on-Trent, England, 20 September, 1993

League Club	Source	Date Signed	Seasons Played	Apps	Subs	Gls
Northampton T	Port Vale (Am)	05/37	37-48	87	-	2
Accrington Stan	Tr	07/49	49	9	-	1

BLUNT Jason John
Born: Penzance, Cornwall, England, 16 August, 1977 M

League Club	Source	Date Signed	Seasons Played	Apps	Subs	Gls
Leeds U	YT	01/95	95-96	2	2	0
Blackpool	Tr	07/98	98	1	1	0

BLY Terence Geoffrey (Terry)
Born: Fincham, Norfolk, England, 22 October, 1935 CF
Died: Grantham, Lincolnshire, England, 24 September, 2009

League Club	Source	Date Signed	Seasons Played	Apps	Subs	Gls
Norwich C	Bury T	08/56	56-59	57	-	31
Peterborough U	Tr	06/60	60-61	88	-	81
Coventry C	Tr	07/62	62	32	-	25
Notts Co	Tr	08/63	63-64	29	-	4

BLY William (Billy)
Born: Newcastle-upon-Tyne, England, 15 May, 1920 G
Died: Hull, England, 24 March, 1982

League Club	Source	Date Signed	Seasons Played	Apps	Subs	Gls
Hull C	Walker Celtic	08/37	38-59	403	-	0

BLYTH Jacob Mathew
Born: Nuneaton, Warwickshire, England, 14 August, 1992 F

League Club	Source	Date Signed	Seasons Played	Apps	Subs	Gls
Leicester C	Leamington	05/12				
Burton A	L	11/12	12	0	2	0
Notts Co	L	02/13	12	2	2	0
Northampton T	L	08/13	13	8	3	3
Burton A	L	08/14	14	15	7	5

BLYTH James Anton (Jim)
Born: Perth, Scotland, 2 February, 1955 G
Scotland: 2

League Club	Source	Date Signed	Seasons Played	Apps	Subs	Gls
Preston NE	App	10/72	71	1	0	0
Coventry C	Tr	10/72	75-81	151	0	0
Hereford U	L	03/75	74	7	0	0
Birmingham C	Tr	08/82	82	14	0	0

BLYTH John William (Ian)
Born: Edinburgh, Scotland, 26 May, 1947 M

League Club	Source	Date Signed	Seasons Played	Apps	Subs	Gls
Rotherham U	Heart of Midlothian	01/67				
Halifax T	Tr	05/67	66-67	5	0	0

BLYTH Melvyn Bernard (Mel)
Born: Norwich, England, 28 July, 1944 CD

League Club	Source	Date Signed	Seasons Played	Apps	Subs	Gls
Scunthorpe U	Yarmouth T	11/67	67	27	0	3
Crystal Palace	Tr	07/68	68-74	213	3	9
Southampton	Tr	09/74	74-76	104	1	6
Crystal Palace	L	11/77	77	6	0	0
Millwall	Margate	11/78	78-80	75	0	0

BLYTHE John Alfred
Born: Darlington, County Durham, England, 31 January, 1924 CH
Died: Durham, England, June, 2007

League Club	Source	Date Signed	Seasons Played	Apps	Subs	Gls
Darlington		06/46	46-48	17	-	0

BLYTHE John David (David)
Born: Huddersfield, West Yorkshire, England, 21 July, 1947 F

League Club	Source	Date Signed	Seasons Played	Apps	Subs	Gls
Hartlepool U	Crook T	01/70	69	1	1	0

BOAG James (Jimmy)
Born: Blairhall, Fife, Scotland, 12 November, 1937 G

League Club	Source	Date Signed	Seasons Played	Apps	Subs	Gls
Exeter C	Bath C	10/62	62	2	-	0

BOAGEY Zak
Born: Hartlepool, Cleveland, England, 11 October, 1994 F

League Club	Source	Date Signed	Seasons Played	Apps	Subs	Gls
Hartlepool U	Middlesbrough (Sch)	11/12	12	0	1	0

BOAKYE-YIADOM Nana Emeka
Born: Hackney, E London, England, 13 May, 1996 W

League Club	Source	Date Signed	Seasons Played	Apps	Subs	Gls
Barnsley	Sch	05/14	14	0	1	0

BOAM Stuart William
Born: Kirkby-in-Ashfield, Nottinghamshire, England, 28 January, 1948 CD

League Club	Source	Date Signed	Seasons Played	Apps	Subs	Gls
Mansfield T	Kirkby BC	07/66	66-70	175	0	3
Middlesbrough	Tr	06/71	71-78	322	0	14
Newcastle U	Tr	08/79	79-80	69	0	1
Mansfield T	Tr	07/81	81-82	11	4	1
Hartlepool U	Tr	03/83	82	1	0	0

BOA MORTE Luis
Born: Lisbon, Portugal, 4 August, 1977 LW
Portugal: 28/U21-10/Youth

League Club	Source	Date Signed	Seasons Played	Apps	Subs	Gls
Arsenal	Sporting Lisbon (POR)	06/97	97-99	6	19	0
Southampton	Tr	08/99	99	6	8	1
Fulham	Tr	07/00	00-06	169	36	44
West Ham U	Tr	01/07	06-10	59	32	2
Chesterfield	Orlando Pirates (USA)	10/12	12	8	4	0

BOARDLEY Stuart James
Born: Ipswich, England, 14 February, 1985 — M

League Club	Source	Date Signed	Seasons Played	Apps	Subs	Gls
Torquay U	Ipswich T (Sch)	09/04	04	2	4	0

BOARDMAN Craig George
Born: Barnsley, South Yorkshire, England, 30 November, 1970 — CD

League Club	Source	Date Signed	Seasons Played	Apps	Subs	Gls
Nottingham F	YT	05/89				
Peterborough U	Tr	08/93				
Scarborough	Halifax T	08/95	95	6	3	0

BOARDMAN George
Born: Glasgow, Scotland, 14 August, 1943 — M
Scotland: Amateur

League Club	Source	Date Signed	Seasons Played	Apps	Subs	Gls
Shrewsbury T	Queen's Park	06/63	63-68	172	4	48
Barnsley	Tr	06/69	69-72	123	3	14

BOARDMAN Jonathan George (Jon)
Born: Reading, England, 27 January, 1981 — CD
England: Semi Pro-5

League Club	Source	Date Signed	Seasons Played	Apps	Subs	Gls
Crystal Palace	YT	06/99				
Rochdale	Woking	05/05	05-06	20	5	1
Dagenham & Red	Tr	01/07	07	22	5	0

BOARDMAN Paul
Born: Tottenham, N London, England, 6 November, 1967 — F

League Club	Source	Date Signed	Seasons Played	Apps	Subs	Gls
Plymouth Arg	Knowsley U	08/92	92-93	2	1	1

BOATENG Daniel Jesse
Born: Enfield, N London, England, 2 September, 1992 — CD

League Club	Source	Date Signed	Seasons Played	Apps	Subs	Gls
Arsenal	Sch	07/10				
Swindon T	L	01/12	11	2	0	0
Oxford U	L	08/12	12	1	1	0

BOATENG Derek Owusu
Born: Accra, Ghana, 2 May, 1983 — M
Ghana: 46

League Club	Source	Date Signed	Seasons Played	Apps	Subs	Gls
Fulham	FC Dnipro (UKR)	05/13	13	2	1	0

BOATENG George
Born: Nkawkaw, Ghana, 5 September, 1975 — M
Netherlands: 4/U21-18

League Club	Source	Date Signed	Seasons Played	Apps	Subs	Gls
Coventry C	Feyenoord (NED)	12/97	97-98	43	4	5
Aston Villa	Tr	07/99	99-01	96	7	4
Middlesbrough	Tr	08/02	02-07	177	5	7
Hull C	Tr	07/08	08-09	47	5	1
Nottingham F	Skoda Xanthi (GRE)	07/11	11	5	0	1

BOATENG Hiram Kojo Kwarteng
Born: Wandsworth, SW London, England, 8 January, 1996 — M

League Club	Source	Date Signed	Seasons Played	Apps	Subs	Gls
Crystal Palace	Sch	01/13				
Crawley T	L	02/14	13	1	0	0

BOATENG Jerome Agyenim
Born: Berlin, Germany, 3 September, 1988 — CD
Germany: 52/U21-15

League Club	Source	Date Signed	Seasons Played	Apps	Subs	Gls
Manchester C	Hamburger SV (GER)	08/10	10	14	2	0

BOATENG Kevin-Prince (Kevin)
Born: Berlin, Germany, 6 March, 1987 — M
Germany: U21-6/Youth//Ghana: 15

League Club	Source	Date Signed	Seasons Played	Apps	Subs	Gls
Tottenham H	Hertha Berlin (GER)	07/07	07-08	7	7	0
Portsmouth	Tr	08/09	09	20	2	3

BOBIC Fredi
Born: Maribor, Slovenia, 30 October, 1971 — F
Germany: 37

League Club	Source	Date Signed	Seasons Played	Apps	Subs	Gls
Bolton W (L)	Bor Dortmund (GER)	01/02	01	14	2	4

BOCANEGRA Carlos Manuel
Born: Alta Loma, California, USA, 25 May, 1979 — CD
USA: 110/U23-7/Youth

League Club	Source	Date Signed	Seasons Played	Apps	Subs	Gls
Fulham	Chicago Fire (USA)	01/04	03-07	105	11	8

BOCHENSKI Simon
Born: Worksop, Nottinghamshire, England, 6 December, 1975 — F

League Club	Source	Date Signed	Seasons Played	Apps	Subs	Gls
Barnsley	YT	07/94	95	0	1	0
Scarborough	Tr	08/96	96	5	14	1

BOCO Romuald
Born: Bernay, France, 8 July, 1985 — M
Benin: 48

League Club	Source	Date Signed	Seasons Played	Apps	Subs	Gls
Accrington Stan	Chamois Niortais (FRA)	08/05	06-07	34	9	3
Burton A (L)	Sligo Rov (ROI)	02/10	09	3	5	0
Accrington Stan	Sligo Rov (ROI)	08/12	12	42	0	10
Plymouth Arg	Tr	07/13	13	22	5	1
Chesterfield	Tr	08/14	14	11	2	1

BODAK Peter John
Born: Birmingham, England, 12 August, 1961 — M

League Club	Source	Date Signed	Seasons Played	Apps	Subs	Gls
Coventry C	App	05/79	80-81	30	2	5
Manchester U	Tr	08/82				
Manchester C	Tr	12/82	82	12	2	1
Crewe Alex	Royal Antwerp (BEL)	12/86	86-87	49	4	7
Swansea C	Tr	03/88	87-88	25	6	4
Walsall	Happy Valley (HKG)	08/90	90	3	1	1

BODDE Ferrie
Born: Den Haag, Netherlands, 5 May, 1982 — M
Netherlands: U21-1

League Club	Source	Date Signed	Seasons Played	Apps	Subs	Gls
Swansea C	ADO Den Haag (NED)	08/07	07-09	52	2	13

BODEL Andrew Cunningham (Andy)
Born: Clydebank, Dunbartonshire, Scotland, 12 February, 1957 — CD

League Club	Source	Date Signed	Seasons Played	Apps	Subs	Gls
Oxford U	App	02/75	75-79	128	0	11

BODELL Norman
Born: Manchester, England, 29 January, 1938 — D

League Club	Source	Date Signed	Seasons Played	Apps	Subs	Gls
Rochdale		09/56	58-62	79	-	1
Crewe Alex	Tr	05/63	63-66	108	1	2
Halifax T	Tr	10/66	66-67	36	0	0

BODEN Christopher Desmond (Chris)
Born: Wolverhampton, England, 13 October, 1973 — LB

League Club	Source	Date Signed	Seasons Played	Apps	Subs	Gls
Aston Villa	YT	12/91	94	0	1	0
Barnsley	L	10/93	93	4	0	0
Derby Co	Tr	03/95	94-95	8	2	0
Shrewsbury T	L	01/96	95	5	0	0

BODEN John Gilbert (Jackie)
Born: Cleethorpes, North Lincolnshire, England, 4 October, 1926 — CF
Died: Grimsby, North Lincolnshire, England, 22 April, 2006

League Club	Source	Date Signed	Seasons Played	Apps	Subs	Gls
Lincoln C	Skegness T	04/50	49-50	3	-	2

BODEN Kenneth (Ken)
Born: Thrybergh, South Yorkshire, England, 5 July, 1950 — M

League Club	Source	Date Signed	Seasons Played	Apps	Subs	Gls
Doncaster Rov	Bridlington T	03/77	76	1	0	0

BODEN Luke
Born: Sheffield, England, 26 November, 1988 — W

League Club	Source	Date Signed	Seasons Played	Apps	Subs	Gls
Sheffield Wed	Sch	07/07	06-08	2	13	0
Chesterfield	L	09/08	08	4	0	0
Northampton T	L	08/09	09	4	0	0

BODEN Scott David
Born: Sheffield, England, 19 December, 1989 — F

League Club	Source	Date Signed	Seasons Played	Apps	Subs	Gls
Chesterfield	Sheffield U (Sch)	08/08	08-12	21	83	15
Macclesfield T	L	10/11	11	6	1	0

BODIN Billy Paul
Born: Swindon, England, 24 March, 1992 — LW
Wales: U21-21/Youth

League Club	Source	Date Signed	Seasons Played	Apps	Subs	Gls
Swindon T	Sch	07/10	10-11	11	5	3
Torquay U	L	08/11	11	15	2	5
Crewe Alex	L	03/12	11	8	0	0
Torquay U	Tr	07/12	12-13	63	7	6
Northampton T	Tr	01/15	14	0	4	0

BODIN Paul John
Born: Cardiff, Wales, 13 September, 1964 — LB
Wales: 23/U21-1/Youth

League Club	Source	Date Signed	Seasons Played	Apps	Subs	Gls
Newport Co	Chelsea (Jnr)	01/82				
Cardiff C	Tr	08/82	82-84	68	7	4
Newport Co	Bath C	01/88	87	6	0	1
Swindon T	Tr	03/88	87-90	87	6	9
Crystal Palace	Tr	03/91	90-91	8	1	0
Newcastle U	L	12/91	91	6	0	0
Swindon T	Tr	01/92	91-95	140	6	28
Reading	Tr	06/96	96-97	40	1	1
Wycombe W	L	09/97	97	5	0	0

BODKIN Matthew James (Matt)
Born: Chatham, Kent, England, 23 November, 1983 — W

League Club	Source	Date Signed	Seasons Played	Apps	Subs	Gls
Nottingham F	Sch	01/03				
Gillingham	Tr	08/04	04	0	2	0

BODLE Harold
Born: Adwick-le-Street, South Yorkshire, England, 4 October, 1920 — IF
Died: Bournemouth, England, 1 January, 2005

League Club	Source	Date Signed	Seasons Played	Apps	Subs	Gls
Rotherham U	Ridgehill Ath	05/38	38	9	-	0
Birmingham C	Tr	12/38	38-48	94	-	32
Bury	Tr	03/49	48-51	119	-	40
Stockport Co	Tr	10/52	52	29	-	6
Accrington Stan	Tr	08/53	53-56	94	-	13

BODLEY Michael John (Mick)
Born: Hayes, W London, England, 14 September, 1967 — CD

League Club	Source	Date Signed	Seasons Played	Apps	Subs	Gls
Chelsea	App	09/85	87	6	0	1
Northampton T	Tr	01/89	88	20	0	0
Barnet	Tr	10/89	91-92	69	0	3
Southend U	Tr	07/93	93-95	66	1	2
Gillingham	L	11/94	94	6	1	0

League Club	Source	Date Signed	Seasons Played	Apps	Subs	Gls
Birmingham C	L	01/95	94	3	0	0
Peterborough U	Tr	08/96	96-98	86	0	1

BODUROV Nikolay Georgiev
Born: Blagoevgrad, Bulgaria, 30 May, 1986 CD
Bulgaria: 31

League Club	Source	Date Signed	Seasons Played	Apps	Subs	Gls
Fulham	Liteks Lovech (BUL)	08/14	14	36	2	1

BOERE Jeroen Willem
Born: Arnhem, Netherlands, 18 November, 1967 F
Died: Marbella, Spain, 16 August, 2007

League Club	Source	Date Signed	Seasons Played	Apps	Subs	Gls
West Ham U	GAE Deventer (NED)	09/93	93-95	15	10	6
Portsmouth	L	03/94	93	4	1	0
West Bromwich A	L	09/94	94	5	0	0
Crystal Palace	Tr	09/95	95	0	8	1
Southend U	Tr	03/96	95-97	61	12	25

BOERSMA Philip (Phil)
Born: Kirkby, Merseyside, England, 24 September, 1949 M/F

League Club	Source	Date Signed	Seasons Played	Apps	Subs	Gls
Liverpool	Jnr	09/68	69-75	73	9	17
Wrexham	L	03/70	69	4	3	0
Middlesbrough	Tr	12/75	75-76	41	6	3
Luton T	Tr	08/77	77-78	35	1	8
Swansea C	Tr	09/78	78	15	3	1

BOERTIEN Paul
Born: Haltwhistle, Northumberland, England, 21 January, 1979 LB

League Club	Source	Date Signed	Seasons Played	Apps	Subs	Gls
Carlisle U	YT	05/97	97-98	16	1	1
Derby Co	Tr	03/99	98-06	92	22	2
Crewe Alex	L	02/00	99	2	0	0
Notts Co	L	01/04	03	5	0	0
Chesterfield	L	03/07	06	4	0	0
Walsall	Tr	07/07	07-08	45	6	0
Burton A	Tr	07/09	09-10	48	2	1

BOFFIN Ruud
Born: Maastricht, Netherlands, 5 November, 1987 G

League Club	Source	Date Signed	Seasons Played	Apps	Subs	Gls
West Ham U	MVV Maastricht (NED)	09/10	10	1	0	0

BOGAN Thomas (Tommy)
Born: Glasgow, Scotland, 18 May, 1920 IF
Died: Alderley Edge, Cheshire, England, 23 September, 1993
Scotland: SLge-1/War-1

League Club	Source	Date Signed	Seasons Played	Apps	Subs	Gls
Preston NE	Glasgow Celtic	10/48	48	11	-	0
Manchester U	Tr	08/49	49-50	29	-	7
Southampton	Aberdeen	12/51	51-52	8	-	2
Blackburn Rov	Tr	08/53	53	1	-	0

BOGARDE Winston
Born: Rotterdam, Netherlands, 22 October, 1970 CD
Netherlands: 20

League Club	Source	Date Signed	Seasons Played	Apps	Subs	Gls
Chelsea	Barcelona (SPN)	09/00	00	2	7	0

BOGDAN Adam
Born: Budapest, Hungary, 27 September, 1987 G
Hungary: 19/U21-7/Youth

League Club	Source	Date Signed	Seasons Played	Apps	Subs	Gls
Bolton W	Vasas SC (HUN)	08/07	10-14	103	1	0
Crewe Alex	L	09/09	09	1	0	0

BOGDANOVIC Daniel
Born: Misrata, Libya, 26 March, 1980 F
Malta: 40

League Club	Source	Date Signed	Seasons Played	Apps	Subs	Gls
Barnsley	Lokomotiv Sofia (BUL)	01/09	08-09	33	12	16
Sheffield U	Tr	07/10	10-11	12	22	5
Blackpool	Tr	08/11	11	1	7	2
Rochdale	L	01/12	11	5	0	1
Notts Co	L	03/12	11	8	0	2

BOGIE Ian
Born: Newcastle-upon-Tyne, England, 6 December, 1967 M
England: Schools

League Club	Source	Date Signed	Seasons Played	Apps	Subs	Gls
Newcastle U	App	12/85	86-88	7	7	0
Preston NE	Tr	02/89	88-90	67	12	12
Millwall	Tr	08/91	91-93	44	7	1
Leyton Orient	Tr	10/93	93-94	62	3	5
Port Vale	Tr	03/95	94-99	133	21	9
Kidderminster Hrs	Tr	08/00	00	14	7	1

BOGIE Malcolm Fisher McKenzie
Born: Edinburgh, Scotland, 26 December, 1939 IF
Scotland: Schools

League Club	Source	Date Signed	Seasons Played	Apps	Subs	Gls
Grimsby T	Hibernian	07/63	63	1	-	0
Aldershot	Tr	07/64	64	2	-	1

BOHINEN Lars Roar
Born: Vadso, Norway, 8 September, 1969 M
Norway: 49/U21-8/Youth

League Club	Source	Date Signed	Seasons Played	Apps	Subs	Gls
Nottingham F	Young Boys Bern (SUI)	11/93	93-95	59	5	7
Blackburn Rov	Tr	10/95	95-97	40	18	7
Derby Co	Tr	03/98	97-00	47	9	1

[BOJAN] KRKIC Bojan
Born: Balaguer, Lerida, Spain, 28 August, 1990 F/W
Spain: 1/U21-21/Youth

League Club	Source	Date Signed	Seasons Played	Apps	Subs	Gls
Stoke C	AS Roma (ITA)	07/14	14	14	2	4

BOJIC Pedrag (Pedj)
Born: Sydney, Australia, 9 April, 1984 RB
Australia: Youth

League Club	Source	Date Signed	Seasons Played	Apps	Subs	Gls
Northampton T	Sydney Olympic (AUS)	08/04	04-06	62	36	4

BOJINOV Valeri Emilov
Born: Gorna Oryahovitsa, Bulgaria, 15 February, 1986 F
Bulgaria: 43

League Club	Source	Date Signed	Seasons Played	Apps	Subs	Gls
Manchester C	Fiorentina (ITA)	08/07	07-08	3	8	1

BOKSIC Alen
Born: Makarska, Croatia, 21 January, 1970 F
Croatia: 40

League Club	Source	Date Signed	Seasons Played	Apps	Subs	Gls
Middlesbrough	SS Lazio (ITA)	08/00	00-02	59	9	22

BOLAM Thomas Edward (Tom)
Born: Newcastle-upon-Tyne, England, 8 July, 1924 WH
Died: Newcastle-upon-Tyne, England, 12 February, 2005

League Club	Source	Date Signed	Seasons Played	Apps	Subs	Gls
Barrow		08/50	50-51	35	-	0

BOLAND William John (Willie)
Born: Ennis, Republic of Ireland, 6 August, 1975 DM
Republic of Ireland: B-1/U21-11/Youth/Schools

League Club	Source	Date Signed	Seasons Played	Apps	Subs	Gls
Coventry C	Jnr	11/92	92-97	43	20	0
Cardiff C	Tr	06/99	99-05	187	22	3
Hartlepool U	Tr	08/06	06-08	60	4	1

BOLASIE Yannick (Yala)
Born: Lyon, France, 24 May, 1989 LW
DR Congo: 18

League Club	Source	Date Signed	Seasons Played	Apps	Subs	Gls
Plymouth Arg	Floriana (MLT)	07/08	09-10	33	18	8
Barnet	L	01/09	08	17	3	3
Barnet	L	07/09	09	14	8	2
Bristol C	Tr	06/11	11	7	16	1
Crystal Palace	Tr	08/12	12-14	93	13	7

BOLDER Adam Peter
Born: Hull, England, 25 October, 1980 M

League Club	Source	Date Signed	Seasons Played	Apps	Subs	Gls
Hull C	YT	07/99	98-99	18	2	0
Derby Co	Tr	04/00	00-06	109	57	11
Queens Park Rgrs	Tr	01/07	06-07	36	4	2
Sheffield Wed	L	02/08	07	11	2	2
Millwall	Tr	11/08	08-09	33	6	0
Bradford C	L	03/10	09	14	0	1
Burton A	Tr	07/10	10-11	73	8	4

BOLDER Christopher James (Chris)
Born: Hull, England, 19 August, 1982 M

League Club	Source	Date Signed	Seasons Played	Apps	Subs	Gls
Grimsby T	Hull C (YT)	07/01	02-03	13	6	0

BOLDER Robert John (Bob)
Born: Dover, Kent, England, 2 October, 1958 G

League Club	Source	Date Signed	Seasons Played	Apps	Subs	Gls
Sheffield Wed	Dover	03/77	77-82	196	0	0
Liverpool	Tr	08/83				
Sunderland	Tr	09/85	85	22	0	0
Charlton Ath	Tr	08/86	86-92	249	0	0

BOLESAN Mirko
Born: Genoa, Italy, 6 May, 1975 M

League Club	Source	Date Signed	Seasons Played	Apps	Subs	Gls
Cardiff C	Sestrese (ITA)	10/95	95	0	1	0

BOLGER Cian Thomas
Born: Celbridge, Co. Kildare, Republic of Ireland, 12 March, 1992 CD
Republic of Ireland: U21-2/Youth

League Club	Source	Date Signed	Seasons Played	Apps	Subs	Gls
Leicester C	Sch	07/09				
Bristol Rov	L	01/11	10	4	2	0
Bristol Rov	L	07/11	11	38	1	2
Bristol Rov	L	08/12	12	3	0	0
Bolton W	Tr	01/13				
Colchester U	L	10/13	13	4	0	0
Southend U	L	02/14	13	1	0	0
Southend U	Tr	08/14	14	21	2	1

BOLI Roger Zokou
Born: Adjame, Ivory Coast, 29 June, 1965 F

League Club	Source	Date Signed	Seasons Played	Apps	Subs	Gls
Walsall	RC Lens (FRA)	08/97	97	41	0	12
Bournemouth	Dundee U	10/98	98	5	1	0

BOLIMA Cedric
Born: Kinshasa, Congo, 26 September, 1979 F

League Club	Source	Date Signed	Seasons Played	Apps	Subs	Gls
Rotherham U	RC Lens (FRA)	10/00	00	0	1	0

BOLLAND Gordon Edward
Born: Boston, Lincolnshire, England, 12 August, 1943 M/F

League Club	Source	Date Signed	Seasons Played	Apps	Subs	Gls
Chelsea	Jnr	08/60	61	2	-	0
Leyton Orient	Tr	03/62	61-63	63	-	19

League Club	Source	Date Signed	Seasons Played	Apps	Subs	Gls
Norwich C	Tr	03/64	63-67	104	1	29
Charlton Ath	Tr	11/67	67-68	9	2	2
Millwall	Tr	10/68	68-74	239	5	62

BOLLAND Paul Graham Arthur
Born: Bradford, England, 23 December, 1979 — M

League Club	Source	Date Signed	Seasons Played	Apps	Subs	Gls
Bradford C	YT	03/98	97-98	4	8	0
Notts Co	Tr	01/99	98-04	153	19	6
Grimsby T	Tr	08/05	05-07	114	4	13
Macclesfield T	Tr	07/09	09-10	48	11	3

BOLLAND Philip Christopher (Phil)
Born: Liverpool, England, 26 August, 1976 — CD

League Club	Source	Date Signed	Seasons Played	Apps	Subs	Gls
Oxford U	Southport	07/01	01	20	0	1
Chester C	Tr	03/02	04-05	54	4	2
Peterborough U	Tr	01/06	05	17	0	0
Chester C	Tr	07/06	06-07	25	3	1
Wrexham	Tr	01/08	07	18	0	0

BOLLANDS John Frederick
Born: Middlesbrough, England, 11 July, 1935 — G

League Club	Source	Date Signed	Seasons Played	Apps	Subs	Gls
Oldham Ath	South Bank	05/53	54-55	23	-	0
Sunderland	Tr	03/56	55-59	61	-	0
Bolton W	Tr	02/60	59	13	-	0
Oldham Ath	Tr	09/61	61-65	131	0	0

BOLT Daniel Anthony (Danny)
Born: Wandsworth, SW London, England, 5 February, 1976 — LM

League Club	Source	Date Signed	Seasons Played	Apps	Subs	Gls
Fulham	YT	07/94	94-95	9	4	2

BOLTON Anthony Gordon (Tony)
Born: Newport, Wales, 15 January, 1968 — W

League Club	Source	Date Signed	Seasons Played	Apps	Subs	Gls
Charlton Ath	Jnr	01/85				
Newport Co	Tr	08/86	86	6	2	0

BOLTON Ian Robert
Born: Leicester, England, 13 July, 1953 — CD

League Club	Source	Date Signed	Seasons Played	Apps	Subs	Gls
Notts Co	Birmingham C (App)	09/70	71-76	61	9	4
Lincoln C	L	08/76	76	1	0	0
Watford	Tr	08/77	77-83	233	1	28
Brentford	Tr	12/83	83	14	0	1

BOLTON John McCaig (Jack)
Born: Lesmahagow, Lanarkshire, Scotland, 26 October, 1941 — D

League Club	Source	Date Signed	Seasons Played	Apps	Subs	Gls
Ipswich T	Raith Rov	07/63	63-65	69	0	2

BOLTON Joseph (Joe)
Born: Birtley, Tyne and Wear, England, 2 February, 1955 — LB

League Club	Source	Date Signed	Seasons Played	Apps	Subs	Gls
Sunderland	App	02/72	71-80	264	9	11
Middlesbrough	Tr	07/81	81-82	59	0	1
Sheffield U	Tr	08/83	83-85	109	0	3

BOLTON Lyall (Laurie)
Born: Gateshead, Tyne and Wear, England, 11 July, 1932 — WH

League Club	Source	Date Signed	Seasons Played	Apps	Subs	Gls
Sunderland	Close House	08/50	55-56	3	-	0

BOLTON Nigel Alan
Born: Bishop Auckland, County Durham, England, 14 January, 1975 — F

League Club	Source	Date Signed	Seasons Played	Apps	Subs	Gls
Darlington	Shildon	08/94	94	1	1	0

BOLTON Ronald (Danny)
Born: Rotherham, South Yorkshire, England, 1 September, 1921 — G
Died: Rotherham, South Yorkshire, England, May, 1997

League Club	Source	Date Signed	Seasons Played	Apps	Subs	Gls
Bolton W		05/39				
Rotherham U	Owen & Dyson	06/48	48-54	151	-	0

BOLTON Ronald (Ronnie)
Born: Golborne, Greater Manchester, England, 21 January, 1938 — WH/IF

League Club	Source	Date Signed	Seasons Played	Apps	Subs	Gls
Bournemouth	Crompton's Rec	04/58	58-65	199	0	31
Ipswich T	Tr	10/65	65-67	21	1	0
Bournemouth	Tr	09/67	67-68	61	4	17

BONALAIR Thierry
Born: Paris, France, 14 June, 1966 — RB/M

League Club	Source	Date Signed	Seasons Played	Apps	Subs	Gls
Nottingham F	Neuchatel Xamax (SUI)	07/97	97-99	58	13	5

BOND Andrew Mark (Andy)
Born: Wigan, Greater Manchester, England, 16 March, 1986 — M

League Club	Source	Date Signed	Seasons Played	Apps	Subs	Gls
Crewe Alex	Sch	06/05				
Colchester U	Barrow	07/10	10-13	80	38	11
Crewe Alex	L	09/12	12	4	0	0
Bristol Rov	L	09/13	13	5	0	0
Stevenage	Chester FC	06/14	14	16	4	0

BOND Anthony (Tony)
Born: Preston, Lancashire, England, 27 December, 1913 — W
Died: Preston, Lancashire, England, 6 July, 1993

League Club	Source	Date Signed	Seasons Played	Apps	Subs	Gls
Blackburn Rov	Dick Kerr's XI	04/32				
Wolverhampton W	Chorley	11/36				
Torquay U	Tr	06/37	37	15	-	0
Preston NE	Leyland Motors	08/44				
Southport	Tr	08/45				
Accrington Stan	Tr	05/46	46	29	-	4

BOND Chad David
Born: Neath, Wales, 20 April, 1987 — F

League Club	Source	Date Signed	Seasons Played	Apps	Subs	Gls
Swansea C	Sch	07/05				
Swansea C	Port Talbot T	08/08	09	1	0	0

BOND Dennis Joseph Thomas
Born: Walthamstow, NE London, England, 17 March, 1947 — M
England: Youth/Schools

League Club	Source	Date Signed	Seasons Played	Apps	Subs	Gls
Watford	App	03/64	64-66	93	0	17
Tottenham H	Tr	03/67	66-70	20	3	1
Charlton Ath	Tr	10/70	70-72	70	5	3
Watford	Tr	02/73	72-77	178	1	21

BOND Graham Charles
Born: Torquay, Devon, England, 30 December, 1932 — IF/W
Died: Torbay, Devon, England, June, 1998

League Club	Source	Date Signed	Seasons Played	Apps	Subs	Gls
Torquay U	Hele Spurs	09/51	53-60	128	-	46
Exeter C	Tr	10/60	60	10	-	4
Torquay U	Weymouth	10/61	61	5	-	1

BOND James Ernest (Ernie)
Born: Preston, Lancashire, England, 4 May, 1929 — LW

League Club	Source	Date Signed	Seasons Played	Apps	Subs	Gls
Manchester U	Leyland Motors	12/50	51-52	20	-	4
Carlisle U	Tr	09/52	52-58	192	-	24

BOND John Frederick
Born: Dedham, Essex, England, 17 December, 1932 — FB
Died: Manchester, England, 25 September, 2012
England: FLge-2

League Club	Source	Date Signed	Seasons Played	Apps	Subs	Gls
West Ham U	Colchester Casuals	03/50	51-64	381	-	32
Torquay U	Tr	01/66	65-68	129	1	12

BOND Jonathan Henry
Born: Hemel Hempstead, Hertfordshire, England, 19 May, 1993 — G
England: U21-5//Wales: U21-1/Youth

League Club	Source	Date Signed	Seasons Played	Apps	Subs	Gls
Watford	Sch	07/10	11-14	18	4	0
Dagenham & Red	L	02/12	11	5	0	0
Bury	L	03/12	11	6	0	0

BOND Kain
Born: Torquay, Devon, England, 19 June, 1985 — F

League Club	Source	Date Signed	Seasons Played	Apps	Subs	Gls
Torquay U	Sch	07/03	02-04	0	3	0

BOND Kevin John
Born: West Ham, E London, England, 22 June, 1957 — CD
England: B-2

League Club	Source	Date Signed	Seasons Played	Apps	Subs	Gls
Norwich C	Bournemouth (App)	07/74	75-80	137	5	12
Manchester C	Seattle Sounders (USA)	09/81	81-84	108	2	11
Southampton	Tr	09/84	84-87	139	1	6
Bournemouth	Tr	08/88	88-91	121	5	4
Exeter C	Tr	08/92	92-93	18	1	0

BOND Leonard Allan (Len)
Born: Ilminster, Somerset, England, 12 February, 1954 — G

League Club	Source	Date Signed	Seasons Played	Apps	Subs	Gls
Bristol C	App	09/71	70-76	30	0	0
Exeter C	L	11/74	74	30	0	0
Torquay U	L	10/75	75	3	0	0
Scunthorpe U	L	12/75	75	8	0	0
Colchester U	L	01/76	75	3	0	0
Brentford	Tr	08/77	77-79	122	0	0
Exeter C	Tr	10/80	80-83	138	0	0

BOND Richard (Richie)
Born: Blyth, Northumberland, England, 27 October, 1965 — F

League Club	Source	Date Signed	Seasons Played	Apps	Subs	Gls
Blackpool	Blyth Spartans	12/91	92	0	1	0

BONDS William Arthur (Billy)
Born: Woolwich, SE London, England, 17 September, 1946 — D/M
England: U23-2

League Club	Source	Date Signed	Seasons Played	Apps	Subs	Gls
Charlton Ath	App	09/64	64-66	95	0	1
West Ham U	Tr	05/67	67-87	655	8	48

BONE James (Jimmy)
Born: Bridge of Allan, Stirlingshire, Scotland, 22 September, 1949 — F
Scotland: 2/U23-3

League Club	Source	Date Signed	Seasons Played	Apps	Subs	Gls
Norwich C	Partick Thistle	02/72	71-72	39	0	9
Sheffield U	Tr	02/73	72-73	30	1	9

BONE John
Born: Hartlepool, Cleveland, England, 19 December, 1930 — CH
Died: Hartlepool, Cleveland, England, January, 2002

League Club	Source	Date Signed	Seasons Played	Apps	Subs	Gls
Sunderland	Wingate	01/51	54-56	11	-	0

BONER David
Born: South Queensferry, Edinburgh, Scotland, 12 October, 1941 — RW
Scotland: Schools

League Club	Source	Date Signed	Seasons Played	Apps	Subs	Gls
Everton	Jnr	10/58				
Mansfield T	Raith Rov	07/63	63	12	-	1

League Club	Source	Date Signed	Seasons Played	Career Record Apps	Subs	Gls
BONETTI Ivano						
Born: Brescia, Italy, 1 August, 1964						M
Grimsby T	Torino (ITA)	09/95	95	19	0	3
Tranmere Rov	Tr	08/96	96	9	4	1
Crystal Palace	Bologna (ITA)	10/97	97	0	2	0
BONETTI Peter Philip						
Born: Putney, SW London, England, 27 September, 1941						G
England: 7/FLge-4/U23-12						
Chelsea	Jnr	05/59	59-78	600	0	0
BONG Thomas Gaetan (Gaetan)						
Born: Sakbayeme, Cameroon, 25 April, 1988						LB
Cameroon: 12//France: U21-1						
Wigan Ath	Olympiakos (GRE)	02/15	14	14	0	0
BONHAM Jack Elliott						
Born: Stevenage, Hertfordshire, England, 14 September, 1993						G
Republic of Ireland: Youth						
Watford	Sch	09/10	12	0	1	0
Brentford	Tr	07/13	13	0	1	0
BONNAR Patrick (Paddy)						
Born: Ballymena, Antrim, Northern Ireland, 27 November, 1920						RW
Northern Ireland: NILge-3/War-2						
Barnsley	Belfast Celtic	08/49	49	5	-	1
Aldershot	Tr	06/50	50-52	63	-	19
BONNE Macauley Miles						
Born: Ipswich, England, 26 October, 1995						F
Colchester U	Sch	10/13	13-14	5	19	3
BONNELL Arnold						
Born: Barnsley, South Yorkshire, England, 23 March, 1921						FB
Barnsley	Jnr	04/38	46-47	7	-	0
Rochdale	Tr	07/48	48	5	-	0
BONNER Bernard						
Born: Motherwell, Lanarkshire, Scotland, 22 July, 1927						CF
Died: East Kilbride, Lanarkshire, Scotland, 14 February, 2005						
Wrexham	Airdrieonians	02/52	51	1	-	0
BONNER Mark						
Born: Ormskirk, Lancashire, England, 7 June, 1974						M
Blackpool	YT	06/92	91-97	156	22	14
Cardiff C	Tr	07/98	98-03	113	30	2
Hull C	L	01/99	98	1	0	1
Oldham Ath	Tr	03/04	03-05	26	7	1
BONNER Thomas Ernest (Tom)						
Born: Camden, N London, England, 6 February, 1988						CD
Cambridge U	Dartford	05/13	14	4	0	0
BONNISSEL Jerome						
Born: Montpellier, France, 16 April, 1973						LB
Fulham	Glasgow Rangers	08/03	03	16	0	0
BONNOT Alexandre (Alex)						
Born: Paris, France, 31 July, 1973						M
Watford	SCO Angiers (FRA)	11/98	98-99	8	8	0
Queens Park Rgrs	Tr	08/01	01	17	5	1
BONNYMAN Philip (Phil)						
Born: Glasgow, Scotland, 6 February, 1954						M
Carlisle U	Hamilton Academical	03/76	75-79	149	3	26
Chesterfield	Tr	03/80	79-81	98	1	25
Grimsby T	Tr	08/82	82-86	146	5	15
Stoke C	L	03/86	85	7	0	0
Darlington	Tr	07/87	87-88	49	1	5
BONSON Joseph (Joe)						
Born: Barnsley, South Yorkshire, England, 19 June, 1936						CF
Died: Wolverhampton, England, 29 November, 1991						
Wolverhampton W	Jnr	07/53	56	10	-	4
Cardiff C	Tr	11/57	57-59	72	-	36
Scunthorpe U	Tr	06/60	60-61	52	-	11
Doncaster Rov	Tr	02/62	61	14	-	4
Newport Co	Tr	06/62	62-63	83	-	47
Brentford	Tr	06/64	64-65	35	0	13
Lincoln C	Tr	01/66	65-66	46	1	16
BONVIN Pablo Facundo						
Born: Concepcion, Argentina, 15 April, 1981						F
Newcastle U	Boca Juniors (ARG)	08/00				
Sheffield Wed	Tr	08/01	01	7	16	4
BONY Wilfried Guemiand						
Born: Bingerville, Ivory Coast, 10 December, 1988						F
Ivory Coast: 42						
Swansea C	Vitesse Arnhem (NED)	07/13	13-14	43	11	25
Manchester C	Tr	01/15	14	2	8	2

League Club	Source	Date Signed	Seasons Played	Career Record Apps	Subs	Gls
BOOGERS Marco						
Born: Dordrecht, Netherlands, 12 January, 1967						F
West Ham U	Sparta Rotterdam (NED)	07/95	95	0	4	0
BOOK Anthony Keith (Tony)						
Born: Bath, England, 4 September, 1934						RB
Plymouth Arg	Bath C	08/64	64-65	81	0	3
Manchester C	Tr	07/66	66-73	242	2	4
BOOK Kim Alistair						
Born: Bath, England, 12 February, 1946						G
Bournemouth	Frome T	07/67	67-68	2	0	0
Northampton T	Tr	10/69	69-71	78	0	0
Mansfield T	L	09/71	71	4	0	0
Doncaster Rov	Tr	12/71	71-73	84	0	0
BOOK Steven Kim (Steve)						
Born: Bournemouth, England, 7 July, 1969						G
England: Semi Pro-3						
Cheltenham T	Forest Green Rov	07/97	99-03	171	1	0
Swindon T	Tr	08/04	04	1	1	0
Bristol Rov	Cirencester T	12/05	05	1	0	0
BOOKER Kenneth (Ken)						
Born: Sheffield, England, 3 March, 1918						CH
Died: Worksop, Nottinghamshire, England, 14 December, 1997						
Chesterfield	Dronfield T	04/36	38-51	183	-	4
Shrewsbury T	Tr	07/52	52	9	-	0
BOOKER Michael (Mike)						
Born: Barnsley, South Yorkshire, England, 22 October, 1947						LB
England: Schools						
Barnsley	App	10/65	66	0	2	0
Bradford Park Ave	Tr	06/68	68	11	2	0
BOOKER Robert (Bob)						
Born: Watford, Hertfordshire, England, 25 January, 1958						M
Brentford	Bedmond Social	10/78	78-88	207	44	42
Sheffield U	Tr	11/88	88-91	91	18	13
Brentford	Tr	11/91	91-92	15	4	2
BOOKER Trevor Christopher						
Born: Lambeth, S London, England, 26 February, 1969						F
Millwall	Jnr	07/86	86	1	2	0
BOORN Alan						
Born: Folkestone, Kent, England, 11 April, 1953						M
England: Youth						
Brighton & HA	Folkestone T	08/71	72	2	0	0
BOOT Edmund (Eddie)						
Born: Laughton Common, South Yorkshire, England, 13 October, 1915						LB
Died: Reading, England, August, 1999						
Sheffield U	Denaby U	10/35	35-36	41	-	0
Huddersfield T	Tr	03/37	36-51	305	-	5
BOOT Michael Colin (Mickey)						
Born: Leicester, England, 17 December, 1947						M
England: Schools						
Arsenal	App	12/64	66	3	1	2
BOOTH Andrew David (Andy)						
Born: Huddersfield, West Yorkshire, England, 6 December, 1973						F
England: U21-3						
Huddersfield T	YT	07/92	91-95	109	14	54
Sheffield Wed	Tr	07/96	96-00	124	9	28
Tottenham H	L	01/01	00	3	1	0
Huddersfield T	Tr	03/01	00-08	229	42	80
BOOTH Anthony John (Tony)						
Born: Biggin Hill, Kent, England, 20 June, 1961						M
Charlton Ath	Jnr	06/78	78-79	2	6	0
BOOTH Colin						
Born: Manchester, England, 30 December, 1934						IF
England: U23-1/Schools						
Wolverhampton W	Jnr	01/52	54-59	78	-	26
Nottingham F	Tr	10/59	59-61	87	-	39
Doncaster Rov	Tr	08/62	62-63	88	-	57
Oxford U	Tr	07/64	64-65	48	0	23
BOOTH David						
Born: Kexbrough, South Yorkshire, England, 2 October, 1948						LB
Barnsley	Higham Rov	05/67	68-71	161	3	8
Grimsby T	Tr	06/72	72-77	199	1	7
BOOTH David Christopher						
Born: Wilmslow, Cheshire, England, 25 October, 1962						M
Stockport Co	Jnr	04/80	79-80	20	8	4

BOOTH Dennis
Born: Stanley Common, Derbyshire, England, 9 April, 1949 M/D

League Club	Source	Date Signed	Seasons Played	Apps	Subs	Gls
Charlton Ath	App	04/66	66-70	67	10	5
Blackpool	Tr	07/71	71	12	0	0
Southend U	Tr	03/72	71-73	77	1	1
Lincoln C	Tr	02/74	73-77	162	0	9
Watford	Tr	10/77	77-79	97	3	2
Hull C	Tr	05/80	80-84	121	2	2

BOOTH Grenville Vincent
Born: Chester, England, 2 April, 1925 LH
Died: Chester, England, May, 1991

League Club	Source	Date Signed	Seasons Played	Apps	Subs	Gls
Chester C	Jnr	08/48	48	8	-	0

BOOTH Kenneth Kershaw (Ken)
Born: Blackpool, Lancashire, England, 22 November, 1934 IF

League Club	Source	Date Signed	Seasons Played	Apps	Subs	Gls
Blackpool	St Peter's YC	01/52	56	1	-	1
Bradford Park Ave	Tr	05/57	57-58	45	-	14
Workington	Tr	06/59	59	30	-	13
Southport	Tr	07/60	60	26	-	7

BOOTH Paul
Born: Bolton, Greater Manchester, England, 7 December, 1965 D
England: Schools

League Club	Source	Date Signed	Seasons Played	Apps	Subs	Gls
Bolton W	App	12/83	84	1	0	0
Crewe Alex	Tr	07/85	85	23	4	0

BOOTH Raymond (Ray)
Born: Wrexham, Wales, 5 December, 1949 W

League Club	Source	Date Signed	Seasons Played	Apps	Subs	Gls
Wrexham	Jnr	10/67	66-68	5	0	0

BOOTH Robert Paul (Robbie)
Born: Liverpool, England, 30 December, 1985 M

League Club	Source	Date Signed	Seasons Played	Apps	Subs	Gls
Chester C	Everton (Sch)	05/05	04	7	4	1

BOOTH Samuel Stewart (Sam)
Born: Shotts, Lanarkshire, Scotland, 20 April, 1926 WH
Died: Carluke, Lanarkshire, Scotland, 25 September, 1968

League Club	Source	Date Signed	Seasons Played	Apps	Subs	Gls
Exeter C	Derry C (ROI)	08/51	51-53	62	-	0
Bradford C	Tr	07/54	54	15	-	0

BOOTH Thomas Anthony (Tommy)
Born: Middleton, Greater Manchester, England, 9 November, 1949 CD
England: U23-4

League Club	Source	Date Signed	Seasons Played	Apps	Subs	Gls
Manchester C	Jnr	08/67	68-81	380	2	25
Preston NE	Tr	10/81	81-84	84	0	2

BOOTH Wilfred (Wilf)
Born: Darton, South Yorkshire, England, 26 December, 1918 CF
Died: Bury, Greater Manchester, England, 24 August, 2009

League Club	Source	Date Signed	Seasons Played	Apps	Subs	Gls
Halifax T	Wombwell Ath	12/47	47	6	-	2

BOOTH William Samuel (Sam)
Born: Hove, East Sussex, England, 7 July, 1920 CH/F
Died: Eastbourne, East Sussex, England, 18 February, 1990

League Club	Source	Date Signed	Seasons Played	Apps	Subs	Gls
Port Vale	Brighton & HA (Am)	02/39	38	9	-	0
Cardiff C	Tr	05/39				
Brighton & HA	Tr	08/47	47-48	28	-	6

BOOTHMAN James (Jerry)
Born: Great Harwood, Lancashire, England, 2 December, 1920 FB
Died: Keighley, West Yorkshire, England, 1980

League Club	Source	Date Signed	Seasons Played	Apps	Subs	Gls
Oldham Ath	Fleet Air Arm	01/46	46-47	44	-	0

BOOTHROYD Adrian Neil (Adie)
Born: Bradford, England, 8 February, 1971 RB

League Club	Source	Date Signed	Seasons Played	Apps	Subs	Gls
Huddersfield T	YT	07/89	89	9	1	0
Bristol Rov	Tr	06/90	90-91	10	6	0
Mansfield T	Heart of Midlothian	12/93	93-95	99	3	3
Peterborough U	Tr	06/96	96	24	2	1

BOOTHWAY John (Jack)
Born: Manchester, England, 4 February, 1919 CF
Died: Runcorn, Cheshire, England, 7 April, 1979

League Club	Source	Date Signed	Seasons Played	Apps	Subs	Gls
Manchester C	Great Harwood	07/41				
Crewe Alex	Tr	07/44	46	12	-	5
Wrexham	Tr	10/46	46-49	95	-	55

BOOTLE William
Born: Ashton-under-Lyne, Greater Manchester, England, 9 January, 1926 LW
Died: Urmston, Greater Manchester, England, 10 August, 2012

League Club	Source	Date Signed	Seasons Played	Apps	Subs	Gls
Manchester C	Jnr	06/43	48-49	5	-	0
Crewe Alex	Wigan Ath	03/54	53-54	14	-	4

BOOTY Justin
Born: Colchester, Essex, England, 2 June, 1976 F

League Club	Source	Date Signed	Seasons Played	Apps	Subs	Gls
Colchester U	YT	08/94	93	0	1	0

BOOTY Martyn James
Born: Anstey, Leicestershire, England, 30 May, 1971 RB

League Club	Source	Date Signed	Seasons Played	Apps	Subs	Gls
Coventry C	YT	05/89	91-93	4	1	0
Crewe Alex	Tr	10/93	93-95	95	1	5
Reading	Tr	01/96	95-98	62	2	1
Southend U	Tr	01/99	98-00	78	2	0
Chesterfield	Tr	08/01	01-02	75	3	2
Huddersfield T	Tr	08/03	03	3	1	0

BOPP Eugene
Born: Kiev, Ukraine, 5 September, 1983 M

League Club	Source	Date Signed	Seasons Played	Apps	Subs	Gls
Nottingham F	YT	09/00	01-05	39	38	8
Rotherham U	Tr	08/06	06	24	5	5
Crewe Alex	Tr	07/07	07-08	9	8	2

BORBOKIS Vassilios (Vas)
Born: Serres, Greece, 10 February, 1969 RB/M
Greece: 2

League Club	Source	Date Signed	Seasons Played	Apps	Subs	Gls
Sheffield U	AEK Athens (GRE)	07/97	97-98	55	0	4
Derby Co	Tr	03/99	98-99	9	7	0

BORE Peter Charles
Born: Grimsby, North Lincolnshire, England, 4 November, 1987 RM

League Club	Source	Date Signed	Seasons Played	Apps	Subs	Gls
Grimsby T	Sch	08/06	06-09	72	44	11

BORG John Carmel Adam
Born: Salford, England, 22 February, 1980 M

League Club	Source	Date Signed	Seasons Played	Apps	Subs	Gls
Doncaster Rov	YT	-	97	1	0	0
Bury	Tr	07/98				

BORGETTI Jared Francisco
Born: Culiacan, Mexico, 14 August, 1973 F
Mexico: 89

League Club	Source	Date Signed	Seasons Played	Apps	Subs	Gls
Bolton W	Pachuca (MEX)	08/05	05	5	14	2

BORI Gabor
Born: Szombathely, Hungary, 16 January, 1984 RW
Hungary: 1/Youth

League Club	Source	Date Signed	Seasons Played	Apps	Subs	Gls
Leicester C (L)	MTK Budapest (HUN)	01/08	07	4	2	0

BORINI Fabio
Born: Bologna, Italy, 23 March, 1991 F
Italy: 1/U21-18/Youth

League Club	Source	Date Signed	Seasons Played	Apps	Subs	Gls
Chelsea	Sch	07/08	09	0	4	0
Swansea C	L	03/11	10	8	1	6
Liverpool	Parma (ITA)	07/12	12-14	8	17	2
Sunderland	L	09/13	13	25	7	7

BORLAND John Robert
Born: Lancaster, England, 28 January, 1977 M

League Club	Source	Date Signed	Seasons Played	Apps	Subs	Gls
Burnley	YT	07/95	95	1	0	0
Scunthorpe U	Tr	08/96	96	0	2	0

BORLEY David
Born: Newcastle-upon-Tyne, England, 14 April, 1983 M
England: Schools

League Club	Source	Date Signed	Seasons Played	Apps	Subs	Gls
Bury	YT	07/01	01	16	5	3

BOROTA Petar
Born: Belgrade, Yugoslavia, 5 March, 1952 G
Died: Genoa, Italy, 12 February, 2010
Yugoslavia: 4

League Club	Source	Date Signed	Seasons Played	Apps	Subs	Gls
Chelsea	Part'n Belgrade (YUG)	03/79	78-81	107	0	0

BORRIELLO Marco
Born: Naples, Italy, 18 June, 1982 F
Italy: 7/U21-12/Youth

League Club	Source	Date Signed	Seasons Played	Apps	Subs	Gls
West Ham U (L)	AS Roma (ITA)	01/14	13	0	2	0

BORROWDALE Gary Ian
Born: Malden, SW London, England, 16 July, 1985 LB
England: Youth

League Club	Source	Date Signed	Seasons Played	Apps	Subs	Gls
Crystal Palace	Sch	12/02	02-06	74	24	0
Coventry C	Tr	07/07	07	20	1	0
Colchester U	L	09/08	08	4	0	0
Queens Park Rgrs	Tr	11/08	09-10	18	4	0
Brighton & HA	L	03/09	08	11	1	0
Charlton Ath	L	03/10	09	10	0	0
Carlisle U	L	02/11	10	1	0	0
Barnet	L	09/11	11	11	0	0

BORROWS Brian
Born: Liverpool, England, 20 December, 1960 RB
England: B-1

League Club	Source	Date Signed	Seasons Played	Apps	Subs	Gls
Everton	Jnr	04/80	81-82	27	0	0
Bolton W	Tr	03/83	82-84	95	0	0
Coventry C	Tr	06/85	85-96	396	13	11
Bristol C	L	09/93	93	6	0	0
Swindon T	Tr	09/97	97-98	80	0	0

BORTHWICK Gary Michael
Born: Slough, Berkshire, England, 30 November, 1955 M

League Club	Source	Date Signed	Seasons Played	Apps	Subs	Gls
Bournemouth	Barnet	03/78	77-79	66	8	4

BORTHWICK John Robert
Born: Hartlepool, Cleveland, England, 24 March, 1964 — F

League Club	Source	Date Signed	Seasons Played	Apps	Subs	Gls
Hartlepool U	Owton Manor SC	12/82	82-88	96	21	14
Darlington	Tr	08/89	90-91	57	18	15
York C	Tr	07/92	92	28	5	8

BORTHWICK Walter Ross
Born: Edinburgh, Scotland, 4 April, 1948 — IF

League Club	Source	Date Signed	Seasons Played	Apps	Subs	Gls
Brighton & HA	Greenock Morton	05/67	66	1	0	0

BORTOLAZZI Mario
Born: Verona, Italy, 10 January, 1965 — M

League Club	Source	Date Signed	Seasons Played	Apps	Subs	Gls
West Bromwich A	Genoa (ITA)	08/98	98	25	10	2

BORUC Artur
Born: Siedlce, Poland, 20 February, 1980 — G
Poland: 60

League Club	Source	Date Signed	Seasons Played	Apps	Subs	Gls
Southampton	Fiorentina (ITA)	09/12	12-13	49	0	0
Bournemouth	L	09/14	14	37	0	0

BOS Gijsbert
Born: Spakenburg, Netherlands, 22 February, 1973 — F

League Club	Source	Date Signed	Seasons Played	Apps	Subs	Gls
Lincoln C	Ijsselmeervogels (NED)	03/96	95-96	28	6	6
Rotherham U	Tr	08/97	97-98	7	11	4

BOSANCIC Jovica (Jovo)
Born: Novi Sad, Yugoslavia, 7 August, 1970 — M
Yugoslavia: U21

League Club	Source	Date Signed	Seasons Played	Apps	Subs	Gls
Barnsley	Uniao Madeira (POR)	08/96	96-97	30	12	3

BOSELLI Mauro
Born: Buenos Aires, Argentina, 22 May, 1985 — F
Argentina: 4/Youth

League Club	Source	Date Signed	Seasons Played	Apps	Subs	Gls
Wigan Ath	Estudiantes (ARG)	08/10	10-12	6	9	0

BOSHELL Daniel Kevin (Danny)
Born: Bradford, England, 30 May, 1981 — M

League Club	Source	Date Signed	Seasons Played	Apps	Subs	Gls
Oldham Ath	YT	07/98	99-04	45	25	2
Bury	L	03/05	04	2	4	0
Stockport Co	Tr	07/05	05	28	5	1
Grimsby T	Tr	08/06	06-09	84	15	10
Chesterfield	Tr	02/10	09	3	6	0

BOSINGWA Jose
Born: Mbandaka, DR Congo, 24 August, 1982 — RB
Portugal: 24/U21-18

League Club	Source	Date Signed	Seasons Played	Apps	Subs	Gls
Chelsea	FC Porto (POR)	06/08	08-11	79	10	3
Queens Park Rgrs	Tr	08/12	12	22	1	0

BOSLEM William (Billy)
Born: Middleton, Greater Manchester, England, 11 January, 1958 — CD

League Club	Source	Date Signed	Seasons Played	Apps	Subs	Gls
Rochdale	Jnr	11/75	75-77	42	3	1

BOSNICH Mark John
Born: Sydney, Australia, 13 January, 1972 — G
Australia: 17/U23-6/Youth

League Club	Source	Date Signed	Seasons Played	Apps	Subs	Gls
Manchester U	Sydney Croatia (AUS)	06/89	89-90	3	0	0
Aston Villa	Sydney Croatia (AUS)	02/92	91-98	179	0	0
Manchester U	Tr	07/99	99	23	0	0
Chelsea	Tr	01/01	01	5	0	0

BOSSONS Percy Lawrence Powell
Born: Crewe, Cheshire, England, 10 January, 1924 — D
Died: Stoke-on-Trent, England, 5 December, 1950

League Club	Source	Date Signed	Seasons Played	Apps	Subs	Gls
Crewe Alex	West Ham U (Am)	06/46	46-48	29	-	2

BOSSU Bertrand (Bert)
Born: Calais, France, 14 October, 1980 — G

League Club	Source	Date Signed	Seasons Played	Apps	Subs	Gls
Barnet	RC Lens (FRA)	10/99				
Gillingham	Hayes	09/03	03-04	4	2	0
Torquay U	L	08/04	04	2	0	0
Darlington	Tr	07/05	05	9	0	0
Walsall	Tr	09/06	06	1	0	0

BOSSY Fabien
Born: Marseille, France, 1 October, 1977 — CD

League Club	Source	Date Signed	Seasons Played	Apps	Subs	Gls
Darlington	Clyde	08/03	03	4	2	0

BOSTOCK Benjamin Roy (Ben)
Born: Mansfield, Nottinghamshire, England, 19 April, 1929 — W
Died: Canterbury, England, 14 January, 1993

League Club	Source	Date Signed	Seasons Played	Apps	Subs	Gls
Crystal Palace	Jnr	05/46	48	4	-	0

BOSTOCK John Joseph
Born: Camberwell, S London, England, 15 January, 1992 — M
England: Youth

League Club	Source	Date Signed	Seasons Played	Apps	Subs	Gls
Crystal Palace	Jnr	-	07	1	3	0
Tottenham H	Sch	01/09				
Brentford	L	11/09	09	9	0	2
Hull C	L	08/10	10	8	3	2
Sheffield Wed	L	01/12	11	2	2	0

League Club	Source	Date Signed	Seasons Played	Apps	Subs	Gls
Swindon T	L	03/12	11	3	0	0
Swindon T	L	08/12	12	6	2	0

BOSTWICK Michael Paul Trevor
Born: Eltham, SE London, England, 17 May, 1988 — M
England: Semi Pro-1

League Club	Source	Date Signed	Seasons Played	Apps	Subs	Gls
Millwall	Sch	05/06				
Stevenage	Ebbsfleet U	08/08	10-11	84	0	9
Peterborough U	Tr	07/12	12-14	116	3	16

BOSVELT Paul
Born: Doetinchem, Netherlands, 26 March, 1970 — DM
Netherlands: 24

League Club	Source	Date Signed	Seasons Played	Apps	Subs	Gls
Manchester C	Feyenoord (NED)	07/03	03-04	50	3	2

BOSWELL Alan Henry
Born: West Bromwich, West Midlands, England, 8 August, 1943 — G

League Club	Source	Date Signed	Seasons Played	Apps	Subs	Gls
Walsall	Jnr	08/60	61-62	66	-	0
Shrewsbury T	Tr	08/63	63-68	222	0	0
Wolverhampton W	Tr	09/68	68	10	0	0
Bolton W	Tr	10/69	69-70	51	0	0
Port Vale	Tr	08/72	72-73	86	0	0

BOSWELL James (Jimmy)
Born: Chester, England, 13 March, 1922 — WH
Died: Stafford, England, 25 May, 2010

League Club	Source	Date Signed	Seasons Played	Apps	Subs	Gls
Gillingham	Chester C (Am)	07/46	50-57	342	-	6

BOTHAM Ian Terence
Born: Heswall, Wirral, England, 24 November, 1955 — CD

League Club	Source	Date Signed	Seasons Played	Apps	Subs	Gls
Scunthorpe U	Yeovil T	03/80	79-84	7	4	0

BOTHROYD Jay
Born: Islington, N London, England, 7 May, 1982 — F
England: 1/U21-1/Youth/Schools

League Club	Source	Date Signed	Seasons Played	Apps	Subs	Gls
Arsenal	YT	07/99				
Coventry C	Tr	07/00	00-02	51	21	14
Blackburn Rov (L)	Perugia (ITA)	09/04	04	6	5	1
Charlton Ath	Tr	08/05	05	3	15	2
Wolverhampton W	Tr	07/06	06-07	32	23	12
Stoke C	L	03/08	07	1	3	0
Cardiff C	Tr	08/08	08-10	112	4	41
Queens Park Rgrs	Tr	07/11	11-12	14	11	3
Sheffield Wed	L	08/12	12	14	0	1

BOTTIGLIERI Antonio (Tony)
Born: Chatham, Kent, England, 29 May, 1962 — M

League Club	Source	Date Signed	Seasons Played	Apps	Subs	Gls
Gillingham	App	04/80	79-81	5	4	0

BOTTOM Arthur Edwin
Born: Sheffield, England, 28 February, 1930 — CF
Died: Sheffield, England, 18 April, 2012

League Club	Source	Date Signed	Seasons Played	Apps	Subs	Gls
Sheffield U	Sheffield YMCA	04/47	48-53	24	-	7
York C	Tr	06/54	54-57	137	-	92
Newcastle U	Tr	01/58	57-58	11	-	10
Chesterfield	Tr	11/58	58-59	33	-	6

BOTTOMLEY Paul
Born: Harrogate, North Yorkshire, England, 11 September, 1965 — CD

League Club	Source	Date Signed	Seasons Played	Apps	Subs	Gls
Doncaster Rov	Bridlington T	08/93	93	10	0	1

BOTTOMS Michael Charles (Mike)
Born: Fulham, W London, England, 11 January, 1939 — IF

League Club	Source	Date Signed	Seasons Played	Apps	Subs	Gls
Queens Park Rgrs	Harrow T	07/60	60	2	-	0

BOUANANE Emad
Born: Paris, France, 22 November, 1976 — D

League Club	Source	Date Signed	Seasons Played	Apps	Subs	Gls
Wrexham	Avranches (FRA)	08/00	00	13	4	0

BOUAZZA Hameur
Born: Evry, France, 22 February, 1985 — LW
Algeria: 21

League Club	Source	Date Signed	Seasons Played	Apps	Subs	Gls
Watford	Sch	07/04	03-06	46	37	9
Swindon T	L	10/05	05	11	2	2
Fulham	Tr	08/07	07	15	5	1
Charlton Ath	L	08/08	08	22	3	4
Birmingham C	L	01/09	08	9	7	1
Blackpool	Sivasspor (TKY)	09/09	09	11	8	1
Millwall	Arles-Avignon (FRA)	01/11	10-11	22	16	3

BOUCAUD Andre Christopher
Born: Enfield, N London, England, 9 October, 1984 — M
Trinidad & Tobago: 24

League Club	Source	Date Signed	Seasons Played	Apps	Subs	Gls
Reading	Sch	03/02				
Peterborough U	L	03/03	02	5	1	0
Peterborough U	L	07/03	03	7	1	1
Peterborough U	Tr	07/04	04-05	15	10	1
Wycombe W	Kettering T	08/07	07	2	8	0
Notts Co	Luton T	07/12	12-13	64	4	1
Dagenham & Red	Tr	07/14	14	36	5	0

League Club	Source	Date Signed	Seasons Played	Career Record Apps	Subs	Gls
BOUGHEN Dean						
Born: Hemsworth, West Yorkshire, England, 25 July, 1971						FB
Newport Co	YT	-	87	1	0	0
BOUGHEN Paul						
Born: South Kirkby, West Yorkshire, England, 17 September, 1949						CD
Barnsley	App	10/67	70	3	5	0
BOUGHERRA Madjid						
Born: Dijon, France, 7 October, 1982						CD
Algeria: 70/U23-3						
Crewe Alex (L)	Gueugnon (FRA)	01/06	05	11	0	1
Sheffield Wed	Gueugnon (FRA)	07/06	06	28	0	2
Charlton Ath	Tr	01/07	06-07	26	8	2
BOUGHEY Darren John						
Born: Stoke-on-Trent, England, 30 November, 1970						RW
Stoke C	YT	07/89	89	4	3	0
Wigan Ath	L	01/91	90	2	0	2
Exeter C	L	03/91	90	8	0	1
BOUKARI Abdoulrazak (Razak)						
Born: Lome, Togo, 25 April, 1987						RW
France: U21-1//Togo: 4						
Wolverhampton W	Stade Rennais (FRA)	08/12	12	2	2	0
BOULAHROUZ Khalid						
Born: Maassluis, Netherlands, 28 December, 1981						CD
Netherlands: 35						
Chelsea	Hamburger SV (GER)	08/06	06	10	3	0
BOULD Stephen Andrew (Steve)						
Born: Stoke-on-Trent, England, 16 November, 1962						CD
England: 2/B-1						
Stoke C	App	11/80	81-87	179	4	6
Torquay U	L	10/82	82	9	0	0
Arsenal	Tr	06/88	88-98	271	16	5
Sunderland	Tr	07/99	99-00	19	2	0
BOULDING Michael Thomas (Mike)						
Born: Sheffield, England, 8 February, 1976						F
Mansfield T	Hallam	08/99	99-00	28	38	12
Grimsby T	Tr	08/01	01	24	11	11
Aston Villa	Tr	07/02				
Sheffield U	L	09/02	02	3	3	0
Grimsby T	Tr	01/03	02-03	37	2	16
Barnsley	Tr	02/04	03-04	27	8	10
Cardiff C	L	03/05	04	0	4	0
Mansfield T	Rotherham U (NC)	08/06	06-07	68	14	27
Bradford C	Tr	08/08	08-09	44	21	15
BOULDING Rory Joseph						
Born: Sheffield, England, 4 March, 1987						F
Mansfield T	Rotherham U (Jnr)	08/06	06-07	4	16	0
Bradford C	Tr	08/08	08-09	1	2	0
Accrington Stan	Tr	08/10	10	6	9	2
BOULTER David Arthur						
Born: Stepney, E London, England, 5 October, 1962						LB
Crystal Palace	App	07/80	81	16	0	0
BOULTON Clinton William (Clint)						
Born: Stoke-on-Trent, England, 6 January, 1948						D/M
Port Vale	App	08/65	64-71	244	0	11
Torquay U	Tr	11/71	71-78	260	2	34
BOULTON Colin Donald						
Born: Cheltenham, Gloucestershire, England, 12 September, 1945						G
Derby Co	Cheltenham Police	08/64	64-77	272	0	0
Southampton	L	09/76	76	5	0	0
Lincoln C	Los Angeles Azt (USA)	07/80	80	4	0	0
BOULTON Frank Preece						
Born: Chipping Sodbury, Avon, England, 12 August, 1917						G
Died: Swindon, England, 12 June, 1987						
Arsenal	Bath C	10/36	36-37	36	-	0
Derby Co	Tr	08/38	38	39	-	0
Swindon T	Tr	08/46	46-49	97	-	0
Crystal Palace	Tr	10/50				
BOULTON Ralph						
Born: Grimsby, North Lincolnshire, England, 22 July, 1923						IF
Died: Grimsby, North Lincolnshire, England, October, 1992						
Grimsby T	Immingham T	04/48	47-48	3	-	0
BOUMA Wilfred						
Born: Helmond, Netherlands, 15 June, 1978						LB
Netherlands: 37						
Aston Villa	PSV Eindhoven (NED)	08/05	05-07	81	2	1

League Club	Source	Date Signed	Seasons Played	Career Record Apps	Subs	Gls
BOUMSONG Jean-Alain Somkong						
Born: Douala, Cameroon, 14 December, 1979						CD
France: 27						
Newcastle U	Glasgow Rangers	01/05	04-05	44	3	0
BOUND Matthew Terence						
Born: Melksham, Wiltshire, England, 9 November, 1972						CD
Southampton	YT	05/91	91-93	2	3	0
Hull C	L	08/93	93	7	0	1
Stockport Co	Tr	10/94	94-96	44	0	5
Lincoln C	L	09/95	95	3	1	0
Swansea C	Tr	11/97	97-01	173	1	9
Oxford U	Tr	12/01	01-03	96	4	2
BOURNE Albert						
Born: Golborne, Greater Manchester, England, 30 September, 1934						IF
Manchester C		08/52				
Oldham Ath	Tr	06/58	58-59	35	-	9
BOURNE George Frederick						
Born: Burslem, Potteries, England, 5 March, 1932						FB
Died: Stoke-on-Trent, England, 7 October, 2004						
Stoke C	Burslem A	06/50	52-55	100	-	1
BOURNE Jeffrey Albert (Jeff)						
Born: Linton, Derbyshire, England, 19 June, 1948						F
Died: Swadlincote, Derbyshire, England, 31 July, 2014						
Derby Co	Burton A	06/69	70-76	35	14	9
Crystal Palace	Tr	03/77	76-77	32	0	10
Sheffield U	Atlanta Chiefs (USA)	09/79	79	25	1	11
BOURNE Richard Adrian						
Born: Colchester, Essex, England, 9 December, 1954						CD
Colchester U	Jnr	04/73	71-72	3	1	0
Torquay U	Bath C	06/79	79-81	64	4	7
BOUSSATTA Idriss (Dries)						
Born: Amsterdam, Netherlands, 23 December, 1972						RW
Netherlands: 3						
Sheffield U	Excelsior (NED)	11/03	03	3	3	0
BOUSTON Bryan John						
Born: Hereford, England, 3 October, 1960						RB
Hereford U	App	10/78	77	4	2	0
BOUZANIS Dean Anthony						
Born: Sydney, Australia, 2 October, 1990						G
Australia: U23-3/Youth						
Liverpool	Jnr	10/07				
Accrington Stan	L	11/09	09	12	2	0
Oldham Ath	Melbourne Vic (AUS)	02/12	11-12	44	1	0
Carlisle U	Aris Salonika (GRE)	01/14				
BOVE Jordan Lee						
Born: Manchester, England, 12 December, 1995						F
Oldham Ath	Sch	06/14	14	0	5	0
BOVINGTON Edward Ernest Perrian (Eddie)						
Born: Edmonton, N London, England, 23 April, 1941						RH
West Ham U	Jnr	05/59	59-67	138	0	1
BOWATER Jason Joseph Barry						
Born: Chesterfield, Derbyshire, England, 5 April, 1978						M
Chesterfield	YT	-	96	0	1	0
BOWDEN John (Jack)						
Born: Manchester, England, 25 August, 1921						WH
Died: Manchester, England, 15 July, 1981						
Oldham Ath	Jnr	09/45	46-48	72	-	1
BOWDEN Jonathan Lee (Jon)						
Born: Stockport, Greater Manchester, England, 21 January, 1963						M
Oldham Ath	Jnr	01/80	81-84	73	9	5
Port Vale	Tr	09/85	85-86	64	6	7
Wrexham	Tr	07/87	87-91	137	10	20
Rochdale	Tr	09/91	91-94	73	33	17
BOWDEN Peter William						
Born: Liverpool, England, 23 July, 1959						M
Doncaster Rov	Jnr	08/77	76-78	22	6	1
BOWDITCH Benjamin Edward (Ben)						
Born: Harlow, Essex, England, 19 February, 1984						M
England: Youth						
Tottenham H	YT	02/01				
Colchester U	Tr	08/04	04	0	5	0
Barnet	Tr	08/05	05	3	3	0
BOWDITCH Dean Peter						
Born: Harlow, Essex, England, 15 June, 1986						F

England: Youth

League Club	Source	Date Signed	Seasons Played	Apps	Subs	Gls
Ipswich T	Sch	07/03	02-08	30	43	8
Burnley	L	03/05	04	8	2	1
Wycombe W	L	01/06	05	9	2	1
Brighton & HA	L	11/06	06	1	2	1
Northampton T	L	11/07	07	7	3	2
Brighton & HA	L	02/08	07	5	0	0
Brentford	L	10/08	08	8	1	2
Yeovil T	Tr	07/09	09-10	66	5	25
MK Dons	Tr	06/11	11-14	100	27	28

BOWEN Daniel (Danny)
Born: Mountain Ash, Rhondda Cynon Taff, Wales, 16 November, 1921 — RW
Died: Bridgend, Wales, 23 September, 2000

League Club	Source	Date Signed	Seasons Played	Apps	Subs	Gls
Scunthorpe U	Treharris	07/50	50	5	-	0

BOWEN David Lloyd
Born: Maesteg, Bridgend, Wales, 7 June, 1928 — LH
Died: Northampton, England, 25 September, 1995
Wales: 19

League Club	Source	Date Signed	Seasons Played	Apps	Subs	Gls
Northampton T	Roadmender's BC	07/47	47-48	12	-	0
Arsenal	Tr	07/50	50-58	146	-	2
Northampton T	Tr	07/59	59	22	-	1

BOWEN James Malcolm Robert
Born: Birmingham, England, 4 February, 1996 — LB

League Club	Source	Date Signed	Seasons Played	Apps	Subs	Gls
Cheltenham T	Sch	07/14	14	1	2	0

BOWEN Jason Peter
Born: Merthyr Tydfil, Wales, 24 August, 1972 — F
Wales: 2/B-1/U21-5/Youth/Schools

League Club	Source	Date Signed	Seasons Played	Apps	Subs	Gls
Swansea C	YT	07/90	90-94	93	31	26
Birmingham C	Tr	07/95	95-96	35	13	7
Southampton	L	09/97	97	1	2	0
Reading	Tr	12/97	97-98	12	3	1
Cardiff C	Tr	01/99	98-03	105	29	34

BOWEN Keith Bryn
Born: Northampton, England, 26 February, 1958 — F
Wales: Schools

League Club	Source	Date Signed	Seasons Played	Apps	Subs	Gls
Northampton T	Jnr	08/76	76-81	61	4	24
Brentford	Tr	09/81	81-82	42	9	9
Colchester U	Tr	03/83	82-85	115	1	38

BOWEN Mark Rosslyn
Born: Neath, Wales, 7 December, 1963 — LB
Wales: 41/U21-3/Youth/Schools

League Club	Source	Date Signed	Seasons Played	Apps	Subs	Gls
Tottenham H	App	12/81	83-86	14	3	2
Norwich C	Tr	07/87	87-95	315	5	24
West Ham U	Tr	07/96	96	15	2	1
Charlton Ath	Shimizu S-Pulse (JPN)	09/97	97-98	36	6	0
Wigan Ath	Tr	08/99	99	7	0	0

BOWEN Stewart Anthony
Born: West Bromwich, West Midlands, England, 12 December, 1972 — LB

League Club	Source	Date Signed	Seasons Played	Apps	Subs	Gls
West Bromwich A	YT	07/91	91	8	0	1

BOWEN Thomas Henry (Tommy)
Born: West Bromwich, West Midlands, England, 21 August, 1924 — RW
Died: Sandwell, West Midlands, England, April, 2009

League Club	Source	Date Signed	Seasons Played	Apps	Subs	Gls
West Bromwich A	West Bromwich Ath	04/44				
Newport Co	Tr	07/46	46-49	37	-	6
Walsall	Tr	07/50	50-52	94	-	7

BOWER Daniel Neil (Danny)
Born: Woolwich, SE London, England, 20 November, 1976 — CD

League Club	Source	Date Signed	Seasons Played	Apps	Subs	Gls
Fulham	YT	11/95	95	4	0	0

BOWER Kenneth (Ken)
Born: Huddersfield, West Yorkshire, England, 18 March, 1926 — CF
Died: Huddersfield, West Yorkshire, England, August, 2002

League Club	Source	Date Signed	Seasons Played	Apps	Subs	Gls
Darlington	Army	01/47	46-48	75	-	35
Rotherham U	Tr	07/49	49	27	-	10

BOWER Mark James
Born: Bradford, England, 23 January, 1980 — CD

League Club	Source	Date Signed	Seasons Played	Apps	Subs	Gls
Bradford C	YT	03/98	97-08	219	12	12
York C	L	02/00	99	15	0	1
York C	L	11/00	00	21	0	1
Luton T	L	01/09	08	16	0	1
Darlington	Tr	08/09	09	12	1	0

BOWERING Michael (Mike)
Born: Hull, England, 15 November, 1936 — W
Died: Cottingham, East Riding of Yorkshire, England, 4 June, 2015

League Club	Source	Date Signed	Seasons Played	Apps	Subs	Gls
Hull C		09/58	58-59	45	-	7
Chesterfield	Tr	06/60	60	16	-	1

BOWERMAN George Oliver
Born: Sedgley, West Midlands, England, 6 November, 1991 — F

League Club	Source	Date Signed	Seasons Played	Apps	Subs	Gls
Walsall	Sch	07/10	11-12	13	37	9
Accrington Stan	Woking	10/13	13-14	12	5	3

BOWERS Ian (Danny)
Born: Newcastle-under-Lyme, Potteries, England, 16 January, 1955 — LB

League Club	Source	Date Signed	Seasons Played	Apps	Subs	Gls
Stoke C	Jnr	06/73	74-77	35	4	2
Shrewsbury T	L	03/78	77	6	0	0
Crewe Alex	Tr	07/79	79-83	170	5	2

BOWERS John Anslow (Jack)
Born: Leicester, England, 14 November, 1939 — W

League Club	Source	Date Signed	Seasons Played	Apps	Subs	Gls
Derby Co	Derby Corinthians	02/57	59-65	65	0	19
Notts Co	Tr	06/66	66	5	0	0

BOWERY Bertram Nathanial (Bert)
Born: St Kitts, 29 October, 1954 — F

League Club	Source	Date Signed	Seasons Played	Apps	Subs	Gls
Nottingham F	Worksop T	01/75	75-76	2	0	2
Lincoln C	L	02/76	75	2	2	1

BOWERY Jordan Nathaniel
Born: Nottingham, England, 2 July, 1991 — F

League Club	Source	Date Signed	Seasons Played	Apps	Subs	Gls
Chesterfield	Sch	07/09	08-12	33	50	10
Aston Villa	Tr	08/12	12-13	5	14	0
Doncaster Rov	L	02/14	13	3	0	0
Rotherham U	Tr	06/14	14	6	27	5

BOWES Gary Tyron
Born: Ilford, E London, England, 18 October, 1989 — W

League Club	Source	Date Signed	Seasons Played	Apps	Subs	Gls
Millwall	Sch	04/08	07	0	1	0

BOWEY Keith Alan
Born: Newcastle-upon-Tyne, England, 9 May, 1960 — M

League Club	Source	Date Signed	Seasons Played	Apps	Subs	Gls
Blackpool	App	03/78	78-79	3	0	1

BOWGETT Paul
Born: Hitchin, Hertfordshire, England, 17 June, 1955 — CD

League Club	Source	Date Signed	Seasons Played	Apps	Subs	Gls
Tottenham H	Letchworth Garden C	02/78				
Wimbledon	Tr	03/79	78-79	41	0	0

BOWIE James Duncan (Jimmy)
Born: Aberdeen, Scotland, 9 August, 1924 — IF
Died: Southend, England, August, 2000

League Club	Source	Date Signed	Seasons Played	Apps	Subs	Gls
Chelsea	Parkvale	01/44	47-50	76	-	18
Fulham	Tr	01/51	50-51	34	-	7
Brentford	Tr	03/52	51	9	-	0
Watford	Tr	07/52	52-55	125	-	39

BOWIE James McAvoy (Jim)
Born: Howwood, Renfrewshire, Scotland, 11 October, 1941 — M

League Club	Source	Date Signed	Seasons Played	Apps	Subs	Gls
Oldham Ath	Arthurlie Jnrs	07/62	62-71	331	2	37
Rochdale	Tr	10/72	72	1	2	0

BOWKER Keith
Born: West Bromwich, West Midlands, England, 18 April, 1951 — F

League Club	Source	Date Signed	Seasons Played	Apps	Subs	Gls
Birmingham C	App	08/68	70-72	19	2	5
Exeter C	Tr	12/73	73-75	110	0	38
Cambridge U	Tr	05/76	76	12	5	1
Northampton T	L	12/76	76	4	0	0
Exeter C	Tr	08/77	77-79	93	9	28
Torquay U	Tr	08/80	80-81	50	3	9

BOWLER Gerard Columba (Gerry)
Born: Derry, Northern Ireland, 8 June, 1919 — CH
Died: Redhill, Surrey, England, 26 March, 2006
Northern Ireland: 3/NILge-3

League Club	Source	Date Signed	Seasons Played	Apps	Subs	Gls
Portsmouth	Distillery	08/46	46-48	8	-	0
Hull C	Tr	08/49	49	38	-	0
Millwall	Tr	06/50	50-54	165	-	0

BOWLER Michael James
Born: Glossop, Derbyshire, England, 8 September, 1987 — RB

League Club	Source	Date Signed	Seasons Played	Apps	Subs	Gls
Stockport Co	Sch	07/06	06-07	9	4	0

BOWLES John Charles (Jack)
Born: Cheltenham, Gloucestershire, England, 4 August, 1914 — G
Died: Shrewsbury, Shropshire, England, March, 1987

League Club	Source	Date Signed	Seasons Played	Apps	Subs	Gls
Newport Co	Cheltenham T	05/36	36	4	-	0
Accrington Stan	Tr	06/37	37	12	-	0
Stockport Co	Tr	07/38	38-52	275	-	0

BOWLES Paul Michael Anthony
Born: Manchester, England, 31 May, 1957 — CD

League Club	Source	Date Signed	Seasons Played	Apps	Subs	Gls
Crewe Alex	App	05/75	74-79	174	4	20
Port Vale	Tr	10/79	79-81	98	0	8
Stockport Co	Tr	06/82	82-84	67	3	0

BOWLES Stanley (Stan)
Born: Manchester, England, 24 December, 1948 — M/F
England: 5/FLge-1

League Club	Source	Date Signed	Seasons Played	Apps	Subs	Gls
Manchester C	App	01/67	67-69	15	2	2
Bury	L	07/70	70	5	0	0

League Club	Source	Date Signed	Seasons Played	Career Record Apps	Subs	Gls
Crewe Alex	Tr	09/70	70-71	51	0	18
Carlisle U	Tr	10/71	71-72	33	0	12
Queens Park Rgrs	Tr	09/72	72-79	255	0	71
Nottingham F	Tr	12/79	79	19	0	2
Leyton Orient	Tr	07/80	80-81	46	0	7
Brentford	Tr	10/81	81-82	73	0	16
Brentford	Hounslow T	11/83	83	7	1	0
BOWLING Ian						
Born: Sheffield, England, 27 July, 1965						G
Lincoln C	Gainsborough Trinity	10/88	88-92	59	0	0
Hartlepool U	L	08/89	89	1	0	0
Bradford C	L	03/93	92	7	0	0
Bradford C	Tr	07/93	93-94	29	0	0
Mansfield T	Tr	08/95	95-00	174	0	0
BOWMAN Andrew (Andy)						
Born: Pittenweem, Fife, Scotland, 7 March, 1934						WH
Died: Dundee, Scotland, 4 March, 2009						
Scotland: Schools						
Chelsea	Jnr	06/51	53	1	-	0
Newport Co	Heart of Midlothian	08/61	61-62	69	-	7
BOWMAN David						
Born: Tunbridge Wells, Kent, England, 10 March, 1964						M
Scotland: 6/U21-1						
Coventry C	Heart of Midlothian	12/84	84-85	38	2	2
BOWMAN David Michael						
Born: Scarborough, North Yorkshire, England, 16 December, 1960						F
Scarborough	Bridlington T	08/87	87	4	0	2
BOWMAN Richard David (Richie)						
Born: Lewisham, SE London, England, 25 September, 1954						M
Charlton Ath	App	09/72	72-76	93	3	7
Reading	Tr	12/76	76-80	194	1	30
Gillingham	Tr	08/81	81-82	26	0	6
BOWMAN Robert Alexander (Rob)						
Born: Durham, England, 21 November, 1975						RB
England: Youth						
Leeds U	YT	11/92	92-95	4	3	0
Rotherham U	Tr	02/97	96	13	0	0
Carlisle U	Tr	08/97	97-99	42	4	2
BOWMAN Robert Craig Caldwell (Bob)						
Born: Motherwell, Lanarkshire, Scotland, 21 October, 1920						FB
Died: Glasgow, Scotland, 30 October, 1991						
New Brighton	Kilmarnock	01/49	48	18	-	0
BOWMAN Ryan Michael						
Born: Carlisle, Cumbria, England, 30 November, 1991						F
Carlisle U	Sch	07/10	09-10	0	9	0
York C	Hereford U	05/13	13	22	15	8
BOWRON Kenneth (Ken)						
Born: Newcastle-upon-Tyne, England, 10 April, 1939						CF
Workington	Berwick Rgrs	12/65	65-66	8	1	2
BOWRY Robert John (Bobby)						
Born: Hampstead, NW London, England, 19 May, 1971						M
St Kitts & Nevis: 2						
Queens Park Rgrs	Carshalton Ath	08/90				
Crystal Palace	Tr	04/92	92-94	36	14	1
Millwall	Tr	07/95	95-00	125	15	5
Colchester U	Tr	07/01	01-04	85	21	2
BOWSTEAD Peter Edward						
Born: Cambridge, England, 10 May, 1944						IF
Oxford U	Cambridge U	10/62	62-63	8	-	2
BOWTELL Stephen John (Steve)						
Born: Bethnal Green, E London, England, 2 December, 1950						G
England: Youth/Schools						
Leyton Orient	App	01/68	67-71	8	0	0
BOWYER Francis (Frank)						
Born: Chesterton, Potteries, England, 10 April, 1922						IF
Died: Truro, Cornwall, England, November, 1999						
Stoke C	Jnr	04/39	47-59	398	-	137
BOWYER Gary David						
Born: Manchester, England, 22 June, 1971						LB/M
Hereford U	Westfields	12/89	89	12	2	2
Nottingham F	Tr	09/90				
Rotherham U	Tr	08/95	95-96	33	5	2
BOWYER George						
Born: Stockport, Greater Manchester, England, 11 November, 1990						RB
Rochdale	Sch	-	07	0	1	0

League Club	Source	Date Signed	Seasons Played	Career Record Apps	Subs	Gls
BOWYER Ian						
Born: Ellesmere Port, Merseyside, England, 6 June, 1951						M
Manchester C	App	08/68	68-70	42	7	13
Leyton Orient	Tr	06/71	71-72	75	3	19
Nottingham F	Tr	10/73	73-80	222	17	49
Sunderland	Tr	01/81	80-81	15	0	1
Nottingham F	Tr	01/82	81-86	203	3	19
Hereford U	Tr	07/87	87-89	33	7	1
BOWYER Lee David						
Born: Canning Town, E London, England, 3 January, 1977						M
England: 1/U21-13/Youth						
Charlton Ath	YT	04/94	94-95	46	0	8
Leeds U	Tr	07/96	96-02	196	7	38
West Ham U	Tr	01/03	02	10	0	0
Newcastle U	Tr	07/03	03-05	61	18	6
West Ham U	Tr	06/06	06-08	34	7	4
Birmingham C	Tr	01/09	08-10	75	6	10
Ipswich T	Tr	07/11	11	24	5	2
BOXALL Alan Ronald						
Born: Woolwich, SE London, England, 11 May, 1953						CD
Scunthorpe U	Barton T	08/80	80-83	50	4	1
Chesterfield	Tr	11/83	83	4	1	0
BOXALL Daniel James (Danny)						
Born: Croydon, S London, England, 24 August, 1977						CD
Republic of Ireland: U21-8						
Crystal Palace	YT	04/95	95-97	5	3	0
Oldham Ath	L	11/97	97	6	0	0
Oldham Ath	L	02/98	97	12	0	0
Brentford	Tr	07/98	98-01	62	6	1
Bristol Rov	Tr	07/02	02-03	58	5	0
BOXLEY John (Jack)						
Born: Cradley, West Midlands, England, 31 May, 1931						LW
Bristol C	Stourbridge	10/50	50-56	193	-	34
Coventry C	Tr	12/56	56-59	92	-	17
Bristol C	Tr	08/60	60	12	-	0
BOXSHALL Daniel (Danny)						
Born: Bradford, England, 2 April, 1920						W
Died: Bradford, England, November, 2009						
Queens Park Rgrs	Salem Ath	01/46	46-47	29	-	14
Bristol C	Tr	05/48	48-49	52	-	10
Bournemouth	Tr	07/50	50-51	51	-	8
Rochdale	Tr	07/52	52-53	11	-	3
BOYACK Steven Robert						
Born: Edinburgh, Scotland, 4 September, 1976						M
Scotland: U21-1						
Hull C (L)	Glasgow Rangers	02/98	97	12	0	3
Boston U	Livingston	01/05	04	2	2	0
Blackpool	Tr	03/05	04	0	1	0
BOYATA Anga Dedryck (Dedryck)						
Born: Brussels, Belgium, 8 September, 1990						CD
Belgium: 1/U21-11/Youth						
Manchester C	Sch	07/08	09-14	8	5	0
Bolton W	L	08/11	11	13	1	1
BOYCE Andrew Thomas						
Born: Doncaster, South Yorkshire, England, 5 November, 1989						CD
Doncaster Rov	Sch	07/08				
Scunthorpe U	Lincoln C	11/13	13-14	25	6	1
BOYCE Emmerson Orlando						
Born: Aylesbury, Buckinghamshire, England, 24 September, 1979						D
Barbados: 8						
Luton T	YT	04/98	98-03	171	15	8
Crystal Palace	Tr	07/04	04-05	68	1	2
Wigan Ath	Tr	08/06	06-14	254	9	13
BOYCE Robert Alexander						
Born: Islington, N London, England, 7 January, 1974						M
Colchester U	Enfield	10/95	95	0	2	0
BOYCE Ronald William (Ronnie)						
Born: West Ham, E London, England, 6 January, 1943						M
England: Youth/Schools						
West Ham U	Jnr	05/60	60-72	275	7	21
BOYD Adam Mark						
Born: Hartlepool, Cleveland, England, 25 May, 1982						F
Hartlepool U	YT	09/99	99-05	89	55	53
Boston U	L	11/03	03	14	0	4
Luton T	Tr	07/06	06	5	14	1
Leyton Orient	Tr	07/07	07-08	67	10	23
Hartlepool U	Tr	07/09	09-11	47	45	16

BOYD Brian George
Born: Carlisle, Cumbria, England, 4 January, 1938 — IF

League Club	Source	Date Signed	Seasons Played	Apps	Subs	Gls
Carlisle U	Raffles Rov	08/55	55-58	6	-	0

BOYD Charles Michael (Charlie)
Born: Liverpool, England, 20 September, 1969 — M

League Club	Source	Date Signed	Seasons Played	Apps	Subs	Gls
Liverpool	App	05/87				
Chesterfield	Bristol Rov (NC)	11/90	90	0	1	0

BOYD George Jan
Born: Chatham, Kent, England, 2 October, 1985 — LW
England: Semi Pro-6//Scotland: 2/B-1

League Club	Source	Date Signed	Seasons Played	Apps	Subs	Gls
Peterborough U	Stevenage Bor	01/07	06-12	255	8	64
Nottingham F	L	03/10	09	5	1	1
Hull C	Tr	02/13	12-14	21	22	6
Burnley	Tr	09/14	14	35	0	5

BOYD Gordon
Born: Glasgow, Scotland, 27 March, 1958 — M
Scotland: Youth/Schools

League Club	Source	Date Signed	Seasons Played	Apps	Subs	Gls
Fulham	Glasgow Rangers	05/78	78	1	2	0
Barnsley	Glasgow Rangers	06/80	80	1	1	0
Scunthorpe U	Tr	03/82	81	10	1	0

BOYD John
Born: Massachusetts, USA, 10 September, 1926 — RW
Died: Horsham, West Sussex, England, May, 2007

League Club	Source	Date Signed	Seasons Played	Apps	Subs	Gls
Bristol C	Gloucester C	12/50	50-51	31	-	6

BOYD John (Jack)
Born: Consett, County Durham, England, 10 April, 1925 — FB
Died: Gateshead, Tyne and Wear, England, 4 September, 2009

League Club	Source	Date Signed	Seasons Played	Apps	Subs	Gls
Sunderland	Medomsley Jnrs	05/45				
West Bromwich A	Tr	06/48	48	1	-	0

BOYD John Robertson (Jock)
Born: Bo'ness, Falkirk, Scotland, 7 March, 1926 — CH
Died: Chippenham, Wiltshire, England, January, 2007

League Club	Source	Date Signed	Seasons Played	Apps	Subs	Gls
Newport Co	Bo'ness Jnrs	03/47	47	1	-	0

BOYD Kris
Born: Tarbolton, Ayrshire, Scotland, 18 August, 1983 — F
Scotland: 18/B-3/U21-8

League Club	Source	Date Signed	Seasons Played	Apps	Subs	Gls
Middlesbrough	Glasgow Rangers	07/10	10	18	9	6
Nottingham F	L	03/11	10	7	3	6

BOYD Leonard Arthur Miller (Len)
Born: Plaistow, E London, England, 11 November, 1923 — RH
Died: Melton Mowbray, Leicestershire, England, 14 February, 2008
England: B-1

League Club	Source	Date Signed	Seasons Played	Apps	Subs	Gls
Plymouth Arg	Ilford	12/45	46-48	78	-	5
Birmingham C	Tr	01/49	48-55	255	-	14

BOYD Marc Edward
Born: Carlisle, Cumbria, England, 22 October, 1981 — RW

League Club	Source	Date Signed	Seasons Played	Apps	Subs	Gls
Newcastle U	YT	10/98				
Port Vale	Tr	07/02	02-03	39	3	3
Carlisle U	Tr	03/04	03	9	0	1
Macclesfield T (L)	Gretna	01/05	04	4	1	0

BOYD Stuart
Born: Workington, Cumbria, England, 22 December, 1954 — RB

League Club	Source	Date Signed	Seasons Played	Apps	Subs	Gls
Workington (Am)	Jnr	08/73	72-73	1	4	0

BOYD Thomas (Tom)
Born: Glasgow, Scotland, 24 November, 1965 — LB
Scotland: 72/B/U21-5/Youth

League Club	Source	Date Signed	Seasons Played	Apps	Subs	Gls
Chelsea	Motherwell	06/91	91	22	1	0

BOYD Walter
Born: Kingston, Jamaica, 1 January, 1972 — F
Jamaica: 66

League Club	Source	Date Signed	Seasons Played	Apps	Subs	Gls
Swansea C	Arnett Gardens (JAM)	10/99	99-00	35	9	10

BOYD William (Willie)
Born: Hamilton, Lanarkshire, Scotland, 18 October, 1958 — G
Scotland: Youth

League Club	Source	Date Signed	Seasons Played	Apps	Subs	Gls
Hull C	App	10/77				
Doncaster Rov	Tr	02/80	79-83	104	0	0

BOYDEN Joseph (Joe)
Born: Willenhall, West Midlands, England, 12 February, 1929 — LB

League Club	Source	Date Signed	Seasons Played	Apps	Subs	Gls
Walsall	Jnr	12/48	52	4	-	0

BOYER Philip John (Phil)
Born: Nottingham, England, 25 January, 1949 — F
England: 1/U23-2

League Club	Source	Date Signed	Seasons Played	Apps	Subs	Gls
Derby Co	App	11/66				
York C	Tr	07/68	68-70	108	1	27
Bournemouth	Tr	12/70	70-73	139	1	46
Norwich C	Tr	12/74	73-76	115	1	34
Southampton	Tr	08/77	77-80	138	0	49
Manchester C	Tr	11/80	80-82	17	3	3

BOYES Kenneth (Ken)
Born: York, England, 4 February, 1935 — CH
Died: Scarborough, North Yorkshire, England, 8 August, 2010

League Club	Source	Date Signed	Seasons Played	Apps	Subs	Gls
York C	Scarborough	10/55	57-65	53	0	2

BOYES Walter Edward (Wally)
Born: Killamarsh, Derbyshire, England, 5 January, 1913 — LW
Died: Sheffield, England, 16 September, 1960
England: 3/FLge-2

League Club	Source	Date Signed	Seasons Played	Apps	Subs	Gls
West Bromwich A	Woodhouse Mills U	02/31	31-37	151	-	35
Everton	Tr	02/38	37-48	66	-	11
Notts Co	Tr	08/49	49	3	-	1
Scunthorpe U	Tr	08/50	50	13	-	2

BOYLAN Anthony (Tony)
Born: Hartlepool, Cleveland, England, 19 February, 1950 — M

League Club	Source	Date Signed	Seasons Played	Apps	Subs	Gls
Hartlepool U (Am)	Bishop Auckland	09/68	69-71	10	1	0

BOYLAN Lee Martin
Born: Witham, Essex, England, 2 September, 1978 — F
Republic of Ireland: Youth

League Club	Source	Date Signed	Seasons Played	Apps	Subs	Gls
West Ham U	YT	07/97	96	0	1	0
Exeter C	Trelleborgs (SWE)	11/99	99	3	3	1
Stevenage	Cambridge U	06/08	10	0	1	0

BOYLE David Walker
Born: North Shields, Tyne and Wear, England, 24 April, 1929 — IF/W
Died: Bradford, England, 16 November, 2009

League Club	Source	Date Signed	Seasons Played	Apps	Subs	Gls
Newcastle U		10/47				
Barnsley	Berwick Rgrs	03/51				
Crewe Alex	Tr	06/52	52-53	35	-	3
Chesterfield	Tr	07/54	54-55	42	-	10
Bradford C	Tr	07/56	56-60	92	-	13

BOYLE Henry (Harry)
Born: Possilpark, Glasgow, Scotland, 22 April, 1924 — LB
Died: Southport, Merseyside, England, 9 April, 2012

League Club	Source	Date Signed	Seasons Played	Apps	Subs	Gls
Southport	Murton CW	07/47	47-49	88	-	0
Rochdale	Tr	06/50	50	17	-	0
Rochdale	Bangor C	07/52	52-55	158	-	0

BOYLE Ian Richard
Born: Barnsley, South Yorkshire, England, 7 December, 1953 — CD

League Club	Source	Date Signed	Seasons Played	Apps	Subs	Gls
Barnsley	App	12/71	72-73	19	2	0

BOYLE John
Born: Motherwell, Lanarkshire, Scotland, 25 December, 1946 — DM

League Club	Source	Date Signed	Seasons Played	Apps	Subs	Gls
Chelsea	Jnr	08/64	64-73	188	10	10
Brighton & HA	L	09/73	73	10	0	0
Leyton Orient	Tr	12/73	73-74	18	0	0

BOYLE Lee David
Born: North Shields, Tyne and Wear, England, 22 January, 1972 — CD

League Club	Source	Date Signed	Seasons Played	Apps	Subs	Gls
Doncaster Rov	Ipswich T (YT)	07/90	91	2	1	0

BOYLE Patrick Joseph Gerard (Pat)
Born: Livingston, West Lothian, Scotland, 20 March, 1987 — D
Scotland: Youth

League Club	Source	Date Signed	Seasons Played	Apps	Subs	Gls
Everton	Sch	07/05				
Norwich C	L	09/06	06	3	0	0
Crewe Alex	L	01/08	07	17	0	0

BOYLE Terence David John (Terry)
Born: Ammanford, Carmarthenshire, Wales, 29 October, 1958 — CD
Wales: 2/U21-1/Schools

League Club	Source	Date Signed	Seasons Played	Apps	Subs	Gls
Tottenham H	App	11/75				
Crystal Palace	Tr	01/78	77-80	24	2	1
Wimbledon	L	09/81	81	5	0	1
Bristol C	Tr	10/81	81-82	36	1	0
Newport Co	Tr	11/82	82-85	165	1	11
Cardiff C	Tr	08/86	86-88	126	2	7
Swansea C	Tr	08/89	89	27	0	1

BOYLE Wesley Samuel
Born: Portadown, Armagh, Northern Ireland, 30 March, 1979 — M
Northern Ireland: U21-7/Youth/Schools

League Club	Source	Date Signed	Seasons Played	Apps	Subs	Gls
Leeds U	YT	05/95	96	0	1	0

BOYLE William Samuel Douglas
Born: Garforth, West Yorkshire, England, 1 September, 1995 — CD

League Club	Source	Date Signed	Seasons Played	Apps	Subs	Gls
Huddersfield T	Sch	07/14	14	0	1	0

BOYLEN David
Born: Prestbury, Cheshire, England, 26 October, 1947 — M

League Club	Source	Date Signed	Seasons Played	Apps	Subs	Gls
Grimsby T	Ryder Brow BC	07/65	66-77	370	14	34

BOZANIC Oliver John (Olly)
Born: Sydney, Australia, 8 January, 1989 — M
Australia: 5/U23-13/Youth

League Club	Source	Date Signed	Seasons Played	Apps	Subs	Gls
Reading	Central Coast M (AUS)	01/07				
Cheltenham T	L	07/09	09	4	0	0
Aldershot T	L	11/09	09	19	6	2

BOZINOSKI Vlado
Born: Skopje, Macedonia, 30 March, 1964 — M
Australia: 6/U23-3

League Club	Source	Date Signed	Seasons Played	Apps	Subs	Gls
Ipswich T	Beira Mar (POR)	12/92	92	3	6	0

BRAATEN Daniel Omoya
Born: Oslo, Norway, 25 May, 1982 — W
Norway: 52/U21-2

League Club	Source	Date Signed	Seasons Played	Apps	Subs	Gls
Bolton W	Rosenborg (NOR)	08/07	07	0	6	1

BRABIN Gary
Born: Liverpool, England, 9 December, 1970 — M
England: Semi Pro-3

League Club	Source	Date Signed	Seasons Played	Apps	Subs	Gls
Stockport Co	YT	12/89	89-90	1	1	0
Doncaster Rov	Runcorn	07/94	94-95	58	1	11
Bury	Tr	03/96	95	5	0	0
Blackpool	Tr	07/96	96-98	50	13	5
Lincoln C	L	12/98	98	3	1	0
Hull C	Tr	01/99	98-00	89	6	9
Torquay U	Boston U	10/01	01	6	0	0

BRABROOK Peter
Born: Greenwich, SE London, England, 8 November, 1937 — RW
England: 3/FLge-3/U23-9/Youth

League Club	Source	Date Signed	Seasons Played	Apps	Subs	Gls
Chelsea	Jnr	03/55	54-61	251	-	47
West Ham U	Tr	10/62	62-67	167	0	33
Leyton Orient	Tr	07/68	68-70	70	2	6

BRACE Deryn Paul John
Born: Tenby, Pembrokeshire, Wales, 15 March, 1975 — LB
Wales: U21-8/Youth

League Club	Source	Date Signed	Seasons Played	Apps	Subs	Gls
Norwich C	YT	07/93				
Wrexham	Tr	04/94	93-99	79	9	2

BRACE Robert Leon (Robbie)
Born: Edmonton, N London, England, 19 December, 1964 — F

League Club	Source	Date Signed	Seasons Played	Apps	Subs	Gls
Tottenham H	App	12/82	83	0	1	0

BRACE Stuart Clive
Born: Taunton, Somerset, England, 21 September, 1942 — RW/F

League Club	Source	Date Signed	Seasons Played	Apps	Subs	Gls
Plymouth Arg	Taunton T	11/60	62-65	9	0	0
Watford	Tr	09/65	65	16	0	4
Mansfield T	Tr	07/66	66-67	55	2	25
Peterborough U	Tr	11/67	67-68	22	1	6
Grimsby T	Tr	10/68	68-73	205	1	81
Southend U	Tr	10/73	73-75	106	6	39

BRACEWELL Kenneth (Ken)
Born: Colne, Lancashire, England, 5 October, 1936 — RB

League Club	Source	Date Signed	Seasons Played	Apps	Subs	Gls
Burnley	Trawden	04/57				
Tranmere Rov	Tr	05/59	59-60	28	-	1
Lincoln C	Toronto Italia (CAN)	11/63	63-64	23	-	1
Bury	Margate	12/66	66	1	0	0
Rochdale	Toronto Falcons (CAN)	03/68	67	5	0	0

BRACEWELL Paul William
Born: Heswall, Wirral, England, 19 July, 1962 — M
England: 3/U21-13

League Club	Source	Date Signed	Seasons Played	Apps	Subs	Gls
Stoke C	App	02/80	79-82	123	6	5
Sunderland	Tr	07/83	83	38	0	4
Everton	Tr	05/84	84-88	95	0	7
Sunderland	Tr	08/89	89-91	112	1	2
Newcastle U	Tr	06/92	92-94	64	9	3
Sunderland	Tr	05/95	95-97	76	1	0
Fulham	Tr	10/97	97-98	61	1	1

BRACEY Lee Michael Ian
Born: Barking, E London, England, 11 September, 1968 — G

League Club	Source	Date Signed	Seasons Played	Apps	Subs	Gls
West Ham U	YT	07/87				
Swansea C	Tr	08/88	88-91	99	0	0
Halifax T	Tr	10/91	91-92	73	0	0
Bury	Tr	08/93	93-95	65	2	0
Ipswich T	Tr	08/97				
Hull C	Tr	07/99	99-00	19	1	0

BRACK Alistair Holland
Born: Aberdeen, Scotland, 27 January, 1940 — FB
Died: Worcester, England, 8 May, 2014

League Club	Source	Date Signed	Seasons Played	Apps	Subs	Gls
Cardiff C	Stonehaven	09/61	62	1	-	0

BRACKENRIDGE Stephen James (Steve)
Born: Rochdale, Greater Manchester, England, 31 July, 1984 — RM

League Club	Source	Date Signed	Seasons Played	Apps	Subs	Gls
Macclesfield T	Sch	07/03	02-03	2	7	2

BRACKSTONE John
Born: Hartlepool, Cleveland, England, 9 February, 1985 — LB

League Club	Source	Date Signed	Seasons Played	Apps	Subs	Gls
Hartlepool U	Sch	03/04	03-06	21	4	0
Darlington	Tr	07/07	07	3	0	0

BRACKSTONE Stephen (Steve)
Born: Hartlepool, Cleveland, England, 19 September, 1982 — M
England: Youth

League Club	Source	Date Signed	Seasons Played	Apps	Subs	Gls
Middlesbrough	YT	07/00				
York C	Tr	02/02	01-03	32	12	4

BRADBURY Allen
Born: Barnsley, South Yorkshire, England, 23 January, 1947 — M
Died: Barnsley, South Yorkshire, England, September, 1999

League Club	Source	Date Signed	Seasons Played	Apps	Subs	Gls
Barnsley	App	01/65	64-69	68	1	9
Hartlepool U	Kettering T	01/71	70	7	0	0

BRADBURY Barry
Born: Rochdale, Greater Manchester, England, 5 August, 1952 — RB

League Club	Source	Date Signed	Seasons Played	Apps	Subs	Gls
Rochdale	Matthew Moss	08/72	72-73	12	3	0

BRADBURY Lee Michael
Born: Cowes, Isle of Wight, England, 3 July, 1975 — F/M
England: U21-3

League Club	Source	Date Signed	Seasons Played	Apps	Subs	Gls
Portsmouth	Cowes	08/95	95-96	41	13	15
Exeter C	L	12/95	95	14	0	5
Manchester C	Tr	08/97	97-98	34	6	10
Crystal Palace	Tr	10/98	98-99	28	4	6
Birmingham C	L	03/99	98	6	1	0
Portsmouth	Tr	10/99	99-02	90	9	28
Sheffield Wed	L	12/02	02	2	1	0
Sheffield Wed	L	03/03	02	8	0	3
Derby Co	L	08/03	03	1	0	0
Derby Co	L	11/03	03	6	0	0
Walsall	Tr	03/04	03	7	1	1
Oxford U	Tr	07/04	04-05	57	6	9
Southend U	Tr	01/06	05-07	40	7	5
Bournemouth	Tr	08/07	07-10	112	15	10

BRADBURY Shaun
Born: Birmingham, England, 11 February, 1974 — F

League Club	Source	Date Signed	Seasons Played	Apps	Subs	Gls
Wolverhampton W	YT	11/92	92	2	0	2

BRADBURY Terence Eugene (Terry)
Born: Paddington, Central London, England, 15 November, 1939 — LH
England: Schools

League Club	Source	Date Signed	Seasons Played	Apps	Subs	Gls
Chelsea	Jnr	07/57	60-61	29	-	1
Southend U	Tr	09/62	62-65	160	1	19
Leyton Orient	Tr	06/66	66	25	2	0
Wrexham	Tr	06/67	67-68	77	1	3
Chester C	Tr	06/69	69-70	90	0	2

BRADBURY William (Bill)
Born: Matlock, Derbyshire, England, 3 April, 1933 — IF
Died: Chesterfield, Derbyshire, England, 9 August, 1999

League Club	Source	Date Signed	Seasons Played	Apps	Subs	Gls
Coventry C	Jnr	05/50	51-54	24	-	7
Birmingham C	Tr	11/54	54-55	3	-	2
Hull C	Tr	10/55	55-59	178	-	82
Bury	Tr	02/60	59-60	18	-	4
Workington	Tr	11/60	60	23	-	5
Southport	Tr	08/61	61	11	-	2

BRADD Leslie John (Les)
Born: Buxton, Derbyshire, England, 6 November, 1947 — F

League Club	Source	Date Signed	Seasons Played	Apps	Subs	Gls
Rotherham U	Earl Sterndale	03/66	67	3	0	0
Notts Co	Tr	10/67	67-77	379	16	125
Stockport Co	Tr	08/78	78-80	116	1	31
Wigan Ath	Tr	07/81	81-82	57	6	25
Bristol Rov	L	12/82	82	1	0	1

BRADER Alec
Born: Horncastle, Lincolnshire, England, 6 October, 1942 — IF

League Club	Source	Date Signed	Seasons Played	Apps	Subs	Gls
Grimsby T	Horncastle U	05/60	60	2	-	0

BRADFORD David William
Born: Manchester, England, 22 February, 1953 — M

League Club	Source	Date Signed	Seasons Played	Apps	Subs	Gls
Blackburn Rov	App	08/71	71-73	58	6	3
Sheffield U	Tr	07/74	74-76	54	6	2
Peterborough U	L	10/76	76	4	0	0
West Bromwich A	Tr	02/77				
Coventry C	Detroit Express (USA)	10/81	81	6	0	1

BRADFORD Geoffrey Reginald William (Geoff)
Born: Bristol, England, 18 July, 1927 — CF
Died: Bristol, England, 31 December, 1994
England: 1

League Club	Source	Date Signed	Seasons Played	Apps	Subs	Gls
Bristol Rov	Soundwell	05/49	49-63	461	-	242

BRADFORD Lewis (Lew)
Born: Swadlincote, Derbyshire, England, 24 November, 1916 — CH

Died: Chorley, Lancashire, England, October, 1984

League Club	Source	Date Signed	Seasons Played	Apps	Subs	Gls
Preston NE	Gresley Rov	12/34				
Bradford C	Kilmarnock	10/46	46-48	68	-	1
Newport Co	Tr	11/48	48	24	-	0

BRADLEY Brendan Colin
Born: Derry, Northern Ireland, 7 June, 1950 F
Republic of Ireland: LoI-3

League Club	Source	Date Signed	Seasons Played	Apps	Subs	Gls
Lincoln C	Finn Harps (ROI)	07/72	72	31	0	12

BRADLEY Charles
Born: York, England, 15 May, 1922 IF
Died: York, England, 23 July, 1984

League Club	Source	Date Signed	Seasons Played	Apps	Subs	Gls
York C	York RI	10/41	46	10	-	2

BRADLEY Darren Michael
Born: Birmingham, England, 24 November, 1965 D/M
England: Youth

League Club	Source	Date Signed	Seasons Played	Apps	Subs	Gls
Aston Villa	App	12/83	84-85	16	4	0
West Bromwich A	Tr	03/86	85-94	236	18	9
Walsall	Tr	08/95	95-96	66	5	1

BRADLEY David
Born: Salford, England, 16 January, 1958 CD
England: Schools

League Club	Source	Date Signed	Seasons Played	Apps	Subs	Gls
Manchester U	App	01/75				
Wimbledon	L	03/78	77	7	0	0
Doncaster Rov	Tr	08/78	78-79	67	0	5
Bury	Tr	08/80	80	8	0	0

BRADLEY David Hughes
Born: Bolton, Greater Manchester, England, 6 December, 1953 F

League Club	Source	Date Signed	Seasons Played	Apps	Subs	Gls
Workington	Silcoms	09/75	75	8	0	1

BRADLEY Donald John (Don)
Born: Annesley, Nottinghamshire, England, 11 September, 1924 LB
Died: Mansfield, Nottinghamshire, England, 23 July, 1997

League Club	Source	Date Signed	Seasons Played	Apps	Subs	Gls
West Bromwich A	Clipstone Welfare	09/43				
Mansfield T	Tr	08/49	49-61	384	-	6

BRADLEY George Joseph
Born: Maltby, South Yorkshire, England, 7 January, 1917 WH
Died: Guildford, Surrey, England, 8 December, 1998

League Club	Source	Date Signed	Seasons Played	Apps	Subs	Gls
Rotherham U	Maltby Hall OB	03/37	37-38	28	-	0
Newcastle U	Tr	11/38	38	1	-	0
Millwall	Tr	09/46	46-49	74	-	2

BRADLEY Gordon
Born: Easington, County Durham, England, 23 November, 1933 WH
Died: Manassas,Virginia, USA, 29 April, 2008
USA: 1

League Club	Source	Date Signed	Seasons Played	Apps	Subs	Gls
Bradford Park Ave	Stanley U	01/56	55-56	18	-	1
Carlisle U	Tr	09/57	57-60	133	-	3

BRADLEY Gordon
Born: Scunthorpe, North Lincolnshire, England, 20 May, 1925 G
Died: Poole, Dorset, England, 2 May, 2006

League Club	Source	Date Signed	Seasons Played	Apps	Subs	Gls
Leicester C	Scunthorpe U	11/42	46-49	69	-	0
Notts Co	Tr	02/50	50-57	192	-	1

BRADLEY James (Jimmy)
Born: Greenock, Inverclyde, Scotland, 21 March, 1927 IF
Died: New Jersey, USA, 26 November, 2008

League Club	Source	Date Signed	Seasons Played	Apps	Subs	Gls
Shrewsbury T	Third Lanark	07/52	52	1	-	0

BRADLEY John (Jack)
Born: Hemsworth, West Yorkshire, England, 27 November, 1916 IF
Died: Gorleston, Norfolk, England, 14 December, 2002

League Club	Source	Date Signed	Seasons Played	Apps	Subs	Gls
Huddersfield T	South Kirkby Colliery	11/35				
Swindon T	Tr	08/36	36-37	25	-	6
Chelsea	Tr	06/38				
Southampton	Tr	05/39	46-47	49	-	22
Bolton W	Tr	10/47	47-50	92	-	19
Norwich C	Tr	11/50	50-51	6	-	0

BRADLEY Keith
Born: Ellesmere Port, Cheshire, England, 31 January, 1946 RB

League Club	Source	Date Signed	Seasons Played	Apps	Subs	Gls
Aston Villa	App	06/63	64-71	115	7	2
Peterborough U	Tr	11/72	72-75	106	3	0

BRADLEY Lee Herbert
Born: Manchester, England, 27 May, 1957 D

League Club	Source	Date Signed	Seasons Played	Apps	Subs	Gls
Stockport Co	App	08/75	75	39	1	4
Halifax T	Tr	10/76	76-78	62	10	4

BRADLEY Mark Simon
Born: Dudley, West Midlands, England, 14 January, 1988 RB/M
Wales: 1/U21-17/Youth

League Club	Source	Date Signed	Seasons Played	Apps	Subs	Gls
Walsall	Sch	07/06	04-09	65	31	5
Rotherham U	Tr	07/10	10-13	73	18	4

BRADLEY Michael Sheehan
Born: Princeton, New Jersey, USA, 31 July, 1987 M
USA: 98/U23-4/Youth

League Club	Source	Date Signed	Seasons Played	Apps	Subs	Gls
Aston Villa (L)	Borussia M'bach (GER)	01/11	10	0	3	0

BRADLEY Noel Bernard
Born: Manchester, England, 17 December, 1957 D

League Club	Source	Date Signed	Seasons Played	Apps	Subs	Gls
Manchester C	St Robert's BC	11/78				
Bury	L	03/80	79	9	0	0
Bury	Tr	08/81	81	15	3	1
Chester C	Tr	08/82	82	27	1	0

BRADLEY Patrick (Pat)
Born: Sydney, Australia, 27 April, 1972 FB
England: Youth

League Club	Source	Date Signed	Seasons Played	Apps	Subs	Gls
Bury	YT	07/90	90	0	1	0

BRADLEY Peter Kenneth
Born: Donnington, Telford & Wrekin, England, 18 March, 1955 CD

League Club	Source	Date Signed	Seasons Played	Apps	Subs	Gls
Shrewsbury T	App	07/73	73	3	0	0

BRADLEY Ronald John (Ron)
Born: Wolverhampton, England, 24 April, 1939 LH
England: Youth

League Club	Source	Date Signed	Seasons Played	Apps	Subs	Gls
West Bromwich A	Jnr	06/56	62	13	-	0
Norwich C	Tr	07/64	64-65	4	0	0

BRADLEY Russell
Born: Birmingham, England, 28 March, 1966 CD

League Club	Source	Date Signed	Seasons Played	Apps	Subs	Gls
Nottingham F	Dudley T	05/88				
Hereford U	L	11/88	88	12	0	1
Hereford U	Tr	07/89	89-91	75	2	3
Halifax T	Tr	09/91	91-92	54	2	3
Scunthorpe U	Tr	06/93	93-96	116	3	5
Hartlepool U	L	02/97	96	12	0	1
Hartlepool U	Tr	07/97	97	43	0	1

BRADLEY Shayne
Born: Gloucester, England, 8 December, 1979 F
England: Schools

League Club	Source	Date Signed	Seasons Played	Apps	Subs	Gls
Southampton	YT	01/98	98-99	0	4	0
Swindon T	L	03/99	98	6	1	0
Exeter C	L	09/99	99	6	2	1
Mansfield T	Tr	08/00	00-01	28	14	10
Chesterfield	Eastwood T	12/02	02	1	8	2
Lincoln C	L	03/03	02	3	0	1

BRADLEY Sonny
Born: Hedon, East Riding of Yorkshire, England, 14 June, 1992 CD

League Club	Source	Date Signed	Seasons Played	Apps	Subs	Gls
Hull C	Sch	06/11	11	1	1	0
Aldershot T	L	01/12	11	13	1	0
Aldershot T	L	08/12	12	42	0	1
Portsmouth	Tr	07/13	13	29	4	2
Crawley T	Tr	06/14	14	25	1	1

BRADLEY Warren
Born: Hyde, Greater Manchester, England, 20 June, 1933 RW
Died: Bolton, Greater Manchester, England, 6 June, 2007
England: 3/Amateur-11

League Club	Source	Date Signed	Seasons Played	Apps	Subs	Gls
Manchester U	Bishop Auckland	11/58	58-61	63	-	20
Bury	Tr	03/62	61-62	13	-	1

BRADLEY William (Willie)
Born: Glasgow, Scotland, 26 June, 1937 W
Died: Bishopbriggs, Glasgow, Scotland, 21 January, 2003

League Club	Source	Date Signed	Seasons Played	Apps	Subs	Gls
Hartlepool U	Ayr U	07/63	63-65	98	0	15

BRADSHAW Alan
Born: Blackburn, Greater Manchester, England, 14 September, 1941 M

League Club	Source	Date Signed	Seasons Played	Apps	Subs	Gls
Blackburn Rov	Jnr	07/63	62-64	11	-	2
Crewe Alex	Tr	05/65	65-72	287	7	51

BRADSHAW Carl
Born: Sheffield, England, 2 October, 1968 RB
England: Youth

League Club	Source	Date Signed	Seasons Played	Apps	Subs	Gls
Sheffield Wed	App	08/86	86-88	16	16	4
Barnsley	L	08/86	86	6	0	1
Manchester C	Tr	09/88	88	1	4	0
Sheffield U	Tr	09/89	89-93	122	25	8
Norwich C	Tr	07/94	94-97	55	10	2
Wigan Ath	Tr	10/97	97-00	109	11	11
Scunthorpe U	Tr	07/01	01	18	3	1

BRADSHAW Darren Shaun
Born: Sheffield, England, 19 March, 1967 CD
England: Youth

League Club	Source	Date Signed	Seasons Played	Apps	Subs	Gls
Chesterfield (L)	Matlock T	08/87	87	18	0	0
York C	Matlock T	11/87	87-88	58	1	3
Newcastle U	Tr	08/89	89-91	32	6	0
Peterborough U	Tr	08/92	92-93	70	3	1

League Club	Source	Date Signed	Seasons Played	Apps	Subs	Gls
Plymouth Arg	L	08/94	94	5	1	1
Blackpool	Tr	10/94	94-97	61	6	1

BRADSHAW Gary
Born: Beverley, East Riding of Yorkshire, England, 30 December, 1982 — F

League Club	Source	Date Signed	Seasons Played	Apps	Subs	Gls
Hull C	YT	07/00	99-02	10	12	1
Cheltenham T	North Ferriby U	10/05	05	0	3	0

BRADSHAW George Frederick
Born: Southport, Merseyside, England, 10 March, 1913 — G
Died: Southport, Merseyside, England, 28 August, 1989

League Club	Source	Date Signed	Seasons Played	Apps	Subs	Gls
New Brighton	High Park Villa	09/33	32-34	83	-	0
Everton	Tr	11/34	34	2	-	0
Arsenal	Tr	05/35				
Doncaster Rov	Tr	05/36	36-37	53	-	0
Bury	Tr	06/38	38-49	118	-	0
Oldham Ath	Tr	07/50	50	1	-	0

BRADSHAW George Henry
Born: Clay Cross, Derbyshire, England, 24 March, 1920 — CF
Died: Bridlington, East Riding of Yorkshire, England, February, 1994

League Club	Source	Date Signed	Seasons Played	Apps	Subs	Gls
Chesterfield	Newstead Colliery	04/46	47	7	-	1

BRADSHAW Mark
Born: Ashton-under-Lyne, Greater Manchester, England, 7 June, 1969 — LB
England: Semi Pro-1

League Club	Source	Date Signed	Seasons Played	Apps	Subs	Gls
Blackpool	YT	12/87	86-90	34	8	1
York C	L	04/91	90	0	1	0
Halifax T	Macclesfield T	05/95	98-00	73	10	7

BRADSHAW Paul
Born: Sheffield, England, 2 October, 1953 — LW
England: Youth/Schools

League Club	Source	Date Signed	Seasons Played	Apps	Subs	Gls
Burnley	App	10/70	74-76	11	2	2
Sheffield Wed	Tr	09/76	76-77	62	2	9

BRADSHAW Paul William
Born: Altrincham, Greater Manchester, England, 28 April, 1956 — G
England: U21-4/Youth

League Club	Source	Date Signed	Seasons Played	Apps	Subs	Gls
Blackburn Rov	App	07/73	73-77	78	0	0
Wolverhampton W	Tr	09/77	77-83	200	0	0
West Bromwich A	Vancouver W'caps (CAN)	04/85	85	8	0	0
Bristol Rov	Walsall (Coach)	03/87	86	5	0	0
Newport Co	Tr	07/87	87	23	0	0
West Bromwich A	Tr	08/88	88-89	6	0	0
Peterborough U	Tr	06/90	90	39	0	0

BRADSHAW Thomas William (Tom)
Born: Shrewsbury, Shropshire, England, 27 July, 1992 — F
Wales: U21-8/Youth

League Club	Source	Date Signed	Seasons Played	Apps	Subs	Gls
Shrewsbury T	Aberystwyth T	08/09	09-13	42	47	17
Walsall	Tr	06/14	14	29	0	17

BRADY Garry
Born: Glasgow, Scotland, 7 September, 1976 — M
Scotland: Youth/Schools

League Club	Source	Date Signed	Seasons Played	Apps	Subs	Gls
Tottenham H	YT	09/93	97	0	9	0
Newcastle U	Tr	07/98	98	3	6	0
Norwich C	L	03/00	99	6	0	0
Norwich C	L	09/00	00	2	0	0
Portsmouth	Tr	03/01	00-01	9	5	0

BRADY Jonathan Edmund Alexander (Jon)
Born: Newcastle, N.S.W, Australia, 14 January, 1975 — M

League Club	Source	Date Signed	Seasons Played	Apps	Subs	Gls
Swansea C	Brentford (YT)	07/93				
Rushden & D	Hayes	07/98	01	9	13	1

BRADY Kieron
Born: Glasgow, Scotland, 17 September, 1971 — M
Republic of Ireland: U21-4

League Club	Source	Date Signed	Seasons Played	Apps	Subs	Gls
Sunderland	YT	07/89	89-91	17	16	7
Doncaster Rov	L	10/92	92	4	0	3

BRADY Matthew John (Matt)
Born: Marylebone, Central London, England, 27 October, 1977 — M

League Club	Source	Date Signed	Seasons Played	Apps	Subs	Gls
Barnet	YT	07/96	94-96	2	8	0
Wycombe W	Boreham Wood	11/99	99-00	6	6	2

BRADY Patrick Joseph (Pat)
Born: Dublin, Republic of Ireland, 11 March, 1936 — FB

League Club	Source	Date Signed	Seasons Played	Apps	Subs	Gls
Millwall	Home Farm (ROI)	01/59	58-62	148	-	1
Queens Park Rgrs	Tr	07/63	63-64	62	-	0

BRADY Paul James
Born: Marston Green, West Midlands, England, 26 March, 1961 — RB

League Club	Source	Date Signed	Seasons Played	Apps	Subs	Gls
Birmingham C	App	08/78				
Northampton T	Tr	08/81	81-82	49	2	3
Crewe Alex	Tr	02/83	82-83	42	1	1

BRADY Robert (Robbie)
Born: Dublin, Republic of Ireland, 14 January, 1992 — LW
Republic of Ireland: 13/U21-12/Youth

League Club	Source	Date Signed	Seasons Played	Apps	Subs	Gls
Manchester U	Sch	01/09				
Hull C	L	07/11	11	24	15	3
Hull C	Tr	11/12	12-14	56	19	7

BRADY Thomas Raymond (Ray)
Born: Dublin, Republic of Ireland, 3 June, 1937 — CH
Republic of Ireland: 6

League Club	Source	Date Signed	Seasons Played	Apps	Subs	Gls
Millwall	Transport (ROI)	07/57	57-62	165	-	4
Queens Park Rgrs	Tr	07/63	63-65	88	0	0

BRADY William (Liam)
Born: Dublin, Republic of Ireland, 13 February, 1956 — M
Republic of Ireland: 72

League Club	Source	Date Signed	Seasons Played	Apps	Subs	Gls
Arsenal	App	08/73	73-79	227	8	43
West Ham U	Ascoli (ITA)	03/87	86-89	79	10	9

BRAGG Walter Leonard (Wally)
Born: Twickenham, W London, England, 8 July, 1929 — CH

League Club	Source	Date Signed	Seasons Played	Apps	Subs	Gls
Brentford	Jnr	01/47	46-56	161	-	6

BRAGSTAD Bjorn Otto
Born: Trondheim, Norway, 15 January, 1971 — CD
Norway: 15

League Club	Source	Date Signed	Seasons Played	Apps	Subs	Gls
Derby Co	Rosenborg (NOR)	08/00	00	10	2	0
Birmingham C	L	09/01	01	3	0	0

BRAHAM-BARRETT Craig Michael
Born: Greenwich, SE London, England, 1 September, 1988 — CD

League Club	Source	Date Signed	Seasons Played	Apps	Subs	Gls
Peterborough U	Welling U	10/08				
Cheltenham T	Macclesfield T	08/13	13-14	74	0	0

BRAHAN Marcel Eric Louis (Lou)
Born: Stepney, E London, England, 3 December, 1926 — CH
Died: Epping Forest, Essex, England, December, 1995

League Club	Source	Date Signed	Seasons Played	Apps	Subs	Gls
Leyton Orient (Am)	Walthamstow Ave	07/55	55	1	-	0

BRAIN Jonathan Robert (Jonny)
Born: Carlisle, Cumbria, England, 11 February, 1983 — G

League Club	Source	Date Signed	Seasons Played	Apps	Subs	Gls
Port Vale	Newcastle U (YT)	08/03	03-04	58	1	0
Macclesfield T	Tr	07/06	06-09	125	0	0
Walsall	Tr	07/10	10	16	0	0

BRAIN Simon Anthony John
Born: Evesham, Worcestershire, England, 31 March, 1966 — F

League Club	Source	Date Signed	Seasons Played	Apps	Subs	Gls
Hereford U	Cheltenham T	12/90	90-93	81	6	20

BRAITHWAITE Leon Jerome
Born: Hackney, E London, England, 17 December, 1972 — F

League Club	Source	Date Signed	Seasons Played	Apps	Subs	Gls
Exeter C	Bishops Stortford	11/95	95-97	40	26	9

BRAITHWAITE Robert Munn (Bobby)
Born: Belfast, Northern Ireland, 24 February, 1937 — LW
Northern Ireland: 10/NILge-8/Schools

League Club	Source	Date Signed	Seasons Played	Apps	Subs	Gls
Middlesbrough	Linfield	06/63	63-66	67	1	12

BRAMBLE Tesfaye Walda Simeon (Tes)
Born: Ipswich, England, 20 July, 1980 — F

League Club	Source	Date Signed	Seasons Played	Apps	Subs	Gls
Southend U	Cambridge C	01/01	00-04	101	38	29
Cambridge U	L	03/05	04	9	0	3
Stockport Co	Tr	07/05	05-06	52	16	11

BRAMBLE Titus Malachi
Born: Ipswich, England, 21 July, 1981 — CD
England: U21-10

League Club	Source	Date Signed	Seasons Played	Apps	Subs	Gls
Ipswich T	YT	08/98	98-01	41	7	1
Colchester U	L	12/99	99	2	0	0
Newcastle U	Tr	07/02	02-06	96	9	3
Wigan Ath	Tr	06/07	07-09	96	0	5
Sunderland	Tr	07/10	10-12	42	5	1

BRAMHALL John
Born: Warrington, Cheshire, England, 20 November, 1956 — CD

League Club	Source	Date Signed	Seasons Played	Apps	Subs	Gls
Tranmere Rov	Stockton Heath	07/76	76-81	164	6	7
Bury	Tr	03/82	81-85	165	2	17
Chester C	L	11/85	85	4	0	0
Rochdale	Tr	08/86	86-87	86	0	13
Halifax T	Tr	08/88	88-89	62	0	5
Scunthorpe U	Tr	01/90	89-90	32	0	0

BRAMHALL Neil
Born: Blackpool, Lancashire, England, 16 October, 1965 — F

League Club	Source	Date Signed	Seasons Played	Apps	Subs	Gls
Blackpool	App	10/83	82	0	3	0

BRAMLEY Arthur
Born: Mansfield, Nottinghamshire, England, 25 March, 1929 — G

League Club	Source	Date Signed	Seasons Played	Apps	Subs	Gls
Mansfield T	Bentinck CW	10/49	49-52	19	-	0

BRAMLEY Ernest
Born: Mansfield, Nottinghamshire, England, 29 August, 1920 — RB
Died: Shuttlewood, Derbyshire, England, December, 1993

League Club	Source	Date Signed	Seasons Played	Apps	Subs	Gls
Mansfield T	Bolsover Colliery	12/38	38-47	45	-	1

BRAMLEY John Stewart (Stewart)
Born: Scunthorpe, North Lincolnshire, England, 19 April, 1946 — IF

League Club	Source	Date Signed	Seasons Played	Apps	Subs	Gls
Scunthorpe U	App	04/64	64-66	35	0	3
Plymouth Arg	Tr	08/67				

BRAMMER David (Dave)
Born: Bromborough, Wirral, England, 28 February, 1975 — M

League Club	Source	Date Signed	Seasons Played	Apps	Subs	Gls
Wrexham	YT	07/93	92-98	118	19	12
Port Vale	Tr	03/99	98-00	71	2	3
Crewe Alex	Tr	08/01	01-03	86	1	4
Stoke C	Tr	07/04	04-06	91	14	2
Millwall	Tr	01/07	06-07	40	0	1
Port Vale	Tr	10/08	08	13	0	0

BRAMWELL John
Born: Ashton-in-Makerfield, Greater Manchester, England, 1 March, 1937 — LB

League Club	Source	Date Signed	Seasons Played	Apps	Subs	Gls
Everton	Wigan Ath	04/58	58-59	52	-	0
Luton T	Tr	10/60	60-64	187	-	0

BRAMWELL Steven (Steve)
Born: Stockport, Greater Manchester, England, 9 October, 1970 — M

League Club	Source	Date Signed	Seasons Played	Apps	Subs	Gls
Oldham Ath	YT	07/89	88	0	1	0
Crewe Alex	Tr	05/90				

BRANAGAN James Kenneth (Ken)
Born: Salford, England, 27 July, 1930 — RB
Died: Salford, England, 9 August, 2008

League Club	Source	Date Signed	Seasons Played	Apps	Subs	Gls
Manchester C	North Salford BC	11/48	50-59	196	-	3
Oldham Ath	Tr	10/60	60-65	177	0	5

BRANAGAN James Patrick Stephen (Jim)
Born: Urmston, Greater Manchester, England, 3 July, 1955 — RB

League Club	Source	Date Signed	Seasons Played	Apps	Subs	Gls
Oldham Ath	Jnr	07/73	74-76	24	3	0
Huddersfield T	Cape Town C (RSA)	11/77	77-78	37	1	0
Blackburn Rov	Tr	10/79	79-86	290	4	5
Preston NE	Tr	05/87	87	3	0	0
York C	Tr	10/87	87-88	40	2	1

BRANAGAN Keith Graham
Born: Fulham, W London, England, 10 July, 1966 — G
Republic of Ireland: 1/B-2

League Club	Source	Date Signed	Seasons Played	Apps	Subs	Gls
Cambridge U	Jnr	08/83	83-87	110	0	0
Millwall	Tr	03/88	89-91	46	0	0
Brentford	L	11/89	89	2	0	0
Gillingham	L	10/91	91	1	0	0
Bolton W	Tr	07/92	92-99	214	0	0
Ipswich T	Tr	04/00	00-01	2	1	0

BRANAGAN Richie Peter
Born: Gravesend, Kent, England, 20 October, 1991 — G
Republic of Ireland: U21-1

League Club	Source	Date Signed	Seasons Played	Apps	Subs	Gls
Bury	Sch	07/10	10	1	1	0

BRANCA Marco
Born: Grosseto, Italy, 6 January, 1965 — F
Italy: U23-3

League Club	Source	Date Signed	Seasons Played	Apps	Subs	Gls
Middlesbrough	Inter Milan (ITA)	02/98	97-98	11	1	9

BRANCH Graham
Born: Liverpool, England, 12 February, 1972 — LB/M

League Club	Source	Date Signed	Seasons Played	Apps	Subs	Gls
Tranmere Rov	Heswall	07/91	91-97	55	47	10
Bury	L	11/92	92	3	1	1
Wigan Ath	L	12/97	97	2	1	0
Stockport Co	Tr	07/98	98	10	4	3
Burnley	Tr	12/98	98-06	208	56	17
Accrington Stan	Tr	07/07	07	19	3	0

BRANCH Paul Michael (Michael)
Born: Liverpool, England, 18 October, 1978 — F
England: U21-1/Youth/Schools

League Club	Source	Date Signed	Seasons Played	Apps	Subs	Gls
Everton	YT	10/95	95-98	16	25	3
Manchester C	L	10/98	98	4	0	0
Wolverhampton W	Tr	11/99	99-01	61	11	10
Reading	L	03/02	01	0	2	0
Hull C	L	10/02	02	6	1	3
Bradford C	Tr	07/03	03	29	4	6
Chester C	Tr	07/04	04-05	54	6	16

[BRANCO] VAZ LEAL Claudio Ibraim
Born: Bage, Brazil, 4 April, 1964 — FB
Brazil: 72

League Club	Source	Date Signed	Seasons Played	Apps	Subs	Gls
Middlesbrough	Genoa (ITA)	03/96	95-96	6	3	0

BRANCO Rodrigo
Born: Sao Bernardo, Brazil, 14 July, 1991 — F

League Club	Source	Date Signed	Seasons Played	Apps	Subs	Gls
Fleetwood T	Brazil	08/12	12	0	1	0

BRANCO Serge
Born: Douala, Cameroon, 11 October, 1980 — DM
Cameroon: 1/U23-5

League Club	Source	Date Signed	Seasons Played	Apps	Subs	Gls
Queens Park Rgrs	VfB Stuttgart (GER)	09/04	04	3	4	0

BRAND Andrew Scougal (Drew)
Born: Edinburgh, Scotland, 8 November, 1957 — G

League Club	Source	Date Signed	Seasons Played	Apps	Subs	Gls
Everton	App	11/75	75-76	2	0	0
Crewe Alex	L	02/77	76	14	0	0
Crewe Alex	L	08/78	78	1	0	0
Hereford U	Tr	05/80	80-81	54	0	0
Wrexham	L	11/82	82	1	0	0
Blackpool	Witton A	03/84	83	3	0	0

BRAND Kenneth Reginald (Ken)
Born: Whitechapel, Central London, England, 28 April, 1938 — LB

League Club	Source	Date Signed	Seasons Played	Apps	Subs	Gls
Millwall	Eton Manor	09/56	56-57	13	-	0

BRAND Ralph Laidlaw
Born: Edinburgh, Scotland, 18 December, 1936 — F
Scotland: 8/SLge-5/U23-1/Schools

League Club	Source	Date Signed	Seasons Played	Apps	Subs	Gls
Manchester C	Glasgow Rangers	08/65	65-66	20	0	2
Sunderland	Tr	08/67	67-68	31	0	7

BRAND Raymond Ernest (Ray)
Born: Islington, N London, England, 2 October, 1934 — CH

League Club	Source	Date Signed	Seasons Played	Apps	Subs	Gls
Millwall	Hatfield T	10/51	55-60	150	-	8
Southend U	Tr	08/61	61-62	22	-	9

BRANDER George Milne
Born: Aberdeen, Scotland, 1 November, 1929 — W
Died: Aberdeen, Scotland, 18 June, 1995

League Club	Source	Date Signed	Seasons Played	Apps	Subs	Gls
Newcastle U	Raith Rov	03/52	52	5	-	2

BRANDON Christopher William (Chris)
Born: Bradford, England, 7 April, 1976 — RW

League Club	Source	Date Signed	Seasons Played	Apps	Subs	Gls
Torquay U	Bradford Park Ave	08/99	99-01	64	7	8
Chesterfield	Tr	07/02	02-03	74	5	11
Huddersfield T	Tr	07/04	04-07	120	15	12
Blackpool	L	03/07	06	4	1	2
Bradford C	Tr	07/08	08-09	18	9	2

BRANDON Kenneth Alfred (Ken)
Born: Birmingham, England, 8 February, 1934 — LW
Died: Birmingham, England, May, 1994

League Club	Source	Date Signed	Seasons Played	Apps	Subs	Gls
Swindon T (Am)	Roundway Hospital	01/53	52	5	-	0
Chester C	Tr	06/53	53-55	39	-	7
Leicester C	Tr	07/56				
Darlington	Tr	06/58	58	16	-	1

BRANDY Febian Earlston
Born: Manchester, England, 4 February, 1989 — F
England: Youth

League Club	Source	Date Signed	Seasons Played	Apps	Subs	Gls
Manchester U	Sch	07/06				
Swansea C	L	01/08	07	2	17	3
Swansea C	L	07/08	08	0	14	0
Hereford U	L	02/09	08	14	1	4
Gillingham	L	11/09	09	5	2	1
Notts Co		02/11	10	5	4	0
Walsall	Panetolikos (GRE)	07/12	12	27	7	7
Sheffield U	Tr	07/13	13	10	4	0
Walsall	L	01/14	13	20	0	4
Rotherham U	Tr	06/14	14	0	1	0
Crewe Alex	L	09/14	14	6	2	1
Rochdale	Tr	01/15	14	1	3	0

BRANFOOT Ian Grant
Born: Gateshead, Tyne and Wear, England, 26 January, 1947 — RB

League Club	Source	Date Signed	Seasons Played	Apps	Subs	Gls
Sheffield Wed	Gateshead	07/65	65-69	33	3	0
Doncaster Rov	Tr	12/69	69-72	156	0	5
Lincoln C	Tr	07/73	73-77	166	0	11

BRANIFF Kevin Robert
Born: Belfast, Northern Ireland, 4 March, 1983 — F
Northern Ireland: U23-1/U21-10/Youth/Schools

League Club	Source	Date Signed	Seasons Played	Apps	Subs	Gls
Millwall	YT	04/00	00-06	28	27	2
Rushden & D	L	08/04	04	11	1	3

BRANNAN Gerard Daniel (Ged)
Born: Prescot, Merseyside, England, 15 January, 1972 — M

League Club	Source	Date Signed	Seasons Played	Apps	Subs	Gls
Tranmere Rov	YT	07/90	90-96	227	11	20
Manchester C	Tr	03/97	96-97	38	5	4
Norwich C	L	08/98	98	10	1	1
Wigan Ath	Motherwell	02/01	00-02	49	3	0
Rochdale	L	09/03	03	11	0	1

BRANNAN Peter
Born: Bradford, England, 7 April, 1947 — M

League Club	Source	Date Signed	Seasons Played	Apps	Subs	Gls
Bradford Park Ave		09/68	68-69	38	4	2

BRANNAN Robert
Born: Bradford, England, 27 August, 1924 — RW
Died: Bradford, England, January, 1986

League Club	Source	Date Signed	Seasons Played	Apps	Subs	Gls
Bradford C		09/47	47	9	-	2
Bradford C	Scarborough	02/49	48	2	-	0

BRANNIGAN Kenneth (Ken)
Born: Glasgow, Scotland, 8 June, 1965 — CD

League Club	Source	Date Signed	Seasons Played	Apps	Subs	Gls
Sheffield Wed	Queen's Park	08/86	86	1	0	0
Stockport Co	L	08/86	86	8	0	0
Doncaster Rov	L	12/87	87	15	0	1

BRANSTON Guy Peter Bromley
Born: Leicester, England, 9 January, 1979 — CD

League Club	Source	Date Signed	Seasons Played	Apps	Subs	Gls
Leicester C	YT	07/97				
Colchester U	L	02/98	97	12	0	1
Colchester U	L	08/98	98	0	1	0
Plymouth Arg	L	11/98	98	7	0	1
Lincoln C	L	08/99	99	4	0	0
Rotherham U	Tr	10/99	99-03	101	3	13
Wycombe W	L	09/03	03	9	0	0
Peterborough U	L	02/04	03	14	0	0
Sheffield Wed	Tr	07/04	04	10	1	0
Peterborough U	L	12/04	04	4	0	1
Oldham Ath	Tr	02/05	04-05	44	1	2
Peterborough U	Tr	07/06	06-07	24	2	0
Rochdale	L	08/07	07	4	0	0
Northampton T	L	10/07	07	3	0	0
Notts Co	Tr	01/08	07	1	0	0
Burton A	Kettering T	07/09	09	18	1	0
Torquay U	Tr	01/10	09-10	61	0	2
Bradford C	Tr	07/11	11	15	1	1
Rotherham U	L	10/11	11	2	0	0
Aldershot T	Tr	07/12	12	3	0	0
Bristol Rov	L	11/12	12	4	0	1
Plymouth Arg	Tr	01/13	12-13	30	1	0

BRANSTON Terence George (Terry)
Born: Rugby, Warwickshire, England, 25 July, 1938 — CD
Died: Coventry, England, 22 December, 2010

League Club	Source	Date Signed	Seasons Played	Apps	Subs	Gls
Northampton T	Thomson-Houston	10/58	60-66	244	2	2
Luton T	Tr	06/67	67-70	100	1	9
Lincoln C	Tr	09/70	70-72	99	1	1

BRASS Christopher Paul (Chris)
Born: Easington, County Durham, England, 24 July, 1975 — CD

League Club	Source	Date Signed	Seasons Played	Apps	Subs	Gls
Burnley	YT	07/93	94-99	120	14	1
Torquay U	L	10/94	94	7	0	0
Halifax T	L	09/00	00	6	0	0
York C	Tr	03/01	00-03	128	2	5
Bury	Tr	01/06	05-06	26	3	0

BRASS Robert Albert (Bobby)
Born: Middlesbrough, England, 9 November, 1943 — WH

League Club	Source	Date Signed	Seasons Played	Apps	Subs	Gls
Middlesbrough	Jnr	06/62				
Hartlepool U	Tr	10/64	64-65	27	1	0

BRASTED Gordon Albert
Born: Burnham-on-Crouch, Essex, England, 30 June, 1933 — CF
Died: Burnham-on-Crouch, Essex, England, 21 February, 2000

League Club	Source	Date Signed	Seasons Played	Apps	Subs	Gls
Arsenal	Burnham Ramblers	12/53				
Gillingham	Tr	07/56	56	5	-	4

BRATHWAITE John Roderick (Rod)
Born: Isleworth, W London, England, 19 December, 1965 — F
England: Schools

League Club	Source	Date Signed	Seasons Played	Apps	Subs	Gls
Fulham	Jnr	07/84	85-86	7	4	2

BRATLEY Charles Tony (Tony)
Born: Spalding, Lincolnshire, England, 30 April, 1939 — FB

League Club	Source	Date Signed	Seasons Played	Apps	Subs	Gls
Grimsby T		08/57	58	2	-	0

BRATT Harold
Born: Salford, England, 8 October, 1939 — WH
England: Schools

League Club	Source	Date Signed	Seasons Played	Apps	Subs	Gls
Manchester U	Jnr	11/57				
Doncaster Rov	Tr	05/61	61-62	54	-	0

BRATTAN Gary
Born: Hull, England, 1 January, 1960 — M

League Club	Source	Date Signed	Seasons Played	Apps	Subs	Gls
Hull C	App	01/78				
Cambridge U	North Ferriby U	08/87	87	7	1	0

BRAVO Raul
Born: Gandia, Spain, 14 April, 1981 — LB
Spain: 14/U21-3/Youth

League Club	Source	Date Signed	Seasons Played	Apps	Subs	Gls
Leeds U (L)	Real Madrid (SPN)	02/03	02	5	0	0

BRAY Alex George
Born: Corsham, Wiltshire, England, 25 July, 1995 — RW
Wales: Youth

League Club	Source	Date Signed	Seasons Played	Apps	Subs	Gls
Swansea C	Sch	07/13				
Plymouth Arg	L	09/14	14	0	1	0

BRAY Geoffrey Charles (Geoff)
Born: Chatham, Kent, England, 30 May, 1951 — F

League Club	Source	Date Signed	Seasons Played	Apps	Subs	Gls
Gillingham	App	06/69				
Oxford U	Erith & Belvedere	07/71	72-74	22	11	6
Swansea C	Tr	07/75	75-76	43	3	20
Torquay U	Tr	11/76	76	7	0	2

BRAY George
Born: Oswaldtwistle, Lancashire, England, 11 November, 1918 — LH
Died: Hapton, Lancashire, England, 13 February, 2002

League Club	Source	Date Signed	Seasons Played	Apps	Subs	Gls
Burnley	Great Harwood	10/37	38-51	241	-	8

BRAY Ian Michael
Born: Neath, Wales, 6 December, 1962 — LB

League Club	Source	Date Signed	Seasons Played	Apps	Subs	Gls
Hereford U	App	12/80	81-84	105	3	4
Huddersfield T	Tr	07/85	85-89	87	2	1
Burnley	Tr	07/90	90-91	15	2	0

BRAY John
Born: Rishton, Lancashire, England, 16 March, 1937 — FB
Died: Rainford, Merseyside, England, 29 September, 1992

League Club	Source	Date Signed	Seasons Played	Apps	Subs	Gls
Blackburn Rov	Jnr	03/54	59-64	153	-	2
Bury	Tr	04/65	65	32	0	0

BRAY Wayne
Born: Bristol, England, 17 November, 1964 — M
England: Schools

League Club	Source	Date Signed	Seasons Played	Apps	Subs	Gls
Bristol C	App	11/81	81-82	28	1	2

BRAYFORD John Robert
Born: Stoke-on-Trent, England, 29 December, 1987 — RB
England: Semi Pro-7

League Club	Source	Date Signed	Seasons Played	Apps	Subs	Gls
Crewe Alex	Burton A	09/08	08-09	79	2	2
Derby Co	Tr	06/10	10-12	108	1	2
Cardiff C	Tr	07/13	14	26	0	0
Sheffield U	L	01/14	13	15	0	1
Sheffield U	Tr	01/15	14	22	0	1

BRAYLEY Albert (Bertie)
Born: Basildon, England, 5 September, 1981 — F

League Club	Source	Date Signed	Seasons Played	Apps	Subs	Gls
Queens Park Rgrs	West Ham U (YT)	08/00				
Swindon T	Tr	08/01	01	0	7	0

BRAYSON Paul
Born: Newcastle-upon-Tyne, England, 16 September, 1977 — F
England: Youth

League Club	Source	Date Signed	Seasons Played	Apps	Subs	Gls
Newcastle U	YT	08/95				
Swansea C	L	01/97	96	11	0	5
Reading	Tr	03/98	97-99	15	26	1
Cardiff C	Tr	03/00	99-01	48	36	19
Cheltenham T	Tr	08/02	02-03	34	17	8

BRAYTON Barry James
Born: Carlisle, Cumbria, England, 29 September, 1938 — IF/W
Died: 20 January, 2015

League Club	Source	Date Signed	Seasons Played	Apps	Subs	Gls
Carlisle U		01/60	59-66	160	1	35
Workington	Tr	02/67	66-67	43	0	8

BRAZIER Colin James
Born: Solihull, West Midlands, England, 6 June, 1957 — CD
England: Semi Pro

League Club	Source	Date Signed	Seasons Played	Apps	Subs	Gls
Wolverhampton W	Northfield T	08/75	76-81	69	9	2
Birmingham C	Tr	09/82	82	10	1	1
Lincoln C	AP Leamington	04/83	82	9	0	0
Walsall	Tr	08/83	83-86	114	1	4

BRAZIER Matthew Ronald (Matt)
Born: Leytonstone, NE London, England, 2 July, 1976 — M/LB

League Club	Source	Date Signed	Seasons Played	Apps	Subs	Gls
Queens Park Rgrs	YT	07/94	95-97	36	13	2
Fulham	Tr	03/98	97-98	4	5	1
Cardiff C	L	08/98	98	11	0	2
Cardiff C	Tr	07/99	99-00	43	13	3
Leyton Orient	Tr	01/02	01-03	46	0	2

BRAZIL Alan Bernard
Born: Glasgow, Scotland, 15 June, 1959 — F
Scotland: 13/U21-8

League Club	Source	Date Signed	Seasons Played	Apps	Subs	Gls
Ipswich T	App	05/77	77-82	143	11	70
Tottenham H	Tr	03/83	82-83	29	2	9
Manchester U	Tr	06/84	84-85	18	13	8
Coventry C	Tr	01/86	85	15	0	2
Queens Park Rgrs	Tr	06/86	86	1	3	0

BRAZIL Derek Michael
Born: Dublin, Republic of Ireland, 14 December, 1968 — D
Republic of Ireland: B/U21-9/Youth/Schools

League Club	Source	Date Signed	Seasons Played	Apps	Subs	Gls
Manchester U	Rivermount BC (ROI)	03/86	88-89	0	2	0
Oldham Ath	L	11/90	90	1	0	0
Swansea C	L	09/91	91	12	0	1
Cardiff C	Tr	08/92	92-95	109	6	1

BRAZIL Gary Nicholas

Born: Tunbridge Wells, Kent, England, 19 September, 1962   F

League Club	Source	Date Signed	Seasons Played	Apps	Subs	Gls
Sheffield U	Crystal Palace (App)	08/80	80-84	39	23	9
Port Vale	L	08/84	84	6	0	3
Preston NE	L	02/85	84	6	0	1
Preston NE	Tr	03/85	84-88	157	3	56
Newcastle U	Tr	02/89	88-89	7	16	2
Fulham	Tr	09/90	90-95	207	7	47
Cambridge U	Tr	08/96	96	1	0	1
Barnet	Tr	09/96	96	15	4	2

BREACKER Timothy Sean (Tim)

Born: Bicester, Oxfordshire, England, 2 July, 1965   RB

England: U21-2

League Club	Source	Date Signed	Seasons Played	Apps	Subs	Gls
Luton T	App	05/83	83-90	204	6	3
West Ham U	Tr	10/90	90-98	229	11	8
Queens Park Rgrs	L	10/98	98	2	0	0
Queens Park Rgrs	Tr	02/99	98-00	39	3	2

BREAKS Edward (Teddy)

Born: Halifax, West Yorkshire, England, 29 December, 1919   LB

Died: Halifax, West Yorkshire, England, November, 2000

League Club	Source	Date Signed	Seasons Played	Apps	Subs	Gls
Halifax T	Shaw Lodge Mills	07/48	48-54	179	-	1

BREARS Paul Arthur

Born: Oldham, Greater Manchester, England, 25 September, 1954   M

League Club	Source	Date Signed	Seasons Played	Apps	Subs	Gls
Rochdale	Oldham Ath (Am)	08/73	73-75	26	1	0

BREBNER Grant Iain

Born: Edinburgh, Scotland, 6 December, 1977   M

Scotland: U21-17/Schools

League Club	Source	Date Signed	Seasons Played	Apps	Subs	Gls
Manchester U	Hutchison Vale BC	03/95				
Cambridge U	L	01/98	97	6	0	1
Reading	Tr	06/98	98-99	38	3	10
Stockport Co (L)	Hibernian	10/00	00	3	3	0

BRECKIN Ian

Born: Rotherham, South Yorkshire, England, 24 February, 1975   CD

League Club	Source	Date Signed	Seasons Played	Apps	Subs	Gls
Rotherham U	YT	11/93	93-96	130	2	6
Chesterfield	Tr	07/97	97-01	208	4	8
Wigan Ath	Tr	06/02	02-04	92	4	0
Nottingham F	Tr	07/05	05-08	131	12	12
Chesterfield	Tr	07/09	09-10	60	7	0

BRECKIN John

Born: Sheffield, England, 27 July, 1953   LB

League Club	Source	Date Signed	Seasons Played	Apps	Subs	Gls
Rotherham U	App	07/71	71-82	405	4	8
Darlington	L	10/72	72	4	0	0
Bury	Tr	02/83	82	17	0	0
Doncaster Rov	Tr	08/83	83	17	1	0

BREE James Patrick

Born: Wakefield, England, 11 December, 1997   RB

League Club	Source	Date Signed	Seasons Played	Apps	Subs	Gls
Barnsley	Sch	12/14	13-14	6	6	0

BREEN Gary Patrick

Born: Hendon, N London, England, 12 December, 1973   CD

Republic of Ireland: 63/U21-9

League Club	Source	Date Signed	Seasons Played	Apps	Subs	Gls
Maidstone U	Charlton Ath (Jnr)	03/91	91	19	0	0
Gillingham	Tr	07/92	92-93	45	6	0
Peterborough U	Tr	08/94	94-95	68	1	1
Birmingham C	Tr	02/96	95-96	37	3	2
Coventry C	Tr	02/97	96-01	138	8	2
West Ham U	Tr	07/02	02	9	5	0
Sunderland	Tr	08/03	03-05	105	2	7
Wolverhampton W	Tr	07/06	06-07	58	1	1
Barnet		12/08	08-09	47	0	0

BREITENFELDER Friedrich Johann

Born: Vienna, Austria, 16 June, 1980   M

League Club	Source	Date Signed	Seasons Played	Apps	Subs	Gls
Luton T	FCM St Polten (AUT)	08/00	00	2	3	0

BREITKREUTZ Matthias

Born: Schwerin, Germany, 12 May, 1971   M

League Club	Source	Date Signed	Seasons Played	Apps	Subs	Gls
Aston Villa	Bergmann Borsig (GER)	10/91	91-93	10	3	0

BREKKE-SKARD Vemund

Born: Hamar, Norway, 11 September, 1981   M

League Club	Source	Date Signed	Seasons Played	Apps	Subs	Gls
Ipswich T	Brumundaal (NOR)	10/05	05	2	1	0

BRELLIER Julien

Born: Grenoble, France, 10 January, 1982   M

League Club	Source	Date Signed	Seasons Played	Apps	Subs	Gls
Norwich C	Heart of Midlothian	07/07	07	8	2	0

BREMNER Desmond George (Des)

Born: Aberchirder, Aberdeenshire, Scotland, 7 September, 1952   M

Scotland: 1/SLge-1/U23-9

League Club	Source	Date Signed	Seasons Played	Apps	Subs	Gls
Aston Villa	Hibernian	09/79	79-84	170	4	9
Birmingham C	Tr	09/84	84-88	167	1	5
Fulham	Tr	08/89	89	7	9	0
Walsall	Tr	03/90	89	2	4	0

BREMNER Kevin Johnston

Born: Banff, Aberdeenshire, Scotland, 7 October, 1957   F

League Club	Source	Date Signed	Seasons Played	Apps	Subs	Gls
Colchester U	Keith	10/80	80-82	89	6	31
Birmingham C	L	10/82	82	3	1	1
Wrexham	L	12/82	82	4	0	1
Plymouth Arg	L	01/83	82	5	0	1
Millwall	Tr	02/83	82-84	87	9	32
Reading	Tr	08/85	85-86	60	4	21
Brighton & HA	Tr	07/87	87-89	125	3	36
Peterborough U	Tr	07/90	90	13	4	3
Shrewsbury T (L)	Dundee	03/92	91	7	0	2

BREMNER William John (Billy)

Born: Stirling, Scotland, 9 December, 1942   M

Died: Doncaster, South Yorkshire, England, 5 March, 1997

Scotland: 54/U23-4/Schools

League Club	Source	Date Signed	Seasons Played	Apps	Subs	Gls
Leeds U	Jnr	12/59	59-76	586	1	90
Hull C	Tr	09/76	76-77	61	0	6
Doncaster Rov	Tr	09/79	79-81	2	3	0

BRENEN Albert (Bert)

Born: South Shields, Tyne and Wear, England, 5 October, 1915   WH

Died: York, England, February, 1995

League Club	Source	Date Signed	Seasons Played	Apps	Subs	Gls
York C	St John's College	08/38	38-50	204	-	13

BRENNAN Bryan

Born: Halifax, West Yorkshire, England, 25 May, 1933   CF

Died: Halifax, West Yorkshire, England, 9 January, 2015

England: Schools

League Club	Source	Date Signed	Seasons Played	Apps	Subs	Gls
Stockport Co	Jnr	06/50	50	4	-	0

BRENNAN Dean James Gary

Born: Dublin, Republic of Ireland, 17 June, 1980   M

League Club	Source	Date Signed	Seasons Played	Apps	Subs	Gls
Sheffield Wed	Stella Maris (ROI)	11/97				
Luton T	Tr	08/00	00	2	7	0

BRENNAN Francis (Frank)

Born: Annathill, Lanarkshire, Scotland, 23 April, 1924   CH

Died: Newcastle-upon-Tyne, England, 5 March, 1997

Scotland: 7/War-2

League Club	Source	Date Signed	Seasons Played	Apps	Subs	Gls
Newcastle U	Airdrieonians	05/46	46-55	318	-	3

BRENNAN Harry

Born: Derby, England, 17 November, 1930   IF

League Club	Source	Date Signed	Seasons Played	Apps	Subs	Gls
Shrewsbury T	Gresley Rov	12/53	53-54	19	-	3

BRENNAN Ian

Born: Easington, County Durham, England, 25 March, 1953   LB

League Club	Source	Date Signed	Seasons Played	Apps	Subs	Gls
Burnley	App	10/70	73-79	173	2	11
Bolton W	Tr	12/80	80-81	16	1	0

BRENNAN James (Jim)

Born: Downpatrick, Northern Ireland, 29 February, 1932   LW

League Club	Source	Date Signed	Seasons Played	Apps	Subs	Gls
Birmingham C	Glentoran	06/52				
Swindon T	Tr	06/54	54-55	16	-	1

BRENNAN James Gerald (Jim)

Born: Toronto, Canada, 8 May, 1977   LB

Canada: 43/U23-1

League Club	Source	Date Signed	Seasons Played	Apps	Subs	Gls
Bristol C	Sora Lazio (CAN)	10/94	96-99	51	4	3
Nottingham F	Tr	10/99	99-02	117	6	1
Huddersfield T	L	03/01	00	0	2	0
Norwich C	Tr	07/03	03-05	25	18	1
Southampton	Tr	01/06	05	13	1	0

BRENNAN James Seamus Anthony (Shay)

Born: Manchester, England, 6 May, 1937   RB

Died: Waterford, Republic of Ireland, 9 June, 2000

Republic of Ireland: 19/LoI-1

League Club	Source	Date Signed	Seasons Played	Apps	Subs	Gls
Manchester U	Jnr	04/55	57-69	291	1	3

BRENNAN Malcolm

Born: Manchester, England, 11 November, 1934   IF

League Club	Source	Date Signed	Seasons Played	Apps	Subs	Gls
Crewe Alex		12/52	56	1	-	0

BRENNAN Mark Robert

Born: Rawtenstall, Lancashire, England, 4 October, 1965   M

England: U21-5/Youth

League Club	Source	Date Signed	Seasons Played	Apps	Subs	Gls
Ipswich T	App	04/83	83-87	165	3	19
Middlesbrough	Tr	07/88	88-89	61	4	6
Manchester C	Tr	07/90	90-91	25	4	6
Oldham Ath	Tr	11/92	92-95	82	8	7

BRENNAN Martin Ian

Born: Leytonstone, NE London, England, 14 September, 1982   G

League Club	Source	Date Signed	Seasons Played	Apps	Subs	Gls
Charlton Ath	Tottenham H (YT)	11/00				
Cambridge U	Tr	08/02	02	1	0	0

BRENNAN Matthew Hyland (Matt)

Born: Glasgow, Scotland, 3 January, 1943   IF

League Club	Source	Date Signed	Seasons Played	Apps	Subs	Gls
Luton T	St Roch's	06/62	62	4	-	1

League Club | Source | Date Signed | Seasons Played | Career Record Apps | Subs | Gls

BRENNAN Michael (Mike)
Born: Salford, England, 17 May, 1952 F

League Club	Source	Date Signed	Seasons Played	Apps	Subs	Gls
Manchester C	App	12/69	70-72	1	3	0
Stockport Co	L	02/72	71	18	0	3
Rochdale	Tr	10/73	73-74	35	2	4

BRENNAN Patrick Joseph (Paddy)
Born: Dublin, Republic of Ireland, 1 March, 1924 WH
Died: Hove, East Sussex, England, 11 January, 1991

League Club	Source	Date Signed	Seasons Played	Apps	Subs	Gls
Brighton & HA	Shelbourne (ROI)	08/48	48-50	45	-	0

BRENNAN Raymond John (Ray)
Born: Blackpool, Lancashire, England, 13 November, 1944 IF

League Club	Source	Date Signed	Seasons Played	Apps	Subs	Gls
Blackburn Rov	Wolverhampton W (Am)	07/62				
Barrow	Tr	03/64	63-64	46	-	10
Norwich C	Tr	07/65				

BRENNAN Robert Anderson (Bobby)
Born: Belfast, Northern Ireland, 14 March, 1925 IF
Died: Norwich, England, 1 January, 2002
Northern Ireland: 5/NILge-1

League Club	Source	Date Signed	Seasons Played	Apps	Subs	Gls
Luton T	Distillery	10/47	47-48	69	-	22
Birmingham C	Tr	07/49	49	39	-	7
Fulham	Tr	06/50	50-52	73	-	13
Norwich C	Tr	07/53	53-55	117	-	30
Norwich C	Yarmouth T	03/57	56-59	108	-	14

BRENNAN Stephen Anthony (Steve)
Born: Mile End, E London, England, 3 September, 1958 M

League Club	Source	Date Signed	Seasons Played	Apps	Subs	Gls
Crystal Palace	App	02/76	76-77	2	1	1
Plymouth Arg	Tr	08/78	78	6	0	0

BRENT Peter
Born: Staveley, Derbyshire, England, 18 November, 1937 WH
Died: Chesterfield, Derbyshire, England, December, 1988

League Club	Source	Date Signed	Seasons Played	Apps	Subs	Gls
Chesterfield	Jnr	05/55	59	2	-	0

BRENTANO Stephen Ronald
Born: Hull, England, 9 September, 1961 RB

League Club	Source	Date Signed	Seasons Played	Apps	Subs	Gls
Hull C	North Ferriby U	03/82	84-86	11	1	0
Doncaster Rov	Bridlington T	08/93	93	1	0	0

BRESLAN Geoffrey Francis (Geoff)
Born: Torquay, Devon, England, 4 June, 1980 M

League Club	Source	Date Signed	Seasons Played	Apps	Subs	Gls
Exeter C	YT	01/99	97-02	61	48	6

BRESSINGTON Graham
Born: Eton, Berkshire, England, 8 July, 1966 M/CD

League Club	Source	Date Signed	Seasons Played	Apps	Subs	Gls
Lincoln C	Wycombe W	10/87	88-92	136	5	7
Southend U	Tr	07/93	93-94	46	2	5

BRETHERTON Thomas Alexander (Tom)
Born: Chorley, Lancashire, England, 9 April, 1920 IF
Died: Chorley, Lancashire, England, 13 April, 1998

League Club	Source	Date Signed	Seasons Played	Apps	Subs	Gls
Accrington Stan	Leyland Motors	02/47	46	4	-	0

BRETT David Stephen
Born: Chester, England, 8 April, 1961 M

League Club	Source	Date Signed	Seasons Played	Apps	Subs	Gls
Chester C	Colwyn Bay	08/83	83-85	52	15	6

BRETT Ronald Alexander (Ron)
Born: Stanford-le-Hope, Essex, England, 4 September, 1937 F
Died: Clerkenwell, Central London, England, 30 August, 1962

League Club	Source	Date Signed	Seasons Played	Apps	Subs	Gls
Crystal Palace	Jnr	09/54	55-58	36	-	12
West Ham U	Tr	06/59	59-60	12	-	4
Crystal Palace	Tr	03/62	61	8	-	1

BRETTELL Raymond (Ray)
Born: Strood, Kent, England, 22 August, 1935 RW

League Club	Source	Date Signed	Seasons Played	Apps	Subs	Gls
Doncaster Rov (Am)	RAF Finningley	01/61	60	9	-	1

BREVETT Rupis Emanuel (Rufus)
Born: Derby, England, 24 September, 1969 LB

League Club	Source	Date Signed	Seasons Played	Apps	Subs	Gls
Doncaster Rov	YT	07/88	87-90	106	3	3
Queens Park Rgrs	Tr	02/91	90-97	141	11	1
Fulham	Tr	01/98	97-02	171	2	1
West Ham U	Tr	01/03	02-04	24	1	1
Plymouth Arg	Tr	07/05	05	12	1	0
Leicester C	L	02/06	05	0	1	0

BREWER Anthony Peter (Tony)
Born: Edmonton, N London, England, 20 May, 1932 G
Died: Northampton, England, September, 1989

League Club	Source	Date Signed	Seasons Played	Apps	Subs	Gls
Millwall	Jnr	10/49	50-57	47	-	0
Northampton T	Tr	02/57	58-60	87	-	0

BREWSTER George
Born: Barlborough, Derbyshire, England, 19 October, 1925 IF

League Club	Source	Date Signed	Seasons Played	Apps	Subs	Gls
Bristol C	Retford T	09/49	49-50	13	-	3

League Club | Source | Date Signed | Seasons Played | Career Record Apps | Subs | Gls

BREWSTER John Robert
Born: Creswell, Derbyshire, England, 19 August, 1942 IF

League Club	Source	Date Signed	Seasons Played	Apps	Subs	Gls
Sheffield U	Jnr	04/60				
Torquay U	Tr	08/64	64-65	21	0	2

BREWSTER William Clark (Bill)
Born: Kinglassie, Fife, Scotland, 4 August, 1933 G
Died: Sutton, S London, England, 29 November, 2005

League Club	Source	Date Signed	Seasons Played	Apps	Subs	Gls
Chelsea	Dundonald Bluebell	08/51				
Southend U	Tr	08/55	55	2	-	0

BREZOVAN Petr
Born: Bratislava, Slovakia, 9 December, 1979 G
Slovakia: U21

League Club	Source	Date Signed	Seasons Played	Apps	Subs	Gls
Swindon T	FC Brno (CZE)	08/06	06-08	66	0	0
Brighton & HA	Tr	12/09	09-13	46	1	0
Tranmere Rov	Portsmouth (NC)	09/14	14	8	0	0

BRICE Gordon Harry Joseph
Born: Bedford, England, 4 May, 1924 CH
Died: Bedford, England, 3 March, 2003

League Club	Source	Date Signed	Seasons Played	Apps	Subs	Gls
Luton T	Bedford St Clement's	10/44	46	13	-	0
Wolverhampton W	Tr	05/47	47	12	-	0
Reading	Tr	03/48	47-52	198	-	9
Fulham	Tr	12/52	52-55	87	-	1

BRICKLEY Dennis
Born: Bradford, England, 9 September, 1929 RW
Died: Bradford, England, 12 June, 1983
England: Youth

League Club	Source	Date Signed	Seasons Played	Apps	Subs	Gls
Bradford Park Ave	Huddersfield T (Am)	08/49	50-56	169	-	24

BRIDCUTT Liam Robert
Born: Reading, England, 8 May, 1989 DM

League Club	Source	Date Signed	Seasons Played	Apps	Subs	Gls
Chelsea	Sch	07/07				
Yeovil T	L	02/08	07	6	3	0
Watford	L	11/08	08	4	2	0
Stockport Co	L	08/09	09	15	0	0
Brighton & HA	Tr	08/10	10-13	123	9	2
Sunderland	Tr	01/14	13-14	19	11	0

BRIDDON Samuel (Sam)
Born: Alfreton, Derbyshire, England, 26 July, 1915 WH
Died: Mansfield, Nottinghamshire, England, 1975

League Club	Source	Date Signed	Seasons Played	Apps	Subs	Gls
Brentford	Stanton Hill	08/35	38	6	-	0
Swindon T	Tr	06/39				
Swansea C	Tr	07/39	46	18	-	0

BRIDGE Michael John (Jackie)
Born: Great Wakering, Essex, England, 30 May, 1932 WH

League Club	Source	Date Signed	Seasons Played	Apps	Subs	Gls
Southend U	Jnr	08/50	52-55	53	-	3

BRIDGE Wayne Michael
Born: Southampton, England, 5 August, 1980 LB
England: 36/U21-8/Youth

League Club	Source	Date Signed	Seasons Played	Apps	Subs	Gls
Southampton	YT	01/98	98-02	140	12	2
Chelsea	Tr	07/03	03-08	74	13	1
Fulham	L	01/06	05	12	0	0
Manchester C	Tr	01/09	08-10	40	2	0
West Ham U	L	01/11	10	15	0	0
Sunderland	L	01/12	11	3	5	0
Brighton & HA	L	07/12	12	37	0	3
Reading	Tr	07/13	13	11	1	0

BRIDGE-WILKINSON Marc
Born: Nuneaton, Warwickshire, England, 16 March, 1979 M

League Club	Source	Date Signed	Seasons Played	Apps	Subs	Gls
Derby Co	YT	03/97	98	0	1	0
Carlisle U	L	03/99	98	4	3	0
Port Vale	Tr	07/00	00-03	111	13	31
Stockport Co	Tr	08/04	04	19	3	2
Bradford C	Tr	02/05	04-06	87	0	12
Carlisle U	Tr	07/07	07-10	70	20	11

BRIDGER David James (Dave)
Born: Hartley Wintney, Hampshire, England, 8 November, 1941 D

League Club	Source	Date Signed	Seasons Played	Apps	Subs	Gls
Reading		03/62	62-64	10	-	0

BRIDGES Barry John
Born: Horsford, Norfolk, England, 29 April, 1941 F
England: 4/FLge-1/Youth/Schools

League Club	Source	Date Signed	Seasons Played	Apps	Subs	Gls
Chelsea	Jnr	05/58	58-65	174	2	80
Birmingham C	Tr	05/66	66-68	83	0	37
Queens Park Rgrs	Tr	08/68	68-70	72	0	31
Millwall	Tr	09/70	70-71	77	0	27
Brighton & HA	Tr	09/72	72-73	56	10	14

BRIDGES Benjamin (Ben)
Born: Hull, England, 3 February, 1937 IF

League Club	Source	Date Signed	Seasons Played	Apps	Subs	Gls
Hull C	Jnr	08/55	57	1	-	0

BRIDGES Bernard
Born: Doncaster, South Yorkshire, England, 28 February, 1959 — CD

League Club	Source	Date Signed	Seasons Played	Apps	Subs	Gls
Scunthorpe U	Jnr	07/76	76-77	22	1	0

BRIDGES David Stephen
Born: Huntingdon, Cambridgeshire, England, 22 September, 1982 — M
England: Semi Pro-1

League Club	Source	Date Signed	Seasons Played	Apps	Subs	Gls
Cambridge U	Sch	03/02	01-03	18	27	5
Stevenage	Kettering T	05/08	10	8	11	1

BRIDGES Harold
Born: Burton-on-Trent, Staffordshire, England, 30 June, 1915 — IF
Died: Stockport, Greater Manchester, England, March, 1989

League Club	Source	Date Signed	Seasons Played	Apps	Subs	Gls
Manchester C	Burton T	04/37				
Tranmere Rov	Tr	07/39	46-47	33	-	9

BRIDGES Michael
Born: North Shields, Tyne and Wear, England, 5 August, 1978 — F
England: U21-3/Youth/Schools

League Club	Source	Date Signed	Seasons Played	Apps	Subs	Gls
Sunderland	YT	11/95	95-98	31	48	16
Leeds U	Tr	07/99	99-03	40	16	19
Newcastle U	L	02/04	03	0	6	0
Bolton W	Tr	07/04				
Sunderland	Tr	09/04	04	5	14	1
Bristol C	Tr	07/05	05	4	7	0
Carlisle U	Tr	11/05	05-06	28	2	15
Hull C	Tr	08/06	06-07	9	13	2
Carlisle U	L	07/08	08	12	18	7
MK Dons	Tr	08/09	09	0	1	0

BRIDGETT John (Jack)
Born: Walsall, West Midlands, England, 10 April, 1929 — CH

League Club	Source	Date Signed	Seasons Played	Apps	Subs	Gls
West Bromwich A	Jnr	05/46				
Walsall	Tr	08/50	50-54	106	-	18

BRIDGETT Raymond Alwyne (Ray)
Born: Nottingham, England, 5 April, 1947 — FB
Died: Walsall, West Midlands, England, October, 1997

League Club	Source	Date Signed	Seasons Played	Apps	Subs	Gls
Nottingham F	Jnr	05/64	67-69	2	2	0

BRIDGWOOD Gerald (Gerry)
Born: Stoke-on-Trent, England, 17 October, 1944 — M
Died: Goostrey, Cheshire, England, 2 March, 2012

League Club	Source	Date Signed	Seasons Played	Apps	Subs	Gls
Stoke C	App	10/61	60-68	90	5	6
Shrewsbury T	Tr	02/69	68-72	113	4	7

BRIEN Anthony James (Tony)
Born: Dublin, Republic of Ireland, 10 February, 1969 — CD
Republic of Ireland: Youth

League Club	Source	Date Signed	Seasons Played	Apps	Subs	Gls
Leicester C	App	02/87	87-88	12	4	1
Chesterfield	Tr	12/88	88-93	201	3	8
Rotherham U	Tr	10/93	93-94	41	2	2
West Bromwich A	Tr	07/95	95	2	0	0
Mansfield T	L	02/96	95	4	0	0
Chester C	L	03/96	95	8	0	0
Hull C	Tr	07/96	96-97	43	4	1

BRIEN William Roy (Roy)
Born: Stoke-on-Trent, England, 11 November, 1930 — WH
Died: Rochdale, Greater Manchester, England, 27 January, 1987

League Club	Source	Date Signed	Seasons Played	Apps	Subs	Gls
Port Vale		05/51	53	1	-	0

BRIER John David
Born: Halifax, West Yorkshire, England, 3 April, 1941 — D

League Club	Source	Date Signed	Seasons Played	Apps	Subs	Gls
Burnley	Jnr	06/58				
Halifax T	Tr	08/61	61-65	78	2	0

BRIERLEY Keith
Born: Dewsbury, West Yorkshire, England, 14 December, 1951 — F

League Club	Source	Date Signed	Seasons Played	Apps	Subs	Gls
Halifax T	Jnr	12/69	69-72	51	4	11

BRIERLEY Kenneth (Ken)
Born: Ashton-under-Lyne, Greater Manchester, England, 3 April, 1926 — LW
Died: Blackpool, Lancashire, England, February, 2004

League Club	Source	Date Signed	Seasons Played	Apps	Subs	Gls
Oldham Ath	Range Boilers	04/45	46-47	58	-	5
Liverpool	Tr	02/48	47-52	58	-	8
Oldham Ath	Tr	03/53	52-54	67	-	5

BRIGGS Alec Michael
Born: Sheffield, England, 21 June, 1939 — FB

League Club	Source	Date Signed	Seasons Played	Apps	Subs	Gls
Bristol C	Jnr	04/57	57-69	349	2	1

BRIGGS Charles Edward (Charlie)
Born: Liphook, Hampshire, England, 4 April, 1911 — G

League Club	Source	Date Signed	Seasons Played	Apps	Subs	Gls
Fulham	Guildford C	12/35				
Crystal Palace	Guildford C	05/36				
Bradford Park Ave	Guildford C	05/37				
Halifax T	Tr	03/38	37-38	53	-	0
Rochdale	Clyde	05/47	46-47	12	-	0
Chesterfield	Tr	12/47				

BRIGGS Gary
Born: Leeds, England, 21 June, 1959 — CD

League Club	Source	Date Signed	Seasons Played	Apps	Subs	Gls
Middlesbrough	App	05/77				
Oxford U	Tr	01/78	77-88	418	2	18
Blackpool	Tr	06/89	89-94	137	0	4

BRIGGS George Henry
Born: Easington, County Durham, England, 26 February, 1923 — CH
Died: Peterlee, County Durham, England, 2005

League Club	Source	Date Signed	Seasons Played	Apps	Subs	Gls
Crystal Palace	Shotton CW	11/47	48-54	150	-	4

BRIGGS John (Jackie)
Born: Barnsley, South Yorkshire, England, 27 October, 1924 — LW
Died: Slough, Berkshire, England, October, 1992

League Club	Source	Date Signed	Seasons Played	Apps	Subs	Gls
Gillingham	Southall	10/46	50-52	52	-	14

BRIGGS John Cyril (Cyril)
Born: Salford, England, 24 November, 1918 — CH
Died: Perth, Australia, 26 November, 1998
England: Schools

League Club	Source	Date Signed	Seasons Played	Apps	Subs	Gls
Manchester U	Darwen	10/44				
Accrington Stan	Tr	08/45	46-49	135	-	1
Southport	Tr	03/50	49	3	-	0

BRIGGS Keith
Born: Glossop, Derbyshire, England, 11 December, 1981 — M

League Club	Source	Date Signed	Seasons Played	Apps	Subs	Gls
Stockport Co	YT	08/99	99-02	47	11	2
Norwich C	Tr	01/03	02-03	2	3	0
Crewe Alex	L	08/04	04	3	0	0
Stockport Co	Sheffield U (NC)	01/05	04-07	74	16	8
Shrewsbury T	Tr	01/08	07	1	1	1
Mansfield T	Tr	02/08	07	10	3	0

BRIGGS Malcolm Douglas
Born: Sunderland, England, 14 September, 1961 — M

League Club	Source	Date Signed	Seasons Played	Apps	Subs	Gls
Birmingham C	App	08/79	78	0	1	0

BRIGGS Matthew Anthony (Matt)
Born: Wandsworth, SW London, England, 6 March, 1991 — LB
England: U21-2/Youth//Guyana: 1

League Club	Source	Date Signed	Seasons Played	Apps	Subs	Gls
Fulham	Sch	06/09	06-13	7	6	0
Leyton Orient	L	01/10	09	1	0	0
Peterborough U	L	02/12	11	5	0	0
Bristol C	L	10/12	12	4	0	0
Watford	L	02/13	12	5	2	1
Millwall	Tr	08/14	14	7	1	0
Colchester U	L	01/15	14	17	1	0

BRIGGS Maxwell Francis (Max)
Born: Bramerton, Norfolk, England, 9 September, 1948 — M

League Club	Source	Date Signed	Seasons Played	Apps	Subs	Gls
Norwich C	Jnr	12/67	68-73	127	8	1
Oxford U	Tr	02/74	73-77	94	3	1

BRIGGS Stephen (Steve)
Born: Leeds, England, 2 December, 1946 — F

League Club	Source	Date Signed	Seasons Played	Apps	Subs	Gls
Leeds U	Jnr	10/65				
Doncaster Rov	Tr	02/69	68-72	114	10	34

BRIGGS Thomas Henry (Tommy)
Born: Chesterfield, Derbyshire, England, 27 November, 1923 — CF
Died: Grimsby, North Lincolnshire, England, 10 February, 1984
England: B-1

League Club	Source	Date Signed	Seasons Played	Apps	Subs	Gls
Plymouth Arg	Royal Navy	03/46				
Grimsby T	Tr	05/47	47-50	116	-	78
Coventry C	Tr	01/51	50-51	11	-	7
Birmingham C	Tr	09/51	51-52	50	-	22
Blackburn Rov	Tr	12/52	52-57	194	-	140
Grimsby T	Tr	03/58	57-58	19	-	9

BRIGGS Thomas Raymond (Tom)
Born: Rotherham, South Yorkshire, England, 11 May, 1919 — D
Died: Crewe, Cheshire, England, 7 November, 1999

League Club	Source	Date Signed	Seasons Played	Apps	Subs	Gls
Huddersfield T	Army	02/46	46-49	45	-	0
Crewe Alex	Tr	12/49	49-55	206	-	2

BRIGGS Walter (Wally)
Born: Middlesbrough, England, 29 November, 1922 — G
Died: Middlesbrough, England, 10 January, 1990

League Club	Source	Date Signed	Seasons Played	Apps	Subs	Gls
Middlesbrough	Cochranes	05/47	46-47	2	-	0
Southport	Tr	06/48	48	4	-	0
Hartlepool U	Tr	09/49	49-51	44	-	0

BRIGGS William Roland (Ronnie)
Born: Belfast, Northern Ireland, 29 March, 1943 — G
Died: Bristol, England, 28 August, 2008
Northern Ireland: 2

League Club	Source	Date Signed	Seasons Played	Apps	Subs	Gls
Manchester U	Jnr	03/60	60-61	9	-	0
Swansea C	Tr	05/64	64	27	-	0
Bristol Rov	Tr	06/65	65-67	35	0	0

BRIGGS Wilson Waite
Born: Gorebridge, Midlothian, Scotland, 15 May, 1942 — FB
Died: Birmingham, England, February, 2005

League Club	Source	Date Signed	Seasons Played	Apps	Subs	Gls
Aston Villa	Arniston Rgrs	08/59	61-62	2	-	0

BRIGHAM Harold (Harry)
Born: Selby, North Yorkshire, England, 19 November, 1914 — RB
Died: York, England, May, 1978

League Club	Source	Date Signed	Seasons Played	Apps	Subs	Gls
Stoke C	Frickley Colliery	05/36	36-46	104	-	0
Nottingham F	Tr	11/46	46-47	35	-	2
York C	Tr	07/48	48-49	56	-	5

BRIGHT David
Born: Prudhoe, Northumberland, England, 24 December, 1946 — FB

League Club	Source	Date Signed	Seasons Played	Apps	Subs	Gls
Sunderland	West Wylam Jnrs	08/65				
Preston NE	Tr	08/67	68	1	0	0
Oldham Ath	Tr	03/69	68-69	19	0	0

BRIGHT David John
Born: Bath, England, 5 September, 1972 — F

League Club	Source	Date Signed	Seasons Played	Apps	Subs	Gls
Stoke C	YT	07/91	90	0	1	0

BRIGHT Gerald (Gerry)
Born: Northampton, England, 2 December, 1934 — CF

League Club	Source	Date Signed	Seasons Played	Apps	Subs	Gls
Northampton T		02/57	56-57	4	-	0

BRIGHT Kris
Born: Auckland, New Zealand, 5 September, 1986 — F
New Zealand: 4

League Club	Source	Date Signed	Seasons Played	Apps	Subs	Gls
Shrewsbury T	Panserraikos (GRE)	08/09	09-10	4	23	2

BRIGHT Mark Abraham
Born: Stoke-on-Trent, England, 6 June, 1962 — F

League Club	Source	Date Signed	Seasons Played	Apps	Subs	Gls
Port Vale	Leek T	10/81	81-83	18	11	10
Leicester C	Tr	07/84	84-86	26	16	6
Crystal Palace	Tr	11/86	86-92	224	3	91
Sheffield Wed	Tr	09/92	92-96	112	21	48
Millwall	L	12/96	96	3	0	1
Charlton Ath	FC Sion (SUI)	04/97	96-98	18	9	10

BRIGHT Stewart Linden
Born: Colchester, Essex, England, 13 October, 1957 — RB

League Club	Source	Date Signed	Seasons Played	Apps	Subs	Gls
Colchester U	App	10/75	75-76	23	2	0

BRIGHTON Thomas James (Tom)
Born: Irvine, Ayrshire, Scotland, 28 March, 1984 — LW
Scotland: U21-7/Youth

League Club	Source	Date Signed	Seasons Played	Apps	Subs	Gls
Scunthorpe U (L)	Glasgow Rangers	08/04	04	2	3	0
Millwall	Clyde	06/06	06	13	3	1

BRIGHTWELL David John
Born: Lutterworth, Leicestershire, England, 7 January, 1971 — CD

League Club	Source	Date Signed	Seasons Played	Apps	Subs	Gls
Manchester C	Jnr	04/88	91-94	35	8	1
Chester C	L	03/91	90	6	0	0
Lincoln C	L	08/95	95	5	0	0
Stoke C	L	09/95	95	0	1	0
Bradford C	Tr	12/95	95-96	23	1	0
Blackpool	L	12/96	96	1	1	0
Northampton T	Tr	07/97	97	34	1	1
Carlisle U	Tr	07/98	98-99	78	0	4
Hull C	Tr	06/00	00	24	3	2
Darlington	Tr	02/01	00-01	34	2	0

BRIGHTWELL Ian Robert
Born: Lutterworth, Leicestershire, England, 9 April, 1968 — RB/M
England: U21-4/Youth

League Club	Source	Date Signed	Seasons Played	Apps	Subs	Gls
Manchester C	Congleton T	05/86	86-97	285	36	18
Coventry C	Tr	07/98				
Walsall	Tr	02/00	99-01	77	4	0
Stoke C	Tr	03/02	01	3	1	0
Port Vale	Tr	08/02	02-03	36	1	0
Macclesfield T	Tr	07/04	04-06	17	4	0

BRIGHTWELL Stuart
Born: Easington, County Durham, England, 31 January, 1979 — W
England: Schools

League Club	Source	Date Signed	Seasons Played	Apps	Subs	Gls
Manchester U	YT	02/96				
Hartlepool U	Tr	07/98	98	8	9	1

BRIGNALL Stephen James Charles (Steve)
Born: Tenterden, Kent, England, 12 June, 1960 — CD

League Club	Source	Date Signed	Seasons Played	Apps	Subs	Gls
Arsenal	App	05/78	78	0	2	0

BRIGNULL Philip Arthur (Phil)
Born: Stratford, E London, England, 2 October, 1960 — CD
England: Schools

League Club	Source	Date Signed	Seasons Played	Apps	Subs	Gls
West Ham U	App	09/78	78	0	1	0
Bournemouth	Tr	08/81	81-84	128	1	11
Wrexham	L	12/85	85	5	0	1
Cardiff C	Tr	02/86	85-86	49	0	0
Newport Co	Tr	08/87	87	3	0	0

BRILEY Leslie (Les)
Born: Lambeth, S London, England, 2 October, 1956 — M

League Club	Source	Date Signed	Seasons Played	Apps	Subs	Gls
Chelsea	App	06/74				
Hereford U	Tr	05/76	76-77	60	1	2
Wimbledon	Tr	02/78	77-79	59	2	2
Aldershot	Tr	03/80	79-83	157	0	11
Millwall	Tr	05/84	84-90	225	2	13
Brighton & HA	Tr	08/91	91	11	4	0

BRILL Dean Michael
Born: Luton, England, 2 December, 1985 — G

League Club	Source	Date Signed	Seasons Played	Apps	Subs	Gls
Luton T	Sch	03/05	03-08	78	3	0
Gillingham	L	12/06	06	8	0	0
Oldham Ath	Tr	07/09	09-10	58	0	0
Barnet	Tr	08/11	11	36	0	0

BRIMACOMBE Anthony (Tony)
Born: Plymouth, England, 6 August, 1939 — IF

League Club	Source	Date Signed	Seasons Played	Apps	Subs	Gls
Plymouth Arg (Am)	Barnet	12/65	65-67	15	1	0

BRIMACOMBE John
Born: Plymouth, England, 25 November, 1965 — FB/M

League Club	Source	Date Signed	Seasons Played	Apps	Subs	Gls
Plymouth Arg	Saltash U	08/85	85-89	93	5	3

BRIMS Donald William (Don)
Born: Blackheath, Staffordshire, England, 8 January, 1936 — WH
Died: Bridgnorth, Shropshire, England, July, 1987

League Club	Source	Date Signed	Seasons Played	Apps	Subs	Gls
Bradford Park Ave	Motherwell	05/58	58-59	76	-	3

BRINDLE John James (Jack)
Born: Blackburn, Greater Manchester, England, 12 July, 1917 — IF
Died: Blackburn, Greater Manchester, England, 1975

League Club	Source	Date Signed	Seasons Played	Apps	Subs	Gls
Burnley	Blackburn Rov (Am)	03/43				
Rochdale	Howard & Bullough	09/45				
Chelsea	Tr	03/46				
Rochdale	Tr	08/47	47	1	-	0
New Brighton	Tr	03/48	47	9	-	3

BRINDLE William (Billy)
Born: Liverpool, England, 29 January, 1950 — M

League Club	Source	Date Signed	Seasons Played	Apps	Subs	Gls
Everton	App	08/67	67	1	0	0
Barnsley	Tr	05/70	70	0	1	0

BRINDLEY Christopher Peter (Chris)
Born: Stoke-on-Trent, England, 5 July, 1969 — CD

League Club	Source	Date Signed	Seasons Played	Apps	Subs	Gls
Wolverhampton W	Hednesford T	11/86	86	7	0	0

BRINDLEY John
Born: Ashbourne, Derbyshire, England, 2 May, 1931 — IF
Died: Stockport, Greater Manchester, England, 1978

League Club	Source	Date Signed	Seasons Played	Apps	Subs	Gls
Chesterfield	Buxton	12/53	53	1	-	0

BRINDLEY John Charles (Bill)
Born: Nottingham, England, 29 January, 1947 — RB
Died: Rushcliffe, Nottinghamshire, England, 6 April, 2007
England: Youth/Schools

League Club	Source	Date Signed	Seasons Played	Apps	Subs	Gls
Nottingham F	Jnr	02/64	65-69	7	7	1
Notts Co	Tr	05/70	70-75	221	2	0
Gillingham	Tr	07/76	76	19	1	1

BRINDLEY Richard Michael
Born: Colchester, Essex, England, 5 May, 1993 — RB

League Club	Source	Date Signed	Seasons Played	Apps	Subs	Gls
Chesterfield	Chelmsford C	01/13	12	10	2	0
Rotherham U	Tr	07/13	13-14	12	6	0
Scunthorpe U	L	11/14	14	3	0	0
Oxford U	L	01/15	14	3	0	0
Colchester U	L	03/15	14	7	1	0

BRINE Peter Kenneth
Born: Greenwich, SE London, England, 18 July, 1953 — M

League Club	Source	Date Signed	Seasons Played	Apps	Subs	Gls
Middlesbrough	App	09/70	72-77	59	20	6

BRINTON Ernest James (Ernie)
Born: Avonmouth, Avon, England, 26 May, 1908 — WH
Died: Bristol, England, 17 September, 1981

League Club	Source	Date Signed	Seasons Played	Apps	Subs	Gls
Bristol C	Avonmouth T	02/30	29-36	249	-	7
Newport Co	Tr	06/37	37-38	75	-	3
Aldershot	Tr	08/46	46	12	-	0

BRINTON John Victor (Jack)
Born: Avonmouth, Avon, England, 11 July, 1916 — W
Died: Abbot's Leigh, Avon, England, 22 February, 1997

League Club	Source	Date Signed	Seasons Played	Apps	Subs	Gls
Bristol C	Avonmouth T	08/35	35-36	12	-	1
Newport Co	Tr	07/37	37	6	-	0
Derby Co	Tr	01/38	37	8	-	2
Stockport Co	Tr	07/46	46-47	58	-	9
Leyton Orient	Tr	08/48	48	4	-	1

BRISCO Neil Anthony
Born: Wigan, Greater Manchester, England, 26 January, 1978 — M

League Club	Source	Date Signed	Seasons Played	Apps	Subs	Gls
Manchester C	YT	03/97				

League Club	Source	Date Signed	Seasons Played	Apps	Subs	Gls
Port Vale	Tr	08/98	98-03	105	13	2
Rochdale	Tr	07/04	04-05	20	7	0

BRISCOE Anthony Maurice (Tony)
Born: Birmingham, England, 16 August, 1978 — F

League Club	Source	Date Signed	Seasons Played	Apps	Subs	Gls
Shrewsbury T	YT	-	96	0	1	0

BRISCOE James Edward
Born: Clock Face, Merseyside, England, 23 April, 1917 — CF/RW
Died: Northampton, England, 17 April, 1981

League Club	Source	Date Signed	Seasons Played	Apps	Subs	Gls
Preston NE	St Helens T	05/34	36	5	-	0
Northampton T	Heart of Midlothian	09/46	46-48	53	-	17

BRISCOE James Patrick
Born: Swinton-on-Dearne, South Yorkshire, England, 14 October, 1923 — CF
Died: Stevenage, Hertfordshire, England, 27 August, 2014

League Club	Source	Date Signed	Seasons Played	Apps	Subs	Gls
Sheffield Wed	Fleet Air Arm	08/46	46	5	-	3

BRISCOE John
Born: Huddersfield, West Yorkshire, England, 31 May, 1947 — CF

League Club	Source	Date Signed	Seasons Played	Apps	Subs	Gls
Barnsley	Jnr	10/66	66-67	11	0	5

BRISCOE Lee Stephen
Born: Pontefract, West Yorkshire, England, 30 September, 1975 — LB
England: U21-5

League Club	Source	Date Signed	Seasons Played	Apps	Subs	Gls
Sheffield Wed	YT	05/94	93-99	48	30	1
Manchester C	L	02/98	97	5	0	1
Burnley	Tr	07/00	00-02	100	6	7
Preston NE	Tr	07/03	03	2	0	0

BRISCOE Louis Andrew
Born: Burton-on-Trent, Staffordshire, England, 2 April, 1988 — RW
England: Semi Pro-1

League Club	Source	Date Signed	Seasons Played	Apps	Subs	Gls
Port Vale	Sch	07/06	05	0	4	0
Mansfield T	Ilkeston T	01/09	13	0	2	0

BRISCOE Michael James
Born: Northampton, England, 4 July, 1983 — D

League Club	Source	Date Signed	Seasons Played	Apps	Subs	Gls
Coventry C	Harpole	04/03				
Macclesfield T	Tr	07/04	04-05	23	4	1

BRISCOE Robert Dean
Born: Derby, England, 4 September, 1969 — LB

League Club	Source	Date Signed	Seasons Played	Apps	Subs	Gls
Derby Co	YT	09/87	89-90	10	3	1

BRISLEY Shaun Richard
Born: Macclesfield, Cheshire, England, 6 May, 1990 — CD

League Club	Source	Date Signed	Seasons Played	Apps	Subs	Gls
Macclesfield T	Sch	07/08	07-11	117	7	6
Peterborough U	Tr	02/12	11-14	65	11	1
Scunthorpe U	L	09/14	14	6	1	0

BRISLEY Terence William (Terry)
Born: Stepney, E London, England, 4 July, 1950 — M

League Club	Source	Date Signed	Seasons Played	Apps	Subs	Gls
Leyton Orient	App	07/68	70-74	133	9	9
Southend U	L	03/75	74	8	0	0
Millwall	Tr	07/75	75-77	106	1	14
Charlton Ath	Tr	01/78	77-78	44	4	5
Portsmouth	Tr	07/79	79-80	55	0	13

BRISSETT Jason Curtis
Born: Wanstead, NE London, England, 7 September, 1974 — LM

League Club	Source	Date Signed	Seasons Played	Apps	Subs	Gls
Peterborough U	Arsenal (YT)	06/93	93-94	27	8	0
Bournemouth	Tr	12/94	94-97	96	28	8
Walsall	Tr	07/98	98-99	32	10	2
Cheltenham T	L	11/99	99	5	3	0
Leyton Orient	Tr	07/00	00	2	2	0

BRISSETT Trevor Anthony
Born: Stoke-on-Trent, England, 2 January, 1961 — RB
Died: Birmingham, England, 17 May, 2010

League Club	Source	Date Signed	Seasons Played	Apps	Subs	Gls
Stoke C	Jnr	04/78				
Port Vale	Tr	05/80	80-81	47	8	0
Darlington	Tr	08/82	82	10	2	0

BRISTOW George Andrew
Born: Chiswick, W London, England, 25 June, 1933 — RH
Died: Wiltshire, England, January, 2010

League Club	Source	Date Signed	Seasons Played	Apps	Subs	Gls
Brentford	Jnr	07/50	50-60	245	-	8

BRISTOW Guy Austin
Born: Kingsbury, NW London, England, 23 October, 1955 — CD

League Club	Source	Date Signed	Seasons Played	Apps	Subs	Gls
Watford	App	07/73	74-76	18	5	0

BRITT Martin Charles
Born: Leigh-on-Sea, Essex, England, 17 January, 1946 — CF
England: Youth

League Club	Source	Date Signed	Seasons Played	Apps	Subs	Gls
West Ham U	App	01/63	62-65	20	0	6
Blackburn Rov	Tr	03/66	65	8	0	0

BRITTAIN Martin
Born: Cramlington, Northumberland, England, 29 December, 1984 — RW

League Club	Source	Date Signed	Seasons Played	Apps	Subs	Gls
Newcastle U	Sch	09/03	03	0	1	0
Ipswich T	Tr	08/06				
Yeovil T	L	10/06	06	12	3	0
Carlisle U	Tr	08/07	07	0	1	0
Walsall	Scunthorpe U (NC)	01/08	07	0	1	0

BRITTAN Colin
Born: Bristol, England, 2 June, 1927 — WH
Died: Bristol, England, 4 April, 2013

League Club	Source	Date Signed	Seasons Played	Apps	Subs	Gls
Tottenham H	Bristol North OB	10/48	50-57	41	-	1

BRITTEN Martyn Edward Walter
Born: Bristol, England, 1 May, 1955 — LW

League Club	Source	Date Signed	Seasons Played	Apps	Subs	Gls
Bristol Rov	App	05/73	74-76	17	3	2
Reading	Tr	08/77	77-78	6	2	0

BRITTON Gerard Joseph (Gerry)
Born: Glasgow, Scotland, 20 October, 1970 — F

League Club	Source	Date Signed	Seasons Played	Apps	Subs	Gls
Reading (L)	Glasgow Celtic	11/91	91	0	2	0

BRITTON Ian
Born: Dundee, Scotland, 19 May, 1954 — RM

League Club	Source	Date Signed	Seasons Played	Apps	Subs	Gls
Chelsea	App	07/71	72-81	253	10	33
Blackpool	Arbroath	12/83	83-85	100	6	15
Burnley	Tr	08/86	86-88	102	6	10

BRITTON James (Jimmy)
Born: Salford, England, 27 May, 1920 — LH

League Club	Source	Date Signed	Seasons Played	Apps	Subs	Gls
Bradford Park Ave	Lowestoft T	01/46	46	1	-	0
Rochdale	Tr	12/47	47-48	20	-	0

BRITTON Leon James
Born: Merton, SW London, England, 16 September, 1982 — DM
England: Youth

League Club	Source	Date Signed	Seasons Played	Apps	Subs	Gls
West Ham U	YT	09/99				
Swansea C	Tr	12/02	02-09	270	25	10
Sheffield U	Tr	07/10	10	22	2	0
Swansea C	Tr	01/11	10-14	105	15	1

BRKOVIC Ahmet
Born: Dubrovnik, Croatia, 23 September, 1974 — M

League Club	Source	Date Signed	Seasons Played	Apps	Subs	Gls
Leyton Orient	HNK Dubrovnik (CRO)	10/99	99-00	59	10	8
Luton T	Tr	10/01	01-07	162	32	31
Millwall	Tr	10/07	07-08	18	13	3

BROAD Joseph Reginald (Joe)
Born: Bristol, England, 24 August, 1982 — M

League Club	Source	Date Signed	Seasons Played	Apps	Subs	Gls
Plymouth Arg	Sch	02/02	01-02	2	10	0
Torquay U	Tr	09/03	03	4	10	0
Walsall	Tr	08/04	04-05	7	5	0

BROAD Ronald (Ron)
Born: Sandbach, Cheshire, England, 18 August, 1933 — LW

League Club	Source	Date Signed	Seasons Played	Apps	Subs	Gls
Crewe Alex (Am)	Congleton T	12/55	55	6	-	0

BROAD Stephen
Born: Epsom, Surrey, England, 10 June, 1980 — CD

League Club	Source	Date Signed	Seasons Played	Apps	Subs	Gls
Chelsea	YT	02/98				
Southend U	Tr	03/01	00-02	57	2	3

BROADBENT Albert Henry
Born: Dudley, West Midlands, England, 20 August, 1934 — IF
Died: Sheffield, England, October, 2006

League Club	Source	Date Signed	Seasons Played	Apps	Subs	Gls
Notts Co	Dudley T	03/52	53-54	31	-	11
Sheffield Wed	Tr	07/55	55-57	81	-	17
Rotherham U	Tr	12/57	57-58	48	-	14
Doncaster Rov	Tr	06/59	59-61	100	-	21
Lincoln C	Tr	11/61	61-62	38	-	4
Doncaster Rov	Tr	01/63	62-65	106	0	19
Bradford Park Ave	Tr	10/65	65-66	56	0	11
Hartlepool U	Tr	02/67	66-67	25	0	3
Rotherham U	Tr	03/68				

BROADBENT Daniel James (Danny)
Born: Leeds, England, 2 March, 1990 — F

League Club	Source	Date Signed	Seasons Played	Apps	Subs	Gls
Huddersfield T	Sch	03/07	07-08	0	6	0

BROADBENT Graham
Born: Halifax, West Yorkshire, England, 20 December, 1958 — F

League Club	Source	Date Signed	Seasons Played	Apps	Subs	Gls
Halifax T	Emley	09/88	88-90	13	19	3

BROADBENT Peter Frank
Born: Elvington, Kent, England, 15 May, 1933 — IF
Died: Himley, Staffordshire, England, 1 April, 2013
England: 7/B-1/FLge-2/U23-1

League Club	Source	Date Signed	Seasons Played	Apps	Subs	Gls
Brentford	Dover	05/50	50	16	-	2
Wolverhampton W	Tr	02/51	50-64	452	-	127
Shrewsbury T	Tr	01/65	64-66	69	0	8
Aston Villa	Tr	10/66	66-68	60	4	0
Stockport Co	Tr	10/69	69	31	0	1

BROADFOOT Joseph James (Joe)
Born: Lewisham, SE London, England, 4 March, 1940 — RW

League Club	Source	Date Signed	Seasons Played	Apps	Subs	Gls
Millwall	Jnr	01/58	58-63	225	-	60
Ipswich T	Tr	10/63	63-65	81	0	17
Northampton T	Tr	11/65	65	17	0	1
Millwall	Tr	07/66	66	26	0	5
Ipswich T	Tr	02/67	66-67	19	1	2

BROADFOOT Kirk John
Born: Drongan, Ayrshire, Scotland, 8 August, 1984 — D
Scotland: 4/B-3/U21-5

League Club	Source	Date Signed	Seasons Played	Apps	Subs	Gls
Blackpool	Glasgow Rangers	09/12	12-13	65	0	2
Rotherham U	Tr	06/14	14	24	1	0

BROADHEAD Jack Patrick
Born: Mansfield, Nottinghamshire, England, 2 October, 1994 — CD

League Club	Source	Date Signed	Seasons Played	Apps	Subs	Gls
Chesterfield	Sch	11/12	14	0	1	0

BROADHURST Brian Walter
Born: Sheffield, England, 24 November, 1938 — IF
Died: Sheffield, England, January, 2006

League Club	Source	Date Signed	Seasons Played	Apps	Subs	Gls
Chesterfield	Hallam	10/61	61	7	-	0

BROADHURST Karl Matthew
Born: Portsmouth, England, 18 March, 1980 — CD

League Club	Source	Date Signed	Seasons Played	Apps	Subs	Gls
Bournemouth	YT	07/98	99-06	176	16	3
Hereford U	Tr	07/07	07-08	45	3	1

BROADHURST Kevan
Born: Dewsbury, West Yorkshire, England, 3 June, 1959 — D/M

League Club	Source	Date Signed	Seasons Played	Apps	Subs	Gls
Birmingham C	App	03/77	76-83	147	6	10
Walsall	L	11/79	79	3	0	0

BROADIS Ivan Arthur (Ivor)
Born: Poplar, E London, England, 18 December, 1922 — IF
England: 14/FLge-3

League Club	Source	Date Signed	Seasons Played	Apps	Subs	Gls
Carlisle U	Tottenham H (Am)	08/46	46-48	90	-	53
Sunderland	Tr	02/49	48-51	79	-	25
Manchester C	Tr	10/51	51-53	74	-	10
Newcastle U	Tr	10/53	53-54	42	-	15
Carlisle U	Tr	07/55	55-58	157	-	32

BROADLEY Leslie (Les)
Born: Goole, East Riding of Yorkshire, England, 10 August, 1930 — CF

League Club	Source	Date Signed	Seasons Played	Apps	Subs	Gls
Scunthorpe U	Goole T	08/52	52	5	-	2

BROADLEY Patrick Joseph (Pat)
Born: Croy, Lanarkshire, Scotland, 13 May, 1926 — LH
Died: Manchester, England, June, 2005
Republic of Ireland: LoI-3

League Club	Source	Date Signed	Seasons Played	Apps	Subs	Gls
Oldham Ath	Sligo Rov (ROI)	06/51	51	4	-	0

BROBBEL Ryan
Born: Hartlepool, Cleveland, England, 5 March, 1993 — W
Northern Ireland: U21-9/Youth

League Club	Source	Date Signed	Seasons Played	Apps	Subs	Gls
Middlesbrough	Sch	07/11				
York C	L	08/13	13	9	3	3
York C	L	03/14	13	7	0	1
Hartlepool U	L	08/14	14	13	2	0

BROCK Kevin Stanley
Born: Middleton Stoney, Oxfordshire, England, 9 September, 1962 — M
England: B-1/U21-4/Schools

League Club	Source	Date Signed	Seasons Played	Apps	Subs	Gls
Oxford U	App	09/79	79-86	229	17	26
Queens Park Rgrs	Tr	08/87	87-88	38	2	2
Newcastle U	Tr	12/88	88-92	135	10	15
Cardiff C	L	02/94	93	14	0	2

BROCK Stuart Alan
Born: West Bromwich, West Midlands, England, 26 September, 1976 — G

League Club	Source	Date Signed	Seasons Played	Apps	Subs	Gls
Aston Villa	YT	05/95				
Northampton T	Tr	03/97				
Kidderminster Hrs	Solihull Bor	09/97	00-03	135	0	0

BROCKBANK Andrew (Andy)
Born: Millom, Cumbria, England, 23 September, 1961 — LB

League Club	Source	Date Signed	Seasons Played	Apps	Subs	Gls
Blackpool	App	12/79	79-82	32	4	1

BROCKEN Budde Jan Peter Maria (Bud)
Born: Tilburg, Netherlands, 12 September, 1957 — RM
Netherlands: 5

League Club	Source	Date Signed	Seasons Played	Apps	Subs	Gls
Birmingham C	Willem II (NED)	08/81	81	17	0	0

BROCKIE Vincent (Vince)
Born: Greenock, Inverclyde, Scotland, 2 February, 1969 — RB/M

League Club	Source	Date Signed	Seasons Played	Apps	Subs	Gls
Leeds U	YT	07/87	87	2	0	0
Doncaster Rov	Tr	12/88	88-90	43	11	7

BROCKLEHURST John Fletcher
Born: Horwich, Greater Manchester, England, 15 December, 1927 — RH
Died: Lancashire, England, September, 2005

League Club	Source	Date Signed	Seasons Played	Apps	Subs	Gls
Accrington Stan	Stalybridge Celtic	05/52	52	34	-	0
Bradford Park Ave	Stalybridge Celtic	08/54	54-55	47	-	1

BRODDLE Julian Raymond
Born: Laughton, South Yorkshire, England, 1 November, 1964 — LB/M

League Club	Source	Date Signed	Seasons Played	Apps	Subs	Gls
Sheffield U	App	11/82	81	1	0	0
Scunthorpe U	Tr	08/83	83-87	126	18	32
Barnsley	Tr	08/87	87-89	63	14	4
Plymouth Arg	Tr	01/90	89	9	0	0
Scunthorpe U (L)	St Mirren	09/92	92	5	0	0

BRODERICK Mortimer
Born: Cork, Republic of Ireland, 1 September, 1923 — IF
Republic of Ireland: LoI-2

League Club	Source	Date Signed	Seasons Played	Apps	Subs	Gls
Sheffield U	Cork Ath (ROI)	08/50	50	2	-	0

BRODIE Charles Thomas George (Chic)
Born: Duntocher, Dunbartonshire, Scotland, 22 February, 1937 — G
Died: Ealing, W London, England, April, 2000
Scotland: Schools

League Club	Source	Date Signed	Seasons Played	Apps	Subs	Gls
Manchester C	Partick Avondale	03/54				
Gillingham	Tr	07/57	57	18	-	0
Aldershot	Tr	07/58	58-60	95	-	0
Wolverhampton W	Tr	02/61	60	1	-	0
Northampton T	Tr	09/61	61-63	87	-	0
Brentford	Tr	11/63	63-70	201	0	0

BRODIE Eric
Born: Rattray, Perthshire, Scotland, 8 November, 1940 — LH

League Club	Source	Date Signed	Seasons Played	Apps	Subs	Gls
Shrewsbury T	Dundee U	06/63	63-67	181	4	24
Chester C	Tr	05/68	68-69	43	1	4
Tranmere Rov	Tr	10/69	69-71	81	3	3

BRODIE John
Born: Bedlington, Northumberland, England, 8 September, 1947 — FB

League Club	Source	Date Signed	Seasons Played	Apps	Subs	Gls
Carlisle U	Whitley Bay	12/67	67-68	8	0	0
Bradford Park Ave	Tr	06/69	69	43	0	0
Port Vale	Tr	01/71	70-76	175	4	2

BRODIE Murray
Born: Glasgow, Scotland, 26 September, 1950 — M

League Club	Source	Date Signed	Seasons Played	Apps	Subs	Gls
Leicester C	Cumbernauld U	10/69	69	3	0	2
Aldershot	Tr	09/70	70-82	449	11	84

BRODIE Richard Jon
Born: Gateshead, Tyne and Wear, England, 8 July, 1987 — F
England: Semi Pro-2

League Club	Source	Date Signed	Seasons Played	Apps	Subs	Gls
Crawley T	York C	08/10				
Morecambe (L)	Crawley T	07/12	12	15	8	5

BRODIE Stephen Eric (Steve)
Born: Sunderland, England, 14 January, 1973 — F

League Club	Source	Date Signed	Seasons Played	Apps	Subs	Gls
Sunderland	YT	07/91	93-94	1	11	0
Doncaster Rov	L	08/95	95	5	0	1
Scarborough	Tr	12/96	96-98	109	2	27
Swansea C	Tr	11/01	01	21	5	2

BROGAN David (Dave)
Born: Glasgow, Scotland, 11 January, 1939 — IF

League Club	Source	Date Signed	Seasons Played	Apps	Subs	Gls
Luton T	St Anthony's	09/60	60	4	-	0

BROGAN Frank Anthony
Born: Stepps, Glasgow, Scotland, 3 August, 1942 — LW

League Club	Source	Date Signed	Seasons Played	Apps	Subs	Gls
Ipswich T	Glasgow Celtic	06/64	64-69	201	2	58
Halifax T	Greenock Morton	11/71	71-72	25	2	6

BROGAN James Andrew (Jim)
Born: Glasgow, Scotland, 5 June, 1944 — LB
Scotland: 4/SLge-1

League Club	Source	Date Signed	Seasons Played	Apps	Subs	Gls
Coventry C	Glasgow Celtic	08/75	75	28	0	0

BROGAN Stephen Patrick
Born: Rotherham, South Yorkshire, England, 12 April, 1988 — LB/M
England: Semi Pro-2

League Club	Source	Date Signed	Seasons Played	Apps	Subs	Gls
Rotherham U	Sch	07/06	05-10	49	13	4

BROGDEN Lee Anthony
Born: Leeds, England, 18 October, 1949 — RW

League Club	Source	Date Signed	Seasons Played	Apps	Subs	Gls
Rotherham U	Leeds Ashley Road	12/67	67-71	79	6	17
Rochdale	Tr	03/72	71-73	48	9	7

BROGHAMMER Fabian
Born: Heppenheim, Germany, 14 January, 1990 — LW

League Club	Source	Date Signed	Seasons Played	Apps	Subs	Gls
Bristol Rov	Bayern Alzenau (GER)	08/12	12-13	26	14	3

BROLIN Tomas
Born: Hudiksvall, Sweden, 29 November, 1969 — F
Sweden: 47/U23-4

League Club	Source	Date Signed	Seasons Played	Apps	Subs	Gls
Leeds U	Parma (ITA)	11/95	95	17	2	4
Crystal Palace	Tr	01/98	97	13	0	0

BROLLS Norman McCall
Born: Wigtown, Dumfries & Galloway, Scotland, 26 September, 1933 RW
Died: Dumfries, Scotland, 31 May, 2013

League Club	Source	Date Signed	Seasons Played	Apps	Subs	Gls
Bradford Park Ave	Third Lanark	06/56	56	11	-	0

BROLLY Michael Joseph (Mike)
Born: Galston, Ayrshire, Scotland, 6 October, 1954 W
Scotland: Schools

League Club	Source	Date Signed	Seasons Played	Apps	Subs	Gls
Chelsea	Kilmarnock Star	10/71	72-73	7	1	1
Bristol C	Tr	06/74	74-75	27	3	2
Grimsby T	Tr	09/76	76-81	246	8	27
Derby Co	Tr	08/82	82	41	1	4
Scunthorpe U	Tr	08/83	83-85	92	3	15

BROLLY Richard
Born: York, England, 5 October, 1969 W
England: Schools

League Club	Source	Date Signed	Seasons Played	Apps	Subs	Gls
Wigan Ath	Illinois Univ (USA)	12/92	92	2	0	1

BROLLY Thomas Henry (Tom)
Born: Belfast, Northern Ireland, 1 June, 1912 D
Died: Sutton, S London, England, June, 1986
Northern Ireland: 4/NILge-4

League Club	Source	Date Signed	Seasons Played	Apps	Subs	Gls
Sheffield Wed	Glenavon	05/33	33	2	-	0
Millwall	Tr	07/35	35-49	229	-	8

BROMAGE Russell
Born: Stoke-on-Trent, England, 9 November, 1959 LB

League Club	Source	Date Signed	Seasons Played	Apps	Subs	Gls
Port Vale	App	11/77	77-86	339	8	13
Oldham Ath	L	10/83	83	2	0	0
Bristol C	Tr	08/87	87-89	44	2	1
Brighton & HA	Tr	08/90	90	1	0	0
Maidstone U	L	01/91	90	3	0	0

BROMBY Leigh David
Born: Dewsbury, West Yorkshire, England, 2 June, 1980 CD
England: Schools

League Club	Source	Date Signed	Seasons Played	Apps	Subs	Gls
Sheffield Wed	Liversedge	07/98	00-03	98	2	2
Mansfield T	L	12/99	99	10	0	1
Norwich C	L	02/03	02	5	0	0
Sheffield U	Tr	07/04	04-07	104	5	6
Watford	Tr	01/08	07-08	35	3	1
Sheffield U	Tr	01/09	08	6	6	1
Leeds U	Tr	09/09	09-11	47	8	1

BROMILOW Geoffrey (Geoff)
Born: Farnworth, Greater Manchester, England, 14 September, 1945 IF

League Club	Source	Date Signed	Seasons Played	Apps	Subs	Gls
Bolton W (Am)	Manchester Univ	10/68	68	3	2	0

BROMILOW George Joseph
Born: Southport, Merseyside, England, 4 December, 1930 CF
Died: Southport, Merseyside, England, 19 November, 2005
England: Amateur-5/Youth

League Club	Source	Date Signed	Seasons Played	Apps	Subs	Gls
Southport (Am)	Northern Nomads	06/55	55-58	84	-	37

BROMLEY Brian
Born: Burnley, Lancashire, England, 20 March, 1946 M
Died: Southampton, England, 9 March, 2012
England: Youth

League Club	Source	Date Signed	Seasons Played	Apps	Subs	Gls
Bolton W	App	03/63	62-68	165	1	25
Portsmouth	Tr	11/68	68-71	88	1	3
Brighton & HA	Tr	11/71	71-73	47	3	3
Reading	Tr	09/73	73-74	13	1	1
Darlington	L	02/75	74	3	0	0

BROMLEY Thomas Charles (Tom)
Born: West Bromwich, West Midlands, England, 30 April, 1933 IF

League Club	Source	Date Signed	Seasons Played	Apps	Subs	Gls
Walsall (Am)	Swan Village	07/53	53	13	-	1

BROOK Daryl
Born: Holmfirth, West Yorkshire, England, 19 November, 1960 M

League Club	Source	Date Signed	Seasons Played	Apps	Subs	Gls
Huddersfield T	App	11/78	78	1	0	0

BROOK Gary
Born: Dewsbury, West Yorkshire, England, 9 May, 1964 F

League Club	Source	Date Signed	Seasons Played	Apps	Subs	Gls
Newport Co	Frickley Ath	12/87	87	14	0	2
Scarborough	Tr	03/88	87-89	59	5	15
Blackpool	Tr	11/89	89-91	27	3	6
Notts Co	L	09/90	90	0	1	0
Scarborough	L	10/90	90	8	0	0

BROOK Harold
Born: Sheffield, England, 15 October, 1921 IF
Died: Sheffield, England, November, 1998

League Club	Source	Date Signed	Seasons Played	Apps	Subs	Gls
Sheffield U	Hallam	04/43	46-53	229	-	90
Leeds U	Tr	07/54	54-57	103	-	46
Lincoln C	Tr	03/58	57	4	-	1

BROOK Lewis
Born: Northowram, West Yorkshire, England, 27 July, 1918 FB
Died: Halifax, West Yorkshire, England, July, 1996

League Club	Source	Date Signed	Seasons Played	Apps	Subs	Gls
Huddersfield T	Halifax T (Am)	05/36	37-46	18	-	6
Oldham Ath	Tr	03/48	47-56	189	-	14

BROOKE David
Born: Barnsley, South Yorkshire, England, 23 November, 1975 M

League Club	Source	Date Signed	Seasons Played	Apps	Subs	Gls
Barnsley	YT	07/93				
Scarborough	Tr	08/96	96	28	6	2

BROOKE Garry James
Born: Bethnal Green, E London, England, 24 November, 1960 M

League Club	Source	Date Signed	Seasons Played	Apps	Subs	Gls
Tottenham H	App	10/78	80-84	49	24	15
Norwich C	Tr	07/85	85-86	8	6	2
Wimbledon	Groningen (NED)	08/88	88-89	5	7	0
Stoke C	L	03/90	89	6	2	0
Brentford	Tr	08/90	90	8	3	1
Reading	Baldock T	03/91	90	1	3	0

BROOKE Maurice
Born: Thurcroft, South Yorkshire, England, 4 June, 1925 CF

League Club	Source	Date Signed	Seasons Played	Apps	Subs	Gls
Stockport Co	Buxton	01/51	50	1	-	0

BROOKE Ryan Michael
Born: Congleton, Cheshire, England, 4 October, 1990 F

League Club	Source	Date Signed	Seasons Played	Apps	Subs	Gls
Oldham Ath	Sch	07/09	08-10	4	25	2

BROOKER Paul
Born: Hammersmith, W London, England, 25 November, 1976 RW

League Club	Source	Date Signed	Seasons Played	Apps	Subs	Gls
Fulham	YT	07/95	95-98	13	43	4
Brighton & HA	Tr	02/00	99-02	102	32	15
Leicester C	Tr	07/03	03	0	3	0
Reading	L	02/04	03	5	6	0
Reading	Tr	07/04	04	22	9	0
Brentford	Tr	07/05	05-07	56	15	4

BROOKER Stephen Michael Lord (Steve)
Born: Newport Pagnell, Buckinghamshire, England, 21 May, 1981 F

League Club	Source	Date Signed	Seasons Played	Apps	Subs	Gls
Watford	YT	07/99	99	0	1	0
Port Vale	Tr	01/01	00-04	120	11	35
Bristol C	Tr	09/04	04-08	87	14	37
Cheltenham T	L	01/08	07	14	0	5
Doncaster Rov	Tr	11/08	08-10	1	13	2

BROOKES Colin
Born: Barnsley, South Yorkshire, England, 2 January, 1942 LW
England: Schools

League Club	Source	Date Signed	Seasons Played	Apps	Subs	Gls
Barnsley	Manchester U (Jnr)	05/59	59-60	47	-	5
West Bromwich A	Tr	06/61				
Peterborough U	Tr	06/62				
Southport	Tr	07/63	63	20	-	2

BROOKES Darren Paul
Born: Sheffield, England, 7 July, 1978 CD

League Club	Source	Date Signed	Seasons Played	Apps	Subs	Gls
Doncaster Rov	Worksop T	07/97	97	9	2	0

BROOKES Eric
Born: Darton, South Yorkshire, England, 3 February, 1944 LB
England: Youth

League Club	Source	Date Signed	Seasons Played	Apps	Subs	Gls
Barnsley	Jnr	04/61	60-68	325	1	1
Northampton T	Tr	07/69	69-70	81	0	1
Peterborough U	Tr	06/71	71-72	41	1	1

BROOKES John Vincent (Johnny)
Born: Staveley, Derbyshire, England, 18 October, 1943 IF

League Club	Source	Date Signed	Seasons Played	Apps	Subs	Gls
Sheffield Wed	Sheffield U (Am)	09/64				
Southport	Tr	07/65	65	14	0	5
York C	Tr	08/66	66	1	0	0
Stockport Co	Sligo Rov (ROI)	08/70	70	18	3	3

BROOKES Stanley Kevin (Stan)
Born: Doncaster, South Yorkshire, England, 2 February, 1953 CD

League Club	Source	Date Signed	Seasons Played	Apps	Subs	Gls
Doncaster Rov	App	02/71	71-76	230	6	7

BROOKES William Amos (Billy)
Born: Dudley, West Midlands, England, 19 April, 1931 WH

League Club	Source	Date Signed	Seasons Played	Apps	Subs	Gls
West Bromwich A	Churchfields	05/49	53-56	19	-	0

BROOKFIELD Anthony John (Tony)
Born: Southport, Merseyside, England, 11 April, 1959 F

League Club	Source	Date Signed	Seasons Played	Apps	Subs	Gls
Southport	Jnr	07/76	76-77	14	5	1

BROOKFIELD Ryan
Born: Liverpool, England, 10 May, 1987 G

League Club	Source	Date Signed	Seasons Played	Apps	Subs	Gls
Chester C	Sch	08/05	05	0	1	0

BROOKIN William James (Bill)
Born: Tilehurst, Berkshire, England, 14 June, 1919 G
Died: Warrington, Cheshire, England, 2 May, 1976

League Club	Source	Date Signed	Seasons Played	Apps	Subs	Gls
Newport Co	RAF Hereford	08/46	46	2	-	0

BROOKING Trevor David
Born: Barking, E London, England, 2 October, 1948 M
England: 47/FLge-1/U23-1/Youth/Schools

League Club	Source	Date Signed	Seasons Played	Apps	Subs	Gls
West Ham U	App	05/66	67-83	521	7	88

BROOKMAN Nicholas Anthony (Nicky)
Born: Manchester, England, 28 October, 1968 M

League Club	Source	Date Signed	Seasons Played	Apps	Subs	Gls
Bolton W	Wrexham (NC)	11/86	86-89	47	10	10
Stockport Co	Tr	03/90	89	4	2	0

BROOKS Anthony (Tony)
Born: Wigan, Greater Manchester, England, 12 March, 1944 IF

League Club	Source	Date Signed	Seasons Played	Apps	Subs	Gls
Blackpool	Jnr	03/62				
Preston NE	Tr	08/62				
Bury		08/63	63	1	-	0
Stockport Co	Tr	06/64	64	2	-	0

BROOKS Christopher (Chris)
Born: Huthwaite, Nottinghamshire, England, 6 June, 1972 F

League Club	Source	Date Signed	Seasons Played	Apps	Subs	Gls
Luton T	Ilkeston T	07/92				
Shrewsbury T	L	02/93	92	1	0	0

BROOKS Harry
Born: Tibshelf, Derbyshire, England, 2 June, 1915 CF
Died: Derby, England, February, 1994

League Club	Source	Date Signed	Seasons Played	Apps	Subs	Gls
Doncaster Rov	Heanor T	01/37	36-38	5	-	0
Aldershot	Tr	06/39	46-47	23	-	14

BROOKS Jamie Paul
Born: Oxford, England, 12 August, 1983 F

League Club	Source	Date Signed	Seasons Played	Apps	Subs	Gls
Oxford U	YT	12/00	00-05	31	19	13

BROOKS John (Johnny)
Born: Reading, England, 23 December, 1931 IF
England: 3

League Club	Source	Date Signed	Seasons Played	Apps	Subs	Gls
Reading	Mount Pleasant	04/49	49-52	46	-	5
Tottenham H	Tr	02/53	52-59	166	-	46
Chelsea	Tr	12/59	59-60	46	-	6
Brentford	Tr	09/61	61-63	83	-	36
Crystal Palace	Tr	01/64	63	7	-	0

BROOKS John
Born: Stoke-on-Trent, England, 8 March, 1927 WH

League Club	Source	Date Signed	Seasons Played	Apps	Subs	Gls
Stoke C		12/46	50	2	-	0

BROOKS John Terence
Born: Paddington, Central London, England, 23 August, 1947 G

League Club	Source	Date Signed	Seasons Played	Apps	Subs	Gls
Queens Park Rgrs	App	08/65				
Ipswich T	Tr	12/66				
Northampton T	Tr	10/67	67	1	0	0

BROOKS Lewis Raymond
Born: Boston, Lincolnshire, England, 4 September, 1987 M

League Club	Source	Date Signed	Seasons Played	Apps	Subs	Gls
Boston U	Jnr	-	04	1	1	0

BROOKS Norman Harry
Born: Reading, England, 28 May, 1920 LW
Died: Reading, England, 20 February, 1973

League Club	Source	Date Signed	Seasons Played	Apps	Subs	Gls
Reading (Am)	Huntley & Palmers	11/46	46	1	-	0

BROOKS Shaun
Born: Reading, England, 9 October, 1962 M
England: Youth/Schools

League Club	Source	Date Signed	Seasons Played	Apps	Subs	Gls
Crystal Palace	App	10/79	79-83	47	7	4
Leyton Orient	Tr	10/83	83-86	140	8	26
Bournemouth	Tr	06/87	87-91	114	14	13
Bournemouth	Dorchester T	10/94	94	1	0	0
Leyton Orient	Tr	11/94	94-95	42	8	2

BROOKS Stephen Michael (Steve)
Born: Liverpool, England, 18 June, 1955 CD

League Club	Source	Date Signed	Seasons Played	Apps	Subs	Gls
Southport	Marine	02/77	76-77	65	0	3
Hartlepool U	Tr	07/78	78-79	62	1	2
Halifax T	Skelmersdale U	03/85	84	16	0	0

BROOKS Thomas William (Tommy)
Born: Wallsend, Tyne and Wear, England, 2 February, 1948 D

League Club	Source	Date Signed	Seasons Played	Apps	Subs	Gls
Lincoln C	App	02/65	64-70	103	10	1

BROOME Frank Henry
Born: Berkhamsted, Hertfordshire, England, 11 June, 1915 CF
Died: Exeter, England, 5 September, 1994
England: 7/War-1

League Club	Source	Date Signed	Seasons Played	Apps	Subs	Gls
Aston Villa	Berkhamsted T	11/34	34-46	133	-	78
Derby Co	Tr	09/46	46-49	112	-	45
Notts Co	Tr	10/49	49-52	105	-	35
Brentford	Tr	07/53	53	6	-	1
Crewe Alex	Tr	10/53	53-54	36	-	17

BROOMES Marlon Charles
Born: Birmingham, England, 28 November, 1977 CD
England: U21-2/Youth/Schools

League Club	Source	Date Signed	Seasons Played	Apps	Subs	Gls
Blackburn Rov	YT	11/94	97-00	24	7	1
Swindon T	L	01/97	96	12	0	1
Queens Park Rgrs	L	10/00	00	5	0	0
Grimsby T	L	09/01	01	13	2	0
Sheffield Wed	Tr	12/01	01	18	1	0
Preston NE	Tr	08/02	02-04	59	10	0
Stoke C	Tr	08/05	05	36	1	2
Blackpool	Tr	07/08	08	0	1	0
Crewe Alex	L	01/09	08	19	0	0
Tranmere Rov	Tr	08/09	09-10	36	0	1

BROOMFIELD Desmond Stretton (Des)
Born: Hove, East Sussex, England, 6 October, 1921 WH
Died: Burgess Hill, West Sussex, England, 5 June, 2007

League Club	Source	Date Signed	Seasons Played	Apps	Subs	Gls
Brighton & HA	Coastal Command	04/46	46-47	20	-	0

BROOMFIELD Ian Lewis
Born: Bristol, England, 17 December, 1950 F

League Club	Source	Date Signed	Seasons Played	Apps	Subs	Gls
Bristol C	App	08/68	68-72	18	3	2
Stockport Co	Tr	12/72	72-74	22	5	1
Workington	Durban C (RSA)	10/75	75	3	0	0

BROOMFIELD John
Born: Crewe, Cheshire, England, 6 June, 1934 CH

League Club	Source	Date Signed	Seasons Played	Apps	Subs	Gls
Crewe Alex (Am)		10/56	56	1	-	0

BROOMHALL Keith Leslie
Born: Stoke-on-Trent, England, 21 May, 1951 FB

League Club	Source	Date Signed	Seasons Played	Apps	Subs	Gls
Port Vale	App	-	68	1	1	0

BROPHY Hugh
Born: Dublin, Republic of Ireland, 2 September, 1948 F
Northern Ireland: Amateur

League Club	Source	Date Signed	Seasons Played	Apps	Subs	Gls
Crystal Palace	Shamrock Rov (ROI)	07/66	66	0	1	0

BROTHERSTON Noel
Born: Dundonald, Belfast, Northern Ireland, 18 November, 1956 W
Died: Blackburn, Greater Manchester, England, 6 May, 1995
Northern Ireland: 27/U21-1

League Club	Source	Date Signed	Seasons Played	Apps	Subs	Gls
Tottenham H	App	04/74	75	1	0	0
Blackburn Rov	Tr	07/77	77-86	307	10	40
Bury	Tr	06/87	87-88	32	6	4
Scarborough	L	10/88	88	5	0	0

BROUGH John Robert
Born: Heanor, Derbyshire, England, 8 January, 1973 CD

League Club	Source	Date Signed	Seasons Played	Apps	Subs	Gls
Notts Co	YT	07/91				
Shrewsbury T	Tr	07/92	92-93	7	9	1
Hereford U	Telford U	11/94	94-96	70	9	3
Cheltenham T	Tr	07/98	99-04	83	53	6

BROUGH Michael
Born: Nottingham, England, 1 August, 1981 M
Wales: U21-3/Youth

League Club	Source	Date Signed	Seasons Played	Apps	Subs	Gls
Notts Co	YT	07/99	99-03	67	22	2
Torquay U	Forest Green Rov	06/08	09	0	1	0

BROUGH Neil Keith
Born: Daventry, Northamptonshire, England, 22 December, 1965 RW

League Club	Source	Date Signed	Seasons Played	Apps	Subs	Gls
Northampton T	App	12/83	83-84	6	6	0

BROUGH Patrick John
Born: Carlisle, Cumbria, England, 20 February, 1996 LB/M

League Club	Source	Date Signed	Seasons Played	Apps	Subs	Gls
Carlisle U	Sch	06/14	13-14	28	4	0

BROUGH Paul
Born: York, England, 24 January, 1965 F

League Club	Source	Date Signed	Seasons Played	Apps	Subs	Gls
York C	York RI	08/87	87	0	1	0

BROUGH Scott
Born: Scunthorpe, North Lincolnshire, England, 10 February, 1983 W

League Club	Source	Date Signed	Seasons Played	Apps	Subs	Gls
Scunthorpe U	Jnr	11/00	00-02	15	31	3

BROUGHTON Drewe Oliver
Born: Hitchin, Hertfordshire, England, 25 October, 1978 F

League Club	Source	Date Signed	Seasons Played	Apps	Subs	Gls
Norwich C	YT	05/97	96-97	3	6	1
Wigan Ath	L	08/97	97	1	3	0
Brentford	Tr	10/98	98	1	0	0
Peterborough U	Tr	11/98	98-99	19	16	8
Kidderminster Hrs	Tr	01/01	00-02	70	24	19
Southend U	Tr	06/03	03-04	31	13	2
Rushden & D	L	10/04	04	9	0	4
Wycombe W	L	12/04	04	2	1	0
Rushden & D	Tr	02/05	04-05	43	6	12
Chester C	Tr	06/06	06	9	5	2
Boston U	L	10/06	06	25	0	8
MK Dons	Tr	07/07	07	2	11	0
Wrexham	L	01/08	07	16	0	2
Rotherham U	Tr	08/08	08-09	39	17	9

League Club	Source	Date Signed	Seasons Played	Apps	Subs	Gls
Lincoln C	L	02/10	09	7	0	0
Lincoln C	Tr	07/10	10	9	14	0

BROUGHTON Edward (Ted)
Born: Bradford, England, 9 February, 1925 RW

League Club	Source	Date Signed	Seasons Played	Apps	Subs	Gls
Bradford C		09/45				
New Brighton	Tr	07/47	47	4	-	0
Crystal Palace	Tr	08/48	48-52	96	-	6

BROWN Aaron Anthony
Born: Birmingham, England, 23 June, 1983 CD

League Club	Source	Date Signed	Seasons Played	Apps	Subs	Gls
Reading	Tamworth	11/05				
Bournemouth	L	02/06	06	3	1	0
Yeovil T	Tr	08/08	08	16	7	3
Burton A	Tr	09/09	09	1	0	0
Aldershot T	Truro C	03/10	09	12	0	1
Leyton Orient	Tr	07/10	10	4	1	0
Stockport Co	L	01/11	10	17	0	1
Aldershot T	Tr	05/11	11	6	5	0
Preston NE	Tr	02/12	11	4	0	0

BROWN Aaron Wesley
Born: Bristol, England, 14 March, 1980 M/LB
England: Schools

League Club	Source	Date Signed	Seasons Played	Apps	Subs	Gls
Bristol C	YT	11/97	98-03	135	25	12
Exeter C	L	01/00	99	4	1	1
Queens Park Rgrs	Tr	01/05	04-05	1	2	0
Torquay U	L	03/05	04	5	0	0
Cheltenham T	L	09/05	05	3	0	0
Swindon T	Tr	11/05	05-06	36	21	4
Gillingham	Tr	07/07	07	10	1	1
Lincoln C	Tr	07/08	08-09	47	9	2

BROWN Adam James
Born: Sunderland, England, 17 December, 1987 F

League Club	Source	Date Signed	Seasons Played	Apps	Subs	Gls
Doncaster Rov	Sch	06/06	04	0	3	1

BROWN Alan
Born: Lewes, Sussex, England, 11 December, 1937 CF

League Club	Source	Date Signed	Seasons Played	Apps	Subs	Gls
Brighton & HA	Portslade	09/58	61	7	-	2
Exeter C	Tr	01/62	61	11	-	3

BROWN Alan
Born: Easington, County Durham, England, 22 May, 1959 F

League Club	Source	Date Signed	Seasons Played	Apps	Subs	Gls
Sunderland	App	07/76	76-81	87	26	21
Newcastle U	L	11/81	81	5	0	3
Shrewsbury T	Tr	08/82	82-83	65	0	15
Doncaster Rov	Tr	03/84	83-85	15	0	6

BROWN Alan Winston
Born: Corbridge, Northumberland, England, 26 August, 1914 CH
Died: Barnstaple, Devon, England, 9 March, 1996
England: FLge-1

League Club	Source	Date Signed	Seasons Played	Apps	Subs	Gls
Huddersfield T	Spen Black & White	03/33	34-38	57	-	0
Burnley	Tr	02/46	46-48	88	-	0
Notts Co	Tr	10/48	48	13	-	0

BROWN Albert Edward (Bert)
Born: Bristol, England, 4 March, 1934 WH

League Club	Source	Date Signed	Seasons Played	Apps	Subs	Gls
Crystal Palace	Exeter Univ	08/56	57	3	-	0
Queens Park Rgrs	Bath C	07/59				

BROWN Albert Roy (Roy)
Born: Nottingham, England, 14 August, 1917 W
Died: Mansfield, Nottinghamshire, England, 31 January, 2005

League Club	Source	Date Signed	Seasons Played	Apps	Subs	Gls
Nottingham F	Sneinton	02/36	36-38	51	-	7
Wrexham	Tr	06/39	46	24	-	3
Mansfield T	Tr	07/47	47	17	-	2

BROWN Alex Stuart
Born: South Woodham Ferrers, Essex, England, 30 September, 1992 M

League Club	Source	Date Signed	Seasons Played	Apps	Subs	Gls
Gillingham	Sch	07/11	11	0	1	0

BROWN Alexander Dewar (Sandy)
Born: Grangemouth, Falkirk, Scotland, 24 March, 1939 FB
Died: Blackpool, Lancashire, England, 8 April, 2014
Scotland: SLge-1

League Club	Source	Date Signed	Seasons Played	Apps	Subs	Gls
Everton	Partick Thistle	09/63	63-70	176	33	9
Shrewsbury T	Tr	05/71	71	21	0	0
Southport	Tr	07/72	72	17	2	0

BROWN Alexander Masterson (Alex)
Born: Glasgow, Scotland, 15 August, 1930 RB
Died: Carlisle, Cumbria, England, 19 June, 2004
Scotland: Youth

League Club	Source	Date Signed	Seasons Played	Apps	Subs	Gls
Preston NE	Partick Thistle	06/57				
Carlisle U	Tr	06/58	58-60	102	-	0

BROWN Alexander Roy (Alex)
Born: Seghill, Northumberland, England, 21 November, 1914 W
Died: Chesterfield, Derbyshire, England, August, 2006

League Club	Source	Date Signed	Seasons Played	Apps	Subs	Gls
Chesterfield	Seghill CW	12/33	34	8	-	1
Darlington	Tr	06/35	35	5	-	0
Gateshead	Shrewsbury T	05/39				
Mansfield T	Tr	11/46	46	5	-	0

BROWN Alistair (Ally)
Born: Musselburgh, East Lothian, Scotland, 12 April, 1951 F

League Club	Source	Date Signed	Seasons Played	Apps	Subs	Gls
Leicester C	Jnr	04/68	68-71	93	8	31
West Bromwich A	Tr	03/72	71-82	254	25	72
Crystal Palace	Tr	03/83	82	11	0	2
Walsall	Tr	08/83	83	37	1	13
Port Vale	Tr	07/84	84-85	62	5	22

BROWN Allan Duncan
Born: Kennoway, Fife, Scotland, 12 October, 1926 IF
Died: Blackpool, Lancashire, England, 19 April, 2011
Scotland: 14/SLge-1

League Club	Source	Date Signed	Seasons Played	Apps	Subs	Gls
Blackpool	East Fife	12/50	50-56	158	-	68
Luton T	Tr	02/57	56-60	151	-	51
Portsmouth	Tr	03/61	60-62	69	-	8

BROWN Andrew (Andy)
Born: Liverpool, England, 17 August, 1963 FB

League Club	Source	Date Signed	Seasons Played	Apps	Subs	Gls
Tranmere Rov	Jnr	08/82	82	1	0	0

BROWN Andrew
Born: Coatbridge, Lanarkshire, Scotland, 20 February, 1915 IF
Died: Colchester, Essex, England, 1973

League Club	Source	Date Signed	Seasons Played	Apps	Subs	Gls
Cardiff C	Cumbernauld Thistle	12/36	36-37	2	-	0
Torquay U	Tr	06/38	38-46	34	-	5

BROWN Andrew Stewart
Born: Edinburgh, Scotland, 11 October, 1976 F

League Club	Source	Date Signed	Seasons Played	Apps	Subs	Gls
Leeds U	St Johnstone (Jnr)	04/95				
Hull C	Tr	05/96	96-97	7	22	1

BROWN Anthony John (Tony)
Born: Oldham, Greater Manchester, England, 3 October, 1945 M/F
England: 1/FLge-1

League Club	Source	Date Signed	Seasons Played	Apps	Subs	Gls
West Bromwich A	App	10/63	63-79	561	13	218
Torquay U	Jacksonville TM (USA)	10/81	81-82	38	7	11

BROWN Anthony John (Tony)
Born: Bradford, England, 17 September, 1958 CD

League Club	Source	Date Signed	Seasons Played	Apps	Subs	Gls
Leeds U	Thackley	03/83	82-84	24	0	1
Doncaster Rov	L	11/84	84	5	0	0
Doncaster Rov	Tr	03/85	84-86	80	2	2
Scunthorpe U	Tr	07/87	87-88	46	8	2
Rochdale	Tr	08/89	89-92	111	3	0

BROWN Brian David
Born: Shoreditch, Central London, England, 10 September, 1949 RB

League Club	Source	Date Signed	Seasons Played	Apps	Subs	Gls
Chelsea	App	11/66				
Millwall	Tr	03/68	68-74	186	4	5

BROWN Christopher Alan (Chris)
Born: Doncaster, South Yorkshire, England, 11 December, 1984 F
England: Youth

League Club	Source	Date Signed	Seasons Played	Apps	Subs	Gls
Sunderland	Sch	08/02	04-06	33	33	9
Doncaster Rov	L	10/03	03	17	5	10
Hull C	L	09/05	05	13	0	1
Norwich C	Tr	01/07	06-07	11	7	1
Preston NE	Tr	01/08	07-10	68	38	18
Doncaster Rov	Tr	07/11	11-13	73	14	19
Blackburn Rov	Tr	06/14	14	11	9	0

BROWN Connor Anton
Born: Sheffield, England, 2 October, 1991 RB

League Club	Source	Date Signed	Seasons Played	Apps	Subs	Gls
Sheffield U	Sch	07/10				
Oldham Ath	Tr	07/12	12-14	66	10	1
Carlisle U	L	11/14	14	8	0	0

BROWN Cyril
Born: Ashington, Northumberland, England, 25 May, 1918 IF
Died: Dover, Kent, England, 15 April, 1990

League Club	Source	Date Signed	Seasons Played	Apps	Subs	Gls
Brentford	Felixstowe	01/39				
Sunderland	Tr	04/45				
Notts Co	Tr	08/46	46	13	-	5
Rochdale	Boston U	08/48	48-50	61	-	11

BROWN Daniel (Danny)
Born: Bethnal Green, E London, England, 12 September, 1980 M

League Club	Source	Date Signed	Seasons Played	Apps	Subs	Gls
Leyton Orient	YT	05/98				
Barnet	Tr	05/99	99-00	42	11	3
Oxford U	Tr	07/03	03-04	15	1	0

BROWN David (Dave)
Born: Wallasey, Wirral, England, 21 October, 1963 FB

League Club	Source	Date Signed	Seasons Played	Apps	Subs	Gls
Tranmere Rov		08/82	82	1	0	0

BROWN David Alistair
Born: Bolton, Greater Manchester, England, 2 October, 1978 — F

League Club	Source	Date Signed	Seasons Played	Apps	Subs	Gls
Manchester U	YT	10/95				
Hull C	Tr	03/98	97-00	108	23	23
Torquay U	Tr	11/01	01	2	0	0
Accrington Stan	Hereford U	03/05	06-07	16	16	5

BROWN David James
Born: Hartlepool, Cleveland, England, 28 January, 1957 — G

League Club	Source	Date Signed	Seasons Played	Apps	Subs	Gls
Middlesbrough	Horden CW	02/77	77	10	0	0
Plymouth Arg	L	08/79	79	5	0	0
Oxford U	Tr	10/79	79-80	21	0	0
Bury	Tr	09/81	81-84	146	0	0
Preston NE	Tr	06/86	86-88	74	0	0
Scunthorpe U	L	01/89	88	5	0	0
Halifax T	Tr	07/89	89-90	38	0	0

BROWN David Patrick
Born: Tadcaster, North Yorkshire, England, 29 May, 1989 — F

League Club	Source	Date Signed	Seasons Played	Apps	Subs	Gls
Nottingham F	Leeds U (Sch)	07/07				
Bradford C	Tr	01/08	07	0	5	1

BROWN Dennis John
Born: Reading, England, 8 February, 1944 — F/M

League Club	Source	Date Signed	Seasons Played	Apps	Subs	Gls
Chelsea	Jnr	06/62	63	10	-	1
Swindon T	Tr	11/64	64-66	92	0	38
Northampton T	Tr	02/67	66-68	41	5	10
Aldershot	Tr	07/69	69-74	237	8	55

BROWN Douglas Alexander (Duggie)
Born: Airdrie, Lanarkshire, Scotland, 21 March, 1958 — F

League Club	Source	Date Signed	Seasons Played	Apps	Subs	Gls
Sheffield U	Clydebank	03/79	78-79	17	8	2

BROWN Edward Alfred Cecil Henry (Eddie)
Born: St Pancras, Central London, England, 4 October, 1927 — CF
Died: Woking, Surrey, England, 4 April, 1996

League Club	Source	Date Signed	Seasons Played	Apps	Subs	Gls
Brentford		02/50				
Torquay U	Tr	08/50				
Aldershot		08/53	53	3	-	0

BROWN Edwin (Eddie)
Born: Preston, Lancashire, England, 28 February, 1926 — CF
Died: Preston, Lancashire, England, 12 July, 2012

League Club	Source	Date Signed	Seasons Played	Apps	Subs	Gls
Preston NE		08/48	48-50	36	-	16
Southampton	Tr	09/50	50-51	57	-	32
Coventry C	Tr	03/52	51-54	85	-	50
Birmingham C	Tr	10/54	54-58	158	-	74
Leyton Orient	Tr	01/59	58-60	63	-	28

BROWN Ernest (Ernie)
Born: Stockport, Greater Manchester, England, 30 May, 1923 — LH
Died: Chester, England, December, 1980

League Club	Source	Date Signed	Seasons Played	Apps	Subs	Gls
Manchester C		04/44				
Aldershot	Tr	06/46	46	12	-	0
Accrington Stan	Tr	08/49	49	2	-	0

BROWN Ernest Charles (Ernie)
Born: South Shields, Tyne and Wear, England, 3 February, 1921 — IF
Died: Newcastle-upon-Tyne, England, 3 December, 1976

League Club	Source	Date Signed	Seasons Played	Apps	Subs	Gls
Newcastle U	South Shields	12/45				
Southend U	Tr	02/47	46-47	6	-	0
Hartlepool U	South Shields	01/57				

BROWN Frederick (Fred)
Born: Leyton, NE London, England, 6 December, 1931 — G
Died: Surrey, England, November, 2013

League Club	Source	Date Signed	Seasons Played	Apps	Subs	Gls
Aldershot	Leytonstone	06/52	52-54	106	-	0
West Bromwich A	Tr	05/55	55-57	11	-	0
Portsmouth	Tr	06/58	58-59	18	-	0

BROWN Gary
Born: Darwen, Lancashire, England, 29 October, 1985 — RB

League Club	Source	Date Signed	Seasons Played	Apps	Subs	Gls
Rochdale	Sch	07/05	04-06	21	17	0

BROWN George
Born: Sheffield, England, 18 October, 1934 — RH
Died: Sheffield, England, April, 1995
England: Schools

League Club	Source	Date Signed	Seasons Played	Apps	Subs	Gls
Liverpool	Jnr	10/51				
Chesterfield	Tr	05/53	53-54	66	-	5

BROWN George
Born: Bonnybridge, Falkirk, Scotland, 12 January, 1932 — G

League Club	Source	Date Signed	Seasons Played	Apps	Subs	Gls
Crewe Alex	Stenhousemuir	06/57	57	40	-	0

BROWN George Donaldson
Born: Airdrie, Lanarkshire, Scotland, 8 May, 1928 — IF
Died: Airdrie, Lanarkshire, Scotland, 22 October, 2011

League Club	Source	Date Signed	Seasons Played	Apps	Subs	Gls
Southport	Airdrieonians	04/51	50	1	-	0
Bradford Park Ave	Clyde	07/56	56	17	-	2

BROWN Gordon
Born: Ellesmere Port, Cheshire, England, 30 June, 1933 — IF
Died: Chester, England, August, 2005

League Club	Source	Date Signed	Seasons Played	Apps	Subs	Gls
Wolverhampton W	Ellesmere Port T	09/51				
Scunthorpe U	Tr	12/52	52-56	154	-	72
Derby Co	Tr	01/57	56-59	53	-	20
Southampton	Tr	03/60	59-60	8	-	2
Barrow	Tr	07/61	61-63	39	-	16
Southport	Tr	01/64	63	4	-	1

BROWN Gordon
Born: Dunfermline, Fife, Scotland, 4 February, 1932 — LW
Died: Blackburn, Greater Manchester, England, 30 December, 1999

League Club	Source	Date Signed	Seasons Played	Apps	Subs	Gls
Blackburn Rov	Blairhall Colliery	04/51				
Newport Co	Tr	08/55	55-58	137	-	14
Gillingham	Tr	06/59	59-60	67	-	13

BROWN Gordon Alexander
Born: East Kilbride, Lanarkshire, Scotland, 7 December, 1965 — CD

League Club	Source	Date Signed	Seasons Played	Apps	Subs	Gls
Rotherham U	App	12/83	83	1	0	0

BROWN Gordon Steele
Born: Warsop, Nottinghamshire, England, 21 March, 1929 — RH/IF
Died: Nottingham, England, August, 2010

League Club	Source	Date Signed	Seasons Played	Apps	Subs	Gls
Nottingham F	Jnr	12/46	46	1	-	0
York C	Tr	06/50	50-57	322	-	25

BROWN Graham Cummings
Born: Matlock, Derbyshire, England, 21 March, 1944 — G

League Club	Source	Date Signed	Seasons Played	Apps	Subs	Gls
Millwall		12/64				
Mansfield T	Crawley T	08/69	69-73	142	0	0
Doncaster Rov	Tr	07/74	74-75	53	0	0
Swansea C	Portland Timbers (USA)	09/76	76	4	0	0
York C	Portland Timbers (USA)	08/77	77-79	69	0	0
Rotherham U	Tr	02/80	79-80	31	0	0
Mansfield T	Tr	01/82	81	1	0	0

BROWN Graham Frederick
Born: Leicester, England, 5 November, 1950 — F

League Club	Source	Date Signed	Seasons Played	Apps	Subs	Gls
Leicester C	App	11/68	69	0	2	0

BROWN Grant Ashley
Born: Sunderland, England, 19 November, 1969 — CD

League Club	Source	Date Signed	Seasons Played	Apps	Subs	Gls
Leicester C	YT	07/88	87-88	14	0	0
Lincoln C	Tr	08/89	89-01	401	6	15

BROWN Gregory Jonathan (Greg)
Born: Wythenshawe, Greater Manchester, England, 31 July, 1978 — LB

League Club	Source	Date Signed	Seasons Played	Apps	Subs	Gls
Chester C	YT	06/96	95-96	1	3	0
Macclesfield T	Tr	12/97	97-99	9	3	0

BROWN Harold Thomas (Harry)
Born: Kingsbury, NW London, England, 9 April, 1924 — G
Died: Abingdon, Oxfordshire, England, June, 1982

League Club	Source	Date Signed	Seasons Played	Apps	Subs	Gls
Queens Park Rgrs	Jnr	04/41				
Notts Co	Tr	04/46	46-48	93	-	0
Derby Co	Tr	10/49	49-50	37	-	0
Queens Park Rgrs	Tr	08/51	51-55	189	-	0
Plymouth Arg	Tr	08/56	56-57	66	-	0
Exeter C	Tr	09/58				

BROWN Henry Roy (Roy)
Born: Stoke-on-Trent, England, 20 December, 1923 — CF/CH
Died: Bushey, Hertfordshire, England, 8 November, 1989

League Club	Source	Date Signed	Seasons Played	Apps	Subs	Gls
Stoke C	Jnr	08/42	46-52	70	-	14
Watford	Tr	07/53	53-57	142	-	40

BROWN Henry Stanford (Harry)
Born: Workington, Cumbria, England, 23 May, 1918 — CH
Died: Grantham, Lincolnshire, England, 27 April, 1963

League Club	Source	Date Signed	Seasons Played	Apps	Subs	Gls
Wolverhampton W	Workington	02/37	38	2	-	0
Hull C	Tr	05/46	46	22	-	0

BROWN Hugh
Born: Carmyle, Glasgow, Scotland, 7 December, 1921 — RH
Died: Surrey, England, July, 1994
Scotland: 3/SLge-2

League Club	Source	Date Signed	Seasons Played	Apps	Subs	Gls
Torquay U	Partick Thistle	11/50	50-51	55	-	0

BROWN Ian O'Neill
Born: Ipswich, England, 11 September, 1965 — F

League Club	Source	Date Signed	Seasons Played	Apps	Subs	Gls
Birmingham C	App	09/84				
Bristol C	Chelmsford C	05/93	93-94	5	7	1
Colchester U	L	03/94	93	4	0	1
Northampton T	Tr	12/94	94	23	0	4

BROWN Irvin
Born: Lewes, Sussex, England, 20 September, 1935 — D
Died: Poole, Dorset, England, 20 November, 2005

League Club	Source	Date Signed	Seasons Played	Apps	Subs	Gls
Brighton & HA	Jnr	10/52	57	3	-	0
Bournemouth	Tr	09/58	58-62	65	-	2

BROWN Isaiah Jay (Izzy)
Born: Peterborough, England, 7 January, 1997 — F
England: Youth

League Club	Source	Date Signed	Seasons Played	Apps	Subs	Gls
West Bromwich A	Sch	-	12	0	1	0
Chelsea	Tr	01/14	14	0	1	0

BROWN James (Jim)
Born: Manchester, England, 5 October, 1935 — W

League Club	Source	Date Signed	Seasons Played	Apps	Subs	Gls
Rochdale	Altrincham	04/57	56-60	52	-	4

BROWN James
Born: Cumnock, Ayrshire, Scotland, 16 February, 1924 — CF
Died: New Cumnock, Ayrshire, Scotland, 17 January, 2002

League Club	Source	Date Signed	Seasons Played	Apps	Subs	Gls
Chesterfield	Motherwell	05/48	48	5	-	2
Bradford C	Tr	11/48	48	20	-	11
Carlisle U	Queen of the South	09/50	50-51	15	-	9

BROWN James Birrell
Born: Stirling, Scotland, 7 June, 1939 — WH

League Club	Source	Date Signed	Seasons Played	Apps	Subs	Gls
Darlington	Dumbarton	09/60	60-62	14	-	0

BROWN James Grady (Jim)
Born: Coatbridge, Lanarkshire, Scotland, 11 May, 1952 — G
Scotland: 1/U23-4

League Club	Source	Date Signed	Seasons Played	Apps	Subs	Gls
Chesterfield	Albion Rov	12/72	72-73	47	0	0
Sheffield U	Tr	03/74	73-77	170	0	0
Cardiff C	Chicago Sting (USA)	12/82	82	3	0	0
Chesterfield	Kettering T	07/83	83-88	135	0	1

BROWN James Keith (Jim)
Born: Musselburgh, East Lothian, Scotland, 3 October, 1953 — M

League Club	Source	Date Signed	Seasons Played	Apps	Subs	Gls
Aston Villa	App	10/70	69-74	73	2	1
Preston NE	Tr	10/75	75-77	64	0	3
Portsmouth	Ethnikos (GRE)	02/80	79	5	0	0

BROWN James Peter
Born: Cramlington, Northumberland, England, 3 January, 1987 — RW

League Club	Source	Date Signed	Seasons Played	Apps	Subs	Gls
Hartlepool U	Sch	09/04	05-11	124	51	29

BROWN Jason Roy
Born: Southwark, S London, England, 18 May, 1982 — G
Wales: 3/U21-7/Youth

League Club	Source	Date Signed	Seasons Played	Apps	Subs	Gls
Gillingham	Charlton Ath (YT)	03/01	01-05	126	0	0
Blackburn Rov	Tr	07/06	06-09	6	3	0
Leeds U	L	09/10	10	3	1	0
Leyton Orient	L	11/10	10	3	0	0
Ipswich T	Aberdeen	03/13				

BROWN Jeremy
Born: Newport, Wales, 13 June, 1961 — F

League Club	Source	Date Signed	Seasons Played	Apps	Subs	Gls
Newport Co	App	06/78	78	2	1	0

BROWN Jermaine Anthony Alexander
Born: Lambeth, S London, England, 12 January, 1983 — W

League Club	Source	Date Signed	Seasons Played	Apps	Subs	Gls
Arsenal	YT	07/01				
Colchester U	Tr	10/03				
Boston U	Tr	02/04	03	3	2	0

BROWN John (Jackie)
Born: Belfast, Northern Ireland, 8 November, 1914 — RW
Died: 1990
Republic of Ireland: 1//Northern Ireland: 10/NILge-2

League Club	Source	Date Signed	Seasons Played	Apps	Subs	Gls
Wolverhampton W	Belfast Celtic	12/34	34-36	27	-	6
Coventry C	Tr	10/36	36-37	69	-	26
Birmingham C	Tr	09/38	38	34	-	6
Ipswich T	Barry T	05/48	48-50	98	-	25

BROWN John (Johnny)
Born: St Kew, Cornwall, England, 29 July, 1940 — IF

League Club	Source	Date Signed	Seasons Played	Apps	Subs	Gls
Plymouth Arg	Wadebridge T	10/60	60-62	9	-	2
Bristol Rov	Tr	07/63	63-67	156	0	32

BROWN John
Born: Edinburgh, Scotland, 6 March, 1940 — WH

League Club	Source	Date Signed	Seasons Played	Apps	Subs	Gls
Colchester U	Dunbar U	09/61	62	1	-	0

BROWN John Christopher
Born: Bradford, England, 30 December, 1947 — G

League Club	Source	Date Signed	Seasons Played	Apps	Subs	Gls
Preston NE	App	03/65	66-74	67	0	0
Stockport Co	L	11/70	70	26	0	0
Stockport Co	Tr	07/75	75	15	0	0
Wigan Ath	Tr	07/76	78-81	93	0	0

BROWN John Keith (Keith)
Born: Edinburgh, Scotland, 24 December, 1979 — CD
Scotland: Youth

League Club	Source	Date Signed	Seasons Played	Apps	Subs	Gls
Blackburn Rov	YT	01/97				
Barnsley	Tr	09/99	99-00	8	3	0
Oxford U	L	11/00	00	3	0	0

BROWN John Lewis
Born: Crook, County Durham, England, 23 March, 1921 — RB
Died: York, England, 10 January, 1989

League Club	Source	Date Signed	Seasons Played	Apps	Subs	Gls
York C	Stanley U	02/48	47-49	22	-	0

BROWN John Michael
Born: Streatham, S London, England, 2 February, 1934 — IF

League Club	Source	Date Signed	Seasons Played	Apps	Subs	Gls
Shrewsbury T (Am)	Queens Park	05/53	53	5	-	3

BROWN John Thomas (Jock)
Born: Edinburgh, Scotland, 2 April, 1935 — LB
Died: Hartlepool, Cleveland, England, 9 April, 2000
Scotland: Schools

League Club	Source	Date Signed	Seasons Played	Apps	Subs	Gls
Tranmere Rov	Third Lanark	01/61	60-61	33	-	0
Hartlepool U	Tr	07/62	62-63	68	-	10

BROWN Jonathan (Jon)
Born: Barnsley, South Yorkshire, England, 8 September, 1966 — D/M

League Club	Source	Date Signed	Seasons Played	Apps	Subs	Gls
Exeter C	Denaby U	07/90	90-94	149	15	3
Halifax T	Tr	07/95	98	32	8	0

BROWN Jonathan David (Jon)
Born: Bridgend, Wales, 17 April, 1990 — RW
Wales: U21-6/Youth

League Club	Source	Date Signed	Seasons Played	Apps	Subs	Gls
Cardiff C	Sch	07/08	07	0	2	0

BROWN Jordan
Born: Benfleet, Essex, England, 11 October, 1991 — LB

League Club	Source	Date Signed	Seasons Played	Apps	Subs	Gls
West Ham U	Sch	07/10				
Aldershot T	L	08/11	11	2	1	0
Crewe Alex	Tr	02/12	11	2	5	0
Barnet	Tr	06/12	12	21	0	0

BROWN Joseph (Joe)
Born: Cramlington, Northumberland, England, 26 April, 1929 — LH
Died: Burnley, Lancashire, England, 30 October, 2014

League Club	Source	Date Signed	Seasons Played	Apps	Subs	Gls
Middlesbrough	Jnr	04/46	49-50	11	-	0
Burnley	Tr	08/52	52	6	-	0
Bournemouth	Tr	06/54	54-59	215	-	5
Aldershot	Tr	07/60	60	5	-	0

BROWN Joseph Samuel (Joe)
Born: Bebington, Wirral, England, 7 May, 1920 — LW
Died: Stoke-on-Trent, England, May, 2004

League Club	Source	Date Signed	Seasons Played	Apps	Subs	Gls
Chester C	Port Sunlight	05/47	46-47	15	-	2

BROWN Joseph William (Joe)
Born: Bradford, England, 3 April, 1988 — F

League Club	Source	Date Signed	Seasons Played	Apps	Subs	Gls
Bradford C	Sch	07/06	05-06	3	16	1

BROWN Junior
Born: Crewe, Cheshire, England, 7 May, 1989 — LM
England: Semi Pro-2

League Club	Source	Date Signed	Seasons Played	Apps	Subs	Gls
Crewe Alex	Sch	05/07	07	0	1	0
Fleetwood T	Northwich Victoria	06/10	12-13	51	13	11
Tranmere Rov	L	03/14	13	8	1	1
Oxford U	Tr	07/14	14	6	5	0
Mansfield T	Tr	11/14	14	21	3	2

BROWN Kayleden Courtney
Born: Derry, Northern Ireland, 15 April, 1992 — LW
Wales: Youth

League Club	Source	Date Signed	Seasons Played	Apps	Subs	Gls
West Bromwich A	Sch	07/10				
Tranmere Rov	L	08/10	10	1	3	0
Dagenham & Red	L	11/10	10	3	0	0
Port Vale	L	01/11	10	0	4	0

BROWN Keith
Born: Bootle, Merseyside, England, 19 October, 1957 — FB

League Club	Source	Date Signed	Seasons Played	Apps	Subs	Gls
Southport	East Villa	11/76	76	4	0	0

BROWN Keith
Born: Grimsby, North Lincolnshire, England, 23 September, 1954 — LW

League Club	Source	Date Signed	Seasons Played	Apps	Subs	Gls
Nottingham F	App	09/72				
Grimsby T	Tr	10/73	73-75	32	7	5

BROWN Keith
Born: Hucknall, Nottinghamshire, England, 1 January, 1942 — CF
England: Schools

League Club	Source	Date Signed	Seasons Played	Apps	Subs	Gls
Notts Co	Jnr	01/59	58	8	-	4
Rotherham U	Tr	07/59				

BROWN Keith Gordon
Born: Coseley, West Midlands, England, 16 July, 1954 — RB

League Club	Source	Date Signed	Seasons Played	Apps	Subs	Gls
Walsall	Jnr	07/73	73-74	8	2	0

BROWN Keith Jack
Born: Bournemouth, England, 29 January, 1942 — FB

League Club	Source	Date Signed	Seasons Played	Apps	Subs	Gls
Bournemouth	Pokesdown	09/60	63-64	15	-	0

BROWN Keith Timothy
Born: Bristol, England, 28 September, 1959 — F

League Club	Source	Date Signed	Seasons Played	Apps	Subs	Gls
Bristol Rov	Bristol St George	10/77	78-80	4	3	0

BROWN Kenneth (Ken)
Born: Forest Gate, E London, England, 16 February, 1934 — CH
England: 1

League Club	Source	Date Signed	Seasons Played	Apps	Subs	Gls
West Ham U	Neville U	10/51	52-66	386	0	4
Torquay U	Tr	05/67	67-68	40	2	1

BROWN Kenneth Geoffrey (Kenny)
Born: Barnsley, South Yorkshire, England, 21 March, 1952 — M

League Club	Source	Date Signed	Seasons Played	Apps	Subs	Gls
Barnsley	App	04/70	69-77	267	10	24
Bournemouth	Tr	06/78	78-79	29	3	4

BROWN Kenneth James (Ken)
Born: Coventry, England, 18 October, 1933 — RW

League Club	Source	Date Signed	Seasons Played	Apps	Subs	Gls
Coventry C		01/56				
Nottingham F	Corby T	11/56				
Bournemouth	Tr	07/57	57	6	-	1
Torquay U	Tr	07/58	58	9	-	1

BROWN Kenneth James (Kenny)
Born: Upminster, E London, England, 11 July, 1967 — RB

League Club	Source	Date Signed	Seasons Played	Apps	Subs	Gls
Norwich C	Jnr	07/85	86-87	24	1	0
Plymouth Arg	Tr	08/88	88-90	126	0	4
West Ham U	Tr	08/91	91-95	55	8	5
Huddersfield T	L	09/95	95	5	0	0
Reading	L	10/95	95	12	0	1
Southend U	L	03/96	95	6	0	0
Crystal Palace	L	03/96	95	5	1	2
Reading	L	09/96	96	5	0	0
Birmingham C	Tr	12/96	96	11	0	0
Millwall	Tr	07/97	97	45	0	0
Gillingham	Tr	03/99	98	2	2	0

BROWN Kevan Barry
Born: Andover, Hampshire, England, 2 January, 1966 — RB

League Club	Source	Date Signed	Seasons Played	Apps	Subs	Gls
Southampton	Jnr	07/84				
Brighton & HA	Tr	02/87	86-88	52	1	0
Aldershot	Tr	11/88	88-90	108	2	2

BROWN Laurence (Laurie)
Born: Shildon, County Durham, England, 22 August, 1937 — CH/CF
Died: Newton Aycliffe, County Durham, England, 30 September, 1998
England: Amateur-3

League Club	Source	Date Signed	Seasons Played	Apps	Subs	Gls
Darlington (Am)	Bishop Auckland	03/59	58	3	-	0
Northampton T	Bishop Auckland	10/60	60	33	-	22
Arsenal	Tr	08/61	61-63	101	-	2
Tottenham H	Tr	04/63	63-65	62	0	3
Norwich C	Tr	09/66	66-68	80	1	2
Bradford Park Ave	Tr	12/68	68-69	36	0	1

BROWN Lee James
Born: Bromley, SE London, England, 10 August, 1990 — LB

League Club	Source	Date Signed	Seasons Played	Apps	Subs	Gls
Queens Park Rgrs	Sch	07/08	09	0	1	0
Bristol Rov	Tr	06/11	11-13	109	13	12

BROWN Linton James
Born: Driffield, East Riding of Yorkshire, England, 12 April, 1968 — F

League Club	Source	Date Signed	Seasons Played	Apps	Subs	Gls
Halifax T	Guiseley	12/92	92	3	0	0
Hull C	Tr	01/93	92-95	111	10	23
Swansea C	Tr	03/96	95-97	16	11	3
Scarborough	L	08/97	97	4	0	1

BROWN Malcolm
Born: Salford, England, 13 December, 1956 — RB

League Club	Source	Date Signed	Seasons Played	Apps	Subs	Gls
Bury	App	12/74	73-76	10	1	0
Huddersfield T	Tr	05/77	77-82	256	0	16
Newcastle U	Tr	08/83	84	39	0	0
Huddersfield T	Tr	06/85	85-88	93	3	1
Rochdale	Tr	02/89	88	11	0	0
Stockport Co	Tr	07/89	89-90	71	0	3
Rochdale	Tr	08/91	91	18	0	1

BROWN Marvin Robert
Born: Bristol, England, 6 July, 1983 — F
England: Youth

League Club	Source	Date Signed	Seasons Played	Apps	Subs	Gls
Bristol C	YT	07/00	99-03	2	17	0
Torquay U	L	09/02	02	2	2	0
Cheltenham T	L	01/03	02	11	4	2
Yeovil T	Weymouth	03/05	04	0	2	0

BROWN Matthew Anthony (Matty)
Born: Liverpool, England, 15 March, 1990 — CD

League Club	Source	Date Signed	Seasons Played	Apps	Subs	Gls
Manchester C	Sch	07/07				
Chesterfield	Marine	07/13	13	2	1	1

BROWN Michael
Born: Preston, Lancashire, England, 27 February, 1985 — M

League Club	Source	Date Signed	Seasons Played	Apps	Subs	Gls
Preston NE	Sch	08/04				
Chester C	L	12/04	04	11	7	0

BROWN Michael Antony (Mike)
Born: Birmingham, England, 8 February, 1968 — RW

League Club	Source	Date Signed	Seasons Played	Apps	Subs	Gls
Shrewsbury T	App	02/86	86-90	174	16	9
Bolton W	Tr	08/91	91-92	27	6	3
Shrewsbury T	Tr	12/92	92-94	66	1	11
Preston NE	Tr	11/94	95-96	11	5	1
Rochdale	L	09/96	96	5	0	0
Shrewsbury T	Tr	12/96	96-00	111	50	16

BROWN Michael John (Mick)
Born: Walsall, West Midlands, England, 11 July, 1939 — RB

League Club	Source	Date Signed	Seasons Played	Apps	Subs	Gls
Hull C	Jnr	10/58	59-65	8	0	0
Lincoln C	Tr	07/67	67	38	0	0

BROWN Michael John (Mick)
Born: Slough, Berkshire, England, 11 April, 1944 — F

League Club	Source	Date Signed	Seasons Played	Apps	Subs	Gls
Fulham	App	09/61	61-62	4	-	0
Millwall	Tr	02/65	64-66	47	5	11
Luton T	Tr	07/67	67-68	9	5	2
Colchester U	Tr	10/68	68-69	47	5	12

BROWN Michael John Leslie (Mick)
Born: Swansea, Wales, 27 September, 1951 — CD
Wales: Schools

League Club	Source	Date Signed	Seasons Played	Apps	Subs	Gls
Crystal Palace	App	09/69				
Brighton & HA	Tr	06/73	73	5	3	1
Brentford	L	09/73	73	3	0	0

BROWN Michael Robert
Born: Hartlepool, Cleveland, England, 25 January, 1977 — M
England: U21-4

League Club	Source	Date Signed	Seasons Played	Apps	Subs	Gls
Manchester C	YT	09/94	95-98	67	22	2
Hartlepool U	L	03/97	96	6	0	1
Portsmouth	L	11/99	99	4	0	0
Sheffield U	Tr	12/99	99-03	146	5	27
Tottenham H	Tr	12/03	03-05	39	11	2
Fulham	Tr	01/06	05-06	40	1	0
Wigan Ath	Tr	07/07	07-09	47	11	0
Portsmouth	Tr	08/09	09-10	42	3	4
Leeds U	Tr	07/11	11-13	48	18	2
Port Vale	Tr	07/14	14	30	6	4

BROWN Monty Raymond
Born: Grimsby, North Lincolnshire, England, 7 September, 1943 — CF

League Club	Source	Date Signed	Seasons Played	Apps	Subs	Gls
Scunthorpe U	Jnr	07/63	64-65	19	0	6

BROWN Nathaniel Levi (Nat)
Born: Sheffield, England, 15 June, 1981 — CD

League Club	Source	Date Signed	Seasons Played	Apps	Subs	Gls
Huddersfield T	YT	07/99	02-04	56	20	0
Lincoln C	Tr	08/05	05-07	86	8	8
Macclesfield T	Wrexham	11/08	08-11	147	2	12

BROWN Neil Richard
Born: Sheffield, England, 16 January, 1966 — LB

League Club	Source	Date Signed	Seasons Played	Apps	Subs	Gls
Chesterfield	App	11/83	83	5	0	0

BROWN Nicholas James (Nicky)
Born: Northampton, England, 25 January, 1973 — G

League Club	Source	Date Signed	Seasons Played	Apps	Subs	Gls
Halifax T	Norwich C (YT)	07/91	91-92	2	0	0

BROWN Nicholas Lee (Nicky)
Born: Hull, England, 16 October, 1966 — RB

League Club	Source	Date Signed	Seasons Played	Apps	Subs	Gls
Hull C	App	08/85	85-91	80	6	3

BROWN Owen John
Born: Liverpool, England, 4 September, 1960 — F
England: Schools

League Club	Source	Date Signed	Seasons Played	Apps	Subs	Gls
Liverpool	Jnr	11/78				
Carlisle U	Tr	06/80	80	4	0	2
Tranmere Rov	Tr	08/81	81	29	8	8
Crewe Alex	Tr	08/82	82	1	0	0
Tranmere Rov	Tr	10/82	82-83	47	9	12
Chester C	Tr	08/84	84	9	1	3

BROWN Paul Henry
Born: Liverpool, England, 10 September, 1984 — W

League Club	Source	Date Signed	Seasons Played	Apps	Subs	Gls
Tranmere Rov	Sch	06/04	04	1	3	0

BROWN Peter Barry
Born: Andover, Hampshire, England, 13 July, 1934 — RW
Died: Andover, Hampshire, England, 8 December, 2011

League Club	Source	Date Signed	Seasons Played	Apps	Subs	Gls
Southampton	Jnr	01/52	53-57	16	-	3
Wrexham	Tr	07/58	58-59	33	-	9

BROWN Peter Ronald
Born: Hemel Hempstead, Hertfordshire, England, 1 September, 1961 — RB

League Club	Source	Date Signed	Seasons Played	Apps	Subs	Gls
Wimbledon	Chelsea (App)	08/80	80-81	53	2	3

BROWN Philip (Phil)
Born: South Shields, Tyne and Wear, England, 30 May, 1959 — RB

League Club	Source	Date Signed	Seasons Played	Apps	Subs	Gls
Hartlepool U	St Hilda's Jnrs	07/78	79-84	210	7	8
Halifax T	Tr	07/85	85-87	135	0	19
Bolton W	Tr	06/88	88-93	254	2	14
Blackpool	Tr	07/94	94-95	33	11	5

BROWN Philip James (Phil)
Born: Sheffield, England, 16 January, 1966 — W

League Club	Source	Date Signed	Seasons Played	Apps	Subs	Gls
Chesterfield	App	10/83	82-86	82	5	19
Stockport Co	Tr	12/86	86	23	0	1
Lincoln C	Tr	08/87	88-89	32	11	3

BROWN Ralph
Born: Ilkeston, Derbyshire, England, 26 February, 1944 — IF

League Club	Source	Date Signed	Seasons Played	Apps	Subs	Gls
Aston Villa	App	03/61				
Notts Co	Tr	05/62	62	18	-	3

BROWN Raymond Moscrop (Ray)
Born: Carlisle, Cumbria, England, 11 February, 1928 — W

League Club	Source	Date Signed	Seasons Played	Apps	Subs	Gls
Notts Co	Queen's Park	08/51	51	7	-	0

BROWN Reece
Born: Manchester, England, 1 November, 1991 — CD
England: Youth

League Club	Source	Date Signed	Seasons Played	Apps	Subs	Gls
Manchester U	Sch	07/10				
Bradford C	L	09/10	10	3	0	0
Doncaster Rov	L	08/11	11	1	2	0
Oldham Ath	L	03/12	11	15	0	0
Coventry C	L	07/12	12	6	0	0
Ipswich T	L	02/13	12	0	1	0
Watford	Tr	07/13	13	0	1	0
Carlisle U	L	03/14	13	9	3	0
Barnsley	Tr	07/14	14	10	3	0

BROWN Reece
Born: Dudley, West Midlands, England, 3 March, 1996 — LM
England: Youth

League Club	Source	Date Signed	Seasons Played	Apps	Subs	Gls
Birmingham C	Sch	01/14	13-14	3	4	0
Notts Co	L	08/14	14	3	0	0

BROWN Richard Anthony
Born: Nottingham, England, 13 January, 1967 — RB

League Club	Source	Date Signed	Seasons Played	Apps	Subs	Gls
Sheffield Wed	Ilkeston T	01/85				
Blackburn Rov	Kettering T	09/90	91-92	26	2	0
Maidstone U	L	02/91	90	3	0	0
Stockport Co	Tr	03/95	94	1	0	0
Blackpool	Tr	08/95	95	2	1	0

BROWN Richard Colin
Born: Sutton Coldfield, West Midlands, England, 25 December, 1973 — LB

League Club	Source	Date Signed	Seasons Played	Apps	Subs	Gls
Walsall	YT	03/92	91	6	3	0

BROWN Robert (Bobby)
Born: Bristol, England, 14 May, 1949 — M

League Club	Source	Date Signed	Seasons Played	Apps	Subs	Gls
Bristol Rov	App	05/67	68-71	28	7	4
Newport Co	L	03/70	69	8	1	0

BROWN Robert (Bob)
Born: Motherwell, Lanarkshire, Scotland, 2 December, 1931 — D

League Club	Source	Date Signed	Seasons Played	Apps	Subs	Gls
Workington	Motherwell	05/56	56-67	419	1	2

BROWN Robert (Bobby)
Born: Glasgow, Scotland, 9 August, 1924 — IF
Died: Rotherham, South Yorkshire, England, 12 January, 2005

League Club	Source	Date Signed	Seasons Played	Apps	Subs	Gls
Derby Co	Camerons	10/47				
Southend U	Tr	07/48	48-49	12	-	0
Shrewsbury T	Tr	07/50	50-52	104	-	41
Barnsley	Tr	07/53	53-56	120	-	55
Rotherham U	Tr	09/56	56-57	42	-	12

BROWN Robert (Bobby)
Born: Carluke, Lanarkshire, Scotland, 23 November, 1955 — D

League Club	Source	Date Signed	Seasons Played	Apps	Subs	Gls
Workington	Jnr	08/74	74-76	44	0	0

BROWN Robert Alan John (Sailor)
Born: Great Yarmouth, Norfolk, England, 7 November, 1915 — IF
Died: Forres, Moray, Scotland, 27 December, 2008
England: War-6

League Club	Source	Date Signed	Seasons Played	Apps	Subs	Gls
Charlton Ath	Gorleston	08/34	37-38	47	-	21
Nottingham F	Tr	05/46	46-47	45	-	17
Aston Villa	Tr	10/47	47-48	30	-	9

BROWN Robert Beresford (Berry)
Born: Hartlepool, Cleveland, England, 6 September, 1927 — G
Died: Hartlepool, Cleveland, England, July, 2001

League Club	Source	Date Signed	Seasons Played	Apps	Subs	Gls
Manchester U	Blackhall CW	08/46	47-48	4	-	0
Doncaster Rov	Tr	01/49	48	4	-	0
Hartlepool U	Stockton	08/51	51-55	126	-	0

BROWN Robert Christopher (Bobby)
Born: Plymouth, England, 24 November, 1953 — M
England: Schools

League Club	Source	Date Signed	Seasons Played	Apps	Subs	Gls
Chelsea	Jnr	08/72				
Sheffield Wed	Tr	08/74	74-75	17	4	3
Aldershot	L	02/76	75	3	2	0

BROWN Robert Henry (Bobby)
Born: Streatham, S London, England, 2 May, 1940 — CF
England: Amateur-14

League Club	Source	Date Signed	Seasons Played	Apps	Subs	Gls
Fulham (Am)	Barnet	09/60	60-61	8	-	4
Watford	Tr	11/61	61-62	28	-	10
Northampton T	Tr	12/63	63-66	50	0	22
Cardiff C	Tr	10/66	66-67	50	0	23

BROWN Roger William
Born: Tamworth, Staffordshire, England, 12 December, 1952 — CD
Died: Tamworth, Staffordshire, England, 16 August, 2011

League Club	Source	Date Signed	Seasons Played	Apps	Subs	Gls
Bournemouth	AP Leamington	02/78	77-78	63	0	3
Norwich C	Tr	07/79	79	16	0	0
Fulham	Tr	03/80	79-83	141	0	18
Bournemouth	Tr	12/83	83-86	83	1	5

BROWN Ronald (Ronnie)
Born: Sunderland, England, 26 December, 1944 — RW

League Club	Source	Date Signed	Seasons Played	Apps	Subs	Gls
Blackpool	Whitley Bay	11/65	65-70	54	7	13
Plymouth Arg	Tr	02/71	70-72	31	5	3
Bradford C	Tr	09/72	72-74	90	7	11

BROWN Ronald (Ron)
Born: Ballymoney, Antrim, Northern Ireland, 20 March, 1923 — CF

League Club	Source	Date Signed	Seasons Played	Apps	Subs	Gls
Plymouth Arg	Linfield	04/45				
Hull C	Tr	03/47	46	7	-	3

BROWN Roy
Born: Stockton-on-Tees, Cleveland, England, 10 June, 1925 — RB/CF
Died: Middlesbrough, England, December, 2004

League Club	Source	Date Signed	Seasons Played	Apps	Subs	Gls
Darlington	Stockton West End	11/46	46-55	158	-	20

BROWN Roy
Born: Stretford, Greater Manchester, England, 17 June, 1932 — IF

League Club	Source	Date Signed	Seasons Played	Apps	Subs	Gls
Doncaster Rov	Gainsborough Trinity	05/53	53-56	26	-	6

BROWN Roy Ernest Eric
Born: Shoreham-by-Sea, West Sussex, England, 5 October, 1945 — G

League Club	Source	Date Signed	Seasons Played	Apps	Subs	Gls
Tottenham H	App	10/62	66	1	0	0
Reading	Tr	07/68	68-69	63	0	0
Notts Co	Tr	07/70	70-74	113	0	0
Mansfield T	Tr	11/75	75	1	0	0

BROWN Ryan Anthony
Born: Stoke-on-Trent, England, 15 March, 1985 — LB

League Club	Source	Date Signed	Seasons Played	Apps	Subs	Gls
Port Vale	Sch	08/03	02-04	33	5	0

BROWN Scott
Born: Runcorn, Cheshire, England, 8 May, 1985 — M
England: Youth

League Club	Source	Date Signed	Seasons Played	Apps	Subs	Gls
Everton	Sch	05/02				
Bristol C	Tr	08/04	04-06	48	15	5
Cheltenham T	Tr	01/07	06-07	13	11	0
Port Vale	Tr	11/08	08	18	0	1
Cheltenham T	Tr	03/10	09	0	1	0
Morecambe	Tr	09/10	10	19	13	3

BROWN Scott Peter Andrew
Born: Wolverhampton, England, 26 April, 1985 — G

League Club	Source	Date Signed	Seasons Played	Apps	Subs	Gls
Bristol C	Welshpool T	01/04				
Cheltenham T	Tr	07/04	05-13	251	1	0

BROWN Sebastian Alexander (Seb)
Born: Sutton, S London, England, 24 November, 1989 — G
England: Semi Pro-3

League Club	Source	Date Signed	Seasons Played	Apps	Subs	Gls
Brentford	Sch	07/08	08	0	1	0
AFC Wimbledon	Tr	08/09	11-13	61	0	0

BROWN Simon Alexander
Born: West Bromwich, West Midlands, England, 18 September, 1983 — F

League Club	Source	Date Signed	Seasons Played	Apps	Subs	Gls
West Bromwich A	Sch	07/03				
Kidderminster Hrs	L	03/04	03	8	0	2
Kidderminster Hrs	L	07/04	04	11	2	0
Mansfield T	Tr	12/04	04-07	76	37	21

BROWN Simon James
Born: Chelmsford, England, 3 December, 1976 — G

League Club	Source	Date Signed	Seasons Played	Apps	Subs	Gls
Tottenham H	YT	07/95				
Lincoln C	L	12/97	97	1	0	0
Colchester U	Tr	07/99	99-03	141	1	0
Brentford	Hibernian	07/07	07	26	0	0
Darlington	L	08/08	08	22	0	0
Northampton T	Tr	09/09	09	2	0	0

BROWN Stanley (Stan)
Born: Lewes, Sussex, England, 15 September, 1941 — M

League Club	Source	Date Signed	Seasons Played	Apps	Subs	Gls
Fulham	Jnr	05/59	60-72	348	5	16
Brighton & HA	L	10/72	72	9	0	0
Colchester U	Tr	12/72	72	23	0	0

BROWN Steven Andrew John (Steve)
Born: Peckham, SE London, England, 13 July, 1952 — W

League Club	Source	Date Signed	Seasons Played	Apps	Subs	Gls
Millwall	App	06/70	69-74	47	22	5

BROWN Steven Byron (Steve)
Born: Brighton, England, 13 May, 1972 — D

League Club	Source	Date Signed	Seasons Played	Apps	Subs	Gls
Charlton Ath	YT	07/90	91-02	194	48	9
Reading	Tr	12/02	02-03	40	0	1

BROWN Steven Ferold (Steve)
Born: Northampton, England, 6 July, 1966 — LM

League Club	Source	Date Signed	Seasons Played	Apps	Subs	Gls
Northampton T	Jnr	08/83	83-84	14	1	3
Northampton T	Irthlingborough D	07/89	89-93	145	13	19
Wycombe W	Tr	02/94	93-03	332	39	35

BROWN Steven Robert (Steve)
Born: Southend-on-Sea, England, 6 December, 1973 — F

League Club	Source	Date Signed	Seasons Played	Apps	Subs	Gls
Southend U	YT	07/92	92	10	0	2
Scunthorpe U	Tr	07/93				
Colchester U	Tr	08/93	93-94	56	6	17
Gillingham	Tr	03/95	94-95	8	1	2
Lincoln C	Tr	10/95	95-97	47	25	8
Macclesfield T	Tr	07/98	98	1	1	0

BROWN Thomas (Tom)
Born: Troon, Ayrshire, Scotland, 26 October, 1919 — G

League Club	Source	Date Signed	Seasons Played	Apps	Subs	Gls
Ipswich T	Glenafton Ath	10/38	46-50	111	-	0

BROWN Thomas (Tom)
Born: Leven, Fife, Scotland, 17 November, 1933 — CF

League Club	Source	Date Signed	Seasons Played	Apps	Subs	Gls
Lincoln C	Newburgh West End	04/56	57	3	-	0

BROWN Thomas (Tommy)
Born: Galashiels, Borders, Scotland, 7 June, 1929 — IF
Died: Ipswich, England, May, 2000

League Club	Source	Date Signed	Seasons Played	Apps	Subs	Gls
Ipswich T	Annbank Jnrs	07/52	52-55	84	-	17
Walsall	Tr	06/56	56-57	38	-	9

BROWN Thomas Emmerson (Tom)
Born: Throckley, Tyne and Wear, England, 8 September, 1935 — FB

League Club	Source	Date Signed	Seasons Played	Apps	Subs	Gls
Middlesbrough	Jnr	04/53	54-57	44	-	0

BROWN Thomas Graham (Tommy)
Born: Cowdenbeath, Fife, Scotland, 11 August, 1924 — IF
Died: Blackpool, Lancashire, England, December, 2005

League Club	Source	Date Signed	Seasons Played	Apps	Subs	Gls
Portsmouth	Worcester C	10/46	47	17	-	1
Watford	Tr	08/49	49-53	108	-	11

BROWN Thomas Hugh (Tommy)
Born: Liverpool, England, 8 May, 1930 — RH
England: Youth

League Club	Source	Date Signed	Seasons Played	Apps	Subs	Gls
Doncaster Rov	South Liverpool	02/51	51-53	86	-	1
Swansea C	Tr	12/55	55-58	68	-	0

BROWN Thomas Law (Tommy)
Born: Glenbuck, Ayrshire, Scotland, 17 April, 1921 — WH
Died: Edinburgh, Scotland, 10 May, 1966
Scotland: SLge-1/War-3

League Club	Source	Date Signed	Seasons Played	Apps	Subs	Gls
Millwall	Heart of Midlothian	01/45	46-48	68	-	7
Charlton Ath	Tr	10/48	48-49	34	-	1
Leyton Orient	Tr	08/50	50-52	99	-	5

BROWN Troy Anthony Fraser
Born: Croydon, S London, England, 17 September, 1990 — CD
Wales: U21-10/Youth

League Club	Source	Date Signed	Seasons Played	Apps	Subs	Gls
Ipswich T	Fulham (Sch)	07/09	09-10	6	7	0
Rotherham U	Tr	07/11	11	4	2	1
Aldershot T	Tr	01/12	11-12	48	3	5
Cheltenham T	Tr	06/13	13-14	81	1	5

BROWN Walter Sidney (Wally)
Born: Oakengates, Telford & Wrekin, England, 8 February, 1921 — RW
Died: Oakengates, Telford & Wrekin, England, March, 1989

League Club	Source	Date Signed	Seasons Played	Apps	Subs	Gls
Walsall	Oakengates T	10/40	46-47	20	-	4

BROWN Wayne Jonathan
Born: Kingston-on-Thames, SW London, England, 6 August, 1988 — M

League Club	Source	Date Signed	Seasons Played	Apps	Subs	Gls
Fulham	Sch	02/07	08	0	1	0
Brentford	L	02/08	07	7	4	1
Bristol Rov	L	02/10	09	3	1	0
Bristol Rov	Tr	07/10	10-12	28	27	0

BROWN Wayne Larry
Born: Southampton, England, 14 January, 1977 — G
England: Semi Pro-7

League Club	Source	Date Signed	Seasons Played	Apps	Subs	Gls
Bristol C	YT	07/95	93	1	0	0
Chester C	Weston-super-Mare	09/96	96-04	107	0	0
Hereford U	Tr	08/05	06-07	83	0	0
Bury	Tr	07/08	08-09	76	0	0
Oxford U	Supersport U (RSA)	07/11	11-12	6	0	0

BROWN Wayne Lawrence
Born: Barking, E London, England, 20 August, 1977 — CD

League Club	Source	Date Signed	Seasons Played	Apps	Subs	Gls
Ipswich T	YT	05/96	97-02	28	12	0
Colchester U	L	10/97	97	0	2	0
Queens Park Rgrs	L	03/01	00	2	0	0
Wimbledon	L	09/01	01	17	0	1
Watford	L	01/02	01	10	1	3
Watford	Tr	12/02	02-03	24	1	1
Gillingham	L	09/03	03	4	0	1
Colchester U	Tr	02/04	03-06	138	2	4
Hull C	Tr	07/07	07-08	42	0	1
Preston NE	L	10/08	08	6	0	0
Leicester C	Tr	01/09	08-09	45	3	0
Preston NE	Tr	07/10	10	12	1	0

BROWN Wesley Michael (Wes)
Born: Manchester, England, 13 October, 1979 — CD
England: 23/U21-8/Youth/Schools

League Club	Source	Date Signed	Seasons Played	Apps	Subs	Gls
Manchester U	YT	11/96	97-10	203	29	3
Sunderland	Tr	07/11	11-14	67	3	1

BROWN William
Born: Seaham, County Durham, England, 27 March, 1928 — D
Died: Durham, England, May, 2010

League Club	Source	Date Signed	Seasons Played	Apps	Subs	Gls
Gateshead	Murton CW	09/50	50-57	216	-	7

BROWN William
Born: Kilsyth, Lanarkshire, Scotland, 21 February, 1929 — IF
Died: Cheltenham, Gloucestershire, England, August, 1987

League Club	Source	Date Signed	Seasons Played	Apps	Subs	Gls
Reading	Bridgeton Waverley	02/50				
Exeter C	Tr	08/51	51	7	-	0

BROWN William (Willie)
Born: Falkirk, Scotland, 5 February, 1950 — F

League Club	Source	Date Signed	Seasons Played	Apps	Subs	Gls
Burnley	Jnr	02/67	68	0	1	0
Carlisle U	Tr	07/69	69	16	1	8
Barrow	L	09/69	69	6	0	1
Newport Co	Tr	08/70	70-74	166	2	50
Hereford U	L	03/74	73	9	0	6
Brentford	Tr	11/74	74	16	0	9
Torquay U	Tr	03/75	74-77	137	2	47

BROWN William (Willie)
Born: Forfar, Angus, Scotland, 17 September, 1928 — CF

League Club	Source	Date Signed	Seasons Played	Apps	Subs	Gls
Accrington Stan	Forfar Ath	08/53	53	6	-	2

BROWN William Charles (Bill)
Born: Canning Town, E London, England, 24 February, 1920 — CF
Died: 1982

League Club	Source	Date Signed	Seasons Played	Apps	Subs	Gls
Leyton Orient	Romford	08/46	46	2	-	1

BROWN William Dallas Fyfe (Bill)
Born: Arbroath, Angus, Scotland, 8 October, 1931 — G
Died: Simcoe, Canada, 30 November, 2004
Scotland: 28/B-1/SLge-8

League Club	Source	Date Signed	Seasons Played	Apps	Subs	Gls
Tottenham H	Dundee	06/59	59-65	222	0	0
Northampton T	Tr	10/66	66	17	0	0

BROWN William Dewis (Dewis)
Born: Rotherham, South Yorkshire, England, 4 June, 1919 — IF

League Club	Source	Date Signed	Seasons Played	Apps	Subs	Gls
Stockport Co		08/45	46-49	65	-	15
Rotherham U	Tr	08/50	51	1	-	0

BROWN William Falconer (Willie)
Born: Larkhall, Lanarkshire, Scotland, 20 October, 1922 — RB
Died: Ronaldsay, Orkney, Scotland, 27 May, 1978

League Club	Source	Date Signed	Seasons Played	Apps	Subs	Gls
Preston NE	Larkhall Thistle	01/42	46-49	40	-	0
Grimsby T	Elgin C	06/51	51-57	265	-	1

BROWN William Frederick Thomas (Billy)
Born: Croydon, S London, England, 7 February, 1943 — F

League Club	Source	Date Signed	Seasons Played	Apps	Subs	Gls
Southampton		09/60				
Charlton Ath	Tr	07/61				
Gillingham	Bedford T	02/66	65-67	104	1	33
Portsmouth	Tr	06/68	68	8	0	2
Brentford	Tr	07/69	69	4	0	0

BROWN William Hutchinson (Billy)
Born: Bedlington, Northumberland, England, 11 March, 1909 — RB
Died: Gateshead, Tyne and Wear, England, December, 1996

League Club	Source	Date Signed	Seasons Played	Apps	Subs	Gls
Middlesbrough	West Stanley	12/28	31-38	256	-	2
Hartlepool U	Tr	06/46	46-47	80	-	0

BROWN William Ian (Billy)
Born: Silvertown, E London, England, 6 September, 1910 RH
Died: Ealing, W London, England, 15 January, 1993

League Club	Source	Date Signed	Seasons Played	Apps	Subs	Gls
Luton T	Silvertown	03/30	30-34	49	-	4
Huddersfield T	Tr	03/35	34-35	20	-	2
Brentford	Tr	03/37	36-46	92	-	2
Leyton Orient	Tr	05/47	46-47	26	-	0

BROWN William Inglis (Bill)
Born: Clydebank, Dunbartonshire, Scotland, 25 November, 1938 G

League Club	Source	Date Signed	Seasons Played	Apps	Subs	Gls
Accrington Stan	St Mirren	08/59	59	29	-	0
Chester C	Tr	06/60	60	41	-	0

BROWNBILL Derek Anthony
Born: Liverpool, England, 4 February, 1954 F

League Club	Source	Date Signed	Seasons Played	Apps	Subs	Gls
Liverpool	Jnr	02/72	73	1	0	0
Port Vale	Tr	02/75	74-77	84	8	13
Wigan Ath	Tr	09/78	78-79	32	16	8

BROWNE Alan James
Born: Cork, Republic of Ireland, 15 April, 1995 M
Republic of Ireland: U21-3/Youth

League Club	Source	Date Signed	Seasons Played	Apps	Subs	Gls
Preston NE	Cork C (ROI)	01/14	13-14	18	10	4

BROWNE Anthony (Tony)
Born: Sheerness, Kent, England, 12 February, 1977 RB

League Club	Source	Date Signed	Seasons Played	Apps	Subs	Gls
Brighton & HA	Gravesend & Northfleet	10/98	98	13	0	0

BROWNE Corey Anthony
Born: Enfield, N London, England, 2 July, 1970 M

League Club	Source	Date Signed	Seasons Played	Apps	Subs	Gls
Fulham	Kingsbury T	08/91	91	1	0	0

BROWNE Gary
Born: Dundonald, Belfast, Northern Ireland, 17 January, 1983 W
Northern Ireland: U21-5

League Club	Source	Date Signed	Seasons Played	Apps	Subs	Gls
Manchester C	YT	07/00				
York C	Whitby T	11/03	03	2	4	0

BROWNE Paul Gerard
Born: Glasgow, Scotland, 17 February, 1975 CD

League Club	Source	Date Signed	Seasons Played	Apps	Subs	Gls
Aston Villa	YT	07/93	95	2	0	0

BROWNE Robert James (Bobby)
Born: Derry, Northern Ireland, 2 February, 1912 WH
Died: Leeds, England, August, 1994
Northern Ireland: 6/NILge-1

League Club	Source	Date Signed	Seasons Played	Apps	Subs	Gls
Leeds U	Derry C (ROI)	10/35	35-46	107	-	0
York C	Tr	08/47	47	5	-	0

BROWNE Stafford Ernest
Born: Hastings, East Sussex, England, 4 January, 1972 F

League Club	Source	Date Signed	Seasons Played	Apps	Subs	Gls
Brighton & HA	Hastings T	07/98	98	2	1	0

BROWNE Stephen Logan
Born: Hackney, E London, England, 21 June, 1964 M

League Club	Source	Date Signed	Seasons Played	Apps	Subs	Gls
Charlton Ath	App	06/82	81	0	1	0

BROWNHILL Joshua (Josh)
Born: Warrington, Cheshire, England, 19 December, 1995 M

League Club	Source	Date Signed	Seasons Played	Apps	Subs	Gls
Preston NE	Sch	01/14	13-14	24	18	5

BROWNING Leonard James (Len)
Born: Doncaster, South Yorkshire, England, 30 March, 1928 CF
Died: Leeds, England, 27 September, 2008

League Club	Source	Date Signed	Seasons Played	Apps	Subs	Gls
Leeds U	Headingley Rgrs	08/46	46-51	97	-	43
Sheffield U	Tr	11/51	51-53	65	-	25

BROWNING Marcus Trevor
Born: Bristol, England, 22 April, 1971 M
Wales: 5

League Club	Source	Date Signed	Seasons Played	Apps	Subs	Gls
Bristol Rov	YT	07/89	89-96	152	22	13
Hereford U	L	09/92	92	7	0	5
Huddersfield T	Tr	02/97	96-98	25	8	0
Gillingham	L	11/98	98	1	0	0
Gillingham	Tr	03/99	98-01	60	17	3
Bournemouth	Tr	08/02	02-06	156	32	3

BROWNING Tyias
Born: Liverpool, England, 27 May, 1994 RB
England: U21-5/Youth

League Club	Source	Date Signed	Seasons Played	Apps	Subs	Gls
Everton	Sch	06/11	14	0	2	0
Wigan Ath	L	01/14	13	1	1	0

BROWNLEE Thomas Courtenay (Tommy)
Born: Carnwath, Lanarkshire, Scotland, 21 May, 1935 CF

League Club	Source	Date Signed	Seasons Played	Apps	Subs	Gls
Walsall	Broxburn	09/56	57-58	30	-	14
York C	Tr	12/58	58	9	-	2
Workington	Tr	06/59	59-60	25	-	2
Bradford C	Netherfield	01/65	64-65	25	0	15

BROWNLIE John
Born: Caldercruix, Lanarkshire, Scotland, 11 March, 1952 RB
Scotland: 7/SLge-1/U23-5

League Club	Source	Date Signed	Seasons Played	Apps	Subs	Gls
Newcastle U	Hibernian	08/78	78-81	124	0	2
Middlesbrough	Tr	08/82	82	12	0	0
Hartlepool U	Tr	08/84	84	19	0	1

BROWNLIE Royce
Born: Coffs Harbour, N.S.W., Australia, 28 January, 1980 F

League Club	Source	Date Signed	Seasons Played	Apps	Subs	Gls
Swindon T	Queensland Roar (AUS)	08/06	06	6	8	0
Chester C	L	03/07	06	3	1	0

BROWNLOW John Martin (Jackie)
Born: Belfast, Northern Ireland, 18 June, 1916 RW
Died: Hastings, East Sussex, England, 19 May, 1989

League Club	Source	Date Signed	Seasons Played	Apps	Subs	Gls
Ipswich T	Gravesend U	05/46	46	1	-	0
Hartlepool U	Tr	10/48	48	3	-	0

BROWNRIGG Andrew David (Andy)
Born: Sheffield, England, 2 August, 1976 CD
Scotland: Schools

League Club	Source	Date Signed	Seasons Played	Apps	Subs	Gls
Hereford U	YT	01/95	94	8	0	0
Norwich C	Tr	03/95				
Rotherham U	Tr	07/98				

BROWNSWORD Nathan John (Jack)
Born: Campsall, South Yorkshire, England, 15 May, 1923 FB
Died: Burton-upon-Stather, Lincolnshire, England, 20 December, 2009

League Club	Source	Date Signed	Seasons Played	Apps	Subs	Gls
Hull C	Frickley Colliery	09/46	46	10	-	0
Scunthorpe U	Frickley Colliery	07/47	50-64	597	-	50

BRU Kevin
Born: Paris, France, 12 December, 1988 M
France: Youth//Mauritius: 1

League Club	Source	Date Signed	Seasons Played	Apps	Subs	Gls
Ipswich T	Levski Sofia (BUL)	07/14	14	16	15	1

BRUCE Alexander Robert (Alex)
Born: Dundee, Scotland, 23 December, 1952 F
Scotland: U23-1

League Club	Source	Date Signed	Seasons Played	Apps	Subs	Gls
Preston NE	App	05/70	71-73	55	7	22
Newcastle U	Tr	01/74	73-75	16	4	3
Preston NE	Tr	08/75	75-82	288	13	135
Wigan Ath	Tr	08/83	83-84	35	8	7

BRUCE Alexander Stephen (Alex)
Born: Norwich, England, 28 September, 1984 CD
Republic of Ireland: 2/B-1/U21-5

League Club	Source	Date Signed	Seasons Played	Apps	Subs	Gls
Blackburn Rov	Sch	07/02				
Oldham Ath	L	12/04	04	3	3	0
Birmingham C	Tr	01/05				
Oldham Ath	L	01/05	04	5	1	0
Sheffield Wed	L	03/05	04	5	1	0
Tranmere Rov	L	08/05	05	10	1	0
Ipswich T	Tr	08/06	06-09	112	3	2
Leicester C	L	02/10	09	2	1	0
Leeds U	Tr	07/10	10-11	29	0	1
Huddersfield T	L	11/11	11	3	0	0
Hull C	Tr	07/12	12-14	65	9	0

BRUCE Marcelle Eugene
Born: Detroit, Michigan, USA, 15 March, 1971 RB

League Club	Source	Date Signed	Seasons Played	Apps	Subs	Gls
Colchester U	YT	07/89	89	28	1	1

BRUCE Paul Mark
Born: Lambeth, S London, England, 18 February, 1978 LM

League Club	Source	Date Signed	Seasons Played	Apps	Subs	Gls
Queens Park Rgrs	YT	07/96	97-01	30	7	3
Cambridge U	L	03/99	98	2	2	0

BRUCE Robert (Bobby)
Born: Belfast, Northern Ireland, 14 October, 1928 LW

League Club	Source	Date Signed	Seasons Played	Apps	Subs	Gls
Leicester C	Larne T	03/50				
Leyton Orient		11/51	51	1	-	0

BRUCE Stephen Roger (Steve)
Born: Corbridge, Northumberland, England, 31 December, 1960 CD
England: B-1/FLge/Youth

League Club	Source	Date Signed	Seasons Played	Apps	Subs	Gls
Gillingham	App	10/78	79-83	203	2	29
Norwich C	Tr	08/84	84-87	141	0	14
Manchester U	Tr	12/87	87-95	309	0	36
Birmingham C	Tr	06/96	96-97	70	2	2
Sheffield U	Tr	07/98	98	10	0	0

BRUCK Dietmar Jurgen
Born: Danzig, Germany, 19 April, 1944 D

League Club	Source	Date Signed	Seasons Played	Apps	Subs	Gls
Coventry C	App	05/62	60-70	181	8	7
Charlton Ath	Tr	10/70	70-71	54	2	0
Northampton T	Tr	06/72	72-73	41	0	0

BRUMA Jeffrey Van Homoet
Born: Rotterdam, Netherlands, 13 November, 1991 CD

League Club	Source	Date Signed	Seasons Played	Career Record Apps	Subs	Gls

Netherlands: 7/U21-19

League Club	Source	Date Signed	Seasons Played	Apps	Subs	Gls
Chelsea	Sch	07/09	09-10	1	3	0
Leicester C	L	02/11	10	10	1	2

BRUMFIELD Peter Stanley
Born: Treeton, South Yorkshire, England, 5 September, 1944 — WH

League Club	Source	Date Signed	Seasons Played	Apps	Subs	Gls
Chesterfield	Sheffield U (Am)	07/64	64	1	-	0

BRUMWELL Philip (Phil)
Born: Darlington, County Durham, England, 8 August, 1975 — M/D

League Club	Source	Date Signed	Seasons Played	Apps	Subs	Gls
Sunderland	YT	06/94				
Darlington	Tr	08/95	95-99	106	50	1
Hull C	Tr	08/00	00	1	3	0
Darlington	Tr	11/00	00-01	35	8	0

BRUNA Gerardo Alfredo
Born: Mendoza, Argentina, 29 January, 1991 — LW
Spain: Youth

League Club	Source	Date Signed	Seasons Played	Apps	Subs	Gls
Liverpool	Sch	03/08				
Blackpool	Tr	07/11	11-12	0	2	0
Accrington Stan	Whitehawk	02/15	14	6	0	0

BRUNDLE Mitchell Ronnie (Mitch)
Born: Croydon, S London, England, 4 December, 1994 — RB

League Club	Source	Date Signed	Seasons Played	Apps	Subs	Gls
Bristol C	Yeovil T (Sch)	07/13				
Cheltenham T	L	01/14	13	7	0	0

BRUNO Pasquale
Born: Lecce, Italy, 19 June, 1962 — CD

League Club	Source	Date Signed	Seasons Played	Apps	Subs	Gls
Wigan Ath (L)	Heart of Midlothian	02/98	97	1	0	0

BRUNSKILL Joseph (Joe)
Born: Shildon, County Durham, England, 22 April, 1932 — CF
Died: Middlesbrough, England, August, 1989

League Club	Source	Date Signed	Seasons Played	Apps	Subs	Gls
Sunderland	Shildon Works Jnrs	04/50				
Oldham Ath	Tr	05/54	54	12	-	2

BRUNT Christopher (Chris)
Born: Belfast, Northern Ireland, 14 December, 1984 — LM
Northern Ireland: 51/U23-1/U21-2/Youth

League Club	Source	Date Signed	Seasons Played	Apps	Subs	Gls
Middlesbrough	Sch	07/02				
Sheffield Wed	Tr	03/04	03-07	113	27	24
West Bromwich A	Tr	08/07	07-14	229	35	38

BRUNT Geoffrey Reginald (Geoff)
Born: Nottingham, England, 24 November, 1926 — WH
Died: Huntingdon, Cambridgeshire, England, June, 2006

League Club	Source	Date Signed	Seasons Played	Apps	Subs	Gls
Notts Co	Jnr	09/49	49-53	29	-	1

BRUNT Malcolm Eric
Born: Sheffield, England, 5 December, 1946 — G

League Club	Source	Date Signed	Seasons Played	Apps	Subs	Gls
Chesterfield	Sheffield Wed (Am)	07/66	66	7	0	0

BRUNT Ryan Samuel
Born: Birmingham, England, 26 May, 1993 — F

League Club	Source	Date Signed	Seasons Played	Apps	Subs	Gls
Stoke C	Sch	11/11				
Tranmere Rov	L	01/12	11	11	4	1
Leyton Orient	L	07/12	12	8	10	3
Bristol Rov	Tr	01/13	12-13	26	3	5
York C	L	10/14	14	5	1	0
Stevenage	L	11/14	14	3	2	0
Plymouth Arg	Tr	01/15	14	4	12	2

BRUSH Paul
Born: Plaistow, E London, England, 22 February, 1958 — LB

League Club	Source	Date Signed	Seasons Played	Apps	Subs	Gls
West Ham U	App	02/76	77-84	144	7	1
Crystal Palace	Tr	09/85	85-87	50	0	3
Southend U	Tr	01/88	87-89	69	4	1

BRUTON David Edward
Born: Dursley, Gloucestershire, England, 31 October, 1952 — CD

League Club	Source	Date Signed	Seasons Played	Apps	Subs	Gls
Bristol C	App	07/71	71-72	16	1	0
Swansea C	Tr	08/73	73-78	185	8	19
Newport Co	L	02/77	76	6	0	1
Newport Co	Tr	10/78	78-80	79	3	9

BRUTON Michael (Mike)
Born: Dursley, Gloucestershire, England, 6 May, 1958 — F

League Club	Source	Date Signed	Seasons Played	Apps	Subs	Gls
Newport Co	Gloucester C	08/79	79	3	6	1

BRYAN Derek Kirk
Born: Hammersmith, W London, England, 11 November, 1974 — F

League Club	Source	Date Signed	Seasons Played	Apps	Subs	Gls
Brentford	Hampton	08/97	97-01	16	34	7

BRYAN Ernest Newton (Ernie)
Born: Hawarden, Flintshire, Wales, 6 June, 1926 — RB
Died: Flintshire, Wales, March, 2008

League Club	Source	Date Signed	Seasons Played	Apps	Subs	Gls
Chester C	Jnr	11/45	48	1	-	0

BRYAN Joseph Edward (Joe)
Born: Bristol, England, 17 September, 1993 — LB/M

League Club	Source	Date Signed	Seasons Played	Apps	Subs	Gls
Bristol C	Sch	07/11	11-14	60	16	8
Plymouth Arg	L	03/13	12	10	0	1

League Club	Source	Date Signed	Seasons Played	Career Record Apps	Subs	Gls

BRYAN Marvin Lee
Born: Paddington, Central London, England, 2 August, 1975 — RB

League Club	Source	Date Signed	Seasons Played	Apps	Subs	Gls
Queens Park Rgrs	YT	08/92				
Doncaster Rov	L	12/94	94	5	0	1
Blackpool	Tr	08/95	95-99	172	10	4
Bury	Tr	03/00	99	6	3	0
Rotherham U	Tr	07/00	00-02	54	9	0

BRYAN Michael Anthony
Born: Hayes, W London, England, 21 February, 1990 — W
Northern Ireland: 2/U21-4/Youth

League Club	Source	Date Signed	Seasons Played	Apps	Subs	Gls
Watford	Sch	11/08	09-10	5	7	0
Bradford C	L	08/11	11	5	3	0

BRYAN Peter
Born: Oxford, England, 30 April, 1944 — RB
Republic of Ireland: LoI-3

League Club	Source	Date Signed	Seasons Played	Apps	Subs	Gls
Oxford U	Botley Minors	07/61	62-65	18	0	0

BRYAN Peter Anthony
Born: Birmingham, England, 22 June, 1943 — FB

League Club	Source	Date Signed	Seasons Played	Apps	Subs	Gls
Middlesbrough		08/61	64	4	-	0
Oldham Ath	Tr	07/65	65	5	1	0

BRYANT Eric
Born: Birmingham, England, 18 November, 1921 — CF
Died: Poole, Dorset, England, December, 1995

League Club	Source	Date Signed	Seasons Played	Apps	Subs	Gls
Mansfield T	Army	05/46	46-47	35	-	17
Plymouth Arg	Yeovil T	10/49	49-50	11	-	4
Leyton Orient	Tr	07/51	51	12	-	1

BRYANT Jeffrey Stephen (Jeff)
Born: Redhill, Surrey, England, 27 November, 1953 — D
England: Youth

League Club	Source	Date Signed	Seasons Played	Apps	Subs	Gls
Wimbledon	Walton & Hersham	08/72	77-78	70	3	9
Bournemouth	Tr	06/79	79	16	0	2

BRYANT Matthew (Matt)
Born: Bristol, England, 21 September, 1970 — CD

League Club	Source	Date Signed	Seasons Played	Apps	Subs	Gls
Bristol C	YT	07/89	90-95	201	2	7
Walsall	L	08/90	90	13	0	0
Gillingham	Tr	08/96	96-99	82	21	0

BRYANT Richard John
Born: Bristol, England, 20 June, 1963 — CD

League Club	Source	Date Signed	Seasons Played	Apps	Subs	Gls
Bristol C	Robinson's DRG	12/85	85	2	0	1

BRYANT Simon Christopher
Born: Bristol, England, 22 November, 1982 — M
England: Youth

League Club	Source	Date Signed	Seasons Played	Apps	Subs	Gls
Bristol Rov	YT	01/00	99-03	65	22	2

BRYANT Steven Paul (Steve)
Born: Islington, N London, England, 5 September, 1953 — LB

League Club	Source	Date Signed	Seasons Played	Apps	Subs	Gls
Birmingham C	App	07/71	74-75	34	2	1
Sheffield Wed	L	08/76	76	2	1	0
Northampton T	Tr	12/76	76-78	95	2	5
Portsmouth	Tr	03/79	78-81	111	0	5
Northampton T	Tr	03/82	81	10	0	0

BRYCELAND Thomas (Tommy)
Born: Greenock, Inverclyde, Scotland, 1 March, 1939 — M
Scotland: Schools

League Club	Source	Date Signed	Seasons Played	Apps	Subs	Gls
Norwich C	St Mirren	09/62	62-69	253	1	49
Oldham Ath	Tr	03/70	69-71	66	0	10

BRYDON Ian Forrester
Born: Edinburgh, Scotland, 22 March, 1927 — CF
Died: Spain, 22 July, 1973

League Club	Source	Date Signed	Seasons Played	Apps	Subs	Gls
Darlington	Alloa Ath	09/53	53	1	-	0
Accrington Stan	Tr	11/53	53-54	27	-	19
Bradford Park Ave	Tr	06/55	55	12	-	3

BRYDON Lee
Born: Stockton-on-Tees, Cleveland, England, 15 November, 1974 — M
England: Schools

League Club	Source	Date Signed	Seasons Played	Apps	Subs	Gls
Liverpool	YT	06/92				
Darlington	Tr	08/96	96-97	28	12	0

BRYNGELSSON Fredrik
Born: Gothenburg, Sweden, 10 April, 1975 — RB

League Club	Source	Date Signed	Seasons Played	Apps	Subs	Gls
Stockport Co	BK Hacken (SWE)	07/00	00-01	7	1	0

BRYSON Craig James
Born: Rutherglen, Glasgow, Scotland, 6 November, 1986 — M
Scotland: 2/U21-1

League Club	Source	Date Signed	Seasons Played	Apps	Subs	Gls
Derby Co	Kilmarnock	06/11	11-14	149	15	31

BRYSON James Ian Cook (Ian)
Born: Kilmarnock, Ayrshire, Scotland, 26 November, 1962 — LW/M

League Club	Source	Date Signed	Seasons Played	Apps	Subs	Gls
Sheffield U	Kilmarnock	08/88	88-92	138	17	36
Barnsley	Tr	08/93	93	16	0	3
Preston NE	Tr	11/93	93-96	141	10	19
Rochdale	Tr	07/97	97-98	43	11	1
BUABEN Prince Christian Abankwah						
Born: Akosombo, Ghana, 23 April, 1988						M
Ghana: 2						
Watford	Dundee U	07/11	11-12	21	10	0
Carlisle U	Tr	10/13	13	10	2	1
BUARI Malik						
Born: Accra, Ghana, 21 January, 1984						M
Fulham	Sch	07/03	03	1	2	0
BUBB Alvin Ryan						
Born: Paddington, Central London, England, 11 October, 1980						M
Queens Park Rgrs	YT	11/98	00	0	1	0
Bristol Rov	Tr	07/01	01	3	10	0
BUBB Bradley Joseph						
Born: Harrow, NW London, England, 30 May, 1988						F
Grenada: 11						
Aldershot T	Farnborough T	06/11	11	1	8	0
BUBB Byron James						
Born: Harrow, NW London, England, 17 December, 1981						W
Millwall	YT	12/98	98-00	3	5	0
BUCHAN Alastair Reid						
Born: Aberdeen, Scotland, 27 May, 1926						LH
Died: Aberdeen, Scotland, 25 May, 2004						
Rochdale	Huntly	02/51	50-53	107	-	2
BUCHAN George						
Born: Aberdeen, Scotland, 2 May, 1950						RW
Manchester U	Aberdeen	05/73	73	0	3	0
Bury	Tr	08/74	74-75	57	8	6
BUCHAN Martin McLean						
Born: Aberdeen, Scotland, 6 March, 1949						CD
Scotland: 34/U23-3						
Manchester U	Aberdeen	03/72	71-82	376	0	4
Oldham Ath	Tr	08/83	83-84	28	0	0
BUCHAN Thomas (Tom)						
Born: Edinburgh, Scotland, 6 December, 1915						WH
Died: Blackpool, Lancashire, England, 12 July, 1980						
Blackpool	Woodhall Thistle	05/38	46-47	12	-	0
Carlisle U	Tr	08/49	49	30	-	0
BUCHAN William Ralston Murray (Willie)						
Born: Grangemouth, Falkirk, Scotland, 17 October, 1914						IF
Died: Polmont, Falkirk, Scotland, 6 July, 2003						
Scotland: SLge-2/War-1						
Blackpool	Glasgow Celtic	11/37	37-47	94	-	35
Hull C	Tr	01/48	47-48	40	-	12
Gateshead	Tr	11/49	49-51	89	-	16
BUCHANAN Cameron Campbell						
Born: Holytown, Lanarkshire, Scotland, 31 July, 1928						IF
Died: Kirkcaldy, Fife, Scotland, 10 September, 2008						
Wolverhampton W	Jnr	09/45				
Bournemouth	Tr	08/49	49-54	83	-	18
Norwich C	Montreal Ukr'ia (CAN)	10/56	56	3	-	0
BUCHANAN David						
Born: Newcastle-upon-Tyne, England, 23 June, 1962						F
England: Semi Pro/Youth						
Leicester C	App	06/79	78-82	24	9	7
Northampton T	L	10/82	82	3	2	0
Peterborough U	Tr	08/83	83	13	3	4
Sunderland	Blyth Spartans	08/86	86-87	25	9	8
York C	L	09/87	87	7	0	2
BUCHANAN David Thomas Hugh						
Born: Rochdale, Greater Manchester, England, 6 May, 1986						LB
Northern Ireland: U21-15/Youth						
Bury	Sch	07/05	04-09	165	21	0
Tranmere Rov	Hamilton Academical	07/11	11	41	0	1
Preston NE	Tr	07/12	12-14	60	9	0
BUCHANAN John (Jock)						
Born: Bonnybridge, Falkirk, Scotland, 9 June, 1928						CF
Died: Bradford, England, December, 2000						
Derby Co	Clyde	02/55	54-56	32	-	12
Bradford Park Ave	Tr	12/57	57-62	164	-	67
BUCHANAN John						
Born: Dingwall, Highlands, Scotland, 19 September, 1951						M

League Club	Source	Date Signed	Seasons Played	Apps	Subs	Gls
Northampton T	Ross Co	11/70	70-74	104	10	25
Cardiff C	Tr	10/74	74-81	217	14	54
Northampton T	Tr	09/81	81-82	66	3	6
BUCHANAN John (Jock)						
Born: Cumbernauld, Lanarkshire, Scotland, 3 January, 1935						CF
Died: Edinburgh, Scotland, 1 January, 2009						
Newport Co	Raith Rov	08/61	61	31	-	8
BUCHANAN Peter Symington						
Born: Glasgow, Scotland, 13 October, 1915						RW
Died: Strathaven, Lanarkshire, Scotland, 26 June, 1977						
Scotland: 1						
Chelsea	Wishaw Jnrs	11/35	36-38	39	-	6
Fulham	Tr	03/46	46	20	-	1
Brentford	Tr	08/47	47-48	74	-	13
BUCHANAN Wayne Bernard						
Born: Banbridge, Down, Northern Ireland, 12 January, 1982						CD
Northern Ireland: U21/Youth/Schools						
Bolton W	YT	07/01				
Chesterfield	L	03/02	01	3	0	0
BUCHANAN William Mack (Billy)						
Born: Tannochside, Lanarkshire, Scotland, 29 July, 1924						LB
Died: Carlisle, Cumbria, England, 14 June, 1999						
Carlisle U	Motherwell	07/49	49	9	-	0
Barrow	Tr	10/49	49-55	242	-	0
BUCK Alan Michael						
Born: Colchester, Essex, England, 25 August, 1946						G
Colchester U	Jnr	07/64	64-68	39	0	0
BUCK Anthony Rowland (Tony)						
Born: Clowne, Derbyshire, England, 18 August, 1944						F
Oxford U	Eastbourne	08/62	62-67	30	5	6
Newport Co	Tr	12/67	67-68	49	0	16
Rochdale	Tr	02/69	68-72	73	10	29
Bradford C	L	01/72	71	3	0	0
Northampton T	Tr	01/73	72-73	16	1	3
BUCK David Colin						
Born: Colchester, Essex, England, 25 August, 1946						WH
Died: Debenham, Suffolk, England, May, 1996						
Colchester U	Jnr	05/65	65	0	1	0
BUCK George William						
Born: Abingdon, Oxfordshire, England, 25 January, 1941						W
Reading	Jnr	01/58	58-60	31	-	4
Stockport Co	Tr	07/62	62	3	-	0
BUCKINGHAM Colin Maurice Ernest						
Born: Plymouth, England, 12 August, 1943						LH
Plymouth Arg	App	08/61	62-65	16	0	0
Exeter C	Tr	09/65	65-66	29	0	0
BUCKINGHAM Victor Frederick (Vic)						
Born: Greenwich, SE London, England, 23 October, 1915						LB/LH
Died: Chichester, West Sussex, England, 26 January, 1995						
England: War-2						
Tottenham H	Jnr	05/35	35-48	204	-	1
BUCKLAND Mark Christopher						
Born: Cheltenham, Gloucestershire, England, 18 August, 1961						M
Wolverhampton W	AP Leamington	02/84	83-84	44	6	5
BUCKLE Herbert Edward William (Ted)						
Born: Southwark, S London, England, 28 October, 1924						W
Died: Trafford, Greater Manchester, England, 14 June, 1990						
Manchester U	Royal Navy	11/45	46-49	20	-	6
Everton	Tr	11/49	49-54	97	-	31
Exeter C	Tr	07/55	55-56	65	-	12
BUCKLE Paul John						
Born: Hatfield, Hertfordshire, England, 16 December, 1970						M
Brentford	YT	07/89	87-92	42	15	1
Torquay U	Tr	02/94	93-95	57	2	9
Exeter C	Tr	10/95	95	22	0	2
Colchester U	Wycombe W (NC)	11/96	96-98	96	9	7
Exeter C	Tr	07/99	99-01	85	8	5
BUCKLEY Adam Christian						
Born: Nottingham, England, 2 August, 1979						M
Grimsby T	West Bromwich A (YT)	08/97	98-99	8	7	0
Lincoln C	Tr	07/01	01-02	19	15	0
BUCKLEY Alan Peter						
Born: Eastwood, Nottinghamshire, England, 20 April, 1951						F
Nottingham F	App	04/68	71-72	16	2	1
Walsall	Tr	08/73	73-78	241	0	125
Birmingham C	Tr	10/78	78	24	4	8
Walsall	Tr	07/79	79-84	161	17	49

BUCKLEY Ambrose (Amby)
Born: Brinsley, Nottinghamshire, England, 31 January, 1909 LB
Died: Manchester, England, 2 September, 1968

League Club	Source	Date Signed	Seasons Played	Apps	Subs	Gls
Fulham	Sherwood Foresters	03/33	34-38	6	-	0
Doncaster Rov	Tr	05/39				
Stockport Co	Dartford	11/45	46	11	-	0

BUCKLEY Frank Leslie
Born: Lichfield, Staffordshire, England, 11 May, 1922 WH
Died: Woking, Surrey, England, 26 February, 1973

League Club	Source	Date Signed	Seasons Played	Apps	Subs	Gls
Notts Co	Jnr	08/39				
Crystal Palace	Tr	11/46	47-50	69	-	0

BUCKLEY Gary
Born: Manchester, England, 3 March, 1961 M

League Club	Source	Date Signed	Seasons Played	Apps	Subs	Gls
Manchester C	App	04/78	80	4	2	0
Preston NE	Tr	10/81	81-82	27	7	0
Bury	Chorley	03/84	83-85	23	8	1

BUCKLEY Glen
Born: Wigan, Greater Manchester, England, 31 August, 1960 F

League Club	Source	Date Signed	Seasons Played	Apps	Subs	Gls
Wigan Ath	Preston NE (NC)	10/79	79	1	0	0

BUCKLEY Ian
Born: Oldham, Greater Manchester, England, 8 October, 1953 LB
England: Youth

League Club	Source	Date Signed	Seasons Played	Apps	Subs	Gls
Oldham Ath	App	12/71	71	5	0	0
Rochdale	L	02/74	73	6	0	0
Stockport Co	Tr	08/75	75-76	55	10	2
Cambridge U	Durban C (RSA)	11/77	77-80	51	6	2

BUCKLEY John William
Born: East Kilbride, Lanarkshire, Scotland, 18 May, 1962 RW

League Club	Source	Date Signed	Seasons Played	Apps	Subs	Gls
Doncaster Rov	Partick Thistle	07/84	84-85	79	5	11
Leeds U	Tr	06/86	86-87	6	4	1
Leicester C	L	03/87	86	1	4	0
Doncaster Rov	L	10/87	87	6	0	0
Rotherham U	Tr	11/87	87-90	85	20	13
Scunthorpe U	Partick Thistle	08/91	91-92	39	4	8
Rotherham U	Tr	02/93	92	2	2	0

BUCKLEY Michael John (Mick)
Born: Manchester, England, 4 November, 1953 M
Died: Whitefield, Greater Manchester, England, 7 October, 2013
England: U23-1/Youth/Schools

League Club	Source	Date Signed	Seasons Played	Apps	Subs	Gls
Everton	App	06/71	71-77	128	7	10
Sunderland	Tr	08/78	78-82	117	4	7
Hartlepool U	Tr	08/83	83	6	0	0
Carlisle U	Tr	09/83	83	24	1	2
Middlesbrough	Tr	06/84	84	27	0	0

BUCKLEY Neil Anthony
Born: Hull, England, 25 September, 1968 CD

League Club	Source	Date Signed	Seasons Played	Apps	Subs	Gls
Hull C	App	12/86	86-91	55	5	3
Burnley	L	03/90	89	5	0	0

BUCKLEY Patrick McCabe (Pat)
Born: Leith, Edinburgh, Scotland, 12 August, 1946 LW

League Club	Source	Date Signed	Seasons Played	Apps	Subs	Gls
Wolverhampton W	Third Lanark	02/64	64-67	28	1	8
Sheffield U	Tr	01/68	67-70	9	6	2
Rotherham U	Tr	06/72	72	1	2	0

BUCKLEY Steven (Steve)
Born: Eastwood, Nottinghamshire, England, 16 October, 1953 LB

League Club	Source	Date Signed	Seasons Played	Apps	Subs	Gls
Luton T	Burton A	04/74	74-77	123	0	9
Derby Co	Tr	01/78	77-85	323	0	21
Lincoln C	Tr	08/86	86	36	0	2

BUCKLEY William Edward (Will)
Born: Oldham, Greater Manchester, England, 21 November, 1989 LW

League Club	Source	Date Signed	Seasons Played	Apps	Subs	Gls
Rochdale	Curzon Ashton	09/07	07-09	41	18	14
Watford	Tr	01/10	09-10	31	8	5
Brighton & HA	Tr	06/11	11-14	64	32	19
Sunderland	Tr	08/14	14	9	13	0

BUDD Kevin John
Born: Hillingdon, W London, England, 20 March, 1962 FB

League Club	Source	Date Signed	Seasons Played	Apps	Subs	Gls
Norwich C	Bournemouth (App)	10/79				
Manchester C	Tr	02/81				
Swansea C	Hillingdon Bor	11/85	85	1	0	0

BUDDLE Nathan John
Born: Amble, Northumberland, England, 29 September, 1993 CD

League Club	Source	Date Signed	Seasons Played	Apps	Subs	Gls
Hartlepool U	Sch	07/12				
Carlisle U	Blyth Spartans	02/15	14	1	2	0

BUDTZ Jan
Born: Fanum, Denmark, 20 April, 1979 G

League Club	Source	Date Signed	Seasons Played	Apps	Subs	Gls
Doncaster Rov	Nordsjaelland (DEN)	07/05	05-06	26	1	0
Wolverhampton W	L	01/07	06	2	2	0
Hartlepool U	Tr	07/07	07-08	37	1	0
Oldham Ath	L	02/09	08	3	0	0

BUENO Alberto
Born: Madrid, Spain, 20 March, 1988 W
Spain: U21-1/Youth

League Club	Source	Date Signed	Seasons Played	Apps	Subs	Gls
Derby Co (L)	Real Valladolid (SPN)	08/10	10	25	4	5

BUGG Alec Alfred
Born: Needham Market, Suffolk, England, 27 November, 1948 G

League Club	Source	Date Signed	Seasons Played	Apps	Subs	Gls
Ipswich T	Jnr	06/67	68-69	4	0	0
Bournemouth	L	02/70	69	4	0	0

BUGGIE Lee David
Born: Bury, Greater Manchester, England, 11 February, 1981 F

League Club	Source	Date Signed	Seasons Played	Apps	Subs	Gls
Bolton W	YT	02/98				
Bury	Tr	05/99	99	0	1	0
Rochdale	L	09/00	00	0	2	0

BUGNO Alessio
Born: Milan, Italy, 23 March, 1990 LB

League Club	Source	Date Signed	Seasons Played	Apps	Subs	Gls
Carlisle U	Monza (ITA)	08/12	12	2	0	0

BUICK Joseph Arnot Lorimer (Joe)
Born: Broughty Ferry, Angus, Scotland, 1 July, 1933 WH

League Club	Source	Date Signed	Seasons Played	Apps	Subs	Gls
Lincoln C	Broughty Ath	10/55	55-61	31	-	3

BUIST James Gibb (Jimmy)
Born: Falkirk, Scotland, 19 June, 1918 W
Died: Inverness, Scotland, 6 September, 1999

League Club	Source	Date Signed	Seasons Played	Apps	Subs	Gls
New Brighton	Dundee	08/46	46	21	-	6
Plymouth Arg	Tr	06/47	48	1	-	0

BUKOVINA John Frank
Born: Barnsley, South Yorkshire, England, 2 February, 1964 F

League Club	Source	Date Signed	Seasons Played	Apps	Subs	Gls
Barnsley	App	02/82				
Doncaster Rov	Tr	08/83	83	1	0	0

BUKOWSKI David
Born: Willington, County Durham, England, 2 November, 1952 CD

League Club	Source	Date Signed	Seasons Played	Apps	Subs	Gls
Northampton T	App	11/70	71-72	10	3	0

BUKRAN Gabor
Born: Eger, Hungary, 16 November, 1975 M
Hungary: 1/U21-2/Youth

League Club	Source	Date Signed	Seasons Played	Apps	Subs	Gls
Walsall	Xerez CD (SPN)	08/99	99-00	63	10	4
Wigan Ath	Tr	08/01	01	1	0	0

BULCH Robert Stephen (Bobby)
Born: Washington, Tyne and Wear, England, 1 January, 1933 WH
Died: Sunderland, England, May, 2012

League Club	Source	Date Signed	Seasons Played	Apps	Subs	Gls
Notts Co	Washington	03/53	55-57	27	-	1
Darlington	Tr	06/58	58-59	45	-	1
Hartlepool U	Tr	11/60				

BULL Gary William
Born: West Bromwich, West Midlands, England, 12 June, 1966 F

League Club	Source	Date Signed	Seasons Played	Apps	Subs	Gls
Southampton	Paget Rgrs	10/86				
Cambridge U	Tr	03/88	87-88	13	6	4
Barnet	Tr	03/89	91-92	83	0	37
Nottingham F	Tr	07/93	93-94	4	8	1
Birmingham C	L	09/94	94	10	0	6
Brighton & HA	L	08/95	95	10	0	2
Birmingham C	Tr	12/95	95	3	3	0
York C	Tr	03/96	95-97	66	17	11
Scunthorpe U	Tr	07/98	98-99	7	23	1

BULL Michael Frederick (Mickey)
Born: Twickenham, W London, England, 3 April, 1930 W
Died: Hull, England, December, 2011

League Club	Source	Date Signed	Seasons Played	Apps	Subs	Gls
Brentford		09/48	52	3	-	0
Swindon T	Tr	06/53	53-54	69	-	15

BULL Nikki
Born: Hastings, East Sussex, England, 2 October, 1981 G
England: Semi Pro-4

League Club	Source	Date Signed	Seasons Played	Apps	Subs	Gls
Queens Park Rgrs	YT	07/99				
Aldershot T	Tr	05/02	08	30	0	0
Brentford	Tr	08/09	09	5	1	0
Wycombe W	Tr	07/10	10-12	101	0	0

BULL Ronald Rodney (Ronnie)
Born: Hackney, E London, England, 26 December, 1980 LB

League Club	Source	Date Signed	Seasons Played	Apps	Subs	Gls
Millwall	YT	05/99	98-02	37	13	0
Yeovil T	L	09/03	03	7	0	0
Brentford	L	01/04	03	20	0	0
Grimsby T	Tr	07/04	04	22	5	2
Rushden & D	NZ Knights (NZL)	01/06	05	19	0	0
Exeter C	Hayes & Yeading U	12/08				

BULL Stephen George (Steve)
Born: Tipton, West Midlands, England, 28 March, 1965 — F
England: 13/B-5/U21-5

League Club	Source	Date Signed	Seasons Played	Apps	Subs	Gls
West Bromwich A	Tipton T	08/85	85-86	2	2	2
Wolverhampton W	Tr	11/86	86-98	461	13	250

BULL William Henry (Bill)
Born: Birmingham, England, 1 April, 1926 — CF
Died: Rushcliffe, Nottinghamshire, England, April, 2006

League Club	Source	Date Signed	Seasons Played	Apps	Subs	Gls
Coventry C		03/48	48	1	-	0

BULLARD James Richard (Jimmy)
Born: East Ham, E London, England, 23 October, 1978 — M

League Club	Source	Date Signed	Seasons Played	Apps	Subs	Gls
West Ham U	Gravesend & Northfleet	02/99				
Peterborough U	Tr	07/01	01-02	62	4	11
Wigan Ath	Tr	01/03	02-05	144	1	10
Fulham	Tr	05/06	06-08	37	2	6
Hull C	Tr	01/09	08-10	18	5	7
Ipswich T	L	01/11	10	16	0	5
Ipswich T	Tr	08/11	11	12	9	1
MK Dons	Tr	08/12	12	0	2	0

BULLEN Lee
Born: Edinburgh, Scotland, 29 March, 1971 — D

League Club	Source	Date Signed	Seasons Played	Apps	Subs	Gls
Sheffield Wed	Dunfermline Ath	07/04	04-07	108	26	8

BULLESS Brian
Born: Hull, England, 4 September, 1933 — LH/LB

League Club	Source	Date Signed	Seasons Played	Apps	Subs	Gls
Hull C	Jnr	10/50	52-63	326	-	30

BULLIMORE Alwyn Arthur (Alan)
Born: Norwich, England, 22 October, 1933 — WH
Died: Norwich, England, 24 October, 2001

League Club	Source	Date Signed	Seasons Played	Apps	Subs	Gls
Norwich C	Jnr	10/53	56	1	-	0

BULLIMORE Wayne Alan
Born: Sutton-in-Ashfield, Nottinghamshire, England, 12 September, 1970 — M
England: Youth

League Club	Source	Date Signed	Seasons Played	Apps	Subs	Gls
Manchester U	YT	09/88				
Barnsley	Tr	03/91	91-92	27	8	1
Scunthorpe U	Stockport Co (NC)	11/93	93-95	62	5	11
Bradford C	Tr	12/95	95	1	1	0
Doncaster Rov	L	09/96	96	4	0	0
Peterborough U	Tr	03/97	96-97	10	11	1
Scarborough	Tr	08/98	98	33	2	1

BULLIONS James Law (Jimmy)
Born: Dennyloanhead, Falkirk, Scotland, 12 March, 1924 — WH
Died: Barlborough, Derbyshire, England, 27 January, 2014

League Club	Source	Date Signed	Seasons Played	Apps	Subs	Gls
Derby Co	Chesterfield (Am)	10/44	46-47	17	-	0
Leeds U	Tr	11/47	47-49	35	-	0
Shrewsbury T	Tr	09/50	50-53	131	-	2

BULLIVANT Terence Paul (Terry)
Born: Lambeth, S London, England, 23 September, 1956 — M

League Club	Source	Date Signed	Seasons Played	Apps	Subs	Gls
Fulham	App	05/74	74-79	94	7	2
Aston Villa	Tr	11/79	79-81	10	2	0
Charlton Ath	Tr	07/82	82	30	0	3
Brentford	Tr	07/83	83-85	36	1	2

BULLOCK Anthony Brian (Tony)
Born: Warrington, Cheshire, England, 18 February, 1972 — G

League Club	Source	Date Signed	Seasons Played	Apps	Subs	Gls
Barnsley	Leek T	03/97	98-99	37	1	0
Macclesfield T	Tr	07/00	00	24	0	0
Lincoln C	Tr	03/01	00	2	0	0
Gillingham	Dundee U	08/05	05	6	0	0

BULLOCK Darren John
Born: Worcester, England, 12 February, 1969 — M

League Club	Source	Date Signed	Seasons Played	Apps	Subs	Gls
Huddersfield T	Nuneaton Bor	11/93	93-96	127	1	16
Swindon T	Tr	02/97	96-98	55	11	2
Bury	Tr	02/99	98-01	45	8	5
Sheffield U	L	03/01	00	6	0	0

BULLOCK Lee
Born: Stockton-on-Tees, Cleveland, England, 22 May, 1981 — M

League Club	Source	Date Signed	Seasons Played	Apps	Subs	Gls
York C	YT	06/99	99-03	156	15	24
Cardiff C	Tr	03/04	03-04	12	20	6
Hartlepool U	Tr	07/05	05-07	30	27	5
Mansfield T	L	08/07	07	5	0	0
Bury	L	10/07	07	8	0	0
Bradford C	Tr	01/08	07-11	104	17	5
York C	Tr	07/12	12	1	11	0

BULLOCK Martin John
Born: Derby, England, 5 March, 1975 — RW
England: U21-1

League Club	Source	Date Signed	Seasons Played	Apps	Subs	Gls
Barnsley	Eastwood T	09/93	94-00	108	77	4
Port Vale	L	01/00	99	6	0	1
Blackpool	Tr	08/01	01-04	128	25	4
Macclesfield T	Tr	07/05	05-06	76	7	11
Wycombe W	Tr	07/07	07	17	8	0

BULLOCK Matthew
Born: Stoke-on-Trent, England, 1 November, 1980 — M
England: Youth

League Club	Source	Date Signed	Seasons Played	Apps	Subs	Gls
Stoke C	YT	11/97	99	4	3	0
Macclesfield T	L	10/01	01	2	1	0

BULLOCK Michael Edwin (Mickey)
Born: Stoke-on-Trent, England, 2 October, 1946 — F
England: Schools

League Club	Source	Date Signed	Seasons Played	Apps	Subs	Gls
Birmingham C	App	10/63	63-66	27	0	10
Oxford U	Tr	06/67	67-68	58	1	15
Leyton Orient	Tr	10/68	68-75	267	10	65
Halifax T	Tr	02/76	75-78	98	8	19

BULLOCK Norman
Born: Nuneaton, Warwickshire, England, 26 March, 1932 — W
Died: Chester, England, 2 October, 2003

League Club	Source	Date Signed	Seasons Played	Apps	Subs	Gls
Aston Villa	Nuneaton Bor	09/49				
Chester C	Tr	07/52	52-59	187	-	41

BULLOCK Peter Leonard
Born: Stoke-on-Trent, England, 17 November, 1941 — IF
England: Youth/Schools

League Club	Source	Date Signed	Seasons Played	Apps	Subs	Gls
Stoke C	Jnr	11/58	57-61	44	-	13
Birmingham C	Tr	03/62	61-64	27	-	3
Southend U	Tr	02/65	64-65	12	0	2
Colchester U	Tr	10/65	65-67	94	1	33
Exeter C	Tr	07/68	68	14	0	2
Walsall	Tr	12/68	68	7	0	0

BULLOCK Simon John
Born: Stoke-on-Trent, England, 28 September, 1962 — LW

League Club	Source	Date Signed	Seasons Played	Apps	Subs	Gls
Halifax T	Stoke C (App)	09/80	80-81	15	2	1

BULLOCK Steven (Steve)
Born: Stockport, Greater Manchester, England, 5 October, 1966 — D/M

League Club	Source	Date Signed	Seasons Played	Apps	Subs	Gls
Oldham Ath	Jnr	07/84	83-85	10	8	0
Tranmere Rov	Tr	08/86	86	25	5	1
Stockport Co	Tr	08/87	87-90	106	14	0

BULMAN Dannie
Born: Ashford, Surrey, England, 24 January, 1979 — M

League Club	Source	Date Signed	Seasons Played	Apps	Subs	Gls
Wycombe W	Ashford T, Kent	06/98	98-03	160	42	14
Oxford U	Crawley T	07/09	10	4	1	0
Crawley T	Oxford U	09/10	11-13	101	15	4
AFC Wimbledon	Tr	06/14	14	40	1	1

BULMER Peter
Born: Liverpool, England, 31 August, 1965 — LB/M

League Club	Source	Date Signed	Seasons Played	Apps	Subs	Gls
Chester C	App	08/83	82-84	56	15	2
Preston NE	Rhyl	07/86	86	4	0	0

BULOT Frederic
Born: Libreville, Gabon, 27 September, 1990 — M
France: U21-9/Youth//Gabon: 11

League Club	Source	Date Signed	Seasons Played	Apps	Subs	Gls
Charlton Ath (L)	Standard Liege (BEL)	08/14	14	19	9	5

BULZIS Riccardo
Born: Bedford, England, 22 November, 1974 — F

League Club	Source	Date Signed	Seasons Played	Apps	Subs	Gls
Northampton T	YT	-	91	1	3	0

BUMPSTEAD David John (Dave)
Born: Rainham, E London, England, 6 November, 1935 — RH
England: Amateur-1

League Club	Source	Date Signed	Seasons Played	Apps	Subs	Gls
Millwall	Tooting & Mitcham U	06/58	57-61	84	-	8
Bristol Rov	Tr	12/61	61-63	40	-	0

BUMSTEAD Charles Henry (Charlie)
Born: Croydon, S London, England, 8 January, 1922 — G
Died: Lambeth, S London, England, 6 May, 1974

League Club	Source	Date Signed	Seasons Played	Apps	Subs	Gls
Millwall		03/43	46-47	12	-	0
Crystal Palace	Tr	08/48	48-51	53	-	0

BUMSTEAD John
Born: Rotherhithe, SE London, England, 27 November, 1958 — M

League Club	Source	Date Signed	Seasons Played	Apps	Subs	Gls
Chelsea	App	11/76	78-90	314	25	38
Charlton Ath	Tr	07/91	91-92	54	2	3

BUMSTEAD Raymond George (Ray)
Born: Ringwood, Hampshire, England, 27 January, 1936 — RW
Died: Bournemouth, England, 17 January, 2013

League Club	Source	Date Signed	Seasons Played	Apps	Subs	Gls
Bournemouth	Ringwood T	05/58	58-69	412	3	55

BUNBURY Alexander (Alex)
Born: Georgetown, Guyana, 18 June, 1967 — F
Canada: 65/Youth

League Club	Source	Date Signed	Seasons Played	Apps	Subs	Gls
West Ham U	Montreal Supra (CAN)	12/92	92	2	2	0

BUNCE Frederick (Freddie)
Born: Watford, Hertfordshire, England, 16 February, 1938 — LW
Died: Victoria, Australia, 9 October, 1991
England: Youth

League Club	Source	Date Signed	Seasons Played	Apps	Subs	Gls
Watford	Jnr	10/55	55-62	150	-	34

BUNCE Paul Eric
Born: Coalville, Leicestershire, England, 7 January, 1967 — RW

League Club	Source	Date Signed	Seasons Played	Apps	Subs	Gls
Leicester C	App	01/85	86	5	1	0
Northampton T	Tr	03/87	86-87	6	6	2

BUNCLARK Cyril
Born: Rotherham, South Yorkshire, England, 27 March, 1931 — W

League Club	Source	Date Signed	Seasons Played	Apps	Subs	Gls
Rotherham U		11/53	54	2	-	1

BUNJEVCEVIC Goran Petar
Born: Karlovac, Croatia, 17 February, 1973 — CD
Yugoslavia: 16

League Club	Source	Date Signed	Seasons Played	Apps	Subs	Gls
Tottenham H	R Star Belgrade (YUG)	07/01	01-04	41	10	0

BUNKELL Raymond Keith (Ray)
Born: Edmonton, N London, England, 18 September, 1949 — M
Died: Gresford, Wrexham, Wales, 15 March, 2000

League Club	Source	Date Signed	Seasons Played	Apps	Subs	Gls
Tottenham H	App	06/67				
Swindon T	Tr	06/71	71-73	52	4	3
Colchester U	Tr	12/73	73-79	117	12	9

BUNN Frank Stephen (Frankie)
Born: Birmingham, England, 6 November, 1962 — F

League Club	Source	Date Signed	Seasons Played	Apps	Subs	Gls
Luton T	App	05/80	80-84	52	7	9
Hull C	Tr	07/85	85-87	89	6	23
Oldham Ath	Tr	12/87	87-89	75	3	26

BUNN Harry Charles
Born: Oldham, Greater Manchester, England, 25 November, 1992 — F

League Club	Source	Date Signed	Seasons Played	Apps	Subs	Gls
Manchester C	Sch	07/10				
Rochdale	L	11/11	11	5	1	0
Preston NE	L	01/12	11	1	0	1
Oldham Ath	L	03/12	11	8	3	0
Crewe Alex	L	08/12	12	2	2	0
Sheffield U	L	09/13	13	0	2	0
Huddersfield T	Tr	01/14	13-14	24	9	9

BUNN Mark John
Born: Southgate, N London, England, 16 November, 1984 — G

League Club	Source	Date Signed	Seasons Played	Apps	Subs	Gls
Northampton T	Sch	07/04	06-08	90	0	0
Blackburn Rov	Tr	09/08	10-11	5	1	0
Leicester C	L	02/09	08	3	0	0
Sheffield U	L	07/09	09	31	1	0
Norwich C	Tr	08/12	12	22	1	0

BUNNER Henry Francis (Harry)
Born: Manchester, England, 18 September, 1936 — CH

League Club	Source	Date Signed	Seasons Played	Apps	Subs	Gls
Bury	Bury Amats	04/57	57-64	105	-	0
Stockport Co	Tr	04/65	65	3	0	0

BUNNEY Joseph Elliott (Joe)
Born: Manchester, England, 26 September, 1993 — F

League Club	Source	Date Signed	Seasons Played	Apps	Subs	Gls
Rochdale	Northwich Victoria	03/13	12-14	17	24	6

BUNTING Benjamin (Ben)
Born: Rochdale, Greater Manchester, England, 14 February, 1923 — FB
Died: Rochdale, Greater Manchester, England, August, 2007

League Club	Source	Date Signed	Seasons Played	Apps	Subs	Gls
Oldham Ath	Rochdale (Am)	08/46	46-47	32	-	0

BURBANKS William Edwin (Eddie)
Born: Campsall, South Yorkshire, England, 1 April, 1913 — LW
Died: Hull, England, 26 July, 1983

League Club	Source	Date Signed	Seasons Played	Apps	Subs	Gls
Sunderland	Denaby U	02/35	34-47	131	-	25
Hull C	Tr	06/48	48-52	143	-	21
Leeds U	Tr	07/53	53	13	-	1

BURBECK Ronald Thomas (Ron)
Born: Leicester, England, 27 February, 1934 — LW
England: Youth

League Club	Source	Date Signed	Seasons Played	Apps	Subs	Gls
Leicester C	Jnr	05/52	52-55	3	-	0
Middlesbrough	Tr	10/56	56-62	139	-	24
Darlington	Tr	08/63	63	18	-	1

BURCH Robert Keith (Rob)
Born: Yeovil, Somerset, England, 8 October, 1993 — G
England: Youth

League Club	Source	Date Signed	Seasons Played	Apps	Subs	Gls
Tottenham H	Sch	07/02				
Barnet	L	01/07	06	6	0	0
Sheffield Wed	Tr	07/07	07	2	0	0
Lincoln C	Tr	07/08	08-09	92	0	0
Notts Co	Tr	07/10	10	14	1	0

BURCHILL Mark James
Born: Broxburn, West Lothian, Scotland, 18 August, 1980 — F
Scotland: 6/U21-15/Schools

League Club	Source	Date Signed	Seasons Played	Apps	Subs	Gls
Birmingham C (L)	Glasgow Celtic	09/00	00	4	9	4
Ipswich T (L)	Glasgow Celtic	01/01	00	2	5	1
Portsmouth	Glasgow Celtic	08/01	01-02	9	15	8
Wigan Ath	L	08/03	03	1	3	0
Sheffield Wed	L	12/03	03	4	1	0
Rotherham U	L	09/04	04	3	0	1
Rotherham U	Dunfermline Ath	07/08	08	10	14	5

BURCKITT John David (Jack)
Born: Coventry, England, 16 December, 1946 — LB
Died: Nuneaton, Warwickshire, England, 1 November, 1999
England: Youth

League Club	Source	Date Signed	Seasons Played	Apps	Subs	Gls
Coventry C	Jnr	07/64	64	5	-	0
Bradford C	L	03/67	66	9	0	0
Walsall	Tr	06/68				

BURDEN Brian
Born: West Stockwith, Lincolnshire, England, 26 November, 1939 — G

League Club	Source	Date Signed	Seasons Played	Apps	Subs	Gls
Lincoln C	West Stockwith	03/61	60	1	-	0

BURDEN Ian
Born: Bradford, England, 27 May, 1944 — CF

League Club	Source	Date Signed	Seasons Played	Apps	Subs	Gls
York C (Am)	Poppleton Road	10/65	65	3	0	2

BURDEN Thomas David (Tommy)
Born: Andover, Hampshire, England, 21 February, 1924 — WH/IF
Died: Street, Somerset, England, 1 October, 2001

League Club	Source	Date Signed	Seasons Played	Apps	Subs	Gls
Wolverhampton W	Jnr	08/41				
Chester C	Tr	11/45	46-47	82	-	40
Leeds U	Tr	07/48	48-54	243	-	13
Bristol C	Tr	10/54	54-60	231	-	20

BURDESS John
Born: East Rainton, Tyne and Wear, England, 10 April, 1946 — IF

League Club	Source	Date Signed	Seasons Played	Apps	Subs	Gls
Oldham Ath	App	04/64	63-64	3	-	0

BURGE Lee Stephen
Born: Hereford, England, 9 January, 1993 — G

League Club	Source	Date Signed	Seasons Played	Apps	Subs	Gls
Coventry C	Sch	06/11	14	18	0	0

BURGE Ryan James
Born: Cheltenham, Gloucestershire, England, 9 November, 1981 — RM

League Club	Source	Date Signed	Seasons Played	Apps	Subs	Gls
Birmingham C	Sch	10/05				
Barnet	Cheltenham T (NC)	11/08	08	1	1	0
Doncaster Rov	Jerez Industrial (SPN)	02/11	10	0	1	0
Oxford U	L	03/11	10	5	0	0
Port Vale	Hyde FC	08/11	12	23	7	2
Newport Co	Tr	08/13	13	12	5	2

BURGESS Albert Campbell (Cam)
Born: Birkenhead, Wirral, England, 21 September, 1919 — CF
Died: Birkenhead, Wirral, England, 1978

League Club	Source	Date Signed	Seasons Played	Apps	Subs	Gls
Bolton W	Bromborough	02/38	46-47	5	-	3
Chester C	Tr	10/48	48-51	111	-	64
Crystal Palace	Tr	09/51	51-52	47	-	40
York C	Tr	07/53	53	32	-	14

BURGESS Andrew John (Andy)
Born: Bozeat, Northamptonshire, England, 10 August, 1981 — LW
England: Semi Pro-8

League Club	Source	Date Signed	Seasons Played	Apps	Subs	Gls
Rushden & D	Jnr	07/99	01-05	128	19	10
Oxford U	Tr	01/06	05	12	4	1

BURGESS Benjamin Keiron (Ben)
Born: Buxton, Derbyshire, England, 9 November, 1981 — F
Republic of Ireland: U21-4/Youth

League Club	Source	Date Signed	Seasons Played	Apps	Subs	Gls
Blackburn Rov	YT	11/98	99	1	1	0
Brentford	L	08/01	01	43	0	17
Stockport Co	Tr	08/02	02	17	2	4
Oldham Ath	L	01/03	02	6	1	0
Hull C	Tr	03/03	02-05	54	16	24
Blackpool	Tr	08/06	06-09	83	43	23
Notts Co	Tr	07/10	10-11	28	17	5
Cheltenham T	L	03/12	11	6	1	2
Tranmere Rov	Tr	07/12				

BURGESS Cameron
Born: Aberdeen, Scotland, 21 October, 1995 — CD
Scotland: Youth

League Club	Source	Date Signed	Seasons Played	Apps	Subs	Gls
Fulham	Sch	07/13	14	4	0	0

BURGESS Christian Albert
Born: Hainault, NE London, England, 7 October, 1991 — CD

League Club	Source	Date Signed	Seasons Played	Apps	Subs	Gls
Middlesbrough	Birmingham Univ	07/12	12	1	0	0
Hartlepool U	L	08/13	13	41	0	0
Peterborough U	Tr	08/14	14	28	2	2

BURGESS Daryl
Born: Marston Green, West Midlands, England, 24 January, 1971 — CD

League Club	Source	Date Signed	Seasons Played	Apps	Subs	Gls
West Bromwich A	YT	07/89	89-00	317	15	10
Northampton T	Tr	07/01	01-02	60	1	2
Rochdale	Tr	08/03	03-04	52	4	0

BURGESS David John (Dave)
Born: Liverpool, England, 20 January, 1960 — FB

League Club	Source	Date Signed	Seasons Played	Apps	Subs	Gls
Tranmere Rov	Jnr	08/81	81-85	217	1	1
Grimsby T	Tr	08/86	86-87	66	3	0
Blackpool	Tr	07/88	88-92	101	0	1
Carlisle U	L	02/93	92	6	0	0
Carlisle U	Tr	06/93	93	36	4	1
Hartlepool U	L	09/94	94	11	0	0

BURGESS Eric Robert Charles
Born: Edgware, NW London, England, 27 October, 1944 — RB

League Club	Source	Date Signed	Seasons Played	Apps	Subs	Gls
Watford	App	07/62	63-64	3	-	0
Torquay U	Tr	07/65	65-67	73	1	0
Plymouth Arg	Tr	07/68	68-69	14	1	0
Colchester U	Plymouth C	12/70	70-71	46	2	9

BURGESS Kevin Matthew
Born: Middlesbrough, England, 8 January, 1988 — CD

League Club	Source	Date Signed	Seasons Played	Apps	Subs	Gls
Darlington	Middlesbrough (Sch)	01/07	06	0	1	0

BURGESS Michael (Mike)
Born: Montreal, Canada, 17 April, 1932 — CF/CH

League Club	Source	Date Signed	Seasons Played	Apps	Subs	Gls
Bradford Park Ave	Frickley Colliery	08/52				
Leyton Orient	Tr	07/53	53-55	31	-	12
Newport Co	Tr	02/56	55-56	25	-	7
Bournemouth	Tr	06/57	57-60	109	-	34
Halifax T	Tr	07/61	61-62	34	-	3
Gillingham	Tr	03/63	62-65	109	1	2
Aldershot	Tr	11/65	65	6	0	0

BURGESS Oliver David (Ollie)
Born: Bracknell, Berkshire, England, 12 October, 1981 — W

League Club	Source	Date Signed	Seasons Played	Apps	Subs	Gls
Queens Park Rgrs	YT	07/01	00-02	6	4	1
Northampton T	Tr	07/03	03	3	6	0

BURGESS Richard Daniel
Born: Bromsgrove, Worcestershire, England, 18 August, 1978 — F

League Club	Source	Date Signed	Seasons Played	Apps	Subs	Gls
Aston Villa	YT	07/96				
Stoke C	Tr	05/97				
Port Vale	Bromsgrove Rov	03/01	00-01	1	2	0

BURGESS Robert Buchanan Benwood (Bob)
Born: Glasgow, Scotland, 1 April, 1927 — CF
Died: Birmingham, England, July, 2005

League Club	Source	Date Signed	Seasons Played	Apps	Subs	Gls
Walsall (Am)	Third Lanark	09/53	53	2	-	1

BURGESS Scott
Born: Warrington, Cheshire, England, 27 June, 1996 — RM

League Club	Source	Date Signed	Seasons Played	Apps	Subs	Gls
Bury	Sch	02/15	13	1	0	0

BURGESS Walter
Born: Golborne, Greater Manchester, England, 19 June, 1921 — LB/CF
Died: Coventry, England, June, 1988

League Club	Source	Date Signed	Seasons Played	Apps	Subs	Gls
Halifax T	Coleraine	11/46	46	13	-	2

BURGESS William Arthur Ronald (Ron)
Born: Cwm, Blaenau Gwent, Wales, 9 April, 1917 — LH
Died: Swansea, Wales, 16 February, 2005
England: FLge-1//Wales: 32/War-10

League Club	Source	Date Signed	Seasons Played	Apps	Subs	Gls
Tottenham H	Cardiff C (Am)	05/36	38-53	297	-	15
Swansea C	Tr	08/54	54-55	46	-	1

BURGHER Symon George
Born: Birmingham, England, 29 October, 1966 — M

League Club	Source	Date Signed	Seasons Played	Apps	Subs	Gls
Exeter C	YT	02/85	84	11	3	0

BURGIN Andrew (Andy)
Born: Sheffield, England, 6 March, 1947 — RB

League Club	Source	Date Signed	Seasons Played	Apps	Subs	Gls
Sheffield Wed	App	03/64	64	1	-	0
Rotherham U	Tr	08/67	67	9	1	0
Halifax T	Detroit Cougars (USA)	12/68	68-74	243	0	9
Blackburn Rov	Tr	09/74	74-75	45	0	1

BURGIN Edward (Ted)
Born: Bradfield, South Yorkshire, England, 29 April, 1927 — G
England: B-2

League Club	Source	Date Signed	Seasons Played	Apps	Subs	Gls
Sheffield U	Alford T	03/49	49-56	281	-	0
Doncaster Rov	Tr	12/57	57	5	-	0
Leeds U	Tr	03/58	58-60	58	-	0
Rochdale	Tr	01/61	60-65	207	0	0

BURGIN Eric
Born: Sheffield, England, 4 January, 1924 — CH
Died: Sheffield, England, 16 November, 2012

League Club	Source	Date Signed	Seasons Played	Apps	Subs	Gls
Sheffield U		12/46				
York C	Tr	05/49	49-50	23	-	0

BURGIN Terence (Terry)
Born: Nottingham, England, 9 October, 1938 — CF

League Club	Source	Date Signed	Seasons Played	Apps	Subs	Gls
Reading		11/59	60	2	-	0

BURGIN Trevor
Born: Darfield, South Yorkshire, England, 28 August, 1943 — CD

League Club	Source	Date Signed	Seasons Played	Apps	Subs	Gls
Bradford Park Ave	Wombwell	07/67	67	12	5	0

BURGMEIER Franz
Born: Triesen, Liechtenstein, 7 April, 1982 — LM
Liechtenstein: 69

League Club	Source	Date Signed	Seasons Played	Apps	Subs	Gls
Darlington	FC Basel (SUI)	08/08	08	30	5	2

BURGSTALLER Guido
Born: Villach, Austria, 29 April, 1989 — W
Austria: 7/U21-11/Youth

League Club	Source	Date Signed	Seasons Played	Apps	Subs	Gls
Cardiff C	Rapid Vienna (AUT)	05/14	14	1	2	0

BURKE Charles (Charlie)
Born: Isle of Arran, Ayrshire, Scotland, 13 September, 1921 — RH/CF
Died: Bournemouth, England, October, 1995

League Club	Source	Date Signed	Seasons Played	Apps	Subs	Gls
Bournemouth	Ardeer Rec	06/39	46	25	-	7

BURKE Christopher Robert (Chris)
Born: Glasgow, Scotland, 2 December, 1983 — RW
Scotland: 7/B-1/U21-3

League Club	Source	Date Signed	Seasons Played	Apps	Subs	Gls
Cardiff C	Glasgow Rangers	01/09	08-10	77	25	15
Birmingham C	Tr	07/11	11-13	111	20	24
Nottingham F	Tr	07/14	14	34	7	6

BURKE David Ian
Born: Liverpool, England, 6 August, 1960 — LB
England: Youth

League Club	Source	Date Signed	Seasons Played	Apps	Subs	Gls
Bolton W	App	08/77	78-80	65	4	1
Huddersfield T	Tr	06/81	81-87	189	0	3
Crystal Palace	Tr	10/87	87-89	80	1	0
Bolton W	Tr	07/90	90-93	104	2	0
Blackpool	Tr	07/94	94	23	0	0

BURKE Graham Dylan
Born: Dublin, Republic of Ireland, 21 September, 1993 — F
Republic of Ireland: U21-3/Youth

League Club	Source	Date Signed	Seasons Played	Apps	Subs	Gls
Aston Villa	Sch	09/10				
Shrewsbury T	L	08/13	13	1	2	0
Notts Co	L	03/15	14	6	1	1

BURKE James Oliver
Born: Shepley, West Yorkshire, England, 16 April, 1994 — RB

League Club	Source	Date Signed	Seasons Played	Apps	Subs	Gls
Huddersfield T	Sch	07/12				
Bury	Tr	01/14	13	2	0	0

BURKE John
Born: Motherwell, Lanarkshire, Scotland, 10 August, 1962 — W
Scotland: Schools

League Club	Source	Date Signed	Seasons Played	Apps	Subs	Gls
Sheffield U	Motherwell	07/80				
Exeter C	Tr	03/83	82	3	0	0
Chester C	Tr	08/83	83	3	0	0

BURKE John Joseph (Johnny)
Born: Dublin, Republic of Ireland, 28 May, 1911 — G
Died: Southport, Merseyside, England, November, 1987

League Club	Source	Date Signed	Seasons Played	Apps	Subs	Gls
Chester C	Shelbourne (ROI)	07/31	31-35	91	-	0
Millwall	Tr	06/36	36-46	24	-	0
Gillingham	Tr	09/47	50	5	-	0

BURKE Mark Stephen
Born: Solihull, West Midlands, England, 12 February, 1969 — M
England: Youth/Schools

League Club	Source	Date Signed	Seasons Played	Apps	Subs	Gls
Aston Villa	App	02/87	86-87	5	2	0
Middlesbrough	Tr	12/87	87-89	32	25	6
Darlington	L	10/90	90	5	0	1
Wolverhampton W	Tr	03/91	90-93	53	15	11
Luton T	L	03/94	93	2	1	0
Port Vale	Tr	08/94	94	4	11	2

BURKE Marshall
Born: Glasgow, Scotland, 26 March, 1959 — M
Scotland: Schools

League Club	Source	Date Signed	Seasons Played	Apps	Subs	Gls
Burnley	App	03/77	77-79	22	2	5
Leeds U	Tr	05/80				
Blackburn Rov	Tr	12/80	80-81	34	5	7
Lincoln C	Tr	10/82	82-83	49	1	7
Cardiff C	L	12/83	83	3	0	0
Tranmere Rov	Scarborough	09/84	84	3	0	0

BURKE Oliver
Born: Kirkcaldy, Fife, Scotland, 7 April, 1997 — W

League Club	Source	Date Signed	Seasons Played	Apps	Subs	Gls
Nottingham F	Sch	09/14	14	0	2	0
Bradford C	L	02/15	14	2	0	0

League Club	Source	Date Signed	Seasons Played	Career Record Apps	Subs	Gls

BURKE Peter
Born: Rotherham, South Yorkshire, England, 26 April, 1957 CD

League Club	Source	Date Signed	Seasons Played	Apps	Subs	Gls
Barnsley	App	04/75	74-76	36	0	1
Halifax T	Tr	03/78	77-79	79	6	9
Rochdale	Tr	07/80	80-81	68	0	2

BURKE Peter Joseph
Born: Kirkby, Merseyside, England, 1 February, 1912 CH
Died: Liverpool, England, 18 November, 1979

League Club	Source	Date Signed	Seasons Played	Apps	Subs	Gls
Oldham Ath	Prescot Cables	05/33	33-35	93	-	6
Norwich C	Tr	12/35	35-38	114	-	0
Luton T	Tr	06/39				
Southport	Tr	07/46	46	1	-	0

BURKE Reece Frederick James
Born: Newham, E London, England, 2 September, 1996 CD
England: Youth

League Club	Source	Date Signed	Seasons Played	Apps	Subs	Gls
West Ham U	Sch	10/14	14	4	1	0

BURKE Richard (Dick)
Born: Ashton-under-Lyne, Greater Manchester, England, 28 October, 1920 FB
Died: Blackpool, Lancashire, England, 4 January, 2004

League Club	Source	Date Signed	Seasons Played	Apps	Subs	Gls
Blackpool	Droylsden	07/38	38	1	-	0
Newcastle U	Tr	12/46	46	15	-	0
Carlisle U	Tr	08/47	47-48	77	-	8

BURKE Robert Gallee
Born: Ballymena, Antrim, Northern Ireland, 5 November, 1934 IF
Northern Ireland: NILge-1

League Club	Source	Date Signed	Seasons Played	Apps	Subs	Gls
Burnley	Albertville U	09/55	55	19	-	5
Chester C	Tr	06/58				

BURKE Ronald Stewart (Ronnie)
Born: Marske, Cleveland, England, 13 August, 1921 CF
Died: Watford, Hertfordshire, England, January, 2004

League Club	Source	Date Signed	Seasons Played	Apps	Subs	Gls
Manchester U	St Albans C	08/46	46-48	28	-	16
Huddersfield T	Tr	06/49	49-51	27	-	6
Rotherham U	Tr	03/53	52-54	73	-	56
Exeter C	Tr	06/55	55-56	42	-	14

BURKE Steven James (Steve)
Born: Nottingham, England, 29 September, 1960 LW
England: Youth

League Club	Source	Date Signed	Seasons Played	Apps	Subs	Gls
Nottingham F	App	03/78				
Queens Park Rgrs	Tr	09/79	79-83	43	24	5
Millwall	L	10/83	83	7	0	1
Notts Co	L	10/84	84	4	1	0
Lincoln C	L	08/85	85	4	1	0
Brentford	L	03/86	85	10	0	1
Doncaster Rov	Tr	08/86	86-87	50	7	8
Stockport Co	L	10/87	87	5	0	0

BURKE Steven Paul (Steve)
Born: Bolton, Greater Manchester, England, 13 January, 1988 F

League Club	Source	Date Signed	Seasons Played	Apps	Subs	Gls
Bury	Sch	-	05	0	1	0

BURKE Thomas (Tommy)
Born: Greenock, Inverclyde, Scotland, 18 October, 1939 IF

League Club	Source	Date Signed	Seasons Played	Apps	Subs	Gls
Barnsley	Clyde	02/63	62	1	-	0

BURKETT Jack William
Born: Edmonton, N London, England, 21 August, 1942 LB

League Club	Source	Date Signed	Seasons Played	Apps	Subs	Gls
West Ham U	Jnr	10/59	61-67	141	1	4
Charlton Ath	Tr	06/68	68-69	8	0	0
Millwall	Tr	07/70				

BURKINSHAW George Allen
Born: Barnsley, South Yorkshire, England, 1 October, 1922 CH
Died: Barnsley, South Yorkshire, England, 1982

League Club	Source	Date Signed	Seasons Played	Apps	Subs	Gls
Barnsley	Woolley Colliery	03/42				
Carlisle U	Tr	09/46	46	24	-	0
Barnsley	Tr	06/47				
Grimsby T	Tr	09/48				
Bradford C	Tr	11/48	48	12	-	0

BURKINSHAW Harry Keith (Keith)
Born: Darton, South Yorkshire, England, 23 June, 1935 LH

League Club	Source	Date Signed	Seasons Played	Apps	Subs	Gls
Liverpool	Denaby U	11/53	54	1	-	0
Workington	Tr	12/57	57-64	295	-	9
Scunthorpe U	Tr	05/65	65-67	107	1	3

BURKITT John Orgill (Jack)
Born: Wednesbury, West Midlands, England, 19 January, 1926 LH
Died: Brighouse, Yorkshire, England, 12 September, 2003

League Club	Source	Date Signed	Seasons Played	Apps	Subs	Gls
Nottingham F	Darlaston	05/47	48-61	463	-	14

BURLEIGH Martin Stewart
Born: Newcastle-upon-Tyne, England, 2 February, 1951 G

League Club	Source	Date Signed	Seasons Played	Apps	Subs	Gls
Newcastle U	Willington	12/68	70-73	11	0	0
Darlington	Tr	10/74	74	30	0	0
Carlisle U	Tr	06/75	75-76	26	0	0
Darlington	Tr	08/77	77-78	71	0	0
Hartlepool U	Tr	10/79	79-81	84	0	0

BURLEY Adam Gareth
Born: Sheffield, England, 27 November, 1980 LB

League Club	Source	Date Signed	Seasons Played	Apps	Subs	Gls
Sheffield U	YT	07/99	99-00	0	3	1

BURLEY Craig William
Born: Ayr, Scotland, 24 September, 1971 M
Scotland: 46/U21-7/Youth/Schools

League Club	Source	Date Signed	Seasons Played	Apps	Subs	Gls
Chelsea	YT	09/89	90-96	85	28	7
Derby Co	Glasgow Celtic	12/99	99-02	73	0	10
Preston NE	Dundee	01/04	03	1	3	0
Walsall	Tr	03/04	03	5	0	0

BURLEY George Elder
Born: Cumnock, Ayrshire, Scotland, 3 June, 1956 RB
Scotland: 11/U23-2/U21-5/Youth/Schools

League Club	Source	Date Signed	Seasons Played	Apps	Subs	Gls
Ipswich T	App	06/73	73-85	394	0	6
Sunderland	Tr	09/85	85-86	54	0	0
Gillingham	Tr	07/88	88	46	0	2
Colchester U	Motherwell	08/94	94	5	2	0

BURLISON Robert Lyle (Bob)
Born: Newcastle-upon-Tyne, England, 29 March, 1920 W
Died: Barnet, N London, England, February, 1987

League Club	Source	Date Signed	Seasons Played	Apps	Subs	Gls
Charlton Ath	Horden CW	09/39	46	1	-	0

BURLISON Thomas Henry (Tom)
Born: Edmondsley, County Durham, England, 23 May, 1936 WH/LW
Died: Rowlands Gill, Tyne and Wear, England, 20 May, 2008

League Club	Source	Date Signed	Seasons Played	Apps	Subs	Gls
Lincoln C	Ouston Jnrs	12/53				
Hartlepool U	Tr	07/57	57-63	148	-	5
Darlington	Tr	08/64	64	26	-	2

BURLURAUX Donald (Don)
Born: Skelton, Cleveland, England, 8 June, 1951 W

League Club	Source	Date Signed	Seasons Played	Apps	Subs	Gls
Middlesbrough	Jnr	07/68	70-71	4	1	0
York C	L	12/71	71	3	0	1
Darlington	Tr	07/72	72-74	105	7	13

BURMAN Anthony Paul (Tony)
Born: Stockwell, S London, England, 3 June, 1958 F

League Club	Source	Date Signed	Seasons Played	Apps	Subs	Gls
Charlton Ath	Queens Park Rgrs (App)	08/76	76-77	16	3	3

BURMAN Simon John
Born: Ipswich, England, 26 November, 1965 W

League Club	Source	Date Signed	Seasons Played	Apps	Subs	Gls
Colchester U	App	11/83	84-86	28	4	3

BURN Daniel Johnson (Dan)
Born: Blyth, Northumberland, England, 1 May, 1992 CD

League Club	Source	Date Signed	Seasons Played	Apps	Subs	Gls
Darlington	Sch	07/10	09	2	2	0
Fulham	Tr	05/11	13-14	26	3	1
Yeovil T	L	09/12	12	34	0	2
Birmingham C	L	07/13	13	23	1	0

BURN John Haytor
Born: South Shields, Tyne and Wear, England, 21 January, 1930 G
Died: South Shields, Tyne and Wear, England, 31 January, 2015

League Club	Source	Date Signed	Seasons Played	Apps	Subs	Gls
Chelsea	South Shields ESB	10/48				
Chesterfield	Tr	08/50				
Carlisle U	Tr	06/55	55	26	-	0

BURN Ralph Gordon (Gordon)
Born: Alnwick, Northumberland, England, 9 November, 1931 IF
Died: Weston Favell, Northamptonshire, England, 11 April, 1984

League Club	Source	Date Signed	Seasons Played	Apps	Subs	Gls
Northampton T	Alnwick Jnrs	08/50	50	1	-	0
Crewe Alex	Tr	07/54	54	1	-	0

BURNDRED John Nigel
Born: Stoke-on-Trent, England, 22 March, 1968 F

League Club	Source	Date Signed	Seasons Played	Apps	Subs	Gls
Port Vale	Knypersley Victoria	02/95	94	1	0	0

BURNELL Joseph Michael (Joe)
Born: Bristol, England, 10 October, 1980 D/M

League Club	Source	Date Signed	Seasons Played	Apps	Subs	Gls
Bristol C	YT	07/99	99-03	117	14	1
Wycombe W	Tr	07/04	04-05	50	7	0
Northampton T	Tr	07/06	06-07	50	7	1
Exeter C	Oxford U	07/09	09	4	4	0

BURNETT Alfred Price (Alf)
Born: Aberdeen, Scotland, 23 July, 1922 CF
Died: Lincoln, England, February, 1977

League Club	Source	Date Signed	Seasons Played	Apps	Subs	Gls
Barrow	Dundee	12/46	46-49	87	-	32
Lincoln C	Tr	11/49	49	4	-	1

BURNETT Dennis Henry
Born: Bermondsey, SE London, England, 27 September, 1944 D

League Club	Source	Date Signed	Seasons Played	Apps	Subs	Gls
West Ham U	Jnr	10/62	65-66	48	2	0

League Club	Source	Date Signed	Seasons Played	Apps	Subs	Gls
Millwall	Tr	08/67	67-73	257	0	3
Hull C	Tr	10/73	73-74	46	0	2
Millwall	L	03/75	74	6	0	2
Brighton & HA	St Louis AS (USA)	09/75	75-76	41	3	1

BURNETT George Gordon
Born: Liverpool, England, 11 February, 1920 — G
Died: Birkenhead, Wirral, England, 29 April, 1985

League Club	Source	Date Signed	Seasons Played	Apps	Subs	Gls
Everton	Litherland BC	09/38	46-50	47	-	0
Oldham Ath	Tr	10/51	51-54	100	-	0

BURNETT John
Born: Market Rasen, Lincolnshire, England, 24 June, 1939 — LB

League Club	Source	Date Signed	Seasons Played	Apps	Subs	Gls
Grimsby T	Gainsborough Trinity	07/58	58	1	-	0

BURNETT Wayne
Born: Lambeth, S London, England, 4 September, 1971 — M
England: Youth

League Club	Source	Date Signed	Seasons Played	Apps	Subs	Gls
Leyton Orient	YT	11/89	89-91	34	6	0
Blackburn Rov	Tr	08/92				
Plymouth Arg	Tr	08/93	93-95	61	9	3
Bolton W	Tr	10/95	95-96	0	2	0
Huddersfield T	Tr	09/96	96-97	44	6	0
Grimsby T	Tr	01/98	97-01	80	26	6

BURNETT William John (Billy)
Born: Pelaw, Tyne and Wear, England, 1 March, 1926 — RW
Died: Pelaw, Tyne and Wear, England, December, 1988

League Club	Source	Date Signed	Seasons Played	Apps	Subs	Gls
Grimsby T	Wardley CW	07/46	47	10	-	0
Hartlepool U	Tr	11/48	48-53	194	-	17

BURNHAM Jason John
Born: Mansfield, Nottinghamshire, England, 8 May, 1973 — LB

League Club	Source	Date Signed	Seasons Played	Apps	Subs	Gls
Northampton T	YT	07/91	91-93	79	9	2
Chester C	Tr	07/94	94-95	62	2	1

BURNS Alexander (Alex)
Born: Bellshill, Lanarkshire, Scotland, 4 August, 1973 — M

League Club	Source	Date Signed	Seasons Played	Apps	Subs	Gls
Southend U	SC Heracles (NED)	07/98	98	26	5	5

BURNS Anthony John (Tony)
Born: Edenbridge, Kent, England, 27 March, 1944 — G

League Club	Source	Date Signed	Seasons Played	Apps	Subs	Gls
Arsenal	Tonbridge	03/63	64-65	31	0	0
Brighton & HA	Tr	07/66	66-68	54	0	0
Charlton Ath	Tr	03/69	68-69	10	0	0
Crystal Palace	Durban U (RSA)	10/73	74-77	90	0	0
Brentford	L	01/77	76	6	0	0
Plymouth Arg	Tr	08/78	78	8	0	0

BURNS Barry Ross
Born: Doncaster, South Yorkshire, England, 19 June, 1937 — IF
Died: Tameside, Greater Manchester, England, April, 2009

League Club	Source	Date Signed	Seasons Played	Apps	Subs	Gls
Rotherham U	Dunscroft	10/54	57	5	-	4

BURNS Charlie Peter John
Born: Croydon, S London, England, 27 May, 1995 — G

League Club	Source	Date Signed	Seasons Played	Apps	Subs	Gls
MK Dons	Sch	-	13	0	1	0

BURNS Christopher (Chris)
Born: Manchester, England, 9 November, 1967 — M

League Club	Source	Date Signed	Seasons Played	Apps	Subs	Gls
Portsmouth	Cheltenham T	03/91	91-93	78	12	9
Swansea C	L	12/93	93	4	0	0
Bournemouth	L	03/94	93	13	1	1
Swansea C	Tr	11/94	94	3	2	0
Northampton T	Tr	01/95	94-96	62	4	9

BURNS David
Born: Ellesmere Port, Cheshire, England, 12 November, 1958 — LB

League Club	Source	Date Signed	Seasons Played	Apps	Subs	Gls
Chester C	App	10/76	76-81	66	12	1

BURNS Derek George
Born: Bournemouth, England, 23 January, 1950 — M

League Club	Source	Date Signed	Seasons Played	Apps	Subs	Gls
Bournemouth	App	01/68	68	3	1	0

BURNS Eric Owen
Born: Newton Stewart, Dumfries & Galloway, Scotland, 8 March, 1945 — RW

League Club	Source	Date Signed	Seasons Played	Apps	Subs	Gls
Bradford Park Ave	App	03/62	63-65	26	2	3
Barnsley	Tr	08/66	66	3	0	0

BURNS Francis
Born: Glenboig, Lanarkshire, Scotland, 17 October, 1948 — LB
Scotland: 1/U23-1/Schools

League Club	Source	Date Signed	Seasons Played	Apps	Subs	Gls
Manchester U	Jnr	10/65	67-71	111	10	6
Southampton	Tr	06/72	72	20	1	0
Preston NE	Tr	08/73	73-80	271	2	9

BURNS Francis Joseph (Frank)
Born: Workington, Cumbria, England, 11 November, 1924 — WH
Died: Southend, England, April, 1987

League Club	Source	Date Signed	Seasons Played	Apps	Subs	Gls
Swansea C	Wolverhampton W (Am)	08/44	46-51	172	-	9
Southend U	Tr	07/52	52-54	89	-	14
Crewe Alex	Tr	11/56	56-57	31	-	7

BURNS Hugh
Born: Lanark, Scotland, 13 December, 1965 — LB
Scotland: U21-2

League Club	Source	Date Signed	Seasons Played	Apps	Subs	Gls
Fulham (L)	Dunfermline Ath	12/89	89	6	0	0

BURNS Jacob Geoffrey
Born: Sydney, Australia, 21 January, 1978 — M
Australia: 11/U23-10

League Club	Source	Date Signed	Seasons Played	Apps	Subs	Gls
Leeds U	Parramatta Power (AUS)	08/00	00-02	5	1	0
Barnsley	Tr	10/03	03-05	81	8	6

BURNS Jamie Daniel
Born: Blackpool, Lancashire, England, 6 March, 1984 — M/LB

League Club	Source	Date Signed	Seasons Played	Apps	Subs	Gls
Blackpool	Sch	07/03	02-05	30	17	1
Bury	L	03/06	05	1	0	0
Morecambe	Tr	11/06	07	4	3	0

BURNS John Christopher
Born: Dublin, Republic of Ireland, 4 December, 1977 — M
Republic of Ireland: U21-2/Youth

League Club	Source	Date Signed	Seasons Played	Apps	Subs	Gls
Nottingham F	Belvedere (ROI)	12/94	99	3	0	0
Bristol C	Tr	11/99	99	6	5	0
Carlisle U	Tr	08/02	02	4	1	0

BURNS Kenneth (Kenny)
Born: Glasgow, Scotland, 23 September, 1953 — CD/F
Scotland: 20/U23-2

League Club	Source	Date Signed	Seasons Played	Apps	Subs	Gls
Birmingham C	App	07/71	71-76	163	7	45
Nottingham F	Tr	07/77	77-81	137	0	13
Leeds U	Tr	10/81	81-83	54	2	2
Derby Co	L	03/83	82	6	1	1
Derby Co	Tr	02/84	83-84	30	1	1
Notts Co	L	02/85	84	2	0	0
Barnsley	Tr	08/85	85	19	3	0

BURNS Kinear (Ken)
Born: Ramsey, Isle of Man, England, 24 September, 1923 — IF
Died: Ramsey, Isle of Man, England, 5 May, 2006

League Club	Source	Date Signed	Seasons Played	Apps	Subs	Gls
Tranmere Rov	Ramsey	09/46	46	14	-	4
Southport	Runcorn	11/47	47	5	-	0

BURNS Leo Francis
Born: Manchester, England, 3 August, 1932 — WH

League Club	Source	Date Signed	Seasons Played	Apps	Subs	Gls
Oldham Ath	Manchester C (Am)	09/53	55	4	-	0

BURNS Leslie George Henry (Les)
Born: Shepherds Bush, W London, England, 22 June, 1944 — CD

League Club	Source	Date Signed	Seasons Played	Apps	Subs	Gls
Charlton Ath	Carshalton Ath	03/67	66-67	8	0	0

BURNS Liam
Born: Belfast, Northern Ireland, 30 October, 1978 — CD
Northern Ireland: U21-13/Youth

League Club	Source	Date Signed	Seasons Played	Apps	Subs	Gls
Port Vale	YT	07/97	97-03	94	24	0
Bristol Rov	Tr	08/04	04	3	0	0
Shrewsbury T	Tr	12/04	04	1	1	0
Kidderminster Hrs	Tr	12/04	04	0	1	0

BURNS Michael Edward (Micky)
Born: Preston, Lancashire, England, 21 December, 1946 — F
England: Amateur-1

League Club	Source	Date Signed	Seasons Played	Apps	Subs	Gls
Blackpool	Skelmersdale U	05/69	69-73	174	7	53
Newcastle U	Tr	07/74	74-77	143	2	39
Cardiff C	Tr	08/78	78	6	0	0
Middlesbrough	Tr	10/78	78-80	58	3	24

BURNS Michael John
Born: Huyton, Merseyside, England, 4 October, 1988 — M
England: Youth

League Club	Source	Date Signed	Seasons Played	Apps	Subs	Gls
Bolton W	Liverpool (Sch)	07/07				
Carlisle U	Tr	01/09	08	0	1	0

BURNS Michael Thomas (Mick)
Born: Coundon, County Durham, England, 7 June, 1908 — G
Died: Sherburn Hill, County Durham, England, 5 September, 1982

League Club	Source	Date Signed	Seasons Played	Apps	Subs	Gls
Newcastle U	Chilton Colliery Rec	09/27	27-35	104	-	0
Preston NE	Tr	07/36	36-37	12	-	0
Ipswich T	Tr	05/38	38-51	157	-	0

BURNS Neil James
Born: Bellshill, Lanarkshire, Scotland, 11 June, 1945 — F

League Club	Source	Date Signed	Seasons Played	Apps	Subs	Gls
Crewe Alex		03/64				
Mansfield T	Bethesda	11/65	65-66	7	3	0

BURNS Oliver Houston (Ollie)
Born: Larkhall, Lanarkshire, Scotland, 16 May, 1914 — IF
Died: Halifax, West Yorkshire, England, December, 1989

League Club	Source	Date Signed	Seasons Played	Apps	Subs	Gls
Burnley	Glenavon	03/39				

League Club	Source	Date Signed	Seasons Played	Apps	Subs	Gls
Oldham Ath	Tr	10/46	46	25	-	5
Halifax T	Tr	09/47	47	27	-	5

BURNS Peter
Born: Ulverston, Cumbria, England, 17 April, 1931 CF
Died: South Cheshire, England, February, 2002

League Club	Source	Date Signed	Seasons Played	Apps	Subs	Gls
Barrow	Askam U	02/52	51	8	-	2
Blackburn Rov	Tr	09/53				

BURNS Philip Martin (Phil)
Born: Stockport, Greater Manchester, England, 18 December, 1966 G

League Club	Source	Date Signed	Seasons Played	Apps	Subs	Gls
Reading	REME	03/89	90	12	0	0

BURNS Robbie Lee
Born: Milton Keynes, England, 15 November, 1990 W

League Club	Source	Date Signed	Seasons Played	Apps	Subs	Gls
Leicester C	Sch	02/09				
Tranmere Rov	L	03/09	08	0	2	0

BURNS Ryan Colum
Born: Belfast, Northern Ireland, 8 September, 1992 RW
Northern Ireland: Youth

League Club	Source	Date Signed	Seasons Played	Apps	Subs	Gls
Oldham Ath	Sch	09/10	10	1	0	0

BURNS Wesley James (Wes)
Born: Barry, Vale of Glamorgan, Wales, 28 October, 1994 F
Wales: U21-11

League Club	Source	Date Signed	Seasons Played	Apps	Subs	Gls
Bristol C	Sch	12/12	12-14	1	29	2
Oxford U	L	11/14	14	6	3	1
Cheltenham T	L	02/15	14	14	0	4

BURNS William (Willie)
Born: Motherwell, Lanarkshire, Scotland, 10 December, 1969 D/M

League Club	Source	Date Signed	Seasons Played	Apps	Subs	Gls
Manchester C	YT	01/88				
Rochdale	Tr	07/89	89-90	68	4	2

BURNSIDE David Gort
Born: Kingswood, Avon, England, 10 December, 1939 IF
Died: Bristol, England, 17 October, 2009
England: U23-1/Youth

League Club	Source	Date Signed	Seasons Played	Apps	Subs	Gls
West Bromwich A	Bristol C (Am)	02/57	57-62	127	-	39
Southampton	Tr	10/62	62-64	61	-	22
Crystal Palace	Tr	12/64	64-66	54	4	8
Wolverhampton W	Tr	09/66	66-67	38	2	5
Plymouth Arg	Tr	03/68	67-70	105	0	15
Bristol C	Tr	12/71	71	1	0	0
Colchester U	Tr	03/72	71	13	0	0

BURRELL Gerald (Gerry)
Born: Belfast, Northern Ireland, 6 September, 1924 W
Died: Belfast, Northern Ireland, 25 October, 2014

League Club	Source	Date Signed	Seasons Played	Apps	Subs	Gls
Huddersfield T	Dundee	12/53	53-55	59	-	9
Chesterfield	Tr	07/56	56-57	51	-	4

BURRELL Lester Frank (Les)
Born: New Brighton, Wirral, England, 8 August, 1917 IF
Died: Brighton, England, 29 April, 2008

League Club	Source	Date Signed	Seasons Played	Apps	Subs	Gls
Crystal Palace	Margate	02/46	46-47	19	-	5
Kidderminster Hrs	Tr	05/48				

BURRELL Warren Matthew
Born: Sheffield, England, 3 June, 1990 M

League Club	Source	Date Signed	Seasons Played	Apps	Subs	Gls
Mansfield T	Sch	-	07	0	1	0

BURRIDGE John
Born: Workington, Cumbria, England, 3 December, 1951 G

League Club	Source	Date Signed	Seasons Played	Apps	Subs	Gls
Workington	App	01/70	68-70	27	0	0
Blackpool	Tr	04/71	70-75	134	0	0
Aston Villa	Tr	09/75	75-76	65	0	0
Southend U	L	01/78	77	6	0	0
Crystal Palace	Tr	03/78	77-79	88	0	0
Queens Park Rgrs	Tr	12/80	80-81	39	0	0
Wolverhampton W	Tr	08/82	82-83	74	0	0
Derby Co	L	09/84	84	6	0	0
Sheffield U	Tr	10/84	84-86	109	0	0
Southampton	Tr	08/87	87-88	62	0	0
Newcastle U	Tr	10/89	89-90	67	0	0
Newcastle U	Hibernian	08/93				
Scarborough	Tr	10/93	93	3	0	0
Lincoln C	Tr	12/93	93	4	0	0
Manchester C	Dumbarton	12/94	94	3	1	0
Notts Co	Tr	08/95				
Darlington	Witton A	11/95	95	3	0	0

BURRIDGE Peter John
Born: Harlow, Essex, England, 30 December, 1933 IF

League Club	Source	Date Signed	Seasons Played	Apps	Subs	Gls
Leyton Orient	Barnet	04/58	58-59	6	-	2
Millwall	Tr	08/60	60-61	87	-	58
Crystal Palace	Tr	06/62	62-65	114	0	42
Charlton Ath	Tr	11/65	65-66	42	2	4

BURROW Jordan
Born: Sheffield, England, 12 September, 1992 F

League Club	Source	Date Signed	Seasons Played	Apps	Subs	Gls
Chesterfield	Sch	07/11				
Morecambe	Tr	01/12	11-12	26	25	5
Stevenage	Tr	07/13	13	9	11	2

BURROWS Adrian Mark
Born: Sutton-in-Ashfield, Nottinghamshire, England, 16 January, 1959 CD

League Club	Source	Date Signed	Seasons Played	Apps	Subs	Gls
Mansfield T		05/79	79-81	77	1	6
Northampton T	Tr	08/82	82-83	88	0	4
Plymouth Arg	Tr	07/84	84-93	272	5	14
Southend U	L	09/87	87	6	0	0

BURROWS Alan
Born: Thorne, South Yorkshire, England, 20 October, 1941 RB

League Club	Source	Date Signed	Seasons Played	Apps	Subs	Gls
Blackpool	Stockport Co (Am)	05/59	59	1	-	0

BURROWS Arthur
Born: Stockport, Greater Manchester, England, 4 December, 1919 WH
Died: Stockport, Greater Manchester, England, March, 2005

League Club	Source	Date Signed	Seasons Played	Apps	Subs	Gls
Stockport Co	Jnr	11/37	38-46	5	-	1
Accrington Stan	Ashton U	03/48	48	9	-	0

BURROWS David
Born: Dudley, West Midlands, England, 25 October, 1968 LB
England: B-3/FLge/U21-7

League Club	Source	Date Signed	Seasons Played	Apps	Subs	Gls
West Bromwich A	App	11/86	85-88	37	9	1
Liverpool	Tr	10/88	88-93	135	11	3
West Ham U	Tr	09/93	93-94	29	0	1
Everton	Tr	09/94	94	19	0	0
Coventry C	Tr	03/95	94-99	106	5	0
Birmingham C	Tr	07/00	00-01	17	8	0
Sheffield Wed	Tr	03/02	01-02	21	0	0

BURROWS David Williams
Born: Bilsthorpe, Nottinghamshire, England, 7 April, 1961 FB

League Club	Source	Date Signed	Seasons Played	Apps	Subs	Gls
Lincoln C	App	04/79	78	1	0	0

BURROWS Frank
Born: Larkhall, Lanarkshire, Scotland, 30 January, 1944 CD

League Club	Source	Date Signed	Seasons Played	Apps	Subs	Gls
Scunthorpe U	Raith Rov	06/65	65-67	106	0	4
Swindon T	Tr	07/68	68-76	293	4	9
Mansfield T	L	03/74	73	6	0	0

BURROWS Harold (Harry)
Born: Haydock, Merseyside, England, 17 March, 1941 LW
England: U23-1

League Club	Source	Date Signed	Seasons Played	Apps	Subs	Gls
Aston Villa	Jnr	03/58	59-64	147	-	53
Stoke C	Tr	03/65	64-72	239	6	68
Plymouth Arg	Tr	08/73	73-74	18	1	3

BURROWS Mark
Born: Kettering, Northamptonshire, England, 14 August, 1980 CD

League Club	Source	Date Signed	Seasons Played	Apps	Subs	Gls
Coventry C	YT	01/98				
Exeter C	Tr	07/00	00-01	27	11	0

BURROWS Paul Samuel
Born: Swansea, Wales, 2 October, 1967 F
Wales: Youth

League Club	Source	Date Signed	Seasons Played	Apps	Subs	Gls
Swansea C	App	10/85	85	1	2	0

BURROWS Philip Arthur (Phil)
Born: Stockport, Greater Manchester, England, 8 April, 1946 LB

League Club	Source	Date Signed	Seasons Played	Apps	Subs	Gls
Manchester C	Jnr	07/64				
York C	Tr	06/66	66-73	333	4	14
Plymouth Arg	Tr	07/74	74-75	81	0	2
Hereford U	Tr	08/76	76-79	110	0	2
Gillingham	L	10/77	77	5	0	0

BURSELL John Clifford (Cliff)
Born: Hull, England, 16 January, 1935 IF
Died: Hull, England, 27 July, 1973

League Club	Source	Date Signed	Seasons Played	Apps	Subs	Gls
Hull C	Jnr	11/52	52	2	-	2

BURT James Hamilton Laird (Jimmy)
Born: Harthill, Lanarkshire, Scotland, 5 April, 1950 LB

League Club	Source	Date Signed	Seasons Played	Apps	Subs	Gls
Leicester C	Whitburn Jnrs	06/67				
Aldershot	Tr	09/70	70-71	22	3	0
Northampton T	Tr	07/72	72	16	5	0
Rochdale	Tr	09/73	73	4	0	0

BURT Jamie Paul
Born: Blyth, Northumberland, England, 29 September, 1979 F
England: Schools

League Club	Source	Date Signed	Seasons Played	Apps	Subs	Gls
Chesterfield	Whitby T	12/01	01-03	29	12	8
Carlisle U	L	12/02	02	4	0	1

BURTENSHAW Charles Edward (Charlie)
Born: Hove, East Sussex, England, 16 October, 1922 RW
Died: Medway, Kent, England, May, 2013

League Club	Source	Date Signed	Seasons Played	Apps	Subs	Gls
Luton T	Southwick	01/48	48-49	11	-	1
Gillingham	Tr	10/49	50-51	28	-	4

League Club	Source	Date Signed	Seasons Played	Apps	Subs	Gls
BURTON Steven Peter Graham (Steve)						
Born: Hove, East Sussex, England, 23 November, 1935						WH
Brighton & HA	Jnr	11/52	52-66	237	0	3
BURTEN SHAW William Frederick (Bill)						
Born: Hove, East Sussex, England, 13 December, 1925						IF
Died: Brighton, England, 23 February, 2010						
Luton T	Southwick	08/48	48	1	-	0
Gillingham	Tr	10/49	50-51	39	-	8
BURTON Alan Michael						
Born: Blackpool, Lancashire, England, 22 February, 1991						M
Accrington Stan	Sch	02/10	10-11	1	1	0
BURTON Alan Richard						
Born: Aldershot, Hampshire, England, 11 January, 1939						W
Aldershot	Alton T	01/61	60-69	225	5	47
BURTON Alwyn Derek (Ollie)						
Born: Chepstow, Monmouthshire, Wales, 11 November, 1941						RH
Wales: 9/U23-5/Schools						
Newport Co	Bulwark YC	12/58	58-60	53	-	8
Norwich C	Tr	03/61	60-62	57	-	8
Newcastle U	Tr	06/63	63-71	181	7	6
BURTON Bruce Brian (Brian)						
Born: Nottingham, England, 28 December, 1932						LW
Nottingham F	Basford BC	07/51	54	1	-	0
BURTON Deon John						
Born: Reading, England, 25 October, 1976						F
Jamaica: 56						
Portsmouth	YT	02/94	93-96	42	20	10
Cardiff C	L	12/96	96	5	0	2
Derby Co	Tr	08/97	97-02	78	47	25
Barnsley	L	12/98	98	3	0	0
Stoke C	L	02/02	01	11	1	2
Portsmouth	L	08/02	02	6	0	3
Portsmouth	Tr	12/02	02-03	5	5	1
Walsall	L	09/03	03	2	1	0
Swindon T	L	10/03	03	4	0	1
Brentford	Tr	08/04	04	38	2	10
Rotherham U	Tr	07/05	05	24	0	12
Sheffield Wed	Tr	01/06	05-08	82	34	23
Charlton Ath	Tr	11/08	08-09	47	12	18
Gillingham	Qabala (AZE)	08/12	12	31	9	12
Scunthorpe U	Tr	07/13	13-14	20	14	6
York C	L	10/14	14	1	0	0
BURTON Ernest (Ernie)						
Born: Sheffield, England, 2 September, 1921						RW
Died: Sheffield, England, July, 1999						
Sheffield Wed	Atlas & Norfolk	11/47				
York C	Tr	08/48	48	3	-	0
BURTON Kenneth Owen (Ken)						
Born: Sheffield, England, 11 February, 1950						LB
Sheffield Wed	App	05/67	68-71	55	2	2
Peterborough U	L	03/73	72	3	1	0
Chesterfield	Tr	07/73	73-78	234	3	6
Halifax T	Tr	08/80	80	26	1	1
BURTON Mark Anthony						
Born: Penistone, South Yorkshire, England, 7 May, 1973						M
Barnsley	YT	06/91	92	5	0	0
BURTON Michael James (Micky)						
Born: Tamworth, Staffordshire, England, 5 November, 1969						M
Birmingham C	YT	07/88	88	0	4	0
Shrewsbury T	Sheffield Wed (NC)	03/91	90	3	3	0
BURTON Nicholas John (Nick)						
Born: Bury St Edmunds, Suffolk, England, 10 February, 1975						CD
Torquay U	Portsmouth (YT)	08/93	93-94	14	2	2
BURTON Paul David						
Born: Enfield, N London, England, 30 November, 1985						M
Oxford U	YT	05/04	04	0	1	0
BURTON Paul Stewart						
Born: Hereford, England, 6 August, 1973						F
Hereford U	YT	07/91	89-91	1	4	1
BURTON Royston (Roy)						
Born: Wantage, Oxfordshire, England, 13 March, 1951						G
Oxford U	Jnr	09/70	71-82	397	0	0
BURTON Samuel (Sam)						
Born: Swindon, England, 10 November, 1926						G
Swindon T	Jnr	06/45	46-61	463	-	0

League Club	Source	Date Signed	Seasons Played	Apps	Subs	Gls
BURTON Simon Paul						
Born: Farnworth, Greater Manchester, England, 29 December, 1973						F
Preston NE	YT	05/92	92-93	19	5	3
BURTON Steven Paul (Steve)						
Born: Doncaster, South Yorkshire, England, 9 October, 1983						F
Ipswich T	Sch	08/02				
Boston U	L	08/02	02	6	2	0
Doncaster Rov	Tr	03/03	03	1	5	0
BURTON Steven Peter Graham (Steve)						
Born: Hull, England, 10 October, 1982						LB
Hull C	Sch	07/02	02	2	9	0
Kidderminster Hrs	L	10/03	03	6	1	0
Kidderminster Hrs	Tr	03/04	03-04	19	1	0
BURTON-GODWIN Osagyefo Lenin Ernesto (Sagi)						
Born: Birmingham, England, 25 November, 1977						D
St Kitts & Nevis: 3						
Crystal Palace	YT	01/96	97-98	19	6	1
Colchester U	Tr	05/99	99	9	0	0
Port Vale	Sheffield U (NC)	01/00	99-01	76	10	2
Crewe Alex	Tr	08/02	02	1	0	0
Peterborough U	Tr	08/02	02-05	88	8	4
Shrewsbury T	Tr	01/06	05-06	41	3	5
Barnet	Tr	08/07	07	29	1	1
BURVILL Glenn						
Born: Canning Town, E London, England, 26 October, 1962						M
West Ham U	App	09/80				
Aldershot	Tr	08/83	83-84	57	8	15
Reading	Tr	03/85	84-85	24	6	0
Fulham	L	03/86	85	9	0	2
Aldershot	Tr	07/86	86-90	176	19	23
BUS Sergiu Florin						
Born: Cluj, Romania, 2 November, 1992						F
Romania: U21-5						
Sheffield Wed	CSKA Sofia (BUL)	02/15	14	2	5	1
BUSBY David Everett						
Born: Paddington, Central London, England, 27 July, 1956						F
Brighton & HA	App	08/74	73-74	1	2	0
BUSBY Hubert George Albert						
Born: Kingston, Canada, 18 June, 1969						G
Jamaica:						
Oxford U	SC Caldas (POR)	08/00	00	0	1	0
BUSBY Martyn George						
Born: High Wycombe, Buckinghamshire, England, 24 March, 1953						M
England: Youth						
Queens Park Rgrs	App	07/70	69-76	72	7	6
Portsmouth	L	02/76	75	6	0	1
Notts Co	Tr	10/76	76-77	37	0	4
Queens Park Rgrs	Tr	09/77	77-79	56	10	11
Burnley	L	02/80	79	4	0	1
BUSBY Vivian Dennis (Viv)						
Born: High Wycombe, Buckinghamshire, England, 19 June, 1949						F
Luton T	Wycombe W	01/70	69-72	64	13	16
Newcastle U	L	12/71	71	4	0	2
Fulham	Tr	08/73	73-76	114	4	29
Norwich C	Tr	09/76	76-77	22	0	11
Stoke C	Tr	11/77	77-79	33	17	10
Sheffield U	L	01/80	79	3	0	1
Blackburn Rov	Tulsa Roughnecks (USA)	02/81	80	8	0	1
York C	Tr	08/82	82-83	9	10	4
BUSH Bryan						
Born: Bristol, England, 25 April, 1925						W/IF
Died: Bristol, England, 25 August, 2008						
Bristol Rov	Soundwell	10/47	47-54	114	-	19
BUSH Christopher Miles (Chris)						
Born: Leytonstone, NE London, England, 12 June, 1992						LB
AFC Wimbledon	Brentford (Sch)	06/11	11	16	6	0
BUSH Terence Douglas (Terry)						
Born: Dersingham, Norfolk, England, 29 January, 1943						CF/LH
Bristol C	Jnr	02/60	60-69	147	15	43
BUSH William Thomas (Tom)						
Born: Hodnet, Shropshire, England, 22 February, 1914						CH
Died: Liverpool, England, 20 December, 1969						
Liverpool	Shrewsbury Amats	03/33	33-46	61	-	1
BUSHBY Alan						
Born: Stainforth, South Yorkshire, England, 15 January, 1932						LH

Died: New York, USA, 1967

League Club	Source	Date Signed	Seasons Played	Apps	Subs	Gls
Scunthorpe U		08/52	52-58	218	-	10
Rochdale	Tr	07/59	59-60	66	-	0

BUSHBY Dennis Christopher
Born: Poole, Dorset, England, 25 December, 1933 — WH

League Club	Source	Date Signed	Seasons Played	Apps	Subs	Gls
Bournemouth	Branksome Gasworks	11/57	57	6	-	0

BUSHBY Thomas William (Billy)
Born: Shildon, County Durham, England, 21 August, 1914 — CF
Died: Warsash, Hampshire, England, 25 December, 1997

League Club	Source	Date Signed	Seasons Played	Apps	Subs	Gls
Southend U	Shildon	10/34	34-38	40	-	12
Portsmouth	Tr	06/39				
Southampton	Tr	09/46	46	2	-	0

BUSHELL Allan
Born: Burnley, Lancashire, England, 4 September, 1932 — W
Died: Blackburn, Greater Manchester, England, 12 October, 2013

League Club	Source	Date Signed	Seasons Played	Apps	Subs	Gls
Accrington Stan (Am)	Wood Top	05/52	52	8	-	1

BUSHELL Mark John
Born: Northampton, England, 5 June, 1968 — FB

League Club	Source	Date Signed	Seasons Played	Apps	Subs	Gls
Northampton T	App	09/85	84	1	0	0

BUSHELL Stephen Paul (Steve)
Born: Manchester, England, 28 December, 1972 — M

League Club	Source	Date Signed	Seasons Played	Apps	Subs	Gls
York C	YT	02/91	90-97	156	18	10
Blackpool	Tr	07/98	98-00	64	15	6
Halifax T	Stalybridge Celtic	11/01	01	25	0	1

BUSSCHER Robby
Born: Leidschendam, Netherlands, 23 November, 1982 — M
Netherlands: Youth

League Club	Source	Date Signed	Seasons Played	Apps	Subs	Gls
Grimsby T	Feyenoord (NED)	07/01	01	0	1	0

BUSST David John (Dave)
Born: Birmingham, England, 30 June, 1967 — CD

League Club	Source	Date Signed	Seasons Played	Apps	Subs	Gls
Coventry C	Moor Green	01/92	92-95	48	2	4

BUTCHER Callum James
Born: Leigh-on-Sea, Essex, England, 26 February, 1991 — CD

League Club	Source	Date Signed	Seasons Played	Apps	Subs	Gls
Tottenham H	Sch	03/09				
Barnet	L	11/09	09	3	0	0

BUTCHER John Melvin
Born: Newcastle-upon-Tyne, England, 27 May, 1956 — G

League Club	Source	Date Signed	Seasons Played	Apps	Subs	Gls
Blackburn Rov		03/76	76-81	104	0	0
Oxford U	Tr	07/82	82	16	0	0
Halifax T	L	09/82	82	5	0	0
Bury	L	12/83	83	11	0	0
Chester C	Tr	08/84	84-86	84	0	0
Bury	L	10/85	85	5	0	0

BUTCHER Lee Anthony
Born: Walthamstow, NE London, England, 11 October, 1988 — G

League Club	Source	Date Signed	Seasons Played	Apps	Subs	Gls
Tottenham H	Arsenal (Sch)	07/07				
Leyton Orient	Tr	07/10	10-11	31	1	0

BUTCHER Reginald (Reg)
Born: Prescot, Merseyside, England, 13 February, 1916 — FB
Died: Birkenhead, Wirral, England, 3 October, 2000

League Club	Source	Date Signed	Seasons Played	Apps	Subs	Gls
Chester C	Liverpool (Am)	11/38	38-49	155	-	1

BUTCHER Richard Tony
Born: Peterborough, England, 22 January, 1981 — M
Died: Manchester, England, 9 January, 2011

League Club	Source	Date Signed	Seasons Played	Apps	Subs	Gls
Rushden & D	Northampton T (YT)	11/99				
Lincoln C	Kettering T	11/02	02-04	95	9	11
Oldham Ath	Tr	07/05	05	32	4	4
Lincoln C	L	10/05	05	4	0	1
Peterborough U	Tr	06/06	06	35	8	4
Notts Co	Tr	07/07	07-08	75	5	18
Lincoln C	Tr	06/09	09	10	5	0
Macclesfield T	Tr	02/10	09-10	13	2	3

BUTCHER Stephen James
Born: Dover, Kent, England, 19 November, 1994 — RB

League Club	Source	Date Signed	Seasons Played	Apps	Subs	Gls
Gillingham	Sch	07/13	13	0	1	0

BUTCHER Terence Ian (Terry)
Born: Singapore, 28 December, 1958 — CD
England: 77/B-1/U21-7

League Club	Source	Date Signed	Seasons Played	Apps	Subs	Gls
Ipswich T	Jnr	08/76	77-85	271	0	16
Coventry C	Glasgow Rangers	11/90	90	6	0	0
Sunderland	Rtd	07/92	92	37	1	0

BUTLAND Jack
Born: Clevedon, Somerset, England, 10 March, 1993 — G
England: 1/U21-28/Youth

League Club	Source	Date Signed	Seasons Played	Apps	Subs	Gls
Birmingham C	Sch	03/10	12	46	0	0
Cheltenham T	L	09/11	11	12	0	0
Cheltenham T	L	02/12	11	12	0	0
Stoke C	Tr	05/13	13-14	5	1	0
Barnsley	L	09/13	13	13	0	0
Leeds U	L	02/14	13	16	0	0
Derby Co	L	10/14	14	6	0	0

BUTLER Andrew Peter (Andy)
Born: Doncaster, South Yorkshire, England, 4 November, 1983 — CD

League Club	Source	Date Signed	Seasons Played	Apps	Subs	Gls
Scunthorpe U	Sch	07/03	03-07	123	12	16
Grimsby T	L	10/06	06	4	0	0
Huddersfield T	Tr	07/08	08-09	52	1	4
Blackpool	L	01/10	09	4	3	0
Walsall	Rochdale (NC)	11/10	10-13	159	0	14
Sheffield U	Tr	06/14				
Walsall	L	09/14	14	7	0	0
Doncaster Rov	Tr	10/14	14	33	0	3

BUTLER Barry
Born: Stockton-on-Tees, Cleveland, England, 30 July, 1934 — CH
Died: Norwich, England, 9 April, 1966

League Club	Source	Date Signed	Seasons Played	Apps	Subs	Gls
Sheffield Wed	South Bank	09/52	53-54	26	-	1
Norwich C	Tr	07/57	57-65	303	0	3

BUTLER Barry Geoffrey
Born: Farnworth, Greater Manchester, England, 4 June, 1962 — M

League Club	Source	Date Signed	Seasons Played	Apps	Subs	Gls
Chester C	Atherton Laburnum Rov	12/85	85-92	255	13	15

BUTLER Brian Francis
Born: Salford, England, 4 July, 1966 — LB/M

League Club	Source	Date Signed	Seasons Played	Apps	Subs	Gls
Blackpool	App	07/84	85-87	58	16	5
Stockport Co	Tr	07/88	88	32	0	2
Halifax T	Tr	07/89	89-90	44	12	4

BUTLER Daniel (Dan)
Born: Cowes, Isle of Wight, England, 26 August, 1994 — LB

League Club	Source	Date Signed	Seasons Played	Apps	Subs	Gls
Portsmouth	Sch	07/12	12-14	42	6	0

BUTLER David
Born: Thornaby, Cleveland, England, 23 March, 1945 — LB/M

League Club	Source	Date Signed	Seasons Played	Apps	Subs	Gls
Workington	Stockton	11/64	64-70	195	3	8
Watford	Tr	11/70	70-75	168	0	2

BUTLER David John (Dave)
Born: Wolverhampton, England, 1 September, 1962 — F

League Club	Source	Date Signed	Seasons Played	Apps	Subs	Gls
Wolverhampton W	App	04/80				
Torquay U	Tr	12/81	81	5	1	0

BUTLER David Joseph
Born: Wednesbury, West Midlands, England, 30 March, 1953 — RW

League Club	Source	Date Signed	Seasons Played	Apps	Subs	Gls
West Bromwich A	App	04/71				
Shrewsbury T	Tr	06/73	73	5	5	0
Workington	L	03/74	73	10	0	0

BUTLER Dennis Anthony
Born: Macclesfield, Cheshire, England, 24 April, 1944 — LW

League Club	Source	Date Signed	Seasons Played	Apps	Subs	Gls
Bolton W	Jnr	06/61	62-67	62	3	11
Rochdale	Tr	02/68	67-72	153	4	36

BUTLER Dennis George
Born: Compton, Berkshire, England, 4 August, 1952 — M

League Club	Source	Date Signed	Seasons Played	Apps	Subs	Gls
Reading	App	05/70	69-70	7	3	1

BUTLER Dennis Michael
Born: Fulham, W London, England, 7 March, 1943 — LB

League Club	Source	Date Signed	Seasons Played	Apps	Subs	Gls
Chelsea	Jnr	06/60	61-62	18	-	0
Hull C	Tr	06/63	63-69	215	2	0
Reading	Tr	12/69	69-73	169	0	0

BUTLER Ernest (Ernie)
Born: Middlesbrough, England, 28 August, 1924 — RW

League Club	Source	Date Signed	Seasons Played	Apps	Subs	Gls
Southend U	Stockton	08/48	48-51	36	-	3
Darlington	Tr	06/53	53	6	-	0

BUTLER Ernest Albert Edward (Ernie)
Born: Box, Wiltshire, England, 13 May, 1919 — G
Died: Portsmouth, England, 24 January, 2002

League Club	Source	Date Signed	Seasons Played	Apps	Subs	Gls
Portsmouth	Bath C	05/38	46-52	222	-	0

BUTLER Geoffrey (Geoff)
Born: Middlesbrough, England, 26 September, 1946 — FB

League Club	Source	Date Signed	Seasons Played	Apps	Subs	Gls
Middlesbrough	App	05/64	65-67	54	1	1
Chelsea	Tr	09/67	67	8	1	0
Sunderland	Tr	01/68	67-68	1	2	0
Norwich C	Tr	10/68	68-75	151	2	1
Bournemouth	Tr	03/76	75-80	118	1	1
Peterborough U	Tr	08/81	81	39	0	0

BUTLER Ian
Born: Darton, South Yorkshire, England, 1 February, 1944 — LW

League Club	Source	Date Signed	Seasons Played	Apps	Subs	Gls

England: Youth

League Club	Source	Date Signed	Seasons Played	Apps	Subs	Gls
Rotherham U	App	08/61	60-64	102	-	27
Hull C	Tr	01/65	64-72	300	5	66
York C	Tr	06/73	73-74	43	3	2
Barnsley	L	10/75	75	5	0	1

BUTLER John (Jackie)
Born: Dawley, Telford & Wrekin, England, 16 October, 1920 LW
Died: Dawley, West Midlands, England, 11 September, 1984

League Club	Source	Date Signed	Seasons Played	Apps	Subs	Gls
Shrewsbury T	Dawley	08/39	50-53	58	-	8

BUTLER John Edward
Born: Liverpool, England, 7 February, 1962 RB

League Club	Source	Date Signed	Seasons Played	Apps	Subs	Gls
Wigan Ath	Prescot Cables	01/82	81-88	238	7	14
Stoke C	Tr	12/88	88-94	258	4	7
Wigan Ath	Tr	06/95	95-96	53	4	1

BUTLER John Herbert
Born: Birmingham, England, 10 March, 1937 CH
Died: Nottingham, England, November, 2010

League Club	Source	Date Signed	Seasons Played	Apps	Subs	Gls
Notts Co	Bestwood Colliery	10/57	58-61	109	-	0
Chester C	Tr	05/62	62-67	220	2	0

BUTLER John Paul
Born: Salford, England, 7 September, 1964 M

League Club	Source	Date Signed	Seasons Played	Apps	Subs	Gls
Blackpool	App	09/82	81-82	4	1	0

BUTLER Joseph William (Joe)
Born: Newcastle-upon-Tyne, England, 7 February, 1943 M/LB

League Club	Source	Date Signed	Seasons Played	Apps	Subs	Gls
Newcastle U	Jnr	09/60	63	3	-	0
Swindon T	Tr	08/65	65-75	355	7	18
Aldershot	Tr	08/76	76-77	31	8	0

BUTLER Kenneth (Ken)
Born: Sunderland, England, 23 August, 1936 LW

League Club	Source	Date Signed	Seasons Played	Apps	Subs	Gls
Hartlepool U	Whitburn	01/60	59-60	20	-	2

BUTLER Lee Simon
Born: Sheffield, England, 30 May, 1966 G

League Club	Source	Date Signed	Seasons Played	Apps	Subs	Gls
Lincoln C	Harworth CI	08/86	86	30	0	0
Aston Villa	Tr	08/87	88-90	8	0	0
Hull C	L	03/91	90	4	0	0
Barnsley	Tr	07/91	91-95	118	2	0
Scunthorpe U	L	02/96	95	2	0	0
Wigan Ath	Tr	07/96	96-97	63	0	0
Halifax T	Dunfermline Ath	09/99	99-01	92	1	0

BUTLER Malcolm Partridge
Born: Belfast, Northern Ireland, 6 August, 1913 FB
Died: Halifax, West Yorkshire, England, December, 1987
Northern Ireland: 1

League Club	Source	Date Signed	Seasons Played	Apps	Subs	Gls
Blackpool	Bangor	01/35	35-38	22	-	0
Accrington Stan	Tr	07/47	47	32	-	0

BUTLER Martin
Born: Hessle, East Riding of Yorkshire, England, 3 March, 1966 F

League Club	Source	Date Signed	Seasons Played	Apps	Subs	Gls
York C	App	10/84	84-88	40	25	9
Aldershot	L	12/85	85	2	0	1
Exeter C	L	02/87	86	4	0	1
Carlisle U	L	12/88	88	1	0	0
Scunthorpe U	Tr	08/89	89	2	0	0
Scarborough	Macclesfield T	11/89	89	1	5	0

BUTLER Martin Neil
Born: Dudley, West Midlands, England, 15 September, 1974 F

League Club	Source	Date Signed	Seasons Played	Apps	Subs	Gls
Walsall	YT	05/93	93-96	43	31	8
Cambridge U	Tr	08/97	97-99	100	3	41
Reading	Tr	02/00	99-03	85	18	32
Rotherham U	Tr	09/03	03-05	90	7	28
Walsall	Tr	07/06	06-07	49	0	12
Grimsby T	Tr	10/07	07-08	18	6	6

BUTLER Michael Anthony (Mick)
Born: Barnsley, South Yorkshire, England, 27 January, 1951 F

League Club	Source	Date Signed	Seasons Played	Apps	Subs	Gls
Barnsley	Worsbrough Bridge MW	07/73	72-75	118	2	57
Huddersfield T	Tr	03/76	75-77	73	6	22
Bournemouth	Tr	07/78	78-79	68	1	19
Bury	Tr	08/80	80-81	80	2	15

BUTLER Paul John
Born: Stockton-on-Tees, Cleveland, England, 9 June, 1964 LW

League Club	Source	Date Signed	Seasons Played	Apps	Subs	Gls
Wolverhampton W	App	06/82	82-84	18	11	2
Hereford U	L	01/84	83	16	0	2
Hereford U	Tr	02/85	84-86	49	15	2
Hartlepool U	Tr	07/87	87	6	3	0

BUTLER Paul John
Born: Manchester, England, 2 November, 1972 CD
Republic of Ireland: 1/B-1

League Club	Source	Date Signed	Seasons Played	Apps	Subs	Gls
Rochdale	YT	07/91	90-95	151	7	10
Bury	Tr	07/96	96-97	83	1	4
Sunderland	Tr	07/98	98-00	78	1	3
Wolverhampton W	L	11/00	00	5	0	0
Wolverhampton W	Tr	01/01	00-03	118	1	3
Leeds U	Tr	07/04	04-06	99	0	4
MK Dons	Tr	11/06	06	17	0	0
Chester C	Tr	07/07	07-08	36	0	2

BUTLER Peter James
Born: Halifax, West Yorkshire, England, 27 August, 1966 M

League Club	Source	Date Signed	Seasons Played	Apps	Subs	Gls
Huddersfield T	App	08/84	84-85	0	5	0
Cambridge U	L	01/86	85	14	0	1
Bury	Tr	07/86	86	9	2	0
Cambridge U	Tr	12/86	86-87	55	0	9
Southend U	Tr	02/88	87-91	135	7	9
Huddersfield T	L	03/92	91	7	0	0
West Ham U	Tr	08/92	92-94	70	0	3
Notts Co	Tr	10/94	94	20	0	0
Grimsby T	L	01/96	95	3	0	0
West Bromwich A	Tr	03/96	95-97	52	8	0
Halifax T	Tr	08/98	98-99	63	0	1

BUTLER Peter Leslie
Born: Nottingham, England, 3 October, 1942 G

League Club	Source	Date Signed	Seasons Played	Apps	Subs	Gls
Notts Co	Jnr	11/60	61-65	44	0	0
Bradford C	Tr	08/66	66	17	0	0

BUTLER Philip Anthony (Tony)
Born: Stockport, Greater Manchester, England, 28 September, 1972 CD

League Club	Source	Date Signed	Seasons Played	Apps	Subs	Gls
Gillingham	YT	05/91	90-95	142	6	5
Blackpool	Tr	07/96	96-98	98	1	0
Port Vale	Tr	03/99	98-99	19	0	0
West Bromwich A	Tr	03/00	99-01	65	5	1
Bristol C	Tr	08/02	02-04	97	1	4
Blackpool	Tr	02/05	04-05	25	7	1

BUTLER Stanley (Stan)
Born: Stillington, North Yorkshire, England, 7 January, 1919 LW
Died: Scunthorpe, North Lincolnshire, England, 16 January, 1979

League Club	Source	Date Signed	Seasons Played	Apps	Subs	Gls
West Bromwich A	Scunthorpe U	05/38	38-46	4	-	0
Southport	Tr	07/47	47	4	-	1

BUTLER Stephen (Steve)
Born: Birmingham, England, 27 January, 1962 F
England: Semi Pro-3

League Club	Source	Date Signed	Seasons Played	Apps	Subs	Gls
Brentford	Windsor & Eton	12/84	84-85	18	3	3
Maidstone U	Tr	08/86	89-90	76	0	41
Watford	Tr	03/91	90-92	40	22	9
Bournemouth	L	12/92	92	1	0	0
Cambridge U	Tr	12/92	92-95	107	2	51
Gillingham	Tr	12/95	95-98	77	31	20
Peterborough U	Tr	10/98	98	13	1	2
Gillingham	Tr	07/99	99	2	8	2

BUTLER Thomas (Tommy)
Born: Atherton, Greater Manchester, England, 28 April, 1918 W
Died: Wigan, Greater Manchester, England, 11 September, 2009

League Club	Source	Date Signed	Seasons Played	Apps	Subs	Gls
Bolton W	Astley & Tyldesley C's	09/36				
Oldham Ath	Macclesfield	02/38	37-38	45	-	9
Middlesbrough	Tr	03/39	38	2	-	0
Oldham Ath	Tr	08/46	46	30	-	3
Accrington Stan	Tr	07/47	47-52	218	-	26

BUTLER Thomas Anthony
Born: Dublin, Republic of Ireland, 25 April, 1981 LM
Republic of Ireland: 2/U21-13/Youth

League Club	Source	Date Signed	Seasons Played	Apps	Subs	Gls
Sunderland	YT	06/98	99-03	16	15	0
Darlington	L	10/00	00	8	0	0
Hartlepool U	Dunfermline Ath	03/05	04-05	31	6	2
Swansea C	Tr	08/06	06-09	75	51	9

BUTLER Walter Garth (Garth)
Born: Birmingham, England, 7 February, 1923 FB
Died: Barnstaple, Devon, England, 13 July, 1995

League Club	Source	Date Signed	Seasons Played	Apps	Subs	Gls
Derby Co	Derby Corinthians	12/42				
Port Vale	Tr	06/46	46-50	128	-	0

BUTLIN Barry Desmond
Born: Rosliston, Derbyshire, England, 9 November, 1949 F

League Club	Source	Date Signed	Seasons Played	Apps	Subs	Gls
Derby Co	Jnr	01/67	67-72	4	0	0
Notts Co	L	01/69	68	20	0	8
Notts Co	L	08/69	69	9	1	5
Luton T	Tr	11/72	72-74	56	1	24
Nottingham F	Tr	10/74	74-76	71	3	17
Brighton & HA	L	09/75	75	5	0	2
Reading	L	01/77	76	5	0	0
Peterborough U	Tr	08/77	77-78	64	0	12
Sheffield U	Tr	08/79	79-80	50	3	12

BUTT Leonard (Len)
Born: Wilmslow, Cheshire, England, 26 August, 1910 — IF
Died: Macclesfield, Cheshire, England, June, 1994

League Club	Source	Date Signed	Seasons Played	Apps	Subs	Gls
Stockport Co	Ashton National	08/28	29-30	8	-	1
Huddersfield T	Macclesfield	05/35	35-36	67	-	11
Blackburn Rov	Tr	01/37	36-46	110	-	44
York C	Tr	01/47	46-47	25	-	2
Mansfield T	Tr	10/47	47	15	-	4

BUTT Nicholas (Nicky)
Born: Manchester, England, 21 January, 1975 — M
England: 39/U21-7/Youth/Schools

League Club	Source	Date Signed	Seasons Played	Apps	Subs	Gls
Manchester U	YT	01/93	92-03	210	60	21
Newcastle U	Tr	07/04	04-09	121	13	5
Birmingham C	L	08/05	05	22	2	3

BUTT Robert
Born: Chester, England, 27 March, 1946 — W

League Club	Source	Date Signed	Seasons Played	Apps	Subs	Gls
Wrexham (Am)	Jnr	01/65	64	3	-	0

BUTTERFIELD Daniel Paul (Danny)
Born: Boston, Lincolnshire, England, 21 November, 1979 — RB
England: Youth

League Club	Source	Date Signed	Seasons Played	Apps	Subs	Gls
Grimsby T	YT	08/97	97-01	100	24	3
Crystal Palace	Tr	08/02	02-09	210	22	6
Charlton Ath	L	03/09	08	12	0	0
Southampton	Tr	07/10	10-11	41	3	0
Bolton W	L	03/13	12	2	4	0
Carlisle U	Tr	08/13	13	1	0	0
Exeter C	Tr	10/13	13-14	52	7	0

BUTTERFIELD Jacob Luke (Jake)
Born: Bradford, England, 10 June, 1990 — M

League Club	Source	Date Signed	Seasons Played	Apps	Subs	Gls
Barnsley	Sch	10/07	07-11	53	37	8
Norwich C	Tr	07/12				
Bolton W	L	11/12	12	4	4	0
Crystal Palace	L	01/13	12	4	5	0
Middlesbrough	Tr	09/13	13	20	11	3
Huddersfield T	Tr	08/14	14	45	0	6

BUTTERFIELD John (Jack)
Born: Barnsley, South Yorkshire, England, 30 August, 1922 — RB
Died: Burnley, Lancashire, England, March, 2001

League Club	Source	Date Signed	Seasons Played	Apps	Subs	Gls
Burnley	Tamworth	02/46	47	3	-	0

BUTTERS Guy
Born: Hillingdon, W London, England, 30 October, 1969 — CD
England: U21-3

League Club	Source	Date Signed	Seasons Played	Apps	Subs	Gls
Tottenham H	YT	08/88	88-89	34	1	1
Southend U	L	01/90	89	16	0	3
Portsmouth	Tr	09/90	90-96	148	6	6
Oxford U	L	11/94	94	3	0	1
Gillingham	Tr	10/96	96-01	155	4	16
Brighton & HA	Tr	08/02	02-07	183	4	8

BUTTERWORTH Adam Lawrence
Born: Paignton, Devon, England, 9 August, 1982 — FB

League Club	Source	Date Signed	Seasons Played	Apps	Subs	Gls
Cambridge U	Torquay U (Jnr)	07/00	00	0	1	0

BUTTERWORTH Aidan James
Born: Leeds, England, 7 November, 1961 — F
England: Schools

League Club	Source	Date Signed	Seasons Played	Apps	Subs	Gls
Leeds U	Jnr	05/80	80-83	54	10	15
Doncaster Rov	Tr	08/84	84-85	35	15	5

BUTTERWORTH David Albert (Dave)
Born: Bristol, England, 4 May, 1937 — WH

League Club	Source	Date Signed	Seasons Played	Apps	Subs	Gls
Exeter C	Guildford C	12/57	57-59	26	-	0

BUTTERWORTH Garry Jeffrey
Born: Whittlesey, Cambridgeshire, England, 8 September, 1969 — M/LB

League Club	Source	Date Signed	Seasons Played	Apps	Subs	Gls
Peterborough U	YT	06/88	86-91	101	23	4
Rushden & D	Dagenham & Red	08/94	01	28	1	1

BUTTERWORTH Ian Stewart
Born: Crewe, Cheshire, England, 25 January, 1964 — CD
England: U21-8

League Club	Source	Date Signed	Seasons Played	Apps	Subs	Gls
Coventry C	App	08/81	81-84	80	10	0
Nottingham F	Tr	06/85	85-86	26	1	0
Norwich C	Tr	09/86	86-93	230	5	4

BUTTIGIEG John
Born: Sliema, Malta, 5 October, 1963 — D
Malta: 97/Youth

League Club	Source	Date Signed	Seasons Played	Apps	Subs	Gls
Brentford	Sliema W (MLT)	11/88	88-89	24	16	0
Swindon T	L	09/90	90	2	1	0

BUTTLE Stephen Arthur (Steve)
Born: Norwich, England, 1 January, 1953 — M
Died: Norwich, England, 5 June, 2012

League Club	Source	Date Signed	Seasons Played	Apps	Subs	Gls
Ipswich T	App	01/71				
Bournemouth	Tr	08/73	73-76	136	3	12

BUTTNER Alexander
Born: Doetinchem, Netherlands, 11 February, 1989 — LB
Netherlands: U21-1

League Club	Source	Date Signed	Seasons Played	Apps	Subs	Gls
Manchester U	Vitesse Arnhem (NED)	08/12	12-13	9	4	2

BUTTON David Robert Edmund
Born: Stevenage, Hertfordshire, England, 27 February, 1989 — G
England: Youth

League Club	Source	Date Signed	Seasons Played	Apps	Subs	Gls
Tottenham H	Sch	03/06				
Bournemouth	L	01/09	08	4	0	0
Dagenham & Red	L	04/09	08	3	0	0
Crewe Alex	L	07/09	09	10	0	0
Shrewsbury T	L	11/09	09	26	0	0
Plymouth Arg	L	08/10	10	29	1	0
Leyton Orient	L	08/11	11	1	0	0
Doncaster Rov	L	01/12	11	7	0	0
Barnsley	L	03/12	11	9	0	0
Charlton Ath	Tr	08/12	12	5	0	0
Brentford	Tr	07/13	13-14	88	0	0

BUTTRESS Michael David (Mike)
Born: Peterborough, England, 23 March, 1958 — LB

League Club	Source	Date Signed	Seasons Played	Apps	Subs	Gls
Aston Villa	App	02/76	76-77	1	2	0
Gillingham	Tr	03/78	77-78	5	2	0

BUXTON Adam Mark
Born: Liverpool, England, 12 May, 1992 — FB

League Club	Source	Date Signed	Seasons Played	Apps	Subs	Gls
Wigan Ath	Sch	07/10				
Accrington Stan	Tr	03/14	13-14	26	2	1

BUXTON Ian Raymond
Born: Cromford, Derbyshire, England, 17 April, 1938 — CF
Died: Matlock, Derbyshire, England, 1 October, 2010

League Club	Source	Date Signed	Seasons Played	Apps	Subs	Gls
Derby Co	Matlock T	03/59	59-67	144	1	41
Luton T	Tr	09/67	67-68	46	1	14
Notts Co	Tr	07/69	69	4	1	1
Port Vale	Tr	12/69	69	16	2	6

BUXTON Jake Fred
Born: Sutton-in-Ashfield, Nottinghamshire, England, 4 March, 1985 — CD

League Club	Source	Date Signed	Seasons Played	Apps	Subs	Gls
Mansfield T	Jnr	10/02	02-07	144	7	5
Derby Co	Burton A	05/09	09-14	118	18	11

BUXTON Lewis Edward
Born: Newport, Isle of Wight, England, 10 December, 1983 — RB

League Club	Source	Date Signed	Seasons Played	Apps	Subs	Gls
Portsmouth	YT	04/01	01-02	27	3	0
Exeter C	L	10/02	02	4	0	0
Bournemouth	L	01/03	02	15	2	0
Bournemouth	L	10/03	03	24	2	0
Stoke C	Tr	12/04	04-07	40	13	1
Sheffield Wed	Tr	10/08	08-14	192	4	6

BUXTON Michael James (Mick)
Born: Corbridge, Northumberland, England, 29 May, 1943 — LB

League Club	Source	Date Signed	Seasons Played	Apps	Subs	Gls
Burnley	Jnr	06/60	62-67	16	2	0
Halifax T	Tr	06/68	68-70	36	0	0

BUXTON Nicholas Gareth (Nick)
Born: Doncaster, South Yorkshire, England, 6 September, 1976 — G

League Club	Source	Date Signed	Seasons Played	Apps	Subs	Gls
Scarborough	Goole T	10/97	97	3	0	0

BUXTON Stephen Christopher (Steve)
Born: Birmingham, England, 13 March, 1960 — F

League Club	Source	Date Signed	Seasons Played	Apps	Subs	Gls
Wrexham	Jnr	07/78	77-83	93	16	21
Stockport Co	Tr	07/84	84	12	6	1
Wrexham	Altrincham	10/85	85-89	86	35	25

BUYENS Yoni
Born: Duffel, Belgium, 10 March, 1988 — DM
Belgium: U21-2/Youth

League Club	Source	Date Signed	Seasons Played	Apps	Subs	Gls
Charlton Ath (L)	Standard Liege (BEL)	06/14	14	38	2	8

BUZSAKY Akos
Born: Budapest, Hungary, 7 May, 1982 — M
Hungary: 20

League Club	Source	Date Signed	Seasons Played	Apps	Subs	Gls
Plymouth Arg	FC Porto (POR)	01/05	04-07	65	31	8
Queens Park Rgrs	Tr	10/07	07-11	77	37	23
Portsmouth	Videoton (HUN)	10/12	12	5	1	0
Barnsley	L	11/12	12	4	1	0

BYATT Dennis John
Born: Hillingdon, W London, England, 8 August, 1958 — CD

League Club	Source	Date Signed	Seasons Played	Apps	Subs	Gls
Fulham	App	05/76				
Peterborough U	Tr	07/78	78	2	1	0
Northampton T	Tr	06/79	79-80	46	1	3

BYCROFT Sydney (Syd)
Born: Lincoln, England, 19 February, 1912 — CH
Died: Doncaster, South Yorkshire, England, 4 October, 2004

League Club	Source	Date Signed	Seasons Played	Apps	Subs	Gls
Bradford C	Grantham	07/32				
Hull C	Tr	10/32				
Doncaster Rov	Newark T	01/36	35-51	333	-	2

BYERS George William
Born: Ilford, E London, England, 29 May, 1996 — M
Scotland: Youth

League Club	Source	Date Signed	Seasons Played	Apps	Subs	Gls
Watford	Sch	05/14	14	0	1	0

BYERS Richard
Born: Haltwhistle, Northumberland, England, 19 December, 1951 — F

League Club	Source	Date Signed	Seasons Played	Apps	Subs	Gls
Workington (Am)	Hadrian Paints	10/71	71	1	0	0

BYFIELD Darren Asherton
Born: Sutton Coldfield, West Midlands, England, 29 September, 1976 — F
Jamaica: 6

League Club	Source	Date Signed	Seasons Played	Apps	Subs	Gls
Aston Villa	YT	02/94	97	1	6	0
Preston NE	L	11/98	98	3	2	1
Northampton T	L	08/99	99	6	0	1
Cambridge U	L	09/99	99	3	1	0
Blackpool	L	03/00	99	3	0	0
Walsall	Tr	06/00	00-01	45	32	13
Rotherham U	Tr	03/02	01-03	53	15	22
Sunderland	Tr	02/04	03	8	9	5
Gillingham	Tr	07/04	04-05	54	13	19
Millwall	Tr	06/06	06	28	3	16
Bristol C	Tr	08/07	07	17	16	8
Doncaster Rov	Tr	07/08	08	3	12	0
Oldham Ath	L	11/08	08	8	0	1
Oldham Ath	Tr	08/09	09	0	3	0
Walsall	Tr	08/09	09-10	39	17	12

BYGRAVE Adam Michael
Born: Walthamstow, NE London, England, 24 February, 1989 — CD

League Club	Source	Date Signed	Seasons Played	Apps	Subs	Gls
Reading	Sch	07/07				
Gillingham	L	11/07	07	13	2	0

BYNG David Graeme (Dave)
Born: Coventry, England, 9 July, 1977 — F

League Club	Source	Date Signed	Seasons Played	Apps	Subs	Gls
Torquay U	YT	07/95	93-95	12	12	3

BYRAM Samuel Mark (Sam)
Born: Thurrock, Essex, England, 16 September, 1993 — RB/M

League Club	Source	Date Signed	Seasons Played	Apps	Subs	Gls
Leeds U	Sch	07/12	12-14	95	13	6

BYRNE Anthony Brendan (Tony)
Born: Rathdowney, Co. Laois, Republic of Ireland, 2 February, 1946 — D
Republic of Ireland: 14

League Club	Source	Date Signed	Seasons Played	Apps	Subs	Gls
Millwall	Jnr	08/63	63	1	-	0
Southampton	Tr	08/64	66-73	81	12	3
Hereford U	Tr	08/74	74-76	54	1	0
Newport Co	Tr	03/77	76-78	80	0	1

BYRNE Christopher Thomas (Chris)
Born: Manchester, England, 9 February, 1975 — W
England: Semi Pro-1

League Club	Source	Date Signed	Seasons Played	Apps	Subs	Gls
Crewe Alex	YT	06/93				
Sunderland	Macclesfield T	06/97	97	4	4	0
Stockport Co	Tr	11/97	97-00	43	13	11
Macclesfield T	L	08/99	99	5	0	0
Macclesfield T	Tr	07/01	01-02	28	7	7

BYRNE Clifford (Cliff)
Born: Dublin, Republic of Ireland, 27 April, 1982 — RB
Republic of Ireland: U21-10/Youth

League Club	Source	Date Signed	Seasons Played	Apps	Subs	Gls
Sunderland	YT	05/99				
Scunthorpe U	L	11/02	02	13	0	0
Scunthorpe U	Tr	07/03	03-11	241	22	9
Oldham Ath	Tr	07/12	12-13	32	6	1
Scunthorpe U	L	09/13	13	7	3	0

BYRNE Daniel Thomas (Danny)
Born: Frimley, Surrey, England, 30 November, 1984 — M
Republic of Ireland: Youth

League Club	Source	Date Signed	Seasons Played	Apps	Subs	Gls
Manchester U	Sch	09/03				
Hartlepool U	L	11/03	03	2	0	0

BYRNE David Stuart
Born: Hammersmith, W London, England, 5 March, 1961 — W

League Club	Source	Date Signed	Seasons Played	Apps	Subs	Gls
Gillingham	Kingstonian	07/85	85	18	5	3
Millwall	Tr	07/86	86-87	52	11	6
Cambridge U	L	09/88	88	4	0	0
Blackburn Rov	L	02/89	88	4	0	0
Plymouth Arg	Tr	03/89	88-90	52	7	2
Bristol Rov	L	02/90	89	0	2	0
Watford	Tr	11/90	90	16	1	2
Reading	L	08/91	91	7	0	2
Fulham	L	01/92	91	5	0	0
Walsall (L)	Partick Thistle	02/94	93	5	0	0

BYRNE Desmond (Des)
Born: Dublin, Republic of Ireland, 10 April, 1981 — LB/M
Republic of Ireland: Youth

League Club	Source	Date Signed	Seasons Played	Apps	Subs	Gls
Stockport Co	YT	-	98	2	0	0
Wimbledon	St Patrick's Ath (ROI)	08/00	01	0	1	0
Cambridge U	L	08/01	01	3	1	0
Carlisle U	Tr	10/02	02-03	18	3	0

BYRNE Gerald (Gerry)
Born: Glasgow, Scotland, 10 April, 1957 — M

League Club	Source	Date Signed	Seasons Played	Apps	Subs	Gls
Cardiff C	App	04/75	77-78	11	4	0

BYRNE Gerald (Gerry)
Born: Liverpool, England, 29 August, 1938 — LB
England: 2/U23-1

League Club	Source	Date Signed	Seasons Played	Apps	Subs	Gls
Liverpool	Jnr	08/55	57-68	273	1	2

BYRNE Jason Noel
Born: Dublin, Republic of Ireland, 23 February, 1978 — F
Republic of Ireland: 2

League Club	Source	Date Signed	Seasons Played	Apps	Subs	Gls
Cardiff C	Shelbourne (ROI)	01/07	06	2	8	1

BYRNE John
Born: Cambuslang, Glasgow, Scotland, 20 May, 1939 — IF

League Club	Source	Date Signed	Seasons Played	Apps	Subs	Gls
Preston NE	Pollok Jnrs	03/58				
Tranmere Rov	Queen of the South	05/61	61	27	-	4
Barnsley	Hibernian	11/63	63-64	68	-	13
Peterborough U	Tr	07/65	65-67	106	1	28
Northampton T	Tr	12/67	67-68	40	0	4

BYRNE John Frederick
Born: Manchester, England, 1 February, 1961 — F
Republic of Ireland: 23

League Club	Source	Date Signed	Seasons Played	Apps	Subs	Gls
York C	App	01/79	79-84	167	8	55
Queens Park Rgrs	Tr	10/84	84-87	108	18	30
Brighton & HA	Le Havre (FRA)	09/90	90-91	47	4	14
Sunderland	Tr	10/91	91-92	33	0	8
Millwall	Tr	10/92	92-93	12	5	1
Brighton & HA	L	03/93	92	5	2	2
Oxford U	Tr	11/93	93-94	52	3	18
Brighton & HA	Tr	02/95	94-95	29	10	6

BYRNE John Joseph (Johnny)
Born: West Horsley, Surrey, England, 13 May, 1939 — CF
Died: Cape Town, South Africa, 27 October, 1999
England: 11/FLge-4/U23-7/Youth

League Club	Source	Date Signed	Seasons Played	Apps	Subs	Gls
Crystal Palace	Guildford C	05/56	56-61	203	-	85
West Ham U	Tr	03/62	61-66	156	0	79
Crystal Palace	Tr	02/67	66-67	36	0	5
Fulham	Tr	03/68	67-68	16	3	2

BYRNE John Joseph Anthony
Born: Wallasey, Wirral, England, 24 March, 1949 — RW

League Club	Source	Date Signed	Seasons Played	Apps	Subs	Gls
Tranmere Rov (Am)	Cammell Laird	11/68	68	1	0	0

BYRNE Joseph (Joe)
Born: Workington, Cumbria, England, 24 April, 1929 — G
Died: Cockermouth, Cumbria, England, December, 1993

League Club	Source	Date Signed	Seasons Played	Apps	Subs	Gls
Workington (Am)	Frizington White Star	09/52	52	2	-	0

BYRNE Mark
Born: Dublin, Republic of Ireland, 9 November, 1988 — M

League Club	Source	Date Signed	Seasons Played	Apps	Subs	Gls
Nottingham F	Crumlin U	01/07	07	0	2	0
Barnet	L	07/10	10	15	1	4
Barnet	L	03/11	10	11	1	2
Barnet	Tr	06/11	11-12	74	9	8
Newport Co	Tr	07/14	14	39	3	4

BYRNE Mark John
Born: Billinge, Merseyside, England, 8 May, 1983 — LW

League Club	Source	Date Signed	Seasons Played	Apps	Subs	Gls
Blackburn Rov	YT	07/01				
Stockport Co	Tr	03/02	01	1	4	0

BYRNE Michael (Mick)
Born: Dublin, Republic of Ireland, 14 January, 1960 — F

League Club	Source	Date Signed	Seasons Played	Apps	Subs	Gls
Huddersfield T	Shamrock Rov (ROI)	09/88	88-89	46	10	11

BYRNE Michael Thomas
Born: Huddersfield, West Yorkshire, England, 14 May, 1985 — F

League Club	Source	Date Signed	Seasons Played	Apps	Subs	Gls
Stockport Co	Bolton W (YT)	10/03	03	1	0	1

BYRNE Nathan William
Born: St Albans, Hertfordshire, England, 5 June, 1992 — RB/M

League Club	Source	Date Signed	Seasons Played	Apps	Subs	Gls
Tottenham H	Sch	07/10				
Brentford	L	02/11	10	4	7	0
Bournemouth	L	07/11	11	9	0	0

League Club	Source	Date Signed	Seasons Played	Apps	Subs	Gls
Crawley T	L	09/12	12	11	1	1
Swindon T	Tr	03/13	12-14	78	7	7

BYRNE Neill
Born: Dublin, Republic of Ireland, 2 February, 1993 RB
Republic of Ireland: Youth

League Club	Source	Date Signed	Seasons Played	Apps	Subs	Gls
Nottingham F	Sch	07/10				
Rochdale	Tr	01/12	11	2	1	0

BYRNE Patrick Joseph (Pat)
Born: Dublin, Republic of Ireland, 15 May, 1956 M
Republic of Ireland: 8

League Club	Source	Date Signed	Seasons Played	Apps	Subs	Gls
Leicester C	Shelbourne (ROI)	07/79	79-80	31	5	3

BYRNE Paul
Born: Natal, South Africa, 26 November, 1982 LB

League Club	Source	Date Signed	Seasons Played	Apps	Subs	Gls
Port Vale	Sch	07/02	00-02	8	3	0

BYRNE Paul Peter
Born: Dublin, Republic of Ireland, 30 June, 1972 M
Republic of Ireland: U21-1/Youth/Schools

League Club	Source	Date Signed	Seasons Played	Apps	Subs	Gls
Oxford U	YT	07/89	89-91	4	2	0
Brighton & HA (L)	Glasgow Celtic	03/95	94	8	0	1
Southend U	Glasgow Celtic	08/95	95-97	70	13	6

BYRNE Raymond (Ray)
Born: Newry, Armagh, Northern Ireland, 4 July, 1972 M

League Club	Source	Date Signed	Seasons Played	Apps	Subs	Gls
Nottingham F	Newry T	02/91				
Northampton T	Tr	08/94	94	2	0	0

BYRNE Richard Philip (Richie)
Born: Dublin, Republic of Ireland, 24 September, 1981 LB
Republic of Ireland: B-1

League Club	Source	Date Signed	Seasons Played	Apps	Subs	Gls
Oldham Ath	Aberdeen	09/08	08	3	1	0
Darlington	Inverness CT	02/10	09	2	2	0

BYRNE Roger William
Born: Manchester, England, 8 September, 1929 LB
Died: Munich, Germany, 6 February, 1958
England: 33/B-3/FLge-6

League Club	Source	Date Signed	Seasons Played	Apps	Subs	Gls
Manchester U	Ryder Brow BC	03/49	51-57	245	-	17

BYRNE Sam John
Born: Dublin, Republic of Ireland, 23 July, 1995 F
Republic of Ireland: Youth

League Club	Source	Date Signed	Seasons Played	Apps	Subs	Gls
Manchester U	Sch	07/12				
Carlisle U	L	01/14	13	4	13	1
Everton	Tr	07/14				

BYRNE Shane William
Born: Dublin, Republic of Ireland, 25 April, 1993 M
Republic of Ireland: Youth

League Club	Source	Date Signed	Seasons Played	Apps	Subs	Gls
Leicester C	Sch	07/10				
Bury	L	08/11	11	10	4	0
Bury	Tr	08/12	12	1	2	0

BYRNE Shaun Ryan
Born: Chesham, Buckinghamshire, England, 21 January, 1981 RB
Republic of Ireland: U21-10/Youth

League Club	Source	Date Signed	Seasons Played	Apps	Subs	Gls
West Ham U	YT	07/99	99-01	0	2	0
Bristol Rov	L	01/00	99	1	1	0
Swansea C	L	01/04	03	9	0	0

BYRNE Wesley John
Born: Dublin, Republic of Ireland, 9 February, 1977 FB
Republic of Ireland: Youth/Schools

League Club	Source	Date Signed	Seasons Played	Apps	Subs	Gls
Middlesbrough	YT	02/94				
Stoke C	Tr	07/96				
Darlington	Tr	12/96	96	1	1	0

BYRNE William (Billy)
Born: Newcastle-under-Lyme, Potteries, England, 22 October, 1918 RW
Died: Newcastle-under-Lyme, Potteries, England, 20 August, 2001

League Club	Source	Date Signed	Seasons Played	Apps	Subs	Gls
Port Vale	Blackpool (Am)	05/46	46	15	-	2
Crewe Alex	Tr	07/47	47-48	17	-	1

BYROM David John
Born: Padiham, Lancashire, England, 6 January, 1965 LB
England: Schools

League Club	Source	Date Signed	Seasons Played	Apps	Subs	Gls
Blackburn Rov	App	01/83				
Stockport Co	Tr	10/84	84	3	0	0

BYROM Joel Alan
Born: Accrington, Lancashire, England, 14 September, 1986 M
England: Semi Pro-1

League Club	Source	Date Signed	Seasons Played	Apps	Subs	Gls
Blackburn Rov	Sch	10/04				
Accrington Stan	Tr	08/06	06	0	1	0
Stevenage	Northwich Victoria	05/09	10-11	34	5	4
Preston NE	Tr	08/12	12-13	19	14	4
Oldham Ath	L	03/14	13	2	2	0
Northampton T	Tr	08/14	14	37	2	3

BYROM John
Born: Blackburn, Greater Manchester, England, 28 July, 1944 F
England: Youth

League Club	Source	Date Signed	Seasons Played	Apps	Subs	Gls
Blackburn Rov	Jnr	08/61	61-65	106	2	45
Bolton W	Tr	06/66	66-75	296	8	113
Blackburn Rov	Tr	09/76	76	15	1	5

BYROM Raymond (Ray)
Born: Blackburn, Greater Manchester, England, 2 January, 1935 LW

League Club	Source	Date Signed	Seasons Played	Apps	Subs	Gls
Accrington Stan	Blackburn Rov (Am)	01/56	57-58	9	-	1
Bradford Park Ave	Tr	12/58	58-60	70	-	14

BYROM Thomas (Tom)
Born: Upton, Wirral, England, 17 March, 1920 LH

League Club	Source	Date Signed	Seasons Played	Apps	Subs	Gls
Tranmere Rov	Heswall	05/39	46	3	-	0

BYROM William (Bill)
Born: Blackburn, Greater Manchester, England, 30 March, 1915 FB
Died: Surrey, England, March, 1989

League Club	Source	Date Signed	Seasons Played	Apps	Subs	Gls
Burnley	Rossendale U	08/37				
Queens Park Rgrs	Tr	05/39				
Rochdale	Tr	06/46	46-47	30	-	0

BYRON Gordon Frank
Born: Prescot, Merseyside, England, 4 September, 1953 M

League Club	Source	Date Signed	Seasons Played	Apps	Subs	Gls
Sheffield Wed	App	07/71				
Lincoln C	Tr	08/74	74	3	3	0

BYRON Michael John
Born: Crosby, Merseyside, England, 16 August, 1987 CD

League Club	Source	Date Signed	Seasons Played	Apps	Subs	Gls
Hull C	Sch	07/06				
Notts Co	L	03/07	06	2	1	0
Notts Co	Tr	09/07				

BYRON Paul
Born: Preston, Lancashire, England, 9 May, 1965 CD

League Club	Source	Date Signed	Seasons Played	Apps	Subs	Gls
Hartlepool U	Blackburn Rov (NC)	08/86	86	1	0	0

BYWATER Noel Leslie (Les)
Born: Lichfield, Staffordshire, England, 8 February, 1920 G
Died: Rochdale, Greater Manchester, England, 9 November, 1998

League Club	Source	Date Signed	Seasons Played	Apps	Subs	Gls
Huddersfield T	Tuke & Bell, Lichfield	03/45				
Luton T	Tr	09/46	46	19	-	0
Rochdale	Tr	12/47	47-48	34	-	0

BYWATER Stephen Michael (Steve)
Born: Manchester, England, 7 June, 1981 G
England: U21-6/Youth

League Club	Source	Date Signed	Seasons Played	Apps	Subs	Gls
West Ham U	Rochdale (YT)	08/98	99-05	57	2	0
Wycombe W	L	09/99	99	2	0	0
Hull C	L	11/99	99	4	0	0
Coventry C	L	08/05	05	14	0	0
Derby Co	Tr	08/06	06-10	149	1	0
Ipswich T	L	01/08	07	17	0	0
Cardiff C	L	03/11	10	8	0	0
Sheffield Wed	Tr	09/11	11	32	0	0
Millwall	Tr	07/13	13	6	1	0
Gillingham	L	08/14	14	13	0	0
Doncaster Rov	Tr	01/15	14	21	0	0

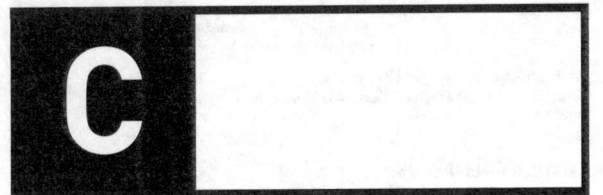

League Club	Source	Date Signed	Seasons Played	Apps	Subs	Gls
CABALLERO Fabian Orlando						
Born: Misiones, Argentina, 31 January, 1978						F
Arsenal (L)	Cerro Porteno (PAR)	10/98	98	0	1	0
CABALLERO Wilfredo Daniel (Willy)						
Born: Entre Rios, Argentina, 28 September, 1981						G
Argentina: U23/Youth						
Manchester C	Malaga (SPN)	07/14	14	2	0	0
CABAYE Yohan						
Born: Tourcoing, France, 14 January, 1986						M
France: 38/U21-15/Youth						
Newcastle U	Lille OSC (FRA)	06/11	11-13	76	3	17
CABELLA Remy						
Born: Ajaccio, France, 8 March, 1990						RW
France: 4/U21-17						
Newcastle U	Montpellier (FRA)	07/14	14	21	10	1
[CABRAL] TAVAREA Adilson						
Born: Praia, Cape Verde Islands, 22 October, 1988						DM
Switzerland: U21-8/Youth						
Sunderland	FC Basel (SUI)	06/13	13	1	0	0
CABRIE David McArthur						
Born: Port Glasgow, Inverclyde, Scotland, 3 June, 1918						WH
Died: Cardiff, Wales, 19 July, 1985						
Newport Co	St Mirren	05/46	46	9	-	0
[CACAPA] DA SILVA Claudio Roberto						
Born: Lavras, Brazil, 29 May, 1976						CD
Brazil: 4						
Newcastle U	Olymp Lyonnais (FRA)	08/07	07-08	20	5	1
CACERES Adrian Claudio						
Born: Buenos Aires, Argentina, 10 January, 1982						W
Southampton	Perth Glory (AUS)	09/00				
Brentford	L	09/01	01	5	0	0
Hull C	Tr	03/02	01	1	3	0
Yeovil T	Perth Glory (AUS)	06/04	04	7	14	3
Wycombe W	Aldershot T	03/05	04	1	2	0
CADAMARTERI Daniel Leon (Danny)						
Born: Cleckheaton, West Yorkshire, England, 12 October, 1979						F
England: U21-3/Youth						
Everton	YT	10/96	96-01	38	55	13
Fulham	L	11/99	99	3	2	1
Bradford C	Tr	02/02	01-03	42	10	5
Leeds U	Tr	07/04				
Sheffield U	Tr	09/04	04	14	7	1
Bradford C	Tr	06/05	05	25	14	2
Leicester C		12/06	06	0	9	0
Doncaster Rov	L	03/07	06	6	0	1
Huddersfield T	Tr	06/07	07-08	34	10	5
Huddersfield T	Dundee U	01/11	10-11	8	18	3
Carlisle U	Tr	07/12	12	14	11	2
CADDEN Joseph Young (Joe)						
Born: Glasgow, Scotland, 13 April, 1920						CH
Died: Liverpool, England, 5 June, 1981						
Liverpool	Brooklyn W (USA)	07/48	50	4	-	0
Grimsby T	Tr	02/52	52	1	-	0
Accrington Stan	Tr	06/53	53	17	-	0
CADDIS Paul McLean						
Born: Kilmarnock, Ayrshire, Scotland, 19 April, 1988						RB/M
Scotland: U21-13/Youth						
Swindon T	Glasgow Celtic	08/10	10-11	75	2	5
Birmingham C	L	09/12	12	27	0	0
Birmingham C	Tr	09/13	13-14	79	4	11
CADE David						
Born: Hemsworth, West Yorkshire, England, 29 September, 1938						W
England: Schools						
Barnsley	Doncaster Rov (Am)	05/57				
Bradford Park Ave	Tr	07/59	59	1	-	0

League Club	Source	Date Signed	Seasons Played	Apps	Subs	Gls
CADE Jamie William						
Born: Durham, England, 15 January, 1984						M
England: Youth						
Middlesbrough	YT	07/01				
Chesterfield	L	09/03	03	9	1	2
Colchester U	Tr	11/03	03-04	10	14	0
CADETE Santos Reis Jorge (Jorge)						
Born: Pemba, Mozambique, 27 August, 1968						F
Portugal: 33/U21-2						
Bradford C (L)	Benfica (POR)	02/00	99	2	5	0
CADETTE Nathan Daniel						
Born: Cardiff, Wales, 6 January, 1980						M
Wales: Youth						
Cardiff C	YT	06/98	97	0	4	0
CADETTE Richard Raymond						
Born: Hammersmith, W London, England, 21 March, 1965						F
Leyton Orient	Wembley	08/84	84	19	2	4
Southend U	Tr	08/85	85-86	90	0	49
Sheffield U	Tr	07/87	87	26	2	7
Brentford	Tr	07/88	88-91	67	20	20
Bournemouth	L	03/90	89	4	4	1
Millwall	Falkirk	10/94	94-96	19	5	5
CADIOU Frederic (Freddie)						
Born: Paris, France, 20 April, 1969						F
Leyton Orient	Wasquehal (FRA)	10/00	00	0	3	0
CADOGAN Kieran James Nathan						
Born: Tooting, SW London, England, 19 April, 1988						RW
Crystal Palace	Sch	08/08	08-11	8	13	2
Burton A	L	11/09	09	2	0	0
Rotherham U	L	01/12	11	7	6	1
Aldershot T	Tr	09/12	12	20	3	1
CADWALLADER Gavin James						
Born: Shrewsbury, Shropshire, England, 18 April, 1986						CD
Shrewsbury T	Sch	07/05	05	0	2	0
CAESAR Gus Cassius						
Born: Tottenham, N London, England, 5 March, 1966						CD
England: U21-3						
Arsenal	App	02/84	85-89	27	17	0
Queens Park Rgrs	L	11/90	90	5	0	0
Cambridge U	Tr	07/91				
Bristol C	Tr	09/91	91	9	1	0
Colchester U	Airdrieonians	08/94	94-95	62	0	3
CAFFREY Henry (Harry)						
Born: Paisley, Renfrewshire, Scotland, 15 February, 1966						LW
Hereford U	Clydebank	07/91	91	12	5	2
CAGIGAO Francisco						
Born: Paddington, Central London, England, 10 November, 1969						F
Southend U	Barcelona (SPN)	09/91	92	0	1	0
CAHILL Gary James						
Born: Dronfield, Derbyshire, England, 19 December, 1985						CD
England: 36/U21-3/Youth						
Aston Villa	Sch	12/03	05-07	25	3	1
Burnley	L	11/04	04	27	0	1
Sheffield U	L	09/07	07	16	0	2
Bolton W	Tr	01/08	07-11	130	0	13
Chelsea	Tr	01/12	11-14	95	7	5
CAHILL Oliver Francis (Ollie)						
Born: Clonmel, Co. Tipperary, Republic of Ireland, 29 September, 1975						W
Northampton T	Clonmel T (ROI)	09/94	94-95	7	4	1
CAHILL Paul Gerard						
Born: Liverpool, England, 29 September, 1955						CD
England: Youth						
Coventry C	App	01/73				
Portsmouth	Tr	02/75	74-77	95	2	2
Aldershot	L	01/78	77	2	0	0
Tranmere Rov	California Surf (USA)	10/78	78	5	0	0
Stockport Co	Tr	02/79	78	3	0	0
CAHILL Thomas (Tommy)						
Born: Glasgow, Scotland, 14 June, 1931						LB
Died: Spain, 27 January, 2003						
Newcastle U	Vale of Leven	12/51	52-53	4	-	0
Barrow	Tr	08/55	55-64	285	-	3
CAHILL Thomas Christopher (Tom)						
Born: Leyland, Lancashire, England, 21 November, 1986						F
Rotherham U	Matlock T	07/07	07	5	2	0

League Club	Source	Date Signed	Seasons Played	Apps	Subs	Gls

CAHILL Timothy (Tim)
Born: Sydney, Australia, 6 December, 1979 — M/F
Australia: 82/U23-3//Samoa: Youth

League Club	Source	Date Signed	Seasons Played	Apps	Subs	Gls
Millwall	Sydney U (AUS)	07/97	97-03	212	5	52
Everton	Tr	07/04	04-11	210	16	56

CAICEDO Felipe Salvador
Born: Guayaquil, Ecuador, 5 September, 1988 — F
Ecuador: 55

League Club	Source	Date Signed	Seasons Played	Apps	Subs	Gls
Manchester C	FC Basel (SUI)	01/08	07-08	10	17	4

CAIG Antony (Tony)
Born: Whitehaven, Cumbria, England, 11 April, 1974 — G

League Club	Source	Date Signed	Seasons Played	Apps	Subs	Gls
Carlisle U	YT	07/92	92-98	223	0	0
Blackpool	Tr	03/99	98-00	49	0	0
Charlton Ath	Tr	11/00	00	0	1	0
Newcastle U	Hibernian	01/03				
Barnsley	L	01/04	03	3	0	0

CAIN Ashley Thomas
Born: Nuneaton, Warwickshire, England, 27 September, 1990 — RW

League Club	Source	Date Signed	Seasons Played	Apps	Subs	Gls
Coventry C	Sch	06/09	08-09	0	7	0

CAIN James Patrick (Jimmy)
Born: Fishburn, County Durham, England, 29 December, 1933 — WH
Died: Sedgefield, County Durham, England, 20 May, 2015

League Club	Source	Date Signed	Seasons Played	Apps	Subs	Gls
Bristol C	Stockton	05/57				
Hartlepool U	South Shields	08/60	60-61	30	-	0

CAIN Michael Dean
Born: Luton, England, 18 February, 1994 — M

League Club	Source	Date Signed	Seasons Played	Apps	Subs	Gls
Leicester C	Sch	12/11				
Mansfield T	L	02/14	13	0	2	0
Walsall	L	10/14	14	28	4	2

CAINE Brian
Born: Nelson, Lancashire, England, 20 June, 1936 — G

League Club	Source	Date Signed	Seasons Played	Apps	Subs	Gls
Blackpool	Accrington Stan (Am)	02/57	57	1	-	0
Coventry C	Tr	09/59	60	1	-	0
Northampton T	Tr	07/61				
Barrow	Tr	10/61	61-63	109	-	0

CAINE William George (Billy)
Born: Barrow, Cumbria, England, 1 July, 1927 — D
Died: Lancashire, England, January, 2009

League Club	Source	Date Signed	Seasons Played	Apps	Subs	Gls
Barrow	Barrow RFC	04/52	51-54	12	-	0

CAINES Gavin Liam
Born: Birmingham, England, 20 September, 1983 — CD

League Club	Source	Date Signed	Seasons Played	Apps	Subs	Gls
Walsall	Sch	07/03				
Cheltenham T	Tr	07/04	04-08	115	28	7

CAIRNEY Charles (Chic)
Born: Blantyre, Lanarkshire, Scotland, 21 September, 1926 — RH
Died: Airdrie, Lanarkshire, Scotland, 25 March, 1995

League Club	Source	Date Signed	Seasons Played	Apps	Subs	Gls
Leyton Orient	Glasgow Celtic	10/50	50	4	-	0
Bristol Rov	Barry T	07/53	53-54	14	-	1

CAIRNEY James (Jim)
Born: Glasgow, Scotland, 13 July, 1931 — CH

League Club	Source	Date Signed	Seasons Played	Apps	Subs	Gls
Portsmouth	Shawfield Jnrs	09/49				
York C	Tr	07/56	56-57	53	-	0

CAIRNEY Thomas (Tom)
Born: Nottingham, England, 20 January, 1991 — M
Scotland: U21-6/Youth

League Club	Source	Date Signed	Seasons Played	Apps	Subs	Gls
Hull C	Sch	07/09	09-12	44	26	2
Blackburn Rov	Tr	08/13	13-14	68	8	8

CAIRNS Alexander Thomas (Alex)
Born: Leeds, England, 4 January, 1993 — G

League Club	Source	Date Signed	Seasons Played	Apps	Subs	Gls
Leeds U	Sch	07/11	11	0	1	0

CAIRNS Colin
Born: Alloa, Stirlingshire, Scotland, 17 September, 1936 — IF

League Club	Source	Date Signed	Seasons Played	Apps	Subs	Gls
Southend U	Heart of Midlothian	02/58	58	2	-	0

CAIRNS John Greenfield (Jackie)
Born: Newcastle-upon-Tyne, England, 13 April, 1922 — IF
Died: Chichester, West Sussex, England, September, 1988

League Club	Source	Date Signed	Seasons Played	Apps	Subs	Gls
Hartlepool U	Heaton Stannington	03/48	47-49	16	-	2

CAIRNS Kevin William
Born: Preston, Lancashire, England, 29 June, 1937 — LB

League Club	Source	Date Signed	Seasons Played	Apps	Subs	Gls
Southport	Dundee U	08/62	62-67	204	2	1

CAIRNS Robert Lynn
Born: Choppington, Northumberland, England, 25 December, 1927 — RB
Died: Bedlington, Northumberland, England, 4 January, 1958

League Club	Source	Date Signed	Seasons Played	Apps	Subs	Gls
Gateshead	Sunderland (Am)	09/48	48-56	139	-	0

CAIRNS Robert Seggie (Bobby)
Born: Glenboig, Lanarkshire, Scotland, 27 May, 1929 — WH
Died: Stoke-on-Trent, England, 26 June, 1998

League Club	Source	Date Signed	Seasons Played	Apps	Subs	Gls
Stoke C	Ayr U	12/53	53-60	175	-	9

CAIRNS Ronald (Ronnie)
Born: Chopwell, Tyne and Wear, England, 4 April, 1934 — IF

League Club	Source	Date Signed	Seasons Played	Apps	Subs	Gls
Blackburn Rov	Consett	09/53	55-58	26	-	7
Rochdale	Tr	06/59	59-63	195	-	66
Southport	Tr	07/64	64	34	-	13

CAIRNS William Hart (Billy)
Born: Newcastle-upon-Tyne, England, 7 October, 1914 — CF
Died: Cleethorpes, North Lincolnshire, England, 9 January, 1988

League Club	Source	Date Signed	Seasons Played	Apps	Subs	Gls
Newcastle U	Stargate Rov	05/33	34-38	87	-	51
Gateshead	Tr	11/44				
Grimsby T	Tr	05/46	46-53	221	-	121

CAIRO Ellery Francois
Born: Rotterdam, Netherlands, 3 August, 1978 — RW

League Club	Source	Date Signed	Seasons Played	Apps	Subs	Gls
Coventry C	Hertha Berlin (GER)	07/07	07	4	3	0

CAIZLEY Kevin
Born: Jarrow, Tyne and Wear, England, 2 December, 1968 — M

League Club	Source	Date Signed	Seasons Played	Apps	Subs	Gls
Newcastle U	YT	08/87				
Darlington	Tr	07/88	88	8	4	1

CAKEBREAD Gerald (Gerry)
Born: Acton, W London, England, 1 April, 1936 — G
Died: Taunton, Somerset, England, 16 September, 2009
England: Youth

League Club	Source	Date Signed	Seasons Played	Apps	Subs	Gls
Brentford	Jnr	06/55	54-63	348	-	0

[CALA] TORRES Juan
Born: Lebrija, Spain, 26 November, 1989 — CD
Spain: Youth

League Club	Source	Date Signed	Seasons Played	Apps	Subs	Gls
Cardiff C	Sevilla (SPN)	02/14	13-14	8	0	2

CALCUTT Connor
Born: Hemel Hempstead, Hertfordshire, England, 10 October, 1993 — F

League Club	Source	Date Signed	Seasons Played	Apps	Subs	Gls
Stevenage	Berkhamsted T	08/14	14	0	8	1

CALDER William Carson (Bill)
Born: Glasgow, Scotland, 28 September, 1934 — CF

League Club	Source	Date Signed	Seasons Played	Apps	Subs	Gls
Leicester C	Port Glasgow	08/55	58	3	-	0
Bury	Tr	05/59	59-63	174	-	67
Oxford U	Tr	11/63	63-66	66	1	28
Rochdale	Tr	11/66	66	7	1	1

CALDERBANK George Raymond (Ray)
Born: Manchester, England, 8 February, 1936 — IF

League Club	Source	Date Signed	Seasons Played	Apps	Subs	Gls
Rochdale (Am)	Hyde U	08/53	53	1	-	0

CALDERON Inigo
Born: Vitoria-Gasteiz, Spain, 4 January, 1982 — RB

League Club	Source	Date Signed	Seasons Played	Apps	Subs	Gls
Brighton & HA	Dep Alaves (SPN)	01/10	09-14	159	22	18

CALDERWOOD Colin
Born: Stranraer, Dumfries & Galloway, Scotland, 20 January, 1965 — CD
Scotland: 36/Schools

League Club	Source	Date Signed	Seasons Played	Apps	Subs	Gls
Mansfield T	Inverness CT	03/82	81-84	97	3	1
Swindon T	Tr	07/85	85-92	328	2	20
Tottenham H	Tr	07/93	93-98	152	11	6
Aston Villa	Tr	03/99	98-99	23	3	0
Nottingham F	Tr	03/00	99-00	7	1	0
Notts Co	L	03/01	00	5	0	0

CALDERWOOD James (Jimmy)
Born: Glasgow, Scotland, 28 February, 1955 — RB/M
Scotland: U23-1

League Club	Source	Date Signed	Seasons Played	Apps	Subs	Gls
Birmingham C	App	07/72	72-79	135	10	4
Cambridge U	L	11/79	79	8	0	0

CALDWELL Anthony (Tony)
Born: Salford, England, 21 March, 1958 — F

League Club	Source	Date Signed	Seasons Played	Apps	Subs	Gls
Bolton W	Horwich RMI	06/83	83-86	131	8	58
Bristol C	Tr	07/87	87-88	9	8	3
Chester C	L	01/88	87	4	0	0
Grimsby T	Tr	09/88	88	2	1	0
Stockport Co	Tr	10/88	88-89	23	3	5

CALDWELL David Lees
Born: Clydebank, Dunbartonshire, Scotland, 7 May, 1932 — FB

League Club	Source	Date Signed	Seasons Played	Apps	Subs	Gls
Rotherham U	Aberdeen	05/60	60	1	-	0

CALDWELL David Wilson (Dave)
Born: Aberdeen, Scotland, 31 July, 1960 — F

League Club	Source	Date Signed	Seasons Played	Apps	Subs	Gls
Mansfield T	Inverness Caledonian	06/79	79-84	145	12	57
Carlisle U	L	12/84	84	4	0	0
Swindon T	L	02/85	84	5	0	0

League Club	Source	Date Signed	Seasons Played	Apps	Subs	Gls
Chesterfield	Tr	07/85	85-87	64	4	17
Torquay U	Tr	11/87	87	24	0	4
Torquay U (L)	KW Overpelt (BEL)	12/89	89	17	0	6
Chesterfield	KW Overpelt (BEL)	10/90	90-91	27	5	4

CALDWELL Garrett Evan James
Born: Princeton, New Jersey, USA, 6 November, 1973 — G

League Club	Source	Date Signed	Seasons Played	Apps	Subs	Gls
Colchester U	Princeton Univ (USA)	09/95	96	6	0	0

CALDWELL Gary Robert
Born: Stirling, Scotland, 12 April, 1982 — CD
Scotland: 55/B-4/U21-19/Youth/Schools

League Club	Source	Date Signed	Seasons Played	Apps	Subs	Gls
Newcastle U	YT	04/99				
Darlington	L	11/01	01	4	0	0
Coventry C	L	07/02	02	36	0	0
Derby Co	L	08/03	03	6	3	0
Wigan Ath	Glasgow Celtic	01/10	09-13	102	0	6

CALDWELL Peter James
Born: Dorchester-on-Thames, Oxfordshire, England, 5 June, 1972 — G
England: Schools

League Club	Source	Date Signed	Seasons Played	Apps	Subs	Gls
Queens Park Rgrs	YT	03/90				
Leyton Orient	Tr	07/95	95-96	31	0	0

CALDWELL Stephen (Steve)
Born: Stirling, Scotland, 12 September, 1980 — CD
Scotland: 12/B-3/U21-4/Youth

League Club	Source	Date Signed	Seasons Played	Apps	Subs	Gls
Newcastle U	YT	10/97	00-03	20	8	1
Blackpool	L	10/01	01	6	0	0
Bradford C	L	12/01	01	9	0	0
Leeds U	L	02/04	03	13	0	1
Sunderland	Tr	07/04	04-06	75	1	4
Burnley	Tr	01/07	06-09	99	5	5
Wigan Ath	Tr	08/10	10	8	2	0
Birmingham C	Tr	07/11	11-12	76	1	1

CALDWELL Terence (Terry)
Born: Sharlston Common, West Yorkshire, England, 5 December, 1938 — LB
England: Youth

League Club	Source	Date Signed	Seasons Played	Apps	Subs	Gls
Huddersfield T	Jnr	06/57	59	4	-	0
Leeds U	Tr	12/59	59-60	20	-	0
Carlisle U	Tr	07/61	61-69	339	4	1
Barrow	Tr	07/70	70-71	29	1	0

CALEB Graham Stuart
Born: Oxford, England, 25 May, 1945 — CH

League Club	Source	Date Signed	Seasons Played	Apps	Subs	Gls
Luton T	App	05/63	63-64	20	-	0

CALERO Ivan
Born: Madrid, Spain, 21 April, 1995 — W
Spain: Youth

League Club	Source	Date Signed	Seasons Played	Apps	Subs	Gls
Derby Co	Atletico Madrid (SPN)	07/14	14	0	2	0
Burton A	L	02/15	14	3	3	0

CALLACHAN Ralph
Born: Edinburgh, Scotland, 29 April, 1955 — M

League Club	Source	Date Signed	Seasons Played	Apps	Subs	Gls
Newcastle U	Heart of Midlothian	02/77	77	9	0	0

CALLAGHAN Aaron Joseph
Born: Dublin, Republic of Ireland, 8 October, 1966 — CD
Republic of Ireland: U21-2/Youth

League Club	Source	Date Signed	Seasons Played	Apps	Subs	Gls
Stoke C	App	10/84	84-86	10	5	0
Crewe Alex	L	11/85	85	8	0	0
Oldham Ath	Tr	10/86	86-87	11	5	2
Crewe Alex	Tr	05/88	88-91	148	10	6
Preston NE	Tr	08/92	92-93	34	2	2

CALLAGHAN Christopher (Chris)
Born: Sandbach, Cheshire, England, 25 August, 1930 — LB
Died: Cheshire, England, August, 2002

League Club	Source	Date Signed	Seasons Played	Apps	Subs	Gls
Crewe Alex	Bideford	12/52	53-56	44	-	0

CALLAGHAN Ernest (Ernie)
Born: Birmingham, England, 21 January, 1910 — RB
Died: Birmingham, England, 5 May, 1972

League Club	Source	Date Signed	Seasons Played	Apps	Subs	Gls
Aston Villa	Atherstone T	09/30	32-46	125	-	0

CALLAGHAN Frederick John (Fred)
Born: Fulham, W London, England, 19 December, 1944 — LB

League Club	Source	Date Signed	Seasons Played	Apps	Subs	Gls
Fulham	App	08/62	63-73	291	4	9

CALLAGHAN Henry William (Harry)
Born: Glasgow, Scotland, 20 March, 1929 — LW
Died: Paisley, Renfrewshire, Scotland, 25 July, 2014

League Club	Source	Date Signed	Seasons Played	Apps	Subs	Gls
Ipswich T	Kirkintilloch Rob Roy	09/54	54	1	-	0

CALLAGHAN Ian Michael
Born: Prescot, Merseyside, England, 5 August, 1969 — M

League Club	Source	Date Signed	Seasons Played	Apps	Subs	Gls
Bolton W	YT	07/87	87	1	0	0

CALLAGHAN Ian Robert
Born: Liverpool, England, 10 April, 1942 — RW
England: 4/FLge-2/U23-4

League Club	Source	Date Signed	Seasons Played	Apps	Subs	Gls
Liverpool	Jnr	03/60	59-77	637	3	50
Swansea C	Tr	09/78	78-79	76	0	1
Crewe Alex	Cork U (RoI)	10/81	81	15	0	0

CALLAGHAN Nigel Ian
Born: Singapore, 12 September, 1962 — W
England: B-1/U21-9

League Club	Source	Date Signed	Seasons Played	Apps	Subs	Gls
Watford	App	07/80	79-86	209	13	41
Derby Co	Tr	02/87	86-88	76	0	10
Aston Villa	Tr	02/89	88-90	24	2	1
Derby Co	L	09/90	90	12	0	1
Watford	L	03/91	90	6	6	1
Huddersfield T	L	01/92	91	8	0	0

CALLAGHAN Robert (Bobby)
Born: Glasgow, Scotland, 5 October, 1931 — RW
Died: Scunthorpe, North Lincolnshire, England, May, 1991

League Club	Source	Date Signed	Seasons Played	Apps	Subs	Gls
Scunthorpe U	Duntocher Hibernian	08/55	55	19	-	6
Barrow	Tr	10/56	56-57	40	-	10

CALLAGHAN William (Willie)
Born: Glasgow, Scotland, 7 February, 1930 — IF

League Club	Source	Date Signed	Seasons Played	Apps	Subs	Gls
Ipswich T	Glasgow Perthshire	07/52	52-54	21	-	7

CALLAGHAN William Andrew (Willie)
Born: Glasgow, Scotland, 9 December, 1941 — RW

League Club	Source	Date Signed	Seasons Played	Apps	Subs	Gls
Barnsley	Dumbarton	08/64	64	15	-	0

CALLAGHAN William Francis (Bill)
Born: Ebbw Vale, Blaenau Gwent, Wales, 26 February, 1924 — LB
Died: Pontefract, West Yorkshire, England, 16 March, 1981

League Club	Source	Date Signed	Seasons Played	Apps	Subs	Gls
Aldershot	Frickley Colliery	06/49	49	1	-	0

CALLAGHAN William Thomas (Willie)
Born: Dunfermline, Fife, Scotland, 23 March, 1967 — F

League Club	Source	Date Signed	Seasons Played	Apps	Subs	Gls
Walsall (L)	Dunfermline Ath	09/88	88	2	0	1

CALLAN Dennis
Born: Merthyr Tydfil, Wales, 27 July, 1932 — W
Died: Merthyr Tydfil, Wales, October, 2006

League Club	Source	Date Signed	Seasons Played	Apps	Subs	Gls
Cardiff C	Troedyrhiw	07/52	55	1	-	0
Exeter C	L	05/54	54	10	-	1

CALLAN Francis Thomas Moore
Born: Belfast, Northern Ireland, 24 May, 1935 — IF

League Club	Source	Date Signed	Seasons Played	Apps	Subs	Gls
Doncaster Rov	Dundalk (ROI)	11/57	57-58	28	-	6

CALLAND Albert
Born: Lanchester, County Durham, England, 10 September, 1929 — CF
Died: Torbay, Devon, England, 3 January, 2014

League Club	Source	Date Signed	Seasons Played	Apps	Subs	Gls
Torquay U	Langley Park	03/50	51-53	24	-	11

CALLAND Edward (Ted)
Born: Lanchester, County Durham, England, 15 June, 1932 — CF
Died: Torquay, Devon, England, 25 May, 1995

League Club	Source	Date Signed	Seasons Played	Apps	Subs	Gls
Fulham	Durham C	04/52				
Torquay U	Cornsay Park A	09/52	52-56	47	-	21
Exeter C	Tr	07/57	57-59	105	-	49
Port Vale	Tr	08/60	60	12	-	3
Lincoln C	Tr	07/61	61	7	-	3

CALLAND Ralph
Born: Lanchester, County Durham, England, 5 July, 1916 — LB
Died: Torbay, Devon, England, August, 2005

League Club	Source	Date Signed	Seasons Played	Apps	Subs	Gls
Charlton Ath	Bexley U	05/37				
Torquay U	Tr	05/39	46-53	207	-	14

CALLENDER John (Jack)
Born: Prudhoe, Northumberland, England, 2 April, 1923 — WH
Died: Gateshead, Tyne and Wear, England, 22 May, 2001

League Club	Source	Date Signed	Seasons Played	Apps	Subs	Gls
Gateshead	Spen Black & White	05/45	46-57	471	-	42

CALLENDER Norman
Born: Newburn, Tyne and Wear, England, 9 June, 1924 — RH
Died: Northallerton, North Yorkshire, England, July, 1990

League Club	Source	Date Signed	Seasons Played	Apps	Subs	Gls
Darlington	Ashington	06/46	46-48	26	-	1

CALLENDER Thomas Sanderson (Tom)
Born: Prudhoe, Northumberland, England, 20 September, 1920 — CH
Died: Lobley Hill, Tyne and Wear, England, 25 February, 2002
England: Schools

League Club	Source	Date Signed	Seasons Played	Apps	Subs	Gls
Lincoln C	Crawcrook A	09/37	38	23	-	0
Gateshead	Tr	11/45	46-56	439	-	58

CALLOWAY Laurence John (Laurie)
Born: Birmingham, England, 17 June, 1945 — LB/M

League Club	Source	Date Signed	Seasons Played	Apps	Subs	Gls
Wolverhampton W	App	10/62				

League Club	Source	Date Signed	Seasons Played	Apps	Subs	Gls
Rochdale	Tr	07/64	64-67	161	1	4
Blackburn Rov	Tr	03/68	67-69	17	8	1
Southport	Tr	08/70	70	45	0	7
York C	Tr	06/71	71-72	54	1	3
Shrewsbury T	Tr	12/72	72-74	77	5	3

CALOW Charles John Herbert (Charlie)
Born: Belfast, Northern Ireland, 30 September, 1931 — G
Northern Ireland: Amateur

League Club	Source	Date Signed	Seasons Played	Apps	Subs	Gls
Bradford Park Ave	Cliftonville	06/52	52	1	-	0

CALVE Jean
Born: Paris, France, 30 April, 1984 — RB

League Club	Source	Date Signed	Seasons Played	Apps	Subs	Gls
Sheffield U (L)	AS Nancy (FRA)	08/10	10	16	2	1

CALVER Craig Tony
Born: Cambridge, England, 20 January, 1991 — F

League Club	Source	Date Signed	Seasons Played	Apps	Subs	Gls
Southend U	Sch	07/09				
Yeovil T	AFC Sudbury	08/10	10	0	6	0

CALVER Reginald John (John)
Born: Cathcart, Glasgow, Scotland, 22 September, 1938 — LH

League Club	Source	Date Signed	Seasons Played	Apps	Subs	Gls
Burnley	Jnr	09/55				
Southport	Tr	07/61	61	2	-	0

CALVERLEY Alfred (Alf)
Born: Huddersfield, West Yorkshire, England, 24 November, 1917 — LW
Died: Sheffield, England, October, 1991

League Club	Source	Date Signed	Seasons Played	Apps	Subs	Gls
Huddersfield T	Jnr	11/43				
Mansfield T	Tr	06/46	46	30	-	1
Arsenal	Tr	03/47	46	11	-	0
Preston NE	Tr	07/47	47	13	-	0
Doncaster Rov	Tr	12/47	47-52	142	-	11

CALVERT Clifford Alistair (Cliff)
Born: York, England, 21 April, 1954 — FB/M
England: Youth

League Club	Source	Date Signed	Seasons Played	Apps	Subs	Gls
York C	Jnr	07/72	72-75	62	5	0
Sheffield U	Tr	09/75	75-78	78	3	5

CALVERT John Steven (Steve)
Born: Barrow, Cumbria, England, 2 April, 1952 — M

League Club	Source	Date Signed	Seasons Played	Apps	Subs	Gls
Barrow (Am)	Jnr	08/70	71	22	0	4

CALVERT Joseph William Herbert (Joe)
Born: Beighton, South Yorkshire, England, 3 February, 1907 — G
Died: Leicester, England, 23 December, 1999

League Club	Source	Date Signed	Seasons Played	Apps	Subs	Gls
Bristol Rov	Frickley Colliery	05/31	31	42	-	0
Leicester C	Tr	05/32	32-47	72	-	0
Watford	Tr	02/48	47	5	-	0

CALVERT Mark Robert
Born: Consett, County Durham, England, 11 September, 1970 — M

League Club	Source	Date Signed	Seasons Played	Apps	Subs	Gls
Hull C	YT	07/89	88-92	24	6	1
Scarborough	Tr	08/93	93-94	68	4	5

CALVERT-LEWIN Dominic Nathaniel
Born: Sheffield, England, 16 March, 1997 — M

League Club	Source	Date Signed	Seasons Played	Apps	Subs	Gls
Sheffield U	Sch	04/15	14	0	2	0

CALVO-GARCIA Alexander (Alex)
Born: Ordizia, Spain, 1 January, 1972 — M

League Club	Source	Date Signed	Seasons Played	Apps	Subs	Gls
Scunthorpe U	SD Eibar (SPN)	10/96	96-03	205	28	32

CAMARA Aboubacar Sidiki (Titi)
Born: Donka, Guinea, 17 November, 1972 — F
Guinea: 38

League Club	Source	Date Signed	Seasons Played	Apps	Subs	Gls
Liverpool	Olymp Marseille (FRA)	06/99	99	22	11	9
West Ham U	Tr	12/00	00-02	5	6	0

CAMARA Ben Ibrahim
Born: Bonn, Germany, 19 June, 1985 — F

League Club	Source	Date Signed	Seasons Played	Apps	Subs	Gls
Torquay U	Sch	07/03	02	0	2	0

CAMARA Henri
Born: Dakar, Senegal, 10 May, 1977 — F
Senegal: 99

League Club	Source	Date Signed	Seasons Played	Apps	Subs	Gls
Wolverhampton W	CS Sedan (FRA)	08/03	03	29	1	7
Southampton	L	01/05	04	10	3	4
Wigan Ath	Tr	08/05	05-08	46	23	20
West Ham U	L	08/07	07	3	7	0
Stoke C	L	02/09	08	0	4	0
Sheffield U	Hull C (NC)	10/09	09	9	14	4

CAMARA Mohamed (Mo)
Born: Conakry, Guinea, 25 June, 1975 — LB
Guinea: 79

League Club	Source	Date Signed	Seasons Played	Apps	Subs	Gls
Wolverhampton W	Le Havre (FRA)	08/00	00-01	27	18	0
Burnley	Tr	07/03	03-04	90	0	0
Derby Co	Glasgow Celtic	08/06	06-08	21	0	0
Norwich C	L	11/07	07	20	1	0
Blackpool	L	08/08	08	14	0	0
Torquay U	St Mirren	02/10	09	2	0	0

CAMARA Zoumana
Born: Paris, France, 3 April, 1979 — CD
France: 1/B-2

League Club	Source	Date Signed	Seasons Played	Apps	Subs	Gls
Leeds U (L)	RC Lens (FRA)	08/03	03	13	0	1

CAMBIASSO Esteban Matias
Born: Buenos Aires, Argentina, 18 August, 1980 — M
Argentina: 52/Youth

League Club	Source	Date Signed	Seasons Played	Apps	Subs	Gls
Leicester C	Inter Milan (ITA)	08/14	14	27	4	5

CAMDEN Christopher Eric (Chris)
Born: Birkenhead, Wirral, England, 28 May, 1963 — F

League Club	Source	Date Signed	Seasons Played	Apps	Subs	Gls
Chester C	Poulton Victoria	12/83	83	9	0	2
Tranmere Rov	Oswestry T	03/87	86	2	1	1

CAME Mark Raymond
Born: Exeter, England, 14 September, 1961 — CD

League Club	Source	Date Signed	Seasons Played	Apps	Subs	Gls
Bolton W	Winsford U	04/84	84-92	188	7	7
Chester C	Tr	12/92	92-93	47	0	1
Exeter C	Tr	07/94	94-95	70	0	5

CAME Shaun Raymond
Born: Winsford, Cheshire, England, 15 June, 1983 — CD

League Club	Source	Date Signed	Seasons Played	Apps	Subs	Gls
Macclesfield T	YT	07/00	00-02	5	4	0

CAMERON Alexander Ramsey (Alex)
Born: Leith, Edinburgh, Scotland, 5 October, 1943 — RB
Died: Edinburgh, Scotland, 2 April, 1981

League Club	Source	Date Signed	Seasons Played	Apps	Subs	Gls
Oldham Ath	Hibernian	05/64	64	15	-	0

CAMERON Colin
Born: Kirkcaldy, Fife, Scotland, 23 October, 1972 — M
Scotland: 29/B-1

League Club	Source	Date Signed	Seasons Played	Apps	Subs	Gls
Wolverhampton W	Heart of Midlothian	08/01	01-05	136	32	22
Millwall	L	03/06	05	5	0	0
Coventry C	Tr	07/06	06	16	8	2
MK Dons	Tr	07/07	07	21	8	3

CAMERON Courtney Lee
Born: Northampton, England, 22 January, 1993 — W/LB

League Club	Source	Date Signed	Seasons Played	Apps	Subs	Gls
Aston Villa	Sch	07/11				
Rotherham U	L	11/12	12	5	10	1
Torquay U	Tr	07/13	13	15	9	1

CAMERON Daniel (Danny)
Born: Dundee, Scotland, 9 November, 1953 — FB

League Club	Source	Date Signed	Seasons Played	Apps	Subs	Gls
Sheffield Wed	App	07/71	73-75	31	0	1
Colchester U	L	02/75	74	5	0	0
Preston NE	Tr	04/76	75-80	120	2	0

CAMERON Daniel
Born: Dublin, Republic of Ireland, 16 June, 1922 — CH
Republic of Ireland: LoI-1

League Club	Source	Date Signed	Seasons Played	Apps	Subs	Gls
Everton	Shelbourne (ROI)	07/48	48	1	-	0

CAMERON David (Davie)
Born: Glasgow, Scotland, 10 March, 1936 — IF
Died: Glasgow, Scotland, 27 June, 2006

League Club	Source	Date Signed	Seasons Played	Apps	Subs	Gls
Bradford C	Rutherglen Glencairn	04/58	58	7	-	2

CAMERON David Anthony (Dave)
Born: Bangor, Gwynedd, Wales, 24 August, 1975 — F

League Club	Source	Date Signed	Seasons Played	Apps	Subs	Gls
Brighton & HA	St Mirren	07/99	99	6	11	0
Lincoln C	Worthing	07/00	00-01	33	27	8

CAMERON Duncan George Brown
Born: Uddingston, Lanarkshire, Scotland, 1 February, 1936 — RW

League Club	Source	Date Signed	Seasons Played	Apps	Subs	Gls
Swindon T	Burnbank Ath	08/56	56-57	2	-	0

CAMERON Geoffrey Scott (Geoff)
Born: Attleboro, Massachusetts, USA, 11 July, 1985 — RB
USA: 31

League Club	Source	Date Signed	Seasons Played	Apps	Subs	Gls
Stoke C	Houston Dynamo (USA)	08/12	12-14	87	12	2

CAMERON Henry Anthony
Born: Lytham St Annes, Lancashire, England, 28 June, 1997 — M

League Club	Source	Date Signed	Seasons Played	Apps	Subs	Gls
Blackpool	Sch	01/15	14	10	1	1

CAMERON Hugh Gibson
Born: Hamilton, Lanarkshire, Scotland, 1 February, 1927 — LW
Died: Wishaw, Lanarkshire, Scotland, 9 December, 2009

League Club	Source	Date Signed	Seasons Played	Apps	Subs	Gls
Torquay U	Clyde	05/48	48-50	120	-	17
Newcastle U	Tr	04/51	51	2	-	0
Bury	Tr	03/52	51-53	29	-	1
Workington	Tr	11/53	53-55	54	-	5

CAMERON John (Jack)
Born: Clydebank, Dunbartonshire, Scotland, 7 March, 1931 — RB

League Club	Source	Date Signed	Seasons Played	Apps	Subs	Gls
Hartlepool U	Dumbarton	11/53	53-59	175	-	0

CAMERON John Alexander (Johnny)
Born: Greenock, Inverclyde, Scotland, 29 November, 1929 — WH
Died: Greenock, Inverclyde, Scotland, 13 July, 2008

League Club	Source	Date Signed	Seasons Played	Apps	Subs	Gls
Bradford Park Ave	Motherwell	07/56	56	3	-	0

CAMERON Martin George William
Born: Dunfermline, Fife, Scotland, 16 August, 1978 — F

League Club	Source	Date Signed	Seasons Played	Apps	Subs	Gls
Bristol Rov	Alloa Ath	07/00	00-01	16	23	6

CAMERON Nathan Benjamin
Born: Birmingham, England, 21 November, 1991 — CD
England: Youth

League Club	Source	Date Signed	Seasons Played	Apps	Subs	Gls
Coventry C	Sch	06/10	10-12	41	7	0
Northampton T	L	03/13	12	2	1	0
Bury	Tr	06/13	13-14	70	3	6

CAMERON Robert (Bobby)
Born: Greenock, Inverclyde, Scotland, 23 November, 1932 — IF
Scotland: Schools

League Club	Source	Date Signed	Seasons Played	Apps	Subs	Gls
Queens Park Rgrs	Port Glasgow	06/50	50-58	256	-	59
Leeds U	Tr	07/59	59-61	58	-	9
Southend U	Gravesend & Northfleet	10/63	63	3	-	0

CAMERON Rodney Peter (Rod)
Born: Newcastle-upon-Tyne, England, 11 April, 1939 — FB

League Club	Source	Date Signed	Seasons Played	Apps	Subs	Gls
Bradford C	Newcastle West End BC	08/57	58	1	-	0

CAMERON Stuart John
Born: Liverpool, England, 28 November, 1966 — G

League Club	Source	Date Signed	Seasons Played	Apps	Subs	Gls
Preston NE	App	08/83	83	1	0	0

CAMILIERI-GIOIA Carlo
Born: Brussels, Belgium, 14 May, 1975 — M

League Club	Source	Date Signed	Seasons Played	Apps	Subs	Gls
Mansfield T	RSC Charleroi (BEL)	09/99	99	0	2	0

CAMM Mark Liam
Born: Mansfield, Nottinghamshire, England, 1 October, 1981 — RB/M

League Club	Source	Date Signed	Seasons Played	Apps	Subs	Gls
Sheffield U	YT	07/99				
Lincoln C	Tr	08/00	00-02	11	21	0

CAMMACK Stephen Richard (Steve)
Born: Sheffield, England, 20 March, 1954 — F
England: Youth

League Club	Source	Date Signed	Seasons Played	Apps	Subs	Gls
Sheffield U	App	05/71	71-75	21	15	5
Chesterfield	Tr	01/76	75-78	95	18	21
Scunthorpe U	Tr	09/79	79-80	84	0	27
Lincoln C	Tr	07/81	81	18	0	6
Scunthorpe U	Tr	03/82	81-86	159	2	83
Port Vale	L	12/85	85	1	2	0
Stockport Co	L	01/86	85	3	1	1

CAMP Lee Michael John
Born: Derby, England, 22 August, 1984 — G
England: U21-5/Youth//Northern Ireland: 9

League Club	Source	Date Signed	Seasons Played	Apps	Subs	Gls
Derby Co	Sch	07/02	02-06	88	1	0
Queens Park Rgrs	L	03/04	03	12	0	0
Norwich C	L	09/06	06	3	0	0
Queens Park Rgrs	Tr	02/07	06-08	61	0	0
Nottingham F	L	10/08	08	15	0	0
Nottingham F	Tr	07/09	09-11	163	0	0
Norwich C	Tr	01/13	12	1	2	0
West Bromwich A	Tr	09/13				
Bournemouth	Tr	10/13	13-14	42	0	0

CAMP Stephen (Steve)
Born: Manchester, England, 8 February, 1954 — F

League Club	Source	Date Signed	Seasons Played	Apps	Subs	Gls
Fulham	Leatherhead	09/75	75-76	4	1	0
Peterborough U	Tr	08/77	77	6	1	1

CAMPABADEL Eduardo (Edu)
Born: Tarragona, Spain, 26 January, 1993 — CD
Spain: Youth

League Club	Source	Date Signed	Seasons Played	Apps	Subs	Gls
Wigan Ath	Barcelona Jnrs (SPN)	07/12	12	0	1	0

CAMPAGNA Samuel Patrick Philip (Sam)
Born: Worcester, England, 19 November, 1980 — FB

League Club	Source	Date Signed	Seasons Played	Apps	Subs	Gls
Swindon T	YT	07/99	98-99	1	4	0

CAMPANA Jose Angel Gomez
Born: Seville, Spain, 31 May, 1993 — M
Spain: U21-2/Youth

League Club	Source	Date Signed	Seasons Played	Apps	Subs	Gls
Crystal Palace	Sevilla (SPN)	07/13	13	4	2	0

CAMPBELL Adam
Born: North Shields, Tyne and Wear, England, 22 August, 1984 — F
England: Youth

League Club	Source	Date Signed	Seasons Played	Apps	Subs	Gls
Newcastle U	Sch	07/12	12	0	3	0
Carlisle U	L	08/13	13	0	1	0
Fleetwood T	L	08/14	14	0	2	0
Hartlepool U	L	11/14	14	1	1	0

CAMPBELL Alan James
Born: Arbroath, Angus, Scotland, 21 January, 1948 — M
Scotland: U23-1/Youth

League Club	Source	Date Signed	Seasons Played	Apps	Subs	Gls
Charlton Ath	Jnr	02/65	65-70	196	2	28
Birmingham C	Tr	10/70	70-75	169	6	11
Cardiff C	Tr	03/76	75-80	165	2	2
Carlisle U	Tr	11/80	80-81	29	2	2

CAMPBELL Andrew Paul (Andy)
Born: Stockton-on-Tees, Cleveland, England, 18 April, 1979 — F
England: U21-4/Youth

League Club	Source	Date Signed	Seasons Played	Apps	Subs	Gls
Middlesbrough	YT	07/96	95-01	28	28	4
Sheffield U	L	12/98	98	5	0	1
Sheffield U	L	03/99	98	6	0	2
Bolton W	L	03/01	00	3	3	0
Cardiff C	Tr	02/02	01-04	30	43	12
Doncaster Rov	L	01/05	04	1	2	0
Oxford U	L	08/05	05	3	2	0

CAMPBELL Anthony Glen (Glen)
Born: Leyland, Lancashire, England, 26 February, 1965 — G

League Club	Source	Date Signed	Seasons Played	Apps	Subs	Gls
Preston NE	App	02/83	82-84	18	0	0

CAMPBELL Charles
Born: Oban, Argyll & Bute, Scotland, 27 February, 1928 — WH

League Club	Source	Date Signed	Seasons Played	Apps	Subs	Gls
Oldham Ath	Rutherglen Glencairn	11/49	49	2	-	0

CAMPBELL Daniel (Danny)
Born: Oldham, Greater Manchester, England, 3 February, 1944 — CD

League Club	Source	Date Signed	Seasons Played	Apps	Subs	Gls
West Bromwich A	Droylsden	11/62	65-67	8	0	0
Stockport Co	Los Angeles Wolv (USA)	01/69	68-69	31	0	3
Bradford Park Ave	Tr	03/70	69	10	0	1

CAMPBELL Darren Archibald
Born: Huntingdon, Cambridgeshire, England, 16 April, 1986 — W
Scotland: Youth

League Club	Source	Date Signed	Seasons Played	Apps	Subs	Gls
Reading	Sch	04/03	02	0	1	0

CAMPBELL David
Born: Wrexham, Wales, 18 February, 1947 — LW
Died: Wrexham, Wales, 7 December, 2013

League Club	Source	Date Signed	Seasons Played	Apps	Subs	Gls
Wrexham	Jnr	07/65	64-66	41	2	7

CAMPBELL David Alistair
Born: Edinburgh, Scotland, 2 November, 1958 — D

League Club	Source	Date Signed	Seasons Played	Apps	Subs	Gls
Charlton Ath	Jnr	06/77	75-79	71	5	3

CAMPBELL David Anthony
Born: Eglinton, Derry, Northern Ireland, 2 June, 1965 — M
Northern Ireland: 10

League Club	Source	Date Signed	Seasons Played	Apps	Subs	Gls
Nottingham F	App	06/83	84-87	35	6	3
Notts Co	L	02/87	86	18	0	2
Charlton Ath	Tr	10/87	87-88	26	4	1
Plymouth Arg	L	03/89	88	1	0	0
Bradford C	Tr	03/89	88-89	27	8	4
Rotherham U	Shamrock Rov (ROI)	11/92	92	0	1	0
Burnley	West Bromwich A (NC)	03/93	92	7	1	0
Lincoln C	L	02/94	93	2	2	1
Wigan Ath	Tr	08/94	94	7	0	0
Cambridge U	Tr	01/95	94	1	0	0

CAMPBELL David Martin
Born: Dublin, Republic of Ireland, 13 September, 1969 — CD

League Club	Source	Date Signed	Seasons Played	Apps	Subs	Gls
Huddersfield T	Bohemians (ROI)	08/90	90-91	4	0	0

CAMPBELL Donald (Don)
Born: Bootle, Merseyside, England, 19 October, 1932 — LB
England: Youth

League Club	Source	Date Signed	Seasons Played	Apps	Subs	Gls
Liverpool	Jnr	11/50	53-57	47	-	2
Crewe Alex	Tr	07/58	58-61	150	-	1
Gillingham	Tr	09/62	62-63	29	-	0

CAMPBELL Dougald
Born: Kirkintilloch, Dunbartonshire, Scotland, 14 December, 1922 — RW

League Club	Source	Date Signed	Seasons Played	Apps	Subs	Gls
Queens Park Rgrs	RAF Spitalgate	03/48				
Crewe Alex	Tr	07/49	49	33	-	0
Barrow	Tr	08/50	50-51	29	-	3
Grimsby T	Tr	10/51	51	6	-	0

CAMPBELL Dudley Junior (DJ)
Born: Hammersmith, W London, England, 12 November, 1981 — F
England: Semi Pro-2

League Club	Source	Date Signed	Seasons Played	Apps	Subs	Gls
Brentford	Yeading	06/05	05	13	10	9
Birmingham C	Tr	01/06	05-06	19	24	9
Leicester C	Tr	07/07	07-10	22	19	5

League Club	Source	Date Signed	Seasons Played	Apps	Subs	Gls
Blackpool	L	01/09	08	20	0	9
Derby Co	L	11/09	09	6	2	3
Blackpool	L	02/10	09	14	1	8
Blackpool	Tr	08/10	10	30	1	13
Queens Park Rgrs	Tr	08/11	11	2	9	1
Ipswich T	L	10/12	12	17	0	10
Blackburn Rov	L	02/13	12	5	2	0
Blackburn Rov	Tr	07/13	13	2	5	0
Millwall	L	01/14	13	6	3	2

CAMPBELL Fraizer Lee
Born: Huddersfield, West Yorkshire, England, 13 September, 1987 — F
England: 1/U21-14/Youth

League Club	Source	Date Signed	Seasons Played	Apps	Subs	Gls
Manchester U	Sch	03/06	07-08	1	1	0
Hull C	L	10/07	07	32	2	15
Tottenham H	L	09/08	08	1	9	1
Sunderland	Tr	07/09	09-12	29	29	6
Cardiff C	Tr	01/13	12-13	41	8	13
Crystal Palace	Tr	07/14	14	13	7	4

CAMPBELL Frank
Born: Dunkeld, Perthshire, Scotland, 23 December, 1950 — M

League Club	Source	Date Signed	Seasons Played	Apps	Subs	Gls
Grimsby T	Jnr	03/68	68	4	0	0

CAMPBELL Gary
Born: Belfast, Northern Ireland, 4 April, 1966 — M

League Club	Source	Date Signed	Seasons Played	Apps	Subs	Gls
Arsenal	App	01/84				
Leyton Orient	Leyton Wingate	01/90	89	4	4	0

CAMPBELL Gregory Robert (Greg)
Born: Portsmouth, England, 13 July, 1965 — F

League Club	Source	Date Signed	Seasons Played	Apps	Subs	Gls
West Ham U	App	10/82	84-85	3	2	0
Brighton & HA	L	02/87	86	0	2	0
Plymouth Arg	Sparta Rotterdam (NED)	11/88	88-89	21	14	6
Northampton T	Tr	07/90	90-91	32	15	7

CAMPBELL James (Jock)
Born: East Kilbride, Lanarkshire, Scotland, 11 November, 1922 — RB
Died: Cambridge, England, 7 July, 1983

League Club	Source	Date Signed	Seasons Played	Apps	Subs	Gls
Charlton Ath	RAF Brize Norton	01/45	46-57	255	-	1

CAMPBELL James (Jim)
Born: Glasgow, Scotland, 25 November, 1918 — RW
Died: Glasgow, Scotland, 12 January, 2011

League Club	Source	Date Signed	Seasons Played	Apps	Subs	Gls
Leicester C	St Anthony's	10/43				
Walsall	Tr	10/46	46-47	14	-	1

CAMPBELL James Charles (Jimmy)
Born: St Pancras, Central London, England, 11 April, 1937 — RW
Died: Dudley, West Midlands, England, 30 January, 1994

League Club	Source	Date Signed	Seasons Played	Apps	Subs	Gls
West Bromwich A	Maidenhead U	10/55	57-58	31	-	9
Portsmouth	Tr	07/59	59-61	50	-	12
Lincoln C	Tr	05/62	62-63	63	-	16

CAMPBELL Jamie
Born: Birmingham, England, 21 October, 1972 — M/D

League Club	Source	Date Signed	Seasons Played	Apps	Subs	Gls
Luton T	YT	07/91	91-93	10	26	1
Mansfield T	L	11/94	94	3	0	1
Cambridge U	L	03/95	94	12	0	0
Barnet	Tr	07/95	95-96	50	17	5
Cambridge U	Tr	08/97	97-98	91	0	6
Brighton & HA	Tr	07/99	99	22	1	1
Exeter C	Tr	07/00	00-01	56	2	3

CAMPBELL Joel Nathaniel
Born: San Jose, Costa Rica, 26 June, 1992 — F
Costa Rica: 42/Youth

League Club	Source	Date Signed	Seasons Played	Apps	Subs	Gls
Arsenal	Saprissa (CRC)	08/11	14	0	4	0

CAMPBELL John
Born: Prudhoe, Northumberland, England, 23 July, 1928 — LW/CF
Died: February, 2015

League Club	Source	Date Signed	Seasons Played	Apps	Subs	Gls
Gateshead	Ashington	11/49	49-55	181	-	45

CAMPBELL John
Born: Alexandria, Dunbartonshire, Scotland, 22 September, 1934 — LW
Died: Alexandria, Dunbartonshire, Scotland, 26 April, 2010

League Club	Source	Date Signed	Seasons Played	Apps	Subs	Gls
Chesterfield	Motherwell	08/59	59	1	-	0

CAMPBELL John (Jackie)
Born: Liverpool, England, 17 March, 1922 — WH
Died: Spain, October, 2007

League Club	Source	Date Signed	Seasons Played	Apps	Subs	Gls
Liverpool		04/43				
Blackburn Rov	Tr	12/45	46-55	224	-	19
Oldham Ath	Tr	07/56	56	26	-	5

CAMPBELL John Peter (Johnny)
Born: Belfast, Northern Ireland, 28 June, 1923 — LW
Died: Belfast, Northern Ireland, January, 1968
Northern Ireland: 2/NILge-4

League Club	Source	Date Signed	Seasons Played	Apps	Subs	Gls
Fulham	Belfast Celtic	03/49	49-52	62	-	4

CAMPBELL John Terence
Born: Newcastle-on-Tyne, England, 23 November, 1988 — F

League Club	Source	Date Signed	Seasons Played	Apps	Subs	Gls
Oxford U (L)	Jarrow Roofing	11/14	14	1	2	1

CAMPBELL Joseph (Joe)
Born: Glasgow, Scotland, 28 March, 1925 — IF
Died: Glasgow, Scotland, 7 September, 1980

League Club	Source	Date Signed	Seasons Played	Apps	Subs	Gls
Leyton Orient	Glasgow Celtic	07/49	49	5	-	1
Gillingham	Tr	09/50	50	12	-	2

CAMPBELL Kevin Joseph
Born: Lambeth, S London, England, 4 February, 1970 — F
England: B-1/U21-4

League Club	Source	Date Signed	Seasons Played	Apps	Subs	Gls
Arsenal	YT	02/88	87-94	124	42	46
Leyton Orient	L	01/89	88	16	0	9
Leicester C	L	11/89	89	11	0	5
Nottingham F	Tr	07/95	95-97	79	1	32
Everton	Trabzonspor (TKY)	03/99	98-04	125	20	45
West Bromwich A	Tr	01/05	04-05	35	10	6
Cardiff C	Tr	08/06	06	4	15	0

CAMPBELL Leslie (Les)
Born: Wigan, Greater Manchester, England, 26 July, 1935 — RW

League Club	Source	Date Signed	Seasons Played	Apps	Subs	Gls
Preston NE	Wigan Ath	06/53	53-59	64	-	6
Blackpool	Tr	07/60	60	11	-	0
Tranmere Rov	Tr	06/61	61-63	102	-	9

CAMPBELL Michael (Mike)
Born: Oban, Argyll & Bute, Scotland, 19 November, 1966 — M

League Club	Source	Date Signed	Seasons Played	Apps	Subs	Gls
Hereford U	Army	08/88	88	1	0	0

CAMPBELL Neil Andrew
Born: Middlesbrough, England, 26 January, 1977 — F

League Club	Source	Date Signed	Seasons Played	Apps	Subs	Gls
York C	YT	06/95	96-97	6	6	1
Scarborough	Tr	09/97	97-98	23	22	7
Southend U	Tr	01/99	98-99	15	9	3

CAMPBELL Paul Andrew
Born: Middlesbrough, England, 29 January, 1980 — M

League Club	Source	Date Signed	Seasons Played	Apps	Subs	Gls
Darlington	YT	07/98	97-02	35	26	6

CAMPBELL Paul John
Born: Newcastle-upon-Tyne, England, 7 October, 1964 — M

League Club	Source	Date Signed	Seasons Played	Apps	Subs	Gls
Hartlepool U	Gateshead	10/83	83	1	2	0

CAMPBELL Philip Anthony (Phil)
Born: Barnsley, South Yorkshire, England, 16 October, 1961 — W

League Club	Source	Date Signed	Seasons Played	Apps	Subs	Gls
Sheffield Wed	App	10/79	80	0	1	0

CAMPBELL Raymond Martin John (Ray)
Born: Downpatrick, Northern Ireland, 3 October, 1968 — W

League Club	Source	Date Signed	Seasons Played	Apps	Subs	Gls
Nottingham F	App	10/86				
Hereford U	L	01/88	87	4	0	0

CAMPBELL Robert (Bobby)
Born: Liverpool, England, 23 April, 1937 — WH
England: Youth

League Club	Source	Date Signed	Seasons Played	Apps	Subs	Gls
Liverpool	Jnr	05/54	58-60	24	-	2
Portsmouth	Wigan Ath	11/61	61-65	60	1	2
Aldershot	Tr	07/66	66	2	3	0

CAMPBELL Robert Inglis (Bobby)
Born: Glasgow, Scotland, 28 June, 1922 — RW/IF
Died: Bristol, England, 4 May, 2009
Scotland: 5

League Club	Source	Date Signed	Seasons Played	Apps	Subs	Gls
Chelsea	Falkirk	05/47	47-53	188	-	36
Reading	Tr	08/54	54-57	94	-	12

CAMPBELL Robert McFaul (Bobby)
Born: Belfast, Northern Ireland, 13 September, 1956 — F
Northern Ireland: 2/Youth

League Club	Source	Date Signed	Seasons Played	Apps	Subs	Gls
Aston Villa	App	01/74	73-74	7	3	1
Halifax T	L	02/75	74	14	1	0
Huddersfield T	Tr	04/75	75-76	30	1	9
Sheffield U	Tr	07/77	77	35	2	11
Huddersfield T	Vancouver W'caps (CAN)	09/78	78	7	0	3
Halifax T	Tr	10/78	78	19	3	3
Bradford C	Brisbane C (AUS)	12/79	79-82	147	1	76
Derby Co	Tr	08/83	83	11	0	4
Bradford C	Tr	11/83	83-86	126	0	45
Wigan Ath	Tr	10/86	86-87	61	8	27

CAMPBELL Roy
Born: Congleton, Cheshire, England, 19 October, 1934 — WH

League Club	Source	Date Signed	Seasons Played	Apps	Subs	Gls
Crewe Alex		12/55	55-56	14	-	0

CAMPBELL Sean Martin
Born: Bristol, England, 31 December, 1974 — W

League Club	Source	Date Signed	Seasons Played	Apps	Subs	Gls
Colchester U	YT	07/93	93	1	3	0

League Club	Source	Date Signed	Seasons Played	Career Record Apps	Subs	Gls
CAMPBELL Stuart Pearson						
Born: Corby, Northamptonshire, England, 9 December, 1977						DM
Scotland: U21-14						
Leicester C	YT	07/96	96-99	12	25	0
Birmingham C	L	03/00	99	0	2	0
Grimsby T	Tr	09/00	00-03	154	1	12
Bristol Rov	Tr	07/04	04-11	268	20	2
CAMPBELL Sulzeer Jeremiah (Sol)						
Born: Plaistow, E London, England, 18 September, 1974						CD
England: 73/B-1/U21-11/Youth						
Tottenham H	YT	09/92	92-00	246	9	10
Arsenal	Tr	07/01	01-05	133	2	8
Portsmouth	Tr	08/06	06-08	95	0	2
Notts Co	Rtd	08/09	09	1	0	0
Arsenal	Rtd	01/10	09	10	1	0
Newcastle U	Tr	07/10	10	4	3	0
CAMPBELL Thomas Alan (Alan)						
Born: Belfast, Northern Ireland, 11 September, 1944						LB
Northern Ireland: NILge-10						
Grimsby T	Coleraine	10/70	70-72	84	1	0
CAMPBELL Thomas McMillan (Tommy)						
Born: Glasgow, Scotland, 20 February, 1935						CF
Tranmere Rov	Dundee U	06/61	61	1	-	0
CAMPBELL William Gibson (Billy)						
Born: Belfast, Northern Ireland, 2 July, 1944						RW
Northern Ireland: 6/NILge-3						
Sunderland	Distillery	09/64	64-65	5	0	0
CAMPBELL Winston Richard						
Born: Sheffield, England, 9 October, 1962						LW
Barnsley	App	10/80	79-86	121	7	9
Doncaster Rov	L	01/83	82	3	0	0
Rotherham U	Tr	09/86	86-87	67	2	9
CAMPBELL-RYCE Jamal Julian						
Born: Lambeth, S London, England, 6 April, 1983						RW
Jamaica: 22						
Charlton Ath	Sch	07/02	02-03	0	3	0
Leyton Orient	L	08/02	02	16	1	2
Wimbledon	L	02/04	03	3	1	0
Chesterfield	L	08/04	04	14	0	0
Rotherham U	Tr	11/04	04-05	27	4	0
Southend U	L	09/05	05	7	6	0
Colchester U	L	03/06	05	1	3	0
Southend U	Tr	06/06	06-07	40	5	2
Barnsley	Tr	08/07	07-09	81	9	12
Bristol C	Tr	01/10	09-11	46	16	2
Leyton Orient	L	03/12	11	7	1	1
Notts Co	Tr	07/12	12-13	70	3	11
Sheffield U	Tr	07/14	14	14	5	4
Notts Co	L	02/15	14	3	1	0
CAMPION Achille Pierre Camille						
Born: Paris, France, 10 March, 1990						F
Port Vale	Norrby IF (SWE)	09/14	14	4	8	1
CAMPION Darren						
Born: Birmingham, England, 17 October, 1988						LB
Carlisle U	Birmingham C (Sch)	09/07	07-08	3	1	0
CAMPO Ramos Ivan (Ivan)						
Born: San Sebastian, Spain, 21 February, 1974						CD/M
Spain: 4						
Bolton W	Real Madrid (SPN)	08/02	02-07	149	23	13
Ipswich T	Tr	08/08	08	14	3	1
CAMPS Callum Jason Noel						
Born: Stockport, Greater Manchester, England, 30 November, 1995						M
Northern Ireland: Youth						
Rochdale	Sch	09/13	12-14	6	8	1
CAN Emre						
Born: Frankfurt, Germany, 12 January, 1994						D/M
Germany: U21-13/Youth						
Liverpool	Bayer Leverkusen (GER)	07/14	14	23	4	1
CANA Lorik						
Born: Pristina, Kosovo, 27 July, 1983						DM
Albania: 84						
Sunderland	Olymp Marseille (FRA)	07/09	09	29	2	0
CANAS Jose Alberto						
Born: Jerez de la Frontera, Spain, 27 May, 1987						DM
Swansea C	Real Betis (SPN)	07/13	13	19	4	0

League Club	Source	Date Signed	Seasons Played	Career Record Apps	Subs	Gls
CANAVAN Niall David Stephen						
Born: Bramley, Leeds, England, 11 April, 1991						CD
Republic of Ireland: U21-4						
Scunthorpe U	Sch	07/09	09-14	135	9	15
Shrewsbury T	L	03/11	10	3	0	0
CANDELA Vincent Philippe Antoine						
Born: Bedarieux, France, 24 October, 1973						LB
France: 40						
Bolton W	AS Roma (ITA)	01/05	04	9	1	0
CANDLIN Maurice Hall						
Born: Jarrow, Tyne and Wear, England, 11 November, 1921						RH
Died: Carlisle, Cumbria, England, 31 December, 1992						
Northampton T	Stirling A	02/49	49-52	139	-	1
Shrewsbury T	Tr	07/53	53-54	69	-	2
CANE Jacob Jagger						
Born: Exeter, England, 20 May, 1994						M
Exeter C	Sch	07/12	12	0	1	0
CANERO Peter						
Born: Glasgow, Scotland, 18 January, 1981						RB/M
Scotland: 1/B-3/U21-17						
Leicester C	Kilmarnock	01/04	03-04	8	5	0
CANHAM Anthony (Tony)						
Born: Leeds, England, 8 June, 1960						LW
York C	Harrogate RI	01/85	84-94	309	38	57
Hartlepool U	Tr	08/95	95	25	4	1
CANHAM Marc David						
Born: Wegburg, Germany, 11 September, 1982						M
Colchester U	Sch	07/02	01-02	2	2	0
CANHAM Scott Walter						
Born: Stratford, E London, England, 5 November, 1974						M
West Ham U	YT	07/93				
Torquay U	L	11/95	95	3	0	0
Brentford	L	01/96	95	14	0	0
Brentford	Tr	08/96	96-97	24	11	1
Leyton Orient	Tr	08/98	98-99	3	6	0
Leyton Orient	Chesham U	07/01	01-02	32	8	6
CANHAM Sean Thomas						
Born: Exeter, England, 26 September, 1984						F
Notts Co	Team Bath	08/08	08-09	7	17	3
Hereford U	Tr	07/10	10	7	9	2
CANI Edgar Junior						
Born: Tirana, Albania, 22 July, 1989						F
Albania: 15						
Leeds U (L)	Catania (ITA)	02/15	14	0	4	0
CANN Darren John						
Born: Torquay, Devon, England, 17 June, 1968						CD
Torquay U	App	06/87	86-87	12	1	0
CANN Ralph Graham						
Born: Sheffield, England, 17 November, 1934						CH
Mansfield T	Sheffield FC	05/57	57	1	-	0
CANN Steven Michael (Steve)						
Born: Benoni, South Africa, 20 January, 1988						G
Wales: Youth						
Derby Co	Sch	06/06				
Rotherham U	Tr	08/07	08	0	1	0
CANNELL Paul Anthony						
Born: Newcastle-upon-Tyne, England, 2 September, 1953						F
England: Schools						
Newcastle U	Jnr	07/72	73-77	48	1	13
Mansfield T	North Shields	01/82	81-82	29	1	4
CANNELL Stuart						
Born: Doncaster, South Yorkshire, England, 31 December, 1958						CD
Doncaster Rov	Bentley Victoria	03/78	77-78	22	4	0
CANNING Lawrence Joseph (Larry)						
Born: Cowdenbeath, Fife, Scotland, 1 November, 1925						RH
Died: Nottingham, England, 6 April, 2012						
Aston Villa	Paget Rgrs	10/47	48-53	39	-	3
Northampton T	Kettering T	06/56	56	2	-	0
CANNING Leslie Daniel (Danny)						
Born: Pontypridd, Rhondda Cynon Taff, Wales, 21 February, 1926						G
Died: Saundersfoot, Pembrokeshire, Wales, 30 July, 2014						
Cardiff C	Abercynon	07/45	46-47	80	-	0
Swansea C	Tr	01/49	48-50	47	-	0
Nottingham F	Tr	07/51	51	5	-	0
Newport Co	Yarmouth T	08/55				

CANNON Andrew Francis (Andy)
Born: Ashton-under-Lyne, Greater Manchester, England, 14 March, 1996 RB/M

League Club	Source	Date Signed	Seasons Played	Apps	Subs	Gls
Rochdale	Sch	07/14	14	16	2	0

CANNON James (Jim)
Born: Coatbridge, Lanarkshire, Scotland, 19 March, 1927 IF
Died: Airdrie, Lanarkshire, Scotland, 26 January, 1991

League Club	Source	Date Signed	Seasons Played	Apps	Subs	Gls
Darlington	Third Lanark	06/56	56	12	-	1

CANNON James Anthony (Jim)
Born: Glasgow, Scotland, 2 October, 1953 CD

League Club	Source	Date Signed	Seasons Played	Apps	Subs	Gls
Crystal Palace	App	05/71	72-87	568	3	30

CANOVILLE Dean
Born: Perivale, W London, England, 30 November, 1978 M

League Club	Source	Date Signed	Seasons Played	Apps	Subs	Gls
Millwall	Jnr	12/95	96	0	2	0

CANOVILLE Leroy Paul (Lee)
Born: Ealing, W London, England, 14 March, 1981 RB
England: Youth/Schools

League Club	Source	Date Signed	Seasons Played	Apps	Subs	Gls
Arsenal	YT	07/98				
Northampton T	L	01/01	00	2	0	0
Torquay U	Tr	09/01	01-04	107	5	2
Boston U	Tr	07/05	05-06	57	2	1
Shrewsbury T	L	01/07	06	6	1	0
Notts Co	Tr	07/07	07	32	3	0

CANOVILLE Paul Kenneth
Born: Hillingdon, W London, England, 4 March, 1962 LW

League Club	Source	Date Signed	Seasons Played	Apps	Subs	Gls
Chelsea	Hillingdon Bor	12/81	81-85	53	26	11
Reading	Tr	08/86	86-87	16	0	4

CANSDELL-SHERIFF Shane Lewis
Born: Sydney, Australia, 10 November, 1982 CD
Australia: Youth

League Club	Source	Date Signed	Seasons Played	Apps	Subs	Gls
Leeds U	NSW Soccer Acad (AUS)	02/00				
Rochdale	L	11/02	02	3	0	0
Tranmere Rov	Aarhus GF (DEN)	07/06	06-07	83	4	6
Shrewsbury T	Tr	08/09	08-11	142	8	9
Preston NE	Tr	07/12	12	14	1	1
Rochdale	L	01/13	12	16	1	0
Burton A	L	09/13	13	32	0	0
Burton A	Tr	07/14	14	37	0	2

CANTELLO Leonard (Len)
Born: Manchester, England, 11 September, 1951 M
England: U23-8/Youth/Schools

League Club	Source	Date Signed	Seasons Played	Apps	Subs	Gls
West Bromwich A	App	10/68	68-78	297	4	13
Bolton W	Tr	06/79	79-81	89	1	3
Hereford U	Eastern AA (HKG)	01/83	82	1	0	0
Bury	Tr	02/83	82	8	1	1

CANTONA Eric Daniel Pierre
Born: Paris, France, 24 May, 1966 F
France: 45

League Club	Source	Date Signed	Seasons Played	Apps	Subs	Gls
Leeds U	Nimes (FRA)	02/92	91-92	18	10	9
Manchester U	Tr	11/92	92-96	142	1	64

CANTONA Joel
Born: Paris, France, 26 October, 1967 M

League Club	Source	Date Signed	Seasons Played	Apps	Subs	Gls
Stockport Co	Ujpest (HUN)	03/94	93	0	3	0

CANTWELL Noel Eucharia Cornelius
Born: Cork, Republic of Ireland, 28 December, 1932 LB
Died: Peterborough, England, 7 September, 2005
Republic of Ireland: 36

League Club	Source	Date Signed	Seasons Played	Apps	Subs	Gls
West Ham U	Cork Celtic (ROI)	09/52	52-60	248	-	11
Manchester U	Tr	11/60	60-66	123	0	6

CANVIN Cyril Edward
Born: Hemel Hempstead, Hertfordshire, England, 23 January, 1924 IF
Died: Hemel Hempstead, Hertfordshire, England, 3 November, 1950

League Club	Source	Date Signed	Seasons Played	Apps	Subs	Gls
Leyton Orient	Apsley	03/47	46	3	-	0

CAPALDI Anthony Charles (Tony)
Born: Porsgrunn, Norway, 12 August, 1981 LB
Northern Ireland: 22/U21-14/Youth

League Club	Source	Date Signed	Seasons Played	Apps	Subs	Gls
Birmingham C	YT	07/99				
Plymouth Arg	Tr	05/03	02-06	122	9	12
Cardiff C	Tr	07/07	07-09	56	6	0
Leeds U	L	11/09	09	3	0	0
Morecambe	Tr	09/10	10	17	1	0
Oxford U	Tr	07/11	11-12	25	5	0

CAPE John Phillips (Jackie)
Born: Carlisle, Cumbria, England, 16 November, 1911 RW
Died: Carlisle, Cumbria, England, 6 June, 1994

League Club	Source	Date Signed	Seasons Played	Apps	Subs	Gls
Carlisle U	Penrith	05/29	29	15	-	2
Newcastle U	Tr	01/30	29-33	51	-	18
Manchester U	Tr	01/34	33-36	59	-	18
Queens Park Rgrs	Tr	06/37	37-38	61	-	12
Carlisle U	Tr	08/39				
Carlisle U	Scarborough	10/46	46	3	-	0

CAPEL Frederick John (Fred)
Born: Manchester, England, 14 January, 1927 LB
Died: Chesterfield, Derbyshire, England, 17 September, 1990

League Club	Source	Date Signed	Seasons Played	Apps	Subs	Gls
Chesterfield	Goslings	06/48	49-56	285	-	16

CAPEL John Elwyn
Born: Newport, Wales, 31 March, 1937 RW
Wales: Schools

League Club	Source	Date Signed	Seasons Played	Apps	Subs	Gls
Newport Co	Jnr	12/55	55	3	-	0

CAPEL Maurice John
Born: Crewe, Cheshire, England, 15 February, 1935 CF

League Club	Source	Date Signed	Seasons Played	Apps	Subs	Gls
Crewe Alex	Whitchurch Alport	04/56	55-56	6	-	0

CAPEL Thomas Arthur (Tommy)
Born: Chorlton, Greater Manchester, England, 27 June, 1922 IF
Died: Basford, Nottinghamshire, England, 5 October, 2009

League Club	Source	Date Signed	Seasons Played	Apps	Subs	Gls
Manchester C	Droylsden	11/41	46-47	9	-	2
Chesterfield	Tr	10/47	47-48	62	-	27
Birmingham C	Tr	06/49	49	8	-	2
Nottingham F	Tr	11/49	49-53	154	-	69
Coventry C	Tr	06/54	54-55	36	-	19
Halifax T	Tr	10/55	55	7	-	1

CAPEWELL Ronald (Ron)
Born: Sheffield, England, 26 July, 1929 G

League Club	Source	Date Signed	Seasons Played	Apps	Subs	Gls
Sheffield Wed	Kiveton Park	03/50	52-53	29	-	0
Hull C	Tr	07/54	54	1	-	0

CAPLETON Melvyn David (Mel)
Born: Hackney, E London, England, 24 October, 1973 G

League Club	Source	Date Signed	Seasons Played	Apps	Subs	Gls
Southend U	YT	07/92				
Blackpool	Tr	08/93	94-95	9	2	0
Leyton Orient	Grays Ath	09/98				
Southend U	Tr	10/98	98-00	54	3	0

CAPOUE Etienne
Born: Niort, France, 11 July, 1988 DM
France: 7/U21-12/Youth

League Club	Source	Date Signed	Seasons Played	Apps	Subs	Gls
Tottenham H	Toulouse (FRA)	08/13	13-14	19	5	1

CAPPER John (Jack)
Born: Wrexham, Wales, 23 July, 1931 CH
Died: Wrexham, Wales, 10 March, 2009

League Club	Source	Date Signed	Seasons Played	Apps	Subs	Gls
Wrexham	Jnr	11/49	52-54	48	-	0
Lincoln C	Headington U	01/56	55-58	21	-	0
Chester C	Tr	09/59	59-60	37	-	0

CAPRICE Jake Lenox
Born: Lambeth, S London, England, 11 November, 1992 LB

League Club	Source	Date Signed	Seasons Played	Apps	Subs	Gls
Crystal Palace	Sch	07/11				
Blackpool	Tr	07/12				
Dagenham & Red	L	11/12	12	0	8	0

CAPSTICK Albert Lewin
Born: South Kirkby, West Yorkshire, England, 2 January, 1928 WH

League Club	Source	Date Signed	Seasons Played	Apps	Subs	Gls
Accrington Stan	Fleetwood	08/48	48	1	-	0

CARAYOL Mustapha Soon
Born: Banjul, Gambia, 10 June, 1989 LW

League Club	Source	Date Signed	Seasons Played	Apps	Subs	Gls
MK Dons	Macclesfield T (Sch)	08/07				
Torquay U	Tr	07/08	09	11	9	6
Lincoln C	Tr	07/10	10	24	9	3
Bristol Rov	Tr	07/11	11	24	6	4
Middlesbrough	Tr	08/12	12-13	36	14	11
Brighton & HA	L	03/15	14	4	1	0

CARBERRY James (Jimmy)
Born: Liverpool, England, 13 October, 1969 M

League Club	Source	Date Signed	Seasons Played	Apps	Subs	Gls
Everton	YT	06/88				
Wigan Ath	Tr	06/89	89-91	30	35	6

CARBERRY Lawrence James (Larry)
Born: Liverpool, England, 18 January, 1936 RB
Died: 26 June, 2015

League Club	Source	Date Signed	Seasons Played	Apps	Subs	Gls
Ipswich T	Bootle	05/56	56-64	257	-	0
Barrow	Tr	07/65	65-66	17	0	0

CARBERRY Robert (Bert)
Born: Glasgow, Scotland, 16 January, 1931 CH

League Club	Source	Date Signed	Seasons Played	Apps	Subs	Gls
Norwich C	Avondale	01/49	53-54	5	-	0
Gillingham	Bedford T	07/56	56	1	-	0
Port Vale	Tr	07/57	57	29	-	0
Exeter C	Tr	08/58				

CARBON Matthew Philip (Matt)
Born: Nottingham, England, 8 June, 1975 — CD
England: U21-4

League Club	Source	Date Signed	Seasons Played	Apps	Subs	Gls
Lincoln C	YT	04/93	92-95	66	3	10
Derby Co	Tr	03/96	95-97	11	9	0
West Bromwich A	Tr	01/98	97-00	106	7	5
Walsall	Tr	07/01	01-03	49	6	2
Lincoln C	L	10/03	03	1	0	0
Barnsley	Tr	07/04	04-05	37	13	1
MK Dons	NZ Knights (NZL)	12/07	07	0	3	0

CARBONARI Horacio Angel
Born: Rosario, Argentina, 2 May, 1973 — CD

League Club	Source	Date Signed	Seasons Played	Apps	Subs	Gls
Derby Co	Rosario Central (ARG)	07/98	98-02	89	1	9
Coventry C	L	03/02	01	5	0	0

CARBONE Benito
Born: Bagnara Calabra, Italy, 14 August, 1971 — F
Italy: U21-8

League Club	Source	Date Signed	Seasons Played	Apps	Subs	Gls
Sheffield Wed	Inter Milan (ITA)	10/96	96-99	86	10	25
Aston Villa	Tr	10/99	99	22	2	3
Bradford C	Tr	08/00	00-01	39	3	10
Derby Co	L	10/01	01	13	0	1
Middlesbrough	L	02/02	01	13	0	1

CARDEN Paul Andrew
Born: Liverpool, England, 29 March, 1979 — DM
England: Semi Pro-2

League Club	Source	Date Signed	Seasons Played	Apps	Subs	Gls
Blackpool	YT	07/97	96	0	1	0
Rochdale	Tr	03/98	97-99	30	15	0
Chester C	Tr	03/00	99	9	2	0
Chester C	Doncaster Rov	11/01	04	36	4	0
Peterborough U	Tr	07/05	05-06	43	1	0
Accrington Stan	Burton A	07/07	07	4	0	0

CARDER-ANDREWS Karle
Born: Feltham, SW London, England, 13 March, 1989 — M

League Club	Source	Date Signed	Seasons Played	Apps	Subs	Gls
Brentford	Sch	08/06	06	2	3	0

CARDEW Norman
Born: South Shields, Tyne and Wear, England, 7 November, 1938 — IF

League Club	Source	Date Signed	Seasons Played	Apps	Subs	Gls
Darlington (Am)	South Shields	07/65	65	5	0	1

CARDLE Joseph (Joe)
Born: Blackpool, Lancashire, England, 7 February, 1987 — LW

League Club	Source	Date Signed	Seasons Played	Apps	Subs	Gls
Port Vale	Sch	07/06	05-07	6	16	0

CARDWELL Louis
Born: Blackpool, Lancashire, England, 20 August, 1912 — CH
Died: Blackpool, Lancashire, England, 23 April, 1986

League Club	Source	Date Signed	Seasons Played	Apps	Subs	Gls
Blackpool	Whitegate Jnrs	04/30	30-37	132	-	6
Manchester C	Tr	09/38	38-46	39	-	0
Crewe Alex	Netherfield	10/47	47-48	25	-	0

CAREW Ashley Wayne
Born: Lambeth, S London, England, 17 December, 1985 — RW

League Club	Source	Date Signed	Seasons Played	Apps	Subs	Gls
Barnet	Fisher Ath	05/07	07-08	28	15	2

CAREW John Alieu
Born: Strommen, Norway, 5 September, 1979 — F
Norway: 91/U21-24/Youth

League Club	Source	Date Signed	Seasons Played	Apps	Subs	Gls
Aston Villa	Olymp Lyonnais (FRA)	01/07	06-10	89	24	37
Stoke C	L	01/11	10	7	3	1
West Ham U	Tr	08/11	11	7	12	2

CAREY Alan William
Born: Greenwich, SE London, England, 21 August, 1975 — F

League Club	Source	Date Signed	Seasons Played	Apps	Subs	Gls
Reading	YT	07/94	93-94	0	3	0

CAREY Brian Patrick
Born: Cork, Republic of Ireland, 31 May, 1968 — CD
Republic of Ireland: 3/U21-1

League Club	Source	Date Signed	Seasons Played	Apps	Subs	Gls
Manchester U	Cork C (ROI)	09/89				
Wrexham	L	01/91	90	3	0	0
Wrexham	L	12/91	91	13	0	1
Leicester C	Tr	07/93	93-95	51	7	1
Wrexham	Tr	07/96	96-04	282	6	15

CAREY Graham
Born: Dublin, Republic of Ireland, 20 May, 1989 — LW
Republic of Ireland: U21-6

League Club	Source	Date Signed	Seasons Played	Apps	Subs	Gls
Huddersfield T (L)	Glasgow Celtic	07/10	10	18	1	2

CAREY John Joseph (Johnny)
Born: Dublin, Republic of Ireland, 23 February, 1919 — FB/IF
Died: Wilmslow, Cheshire, England, 23 August, 1995
Republic of Ireland: 29//Northern Ireland: 7/War-2

League Club	Source	Date Signed	Seasons Played	Apps	Subs	Gls
Manchester U	St James' Gate (ROI)	11/36	37-52	304	-	16

CAREY Louis Anthony
Born: Bristol, England, 20 January, 1977 — D
Scotland: U21-1

League Club	Source	Date Signed	Seasons Played	Apps	Subs	Gls
Bristol C	YT	07/95	95-03	301	11	5
Coventry C	Tr	07/04	04	23	0	0
Bristol C	Tr	02/05	04-13	237	10	7

CAREY Peter Richard
Born: Barking, E London, England, 14 April, 1933 — LB/WH

League Club	Source	Date Signed	Seasons Played	Apps	Subs	Gls
Leyton Orient	Barking	10/57	56-59	34	-	2
Queens Park Rgrs	Tr	07/60	60	15	-	1
Colchester U	Tr	11/60	60	10	-	0
Aldershot	Tr	08/61	61-62	47	-	0

CAREY Richard (Dick)
Born: Paisley, Renfrewshire, Scotland, 19 November, 1927 — WH
Died: Renfrew, Renfrewshire, Scotland, 16 December, 2004

League Club	Source	Date Signed	Seasons Played	Apps	Subs	Gls
Southport	Cowdenbeath	07/49	49	1	-	0

CAREY Shaun Peter
Born: Rushden, Northamptonshire, England, 13 May, 1976 — M
Republic of Ireland: U21-2

League Club	Source	Date Signed	Seasons Played	Apps	Subs	Gls
Norwich C	YT	07/94	95-99	50	18	0
Rushden & D	Tr	08/00	01	7	1	0

CARGILL Baily James
Born: Eastleigh, Hampshire, England, 13 October, 1995 — CD
England: Youth

League Club	Source	Date Signed	Seasons Played	Apps	Subs	Gls
Bournemouth	Jnr	07/13				
Torquay U	L	03/14	13	5	0	0

CARGILL David Anderson
Born: Arbroath, Angus, Scotland, 21 July, 1936 — LW
Died: Arbroath, Angus, Scotland, 20 November, 2011

League Club	Source	Date Signed	Seasons Played	Apps	Subs	Gls
Burnley	Jnr	07/53	53-55	5	-	0
Sheffield Wed	Tr	09/56	56-57	10	-	0
Derby Co	Tr	04/58	58-60	56	-	8
Lincoln C	Tr	12/60	60	9	-	0

CARGILL James Gordon (Jim)
Born: Alyth, Perthshire, Scotland, 22 September, 1945 — G
Scotland: Schools

League Club	Source	Date Signed	Seasons Played	Apps	Subs	Gls
Nottingham F	Dundee North End	09/62	64-65	2	0	0
Notts Co	Tr	07/66	66	10	0	0

CARLE Nicholas Alberto (Nick)
Born: Sydney, Australia, 23 November, 1981 — M
Australia: 13/U23-16/Youth

League Club	Source	Date Signed	Seasons Played	Apps	Subs	Gls
Bristol C	Genclerbirligi (TKY)	01/08	07	14	3	0
Crystal Palace	Tr	07/08	08-09	49	10	4

CARLESS Ernest Francis (Ernie)
Born: Barry, Vale of Glamorgan, Wales, 9 September, 1912 — IF
Died: Barry, Vale of Glamorgan, Wales, 26 September, 1987

League Club	Source	Date Signed	Seasons Played	Apps	Subs	Gls
Cardiff C	Barry T	10/32	32	1	-	0
Plymouth Arg	Barry T	12/46	46	4	-	0

CARLIN Patrick (Pat)
Born: Dunscroft, South Yorkshire, England, 17 December, 1929 — RB
Died: Doncaster, South Yorkshire, England, 8 April, 2012

League Club	Source	Date Signed	Seasons Played	Apps	Subs	Gls
Bradford Park Ave	Dunscroft	07/53	53	6	-	0

CARLIN William (Willie)
Born: Liverpool, England, 6 October, 1940 — M
England: Youth/Schools

League Club	Source	Date Signed	Seasons Played	Apps	Subs	Gls
Liverpool	Jnr	05/58	59	1	-	0
Halifax T	Tr	08/62	62-64	95	-	31
Carlisle U	Tr	10/64	64-67	93	0	20
Sheffield U	Tr	09/67	67-68	36	0	3
Derby Co	Tr	08/68	68-70	89	0	14
Leicester C	Tr	10/70	70-71	31	0	1
Notts Co	Tr	09/71	71-73	57	3	2
Cardiff C	Tr	11/73	73	22	0	1

CARLINE Peter
Born: Chesterfield, Derbyshire, England, 2 March, 1951 — CD
Died: Skegby, Nottinghamshire, England, 27 November, 2001

League Club	Source	Date Signed	Seasons Played	Apps	Subs	Gls
Chesterfield	Jnr	09/70	70	1	0	0

CARLING Terence Patrick (Terry)
Born: Otley, West Yorkshire, England, 26 February, 1939 — G

League Club	Source	Date Signed	Seasons Played	Apps	Subs	Gls
Leeds U	Dawson's PE	11/56	60-61	5	-	0
Lincoln C	Tr	07/62	62-63	84	-	0
Walsall	Tr	06/64	64-66	101	0	0
Chester C	Tr	12/66	66-70	199	0	0

CARLISLE Clarke James
Born: Preston, Lancashire, England, 14 October, 1979 — CD
England: U21-3

League Club	Source	Date Signed	Seasons Played	Apps	Subs	Gls
Blackpool	YT	08/97	97-99	85	8	7
Queens Park Rgrs	Tr	05/00	00-03	93	3	6
Leeds U	Tr	07/04	04	29	6	4
Watford	Tr	08/05	05-06	34	2	3
Luton T	L	03/07	06	4	1	0
Burnley	Tr	08/07	07-10	128	3	6
Preston NE	L	07/11	11	20	0	3
Northampton T	L	01/12	11	18	0	1
York C	Tr	08/12	12	10	0	0
Northampton T	Tr	11/12	12	26	0	3

CARLISLE Wayne Thomas
Born: Lisburn, Belfast, Northern Ireland, 9 September, 1979 — RW
Northern Ireland: U21-9/Youth/Schools

League Club	Source	Date Signed	Seasons Played	Apps	Subs	Gls
Crystal Palace	YT	09/96	98-00	29	17	3
Swindon T	L	10/01	01	10	1	2
Bristol Rov	Tr	03/02	01-03	62	9	14
Leyton Orient	Tr	07/04	04-05	27	13	3
Torquay U	Exeter C	06/08	09-10	23	11	2

CARLOS Joao Miguel Martins Pais
Born: Portugal, 2 April, 1989 — W

League Club	Source	Date Signed	Seasons Played	Apps	Subs	Gls
Dagenham & Red	Dartford	11/09	09	0	1	0

CARLSON George Edward
Born: Liverpool, England, 27 July, 1925 — CF
Died: Liverpool, England, August, 2006

League Club	Source	Date Signed	Seasons Played	Apps	Subs	Gls
Tranmere Rov	Army	09/47	47-48	2	-	0

CARLTON Daniel Andrew (Danny)
Born: Leeds, England, 22 December, 1983 — F
England: Semi Pro-1

League Club	Source	Date Signed	Seasons Played	Apps	Subs	Gls
Carlisle U	Morecambe	07/07	07-08	17	26	3
Morecambe	L	11/08	08	8	0	2
Darlington	L	01/09	08	16	1	4
Bury	Tr	07/09	09-10	1	9	0
Morecambe	Tr	02/11	10-12	45	17	12

CARLTON David George
Born: Stepney, E London, England, 24 November, 1952 — M

League Club	Source	Date Signed	Seasons Played	Apps	Subs	Gls
Fulham	App	12/69	71-72	5	4	0
Northampton T	Tr	10/73	73-76	99	5	6
Brentford	Tr	10/76	76-79	138	2	7
Northampton T	Tr	09/80	80-81	76	0	1

CARMICHAEL John (Jack)
Born: Newcastle-upon-Tyne, England, 11 November, 1948 — CD

League Club	Source	Date Signed	Seasons Played	Apps	Subs	Gls
Arsenal	Possilpark Jnrs	11/66				
Peterborough U	Tr	01/71	70-79	331	21	5
Swindon T	New England TM (USA)	09/80				
Peterborough U	Jacksonville TM (USA)	01/83	82	5	1	0

CARMICHAEL Joshua Lewis (Josh)
Born: Poole, Dorset, England, 27 September, 1994 — M
Scotland: Youth

League Club	Source	Date Signed	Seasons Played	Apps	Subs	Gls
Bournemouth	Jnr	10/11	11-12	2	2	0

CARMICHAEL Matthew (Matt)
Born: Singapore, 13 May, 1964 — F

League Club	Source	Date Signed	Seasons Played	Apps	Subs	Gls
Lincoln C	Basingstoke T	08/89	89-92	113	20	18
Scunthorpe U	Tr	07/93	93-94	51	11	20
Barnet	L	09/94	94	2	1	0
Preston NE	Tr	03/95	94	7	3	3
Mansfield T	Tr	08/95	95	1	0	1
Doncaster Rov	Tr	08/95	95	19	8	4
Darlington	Tr	02/96	95	11	2	2

CARMODY Michael Joseph (Mike)
Born: Huddersfield, West Yorkshire, England, 9 February, 1966 — LB

League Club	Source	Date Signed	Seasons Played	Apps	Subs	Gls
Huddersfield T	Emley	12/84	84	8	0	0
Tranmere Rov	Emley	09/86	86	2	0	0

CARNABY Brian James
Born: Plymouth, England, 14 December, 1947 — M

League Club	Source	Date Signed	Seasons Played	Apps	Subs	Gls
Reading	Arcadia Shep's (RSA)	07/72	72-76	136	9	10

CARNEIRO Carlos Paulo Martins
Born: Pacos de Ferreira, Portugal, 27 December, 1974 — F

League Club	Source	Date Signed	Seasons Played	Apps	Subs	Gls
Walsall	Panionis (GRE)	07/07	07	2	1	0

CARNEY David Raymond (Dave)
Born: Sydney, Australia, 30 November, 1983 — LB
Australia: 48/Youth

League Club	Source	Date Signed	Seasons Played	Apps	Subs	Gls
Everton	Sch	01/01				
Oldham Ath	Tr	08/03				
Sheffield U	Sydney FC (AUS)	08/07	07	18	3	2
Norwich C	L	01/09	08	4	5	0
Blackpool	FC Twente (NED)	09/10	10	5	6	0

CARNEY Leonard Francis (Len)
Born: Liverpool, England, 30 May, 1915 — IF
Died: Liverpool, England, March, 1996

League Club	Source	Date Signed	Seasons Played	Apps	Subs	Gls
Liverpool (Am)	Collegiate OB	09/39	46-47	6	-	1

CARNEY Stephen (Steve)
Born: Wallsend, Tyne and Wear, England, 22 September, 1957 — D
Died: Newcastle-upon-Tyne, England, 6 May, 2013

League Club	Source	Date Signed	Seasons Played	Apps	Subs	Gls
Newcastle U	Blyth Spartans	10/79	79-84	125	9	1
Carlisle U	L	03/85	84	6	0	0
Darlington	Tr	08/85	85	10	2	0
Rochdale	L	01/86	85	4	0	0
Hartlepool U	Tr	03/86	85	7	0	0

CAROLAN Joseph Francis (Joe)
Born: Dublin, Republic of Ireland, 8 September, 1937 — LB
Republic of Ireland: 2

League Club	Source	Date Signed	Seasons Played	Apps	Subs	Gls
Manchester U	Home Farm (ROI)	02/56	58-60	66	-	0
Brighton & HA	Tr	12/60	60-61	33	-	0

CAROLE Sebastien
Born: Pontoise, France, 8 September, 1982 — RW

League Club	Source	Date Signed	Seasons Played	Apps	Subs	Gls
West Ham U (L)	AS Monaco (FRA)	01/04	03	0	1	0
Brighton & HA	AS Monaco (FRA)	08/05	05	34	6	2
Leeds U	Tr	07/06	06-07	24	21	3
Darlington	Bradford C (NC)	11/08	08	3	3	0
Brighton & HA	Tr	01/09	08	5	7	0
Tranmere Rov	Tr	08/09	09	4	0	0
Brighton & HA	Tr	01/10	09	7	2	0
Bury	OGC Nice (FRA)	11/12	12	0	4	0

CAROLIN Brian
Born: Ashington, Northumberland, England, 6 December, 1939 — RH

League Club	Source	Date Signed	Seasons Played	Apps	Subs	Gls
Gateshead	Ashington CW	08/57	57-59	17	-	0

CARPENTER Richard
Born: Sheerness, Kent, England, 30 September, 1972 — M

League Club	Source	Date Signed	Seasons Played	Apps	Subs	Gls
Gillingham	YT	05/91	90-96	107	15	4
Fulham	Tr	09/96	96-97	49	9	7
Cardiff C	Tr	07/98	98-99	69	6	2
Brighton & HA	Tr	07/00	00-06	241	11	19

CARPENTER Stephen (Steve)
Born: Torquay, Devon, England, 23 September, 1960 — M

League Club	Source	Date Signed	Seasons Played	Apps	Subs	Gls
Torquay U	STC Paignton	04/86	85	2	0	0

CARPENTER Thomas Albert Edward (Tommy)
Born: Carshalton, S London, England, 11 March, 1925 — G

League Club	Source	Date Signed	Seasons Played	Apps	Subs	Gls
Watford	Harrow T	11/50	50	4	-	0

CARR Ashley
Born: Crowland, Lincolnshire, England, 15 August, 1968 — M

League Club	Source	Date Signed	Seasons Played	Apps	Subs	Gls
Peterborough U	Jnr	08/86	86-88	9	6	0

CARR Christopher Paul (Chris)
Born: Newcastle-upon-Tyne, England, 14 December, 1984 — FB

League Club	Source	Date Signed	Seasons Played	Apps	Subs	Gls
Sheffield Wed	Newcastle U (Sch)	03/04	03	0	2	0

CARR Clifford Paul (Cliff)
Born: Clapton, NE London, England, 19 June, 1964 — LB
England: U21-1

League Club	Source	Date Signed	Seasons Played	Apps	Subs	Gls
Fulham	App	06/82	82-86	136	9	14
Stoke C	Tr	07/87	87-90	116	8	1
Shrewsbury T	Tr	08/91	91	1	0	1
Mansfield T	Telford U	10/91	91	20	0	0
Chesterfield	Tr	08/92	92-93	62	3	1

CARR Daniel Clive (Danny)
Born: Lambeth, S London, England, 30 November, 1993 — F

League Club	Source	Date Signed	Seasons Played	Apps	Subs	Gls
Huddersfield T	Dulwich Hamlet	07/13	13	0	2	0
Fleetwood T	L	11/13	13	1	3	1
Mansfield T	L	10/14	14	3	1	1
Dagenham & Red	L	02/15	14	0	6	0

CARR Darren John
Born: Bristol, England, 4 September, 1968 — CD

League Club	Source	Date Signed	Seasons Played	Apps	Subs	Gls
Bristol Rov	App	08/86	85-87	26	4	0
Newport Co	Tr	10/87	87	9	0	0
Sheffield U	Tr	03/88	87-88	12	1	1
Crewe Alex	Tr	09/90	90-92	96	8	5
Chesterfield	Tr	07/93	93-97	84	2	4
Gillingham	Tr	08/98	98	22	8	2
Brighton & HA	Tr	07/99	99-00	18	3	0
Rotherham U	L	11/00	00	1	0	0
Lincoln C	L	01/01	00	3	0	0
Carlisle U	L	02/01	00	10	0	0
Rushden & D	Tr	01/02	01	1	0	0

CARR David (Dave)
Born: Wheatley Hill, County Durham, England, 19 January, 1937 — IF

Died: Blackhall, County Durham, England, 12 November, 2013

League Club	Source	Date Signed	Seasons Played	Apps	Subs	Gls
Darlington	Spennymoor U	05/57	57-61	132	-	50
Workington	Tr	07/62	62-64	108	-	47
Watford	Tr	02/65	64-65	10	0	3

CARR David (Dave)
Born: Aylesham, Kent, England, 31 January, 1957 M/D
Died: Maidstone, Kent, England, 19 June, 2005

League Club	Source	Date Signed	Seasons Played	Apps	Subs	Gls
Luton T	App	01/75	76-78	39	4	0
Lincoln C	Tr	07/79	79-82	165	3	4
Torquay U	Tr	08/83	83	34	0	0

CARR Derek Henry
Born: Blidworth, Nottinghamshire, England, 1 September, 1927 RH
Died: Birmingham, England, 6 July, 2004

League Club	Source	Date Signed	Seasons Played	Apps	Subs	Gls
Birmingham C	Lockheed Leamington	02/48	49	3	-	0

CARR Edward Miller (Eddie)
Born: Wheatley Hill, County Durham, England, 3 October, 1917 CF
Died: Hartlepool, Cleveland, England, June, 1998

League Club	Source	Date Signed	Seasons Played	Apps	Subs	Gls
Arsenal	Wheatley Hill Welfare	05/35	37-38	12	-	7
Huddersfield T	Tr	10/45	46	2	-	0
Newport Co	Tr	10/46	46-49	98	-	48
Bradford C	Tr	10/49	49-52	94	-	49
Darlington	Tr	08/53	53	7	-	0

CARR Everton Dale
Born: Antigua & Barbuda, 11 January, 1961 LB

League Club	Source	Date Signed	Seasons Played	Apps	Subs	Gls
Leicester C	App	01/79	78-80	11	1	0
Halifax T	Tr	08/81	81-82	49	4	0
Rochdale	Tr	03/83	82	9	0	0

CARR Francis Joseph (Frank)
Born: Maltby, South Yorkshire, England, 21 April, 1919 IF
Died: North Yorkshire, England, July, 2010

League Club	Source	Date Signed	Seasons Played	Apps	Subs	Gls
Rotherham U		09/41				
York C	Tr	08/46	46	7	-	3

CARR Franz Alexander
Born: Preston, Lancashire, England, 24 September, 1966 RW
England: U21-9/Youth

League Club	Source	Date Signed	Seasons Played	Apps	Subs	Gls
Blackburn Rov	App	07/84				
Nottingham F	Tr	08/84	85-90	122	9	17
Sheffield Wed	L	12/89	89	9	3	0
West Ham U	L	03/91	90	1	2	0
Newcastle U	Tr	06/91	91-92	20	5	3
Sheffield U	Tr	01/93	92-93	18	0	4
Leicester C	Tr	09/94	94	12	1	1
Aston Villa	Tr	02/95	94-95	1	2	0
Bolton W	Reggiana (ITA)	10/97	97	0	5	0
West Bromwich A	Tr	02/98	97	1	3	0

CARR Graeme
Born: Chester-le-Street, County Durham, England, 28 October, 1978 M

League Club	Source	Date Signed	Seasons Played	Apps	Subs	Gls
Scarborough	YT	09/97	98	5	5	0

CARR Graham Gordon
Born: Darlington, County Durham, England, 8 December, 1970 G

League Club	Source	Date Signed	Seasons Played	Apps	Subs	Gls
Hartlepool U	YT	08/89	89	1	0	0

CARR John (Jackie)
Born: Bishopbriggs, Glasgow, Scotland, 12 January, 1924 W
Died: Glasgow, Scotland, 18 December, 1990

League Club	Source	Date Signed	Seasons Played	Apps	Subs	Gls
Gillingham	Alloa Ath	06/48	50	11	-	2

CARR John William
Born: Durban, South Africa, 10 June, 1926 LW

League Club	Source	Date Signed	Seasons Played	Apps	Subs	Gls
Huddersfield T	Durban Railway (RSA)	10/50	50	1	-	0

CARR Kevin
Born: Morpeth, Northumberland, England, 6 November, 1958 G

League Club	Source	Date Signed	Seasons Played	Apps	Subs	Gls
Newcastle U	Burnley (App)	07/76	77-84	173	0	0
Carlisle U	Tr	08/85	85-86	17	0	0
Darlington	L	11/86	86	3	0	0
Hartlepool U	Middlesbrough (NC)	07/87	87	31	0	0

CARR Lance Lanyon
Born: Johannesburg, South Africa, 18 February, 1910 LW
Died: Greenwich, SE London, England, 1983

League Club	Source	Date Signed	Seasons Played	Apps	Subs	Gls
Liverpool	Boksburg (RSA)	08/33	33-35	31	-	8
Newport Co	Tr	10/36	36	25	-	5
Newport Co	South Liverpool	07/38	38	39	-	9
Bristol Rov	Tr	08/46	46	42	-	8

CARR Michael Andrew
Born: Crewe, Cheshire, England, 6 December, 1983 M
England: Semi Pro-7

League Club	Source	Date Signed	Seasons Played	Apps	Subs	Gls
Macclesfield T	Sch	07/03	02-03	11	0	0
Morecambe	Northwich Victoria	06/08	08	4	3	0

CARR Peter
Born: Bishop Middleham, County Durham, England, 25 August, 1951 D

League Club	Source	Date Signed	Seasons Played	Apps	Subs	Gls
Darlington	App	08/69	67-72	131	4	1
Carlisle U	Tr	11/72	72-77	202	2	1
Hartlepool U	New England TM (USA)	10/79	79	22	0	0

CARR Peter
Born: Rawmarsh, South Yorkshire, England, 16 November, 1960 M

League Club	Source	Date Signed	Seasons Played	Apps	Subs	Gls
Rotherham U	App	11/78	78-81	31	5	3

CARR Stanley Rushton (Stan)
Born: Southport, Merseyside, England, 1 June, 1926 FB

League Club	Source	Date Signed	Seasons Played	Apps	Subs	Gls
Southport	Brockhouse	10/45				
New Brighton	Tr	08/48	48	1	-	0

CARR Stephen (Steve)
Born: Dublin, Republic of Ireland, 29 August, 1976 RB
Republic of Ireland: 44/U21-12/Youth/Schools

League Club	Source	Date Signed	Seasons Played	Apps	Subs	Gls
Tottenham H	YT	09/93	93-03	222	4	7
Newcastle U	Tr	08/04	04-07	76	2	1
Birmingham C	Tr	02/09	08-11	106	0	0

CARR William Graham (Graham)
Born: Corbridge, Northumberland, England, 25 October, 1944 CD
England: Youth

League Club	Source	Date Signed	Seasons Played	Apps	Subs	Gls
Northampton T	Jnr	08/62	62-67	84	1	0
York C	Tr	06/68	68	32	1	1
Bradford Park Ave	Tr	07/69	69	42	0	2

CARR William McInanny (Willie)
Born: Glasgow, Scotland, 6 January, 1950 M
Scotland: 6/U23-4

League Club	Source	Date Signed	Seasons Played	Apps	Subs	Gls
Coventry C	App	07/67	67-74	245	7	33
Wolverhampton W	Tr	03/75	74-81	231	6	21
Millwall	Tr	08/82	82	8	0	1

CARR-LAWTON Colin
Born: South Shields, Tyne and Wear, England, 5 September, 1978 F

League Club	Source	Date Signed	Seasons Played	Apps	Subs	Gls
Burnley	YT	01/97	97-98	2	3	0

CARRAGHER James Lee Duncan (Jamie)
Born: Bootle, Merseyside, England, 28 January, 1978 CD
England: 38/B-2/U21-27/Youth

League Club	Source	Date Signed	Seasons Played	Apps	Subs	Gls
Liverpool	YT	10/96	96-12	484	24	3

CARRAGHER Matthew
Born: Liverpool, England, 14 January, 1976 RB

League Club	Source	Date Signed	Seasons Played	Apps	Subs	Gls
Wigan Ath	YT	11/93	93-96	102	17	0
Port Vale	Tr	07/97	97-02	190	4	1
Macclesfield T	Stafford Rgrs	11/03	03-04	44	5	0

CARRASSO Cedric
Born: Avignon, France, 30 December, 1981 G

League Club	Source	Date Signed	Seasons Played	Apps	Subs	Gls
Crystal Palace (L)	Olymp Marseille (FRA)	12/01	01	0	1	0

CARRATT Philip Edward (Phil)
Born: Stockport, Greater Manchester, England, 22 October, 1981 F

League Club	Source	Date Signed	Seasons Played	Apps	Subs	Gls
Stockport Co	YT	09/00	00-01	0	4	0

CARRICK Matthew David (Dave)
Born: Evenwood, County Durham, England, 5 December, 1946 M
Died: Manchester, England, 1 July, 1989

League Club	Source	Date Signed	Seasons Played	Apps	Subs	Gls
Wolverhampton W	App	12/64				
Wrexham	Tr	07/66	66-67	20	4	3
Port Vale	Altrincham	01/69	68	14	2	1
Preston NE	Witton A	11/73	73	0	2	0
Rochdale	Tr	03/74	73-74	25	1	4

CARRICK Michael
Born: Wallsend, Tyne and Wear, England, 28 July, 1981 DM
England: 33/B-1/U21-14/Youth

League Club	Source	Date Signed	Seasons Played	Apps	Subs	Gls
West Ham U	YT	08/98	99-03	128	8	6
Swindon T	L	11/99	99	6	0	2
Birmingham C	L	02/00	99	1	1	0
Tottenham H	Tr	08/04	04-05	61	3	2
Manchester U	Tr	08/06	06-14	225	38	17

CARRICK William Francis (Willie)
Born: Dublin, Republic of Ireland, 26 September, 1952 G

League Club	Source	Date Signed	Seasons Played	Apps	Subs	Gls
Manchester U	App	09/70				
Luton T	Tr	07/72	72	4	0	0

CARRICO Daniel Felipe Martins
Born: Cascais, Portugal, 4 August, 1988 LB
Portugal: U21-16

League Club	Source	Date Signed	Seasons Played	Apps	Subs	Gls
Reading	Sporting Lisbon (POR)	01/13	12	1	2	0

CARRIGAN Brian Eric
Born: Glasgow, Scotland, 26 September, 1979 F
Scotland: U21-1

League Club	Source	Date Signed	Seasons Played	Apps	Subs	Gls
Stockport Co	Clyde	08/00	00	3	10	1

League Club	Source	Date Signed	Seasons Played	Apps	Subs	Gls

CARRILHO Mirano
Born: Amsterdam, Netherlands, 17 July, 1975 — LB

League Club	Source	Date Signed	Seasons Played	Apps	Subs	Gls
MK Dons	SVV Dordrecht (NED)	08/05	05	1	2	0

CARRINGTON Andrew (Andy)
Born: Grimsby, North Lincolnshire, England, 14 November, 1936 — CH

League Club	Source	Date Signed	Seasons Played	Apps	Subs	Gls
Grimsby T	Jnr	09/55	59-60	4	-	0

CARRINGTON Mark Richard
Born: Warrington, Cheshire, England, 4 May, 1987 — M

League Club	Source	Date Signed	Seasons Played	Apps	Subs	Gls
Crewe Alex	Sch	07/06	06-08	15	14	2
MK Dons	Tr	07/09	09-10	22	10	6
Bury	Hamilton Academical	09/11	11-12	32	16	1

CARRODUS Frank
Born: Manchester, England, 31 May, 1949 — LW

League Club	Source	Date Signed	Seasons Played	Apps	Subs	Gls
Manchester C	Altrincham	11/69	69-73	33	8	1
Aston Villa	Tr	08/74	74-78	150	0	7
Wrexham	Tr	12/79	79-81	97	0	6
Birmingham C	Tr	08/82	82	7	1	0
Bury	Tr	10/83	83	31	3	1

CARROLL Alfred (Alf)
Born: Bradford, England, 6 March, 1920 — CH
Died: Keighley, West Yorkshire, England, November, 1994

League Club	Source	Date Signed	Seasons Played	Apps	Subs	Gls
Bradford C	US Metallic Packing	03/48	48-49	28	-	0

CARROLL Andrew Thomas (Andy)
Born: Gateshead, Tyne and Wear, England, 6 January, 1989 — F
England: 9/U21-5/Youth

League Club	Source	Date Signed	Seasons Played	Apps	Subs	Gls
Newcastle U	Sch	07/06	06-10	57	23	31
Preston NE	L	08/07	07	7	4	1
Liverpool	Tr	01/11	10-12	26	18	6
West Ham U	Tr	08/12	12-14	46	7	14

CARROLL David Francis (Dave)
Born: Paisley, Renfrewshire, Scotland, 20 September, 1966 — M
England: Schools

League Club	Source	Date Signed	Seasons Played	Apps	Subs	Gls
Wycombe W	Ruislip Manor	07/88	93-01	277	25	40

CARROLL Jake
Born: Dublin, Republic of Ireland, 11 August, 1991 — LB/M
Republic of Ireland: Schools

League Club	Source	Date Signed	Seasons Played	Apps	Subs	Gls
Huddersfield T	St Patricks Ath (ROI)	07/13	13-14	5	1	0
Bury	L	02/14	13	5	1	1

CARROLL John (Johnny)
Born: Limerick, Republic of Ireland, 11 May, 1923 — CF

League Club	Source	Date Signed	Seasons Played	Apps	Subs	Gls
West Ham U	Limerick (ROI)	05/48	48	5	-	0

CARROLL Joseph (Joe)
Born: Radcliffe, Greater Manchester, England, 6 January, 1957 — F

League Club	Source	Date Signed	Seasons Played	Apps	Subs	Gls
Oldham Ath	Jnr	07/75	75	3	1	0
Halifax T	Tr	09/76	76-78	76	6	14

CARROLL Michael (Micky)
Born: Blaydon, Tyne and Wear, England, 4 October, 1961 — W

League Club	Source	Date Signed	Seasons Played	Apps	Subs	Gls
Chesterfield	Whickham	09/81	81-82	5	1	1

CARROLL Michael (Mike)
Born: Aberdeen, Scotland, 10 September, 1952 — F
Scotland: Schools

League Club	Source	Date Signed	Seasons Played	Apps	Subs	Gls
Grimsby T	Liverpool (App)	03/71	70	0	1	0

CARROLL Neil Adam
Born: Cheltenham, Gloucestershire, England, 21 September, 1988 — M

League Club	Source	Date Signed	Seasons Played	Apps	Subs	Gls
Chester C	Sch	05/07	07	1	0	0

CARROLL Robert (Robbie)
Born: Greenford, W London, England, 15 February, 1968 — F

League Club	Source	Date Signed	Seasons Played	Apps	Subs	Gls
Southampton	App	02/86				
Brentford	Gosport Bor	09/86	86-87	24	10	8

CARROLL Roy Eric
Born: Enniskillen, Fermanagh, Northern Ireland, 30 September, 1977 — G
Northern Ireland: 41/U21-11/Youth

League Club	Source	Date Signed	Seasons Played	Apps	Subs	Gls
Hull C	YT	09/95	95-96	46	0	0
Wigan Ath	Tr	04/97	97-00	135	0	0
Manchester U	Tr	07/01	01-04	46	3	0
West Ham U	Tr	06/05	05-06	31	0	0
Derby Co	Glasgow Rangers	01/08	07-08	30	0	0
Notts Co	Olympiakos (GRE)	08/14	14	45	0	0

CARROLL Thomas James (Tom)
Born: Watford, Hertfordshire, England, 28 May, 1992 — M
England: U21-17/Youth

League Club	Source	Date Signed	Seasons Played	Apps	Subs	Gls
Tottenham H	Sch	07/10	12	0	7	0
Leyton Orient	L	01/11	10	8	4	0
Derby Co	L	01/12	11	8	4	1
Queens Park Rgrs	L	09/13	13	23	3	0
Swansea C	L	08/14	14	8	5	0

CARROLL Thomas Roger (Tommy)
Born: Dublin, Republic of Ireland, 18 August, 1942 — RB
Republic of Ireland: 17/LoI-7/U23-1/Amateur

League Club	Source	Date Signed	Seasons Played	Apps	Subs	Gls
Ipswich T	Cambridge C	07/66	66-71	115	2	2
Birmingham C	Tr	10/71	71-72	38	0	0

CARRUTHERS Alexander Neilson (Alec)
Born: Loganlea, West Lothian, Scotland, 12 May, 1915 — RW
Died: Bolton, Greater Manchester, England, 1977

League Club	Source	Date Signed	Seasons Played	Apps	Subs	Gls
Bolton W	Falkirk	02/37	36-37	26	-	4
Rochdale	Falkirk	05/46	46	13	-	4

CARRUTHERS Christopher Paul (Chris)
Born: Kettering, Northamptonshire, England, 19 August, 1983 — LB
England: Youth

League Club	Source	Date Signed	Seasons Played	Apps	Subs	Gls
Northampton T	Sch	04/02	00-04	52	22	1
Bristol Rov	L	03/05	04-07	87	13	1

CARRUTHERS Eric
Born: Edinburgh, Scotland, 2 February, 1953 — F

League Club	Source	Date Signed	Seasons Played	Apps	Subs	Gls
Derby Co	Heart of Midlothian	01/75	76	0	1	0

CARRUTHERS John Parker
Born: Dumfries, Scotland, 2 August, 1926 — W
Died: Gateshead, Tyne and Wear, England, 14 September, 1997

League Club	Source	Date Signed	Seasons Played	Apps	Subs	Gls
Carlisle U		07/49	49	2	-	0
Workington	Tr	07/50	51	3	-	0

CARRUTHERS Martin George
Born: Nottingham, England, 7 August, 1972 — F

League Club	Source	Date Signed	Seasons Played	Apps	Subs	Gls
Aston Villa	YT	07/90	91-92	2	2	0
Hull C	L	10/92	92	13	0	6
Stoke C	Tr	07/93	93-96	60	31	13
Peterborough U	Tr	11/96	96-98	63	4	21
York C	L	01/99	98	3	3	0
Darlington	Tr	03/99	98-99	11	6	2
Southend U	Tr	09/99	99-00	69	1	26
Scunthorpe U	Tr	03/01	00-02	80	6	34
Macclesfield T	Tr	07/03	03	30	9	8
Boston U	Tr	08/04	04	4	2	0
Lincoln C	Tr	09/04	04	7	4	0
Cambridge U	L	01/05	04	5	0	0

CARRUTHERS Matthew (Matt)
Born: Dover, Kent, England, 22 July, 1976 — F

League Club	Source	Date Signed	Seasons Played	Apps	Subs	Gls
Mansfield T	Dover Ath	02/99	98	0	5	0

CARRUTHERS Samir Badre
Born: Islington, N London, England, 4 April, 1993 — M
Republic of Ireland: U21-10/Youth

League Club	Source	Date Signed	Seasons Played	Apps	Subs	Gls
Aston Villa	Sch	07/11	11	0	3	0
MK Dons	L	08/13	13	19	4	2
MK Dons	Tr	08/14	14	20	12	2

CARSLEY Lee Kevin
Born: Birmingham, England, 28 February, 1974 — DM
Republic of Ireland: 39/U21-1

League Club	Source	Date Signed	Seasons Played	Apps	Subs	Gls
Derby Co	YT	07/92	94-98	122	16	5
Blackburn Rov	Tr	03/99	98-00	40	6	10
Coventry C	Tr	12/00	00-01	46	1	4
Everton	Tr	02/02	01-07	153	13	12
Birmingham C	Tr	07/08	08-09	44	4	2
Coventry C	Tr	07/10	10	25	0	0

CARSON Alexander McPhee (Alec)
Born: Clarkston, Renfrewshire, Scotland, 12 November, 1942 — WH

League Club	Source	Date Signed	Seasons Played	Apps	Subs	Gls
Northampton T	Jnr	11/59	60-61	8	-	0
Aldershot	Tr	05/63	63-64	5	-	0

CARSON Daniel (Danny)
Born: Huyton, Merseyside, England, 2 February, 1981 — M

League Club	Source	Date Signed	Seasons Played	Apps	Subs	Gls
Chester C	YT	07/99	98	1	1	0

CARSON Joshua Glyn (Josh)
Born: Newtownabbey, Antrim, Northern Ireland, 3 June, 1993 — RW
Northern Ireland: 4/U21-12/Youth

League Club	Source	Date Signed	Seasons Played	Apps	Subs	Gls
Ipswich T	Sch	08/10	10-12	16	15	5
York C	L	03/13	12	5	0	0
York C	Tr	09/13	13-14	47	6	6

CARSON Scott Paul
Born: Whitehaven, Cumbria, England, 3 September, 1985 — G
England: 4/B-2/U21-29/Youth

League Club	Source	Date Signed	Seasons Played	Apps	Subs	Gls
Leeds U	Sch	09/02	03	2	1	0
Liverpool	Tr	01/05	04	4	0	0
Sheffield Wed	L	03/06	05	9	0	0
Charlton Ath	L	08/06	06	36	0	0
Aston Villa	L	08/07	07	35	0	0
West Bromwich A	Tr	07/08	08-10	110	0	0
Wigan Ath	Bursaspor (TKY)	07/13	13-14	50	0	0

League Club	Source	Date Signed	Seasons Played	Apps	Subs	Gls

CARSON Stephen
Born: Ballymoney, Antrim, Northern Ireland, 6 October, 1980 — M
Northern Ireland: 1/U21-2

League Club	Source	Date Signed	Seasons Played	Apps	Subs	Gls
Barnsley	Dundee U	09/03	03	9	2	1
Hartlepool U	Tr	02/04	03	1	2	0

CARSON Thomas (Tom)
Born: Alexandria, Dunbartonshire, Scotland, 26 March, 1959 — G

League Club	Source	Date Signed	Seasons Played	Apps	Subs	Gls
Ipswich T (L)	Dundee U	01/88	87	1	0	0

CARSON Trevor
Born: Downpatrick, Northern Ireland, 5 March, 1988 — G
Northern Ireland: B-1/U21-15/Youth

League Club	Source	Date Signed	Seasons Played	Apps	Subs	Gls
Sunderland	Sch	07/06				
Chesterfield	L	08/08	08	18	0	0
Lincoln C	L	01/11	10	16	0	0
Brentford	L	03/11	10	1	0	0
Bury	L	09/11	11	8	0	0
Bury	Tr	02/12	11-13	53	0	0
Portsmouth	L	10/13	13	36	0	0
Cheltenham T	Tr	06/14	14	46	0	0

CARSS Anthony John (Tony)
Born: Alnwick, Northumberland, England, 31 March, 1976 — LM

League Club	Source	Date Signed	Seasons Played	Apps	Subs	Gls
Blackburn Rov	Bradford C (YT)	08/94				
Darlington	Tr	08/95	95-96	33	24	2
Cardiff C	Tr	07/97	97	36	6	1
Chesterfield	Tr	09/98	98-99	26	9	1
Carlisle U	Tr	08/00	00	6	1	0
Oldham Ath	Tr	10/00	00-02	58	17	5
Huddersfield T	Tr	08/03	03-05	68	12	3

CARSTAIRS James Wood (Jim)
Born: St Andrews, Fife, Scotland, 29 January, 1971 — LB

League Club	Source	Date Signed	Seasons Played	Apps	Subs	Gls
Arsenal	YT	03/89				
Brentford	L	02/91	90	8	0	0
Cambridge U	Tr	07/91				
Stockport Co	Tr	11/91	91-92	33	1	1

CARTER Alfonso Jermaine (Alfie)
Born: Birmingham, England, 23 August, 1980 — F

League Club	Source	Date Signed	Seasons Played	Apps	Subs	Gls
Walsall	YT	04/99	98-00	1	2	0

CARTER Ashley Robert
Born: Birmingham, England, 12 September, 1995 — CD

League Club	Source	Date Signed	Seasons Played	Apps	Subs	Gls
Wolverhampton W	Coventry C (Sch)	09/13				
Chesterfield	L	02/15	14	2	0	0

CARTER Brian
Born: Dorchester, Dorset, England, 17 November, 1938 — LH

League Club	Source	Date Signed	Seasons Played	Apps	Subs	Gls
Portsmouth	Weymouth	01/56	57-60	44	-	0
Bristol Rov	Tr	07/61	61	4	-	0

CARTER Daniel Stephen (Danny)
Born: Hackney, E London, England, 29 June, 1969 — LW

League Club	Source	Date Signed	Seasons Played	Apps	Subs	Gls
Leyton Orient	Billericay T	07/88	88-94	168	20	22
Peterborough U	Tr	06/95	95-96	33	12	1

CARTER Darren Anthony
Born: Solihull, West Midlands, England, 18 December, 1983 — M
England: Youth

League Club	Source	Date Signed	Seasons Played	Apps	Subs	Gls
Birmingham C	YT	11/01	01-04	28	17	3
Sunderland	L	09/04	04	8	2	1
West Bromwich A	Tr	07/05	05-06	30	23	4
Preston NE	Tr	08/07	07-10	62	32	4
Millwall	L	08/10	10	5	5	0
Cheltenham T	Tr	08/12	12	27	7	6
Northampton T	Tr	07/13	13-14	49	11	6

CARTER Donald Frederick (Don)
Born: Midsomer Norton, Somerset, England, 11 September, 1921 — IF

League Club	Source	Date Signed	Seasons Played	Apps	Subs	Gls
Bury	Stourbridge	01/39	46-47	56	-	27
Blackburn Rov	Tr	06/48	48	2	-	0
New Brighton	Tr	11/48	48-50	105	-	19

CARTER Geoffrey (Geoff)
Born: Northwich, Cheshire, England, 14 February, 1943 — LW

League Club	Source	Date Signed	Seasons Played	Apps	Subs	Gls
West Bromwich A	Moulton	02/60	59-64	25	-	3
Bury	Tr	07/66	66	4	0	0
Bradford C	Tr	08/67	67	1	0	0

CARTER Horatio Stratton (Raich)
Born: Sunderland, England, 21 December, 1913 — IF
Died: Hull, England, 9 October, 1994
England: 13/FLge-4/Schools/War-17//Republic of Ireland: LoI-2

League Club	Source	Date Signed	Seasons Played	Apps	Subs	Gls
Sunderland	Esh Winning	11/31	32-38	245	-	118
Derby Co	Tr	12/45	46-47	63	-	34
Hull C	Tr	04/48	47-51	136	-	57

CARTER Ian Noel
Born: Birmingham, England, 20 September, 1967 — LB
Canada: 8/Youth

League Club	Source	Date Signed	Seasons Played	Apps	Subs	Gls
Peterborough U	Toronto Blizzard (CAN)	02/94	93	9	2	0

CARTER James William Charles (Jimmy)
Born: Hammersmith, W London, England, 9 November, 1965 — RW

League Club	Source	Date Signed	Seasons Played	Apps	Subs	Gls
Crystal Palace	App	11/83				
Queens Park Rgrs	Tr	09/85				
Millwall	Tr	03/87	86-90	99	11	11
Liverpool	Tr	01/91	90	2	3	0
Arsenal	Tr	10/91	91-94	18	7	2
Oxford U	L	03/94	93	5	0	0
Oxford U	L	12/94	94	3	1	0
Portsmouth	Tr	07/95	95-97	60	12	5
Millwall	Tr	07/98	98	16	0	0

CARTER Joseph (Joe)
Born: Bingley, West Yorkshire, England, 23 April, 1920 — G
Died: Hemel Hempstead, Hertfordshire, England, December, 1978

League Club	Source	Date Signed	Seasons Played	Apps	Subs	Gls
Notts Co	Queens Park Rgrs (Am)	09/44				
Hull C	Tr	06/46	46	5	-	0
Bournemouth	Tr	03/47				

CARTER Lee Richard
Born: Dartford, Kent, England, 22 March, 1970 — FB

League Club	Source	Date Signed	Seasons Played	Apps	Subs	Gls
Northampton T	YT	07/88	87	0	1	0

CARTER Leslie Alan (Les)
Born: Bromley, SE London, England, 24 October, 1960 — F
England: Schools

League Club	Source	Date Signed	Seasons Played	Apps	Subs	Gls
Crystal Palace	App	11/77	80	1	1	0
Bristol C	Tr	02/82	81	16	0	0

CARTER Mark Colin
Born: Liverpool, England, 17 December, 1960 — F
England: Semi Pro

League Club	Source	Date Signed	Seasons Played	Apps	Subs	Gls
Barnet	Runcorn	02/91	91-93	62	20	30
Bury	Tr	09/93	93-96	113	21	62
Rochdale	Tr	07/97	97	7	4	2

CARTER Michael (Mike)
Born: Warrington, Cheshire, England, 18 April, 1960 — LW

League Club	Source	Date Signed	Seasons Played	Apps	Subs	Gls
Bolton W	App	07/77	79-81	37	12	8
Mansfield T	L	03/79	78	18	0	4
Swindon T	L	03/82	81	4	1	0
Plymouth Arg	Tr	08/82	82	6	6	1
Hereford U	L	03/83	82	10	0	0
Hereford U	Tr	06/83	84-86	81	6	11
Wrexham	Tr	07/87	87-88	25	9	7

CARTER Michael David
Born: Darlington, County Durham, England, 13 November, 1980 — F

League Club	Source	Date Signed	Seasons Played	Apps	Subs	Gls
Darlington	YT	07/99	98	1	0	1

CARTER Raymond (Ray)
Born: Chester, England, 1 May, 1951 — M

League Club	Source	Date Signed	Seasons Played	Apps	Subs	Gls
Chester C	Jnr	09/71	71-73	56	6	0
Crewe Alex	Tr	07/74	74	26	0	3

CARTER Raymond (Ray)
Born: West Hoathly, West Sussex, England, 1 June, 1933 — IF

League Club	Source	Date Signed	Seasons Played	Apps	Subs	Gls
Torquay U	Brixham	08/58	58-59	3	-	1
Exeter C	Tr	10/60	60-62	105	-	50

CARTER Robert Hector Andrew (Rob)
Born: Stepney, E London, England, 23 April, 1982 — M

League Club	Source	Date Signed	Seasons Played	Apps	Subs	Gls
Leyton Orient	YT	-	99	0	2	0

CARTER Roger Frank
Born: Great Yarmouth, Norfolk, England, 11 October, 1937 — IF

League Club	Source	Date Signed	Seasons Played	Apps	Subs	Gls
Aston Villa	Gorleston	12/55				
Torquay U	Tr	07/60	60	5	-	0

CARTER Roy William
Born: Torpoint, Cornwall, England, 19 February, 1954 — M

League Club	Source	Date Signed	Seasons Played	Apps	Subs	Gls
Hereford U	Falmouth	04/75	74-77	64	7	9
Swindon T	Tr	12/77	77-82	193	7	34
Torquay U	L	10/82	82	6	0	5
Bristol Rov	L	12/82	82	4	0	1
Torquay U	Tr	02/83	82-83	21	0	3
Newport Co	Tr	09/83	83-86	150	2	22
Exeter C	Tr	06/87	87	37	4	2

CARTER Stanley Albert (Stan)
Born: Exeter, England, 6 September, 1928 — CH

League Club	Source	Date Signed	Seasons Played	Apps	Subs	Gls
Exeter C	Heavitree U	11/49	50-51	2	-	0

CARTER Stephen Charles (Steve)
Born: Great Yarmouth, Norfolk, England, 23 April, 1953 — RW

League Club	Source	Date Signed	Seasons Played	Apps	Subs	Gls
Manchester C	App	08/70	70-71	4	2	2
Notts Co	Tr	02/72	71-78	172	16	21
Derby Co	Tr	08/78	78-79	32	1	1
Bournemouth	Notts Co (NC)	03/82	81-83	42	4	1
Torquay U	Tr	07/84	84	16	0	1

CARTER Stephen George (Steve)
Born: Sunderland, England, 13 April, 1972 — LW

League Club	Source	Date Signed	Seasons Played	Apps	Subs	Gls
Scarborough	Manchester U (YT)	07/90	90-91	33	4	3

CARTER Sydney Youles (Syd)
Born: Chesterfield, Derbyshire, England, 28 July, 1916 — CF
Died: Mansfield, Nottinghamshire, England, 15 September, 1978

League Club	Source	Date Signed	Seasons Played	Apps	Subs	Gls
Mansfield T	Macclesfield	05/38	38-46	39	-	10

CARTER Timothy Douglas (Tim)
Born: Bristol, England, 5 October, 1967 — G
Died: Stretford, Greater Manchester, England, 19 June, 2008
England: Youth

League Club	Source	Date Signed	Seasons Played	Apps	Subs	Gls
Bristol Rov	App	10/85	85-87	47	0	0
Newport Co	L	12/87	87	1	0	0
Sunderland	Tr	12/87	87-92	37	0	0
Carlisle U	L	03/88	87	4	0	0
Bristol C	L	09/88	88	3	0	0
Birmingham C	L	11/91	91	2	0	0
Hartlepool U	Tr	08/92	93	18	0	0
Millwall	Tr	01/94	93-94	4	0	0
Oxford U	Tr	08/95	95	12	0	0
Millwall	Tr	12/95	95-97	62	0	0
Halifax T	Tr	07/98	98	9	1	0

CARTER Wilfred (Wilf)
Born: Wednesbury, West Midlands, England, 4 October, 1933 — IF
Died: Bath, England, 4 August, 2013

League Club	Source	Date Signed	Seasons Played	Apps	Subs	Gls
West Bromwich A	Jnr	01/51	51-56	57	-	12
Plymouth Arg	Tr	03/57	57-63	254	-	134
Exeter C	Tr	05/64	64-65	48	0	6

CARTER William Henry John (Billy)
Born: Wokingham, Berkshire, England, 14 September, 1945 — M

League Club	Source	Date Signed	Seasons Played	Apps	Subs	Gls
Leyton Orient	Jnr	10/64	65-66	26	3	3

CARTERON Patrice
Born: St Brieuc, France, 30 July, 1970 — RB

League Club	Source	Date Signed	Seasons Played	Apps	Subs	Gls
Sunderland (L)	Saint-Etienne (FRA)	03/01	00	8	0	1

CARTLEDGE Jonathan Robert (Jon)
Born: Carshalton, S London, England, 27 November, 1984 — CD

League Club	Source	Date Signed	Seasons Played	Apps	Subs	Gls
Bury	Sch	08/04	03-04	8	8	1

CARTLIDGE David Thomas
Born: Leicester, England, 9 April, 1940 — LH/IF

League Club	Source	Date Signed	Seasons Played	Apps	Subs	Gls
Leicester C	Jnr	10/57				
Bradford C	Tr	06/61	61	6	-	3
Chester C	Tr	11/61	61-62	20	-	0

CARTWRIGHT Ian James
Born: Brierley Hill, West Midlands, England, 13 November, 1964 — M

League Club	Source	Date Signed	Seasons Played	Apps	Subs	Gls
Wolverhampton W	App	09/82	82-85	59	2	3

CARTWRIGHT John William
Born: Brixworth, Northamptonshire, England, 5 November, 1940 — IF
England: Youth

League Club	Source	Date Signed	Seasons Played	Apps	Subs	Gls
West Ham U	Jnr	11/57	59-60	4	-	0
Crystal Palace	Tr	05/61	61-62	11	-	1

CARTWRIGHT Lee
Born: Rawtenstall, Lancashire, England, 19 September, 1972 — M

League Club	Source	Date Signed	Seasons Played	Apps	Subs	Gls
Preston NE	YT	07/91	90-03	312	85	22
Stockport Co	Tr	01/04	03-04	32	2	1
Rochdale	Tr	07/05	05	21	6	1

CARTWRIGHT Leslie (Les)
Born: Aberdare, Rhondda Cynon Taff, Wales, 4 April, 1952 — M
Wales: 7/U23-4

League Club	Source	Date Signed	Seasons Played	Apps	Subs	Gls
Coventry C	Jnr	05/70	73-76	50	18	4
Wrexham	Tr	06/77	77-81	111	4	6
Cambridge U	Tr	03/82	81-84	52	8	1
Southend U	L	09/83	83	2	2	0

CARTWRIGHT Mark Neville
Born: Runcorn, Cheshire, England, 13 January, 1973 — G

League Club	Source	Date Signed	Seasons Played	Apps	Subs	Gls
Stockport Co	York C (YT)	08/91				
Wrexham	Runcorn	03/94	96-98	37	0	0
Brighton & HA	Tr	08/00	00	12	1	0
Shrewsbury T	Tr	07/01	01	14	0	0
Shrewsbury T	L Wilson College (USA)	02/03	02	13	0	0

CARTWRIGHT Michael (Mick)
Born: Birmingham, England, 9 October, 1946 — RB

League Club	Source	Date Signed	Seasons Played	Apps	Subs	Gls
Coventry C		08/65				
Notts Co	Tr	06/67	67-68	15	1	0
Bradford C	L	11/67	67	1	0	0

CARTWRIGHT Neil Andrew
Born: Stourbridge, West Midlands, England, 20 February, 1971 — M

League Club	Source	Date Signed	Seasons Played	Apps	Subs	Gls
West Bromwich A	YT	07/89	88-91	5	6	0

CARTWRIGHT Peter
Born: Newcastle-upon-Tyne, England, 23 August, 1957 — M

League Club	Source	Date Signed	Seasons Played	Apps	Subs	Gls
Newcastle U	North Shields	06/79	79-82	57	8	3
Scunthorpe U	L	12/82	82	2	2	1
Darlington	Tr	03/83	82-83	48	2	5

CARTWRIGHT Stephen Raymond (Steve)
Born: Tamworth, Staffordshire, England, 8 January, 1965 — LB

League Club	Source	Date Signed	Seasons Played	Apps	Subs	Gls
Colchester U	Tamworth	08/88	88	10	0	0

CARTWRIGHT William John
Born: Malpas, Cheshire, England, 11 June, 1922 — WH
Died: Birkenhead, Wirral, England, June, 1992

League Club	Source	Date Signed	Seasons Played	Apps	Subs	Gls
Tranmere Rov	Jnr	02/41	46-47	9	-	1

CARTY Stephen Francis (Steve)
Born: Dunfermline, Fife, Scotland, 12 January, 1934 — FB

League Club	Source	Date Signed	Seasons Played	Apps	Subs	Gls
Crewe Alex	Blair Hall	03/57	56-59	37	-	0

CARVALHO Alberto Ricardo (Ricardo)
Born: Amarante, Portugal, 18 May, 1978 — CD
Portugal: 75/U21-14

League Club	Source	Date Signed	Seasons Played	Apps	Subs	Gls
Chelsea	FC Porto (POR)	07/04	04-09	129	6	7

CARVALHO Rogerio
Born: Sao Paulo, Brazil, 28 May, 1980 — F

League Club	Source	Date Signed	Seasons Played	Apps	Subs	Gls
York C	Ituano (BRA)	08/02	02	0	4	0

CARVER David Francis
Born: Wickersley, South Yorkshire, England, 16 April, 1944 — RB

League Club	Source	Date Signed	Seasons Played	Apps	Subs	Gls
Rotherham U	App	01/62	61-64	82	-	0
Cardiff C	Tr	01/66	65-72	210	0	1
Swansea C	L	12/72	72	3	0	0
Hereford U	Tr	08/73	73	14	0	0
Doncaster Rov	Tr	03/74	73-74	29	1	0

CARVER Gerald Francis (Gerry)
Born: Worcester, England, 27 June, 1935 — LH

League Club	Source	Date Signed	Seasons Played	Apps	Subs	Gls
Notts Co	Boldmere St Michael's	08/52	53-65	279	1	10

CARVER John William
Born: Newcastle-upon-Tyne, England, 16 January, 1965 — LB

League Club	Source	Date Signed	Seasons Played	Apps	Subs	Gls
Newcastle U	App	01/83				
Cardiff C	Tr	07/85	85	13	0	0

CARVER Joseph Anthony (Joe)
Born: Illinois, USA, 11 June, 1971 — CD

League Club	Source	Date Signed	Seasons Played	Apps	Subs	Gls
Chester C	Hampton Road M's (USA)	09/99	99	1	1	0

CARVER Marcus Alan Edward
Born: Blackburn, Greater Manchester, England, 22 October, 1993 — F

League Club	Source	Date Signed	Seasons Played	Apps	Subs	Gls
Accrington Stan	Sch	07/12	11-14	9	27	1

CARVILL Michael Desmond
Born: Belfast, Northern Ireland, 3 April, 1988 — M
Northern Ireland: U21-8/Youth

League Club	Source	Date Signed	Seasons Played	Apps	Subs	Gls
Charlton Ath	Sch	05/06				
Wrexham	Tr	02/07	06-07	6	8	0

CAS Marcel
Born: Breda, Netherlands, 30 April, 1972 — RW

League Club	Source	Date Signed	Seasons Played	Apps	Subs	Gls
Notts Co	RBC Roosendaal (NED)	07/01	01-02	49	9	8
Sheffield U	Tr	02/03	02	3	3	0
Grimsby T	Tr	07/03	03	13	7	2

CASAL Kasali Olatunda (Yinka)
Born: Hendon, N London, England, 21 October, 1987 — LB

League Club	Source	Date Signed	Seasons Played	Apps	Subs	Gls
Swindon T	Cambuur (NED)	08/08	08	4	1	0

CASCARINO Anthony Guy (Tony)
Born: St Pauls Cray, SE London, England, 1 September, 1962 — F
Republic of Ireland: 76

League Club	Source	Date Signed	Seasons Played	Apps	Subs	Gls
Gillingham	Crockenhill	01/82	81-86	209	10	77
Millwall	Tr	06/87	87-89	105	0	42
Aston Villa	Tr	03/90	89-90	43	3	11
Chelsea	Glasgow Celtic	02/92	91-93	35	5	8

CASE James Robert (Jimmy)
Born: Liverpool, England, 18 May, 1954 — M
England: U23-1

League Club	Source	Date Signed	Seasons Played	Apps	Subs	Gls
Liverpool	South Liverpool	05/73	74-80	170	16	23

League Club	Source	Date Signed	Seasons Played	Apps	Subs	Gls
Brighton & HA	Tr	08/81	81-84	124	3	10
Southampton	Tr	03/85	84-90	213	2	10
Bournemouth	Tr	07/91	91	38	2	1
Halifax T	Tr	05/92	92	17	4	2
Wrexham	Tr	02/93	92	1	3	0
Darlington	Wanneroo British (AUS)	10/93	93	1	0	0
Brighton & HA	Sittingbourne	12/93	93-95	30	2	0

CASE Norman
Born: Prescot, Merseyside, England, 1 September, 1925 — CF
Died: Watford, Hertfordshire, England, 1973
Northern Ireland: NILge-1

League Club	Source	Date Signed	Seasons Played	Apps	Subs	Gls
Sunderland	Ards	09/49	49-50	4	-	2
Watford	Tr	12/50	50	10	-	4
Rochdale	Yeovil T	02/52	51	2	-	0

CASEMENT Christopher (Chris)
Born: Belfast, Northern Ireland, 12 January, 1988 — CD
Northern Ireland: 1/B-1/U21-17/Youth

League Club	Source	Date Signed	Seasons Played	Apps	Subs	Gls
Ipswich T	Sch	03/06	05-07	4	4	0
Wycombe W	L	01/09	08	12	0	0

CASEY Gerald Hugh (Gerry)
Born: Birkenhead, Wirral, England, 25 August, 1941 — M

League Club	Source	Date Signed	Seasons Played	Apps	Subs	Gls
Tranmere Rov	Holyhead T	08/67	67-69	49	3	5

CASEY Leonard John (Len)
Born: Hackney, E London, England, 24 May, 1931 — LH

League Club	Source	Date Signed	Seasons Played	Apps	Subs	Gls
Chelsea	Leyton	02/54	55-58	34	-	0
Plymouth Arg	Tr	12/58	58-59	44	-	0

CASEY Paul
Born: Rinteln, Germany, 6 October, 1961 — RB/M

League Club	Source	Date Signed	Seasons Played	Apps	Subs	Gls
Sheffield U	App	06/79	79-81	23	2	1
Lincoln C	Boston U	03/88	88-90	44	5	4

CASEY Paul
Born: Great Yarmouth, Norfolk, England, 29 July, 1969 — G

League Club	Source	Date Signed	Seasons Played	Apps	Subs	Gls
Cambridge U	YT	07/87	87	1	0	0

CASEY Ryan Peter
Born: Coventry, England, 3 January, 1979 — W
Republic of Ireland: U21/Youth

League Club	Source	Date Signed	Seasons Played	Apps	Subs	Gls
Swansea C	YT	05/97	96-01	19	43	2

CASEY Terence David (Terry)
Born: Abergwynfi, Neath Port Talbot, Wales, 5 September, 1943 — RH
Died: Bridgend, Wales, June, 2005

League Club	Source	Date Signed	Seasons Played	Apps	Subs	Gls
Leeds U	Jnr	10/60	61	3	-	0

CASEY Thomas (Tommy)
Born: Comber, Down, Northern Ireland, 11 March, 1930 — LH
Died: Nailsea, Somerset, England, 13 January, 2009
Northern Ireland: 12

League Club	Source	Date Signed	Seasons Played	Apps	Subs	Gls
Leeds U	Bangor	05/49	49	4	-	0
Bournemouth	Tr	08/50	50-51	66	-	1
Newcastle U	Tr	08/52	52-57	116	-	8
Portsmouth	Tr	07/58	58	24	-	1
Bristol C	Tr	03/59	58-62	122	-	9

CASH Brian Dominick
Born: Dublin, Republic of Ireland, 24 November, 1982 — M
Republic of Ireland: U21-4/Youth

League Club	Source	Date Signed	Seasons Played	Apps	Subs	Gls
Nottingham F	YT	12/99	01-03	0	7	0
Swansea C	L	10/02	02	5	0	0
Rochdale	L	08/04	04	6	0	0
Bristol Rov	Tr	12/04	04	0	1	0

CASH Stuart Paul
Born: Tipton, West Midlands, England, 5 September, 1965 — LB

League Club	Source	Date Signed	Seasons Played	Apps	Subs	Gls
Nottingham F	Halesowen T	09/89				
Rotherham U	L	03/90	89	8	0	1
Brentford	L	09/90	90	11	0	0
Shrewsbury T	L	09/91	91	8	0	1
Chesterfield	Tr	08/92	92-93	27	2	0

CASHLEY Alec Raymond (Ray)
Born: Bristol, England, 23 October, 1951 — G

League Club	Source	Date Signed	Seasons Played	Apps	Subs	Gls
Bristol C	Jnr	09/70	70-80	227	0	1
Hereford U	L	01/81	80	20	0	0
Bristol Rov	Clevedon T	08/82	83-84	53	0	0
Chester C	Trowbridge T	10/85	85	9	0	0

CASHMORE Norman
Born: Aldershot, Hampshire, England, 24 March, 1939 — RH

League Club	Source	Date Signed	Seasons Played	Apps	Subs	Gls
Aldershot	Woking	07/63	64	7	-	0

CASIRAGHI Pierluigi
Born: Monza, Italy, 4 March, 1969 — F
Italy: 44

League Club	Source	Date Signed	Seasons Played	Apps	Subs	Gls
Chelsea	SS Lazio (ITA)	07/98	98	10	0	1

CASKEY Darren Mark
Born: Basildon, England, 21 August, 1974 — M
England: Youth/Schools

League Club	Source	Date Signed	Seasons Played	Apps	Subs	Gls
Tottenham H	YT	03/92	93-95	20	12	4
Watford	L	10/95	95	6	0	1
Reading	Tr	02/96	95-00	180	22	35
Notts Co	Tr	07/01	01-03	101	13	10
Peterborough U	Hornchurch	11/04	04	2	2	0
Rushden & D	Virginia Beach (USA)	01/06	05	17	1	1

CASKEY William Thomas (Billy)
Born: Belfast, Northern Ireland, 12 October, 1953 — F
Northern Ireland: 7

League Club	Source	Date Signed	Seasons Played	Apps	Subs	Gls
Derby Co	Glentoran	09/78	78-79	26	2	3

CASLEY John Ernest (Jack)
Born: Torquay, Devon, England, 27 April, 1926 — G
Died: Oxford, England, 31 May, 2014

League Club	Source	Date Signed	Seasons Played	Apps	Subs	Gls
Torquay U		06/47	47	1	-	0

CASPER Christopher Martin (Chris)
Born: Burnley, Lancashire, England, 28 April, 1975 — CD
England: U21-1/Youth

League Club	Source	Date Signed	Seasons Played	Apps	Subs	Gls
Manchester U	YT	02/93	96	0	2	0
Bournemouth	L	01/96	95	16	0	1
Swindon T	L	09/97	97	8	1	1
Reading	Tr	09/98	98-99	46	1	0

CASPER Frank
Born: Barnsley, South Yorkshire, England, 9 December, 1944 — F
England: FLge-1

League Club	Source	Date Signed	Seasons Played	Apps	Subs	Gls
Rotherham U	App	07/62	62-66	101	1	25
Burnley	Tr	06/67	67-75	230	7	74

CASS David William Royce
Born: Forest Gate, E London, England, 27 March, 1962 — G

League Club	Source	Date Signed	Seasons Played	Apps	Subs	Gls
Leyton Orient	Billericay T	03/87	86	7	0	0

CASSELL James (Jim)
Born: Prestwich, Greater Manchester, England, 23 April, 1947 — M

League Club	Source	Date Signed	Seasons Played	Apps	Subs	Gls
Bury		07/70	70	2	1	0

CASSELLS Keith Barrington
Born: Islington, N London, England, 10 July, 1957 — F

League Club	Source	Date Signed	Seasons Played	Apps	Subs	Gls
Watford	Wembley	11/77	78-80	6	6	0
Peterborough U	L	01/80	79	8	0	0
Oxford U	Tr	11/80	80-81	43	2	13
Southampton	Tr	03/82	81-82	13	6	4
Brentford	Tr	02/83	82-84	80	6	29
Mansfield T	Tr	08/85	85-88	162	1	52

CASSETTI Marco
Born: Brescia, Italy, 29 May, 1977 — D/M
Italy: 5

League Club	Source	Date Signed	Seasons Played	Apps	Subs	Gls
Watford (L)	Udinese (ITA)	08/12	12	36	2	0
Watford	Udinese (ITA)	07/13	13	32	3	1

CASSIDY Andrew Duncan (Andy)
Born: Leeds, England, 1 March, 1959 — G

League Club	Source	Date Signed	Seasons Played	Apps	Subs	Gls
Stockport Co	Manchester C (Jnr)	02/77	77-78	5	0	0

CASSIDY Francis James Augustine
Born: Watford, Hertfordshire, England, 20 August, 1964 — M

League Club	Source	Date Signed	Seasons Played	Apps	Subs	Gls
Watford	App	08/82				
Plymouth Arg	L	02/84	83	1	0	0
Peterborough U	Tr	08/84	84-85	44	2	9

CASSIDY Jake Ashley
Born: Glan Conwy, Wales, 9 February, 1993 — F
Wales: U21-8/Youth

League Club	Source	Date Signed	Seasons Played	Apps	Subs	Gls
Wolverhampton W	Airbus UK	08/10	12-13	7	13	0
Tranmere Rov	L	03/12	11	7	3	5
Tranmere Rov	L	08/12	12	26	0	11
Tranmere Rov	L	01/14	13	19	0	1
Notts Co	L	07/14	14	15	1	3
Southend U	L	01/15	14	12	5	0

CASSIDY James Toner (Jimmy)
Born: Falkirk, Scotland, 1 December, 1943 — FB

League Club	Source	Date Signed	Seasons Played	Apps	Subs	Gls
Oxford U	Stirling A	07/63	63	5	-	0
Barrow	Tr	03/65	64	5	-	0

CASSIDY Jamie
Born: Liverpool, England, 21 November, 1977 — M
England: Youth/Schools

League Club	Source	Date Signed	Seasons Played	Apps	Subs	Gls
Liverpool	YT	03/95				
Cambridge U	Tr	08/99	99	4	4	0

CASSIDY Laurence (Laurie)
Born: Manchester, England, 10 March, 1923 — IF
Died: Stafford, England, November, 2010

League Club	Source	Date Signed	Seasons Played	Apps	Subs	Gls
Manchester U		02/47	47-51	4	-	0
Oldham Ath	Tr	07/56	56	4	-	1

CASSIDY Nigel
Born: Sudbury, Suffolk, England, 7 December, 1945 — F
Died: Wadebridge, Cornwall, England, 19 May, 2008

League Club	Source	Date Signed	Seasons Played	Apps	Subs	Gls
Norwich C	Lowestoft T	07/67	67-68	2	1	0
Scunthorpe U	Tr	12/68	68-70	88	0	35
Oxford U	Tr	11/70	70-73	113	3	33
Cambridge U	Tr	03/74	73-75	52	2	13

CASSIDY Thomas (Tommy)
Born: Belfast, Northern Ireland, 18 November, 1950 — M
Northern Ireland: 24

League Club	Source	Date Signed	Seasons Played	Apps	Subs	Gls
Newcastle U	Glentoran	10/70	70-79	170	10	22
Burnley	Tr	07/80	80-82	70	2	4

CASSIDY William (Bill)
Born: Gateshead, Tyne and Wear, England, 30 June, 1917 — WH

League Club	Source	Date Signed	Seasons Played	Apps	Subs	Gls
Gateshead	Close Works	01/36	35-52	133	-	6

CASSIDY William Pitt (Billy)
Born: Hamilton, Lanarkshire, Scotland, 4 October, 1940 — M
Died: Oxford, England, March, 1995

League Club	Source	Date Signed	Seasons Played	Apps	Subs	Gls
Rotherham U	Glasgow Rangers	08/61	61-62	25	-	1
Brighton & HA	Tr	11/62	62-66	113	5	25
Cambridge U	Detroit Cougars (USA)	10/68	70	27	5	6

CASTILLO Nery Alberto
Born: San Luis Potosi, Mexico, 13 June, 1984 — F
Mexico: 21

League Club	Source	Date Signed	Seasons Played	Apps	Subs	Gls
Manchester C (L)	Shakhtar Donetsk (UKR)	01/08	07	2	5	0

CASTILLO Segundo Alejandro
Born: San Lorenzo, Ecuador, 15 May, 1982 — M
Ecuador: 81

League Club	Source	Date Signed	Seasons Played	Apps	Subs	Gls
Everton (L)	R Star Belgrade (SRB)	08/08	08	5	4	0
Wolverhampton W (L)	R Star Belgrade (SRB)	08/09	09	7	1	0

CASTLE Peter James
Born: Southampton, England, 12 March, 1987 — CD
England: Youth

League Club	Source	Date Signed	Seasons Played	Apps	Subs	Gls
Reading	Jnr	03/04	02	0	1	0
Rushden & D	L	01/06	05	1	0	0

CASTLE Stephen Charles (Steve)
Born: Barkingside, E London, England, 17 May, 1966 — M

League Club	Source	Date Signed	Seasons Played	Apps	Subs	Gls
Leyton Orient	App	05/84	84-91	232	11	55
Plymouth Arg	Tr	06/92	92-94	98	3	35
Birmingham C	Tr	07/95	95-96	16	7	1
Gillingham	L	02/96	95	5	1	1
Leyton Orient	L	02/97	96	4	0	1
Peterborough U	Tr	05/97	97-99	96	6	17
Leyton Orient	Tr	07/00	00-01	2	8	0

CASTLEDINE Gary John
Born: Dumfries, Scotland, 27 March, 1970 — M

League Club	Source	Date Signed	Seasons Played	Apps	Subs	Gls
Mansfield T	Shirebrook Colliery	01/91	91-94	43	23	3

CASTLEDINE Stewart Mark
Born: Wandsworth, SW London, England, 22 January, 1973 — M

League Club	Source	Date Signed	Seasons Played	Apps	Subs	Gls
Wimbledon	YT	07/91	91-98	18	10	4
Wycombe W	L	08/95	95	7	0	3
Wycombe W	Tr	07/00	00	6	11	0

CASWELL Brian Leonard
Born: Wednesbury, West Midlands, England, 14 February, 1956 — LB/M

League Club	Source	Date Signed	Seasons Played	Apps	Subs	Gls
Walsall	App	09/73	72-84	388	12	17
Doncaster Rov	Tr	08/85	85	15	0	2
Leeds U	Tr	11/85	85-86	9	0	0
Wolverhampton W	L	01/87	86	1	0	0

CASWELL Peter Donald
Born: Leatherhead, Surrey, England, 16 January, 1957 — G

League Club	Source	Date Signed	Seasons Played	Apps	Subs	Gls
Crystal Palace	App	08/75	76-77	3	0	0
Crewe Alex	Tr	08/78	78	22	0	0

CATER Ronald (Ron)
Born: Fulham, W London, England, 2 February, 1922 — WH

League Club	Source	Date Signed	Seasons Played	Apps	Subs	Gls
West Ham U	Leytonstone	01/44	46-49	63	-	0
Leyton Orient	Tr	06/51	51	13	-	0

CATERER Brian John
Born: Hayes, W London, England, 23 January, 1943 — CD
Died: Barnet, N London, England, 21 January, 2010

League Club	Source	Date Signed	Seasons Played	Apps	Subs	Gls
Brentford (Am)	Leatherhead	05/68	68	1	0	0

CATHALINA Timothy Benjamin David
Born: Willemstad, Curacao, 24 January, 1985 — RB

League Club	Source	Date Signed	Seasons Played	Apps	Subs	Gls
Tranmere Rov	FC Emmen (NED)	08/10	10	6	1	0

CATHCART Craig George
Born: Belfast, Northern Ireland, 6 February, 1989 — CD
Northern Ireland: 20/U21-15/Youth

League Club	Source	Date Signed	Seasons Played	Apps	Subs	Gls
Manchester U	Sch	02/06				
Plymouth Arg	L	08/08	08	30	1	1
Watford	L	09/09	09	12	0	0
Blackpool	Tr	08/10	10-13	106	6	3
Watford	Tr	07/14	14	28	1	3

CATLEUGH George Charles
Born: Horden, County Durham, England, 11 June, 1932 — RH
Died: Hillingdon, W London, England, 5 April, 1996

League Club	Source	Date Signed	Seasons Played	Apps	Subs	Gls
Watford	Nuneaton Bor	05/54	54-64	293	-	15

CATLEY John William (Jack)
Born: Grimsby, North Lincolnshire, England, 16 March, 1945 — W

League Club	Source	Date Signed	Seasons Played	Apps	Subs	Gls
Grimsby T	Jnr	07/62	62	2	-	0

CATLIN Robert (Bob)
Born: Wembley, NW London, England, 22 June, 1965 — G

League Club	Source	Date Signed	Seasons Played	Apps	Subs	Gls
Notts Co	Marconi (AUS)	08/92	92-93	3	0	0
Birmingham C	L	03/93	92	8	0	0

CATON Andrew James (Andy)
Born: Oxford, England, 3 December, 1987 — F

League Club	Source	Date Signed	Seasons Played	Apps	Subs	Gls
Swindon T	Sch	03/07	04-06	4	9	1

CATON James Alan Kenneth
Born: Widnes, Cheshire, England, 4 January, 1994 — W

League Club	Source	Date Signed	Seasons Played	Apps	Subs	Gls
Blackpool	Bolton W (Sch)	08/12	13	0	2	0
Accrington Stan	L	10/13	13	1	1	0
Shrewsbury T	Tr	06/14	14	0	2	0

CATON Thomas Stephen (Tommy)
Born: Liverpool, England, 6 October, 1962 — CD
Died: Bampton, Oxfordshire, England, 29 April, 1993
England: U21-14/Youth/Schools

League Club	Source	Date Signed	Seasons Played	Apps	Subs	Gls
Manchester C	App	10/79	79-83	164	1	8
Arsenal	Tr	12/83	83-85	81	0	2
Oxford U	Tr	02/87	86-87	50	3	3
Charlton Ath	Tr	11/88	88-90	56	1	5

CATON William Clifford (Bill)
Born: Stoke-on-Trent, England, 11 September, 1924 — IF
Died: Stoke-on-Trent, England, August, 2011

League Club	Source	Date Signed	Seasons Played	Apps	Subs	Gls
Stoke C	Jnr	09/41	47-49	22	-	2
Carlisle U	Tr	04/50	49-51	61	-	15
Chesterfield	Tr	10/52	52	7	-	0
Crewe Alex	Worcester C	07/54	54	39	-	9

CATTERICK Harry
Born: Darlington, County Durham, England, 26 November, 1919 — CF
Died: Liverpool, England, 9 March, 1985

League Club	Source	Date Signed	Seasons Played	Apps	Subs	Gls
Everton	Cheadle Heath	03/37	46-51	59	-	19
Crewe Alex	Tr	12/51	51-52	25	-	11

CATTERMOLE Lee Barry
Born: Stockton-on-Tees, Cleveland, England, 21 March, 1988 — DM
England: U21-16/Youth

League Club	Source	Date Signed	Seasons Played	Apps	Subs	Gls
Middlesbrough	Sch	07/05	05-07	42	27	3
Wigan Ath	Tr	07/08	08	33	0	1
Sunderland	Tr	08/09	09-14	121	9	2

CATTLIN Christopher John (Chris)
Born: Milnrow, Greater Manchester, England, 25 June, 1946 — LB
England: U23-1

League Club	Source	Date Signed	Seasons Played	Apps	Subs	Gls
Huddersfield T	Burnley (Am)	08/64	64-67	59	2	1
Coventry C	Tr	03/68	67-75	213	4	0
Brighton & HA	Tr	06/76	76-78	95	0	1

CATTRELL Gordon William
Born: Sunderland, England, 18 December, 1954 — M
England: Schools

League Club	Source	Date Signed	Seasons Played	Apps	Subs	Gls
Leeds U	App	01/72				
Darlington	Tr	08/73	73-75	96	6	5

CAU Jean-Michel
Born: Ajaccio, France, 27 October, 1980 — F

League Club	Source	Date Signed	Seasons Played	Apps	Subs	Gls
Darlington	Gazelec Ajaccio (FRA)	03/01	00	0	1	0

CAUGHEY Mark
Born: Belfast, Northern Ireland, 27 August, 1960 — F
Northern Ireland: 2/NILge-2

League Club	Source	Date Signed	Seasons Played	Apps	Subs	Gls
Burnley (L)	Hibernian	02/87	86	8	0	0

CAUGHTER Alan David
Born: Bangor, Gwynedd, Wales, 19 February, 1946 — FB

League Club	Source	Date Signed	Seasons Played	Apps	Subs	Gls
Chester C		08/69	69	1	1	0

CAULFIELD Graham William
Born: Leeds, England, 18 July, 1943 — F

League Club	Source	Date Signed	Seasons Played	Career Record Apps	Subs	Gls
York C (Am)	Frickley Colliery	02/67	66	9	0	2
Bradford C (Am)	Tr	07/67	67	1	0	0
CAULKER Steven Roy						
Born: Feltham, SW London, England, 29 December, 1991						CD
England: 1/U21-10/Youth						
Tottenham H	Sch	06/09	12	17	1	2
Yeovil T	L	08/09	09	44	0	0
Bristol C	L	09/10	10	29	0	2
Swansea C	L	07/11	11	26	0	0
Cardiff C	Tr	07/13	13	38	0	5
Queens Park Rgrs	Tr	07/14	14	34	1	1
CAUNA Aleksandrs (Alex)						
Born: Riga, Latvia, 19 January, 1988						M
Latvia: 40						
Watford (L)	Skonto Riga (LAT)	02/09	08	2	3	1
CAVACO Luis Miguel Pasaro						
Born: Almada, Portugal, 1 March, 1972						W
Stockport Co	Estoril (POR)	08/96	96-97	19	10	5
CAVALLI Johan Etienne Anthony						
Born: Ajaccio, Corsica, France, 12 September, 1981						M
Watford	Istres (FRA)	01/07	06	2	1	0
CAVANAGH Irvin						
Born: Rochdale, Greater Manchester, England, 31 July, 1924						IF
Died: Rochdale, Greater Manchester, England, May, 2010						
Bury		05/48	49	1	-	0
CAVANAGH John						
Born: Salford, England, 4 August, 1961						RB
Rochdale	Barrow	09/84	84	14	3	0
CAVANAGH Peter Joseph						
Born: Bootle, Merseyside, England, 14 October, 1981						D
England: Semi Pro-3						
Accrington Stan	Liverpool (Sch)	07/01	06-08	73	1	6
Rochdale	Fleetwood T	06/12	12-13	47	4	2
CAVANAGH Thomas Henry (Tommy)						
Born: Liverpool, England, 29 June, 1928						IF/WH
Died: Driffield, East Riding of Yorkshire, England, 14 March, 2007						
Preston NE		08/49				
Stockport Co	Tr	01/50	49-51	32	-	2
Huddersfield T	Tr	05/52	52-55	93	-	29
Doncaster Rov	Tr	05/56	56-58	119	-	16
Bristol C	Tr	07/59	59	24	-	6
Carlisle U	Tr	06/60	60	33	-	4
CAVE Michael John (Micky)						
Born: Weymouth, Dorset, England, 28 January, 1949						M
Died: Pittsburgh, USA, 6 November, 1985						
Torquay U	Weymouth	07/68	68-70	106	8	17
Bournemouth	Tr	07/71	71-73	91	8	17
Plymouth Arg	L	03/72	71	8	0	4
York C	Tr	08/74	74-76	94	2	13
Bournemouth	Tr	02/77	76-77	42	0	3
CAVE-BROWN Andrew Robert (Andy)						
Born: Gravesend, Kent, England, 5 August, 1988						FB
Scotland: Youth						
Norwich C	Sch	07/06				
Leyton Orient	Tr	07/08	08-09	22	7	0
CAVEN John						
Born: Edinburgh, Scotland, 6 July, 1934						LW
Brentford	Kilmarnock	10/57	57-58	7	-	1
CAVEN John Brown (Joe)						
Born: Kirkintilloch, Dunbartonshire, Scotland, 11 October, 1936						CF
Brighton & HA	Airdrieonians	03/62	61-62	10	-	0
CAVENER Philip (Phil)						
Born: Tynemouth, Tyne and Wear, England, 2 June, 1961						M
Burnley	App	05/79	79-82	55	14	4
Bradford C	L	03/83	82	9	0	2
Gillingham	Tr	10/83	83	4	6	1
Northampton T	Tr	08/84	84-85	41	4	11
Peterborough U	Tr	03/86	85	9	1	0
CAVILL Aaran						
Born: Bedford, England, 5 March, 1984						M
Northampton T	Sch	07/03	01	0	1	0
CAWLEY Peter						
Born: Walton-on-Thames, Surrey, England, 15 September, 1965						CD
Wimbledon	Chertsey T	01/87	88	1	0	0
Bristol Rov	L	02/87	86	9	1	0
Fulham	L	12/88	88	3	2	0

League Club	Source	Date Signed	Seasons Played	Career Record Apps	Subs	Gls
Bristol Rov	Tr	07/89	89	1	2	0
Southend U	Tr	07/90	90	6	1	1
Exeter C	Tr	11/90	90	7	0	0
Barnet	Tr	11/91	91	3	0	0
Colchester U	Tr	10/92	92-97	178	2	8
CAWSTON Mervyn William						
Born: Diss, Norfolk, England, 4 February, 1952						G
England: Schools						
Norwich C	App	07/69	70	4	0	0
Southend U	L	08/74	74	10	0	0
Newport Co	L	01/76	75	4	0	0
Gillingham	Tr	05/76	76	19	0	0
Southend U	Chicago Sting (USA)	08/78	78-83	189	0	0
Stoke C	Tr	03/84				
Southend U	Chelmsford C	11/84	84	9	0	0
CAWTHORN Paul James						
Born: Pontefract, West Yorkshire, England, 26 May, 1975						W
Scarborough	YT	12/93	92-93	8	3	1
CAWTHORNE Graham John						
Born: Doncaster, South Yorkshire, England, 30 September, 1958						CD
Grimsby T	Harworth CI	11/79	79	1	0	0
Doncaster Rov	Tr	03/82	81-82	33	0	1
CAZORLA Santiago (Santi)						
Born: Oviedo, Spain, 13 December, 1984						M/W
Spain: 73/U21-7						
Arsenal	Malaga (SPN)	08/12	12-14	100	6	23
CECERE Michele Joseph (Mike)						
Born: Chester, England, 4 January, 1968						F
Oldham Ath	App	01/86	86-88	35	17	8
Huddersfield T	Tr	11/88	88-89	50	4	8
Stockport Co	L	03/90	89	0	1	0
Walsall	Tr	08/90	90-93	92	20	32
Exeter C	Tr	01/94	93-95	34	9	11
Rochdale	Tr	07/96	96	2	2	1
CECH Marek						
Born: Trebisov, Slovakia, 26 January, 1983						LB/M
Slovakia: 52						
West Bromwich A	FC Porto (POR)	07/08	08-10	46	10	2
CECH Petr						
Born: Plzen, Czech Republic, 20 May, 1982						G
Czech Republic: 115/U21-15/Youth						
Chelsea	Stade Rennais (FRA)	07/04	04-14	332	1	0
CEDERQVIST Paer						
Born: Vaernamo, Sweden, 10 March, 1980						F
Walsall	Raufoss (NOR)	01/07	06	3	8	0
CEGIELSKI Wayne						
Born: Tredegar, Blaenau Gwent, Wales, 11 January, 1956						CD
Wales: U21-2						
Tottenham H	App	05/73				
Northampton T	L	03/75	74	11	0	0
Wrexham	Schalke 04 (GER)	09/76	76-81	112	11	0
Port Vale	Tr	08/82	82-84	91	1	5
Blackpool	Tr	03/85	84	5	1	1
Hereford U	Tr	07/85	85-86	46	4	2
CELUSTKA Ondrej						
Born: Zlin, Czech Republic, 18 June, 1989						RB
Czech Republic: 1/U21-18/Youth						
Sunderland (L)	Trabzonspor (TKY)	08/13	13	14	7	0
CERNY Radek						
Born: Prague, Czech Republic, 18 February, 1974						G
Czech Republic: 3						
Tottenham H	Slavia Prague (CZE)	01/05	04-07	15	1	0
Queens Park Rgrs	Tr	07/08	08-11	78	0	0
[CESAR] MARTIN VILLAR Cesar						
Born: Oviedo, Spain, 3 April, 1977						CD
Spain: 12						
Bolton W (L)	Levante (SPN)	02/07	06	0	1	0
CESAR Bostjan						
Born: Ljubljana, Slovenia, 9 July, 1982						CD
Slovenia: 83/U21-15						
West Bromwich A (L)	Olymp Marseille (FRA)	08/07	07	19	1	1
CESTOR Mike Botuli						
Born: Paris, France, 30 April, 1992						CD
Leyton Orient	Jnr	07/10	10-11	3	0	0

CHADBOURN William Gordon
Born: Mansfield, Nottinghamshire, England, 29 October, 1922 — IF
Died: Mansfield, Nottinghamshire, England, 1988

League Club	Source	Date Signed	Seasons Played	Apps	Subs	Gls
Mansfield T	South Normanton MW	04/47	46-47	9	-	3

CHADLI Nacer
Born: Liege, Belgium, 2 August, 1989 — LW
Belgium: 29//Morocco: 1

League Club	Source	Date Signed	Seasons Played	Apps	Subs	Gls
Tottenham H	FC Twente (NED)	07/13	13-14	43	16	12

CHADWICK Clifton (Cliff)
Born: Bolton, Greater Manchester, England, 26 January, 1914 — LW

League Club	Source	Date Signed	Seasons Played	Apps	Subs	Gls
Oldham Ath	Fleetwood	10/33	33	18	-	6
Middlesbrough	Tr	02/34	33-38	93	-	27
Hull C	Tr	09/46	46	23	-	7
Darlington	Tr	07/47	47	37	-	5

CHADWICK David Edwin (Dave)
Born: Ootamund, India, 19 August, 1943 — RW

League Club	Source	Date Signed	Seasons Played	Apps	Subs	Gls
Southampton	Jnr	10/60	61-65	25	0	1
Middlesbrough	Tr	07/66	66-69	100	2	3
Halifax T	Tr	01/70	69-71	95	0	15
Bournemouth	Tr	02/72	71-73	29	7	4
Torquay U	L	12/72	72	10	0	0
Gillingham	Tr	09/74	74	35	0	3

CHADWICK Frank Robert
Born: Blackburn, Greater Manchester, England, 9 November, 1927 — WH

League Club	Source	Date Signed	Seasons Played	Apps	Subs	Gls
Blackburn Rov	Jnr	06/46	48-52	11	-	1
York C	Tr	07/55				

CHADWICK Frederick William (Fred)
Born: Manchester, England, 8 September, 1913 — CF
Died: Bristol, England, September, 1987

League Club	Source	Date Signed	Seasons Played	Apps	Subs	Gls
Wolverhampton W	British Dyes	05/35				
Newport Co	Tr	09/36	36-37	40	-	19
Ipswich T	Tr	06/38	38-46	40	-	18
Bristol Rov	Tr	07/47	47	6	-	1

CHADWICK Graham
Born: Oldham, Greater Manchester, England, 8 April, 1942 — WH

League Club	Source	Date Signed	Seasons Played	Apps	Subs	Gls
Manchester C	Jnr	03/62	62-63	12	-	0
Walsall	Tr	08/64	64	9	-	0
Chester C	Tr	07/65	65-66	11	1	0

CHADWICK Harold
Born: Oldham, Greater Manchester, England, 25 January, 1919 — RW
Died: Chadderton, Greater Manchester, England, 2 December, 1987

League Club	Source	Date Signed	Seasons Played	Apps	Subs	Gls
Grimsby T	Goslings	05/45				
Tranmere Rov	Hurst	03/48	47-48	9	-	0

CHADWICK Keith Michael
Born: Kidsgrove, Potteries, England, 10 March, 1953 — F

League Club	Source	Date Signed	Seasons Played	Apps	Subs	Gls
Port Vale	Nantwich T	09/73	73-75	29	12	7

CHADWICK Luke Harry
Born: Cambridge, England, 18 November, 1980 — W
England: U21-13/Youth

League Club	Source	Date Signed	Seasons Played	Apps	Subs	Gls
Manchester U	YT	02/99	00-02	11	14	2
Reading	L	02/03	02	15	0	1
Burnley	L	07/03	03	23	13	5
West Ham U	Tr	08/04	04	22	10	1
Stoke C	Tr	08/05	05-06	46	5	5
Norwich C	Tr	11/06	06	10	7	2
MK Dons	Tr	10/08	08-13	177	31	17
Cambridge U	Tr	06/14	14	8	14	1

CHADWICK Nicholas Gerald (Nick)
Born: Market Drayton, Shropshire, England, 26 October, 1982 — F

League Club	Source	Date Signed	Seasons Played	Apps	Subs	Gls
Everton	YT	10/99	01-04	3	11	3
Derby Co	L	02/03	02	4	2	0
Millwall	L	11/03	03	6	0	2
Millwall	L	03/04	03	5	4	2
Plymouth Arg	Tr	02/05	04-07	49	28	10
Hereford U	Tr	09/08	08	5	5	1
Shrewsbury T	Tr	01/09	08	9	6	2
Plymouth Arg	Stockport Co	11/11	11-12	29	21	6

CHADWICK Simon Leslie
Born: Liverpool, England, 15 March, 1968 — F

League Club	Source	Date Signed	Seasons Played	Apps	Subs	Gls
Wrexham	Jnr	08/85	85	1	1	0

CHAIGNEAU Florent
Born: La Roche-sur-Yon, France, 21 March, 1984 — G

League Club	Source	Date Signed	Seasons Played	Apps	Subs	Gls
Brighton & HA (L)	Rennes (FRA)	08/05	05	1	0	0

CHALK Martyn Peter Glyn
Born: Swindon, England, 30 August, 1969 — W

League Club	Source	Date Signed	Seasons Played	Apps	Subs	Gls
Derby Co	Louth U	01/90	91	4	3	1
Stockport Co	Tr	06/94	94-95	29	14	6
Wrexham	Tr	02/96	95-01	136	48	13

CHALK Stephen Roger (Steve)
Born: Southampton, England, 15 October, 1957 — G

League Club	Source	Date Signed	Seasons Played	Apps	Subs	Gls
Bournemouth	App	10/75	75-77	11	0	0
Charlton Ath	Tr	06/78				

CHALKIAS Konstantinos
Born: Larisa, Greece, 30 May, 1974 — G
Greece: 32

League Club	Source	Date Signed	Seasons Played	Apps	Subs	Gls
Portsmouth	Panathinaikos (GRE)	01/05	04	5	0	0

CHALKLIN Geoffrey (Geoff)
Born: Swindon, England, 1 October, 1956 — CD
England: Schools

League Club	Source	Date Signed	Seasons Played	Apps	Subs	Gls
Swindon T	App	10/74	75	3	0	0

CHALLENDER Gregory Louis (Greg)
Born: Rochdale, Greater Manchester, England, 5 February, 1973 — M

League Club	Source	Date Signed	Seasons Played	Apps	Subs	Gls
Preston NE	Mossley	05/93	93	5	5	2

CHALLINOR David Paul (Dave)
Born: Chester, England, 2 October, 1975 — CD
England: Youth/Schools

League Club	Source	Date Signed	Seasons Played	Apps	Subs	Gls
Tranmere Rov	Bromborough Pool	07/94	96-01	124	16	6
Stockport Co	Tr	01/02	01-03	78	3	1
Bury	L	01/04	03	15	0	0
Bury	Tr	07/04	04-07	158	0	2

CHALLINOR Jon
Born: Northampton, England, 2 December, 1980 — M
England: Semi Pro-2

League Club	Source	Date Signed	Seasons Played	Apps	Subs	Gls
York C	Kettering T	08/11	12	5	13	0

CHALLINOR Paul
Born: Newcastle-under-Lyme, Potteries, England, 6 April, 1976 — CD

League Club	Source	Date Signed	Seasons Played	Apps	Subs	Gls
Birmingham C	YT	07/94				
Bury	Telford U	08/99	99	0	1	0

CHALLIS Roger Leonard Alfred
Born: Rochester, Kent, England, 3 August, 1943 — FB
England: Youth

League Club	Source	Date Signed	Seasons Played	Apps	Subs	Gls
Gillingham	Jnr	09/60	60-62	10	-	0
Crewe Alex	Tr	08/64	64	3	-	0

CHALLIS Stanley Marcel Douglas (Stan)
Born: Lympstone, Devon, England, 22 April, 1918 — LW
Died: Devon, England, 16 October, 2008

League Club	Source	Date Signed	Seasons Played	Apps	Subs	Gls
Exeter C	Lympstone	09/45	46	4	-	1

CHALLIS Trevor Michael
Born: Paddington, Central London, England, 23 October, 1975 — LB
England: U21-2/Youth

League Club	Source	Date Signed	Seasons Played	Apps	Subs	Gls
Queens Park Rgrs	YT	07/94	95-96	12	1	0
Bristol Rov	Tr	07/98	98-02	137	8	1
Shrewsbury T	Telford U	03/04	04	38	0	0

CHALMERS Aaron Anthony
Born: Manchester, England, 2 February, 1991 — M

League Club	Source	Date Signed	Seasons Played	Apps	Subs	Gls
Oldham Ath	Sch	05/08	07	0	2	0

CHALMERS Grant
Born: Guernsey, Channel Islands, 12 September, 1969 — M

League Club	Source	Date Signed	Seasons Played	Apps	Subs	Gls
Brentford	Northerners, Guernsey	08/92	92	9	2	1

CHALMERS Leonard Austin (Len)
Born: Geddington, Northamptonshire, England, 4 September, 1936 — RB
Died: Northampton, England, 10 February, 2014

League Club	Source	Date Signed	Seasons Played	Apps	Subs	Gls
Leicester C	Corby T	01/56	57-65	171	0	4
Notts Co	Tr	07/66	66-67	51	0	1

CHALMERS Lewis John
Born: Manchester, England, 4 February, 1986 — M
England: Semi Pro-10

League Club	Source	Date Signed	Seasons Played	Apps	Subs	Gls
Aldershot T	Altrincham	05/07	08-09	38	8	1
Macclesfield T	Tr	07/10	10-11	39	14	5

CHALMERS Paul
Born: Glasgow, Scotland, 31 October, 1963 — F
Scotland: Youth

League Club	Source	Date Signed	Seasons Played	Apps	Subs	Gls
Bradford C (L)	Glasgow Celtic	01/86	85	2	0	0
Swansea C	St Mirren	11/89	89-91	39	19	13

CHALOBAH Nathaniel Nyakie
Born: Freetown, Sierra Leone, 12 December, 1994 — DM
England: U21-21/Youth

League Club	Source	Date Signed	Seasons Played	Apps	Subs	Gls
Chelsea	Sch	01/12				
Watford	L	08/12	12	34	4	5
Nottingham F	L	09/13	13	7	5	2
Middlesbrough	L	01/14	13	15	4	1
Burnley	L	09/14	14	0	4	0
Reading	L	01/15	14	15	0	1

League Club	Source	Date Signed	Seasons Played	Apps	Subs	Gls
CHALQI Khalid						
Born: Oujda, Morocco, 28 April, 1971						M
Torquay U	Creteil (FRA)	11/00	00	20	1	1
CHAMAKH Marouane						
Born: Tonneins, France, 10 January, 1984						F
France: Youth//Morocco: 64						
Arsenal	Bordeaux (FRA)	07/10	10-11	19	21	8
West Ham U	L	01/13	12	2	1	0
Crystal Palace	Tr	08/13	13-14	42	8	7
CHAMBERLAIN Alec Francis Roy						
Born: Ramsey, Cambridgeshire, England, 20 June, 1964						G
Ipswich T	Ramsey T	07/81				
Colchester U	Tr	08/82	82-86	188	0	0
Everton	Tr	07/87				
Tranmere Rov	L	11/87	87	15	0	0
Luton T	Tr	07/88	88-92	138	0	0
Sunderland	Tr	07/93	93-95	89	1	0
Watford	Tr	07/96	96-06	242	6	0
CHAMBERLAIN Derek Colin						
Born: Nottingham, England, 6 January, 1933						RB
Died: Nottinghamshire, England, December, 2013						
Aston Villa	Parliament St Meth's	11/53				
Mansfield T	Tr	11/56	56-57	43	-	0
York C	Tr	07/58				
CHAMBERLAIN Elliott Charles						
Born: Paget, Bermuda, 29 April, 1992						F
Wales: U21-9						
Leicester C	Sch	12/09				
Exeter C	Tr	08/12	12	0	4	0
CHAMBERLAIN Glyn						
Born: Chesterfield, Derbyshire, England, 29 July, 1957						D/M
Burnley	App	11/74				
Chesterfield	Tr	12/76	76-78	17	1	0
Halifax T	Tr	08/81	81	35	0	0
CHAMBERLAIN Kenneth Russell (Ken)						
Born: Durban, South Africa, 30 June, 1926						CH
Charlton Ath	Parkhill (RSA)	10/51	52-56	42	-	0
CHAMBERLAIN Mark Valentine						
Born: Stoke-on-Trent, England, 19 November, 1961						W
England: 8/U21-4/Schools						
Port Vale	App	05/79	78-81	90	6	18
Stoke C	Tr	08/82	82-85	109	2	17
Sheffield Wed	Tr	09/85	85-87	32	34	8
Portsmouth	Tr	08/88	88-93	143	24	20
Brighton & HA	Tr	08/94	94	12	7	2
Exeter C	Tr	08/95	95-96	51	8	4
CHAMBERLAIN Neville Patrick						
Born: Stoke-on-Trent, England, 22 January, 1960						F
Port Vale	App	01/78	77-82	133	8	32
Stoke C	Tr	09/82	82-83	7	0	0
Newport Co	L	11/83	83	6	0	2
Plymouth Arg	L	03/84	83	7	4	3
Newport Co	Tr	06/84	84	39	2	13
Mansfield T	Tr	07/85	85-86	56	5	19
Doncaster Rov	Tr	08/87	87	22	7	4
CHAMBERLAIN Peter Michael						
Born: Liverpool, England, 30 June, 1935						CH
Died: Swindon, England, October, 2013						
Leicester C	Everton (Am)	09/56				
Swindon T	Tr	06/57	57-62	80	-	6
Aldershot	Tr	10/62	62-64	46	-	1
CHAMBERLAIN Thomas Liam (Tom)						
Born: Pickering, North Yorkshire, England, 23 May, 1996						W
York C	Sch	-	13	0	2	0
CHAMBERLAIN Trevor Charles (Tosh)						
Born: Camden, N London, England, 11 July, 1934						LW
England: Youth/Schools						
Fulham	Jnr	07/51	54-64	187	-	59
CHAMBERS Adam Craig						
Born: West Bromwich, West Midlands, England, 20 November, 1980						M
England: Youth						
West Bromwich A	YT	01/99	00-02	38	18	1
Sheffield Wed	L	02/04	03	8	3	0
Kidderminster Hrs	Tr	03/05	04	2	0	0
Leyton Orient	Tr	08/06	06-10	163	11	9
Walsall	Tr	07/11	11-14	150	6	2

League Club	Source	Date Signed	Seasons Played	Apps	Subs	Gls
CHAMBERS Ashley Renaldo						
Born: Leicester, England, 1 March, 1990						W/F
England: Semi Pro-2/Youth						
Leicester C	Sch	07/07	07-08	1	5	0
Wycombe W	L	08/09	09	0	3	1
Grimsby T	L	01/10	09	2	2	2
York C	Tr	11/10	12-13	44	9	10
Dagenham & Red	Cambridge U	03/14	13-14	31	7	2
CHAMBERS Brian Mark						
Born: Newcastle-upon-Tyne, England, 31 October, 1949						M
England: Schools						
Sunderland	Jnr	08/67	70-72	53	10	5
Arsenal	Tr	06/73	73	1	0	0
Luton T	Tr	02/74	74-76	73	3	9
Millwall	Tr	07/77	77-78	54	5	9
Bournemouth	Tr	07/79	79-80	39	3	7
Halifax T	Tr	03/81	80	10	0	1
CHAMBERS Calum						
Born: Petersfield, Hampshire, England, 20 January, 1995						D
England: 3/U21-3/Youth						
Southampton	Sch	01/12	13	18	4	0
Arsenal	Tr	07/14	14	17	6	1
CHAMBERS David Martin (Dave)						
Born: Barnsley, South Yorkshire, England, 6 June, 1947						W
Rotherham U	App	06/65	65-67	23	4	4
Southend U	Cambridge U	10/68	68-70	52	10	5
York C	Tr	03/71	70-71	8	8	1
CHAMBERS James Ashley						
Born: West Bromwich, West Midlands, England, 20 November, 1980						RB
England: Youth						
West Bromwich A	YT	01/99	99-03	54	19	0
Watford	Tr	08/04	04-06	74	16	0
Cardiff C	L	10/06	06	7	0	0
Leicester C	Tr	07/07	07	15	9	0
Doncaster Rov	Tr	08/08	08-10	83	4	0
Hereford U	L	03/12	11	7	0	0
Walsall	Tr	08/12	12-14	87	6	1
CHAMBERS John Frederick						
Born: Birmingham, England, 7 October, 1949						M
Aston Villa	App	10/66	68	1	1	0
Southend U	Tr	07/69	69	6	1	0
CHAMBERS Leroy Dean						
Born: Sheffield, England, 25 October, 1972						F
Sheffield Wed	YT	06/91				
Chester C	Tr	08/94	94-95	8	13	1
Macclesfield T	Boston U	12/97	97	17	4	4
CHAMBERS Luke						
Born: Kettering, Northamptonshire, England, 29 August, 1985						CD
Northampton T	Sch	11/03	02-06	109	15	1
Nottingham F	Tr	01/07	06-11	185	20	17
Ipswich T	Tr	07/12	12-14	135	0	7
CHAMBERS Paul Anthony						
Born: Wolverhampton, England, 14 January, 1965						CD
Plymouth Arg	App	01/83				
Torquay U	Saltash U	10/84	84	1	1	0
CHAMBERS Philip Martin (Phil)						
Born: Barnsley, South Yorkshire, England, 10 November, 1953						LB
England: Schools						
Barnsley	App	11/71	70-84	441	1	7
Rochdale	Tr	08/85	85	9	1	0
Hartlepool U	Tr	11/85	85	29	0	0
CHAMBERS Stephen (Steve)						
Born: Worksop, Nottinghamshire, England, 20 July, 1968						RB/M
Mansfield T	Sheffield Wed (App)	11/86	86-90	42	14	0
CHAMBERS Triston Gregory						
Born: Enfield, N London, England, 25 December, 1982						F
Colchester U	Sch	07/02	01	0	1	0
CHAMPELOVIER Leslie William (Les)						
Born: Kensington, Central London, England, 23 April, 1933						IF
England: Amateur-3						
Brighton & HA (Am)	Hayes	05/57	57	1	-	0
CHAMPION Thomas Matthew (Tom)						
Born: Barnet, N London, England, 15 May, 1986						DM
Cambridge U	Dartford	05/13	14	38	0	0
CHANDLER Dean Andrew Robert						
Born: Ilford, E London, England, 6 May, 1976						CD

League Club	Source	Date Signed	Seasons Played	Apps	Subs	Gls
Charlton Ath	YT	04/94	94-95	1	1	1
Torquay U	L	03/97	96	4	0	0

CHANDLER Frederick Ernest John (Fred)
Born: Hythe, Hampshire, England, 2 August, 1912 — IF
Died: Crewe, Cheshire, England, 5 September, 2005

League Club	Source	Date Signed	Seasons Played	Apps	Subs	Gls
Reading	Newport, Isle of Wight	05/32	32-35	41	-	14
Blackpool	Tr	10/35	35	15	-	2
Swindon T	Tr	05/36	36	21	-	7
Crewe Alex	Tr	05/37	37-46	81	-	21

CHANDLER Ian
Born: Sunderland, England, 20 March, 1968 — F
England: Schools

League Club	Source	Date Signed	Seasons Played	Apps	Subs	Gls
Barnsley	Jnr	08/86	86	8	4	4
Stockport Co	L	08/87	87	4	1	0
Aldershot	Tr	08/88	88	5	4	2

CHANDLER Jamie
Born: South Shields, Tyne and Wear, England, 24 March, 1989 — M
England: Youth

League Club	Source	Date Signed	Seasons Played	Apps	Subs	Gls
Sunderland	Sch	07/07				
Darlington	L	08/09	09	12	2	0

CHANDLER Jeffrey George (Jeff)
Born: Hammersmith, W London, England, 19 June, 1959 — W/F
Republic of Ireland: 2/U21-1

League Club	Source	Date Signed	Seasons Played	Apps	Subs	Gls
Blackpool	App	08/76	77-78	31	6	6
Leeds U	Tr	09/79	79-80	21	5	2
Bolton W	Tr	10/81	81-84	152	5	36
Derby Co	Tr	07/85	85-86	45	1	9
Mansfield T	L	11/86	86	6	0	0
Bolton W	Tr	07/87	87-89	18	6	4
Cardiff C	Tr	11/89	89-90	21	4	0

CHANDLER Raymond (Ray)
Born: Bath, England, 14 August, 1931 — G

League Club	Source	Date Signed	Seasons Played	Apps	Subs	Gls
Bristol Rov	Bristol C (Am)	06/53	53-54	12	-	0
Swindon T	Tr	06/56	56-58	35	-	0

CHANDLER Richard David (Ricky)
Born: Bristol, England, 26 September, 1961 — F
England: Schools

League Club	Source	Date Signed	Seasons Played	Apps	Subs	Gls
Bristol C	App	10/78	80-82	57	4	13

CHANDLER Robin Anthony Sydney
Born: Luton, England, 19 December, 1942 — CF
England: Schools

League Club	Source	Date Signed	Seasons Played	Apps	Subs	Gls
Luton T	Jnr	12/61	60-64	13	-	0

CHANNING Justin Andrew
Born: Reading, England, 19 November, 1968 — D/M
England: Youth

League Club	Source	Date Signed	Seasons Played	Apps	Subs	Gls
Queens Park Rgrs	App	08/86	86-92	42	13	5
Bristol Rov	Tr	10/92	92-95	121	9	10
Leyton Orient	Tr	06/96	96-97	69	5	5

CHANNON Michael Roger (Mick)
Born: Orcheston, Wiltshire, England, 28 November, 1948 — F
England: 46/FLge-2/U23-9

League Club	Source	Date Signed	Seasons Played	Apps	Subs	Gls
Southampton	App	12/65	65-76	388	3	157
Manchester C	Tr	07/77	77-79	71	1	24
Southampton	Tr	09/79	79-81	119	0	28
Newcastle U	Carolina Hills (USA)	09/82	82	4	0	1
Bristol Rov	Tr	10/82	82	4	5	0
Norwich C	Tr	12/82	82-84	84	4	16
Portsmouth	Tr	08/85	85	34	0	6

CHANTLER Christopher Steven (Chris)
Born: Cheadle Hulme, Greater Manchester, England, 16 December, 1990 — LB

League Club	Source	Date Signed	Seasons Played	Apps	Subs	Gls
Manchester C	Sch	07/09				
Carlisle U	Tr	11/11	11-13	49	5	0

CHAPELL Jordan Mark
Born: Sheffield, England, 8 September, 1991 — W

League Club	Source	Date Signed	Seasons Played	Apps	Subs	Gls
Sheffield U	Sch	07/10	12	0	2	0
Burton A	L	10/12	12	0	2	1
Torquay U	Tr	03/13	12-13	28	14	5

CHAPLIN Conor Mark
Born: Worthing, West Sussex, England, 16 February, 1997 — F

League Club	Source	Date Signed	Seasons Played	Apps	Subs	Gls
Portsmouth	Sch	10/14	14	1	8	1

CHAPLOW Richard David
Born: Accrington, Lancashire, England, 2 February, 1985 — RM
England: U21-1/Youth

League Club	Source	Date Signed	Seasons Played	Apps	Subs	Gls
Burnley	Sch	09/03	02-04	48	17	7
West Bromwich A	Tr	01/05	04-07	25	19	1
Southampton	L	02/06	05	11	0	1
Preston NE	Tr	01/08	07-09	57	11	8
Southampton	Tr	09/10	10-12	44	17	7
Millwall	L	03/13	12	4	0	0
Millwall	Tr	07/13	13-14	18	8	1
Ipswich T	L	02/15	14	3	3	1

CHAPMAN Aaron James
Born: Rotherham, South Yorkshire, England, 29 May, 1990 — G

League Club	Source	Date Signed	Seasons Played	Apps	Subs	Gls
Chesterfield	Belper T	06/13				
Accrington Stan	L	09/14	14	3	0	0

CHAPMAN Adam Henry
Born: Doncaster, South Yorkshire, England, 29 November, 1989 — M
Northern Ireland: U21-7/Youth

League Club	Source	Date Signed	Seasons Played	Apps	Subs	Gls
Sheffield U	Sch	07/08				
Oxford U	Tr	01/09	11-12	32	8	2
Newport Co	Tr	06/13	13-14	62	13	4

CHAPMAN Benjamin (Ben)
Born: Scunthorpe, North Lincolnshire, England, 2 March, 1979 — LB

League Club	Source	Date Signed	Seasons Played	Apps	Subs	Gls
Grimsby T	YT	07/97	98-01	13	8	0
Boston U	Tr	08/02	02-03	70	4	0

CHAPMAN Campbell
Born: Sutton-in-Ashfield, Nottinghamshire, England, 28 June, 1963 — M

League Club	Source	Date Signed	Seasons Played	Apps	Subs	Gls
Peterborough U	App	06/81				
Wolverhampton W	Bilston T	12/84	84-85	47	6	4
Crewe Alex	Preston NE (NC)	11/86	86	0	1	0

CHAPMAN Cavan
Born: Hemsworth, West Yorkshire, England, 11 September, 1967 — F

League Club	Source	Date Signed	Seasons Played	Apps	Subs	Gls
Wolverhampton W	App	07/84	84	1	0	0

CHAPMAN Daniel Graham (Danny)
Born: Peckham, SE London, England, 21 November, 1974 — M

League Club	Source	Date Signed	Seasons Played	Apps	Subs	Gls
Millwall	YT	03/93	94	4	8	0
Leyton Orient	Tr	07/95	95-96	69	9	4

CHAPMAN Darren Peter
Born: Lincoln, England, 15 November, 1974 — M

League Club	Source	Date Signed	Seasons Played	Apps	Subs	Gls
Lincoln C	YT	07/91	91	0	1	0

CHAPMAN Daryl Mark
Born: Kenilworth, Warwickshire, England, 17 September, 1963 — F

League Club	Source	Date Signed	Seasons Played	Apps	Subs	Gls
Derby Co	Jnr	07/82				
Crewe Alex	Tr	03/83	82	3	3	2

CHAPMAN Edwin (Eddie)
Born: Blackburn, Greater Manchester, England, 2 May, 1919 — CF
Died: Blackburn, Greater Manchester, England, 4 December, 1976

League Club	Source	Date Signed	Seasons Played	Apps	Subs	Gls
Blackburn Rov	Darwen	05/36				
Accrington Stan	Tr	07/38	38	4	-	1
Oldham Ath	Tr	06/39				
Stockport Co	Tr	08/46	46	9	-	3

CHAPMAN Edwin Maude (Eddie)
Born: East Ham, E London, England, 3 August, 1923 — IF
Died: Ilford, E London, England, 6 October, 2002

League Club	Source	Date Signed	Seasons Played	Apps	Subs	Gls
West Ham U	Romford	09/42	48	7	-	3

CHAPMAN Gary Anthony
Born: Bradford, England, 1 May, 1964 — F

League Club	Source	Date Signed	Seasons Played	Apps	Subs	Gls
Bradford C	Frickley Ath	08/88	88-89	2	3	0
Notts Co	Tr	09/89	89-90	13	12	4
Mansfield T	L	10/90	90	6	0	0
Exeter C	Tr	09/91	91-92	20	4	5
Torquay U	Tr	02/93	92	6	2	0
Darlington	Tr	08/93	93-94	57	17	9

CHAPMAN George William
Born: Burton-on-Trent, Staffordshire, England, 8 October, 1920 — IF
Died: Ashby-de-la-Zouch, Leicestershire, England, 27 April, 1998

League Club	Source	Date Signed	Seasons Played	Apps	Subs	Gls
West Bromwich A	Donisthorpe	12/38				
Brighton & HA	Tr	07/46	46-47	43	-	12

CHAPMAN Harold (Harry)
Born: Liverpool, England, 4 March, 1921 — WH
Died: Nottingham, England, August, 1990

League Club	Source	Date Signed	Seasons Played	Apps	Subs	Gls
Aston Villa	Kidderminster Hrs	02/47	47	6	-	0
Notts Co	Tr	03/49	48-50	53	-	1

CHAPMAN Ian Russell
Born: Brighton, England, 31 May, 1970 — LB

League Club	Source	Date Signed	Seasons Played	Apps	Subs	Gls
Brighton & HA	App	06/87	86-95	265	16	13
Gillingham	Tr	08/96	96	20	3	1

CHAPMAN John
Born: Sacriston, County Durham, England, 24 May, 1945 — M/D

League Club	Source	Date Signed	Seasons Played	Apps	Subs	Gls
Workington	Stockton	02/63	63-65	28	0	1
Reading	Tr	06/66	66-68	102	1	2
Stockport Co	Tr	07/69	69-71	87	2	5

CHAPMAN Kenneth Arthur (Ken)
Born: Coventry, England, 25 April, 1932 — LW

League Club	Source	Date Signed	Seasons Played	Apps	Subs	Gls
Blackpool	Jnr	08/49				
Crewe Alex	Tr	07/53	53	25	-	8
Bradford C	Tr	07/54	54	26	-	4

CHAPMAN Kenneth Freeman Raymond (Ken)
Born: Grimsby, North Lincolnshire, England, 16 November, 1948 — W

League Club	Source	Date Signed	Seasons Played	Apps	Subs	Gls
Grimsby T (Am)	Louth U	06/68	69	6	1	0

CHAPMAN Lee Roy
Born: Lincoln, England, 5 December, 1959 — F
England: B-1/U21-1

League Club	Source	Date Signed	Seasons Played	Apps	Subs	Gls
Stoke C	Jnr	06/78	79-81	95	4	34
Plymouth Arg	L	12/78	78	3	1	0
Arsenal	Tr	08/82	82-83	15	8	4
Sunderland	Tr	12/83	83	14	1	3
Sheffield Wed	Tr	08/84	84-87	147	2	63
Nottingham F	Niort (FRA)	10/88	88-89	48	0	15
Leeds U	Tr	01/90	89-92	133	4	63
Portsmouth	Tr	08/93	93	5	0	2
West Ham U	Tr	09/93	93-94	33	7	7
Southend U	L	01/95	94	1	0	1
Ipswich T	Tr	01/95	94-95	11	11	1
Leeds U	L	01/96	95	2	0	0
Swansea C	Tr	03/96	95	7	0	4

CHAPMAN Leslie (Les)
Born: Oldham, Greater Manchester, England, 27 September, 1948 — M

League Club	Source	Date Signed	Seasons Played	Apps	Subs	Gls
Oldham Ath	Huddersfield T (Am)	02/67	66-69	75	1	9
Huddersfield T	Tr	09/69	69-74	120	14	8
Oldham Ath	Tr	12/74	74-78	186	1	11
Stockport Co	Tr	05/79	79	32	0	1
Bradford C	Tr	02/80	79-82	137	2	3
Rochdale	Tr	06/83	83-84	87	1	0
Stockport Co	Tr	07/85	85	38	0	3
Preston NE	Tr	07/86	86-87	50	3	1

CHAPMAN Luke Richard
Born: Cannock, Staffordshire, England, 10 March, 1991 — LW

League Club	Source	Date Signed	Seasons Played	Apps	Subs	Gls
Port Vale	Sch	-	07	0	1	0

CHAPMAN Neville
Born: Cockfield, County Durham, England, 15 September, 1941 — RB
Died: Grangetown, Cleveland, England, 14 October, 1993

League Club	Source	Date Signed	Seasons Played	Apps	Subs	Gls
Middlesbrough	Jnr	11/58	61-66	51	2	0
Darlington	Tr	09/67	67-68	31	1	0

CHAPMAN Paul Christopher
Born: Cardiff, Wales, 28 September, 1951 — CD

League Club	Source	Date Signed	Seasons Played	Apps	Subs	Gls
Plymouth Arg	App	10/69	69	2	1	0

CHAPMAN Philip Edward (Phil)
Born: Chasetown, Staffordshire, England, 27 January, 1925 — CF
Died: Burton-on-Trent, Staffordshire, England, April, 1997

League Club	Source	Date Signed	Seasons Played	Apps	Subs	Gls
Walsall	Cannock T	09/48	48-50	63	-	36

CHAPMAN Reginald (Reg)
Born: Eccles, Greater Manchester, England, 14 June, 1928 — W

League Club	Source	Date Signed	Seasons Played	Apps	Subs	Gls
Crewe Alex	Hereford U	05/50	50-51	21	-	1

CHAPMAN Reginald Frederick James (Reg)
Born: Shepherds Bush, W London, England, 7 September, 1921 — CH
Died: Eastbourne, East Sussex, England, 4 July, 1992

League Club	Source	Date Signed	Seasons Played	Apps	Subs	Gls
Queens Park Rgrs		08/44	46-52	97	-	2

CHAPMAN Robert Dennis (Sammy)
Born: Aldridge, West Midlands, England, 18 August, 1946 — CD

League Club	Source	Date Signed	Seasons Played	Apps	Subs	Gls
Nottingham F	Jnr	08/63	63-76	347	12	17
Notts Co	Tr	08/77	77	42	0	0
Shrewsbury T	Tr	07/78	78-79	36	1	6

CHAPMAN Rodger Anthony
Born: Doncaster, South Yorkshire, England, 20 November, 1944 — G

League Club	Source	Date Signed	Seasons Played	Apps	Subs	Gls
Rotherham U		01/65	64	2	-	0
Doncaster Rov	Tr	12/65	65	5	0	0

CHAPMAN Roy Clifford
Born: Birmingham, England, 18 March, 1934 — IF
Died: Trentham, Potteries, England, 21 March, 1983

League Club	Source	Date Signed	Seasons Played	Apps	Subs	Gls
Aston Villa	Kynoch Works	02/52	53-57	19	-	8
Lincoln C	Tr	11/57	57-61	105	-	45
Mansfield T	Tr	08/61	61-64	136	-	78
Lincoln C	Tr	01/65	64-66	69	1	32
Port Vale	Tr	08/67	67-68	76	0	35
Chester C	Tr	06/69	69	9	0	3

CHAPMAN Samuel Edward Campbell (Sammy)
Born: Belfast, Northern Ireland, 16 February, 1938 — WH/IF
Northern Ireland: B

League Club	Source	Date Signed	Seasons Played	Apps	Subs	Gls
Mansfield T	Shamrock Rov (ROI)	10/56	56-57	50	-	25
Portsmouth	Tr	02/58	57-61	48	-	10
Mansfield T	Tr	12/61	61-63	105	-	15

CHAPMAN Stuart
Born: Lynemouth, Northumberland, England, 6 May, 1951 — F

League Club	Source	Date Signed	Seasons Played	Apps	Subs	Gls
Port Vale	App	07/69	66-69	6	3	0

CHAPMAN Vernon William
Born: Leicester, England, 9 May, 1921 — RW
Died: Leicester, England, 6 June, 2006

League Club	Source	Date Signed	Seasons Played	Apps	Subs	Gls
Leicester C	Bath C	01/42	46	1	-	0
Leyton Orient	Tr	07/47	47-48	31	-	7

CHAPMAN Vincent John (Vinny)
Born: Newcastle-upon-Tyne, England, 5 December, 1967 — LB

League Club	Source	Date Signed	Seasons Played	Apps	Subs	Gls
Huddersfield T	Tow Law T	01/88	87	4	2	0
Rochdale	Tr	07/89	89-90	23	1	1

CHAPPELL Larratt (Lol)
Born: Chapeltown, South Yorkshire, England, 19 December, 1930 — CF
Died: Barnstaple, Devon, England, February, 1988

League Club	Source	Date Signed	Seasons Played	Apps	Subs	Gls
Barnsley	Birdwell Rov	05/49	52-58	218	-	94
Doncaster Rov	Tr	08/59	59-60	33	-	5

CHAPPELL Leslie Alan (Les)
Born: Nottingham, England, 6 February, 1947 — F

League Club	Source	Date Signed	Seasons Played	Apps	Subs	Gls
Rotherham U	App	02/65	65-67	106	2	37
Blackburn Rov	Tr	05/68	68	7	0	0
Reading	Tr	07/69	69-74	193	8	78
Doncaster Rov	Tr	12/74	74-75	57	1	10
Swansea C	Tr	07/76	76-77	65	2	5

CHAPPLE Philip Richard (Phil)
Born: Norwich, England, 26 November, 1966 — CD

League Club	Source	Date Signed	Seasons Played	Apps	Subs	Gls
Norwich C	App	07/85				
Cambridge U	Tr	03/88	87-92	183	4	19
Charlton Ath	Tr	08/93	93-97	128	14	15
Peterborough U	Tr	07/98	98-99	16	1	1

CHAPPLE Shaun Ronald
Born: Swansea, Wales, 14 February, 1973 — M
Wales: B/U21-8/Schools

League Club	Source	Date Signed	Seasons Played	Apps	Subs	Gls
Swansea C	YT	07/91	91-97	72	35	9

CHAPUIS Cyril Sylvain Thierry
Born: Lyon, France, 21 March, 1979 — F
France: U21-9

League Club	Source	Date Signed	Seasons Played	Apps	Subs	Gls
Leeds U (L)	Olymp Marseille (FRA)	09/03	03	0	1	0

CHARD Philip John (Phil)
Born: Corby, Northamptonshire, England, 16 October, 1960 — FB/M

League Club	Source	Date Signed	Seasons Played	Apps	Subs	Gls
Peterborough U	Corby T	01/79	78-84	153	19	18
Northampton T	Tr	08/85	85-87	113	2	27
Wolverhampton W	Tr	03/88	87-89	26	8	5
Northampton T	Tr	10/89	89-93	155	8	19

CHARGE Daniel Martin
Born: Woodford, NE London, England, 10 May, 1988 — F

League Club	Source	Date Signed	Seasons Played	Apps	Subs	Gls
Dagenham & Red	Barking Abbey College	04/08	08	0	1	0

CHARLERY Kenneth Leroy (Ken)
Born: Stepney, E London, England, 28 November, 1964 — F
Saint Lucia: 4

League Club	Source	Date Signed	Seasons Played	Apps	Subs	Gls
Maidstone U	Fisher Ath	03/89	89-90	41	18	11
Peterborough U	Tr	03/91	90-92	45	6	19
Watford	Tr	10/92	92-93	45	3	13
Peterborough U	Tr	12/93	93-94	70	0	24
Birmingham C	Tr	07/95	95	8	9	4
Southend U	L	01/96	95	2	1	0
Peterborough U	Tr	02/96	95-96	55	1	12
Stockport Co	Tr	03/97	96	8	2	0
Barnet	Tr	08/97	97-00	106	18	37

CHARLES Anthony Daniel
Born: Isleworth, W London, England, 11 March, 1981 — CD
England: Semi Pro-2

League Club	Source	Date Signed	Seasons Played	Apps	Subs	Gls
Crewe Alex	Brook House	09/99				
Barnet	Farnborough T	01/05	05-06	52	5	0
Aldershot T	Tr	02/07	08-10	114	1	11
Northampton T	Tr	03/12	11-12	13	5	0
Plymouth Arg	Tr	01/13	12	9	2	0

CHARLES Clive Michael
Born: Bow, E London, England, 3 October, 1951 — LB/M
Died: Portland, Oregon, USA, 26 August, 2003
England: Youth

League Club	Source	Date Signed	Seasons Played	Apps	Subs	Gls
West Ham U	App	08/69	71-73	12	2	0
Cardiff C	Tr	03/74	73-76	75	2	5

CHARLES Elliott Grant
Born: Enfield, N London, England, 23 December, 1990 — F

League Club	Source	Date Signed	Seasons Played	Apps	Subs	Gls
Barnet	Jnr	07/08	08-09	0	8	0

CHARLES Gary Andrew
Born: Newham, E London, England, 13 April, 1970 — RB
England: 2/U21-4

League Club	Source	Date Signed	Seasons Played	Apps	Subs	Gls
Nottingham F	YT	11/87	88-92	54	2	1
Leicester C	L	03/89	88	5	3	0
Derby Co	Tr	07/93	93-94	61	0	3
Aston Villa	Tr	01/95	94-98	72	7	3
West Ham U	Benfica (POR)	10/99	99-00	2	3	0
Birmingham C	L	09/00	00	3	0	0

CHARLES Jake David
Born: Mirfield, West Yorkshire, England, 16 February, 1996 — F

League Club	Source	Date Signed	Seasons Played	Apps	Subs	Gls
Huddersfield T	Sch	10/13	14	0	1	0

CHARLES Jeremy Melvyn
Born: Swansea, Wales, 26 September, 1959 — F
Wales: 19/U21-2

League Club	Source	Date Signed	Seasons Played	Apps	Subs	Gls
Swansea C	App	01/77	76-83	224	23	52
Queens Park Rgrs	Tr	11/83	83	10	2	5
Oxford U	Tr	02/85	84-86	41	5	13

CHARLES John William
Born: Canning Town, E London, England, 20 September, 1944 — LB
Died: Ilford, E London, England, 12 August, 2002
England: Youth

League Club	Source	Date Signed	Seasons Played	Apps	Subs	Gls
West Ham U	App	05/62	62-69	117	1	1

CHARLES Julian
Born: Plaistow, E London, England, 5 February, 1977 — F
St Vincent & The Grenadines

League Club	Source	Date Signed	Seasons Played	Apps	Subs	Gls
Brentford	Hampton & Richmond Bor	12/99	99-00	4	8	0

CHARLES Lee Mercury
Born: Hillingdon, W London, England, 20 August, 1971 — F

League Club	Source	Date Signed	Seasons Played	Apps	Subs	Gls
Queens Park Rgrs	Chertsey T	08/95	95-96	6	10	1
Barnet	L	09/95	95	2	3	0
Cambridge U	L	02/98	97	7	0	1

CHARLES Melvyn (Mel)
Born: Swansea, Wales, 14 May, 1935 — WH/CF/CH
Wales: 31/U23-1

League Club	Source	Date Signed	Seasons Played	Apps	Subs	Gls
Swansea C	Leeds U (Am)	05/52	52-58	233	-	66
Arsenal	Tr	04/59	59-61	60	-	26
Cardiff C	Tr	02/62	61-64	79	-	25
Port Vale	Portmadoc	02/67	66	7	0	0

CHARLES Robert John (Bob)
Born: Bursledon, Hampshire, England, 26 December, 1941 — G
Died: 7 March, 2014
England: Youth/Schools

League Club	Source	Date Signed	Seasons Played	Apps	Subs	Gls
Southampton	Jnr	04/59	59-60	26	-	0

CHARLES Ryan Andrew
Born: Enfield, N London, England, 30 September, 1989 — F

League Club	Source	Date Signed	Seasons Played	Apps	Subs	Gls
Luton T	Sch	08/08	07-08	6	11	2

CHARLES Stephen (Steve)
Born: Sheffield, England, 10 May, 1960 — M
England: Schools

League Club	Source	Date Signed	Seasons Played	Apps	Subs	Gls
Sheffield U	Sheffield Univ	01/80	79-84	112	11	10
Wrexham	Tr	11/84	84-86	111	2	37
Mansfield T	Tr	08/87	87-92	231	6	38
Scunthorpe U	L	11/92	92	4	0	0
Scarborough	Tr	02/93	92-95	134	0	20

CHARLES Wesley Darius Donald (Darius)
Born: Ealing, W London, England, 10 December, 1987 — CD
England: Semi Pro-2

League Club	Source	Date Signed	Seasons Played	Apps	Subs	Gls
Brentford	Sch	06/06	04-07	18	19	1
Stevenage	Ebbsfleet U	07/10	10-14	122	22	13

CHARLES William John (John)
Born: Swansea, Wales, 27 December, 1931 — CH/CF
Died: Wakefield, England, 21 February, 2004
Italy: ILge-4//Wales: 38

League Club	Source	Date Signed	Seasons Played	Apps	Subs	Gls
Leeds U	Jnr	01/49	48-56	297	-	150
Leeds U	Juventus (ITA)	08/62	62	11	-	3
Cardiff C	AS Roma (ITA)	08/63	63-65	68	0	18

CHARLES-COOK Reice Jordan
Born: Lewisham, SE London, England, 8 April, 1994 — G

League Club	Source	Date Signed	Seasons Played	Apps	Subs	Gls
Arsenal	Sch	07/12				
Bury	Tr	07/13	13	1	1	0
Coventry C	Tr	07/14				

CHARLESWORTH Arnold
Born: Sheffield, England, 6 July, 1930 — IF
Died: Retford, Nottinghamshire, England, 1972

League Club	Source	Date Signed	Seasons Played	Apps	Subs	Gls
West Bromwich A	Boston U	03/52				
Rotherham U	Tr	08/53				
York C	Tr	04/54	54	1	-	0

CHARLESWORTH Stanley (Stan)
Born: Conisbrough, South Yorkshire, England, 8 March, 1920 — CH
Died: Plymouth, England, March, 2003

League Club	Source	Date Signed	Seasons Played	Apps	Subs	Gls
Grimsby T	Wath W	12/37	38-46	2	-	0
Barnsley	Tr	12/46	46	7	-	0

CHARLESWORTH Terence (Terry)
Born: Scunthorpe, North Lincolnshire, England, 13 July, 1933 — G

League Club	Source	Date Signed	Seasons Played	Apps	Subs	Gls
Scunthorpe U		06/52	52-56	19	-	0

CHARLTON Asa Edmund
Born: Bridgnorth, Shropshire, England, 7 December, 1977 — LB

League Club	Source	Date Signed	Seasons Played	Apps	Subs	Gls
Mansfield T	Redditch U	11/06	06	3	1	0

CHARLTON Harold (Harry)
Born: Gateshead, Tyne and Wear, England, 22 June, 1951 — M

League Club	Source	Date Signed	Seasons Played	Apps	Subs	Gls
Middlesbrough	App	07/68	70-74	8	2	0
Hartlepool U	L	01/76	75	2	1	0
Chesterfield	Tr	03/76	75-76	17	4	0
Darlington	Buxton	08/79	79-81	69	3	4

CHARLTON John (Jack)
Born: Ashington, Northumberland, England, 8 May, 1935 — CD
England: 35/FLge-6

League Club	Source	Date Signed	Seasons Played	Apps	Subs	Gls
Leeds U	Jnr	05/52	52-72	629	0	70

CHARLTON John Alfred
Born: Gateshead, Tyne and Wear, England, 24 March, 1922 — G
Died: Durham, England, 18 May, 1981

League Club	Source	Date Signed	Seasons Played	Apps	Subs	Gls
Gateshead (Am)		08/49	49	1	-	0

CHARLTON Kevin
Born: Atherstone, Warwickshire, England, 12 September, 1954 — G
England: Semi Pro

League Club	Source	Date Signed	Seasons Played	Apps	Subs	Gls
Wolverhampton W	App	09/72				
Bournemouth	Tr	12/73	73-74	21	0	0
Hereford U	Tr	06/75	75-77	52	0	0
Scarborough	Telford U	09/88	88	3	0	0

CHARLTON Robert (Bobby)
Born: Ashington, Northumberland, England, 11 October, 1937 — M/F
England: 106/FLge-8/U23-6/Youth/Schools

League Club	Source	Date Signed	Seasons Played	Apps	Subs	Gls
Manchester U	Jnr	10/54	56-72	604	2	199
Preston NE	Tr	05/74	74	38	0	8

CHARLTON Simon Thomas
Born: Huddersfield, West Yorkshire, England, 25 October, 1971 — LB
England: Youth

League Club	Source	Date Signed	Seasons Played	Apps	Subs	Gls
Huddersfield T	YT	07/89	89-92	121	3	1
Southampton	Tr	06/93	93-97	104	10	2
Birmingham C	Tr	12/97	97-99	69	3	0
Bolton W	Tr	07/00	00-03	108	12	0
Norwich C	Tr	07/04	04-05	39	6	2
Oldham Ath	Tr	08/06	06	34	0	1

CHARLTON Stanley (Stan)
Born: Exeter, England, 28 June, 1929 — FB
Died: Dorchester, Dorset, England, 20 December, 2012
England: Amateur-4

League Club	Source	Date Signed	Seasons Played	Apps	Subs	Gls
Leyton Orient	Bromley	11/52	52-55	151	-	1
Arsenal	Tr	11/55	55-58	99	-	0
Leyton Orient	Tr	12/58	58-64	216	-	1

CHARLTON Wilfred Sydney (Wilf)
Born: Blyth, Northumberland, England, 12 September, 1933 — WH

League Club	Source	Date Signed	Seasons Played	Apps	Subs	Gls
Huddersfield T	Portsmouth (Am)	11/50				
Southport	Tr	07/54	54-56	109	-	8
Tranmere Rov	Tr	06/57	57-60	92	-	4

CHARNLEY Derek Lawrence
Born: Doncaster, South Yorkshire, England, 7 May, 1954 — F

League Club	Source	Date Signed	Seasons Played	Apps	Subs	Gls
Scunthorpe U		02/73	72-75	28	10	3

CHARNLEY James Callaghan (Chic)
Born: Glasgow, Scotland, 11 June, 1963 — M

League Club	Source	Date Signed	Seasons Played	Apps	Subs	Gls
Bolton W (L)	St Mirren	03/92	91	3	0	0

CHARNLEY Raymond Ogden (Ray)
Born: Lancaster, England, 29 May, 1935 — CF
Died: Fleetwood, Lancashire, England, 15 November, 2009
England: 1

League Club	Source	Date Signed	Seasons Played	Apps	Subs	Gls
Blackpool	Morecambe	05/57	57-67	363	0	193
Preston NE	Tr	12/67	67	23	0	4

League Club	Source	Date Signed	Seasons Played	Apps	Subs	Gls
Wrexham	Tr	07/68	68	19	1	5
Bradford Park Ave	Tr	01/69	68-69	59	0	15
CHARNOCK Kieran James						
Born: Preston, Lancashire, England, 3 August, 1984						CD
England: Semi Pro-11						
Wigan Ath	Sch	07/02				
Peterborough U	Northwich Victoria	07/07	07-08	12	0	0
Accrington Stan	L	10/08	08	33	1	0
Torquay U	Tr	08/09	09-10	23	5	0
Morecambe	Tr	11/10	10-11	20	5	1
Fleetwood T	Tr	11/11	12	1	2	0
CHARNOCK Philip Anthony (Phil)						
Born: Southport, Merseyside, England, 14 February, 1975						M
Liverpool	YT	03/93				
Blackpool	L	02/96	95	0	4	0
Crewe Alex	Tr	09/96	96-01	136	21	8
Port Vale	Tr	08/02	02	14	4	1
Bury	Tr	08/03	03	3	0	0
CHARTER Raymond (Ray)						
Born: Ashton-under-Lyne, Greater Manchester, England, 10 January, 1950						FB/M
Blackburn Rov	App	01/68	69-70	13	5	0
Stockport Co	Tr	07/71	71-73	87	4	2
CHARVET Laurent Jean						
Born: Beziers, France, 8 May, 1973						RB/M
Chelsea (L)	AS Cannes (FRA)	01/98	97	7	4	2
Newcastle U	AS Cannes (FRA)	07/98	98-00	37	3	1
Manchester C	Tr	10/00	00-01	19	4	0
CHASE Charles Thomas (Charlie)						
Born: Steyning, West Sussex, England, 31 January, 1924						WH
Watford	Brighton & HA (Am)	09/46	46-47	16	-	1
Crystal Palace	Tr	07/48	48-49	55	-	2
CHATHAM Alexander Whyte (Alec)						
Born: Glasgow, Scotland, 7 July, 1936						CF
Barrow		12/58	58	1	-	0
CHATHAM Raymond Harold (Ray)						
Born: Wolverhampton, England, 20 July, 1924						CH
Died: Purley, S London, England, 1 June, 1999						
Wolverhampton W	Jnr	06/45	46-53	76	-	0
Notts Co	Tr	01/54	53-58	127	-	4
CHATTERLEY Lawson Colin (Lew)						
Born: Birmingham, England, 15 February, 1945						M
England: Youth						
Aston Villa	App	02/62	62-70	149	4	26
Doncaster Rov	L	03/71	70	9	0	0
Northampton T	Tr	09/71	71	23	0	2
Grimsby T	Tr	02/72	71-73	72	1	16
Southampton	Tr	03/74	73-74	7	2	0
Torquay U	Tr	02/75	74-76	55	2	10
CHATTERTON Nicholas John (Nicky)						
Born: Norwood, S London, England, 18 May, 1954						M
Crystal Palace	Jnr	03/72	73-78	142	9	31
Millwall	Tr	11/78	78-85	258	6	56
Colchester U	Tr	09/86	86-88	47	2	8
CHAYTOR Kenneth (Kenny)						
Born: Trimdon, County Durham, England, 18 November, 1937						IF
Oldham Ath	Jnr	11/54	54-59	77	-	20
CHEADLE Thomas (Tom)						
Born: Stoke-on-Trent, England, 8 April, 1919						CH
Died: Stoke-on-Trent, England, 4 September, 1993						
Port Vale	Royal Artillery	05/46	46-56	333	-	14
Crewe Alex	Tr	07/57	57-58	37	-	0
CHEESEBROUGH Albert						
Born: Burnley, Lancashire, England, 17 January, 1935						IF
England: U23-1						
Burnley	Jnr	01/52	51-58	142	-	35
Leicester C	Tr	06/59	59-62	122	-	40
Port Vale	Tr	07/63	63-64	57	-	13
Mansfield T	Tr	07/65	65-66	24	0	0
CHEESEWRIGHT John Anthony						
Born: Romford, E London, England, 12 January, 1973						G
Southend U	Tottenham H (YT)	03/91				
Birmingham C	Tr	11/91	91	1	0	0
Colchester U	Braintree T	01/94	93-94	40	0	0
Wycombe W	Mansion (HKG)	03/96	96	18	0	0
CHEESLEY Paul Martyn						
Born: Bristol, England, 20 October, 1953						F
Norwich C	App	10/71	72-73	10	3	1
Bristol C	Tr	12/73	73-76	61	3	20
CHEETHAM Hugh David						
Born: Manchester, England, 3 February, 1958						M/LB
Crewe Alex	App	01/76	75-78	90	6	0
Reading	Tr	07/79	79-80	10	2	0
CHEETHAM Michael Martin (Mike)						
Born: Nijmegen, Netherlands, 30 June, 1967						M
Ipswich T	Basingstoke T	10/88	88-89	1	3	0
Cambridge U	Tr	10/89	89-93	123	9	22
Chesterfield	Tr	07/94	94	5	0	0
Colchester U	Tr	03/95	94-95	33	4	3
CHEETHAM Roy Alexander John						
Born: Eccles, Greater Manchester, England, 21 December, 1939						RH
Manchester C	Jnr	12/56	57-67	127	4	4
Charlton Ath	Detroit Cougars (USA)	10/68				
Chester C	Tr	12/68	68-71	122	2	8
CHEETHAM Thomas (Tommy)						
Born: Liverpool, England, 8 December, 1950						F
Died: Liverpool, England, 5 October, 2003						
Southport	Cambridge Park	12/69	69-70	24	2	4
CHEETHAM Thomas Miles (Tommy)						
Born: Newcastle-upon-Tyne, England, 11 October, 1910						CF
Died: Mansfield, Nottinghamshire, England, 23 December, 1993						
Queens Park Rgrs	Royal Artillery	08/35	35-38	115	-	81
Brentford	Tr	02/39	38	17	-	8
Lincoln C	Tr	10/45	46-47	47	-	29
CHENERY Benjamin Roger (Ben)						
Born: Ipswich, England, 28 January, 1977						RB
Luton T	YT	03/95	95	2	0	0
Cambridge U	Tr	07/97	97-99	97	1	2
CHENEY Denis						
Born: Coalville, Leicestershire, England, 30 June, 1924						IF
Died: Bournemouth, England, October, 2008						
Leicester C	Coalville T	11/41	47-48	2	-	0
Watford	L	02/48	47	18	-	4
Bournemouth	Tr	10/48	48-53	158	-	47
Aldershot	Tr	06/54	54-55	53	-	19
CHENHALL John Colin						
Born: Bristol, England, 23 July, 1927						LB
Died: Bristol, England, April, 2011						
Arsenal	Maidenhead U	11/45	51-52	16	-	0
Fulham	Tr	07/53	53-57	91	-	0
CHENOWETH Oliver Ralph (Ollie)						
Born: Liskeard, Cornwall, England, 17 February, 1992						G
Plymouth Arg	Sch	07/10	11	1	0	0
CHEREDNIK Alexei						
Born: Dushanbe, Tajikistan, 12 December, 1960						RB
Soviet Union: 2						
Southampton	Dnepr (URS)	02/90	89-90	19	4	0
CHEREL Julien						
Born: Caen, France, 8 March, 1983						CD
Hartlepool U	Mondeville (FRA)	09/09	09	1	0	0
CHERRY Rex Aubrey						
Born: Penistone, South Yorkshire, England, 11 November, 1933						CF
Gillingham	Military Provost Corps	03/53	52-53	10	-	4
CHERRY Steven Reginald (Steve)						
Born: Nottingham, England, 5 August, 1960						G
England: Youth						
Derby Co	App	03/78	79-83	77	0	0
Port Vale	L	11/80	80	4	0	0
Walsall	Tr	08/84	84-85	71	0	0
Plymouth Arg	Tr	10/86	86-88	73	0	0
Chesterfield	L	12/88	88	10	0	0
Notts Co	Tr	02/89	88-94	266	0	0
Watford	Tr	07/95	95	4	0	0
Plymouth Arg	Tr	02/96	95	16	0	0
Rotherham U	Tr	07/96	96	20	0	0
Notts Co	Stalybridge Celtic	03/98				
Mansfield T	Tr	07/98	98	1	0	0
CHERRY Trevor John						
Born: Huddersfield, West Yorkshire, England, 23 February, 1948						CD
England: 27/FLge-1						
Huddersfield T	Jnr	07/65	66-71	185	3	12
Leeds U	Tr	06/72	72-82	393	6	24
Bradford C	Tr	12/82	82-84	92	0	0

League Club	Source	Date Signed	Seasons Played	Career Record Apps	Subs	Gls

CHESSELL Samuel (Sammy)
Born: Shirebrook, Derbyshire, England, 9 July, 1921 RB
Died: Shirebrook, Derbyshire, England, 14 March, 1996

Mansfield T	Welbeck Colliery	09/45	46-53	256	-	7

CHESTER James Grant
Born: Warrington, Cheshire, England, 23 January, 1989 CD
Wales: 6

Manchester U	Sch	07/07				
Peterborough U	L	02/09	08	5	0	0
Plymouth Arg	L	09/09	09	2	1	0
Carlisle U	L	08/10	10	18	0	2
Hull C	Tr	01/11	10-14	153	3	7

CHESTERS Colin Wayne
Born: Crewe, Cheshire, England, 21 November, 1959 F

Derby Co	App	11/77	77-78	6	3	1
Crewe Alex	Tr	09/79	79-81	52	9	6

CHETTLE Stephen (Steve)
Born: Nottingham, England, 27 September, 1968 CD
England: U21-12

Nottingham F	App	08/86	87-99	398	17	11
Barnsley	Tr	11/99	99-01	91	1	2
Walsall	L	09/01	01	6	0	0
Grimsby T	Tr	08/02	02	18	2	1

CHEUNG Chi-Doy (Chi)
Born: Hong Kong, 30 July, 1941 IF

Blackpool	Tung Wah (HKG)	10/60	60-61	2	-	1

CHEVANTON Ernesto Javier (Javier)
Born: Juan Lacaze, Uruguay, 12 August, 1980 F
Uruguay: 22

Queens Park Rgrs	US Lecce (ITA)	09/13	13	0	2	0

CHEW John (Jackie)
Born: Blackburn, Greater Manchester, England, 13 May, 1920 RW
Died: Blackburn, Greater Manchester, England, 19 October, 2002

Burnley	Blackburn Rov (Am)	05/45	46-53	225	-	39
Bradford C	Tr	06/54	54	36	-	4

CHEW John (Jack)
Born: Longton, Potteries, England, 25 November, 1915 FB
Died: Stoke-on-Trent, England, 5 April, 1984

Luton T		11/42				
Port Vale	Tr	03/46	46	9	-	0

CHEYROU Bruno
Born: Paris, France, 10 May, 1978 M
France: 3

Liverpool	OSC Lille (FRA)	07/02	02-03	17	14	2

CHICKSEN Adam Thomas
Born: Milton Keynes, England, 23 January, 1989 CD

MK Dons	Sch	07/10	08-12	48	25	2
Leyton Orient	L	01/12	11	3	0	0
Brighton & HA	Tr	07/13	13-14	4	2	0
Gillingham	L	11/14	14	3	0	0
Fleetwood T	L	02/15	14	13	0	0

[CHICO] FLORES Jose Manuel
Born: Cadiz, Spain, 6 March, 1987 CD
Spain: U21-3

Swansea C	Genoa (ITA)	07/12	12-13	56	1	2

CHIEDOZIE John Okay
Born: Owerri, Nigeria, 18 April, 1960 RW
Nigeria: 9

Leyton Orient	App	04/77	76-80	131	14	20
Notts Co	Tr	08/81	81-83	110	1	15
Tottenham H	Tr	08/84	84-86	45	8	12
Derby Co	Tr	08/88	88	2	0	0
Notts Co	Tr	01/90	89	0	1	0
Chesterfield	Tr	03/90	89	5	2	0

CHIEDOZIE Jordan Joshua
Born: Bournemouth, England, 1 August, 1994 F

Bournemouth	Sch	07/12				
Cambridge U	Concord Rgrs	11/14	14	2	4	0

CHIHI Adil
Born: Dusseldorf, Germany, 21 February, 1988 RW
Morocco: 2

Fulham	FC Koln (GER)	07/14	14	0	1	0

CHILAKA Chibuzor (Chib)
Born: Nigeria, 21 October, 1986 F

Notts Co	Rushden & D (Sch)	08/05				
Bradford C	Leeds Carnegie College	08/10	10	0	4	0

CHILCOTT Kenneth (Ken)
Born: Ystrad Rhondda, Rhondda Cynon Taff, Wales, 17 March, 1920 RW
Died: Bristol, England, June, 2001

Bristol C	Eastville U	10/37	37-48	46	-	6

CHILDS Albert Robert (Bert)
Born: Liverpool, England, 25 September, 1930 FB
England: Amateur-1

Liverpool (Am)	Northern Nomads	09/53	53	2	-	0

CHILDS Gary Paul Colin
Born: Birmingham, England, 19 April, 1964 W
England: Youth

West Bromwich A	App	02/82	81-83	2	1	0
Walsall	Tr	10/83	83-86	120	11	17
Birmingham C	Tr	07/87	87-88	39	16	2
Grimsby T	Tr	07/89	89-96	204	29	26

CHILLINGWORTH Daniel Thomas (Dan)
Born: Somersham, Cambridgeshire, England, 13 September, 1981 F

Cambridge U	YT	02/00	99-04	53	34	13
Darlington	L	11/01	01	2	2	1
Leyton Orient	L	12/04	04	8	0	2
Rushden & D	Tr	07/05	05	3	3	0
Notts Co	L	02/06	05	8	5	2

CHILTON Allenby
Born: Sunderland, England, 16 September, 1918 CH
Died: Sunderland, England, 15 June, 1996
England: 2

Manchester U	Seaham CW	11/38	46-54	352	-	3
Grimsby T	Tr	03/55	54-56	63	-	0

CHILTON Anthony Julian Thomas (Tony)
Born: Maryport, Cumbria, England, 7 September, 1965 FB

Sunderland	App	09/83				
Burnley	Tr	02/85	84	1	0	0
Hartlepool U	Tr	10/85	85	3	0	0

CHILTON Christopher Roy (Chris)
Born: Sproatley, East Riding of Yorkshire, England, 25 June, 1943 CF

Hull C	Jnr	07/60	60-71	415	0	193
Coventry C	Tr	09/71	71	26	1	3

CHILTON Frederick (Fred)
Born: Washington, Tyne and Wear, England, 10 July, 1935 FB

Sunderland	Usworth Colliery	05/53	56-57	3	-	0

CHILVERS Geoffrey Thomas (Geoff)
Born: Epsom, Surrey, England, 31 January, 1925 WH
Died: Smallfield, Surrey, England, 1 January, 1971
England: Schools

Crystal Palace	Sutton U	03/45	48-53	118	-	1

CHILVERS Gordon Malcolm
Born: Norwich, England, 15 November, 1933 G

Walsall	Fordhouses YC	04/52	51-57	123	-	0

CHILVERS Liam Christopher
Born: Chelmsford, England, 6 November, 1981 CD

Arsenal	YT	07/00				
Northampton T	L	12/00	00	7	0	0
Notts Co	L	11/01	01	9	0	1
Colchester U	L	01/03	02	6	0	0
Colchester U	L	08/03	03	29	3	0
Colchester U	Tr	08/04	04-05	73	2	3
Preston NE	Tr	07/06	06-09	92	5	2
Notts Co	Tr	07/10	10-11	33	5	0
Port Vale	L	09/11	11	12	0	0
Port Vale	AFC Telford U	11/12	12-13	33	1	2

CHIMBONDA Pascal
Born: Les Abymes, Guadeloupe, 21 February, 1979 RB
France: 1//Guadeloupe: 6

Wigan Ath	SC Bastia (FRA)	07/05	05-06	37	1	2
Tottenham H	Tr	08/06	06-07	64	1	3
Sunderland	Tr	07/08	08	13	0	0
Tottenham H	Tr	01/09	08	1	2	0
Blackburn Rov	Tr	08/09	09-10	25	5	1
Queens Park Rgrs	Tr	01/11	10	0	3	0
Doncaster Rov	Tr	09/11	11	16	0	0
Carlisle U	Market Drayton T	10/13	13	25	1	0

CHINAGLIA Giorgio
Born: Carrara, Italy, 24 January, 1947 CF
Died: Florida, USA, 1 April, 2012
Italy: 14/ILge-1

Swansea C	App	04/65	64-65	4	1	1

CHINE Athumani Khamiss
Born: Dar es Salaam, Tanzania, 12 March, 1967 — M

League Club	Source	Date Signed	Seasons Played	Apps	Subs	Gls
Walsall	Young Africans (TAN)	03/92	91	4	1	0

CHIPPENDALE Aidan Luke
Born: Bradford, England, 24 May, 1992 — LW

League Club	Source	Date Signed	Seasons Played	Apps	Subs	Gls
Huddersfield T	Sch	07/10	10	0	1	0
Accrington Stan	Tr	08/12	12	2	4	0
Bury	Tr	07/13				

CHIPPENDALE Brian Albert
Born: Bradford, England, 29 October, 1964 — RW

League Club	Source	Date Signed	Seasons Played	Apps	Subs	Gls
York C	Bradford C (App)	10/83	83-84	2	6	0
Halifax T	L	11/84	84	1	1	0
Burnley	Tr	08/85	85	6	2	0
Preston NE	Tr	10/85	85	5	1	0

CHIPPO Youssef
Born: Boujaad, Morocco, 10 June, 1973 — M
Morocco: 62

League Club	Source	Date Signed	Seasons Played	Apps	Subs	Gls
Coventry C	FC Porto (POR)	07/99	99-02	100	22	6

CHIRICHES Vlad Iulian
Born: Bacau, Romania, 14 November, 1989 — CD
Romania: 32/U21-3

League Club	Source	Date Signed	Seasons Played	Apps	Subs	Gls
Tottenham H	Steaua Bucharest (ROM)	09/13	13-14	24	3	1

CHISHOLM Gordon William
Born: Glasgow, Scotland, 8 April, 1960 — CD

League Club	Source	Date Signed	Seasons Played	Apps	Subs	Gls
Sunderland	App	04/78	78-85	192	5	10

CHISHOLM John Richardson (Jack)
Born: Edmonton, N London, England, 9 October, 1924 — CH
Died: Waltham Forest, NE London, England, September, 1977

League Club	Source	Date Signed	Seasons Played	Apps	Subs	Gls
Tottenham H	Jnr	10/42	47	2	-	0
Brentford	Tr	12/47	47-48	49	-	1
Sheffield U	Tr	03/49	48-49	21	-	1
Plymouth Arg	Tr	12/49	49-53	175	-	2

CHISHOLM Kenneth McTaggart (Ken)
Born: Glasgow, Scotland, 12 April, 1925 — IF
Died: Chester-le-Street, County Durham, England, 30 April, 1990
Scotland: War-1

League Club	Source	Date Signed	Seasons Played	Apps	Subs	Gls
Leeds U	Partick Thistle	01/48	47-48	40	-	17
Leicester C	Tr	01/49	48-49	42	-	17
Coventry C	Tr	03/50	49-51	68	-	34
Cardiff C	Tr	03/52	51-53	62	-	33
Sunderland	Tr	01/54	53-55	78	-	34
Workington	Tr	08/56	56-57	39	-	14

CHISHOLM Ross Stephen
Born: Irvine, Ayrshire, Scotland, 14 January, 1988 — M

League Club	Source	Date Signed	Seasons Played	Apps	Subs	Gls
Darlington	Shamrock Rov (ROI)	03/10	09	2	1	0

CHISHOLM Wilfred (Wilf)
Born: Hebburn, Tyne and Wear, England, 23 May, 1921 — G
Died: Durham, England, December, 1962

League Club	Source	Date Signed	Seasons Played	Apps	Subs	Gls
Grimsby T	Newcastle U (Am)	09/46	46-50	92	-	0

CHISNALL Joseph Philip (Phil)
Born: Manchester, England, 27 October, 1942 — M
England: U23-1/Schools

League Club	Source	Date Signed	Seasons Played	Apps	Subs	Gls
Manchester U	Jnr	11/59	61-63	35	-	8
Liverpool	Tr	04/64	64	6	-	1
Southend U	Tr	08/67	67-70	137	5	28
Stockport Co	Tr	09/71	71	30	0	2

CHISWICK Peter John Henry
Born: Plaistow, E London, England, 19 September, 1929 — G
Died: Plaistow, E London, England, 18 August, 1962

League Club	Source	Date Signed	Seasons Played	Apps	Subs	Gls
West Ham U	Jnr	07/47	53-54	19	-	0
Gillingham	Tr	07/56	56	14	-	0

CHITTY Wilfred Sidney (Wilf)
Born: Walton-on-Thames, Surrey, England, 10 July, 1912 — W
Died: Caterham, Surrey, England, 2 February, 1997

League Club	Source	Date Signed	Seasons Played	Apps	Subs	Gls
Chelsea	Woking	03/30	31-37	45	-	16
Plymouth Arg	Tr	12/38	38	3	-	1
Reading	Tr	08/39	46-47	23	-	7

CHIVERS Gary Paul Stephen
Born: Stockwell, S London, England, 15 May, 1960 — FB

League Club	Source	Date Signed	Seasons Played	Apps	Subs	Gls
Chelsea	App	07/78	78-82	128	5	4
Swansea C	Tr	08/83	83	10	0	0
Queens Park Rgrs	Tr	02/84	84-86	58	2	0
Watford	Tr	09/87	87	14	0	0
Brighton & HA	Tr	03/88	87-92	215	2	13
Bournemouth	Lyn Oslo (NOR)	11/93	93-94	29	2	2

CHIVERS Martin Harcourt
Born: Southampton, England, 27 April, 1945 — F
England: 24/FLge-1/U23-17

League Club	Source	Date Signed	Seasons Played	Apps	Subs	Gls
Southampton	Jnr	09/62	62-67	174	1	97
Tottenham H	Tr	01/68	67-75	268	10	118
Norwich C	Servette (SUI)	07/78	78	11	0	4
Brighton & HA	Tr	03/79	78-79	4	1	1

CHMILOWSKY Roman
Born: Bradford, England, 19 April, 1959 — G

League Club	Source	Date Signed	Seasons Played	Apps	Subs	Gls
Halifax T (Am)	Jnr	04/77	76	1	0	0

CHO Won-Hee
Born: Seoul, South Korea, 17 April, 1983 — M
South Korea: 30

League Club	Source	Date Signed	Seasons Played	Apps	Subs	Gls
Wigan Ath	Suwan Samsung (KOR)	03/09	08-09	2	3	0

CHOLERTON William
Born: Derby, England, 1 January, 1949 — FB

League Club	Source	Date Signed	Seasons Played	Apps	Subs	Gls
Derby Co	App	12/66	66	1	0	0

CHOPRA Rocky Michael (Michael)
Born: Newcastle-upon-Tyne, England, 23 December, 1983 — F
England: U21-1/Youth

League Club	Source	Date Signed	Seasons Played	Apps	Subs	Gls
Newcastle U	YT	01/01	02-05	7	14	1
Watford	L	03/03	02	4	1	5
Nottingham F	L	02/04	03	3	2	0
Barnsley	L	08/04	04	38	1	17
Cardiff C	Tr	07/06	06	42	0	22
Sunderland	Tr	07/07	07-08	22	17	8
Cardiff C	L	11/08	08	10	1	5
Cardiff C	Tr	02/09	08-10	74	15	29
Ipswich T	Tr	06/11	11-12	53	25	18
Blackpool	Tr	08/13	13	5	13	0

CHORLEY Benjamin Francis (Ben)
Born: Sidcup, SE London, England, 30 September, 1982 — CD

League Club	Source	Date Signed	Seasons Played	Apps	Subs	Gls
Arsenal	YT	07/01				
Brentford	L	08/02	02	2	0	0
Wimbledon	Tr	03/03	02-03	41	4	2
MK Dons	Wimbledon relocation	07/04	04-06	78	2	3
Gillingham	L	10/06	06	24	3	1
Tranmere Rov	Tr	07/07	07-08	75	1	2
Leyton Orient	Tr	07/09	09-12	127	4	7
Stevenage	Tr	01/13	12-13	12	0	0
Portsmouth	Tr	01/14	13-14	27	1	0

CHOULES Leonard George (Len)
Born: Orpington, SE London, England, 29 January, 1932 — CH

League Club	Source	Date Signed	Seasons Played	Apps	Subs	Gls
Crystal Palace	Sutton U	05/51	52-61	258	-	2

CHOW Timothy Alexander (Tim)
Born: Wigan, Greater Manchester, England, 18 January, 1994 — M

League Club	Source	Date Signed	Seasons Played	Apps	Subs	Gls
Wigan Ath	Sch	03/12	14	3	1	1

CHRISTANVAL Phillipe Charles Lucien
Born: Paris, France, 31 August, 1978 — LB
France: 6

League Club	Source	Date Signed	Seasons Played	Apps	Subs	Gls
Fulham	Olymp Marseille (FRA)	09/05	05-07	26	10	1

CHRISTENSEN Andreas Bodtker
Born: Copenhagen, Denmark, 10 April, 1996 — D
Denmark: U21-15/Youth

League Club	Source	Date Signed	Seasons Played	Apps	Subs	Gls
Chelsea	Sch	07/13	14	0	1	0

CHRISTENSEN Kim
Born: Fredriksvaerk, Denmark, 8 May, 1980 — F
Denmark: U21-9

League Club	Source	Date Signed	Seasons Played	Apps	Subs	Gls
Barnsley	Odense BK (DEN)	08/07	07	0	12	1

CHRISTENSEN Lasse Vigen
Born: Esbjerg, Denmark, 15 August, 1994 — M
Denmark: U21-12/Youth

League Club	Source	Date Signed	Seasons Played	Apps	Subs	Gls
Fulham	Midtjylland (DEN)	01/12	14	24	1	5

CHRISTENSEN Thomas Anton (Tommy)
Born: Aarhus, Denmark, 20 July, 1961 — W

League Club	Source	Date Signed	Seasons Played	Apps	Subs	Gls
Leicester C	Elche (SPN)	11/85	85	1	1	0
Portsmouth	Tr	11/85	85	3	0	2

CHRISTIANSEN Jesper
Born: Roskilde, Denmark, 18 June, 1980 — F

League Club	Source	Date Signed	Seasons Played	Apps	Subs	Gls
Kidderminster Hrs	OB Odense (DEN)	01/04	03-04	22	16	1

CHRISTIE Cyrus Sylvester Frederick
Born: Coventry, England, 30 September, 1992 — RB
Republic of Ireland: 1

League Club	Source	Date Signed	Seasons Played	Apps	Subs	Gls
Coventry C	Sch	06/11	11-13	91	11	2
Derby Co	Tr	07/14	14	34	4	0

CHRISTIE David
Born: Salford, England, 26 February, 1973 LW

League Club	Source	Date Signed	Seasons Played	Apps	Subs	Gls
Preston NE	YT	07/91	91-92	1	3	0
Halifax T	Tr	01/93	92	6	3	0

CHRISTIE Derrick Hugh Michael
Born: Bletchley, Buckinghamshire, England, 15 March, 1957 W

League Club	Source	Date Signed	Seasons Played	Apps	Subs	Gls
Northampton T	App	03/75	73-78	116	22	18
Cambridge U	Tr	11/78	78-83	132	6	19
Reading	Tr	07/84	84	8	6	1
Cardiff C	Tr	10/85	85	18	1	2
Peterborough U	Tr	08/86	86	6	2	0

CHRISTIE Frank
Born: Scone, Perthshire, Scotland, 17 December, 1927 WH
Died: Perth, Scotland, 12 September, 1996

League Club	Source	Date Signed	Seasons Played	Apps	Subs	Gls
Liverpool	Forfar Ath	03/49	49	4	-	0

CHRISTIE Iyseden
Born: Coventry, England, 14 November, 1976 F

League Club	Source	Date Signed	Seasons Played	Apps	Subs	Gls
Coventry C	YT	05/95	95	0	1	0
Bournemouth	L	11/96	96	3	1	0
Mansfield T	L	02/97	96	8	0	0
Mansfield T	Tr	06/97	97-98	44	37	18
Leyton Orient	Tr	07/99	99-01	32	26	12
Mansfield T	Tr	08/02	02-03	53	11	26
Kidderminster Hrs	Tr	08/04	04	1	7	0
Rochdale	Tr	01/06	05-06	14	5	2

CHRISTIE Jeremy John
Born: Whangarei, New Zealand, 22 May, 1983 M
New Zealand: 28/U23-13/Youth-17

League Club	Source	Date Signed	Seasons Played	Apps	Subs	Gls
Barnsley	YT	-	01	0	1	0

CHRISTIE John Alexander
Born: Fraserburgh, Aberdeenshire, Scotland, 26 September, 1929 G
Died: Chandler's Ford, Hampshire, England, 9 March, 2014

League Club	Source	Date Signed	Seasons Played	Apps	Subs	Gls
Southampton	Ayr U	01/51	50-58	197	-	0
Walsall	Tr	06/59	59-62	102	-	0

CHRISTIE Malcolm Neil
Born: Stamford, Lincolnshire, England, 11 April, 1979 F
England: U21-11

League Club	Source	Date Signed	Seasons Played	Apps	Subs	Gls
Derby Co	Nuneaton Bor	11/98	98-02	90	26	30
Middlesbrough	Tr	01/03	02-06	27	16	7
Leeds U	Tr	11/08	08	1	3	1

CHRISTIE Trevor John
Born: Cresswell, Northumberland, England, 28 February, 1959 F

League Club	Source	Date Signed	Seasons Played	Apps	Subs	Gls
Leicester C	App	12/76	77-78	28	3	8
Notts Co	Tr	06/79	79-83	158	29	64
Nottingham F	Tr	07/84	84	14	0	5
Derby Co	Tr	02/85	84-85	65	0	22
Manchester C	Tr	08/86	86	9	0	3
Walsall	Tr	10/86	86-88	91	8	22
Mansfield T	Tr	03/89	88-90	88	4	24

CHRISTON Lewis John
Born: Milton Keynes, England, 24 January, 1989 CD

League Club	Source	Date Signed	Seasons Played	Apps	Subs	Gls
Wycombe W	Sch	03/06	06-07	7	1	0

CHRISTOPHE Jean-Francois
Born: Creil, France, 27 June, 1987 M

League Club	Source	Date Signed	Seasons Played	Apps	Subs	Gls
Portsmouth	RC Lens (FRA)	07/07				
Bournemouth	L	08/07	07	5	5	1
Yeovil T	L	03/08	07	4	1	0
Southend U	Tr	09/08	08-09	60	9	5
Oldham Ath	Tr	09/10	10	0	1	0

CHRISTOPHER Paul Anthony
Born: Poole, Dorset, England, 19 June, 1954 F

League Club	Source	Date Signed	Seasons Played	Apps	Subs	Gls
Bournemouth	App	11/71				
Mansfield T	Tr	07/73	73	7	1	1

CHUNG Cyril (Sammy)
Born: Abingdon, Oxfordshire, England, 16 July, 1932 WH/CF

League Club	Source	Date Signed	Seasons Played	Apps	Subs	Gls
Reading	Headington U	11/51	53-54	22	-	12
Norwich C	Tr	01/55	54-56	47	-	9
Watford	Tr	06/57	57-64	220	-	22

CHURCH Garry
Born: Pontefract, West Yorkshire, England, 20 September, 1944 RH
Died: Beverley, East Riding of Yorkshire, England, 24 December, 2011

League Club	Source	Date Signed	Seasons Played	Apps	Subs	Gls
Bradford Park Ave	Great Preston Jnrs	07/62	63	4	-	0

CHURCH John
Born: Lowestoft, Suffolk, England, 17 September, 1919 LW
Died: Carlton Colville, Suffolk, England, 6 September, 2004

League Club	Source	Date Signed	Seasons Played	Apps	Subs	Gls
Norwich C	Lowestoft T	09/36	37-49	110	-	16
Colchester U	Tr	07/50	50-53	118	-	21

CHURCH Simon Richard
Born: Amersham, Buckinghamshire, England, 10 December, 1988 F
Wales: 29/U21-15

League Club	Source	Date Signed	Seasons Played	Apps	Subs	Gls
Reading	Sch	07/07	09-11	55	49	22
Crewe Alex	L	10/07	07	11	1	1
Yeovil T	L	01/08	07	2	4	0
Wycombe W	L	08/08	08	6	3	0
Leyton Orient	L	02/09	08	12	1	5
Huddersfield T	L	11/12	12	7	0	1
Charlton Ath	Tr	08/13	13-14	31	24	5

CHURCHILL Trevor
Born: Barnsley, South Yorkshire, England, 20 November, 1923 G

League Club	Source	Date Signed	Seasons Played	Apps	Subs	Gls
Reading	Sheffield U (Am)	09/46	46	10	-	0
Leicester C	Tr	08/47				
Rochdale	Tr	01/49	48-52	110	-	0
Swindon T	Tr	05/53	53	11	-	0

CHURCHOUSE Gary
Born: Wembley, NW London, England, 1 February, 1957 M

League Club	Source	Date Signed	Seasons Played	Apps	Subs	Gls
Charlton Ath	Windsor & Eton	03/79	78-79	13	5	0

CHURMS Dennis John
Born: Rotherham, South Yorkshire, England, 8 May, 1931 IF

League Club	Source	Date Signed	Seasons Played	Apps	Subs	Gls
Rotherham U	Spurley Hey	04/50	53-55	15	-	0
Coventry C	Tr	06/56	56	10	-	2
Exeter C	Tr	03/57	56-57	44	-	8

CIBOCCHI Alessandro (Sandro)
Born: Terni, Italy, 18 September, 1982 LB

League Club	Source	Date Signed	Seasons Played	Apps	Subs	Gls
Swindon T	Porto Summaga (ITA)	07/11	11	11	7	0

CID Gerald
Born: Bordeaux, France, 17 February, 1983 CD

League Club	Source	Date Signed	Seasons Played	Apps	Subs	Gls
Bolton W	Bordeaux (FRA)	07/07	07	6	1	0

CIFTCI Nadir
Born: Den Haag, Netherlands, 12 February, 1992 W
Netherlands: Youth//Turkey: Youth

League Club	Source	Date Signed	Seasons Played	Apps	Subs	Gls
Portsmouth	Sch	02/09	10	4	15	1

CINI Joseph (Joe)
Born: Hamrun, Malta, 20 November, 1936 W
Malta: 16

League Club	Source	Date Signed	Seasons Played	Apps	Subs	Gls
Queens Park Rgrs (Am)	Hibernians (MLT)	08/59	59	7	-	1

CIRCUIT Steven (Steve)
Born: Sheffield, England, 11 April, 1972 M

League Club	Source	Date Signed	Seasons Played	Apps	Subs	Gls
Sheffield U	YT	07/90				
Halifax T	Stafford Rgrs	03/93	92	0	1	0

CISAK Aleksander (Alex)
Born: Krakow, Poland, 19 May, 1989 G
Australia: Youth

League Club	Source	Date Signed	Seasons Played	Apps	Subs	Gls
Leicester C	Sch	07/06				
Accrington Stan	Tr	08/10	10	21	0	0
Oldham Ath	Tr	07/11	11-12	48	0	0
Portsmouth	L	11/12	12	1	0	0
Burnley	Tr	06/13	13	0	1	0
York C	L	10/14	14	10	0	0
Leyton Orient	L	02/15	14	19	0	0

CISSE Aliou
Born: Zinguinchor, Senegal, 24 March, 1976 M
Senegal: 28

League Club	Source	Date Signed	Seasons Played	Apps	Subs	Gls
Birmingham C	Montpellier (FRA)	07/02	02-03	26	10	0
Portsmouth	Tr	08/04	04-05	14	9	0

CISSE Djibril
Born: Arles, France, 12 August, 1981 F
France: 41/U21-4

League Club	Source	Date Signed	Seasons Played	Apps	Subs	Gls
Liverpool	AJ Auxerre (FRA)	07/04	04-05	29	20	13
Sunderland (L)	Olymp Marseille (FRA)	08/08	08	29	6	10
Queens Park Rgrs	SS Lazio (ITA)	01/12	11-12	19	7	9

CISSE Edouard Souleymane Leopold
Born: Pau, France, 30 March, 1978 M
France: U21-14

League Club	Source	Date Signed	Seasons Played	Apps	Subs	Gls
West Ham U (L)	Paris St-Germain (FRA)	08/02	02	18	7	0

CISSE Kalifa
Born: Dreux, France, 9 January, 1984 DM
Mali: 5

League Club	Source	Date Signed	Seasons Played	Apps	Subs	Gls
Reading	Boavista (POR)	07/07	07-09	49	26	7
Bristol C	Tr	07/10	10-11	45	16	2
Derby Co	New England Rev (USA)	11/13	13	1	2	0

CISSE Papiss Demba
Born: Dakar, Senegal, 3 June, 1985 F
Senegal: 33

League Club	Source	Date Signed	Seasons Played	Apps	Subs	Gls
Newcastle U	SC Freiburg (GER)	01/12	11-14	74	22	34

League Club	Source	Date Signed	Seasons Played	Career Record Apps	Subs	Gls

CISSOKHO Aly
Born: Blois, France, 15 September, 1987 — LB
France: 1

League Club	Source	Date Signed	Seasons Played	Apps	Subs	Gls
Liverpool (L)	Valencia (SPN)	08/13	13	12	3	0
Aston Villa	Valencia (SPN)	08/14	14	24	1	0

CITRON Gerald Conrad (Gerry)
Born: Manchester, England, 8 April, 1935 — LW
Died: Fleetwood, Lancashire, England, 8 July, 2005

League Club	Source	Date Signed	Seasons Played	Apps	Subs	Gls
Chester C (Am)	Corinthian Casuals	10/59	59	2	-	0

CIVELLI Luciano
Born: Buenos Aires, Argentina, 6 October, 1986 — W

League Club	Source	Date Signed	Seasons Played	Apps	Subs	Gls
Ipswich T	Atletic Banfield (ARG)	02/09	08-10	8	9	0

CLACK Frank Edward
Born: Witney, Oxfordshire, England, 30 March, 1912 — G
Died: Witney, Oxfordshire, England, 2 June, 1995

League Club	Source	Date Signed	Seasons Played	Apps	Subs	Gls
Birmingham C	Witney T	05/33	33-38	60	-	0
Brentford	Tr	07/39				
Bristol C	Tr	05/47	46-48	67	-	0

CLAESEN Nicolas Pieter Josef (Nico)
Born: Maasmechelen, Belgium, 1 October, 1962 — F
Belgium: 36

League Club	Source	Date Signed	Seasons Played	Apps	Subs	Gls
Tottenham H	Standard Liege (BEL)	10/86	86-87	37	13	18

CLAMP Edward (Ted)
Born: Church Gresley, Derbyshire, England, 13 November, 1922 — G
Died: Church Gresley, Derbyshire, England, 2 June, 1990

League Club	Source	Date Signed	Seasons Played	Apps	Subs	Gls
Derby Co	Gresley Rov	11/47	48	1	-	0
Oldham Ath	Tr	07/49	49	3	-	0

CLAMP Harold Edwin (Eddie)
Born: Coalville, Leicestershire, England, 14 September, 1934 — RH
Died: Wolverhampton, England, 15 December, 1995
England: 4/FLge-1/Schools

League Club	Source	Date Signed	Seasons Played	Apps	Subs	Gls
Wolverhampton W	Jnr	04/52	53-61	214	-	23
Arsenal	Tr	11/61	61-62	22	-	1
Stoke C	Tr	09/62	62-63	50	-	2
Peterborough U	Tr	10/64	64	8	-	0

CLAMP Martin
Born: Coventry, England, 31 January, 1948 — G

League Club	Source	Date Signed	Seasons Played	Apps	Subs	Gls
Coventry C	Jnr	01/66				
Plymouth Arg	Tr	07/68	69	8	0	0

CLANCY John Patrick
Born: Perivale, W London, England, 5 July, 1949 — W

League Club	Source	Date Signed	Seasons Played	Apps	Subs	Gls
Bristol C	Tottenham H (App)	03/67				
Bradford Park Ave	Tr	07/67	67-68	52	4	2

CLANCY Sean Thomas
Born: Liverpool, England, 16 September, 1987 — LB

League Club	Source	Date Signed	Seasons Played	Apps	Subs	Gls
Blackpool	Sch	-	03	1	1	0

CLAPHAM Graham Leslie
Born: Lincoln, England, 23 September, 1947 — M

League Club	Source	Date Signed	Seasons Played	Apps	Subs	Gls
Newcastle U	App	09/65				
Shrewsbury T	Tr	08/67	67-71	73	14	5
Chester C	Tr	01/72	71-72	37	4	5

CLAPHAM James Richard (Jamie)
Born: Lincoln, England, 7 December, 1975 — LB

League Club	Source	Date Signed	Seasons Played	Apps	Subs	Gls
Tottenham H	YT	07/94	96	0	1	0
Leyton Orient	L	01/97	96	6	0	0
Bristol Rov	L	03/97	96	4	1	0
Ipswich T	Tr	01/98	97-02	187	20	10
Birmingham C	Tr	01/03	02-05	69	15	1
Wolverhampton W	Tr	08/06	06	21	5	0
Leeds U	L	08/07	07	12	1	0
Leicester C	Tr	01/08	07	11	0	0
Notts Co	Tr	09/08	08-09	57	13	3
Lincoln C	Tr	07/10	10	21	4	1

CLAPHAM Keith
Born: Fareham, Hampshire, England, 9 September, 1952 — CD

League Club	Source	Date Signed	Seasons Played	Apps	Subs	Gls
Bournemouth	App	09/70				
Exeter C	Tr	07/72	72-76	79	12	0

CLAPTON Daniel Robert (Danny)
Born: Stepney, E London, England, 22 July, 1934 — RW
Died: Hackney, E London, England, June, 1986
England: 1/FLge-1

League Club	Source	Date Signed	Seasons Played	Apps	Subs	Gls
Arsenal	Leytonstone	08/53	54-61	207	-	25
Luton T	Tr	09/62	62	10	-	0

CLAPTON Dennis Patrick
Born: Hackney, E London, England, 12 October, 1939 — CF
England: Youth

League Club	Source	Date Signed	Seasons Played	Apps	Subs	Gls
Arsenal	Bexleyheath	08/58	59-60	4	-	0
Northampton T	Tr	08/61	61	1	-	0

CLARE Daryl Adam
Born: Jersey, Channel Islands, 1 August, 1978 — F
Republic of Ireland: B-1/U21-6

League Club	Source	Date Signed	Seasons Played	Apps	Subs	Gls
Grimsby T	YT	12/95	95-00	34	45	9
Northampton T	L	11/99	99	9	1	3
Northampton T	L	11/00	00	3	1	0
Cheltenham T	L	12/00	00	4	0	0
Boston U	Tr	07/01	02	7	0	1
Chester C	Tr	11/02	04	3	4	1
Boston U	Tr	11/04	04-05	14	6	3

CLARE James Edward (Jimmy)
Born: Islington, N London, England, 6 November, 1959 — F

League Club	Source	Date Signed	Seasons Played	Apps	Subs	Gls
Chelsea	App	08/78	80	0	1	0

CLARE Robert (Rob)
Born: Belper, Derbyshire, England, 28 February, 1983 — D

League Club	Source	Date Signed	Seasons Played	Apps	Subs	Gls
Stockport Co	YT	03/00	00-03	107	10	3
Blackpool	Tr	08/04	04	19	4	0
Stockport Co	Tr	07/05	05-06	60	4	2

CLARIDGE Stephen Edward (Steve)
Born: Portsmouth, England, 10 April, 1966 — F

League Club	Source	Date Signed	Seasons Played	Apps	Subs	Gls
Bournemouth	Fareham T	11/84	84-85	3	4	1
Crystal Palace	Weymouth	10/88				
Aldershot	Tr	10/88	88-89	58	4	19
Cambridge U	Tr	02/90	89-91	56	23	28
Luton T	Tr	07/92	92	15	1	2
Cambridge U	Tr	11/92	92-93	53	0	18
Birmingham C	Tr	01/94	93-95	86	2	35
Leicester C	Tr	03/96	95-97	53	10	16
Portsmouth	L	01/98	97	10	0	2
Wolverhampton W	Tr	03/98	97	4	1	0
Portsmouth	Tr	08/98	98-00	94	10	34
Millwall	Tr	03/01	00-02	76	15	29
Brighton & HA	Weymouth	11/04	04	5	0	0
Brentford	Tr	12/04	04	3	1	0
Wycombe W	Tr	01/05	04	14	5	4
Gillingham	Tr	08/05	05	1	0	0
Bradford C	Tr	08/05	05	14	12	5
Walsall	L	03/06	05	7	0	1
Bournemouth	Rtd	10/06	06	1	0	0

CLARK Albert Henry
Born: Ashington, Northumberland, England, 24 July, 1921 — WH
Died: Newcastle-upon-Tyne, England, 1 December, 1977

League Club	Source	Date Signed	Seasons Played	Apps	Subs	Gls
Newcastle U	North Shields	01/48	48	1	-	0

CLARK Alexander (Sandy)
Born: Airdrie, Lanarkshire, Scotland, 28 October, 1956 — F

League Club	Source	Date Signed	Seasons Played	Apps	Subs	Gls
West Ham U	Airdrieonians	06/82	82	26	0	7

CLARK Anthony Carl
Born: Camden, N London, England, 5 October, 1984 — M

League Club	Source	Date Signed	Seasons Played	Apps	Subs	Gls
Southend U	YT	-	01	0	2	0

CLARK Anthony John (Tony)
Born: Lambeth, S London, England, 7 April, 1977 — F

League Club	Source	Date Signed	Seasons Played	Apps	Subs	Gls
Wycombe W	Jnr	07/95	94-95	2	2	0

CLARK Benjamin (Ben)
Born: Consett, County Durham, England, 24 January, 1983 — CD
England: Youth/Schools

League Club	Source	Date Signed	Seasons Played	Apps	Subs	Gls
Sunderland	YT	07/00	02-04	3	5	0
Hartlepool U	Tr	10/04	04-09	144	18	6

CLARK Benjamin (Ben)
Born: North Shields, Tyne and Wear, England, 14 April, 1933 — WH

League Club	Source	Date Signed	Seasons Played	Apps	Subs	Gls
Sunderland	North Shields	08/50				
Derby Co	Yeovil T	05/54	54-57	16	-	0
Barrow	Tr	02/59	58-63	202	-	7

CLARK Brian Donald
Born: Bristol, England, 13 January, 1943 — F
Died: Cardiff, Wales, 10 August, 2010

League Club	Source	Date Signed	Seasons Played	Apps	Subs	Gls
Bristol C	Jnr	03/60	60-66	195	0	83
Huddersfield T	Tr	10/66	66-67	28	4	11
Cardiff C	Tr	02/68	67-72	177	5	78
Bournemouth	Tr	10/72	72-73	28	2	12
Millwall	Tr	09/73	73-74	66	5	17
Cardiff C	Tr	05/75	75	19	2	1
Newport Co	Tr	08/76	76-78	72	8	18

CLARK Christopher (Chris)
Born: Aberdeen, Scotland, 15 September, 1980 — DM
Scotland: B-3

League Club	Source	Date Signed	Seasons Played	Apps	Subs	Gls
Plymouth Arg	Aberdeen	01/08	07-10	84	23	2

CLARK Christopher James (Chris)
Born: Shoreham-by-Sea, West Sussex, England, 9 June, 1984 — M

League Club	Source	Date Signed	Seasons Played	Apps	Subs	Gls
Portsmouth	Sch	03/03				
Stoke C	L	02/05	04	0	2	0

CLARK Ciaran
Born: Harrow, NW London, England, 26 September, 1989 — CD
England: Youth//Republic of Ireland: 11

League Club	Source	Date Signed	Seasons Played	Apps	Subs	Gls
Aston Villa	Sch	07/08	09-14	103	13	6

CLARK Clive
Born: Leeds, England, 19 December, 1940 — LW
Died: Scarborough, North Yorkshire, England, 1 May, 2014
England: U23-1

League Club	Source	Date Signed	Seasons Played	Apps	Subs	Gls
Leeds U	Ashley Road Meth's	01/58				
Queens Park Rgrs	Tr	08/58	58-60	58	-	7
West Bromwich A	Tr	01/61	60-68	300	1	80
Queens Park Rgrs	Tr	06/69	69	7	1	1
Preston NE	Tr	01/70	69-72	71	1	9
Southport	Tr	07/73	73	7	1	1

CLARK David George
Born: Ilford, E London, England, 19 January, 1938 — CH

League Club	Source	Date Signed	Seasons Played	Apps	Subs	Gls
Leyton Orient	Leyton	12/61	61-62	4	-	0

CLARK Dean Wayne
Born: Hillingdon, W London, England, 31 March, 1980 — M

League Club	Source	Date Signed	Seasons Played	Apps	Subs	Gls
Brentford	YT	10/97	97	0	4	0

CLARK Derek
Born: Newcastle-upon-Tyne, England, 10 August, 1931 — W
Died: Lincolnshire, England, 9 June, 2008

League Club	Source	Date Signed	Seasons Played	Apps	Subs	Gls
Lincoln C	Durham C	12/51	51	4	-	1

CLARK Derrick Bryan
Born: Leyburn, North Yorkshire, England, 27 December, 1935 — RW
Died: Middlesbrough, England, 13 March, 1985

League Club	Source	Date Signed	Seasons Played	Apps	Subs	Gls
Darlington		03/55	54-55	6	-	1

CLARK Frank Albert
Born: Rowlands Gill, Tyne and Wear, England, 9 September, 1943 — LB
England: FLge-1/Amateur-1/Youth

League Club	Source	Date Signed	Seasons Played	Apps	Subs	Gls
Newcastle U	Crook T	11/62	63-74	388	1	0
Nottingham F	Tr	07/75	75-78	116	1	1

CLARK Frederick Donald (Don)
Born: Bristol, England, 25 October, 1917 — CF
Died: Cardiff, Wales, 14 April, 2014

League Club	Source	Date Signed	Seasons Played	Apps	Subs	Gls
Bristol C	North Bristol OB	05/37	38-50	117	-	67

CLARK Graham John
Born: Aberdeen, Scotland, 20 January, 1961 — M
Scotland: Schools

League Club	Source	Date Signed	Seasons Played	Apps	Subs	Gls
Sheffield U	App	10/78				
Darlington	Tr	08/79	79	6	0	0

CLARK Harold (Harry)
Born: Tantobie, County Durham, England, 30 March, 1913 — W
Died: Sunderland, England, 4 January, 2014

League Club	Source	Date Signed	Seasons Played	Apps	Subs	Gls
Accrington Stan	Manchester C (Am)	12/44				
Gateshead	Tr	06/46	46	21	-	1

CLARK Harold Maurice (Harry)
Born: Newcastle-upon-Tyne, England, 29 December, 1932 — IF

League Club	Source	Date Signed	Seasons Played	Apps	Subs	Gls
Darlington	Eastbourne OB	12/50	50-56	141	-	27
Sheffield Wed	Tr	10/57	57	1	-	0
Hartlepool U	Tr	08/58	58-60	118	-	43

CLARK Henry (Harry)
Born: Sunderland, England, 11 September, 1934 — IF

League Club	Source	Date Signed	Seasons Played	Apps	Subs	Gls
Sunderland	Sunderland St Benet's	05/56	56	6	-	0

CLARK Howard William
Born: Coventry, England, 19 September, 1968 — RB/M

League Club	Source	Date Signed	Seasons Played	Apps	Subs	Gls
Coventry C	App	09/86	88-90	9	11	1
Darlington	L	09/91	91	5	0	0
Shrewsbury T	Tr	12/91	91-92	51	5	0
Hereford U	Tr	07/93	93-94	52	3	7

CLARK Ian David
Born: Stockton-on-Tees, Cleveland, England, 23 October, 1974 — LW

League Club	Source	Date Signed	Seasons Played	Apps	Subs	Gls
Doncaster Rov	Stockton	08/95	95-97	23	22	3
Hartlepool U	Tr	10/97	97-01	109	29	17
Darlington	Tr	11/01	01-04	84	35	26

CLARK James Donald (Jim)
Born: Dornoch, Highlands, Scotland, 1 May, 1923 — FB
Died: Forest of Dean, Gloucestershire, England, February, 1994

League Club	Source	Date Signed	Seasons Played	Apps	Subs	Gls
Exeter C	Aberdeen	08/48	48-52	95	-	5
Bradford C	L	09/52	52	6	-	0

CLARK John Brown
Born: Edinburgh, Scotland, 22 September, 1964 — CD
Scotland: Youth

League Club	Source	Date Signed	Seasons Played	Apps	Subs	Gls
Stoke C	Dundee U	02/94	93-94	17	0	0

CLARK Jonathan
Born: Swansea, Wales, 12 November, 1958 — M
Wales: U21-2/Schools

League Club	Source	Date Signed	Seasons Played	Apps	Subs	Gls
Manchester U	App	11/75	76	0	1	0
Derby Co	Tr	09/78	78-80	48	5	3
Preston NE	Tr	08/81	81-86	107	3	10
Bury	Tr	12/86	86	13	1	1
Carlisle U	Tr	08/87	87-88	48	1	2

CLARK Jordan Charles
Born: Barnsley, South Yorkshire, England, 22 September, 1993 — W

League Club	Source	Date Signed	Seasons Played	Apps	Subs	Gls
Barnsley	Sch	02/11	10-11	1	5	0
Chesterfield	L	02/13	12	1	1	0
Scunthorpe U	L	08/13	13	0	1	0
Shrewsbury T	Tr	07/14	14	18	9	3

CLARK Joseph Peter (Peter)
Born: Doncaster, South Yorkshire, England, 22 January, 1938 — WH
Died: Wolverhampton, England, 7 September, 2008

League Club	Source	Date Signed	Seasons Played	Apps	Subs	Gls
Wolverhampton W	Jnr	03/55				
Doncaster Rov	Tr	07/59	59	13	-	8
Mansfield T	Tr	06/60	60	2	-	0
Stockport Co	Hednesford T	08/65	65	21	0	2
Crewe Alex	Tr	07/66	66	2	0	0

CLARK Joseph Thomas Henry (Joe)
Born: Bermondsey, SE London, England, 2 March, 1920 — FB
Died: Ramsgate, Kent, England, 31 January, 2008

League Club	Source	Date Signed	Seasons Played	Apps	Subs	Gls
Leyton Orient	Gravesend U	02/46	46	18	-	0

CLARK Lee Robert
Born: Wallsend, Tyne and Wear, England, 27 October, 1972 — M
England: U21-11/Youth/Schools

League Club	Source	Date Signed	Seasons Played	Apps	Subs	Gls
Newcastle U	YT	12/89	90-96	153	42	23
Sunderland	Tr	06/97	97-98	72	1	16
Fulham	Tr	07/99	99-04	141	8	20
Newcastle U	Tr	08/05	05	8	14	1

CLARK Luke Stephen
Born: Preston, Lancashire, England, 24 May, 1994 — RB/M

League Club	Source	Date Signed	Seasons Played	Apps	Subs	Gls
Preston NE	Sch	-	11	2	0	0
Accrington Stan	Tr	07/12	12-13	2	5	0

CLARK Martin Alan
Born: Haslingden, Lancashire, England, 12 September, 1970 — RB

League Club	Source	Date Signed	Seasons Played	Apps	Subs	Gls
Rotherham U	Southport	06/97	97-98	29	0	0

CLARK Martin John
Born: Uddingston, Glasgow, Scotland, 13 October, 1968 — M

League Club	Source	Date Signed	Seasons Played	Apps	Subs	Gls
Nottingham F	Clyde	02/89				
Mansfield T	L	03/90	89	14	0	1
Mansfield T	Tr	08/90	90-91	31	2	0

CLARK Matthew Alec William (Matt)
Born: Swindon, England, 16 November, 1992 — M

League Club	Source	Date Signed	Seasons Played	Apps	Subs	Gls
Swindon T	Sch	07/11	10	0	1	0

CLARK Neville
Born: Gateshead, Tyne and Wear, England, 9 October, 1930 — RH

League Club	Source	Date Signed	Seasons Played	Apps	Subs	Gls
Grimsby T	Chilton Ath	12/48				
Sunderland		12/49				
Hartlepool U	Tr	08/53	53	2	-	0

CLARK Paul Peterson
Born: Benfleet, Essex, England, 14 September, 1958 — CD
England: Youth/Schools

League Club	Source	Date Signed	Seasons Played	Apps	Subs	Gls
Southend U	App	07/76	76-77	29	4	1
Brighton & HA	Tr	11/77	77-80	69	10	9
Reading	L	10/81	81	2	0	0
Southend U	Tr	08/82	82-90	271	7	3
Gillingham	Tr	07/91	91-93	87	3	1
Cambridge U	Chelmsford C	10/95	95	2	0	0

CLARK Peter James
Born: Romford, E London, England, 10 December, 1979 — LB

League Club	Source	Date Signed	Seasons Played	Apps	Subs	Gls
Carlisle U	Arsenal (YT)	08/98	98-99	77	2	1
Stockport Co	Tr	07/00	00-02	66	6	3
Mansfield T	L	09/02	02	2	1	0
Northampton T	Tr	07/03	03	6	0	0

CLARK Ronald (Ronnie)
Born: Clarkston, Renfrewshire, Scotland, 21 May, 1932 — LW
Died: Hollywood, Worcestershire, England, 13 September, 2013

League Club	Source	Date Signed	Seasons Played	Apps	Subs	Gls
Gillingham	Kilmarnock	07/56	56-57	33	-	6
Oldham Ath	Tr	06/58	58	4	-	0

CLARK Simon
Born: Boston, Lincolnshire, England, 12 March, 1967 CD

League Club	Source	Date Signed	Seasons Played	Apps	Subs	Gls
Peterborough U	Stevenage Bor	03/94	93-96	102	5	4
Leyton Orient	Tr	06/97	97-99	98	0	9
Colchester U	Tr	07/00	00-01	52	3	0

CLARK Steven (Steve)
Born: Baldock, Hertfordshire, England, 20 September, 1964 RB

League Club	Source	Date Signed	Seasons Played	Apps	Subs	Gls
Cambridge U	App	09/82	83-85	63	3	0

CLARK Steven Terence (Steve)
Born: Mile End, E London, England, 10 February, 1982 W

League Club	Source	Date Signed	Seasons Played	Apps	Subs	Gls
West Ham U	YT	07/01				
Southend U	Tr	11/01	01-03	31	20	1
Macclesfield T	L	09/03	03	1	3	0

CLARK Thomas Henry (Tom)
Born: Luton, England, 5 October, 1924 IF
Died: Luton, England, 14 June, 1981

League Club	Source	Date Signed	Seasons Played	Apps	Subs	Gls
Aston Villa	Vauxhall Motors	04/47				
Walsall	Tr	05/48	48	9	-	2

CLARK William (Willie)
Born: Larkhall, Lanarkshire, Scotland, 25 February, 1932 CF
Died: Aberdeen, Scotland, 27 July, 2006

League Club	Source	Date Signed	Seasons Played	Apps	Subs	Gls
Queens Park Rgrs	Petershill	02/54	53-55	95	-	32

CLARK William Charles (Billy)
Born: Ipswich, England, 20 October, 1991 F

League Club	Source	Date Signed	Seasons Played	Apps	Subs	Gls
Ipswich T	Sch	07/10	09	0	3	0

CLARK William Raymond (Billy)
Born: Christchurch, Dorset, England, 19 May, 1967 CD

League Club	Source	Date Signed	Seasons Played	Apps	Subs	Gls
Bournemouth	YT	09/84	84-87	4	0	0
Bristol Rov	Tr	10/87	87-96	235	13	14
Exeter C	Tr	10/97	97-98	39	2	3

CLARKE Adrian James
Born: Cambridge, England, 28 September, 1974 LM
England: Youth/Schools

League Club	Source	Date Signed	Seasons Played	Apps	Subs	Gls
Arsenal	YT	07/93	94-95	4	3	0
Rotherham U	L	12/96	96	1	1	0
Southend U	Tr	03/97	96-99	63	16	8
Carlisle U	L	09/99	99	7	0	0

CLARKE Alan
Born: Houghton Regis, Bedfordshire, England, 10 April, 1942 W

League Club	Source	Date Signed	Seasons Played	Apps	Subs	Gls
Luton T	Jnr	10/61	61-62	9	-	0

CLARKE Alfred (Alf)
Born: Hollinwood, Greater Manchester, England, 23 August, 1926 IF
Died: Eccles, Greater Manchester, England, 17 July, 1971

League Club	Source	Date Signed	Seasons Played	Apps	Subs	Gls
Crewe Alex	Stalybridge Celtic	02/48	47-48	22	-	12
Burnley	Tr	12/48	48-51	24	-	6
Oldham Ath	Tr	08/52	52-53	43	-	12
Halifax T	Tr	03/54	53-55	71	-	22

CLARKE Allan John
Born: Willenhall, West Midlands, England, 31 July, 1946 F
England: 19/FLge-2/U23-6

League Club	Source	Date Signed	Seasons Played	Apps	Subs	Gls
Walsall	App	08/63	63-65	72	0	41
Fulham	Tr	03/66	65-67	85	1	45
Leicester C	Tr	06/68	68	36	0	12
Leeds U	Tr	07/69	69-77	270	3	110
Barnsley	Tr	06/78	78-79	47	0	15

CLARKE Allan Robert (Bobby)
Born: Liverpool, England, 13 October, 1941 IF
Died: Liverpool, England, August, 2008

League Club	Source	Date Signed	Seasons Played	Apps	Subs	Gls
Chester C	Liverpool (Jnr)	10/61	61-62	30	-	5

CLARKE Allen Frederick
Born: Crayford, SE London, England, 2 December, 1952 G

League Club	Source	Date Signed	Seasons Played	Apps	Subs	Gls
Charlton Ath	App	07/71	71	2	0	0
Bristol Rov	L	09/71	71	1	0	0
Exeter C	Tr	02/73	72-73	16	0	0

CLARKE Ambrose
Born: Bootle, Merseyside, England, 10 September, 1945 D

League Club	Source	Date Signed	Seasons Played	Apps	Subs	Gls
Everton	Everton Red Triangle	06/64				
Southport	Tr	01/66	65-70	193	4	4
Barrow	Tr	07/71	71	45	1	0

CLARKE Andre Nathan Jermaine Everton (Jamie)
Born: Hammersmith, W London, England, 11 September, 1988 F

League Club	Source	Date Signed	Seasons Played	Apps	Subs	Gls
Blackburn Rov	Sch	07/07				
Accrington Stan	L	07/08	08	12	3	5
Rotherham U	Tr	02/09	08	7	4	2
Lincoln C	Tr	06/09	09	14	6	1

CLARKE Andrew Weston (Andy)
Born: Islington, N London, England, 22 July, 1967 F
England: Semi Pro-2

League Club	Source	Date Signed	Seasons Played	Apps	Subs	Gls
Wimbledon	Barnet	02/91	90-97	74	96	17
Port Vale	L	08/98	98	2	4	0
Northampton T	L	01/99	98	2	2	0
Peterborough U	Tr	05/99	99-04	170	60	57

CLARKE Bradie Jason
Born: Cambridge, England, 26 May, 1986 G

League Club	Source	Date Signed	Seasons Played	Apps	Subs	Gls
Oxford U	Sch	07/05	04	3	1	0

CLARKE Brian Roy
Born: Eastbourne, East Sussex, England, 10 October, 1968 CD

League Club	Source	Date Signed	Seasons Played	Apps	Subs	Gls
Gillingham	App	06/87	88-91	42	2	0

CLARKE Christopher Edward (Chris)
Born: Leeds, England, 18 December, 1980 LW

League Club	Source	Date Signed	Seasons Played	Apps	Subs	Gls
Halifax T	Wolverhampton W (YT)	07/99	99-01	50	1	1
Blackpool	Tr	02/02	01-03	33	13	2
Cambridge U	Tr	03/04	03	0	1	0

CLARKE Christopher Elliott (Chris)
Born: Battersea, SW London, England, 11 December, 1946 W

League Club	Source	Date Signed	Seasons Played	Apps	Subs	Gls
Millwall	Chelsea (App)	12/63	64-65	19	0	4
Watford	Tr	08/66	66	1	1	0

CLARKE Christopher John (Chris)
Born: Barnsley, South Yorkshire, England, 1 May, 1974 G

League Club	Source	Date Signed	Seasons Played	Apps	Subs	Gls
Bolton W	YT	07/92				
Rochdale	Tr	07/94	94-95	30	0	0

CLARKE Clive Richard Luke
Born: Dublin, Republic of Ireland, 14 January, 1980 LB
Republic of Ireland: 2/U21-11/Youth

League Club	Source	Date Signed	Seasons Played	Apps	Subs	Gls
Stoke C	YT	01/97	98-04	205	18	9
West Ham U	Tr	08/05	05	2	0	0
Sunderland	Tr	08/06	06	2	2	0
Coventry C	L	10/06	06	12	0	0
Leicester C	L	08/07	07	2	0	0

CLARKE Colin
Born: Hillington, Glasgow, Scotland, 4 April, 1946 CD

League Club	Source	Date Signed	Seasons Played	Apps	Subs	Gls
Arsenal	Arthurlie Jnrs	10/63				
Oxford U	Tr	07/65	65-77	443	1	23
Plymouth Arg	Los Angeles Azt (USA)	09/78	78	35	0	3

CLARKE Colin John
Born: Newry, Armagh, Northern Ireland, 30 October, 1962 F
Northern Ireland: 38

League Club	Source	Date Signed	Seasons Played	Apps	Subs	Gls
Ipswich T	App	10/80				
Peterborough U	Tr	07/81	81-83	76	6	18
Gillingham	L	03/84	83	8	0	1
Tranmere Rov	Tr	07/84	84	45	0	22
Bournemouth	Tr	06/85	85	46	0	26
Southampton	Tr	06/86	86-88	82	0	36
Bournemouth	L	12/88	88	3	1	2
Queens Park Rgrs	Tr	03/89	88-89	39	7	11
Portsmouth	Tr	06/90	90-92	68	17	18

CLARKE Darrell James
Born: Mansfield, Nottinghamshire, England, 16 December, 1977 M

League Club	Source	Date Signed	Seasons Played	Apps	Subs	Gls
Mansfield T	YT	07/96	95-00	137	24	24
Hartlepool U	Tr	07/01	01-05	98	25	19
Stockport Co	L	01/05	04	1	0	0
Port Vale	L	09/05	05	0	1	0
Rochdale	L	07/06	06	5	7	1

CLARKE David Alan
Born: Nottingham, England, 3 December, 1964 LB
England: Youth

League Club	Source	Date Signed	Seasons Played	Apps	Subs	Gls
Notts Co	App	12/82	82-86	113	10	7
Lincoln C	Tr	07/87	88-93	141	6	9
Doncaster Rov	Tr	01/94	93	15	1	0

CLARKE David Arthur
Born: Long Eaton, Derbyshire, England, 25 September, 1946 LW

League Club	Source	Date Signed	Seasons Played	Apps	Subs	Gls
Nottingham F	Derby Co (Am)	05/64				
Notts Co	Tr	07/66	66	23	1	0

CLARKE David Leslie
Born: Newcastle-upon-Tyne, England, 24 July, 1949 G
England: Semi Pro

League Club	Source	Date Signed	Seasons Played	Apps	Subs	Gls
Newcastle U	Felham BC	06/67				
Doncaster Rov	Tr	08/69	69	3	0	0
Darlington	L	03/70	69	12	0	0

CLARKE Dean Brian
Born: Hereford, England, 28 July, 1977 RB

League Club	Source	Date Signed	Seasons Played	Apps	Subs	Gls
Hereford U	YT	07/95	93-95	8	3	0

CLARKE Dennis
Born: Stockton-on-Tees, Cleveland, England, 18 January, 1948 RB

League Club	Source	Date Signed	Seasons Played	Apps	Subs	Gls
West Bromwich A	App	02/65	66-68	19	2	0
Huddersfield T	Tr	01/69	68-73	172	0	3
Birmingham C	Tr	09/73	73-74	14	0	0

CLARKE Derek
Born: Willenhall, West Midlands, England, 19 February, 1950 F

League Club	Source	Date Signed	Seasons Played	Apps	Subs	Gls
Walsall	App	12/67	67	6	0	2
Wolverhampton W	Tr	05/68	68-69	2	3	0
Oxford U	Tr	10/70	70-75	172	6	35
Leyton Orient	Tr	08/76	76-78	30	6	6
Carlisle U	L	10/78	78	0	1	0

CLARKE Donald Leslie (Don)
Born: Poole, Dorset, England, 29 June, 1931 IF
Died: Reading, England, October, 1993

League Club	Source	Date Signed	Seasons Played	Apps	Subs	Gls
Cardiff C		08/54				
Brighton & HA	Tr	06/55	55	2	-	0

CLARKE Douglas (Doug)
Born: Bolton, Greater Manchester, England, 19 January, 1934 RW

League Club	Source	Date Signed	Seasons Played	Apps	Subs	Gls
Bury	Darwen	02/52	53-55	37	-	15
Hull C	Tr	11/55	55-64	368	-	79
Torquay U	Tr	07/65	65-67	116	3	21

CLARKE Frank James
Born: Willenhall, West Midlands, England, 15 July, 1942 F

League Club	Source	Date Signed	Seasons Played	Apps	Subs	Gls
Shrewsbury T	Willenhall St Giles	11/61	61-67	188	0	77
Queens Park Rgrs	Tr	02/68	67-69	67	0	17
Ipswich T	Tr	03/70	69-72	62	4	15
Carlisle U	Tr	08/73	73-77	121	5	30

CLARKE Frederick Jeffrey (Jeff)
Born: Crewe, Cheshire, England, 3 January, 1931 CH
Died: Crewe, Cheshire, England, April, 2002

League Club	Source	Date Signed	Seasons Played	Apps	Subs	Gls
Crewe Alex	Royal Navy	11/51	53-54	2	-	0

CLARKE Frederick Robert George (Fred)
Born: Banbridge, Down, Northern Ireland, 4 November, 1941 LB
Northern Ireland: NILge-3/U23-4

League Club	Source	Date Signed	Seasons Played	Apps	Subs	Gls
Arsenal	Glenavon	11/60	61-64	26	-	0

CLARKE Gary
Born: Boston, Lincolnshire, England, 6 November, 1960 LW

League Club	Source	Date Signed	Seasons Played	Apps	Subs	Gls
Bristol Rov	App	11/78	78-79	6	5	0

CLARKE George Edmund
Born: Ipswich, England, 24 April, 1921 CH
Died: Ipswich, England, 17 February, 2011

League Club	Source	Date Signed	Seasons Played	Apps	Subs	Gls
Ipswich T	RAF	11/46	46-52	34	-	1

CLARKE Gerald (Gerry)
Born: Barrow Hill, Derbyshire, England, 4 January, 1936 RB

League Club	Source	Date Signed	Seasons Played	Apps	Subs	Gls
Chesterfield	Oaks Fold	03/55	54-67	382	0	21

CLARKE Graham Peter
Born: Nottingham, England, 11 August, 1935 FB
Died: Southampton, England, 27 April, 2010
England: Youth

League Club	Source	Date Signed	Seasons Played	Apps	Subs	Gls
Southampton		06/53	57-58	3	-	0

CLARKE Henry (Harry)
Born: Sunderland, England, 26 November, 1960 M

League Club	Source	Date Signed	Seasons Played	Apps	Subs	Gls
Hartlepool U	Middlesbrough (NC)	08/79	81	5	2	1

CLARKE Henry Alfred (Harry)
Born: Woodford, NE London, England, 23 February, 1923 CH
Died: Havering, E London, England, 16 April, 2000
England: 1/B-1

League Club	Source	Date Signed	Seasons Played	Apps	Subs	Gls
Tottenham H	Lovells Ath	03/49	48-56	295	-	4

CLARKE Isaac (Ike)
Born: Tipton, West Midlands, England, 9 January, 1915 CF
Died: Canterbury, England, 4 April, 2002

League Club	Source	Date Signed	Seasons Played	Apps	Subs	Gls
West Bromwich A	Toll End Wesley	01/37	37-47	108	-	39
Portsmouth	Tr	11/47	47-52	116	-	49

CLARKE James
Born: West Bromwich, West Midlands, England, 7 December, 1923 LB

League Club	Source	Date Signed	Seasons Played	Apps	Subs	Gls
Nottingham F	Darlaston	05/47	47-53	18	-	0

CLARKE James Henry (Harry)
Born: Darlington, County Durham, England, 27 March, 1921 CF

League Club	Source	Date Signed	Seasons Played	Apps	Subs	Gls
Darlington	Gateshead (Am)	02/45	46	19	-	17
Leeds U	Tr	02/47	46	14	-	1
Darlington	Tr	11/47	47-48	37	-	24
Hartlepool U	Tr	11/49	49	7	-	1
Darlington	Stockton	09/52	52	14	-	6

CLARKE James William (Jamie)
Born: Sunderland, England, 18 September, 1982 RB/M

League Club	Source	Date Signed	Seasons Played	Apps	Subs	Gls
Mansfield T	Sch	07/02	01-03	29	5	1
Rochdale	Tr	07/04	04-05	53	10	1
Boston U	Tr	01/06	05-06	42	10	3
Grimsby T	Tr	07/07	07-09	67	7	3

CLARKE Jeffrey Derek (Jeff)
Born: Hemsworth, West Yorkshire, England, 18 January, 1954 CD
England: Schools

League Club	Source	Date Signed	Seasons Played	Apps	Subs	Gls
Manchester C	Jnr	01/72	74	13	0	0
Sunderland	Tr	06/75	75-81	178	3	6
Newcastle U	Tr	08/82	82-86	124	0	4
Brighton & HA	L	08/84	84	4	0	0

CLARKE John Leslie
Born: Northampton, England, 23 October, 1946 CD
Died: Northampton, England, 1 January, 2011
England: Youth

League Club	Source	Date Signed	Seasons Played	Apps	Subs	Gls
Northampton T	Jnr	07/65	66-74	228	5	1

CLARKE Jordan Lee
Born: Coventry, England, 19 November, 1991 RB
England: Youth

League Club	Source	Date Signed	Seasons Played	Apps	Subs	Gls
Coventry C	Sch	08/09	09-14	99	24	4
Yeovil T	L	10/14	14	5	0	2
Scunthorpe U	Tr	01/15	14	24	0	0

CLARKE Joshua Joseph Jason Ishmel (Josh)
Born: Walthamstow, NE London, England, 5 July, 1994 RB

League Club	Source	Date Signed	Seasons Played	Apps	Subs	Gls
Brentford	Sch	07/13	13	0	1	0
Stevenage	L	10/14	14	0	1	0

CLARKE Kelvin Leslie
Born: Wolverhampton, England, 16 July, 1957 FB

League Club	Source	Date Signed	Seasons Played	Apps	Subs	Gls
Walsall	App	07/75	74-78	4	5	0

CLARKE Kevin Joseph
Born: Drogheda, Republic of Ireland, 29 April, 1921 CF
Died: Barrow, Cumbria, England, 16 March, 2004

League Club	Source	Date Signed	Seasons Played	Apps	Subs	Gls
Barrow	Drogheda (ROI)	12/45	46	12	-	1

CLARKE Lee Colin
Born: Peterborough, England, 28 July, 1983 F
Northern Ireland: U21-4

League Club	Source	Date Signed	Seasons Played	Apps	Subs	Gls
Peterborough U	Yaxley	10/01	01-02	0	2	0

CLARKE Leon Marvin
Born: Birmingham, England, 10 February, 1985 F

League Club	Source	Date Signed	Seasons Played	Apps	Subs	Gls
Wolverhampton W	Sch	03/04	04-06	32	43	13
Kidderminster Hrs	L	03/04	03	3	1	0
Queens Park Rgrs	L	01/06	05	1	0	0
Plymouth Arg	L	03/06	05	5	0	0
Sheffield Wed	Tr	01/07	06-09	43	40	18
Oldham Ath	L	03/07	06	5	0	3
Southend U	L	08/07	07	16	0	8
Queens Park Rgrs	Tr	05/10	10	2	11	0
Preston NE	L	01/11	10	5	1	1
Swindon T	Tr	08/11	11	2	0	0
Chesterfield	L	09/11	11	14	0	9
Charlton Ath	Tr	01/12	11	1	6	0
Crawley T	L	03/12	11	4	0	1
Scunthorpe U	L	09/12	12	14	1	11
Coventry C	Tr	01/13	12-13	33	2	23
Wolverhampton W	Tr	01/14	13-14	9	20	3
Wigan Ath	L	02/15	14	9	1	1

CLARKE Malcolm McQueen Gillespie
Born: Clydebank, Dunbartonshire, Scotland, 29 June, 1944 M
Died: Leicester, England, January, 2004

League Club	Source	Date Signed	Seasons Played	Apps	Subs	Gls
Leicester C	Johnstone Burgh	07/65	65	0	1	0
Cardiff C	Tr	08/67	67-68	44	2	3
Bristol C	Tr	07/69	69	2	1	0
Hartlepool U	Tr	07/70	70-71	29	4	0

CLARKE Matthew Edward
Born: Ipswich, England, 22 September, 1996 LB

League Club	Source	Date Signed	Seasons Played	Apps	Subs	Gls
Ipswich T	Sch	07/14	14	0	4	0

CLARKE Matthew John (Matt)
Born: Sheffield, England, 3 November, 1973 G

League Club	Source	Date Signed	Seasons Played	Apps	Subs	Gls
Rotherham U	YT	07/92	92-95	123	1	0
Sheffield Wed	Tr	07/96	96-97	2	2	0
Bradford C	Tr	07/99	99-00	38	0	0
Bolton W	L	03/01	00	8	0	0
Crystal Palace	Tr	09/01	01-03	38	0	0

CLARKE Matthew Paul
Born: Leeds, England, 18 December, 1980 CD

League Club	Source	Date Signed	Seasons Played	Apps	Subs	Gls
Halifax T	Wolverhampton W (YT)	07/99	99-01	42	27	2

League Club	Source	Date Signed	Seasons Played	Apps	Subs	Gls
Darlington	Tr	07/02	02-05	163	6	13
Bradford C	Tr	07/06	06-09	82	6	4
Darlington	L	10/06	06	2	0	0

CLARKE Michael (Mick)
Born: Sheffield, England, 28 November, 1944 LB

League Club	Source	Date Signed	Seasons Played	Apps	Subs	Gls
Sheffield U	App	01/62				
Aldershot	Tr	06/64	64	5	-	0
Halifax T	Tr	07/65	65-66	50	1	1

CLARKE Michael Darren (Micky)
Born: Marston Green, West Midlands, England, 22 December, 1967 LB/M

League Club	Source	Date Signed	Seasons Played	Apps	Subs	Gls
Barnsley	Birmingham C (App)	11/86	86-88	37	3	3
Scarborough	Tr	08/89	89-90	31	6	1

CLARKE Nathan
Born: Halifax, West Yorkshire, England, 30 November, 1983 CD

League Club	Source	Date Signed	Seasons Played	Apps	Subs	Gls
Huddersfield T	YT	09/01	01-10	260	4	8
Colchester U	L	01/11	10	18	0	0
Oldham Ath	L	08/11	11	16	0	1
Bury	L	03/12	11	11	0	0
Leyton Orient	Tr	07/12	12-14	109	4	2

CLARKE Nicholas John (Nicky)
Born: Walsall, West Midlands, England, 20 August, 1967 CD

League Club	Source	Date Signed	Seasons Played	Apps	Subs	Gls
Wolverhampton W	Jnr	02/85	85-91	73	8	1
Mansfield T	Tr	12/91	91-93	39	4	5
Chesterfield	L	02/93	92	7	0	0
Doncaster Rov	L	12/93	93	5	0	0

CLARKE Norman Frederick Michael (Nobby)
Born: Birmingham, England, 31 October, 1934 WH
Died: Bridgwater, Somerset, England, 11 November, 1997
England: Youth

League Club	Source	Date Signed	Seasons Played	Apps	Subs	Gls
Aston Villa	Jnr	07/53	54	1	-	0
Torquay U	Tr	07/56	56-58	54	-	0

CLARKE Norman Samson
Born: Ballymena, Antrim, Northern Ireland, 1 April, 1942 LW
Northern Ireland: NILge-2/U23-2

League Club	Source	Date Signed	Seasons Played	Apps	Subs	Gls
Sunderland	Ballymena U	02/62	62	4	-	0

CLARKE Oliver Anthony (Ollie)
Born: Bristol, England, 29 June, 1992 M

League Club	Source	Date Signed	Seasons Played	Apps	Subs	Gls
Bristol Rov	Jnr	07/09	10-13	31	7	2

CLARKE Patrick Kevin Noel (Kevin)
Born: Dublin, Republic of Ireland, 3 December, 1921 WH
Died: Gravesend, Kent, England, November, 1990
Republic of Ireland: 2/LoI-9

League Club	Source	Date Signed	Seasons Played	Apps	Subs	Gls
Swansea C	Drumcondra (ROI)	11/48	48-51	10	-	0

CLARKE Paul Stewart
Born: Chesterfield, Derbyshire, England, 25 September, 1950 CD
England: Schools

League Club	Source	Date Signed	Seasons Played	Apps	Subs	Gls
Liverpool	App	10/67				
Rochdale	Tr	08/69	69-71	11	1	0

CLARKE Peter Anthony
Born: Bolton, Greater Manchester, England, 6 July, 1949 G

League Club	Source	Date Signed	Seasons Played	Apps	Subs	Gls
Bolton W	Jnr	06/69	70	13	0	0
Stockport Co	Tr	07/71	71-74	49	0	0

CLARKE Peter Michael
Born: Southport, Merseyside, England, 3 January, 1982 CD
England: U21-8/Youth/Schools

League Club	Source	Date Signed	Seasons Played	Apps	Subs	Gls
Everton	Jnr	01/99	00-03	6	3	0
Blackpool	L	08/02	02	16	0	3
Port Vale	L	02/03	02	13	0	1
Coventry C	L	02/04	03	5	0	0
Blackpool	Tr	09/04	04-05	84	0	11
Southend U	Tr	08/06	06-08	122	4	10
Huddersfield T	Tr	07/09	09-13	189	3	9
Blackpool	Tr	07/14	14	37	2	2

CLARKE Raymond Charles (Ray)
Born: Hackney, E London, England, 25 September, 1952 F
England: Youth

League Club	Source	Date Signed	Seasons Played	Apps	Subs	Gls
Tottenham H	App	10/69	72	0	1	0
Swindon T	Tr	06/73	73	11	3	2
Mansfield T	Tr	08/74	74-75	91	0	52
Brighton & HA	Club Brugge (BEL)	10/79	79	30	0	8
Newcastle U	Tr	07/80	80	14	0	2

CLARKE Richard James
Born: Enfield, N London, England, 15 February, 1980 FB

League Club	Source	Date Signed	Seasons Played	Apps	Subs	Gls
Luton T	YT	11/98				
Scunthorpe U	Stanway Rov	03/00	99	1	0	0

CLARKE Royston James (Roy)
Born: Newport, Wales, 1 June, 1925 LW
Died: Trafford, Greater Manchester, England, 13 March, 2006
Wales: 22/War-1

League Club	Source	Date Signed	Seasons Played	Apps	Subs	Gls
Cardiff C	Albion Rov	12/42	46	39	-	10
Manchester C	Tr	04/47	46-57	349	-	73
Stockport Co	Tr	09/58	58	25	-	5

CLARKE Ryan Anthony
Born: Sutton Coldfield, West Midlands, England, 22 January, 1984 RB

League Club	Source	Date Signed	Seasons Played	Apps	Subs	Gls
Boston U	Notts Co (Sch)	07/03	03	1	3	0

CLARKE Ryan James
Born: Bristol, England, 30 April, 1982 G

League Club	Source	Date Signed	Seasons Played	Apps	Subs	Gls
Bristol Rov	YT	07/01	01-04	22	1	0
Southend U	L	10/04	04	1	0	0
Kidderminster Hrs	L	11/04	04	6	0	0
Oxford U	Northwich Victoria	05/09	10-14	188	1	0

CLARKE Shane Robin
Born: Lincoln, England, 7 November, 1987 M

League Club	Source	Date Signed	Seasons Played	Apps	Subs	Gls
Lincoln C	Sch	07/06	07-09	45	23	0

CLARKE Simon Nathan
Born: Chelmsford, England, 23 September, 1971 LM

League Club	Source	Date Signed	Seasons Played	Apps	Subs	Gls
West Ham U	YT	03/90	90-92	0	3	0

CLARKE Stephen (Steve)
Born: Saltcoats, Ayrshire, Scotland, 29 August, 1963 RB
Scotland: 6/B-2/U21-8/Youth

League Club	Source	Date Signed	Seasons Played	Apps	Subs	Gls
Chelsea	St Mirren	01/87	86-97	321	9	7

CLARKE Stuart Anthony
Born: Torquay, Devon, England, 25 January, 1961 F

League Club	Source	Date Signed	Seasons Played	Apps	Subs	Gls
Torquay U	Jnr	02/78	78	4	1	0

CLARKE Thomas (Tom)
Born: Halifax, West Yorkshire, England, 21 December, 1987 CD
England: Youth

League Club	Source	Date Signed	Seasons Played	Apps	Subs	Gls
Huddersfield T	Sch	01/05	04-11	72	24	3
Bradford C	L	10/08	08	4	2	0
Leyton Orient	L	09/11	11	10	0	0
Preston NE	Tr	07/13	13-14	84	1	5

CLARKE Thomas (Tom)
Born: Ardrossan, Ayrshire, Scotland, 12 April, 1946 G

League Club	Source	Date Signed	Seasons Played	Apps	Subs	Gls
Carlisle U	Airdrieonians	07/70	71-74	23	0	0
Preston NE	Tr	07/75	75	3	0	0

CLARKE Thomas Bridger (Tom)
Born: Worthing, West Sussex, England, 2 January, 1989 F

League Club	Source	Date Signed	Seasons Played	Apps	Subs	Gls
Yeovil T	Jnr	07/06	06	1	0	0

CLARKE Timothy Joseph (Tim)
Born: Stourbridge, West Midlands, England, 19 September, 1968 G

League Club	Source	Date Signed	Seasons Played	Apps	Subs	Gls
Coventry C	Halesowen T	10/90				
Huddersfield T	Tr	07/91	91-92	70	0	0
Rochdale	L	02/93	92	2	0	0
Shrewsbury T	Altrincham	10/93	94-95	30	1	0
York C	Witton A	06/96	96	17	0	0
Scunthorpe U	Tr	02/97	96-98	78	0	0
Kidderminster Hrs	Tr	10/99	00	25	0	0

CLARKE Wayne
Born: Wolverhampton, England, 28 February, 1961 F
England: Youth/Schools

League Club	Source	Date Signed	Seasons Played	Apps	Subs	Gls
Wolverhampton W	App	03/78	77-83	129	19	30
Birmingham C	Tr	08/84	84-86	92	0	38
Everton	Tr	03/87	86-88	46	11	18
Leicester C	Tr	07/89	89	10	1	1
Manchester C	Tr	01/90	89-91	7	14	2
Shrewsbury T	L	10/90	90	7	0	6
Stoke C	L	03/91	90	9	0	3
Wolverhampton W	L	09/91	91	1	0	0
Walsall	Tr	07/92	92	39	0	21
Shrewsbury T	Tr	08/93	93-94	53	6	22

CLARKE William Arthur (Willie)
Born: Newport, Wales, 17 April, 1923 W
Died: Great Yarmouth, Norfolk, England, 16 May, 1994
Wales: Amateur

League Club	Source	Date Signed	Seasons Played	Apps	Subs	Gls
Ipswich T (Am)	Albion Rov	02/47	46	3	-	0

CLARKE William Charles (Billy)
Born: Cork, Republic of Ireland, 13 December, 1987 F
Republic of Ireland: U21-7

League Club	Source	Date Signed	Seasons Played	Apps	Subs	Gls
Ipswich T	Sch	12/04	05-07	20	29	3
Colchester U	L	03/06	05	2	4	0
Darlington	L	08/08	08	18	2	8
Northampton T	L	01/09	08	5	0	3
Brentford	L	03/09	08	8	0	6
Blackpool	Tr	07/09	09-11	13	14	1

League Club	Source	Date Signed	Seasons Played	Apps	Subs	Gls
Sheffield U	L	10/11	11	5	0	1
Crawley T	Tr	01/12	11-13	72	10	20
Bradford C	Tr	06/14	14	32	4	13

CLARKE William John (John)
Born: Bargoed, Caerphilly, Wales, 26 December, 1940 G

League Club	Source	Date Signed	Seasons Played	Apps	Subs	Gls
Newport Co	Bargoed YMCA	05/59	59-61	12	-	0

CLARKE-HARRIS Jonson Scott
Born: Leicester, England, 21 July, 1994 F

League Club	Source	Date Signed	Seasons Played	Apps	Subs	Gls
Peterborough U	Coventry C (Sch)	07/12				
Southend U	L	10/12	12	0	3	0
Bury	L	02/13	12	4	8	4
Oldham Ath	Tr	05/13	13-14	28	17	7
Rotherham U	Tr	09/14	14	5	10	3
MK Dons	L	01/15	14	2	3	0
Doncaster Rov	L	03/15	14	3	6	1

CLARKSON David James
Born: Preston, Lancashire, England, 1 February, 1968 M

League Club	Source	Date Signed	Seasons Played	Apps	Subs	Gls
Brighton & HA	Sunshine GC (AUS)	09/91	91	4	9	0

CLARKSON David Thomas
Born: Airdrie, Lanarkshire, Scotland, 10 September, 1985 F
Scotland: 2/B-1/U21-13

League Club	Source	Date Signed	Seasons Played	Apps	Subs	Gls
Bristol C	Motherwell	07/09	09-11	27	37	11
Brentford	L	09/11	11	4	0	1
Bristol Rov	Tr	07/12	12-13	49	11	12

CLARKSON Ian Stewart
Born: Solihull, West Midlands, England, 4 December, 1970 RB

League Club	Source	Date Signed	Seasons Played	Apps	Subs	Gls
Birmingham C	YT	12/88	88-92	125	11	0
Stoke C	Tr	09/93	93-95	72	3	0
Northampton T	Tr	08/96	96-99	91	3	1
Kidderminster Hrs	Tr	11/99	00-01	73	4	0

CLARKSON Lewis Anthony
Born: Hull, England, 8 November, 1993 F

League Club	Source	Date Signed	Seasons Played	Apps	Subs	Gls
Hull C	Sch	07/12				
Bradford C	Scarborough Ath	11/13	13	0	1	0

CLARKSON Philip Ian (Phil)
Born: Hambleton, Lancashire, England, 13 November, 1968 M

League Club	Source	Date Signed	Seasons Played	Apps	Subs	Gls
Crewe Alex	Fleetwood T	10/91	91-95	76	22	27
Scunthorpe U	L	10/95	95	4	0	1
Scunthorpe U	Tr	02/96	95-96	45	3	18
Blackpool	Tr	02/97	96-01	154	17	35
Bury	Tr	03/02	01	4	0	0

CLAXTON Thomas (Tommy)
Born: Rochdale, Greater Manchester, England, 17 October, 1944 RW

League Club	Source	Date Signed	Seasons Played	Apps	Subs	Gls
Bury	Burnley (Am)	03/63	63-68	98	4	3

CLAY Craig William
Born: Nottingham, England, 5 May, 1992 M

League Club	Source	Date Signed	Seasons Played	Apps	Subs	Gls
Chesterfield	Sch	07/10	10-12	8	19	1
York C	Tr	07/13	13	6	2	0

CLAY John Harfield
Born: Stockport, Greater Manchester, England, 22 November, 1946 IF

League Club	Source	Date Signed	Seasons Played	Apps	Subs	Gls
Manchester C	App	05/64	67	1	1	0

CLAYPOLE Anthony William (Tony)
Born: Weldon, Northamptonshire, England, 13 February, 1937 FB

League Club	Source	Date Signed	Seasons Played	Apps	Subs	Gls
Northampton T	Jnr	03/54	56-61	116	-	1

CLAYTON Adam Stephen
Born: Manchester, England, 14 January, 1989 M
England: Youth

League Club	Source	Date Signed	Seasons Played	Apps	Subs	Gls
Manchester C	Sch	07/07				
Carlisle U	L	11/09	09	28	0	1
Leeds U	Tr	08/10	10-11	42	5	6
Peterborough U	L	11/10	10	6	1	0
MK Dons	L	03/11	10	1	5	1
Huddersfield T	Tr	07/12	12-13	84	1	11
Middlesbrough	Tr	08/14	14	37	4	0

CLAYTON Edward (Eddie)
Born: Bethnal Green, E London, England, 7 May, 1937 IF

League Club	Source	Date Signed	Seasons Played	Apps	Subs	Gls
Tottenham H	Eton Manor	12/57	57-67	88	4	20
Southend U	Tr	03/68	67-69	69	2	16

CLAYTON Gary
Born: Sheffield, England, 2 February, 1963 M/RB
England: Semi Pro-1

League Club	Source	Date Signed	Seasons Played	Apps	Subs	Gls
Doncaster Rov	Burton A	08/86	86	34	1	5
Cambridge U	Tr	07/87	87-93	166	13	14
Peterborough U	L	01/91	90	4	0	0
Huddersfield T	Tr	02/94	93-94	15	4	1
Plymouth Arg	Tr	08/95	95-97	32	6	2
Torquay U	Tr	08/97	97-98	56	0	2

CLAYTON Gordon
Born: Wednesbury, West Midlands, England, 3 November, 1936 G
Died: Stretford, Greater Manchester, England, 29 September, 1991
England: Youth/Schools

League Club	Source	Date Signed	Seasons Played	Apps	Subs	Gls
Manchester U	Jnr	11/53	56	2	-	0
Tranmere Rov	Tr	11/59	59-60	4	-	0

CLAYTON John
Born: Elgin, Moray, Scotland, 20 August, 1961 F

League Club	Source	Date Signed	Seasons Played	Apps	Subs	Gls
Derby Co	App	12/78	78-81	21	3	4
Chesterfield	Bulova (HKG)	06/83	83	25	8	5
Tranmere Rov	Tr	07/84	84-85	47	0	35
Plymouth Arg	Tr	08/85	85-87	68	9	22
Burnley	Volendam (NED)	08/92	92	3	0	1

CLAYTON John Michael (Johnny)
Born: St Asaph, Denbighshire, Wales, 28 March, 1937 CF/RH

League Club	Source	Date Signed	Seasons Played	Apps	Subs	Gls
Everton	Jnr	06/55				
Southport	Tr	07/59	59-60	32	-	3

CLAYTON Kenneth (Ken)
Born: Preston, Lancashire, England, 6 April, 1933 WH
Died: Lancashire, England, 26 November, 2014

League Club	Source	Date Signed	Seasons Played	Apps	Subs	Gls
Blackburn Rov	Jnr	05/50	52-58	72	-	0

CLAYTON Lewis (Lew)
Born: Royston, South Yorkshire, England, 7 June, 1924 RH
Died: Redcar, Cleveland, England, 19 January, 2010

League Club	Source	Date Signed	Seasons Played	Apps	Subs	Gls
Barnsley	Monckton Ath	03/42				
Carlisle U	Tr	09/46	46	24	-	0
Barnsley	Tr	06/47	48-49	15	-	0
Queens Park Rgrs	Tr	08/50	50-53	91	-	5
Bournemouth	Tr	05/55	55-56	40	-	1
Swindon T	Tr	06/57	57-58	35	-	2

CLAYTON Maximilian James (Max)
Born: Crewe, Cheshire, England, 9 August, 1994 F
England: Youth

League Club	Source	Date Signed	Seasons Played	Apps	Subs	Gls
Crewe Alex	Sch	08/11	10-13	32	42	9
Bolton W	Tr	09/14	14	5	4	1

CLAYTON Paul Spencer
Born: Dunstable, Bedfordshire, England, 4 January, 1965 F

League Club	Source	Date Signed	Seasons Played	Apps	Subs	Gls
Norwich C	App	01/83	83-85	8	5	0
Darlington	Tr	03/88	87-88	20	2	3
Crewe Alex	Tr	01/89	88-90	51	9	12

CLAYTON Ronald (Ronnie)
Born: Hull, England, 18 January, 1937 IF

League Club	Source	Date Signed	Seasons Played	Apps	Subs	Gls
Arsenal	Hereford U	01/58				
Brighton & HA	Tr	09/58	58-59	14	-	3

CLAYTON Ronald (Ronnie)
Born: Preston, Lancashire, England, 5 August, 1934 RH
Died: Blackburn, Greater Manchester, England, 29 October, 2010
England: 35/B-1/FLge-10/U23-6

League Club	Source	Date Signed	Seasons Played	Apps	Subs	Gls
Blackburn Rov	Jnr	08/51	50-68	579	2	15

CLAYTON Roy Charles
Born: Dudley, West Midlands, England, 18 February, 1950 F

League Club	Source	Date Signed	Seasons Played	Apps	Subs	Gls
Oxford U	Warley Bor	08/69	69-72	49	4	8

CLEARY George
Born: Bedford, England, 14 May, 1947 F

League Club	Source	Date Signed	Seasons Played	Apps	Subs	Gls
Cambridge U	Dunstable T	12/75	75	5	3	0

CLEARY William (Bill)
Born: Middlesbrough, England, 20 April, 1931 WH
Died: Kings Lynn, Norfolk, England, 12 March, 1991

League Club	Source	Date Signed	Seasons Played	Apps	Subs	Gls
Sunderland	South Bank EE Jnrs	05/49				
Norwich C	Tr	05/52	53-55	18	-	0
Port Vale	Wisbech T	11/57	57	8	-	0

CLEAVER Christopher William (Chris)
Born: Hitchin, Hertfordshire, England, 24 March, 1979 F

League Club	Source	Date Signed	Seasons Played	Apps	Subs	Gls
Peterborough U	YT	03/97	96-98	10	19	3

CLEEVELY Nigel Robert
Born: Cheltenham, Gloucestershire, England, 23 December, 1945 LW

League Club	Source	Date Signed	Seasons Played	Apps	Subs	Gls
Derby Co	Jnr	07/64	64-66	15	1	3

CLEGG David Lee
Born: Liverpool, England, 23 October, 1976 M

League Club	Source	Date Signed	Seasons Played	Apps	Subs	Gls
Liverpool	YT	05/95				
Hartlepool U	Tr	07/96	96	24	11	2

CLEGG Donald (Don)
Born: Huddersfield, West Yorkshire, England, 2 June, 1921 G

Died: Lancaster, England, February, 2005

League Club	Source	Date Signed	Seasons Played	Apps	Subs	Gls
Huddersfield T	Imperial Chemicals	05/40	46-47	3	-	0
Bury	Tr	07/48	48-49	15	-	0
Stoke C	Tr	06/50	50	2	-	0

CLEGG George Gerald
Born: Manchester, England, 16 November, 1980 — LW

League Club	Source	Date Signed	Seasons Played	Apps	Subs	Gls
Manchester U	YT	07/99				
Wycombe W	L	03/01	00	2	8	0
Bury	Tr	08/01	01-03	57	11	9

CLEGG Malcolm Brook
Born: Leeds, England, 9 April, 1936 — F
Died: Ripon, North Yorkshire, England, 5 June, 2004

League Club	Source	Date Signed	Seasons Played	Apps	Subs	Gls
Bradford Park Ave (Am)	Bradford Rov	01/58	57	6	-	0

CLEGG Michael Jaime
Born: Ashton-under-Lyne, Greater Manchester, England, 3 July, 1977 — RB
England: U21-2

League Club	Source	Date Signed	Seasons Played	Apps	Subs	Gls
Manchester U	YT	07/95	96-99	4	5	0
Ipswich T	L	02/00	99	3	0	0
Wigan Ath	L	03/00	99	6	0	0
Oldham Ath	Tr	02/02	01-03	40	6	0

CLEGG Tony
Born: Keighley, West Yorkshire, England, 8 November, 1965 — D

League Club	Source	Date Signed	Seasons Played	Apps	Subs	Gls
Bradford C	App	11/83	83-86	41	7	2
York C	Tr	08/87	87-88	38	3	3

CLELAND Alexander (Alex)
Born: Glasgow, Scotland, 10 December, 1970 — RB
Scotland: B-2/U21-11/Schools

League Club	Source	Date Signed	Seasons Played	Apps	Subs	Gls
Everton	Glasgow Rangers	07/98	98-01	21	14	0

CLELAND Peter Melville
Born: Eaglesham, Renfrewshire, Scotland, 8 May, 1932 — CF
Died: Bedford, England, 23 September, 1990

League Club	Source	Date Signed	Seasons Played	Apps	Subs	Gls
Norwich C	Cheltenham T	08/58	58	3	-	0

CLELLAND Crawford
Born: New Jersey, USA, 3 December, 1930 — IF

League Club	Source	Date Signed	Seasons Played	Apps	Subs	Gls
Plymouth Arg	Aberdeen	06/55	55	2	-	0

CLELLAND David (Dave)
Born: Netherburn, Lanarkshire, Scotland, 18 March, 1924 — CF
Died: Whitburn, Tyne and Wear, England, 8 June, 2004

League Club	Source	Date Signed	Seasons Played	Apps	Subs	Gls
Arsenal	Army	08/46				
Brighton & HA	Tr	01/48	47	8	-	1
Ipswich T	Tr	08/49				
Crystal Palace	Tr	09/49	49	2	-	0
Scunthorpe U	Weymouth	07/50	50	16	-	8

CLEMENCE Raymond Neal (Ray)
Born: Skegness, Lincolnshire, England, 5 August, 1948 — G
England: 61/FLge-2/U23-4

League Club	Source	Date Signed	Seasons Played	Apps	Subs	Gls
Scunthorpe U	Notts Co (Am)	08/65	65-66	48	0	0
Liverpool	Tr	06/67	69-80	470	0	0
Tottenham H	Tr	08/81	81-87	240	0	0

CLEMENCE Stephen Neal
Born: Liverpool, England, 31 March, 1978 — M
England: U21-1/Youth/Schools

League Club	Source	Date Signed	Seasons Played	Apps	Subs	Gls
Tottenham H	YT	04/95	97-01	68	22	2
Birmingham C	Tr	01/03	02-06	104	17	8
Leicester C	Tr	07/07	07	30	1	2

CLEMENT Andrew David (Andy)
Born: Cardiff, Wales, 12 November, 1967 — FB
Wales: Youth

League Club	Source	Date Signed	Seasons Played	Apps	Subs	Gls
Wimbledon	App	10/85	86-88	14	12	0
Bristol Rov	L	03/87	86	5	1	0
Newport Co	L	12/87	87	5	0	1
Plymouth Arg	Woking	12/90	90-91	28	14	0

CLEMENT David Thomas (Dave)
Born: Battersea, SW London, England, 2 February, 1948 — RB
Died: Wandsworth, SW London, England, 31 March, 1982
England: 5/Youth

League Club	Source	Date Signed	Seasons Played	Apps	Subs	Gls
Queens Park Rgrs	Jnr	07/65	66-78	403	4	21
Bolton W	Tr	06/79	79-80	33	0	0
Fulham	Tr	10/80	80	17	1	0
Wimbledon	Tr	10/81	81	9	0	2

CLEMENT Neil
Born: Reading, England, 3 October, 1978 — RB
England: Youth/Schools

League Club	Source	Date Signed	Seasons Played	Apps	Subs	Gls
Chelsea	YT	10/95	96	1	0	0
Reading	L	11/98	98	11	0	1
Preston NE	L	03/99	98	4	0	0
Brentford	L	11/99	99	7	1	0
West Bromwich A	Tr	03/00	99-07	242	22	21
Hull C	L	02/08	07	4	1	0

CLEMENT Philippe
Born: Antwerp, Belgium, 22 March, 1974 — DM
Belgium: 38

League Club	Source	Date Signed	Seasons Played	Apps	Subs	Gls
Coventry C	KRC Genk (BEL)	07/98	98	6	6	0

CLEMENTS Andrew Paul (Andy)
Born: Swinton, Greater Manchester, England, 11 October, 1955 — CD

League Club	Source	Date Signed	Seasons Played	Apps	Subs	Gls
Bolton W	App	10/73	77	1	0	0
Port Vale	L	02/77	76	2	1	0
York C	Tr	11/77	77-80	146	2	6

CLEMENTS Christopher Lee (Chris)
Born: Birmingham, England, 6 February, 1990 — M

League Club	Source	Date Signed	Seasons Played	Apps	Subs	Gls
Crewe Alex	Sch	05/08				
Mansfield T	Hednesford T	05/12	13-14	53	4	2

CLEMENTS David (Dave)
Born: Larne, Antrim, Northern Ireland, 15 September, 1945 — M/LB
Northern Ireland: 48/U23-3/Amateur

League Club	Source	Date Signed	Seasons Played	Apps	Subs	Gls
Wolverhampton W	Portadown	01/63				
Coventry C	Tr	07/64	64-71	228	2	26
Sheffield Wed	Tr	08/71	71-73	78	0	0
Everton	Tr	09/73	73-75	81	2	6

CLEMENTS Kenneth Henry (Kenny)
Born: Middleton, Greater Manchester, England, 9 April, 1955 — CD

League Club	Source	Date Signed	Seasons Played	Apps	Subs	Gls
Manchester C	Jnr	07/75	75-78	116	3	0
Oldham Ath	Tr	09/79	79-84	204	2	2
Manchester C	Tr	03/85	84-87	104	2	1
Bury	Tr	03/88	87-89	66	15	1
Shrewsbury T	Limerick (ROI)	10/90	90	19	1	0

CLEMENTS Matthew Carlton (Matt)
Born: Birmingham, England, 17 September, 1977 — M

League Club	Source	Date Signed	Seasons Played	Apps	Subs	Gls
Cambridge U	Mildenhall T	08/01	01	0	1	0

CLEMENTS Paul Robert
Born: Greenwich, SE London, England, 7 November, 1946 — M
Died: Lytham St Annes, Lancashire, England, 4 January, 2010
England: Amateur-8

League Club	Source	Date Signed	Seasons Played	Apps	Subs	Gls
Oldham Ath	Skelmersdale U	06/71	71-72	32	3	0

CLEMENTS Stanley (Stan)
Born: Portsmouth, England, 25 June, 1923 — CH

League Club	Source	Date Signed	Seasons Played	Apps	Subs	Gls
Southampton	Gosport Bor	07/44	46-54	116	-	1

CLEMENTS Steven (Steve)
Born: Slough, Berkshire, England, 26 September, 1972 — M
England: Schools

League Club	Source	Date Signed	Seasons Played	Apps	Subs	Gls
Arsenal	YT	11/90				
Hereford U	Tr	07/93	93	2	5	0

CLEMPSON Frank
Born: Salford, England, 27 May, 1930 — LH/IF
Died: Eccles, Greater Manchester, England, 24 December, 1970

League Club	Source	Date Signed	Seasons Played	Apps	Subs	Gls
Manchester U	Adelphi BC	09/48	49-52	15	-	2
Stockport Co	Tr	02/53	52-58	246	-	35
Chester C	Tr	07/59	59-60	67	-	8

CLEVERLEY Benjamin Raymond (Ben)
Born: Bristol, England, 12 September, 1981 — M

League Club	Source	Date Signed	Seasons Played	Apps	Subs	Gls
Bristol C	YT	07/01				
Cheltenham T	Tr	08/03	03	2	6	0

CLEVERLEY Thomas William (Tom)
Born: Basingstoke, Hampshire, England, 12 August, 1989 — M
England: 13/U21-16/Youth

League Club	Source	Date Signed	Seasons Played	Apps	Subs	Gls
Manchester U	Sch	07/07	11-14	42	13	3
Leicester C	L	01/09	08	10	5	2
Watford	L	08/09	09	33	0	11
Wigan Ath	L	08/10	10	19	6	3
Aston Villa	L	09/14	14	31	0	3

CLEWLOW Sidney John (Sid)
Born: Wallasey, Wirral, England, 8 November, 1919 — WH
Died: Birkenhead, Wirral, England, January, 1989

League Club	Source	Date Signed	Seasons Played	Apps	Subs	Gls
New Brighton	Poulton Victoria	02/39				
Wolverhampton W	Tr	05/39				
New Brighton	Tr	08/46	46	1	-	0

CLEWS Malcolm Derek (Maxie)
Born: Tipton, West Midlands, England, 12 March, 1931 — LW
Died: Walsall, West Midlands, England, 1 May, 2011

League Club	Source	Date Signed	Seasons Played	Apps	Subs	Gls
Wolverhampton W	Jnr	03/48	51	1	-	0
Lincoln C	Tr	02/54	53-54	7	-	0

CLICHY Gael
Born: Paris, France, 26 February, 1985 — LB
France: 20/U21-13

League Club	Source	Date Signed	Seasons Played	Apps	Subs	Gls
Arsenal	AS Cannes (FRA)	08/03	03-10	168	19	1
Manchester C	Tr	07/11	11-14	95	4	1

CLIFF Edward (Eddie)
Born: Liverpool, England, 30 September, 1951 — LB/M

League Club	Source	Date Signed	Seasons Played	Apps	Subs	Gls
Burnley	App	10/68	70-72	21	0	0
Notts Co	Tr	09/73	73	5	0	0
Lincoln C	L	10/74	74	3	0	0
Tranmere Rov	Chicago Sting (USA)	09/76	76-78	44	6	4
Rochdale	Tr	09/79	79-80	25	1	0

CLIFF John George
Born: Middlesbrough, England, 7 November, 1946 — W

League Club	Source	Date Signed	Seasons Played	Apps	Subs	Gls
Middlesbrough	App	11/63				
Halifax T	Tr	07/66	66	1	0	0

CLIFF Philip Robert (Phil)
Born: Rotherham, South Yorkshire, England, 20 November, 1947 — W
Died: Rotherham, South Yorkshire, England, September, 2012

League Club	Source	Date Signed	Seasons Played	Apps	Subs	Gls
Sheffield U	Jnr	11/65	66-69	16	6	5
Chesterfield	Tr	02/71	70-72	29	0	2

CLIFFORD Billy
Born: Slough, Berkshire, England, 18 October, 1992 — LW

League Club	Source	Date Signed	Seasons Played	Apps	Subs	Gls
Chelsea	Sch	07/10				
Colchester U	L	01/13	12	18	0	1
Walsall	Tr	08/14	14	7	6	0

CLIFFORD Conor Paul
Born: Dublin, Republic of Ireland, 1 October, 1991 — M
Republic of Ireland: U21-12/Youth

League Club	Source	Date Signed	Seasons Played	Apps	Subs	Gls
Chelsea	Sch	10/08				
Plymouth Arg	L	10/10	10	7	0	0
Notts Co	L	02/11	10	5	4	0
Yeovil T	L	11/11	11	6	1	0
Portsmouth	L	08/12	12	0	2	1
Crawley T	L	11/12	12	0	1	0
Leicester C	Tr	02/13				
Southend U	Tr	08/13	13-14	23	12	3

CLIFFORD Darren Robert
Born: Bristol, England, 2 November, 1966 — M

League Club	Source	Date Signed	Seasons Played	Apps	Subs	Gls
Exeter C	App	11/84	84	0	1	0

CLIFFORD Mark Robert
Born: Nottingham, England, 11 September, 1977 — RB

League Club	Source	Date Signed	Seasons Played	Apps	Subs	Gls
Mansfield T	YT	07/96	94-96	4	0	0
Boston U	Ilkeston T	02/01	02	5	2	0

CLIFTON Brian
Born: Whitchurch, Hampshire, England, 15 March, 1934 — WH/IF

League Club	Source	Date Signed	Seasons Played	Apps	Subs	Gls
Southampton	Whitchurch	02/53	57-62	111	-	35
Grimsby T	Tr	10/62	62-65	104	0	5

CLIFTON Bryan
Born: Bentley, South Yorkshire, England, 13 February, 1939 — IF

League Club	Source	Date Signed	Seasons Played	Apps	Subs	Gls
Doncaster Rov	Leeds U (Am)	10/58	58	3	-	0

CLIFTON Henry (Harry)
Born: Sunniside, Tyne and Wear, England, 28 May, 1914 — IF
Died: Newcastle-upon-Tyne, England, October, 1998
England: War-1

League Club	Source	Date Signed	Seasons Played	Apps	Subs	Gls
West Bromwich A	Lintz Colliery	09/32				
Chesterfield	Scotswood	08/33	33-37	121	-	67
Newcastle U	Tr	06/38	38	29	-	15
Grimsby T	Tr	02/46	46-48	69	-	23

CLINCH Peter John
Born: Coventry, England, 15 October, 1950 — CD

League Club	Source	Date Signed	Seasons Played	Apps	Subs	Gls
Oxford U	App	10/68	69	2	0	0

CLINGAN Samuel Gary (Sammy)
Born: Belfast, Northern Ireland, 13 January, 1984 — M
Northern Ireland: 39/U23-1/U21-11/Youth/Schools

League Club	Source	Date Signed	Seasons Played	Apps	Subs	Gls
Wolverhampton W	YT	07/01				
Chesterfield	L	10/04	04	15	0	2
Chesterfield	L	08/05	05	14	7	1
Nottingham F	Tr	01/06	05-07	79	6	1
Norwich C	Tr	07/08	08	40	0	6
Coventry C	Tr	07/09	09-11	92	6	7
Doncaster Rov		10/12	12	1	5	0

CLINTON Thomas Joseph (Tommy)
Born: Dublin, Republic of Ireland, 13 April, 1926 — LB
Died: Liverpool, England, 9 August, 2009
Republic of Ireland: 3

League Club	Source	Date Signed	Seasons Played	Apps	Subs	Gls
Everton	Dundalk (ROI)	03/48	48-53	73	-	4
Blackburn Rov	Tr	04/55	55	6	-	0
Tranmere Rov	Tr	06/56	56	9	-	0

CLISH Colin
Born: Hetton-le-Hole, Tyne and Wear, England, 14 January, 1944 — LB

League Club	Source	Date Signed	Seasons Played	Apps	Subs	Gls
Newcastle U	Jnr	01/61	61-63	20	-	0
Rotherham U	Tr	12/63	63-67	128	0	4
Doncaster Rov	Tr	02/68	67-71	99	1	4

CLISH Thomas Partridge (Tommy)
Born: Wheatley Hill, County Durham, England, 19 October, 1932 — G

League Club	Source	Date Signed	Seasons Played	Apps	Subs	Gls
West Ham U	Wheatley Hill	09/53				
Darlington	Tr	07/55	55-57	52	-	0

CLISS David Laurence
Born: Enfield, N London, England, 15 November, 1939 — IF
England: Youth/Schools

League Club	Source	Date Signed	Seasons Played	Apps	Subs	Gls
Chelsea	Jnr	11/56	57-61	24	-	1

CLISS Tony
Born: March, Cambridgeshire, England, 22 September, 1959 — W

League Club	Source	Date Signed	Seasons Played	Apps	Subs	Gls
Peterborough U	Jnr	08/77	77-82	65	20	11
Crewe Alex	Tr	12/82	82-86	109	4	11

CLIST Simon James
Born: Shaftesbury, Dorset, England, 13 June, 1981 — M

League Club	Source	Date Signed	Seasons Played	Apps	Subs	Gls
Bristol C	Tottenham H (YT)	07/99	99-03	54	17	6
Torquay U	L	02/03	02	11	0	2
Barnet	Tr	01/04	05	12	2	0
Oxford U	Forest Green Rov	02/09	10	16	7	1
Hereford U	Tr	08/11	11	27	1	0

CLITHEROE Lee John
Born: Chorley, Lancashire, England, 18 November, 1978 — RW

League Club	Source	Date Signed	Seasons Played	Apps	Subs	Gls
Oldham Ath	YT	07/97	97-98	2	3	0

CLODE Mark James
Born: Plymouth, England, 24 February, 1973 — FB

League Club	Source	Date Signed	Seasons Played	Apps	Subs	Gls
Plymouth Arg	YT	03/91				
Swansea C	Tr	07/93	93-98	109	10	3

CLOHESSY Sean David
Born: Croydon, S London, England, 12 December, 1986 — RB

League Club	Source	Date Signed	Seasons Played	Apps	Subs	Gls
Gillingham	Arsenal (Sch)	07/06	05-07	37	6	1
Southend U	Salisbury C	08/10	10-12	137	0	4
Colchester U	Kilmarnock	07/14	14	31	1	0

CLOSE Ben Easton
Born: Portsmouth, England, 8 August, 1996 — M

League Club	Source	Date Signed	Seasons Played	Apps	Subs	Gls
Portsmouth	Sch	07/14	14	3	3	0

CLOSE Brian Aidan
Born: Belfast, Northern Ireland, 27 January, 1982 — RB/M
Northern Ireland: U23-1/U21-10/Youth

League Club	Source	Date Signed	Seasons Played	Apps	Subs	Gls
Middlesbrough	St Oliver Plunkett BC	10/99				
Chesterfield	L	03/03	02	8	0	1
Darlington	Tr	03/04	03-06	75	8	0

CLOSE Dennis Brian (Brian)
Born: Rawdon, West Yorkshire, England, 24 January, 1931 — CF
Died: Baildon, West Yorkshire, England, 13 September, 2015
England: Youth

League Club	Source	Date Signed	Seasons Played	Apps	Subs	Gls
Leeds U	Jnr	02/49				
Arsenal	Tr	08/50				
Bradford C	Tr	10/52	52	6	-	2

CLOSE Shaun Charles
Born: Islington, N London, England, 8 September, 1966 — F

League Club	Source	Date Signed	Seasons Played	Apps	Subs	Gls
Tottenham H	App	08/84	86-87	3	6	0
Bournemouth	Tr	01/88	87-88	28	11	8
Swindon T	Tr	09/89	89-92	13	31	1
Barnet	Tr	08/93	93	21	6	2

CLOUGH Brian Howard
Born: Middlesbrough, England, 21 March, 1935 — CF
Died: Derby, England, 20 September, 2004
England: 2/B-1/FLge-2/U23-3

League Club	Source	Date Signed	Seasons Played	Apps	Subs	Gls
Middlesbrough	Great Broughton Jnrs	05/53	55-60	213	-	197
Sunderland	Tr	07/61	61-64	61	-	54

CLOUGH Charles David (Charlie)
Born: Taunton, Somerset, England, 4 September, 1990 — CD
Wales: Youth

League Club	Source	Date Signed	Seasons Played	Apps	Subs	Gls
Bristol Rov	Jnr	08/07	07-10	1	2	0

CLOUGH James (Jimmy)
Born: Hazlerigg, Tyne and Wear, England, 30 August, 1918 — W
Died: Newcastle-upon-Tyne, England, 2 September, 1998

League Club	Source	Date Signed	Seasons Played	Apps	Subs	Gls
Southport	Seaton Burn	02/39	38-46	45	-	10
Crystal Palace	Tr	09/47	47-48	67	-	12

League Club	Source	Date Signed	Seasons Played	Apps	Subs	Gls
Southend U	Tr	05/49	49	34	-	7
Barrow	Tr	07/50	50	18	-	3

CLOUGH Nigel Howard
Born: Sunderland, England, 19 March, 1966 — F
England: 14/B-3/FLge/U21-15

League Club	Source	Date Signed	Seasons Played	Apps	Subs	Gls
Nottingham F	Heanor T	09/84	84-92	307	4	101
Liverpool	Tr	06/93	93-95	29	10	7
Manchester C	Tr	01/96	95-96	33	5	4
Nottingham F	L	12/96	96	10	3	1
Sheffield Wed	L	09/97	97	1	0	0

CLOUGH Zach Paul John
Born: Denton, Greater Manchester, England, 8 March, 1995 — F

League Club	Source	Date Signed	Seasons Played	Apps	Subs	Gls
Bolton W	Sch	07/13	14	6	2	5

CLOVER William Arthur (Bill)
Born: Bracknell, Berkshire, England, 19 February, 1920 — RB
Died: Reading, England, 30 October, 1971

League Club	Source	Date Signed	Seasons Played	Apps	Subs	Gls
Reading	Woodley OB	02/46	46-49	44	-	4

CLOWES John Alan
Born: Alton, Staffordshire, England, 5 November, 1929 — CF

League Club	Source	Date Signed	Seasons Played	Apps	Subs	Gls
Stoke C	Crewe Alex (Am)	06/50	50	2	-	2
Shrewsbury T	Tr	06/52	52-53	11	-	2
Stoke C	Wellington T	08/55	55	2	-	0

CLUCAS Martin Seanan (Seanan)
Born: Dungannon, Tyrone, Northern Ireland, 8 November, 1992 — M
Northern Ireland: U21-11/Youth

League Club	Source	Date Signed	Seasons Played	Apps	Subs	Gls
Preston NE	Sch	07/11	11	0	1	0
Burton A	L	03/12	11	1	1	0
Bristol Rov	Tr	07/12	12-13	25	11	0

CLUCAS Samuel Raymond (Sam)
Born: Lincoln, England, 25 September, 1990 — M

League Club	Source	Date Signed	Seasons Played	Apps	Subs	Gls
Lincoln C	Nettleham	08/09				
Hereford U	Glenn Hoddle Academy	11/11	11	3	14	0
Mansfield T	Tr	06/13	13-14	31	12	8
Chesterfield	Tr	09/14	14	40	1	9

CLUGSTON James Edward (Jimmy)
Born: Belfast, Northern Ireland, 30 October, 1934 — IF
Died: Staines, Surrey, England, August, 2002
Northern Ireland: Schools

League Club	Source	Date Signed	Seasons Played	Apps	Subs	Gls
Liverpool	Distillery	01/52				
Portsmouth	Glentoran	01/57	56	1	-	0

CLUNIE James Robertson (Jim)
Born: Kirkcaldy, Fife, Scotland, 4 September, 1933 — CD
Died: Kilmarnock, Ayrshire, Scotland, 12 May, 2003
Scotland: SLge-1

League Club	Source	Date Signed	Seasons Played	Apps	Subs	Gls
Bury	St Mirren	07/65	65	10	0	0

CLUROE Malcolm
Born: Nottingham, England, 6 February, 1935 — IF
Died: Exeter, England, 26 September, 2006

League Club	Source	Date Signed	Seasons Played	Apps	Subs	Gls
Nottingham F	Chelsea (Jnr)	11/54	54	1	-	0

CLUTTON Nigel
Born: Chester, England, 12 February, 1954 — F

League Club	Source	Date Signed	Seasons Played	Apps	Subs	Gls
Chester C	Blacon	12/77	77	1	0	0

CLYDE Mark Graham
Born: Limavady, Derry, Northern Ireland, 27 December, 1982 — CD
Northern Ireland: 3/U21-5

League Club	Source	Date Signed	Seasons Played	Apps	Subs	Gls
Wolverhampton W	YT	08/01	02-06	41	6	0
Kidderminster Hrs	L	09/02	02	4	0	0

CLYDESDALE William McLay (Bill)
Born: Fallin, Stirlingshire, Scotland, 14 September, 1935 — LB

League Club	Source	Date Signed	Seasons Played	Apps	Subs	Gls
Hartlepool U	Aberdeen	08/60	60	14	-	0

CLYNE Nathaniel Edwin
Born: Stockwell, S London, England, 5 April, 1991 — RB
England: 5/U21-8/Youth

League Club	Source	Date Signed	Seasons Played	Apps	Subs	Gls
Crystal Palace	Sch	10/08	08-11	118	4	1
Southampton	Tr	07/12	12-14	89	5	3

COAD Matthew Paul
Born: Darlington, County Durham, England, 25 September, 1984 — M

League Club	Source	Date Signed	Seasons Played	Apps	Subs	Gls
York C	Sch	07/04	03	0	3	0

COADY Conor David
Born: Liverpool, England, 25 February, 1993 — DM
England: Youth

League Club	Source	Date Signed	Seasons Played	Apps	Subs	Gls
Liverpool	Sch	07/10	12	0	1	0
Sheffield U	L	07/13	13	32	7	5
Huddersfield T	Tr	08/14	14	42	3	3

COADY John
Born: Dublin, Republic of Ireland, 25 August, 1960 — M/LB
Republic of Ireland: LoI-4

League Club	Source	Date Signed	Seasons Played	Apps	Subs	Gls
Chelsea	Shamrock Rov (ROI)	12/86	86-87	9	7	2

COADY Lewis
Born: Liverpool, England, 20 September, 1976 — M

League Club	Source	Date Signed	Seasons Played	Apps	Subs	Gls
Wrexham	YT	07/95	94	2	0	0
Doncaster Rov	Tr	03/97	96	1	0	0

COADY Michael Liam (Mike)
Born: Dipton, County Durham, England, 1 October, 1958 — D

League Club	Source	Date Signed	Seasons Played	Apps	Subs	Gls
Sunderland	App	07/76	76-79	5	2	0
Carlisle U	Tr	07/80	80-81	48	3	1
Wolverhampton W	Sydney Olympic (AUS)	01/85	84-85	14	1	1

COAK Timothy David (Tim)
Born: Southampton, England, 16 January, 1958 — LB

League Club	Source	Date Signed	Seasons Played	Apps	Subs	Gls
Southampton	App	01/76	76-77	4	0	0

COAKLEY Thomas (Tommy)
Born: Bellshill, Lanarkshire, Scotland, 21 May, 1947 — RW

League Club	Source	Date Signed	Seasons Played	Apps	Subs	Gls
Arsenal	Motherwell	05/66	66	9	0	1

COATES David Plews
Born: Newcastle-upon-Tyne, England, 11 April, 1935 — IF/WH

League Club	Source	Date Signed	Seasons Played	Apps	Subs	Gls
Hull C	Shiney Row	10/52	56-59	62	-	13
Mansfield T	Tr	03/60	59-63	159	-	17
Notts Co	Tr	07/64	64-66	66	0	1

COATES Frank
Born: Farington, Lancashire, England, 16 April, 1922 — RW
Died: Huddersfield, West Yorkshire, England, May, 2012

League Club	Source	Date Signed	Seasons Played	Apps	Subs	Gls
Blackburn Rov	Leyland Motors	01/43				
Accrington Stan	Leyland Motors	01/48	47	4	-	0

COATES John Albert
Born: Southport, Merseyside, England, 3 June, 1944 — G

League Club	Source	Date Signed	Seasons Played	Apps	Subs	Gls
Southport	Burscough	02/65	64	5	-	0
Chester C	Tr	08/66	66	1	0	0
Southport	Burscough	07/76	76	16	0	0

COATES John Alfred
Born: Limehouse, E London, England, 13 May, 1920 — RW
Died: Bromley, SE London, England, 4 January, 2008

League Club	Source	Date Signed	Seasons Played	Apps	Subs	Gls
Crystal Palace (Am)		08/46	46	4	-	0

COATES Jonathan Simon
Born: Swansea, Wales, 27 June, 1975 — LW
Wales: B-1/U21-5/Youth

League Club	Source	Date Signed	Seasons Played	Apps	Subs	Gls
Swansea C	YT	07/93	93-01	218	32	23
Cheltenham T	Tr	10/02				
Swansea C	Woking	03/03	02-03	16	14	0

COATES Ralph
Born: Hetton-le-Hole, Tyne and Wear, England, 26 April, 1946 — LW/M
Died: Luton, England, 17 December, 2010
England: 4/FLge-4/U23-8

League Club	Source	Date Signed	Seasons Played	Apps	Subs	Gls
Burnley	App	06/63	64-70	214	2	26
Tottenham H	Tr	05/71	71-77	173	15	14
Leyton Orient	St Georges (AUS)	10/78	78-80	76	0	12

COATES Sebastian
Born: Montevideo, Uruguay, 7 October, 1990 — CD
Uruguay: 17/Youth

League Club	Source	Date Signed	Seasons Played	Apps	Subs	Gls
Liverpool	Nacional (UGY)	08/11	11-12	6	6	1
Sunderland	L	09/14	14	9	1	0

COATSWORTH Frederick William (Fred)
Born: Lincoln, England, 5 July, 1948 — LW

League Club	Source	Date Signed	Seasons Played	Apps	Subs	Gls
Scunthorpe U	Jnr	07/65	65-66	15	0	2

COATSWORTH Gary
Born: Sunderland, England, 7 October, 1968 — D

League Club	Source	Date Signed	Seasons Played	Apps	Subs	Gls
Barnsley		02/87	87	3	3	0
Darlington	Tr	08/89	90-91	15	7	2
Leicester C	Tr	10/91	91-93	27	5	4

COATSWORTH John Robert
Born: Newcastle-upon-Tyne, England, 21 May, 1933 — CF

League Club	Source	Date Signed	Seasons Played	Apps	Subs	Gls
Gateshead	Crook T	08/56	56	16	-	4

COBB Gary Edward
Born: Luton, England, 6 August, 1968 — M

League Club	Source	Date Signed	Seasons Played	Apps	Subs	Gls
Luton T	App	08/86	86-87	6	3	0
Northampton T	L	10/88	88	1	0	0
Swansea C	L	08/89	89	5	0	0
Fulham	Tr	08/90	90-91	8	14	0

COBB Paul Mark
Born: Aveley, Essex, England, 13 December, 1972 — F

League Club	Source	Date Signed	Seasons Played	Apps	Subs	Gls
Leyton Orient	Purfleet	11/90	90-91	3	2	0

COBB Walter William (Billy)
Born: Newark, Nottinghamshire, England, 29 September, 1940 IF/WH

League Club	Source	Date Signed	Seasons Played	Apps	Subs	Gls
Nottingham F	Ransome & Marles	05/59	60-62	30	-	5
Plymouth Arg	Tr	10/63	63-64	31	-	0
Brentford	Tr	10/64	64-66	69	2	23
Lincoln C	Tr	11/66	66-67	67	0	10

COBIAN Juan Manuel
Born: Buenos Aires, Argentina, 11 September, 1975 RB

League Club	Source	Date Signed	Seasons Played	Apps	Subs	Gls
Sheffield Wed	Boca Juniors (ARG)	08/98	98	7	2	0
Charlton Ath	Tr	08/99				
Swindon T	Aberdeen	07/00	00-01	3	1	0

COCHRAN Albert George
Born: Ebbw Vale, Blaenau Gwent, Wales, 26 November, 1939 G
Died: Folkestone, Kent, England, 24 January, 2015

League Club	Source	Date Signed	Seasons Played	Apps	Subs	Gls
Plymouth Arg	Ilford	09/59				
Leyton Orient	Tr	07/60	60	1	-	0

COCHRANE Alan
Born: Belfast, Northern Ireland, 16 March, 1956 W

League Club	Source	Date Signed	Seasons Played	Apps	Subs	Gls
Shrewsbury T	App	03/74	73-74	3	0	0

COCHRANE Colin
Born: Sutton-in-Ashfield, Nottinghamshire, England, 26 August, 1921 IF
Died: Sutton-in-Ashfield, Nottinghamshire, England, 9 February, 1985

League Club	Source	Date Signed	Seasons Played	Apps	Subs	Gls
Mansfield T		09/47	47	1	-	0

COCHRANE David Andrew (Davy)
Born: Portadown, Armagh, Northern Ireland, 14 August, 1920 RW
Died: Leeds, England, 4 June, 2000
Republic of Ireland: LoI-4//Northern Ireland: 12/NILge-8

League Club	Source	Date Signed	Seasons Played	Apps	Subs	Gls
Leeds U	Portadown	08/37	37-38	28	-	3
Leeds U	Shamrock Rov (ROI)	08/46	46-50	144	-	25

COCHRANE George Napier
Born: Glasgow, Scotland, 27 February, 1931 IF

League Club	Source	Date Signed	Seasons Played	Apps	Subs	Gls
New Brighton	Arthurlie	07/50	50	2	-	0

COCHRANE George Terence (Terry)
Born: Killyleagh, Down, Northern Ireland, 23 January, 1953 RW
Northern Ireland: 26

League Club	Source	Date Signed	Seasons Played	Apps	Subs	Gls
Burnley	Coleraine	10/76	76-78	62	5	13
Middlesbrough	Tr	10/78	78-82	96	15	7
Gillingham	Tr	10/83	83-85	105	2	17
Millwall	Dallas Sidekicks (USA)	11/86	86	1	0	0
Hartlepool U	Tr	01/87	86	2	0	0

COCHRANE Hugh
Born: Glasgow, Scotland, 9 February, 1943 IF

League Club	Source	Date Signed	Seasons Played	Apps	Subs	Gls
Barnsley	Dundee U	08/63	63	5	-	0

COCHRANE James
Born: Kingswinford, West Midlands, England, 26 October, 1935 IF

League Club	Source	Date Signed	Seasons Played	Apps	Subs	Gls
Birmingham C	Jnr	10/52	52-53	3	-	1
Walsall	Tr	06/58	58	6	-	1

COCHRANE James Kyle (Jimmy)
Born: Glasgow, Scotland, 14 January, 1954 LB

League Club	Source	Date Signed	Seasons Played	Apps	Subs	Gls
Middlesbrough	Drumchapel Amats	05/71	73	3	0	0
Darlington	Tr	02/75	74-79	222	1	5
Torquay U	Tr	08/80	80	16	0	0

COCHRANE John (Ian)
Born: Bellshill, Lanarkshire, Scotland, 27 April, 1959 W

League Club	Source	Date Signed	Seasons Played	Apps	Subs	Gls
Preston NE	App	02/77	76-78	3	2	2

COCHRANE John James (Johnny)
Born: Belfast, Northern Ireland, 11 May, 1944 IF

League Club	Source	Date Signed	Seasons Played	Apps	Subs	Gls
Brighton & HA	Jnr	10/61	61-62	14	-	3
Exeter C	Tr	08/63	63	2	-	0

COCHRANE Justin Vincent
Born: Hackney, E London, England, 26 January, 1982 M
Antigua & Barbuda: 14

League Club	Source	Date Signed	Seasons Played	Apps	Subs	Gls
Queens Park Rgrs	YT	07/99	00	0	1	0
Crewe Alex	Hayes	07/03	03-05	60	12	0
Gillingham	L	02/06	05	5	0	1
Rotherham U	Tr	07/06	06	29	2	1
Yeovil T	Tr	08/07	07	6	6	2
Millwall	Tr	03/08	07	0	1	0
Aldershot T	Rushden & D	12/08	08	9	1	0

COCKBURN Henry
Born: Ashton-under-Lyne, Greater Manchester, England, 14 September, 1921 LH
Died: Ashton-under-Lyne, Greater Manchester, England, 2 February, 2004
England: 13/B-1/FLge-1

League Club	Source	Date Signed	Seasons Played	Apps	Subs	Gls
Manchester U	Goslings	08/44	46-54	243	-	4
Bury	Tr	10/54	54-55	36	-	0

COCKBURN Keith
Born: Barnsley, South Yorkshire, England, 2 September, 1948 LW

League Club	Source	Date Signed	Seasons Played	Apps	Subs	Gls
Barnsley	Jnr	11/66	66	1	0	0
Bradford Park Ave	Tr	07/68	68	16	0	1
Grimsby T	Tr	01/69	68-69	15	4	2

COCKBURN William Robb (Bill)
Born: Shotton Colliery, County Durham, England, 3 May, 1937 D
Died: Hartlepool, Cleveland, England, August, 1995

League Club	Source	Date Signed	Seasons Played	Apps	Subs	Gls
Burnley	Murton Jnrs	08/55				
Gillingham	Tr	06/60	60-61	62	-	1

COCKCROFT Victor Herbert (Vic)
Born: Birmingham, England, 25 February, 1941 FB
England: Youth

League Club	Source	Date Signed	Seasons Played	Apps	Subs	Gls
Wolverhampton W	Jnr	12/59				
Northampton T	Tr	07/62	62-66	46	1	1
Rochdale	Tr	06/67	67	42	0	0

COCKELL David John (Dave)
Born: Ashford, Surrey, England, 1 February, 1939 RH

League Club	Source	Date Signed	Seasons Played	Apps	Subs	Gls
Queens Park Rgrs	Hounslow T	08/60	60-61	9	-	0

COCKER Leslie (Les)
Born: Stockport, Greater Manchester, England, 13 March, 1924 IF
Died: Doncaster, South Yorkshire, England, 4 October, 1979

League Club	Source	Date Signed	Seasons Played	Apps	Subs	Gls
Stockport Co	Army	08/47	46-52	173	-	43
Accrington Stan	Tr	08/53	53-57	122	-	48

COCKER Leslie James Robert (Les)
Born: Wolverhampton, England, 18 September, 1939 IF
England: Youth

League Club	Source	Date Signed	Seasons Played	Apps	Subs	Gls
Wolverhampton W	Jnr	06/58	60	1	-	0

COCKERILL Glenn
Born: Grimsby, North Lincolnshire, England, 25 August, 1959 M

League Club	Source	Date Signed	Seasons Played	Apps	Subs	Gls
Lincoln C	Louth U	11/76	76-79	65	6	10
Swindon T	Tr	12/79	79-80	23	3	1
Lincoln C	Tr	08/81	81-83	114	1	25
Sheffield U	Tr	03/84	83-85	62	0	10
Southampton	Tr	10/85	85-93	272	15	32
Leyton Orient	Tr	12/93	93-95	89	1	7
Fulham	Tr	06/96	96-97	32	8	1
Brentford	Tr	11/97	97	23	0	0

COCKERILL John
Born: Cleethorpes, North Lincolnshire, England, 12 July, 1961 M

League Club	Source	Date Signed	Seasons Played	Apps	Subs	Gls
Grimsby T	Stafford Rgrs	08/88	88-91	99	8	19

COCKERILL Ronald (Ron)
Born: Chapeltown, South Yorkshire, England, 28 February, 1935 WH
Died: Cleethorpes, North Lincolnshire, England, 4 November, 2010

League Club	Source	Date Signed	Seasons Played	Apps	Subs	Gls
Huddersfield T	High Green Villa	05/52	55-57	40	-	1
Grimsby T	Tr	08/58	58-67	293	1	28

COCKHILL Andrew James (Andy)
Born: Bowdon, Greater Manchester, England, 11 October, 1967 F

League Club	Source	Date Signed	Seasons Played	Apps	Subs	Gls
Stockport Co	Derby Co (App)	08/86	86	3	0	0

COCKRAM Allan Charles
Born: Kensington, Central London, England, 8 October, 1963 M

League Club	Source	Date Signed	Seasons Played	Apps	Subs	Gls
Tottenham H	App	01/81	83	2	0	0
Bristol Rov	Tr	08/85	85	1	0	0
Brentford	St Albans C	03/88	87-90	66	24	14
Reading	Woking	10/91	91	2	4	1

COCKROFT Hubert
Born: Barnsley, South Yorkshire, England, 21 November, 1918 LH
Died: Bradford, England, 2 January, 1979

League Club	Source	Date Signed	Seasons Played	Apps	Subs	Gls
Barnsley	Gainsborough Trinity	06/38				
Bradford C	Tr	08/45	46	27	-	0
Halifax T	Tr	07/47	47	10	-	1

COCKROFT Joseph (Joe)
Born: Barnsley, South Yorkshire, England, 20 June, 1911 LH
Died: Kings Lynn, Norfolk, England, February, 1994

League Club	Source	Date Signed	Seasons Played	Apps	Subs	Gls
Rotherham U	Wombwell	02/31	30-31	3	-	1
West Ham U	Gainsborough Trinity	03/33	32-38	251	-	3
Sheffield Wed	Tr	11/45	46-48	87	-	2
Sheffield U	Tr	11/48	48	12	-	0

COCKS Alan William
Born: Burscough, Lancashire, England, 7 May, 1951 F

League Club	Source	Date Signed	Seasons Played	Apps	Subs	Gls
Chelsea	App	04/69				
Brentford	L	01/70	69	11	0	1
Southport	Tr	07/70	70	24	1	7

CODD Ronald William (Ronnie)
Born: Sheffield, England, 3 December, 1928 RW

League Club	Source	Date Signed	Seasons Played	Apps	Subs	Gls
Bolton W	Meynell YC	03/50	50-53	31	-	5

League Club	Source	Date Signed	Seasons Played	Apps	Subs	Gls
Sheffield Wed	L	03/53	52	2	-	0
Barrow	Tr	10/54	54-55	45	-	11

CODDINGTON John William
Born: Worksop, Nottinghamshire, England, 16 December, 1937 CH

League Club	Source	Date Signed	Seasons Played	Apps	Subs	Gls
Huddersfield T	Worksop BC	01/55	55-66	332	0	17
Blackburn Rov	Tr	06/67	67-69	72	1	3
Stockport Co	Tr	01/70	69-70	52	0	0

CODNER Robert Andrew George
Born: Walthamstow, NE London, England, 23 January, 1965 M
England: SemiPro - 1

League Club	Source	Date Signed	Seasons Played	Apps	Subs	Gls
Leicester C	Tottenham H (Jnr)	09/83				
Brighton & HA	Barnet	09/88	88-94	257	9	39
Reading	Woking	09/95	95	3	1	0
Peterborough U	Tr	03/96	95	1	1	0
Barnet	Tr	03/96	95-96	28	4	1
Southend U	Tr	03/97	96	3	1	0

COE Norman Clive
Born: Swansea, Wales, 6 December, 1940 G
Died: Northampton, England, 24 October, 2001

League Club	Source	Date Signed	Seasons Played	Apps	Subs	Gls
Arsenal	Jnr	08/58				
Northampton T	Tr	07/60	60-65	58	0	0

COEN Lawrence (Laurie)
Born: Lowestoft, Suffolk, England, 4 December, 1914 LB
Died: Dudley, West Midlands, England, June, 1972
England: Schools

League Club	Source	Date Signed	Seasons Played	Apps	Subs	Gls
West Bromwich A	Milford Haven	10/32	36	7	-	4
Coventry C	Tr	06/38	38-47	20	-	3

COFFEY Michael James Joseph (Mike)
Born: Liverpool, England, 29 September, 1958 M

League Club	Source	Date Signed	Seasons Played	Apps	Subs	Gls
Everton	App	07/76				
Mansfield T	Tr	07/78	78	2	1	0

COFFILL Peter Terence
Born: Romford, E London, England, 14 February, 1957 M/W

League Club	Source	Date Signed	Seasons Played	Apps	Subs	Gls
Watford	App	02/75	75-77	56	7	6
Torquay U	Tr	11/77	77-80	101	21	11
Northampton T	Tr	07/81	81-82	64	5	3

COFFIN Geoffrey William (Geoff)
Born: Chester, England, 17 August, 1924 CF/CH
Died: Chester, England, 12 March, 2015

League Club	Source	Date Signed	Seasons Played	Apps	Subs	Gls
Chester C	Heath Rgrs	05/47	47-54	151	-	35

COFIE John Erzuah
Born: Aboso, Ghana, 21 January, 1993 F
England: Youth

League Club	Source	Date Signed	Seasons Played	Apps	Subs	Gls
Manchester U	Sch	07/10				
Sheffield U	L	07/12	12	8	8	2
Notts Co	L	02/13	12	6	1	1
Barnsley	Tr	07/13				
Crawley T	Molde FK (NOR)	03/15	14	0	1	0

COGAN Barry Christopher
Born: Sligo, Republic of Ireland, 4 November, 1984 M
Republic of Ireland: U21-1

League Club	Source	Date Signed	Seasons Played	Apps	Subs	Gls
Millwall	YT	11/01	03-05	8	16	0
Barnet	Tr	08/06	06	33	6	3
Gillingham	Tr	07/07	07	9	7	1

COGGINS Philip Reginald (Phil)
Born: Bristol, England, 10 July, 1940 RW

League Club	Source	Date Signed	Seasons Played	Apps	Subs	Gls
Bristol C	Dorset House BC	10/58	59	4	-	0
Bristol Rov	Tr	07/60	60	4	-	0

COGHLAN Michael James
Born: Sunderland, England, 15 January, 1985 CD

League Club	Source	Date Signed	Seasons Played	Apps	Subs	Gls
Darlington	Sch	08/04	03	0	3	0

COGLAN Alan
Born: Barrow, Cumbria, England, 14 December, 1936 G
Died: Barrow, Cumbria, England, 2 December, 1987

League Club	Source	Date Signed	Seasons Played	Apps	Subs	Gls
Barrow	Jnr	04/54	53-61	52	-	0

COHEN Abraham (Avi)
Born: Tel Aviv, Israel, 14 November, 1956 LB
Died: Tel Aviv, Israel, 28 December, 2010
Israel: 51

League Club	Source	Date Signed	Seasons Played	Apps	Subs	Gls
Liverpool	Maccabi Tel Aviv (ISR)	07/79	79-80	16	2	1

COHEN Christopher David (Chris)
Born: Norwich, England, 5 March, 1987 M
England: Youth

League Club	Source	Date Signed	Seasons Played	Apps	Subs	Gls
West Ham U	Sch	04/04	03-04	2	16	0
Yeovil T	Tr	11/05	05-06	73	1	7
Nottingham F	Tr	07/07	07-14	231	4	12

COHEN Gary Dane
Born: Leyton, NE London, England, 20 January, 1984 RW

League Club	Source	Date Signed	Seasons Played	Apps	Subs	Gls
Watford	Ford U	07/02				
Grimsby T	Workington	07/05	05	32	8	6

COHEN George Reginald
Born: Kensington, Central London, England, 22 October, 1939 RB
England: 37/FLge-4/U23-8

League Club	Source	Date Signed	Seasons Played	Apps	Subs	Gls
Fulham	Jnr	10/56	56-68	408	0	6

COHEN Jacob
Born: Tel Aviv, Israel, 25 September, 1956 LB
Israel: 19

League Club	Source	Date Signed	Seasons Played	Apps	Subs	Gls
Brighton & HA	Maccabi Tel Aviv (ISR)	10/80	80	3	3	0

COHEN Tamir
Born: Tel Aviv, Israel, 4 March, 1984 M
Israel: 21/U21-12

League Club	Source	Date Signed	Seasons Played	Apps	Subs	Gls
Bolton W	Maccabi Netanya (ISR)	01/08	07-10	35	14	6

COID Daniel John (Danny)
Born: Liverpool, England, 3 October, 1981 RB/M

League Club	Source	Date Signed	Seasons Played	Apps	Subs	Gls
Blackpool	YT	07/00	98-09	227	37	9
Rotherham U	L	11/10	10	9	0	0
Accrington Stan	Tr	07/11	11	16	5	1

COKE Giles Christopher
Born: Westminster, Central London, England, 3 June, 1986 M

League Club	Source	Date Signed	Seasons Played	Apps	Subs	Gls
Mansfield T	Kingstonian	03/05	04-06	55	15	5
Northampton T	Tr	07/07	07-08	36	16	7
Sheffield Wed	Motherwell	07/10	10-14	66	18	6
Bury	L	08/11	11	28	2	6
Swindon T	L	08/12	12	1	3	0
Bolton W	L	03/15	14	3	1	0

COKER Adewunmi Olarewaju (Ade)
Born: Lagos, Nigeria, 19 May, 1954 F
USA: 5

League Club	Source	Date Signed	Seasons Played	Apps	Subs	Gls
West Ham U	App	12/71	71-73	9	1	3
Lincoln C	L	12/74	74	6	0	1

COKER Benjamin Leslie (Ben)
Born: Hatfield, Hertfordshire, England, 17 June, 1989 LB

League Club	Source	Date Signed	Seasons Played	Apps	Subs	Gls
Colchester U	Bury T	07/10	10-12	36	5	0
Southend U	Histon	08/13	13-14	77	0	3

COLACE Hugo Roberto
Born: Buenos Aires, Argentina, 6 January, 1984 M
Argentina: Youth

League Club	Source	Date Signed	Seasons Played	Apps	Subs	Gls
Barnsley	Newells Old Boys (ARG)	09/08	08-10	95	6	8

COLBACK Jack Raymond
Born: Killingworth, Tyne and Wear, England, 24 October, 1989 LB/M

League Club	Source	Date Signed	Seasons Played	Apps	Subs	Gls
Sunderland	Sch	07/07	09-13	93	22	4
Ipswich T	L	08/09	09	29	8	4
Ipswich T	L	10/10	10	13	0	0
Newcastle U	Tr	06/14	14	35	0	4

COLBECK Philip Joseph (Joe)
Born: Bradford, England, 29 November, 1986 RW

League Club	Source	Date Signed	Seasons Played	Apps	Subs	Gls
Bradford C	Sch	06/06	05-09	68	41	8
Darlington	L	10/07	07	4	2	2
Oldham Ath	Tr	09/09	09	18	9	1
Hereford U	Tr	07/10	10-11	59	13	6

COLBOURNE Neil
Born: Swinton, Greater Manchester, England, 25 August, 1956 G

League Club	Source	Date Signed	Seasons Played	Apps	Subs	Gls
Rochdale	Hyde U	03/80	79	1	0	0

COLBRIDGE Clive
Born: Hull, England, 27 April, 1934 LW

League Club	Source	Date Signed	Seasons Played	Apps	Subs	Gls
Leeds U	Hull C (Am)	05/52				
York C	Tr	05/55	55-57	37	-	14
Workington	Tr	09/57	57-58	46	-	8
Crewe Alex	Tr	10/58	58	29	-	8
Manchester C	Tr	05/59	59-61	62	-	12
Wrexham	Tr	02/62	61-64	108	-	33

COLCLOUGH Ryan Paul
Born: Stoke-on-Trent, England, 27 December, 1994 W

League Club	Source	Date Signed	Seasons Played	Apps	Subs	Gls
Crewe Alex	Sch	10/12	12-14	13	20	5

COLCOMBE Scott
Born: West Bromwich, West Midlands, England, 15 December, 1971 LB/M

League Club	Source	Date Signed	Seasons Played	Apps	Subs	Gls
West Bromwich A	YT	07/90				
Torquay U	Tr	08/91	91-94	78	11	1
Doncaster Rov	Tr	07/95	95-96	30	12	4

COLDICOTT Stacy
Born: Redditch, Worcestershire, England, 29 April, 1974 M

League Club	Source	Date Signed	Seasons Played	Apps	Subs	Gls
West Bromwich A	YT	03/92	92-97	64	40	3

League Club	Source	Date Signed	Seasons Played	Apps	Subs	Gls
Cardiff C	L	08/96	96	6	0	0
Grimsby T	Tr	08/98	98-04	189	32	4

COLDRICK Graham George
Born: Newport, Wales, 6 November, 1945 — D
Wales: U23-2/Schools

League Club	Source	Date Signed	Seasons Played	Apps	Subs	Gls
Cardiff C	App	11/62	63-69	91	5	2
Newport Co	Tr	03/70	69-74	156	1	10

COLDWELL George Cecil (Cec)
Born: Dungworth, South Yorkshire, England, 12 January, 1929 — RB
Died: Poynton, Cheshire, England, 9 November, 2008

League Club	Source	Date Signed	Seasons Played	Apps	Subs	Gls
Sheffield U	Norton Woodseats	09/51	51-66	409	1	2

COLE Andrew Alexander (Andy)
Born: Nottingham, England, 15 October, 1971 — F
England: 15/B-1/U21-8/Youth/Schools

League Club	Source	Date Signed	Seasons Played	Apps	Subs	Gls
Arsenal	YT	10/89	90	0	1	0
Fulham	L	09/91	91	13	0	3
Bristol C	Tr	03/92	91-92	41	0	20
Newcastle U	Tr	03/93	92-94	69	1	55
Manchester U	Tr	01/95	94-01	161	34	94
Blackburn Rov	Tr	12/01	01-03	74	9	27
Fulham	Tr	07/04	04	29	2	12
Manchester C	Tr	07/05	05	20	2	9
Portsmouth	Tr	08/06	06	5	13	3
Birmingham C	L	03/07	06	5	0	1
Sunderland	Tr	08/07	07	3	4	0
Burnley	L	01/08	07	8	5	6
Nottingham F	Tr	07/08	08	5	5	0

COLE Ashley
Born: Stepney, E London, England, 20 December, 1980 — LB
England: 107/U21-4/Youth

League Club	Source	Date Signed	Seasons Played	Apps	Subs	Gls
Arsenal	YT	11/98	99-05	151	5	8
Crystal Palace	L	02/00	99	14	0	1
Chelsea	Tr	09/06	06-13	221	8	7

COLE Carlton Michael
Born: Croydon, S London, England, 12 November, 1983 — F
England: 7/U21-19/Youth

League Club	Source	Date Signed	Seasons Played	Apps	Subs	Gls
Chelsea	YT	10/00	01-05	4	21	4
Wolverhampton W	L	11/02	02	5	2	1
Charlton Ath	L	08/03	03	8	13	4
Aston Villa	L	07/04	04	18	9	3
West Ham U	Tr	07/06	06-14	158	98	55

COLE David Andrew
Born: Barnsley, South Yorkshire, England, 28 September, 1962 — CD

League Club	Source	Date Signed	Seasons Played	Apps	Subs	Gls
Sunderland	Laxey FC, Isle of Man	10/83				
Swansea C	Tr	09/84	84	7	1	0
Swindon T	Tr	02/85	84-86	69	0	3
Torquay U	Tr	11/86	86-88	107	3	6
Rochdale	Tr	07/89	89-90	73	11	7
Exeter C	Tr	08/91	91	0	2	0

COLE Devante Dewar
Born: Alderley Edge, Cheshire, England, 10 May, 1995 — F
England: Youth

League Club	Source	Date Signed	Seasons Played	Apps	Subs	Gls
Manchester C	Sch	07/13				
Barnsley	L	08/14	14	15	4	5
MK Dons	L	01/15	14	5	10	3

COLE George Douglas (Doug)
Born: Heswall, Wirral, England, 2 July, 1916 — FB
Died: Stannington, Northumberland, England, 30 January, 1959

League Club	Source	Date Signed	Seasons Played	Apps	Subs	Gls
Sheffield Wed	Hessle OB	10/35				
Sheffield U	Tr	05/37	37	1	-	0
Chester C	Tr	05/39	46-47	20	-	0

COLE Jake Stanley
Born: Hammersmith, W London, England, 11 September, 1985 — G

League Club	Source	Date Signed	Seasons Played	Apps	Subs	Gls
Queens Park Rgrs	Sch	07/05	05-06	4	2	0
Barnet	Tr	03/09	08-10	87	0	0
Plymouth Arg	Tr	07/11	11-13	89	2	0

COLE James Edward (Jim)
Born: Wrexham, Wales, 14 August, 1925 — RB
Died: Wrexham, Wales, May, 1997

League Club	Source	Date Signed	Seasons Played	Apps	Subs	Gls
Bolton W	Wrexham (Am)	05/47				
Chester C	Tr	08/49	49	1	-	0

COLE Joseph John (Joe)
Born: Paddington, Central London, England, 8 November, 1981 — M
England: 56/B-1/U21-8/Youth/Schools

League Club	Source	Date Signed	Seasons Played	Apps	Subs	Gls
West Ham U	YT	12/98	98-02	108	18	10
Chelsea	Tr	08/03	03-09	122	61	27
Liverpool	Tr	07/10	10-12	9	17	3
West Ham U	Tr	01/13	12-13	13	18	5
Aston Villa	Tr	06/14	14	3	9	1

COLE Larnell James
Born: Manchester, England, 9 March, 1993 — M
England: Youth

League Club	Source	Date Signed	Seasons Played	Apps	Subs	Gls
Manchester U	Sch	07/11				
Fulham	Tr	01/14	13	0	1	0
MK Dons	L	02/14	13	2	1	0

COLE Michael Edward (Mike)
Born: Ilford, E London, England, 9 June, 1937 — FB

League Club	Source	Date Signed	Seasons Played	Apps	Subs	Gls
Norwich C	Harwich & Parkeston	08/56	55-57	3	-	0

COLE Michael Washington (Mike)
Born: Stepney, E London, England, 3 September, 1966 — F

League Club	Source	Date Signed	Seasons Played	Apps	Subs	Gls
Ipswich T	App	11/83	84-87	24	14	3
Port Vale	L	01/88	87	4	0	1
Fulham	Tr	03/88	87-90	45	3	4

COLE Mitchell James
Born: Shoreditch, Central London, England, 6 October, 1985 — LW
Died: Tower Hamlets, E London, England, 1 December, 2012
England: Semi Pro-12/Youth

League Club	Source	Date Signed	Seasons Played	Apps	Subs	Gls
West Ham U	Sch	12/02				
Southend U	Grays Ath	07/05	05-06	20	13	1
Northampton T	L	09/06	06	6	2	1
Oxford U	Stevenage Bor	07/10	10	0	4	0

COLE Roy
Born: Barnsley, South Yorkshire, England, 8 December, 1953 — CD

League Club	Source	Date Signed	Seasons Played	Apps	Subs	Gls
Barnsley	App	12/71	71-73	6	0	0

COLEMAN Anthony George (Tony)
Born: Crosby, Merseyside, England, 2 May, 1945 — LW

League Club	Source	Date Signed	Seasons Played	Apps	Subs	Gls
Tranmere Rov	Ellesmere Port T	10/62	62-63	8	-	0
Preston NE	Tr	05/64	64	5	-	1
Doncaster Rov	Bangor C	11/65	65-66	58	0	11
Manchester C	Tr	03/67	66-69	82	1	12
Sheffield Wed	Tr	10/69	69	25	1	2
Blackpool	Tr	08/70	70	17	0	0
Southport	Durban C (RSA)	11/73	73	22	1	1
Stockport Co	Tr	06/74	74-75	28	2	3

COLEMAN Christopher (Chris)
Born: Swansea, Wales, 10 June, 1970 — D
Wales: 32/U21-3/Youth/Schools

League Club	Source	Date Signed	Seasons Played	Apps	Subs	Gls
Swansea C	Manchester C (Jnr)	09/87	87-90	159	1	2
Crystal Palace	Tr	07/91	91-95	143	11	13
Blackburn Rov	Tr	12/95	95-96	27	1	0
Fulham	Tr	12/97	97-00	136	0	8

COLEMAN David Houston
Born: Salisbury, Wiltshire, England, 8 April, 1967 — LB
Died: Salisbury, Wiltshire, England, May, 1997

League Club	Source	Date Signed	Seasons Played	Apps	Subs	Gls
Bournemouth	Jnr	09/84	85-90	40	10	2
Colchester U	L	02/88	87	6	0	1

COLEMAN David John
Born: Colchester, Essex, England, 27 March, 1942 — CF

League Club	Source	Date Signed	Seasons Played	Apps	Subs	Gls
Colchester U	Harwich & Parkeston	11/61	61-62	2	-	1

COLEMAN Dean Samuel
Born: Dudley, West Midlands, England, 18 September, 1985 — G

League Club	Source	Date Signed	Seasons Played	Apps	Subs	Gls
Walsall	Jnr	08/03	04	1	1	0

COLEMAN Edward (Ted)
Born: Middlesbrough, England, 23 September, 1957 — F

League Club	Source	Date Signed	Seasons Played	Apps	Subs	Gls
Middlesbrough	App	09/75	75	1	0	0
Workington	L	03/77	76	10	2	1

COLEMAN Geoffrey James (Geoff)
Born: Bedworth, Warwickshire, England, 13 May, 1936 — RB

League Club	Source	Date Signed	Seasons Played	Apps	Subs	Gls
Northampton T	Bedworth T	05/55	55-58	18	-	0

COLEMAN Gordon Michael
Born: Nottingham, England, 11 February, 1954 — M

League Club	Source	Date Signed	Seasons Played	Apps	Subs	Gls
Preston NE	Padstow YC, Nottingham	09/73	73-82	248	21	25
Bury	Tr	08/83	83	24	5	0

COLEMAN Joel
Born: Bolton, Greater Manchester, England, 26 September, 1995 — G

League Club	Source	Date Signed	Seasons Played	Apps	Subs	Gls
Oldham Ath	Sch	07/14	14	10	1	0

COLEMAN John Henry
Born: Hucknall, Nottinghamshire, England, 3 March, 1946 — RB/M

League Club	Source	Date Signed	Seasons Played	Apps	Subs	Gls
Nottingham F	Jnr	03/63				
Mansfield T	Tr	08/66	66-67	43	0	1
York C	Tr	07/68	68	8	3	3

COLEMAN Keith
Born: Washington, Tyne and Wear, England, 24 May, 1951 — RB

League Club	Source	Date Signed	Seasons Played	Apps	Subs	Gls
Sunderland	App	06/68	71-72	49	0	2

League Club	Source	Date Signed	Seasons Played	Apps	Subs	Gls
West Ham U	Tr	09/73	73-76	96	5	0
Darlington	KV Mechelen (BEL)	07/79	79	25	0	0

COLEMAN Kenneth James (Kenny)
Born: Cork, Republic of Ireland, 20 September, 1982 — D
Republic of Ireland: Youth

League Club	Source	Date Signed	Seasons Played	Apps	Subs	Gls
Wolverhampton W	YT	07/00				
Kidderminster Hrs	L	10/02	02	13	2	0
Kidderminster Hrs	Tr	08/03	03	10	0	0

COLEMAN Liam Philip
Born: Colchester, Essex, England, 11 January, 1986 — M

League Club	Source	Date Signed	Seasons Played	Apps	Subs	Gls
Torquay U	Wivenhoe T	07/05	05	7	7	0

COLEMAN Neville James (Tim)
Born: Baschurch, Shropshire, England, 29 January, 1930 — RW
Died: Australia, 1 January, 1981

League Club	Source	Date Signed	Seasons Played	Apps	Subs	Gls
Stoke C	Gorleston	01/55	53-58	114	-	46
Crewe Alex	Tr	02/59	58-60	73	-	17

COLEMAN Nicholas (Nicky)
Born: Crayford, SE London, England, 6 May, 1966 — LB

League Club	Source	Date Signed	Seasons Played	Apps	Subs	Gls
Millwall	App	08/84	84-89	87	1	0
Swindon T	L	09/85	85	13	0	4

COLEMAN Philip (Phil)
Born: Woolwich, SE London, England, 8 September, 1960 — D

League Club	Source	Date Signed	Seasons Played	Apps	Subs	Gls
Millwall	App	08/78	78-80	23	13	1
Colchester U	Tr	02/81	80-83	82	4	6
Wrexham	L	09/83	83	17	0	2
Exeter C	Chelmsford C	12/84	84	6	0	0
Aldershot	Tr	02/85	84-85	45	0	5
Millwall	Dulwich Hamlet	09/86	86	8	2	0
Colchester U	MyPa (FIN)	02/88	88	6	4	0

COLEMAN Seamus
Born: Killybegs, Donegal, Republic of Ireland, 11 October, 1988 — RB
Republic of Ireland: 28/U21-13

League Club	Source	Date Signed	Seasons Played	Apps	Subs	Gls
Everton	Sligo Rov (ROI)	02/09	09-14	133	19	13
Blackpool	L	03/10	09	9	0	1

COLEMAN Simon
Born: Worksop, Nottinghamshire, England, 13 March, 1968 — CD

League Club	Source	Date Signed	Seasons Played	Apps	Subs	Gls
Mansfield T	Jnr	07/85	86-89	96	0	7
Middlesbrough	Tr	09/89	89-90	51	4	2
Derby Co	Tr	08/91	91-93	62	8	2
Sheffield Wed	Tr	01/94	93-94	11	5	1
Bolton W	Tr	10/94	94-95	34	0	5
Wolverhampton W	L	09/97	97	3	1	0
Southend U	Tr	02/98	97-99	98	1	9
Rochdale	Tr	07/00	00-01	13	3	1

COLEMAN Theodore Aaron Anthony (Theo)
Born: Manchester, England, 5 May, 1989 — F

League Club	Source	Date Signed	Seasons Played	Apps	Subs	Gls
Rochdale	Sch	-	05	1	0	0

COLEMAN-CARR Luca Paolo
Born: Epsom, Surrey, England, 11 January, 1991 — LB

League Club	Source	Date Signed	Seasons Played	Apps	Subs	Gls
Lincoln C	Sch	-	08-09	0	2	0

COLES Arthur
Born: Crediton, Devon, England, 27 January, 1914 — D
Died: Weymouth, Dorset, England, 5 September, 1997

League Club	Source	Date Signed	Seasons Played	Apps	Subs	Gls
Exeter C	Copplestone	06/37	37	2	-	0
Exeter C	Coleraine	08/46	46-48	14	-	0

COLES Daniel Richard (Danny)
Born: Bristol, England, 31 October, 1981 — CD

League Club	Source	Date Signed	Seasons Played	Apps	Subs	Gls
Bristol C	YT	06/00	99-04	141	7	5
Hull C	Tr	07/05	05-07	26	5	0
Hartlepool U	L	10/07	07	3	0	0
Bristol Rov	Tr	11/07	07-10	102	0	3
Exeter C	Tr	07/11	11-13	111	3	8

COLES David Andrew (Dave)
Born: Wandsworth, SW London, England, 15 June, 1964 — G

League Club	Source	Date Signed	Seasons Played	Apps	Subs	Gls
Birmingham C	App	04/82				
Mansfield T	Tr	03/83	82	3	0	0
Aldershot	Tr	08/83	83-87	120	0	0
Newport Co	L	01/88	87	14	0	0
Brighton & HA	HJK Helsinki (FIN)	02/89	88	1	0	0
Aldershot	Tr	07/89	89-90	30	0	0

COLEY William Ernest (Bill)
Born: Wolverhampton, England, 17 September, 1916 — LH
Died: Torquay, Devon, England, 1 September, 1974

League Club	Source	Date Signed	Seasons Played	Apps	Subs	Gls
Wolverhampton W	Jnr	09/33	36	2	-	0
Bournemouth	Tr	09/37	37	13	-	0
Torquay U	Tr	07/38	38-46	61	-	1
Northampton T	Tr	08/47	47-50	104	-	7
Exeter C	Tr	07/51	51	8	-	0

COLFAR Raymond Joseph (Ray)
Born: Liverpool, England, 4 December, 1935 — W

League Club	Source	Date Signed	Seasons Played	Apps	Subs	Gls
Crystal Palace	Sutton U	11/58	58-60	41	-	6
Oxford U	Cambridge U	08/62	62-63	18	-	4

COLGAN Nicholas Vincent (Nicky)
Born: Drogheda, Republic of Ireland, 19 September, 1973 — G
Republic of Ireland: 9/B-1/U21-9/Youth/Schools

League Club	Source	Date Signed	Seasons Played	Apps	Subs	Gls
Chelsea	YT	10/92	96	1	0	0
Brentford	L	10/97	97	5	0	0
Reading	L	02/98	97	5	0	0
Bournemouth	Tr	07/98				
Stockport Co (L)	Hibernian	08/03	03	14	1	0
Barnsley	Hibernian	07/04	04-07	99	2	0
Ipswich T	Tr	01/08				
Sunderland	Tr	07/08				
Grimsby T	Tr	07/09	09	35	0	0
Huddersfield T	Tr	01/11				

COLGAN Walter (Wally)
Born: Castleford, West Yorkshire, England, 3 April, 1937 — FB

League Club	Source	Date Signed	Seasons Played	Apps	Subs	Gls
Queens Park Rgrs	Leeds Ashley Road	07/54	57-58	3	-	0

COLIN Jurgen Romano
Born: Utrecht, Netherlands, 20 January, 1981 — RB

League Club	Source	Date Signed	Seasons Played	Apps	Subs	Gls
Norwich C	PSV Eindhoven (NED)	07/05	05-06	54	4	0

COLKIN Lee
Born: Nuneaton, Warwickshire, England, 15 July, 1974 — LB/M

League Club	Source	Date Signed	Seasons Played	Apps	Subs	Gls
Northampton T	YT	08/92	91-96	74	25	3
Leyton Orient	L	08/97	97	5	6	0

COLL Owen Oliver
Born: Donegal, Republic of Ireland, 9 April, 1976 — CD
Republic of Ireland: U21-5

League Club	Source	Date Signed	Seasons Played	Apps	Subs	Gls
Tottenham H	Enfield Rgrs YC	07/94				
Bournemouth	Tr	03/96	95-96	24	0	0

COLL William Sean (Liam)
Born: Carrickmacross, Monaghan, Republic of Ireland, 16 December, 1929 — RW

League Club	Source	Date Signed	Seasons Played	Apps	Subs	Gls
Accrington Stan		08/49	49-50	13	-	0

COLLARD Ian
Born: Hetton-le-Hole, Tyne and Wear, England, 31 August, 1947 — M

League Club	Source	Date Signed	Seasons Played	Apps	Subs	Gls
West Bromwich A	App	11/64	64-68	63	6	7
Ipswich T	Tr	05/69	69-74	83	9	5
Portsmouth	L	09/75	75	1	0	0

COLLARD James Bruce (Bruce)
Born: Hetton-le-Hole, Tyne and Wear, England, 21 August, 1953 — M/D

League Club	Source	Date Signed	Seasons Played	Apps	Subs	Gls
West Bromwich A	App	05/71				
Scunthorpe U	Tr	07/73	73	21	1	0

COLLETER Patrick
Born: Brest, France, 6 November, 1965 — LB
France: B

League Club	Source	Date Signed	Seasons Played	Apps	Subs	Gls
Southampton	Olymp Marseille (FRA)	12/98	98-99	24	0	1

COLLETON Anthony (Tony)
Born: Manchester, England, 17 January, 1974 — F

League Club	Source	Date Signed	Seasons Played	Apps	Subs	Gls
Rochdale	YT	-	90	0	1	0

COLLETT Andrew Alfred (Andy)
Born: Stockton-on-Tees, Cleveland, England, 28 October, 1973 — G

League Club	Source	Date Signed	Seasons Played	Apps	Subs	Gls
Middlesbrough	YT	03/92	92	2	0	0
Bristol Rov	L	10/94	94	4	0	0
Bristol Rov	Tr	03/95	95-98	103	0	0
Darlington	Tr	08/99	99-03	125	0	0

COLLETT Ernest (Ernie)
Born: Sheffield, England, 17 November, 1914 — LH
Died: Islington, N London, England, 11 April, 1980

League Club	Source	Date Signed	Seasons Played	Apps	Subs	Gls
Arsenal	Oughtibridge WMC	04/33	37-46	20	-	0

COLLIER Alan Stanley
Born: Markyate, Hertfordshire, England, 24 March, 1938 — G
England: Youth/Schools

League Club	Source	Date Signed	Seasons Played	Apps	Subs	Gls
Luton T	Jnr	05/55	58-60	10	-	0

COLLIER Austin
Born: Dewsbury, West Yorkshire, England, 24 July, 1914 — LH
Died: Dewsbury, West Yorkshire, England, May, 1991

League Club	Source	Date Signed	Seasons Played	Apps	Subs	Gls
Mansfield T	Frickley Colliery	05/38	38	21	-	0
York C	Tr	05/39	46	10	-	0
Rochdale	Queen of the South	04/47	46-47	6	-	0
Halifax T	Tr	11/47	47	1	-	0

COLLIER Daniel Joseph (Danny)
Born: Eccles, Greater Manchester, England, 15 January, 1974 — CD

League Club	Source	Date Signed	Seasons Played	Apps	Subs	Gls
Wolverhampton W	YT	07/92				
Crewe Alex	Tr	06/94	94-95	5	6	0

COLLIER Darren James
Born: Stockton-on-Tees, Cleveland, England, 1 December, 1967 — G

League Club	Source	Date Signed	Seasons Played	Apps	Subs	Gls
Blackburn Rov	Middlesbrough (NC)	12/87	88-90	27	0	0
Darlington	Tr	09/93	93-94	44	0	0

COLLIER David
Born: Colwyn Bay, Conwy, Wales, 2 October, 1957 — RB

League Club	Source	Date Signed	Seasons Played	Apps	Subs	Gls
Shrewsbury T	App	10/75	74-76	20	0	4
Crewe Alex	Tr	08/77	77	24	2	1

COLLIER Gary Bernard
Born: Bristol, England, 4 February, 1955 — CD

League Club	Source	Date Signed	Seasons Played	Apps	Subs	Gls
Bristol C	App	11/72	72-78	193	0	3
Coventry C	Tr	07/79	79	2	0	0

COLLIER Geoffrey Heywood (Geoff)
Born: Blackpool, Lancashire, England, 25 July, 1950 — F

League Club	Source	Date Signed	Seasons Played	Apps	Subs	Gls
Notts Co	Macclesfield T	07/73	73	0	3	0

COLLIER Graham Ronald
Born: Nottingham, England, 12 September, 1951 — M

League Club	Source	Date Signed	Seasons Played	Apps	Subs	Gls
Nottingham F	App	03/69	69-70	13	2	2
Scunthorpe U	Tr	07/72	72-76	155	6	19
Barnsley	Tr	08/77	77	22	2	2
York C	Buxton	09/78	78	5	0	0

COLLIER James Robert (Jim)
Born: Stockport, Greater Manchester, England, 24 August, 1952 — M

League Club	Source	Date Signed	Seasons Played	Apps	Subs	Gls
Stockport Co	App	03/70	68-73	101	6	12

COLLIN Adam James
Born: Penrith, Cumbria, England, 9 December, 1984 — G

League Club	Source	Date Signed	Seasons Played	Apps	Subs	Gls
Newcastle U	Sch	08/03				
Carlisle U	Workington	07/09	09-12	132	1	0
Rotherham U	Tr	07/13	13-14	70	0	0

COLLIN Francis John Patrick (Frannie)
Born: Chatham, Kent, England, 20 April, 1987 — F

League Club	Source	Date Signed	Seasons Played	Apps	Subs	Gls
Gillingham	Chatham T	05/05	05-06	1	8	1

COLLINDRIDGE Colin
Born: Barnsley, South Yorkshire, England, 15 November, 1920 — LW

League Club	Source	Date Signed	Seasons Played	Apps	Subs	Gls
Sheffield U	Barugh Green	01/39	46-49	142	-	52
Nottingham F	Tr	08/50	50-53	151	-	45
Coventry C	Tr	06/54	54-55	34	-	6

COLLINGS Paul Wallace
Born: Liverpool, England, 30 September, 1968 — G

League Club	Source	Date Signed	Seasons Played	Apps	Subs	Gls
Tranmere Rov	Ellesmere Port T	08/88	88-90	4	0	0
Bury	Altrincham	08/93	93	1	0	0

COLLINGWOOD Graham
Born: South Kirkby, West Yorkshire, England, 8 December, 1954 — M

League Club	Source	Date Signed	Seasons Played	Apps	Subs	Gls
Barnsley	App	12/72	73-74	12	2	0

COLLINS Aaron Graham John
Born: Newport, Wales, 27 May, 1997 — F
Wales: Youth

League Club	Source	Date Signed	Seasons Played	Apps	Subs	Gls
Newport Co	Sch	05/15	14	0	2	0

COLLINS Aidan Arthur
Born: Harlow, Essex, England, 18 October, 1986 — CD

League Club	Source	Date Signed	Seasons Played	Apps	Subs	Gls
Ipswich T	Jnr	11/03	02-05	2	2	0
Wycombe W	L	01/06	05	3	2	1
Stockport Co	L	03/06	05	2	1	0

COLLINS Albert Desmond (Des)
Born: Chesterfield, Derbyshire, England, 15 April, 1923 — RW

League Club	Source	Date Signed	Seasons Played	Apps	Subs	Gls
Chesterfield	Jnr	01/41	46	8	-	0
Halifax T	Tr	11/46	46-47	44	-	10
Carlisle U	Tr	02/48	47-48	19	-	3
Barrow	Tr	12/48	48-49	55	-	7
Bournemouth	Tr	08/50	50	5	-	1
Shrewsbury T	Tr	08/51	51	9	-	2
Accrington Stan	Tr	07/52	52	17	-	2

COLLINS Andrew Balsillie (Andy)
Born: Carlisle, Cumbria, England, 20 October, 1958 — FB

League Club	Source	Date Signed	Seasons Played	Apps	Subs	Gls
Carlisle U	Carlisle Spartans	09/77	77-81	47	7	1

COLLINS Anthony Norman (Tony)
Born: Kensington, Central London, England, 19 March, 1926 — LW

League Club	Source	Date Signed	Seasons Played	Apps	Subs	Gls
Sheffield Wed	Acton U	11/47				
York C	Tr	07/49	49	10	-	1
Watford	Tr	08/50	50-52	90	-	8
Norwich C	Tr	07/53	53-54	29	-	2
Torquay U	Tr	07/55	55-56	85	-	16
Watford	Tr	07/57	57	17	-	1
Crystal Palace	Tr	11/57	57-58	55	-	14
Rochdale	Tr	06/59	59-60	47	-	5

COLLINS Benjamin Victor (Ben)
Born: Kislingbury, Northamptonshire, England, 9 March, 1928 — CH
Died: Northampton, England, 2 March, 2010

League Club	Source	Date Signed	Seasons Played	Apps	Subs	Gls
Northampton T	Jnr	04/48	48-58	213	-	0

COLLINS Charlie John
Born: Hammersmith, W London, England, 22 November, 1991 — F
Republic of Ireland: Youth

League Club	Source	Date Signed	Seasons Played	Apps	Subs	Gls
MK Dons	Sch	07/10	09-10	2	1	0
Aldershot T	L	01/12	11	0	1	0

COLLINS Daniel Lewis (Danny)
Born: Buckley, Flintshire, Wales, 6 August, 1980 — CD
England: Semi Pro-2//Wales: 12

League Club	Source	Date Signed	Seasons Played	Apps	Subs	Gls
Chester C	Buckley T	12/01	04	12	0	1
Sunderland	Tr	10/04	04-09	134	15	3
Stoke C	Tr	09/09	09-10	45	5	0
Ipswich T	L	09/11	11	16	0	3
West Ham U	L	03/12	11	4	7	1
Nottingham F	Tr	07/12	12-14	65	6	2

COLLINS Darren
Born: Winchester, Hampshire, England, 24 May, 1967 — F
England: Semi Pro-4

League Club	Source	Date Signed	Seasons Played	Apps	Subs	Gls
Northampton T	Petersfield U	08/89	88-90	40	11	9

COLLINS David Dennis
Born: Dublin, Republic of Ireland, 30 October, 1971 — D/M
Republic of Ireland: U21-6/Youth

League Club	Source	Date Signed	Seasons Played	Apps	Subs	Gls
Liverpool	YT	11/88				
Wigan Ath	L	01/92	91	9	0	0
Oxford U	Tr	07/92	92-94	33	9	0

COLLINS Eamonn Anthony Stephen
Born: Dublin, Republic of Ireland, 22 October, 1965 — M
Republic of Ireland: U21-5/Youth

League Club	Source	Date Signed	Seasons Played	Apps	Subs	Gls
Southampton	App	10/83	84	1	2	0
Portsmouth	Tr	05/86	86	4	1	0
Exeter C	L	11/87	87	8	1	0
Colchester U	Tr	05/89	89	39	0	2
Exeter C	Tr	07/92	92	8	3	0

COLLINS George Cornelius
Born: Hengoed, Caerphilly, Wales, 6 August, 1935 — CF
Died: Merthyr Tydfil, Wales, 1983

League Club	Source	Date Signed	Seasons Played	Apps	Subs	Gls
Bristol Rov	Ton Pentre	06/60	60	2	-	1

COLLINS Glyn
Born: Hereford, England, 18 January, 1946 — G

League Club	Source	Date Signed	Seasons Played	Apps	Subs	Gls
Brighton & HA (Am)	Cinderford T	03/66	65	2	0	0

COLLINS Graham Frank
Born: Bury, Greater Manchester, England, 5 February, 1947 — LH
Died: Bury, Greater Manchester, England, 11 January, 2004

League Club	Source	Date Signed	Seasons Played	Apps	Subs	Gls
Rochdale	Jnr	09/65	66	7	0	0

COLLINS James (Jimmy)
Born: Catrine, Ayrshire, Scotland, 21 December, 1937 — IF

League Club	Source	Date Signed	Seasons Played	Apps	Subs	Gls
Tottenham H	Lugar Boswell Thistle	06/56	61	2	-	0
Brighton & HA	Tr	10/62	62-66	199	2	44

COLLINS James Edward (Jamie)
Born: Barking, E London, England, 28 September, 1984 — M

League Club	Source	Date Signed	Seasons Played	Apps	Subs	Gls
Watford	Sch	06/04				
Aldershot T	Newport Co	07/11	11	21	4	0

COLLINS James Ian (Jamie)
Born: Liverpool, England, 28 May, 1978 — M

League Club	Source	Date Signed	Seasons Played	Apps	Subs	Gls
Crewe Alex	YT	07/96	97-00	15	9	1

COLLINS James Kenneth (Jim)
Born: Colne, Lancashire, England, 7 November, 1923 — IF
Died: Nottingham, England, 27 March, 1996

League Club	Source	Date Signed	Seasons Played	Apps	Subs	Gls
Barrow	Derby Co (Am)	09/47	47-54	295	-	53
Chester C	Tr	07/55	55-56	48	-	11

COLLINS James Michael
Born: Newport, Wales, 23 August, 1983 — CD
Wales: 45/U21-7/Youth

League Club	Source	Date Signed	Seasons Played	Apps	Subs	Gls
Cardiff C	YT	04/01	00-04	49	17	3
West Ham U	Tr	07/05	05-09	51	3	2
Aston Villa	Tr	09/09	09-11	88	3	5
West Ham U	Tr	08/12	12-14	72	8	1

COLLINS James Patrick (Jimmy)
Born: Urmston, Greater Manchester, England, 27 December, 1966 — RB

League Club	Source	Date Signed	Seasons Played	Apps	Subs	Gls
Oldham Ath	YT	08/84	83	0	1	0
Bury	Tr	10/86	86-87	10	1	0

League Club	Source	Date Signed	Seasons Played	Apps	Subs	Gls
COLLINS James Steven (Jim)						
Born: Coventry, England, 1 December, 1990						F
Republic of Ireland: U21-12/Youth						
Aston Villa	Sch	07/09				
Darlington	L	10/09	09	5	2	2
Burton A	L	10/10	10	9	1	4
Shrewsbury T	Tr	01/11	10-11	54	12	22
Swindon T	Tr	07/12	12	27	18	15
Shrewsbury T	Hibernian	06/14	14	42	3	15
COLLINS Jeremy David						
Born: Plymouth, England, 21 December, 1961						M
Plymouth Arg	App	01/80	80-81	4	0	0
Torquay U	Falmouth	08/83	83	6	1	0
COLLINS John Angus Paul						
Born: Galashiels, Borders, Scotland, 31 January, 1968						M
Scotland: 58/U21-8/Youth						
Everton	AS Monaco (FRA)	08/98	98-99	52	3	3
Fulham	Tr	07/00	00-02	54	12	3
COLLINS John Douglas (Doug)						
Born: Tibshelf, Derbyshire, England, 28 August, 1945						M
Grimsby T	Rotherham U (App)	06/63	63-68	96	7	9
Burnley	Tr	09/68	68-75	172	15	18
Plymouth Arg	Tr	05/76	76	22	1	2
Sunderland	Tr	03/77	76-77	3	2	0
Rochdale	Tulsa Roughnecks (USA)	01/79	78	6	2	0
COLLINS John Joseph						
Born: Manchester, England, 30 January, 1945						D
Blackburn Rov	Jnr	02/63				
Stockport Co	Tr	01/64	63-65	84	0	1
COLLINS John Lindsay						
Born: Rhymney, Caerphilly, Wales, 21 January, 1949						LB
Wales: U23-7/Schools						
Tottenham H	App	03/66	65	2	0	0
Portsmouth	Tr	05/71	71-73	71	3	0
Halifax T	Tr	08/74	74-75	82	0	1
Sheffield Wed	Tr	07/76	76	7	0	0
Barnsley	Tr	12/76	76-79	129	1	1
COLLINS John William						
Born: Chiswick, W London, England, 10 August, 1942						IF
Queens Park Rgrs	Jnr	08/59	59-66	172	0	46
Oldham Ath	Tr	10/66	66	20	1	8
Reading	Tr	08/67	67-68	82	3	27
Luton T	Tr	08/69	69-70	40	2	10
Cambridge U	Tr	02/71	70-72	93	4	16
COLLINS Kenneth John (Ken)						
Born: Pontypridd, Rhondda Cynon Taff, Wales, 11 October, 1933						RB
Died: 1 January, 2010						
Fulham	Ynysybwl	05/52	55-58	32	-	0
COLLINS Kevin						
Born: Birmingham, England, 21 July, 1964						FB
Shrewsbury T	Boldmere St Michael's	01/84	83	1	0	0
COLLINS Lee						
Born: Coatbridge, Lanarkshire, Scotland, 3 February, 1974						M
Swindon T	Albion Rov	11/95	95-99	52	11	2
Blackpool	Tr	07/00	00-02	48	18	2
COLLINS Lee David						
Born: Birmingham, England, 10 September, 1977						CD
Aston Villa	YT	07/96				
Stoke C	Tr	02/99	98	4	0	0
COLLINS Lee Harvey						
Born: Telford, England, 28 September, 1988						CD
Wolverhampton W	Sch	03/07				
Hereford U	L	11/07	07	14	2	0
Port Vale	Tr	08/08	08-11	140	2	4
Barnsley	Tr	03/12	11	4	3	0
Shrewsbury T	L	09/12	12	8	0	0
Northampton T	Tr	02/13	12-14	70	4	1
COLLINS Lyn						
Born: Neath, Wales, 30 April, 1948						FB
Newport Co	Jnr	06/66	66-67	17	0	0
COLLINS Matthew Jeffrey (Matty)						
Born: Merthyr Tydfil, Wales, 31 March, 1986						M
Wales: U21-2/Youth						
Fulham	Sch	04/03				
Swansea C	Tr	07/07	08-09	3	1	0
Wrexham	L	11/07	07	2	0	0
COLLINS Michael Anthony (Mike)						
Born: Johannesburg, South Africa, 27 July, 1953						F
Wolverhampton W	Jnr	08/71				
Swindon T	Chelmsford C	07/73	73	2	4	0
COLLINS Michael Anthony						
Born: Halifax, West Yorkshire, England, 30 April, 1986						M
Republic of Ireland: U21-6/Youth						
Huddersfield T	Sch	05/05	04-09	147	26	19
Scunthorpe U	Tr	01/10	10-13	54	25	2
AFC Wimbledon	L	02/14	13	9	0	0
Oxford U	Tr	07/14	14	38	1	2
COLLINS Michael Joseph Anthony (Mick)						
Born: Bermondsey, SE London, England, 1 February, 1938						CH
Luton T	Jnr	03/55	59-61	8	-	0
COLLINS Michael Thomas						
Born: Belfast, Northern Ireland, 6 September, 1977						M
Northern Ireland: Youth						
Darlington	Coleraine	08/96	96	0	1	0
COLLINS Neill William						
Born: Troon, Ayrshire, Scotland, 2 September, 1983						CD
Scotland: B-1/U21-7						
Sunderland	Dumbarton	08/04	04-06	14	4	1
Hartlepool U	L	08/05	05	22	0	0
Sheffield U	L	02/06	05	2	0	0
Wolverhampton W	Tr	11/06	06-08	74	10	9
Preston NE	Tr	09/09	09	19	2	1
Leeds U	Tr	03/10	09-10	29	1	0
Sheffield U	Tr	01/11	10-14	146	1	8
Port Vale	L	03/15	14	7	0	0
COLLINS Patrick Paul						
Born: Muscat, Oman, 4 February, 1985						CD
England: Youth						
Sunderland	Sch	03/02				
Sheffield Wed	Tr	07/04	04-05	28	3	1
Swindon T	L	08/05	05	13	0	0
Darlington	Tr	07/06	06	28	3	0
COLLINS Paul						
Born: West Ham, E London, England, 11 August, 1966						M
England: Youth						
Gillingham	App	08/84	84-86	30	7	3
COLLINS Peter John						
Born: Chelmsford, England, 29 November, 1948						CD
Tottenham H	Chelmsford C	01/68	68-72	77	6	4
COLLINS Robert Lionel (Bob)						
Born: Winchester, Hampshire, England, 12 August, 1939						G
Newport Co	Winchester C	03/63	62	1	-	0
COLLINS Robert Young (Bobby)						
Born: Govanhill, Glasgow, Scotland, 16 February, 1931						IF
Died: Leeds, England, 13 January, 2014						
Scotland: 31/SLge-16						
Everton	Glasgow Celtic	09/58	58-61	133	-	42
Leeds U	Tr	03/62	61-66	149	0	24
Bury	Tr	02/67	66-68	74	1	6
Oldham Ath	Sydney Hakoah (AUS)	10/72	72	6	1	0
COLLINS Roderick (Roddy)						
Born: Dublin, Republic of Ireland, 7 August, 1962						F
Mansfield T	Dundalk (ROI)	12/85	85-86	11	4	1
Newport Co	Tr	08/87	87	5	2	1
COLLINS Ronald Dudley (Sammy)						
Born: Bristol, England, 13 January, 1923						IF
Died: Bristol, England, 1 June, 1998						
Bristol C		11/44	46-47	14	-	2
Torquay U	Tr	06/48	48-57	356	-	204
COLLINS Ronald Michael (Mike)						
Born: Middlesbrough, England, 8 June, 1933						G
Chelsea	Redcar A	11/51	53	1	-	0
Watford	Tr	07/57	57-58	43	-	0
COLLINS Samuel Jason (Sam)						
Born: Pontefract, West Yorkshire, England, 5 June, 1977						CD
Huddersfield T	YT	07/94	96-98	34	3	0
Bury	Tr	07/99	99-01	78	4	2
Port Vale	Tr	07/02	02-05	135	0	11
Hull C	Tr	11/05	05-06	23	0	0
Swindon T	L	09/07	07	3	1	0
Hartlepool U	Tr	01/08	07-14	239	5	6

COLLINS Simon Jonathan
Born: Pontefract, West Yorkshire, England, 16 December, 1973 — CD

League Club	Source	Date Signed	Seasons Played	Apps	Subs	Gls
Huddersfield T	YT	07/92	92-96	31	21	3
Plymouth Arg	Tr	03/97	96-98	81	3	5
Macclesfield T	Tr	07/99	99-00	52	4	3
Shrewsbury T	L	02/01	00	12	0	0

COLLINS Stephen Mark (Steve)
Born: Stamford, Lincolnshire, England, 21 March, 1962 — LB

League Club	Source	Date Signed	Seasons Played	Apps	Subs	Gls
Peterborough U	App	08/79	78-82	92	2	1
Southend U	Tr	08/83	83-84	51	0	0
Lincoln C	Tr	03/85	84-85	24	0	0
Peterborough U	Tr	12/85	85-88	114	8	2

COLLINS Terence James (Terry)
Born: Penrhiwceiber, Rhondda Cynon Taff, Wales, 8 January, 1943 — IF

League Club	Source	Date Signed	Seasons Played	Apps	Subs	Gls
Swansea C	Ton Pentre	03/67	67	2	0	0

COLLINS Wayne Anthony
Born: Manchester, England, 4 March, 1969 — M

League Club	Source	Date Signed	Seasons Played	Apps	Subs	Gls
Crewe Alex	Winsford U	07/93	93-95	102	15	14
Sheffield Wed	Tr	08/96	96-97	16	15	6
Fulham	Tr	01/98	97-00	37	21	4
Crewe Alex	Tr	08/01	01	13	7	0
Stockport Co	Tr	08/03	03	0	2	0

COLLINS William Hanna (Bill)
Born: Belfast, Northern Ireland, 15 February, 1920 — WH
Died: Gillingham, Kent, England, 3 November, 2010

League Club	Source	Date Signed	Seasons Played	Apps	Subs	Gls
Luton T	Belfast Celtic	02/48	47-48	7	-	0
Gillingham	Tr	10/49	50	13	-	0

COLLINSON Clifford (Cliff)
Born: Middlesbrough, England, 3 March, 1920 — G
Died: Bristol, England, September, 1990

League Club	Source	Date Signed	Seasons Played	Apps	Subs	Gls
Manchester U	Urmston BC	09/46	46	7	-	0

COLLINSON Leslie (Les)
Born: Hull, England, 2 December, 1935 — RH

League Club	Source	Date Signed	Seasons Played	Apps	Subs	Gls
Hull C	Jnr	09/56	56-66	296	1	14
York C	Tr	02/67	66-67	35	0	2

COLLINSON Roger
Born: Rawmarsh, South Yorkshire, England, 5 December, 1940 — RB
Died: Rotherham, South Yorkshire, England, December, 1989
England: Youth/Schools

League Club	Source	Date Signed	Seasons Played	Apps	Subs	Gls
Bristol C	Doncaster Rov (Am)	10/58	59-60	50	-	1
Stockport Co	Tr	07/61	61	2	-	0

COLLIS David John (Dave)
Born: Hornchurch, E London, England, 8 November, 1981 — FB

League Club	Source	Date Signed	Seasons Played	Apps	Subs	Gls
Charlton Ath	YT	05/00				
Barnet	L	03/01	00	1	1	0

COLLIS Stephen Philip (Steve)
Born: Harrow, NW London, England, 18 March, 1981 — G

League Club	Source	Date Signed	Seasons Played	Apps	Subs	Gls
Barnet	Jnr	08/99				
Nottingham F	Tr	07/00				
Yeovil T	Tr	08/01	03-05	41	2	0
Southend U	Tr	06/06	06-07	20	1	0
Crewe Alex	Tr	07/08	08-09	19	0	0
Bristol C	Tr	01/10				
Torquay U	L	05/10	09	1	0	0
Peterborough U	Tr	08/10				
Northampton T	L	03/11	10	3	1	0
Macclesfield T	Tr	09/11				
Rochdale	Buxton	01/13				

COLLISON Jack David
Born: Watford, Hertfordshire, England, 2 October, 1988 — M
Wales: 17/U21-7

League Club	Source	Date Signed	Seasons Played	Apps	Subs	Gls
West Ham U	Sch	08/07	07-13	75	30	11
Bournemouth	L	10/13	13	4	0	0
Wigan Ath	L	03/14	13	5	4	0
Ipswich T	Tr	09/14				

COLLISTER Joseph Douglas (Joe)
Born: Hoylake, Wirral, England, 15 December, 1991 — G

League Club	Source	Date Signed	Seasons Played	Apps	Subs	Gls
Tranmere Rov	Sch	07/09	09-10	8	2	0

COLLYMORE Stanley Victor (Stan)
Born: Cannock, Staffordshire, England, 22 January, 1971 — F
England: 3

League Club	Source	Date Signed	Seasons Played	Apps	Subs	Gls
Wolverhampton W	YT	07/89				
Crystal Palace	Stafford Rgrs	01/91	90-92	4	16	1
Southend U	Tr	11/92	92	30	0	15
Nottingham F	Tr	07/93	93-94	64	1	41
Liverpool	Tr	07/95	95-96	55	6	26
Aston Villa	Tr	05/97	97-98	34	11	7
Fulham	L	07/99	99	3	3	0
Leicester C	Tr	02/00	99-00	7	4	5
Bradford C	Tr	10/00	00	5	2	2

COLMAN Edward (Eddie)
Born: Salford, England, 1 November, 1936 — LH
Died: Munich, Germany, 6 February, 1958

League Club	Source	Date Signed	Seasons Played	Apps	Subs	Gls
Manchester U	Jnr	11/53	55-57	85	-	1

COLOCCINI Fabricio
Born: Cordoba, Argentina, 22 January, 1982 — CD
Argentina: 39

League Club	Source	Date Signed	Seasons Played	Apps	Subs	Gls
Newcastle U	Depo la Coruna (SPN)	08/08	08-14	222	0	5

COLOMBO Donald Simon (Don)
Born: Poplar, E London, England, 26 October, 1928 — LW

League Club	Source	Date Signed	Seasons Played	Apps	Subs	Gls
Portsmouth	Barking	03/53				
Walsall	Tr	12/53	53	20	-	1

COLOSIMO Simon
Born: Melbourne, Australia, 24 August, 1980 — CD
Australia: 26/U23-14

League Club	Source	Date Signed	Seasons Played	Apps	Subs	Gls
Manchester C	South Melbourne (AUS)	07/01	01	0	6	0

COLQUHOUN Edmund Peter Skirving (Eddie)
Born: Prestonpans, East Lothian, Scotland, 29 March, 1945 — CD
Scotland: 9

League Club	Source	Date Signed	Seasons Played	Apps	Subs	Gls
Bury	Jnr	03/62	63-66	81	0	2
West Bromwich A	Tr	02/67	66-68	46	0	1
Sheffield U	Tr	10/68	68-77	360	3	21

COLQUHOUN John
Born: Stirling, Scotland, 3 June, 1940 — W
Died: Stirling, Scotland, 10 June, 1996

League Club	Source	Date Signed	Seasons Played	Apps	Subs	Gls
Oldham Ath	Stirling A	08/61	61-64	163	-	33
Scunthorpe U	Tr	06/65	65-68	149	0	23
Oldham Ath	Tr	11/68	68-69	68	2	6

COLQUHOUN John Mark
Born: Stirling, Scotland, 14 July, 1963 — M
Scotland: 2

League Club	Source	Date Signed	Seasons Played	Apps	Subs	Gls
Millwall	Heart of Midlothian	08/91	91	27	0	3
Sunderland	Tr	07/92	92	12	8	0

COLRAIN John James
Born: Glasgow, Scotland, 4 February, 1937 — IF
Died: Glasgow, Scotland, 14 July, 1984
Scotland: U23-1

League Club	Source	Date Signed	Seasons Played	Apps	Subs	Gls
Ipswich T	Clyde	04/63	63-65	55	1	17

COLUNGA Adrian
Born: Oviedo, Spain, 17 November, 1984 — W/F

League Club	Source	Date Signed	Seasons Played	Apps	Subs	Gls
Brighton & HA	Getafe (SPN)	08/14	14	11	6	3

COLUSSO Cristian Daniel
Born: Buenos Aires, Argentina, 2 July, 1977 — M
Argentina: Youth

League Club	Source	Date Signed	Seasons Played	Apps	Subs	Gls
Oldham Ath	Rosario Central (ARG)	02/02	01	6	7	2

COLVAN Hugh
Born: Port Glasgow, Inverclyde, Scotland, 24 September, 1925 — IF
Died: Port Glasgow, Inverclyde, Scotland, 26 February, 2002

League Club	Source	Date Signed	Seasons Played	Apps	Subs	Gls
Rochdale	Hibernian	02/48	47	1	-	0

COLVILLE Henry (Harry)
Born: Kirkcaldy, Fife, Scotland, 12 February, 1924 — LW
Died: Glenrothes, Fife, Scotland, 16 March, 1999

League Club	Source	Date Signed	Seasons Played	Apps	Subs	Gls
Chester C	Raith Rov	08/47	47	4	-	1

COLVILLE Robert John (Bob)
Born: Nuneaton, Warwickshire, England, 27 April, 1963 — F
Wales: Semi Pro

League Club	Source	Date Signed	Seasons Played	Apps	Subs	Gls
Oldham Ath	Rhos U	02/84	83-86	22	10	4
Bury	Tr	10/86	86-87	5	6	1
Stockport Co	Tr	09/87	87-88	67	4	20
York C	Tr	06/89	89	17	7	0

COLY Ferdinand
Born: Dakar, Senegal, 10 September, 1973 — FB
Senegal: 23

League Club	Source	Date Signed	Seasons Played	Apps	Subs	Gls
Birmingham C (L)	RC Lens (FRA)	01/03	02	1	0	0

COMAZZI Alberto
Born: Novara, Italy, 16 April, 1979 — CD

League Club	Source	Date Signed	Seasons Played	Apps	Subs	Gls
Swindon T	Spezia (ITA)	06/11	11	4	0	0

COMBE Alan
Born: Edinburgh, Scotland, 3 April, 1974 — G
Scotland: B-1

League Club	Source	Date Signed	Seasons Played	Apps	Subs	Gls
Bradford C (L)	Dundee U	02/02	01	16	0	0
Bradford C	Dundee U	07/03	03	21	0	0

COMERFORD Patrick (Pat)
Born: Chester-le-Street, County Durham, England, 30 November, 1925 — WH
Died: Luton, England, January, 2002

League Club	Source	Date Signed	Seasons Played	Apps	Subs	Gls
Shrewsbury T	Bedford T	07/52	52	7	-	0

COMFORT Alan
Born: Aldershot, Hampshire, England, 8 December, 1964 — LW
England: Youth

League Club	Source	Date Signed	Seasons Played	Apps	Subs	Gls
Queens Park Rgrs	App	10/82				
Cambridge U	Tr	09/84	84-85	61	2	5
Leyton Orient	Tr	03/86	85-88	145	5	46
Middlesbrough	Tr	07/89	89	15	0	2

COMINELLI Lucas
Born: Buenos Aires, Argentina, 25 December, 1976 — M

League Club	Source	Date Signed	Seasons Played	Apps	Subs	Gls
Oxford U	Pahang FA (MLY)	01/05	04	11	5	1

COMLEY Brandon
Born: Islington, N London, England, 18 November, 1995 — M

League Club	Source	Date Signed	Seasons Played	Apps	Subs	Gls
Queens Park Rgrs	Sch	03/14	14	0	1	0

COMLEY James Richard
Born: Holloway, N London, England, 24 January, 1991 — M

League Club	Source	Date Signed	Seasons Played	Apps	Subs	Gls
Crystal Palace	Sch	08/08	08	1	3	0

COMLEY Leonard George (Len)
Born: Swansea, Wales, 25 January, 1922 — IF
Died: Swansea, Wales, 5 August, 2007

League Club	Source	Date Signed	Seasons Played	Apps	Subs	Gls
Swansea C	Jnr	10/45	46-47	28	-	7
Newport Co	Milford U	10/48	48-50	76	-	29
Scunthorpe U	Tr	03/51	50	12	-	5

COMMINGES Miguel Gregory
Born: Les Abymes, Guadeloupe, 16 March, 1982 — RB
Guadeloupe: 15

League Club	Source	Date Signed	Seasons Played	Apps	Subs	Gls
Swindon T	Stade de Reims (FRA)	07/07	07	32	8	0
Cardiff C	Tr	07/08	08-09	10	21	0
Southend U	Tr	01/11	10	4	3	0
Stevenage	Colorado Rapids (USA)	09/12	12	19	2	0

COMMON Alan Robert
Born: Stannington, Northumberland, England, 16 December, 1954 — FB

League Club	Source	Date Signed	Seasons Played	Apps	Subs	Gls
West Bromwich A	App	12/72				
Stockport Co	Tr	07/73	73	2	1	0

COMMONS Kristian Arran (Kris)
Born: Mansfield, Nottinghamshire, England, 30 August, 1983 — W/F
Scotland: 12

League Club	Source	Date Signed	Seasons Played	Apps	Subs	Gls
Stoke C	YT	01/01	02-03	20	21	5
Nottingham F	Tr	07/04	04-07	112	26	32
Derby Co	Tr	07/08	08-10	66	14	21

COMMONS Michael (Mike)
Born: Adwick-le-Street, South Yorkshire, England, 18 April, 1940 — CF

League Club	Source	Date Signed	Seasons Played	Apps	Subs	Gls
Lincoln C	Wath W	05/58	59-60	2	-	1
Workington	Tr	07/61	61-63	74	-	36
Chesterfield	Tr	07/64	64	10	-	1

COMPTON Denis Charles Scott
Born: Hendon, N London, England, 23 May, 1918 — LW
Died: Windsor, Berkshire, England, 23 April, 1997
England: War-12

League Club	Source	Date Signed	Seasons Played	Apps	Subs	Gls
Arsenal	Jnr	05/35	36-49	54	-	15

COMPTON Jack Louis Paul
Born: Torquay, Devon, England, 2 September, 1998 — LW

League Club	Source	Date Signed	Seasons Played	Apps	Subs	Gls
West Bromwich A	Sch	07/07				
Brighton & HA	Tr	08/08				
Bradford C (L)	Falkirk	08/11	11	9	5	0
Portsmouth	Falkirk	08/12	12	7	5	0
Colchester U	Tr	01/13	12	1	6	0
Hartlepool U	Tr	06/13	13-14	42	13	4

COMPTON John Frederick
Born: Poplar, E London, England, 27 August, 1937 — LB

League Club	Source	Date Signed	Seasons Played	Apps	Subs	Gls
Chelsea	Jnr	02/55	55-59	12	-	0
Ipswich T	Tr	07/60	60-63	111	-	0
Bournemouth	Tr	07/64	64	27	-	1

COMPTON Leslie Harry (Les)
Born: Woodford, NE London, England, 12 September, 1912 — CH
Died: Hendon, N London, England, 27 December, 1984
England: 2/FLge-1/War-5

League Club	Source	Date Signed	Seasons Played	Apps	Subs	Gls
Arsenal	Hampstead T	02/32	31-51	253	-	5

COMPTON Paul David
Born: Stroud, Gloucestershire, England, 6 June, 1961 — CD

League Club	Source	Date Signed	Seasons Played	Apps	Subs	Gls
Bournemouth	Trowbridge T	10/80	80-82	64	0	0
Aldershot	Tr	12/83	83	13	0	0
Torquay U	Tr	02/84	83-86	95	0	4
Newport Co	Tr	12/86	86	27	0	2
Torquay U	Bashley	08/91	91-92	19	2	0

COMPTON Roy
Born: Lambeth, S London, England, 8 November, 1954 — F

League Club	Source	Date Signed	Seasons Played	Apps	Subs	Gls
Swindon T	Millwall (App)	11/72	73	4	0	2

COMPTON Terence David (Terry)
Born: Bristol, England, 28 November, 1931 — CH
Died: Bristol, England, 6 October, 1991

League Club	Source	Date Signed	Seasons Played	Apps	Subs	Gls
Bristol C	Jnr	12/48	51-57	44	-	0

COMSTIVE Paul Thomas
Born: Southport, Merseyside, England, 25 November, 1961 — M
Died: Southport, Merseyside, England, 29 December, 2013

League Club	Source	Date Signed	Seasons Played	Apps	Subs	Gls
Blackburn Rov	Jnr	10/79	80-82	3	3	0
Rochdale	L	09/82	82	6	0	2
Rochdale	L	02/83	82	3	0	0
Wigan Ath	Tr	08/83	83-84	35	0	2
Wrexham	Tr	11/84	84-86	95	4	8
Burnley	Tr	07/87	87-88	81	1	17
Bolton W	Tr	09/89	89-90	42	7	3
Chester C	Tr	11/91	91-92	55	2	6

COMYN Andrew John (Andy)
Born: Wakefield, England, 2 August, 1968 — CD

League Club	Source	Date Signed	Seasons Played	Apps	Subs	Gls
Aston Villa	Alvechurch	08/89	89-90	12	3	0
Derby Co	Tr	08/91	91-92	59	4	1
Plymouth Arg	Tr	08/93	93-94	76	0	5
West Bromwich A	Tr	03/96	95	3	0	0

COMYN-PLATT Charlie
Born: Manchester, England, 2 October, 1985 — CD

League Club	Source	Date Signed	Seasons Played	Apps	Subs	Gls
Bolton W	Sch	09/04				
Wycombe W	L	09/04	04	3	1	0
Swindon T	Tr	07/05	05-06	15	9	1
Rochdale	Tr	01/07				

CONBOY Francis Joseph Anthony (Frank)
Born: Marylebone, Central London, England, 5 September, 1947 — RH

League Club	Source	Date Signed	Seasons Played	Apps	Subs	Gls
Chelsea	App	07/65				
Luton T	Tr	10/66	66	19	0	1

CONDE James Patrick (Jim)
Born: Creswell, Derbyshire, England, 19 July, 1944 — CF

League Club	Source	Date Signed	Seasons Played	Apps	Subs	Gls
Wolverhampton W	Jnr	05/62				
Scunthorpe U	Tr	06/63	63	4	-	1

CONDIE James Collins Armstrong (Jimmy)
Born: Hamilton, Lanarkshire, Scotland, 24 July, 1926 — W
Died: Walsall, West Midlands, England, February, 1999

League Club	Source	Date Signed	Seasons Played	Apps	Subs	Gls
Walsall	Kilsyth Rgrs	12/47	47-49	49	-	2

CONEY Dean Henry
Born: Dagenham, E London, England, 18 September, 1963 — F
England: U21-4

League Club	Source	Date Signed	Seasons Played	Apps	Subs	Gls
Fulham	App	05/81	80-86	209	2	56
Queens Park Rgrs	Tr	06/87	87-88	36	12	7
Norwich C	Tr	03/89	88-89	12	5	1

CONLEY Brian John
Born: Thurnscoe, South Yorkshire, England, 21 November, 1948 — WH

League Club	Source	Date Signed	Seasons Played	Apps	Subs	Gls
Sheffield U	App	01/66				
Bradford Park Ave	Tr	12/68	68-69	11	2	0

CONLEY John Joseph (Jack)
Born: Whitstable, Kent, England, 27 September, 1920 — CF
Died: Swindon, England, January, 1991

League Club	Source	Date Signed	Seasons Played	Apps	Subs	Gls
Charlton Ath	Canterbury Waverley	08/38				
Torquay U	Tr	05/39	46-50	156	-	72

CONLON Barry John
Born: Drogheda, Republic of Ireland, 1 October, 1978 — F
Republic of Ireland: U21-7

League Club	Source	Date Signed	Seasons Played	Apps	Subs	Gls
Manchester C	Queens Park Rgrs (YT)	08/97	97	1	6	0
Plymouth Arg	L	02/98	97	13	0	2
Southend U	Tr	09/98	98	28	6	7
York C	Tr	07/99	99-00	33	15	11
Colchester U	L	11/00	00	23	3	8
Darlington	Tr	07/01	01-03	114	1	39
Barnsley	Tr	07/04	04-05	25	10	7
Rotherham U	L	10/05	05	3	0	1
Darlington	Tr	07/06	06	12	7	6
Mansfield T	Tr	01/07	06	16	1	6
Bradford C	Tr	07/07	07-08	36	36	17
Grimsby T	Tr	03/09	08-09	15	9	10
Chesterfield	Tr	01/10	09	15	4	7
Stockport Co	Tr	08/10	10	5	4	0

CONLON Bryan
Born: Shildon, County Durham, England, 14 January, 1943 — F

Died: Shildon, County Durham, England, 11 October, 2000

League Club	Source	Date Signed	Seasons Played	Apps	Subs	Gls
Newcastle U	Jnr	05/61				
Darlington	South Shields	08/64	64-67	72	3	27
Millwall	Tr	11/67	67-68	40	1	13
Norwich C	Tr	12/68	68-69	29	0	8
Blackburn Rov	Tr	05/70	70-71	43	2	7
Crewe Alex	L	01/72	71	4	0	1
Cambridge U	Tr	03/72	71-72	17	1	3
Hartlepool U	Tr	09/72	72-73	38	3	3

CONLON Paul Robert
Born: Sunderland, England, 5 January, 1978 — F

League Club	Source	Date Signed	Seasons Played	Apps	Subs	Gls
Hartlepool U	YT	-	95	11	4	4
Sunderland	Tr	07/96				
Doncaster Rov	Tr	08/97	97	4	10	1

CONLON Thomas George Sawyer (Tom)
Born: Newcastle-under-Lyme, Potteries, England, 3 February, 1996 — M

League Club	Source	Date Signed	Seasons Played	Apps	Subs	Gls
Peterborough U	Sch	01/14	13	0	1	0
Stevenage	Tr	09/14	14	6	7	0

CONMY Oliver Martin (Ollie)
Born: Mulrany, Co. Mayo, Republic of Ireland, 13 November, 1939 — M
Died: Southport, Merseyside, England, 26 January, 2014
Republic of Ireland: 5

League Club	Source	Date Signed	Seasons Played	Apps	Subs	Gls
Huddersfield T	St Paulinus YC	05/59	60-62	3	-	0
Peterborough U	Tr	05/64	64-71	251	12	34

CONN Alfred James (Alfie)
Born: Edinburgh, Scotland, 5 April, 1952 — M
Scotland: 2/U23-3

League Club	Source	Date Signed	Seasons Played	Apps	Subs	Gls
Tottenham H	Glasgow Rangers	07/74	74-76	35	3	6
Blackpool	Heart of Midlothian	03/81	80	3	0	0

CONNACHAN Edward Devlin (Eddie)
Born: Prestonpans, East Lothian, Scotland, 27 August, 1935 — G
Scotland: 2/SLge-4

League Club	Source	Date Signed	Seasons Played	Apps	Subs	Gls
Middlesbrough	Dunfermline Ath	08/63	63-65	95	0	0

CONNAUGHTON Patrick John (John)
Born: Wigan, Greater Manchester, England, 23 September, 1949 — G
England: Youth

League Club	Source	Date Signed	Seasons Played	Apps	Subs	Gls
Manchester U	App	10/66	71	3	0	0
Halifax T	L	09/69	69	3	0	0
Torquay U	L	10/71	71	22	0	0
Sheffield U	Tr	10/72	73	12	0	0
Port Vale	Tr	06/74	74-79	191	0	0

CONNEALLY Martin
Born: Lichfield, Staffordshire, England, 2 February, 1962 — G

League Club	Source	Date Signed	Seasons Played	Apps	Subs	Gls
Walsall	App	02/80	80	3	0	0

CONNEELY Seamus Joseph
Born: Lambeth, S London, England, 9 July, 1988 — M/D
Republic of Ireland: U21-4

League Club	Source	Date Signed	Seasons Played	Apps	Subs	Gls
Sheffield U	Galway U (ROI)	01/11				
Accrington Stan	Sligo Rov (ROI)	01/15	14	12	4	3

CONNELL Alan John
Born: Enfield, N London, England, 15 February, 1983 — F

League Club	Source	Date Signed	Seasons Played	Apps	Subs	Gls
Bournemouth	Ipswich T (YT)	07/02	02-04	18	36	8
Torquay U	Tr	07/05	05	12	10	7
Hereford U	Tr	07/06	06	33	11	9
Brentford	Tr	07/07	07-08	36	8	12
Bournemouth	Tr	08/08	08-09	25	25	5
Swindon T	Grimsby T	07/11	11	13	19	11
Bradford C	Tr	07/12	12-13	8	35	8
Northampton T	Tr	01/14	13	11	5	0

CONNELL Darren Stephen
Born: Liverpool, England, 3 February, 1982 — M

League Club	Source	Date Signed	Seasons Played	Apps	Subs	Gls
Blackpool	YT	-	99	1	2	0
Macclesfield T	Tr	09/00	00	0	1	0

CONNELL James David (Jim)
Born: Blackburn, Greater Manchester, England, 24 May, 1951 — LW

League Club	Source	Date Signed	Seasons Played	Apps	Subs	Gls
Bury	Blackburn Rov (App)	02/68	69	9	0	2

CONNELL Lee Anthony
Born: Bury, Greater Manchester, England, 24 June, 1981 — FB/M

League Club	Source	Date Signed	Seasons Played	Apps	Subs	Gls
Bury	YT	07/99	99-03	46	12	9

CONNELL Peter McArthur
Born: East Kilbride, Lanarkshire, Scotland, 26 November, 1927 — RB
Died: Ayr, Scotland, 4 June, 1995

League Club	Source	Date Signed	Seasons Played	Apps	Subs	Gls
Northampton T	Greenock Morton	05/51	51	13	-	0

CONNELL Roger
Born: Seaford, East Sussex, England, 8 September, 1946 — F
England: Amateur-2

League Club	Source	Date Signed	Seasons Played	Apps	Subs	Gls
Wimbledon	Walton & Hersham	08/74	77-78	30	2	14

CONNELL Thomas Eugene (Tom)
Born: Newry, Armagh, Northern Ireland, 25 November, 1957 — LB
Northern Ireland: 1

League Club	Source	Date Signed	Seasons Played	Apps	Subs	Gls
Manchester U	Coleraine	08/78	78	2	0	0

CONNELLY Dean (Dino)
Born: St Helier, Jersey, Channel Islands, 6 January, 1970 — M
Scotland: Youth/Schools

League Club	Source	Date Signed	Seasons Played	Apps	Subs	Gls
Arsenal	YT	02/88				
Barnsley	Tr	06/90	90-92	7	6	0
Wigan Ath	L	10/91	91	12	0	2
Carlisle U	L	08/92	92	0	3	0
Wigan Ath	Tr	02/93	92-93	15	5	1

CONNELLY Edward John (Eddie)
Born: Dumbarton, Dunbartonshire, Scotland, 9 December, 1916 — IF
Died: Luton, England, 16 February, 1990

League Club	Source	Date Signed	Seasons Played	Apps	Subs	Gls
Newcastle U	Rosslyn	03/35	35-37	25	-	8
Luton T	Tr	03/38	37-38	50	-	16
West Bromwich A	Tr	08/39				
Luton T	Tr	04/46	46-47	38	-	8
Leyton Orient	Tr	06/48	48-49	32	-	5
Brighton & HA	Tr	10/49	49	6	-	1

CONNELLY Gordon Paul John
Born: Glasgow, Scotland, 1 November, 1976 — RW
Scotland: Youth/Schools

League Club	Source	Date Signed	Seasons Played	Apps	Subs	Gls
York C	Airdrieonians	08/98	98	28	0	4
Southend U	Tr	07/99	99-00	37	5	2
Carlisle U	Tr	11/00	00	21	7	1

CONNELLY John Michael
Born: St Helens, Merseyside, England, 18 July, 1938 — RW
Died: Barrowford, Lancashire, England, 25 October, 2012
England: 20/FLge-8/U23-1

League Club	Source	Date Signed	Seasons Played	Apps	Subs	Gls
Burnley	St Helens T	11/56	56-63	215	-	86
Manchester U	Tr	04/64	64-66	79	1	22
Blackburn Rov	Tr	09/66	66-69	148	1	36
Bury	Tr	06/70	70-72	129	0	37

CONNELLY Michael
Born: Wigan, Greater Manchester, England, 29 January, 1937 — RW

League Club	Source	Date Signed	Seasons Played	Apps	Subs	Gls
Stockport Co (Am)	Mossley Common	06/58	59	4	-	0

CONNELLY Sean Patrick
Born: Sheffield, England, 26 June, 1970 — RB

League Club	Source	Date Signed	Seasons Played	Apps	Subs	Gls
Stockport Co	Hallam	08/91	92-00	292	10	6
Wolverhampton W	Tr	03/01	00-01	11	3	0
Tranmere Rov	Tr	10/02	02-03	66	4	0
Rushden & D	Tr	07/04	04	40	2	0

CONNER Richard John (Dick)
Born: Jarrow, Tyne and Wear, England, 13 August, 1931 — RH
Died: Jarrow, Tyne and Wear, England, May, 1999

League Club	Source	Date Signed	Seasons Played	Apps	Subs	Gls
Newcastle U	Jnr	01/50				
Grimsby T	South Shields	08/52	53-58	186	-	8
Southampton	Tr	07/59	59-60	78	-	2
Tranmere Rov	Tr	07/61	61	4	-	0
Aldershot	Tr	07/62	62	6	-	0

CONNERTON Jordan Stuart
Born: Lancaster, England, 2 October, 1989 — F

League Club	Source	Date Signed	Seasons Played	Apps	Subs	Gls
Crewe Alex	Lancaster C	03/10	10	0	1	0

CONNING Terence Peter (Peter)
Born: Liverpool, England, 18 October, 1964 — M/FB
England: Schools

League Club	Source	Date Signed	Seasons Played	Apps	Subs	Gls
Rochdale	Altrincham	08/86	86	40	0	1

CONNOLLY Adam James
Born: Manchester, England, 10 April, 1986 — M

League Club	Source	Date Signed	Seasons Played	Apps	Subs	Gls
Cheltenham T	Sch	07/05	04-07	14	18	1

CONNOLLY David James
Born: Willesden, NW London, England, 6 June, 1977 — F
Republic of Ireland: 41

League Club	Source	Date Signed	Seasons Played	Apps	Subs	Gls
Watford	YT	11/94	94-96	19	7	10
Wolverhampton W (L)	Feyenoord (NED)	08/98	98	18	14	6
Wimbledon	Feyenoord (NED)	07/01	01-02	63	0	42
West Ham U	Tr	08/03	03	37	2	10
Leicester C	Tr	07/04	04-05	48	1	17
Wigan Ath	Tr	08/05	05-06	4	15	1
Sunderland	Tr	08/06	06-07	31	8	13
Southampton	Tr	10/09	09-11	34	27	14
Portsmouth		01/13	12-13	26	9	11
Oxford U	L	01/14	13	8	8	4
AFC Wimbledon	Tr	01/15	14	2	6	1

CONNOLLY John
Born: Barrhead, Renfrewshire, Scotland, 13 June, 1950 — LW

League Club	Source	Date Signed	Seasons Played	Apps	Subs	Gls

Scotland: 1/U23-2

League Club	Source	Date Signed	Seasons Played	Apps	Subs	Gls
Everton	St Johnstone	03/72	71-75	105	3	16
Birmingham C	Tr	09/76	76-77	49	8	9
Newcastle U	Tr	05/78	78-79	42	7	10

CONNOLLY Karl Andrew
Born: Prescot, Merseyside, England, 9 February, 1970 — F

League Club	Source	Date Signed	Seasons Played	Apps	Subs	Gls
Wrexham	Napoli, Liverpool	05/91	91-99	337	21	88
Queens Park Rgrs	Tr	05/00	00-02	53	19	12
Swansea C	Tr	08/03	03	4	6	1

CONNOLLY Mark Gerard
Born: Monaghan, Republic of Ireland, 16 December, 1991 — CD
Republic of Ireland: U21-7/Youth

League Club	Source	Date Signed	Seasons Played	Apps	Subs	Gls
Bolton W	Wolverhampton W (Sch)	09/09				
Macclesfield T	L	02/12	11	7	0	0
Crawley T	Tr	07/12	12-13	57	12	3

CONNOLLY Matthew Thomas Martin
Born: Barnet, N London, England, 24 September, 1987 — D
England: Youth

League Club	Source	Date Signed	Seasons Played	Apps	Subs	Gls
Arsenal	Sch	07/05				
Bournemouth	L	11/06	06	3	2	1
Colchester U	L	07/07	07	13	3	2
Queens Park Rgrs	Tr	01/08	07-11	104	12	2
Reading	L	01/12	11	6	0	0
Cardiff C	Tr	08/12	12-14	59	3	5
Watford	L	03/15	14	4	2	1

CONNOLLY Michael (Mike)
Born: Stainforth, South Yorkshire, England, 8 September, 1938 — W

League Club	Source	Date Signed	Seasons Played	Apps	Subs	Gls
Doncaster Rov (Am)	Jnr	03/57	56	3	-	0
Wolverhampton W	Tr	09/59				
Stockport Co	Tr	11/60	60	2	-	0

CONNOLLY Patrick Joseph (Pat)
Born: Newcastle-under-Lyme, Potteries, England, 27 July, 1941 — CF

League Club	Source	Date Signed	Seasons Played	Apps	Subs	Gls
Crewe Alex		01/61	60-62	9	-	3
Colchester U	Macclesfield T	07/64	64	21	-	6

CONNOLLY Paul
Born: Liverpool, England, 29 September, 1983 — RB

League Club	Source	Date Signed	Seasons Played	Apps	Subs	Gls
Plymouth Arg	Sch	07/02	00-04	156	6	1
Derby Co	Tr	07/08	08-09	56	5	1
Sheffield U	L	03/10	09	7	0	0
Leeds U	Tr	06/10	10-11	53	5	0
Portsmouth	L	08/12	12	4	0	0
Preston NE	L	01/13	12	14	1	0
Millwall	Tr	09/13	13	3	1	0
Crawley T	Tr	02/14	13	5	2	0
Luton T	Tr	07/14	14	4	0	0

CONNOLLY Reece William
Born: Farnborough, Hampshire, England, 22 January, 1992 — F

League Club	Source	Date Signed	Seasons Played	Apps	Subs	Gls
Aldershot T	Sch	05/10	09-12	1	15	0

CONNOLLY Ryan Michael
Born: Castlebar, Co. Mayo, Republic of Ireland, 13 January, 1992 — LB
Republic of Ireland: Youth

League Club	Source	Date Signed	Seasons Played	Apps	Subs	Gls
Derby Co	Sch	07/10	09	0	1	0

CONNOR Daniel Brian (Dan)
Born: Dublin, Republic of Ireland, 31 January, 1981 — G
Republic of Ireland: B-1/U21-7/Youth

League Club	Source	Date Signed	Seasons Played	Apps	Subs	Gls
Peterborough U	YT	04/98	98-02	6	2	0
Hereford U	St Patricks Ath (ROI)	08/10	11	1	0	0

CONNOR David Richard (Dave)
Born: Wythenshawe, Greater Manchester, England, 27 October, 1945 — LB/M

League Club	Source	Date Signed	Seasons Played	Apps	Subs	Gls
Manchester C	Jnr	11/62	64-71	130	11	10
Preston NE	Tr	01/72	71-72	29	0	0
Manchester C	Tr	03/74				

CONNOR Harold (Harry)
Born: Liverpool, England, 26 December, 1929 — W

League Club	Source	Date Signed	Seasons Played	Apps	Subs	Gls
Stoke C (Am)	Marine	03/53	52-53	4	-	2

CONNOR James
Born: Sunderland, England, 28 November, 1938 — LW

League Club	Source	Date Signed	Seasons Played	Apps	Subs	Gls
Darlington (Am)	Stanley U	09/65	65	3	0	0

CONNOR James Richard (Jim)
Born: Twickenham, W London, England, 22 August, 1974 — M

League Club	Source	Date Signed	Seasons Played	Apps	Subs	Gls
Millwall	YT	11/92	94-95	8	1	0

CONNOR James Terence
Born: Stockport, Greater Manchester, England, 31 January, 1959 — CD

League Club	Source	Date Signed	Seasons Played	Apps	Subs	Gls
Stockport Co	Jnr	02/79	78	1	1	0

CONNOR John
Born: Ashton-under-Lyne, Greater Manchester, England, 1 February, 1914 — LB
Died: Manchester, England, November, 1978

League Club	Source	Date Signed	Seasons Played	Apps	Subs	Gls
Bolton W	Mossley	10/34	34-38	29	-	0
Tranmere Rov	Mossley	06/47	47-48	46	-	3

CONNOR John
Born: Stockport, Greater Manchester, England, 15 March, 1961 — G

League Club	Source	Date Signed	Seasons Played	Apps	Subs	Gls
Stockport Co		08/80	81	1	0	0

CONNOR John Ferguson (Jack)
Born: Maryport, Cumbria, England, 25 July, 1934 — CH
Died: Formby, Merseyside, England, 9 March, 2010

League Club	Source	Date Signed	Seasons Played	Apps	Subs	Gls
Huddersfield T	Jnr	10/52	54-60	85	-	10
Bristol C	Tr	10/60	60-70	354	1	10

CONNOR John Thomas (Jack)
Born: Todmorden, West Yorkshire, England, 21 December, 1919 — CF
Died: Hackney, E London, England, December, 1998

League Club	Source	Date Signed	Seasons Played	Apps	Subs	Gls
Ipswich T	Albion Rov	11/44	46	12	-	4
Carlisle U	Tr	12/46	46-47	40	-	12
Rochdale	Ards	12/48	48-50	82	-	42
Bradford C	Tr	04/51	50-51	14	-	7
Stockport Co	Tr	10/51	51-56	206	-	132
Crewe Alex	Tr	09/56	56	27	-	4

CONNOR Kevin Holland
Born: Radcliffe, Greater Manchester, England, 12 January, 1945 — RB

League Club	Source	Date Signed	Seasons Played	Apps	Subs	Gls
Rochdale		01/66	65-66	21	2	1

CONNOR Paul
Born: Bishop Auckland, County Durham, England, 12 January, 1979 — F

League Club	Source	Date Signed	Seasons Played	Apps	Subs	Gls
Middlesbrough	YT	07/96				
Hartlepool U	L	02/98	97	4	1	0
Stoke C	Tr	03/99	98-00	18	18	7
Cambridge U	L	11/00	00	12	1	5
Rochdale	Tr	03/01	00-03	76	18	28
Swansea C	Tr	03/04	03-05	51	14	16
Leyton Orient	Tr	01/06	05-06	20	14	7
Cheltenham T	Tr	01/07	06-08	53	26	7
Lincoln C	Tr	07/09	09	8	7	0

CONNOR Robert
Born: Bradford, England, 13 October, 1925 — G

League Club	Source	Date Signed	Seasons Played	Apps	Subs	Gls
Bradford C	Salts	11/49	49-50	28	-	0
Wrexham	Tr	07/51	51-53	77	-	0

CONNOR Terence Fitzroy (Terry)
Born: Leeds, England, 9 November, 1962 — F
England: U21-1/Youth

League Club	Source	Date Signed	Seasons Played	Apps	Subs	Gls
Leeds U	App	11/79	79-82	83	13	19
Brighton & HA	Tr	03/83	82-86	153	3	51
Portsmouth	Tr	06/87	87-89	42	6	12
Swansea C	Tr	08/90	90-91	39	0	6
Bristol C	Tr	09/91	91-92	11	5	1
Swansea C	L	11/92	92	3	0	0

CONNORS Jack Stuart
Born: Brent, NW London, England, 24 October, 1994 — LB
Republic of Ireland: U21-6

League Club	Source	Date Signed	Seasons Played	Apps	Subs	Gls
Dagenham & Red	Jnr	07/13	13-14	37	3	0

CONNORS John Joseph Aloysius (Jack)
Born: Stockton-on-Tees, Cleveland, England, 21 August, 1927 — LH
Died: Corby, Northamptonshire, England, February, 2006

League Club	Source	Date Signed	Seasons Played	Apps	Subs	Gls
Darlington	Stockton	03/48	47-51	65	-	0

CONROY Gerard Anthony Francis (Terry)
Born: Dublin, Republic of Ireland, 2 October, 1946 — F/W
Republic of Ireland: 26

League Club	Source	Date Signed	Seasons Played	Apps	Subs	Gls
Stoke C	Glentoran	03/67	67-78	244	27	49
Crewe Alex	Bulova (HKG)	01/80	79-80	37	0	5

CONROY Michael George (Mike)
Born: Johnstone, Renfrewshire, Scotland, 31 July, 1957 — M

League Club	Source	Date Signed	Seasons Played	Apps	Subs	Gls
Blackpool	Hibernian	08/84	84-85	66	0	2
Wrexham	Tr	07/86	86	23	2	2
Leyton Orient	Tr	07/87	87	2	1	0

CONROY Michael Kevin (Mike)
Born: Glasgow, Scotland, 31 December, 1965 — F

League Club	Source	Date Signed	Seasons Played	Apps	Subs	Gls
Reading	St Mirren	09/88	88-90	65	15	7
Burnley	Tr	07/91	91-92	76	1	30
Preston NE	Tr	08/93	93-94	50	7	22
Fulham	Tr	08/95	95-97	88	6	32
Blackpool	Tr	03/98	97-98	12	2	0
Chester C	L	12/98	98	10	0	3
Chester C	L	03/99	98	1	4	0

CONROY Richard (Dick)
Born: Bradford, England, 29 July, 1927 — CH
Died: Bradford, England, November, 1991

League Club	Source	Date Signed	Seasons Played	Apps	Subs	Gls
Bradford C	Swain House United	02/48	48-52	158	-	0
Bradford Park Ave	Tr	10/53	53-55	57	-	0

CONROY Richard Maurice (Maurice)
Born: Bradford, England, 26 April, 1919 — FB
Died: East Riding of Yorkshire, England, December, 2006

League Club	Source	Date Signed	Seasons Played	Apps	Subs	Gls
Fulham		05/37				
Accrington Stan	Tr	07/39	46-48	87	-	1
Scunthorpe U	Tr	09/50	50	1	-	0

CONROY Robert Bell (Bobby)
Born: Kirkintilloch, Dunbartonshire, Scotland, 20 June, 1929 — LB
Died: Rochdale, Greater Manchester, England, 1978

League Club	Source	Date Signed	Seasons Played	Apps	Subs	Gls
Bury	Ashfield	10/51	55-61	216	-	2
Tranmere Rov	Tr	07/62	62-64	103	-	1

CONROY Steven Harold (Steve)
Born: Chesterfield, Derbyshire, England, 19 December, 1956 — G

League Club	Source	Date Signed	Seasons Played	Apps	Subs	Gls
Sheffield U	App	06/74	77-82	104	0	0
Rotherham U	Tr	02/83	82	5	0	0
Rochdale	Tr	06/83	83-84	49	0	0

CONSTABLE James Ashley
Born: Malmesbury, Wiltshire, England, 5 October, 1984 — F
England: Semi Pro-3

League Club	Source	Date Signed	Seasons Played	Apps	Subs	Gls
Walsall	Chippenham T	11/05	05-06	9	14	3
Shrewsbury T	Kidderminster Hrs	01/08	07	7	7	4
Oxford U	Tr	07/08	10-13	128	39	45

CONSTABLE Shaun
Born: Maidstone, Kent, England, 21 March, 1968 — LW

League Club	Source	Date Signed	Seasons Played	Apps	Subs	Gls
Scunthorpe U	Leeds Univ	02/93	92	2	5	0

CONSTANTINE David (Dave)
Born: Dukinfield, Greater Manchester, England, 2 February, 1957 — RB
England: Semi Pro

League Club	Source	Date Signed	Seasons Played	Apps	Subs	Gls
Bury	Hyde U	02/79	78-81	67	3	2

CONSTANTINE James Joseph (Jimmy)
Born: Ashton-under-Lyne, Greater Manchester, England, 16 February, 1920 — CF
Died: Tunbridge Wells, Kent, England, 4 September, 1998

League Club	Source	Date Signed	Seasons Played	Apps	Subs	Gls
Rochdale	Mossley	01/45				
Manchester C	Tr	04/45	46	18	-	12
Bury	Tr	08/47	47	32	-	14
Millwall	Tr	05/48	48-51	141	-	74

CONSTANTINE Leon
Born: Hackney, E London, England, 24 February, 1978 — F

League Club	Source	Date Signed	Seasons Played	Apps	Subs	Gls
Millwall	Edgware T	08/00	00	0	1	0
Leyton Orient	L	08/01	01	9	1	3
Brentford	Tr	08/02	02	2	15	0
Southend U	Tr	08/03	03	40	3	21
Peterborough U	Tr	07/04	04	5	6	1
Torquay U	L	10/04	04	4	0	3
Torquay U	Tr	12/04	04-05	30	8	7
Port Vale	Tr	11/05	05-06	71	1	32
Leeds U	Tr	07/07	07	1	3	1
Oldham Ath	L	03/08	07	7	1	2
Northampton T	Tr	07/08	08	21	11	3
Cheltenham T	L	03/09	08	4	2	1
Hereford U	Tr	07/09	09	25	10	6

CONSTANTINOU Costakis Khriakou (Costas)
Born: Limassol, Cyprus, 24 September, 1968 — CD
Cyprus: 39

League Club	Source	Date Signed	Seasons Played	Apps	Subs	Gls
Barnet (L)	Omonia Nicosia (CYP)	10/96	96	1	0	0

CONTRA Cosmin Marius
Born: Timisoara, Romania, 15 December, 1975 — RB
Romania: 73

League Club	Source	Date Signed	Seasons Played	Apps	Subs	Gls
West Bromwich A (L)	Atletico Madrid (SPN)	08/04	04	5	0	0

CONVERY Mark Peter
Born: Newcastle-upon-Tyne, England, 29 May, 1981 — M

League Club	Source	Date Signed	Seasons Played	Apps	Subs	Gls
Sunderland	YT	03/99				
Darlington	Tr	01/01	00-04	38	38	3
Darlington	Newcastle Blue Star	08/09	09	9	12	0

CONVEY Robert (Bobby)
Born: Philadelphia, USA, 27 May, 1983 — LW
USA: 46

League Club	Source	Date Signed	Seasons Played	Apps	Subs	Gls
Reading	Washington DC U (USA)	08/04	04-08	72	26	7

CONWAY Andrew (Andy)
Born: South Shields, Tyne and Wear, England, 17 February, 1923 — IF
Died: Lincoln, England, October, 1996

League Club	Source	Date Signed	Seasons Played	Apps	Subs	Gls
Hull C	North Shields	06/47	47-48	6	-	5
Stockport Co	Tr	07/50				

CONWAY Christopher (Chris)
Born: Dundee, Scotland, 23 July, 1928 — G

League Club	Source	Date Signed	Seasons Played	Apps	Subs	Gls
Bury	Ayr U	09/54	54-55	44	-	0

CONWAY Craig Ian
Born: Prestwick, Ayrshire, Scotland, 2 May, 1985 — LW
Scotland: 7

League Club	Source	Date Signed	Seasons Played	Apps	Subs	Gls
Cardiff C	Dundee U	06/11	11-12	45	13	5
Brighton & HA	L	09/13	13	11	2	1
Blackburn Rov	Tr	01/14	13-14	45	11	7

CONWAY James (Jimmy)
Born: Motherwell, Lanarkshire, Scotland, 27 August, 1940 — CF
Northern Ireland: NILge-1//Scotland: Schools

League Club	Source	Date Signed	Seasons Played	Apps	Subs	Gls
Norwich C	Glasgow Celtic	05/61	61-63	42	-	13
Southend U	Tr	10/63	63-64	31	-	9

CONWAY James Patrick (Jim)
Born: Dublin, Republic of Ireland, 10 August, 1946 — RW
Republic of Ireland: 20/LoI-1/Amateur

League Club	Source	Date Signed	Seasons Played	Apps	Subs	Gls
Fulham	Bohemians (ROI)	05/66	66-75	312	4	67
Manchester C	Tr	08/76	76	11	2	1

CONWAY John
Born: Dublin, Republic of Ireland, 11 July, 1951 — RW

League Club	Source	Date Signed	Seasons Played	Apps	Subs	Gls
Fulham	Bohemians (ROI)	08/71	71-74	30	8	6

CONWAY John George
Born: Gateshead, Tyne and Wear, England, 24 January, 1931 — IF
Died: Gateshead, Tyne and Wear, England, 1981

League Club	Source	Date Signed	Seasons Played	Apps	Subs	Gls
Gateshead		05/53	53-54	4	-	0

CONWAY Michael Denis (Mickey)
Born: Sheffield, England, 11 March, 1956 — W

League Club	Source	Date Signed	Seasons Played	Apps	Subs	Gls
Brighton & HA	App	03/74	72-73	1	1	1
Swansea C	Tr	12/75	75-77	56	5	11

CONWAY Patrick (Pat)
Born: Newcastle-upon-Tyne, England, 19 September, 1968 — M

League Club	Source	Date Signed	Seasons Played	Apps	Subs	Gls
Cambridge U	App	10/85	85-86	2	0	0

CONWAY Paul James
Born: Portland, Oregon, USA, 17 April, 1970 — M/F
USA: U21

League Club	Source	Date Signed	Seasons Played	Apps	Subs	Gls
Carlisle U	Brooklyn Ital'ns (USA)	10/93	93-96	75	14	22
Northampton T	Tr	06/97	97	2	1	0
Scarborough	L	12/97	97	13	0	2

CONWAY Thomas (Tom)
Born: Stoke-on-Trent, England, 7 November, 1933 — IF

League Club	Source	Date Signed	Seasons Played	Apps	Subs	Gls
Port Vale	Jnr	05/51	55	15	-	4

CONWELL Anthony (Tony)
Born: Bradford, England, 17 January, 1932 — LB

League Club	Source	Date Signed	Seasons Played	Apps	Subs	Gls
Sheffield Wed	Jnr	02/49	53-54	44	-	0
Huddersfield T	Tr	07/55	55-58	106	-	2
Derby Co	Tr	06/59	59-61	98	-	1
Doncaster Rov	Tr	07/62	62-63	33	-	0

COO-RICHARDS Cavell Stefan
Born: Manchester, England, 7 August, 1987 — CD

League Club	Source	Date Signed	Seasons Played	Apps	Subs	Gls
Crewe Alex	Sch	07/06	06	0	1	0

COOK Aaron
Born: Caerphilly, Wales, 6 December, 1979 — FB

League Club	Source	Date Signed	Seasons Played	Apps	Subs	Gls
Portsmouth	YT	07/98	97	1	0	0

COOK Andrew Charles (Andy)
Born: Romsey, Hampshire, England, 10 August, 1969 — LB

League Club	Source	Date Signed	Seasons Played	Apps	Subs	Gls
Southampton	YT	07/87	87-90	11	5	1
Exeter C	Tr	09/91	91-92	70	0	1
Swansea C	Tr	07/93	93-95	54	8	0
Portsmouth	Tr	12/96	96-97	7	2	0
Millwall	Tr	01/98	97-98	4	1	0

COOK Anthony (Tony)
Born: Bristol, England, 8 October, 1929 — G
Died: Bristol, England, March, 1996

League Club	Source	Date Signed	Seasons Played	Apps	Subs	Gls
Bristol C	Clifton St Vincent's	01/50	52-63	320	-	0

COOK Anthony (Tony)
Born: Hemel Hempstead, Hertfordshire, England, 17 September, 1976 — M

League Club	Source	Date Signed	Seasons Played	Apps	Subs	Gls
Colchester U	YT	-	93	1	1	0

COOK Anthony (Tony)
Born: Crewe, Cheshire, England, 26 December, 1961 — M

League Club	Source	Date Signed	Seasons Played	Apps	Subs	Gls
Crewe Alex	Winsford U	05/81	81	2	1	0

COOK Anthony Lloyd Evans
Born: Hackney, E London, England, 10 August, 1989 — M

League Club	Source	Date Signed	Seasons Played	Apps	Subs	Gls
Dagenham & Red	Croydon Ath	11/07	07	0	1	0

COOK Charles Ivor (Charlie)
Born: Cheltenham, Gloucestershire, England, 28 January, 1937 — FB

League Club	Source	Date Signed	Seasons Played	Apps	Subs	Gls
Bristol C	Gloucester C	02/57	56-57	2	-	0

COOK Garry John
Born: Northampton, England, 31 March, 1978 — W

League Club	Source	Date Signed	Seasons Played	Apps	Subs	Gls
Hereford U	YT	07/96	96	17	3	0

COOK James Steven (Jamie)
Born: Witney, Oxfordshire, England, 2 August, 1979 — W

League Club	Source	Date Signed	Seasons Played	Apps	Subs	Gls
Oxford U	YT	07/97	97-00	33	44	7
Boston U	Tr	02/01	02	6	10	2

COOK Jason Peter
Born: Edmonton, N London, England, 29 December, 1969 — M

League Club	Source	Date Signed	Seasons Played	Apps	Subs	Gls
Tottenham H	YT	07/88				
Southend U	Tr	07/89	89-90	29	1	1
Colchester U	Tr	09/91	92-93	30	5	1

COOK Jeffrey William (Jeff)
Born: Hartlepool, Cleveland, England, 14 March, 1953 — F

League Club	Source	Date Signed	Seasons Played	Apps	Subs	Gls
Stoke C	Hellenic (RSA)	10/77	77-81	22	8	5
Bradford C	L	02/79	78	8	0	1
Plymouth Arg	L	12/79	79	4	3	5
Plymouth Arg	Tr	10/81	81-82	54	1	21
Halifax T	Tr	08/83	83-84	49	7	9

COOK John Albert
Born: Iron Acton, Avon, England, 27 June, 1929 — IF

League Club	Source	Date Signed	Seasons Played	Apps	Subs	Gls
Bristol Rov	Coalpit Heath	09/46	46	2	-	0

COOK Jordan Alan
Born: Hetton-le-Hole, Tyne and Wear, England, 20 March, 1990 — F

League Club	Source	Date Signed	Seasons Played	Apps	Subs	Gls
Sunderland	Sch	07/07	10	0	3	0
Darlington	L	08/09	09	4	1	0
Walsall	L	03/11	10	6	2	1
Carlisle U	L	01/12	11	6	8	4
Charlton Ath	Tr	07/12	12-13	2	8	0
Yeovil T	L	03/13	12	0	1	0
Walsall	Tr	07/14	14	27	5	5

COOK Lee
Born: Hammersmith, W London, England, 3 August, 1982 — LW

League Club	Source	Date Signed	Seasons Played	Apps	Subs	Gls
Watford	Aylesbury U	11/99	00-03	31	28	7
York C	L	10/02	02	7	0	1
Queens Park Rgrs	L	12/02	02	13	0	1
Queens Park Rgrs	Tr	07/04	04-06	109	10	9
Fulham	Tr	07/07				
Charlton Ath	L	01/08	07	4	5	0
Queens Park Rgrs	Tr	08/08	08-09	36	14	2
Leyton Orient	L	11/11	11	9	0	1
Charlton Ath	L	03/12	11	3	1	0
Leyton Orient	Tr	08/12	12	30	8	5

COOK Leslie (Les)
Born: Blackburn, Greater Manchester, England, 11 November, 1924 — WH
Died: Leicester, England, September, 1996
England: Schools

League Club	Source	Date Signed	Seasons Played	Apps	Subs	Gls
Blackburn Rov	Jnr	11/41	46-48	58	-	0
Coventry C	Tr	07/49	49-53	88	-	0

COOK Lewis John
Born: York, England, 3 February, 1997 — M
England: Youth

League Club	Source	Date Signed	Seasons Played	Apps	Subs	Gls
Leeds U	Sch	02/14	14	33	4	0

COOK Lewis Leon
Born: High Wycombe, Buckinghamshire, England, 28 December, 1983 — LW

League Club	Source	Date Signed	Seasons Played	Apps	Subs	Gls
Wycombe W	Sch	01/03	02-03	5	17	0

COOK Malcolm Ian
Born: Glasgow, Scotland, 24 May, 1943 — RH

League Club	Source	Date Signed	Seasons Played	Apps	Subs	Gls
Bradford Park Ave	Motherwell	07/63	63-64	45	-	2
Newport Co	Tr	07/65	65	29	2	0

COOK Mark Richard
Born: Boston, Lincolnshire, England, 7 August, 1970 — M

League Club	Source	Date Signed	Seasons Played	Apps	Subs	Gls
Lincoln C	YT	08/88	88-89	7	0	0

COOK Maurice
Born: Berkhamsted, Hertfordshire, England, 10 December, 1931 — CF
Died: Hemel Hempstead, Hertfordshire, England, 31 December, 2006

League Club	Source	Date Signed	Seasons Played	Apps	Subs	Gls
Watford	Berkhamsted T	05/53	53-57	208	-	68
Fulham	Tr	02/58	57-64	221	-	89
Reading	Tr	05/65	65	12	0	2

COOK Michael (Micky)
Born: Enfield, N London, England, 9 April, 1951 — RB

League Club	Source	Date Signed	Seasons Played	Apps	Subs	Gls
Colchester U	Leyton Orient (Am)	07/69	69-83	609	5	21

COOK Michael John (Mickey)
Born: Sutton, S London, England, 25 January, 1950 — F

League Club	Source	Date Signed	Seasons Played	Apps	Subs	Gls
Crystal Palace	App	02/68	67	1	0	0
Brentford	Tr	08/69	69	16	4	4

COOK Michael John (Mike)
Born: Stroud, Gloucestershire, England, 18 October, 1968 — M

League Club	Source	Date Signed	Seasons Played	Apps	Subs	Gls
Coventry C	App	03/87				
York C	L	08/87	87	6	0	1
Cambridge U	Tr	06/89	89-90	12	5	1
York C	L	11/90	90	3	3	0

COOK Mitchell Christopher (Mitch)
Born: Scarborough, North Yorkshire, England, 15 October, 1961 — LB/M

League Club	Source	Date Signed	Seasons Played	Apps	Subs	Gls
Darlington	Scarborough	08/84	84-85	34	0	4
Middlesbrough	Tr	09/85	85	3	3	0
Scarborough	Tr	08/86	87-88	61	20	10
Halifax T	Tr	08/89	89-90	52	2	2
Scarborough	L	10/90	90	9	0	1
Darlington	Tr	03/91	90-91	35	1	4
Blackpool	Tr	03/92	91-94	66	2	0
Hartlepool U	Tr	11/94	94	22	2	0
Scarborough	Guiseley	03/96	95	2	0	0

COOK Paul Anthony
Born: Liverpool, England, 22 February, 1967 — M

League Club	Source	Date Signed	Seasons Played	Apps	Subs	Gls
Wigan Ath	Marine	07/84	84-87	77	6	14
Norwich C	Tr	05/88	88-89	3	3	0
Wolverhampton W	Tr	11/89	89-93	191	2	19
Coventry C	Tr	08/94	94-95	35	2	3
Tranmere Rov	Tr	02/96	95-97	54	6	4
Stockport Co	Tr	10/97	97-98	48	1	3
Burnley	Tr	03/99	98-02	140	7	12
Wigan Ath	L	11/01	01	6	0	0

COOK Peter Henry
Born: Hull, England, 1 February, 1927 — WH
Died: Hull, England, 4 November, 1960

League Club	Source	Date Signed	Seasons Played	Apps	Subs	Gls
Hull C	Kingston Wolv	06/46	46-47	5	-	0
Bradford C	Scarborough	05/49	49	1	-	0
Crewe Alex	Tr	08/50	50-52	47	-	6

COOK Reuben (Ben)
Born: Gateshead, Tyne and Wear, England, 9 March, 1933 — WH

League Club	Source	Date Signed	Seasons Played	Apps	Subs	Gls
Arsenal	Tow Law T	11/51				
Leyton Orient	Tr	01/56	56	2	-	0

COOK Robert Kenneth (Bobby)
Born: Letchworth, Hertfordshire, England, 13 June, 1924 — W
Died: Ayton, Borders, Scotland, 6 March, 1997

League Club	Source	Date Signed	Seasons Played	Apps	Subs	Gls
Reading	Letchworth T	03/48				
Tottenham H	Tr	07/49	49	3	-	0
Watford	Tr	08/51	51-52	53	-	8

COOK Steve Anthony
Born: Hastings, East Sussex, England, 19 April, 1991 — CD

League Club	Source	Date Signed	Seasons Played	Apps	Subs	Gls
Brighton & HA	Sch	07/09	08-11	1	2	0
Bournemouth	L	10/11	11	8	0	0
Bournemouth	Tr	01/12	11-14	134	1	9

COOK Trevor
Born: Blidworth, Nottinghamshire, England, 2 July, 1956 — F

League Club	Source	Date Signed	Seasons Played	Apps	Subs	Gls
Mansfield T	App	07/74	73	1	0	0

COOKE Alan
Born: Nantwich, Cheshire, England, 28 December, 1930 — LB
Died: Congleton, Cheshire, England, 13 May, 1990

League Club	Source	Date Signed	Seasons Played	Apps	Subs	Gls
Crewe Alex	Nantwich	08/55	55	8	-	0

COOKE Andrew Roy (Andy)
Born: Shrewsbury, Shropshire, England, 20 January, 1974 — F

League Club	Source	Date Signed	Seasons Played	Apps	Subs	Gls
Burnley	Newtown	05/95	95-00	134	37	52
Stoke C	Tr	12/00	00-02	71	17	21
Bradford C	Busan Icons (KOR)	01/05	04-05	30	7	5
Darlington	L	02/06	05	11	3	3
Shrewsbury T	Tr	07/06	06-07	31	17	15

COOKE Barry Anthony
Born: Wolverhampton, England, 22 January, 1938 — RH
Died: Wolverhampton, England, 19 September, 1998
England: Youth

League Club	Source	Date Signed	Seasons Played	Apps	Subs	Gls
West Bromwich A	Erdington	05/55				
Northampton T	Tr	07/59	59-61	58	-	1

COOKE Charles (Charlie)
Born: St Monace, Fife, Scotland, 14 October, 1942 — M
Scotland: 16/SLge-4/U23-4

League Club	Source	Date Signed	Seasons Played	Apps	Subs	Gls
Chelsea	Dundee	04/66	66-72	204	8	15
Crystal Palace	Tr	10/72	72-73	42	2	0
Chelsea	Tr	01/74	73-77	85	2	7

COOKE David Frederick
Born: Birmingham, England, 29 November, 1946 — LB

League Club	Source	Date Signed	Seasons Played	Apps	Subs	Gls
Wolverhampton W	Jnr	07/65				
Stockport Co	Tr	07/68	68	3	0	0

COOKE Edward John
Born: Barnsley, South Yorkshire, England, 18 March, 1942 — G

League Club	Source	Date Signed	Seasons Played	Apps	Subs	Gls
Port Vale	Jnr	06/60	60-63	7	-	0

COOKE Gordon Gregory
Born: Crewe, Cheshire, England, 31 May, 1928 — IF
Died: Cheshire, England, September, 2012

League Club	Source	Date Signed	Seasons Played	Apps	Subs	Gls
Crewe Alex	Jnr	05/48	48	3	-	0

COOKE Jason Lee
Born: Birmingham, England, 13 July, 1971 — F

League Club	Source	Date Signed	Seasons Played	Apps	Subs	Gls
Torquay U	Bilston T	10/95	95	1	0	0

COOKE John
Born: Salford, England, 25 April, 1962 — M
England: Youth

League Club	Source	Date Signed	Seasons Played	Apps	Subs	Gls
Sunderland	App	11/79	79-84	42	13	4
Carlisle U	L	11/84	84	5	1	2
Sheffield Wed	Tr	06/85				
Carlisle U	Tr	10/85	85-87	105	1	11
Stockport Co	Tr	07/88	88-89	54	4	7
Chesterfield	Tr	07/90	90-91	48	5	8

COOKE Joseph (Joe)
Born: Dominica, 15 February, 1955 — CD/F

League Club	Source	Date Signed	Seasons Played	Apps	Subs	Gls
Bradford C	App	05/72	71-78	184	20	62
Peterborough U	Tr	01/79	78	18	0	5
Oxford U	Tr	08/79	79-80	71	1	13
Exeter C	Tr	06/81	81	17	0	3
Bradford C	Tr	01/82	81-83	61	1	6
Rochdale	Tr	07/84	84-85	75	0	4
Wrexham	Tr	07/86	86-87	49	2	4

COOKE Joshua Ian Ronald (Josh)
Born: Birmingham, England, 4 February, 1997 — F

League Club	Source	Date Signed	Seasons Played	Apps	Subs	Gls
Swindon T	Sch	03/15	14	1	1	0

COOKE Peter Charles
Born: Northampton, England, 15 January, 1962 — M

League Club	Source	Date Signed	Seasons Played	Apps	Subs	Gls
Northampton T	Jnr	07/80	80	4	1	1

COOKE Richard Edward
Born: Islington, N London, England, 4 September, 1965 — W
England: U21-1/Youth

League Club	Source	Date Signed	Seasons Played	Apps	Subs	Gls
Tottenham H	App	05/83	83-85	9	2	2
Birmingham C	L	09/86	86	5	0	0
Bournemouth	Tr	01/87	86-88	63	8	15
Luton T	Tr	03/89	88-89	3	14	1
Bournemouth	Tr	03/91	90-92	38	15	2

COOKE Robert Leslie (Robbie)
Born: Rotherham, South Yorkshire, England, 16 February, 1957 — F

League Club	Source	Date Signed	Seasons Played	Apps	Subs	Gls
Mansfield T	App	02/75	76-77	7	8	1
Peterborough U	Grantham	05/80	80-82	115	0	51
Cambridge U	Tr	02/83	82-84	62	3	14
Brentford	Tr	12/84	84-87	122	2	53
Millwall	Tr	12/87	87	4	0	1

COOKE Stephen Lee
Born: Walsall, West Midlands, England, 15 February, 1983 — M
England: Youth

League Club	Source	Date Signed	Seasons Played	Apps	Subs	Gls
Aston Villa	YT	02/00	02	0	3	0
Bournemouth	L	03/02	01	6	1	0
Bournemouth	L	01/04	03	3	0	0
Wycombe W	L	12/04	04	4	2	0
Bournemouth	Tr	07/05	05-06	24	17	3
Torquay U	L	01/07	06	9	4	1

COOKE Terence Arthur (Terry)
Born: Wrexham, Wales, 21 February, 1962 — F

League Club	Source	Date Signed	Seasons Played	Apps	Subs	Gls
Chester C	App	02/80	80-82	37	12	11

COOKE Terence John (Terry)
Born: Marston Green, West Midlands, England, 5 August, 1976 — W
England: U21-4/Youth

League Club	Source	Date Signed	Seasons Played	Apps	Subs	Gls
Manchester U	YT	07/94	95	1	3	0
Sunderland	L	01/96	95	6	0	0
Birmingham C	L	11/96	96	1	3	0
Wrexham	L	10/98	98	10	0	0
Manchester C	Tr	01/99	98-99	27	7	7
Wigan Ath	L	03/00	99	10	0	1
Sheffield Wed	L	09/00	00	12	1	1
Sheffield Wed	L	12/00	00	4	0	0
Grimsby T	Tr	03/02	01-02	18	10	1
Sheffield Wed	Tr	08/03	03	19	4	2

COOKE Wilfred Hudson (Wilf)
Born: Crewe, Cheshire, England, 5 October, 1915 — WH
Died: Whitby, North Yorkshire, England, 18 December, 1985

League Club	Source	Date Signed	Seasons Played	Apps	Subs	Gls
Bradford C	Leeds U (Am)	08/35	36-37	21	-	2
Leeds U	Tr	07/38				
Fulham	Tr	07/39				
Crewe Alex	Tr	02/46	46	9	-	2

COOKE William Henry (Harry)
Born: Oswestry, Shropshire, England, 7 March, 1919 — RB
Died: Luton, England, 22 September, 1992

League Club	Source	Date Signed	Seasons Played	Apps	Subs	Gls
Bournemouth		04/38				
Luton T	Tr	01/46	46-52	210	-	4
Shrewsbury T	Tr	07/53	53	4	-	0
Watford	Tr	07/54	54	10	-	0

COOKSEY Ernest George (Ernie)
Born: Bishops Stortford, Hertfordshire, England, 11 June, 1980 — M
Died: Westminster, Central London, England, 3 July, 2008

League Club	Source	Date Signed	Seasons Played	Apps	Subs	Gls
Oldham Ath	Crawley T	08/03	03-04	23	14	4
Rochdale	Tr	09/04	04-06	64	23	8
Boston U	Tr	01/07	06	11	5	0

COOKSEY Scott Andrew
Born: Birmingham, England, 24 June, 1972 — G
England: Semi Pro-1

League Club	Source	Date Signed	Seasons Played	Apps	Subs	Gls
Derby Co	YT	07/90				
Shrewsbury T	Tr	02/91				
Peterborough U	Bromsgrove Rov	12/93	93-94	15	0	0
Shrewsbury T	Hednesford T	10/98	98	2	0	0

COOKSLEY Harry Edward
Born: Guildford, Surrey, England, 15 November, 1994 — M

League Club	Source	Date Signed	Seasons Played	Apps	Subs	Gls
Aldershot T	Brentford (Jnr)	08/12	12	0	1	0
AFC Wimbledon	Tr	09/13				

COOKSON James (Jimmy)
Born: Litherland, Merseyside, England, 22 August, 1927 — FB
Died: Bootle, Merseyside, England, 23 December, 1993

League Club	Source	Date Signed	Seasons Played	Apps	Subs	Gls
Everton	Jnr	10/45				
Southport	Tr	08/49	49-51	55	-	1

COOKSON Steven John (Steve)
Born: Wolverhampton, England, 19 February, 1972 — F

League Club	Source	Date Signed	Seasons Played	Apps	Subs	Gls
Torquay U	YT	07/90	89-90	7	5	1

COOLE William (Billy)
Born: Manchester, England, 27 January, 1925 — RW
Died: Sale, Greater Manchester, England, 12 April, 2001

League Club	Source	Date Signed	Seasons Played	Apps	Subs	Gls
Mansfield T	Royal Navy	01/48	47-53	182	-	35
Notts Co	Tr	10/53	53-55	42	-	5
Barrow	Tr	07/56	56-58	56	-	4

COOLING Roy
Born: Barnsley, South Yorkshire, England, 9 December, 1921 — IF
Died: Barnsley, South Yorkshire, England, 10 April, 2003

League Club	Source	Date Signed	Seasons Played	Apps	Subs	Gls
Barnsley	Mitchell Main	03/42	46	6	-	3
Mansfield T	Tr	09/47	47-49	65	-	14

COOMBE Mark Andrew
Born: Torquay, Devon, England, 17 September, 1968 — G

League Club	Source	Date Signed	Seasons Played	Apps	Subs	Gls
Bristol C	Bournemouth (YT)	08/87				
Colchester U	Carlisle U (NC)	10/88	88	3	0	0
Torquay U	Tr	12/88	88	8	0	0

COOMBES (PHILLIP) Adam Julian
Born: Carshalton, S London, England, 19 June, 1991 — F
England: Youth

League Club	Source	Date Signed	Seasons Played	Apps	Subs	Gls
Chelsea	Sch	07/09				
Yeovil T	L	11/10	10	0	3	0
Notts Co		08/13	13	3	3	0

COOMBES Jeffrey (Jeff)
Born: Ystrad Rhondda, Rhondda Cynon Taff, Wales, 1 April, 1954 — M
Wales: Schools

League Club	Source	Date Signed	Seasons Played	Apps	Subs	Gls
Bristol Rov	App	04/72	72-74	10	1	1

COOMBES Lee Edward
Born: Dinnington, South Yorkshire, England, 5 July, 1966 — FB

League Club	Source	Date Signed	Seasons Played	Apps	Subs	Gls
Sheffield Wed	App	07/84				
Scunthorpe U	Tr	08/85				
Chesterfield	Tr	07/86	86	1	2	0

COOMBS Francis Henry (Frank)
Born: East Ham, E London, England, 24 April, 1925 — G
Died: Colchester, Essex, England, 26 April, 1998

League Club	Source	Date Signed	Seasons Played	Apps	Subs	Gls
Bristol C	Dartford	06/49	49	24	-	0
Southend U	Tr	06/50	50	20	-	0
Colchester U	Tr	07/51	51-53	38	-	0

COOMBS Paul Andrew
Born: Bristol, England, 4 September, 1970 — RW

League Club	Source	Date Signed	Seasons Played	Apps	Subs	Gls
Aldershot	YT	07/89	88-90	9	7	1

COONEY Sean Patrick
Born: Perth, Australia, 31 October, 1983 — FB
Republic of Ireland: U21-1

League Club	Source	Date Signed	Seasons Played	Apps	Subs	Gls
Coventry C	Sch	01/03	02	0	1	0

COOP James Yates (Jim)
Born: Horwich, Greater Manchester, England, 17 September, 1927 — LW
Died: Doncaster, South Yorkshire, England, March, 1996

League Club	Source	Date Signed	Seasons Played	Apps	Subs	Gls
Sheffield U	Brodsworth Main	05/46	47-48	9	-	1
York C	Tr	07/49	49-50	12	-	4

COOP Michael Anthony (Mick)
Born: Grimsby, North Lincolnshire, England, 10 July, 1948 — RB

League Club	Source	Date Signed	Seasons Played	Apps	Subs	Gls
Coventry C	App	01/66	66-80	413	12	18
York C	L	11/74	74	4	0	0
Derby Co	Tr	07/81	81	17	1	0

COOPER Adrian Stanley John
Born: Reading, England, 16 January, 1957 — M
England: Schools

League Club	Source	Date Signed	Seasons Played	Apps	Subs	Gls
Reading	App	01/75	73-75	14	0	2

COOPER Arthur
Born: Etruria, Potteries, England, 16 March, 1921 — LH
Died: Cheshire, England, December, 2008

League Club	Source	Date Signed	Seasons Played	Apps	Subs	Gls
Port Vale	Shelton St Mark's	08/41	46	4	-	0

COOPER Charles (Charlie)
Born: Farnworth, Greater Manchester, England, 14 June, 1941 — LB

League Club	Source	Date Signed	Seasons Played	Apps	Subs	Gls
Bolton W	Jnr	05/59	60-68	79	4	0
Barrow	Tr	07/69	69-70	54	1	0

COOPER Colin Terence
Born: Trimdon, County Durham, England, 28 February, 1967 — D
England: 2/U21-8

League Club	Source	Date Signed	Seasons Played	Apps	Subs	Gls
Middlesbrough	Jnr	07/84	85-90	183	5	6
Millwall	Tr	07/91	91-92	77	0	6
Nottingham F	Tr	06/93	93-97	179	1	20
Middlesbrough	Tr	08/98	98-05	139	19	5
Sunderland	L	03/04	03	0	3	0

COOPER David Andrew
Born: Lambeth, S London, England, 25 June, 1971 — F

League Club	Source	Date Signed	Seasons Played	Apps	Subs	Gls
Wimbledon	YT	07/89				
Plymouth Arg	Tr	03/91	90	0	3	0

COOPER David Barry Ernest
Born: Welwyn Garden City, Hertfordshire, England, 7 March, 1973 — LB

League Club	Source	Date Signed	Seasons Played	Apps	Subs	Gls
Exeter C	Luton T (YT)	08/91	91-94	39	9	0

COOPER Douglas (Doug)
Born: Eston, Cleveland, England, 18 October, 1936 — CF
Died: Stockton-on-Tees, Cleveland, England, 27 July, 1998

League Club	Source	Date Signed	Seasons Played	Apps	Subs	Gls
Middlesbrough	Grangetown BC	10/53	54-56	5	-	0
Rotherham U	Tr	01/59	58	14	-	5
Hartlepool U	Tr	08/60	60	16	-	6

COOPER Frederick John (Fred)
Born: West Ham, E London, England, 18 November, 1934 — FB
Died: Chelsea, W London, England, April, 1972
England: Schools

League Club	Source	Date Signed	Seasons Played	Apps	Subs	Gls
West Ham U	Jnr	12/51	56-57	4	-	0

COOPER Gary
Born: Hammersmith, W London, England, 20 November, 1965 — M
England: Youth/Schools

League Club	Source	Date Signed	Seasons Played	Apps	Subs	Gls
Queens Park Rgrs	App	06/83	84	1	0	0
Brentford	L	09/85	85	9	1	0
Maidstone U	Fisher Ath	03/89	89-90	53	7	7
Peterborough U	Tr	03/91	90-93	83	5	10
Birmingham C	Tr	12/93	93-95	58	4	2

COOPER Gary Smethurst
Born: Horwich, Greater Manchester, England, 15 February, 1955 — F
England: Schools

League Club	Source	Date Signed	Seasons Played	Apps	Subs	Gls
Rochdale	Horwich RMI	12/73	73-76	81	10	14
Southport	Tr	08/77	77	13	7	5

COOPER Geoffrey Victor (Geoff)
Born: Kingston-on-Thames, SW London, England, 27 December, 1960 — LB

League Club	Source	Date Signed	Seasons Played	Apps	Subs	Gls
Brighton & HA	Bognor Regis T	12/87	87-88	2	5	0
Barnet	Tr	07/89	91-92	30	1	1
Barnet	Wycombe W	08/93	93-94	25	12	3

COOPER George
Born: Kingswinford, West Midlands, England, 1 October, 1932 — IF
Died: Kingswinford, West Midlands, England, May, 1994

League Club	Source	Date Signed	Seasons Played	Apps	Subs	Gls
Crystal Palace	Brierley Hill Alliance	01/55	54-58	69	-	27
Rochdale	Tr	01/59	58-59	32	-	9

COOPER George Iain
Born: Warrington, Cheshire, England, 2 November, 1996 — F

League Club	Source	Date Signed	Seasons Played	Apps	Subs	Gls
Crewe Alex	Sch	03/14	14	5	17	3

COOPER Graham
Born: Huddersfield, West Yorkshire, England, 22 May, 1962 — W/F

League Club	Source	Date Signed	Seasons Played	Apps	Subs	Gls
Huddersfield T	Emley	03/84	83-87	61	13	13
Wrexham	Tr	08/88	88-90	50	13	16
York C	L	11/90	90	2	0	0
Halifax T	Northwich Victoria	01/91	90-91	32	7	4

COOPER Ian Laurence
Born: Bradford, England, 21 September, 1946 — LB

League Club	Source	Date Signed	Seasons Played	Apps	Subs	Gls
Bradford C	Jnr	07/65	65-76	442	1	4

COOPER Jake Matthew
Born: Bracknell, Berkshire, England, 3 February, 1995 — CD
England: Youth

League Club	Source	Date Signed	Seasons Played	Apps	Subs	Gls
Reading	Sch	07/13	14	9	6	2

COOPER James Else (Jim)
Born: Blackpool, Lancashire, England, 13 January, 1928 — W
Died: Blackpool, Lancashire, England, March, 2010

League Club	Source	Date Signed	Seasons Played	Apps	Subs	Gls
Accrington Stan	Fleetwood	06/52	52	7	-	1

COOPER James Ernest (Jimmy)
Born: Chester, England, 19 January, 1942 — W

League Club	Source	Date Signed	Seasons Played	Apps	Subs	Gls
Chester C	Jnr	09/59	59-61	91	-	17
Southport	Tr	06/62	62	28	-	7
Blackpool	Tr	07/63	63	4	-	0
Mansfield T	Tr	05/64	64	7	-	4
Crewe Alex	Tr	07/65	65	6	0	0

COOPER James Thomson (Jim)
Born: Glasgow, Scotland, 28 December, 1939 — W

League Club	Source	Date Signed	Seasons Played	Apps	Subs	Gls
Brighton & HA	Airdrieonians	08/62	62-63	41	-	6
Hartlepool U	Tr	07/65	65	19	0	1

COOPER Joseph (Joe)
Born: Reddish, Greater Manchester, England, 16 February, 1918 — LB
Died: Reddish, Greater Manchester, England, August, 1992

League Club	Source	Date Signed	Seasons Played	Apps	Subs	Gls
Blackpool	Hurst	01/38				
Crewe Alex	Tr	07/39	46	3	-	0

COOPER Joseph (Joe)
Born: Gateshead, Tyne and Wear, England, 15 October, 1934 — WH

League Club	Source	Date Signed	Seasons Played	Apps	Subs	Gls
Newcastle U	Winlaton Mill	09/52	53-57	6	-	0

COOPER Joseph Mark (Joe)
Born: Saddleworth, Greater Manchester, England, 25 September, 1994 — CD

League Club	Source	Date Signed	Seasons Played	Apps	Subs	Gls
Oldham Ath	Sch	07/13	12	1	0	0

COOPER Kenny Scott
Born: Baltimore, Maryland, USA, 21 October, 1984 — F
USA: 10

League Club	Source	Date Signed	Seasons Played	Apps	Subs	Gls
Manchester U	Dallas Mustangs (USA)	01/04				
Oldham Ath	L	01/05	04	5	2	3
Plymouth Arg (L)	1860 Munich (GER)	02/10	09	0	7	0

COOPER Kevin Lee
Born: Derby, England, 8 February, 1975 — LW

League Club	Source	Date Signed	Seasons Played	Apps	Subs	Gls
Derby Co	YT	07/93	94-95	0	2	0
Stockport Co	Tr	03/97	96-00	146	22	21
Wimbledon	Tr	03/01	00-01	50	1	13
Wolverhampton W	Tr	03/02	01-04	32	30	9
Sunderland	L	01/04	03	0	1	0
Norwich C	L	03/04	03	6	4	0
Cardiff C	Tr	07/05	05-06	31	9	2
Yeovil T	L	09/06	06	4	0	0
Walsall	L	02/07	06	8	0	0
Tranmere Rov	L	10/07	07	3	1	0
Chesterfield	Tr	02/08	07	2	5	1

COOPER Leigh Vernon
Born: Reading, England, 7 May, 1961 — LB

League Club	Source	Date Signed	Seasons Played	Apps	Subs	Gls
Plymouth Arg	App	05/79	79-89	316	7	15
Aldershot	Tr	09/90	90	33	0	2

COOPER Leonard Arnold (Len)
Born: Lower Gornal, West Midlands, England, 11 May, 1936 — LW
Died: Birmingham, England, November, 1992
England: Youth

League Club	Source	Date Signed	Seasons Played	Apps	Subs	Gls
Wolverhampton W	Jnr	05/53				
Walsall		02/56	55	5	-	2

COOPER Liam David Ian
Born: Hull, England, 30 August, 1991 — CD
Scotland: Youth

League Club	Source	Date Signed	Seasons Played	Career Record Apps	Subs	Gls
Hull C	Sch	09/08	09-11	10	1	0
Carlisle U	L	01/11	10	6	0	1
Huddersfield T	L	07/11	11	2	2	0
Chesterfield	Tr	11/12	12-14	68	3	5
Leeds U	Tr	08/14	14	25	4	1

COOPER Mark David
Born: Watford, Hertfordshire, England, 5 April, 1967 — F

League Club	Source	Date Signed	Seasons Played	Apps	Subs	Gls
Cambridge U	App	10/84	83-86	61	9	17
Tottenham H	Tr	04/87				
Shrewsbury T	L	09/87	87	6	0	2
Gillingham	Tr	10/87	87-88	38	11	11
Leyton Orient	Tr	02/89	88-93	117	33	45
Barnet	Tr	07/94	94-95	58	9	19
Northampton T	Tr	08/96	96	37	4	10

COOPER Mark Nicholas
Born: Wakefield, England, 18 December, 1968 — M

League Club	Source	Date Signed	Seasons Played	Apps	Subs	Gls
Bristol C	YT	09/87				
Exeter C	Tr	10/89	89-91	46	4	12
Southend U	L	03/90	89	4	1	0
Birmingham C	Tr	09/91	91-92	30	9	4
Fulham	Tr	11/92	92-93	10	4	0
Huddersfield T	L	03/93	92	10	0	4
Wycombe W	Tr	01/94	93	0	2	1
Exeter C	Tr	02/94	93-95	78	10	20
Hartlepool U	Tr	07/96	96	33	0	9
Macclesfield T	L	09/97	97	8	0	2
Leyton Orient	Tr	12/97	97	0	1	0

COOPER Neale James
Born: Darjeeling, India, 24 November, 1963 — DM
Scotland: U21-13/Youth

League Club	Source	Date Signed	Seasons Played	Apps	Subs	Gls
Aston Villa	Aberdeen	07/86	86-87	19	1	0
Reading	Glasgow Rangers	07/91	91	6	1	0

COOPER Neil
Born: Aberdeen, Scotland, 12 August, 1959 — M/D
Scotland: Youth/Schools

League Club	Source	Date Signed	Seasons Played	Apps	Subs	Gls
Barnsley	Aberdeen	01/80	79-81	57	3	6
Grimsby T	Tr	03/82	81-83	47	0	2

COOPER Paul
Born: Darlington, County Durham, England, 24 December, 1975 — M

League Club	Source	Date Signed	Seasons Played	Apps	Subs	Gls
Darlington	YT	07/93	93	1	0	0

COOPER Paul David
Born: Brierley Hill, West Midlands, England, 21 December, 1953 — G

League Club	Source	Date Signed	Seasons Played	Apps	Subs	Gls
Birmingham C	App	07/71	71-73	17	0	0
Ipswich T	Tr	03/74	73-86	447	0	0
Leicester C	Tr	06/87	87-88	56	0	0
Manchester C	Tr	03/89	88-89	15	0	0
Stockport Co	Tr	08/90	90	22	0	0

COOPER Paul Terence
Born: Birmingham, England, 12 July, 1957 — FB

League Club	Source	Date Signed	Seasons Played	Apps	Subs	Gls
Huddersfield T	App	08/75	76	2	0	0
Grimsby T	Tr	07/77	77	3	0	0

COOPER Richard Anthony
Born: Nottingham, England, 27 September, 1979 — M/D
England: Youth/Schools

League Club	Source	Date Signed	Seasons Played	Apps	Subs	Gls
Nottingham F	YT	10/96	99-00	0	3	0
York C	Tr	03/01	00-03	84	16	4

COOPER Richard David
Born: Wembley, NW London, England, 7 May, 1965 — M

League Club	Source	Date Signed	Seasons Played	Apps	Subs	Gls
Sheffield U	App	05/83	82-84	2	4	0
Lincoln C	Tr	08/85	85-86	57	4	2
Exeter C	Tr	07/87	87-88	55	7	2

COOPER Robert Charles (Bobby)
Born: Sutton Coldfield, West Midlands, England, 3 September, 1966 — M

League Club	Source	Date Signed	Seasons Played	Apps	Subs	Gls
Leicester C	App	05/85				
Preston NE	L	12/85	85	3	2	0

COOPER Ronald (Ron)
Born: Peterborough, England, 28 August, 1938 — D

League Club	Source	Date Signed	Seasons Played	Apps	Subs	Gls
Peterborough U	Jnr	07/60	63-67	132	0	1

COOPER Shaun David
Born: Newport, Isle of Wight, England, 5 October, 1983 — FB

League Club	Source	Date Signed	Seasons Played	Apps	Subs	Gls
Portsmouth	YT	04/01	01	3	4	0
Leyton Orient	L	10/03	03	9	0	0
Kidderminster Hrs	L	09/04	04	10	0	0
Bournemouth	Tr	08/05	05-11	194	17	1
Crawley T	Tr	07/12	12	5	3	0
Portsmouth	L	01/13	12	13	1	2
Portsmouth	Tr	09/13	13	7	2	0
Torquay U	Tr	01/14				

COOPER Stephen Brian (Steve)
Born: Birmingham, England, 22 June, 1964 — F
Died: Warley, West Midlands, England, 15 February, 2004

League Club	Source	Date Signed	Seasons Played	Apps	Subs	Gls
Birmingham C	Moor Green	11/83				
Halifax T	L	12/83	83	7	0	1
Newport Co	Tr	09/84	84	38	0	11
Plymouth Arg	Tr	08/85	85-87	58	15	15
Barnsley	Tr	08/88	88-90	62	15	13
Tranmere Rov	Tr	12/90	90-92	16	16	3
Peterborough U	L	03/92	91	2	7	0
Wigan Ath	L	12/92	92	4	0	0
York C	Tr	08/93	93-94	37	1	6

COOPER Steven Milne (Steve)
Born: Stourbridge, West Midlands, England, 14 December, 1955 — F
England: Youth

League Club	Source	Date Signed	Seasons Played	Apps	Subs	Gls
Torquay U	Stourbridge	03/78	77-83	219	15	76

COOPER Terence (Terry)
Born: Brotherton, West Yorkshire, England, 12 July, 1944 — LB
England: 20

League Club	Source	Date Signed	Seasons Played	Apps	Subs	Gls
Leeds U	App	07/62	63-74	240	10	7
Middlesbrough	Tr	03/75	74-77	105	0	1
Bristol C	Tr	07/78	78	11	0	0
Bristol Rov	Tr	08/79	79-81	53	6	0
Doncaster Rov	Tr	11/81	81	20	0	0
Bristol C	Tr	08/82	82-84	38	22	1

COOPER Terence (Terry)
Born: Cwmbran, Torfaen, Wales, 11 March, 1950 — CD

League Club	Source	Date Signed	Seasons Played	Apps	Subs	Gls
Newport Co	Jnr	07/68	67-69	65	3	1
Notts Co	Tr	07/70	71-72	3	6	0
Lincoln C	L	12/71	71	3	0	0
Lincoln C	Tr	08/72	72-78	265	2	12
Scunthorpe U	L	11/77	77	4	0	0
Bradford C	Tr	06/79	79-80	47	1	2
Rochdale	Tr	08/81	81	35	0	2

COOPER William George Edward
Born: York, England, 2 November, 1917 — IF
Died: Halifax, West Yorkshire, England, 1978

League Club	Source	Date Signed	Seasons Played	Apps	Subs	Gls
Halifax T (Am)	Chesterfield (Am)	03/39	38	2	-	0
Bradford C		09/46	46-47	7	-	4
Rochdale	Tr	08/48				

COOTE Adrian
Born: Great Yarmouth, Norfolk, England, 30 September, 1978 — F
Northern Ireland: 6/B-1/U21-12

League Club	Source	Date Signed	Seasons Played	Apps	Subs	Gls
Norwich C	YT	07/97	97-00	20	34	3
Colchester U	Tr	12/01	01-02	12	23	4
Bristol Rov	L	10/02	02	4	1	1

COOTE Kenneth Alexander (Ken)
Born: Paddington, Central London, England, 19 May, 1928 — D
Died: Isleworth, W London, England, 2 August, 2003

League Club	Source	Date Signed	Seasons Played	Apps	Subs	Gls
Brentford	Wembley T	05/49	49-63	514	-	14

COPE Charles Anthony (Tony)
Born: Doncaster, South Yorkshire, England, 17 January, 1941 — WH
Died: Doncaster, South Yorkshire, England, 3 November, 2009

League Club	Source	Date Signed	Seasons Played	Apps	Subs	Gls
Doncaster Rov	Jnr	09/58	58-59	8	-	0

COPE James Andrew
Born: Solihull, West Midlands, England, 4 October, 1977 — M

League Club	Source	Date Signed	Seasons Played	Apps	Subs	Gls
Shrewsbury T	YT	07/96	95-96	3	1	0

COPE Ronald (Ron)
Born: Crewe, Cheshire, England, 5 October, 1934 — CH
England: Schools

League Club	Source	Date Signed	Seasons Played	Apps	Subs	Gls
Manchester U	Jnr	10/51	56-60	93	-	2
Luton T	Tr	08/61	61-62	28	-	0

COPELAND Edward (Teddy)
Born: Hetton-le-Hole, Tyne and Wear, England, 19 May, 1921 — RW
Died: Newcastle-upon-Tyne, England, July, 2001

League Club	Source	Date Signed	Seasons Played	Apps	Subs	Gls
Hartlepool U	Easington CW	06/44	46-47	38	-	9

COPELAND Michael Wilfred (Mike)
Born: Newport, Wales, 31 December, 1954 — FB

League Club	Source	Date Signed	Seasons Played	Apps	Subs	Gls
Newport Co	Jnr	07/73	73	3	1	0

COPELAND Simon Dean
Born: Sheffield, England, 10 October, 1968 — RB

League Club	Source	Date Signed	Seasons Played	Apps	Subs	Gls
Sheffield U	App	06/87				
Rochdale	Tr	07/88	88	27	1	0

COPELAND William Philip (Phil)
Born: Workington, Cumbria, England, 16 September, 1936 — D

League Club	Source	Date Signed	Seasons Played	Apps	Subs	Gls
Workington		02/57	60-62	11	-	0

COPESTAKE Oliver Francis Reginald
Born: Mansfield, Nottinghamshire, England, 1 September, 1921 — IF
Died: Mansfield, Nottinghamshire, England, 25 December, 1953

League Club	Source	Date Signed	Seasons Played	Apps	Subs	Gls
Mansfield T	Church Warsop	01/46	46	33	-	7

COPLEY Dennis Irwin
Born: Misterton, Nottinghamshire, England, 21 December, 1921 — IF
Died: Washingborough, Lincolnshire, England, 18 October, 2006

League Club	Source	Date Signed	Seasons Played	Apps	Subs	Gls
Lincoln C	Lincoln Rov	09/46	46	1	-	0

COPLEY Gary
Born: Rotherham, South Yorkshire, England, 30 December, 1960 — G

League Club	Source	Date Signed	Seasons Played	Apps	Subs	Gls
Barnsley	App	01/79	78	1	0	0

COPP Leonard James Henry (Lenny)
Born: Aberystwyth, Ceredigion, Wales, 7 October, 1940 — IF
Died: Swansea, Wales, January, 2003

League Club	Source	Date Signed	Seasons Played	Apps	Subs	Gls
Leeds U	Jnr	10/57				
Shrewsbury T	Tr	07/58	60	2	-	1

COPPELL Stephen James (Steve)
Born: Liverpool, England, 9 July, 1955 — RW
England: 42/FLge/U23-1

League Club	Source	Date Signed	Seasons Played	Apps	Subs	Gls
Tranmere Rov	Liverpool Univ	01/74	73-74	35	3	10
Manchester U	Tr	02/75	74-82	320	2	54

COPPINGER James
Born: Middlesbrough, England, 10 January, 1981 — RW
England: Youth

League Club	Source	Date Signed	Seasons Played	Apps	Subs	Gls
Newcastle U	Darlington (YT)	03/98	00	0	1	0
Hartlepool U	L	03/00	99	6	4	3
Hartlepool U	L	01/02	01	14	0	2
Exeter C	Tr	08/02	02	35	8	5
Doncaster Rov	Tr	07/04	04-14	346	48	40
Nottingham F	L	08/12	12	2	4	0

COQUELIN Francis
Born: Laval, France, 13 May, 1991 — DM
France: U21-7/Youth

League Club	Source	Date Signed	Seasons Played	Apps	Subs	Gls
Arsenal	Stade Lavallois (FRA)	07/08	11-14	28	15	0
Charlton Ath	L	11/14	14	3	2	0

CORAZZIN Giancarlo Michele (Carlo)
Born: Vancouver, Canada, 25 December, 1971 — F
Canada: 58

League Club	Source	Date Signed	Seasons Played	Apps	Subs	Gls
Cambridge U	Vancouver W'caps (CAN)	12/93	93-95	104	1	39
Plymouth Arg	Tr	03/96	95-97	61	13	22
Northampton T	Tr	07/98	98-99	63	15	30
Oldham Ath	Tr	07/00	00-02	82	28	20

CORBETT Alexander McLennan (Alex)
Born: Saltcoats, Ayrshire, Scotland, 20 April, 1921 — G
Died: Gravesend, Kent, England, March, 2000

League Club	Source	Date Signed	Seasons Played	Apps	Subs	Gls
New Brighton	Ayr U	07/46	46-47	58	-	0
Hull C	Tr	01/48	47	8	-	0
Hartlepool U	Weymouth	07/53	53	7	-	0

CORBETT Andrew John (Andy)
Born: Worcester, England, 20 February, 1982 — RB

League Club	Source	Date Signed	Seasons Played	Apps	Subs	Gls
Kidderminster Hrs	Jnr	07/00	00-01	3	5	0
Burton A	Nuneaton Bor	11/03	09-12	99	13	2

CORBETT Anthony (Tony)
Born: Bilston, West Midlands, England, 28 April, 1940 — FB
England: Youth

League Club	Source	Date Signed	Seasons Played	Apps	Subs	Gls
Wolverhampton W	Jnr	05/59				
Shrewsbury T	Tr	07/60	60-61	8	-	0

CORBETT Arthur Beech
Born: Birmingham, England, 17 August, 1928 — IF
Died: Birmingham, England, September, 2009

League Club	Source	Date Signed	Seasons Played	Apps	Subs	Gls
Walsall	Sutton T	12/49	49-50	25	-	5

CORBETT David Frank (Dave)
Born: Marshfield, Avon, England, 15 May, 1940 — RW

League Club	Source	Date Signed	Seasons Played	Apps	Subs	Gls
Swindon T	Jnr	08/58	58-61	68	-	3
Plymouth Arg	Tr	02/62	61-66	84	0	8

CORBETT George
Born: North Walbottle, Tyne and Wear, England, 11 May, 1925 — LW
Died: Newcastle-upon-Tyne, England, June, 1999

League Club	Source	Date Signed	Seasons Played	Apps	Subs	Gls
Sheffield Wed	Shildon	05/45				
West Bromwich A	Spennymoor U	03/51	51	1	-	0
Workington	Tr	07/53	53	9	-	0

CORBETT James John (Jimmy)
Born: Hackney, E London, England, 6 July, 1980 — W

League Club	Source	Date Signed	Seasons Played	Apps	Subs	Gls
Gillingham	YT	01/98	97	8	8	2
Blackburn Rov	Tr	05/98				
Darlington	L	02/03	02	9	1	2
Southend U	Tr	07/03	03-04	14	9	2

CORBETT John Thomas
Born: Bromley-by-Bow, E London, England, 9 January, 1920 — IF
Died: Gillingham, Dorset, England, 26 August, 2005

League Club	Source	Date Signed	Seasons Played	Apps	Subs	Gls
Hartlepool U	Army	09/43				
Swansea C	Tr	08/45				
Crystal Palace	Tr	09/46	46	1	-	1

CORBETT Luke John
Born: Worcester, England, 10 August, 1984 — F

League Club	Source	Date Signed	Seasons Played	Apps	Subs	Gls
Cheltenham T	Jnr	01/03	03	0	1	0

CORBETT Norman George (Norrie)
Born: Falkirk, Scotland, 23 June, 1919 — RH
Died: Derby, England, June, 1990

League Club	Source	Date Signed	Seasons Played	Apps	Subs	Gls
West Ham U	Heart of Midlothian	04/37	36-49	166	-	3

CORBETT Patrick Avalon (Pat)
Born: Hackney, E London, England, 12 February, 1963 — CD
England: Youth

League Club	Source	Date Signed	Seasons Played	Apps	Subs	Gls
Tottenham H	App	10/80	81-82	3	2	1
Leyton Orient	Tr	08/83	83-85	77	0	2

CORBETT Peter
Born: Preston, Lancashire, England, 5 March, 1934 — G
Died: Longridge, Lancashire, England, 2 July, 2007

League Club	Source	Date Signed	Seasons Played	Apps	Subs	Gls
Preston NE		06/56				
Workington	Tr	08/57	57-58	11	-	0
Oldham Ath	Tr	07/59	59	10	-	0

CORBETT Robert (Bobby)
Born: Throckley, Tyne and Wear, England, 16 March, 1922 — LB
Died: Newcastle-upon-Tyne, England, October, 1988

League Club	Source	Date Signed	Seasons Played	Apps	Subs	Gls
Newcastle U	Throckley Welfare	08/43	46-51	46	-	1
Middlesbrough	Tr	12/51	51-56	92	-	0
Northampton T	Tr	08/57	57	8	-	1

CORBETT William
Born: Wolverhampton, England, 29 July, 1920 — LB
Died: Teignbridge, Devon, England, February, 2007

League Club	Source	Date Signed	Seasons Played	Apps	Subs	Gls
Doncaster Rov		01/42	46-47	37	-	0
Bristol C	Tr	06/48	48	1	-	0

CORBETT William Risk (Willie)
Born: Falkirk, Scotland, 31 August, 1922 — CH
Died: Bonnybridge, Falkirk, Scotland, 1 August, 2011
Scotland: War-1

League Club	Source	Date Signed	Seasons Played	Apps	Subs	Gls
Preston NE	Glasgow Celtic	06/48	48	19	-	0
Leicester C	Tr	08/49	49	16	-	0

CORBIN Kirk DeVere
Born: Barbados, 12 March, 1955 — RB

League Club	Source	Date Signed	Seasons Played	Apps	Subs	Gls
Cambridge U	Wokingham T	01/78	78	3	0	0

CORBISHLEY Colin
Born: Stoke-on-Trent, England, 13 June, 1939 — LH

League Club	Source	Date Signed	Seasons Played	Apps	Subs	Gls
Port Vale		10/59	60-61	11	-	0
Chester C	Tr	08/62	62-64	83	-	11

CORBISIERO Antonio Giovanni
Born: Exeter, England, 17 November, 1984 — M

League Club	Source	Date Signed	Seasons Played	Apps	Subs	Gls
Swansea C	Sch	07/04	03	1	4	0

CORBO Mateo Andres
Born: Montevideo, Uruguay, 21 April, 1976 — M/LB

League Club	Source	Date Signed	Seasons Played	Apps	Subs	Gls
Barnsley	Real Oviedo (SPN)	08/00	00-01	10	8	0
Oxford U	Olimpia Asuncion (PAR)	01/05	04	13	0	0

CORCORAN Samuel Joseph (Sam)
Born: Enfield, N London, England, 5 February, 1991 — M

League Club	Source	Date Signed	Seasons Played	Apps	Subs	Gls
Colchester U	Sch	07/09	08	0	1	0

CORDELL John Graham (Graham)
Born: Walsall, West Midlands, England, 6 December, 1928 — G
Died: Nottingham, England, 9 September, 1984

League Club	Source	Date Signed	Seasons Played	Apps	Subs	Gls
Aston Villa	Walsall Star	09/49	51-52	5	-	0
Rochdale	Tr	05/53	53-54	15	-	0

CORDEN Simon Wayne (Wayne)
Born: Leek, Staffordshire, England, 1 November, 1975 — LW

League Club	Source	Date Signed	Seasons Played	Apps	Subs	Gls
Port Vale	YT	09/94	94-99	30	36	1
Mansfield T	Tr	07/00	00-04	173	19	35
Scunthorpe U	Tr	02/05	04-05	8	9	0
Chester C	L	01/06	05	2	0	0
Leyton Orient	Tr	03/06	05-07	61	15	5
Notts Co	L	03/08	07	7	2	0

CORDEN Stephen (Steve)
Born: Eston, Cleveland, England, 9 January, 1967 — M

League Club	Source	Date Signed	Seasons Played	Apps	Subs	Gls
Middlesbrough	App	06/84	85	1	0	0

League Club	Source	Date Signed	Seasons Played	Career Record Apps	Subs	Gls

CORDER Peter Robert
Born: Loughton, Essex, England, 12 December, 1966 G

Tottenham H	App	10/84				
Peterborough U	L	10/85	85	2	0	0

CORDICE Neil Anthony
Born: Amersham, Buckinghamshire, England, 7 April, 1960 F

Northampton T	Flackwell Heath	07/78	78	4	4	1

CORDJOHN Barry Ronald
Born: Oxford, England, 5 September, 1942 RB

Charlton Ath	Jnr	06/60				
Aldershot	Tr	07/63				
Portsmouth	Tr	07/64	64	14	-	0

CORDNER Scott
Born: Derby, England, 3 August, 1972 M

Chesterfield	YT	-	90	1	3	1

CORDONE Carlos Daniel (Daniel)
Born: Buenos Aires, Argentina, 6 November, 1974 F

Newcastle U (L)	Racing Club (ARG)	08/00	00	12	9	2

CORE Frank
Born: Halifax, West Yorkshire, England, 5 September, 1932 WH

Halifax T (Am)	Nottingham Univ	09/53	53	1	-	0

CORE John
Born: Ripponden, West Yorkshire, England, 29 March, 1929 CF

Halifax T (Am)	Leeds Univ	09/49	49-50	28	-	15

CORFIELD Ernest (Ernie)
Born: Wigan, Greater Manchester, England, 18 January, 1931 IF
Died: Wigan, Greater Manchester, England, 26 October, 2013

Bolton W	Jnr	04/48	49-51	6	-	0
Stockport Co	Tr	07/53	53	2	-	0

CORICA Stephen Christopher (Steve)
Born: Cairns, Queensland, Australia, 24 March, 1973 RW
Australia: 32/U23-7/Youth

Leicester C	Marconi (AUS)	08/95	95	16	0	2
Wolverhampton W	Tr	02/96	95-99	80	20	5
Walsall	San. Hiroshima (JPN)	02/02	01-03	63	10	9

CORISH Robert (Bob)
Born: Liverpool, England, 13 September, 1958 FB

Derby Co	Jnr	08/76	77	0	1	0

CORK Alan Graham
Born: Derby, England, 4 March, 1959 F

Derby Co	Jnr	07/77				
Lincoln C	L	09/77	77	5	0	0
Wimbledon	Tr	02/78	77-91	352	78	145
Sheffield U	Tr	03/92	91-93	25	29	7
Fulham	Tr	08/94	94	11	4	3

CORK David
Born: Doncaster, South Yorkshire, England, 8 October, 1959 M

Manchester U	App	10/76				
Doncaster Rov	Tr	08/78	78-79	9	0	1

CORK David
Born: Doncaster, South Yorkshire, England, 28 October, 1962 F

Arsenal	App	06/80	83	5	2	1
Huddersfield T	Tr	07/85	85-87	104	6	25
West Bromwich A	L	09/88	88	1	3	0
Scunthorpe U	Tr	02/89	88	8	7	0
Darlington	Tr	07/89	90-91	53	11	11

CORK Jack Frank Porteous
Born: Carshalton, S London, England, 25 June, 1989 DM
England: U21-13/Youth

Chelsea	Sch	07/06				
Bournemouth	L	11/06	06	7	0	0
Scunthorpe U	L	08/07	07	32	2	2
Southampton	L	08/08	08	22	1	0
Watford	L	01/09	08	18	1	0
Coventry C	L	08/09	09	20	1	0
Burnley	L	02/10	09	8	3	1
Burnley	L	08/10	10	36	4	3
Southampton	Tr	07/11	11-14	93	21	2
Swansea C	Tr	01/15	14	15	0	1

CORKAIN Stephen (Steve)
Born: Stockton-on-Tees, Cleveland, England, 25 February, 1967 M

Hull C	Jnr	06/85	86	5	0	1

CORKER Ashley James
Born: Marske, Cleveland, England, 18 September, 1990 LB

Northampton T	Horden CW	07/11	11	9	7	0

CORKHILL Robert Douglas
Born: Barrow, Cumbria, England, 20 November, 1943 LW

Barrow	Holker Central OB	08/63	63-64	8	-	1

CORKHILL William Grant (Bill)
Born: Belfast, Northern Ireland, 23 April, 1910 WH
Died: Nottingham, England, 9 August, 1978

Notts Co	Marine	05/31	31-37	166	-	9
Cardiff C	Tr	05/38	38	23	-	0
Notts Co	Tr	11/45	46-51	98	-	0

CORLUKA Vedran
Born: Zagreb, Croatia, 5 February, 1986 RB
Croatia: 82/U21-9/Youth

Manchester C	Dinamo Zagreb (CRO)	08/07	07-08	37	1	1
Tottenham H	Tr	09/08	08-11	76	5	1

CORMACK Peter Barr
Born: Edinburgh, Scotland, 17 July, 1946 M
Scotland: 9/SLge-6/U23-5/Amateur

Nottingham F	Hibernian	03/70	69-71	74	0	15
Liverpool	Tr	07/72	72-75	119	6	21
Bristol C	Tr	11/76	76-79	59	8	15

CORNEILLE Mark Paul
Born: Camberwell, S London, England, 31 May, 1986 RB

Gillingham	Jnr	08/05	05	0	2	0

CORNELIUS Andreas Evald
Born: Copenhagen, Denmark, 16 March, 1993 F
Denmark: 8/U21-5/Youth

Cardiff C	FC Copenhagen (DEN)	06/13	13	0	8	0

CORNELL David Joseph
Born: Gorseinon, Swansea, Wales, 28 March, 1991 G
Wales: U21-4/Youth

Swansea C	Sch	07/09				
Hereford U	L	08/11	11	25	0	0

CORNELLY Christopher (Chris)
Born: Huddersfield, West Yorkshire, England, 7 July, 1976 M

Lincoln C	Ashton U	12/02	02	9	7	0

CORNER Brian
Born: Glasgow, Scotland, 6 January, 1961 M

Fulham	App	01/79	80	1	2	0

CORNER David Edward
Born: Sunderland, England, 15 May, 1966 CD
England: Youth

Sunderland	App	04/84	84-87	33	0	1
Cardiff C	L	09/85	85	6	0	0
Peterborough U	L	03/88	87	9	0	0
Leyton Orient	Tr	07/88	88	4	0	0
Darlington	Tr	07/89	90	13	2	0

CORNER James Norman (Norman)
Born: Horden, County Durham, England, 16 February, 1943 F/CD
Died: Horden, County Durham, England, 19 February, 2011

Hull C	Horden CW	08/62	63-66	5	0	4
Lincoln C	Tr	10/67	67-68	44	1	12
Bradford C	Tr	01/69	68-71	105	5	16

CORNES Christopher Richard (Chris)
Born: Worcester, England, 20 December, 1986 M

Wolverhampton W	Sch	03/05				
Port Vale	L	08/05	05	7	3	3

CORNES James Stuart (Stuart)
Born: Usk, Monmouthshire, Wales, 4 March, 1960 CD

Hereford U	App	01/78	77-81	91	2	3

CORNFIELD Allen Henry
Born: Dudley, West Midlands, England, 19 December, 1940 LW
Died: Dudley, West Midlands, England, December, 2007

Shrewsbury T	Lower Gornal Ath	11/59	59-61	9	-	0

CORNFORTH John Michael
Born: Whitley Bay, Tyne and Wear, England, 7 October, 1967 M
Wales: 2

Sunderland	App	10/85	84-90	21	11	2
Doncaster Rov	L	11/86	86	6	1	3
Shrewsbury T	L	11/89	89	3	0	0
Lincoln C	L	01/90	89	9	0	1
Swansea C	Tr	08/91	91-95	147	2	16
Birmingham C	Tr	03/96	95	8	0	0
Wycombe W	Tr	12/96	96-98	35	12	6
Peterborough U	L	02/98	97	3	1	0
Cardiff C	Tr	08/99	99	6	4	1
Scunthorpe U	Tr	11/99	99	2	2	1
Exeter C	Tr	02/00	99-00	23	1	2

CORNISH Ricky George
Born: Newham, E London, England, 1 December, 1970 LB

League Club	Source	Date Signed	Seasons Played	Apps	Subs	Gls
Aldershot	Cornard U	11/90	90	7	2	0

CORNOCK Walter Berkeley (Wally)
Born: Sydney, Australia, 1 January, 1921 G
Died: New South Wales, Australia, 20 November, 2007

League Club	Source	Date Signed	Seasons Played	Apps	Subs	Gls
Oldham Ath	Royton Amats	01/41				
Rochdale	Hereford U	11/47	47	1	-	0

CORNWALL Lucas Clarence (Luke)
Born: Lambeth, S London, England, 23 July, 1980 F

League Club	Source	Date Signed	Seasons Played	Apps	Subs	Gls
Fulham	YT	07/98	98	1	3	1
Grimsby T	L	03/01	00	9	1	4
Lincoln C	L	01/03	02	1	2	0
Bradford C	Tr	07/03	03	2	1	0

CORNWELL Ellis
Born: Coppull, Lancashire, England, 14 November, 1913 FB
Died: Coppull, Lancashire, England, October, 1986

League Club	Source	Date Signed	Seasons Played	Apps	Subs	Gls
Accrington Stan	RAF Kirkham	11/45	46	5	-	0

CORNWELL John Anthony
Born: Bethnal Green, E London, England, 13 October, 1964 M

League Club	Source	Date Signed	Seasons Played	Apps	Subs	Gls
Leyton Orient	App	10/82	81-86	194	9	35
Newcastle U	Tr	07/87	87-88	28	5	1
Swindon T	Tr	12/88	88-89	7	18	0
Southend U	Tr	08/90	90-92	92	9	5
Cardiff C	L	08/93	93	5	0	2
Brentford	L	09/93	93	4	0	0
Northampton T	L	02/94	93	13	0	1

CORNWELL Kevin John
Born: Birmingham, England, 10 December, 1941 IF

League Club	Source	Date Signed	Seasons Played	Apps	Subs	Gls
Oxford U	Banbury Spencer	07/62	62-63	26	-	10

CORR Barry
Born: Wicklow, Republic of Ireland, 2 April, 1985 F
Republic of Ireland: Youth

League Club	Source	Date Signed	Seasons Played	Apps	Subs	Gls
Leeds U	Sch	04/02				
Sheffield Wed	Tr	04/05	05-06	7	10	0
Bristol C	L	10/06	06	1	2	0
Swindon T	Tr	03/07	06-08	17	19	10
Exeter C	Tr	07/09	09	17	17	3
Southend U	Tr	08/10	10-14	110	45	50

CORR John Joseph
Born: Glasgow, Scotland, 18 December, 1946 W

League Club	Source	Date Signed	Seasons Played	Apps	Subs	Gls
Arsenal	Possilpark Jnrs	07/65				
Exeter C	Tr	07/67	67-70	75	6	19

CORR Patrick Malachy (Pat)
Born: Enniskillen, Fermanagh, Northern Ireland, 31 March, 1927 CF
Northern Ireland: NILge-11/Amateur

League Club	Source	Date Signed	Seasons Played	Apps	Subs	Gls
Burnley	Coleraine	10/51	51	1	-	0

CORR Peter Joseph
Born: Dundalk, Republic of Ireland, 22 June, 1923 RW
Died: Preston, Lancashire, England, 27 May, 2001
Republic of Ireland: 4/LoI-2

League Club	Source	Date Signed	Seasons Played	Apps	Subs	Gls
Preston NE	Dundalk (ROI)	04/47	46	3	-	0
Everton	Tr	08/48	48-49	24	-	2

CORRADI Bernardo
Born: Siena, Italy, 30 March, 1976 F
Italy: 13

League Club	Source	Date Signed	Seasons Played	Apps	Subs	Gls
Manchester C	Valencia (SPN)	07/06	06	19	6	3

CORRIGAN Francis Joseph (Frank)
Born: Liverpool, England, 13 November, 1952 M

League Club	Source	Date Signed	Seasons Played	Apps	Subs	Gls
Blackpool	Ormskirk	08/72				
Walsall	Tr	07/73	73	1	0	0
Wigan Ath	Northwich Victoria	01/77	78-80	113	3	12

CORRIGAN Thomas Joseph (Joe)
Born: Sale, Greater Manchester, England, 18 November, 1948 G
England: 9/B-10/FLge/U21-3

League Club	Source	Date Signed	Seasons Played	Apps	Subs	Gls
Manchester C	Sale Moor	01/67	68-82	476	0	0
Brighton & HA	Seattle Sounders (USA)	09/83	83	36	0	0
Norwich C	L	09/84	84	3	0	0
Stoke C	L	10/84	84	9	0	0

CORRY Paul
Born: Dublin, Republic of Ireland, 3 February, 1991 M
Republic of Ireland: U23-1

League Club	Source	Date Signed	Seasons Played	Apps	Subs	Gls
Sheffield Wed	Belvedere (ROI)	08/12	12-13	6	1	0
Tranmere Rov	L	02/13	12	5	1	0
Carlisle U	L	03/15	14	4	2	1

CORT Carl Edward Richard
Born: Bermondsey, SE London, England, 1 November, 1977 F
England: U21-12

League Club	Source	Date Signed	Seasons Played	Apps	Subs	Gls
Wimbledon	YT	06/96	96-99	54	19	16
Lincoln C	L	02/97	96	5	1	1
Newcastle U	Tr	07/00	00-02	19	3	7
Wolverhampton W	Tr	01/04	03-06	78	16	31
Leicester C	Tr	07/07	07	7	7	0
Norwich C	UD Marbella (SPN)	12/08	08	7	5	1
Brentford	Tr	08/09	09-10	16	15	6

CORT Leon Terence Anthony
Born: Bermondsey, SE London, England, 11 September, 1979 CD
Guyana: 6

League Club	Source	Date Signed	Seasons Played	Apps	Subs	Gls
Millwall	Dulwich Hamlet	01/98				
Southend U	Tr	07/01	01-03	135	2	11
Hull C	Tr	07/04	04-05	85	1	10
Crystal Palace	Tr	06/06	06-07	49	0	7
Stoke C	Tr	11/07	07-08	42	2	8
Burnley	Tr	01/10	09-10	18	1	0
Preston NE	L	11/10	10	13	0	0
Charlton Ath	Tr	08/11	11-13	41	7	2

CORTHINE Peter Alan
Born: Highbury, N London, England, 19 July, 1937 IF

League Club	Source	Date Signed	Seasons Played	Apps	Subs	Gls
Chelsea	Leytonstone	12/57	59	2	-	0
Southend U	Tr	03/60	59-61	73	-	24

COSSLETT Michael Paul (Mike)
Born: Barry, Vale of Glamorgan, Wales, 17 April, 1957 CD

League Club	Source	Date Signed	Seasons Played	Apps	Subs	Gls
Newport Co	Barry T	02/78	77-78	2	0	0

COSTA Candido Alves Moreira
Born: Sao Joao da Madeira, Portugal, 30 April, 1981 M

League Club	Source	Date Signed	Seasons Played	Apps	Subs	Gls
Derby Co (L)	FC Porto (POR)	08/03	03	23	11	1

COSTA Jorge Paulo
Born: Oporto, Portugal, 14 October, 1971 CD
Portugal: 51

League Club	Source	Date Signed	Seasons Played	Apps	Subs	Gls
Charlton Ath (L)	FC Porto (POR)	12/01	01	22	2	0

COSTA Ricardo
Born: Lisbon, Portugal, 10 January, 1973 F

League Club	Source	Date Signed	Seasons Played	Apps	Subs	Gls
Darlington (L)	Boavista (POR)	01/99	98	0	3	1

COSTELLO John
Born: Prestonpans, East Lothian, Scotland, 23 March, 1920 RB

League Club	Source	Date Signed	Seasons Played	Apps	Subs	Gls
Southend U	Prestonpans	08/52				
Barrow	Tr	07/53	53	6	-	0

COSTELLO Matthew (Matt)
Born: Airdrie, Lanarkshire, Scotland, 4 August, 1924 W
Died: Melton Mowbray, Leicestershire, England, 27 November, 1987

League Club	Source	Date Signed	Seasons Played	Apps	Subs	Gls
Chesterfield	New Stevenston	05/49	49-51	18	-	2
Chester C	Tr	07/52	52	9	-	2

COSTELLO Mortimer Daniel (Lou)
Born: Dagenham, E London, England, 8 July, 1936 RH/CF
Died: Doddington, Essex, England, 8 August, 2012

League Club	Source	Date Signed	Seasons Played	Apps	Subs	Gls
Aldershot (Am)	Leytonstone	05/56	56	28	-	7
Southend U	Tr	05/57	57-64	251	-	15

COSTELLO Nigel Graham
Born: Catterick Camp, North Yorkshire, England, 22 November, 1968 W

League Club	Source	Date Signed	Seasons Played	Apps	Subs	Gls
York C	YT	07/87	86-87	2	2	0

COSTELLO Peter
Born: Halifax, West Yorkshire, England, 31 October, 1969 M

League Club	Source	Date Signed	Seasons Played	Apps	Subs	Gls
Bradford C	YT	07/88	88-89	11	9	2
Rochdale	Tr	07/90	90	31	3	10
Peterborough U	Tr	03/91	90-92	3	5	0
Lincoln C	L	09/91	91	3	0	0
Lincoln C	Tr	09/92	92-93	28	10	7
Boston U	Kettering T	08/99	02	13	5	0

COSTLY Carlos Yair
Born: San Pedro Sula, Honduras, 17 July, 1982 F
Honduras: 71

League Club	Source	Date Signed	Seasons Played	Apps	Subs	Gls
Birmingham C (L)	GKS Belchatow (POL)	02/09	08	3	5	0

COTHLIFF Harold Thomas
Born: Liverpool, England, 24 March, 1916 RH
Died: New Zealand, 1976

League Club	Source	Date Signed	Seasons Played	Apps	Subs	Gls
Manchester C	Prescot Cables	04/36				
Nottingham F	Tr	05/37				
Torquay U	Tr	06/38	38-47	65	-	1

COTON Anthony Philip (Tony)
Born: Tamworth, Staffordshire, England, 19 May, 1961 G
England: B-1

League Club	Source	Date Signed	Seasons Played	Apps	Subs	Gls
Birmingham C	Mile Oak Rov	10/78	80-84	94	0	0

League Club	Source	Date Signed	Seasons Played	Apps	Subs	Gls
Watford	Tr	09/84	84-89	233	0	0
Manchester C	Tr	07/90	90-94	162	1	0
Manchester U	Tr	01/96				
Sunderland	Tr	07/96	96	10	0	0

COTON Paul Stanley
Born: Birmingham, England, 9 February, 1949 — FB

League Club	Source	Date Signed	Seasons Played	Apps	Subs	Gls
Walsall	App	02/67	66	1	0	0

COTTAM John Edward
Born: Worksop, Nottinghamshire, England, 5 June, 1950 — CD

League Club	Source	Date Signed	Seasons Played	Apps	Subs	Gls
Nottingham F	App	04/68	70-75	92	3	4
Mansfield T	L	11/72	72	2	0	1
Lincoln C	L	03/73	72	1	0	0
Chesterfield	Tr	08/76	76-78	120	0	7
Chester C	Tr	07/79	79-81	117	3	1

COTTEE Anthony Richard (Tony)
Born: West Ham, E London, England, 11 July, 1965 — F
England: 7/U21-8/Youth

League Club	Source	Date Signed	Seasons Played	Apps	Subs	Gls
West Ham U	App	09/82	82-87	203	9	92
Everton	Tr	08/88	88-94	161	23	72
West Ham U	Tr	09/94	94-96	63	4	23
Leicester C	Selangor (MLY)	08/97	97-00	66	19	27
Birmingham C	L	11/97	97	4	1	1
Norwich C	Tr	09/00	00	5	2	1
Barnet	Tr	10/00	00	16	0	9
Millwall	Tr	03/01	00	0	2	0

COTTERELL Leo Spencer
Born: Cambridge, England, 2 September, 1974 — FB
England: Youth/Schools

League Club	Source	Date Signed	Seasons Played	Apps	Subs	Gls
Ipswich T	YT	07/93	94	0	2	0
Bournemouth	Tr	06/96	96	2	7	0

COTTERILL David Rhys George Best
Born: Cardiff, Wales, 4 December, 1987 — RW
Wales: 22/U21-11/Youth

League Club	Source	Date Signed	Seasons Played	Apps	Subs	Gls
Bristol C	Sch	01/05	04-06	48	14	8
Wigan Ath	Tr	08/06	06-07	7	1	1
Sheffield U	Tr	02/08	07-09	35	19	6
Swansea C	Tr	11/09	09-10	24	11	4
Portsmouth	L	02/11	10	12	3	1
Barnsley	Tr	02/12	11	6	5	1
Doncaster Rov	Tr	07/12	12-13	69	15	14
Birmingham C	Tr	06/14	14	42	0	9

COTTERILL James Michael
Born: Barnsley, South Yorkshire, England, 3 August, 1982 — CD

League Club	Source	Date Signed	Seasons Played	Apps	Subs	Gls
Scunthorpe U	YT	07/01	00-02	19	4	0

COTTERILL Stephen John (Steve)
Born: Cheltenham, Gloucestershire, England, 20 July, 1964 — F

League Club	Source	Date Signed	Seasons Played	Apps	Subs	Gls
Wimbledon	Burton A	02/89	88-92	10	7	6
Brighton & HA	L	08/92	92	11	0	4
Bournemouth	Tr	08/93	93-94	44	1	15

COTTEY Philip Anthony (Tony)
Born: Swansea, Wales, 2 June, 1966 — M

League Club	Source	Date Signed	Seasons Played	Apps	Subs	Gls
Swansea C	App	06/84	84	2	1	0

COTTINGTON Brian Anthony
Born: Hammersmith, W London, England, 14 February, 1965 — D

League Club	Source	Date Signed	Seasons Played	Apps	Subs	Gls
Fulham	App	02/83	83-86	67	6	1

COTTON Daniel Lee (Danny)
Born: Northampton, England, 8 April, 1988 — RW

League Club	Source	Date Signed	Seasons Played	Apps	Subs	Gls
Boston U	Blackstone	10/06	06	0	2	0

COTTON Frederick Joseph (Fred)
Born: Halesowen, West Midlands, England, 12 March, 1932 — IF
Died: Dudley, West Midlands, England, 7 November, 1994

League Club	Source	Date Signed	Seasons Played	Apps	Subs	Gls
Crystal Palace		08/56	56	4	-	0

COTTON John
Born: Stoke-on-Trent, England, 2 March, 1930 — RB

League Club	Source	Date Signed	Seasons Played	Apps	Subs	Gls
Stoke C	Port Vale (Am)	05/52	53	2	-	0
Crewe Alex	Tr	10/55	55	14	-	0

COTTON Perry
Born: Chislehurst, SE London, England, 11 November, 1965 — M
New Zealand: 10

League Club	Source	Date Signed	Seasons Played	Apps	Subs	Gls
Scunthorpe U	Nelson U (NZL)	12/88	88-90	24	9	2

COTTON Roy William
Born: Fulham, W London, England, 14 November, 1955 — W
England: Youth

League Club	Source	Date Signed	Seasons Played	Apps	Subs	Gls
Brentford (Am)	Jnr	09/73	73	1	1	0
Leyton Orient	Tr	07/74	75	0	3	0
Aldershot	Tr	07/76	77	5	0	0

COTTON Russell Andrew
Born: Wellington, New Zealand, 4 April, 1960 — M

League Club	Source	Date Signed	Seasons Played	Apps	Subs	Gls
Colchester U	App	04/78	77-81	33	4	1

COTTON Terence (Terry)
Born: Swansea, Wales, 25 January, 1946 — F
Wales: Amateur

League Club	Source	Date Signed	Seasons Played	Apps	Subs	Gls
Swansea C	Ammanford	06/68	68-70	12	0	1

COUCH Alan
Born: Neath, Wales, 15 March, 1953 — M

League Club	Source	Date Signed	Seasons Played	Apps	Subs	Gls
Cardiff C	Jnr	08/70	71-72	7	4	0

COUCH Geoffrey Raymond (Geoff)
Born: Crowle, North Lincolnshire, England, 3 April, 1953 — F

League Club	Source	Date Signed	Seasons Played	Apps	Subs	Gls
Scunthorpe U	Crowle	03/78	77-79	22	4	5

COUGHLAN Derek James
Born: Cork, Republic of Ireland, 2 January, 1977 — CD

League Club	Source	Date Signed	Seasons Played	Apps	Subs	Gls
Brighton & HA	YT	05/95	95	1	0	0

COUGHLAN Graham
Born: Dublin, Republic of Ireland, 18 November, 1974 — CD

League Club	Source	Date Signed	Seasons Played	Apps	Subs	Gls
Blackburn Rov	Bray W (ROI)	10/95				
Swindon T	L	03/97	96	3	0	0
Plymouth Arg	Livingston	06/01	01-04	177	0	25
Sheffield Wed	Tr	07/05	05-06	47	4	5
Burnley	L	03/07	06	1	1	0
Rotherham U	Tr	07/07	07	45	0	1
Shrewsbury T	Tr	08/08	08-09	78	0	6
Southend U	Tr	08/10	10-12	30	8	0

COUGHLIN Andrew Michael
Born: Bootle, Merseyside, England, 31 January, 1993 — G
England: Semi Pro-1

League Club	Source	Date Signed	Seasons Played	Apps	Subs	Gls
Tranmere Rov	Sch	04/11	11	1	1	0

COUGHLIN Dennis Michael
Born: Houghton-le-Spring, Tyne and Wear, England, 26 November, 1937 — CF

League Club	Source	Date Signed	Seasons Played	Apps	Subs	Gls
Barnsley	Durham C	10/57				
Bournemouth	Yeovil T	03/63	62-65	86	2	40
Swansea C	Tr	08/66	66-67	39	1	10
Exeter C	L	03/68	67	13	0	2

COUGHLIN James (Jim)
Born: Cheltenham, Gloucestershire, England, 26 July, 1953 — F

League Club	Source	Date Signed	Seasons Played	Apps	Subs	Gls
Hereford U	Albion Rov	03/77	76	1	1	1

COUGHLIN Russell James
Born: Swansea, Wales, 15 February, 1960 — M
Wales: Youth/Schools

League Club	Source	Date Signed	Seasons Played	Apps	Subs	Gls
Manchester C	App	03/78				
Blackburn Rov	Tr	03/79	78-80	22	2	0
Carlisle U	Tr	10/80	80-83	114	16	13
Plymouth Arg	Tr	07/84	84-87	128	3	18
Blackpool	Tr	12/87	87-89	100	2	8
Shrewsbury T	L	09/90	90	4	1	0
Swansea C	Tr	10/90	90-92	99	2	2
Exeter C	Tr	07/93	93-95	64	4	0
Torquay U	Tr	10/95	95	22	3	0

COULBAULT Regis Arnaud Vincent
Born: Brignoles, Provence, France, 12 August, 1972 — M

League Club	Source	Date Signed	Seasons Played	Apps	Subs	Gls
Southend U	Toulon (FRA)	10/97	97	30	4	4

COULIBALY Mohamed Aly
Born: Bakel, Senegal, 7 August, 1988 — RM

League Club	Source	Date Signed	Seasons Played	Apps	Subs	Gls
Bournemouth	G'hopper Zurich (SUI)	07/13	13	2	5	0
Coventry C	L	07/14	14	1	3	0
Port Vale	L	03/15	14	1	3	0

COULL George Thomson
Born: Dundee, Scotland, 10 August, 1935 — IF

League Club	Source	Date Signed	Seasons Played	Apps	Subs	Gls
Millwall	Dundee Downfield	08/56	56	6	-	1

COULSON Charlie William
Born: Kettering, Northamptonshire, England, 11 January, 1996 — M

League Club	Source	Date Signed	Seasons Played	Apps	Subs	Gls
Peterborough U	Sch	01/13	11	0	1	0

COULSON Joshua David (Josh)
Born: Cambridge, England, 28 January, 1989 — CD
England: Semi Pro-1

League Club	Source	Date Signed	Seasons Played	Apps	Subs	Gls
Cambridge U	Jnr	08/07	14	46	0	1

COULSON Mark David
Born: Huntingdon, Cambridgeshire, England, 11 February, 1986 — M/D

League Club	Source	Date Signed	Seasons Played	Apps	Subs	Gls
Peterborough U	Sch	03/03	04	2	5	0

COULSON Michael James
Born: Scarborough, North Yorkshire, England, 4 April, 1988 — F
England: Semi Pro-2

League Club	Source	Date Signed	Seasons Played	Apps	Subs	Gls
Barnsley	Scarborough	07/06	06-08	1	15	0
Grimsby T	L	11/09	09	28	1	5
York C	Grimsby T	07/12	12-14	78	17	15

COULSON William John (Willie)
Born: North Shields, Tyne and Wear, England, 14 January, 1950 — W

League Club	Source	Date Signed	Seasons Played	Apps	Subs	Gls
Newcastle U	North Shields	09/71				
Southend U	Tr	10/73	73-75	51	1	4
Aldershot	L	02/75	74	3	0	0
Huddersfield T	L	11/75	75	2	0	0
Darlington	L	01/76	75	11	2	1

COULTHIRST Shaquille Tyshaan
Born: Hackney, E London, England, 2 November, 1994 — F

League Club	Source	Date Signed	Seasons Played	Apps	Subs	Gls
Tottenham H	Sch	04/13				
Leyton Orient	L	01/14	13	0	1	1
Torquay U	L	03/14	13	5	1	2
Southend U	L	08/14	14	12	10	4
York C	L	03/15	14	10	1	2

COULTON Thomas Phillip (Tom)
Born: Hatfield, Hertfordshire, England, 15 November, 1992 — G

League Club	Source	Date Signed	Seasons Played	Apps	Subs	Gls
Barnet	Sch	-	10	1	0	0

COUNAGO Pablo
Born: Pontevedra, Spain, 9 August, 1979 — F
Spain: U21-15/Youth

League Club	Source	Date Signed	Seasons Played	Apps	Subs	Gls
Ipswich T	Celta Vigo (SPN)	07/01	01-04	51	49	31
Ipswich T	Malaga (SPN)	07/07	07-09	72	42	23
Crystal Palace	L	08/10	10	17	13	2

COUPE Joseph Norman (Joe)
Born: Carlisle, Cumbria, England, 15 July, 1924 — LB
Died: Plymouth, England, 22 April, 1998

League Club	Source	Date Signed	Seasons Played	Apps	Subs	Gls
Carlisle U	Swift Rov	09/47	48-50	31	-	0
Rochdale	Tr	10/51	51	8	-	0
Workington	Tr	10/52	52	6	-	0

COUPLAND Joseph (Joe)
Born: Glasgow, Scotland, 10 April, 1920 — FB
Died: Connecticut, USA, 14 March, 1989

League Club	Source	Date Signed	Seasons Played	Apps	Subs	Gls
Bradford C	Ayr U	08/50	50-51	18	-	0
Carlisle U	Tr	07/52	52-53	3	-	0

COURT Colin
Born: Winchester, Hampshire, England, 25 March, 1964 — G

League Club	Source	Date Signed	Seasons Played	Apps	Subs	Gls
Reading	Andover T	07/81	81	1	0	0

COURT Colin Raymond
Born: Ebbw Vale, Blaenau Gwent, Wales, 3 September, 1937 — W
Wales: Schools

League Club	Source	Date Signed	Seasons Played	Apps	Subs	Gls
Chelsea	Jnr	09/54				
Torquay U	Tr	05/59	59-60	27	-	5

COURT David John
Born: Mitcham, S London, England, 1 March, 1944 — M

League Club	Source	Date Signed	Seasons Played	Apps	Subs	Gls
Arsenal	App	01/62	62-69	168	7	17
Luton T	Tr	07/70	70-71	50	2	0
Brentford	Tr	08/72	72	8	4	1

COURT Harold John (Jack)
Born: New Tredegar, Caerphilly, Wales, 13 June, 1919 — IF
Died: Rochester, Kent, England, 29 June, 1975

League Club	Source	Date Signed	Seasons Played	Apps	Subs	Gls
Cardiff C	Llanbradach	03/39	38	1	-	0
Swindon T	Dundee	06/50	50	16	-	2

COURTNEY Duane Jerome
Born: Oldbury, West Midlands, England, 7 January, 1985 — CD

League Club	Source	Date Signed	Seasons Played	Apps	Subs	Gls
Burnley	AFC Telford U	08/05	05	1	6	0

COURTOIS Laurent
Born: Lyon, France, 11 September, 1978 — M

League Club	Source	Date Signed	Seasons Played	Apps	Subs	Gls
West Ham U	Toulouse (FRA)	08/01	01	5	2	0

COURTOIS Thibaut Nicolas Marc
Born: Bree, Belgium, 11 May, 1992 — G
Belgium: 31/Youth

League Club	Source	Date Signed	Seasons Played	Apps	Subs	Gls
Chelsea	KRC Genk (BEL)	07/11	14	32	0	0

COUSANS William Eric (Eric)
Born: Doncaster, South Yorkshire, England, 10 September, 1929 — W

League Club	Source	Date Signed	Seasons Played	Apps	Subs	Gls
Walsall	Goole T	08/54	54	4	-	1
Gillingham	Tr	09/55	55	2	-	0

COUSIN Daniel Michel
Born: Libreville, Gabon, 2 February, 1977 — F
Gabon: 31

League Club	Source	Date Signed	Seasons Played	Apps	Subs	Gls
Hull C	Glasgow Rangers	09/08	08-09	19	11	4

COUSINS Anthony James (Tony)
Born: Dublin, Republic of Ireland, 25 August, 1969 — F
Republic of Ireland: U21-6

League Club	Source	Date Signed	Seasons Played	Apps	Subs	Gls
Liverpool	Dundalk (ROI)	10/90				
Hereford U	L	11/92	92	3	0	0

COUSINS Harold (Harry)
Born: Pilsley, Derbyshire, England, 25 September, 1907 — WH
Died: Swindon, England, 21 October, 1981

League Club	Source	Date Signed	Seasons Played	Apps	Subs	Gls
Chesterfield	North Wingfield	10/26	26-31	86	-	0
Swindon T	Tr	08/32	32-46	272	-	1

COUSINS Jason Michael
Born: Hayes, W London, England, 14 October, 1970 — D

League Club	Source	Date Signed	Seasons Played	Apps	Subs	Gls
Brentford	YT	07/89	89-90	20	1	0
Wycombe W	Tr	07/91	93-01	270	26	6

COUSINS Jordan Paul
Born: Greenwich, SE London, England, 6 March, 1994 — DM
England: Youth

League Club	Source	Date Signed	Seasons Played	Apps	Subs	Gls
Charlton Ath	Sch	07/11	13-14	80	6	5

COUSINS Kenneth Frank (Ken)
Born: Bristol, England, 6 August, 1922 — G
Died: Bristol, England, 11 October, 2007

League Club	Source	Date Signed	Seasons Played	Apps	Subs	Gls
Bristol C	Brislington	03/46	46	3	-	0

COUSINS Mark Richard
Born: Chelmsford, England, 9 January, 1987 — G

League Club	Source	Date Signed	Seasons Played	Apps	Subs	Gls
Colchester U	Sch	07/06	07-12	55	3	0
Dagenham & Red	Tr	06/14	14	37	0	0

COUTINHO Phillipe
Born: Rio de Janeiro, Brazil, 12 June, 1992 — M/F
Brazil: 11/Youth

League Club	Source	Date Signed	Seasons Played	Apps	Subs	Gls
Liverpool	Inter Milan (ITA)	01/13	12-14	72	9	13

COUTTS James Ryan
Born: Weymouth, Dorset, England, 15 April, 1987 — M

League Club	Source	Date Signed	Seasons Played	Apps	Subs	Gls
Bournemouth	Southampton (Jnr)	07/04	04-05	0	12	0

COUTTS Paul Alexander
Born: Aberdeen, Scotland, 22 July, 1988 — M
Scotland: U21-7

League Club	Source	Date Signed	Seasons Played	Apps	Subs	Gls
Peterborough U	Cove Rgrs	07/08	08-09	47	6	0
Preston NE	Tr	02/10	09-11	71	6	4
Derby Co	Tr	07/12	12-14	47	12	3
Sheffield U	Tr	01/15	14	19	1	0

COUTTS Roger Alexander
Born: Barrow, Cumbria, England, 18 December, 1944 — RW

League Club	Source	Date Signed	Seasons Played	Apps	Subs	Gls
Barrow	Walney Rov	08/64	64	2	-	0

COUZENS Andrew (Andy)
Born: Shipley, West Yorkshire, England, 4 June, 1975 — M
England: U21-3

League Club	Source	Date Signed	Seasons Played	Apps	Subs	Gls
Leeds U	YT	03/93	94-96	17	11	1
Carlisle U	Tr	07/97	97-98	28	14	2
Blackpool	Tr	03/99	98-99	18	3	0

COVERDALE Andrew (Drew)
Born: Middlesbrough, England, 20 September, 1969 — LB/M

League Club	Source	Date Signed	Seasons Played	Apps	Subs	Gls
Middlesbrough	YT	07/88				
Darlington	Tr	07/89	90-91	24	6	3

COWAN Donald (Don)
Born: Sherburn, County Durham, England, 17 August, 1931 — G

League Club	Source	Date Signed	Seasons Played	Apps	Subs	Gls
Darlington	Middlesbrough (Am)	11/52	52-53	17	-	0

COWAN Donald (Don)
Born: New York, USA, 16 November, 1989 — F

League Club	Source	Date Signed	Seasons Played	Apps	Subs	Gls
Stevenage	Longford T (ROI)	09/11	11	2	6	0
Southend U	Dundee U	08/13	13	0	2	0
Stevenage	Tr	09/13	13	0	1	0

COWAN Gavin Patrick
Born: Hannover, Germany, 24 May, 1981 — CD
England: Semi Pro-2

League Club	Source	Date Signed	Seasons Played	Apps	Subs	Gls
Shrewsbury T	Canvey Island	03/05	04-06	17	7	1

COWAN Ian
Born: Falkirk, Scotland, 27 November, 1944 — RW

League Club	Source	Date Signed	Seasons Played	Apps	Subs	Gls
Southend U	Dunfermline Ath	07/70	70	3	0	0

COWAN James Clews (Jimmy)
Born: Paisley, Renfrewshire, Scotland, 16 June, 1926 — G
Died: Greenock, Inverclyde, Scotland, 20 June, 1968
Scotland: 25/SLge-3

League Club	Source	Date Signed	Seasons Played	Apps	Subs	Gls
Sunderland	Greenock Morton	06/53	53	28	-	0

COWAN John
Born: Belfast, Northern Ireland, 8 January, 1949 — M
Northern Ireland: 1

League Club	Source	Date Signed	Seasons Played	Apps	Subs	Gls
Newcastle U	Crusaders	02/67	69-72	6	3	0
Darlington	Drogheda (ROI)	08/75	75	10	0	0

COWAN Thomas (Tom)
Born: Motherwell, Lanarkshire, Scotland, 28 August, 1969 LB

League Club	Source	Date Signed	Seasons Played	Apps	Subs	Gls
Sheffield U	Glasgow Rangers	08/91	91-93	45	0	0
Stoke C	L	10/93	93	14	0	0
Huddersfield T	Tr	03/94	93-98	137	0	8
Burnley	Tr	03/99	98-99	17	3	1
Cambridge U	Tr	02/00	99-01	48	2	3
Peterborough U	L	01/02	01	4	1	1
York C	Tr	07/02	02	31	2	1
Carlisle U	Dundee	11/03	03	20	0	1

COWAN-HALL Paris Declan Joseph
Born: Hillingdon, W London, England, 1 October, 1990 W

League Club	Source	Date Signed	Seasons Played	Apps	Subs	Gls
Portsmouth	Sch	07/08				
Grimsby T	L	12/09	09	0	3	0
Scunthorpe U	Oldham Ath (NC)	10/10	10	0	1	0
Plymouth Arg	Woking	07/12	12	25	15	3
Wycombe W	Tr	06/13	13-14	38	7	10
Millwall	Tr	01/15	14	0	5	0

COWANS Gordon Sidney
Born: Cornforth, County Durham, England, 27 October, 1958 M
England: 10/B-2/U21-5/Youth

League Club	Source	Date Signed	Seasons Played	Apps	Subs	Gls
Aston Villa	App	09/76	75-84	276	10	42
Aston Villa	Bari (ITA)	07/88	88-91	114	3	7
Blackburn Rov	Tr	11/91	91-92	49	1	2
Aston Villa	Tr	07/93	93	9	2	0
Derby Co	Tr	02/94	93-94	36	0	0
Wolverhampton W	Tr	12/94	94-95	31	6	0
Sheffield U	Tr	12/95	95	18	2	0
Bradford C	Tr	06/96	96	23	1	0
Stockport Co	Tr	03/97	96	6	1	0
Burnley	Tr	08/97	97	5	1	0

COWDRILL Barry James
Born: Birmingham, England, 3 January, 1957 LB

League Club	Source	Date Signed	Seasons Played	Apps	Subs	Gls
West Bromwich A	Sutton Coldfield T	04/79	79-87	127	4	0
Rotherham U	L	10/85	85	2	0	0
Bolton W	Tr	07/88	88-91	117	2	4
Rochdale	Tr	02/92	91	15	0	1

COWE Steven Mark (Steve)
Born: Gloucester, England, 29 September, 1974 F

League Club	Source	Date Signed	Seasons Played	Apps	Subs	Gls
Aston Villa	YT	07/93				
Swindon T	Tr	03/96	95-00	59	38	11

COWELL George Robert (Bobby)
Born: Trimdon, County Durham, England, 5 December, 1922 RB
Died: Newcastle-upon-Tyne, England, 11 January, 1996

League Club	Source	Date Signed	Seasons Played	Apps	Subs	Gls
Newcastle U	Blackhall CW	10/43	46-54	289	-	0

COWEN John Michael
Born: Lewisham, SE London, England, 1 December, 1944 G
England: Youth

League Club	Source	Date Signed	Seasons Played	Apps	Subs	Gls
Chelsea	App	10/62				
Watford	Tr	10/64	64-66	17	0	0

COWGILL Jack Nicholas
Born: Wakefield, England, 8 January, 1997 CD

League Club	Source	Date Signed	Seasons Played	Apps	Subs	Gls
Barnsley	Sch	08/14	14	1	1	0

COWIE Alexander George (George)
Born: Findochty, Moray, Scotland, 9 May, 1961 M

League Club	Source	Date Signed	Seasons Played	Apps	Subs	Gls
West Ham U	App	08/78	81-82	6	2	0

COWIE Andrew David (Andy)
Born: Motherwell, Lanarkshire, Scotland, 11 March, 1913 WH
Died: Inverness, Scotland, 19 January, 1972
Scotland: SLge-1

League Club	Source	Date Signed	Seasons Played	Apps	Subs	Gls
Swindon T	Aberdeen	07/48	48-50	89	-	4

COWIE Donald McCulloch (Don)
Born: Inverness, Scotland, 15 February, 1983 M
Scotland: 10

League Club	Source	Date Signed	Seasons Played	Apps	Subs	Gls
Watford	Inverness CT	02/09	08-10	87	1	9
Cardiff C	Tr	07/11	11-13	68	18	6
Wigan Ath	Tr	07/14	14	24	8	0

COWLER Samuel Paul (Sam)
Born: Colchester, Essex, England, 26 October, 1992 G

League Club	Source	Date Signed	Seasons Played	Apps	Subs	Gls
Barnet	West Ham U (Sch)	07/12	12	1	1	0

COWLEY Carl
Born: Stepney, E London, England, 10 July, 1965 CD

League Club	Source	Date Signed	Seasons Played	Apps	Subs	Gls
Millwall	App	10/82	83	2	1	0

COWLEY Francis
Born: Stepney, E London, England, 28 November, 1957 W

League Club	Source	Date Signed	Seasons Played	Apps	Subs	Gls
Derby Co	Sutton U	08/77				
Wimbledon	Tr	02/78	77-78	5	3	0

COWLING Christopher (Chris)
Born: Scunthorpe, North Lincolnshire, England, 19 September, 1962 M/F

League Club	Source	Date Signed	Seasons Played	Apps	Subs	Gls
Scunthorpe U	App	12/79	79-84	117	14	26

COWLING David Roy
Born: Doncaster, South Yorkshire, England, 27 November, 1958 LW

League Club	Source	Date Signed	Seasons Played	Apps	Subs	Gls
Mansfield T	App	11/76				
Huddersfield T	Tr	08/77	78-87	331	9	43
Scunthorpe U	L	11/87	87	1	0	0
Reading	Tr	12/87	87	9	1	1
Scunthorpe U	Tr	08/88	88-90	85	4	5

COWLING Jason Paul
Born: Cambridge, England, 12 August, 1969 M

League Club	Source	Date Signed	Seasons Played	Apps	Subs	Gls
Cambridge U	Jnr	07/87	86	0	2	1

COWLING Lee David
Born: Doncaster, South Yorkshire, England, 22 September, 1977 LB

League Club	Source	Date Signed	Seasons Played	Apps	Subs	Gls
Nottingham F	YT	09/94				
Mansfield T	Tr	08/99	99	3	5	0

COWPERTHWAITE Niall Thomas
Born: Barrow, Cumbria, England, 28 January, 1992 LB

League Club	Source	Date Signed	Seasons Played	Apps	Subs	Gls
Morecambe	Jnr	08/10	10-11	7	3	1

COWSILL Charles Mills (Charlie)
Born: Farnworth, Greater Manchester, England, 5 May, 1929 W

League Club	Source	Date Signed	Seasons Played	Apps	Subs	Gls
Bury		05/50				
Workington	Ashton U	11/51	51	1	-	0

COX Alan William
Born: Liverpool, England, 4 September, 1920 IF
Died: Trafford, Greater Manchester, England, March, 1993

League Club	Source	Date Signed	Seasons Played	Apps	Subs	Gls
Tranmere Rov		03/41	46-47	8	-	2

COX Albert Edward Harrison
Born: Treeton, South Yorkshire, England, 24 June, 1917 LB
Died: Rotherham, South Yorkshire, England, April, 2003

League Club	Source	Date Signed	Seasons Played	Apps	Subs	Gls
Sheffield U	Woodhouse Mills U	04/35	35-51	267	-	5
Halifax T	Tr	07/52	52-53	54	-	1

COX Brian Roy
Born: Sheffield, England, 7 May, 1961 G

League Club	Source	Date Signed	Seasons Played	Apps	Subs	Gls
Sheffield Wed	App	02/79	78-80	22	0	0
Huddersfield T	Tr	03/82	81-87	213	0	0
Mansfield T	Tr	08/88	88-89	54	0	0
Hartlepool U	Tr	08/90	90	34	0	0

COX David
Born: Dukinfield, Greater Manchester, England, 16 September, 1936 CF

League Club	Source	Date Signed	Seasons Played	Apps	Subs	Gls
Stockport Co	Oldham Ath (Am)	10/55	56-57	7	-	4

COX Dean Arthur Edward
Born: Haywards Heath, West Sussex, England, 12 August, 1987 LW

League Club	Source	Date Signed	Seasons Played	Apps	Subs	Gls
Brighton & HA	Sch	06/06	05-09	121	25	16
Leyton Orient	Tr	07/10	10-14	189	20	40

COX Frederick James Arthur (Freddie)
Born: Reading, England, 1 November, 1920 W
Died: Bournemouth, England, 7 August, 1973

League Club	Source	Date Signed	Seasons Played	Apps	Subs	Gls
Tottenham H	St George's LC	08/38	38-48	99	-	15
Arsenal	Tr	09/49	49-52	79	-	9
West Bromwich A	Tr	07/53	53	4	-	1

COX Geoffrey (Geoff)
Born: Arley, Warwickshire, England, 30 November, 1934 IF/WH
Died: Torquay, Devon, England, 3 November, 2014

League Club	Source	Date Signed	Seasons Played	Apps	Subs	Gls
Birmingham C	Jnr	12/51	52-56	35	-	3
Torquay U	Tr	12/57	57-66	260	1	62

COX Graham Paul
Born: Willesden, NW London, England, 30 April, 1959 G

League Club	Source	Date Signed	Seasons Played	Apps	Subs	Gls
Brentford	App	04/77	76-77	4	0	0
Aldershot	Wokingham T	01/85	84-85	13	0	0

COX Ian Gary
Born: Croydon, S London, England, 25 March, 1971 CD
Trinidad & Tobago: 16

League Club	Source	Date Signed	Seasons Played	Apps	Subs	Gls
Crystal Palace	Carshalton Ath	03/94	94-95	2	13	0
Bournemouth	Tr	03/96	95-99	172	0	16
Burnley	Tr	02/00	99-02	107	8	5
Gillingham	Tr	08/03	03-07	150	3	6

COX James Darryl (Jimmy)
Born: Gloucester, England, 11 April, 1980 F

League Club	Source	Date Signed	Seasons Played	Apps	Subs	Gls
Luton T	YT	05/98	98	3	5	0

COX Keith
Born: Heanor, Derbyshire, England, 26 January, 1936 — WH

League Club	Source	Date Signed	Seasons Played	Apps	Subs	Gls
Charlton Ath	Heanor T	04/54	56-58	14	-	0

COX Kristian Caleb
Born: Birmingham, England, 28 September, 1992 — F

League Club	Source	Date Signed	Seasons Played	Apps	Subs	Gls
Port Vale	Sch	-	10	0	1	0

COX Lee David
Born: Leicester, England, 26 June, 1990 — M

League Club	Source	Date Signed	Seasons Played	Apps	Subs	Gls
Leicester C	Sch	07/08				
Swindon T	Inverness CT	01/12	11-13	6	6	1
Oxford U	L	07/12	12	14	0	0
Plymouth Arg	L	02/13	12	10	0	0
Plymouth Arg	Tr	05/14	14	21	11	0

COX Mark Louis
Born: Birmingham, England, 4 October, 1959 — F

League Club	Source	Date Signed	Seasons Played	Apps	Subs	Gls
Lincoln C	App	09/77	76-77	3	2	0
Doncaster Rov	Tr	08/78	78	10	5	3

COX Maurice
Born: Torquay, Devon, England, 1 October, 1959 — F
England: Schools

League Club	Source	Date Signed	Seasons Played	Apps	Subs	Gls
Torquay U	Jnr	01/80	78-81	49	13	13
Huddersfield T	Tr	08/82	82	3	1	1

COX Neil James
Born: Scunthorpe, North Lincolnshire, England, 8 October, 1971 — D
England: U21-6

League Club	Source	Date Signed	Seasons Played	Apps	Subs	Gls
Scunthorpe U	YT	03/90	90	17	0	1
Aston Villa	Tr	02/91	91-93	26	16	3
Middlesbrough	Tr	07/94	94-96	103	3	3
Bolton W	Tr	05/97	97-99	77	3	7
Watford	Tr	11/99	99-04	215	4	20
Cardiff C	Tr	08/05	05	21	6	2
Crewe Alex	Tr	06/06	06-07	50	8	1

COX Paul Richard
Born: Nottingham, England, 6 January, 1972 — CD

League Club	Source	Date Signed	Seasons Played	Apps	Subs	Gls
Notts Co	YT	08/89	91-94	39	5	1
Hull C	L	12/94	94	5	0	1

COX Ronald Bert (Ron)
Born: Coventry, England, 2 May, 1919 — CH
Died: Nuneaton, Warwickshire, England, 28 September, 2006

League Club	Source	Date Signed	Seasons Played	Apps	Subs	Gls
Coventry C	RASC Egypt	10/45	46-51	29	-	0

COX Samuel (Sam)
Born: Mexborough, South Yorkshire, England, 30 October, 1920 — FB
Died: Mexborough, South Yorkshire, England, May, 1985

League Club	Source	Date Signed	Seasons Played	Apps	Subs	Gls
West Bromwich A	Denaby U	05/48	48	2	-	0
Accrington Stan	Tr	07/51	51	43	-	0
Scunthorpe U	Tr	07/52	52	3	-	0

COX Samuel Peter (Sam)
Born: Edgware, NW London, England, 10 October, 1990 — D/M

League Club	Source	Date Signed	Seasons Played	Apps	Subs	Gls
Tottenham H	Sch	07/09				
Cheltenham T	L	09/09	09	1	0	0
Torquay U	L	01/10	09	1	2	0
Barnet	Tr	07/10	10	5	5	0

COX Simon Peter
Born: Clapham, SW London, England, 24 March, 1984 — G
Republic of Ireland: 30/Youth

League Club	Source	Date Signed	Seasons Played	Apps	Subs	Gls
Oxford U	Sch	07/03	03-04	7	1	0

COX Simon Richard
Born: Reading, England, 28 April, 1987 — F
Republic of Ireland: 26

League Club	Source	Date Signed	Seasons Played	Apps	Subs	Gls
Reading	Sch	11/05	05	0	2	0
Brentford	L	09/06	06	11	2	0
Northampton T	L	03/07	06	6	2	3
Swindon T	Tr	08/07	07-08	80	1	44
West Bromwich A	Tr	07/09	09-11	32	33	10
Nottingham F	Tr	08/12	12-13	57	16	13
Reading	Tr	08/14	14	28	9	8

COXHILL David
Born: Brentford, W London, England, 10 April, 1952 — M

League Club	Source	Date Signed	Seasons Played	Apps	Subs	Gls
Millwall	Jnr	06/70	70-71	6	2	0
Gillingham	Tr	07/73	73-74	32	2	1

COXON Eric Gary (Gary)
Born: Liverpool, England, 31 May, 1946 — RB

League Club	Source	Date Signed	Seasons Played	Apps	Subs	Gls
Blackburn Rov	Everton (App)	12/63	66-67	10	0	0

COXON John
Born: Whitley Bay, Tyne and Wear, England, 7 April, 1922 — FB
Died: North Tyneside, Tyne and Wear, England, May, 1998

League Club	Source	Date Signed	Seasons Played	Apps	Subs	Gls
Darlington (Am)	Hartley	05/46	46	1	-	0

COXON William George (Billy)
Born: Derby, England, 28 April, 1933 — LW

League Club	Source	Date Signed	Seasons Played	Apps	Subs	Gls
Derby Co	Jnr	05/50				
Norwich C	Ilkeston T	05/52	52-57	98	-	24
Lincoln C	Tr	03/58	57-58	11	-	1
Bournemouth	Tr	11/58	58-65	199	1	37

COY Robert Anthony (Bobby)
Born: Birmingham, England, 30 November, 1961 — CD

League Club	Source	Date Signed	Seasons Played	Apps	Subs	Gls
Wolverhampton W	App	11/79	81-83	40	3	0
Chester C	Tr	03/84	83-85	93	0	2
Northampton T	Tr	08/86	86	15	2	0

COYLE Anthony John (Tony)
Born: Glasgow, Scotland, 17 January, 1960 — W

League Club	Source	Date Signed	Seasons Played	Apps	Subs	Gls
Stockport Co	Albion Rov	12/79	79-85	215	4	28
Chesterfield	Tr	06/86	86-87	71	5	4
Stockport Co	Tr	08/88	88	23	0	3
Exeter C	Northwich Victoria	11/89	89	1	0	0

COYLE Francis (Fay)
Born: Derry, Northern Ireland, 1 April, 1924 — CF
Northern Ireland: 4/NILge-4/Amateur

League Club	Source	Date Signed	Seasons Played	Apps	Subs	Gls
Nottingham F	Coleraine	03/58	57	3	-	0

COYLE Owen Columba
Born: Paisley, Renfrewshire, Scotland, 14 July, 1966 — F
Republic of Ireland: 1/B/U21-2

League Club	Source	Date Signed	Seasons Played	Apps	Subs	Gls
Bolton W	Airdrieonians	06/93	93-95	35	19	12

COYLE Robert Irvine (Roy)
Born: Belfast, Northern Ireland, 31 January, 1948 — M
Northern Ireland: 5

League Club	Source	Date Signed	Seasons Played	Apps	Subs	Gls
Sheffield Wed	Glentoran	03/72	72-73	38	2	2
Grimsby T	Tr	10/74	74	24	0	1

COYLE Ronald Paul (Ronnie)
Born: Glasgow, Scotland, 4 August, 1964 — M
Died: Glasgow, Scotland, 12 April, 2011

League Club	Source	Date Signed	Seasons Played	Apps	Subs	Gls
Middlesbrough	Glasgow Celtic	12/86	86	1	2	0
Rochdale	Tr	08/87	87	23	1	1

COYLE William (Billy)
Born: Newcastle-upon-Tyne, England, 24 October, 1926 — CH
Died: Sunderland, England, May, 2011

League Club	Source	Date Signed	Seasons Played	Apps	Subs	Gls
Darlington	West Auckland T	05/49	49	17	-	0

COYNE Brian
Born: Glasgow, Scotland, 13 December, 1959 — M

League Club	Source	Date Signed	Seasons Played	Apps	Subs	Gls
Shrewsbury T	Glasgow Celtic	06/79	79	1	0	0

COYNE Christopher John (Chris)
Born: Brisbane, Australia, 20 December, 1978 — CD
Australia: 7/U23-8/Youth

League Club	Source	Date Signed	Seasons Played	Apps	Subs	Gls
West Ham U	Perth SC (AUS)	01/96	98	0	1	0
Brentford	L	08/98	98	7	0	0
Southend U	L	03/99	98	0	1	0
Luton T	Dundee	09/01	01-07	207	14	14
Colchester U	Tr	01/08	07-08	33	2	1

COYNE Cyril
Born: Barnsley, South Yorkshire, England, 21 May, 1924 — LH
Died: Leeds, England, 14 December, 1981

League Club	Source	Date Signed	Seasons Played	Apps	Subs	Gls
Leeds U	Barnsley Main	10/44				
Halifax T	Stalybridge Celtic	06/51	51	4	-	0

COYNE Daniel (Danny)
Born: Prestatyn, Denbighshire, Wales, 27 August, 1973 — G
Wales: 16/B-1/U21-9/Youth/Schools

League Club	Source	Date Signed	Seasons Played	Apps	Subs	Gls
Tranmere Rov	YT	05/92	92-98	110	1	0
Grimsby T	Tr	07/99	99-02	181	0	0
Leicester C	Tr	07/03	03	1	3	0
Burnley	Tr	08/04	04-06	39	1	0
Tranmere Rov	Tr	07/07	07-08	80	0	0
Middlesbrough	Tr	07/09	09-11	25	1	0
Sheffield U		11/12				

COYNE Gerard Aloysius (Gerry)
Born: Hebburn, Tyne and Wear, England, 9 August, 1948 — CF

League Club	Source	Date Signed	Seasons Played	Apps	Subs	Gls
York C	Reyrolles	08/66	66	2	0	0

COYNE John David
Born: Liverpool, England, 18 July, 1951 — F

League Club	Source	Date Signed	Seasons Played	Apps	Subs	Gls
Tranmere Rov		08/71	71	12	3	3
Hartlepool U	Tr	07/72	72-73	47	8	10
Stockport Co	Wigan Ath	11/75	75	3	1	0

COYNE Peter David
Born: Hartlepool, Cleveland, England, 13 November, 1958 — F
England: Schools

League Club	Source	Date Signed	Seasons Played	Apps	Subs	Gls
Manchester U	App	11/75	75	1	1	1
Crewe Alex	Ashton U	08/77	77-80	113	21	47
Swindon T	Hyde U	08/84	84-88	99	11	30
Aldershot	L	08/89	89	3	0	0

COYNE Thomas (Tommy)
Born: Glasgow, Scotland, 14 November, 1962 — F
Republic of Ireland: 22/B

League Club	Source	Date Signed	Seasons Played	Apps	Subs	Gls
Tranmere Rov	Glasgow Celtic	03/93	92	9	3	1

COZENS John William
Born: Hammersmith, W London, England, 14 May, 1946 — F

League Club	Source	Date Signed	Seasons Played	Apps	Subs	Gls
Notts Co	Hillingdon Bor	08/70	70-72	41	3	13
Peterborough U	Tr	11/72	72-77	127	5	41
Cambridge U	Tr	12/77	77-79	52	9	4

COZIC Bertrand Edern
Born: Quimper, France, 18 May, 1978 — M

League Club	Source	Date Signed	Seasons Played	Apps	Subs	Gls
Cheltenham T	Team Bath	08/03	03	7	0	1
Northampton T	Hereford U	08/04	04	8	6	0
Kidderminster Hrs	Tr	02/05	04	13	2	0
Exeter C	Team Bath	08/06	08-10	39	21	2

CRABBE Stephen Allan John (John)
Born: Weymouth, Dorset, England, 20 October, 1954 — M

League Club	Source	Date Signed	Seasons Played	Apps	Subs	Gls
Southampton	App	10/72	74-76	8	4	0
Gillingham	Tr	01/76	76-80	181	0	13
Carlisle U	Tr	08/81	81	26	0	4
Hereford U	Tr	08/82	82	15	1	2
Crewe Alex	Tr	08/83	83-85	75	0	7
Torquay U	Tr	09/85	85	27	2	2

CRABTREE Richard Edward
Born: Exeter, England, 6 February, 1955 — G

League Club	Source	Date Signed	Seasons Played	Apps	Subs	Gls
Bristol Rov	App	02/73	71	7	0	0
Doncaster Rov	L	10/74	74	1	0	0
Torquay U	Dawlish T	08/75	75	1	0	0
Exeter C	Dawlish T	07/83	83	1	0	0

CRADDOCK Darren
Born: Bishop Auckland, County Durham, England, 23 February, 1985 — CD

League Club	Source	Date Signed	Seasons Played	Apps	Subs	Gls
Hartlepool U	Sch	07/04	03-05	22	2	0

CRADDOCK Jody Darryl
Born: Redditch, Worcestershire, England, 25 July, 1975 — CD

League Club	Source	Date Signed	Seasons Played	Apps	Subs	Gls
Cambridge U	Christchurch	08/93	93-96	142	3	4
Sunderland	Tr	08/97	97-02	140	6	2
Sheffield U	L	08/99	99	10	0	0
Wolverhampton W	Tr	08/03	03-11	203	12	14
Stoke C	L	08/07	07	4	0	0

CRADDOCK Joshua Glynn (Josh)
Born: Wolverhampton, England, 5 March, 1991 — F

League Club	Source	Date Signed	Seasons Played	Apps	Subs	Gls
Walsall	Sch	05/08	07-08	0	3	0

CRADDOCK Leonard Miller (Miller)
Born: Newent, Gloucestershire, England, 21 September, 1926 — CF
Died: Ledbury, Herefordshire, England, 21 May, 1960

League Club	Source	Date Signed	Seasons Played	Apps	Subs	Gls
Newport Co	Chelsea (Am)	05/46	46	7	-	0
Aston Villa	Hereford U	09/48	48-50	34	-	10

CRADDOCK Thomas (Tom)
Born: Darlington, County Durham, England, 14 October, 1986 — F

League Club	Source	Date Signed	Seasons Played	Apps	Subs	Gls
Middlesbrough	Sch	07/06	05-07	1	3	0
Wrexham	L	10/06	06	1	0	1
Hartlepool U	L	02/08	07	1	3	0
Luton T	Tr	10/08	08	27	0	10
Oxford U	Tr	08/10	10-12	64	16	25
Portsmouth	Tr	05/13	13	2	6	1

CRAGGS John Edward
Born: Flint Hill, County Durham, England, 21 October, 1948 — RB
England: Youth

League Club	Source	Date Signed	Seasons Played	Apps	Subs	Gls
Newcastle U	App	12/65	66-70	50	2	1
Middlesbrough	Tr	08/71	71-81	408	1	12
Newcastle U	Tr	08/82	82	10	2	0
Darlington	Tr	08/83	83-84	53	1	0

CRAIG Albert Hughes
Born: Glasgow, Scotland, 3 January, 1962 — M

League Club	Source	Date Signed	Seasons Played	Apps	Subs	Gls
Newcastle U	Hamilton Academical	02/87	86-88	6	4	0
Northampton T	L	01/89	88	2	0	1

CRAIG Benjamin (Benny)
Born: Consett, County Durham, England, 6 December, 1915 — FB
Died: Newcastle-upon-Tyne, England, 18 January, 1982

League Club	Source	Date Signed	Seasons Played	Apps	Subs	Gls
Huddersfield T	Eden Colliery	01/34	33-38	98	-	0
Newcastle U	Tr	11/38	38-49	66	-	0

CRAIG David James
Born: Belfast, Northern Ireland, 8 June, 1944 — RB
Northern Ireland: 25/U23-1/Youth

League Club	Source	Date Signed	Seasons Played	Apps	Subs	Gls
Newcastle U	App	04/62	63-77	346	5	8

CRAIG Derek Malcolm
Born: Ryton-on-Tyne, Tyne and Wear, England, 28 July, 1952 — CD

League Club	Source	Date Signed	Seasons Played	Apps	Subs	Gls
Newcastle U	Jnr	08/69				
Darlington	San Jose E'quake (USA)	09/75	75-79	186	1	10
York C	Tr	05/80	80-81	53	0	1

CRAIG James Philip (Jim)
Born: Glasgow, Scotland, 30 April, 1943 — RB
Scotland: 1

League Club	Source	Date Signed	Seasons Played	Apps	Subs	Gls
Sheffield Wed	Hellenic (RSA)	12/72	72-73	5	1	0

CRAIG Joseph (Joe)
Born: Bridge of Allan, Stirlingshire, Scotland, 14 May, 1954 — F
Scotland: 1/SLge-1/U23-4

League Club	Source	Date Signed	Seasons Played	Apps	Subs	Gls
Blackburn Rov	Glasgow Celtic	09/78	78-80	44	4	8

CRAIG Nathan Lee
Born: Caernarfon, Gwynedd, Wales, 25 October, 1991 — M
Wales: U21-4/Youth

League Club	Source	Date Signed	Seasons Played	Apps	Subs	Gls
Everton	Sch	10/08				
Torquay U	Caernarfon T	01/12	11-13	34	9	1

CRAIG Robert
Born: Consett, County Durham, England, 16 June, 1928 — FB

League Club	Source	Date Signed	Seasons Played	Apps	Subs	Gls
Sunderland	Leadgate Jnrs	11/45	49	1	-	0

CRAIG Robert McAllister (Bobby)
Born: Airdrie, Lanarkshire, Scotland, 8 April, 1935 — IF
Died: Toronto, Canada, 1 October, 2010

League Club	Source	Date Signed	Seasons Played	Apps	Subs	Gls
Sheffield Wed	Third Lanark	11/59	59-61	84	-	25
Blackburn Rov	Tr	04/62	61-62	8	-	3
Oldham Ath	St Johnstone	03/64	63-64	18	-	4

CRAIG Steven
Born: Bathgate, West Lothian, Scotland, 5 February, 1981 — F

League Club	Source	Date Signed	Seasons Played	Apps	Subs	Gls
Wycombe W	Partick Thistle	07/13	13-14	31	27	6

CRAIG Thomas Brooks (Tommy)
Born: Glasgow, Scotland, 21 November, 1950 — M
Scotland: 1/U23-9/U21-1/Schools

League Club	Source	Date Signed	Seasons Played	Apps	Subs	Gls
Sheffield Wed	Aberdeen	05/69	68-74	210	4	38
Newcastle U	Tr	12/74	74-77	122	2	22
Aston Villa	Tr	01/78	77-78	27	0	2
Swansea C	Tr	07/78	79-80	47	5	9
Carlisle U	Tr	03/82	81-84	92	6	10

CRAIG Tony Andrew
Born: Greenwich, SE London, England, 20 April, 1985 — D

League Club	Source	Date Signed	Seasons Played	Apps	Subs	Gls
Millwall	Sch	03/03	02-06	75	4	2
Wycombe W	L	10/04	04	14	0	0
Crystal Palace	Tr	06/07	07	13	0	0
Millwall	Tr	03/08	07-11	119	7	5
Leyton Orient	L	11/11	11	4	0	0
Brentford	Tr	07/12	12-14	109	2	0

CRAIG William David (David)
Born: Liverpool, England, 27 December, 1921 — RW
Died: Canada, 3 March, 1994

League Club	Source	Date Signed	Seasons Played	Apps	Subs	Gls
Blackpool	Marine	05/46				
Southport	Tr	08/48	48	5	-	2

CRAIG William James
Born: Aberdeen, Scotland, 11 September, 1929 — D
Died: Aberdeen, Scotland, 31 August, 2011

League Club	Source	Date Signed	Seasons Played	Apps	Subs	Gls
Millwall	Dundee	08/56	56-58	21	-	1

CRAINEY Stephen Daniel
Born: Glasgow, Scotland, 22 June, 1981 — LB
Scotland: 12/B-1/U21-7

League Club	Source	Date Signed	Seasons Played	Apps	Subs	Gls
Southampton	Glasgow Celtic	01/04	03	5	0	0
Leeds U	Tr	08/04	04-06	51	1	0
Blackpool	Tr	07/07	07-12	207	7	4
Wigan Ath	Tr	07/13	13	14	6	0
Fleetwood T	Tr	08/14	14	26	2	0

CRAINIE Daniel (Danny)
Born: Kilsyth, Lanarkshire, Scotland, 24 May, 1962 — LW
Scotland: U21-1

League Club	Source	Date Signed	Seasons Played	Apps	Subs	Gls
Wolverhampton W	Glasgow Celtic	12/83	83-85	63	1	4
Blackpool	L	03/85	84	6	0	0

CRAKER Laurence David (Laurie)
Born: Aylesbury, Buckinghamshire, England, 1 March, 1953 — M

League Club	Source	Date Signed	Seasons Played	Apps	Subs	Gls
Chelsea	App	08/70				
Watford	Jewish Guild (RSA)	11/72	72-76	60	6	4

CRAM Robert (Bobby)
Born: Hetton-le-Hole, Tyne and Wear, England, 19 November, 1939 — RB
Died: Vancouver, Canada, 14 April, 2007

League Club	Source	Date Signed	Seasons Played	Apps	Subs	Gls
West Bromwich A	Jnr	01/57	59-66	141	0	25
Colchester U	Vancouver Royals (CAN)	01/70	69-71	99	1	4

CRAMB Colin
Born: Lanark, Scotland, 23 June, 1974 — F

League Club	Source	Date Signed	Seasons Played	Apps	Subs	Gls
Southampton	Hamilton Academical	06/93	93	0	1	0
Doncaster Rov	Heart of Midlothian	12/95	95-96	60	2	25
Bristol C	Tr	07/97	97-98	38	15	9
Walsall	L	02/99	98	4	0	4
Crewe Alex	Tr	08/99	99-00	43	7	10
Notts Co	L	09/00	00	2	1	0
Bury	L	02/01	00	15	0	5
Bury	Fortuna Sittard (NED)	01/03	02	17	1	3
Shrewsbury T	Tr	07/03	04	0	2	0
Grimsby T	Tr	09/04	04	7	4	2

CRAMPTON David William (Dave)
Born: Bearpark, County Durham, England, 9 June, 1949 — G

League Club	Source	Date Signed	Seasons Played	Apps	Subs	Gls
Blackburn Rov	Spennymoor U	03/68				
Darlington	Tr	07/69	69	13	0	0

CRAMPTON Paul
Born: Cleethorpes, North Lincolnshire, England, 28 January, 1953 — FB

League Club	Source	Date Signed	Seasons Played	Apps	Subs	Gls
Grimsby T	App	-	70	0	1	0

CRANE Andrew David (Andy)
Born: Ipswich, England, 3 January, 1967 — LB

League Club	Source	Date Signed	Seasons Played	Apps	Subs	Gls
Ipswich T	App	04/84				
Shrewsbury T	Tr	06/87				
Hereford U	Tr	07/88	88	30	2	0

CRANE Anthony Steven (Tony)
Born: Liverpool, England, 8 September, 1982 — CD
England: Youth

League Club	Source	Date Signed	Seasons Played	Apps	Subs	Gls
Sheffield Wed	YT	09/99	00-02	24	25	4
Grimsby T	Tr	07/03	03-05	42	3	4

CRANE Daniel Peter (Dan)
Born: Bromsgrove, Worcestershire, England, 27 May, 1984 — G

League Club	Source	Date Signed	Seasons Played	Apps	Subs	Gls
West Bromwich A	Sch	07/03				
Rushden & D	Burton A	01/06	05	8	0	0

CRANE Steven John (Steve)
Born: Grays, Essex, England, 3 June, 1972 — F

League Club	Source	Date Signed	Seasons Played	Apps	Subs	Gls
Charlton Ath	YT	07/90				
Gillingham	Aveley	03/93	92-93	3	10	1
Torquay U	Papatoetoe (NZL)	12/96	96	0	2	0

CRANEY Ian Thomas William
Born: Liverpool, England, 21 July, 1982 — M
England: Semi Pro-7

League Club	Source	Date Signed	Seasons Played	Apps	Subs	Gls
Accrington Stan	Altrincham	06/04	06	18	0	5
Swansea C	Tr	11/06	06-07	24	4	0
Accrington Stan	Tr	09/07	07-08	36	0	8
Huddersfield T	Tr	08/08	08	23	11	5
Morecambe	L	08/09	09	16	0	2
Accrington Stan	Fleetwood T	11/10	10-11	29	15	8
Rochdale	Tr	08/12	12	0	6	0

CRANFIELD Harold Richard (Harry)
Born: Cambridge, England, 25 December, 1917 — LW
Died: Kings Lynn, Norfolk, England, 5 December, 1990

League Club	Source	Date Signed	Seasons Played	Apps	Subs	Gls
Fulham	Cambridge T	12/37	46	1	-	0
Bristol Rov	Tr	06/47	47	24	-	2

CRANGLE James Patrick (Jimmy)
Born: Glasgow, Scotland, 4 April, 1953 — W

League Club	Source	Date Signed	Seasons Played	Apps	Subs	Gls
York C	Campsie Black Watch	08/72	72	4	0	0

CRANIE Martin James
Born: Yeovil, Somerset, England, 23 September, 1986 — CD
England: U21-16/Youth

League Club	Source	Date Signed	Seasons Played	Apps	Subs	Gls
Southampton	Sch	09/04	03-06	11	5	0
Bournemouth	L	10/04	04	2	1	0
Yeovil T	L	11/06	06	8	0	0
Yeovil T	L	03/07	06	3	1	0
Portsmouth	Tr	06/07	07	1	1	0
Queens Park Rgrs	L	10/07	07	6	0	0
Charlton Ath	L	09/08	08	19	0	0
Coventry C	Tr	08/09	09-11	108	6	1
Barnsley	Tr	08/12	12-14	107	3	1

CRANSON Ian
Born: Horden, County Durham, England, 2 July, 1964 — CD
England: U21-5

League Club	Source	Date Signed	Seasons Played	Apps	Subs	Gls
Ipswich T	App	07/82	83-87	130	1	5
Sheffield Wed	Tr	03/88	87-88	29	1	0
Stoke C	Tr	07/89	89-96	220	3	9

CRANSTON Jordan Christopher
Born: Wolverhampton, England, 11 November, 1993 — LB
Wales: Youth

League Club	Source	Date Signed	Seasons Played	Apps	Subs	Gls
Wolverhampton W	Sch	07/12				
Notts Co	Tr	09/14	14	9	0	0

CRANSTON Nicholas Geoffrey (Nick)
Born: Carlisle, Cumbria, England, 20 October, 1972 — M

League Club	Source	Date Signed	Seasons Played	Apps	Subs	Gls
Carlisle U	YT	01/92	91	0	2	0

CRANSTON William (Bill)
Born: Kilmarnock, Ayrshire, Scotland, 18 January, 1942 — CD

League Club	Source	Date Signed	Seasons Played	Apps	Subs	Gls
Blackpool	Saxone YC	08/60	61-64	33	-	0
Preston NE	Tr	12/64	64-69	80	6	1
Oldham Ath	Tr	07/70	70-72	98	2	2

CRAVEN Dean
Born: Shrewsbury, Shropshire, England, 17 February, 1979 — RW

League Club	Source	Date Signed	Seasons Played	Apps	Subs	Gls
West Bromwich A	YT	07/97				
Shrewsbury T	Tr	03/98	97-98	7	4	0

CRAVEN John Roland
Born: Lytham St Annes, Lancashire, England, 15 May, 1947 — M/D
Died: California, USA, 14 December, 1996

League Club	Source	Date Signed	Seasons Played	Apps	Subs	Gls
Blackpool	App	01/65	65-71	154	11	24
Crystal Palace	Tr	09/71	71-72	56	7	14
Coventry C	Tr	05/73	73-76	86	3	8
Plymouth Arg	Tr	01/77	76-77	45	0	3

CRAVEN Michael Anthony (Mike)
Born: Birkenhead, Wirral, England, 20 November, 1957 — G

League Club	Source	Date Signed	Seasons Played	Apps	Subs	Gls
Chester C	Cadbury's	09/75	75-76	4	0	0

CRAVEN Peter
Born: Hannover, Germany, 30 June, 1968 — LW

League Club	Source	Date Signed	Seasons Played	Apps	Subs	Gls
Halifax T	Guiseley	03/93	92	7	0	0

CRAVEN Stephen Joseph (Steve)
Born: Birkenhead, Wirral, England, 17 September, 1957 — M

League Club	Source	Date Signed	Seasons Played	Apps	Subs	Gls
Tranmere Rov		03/78	77-81	106	8	17
Crewe Alex	Tr	08/82	82	26	3	3
Tranmere Rov	Caernarfon T	07/87	87	6	7	0

CRAVEN Terence (Terry)
Born: Barnsley, South Yorkshire, England, 27 November, 1944 — LH
England: Youth

League Club	Source	Date Signed	Seasons Played	Apps	Subs	Gls
Barnsley	Jnr	06/63	64	3	-	0

CRAWFORD Alan Paterson
Born: Rotherham, South Yorkshire, England, 30 October, 1953 — LW

League Club	Source	Date Signed	Seasons Played	Apps	Subs	Gls
Rotherham U	App	10/71	73-78	233	4	49
Mansfield T	L	01/73	72	1	1	0
Chesterfield	Tr	08/79	79-81	88	6	20
Bristol C	Tr	08/82	82-84	85	7	26
Exeter C	Tr	07/85	85	33	0	3

CRAWFORD Andrew (Andy)
Born: Filey, North Yorkshire, England, 30 January, 1959 — F

League Club	Source	Date Signed	Seasons Played	Apps	Subs	Gls
Derby Co	App	01/77	77-79	16	5	4
Blackburn Rov	Tr	10/79	79-81	56	0	21
Bournemouth	Tr	11/81	81-82	31	2	10
Cardiff C	Tr	08/83	83	6	0	1
Middlesbrough	Scarborough	10/83	83	8	1	1
Stockport Co		12/84	84	6	0	2
Torquay U	Tr	02/85	84	3	0	0

CRAWFORD Campbell Hackett Rankin
Born: Alexandria, Dunbartonshire, Scotland, 1 December, 1943 — RB
Scotland: Schools

League Club	Source	Date Signed	Seasons Played	Apps	Subs	Gls
West Bromwich A	Jnr	12/60	63-66	10	0	0
Exeter C	Tr	07/67	67-73	224	10	3

CRAWFORD Harrison (Harry)
Born: Watford, Hertfordshire, England, 10 December, 1991 — F

League Club	Source	Date Signed	Seasons Played	Apps	Subs	Gls
Southend U	Sch	07/10	09-11	7	26	3
Barnet	Dartford	01/13	12	3	7	1

CRAWFORD James (Jimmy)
Born: Chicago, Illinois, USA, 1 May, 1973 — M/RB
Republic of Ireland: U21-2

League Club	Source	Date Signed	Seasons Played	Apps	Subs	Gls
Newcastle U	Bohemians (ROI)	03/95	96	0	2	0
Rotherham U	L	09/96	96	11	0	0
Reading	Tr	03/98	97-99	17	4	1

CRAWFORD James Cherrie (Jimmy)
Born: Bellshill, Lanarkshire, Scotland, 27 September, 1930 — IF
Died: Corby, Northamptonshire, England, 20 August, 2012

League Club	Source	Date Signed	Seasons Played	Apps	Subs	Gls
Leicester C	Jnr	10/47	50-53	10	-	2
Plymouth Arg	Tr	03/54	53-55	25	-	4

CRAWFORD John (Ian)
Born: Edinburgh, Scotland, 14 July, 1934 LB/W
Died: Peterborough, England, 30 November, 2007
Scotland: U23-1

League Club	Source	Date Signed	Seasons Played	Apps	Subs	Gls
West Ham U	Greenock Morton	07/61	61-62	24	-	5
Scunthorpe U	Tr	03/63	62-63	35	-	2
Peterborough U	Tr	07/64	64-68	172	0	6

CRAWFORD John Campbell (Ian)
Born: Falkirk, Scotland, 27 June, 1922 IF
Died: Falkirk, Scotland, 28 June, 1996

League Club	Source	Date Signed	Seasons Played	Apps	Subs	Gls
Oldham Ath	Ayr U	07/52	52-53	24	-	8
Halifax T	Tr	07/54	54	11	-	2

CRAWFORD John Robert Bruce (Bruce)
Born: Preston, Lancashire, England, 10 October, 1938 WH/IF
England: U23-1

League Club	Source	Date Signed	Seasons Played	Apps	Subs	Gls
Blackpool	Jnr	05/56	59-64	98	-	11
Tranmere Rov	Tr	09/65	65-66	24	2	5

CRAWFORD Peter Graeme (Graeme)
Born: Falkirk, Scotland, 7 August, 1947 G

League Club	Source	Date Signed	Seasons Played	Apps	Subs	Gls
Sheffield U	East Stirlingshire	09/68	69-70	2	0	0
Mansfield T	L	07/71	71	2	0	0
York C	Tr	10/71	71-76	235	0	0
Scunthorpe U	Tr	08/77	77-79	104	0	0
York C	Tr	01/80	79	17	0	0
Rochdale	Tr	09/80	80-82	70	0	0

CRAWFORD Raymond (Ray)
Born: Portsmouth, England, 13 July, 1936 CF
England: 2/FLge-3

League Club	Source	Date Signed	Seasons Played	Apps	Subs	Gls
Portsmouth	Jnr	12/54	57-58	19	-	9
Ipswich T	Tr	09/58	58-63	197	-	143
Wolverhampton W	Tr	09/63	63-64	57	-	39
West Bromwich A	Tr	02/65	64-65	14	0	6
Ipswich T	Tr	03/66	65-68	123	0	61
Charlton Ath	Tr	03/69	68-69	21	0	7
Colchester U	Kettering T	06/70	70	45	0	25

CRAWFORD Stephen (Stevie)
Born: Dunfermline, Fife, Scotland, 9 January, 1974 F
Scotland: 25/U21-19

League Club	Source	Date Signed	Seasons Played	Apps	Subs	Gls
Millwall	Raith Rov	07/96	96	40	2	11
Plymouth Arg	Dunfermline Ath	07/04	04	19	7	6

CRAWLEY Thomas Andrew (Tommy)
Born: Hamilton, Lanarkshire, Scotland, 10 November, 1911 CF
Died: Coventry, England, 1976

League Club	Source	Date Signed	Seasons Played	Apps	Subs	Gls
Preston NE	Motherwell	05/35	35	2	-	0
Coventry C	Tr	02/36	35-46	45	-	16

CRAWSHAW Cyril
Born: Eccles, Greater Manchester, England, 2 March, 1916 IF
Died: Worsley, Greater Manchester, England, 27 January, 2003

League Club	Source	Date Signed	Seasons Played	Apps	Subs	Gls
Rochdale	Rossendale U	11/36	36	2	-	0
Exeter C	Queen of the South	07/39				
Hull C	Stalybridge Celtic	06/46	46	2	-	2

CREAMER Peter Anthony
Born: Hartlepool, Cleveland, England, 20 September, 1953 D/M
England: Schools

League Club	Source	Date Signed	Seasons Played	Apps	Subs	Gls
Middlesbrough	App	10/70	72-73	9	0	0
York C	L	11/75	75	4	0	0
Doncaster Rov	Tr	12/75	75-76	31	1	0
Hartlepool U	Tr	10/76	76-77	63	0	3
Rochdale	Gateshead	12/78	78	18	2	0

CREANE Gerard Martin (Gerry)
Born: Lincoln, England, 2 February, 1962 CD

League Club	Source	Date Signed	Seasons Played	Apps	Subs	Gls
Lincoln C	App	02/80	78-82	6	1	0

CREANEY Gerard Thomas (Gerry)
Born: Coatbridge, Lanarkshire, Scotland, 13 April, 1970 F
Scotland: B-1/U21-11

League Club	Source	Date Signed	Seasons Played	Apps	Subs	Gls
Portsmouth	Glasgow Celtic	01/94	93-95	60	0	32
Manchester C	Tr	09/95	95-97	8	13	4
Oldham Ath	L	03/96	95	8	1	2
Ipswich T	L	10/96	96	6	0	1
Burnley	L	09/97	97	9	1	8
Chesterfield	L	01/98	97	3	1	0
Notts Co	St Mirren	02/99	98	13	3	3

CREASER Glyn Robert
Born: Camden, N London, England, 1 September, 1959 CD

League Club	Source	Date Signed	Seasons Played	Apps	Subs	Gls
Wycombe W	Barnet	09/88	93-94	17	2	2

CREGG Patrick Anthony
Born: Dublin, Republic of Ireland, 21 February, 1986 M
Republic of Ireland: U21-5

League Club	Source	Date Signed	Seasons Played	Apps	Subs	Gls
Arsenal	Sch	02/03				
Bury	St Mirren	08/11	11	5	2	0

CREIGHTON Mark Adam
Born: Burton-on-Trent, Staffordshire, England, 8 October, 1981 CD

League Club	Source	Date Signed	Seasons Played	Apps	Subs	Gls
Oxford U	Kidderminster Hrs	05/09	10	5	2	0

CRELLIN Andrew
Born: Gainsborough, Lincolnshire, England, 11 October, 1954 LB

League Club	Source	Date Signed	Seasons Played	Apps	Subs	Gls
Scunthorpe U	App	10/72				
Doncaster Rov	Ashby Inst	03/74	74	4	0	0

CRERAND Daniel Bruno (Danny)
Born: Eccles, Greater Manchester, England, 5 May, 1969 M

League Club	Source	Date Signed	Seasons Played	Apps	Subs	Gls
Rochdale	Chapel Villa	02/88	87	3	0	0

CRERAND Patrick Timothy (Pat)
Born: Glasgow, Scotland, 19 February, 1939 RH
Scotland: 16/SLge-7/U23-1

League Club	Source	Date Signed	Seasons Played	Apps	Subs	Gls
Manchester U	Glasgow Celtic	02/63	62-70	304	0	10

CRESPO Hernan Jorge
Born: Buenos Aires, Argentina, 6 July, 1975 F
Argentina: 64/U23-6

League Club	Source	Date Signed	Seasons Played	Apps	Subs	Gls
Chelsea	Inter Milan (ITA)	08/03	03-05	33	16	20

CRESSWELL Aaron William
Born: Liverpool, England, 15 December, 1989 LB

League Club	Source	Date Signed	Seasons Played	Apps	Subs	Gls
Tranmere Rov	Sch	07/08	08-10	63	7	5
Ipswich T	Tr	07/11	11-13	132	0	6
West Ham U	Tr	07/14	14	38	0	2

CRESSWELL Corbett Eric
Born: Birkenhead, Wirral, England, 3 August, 1932 CH
England: Amateur-10

League Club	Source	Date Signed	Seasons Played	Apps	Subs	Gls
Carlisle U	Bishop Auckland	03/58	57-58	14	-	2

CRESSWELL Peter Frank
Born: Hucknall, Nottinghamshire, England, 9 November, 1935 RW

League Club	Source	Date Signed	Seasons Played	Apps	Subs	Gls
Derby Co	Heanor T	04/54	54-56	12	-	2

CRESSWELL Philip
Born: Hucknall, Nottinghamshire, England, 11 May, 1933 RW
Died: Mansfield, Nottinghamshire, England, February, 1993

League Club	Source	Date Signed	Seasons Played	Apps	Subs	Gls
Coventry C	Jnr	05/50	54	2	-	0

CRESSWELL Richard Paul Wesley
Born: Bridlington, East Riding of Yorkshire, England, 20 September, 1977 F
England: U21-4

League Club	Source	Date Signed	Seasons Played	Apps	Subs	Gls
York C	YT	11/95	95-98	72	23	21
Mansfield T	L	03/97	96	5	0	1
Sheffield Wed	Tr	03/99	98-00	7	24	2
Leicester C	Tr	09/00	00	3	5	0
Preston NE	Tr	03/01	00-05	164	23	49
Leeds U	Tr	08/05	05-06	30	8	9
Stoke C	Tr	08/07	07-09	54	21	11
Sheffield U	Tr	09/09	09-12	92	32	27
York C	Tr	03/13	12-13	8	3	2

CRESSWELL Ryan Anthony
Born: Rotherham, South Yorkshire, England, 22 December, 1987 CD

League Club	Source	Date Signed	Seasons Played	Apps	Subs	Gls
Sheffield U	Sch	07/06				
Rotherham U	L	09/07	07	1	2	0
Morecambe	L	11/07	07	2	0	0
Macclesfield T	L	01/08	07	19	0	1
Bury	Tr	07/08	08-09	43	10	1
Rotherham U	Tr	07/10	10-11	34	4	0
Southend U	Tr	08/12	12	42	1	6
Fleetwood T	Tr	07/13	13-14	18	3	1
Northampton T	Tr	09/14	14	31	1	5

CRIBLEY Alexander (Alex)
Born: Liverpool, England, 1 April, 1957 CD

League Club	Source	Date Signed	Seasons Played	Apps	Subs	Gls
Liverpool		06/78				
Wigan Ath	Tr	10/80	80-87	268	4	16

CRICHTON George
Born: Leslie, Fife, Scotland, 11 December, 1925 CH
Died: Workington, Cumbria, England, 13 June, 2011

League Club	Source	Date Signed	Seasons Played	Apps	Subs	Gls
Workington	Loughborough College	07/50	51	4	-	0

CRICHTON Paul Andrew
Born: Pontefract, West Yorkshire, England, 3 October, 1968 G

League Club	Source	Date Signed	Seasons Played	Apps	Subs	Gls
Nottingham F	Jnr	05/86				
Notts Co	L	09/86	86	5	0	0
Darlington	L	01/87	86	5	0	0
Peterborough U	L	03/87	86	4	0	0

League Club	Source	Date Signed	Seasons Played	Apps	Subs	Gls
Darlington	L	09/87	87	3	0	0
Swindon T	L	12/87	87	4	0	0
Rotherham U	L	03/88	87	6	0	0
Torquay U	L	08/88	88	13	0	0
Peterborough U	Tr	11/88	88-89	47	0	0
Doncaster Rov	Tr	08/90	90-92	77	0	0
Grimsby T	Tr	07/93	93-95	133	0	0
West Bromwich A	Tr	09/96	96-97	32	0	0
Burnley	L	08/98	98	1	0	0
Burnley	Tr	11/98	98-00	81	1	0
Norwich C	Tr	06/01	01	5	1	0
Gillingham	Accrington Stan	08/05	05	1	0	0

CRICKETT Norman
Born: Carlisle, Cumbria, England, 13 October, 1932 — RW

League Club	Source	Date Signed	Seasons Played	Apps	Subs	Gls
Carlisle U	Raffles Rov	11/52	55	1	-	0

CRICKMORE Charles Alfred (Charlie)
Born: Hull, England, 11 February, 1942 — LW

League Club	Source	Date Signed	Seasons Played	Apps	Subs	Gls
Hull C	Jnr	02/59	59-61	53	-	13
Bournemouth	Tr	07/62	62-65	128	0	17
Gillingham	Tr	06/66	66-67	53	0	13
Rotherham U	Tr	11/67	67	7	1	1
Norwich C	Tr	01/68	67-69	54	2	9
Notts Co	Tr	03/70	69-71	59	0	11

CRICKSON George Edward (Gerry)
Born: Dover, Kent, England, 21 September, 1934 — RH
Died: Dover, Kent, England, 4 March, 1991
England: Youth/Schools

League Club	Source	Date Signed	Seasons Played	Apps	Subs	Gls
Queens Park Rgrs	Dover	09/51	52-55	5	-	0

CRIPPS Henry Richard (Harry)
Born: Dereham, Norfolk, England, 29 April, 1941 — LB
Died: Wanstead, NE London, England, 29 December, 1995

League Club	Source	Date Signed	Seasons Played	Apps	Subs	Gls
West Ham U	Jnr	09/58				
Millwall	Tr	06/61	61-74	390	10	37
Charlton Ath	Tr	10/74	74-75	17	3	4

CRIPSEY Brian Samuel
Born: Hull, England, 26 June, 1931 — LW

League Club	Source	Date Signed	Seasons Played	Apps	Subs	Gls
Hull C	Brunswick Inst	11/51	52-58	145	-	19
Wrexham	Tr	09/58	58-59	27	-	3

CRISP Richard Ian
Born: Dudley, West Midlands, England, 23 May, 1972 — M

League Club	Source	Date Signed	Seasons Played	Apps	Subs	Gls
Aston Villa	YT	07/90				
Scunthorpe U	L	03/93	92	6	2	0

CRISP Ronald James (Ron)
Born: Datchet, England, 24 September, 1938 — RH/CF

League Club	Source	Date Signed	Seasons Played	Apps	Subs	Gls
Watford	Dulwich Hamlet	01/61	60-64	89	-	14
Brentford	Tr	08/65	65-66	17	1	0

CRISPIN Timothy (Tim)
Born: Leicester, England, 7 June, 1948 — LB

League Club	Source	Date Signed	Seasons Played	Apps	Subs	Gls
Notts Co	Jnr	07/66	66-67	8	0	0

[CRISTIAN] LOPEZ Cristian
Born: Elche, Spain, 27 April, 1989 — F

League Club	Source	Date Signed	Seasons Played	Apps	Subs	Gls
Huddersfield T	Atlet Baleares (SPN)	08/13	13	0	2	0
Shrewsbury T	L	10/13	13	4	1	1
Northampton T	L	03/14	13	0	3	0

CRITCHELL Kyle Andrew Ross
Born: Dorchester, Dorset, England, 18 January, 1987 — RB

League Club	Source	Date Signed	Seasons Played	Apps	Subs	Gls
Southampton	Sch	07/05				
Torquay U	L	10/06	06	6	1	0
Chesterfield	Tr	01/07	06	6	4	0

CRITCHLEY Neil
Born: Crewe, Cheshire, England, 18 October, 1978 — M

League Club	Source	Date Signed	Seasons Played	Apps	Subs	Gls
Crewe Alex	YT	07/97	99	0	1	0

CRITTENDEN Nicholas James (Nicky)
Born: Bracknell, Berkshire, England, 11 November, 1978 — LB
England: Semi Pro-1

League Club	Source	Date Signed	Seasons Played	Apps	Subs	Gls
Chelsea	YT	07/97	97	0	2	0
Plymouth Arg	L	10/98	98	1	1	0
Yeovil T	Tr	08/00	03	20	9	2

CROCI Laurent
Born: Montbeliard, France, 8 December, 1964 — CD

League Club	Source	Date Signed	Seasons Played	Apps	Subs	Gls
Carlisle U	Bordeaux (FRA)	10/97	97	1	0	0

CROCKER Marcus Alan
Born: Plymouth, England, 8 October, 1974 — F

League Club	Source	Date Signed	Seasons Played	Apps	Subs	Gls
Plymouth Arg	YT	06/93	92-94	4	6	0

CROCOMBE Maxime Teremoana (Max)
Born: Auckland, New Zealand, 12 August, 1993 — G

League Club	Source	Date Signed	Seasons Played	Apps	Subs	Gls
Oxford U	Buckingham T	07/12	12	4	0	0

CROFT Alec Robert
Born: Chester, England, 17 June, 1937 — W

League Club	Source	Date Signed	Seasons Played	Apps	Subs	Gls
Chester C	Saltney Jnrs	08/58	58-60	53	-	3

CROFT Brian Graham Alexander
Born: Chester, England, 27 September, 1967 — LW

League Club	Source	Date Signed	Seasons Played	Apps	Subs	Gls
Chester C	App	07/86	85-87	36	23	3
Cambridge U	Tr	10/88	88	12	5	2
Chester C	Tr	08/89	89-91	90	24	3
Queens Park Rgrs	Tr	08/92				
Shrewsbury T	L	12/93	93	4	0	0
Blackpool	Tr	07/95				
Torquay U	Tr	08/95	95	0	1	0
Stockport Co	Southport	10/95	95	0	3	0

CROFT Charles (Charlie)
Born: Dewsbury, West Yorkshire, England, 26 November, 1918 — LH
Died: Robertstown, West Yorkshire, England, 26 July, 2006

League Club	Source	Date Signed	Seasons Played	Apps	Subs	Gls
Huddersfield T	Thornhill Edge	05/39				
Mansfield T	Tr	05/47	47-49	85	-	5

CROFT Gary
Born: Burton-on-Trent, Staffordshire, England, 17 February, 1974 — LB
England: U21-4

League Club	Source	Date Signed	Seasons Played	Apps	Subs	Gls
Grimsby T	YT	07/92	90-95	139	10	3
Blackburn Rov	Tr	03/96	96-98	33	7	1
Ipswich T	Tr	09/99	99-00	20	9	1
Wigan Ath	L	01/02	01	7	0	0
Cardiff C	Tr	03/02	01-04	65	12	3
Grimsby T	Tr	08/05	05-06	52	9	0
Lincoln C	Tr	07/07	07	20	0	0

CROFT Lee David
Born: Orrell, Greater Manchester, England, 21 June, 1985 — RM
England: Youth

League Club	Source	Date Signed	Seasons Played	Apps	Subs	Gls
Manchester C	Sch	07/02	04-05	4	24	1
Oldham Ath	L	11/04	04	11	1	0
Norwich C	Tr	07/06	06-08	86	32	9
Derby Co	Tr	07/09	09-11	18	9	1
Huddersfield T	L	07/10	10	0	3	0
Oldham Ath	Tr	07/12	12	44	1	0

CROFT Stuart Dunbar
Born: Ashington, Northumberland, England, 12 April, 1954 — CD

League Club	Source	Date Signed	Seasons Played	Apps	Subs	Gls
Hull C	App	04/72	72-80	187	3	4
Portsmouth	Tr	03/81	80	6	0	1
York C	Tr	08/81	81	14	0	0

CROFTS Andrew Lawrence (Andy)
Born: Chatham, Kent, England, 29 May, 1984 — M
Wales: 27/U21-10/Youth

League Club	Source	Date Signed	Seasons Played	Apps	Subs	Gls
Gillingham	Sch	08/03	00-08	162	12	17
Peterborough U	L	11/08	08	4	5	0
Brighton & HA	Tr	07/09	09	44	0	5
Norwich C	Tr	05/10	10-11	57	11	8
Brighton & HA	Tr	08/12	12-14	47	7	5

CROKER Edgar Alfred (Ted)
Born: Kingston-on-Thames, SW London, England, 13 February, 1924 — LB
Died: Cheltenham, Gloucestershire, England, 25 December, 1992

League Club	Source	Date Signed	Seasons Played	Apps	Subs	Gls
Charlton Ath	Kingstonian	07/48	50	8	-	0

CROKER Peter Harry Lucas
Born: Kingston-on-Thames, SW London, England, 21 December, 1921 — FB
Died: Bexley, SE London, England, 7 December, 2011

League Club	Source	Date Signed	Seasons Played	Apps	Subs	Gls
Charlton Ath	Bromley	11/45	46-50	59	-	0
Watford	Tr	06/52	52	23	-	0

CROMACK David Charles (Dave)
Born: Leeds, England, 22 December, 1948 — RB

League Club	Source	Date Signed	Seasons Played	Apps	Subs	Gls
Doncaster Rov	Bradford C (Am)	11/66	66	8	0	0

CROMACK Victor (Vic)
Born: Mansfield, Nottinghamshire, England, 17 March, 1920 — G
Died: Mansfield, Nottinghamshire, England, October, 1984

League Club	Source	Date Signed	Seasons Played	Apps	Subs	Gls
Mansfield T	Meadow Foundry	01/46	46	10	-	0

CROMBIE Dean Malcolm
Born: Lincoln, England, 9 August, 1957 — CD

League Club	Source	Date Signed	Seasons Played	Apps	Subs	Gls
Lincoln C	Ruston-Bucyrus	02/77	76-77	33	0	0
Grimsby T	Tr	08/78	78-86	316	4	4
Reading	L	11/86	86	4	0	0
Bolton W	Tr	08/87	87-90	90	5	1
Lincoln C	Tr	01/91	90	0	1	0

CROMBIE Thomas Ronald (Tom)
Born: Kirkcaldy, Fife, Scotland, 3 June, 1930 LB

League Club	Source	Date Signed	Seasons Played	Apps	Subs	Gls
Blackpool	Jeanfield Swifts	08/51				
Gillingham	Tr	07/55	55-56	17	-	0

CROMPTON Alan
Born: Bolton, Greater Manchester, England, 6 March, 1958 M

League Club	Source	Date Signed	Seasons Played	Apps	Subs	Gls
Sunderland	App	03/75				
Blackburn Rov	Tr	07/76	76	2	2	0
Wigan Ath	Tr	07/78	78-79	7	7	0

CROMPTON David Gerald
Born: Wigan, Greater Manchester, England, 6 March, 1945 LM

League Club	Source	Date Signed	Seasons Played	Apps	Subs	Gls
Rochdale (Am)		11/66	66-67	15	2	0

CROMPTON Dennis
Born: Bolton, Greater Manchester, England, 12 March, 1942 WH

League Club	Source	Date Signed	Seasons Played	Apps	Subs	Gls
Bolton W	Wigan Ath	12/59				
Doncaster Rov	Tr	06/63	63	23	-	0

CROMPTON John (Jack)
Born: Chorlton, Greater Manchester, England, 18 December, 1921 G
Died: Hulme, Greater Manchester, England, 4 July, 2013

League Club	Source	Date Signed	Seasons Played	Apps	Subs	Gls
Manchester U	Goslings	01/45	46-55	191	-	0

CROMPTON Paul Jonathan (Jonathan)
Born: Orrell, Greater Manchester, England, 25 January, 1970 F

League Club	Source	Date Signed	Seasons Played	Apps	Subs	Gls
Wigan Ath	YT	07/88	89	1	0	0

CROMPTON Stephen Wynn (Steve)
Born: Wrexham, Wales, 3 December, 1958 F

League Club	Source	Date Signed	Seasons Played	Apps	Subs	Gls
Hereford U	Wolverhampton W (App)	02/77	76-78	30	4	6

CROMPTON Steven Geoffrey (Steve)
Born: Partington, Greater Manchester, England, 20 April, 1968 G

League Club	Source	Date Signed	Seasons Played	Apps	Subs	Gls
Manchester C	Jnr	05/86				
Carlisle U	Tr	07/87	87	10	0	0
Stockport Co	Tr	02/88	87	2	0	0

CRONIN Dennis
Born: Altrincham, Greater Manchester, England, 30 October, 1967 F

League Club	Source	Date Signed	Seasons Played	Apps	Subs	Gls
Manchester U	App	10/85				
Stockport Co	Tr	08/87	87	11	4	1
Crewe Alex	Tr	08/88	88	12	3	2

CRONIN Glenn
Born: Dublin, Republic of Ireland, 14 September, 1981 M
Republic of Ireland: Youth

League Club	Source	Date Signed	Seasons Played	Apps	Subs	Gls
Exeter C	YT	07/00	01-02	52	17	0
Chester C	Tr	07/06	06	1	3	0

CRONIN Lance
Born: Brighton, England, 11 September, 1985 G
England: Semi Pro-7

League Club	Source	Date Signed	Seasons Played	Apps	Subs	Gls
Crystal Palace	Jnr	09/02				
Wycombe W	L	03/05	04	1	0	0
Gillingham	Ebbsfleet U	07/10	10	7	0	0
Bristol Rov	Tr	07/11	11	0	1	0

CRONIN Thomas Patrick (Tommy)
Born: Richmond, SW London, England, 17 December, 1932 IF

League Club	Source	Date Signed	Seasons Played	Apps	Subs	Gls
Fulham	East Sheen Ath	09/50	53-54	2	-	0
Reading	Tr	06/56	56-57	30	-	4

CROOK Alfred Rowland (Alf)
Born: Brewood, Staffordshire, England, 13 August, 1923 FB

League Club	Source	Date Signed	Seasons Played	Apps	Subs	Gls
Wolverhampton W	Boulton & Paul	05/45	48	1	-	0

CROOK George
Born: Hutton Henry, County Durham, England, 30 January, 1935 IF

League Club	Source	Date Signed	Seasons Played	Apps	Subs	Gls
Oldham Ath		02/53	53-57	57	-	13
Middlesbrough	Tr	11/58				

CROOK Ian Stuart
Born: Romford, E London, England, 18 January, 1963 M
England: B-1

League Club	Source	Date Signed	Seasons Played	Apps	Subs	Gls
Tottenham H	App	08/80	81-85	10	10	1
Norwich C	Tr	06/86	86-96	314	27	18

CROOK Leslie Ronald (Les)
Born: Manchester, England, 26 June, 1948 M
Died: Bolton, Greater Manchester, England, October, 2006

League Club	Source	Date Signed	Seasons Played	Apps	Subs	Gls
Oxford U	Manchester Amats	10/68	68	1	0	0
Hartlepool U	Tr	07/70	70	23	2	3

CROOK Walter
Born: Whittle-le-Woods, Lancashire, England, 28 April, 1913 FB
Died: Mellor, Lancashire, England, 27 December, 1988
England: War-1

League Club	Source	Date Signed	Seasons Played	Apps	Subs	Gls
Blackburn Rov	Blackburn Nomads	01/31	31-46	236	-	2
Bolton W	Tr	05/47	47	28	-	0

CROOK William Charles (Billy)
Born: Cannock, Staffordshire, England, 7 June, 1926 RH
Died: Cheshire, England, 30 May, 2011

League Club	Source	Date Signed	Seasons Played	Apps	Subs	Gls
Wolverhampton W	Jnr	08/45	46-52	196	-	2
Walsall	Tr	10/54	54-55	45	-	2

CROOKES Peter
Born: Liverpool, England, 7 May, 1982 G
England: Youth/Schools

League Club	Source	Date Signed	Seasons Played	Apps	Subs	Gls
Halifax T	Liverpool (YT)	03/01	01	1	0	0

CROOKES Robert Eastland (Bobby)
Born: Stretford, Greater Manchester, England, 29 February, 1924 LW

League Club	Source	Date Signed	Seasons Played	Apps	Subs	Gls
Notts Co	Retford T	06/49	49-55	177	-	45

CROOKS Garth Anthony
Born: Stoke-on-Trent, England, 10 March, 1958 F
England: U21-4

League Club	Source	Date Signed	Seasons Played	Apps	Subs	Gls
Stoke C	App	03/76	75-79	141	6	48
Tottenham H	Tr	07/80	80-84	121	4	48
Manchester U	L	11/83	83	6	1	2
West Bromwich A	Tr	08/85	85-86	39	1	16
Charlton Ath	Tr	03/87	86-90	41	15	15

CROOKS Lee Robert
Born: Wakefield, England, 14 January, 1978 D/M
England: Youth

League Club	Source	Date Signed	Seasons Played	Apps	Subs	Gls
Manchester C	YT	01/95	96-00	52	24	2
Northampton T	L	12/00	00	3	0	0
Barnsley	Tr	03/01	01-03	50	17	0
Bradford C	Tr	08/04	04-05	44	3	1
Notts Co	L	01/06	05	18	0	1
Rochdale	Tr	08/06	06-07	31	9	0

CROOKS Leon Everton George
Born: Greenwich, SE London, England, 21 November, 1985 CD

League Club	Source	Date Signed	Seasons Played	Apps	Subs	Gls
MK Dons	Sch	07/04	04-06	40	12	0
Wycombe W	Tr	01/07	06-08	13	0	0

CROOKS Matt Davidson Rider
Born: Huddersfield, West Yorkshire, England, 20 January, 1994 M/D

League Club	Source	Date Signed	Seasons Played	Apps	Subs	Gls
Huddersfield T	Sch	10/11	14	1	0	0
Hartlepool U	L	10/14	14	2	1	0
Accrington Stan	Tr	11/14	14	11	5	0

CROOKS Paul
Born: Durham, England, 12 October, 1966 F

League Club	Source	Date Signed	Seasons Played	Apps	Subs	Gls
Stoke C	Caernarfon T	08/86	86	0	1	0

CROOKS Samuel Dickinson (Sammy)
Born: Bearpark, County Durham, England, 16 January, 1908 RW
Died: Belper, Derbyshire, England, 3 February, 1981
England: 26/FLge-5

League Club	Source	Date Signed	Seasons Played	Apps	Subs	Gls
Durham C	Tow Law T	06/26	26	16		4
Derby Co	Tr	04/27	27-46	408	-	101

CROPLEY Alexander James (Alex)
Born: Aldershot, Hampshire, England, 16 January, 1951 M
Scotland: 2/U23-3

League Club	Source	Date Signed	Seasons Played	Apps	Subs	Gls
Arsenal	Hibernian	12/74	74-76	29	1	5
Aston Villa	Tr	09/78	76-79	65	2	7
Newcastle U	L	02/80	79	3	0	0
Portsmouth	Toronto Blizzard (CAN)	09/81	81	8	2	2

CROPLEY John Thomas (Jack)
Born: Edinburgh, Scotland, 27 September, 1924 LH
Died: Edinburgh, Scotland, 29 October, 2009

League Club	Source	Date Signed	Seasons Played	Apps	Subs	Gls
Aldershot	Tranent Jnrs	10/46	47-53	162	-	3

CROPPER Dene James
Born: Chesterfield, Derbyshire, England, 5 January, 1983 F

League Club	Source	Date Signed	Seasons Played	Apps	Subs	Gls
Lincoln C	Sheffield Wed (YT)	08/02	02-03	29	21	3
Boston U	Tr	03/04	03	4	1	1

CROSBIE Robert Crichton (Bob)
Born: Glasgow, Scotland, 2 September, 1925 CF
Died: Glasgow, Scotland, 18 February, 1994

League Club	Source	Date Signed	Seasons Played	Apps	Subs	Gls
Bury		05/47	47-48	9	-	5
Bradford Park Ave	Tr	05/49	49-53	139	-	72
Hull C	Tr	10/53	53-54	61	-	22
Grimsby T	Tr	07/55	55-56	65	-	45

CROSBY Andrew Keith (Andy)
Born: Rotherham, South Yorkshire, England, 3 March, 1973 CD

League Club	Source	Date Signed	Seasons Played	Apps	Subs	Gls
Doncaster Rov	Leeds U (YT)	07/91	91-92	41	10	0
Darlington	Tr	12/93	93-97	179	2	3

League Club	Source	Date Signed	Seasons Played	Apps	Subs	Gls
Chester C	Tr	07/98	98	41	0	4
Brighton & HA	Tr	07/99	99-01	64	8	5
Oxford U	Tr	12/01	01-03	109	2	12
Scunthorpe U	Tr	08/04	04-08	158	9	15

CROSBY Gary
Born: Sleaford, Lincolnshire, England, 8 May, 1964 — RW

League Club	Source	Date Signed	Seasons Played	Apps	Subs	Gls
Lincoln C	Lincoln U	08/86	86	6	1	0
Nottingham F	Grantham T	12/87	87-93	139	13	12
Grimsby T	L	08/93	93	2	1	0
Huddersfield T	Tr	09/94	94-96	35	9	6

CROSBY Geoffrey John (Geoff)
Born: Stoke-on-Trent, England, 24 August, 1931 — IF
Died: Stoke-on-Trent, England, 5 January, 2000

League Club	Source	Date Signed	Seasons Played	Apps	Subs	Gls
Stockport Co	Leek T	09/52	52-53	5	-	1

CROSBY Malcolm
Born: South Shields, Tyne and Wear, England, 4 July, 1954 — M

League Club	Source	Date Signed	Seasons Played	Apps	Subs	Gls
Aldershot	App	07/72	71-81	272	22	23
York C	Tr	11/81	81-84	99	4	4
Wrexham	L	09/84	84	5	1	0

CROSBY Philip Alan (Phil)
Born: Upton, West Yorkshire, England, 9 November, 1962 — LB
England: Youth

League Club	Source	Date Signed	Seasons Played	Apps	Subs	Gls
Grimsby T	App	09/80	79-82	34	5	1
Rotherham U	Tr	08/83	83-88	181	2	2
Peterborough U	Tr	08/89	89-90	85	2	0
York C	Tr	07/91	91	25	0	0

CROSLAND John Ronald (Johnny)
Born: St Annes, Lancashire, England, 10 November, 1922 — CH
Died: Ely, Cambridgeshire, England, 5 May, 2006
England: B-2

League Club	Source	Date Signed	Seasons Played	Apps	Subs	Gls
Blackpool	Ansdell Rov	05/46	46-53	67	-	0
Bournemouth	Tr	06/54	54-56	106	-	0

CROSS David
Born: Heywood, Greater Manchester, England, 8 December, 1950 — F

League Club	Source	Date Signed	Seasons Played	Apps	Subs	Gls
Rochdale	Jnr	08/69	69-71	50	6	20
Norwich C	Tr	10/71	71-73	83	1	21
Coventry C	Tr	11/73	73-76	90	1	30
West Bromwich A	Tr	11/76	76-77	38	0	18
West Ham U	Tr	12/77	77-81	178	1	77
Manchester C	Tr	08/82	82	31	0	12
Oldham Ath	Vancouver W'caps (CAN)	10/83	83	18	4	6
West Bromwich A	Vancouver W'caps (CAN)	10/84	84	16	0	2
Bolton W	Tr	06/85	85	19	1	8
Bury	L	01/86	85	12	1	0

CROSS David Barron
Born: Bromley, SE London, England, 7 September, 1982 — F

League Club	Source	Date Signed	Seasons Played	Apps	Subs	Gls
Notts Co	YT	-	99	0	1	0

CROSS Garry Robert
Born: Chelmsford, England, 7 October, 1980 — RB

League Club	Source	Date Signed	Seasons Played	Apps	Subs	Gls
Southend U	YT	07/99	99-00	11	5	0

CROSS Graham Frederick
Born: Leicester, England, 15 November, 1943 — CD/M
England: U23-11

League Club	Source	Date Signed	Seasons Played	Apps	Subs	Gls
Leicester C	App	11/60	60-75	496	3	29
Chesterfield	L	03/76	75	12	0	0
Brighton & HA	Tr	06/76	76	46	0	3
Preston NE	Tr	07/77	77-78	45	0	1
Lincoln C	Enderby T	03/79	78	19	0	0

CROSS James Keith (Jimmy)
Born: Liverpool, England, 3 December, 1926 — RH
Died: Swindon, England, 15 December, 1999

League Club	Source	Date Signed	Seasons Played	Apps	Subs	Gls
Everton		10/50				
Swindon T	Tr	07/53	53-57	154	-	5

CROSS John (Jack)
Born: Bury, Greater Manchester, England, 5 February, 1927 — CF
Died: Bournemouth, England, 19 February, 2006

League Club	Source	Date Signed	Seasons Played	Apps	Subs	Gls
Bournemouth	Guildford C	06/47	47-53	136	-	64
Northampton T	Tr	10/53	53	10	-	8
Sheffield U	Tr	02/54	53-55	44	-	16
Reading	Tr	10/55	55	15	-	6

CROSS Jonathan Neil (Jon)
Born: Wallasey, Wirral, England, 2 March, 1975 — LB/M

League Club	Source	Date Signed	Seasons Played	Apps	Subs	Gls
Wrexham	YT	11/92	91-97	92	27	12
Hereford U	L	12/96	96	5	0	1
Chester C	Tr	08/98	98-99	46	6	1

CROSS Mark
Born: Abergavenny, Monmouthshire, Wales, 6 May, 1976 — W

League Club	Source	Date Signed	Seasons Played	Apps	Subs	Gls
Hereford U	YT	-	92	0	1	0

CROSS Michael John (Mike)
Born: Walkden, Greater Manchester, England, 25 April, 1956 — LB

League Club	Source	Date Signed	Seasons Played	Apps	Subs	Gls
Bolton W	App	04/74				
Stockport Co	Tr	07/75	75	27	0	2

CROSS Nicholas Jeremy Rowland (Nicky)
Born: Birmingham, England, 7 February, 1961 — F

League Club	Source	Date Signed	Seasons Played	Apps	Subs	Gls
West Bromwich A	App	02/79	80-84	68	37	15
Walsall	Tr	08/85	85-87	107	2	45
Leicester C	Tr	01/88	87-88	54	4	15
Port Vale	Tr	06/89	89-93	120	24	39
Hereford U	Tr	07/94	94-95	56	9	14

CROSS Paul
Born: Barnsley, South Yorkshire, England, 31 October, 1965 — LB

League Club	Source	Date Signed	Seasons Played	Apps	Subs	Gls
Barnsley	App	10/83	82-91	115	4	0
Preston NE	L	09/91	91	5	0	0
Hartlepool U	Tr	01/92	91-93	73	1	1
Darlington	Tr	11/93	93-94	39	0	2

CROSS Roger George
Born: East Ham, E London, England, 20 October, 1948 — F

League Club	Source	Date Signed	Seasons Played	Apps	Subs	Gls
West Ham U	App	07/64	68-69	5	2	1
Leyton Orient	L	10/68	68	4	2	2
Brentford	Tr	03/70	69-71	62	0	21
Fulham	Tr	09/71	71-72	39	1	8
Brentford	Tr	12/72	72-76	141	4	52
Millwall	Tr	01/77	76-78	14	4	0

CROSS Roy
Born: Wednesbury, West Midlands, England, 4 December, 1947 — CD
England: Schools

League Club	Source	Date Signed	Seasons Played	Apps	Subs	Gls
Walsall	Jnr	07/66	66-69	11	1	0
Port Vale	Tr	07/70	70-74	136	0	1

CROSS Ryan
Born: Plymouth, England, 11 October, 1972 — RB

League Club	Source	Date Signed	Seasons Played	Apps	Subs	Gls
Plymouth Arg	YT	03/91	90-91	18	1	0
Hartlepool U	Tr	06/92	92-93	49	1	2
Bury	Tr	12/93	93-95	40	2	0

CROSS Scott Keith
Born: Northampton, England, 30 October, 1987 — F

League Club	Source	Date Signed	Seasons Played	Apps	Subs	Gls
Northampton T	Sch	07/06	04-05	0	5	0

CROSS Stephen Charles (Steve)
Born: Wolverhampton, England, 22 December, 1959 — M

League Club	Source	Date Signed	Seasons Played	Apps	Subs	Gls
Shrewsbury T	App	12/77	76-85	240	22	33
Derby Co	Tr	06/86	86-91	42	31	3
Bristol Rov	Tr	09/91	91-92	37	6	2

CROSSAN Edward (Eddie)
Born: Derry, Northern Ireland, 17 November, 1925 — IF
Died: Derry, Northern Ireland, 13 June, 2006
Northern Ireland: 3

League Club	Source	Date Signed	Seasons Played	Apps	Subs	Gls
Blackburn Rov	Derry C (ROI)	11/47	47-56	287	-	73
Tranmere Rov	Tr	08/57	57	39	-	6

CROSSAN Errol Gilmour
Born: Montreal, Canada, 6 October, 1930 — RW

League Club	Source	Date Signed	Seasons Played	Apps	Subs	Gls
Manchester C	Gymnasium, Isle of Man	01/54				
Gillingham	Tr	07/55	55-56	76	-	16
Southend U	Tr	08/57	57-58	40	-	11
Norwich C	Tr	09/58	58-60	102	-	28
Leyton Orient	Tr	01/61	60	8	-	2

CROSSAN John Andrew (Johnny)
Born: Derry, Northern Ireland, 29 November, 1938 — IF
Northern Ireland: 24/B-1

League Club	Source	Date Signed	Seasons Played	Apps	Subs	Gls
Sunderland	Standard Liege (BEL)	10/62	62-64	82	-	39
Manchester C	Tr	01/65	64-66	94	0	24
Middlesbrough	Tr	08/67	67-69	54	2	7

CROSSLEY James
Born: Belfast, Northern Ireland, 29 July, 1922 — LB
Died: Whitefield, Greater Manchester, England, 27 November, 2001

League Club	Source	Date Signed	Seasons Played	Apps	Subs	Gls
Portsmouth	Cliftonville	04/45				
Reading	Tr	07/46	46	1	-	0

CROSSLEY Mark Geoffrey
Born: Barnsley, South Yorkshire, England, 16 June, 1969 — G
England: U21-3//Wales: 8/B-1

League Club	Source	Date Signed	Seasons Played	Apps	Subs	Gls
Nottingham F	YT	07/87	88-99	301	2	0
Millwall	L	02/98	97	13	0	0
Middlesbrough	Tr	07/00	00-01	21	2	0
Stoke C	L	11/02	02	1	0	0
Stoke C	L	03/03	02	11	0	0
Fulham	Tr	08/03	03-05	19	1	0
Sheffield Wed	L	11/06	06	17	0	1

League Club	Source	Date Signed	Seasons Played	Career Record Apps	Subs	Gls
Oldham Ath	Tr	08/07	07-08	59	0	0
Chesterfield	Tr	07/09	09	4	0	0

CROSSLEY Matthew John William (Matt)
Born: Basingstoke, Hampshire, England, 18 March, 1968 — CD

League Club	Source	Date Signed	Seasons Played	Apps	Subs	Gls
Wycombe W	Overton U	02/88	93-96	93	3	3

CROSSLEY Paul
Born: Rochdale, Greater Manchester, England, 14 July, 1948 — W
Died: Seattle, Washington, USA, 12 March, 1996

League Club	Source	Date Signed	Seasons Played	Apps	Subs	Gls
Rochdale	St Clement's	09/65	65-66	17	0	2
Preston NE	Tr	11/66	66-67	3	0	0
Southport	L	09/68	68	10	0	2
Tranmere Rov	Tr	06/69	69-75	186	17	37
Chester C	Tr	09/75	75-77	93	6	26

CROSSLEY Richard Mark
Born: Huddersfield, West Yorkshire, England, 5 September, 1970 — CD

League Club	Source	Date Signed	Seasons Played	Apps	Subs	Gls
York C	Huddersfield T (YT)	10/89	89-90	6	0	0

CROSSLEY Roy
Born: Hebden Bridge, West Yorkshire, England, 16 October, 1923 — CF
Died: Calderdale, West Yorkshire, England, July, 2003

League Club	Source	Date Signed	Seasons Played	Apps	Subs	Gls
Huddersfield T	RAF	05/46				
Halifax T	Tr	09/48	48-50	41	-	15

CROSSLEY Russell
Born: Hebden Bridge, West Yorkshire, England, 25 June, 1927 — G

League Club	Source	Date Signed	Seasons Played	Apps	Subs	Gls
Liverpool	Jnr	06/47	50-53	68	-	0
Shrewsbury T	Tr	07/54	54-59	173	-	0

CROSSLEY Terence Gordon (Terry)
Born: Rock Ferry, Wirral, England, 24 February, 1936 — LW
Died: St Helens, Merseyside, England, 7 August, 2009

League Club	Source	Date Signed	Seasons Played	Apps	Subs	Gls
Oldham Ath	Bangor Univ	08/57	57	2	-	1

CROSSON David
Born: Bishop Auckland, County Durham, England, 24 November, 1952 — RB

League Club	Source	Date Signed	Seasons Played	Apps	Subs	Gls
Newcastle U	Jnr	11/70	73-74	6	0	0
Darlington	Tr	08/75	75-79	115	13	2

CROTTY Colin
Born: Aberfan, Merthyr Tydfil, Wales, 12 February, 1951 — F

League Club	Source	Date Signed	Seasons Played	Apps	Subs	Gls
Swansea C (Am)	Jnr	08/68	68	1	1	1

CROUCH Nigel John
Born: Ardleigh, Essex, England, 24 November, 1958 — LB

League Club	Source	Date Signed	Seasons Played	Apps	Subs	Gls
Ipswich T	App	11/76				
Lincoln C	L	08/79	79	7	0	0
Colchester U	Tr	07/80	80	9	1	0

CROUCH Peter James
Born: Macclesfield, Cheshire, England, 30 January, 1981 — F
England: 42/U21-6/Youth

League Club	Source	Date Signed	Seasons Played	Apps	Subs	Gls
Tottenham H	YT	07/98				
Queens Park Rgrs	Tr	07/00	00	38	4	10
Portsmouth	Tr	07/01	01	37	0	18
Aston Villa	Tr	03/02	01-03	20	17	6
Norwich C	L	09/03	03	14	1	4
Southampton	Tr	07/04	04	18	9	12
Liverpool	Tr	07/05	05-07	55	30	22
Portsmouth	Tr	07/08	08	38	0	11
Tottenham H	Tr	07/09	09-11	42	31	12
Stoke C	Tr	08/11	11-14	106	27	33

CROUDSON Steven David (Steve)
Born: Grimsby, North Lincolnshire, England, 14 September, 1979 — G

League Club	Source	Date Signed	Seasons Played	Apps	Subs	Gls
Grimsby T	YT	07/98	98-01	5	1	0
Scunthorpe U	L	08/01	01	4	0	0
Boston U	Tr	08/03				

CROW Daniel Stephen (Danny)
Born: Great Yarmouth, Norfolk, England, 26 January, 1986 — F

League Club	Source	Date Signed	Seasons Played	Apps	Subs	Gls
Norwich C	Sch	09/04	04	0	3	0
Northampton T	L	02/05	04	4	6	2
Peterborough U	Tr	07/05	05-07	58	19	23
Notts Co	L	10/07	07	1	0	0
Notts Co	L	02/08	07	12	1	2
Newport Co	Luton T	06/12	13-14	13	16	3

CROWE Alexander Allan (Alec)
Born: Motherwell, Lanarkshire, Scotland, 24 November, 1924 — IF
Died: Motherwell, Lanarkshire, Scotland, 3 May, 1997

League Club	Source	Date Signed	Seasons Played	Apps	Subs	Gls
Ipswich T	Cowdenbeath	05/53	53-54	50	-	9

CROWE Charles Alfred (Charlie)
Born: Walker, Tyne and Wear, England, 30 October, 1924 — LH
Died: North Shields, Tyne and Wear, England, 27 February, 2010

League Club	Source	Date Signed	Seasons Played	Apps	Subs	Gls
Newcastle U	Heaton & Byker	10/44	46-56	178	-	5
Mansfield T	Tr	02/57	56-57	37	-	0

CROWE Christopher (Chris)
Born: Newcastle-upon-Tyne, England, 11 June, 1939 — IF/RW
Died: Bristol, England, May, 2003
England: 1/U23-4/Youth//Scotland: Schools

League Club	Source	Date Signed	Seasons Played	Apps	Subs	Gls
Leeds U	Jnr	06/56	56-59	95	-	27
Blackburn Rov	Tr	03/60	59-61	51	-	6
Wolverhampton W	Tr	02/62	61-63	83	-	24
Nottingham F	Tr	08/64	64-66	73	0	12
Bristol C	Tr	01/67	66-68	66	1	13
Walsall	Auburn (AUS)	09/69	69	10	3	1

CROWE Dean Anthony
Born: Stockport, Greater Manchester, England, 6 June, 1979 — F

League Club	Source	Date Signed	Seasons Played	Apps	Subs	Gls
Stoke C	YT	09/96	97-99	29	31	12
Northampton T	L	02/00	99	3	2	0
Bury	L	03/00	99	4	0	1
Bury	L	08/00	00	1	6	1
Plymouth Arg	L	08/01	01	0	1	0
Luton T	Tr	09/01	01-03	49	20	17
York C	L	09/03	03	2	3	0
Oldham Ath	Tr	03/04	03	2	3	1
Stockport Co	Leek T	08/05	05	1	5	0

CROWE Glen Michael
Born: Dublin, Republic of Ireland, 25 December, 1977 — F
Republic of Ireland: U21-2/Youth

League Club	Source	Date Signed	Seasons Played	Apps	Subs	Gls
Wolverhampton W	YT	07/96	95-97	6	4	1
Exeter C	L	02/97	96	10	0	5
Cardiff C	L	10/97	97	7	1	1
Exeter C	L	08/98	98	3	6	0
Plymouth Arg	Tr	02/99	98	3	8	1

CROWE Jason William Robert
Born: Sidcup, SE London, England, 30 September, 1978 — RB
England: Youth/Schools

League Club	Source	Date Signed	Seasons Played	Apps	Subs	Gls
Arsenal	YT	05/96				
Crystal Palace	L	11/98	98	8	0	0
Portsmouth	Tr	07/99	99-02	67	19	5
Brentford	L	09/00	00	9	0	0
Grimsby T	Tr	08/03	03-04	64	5	4
Northampton T	Tr	07/05	05-08	170	1	14
Leeds U	Tr	07/09	09	16	1	0
Leyton Orient	Tr	01/11	10	5	7	0
Northampton T		11/11	11	11	0	0

CROWE Mark Anthony
Born: Southwold, Suffolk, England, 21 January, 1965 — CD

League Club	Source	Date Signed	Seasons Played	Apps	Subs	Gls
Norwich C	App	01/83	82	0	1	0
Torquay U	Tr	07/85	85-86	57	0	2
Cambridge U	Tr	12/86	86-87	51	0	0

CROWE Matthew Jackson (Matt)
Born: Bathgate, West Lothian, Scotland, 4 July, 1932 — LH

League Club	Source	Date Signed	Seasons Played	Apps	Subs	Gls
Bradford Park Ave	Partick Thistle	07/49	52	1	-	0
Norwich C	Partick Thistle	05/57	57-61	186	-	14
Brentford	Tr	07/62	62-63	73	-	0

CROWE Michael (Mick)
Born: Ulverston, Cumbria, England, 13 August, 1942 — RW

League Club	Source	Date Signed	Seasons Played	Apps	Subs	Gls
Barrow	Ulverston Ath	08/60	60-62	15	-	1

CROWE Victor Herbert (Vic)
Born: Abercynon, Rhondda Cynon Taff, Wales, 31 January, 1932 — RH
Died: Sutton Coldfield, West Midlands, England, 21 January, 2009
Wales: 16

League Club	Source	Date Signed	Seasons Played	Apps	Subs	Gls
Aston Villa	West Bromwich A (Am)	06/52	54-63	294	-	10
Peterborough U	Tr	07/64	64-66	56	0	0

CROWELL Matthew Thomas (Matty)
Born: Bridgend, Wales, 3 July, 1984 — M
Wales: U21-7/Youth

League Club	Source	Date Signed	Seasons Played	Apps	Subs	Gls
Southampton	YT	07/01				
Wrexham	Tr	07/03	03-07	70	23	4

CROWN David Ian
Born: Enfield, N London, England, 16 February, 1958 — F

League Club	Source	Date Signed	Seasons Played	Apps	Subs	Gls
Brentford	Walthamstow Ave	07/80	80-81	44	2	8
Portsmouth	Tr	10/81	81-82	25	3	2
Exeter C	L	03/83	82	6	1	3
Reading	Tr	08/83	83-84	87	1	14
Cambridge U	Tr	07/85	85-87	106	0	45
Southend U	Tr	11/87	87-89	113	0	61
Gillingham	Tr	06/90	90-92	83	3	38

CROWSHAW Allan Alfred
Born: Bloxwich, West Midlands, England, 12 December, 1932 — LW

League Club	Source	Date Signed	Seasons Played	Apps	Subs	Gls
West Bromwich A	Bloxwich Wesleyans	05/50	54-55	11	-	2
Derby Co	Tr	06/56	56-57	18	-	6
Millwall	Tr	05/58	58-59	49	-	10

CROWTHER Kenneth (Ken)
Born: Halifax, West Yorkshire, England, 17 December, 1924 RH
Died: Halifax, West Yorkshire, England, June, 1994

League Club	Source	Date Signed	Seasons Played	Apps	Subs	Gls
Burnley	Halifax T (Am)	09/45				
Bradford Park Ave	Tr	07/48	48	6	-	1
Rochdale	Tr	08/50	50	2	-	0

CROWTHER Ryan John
Born: Stockport, Greater Manchester, England, 17 September, 1988 RW

League Club	Source	Date Signed	Seasons Played	Apps	Subs	Gls
Stockport Co	Sch	04/07	05-06	1	1	0
Liverpool	Tr	07/07				
Fleetwood T	Hyde FC	11/11	12-13	13	9	2

CROWTHER Stanley (Stan)
Born: Bilston, West Midlands, England, 3 September, 1935 LH
Died: Wolverhampton, England, 28 May, 2014
England: U23-3

League Club	Source	Date Signed	Seasons Played	Apps	Subs	Gls
Aston Villa	Bilston	08/55	56-57	50	-	4
Manchester U	Tr	02/58	57-58	13	-	0
Chelsea	Tr	12/58	58-59	51	-	0
Brighton & HA	Tr	03/61	60	4	-	0

CROWTHER Stephen John (Steve)
Born: Romiley, Greater Manchester, England, 16 January, 1955 FB

League Club	Source	Date Signed	Seasons Played	Apps	Subs	Gls
Stockport Co		11/73	73-74	42	2	4
Hartlepool U	Tr	07/75	75	3	0	0

CROY John
Born: Falkirk, Scotland, 23 February, 1925 CH
Died: Northampton, England, September, 1979

League Club	Source	Date Signed	Seasons Played	Apps	Subs	Gls
Northampton T	Third Lanark	07/50	51-54	25	-	0

CROZIER Joseph (Joe)
Born: Coatbridge, Lanarkshire, Scotland, 2 December, 1914 G
Died: Greenwich, SE London, England, 27 July, 1985
Scotland: War-3

League Club	Source	Date Signed	Seasons Played	Apps	Subs	Gls
Brentford	East Fife	05/37	37-48	200	-	0

CRUDGINGTON Geoffrey (Geoff)
Born: Wolverhampton, England, 14 February, 1952 G
England: Schools

League Club	Source	Date Signed	Seasons Played	Apps	Subs	Gls
Aston Villa	Wolverhampton W (Jnr)	09/69	70-71	4	0	0
Bradford C	L	03/71	70	1	0	0
Crewe Alex	Tr	03/72	71-77	250	0	0
Swansea C	Tr	07/78	78-79	52	0	0
Plymouth Arg	Tr	10/79	79-87	326	0	0

CRUICKSHANK Frank James
Born: Falkirk, Scotland, 20 November, 1931 FB
Died: 20 January, 2015

League Club	Source	Date Signed	Seasons Played	Apps	Subs	Gls
Notts Co	Nuneaton Bor	01/50	53-59	151	-	5

CRUICKSHANK George Philip
Born: Malaysia, 22 July, 1931 LW

League Club	Source	Date Signed	Seasons Played	Apps	Subs	Gls
Carlisle U	Queen of the South	08/57	57	14	-	0

CRUICKSHANK John Paul (Paul)
Born: Oldham, Greater Manchester, England, 18 January, 1960 M

League Club	Source	Date Signed	Seasons Played	Apps	Subs	Gls
Blackpool	App	08/77				
Bury	Tr	07/79	79-82	65	17	4

CRUISE Thomas Daniel
Born: Islington, N London, England, 9 March, 1991 LB
England: Youth

League Club	Source	Date Signed	Seasons Played	Apps	Subs	Gls
Arsenal	Sch	07/08				
Carlisle U	L	11/10	10	3	0	0
Torquay U	New England Rev (USA)	07/12	12-13	24	13	0

CRUMBLEHULME Kevin
Born: Manchester, England, 17 June, 1952 M

League Club	Source	Date Signed	Seasons Played	Apps	Subs	Gls
Oldham Ath	App	07/70	71	2	0	0

CRUMPLIN Ian
Born: Newburn, Tyne and Wear, England, 12 September, 1954 F

League Club	Source	Date Signed	Seasons Played	Apps	Subs	Gls
Hartlepool U	Newcastle Blue Star	06/78	78	25	4	5

CRUMPLIN John Leslie
Born: Bath, England, 26 May, 1967 RB/M

League Club	Source	Date Signed	Seasons Played	Apps	Subs	Gls
Brighton & HA	Bognor Regis T	02/87	86-93	173	34	7

CRUSAT Albert
Born: Barcelona, Spain, 13 May, 1982 LW
Spain: Youth

League Club	Source	Date Signed	Seasons Played	Apps	Subs	Gls
Wigan Ath	UD Almeria (SPN)	08/11	11	4	11	1

CRUSE Peter Leonard
Born: Camden, N London, England, 10 January, 1951 M
England: Amateur-2

League Club	Source	Date Signed	Seasons Played	Apps	Subs	Gls
Arsenal	Slough T	04/72				
Luton T	Tr	07/73	73	3	1	0
Shrewsbury T	L	02/74	73	2	0	0

CRUTCHLEY Wilfred Ronald (Ron)
Born: Walsall, West Midlands, England, 20 June, 1922 WH
Died: Walsall, West Midlands, England, August, 1987

League Club	Source	Date Signed	Seasons Played	Apps	Subs	Gls
Walsall	Hilary Street OB	03/45	46-49	62	-	3
Shrewsbury T	Tr	09/50	50-53	146	-	1

CRUYFF Jordi
Born: Amsterdam, Netherlands, 9 February, 1974 F
Netherlands: 9

League Club	Source	Date Signed	Seasons Played	Apps	Subs	Gls
Manchester U	Barcelona (SPN)	08/96	96-99	15	19	8

CRYAN Colin
Born: Dublin, Republic of Ireland, 23 March, 1981 CD
Republic of Ireland: U21-5

League Club	Source	Date Signed	Seasons Played	Apps	Subs	Gls
Sheffield U	YT	08/99	00-03	0	5	0
Lincoln C	Scarborough	07/05	05-06	37	4	0
Boston U	Tr	01/07	06	15	0	0

CRYLE George
Born: Aberdeen, Scotland, 10 April, 1928 LH
Died: Reading, England, 29 September, 2011

League Club	Source	Date Signed	Seasons Played	Apps	Subs	Gls
Wolverhampton W	Jnr	02/46				
Reading	Tr	06/48	48-50	8	-	2
Swindon T	Ayr U	08/52	52	12	-	0

CUADRADO Juan Guillermo
Born: Turbo, Colombia, 26 May, 1988 RW
Colombia: 44

League Club	Source	Date Signed	Seasons Played	Apps	Subs	Gls
Chelsea	Fiorentina (ITA)	02/15	14	4	8	0

CUBERO Jose Miguel
Born: Alajuela, Costa Rica, 14 February, 1987 M
Costa Rica: 39

League Club	Source	Date Signed	Seasons Played	Apps	Subs	Gls
Blackpool	Herediaro (CRC)	07/14	14	10	2	0

CUBIE Neil George
Born: Cape Town, South Africa, 3 November, 1932 RB

League Club	Source	Date Signed	Seasons Played	Apps	Subs	Gls
Bury	Clyde (RSA)	10/56				
Hull C	Tr	07/57	57	4	-	0

CUDDIHEY Russell Francis
Born: Rawtenstall, Lancashire, England, 8 September, 1939 LH

League Club	Source	Date Signed	Seasons Played	Apps	Subs	Gls
Accrington Stan		09/60	60	10	-	0

CUDDY Paul
Born: Kendal, Cumbria, England, 21 February, 1959 CD
England: Semi Pro

League Club	Source	Date Signed	Seasons Played	Apps	Subs	Gls
Rochdale	Jnr	08/77	77	0	1	0

CUDICINI Carlo
Born: Milan, Italy, 6 September, 1973 G
Italy: U21-1/Youth

League Club	Source	Date Signed	Seasons Played	Apps	Subs	Gls
Chelsea	Castel di Sangro (ITA)	08/99	99-08	138	4	0
Tottenham H	Tr	01/09	08-10	18	1	0

CUELLAR Carlos Javier
Born: Madrid, Spain, 23 August, 1981 CD

League Club	Source	Date Signed	Seasons Played	Apps	Subs	Gls
Aston Villa	Glasgow Rangers	08/08	08-11	87	7	2
Sunderland	Tr	07/12	12-13	30	0	1
Norwich C	Tr	08/14	14	8	0	0

CUERVO Philippe
Born: Paris, France, 13 August, 1969 RM

League Club	Source	Date Signed	Seasons Played	Apps	Subs	Gls
Swindon T	Saint-Etienne (FRA)	08/97	97-99	16	19	0

CUFF Patrick Joseph (Pat)
Born: Middlesbrough, England, 19 March, 1952 G
England: Schools

League Club	Source	Date Signed	Seasons Played	Apps	Subs	Gls
Middlesbrough	App	05/69	73-77	31	0	0
Grimsby T	L	09/71	71	2	0	0
Millwall	Tr	08/78	78	42	0	0
Darlington	Tr	06/80	80-82	110	0	0

CUGGY Michael Steven (Steve)
Born: Wallsend, Tyne and Wear, England, 18 March, 1971 F

League Club	Source	Date Signed	Seasons Played	Apps	Subs	Gls
Maidstone U	Blyth Spartans	06/91	91	1	12	1

CULKIN Nicholas James (Nick)
Born: York, England, 6 July, 1978 G

League Club	Source	Date Signed	Seasons Played	Apps	Subs	Gls
Manchester U	York C (YT)	09/95	99	0	1	0
Hull C	L	12/99	99	4	0	0
Bristol Rov	L	07/00	00	45	0	0
Queens Park Rgrs	Tr	07/02	02-03	22	0	0

CULLEN Anthony Scott (Tony)
Born: Gateshead, Tyne and Wear, England, 30 September, 1969 RW

League Club	Source	Date Signed	Seasons Played	Apps	Subs	Gls
Sunderland	Newcastle U (YT)	09/88	88-91	11	18	0
Carlisle U	L	12/89	89	2	0	1
Rotherham U	L	01/91	90	3	0	1

CULLEN (continued)

League Club	Source	Date Signed	Seasons Played	Apps	Subs	Gls
Bury	L	10/91	91	4	0	0
Swansea C	Tr	08/92	92	20	7	3

CULLEN David Jonathan (Jon)
Born: Bishop Auckland, County Durham, England, 10 January, 1973 M

League Club	Source	Date Signed	Seasons Played	Apps	Subs	Gls
Doncaster Rov	YT	09/91	90-91	8	1	0
Hartlepool U	Morpeth T	03/97	96-97	33	1	12
Sheffield U	Tr	01/98	97-98	0	4	0
Shrewsbury T	L	09/99	99	10	0	1
Halifax T	L	12/99	99	11	0	5
Peterborough U	Tr	03/00	99-01	34	10	5
Carlisle U	L	03/01	00	10	1	0
Darlington	Tr	08/02	02	2	1	0

CULLEN Mark
Born: Ashington, Northumberland, England, 24 April, 1992 F

League Club	Source	Date Signed	Seasons Played	Apps	Subs	Gls
Hull C	Sch	11/09	09-11	6	18	1
Bradford C	L	01/11	10	1	3	0
Bury	L	07/11	11	1	3	0
Bury	L	08/12	12	7	3	1
Luton T	Tr	05/13	14	33	9	13

CULLEN Michael Joseph (Mick)
Born: Glasgow, Scotland, 3 July, 1931 IF/RW
Scotland: 1/B-1

League Club	Source	Date Signed	Seasons Played	Apps	Subs	Gls
Luton T	Douglasdale Jnrs	08/49	51-57	112	-	17
Grimsby T	Tr	04/58	58-62	178	-	35
Derby Co	Tr	12/62	62-64	24	-	5

CULLEN Patrick Joseph (Pat)
Born: Mexborough, South Yorkshire, England, 9 August, 1949 F
Republic of Ireland: Amateur

League Club	Source	Date Signed	Seasons Played	Apps	Subs	Gls
Halifax T	Mexborough	05/68	67-73	1	5	0

CULLEN Shane Jonathan Raymond (Jon)
Born: Oxford, England, 9 October, 1962 FB

League Club	Source	Date Signed	Seasons Played	Apps	Subs	Gls
Reading	App	10/80	79-81	14	6	0

CULLERTON Michael Joseph (Mike)
Born: Edinburgh, Scotland, 25 November, 1948 F

League Club	Source	Date Signed	Seasons Played	Apps	Subs	Gls
Port Vale	Jnr	01/66	65-68	95	2	22
Chester C	L	03/69	68	5	2	0
Derby Co	Tr	07/69				
Port Vale	Stafford Rgrs	07/75	75-77	67	16	28

CULLING Gary
Born: Braintree, Essex, England, 6 April, 1972 RB

League Club	Source	Date Signed	Seasons Played	Apps	Subs	Gls
Colchester U	Braintree T	08/94	94	2	0	0

CULLINGFORD Robert
Born: Bradford, England, 3 December, 1953 CD
England: Schools

League Club	Source	Date Signed	Seasons Played	Apps	Subs	Gls
Bradford C (Am)	Jnr	10/69	69-71	1	1	0

CULLIP Daniel (Danny)
Born: Bracknell, Berkshire, England, 17 September, 1976 CD

League Club	Source	Date Signed	Seasons Played	Apps	Subs	Gls
Oxford U	YT	07/95				
Fulham	Tr	07/96	96-97	41	9	2
Brentford	Tr	02/98	97-98	15	0	0
Brighton & HA	Tr	09/99	99-04	216	1	7
Sheffield U	Tr	12/04	04	11	0	0
Watford	L	03/05	04	4	0	0
Nottingham F	Tr	08/05	05-06	29	2	0
Queens Park Rgrs	Tr	01/07	06-07	18	1	0
Gillingham	Tr	02/08	07	11	0	0

CULLIS Stanley (Stan)
Born: Ellesmere Port, Cheshire, England, 25 October, 1915 CH
Died: Malvern, Worcestershire, England, 28 February, 2001
England: 12/FLge-3/War-20

League Club	Source	Date Signed	Seasons Played	Apps	Subs	Gls
Wolverhampton W	Ellesmere Port Wed	02/34	34-46	152	-	0

CULLUM Arthur Richard (Dick)
Born: Colchester, Essex, England, 28 January, 1931 CF
Died: Hemel Hempstead, Hertfordshire, England, 9 April, 2012

League Club	Source	Date Signed	Seasons Played	Apps	Subs	Gls
Colchester U	Jnr	01/51	50-53	2	-	1

CULLUM Riley Granville
Born: West Ham, E London, England, 2 April, 1923 IF
Died: Barking, E London, England, 31 December, 1996

League Club	Source	Date Signed	Seasons Played	Apps	Subs	Gls
Charlton Ath	Dartford	10/47	49-52	32	-	6

CULPIN Paul
Born: Kirby Muxloe, Leicestershire, England, 8 February, 1962 F
England: Semi Pro-5

League Club	Source	Date Signed	Seasons Played	Apps	Subs	Gls
Leicester C	Jnr	05/81				
Coventry C	Nuneaton Bor	06/85	85-86	5	4	2
Northampton T	Tr	10/87	87-89	52	11	23
Peterborough U	Tr	10/89	89-91	30	17	14
Hereford U	Tr	02/92	91	1	1	0

CULVERHOUSE Ian Brett
Born: Bishops Stortford, Hertfordshire, England, 22 September, 1964 RB
England: Youth

League Club	Source	Date Signed	Seasons Played	Apps	Subs	Gls
Tottenham H	App	09/82	83	1	1	0
Norwich C	Tr	10/85	85-93	295	1	1
Swindon T	Tr	12/94	94-97	95	2	0
Brighton & HA	Kingstonian	09/98	98-99	36	0	0

CUMBERS Luis Cosme
Born: Chelmsford, England, 6 September, 1988 F

League Club	Source	Date Signed	Seasons Played	Apps	Subs	Gls
Gillingham	Sch	05/08	06-08	2	12	1

CUMBES James (Jim)
Born: Manchester, England, 4 May, 1944 G

League Club	Source	Date Signed	Seasons Played	Apps	Subs	Gls
Tranmere Rov	Runcorn	09/65	66-69	136	0	0
West Bromwich A	Tr	08/69	69-71	64	0	0
Aston Villa	Tr	10/71	71-75	157	0	0
Southport	Runcorn	01/78	77	19	0	0

CUMMING David Scott (Dave)
Born: Aberdeen, Scotland, 6 May, 1910 G
Died: Kirriemuir, Angus, Scotland, 18 April, 1993
Scotland: 1/War-1

League Club	Source	Date Signed	Seasons Played	Apps	Subs	Gls
Middlesbrough	Arbroath	10/36	36-46	135	-	0

CUMMING Gordon Robert Riddell
Born: Johnstone, Renfrewshire, Scotland, 23 January, 1948 RM

League Club	Source	Date Signed	Seasons Played	Apps	Subs	Gls
Arsenal	Glasgow U	01/65				
Reading	Tr	12/69	69-77	277	18	51

CUMMING Robert (Bobby)
Born: Airdrie, Lanarkshire, Scotland, 7 December, 1955 LW/FB

League Club	Source	Date Signed	Seasons Played	Apps	Subs	Gls
Grimsby T	Baillieston Jnrs	03/74	74-86	338	27	57
Lincoln C	Tr	07/87	88-89	40	1	5

CUMMINGS George Wilfred
Born: Falkirk, Scotland, 5 June, 1913 LB
Died: Birmingham, England, 9 April, 1987
Scotland: 9/SLge-2/War-1

League Club	Source	Date Signed	Seasons Played	Apps	Subs	Gls
Aston Villa	Partick Thistle	11/35	35-48	210	-	0

CUMMINGS John
Born: Greenock, Inverclyde, Scotland, 5 May, 1944 CF

League Club	Source	Date Signed	Seasons Played	Apps	Subs	Gls
Port Vale	Aberdeen	08/65	65	2	1	0

CUMMINGS Robert Douglas (Bobby)
Born: Ashington, Northumberland, England, 17 November, 1935 CF
Died: Blyth, Northumberland, England, 26 August, 2008

League Club	Source	Date Signed	Seasons Played	Apps	Subs	Gls
Newcastle U	New Hartley Jnrs	05/54				
Newcastle U	Aberdeen	10/63	63-65	43	1	14
Darlington	Tr	10/65	65-67	73	1	43
Hartlepool U	Tr	02/68	67-68	48	4	12

CUMMINGS Shaun Michael
Born: Hammersmith, W London, England, 25 February, 1989 RB
Jamaica: 2

League Club	Source	Date Signed	Seasons Played	Apps	Subs	Gls
Chelsea	Sch	07/07				
MK Dons	L	08/08	08	29	3	0
West Bromwich A	L	08/09	09	3	0	0
Reading	Tr	09/09	09-14	71	6	1
Millwall	Tr	01/15	14	12	0	0

CUMMINGS Thomas Smith (Tommy)
Born: Sunderland, England, 12 September, 1928 CH
Died: Blackburn, Greater Manchester, England, 12 July, 2009
England: B-2/FLge-1

League Club	Source	Date Signed	Seasons Played	Apps	Subs	Gls
Burnley	Hylton Colliery Jnrs	10/47	48-62	434	-	3
Mansfield T	Tr	03/63	62-63	10	-	0

CUMMINGS Warren Thomas
Born: Aberdeen, Scotland, 15 October, 1980 LB
Scotland: 1/U21-9

League Club	Source	Date Signed	Seasons Played	Apps	Subs	Gls
Chelsea	YT	07/99				
Bournemouth	L	10/00	00	10	0	1
West Bromwich A	L	03/01	00	1	2	0
West Bromwich A	L	07/01	01	6	8	0
Bournemouth	Tr	02/03	02-11	222	27	6
Crawley T	L	03/12	11	6	3	0
AFC Wimbledon	Tr	07/12	12	7	2	0

CUMMINS George Patrick
Born: Dublin, Republic of Ireland, 12 March, 1931 IF
Died: Southport, Merseyside, England, 29 November, 2009
Republic of Ireland: 19

League Club	Source	Date Signed	Seasons Played	Apps	Subs	Gls
Everton	St Patrick's Ath (ROI)	11/50	51-52	24	-	0
Luton T	Tr	08/53	53-60	184	-	21
Hull C	Cambridge C	11/62	62-63	21	-	2

CUMMINS Graham Rickard
Born: Cork, Republic of Ireland, 29 December, 1987 F

Republic of Ireland: U23-1

League Club	Source	Date Signed	Seasons Played	Apps	Subs	Gls
Preston NE	Cork C (ROI)	01/12	11-12	18	16	4
Rochdale	L	09/13	13	15	12	4
Exeter C	Tr	08/14	14	26	8	7

CUMMINS James William Heywood (Jimmy)
Born: Hebburn, Tyne and Wear, England, 15 February, 1925 CF
Died: South Shields, Tyne and Wear, England, 27 October, 1981

League Club	Source	Date Signed	Seasons Played	Apps	Subs	Gls
Southport	Horden CW	09/49	49	9	-	1

CUMMINS Michael Thomas (Micky)
Born: Dublin, Republic of Ireland, 1 June, 1978 M
Republic of Ireland: U21-2/Youth

League Club	Source	Date Signed	Seasons Played	Apps	Subs	Gls
Middlesbrough	YT	07/95	98-99	1	1	0
Port Vale	Tr	03/00	99-05	247	6	31
Darlington	Tr	07/06	06-07	69	10	10
Rotherham U	Tr	08/08	08-09	36	14	5

CUMMINS Stanley (Stan)
Born: Ferryhill, County Durham, England, 6 December, 1958 F/M

League Club	Source	Date Signed	Seasons Played	Apps	Subs	Gls
Middlesbrough	App	12/76	76-79	39	4	9
Sunderland	Tr	11/79	79-82	132	1	29
Crystal Palace	Tr	08/83	83-84	27	1	7
Sunderland	Tr	10/84	84	13	4	0

CUMNER Reginald Horace (Horace)
Born: Cwmaman, Rhondda Cynon Taff, Wales, 31 March, 1918 LW
Died: Poole, Dorset, England, 23 January, 1999
Wales: 3/War-10

League Club	Source	Date Signed	Seasons Played	Apps	Subs	Gls
Arsenal	Aberaman Ath	05/36	38	12	-	2
Hull C	L	01/38	37	12	-	4
Notts Co	Tr	08/46	46-47	66	-	11
Watford	Tr	07/48	48-50	62	-	7
Scunthorpe U	Tr	09/50	50-52	102	-	21
Bradford C	Tr	08/53				

CUNDY Jason Victor
Born: Wandsworth, SW London, England, 12 November, 1969 CD
England: U21-3

League Club	Source	Date Signed	Seasons Played	Apps	Subs	Gls
Chelsea	YT	08/88	90-91	40	1	2
Tottenham H	Tr	03/92	91-95	23	3	1
Crystal Palace	L	12/95	95	4	0	0
Bristol C	L	08/96	96	6	0	1
Ipswich T	Tr	10/96	96-98	54	4	5
Portsmouth	Tr	07/99	99	9	0	0

CUNLIFFE Arthur
Born: Blackrod, Greater Manchester, England, 5 February, 1909 LW
Died: Bournemouth, England, 28 August, 1986
England: 2

League Club	Source	Date Signed	Seasons Played	Apps	Subs	Gls
Blackburn Rov	Chorley	01/28	29-32	129	-	47
Aston Villa	Tr	05/33	32-35	69	-	11
Middlesbrough	Tr	12/35	35-36	27	-	5
Burnley	Tr	04/37	37	9	-	0
Hull C	Tr	06/38	38	42	-	20
Rochdale	Tr	08/45	46	23	-	5

CUNLIFFE James Graham (Graham)
Born: Hindley, Greater Manchester, England, 16 June, 1936 LH

League Club	Source	Date Signed	Seasons Played	Apps	Subs	Gls
Bolton W		01/55	57-62	25	-	0
Rochdale	Tr	07/64	64	36	-	0

CUNLIFFE James Nathaniel (Jimmy)
Born: Blackrod, Greater Manchester, England, 5 July, 1912 IF
Died: Blackrod, Greater Manchester, England, 21 November, 1986
England: 1

League Club	Source	Date Signed	Seasons Played	Apps	Subs	Gls
Everton	Adlington	05/30	32-38	174	-	73
Rochdale	Tr	09/46	46	2	-	0

CUNLIFFE James William (Jim)
Born: Adlington, Greater Manchester, England, 4 October, 1941 CF
Died: Chorley, Lancashire, England, 10 October, 2006

League Club	Source	Date Signed	Seasons Played	Apps	Subs	Gls
Stockport Co (Am)	Horwich RMI	11/60	60	1	-	0

CUNLIFFE John (Dickie)
Born: Wigan, Greater Manchester, England, 4 February, 1930 LW
Died: Stoke-on-Trent, England, 15 November, 1975

League Club	Source	Date Signed	Seasons Played	Apps	Subs	Gls
Port Vale		12/50	50-59	283	-	52
Stoke C	Tr	09/59	59	25	-	3

CUNLIFFE Reginald (Reg)
Born: Wigan, Greater Manchester, England, 4 December, 1920 LB
Died: Fleetwood, Lancashire, England, August, 2000

League Club	Source	Date Signed	Seasons Played	Apps	Subs	Gls
Swansea C	Wigan Ath	06/46	46-47	2	-	0

CUNLIFFE Robert (Bobby)
Born: Manchester, England, 17 May, 1945 IF

League Club	Source	Date Signed	Seasons Played	Apps	Subs	Gls
Manchester C	App	08/62	63	3	-	1
York C	Tr	06/65	65	11	1	2

CUNLIFFE Robert Arthur (Bobby)
Born: Garswood, Merseyside, England, 27 December, 1928 LW
Died: Wigan, Greater Manchester, England, 25 January, 2000

League Club	Source	Date Signed	Seasons Played	Apps	Subs	Gls
Manchester C	Haydock C&B	01/46	49-55	44	-	9
Chesterfield	Tr	06/56	56-57	62	-	19
Southport	Tr	07/58	58	17	-	2

CUNNING Robert Robertson Innes (Bobby)
Born: Dunfermline, Fife, Scotland, 12 February, 1930 LW
Died: Dunoon, Argyll & Bute, Scotland, 24 January, 1983

League Club	Source	Date Signed	Seasons Played	Apps	Subs	Gls
Sunderland	Port Glasgow Ath	06/50	50	5	-	0

CUNNINGHAM Anthony Eugene (Tony)
Born: Kingston, Jamaica, 12 November, 1957 F

League Club	Source	Date Signed	Seasons Played	Apps	Subs	Gls
Lincoln C	Stourbridge	05/79	79-82	111	12	32
Barnsley	Tr	09/82	82-83	40	2	11
Sheffield Wed	Tr	11/83	83	26	2	5
Manchester C	Tr	07/84	84	16	2	1
Newcastle U	Tr	02/85	84-86	37	10	4
Blackpool	Tr	07/87	87-88	71	0	17
Bury	Tr	07/89	89-90	55	3	17
Bolton W	Tr	03/91	90	9	0	4
Rotherham U	Tr	08/91	91-92	65	5	24
Doncaster Rov	Tr	07/93	93	19	6	1
Wycombe W	Tr	03/94	93	4	1	0

CUNNINGHAM Daniel Harvey (Harvey)
Born: Manchester, England, 11 September, 1968 RM

League Club	Source	Date Signed	Seasons Played	Apps	Subs	Gls
Doncaster Rov	Droylsden	02/97	96-97	43	1	1

CUNNINGHAM David (Dave)
Born: Kirkcaldy, Fife, Scotland, 10 August, 1953 W

League Club	Source	Date Signed	Seasons Played	Apps	Subs	Gls
Southend U	Brechin C	04/73	73-76	55	4	4
Hartlepool U	L	03/77	76	10	2	1
Swindon T	Tr	06/77	77-78	18	5	3
Peterborough U	L	11/78	78	4	0	1
Aston Villa	Tr	12/78				
Hereford U	Tr	08/79	79	28	2	2

CUNNINGHAM Edward Milburn
Born: South Shields, Tyne and Wear, England, 20 March, 1928 LH

League Club	Source	Date Signed	Seasons Played	Apps	Subs	Gls
Blackburn Rov	North Shields	09/49				
Chesterfield	North Shields	08/52	52-54	56	-	0

CUNNINGHAM Edwin Burnhope
Born: Jarrow, Tyne and Wear, England, 20 September, 1919 W
Died: Burnhope, County Durham, England, April, 1993

League Club	Source	Date Signed	Seasons Played	Apps	Subs	Gls
Bristol C	Luton Amats	05/39	46	1	-	0

CUNNINGHAM Gregory Richard (Greg)
Born: Galway, Republic of Ireland, 31 January, 1991 LB
Republic of Ireland: 4/U21-6/Youth

League Club	Source	Date Signed	Seasons Played	Apps	Subs	Gls
Manchester C	Sch	07/08	09	0	2	0
Leicester C	L	10/10	10	13	0	0
Nottingham F	L	10/11	11	25	2	0
Bristol C	Tr	07/12	12-14	70	21	4

CUNNINGHAM Hugh
Born: Kirkintilloch, Dunbartonshire, Scotland, 5 April, 1947 M

League Club	Source	Date Signed	Seasons Played	Apps	Subs	Gls
Fulham	Glasgow Celtic	05/66	67	0	1	0

CUNNINGHAM Ian
Born: Glasgow, Scotland, 6 September, 1956 RB

League Club	Source	Date Signed	Seasons Played	Apps	Subs	Gls
Bournemouth	App	08/74	74-80	180	8	4

CUNNINGHAM John
Born: Derry, Northern Ireland, 30 November, 1966 W
Northern Ireland: Youth

League Club	Source	Date Signed	Seasons Played	Apps	Subs	Gls
Mansfield T	Jnr	08/84	84	3	1	0

CUNNINGHAM Kenneth Edward (Kenny)
Born: Dublin, Republic of Ireland, 28 June, 1971 D
Republic of Ireland: 72/B-2/U21-4/Youth

League Club	Source	Date Signed	Seasons Played	Apps	Subs	Gls
Millwall	Tolka Rov (ROI)	09/89	89-94	132	4	1
Wimbledon	Tr	11/94	94-01	249	1	0
Birmingham C	Tr	07/02	02-05	134	0	0
Sunderland	Tr	07/06	06	11	0	0

CUNNINGHAM Kenneth Rankin (Ken)
Born: Glasgow, Scotland, 26 October, 1941 CF

League Club	Source	Date Signed	Seasons Played	Apps	Subs	Gls
Hartlepool U	Falkirk	07/63	63	2	-	0

CUNNINGHAM Laurence (Laurie)
Born: Consett, County Durham, England, 20 October, 1921 RB
Died: Bournemouth, England, 3 October, 2013

League Club	Source	Date Signed	Seasons Played	Apps	Subs	Gls
Barnsley	Consett	11/45	46-47	51	-	1
Bournemouth	Tr	06/48	48-56	273	-	0

CUNNINGHAM Lawrence Paul (Laurie)
Born: Hollway, N London, England, 8 March, 1956 W

Died: Madrid, Spain, 15 July, 1989
England: 6/B-1/U21-6

League Club	Source	Date Signed	Seasons Played	Apps	Subs	Gls
Leyton Orient	App	07/74	74-76	72	3	15
West Bromwich A	Tr	03/77	76-78	81	5	21
Manchester U	Real Madrid (SPN)	03/83	82	3	2	1
Leicester C	Olymp Marseille (FRA)	10/85	85	13	2	0
Wimbledon	RSC Charleroi (BEL)	02/88	87	6	0	2

CUNNINGHAM Thomas Edward (Tommy)
Born: Bethnal Green, E London, England, 7 December, 1955 — CD

League Club	Source	Date Signed	Seasons Played	Apps	Subs	Gls
Chelsea	App	10/73				
Queens Park Rgrs	Tr	05/75	76-78	27	3	2
Wimbledon	Tr	03/79	78-81	99	0	12
Leyton Orient	Tr	09/81	81-86	162	0	17

CUNNINGHAM William Carruthers (Willie)
Born: Cowdenbeath, Fife, Scotland, 22 February, 1925 — RB
Died: Preston, Lancashire, England, 28 November, 2000
Scotland: 8

League Club	Source	Date Signed	Seasons Played	Apps	Subs	Gls
Preston NE	Airdrieonians	07/49	49-62	440	-	3
Southport	Tr	03/64	64	12	-	0

CUNNINGHAM William Edward (Willie)
Born: Mallusk, Belfast, Northern Ireland, 20 February, 1930 — FB
Died: Dunfermline, Fife, Scotland, 31 August, 2007
Northern Ireland: 30

League Club	Source	Date Signed	Seasons Played	Apps	Subs	Gls
Leicester C	St Mirren	12/54	54-59	127	-	4

CUNNINGHAM William Livingstone (Willie)
Born: Paisley, Renfrewshire, Scotland, 11 July, 1938 — LH

League Club	Source	Date Signed	Seasons Played	Apps	Subs	Gls
Barnsley	Third Lanark	07/64	64	24	-	0

CUNNINGTON Adam Paul
Born: Leighton Buzzard, Bedfordshire, England, 7 October, 1987 — F

League Club	Source	Date Signed	Seasons Played	Apps	Subs	Gls
Dagenham & Red	Kettering T	11/11	11	2	7	0
Cambridge U	Tamworth	05/13	14	4	3	2

CUNNINGTON Shaun Gary
Born: Bourne, Lincolnshire, England, 4 January, 1966 — M/LB

League Club	Source	Date Signed	Seasons Played	Apps	Subs	Gls
Wrexham	Bourne T	01/84	82-87	196	3	12
Grimsby T	Tr	02/88	87-91	182	0	13
Sunderland	Tr	07/92	92-94	52	6	8
West Bromwich A	Tr	08/95	95-96	8	5	0
Notts Co	Tr	03/97	96-97	9	8	0

CURBISHLEY Llewellyn Charles (Alan)
Born: Forest Gate, E London, England, 8 November, 1957 — M
England: U21-1/Youth/Schools

League Club	Source	Date Signed	Seasons Played	Apps	Subs	Gls
West Ham U	App	08/75	74-78	78	7	5
Birmingham C	Tr	07/79	79-82	128	2	11
Aston Villa	Tr	03/83	82-84	34	2	1
Charlton Ath	Tr	12/84	84-86	62	1	6
Brighton & HA	Tr	08/87	87-89	111	5	13
Charlton Ath	Tr	07/90	90-93	22	6	0

CURCIC Sasa
Born: Belgrade, Yugoslavia, 14 February, 1972 — M
Yugoslavia: 14

League Club	Source	Date Signed	Seasons Played	Apps	Subs	Gls
Bolton W	Part'n Belgrade (YUG)	10/95	95	28	0	4
Aston Villa	Tr	08/96	96-97	20	9	0
Crystal Palace	Tr	03/98	97-98	10	13	5

CURETON Jamie
Born: Bristol, England, 28 August, 1975 — F
England: Youth

League Club	Source	Date Signed	Seasons Played	Apps	Subs	Gls
Norwich C	YT	02/93	94-95	13	16	6
Bournemouth	L	09/95	95	0	5	0
Bristol Rov	Tr	09/96	96-00	165	9	72
Reading	Tr	08/00	00-02	74	34	50
Queens Park Rgrs	Busan Icons (KOR)	02/04	03-04	20	23	6
Swindon T	Tr	07/05	05	22	8	7
Colchester U	L	10/05	05	7	1	4
Colchester U	Tr	06/06	06	44	0	23
Norwich C	Tr	07/07	07-09	42	27	16
Barnsley	L	11/08	08	7	1	2
Shrewsbury T	L	02/10	09	10	2	0
Exeter C	Tr	08/10	10	34	7	17
Leyton Orient	Tr	07/11	11	9	10	1
Exeter C	Tr	03/12	11-12	43	4	22
Cheltenham T	Tr	06/13	13	23	12	11
Dagenham & Red	Tr	07/14	14	40	5	19

CURLE Keith
Born: Bristol, England, 14 November, 1963 — CD
England: 3/B-4/FLge

League Club	Source	Date Signed	Seasons Played	Apps	Subs	Gls
Bristol Rov	App	11/81	81-82	21	11	4
Torquay U	Tr	11/83	83	16	0	5
Bristol C	Tr	03/84	83-87	113	8	1
Reading	Tr	10/87	87-88	40	0	0
Wimbledon	Tr	10/88	88-90	91	2	3
Manchester C	Tr	08/91	91-95	171	0	11
Wolverhampton W	Tr	08/96	96-99	148	2	9
Sheffield U	Tr	07/00	00-01	53	4	1
Barnsley	Tr	08/02	02	11	0	0
Mansfield T	Tr	12/02	02	11	3	0

CURLE Thomas Keith (Tom)
Born: Bristol, England, 3 March, 1986 — M

League Club	Source	Date Signed	Seasons Played	Apps	Subs	Gls
Mansfield T	Sch	-	03	0	1	0
Chester C	Tr	08/05	05	0	2	0

CURLEY Thomas (Tom)
Born: Glasgow, Scotland, 11 June, 1945 — RW

League Club	Source	Date Signed	Seasons Played	Apps	Subs	Gls
Brentford	Glasgow Celtic	08/65	65-66	40	0	6
Crewe Alex	Tr	08/67	67-68	49	3	7

CURLEY William (Billy)
Born: Trimdon, County Durham, England, 20 November, 1945 — LB

League Club	Source	Date Signed	Seasons Played	Apps	Subs	Gls
Darlington	App	11/63	62-64	28	-	1

CURRAN Christopher (Chris)
Born: Birmingham, England, 17 September, 1971 — CD

League Club	Source	Date Signed	Seasons Played	Apps	Subs	Gls
Torquay U	YT	07/90	89-95	144	8	4
Plymouth Arg	Tr	12/95	95-96	26	4	0
Exeter C	Tr	07/97	97-02	146	11	6

CURRAN Christopher Patrick (Chris)
Born: Heywood, Greater Manchester, England, 6 January, 1971 — CD

League Club	Source	Date Signed	Seasons Played	Apps	Subs	Gls
Crewe Alex	YT	09/89	89-90	2	3	0
Scarborough	Tr	03/92	91-92	40	0	4
Carlisle U	Tr	07/93	93	4	2	1

CURRAN Craig
Born: Liverpool, England, 23 August, 1989 — F

League Club	Source	Date Signed	Seasons Played	Apps	Subs	Gls
Tranmere Rov	Sch	08/06	06-09	48	49	14
Carlisle U	Tr	07/10	10-11	38	19	8
Morecambe	L	03/12	11	6	1	1
Rochdale	Tr	08/12	12	0	4	0

CURRAN Daniel Lee James (Danny)
Born: Brentwood, Essex, England, 13 June, 1981 — F

League Club	Source	Date Signed	Seasons Played	Apps	Subs	Gls
Leyton Orient	YT	07/99	98	0	1	0

CURRAN Edward Terence (Terry)
Born: Kinsley, West Yorkshire, England, 20 March, 1955 — W

League Club	Source	Date Signed	Seasons Played	Apps	Subs	Gls
Doncaster Rov	Jnr	07/73	73-75	67	1	11
Nottingham F	Tr	08/75	75-76	46	2	12
Bury	L	10/77	77	2	0	0
Derby Co	Tr	11/77	77	26	0	2
Southampton	Tr	08/78	78	25	1	0
Sheffield Wed	Tr	03/79	78-81	122	3	35
Sheffield U	Tr	08/82	82	31	2	3
Everton	L	12/82	82	7	0	1
Everton	Tr	09/83	83-84	12	4	0
Huddersfield T	Tr	07/85	85	33	1	7
Hull C	Panionios (GRE)	10/86	86	4	0	0
Sunderland	Tr	11/86	86	9	0	1
Grimsby T	Grantham T	11/87	87	10	2	0
Chesterfield	Tr	03/88	87	0	1	0

CURRAN Frank
Born: Ryton-on-Tyne, Tyne and Wear, England, 31 May, 1917 — IF
Died: Southport, Merseyside, England, 24 September, 1998

League Club	Source	Date Signed	Seasons Played	Apps	Subs	Gls
Southport	Washington Colliery	08/35	35-36	16	-	3
Accrington Stan	Tr	02/37	36-37	34	-	14
Bristol Rov	Tr	06/38	38	27	-	21
Bristol C	Tr	05/39				
Bristol Rov	Tr	05/46	46	10	-	3
Tranmere Rov	Shrewsbury T	06/47	47	17	-	7

CURRAN Hugh Patrick
Born: Carstairs, Lanarkshire, Scotland, 25 September, 1943 — F
Scotland: 5

League Club	Source	Date Signed	Seasons Played	Apps	Subs	Gls
Millwall	Corby T	03/64	63-65	57	0	26
Norwich C	Tr	01/66	65-68	112	0	46
Wolverhampton W	Tr	01/69	68-71	77	5	40
Oxford U	Tr	09/72	72-74	69	1	28
Bolton W	Tr	09/74	74-76	40	7	13
Oxford U	Tr	07/77	77-78	30	5	11

CURRAN James (Jimmy)
Born: Macclesfield, Cheshire, England, 24 September, 1947 — G

League Club	Source	Date Signed	Seasons Played	Apps	Subs	Gls
Newcastle U	Jnr	10/64				
Oldham Ath		12/66	66	3	0	0
Crewe Alex	Tr	04/67	68	3	0	0

CURRAN John (Johnny)
Born: Glasgow, Scotland, 22 June, 1924 — G
Died: Milltimber, Aberdeenshire, Scotland, 24 March, 1985

League Club	Source	Date Signed	Seasons Played	Apps	Subs	Gls
Shrewsbury T	East Fife	08/56	56	24	-	0
Watford	Tr	06/57	57	30	-	0

CURRAN Patrick Joseph (Pat)
Born: Sunderland, England, 13 November, 1917 — IF
Died: Sunderland, England, December, 2003

League Club	Source	Date Signed	Seasons Played	Apps	Subs	Gls
Sunderland	Sunderland St Pat's	10/36	37	1	-	0
Ipswich T	Tr	10/38	38	7	-	1
Watford	Tr	06/39				
Bradford C	Tr	06/47	47	5	-	1

CURRAN Terence William (Terry)
Born: Staines, Surrey, England, 29 June, 1940 — IF
Died: Reading, England, May, 2000

League Club	Source	Date Signed	Seasons Played	Apps	Subs	Gls
Brentford	Tottenham H (Am)	09/57	60	5	-	0

CURRIE Anthony William (Tony)
Born: Edgware, NW London, England, 1 January, 1950 — M
England: 17/FLge-3/U23-13/Youth

League Club	Source	Date Signed	Seasons Played	Apps	Subs	Gls
Watford	App	05/67	67	17	1	9
Sheffield U	Tr	02/68	67-75	313	0	54
Leeds U	Tr	06/76	76-78	102	0	11
Queens Park Rgrs	Tr	08/79	79-82	79	2	5
Torquay U	Chesham U	02/84	83-84	14	0	1

CURRIE Charles (Charlie)
Born: Belfast, Northern Ireland, 17 April, 1920 — RH/RB
Northern Ireland: NILge-6

League Club	Source	Date Signed	Seasons Played	Apps	Subs	Gls
Bradford Park Ave	Belfast Celtic	06/49	49-53	118	-	2

CURRIE Darren Paul
Born: Hampstead, NW London, England, 29 November, 1974 — W

League Club	Source	Date Signed	Seasons Played	Apps	Subs	Gls
West Ham U	YT	07/93				
Shrewsbury T	L	09/94	94	10	2	2
Shrewsbury T	L	02/95	94	5	0	0
Leyton Orient	L	11/95	95	9	1	0
Shrewsbury T	Tr	02/96	95-97	46	20	8
Plymouth Arg	Tr	03/98	97	5	2	0
Barnet	Tr	07/98	98-00	120	7	19
Wycombe W	Tr	07/01	01-03	109	17	14
Brighton & HA	Tr	08/04	04	21	1	2
Ipswich T	Tr	12/04	04-06	64	19	9
Coventry C	L	11/06	06	6	2	0
Derby Co	L	03/07	06	4	3	1
Luton T	Tr	07/07	07	25	6	2
Chesterfield	Tr	08/08	08-09	16	15	3
Dagenham & Red	Tr	11/09	09-10	17	21	1

CURRIE David Norman
Born: Stockton-on-Tees, Cleveland, England, 27 November, 1962 — F

League Club	Source	Date Signed	Seasons Played	Apps	Subs	Gls
Middlesbrough		02/82	81-85	94	19	30
Darlington	Tr	06/86	86-87	76	0	33
Barnsley	Tr	02/88	87-89	80	0	30
Nottingham F	Tr	01/90	89	4	4	1
Oldham Ath	Tr	08/90	90-91	17	14	3
Barnsley	Tr	09/91	91-93	53	22	12
Rotherham U	L	10/92	92	5	0	2
Huddersfield T	L	01/94	93	7	0	1
Carlisle U	Tr	07/94	94-96	84	5	14
Scarborough	Tr	01/97	96	16	0	6

CURRIE James Adam Campbell (Jimmy)
Born: Glasgow, Scotland, 25 April, 1932 — CF
Died: Ampthill, Bedfordshire, England, April, 1998

League Club	Source	Date Signed	Seasons Played	Apps	Subs	Gls
Exeter C	Falkirk	06/56	56-57	54	-	19
Workington	Tr	10/57	57-59	23	-	8

CURRIE James Thomson (Jim)
Born: Bridge of Allan, Stirlingshire, Scotland, 6 August, 1948 — M

League Club	Source	Date Signed	Seasons Played	Apps	Subs	Gls
Scunthorpe U	Glasgow Celtic	09/68	68-69	4	2	0

CURRIE John (Jack)
Born: Motherwell, Lanarkshire, Scotland, 19 March, 1935 — IF

League Club	Source	Date Signed	Seasons Played	Apps	Subs	Gls
Accrington Stan	Cleland Jnrs	11/53	53-54	16	-	3

CURRIE John Edward
Born: Liverpool, England, 18 March, 1921 — RW
Died: Bromley, SE London, England, 24 April, 1984

League Club	Source	Date Signed	Seasons Played	Apps	Subs	Gls
Bournemouth (Am)	Stafford Rgrs	10/46	46	7	-	1
Port Vale	Tr	06/47	47	9	-	0

CURRIE John Gemmell
Born: Dumfries, Scotland, 7 April, 1939 — RH
Scotland: Schools

League Club	Source	Date Signed	Seasons Played	Apps	Subs	Gls
Leicester C	Jnr	04/57				
Workington	Tr	07/61	61-62	55	-	2
Chester C	Tr	07/63	63	2	-	0

CURRIE Malcolm
Born: Rutherglen, Glasgow, Scotland, 5 February, 1932 — D
Died: Keighley, West Yorkshire, England, December, 1996

League Club	Source	Date Signed	Seasons Played	Apps	Subs	Gls
Bradford C	Rutherglen Glencairn	07/56	56-60	136	-	1

CURRY Robert (Bob)
Born: Gateshead, Tyne and Wear, England, 2 November, 1918 — IF
Died: Halstead, Essex, England, 23 June, 2001

League Club	Source	Date Signed	Seasons Played	Apps	Subs	Gls
Sheffield Wed		10/37	37	1	-	0
Sheffield U	Gainsborough Trinity	07/43				
Colchester U	Gainsborough Trinity	07/46	50	32	-	13

CURRY Sean Patrick
Born: Liverpool, England, 13 November, 1966 — F

League Club	Source	Date Signed	Seasons Played	Apps	Subs	Gls
Liverpool	App	07/84				
Blackburn Rov	Tr	01/87	86-88	25	13	6
Hartlepool U	Tr	08/89	89	0	1	0

CURRY William Morton (Bill)
Born: Walker, Tyne and Wear, England, 12 October, 1935 — CF
Died: Mansfield, Nottinghamshire, England, 20 August, 1990
England: U23-1

League Club	Source	Date Signed	Seasons Played	Apps	Subs	Gls
Newcastle U	Jnr	10/53	54-58	80	-	36
Brighton & HA	Tr	07/59	59-60	49	-	26
Derby Co	Tr	10/60	60-64	148	-	67
Mansfield T	Tr	02/65	64-67	102	0	53
Chesterfield	Tr	01/68	67-68	14	0	2

CURTIN Douglas James (Doug)
Born: Cardiff, Wales, 15 September, 1947 — LW
Wales: Schools

League Club	Source	Date Signed	Seasons Played	Apps	Subs	Gls
Mansfield T	Cardiff C (App)	11/65	65	3	0	0

CURTIS Alan Thomas
Born: Ton Pentre, Rhondda Cynon Taff, Wales, 16 April, 1954 — F/M
Wales: 35/U23-1/U21-1/Youth

League Club	Source	Date Signed	Seasons Played	Apps	Subs	Gls
Swansea C	Jnr	07/72	72-78	244	4	71
Leeds U	Tr	06/79	79-80	28	0	5
Swansea C	Tr	12/80	80-83	82	8	21
Southampton	Tr	11/83	83-85	43	7	5
Stoke C	L	03/86	85	3	0	0
Cardiff C	Tr	07/86	86-89	122	3	10
Swansea C	Tr	10/89	89	21	5	3

CURTIS Andrew (Andy)
Born: Doncaster, South Yorkshire, England, 2 December, 1972 — LW

League Club	Source	Date Signed	Seasons Played	Apps	Subs	Gls
York C	YT	07/91	90-91	6	6	0
Peterborough U	Kettering T	09/92	92	8	3	1
York C	Rtd	07/95	95	0	1	0
Scarborough	Tr	01/96	95	3	2	0

CURTIS Dermot Patrick
Born: Dublin, Republic of Ireland, 26 August, 1932 — CF
Died: Exeter, England, 1 November, 2008
Republic of Ireland: 17/LoI-2

League Club	Source	Date Signed	Seasons Played	Apps	Subs	Gls
Bristol C	Shelbourne (ROI)	12/56	56-57	26	-	16
Ipswich T	Tr	09/58	58-62	41	-	17
Exeter C	Tr	08/63	63-65	91	0	23
Torquay U	Tr	08/66	66	12	0	1
Exeter C	Tr	06/67	67-68	64	2	10

CURTIS George Edward
Born: Purfleet, Essex, England, 3 December, 1919 — IF/WH
Died: Brentwood, Essex, England, 17 November, 2004

League Club	Source	Date Signed	Seasons Played	Apps	Subs	Gls
Arsenal	Anglo, Purfleet	04/37	38-46	13	-	0
Southampton	Tr	08/47	47-51	174	-	11

CURTIS George William
Born: Dover, Kent, England, 5 May, 1939 — CH
England: Youth

League Club	Source	Date Signed	Seasons Played	Apps	Subs	Gls
Coventry C	Snowdown CW	05/56	55-69	483	4	11
Aston Villa	Tr	12/69	69-71	51	0	3

CURTIS John
Born: Poulton-le-Fylde, Lancashire, England, 2 September, 1954 — RB

League Club	Source	Date Signed	Seasons Played	Apps	Subs	Gls
Blackpool	App	09/72	73-76	96	6	0
Blackburn Rov	Tr	07/77	77-78	9	1	0
Wigan Ath	Tr	03/79	78-80	32	0	0

CURTIS John Charles Keyworth
Born: Nuneaton, Warwickshire, England, 3 September, 1978 — RB
England: B-1/U21-16/Youth/Schools

League Club	Source	Date Signed	Seasons Played	Apps	Subs	Gls
Manchester U	YT	10/95	97-99	4	9	0
Barnsley	L	11/99	99	28	0	2
Blackburn Rov	Tr	06/00	00-02	61	0	0
Sheffield U	L	03/03	02	9	3	0
Leicester C	Tr	08/03	03	14	1	0
Portsmouth	Tr	02/04	03-04	5	2	0
Preston NE	L	09/04	04	12	0	0
Nottingham F	Tr	02/05	04-06	76	3	0
Queens Park Rgrs	Tr	07/07	07	3	1	0
Northampton T	Wrexham	08/09	09	18	1	0

League Club	Source	Date Signed	Seasons Played	Apps	Subs	Gls

CURTIS Mark Wayne (Wayne)
Born: Neath, Wales, 22 February, 1967 RB

League Club	Source	Date Signed	Seasons Played	Apps	Subs	Gls
Cardiff C	Swansea C (Jnr)	10/84	85	24	3	2

CURTIS Paul Anthony Ernest
Born: Woolwich, SE London, England, 1 July, 1963 RB

League Club	Source	Date Signed	Seasons Played	Apps	Subs	Gls
Charlton Ath	App	07/81	82-84	69	3	5
Northampton T	Tr	07/85	85	27	0	1
Northampton T	Corby T	08/92	92	22	0	1

CURTIS Robert Anthony (Robbie)
Born: Mansfield, Nottinghamshire, England, 21 May, 1972 CD

League Club	Source	Date Signed	Seasons Played	Apps	Subs	Gls
Northampton T	Boston U	06/94	94	13	0	0

CURTIS Robert Dennis (Bob)
Born: Langwith, Derbyshire, England, 25 January, 1950 RB
Died: Langwith, Derbyshire, England, 19 March, 2010

League Club	Source	Date Signed	Seasons Played	Apps	Subs	Gls
Charlton Ath	App	02/67	66-77	324	13	35
Mansfield T	Tr	02/78	77-79	69	4	7

CURTIS Thomas David (Tom)
Born: Exeter, England, 1 March, 1973 M

League Club	Source	Date Signed	Seasons Played	Apps	Subs	Gls
Derby Co	Jnr	07/91				
Chesterfield	Tr	08/93	93-99	235	5	12
Portsmouth	Tr	08/00	00-01	7	6	0
Walsall	L	09/01	01	3	1	0
Tranmere Rov	L	08/02	02	8	0	0
Mansfield T	Tr	12/02	02-04	83	10	0
Chester C	Tr	07/05	05	34	6	1
Notts Co	Tr	07/06	06	0	2	0

CURTIS Wayne John
Born: Barrow, Cumbria, England, 6 March, 1978 F

League Club	Source	Date Signed	Seasons Played	Apps	Subs	Gls
Morecambe	Holker Central OB	03/98	07-09	48	55	11

CURTIS William Norman (Norman)
Born: Dinnington, South Yorkshire, England, 10 September, 1924 LB
Died: York, England, 7 September, 2009

League Club	Source	Date Signed	Seasons Played	Apps	Subs	Gls
Sheffield Wed	Gainsborough Trinity	01/50	50-59	310	-	21
Doncaster Rov	Tr	08/60	60	40	-	3

CURWEN Eric
Born: Blackpool, Lancashire, England, 16 September, 1947 FB
England: Schools

League Club	Source	Date Signed	Seasons Played	Apps	Subs	Gls
Everton	App	05/65				
Southport	Tr	12/66	66-68	89	0	0

CURZON Terence (Terry)
Born: Winsford, Cheshire, England, 26 May, 1936 LW

League Club	Source	Date Signed	Seasons Played	Apps	Subs	Gls
Crewe Alex	Bolton W (Am)	10/53	53-56	11	-	1

CUSACK David Stephen (Dave)
Born: Thurcroft, South Yorkshire, England, 6 June, 1956 CD

League Club	Source	Date Signed	Seasons Played	Apps	Subs	Gls
Sheffield Wed	App	06/74	75-77	92	3	1
Southend U	Tr	09/78	78-82	186	0	17
Millwall	Tr	03/83	82-84	98	0	9
Doncaster Rov	Tr	07/85	85-87	100	0	4
Rotherham U	Tr	12/87	87	18	0	0
Doncaster Rov	Boston U	08/89	89	1	0	0

CUSACK Nicholas John (Nick)
Born: Maltby, South Yorkshire, England, 24 December, 1965 M/F

League Club	Source	Date Signed	Seasons Played	Apps	Subs	Gls
Leicester C	Alvechurch	06/87	87	5	11	1
Peterborough U	Tr	07/88	88	44	0	10
Darlington	Motherwell	01/92	91	21	0	6
Oxford U	Tr	07/92	92-94	48	13	10
Wycombe W	L	03/94	93	2	2	1
Fulham	Tr	11/94	94-97	109	7	14
Swansea C	Tr	10/97	97-02	184	14	13

CUSH Wilbur
Born: Lurgan, Armagh, Northern Ireland, 10 June, 1928 WH/IF
Died: Lurgan, Belfast, Northern Ireland, 1981
Northern Ireland: 24/NILge-32

League Club	Source	Date Signed	Seasons Played	Apps	Subs	Gls
Leeds U	Glenavon	11/57	57-59	87	-	9

CUSHIN Edward (Ted)
Born: Whitehaven, Cumbria, England, 27 January, 1927 FB/W
Died: Whitehaven, Cumbria, England, 26 May, 1985

League Club	Source	Date Signed	Seasons Played	Apps	Subs	Gls
Workington	Lowca	07/50	51-55	119	-	4

CUSHLEY John
Born: Blantyre, Lanarkshire, Scotland, 21 January, 1943 CH
Died: Bothwell, Lanarkshire, Scotland, 24 March, 2008

League Club	Source	Date Signed	Seasons Played	Apps	Subs	Gls
West Ham U	Glasgow Celtic	07/67	67-69	38	0	0

CUSHLOW Richard (Dick)
Born: Shotton Colliery, County Durham, England, 15 June, 1920 CH
Died: Chesterfield, Derbyshire, England, 26 June, 2002

League Club	Source	Date Signed	Seasons Played	Apps	Subs	Gls
Chesterfield	Murton CW	05/46	46-47	34	-	0
Sheffield U	Tr	12/47				
Derby Co	Tr	03/48	48-49	2	-	0
Crystal Palace	Tr	02/51	50-51	28	-	0

CUTBUSH William John (John)
Born: Malta, 28 June, 1949 RB

League Club	Source	Date Signed	Seasons Played	Apps	Subs	Gls
Tottenham H	App	09/66				
Fulham	Tr	07/72	72-76	131	3	3
Sheffield U	Tr	03/77	76-80	126	3	1

CUTHBERT Ean Richardson
Born: Hurlford, Ayrshire, Scotland, 5 February, 1942 LB

League Club	Source	Date Signed	Seasons Played	Apps	Subs	Gls
Blackpool	Alyth U	07/59				
Stockport Co	Tr	07/63	63-65	93	0	0
Bristol C	Tr	08/66				
Crewe Alex	Bangor C	11/66	66	1	0	0

CUTHBERT Scott James
Born: Alexandria, Dunbartonshire, Scotland, 15 June, 1987 CD
Scotland: B-1/U21-13/Youth

League Club	Source	Date Signed	Seasons Played	Apps	Subs	Gls
Swindon T	Glasgow Celtic	07/09	09-10	77	3	5
Leyton Orient	Tr	07/11	11-14	129	4	7

CUTHBERTSON James (Jimmy)
Born: Sunderland, England, 7 December, 1947 LW

League Club	Source	Date Signed	Seasons Played	Apps	Subs	Gls
Bradford C	App	07/66	66-67	25	3	7

CUTHBERTSON John
Born: Glasgow, Scotland, 10 March, 1932 IF

League Club	Source	Date Signed	Seasons Played	Apps	Subs	Gls
Mansfield T		10/53	53	3	-	0

CUTLER Christopher Paul (Chris)
Born: Manchester, England, 7 April, 1964 M/F

League Club	Source	Date Signed	Seasons Played	Apps	Subs	Gls
Bury	Jnr	08/81	81-84	8	15	3
Crewe Alex	Tr	08/85	85-89	116	24	24

CUTLER Neil Anthony
Born: Cannock, Staffordshire, England, 3 September, 1976 G
England: Youth/Schools

League Club	Source	Date Signed	Seasons Played	Apps	Subs	Gls
West Bromwich A	YT	09/93				
Chester C	L	03/96	95	1	0	0
Crewe Alex	Tr	07/96				
Chester C	L	08/96	96	5	0	0
Chester C	Tr	07/98	98	23	0	0
Aston Villa	Tr	11/99	99	0	1	0
Oxford U	L	12/00	00	11	0	0
Stoke C	Tr	07/01	01-03	65	4	0
Swansea C	L	02/03	02	13	0	0
Stockport Co	Tr	07/04	04	22	0	0
Rotherham U	Tr	08/05	05-06	63	0	0

CUTLER Paul
Born: Welwyn Garden City, Hertfordshire, England, 18 June, 1946 LW

League Club	Source	Date Signed	Seasons Played	Apps	Subs	Gls
Crystal Palace	App	04/64	64-65	10	0	1

CUTLER Reginald Victor (Reg)
Born: Rowley Regis, West Midlands, England, 17 February, 1935 LW
Died: Kidderminster, Worcestershire, England, 5 May, 2012

League Club	Source	Date Signed	Seasons Played	Apps	Subs	Gls
West Bromwich A	Jnr	02/52	51-54	5	-	0
Bournemouth	Tr	06/56	56-58	96	-	21
Portsmouth	Tr	09/58	58-61	100	-	13
Stockport Co	Tr	07/62	62	34	-	0

CUTTING John Andrew (Jack)
Born: Fleetwood, Lancashire, England, 15 April, 1924 IF
Died: Fleetwood, Lancashire, England, 24 April, 1985

League Club	Source	Date Signed	Seasons Played	Apps	Subs	Gls
Oldham Ath	RAF	11/46	46	4	-	1
Accrington Stan	Fleetwood	06/48	48	23	-	5

CUTTING Noel Frederick Charles (Fred)
Born: North Walsham, Norfolk, England, 4 December, 1921 IF
Died: Plymouth, England, 29 July, 1997

League Club	Source	Date Signed	Seasons Played	Apps	Subs	Gls
Leicester C	Army	01/46				
Norwich C	Tr	09/46				
Colchester U	Tr	09/47	50-51	29	-	12

CUTTING Stanley William (Stan)
Born: Norwich, England, 21 September, 1914 RH
Died: Exeter, England, 24 April, 2004

League Club	Source	Date Signed	Seasons Played	Apps	Subs	Gls
Southampton	Norwich C (Am)	05/37	38	3	-	0
Exeter C	Tr	07/39	46-47	38	-	2

CUVELIER Florent
Born: Brussels, Belgium, 12 September, 1992 M
Belgium: U21-1/Youth

League Club	Source	Date Signed	Seasons Played	Apps	Subs	Gls
Portsmouth	Sch	09/09				
Stoke C	Tr	07/10				
Walsall	L	01/12	11	17	1	4
Walsall	L	07/12	12	16	3	2

League Club	Source	Date Signed	Seasons Played	Career Record Apps	Subs	Gls
Peterborough U	L	03/13	12	0	1	0
Sheffield U	Tr	09/13	13-14	6	4	0
Port Vale	L	01/14	13	1	0	0
Burton A	L	03/15	14	0	1	1

CYGAN Pascal
Born: Lens, France, 19 April, 1974 CD

League Club	Source	Date Signed	Seasons Played	Apps	Subs	Gls
Arsenal	Lille OSC (FRA)	08/02	02-05	52	11	3

CYGAN Paul
Born: Doncaster, South Yorkshire, England, 4 March, 1972 M

League Club	Source	Date Signed	Seasons Played	Apps	Subs	Gls
Doncaster Rov	YT	-	89	0	1	0

CYRUS Andrew Daryl (Andy)
Born: Lambeth, S London, England, 30 September, 1976 LB

League Club	Source	Date Signed	Seasons Played	Apps	Subs	Gls
Crystal Palace	YT	08/95	96	1	0	0
Exeter C	Tr	07/97	97	17	4	0

CYWKA Tomasz
Born: Gliwice, Poland, 27 June, 1988 M
Poland: U21-2/Youth

League Club	Source	Date Signed	Seasons Played	Apps	Subs	Gls
Wigan Ath	Gornik Zabrze (POL)	08/06				
Oldham Ath	L	10/06	06	0	4	0
Derby Co	Tr	03/10	09-11	28	16	5
Reading	Tr	01/12	11	1	3	0
Barnsley	Tr	08/12	12-13	35	24	9
Blackpool	Tr	07/14	14	5	1	1
Rochdale	L	11/14	14	1	2	0

CZERKAS Adam
Born: Sokolow Poblaski, Poland, 13 July, 1984 F

League Club	Source	Date Signed	Seasons Played	Apps	Subs	Gls
Queens Park Rgrs (L)	Odra Wodzislaw (POL)	08/06	06	2	1	0

CZUCZMAN Mychaljo (Mike)
Born: Carlisle, Cumbria, England, 27 May, 1953 D/M

League Club	Source	Date Signed	Seasons Played	Apps	Subs	Gls
Grimsby T	Preston NE (App)	08/71	71-75	107	6	6
Scunthorpe U	Tr	08/76	76-78	115	0	1
Stockport Co	Tr	05/79	79	36	0	7
Grimsby T	San Jose E'quake (USA)	09/80	80-81	9	0	0
York C	Tr	11/81	81	17	0	0

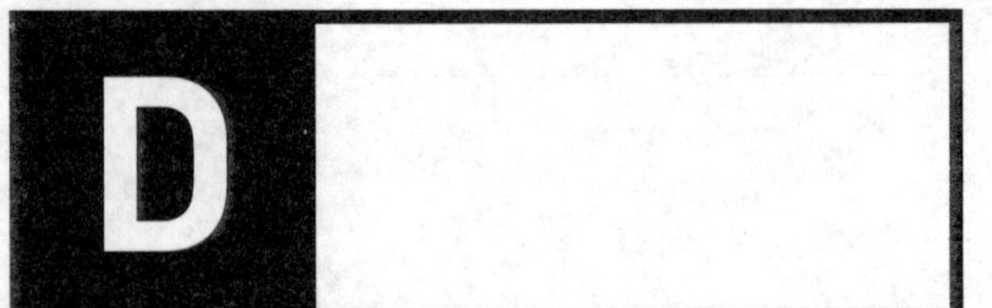

DABELSTEEN Thomas
Born: Copenhagen, Denmark, 6 March, 1973 M

League Club	Source	Date Signed	Seasons Played	Apps	Subs	Gls
Scarborough	Kolding (DEN)	11/98	98	5	0	1

DABIZAS Nikolaos (Nicos)
Born: Amyntaio, Greece, 3 August, 1973 CD
Greece: 70/U21/Youth

League Club	Source	Date Signed	Seasons Played	Apps	Subs	Gls
Newcastle U	Olympiakos (GRE)	03/98	97-02	119	11	10
Leicester C	Tr	01/04	03-04	51	0	1

DABO Ousmane
Born: Laval, France, 5 February, 1977 M
France: 3

League Club	Source	Date Signed	Seasons Played	Apps	Subs	Gls
Manchester C	SS Lazio (ITA)	07/06	06	10	3	0

DACK Bradley Paul
Born: Greenwich, SE London, England, 31 December, 1993 M

League Club	Source	Date Signed	Seasons Played	Apps	Subs	Gls
Gillingham	Sch	08/12	12-14	58	28	13

DA COSTA Filipe
Born: Lisbon, Portugal, 30 August, 1984 LW

League Club	Source	Date Signed	Seasons Played	Apps	Subs	Gls
Leeds U	Ionikos (GRE)	08/07	07	0	4	0

DA COSTA Hugo Alexandre
Born: Abrantes, Portugal, 4 November, 1973 CD

League Club	Source	Date Signed	Seasons Played	Apps	Subs	Gls
Stoke C	Estrela Amadora (POR)	08/96	96	1	1	0

DA COSTA Manuel
Born: Nancy, France, 6 May, 1986 CD
Morocco: 8//Portugal: U21-22/Youth

League Club	Source	Date Signed	Seasons Played	Apps	Subs	Gls
West Ham U	Fiorentina (ITA)	08/09	09-10	26	5	3

DACOURT Olivier Nicolas Andre
Born: Paris, France, 25 September, 1974 M
France: 21/Youth

League Club	Source	Date Signed	Seasons Played	Apps	Subs	Gls
Everton	RC Strasbourg (FRA)	06/98	98	28	2	2
Leeds U	RC Lens (FRA)	07/00	00-02	53	4	3
Fulham (L)	Inter Milan (ITA)	02/09	08	0	9	0

DADASON Rikhardur (Rikki)
Born: Reykjavik, Iceland, 26 April, 1972 F
Iceland: 42/U21-10/Youth

League Club	Source	Date Signed	Seasons Played	Apps	Subs	Gls
Stoke C	Viking Stavanger (NOR)	10/00	00-01	19	20	10

DADI Eugene
Born: Abidjan, Ivory Coast, 20 August, 1973 F
Ivory Coast: 1

League Club	Source	Date Signed	Seasons Played	Apps	Subs	Gls
Tranmere Rov	Livingston	08/03	03-04	44	25	25
Nottingham F	Tr	08/05	05	0	5	0
Notts Co	L	01/06	05	9	2	2

DADLEY Peter Robin
Born: Farnham, Surrey, England, 10 December, 1948 W

League Club	Source	Date Signed	Seasons Played	Apps	Subs	Gls
Aldershot	App	12/66	66	1	0	1

DAEHLI Mats Moller
Born: Oslo, Norway, 2 March, 1995 M
Norway: 11/U21-1/Youth

League Club	Source	Date Signed	Seasons Played	Apps	Subs	Gls
Manchester U	Sch	03/12				
Cardiff C	Molde FK (NOR)	01/14	13-14	12	10	1

DAGG Henry Cable (Harry)
Born: Sunderland, England, 4 March, 1924 CF

League Club	Source	Date Signed	Seasons Played	Apps	Subs	Gls
Lincoln C (Am)	Boston U	12/46	46	1	-	1

DAGGER John Leslie (Les)
Born: Lostock Hall, Lancashire, England, 25 April, 1933 RW
Died: Preston, Lancashire, England, 9 March, 2011

League Club	Source	Date Signed	Seasons Played	Apps	Subs	Gls
Preston NE	West Auckland T	05/56	56-60	61	-	8
Carlisle U	Tr	06/61	61-62	74	-	9
Southport	Tr	07/63	63-64	81	-	9

DAGNALL Christopher (Chris)
Born: Liverpool, England, 15 April, 1986 F

League Club	Source	Date Signed	Seasons Played	Apps	Subs	Gls
Tranmere Rov	Sch	07/03	03-05	18	21	7
Rochdale	Tr	01/06	05-09	124	33	54
Scunthorpe U	Tr	07/10	10-11	50	10	9
Barnsley	Tr	01/12	11-13	34	19	6
Bradford C	L	03/12	11	5	2	1
Coventry C	L	11/13	13	4	2	1
Leyton Orient	Tr	01/14	13-14	45	13	17

DAGNOGO Moussa Moustapha
Born: Paris, France, 30 January, 1972 F

League Club	Source	Date Signed	Seasons Played	Apps	Subs	Gls
Bristol Rov	Uniao Madeira (POR)	09/00	00	0	2	0

D'AGOSTINO Michael Joseph
Born: Vancouver, Canada, 7 January, 1987 W
Canada: Youth

League Club	Source	Date Signed	Seasons Played	Apps	Subs	Gls
Blackpool	Kentucky W'cats (USA)	10/07				
Cheltenham T	L	11/07	07	14	11	0

DAHLIN Dan Martin Nataniel (Martin)
Born: Hogaras, Sweden, 16 April, 1968 F
Sweden: 60

League Club	Source	Date Signed	Seasons Played	Apps	Subs	Gls
Blackburn Rov	AS Roma (ITA)	07/97	97-98	13	13	4

DAILEY James Augustine (Jimmy)
Born: Airdrie, Lanarkshire, Scotland, 8 September, 1927 CF
Died: Weymouth, Dorset, England, January, 2002

League Club	Source	Date Signed	Seasons Played	Apps	Subs	Gls
Sheffield Wed	Third Lanark	10/46	46-48	37	-	24
Birmingham C	Tr	02/49	48-51	41	-	14
Exeter C	Tr	08/52	52-53	45	-	13
Workington	Tr	12/53	53-57	176	-	81
Rochdale	Tr	10/57	57-58	53	-	25

DAILLY Christian Eduard
Born: Dundee, Scotland, 23 October, 1973 CD
Scotland: 67/B-1/U21-34/Youth/Schools

League Club	Source	Date Signed	Seasons Played	Apps	Subs	Gls
Derby Co	Dundee U	08/96	96-98	62	5	4
Blackburn Rov	Tr	08/98	98-00	60	10	4
West Ham U	Tr	01/01	00-06	133	25	2
Southampton	L	09/07	07	11	0	0
Charlton Ath	Glasgow Rangers	08/09	09-10	76	0	1
Portsmouth	Tr	08/11	11	0	1	0
Southend U	Rtd	03/12	11	3	0	0

DAILLY Marcus Graham
Born: Dundee, Scotland, 1 October, 1975 M

League Club	Source	Date Signed	Seasons Played	Apps	Subs	Gls
Exeter C	Dundee	08/96	96	8	9	0

DAINES Barry Raymond
Born: Witham, Essex, England, 30 September, 1951 G
England: Youth

League Club	Source	Date Signed	Seasons Played	Apps	Subs	Gls
Tottenham H	App	09/69	71-80	146	0	0
Mansfield T	Bulova (HKG)	10/83	83	21	0	0

DAINO Daniele (Danny)
Born: Alessandria, Italy, 8 September, 1979 FB
Italy: U21-3/Youth

League Club	Source	Date Signed	Seasons Played	Apps	Subs	Gls
Derby Co (L)	AC Milan (ITA)	08/01	01	2	0	0

DAINTY Albert
Born: Lancaster, England, 4 December, 1923 CF
Died: Lancaster, England, 23 March, 1979

League Club	Source	Date Signed	Seasons Played	Apps	Subs	Gls
Preston NE	Standfast Dyers	10/42	46	1	-	1
Stockport Co	Tr	04/47	46-48	36	-	16
Southport	Tr	02/49	48-50	48	-	11

DAINTY James Anthony (Jim)
Born: Coleshill, Warwickshire, England, 21 January, 1954 W

League Club	Source	Date Signed	Seasons Played	Apps	Subs	Gls
Walsall	Jnr	10/71	71-72	4	1	0

DAIR Jason
Born: Dunfermline, Fife, Scotland, 15 June, 1974 LM
Scotland: Schools

League Club	Source	Date Signed	Seasons Played	Apps	Subs	Gls
Millwall	Raith Rov	07/96	96	21	3	1

DAISH Liam Sean
Born: Portsmouth, England, 23 September, 1968 CD
Republic of Ireland: 5/B-1/U21-5

League Club	Source	Date Signed	Seasons Played	Apps	Subs	Gls
Portsmouth	App	09/86	86	1	0	0
Cambridge U	Tr	07/88	88-93	138	1	4
Birmingham C	Tr	01/94	93-95	72	1	3
Coventry C	Tr	02/96	95-96	31	0	2

DAKIN Simon Mark
Born: Nottingham, England, 30 November, 1974 RB

League Club	Source	Date Signed	Seasons Played	Apps	Subs	Gls
Derby Co	YT	07/93				
Hull C	Tr	03/94	93-95	29	7	1

DAKINAH Yari Kofi Kuranchi (Kofi)
Born: Copenhagen, Denmark, 1 February, 1980 CD
Denmark: Youth

League Club	Source	Date Signed	Seasons Played	Apps	Subs	Gls
Walsall	Herfolge (DEN)	07/04	04	1	0	0

DALE Alan George
Born: Thorne, South Yorkshire, England, 20 September, 1958 F

League Club	Source	Date Signed	Seasons Played	Apps	Subs	Gls
Scunthorpe U	App	09/76	75-76	1	2	0

League Club	Source	Date Signed	Seasons Played	Career Record Apps	Subs	Gls
DALE Carl						
Born: Colwyn Bay, Conwy, Wales, 29 April, 1966						F
Chester C	Bangor C	05/88	88-90	106	10	40
Cardiff C	Tr	08/91	91-97	188	25	71
DALE Christopher (Chris)						
Born: York, England, 16 April, 1950						LW
York C (Am)	Hull C (Am)	05/68	68	5	0	0
DALE Eric						
Born: Manchester, England, 6 July, 1924						W
Shrewsbury T		03/50	50	1	-	0
DALE Frederick William (Billy)						
Born: Doncaster, South Yorkshire, England, 26 October, 1925						RW
Halifax T	Scunthorpe U	08/49	49-51	70	-	16
Southport	Tr	07/52	52-53	47	-	5
Accrington Stan	Tr	07/54	54	1	-	0
Crewe Alex	Tr	10/54	54	4	-	3
DALE Gordon						
Born: Worksop, Nottinghamshire, England, 20 May, 1928						LW
Died: Portsmouth, England, 14 March, 1996						
Chesterfield	Worksop T	02/48	48-50	92	-	3
Portsmouth	Tr	07/51	51-56	114	-	18
Exeter C	Tr	10/57	57-60	124	-	8
DALE Joseph (Joe)						
Born: Northwich, Cheshire, England, 3 July, 1921						RW
Died: Northwich, Cheshire, England, 11 September, 2000						
Manchester U	Witton A	06/47	47	2	-	0
Port Vale	Tr	04/48	47-48	9	-	1
DALE Leo						
Born: Esh Winning, County Durham, England, 11 October, 1933						W
Died: Doncaster, South Yorkshire, England, 30 December, 2003						
Doncaster Rov	Durham C	02/54	54	1	-	0
DALE Robert Jenkins (Bobby)						
Born: Irlam, Greater Manchester, England, 31 October, 1931						WH/IF
Died: Colchester, Essex, England, 12 January, 2007						
Bury	Altrincham	09/51	52-53	15	-	2
Colchester U	Tr	12/53	53-56	127	-	12
DALE Robson Louis (Bobby)						
Born: Worcester, England, 25 November, 1995						F
Cheltenham T	Sch	07/14	13-14	1	2	0
D'ALESSANDRO Andres Nicol						
Born: Buenos Aires, Argentina, 15 April, 1981						LW
Argentina: 28						
Portsmouth (L)	VfL Wolfsburg (GER)	01/06	05	13	0	1
DALEY Alan James						
Born: Mansfield, Nottinghamshire, England, 11 October, 1927						W
Died: Bedford, England, 24 June, 2008						
Mansfield T	Pleasley BC	09/46				
Hull C	Tr	07/47	47	7	-	0
Doncaster Rov	Worksop T	03/50	49	1	-	1
Scunthorpe U	Boston U	07/52	52	35	-	8
Mansfield T	Corby T	11/53	53-55	97	-	26
Stockport Co	Tr	02/56	55-57	73	-	17
Crewe Alex	Tr	06/58	58	14	-	1
Coventry C	Tr	11/58	58-60	56	-	10
DALEY Anthony Mark (Tony)						
Born: Birmingham, England, 18 October, 1967						RW
England: 7/B-1/Youth						
Aston Villa	App	05/85	84-93	189	44	31
Wolverhampton W	Tr	06/94	94-97	16	5	3
Watford	Tr	08/98	98	6	6	1
Walsall	Tr	06/99	99	3	4	0
DALEY Keammar Rudolph						
Born: Kingston, Jamaica, 18 February, 1988						W
Jamaica: 27/U23-2/Youth						
Preston NE	Tivoli Gardens (JAM)	08/11	11	0	8	1
DALEY Luke Aaron						
Born: Northampton, England, 10 November, 1989						W
Norwich C	Sch	04/08	08-10	3	8	0
Stevenage	L	01/11	10	0	2	0
Plymouth Arg	Tr	07/11	11	14	4	1
DALEY Omar						
Born: Kingston, Jamaica, 25 April, 1981						W
Jamaica: 72						
Reading	Portmore U (JAM)	08/03	03	0	6	0
Preston NE	Tr	08/04	04	1	13	0
Bradford C	Charleston Bat'y (USA)	01/07	06-10	104	19	15
Rotherham U	L	02/11	10	2	6	1
DALEY Peter John						
Born: Liverpool, England, 14 February, 1970						M
Southend U	Knowsley U	09/89	89	0	5	1
DALEY Philip (Phil)						
Born: Liverpool, England, 12 April, 1967						F
Wigan Ath	Newton	10/89	89-93	152	9	39
Lincoln C	Tr	08/94	94-95	25	7	5
DALEY Stephen (Steve)						
Born: Barnsley, South Yorkshire, England, 15 April, 1953						M
England: B-6/Youth						
Wolverhampton W	App	06/71	71-78	191	21	38
Manchester C	Tr	09/79	79-80	47	1	4
Burnley	Seattle Sounders (USA)	11/83	83	20	3	4
Walsall	San Diego Sock's (USA)	08/85	85	28	0	1
DALEY Thomas Edward (Tom)						
Born: Grimsby, North Lincolnshire, England, 15 November, 1933						G
Grimsby T	Jnr	08/51	51-56	14	-	0
Huddersfield T	Tr	03/57	56	1	-	0
West Bromwich A	Tr	08/58				
DALGLISH Kenneth Mathieson (Kenny)						
Born: Dalmarnock, Glasgow, Scotland, 4 March, 1951						F
Scotland: 102/U23-4						
Liverpool	Glasgow Celtic	08/77	77-89	342	13	118
DALGLISH Paul Kenneth						
Born: Glasgow, Scotland, 18 February, 1977						F
Scotland: U21-6						
Liverpool	Glasgow Celtic	08/96				
Newcastle U	Tr	11/97	98	6	5	1
Bury	L	11/97	97	1	11	0
Norwich C	Tr	03/99	98-00	25	18	2
Wigan Ath	L	03/01	00	5	1	0
Wigan Ath	Tr	08/01	01	17	12	2
Blackpool	Tr	08/02	02	20	7	1
Scunthorpe U	L	03/03	02	5	3	3
DALIBARD Benoit						
Born: Landerneau, France, 26 March, 1991						D
Hereford U	EA Guingamp (FRA)	08/11	11	9	1	0
DALL David Graham						
Born: St Andrews, Fife, Scotland, 10 October, 1957						CD
Scunthorpe U	Grantham	10/79	79-81	77	0	2
DALLA BONA Samuele (Sam)						
Born: Venice, Italy, 6 February, 1981						M
Italy: U21-9/Youth						
Chelsea	Atalanta (ITA)	10/98	99-01	42	13	6
DALLAS Stuart Alan						
Born: Cookstown, Tyrone, Northern Ireland, 19 April, 1991						W
Northern Ireland: 5/U21-2/Youth						
Brentford	Crusaders	07/12	12-14	32	31	7
Northampton T	L	10/13	13	10	2	3
DALLAS William Robert Dempster						
Born: Glasgow, Scotland, 6 March, 1931						CH
Luton T	Caledonian Amats	09/52				
Wrexham	St Mirren	07/57	57	8	-	0
DALLA VALLE Lauri						
Born: Joensuu, Finland, 14 September, 1991						F
Finland: U21-10/Youth						
Liverpool	JIPPO Joensuu (FIN)	09/08				
Fulham	Tr	08/10				
Bournemouth	L	03/11	10	5	3	2
Exeter C	L	03/12	11	4	1	0
Crewe Alex	L	11/12	12	10	0	5
Crewe Alex	Sint-Truiden (BEL)	12/14	14	10	7	4
DALLI Jean						
Born: Enfield, N London, England, 13 August, 1976						FB
Colchester U	Jnr	08/94	94	1	0	0
DALLING Nigel Aubrey						
Born: Swansea, Wales, 20 February, 1959						M
Swansea C	App	02/77	74-77	2	6	0
DALLMAN William (Bill)						
Born: Mansfield, Nottinghamshire, England, 8 August, 1918						CH
Died: Mansfield, Nottinghamshire, England, December, 1988						
Mansfield T	Rufford Colliery	03/47	46-47	5	-	0
DALMAT Stephane						
Born: Tours, France, 16 February, 1979						M
France: U21-27						
Tottenham H (L)	Inter Milan (ITA)	09/03	03	12	10	3

DALRYMPLE Malcolm Owen
Born: Bedford, England, 8 October, 1951 — G
England: Youth

League Club	Source	Date Signed	Seasons Played	Apps	Subs	Gls
Luton T	Jnr	07/70				
Bristol Rov	Margate	10/71	71-72	7	0	0
Watford	Tr	07/73	73	5	0	0

DALTON George
Born: Longbenton, Tyne and Wear, England, 4 September, 1941 — LB

League Club	Source	Date Signed	Seasons Played	Apps	Subs	Gls
Newcastle U	Jnr	11/58	60-66	85	0	2
Brighton & HA	Tr	06/67	67	24	0	0

DALTON Paul
Born: Middlesbrough, England, 25 April, 1967 — LW

League Club	Source	Date Signed	Seasons Played	Apps	Subs	Gls
Manchester U	Brandon U	05/88				
Hartlepool U	Tr	03/89	88-91	140	11	37
Plymouth Arg	Tr	06/92	92-94	93	5	25
Huddersfield T	Tr	08/95	95-98	79	19	25
Carlisle U	L	12/99	99	3	0	1

DALTON Richard Timothy (Tim)
Born: Waterford, Republic of Ireland, 14 October, 1965 — G

League Club	Source	Date Signed	Seasons Played	Apps	Subs	Gls
Coventry C	App	09/83				
Notts Co	Tr	07/84	85	1	0	0
Bradford C	Boston U	09/86				
Tranmere Rov	L	12/86	86	1	0	0

DALY George Jeffrey
Born: Westminster, Central London, England, 5 November, 1990 — F

League Club	Source	Date Signed	Seasons Played	Apps	Subs	Gls
Wycombe W	Sch	07/09	07	0	2	0

DALY Gerard Anthony (Gerry)
Born: Dublin, Republic of Ireland, 30 April, 1954 — M
Republic of Ireland: 48/LoI-1/U21-1

League Club	Source	Date Signed	Seasons Played	Apps	Subs	Gls
Manchester U	Bohemians (ROI)	04/73	73-76	107	4	23
Derby Co	Tr	03/77	76-79	111	1	30
Coventry C	Tr	08/80	80-83	82	2	19
Leicester C	L	01/83	82	17	0	1
Birmingham C	Tr	08/84	84-85	31	1	1
Shrewsbury T	Tr	10/85	85-86	55	0	8
Stoke C	Tr	03/87	86-87	17	5	1
Doncaster Rov	Tr	07/88	88	37	2	4

DALY Jonathan Marvin (Jon)
Born: Dublin, Republic of Ireland, 8 January, 1983 — F
Republic of Ireland: U21-9/Youth

League Club	Source	Date Signed	Seasons Played	Apps	Subs	Gls
Stockport Co	YT	01/00	99-04	65	26	14
Bury	L	01/04	03	7	0	1
Grimsby T	L	10/04	04	3	0	1
Hartlepool U	Tr	02/05	04-06	36	25	12
Bury	L	03/06	05	11	0	2

DALY Maurice Celsus
Born: Dublin, Republic of Ireland, 28 November, 1955 — LB/M
Republic of Ireland: 2/U21-4

League Club	Source	Date Signed	Seasons Played	Apps	Subs	Gls
Wolverhampton W	Home Farm (ROI)	07/73	75-77	28	4	0

DALY Patrick (Pat)
Born: Dublin, Republic of Ireland, 4 December, 1927 — FB
Republic of Ireland: 1/LoI-1

League Club	Source	Date Signed	Seasons Played	Apps	Subs	Gls
Aston Villa	Shamrock Rov (ROI)	11/49	49	3	-	0

DALY Patrick John (Paddy)
Born: Manchester, England, 3 January, 1941 — LW

League Club	Source	Date Signed	Seasons Played	Apps	Subs	Gls
Blackburn Rov	Jnr	01/58	59-60	3	-	0
Southport	Tr	02/62	61	10	-	0

DALY Ronald George (Ron)
Born: Clerkenwell, Central London, England, 22 July, 1930 — IF
Died: High Wycombe, Buckinghamshire, England, 4 August, 1996

League Club	Source	Date Signed	Seasons Played	Apps	Subs	Gls
Watford		10/50	50	3	-	0

DALY Wesley James Patrick (Wes)
Born: Hammersmith, W London, England, 7 March, 1984 — M

League Club	Source	Date Signed	Seasons Played	Apps	Subs	Gls
Queens Park Rgrs	Sch	08/04	01-03	4	5	0

DALZIEL Gordon
Born: Motherwell, Lanarkshire, Scotland, 16 March, 1962 — F

League Club	Source	Date Signed	Seasons Played	Apps	Subs	Gls
Manchester C	Glasgow Rangers	12/83	83	4	1	0

DALZIEL Ian
Born: South Shields, Tyne and Wear, England, 24 October, 1962 — FB

League Club	Source	Date Signed	Seasons Played	Apps	Subs	Gls
Derby Co	App	10/79	81-82	22	0	4
Hereford U	Tr	05/83	83-87	137	13	8
Carlisle U	Tr	07/88	88-92	90	1	2

DAMERELL Mark Anthony
Born: Plymouth, England, 31 July, 1965 — W

League Club	Source	Date Signed	Seasons Played	Apps	Subs	Gls
Plymouth Arg	St Blazey	11/89	89-91	0	6	0
Exeter C	Tr	12/91	91	1	0	0

[DAMIA] ABELLA Damia
Born: Olot, Spain, 15 April, 1982 — RB

League Club	Source	Date Signed	Seasons Played	Apps	Subs	Gls
Middlesbrough	Osasuna (SPN)	08/14	14	6	0	0

DANBY John Robert
Born: Stoke-on-Trent, England, 20 September, 1983 — G

League Club	Source	Date Signed	Seasons Played	Apps	Subs	Gls
Kidderminster Hrs	Jnr	12/01	01-04	46	2	0
Chester C	Tr	08/06	06-08	133	0	0

DANCE Trevor
Born: Hetton-le-Hole, Tyne and Wear, England, 31 July, 1958 — G

League Club	Source	Date Signed	Seasons Played	Apps	Subs	Gls
Port Vale	App	07/76	76-80	84	0	0

DANDO Philip (Phil)
Born: Liverpool, England, 8 June, 1952 — G

League Club	Source	Date Signed	Seasons Played	Apps	Subs	Gls
Liverpool	Jnr	09/69				
Barrow	L	10/70	70	9	0	0

DANGERFIELD Christopher George (Chris)
Born: Coleshill, Warwickshire, England, 9 August, 1955 — F

League Club	Source	Date Signed	Seasons Played	Apps	Subs	Gls
Wolverhampton W	App	08/73				
Port Vale	Portland Timbers (USA)	09/76	76	0	2	0

DANGERFIELD David Anthony
Born: Tetbury, Gloucestershire, England, 27 September, 1951 — M
England: Schools

League Club	Source	Date Signed	Seasons Played	Apps	Subs	Gls
Swindon T	App	08/69	68-72	16	4	0
Charlton Ath	Tr	06/73				

[DANI] CARVALHO DA CRUZ Daniel
Born: Lisbon, Portugal, 2 November, 1976 — F
Portugal: 9/U21-11/Youth

League Club	Source	Date Signed	Seasons Played	Apps	Subs	Gls
West Ham U (L)	Sporting Lisbon (POR)	02/96	95	3	6	2

[DANI] FERREIRA RODRIGUES Daniel
Born: Sao Joao da Madeira, Portugal, 3 March, 1980 — F
Portugal: U21-2

League Club	Source	Date Signed	Seasons Played	Apps	Subs	Gls
Bournemouth (L)	Depo Farense (POR)	10/98	98	0	5	0
Southampton	Depo Farense (POR)	03/99	99	0	2	0
Bristol C	L	10/00	00	3	1	0
Bristol C	L	12/01	01	0	4	0
Walsall	Tr	08/02	02	0	1	0
Yeovil T	Ionikos (GRE)	03/04	03	3	1	4
Bournemouth	Tr	07/04	04-05	23	29	6

DANIEL Alan Winstone
Born: Ashford, Kent, England, 5 April, 1940 — FB

League Club	Source	Date Signed	Seasons Played	Apps	Subs	Gls
Luton T	Bexleyheath & Welling	01/58	58-63	50	-	3

DANIEL Colin Alan (Junior)
Born: Eastwood, Nottinghamshire, England, 15 February, 1988 — LM

League Club	Source	Date Signed	Seasons Played	Apps	Subs	Gls
Crewe Alex	Eastwood T	05/07	07-08	9	5	1
Macclesfield T	Tr	03/09	08-11	118	17	13
Mansfield T	Tr	08/12	13	18	10	2
Port Vale	Tr	06/14	14	8	20	4

DANIEL Melville Verdun Reginald John (Mel)
Born: Llanelli, Carmarthenshire, Wales, 26 January, 1916 — IF
Died: Ashford, Kent, England, 15 September, 1997

League Club	Source	Date Signed	Seasons Played	Apps	Subs	Gls
Luton T	Ashford T, Kent	09/44	46-48	53	-	20
Aldershot	Tr	06/49	49	28	-	1

DANIEL Peter Aylmer
Born: Ripley, Derbyshire, England, 22 December, 1946 — CD

League Club	Source	Date Signed	Seasons Played	Apps	Subs	Gls
Derby Co	App	12/64	65-78	188	7	7

DANIEL Peter William
Born: Hull, England, 12 December, 1955 — M/RB
England: U23-3/U21-7

League Club	Source	Date Signed	Seasons Played	Apps	Subs	Gls
Hull C	Jnr	09/73	74-77	113	0	9
Wolverhampton W	Tr	05/78	78-83	157	0	13
Sunderland	Minnesota S'kers (USA)	08/84	84-85	33	1	0
Lincoln C	Tr	11/85	85-86	55	0	2
Burnley	Tr	07/87	87-88	40	1	0

DANIEL Raymond Christopher (Ray)
Born: Luton, England, 10 December, 1964 — LB

League Club	Source	Date Signed	Seasons Played	Apps	Subs	Gls
Luton T	App	09/82	82-85	14	8	4
Gillingham	L	09/83	83	5	0	0
Hull C	Tr	06/86	86-88	55	3	3
Cardiff C	Tr	08/89	89-90	56	0	1
Portsmouth	Tr	11/90	90-94	91	9	4
Notts Co	L	10/94	94	5	0	0
Walsall	Tr	08/95	95-96	31	4	0

DANIEL Thomas (Tommy)
Born: Middleton, Greater Manchester, England, 14 April, 1923 — RH/IF

League Club	Source	Date Signed	Seasons Played	Apps	Subs	Gls
Bury	Castleton Gabriels	12/46	47-57	276	-	57

DANIEL William Raymond (Ray)
Born: Swansea, Wales, 2 November, 1928 — CH
Died: Clevedon, Somerset, England, 7 November, 1997
Wales: 21

League Club	Source	Date Signed	Seasons Played	Apps	Subs	Gls
Arsenal	Swansea C (Am)	10/46	48-52	87	-	5
Sunderland	Tr	06/53	53-56	136	-	6
Cardiff C	Tr	10/57	57	6	-	0
Swansea C	Tr	03/58	57-59	44	-	7

DANIELS Bernard Joseph (Barney)
Born: Salford, England, 24 November, 1950 — F

League Club	Source	Date Signed	Seasons Played	Apps	Subs	Gls
Manchester U	Jnr	04/69				
Manchester C	Ashton U	04/73	73-74	9	4	2
Chester C	Tr	07/75	75	8	1	1
Stockport Co	Tr	07/76	76-77	45	2	17

DANIELS Billy Jordan
Born: Bristol, England, 3 July, 1994 — M/F

League Club	Source	Date Signed	Seasons Played	Apps	Subs	Gls
Coventry C	Sch	06/12	12-14	13	12	3
Cheltenham T	L	03/14	13	2	0	0
Notts Co	Tr	01/15	14	1	2	1

DANIELS Brendon George Kofi Nana Osei Manoo
Born: Stoke-on-Trent, England, 24 September, 1993 — W

League Club	Source	Date Signed	Seasons Played	Apps	Subs	Gls
Crewe Alex	Sch	07/11	12	2	5	0

DANIELS Charlie John
Born: Harlow, Essex, England, 7 September, 1986 — LB

League Club	Source	Date Signed	Seasons Played	Apps	Subs	Gls
Tottenham H	Sch	07/05				
Chesterfield	L	03/07	06	2	0	0
Leyton Orient	L	08/07	07	24	7	2
Gillingham	L	08/08	08	5	0	1
Leyton Orient	Tr	01/09	08-11	115	2	2
Bournemouth	Tr	11/11	11-14	116	4	7

DANIELS David William (Dave)
Born: Bedford, England, 14 September, 1985 — F

League Club	Source	Date Signed	Seasons Played	Apps	Subs	Gls
Cambridge U	Sch	-	03	0	1	0

DANIELS Donervon Joseph
Born: Montserrat, 24 November, 1993 — CD

League Club	Source	Date Signed	Seasons Played	Apps	Subs	Gls
West Bromwich A	Sch	11/11				
Tranmere Rov	L	11/12	12	10	3	1
Gillingham	L	11/13	13	3	0	1
Blackpool	L	08/14	14	19	0	1

DANIELS Douglas (Doug)
Born: Salford, England, 21 August, 1924 — G
Died: Salford, England, 7 November, 2004

League Club	Source	Date Signed	Seasons Played	Apps	Subs	Gls
New Brighton	Manchester C (Am)	08/47	47	25	-	0
Chesterfield	Tr	07/48				
Accrington Stan	Tr	10/49	49-52	112	-	0

DANIELS Graham David
Born: Farnborough, Hampshire, England, 9 April, 1962 — LW

League Club	Source	Date Signed	Seasons Played	Apps	Subs	Gls
Cambridge U	Cardiff Corinthians	11/83	83-84	37	2	4

DANIELS Henry Augustus George (Harry)
Born: Kensington, Central London, England, 25 June, 1920 — LH
Died: Ham, SW London, England, October, 2002

League Club	Source	Date Signed	Seasons Played	Apps	Subs	Gls
Queens Park Rgrs	Kensington Sports	10/44	46-47	14	-	0
Brighton & HA	Tr	08/48	48-49	32	-	0
York C	Tr	08/50	50	4	-	2

DANIELS John
Born: St Helens, Merseyside, England, 8 January, 1925 — G
Died: St Helens, Merseyside, England, June, 1994

League Club	Source	Date Signed	Seasons Played	Apps	Subs	Gls
New Brighton	British Cidac	03/48	48	3	-	0

DANIELS John Francis (Jack)
Born: Prestwich, Greater Manchester, England, 6 October, 1913 — G
Died: Canada, 1970

League Club	Source	Date Signed	Seasons Played	Apps	Subs	Gls
Leeds U	Ashton National	04/34	34	1	-	0
Stockport Co	Tr	06/35	35-37	9	-	0
Accrington Stan	Tr	07/38	38	10	-	0
Tranmere Rov	Tr	06/39				
Leeds U	Tr	12/40				
Bradford C	Tr	07/45				
Lincoln C	Tr	07/46	46	17	-	0

DANIELS Luke Matthew
Born: Bolton, Greater Manchester, England, 5 January, 1988 — G
England: Youth

League Club	Source	Date Signed	Seasons Played	Apps	Subs	Gls
West Bromwich A	Sch	07/06	13	0	1	0
Shrewsbury T	L	08/08	08	38	0	0
Tranmere Rov	L	07/09	09	37	0	0
Rochdale	L	11/10	10	1	0	0
Bristol Rov	L	01/11	10	9	0	0
Southend U	L	10/11	11	9	0	0
Scunthorpe U	Tr	01/15	14	23	0	0

DANIELS Scott Charles
Born: Benfleet, Essex, England, 22 November, 1969 — CD

League Club	Source	Date Signed	Seasons Played	Apps	Subs	Gls
Colchester U	YT	06/88	87-89	64	9	0
Exeter C	Tr	08/91	91-94	114	3	7
Northampton T	Tr	01/95	94	5	3	0

DANIELS Stephen Richard
Born: Leeds, England, 17 December, 1961 — FB

League Club	Source	Date Signed	Seasons Played	Apps	Subs	Gls
Doncaster Rov	App	10/79	79	0	1	0

DANIELSSON Einar Thor
Born: Reykjavik, Iceland, 19 January, 1970 — M
Iceland: 21/U21-1

League Club	Source	Date Signed	Seasons Played	Apps	Subs	Gls
Stoke C (L)	KR Reykjavik (ICE)	11/99	99	3	5	1

DANIELSSON Helgi Valur
Born: Reykjavik, Iceland, 13 July, 1981 — DM
Iceland: 32/U21-17/Youth

League Club	Source	Date Signed	Seasons Played	Apps	Subs	Gls
Peterborough U	Fylkir (ICE)	10/98	00-02	38	17	2

DANILEVICIUS Tomas
Born: Klaipeda, Lithuania, 18 July, 1978 — F
Lithuania: 71

League Club	Source	Date Signed	Seasons Played	Apps	Subs	Gls
Arsenal	FC Lausanne (SUI)	12/00	00	0	2	0

DANKS Derek Peter
Born: Cheadle, Staffordshire, England, 15 February, 1931 — IF
Died: Staffordshire, England, 7 July, 2012

League Club	Source	Date Signed	Seasons Played	Apps	Subs	Gls
Northampton T		11/53	54	1	-	0

DANKS Mark James
Born: Warley, West Midlands, England, 8 February, 1984 — F

League Club	Source	Date Signed	Seasons Played	Apps	Subs	Gls
Bradford C	Wolverhampton W (YT)	11/02	02	0	3	0

DANN Scott
Born: Liverpool, England, 14 February, 1987 — CD
England: U21-2

League Club	Source	Date Signed	Seasons Played	Apps	Subs	Gls
Walsall	Sch	08/04	04-07	52	7	7
Coventry C	Tr	01/08	07-08	45	2	3
Birmingham C	Tr	06/09	09-10	50	0	2
Blackburn Rov	Tr	08/11	11-13	98	0	5
Crystal Palace	Tr	01/14	13-14	48	0	3

DANN Terence Edward (Terry)
Born: Finsbury, Central London, England, 6 July, 1936 — IF

League Club	Source	Date Signed	Seasons Played	Apps	Subs	Gls
Plymouth Arg	Penzance	07/59	59	8	-	0
Torquay U	Sittingbourne	07/62	62	1	-	0

DANNS Neil Alexander
Born: Liverpool, England, 23 November, 1982 — M
Guyana: 1

League Club	Source	Date Signed	Seasons Played	Apps	Subs	Gls
Blackburn Rov	YT	07/00	02-03	1	2	0
Blackpool	L	08/03	03	12	0	2
Hartlepool U	L	03/04	03	8	1	1
Colchester U	Tr	09/04	04-05	70	3	19
Birmingham C	Tr	06/06	06-07	11	20	3
Crystal Palace	Tr	01/08	07-10	93	10	18
Leicester C	Tr	07/11	11-12	22	8	5
Bristol C	L	11/12	12	9	0	2
Huddersfield T	L	01/13	12	17	0	2
Bolton W	Tr	09/13	13-14	62	12	7

DANSKIN Jason
Born: Winsford, Cheshire, England, 28 December, 1967 — M

League Club	Source	Date Signed	Seasons Played	Apps	Subs	Gls
Everton	App	07/85	84	1	0	0
Mansfield T	Tr	03/87	86	10	0	0
Hartlepool U	L	01/88	87	3	0	0

DANSKIN Robert (Bob)
Born: Scotswood, Tyne and Wear, England, 28 May, 1908 — CH
Died: Shelf, West Yorkshire, England, 14 September, 1985

League Club	Source	Date Signed	Seasons Played	Apps	Subs	Gls
Leeds U	Wallsend U	05/29	30-31	5	-	1
Bradford Park Ave	Tr	12/32	32-47	260	-	6

DANZE Anthony
Born: Perth, Australia, 15 March, 1984 — M
Australia: U23-7/Youth

League Club	Source	Date Signed	Seasons Played	Apps	Subs	Gls
Crystal Palace	Perth Glory (AUS)	10/04				
MK Dons	L	12/04	04	2	0	0

DANZEY Michael James (Mike)
Born: Widnes, Cheshire, England, 8 February, 1971 — F

League Club	Source	Date Signed	Seasons Played	Apps	Subs	Gls
Nottingham F	YT	05/89				
Chester C	L	02/90	89	0	2	0
Peterborough U	Boston U	01/91	90	0	1	0
Cambridge U	St Albans C	10/92	92-94	18	9	3
Scunthorpe U	L	02/93	93	3	0	1

DAPRELA Fabio
Born: Zurich, Switzerland, 19 February, 1991 — LB

Switzerland: U21-18/Youth

League Club	Source	Date Signed	Seasons Played	Apps	Subs	Gls
West Ham U	G'hopper Zurich (SUI)	08/09	09	4	3	0

DARBY Alan
Born: Sheffield, England, 3 June, 1942 — G

League Club	Source	Date Signed	Seasons Played	Apps	Subs	Gls
Doncaster Rov	Goole T	06/59	60	1	-	0

DARBY Brett Thomas
Born: Leicester, England, 10 November, 1983 — W

League Club	Source	Date Signed	Seasons Played	Apps	Subs	Gls
Leicester C	YT	12/00				
Southend U	Tr	02/03	02	6	4	0

DARBY Douglas (Doug)
Born: Bolton-on-Dearne, South Yorkshire, England, 26 December, 1919 — CF
Died: Rotherham, South Yorkshire, England, 26 February, 1963

League Club	Source	Date Signed	Seasons Played	Apps	Subs	Gls
Wolverhampton W	Wath W	09/41				
Walsall	Tr	05/46	46	15	-	4

DARBY Duane Anthony
Born: Warley, West Midlands, England, 17 October, 1973 — F

League Club	Source	Date Signed	Seasons Played	Apps	Subs	Gls
Torquay U	YT	07/92	91-94	60	48	26
Doncaster Rov	Tr	07/95	95	8	9	4
Hull C	Tr	03/96	95-97	75	3	27
Notts Co	Tr	07/98	99	22	6	5
Hull C	L	03/99	98	4	4	0
Rushden & D	Tr	06/00	01-03	61	18	23
Shrewsbury T	Tr	11/03	04-05	15	12	3

DARBY Julian Timothy
Born: Farnworth, Greater Manchester, England, 3 October, 1967 — M
England: Schools

League Club	Source	Date Signed	Seasons Played	Apps	Subs	Gls
Bolton W	App	07/86	85-93	258	12	36
Coventry C	Tr	10/93	93-94	52	3	5
West Bromwich A	Tr	11/95	95-96	32	7	1
Preston NE	Tr	06/97	97-99	20	15	1
Rotherham U	L	03/98	97	3	0	0
Carlisle U	Tr	08/00	00	15	3	1

DARBY Lee Alan
Born: Salford, England, 20 September, 1969 — M
England: Schools

League Club	Source	Date Signed	Seasons Played	Apps	Subs	Gls
Portsmouth	App	10/86	87	1	0	0

DARBY Stephen Mark
Born: Liverpool, England, 6 October, 1988 — RB
England: Youth

League Club	Source	Date Signed	Seasons Played	Apps	Subs	Gls
Liverpool	Sch	07/06	09	0	1	0
Swindon T	L	03/10	09	12	0	0
Notts Co	L	11/10	10	23	0	0
Rochdale	L	07/11	11	34	1	0
Bradford C	Tr	07/12	12-14	124	2	0

DARBYSHIRE Harold (Harry)
Born: Leeds, England, 22 October, 1931 — CF/RH
Died: Leeds, England, 17 June, 1991

League Club	Source	Date Signed	Seasons Played	Apps	Subs	Gls
Leeds U	Jnr	02/50				
Halifax T	Tr	07/52	52-56	162	-	32
Bury	Tr	08/57	57-58	29	-	12
Darlington	Tr	06/59	59	15	-	2

DARCHEVILLE Jean-Claude Ducan
Born: Sinnamary, France, 25 July, 1975 — F
France: U21-1//French Guiana: 7

League Club	Source	Date Signed	Seasons Played	Apps	Subs	Gls
Nottingham F (L)	Stade Rennais (FRA)	07/98	98	14	2	2

D'ARCY Arnold Joseph (Arnie)
Born: Blackburn, Greater Manchester, England, 13 January, 1933 — LW

League Club	Source	Date Signed	Seasons Played	Apps	Subs	Gls
Accrington Stan	St Matthew's BC	03/52	51-52	38	-	9
Swindon T	Wigan Ath	11/56	56-63	223	-	29

D'ARCY Colin Robert
Born: Greasby, Wirral, England, 5 August, 1954 — G

League Club	Source	Date Signed	Seasons Played	Apps	Subs	Gls
Everton		04/73				
Bury	Tr	01/75	74	4	0	0

D'ARCY Francis Anthony (Frank)
Born: Liverpool, England, 8 December, 1946 — LB/M

League Club	Source	Date Signed	Seasons Played	Apps	Subs	Gls
Everton	App	08/64	65-70	8	8	0
Tranmere Rov	Tr	07/72	72	7	1	1

D'ARCY Michael Edmund
Born: Dublin, Republic of Ireland, 8 March, 1933 — G
Republic of Ireland: LoI-10

League Club	Source	Date Signed	Seasons Played	Apps	Subs	Gls
Oldham Ath	Dundalk (ROI)	09/54	54-55	45	-	0

D'ARCY Ross
Born: Balbriggan, Co.Fingal, Republic of Ireland, 21 March, 1978 — CD
Republic of Ireland: U21-6

League Club	Source	Date Signed	Seasons Played	Apps	Subs	Gls
Tottenham H	YT	07/95				
Barnet	Tr	12/99	99-00	1	5	0

D'ARCY Seamus Donal (Jimmy)
Born: Newry, Armagh, Northern Ireland, 14 December, 1921 — IF
Died: Harrow, NW London, England, 22 February, 1985
Northern Ireland: 5

League Club	Source	Date Signed	Seasons Played	Apps	Subs	Gls
Charlton Ath	Ballymena U	03/48	47-50	13	-	1
Chelsea	Tr	10/51	51-52	23	-	12
Brentford	Tr	10/52	52	13	-	3

D'ARCY Thomas McDonald (Tommy)
Born: Edinburgh, Scotland, 22 June, 1932 — CF
Died: Sudbury, Suffolk, England, 20 September, 1985

League Club	Source	Date Signed	Seasons Played	Apps	Subs	Gls
Bournemouth	Hibernian	09/54				
Southend U	Hibernian	05/56	56-57	4	-	0

DARE Kevin John
Born: Finchley, N London, England, 15 November, 1959 — LB

League Club	Source	Date Signed	Seasons Played	Apps	Subs	Gls
Crystal Palace	App	02/77	80-81	6	0	0

DARE Reginald Arthur (Reg)
Born: Blandford Forum, Dorset, England, 26 November, 1921 — CF
Died: Bournemouth, England, October, 1993

League Club	Source	Date Signed	Seasons Played	Apps	Subs	Gls
Southampton	Windsor & Eton	06/49				
Exeter C	Tr	08/50	50	6	-	0

DARE William Thomas Charles (Billy)
Born: Willesden, NW London, England, 14 February, 1927 — CF
Died: Hillingdon, W London, England, 8 May, 1994

League Club	Source	Date Signed	Seasons Played	Apps	Subs	Gls
Brentford	Hendon	11/48	48-54	208	-	62
West Ham U	Tr	01/55	54-58	111	-	44

DAREY Jeffrey Arthur (Jeff)
Born: Hammersmith, W London, England, 26 February, 1934 — CF
Died: Brighton, England, January, 2014
England: Amateur-4

League Club	Source	Date Signed	Seasons Played	Apps	Subs	Gls
Brighton & HA	Hendon	03/57	56-60	10	-	2

DARFIELD Stuart Charles
Born: Leeds, England, 12 April, 1950 — M

League Club	Source	Date Signed	Seasons Played	Apps	Subs	Gls
Bradford Park Ave	Wolverhampton W (App)	07/68	68	15	2	0

DARGIE Ian Charles
Born: Camberwell, S London, England, 3 October, 1931 — CD

League Club	Source	Date Signed	Seasons Played	Apps	Subs	Gls
Brentford	Tonbridge	02/52	51-62	263	-	2

DARIKWA Tendayi David
Born: Nottingham, England, 13 December, 1991 — M/RB

League Club	Source	Date Signed	Seasons Played	Apps	Subs	Gls
Chesterfield	Sch	07/10	11-14	111	14	9

DARK Lewis Kenneth
Born: Harlow, Essex, England, 10 April, 1988 — RB

League Club	Source	Date Signed	Seasons Played	Apps	Subs	Gls
Brentford	Sch	06/07	06	2	1	0

DARK Trevor Charles
Born: Morden, S London, England, 29 January, 1961 — W

League Club	Source	Date Signed	Seasons Played	Apps	Subs	Gls
Birmingham C	App	01/79	78	2	3	1

DARKE Peter George
Born: Exeter, England, 21 December, 1953 — D

League Club	Source	Date Signed	Seasons Played	Apps	Subs	Gls
Plymouth Arg	App	12/71	71-76	94	5	2
Exeter C	L	10/76	76	5	0	0
Torquay U	Tr	07/77	77-78	58	1	0

DARKO Jesse Asieddu
Born: Austria, 13 March, 1993 — F

League Club	Source	Date Signed	Seasons Played	Apps	Subs	Gls
Cardiff C	Sch	07/12				
AFC Wimbledon	L	03/13	12	2	10	0

DARKWAH Cameron Kwaku
Born: Manchester, England, 2 September, 1992 — F

League Club	Source	Date Signed	Seasons Played	Apps	Subs	Gls
Stockport Co	Sch	07/11	10	0	6	0

DARLING Henry Leonard (Len)
Born: Gillingham, Kent, England, 9 August, 1911 — WH
Died: Felixstowe, Suffolk, England, 6 February, 1958

League Club	Source	Date Signed	Seasons Played	Apps	Subs	Gls
Gillingham	Chatham T	05/32	32	14	-	0
Brighton & HA	Tr	08/33	33-47	199	-	5

DARLING Malcolm
Born: Arbroath, Angus, Scotland, 4 July, 1947 — F/W

League Club	Source	Date Signed	Seasons Played	Apps	Subs	Gls
Blackburn Rov	Luncarty Jnrs	10/64	65-69	115	14	30
Norwich C	Tr	05/70	70-71	16	0	5
Rochdale	Tr	10/71	71-73	82	4	16
Bolton W	Tr	09/73	73	6	2	0
Chesterfield	Tr	08/74	74-76	100	4	33
Stockport Co	L	03/77	76	11	0	2
Sheffield Wed	Tr	08/77	77	1	1	0
Hartlepool U	Tr	09/77	77	2	2	0
Bury	Morecambe	03/78	77	1	1	0

DARLINGTON Jermaine Christopher
Born: Hackney, E London, England, 11 April, 1974 — LB

League Club	Source	Date Signed	Seasons Played	Apps	Subs	Gls
Charlton Ath	YT	06/92	91	1	1	0
Queens Park Rgrs	Aylesbury U	03/99	98-00	70	1	2
Wimbledon	Tr	07/01	01-03	97	8	3
Watford	Tr	08/04	04	25	1	0
Cardiff C	Tr	07/05	05	7	2	0

DARLOW Karl
Born: Northampton, England, 8 October, 1990 — G

League Club	Source	Date Signed	Seasons Played	Apps	Subs	Gls
Nottingham F	Sch	07/09	10-13	63	1	0
Walsall	L	09/12	12	9	0	0
Newcastle U	Tr	07/14				
Nottingham F	L	08/14	14	42	0	0

DARLOW Kieran Brian
Born: Bedford, England, 9 November, 1982 — FB

League Club	Source	Date Signed	Seasons Played	Apps	Subs	Gls
York C	YT	-	99-01	1	4	0

DARMODY Aubrey
Born: Swansea, Wales, 17 May, 1921 — FB
Died: Great Yarmouth, Norfolk, England, March, 2006

League Club	Source	Date Signed	Seasons Played	Apps	Subs	Gls
Norwich C	Cardiff Nomads	10/46	46	2	-	0

DARRACOTT Terence Michael (Terry)
Born: Liverpool, England, 6 December, 1950 — D

League Club	Source	Date Signed	Seasons Played	Apps	Subs	Gls
Everton	App	07/68	67-78	138	10	0
Wrexham	Tulsa Roughnecks (USA)	09/79	79	22	0	0

DARRAS Frederic Guy Albert
Born: Calais, France, 19 August, 1966 — RB/M
Died: Maligny,France, France, 27 October, 2010

League Club	Source	Date Signed	Seasons Played	Apps	Subs	Gls
Swindon T	SC Bastia (FRA)	08/96	96-97	42	7	0

DARRELL Michael Alan (Mike)
Born: Bilston, West Midlands, England, 14 January, 1947 — M

League Club	Source	Date Signed	Seasons Played	Apps	Subs	Gls
Birmingham C	App	01/65	65-69	10	4	2
Newport Co	L	10/70	70	7	0	0
Gillingham	L	12/70	70	19	3	1
Peterborough U	Tr	05/71	71-72	32	10	6

DARTON Scott Richard
Born: Ipswich, England, 27 March, 1975 — LB

League Club	Source	Date Signed	Seasons Played	Apps	Subs	Gls
West Bromwich A	YT	10/92	92-94	15	0	0
Blackpool	Tr	01/95	94-96	31	11	1

DARVELL Roger Derek
Born: High Wycombe, Buckinghamshire, England, 10 February, 1931 — CH
Died: Banbury, Oxfordshire, England, 21 October, 2014

League Club	Source	Date Signed	Seasons Played	Apps	Subs	Gls
Charlton Ath	Rickmansworth T	12/53				
Gillingham	Tr	07/57	57	3	-	0
Southport	Tr	07/58	58-64	256	-	1

DARVILLE Liam Thomas
Born: Leyburn, North Yorkshire, England, 26 October, 1990 — RB
England: Youth

League Club	Source	Date Signed	Seasons Played	Apps	Subs	Gls
Leeds U	Sch	08/08				
Tranmere Rov	L	08/10	10	8	1	0

DARWIN George Hedworth
Born: Chester-le-Street, County Durham, England, 16 May, 1932 — IF

League Club	Source	Date Signed	Seasons Played	Apps	Subs	Gls
Huddersfield T	Kimblesworth Jnrs	05/50				
Mansfield T	Tr	11/53	53-56	126	-	63
Derby Co	Tr	05/57	57-60	94	-	32
Rotherham U	Tr	10/60	60	2	-	2
Barrow	Tr	07/61	61-63	92	-	28

DA SILVA Leonardo
Born: Lisbon, Portugal, 30 November, 1998 — LM

League Club	Source	Date Signed	Seasons Played	Apps	Subs	Gls
Peterborough U	Sch	-	14	2	0	0

DA SILVA Paulo Cesar
Born: Asuncion, Paraguay, 1 February, 1980 — CD
Paraguay: 103

League Club	Source	Date Signed	Seasons Played	Apps	Subs	Gls
Sunderland	Toluca (MEX)	07/09	09-10	13	4	0

D'ATH Lawson Marc
Born: Witney, Oxfordshire, England, 24 December, 1992 — M

League Club	Source	Date Signed	Seasons Played	Apps	Subs	Gls
Reading	Sch	02/11				
Yeovil T	L	02/12	11	12	2	1
Cheltenham T	L	10/12	12	1	1	1
Exeter C	L	03/13	12	7	1	1
Dagenham & Red	L	11/13	13	17	4	1
Northampton T	Tr	08/14	14	31	10	7

DAUBNEY Raymond (Ray)
Born: Oldham, Greater Manchester, England, 7 December, 1946 — RW

League Club	Source	Date Signed	Seasons Played	Apps	Subs	Gls
Rochdale	Hathershaw School OB	12/66	66-67	12	0	2

DAUGHTRY Paul William
Born: Oldham, Greater Manchester, England, 14 February, 1973 — RW

League Club	Source	Date Signed	Seasons Played	Apps	Subs	Gls
Stockport Co	Winsford U	01/94				
Hartlepool U	Droylsden	11/94	94	14	1	0

D'AURIA David Alan
Born: Swansea, Wales, 26 March, 1970 — M
Wales: Youth

League Club	Source	Date Signed	Seasons Played	Apps	Subs	Gls
Swansea C	YT	08/88	87-90	27	18	6
Scarborough	Barry T	08/94	94-95	49	3	8
Scunthorpe U	Tr	12/95	95-97	103	4	18
Hull C	Tr	07/98	98-99	52	2	4
Chesterfield	Tr	11/99	99-01	18	7	1

DAVENPORT Calum Raymond Paul
Born: Bedford, England, 1 January, 1983 — CD
England: U21-8/Youth

League Club	Source	Date Signed	Seasons Played	Apps	Subs	Gls
Coventry C	YT	01/00	00-04	64	11	3
Tottenham H	Tr	08/04	04-06	9	6	1
West Ham U	L	09/04	04	10	0	0
Southampton	L	01/05	04	5	2	0
Norwich C	L	09/05	05	14	1	1
West Ham U	Tr	01/07	06-08	12	1	1
Watford	L	01/08	07	1	0	0
Sunderland	L	02/09	08	7	1	0

DAVENPORT Carl
Born: Farnworth, Greater Manchester, England, 30 May, 1944 — CF
Republic of Ireland: LoI-2

League Club	Source	Date Signed	Seasons Played	Apps	Subs	Gls
Preston NE	App	05/62				
Stockport Co	Tr	03/63	62-63	16	-	3

DAVENPORT Peter
Born: Birkenhead, Wirral, England, 24 March, 1961 — F
England: 1/B-1

League Club	Source	Date Signed	Seasons Played	Apps	Subs	Gls
Nottingham F	Cammell Laird	01/82	81-85	114	4	54
Manchester U	Tr	03/86	85-88	73	19	22
Middlesbrough	Tr	11/88	88-89	53	6	7
Sunderland	Tr	07/90	90-92	72	27	15
Stockport Co	St Johnstone	03/95	94	3	3	1
Macclesfield T	Southport	01/97	97-98	2	3	1

DAVEY Alexander James (Alex)
Born: Welwyn Garden City, Hertfordshire, England, 24 November, 1994 — CD
Scotland: Youth

League Club	Source	Date Signed	Seasons Played	Apps	Subs	Gls
Chelsea	Sch	07/12				
Scunthorpe U	L	11/14	14	13	0	0

DAVEY Frederick Albert (Fred)
Born: Crediton, Devon, England, 13 April, 1924 — WH
Died: Peterborough, England, April, 2000

League Club	Source	Date Signed	Seasons Played	Apps	Subs	Gls
Exeter C	Crediton T	08/47	47-55	276	-	3

DAVEY Nigel Geoffrey
Born: Garforth, West Yorkshire, England, 20 June, 1946 — FB

League Club	Source	Date Signed	Seasons Played	Apps	Subs	Gls
Leeds U	Great Preston Jnrs	02/64	67-70	13	1	0
Rotherham U	Tr	07/74				

DAVEY Simon
Born: Swansea, Wales, 1 October, 1970 — M

League Club	Source	Date Signed	Seasons Played	Apps	Subs	Gls
Swansea C	YT	07/89	86-91	37	12	4
Carlisle U	Tr	08/92	92-94	105	0	18
Preston NE	Tr	02/95	94-97	97	9	21
Darlington	L	09/97	97	10	1	0

DAVEY Stephen Gilbert Richard (Steve)
Born: Plymouth, England, 5 September, 1948 — M/F
England: Youth

League Club	Source	Date Signed	Seasons Played	Apps	Subs	Gls
Plymouth Arg	App	07/66	66-74	213	11	47
Hereford U	Tr	08/75	75-77	104	3	32
Portsmouth	Tr	06/78	78-80	82	10	8
Exeter C	Tr	08/81	81	15	0	0

DAVEY Stuart
Born: Haslington, Cheshire, England, 4 January, 1938 — FB
Died: Cheshire, England, April, 2013

League Club	Source	Date Signed	Seasons Played	Apps	Subs	Gls
Crewe Alex	Jnr	08/56	56	1	-	0

DAVID Christofer Gerkan (Chris)
Born: Amsterdam, Netherlands, 6 March, 1993 — M
Netherlands: Youth

League Club	Source	Date Signed	Seasons Played	Apps	Subs	Gls
Fulham	FC Twente (NED)	01/13	13-14	3	3	1

[DAVID LUIZ] MOREIRA David Luiz
Born: Sao Paulo, Brazil, 22 April, 1987 — CD/DM
Brazil: 43/Youth

League Club	Source	Date Signed	Seasons Played	Apps	Subs	Gls
Chelsea	Benfica (POR)	01/11	10-13	73	8	6

DAVIDS Edgar Steven
Born: Paramaribo, Suriname, 13 March, 1973 — M

Netherlands: 74/U21-8/Youth

League Club	Source	Date Signed	Seasons Played	Apps	Subs	Gls
Tottenham H	Inter Milan (ITA)	08/05	05-06	34	6	1
Crystal Palace	Rtd	08/10	10	6	0	0
Barnet	Rtd	10/12	12	28	0	1

DAVIDS Lorenzo
Born: Paramaribo, Suriname, 4 September, 1986 M
Netherlands: U21-3

League Club	Source	Date Signed	Seasons Played	Apps	Subs	Gls
Bournemouth	Augsburg (GER)	09/12	12	2	1	0

DAVIDS Neil Graham
Born: Bingley, West Yorkshire, England, 22 September, 1955 CD
Died: Blackpool, Lancashire, England, 23 December, 2011
England: Youth

League Club	Source	Date Signed	Seasons Played	Apps	Subs	Gls
Leeds U	App	08/73				
Norwich C	Tr	04/75	75	2	0	0
Northampton T	L	09/75	75	9	0	0
Stockport Co	L	01/76	75	5	0	1
Swansea C	Tr	07/77	77	9	0	0
Wigan Ath	Tr	07/78	78-80	66	2	1

DAVIDSON Adam Richmond
Born: Dundee, Scotland, 28 November, 1929 RW
Died: Portsmouth, England, September, 2007

League Club	Source	Date Signed	Seasons Played	Apps	Subs	Gls
Sheffield Wed	Elmwood	03/48				
Colchester U	Tr	08/51	51	19	-	0

DAVIDSON Alan Edward
Born: Melbourne, Australia, 1 June, 1960 FB
Australia: 79/U23-11/Youth

League Club	Source	Date Signed	Seasons Played	Apps	Subs	Gls
Nottingham F	S Melbourne H's (AUS)	11/84	84	3	0	0

DAVIDSON Alexander Morrison (Alex)
Born: Langholm, Dumfries & Galloway, Scotland, 6 June, 1920 IF
Died: Helensburgh, Argyll & Bute, Scotland, 11 February, 2005

League Club	Source	Date Signed	Seasons Played	Apps	Subs	Gls
Chelsea	Hibernian	08/46	46	2	-	0
Crystal Palace	Tr	08/48	48	10	-	2

DAVIDSON Andrew (Andy)
Born: Douglas Water, Lanarkshire, Scotland, 13 July, 1932 RB
Died: Beverley, East Riding of Yorkshire, England, 5 April, 2014

League Club	Source	Date Signed	Seasons Played	Apps	Subs	Gls
Hull C	Douglas Water Thistle	09/49	52-67	520	0	18

DAVIDSON Angus Gordon
Born: Forfar, Angus, Scotland, 2 October, 1948 M

League Club	Source	Date Signed	Seasons Played	Apps	Subs	Gls
Grimsby T	Arbroath Lads	11/65	65-68	46	5	1
Scunthorpe U	Tr	07/69	69-76	304	15	44

DAVIDSON Brian
Born: Workington, Cumbria, England, 23 August, 1951 W

League Club	Source	Date Signed	Seasons Played	Apps	Subs	Gls
Workington (Am)	Jnr	08/72	72	1	0	0

DAVIDSON Callum Iain
Born: Stirling, Scotland, 25 June, 1976 LB/M
Scotland: 19/U21-2

League Club	Source	Date Signed	Seasons Played	Apps	Subs	Gls
Blackburn Rov	St Johnstone	02/98	97-99	63	2	1
Leicester C	Tr	07/00	00-03	90	11	2
Preston NE	Tr	08/04	04-10	153	13	21

DAVIDSON David
Born: Govanhill, Glasgow, Scotland, 20 August, 1934 WH

League Club	Source	Date Signed	Seasons Played	Apps	Subs	Gls
Manchester C	Glentyne Thistle	08/51	53	1	-	0
Workington	Tr	07/58	58	3	-	0

DAVIDSON David Blyth Logie (Dave)
Born: Lanark, Scotland, 25 March, 1920 FB
Died: Hackney, E London, England, 1954

League Club	Source	Date Signed	Seasons Played	Apps	Subs	Gls
Bradford Park Ave	Douglas Water Thistle	05/38	46	13	-	0
Leyton Orient	Tr	01/47	46-49	84	-	1

DAVIDSON David Craiglogie
Born: Douglas Water, Lanarkshire, Scotland, 19 March, 1926 RW
Died: Hull, England, March, 1996

League Club	Source	Date Signed	Seasons Played	Apps	Subs	Gls
Hull C	Douglas Water Thistle	10/46	46-47	22	-	4

DAVIDSON Dennis James
Born: Aberdeen, Scotland, 18 May, 1937 WH

League Club	Source	Date Signed	Seasons Played	Apps	Subs	Gls
Portsmouth	Torry Rgrs	05/54	59	1	-	0

DAVIDSON Douglas Bell
Born: Dundee, Scotland, 2 December, 1918 IF
Died: Southsea, Hampshire, England, 17 July, 1968

League Club	Source	Date Signed	Seasons Played	Apps	Subs	Gls
Blackpool	East Fife	10/48	48-49	14	-	0
Reading	Tr	04/50	49-50	11	-	1

DAVIDSON Duncan
Born: Elgin, Moray, Scotland, 5 July, 1954 F

League Club	Source	Date Signed	Seasons Played	Apps	Subs	Gls
Manchester C	Sea Bee (HKG)	09/83	83	2	4	1

DAVIDSON Ian
Born: Pencaitland, East Lothian, Scotland, 8 September, 1937 WH

League Club	Source	Date Signed	Seasons Played	Apps	Subs	Gls
Preston NE	Kilmarnock	12/62	62-64	67	-	1
Middlesbrough	Tr	02/65	64-66	46	0	0
Darlington	Tr	09/67	67	27	0	0

DAVIDSON Ian
Born: Goole, East Riding of Yorkshire, England, 31 January, 1947 M

League Club	Source	Date Signed	Seasons Played	Apps	Subs	Gls
Hull C	Jnr	02/65	66-67	5	1	1
Scunthorpe U	L	09/68	68	32	3	0
York C	Tr	06/69	69-70	82	4	4
Bournemouth	Tr	07/71	71	7	2	0
Stockport Co	Tr	05/72	72-73	74	4	6

DAVIDSON Jason Alan
Born: Melbourne, Australia, 29 June, 1991 LB
Australia: 18/Youth

League Club	Source	Date Signed	Seasons Played	Apps	Subs	Gls
West Bromwich A	Heracles Almelo (NED)	08/14	14	1	1	0

DAVIDSON John Summers (Johnny)
Born: Stonehouse, Lanarkshire, Scotland, 6 November, 1931 IF

League Club	Source	Date Signed	Seasons Played	Apps	Subs	Gls
Walsall	Alloa Ath	08/55	55	5	-	0

DAVIDSON Jonathan Stewart (Jon)
Born: Cheadle, Staffordshire, England, 1 March, 1970 FB

League Club	Source	Date Signed	Seasons Played	Apps	Subs	Gls
Derby Co	YT	07/88	89-91	7	5	0
Preston NE	Tr	07/92	92	18	3	1
Chesterfield	L	03/93	92	0	1	0

DAVIDSON Peter Edward
Born: Newcastle-upon-Tyne, England, 31 October, 1956 W

League Club	Source	Date Signed	Seasons Played	Apps	Subs	Gls
Queens Park Rgrs	Berwick Rgrs	07/79	79	0	1	0

DAVIDSON Robert (Bob)
Born: Rutherglen, Glasgow, Scotland, 25 March, 1986 F

League Club	Source	Date Signed	Seasons Played	Apps	Subs	Gls
Boston U (L)	Glasgow Rangers	08/06	06	3	6	0

DAVIDSON Robert Trimming (Bobby)
Born: Lochgelly, Fife, Scotland, 27 April, 1913 IF
Died: Coventry, England, October, 1988
Scotland: SLge-1

League Club	Source	Date Signed	Seasons Played	Apps	Subs	Gls
Arsenal	St Johnstone	02/35	34-37	57	-	13
Coventry C	Tr	11/37	37-47	47	-	9

DAVIDSON Roger
Born: Islington, N London, England, 27 October, 1948 M
England: Schools

League Club	Source	Date Signed	Seasons Played	Apps	Subs	Gls
Arsenal	App	11/65	67	0	1	0
Portsmouth	Tr	06/69	69	3	0	0
Fulham	Tr	08/70	70	1	0	0
Lincoln C	Tr	10/71	71	6	0	0
Aldershot	L	02/72	71	12	0	2

DAVIDSON Ross
Born: Burton-on-Trent, Staffordshire, England, 6 September, 1989 M

League Club	Source	Date Signed	Seasons Played	Apps	Subs	Gls
Port Vale	Sch	05/08	07-08	15	11	0

DAVIDSON Ross James
Born: Chertsey, Surrey, England, 13 November, 1973 RB

League Club	Source	Date Signed	Seasons Played	Apps	Subs	Gls
Sheffield U	Walton & Hersham	06/93	94-95	2	0	0
Chester C	Tr	01/96	95-99	132	0	5
Barnet	Tr	11/99	99	8	1	0
Shrewsbury T	Tr	03/00	99-00	40	3	0

DAVIDSON Victor Salvatore Ferla (Vic)
Born: Glasgow, Scotland, 8 November, 1950 F

League Club	Source	Date Signed	Seasons Played	Apps	Subs	Gls
Blackpool	Motherwell	07/78	78	23	2	3

DAVIE Alexander Grimmond (Sandy)
Born: Dundee, Scotland, 10 June, 1945 G

League Club	Source	Date Signed	Seasons Played	Apps	Subs	Gls
Luton T	Dundee U	09/68	68-69	58	0	0
Southampton	Tr	05/70	70	1	0	0

DAVIE James Graham (Jim)
Born: Cambuslang, Glasgow, Scotland, 7 September, 1922 WH
Died: Glasgow, Scotland, 31 January, 1984

League Club	Source	Date Signed	Seasons Played	Apps	Subs	Gls
Preston NE	Kilmarnock	06/48	48-49	28	-	0
Northampton T	Tr	07/50	50-52	75	-	1
Shrewsbury T	Tr	07/53				

DAVIE John (Jock)
Born: Dunfermline, Fife, Scotland, 19 February, 1913 CF
Died: Shrewsbury, Shropshire, England, June, 1994

League Club	Source	Date Signed	Seasons Played	Apps	Subs	Gls
Brighton & HA	Margate	05/36	36-38	89	-	39
Barnsley	Stockton	12/46	46	6	-	0

DAVIE William Clark (Willie)
Born: Paisley, Renfrewshire, Scotland, 7 January, 1925 IF
Died: Huddersfield, West Yorkshire, England, 29 January, 1996

League Club	Source	Date Signed	Seasons Played	Apps	Subs	Gls
Luton T	St Mirren	12/50	50-51	42	-	11
Huddersfield T	Tr	12/51	51-56	113	-	16
Walsall	Tr	07/57	57	7	-	0

DAVIES Adam Glen
Born: Peterborough, England, 27 March, 1987 — CD
Wales: Youth

League Club	Source	Date Signed	Seasons Played	Apps	Subs	Gls
Cambridge U	Sch	-	04	0	2	0

DAVIES Adam Rhys
Born: Rinteln, Germany, 17 July, 1992 — G

League Club	Source	Date Signed	Seasons Played	Apps	Subs	Gls
Everton	Sch	08/09				
Sheffield Wed	Tr	10/12				
Barnsley	Tr	06/14	14	22	1	0

DAVIES Alan
Born: Manchester, England, 5 December, 1961 — M
Died: Gower, Swansea, Wales, 4 April, 1992
Wales: 13/U21-6

League Club	Source	Date Signed	Seasons Played	Apps	Subs	Gls
Manchester U	App	12/78	81-83	6	1	0
Newcastle U	Tr	08/85	85-86	20	1	1
Charlton Ath	L	03/86	85	1	0	0
Carlisle U	L	11/86	86	4	0	1
Swansea C	Tr	07/87	87-88	84	0	8
Bradford C	Tr	06/89	89	24	2	1
Swansea C	Tr	08/90	90-91	41	2	4

DAVIES Albert John Victor
Born: Greenwich, SE London, England, 19 April, 1935 — G

League Club	Source	Date Signed	Seasons Played	Apps	Subs	Gls
Millwall	Plumstead Maybloom	10/56	57	1	-	0

DAVIES Albert Llewellyn
Born: Pontypridd, Rhondda Cynon Taff, Wales, 11 March, 1933 — W

League Club	Source	Date Signed	Seasons Played	Apps	Subs	Gls
Newport Co	Merthyr Tydfil	04/51	50	1	-	0

DAVIES Alexander John (Alex)
Born: Swansea, Wales, 2 November, 1982 — G

League Club	Source	Date Signed	Seasons Played	Apps	Subs	Gls
Swansea C	YT	-	00	0	1	0

DAVIES Alexander McLean (Alec)
Born: Dundonald, Ayrshire, Scotland, 21 May, 1920 — RW
Died: Christchurch, New Zealand, 1964

League Club	Source	Date Signed	Seasons Played	Apps	Subs	Gls
Sheffield Wed	Kiveton Park	04/45				
Lincoln C	Tr	07/45	46-48	37	-	9

DAVIES Andrew John
Born: Stockton-on-Tees, Cleveland, England, 17 December, 1984 — CD
England: U21-1/Youth

League Club	Source	Date Signed	Seasons Played	Apps	Subs	Gls
Middlesbrough	Sch	07/02	02-07	39	14	0
Queens Park Rgrs	L	01/05	04	9	0	0
Derby Co	L	07/05	05	22	1	3
Southampton	Tr	10/07	07	22	1	0
Stoke C	Tr	08/08	08	0	2	0
Preston NE	L	02/09	08	5	0	0
Sheffield U	L	09/09	09	7	1	0
Walsall	L	10/10	10	3	0	0
Middlesbrough	L	02/11	10	5	1	0
Crystal Palace	L	08/11	11	1	0	0
Bradford C	L	09/11	11	26	0	2
Bradford C	Tr	07/12	12-14	83	1	5

DAVIES Andrew Jonathan (Andy)
Born: Wolverhampton, England, 6 June, 1972 — CD

League Club	Source	Date Signed	Seasons Played	Apps	Subs	Gls
Torquay U	YT	07/88	88-89	9	4	0
Hartlepool U	Tr	06/90	90-91	4	3	0
Torquay U	Tr	08/92	92	1	2	0

DAVIES Arron Rhys
Born: Cardiff, Wales, 22 June, 1984 — W
Wales: 1/U21-14

League Club	Source	Date Signed	Seasons Played	Apps	Subs	Gls
Southampton	Sch	07/02				
Barnsley	L	02/04	03	1	3	0
Yeovil T	Tr	12/04	04-06	76	25	22
Nottingham F	Tr	07/07	07-08	12	20	1
Brighton & HA	L	09/09	09	7	0	0
Yeovil T	L	02/10	09	4	6	0
Peterborough U	Tr	07/10	10	12	10	1
Northampton T	Tr	07/11	11	15	0	4
Exeter C	Tr	07/12	12-14	93	15	9

DAVIES Benjamin James (Ben)
Born: Birmingham, England, 27 May, 1981 — M

League Club	Source	Date Signed	Seasons Played	Apps	Subs	Gls
Walsall	Stoke C (YT)	08/99				
Kidderminster Hrs	Tr	03/00	00-01	11	1	0
Chester C	Tr	05/02	04-05	80	9	9
Shrewsbury T	Tr	06/06	06-08	111	1	30
Notts Co	Tr	07/09	09-10	67	0	20
Derby Co	Tr	01/11	10-13	49	26	7
Sheffield U	Tr	02/14	13-14	19	13	7

DAVIES Benjamin Keith (Ben)
Born: Barrow, Cumbria, England, 11 August, 1995 — LB

League Club	Source	Date Signed	Seasons Played	Apps	Subs	Gls
Preston NE	Sch	05/13	12-14	7	0	0
York C	L	07/13	13	44	0	0
Tranmere Rov	L	09/14	14	3	0	0

DAVIES Benjamin Thomas (Ben)
Born: Neath, Wales, 24 April, 1993 — LB
Wales: 13/Youth

League Club	Source	Date Signed	Seasons Played	Apps	Subs	Gls
Swansea C	Sch	07/11	12-13	65	6	3
Tottenham H	Tr	07/14	14	9	5	0

DAVIES Brian
Born: Doncaster, South Yorkshire, England, 21 August, 1947 — IF

League Club	Source	Date Signed	Seasons Played	Apps	Subs	Gls
Sheffield Wed	App	08/64	65	3	0	1

DAVIES Byron
Born: Llanelli, Carmarthenshire, Wales, 5 February, 1932 — CH

League Club	Source	Date Signed	Seasons Played	Apps	Subs	Gls
Leeds U	Llanelli	05/52	53	1	-	0
Newport Co	Tr	06/56				

DAVIES Callum Joshua
Born: Sittingbourne, Kent, England, 8 February, 1993 — CD

League Club	Source	Date Signed	Seasons Played	Apps	Subs	Gls
Gillingham	Sch	07/11	10-14	22	7	0

DAVIES Cecil Joseph
Born: Fleur-de-Lys, Caerphilly, Wales, 26 March, 1918 — WH
Died: Greenwich, SE London, England, 23 October, 1994
Wales: Schools

League Club	Source	Date Signed	Seasons Played	Apps	Subs	Gls
Charlton Ath	Lovells Ath	03/35				
Barrow	Tr	06/38	38-46	75	-	3
Millwall	Tr	07/47	47-48	31	-	0

DAVIES Clint Aaron
Born: Perth, Australia, 24 April, 1983 — G

League Club	Source	Date Signed	Seasons Played	Apps	Subs	Gls
Birmingham C	Sch	07/02				
Bradford C	Tr	07/03	03	1	1	0
Bristol C	Tr	08/04				

DAVIES Colin Frank
Born: Shrewsbury, Shropshire, England, 12 April, 1936 — CH

League Club	Source	Date Signed	Seasons Played	Apps	Subs	Gls
Port Vale		06/59	59-60	13	-	0

DAVIES Craig Martin
Born: Burton-on-Trent, Staffordshire, England, 9 January, 1986 — F
Wales: 8/U21-9/Youth

League Club	Source	Date Signed	Seasons Played	Apps	Subs	Gls
Oxford U	Sch	02/05	04-05	23	25	8
Wolverhampton W (L)	Verona (ITA)	08/06	06	6	17	0
Oldham Ath	Verona (ITA)	07/07	07-08	36	8	10
Stockport Co	L	10/08	08	9	0	5
Brighton & HA	Tr	02/09	08-09	10	11	1
Yeovil T	L	09/09	09	2	2	0
Port Vale	L	01/10	09	22	2	7
Chesterfield	Tr	07/10	10	41	0	23
Barnsley	Tr	07/11	11-12	52	8	19
Bolton W	Tr	01/13	12-14	24	29	10
Preston NE	L	01/14	13	12	3	5

DAVIES Curtis Eugene
Born: Leytonstone, NE London, England, 15 March, 1985 — CD
England: U21-3

League Club	Source	Date Signed	Seasons Played	Apps	Subs	Gls
Luton T	Sch	07/04	03-05	54	2	2
West Bromwich A	Tr	08/05	05-06	65	0	2
Aston Villa	Tr	08/07	07-09	45	4	3
Leicester C	L	10/10	10	12	0	0
Birmingham C	Tr	01/11	10-12	84	5	11
Hull C	Tr	06/13	13-14	58	0	2

DAVIES Cyril
Born: Swansea, Wales, 7 September, 1948 — M
Wales: 1/U23-4/Schools

League Club	Source	Date Signed	Seasons Played	Apps	Subs	Gls
Swansea C	App	09/66				
Carlisle U	Tr	06/68	68	1	1	0
Charlton Ath	Yeovil T	05/70	70-72	70	6	5

DAVIES David Daniel (Dai)
Born: Aberdare, Rhondda Cynon Taff, Wales, 5 December, 1914 — IF
Died: Hull, England, 13 October, 1984

League Club	Source	Date Signed	Seasons Played	Apps	Subs	Gls
Hull C	Aberaman Ath	08/35	35-46	141	-	30

DAVIES David Ivor (Dai)
Born: Bridgend, Wales, 21 July, 1932 — CF
Died: Bridgend, Wales, 26 February, 2012

League Club	Source	Date Signed	Seasons Played	Apps	Subs	Gls
Leyton Orient	Pyle	04/53	53	4	-	0

DAVIES David John
Born: Neath, Wales, 21 May, 1952 — CD

League Club	Source	Date Signed	Seasons Played	Apps	Subs	Gls
Swansea C	Afan Lido	07/73	73-74	27	1	0

DAVIES David Lamb
Born: Pontypridd, Rhondda Cynon Taff, Wales, 11 July, 1956 — W

League Club	Source	Date Signed	Seasons Played	Apps	Subs	Gls
Swansea C	App	07/74	72	0	1	0
Crewe Alex	Tr	03/75	74-80	196	13	26

DAVIES David Lyn (Lyn)
Born: Neath, Wales, 29 September, 1947 — G
Wales: U23-1/Schools

League Club	Source	Date Signed	Seasons Played	Apps	Subs	Gls
Cardiff C	App	10/65	65-66	16	0	0
Swansea C	Llanelli	07/72	72	3	0	0

DAVIES Dudley
Born: Shoreham-by-Sea, West Sussex, England, 27 December, 1924 — RW
Died: 12 February, 2015

League Club	Source	Date Signed	Seasons Played	Apps	Subs	Gls
Charlton Ath	Lancing T	01/48				
Leyton Orient	Tr	05/50	50-51	17	-	2

DAVIES Edmund (Eddie)
Born: Oswestry, Shropshire, England, 5 June, 1927 — W

League Club	Source	Date Signed	Seasons Played	Apps	Subs	Gls
Arsenal	Liverpool (Am)	08/48				
Queens Park Rgrs	Tr	04/50	50	1	-	1
Crewe Alex	Tr	07/51	51	7	-	0

DAVIES Edward (Eddie)
Born: Burslem, Potteries, England, 3 May, 1923 — CF
Died: Herne Bay, Kent, England, 26 March, 1995

League Club	Source	Date Signed	Seasons Played	Apps	Subs	Gls
Port Vale		01/43	46	3	-	0

DAVIES Edward George Gladstone (Glen)
Born: Swansea, Wales, 30 June, 1950 — CD

League Club	Source	Date Signed	Seasons Played	Apps	Subs	Gls
Swansea C	Jnr	07/70	70-75	139	8	13

DAVIES Edward Keith (Keith)
Born: Birkenhead, Wirral, England, 19 February, 1934 — IF

League Club	Source	Date Signed	Seasons Played	Apps	Subs	Gls
Tranmere Rov		07/53	53	1	-	0

DAVIES Ellis Reginald (Reg)
Born: Cymmer Afan, Neath Port Talbot, Wales, 27 May, 1929 — IF
Died: Perth, Australia, 9 February, 2009
Wales: 6

League Club	Source	Date Signed	Seasons Played	Apps	Subs	Gls
Southend U	Southampton (Am)	07/49	49-50	41	-	18
Newcastle U	Tr	04/51	51-58	157	-	49
Swansea C	Tr	10/58	58-61	111	-	29
Carlisle U	Tr	06/62	62-63	65	-	13

DAVIES Eric
Born: Crumpsall, Greater Manchester, England, 20 February, 1943 — CF
Died: Stainmore, Cumbria, England, 10 March, 1988

League Club	Source	Date Signed	Seasons Played	Apps	Subs	Gls
Southport	Southport Trinity	03/62	61-64	3	-	0

DAVIES Frederick (Fred)
Born: Liverpool, England, 22 August, 1939 — G

League Club	Source	Date Signed	Seasons Played	Apps	Subs	Gls
Wolverhampton W	Llandudno	04/57	61-67	156	0	0
Cardiff C	Tr	01/68	67-69	98	0	0
Bournemouth	Tr	07/70	70-73	134	0	0

DAVIES Gareth
Born: Cardiff, Wales, 6 October, 1959 — M

League Club	Source	Date Signed	Seasons Played	Apps	Subs	Gls
Cardiff C	Sully	11/86	86	1	1	0

DAVIES Gareth Melville
Born: Hereford, England, 11 December, 1973 — CD
Wales: U21-8

League Club	Source	Date Signed	Seasons Played	Apps	Subs	Gls
Hereford U	YT	04/92	91-94	91	4	2
Crystal Palace	Tr	07/95	95-97	22	5	2
Cardiff C	L	02/97	96	6	0	2
Reading	Tr	12/97	97-98	18	1	0
Swindon T	Tr	03/99	98-01	23	2	0

DAVIES Gareth Michael John
Born: Chesterfield, Derbyshire, England, 4 February, 1983 — M

League Club	Source	Date Signed	Seasons Played	Apps	Subs	Gls
Chesterfield	Buxton	08/01	02-07	73	43	2

DAVIES Geoffrey Peter (Geoff)
Born: Ellesmere Port, Cheshire, England, 1 July, 1947 — F

League Club	Source	Date Signed	Seasons Played	Apps	Subs	Gls
Chester C	Wigan Ath	08/72	72-73	18	14	5
Wrexham	Tr	10/73	73-75	64	3	15
Port Vale	Chicago Sting (USA)	08/76	76	7	0	0
Hartlepool U	L	11/76	76	5	0	1
Wimbledon	San Jose E'quake (USA)	08/77	77	23	0	1

DAVIES George
Born: Rednal, Shropshire, England, 1 March, 1927 — WH

League Club	Source	Date Signed	Seasons Played	Apps	Subs	Gls
Sheffield Wed	Oswestry T	06/50	50-54	98	-	1
Chester C	Tr	07/56	56-57	35	-	4

DAVIES Glen
Born: Brighton, England, 20 July, 1976 — CD

League Club	Source	Date Signed	Seasons Played	Apps	Subs	Gls
Burnley	YT	07/94				
Hartlepool U	Tr	06/96	96-97	48	4	1

DAVIES Glyn
Born: Swansea, Wales, 31 May, 1932 — LH/LB
Died: Swansea, Wales, 7 February, 2013

League Club	Source	Date Signed	Seasons Played	Apps	Subs	Gls
Derby Co	Jnr	07/49	53-61	200	-	5
Swansea C	Tr	07/62	62	18	-	1

DAVIES Gordon
Born: Manchester, England, 4 September, 1932 — IF

League Club	Source	Date Signed	Seasons Played	Apps	Subs	Gls
Manchester C	Ashton U	12/51	51-54	13	-	5
Chester C	Tr	06/57	57	22	-	5
Southport	Tr	08/58	58	11	-	1

DAVIES Gordon John
Born: Merthyr Tydfil, Wales, 3 August, 1955 — F
Wales: 16/Schools

League Club	Source	Date Signed	Seasons Played	Apps	Subs	Gls
Fulham	Merthyr Tydfil	03/78	77-84	244	3	114
Chelsea	Tr	11/84	84-85	11	2	6
Manchester C	Tr	10/85	85-86	31	0	9
Fulham	Tr	10/86	86-90	120	27	45
Wrexham	Tr	08/91	91	21	1	4

DAVIES Graham Gilding
Born: Swansea, Wales, 3 October, 1921 — G
Died: Swansea, Wales, 12 November, 2003
Wales: Schools

League Club	Source	Date Signed	Seasons Played	Apps	Subs	Gls
Swansea C		02/42				
Watford	Tr	06/47	47-48	9	-	0

DAVIES Grant
Born: Barrow, Cumbria, England, 13 October, 1959 — CD

League Club	Source	Date Signed	Seasons Played	Apps	Subs	Gls
Preston NE	App	10/77				
Newport Co	Tr	07/78	78-82	147	3	1
Exeter C	L	02/83	82	7	0	0

DAVIES Ian Claude
Born: Bristol, England, 29 March, 1957 — LB
Wales: U21-1

League Club	Source	Date Signed	Seasons Played	Apps	Subs	Gls
Norwich C	App	03/75	73-78	29	3	2
Newcastle U	Tr	06/79	79-81	74	1	3
Manchester C	Tr	08/82	82-83	7	0	0
Bury	L	11/82	82	14	0	0
Brentford	L	11/83	83	2	0	0
Cambridge U	L	02/84	83	5	0	0
Carlisle U	Tr	08/84	84	4	0	0
Exeter C	Tr	12/84	84	5	0	0
Bristol Rov	Diss T	08/85	85	13	1	1
Swansea C	Tr	11/85	85	11	0	0

DAVIES Jamie
Born: Swansea, Wales, 12 February, 1980 — F

League Club	Source	Date Signed	Seasons Played	Apps	Subs	Gls
Swansea C	YT	07/98	98	0	1	0

DAVIES John Gerwyn
Born: Llandysul, Ceredigion, Wales, 18 November, 1959 — G

League Club	Source	Date Signed	Seasons Played	Apps	Subs	Gls
Cardiff C	App	11/77	78-79	7	0	0
Hull C	Tr	07/80	80-82	24	0	0
Notts Co	L	03/86	85	10	0	0

DAVIES John Robert
Born: Portsmouth, England, 26 September, 1933 — RW

League Club	Source	Date Signed	Seasons Played	Apps	Subs	Gls
Portsmouth	Jnr	05/52	53-54	2	-	0
Scunthorpe U	Tr	07/55	55-57	67	-	10
Walsall	Tr	01/59	58-60	65	-	17

DAVIES John William (Jack)
Born: Northolt, W London, England, 14 November, 1916 — WH
Wales: Schools

League Club	Source	Date Signed	Seasons Played	Apps	Subs	Gls
Chester C	Ruthin T	12/34	35-36	18	-	1
Everton	Tr	07/37	46	1	-	0
Plymouth Arg	Tr	02/47	46-47	33	-	0
Bristol C	Tr	05/48	48	30	-	1

DAVIES Joseph (Joe)
Born: Birkenhead, Wirral, England, 30 January, 1926 — W
Died: Birkenhead, Wirral, England, 12 June, 1973

League Club	Source	Date Signed	Seasons Played	Apps	Subs	Gls
Chester C	Bromborough	04/48	47-51	55	-	10

DAVIES Kenneth (Ken)
Born: Doncaster, South Yorkshire, England, 20 September, 1923 — LW
Died: Exeter, England, 14 November, 2008

League Club	Source	Date Signed	Seasons Played	Apps	Subs	Gls
Wolverhampton W		01/44				
Walsall	Tr	06/46	46-47	28	-	5
Brighton & HA	Tr	05/48	48-49	36	-	5

DAVIES Kenneth Frank (Kenny)
Born: Stockton-on-Tees, Cleveland, England, 22 December, 1970 — M

League Club	Source	Date Signed	Seasons Played	Apps	Subs	Gls
Hartlepool U	YT	07/89	89-90	4	2	0

DAVIES Kevin
Born: Hereford, England, 1 April, 1963 — M

League Club	Source	Date Signed	Seasons Played	Apps	Subs	Gls
Hereford U	Westfields	07/85	85	0	1	0

DAVIES Kevin Cyril
Born: Sheffield, England, 26 March, 1977 — F
England: 1/U21-3/Youth

League Club	Source	Date Signed	Seasons Played	Apps	Subs	Gls
Chesterfield	YT	04/94	93-96	113	16	22

League Club	Source	Date Signed	Seasons Played	Apps	Subs	Gls
Southampton	Tr	05/97	97	20	5	9
Blackburn Rov	Tr	06/98	98-99	11	12	1
Southampton	Tr	08/99	99-02	59	23	10
Millwall	L	09/02	02	6	3	3
Bolton W	Tr	07/03	03-12	330	21	73
Preston NE	Tr	07/13	13-14	34	36	4

DAVIES Lawrence
Born: Abergavenny, Monmouthshire, Wales, 3 September, 1977 — F
Wales: Youth

League Club	Source	Date Signed	Seasons Played	Apps	Subs	Gls
Leeds U	YT	08/96				
Bradford C	Tr	07/97	97	1	3	0
Darlington	L	12/97	97	2	0	0
Hartlepool U	L	09/98	98	2	1	0
Brighton & HA	Tr	02/99	98	2	6	0

DAVIES Leonard Raymond (Ray)
Born: Wallasey, Wirral, England, 3 October, 1931 — RW

League Club	Source	Date Signed	Seasons Played	Apps	Subs	Gls
Tranmere Rov		10/49	51-57	120	-	28

DAVIES Malcolm
Born: Aberdare, Rhondda Cynon Taff, Wales, 26 June, 1931 — RW
Died: Merthyr Tydfil, Wales, 31 July, 2012

League Club	Source	Date Signed	Seasons Played	Apps	Subs	Gls
Plymouth Arg	Aberaman Ath	04/49	52-56	84	-	15

DAVIES Mark
Born: Swansea, Wales, 9 August, 1972 — FB

League Club	Source	Date Signed	Seasons Played	Apps	Subs	Gls
Swansea C	YT	07/91	91	1	0	0

DAVIES Mark Nicholas
Born: Willenhall, West Midlands, England, 18 February, 1988 — M
England: Youth

League Club	Source	Date Signed	Seasons Played	Apps	Subs	Gls
Wolverhampton W	Sch	02/05	05-06	12	15	1
Leicester C	L	11/08	08	5	2	1
Bolton W	Tr	01/09	08-14	97	46	14

DAVIES Martin Lemuel
Born: Swansea, Wales, 28 June, 1974 — G
Wales: Youth

League Club	Source	Date Signed	Seasons Played	Apps	Subs	Gls
Coventry C	YT	07/92				
Cambridge U	Stafford Rgrs	08/95	95	15	0	0

DAVIES Michael John (Mike)
Born: Stretford, Greater Manchester, England, 19 January, 1966 — RB/M

League Club	Source	Date Signed	Seasons Played	Apps	Subs	Gls
Blackpool	App	01/84	83-94	276	34	16

DAVIES Paul
Born: Holywell, Flintshire, Wales, 10 October, 1952 — F
Wales: Schools

League Club	Source	Date Signed	Seasons Played	Apps	Subs	Gls
Arsenal	App	11/69	71	0	1	0
Charlton Ath	Tr	08/72	72-74	51	6	9

DAVIES Paul Andrew
Born: Kidderminster, Worcestershire, England, 9 October, 1960 — F
England: Semi Pro-6

League Club	Source	Date Signed	Seasons Played	Apps	Subs	Gls
Cardiff C	Oldswinford	10/78	79-80	1	1	0

DAVIES Peter
Born: Llanelli, Carmarthenshire, Wales, 8 March, 1936 — WH
Wales: Amateur

League Club	Source	Date Signed	Seasons Played	Apps	Subs	Gls
Arsenal	Llanelli	11/57				
Swansea C	Tr	03/59	58-64	134	-	5
Brighton & HA	Tr	07/65	65	6	0	0

DAVIES Peter
Born: Merthyr Tydfil, Wales, 1 July, 1942 — IF
Wales: Amateur

League Club	Source	Date Signed	Seasons Played	Apps	Subs	Gls
Newport Co	Merthyr Tydfil	05/64	64	1	-	0

DAVIES Reginald Walter (Reg)
Born: Tipton, West Midlands, England, 10 October, 1933 — G

League Club	Source	Date Signed	Seasons Played	Apps	Subs	Gls
West Bromwich A	Palethorpes	01/51	53-54	4	-	0
Walsall	Tr	07/55	55-56	53	-	0
Millwall	Tr	05/58	58-62	199	-	0
Leyton Orient	Tr	07/63	63	11	-	0
Port Vale	Tr	07/64	64	13	-	0
Leyton Orient	Tr	03/65	64-65	16	0	0

DAVIES Richard Peter
Born: Walsall, West Midlands, England, 14 May, 1990 — M

League Club	Source	Date Signed	Seasons Played	Apps	Subs	Gls
Walsall	Sch	07/08	08	0	3	0

DAVIES Robert Griffith
Born: Blaenau Ffestiniog, Gwynedd, Wales, 19 October, 1913 — CH
Died: Nottingham, England, 10 May, 1978
Wales: War-6

League Club	Source	Date Signed	Seasons Played	Apps	Subs	Gls
Nottingham F	Blaenau Ffestiniog	11/36	36-46	55	-	0

DAVIES Roger
Born: Wolverhampton, England, 25 October, 1950 — F

England: U23-1

League Club	Source	Date Signed	Seasons Played	Apps	Subs	Gls
Derby Co	Worcester C	09/71	72-75	98	16	31
Preston NE	L	08/72	72	2	0	0
Leicester C	Club Brugge (BEL)	12/77	77-78	22	4	6
Derby Co	Tulsa Roughnecks (USA)	09/79	79	22	0	3
Darlington	Burnley (NC)	11/83	83	10	0	1

DAVIES Ronald Alfred (Roy)
Born: Cape Town, South Africa, 23 August, 1924 — RW
Died: Hitchin, Hertfordshire, England, 10 December, 1973
South Africa:

League Club	Source	Date Signed	Seasons Played	Apps	Subs	Gls
Luton T	Clyde	05/51	51-56	150	-	24

DAVIES Ronald George (Ron)
Born: Swansea, Wales, 13 November, 1935 — WH

League Club	Source	Date Signed	Seasons Played	Apps	Subs	Gls
Swansea C	Tower U	05/58	58	2	-	0
Plymouth Arg	Tr	06/59				

DAVIES Ronald Thomas (Ron)
Born: Merthyr Tydfil, Wales, 21 September, 1932 — RB
Died: Tredegar, Blaenau Gwent, Wales, 8 December, 2007

League Club	Source	Date Signed	Seasons Played	Apps	Subs	Gls
Cardiff C	Merthyr Tydfil	10/52	55-57	32	-	3
Southampton	Tr	03/58	57-63	161	-	0
Aldershot	Tr	08/64	64-66	84	1	1

DAVIES Ronald Tudor (Ron)
Born: Holywell, Flintshire, Wales, 25 May, 1942 — F
Died: Albuquerque, New Mexico, USA, 24 May, 2013
Wales: 29/U23-3

League Club	Source	Date Signed	Seasons Played	Apps	Subs	Gls
Chester C	Jnr	07/59	59-62	94	-	44
Luton T	Tr	10/62	62-63	32	-	21
Norwich C	Tr	09/63	63-65	113	0	58
Southampton	Tr	08/66	66-72	239	1	134
Portsmouth	Tr	04/73	73-74	59	0	18
Manchester U	Tr	11/74	74	0	8	0
Millwall	L	11/75	75	3	0	0

DAVIES Ronald Wyn (Wyn)
Born: Caernarfon, Gwynedd, Wales, 20 March, 1942 — F
Wales: 34/U23-4

League Club	Source	Date Signed	Seasons Played	Apps	Subs	Gls
Wrexham	Caernarvon T	04/60	60-61	55	-	21
Bolton W	Tr	03/62	61-66	155	0	66
Newcastle U	Tr	10/66	66-70	181	0	40
Manchester C	Tr	08/71	71-72	45	0	8
Manchester U	Tr	09/72	72	15	1	4
Blackpool	Tr	06/73	73-74	34	2	5
Crystal Palace	L	08/74	74	3	0	0
Stockport Co	Tr	08/75	75	28	2	7
Crewe Alex	Arcadia Shep's (RSA)	08/76	76-77	50	5	13

DAVIES Roy
Born: Ealing, W London, England, 25 October, 1953 — M

League Club	Source	Date Signed	Seasons Played	Apps	Subs	Gls
Reading	Slough T	09/77	77	37	0	2
Torquay U	Tr	08/78	78-79	65	5	6
Wimbledon	Tr	08/80	80	6	3	0

DAVIES Roy Martin
Born: Cardiff, Wales, 19 August, 1971 — RB
Wales: Youth

League Club	Source	Date Signed	Seasons Played	Apps	Subs	Gls
Newport Co	YT	-	87	0	2	0
Chelsea	Tr	07/89				

DAVIES Scott David
Born: Blackpool, Lancashire, England, 27 February, 1987 — G

League Club	Source	Date Signed	Seasons Played	Apps	Subs	Gls
Morecambe	Jnr	07/05	07-09	11	0	0
Fleetwood T	Tr	08/10	12-13	73	0	0
Morecambe	L	10/14	14	10	0	0
Accrington Stan	L	02/15	14	19	0	0

DAVIES Scott Myles Edward
Born: Aylesbury, Buckinghamshire, England, 10 March, 1988 — M
Republic of Ireland: U21-3/Youth

League Club	Source	Date Signed	Seasons Played	Apps	Subs	Gls
Reading	Sch	07/06	09	3	1	0
Aldershot T	L	07/08	08	37	4	13
Wycombe W	L	10/09	09	14	1	3
Yeovil T	L	03/10	09	4	0	0
Wycombe W	L	09/10	10	5	3	1
Bristol Rov	L	01/11	10	4	3	0
Crawley T	Tr	07/11	11	17	3	2
Aldershot T	L	10/11	11	3	5	1
Oxford U	Tr	03/13	12-13	17	17	1

DAVIES Sean Graham
Born: Middlesbrough, England, 27 February, 1985 — FB

League Club	Source	Date Signed	Seasons Played	Apps	Subs	Gls
York C	Sch	07/04	03	6	2	0

DAVIES Simon
Born: Haverfordwest, Pembrokeshire, Wales, 23 October, 1979 — RM
Wales: 58/B-1/U21-10/Youth

League Club	Source	Date Signed	Seasons Played	Apps	Subs	Gls
Peterborough U	YT	07/97	97-99	63	2	6
Tottenham H	Tr	01/00	99-04	99	22	13
Everton	Tr	08/05	05-06	35	10	1
Fulham	Tr	01/07	06-11	123	14	13

DAVIES Simon Ithel
Born: Winsford, Cheshire, England, 23 April, 1974 — M
Wales: 1

League Club	Source	Date Signed	Seasons Played	Apps	Subs	Gls
Manchester U	YT	07/92	94-95	4	7	0
Exeter C	L	12/93	93	5	1	1
Huddersfield T	L	10/96	96	3	0	0
Luton T	Tr	08/97	97-98	10	12	1
Macclesfield T	Tr	12/98	98-99	39	9	3
Rochdale	Tr	08/00	00	7	5	1

DAVIES Steven Easman (Steve)
Born: Liverpool, England, 16 July, 1960 — W

League Club	Source	Date Signed	Seasons Played	Apps	Subs	Gls
Port Vale	Congleton T	12/87	87	1	5	0

DAVIES Steven Gary (Steve)
Born: Liverpool, England, 29 December, 1987 — F

League Club	Source	Date Signed	Seasons Played	Apps	Subs	Gls
Tranmere Rov	Sch	07/05	05-07	30	30	5
Derby Co	Tr	07/08	08-11	49	34	20
Bristol C	Tr	08/12	12	21	16	13
Blackpool	Tr	07/13	13-14	24	21	8
Sheffield U	L	03/15	14	10	3	2

DAVIES Wilford Gordon (Gordon)
Born: Swansea, Wales, 31 July, 1915 — RB
Died: Swansea, Wales, February, 1992

League Club	Source	Date Signed	Seasons Played	Apps	Subs	Gls
Swansea C		03/34	34-46	54	-	0

DAVIES William
Born: United Kingdom — RW

League Club	Source	Date Signed	Seasons Played	Apps	Subs	Gls
Crewe Alex	Droylsden	02/47	46	11	-	3

DAVIES William (Will)
Born: Wirksworth, Derbyshire, England, 27 September, 1975 — CD

League Club	Source	Date Signed	Seasons Played	Apps	Subs	Gls
Derby Co	YT	07/94	94	1	1	0

DAVIES William (Bill)
Born: Middlesbrough, England, 16 May, 1930 — CH

League Club	Source	Date Signed	Seasons Played	Apps	Subs	Gls
Hull C	St Mary's College OB	04/49				
Leeds U	Tr	08/50				
Reading	Scarborough	12/52	54-60	202	-	0

DAVIES William
Born: Troedyrhiw, Merthyr Tydfil, Wales, 22 June, 1910 — LW
Died: Watford, Hertfordshire, England, 30 October, 1995
Wales: War-1

League Club	Source	Date Signed	Seasons Played	Apps	Subs	Gls
Watford	New Tredegar	07/30	30-49	283	-	69

DAVIES William David (Dai)
Born: Ammanford, Carmarthenshire, Wales, 1 April, 1948 — RW
Wales: 52/U23-3

League Club	Source	Date Signed	Seasons Played	Apps	Subs	Gls
Swansea C	Ammanford	08/69	69-70	9	0	0
Everton	Tr	12/70	70-76	82	0	0
Swansea C	L	02/74	73	6	0	0
Wrexham	Tr	09/77	77-80	144	0	0
Swansea C	Tr	07/81	81-82	71	0	0
Tranmere Rov	Tr	06/83	83	42	0	0

DAVIES William McIntosh (Billy)
Born: Glasgow, Scotland, 31 May, 1964 — M

League Club	Source	Date Signed	Seasons Played	Apps	Subs	Gls
Leicester C	St Mirren	08/90	90	5	1	0

DAVIN Joseph James (Joe)
Born: Dumbarton, Dunbartonshire, Scotland, 13 February, 1942 — RB
Died: Dumbarton, Dunbartonshire, Scotland, 30 September, 2013
Scotland: Schools

League Club	Source	Date Signed	Seasons Played	Apps	Subs	Gls
Ipswich T	Hibernian	07/63	63-65	77	0	0

DAVIS Arron Spencer
Born: Wanstead, NE London, England, 11 February, 1972 — LB

League Club	Source	Date Signed	Seasons Played	Apps	Subs	Gls
Torquay U	YT	08/91	91-92	20	4	0
Colchester U	Dorchester T	08/94	94	4	0	0

DAVIS Claude
Born: Kingston, Jamaica, 6 March, 1979 — CD
Jamaica: 64

League Club	Source	Date Signed	Seasons Played	Apps	Subs	Gls
Preston NE	Portmore U (JAM)	08/03	03-05	74	20	4
Sheffield U	Tr	06/06	06	18	3	0
Derby Co	Tr	07/07	07-08	25	2	0
Crystal Palace	L	02/09	08	7	0	0
Crystal Palace	Tr	09/09	09-10	36	9	0
Crawley T	Tr	09/11	11-12	43	2	3
Rotherham U	Tr	01/13	12-13	29	2	1

DAVIS Craig
Born: Rotherham, South Yorkshire, England, 12 October, 1977 — G

League Club	Source	Date Signed	Seasons Played	Apps	Subs	Gls
Rotherham U	YT	06/96				
Doncaster Rov	Denaby U	11/97	97	15	0	0

DAVIS Cyril
Born: Birmingham, England, 21 July, 1925 — CF
Died: Birmingham, England, 3 March, 1992

League Club	Source	Date Signed	Seasons Played	Apps	Subs	Gls
Walsall (Am)	Hednesford T	05/48	48	1	-	0

DAVIS Daniel Jonathan Steven (Danny)
Born: Brighton, England, 3 October, 1980 — M

League Club	Source	Date Signed	Seasons Played	Apps	Subs	Gls
Brighton & HA	YT	06/99	98	0	1	0

DAVIS Darren John
Born: Sutton-in-Ashfield, Nottinghamshire, England, 5 February, 1967 — D
England: Youth

League Club	Source	Date Signed	Seasons Played	Apps	Subs	Gls
Notts Co	App	02/85	83-87	90	2	1
Lincoln C	Tr	08/88	88-90	97	5	4
Maidstone U	Tr	03/91	90-91	31	0	2
Scarborough	Frickley Ath	08/93	93-94	46	2	3
Lincoln C	Grantham T	07/95	95	3	0	0

DAVIS David Lowell
Born: Smethwick, West Midlands, England, 20 February, 1991 — M

League Club	Source	Date Signed	Seasons Played	Apps	Subs	Gls
Wolverhampton W	Sch	07/09	11-13	30	23	0
Darlington	L	10/09	09	5	0	0
Walsall	L	09/10	10	7	0	0
Shrewsbury T	L	01/11	10	19	0	2
Chesterfield	L	01/12	11	9	0	0
Birmingham C	Tr	08/14	14	36	6	3

DAVIS Derek Edgar Counsell
Born: Colwyn Bay, Conwy, Wales, 19 June, 1922 — G
Died: Plymouth, England, 7 March, 1985

League Club	Source	Date Signed	Seasons Played	Apps	Subs	Gls
Norwich C	Plymouth Arg (Am)	10/45	46-47	26	-	0
Torquay U	Tr	08/48	48-50	89	-	0

DAVIS Edward
Born: Brackley, Northamptonshire, England, 8 March, 1922 — W
Died: Wisbech, Cambridgeshire, England, 16 July, 2011

League Club	Source	Date Signed	Seasons Played	Apps	Subs	Gls
Newport Co	RAF Hereford	10/46	46	3	-	1
Northampton T	Tr	07/47				

DAVIS Eric William Charles
Born: Plymouth, England, 26 February, 1932 — CF
Died: Plymouth, England, 21 July, 2007

League Club	Source	Date Signed	Seasons Played	Apps	Subs	Gls
Plymouth Arg	Tavistock T	08/52	52-56	64	-	29
Scunthorpe U	Tr	07/57	57-58	40	-	20
Chester C	Tr	02/59	58-59	31	-	11
Oldham Ath	Tr	09/60	60	2	-	1

DAVIS Gareth
Born: Bangor, Gwynedd, Wales, 11 July, 1949 — CD
Wales: 3/U23-4

League Club	Source	Date Signed	Seasons Played	Apps	Subs	Gls
Wrexham	Colwyn Bay	10/67	67-82	482	8	9

DAVIS Gordon
Born: Newcastle-upon-Tyne, England, 14 December, 1930 — CH
Died: North Tyneside, Tyne and Wear, England, 1977

League Club	Source	Date Signed	Seasons Played	Apps	Subs	Gls
Gateshead	Everton (Am)	11/49	51-56	87	-	0

DAVIS Harry Spencer
Born: Burnley, Lancashire, England, 24 September, 1991 — LB

League Club	Source	Date Signed	Seasons Played	Apps	Subs	Gls
Crewe Alex	Sch	06/10	09-14	144	4	10

DAVIS Ian
Born: Hull, England, 1 February, 1965 — M

League Club	Source	Date Signed	Seasons Played	Apps	Subs	Gls
Hull C	App	02/83	81-82	25	3	1

DAVIS James Roger William (Jimmy)
Born: Redditch, Worcestershire, England, 6 February, 1982 — W
Died: Oxfordshire, England, 9 August, 2003
England: Youth/Schools

League Club	Source	Date Signed	Seasons Played	Apps	Subs	Gls
Manchester U	YT	09/99				
Swindon T	L	08/02	02	10	3	2

DAVIS John Leslie
Born: Hackney, E London, England, 31 March, 1957 — FB

League Club	Source	Date Signed	Seasons Played	Apps	Subs	Gls
Gillingham	Arsenal (App)	07/75	75	2	1	0
Sheffield Wed	Tr	10/76	76	1	0	0

DAVIS Joseph (Joe)
Born: Bristol, England, 24 August, 1938 — CH

League Club	Source	Date Signed	Seasons Played	Apps	Subs	Gls
Bristol Rov	Soundwell	03/56	60-66	210	1	4
Swansea C	Tr	03/67	66-67	36	0	0

DAVIS Joseph (Joe)
Born: Glasgow, Scotland, 22 May, 1941 — LB

League Club	Source	Date Signed	Seasons Played	Apps	Subs	Gls
Carlisle U	Hibernian	12/69	69-71	75	4	0

DAVIS Joseph Frederick (Fred)
Born: Bloxwich, West Midlands, England, 23 May, 1929 — WH

Died: Surrey, England, 10 September, 1996

League Club	Source	Date Signed	Seasons Played	Apps	Subs	Gls
Reading	Bloxwich Strollers	12/52	53-54	63	-	1
Wrexham	Tr	07/55	55-60	230	-	12

DAVIS Joseph Steven (Joe)
Born: Burnley, Lancashire, England, 10 November, 1993 CD

League Club	Source	Date Signed	Seasons Played	Apps	Subs	Gls
Port Vale	Sch	07/12	10-13	21	6	0
Leicester C	Tr	06/14				

DAVIS Kelvin Geoffrey
Born: Bedford, England, 29 September, 1976 G
England: U21-3/Youth

League Club	Source	Date Signed	Seasons Played	Apps	Subs	Gls
Luton T	YT	07/94	93-98	92	0	0
Torquay U	L	09/94	94	2	0	0
Hartlepool U	L	08/97	97	2	0	0
Wimbledon	Tr	07/99	00-02	131	0	0
Ipswich T	Tr	08/03	03-04	84	0	0
Sunderland	Tr	07/05	05	33	0	0
Southampton	Tr	07/06	06-14	267	2	0

DAVIS Kenneth Edward (Ken)
Born: Romsey, Hampshire, England, 6 February, 1933 W

League Club	Source	Date Signed	Seasons Played	Apps	Subs	Gls
Bristol C	Jnr	05/52	52	1	-	0

DAVIS Leonard (Len)
Born: United Kingdom G

League Club	Source	Date Signed	Seasons Played	Apps	Subs	Gls
Southend U	Army	11/45	46	3	-	0

DAVIS Leonard Philip (Len)
Born: Cork, Republic of Ireland, 31 July, 1931 CF

League Club	Source	Date Signed	Seasons Played	Apps	Subs	Gls
Arsenal	Evergreen U (ROI)	11/49				
Walsall	Tr	02/54	53-54	25	-	5

DAVIS Liam Lloyd
Born: Wandsworth, SW London, England, 23 November, 1986 LB/M

League Club	Source	Date Signed	Seasons Played	Apps	Subs	Gls
Coventry C	Sch	07/06	05-07	3	8	0
Peterborough U	L	09/06	06	7	0	0
Northampton T	Tr	07/08	08-10	66	13	8
Oxford U	Tr	08/11	11-12	60	7	3
Yeovil T	Tr	07/13	13-14	26	9	1

DAVIS Mark Ronald
Born: Wallsend, Tyne and Wear, England, 12 October, 1969 M

League Club	Source	Date Signed	Seasons Played	Apps	Subs	Gls
Darlington	App	-	86	0	2	0

DAVIS Michael Vernon (Mike)
Born: Bristol, England, 19 October, 1974 F

League Club	Source	Date Signed	Seasons Played	Apps	Subs	Gls
Bristol Rov	Yate T	04/93	92-95	3	14	1
Hereford U	L	08/94	94	1	0	0

DAVIS Neil Leonard
Born: Bloxwich, West Midlands, England, 15 August, 1973 F

League Club	Source	Date Signed	Seasons Played	Apps	Subs	Gls
Aston Villa	Redditch U	05/91	95	0	2	0
Wycombe W	L	10/96	96	13	0	0
Walsall	Tr	08/98	98	0	1	0

DAVIS Paul Edward
Born: Newham, E London, England, 31 January, 1968 FB

League Club	Source	Date Signed	Seasons Played	Apps	Subs	Gls
Queens Park Rgrs	App	12/85				
Aldershot	Tr	08/87	87	1	0	0

DAVIS Paul Vincent
Born: Dulwich, S London, England, 9 December, 1961 M
England: B-1/FLge/U21-11

League Club	Source	Date Signed	Seasons Played	Apps	Subs	Gls
Arsenal	App	07/79	79-94	331	20	30
Brentford	Tr	09/95	95	5	0	0

DAVIS Richard Daniel (Dickie)
Born: Birmingham, England, 22 January, 1922 CF
Died: Bishops Stortford, Hertfordshire, England, 11 August, 1999
England: Schools

League Club	Source	Date Signed	Seasons Played	Apps	Subs	Gls
Sunderland	Morris Motors	02/39	46-53	144	-	73
Darlington	Tr	05/54	54-56	93	-	32

DAVIS Richard Frederick
Born: Plymouth, England, 14 November, 1943 LB

League Club	Source	Date Signed	Seasons Played	Apps	Subs	Gls
Plymouth Arg	App	11/61	62-63	23	-	0
Southampton	Tr	07/64	64	1	-	0
Bristol C	Tr	07/65	67-68	8	0	0
Barrow	Tr	03/69	68-69	50	0	0

DAVIS Sean
Born: Clapham, SW London, England, 20 September, 1979 M
England: U21-11

League Club	Source	Date Signed	Seasons Played	Apps	Subs	Gls
Fulham	YT	07/98	96-03	128	27	14
Tottenham H	Tr	07/04	04	11	4	0
Portsmouth	Tr	01/06	05-08	94	8	2
Bolton W	Tr	07/09	09	3	0	0
Bristol C	L	02/12	11	2	1	0

DAVIS Solomon Sebastian (Sol)
Born: Cheltenham, Gloucestershire, England, 4 September, 1979 LB

League Club	Source	Date Signed	Seasons Played	Apps	Subs	Gls
Swindon T	YT	05/98	97-01	100	17	0
Luton T	Tr	08/02	02-08	187	12	3
MK Dons	Tr	08/09	09	5	5	0

DAVIS Stephen Mark (Steve)
Born: Hexham, Northumberland, England, 30 October, 1968 CD

League Club	Source	Date Signed	Seasons Played	Apps	Subs	Gls
Southampton	YT	07/87	89-90	5	1	0
Burnley	L	11/89	89	7	2	0
Notts Co	L	03/91	90	0	2	0
Burnley	Tr	08/91	91-94	162	0	22
Luton T	Tr	07/95	95-98	137	1	21
Burnley	Tr	12/98	98-02	152	4	20
Blackpool	Tr	07/03	03	22	7	1

DAVIS Steven Peter (Steve)
Born: Birmingham, England, 26 July, 1965 CD
England: Youth

League Club	Source	Date Signed	Seasons Played	Apps	Subs	Gls
Crewe Alex	Stoke C (App)	08/83	83-87	140	5	1
Burnley	Tr	10/87	87-90	147	0	11
Barnsley	Tr	07/91	91-96	103	4	10
York C	L	09/97	97	2	0	1
Oxford U	Tr	02/98	97-99	38	4	3

DAVIS Steven William
Born: Ballymena, Antrim, Northern Ireland, 1 January, 1985 M
Northern Ireland: 74/U23-1/U21-3/Youth/Schools

League Club	Source	Date Signed	Seasons Played	Apps	Subs	Gls
Aston Villa	Sch	01/02	04-06	70	21	5
Fulham	Tr	07/07	07	22	0	0
Southampton	Glasgow Rangers	07/12	12-14	82	19	4

DAVISON Aidan John
Born: Sedgefield, County Durham, England, 11 May, 1968 G
Northern Ireland: 3/B-1

League Club	Source	Date Signed	Seasons Played	Apps	Subs	Gls
Notts Co	Billingham Synthonia	03/88	88	1	0	0
Bury	Tr	10/89				
Millwall	Tr	08/91	91-92	34	0	0
Bolton W	Tr	07/93	93-95	35	2	0
Hull C	L	11/96	96	9	0	0
Bradford C	Tr	03/97	96	10	0	0
Grimsby T	Tr	07/97	97-98	77	0	0
Sheffield U	Tr	08/99	99	1	1	0
Bradford C	Tr	01/00	99-02	49	2	0
Grimsby T	Tr	08/03	03	32	0	0
Colchester U	Tr	07/04	04-07	99	0	0

DAVISON Arthur
Born: Hackney, E London, England, 21 December, 1915 FB

League Club	Source	Date Signed	Seasons Played	Apps	Subs	Gls
Stockport Co		09/45				
Torquay U	Tr	11/46	46	1	-	0

DAVISON Daniel (Danny)
Born: Newcastle-upon-Tyne, England, 11 November, 1947 LB

League Club	Source	Date Signed	Seasons Played	Apps	Subs	Gls
Barrow	Newcastle U (Am)	09/65	66-69	6	1	0

DAVISON Edward (Ted)
Born: Seaham, County Durham, England, 15 April, 1933 CH
Died: County Durham, England, 1976

League Club	Source	Date Signed	Seasons Played	Apps	Subs	Gls
Hartlepool U	Seaham Jnrs	08/53	53	1	-	0

DAVISON James Hawkins (Jimmy)
Born: Sunderland, England, 1 November, 1942 RW
Died: Sunderland, England, 1 February, 1987

League Club	Source	Date Signed	Seasons Played	Apps	Subs	Gls
Sunderland	Jnr	11/59	59-62	62	-	10
Bolton W	Tr	11/63	63	21	-	1

DAVISON Joseph Henry (Joe)
Born: Newcastle-upon-Tyne, England, 29 July, 1919 RB
Died: Darlington, County Durham, England, 1983

League Club	Source	Date Signed	Seasons Played	Apps	Subs	Gls
Darlington	Throckley Welfare	01/47	46-53	240	-	8

DAVISON Robert (Bobby)
Born: South Shields, Tyne and Wear, England, 17 July, 1959 F

League Club	Source	Date Signed	Seasons Played	Apps	Subs	Gls
Huddersfield T	Seaham CW	07/80	80	1	1	0
Halifax T	Tr	08/81	81-82	63	0	29
Derby Co	Tr	12/82	82-87	203	3	83
Leeds U	Tr	11/87	87-91	79	12	31
Derby Co	L	09/91	91	10	0	8
Sheffield U	L	03/92	91	6	5	4
Leicester C	Tr	08/92	92	21	4	6
Sheffield U	Tr	11/93	93	9	3	1
Rotherham U	Tr	10/94	94-95	20	2	4
Hull C	L	11/95	95	11	0	4

DAVOCK Michael (Mike)
Born: St Helens, Merseyside, England, 27 April, 1935 LW

League Club	Source	Date Signed	Seasons Played	Apps	Subs	Gls
Stockport Co	St Helens T	01/57	56-63	235	-	41

D'AVRAY Jean Michel (Mich)
Born: Johannesburg, South Africa, 19 February, 1962 — F
England: U21-2

League Club	Source	Date Signed	Seasons Played	Apps	Subs	Gls
Ipswich T	App	05/79	79-89	170	41	37
Leicester C	L	02/87	86	3	0	0

DAVY Stephen (Steve)
Born: Norwich, England, 9 April, 1955 — RB

League Club	Source	Date Signed	Seasons Played	Apps	Subs	Gls
Scunthorpe U	West Ham U (NC)	08/77	77-81	126	8	1

DAWBER Andrew John
Born: Wigan, Greater Manchester, England, 20 November, 1994 — G

League Club	Source	Date Signed	Seasons Played	Apps	Subs	Gls
Accrington Stan	Sch	01/13	12-13	3	2	0

DAWE Simon
Born: Plymouth, England, 16 March, 1977 — M

League Club	Source	Date Signed	Seasons Played	Apps	Subs	Gls
Plymouth Arg	YT	07/95	94	3	1	0

DAWES Derek Malcolm
Born: Dawley, Telford & Wrekin, England, 23 June, 1944 — IF

League Club	Source	Date Signed	Seasons Played	Apps	Subs	Gls
Shrewsbury T	App	06/62	61-62	9	-	0

DAWES Frederick William (Fred)
Born: Frimley Green, Surrey, England, 2 May, 1911 — LB
Died: Croydon, S London, England, 12 August, 1989

League Club	Source	Date Signed	Seasons Played	Apps	Subs	Gls
Northampton T	Aldershot	03/30	29-35	162	-	1
Crystal Palace	Tr	02/36	35-49	222	-	2

DAWES Ian Michael
Born: Aldershot, Hampshire, England, 5 January, 1965 — CD
England: Schools

League Club	Source	Date Signed	Seasons Played	Apps	Subs	Gls
Newcastle U	Jnr	06/83				
Northampton T	Tr	06/85	85	3	2	0

DAWES Ian Robert
Born: Croydon, S London, England, 22 February, 1963 — LB
England: Schools

League Club	Source	Date Signed	Seasons Played	Apps	Subs	Gls
Queens Park Rgrs	App	12/80	81-87	229	0	3
Millwall	Tr	08/88	88-94	219	6	5

DAWES Malcolm
Born: Trimdon, County Durham, England, 3 March, 1944 — CD

League Club	Source	Date Signed	Seasons Played	Apps	Subs	Gls
Darlington	Fishburn Jnrs	03/62				
Aldershot	Horden CW	08/65	65-69	160	4	2
Hartlepool U	Tr	07/70	70-75	193	2	12
Workington	Tr	11/75	75-76	49	2	1

DAWKINS Derek Anthony
Born: Edmonton, N London, England, 29 November, 1959 — M/D

League Club	Source	Date Signed	Seasons Played	Apps	Subs	Gls
Leicester C	App	11/77	77	3	0	0
Mansfield T	Tr	12/78	78-80	73	0	0
Bournemouth	Tr	08/81	81-82	4	4	0
Torquay U	Weymouth	02/84	83-88	153	22	7

DAWKINS Simon Jonathan
Born: Edgware, NW London, England, 1 December, 1987 — M
Jamaica: 11

League Club	Source	Date Signed	Seasons Played	Apps	Subs	Gls
Tottenham H	Sch	07/05				
Leyton Orient	L	07/08	08	2	9	0
Aston Villa	L	01/13	12	0	4	0
Derby Co	L	10/13	13-14	35	25	7

DAWKINS Trevor Andrew
Born: Thorpe Bay, Southend, Essex, England, 7 October, 1945 — M
England: Youth/Schools

League Club	Source	Date Signed	Seasons Played	Apps	Subs	Gls
West Ham U	App	10/62	64-66	5	1	0
Crystal Palace	Tr	10/67	67-70	24	1	3
Brentford	L	09/71	71	3	1	0

DAWS Anthony (Tony)
Born: Sheffield, England, 10 September, 1966 — F
England: Youth/Schools

League Club	Source	Date Signed	Seasons Played	Apps	Subs	Gls
Notts Co	App	09/84	84-85	6	2	1
Sheffield U	Tr	08/86	86	7	4	3
Scunthorpe U	Tr	07/87	87-92	166	17	63
Grimsby T	Tr	03/93	92-93	14	2	1
Lincoln C	Tr	02/94	93-95	42	9	13
Scarborough	Tr	08/96	96	4	2	0

DAWS Nicholas John (Nick)
Born: Manchester, England, 15 March, 1970 — M

League Club	Source	Date Signed	Seasons Played	Apps	Subs	Gls
Bury	Altrincham	08/92	92-00	356	13	16
Rotherham U	Tr	07/01	01-03	54	18	2
Grimsby T	L	09/03	03	7	0	0
Grimsby T	L	01/04	03	10	0	0

DAWSON Aaron Peter
Born: Exmouth, Devon, England, 24 March, 1992 — M/RB

League Club	Source	Date Signed	Seasons Played	Apps	Subs	Gls
Exeter C	Sch	07/10	11-14	10	7	0

DAWSON Adam Ryan
Born: Bury, Greater Manchester, England, 5 October, 1992 — W

League Club	Source	Date Signed	Seasons Played	Apps	Subs	Gls
Wigan Ath	Bury (Sch)	07/11				
Leicester C	Nelson	10/13				
Notts Co	L	08/14	14	1	1	0

DAWSON Alexander (Alec)
Born: Glasgow, Scotland, 23 October, 1933 — RW
Died: Westminster, Central London, England, October, 1986

League Club	Source	Date Signed	Seasons Played	Apps	Subs	Gls
Queens Park Rgrs	Gourock Jnrs	02/57	56-58	59	-	5

DAWSON Alexander Downie (Alex)
Born: Aberdeen, Scotland, 21 February, 1940 — CF
Scotland: Schools

League Club	Source	Date Signed	Seasons Played	Apps	Subs	Gls
Manchester U	Jnr	04/57	56-61	80	-	45
Preston NE	Tr	10/61	61-66	199	0	114
Bury	Tr	03/67	66-68	49	1	21
Brighton & HA	Tr	12/68	68-70	53	4	26
Brentford	L	09/70	70	10	0	6

DAWSON Alistair John (Ally)
Born: Glasgow, Scotland, 25 February, 1958 — D
Scotland: 5/U21-8/Youth

League Club	Source	Date Signed	Seasons Played	Apps	Subs	Gls
Blackburn Rov	Glasgow Rangers	08/87	87-89	32	8	0

DAWSON Andrew Stephen (Andy)
Born: York, England, 8 December, 1979 — RB/M

League Club	Source	Date Signed	Seasons Played	Apps	Subs	Gls
York C	YT	07/98	98-99	18	10	1

DAWSON Andrew Stuart (Andy)
Born: Leyburn, North Yorkshire, England, 20 October, 1978 — LB

League Club	Source	Date Signed	Seasons Played	Apps	Subs	Gls
Nottingham F	YT	10/95				
Scunthorpe U	Tr	12/98	98-02	192	3	8
Hull C	Tr	07/03	03-12	284	9	8
Scunthorpe U	Tr	08/13	13-14	21	0	0

DAWSON Carl Michael
Born: Harwich, Essex, England, 24 June, 1934 — G
Died: Nottingham, England, 24 May, 1991

League Club	Source	Date Signed	Seasons Played	Apps	Subs	Gls
Lincoln C (Am)	Jnr	05/50	50	1	-	0

DAWSON Christopher Gary (Chris)
Born: Ossett, West Yorkshire, England, 2 September, 1994 — M
Wales: U21-2

League Club	Source	Date Signed	Seasons Played	Apps	Subs	Gls
Leeds U	Sch	10/12	12-14	1	3	0

DAWSON Craig
Born: Rochdale, Greater Manchester, England, 6 May, 1990 — CD
England: U21-15

League Club	Source	Date Signed	Seasons Played	Apps	Subs	Gls
Rochdale	Radcliffe Bor	02/09	09-10	44	2	10
West Bromwich A	Tr	08/10	11-14	46	4	2
Rochdale	L	09/10	10	40	1	9
Bolton W	L	01/13	12	16	0	4

DAWSON Edward
Born: Chester-le-Street, County Durham, England, 16 January, 1913 — G
Died: Darlington, County Durham, England, December, 1970

League Club	Source	Date Signed	Seasons Played	Apps	Subs	Gls
Manchester C	Blyth Spartans	12/34				
Bristol C	Tr	05/36	36-38	66	-	0
Gateshead	Tr	08/46	46-48	83	-	0

DAWSON George
Born: Glasgow, Scotland, 13 September, 1930 — WH
Died: Glasgow, Scotland, 18 November, 2000

League Club	Source	Date Signed	Seasons Played	Apps	Subs	Gls
Queens Park Rgrs	Motherwell	05/55	55	1	-	0

DAWSON James Emslie Irvine Bannerman (Jimmy)
Born: Stoneyburn, West Lothian, Scotland, 21 December, 1927 — LW
Died: Leicester, England, 7 February, 2005

League Club	Source	Date Signed	Seasons Played	Apps	Subs	Gls
Leicester C	Polkemmet	05/46	46-48	5	-	0
Portsmouth	Tr	06/49	49	1	-	0

DAWSON Jason
Born: Burslem, Potteries, England, 9 February, 1971 — F

League Club	Source	Date Signed	Seasons Played	Apps	Subs	Gls
Rochdale	Port Vale (YT)	07/89	89-90	37	18	7

DAWSON Joseph Reginald (Reg)
Born: Sheffield, England, 4 October, 1914 — LW
Died: Sheffield, England, 25 July, 1973

League Club	Source	Date Signed	Seasons Played	Apps	Subs	Gls
Rotherham U	Dinnington Ath	01/39	38-46	32	-	2

DAWSON Kevin Edward
Born: Leyburn, North Yorkshire, England, 18 June, 1981 — CD

League Club	Source	Date Signed	Seasons Played	Apps	Subs	Gls
Nottingham F	YT	06/98	99-01	8	3	0
Barnet	L	03/01	00	5	0	0
Chesterfield	Tr	08/02	02-04	49	2	1

DAWSON Kevin Patrick
Born: Dublin, Republic of Ireland, 30 June, 1990 — M
Republic of Ireland: Youth

League Club	Source	Date Signed	Seasons Played	Apps	Subs	Gls
Yeovil T	Shelbourne (ROI)	01/13	12-14	49	23	4

DAWSON Lucas Jay
Born: Stoke-on-Trent, England, 12 November, 1993 M

League Club	Source	Date Signed	Seasons Played	Apps	Subs	Gls
Stoke C	Sch	07/12				
Carlisle U	L	03/14	13	1	0	0

DAWSON Michael Richard
Born: Leyburn, North Yorkshire, England, 18 November, 1983 CD
England: 4/B-2/U21-13/Youth

League Club	Source	Date Signed	Seasons Played	Apps	Subs	Gls
Nottingham F	YT	11/00	01-04	82	1	7
Tottenham H	Tr	01/05	04-13	221	15	7
Hull C	Tr	08/14	14	28	0	1

DAWSON Owen John
Born: Christchurch, Dorset, England, 7 March, 1943 RB
England: Youth

League Club	Source	Date Signed	Seasons Played	Apps	Subs	Gls
Portsmouth	Jnr	06/60				
Swindon T	Tr	06/62	62-70	196	6	4

DAWSON Peter
Born: Crewe, Cheshire, England, 19 January, 1933 RB

League Club	Source	Date Signed	Seasons Played	Apps	Subs	Gls
Crewe Alex		01/54	55	2	-	0

DAWSON Richard
Born: Chesterfield, Derbyshire, England, 19 January, 1960 F

League Club	Source	Date Signed	Seasons Played	Apps	Subs	Gls
Rotherham U	App	01/78	77-79	21	3	3
Doncaster Rov	Tr	02/81	80-81	39	4	14
Chesterfield	Tr	08/82	82	6	6	0

DAWSON Richard
Born: York, England, 6 July, 1962 D

League Club	Source	Date Signed	Seasons Played	Apps	Subs	Gls
York C	New Earswick	07/80	81-82	45	0	0

DAWSON Richard
Born: Sheffield, England, 12 April, 1967 G

League Club	Source	Date Signed	Seasons Played	Apps	Subs	Gls
Grimsby T	Stoke C (App)	08/84	84	1	0	0

DAWSON Robert (Bobby)
Born: South Shields, Tyne and Wear, England, 31 January, 1935 RB
Died: Gateshead, Tyne and Wear, England, 1980

League Club	Source	Date Signed	Seasons Played	Apps	Subs	Gls
Leeds U	South Shields	11/53	53	1	-	0
Gateshead	Tr	11/55	55-59	118	-	1

DAWSON Robert Anthony
Born: Bentley, South Yorkshire, England, 21 June, 1944 G

League Club	Source	Date Signed	Seasons Played	Apps	Subs	Gls
Doncaster Rov		12/64	65-66	28	0	0

DAWSON Stephen John
Born: Dublin, Republic of Ireland, 4 December, 1985 RM
Republic of Ireland: U21-2

League Club	Source	Date Signed	Seasons Played	Apps	Subs	Gls
Leicester C	Sch	07/03				
Mansfield T	Tr	07/05	05-07	106	11	4
Bury	Tr	07/08	08-09	87	1	6
Leyton Orient	Tr	07/10	10-11	59	1	3
Barnsley	Tr	01/12	11-13	67	14	5
Rochdale	Tr	08/14	14	27	3	0

DAWSON Thomas (Tommy)
Born: Middlesbrough, England, 6 February, 1915 IF
Died: Middlesbrough, England, 20 December, 1972

League Club	Source	Date Signed	Seasons Played	Apps	Subs	Gls
Darlington	Whitby U	12/36	36-37	23	-	3
Charlton Ath	Spennymoor U	02/39	38-46	23	-	2
Brentford	Tr	08/47	47	36	-	10
Swindon T	Tr	05/48	48-49	65	-	15

DAWSON William
Born: Glasgow, Scotland, 5 February, 1931 CF
Died: Corby, Northamptonshire, England, January, 1991

League Club	Source	Date Signed	Seasons Played	Apps	Subs	Gls
Northampton T	Ashfield	03/55	54-55	14	-	7

DAWTRY Kevin Austin
Born: Hythe, Hampshire, England, 15 June, 1958 M

League Club	Source	Date Signed	Seasons Played	Apps	Subs	Gls
Southampton	App	06/76	78	0	1	0
Crystal Palace	Tr	05/80				
Bournemouth	Tr	03/81	80-83	58	5	11
Reading	L	09/82	82	4	0	0

DAY Albert
Born: Camberwell, S London, England, 7 March, 1918 F
Died: Brighton, England, March, 1983

League Club	Source	Date Signed	Seasons Played	Apps	Subs	Gls
Brighton & HA	Hastings & St Leonard	08/38				
Ipswich T	Tr	05/46	46-48	63	-	25
Watford	Tr	08/49	49	4	-	1

DAY Burcombe James (Jimmy)
Born: Watford, Hertfordshire, England, 9 May, 1931 IF

League Club	Source	Date Signed	Seasons Played	Apps	Subs	Gls
Watford	Berkhamsted T	12/51	51	3	-	0

DAY Christopher Nicholas (Chris)
Born: Leytonstone, NE London, England, 28 July, 1975 G
England: U21-6/Youth

League Club	Source	Date Signed	Seasons Played	Apps	Subs	Gls
Tottenham H	YT	04/93				
Crystal Palace	Tr	08/96	96	24	0	0
Watford	Tr	07/97	99	11	0	0
Lincoln C	L	12/00	00	14	0	0
Queens Park Rgrs	Tr	07/01	01-04	87	0	0
Preston NE	L	02/05	04	6	0	0
Oldham Ath	Tr	08/05	05	30	0	0
Millwall	Tr	07/06	06-07	9	1	0
Stevenage	Tr	08/08	10-14	188	1	0

DAY Clive Anthony
Born: Thurrock, Essex, England, 27 January, 1961 FB

League Club	Source	Date Signed	Seasons Played	Apps	Subs	Gls
Fulham	App	08/78	80-81	2	8	0
Mansfield T	L	08/82	82	10	2	1
Aldershot	Tr	08/83	83-84	53	7	0

DAY Eric Charles
Born: Dartford, Kent, England, 6 November, 1921 RW
Died: Broughton Gifford, Wiltshire, England, 10 November, 2012

League Club	Source	Date Signed	Seasons Played	Apps	Subs	Gls
Southampton	RAF Ford	04/45	46-56	398	-	145

DAY Graham George
Born: Bristol, England, 22 November, 1953 CD

League Club	Source	Date Signed	Seasons Played	Apps	Subs	Gls
Bristol Rov	Bristol St George	05/73	74-78	129	1	1

DAY James Russell (Jamie)
Born: Bexley, SE London, England, 13 September, 1979 M
England: Schools

League Club	Source	Date Signed	Seasons Played	Apps	Subs	Gls
Arsenal	YT	07/97				
Bournemouth	Tr	03/99	98-00	15	5	1

DAY Jamie Robert
Born: High Wycombe, Buckinghamshire, England, 7 May, 1986 LB
England: Semi Pro-1

League Club	Source	Date Signed	Seasons Played	Apps	Subs	Gls
Peterborough U	Sch	08/03	04-09	85	17	5
Dagenham & Red	L	11/09	09	8	0	0
Crawley T	Rushden & D	07/11				

DAY John Norman (Jack)
Born: Northfleet, Kent, England, 21 January, 1924 G

League Club	Source	Date Signed	Seasons Played	Apps	Subs	Gls
Fulham	Shrewsbury T	11/48				
Brighton & HA	Tr	03/49				
Gillingham	Tr	07/49	50	1	-	0

DAY Joseph David (Joe)
Born: Brighton, England, 13 August, 1990 G

League Club	Source	Date Signed	Seasons Played	Apps	Subs	Gls
Peterborough U	Rushden & D	05/11	13	4	0	0
Newport Co	L	08/14	14	16	0	0
Newport Co	Tr	01/15	14	20	0	0

DAY Keith David
Born: Grays, Essex, England, 29 November, 1962 CD

League Club	Source	Date Signed	Seasons Played	Apps	Subs	Gls
Colchester U	Aveley	08/84	84-86	113	0	12
Leyton Orient	Tr	07/87	87-92	184	8	9

DAY Mervyn Richard
Born: Chelmsford, England, 26 June, 1955 G
England: U23-5/Youth

League Club	Source	Date Signed	Seasons Played	Apps	Subs	Gls
West Ham U	App	03/73	73-78	194	0	0
Leyton Orient	Tr	07/79	79-82	170	0	0
Aston Villa	Tr	08/83	83-84	30	0	0
Leeds U	Tr	01/85	84-92	227	0	0
Luton T	L	03/92	91	4	0	0
Sheffield U	L	04/92	91	1	0	0
Carlisle U	Tr	07/93	93	16	0	0

DAY Rhys
Born: Bridgend, Wales, 31 August, 1982 CD
Wales: U21-11/Youth

League Club	Source	Date Signed	Seasons Played	Apps	Subs	Gls
Manchester C	YT	09/99				
Blackpool	L	12/01	01	4	5	0
Mansfield T	Tr	11/02	02-05	95	8	12
Aldershot T	Tr	07/06	08	16	1	0

DAY Roger Arthur
Born: Romford, E London, England, 3 December, 1939 IF
England: Amateur-43

League Club	Source	Date Signed	Seasons Played	Apps	Subs	Gls
Watford (Am)	Enfield	12/61	61	1	-	0

DAY William (Billy)
Born: South Bank, Cleveland, England, 27 December, 1936 RW

League Club	Source	Date Signed	Seasons Played	Apps	Subs	Gls
Middlesbrough	South Bank Jnrs	05/55	55-61	120	-	18
Newcastle U	Tr	03/62	61-62	13	-	1
Peterborough U	Tr	04/63	62-63	18	-	2

DAYKIN Reginald Brian (Brian)
Born: Long Eaton, Derbyshire, England, 4 August, 1937 WH

League Club	Source	Date Signed	Seasons Played	Apps	Subs	Gls
Derby Co	Long Eaton T	11/55	59-61	4	-	1
Notts Co	Tr	07/62	62	3	-	0

DAYTON James Francis
Born: Cheshunt, Hertfordshire, England, 12 December, 1988 — W

League Club	Source	Date Signed	Seasons Played	Apps	Subs	Gls
Crystal Palace	Sch	07/07				
Yeovil T	L	08/08	08	0	2	0
Oldham Ath	Kilmarnock	05/13	13-14	29	22	4

DE-VULGT Leigh Stuart
Born: Swansea, Wales, 17 March, 1981 — CD
Wales: U21-2/Youth

League Club	Source	Date Signed	Seasons Played	Apps	Subs	Gls
Swansea C	YT	07/99	99-02	16	7	0

DEACON David Benjamin
Born: Broome, Norfolk, England, 10 March, 1929 — FB
Died: Cambridge, England, 23 July, 1990

League Club	Source	Date Signed	Seasons Played	Apps	Subs	Gls
Ipswich T	Bungay T	11/50	50-59	66	-	0

DEACON Roarie Milton Ryan
Born: Wandsworth, SW London, England, 12 October, 1991 — LB
England: Youth

League Club	Source	Date Signed	Seasons Played	Apps	Subs	Gls
Arsenal	Sch	07/10				
Sunderland	Tr	07/11				
Stevenage	Tr	03/13	12-14	23	25	1

DEACY Eamonn Stephen
Born: Galway, Republic of Ireland, 1 October, 1958 — FB
Died: Galway, Republic of Ireland, 13 February, 2012
Republic of Ireland: 4/LoI-1

League Club	Source	Date Signed	Seasons Played	Apps	Subs	Gls
Aston Villa	Galway Rov (ROI)	03/79	79-83	27	6	1
Derby Co	L	10/83	83	5	0	0

DEACY Michael (Mike)
Born: Cardiff, Wales, 29 November, 1943 — CD

League Club	Source	Date Signed	Seasons Played	Apps	Subs	Gls
Newport Co		08/66	66-69	46	1	2

DEACY Nicholas Simon (Nick)
Born: Cardiff, Wales, 19 July, 1953 — CD/CF
Wales: 12/U23-1/U21-1

League Club	Source	Date Signed	Seasons Played	Apps	Subs	Gls
Hereford U	Merthyr Tydfil	09/74	74	13	4	2
Workington	L	12/74	74	5	0	1
Hull C	Vitesse Arnhem (NED)	02/80	79-81	80	7	7
Bury	Happy Valley (HKG)	10/83	83	30	1	0

DEAKIN Alan Roy
Born: Birmingham, England, 27 November, 1941 — LH
England: U23-6

League Club	Source	Date Signed	Seasons Played	Apps	Subs	Gls
Aston Villa	Jnr	12/58	59-69	230	1	9
Walsall	Tr	10/69	69-71	46	4	0

DEAKIN Frederick Arthur (Fred)
Born: Birmingham, England, 5 February, 1920 — FB
Died: Birmingham, England, 5 June, 2000

League Club	Source	Date Signed	Seasons Played	Apps	Subs	Gls
Birmingham C		01/38				
Crystal Palace	Tr	09/46	46-47	6	-	0

DEAKIN John
Born: Stocksbridge, South Yorkshire, England, 29 September, 1966 — M

League Club	Source	Date Signed	Seasons Played	Apps	Subs	Gls
Doncaster Rov	Barnsley (App)	08/85	85-86	21	2	0
Birmingham C	Shepshed Charterhouse	09/89	89	3	4	0
Carlisle U	Tr	08/91	91	3	0	0

DEAKIN Michael Raymond Frederick (Mike)
Born: Birmingham, England, 25 October, 1933 — CF

League Club	Source	Date Signed	Seasons Played	Apps	Subs	Gls
Crystal Palace	Bromsgrove Rov	11/54	54-59	143	-	56
Northampton T	Tr	10/59	59-60	44	-	31
Aldershot	Tr	01/61	60-61	17	-	5

DEAKIN Peter
Born: Normanton, West Yorkshire, England, 25 March, 1938 — IF

League Club	Source	Date Signed	Seasons Played	Apps	Subs	Gls
Bolton W	Jnr	05/55	57-63	63	-	13
Peterborough U	Tr	06/64	64-66	74	1	34
Bradford Park Ave	Tr	09/66	66-67	36	0	9
Peterborough U	Tr	09/67	67	16	0	1
Brentford	Tr	07/68	68	7	1	2

DEAKIN Raymond John (Ray)
Born: Liverpool, England, 19 June, 1959 — LB
Died: York, England, 24 December, 2008
England: Schools

League Club	Source	Date Signed	Seasons Played	Apps	Subs	Gls
Everton	App	06/77				
Port Vale	Tr	08/81	81	21	2	6
Bolton W	Tr	08/82	82-84	104	1	2
Burnley	Tr	07/85	85-90	212	1	6

DEAKIN William Edward (Billy)
Born: Maltby, South Yorkshire, England, 19 January, 1925 — W

League Club	Source	Date Signed	Seasons Played	Apps	Subs	Gls
Barnsley	Sunnyside WMC	05/49	49-51	25	-	3
Chester C	Tr	07/52	52	27	-	5

DEAMAN Jack Edward
Born: Camden, N London, England, 18 May, 1993 — CD

League Club	Source	Date Signed	Seasons Played	Apps	Subs	Gls
Birmingham C	Wrexham (Sch)	08/11				
Cheltenham T	Eastbourne Bor	07/14	14	13	6	0

DEAN Alan John
Born: Aldershot, Hampshire, England, 20 January, 1950 — FB

League Club	Source	Date Signed	Seasons Played	Apps	Subs	Gls
Aldershot	App	01/68	66-67	3	0	0

DEAN Andrew Geoffrey (Andy)
Born: Salford, England, 27 November, 1966 — FB

League Club	Source	Date Signed	Seasons Played	Apps	Subs	Gls
Rochdale	Burnley (Jnr)	10/83	83	1	0	0

DEAN Brian Robert
Born: Stockport, Greater Manchester, England, 10 September, 1947 — RB

League Club	Source	Date Signed	Seasons Played	Apps	Subs	Gls
Blackpool	Jnr	09/64	67	0	1	0
Barrow	Tr	07/69	69-70	44	3	0

DEAN George Charles
Born: Walsall, West Midlands, England, 22 February, 1930 — WH

League Club	Source	Date Signed	Seasons Played	Apps	Subs	Gls
Walsall	Hilary Street OB	05/50	50-53	72	-	13

DEAN Harlee James
Born: Basingstoke, Hampshire, England, 26 July, 1991 — CD

League Club	Source	Date Signed	Seasons Played	Apps	Subs	Gls
Dagenham & Red	Jnr	07/08	09	0	1	0
Southampton	Tr	08/10				
Brentford	Tr	11/11	11-14	130	7	5

DEAN James
Born: Blackburn, Greater Manchester, England, 15 May, 1985 — F

League Club	Source	Date Signed	Seasons Played	Apps	Subs	Gls
Bury	Northwich Victoria	08/07	07	3	1	0

DEAN Joby
Born: Edwinstowe, Nottinghamshire, England, 25 November, 1934 — D

League Club	Source	Date Signed	Seasons Played	Apps	Subs	Gls
Queens Park Rgrs	Thoresby CW	11/52	55-56	16	-	0
Bradford Park Ave	Sutton T	12/57	57-58	53	-	1

DEAN Joseph (Joe)
Born: Manchester, England, 4 April, 1939 — G
England: Youth/Schools

League Club	Source	Date Signed	Seasons Played	Apps	Subs	Gls
Bolton W	Jnr	04/56	55-59	17	-	0
Carlisle U	Tr	07/62	62-69	137	0	0
Barrow	Tr	07/70	70-71	41	0	0

DEAN Luke Adam
Born: Cleckheaton, West Yorkshire, England, 14 May, 1991 — M

League Club	Source	Date Signed	Seasons Played	Apps	Subs	Gls
Bradford C	Sch	07/09	09-11	0	3	0

DEAN Mark Christopher
Born: Northwich, Cheshire, England, 18 November, 1964 — D

League Club	Source	Date Signed	Seasons Played	Apps	Subs	Gls
Chester C	App	10/82	81-82	23	2	0

DEAN Michael James (Mike)
Born: Weymouth, Dorset, England, 9 March, 1978 — M

League Club	Source	Date Signed	Seasons Played	Apps	Subs	Gls
Bournemouth	YT	07/96	95-98	18	16	0

DEAN Norman
Born: Corby, Northamptonshire, England, 13 September, 1944 — F

League Club	Source	Date Signed	Seasons Played	Apps	Subs	Gls
Southampton	Corby T	04/63	65	18	0	11
Cardiff C	Tr	03/67	66-68	20	1	3
Barnsley	Tr	09/68	68-72	58	2	19

DEAN Raymond George (Ray)
Born: Steventon, Oxfordshire, England, 15 December, 1945 — CD

League Club	Source	Date Signed	Seasons Played	Apps	Subs	Gls
Reading	Cheltenham T	05/66	66-68	50	4	0
Aldershot	Tr	07/69	69-74	256	0	7

DEANE Brian Christopher
Born: Leeds, England, 7 February, 1968 — F
England: 3/B-3

League Club	Source	Date Signed	Seasons Played	Apps	Subs	Gls
Doncaster Rov	Jnr	12/85	85-87	59	7	12
Sheffield U	Tr	07/88	88-92	197	0	82
Leeds U	Tr	07/93	93-96	131	7	32
Sheffield U	Tr	07/97	97	24	0	11
Middlesbrough	Benfica (POR)	10/98	98-01	72	15	18
Leicester C	Tr	11/01	01-03	44	8	19
West Ham U	Tr	10/03	03	9	17	6
Leeds U	Tr	07/04	04	23	8	6
Sunderland	Tr	03/05	04	0	4	0
Sheffield U	Perth Glory (AUS)	01/06	05	0	2	0

DEANE Patrick Martin
Born: Perth, Scotland, 16 April, 1990 — F

League Club	Source	Date Signed	Seasons Played	Apps	Subs	Gls
Darlington	Hibernian (Jnr)	01/10	09	0	10	0

DEANS John Kelly (Dixie)
Born: Johnstone, Renfrewshire, Scotland, 30 July, 1946 — F
Scotland: 2

League Club	Source	Date Signed	Seasons Played	Apps	Subs	Gls
Luton T	Glasgow Celtic	06/76	76	13	1	6
Carlisle U	L	02/77	76	4	0	2

DEANS Raymond Alexander (Ray)
Born: Lanark, Scotland, 24 January, 1966 — F

Scotland: Youth

League Club	Source	Date Signed	Seasons Played	Apps	Subs	Gls
Doncaster Rov	Clyde	02/85	84-85	18	1	5

DEANS Thomas Sneddon (Tommy)
Born: Shieldhall, Falkirk, Scotland, 7 January, 1922 LB
Died: Nottingham, England, 30 December, 2000
Scotland: SLge-1

League Club	Source	Date Signed	Seasons Played	Apps	Subs	Gls
Notts Co	Clyde	10/49	49-55	239	-	0

DEAR Brian Charles
Born: Plaistow, E London, England, 18 September, 1943 F
England: Schools

League Club	Source	Date Signed	Seasons Played	Apps	Subs	Gls
West Ham U	App	11/60	62-68	63	2	33
Brighton & HA	L	03/67	66	7	0	5
Fulham	Tr	02/69	68	13	0	7
Millwall	Tr	07/69	69	5	1	0
West Ham U	Tr	08/70	70	4	0	0

DEAR Gerald Albert (Gerry)
Born: Kensington, Central London, England, 5 January, 1937 FB

League Club	Source	Date Signed	Seasons Played	Apps	Subs	Gls
Swindon T	RAPC Devizes	07/56	56	4	-	0

DEARDEN Kevin Charles
Born: Luton, England, 8 March, 1970 G

League Club	Source	Date Signed	Seasons Played	Apps	Subs	Gls
Tottenham H	YT	08/88	92	0	1	0
Cambridge U	L	03/89	88	15	0	0
Hartlepool U	L	08/89	89	10	0	0
Swindon T	L	03/90	89	1	0	0
Peterborough U	L	08/90	90	7	0	0
Hull C	L	01/91	90	3	0	0
Rochdale	L	08/91	91	2	0	0
Birmingham C	L	03/92	91	12	0	0
Brentford	Tr	09/93	93-98	205	0	0
Barnet	L	02/99	98	1	0	0
Wrexham	Tr	06/99	99-00	81	0	0
Torquay U	Tr	08/01	01-04	98	2	0

DEARDEN William (Billy)
Born: Oldham, Greater Manchester, England, 11 February, 1944 F/W

League Club	Source	Date Signed	Seasons Played	Apps	Subs	Gls
Oldham Ath	Jnr	09/63	64-66	32	3	2
Crewe Alex	Tr	12/66	66-67	44	3	5
Chester C	Tr	06/68	68-69	85	0	22
Sheffield U	Tr	04/70	70-75	170	5	61
Chester C	Tr	02/76	75-76	35	1	7
Chesterfield	Tr	08/77	77-78	18	9	2

DEARSON Donald John (Don)
Born: Ynysybwl, Rhondda Cynon Taff, Wales, 13 May, 1914 IF
Died: Birmingham, England, 24 December, 1990
Wales: 3/Amateur/War-15

League Club	Source	Date Signed	Seasons Played	Apps	Subs	Gls
Birmingham C	Barry T	04/34	34-46	131	-	17
Coventry C	Tr	02/47	46-49	84	-	10
Walsall	Tr	03/50	49-50	51	-	12

DEARY John Steele
Born: Ormskirk, Lancashire, England, 18 October, 1962 M

League Club	Source	Date Signed	Seasons Played	Apps	Subs	Gls
Blackpool	App	03/80	80-88	285	18	43
Burnley	Tr	07/89	89-94	209	6	23
Rochdale	Tr	01/95	94-96	90	1	10

DEASY Timothy (Tim)
Born: Salford, England, 1 October, 1985 G

League Club	Source	Date Signed	Seasons Played	Apps	Subs	Gls
Macclesfield T	Sch	07/05	05	2	1	0
Stockport Co	Tr	08/06				

DEATH Stephen Victor (Steve)
Born: Elmswell, Suffolk, England, 19 September, 1949 G
Died: Reading, England, 26 October, 2003
England: Schools

League Club	Source	Date Signed	Seasons Played	Apps	Subs	Gls
West Ham U	App	06/67	68	1	0	0
Reading	Tr	11/69	69-81	471	0	0

DEBEC Fabien
Born: Lyon, France, 18 January, 1976 G

League Club	Source	Date Signed	Seasons Played	Apps	Subs	Gls
Coventry C	Stade Rennais (FRA)	08/02	02	11	0	0

DEBENHAM Robert Karl (Rob)
Born: Doncaster, South Yorkshire, England, 28 November, 1979 FB

League Club	Source	Date Signed	Seasons Played	Apps	Subs	Gls
Doncaster Rov	YT	-	97	4	2	0
Bury	Tr	07/98				

DEBEVE Mickael
Born: Abbeville, France, 1 December, 1970 M

League Club	Source	Date Signed	Seasons Played	Apps	Subs	Gls
Middlesbrough	RC Lens (FRA)	02/02	01	1	3	0

DE BILDE Gilles Roger Gerard
Born: Asse, Belgium, 9 June, 1971 F
Belgium: 25

League Club	Source	Date Signed	Seasons Played	Apps	Subs	Gls
Sheffield Wed	PSV Eindhoven (NED)	07/99	99-00	50	9	13
Aston Villa	L	10/00	00	4	0	0

DE BLASIIS Jean-Yves
Born: Bordeaux, France, 25 September, 1973 M
France: Youth

League Club	Source	Date Signed	Seasons Played	Apps	Subs	Gls
Norwich C	Red Star 93 (FRA)	07/99	99-00	28	7	0

DE BOLLA Grant Marcus (Mark)
Born: Camberwell, S London, England, 1 January, 1983 F

League Club	Source	Date Signed	Seasons Played	Apps	Subs	Gls
Aston Villa	YT	04/00				
Charlton Ath	Tr	01/01				
Chesterfield	L	09/03	03	2	1	0
Chesterfield	Tr	03/04	03-05	18	19	5
Notts Co	Tr	11/05	05	8	6	1

DE BONT Andrew Cornelius (Andy)
Born: Wolverhampton, England, 7 February, 1974 G

League Club	Source	Date Signed	Seasons Played	Apps	Subs	Gls
Wolverhampton W	YT	07/92				
Hartlepool U	L	10/95	95	1	0	0
Hereford U	L	03/96	95	8	0	0
Hereford U	Tr	08/96	96	27	0	0

DE BRUYNE Kevin
Born: Ghent, Belgium, 1 January, 2012 W
Belgium: 30/U21-2/Youth

League Club	Source	Date Signed	Seasons Played	Apps	Subs	Gls
Chelsea	KRC Genk (BEL)	01/12	13	2	1	0

DEBUCHY Mathieu
Born: Lille, France, 28 July, 1985 RB
France: 26

League Club	Source	Date Signed	Seasons Played	Apps	Subs	Gls
Newcastle U	Lille OSC (FRA)	01/13	12-13	42	1	1
Arsenal	Tr	07/14	14	10	0	1

[DECO] DE SOUZA Anderson Luis
Born: Sao Paulo, Brazil, 27 August, 1977 M
Portugal: 75

League Club	Source	Date Signed	Seasons Played	Apps	Subs	Gls
Chelsea	Barcelona (SPN)	08/08	08-09	31	12	5

DEEGAN Gary
Born: Dublin, Republic of Ireland, 28 September, 1987 M
Republic of Ireland: U21-2

League Club	Source	Date Signed	Seasons Played	Apps	Subs	Gls
Coventry C	Bohemians (ROI)	01/10	09-11	28	14	5
Northampton T	Hibernian	07/13	13	22	5	1
Southend U	Tr	08/14	14	19	3	0

DEEGAN Mark
Born: Liverpool, England, 12 November, 1971 G
Wales: Semi Pro

League Club	Source	Date Signed	Seasons Played	Apps	Subs	Gls
Oxford U	Holywell T	08/94	94	2	0	0

DEEHAN John Matthew
Born: Solihull, West Midlands, England, 6 August, 1957 F
England: U21-7/Youth

League Club	Source	Date Signed	Seasons Played	Apps	Subs	Gls
Aston Villa	App	04/75	75-79	107	3	40
West Bromwich A	Tr	09/79	79-81	44	3	5
Norwich C	Tr	12/81	81-85	158	4	62
Ipswich T	Tr	06/86	86-87	45	4	11
Manchester C	Tr	07/88				
Barnsley	Tr	01/90	90	3	8	2

DEELEY Norman Victor
Born: Wednesbury, West Midlands, England, 30 November, 1933 RW
Died: Wednesbury, West Midlands, England, 7 September, 2007
England: 2/Schools

League Club	Source	Date Signed	Seasons Played	Apps	Subs	Gls
Wolverhampton W	Jnr	12/50	51-61	206	-	66
Leyton Orient	Tr	02/62	61-63	73	-	9

DEEN Ahmed Nuru
Born: Freetown, Sierra Leone, 30 June, 1985 LB/M
Sierra Leone: 10

League Club	Source	Date Signed	Seasons Played	Apps	Subs	Gls
Peterborough U	Leicester C (Sch)	08/04	04	4	1	0
Macclesfield T	Bishops Stortford	07/08	08	19	9	0
Barnet	Tr	08/09	09	12	4	1

DEENEY Saul
Born: Derry, Northern Ireland, 12 March, 1983 G
Republic of Ireland: U21-2/Youth

League Club	Source	Date Signed	Seasons Played	Apps	Subs	Gls
Notts Co	YT	09/00	02-04	41	1	0
Notts Co	Burton A	07/06	06	7	0	0
Derby Co	Burton A	08/09	09	2	1	0

DEENEY Troy Matthew
Born: Solihull, West Midlands, England, 29 June, 1988 F

League Club	Source	Date Signed	Seasons Played	Apps	Subs	Gls
Walsall	Chelmsley T	12/06	06-09	95	28	27
Watford	Tr	08/10	10-14	159	46	78

DEERE Stephen Herbert (Steve)
Born: Burnham Market, Norfolk, England, 31 March, 1948 CD

League Club	Source	Date Signed	Seasons Played	Apps	Subs	Gls
Scunthorpe U	Norwich C (Am)	11/67	67-72	232	4	21
Hull C	Tr	06/73	73-74	65	1	2
Barnsley	L	10/75	75	4	0	0
Stockport Co	L	12/75	75	6	0	0
Scunthorpe U	Scarborough	02/78	77-79	105	0	2

DEERING Sam
Born: Stepney, E London, England, 26 February, 1991 — W
England: Semi Pro-1

League Club	Source	Date Signed	Seasons Played	Apps	Subs	Gls
Oxford U	Sch	10/08	10	0	6	0
Barnet	Tr	02/11	10-11	53	7	5
Cheltenham T	Tr	07/12	12-13	46	21	0

DEFOE Jermain Colin
Born: Beckton, E London, England, 7 October, 1982 — F
England: 55/U21-23/Youth/Schools

League Club	Source	Date Signed	Seasons Played	Apps	Subs	Gls
West Ham U	Charlton Ath (YT)	10/99	00-03	62	31	29
Bournemouth	L	10/00	00	27	2	18
Tottenham H	Tr	02/04	03-07	88	51	43
Portsmouth	Tr	01/08	07-08	29	2	15
Tottenham H	Tr	01/09	08-13	94	43	48
Sunderland	Toronto FC (CAN)	01/15	14	17	0	4

DE FREITAS Fabian
Born: Paramaribo, Suriname, 28 July, 1972 — F

League Club	Source	Date Signed	Seasons Played	Apps	Subs	Gls
Bolton W	Volendam (NED)	08/94	94-95	24	16	7
West Bromwich A	CA Osasuna (SPN)	08/98	98-99	34	27	8

DE GARIS James Frederick (Jim)
Born: Worcester, England, 9 October, 1952 — M

League Club	Source	Date Signed	Seasons Played	Apps	Subs	Gls
Arsenal	App	06/70				
Bournemouth	Tr	09/71	71-73	8	4	0
Torquay U	Tr	03/74	73	7	2	0

DE GEA David
Born: Madrid, Spain, 7 November, 1990 — G
Spain: 5/U23-5/U21-27/Youth

League Club	Source	Date Signed	Seasons Played	Apps	Subs	Gls
Manchester U	Atletico Madrid (SPN)	06/11	11-14	131	0	0

DEGEN Philipp
Born: Holstein, Switzerland, 15 February, 1983 — RB
Switzerland: 32/U21-14

League Club	Source	Date Signed	Seasons Played	Apps	Subs	Gls
Liverpool	Bor Dortmund (GER)	07/08	09	3	4	0

DE GIROLAMO Diego Raymond
Born: Chesterfield, Derbyshire, England, 5 October, 1995 — F
Italy: Youth

League Club	Source	Date Signed	Seasons Played	Apps	Subs	Gls
Sheffield U	Jnr	10/12	12	0	2	0
York C	L	10/14	14	7	1	4
York C	L	02/15	14	2	2	0
Northampton T	L	03/15	14	5	1	0

DEGN Peter
Born: Ebeltoft, Denmark, 6 April, 1977 — M
Denmark: U21-25/Youth

League Club	Source	Date Signed	Seasons Played	Apps	Subs	Gls
Everton	Aarhus GF (DEN)	02/99	98	0	4	0

DE GOEY Eduard Franciscus (Ed)
Born: Gouda, Netherlands, 20 December, 1966 — G
Netherlands: 31/U21-16/Youth

League Club	Source	Date Signed	Seasons Played	Apps	Subs	Gls
Chelsea	Feyenoord (NED)	07/97	97-02	123	0	0
Stoke C	Tr	08/03	03-05	55	1	0

DE GOEY Leendert (Len)
Born: Amsterdam, Netherlands, 29 February, 1952 — M

League Club	Source	Date Signed	Seasons Played	Apps	Subs	Gls
Sheffield U	Sparta Rotterdam (NED)	08/79	79	33	0	5

DE GRUCHY Raymond Philip (Ray)
Born: Guernsey, Channel Islands, 18 May, 1932 — LB

League Club	Source	Date Signed	Seasons Played	Apps	Subs	Gls
Nottingham F		08/53				
Grimsby T	Tr	05/54	54-57	74	-	2
Chesterfield	Tr	06/58	58	1	-	0

DEGRYSE Marc
Born: Roeselare, Belgium, 4 September, 1965 — F
Belgium: 63/U21-4/Youth

League Club	Source	Date Signed	Seasons Played	Apps	Subs	Gls
Sheffield Wed	Anderlecht (BEL)	08/95	95	30	4	8

DE GUZMAN Jonathan Alexander
Born: Toronto, Canada, 13 September, 1987 — M
Netherlands: 14/U23-6/U21-4

League Club	Source	Date Signed	Seasons Played	Apps	Subs	Gls
Swansea C (L)	Villarreal (SPN)	08/12	12-13	59	12	9

DEJAGAH Sayed Ashkan (Ashkan)
Born: Tehran, Iran, 5 July, 1986 — RW
Germany: U21-20/Youth//Iran: 25

League Club	Source	Date Signed	Seasons Played	Apps	Subs	Gls
Fulham	VfL Wolfsburg (GER)	08/12	12-13	26	17	5

DE JONG Luuk
Born: Aigle, Switzerland, 27 August, 1990 — F
Netherlands: 7/U21-18/Youth

League Club	Source	Date Signed	Seasons Played	Apps	Subs	Gls
Newcastle U (L)	Borussia M'bach (GER)	01/14	13	8	4	0

DE JONG Nigel
Born: Amsterdam, Netherlands, 30 November, 1984 — DM
Netherlands: 80/U21-10

League Club	Source	Date Signed	Seasons Played	Apps	Subs	Gls
Manchester C	Hamburger SV (GER)	01/09	08-12	88	16	1

DE JONG Siem
Born: Aigle, Switzerland, 28 January, 1989 — F
Netherlands: 6/B-3/U21-12/Youth

League Club	Source	Date Signed	Seasons Played	Apps	Subs	Gls
Newcastle U	Ajax (NED)	07/14	14	1	3	1

DE LA CRUZ Bernardo Ulises (Ulises)
Born: El Chota, Ecuador, 8 February, 1974 — RB
Ecuador: 78

League Club	Source	Date Signed	Seasons Played	Apps	Subs	Gls
Aston Villa	Hibernian	08/02	02-05	66	23	1
Reading	Tr	08/06	06-07	12	3	1
Birmingham C	Tr	03/09	08	0	1	0

DE LAET Ritchie Ria Alfons
Born: Antwerp, Belgium, 28 November, 1988 — RB
Belgium: 2/U21-5

League Club	Source	Date Signed	Seasons Played	Apps	Subs	Gls
Stoke C	Royal Antwerp (BEL)	08/07				
Manchester U	Tr	01/09	08-09	3	0	0
Sheffield U	L	09/10	10	4	2	0
Preston NE	L	11/10	10	5	0	0
Portsmouth	L	01/11	10	22	0	0
Norwich C	L	07/11	11	6	0	1
Leicester C	Tr	05/12	12-14	94	9	3

DELANEY Damien Finbarr
Born: Cork, Republic of Ireland, 20 July, 1981 — CD
Republic of Ireland: 9/U21-1/Youth

League Club	Source	Date Signed	Seasons Played	Apps	Subs	Gls
Leicester C	Cork C (ROI)	11/00	00-01	5	3	0
Stockport Co	L	11/01	01	10	2	1
Huddersfield T	L	03/02	01	1	1	0
Mansfield T	L	09/02	02	7	0	0
Hull C	Tr	10/02	02-07	220	4	5
Queens Park Rgrs	Tr	01/08	07-08	52	2	2
Ipswich T	Tr	07/09	09-12	94	4	2
Crystal Palace	Tr	08/12	12-14	105	1	4

DELANEY James (Jimmy)
Born: Stoneyburn, West Lothian, Scotland, 3 September, 1914 — RW
Died: Cleland, Lanarkshire, Scotland, 26 September, 1989
Scotland: 13/SLge-6/War-5

League Club	Source	Date Signed	Seasons Played	Apps	Subs	Gls
Manchester U	Glasgow Celtic	02/46	46-50	164	-	25

DELANEY James Christopher (Jim)
Born: London, England, 22 July, 1945 — F

League Club	Source	Date Signed	Seasons Played	Apps	Subs	Gls
Newport Co	Port Talbot	07/69	69	1	0	0

DELANEY John Joseph
Born: Slough, Berkshire, England, 3 February, 1942 — CD
England: Amateur-17

League Club	Source	Date Signed	Seasons Played	Apps	Subs	Gls
Bournemouth	Wycombe W	08/73	73-74	25	0	0

DELANEY Lewis Peter
Born: Bothwell, Lanarkshire, Scotland, 28 February, 1921 — FB
Died: Twyford, Berkshire, England, 16 December, 1968

League Club	Source	Date Signed	Seasons Played	Apps	Subs	Gls
Arsenal	Nunhead	05/43				
Crystal Palace	Tr	11/49	49	3	-	0

DELANEY Mark Anthony
Born: Fishguard, Pembrokeshire, Wales, 13 May, 1976 — RB
Wales: 36

League Club	Source	Date Signed	Seasons Played	Apps	Subs	Gls
Cardiff C	Carmarthen T	07/98	98	28	0	0
Aston Villa	Tr	03/99	98-05	144	14	2

DELANY Dean
Born: Dublin, Republic of Ireland, 15 September, 1980 — G
Republic of Ireland: U21-6

League Club	Source	Date Signed	Seasons Played	Apps	Subs	Gls
Everton	YT	09/97				
Port Vale	Tr	06/00	00-03	34	2	0

DELAP Rory John
Born: Sutton Coldfield, West Midlands, England, 6 July, 1976 — M
Republic of Ireland: 11/B-1/U21-4

League Club	Source	Date Signed	Seasons Played	Apps	Subs	Gls
Carlisle U	YT	07/94	92-97	40	25	7
Derby Co	Tr	02/98	97-00	97	6	11
Southampton	Tr	07/01	01-05	118	14	5
Sunderland	Tr	01/06	05-06	11	1	1
Stoke C	Tr	10/06	06-12	165	15	8
Barnsley	L	01/13	12	6	0	0
Burton A	Tr	07/13	13	6	0	1

DELAPENHA Lloyd Lindbergh (Lindy)
Born: Kingston, Jamaica, 20 May, 1927 — W

League Club	Source	Date Signed	Seasons Played	Apps	Subs	Gls
Portsmouth	Arsenal (Am)	04/48	48-49	7	-	0
Middlesbrough	Tr	04/50	49-57	260	-	90
Mansfield T	Tr	06/58	58-60	115	-	27

DELF Barrie
Born: Leigh-on-Sea, Essex, England, 5 June, 1961 — G

League Club	Source	Date Signed	Seasons Played	Apps	Subs	Gls
Southend U	Trinity, Southend	03/83	82	1	0	0

DELFOUNESO Nathan Abayomi
Born: Birmingham, England, 2 February, 1991 — F
England: U21-17/Youth

League Club	Source	Date Signed	Seasons Played	Apps	Subs	Gls
Aston Villa	Sch	02/08	08-12	4	27	2
Burnley	L	03/11	10	7	4	1
Leicester C	L	01/12	11	0	4	0
Blackpool	L	08/12	12	22	18	6
Blackpool	L	08/13	13	3	8	0
Coventry C	L	01/14	13	8	6	3
Blackpool	Tr	07/14	14	21	17	3

DELGADO Chala Agustin (Agustin)
Born: Ibarra, Ecuador, 23 December, 1974 — F
Ecuador: 71

League Club	Source	Date Signed	Seasons Played	Apps	Subs	Gls
Southampton	Necaxa (MEX)	11/01	01-03	2	9	0

DELGADO Robert Allan (Bob)
Born: Cardiff, Wales, 29 January, 1949 — CD

League Club	Source	Date Signed	Seasons Played	Apps	Subs	Gls
Luton T	Barry T	02/70				
Carlisle U	Tr	07/71	71-73	25	10	3
Workington	L	10/73	73	7	0	0
Rotherham U	Tr	12/73	73-75	69	1	5
Chester C	Tr	10/75	75-78	125	3	8
Port Vale	Tr	12/78	78-79	41	0	0

DEL HORNO Asier
Born: Barrakaldo, Spain, 19 January, 1981 — LB
Spain: 10/U21-16/Youth

League Club	Source	Date Signed	Seasons Played	Apps	Subs	Gls
Chelsea	Atletico Bilbao (SPN)	07/05	05	25	0	1

DELL Steven Bradley
Born: Acton, W London, England, 6 February, 1980 — RB

League Club	Source	Date Signed	Seasons Played	Apps	Subs	Gls
Wycombe W	Beaconsfield SYCOB	08/03	03	3	1	0

DELLAS Traianos
Born: Thessalonika, Greece, 31 January, 1976 — CD
Greece: 53

League Club	Source	Date Signed	Seasons Played	Apps	Subs	Gls
Sheffield U	Aris Salonika (GRE)	08/97	97-98	14	12	3

DELLOW Ronald William (Ron)
Born: Crosby, Merseyside, England, 13 July, 1914 — RW
Died: Almelo, Netherlands, 7 November, 2013

League Club	Source	Date Signed	Seasons Played	Apps	Subs	Gls
Blackburn Rov	Bootle Celtic	08/33				
Mansfield T	Tr	06/34	34	24	-	10
Manchester C	Tr	01/35	34	10	-	4
Tranmere Rov	Tr	03/36	35-38	105	-	29
Carlisle U	Tr	08/39	46	16	-	5

DELORGE Laurent Jan
Born: Leuven, Belgium, 21 July, 1979 — M
Belgium: U21-2/Youth

League Club	Source	Date Signed	Seasons Played	Apps	Subs	Gls
Coventry C	KAA Gent (BEL)	11/98	01-02	23	7	4

DELORT Andy
Born: Sete, Herault, France, 9 October, 1991 — F

League Club	Source	Date Signed	Seasons Played	Apps	Subs	Gls
Wigan Ath	FC Tours (FRA)	09/14	14	4	7	0

DELOUMEAUX Eric Jean
Born: Montbeliard, France, 12 May, 1973 — D

League Club	Source	Date Signed	Seasons Played	Apps	Subs	Gls
Coventry C	Aberdeen	01/04	03-04	20	1	1

DELPH Fabian
Born: Bradford, England, 21 November, 1989 — M
England: 6/U21-4/Youth

League Club	Source	Date Signed	Seasons Played	Apps	Subs	Gls
Leeds U	Sch	01/08	06-08	40	4	6
Aston Villa	Tr	08/09	09-14	97	15	3
Leeds U	L	01/12	11	5	0	0

DEL RIO Walter Jose
Born: Buenos Aires, Argentina, 16 June, 1976 — CD

League Club	Source	Date Signed	Seasons Played	Apps	Subs	Gls
Crystal Palace (L)	Boca Juniors (ARG)	09/98	98	1	1	0

DE LUCAS Enrique
Born: Llobregat, Spain, 17 August, 1978 — M
Spain: U21-4

League Club	Source	Date Signed	Seasons Played	Apps	Subs	Gls
Chelsea	RCD Espanyol (SPN)	07/02	02	17	8	0

DELVE John Frederick
Born: Ealing, W London, England, 27 September, 1953 — M
England: Schools

League Club	Source	Date Signed	Seasons Played	Apps	Subs	Gls
Queens Park Rgrs	App	07/71	72-73	9	6	0
Plymouth Arg	Tr	07/74	74-77	127	5	6
Exeter C	Tr	03/78	77-82	215	0	20
Hereford U	Tr	06/83	83-86	116	2	11
Exeter C	Gloucester C	10/87	87	12	1	1

DE MAGALHAES Jeremy
Born: Paris, France, 21 November, 1983 — CD

League Club	Source	Date Signed	Seasons Played	Apps	Subs	Gls
Barnet	AS Cannes (FRA)	08/08	08	4	0	0

DEMAINE David Jack (Dave)
Born: Cleveleys, Lancashire, England, 7 May, 1942 — W

League Club	Source	Date Signed	Seasons Played	Apps	Subs	Gls
Blackpool	Jnr	07/60				
Tranmere Rov	Tr	08/61	61	2	-	0
Southport	Tr	07/62	62	5	-	0

DE MANGE Kenneth John Philip Petit (Ken)
Born: Dublin, Republic of Ireland, 3 September, 1964 — M
Republic of Ireland: 2/U21-5/Youth

League Club	Source	Date Signed	Seasons Played	Apps	Subs	Gls
Liverpool	Home Farm (ROI)	08/83				
Scunthorpe U	L	12/86	86	3	0	2
Leeds U	Tr	09/87	87	14	1	1
Hull C	Tr	03/88	87-90	48	20	1
Cardiff C	L	11/90	90	5	0	0
Cardiff C	L	03/91	90	10	0	0

DEMBA-NYREN Njogu
Born: Bakau, Gambia, 26 June, 1979 — F
Gambia: 11

League Club	Source	Date Signed	Seasons Played	Apps	Subs	Gls
Notts Co	Odense BK (DEN)	03/11	10	5	7	1

DEMBELE Bira
Born: Paris, France, 22 March, 1988 — D
France: U21-4

League Club	Source	Date Signed	Seasons Played	Apps	Subs	Gls
Stevenage	CS Sedan (FRA)	02/14	13-14	38	2	3

DEMBELE Mousa Sidi Yaya
Born: Antwerp, Belgium, 16 July, 1987 — M
Belgium: 61

League Club	Source	Date Signed	Seasons Played	Apps	Subs	Gls
Fulham	AZ Alkmaar (NED)	08/10	10-12	57	5	5
Tottenham H	Tr	08/12	12-14	58	26	3

DEMBELE Moussa
Born: Pontoise, France, 12 July, 1996 — F
France: Youth

League Club	Source	Date Signed	Seasons Played	Apps	Subs	Gls
Fulham	Sch	07/13	13-14	3	10	0

DEMEL Guy Roland
Born: Paris, France, 13 June, 1981 — RB
Ivory Coast: 35

League Club	Source	Date Signed	Seasons Played	Apps	Subs	Gls
Arsenal	Nimes (FRA)	07/00				
West Ham U	Hamburger SV (GER)	08/11	11-14	68	8	1

DEMERIT Jay Michael
Born: Green Bay, Wisconsin, USA, 4 December, 1979 — CD
USA: 25

League Club	Source	Date Signed	Seasons Played	Apps	Subs	Gls
Watford	Northwood	08/04	04-09	164	18	8

DEMETRIOS Cristakis (Chris)
Born: Dudley, West Midlands, England, 26 October, 1973 — LB

League Club	Source	Date Signed	Seasons Played	Apps	Subs	Gls
Walsall	YT	08/92	92	3	4	1

DEMETRIOU Jason
Born: Newham, E London, England, 18 November, 1987 — LW
Cyprus: 20

League Club	Source	Date Signed	Seasons Played	Apps	Subs	Gls
Leyton Orient	Sch	07/06	05-09	105	38	10

DEMETRIOU Michael David (Mickey)
Born: Worthing, West Sussex, England, 12 March, 1990 — LB/M
England: Semi Pro-3

League Club	Source	Date Signed	Seasons Played	Apps	Subs	Gls
Shrewsbury T	Kidderminster Hrs	06/14	14	40	2	3

DEMICHELIS Martin Gaston
Born: Cordoba, Argentina, 20 December, 1980 — CD
Argentina: 47

League Club	Source	Date Signed	Seasons Played	Apps	Subs	Gls
Manchester C	Atletico Madrid (SPN)	09/13	13-14	55	3	3

DEMONTAGNAC Ishmel Abendigo
Born: Newham, E London, England, 15 June, 1988 — LW
England: Youth

League Club	Source	Date Signed	Seasons Played	Apps	Subs	Gls
Walsall	Sch	12/05	05-08	28	55	9
Blackpool	Sheffield U (NC)	08/09	09-10	1	8	0
Chesterfield	L	03/10	09	10	0	3
Stockport Co	L	01/11	10	7	0	2
Notts Co	Tr	07/11	11	2	15	0
Northampton T	Tr	07/12	12-13	19	18	1

DEMOUGE Frank
Born: Nijmegen, Netherlands, 25 June, 1982 — F
Netherlands: U21-4

League Club	Source	Date Signed	Seasons Played	Apps	Subs	Gls
Bournemouth	FC Utrecht (NED)	07/12	12	2	0	0

DEMPSEY Clinton Drew (Clint)
Born: Nacogdoches, Texas, USA, 9 March, 1983 — M/F
USA: 112

League Club	Source	Date Signed	Seasons Played	Apps	Subs	Gls
Fulham	New England Rev (USA)	01/07	06-11	157	27	50
Tottenham H	Tr	08/12	12	22	7	7
Fulham (L)	Seattle Sounders (USA)	12/13	13	4	1	0

DEMPSEY Gary William
Born: Wexford, Republic of Ireland, 15 January, 1981 — M
Republic of Ireland: Youth

League Club	Source	Date Signed	Seasons Played	Apps	Subs	Gls
Everton	YT	01/98				
Yeovil T	Aberdeen	07/07	07	10	6	2
Darlington	St Patricks Ath (ROI)	01/10	09	24	0	1

DEMPSEY John
Born: Cumbernauld, Lanarkshire, Scotland, 22 June, 1913 — IF
Died: Carluke, Lanarkshire, Scotland, 27 September, 1998

League Club	Source	Date Signed	Seasons Played	Apps	Subs	Gls
Ipswich T	Queen of the South	06/48	48	22	-	5

DEMPSEY John Thomas
Born: Hampstead, NW London, England, 15 March, 1946 — CD
Republic of Ireland: 19

League Club	Source	Date Signed	Seasons Played	Apps	Subs	Gls
Fulham	App	03/64	64-68	149	0	4
Chelsea	Tr	01/69	68-75	161	4	4

DEMPSEY John William
Born: Birkenhead, Wirral, England, 2 April, 1951 — LB

League Club	Source	Date Signed	Seasons Played	Apps	Subs	Gls
Tranmere Rov	App	04/69	67-71	52	2	1

DEMPSEY Kyle Michael
Born: Whitehaven, Cumbria, England, 17 September, 1995 — M

League Club	Source	Date Signed	Seasons Played	Apps	Subs	Gls
Carlisle U	Sch	06/14	13-14	41	6	10

DEMPSEY Mark Anthony
Born: Dublin, Republic of Ireland, 10 December, 1972 — LW
Republic of Ireland: U21-5/Youth

League Club	Source	Date Signed	Seasons Played	Apps	Subs	Gls
Gillingham	YT	08/90	90-92	27	21	2
Leyton Orient	Tr	07/94	94	43	0	1
Shrewsbury T	Tr	07/95	95-97	62	18	3

DEMPSEY Mark James
Born: Manchester, England, 14 January, 1964 — M

League Club	Source	Date Signed	Seasons Played	Apps	Subs	Gls
Manchester U	App	01/82	85	1	0	0
Swindon T	L	01/85	84	5	0	0
Sheffield U	Tr	08/86	86-87	60	3	9
Chesterfield	L	09/88	88	3	0	0
Rotherham U	Tr	10/88	88-90	71	4	7

DEMPSEY Paul
Born: Birkenhead, Wirral, England, 3 December, 1981 — FB

League Club	Source	Date Signed	Seasons Played	Apps	Subs	Gls
Sheffield U	YT	07/00				
Northampton T	Tr	03/01	00-01	18	8	0

DEMPSTER John
Born: Kettering, Northamptonshire, England, 1 April, 1983 — CD
Scotland: U21-1/Youth

League Club	Source	Date Signed	Seasons Played	Apps	Subs	Gls
Rushden & D	Jnr	07/01	01-05	44	22	4
Oxford U	Tr	01/06	05	6	0	0
Crawley T	Kettering T	01/11	11	6	1	1
Mansfield T	Tr	07/12	13-14	39	1	0

DENHAM Charles (Charlie)
Born: Hartlepool, Cleveland, England, 28 April, 1937 — RW

League Club	Source	Date Signed	Seasons Played	Apps	Subs	Gls
Hartlepool U (Am)	West Amats	11/58	58	5	-	3

DENHAM John William
Born: Middleton, West Yorkshire, England, 6 November, 1925 — FB
Died: Redcar, Cleveland, England, 30 June, 1972

League Club	Source	Date Signed	Seasons Played	Apps	Subs	Gls
Hull C	Yorkshire Amats	06/48				
Hartlepool U	Tr	08/49	49	1	-	0

DENIAL Geoffrey (Geoff)
Born: Stocksbridge, South Yorkshire, England, 31 January, 1932 — LH

League Club	Source	Date Signed	Seasons Played	Apps	Subs	Gls
Sheffield U		01/52	52-54	10	-	0
Oxford U	Tr	09/56	62	6	-	0

[DENILSON] PEREIRA NEVES Denilson
Born: Sao Paulo, Brazil, 16 February, 1988 — M
Brazil: Youth

League Club	Source	Date Signed	Seasons Played	Apps	Subs	Gls
Arsenal	Sao Paulo (BRA)	08/06	06-10	69	27	6

DENNEHY Billy Michael
Born: Tralee, Republic of Ireland, 17 February, 1987 — LW
Republic of Ireland: U21-2

League Club	Source	Date Signed	Seasons Played	Apps	Subs	Gls
Sunderland	Shelbourne (ROI)	01/05				
Accrington Stan	L	11/07	07	2	5	0

DENNEHY Darren John
Born: Tralee, Republic of Ireland, 21 September, 1988 — CD
Republic of Ireland: U21-8

League Club	Source	Date Signed	Seasons Played	Apps	Subs	Gls
Cardiff C	Everton (Sch)	07/08				
Hereford U	L	03/09	08	3	0	0
Hereford U	L	07/09	09	6	1	0
Gillingham	L	01/10	09	19	0	0
Barnet	Tr	08/10	10-11	22	2	0

DENNEHY Jeremiah (Miah)
Born: Cork, Republic of Ireland, 29 March, 1950 — RW
Republic of Ireland: 11/U23-1

League Club	Source	Date Signed	Seasons Played	Apps	Subs	Gls
Nottingham F	Cork Hibernian (ROI)	01/73	72-74	37	4	4
Walsall	Tr	07/75	75-77	123	5	22
Bristol Rov	Tr	07/78	78-79	47	5	6

DENNIS Alan George
Born: Colchester, Essex, England, 22 December, 1951 — CD

League Club	Source	Date Signed	Seasons Played	Apps	Subs	Gls
Colchester U	Jnr	08/70	69-70	2	3	0

DENNIS John Anthony (Tony)
Born: Eton, Berkshire, England, 1 December, 1963 — RW/M

League Club	Source	Date Signed	Seasons Played	Apps	Subs	Gls
Plymouth Arg	App	12/81	81-82	7	2	0
Exeter C	Tr	08/83	83	3	1	0
Cambridge U	Slough T	02/89	88-92	89	22	10
Chesterfield	Tr	06/93	93	4	6	0
Colchester U	Tr	08/94	94-95	56	9	5
Lincoln C	Tr	07/96	96	23	5	2

DENNIS Kevin Jason
Born: Islington, N London, England, 14 December, 1976 — LW

League Club	Source	Date Signed	Seasons Played	Apps	Subs	Gls
Brentford	Arsenal (YT)	07/96	96-97	9	8	0

DENNIS Kristian
Born: Manchester, England, 12 March, 1990 — F

League Club	Source	Date Signed	Seasons Played	Apps	Subs	Gls
Macclesfield T	Sch	07/08	07-08	0	4	1

DENNIS Louis Hugh
Born: Hendon, N London, England, 9 October, 1992 — F

League Club	Source	Date Signed	Seasons Played	Apps	Subs	Gls
Dagenham & Red	Jnr	07/11	12-13	0	8	0

DENNIS Mark Earl
Born: Streatham, S London, England, 2 May, 1961 — LB
England: U21-3/Youth

League Club	Source	Date Signed	Seasons Played	Apps	Subs	Gls
Birmingham C	App	08/78	78-82	130	0	1
Southampton	Tr	11/83	83-86	95	0	2
Queens Park Rgrs	Tr	05/87	87-88	26	2	0
Crystal Palace	Tr	08/89	89-90	8	1	0

DENNISON Charles Robert (Bob)
Born: Hull, England, 12 September, 1932 — RB

League Club	Source	Date Signed	Seasons Played	Apps	Subs	Gls
Hull C	Jnr	07/54	54-57	24	-	1

DENNISON Robert (Robbie)
Born: Banbridge, Down, Northern Ireland, 30 April, 1963 — LW
Northern Ireland: 18/B-3/Youth

League Club	Source	Date Signed	Seasons Played	Apps	Subs	Gls
West Bromwich A	Glenavon	09/85	85-86	9	7	1
Wolverhampton W	Tr	03/87	86-96	264	29	40
Swansea C	L	10/95	95	9	0	0

DENNISON Robert Smith (Bob)
Born: Amble, Northumberland, England, 6 March, 1912 — CH
Died: Gillingham, Kent, England, 19 June, 1996

League Club	Source	Date Signed	Seasons Played	Apps	Subs	Gls
Newcastle U	Radcliffe Welfare U	05/29	32-33	11	-	2
Nottingham F	Tr	05/34	34	15	-	5
Fulham	Tr	06/35	35-38	31	-	0
Northampton T	Tr	09/45	46-47	55	-	0

DENNY Jay
Born: Los Angeles, California, USA, 6 January, 1986 — M

League Club	Source	Date Signed	Seasons Played	Apps	Subs	Gls
Stoke C	Sch	06/04				
Shrewsbury T	Tr	07/05	05	7	7	0

DENNY Paul Nicholas
Born: Croydon, S London, England, 5 September, 1957 — M

League Club	Source	Date Signed	Seasons Played	Apps	Subs	Gls
Southend U	App	09/75	76	8	1	2
Wimbledon	Tr	08/77	77-80	87	16	11

DENTON Alec Sam
Born: Sheffield, England, 30 July, 1994 — F

League Club	Source	Date Signed	Seasons Played	Apps	Subs	Gls
Rotherham U	Sch	07/12	11-12	0	2	0

DENTON Edward John (Eddie)
Born: Oxford, England, 18 September, 1970 — M

League Club	Source	Date Signed	Seasons Played	Apps	Subs	Gls
Oxford U	YT	07/88	87	0	2	0
Watford	Witney T	02/91	90	0	2	0

DENTON Peter Robert
Born: Gorleston, Norfolk, England, 1 March, 1946 — RW

League Club	Source	Date Signed	Seasons Played	Apps	Subs	Gls
Coventry C	App	03/64	65-67	10	0	1
Luton T	Tr	01/68	67-68	4	1	0

DENTON Roger William
Born: Stretford, Greater Manchester, England, 6 January, 1953 — LB/M

League Club	Source	Date Signed	Seasons Played	Apps	Subs	Gls
Bolton W	Jnr	05/71	71	3	1	0
Bradford C	Tr	07/72	72-73	25	5	0
Rochdale	L	02/74	73	2	0	0

League Club	Source	Date Signed	Seasons Played	Career Record Apps	Subs	Gls
DENTON Thomas Ashley (Tom)						
Born: Shepley, West Yorkshire, England, 24 July, 1989						F
Huddersfield T	Wakefield	08/08				
Cheltenham T	L	07/09	09	1	1	0
DENYER Albert Thomas Frederick (Bertie)						
Born: Swindon, England, 6 December, 1924						W
Swindon T	Garrards Ath	10/45	46	7	-	1
Cardiff C	Tr	05/48				
DENYER Peter Russell						
Born: Chiddingfold, Surrey, England, 26 November, 1957						M
Portsmouth	App	12/75	75-78	123	8	15
Northampton T	Tr	07/79	79-82	138	9	27
DENYS Ryan Hayden						
Born: Brentford, W London, England, 16 August, 1978						RW
Brentford	YT	07/97	97	12	7	1
DE ORNELAS Fernando Franco						
Born: Caracas, Venezuela, 29 July, 1976						W
Venezuela: 13						
Crystal Palace	Happy Valley (HKG)	09/99	99	5	4	0
Queens Park Rgrs	South China (HKG)	10/01	01	1	1	0
DEPEAR Ernest Roland (Roly)						
Born: Spalding, Lincolnshire, England, 10 December, 1923						CH
Died: Barton in Fabis, Nottinghamshire, England, January, 2001						
Leeds U	Boston U	05/48	48	4	-	0
Newport Co	Tr	06/49	49	16	-	0
Shrewsbury T	Tr	07/50	50-51	74	-	5
DE PEDRO Javier Francisco						
Born: Logrono, Spain, 4 August, 1973						M
Spain: 12/U21-4/Youth						
Blackburn Rov	Real Sociedad (SPN)	07/04	04	1	1	0
DE PLACIDO Michael Stephen (Mike)						
Born: Scarborough, North Yorkshire, England, 9 March, 1954						W
England: Youth						
York C	Jnr	03/72	71-72	4	7	0
DEPLEDGE William (Bill)						
Born: Bradford, England, 24 June, 1924						LH/IF
Died: Bradford, England, 1985						
Bradford Park Ave	Jnr	08/42	46-55	274	-	62
DERBYSHIRE Matthew Anthony (Matt)						
Born: Great Harwood, Lancashire, England, 14 April, 1986						F
England: U21-14						
Blackburn Rov	Great Harwood T	11/03	04-08	17	46	10
Plymouth Arg	L	08/05	05	2	10	0
Wrexham	L	02/06	05	16	0	10
Birmingham C (L)	Olympiakos (GRE)	08/10	10	4	9	0
Nottingham F	Olympiakos (GRE)	08/11	11-13	15	29	8
Oldham Ath	L	09/12	12	18	0	4
Blackpool	L	01/13	12	4	8	0
Rotherham U	Tr	05/14	14	28	6	9
DERBYSHIRE Thomas (Tommy)						
Born: Manchester, England, 10 December, 1930						G
Hartlepool U (Am)	East Yorks Regiment	08/50	50	1	-	0
DE RIDDER Daniel Robin Frede						
Born: Amsterdam, Netherlands, 6 March, 1984						W
Netherlands: U21-30						
Birmingham C	Ajax (NED)	07/07	07	6	4	0
Wigan Ath	Tr	07/08	08	5	13	0
DE RIDDER Steve Danny Marc						
Born: Ghent, Belgium, 25 February, 1987						W
Belgium: Youth						
Southampton	De Graafschap (NED)	07/11	11-12	5	31	3
Bolton W	L	01/13	12	2	1	0
DERKO Tadeusz Franciszek (Franco)						
Born: Italy, 22 December, 1946						WH
Mansfield T	App	01/65	66	1	0	0
DERRETT Stephen Clifford (Steve)						
Born: Cardiff, Wales, 16 October, 1947						D
Wales: 4/U23-3/Schools						
Cardiff C	App	10/65	66-71	61	6	1
Carlisle U	Tr	04/72	72	13	0	0
Aldershot	L	10/73	73	4	0	0
Rotherham U	Tr	12/73	73-75	79	2	2
Newport Co	Tr	06/76	76-77	61	0	0
DERRICK Albert Edward						
Born: Newport, Wales, 8 September, 1908						CF

League Club	Source	Date Signed	Seasons Played	Career Record Apps	Subs	Gls
Died: Newport, Wales, 5 June, 1975						
Newport Co		10/35	35-38	125	-	43
Swindon T	Tr	01/46	46	1	-	0
DERRICK Edward Albert (Albert)						
Born: Newport, Wales, 6 August, 1939						IF
Newport Co	Army	12/60	60	3	-	1
Newport Co	Hereford U	07/69	69	25	1	8
DERRICK Jantzen Stuart						
Born: Bristol, England, 10 January, 1943						LW
England: Schools						
Bristol C	Jnr	01/60	59-70	253	6	31
Mansfield T	L	03/71	70	2	1	0
DERRY Shaun Peter						
Born: Nottingham, England, 6 December, 1977						DM
Notts Co	YT	04/96	95-97	76	3	4
Sheffield U	Tr	01/98	97-99	62	10	0
Portsmouth	Tr	03/00	99-01	48	1	1
Crystal Palace	Tr	08/02	02-04	62	21	3
Nottingham F	L	12/04	04	7	0	0
Leeds U	Tr	02/05	04-06	71	0	3
Crystal Palace	Tr	11/07	07-09	111	4	0
Queens Park Rgrs	Tr	07/10	10-12	83	9	1
Millwall	L	08/13	13	7	0	0
DERVELD Fernando						
Born: Vlissingen, Netherlands, 22 October, 1976						LB
Norwich C	Haarlem (NED)	03/00	99-00	20	2	1
West Bromwich A	L	02/01	00	1	1	0
DERVITE Dorian Pierre						
Born: Lille, France, 25 July, 1988						CD
France: U21-8/Youth						
Tottenham H	Lille OSC Jnrs (FRA)	08/06				
Southend U	L	01/09	08	18	0	0
Charlton Ath	Villarreal (SPN)	08/12	12-13	53	17	5
Bolton W	Tr	05/14	14	34	3	0
DESAILLY Marcel						
Born: Accra, Ghana, 7 September, 1968						CD
France: 116/B-1						
Chelsea	AC Milan (ITA)	07/98	98-03	156	2	6
DESBOROUGH Michael (Mike)						
Born: Newham, E London, England, 28 November, 1969						G
Colchester U	Chelmsford C	10/93	93	1	0	0
DESCHAMPS Didier Claude						
Born: Bayonne, France, 15 October, 1968						DM
France: 103/U21-18						
Chelsea	Juventus (ITA)	06/99	99	24	3	0
DE SILVA Kyle Matthew						
Born: Croydon, S London, England, 29 November, 1993						M
Crystal Palace	Sch	11/10	11-12	2	5	0
Barnet	L	03/13	12	1	2	0
DESMEULES Rodney Leo (Rod)						
Born: Newbury, Berkshire, England, 23 September, 1948						RH
Swindon T	App	10/66	66-67	4	0	0
DESMOND Peter						
Born: Cork, Republic of Ireland, 23 November, 1926						IF
Died: Dawlish, Devon, England, 16 September, 1990						
Republic of Ireland: 4/LoI-2						
Middlesbrough	Shelbourne (ROI)	05/49	49	2	-	0
Southport	Tr	08/50	50	12	-	2
York C	Fleetwood	12/51	51	1	-	0
Hartlepool U	Stockton	08/53	53	1	-	0
DE SOUZA Miguel Juan (Juan)						
Born: Newham, E London, England, 11 February, 1970						F
Charlton Ath	Clapton	07/89				
Bristol C	Tr	08/90				
Birmingham C	Dagenham & Red	02/94	93-94	5	10	0
Bury	L	11/94	94	2	1	0
Wycombe W	Tr	01/95	94-96	73	10	29
Peterborough U	Tr	03/97	96-98	19	16	5
Southend U	L	08/98	98	2	0	0
Rochdale	L	10/98	98	5	0	0
DEUCHAR Kenneth Robert John (Kenny)						
Born: Stirling, Scotland, 8 June, 1980						F
Northampton T (L)	Gretna	01/07	06	14	3	3
DEULOFEU Gerard						
Born: Girona, Spain, 13 March, 1994						LW
Spain: 1/U21-19/Youth						
Everton (L)	Barcelona (SPN)	07/13	13	9	16	3

DE VAL Marc
Born: Blanes, Spain, 15 February, 1990 — M

League Club	Source	Date Signed	Seasons Played	Apps	Subs	Gls
Doncaster Rov	Real Madrid B (SPN)	07/13	13-14	10	6	0

DEVANEY Martin Thomas
Born: Cheltenham, Gloucestershire, England, 1 June, 1980 — RW

League Club	Source	Date Signed	Seasons Played	Apps	Subs	Gls
Coventry C	YT	06/97				
Cheltenham T	Tr	08/99	99-04	154	49	38
Watford	Tr	07/05				
Barnsley	Tr	08/05	05-10	118	38	15
MK Dons	L	10/09	09	4	1	0
Walsall	L	10/10	10	4	0	1
Tranmere Rov	Tr	08/11	11	16	4	2

DEVANEY Philip Charles (Phil)
Born: Huyton, Merseyside, England, 12 February, 1969 — F

League Club	Source	Date Signed	Seasons Played	Apps	Subs	Gls
Burnley	App	02/87	86-87	8	5	1

DEVANNEY Allan
Born: Otley, West Yorkshire, England, 5 September, 1941 — CF
Died: Leeds, England, July, 1992

League Club	Source	Date Signed	Seasons Played	Apps	Subs	Gls
Bradford C	Jnr	02/59	59-61	12	-	4

DEVERA Joseph (Joe)
Born: Southgate, N London, England, 6 February, 1987 — D

League Club	Source	Date Signed	Seasons Played	Apps	Subs	Gls
Barnet	Jnr	08/06	06-10	171	6	2
Swindon T	Tr	07/11	11-12	51	2	2
Portsmouth	Tr	07/13	13-14	70	2	1

DEVERALL Harold Reginald (Jackie)
Born: Petersfield, Hampshire, England, 5 May, 1916 — LH/LW
Died: Basingstoke, Hampshire, England, 11 June, 1999
England: Schools

League Club	Source	Date Signed	Seasons Played	Apps	Subs	Gls
Reading	Maidenhead U	11/37	38-47	74	-	9
Leyton Orient	Tr	08/48	48-52	115	-	2

DEVERDICS Nicholas Ferenc (Nicky)
Born: Gateshead, Tyne and Wear, England, 24 November, 1987 — M

League Club	Source	Date Signed	Seasons Played	Apps	Subs	Gls
Barnet	Gretna	07/08	08-09	26	19	2

DEVEREUX Anthony William John (Tony)
Born: Gibraltar, 6 January, 1940 — FB

League Club	Source	Date Signed	Seasons Played	Apps	Subs	Gls
Aldershot	Chelsea (Am)	11/58	59-65	132	0	0

DEVEREUX James Anthony (Jimmy)
Born: Fleet, Hampshire, England, 20 February, 1970 — FB

League Club	Source	Date Signed	Seasons Played	Apps	Subs	Gls
Aldershot	YT	07/88	88-89	0	2	0

DEVEREUX Robert (Robbie)
Born: Sudbury, Suffolk, England, 13 January, 1971 — M

League Club	Source	Date Signed	Seasons Played	Apps	Subs	Gls
Colchester U	Ipswich T (YT)	05/89	89	1	1	0
Colchester U	Cornard U	08/92	92	3	3	0

DEVEY Raymond (Ray)
Born: Birmingham, England, 19 December, 1917 — CH
Died: Coventry, England, June, 2001

League Club	Source	Date Signed	Seasons Played	Apps	Subs	Gls
Birmingham C	Shirley Jnrs	08/37	46	1	-	0
Mansfield T	Tr	08/47	47-49	76	-	4

DEVINE Daniel Gerard
Born: Belfast, Northern Ireland, 7 September, 1992 — CD
Northern Ireland: U21-2

League Club	Source	Date Signed	Seasons Played	Apps	Subs	Gls
Preston NE	Sch	07/11	10-11	15	0	1
Fleetwood T	Tr	07/12				

DEVINE John Anthony
Born: Dublin, Republic of Ireland, 11 November, 1958 — RB/M
Republic of Ireland: 13/U21-2

League Club	Source	Date Signed	Seasons Played	Apps	Subs	Gls
Arsenal	App	10/76	77-82	86	3	0
Norwich C	Tr	08/83	83-84	51	2	3
Stoke C	Tr	11/85	85	15	0	1

DEVINE John Henry
Born: Liverpool, England, 9 July, 1933 — W

League Club	Source	Date Signed	Seasons Played	Apps	Subs	Gls
Chester C	Rhyl	07/55	55	1	-	0

DEVINE Peter
Born: Blackburn, Greater Manchester, England, 25 May, 1960 — W

League Club	Source	Date Signed	Seasons Played	Apps	Subs	Gls
Bristol C	Vancouver W'caps (CAN)	07/81	81	19	2	1
Blackburn Rov	Tr	09/82	82-83	8	0	2
Burnley	Chorley	06/84	84-85	46	10	4

DEVINE Sean Thomas
Born: Lewisham, SE London, England, 6 September, 1972 — F
Republic of Ireland: B-1

League Club	Source	Date Signed	Seasons Played	Apps	Subs	Gls
Millwall	YT	05/91				
Barnet	Famagusta (CYP)	10/95	95-98	112	14	47
Wycombe W	Tr	03/99	98-02	82	7	41
Exeter C	Tr	01/03	02	21	2	8

DEVINE Stephen Bernard (Steve)
Born: Strabane, Tyrone, Northern Ireland, 11 December, 1964 — D
Northern Ireland: Youth

League Club	Source	Date Signed	Seasons Played	Apps	Subs	Gls
Wolverhampton W	App	12/82				
Derby Co	Tr	03/83	83-84	10	1	0
Stockport Co	Tr	08/85	85	2	0	0
Hereford U	Tr	10/85	85-92	261	11	4

DEVINE William (Willie)
Born: Ayr, Scotland, 22 August, 1933 — LW
Died: Stevenston, Ayrshire, Scotland, 16 April, 1997

League Club	Source	Date Signed	Seasons Played	Apps	Subs	Gls
Watford	St Mirren	03/58	57-58	30	-	6
Accrington Stan	Partick Thistle	05/60	60	46	-	6

DE VITA Raffaele
Born: Rome, Italy, 23 September, 1987 — RW

League Club	Source	Date Signed	Seasons Played	Apps	Subs	Gls
Blackburn Rov	Sch	09/05				
Swindon T	Livingston	07/11	11-12	54	20	12
Bradford C	Tr	07/13	13	6	14	1
Cheltenham T	Tr	09/14	14	7	3	0

DE VITO Claudio Gaetano
Born: Peterborough, England, 21 July, 1978 — F

League Club	Source	Date Signed	Seasons Played	Apps	Subs	Gls
Northampton T	YT	07/96				
Barnet	Tr	03/98	97	0	1	0

DEVITT Bernard Malcolm (Malcolm)
Born: Bradford, England, 26 January, 1937 — IF/RH
Died: Cyprus, 12 February, 2012

League Club	Source	Date Signed	Seasons Played	Apps	Subs	Gls
Bradford C	Bradford Rov	03/59	58-62	100	-	13

DEVITT Jamie Martin
Born: Dublin, Republic of Ireland, 6 July, 1990 — M/W
Republic of Ireland: U21-1/Youth

League Club	Source	Date Signed	Seasons Played	Apps	Subs	Gls
Hull C	Sch	01/08	10	7	9	0
Darlington	L	09/09	09	5	1	1
Shrewsbury T	L	10/09	09	8	1	2
Grimsby T	L	02/10	09	15	0	5
Bradford C	L	08/11	11	5	2	1
Accrington Stan	L	02/12	11	15	1	2
Rotherham U	L	11/12	12	1	0	0
Chesterfield	Tr	07/13	13	3	4	0
Morecambe	Tr	01/14	13-14	44	6	5

DEVLIN Alan Thomas
Born: Edinburgh, Scotland, 10 October, 1953 — F

League Club	Source	Date Signed	Seasons Played	Apps	Subs	Gls
Exeter C	Dundee U	11/73	73	1	0	0

DEVLIN Douglas Paul Keith (Doug)
Born: Glasgow, Scotland, 17 March, 1953 — M

League Club	Source	Date Signed	Seasons Played	Apps	Subs	Gls
Wolverhampton W	App	06/71				
Walsall	Tr	07/72	72	15	3	0

DEVLIN Ernest (Joe)
Born: Gateshead, Tyne and Wear, England, 6 March, 1920 — RB
Died: Gateshead, Tyne and Wear, England, 1976

League Club	Source	Date Signed	Seasons Played	Apps	Subs	Gls
Gateshead		08/42				
West Ham U	Tr	06/46	46-52	70	-	0
Darlington	Tr	02/54	53-56	115	-	1

DEVLIN John (Johnny)
Born: Airdrie, Lanarkshire, Scotland, 11 December, 1917 — IF
Died: Walsall, West Midlands, England, 26 January, 2001

League Club	Source	Date Signed	Seasons Played	Apps	Subs	Gls
Walsall	Kilmarnock	12/47	47-51	159	-	51

DEVLIN Joseph (Joe)
Born: Cleland, Lanarkshire, Scotland, 12 March, 1931 — RW

League Club	Source	Date Signed	Seasons Played	Apps	Subs	Gls
Accrington Stan	Falkirk	07/53	53-56	114	-	18
Rochdale	Tr	09/56	56-57	38	-	7
Bradford Park Ave	Tr	11/57	57-58	34	-	3
Carlisle U	Tr	07/59	59	3	-	0

DEVLIN Mark Andrew
Born: Kilmarnock, Ayrshire, Scotland, 18 January, 1973 — M
Scotland: Youth

League Club	Source	Date Signed	Seasons Played	Apps	Subs	Gls
Stoke C	YT	04/91	90-96	39	16	2
Exeter C	Tr	10/97	97	31	2	2

DEVLIN Paul John
Born: Birmingham, England, 14 April, 1972 — RW/F
Scotland: 10/B-1

League Club	Source	Date Signed	Seasons Played	Apps	Subs	Gls
Notts Co	Stafford Rgrs	02/92	91-95	132	9	25
Birmingham C	Tr	02/96	95-97	61	15	28
Sheffield U	Tr	03/98	97-01	122	25	24
Notts Co	L	10/98	98	5	0	0
Birmingham C	Tr	02/02	01-03	31	16	4
Watford	Tr	09/03	03-05	75	4	6
Walsall	Tr	01/06	05	8	0	1

League Club	Source	Date Signed	Seasons Played	Career Record Apps	Subs	Gls

DEVLIN William
Born: Glasgow, Scotland, 30 May, 1931 — LW

League Club	Source	Date Signed	Seasons Played	Apps	Subs	Gls
Carlisle U	Peterborough U	08/56	56	28	-	6

DE VOGT Wilko
Born: Breda, Netherlands, 17 September, 1975 — G

League Club	Source	Date Signed	Seasons Played	Apps	Subs	Gls
Sheffield U	NAC Breda (NED)	07/01	01	5	1	0

DEVONSHIRE Alan Ernest
Born: Acton, W London, England, 13 April, 1956 — M
England: 8/B-1

League Club	Source	Date Signed	Seasons Played	Apps	Subs	Gls
West Ham U	Southall	10/76	76-89	345	13	29
Watford	Tr	07/90	90-91	23	2	1

DEVONSHIRE Leslie Ernest Edward (Les)
Born: Acton, W London, England, 13 June, 1926 — W
Died: Southall, W London, England, 19 December, 2012

League Club	Source	Date Signed	Seasons Played	Apps	Subs	Gls
Brentford	Wealdstone	05/48				
Chester C	Tr	06/50	50	44	-	4
Crystal Palace	Tr	08/51	51-54	83	-	12

DE VOS Jason Richard
Born: London, Ontario, Canada, 2 January, 1974 — CD
Canada: 49/U23-14/Youth

League Club	Source	Date Signed	Seasons Played	Apps	Subs	Gls
Darlington	Montreal Impact (CAN)	11/96	96-98	43	1	5
Wigan Ath	Dundee U	08/01	01-03	87	3	15
Ipswich T	Tr	06/04	04-07	171	0	10

DE VRIES Dorus
Born: Bewerwijk, Netherlands, 29 December, 1980 — G

League Club	Source	Date Signed	Seasons Played	Apps	Subs	Gls
Swansea C	Dunfermline Ath	07/07	07-10	178	0	0
Wolverhampton W	Tr	07/11	11-12	12	2	0
Nottingham F	Tr	07/13	13-14	7	0	0

DE VRIES Mark Lyndon Patrick
Born: Paramaribo, Suriname, 24 August, 1975 — F

League Club	Source	Date Signed	Seasons Played	Apps	Subs	Gls
Leicester C	Heart of Midlothian	01/05	04-07	34	17	8
Leeds U	L	10/07	07	1	5	1

DEVRIES Roger Stuart
Born: Hull, England, 25 October, 1950 — FB

League Club	Source	Date Signed	Seasons Played	Apps	Subs	Gls
Hull C	Jnr	09/67	70-79	314	4	0
Blackburn Rov	Tr	07/80	80	13	0	0
Scunthorpe U	Tr	10/81	81	6	0	1

DE WAARD Raymond Marienus
Born: Rotterdam, Netherlands, 27 March, 1973 — F

League Club	Source	Date Signed	Seasons Played	Apps	Subs	Gls
Norwich C	SC Cambuur (NED)	03/00	99-00	4	6	0

DEWHURST Robert Matthew (Rob)
Born: Keighley, West Yorkshire, England, 10 September, 1971 — CD

League Club	Source	Date Signed	Seasons Played	Apps	Subs	Gls
Blackburn Rov	YT	10/90	90	13	0	0
Darlington	L	12/91	91	11	0	1
Huddersfield T	L	10/92	92	7	0	0
Hull C	Tr	11/93	93-98	132	6	13
Exeter C	Tr	08/99	99	21	2	2

DEWICK John Albert
Born: Rotherham, South Yorkshire, England, 28 November, 1919 — G
Died: Bracknell, Berkshire, England, June, 1997

League Club	Source	Date Signed	Seasons Played	Apps	Subs	Gls
Notts Co		10/46	46	1	-	0

DEWIS George Renger
Born: Hinckley, Leicestershire, England, 22 January, 1913 — CF
Died: Hinckley, Leicestershire, England, 23 October, 1994

League Club	Source	Date Signed	Seasons Played	Apps	Subs	Gls
Leicester C	Nuneaton T	10/33	33-49	116	-	45

DE WOLF Johannes Hildebrand (John)
Born: Schiedam, Netherlands, 10 December, 1962 — CD
Netherlands:

League Club	Source	Date Signed	Seasons Played	Apps	Subs	Gls
Wolverhampton W	Feyenoord (NED)	12/94	94-95	27	1	5

DEWS George
Born: Ossett, West Yorkshire, England, 5 June, 1921 — IF
Died: Brierley Hill, West Midlands, England, 29 January, 2003

League Club	Source	Date Signed	Seasons Played	Apps	Subs	Gls
Middlesbrough	Ossett T	08/46	46-47	33	-	8
Plymouth Arg	Tr	10/47	47-54	257	-	76
Walsall	Tr	06/55	55	9	-	1

DEWSBURY John
Born: Swansea, Wales, 16 February, 1932 — FB
Died: Swansea, Wales, 16 October, 2007

League Club	Source	Date Signed	Seasons Played	Apps	Subs	Gls
Swansea C	Jnr	07/50	52	9	-	0
Newport Co	Tr	08/55	55	2	-	0

DEWSNIP George Edward
Born: Salford, England, 6 May, 1956 — W

League Club	Source	Date Signed	Seasons Played	Apps	Subs	Gls
Southport	Preston NE (App)	06/74	74-76	83	4	11

DEY Geoffrey (Geoff)
Born: Chesterfield, Derbyshire, England, 11 January, 1964 — M
England: Youth

League Club	Source	Date Signed	Seasons Played	Apps	Subs	Gls
Sheffield U	App	01/82				
Scunthorpe U	Tr	08/83	83-84	17	0	1

DEYNA Kazimierz
Born: Starogard Gdanski, Poland, 23 October, 1947 — F/M
Died: San Diego,California, USA, 1 September, 1989
Poland: 97

League Club	Source	Date Signed	Seasons Played	Apps	Subs	Gls
Manchester C	Legia Warsaw (POL)	11/78	78-80	34	4	12

DE ZEEUW Adrianus Johannes (Arjan)
Born: Castricum, Netherlands, 16 April, 1970 — CD

League Club	Source	Date Signed	Seasons Played	Apps	Subs	Gls
Barnsley	Telstar (NED)	11/95	95-98	138	0	7
Wigan Ath	Tr	07/99	99-01	126	0	6
Portsmouth	Tr	07/02	02-04	103	3	5
Wigan Ath	Tr	08/05	05-06	52	0	0
Coventry C	Tr	07/07	07	16	1	0

DIA Aly
Born: Dakar, Senegal, 20 August, 1965 — F

League Club	Source	Date Signed	Seasons Played	Apps	Subs	Gls
Southampton	VfB Lubeck (GER)	11/96	96	0	1	0

DIABATE Lassina
Born: Bouake, Ivory Coast, 16 September, 1974 — DM
Ivory Coast: 34

League Club	Source	Date Signed	Seasons Played	Apps	Subs	Gls
Portsmouth	AJ Auxerre (FRA)	10/02	02	16	9	0

DIABY Vassiriki Abou (Abou)
Born: Paris, France, 11 May, 1986 — M
France: 16/U21-2/Youth

League Club	Source	Date Signed	Seasons Played	Apps	Subs	Gls
Arsenal	AJ Auxerre (FRA)	01/06	05-13	92	32	14

DIAF Farid
Born: Carcassonne, France, 19 April, 1971 — M

League Club	Source	Date Signed	Seasons Played	Apps	Subs	Gls
Preston NE	Stade Lavallois (FRA)	07/99	99	1	2	0

DIAGNE Anthony (Tony)
Born: Mantes-la-Jolie, France, 17 September, 1990 — D/M

League Club	Source	Date Signed	Seasons Played	Apps	Subs	Gls
Nottingham F	Sch	08/08				
Macclesfield T	Aubervilliers (FRA)	01/11	10-11	59	2	4
Morecambe	Tr	07/13	13	15	12	1

DIAGOURAGA Toumani
Born: Paris, France, 10 June, 1987 — DM

League Club	Source	Date Signed	Seasons Played	Apps	Subs	Gls
Watford	Sch	11/04	05	1	0	0
Swindon T	L	03/06	05	5	3	0
Rotherham U	L	01/07	06	4	3	0
Hereford U	L	08/07	07	41	0	2
Hereford U	Tr	07/08	08	45	0	2
Peterborough U	Tr	06/09	09	18	1	0
Brentford	Tr	01/10	09-14	151	32	6
Portsmouth	L	02/14	13	8	0	0

DIAKITE Modibo
Born: Paris, France, 2 March, 1987 — CD

League Club	Source	Date Signed	Seasons Played	Apps	Subs	Gls
Sunderland	SS Lazio (ITA)	07/13	13	7	0	0

DIAKITE Samba
Born: Paris, France, 24 January, 1989 — M
Mali: 19

League Club	Source	Date Signed	Seasons Played	Apps	Subs	Gls
Queens Park Rgrs	AS Nancy (FRA)	01/12	11-12	20	3	1
Watford	L	01/14	13	1	5	0

DIALLO Bradley
Born: Paris, France, 20 July, 1990 — LB

League Club	Source	Date Signed	Seasons Played	Apps	Subs	Gls
Oldham Ath	Olymp Marseille (FRA)	08/11	11	12	3	0

DIALLO Cherif
Born: Dakar, Senegal, 23 December, 1976 — F

League Club	Source	Date Signed	Seasons Played	Apps	Subs	Gls
Exeter C	Scarborough	09/01	01	0	2	0

DIALLO Drissa
Born: Nouadhibou, Mauritania, 4 January, 1973 — CD
Guinea: 7

League Club	Source	Date Signed	Seasons Played	Apps	Subs	Gls
Burnley	KV Mechelen (BEL)	01/03	02	14	0	1
Ipswich T	Tr	06/03	03-04	39	6	0
Sheffield Wed	Tr	07/05	05	8	3	0
MK Dons	Tr	07/06	06-07	70	0	2
Cheltenham T	Tr	09/08	08-09	44	1	2

DIALLO Issago
Born: Montceau-les-Mines, France, 26 January, 1987 — DM

League Club	Source	Date Signed	Seasons Played	Apps	Subs	Gls
Cambridge U	Kaposvar (HUN)	08/14	14	7	1	1

DIAMANTI Alessandro
Born: Prato, Italy, 2 May, 1983 — M/F
Italy: 17

League Club	Source	Date Signed	Seasons Played	Apps	Subs	Gls
West Ham U	Livorno (ITA)	09/09	09-10	18	10	7

DIAME Mohamed
Born: Creteil, France, 14 June, 1987 — DM
Senegal: 22

League Club	Source	Date Signed	Seasons Played	Apps	Subs	Gls
Wigan Ath	Rayo Vallecano (SPN)	08/09	09-11	82	14	5
West Ham U	Tr	07/12	12-14	60	11	7
Hull C	Tr	09/14	14	10	2	4

DIAMOND Alexander Kevin (Zander)
Born: Dumbarton, Dunbartonshire, Scotland, 12 March, 1985 — CD
Scotland: U21-12

League Club	Source	Date Signed	Seasons Played	Apps	Subs	Gls
Oldham Ath	Aberdeen	07/11	11	21	2	2
Burton A	Tr	07/12	12-13	43	4	5
Northampton T	Tr	02/14	13-14	32	3	2

DIAMOND Anthony John (Tony)
Born: Rochdale, Greater Manchester, England, 23 August, 1968 — F
Northern Ireland: U23-1

League Club	Source	Date Signed	Seasons Played	Apps	Subs	Gls
Blackburn Rov	App	06/86	86-88	9	17	3
Wigan Ath	L	10/88	88	6	0	2
Blackpool	Tr	08/89	89	2	1	1

DIAMOND Barry
Born: Dumbarton, Dunbartonshire, Scotland, 20 February, 1960 — F

League Club	Source	Date Signed	Seasons Played	Apps	Subs	Gls
Rochdale	Barrow	07/84	84-85	50	2	16
Stockport Co	L	12/85	85	6	0	0
Halifax T	Tr	02/86	85-86	17	5	3
Wrexham	L	01/87	86	2	2	0

DIAO Salif Alassane
Born: Kedougou, Senegal, 10 February, 1977 — DM
Senegal: 39

League Club	Source	Date Signed	Seasons Played	Apps	Subs	Gls
Liverpool	CS Sedan (FRA)	08/02	02-04	19	18	1
Birmingham C	L	01/05	04	2	0	0
Portsmouth	L	08/05	05	7	4	0
Stoke C	Tr	10/06	06-11	69	19	1

DIARRA Alou
Born: Paris, France, 15 July, 1981 — DM
France: 44/U21-14/Youth

League Club	Source	Date Signed	Seasons Played	Apps	Subs	Gls
Liverpool	Bayern Munich (GER)	07/02				
West Ham U	Olymp Marseille (FRA)	08/12	12-13	2	4	0
Charlton Ath		02/15	14	8	4	1

DIARRA Lassana
Born: Paris, France, 10 March, 1985 — DM
France: 28/U21-18

League Club	Source	Date Signed	Seasons Played	Apps	Subs	Gls
Chelsea	Le Havre (FRA)	07/05	05-06	9	4	0
Arsenal	Tr	08/07	07	4	3	0
Portsmouth	Tr	01/08	07-08	22	2	1

DIARRA Mahamadou
Born: Bamako, Mali, 18 May, 1981 — DM
Mali: 64

League Club	Source	Date Signed	Seasons Played	Apps	Subs	Gls
Fulham	AS Monaco (FRA)	02/12	11-13	19	4	1

DIAS Claudio Franca
Born: Milton Keynes, England, 10 November, 1994 — M

League Club	Source	Date Signed	Seasons Played	Apps	Subs	Gls
Northampton T	Sch	06/13	12	0	1	0

DIATTA Lamine
Born: Dakar, Senegal, 2 July, 1975 — CD
Senegal: 40

League Club	Source	Date Signed	Seasons Played	Apps	Subs	Gls
Newcastle U (L)	Besiktas (TKY)	03/08	07	0	2	0

DIAWARA Djibril
Born: Dakar, Senegal, 3 January, 1975 — CD
France: Youth//Senegal: 1

League Club	Source	Date Signed	Seasons Played	Apps	Subs	Gls
Bolton W (L)	Torino (ITA)	07/01	01	4	5	0

DIAWARA Kaba
Born: Toulon, France, 16 December, 1975 — F
France: U21-1//Guinea: 16

League Club	Source	Date Signed	Seasons Played	Apps	Subs	Gls
Arsenal	Bordeaux (FRA)	01/99	98	2	10	0
Blackburn Rov (L)	Paris St-Germain (FRA)	08/00	00	1	4	0
West Ham U (L)	Paris St-Germain (FRA)	09/00	00	6	5	0

DIAWARA Souleymane
Born: Dakar, Senegal, 24 December, 1978 — CD
Senegal: 48

League Club	Source	Date Signed	Seasons Played	Apps	Subs	Gls
Charlton Ath	Sochaux (FRA)	08/06	06	18	5	0

DIAZ Isidro
Born: Valencia, Spain, 15 May, 1972 — RW

League Club	Source	Date Signed	Seasons Played	Apps	Subs	Gls
Wigan Ath	FC Balaguer (SPN)	07/95	95-96	57	19	16
Wolverhampton W	Tr	08/97	97	1	0	0
Wigan Ath	Tr	12/97	97	1	1	0
Rochdale	Tr	08/98	98	12	2	2

DIAZ Ramon Emilliano (Emilliano)
Born: Napoli, Italy, 22 June, 1983 — M

League Club	Source	Date Signed	Seasons Played	Apps	Subs	Gls
Oxford U	Depo Colonia (UGY)	02/05	04	2	5	0

DIBA-MUSANGU Jonathan (Jonny)
Born: Mbuji-Mayi, DR Congo, 12 October, 1997 — G

League Club	Source	Date Signed	Seasons Played	Apps	Subs	Gls
Rochdale	Sch	11/14	14	0	1	0

DIBBLE Andrew Gerald (Andy)
Born: Cwmbran, Torfaen, Wales, 8 May, 1965 — G
Wales: 3/U21-3/Youth/Schools

League Club	Source	Date Signed	Seasons Played	Apps	Subs	Gls
Cardiff C	App	08/82	81-83	62	0	0
Luton T	Tr	07/84	84-87	30	0	0
Sunderland	L	02/86	85	12	0	0
Huddersfield T	L	03/87	86	5	0	0
Manchester C	Tr	07/88	88-96	113	3	0
Middlesbrough	L	02/91	90	19	0	0
Bolton W	L	09/91	91	4	0	0
Bolton W	L	09/91	91	9	0	0
West Bromwich A	L	02/92	91	9	0	0
Luton T	Glasgow Rangers	09/97	97	1	0	0
Middlesbrough	Tr	01/98	97	2	0	0
Hartlepool U	Altrincham	03/99	99	6	0	0
Carlisle U	L	10/99	99	2	0	0
Stockport Co	Tr	08/00	00-01	22	1	0
Wrexham	Tr	08/02	02-04	83	0	0

DIBBLE Christopher (Chris)
Born: Morden, S London, England, 10 October, 1960 — M
England: Schools

League Club	Source	Date Signed	Seasons Played	Apps	Subs	Gls
Millwall	App	11/77	77-81	49	14	5
Wimbledon	Tr	07/82	82-83	7	2	0

DIBDEN William Keith (Keith)
Born: Totton, Hampshire, England, 17 December, 1933 — IF

League Club	Source	Date Signed	Seasons Played	Apps	Subs	Gls
Southampton	Jnr	01/52				
Gillingham	Tr	07/57	57	1	-	0

DI CANIO Paolo
Born: Rome, Italy, 9 July, 1968 — F
Italy: U21-9

League Club	Source	Date Signed	Seasons Played	Apps	Subs	Gls
Sheffield Wed	Glasgow Celtic	08/97	97-98	39	2	15
West Ham U	Tr	01/99	98-02	114	4	47
Charlton Ath	Tr	08/03	03	23	8	4

DI CARMINE Samuel
Born: Florence, Italy, 29 September, 1988 — F

League Club	Source	Date Signed	Seasons Played	Apps	Subs	Gls
Queens Park Rgrs (L)	Fiorentina (ITA)	07/08	08	15	12	2

DICHIO Daniele Salvatore Ernest (Danny)
Born: Hammersmith, W London, England, 19 October, 1974 — F
England: U21-1/Schools

League Club	Source	Date Signed	Seasons Played	Apps	Subs	Gls
Queens Park Rgrs	YT	05/93	94-96	56	19	20
Barnet	L	03/94	93	9	0	2
Sunderland	Sampdoria (ITA)	01/98	97-00	20	56	11
West Bromwich A	L	08/01	01	3	0	2
West Bromwich A	Tr	11/01	01-03	47	16	12
Derby Co	L	10/03	03	6	0	1
Millwall	Tr	01/04	03-04	42	4	17
Preston NE	Tr	07/05	05-06	34	29	5

DICK Alistair John (Ally)
Born: Stirling, Scotland, 25 April, 1965 — W
Scotland: Youth/Schools

League Club	Source	Date Signed	Seasons Played	Apps	Subs	Gls
Tottenham H	App	05/82	81-85	16	1	2

DICK George White
Born: Torphichen, West Lothian, Scotland, 12 June, 1921 — IF
Died: Carlisle, Cumbria, England, 7 September, 1960

League Club	Source	Date Signed	Seasons Played	Apps	Subs	Gls
Blackpool	BAOR Germany	08/46	46-47	45	-	13
West Ham U	Tr	10/48	48	14	-	1
Carlisle U	Tr	07/49	49-50	52	-	25
Stockport Co	Tr	10/50	50	25	-	12
Workington	Tr	10/51	51-52	56	-	17

DICK John Hart
Born: Glasgow, Scotland, 19 March, 1930 — IF
Died: Chigwell, Essex, England, September, 2000
Scotland: 1/B-1

League Club	Source	Date Signed	Seasons Played	Apps	Subs	Gls
West Ham U	Crittall Ath	06/53	53-62	326	-	153
Brentford	Tr	09/62	62-64	72	-	45

DICK Peter Watt (Wattie)
Born: Newmains, Lanarkshire, Scotland, 20 August, 1927 — LH/IF
Died: Castleford, West Yorkshire, England, 22 December, 2012

League Club	Source	Date Signed	Seasons Played	Apps	Subs	Gls
Accrington Stan	Third Lanark	06/55	55-58	125	-	37
Bradford Park Ave	Tr	12/58	58-62	155	-	2

DICK Thomas Woods (Tommy)
Born: Glasgow, Scotland, 19 July, 1936 — CF

League Club	Source	Date Signed	Seasons Played	Apps	Subs	Gls
Bradford Park Ave	Third Lanark	06/60	60	4	-	0

DICKENS Alan William
Born: Plaistow, E London, England, 3 September, 1964 — M
England: U21-1/Youth

League Club	Source	Date Signed	Seasons Played	Apps	Subs	Gls
West Ham U	App	08/82	82-88	173	19	23
Chelsea	Tr	08/89	89-91	39	9	1
West Bromwich A	L	12/92	92	3	0	1
Brentford	Tr	02/93	92	13	2	1
Colchester U	Tr	09/93	93	28	4	3

DICKENS Leo
Born: Hemsworth, West Yorkshire, England, 16 March, 1927 — RB

League Club	Source	Date Signed	Seasons Played	Apps	Subs	Gls
Rotherham U	Frickley Colliery	07/50				
Chester C	Tr	07/52	52	7	-	0

DICKENSON Brennan Peter (Ben)
Born: Ferndown, Hampshire, England, 9 August, 1993 — LW

League Club	Source	Date Signed	Seasons Played	Apps	Subs	Gls
Brighton & HA	Dorchester T	01/12				
Chesterfield	L	11/12	12	5	6	1
AFC Wimbledon	L	02/13	12	5	2	2
Northampton T	L	02/14	13	8	5	1
Gillingham	Tr	06/14	14	17	17	1

DICKENSON Kevin James
Born: Hackney, E London, England, 24 November, 1962 — LB

League Club	Source	Date Signed	Seasons Played	Apps	Subs	Gls
Charlton Ath	Tottenham H (App)	04/80	79-84	72	3	1
Leyton Orient	Tr	07/85	85-91	190	2	3

DICKER Gary Richard Perry
Born: Dublin, Republic of Ireland, 31 July, 1986 — DM
Republic of Ireland: U21-1

League Club	Source	Date Signed	Seasons Played	Apps	Subs	Gls
Birmingham C	UC Dublin (ROI)	01/07				
Stockport Co	Tr	08/07	07-08	51	4	0
Brighton & HA	Tr	03/09	08-12	109	29	6
Rochdale	Tr	09/13	13	10	2	1
Crawley T	Tr	01/14	13	9	2	0
Carlisle U	Tr	06/14	14	16	4	1

DICKER Leslie Raymond (Les)
Born: Stockwell, S London, England, 20 December, 1926 — LW

League Club	Source	Date Signed	Seasons Played	Apps	Subs	Gls
Tottenham H	Chelmsford C	06/51	52	10	-	2
Southend U	Tr	07/53	53-54	17	-	7

DICKIE Alan Leonard
Born: Charlton, SE London, England, 30 January, 1944 — G

League Club	Source	Date Signed	Seasons Played	Apps	Subs	Gls
West Ham U	App	02/62	61-65	12	0	0
Coventry C	Tr	03/67	67	2	0	0
Aldershot	Tr	07/68	68	7	0	0

DICKIE Murdoch McFarlane
Born: Dumbarton, Dunbartonshire, Scotland, 28 December, 1919 — RW
Died: Leicester, England, February, 2004

League Club	Source	Date Signed	Seasons Played	Apps	Subs	Gls
Plymouth Arg	Dumbarton Harp	06/37				
Crewe Alex	Linfield	10/38				
Port Vale	Tr	05/39				
Walsall	St Mirren	01/43				
Port Vale	Tr	10/44				
Chelsea	Guildford C	04/45	46	1	-	0
Bournemouth	Tr	02/47	46-47	17	-	1

DICKINS Matthew James (Matt)
Born: Sheffield, England, 3 September, 1970 — G

League Club	Source	Date Signed	Seasons Played	Apps	Subs	Gls
Sheffield U	YT	07/89				
Lincoln C	Tr	02/91	90-91	27	0	0
Blackburn Rov	Tr	03/92	91	1	0	0
Blackpool	L	01/93	92	19	0	0
Rochdale	L	10/94	94	4	0	0
Stockport Co	Tr	02/95	94-95	12	1	0

DICKINSON Carl Matthew
Born: Swadlincote, Derbyshire, England, 31 March, 1987 — LB

League Club	Source	Date Signed	Seasons Played	Apps	Subs	Gls
Stoke C	Sch	06/06	04-08	31	20	0
Blackpool	L	10/06	06	7	0	0
Leeds U	L	01/09	08	7	0	0
Barnsley	L	09/09	09	27	1	1
Portsmouth	L	08/10	10	23	13	0
Watford	Tr	07/11	11-12	40	3	2
Portsmouth	L	10/12	12	6	0	0
Coventry C	L	02/13	12	6	0	0
Port Vale	Tr	07/13	13-14	83	0	1

DICKINSON Christopher Neil (Chris)
Born: Stockton-on-Tees, Cleveland, England, 4 November, 1994 — F

League Club	Source	Date Signed	Seasons Played	Apps	Subs	Gls
York C	Sch	07/13	13	0	2	0

DICKINSON James Arthur (Jimmy)
Born: South Elmsall, West Yorkshire, England, 26 September, 1931 — RB
Died: Pontefract, West Yorkshire, England, 6 December, 2002

League Club	Source	Date Signed	Seasons Played	Apps	Subs	Gls
Barrow	Pontefract	08/51	51-57	67	-	0

DICKINSON James William (Jimmy)
Born: Alton, Hampshire, England, 24 April, 1925 — LH
Died: Alton, Hampshire, England, 9 November, 1982
England: 48/B-3/FLge-11

League Club	Source	Date Signed	Seasons Played	Apps	Subs	Gls
Portsmouth	Jnr	01/44	46-64	764	-	9

DICKINSON Leonard (Len)
Born: South Elmsall, West Yorkshire, England, 6 March, 1942 — IF

League Club	Source	Date Signed	Seasons Played	Apps	Subs	Gls
Sheffield Wed	Jnr	02/60				
Oldham Ath	Tr	06/61	61	5	-	2

DICKINSON Liam Michael
Born: Salford, England, 4 October, 1985 — F

League Club	Source	Date Signed	Seasons Played	Apps	Subs	Gls
Stockport Co	Woodley Sports	12/05	05-07	57	37	33
Derby Co	Tr	07/08				
Huddersfield T	L	08/08	08	13	0	6
Blackpool	L	11/08	08	5	2	4
Leeds U	L	03/09	08	4	4	0
Brighton & HA	Tr	07/09	09	17	10	4
Peterborough U	L	02/10	09	9	0	3
Barnsley	Tr	07/10	10	0	3	0
Walsall	L	11/10	10	2	2	0
Rochdale	L	01/11	10	7	7	0
Southend U	Tr	07/11	11	28	2	10

DICKINSON Martin John
Born: Leeds, England, 14 March, 1963 — CD

League Club	Source	Date Signed	Seasons Played	Apps	Subs	Gls
Leeds U	App	05/80	79-85	100	3	2
West Bromwich A	Tr	02/86	85-87	46	4	2
Sheffield U	Tr	07/88	88	0	1	0

DICKINSON Michael James (Mike)
Born: Newcastle-upon-Tyne, England, 4 May, 1984 — F

League Club	Source	Date Signed	Seasons Played	Apps	Subs	Gls
Carlisle U	Sch	07/02	01	0	1	0

DICKINSON Patrick James
Born: Vancouver, Canada, 6 May, 1978 — M

League Club	Source	Date Signed	Seasons Played	Apps	Subs	Gls
Hull C	YT	07/97	96-97	2	2	0

DICKINSON Ronald Arthur (Ron)
Born: Coventry, England, 29 June, 1930 — CH

League Club	Source	Date Signed	Seasons Played	Apps	Subs	Gls
Shrewsbury T (Am)	Nuneaton Bor	05/53	53	11	-	0
Coventry C	Tr	06/54				

DICKMAN Jonjo
Born: Hexham, Northumberland, England, 22 September, 1981 — M

League Club	Source	Date Signed	Seasons Played	Apps	Subs	Gls
Sunderland	Jnr	11/98	02	0	1	0
York C	L	02/04	03	2	0	0
Darlington	Tr	02/05	04-05	43	3	3

DICKO Nouha
Born: Paris, France, 14 May, 1992 — F

League Club	Source	Date Signed	Seasons Played	Apps	Subs	Gls
Wigan Ath	Strasbourg Jnrs (FRA)	08/11				
Blackpool	L	01/12	11	4	6	4
Blackpool	L	08/12	12	2	20	5
Wolverhampton W	L	03/13	12	1	3	1
Rotherham U	L	11/13	13	4	1	5
Wolverhampton W	Tr	01/14	13-14	46	10	27

DICKOV Paul
Born: Livingston, West Lothian, Scotland, 1 November, 1972 — F
Scotland: 10/U21-4/Youth/Schools

League Club	Source	Date Signed	Seasons Played	Apps	Subs	Gls
Arsenal	YT	12/90	92-96	6	15	3
Luton T	L	10/93	93	8	7	1
Brighton & HA	L	03/94	93	8	0	5
Manchester C	Tr	08/96	96-01	105	51	33
Leicester C	Tr	02/02	01-03	81	8	32
Blackburn Rov	Tr	06/04	04-05	44	6	14
Manchester C	Tr	07/06	06	9	7	0
Crystal Palace	L	08/07	07	6	3	0
Blackpool	L	01/08	07	7	4	0
Leicester C	Tr	08/08	08	4	17	2
Derby Co	Tr	08/09	09	10	6	2
Leeds U	L	03/10	09	1	3	0
Oldham Ath	Tr	07/10	10	0	2	0

DICKS Alan Victor
Born: Kennington, S London, England, 29 August, 1934 — CH

League Club	Source	Date Signed	Seasons Played	Apps	Subs	Gls
Chelsea	Jnr	09/51	52-57	33	-	1
Southend U	Tr	11/58	58-61	85	-	2

DICKS Julian Andrew
Born: Bristol, England, 8 August, 1968 — LB
England: B-2/U21-4

League Club	Source	Date Signed	Seasons Played	Apps	Subs	Gls
Birmingham C	App	04/86	85-87	83	6	1
West Ham U	Tr	03/88	87-93	159	0	29
Liverpool	Tr	09/93	93	24	0	3
West Ham U	Tr	10/94	94-98	103	0	21

League Club	Source	Date Signed	Seasons Played	Career Record Apps	Subs	Gls

DICKS Ronald William (Ronnie)
Born: Kennington, S London, England, 13 April, 1924 — LH
Died: Middlesbrough, England, 30 January, 2004

League Club	Source	Date Signed	Seasons Played	Apps	Subs	Gls
Middlesbrough	Dulwich Hamlet	05/43	47-58	316	-	10

DICKSON Adam
Born: Hamilton, Lanarkshire, Scotland, 4 January, 1929 — G
Died: Leicester, England, November, 2006

League Club	Source	Date Signed	Seasons Played	Apps	Subs	Gls
Leicester C	Thorniewood U	06/51	51-54	16	-	0

DICKSON Chris Alexander Kofi
Born: Plumstead, SE London, England, 28 December, 1984 — F
Ghana: 2

League Club	Source	Date Signed	Seasons Played	Apps	Subs	Gls
Charlton Ath	Dulwich Hamlet	03/07	07-09	7	21	0
Crewe Alex	L	08/07	07	2	1	0
Gillingham	L	09/07	07	9	3	7
Bristol Rov	L	09/09	09	10	4	4
Gillingham	L	02/10	09	4	5	1
Dagenham & Red	Shanghai Dongya (CHN)	10/13	13	3	22	1

DICKSON Hugh Robinson
Born: Downpatrick, Northern Ireland, 28 August, 1981 — CD
Northern Ireland: U21

League Club	Source	Date Signed	Seasons Played	Apps	Subs	Gls
Wigan Ath	Glentoran	08/00	00	0	1	0

DICKSON Joseph James March (Joe)
Born: Liverpool, England, 31 January, 1934 — IF
Died: 1990
England: Youth

League Club	Source	Date Signed	Seasons Played	Apps	Subs	Gls
Liverpool	Jnr	06/52	55	6	-	3

DICKSON Ryan Anthony
Born: Saltash, Cornwall, England, 14 December, 1986 — LB

League Club	Source	Date Signed	Seasons Played	Apps	Subs	Gls
Plymouth Arg	Sch	07/05	04-06	2	3	0
Torquay U	L	01/07	06	7	2	1
Brentford	Tr	11/07	07-09	87	10	3
Southampton	Tr	07/10	10	15	8	1
Yeovil T	L	01/12	11	5	0	1
Leyton Orient	L	02/12	11	9	0	0
Bradford C	L	01/13	12	3	2	1
Colchester U	Tr	07/13	13	28	4	0
Crawley T	Tr	06/14	14	30	2	1

DICKSON William (Bill)
Born: Lurgan, Armagh, Northern Ireland, 15 April, 1923 — WH
Died: Lurgan, Armagh, Northern Ireland, June, 2002
Northern Ireland: 12

League Club	Source	Date Signed	Seasons Played	Apps	Subs	Gls
Notts Co	Glenavon	11/45	46-47	21	-	2
Chelsea	Tr	11/47	47-52	101	-	4
Arsenal	Tr	10/53	53-55	29	-	1
Mansfield T	Tr	07/56	56	19	-	0

[DIEGO COSTA] COSTA DA SILVA Diego
Born: Lagarto, Sergipe, Brazil, 7 October, 1988 — F
Brazil: 2//Spain: 7

League Club	Source	Date Signed	Seasons Played	Apps	Subs	Gls
Chelsea	Atletico Madrid (SPN)	07/14	14	24	2	20

DIELNA Claude Pierre Marie
Born: Paris, France, 14 December, 1987 — D

League Club	Source	Date Signed	Seasons Played	Apps	Subs	Gls
Sheffield Wed	Olympiakos (GRE)	08/14	14	14	9	1

DIELNA Joel David Lionel
Born: Sainte-Rose, Guadeloupe, 27 December, 1990 — FB

League Club	Source	Date Signed	Seasons Played	Apps	Subs	Gls
Blackpool	Vannes OC (FRA)	08/14	14	1	1	0

DIENG Timothee
Born: Grenoble, France, 9 April, 1992 — CD/M

League Club	Source	Date Signed	Seasons Played	Apps	Subs	Gls
Oldham Ath	Stade Brest (FRA)	07/14	14	15	7	0

DIER Eric Jeremy Edgar
Born: Cheltenham, Gloucestershire, England, 15 January, 1994 — D
England: U21-9/Youth

League Club	Source	Date Signed	Seasons Played	Apps	Subs	Gls
Tottenham H	Sporting Lisbon (POR)	08/14	14	25	3	2

DIESERUVWE Emmanuel Aghogo Oluwafemi
Born: Bradford, England, 20 February, 1995 — F

League Club	Source	Date Signed	Seasons Played	Apps	Subs	Gls
Sheffield Wed	Sch	04/13				
Fleetwood T	L	11/13	13	0	4	0
Chesterfield	Tr	01/15	14	0	9	0

DIGARD Didier Frederic
Born: Lyon, France, 12 July, 1986 — M
France: U21-4

League Club	Source	Date Signed	Seasons Played	Apps	Subs	Gls
Middlesbrough	Paris St-Germain (FRA)	07/08	08-09	19	13	0

DIGBY Derek Francis
Born: Teignmouth, Devon, England, 14 May, 1931 — W
Died: Ledbury, Herefordshire, England, 27 September, 2005

League Club	Source	Date Signed	Seasons Played	Apps	Subs	Gls
Exeter C	Dawlish T	08/49	51-52	31	-	2
Southampton	Tr	09/53	53-54	15	-	2

DIGBY Fraser Charles
Born: Sheffield, England, 23 April, 1967 — G
England: U21-5/Youth/Schools

League Club	Source	Date Signed	Seasons Played	Apps	Subs	Gls
Manchester U	App	04/85				
Swindon T	Tr	09/86	86-97	417	0	0
Crystal Palace	Tr	08/98	98-99	56	0	0
Huddersfield T	Barry T	08/01				
Queens Park Rgrs	Tr	10/01	01-02	20	2	0
Kidderminster Hrs	Tr	01/03	02	11	0	0

DIGBY Paul Andrew
Born: Rotherham, South Yorkshire, England, 2 February, 1995 — M

League Club	Source	Date Signed	Seasons Played	Apps	Subs	Gls
Barnsley	Sch	08/12	11-14	9	11	0

DIGHTON Richard Anthony (Dick)
Born: Corby, Northamptonshire, England, 26 July, 1951 — G

League Club	Source	Date Signed	Seasons Played	Apps	Subs	Gls
Peterborough U	Coventry C (App)	11/69	70-71	8	0	0
Stockport Co	L	10/70	70	1	0	0

DIGNAM Joseph Colquhoun (Joe)
Born: Glasgow, Scotland, 10 January, 1931 — IF
Died: Glasgow, Scotland, 7 July, 1999

League Club	Source	Date Signed	Seasons Played	Apps	Subs	Gls
Wrexham	Alloa Ath	07/57	57	8	-	0

DIGWEED Perry Michael
Born: Westminster, Central London, England, 26 October, 1959 — G

League Club	Source	Date Signed	Seasons Played	Apps	Subs	Gls
Fulham	App	08/77	76-80	15	0	0
Brighton & HA	Tr	01/81	80-92	179	0	0
Chelsea	L	02/88	87	3	0	0
Wimbledon	Tr	08/93				
Watford	Tr	12/93	93-94	28	1	0

DIJKSTRA Meindert
Born: Eindhoven, Netherlands, 28 February, 1967 — RB

League Club	Source	Date Signed	Seasons Played	Apps	Subs	Gls
Notts Co	Willem II (NED)	08/92	92-93	27	2	1

DIJKSTRA Sybrandus Johannes Andreas (Sieb)
Born: Kerkrade, Netherlands, 20 October, 1966 — G

League Club	Source	Date Signed	Seasons Played	Apps	Subs	Gls
Queens Park Rgrs	Motherwell	07/94	94	11	0	0
Bristol C	L	09/95	95	8	0	0
Wycombe W	L	03/96	95	13	0	0

DIKABA Rodrigue
Born: Toulouse, France, 28 October, 1985 — D
DR Congo: 11

League Club	Source	Date Signed	Seasons Played	Apps	Subs	Gls
Oldham Ath	FC Ceahloul PN (ROM)	08/10	10	1	0	0

DIKGACOI Kagisho Evidence
Born: Brandfort, South Africa, 24 November, 1984 — DM
South Africa: 54

League Club	Source	Date Signed	Seasons Played	Apps	Subs	Gls
Fulham	Golden Arrows (RSA)	08/09	09-10	7	6	0
Crystal Palace	L	02/11	10	13	0	1
Crystal Palace	Tr	08/11	11-13	88	4	6
Cardiff C	Tr	06/14	14	1	1	0

DI LELLA Gustavo Martin
Born: Buenos Aires, Argentina, 6 October, 1973 — M/F

League Club	Source	Date Signed	Seasons Played	Apps	Subs	Gls
Darlington	Blyth Spartans	12/97	97	0	5	0
Hartlepool U	Blyth Spartans	03/98	97-99	22	9	4

DILLON Andrew (Andy)
Born: Caerphilly, Wales, 20 January, 1969 — G

League Club	Source	Date Signed	Seasons Played	Apps	Subs	Gls
Newport Co	YT	07/87	86-87	15	0	0

DILLON Daniel Martin
Born: Hillingdon, W London, England, 6 September, 1986 — M

League Club	Source	Date Signed	Seasons Played	Apps	Subs	Gls
Carlisle U	Sch	07/05	02	0	1	0

DILLON John
Born: Coatbridge, Lanarkshire, Scotland, 9 November, 1942 — LW

League Club	Source	Date Signed	Seasons Played	Apps	Subs	Gls
Sunderland	Jnr	11/59	60-61	18	-	1
Brighton & HA	Tr	07/62	62	21	-	3
Crewe Alex	Tr	07/63	63	5	-	1

DILLON Kevin Paul
Born: Sunderland, England, 18 December, 1959 — M
England: U21-1/Youth

League Club	Source	Date Signed	Seasons Played	Apps	Subs	Gls
Birmingham C	App	07/77	77-82	181	5	15
Portsmouth	Tr	03/83	82-88	206	9	45
Newcastle U	Tr	07/89	89-90	62	0	0
Reading	Tr	07/91	91-93	100	1	4

DILLON Michael Leslie (Mike)
Born: Highgate, N London, England, 29 September, 1952 — CD
England: Youth/Schools

League Club	Source	Date Signed	Seasons Played	Apps	Subs	Gls
Tottenham H	App	12/69	72-73	21	3	1
Millwall	L	12/74	74	4	0	0
Swindon T	L	03/75	74	7	2	0

DILLON Paul William
Born: Limerick, Republic of Ireland, 22 October, 1978 CD
Republic of Ireland: U21-1/Youth

League Club	Source	Date Signed	Seasons Played	Apps	Subs	Gls
Rotherham U	YT	03/97	96-99	65	5	2

DILLON Vincent (Vince)
Born: Manchester, England, 2 October, 1923 CF
Died: Truro, Cornwall, England, September, 2005

League Club	Source	Date Signed	Seasons Played	Apps	Subs	Gls
Bolton W		04/48	47-50	17	-	2
Tranmere Rov	Tr	02/51	50-52	34	-	17

DILLSWORTH Edward (Eddie)
Born: Freetown, Sierra Leone, 16 April, 1946 WH

League Club	Source	Date Signed	Seasons Played	Apps	Subs	Gls
Lincoln C (Am)	Wealdstone	03/67	66	2	0	0

DIMAIO Connor James
Born: Chesterfield, Derbyshire, England, 28 January, 1996 M
Republic of Ireland: Youth

League Club	Source	Date Signed	Seasons Played	Apps	Subs	Gls
Sheffield U	Sch	-	13	2	1	0

DI MARIA Angel Fabian
Born: Rosario, Argentina, 14 February, 1988 M/W
Argentina: 65/U23-6/Youth

League Club	Source	Date Signed	Seasons Played	Apps	Subs	Gls
Manchester U	Real Madrid (SPN)	08/14	14	20	7	3

DI MATTEO Roberto
Born: Schaffhausen, Switzerland, 29 May, 1970 M
Italy: 34

League Club	Source	Date Signed	Seasons Played	Apps	Subs	Gls
Chelsea	SS Lazio (ITA)	07/96	96-00	108	11	15

DIMECH Luke Anthony
Born: Floriana, Malta, 11 January, 1977 CD
Malta: 56

League Club	Source	Date Signed	Seasons Played	Apps	Subs	Gls
Mansfield T	Shamrock Rov (ROI)	08/03	03-04	36	9	1
Chester C	Tr	07/05	05	27	3	0
Macclesfield T	Marsaxlokk (MLT)	07/07	07	23	3	0

DI MICHELE David
Born: Rome, Italy, 6 January, 1976 F
Italy: 6

League Club	Source	Date Signed	Seasons Played	Apps	Subs	Gls
West Ham U (L)	Torino (ITA)	09/08	08	22	8	4

DIMMER Hyam
Born: Glasgow, Scotland, 14 March, 1914 IF
Died: Daventry, Northamptonshire, England, June, 1990

League Club	Source	Date Signed	Seasons Played	Apps	Subs	Gls
Aldershot	Ayr U	08/46	46	7	-	1
Bristol C	Tr	05/47	47	1	-	0

DIMOND Stuart
Born: Chorlton, Greater Manchester, England, 3 January, 1920 CF
Died: Manchester, England, November, 2004

League Club	Source	Date Signed	Seasons Played	Apps	Subs	Gls
Manchester U		12/42				
Bradford C	Tr	11/45	46	9	-	1

DINDANE Aruna
Born: Abidjan, Ivory Coast, 26 November, 1980 F
Ivory Coast: 67

League Club	Source	Date Signed	Seasons Played	Apps	Subs	Gls
Portsmouth (L)	RC Lens (FRA)	09/09	09	18	1	8
Crystal Palace	Al Sailiya (QAT)	03/13				

DINE John McQuade
Born: Newton Stewart, Dumfries & Galloway, Scotland, 3 May, 1940 G
Died: Southend-on-Sea, England, January, 2006

League Club	Source	Date Signed	Seasons Played	Apps	Subs	Gls
Bradford Park Ave	Bulford U	08/62	62-64	32	-	0

DINEEN Jack Anthony
Born: Brighton, England, 29 September, 1970 M

League Club	Source	Date Signed	Seasons Played	Apps	Subs	Gls
Brighton & HA	YT	09/87				
Scarborough	Crawley T	01/94	93	1	1	0

DINGWALL William Norman (Norman)
Born: Gateshead, Tyne and Wear, England, 29 July, 1923 WH
Died: Sheffield, England, 22 June, 2009

League Club	Source	Date Signed	Seasons Played	Apps	Subs	Gls
Sheffield U		03/46				
Halifax T	Tr	07/47	47	9	-	0

DINNING Tony
Born: Wallsend, Tyne and Wear, England, 12 April, 1975 M

League Club	Source	Date Signed	Seasons Played	Apps	Subs	Gls
Newcastle U	YT	10/93				
Stockport Co	Tr	06/94	94-00	159	32	25
Wolverhampton W	Tr	09/00	00-01	35	0	6
Wigan Ath	Tr	09/01	01-03	79	5	12
Stoke C	L	03/02	01	5	0	0
Walsall	L	11/03	03	2	3	0
Blackpool	L	01/04	03	10	0	3
Ipswich T	L	08/04	04	3	4	0
Bristol C	Tr	10/04	04	15	4	0
Port Vale	Tr	03/05	04-05	40	2	5
Stockport Co	Tr	06/06	06	27	5	2
Chester C	Tr	10/07	07-08	23	1	2

DINSDALE Peter
Born: Bradford, England, 19 October, 1938 LH
Died: British Columbia, Canada, 5 June, 2004

League Club	Source	Date Signed	Seasons Played	Apps	Subs	Gls
Huddersfield T	Yorkshire Amats	01/56	59-66	213	1	8
Bradford Park Ave	Tr	08/67	67	9	0	0

DIOMEDE Bernard
Born: Bourges, France, 23 January, 1974 W
France: 8

League Club	Source	Date Signed	Seasons Played	Apps	Subs	Gls
Liverpool	AJ Auxerre (FRA)	07/00	00	1	1	0

DIOP Pape Bouba
Born: Dakar, Senegal, 28 January, 1978 M
Senegal: 63

League Club	Source	Date Signed	Seasons Played	Apps	Subs	Gls
Fulham	RC Lens (FRA)	07/04	04-07	70	6	8
Portsmouth	Tr	08/07	07-09	49	4	0
West Ham U	AEK Athens (GRE)	08/11	11	14	2	1
Birmingham C	Tr	10/12	12	1	1	1

DIOP Pape Seydou
Born: Dakar, Senegal, 12 January, 1979 FB
Senegal: 3

League Club	Source	Date Signed	Seasons Played	Apps	Subs	Gls
Norwich C (L)	RC Lens (FRA)	08/99	99	2	5	0

DIOP Serigne Mor
Born: Paris, France, 29 September, 1988 F

League Club	Source	Date Signed	Seasons Played	Apps	Subs	Gls
Darlington	Ibiza (SPN)	10/09	09	18	5	2

DIOP Youssouph (Youssou)
Born: Ziguinchor, Senegal, 5 May, 1980 M

League Club	Source	Date Signed	Seasons Played	Apps	Subs	Gls
Kidderminster Hrs	Albi (FRA)	07/04	04	7	3	0

DIOUF El Hadji Ousseynou
Born: Dakar, Senegal, 15 January, 1981 W/F
Senegal: 69

League Club	Source	Date Signed	Seasons Played	Apps	Subs	Gls
Liverpool	RC Lens (FRA)	07/02	02-03	41	14	3
Bolton W	Tr	08/04	04-07	102	12	21
Sunderland	Tr	07/08	08	11	3	0
Blackburn Rov	Tr	01/09	08-10	55	5	4
Doncaster Rov	West Ham U (NC)	10/11	11	22	0	6
Leeds U	Tr	08/12	12-13	30	12	5

DIOUF Mame Biram (Biram)
Born: Dakar, Senegal, 16 December, 1987 F
Senegal: 24

League Club	Source	Date Signed	Seasons Played	Apps	Subs	Gls
Manchester U	Molde FK (NOR)	08/09	09	0	5	1
Blackburn Rov	L	08/10	10	17	9	3
Stoke C	Hannover 96 (GER)	07/14	14	28	6	11

DI PIEDI Michele
Born: Palermo, Sicily, Italy, 4 December, 1980 F

League Club	Source	Date Signed	Seasons Played	Apps	Subs	Gls
Sheffield Wed	Perugia (ITA)	08/00	00-02	9	30	5
Bristol Rov	L	02/03	02	3	2	0
Doncaster Rov	Gela (ITA)	08/06	06	1	2	0

DI SANTO Franco Matias
Born: Mendoza, Argentina, 7 April, 1989 F
Argentina: 3/Youth

League Club	Source	Date Signed	Seasons Played	Apps	Subs	Gls
Chelsea	Audax Italiana (CHL)	01/08	08	0	8	0
Blackburn Rov	L	08/09	09	15	7	1
Wigan Ath	Tr	08/10	10-12	57	35	13

DISLEY Craig Edward
Born: Worksop, Nottinghamshire, England, 24 August, 1981 M

League Club	Source	Date Signed	Seasons Played	Apps	Subs	Gls
Mansfield T	YT	06/99	99-03	106	35	16
Bristol Rov	Tr	07/04	04-08	171	32	25
Shrewsbury T	Tr	07/09	09-10	38	4	3

DISLEY Martin
Born: Ormskirk, Lancashire, England, 24 June, 1971 F

League Club	Source	Date Signed	Seasons Played	Apps	Subs	Gls
Crewe Alex	YT	09/89	89-91	0	2	0

DISTIN Sylvain
Born: Paris, France, 16 December, 1977 CD

League Club	Source	Date Signed	Seasons Played	Apps	Subs	Gls
Newcastle U (L)	Paris St-Germain (FRA)	09/01	01	20	8	0
Manchester C	Paris St-Germain (FRA)	07/02	02-06	178	0	5
Portsmouth	Tr	05/07	07-09	77	0	0
Everton	Tr	08/09	09-14	167	7	2

DITCHBURN Edwin George (Ted)
Born: Gillingham, Kent, England, 24 October, 1921 G
Died: Ipswich, England, 26 December, 2005
England: 6/B-2/FLge-6/War-2

League Club	Source	Date Signed	Seasons Played	Apps	Subs	Gls
Tottenham H	Jnr	05/39	46-58	418	-	0

DIUK Wayne John
Born: Nottingham, England, 26 May, 1980 M

League Club	Source	Date Signed	Seasons Played	Apps	Subs	Gls
Notts Co	YT	07/98	96-97	0	2	0

DIVERS John
Born: Clydebank, Dunbartonshire, Scotland, 6 August, 1911 — IF
Died: Glasgow, Scotland, 8 June, 1984
Scotland: 1

League Club	Source	Date Signed	Seasons Played	Apps	Subs	Gls
Oldham Ath	Greenock Morton	08/47	47	1	-	0

DIVERS John Rice
Born: Glasgow, Scotland, 24 November, 1931 — LW
Died: Glasgow, Scotland, 9 November, 2005

League Club	Source	Date Signed	Seasons Played	Apps	Subs	Gls
Exeter C	Clyde	05/56	56	12	-	1

DIX Richard
Born: South Shields, Tyne and Wear, England, 17 January, 1924 — LW
Died: Leeds, England, 2 July, 1990

League Club	Source	Date Signed	Seasons Played	Apps	Subs	Gls
Bradford Park Ave	North Shields	08/44	46-47	18	-	5
Bradford C	King's Lynn	08/52	52	8	-	1

DIX Ronald William (Ronnie)
Born: Bristol, England, 5 September, 1912 — IF
Died: Bristol, England, 2 April, 1998
England: 1/FLge-1/Schools

League Club	Source	Date Signed	Seasons Played	Apps	Subs	Gls
Bristol Rov	Jnr	02/28	27-31	100	-	33
Blackburn Rov	Tr	05/32	32	38	-	14
Aston Villa	Tr	05/33	32-36	97	-	30
Derby Co	Tr	02/37	36-38	94	-	35
Tottenham H	Tr	06/39	46-47	36	-	5
Reading	Tr	11/47	47-48	44	-	13

DIXEY Richard
Born: Wigston, Leicestershire, England, 2 September, 1956 — CD

League Club	Source	Date Signed	Seasons Played	Apps	Subs	Gls
Burnley	Enderby T	12/74	74	3	0	0
Stockport Co	L	02/76	75	14	0	1

DIXON Andrew (Andy)
Born: Louth, Lincolnshire, England, 19 April, 1968 — RB

League Club	Source	Date Signed	Seasons Played	Apps	Subs	Gls
Grimsby T	App	05/86	86-88	35	3	0
Southend U	Tr	08/89	89	24	0	0

DIXON Andrew Paul (Andy)
Born: Hartlepool, Cleveland, England, 5 August, 1968 — F

League Club	Source	Date Signed	Seasons Played	Apps	Subs	Gls
Hartlepool U	Seaton Holy Trinity	07/87	86-87	7	7	1
Hartlepool U	RAEC Mons (BEL)	11/95	95	3	0	0

DIXON Arthur
Born: Middleton, Greater Manchester, England, 17 November, 1921 — IF
Died: Glasgow, Scotland, 3 May, 2006

League Club	Source	Date Signed	Seasons Played	Apps	Subs	Gls
Northampton T	Heart of Midlothian	11/49	49-51	68	-	21
Leicester C	Tr	10/51	51-52	11	-	0

DIXON Benjamin Marcus Alexander (Ben)
Born: Lincoln, England, 16 September, 1974 — LB

League Club	Source	Date Signed	Seasons Played	Apps	Subs	Gls
Lincoln C	YT	11/92	91-95	33	10	0
Blackpool	Tr	07/96	96-97	9	9	0

DIXON Bohan Soloman Cheidu
Born: Liverpool, England, 17 October, 1989 — M

League Club	Source	Date Signed	Seasons Played	Apps	Subs	Gls
Accrington Stan	Burscough	07/12	12	1	5	0

DIXON Cecil Hubert
Born: Trowbridge, Wiltshire, England, 28 March, 1935 — RW

League Club	Source	Date Signed	Seasons Played	Apps	Subs	Gls
Cardiff C	Trowbridge T	07/54	54-56	21	-	1
Newport Co	Tr	07/57	57-60	108	-	16
Northampton T	Tr	08/61	61	15	-	4

DIXON Colin
Born: Newcastle-upon-Tyne, England, 24 September, 1963 — CD

League Club	Source	Date Signed	Seasons Played	Apps	Subs	Gls
Southampton	App	09/81				
Hartlepool U	Gateshead	11/83	83	1	0	0

DIXON John Thomas (Johnny)
Born: Hebburn, Tyne and Wear, England, 10 December, 1923 — IF
Died: Sutton Coldfield, West Midlands, England, 20 January, 2009

League Club	Source	Date Signed	Seasons Played	Apps	Subs	Gls
Aston Villa	Spennymoor U	01/46	46-60	392	-	132

DIXON John William (Johnny)
Born: Hartlepool, Cleveland, England, 12 March, 1934 — D
Died: Sunderland, England, December, 2014

League Club	Source	Date Signed	Seasons Played	Apps	Subs	Gls
Hartlepool U	Throston W	10/57	58-60	35	-	2

DIXON Jonathan James (Jonny)
Born: Murcia, Spain, 16 January, 1984 — F

League Club	Source	Date Signed	Seasons Played	Apps	Subs	Gls
Wycombe W	Sch	02/03	02-06	21	52	7
Brighton & HA	Aldershot T	01/08	07-08	2	3	0

DIXON Joseph (Joe)
Born: Newcastle-under-Lyme, Potteries, England, 24 September, 1915 — CF
Died: Newcastle-under-Lyme, Potteries, England, December, 2001

League Club	Source	Date Signed	Seasons Played	Apps	Subs	Gls
Northampton T	Audley U	04/45				
Port Vale	Tr	10/46	46	1	-	0

DIXON Kerry Michael
Born: Luton, England, 24 July, 1961 — F
England: 8/U21-1

League Club	Source	Date Signed	Seasons Played	Apps	Subs	Gls
Tottenham H	Chesham U	07/78				
Reading	Dunstable T	07/80	80-82	110	6	51
Chelsea	Tr	08/83	83-91	331	3	147
Southampton	Tr	07/92	92	8	1	2
Luton T	Tr	02/93	92-94	66	9	19
Millwall	Tr	03/95	94-95	24	7	9
Watford	Tr	01/96	95	8	3	0
Doncaster Rov	Tr	08/96	96	13	3	3

DIXON Kevin Lynton
Born: Consett, County Durham, England, 27 July, 1960 — W/F

League Club	Source	Date Signed	Seasons Played	Apps	Subs	Gls
Carlisle U	Tow Law T	08/83	83	5	4	0
Hartlepool U	L	10/83	83	6	0	3
Hartlepool U	Tr	08/84	84-86	103	4	26
Scunthorpe U	L	01/86	85	14	0	2
Scunthorpe U	Tr	08/87	87	37	4	4
Hartlepool U	Tr	06/88	88	14	0	4
York C	Tr	11/88	88-89	33	5	8
Scarborough	L	02/90	89	3	0	0

DIXON Kevin Robert
Born: Easington, County Durham, England, 27 June, 1980 — M
England: Youth

League Club	Source	Date Signed	Seasons Played	Apps	Subs	Gls
Leeds U	YT	07/97				
York C	L	08/99	99	3	0	0
Barnsley	Tr	07/01				

DIXON Kyle Anthony
Born: Nottingham, England, 20 December, 1994 — M

League Club	Source	Date Signed	Seasons Played	Apps	Subs	Gls
Notts Co	Sch	07/13	13	0	1	0

DIXON Lee Michael
Born: Manchester, England, 17 March, 1964 — RB
England: 22/B-4/FLge

League Club	Source	Date Signed	Seasons Played	Apps	Subs	Gls
Burnley	Jnr	07/82	82-83	4	0	0
Chester C	Tr	02/84	83-84	56	1	1
Bury	Tr	07/85	85	45	0	6
Stoke C	Tr	07/86	86-87	71	0	5
Arsenal	Tr	01/88	87-01	439	19	25

DIXON Michael (Mike)
Born: Willesden, NW London, England, 14 March, 1937 — CF

League Club	Source	Date Signed	Seasons Played	Apps	Subs	Gls
Luton T	Hitchin T	04/57	58-60	3	-	1
Coventry C	Tr	05/61	61	18	-	12

DIXON Michael George (Mike)
Born: Reading, England, 12 October, 1943 — G
Died: Hammersmith, W London, England, 30 January, 1993
England: Schools

League Club	Source	Date Signed	Seasons Played	Apps	Subs	Gls
Reading	Jnr	08/61	62-67	113	0	0
Aldershot	Tr	07/69	69-70	38	0	0

DIXON Milton
Born: Manchester, England, 30 March, 1925 — RW
Died: Tameside, Greater Manchester, England, June, 2008

League Club	Source	Date Signed	Seasons Played	Apps	Subs	Gls
Huddersfield T	Droylsden	02/48				
Stockport Co	Tr	10/50	50	21	-	2

DIXON Paul Andrew
Born: Aberdeen, Scotland, 22 November, 1986 — LB
Scotland: 3/U21-2

League Club	Source	Date Signed	Seasons Played	Apps	Subs	Gls
Huddersfield T	Dundee U	07/12	12-14	74	11	0

DIXON Paul Kenneth
Born: Derry, Northern Ireland, 22 February, 1960 — CD

League Club	Source	Date Signed	Seasons Played	Apps	Subs	Gls
Burnley	App	02/78	79-81	23	1	1

DIXON Raymond (Ray)
Born: Denaby, South Yorkshire, England, 31 December, 1930 — CF
Died: Mexborough, South Yorkshire, England, 10 April, 2008

League Club	Source	Date Signed	Seasons Played	Apps	Subs	Gls
Rotherham U	Denaby U	06/55	55-56	14	-	4

DIXON Robert
Born: Felling, Tyne and Wear, England, 11 January, 1936 — LW

League Club	Source	Date Signed	Seasons Played	Apps	Subs	Gls
Arsenal	Crook T	08/57				
Workington	Tr	11/58	58	28	-	5
West Bromwich A	Tr	05/59	59	7	-	1

DIXON Stanley (Stan)
Born: Burnley, Lancashire, England, 28 August, 1920 — CH
Died: Bournemouth, England, 26 July, 1996

League Club	Source	Date Signed	Seasons Played	Apps	Subs	Gls
Plymouth Arg	Hapton U	12/38	46-50	60	-	1

DIXON Terry Noel
Born: Holloway, N London, England, 15 January, 1990 — F
Republic of Ireland: Youth

League Club	Source	Date Signed	Seasons Played	Apps	Subs	Gls
Tottenham H	Sch	01/07				

League Club	Source	Date Signed	Seasons Played	Apps	Subs	Gls
West Ham U	Tr	02/09				
Stevenage		09/10	10	0	1	0
Bradford C	Tooting & Mitcham U	08/11				

DIXON Thomas Charles (Tommy)
Born: Newcastle-upon-Tyne, England, 8 June, 1929 — CF
Died: Watford, Hertfordshire, England, 6 February, 2014

League Club	Source	Date Signed	Seasons Played	Apps	Subs	Gls
West Ham U	Newcastle U (Am)	02/51	52-54	39	-	21
Reading	Tr	03/55	54-58	123	-	63
Brighton & HA	Tr	10/58	58-59	35	-	12
Workington	Tr	07/60	60-61	53	-	17
Barrow	Tr	10/61	61-62	62	-	23

DIXON Wilfred Edward (Will)
Born: Wood Green, N London, England, 20 February, 1950 — RB

League Club	Source	Date Signed	Seasons Played	Apps	Subs	Gls
Arsenal	App	02/68				
Reading	Tr	07/69	69-72	150	3	0
Colchester U	Tr	08/73				
Swindon T	Tr	09/73	73-76	134	6	10
Aldershot	Tr	07/77	77-79	114	6	6

D'JAFFO Laurent
Born: Bazas, Gironde, France, 5 November, 1970 — F
Benin: 3

League Club	Source	Date Signed	Seasons Played	Apps	Subs	Gls
Bury	Ayr U	07/98	98	35	2	8
Stockport Co	Tr	08/99	99	20	1	7
Sheffield U	Tr	02/00	99-01	45	24	11
Mansfield T	Aberdeen	03/04	03	4	4	1

DJE Ludovic
Born: Paris, France, 22 July, 1977 — D/F

League Club	Source	Date Signed	Seasons Played	Apps	Subs	Gls
Stockport Co	UT Arad (ROM)	03/05	04-05	7	3	0

DJEBBOUR Rafik Zoheir
Born: Grenoble, France, 8 March, 1984 — F
Algeria: 33

League Club	Source	Date Signed	Seasons Played	Apps	Subs	Gls
Nottingham F	Olympiakos (GRE)	01/14	13	3	4	1

DJEMBA-DJEMBA Eric Daniel
Born: Douala, Cameroon, 4 May, 1981 — M
Cameroon: 24

League Club	Source	Date Signed	Seasons Played	Apps	Subs	Gls
Manchester U	FC Nantes (FRA)	07/03	03-04	13	7	0
Aston Villa	Tr	01/05	04-06	4	7	0
Burnley	L	01/07	06	13	2	0

DJETOU Martin Okelo
Born: Abidjan, Ivory Coast, 15 December, 1974 — M/D
France: 6/B-2

League Club	Source	Date Signed	Seasons Played	Apps	Subs	Gls
Fulham (L)	Parma (ITA)	07/02	02	22	3	1
Fulham (L)	Parma (ITA)	07/03	03	19	7	0
Bolton W	Parma (ITA)	10/05	05	1	2	0

DJEZIRI Adda
Born: Copenhagen, Denmark, 3 August, 1988 — F

League Club	Source	Date Signed	Seasons Played	Apps	Subs	Gls
Blackpool	Viborg FF (DEN)	08/12				
Scunthorpe U	L	11/12	12	1	3	0

DJILALI Kieran Stephen Larbi
Born: Lambeth, S London, England, 22 January, 1991 — W

League Club	Source	Date Signed	Seasons Played	Apps	Subs	Gls
Crystal Palace	Sch	08/08	08-10	14	14	1
Chesterfield	L	11/09	09	8	0	1
Chesterfield	L	02/11	10	7	3	1
AFC Wimbledon	Tr	08/11	11	4	8	1
Portsmouth	Tr	08/12	12	1	0	0
AFC Wimbledon	Tr	11/12	12	0	5	0

DJORDJIC Bojan
Born: Belgrade, Yugoslavia, 6 February, 1982 — LW
Sweden: U21-9

League Club	Source	Date Signed	Seasons Played	Apps	Subs	Gls
Manchester U	Brommapojkarna (SWE)	02/99	00	0	1	0
Sheffield Wed	L	12/01	01	4	1	0
Plymouth Arg	Glasgow Rangers	07/05	05-07	18	22	4
Blackpool	Videoton (HUN)	07/11				

DJORKAEFF Youri
Born: Lyon, France, 9 March, 1968 — F
France: 82

League Club	Source	Date Signed	Seasons Played	Apps	Subs	Gls
Bolton W	Kaiserslautern (GER)	02/02	01-03	72	3	19
Blackburn Rov	Tr	09/04	04	3	0	0

DJOUROU Yohan Danon
Born: Abidjan, Ivory Coast, 18 January, 1987 — CD
Switzerland: 51/U21-2/Youth

League Club	Source	Date Signed	Seasons Played	Apps	Subs	Gls
Arsenal	Sch	08/04	05-11	72	14	1
Birmingham C	L	08/07	07	13	0	0

DJURICIC Filip
Born: Obrenovac, Serbia, 30 January, 1992 — M
Serbia: 22/U21-17

League Club	Source	Date Signed	Seasons Played	Apps	Subs	Gls
Southampton (L)	Benfica (POR)	02/15	14	3	6	0

D'LARYEA Jonathan Amar
Born: Manchester, England, 3 September, 1985 — DM
England: Semi Pro-2

League Club	Source	Date Signed	Seasons Played	Apps	Subs	Gls
Manchester C	Sch	07/03				
Mansfield T	Tr	10/05	05-07	89	6	1

D'LARYEA Nathan Amarkine
Born: Manchester, England, 3 September, 1985 — RB

League Club	Source	Date Signed	Seasons Played	Apps	Subs	Gls
Manchester C	Sch	07/03				
Macclesfield T	L	01/07	06	1	0	0
Rochdale	Tr	07/07	07	2	4	0

DMITROVIC Marko
Born: Subotica, Serbia, 24 January, 1992 — G
Serbia: U21-5/Youth

League Club	Source	Date Signed	Seasons Played	Apps	Subs	Gls
Charlton Ath	Ujpest (HUN)	01/15	14	4	1	0

DOANE Benjamin Nigel David (Ben)
Born: Sheffield, England, 22 December, 1979 — RB

League Club	Source	Date Signed	Seasons Played	Apps	Subs	Gls
Sheffield U	YT	07/98	99-02	19	4	1
Mansfield T	L	01/03	02	11	0	0

DOBBIE Harold
Born: Bishop Auckland, County Durham, England, 20 February, 1923 — CF
Died: Middlesbrough, England, July, 1988

League Club	Source	Date Signed	Seasons Played	Apps	Subs	Gls
Middlesbrough	South Bank St Peter's	12/46	46-49	23	-	6
Plymouth Arg	Tr	03/50	49-53	30	-	6
Torquay U	Tr	10/53	53-56	113	-	46

DOBBIE Stephen
Born: Glasgow, Scotland, 5 December, 1982 — F

League Club	Source	Date Signed	Seasons Played	Apps	Subs	Gls
Swansea C	Queen of the South	07/09	09-11	29	26	9
Blackpool	L	02/10	09	6	10	4
Blackpool	L	03/12	11	5	2	5
Brighton & HA	Tr	08/12	12	5	10	2
Crystal Palace	Tr	01/13	12-13	9	7	3
Blackpool	L	09/13	13	23	4	4
Fleetwood T	L	08/14	14	18	9	4

DOBBIN James (Jim)
Born: Dunfermline, Fife, Scotland, 17 September, 1963 — M
Scotland: Youth

League Club	Source	Date Signed	Seasons Played	Apps	Subs	Gls
Doncaster Rov	Glasgow Celtic	03/84	83-86	56	8	13
Barnsley	Tr	09/86	86-90	116	13	12
Grimsby T	Tr	07/91	91-95	154	10	21
Rotherham U	Tr	08/96	96	17	2	0
Doncaster Rov	Tr	08/97	97	28	3	0
Scarborough	Tr	03/98	97	1	0	0
Grimsby T	Tr	03/98	97-98	1	5	0

DOBBING Robert (Bobby)
Born: Sunderland, England, 27 June, 1949 — LB

League Club	Source	Date Signed	Seasons Played	Apps	Subs	Gls
Coventry C	App	06/67				
Hartlepool U	Tr	07/69	69	34	0	1

DOBBINS Lionel Wayne (Wayne)
Born: Bromsgrove, Worcestershire, England, 30 August, 1968 — FB/M

League Club	Source	Date Signed	Seasons Played	Apps	Subs	Gls
West Bromwich A	App	08/86	86-90	30	15	0
Torquay U	Tr	07/91	91	18	3	1

DOBBS Eric
Born: Hingham, Norfolk, England, 15 October, 1920 — FB
Died: Coventry, England, February, 2011

League Club	Source	Date Signed	Seasons Played	Apps	Subs	Gls
Coventry C	Miners Arms	08/46	46-47	5	-	0
Bristol Rov	Tr	07/48				

DOBBS Gerald Francis
Born: Lambeth, S London, England, 24 January, 1971 — M

League Club	Source	Date Signed	Seasons Played	Apps	Subs	Gls
Wimbledon	YT	07/89	91-93	21	12	1
Cardiff C	L	09/95	95	3	0	0

DOBIE Luke Jeffrey
Born: Ormskirk, Lancashire, England, 7 October, 1992 — M

League Club	Source	Date Signed	Seasons Played	Apps	Subs	Gls
Middlesbrough	Everton (Sch)	07/11				
Accrington Stan	L	10/11	11	0	4	0
Bristol C	Tr	10/12				
Wigan Ath		11/13				

DOBIE Mark Walter Graham
Born: Carlisle, Cumbria, England, 8 November, 1963 — F

League Club	Source	Date Signed	Seasons Played	Apps	Subs	Gls
Carlisle U	Workington	12/86	86	2	4	0
Cambridge U	Gretna	12/90				
Torquay U	Tr	08/91	91	18	2	2
Darlington	Tr	08/92	92	35	1	8

DOBIE Robert Scott (Scott)
Born: Workington, Cumbria, England, 10 October, 1978 — F
Scotland: 6

League Club	Source	Date Signed	Seasons Played	Apps	Subs	Gls
Carlisle U	YT	05/97	96-00	101	35	24
West Bromwich A	Tr	07/01	01-04	57	53	21

League Club	Source	Date Signed	Seasons Played	Apps	Subs	Gls
Millwall	Tr	11/04	04	15	1	3
Nottingham F	Tr	02/05	04-07	20	21	3
Carlisle U	Tr	01/08	07-09	43	41	12
Bradford C (L)	St Johnstone	01/11	10	8	5	0

DOBING Brian George
Born: Sheffield, England, 29 December, 1937 — G
Died: Whitchurch, Shropshire, England, 4 January, 1995

League Club	Source	Date Signed	Seasons Played	Apps	Subs	Gls
Crewe Alex	Knutsford	04/59	58	1	-	0

DOBING Peter Alan
Born: Manchester, England, 1 December, 1938 — IF
England: FLge-3/U23-7

League Club	Source	Date Signed	Seasons Played	Apps	Subs	Gls
Blackburn Rov	Jnr	12/55	56-60	179	-	88
Manchester C	Tr	07/61	61-62	82	-	31
Stoke C	Tr	08/63	63-72	303	4	82

DOBLE Ryan Alan
Born: Blaenavon, Torfaen, Wales, 1 February, 1991 — F
Wales: U21-10/Youth

League Club	Source	Date Signed	Seasons Played	Apps	Subs	Gls
Southampton	Sch	02/09				
Stockport Co	L	02/11	10	3	0	1
Oxford U	L	03/11	10	1	2	0
Bournemouth	L	08/11	11	4	3	0
Bury	L	01/12	11	3	2	0
Shrewsbury T	Tr	07/12	12	1	4	0

DOBSON Anthony John (Tony)
Born: Coventry, England, 5 February, 1969 — D
England: U21-4

League Club	Source	Date Signed	Seasons Played	Apps	Subs	Gls
Coventry C	App	07/86	86-90	51	3	1
Blackburn Rov	Tr	01/91	90-92	36	5	0
Portsmouth	Tr	09/93	93-96	48	5	2
Oxford U	L	12/94	94	5	0	0
Peterborough U	L	01/96	95	4	0	0
West Bromwich A	Tr	08/97	97	6	5	0
Gillingham	L	09/98	98	2	0	0
Northampton T	Tr	09/98	98-99	9	3	0

DOBSON Brian Ashley
Born: Colchester, Essex, England, 1 March, 1934 — CH

League Club	Source	Date Signed	Seasons Played	Apps	Subs	Gls
Colchester U	Colchester Casuals	01/56	55-59	24	-	0

DOBSON Colin
Born: Eston, Cleveland, England, 9 May, 1940 — LW/IF
England: U23-2

League Club	Source	Date Signed	Seasons Played	Apps	Subs	Gls
Sheffield Wed	Jnr	11/57	61-65	177	0	49
Huddersfield T	Tr	08/66	66-70	149	6	50
Brighton & HA	L	01/72	71	2	2	0
Bristol Rov	Tr	07/72	72-75	62	0	4

DOBSON Craig Gregory
Born: Chingford, NE London, England, 23 January, 1984 — W
Jamaica: 1

League Club	Source	Date Signed	Seasons Played	Apps	Subs	Gls
Cheltenham T	Crystal Palace (Sch)	07/03	03	0	2	0
MK Dons	Stevenage Bor	01/08	07	1	0	0
Brentford	Tr	03/09				
Barnet	Thurrock	11/10	10	0	1	0

DOBSON George Richard
Born: Chiswick, W London, England, 24 August, 1949 — RW
Died: Barton-on-Sea, Hampshire, England, 10 September, 2007

League Club	Source	Date Signed	Seasons Played	Apps	Subs	Gls
Brentford	App	08/67	66-69	75	11	10

DOBSON Ian
Born: Hull, England, 3 October, 1957 — CD

League Club	Source	Date Signed	Seasons Played	Apps	Subs	Gls
Hull C	App	10/75	75-79	86	6	7
Hereford U	Tr	06/80	80-81	41	0	5

DOBSON John Martin (Martin)
Born: Rishton, Lancashire, England, 14 February, 1948 — M
England: 5/FLge-1/Schools

League Club	Source	Date Signed	Seasons Played	Apps	Subs	Gls
Bolton W	Jnr	07/66				
Burnley	Tr	08/67	67-74	220	4	43
Everton	Tr	08/74	74-78	190	0	29
Burnley	Tr	08/79	79-83	186	0	20
Bury	Tr	03/84	83-85	60	1	4

DOBSON Michael William
Born: Isleworth, W London, England, 9 April, 1981 — RB/M

League Club	Source	Date Signed	Seasons Played	Apps	Subs	Gls
Brentford	YT	06/99	00-05	164	13	3
Reading	L	11/05	05	0	1	0
Walsall	Tr	07/06	06-07	60	3	4

DOBSON Paul
Born: Hartlepool, Cleveland, England, 17 December, 1962 — F

League Club	Source	Date Signed	Seasons Played	Apps	Subs	Gls
Hartlepool U	Newcastle U (Jnr)	11/81	81-82	23	8	8
Hartlepool U	Horden CW	12/83	83-85	60	20	24
Torquay U	Tr	07/86	86-87	63	14	38
Doncaster Rov	Tr	08/88	88	22	2	10
Scarborough	Tr	02/89	88-90	54	7	22
Halifax T	L	10/90	90	1	0	1
Hereford U	L	11/90	90	6	0	1
Lincoln C	Tr	01/91	90-91	13	8	5
Darlington	Tr	08/92	92	4	10	2

DOBSON Robert Peter (Peter)
Born: Frimley, Surrey, England, 13 June, 1925 — IF
Died: Cambridge, England, 5 February, 2008

League Club	Source	Date Signed	Seasons Played	Apps	Subs	Gls
Ipswich T	Wisbech T	10/49	49-53	30	-	5

DOBSON Ryan Adam
Born: Wellington, Telford & Wrekin, England, 24 September, 1978 — RB

League Club	Source	Date Signed	Seasons Played	Apps	Subs	Gls
Chester C	YT	07/97	97	6	0	0

DOBSON Warren Edward
Born: North Shields, Tyne and Wear, England, 5 November, 1978 — G

League Club	Source	Date Signed	Seasons Played	Apps	Subs	Gls
Hartlepool U	Queens Park Rgrs (YT)	08/97	97	1	0	0

DOCHERTY Bernard (Benny)
Born: Hamilton, Lanarkshire, Scotland, 11 August, 1941 — IF

League Club	Source	Date Signed	Seasons Played	Apps	Subs	Gls
Notts Co	Cowdenbeath	08/64	64	25	-	2

DOCHERTY James (Jim)
Born: Broxburn, West Lothian, Scotland, 8 November, 1956 — F

League Club	Source	Date Signed	Seasons Played	Apps	Subs	Gls
Chelsea	East Stirlingshire	03/79	78	2	1	0

DOCHERTY James (Jimmy)
Born: Clydebank, Dunbartonshire, Scotland, 22 April, 1929 — IF

League Club	Source	Date Signed	Seasons Played	Apps	Subs	Gls
Doncaster Rov	Airdrieonians	05/51	51	11	-	4
Crewe Alex	Limerick C (ROI)	02/57	56	2	-	0

DOCHERTY James (Jimmy)
Born: Greenock, Inverclyde, Scotland, 21 April, 1926 — IF
Died: Kettering, Northamptonshire, England, July, 2002

League Club	Source	Date Signed	Seasons Played	Apps	Subs	Gls
Plymouth Arg	Glasgow Celtic	05/50				
Northampton T	Tr	07/50	50	1	-	0

DOCHERTY John
Born: Glasgow, Scotland, 28 February, 1935 — LH

League Club	Source	Date Signed	Seasons Played	Apps	Subs	Gls
Colchester U	Heart of Midlothian	06/63	63-64	76	-	2

DOCHERTY John
Born: Glasgow, Scotland, 29 April, 1940 — RW

League Club	Source	Date Signed	Seasons Played	Apps	Subs	Gls
Brentford	St Roch's	07/59	60	17	-	2
Sheffield U	Tr	03/61	60-65	41	0	9
Brentford	Tr	12/65	65-67	97	0	31
Reading	Tr	02/68	67-69	45	1	8
Brentford	Tr	03/70	69-73	137	4	34
Queens Park Rgrs	Tr	07/74				

DOCHERTY Michael (Mike)
Born: Preston, Lancashire, England, 29 October, 1950 — RB
England: Youth

League Club	Source	Date Signed	Seasons Played	Apps	Subs	Gls
Burnley	App	11/67	68-75	149	4	0
Manchester C	Tr	04/76	75-76	8	0	0
Sunderland	Tr	12/76	76-78	72	1	6

DOCHERTY Peter
Born: Hebburn, Tyne and Wear, England, 14 February, 1929 — LW

League Club	Source	Date Signed	Seasons Played	Apps	Subs	Gls
Fulham		09/49				
Darlington	Tr	09/50	50	3	-	1

DOCHERTY Thomas (Tom)
Born: Penshaw, Tyne and Wear, England, 15 April, 1924 — LH/LW

League Club	Source	Date Signed	Seasons Played	Apps	Subs	Gls
Lincoln C	Murton CW	07/47	47-49	45	-	3
Norwich C	Tr	06/50	50-52	85	-	4
Reading	Tr	07/53	53-54	53	-	2
Newport Co	Tr	06/55	55-57	108	-	1

DOCHERTY Thomas Henderson (Tommy)
Born: Glasgow, Scotland, 24 August, 1928 — WH
Scotland: 25/B-2

League Club	Source	Date Signed	Seasons Played	Apps	Subs	Gls
Preston NE	Glasgow Celtic	11/49	49-57	323	-	5
Arsenal	Tr	08/58	58-60	83	-	1
Chelsea	Tr	09/61	61	4	-	0

DOCKER Ian
Born: Gravesend, Kent, England, 12 September, 1969 — M
England: Schools

League Club	Source	Date Signed	Seasons Played	Apps	Subs	Gls
Gillingham	YT	09/87	87-90	73	14	3

DOCKER John Barry
Born: Coventry, England, 25 September, 1947 — LW

League Club	Source	Date Signed	Seasons Played	Apps	Subs	Gls
Coventry C	Jnr	08/65				
Torquay U	L	07/67	67	4	1	0

DODD Alan
Born: Stoke-on-Trent, England, 20 September, 1953 — D
England: FLge-1/U23-6

League Club	Source	Date Signed	Seasons Played	Apps	Subs	Gls
Stoke C	App	10/70	72-82	349	9	3

League Club	Source	Date Signed	Seasons Played	Apps	Subs	Gls
Wolverhampton W	Tr	11/82	82-84	88	0	5
Stoke C	Tr	01/85	84	16	0	0
Port Vale	Elfsborg (SWE)	11/86	86	2	0	0

DODD Ashley Michael
Born: Stafford, England, 7 January, 1982 — M
England: Schools

League Club	Source	Date Signed	Seasons Played	Apps	Subs	Gls
Manchester U	YT	09/99				
Port Vale	Tr	03/01	00-01	8	4	1

DODD James Edward (Jim)
Born: Wallasey, Wirral, England, 12 December, 1933 — CF

League Club	Source	Date Signed	Seasons Played	Apps	Subs	Gls
Tranmere Rov	Upton	05/56	56-59	63	-	22

DODD Jason Robert
Born: Bath, England, 2 November, 1970 — RB
England: U21-8

League Club	Source	Date Signed	Seasons Played	Apps	Subs	Gls
Southampton	Bath C	03/89	89-04	371	27	9
Plymouth Arg	L	03/05	04	4	0	0
Brighton & HA	Tr	07/05	05	6	1	0

DODD William
Born: Bedlington, Northumberland, England, 30 September, 1936 — CF
Died: Burnley, Lancashire, England, 14 January, 2015

League Club	Source	Date Signed	Seasons Played	Apps	Subs	Gls
Burnley	Whitley Bay	02/56				
Workington	Tr	09/58	58	1	-	0

DODD William Dickinson (Billy)
Born: Chester-le-Street, County Durham, England, 25 August, 1933 — RB
Died: Shrewsbury, Shropshire, England, 25 September, 1982

League Club	Source	Date Signed	Seasons Played	Apps	Subs	Gls
Shrewsbury T	Derby Co (Am)	08/50	50-54	28	-	1
Southport	Banbury Spencer	06/57	57-58	70	-	2

DODDS Ephraim (Jock)
Born: Grangemouth, Falkirk, Scotland, 7 September, 1915 — CF
Died: Lytham St Annes, Lancashire, England, 23 February, 2007
Scotland: War-8

League Club	Source	Date Signed	Seasons Played	Apps	Subs	Gls
Huddersfield T	Medomsley Jnrs	02/33				
Lincoln C	Tr	03/33				
Sheffield U	Tr	05/34	34-38	178	-	114
Blackpool	Tr	03/39	38	12	-	10
Everton	Shamrock Rov (ROI)	11/46	46-48	55	-	36
Lincoln C	Tr	10/48	48-49	60	-	39

DODDS Gerald (Gerry)
Born: Sheffield, England, 4 January, 1935 — RW

League Club	Source	Date Signed	Seasons Played	Apps	Subs	Gls
Sheffield U	Jnr	02/52				
Chesterfield	Tr	06/55	55	4	-	0
Scunthorpe U	Salisbury C	05/59				

DODDS Leslie (Les)
Born: Newcastle-upon-Tyne, England, 12 October, 1936 — G
England: Schools

League Club	Source	Date Signed	Seasons Played	Apps	Subs	Gls
Sunderland	Jnr	10/53	54-55	6	-	0

DODDS Louis Bartholomew
Born: Sheffield, England, 8 October, 1986 — W/F

League Club	Source	Date Signed	Seasons Played	Apps	Subs	Gls
Leicester C	Sch	07/05				
Rochdale	L	02/07	06	6	6	2
Lincoln C	L	07/07	07	38	3	9
Port Vale	Tr	07/08	08-14	170	82	43

DODDS Robert
Born: Gateshead, Tyne and Wear, England, 1 July, 1923 — WH
Died: Darlington, County Durham, England, May, 2011

League Club	Source	Date Signed	Seasons Played	Apps	Subs	Gls
Darlington	Liverpool (Am)	02/47	46-48	35	-	1

DODDS Thomas Black (Tom)
Born: South Shields, Tyne and Wear, England, 20 December, 1918 — IF
Died: South Shields, Tyne and Wear, England, April, 1998

League Club	Source	Date Signed	Seasons Played	Apps	Subs	Gls
Aston Villa	North Shields	01/39	46	1	-	0
Swansea C	Tr	01/47	46-47	11	-	2

DODDS William (Billy)
Born: New Cumnock, Ayrshire, Scotland, 5 February, 1969 — F
Scotland: 26

League Club	Source	Date Signed	Seasons Played	Apps	Subs	Gls
Chelsea	App	05/86	86-88	0	3	0

DODGE William Charles (Bill)
Born: Hackney, E London, England, 10 March, 1937 — RH

League Club	Source	Date Signed	Seasons Played	Apps	Subs	Gls
Tottenham H	Eton Manor	10/57	58-59	6	-	0
Crystal Palace	Tr	07/62	62	3	-	0

DODGIN Norman
Born: Gateshead, Tyne and Wear, England, 1 November, 1921 — WH
Died: Peterborough, England, April, 2000

League Club	Source	Date Signed	Seasons Played	Apps	Subs	Gls
Newcastle U	Whitehall BC	08/40	47-49	84	-	1
Reading	Tr	06/50	50	13	-	1
Northampton T	Tr	09/51	51-52	19	-	1
Exeter C	Tr	08/53	53-54	33	-	1

DODGIN William (Bill)
Born: Wardley, Tyne and Wear, England, 4 November, 1931 — CH
Died: Woking, Surrey, England, June, 2000
England: U23-1

League Club	Source	Date Signed	Seasons Played	Apps	Subs	Gls
Fulham	Southampton (Am)	09/49	51-52	35	-	0
Arsenal	Tr	12/52	52-59	191	-	0
Fulham	Tr	03/61	60-63	69	-	0

DODSON David Alfred (Dave)
Born: Gravesend, Kent, England, 20 January, 1940 — LW
England: Youth

League Club	Source	Date Signed	Seasons Played	Apps	Subs	Gls
Arsenal	Jnr	11/57				
Swansea C	Tr	07/59	59-61	30	-	11
Portsmouth	Tr	12/61	61-64	53	-	15
Aldershot	Tr	01/65	64-66	59	0	12

DOE Scott Mark
Born: Reading, England, 6 November, 1988 — CD
England: Semi Pro-1

League Club	Source	Date Signed	Seasons Played	Apps	Subs	Gls
Dagenham & Red	Weymouth	03/09	09-14	240	3	11

DOHERTY Gary Michael Thomas
Born: Carndonagh, Donegal, Republic of Ireland, 31 January, 1980 — CD
Republic of Ireland: 34/U21-7/Youth

League Club	Source	Date Signed	Seasons Played	Apps	Subs	Gls
Luton T	YT	07/97	97-99	46	24	12
Tottenham H	Tr	04/00	99-04	45	19	4
Norwich C	Tr	08/04	04-09	192	10	11
Charlton Ath	Tr	07/10	10-11	35	6	0
Wycombe W	Tr	02/12	11-13	54	2	3

DOHERTY James Clarkson (Jim)
Born: Douglas, Lanarkshire, Scotland, 31 January, 1957 — F

League Club	Source	Date Signed	Seasons Played	Apps	Subs	Gls
Notts Co	Cumnock Jnrs	07/79	79-80	6	2	0

DOHERTY John Herbert
Born: Manchester, England, 12 March, 1935 — IF
Died: Heald Green, Greater Manchester, England, 13 November, 2007

League Club	Source	Date Signed	Seasons Played	Apps	Subs	Gls
Manchester U	Jnr	03/52	52-57	25	-	7
Leicester C	Tr	10/57	57	12	-	5

DOHERTY John Michael
Born: Stoneleigh, Surrey, England, 26 April, 1936 — CF

League Club	Source	Date Signed	Seasons Played	Apps	Subs	Gls
Fulham	Chelsea (Am)	09/54	56-61	49	-	7
Aldershot	South Coast U (AUS)	01/65	64-65	18	0	1

DOHERTY Joshua Edward (Josh)
Born: Newtownards, Down, Northern Ireland, 15 March, 1996 — M/FB
Northern Ireland: U21-1/Youth

League Club	Source	Date Signed	Seasons Played	Apps	Subs	Gls
Watford	Sch	06/14	13	0	1	0

DOHERTY Lee Joseph
Born: Camden, N London, England, 6 February, 1980 — CD

League Club	Source	Date Signed	Seasons Played	Apps	Subs	Gls
Charlton Ath	Arsenal (YT)	10/98				
Brighton & HA	Tr	03/99	98	3	0	0

DOHERTY Matthew James (Matt)
Born: Dublin, Republic of Ireland, 17 January, 1992 — RB
Republic of Ireland: U21-8/Youth

League Club	Source	Date Signed	Seasons Played	Apps	Subs	Gls
Wolverhampton W	Bohemians (ROI)	08/10	11-14	54	11	2
Bury	L	10/12	12	17	0	1

DOHERTY Michael (Mike)
Born: Liverpool, England, 8 March, 1961 — F
England: Semi Pro

League Club	Source	Date Signed	Seasons Played	Apps	Subs	Gls
Reading	Basingstoke T	10/82	82	23	2	5

DOHERTY Neil
Born: Barrow, Cumbria, England, 21 February, 1969 — LW

League Club	Source	Date Signed	Seasons Played	Apps	Subs	Gls
Watford	App	03/87				
Birmingham C	Barrow	02/94	93-95	15	8	2
Northampton T	L	02/96	95	3	6	1

DOHERTY Peter Dermont
Born: Magherafelt, Derry, Northern Ireland, 5 June, 1913 — IF
Died: Blackpool, Lancashire, England, 5 April, 1990
England: FLge-1//Northern Ireland: 16/War-2

League Club	Source	Date Signed	Seasons Played	Apps	Subs	Gls
Blackpool	Glentoran	11/33	33-35	83	-	28
Manchester C	Tr	02/36	35-38	119	-	74
Derby Co	Tr	12/45	46	15	-	7
Huddersfield T	Tr	12/46	46-48	83	-	33
Doncaster Rov	Tr	06/49	49-52	103	-	56

DOHERTY Sean Anthony
Born: Basingstoke, Hampshire, England, 10 May, 1985 — LW
England: Youth/Schools

League Club	Source	Date Signed	Seasons Played	Apps	Subs	Gls
Fulham	Sch	02/02				
Blackpool	L	09/03	03	0	1	0
Port Vale	ADO Den Haag (NED)	01/06	05	3	3	0
Accrington Stan	Tr	07/06	06	14	6	1

DOHERTY Thomas Edward (Tommy)
Born: Bristol, England, 17 March, 1979 — M
Northern Ireland: 9/B-1

League Club	Source	Date Signed	Seasons Played	Apps	Subs	Gls
Bristol C	YT	07/97	97-04	155	33	7
Queens Park Rgrs	Tr	06/05	05	14	1	0
Yeovil T	L	03/06	05	1	0	0
Wycombe W	L	09/06	06	23	3	2
Wycombe W	Tr	10/07	07-09	66	4	0
Bradford C	Ferencvaros (HUN)	08/10	10	17	1	0
Exeter C	Bath C	07/12	12-13	31	9	0

DOIDGE Christian Rhys
Born: Cwmbran, Torfaen, Wales, 25 August, 1992 — F

League Club	Source	Date Signed	Seasons Played	Apps	Subs	Gls
Dagenham & Red	Carmarthen T	08/14	14	3	8	2

DOIG Christopher Ross (Chris)
Born: Dumfries, Scotland, 13 February, 1981 — CD
Scotland: U21-13/Youth/Schools

League Club	Source	Date Signed	Seasons Played	Apps	Subs	Gls
Nottingham F	YT	03/98	98-04	62	15	1
Northampton T	L	09/03	03	9	0	0
Northampton T	Tr	07/05	05-08	116	4	4
Aldershot T	Pelit Jaya (INA)	12/11	11	2	0	0
York C	Tr	02/12	12	13	1	0

DOIG Russell
Born: Millport, Cumbrae, Ayrshire, Scotland, 17 January, 1964 — M

League Club	Source	Date Signed	Seasons Played	Apps	Subs	Gls
Leeds U	East Stirlingshire	07/86	86-87	3	3	0
Peterborough U	L	10/86	86	7	0	0
Hartlepool U	Tr	03/88	87-89	22	11	2

DOLAN Andrew (Andy)
Born: Glasgow, Scotland, 2 August, 1920 — IF
Died: Glasgow, Scotland, 1 January, 1971

League Club	Source	Date Signed	Seasons Played	Apps	Subs	Gls
Bury	Raith Rov	08/48	48	10	-	2
Accrington Stan	Tr	09/49	49	19	-	4

DOLAN Eamonn John
Born: Dagenham, E London, England, 20 September, 1967 — F
Republic of Ireland: U21-5/Youth

League Club	Source	Date Signed	Seasons Played	Apps	Subs	Gls
West Ham U	App	03/85	86-89	9	6	3
Bristol C	L	02/89	88	3	0	0
Birmingham C	Tr	12/90	90-91	6	6	1
Exeter C	Tr	09/91	91-92	15	11	4

DOLAN Joseph Thomas (Joe)
Born: Harrow, NW London, England, 27 May, 1980 — CD
Northern Ireland: U21-6/Youth

League Club	Source	Date Signed	Seasons Played	Apps	Subs	Gls
Millwall	Chelsea (Jnr)	04/98	98-03	47	2	3
Stockport Co	L	01/05	04	11	0	1
Brighton & HA	L	03/05	04	3	0	0
Leyton Orient	Tr	07/05	05	1	0	0
Stockport Co	L	10/05	05	2	0	0

DOLAN Matthew Alexander
Born: Hartlepool, Cleveland, England, 11 February, 1993 — LB/M

League Club	Source	Date Signed	Seasons Played	Apps	Subs	Gls
Middlesbrough	Sch	07/10				
Yeovil T	L	01/13	12	6	2	1
Hartlepool U	L	08/13	13	20	0	2
Bradford C	L	02/14	13-14	12	12	0
Hartlepool U	L	11/14	14	2	0	0

DOLAN Patrick Daniel (Pat)
Born: Dagenham, E London, England, 20 September, 1967 — CD
Republic of Ireland: U21-3/Youth

League Club	Source	Date Signed	Seasons Played	Apps	Subs	Gls
Arsenal	App	07/85				
Walsall	Tr	08/86	86	1	0	0

DOLAN Terence Peter (Terry)
Born: Bradford, England, 11 June, 1950 — M/D

League Club	Source	Date Signed	Seasons Played	Apps	Subs	Gls
Bradford Park Ave	Bradford C (Am)	03/69	68-69	46	2	0
Huddersfield T	Tr	10/70	71-75	157	5	14
Bradford C	Tr	08/76	76-80	191	4	43
Rochdale	Tr	08/81	81	42	1	1

DOLBY Anthony Christopher (Tony)
Born: Greenwich, SE London, England, 16 June, 1974 — LM

League Club	Source	Date Signed	Seasons Played	Apps	Subs	Gls
Millwall	YT	10/91	92-96	38	28	3
Barnet	L	02/94	93	13	3	2

DOLBY Christopher John (Chris)
Born: Dewsbury, West Yorkshire, England, 4 September, 1974 — W

League Club	Source	Date Signed	Seasons Played	Apps	Subs	Gls
Rotherham U	YT	08/93	93-94	0	3	0

DOLBY Peter
Born: Derby, England, 18 May, 1940 — CD

League Club	Source	Date Signed	Seasons Played	Apps	Subs	Gls
Shrewsbury T	Heanor T	02/60	60-75	303	21	21

DOLDING Desmond Leonard (Len)
Born: Kolar, India, 13 December, 1922 — W
Died: Wembley, NW London, England, 23 November, 1954

League Club	Source	Date Signed	Seasons Played	Apps	Subs	Gls
Chelsea	Wealdstone	07/45	46-47	26	-	2
Norwich C	Tr	07/48	48-49	12	-	1

DOLING Stuart James
Born: Newport, Isle of Wight, England, 28 October, 1972 — M/FB
England: Youth

League Club	Source	Date Signed	Seasons Played	Apps	Subs	Gls
Portsmouth	YT	06/90	91-94	20	17	4
Doncaster Rov	AFC Lymington	10/95	95-96	3	3	0

DOLMAN Liam Edward Lewis
Born: Brixworth, Northamptonshire, England, 26 September, 1987 — CD

League Club	Source	Date Signed	Seasons Played	Apps	Subs	Gls
Northampton T	Sch	07/06	06-08	37	8	1

DOMI Didier
Born: Paris, France, 2 May, 1978 — LB
France: U21-14/Youth

League Club	Source	Date Signed	Seasons Played	Apps	Subs	Gls
Newcastle U	Paris St-Germain (FRA)	01/99	98-00	44	11	3
Leeds U (L)	Paris St-Germain (FRA)	08/03	03	9	3	0

DOMINEY Barry William
Born: Edmonton, N London, England, 21 October, 1955 — CD
Died: Colchester, Essex, England, March, 2005

League Club	Source	Date Signed	Seasons Played	Apps	Subs	Gls
Colchester U	Enfield WMC	01/74	73-76	56	15	3

DOMINGUEZ Jose Manuel Martins
Born: Lisbon, Portugal, 16 February, 1974 — W
Portugal: 3/U21-8/Youth

League Club	Source	Date Signed	Seasons Played	Apps	Subs	Gls
Birmingham C	Benfica (POR)	03/94	93-94	15	20	3
Tottenham H	Sporting Lisbon (POR)	08/97	97-00	12	33	4

DOMORAUD Wilfried
Born: Paris, France, 18 August, 1988 — F

League Club	Source	Date Signed	Seasons Played	Apps	Subs	Gls
Yeovil T	AS Nancy (FRA)	08/07	07	0	5	0

DONACHIE Daniel James (Danny)
Born: Manchester, England, 17 May, 1973 — FB

League Club	Source	Date Signed	Seasons Played	Apps	Subs	Gls
Carlisle U	Radcliffe Bor	01/96	95	0	1	0

DONACHIE William (Willie)
Born: Glasgow, Scotland, 5 October, 1951 — LB
Scotland: 35/U23-2

League Club	Source	Date Signed	Seasons Played	Apps	Subs	Gls
Manchester C	Jnr	12/68	69-79	347	4	2
Norwich C	Portland Timbers (USA)	09/81	81	11	0	0
Burnley	Portland Timbers (USA)	11/82	82-83	60	0	3
Oldham Ath	Tr	07/84	84-90	158	11	3

DONACIEN Janoi Denzil Naime
Born: Castries, Saint Lucia, 3 November, 1993 — D

League Club	Source	Date Signed	Seasons Played	Apps	Subs	Gls
Aston Villa	Sch	07/14				
Tranmere Rov	L	08/14	14	31	0	0

DONAGHY Barry
Born: Consett, County Durham, England, 21 March, 1956 — F
England: Youth

League Club	Source	Date Signed	Seasons Played	Apps	Subs	Gls
West Bromwich A	App	05/73	73-74	4	2	1
Workington	Tr	12/75	75-76	40	4	3

DONAGHY Malachy Martin (Mal)
Born: Belfast, Northern Ireland, 13 September, 1957 — CD
Northern Ireland: 91/U21-1

League Club	Source	Date Signed	Seasons Played	Apps	Subs	Gls
Luton T	Larne T	06/78	78-88	410	0	16
Manchester U	Tr	10/88	88-91	76	13	0
Luton T	L	12/89	89	5	0	0
Chelsea	Tr	08/92	92-93	63	5	3

DONALD Alexander (Alex)
Born: Kirkliston, Edinburgh, Scotland, 5 June, 1948 — RW

League Club	Source	Date Signed	Seasons Played	Apps	Subs	Gls
Port Vale	Jnr	10/65	65-67	41	2	0

DONALD Ian Richard
Born: Aberdeen, Scotland, 28 November, 1951 — RB
Scotland: Schools

League Club	Source	Date Signed	Seasons Played	Apps	Subs	Gls
Manchester U	Banks o' Dee	07/69	72	4	0	0

DONALD Warren Ramsay
Born: Hillingdon, W London, England, 7 October, 1964 — M
England: Schools

League Club	Source	Date Signed	Seasons Played	Apps	Subs	Gls
West Ham U	App	10/82	83	1	1	0
Northampton T	L	03/85	84	11	0	2
Northampton T	Tr	10/85	85-89	169	8	11
Colchester U	Tr	07/90	92	8	2	0

DONALDSON Andrew (Andy)
Born: Newcastle-upon-Tyne, England, 22 March, 1925 — CF
Died: Peterborough, England, 20 June, 1987

League Club	Source	Date Signed	Seasons Played	Apps	Subs	Gls
Newcastle U	Vickers Armstrong	09/43	46-48	19	-	6
Middlesbrough	Tr	01/49	48-50	21	-	7
Exeter C	Peterborough U	09/53	53-54	39	-	16

DONALDSON Brian Leslie
Born: Hove, East Sussex, England, 3 April, 1936 — RW

Died: Brighton, England, December, 2009

League Club	Source	Date Signed	Seasons Played	Apps	Subs	Gls
Chelsea	Jnr	07/53				
Swindon T	Tr	10/57	57	1	-	0

DONALDSON Clayton Andrew
Born: Bradford, England, 7 February, 1984 — F
England: Semi Pro-2

League Club	Source	Date Signed	Seasons Played	Apps	Subs	Gls
Hull C	Sch	02/03	02	0	2	0
Crewe Alex	Hibernian	08/08	08-10	98	19	47
Brentford	Tr	07/11	11-13	129	7	46
Birmingham C	Tr	07/14	14	44	2	15

DONALDSON Coll
Born: Edinburgh, Scotland, 9 April, 1995 — CD

League Club	Source	Date Signed	Seasons Played	Apps	Subs	Gls
Queens Park Rgrs	Livingston	01/14	13	1	0	0

DONALDSON David (Dave)
Born: Hillingdon, W London, England, 28 December, 1941 — CD

League Club	Source	Date Signed	Seasons Played	Apps	Subs	Gls
Wimbledon	Walton & Hersham	08/74	77-78	61	0	0

DONALDSON David John (Dave)
Born: Islington, N London, England, 12 November, 1954 — RB
England: Schools

League Club	Source	Date Signed	Seasons Played	Apps	Subs	Gls
Arsenal	App	07/72				
Millwall	Tr	06/73	73-79	215	1	1
Cambridge U	Tr	02/80	79-83	130	2	0

DONALDSON Frederick Lewis (Fred)
Born: Stoke-on-Trent, England, 7 April, 1937 — FB/F

League Club	Source	Date Signed	Seasons Played	Apps	Subs	Gls
Port Vale	Jnr	07/54	54-59	47	-	4
Exeter C	Tr	08/60	60	36	-	6
Chester C	Tr	07/61	61	21	-	0

DONALDSON James Dent (Jimmy)
Born: South Shields, Tyne and Wear, England, 11 June, 1927 — LH
Died: South Shields, Tyne and Wear, England, 20 March, 1980

League Club	Source	Date Signed	Seasons Played	Apps	Subs	Gls
Chesterfield	South Shields	11/48	49-50	17	-	4
Newport Co	Tr	08/51	51-52	36	-	1

DONALDSON Leslie Darcy Robert (Les)
Born: Glasgow, Scotland, 30 July, 1922 — IF
Died: Rhyl, Denbighshire, Wales, 8 January, 1995

League Club	Source	Date Signed	Seasons Played	Apps	Subs	Gls
Wrexham	Rhyl	06/50	50-51	30	-	6

DONALDSON O'Neill McKay
Born: Birmingham, England, 24 November, 1969 — F

League Club	Source	Date Signed	Seasons Played	Apps	Subs	Gls
Shrewsbury T	Hinckley U	11/91	91-93	15	13	4
Doncaster Rov	Tr	08/94	94	7	2	2
Mansfield T	L	12/94	94	4	0	6
Sheffield Wed	Tr	01/95	94-97	4	10	3
Oxford U	L	01/98	97	6	0	2
Stoke C	Tr	03/98	97	2	0	0
Torquay U	Tr	09/98	98-99	11	16	1

DONALDSON Robert Steve (Bobby)
Born: South Shields, Tyne and Wear, England, 26 February, 1921 — RH
Died: North Tyneside, Tyne and Wear, England, 16 September, 1990

League Club	Source	Date Signed	Seasons Played	Apps	Subs	Gls
Newcastle U		01/43				
Hartlepool U	Tr	07/47	47-51	131	-	4

DONALDSON Ryan Mark
Born: Newcastle-upon-Tyne, England, 1 May, 1991 — W
England: Youth

League Club	Source	Date Signed	Seasons Played	Apps	Subs	Gls
Newcastle U	Sch	11/08	09	0	2	0
Hartlepool U	L	01/11	10	11	1	0
Tranmere Rov	L	09/11	11	1	0	0
Cambridge U	Gateshead	05/13	14	38	0	5

DONALDSON William (Willie)
Born: Edinburgh, Scotland, 20 January, 1920 — LW
Died: Bradford, England, 9 January, 1977

League Club	Source	Date Signed	Seasons Played	Apps	Subs	Gls
Bradford Park Ave	Leith Ath	05/46	46-50	45	-	6
Mansfield T	Tr	10/50	50-51	52	-	10

DONCEL-VARCARCEL Antonio
Born: Lugo, Spain, 31 January, 1967 — CD

League Club	Source	Date Signed	Seasons Played	Apps	Subs	Gls
Hull C	Racing Ferrol (SPN)	08/96	96-97	30	8	2

DONE Cyril Charles
Born: Liverpool, England, 21 October, 1920 — CF
Died: Southport, Merseyside, England, 24 December, 1993

League Club	Source	Date Signed	Seasons Played	Apps	Subs	Gls
Liverpool	Bootle Boys Brigade	01/38	46-51	93	-	32
Tranmere Rov	Tr	05/52	52-54	87	-	61
Port Vale	Tr	12/54	54-56	52	-	34

DONE Matthew (Matty)
Born: Oswestry, Shropshire, England, 22 June, 1988 — LW/F

League Club	Source	Date Signed	Seasons Played	Apps	Subs	Gls
Wrexham	Sch	08/06	05-07	41	25	1
Hereford U	Tr	08/08	08-09	31	25	0
Rochdale	Tr	07/10	10	16	17	5
Barnsley	Tr	06/11	11-12	28	16	4
Rochdale	Tr	07/13	13-14	48	13	10
Sheffield U	Tr	02/15	14	12	3	7

DONEGAL Glenville Paul (Glen)
Born: Northampton, England, 20 June, 1969 — F

League Club	Source	Date Signed	Seasons Played	Apps	Subs	Gls
Northampton T	YT	08/87	87-89	7	13	3
Maidstone U	Aylesbury U	08/91	91	9	5	1

DONG FANG ZHUO (Dong)
Born: Dalian, China, 23 January, 1985 — F
China: 13

League Club	Source	Date Signed	Seasons Played	Apps	Subs	Gls
Manchester U	Dalian Shide (CHN)	01/04	06	1	0	0

[DONI] MARANGON Donieber Alexander
Born: Sao Paulo, Brazil, 22 October, 1979 — G
Brazil: 10

League Club	Source	Date Signed	Seasons Played	Apps	Subs	Gls
Liverpool	AS Roma (ITA)	07/11	11	4	0	0

DONIS Georgios Yorgos (George)
Born: Frankfurt, Germany, 29 October, 1969 — LW
Greece: 24

League Club	Source	Date Signed	Seasons Played	Apps	Subs	Gls
Blackburn Rov	Panathinaikos (GRE)	07/96	96	11	11	2
Sheffield U	AEK Athens (GRE)	03/99	98	5	2	1
Huddersfield T	Tr	06/99	99	10	10	0

DONK Ryan
Born: Amsterdam, Netherlands, 30 March, 1986 — CD
Netherlands: U21-15

League Club	Source	Date Signed	Seasons Played	Apps	Subs	Gls
West Bromwich A (L)	AZ Alkmaar (NED)	09/08	08	14	2	0

DONN Alan Nigel (Nigel)
Born: Maidstone, Kent, England, 2 March, 1962 — M

League Club	Source	Date Signed	Seasons Played	Apps	Subs	Gls
Gillingham	App	02/80	80-81	2	1	0
Leyton Orient	Karpalo (FIN)	08/82	82	22	1	2

DONNELLAN Gary
Born: Kensington, Central London, England, 3 July, 1962 — LW

League Club	Source	Date Signed	Seasons Played	Apps	Subs	Gls
Chelsea	App	07/80				
Watford	Tr	11/80				
Reading	Tr	11/81	81-82	33	8	5

DONNELLAN Leo John
Born: Willesden, NW London, England, 19 January, 1965 — M
Republic of Ireland: U21-1

League Club	Source	Date Signed	Seasons Played	Apps	Subs	Gls
Chelsea	App	08/82				
Leyton Orient	L	12/84	84	6	0	0
Fulham	Tr	08/85	85-89	54	25	4

DONNELLY Andrew (Andy)
Born: Lanark, Scotland, 1 May, 1943 — G

League Club	Source	Date Signed	Seasons Played	Apps	Subs	Gls
Millwall	Clyde	05/63				
Torquay U	Weymouth	08/67	67-71	160	0	0

DONNELLY Ciaran
Born: Blackpool, Lancashire, England, 2 April, 1984 — M
England: Youth

League Club	Source	Date Signed	Seasons Played	Apps	Subs	Gls
Blackburn Rov	YT	07/01				
Blackpool	L	03/04	03	8	1	0
Blackpool	Tr	03/05	04-05	21	11	2

DONNELLY Darren Charles
Born: Liverpool, England, 28 December, 1971 — F

League Club	Source	Date Signed	Seasons Played	Apps	Subs	Gls
Blackburn Rov	YT	06/90	90	1	1	0
Chester C	Tr	08/93	93	0	9	0

DONNELLY George John
Born: Liverpool, England, 28 May, 1988 — F
England: Semi Pro-1

League Club	Source	Date Signed	Seasons Played	Apps	Subs	Gls
Plymouth Arg	Skelmersdale U	03/09	08	0	2	0
Stockport Co	L	01/10	09	16	3	4
Stockport Co	L	08/10	10	23	0	8
Macclesfield T	Fleetwood T	09/11	11	28	0	6
Rochdale	Tr	05/12	12-14	43	35	13
Tranmere Rov	Tr	09/14	14	4	7	0

DONNELLY James (Jim)
Born: Cork, Republic of Ireland, 6 May, 1919 — IF

League Club	Source	Date Signed	Seasons Played	Apps	Subs	Gls
Accrington Stan	Sligo Rov (ROI)	08/51	51	4	-	1

DONNELLY John
Born: Glasgow, Scotland, 8 March, 1961 — M

League Club	Source	Date Signed	Seasons Played	Apps	Subs	Gls
Leeds U	Dumbarton	03/83	82-84	36	4	4

DONNELLY John
Born: Broxburn, West Lothian, Scotland, 17 December, 1936 — RB
Died: Broxburn, West Lothian, Scotland, 31 July, 2009

League Club	Source	Date Signed	Seasons Played	Apps	Subs	Gls
Preston NE	Glasgow Celtic	04/62	62-66	56	2	1

DONNELLY Mark Paul
Born: Leeds, England, 22 December, 1979 — M

League Club	Source	Date Signed	Seasons Played	Apps	Subs	Gls
Doncaster Rov	YT	-	96-97	8	3	1
Bury	Tr	07/98				

DONNELLY Paul Anthony
Born: Liverpool, England, 23 December, 1971 — W

League Club	Source	Date Signed	Seasons Played	Apps	Subs	Gls
Halifax T	YT	03/90	88-90	9	4	0

DONNELLY Paul Michael
Born: Newcastle-under-Lyme, Potteries, England, 16 February, 1981 — CD

League Club	Source	Date Signed	Seasons Played	Apps	Subs	Gls
Port Vale	YT	07/99	99-01	5	6	0

DONNELLY Peter
Born: Hull, England, 22 September, 1936 — IF

League Club	Source	Date Signed	Seasons Played	Apps	Subs	Gls
Doncaster Rov	Jnr	03/54	53-56	6	-	1
Scunthorpe U	Tr	07/58	58-59	39	-	19
Cardiff C	Tr	06/60	60-61	31	-	8
Swansea C	Tr	10/61	61	16	-	3
Brighton & HA	Tr	07/62	62-64	56	-	13
Bradford C	Tr	03/65	64-65	13	0	5

DONNELLY Peter James
Born: Chester, England, 11 May, 1965 — M

League Club	Source	Date Signed	Seasons Played	Apps	Subs	Gls
Chester C	YT	08/83	83	1	0	0

DONNELLY Rory
Born: Belfast, Northern Ireland, 18 February, 1992 — F
Northern Ireland: U21-1

League Club	Source	Date Signed	Seasons Played	Apps	Subs	Gls
Swansea C	Cliftonville	01/12				
Tranmere Rov	L	01/15	14	15	5	5

DONNELLY Scott Paul
Born: Hammersmith, W London, England, 25 December, 1987 — M

League Club	Source	Date Signed	Seasons Played	Apps	Subs	Gls
Queens Park Rgrs	Sch	03/06	04-06	3	10	0
Aldershot T	Wealdstone	06/08	08-09	54	9	14
Swansea C	Tr	07/10	10	0	1	0
Wycombe W	L	01/11	10	11	7	3
Wycombe W	L	07/11	11	16	2	4
Aldershot T	Tr	09/12	12	4	0	0
Southend U	L	11/12	12	0	2	0

DONNELLY Simon Thomas
Born: Glasgow, Scotland, 1 December, 1974 — M
Scotland: 10/U21-11

League Club	Source	Date Signed	Seasons Played	Apps	Subs	Gls
Sheffield Wed	Glasgow Celtic	07/99	99-02	27	26	8

DONOVAN Donal Christopher (Don)
Born: Cork, Republic of Ireland, 23 December, 1929 — FB
Died: Grimsby, North Lincolnshire, England, 26 September, 2013
Republic of Ireland: 5

League Club	Source	Date Signed	Seasons Played	Apps	Subs	Gls
Everton	Dalymount Rov (ROI)	05/49	51-57	179	-	2
Grimsby T	Tr	08/58	58-63	238	-	1

DONOVAN Francis James (Frank)
Born: Pembroke, Wales, 26 February, 1919 — RW
Died: Pembroke, Wales, 17 April, 2003
Wales: Amateur

League Club	Source	Date Signed	Seasons Played	Apps	Subs	Gls
Swansea C	Pembroke Bor	05/50	50	15	-	2

DONOVAN Kevin
Born: Halifax, West Yorkshire, England, 17 December, 1971 — RW

League Club	Source	Date Signed	Seasons Played	Apps	Subs	Gls
Huddersfield T	YT	10/89	89-92	11	9	1
Halifax T	L	02/92	91	6	0	0
West Bromwich A	Tr	10/92	92-96	139	29	19
Grimsby T	Tr	07/97	97-00	150	6	24
Barnsley	Tr	07/01	01-02	48	6	1
Rochdale	Tr	12/03	03	4	3	0

DONOVAN Landon Timothy
Born: San Bernardino, California, USA, 4 March, 1982 — F
USA: 157/U23-15/Youth

League Club	Source	Date Signed	Seasons Played	Apps	Subs	Gls
Everton (L)	Los Angeles G'xy (USA)	01/10	09	7	3	2
Everton (L)	Los Angeles G'xy (USA)	01/12	11	7	0	0

DONOVAN Terence Christopher (Terry)
Born: Liverpool, England, 27 February, 1958 — F
England: Schools//Republic of Ireland: 1/U21-1

League Club	Source	Date Signed	Seasons Played	Apps	Subs	Gls
Grimsby T	Louth U	08/76	76-78	52	12	23
Aston Villa	Tr	09/79	79-81	17	0	6
Oxford U	L	02/83	82	3	0	0
Burnley	Tr	02/83	82-83	13	2	6
Rotherham U	Tr	09/83	83-84	9	4	0
Blackpool	L	10/84	84	2	0	0

DONOWA Brian Louie (Louie)
Born: Ipswich, England, 24 September, 1964 — W
England: U21-3

League Club	Source	Date Signed	Seasons Played	Apps	Subs	Gls
Norwich C	App	09/82	82-85	56	6	11
Stoke C	L	12/85	85	4	0	1
Ipswich T	Willem II (NED)	04/89	89	17	6	1
Bristol C	Tr	08/90	90	11	13	3
Birmingham C	Tr	08/91	91-96	78	38	18
Burnley	L	01/93	92	4	0	0
Shrewsbury T	L	01/94	93	4	0	0
Walsall	L	10/96	96	6	0	1
Peterborough U	Tr	12/96	96	16	6	1
Walsall	Tr	08/97	97	5	1	0

DOOLAN John
Born: Liverpool, England, 10 November, 1968 — M/D

League Club	Source	Date Signed	Seasons Played	Apps	Subs	Gls
Wigan Ath	Knowsley U	03/92	91-95	29	9	1

DOOLAN John
Born: Liverpool, England, 7 May, 1974 — M

League Club	Source	Date Signed	Seasons Played	Apps	Subs	Gls
Everton	YT	06/92				
Mansfield T	Witton A	09/94	94-97	128	3	10
Barnet	Tr	01/98	97-00	132	2	7
Doncaster Rov	Tr	03/03	03-04	68	9	2
Blackpool	Tr	07/05	05	15	4	0
Rochdale	Tr	01/06	05-07	75	8	3

DOOLEY Derek
Born: Sheffield, England, 13 December, 1929 — CF
Died: Sheffield, England, 5 August, 2008

League Club	Source	Date Signed	Seasons Played	Apps	Subs	Gls
Lincoln C (Am)	Sheffield YMCA	09/46	46	2	-	2
Sheffield Wed	Tr	06/47	49-52	61	-	62

DOOLEY George William
Born: Chesterfield, Derbyshire, England, 29 December, 1922 — IF
Died: Chesterfield, Derbyshire, England, April, 2004

League Club	Source	Date Signed	Seasons Played	Apps	Subs	Gls
Chesterfield	Parkhouse Colliery	06/45				
Halifax T	Tr	12/46	46	11	-	2
Chesterfield	Tr	06/47				

DOONAN Thomas (Tom)
Born: West Calder, West Lothian, Scotland, 5 October, 1922 — CF
Died: Bradford, England, December, 1998

League Club	Source	Date Signed	Seasons Played	Apps	Subs	Gls
Bradford C	Albion Rov	06/49	49	13	-	7
Tranmere Rov	Tr	07/50	50	4	-	2

DOONER Gary James
Born: St Helens, Merseyside, England, 14 September, 1970 — W

League Club	Source	Date Signed	Seasons Played	Apps	Subs	Gls
Stockport Co	YT	07/89	88	1	0	0

DOOTSON Craig Robert
Born: Chorley, Lancashire, England, 23 May, 1979 — G

League Club	Source	Date Signed	Seasons Played	Apps	Subs	Gls
Bury	Stalybridge Celtic	07/05	05	4	1	0

DO PRADO Guilherme (Guly)
Born: Campinas, Brazil, 31 December, 1981 — W/F

League Club	Source	Date Signed	Seasons Played	Apps	Subs	Gls
Southampton	Cesena (ITA)	08/10	10-13	67	36	19

DORAN Robert Rennie
Born: Carlisle, Cumbria, England, 26 December, 1933 — CD

League Club	Source	Date Signed	Seasons Played	Apps	Subs	Gls
Carlisle U		10/52	53-61	107	-	0

DORAN Terence (Terry)
Born: Jarrow, Tyne and Wear, England, 2 April, 1940 — LB

League Club	Source	Date Signed	Seasons Played	Apps	Subs	Gls
Gateshead (Am)	St Mary's BC	09/59	59	1	-	0

DORAN-COGAN Aaron Brian
Born: Dublin, Republic of Ireland, 13 May, 1991 — M
Republic of Ireland: U21-5/Youth

League Club	Source	Date Signed	Seasons Played	Apps	Subs	Gls
Blackburn Rov	Sch	05/08	08	0	3	0
MK Dons	L	10/09	09	2	2	0
Leyton Orient	L	02/10	09	6	0	0

DORE Leslie Charles Albert (Charlie)
Born: Gosport, Hampshire, England, 22 January, 1931 — G
Died: Hampshire, England, 3 November, 2011

League Club	Source	Date Signed	Seasons Played	Apps	Subs	Gls
Portsmouth	Hillside YC	05/50	51-53	18	-	0

DORIGO Anthony Robert (Tony)
Born: Melbourne, Australia, 31 December, 1965 — LB
England: 15/B-7/U21-11

League Club	Source	Date Signed	Seasons Played	Apps	Subs	Gls
Aston Villa	App	07/83	83-86	106	5	1
Chelsea	Tr	07/87	87-90	146	0	11
Leeds U	Tr	06/91	91-96	168	3	5
Derby Co	Torino (ITA)	10/98	98-99	37	4	1
Stoke C	Tr	07/00	00	34	2	0

[DORIVA] GHIDONI Dorival
Born: Nhandeara, Sao Paulo, Brazil, 28 May, 1972 — DM
Brazil: 12

League Club	Source	Date Signed	Seasons Played	Apps	Subs	Gls
Middlesbrough	Celta Vigo (SPN)	02/03	02-05	56	23	0

DORLING George John
Born: Edmonton, N London, England, 27 July, 1918 — RB
Died: Enfield, N London, England, October, 1987

League Club	Source	Date Signed	Seasons Played	Apps	Subs	Gls
Tottenham H	Jnr	03/46				
Gillingham	Tr	05/47	50	10	-	0

DORMAN Andrew (Andy)
Born: Chester, England, 1 May, 1982 M
Wales: 3

League Club	Source	Date Signed	Seasons Played	Apps	Subs	Gls
Crystal Palace	St Mirren	07/10	10-11	14	7	1
Bristol Rov	L	11/11	11	20	5	2

DORMAN Donald (Don)
Born: Hall Green, West Midlands, England, 18 September, 1922 IF/WH
Died: Worcester, England, 12 January, 1997

League Club	Source	Date Signed	Seasons Played	Apps	Subs	Gls
Birmingham C	Shirley Jnrs	05/46	46-51	59	-	4
Coventry C	Tr	09/51	51-54	90	-	29
Walsall	Tr	10/54	54-56	116	-	34

DORNAN Andrew (Andy)
Born: Aberdeen, Scotland, 19 August, 1961 RB
Scotland: Youth/Schools

League Club	Source	Date Signed	Seasons Played	Apps	Subs	Gls
Walsall	Motherwell	08/86	86-89	117	1	1

DORNAN Peter
Born: Belfast, Northern Ireland, 30 June, 1953 M
Northern Ireland: NILge-3

League Club	Source	Date Signed	Seasons Played	Apps	Subs	Gls
Sheffield U	Linfield	12/76	76	1	2	0
Swindon T	Linfield	02/79	78	0	1	0

DORNER Mario
Born: Baden bei Wien, Austria, 21 March, 1970 F

League Club	Source	Date Signed	Seasons Played	Apps	Subs	Gls
Darlington	Motherwell	10/97	97-98	34	15	13

DORNEY Alan John
Born: Bermondsey, SE London, England, 18 May, 1947 CD

League Club	Source	Date Signed	Seasons Played	Apps	Subs	Gls
Millwall	Jnr	05/65	68-76	249	3	1

DORNEY Jack Christopher
Born: Ashton-under-Lyne, Greater Manchester, England, 9 January, 1990 M

League Club	Source	Date Signed	Seasons Played	Apps	Subs	Gls
Bury	Sch	12/07	07	3	4	0

DORRANS Graham
Born: Glasgow, Scotland, 5 May, 1987 M
Scotland: 10/U21-6/Youth

League Club	Source	Date Signed	Seasons Played	Apps	Subs	Gls
West Bromwich A	Livingston	07/08	08-14	131	35	21
Norwich C	L	02/15	14	12	3	3

DORRIAN Christopher Stewart (Chris)
Born: Harlow, Essex, England, 3 April, 1982 RB

League Club	Source	Date Signed	Seasons Played	Apps	Subs	Gls
Leyton Orient	YT	07/00	00-01	4	1	0

DORSETT Richard (Dickie)
Born: Brownhills, West Midlands, England, 3 December, 1919 WH/CF
Died: Walsall, West Midlands, England, December, 1999

League Club	Source	Date Signed	Seasons Played	Apps	Subs	Gls
Wolverhampton W	Jnr	12/36	37-46	46	-	32
Aston Villa	Tr	09/46	46-52	257	-	32

DOSSENA Andrea
Born: Lodi, Italy, 11 September, 1981 LB
Italy: 10

League Club	Source	Date Signed	Seasons Played	Apps	Subs	Gls
Liverpool	Udinese (ITA)	07/08	08-09	13	5	1
Sunderland	Napoli (ITA)	09/13	13	6	1	0
Leyton Orient		11/14	14	13	2	1

DOSSEVI Thomas Folivi
Born: Tours, France, 6 March, 1979 F
Togo: 27

League Club	Source	Date Signed	Seasons Played	Apps	Subs	Gls
Swindon T	FC Nantes (FRA)	08/10	10	16	11	3

DOUALA Roudolphe Douala
Born: Douala, Cameroon, 25 September, 1978 W
Cameroon: 17

League Club	Source	Date Signed	Seasons Played	Apps	Subs	Gls
Portsmouth (L)	Sporting Lisbon (POR)	08/06	06	1	6	0
Plymouth Arg	Asteras Tripolis (GRE)	03/09	08	1	1	0

[DOUDOU] M'BOMBO Aziana Ebele
Born: Kinshasa, DR Congo, 11 September, 1980 W/W

League Club	Source	Date Signed	Seasons Played	Apps	Subs	Gls
Queens Park Rgrs	AS Monaco (FRA)	08/01	01-02	23	23	3
Oxford U	Farnborough T	12/04	04	0	1	0

DOUGAL Cornelius (Neil)
Born: Falkirk, Scotland, 7 November, 1921 RH/IF
Died: Plymouth, England, 2 December, 2009
Scotland: 1/War-1

League Club	Source	Date Signed	Seasons Played	Apps	Subs	Gls
Burnley	Jnr	03/40				
Birmingham C	Tr	10/45	46-48	93	-	15
Plymouth Arg	Tr	03/49	48-58	274	-	26

DOUGAL James (Jimmy)
Born: Denny, Falkirk, Scotland, 3 October, 1913 IF
Died: Walton-on-Thames, Surrey, England, 17 October, 1999
Scotland: 1/War-1

League Club	Source	Date Signed	Seasons Played	Apps	Subs	Gls
Preston NE	Falkirk	01/34	33-46	170	-	51
Carlisle U	Tr	10/46	46-48	71	-	13
Halifax T	Tr	10/48	48	21	-	2

DOUGAL John (Jack)
Born: Falkirk, Scotland, 7 August, 1934 FB
England: Amateur-6

League Club	Source	Date Signed	Seasons Played	Apps	Subs	Gls
Halifax T (Am)	Pegasus	05/56	55-56	3	-	0

DOUGAL William (Willie)
Born: Falkirk, Scotland, 30 October, 1923 LH
Died: Glasgow, Scotland, 28 October, 1981

League Club	Source	Date Signed	Seasons Played	Apps	Subs	Gls
Preston NE	Glasgow Rangers	12/47	47-48	22	-	2
Barnsley	Tr	08/52	52	21	-	0

DOUGALL Thomas (Tom)
Born: Wishaw, Lanarkshire, Scotland, 17 May, 1921 RW
Died: Kingston-on-Thames, SW London, England, January, 1997

League Club	Source	Date Signed	Seasons Played	Apps	Subs	Gls
Coventry C	Leicester C (Am)	09/45				
Brentford	Tr	08/47	47	2	-	0
Sunderland	Tr	11/48	48	3	-	0

DOUGAN Alexander Derek (Derek)
Born: Belfast, Northern Ireland, 20 January, 1938 CF
Died: Wolverhampton, England, 24 June, 2007
Northern Ireland: 43/B/Schools

League Club	Source	Date Signed	Seasons Played	Apps	Subs	Gls
Portsmouth	Distillery	08/57	57-58	33	-	9
Blackburn Rov	Tr	03/59	58-60	59	-	26
Aston Villa	Tr	08/61	61-62	51	-	19
Peterborough U	Tr	06/63	63-64	77	-	38
Leicester C	Tr	05/65	65-66	68	0	35
Wolverhampton W	Tr	03/67	66-74	244	14	95

DOUGAN George
Born: Glasgow, Scotland, 22 March, 1939 LH

League Club	Source	Date Signed	Seasons Played	Apps	Subs	Gls
Ipswich T	Yiewsley	03/63	62-63	17	-	0

DOUGAN John McKechnie
Born: Glasgow, Scotland, 12 January, 1931 IF
Died: Brighton, England, January, 1995

League Club	Source	Date Signed	Seasons Played	Apps	Subs	Gls
Brighton & HA	Bellshill Ath	12/51				
Torquay U	Tr	02/54	53-54	21	-	3

DOUGAN Maxwell Spalding (Max)
Born: Stoneyburn, West Lothian, Scotland, 23 May, 1938 D
Scotland: Amateur

League Club	Source	Date Signed	Seasons Played	Apps	Subs	Gls
Leicester C	Queen's Park	09/63	63-66	9	0	0
Luton T	Tr	12/66	66-69	117	1	0

DOUGHERTY Paul
Born: Leamington Spa, Warwickshire, England, 12 May, 1966 M

League Club	Source	Date Signed	Seasons Played	Apps	Subs	Gls
Wolverhampton W	App	05/84	83-86	24	17	3
Torquay U	L	02/85	84	5	0	0

DOUGHERTY Victor Robert (Vic)
Born: Glasgow, Scotland, 17 January, 1955 RB

League Club	Source	Date Signed	Seasons Played	Apps	Subs	Gls
Bury	App	01/73	72	9	0	0

DOUGHTY Eric
Born: Radstock, Somerset, England, 9 April, 1932 LB

League Club	Source	Date Signed	Seasons Played	Apps	Subs	Gls
Arsenal	Peasedown	05/51				
Plymouth Arg	Tr	07/58	58	1	-	0

DOUGHTY Matthew Liam (Matt)
Born: Warrington, Cheshire, England, 2 November, 1981 LB

League Club	Source	Date Signed	Seasons Played	Apps	Subs	Gls
Chester C	YT	07/00	99	19	14	1
Rochdale	Tr	07/01	01-03	96	12	1

DOUGHTY Michael Edward
Born: Westminster, Central London, England, 20 November, 1992 M
Wales: U21-1/Youth

League Club	Source	Date Signed	Seasons Played	Apps	Subs	Gls
Queens Park Rgrs	Sch	01/11	14	0	3	0
Crawley T	L	08/11	11	2	14	0
Aldershot T	L	03/12	11	2	3	0
Stevenage	L	08/13	13	28	8	2
Gillingham	L	10/14	14	9	0	0

DOUGHTY Philip Michael (Phil)
Born: Kirkham, Lancashire, England, 6 September, 1986 CD

League Club	Source	Date Signed	Seasons Played	Apps	Subs	Gls
Blackpool	Sch	10/04				
Macclesfield T	L	11/07	07	5	1	0
Accrington Stan	L	01/08	07	3	0	0

DOUGLAS Andrew Stephen (Andy)
Born: Penrith, Cumbria, England, 27 May, 1980 F

League Club	Source	Date Signed	Seasons Played	Apps	Subs	Gls
Carlisle U	YT	07/98	98	0	1	0

DOUGLAS Bryan
Born: Blackburn, Greater Manchester, England, 27 May, 1934 RW
England: 36/B-1/FLge-4/U23-5

League Club	Source	Date Signed	Seasons Played	Apps	Subs	Gls
Blackburn Rov	Lower Darwen YC	04/52	54-68	438	0	100

DOUGLAS Colin Francis
Born: Hurlford, Ayrshire, Scotland, 9 September, 1962 RB/F

League Club	Source	Date Signed	Seasons Played	Apps	Subs	Gls
Doncaster Rov	Glasgow Celtic	08/81	81-85	202	10	48
Rotherham U	Tr	07/86	86-87	82	1	4
Doncaster Rov	Tr	08/88	88-92	182	10	5

DOUGLAS James Stewart (Jimmy)
Born: Sunderland, England, 16 September, 1941 CF

League Club	Source	Date Signed	Seasons Played	Apps	Subs	Gls
Hartlepool U (Am)	Willington	10/62	62	13	-	4

DOUGLAS Jamie Trevor
Born: Cookstown, Derry, Northern Ireland, 4 July, 1992 F

League Club	Source	Date Signed	Seasons Played	Apps	Subs	Gls
Preston NE	Sch	07/10	10-11	0	6	1

DOUGLAS John
Born: Stockton-on-Tees, Cleveland, England, 13 March, 1961 F

League Club	Source	Date Signed	Seasons Played	Apps	Subs	Gls
Darlington	Stockton	01/86	85	3	0	0

DOUGLAS John Stewart
Born: West Hartlepool, County Durham, England, 1 December, 1917 D
Died: Hartlepool, Cleveland, England, 31 January, 2001

League Club	Source	Date Signed	Seasons Played	Apps	Subs	Gls
Hartlepool U (Am)	Houghton CW	09/38	38	5	-	0
Middlesbrough	Tr	09/45	46	2	-	0
Hartlepool U	Tr	11/48	48-49	27	-	1
Halifax T	Tr	10/50				

DOUGLAS Jonathan Michael
Born: Monaghan, Republic of Ireland, 22 November, 1981 M
Republic of Ireland: 8/U21-1/Youth

League Club	Source	Date Signed	Seasons Played	Apps	Subs	Gls
Blackburn Rov	YT	02/00	02-04	14	2	1
Chesterfield	L	03/03	02	7	0	1
Blackpool	L	08/03	03	15	1	3
Gillingham	L	03/05	04	10	0	0
Leeds U	L	08/05	05	32	8	5
Leeds U	Tr	08/06	06-08	98	4	5
Swindon T	Tr	07/09	09-10	81	1	1
Brentford	Tr	07/11	11-14	169	0	17

DOUGLAS Patrick George (Pat)
Born: Baschurch, Shropshire, England, 17 September, 1951 M

League Club	Source	Date Signed	Seasons Played	Apps	Subs	Gls
Shrewsbury T	App	07/69	68	12	1	1

DOUGLAS Robert James (Rab)
Born: Forth, Lanarkshire, Scotland, 24 April, 1972 G
Scotland: 19

League Club	Source	Date Signed	Seasons Played	Apps	Subs	Gls
Leicester C	Glasgow Celtic	06/05	05	32	0	0
Millwall	L	09/07	07	7	0	0
Wycombe W	L	10/07	07	3	0	0
Plymouth Arg	L	03/08	07	1	0	0

DOUGLAS Stuart Anthony
Born: Enfield, N London, England, 9 April, 1978 F

League Club	Source	Date Signed	Seasons Played	Apps	Subs	Gls
Luton T	YT	05/96	95-01	104	42	18
Oxford U	L	10/01	01	1	3	0
Rushden & D	L	01/02	01	4	5	0
Boston U	Tr	08/02	02-03	28	30	8

DOUGLASS Norman
Born: Sunderland, England, 14 May, 1930 FB
Died: Ashtead, Surrey, England, 28 April, 1987

League Club	Source	Date Signed	Seasons Played	Apps	Subs	Gls
Chelsea	Crook T	03/52				
Exeter C	Tr	06/53	53-54	63	-	0

DOUGLIN Troy Alexander
Born: Coventry, England, 7 May, 1982 D

League Club	Source	Date Signed	Seasons Played	Apps	Subs	Gls
Torquay U	YT	07/00	00-02	9	5	0

DOUKARA Souleymane
Born: Meudon, France, 29 September, 1991 F

League Club	Source	Date Signed	Seasons Played	Apps	Subs	Gls
Leeds U	Catania (ITA)	07/14	14	17	8	5

DOUMBE Mathias Kouo
Born: Paris, France, 28 October, 1979 CD

League Club	Source	Date Signed	Seasons Played	Apps	Subs	Gls
Plymouth Arg	Hibernian	06/04	04-08	127	7	4
MK Dons	Tr	09/09	09-12	105	16	11
Northampton T	Tr	09/13	13	30	2	3

DOUMBIA Tongo Hened
Born: Vernon, France, 6 August, 1989 M
Mali: 13/U21-19

League Club	Source	Date Signed	Seasons Played	Apps	Subs	Gls
Wolverhampton W	Stade Rennais (FRA)	08/12	12	27	6	2

DOVE Craig
Born: Hartlepool, Cleveland, England, 16 August, 1983 M
England: Youth

League Club	Source	Date Signed	Seasons Played	Apps	Subs	Gls
Middlesbrough	YT	07/00				
York C	L	10/03	03	1	0	0
Rushden & D	Tr	07/04	04	31	5	6
Chester C	Tr	07/05	05	2	3	0

DOVE Henry William
Born: Stepney, E London, England, 11 March, 1932 CH
Died: Hemel Hempstead, Hertfordshire, England, 22 July, 2012

League Club	Source	Date Signed	Seasons Played	Apps	Subs	Gls
Arsenal	Essex Company Cadets	08/50				
Millwall	Tr	04/58	58	7	-	0

DOVEY Alan Raymond
Born: Stepney, E London, England, 18 July, 1952 G

League Club	Source	Date Signed	Seasons Played	Apps	Subs	Gls
Chelsea	App	07/69				
Brighton & HA	Tr	03/71	70-72	6	0	0

DOW Andrew James (Andy)
Born: Dundee, Scotland, 7 February, 1973 CD
Scotland: U21-3

League Club	Source	Date Signed	Seasons Played	Apps	Subs	Gls
Chelsea	Dundee	07/93	93-95	14	1	0
Bradford C	L	10/94	94	5	0	0

DOW David
Born: Manchester, England, 10 June, 1947 CD

League Club	Source	Date Signed	Seasons Played	Apps	Subs	Gls
Rochdale (Am)	Avorton	02/66	66-67	8	0	0

DOWD Henry William (Harry)
Born: Salford, England, 4 July, 1938 G
Died: 7 April, 2015

League Club	Source	Date Signed	Seasons Played	Apps	Subs	Gls
Manchester C	ICI Blackley	07/60	61-69	181	0	1
Stoke C	L	10/69	69	3	0	0
Oldham Ath	Tr	12/70	70-73	121	0	0

DOWD Hugh Oliver
Born: Lurgan, Armagh, Northern Ireland, 19 May, 1951 CD
Northern Ireland: 3

League Club	Source	Date Signed	Seasons Played	Apps	Subs	Gls
Sheffield Wed	Glenavon	07/74	74-78	110	2	0
Doncaster Rov	Tr	08/79	79-82	94	0	3

DOWE Jens
Born: Rostock, Germany, 1 June, 1968 M

League Club	Source	Date Signed	Seasons Played	Apps	Subs	Gls
Wolverhampton W (L)	Hamburger SV (GER)	10/96	96	5	3	0

DOWE Julian Whytus Lennox
Born: Manchester, England, 9 September, 1975 F

League Club	Source	Date Signed	Seasons Played	Apps	Subs	Gls
Wigan Ath	YT	09/92				
Rochdale	Colne	08/99	99	1	6	0

DOWELL Wayne Anthony
Born: Easington, County Durham, England, 28 December, 1973 LB

League Club	Source	Date Signed	Seasons Played	Apps	Subs	Gls
Burnley	YT	03/93	94-95	6	0	0
Carlisle U	L	03/96	95	2	5	0
Rochdale	Tr	07/96	96	6	1	0
Doncaster Rov	Tr	08/97	97	1	0	0

DOWEY Walter Leslie
Born: Lockton, North Yorkshire, England, 12 June, 1923 LB
Died: Cheshire, England, November, 2014

League Club	Source	Date Signed	Seasons Played	Apps	Subs	Gls
Crewe Alex		04/45	47-48	17	-	0

DOWIE Iain
Born: Hatfield, Hertfordshire, England, 9 January, 1965 F
Northern Ireland: 59/U23-1/U21-1

League Club	Source	Date Signed	Seasons Played	Apps	Subs	Gls
Luton T	Hendon	12/88	88-90	53	13	15
Fulham	L	09/89	89	5	0	1
West Ham U	Tr	03/91	90	12	0	4
Southampton	Tr	09/91	91-94	115	7	30
Crystal Palace	Tr	01/95	94-95	19	0	6
West Ham U	Tr	09/95	95-97	58	10	8
Queens Park Rgrs	Tr	01/98	97-00	16	15	2

DOWIE John
Born: Hamilton, Lanarkshire, Scotland, 12 December, 1955 M

League Club	Source	Date Signed	Seasons Played	Apps	Subs	Gls
Fulham	App	05/73	73-76	32	5	2
Doncaster Rov	Glasgow Celtic	07/79	79-80	21	0	0

DOWKER Thomas (Tom)
Born: Liverpool, England, 7 November, 1922 LW
Died: Wigan, Greater Manchester, England, December, 2001

League Club	Source	Date Signed	Seasons Played	Apps	Subs	Gls
Oldham Ath	South Liverpool	07/47	47	1	-	0

DOWLER Michael (Mike)
Born: Caldicot, Monmouthshire, Wales, 12 October, 1957 G
Wales: Schools

League Club	Source	Date Signed	Seasons Played	Apps	Subs	Gls
Newport Co	Hereford U (App)	10/75	75-80	19	0	0

DOWLING Michael Leslie (Mike)
Born: Bodmin, Cornwall, England, 3 October, 1952 RB/M

League Club	Source	Date Signed	Seasons Played	Apps	Subs	Gls
Plymouth Arg	App	10/70	69-73	27	4	0

DOWMAN Stephen John (Steve)
Born: East Ham, E London, England, 15 April, 1958 CD

League Club	Source	Date Signed	Seasons Played	Apps	Subs	Gls
Colchester U	App	04/76	76-79	150	4	21
Wrexham	Tr	07/80	80-82	87	0	2
Charlton Ath	Tr	08/83	83-84	60	1	5
Newport Co	Tr	08/85	85	9	0	1
Cambridge U	Tr	10/85	85-86	45	0	3

DOWN David Frederick
Born: Bristol, England, 7 July, 1948 F

League Club	Source	Date Signed	Seasons Played	Apps	Subs	Gls
Bristol C	App	09/65	66-67	6	1	3
Bradford Park Ave	Tr	10/67	67-68	39	0	7
Oldham Ath	Tr	09/68	68	9	0	1
Swindon T	Tr	08/69	69-70	1	1	0

DOWN William Frederick (Billy)
Born: Bristol, England, 8 November, 1963 FB

League Club	Source	Date Signed	Seasons Played	Apps	Subs	Gls
Bristol C	App	10/81	81	1	0	0

DOWNER Simon
Born: Romford, E London, England, 19 October, 1981 CD

League Club	Source	Date Signed	Seasons Played	Apps	Subs	Gls
Leyton Orient	YT	10/99	98-03	64	15	0

DOWNES Aaron Terence
Born: Mudgee, NSW, Australia, 15 May, 1985 CD
Australia: U23-8/Youth

League Club	Source	Date Signed	Seasons Played	Apps	Subs	Gls
Chesterfield	Australian IOS (AUS)	07/04	04-11	165	9	10
Bristol Rov	L	01/12	11	8	0	0
Torquay U	Tr	07/12	12-13	68	2	9

DOWNES Aidan
Born: Dublin, Republic of Ireland, 24 July, 1988 M
Republic of Ireland: U21-3/Youth

League Club	Source	Date Signed	Seasons Played	Apps	Subs	Gls
Everton	Sch	01/06				
Yeovil T	Tr	03/08	07-09	20	14	1

DOWNES Christopher Bryan (Chris)
Born: Sheffield, England, 17 January, 1969 M

League Club	Source	Date Signed	Seasons Played	Apps	Subs	Gls
Sheffield U	App	06/87	88	2	0	0
Scarborough	L	03/88	87	2	0	0
Stockport Co	Tr	08/89	89	10	1	1
Crewe Alex	Tr	08/91	91	1	1	0

DOWNES Eric
Born: Wigan, Greater Manchester, England, 25 August, 1926 CH

League Club	Source	Date Signed	Seasons Played	Apps	Subs	Gls
Rochdale	Chester C (Am)	05/49	50-53	54	-	0

DOWNES Robert David (Bobby)
Born: Bloxwich, West Midlands, England, 18 August, 1949 W/M

League Club	Source	Date Signed	Seasons Played	Apps	Subs	Gls
West Bromwich A	Jnr	08/66				
Peterborough U	Tr	09/67	67-68	23	3	3
Rochdale	Tr	08/69	69-73	164	10	10
Watford	Tr	05/74	74-79	192	7	18
Barnsley	Tr	03/80	79-80	43	0	1
Blackpool	Tr	07/82	82-83	27	1	3

DOWNES Stephen
Born: Leeds, England, 22 November, 1981 RB

League Club	Source	Date Signed	Seasons Played	Apps	Subs	Gls
Grimsby T	Ossett A	09/01				
York C	Tr	07/03	03	4	2	0

DOWNES Steven Fleming (Steve)
Born: Leeds, England, 2 December, 1949 F

League Club	Source	Date Signed	Seasons Played	Apps	Subs	Gls
Rotherham U	Leeds Mkt District BC	04/67	67-69	54	5	18
Sheffield Wed	Tr	12/69	69-71	26	4	4
Chesterfield	Tr	08/72	72-73	37	4	11
Halifax T	Tr	07/74	74-75	38	12	12
Blackburn Rov	L	03/76	75	6	0	0

DOWNES Walter John (Wally)
Born: Hammersmith, W London, England, 9 June, 1961 M

League Club	Source	Date Signed	Seasons Played	Apps	Subs	Gls
Wimbledon	App	01/79	78-86	194	13	15
Newport Co	L	12/87	87	4	0	2
Sheffield U	Tr	02/88	87	6	3	1

DOWNEY Christopher Anthony (Chris)
Born: Warrington, Cheshire, England, 19 April, 1983 F

League Club	Source	Date Signed	Seasons Played	Apps	Subs	Gls
Bolton W	YT	07/01	00	0	1	0

DOWNEY Glen
Born: Sunderland, England, 20 September, 1978 CD

League Club	Source	Date Signed	Seasons Played	Apps	Subs	Gls
Hartlepool U	YT	07/97				
Grimsby T	Scarborough	08/04	04-05	0	2	1

DOWNIE John Dennis (Johnny)
Born: Lanark, Scotland, 19 July, 1925 IF
Died: Tynemouth, Tyne and Wear, England, 19 February, 2013

League Club	Source	Date Signed	Seasons Played	Apps	Subs	Gls
Bradford Park Ave	Lanark ATC	12/44	46-48	86	-	33
Manchester U	Tr	03/49	48-52	110	-	35
Luton T	Tr	08/53	53	26	-	12
Hull C	Tr	07/54	54	27	-	5
Mansfield T	Wisbech T	10/58	58	18	-	4
Darlington	Tr	05/59	59	15	-	2

DOWNIE Mitchell (Mitch)
Born: Troon, Ayrshire, Scotland, 9 February, 1923 G
Died: Bradford, England, 12 July, 2001

League Club	Source	Date Signed	Seasons Played	Apps	Subs	Gls
Bradford Park Ave	Airdrieonians	08/50	50-53	156	-	0
Lincoln C	Tr	05/54	54-58	157	-	0
Bradford C	Goole T	09/59	59-62	134	-	0
Doncaster Rov	Tr	09/63	63	7	-	0

DOWNING David William
Born: Bideford, Devon, England, 6 October, 1969 W

League Club	Source	Date Signed	Seasons Played	Apps	Subs	Gls
York C	YT	-	87	1	0	0

DOWNING Derrick Graham
Born: Doncaster, South Yorkshire, England, 3 November, 1945 W

League Club	Source	Date Signed	Seasons Played	Apps	Subs	Gls
Middlesbrough	Frickley Colliery	02/65	65-71	172	10	39
Leyton Orient	Tr	05/72	72-74	100	4	12
York C	Tr	07/75	75-76	44	3	2
Hartlepool U	Tr	07/77	77	40	0	4

DOWNING Keith Gordon
Born: Oldbury, West Midlands, England, 23 July, 1965 DM

League Club	Source	Date Signed	Seasons Played	Apps	Subs	Gls
Notts Co	Mile Oak Rov	05/84	84-86	23	0	1
Wolverhampton W	Tr	08/87	87-92	169	22	8
Birmingham C	Tr	07/93	93	1	0	0
Stoke C	Tr	08/94	94	16	0	0
Cardiff C	Tr	08/95	95	3	1	0
Hereford U	Tr	09/95	95-96	45	0	0

DOWNING Paul Michael
Born: Taunton, Somerset, England, 26 October, 1991 CD

League Club	Source	Date Signed	Seasons Played	Apps	Subs	Gls
West Bromwich A	Sch	02/10				
Hereford U	L	03/10	09	6	0	0
Barnet	L	11/11	11	25	1	0
Walsall	Tr	07/12	12-14	103	7	3

DOWNING Stewart
Born: Middlesbrough, England, 22 July, 1984 LW
England: 35/B-2/U21-8/Youth

League Club	Source	Date Signed	Seasons Played	Apps	Subs	Gls
Middlesbrough	YT	09/01	01-08	157	24	17
Sunderland	L	10/03	03	7	0	3
Aston Villa	Tr	07/09	09-10	61	2	9
Liverpool	Tr	07/11	11-12	53	12	3
West Ham U	Tr	08/13	13-14	66	3	7

DOWNS David
Born: Glasgow, Scotland, 7 March, 1934 LB
Died: Torquay, Devon, England, 17 February, 1978

League Club	Source	Date Signed	Seasons Played	Apps	Subs	Gls
Plymouth Arg	Queens Park	11/57				
Torquay U	Tr	07/59	59	3	-	0

DOWNS Gregory (Greg)
Born: Carlton, Nottinghamshire, England, 13 December, 1958 LB

League Club	Source	Date Signed	Seasons Played	Apps	Subs	Gls
Norwich C	App	12/76	77-84	162	7	7
Torquay U	L	11/77	77	1	0	1
Coventry C	Tr	07/85	85-89	142	4	4
Birmingham C	Tr	07/90	90	16	1	0
Hereford U	Tr	06/91	91-94	105	3	2

DOWNS Ronald Henry (Ronnie)
Born: Southwark, S London, England, 27 August, 1932 W
Died: North West Surrey, England, March, 1994

League Club	Source	Date Signed	Seasons Played	Apps	Subs	Gls
Crystal Palace	Grove U	12/52	52-53	23	-	2

DOWNSBOROUGH Peter
Born: Halifax, West Yorkshire, England, 13 September, 1943 G

League Club	Source	Date Signed	Seasons Played	Apps	Subs	Gls
Halifax T	Jnr	09/60	59-64	148	-	0
Swindon T	Tr	08/65	65-72	274	0	0
Brighton & HA	L	08/73	73	3	0	0
Bradford C	Tr	11/73	73-78	225	0	0

DOWSETT Gilbert James (Dickie)
Born: Chelmsford, England, 3 July, 1931 CF

League Club	Source	Date Signed	Seasons Played	Apps	Subs	Gls
Tottenham H	Sudbury T	05/52	54	1	-	1
Southend U	Tr	05/55	55	20	-	4
Southampton	Tr	07/56	56	2	-	0
Bournemouth	Tr	06/57	57-62	169	-	79
Crystal Palace	Tr	11/62	62-64	54	-	22

DOWSON Alan Paul
Born: Gateshead, Tyne and Wear, England, 17 June, 1970 LB

League Club	Source	Date Signed	Seasons Played	Apps	Subs	Gls
Millwall	YT	05/88	90	1	0	0
Fulham	L	01/90	89	4	0	0
Bradford C	Tr	07/91	91	16	2	0
Darlington	Tr	08/92	92	30	2	0

DOWSON David
Born: Bishop Auckland, County Durham, England, 12 September, 1988 F

League Club	Source	Date Signed	Seasons Played	Apps	Subs	Gls
Sunderland	Sch	07/07				
Chesterfield	L	02/08	07	9	3	3
Darlington	L	08/09	09	6	4	1

DOWSON John Simpson
Born: Ashington, Northumberland, England, 18 September, 1926 RW
Died: Ashington, Northumberland, England, January, 1989

League Club	Source	Date Signed	Seasons Played	Apps	Subs	Gls
Manchester C	Murton CW	03/50				
Darlington	Peterborough U	06/52	52-53	65	-	11

DOYLE Christopher John (Chris)
Born: Liverpool, England, 17 February, 1995 CD

League Club	Source	Date Signed	Seasons Played	Apps	Subs	Gls
Morecambe	Jnr	07/12	12-14	3	6	0

DOYLE Colin Anthony
Born: Cork, Republic of Ireland, 12 August, 1985 G
Republic of Ireland: 1/B-1/U21-4

League Club	Source	Date Signed	Seasons Played	Apps	Subs	Gls
Birmingham C	Sch	07/04	06-14	28	3	0
Nottingham F	L	12/04	04	2	1	0
Millwall	L	11/05	05	14	0	0

DOYLE Conor Joseph
Born: McKinney, Texas, USA, 13 October, 1991 F

League Club	Source	Date Signed	Seasons Played	Apps	Subs	Gls
Derby Co	Creighton Blue's (USA)	08/10	10-12	7	15	0

DOYLE Daire Michael
Born: Dublin, Republic of Ireland, 18 October, 1980 M

League Club	Source	Date Signed	Seasons Played	Apps	Subs	Gls
Coventry C	Cherry Orchard (ROI)	09/98				
Kidderminster Hrs	Tr	01/01	00-02	14	7	0

DOYLE Eoin
Born: Dublin, Republic of Ireland, 12 March, 1988 F
Republic of Ireland: Youth

League Club	Source	Date Signed	Seasons Played	Apps	Subs	Gls
Chesterfield	Hibernian	06/13	13-14	52	17	32
Cardiff C	Tr	02/15	14	11	5	5

DOYLE Ian Patrick
Born: Torquay, Devon, England, 27 February, 1959 W

League Club	Source	Date Signed	Seasons Played	Apps	Subs	Gls
Bristol C	Barnstaple T	12/78	79-80	2	1	0

DOYLE Jeffrey Noel (Jeff)
Born: Dublin, Republic of Ireland, 25 February, 1967 M

League Club	Source	Date Signed	Seasons Played	Apps	Subs	Gls
Coventry C	App	02/85				
Peterborough U	Tr	08/86	86	13	1	0

DOYLE John Alexander (Ally)
Born: Limavady, Derry, Northern Ireland, 25 October, 1949 RB

League Club	Source	Date Signed	Seasons Played	Apps	Subs	Gls
Oldham Ath	Coleraine	11/66	67-68	31	2	0

DOYLE John Joseph
Born: Oxford, England, 8 February, 1960 RB

League Club	Source	Date Signed	Seasons Played	Apps	Subs	Gls
Oxford U	App	02/78	77-81	66	0	0
Torquay U	Tr	08/82	82	40	1	3

DOYLE Joseph Brian (Brian)
Born: Manchester, England, 15 July, 1930 FB
Died: Blackpool, Lancashire, England, 22 December, 1992

League Club	Source	Date Signed	Seasons Played	Apps	Subs	Gls
Stoke C	Winsford U	03/51	52	17	-	0
Exeter C	Tr	04/54	54-56	100	-	0
Bristol Rov	Tr	08/57	57-59	43	-	1

DOYLE Kevin Edward
Born: Adamstown, Wexford, Republic of Ireland, 18 September, 1983 F
Republic of Ireland: 61/U21-11

League Club	Source	Date Signed	Seasons Played	Apps	Subs	Gls
Reading	Cork C (ROI)	06/05	05-08	142	12	55
Wolverhampton W	Tr	07/09	09-14	140	24	30
Queens Park Rgrs	L	01/14	13	8	1	2
Crystal Palace	L	09/14	14	0	3	0

DOYLE Maurice
Born: Ellesmere Port, Cheshire, England, 17 October, 1969 M

League Club	Source	Date Signed	Seasons Played	Apps	Subs	Gls
Crewe Alex	YT	07/88	87-88	6	2	2
Queens Park Rgrs	Tr	04/89	92-93	6	0	0
Crewe Alex	L	01/91	90	6	1	2
Millwall	Tr	05/95	95-97	42	24	1

DOYLE Michael (Mike)
Born: Manchester, England, 25 November, 1946 CD
Died: Ashton-under-Lyne, Greater Manchester, England, 27 June, 2011
England: 5/FLge-2/U23-8

League Club	Source	Date Signed	Seasons Played	Apps	Subs	Gls
Manchester C	App	05/64	64-77	441	7	32
Stoke C	Tr	06/78	78-81	115	0	5
Bolton W	Tr	01/82	81-82	40	0	2
Rochdale	Tr	08/83	83	24	0	1

DOYLE Michael Paul (Micky)
Born: Dublin, Republic of Ireland, 8 July, 1981 DM
Republic of Ireland: 1/B-1/U21-8

League Club	Source	Date Signed	Seasons Played	Apps	Subs	Gls
Coventry C	Glasgow Celtic	07/03	03-10	256	9	20
Leeds U	L	08/09	09	42	0	0
Sheffield U	Tr	01/11	10-14	175	13	9

DOYLE Nathan Luke Robert
Born: Derby, England, 12 January, 1987 DM
England: Youth

League Club	Source	Date Signed	Seasons Played	Apps	Subs	Gls
Derby Co	Sch	01/04	03-05	4	5	0
Notts Co	L	02/06	05	12	0	0
Bradford C	L	08/06	06	25	3	0
Hull C	Tr	01/07	06-07	3	2	0
Barnsley	Tr	09/09	09-11	83	15	2
Preston NE	L	11/11	11	5	0	0
Bradford C	Tr	08/12	12-13	67	8	2
Luton T	Tr	09/14	14	27	0	0

DOYLE Robert (Bobby)
Born: Dumbarton, Dunbartonshire, Scotland, 27 December, 1953 M

League Club	Source	Date Signed	Seasons Played	Apps	Subs	Gls
Barnsley	Jnr	12/72	72-75	148	1	16
Peterborough U	Tr	07/76	76-78	130	0	10
Blackpool	Tr	07/79	79-80	47	2	2
Portsmouth	Tr	12/80	80-85	169	8	16
Hull C	Tr	08/85	85-86	43	0	2

DOYLE Robert (Robbie)
Born: Bray, Republic of Ireland, 15 April, 1982 F
Republic of Ireland: U21-1

League Club	Source	Date Signed	Seasons Played	Apps	Subs	Gls
Blackburn Rov	YT	04/99				
Macclesfield T	Bray W (ROI)	01/07	06	0	2	0

DOYLE Robert Leslie (Les)
Born: Liverpool, England, 28 June, 1927 CH
Died: Yeovil, Somerset, England, September, 1998

League Club	Source	Date Signed	Seasons Played	Apps	Subs	Gls
Everton	Jnr	05/45				
Exeter C	Tr	08/49	49-54	82	-	0

DOYLE Stephen Charles (Steve)
Born: Neath, Wales, 2 June, 1958 M
Wales: U21-2/Youth

League Club	Source	Date Signed	Seasons Played	Apps	Subs	Gls
Preston NE	App	06/75	74-81	178	19	8
Huddersfield T	Tr	09/82	82-86	158	3	6
Sunderland	Tr	09/86	86-88	99	1	2
Hull C	Tr	08/89	89-90	47	0	2
Rochdale	Tr	11/90	90-94	115	6	1

DOYLEY Lloyd Colin
Born: Whitechapel, Central London, England, 1 December, 1982 LB
Jamaica: 9

League Club	Source	Date Signed	Seasons Played	Apps	Subs	Gls
Watford	YT	03/01	01-14	360	35	2

DOZZELL Jason Alvin Winans
Born: Ipswich, England, 9 December, 1967 M/F
England: U21-9/Youth

League Club	Source	Date Signed	Seasons Played	Apps	Subs	Gls
Ipswich T	App	12/84	83-92	312	20	52
Tottenham H	Tr	08/93	93-96	68	16	13
Ipswich T	Tr	10/97	97	8	0	1
Northampton T	Tr	12/97	97	18	3	4
Colchester U	Tr	10/98	98-00	83	7	9

DRAKE Kenneth Lawrence (Ken)
Born: Skipton, North Yorkshire, England, 17 February, 1922 D
Died: York, England, 8 December, 2010

League Club	Source	Date Signed	Seasons Played	Apps	Subs	Gls
Halifax T	RAF	01/47	46-51	132	-	0

DRAKE Leonard George (Len)
Born: Dorchester, Dorset, England, 26 July, 1937 IF

League Club	Source	Date Signed	Seasons Played	Apps	Subs	Gls
Bristol Rov	Dorchester T	08/57	58-59	8	-	1

DRAKE Raymond Bradwell (Ray)
Born: Stockport, Greater Manchester, England, 24 October, 1934 CF
Died: Stockport, Greater Manchester, England, 30 March, 2013

League Club	Source	Date Signed	Seasons Played	Apps	Subs	Gls
Stockport Co	Bramhall	03/55	56-57	23	-	19

DRAKE Robert James (Bobby)
Born: Southgate, N London, England, 7 September, 1943 FB

League Club	Source	Date Signed	Seasons Played	Apps	Subs	Gls
Fulham	Chelsea (Am)	02/61	63-67	15	0	0

DRAKE Stephen (Steve)
Born: Goole, East Riding of Yorkshire, England, 27 August, 1948 G

League Club	Source	Date Signed	Seasons Played	Apps	Subs	Gls
Huddersfield T	Leeds U (Am)	06/66				
Scunthorpe U	Tr	07/67	67-69	23	0	0

DRAPER Craig James Edwin
Born: Swansea, Wales, 4 December, 1982 M

League Club	Source	Date Signed	Seasons Played	Apps	Subs	Gls
Swansea C	YT	07/01	01	0	2	0

DRAPER Derek
Born: Swansea, Wales, 11 May, 1943 M
Wales: U23-1

League Club	Source	Date Signed	Seasons Played	Apps	Subs	Gls
Swansea C	Jnr	05/62	62-65	61	0	10
Derby Co	Tr	04/66	66	8	0	1
Bradford Park Ave	Tr	09/67	67-68	60	3	9
Chester C	Tr	01/69	68-76	316	6	54

DRAPER Mark Andrew
Born: Long Eaton, Derbyshire, England, 11 November, 1970 M
England: U21-3

League Club	Source	Date Signed	Seasons Played	Apps	Subs	Gls
Notts Co	YT	12/88	88-93	206	15	40
Leicester C	Tr	07/94	94	39	0	5
Aston Villa	Tr	07/95	95-99	108	12	7
Southampton	Tr	07/00	00-01	17	7	1

DRAPER Richard Walter William (Bill)
Born: Leamington Spa, Warwickshire, England, 26 September, 1932 — CF

League Club	Source	Date Signed	Seasons Played	Apps	Subs	Gls
Northampton T	Lockheed Leamington	06/55	55-56	49	-	20

DRAPER Ross James
Born: Wolverhampton, England, 20 October, 1988 — M

League Club	Source	Date Signed	Seasons Played	Apps	Subs	Gls
Macclesfield T	Hednesford T	07/09	09-11	89	8	10

DRENCH Steven Mark
Born: Salford, England, 11 September, 1985 — G

League Club	Source	Date Signed	Seasons Played	Apps	Subs	Gls
Blackburn Rov	Sch	09/02				
Morecambe	Tr	07/06	07	3	1	0

DRENNAN Michael Joseph
Born: Kilkenny, Republic of Ireland, 2 February, 1994 — F
Republic of Ireland: U21-1/Youth

League Club	Source	Date Signed	Seasons Played	Apps	Subs	Gls
Aston Villa	Sch	02/11				
Carlisle U	L	01/14	13	3	3	0
Portsmouth	L	02/14	13	5	5	3
Portsmouth	L	09/14	14	3	1	0

DRENTHE Roysten Rickie
Born: Rotterdam, Netherlands, 8 April, 1987 — W
Netherlands: 1/B-1/U21-17/Youth

League Club	Source	Date Signed	Seasons Played	Apps	Subs	Gls
Everton (L)	Real Madrid (SPN)	08/11	11	10	11	3
Reading	FCA Vladikavkaz (RUS)	07/13	13	17	6	2
Sheffield Wed	L	09/14	14	7	8	1

DREWERY Michael Stephen (Mike)
Born: Snettisham, Norfolk, England, 16 January, 1949 — G

League Club	Source	Date Signed	Seasons Played	Apps	Subs	Gls
Peterborough U	Snettisham	07/67	68-73	209	0	0

DREYER John Brian
Born: Alnwick, Northumberland, England, 11 June, 1963 — CD

League Club	Source	Date Signed	Seasons Played	Apps	Subs	Gls
Oxford U	Wallingford T	01/85	86-87	57	3	2
Torquay U	L	12/85	85	5	0	0
Fulham	L	03/86	85	12	0	2
Luton T	Tr	06/88	88-93	212	2	13
Stoke C	Tr	07/94	94-96	32	17	3
Bolton W	L	03/95	94	1	1	0
Bradford C	Tr	11/96	96-99	72	8	2
Cambridge U	Tr	07/00	00	40	0	0

DRING Raymond (Ray)
Born: Lincoln, England, 13 February, 1924 — G
Died: Lincoln, England, 21 October, 2003
England: Schools

League Club	Source	Date Signed	Seasons Played	Apps	Subs	Gls
Huddersfield T (Am)	Scarborough High ATC	06/47	47	4	-	0

DRINKELL Kevin Smith
Born: Grimsby, North Lincolnshire, England, 18 June, 1960 — F

League Club	Source	Date Signed	Seasons Played	Apps	Subs	Gls
Grimsby T	App	06/78	76-84	242	30	89
Norwich C	Tr	08/85	85-87	121	0	50
Coventry C	Glasgow Rangers	10/89	89-91	34	7	5
Birmingham C	L	10/91	91	5	0	2

DRINKWATER Charles John (Charlie)
Born: Willesden, NW London, England, 25 June, 1914 — LW
Died: Denham, Buckinghamshire, England, 8 April, 1998

League Club	Source	Date Signed	Seasons Played	Apps	Subs	Gls
Aston Villa	Walthamstow Ave	11/35	35	2	-	1
Charlton Ath	Tr	07/38	38	3	-	0
Watford	Tr	01/45	46	1	-	0

DRINKWATER Daniel Noel (Danny)
Born: Manchester, England, 5 March, 1990 — M
England: Youth

League Club	Source	Date Signed	Seasons Played	Apps	Subs	Gls
Manchester U	Sch	07/08				
Huddersfield T	L	08/09	09	27	6	2
Cardiff C	L	08/10	10	7	2	0
Watford	L	01/11	10	3	9	0
Barnsley	L	08/11	11	16	1	1
Leicester C	Tr	01/12	11-14	113	16	10

DRINKWATER James Arthur (Jimmy)
Born: Northwich, Cheshire, England, 10 February, 1918 — FB
Died: Hythe, Hampshire, England, January, 1996

League Club	Source	Date Signed	Seasons Played	Apps	Subs	Gls
Torquay U	St Mirren	06/52	52-53	67	-	1

DRINKWATER Raymond (Ray)
Born: Jarrow, Tyne and Wear, England, 18 May, 1931 — G
Died: Guildford, Surrey, England, 24 March, 2008

League Club	Source	Date Signed	Seasons Played	Apps	Subs	Gls
Portsmouth	Guildford C	11/55	56	8	-	0
Queens Park Rgrs	Tr	02/58	57-62	199	-	0

DRINKWATER Roy
Born: Altrincham, Greater Manchester, England, 25 December, 1954 — M

League Club	Source	Date Signed	Seasons Played	Apps	Subs	Gls
Crewe Alex	App	-	70	0	1	0

DRISCOLL Andrew (Andy)
Born: Staines, Surrey, England, 21 October, 1971 — RW

League Club	Source	Date Signed	Seasons Played	Apps	Subs	Gls
Brentford	YT	03/90	88-91	10	4	2

DRIVER Allenby
Born: Blackwell, Derbyshire, England, 29 December, 1918 — IF
Died: Sheffield, England, 31 March, 1997

League Club	Source	Date Signed	Seasons Played	Apps	Subs	Gls
Sheffield Wed	Mansfield Shoes	04/36	37-38	6	-	3
Luton T	Tr	10/46	46-47	41	-	13
Norwich C	Tr	01/48	47-49	49	-	19
Ipswich T	Tr	01/50	49-51	86	-	25
Walsall	Tr	07/52	52	26	-	2

DRIVER Callum Charles John
Born: Sidcup, SE London, England, 23 October, 1992 — LB

League Club	Source	Date Signed	Seasons Played	Apps	Subs	Gls
West Ham U	Sch	07/11				
Burton A	L	01/12	11	8	0	1

DRIVER Philip Anthony (Phil)
Born: Huddersfield, West Yorkshire, England, 10 August, 1959 — RW

League Club	Source	Date Signed	Seasons Played	Apps	Subs	Gls
Wimbledon	Bedford T	12/78	78-80	7	9	3
Chelsea	Tr	09/80	80-82	25	19	4
Wimbledon	Tr	07/83	83-84	2	2	0

DROGBA Didier Yves Tebily
Born: Abidjan, Ivory Coast, 11 March, 1978 — F
Ivory Coast: 104

League Club	Source	Date Signed	Seasons Played	Apps	Subs	Gls
Chelsea	Olymp Marseille (FRA)	07/04	04-11	179	47	100
Chelsea	Galatasaray (TKY)	07/14	14	8	20	4

DROY Michael Robert (Micky)
Born: Highbury, N London, England, 7 May, 1951 — CD

League Club	Source	Date Signed	Seasons Played	Apps	Subs	Gls
Chelsea	Slough T	09/70	70-84	263	9	13
Luton T	L	11/84	84	2	0	0
Crystal Palace	Tr	03/85	84-86	49	0	7
Brentford	Tr	11/86	86	19	0	3

DRUCE Mark Andrew
Born: Oxford, England, 3 March, 1974 — F

League Club	Source	Date Signed	Seasons Played	Apps	Subs	Gls
Oxford U	YT	12/91	91-95	18	34	4
Rotherham U	Tr	09/96	96-97	21	13	4

DRUMMOND Ian Philip
Born: Brechin, Angus, Scotland, 27 August, 1923 — FB
Died: Poole, Dorset, England, April, 2010

League Club	Source	Date Signed	Seasons Played	Apps	Subs	Gls
Portsmouth	Jeanfield Swifts	05/45				
Bournemouth	Tr	06/49	49-55	265	-	2

DRUMMOND Stewart James
Born: Preston, Lancashire, England, 11 December, 1975 — M
England: Semi Pro-13

League Club	Source	Date Signed	Seasons Played	Apps	Subs	Gls
Chester C	Morecambe	06/04	04-05	85	2	12
Shrewsbury T	Tr	07/06	06-07	65	2	7
Morecambe	Tr	01/08	07-14	257	20	34

DRUMMY Dermot
Born: Hackney, E London, England, 16 January, 1961 — M

League Club	Source	Date Signed	Seasons Played	Apps	Subs	Gls
Arsenal	App	01/79				
Blackpool	L	03/80	79	4	1	0

DRURY Adam James
Born: Cottenham, Cambridgeshire, England, 29 August, 1978 — LB

League Club	Source	Date Signed	Seasons Played	Apps	Subs	Gls
Peterborough U	YT	07/96	95-00	138	10	2
Norwich C	Tr	03/01	00-11	322	4	4
Leeds U	Tr	07/12	12-13	11	2	0
Bradford C	L	03/14	13	11	1	0

DRURY Adam John
Born: Grimsby, North Lincolnshire, England, 21 September, 1993 — RM

League Club	Source	Date Signed	Seasons Played	Apps	Subs	Gls
Manchester C	Sch	09/10				
Burton A	L	01/13	12	6	6	0

DRURY Andrew Mark (Andy)
Born: Sittingbourne, Kent, England, 28 November, 1983 — RW

League Club	Source	Date Signed	Seasons Played	Apps	Subs	Gls
Ipswich T	Luton T	01/11	10-12	44	18	2
Crawley T	L	09/11	11	13	0	3
Crawley T	Tr	06/13	13	36	5	5
Luton T	Tr	06/14	14	30	5	2

DRURY Charles Edward (Chuck)
Born: Darlaston, West Midlands, England, 4 July, 1937 — WH
England: Youth

League Club	Source	Date Signed	Seasons Played	Apps	Subs	Gls
West Bromwich A	FH Lloyds	02/55	57-63	146	-	1
Bristol C	Tr	08/64	64-66	51	0	2
Bradford Park Ave	Tr	03/68	67-68	31	0	1

DRURY George Benjamin
Born: Hucknall, Nottinghamshire, England, 22 January, 1914 — IF
Died: Hucknall, Nottinghamshire, England, 19 June, 1972

League Club	Source	Date Signed	Seasons Played	Apps	Subs	Gls
Sheffield Wed	Heanor T	09/34	36-37	44	-	9
Arsenal	Tr	03/38	37-46	38	-	3
West Bromwich A	Tr	10/46	46-47	29	-	8
Watford	Tr	07/48	48-49	35	-	3

DRURY James Welsh (Jim)
Born: Cumnock, Ayrshire, Scotland, 29 May, 1924 — LW
Died: Cumnock, Ayrshire, Scotland, 26 July, 2000

League Club	Source	Date Signed	Seasons Played	Apps	Subs	Gls
Rochdale	Stirling A	05/51	51	4	-	1
Carlisle U	Tr	08/52	52-53	35	-	5
Southport	Tr	07/54	54	24	-	2

DRYBURGH Thomas James Douglas (Tom)
Born: Kirkcaldy, Fife, Scotland, 23 April, 1923 — LW
Died: Rochdale, Greater Manchester, England, 15 May, 2008

League Club	Source	Date Signed	Seasons Played	Apps	Subs	Gls
Aldershot	Lochgelly Albert	06/47	47	19	-	2
Rochdale	Tr	07/48	48-49	77	-	17
Leicester C	Tr	09/50	50-53	95	-	29
Hull C	Tr	05/54	54	23	-	3
Oldham Ath	Kings Lynn	08/57	57	1	-	0
Rochdale	Tr	11/57	57	5	-	0

DRYDEN John George (Jackie)
Born: Sunderland, England, 16 September, 1919 — RW
Died: Eastbourne, East Sussex, England, 3 April, 2004

League Club	Source	Date Signed	Seasons Played	Apps	Subs	Gls
Charlton Ath	Washington Chemicals	03/46				
Swindon T	Hylton CW	05/47	47	21	-	3
Leyton Orient	Tr	06/48	48-49	40	-	10

DRYDEN Richard Andrew
Born: Stroud, Gloucestershire, England, 14 June, 1969 — CD

League Club	Source	Date Signed	Seasons Played	Apps	Subs	Gls
Bristol Rov	YT	07/87	86-88	12	1	0
Exeter C	Tr	09/88	88-90	92	0	13
Notts Co	Tr	08/91	91-92	30	1	1
Plymouth Arg	L	11/92	92	5	0	0
Birmingham C	Tr	03/93	92-94	48	0	0
Bristol C	Tr	12/94	94-95	32	5	2
Southampton	Tr	08/98	96-99	44	3	1
Stoke C	L	11/99	99	3	0	0
Stoke C	L	03/00	99	8	2	0
Northampton T	L	09/00	00	9	1	0
Swindon T	L	11/00	00	7	0	0
Luton T	Tr	02/01	00-01	22	1	0

DRYHURST Carl David
Born: Sutton Coldfield, West Midlands, England, 8 November, 1960 — F

League Club	Source	Date Signed	Seasons Played	Apps	Subs	Gls
Halifax T	Sutton Coldfield T	11/79	79	4	4	0

DRYSDALE Brian
Born: Wingate, County Durham, England, 24 February, 1943 — LB

League Club	Source	Date Signed	Seasons Played	Apps	Subs	Gls
Lincoln C	Jnr	09/60	59-64	21	-	0
Hartlepool U	Tr	07/65	65-68	169	1	2
Bristol C	Tr	05/69	69-76	280	2	3
Reading	L	02/77	76	16	0	0
Oxford U	Tr	07/77	77	15	0	0

DRYSDALE Jason
Born: Bristol, England, 17 November, 1970 — LB
England: Youth

League Club	Source	Date Signed	Seasons Played	Apps	Subs	Gls
Watford	YT	09/88	89-93	135	10	11
Newcastle U	Tr	08/94				
Swindon T	Tr	03/95	94-97	35	7	0
Northampton T	Tr	03/98	97	1	0	0

DRYSDALE Leon Anthony
Born: Walsall, West Midlands, England, 3 February, 1981 — FB

League Club	Source	Date Signed	Seasons Played	Apps	Subs	Gls
Shrewsbury T	YT	07/99	98-02	51	14	1

D'SANE Roscoe Niquaye
Born: Epsom, Surrey, England, 16 October, 1980 — F
England: Semi Pro-7

League Club	Source	Date Signed	Seasons Played	Apps	Subs	Gls
Crystal Palace	YT	06/99				
Southend U	Slough T	11/01	01	1	1	0
Accrington Stan	AFC Wimbledon	07/07	07	18	4	7

DUBERRY Michael Wayne
Born: Enfield, N London, England, 14 October, 1975 — CD
England: U21-5

League Club	Source	Date Signed	Seasons Played	Apps	Subs	Gls
Chelsea	YT	06/93	93-98	77	9	1
Bournemouth	L	09/95	95	7	0	0
Leeds U	Tr	07/99	99-04	54	4	4
Stoke C	Tr	10/04	04-06	95	0	1
Reading	Tr	01/07	06-08	47	1	0
Wycombe W	Tr	07/09	09	18	0	0
Oxford U	St Johnstone	07/11	11-12	45	2	3

DUBLIN Dion
Born: Leicester, England, 22 April, 1969 — F
England: 4

League Club	Source	Date Signed	Seasons Played	Apps	Subs	Gls
Norwich C	Oakham U	03/88				
Cambridge U	Tr	08/88	88-91	133	23	52
Manchester U	Tr	08/92	92-93	4	8	2
Coventry C	Tr	09/94	94-98	144	1	61
Aston Villa	Tr	11/98	98-03	120	35	48
Millwall	L	03/02	01	5	0	2
Leicester C	Tr	07/04	04-05	49	9	5
Norwich C	Glasgow Celtic	09/06	06-07	50	20	12

DUBLIN Keith Barry Lennox
Born: High Wycombe, Buckinghamshire, England, 29 January, 1966 — CD
England: Youth

League Club	Source	Date Signed	Seasons Played	Apps	Subs	Gls
Chelsea	App	01/84	83-86	50	1	0
Brighton & HA	Tr	08/87	87-89	132	0	5
Watford	Tr	07/90	90-93	165	3	2
Southend U	Tr	07/94	94-98	175	4	9
Colchester U	L	11/98	98	2	0	0

DUBOIS Joseph Martin (Joe)
Born: Newtownabbey, Antrim, Northern Ireland, 27 December, 1927 — W
Died: Doncaster, South Yorkshire, England, July, 1987
Northern Ireland: Amateur

League Club	Source	Date Signed	Seasons Played	Apps	Subs	Gls
Doncaster Rov	Brantwood	05/49	49-51	31	-	5
Grimsby T	Bedford T	07/53	53	6	-	1
Halifax T	Tr	07/54	54-56	78	-	10

DUCHART Alexander (Alex)
Born: Falkirk, Scotland, 3 May, 1933 — LW

League Club	Source	Date Signed	Seasons Played	Apps	Subs	Gls
Southend U	Third Lanark	05/56	56	8	-	2

DUCK George Thomas
Born: Tottenham, N London, England, 22 February, 1952 — F

League Club	Source	Date Signed	Seasons Played	Apps	Subs	Gls
Millwall	App	02/70				
Southend U	Tr	06/71	71	3	0	0

DUCKHOUSE Edward (Ted)
Born: Walsall, West Midlands, England, 9 April, 1918 — CH
Died: Walsall, West Midlands, England, 1978

League Club	Source	Date Signed	Seasons Played	Apps	Subs	Gls
Birmingham C	West Bromwich A (Am)	08/38	38-49	119	-	4
Northampton T	Tr	08/50	50-51	68	-	0

DUCKWORTH Michael James
Born: Rinteln, Germany, 28 April, 1992 — RB

League Club	Source	Date Signed	Seasons Played	Apps	Subs	Gls
Hartlepool U	Bradford Park Ave	08/13	13-14	67	0	3

DUCROCQ Pierre
Born: Pontoise, France, 18 December, 1976 — DM

League Club	Source	Date Signed	Seasons Played	Apps	Subs	Gls
Derby Co (L)	Paris St-Germain (FRA)	10/01	01	19	0	0

DUCROS Andrew John (Andy)
Born: Evesham, Worcestershire, England, 16 September, 1977 — LW
England: Youth/Schools

League Club	Source	Date Signed	Seasons Played	Apps	Subs	Gls
Coventry C	YT	09/94	96-97	2	6	0
Kidderminster Hrs	Nuneaton Bor	07/00	00-02	38	12	4

DUDDY John Michael
Born: Manchester, England, 8 February, 1956 — M

League Club	Source	Date Signed	Seasons Played	Apps	Subs	Gls
Oldham Ath	App	02/74				
Stockport Co	Tr	03/76	75	6	0	0

DUDEK Jerzy
Born: Rybnik, Poland, 23 March, 1973 — G
Poland: 59

League Club	Source	Date Signed	Seasons Played	Apps	Subs	Gls
Liverpool	Feyenoord (NED)	08/01	01-06	126	1	0

DUDFIELD Lawrence George (Lawrie)
Born: Southwark, S London, England, 7 May, 1980 — F

League Club	Source	Date Signed	Seasons Played	Apps	Subs	Gls
Leicester C	Kettering T	06/97	99	0	2	0
Lincoln C	L	09/00	00	2	1	0
Chesterfield	L	12/00	00	4	10	3
Hull C	Tr	07/01	01-02	39	20	13
Northampton T	Tr	03/03	02-03	20	9	4
Southend U	Tr	02/04	03-04	29	20	9
Northampton T	Tr	08/05	05	2	4	1
Boston U	Tr	09/05	05	21	15	5
Notts Co	Tr	07/06	06-07	55	19	8

DUDGEON James Fleming
Born: Newcastle-upon-Tyne, England, 19 March, 1981 — CD
Scotland: Youth

League Club	Source	Date Signed	Seasons Played	Apps	Subs	Gls
Barnsley	YT	07/99				
Lincoln C	L	11/00	00	20	2	3

DUDGEON Joseph Patrick (Joe)
Born: Leeds, England, 26 November, 1990 — LB
Northern Ireland: U21-4

League Club	Source	Date Signed	Seasons Played	Apps	Subs	Gls
Manchester U	Sch	07/09				
Carlisle U	L	01/11	10	1	1	0
Hull C	Tr	05/11	11-12	26	7	0
Barnsley	L	07/14	14	14	0	0

DUDKA Dariusz
Born: Kostrzyn, Poland, 9 December, 1983 — DM
Poland: 65

League Club	Source	Date Signed	Seasons Played	Apps	Subs	Gls
Birmingham C	Levante (SPN)	11/13	13	1	1	0

DUDLEY Anthony
Born: Manchester, England, 3 January, 1996 — F

League Club	Source	Date Signed	Seasons Played	Apps	Subs	Gls
Bury	Sch	01/15	13-14	0	3	0

DUDLEY Craig Bryan
Born: Ollerton, Nottinghamshire, England, 12 September, 1979 — F
England: Youth

League Club	Source	Date Signed	Seasons Played	Apps	Subs	Gls
Notts Co	YT	04/97	96-98	11	20	3
Shrewsbury T	L	01/98	97	3	1	0
Hull C	L	11/98	98	4	3	2
Oldham Ath	Tr	03/99	99-01	34	26	10
Chesterfield	L	08/99	99	0	2	0
Scunthorpe U	L	02/02	01	1	3	0

DUDLEY Frank Ernest
Born: Southend-on-Sea, England, 9 May, 1925 — CF
Died: Southend-on-Sea, England, 14 September, 2012

League Club	Source	Date Signed	Seasons Played	Apps	Subs	Gls
Southend U	Jnr	10/45	46-48	88	-	32
Leeds U	Tr	08/49	49-50	64	-	23
Southampton	Tr	02/51	50-53	67	-	32
Cardiff C	Tr	09/53	53	5	-	1
Brentford	Tr	12/53	53-56	72	-	32

DUDLEY James George (Jimmy)
Born: Gartcosh, Lanarkshire, Scotland, 24 August, 1928 — WH
Died: West Bromwich, West Midlands, England, 25 April, 2006
Scotland: B

League Club	Source	Date Signed	Seasons Played	Apps	Subs	Gls
West Bromwich A	Albright YC	05/46	49-59	285	-	9
Walsall	Tr	12/59	59-63	167	-	3

DUDLEY Mark
Born: Doncaster, South Yorkshire, England, 29 January, 1990 — LB

League Club	Source	Date Signed	Seasons Played	Apps	Subs	Gls
Derby Co	Sch	07/08	08	0	1	0

DUDLEY Philip William (Phil)
Born: Basildon, England, 17 February, 1959 — RB

League Club	Source	Date Signed	Seasons Played	Apps	Subs	Gls
Southend U	App	02/77	77-82	109	3	3

DUDLEY Reginald Arthur (Reg)
Born: Hemel Hempstead, Hertfordshire, England, 3 February, 1915 — RB
Died: Cambridge, England, February, 1994
England: Amateur

League Club	Source	Date Signed	Seasons Played	Apps	Subs	Gls
Millwall	Apsley	03/35	35-46	42	-	0
Queens Park Rgrs	Tr	12/46	46-49	58	-	0
Watford	Tr	07/50	50	1	-	0

DUERDEN Harold (Harry)
Born: Barnsley, South Yorkshire, England, 5 March, 1948 — LH

League Club	Source	Date Signed	Seasons Played	Apps	Subs	Gls
Barnsley	App	09/65	65-66	24	1	1

DUERDEN Ian Christopher
Born: Burnley, Lancashire, England, 27 March, 1978 — F

League Club	Source	Date Signed	Seasons Played	Apps	Subs	Gls
Burnley	YT	07/96	97	1	0	0
Halifax T	Tr	08/98	98	1	1	0

DUFF Damien Anthony
Born: Dublin, Republic of Ireland, 2 March, 1979 — W
Republic of Ireland: 100/B-1/Youth/Schools

League Club	Source	Date Signed	Seasons Played	Apps	Subs	Gls
Blackburn Rov	Lourdes Celtic (ROI)	03/96	96-02	157	27	27
Chelsea	Tr	07/03	03-05	63	18	14
Newcastle U	Tr	06/06	06-09	61	8	5
Fulham	Tr	08/09	09-13	111	19	15

DUFF Michael James
Born: Belfast, Northern Ireland, 11 January, 1978 — CD
Northern Ireland: 24/B-1

League Club	Source	Date Signed	Seasons Played	Apps	Subs	Gls
Cheltenham T	YT	08/96	99-03	201	0	12
Burnley	Tr	07/04	04-14	300	18	7

DUFF Shane Joseph
Born: Wroughton, Wiltshire, England, 2 April, 1982 — CD
Northern Ireland: U21-1

League Club	Source	Date Signed	Seasons Played	Apps	Subs	Gls
Cheltenham T	Jnr	10/00	02-09	184	9	2
Bradford C	Tr	07/10	10	14	0	1

DUFF William (Willie)
Born: Winchburgh, West Lothian, Scotland, 6 February, 1935 — G
Died: Edinburgh, Scotland, 30 August, 2004
Scotland: SLge-1/U23-1

League Club	Source	Date Signed	Seasons Played	Apps	Subs	Gls
Charlton Ath	Heart of Midlothian	12/56	56-61	213	-	0
Peterborough U	Tr	05/63	63-66	118	0	0

DUFF William Francis Andrew (Billy)
Born: Littleborough, Greater Manchester, England, 16 December, 1938 — LW
Died: Rochdale, Greater Manchester, England, 25 March, 2002

League Club	Source	Date Signed	Seasons Played	Apps	Subs	Gls
Rochdale	Jnr	05/56				
Scunthorpe U	Tr	10/58				
Grimsby T	Tr	10/59	59	3	-	1
Accrington Stan	Toronto WE (CAN)	10/60	60	14	-	3

DUFFETT Edgar
Born: Worcester, England, 29 August, 1926 — IF
Died: Bedford, England, October, 2006

League Club	Source	Date Signed	Seasons Played	Apps	Subs	Gls
Norwich C	West Bromwich A (Am)	11/47				
Carlisle U	Tr	08/50	50-52	47	-	8

DUFFEY Christopher Paul (Chris)
Born: Kirkby, Merseyside, England, 8 January, 1952 — LW

League Club	Source	Date Signed	Seasons Played	Apps	Subs	Gls
Bolton W	App	09/69	69-71	8	0	0
Crewe Alex	L	09/72	72	6	0	3
Crewe Alex	Tr	07/73	73-74	54	3	12
Bury	Tr	10/74	74	17	4	8
Shrewsbury T	Tr	05/75	75	4	4	1
Rochdale	L	11/75	75	2	0	0

DUFFIELD Martin John
Born: Acton, W London, England, 28 February, 1964 — M
England: Youth

League Club	Source	Date Signed	Seasons Played	Apps	Subs	Gls
Queens Park Rgrs	App	01/82	82	0	1	0
Bournemouth	L	09/83	83	6	0	1
Charlton Ath	L	11/84	84	1	0	0

DUFFIELD Peter
Born: Middlesbrough, England, 4 February, 1969 — F

League Club	Source	Date Signed	Seasons Played	Apps	Subs	Gls
Middlesbrough	App	11/86				
Sheffield U	Tr	08/87	87-91	34	24	16
Halifax T	L	03/88	87	12	0	6
Rotherham U	L	03/91	90	17	0	5
Blackpool	L	07/92	92	3	2	1
Crewe Alex	L	01/93	92	0	2	0
Stockport Co	L	03/93	92	6	1	4
Darlington	Falkirk	01/99	98-99	31	16	14
York C	Tr	07/00	00-02	41	4	19
Boston U	Tr	01/03	02-03	24	21	9
Carlisle U	Tr	03/04	03	10	0	3

DUFFIN Lionel Joseph
Born: Ulverston, Cumbria, England, 8 August, 1945 — G

League Club	Source	Date Signed	Seasons Played	Apps	Subs	Gls
Barrow	Jnr	07/64	64-67	46	0	0

DUFFUS Courtney John
Born: Cheltenham, Gloucestershire, England, 24 October, 1995 — F

League Club	Source	Date Signed	Seasons Played	Apps	Subs	Gls
Everton	Sch	10/12				
Bury	L	10/14	14	1	2	0

DUFFY Alan
Born: Stanley, County Durham, England, 20 December, 1949 — M
England: Youth

League Club	Source	Date Signed	Seasons Played	Apps	Subs	Gls
Newcastle U	App	03/67	68-69	2	2	0
Brighton & HA	Tr	01/70	69-71	34	16	8
Tranmere Rov	Tr	03/72	71-72	29	4	2
Darlington	Tr	08/73	73	19	5	0

DUFFY Ayden Stuart
Born: Kettering, Northamptonshire, England, 16 January, 1986 — G

League Club	Source	Date Signed	Seasons Played	Apps	Subs	Gls
Lincoln C	Sch	07/06	07-08	3	2	0

DUFFY Christopher (Chris)
Born: Methil, Fife, Scotland, 21 October, 1918 — LW
Died: Consett, County Durham, England, 20 February, 1978

League Club	Source	Date Signed	Seasons Played	Apps	Subs	Gls
Charlton Ath	Leith Ath	09/45	46-52	162	-	33

DUFFY Christopher John (Chris)
Born: Eccles, Greater Manchester, England, 31 October, 1973 — M/FB

League Club	Source	Date Signed	Seasons Played	Apps	Subs	Gls
Crewe Alex	YT	06/92				
Wigan Ath	Tr	07/93	93-94	15	16	1

DUFFY Darrell Gerald
Born: Birmingham, England, 18 January, 1971 — CD
England: Youth/Schools

League Club	Source	Date Signed	Seasons Played	Apps	Subs	Gls
Aston Villa	YT	07/89	88	1	0	0
Scunthorpe U	Moor Green	02/93	92	4	0	0

DUFFY Darryl Alexander
Born: Glasgow, Scotland, 16 April, 1984 — F
Scotland: B-1/U21-8

League Club	Source	Date Signed	Seasons Played	Apps	Subs	Gls
Hull C	Falkirk	01/06	05-06	9	15	3
Hartlepool U	L	11/06	06	10	0	5
Swansea C	Tr	03/07	06-07	17	11	6
Bristol Rov	Tr	07/08	08-10	43	33	17
Carlisle U	L	02/10	09	7	1	1
Cheltenham T	Tr	07/11	11-12	28	37	13

DUFFY Gerald (Gerry)
Born: Middlewich, Cheshire, England, 12 September, 1934 — CF

League Club	Source	Date Signed	Seasons Played	Apps	Subs	Gls
Oldham Ath	Middlewich	05/56	56-58	58	-	21

DUFFY John
Born: Dunfermline, Fife, Scotland, 6 September, 1943 — LH

League Club	Source	Date Signed	Seasons Played	Apps	Subs	Gls
Darlington	Dunfermline Ath	08/63	63	10	-	1

DUFFY John
Born: Glasgow, Scotland, 24 April, 1922 — RB
Died: Strathclyde, Glasgow, Scotland, 10 April, 1996

League Club	Source	Date Signed	Seasons Played	Apps	Subs	Gls
Norwich C	Raith Rov	03/49	49-53	78	-	0

DUFFY John Gerard
Born: Dundee, Scotland, 24 August, 1929 — LH
Died: Dundee, Scotland, 4 May, 2004

League Club	Source	Date Signed	Seasons Played	Apps	Subs	Gls
Southend U	Glasgow Celtic	05/54	54-59	114	-	4

DUFFY Lee Alan
Born: Oldham, Greater Manchester, England, 24 July, 1982 — RB

League Club	Source	Date Signed	Seasons Played	Apps	Subs	Gls
Rochdale	YT	09/01	01-02	20	8	0

DUFFY Mark James
Born: Liverpool, England, 7 October, 1985 — RW

League Club	Source	Date Signed	Seasons Played	Apps	Subs	Gls
Morecambe	Southport	02/09	08-10	44	22	5
Scunthorpe U	Tr	01/11	10-12	89	13	8
Doncaster Rov	Tr	07/13	13	28	8	2
Birmingham C	Tr	06/14	14	1	3	0
Chesterfield	L	02/15	14	1	2	0

DUFFY Michael Kevin (Mike)
Born: Leicester, England, 12 June, 1961 — M

League Club	Source	Date Signed	Seasons Played	Apps	Subs	Gls
Leicester C	Jnr	07/78	78-79	7	5	1

DUFFY Richard Michael
Born: Swansea, Wales, 30 August, 1985 — RB
Wales: 13/U21-8/Youth

League Club	Source	Date Signed	Seasons Played	Apps	Subs	Gls
Swansea C	Sch	09/02	03	16	2	1
Portsmouth	Tr	01/04	03	0	1	0
Burnley	L	09/04	04	3	4	1
Coventry C	L	01/05	04	14	0	0
Coventry C	L	07/05	05	30	2	0
Coventry C	L	10/06	06	13	0	0
Swansea C	L	01/07	06	8	3	0
Coventry C	L	03/08	07	2	0	0
Millwall	Tr	02/09	08	11	1	0
Exeter C	Tr	08/09	09-11	104	8	3
Port Vale	Tr	07/12	12-14	88	3	1

DUFFY Robert James
Born: Swansea, Wales, 2 December, 1982 — F
Wales: Youth

League Club	Source	Date Signed	Seasons Played	Apps	Subs	Gls
Rushden & D	Jnr	07/00	01-04	8	21	1
Wrexham (L)	Oxford U	01/08	07	0	6	0

DUFFY Shane Patrick Michael
Born: Derry, Northern Ireland, 1 January, 1992 — CD
Republic of Ireland: 1/U21-20//Northern Ireland: B-1/U21-3/Youth

League Club	Source	Date Signed	Seasons Played	Apps	Subs	Gls
Everton	Sch	01/09	11-12	2	3	0
Burnley	L	03/11	10	1	0	0
Scunthorpe U	L	08/11	11	18	0	2
Yeovil T	L	09/13	13	37	0	1
Blackburn Rov	Tr	09/14	14	18	1	1

DUFFY Vincent Gerard (Vince)
Born: Nottingham, England, 21 September, 1962 — M

League Club	Source	Date Signed	Seasons Played	Apps	Subs	Gls
Scunthorpe U	Nottingham F (App)	12/80	80-81	3	5	0

DUGARRY Christophe Jerome
Born: Bordeaux, France, 24 March, 1972 — F
France: 55

League Club	Source	Date Signed	Seasons Played	Apps	Subs	Gls
Birmingham C	Bordeaux (FRA)	01/03	02-03	28	2	6

DUGDALE Adam
Born: Liverpool, England, 12 September, 1987 — CD

League Club	Source	Date Signed	Seasons Played	Apps	Subs	Gls
Crewe Alex	Sch	07/06				
Accrington Stan	L	11/06	06	2	0	0
Crewe Alex	AFC Telford U	07/10	10-14	109	11	6
Tranmere Rov	L	08/13	13	4	0	1
Tranmere Rov	Tr	01/15	14	15	1	0

DUGDALE Alan
Born: Liverpool, England, 11 September, 1952 — CD
England: Youth

League Club	Source	Date Signed	Seasons Played	Apps	Subs	Gls
Coventry C	App	11/69	72-77	139	3	0
Charlton Ath	Tr	10/77	77-78	34	0	0
Barnsley	L	08/79	79	7	0	0

DUGDALE Gordon
Born: Liverpool, England, 21 February, 1924 — LB
Died: Liverpool, England, 23 May, 1986

League Club	Source	Date Signed	Seasons Played	Apps	Subs	Gls
Everton	Jnr	06/47	47-49	58	-	0

DUGDALE James Robert (Jimmy)
Born: Liverpool, England, 15 January, 1932 — CH
Died: Birmingham, England, 25 February, 2008
England: B/FLge-1

League Club	Source	Date Signed	Seasons Played	Apps	Subs	Gls
West Bromwich A	Harrowby	06/52	52-55	63	-	0
Aston Villa	Tr	01/56	55-61	215	-	3
Queens Park Rgrs	Tr	10/62	62	10	-	0

DUGGAN Andrew James (Andy)
Born: Bradford, England, 19 September, 1967 — CD

League Club	Source	Date Signed	Seasons Played	Apps	Subs	Gls
Barnsley	App	07/85	86	1	1	1
Rochdale	L	11/87	87	3	0	0
Huddersfield T	Tr	09/88	88-89	29	0	3
Hartlepool U	L	08/90	90	2	0	0
Rochdale	Tr	03/91	90	1	0	0

DUGGAN Edward John (Ted)
Born: Plaistow, E London, England, 27 July, 1922 — IF
Died: Luton, England, 11 September, 1982

League Club	Source	Date Signed	Seasons Played	Apps	Subs	Gls
Luton T	Jnr	08/39	46-48	48	-	20
Queens Park Rgrs	Tr	02/49	48-50	47	-	5
Luton T	Bedford T	02/56				

DUGGAN James (Jim)
Born: Droitwich, Worcestershire, England, 17 November, 1920 — IF
Died: Droitwich, Worcestershire, England, 1982

League Club	Source	Date Signed	Seasons Played	Apps	Subs	Gls
West Bromwich A	Droitwich OB	12/39	46	25	-	8

DUGGAN Mitchell James (Mitch)
Born: Upton, Wirral, England, 20 March, 1997 — M

League Club	Source	Date Signed	Seasons Played	Apps	Subs	Gls
Tranmere Rov	Sch	05/15	14	0	1	0

DUGGINS Eric Edward
Born: Tamworth, Staffordshire, England, 24 November, 1928 — FB
Died: Lichfield, Staffordshire, England, November, 1992

League Club	Source	Date Signed	Seasons Played	Apps	Subs	Gls
Portsmouth	Atherstone T	08/48				
Southend U	Tr	07/52	52-53	28	-	0

DUGGINS Gordon
Born: Tamworth, Staffordshire, England, 8 December, 1932 — CF
Died: Stafford, England, 31 March, 2010

League Club	Source	Date Signed	Seasons Played	Apps	Subs	Gls
Barnsley	Gresley Rov	11/55	55-57	17	-	6

DUGGINS John Austin
Born: Tamworth, Staffordshire, England, 4 August, 1931 — IF

League Club	Source	Date Signed	Seasons Played	Apps	Subs	Gls
Portsmouth	Atherstone T	06/50				
Walsall	Tr	08/52	52	16	-	3

DUGNOLLE John Henry (Jack)
Born: Peshawar, India, 24 March, 1914 — WH
Died: Shoreham-by-Sea, West Sussex, England, 31 August, 1977

League Club	Source	Date Signed	Seasons Played	Apps	Subs	Gls
Brighton & HA	Southwick	10/34	35-37	7	-	0
Plymouth Arg	Tunbridge Wells Rgrs	02/39	38	4	-	0
Brighton & HA	Tr	08/46	46-47	59	-	0

DUGUID Karl Anthony
Born: Letchworth, Hertfordshire, England, 21 March, 1978 — M/RB

League Club	Source	Date Signed	Seasons Played	Apps	Subs	Gls
Colchester U	YT	07/96	95-07	317	68	42
Plymouth Arg	Tr	06/08	08-10	98	9	2
Colchester U	Tr	07/11	11-13	19	12	3

DUKE David
Born: Inverness, Scotland, 7 November, 1978 — LB

League Club	Source	Date Signed	Seasons Played	Apps	Subs	Gls
Sunderland	Redby CA	07/97				
Swindon T	Tr	08/00	00-04	181	23	7
Darlington	Tr	08/05	05-06	21	12	1

DUKE George Edward
Born: Chichester, West Sussex, England, 6 September, 1920 — G
Died: Worthing, West Sussex, England, 19 March, 1988

League Club	Source	Date Signed	Seasons Played	Apps	Subs	Gls
Luton T	Southwick	01/39	46-48	16	-	0
Bournemouth	Tr	05/49	49	10	-	0

DUKE Matthew (Matt)
Born: Sheffield, England, 16 June, 1977 — G

League Club	Source	Date Signed	Seasons Played	Apps	Subs	Gls
Sheffield U	Matlock T	08/99				
Hull C	Burton A	07/04	04-10	46	4	0
Stockport Co	L	08/05	05	3	0	0
Wycombe W	L	01/06	05	5	0	0
Bradford C	Tr	08/11	11-12	41	1	0
Northampton T	L	02/12	11	9	0	0
Northampton T	Tr	06/13	13-14	75	1	0

DUKES Harold Parkinson (Harry)
Born: Portsmouth, England, 31 March, 1912 — G
Died: Cambridge, England, 13 August, 1988

League Club	Source	Date Signed	Seasons Played	Apps	Subs	Gls
Norwich C	Ipswich T	08/34	34-38	105	-	0
Norwich C	Bedford T	09/46	46	13	-	0

DULIN Michael Charles (Micky)
Born: Stepney, E London, England, 25 October, 1935 — RW

League Club	Source	Date Signed	Seasons Played	Apps	Subs	Gls
Tottenham H	Welwyn Garden C	11/52	55-57	10	-	2

DULSON Garry
Born: Nottingham, England, 21 December, 1953 — D

League Club	Source	Date Signed	Seasons Played	Apps	Subs	Gls
Nottingham F	App	10/71				

League Club	Source	Date Signed	Seasons Played	Apps	Subs	Gls
Port Vale	Tr	10/74	74-77	108	2	3
Crewe Alex	Tr	11/78	78-79	33	5	0

DUMAS Franck
Born: Bayeux, France, 9 January, 1968 — CD

League Club	Source	Date Signed	Seasons Played	Apps	Subs	Gls
Newcastle U	AS Monaco (FRA)	06/99	99	6	0	0

DUMBUYA Mustapha Sima Michael
Born: Freetown, Sierra Leone, 7 August, 1987 — RB
Sierra Leone: 7

League Club	Source	Date Signed	Seasons Played	Apps	Subs	Gls
Doncaster Rov	Potters Bar T	08/09	09-11	23	13	0
Crystal Palace	L	01/12	11	2	0	0
Portsmouth	Tr	08/12	12	22	1	0
Crawley T	Tr	01/13	12	14	1	0
Notts Co	Tr	07/13	13-14	50	3	0

DUMIGHAN Joseph (Joe)
Born: Langley Park, County Durham, England, 25 September, 1938 — CF

League Club	Source	Date Signed	Seasons Played	Apps	Subs	Gls
Sunderland	Jnr	11/55				
Darlington	Tr	07/58	58	4	-	1

DUMITRESCU Ilie
Born: Bucharest, Romania, 6 January, 1969 — F
Romania: 62

League Club	Source	Date Signed	Seasons Played	Apps	Subs	Gls
Tottenham H	Steaua Bucharest (ROM)	08/94	94-95	16	2	4
West Ham U	Tr	03/96	95-96	5	5	0

DUMMETT Paul
Born: Newcastle-upon-Tyne, England, 26 September, 1991 — LB
Wales: 1/U21-3

League Club	Source	Date Signed	Seasons Played	Apps	Subs	Gls
Newcastle U	Sch	07/10	13-14	35	8	1

DUNBAR Ian
Born: Newcastle-upon-Tyne, England, 6 June, 1971 — F
England: Schools

League Club	Source	Date Signed	Seasons Played	Apps	Subs	Gls
Hartlepool U	Jnr	08/89	89-90	1	2	0

DUNBAVIN Ian Stuart
Born: Huyton, Merseyside, England, 27 May, 1980 — G

League Club	Source	Date Signed	Seasons Played	Apps	Subs	Gls
Liverpool	YT	11/98				
Shrewsbury T	Tr	01/00	99-02	91	5	0
Accrington Stan	Scarborough	08/06	06-13	149	2	0

DUNCAN Andrew (Andy)
Born: Hexham, Northumberland, England, 20 October, 1977 — CD
England: Schools

League Club	Source	Date Signed	Seasons Played	Apps	Subs	Gls
Manchester U	YT	07/96				
Cambridge U	Tr	01/98	97-04	233	9	6

DUNCAN Cameron
Born: Shotts, Lanarkshire, Scotland, 4 August, 1965 — G
Scotland: Youth

League Club	Source	Date Signed	Seasons Played	Apps	Subs	Gls
Sunderland	Shotts	07/84	85	1	0	0

DUNCAN Colin John
Born: Plymstock, Devon, England, 5 August, 1957 — M

League Club	Source	Date Signed	Seasons Played	Apps	Subs	Gls
Oxford U	App	12/74	74-79	188	1	6
Gillingham	Tr	01/80	79-83	83	2	5
Reading	Tr	09/83	83-84	56	0	3
Aldershot	Tr	08/85	85	15	0	0

DUNCAN David Millar
Born: Markinch, Fife, Scotland, 21 November, 1921 — LW
Died: Kirkcaldy, Fife, Scotland, 11 January, 1991
Scotland: 3/SLge-1

League Club	Source	Date Signed	Seasons Played	Apps	Subs	Gls
Crewe Alex	Raith Rov	08/55	55	22	-	0

DUNCAN Derek Henry Junior
Born: West Ham, E London, England, 23 April, 1987 — LW

League Club	Source	Date Signed	Seasons Played	Apps	Subs	Gls
Leyton Orient	Sch	08/06	03-06	6	14	0
Wycombe W	Tr	07/07				

DUNCAN Douglas (Dally)
Born: Aberdeen, Scotland, 14 October, 1909 — LW
Died: Brighton, England, 2 January, 1990
Scotland: 14

League Club	Source	Date Signed	Seasons Played	Apps	Subs	Gls
Hull C	Aberdeen Richmond	08/28	28-31	111	-	47
Derby Co	Tr	03/32	31-46	261	-	63
Luton T	Tr	10/46	46-47	32	-	4

DUNCAN George
Born: Glasgow, Scotland, 16 January, 1937 — RW
Died: Chelmsford, England, 4 February, 2012

League Club	Source	Date Signed	Seasons Played	Apps	Subs	Gls
Southend U	Glasgow Rangers	06/60	60	6	-	2
Chesterfield	Tr	08/61	61-64	140	-	13

DUNCAN James Robert
Born: Hull, England, 2 April, 1938 — F

League Club	Source	Date Signed	Seasons Played	Apps	Subs	Gls
Hull C	Jnr	04/55	55-59	26	-	3
Bradford C	Tr	06/60	60	18	-	5

DUNCAN John Gilhespie
Born: Glasgow, Scotland, 10 December, 1926 — CF
Died: Glasgow, Scotland, 22 February, 1984

League Club	Source	Date Signed	Seasons Played	Apps	Subs	Gls
Newcastle U	Ayr U	11/50	51-52	5	-	3

DUNCAN John Pearson
Born: Dundee, Scotland, 22 February, 1949 — F
Scotland: SLge-1

League Club	Source	Date Signed	Seasons Played	Apps	Subs	Gls
Tottenham H	Dundee	10/74	74-78	101	2	53
Derby Co	Tr	09/78	78-80	35	1	12
Scunthorpe U	Tr	06/81	81-82	3	6	0

DUNCAN Joseph James (Joe)
Born: Huyton, Merseyside, England, 24 February, 1950 — RW

League Club	Source	Date Signed	Seasons Played	Apps	Subs	Gls
Wrexham (Am)	Jnr	12/68	68	1	0	0

DUNCAN Robert (Bob)
Born: Kirkcaldy, Fife, Scotland, 2 November, 1943 — LB

League Club	Source	Date Signed	Seasons Played	Apps	Subs	Gls
Southend U	Dunfermline Ath	08/61	61	1	-	0

DUNCAN Thomas Montgomerie (Tommy)
Born: Portsoy, Aberdeenshire, Scotland, 15 July, 1936 — LW

League Club	Source	Date Signed	Seasons Played	Apps	Subs	Gls
Newport Co (L)	Airdrieonians	03/58	57	1	-	0

DUNCLIFFE Michael John (John)
Born: Brighton, England, 17 September, 1947 — LB

League Club	Source	Date Signed	Seasons Played	Apps	Subs	Gls
Brighton & HA	App	09/65	66-67	22	0	0
Grimsby T	Tr	06/68	68-69	71	1	0
Peterborough U	Tr	07/70	70-72	120	0	0

DUNCUM Samuel (Sam)
Born: Sheffield, England, 18 February, 1987 — LW

League Club	Source	Date Signed	Seasons Played	Apps	Subs	Gls
Rotherham U	Sch	07/06	04-07	2	5	0

DUNDEE Sean William
Born: Durban, South Africa, 7 December, 1972 — F
Germany: B-1

League Club	Source	Date Signed	Seasons Played	Apps	Subs	Gls
Liverpool	Karlsruhe (GER)	06/98	98	0	3	0

DUNDERDALE William Leonard (Len)
Born: Willingham-by-Stow, Lincolnshire, England, 6 February, 1915 — CF
Died: Saxilby, Lincolnshire, England, 10 January, 1989

League Club	Source	Date Signed	Seasons Played	Apps	Subs	Gls
Sheffield Wed	Goole T	03/34				
Walsall	Tr	03/36	35-37	32	-	19
Watford	Tr	05/38	38	30	-	19
Leeds U	Tr	03/39	38	3	-	0
Watford	Tr	04/46	46-47	44	-	15

DUNFIELD Terence (Terry)
Born: Vancouver, Canada, 20 February, 1982 — M
Canada: 12/U23-1/Youth//England: Youth

League Club	Source	Date Signed	Seasons Played	Apps	Subs	Gls
Manchester C	YT	05/99	00	0	1	0
Bury	L	08/02	02	15	0	2
Bury	Tr	12/02	02-04	48	11	3
Macclesfield T	Rtd	07/07	07-08	59	2	2
Shrewsbury T	Tr	02/09	08-09	43	4	2
Oldham Ath	Toronto FC (CAN)	02/14	13	1	1	0

DUNFORD Neil
Born: Rochdale, Greater Manchester, England, 18 July, 1967 — G

League Club	Source	Date Signed	Seasons Played	Apps	Subs	Gls
Rochdale	Castleton Gabriels	09/93	94	2	0	0

DUNGEY James Andrew
Born: Plymouth, England, 7 February, 1978 — G
England: Youth/Schools

League Club	Source	Date Signed	Seasons Played	Apps	Subs	Gls
Plymouth Arg	YT	10/95	94-96	9	1	0
Exeter C	Tr	12/97	97	1	0	0
Plymouth Arg	Bodmin T	08/98	98	7	0	0

DUNGWORTH John Henry
Born: Brampton, South Yorkshire, England, 30 March, 1955 — F/CD

League Club	Source	Date Signed	Seasons Played	Apps	Subs	Gls
Huddersfield T	App	04/72	72-74	18	5	1
Barnsley	L	10/74	74	2	1	1
Oldham Ath	Tr	03/75	75	2	2	0
Rochdale	L	03/77	76	14	0	3
Aldershot	Tr	09/77	77-79	105	0	58
Shrewsbury T	Tr	11/79	79-81	81	5	17
Hereford U	L	10/81	81	7	0	3
Mansfield T	Tr	08/82	82-83	50	6	16
Rotherham U	Tr	02/84	83-87	177	11	16

DUNK Harrison Charles
Born: Hammersmith, W London, England, 25 October, 1990 — M/LB

League Club	Source	Date Signed	Seasons Played	Apps	Subs	Gls
Cambridge U	Bromley	06/11	14	21	11	2

DUNK Lewis Carl
Born: Brighton, England, 1 December, 1991 — CD

League Club	Source	Date Signed	Seasons Played	Apps	Subs	Gls
Brighton & HA	Sch	06/10	09-14	83	6	5
Bristol C	L	10/13	13	2	0	0

DUNKLEY Cheyenne Armani Keanu Rama
Born: Wolverhampton, England, 13 February, 1992 — CD

League Club	Source	Date Signed	Seasons Played	Apps	Subs	Gls
Oxford U	Kidderminster Hrs	11/14	14	7	2	0

DUNKLEY Malcolm Mark
Born: Wolverhampton, England, 12 July, 1961 — F
Died: Sandwell, West Midlands, England, 24 September, 2005

League Club	Source	Date Signed	Seasons Played	Apps	Subs	Gls
Lincoln C	Bromsgrove Rov	02/89	88	9	2	4

DUNKLEY Maurice Edward Frank
Born: Kettering, Northamptonshire, England, 19 February, 1914 — RW
Died: Uppingham, Rutland, England, 27 December, 1989

League Club	Source	Date Signed	Seasons Played	Apps	Subs	Gls
Northampton T	Kettering T	12/36	36-37	26	-	5
Manchester C	Tr	03/38	37-46	51	-	5
Northampton T	Kettering T	07/49	49	4	-	0

DUNKLEY Robert (Bob)
Born: Stoke-on-Trent, England, 6 April, 1922 — LW

League Club	Source	Date Signed	Seasons Played	Apps	Subs	Gls
Stoke C		01/41				
Barrow	Tr	08/46	46	11	-	0

DUNLEAVY Christopher (Chris)
Born: Liverpool, England, 30 December, 1949 — CD

League Club	Source	Date Signed	Seasons Played	Apps	Subs	Gls
Everton	Jnr	03/68				
Southport	Tr	07/69	69-73	145	2	9
Chester C	Tr	09/73	73-76	74	2	0
Halifax T	Tr	10/76	76-80	181	0	13

DUNLEAVY John Francis
Born: Ballybofey, Donegal, Republic of Ireland, 3 July, 1991 — CD
Republic of Ireland: U21-2/Youth

League Club	Source	Date Signed	Seasons Played	Apps	Subs	Gls
Wolverhampton W	Sch	07/09				
Barnet	L	01/11	10	1	2	0

DUNLOP Albert
Born: Liverpool, England, 21 April, 1932 — G
Died: Liverpool, England, 6 March, 1990

League Club	Source	Date Signed	Seasons Played	Apps	Subs	Gls
Everton	Jnr	08/49	56-62	211	-	0
Wrexham	Tr	11/63	63-64	15	-	0

DUNLOP William Lumsden (Billy)
Born: Airdrie, Lanarkshire, Scotland, 20 February, 1926 — IF
Died: Torbay, Devon, England, August, 1994

League Club	Source	Date Signed	Seasons Played	Apps	Subs	Gls
Exeter C	Dunfermline Ath	07/50	50	4	-	0
Bristol Rov	Ilfracombe	05/52				
Bradford Park Ave	Tr	05/53	53	36	-	12
Darlington	Tr	10/54	54	18	-	2

DUNLOP William Rex (Rex)
Born: Dumfries, Scotland, 21 September, 1927 — LH

League Club	Source	Date Signed	Seasons Played	Apps	Subs	Gls
Workington	Glasgow Rangers	11/53	53-55	110	-	19

DUNMORE David Gerald Ivor (Dave)
Born: Whitehaven, Cumbria, England, 8 February, 1934 — CF

League Club	Source	Date Signed	Seasons Played	Apps	Subs	Gls
York C	Cliftonville Minors	05/52	51-53	48	-	25
Tottenham H	Tr	02/54	53-59	75	-	23
West Ham U	Tr	03/60	59-60	36	-	16
Leyton Orient	Tr	03/61	60-64	147	-	54
York C	Tr	06/65	65-66	61	2	13

DUNN Barry
Born: Middlesbrough, England, 17 December, 1939 — RW

League Club	Source	Date Signed	Seasons Played	Apps	Subs	Gls
Doncaster Rov		02/58				
Halifax T	Tr	09/59	59-60	7	-	1

DUNN Barry
Born: Sunderland, England, 15 February, 1952 — LW

League Club	Source	Date Signed	Seasons Played	Apps	Subs	Gls
Sunderland	Newcastle Blue Star	09/79	79-80	16	7	2
Preston NE	Tr	10/81	81	8	0	1
Darlington	Tr	08/82	82	16	0	4

DUNN Brian James
Born: Boston, Lincolnshire, England, 4 October, 1940 — LW

League Club	Source	Date Signed	Seasons Played	Apps	Subs	Gls
Grimsby T	Jnr	10/57				
Hartlepool U	Tr	06/58	58-60	27	-	1

DUNN Christopher Michael (Chris)
Born: Brentwood, Essex, England, 23 October, 1987 — G

League Club	Source	Date Signed	Seasons Played	Apps	Subs	Gls
Northampton T	Sch	01/07	07-10	98	0	0
Coventry C	Tr	07/11	11-12	1	2	0
Yeovil T	Tr	08/13	13	7	1	0
Cambridge U	Tr	06/14	14	43	0	0

DUNN David John Ian
Born: Great Harwood, Lancashire, England, 27 December, 1979 — M
England: 1/U21-20/Youth

League Club	Source	Date Signed	Seasons Played	Apps	Subs	Gls
Blackburn Rov	YT	09/97	98-02	120	16	30
Birmingham C	Tr	07/03	03-06	46	12	7
Blackburn Rov	Tr	01/07	06-14	121	59	20

DUNN Iain George William
Born: Goole, East Riding of Yorkshire, England, 1 April, 1970 — W
England: Youth/Schools

League Club	Source	Date Signed	Seasons Played	Apps	Subs	Gls
York C	Jnr	07/88	88-90	46	31	11
Chesterfield	Tr	08/91	91	8	5	1
Huddersfield T	Goole T	12/92	92-96	62	58	14
Scunthorpe U	L	09/96	96	3	0	0
Chesterfield	Tr	02/97	96-97	10	8	0

DUNN Jack Anthony
Born: Liverpool, England, 19 November, 1994 — F
England: Youth

League Club	Source	Date Signed	Seasons Played	Apps	Subs	Gls
Liverpool	Sch	11/11				
Cheltenham T	L	01/15	14	5	0	3
Burton A	L	03/15	14	0	1	0

DUNN James (Jimmy)
Born: Rutherglen, Glasgow, Scotland, 23 October, 1922 — RB
Died: Leeds, England, 24 January, 2005

League Club	Source	Date Signed	Seasons Played	Apps	Subs	Gls
Leeds U	Rutherglen Glencairn	06/47	47-58	422	-	1
Darlington	Tr	07/59	59	27	-	0

DUNN James (Jimmy)
Born: Edinburgh, Scotland, 25 November, 1923 — IF
Died: 31 December, 2014

League Club	Source	Date Signed	Seasons Played	Apps	Subs	Gls
Wolverhampton W	Maghull Ath	11/42	46-52	123	-	33
Derby Co	Tr	11/52	52-54	57	-	21

DUNN John Alfred
Born: Barking, E London, England, 21 June, 1944 — G

League Club	Source	Date Signed	Seasons Played	Apps	Subs	Gls
Chelsea	App	02/62	62-65	13	0	0
Torquay U	Tr	10/66	66-67	44	0	0
Aston Villa	Tr	01/68	67-70	101	0	0
Charlton Ath	Tr	07/71	71-74	104	0	0

DUNN Joseph (Joe)
Born: Glasgow, Scotland, 20 September, 1925 — CH
Died: Lancashire, England, December, 2005

League Club	Source	Date Signed	Seasons Played	Apps	Subs	Gls
Preston NE	Clyde	08/51	51-60	224	-	2

DUNN Richard (Dick)
Born: Easington, County Durham, England, 23 December, 1919 — IF
Died: Durham, England, January, 1986

League Club	Source	Date Signed	Seasons Played	Apps	Subs	Gls
West Ham U	Ferryhill Ath	02/38	46-47	11	-	2
Hartlepool U	Tr	08/49	49	13	-	2

DUNN William Charles (Billy)
Born: Hebburn, Tyne and Wear, England, 25 March, 1920 — G
Died: Jarrow, Tyne and Wear, England, 1982

League Club	Source	Date Signed	Seasons Played	Apps	Subs	Gls
Darlington	RAF	05/46	46-55	340	-	0

DUNNE Alan James
Born: Dublin, Republic of Ireland, 23 August, 1982 — RB

League Club	Source	Date Signed	Seasons Played	Apps	Subs	Gls
Millwall	YT	03/00	01-14	305	36	17

DUNNE Anthony Peter (Tony)
Born: Dublin, Republic of Ireland, 24 July, 1941 — LB
Republic of Ireland: 33

League Club	Source	Date Signed	Seasons Played	Apps	Subs	Gls
Manchester U	Shelbourne (ROI)	04/60	60-72	414	0	2
Bolton W	Tr	08/73	73-78	166	4	0

DUNNE Augustine (Austin)
Born: Limerick, Republic of Ireland, 31 July, 1934 — WH
Died: Tonbridge, Kent, England, 5 March, 2007

League Club	Source	Date Signed	Seasons Played	Apps	Subs	Gls
Colchester U	Limerick (ROI)	10/53	54	1	-	0

DUNNE Charles
Born: Lambeth, S London, England, 13 February, 1993 — LB
Republic of Ireland: U21-1

League Club	Source	Date Signed	Seasons Played	Apps	Subs	Gls
Wycombe W	Sch	10/11	11-12	38	3	0
Blackpool	Tr	07/13	14	21	1	0
Wycombe W	L	08/13	13	9	0	0

DUNNE James Christopher (Jimmy)
Born: Dublin, Republic of Ireland, 1 December, 1947 — CD
Republic of Ireland: 1

League Club	Source	Date Signed	Seasons Played	Apps	Subs	Gls
Millwall	Shelbourne (ROI)	02/66				
Torquay U	Tr	07/67	67-69	125	1	13
Fulham	Tr	07/70	70-73	142	1	2
Torquay U	Durban C (RSA)	04/76	75-78	119	3	5

DUNNE James Patrick (Jimmy)
Born: Dublin, Republic of Ireland, 16 March, 1935 — IF
Died: Dunstable, Bedfordshire, England, June, 1985
Republic of Ireland: 3

League Club	Source	Date Signed	Seasons Played	Apps	Subs	Gls
Leicester C		09/53	54-55	4	-	0
Peterborough U	St Patrick's Ath (ROI)	07/60	60-61	4	-	0

DUNNE James William
Born: Bromley, SE London, England, 18 September, 1989 — M

League Club	Source	Date Signed	Seasons Played	Apps	Subs	Gls
Arsenal	Sch	09/07				
Exeter C	Tr	07/09	09-11	98	12	6
Stevenage	Tr	07/12	12-13	46	9	5
Portsmouth	Tr	06/14	14	34	2	1

DUNNE Joseph John (Joe)
Born: Dublin, Republic of Ireland, 25 May, 1973 — RB
Republic of Ireland: U21-1/Youth/Schools

League Club	Source	Date Signed	Seasons Played	Apps	Subs	Gls
Gillingham	YT	08/90	90-95	108	7	1
Colchester U	Tr	03/96	95-98	79	22	3
Colchester U	Dover Ath	12/99	99-01	56	6	3

DUNNE Patrick Anthony Joseph (Pat)
Born: Dublin, Republic of Ireland, 9 February, 1943 — G
Republic of Ireland: 5/U23-1

League Club	Source	Date Signed	Seasons Played	Apps	Subs	Gls
Everton	Jnr	05/60				
Manchester U	Shamrock Rov (ROI)	05/64	64-65	45	0	0
Plymouth Arg	Tr	02/67	66-70	152	0	0

DUNNE Richard Patrick
Born: Dublin, Republic of Ireland, 21 September, 1979 — CD
Republic of Ireland: 80/B-1/U21-4/Youth/Schools

League Club	Source	Date Signed	Seasons Played	Apps	Subs	Gls
Everton	YT	10/96	96-00	53	7	0
Manchester C	Tr	10/00	00-09	290	6	8
Aston Villa	Tr	09/09	09-11	95	0	4
Queens Park Rgrs	Tr	07/13	13-14	63	1	1

DUNNE Seamus (Shay)
Born: Wicklow, Republic of Ireland, 13 April, 1930 — RB
Republic of Ireland: 15

League Club	Source	Date Signed	Seasons Played	Apps	Subs	Gls
Luton T	Shelbourne (ROI)	07/50	51-60	301	-	0

DUNNE Thomas (Tommy)
Born: Dublin, Republic of Ireland, 19 March, 1927 — WH
Died: Fazakerley, Merseyside, England, 23 January, 1988

League Club	Source	Date Signed	Seasons Played	Apps	Subs	Gls
Leicester C	Shamrock Rov (ROI)	11/49	50-53	33	-	0
Exeter C	Tr	07/54	54-55	37	-	1
Shrewsbury T	Tr	08/56	56	3	-	0
Southport	Tr	07/57	57	21	-	0

DUNNE Thomas Joseph (Tommy)
Born: Glasgow, Scotland, 22 June, 1946 — IF
Died: Glasgow, Scotland, 25 August, 2001

League Club	Source	Date Signed	Seasons Played	Apps	Subs	Gls
Leyton Orient	Glasgow Celtic	05/64	64	1	-	0

DUNNIGAN John Young
Born: Dalmuir, Dunbartonshire, Scotland, 30 November, 1920 — RW
Died: Glasgow, Scotland, 26 April, 2008

League Club	Source	Date Signed	Seasons Played	Apps	Subs	Gls
Barrow	Bridgeton Waverley	09/45	46	1	-	0

DUNNING Darren
Born: Scarborough, North Yorkshire, England, 8 January, 1981 — M

League Club	Source	Date Signed	Seasons Played	Apps	Subs	Gls
Blackburn Rov	YT	02/99	00	1	0	0
Bristol C	L	08/00	00	9	0	0
Rochdale	L	11/01	01	4	1	0
Blackpool	L	03/02	01	5	0	0
Torquay U	L	11/02	02	4	3	1
Macclesfield T	L	01/03	02	17	0	0
York C	Tr	07/03	03	42	0	3

DUNNING William Samuel (Bill)
Born: Bury, Greater Manchester, England, 15 November, 1952 — W

League Club	Source	Date Signed	Seasons Played	Apps	Subs	Gls
Blackburn Rov	App	11/70	70-71	10	3	2

DUNPHY Eamon Martin
Born: Dublin, Republic of Ireland, 3 August, 1945 — M
Republic of Ireland: 23/U23-1

League Club	Source	Date Signed	Seasons Played	Apps	Subs	Gls
Manchester U	App	08/62				
York C	Tr	08/65	65	22	0	3
Millwall	Tr	01/66	65-73	267	7	24
Charlton Ath	Tr	11/73	73-74	39	3	3
Reading	Tr	07/75	75-76	74	3	3

DUNPHY Nicholas Owen (Nick)
Born: Sutton Coldfield, West Midlands, England, 3 August, 1974 — CD

League Club	Source	Date Signed	Seasons Played	Apps	Subs	Gls
Peterborough U	Hednesford T	08/94	94	0	2	0

DUNPHY Sean
Born: Maltby, South Yorkshire, England, 5 November, 1970 — CD

League Club	Source	Date Signed	Seasons Played	Apps	Subs	Gls
Barnsley	YT	06/89	89	5	1	0
Lincoln C	Tr	07/90	91-93	48	5	2
Doncaster Rov	L	10/93	93	1	0	0
Scarborough	L	08/94	94	10	0	0

DUNS Leonard (Len)
Born: Newcastle-upon-Tyne, England, 28 September, 1916 — RW
Died: Ponteland, Northumberland, England, 29 April, 1989

League Club	Source	Date Signed	Seasons Played	Apps	Subs	Gls
Sunderland	Newcastle West End	10/33	35-51	215	-	45

DUNWELL Michael (Mike)
Born: Stockton-on-Tees, Cleveland, England, 6 January, 1980 — F

League Club	Source	Date Signed	Seasons Played	Apps	Subs	Gls
Hartlepool U	YT	07/98	98	0	1	0

DUNWELL Peter Matthew
Born: Ecclesfield, South Yorkshire, England, 22 November, 1938 — W

League Club	Source	Date Signed	Seasons Played	Apps	Subs	Gls
Lincoln C	Ecclesfield	09/58	59-60	14	-	1

DUNWELL Richard Kirk
Born: Islington, N London, England, 17 June, 1971 — F

League Club	Source	Date Signed	Seasons Played	Apps	Subs	Gls
Aldershot	Millwall (NC)	11/90	90	0	1	0
Barnet	Collier Row	10/95	95-96	4	10	1

DUQUEMIN Leonard Stanley (Len)
Born: Guernsey, Channel Islands, 17 July, 1924 — CF
Died: Buckhurst Hill, Essex, England, 20 April, 2003

League Club	Source	Date Signed	Seasons Played	Apps	Subs	Gls
Tottenham H	Vauxbelet, Guernsey	09/46	47-56	274	-	114

DURANDT Clifford Michael (Cliff)
Born: Johannesburg, South Africa, 16 April, 1940 — IF/LW
Died: South Africa, 9 October, 2002

League Club	Source	Date Signed	Seasons Played	Apps	Subs	Gls
Wolverhampton W	Marist Brothers (RSA)	06/57	58-61	43	-	9
Charlton Ath	Tr	03/63	62-64	36	-	4

DURBAN William Alan (Alan)
Born: Port Talbot, Wales, 7 July, 1941 — M
Wales: 27/U23-1

League Club	Source	Date Signed	Seasons Played	Apps	Subs	Gls
Cardiff C	Jnr	09/58	59-62	52	-	9
Derby Co	Tr	07/63	63-72	336	10	93
Shrewsbury T	Tr	09/73	73-77	150	6	33

DURHAM Jonathan Simon
Born: Wombwell, South Yorkshire, England, 12 June, 1965 — F

League Club	Source	Date Signed	Seasons Played	Apps	Subs	Gls
Rotherham U	App	06/83	83	3	3	1
Torquay U	Tr	03/85	84-85	20	4	2

DURHAM Raymond Denis (Denis)
Born: East Halton, North Lincolnshire, England, 26 September, 1923 — LH
Died: East Riding of Yorkshire, England, August, 2014

League Club	Source	Date Signed	Seasons Played	Apps	Subs	Gls
Hull C	East Halton U	04/47	46-58	267	-	7

DURIE David George (Dave)
Born: Blackpool, Lancashire, England, 13 August, 1931 — IF/WH

League Club	Source	Date Signed	Seasons Played	Apps	Subs	Gls
Blackpool	Oxford Amats, Blackp'l	05/52	52-63	301	-	84
Chester C	Tr	09/64	64-66	87	2	4

DURIE Gordon Scott
Born: Paisley, Renfrewshire, Scotland, 6 December, 1965 — F
Scotland: 43/B-2/U21-4

League Club	Source	Date Signed	Seasons Played	Apps	Subs	Gls
Chelsea	Hibernian	04/86	85-90	115	8	51
Tottenham H	Tr	08/91	91-93	58	0	11

DURKAN Kieron John
Born: Runcorn, Cheshire, England, 1 December, 1973 — W
Republic of Ireland: U21-3

League Club	Source	Date Signed	Seasons Played	Apps	Subs	Gls
Wrexham	YT	07/92	91-95	43	7	3
Stockport Co	Tr	02/96	95-97	52	12	4
Macclesfield T	Tr	03/98	97-00	92	11	13
York C	L	10/00	00	7	0	0
Rochdale	Tr	07/01	01	16	14	1
Swansea C	Tr	01/03	02-03	15	6	1

DURKIN John
Born: Cowdenbeath, Fife, Scotland, 18 April, 1930 — RW/CF

League Club	Source	Date Signed	Seasons Played	Apps	Subs	Gls
Gillingham	Heart of Midlothian	08/53	53-54	30	-	5

DURKIN William (Billy)
Born: Bradford, England, 29 September, 1921 — IF
Died: Dorset, England, August, 2000

League Club	Source	Date Signed	Seasons Played	Apps	Subs	Gls
Bradford C		01/47	46-47	28	-	1
Rotherham U	Tr	08/48	48	1	-	0
Aldershot	Tr	08/49	49-53	129	-	17

DURNIN John Paul
Born: Bootle, Merseyside, England, 18 August, 1965 — F

League Club	Source	Date Signed	Seasons Played	Apps	Subs	Gls
Liverpool	Waterloo Dock	03/86				
West Bromwich A	L	10/88	88	5	0	2
Oxford U	Tr	02/89	88-92	140	21	44
Portsmouth	Tr	07/93	93-99	118	63	31
Blackpool	L	11/99	99	4	1	1
Carlisle U	Tr	12/99	99	20	2	2
Kidderminster Hrs	Tr	10/00	00	28	3	9
Port Vale	Rhyl	12/01	01-02	43	4	2

DURRANT Frederick Harry (Fred)
Born: Dover, Kent, England, 19 June, 1921 — CF
Died: Dover, Kent, England, 5 March, 2010

League Club	Source	Date Signed	Seasons Played	Apps	Subs	Gls
Brentford	Folkestone	05/39	46	4	-	3
Queens Park Rgrs	Tr	09/46	46-48	51	-	26
Exeter C	Tr	02/49	48-49	17	-	5

DURRANT Ian
Born: Glasgow, Scotland, 29 October, 1966 — M
Scotland: 20/U21-4/Youth

League Club	Source	Date Signed	Seasons Played	Apps	Subs	Gls
Everton (L)	Glasgow Rangers	10/94	94	4	1	0

DURRANT Jack William
Born: Bristol, England, 6 May, 1991 — CD

League Club	Source	Date Signed	Seasons Played	Apps	Subs	Gls
Cheltenham T	Sch	07/09	08	0	4	0

DURRANT Lee Roger
Born: Great Yarmouth, Norfolk, England, 18 December, 1973 — LM
England: Schools

League Club	Source	Date Signed	Seasons Played	Apps	Subs	Gls
Ipswich T	YT	07/92	93	3	4	0

DURRANT Paul
Born: North Shields, Tyne and Wear, England, 21 February, 1943 — LW

League Club	Source	Date Signed	Seasons Played	Apps	Subs	Gls
Wolverhampton W	Sunderland (Am)	07/61				
Bury	Tr	07/62	63-64	21	-	6
Doncaster Rov	Tr	07/65	65-66	13	2	1

DURRELL Joseph Timothy (Joe)
Born: Stepney, E London, England, 15 March, 1953 — LW

League Club	Source	Date Signed	Seasons Played	Apps	Subs	Gls
West Ham U	App	10/70	71	5	1	0
Bristol C	Tr	07/73	73-74	5	3	0
Cardiff C	L	08/75	75	2	0	0
Gillingham	Tr	11/75	75-76	43	6	9

DURSUN Peter Muhamet Ali
Born: Aarhus, Denmark, 8 January, 1975 — F

League Club	Source	Date Signed	Seasons Played	Apps	Subs	Gls
Southend U	Aarhus Fremad (DEN)	11/96	96	0	1	0

DUTHIE Ian Martin
Born: Forfar, Angus, Scotland, 18 January, 1930 — CF
Died: Huddersfield, West Yorkshire, England, 27 June, 2010

League Club	Source	Date Signed	Seasons Played	Apps	Subs	Gls
Huddersfield T	Forfar Celtic	06/49	49-52	7	-	0
Bradford C	Tr	06/54	54-55	28	-	4

DUTHIE James (Jim)
Born: Forfar, Angus, Scotland, 23 September, 1923 — RH
Died: Bury St Edmunds, Suffolk, England, 8 February, 1972

League Club	Source	Date Signed	Seasons Played	Apps	Subs	Gls
Grimsby T	Lincoln C (Am)	09/49	48-50	40	-	0
Hull C	Tr	06/51	51-52	17	-	3
Southend U	Tr	05/53	53-57	160	-	8

DUTHOIT John (Jack)
Born: Leeds, England, 4 November, 1918 — LB
Died: Burton-on-Trent, Staffordshire, England, November, 2001

League Club	Source	Date Signed	Seasons Played	Apps	Subs	Gls
Leeds U	Carlton U	04/45				
York C	Tr	05/46	46-49	36	-	0

DUTTON Brian
Born: Malton, North Yorkshire, England, 12 April, 1985 — M

League Club	Source	Date Signed	Seasons Played	Apps	Subs	Gls
Cambridge U	Pickering T	11/03	03	0	3	0

DUTTON Charles Alfred (Charlie)
Born: Rugeley, Staffordshire, England, 10 April, 1934 — CF
Died: Stafford, England, 30 October, 2009

League Club	Source	Date Signed	Seasons Played	Apps	Subs	Gls
Coventry C	Derby Co (Am)	10/52	53-55	27	-	8
Northampton T	Tr	03/56	55-56	10	-	2

DUTTON Leonard Lewis (Len)
Born: Cardiff, Wales, 17 January, 1922 — LH
Died: Norwich, England, 19 October, 1998
Wales: Schools

League Club	Source	Date Signed	Seasons Played	Apps	Subs	Gls
Arsenal	Jnr	05/39				
Norwich C	Tr	08/46	46-52	139	-	11

DUXBURY Lee Edward
Born: Keighley, West Yorkshire, England, 7 October, 1969 — M

League Club	Source	Date Signed	Seasons Played	Apps	Subs	Gls
Bradford C	YT	07/88	88-94	204	5	25
Rochdale	L	01/90	89	9	1	0
Huddersfield T	Tr	12/94	94-95	29	0	2
Bradford C	Tr	11/95	95-96	63	0	7
Oldham Ath	Tr	03/97	96-02	222	26	32
Bury	Tr	08/03	03	36	1	0

DUXBURY Michael (Mike)
Born: Accrington, Lancashire, England, 1 September, 1959 — D/M
England: 10/U21-7

League Club	Source	Date Signed	Seasons Played	Apps	Subs	Gls
Manchester U	App	10/76	80-89	274	25	6
Blackburn Rov	Tr	08/90	90-91	25	2	0
Bradford C	Tr	01/92	91-93	64	1	0

DWIGHT Royston Edward (Roy)
Born: Belvedere, SE London, England, 9 January, 1933 — RW
Died: Woolwich, SE London, England, 9 April, 2002

League Club	Source	Date Signed	Seasons Played	Apps	Subs	Gls
Fulham	Hastings U	06/50	54-57	72	-	54
Nottingham F	Tr	07/58	58-59	44	-	21
Coventry C	Gravesend & Northfleet	01/62	61-62	31	-	8
Millwall	Tr	01/64	63-64	7	-	2

DWYER Noel Michael
Born: Dublin, Republic of Ireland, 30 October, 1934 — G
Died: Wolverhampton, England, 6 December, 1992
Republic of Ireland: 14/B

League Club	Source	Date Signed	Seasons Played	Apps	Subs	Gls
Wolverhampton W	Ormeau (ROI)	08/53	57	5	-	0
West Ham U	Tr	12/58	58-59	36	-	0
Swansea C	Tr	08/60	60-64	140	-	0
Plymouth Arg	Tr	01/65	64-65	26	0	0
Charlton Ath	Tr	12/65	65	6	0	0

DWYER Philip John (Phil)
Born: Cardiff, Wales, 28 October, 1953 — D
Wales: 10/U23-5/U21-1/Youth/Schools

League Club	Source	Date Signed	Seasons Played	Apps	Subs	Gls
Cardiff C	Jnr	10/71	72-84	466	5	41
Rochdale	L	03/85	84	15	0	1

DWYER Robert Alan (Alan)
Born: Liverpool, England, 5 October, 1952 — LB

League Club	Source	Date Signed	Seasons Played	Apps	Subs	Gls
Wrexham	Halewood YC	10/73	74-80	169	11	2
Stockport Co	Tr	10/81	81	4	0	0

DYAS Gordon
Born: Hednesford, Staffordshire, England, 17 May, 1936 — LH
Died: Pye Green, Hednesford, Staffordshire, England, January, 2012

League Club	Source	Date Signed	Seasons Played	Apps	Subs	Gls
Walsall	Hednesford T	06/55	55	12	-	0

DYCHE Sean Mark
Born: Kettering, Northamptonshire, England, 28 June, 1971 — CD

League Club	Source	Date Signed	Seasons Played	Apps	Subs	Gls
Nottingham F	YT	05/89				
Chesterfield	Tr	02/90	89-96	219	12	8
Bristol C	Tr	07/97	97-98	14	3	0
Luton T	L	01/99	98	14	0	1
Millwall	Tr	07/99	99-01	69	0	3
Watford	Tr	07/02	02-04	68	4	0
Northampton T	Tr	07/05	05-06	54	2	0

DYE Dean Charles
Born: Lincoln, England, 4 March, 1969 — F

League Club	Source	Date Signed	Seasons Played	Apps	Subs	Gls
Charlton Ath	Lincoln U	06/91				
Lincoln C	Tr	10/91	91	0	2	0

DYER Alex Craig
Born: Edmonton, N London, England, 1 June, 1990 — M

League Club	Source	Date Signed	Seasons Played	Apps	Subs	Gls
Northampton T	Sch	02/09	07-09	12	22	3

DYER Alexander Constantine (Alex)
Born: Forest Gate, E London, England, 14 November, 1965 — LW/F

League Club	Source	Date Signed	Seasons Played	Apps	Subs	Gls
Blackpool	Watford (App)	10/83	83-86	101	7	19
Hull C	Tr	02/87	86-88	59	1	14
Crystal Palace	Tr	11/88	88-89	16	1	2
Charlton Ath	Tr	11/90	90-92	60	18	13
Oxford U	Tr	07/93	93-94	62	14	6
Lincoln C	Tr	08/95	95	1	0	0
Barnet	Tr	09/95	95	30	5	2
Huddersfield T	FC Maia (POR)	08/97	97	8	4	1
Notts Co	Tr	03/98	97-00	58	20	6

DYER Bruce Antonio
Born: Ilford, E London, England, 13 April, 1975 — F
England: U21-10

League Club	Source	Date Signed	Seasons Played	Apps	Subs	Gls
Watford	YT	04/93	92-93	29	2	6
Crystal Palace	Tr	03/94	93-98	95	40	37
Barnsley	Tr	10/98	98-02	149	33	59
Watford	Tr	07/03	03-04	39	29	12
Stoke C	Tr	08/05	05	2	9	0
Millwall	L	11/05	05	9	1	2
Sheffield U	Tr	01/06	05	3	2	1
Doncaster Rov	Tr	06/06	06	9	6	1
Bradford C	L	01/07	06	2	3	1
Rotherham U	L	09/07	07	3	0	0
Chesterfield	Tr	03/08	07	0	3	0

DYER Jack Robert
Born: Aldridge, West Midlands, England, 11 December, 1991 — W

League Club	Source	Date Signed	Seasons Played	Apps	Subs	Gls
Burton A	Aston Villa (Sch)	07/10	10-13	35	19	1

DYER Joseph Alexander (Alec)
Born: Crewe, Cheshire, England, 13 April, 1913 — LW
Died: Wistaston, Cheshire, England, 11 August, 1984

League Club	Source	Date Signed	Seasons Played	Apps	Subs	Gls
Crewe Alex		10/33	33-36	51	-	10
Plymouth Arg	Tr	02/37	36-46	53	-	3

DYER Kieron Courtney
Born: Ipswich, England, 29 December, 1978 — M
England: 33/B-2/U21-11/Youth

League Club	Source	Date Signed	Seasons Played	Apps	Subs	Gls
Ipswich T	YT	01/97	96-98	79	12	9
Newcastle U	Tr	07/99	99-06	169	21	23
West Ham U	Tr	08/07	07-10	15	15	0
Ipswich T	L	03/11	10	1	3	0
Queens Park Rgrs	Tr	07/11	11-12	2	3	0
Middlesbrough	Tr	01/13	12	7	2	2

DYER Lloyd Richard
Born: Birmingham, England, 13 September, 1982 — LW

League Club	Source	Date Signed	Seasons Played	Apps	Subs	Gls
West Bromwich A	Aston Villa (Jnr)	07/01	03-04	2	19	2
Kidderminster Hrs	L	09/03	03	5	2	1
Coventry C	L	03/05	04	6	0	0
Queens Park Rgrs	L	09/05	05	15	0	0
Millwall	Tr	01/06	05	2	4	0
MK Dons	Tr	08/06	06-07	82	4	16
Leicester C	Tr	07/08	08-13	171	59	30
Watford	Tr	06/14	14	4	10	1
Birmingham C	L	01/15	14	7	11	1

DYER Nathan Antone Jonah
Born: Trowbridge, Wiltshire, England, 29 November, 1987 LW
England: Youth

League Club	Source	Date Signed	Seasons Played	Apps	Subs	Gls
Southampton	Sch	07/05	05-08	36	20	1
Burnley	L	10/05	05	4	1	2
Sheffield U	L	09/08	08	3	4	1
Swansea C	Tr	01/09	08-14	191	42	23

DYER Paul David
Born: Leicester, England, 24 January, 1953 M

League Club	Source	Date Signed	Seasons Played	Apps	Subs	Gls
Notts Co	Jnr	08/71	72-73	1	6	0
Colchester U	Tr	07/75	75-79	124	20	4

DYER Peter Robert Francis
Born: Devonport, Devon, England, 12 October, 1937 G

League Club	Source	Date Signed	Seasons Played	Apps	Subs	Gls
Plymouth Arg	Oak Villa	06/55	55-56	8	-	0

DYER Raymond (Ray)
Born: Stockport, Greater Manchester, England, 12 May, 1938 LW

League Club	Source	Date Signed	Seasons Played	Apps	Subs	Gls
Stockport Co	Bolton W (Am)	09/56	56	1	-	0

DYER Ross David
Born: Cannock, Staffordshire, England, 12 May, 1988 F

League Club	Source	Date Signed	Seasons Played	Apps	Subs	Gls
Mansfield T	Forest Green Rov	06/11	13	7	5	2

DYER Stephen Paul (Steve)
Born: Chelmsford, England, 21 March, 1954 D

League Club	Source	Date Signed	Seasons Played	Apps	Subs	Gls
Southend U	App	03/72	72-76	60	8	0

DYER Wayne
Born: Birmingham, England, 24 November, 1977 M
Montserrat:

League Club	Source	Date Signed	Seasons Played	Apps	Subs	Gls
Birmingham C	YT	07/96				
Walsall	Moor Green	08/98	98	0	1	0

DYKE Charles (Charlie)
Born: Caerphilly, Wales, 23 September, 1926 RW
Died: Penarth, Vale of Glamorgan, Wales, 4 January, 2013

League Club	Source	Date Signed	Seasons Played	Apps	Subs	Gls
Chelsea	Troedyrhiw	11/47	47-50	24	-	2

DYKES Darren Lewis
Born: Aylesbury, Buckinghamshire, England, 27 June, 1984 F

League Club	Source	Date Signed	Seasons Played	Apps	Subs	Gls
Swindon T	Buckingham T	08/02	02	1	1	0
Lincoln C	L	12/02	02	2	1	0

DYKES Donald William (Don)
Born: Spilsby, Lincolnshire, England, 8 June, 1930 FB

League Club	Source	Date Signed	Seasons Played	Apps	Subs	Gls
Lincoln C	Metheringham BC	06/49	49-58	95	-	4

DYMOND William Henry (Bill)
Born: Dawlish, Devon, England, 13 February, 1920 RW
Died: Exeter, England, 10 September, 2004

League Club	Source	Date Signed	Seasons Played	Apps	Subs	Gls
Bristol C	Exeter C (Am)	09/45	46	8	-	1
Exeter C	Tr	06/47	47-48	41	-	7

DYSON Geoffrey (Geoff)
Born: Huddersfield, West Yorkshire, England, 16 March, 1923 IF
Died: Huddersfield, West Yorkshire, England, April, 1989

League Club	Source	Date Signed	Seasons Played	Apps	Subs	Gls
Huddersfield T	Jnr	03/46				
Bradford C	Tr	06/47	47	1	-	0
Accrington Stan	Tr	01/48	47-48	20	-	1

DYSON Jack
Born: Oldham, Greater Manchester, England, 8 July, 1934 IF
Died: Oldham, Greater Manchester, England, 16 November, 2000
England: U23-1

League Club	Source	Date Signed	Seasons Played	Apps	Subs	Gls
Manchester C	Nelson	05/52	55-59	63	-	26
Oldham Ath	Stirling A	01/62				

DYSON James (Jim)
Born: Ryhope, Tyne and Wear, England, 16 February, 1935 G
Died: 12 July, 2014

League Club	Source	Date Signed	Seasons Played	Apps	Subs	Gls
Hartlepool U	Seaham CW	04/55	54-58	63	-	0

DYSON James Gareth
Born: Dudley, West Midlands, England, 20 April, 1979 M

League Club	Source	Date Signed	Seasons Played	Apps	Subs	Gls
Birmingham C	YT	07/97	99	0	2	0

DYSON John Barry (Barry)
Born: Oldham, Greater Manchester, England, 6 September, 1942 F/M
Died: Colchester, Essex, England, 26 February, 1995

League Club	Source	Date Signed	Seasons Played	Apps	Subs	Gls
Bury	Jnr	09/60				
Tranmere Rov	Tr	07/62	62-66	174	0	100
Crystal Palace	Tr	09/66	66-67	33	1	9
Watford	Tr	01/68	67-68	38	0	19
Leyton Orient	Tr	12/68	68-72	154	6	28
Colchester U	Tr	07/73	73-74	41	1	6

DYSON Jonathan Paul (Jon)
Born: Mirfield, West Yorkshire, England, 18 December, 1971 CD

League Club	Source	Date Signed	Seasons Played	Apps	Subs	Gls
Huddersfield T	Jnr	12/90	92-02	184	32	9

DYSON Keith
Born: Consett, County Durham, England, 10 February, 1950 F
England: U23-1/Schools

League Club	Source	Date Signed	Seasons Played	Apps	Subs	Gls
Newcastle U	Jnr	08/68	68-71	74	2	22
Blackpool	Tr	10/71	71-75	91	3	30

DYSON Paul Ian
Born: Birmingham, England, 27 December, 1959 CD
England: U21-4

League Club	Source	Date Signed	Seasons Played	Apps	Subs	Gls
Coventry C	App	06/77	78-82	140	0	5
Stoke C	Tr	07/83	83-85	106	0	5
West Bromwich A	Tr	03/86	85-88	64	0	5
Darlington	Tr	03/89	88	12	0	3
Crewe Alex	Tr	08/89	89	30	1	2

DYSON Terence Kent (Terry)
Born: Malton, North Yorkshire, England, 29 November, 1934 LW

League Club	Source	Date Signed	Seasons Played	Apps	Subs	Gls
Tottenham H	Scarborough	04/55	54-64	184	-	41
Fulham	Tr	06/65	65-66	21	2	3
Colchester U	Tr	08/68	68-69	53	3	4

DZEKO Edin
Born: Sarajevo, Bosnia & Herzegovina, 17 March, 1986 F
Bosnia & Herzegovina: 72/U21-5/Youth

League Club	Source	Date Signed	Seasons Played	Apps	Subs	Gls
Manchester C	VfL Wolfsburg (GER)	01/11	10-14	74	56	50

DZIADULEWICZ Mieczyslaw (Mark)
Born: Wimbledon, SW London, England, 29 January, 1960 M

League Club	Source	Date Signed	Seasons Played	Apps	Subs	Gls
Southend U	App	02/78				
Wimbledon	Chelmsford C	02/79	78-79	22	6	1

DZIEKANOWSKI Dariusz Pawel (Jackie)
Born: Warsaw, Poland, 30 September, 1962 F
Poland: 62

League Club	Source	Date Signed	Seasons Played	Apps	Subs	Gls
Bristol C	Glasgow Celtic	01/92	91-92	40	3	7

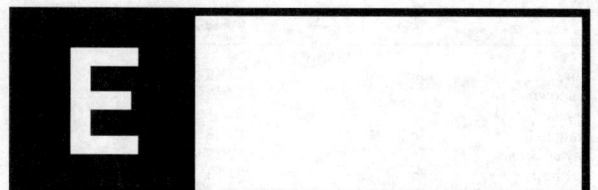

League Club	Source	Date Signed	Seasons Played	Career Record Apps	Subs	Gls

EADEN Nicholas Jeremy (Nicky)
Born: Sheffield, England, 12 December, 1972 — RB

League Club	Source	Date Signed	Seasons Played	Apps	Subs	Gls
Barnsley	Jnr	06/91	92-99	281	12	10
Birmingham C	Tr	07/00	00-01	68	6	3
Wigan Ath	Tr	09/02	02-04	116	6	0
Nottingham F	Tr	07/05	05	26	2	0
Lincoln C	L	08/06	06	32	1	0

EADES Kevin Michael
Born: Rotherham, South Yorkshire, England, 11 March, 1959 — RW

League Club	Source	Date Signed	Seasons Played	Apps	Subs	Gls
Rotherham U	App	03/77	75	1	0	0

EADES Terence Gerald (Terry)
Born: Banbridge, Down, Northern Ireland, 5 March, 1944 — CD

League Club	Source	Date Signed	Seasons Played	Apps	Subs	Gls
Cambridge U	Chelmsford C	03/69	70-76	248	0	5
Watford	L	09/76	76	4	0	0

EADIE Darren Malcolm
Born: Chippenham, Wiltshire, England, 10 June, 1975 — LW
England: U21-7/Youth

League Club	Source	Date Signed	Seasons Played	Apps	Subs	Gls
Norwich C	YT	02/93	93-99	153	15	35
Leicester C	Tr	12/99	99-00	31	9	2

EADIE Douglas (Doug)
Born: Edinburgh, Scotland, 22 September, 1946 — LW
Died: Glasgow, Scotland, 9 January, 2013

League Club	Source	Date Signed	Seasons Played	Apps	Subs	Gls
West Ham U	Possil YMCA	09/66	66	2	0	0
Leyton Orient	L	09/67	67	2	0	0

EADIE Gordon
Born: Glasgow, Scotland, 17 November, 1950 — LW

League Club	Source	Date Signed	Seasons Played	Apps	Subs	Gls
Bury (Am)	Glasgow U	06/67	67	2	0	0

EADIE James (Jim)
Born: Kirkintilloch, Dunbartonshire, Scotland, 4 February, 1947 — G

League Club	Source	Date Signed	Seasons Played	Apps	Subs	Gls
Cardiff C	Dumbarton	09/66	69-71	43	0	0
Chester C	L	08/72	72	6	0	0
Bristol Rov	Tr	02/73	72-76	183	0	0

EAGLE Robert John
Born: Leiston, Suffolk, England, 23 February, 1987 — W

League Club	Source	Date Signed	Seasons Played	Apps	Subs	Gls
Norwich C	Sch	07/06	06	3	7	0

EAGLES Alan James
Born: Edgware, NW London, England, 6 September, 1933 — RB
Died: Tenby, Pembrokeshire, Wales, 6 November, 1995

League Club	Source	Date Signed	Seasons Played	Apps	Subs	Gls
Leyton Orient	Carshalton Ath	09/57	57-60	75	-	0
Colchester U	Tr	01/61	60	16	-	1
Queens Park Rgrs	Tr	08/61				
Aldershot	Tr	11/61	61-62	15	-	1

EAGLES Christopher Mark (Chris)
Born: Hemel Hempstead, Hertfordshire, England, 19 November, 1985 — W
England: Youth

League Club	Source	Date Signed	Seasons Played	Apps	Subs	Gls
Manchester U	Sch	07/03	06-07	2	4	1
Watford	L	01/05	04	10	3	1
Sheffield Wed	L	07/05	05	21	4	3
Watford	L	01/06	05	16	1	3
Burnley	Tr	08/08	08-10	87	33	21
Bolton W	Tr	07/11	11-13	79	14	17
Blackpool		11/14	14	7	0	1
Charlton Ath	Tr	02/15	14	5	10	2

EALING William Henry
Born: Tamworth, Staffordshire, England, 12 March, 1930 — CF
Died: Sutton Coldfield, West Midlands, England, June, 2009

League Club	Source	Date Signed	Seasons Played	Apps	Subs	Gls
Blackburn Rov	Tamworth	02/50				
Walsall	Tr	07/52	52	1	-	0

EAMES Terence (Terry)
Born: Croydon, S London, England, 13 October, 1957 — FB

League Club	Source	Date Signed	Seasons Played	Apps	Subs	Gls
Wimbledon	Crystal Palace (NC)	01/77	77-79	46	1	1

EAMES William Alan (Billy)
Born: Emsworth, Hampshire, England, 20 September, 1957 — M

League Club	Source	Date Signed	Seasons Played	Apps	Subs	Gls
Portsmouth	App	09/75	75	9	3	1
Brentford	Tr	08/78	78	2	0	1

League Club Source Date Signed Seasons Played Career Record Apps Subs Gls

EARDLEY Neal James
Born: Llandudno, Conwy, Wales, 6 November, 1988 — RB
Wales: 16/U21-11/Youth

League Club	Source	Date Signed	Seasons Played	Apps	Subs	Gls
Oldham Ath	Sch	09/06	05-08	108	5	10
Blackpool	Tr	08/09	09-12	94	10	2
Birmingham C	Tr	07/13	13-14	9	0	0
Leyton Orient	L	01/15	14	1	0	0

EARL Albert Thomas (Stan)
Born: Gateshead, Tyne and Wear, England, 10 February, 1915 — IF
Died: Bury, Greater Manchester, England, November, 2000

League Club	Source	Date Signed	Seasons Played	Apps	Subs	Gls
Bury	Dunston Soap Works	03/32	33-35	35	-	7
York C	Rhyl Ath	07/37	37-38	58	-	9
Hartlepool U	Tr	07/39				
Stockport Co	Tr	08/46	46-47	42	-	12
Rochdale	Tr	11/47	47	4	-	1
New Brighton	Tr	03/48	47	9	-	1

EARL Stanley James William (Stan)
Born: Alton, Hampshire, England, 9 July, 1929 — LB
Died: Yeovil, Somerset, England, 26 February, 2012

League Club	Source	Date Signed	Seasons Played	Apps	Subs	Gls
Portsmouth	Alton T	11/49	50-51	8	-	0
Leyton Orient	Tr	07/53	53-55	33	-	0
Swindon T	Tr	11/56	56-57	23	-	0

EARL Steven (Steve)
Born: Scunthorpe, North Lincolnshire, England, 31 August, 1956 — F
Died: Chiltern, Buckinghamshire, England, 3 November, 2004

League Club	Source	Date Signed	Seasons Played	Apps	Subs	Gls
Scunthorpe U (Am)	Appleby Frodingham	09/74	74	7	0	1
Scunthorpe U	Appleby Frodingham	11/78	78-79	30	2	9

EARLAM Donald Stuart (Don)
Born: Altrincham, Greater Manchester, England, 25 June, 1931 — WH
Died: Trafford, Greater Manchester, England, 25 March, 1988

League Club	Source	Date Signed	Seasons Played	Apps	Subs	Gls
Southport (Am)	Broadheath Central	08/54	54	2	-	0

EARLE Robert Fitzgerald (Robbie)
Born: Newcastle-under-Lyme, Potteries, England, 27 January, 1965 — M/F
Jamaica: 33

League Club	Source	Date Signed	Seasons Played	Apps	Subs	Gls
Port Vale	Jnr	07/82	82-90	284	10	77
Wimbledon	Tr	07/91	91-99	280	4	59

EARLE Stephen John (Steve)
Born: Feltham, SW London, England, 1 November, 1945 — F

League Club	Source	Date Signed	Seasons Played	Apps	Subs	Gls
Fulham	App	11/63	63-73	285	6	98
Leicester C	Tr	11/73	73-77	91	8	20
Peterborough U	L	11/77	77	1	0	0

EARLES Patrick John Earles (Pat)
Born: Titchfield, Hampshire, England, 22 March, 1955 — RW
England: Schools

League Club	Source	Date Signed	Seasons Played	Apps	Subs	Gls
Southampton	App	11/72	74-76	4	8	1
Reading	Tr	01/77	76-82	240	7	68

EARLS Michael Patrick Marien (Mike)
Born: Limerick, Republic of Ireland, 25 March, 1954 — D

League Club	Source	Date Signed	Seasons Played	Apps	Subs	Gls
Southampton	App	11/72	73-74	8	0	0
Aldershot	Tr	06/75	75-78	68	5	0

EARLY Michael (Mike)
Born: Dumbarton, Dunbartonshire, Scotland, 4 April, 1928 — RW
Died: Dumbarton, Dunbartonshire, Scotland, 26 May, 1995

League Club	Source	Date Signed	Seasons Played	Apps	Subs	Gls
Watford	Strathleven	06/46	46	5	-	1

EARNSHAW Robert (Rob)
Born: Mufulira, Zambia, 6 April, 1981 — F
Wales: 59/U21-10/Youth

League Club	Source	Date Signed	Seasons Played	Apps	Subs	Gls
Cardiff C	YT	08/98	97-04	141	37	85
West Bromwich A	Tr	08/04	04-05	22	21	12
Norwich C	Tr	01/06	05-06	41	4	27
Derby Co	Tr	06/07	07	7	15	1
Nottingham F	Tr	05/08	08-10	72	26	35
Cardiff C	Tr	07/11	11	8	11	3
Blackpool	Toronto FC (CAN)	03/14	13	0	1	0

EARNSHAW Robert Ian (Bob)
Born: Rotherham, South Yorkshire, England, 15 March, 1943 — RW

League Club	Source	Date Signed	Seasons Played	Apps	Subs	Gls
Barnsley	Jnr	06/62	62-72	219	6	35

EASDALE John Hollywood Millar
Born: Dumbarton, Dunbartonshire, Scotland, 16 January, 1919 — CH

League Club	Source	Date Signed	Seasons Played	Apps	Subs	Gls
Liverpool		02/37	46	2	-	0
Stockport Co	Tr	09/48	48	6	-	0

EAST Daniel (Danny)
Born: Hessle, East Riding of Yorkshire, England, 26 December, 1991 — RB

League Club	Source	Date Signed	Seasons Played	Apps	Subs	Gls
Hull C	Sch	05/11				
Northampton T	L	08/12	12	12	2	0
Gillingham	L	03/13	12	1	1	0
Portsmouth	Tr	06/13	13-14	14	5	1

EAST Keith Michael George
Born: Southampton, England, 31 October, 1944 — CF

League Club	Source	Date Signed	Seasons Played	Apps	Subs	Gls
Portsmouth	App	06/63				
Swindon T	Tr	05/64	64-66	43	2	21
Stockport Co	Tr	12/66	66-67	23	2	7
Bournemouth	Tr	11/67	67-69	93	1	34
Northampton T	Tr	07/70	70	26	3	7
Crewe Alex	Tr	07/71	71	32	2	8

EASTER Derwain Jamal (Jamal)
Born: Cardiff, Wales, 15 November, 1987 — F
Wales: U21-1/Youth

League Club	Source	Date Signed	Seasons Played	Apps	Subs	Gls
Cardiff C	Sch	09/06				
Bristol Rov	L	10/06	06	1	2	0
Torquay U	L	01/07	06	8	2	0

EASTER Graham Paul
Born: Epsom, Surrey, England, 26 September, 1969 — W

League Club	Source	Date Signed	Seasons Played	Apps	Subs	Gls
West Bromwich A	YT	07/88				
Huddersfield T	Tr	03/89				
Crewe Alex	Tr	07/89	89	0	3	0
Preston NE	Viborg FF (FIN)	10/90	90	1	0	0

EASTER Jermaine Maurice
Born: Cardiff, Wales, 15 January, 1982 — F
Wales: 12/Youth

League Club	Source	Date Signed	Seasons Played	Apps	Subs	Gls
Wolverhampton W	YT	07/00				
Hartlepool U	Tr	03/01	00-03	0	27	2
Cambridge U	Tr	02/04	03-04	25	14	8
Boston U	Tr	03/05	04	5	4	3
Stockport Co	Tr	07/05	05	18	1	8
Wycombe W	Tr	01/06	05-07	44	15	21
Plymouth Arg	Tr	10/07	07-08	22	14	6
Millwall	L	09/08	08	2	3	1
Colchester U	L	10/08	08	5	0	2
MK Dons	Tr	08/09	09-10	43	7	14
Swansea C	L	11/10	10	2	4	1
Crystal Palace	Tr	01/11	10-12	26	29	8
Millwall	Tr	03/13	12-14	13	25	5

EASTHAM Ashley Thomas
Born: Preston, Lancashire, England, 22 March, 1991 — CD

League Club	Source	Date Signed	Seasons Played	Apps	Subs	Gls
Blackpool	Sch	05/09	09	0	1	0
Cheltenham T	L	11/09	09	18	2	0
Cheltenham T	L	01/11	10	8	1	0
Bury	L	08/11	11	22	3	2
Fleetwood T	L	08/12	12	1	0	0
Notts Co	L	10/12	12	3	1	0
Bury	L	01/13	12	18	1	0
Rochdale	Tr	06/13	13-14	55	1	2

EASTHAM Brian
Born: Bolton, Greater Manchester, England, 26 April, 1937 — LB

League Club	Source	Date Signed	Seasons Played	Apps	Subs	Gls
Bury	Chorley	09/58	58-66	188	1	3
Rochdale	Toronto Falcons (CAN)	07/67	67	13	0	0

EASTHAM George Edward
Born: Blackpool, Lancashire, England, 23 September, 1936 — IF
England: 19/FLge-3/U23-6//Northern Ireland: NILge-3

League Club	Source	Date Signed	Seasons Played	Apps	Subs	Gls
Newcastle U	Ards	05/56	56-59	124	-	29
Arsenal	Tr	10/60	60-65	207	0	41
Stoke C	Tr	08/66	66-73	184	10	4

EASTHAM George Richard
Born: Blackpool, Lancashire, England, 13 September, 1914 — IF
Died: South Africa, 2000
England: 1

League Club	Source	Date Signed	Seasons Played	Apps	Subs	Gls
Bolton W	South Shore Wed	08/32	32-36	114	-	16
Brentford	Tr	05/37	37-38	49	-	1
Blackpool	Tr	11/38	38-46	44	-	9
Swansea C	Tr	08/47	47	15	-	0
Rochdale	Tr	06/48	48	2	-	0
Lincoln C	Tr	01/49	48-49	27	-	1

EASTHAM Henry (Harry)
Born: Blackpool, Lancashire, England, 30 June, 1917 — RH
Died: Middlesbrough, England, September, 1998

League Club	Source	Date Signed	Seasons Played	Apps	Subs	Gls
Blackpool	Jnr	06/34				
Liverpool	Tr	02/36	36-46	63	-	3
Tranmere Rov	Tr	05/48	48-52	154	-	12
Accrington Stan	Tr	07/53	53	42	-	3

EASTHAM Stanley (Stan)
Born: Bolton, Greater Manchester, England, 26 November, 1913 — WH
England: Amateur

League Club	Source	Date Signed	Seasons Played	Apps	Subs	Gls
Liverpool	Kingstonian	05/38				
Exeter C	Tr	04/46				
Stockport Co	Tr	06/46	46	14	-	1

EASTHOPE Joseph Donald (Don)
Born: Liverpool, England, 26 September, 1929 — LW
Died: Liverpool, England, 15 February, 1993

League Club	Source	Date Signed	Seasons Played	Apps	Subs	Gls
Everton		04/50	52	2	-	0
Stockport Co	Tr	06/54	54	9	-	2

EASTMAN Donald John (Don)
Born: Eastry, Kent, England, 9 August, 1923 — FB
Died: Bournemouth, England, 16 August, 2010

League Club	Source	Date Signed	Seasons Played	Apps	Subs	Gls
Crystal Palace (Am)	Jnr	08/46	46	1	-	0

EASTMAN Thomas Michael (Tom)
Born: Clacton, Essex, England, 21 October, 1991 — CD

League Club	Source	Date Signed	Seasons Played	Apps	Subs	Gls
Ipswich T	Sch	07/10	09-10	9	1	0
Colchester U	Tr	07/11	11-14	132	4	6
Crawley T	L	09/11	11	6	0	0

EASTMOND Craig Leon
Born: Wandsworth, SW London, England, 9 December, 1990 — M

League Club	Source	Date Signed	Seasons Played	Apps	Subs	Gls
Arsenal	Sch	07/09	09	2	2	0
Millwall	L	01/11	10	4	2	0
Wycombe W	L	02/12	11	14	0	0
Colchester U	L	09/12	12	12	0	2
Colchester U	Tr	07/13	13-14	38	11	5
Yeovil T	Tr	02/15	14	0	1	0

EASTOE Peter Robert
Born: Tamworth, Staffordshire, England, 2 August, 1953 — F
England: Youth

League Club	Source	Date Signed	Seasons Played	Apps	Subs	Gls
Wolverhampton W	App	06/71	71-73	4	2	0
Swindon T	L	11/73	73	11	0	7
Swindon T	Tr	03/74	73-75	80	0	36
Queens Park Rgrs	Tr	03/76	76-78	69	3	15
Everton	Tr	03/79	78-81	88	7	26
West Bromwich A	Tr	08/82	82	30	1	8
Leicester C	L	10/83	83	5	0	1
Huddersfield T	L	03/84	83	8	2	0
Walsall	L	08/84	84	6	0	1
Leicester C	L	10/84	84	6	0	1
Wolverhampton W	L	02/85	84	8	0	0

EASTON Brian Neil
Born: Glasgow, Scotland, 5 March, 1988 — LB
Scotland: B-1/U21-3

League Club	Source	Date Signed	Seasons Played	Apps	Subs	Gls
Burnley	Hamilton Academical	07/09	09-11	28	5	1

EASTON Clint Jude
Born: Barking, E London, England, 1 October, 1977 — M/LB
England: Youth

League Club	Source	Date Signed	Seasons Played	Apps	Subs	Gls
Watford	YT	07/96	96-00	50	14	1
Norwich C	Tr	06/01	01-03	41	9	5
Wycombe W	Tr	07/04	04-05	69	8	2
Gillingham	Tr	07/06	06	26	6	1
Hereford U	Tr	07/07	07-08	45	6	3

EASTON Craig
Born: Airdrie, Lanarkshire, Scotland, 26 February, 1979 — M
Scotland: U21-21

League Club	Source	Date Signed	Seasons Played	Apps	Subs	Gls
Leyton Orient	Livingston	07/05	05-06	65	6	5
Swindon T	Tr	07/07	07-09	56	19	8
Southend U	Tr	08/10	10	32	0	4
Torquay U		06/12	12	18	3	0

EASTON Henry Blair (Harry)
Born: Shoreham-by-Sea, West Sussex, England, 12 September, 1938 — IF

League Club	Source	Date Signed	Seasons Played	Apps	Subs	Gls
Crystal Palace	Jnr	11/56	59-61	8	-	1

EASTWAY Raymond John (Ray)
Born: Croydon, S London, England, 12 April, 1929 — RB
Died: Wandsworth, SW London, England, January, 1989

League Club	Source	Date Signed	Seasons Played	Apps	Subs	Gls
Watford	Manchester U (Jnr)	08/49	51	12	-	0

EASTWOOD Eric
Born: Heywood, Greater Manchester, England, 24 March, 1916 — CH
Died: Bolton, Greater Manchester, England, October, 1991

League Club	Source	Date Signed	Seasons Played	Apps	Subs	Gls
Manchester C	Heywood St James'	04/35	38-46	16	-	0
Port Vale	Tr	03/47	46-48	28	-	1

EASTWOOD Freddy
Born: Epsom, Surrey, England, 29 October, 1983 — F
Wales: 11

League Club	Source	Date Signed	Seasons Played	Apps	Subs	Gls
Southend U	Grays Ath	10/04	04-06	106	9	53
Wolverhampton W	Tr	07/07	07	10	21	3
Coventry C	Tr	07/08	08-11	72	41	17
Southend U	Tr	03/12	11-13	27	36	11

EASTWOOD Philip John (Phil)
Born: Blackburn, Greater Manchester, England, 6 April, 1978 — F

League Club	Source	Date Signed	Seasons Played	Apps	Subs	Gls
Burnley	YT	07/96	97-98	7	9	1

EASTWOOD Raymond (Ray)
Born: Moston, Greater Manchester, England, 1 January, 1915 — RB
Died: Manchester, England, February, 1999

League Club	Source	Date Signed	Seasons Played	Apps	Subs	Gls
Aldershot	Altrincham	06/38	38	9	-	0
Accrington Stan	Tr	07/46	46	3	-	0

EASTWOOD Simon Christopher
Born: Luton, England, 26 June, 1989 — G
England: Youth

League Club	Source	Date Signed	Seasons Played	Apps	Subs	Gls
Huddersfield T	Sch	07/07	08	1	0	0
Bradford C	L	07/09	09	22	0	0
Oxford U	Tr	07/10				
Portsmouth	FC Halifax T	08/12	12	27	0	0
Blackburn Rov	Tr	05/13	13-14	13	0	0

EATON Adam Paul
Born: Wigan, Greater Manchester, England, 2 May, 1980 — LB

League Club	Source	Date Signed	Seasons Played	Apps	Subs	Gls
Everton	YT	06/97				
Preston NE	Tr	06/99	00-02	7	7	0
Mansfield T	L	12/02	02	6	0	0
Mansfield T	Tr	02/03	02-04	19	0	0

EATON David Franklin
Born: Liverpool, England, 30 September, 1981 — F

League Club	Source	Date Signed	Seasons Played	Apps	Subs	Gls
Everton	YT	07/01				
Macclesfield T	Tr	09/02	02	8	12	5

EATON Jason Cord
Born: Bristol, England, 29 January, 1969 — F

League Club	Source	Date Signed	Seasons Played	Apps	Subs	Gls
Bristol Rov	YT	06/87	87	0	3	0
Bristol C	Trowbridge T	03/89	88-89	6	7	1

EATON Joseph David (Joe)
Born: Cuckney, Nottinghamshire, England, 16 May, 1931 — IF

League Club	Source	Date Signed	Seasons Played	Apps	Subs	Gls
Mansfield T	Langwith BC	08/51	52-53	4	-	1

EATON Stephen Paul (Steve)
Born: Liverpool, England, 25 December, 1959 — FB

League Club	Source	Date Signed	Seasons Played	Apps	Subs	Gls
Tranmere Rov	Jnr	03/79	78	1	0	0

EAVES David Michael Curtis
Born: Blackpool, Lancashire, England, 13 February, 1973 — M

League Club	Source	Date Signed	Seasons Played	Apps	Subs	Gls
Preston NE	YT	07/91	90-92	2	5	0

EAVES Ernest (Ernie)
Born: Bryn, Greater Manchester, England, 4 January, 1927 — CF
Died: St Helens, Merseyside, England, July, 2014

League Club	Source	Date Signed	Seasons Played	Apps	Subs	Gls
New Brighton	Newton-le-Willows	10/48	48-50	14	-	3

EAVES Thomas James (Tom)
Born: Liverpool, England, 14 January, 1992 — F

League Club	Source	Date Signed	Seasons Played	Apps	Subs	Gls
Oldham Ath	Sch	05/10	09	0	15	0
Bolton W	Tr	08/10	12-14	0	4	0
Bristol Rov	L	09/12	12	16	0	7
Shrewsbury T	L	02/13	12	10	0	6
Rotherham U	L	09/13	13	1	7	0
Shrewsbury T	L	11/13	13	20	5	2
Yeovil T	L	11/14	14	4	1	0
Bury	L	03/15	14	7	2	1

EBANKS Michael Wayne Anthony (Wayne)
Born: Longbridge, West Midlands, England, 2 October, 1964 — RB/M

League Club	Source	Date Signed	Seasons Played	Apps	Subs	Gls
West Bromwich A	App	04/82	83	6	1	0
Stoke C	L	08/84	84	10	0	0
Port Vale	Tr	03/85	84-86	36	3	0
Cambridge U	Tr	08/87	87	3	1	0

EBANKS-BLAKE Sylvan Augustus
Born: Cambridge, England, 29 March, 1986 — F
England: U21-1

League Club	Source	Date Signed	Seasons Played	Apps	Subs	Gls
Manchester U	Sch	02/05				
Plymouth Arg	Tr	07/06	06-07	49	17	21
Wolverhampton W	Tr	01/08	07-12	123	54	61
Ipswich T		12/13	13	1	8	0
Preston NE		01/15	14	1	8	1

EBANKS-LANDELL Ethan Reid
Born: Oldbury, West Midlands, England, 16 December, 1992 — CD

League Club	Source	Date Signed	Seasons Played	Apps	Subs	Gls
Wolverhampton W	Sch	12/09	13-14	13	8	4
Bury	L	11/12	12	24	0	0

EBBRELL John Keith
Born: Bromborough, Wirral, England, 1 October, 1969 — M
England: B-1/U21-14/Youth/Schools

League Club	Source	Date Signed	Seasons Played	Apps	Subs	Gls
Everton	App	11/86	88-96	207	10	13
Sheffield U	Tr	03/97	96	1	0	0

EBDON Marcus
Born: Pontypool, Torfaen, Wales, 17 October, 1970 — M
Wales: U21-2/Youth

League Club	Source	Date Signed	Seasons Played	Apps	Subs	Gls
Everton	YT	08/89				
Peterborough U	Tr	07/91	91-96	136	11	15
Chesterfield	Tr	03/97	96-02	180	12	13
Leyton Orient	Tr	08/03	03	10	4	0

EBDON Richard George (Dick)
Born: Ottery St Mary, Devon, England, 3 May, 1913 — CF
Died: Ottery St Mary, Devon, England, 27 April, 1987

League Club	Source	Date Signed	Seasons Played	Apps	Subs	Gls
Exeter C	Ottery St Mary	12/35	35-47	138	-	50
Torquay U	Tr	07/48	48	5	-	1

E'BEYER Mark Edward
Born: Stevenage, Hertfordshire, England, 21 September, 1984 — LW

League Club	Source	Date Signed	Seasons Played	Apps	Subs	Gls
Oxford U	MK Dons (Sch)	07/04	04-05	9	7	3

EBOUE Emmanuel
Born: Abidjan, Ivory Coast, 4 June, 1983 — RB
Ivory Coast: 79

League Club	Source	Date Signed	Seasons Played	Apps	Subs	Gls
Arsenal	Beveren (BEL)	01/05	04-10	96	36	5

ECCLES Peter Edward
Born: Dublin, Republic of Ireland, 24 August, 1962 — CD
Republic of Ireland: 1

League Club	Source	Date Signed	Seasons Played	Apps	Subs	Gls
Leicester C	Dundalk (ROI)	10/88	88	1	0	0

ECCLES Terence Stuart (Terry)
Born: Leeds, England, 2 March, 1952 — F

League Club	Source	Date Signed	Seasons Played	Apps	Subs	Gls
Blackburn Rov	App	08/69	69-72	33	13	6
Mansfield T	Tr	07/73	73-76	115	3	47
Huddersfield T	Tr	01/77	76-77	41	5	6
York C	Ethnikos (GRE)	09/79	79-80	64	0	18

ECCLESHARE Keith
Born: Bolton, Greater Manchester, England, 14 December, 1950 — RB
England: Youth

League Club	Source	Date Signed	Seasons Played	Apps	Subs	Gls
Bury	App	12/68	68-71	79	4	0

ECCLESTON Nathan Geoffrey
Born: Manchester, England, 30 December, 1990 — F
England: Youth

League Club	Source	Date Signed	Seasons Played	Apps	Subs	Gls
Liverpool	Sch	02/08	09-10	0	2	0
Huddersfield T	L	01/10	09	4	7	1
Charlton Ath	L	01/11	10	8	13	3
Rochdale	L	10/11	11	3	2	1
Blackpool	Tr	08/12	12-13	2	8	1
Tranmere Rov	L	10/12	12	1	0	0
Carlisle U	L	10/13	13	0	2	0
Coventry C	L	03/14	13	4	4	0

ECCLESTON Stuart Ian
Born: Stoke-on-Trent, England, 4 October, 1961 — CD

League Club	Source	Date Signed	Seasons Played	Apps	Subs	Gls
Stoke C	App	10/79				
Hull C	Tr	01/81	80-81	22	1	0

ECHANOMI Efe
Born: Nigeria, 27 September, 1986 — F

League Club	Source	Date Signed	Seasons Played	Apps	Subs	Gls
Leyton Orient	Sch	07/06	04-07	4	47	8

ECKERSALL Michael William (Mike)
Born: Bury, Greater Manchester, England, 3 February, 1939 — WH

League Club	Source	Date Signed	Seasons Played	Apps	Subs	Gls
Torquay U	Mossley	10/59	60-62	28	-	2
Stockport Co	Tr	07/63	63-65	39	1	2

ECKERSLEY Adam James
Born: Worsley, Greater Manchester, England, 7 September, 1985 — LB
England: Youth

League Club	Source	Date Signed	Seasons Played	Apps	Subs	Gls
Manchester U	Sch	07/04				
Barnsley	L	01/07	06	6	0	0
Port Vale	Tr	10/07	07	18	0	1

ECKERSLEY Richard Jon
Born: Worsley, Greater Manchester, England, 12 March, 1989 — RB

League Club	Source	Date Signed	Seasons Played	Apps	Subs	Gls
Manchester U	Sch	07/06	08	0	2	0
Burnley	Tr	07/09				
Plymouth Arg	L	03/10	09	7	0	0
Bradford C	L	11/10	10	12	0	0
Bury	L	03/11	10	3	0	0

ECKERSLEY Thomas Scott (Tom)
Born: Sale, Greater Manchester, England, 6 December, 1991 — CD

League Club	Source	Date Signed	Seasons Played	Apps	Subs	Gls
Bolton W	Sch	08/11				
Accrington Stan	Tr	08/12	12	1	1	0

ECKERSLEY William (Bill)
Born: Southport, Merseyside, England, 16 July, 1925 — LB
Died: Blackburn, Greater Manchester, England, 25 December, 1982
England: 17/B-3/FLge-6

League Club	Source	Date Signed	Seasons Played	Apps	Subs	Gls
Blackburn Rov	High Park	03/48	47-60	406	-	20

League Club	Source	Date Signed	Seasons Played	Apps	Subs	Gls

ECKHARDT Jeffrey Edward (Jeff)
Born: Sheffield, England, 7 October, 1965 — CD/M

League Club	Source	Date Signed	Seasons Played	Apps	Subs	Gls
Sheffield U	Jnr	08/84	84-87	73	1	2
Fulham	Tr	11/87	87-93	245	4	25
Stockport Co	Tr	07/94	94-95	56	6	7
Cardiff C	Tr	08/96	96-00	129	11	14

ECONOMOU Jon (Joe)
Born: Holloway, N London, England, 25 October, 1961 — M

League Club	Source	Date Signed	Seasons Played	Apps	Subs	Gls
Bristol C	App	10/79	81-83	62	3	3

ECUELE MANGA Bruno
Born: Libreville, Gabon, 16 July, 1988 — CD
Gabon: 41

League Club	Source	Date Signed	Seasons Played	Apps	Subs	Gls
Cardiff C	Lorient (FRA)	09/14	14	29	0	3

EDDOLLS John Douglas
Born: Bristol, England, 19 August, 1919 — G
Died: Bath, England, August, 1994

League Club	Source	Date Signed	Seasons Played	Apps	Subs	Gls
Bristol C	Peasedown	09/45	46	6	-	0

EDDS Ernest Frederick (Ernie)
Born: Plymouth, England, 19 March, 1926 — LW

League Club	Source	Date Signed	Seasons Played	Apps	Subs	Gls
Plymouth Arg	Portsmouth (Am)	10/46	46-49	59	-	18
Blackburn Rov	Tr	12/49	49-50	18	-	3
Torquay U	Tr	06/51	51-53	84	-	34
Plymouth Arg	Tr	10/53	53-54	26	-	4
Swindon T	Tr	07/55	55	3	-	0

EDDS Gareth James
Born: Sydney, Australia, 3 February, 1981 — RB/M
Australia: U23-2/Youth

League Club	Source	Date Signed	Seasons Played	Apps	Subs	Gls
Nottingham F	YT	02/98	99-01	11	5	1
Swindon T	Tr	08/02	02	8	6	0
Bradford C	Tr	07/03	03	19	4	0
MK Dons	Tr	07/04	04-07	97	25	10
Tranmere Rov	Tr	07/08	08-09	46	23	5

EDDY Keith
Born: Barrow, Cumbria, England, 23 October, 1944 — M

League Club	Source	Date Signed	Seasons Played	Apps	Subs	Gls
Barrow	Holker Central OB	06/62	62-65	127	1	5
Watford	Tr	07/66	66-71	239	1	26
Sheffield U	Tr	08/72	72-75	113	1	16

EDELSTON Maurice
Born: Hull, England, 27 April, 1918 — IF
Died: Tilehurst, Berkshire, England, 30 January, 1976
England: Amateur-3/War-5

League Club	Source	Date Signed	Seasons Played	Apps	Subs	Gls
Fulham (Am)	Jnr	07/35	35-37	3	-	0
Brentford (Am)	Wimbledon	12/37	37-38	21	-	6
Reading	Corinthians	05/39	46-51	202	-	70
Northampton T	Tr	07/52	52-53	40	-	17

EDEN Alan
Born: Sunderland, England, 8 October, 1958 — M

League Club	Source	Date Signed	Seasons Played	Apps	Subs	Gls
Lincoln C	Lambton Street BC	08/77	77-78	5	2	0

EDEN Anthony Frederick
Born: Birmingham, England, 15 March, 1941 — CH

League Club	Source	Date Signed	Seasons Played	Apps	Subs	Gls
Aston Villa	Jnr	04/58				
Walsall	Tr	07/60	60-62	14	-	0

EDESON Matthew Kirk (Matt)
Born: Beverley, East Riding of Yorkshire, England, 11 August, 1976 — F

League Club	Source	Date Signed	Seasons Played	Apps	Subs	Gls
Hull C	YT	07/94	92-94	0	5	0

EDEY Cecil (Cec)
Born: Manchester, England, 12 March, 1965 — D

League Club	Source	Date Signed	Seasons Played	Apps	Subs	Gls
Macclesfield T	Witton A	10/95	97	9	4	0

EDGAR Anthony James
Born: Newham, E London, England, 30 September, 1990 — M

League Club	Source	Date Signed	Seasons Played	Apps	Subs	Gls
West Ham U	Sch	07/09				
Bournemouth	L	10/09	09	2	1	0
Yeovil T	Tr	07/11	11	5	5	1
Barnet	Tr	07/12	12	7	4	1
Dagenham & Red		11/13	13	0	7	0

EDGAR David Edward
Born: Kitchener, Ontario, Canada, 19 May, 1987 — CD
Canada: 29/Youth

League Club	Source	Date Signed	Seasons Played	Apps	Subs	Gls
Newcastle U	Sch	09/05	06-08	11	8	2
Burnley	Tr	07/09	09-13	74	25	4
Swansea C	L	03/10	09	5	0	1
Birmingham C	Tr	06/14	14	14	2	1
Huddersfield T	L	01/15	14	9	3	0

EDGAR Edward (Eddie)
Born: Jarrow, Tyne and Wear, England, 31 October, 1956 — G

League Club	Source	Date Signed	Seasons Played	Apps	Subs	Gls
Newcastle U	App	08/74				
Hartlepool U	Tr	07/76	76-78	75	0	0

EDGAR John (Johnny)
Born: Barnsley, South Yorkshire, England, 9 April, 1936 — IF
Died: Barnsley, South Yorkshire, England, 1 February, 2008

League Club	Source	Date Signed	Seasons Played	Apps	Subs	Gls
Barnsley	Jnr	05/54	55-57	22	-	6
Gillingham	Tr	06/58	58	45	-	23
York C	Tr	06/59	59-60	47	-	16
Hartlepool U	Tr	06/61	61-62	72	-	31
Exeter C	Tr	07/63	63	6	-	0

EDGAR John David
Born: Aldershot, Hampshire, England, 1 December, 1930 — IF/RH
Died: Hurworth, County Durham, England, 9 September, 2006

League Club	Source	Date Signed	Seasons Played	Apps	Subs	Gls
Darlington	Ferryhill Ath	12/54	54-55	12	-	0

EDGE Declan John
Born: Malacca, Malaysia, 18 September, 1965 — F
New Zealand:

League Club	Source	Date Signed	Seasons Played	Apps	Subs	Gls
Notts Co	Gisborne C (NZL)	12/85	85	7	3	2

EDGE Derek
Born: Hanley, Potteries, England, 14 February, 1942 — RW
Died: Stoke-on-Trent, England, 23 October, 1991

League Club	Source	Date Signed	Seasons Played	Apps	Subs	Gls
Port Vale	Stoke C (Am)	09/60	61	2	-	0

EDGE Harold Anthony (Tony)
Born: Hoylake, Wirral, England, 14 March, 1937 — CF

League Club	Source	Date Signed	Seasons Played	Apps	Subs	Gls
Bristol Rov	Devizes T	08/59	59-60	13	-	4

EDGE Lewis John Spencer
Born: Lancaster, England, 12 January, 1987 — G

League Club	Source	Date Signed	Seasons Played	Apps	Subs	Gls
Blackpool	Sch	07/06	03-06	2	1	0
Bury	L	10/06	06	1	0	0
Morecambe	Tr	10/08				

EDGE Roland
Born: Gillingham, Kent, England, 25 November, 1978 — LB

League Club	Source	Date Signed	Seasons Played	Apps	Subs	Gls
Gillingham	YT	07/97	98-02	93	9	1
Hull C	Hibernian	07/04	04-05	21	1	0

EDGHILL Richard Arlon
Born: Oldham, Greater Manchester, England, 23 September, 1974 — RB
England: B-1/U21-3

League Club	Source	Date Signed	Seasons Played	Apps	Subs	Gls
Manchester C	YT	07/92	93-01	178	3	1
Birmingham C	L	11/00	00	3	0	0
Wigan Ath	Tr	10/02				
Sheffield U	Tr	01/03	02	0	1	0
Queens Park Rgrs	Tr	08/03	03-04	28	12	0
Bradford C	Tr	08/05	05-06	39	4	1
Macclesfield T	Tr	07/07	07	13	2	0

EDGLEY Brian Kenneth
Born: Shrewsbury, Shropshire, England, 26 August, 1937 — IF/W

League Club	Source	Date Signed	Seasons Played	Apps	Subs	Gls
Shrewsbury T	Jnr	02/56	55-59	113	-	12
Cardiff C	Tr	07/60	60	10	-	1
Brentford	Tr	06/61	61-62	31	-	9
Barnsley	Tr	11/62	62	4	-	0

EDINBURGH Justin Charles
Born: Basildon, England, 18 December, 1969 — LB

League Club	Source	Date Signed	Seasons Played	Apps	Subs	Gls
Southend U	YT	08/88	88-89	36	1	0
Tottenham H	Tr	07/90	90-99	190	23	1
Portsmouth	Tr	03/00	99-01	34	1	1

[EDINHO] AMARAL Neto Edon
Born: Arapiraca, Brazil, 21 February, 1967 — F

League Club	Source	Date Signed	Seasons Played	Apps	Subs	Gls
Bradford C	Vit Guimaraes (POR)	02/97	96-98	50	9	15

[EDINHO JUNIOR] AMARAL Edon Junior Viegas
Born: Faro, Portugal, 7 March, 1994 — F
Portugal: Youth

League Club	Source	Date Signed	Seasons Played	Apps	Subs	Gls
Blackburn Rov	Olhanense (POR)	08/12	12	1	0	0

EDISBURY William
Born: Tyldesley, Greater Manchester, England, 12 November, 1937 — LB

League Club	Source	Date Signed	Seasons Played	Apps	Subs	Gls
Bolton W	Jnr	10/56	56-57	2	-	0

EDJENGUELE William Emery
Born: Paris, France, 7 May, 1987 — CD

League Club	Source	Date Signed	Seasons Played	Apps	Subs	Gls
Coventry C	Panetolikos (GRE)	07/12	12	30	3	1
Bury	Tr	08/13	13	18	1	2

EDKINS Ashley Michael
Born: Coalville, Leicestershire, England, 23 December, 1986 — RB/M

League Club	Source	Date Signed	Seasons Played	Apps	Subs	Gls
Boston U	Aston Villa (Sch)	-	05	0	1	0

EDMAN Erik Kenneth
Born: Huskvarna, Sweden, 11 November, 1978 — LB
Sweden: 57/U21-19/Youth

League Club	Source	Date Signed	Seasons Played	Apps	Subs	Gls
Tottenham H	Heerenveen (NED)	07/04	04-05	31	0	1
Wigan Ath	Stade Rennais (FRA)	01/08	07-09	7	3	0

League Club	Source	Date Signed	Seasons Played	Apps	Subs	Gls
EDMANS Robert Michael (Rob)						
Born: Greenwich, SE London, England, 25 January, 1987						F
Dagenham & Red	Chelmsford C	07/11	11-12	0	4	0
EDMONDS Darren						
Born: Watford, Hertfordshire, England, 12 April, 1971						W
Leeds U	YT	05/89				
Ipswich T	Tr	09/91	91	0	2	0
Scarborough	Tr	08/92	92	0	1	0
Halifax T	Mossley	11/92	92	0	2	0
EDMONDS Derek James						
Born: Hexham, Northumberland, England, 9 October, 1950						G
Died: Leeds, England, August, 2013						
England: Youth						
Leeds U	App	11/67				
Watford	Tr	05/70	70-71	15	0	0
Southport	Cape Town C (RSA)	07/74	74	2	0	0
EDMONDS Neil Anthony						
Born: Accrington, Lancashire, England, 18 October, 1968						M
Oldham Ath	App	06/86	86-87	3	2	0
Rochdale	Tr	09/88	88-89	36	7	8
EDMONDSON Darren Stephen						
Born: Coniston, Cumbria, England, 4 November, 1971						D
Carlisle U	YT	07/90	90-96	205	9	9
Huddersfield T	Tr	03/97	96-99	28	9	0
Plymouth Arg	L	09/98	98	4	0	0
York C	Tr	03/00	99-03	126	5	6
Chester C	Tr	08/04	04	26	1	0
EDMONDSON Douglas Barry (Barry)						
Born: Southport, Merseyside, England, 10 February, 1943						WH
Southport	Blackpool (Am)	12/61	61	1	-	0
EDMONDSON Stanley Glasgow (Stan)						
Born: Bacup, Lancashire, England, 10 August, 1922						RW
Died: Accrington, Lancashire, England, 1977						
Bradford C (Am)	Bacup Bor	05/46	46	3	-	0
EDMUNDS Paul						
Born: Doncaster, South Yorkshire, England, 2 December, 1957						RW
Leicester C	Troston Welfare	04/79	79-80	8	0	2
Bournemouth	Tr	07/81	81	13	1	2
EDMUNDS Redvern Esmond						
Born: Newport, Wales, 10 January, 1943						LW
Wales: Schools						
Portsmouth	Jnr	06/60	60	5	-	0
Newport Co	Tr	07/61	61	4	-	0
[EDU] GASPAR Eduardo Cesar Daud						
Born: Sao Paulo, Brazil, 15 May, 1978						M
Brazil: 15						
Arsenal	Corinthians (BRA)	01/01	00-04	41	38	7
EDU Maurice						
Born: San Bernardino, California, USA, 18 April, 1986						DM
USA: 46/U23-6						
Stoke C	Glasgow Rangers	08/12	12	0	1	0
[EDUARDO] DA SILVA Eduardo Alves						
Born: Rio de Janeiro, Brazil, 25 February, 1983						F
Croatia: 64/U21-12						
Arsenal	Dinamo Zagreb (CRO)	06/07	07-09	26	15	6
EDUSEI Akwasi Fobi						
Born: Camberwell, S London, England, 12 September, 1986						W
Gillingham	Sch	07/05	02-05	6	3	0
EDWARDS Akenhaton Carlos (Carlos)						
Born: Port of Spain, Trinidad, 24 October, 1978						RW
Trinidad And Tobago: 86						
Wrexham	Defence Force (TRD)	08/00	00-04	144	22	23
Luton T	Tr	07/05	05-06	64	4	8
Sunderland	Tr	01/07	06-08	32	18	5
Wolverhampton W	L	10/08	08	5	1	0
Ipswich T	Tr	09/09	09-13	159	17	9
Millwall	Tr	03/14	13-14	16	0	1
EDWARDS Alistair Martin						
Born: Whyalla, S Australia, Australia, 21 June, 1968						F
Australia: 19/Youth						
Brighton & HA	Sydney Olympic (AUS)	11/89	89	1	0	0
Millwall	Selangor (MLY)	12/94	94	3	1	0
EDWARDS Andrew David (Andy)						
Born: Loughton, Essex, England, 17 September, 1971						CD
Southend U	YT	12/89	88-94	141	6	5
Birmingham C	Tr	07/95	95-96	37	3	1
Peterborough U	Tr	11/96	96-02	266	0	10
Rushden & D	Tr	03/03	02-03	40	1	4
Southend U	Tr	07/04	04-05	28	4	1
EDWARDS Andrew John (Andy)						
Born: Wrexham, Wales, 28 March, 1965						W/F
Wales: Youth						
Wrexham	Jnr	08/83	82-85	89	25	27
EDWARDS Brian Allan						
Born: Portsmouth, England, 6 October, 1930						FB
Portsmouth	Jnr	10/48	51	1	-	0
EDWARDS Christian Nicholas Howells						
Born: Caerphilly, Wales, 23 November, 1975						CD
Wales: 1/B-2/U21-7						
Swansea C	YT	07/94	94-97	113	2	4
Nottingham F	Tr	03/98	98-01	44	10	3
Bristol C	L	12/98	98	3	0	0
Oxford U	L	02/00	99	5	0	1
Crystal Palace	L	11/01	01	9	0	0
Tranmere Rov	L	09/02	02	12	0	0
Oxford U	L	01/03	02	5	1	0
Bristol Rov	Tr	07/03	03-05	91	8	3
Swansea C	L	08/05	05	1	1	0
EDWARDS Clifford (Cliff)						
Born: Carmarthen, Wales, 4 December, 1928						G
Died: Swansea, Wales, July, 2008						
Swansea C	Grovesend Welfare	10/51	52	1	-	0
EDWARDS Clifford Ivor (Cliff)						
Born: Burntwood, Staffordshire, England, 8 March, 1921						WH
Died: Walsall, West Midlands, England, March, 1989						
West Bromwich A	Cannock T	06/39	46-47	40	-	1
Bristol C	Tr	06/48	48-49	33	-	3
EDWARDS Craig Alfred						
Born: Dagenham, E London, England, 8 July, 1982						M
Southend U	YT	-	00	0	1	0
EDWARDS David Alexander						
Born: Pontesbury, Shropshire, England, 3 February, 1986						M
Wales: 28/U21-9/Youth						
Shrewsbury T	Sch	01/04	02-06	82	21	12
Luton T	Tr	07/07	07	18	1	4
Wolverhampton W	Tr	01/08	07-14	153	57	26
EDWARDS David Arthur						
Born: Llangollen, Denbighshire, Wales, 14 December, 1925						CF
Died: Harrogate, North Yorkshire, England, 4 March, 2001						
Wrexham (Am)		11/49	49	1	-	1
EDWARDS David James						
Born: Treharris, Merthyr Tydfil, Wales, 10 December, 1934						WH
Fulham	Treharris	05/52	56-63	38	-	0
EDWARDS David John						
Born: Bridgnorth, Shropshire, England, 13 January, 1974						M
Walsall	YT	01/92	91-92	16	11	1
EDWARDS David Samuel (Dai)						
Born: Bargoed, Caerphilly, Wales, 11 September, 1916						LW
Died: Canterbury, England, September, 1990						
Newport Co	Deri	09/37	37	2	-	0
Ipswich T	Gloucester C	06/39				
Swindon T	Tr	06/46	46	3	-	1
EDWARDS Dean Stephen						
Born: Wolverhampton, England, 25 February, 1962						F
Shrewsbury T	App	02/80	79-81	7	6	1
Wolverhampton W	Telford U	10/85	85-86	28	3	9
Exeter C	Tr	03/87	86-87	51	3	17
Torquay U	Tr	08/88	88-91	98	18	26
Exeter C	Tr	12/91	91	4	0	0
Northampton T	Tr	02/92	91	7	0	0
EDWARDS Declan						
Born: Dublin, Republic of Ireland, 23 December, 1989						F
Republic of Ireland: Youth						
Stockport Co	St Josephs BC (ROI)	07/08	09	0	1	0
EDWARDS Dennis						
Born: Slough, Berkshire, England, 19 January, 1937						IF
England: Amateur-2						
Charlton Ath	Wycombe W	02/59	58-64	171	-	61
Portsmouth	Tr	01/65	64-67	69	2	14
Brentford	L	09/67	67	11	0	2
Aldershot	Tr	12/67	67	11	3	1

League Club	Source	Date Signed	Seasons Played	Apps	Subs	Gls

EDWARDS Donald (Don)
Born: Wrexham, Wales, 2 August, 1930 G
Died: Great Yarmouth, Norfolk, England, 24 March, 1995

Norwich C	Wrexham Victoria	09/47	47	2	-	0

EDWARDS Duncan
Born: Dudley, West Midlands, England, 1 October, 1936 LH
Died: Munich, Germany, 21 February, 1958
England: 18/B-4/FLge-4/U23-6/Youth/Schools

Manchester U	Jnr	10/53	52-57	151	-	20

EDWARDS Edward (Ted)
Born: Seaham, County Durham, England, 13 February, 1936 FB

Hartlepool U	Dawdon Jnrs	02/57	57	1	-	0

EDWARDS Emmanuel Conroy (Roy)
Born: Sheffield, England, 26 November, 1920 IF
Died: Lincolnshire, England, January, 1999

Lincoln C	Army	06/47	47-48	6	-	0

EDWARDS George
Born: Treherbert, Rhondda Cynon Taff, Wales, 2 December, 1920 LW
Died: Cardiff, Wales, 22 October, 2008
Wales: 12/WLge-3/Amateur/War-3

Swansea C (Am)	Jnr	05/38	38	2	-	0
Birmingham C	Tr	07/44	46-48	84	-	9
Cardiff C	Tr	12/48	48-54	195	-	36

EDWARDS George Bryan (Bryan)
Born: Leeds, England, 27 October, 1930 D

Bolton W	Oulton YC	10/47	50-64	482	-	8

EDWARDS George Robert
Born: Great Yarmouth, Norfolk, England, 1 April, 1918 W
Died: 1993

Norwich C	Yarmouth Caledonians	04/36	35-37	9	-	1
Aston Villa	Tr	06/38	38-50	138	-	34

EDWARDS Gwion Dafydd Rhys
Born: Lampeter, Ceredigion, Wales, 1 March, 1993 W
Wales: U21-6/Youth

Swansea C	Sch	07/11				
Crawley T	Tr	03/14	13-14	34	9	6

EDWARDS Henry Patrick (Harry)
Born: Wigan, Greater Manchester, England, 13 February, 1932 IF
Died: Ormskirk, Lancashire, England, February, 2003

Blackpool	Wigan BC	06/51				
Southport	Tr	08/53	54	1	-	0

EDWARDS Howard
Born: Tipton, West Midlands, England, 2 June, 1919 WH
Died: Stourbridge, West Midlands, England, 22 November, 1992

Derby Co	Stourbridge	01/47				
Crewe Alex	Tr	06/52	52	5	-	0

EDWARDS Jake
Born: Prestwich, Greater Manchester, England, 11 May, 1976 F

Wrexham	J Maddison Univ (USA)	08/98	98-99	4	7	2
Yeovil T	Telford U	08/03	03	17	10	6
Chester C (L)	Exeter C	03/06	05	10	0	1

EDWARDS James Elfyn (Elfyn)
Born: Aberystwyth, Ceredigion, Wales, 4 May, 1960 CD

Wrexham	Jnr	07/78				
Tranmere Rov	Tr	07/79	79-80	62	0	1

EDWARDS Jeffrey Gordon (Gordon)
Born: Wrexham, Wales, 14 October, 1935 CH
Died: Wrexham, Wales, June, 2009
Wales: Schools

Bolton W	Jnr	10/52	58	3	-	0

EDWARDS John
Born: Wrexham, Wales, 23 May, 1940 G

Wrexham (Am)	Bradley Sports	10/65	65	1	0	0

EDWARDS John (Jack)
Born: Salford, England, 23 February, 1924 IF
Died: Derby, England, January, 1979

Nottingham F	Long Eaton U	05/44	46-48	77	-	20
Southampton	Tr	06/49	49-51	82	-	16
Notts Co	Kidderminster Hrs	11/52	52-53	25	-	3

EDWARDS John Francis (Jack)
Born: Wath-on-Dearne, South Yorkshire, England, 27 December, 1921 WH
Died: Rotherham, South Yorkshire, England, March, 2009

Rotherham U	Manvers Main	09/44	46-53	296	-	9

EDWARDS John William (Jack)
Born: Risca, Caerphilly, Wales, 6 July, 1929 RB
Died: Plymouth, England, May, 2014

Crystal Palace	Lovells Ath	09/49	49-58	223	-	0
Rochdale	Tr	06/59	59-60	68	-	1

EDWARDS Jonathan Devonte (Jonny)
Born: Luton, England, 24 November, 1996 F

Peterborough U	Sch	03/15	14	1	2	0

EDWARDS Joseph Robert (Joe)
Born: Gloucester, England, 31 October, 1990 FB/M

Bristol C	Sch	07/09	10-11	2	2	0
Yeovil T	L	01/12	11	4	0	1
Yeovil T	Tr	09/12	12-14	111	4	3

EDWARDS Keith
Born: Stockton-on-Tees, Cleveland, England, 16 July, 1957 F

Sheffield U	Middlesbrough (Jnr)	08/75	75-77	64	6	29
Hull C	Tr	08/78	78-81	130	2	57
Sheffield U	Tr	09/81	81-85	183	8	114
Leeds U	Tr	08/86	86-87	28	10	6
Hull C	Aberdeen	03/88	87-89	55	0	29
Stockport Co	Tr	09/89	89	26	1	10
Huddersfield T	L	03/90	89	6	4	4
Huddersfield T	Tr	08/90	90	10	8	4
Plymouth Arg	L	12/90	90	3	0	1

EDWARDS Keith Barry
Born: Chester, England, 10 June, 1944 CF

Chester C (Am)	Buckley W	03/66	65-66	3	0	0

EDWARDS Leonard Owen (Len)
Born: Wrexham, Wales, 30 May, 1930 WH

Sheffield Wed	Wrexham (Am)	01/51	51	2	-	0
Brighton & HA	Tr	03/54	54	6	-	0
Crewe Alex	Tr	12/55	55-56	40	-	0

EDWARDS Leonard Trevor (Trevor)
Born: Ystrad Rhondda, Rhondda Cynon Taff, Wales, 24 January, 1937 FB
Wales: 2/U23-2

Charlton Ath	Jnr	05/55	56-59	64	-	0
Cardiff C	Tr	06/60	60-63	73	-	3

EDWARDS Leslie Raymond (Les)
Born: Guildford, Surrey, England, 12 April, 1924 LB
Died: Somerset, United Kingdom, August, 2014

Bristol Rov	Yeovil T	05/48	50-56	47	-	0

EDWARDS Levi Wilfred
Born: Manchester, England, 10 September, 1961 M

Crewe Alex	Ashton U	08/85	85	10	3	0
Stockport Co	Altrincham	09/86	86-87	40	9	5

EDWARDS Malcolm
Born: Wrexham, Wales, 25 October, 1939 LB
Wales: U23-2/Schools

Bolton W	Jnr	11/56	56-60	14	-	1
Chester C	Tr	02/61	60-61	43	-	5
Tranmere Rov	Tr	07/62	62-63	34	-	2
Barrow	Tr	07/64	64-68	177	0	9

EDWARDS Malcolm Keith (Keith)
Born: Briton Ferry, Neath Port Talbot, Wales, 26 September, 1952 CD
Wales: Schools

Leeds U	App	10/69	71	0	1	0

EDWARDS Matthew David
Born: Hammersmith, W London, England, 15 June, 1971 W

Tottenham H	YT	07/89				
Reading	L	03/91	90	6	2	0
Peterborough U	Tr	03/92				
Brighton & HA	Tr	08/92	92-93	49	11	6

EDWARDS Matthew Philip (Matty)
Born: Birkenhead, Wirral, England, 22 August, 1990 G
Scotland: U21-1

Leeds U	Sch	07/08				
Rochdale	Tr	07/09	10-11	5	3	0

EDWARDS Michael (Mike)
Born: Bebington, Wirral, England, 10 September, 1974 M

Tranmere Rov	YT	07/93	94	2	1	0

EDWARDS Michael (Mike)
Born: Hessle, Hull, East Riding of Yorkshire, England, 25 April, 1980 CD

Hull C	YT	07/98	97-02	165	13	6
Colchester U	Tr	03/03	02	3	2	0
Grimsby T	Tr	08/03	03	32	1	1
Notts Co	Tr	07/04	04-11	258	11	20

League Club	Source	Date Signed	Seasons Played	Apps	Subs	Gls
Carlisle U	Tr	07/12	12-13	23	1	0
Notts Co	Tr	08/14	14	17	1	3

EDWARDS Nathan Mark
Born: Lincoln, England, 8 April, 1983 — M

League Club	Source	Date Signed	Seasons Played	Apps	Subs	Gls
Swindon T	Sch	07/02	01-02	2	8	0

EDWARDS Neil Anthony
Born: Rowley Regis, West Midlands, England, 14 March, 1966 — F

League Club	Source	Date Signed	Seasons Played	Apps	Subs	Gls
Wolverhampton W	Oldswinford	08/85	85-87	26	3	7

EDWARDS Neil Robert
Born: Liverpool, England, 2 July, 1967 — F

League Club	Source	Date Signed	Seasons Played	Apps	Subs	Gls
Burnley	Liverpool (YT)	08/85	85	0	1	0

EDWARDS Neil Ryan
Born: Aberdare, Rhondda Cynon Taff, Wales, 5 December, 1970 — G
Wales: U21-1/Youth/Schools

League Club	Source	Date Signed	Seasons Played	Apps	Subs	Gls
Leeds U	YT	03/89				
Stockport Co	Tr	09/91	91-95	163	1	0
Rochdale	Tr	11/97	97-04	239	0	0
Bury	Tr	07/05	05	24	0	0

EDWARDS Nigel Steven
Born: Wrexham, Wales, 31 December, 1950 — RB
Wales: U23-3

League Club	Source	Date Signed	Seasons Played	Apps	Subs	Gls
Chester C	Blackburn Rov (Am)	09/68	68-77	281	10	15
Aldershot	Tr	07/78	78-81	137	0	6
Chester C	Tr	06/82	82	8	0	1

EDWARDS Patrick Kenneth
Born: Wolverhampton, England, 9 December, 1939 — W

League Club	Source	Date Signed	Seasons Played	Apps	Subs	Gls
Walsall	Jnr	10/57	58	1	-	0

EDWARDS Paul
Born: Derby, England, 10 November, 1982 — F

League Club	Source	Date Signed	Seasons Played	Apps	Subs	Gls
Crewe Alex	YT	02/01	02-03	2	10	0

EDWARDS Paul
Born: Manchester, England, 1 January, 1980 — LB

League Club	Source	Date Signed	Seasons Played	Apps	Subs	Gls
Doncaster Rov	Ashton U	02/98	97	5	4	0
Swindon T	Altrincham	08/01	01	14	6	0
Wrexham	Tr	07/02	02-03	73	6	4
Blackpool	Tr	07/04	04	22	6	3
Oldham Ath	Tr	07/05	05-06	39	21	0
Port Vale	Tr	07/07	07-08	46	10	2

EDWARDS Paul
Born: Liverpool, England, 22 February, 1965 — G

League Club	Source	Date Signed	Seasons Played	Apps	Subs	Gls
Crewe Alex	Leek T	03/87	88-91	29	0	0
Shrewsbury T	Tr	08/92	92-00	312	0	0

EDWARDS Paul Francis
Born: Shaw, Greater Manchester, England, 7 October, 1947 — CD
England: FLge-1/U23-3

League Club	Source	Date Signed	Seasons Played	Apps	Subs	Gls
Manchester U	Jnr	02/65	69-72	52	2	0
Oldham Ath	Tr	09/72	72-77	108	4	7
Stockport Co	L	01/77	76	2	0	0
Stockport Co	Tr	08/78	78-79	64	3	2

EDWARDS Paul Ronald
Born: Birkenhead, Wirral, England, 25 December, 1963 — LB

League Club	Source	Date Signed	Seasons Played	Apps	Subs	Gls
Crewe Alex	Altrincham	01/88	87-89	82	4	6
Coventry C	Tr	03/90	89-91	32	4	0
Wolverhampton W	Tr	08/92	92-93	43	3	0
West Bromwich A	Tr	01/94	93-95	48	3	0
Bury	L	02/96	95	4	0	0

EDWARDS Philip Lee (Phil)
Born: Bootle, Merseyside, England, 8 November, 1985 — CD

League Club	Source	Date Signed	Seasons Played	Apps	Subs	Gls
Wigan Ath	Sch	07/05				
Accrington Stan	Tr	07/06	06-10	193	7	23
Stevenage	Tr	07/11	11	11	11	0
Rochdale	L	03/12	11	1	2	0
Rochdale	Tr	08/12	12	43	1	0
Burton A	Tr	06/13	13-14	84	2	8

EDWARDS Preston Matthew
Born: Cheshunt, Hertfordshire, England, 5 September, 1989 — G
England: Youth

League Club	Source	Date Signed	Seasons Played	Apps	Subs	Gls
Millwall	Sch	11/06	07	0	1	0

EDWARDS Reginald Charles (Reg)
Born: Newton-le-Willows, Merseyside, England, 24 July, 1919 — W
Died: Warrington, Cheshire, England, April, 2002

League Club	Source	Date Signed	Seasons Played	Apps	Subs	Gls
Luton T	Alloa Ath	11/45				
Accrington Stan	Tr	08/46	46-48	66	-	10

EDWARDS Reginald Ernest (Reg)
Born: Rugeley, Staffordshire, England, 28 January, 1953 — LW

League Club	Source	Date Signed	Seasons Played	Apps	Subs	Gls
Port Vale	Nuneaton Bor	08/72	72-74	8	0	0

EDWARDS Richard (Richie)
Born: Hartlepool, Cleveland, England, 9 September, 1964 — G

League Club	Source	Date Signed	Seasons Played	Apps	Subs	Gls
Hartlepool U		08/86	86	1	0	0

EDWARDS Richard Leonard (Dick)
Born: Kingsbury, NW London, England, 5 November, 1943 — FB

League Club	Source	Date Signed	Seasons Played	Apps	Subs	Gls
Luton T	Addmult FC	06/64	64-65	15	2	1

EDWARDS Richard Thomas (Dick)
Born: Kirkby-in-Ashfield, Nottinghamshire, England, 20 November, 1942 — D

League Club	Source	Date Signed	Seasons Played	Apps	Subs	Gls
Notts Co	East Kirkby MW	10/59	59-66	221	0	20
Mansfield T	Tr	03/67	66-67	45	0	1
Aston Villa	Tr	03/68	67-69	68	0	2
Torquay U	Tr	06/70	70-72	99	6	5
Mansfield T	Tr	07/73	73	31	2	1

EDWARDS Robert (Rob)
Born: Manchester, England, 23 February, 1970 — LB/W

League Club	Source	Date Signed	Seasons Played	Apps	Subs	Gls
Crewe Alex	YT	07/88	87-95	110	45	44
Huddersfield T	Tr	03/96	95-99	109	29	14
Chesterfield	Tr	09/00	00-02	89	5	7
Huddersfield T	Tr	08/03	03-04	32	9	3

EDWARDS Robert Henry (Bob)
Born: Guildford, Surrey, England, 22 May, 1931 — IF

League Club	Source	Date Signed	Seasons Played	Apps	Subs	Gls
Chelsea	Woking	11/51	52-54	13	-	2
Swindon T	Tr	07/55	55-59	173	-	65
Norwich C	Tr	12/59	59	1	-	0
Northampton T	Tr	03/61	60-61	23	-	10

EDWARDS Robert Ian (Ian)
Born: Rossett, Wrexham, Wales, 30 January, 1955 — F
Wales: 4/U21-2

League Club	Source	Date Signed	Seasons Played	Apps	Subs	Gls
West Bromwich A	Rhyl Ath	02/73	74-76	13	3	3
Chester C	Tr	11/76	76-79	104	0	36
Wrexham	Tr	11/79	79-81	72	4	20
Crystal Palace	Tr	07/82	82	16	2	4

EDWARDS Robert Owen (Rob)
Born: Telford, England, 25 December, 1982 — CD
Wales: 15/Youth

League Club	Source	Date Signed	Seasons Played	Apps	Subs	Gls
Aston Villa	YT	01/00	02	7	1	0
Crystal Palace	L	11/03	03	6	1	1
Derby Co	L	01/04	03	10	1	1
Wolverhampton W	Tr	07/04	04-07	82	18	1
Blackpool	Tr	08/08	08-10	55	4	2
Norwich C	L	02/11	10	0	3	0
Barnsley	Tr	07/11	11	17	0	0
Fleetwood T	L	10/12	12	4	0	0
Shrewsbury T	L	01/13	12	4	0	0

EDWARDS Robert William (Rob)
Born: Kendal, Cumbria, England, 1 July, 1973 — DM
Wales: 4/B-2/U21-17/Youth

League Club	Source	Date Signed	Seasons Played	Apps	Subs	Gls
Carlisle U	YT	04/90	89-90	48	0	5
Bristol C	Tr	03/91	91-98	188	28	5
Preston NE	Tr	08/99	99-03	156	13	4
Blackpool	Tr	08/04	04-05	52	6	1
Exeter C	Tr	08/06	08-10	67	7	0

EDWARDS Ronald (Ron)
Born: Liverpool, England, 11 July, 1927 — RW
Died: Liverpool, England, 24 October, 2001

League Club	Source	Date Signed	Seasons Played	Apps	Subs	Gls
Chesterfield	South Liverpool	07/53	53	13	-	2

EDWARDS Russell James
Born: Beckenham, SE London, England, 21 December, 1973 — CD

League Club	Source	Date Signed	Seasons Played	Apps	Subs	Gls
Crystal Palace	Jnr	06/92				
Barnet	Tr	03/94	93	5	0	1

EDWARDS Ryan Christopher
Born: Liverpool, England, 7 October, 1993 — CD

League Club	Source	Date Signed	Seasons Played	Apps	Subs	Gls
Blackburn Rov	Sch	04/12				
Rochdale	L	07/12	12	25	1	0
Fleetwood T	L	02/13	12	9	0	0
Chesterfield	L	07/13	13	4	1	0
Morecambe	Tr	03/14	13-14	39	1	0

EDWARDS Ryan Marc
Born: Sydney, Australia, 17 November, 1993 — M
Australia: U23-8/Youth

League Club	Source	Date Signed	Seasons Played	Apps	Subs	Gls
Reading	Australian IOS (AUS)	04/11	14	4	3	0

EDWARDS Stanley (Stan)
Born: West Bromwich, West Midlands, England, 11 December, 1942 — LW

League Club	Source	Date Signed	Seasons Played	Apps	Subs	Gls
Everton	Jnr	12/59				
Port Vale	Tr	05/61	61-62	49	-	9

EDWARDS Stanley Llewellyn (Stan)
Born: Seaham, County Durham, England, 17 October, 1926 CF
Died: Bromley, SE London, England, 14 January, 1989

League Club	Source	Date Signed	Seasons Played	Apps	Subs	Gls
Chelsea	Horden CW	10/49				
Colchester U	Tr	06/52	52	16	-	5
Leyton Orient	Tr	06/53	53	2	-	1

EDWARDS Stephen Gerald (Steve)
Born: Birkenhead, Wirral, England, 11 January, 1958 D

League Club	Source	Date Signed	Seasons Played	Apps	Subs	Gls
Oldham Ath	App	01/76	77-82	77	3	0
Crewe Alex	Tr	02/83	82-83	57	1	1
Rochdale	Tr	07/84	84	4	0	0
Tranmere Rov	Tr	10/84	84-86	70	0	6

EDWARDS Walter
Born: Mansfield, Nottinghamshire, England, 26 June, 1924 W

League Club	Source	Date Signed	Seasons Played	Apps	Subs	Gls
Mansfield T	Woodhouse	11/47	47-48	25	-	5
Leeds U	Tr	03/49	48	2	-	0
Leicester C	Tr	08/49				

EDWARDS Walter Thomas (Tommy)
Born: Llanelli, Carmarthenshire, Wales, 11 March, 1923 LW
Died: Lambeth, S London, England, October, 2000

League Club	Source	Date Signed	Seasons Played	Apps	Subs	Gls
Fulham	Workington	08/46	47	2	-	0
Southend U	Tr	03/48	47-48	12	-	1
Leicester C	Tr	12/48	48	3	-	1
Walsall	Bath C	05/52	52	12	-	0

EDWARDS William (Billy)
Born: Paddington, Central London, England, 8 January, 1952 CD

League Club	Source	Date Signed	Seasons Played	Apps	Subs	Gls
Wimbledon	Walton & Hersham	08/74	77	21	0	2

EDWARDS William Inman
Born: Bowburn, County Durham, England, 10 December, 1933 CF
Died: Durham, England, December, 2010

League Club	Source	Date Signed	Seasons Played	Apps	Subs	Gls
Middlesbrough	Bowburn	03/52	52-54	16	-	4

EDWARDSON Barry John
Born: Hindley, Greater Manchester, England, 4 November, 1972 M

League Club	Source	Date Signed	Seasons Played	Apps	Subs	Gls
Wigan Ath	YT	07/91	91	0	1	0

EDWARDSON John Philemon
Born: Manchester, England, 9 March, 1944 W

League Club	Source	Date Signed	Seasons Played	Apps	Subs	Gls
Crystal Palace	Bethesda	11/66				
Crewe Alex	L	01/68	67	1	0	0

EDWORTHY Marc
Born: Bideford, Devon, England, 24 December, 1972 RB

League Club	Source	Date Signed	Seasons Played	Apps	Subs	Gls
Plymouth Arg	YT	03/91	91-94	52	17	1
Crystal Palace	Tr	06/95	95-98	120	6	0
Coventry C	Tr	08/98	98-01	62	14	1
Wolverhampton W	Tr	08/02	02	18	4	0
Norwich C	Tr	08/03	03-04	69	2	0
Derby Co	Tr	07/05	05-07	75	2	0
Leicester C	Tr	10/08	08	5	0	0
Burton A	Tr	08/09	09	1	0	0

EELES Anthony George (Tony)
Born: Chatham, Kent, England, 15 November, 1970 M

League Club	Source	Date Signed	Seasons Played	Apps	Subs	Gls
Gillingham	YT	07/89	88-92	54	19	5

EGAN Christopher Anthony (Chris)
Born: Limerick, Republic of Ireland, 6 August, 1953 LW

League Club	Source	Date Signed	Seasons Played	Apps	Subs	Gls
Derby Co	Sligo Rov (ROI)	10/73				
Newport Co	Tr	08/76	76	5	2	0

EGAN John
Born: Kilsyth, Lanarkshire, Scotland, 19 August, 1937 W

League Club	Source	Date Signed	Seasons Played	Apps	Subs	Gls
Halifax T	Berwick Rgrs	10/59	59	5	-	0
Accrington Stan	Tr	08/60	60	1	-	0

EGAN John
Born: Cork, Republic of Ireland, 20 October, 1992 CD
Republic of Ireland: U21-6/Youth

League Club	Source	Date Signed	Seasons Played	Apps	Subs	Gls
Sunderland	Sch	10/09				
Crystal Palace	L	01/12	11	1	0	0
Sheffield U	L	03/12	11	1	0	0
Bradford C	L	11/12	12	4	0	0
Southend U	L	02/14	13	13	0	1
Gillingham	Tr	07/14	14	45	0	4

EGDELL Ernest (Ernie)
Born: Newcastle-upon-Tyne, England, 29 May, 1922 FB
Died: Salford, England, 27 February, 1976

League Club	Source	Date Signed	Seasons Played	Apps	Subs	Gls
Darlington (Am)	Consett	08/46	46	1	-	0

EGER Marcel
Born: Nuremberg, Germany, 23 March, 1983 CD

League Club	Source	Date Signed	Seasons Played	Apps	Subs	Gls
Brentford	St Pauli (GER)	07/11	11	13	3	0

EGERTON Frank
Born: Atherton, Greater Manchester, England, 5 April, 1926 FB
Died: Trafford, Greater Manchester, England, 15 April, 2002

League Club	Source	Date Signed	Seasons Played	Apps	Subs	Gls
Blackburn Rov	Atherton Collieries	04/44				
Accrington Stan	Tr	06/47	47-48	8	-	0

EGGLESTON Thomas (Tommy)
Born: Consett, County Durham, England, 21 February, 1920 LH
Died: Tockwith, North Yorkshire, England, January, 2004Jan

League Club	Source	Date Signed	Seasons Played	Apps	Subs	Gls
Derby Co	Medomsley Jnrs	02/37				
Leicester C	Tr	08/46	46-47	34	-	2
Watford	Tr	02/48	47-52	177	-	6

EGGLESTONE Patrick (Pat)
Born: Penrith, Cumbria, England, 17 March, 1927 G

League Club	Source	Date Signed	Seasons Played	Apps	Subs	Gls
Bradford C	Portsmouth (Am)	05/48	48	2	-	0
Halifax T	Tr	09/49	49	20	-	0
Shrewsbury T	Tr	08/50	50-52	109	-	0
Wrexham	Tr	02/53	52-55	84	-	0

EGLINGTON Thomas Joseph (Tommy)
Born: Dublin, Republic of Ireland, 15 January, 1923 LW
Died: Dublin, Republic of Ireland, 18 February, 2004
Republic of Ireland: 24/LoI-4//Northern Ireland: 6

League Club	Source	Date Signed	Seasons Played	Apps	Subs	Gls
Everton	Shamrock Rov (ROI)	07/46	46-56	394	-	76
Tranmere Rov	Tr	06/57	57-60	171	-	36

EHIOGU Ugochuku (Ugo)
Born: Hackney, E London, England, 3 November, 1972 CD
England: 4/B-1/U21-15

League Club	Source	Date Signed	Seasons Played	Apps	Subs	Gls
West Bromwich A	YT	-	90	0	2	0
Aston Villa	Tr	07/91	91-00	223	14	12
Middlesbrough	Tr	10/00	00-05	122	4	7
Leeds U	L	11/06	06	6	0	1
Sheffield U	Glasgow Rangers	01/08	07-08	16	10	1

EHMER Maximilian Andreas (Max)
Born: Frankfurt, Germany, 3 February, 1992 CD

League Club	Source	Date Signed	Seasons Played	Apps	Subs	Gls
Queens Park Rgrs	Sch	07/09	13	0	1	0
Yeovil T	L	12/10	10	26	1	0
Yeovil T	L	07/11	11	24	0	0
Preston NE	L	03/12	11	7	2	0
Stevenage	L	03/13	12	5	1	1
Carlisle U	L	11/13	13	12	0	1
Gillingham	L	11/14	14	27	0	1

EHUI Ismael
Born: Lille, France, 10 December, 1986 F

League Club	Source	Date Signed	Seasons Played	Apps	Subs	Gls
Fulham	Jnr	09/04				
Scunthorpe U	L	02/06	05	0	3	0

EHUI Kouadio Georges (Georges)
Born: Abidjan, Ivory Coast, 2 February, 1994 M

League Club	Source	Date Signed	Seasons Played	Apps	Subs	Gls
Wycombe W	Sch	07/12	12	0	2	0

EIKREM Magnus Wolff
Born: Molde, Norway, 8 August, 1990 M
Norway: 15/U21-12/Youth

League Club	Source	Date Signed	Seasons Played	Apps	Subs	Gls
Manchester U	Sch	07/08				
Cardiff C	Heerenveen (NED)	01/14	13-14	1	8	0

EINARSSON Gunnar
Born: Reykjavik, Iceland, 7 July, 1976 FB
Iceland: 1/U21-6/Youth

League Club	Source	Date Signed	Seasons Played	Apps	Subs	Gls
Brentford (L)	Roda JC (NED)	01/00	99	1	2	0

EINARSSON Gylfi
Born: Reykjavik, Iceland, 27 October, 1978 M
Iceland: 24/Youth

League Club	Source	Date Signed	Seasons Played	Apps	Subs	Gls
Leeds U	Lillestrom (NOR)	12/04	04-06	12	9	1

EISENTRAGER Alois Bernhard (Alec)
Born: Hamburg, Germany, 20 July, 1927 IF

League Club	Source	Date Signed	Seasons Played	Apps	Subs	Gls
Bristol C	Trowbridge T	01/50	49-57	228	-	47

EISFELD Thomas
Born: Finsterwalde, Germany, 18 January, 1993 M
Germany: Youth

League Club	Source	Date Signed	Seasons Played	Apps	Subs	Gls
Arsenal	Bor Dortmund (GER)	01/12				
Fulham	Tr	07/14	14	2	5	0

EKANGAMENE Charni
Born: Antwerp, Belgium, 16 February, 1994 M
Belgium: Youth

League Club	Source	Date Signed	Seasons Played	Apps	Subs	Gls
Manchester U	Sch	07/11				
Carlisle U	L	01/14	13	4	0	0

EKELUND Ronald Michael (Ronnie)
Born: Glostrup, Denmark, 21 August, 1972 M
Denmark: U21-21/Youth

League Club	Source	Date Signed	Seasons Played	Apps	Subs	Gls
Southampton (L)	Barcelona (SPN)	09/94	94	15	2	5
Manchester C (L)	Barcelona (SPN)	12/95	95	2	2	0
Walsall	Toulouse (FRA)	12/00	00	2	7	1

EKNER Daniel Heimer (Dan)
Born: Gothenburg, Sweden, 5 February, 1927 — CF
Died: Gothenburg, Sweden, 1975

League Club	Source	Date Signed	Seasons Played	Apps	Subs	Gls
Portsmouth (Am)	IFK Goteberg (SWE)	11/49	49	5	-	0

EKOKU Efangwu Goziem (Efan)
Born: Manchester, England, 8 June, 1967 — F
Nigeria: 20

League Club	Source	Date Signed	Seasons Played	Apps	Subs	Gls
Bournemouth	Sutton U	05/90	90-92	43	19	21
Norwich C	Tr	03/93	92-94	26	11	15
Wimbledon	Tr	10/94	94-98	102	21	37
Sheffield Wed	G'hopper Zurich (SUI)	10/00	00-01	52	7	14

EKSTRAND Lars Henning Joel (Joel)
Born: Lund, Sweden, 4 February, 1989 — CD
Sweden: 2/U21-9

League Club	Source	Date Signed	Seasons Played	Apps	Subs	Gls
Watford	Udinese (ITA)	08/12	12-14	83	6	2

EL-ABD Adam Mohamad
Born: Brighton, England, 11 September, 1984 — CD
Egypt: 7

League Club	Source	Date Signed	Seasons Played	Apps	Subs	Gls
Brighton & HA	Sch	12/03	03-13	264	36	5
Bristol C	Tr	01/14	13-14	13	3	0
Bury	L	11/14	14	24	0	1

ELAD Diodene Efon (Efon)
Born: Hillingdon, W London, England, 5 September, 1970 — W

League Club	Source	Date Signed	Seasons Played	Apps	Subs	Gls
Northampton T	Fortuna Koln (GER)	01/94	93	8	2	0
Cambridge U	Tr	08/94	94	2	1	0
Mansfield T	Tr	02/95	94	0	2	0

EL AHMADI Karim
Born: Enschede, Netherlands, 27 January, 1985 — DM
Morocco: 20

League Club	Source	Date Signed	Seasons Played	Apps	Subs	Gls
Aston Villa	Feyenoord (NED)	07/12	12-13	38	13	3

EL ALAGUI Farid
Born: Bordeaux, France, 10 February, 1985 — F

League Club	Source	Date Signed	Seasons Played	Apps	Subs	Gls
Brentford	Falkirk	07/12	12-13	8	15	4

ELAM Lee Patrick George
Born: Bradford, England, 24 September, 1976 — W
England: Semi Pro-4

League Club	Source	Date Signed	Seasons Played	Apps	Subs	Gls
Yeovil T	Halifax T	10/03	03	6	6	1

[ELANO] BLUMER Elano Ralph
Born: Sao Paulo, Brazil, 14 June, 1981 — M
Brazil: 50

League Club	Source	Date Signed	Seasons Played	Apps	Subs	Gls
Manchester C	Shakhtar Donetsk (UKR)	08/07	07-08	50	12	14

ELDER Alexander Russell (Alex)
Born: Lisburn, Belfast, Northern Ireland, 25 April, 1941 — LB
Northern Ireland: 40/U23-1/Schools

League Club	Source	Date Signed	Seasons Played	Apps	Subs	Gls
Burnley	Glentoran	01/59	59-66	271	0	15
Stoke C	Tr	08/67	67-72	80	3	1

ELDER Alexander Yeoman Pirrie (Alex)
Born: Perth, Scotland, 11 September, 1923 — IF

League Club	Source	Date Signed	Seasons Played	Apps	Subs	Gls
Hartlepool U	Dundee U	08/51	51-52	65	-	20

ELDER Callum Roddie
Born: Sydney, Australia, 27 January, 1995 — LB
Australia: Youth

League Club	Source	Date Signed	Seasons Played	Apps	Subs	Gls
Leicester C	Sch	07/13				
Mansfield T	L	01/15	14	21	0	0

ELDER James (Jimmy)
Born: Scone, Perthshire, Scotland, 5 March, 1928 — WH

League Club	Source	Date Signed	Seasons Played	Apps	Subs	Gls
Portsmouth	Jeanfield Swifts	09/45	49	1	-	0
Colchester U	Tr	07/50	50-54	199	-	15

ELDER Nathan John
Born: Hornchurch, E London, England, 5 April, 1985 — F

League Club	Source	Date Signed	Seasons Played	Apps	Subs	Gls
Brighton & HA	Billericay T	12/06	06-07	2	20	2
Brentford	Tr	01/08	07-08	34	10	10
Shrewsbury T	Tr	08/09	09	9	10	2
Hereford U	Hayes & Yeading U	09/11	11	13	13	3

ELDERSHAW Simon
Born: Stoke-on-Trent, England, 2 December, 1983 — F

League Club	Source	Date Signed	Seasons Played	Apps	Subs	Gls
Port Vale	Sch	07/03	02-04	5	10	1

ELDING Anthony Lee
Born: Boston, Lincolnshire, England, 16 April, 1982 — F
England: Semi Pro-6

League Club	Source	Date Signed	Seasons Played	Apps	Subs	Gls
Boston U	Jnr	07/01	02	3	5	0
Boston U	Kettering T	07/06	06	18	1	5
Stockport Co	Tr	01/07	06-07	38	7	24
Leeds U	Tr	01/08	07	4	5	1
Crewe Alex	Tr	07/08	08-09	14	12	1
Lincoln C	L	01/09	08	15	0	3
Rochdale	Ferencvaros (HUN)	08/10	10	9	8	3
Stockport Co	L	01/11	10	18	3	3
Preston NE (L)	Grimsby T	11/12	12	2	3	0

ELEY Kevin
Born: Mexborough, South Yorkshire, England, 4 March, 1968 — W

League Club	Source	Date Signed	Seasons Played	Apps	Subs	Gls
Rotherham U	App	03/86	83-86	3	10	0
Chesterfield	Tr	08/87	87-89	72	9	2

ELFORD-ALLIYU Lateef
Born: Ibadan, Nigeria, 1 June, 1992 — F

League Club	Source	Date Signed	Seasons Played	Apps	Subs	Gls
West Bromwich A	Sch	06/09				
Hereford U	L	01/10	09	1	0	0
Tranmere Rov	L	11/10	10	13	3	5
Tranmere Rov	L	01/12	11	2	2	0
Bury	Tr	02/12	11-12	2	13	2
Crawley T	Tr	01/13	12	0	6	0

EL GABBAS Mohamed (Dodo)
Born: Port Said, Egypt, 21 July, 1988 — W
Egypt: 6

League Club	Source	Date Signed	Seasons Played	Apps	Subs	Gls
Swindon T	Lierse SK (BEL)	08/13	13	0	6	0

ELGIN Robert Brown
Born: Edinburgh, Scotland, 23 June, 1949 — M

League Club	Source	Date Signed	Seasons Played	Apps	Subs	Gls
Stockport Co	Heart of Midlothian	07/69	69-70	30	5	3

EL HAIMOUR Mounir
Born: Limoges, France, 29 October, 1980 — LB/M

League Club	Source	Date Signed	Seasons Played	Apps	Subs	Gls
Barnsley	Neuchatel Xamax (SUI)	07/08	08-09	10	8	0

EL HAMDAOUI Mounir
Born: Rotterdam, Netherlands, 14 July, 1984 — F
Morocco: 15//Netherlands: U21-3

League Club	Source	Date Signed	Seasons Played	Apps	Subs	Gls
Tottenham H	Excelsior (NED)	01/05				
Derby Co	L	09/05	05	2	4	2
Derby Co	L	01/06	05	3	0	1

ELI Roger
Born: Bradford, England, 11 September, 1965 — W

League Club	Source	Date Signed	Seasons Played	Apps	Subs	Gls
Leeds U	App	09/83	84-85	1	1	0
Wolverhampton W	Tr	01/86	85-86	16	2	0
Crewe Alex	Cambridge U	09/87	87	20	7	1
York C	Pontefract Collieries	11/88	88	3	1	1
Bury	Tr	12/88	88	0	2	0
Burnley	Northwich Victoria	07/89	89-92	70	29	20
Scunthorpe U	Foshan Fosti (HKG)	02/95	94	0	2	0

ELIA Eljero George Rinaldo
Born: Voorburg, Netherlands, 13 February, 1987 — LW
Netherlands: 27/B-1/U21-7

League Club	Source	Date Signed	Seasons Played	Apps	Subs	Gls
Southampton (L)	Werder Bremen (GER)	01/15	14	9	7	2

EL IDRISSI Mustapha Faysal (Moussa)
Born: Lille, France, 16 November, 1977 — M

League Club	Source	Date Signed	Seasons Played	Apps	Subs	Gls
Coventry C	Al-Nasr (BRN)	08/06	06	0	1	0

ELITO Medy Efoko
Born: Kinshasa, DR Congo, 20 March, 1990 — LW
England: Youth

League Club	Source	Date Signed	Seasons Played	Apps	Subs	Gls
Colchester U	Sch	07/07	07-09	7	12	1
Cheltenham T	L	03/10	09	12	0	3
Dagenham & Red	L	11/10	10	8	2	2
Cheltenham T	L	02/11	10	1	1	0
Dagenham & Red	Tr	07/11	11-13	99	16	17

EL KARKOURI Talal
Born: Casablanca, Morocco, 8 July, 1976 — DM
Morocco: 53

League Club	Source	Date Signed	Seasons Played	Apps	Subs	Gls
Sunderland (L)	Paris St-Germain (FRA)	01/03	02	8	0	0
Charlton Ath	Paris St-Germain (FRA)	07/04	04-06	68	10	8

EL KHALEJ Tahar
Born: Marrakesh, Morocco, 16 June, 1968 — CD
Morocco: 72

League Club	Source	Date Signed	Seasons Played	Apps	Subs	Gls
Southampton	Benfica (POR)	03/00	99-02	48	10	3
Charlton Ath	Tr	01/03	02	2	1	0

EL KHAYATI Abdenassar
Born: Rotterdam, Netherlands, 7 February, 1989 — F

League Club	Source	Date Signed	Seasons Played	Apps	Subs	Gls
Burton A	Kozakken Boys (NED)	01/15	14	9	9	3

EL KHOLTI Abdelhalim (Abdou)
Born: Annemasse, France, 17 October, 1980 — LB/M

League Club	Source	Date Signed	Seasons Played	Apps	Subs	Gls
Yeovil T	Raja Casablanca (MOR)	10/02	03	19	4	1

League Club	Source	Date Signed	Seasons Played	Apps	Subs	Gls
Cambridge U	Tr	07/04	04	13	2	0
Chester C	Tr	07/05	05	7	15	0

ELKINS Gary
Born: Wallingford, Oxfordshire, England, 4 May, 1966 — LB
England: Youth

League Club	Source	Date Signed	Seasons Played	Apps	Subs	Gls
Fulham	App	12/83	84-89	100	4	2
Exeter C	L	12/89	89	5	0	0
Wimbledon	Tr	08/90	90-95	100	10	3
Swindon T	Tr	09/96	96	19	4	1

ELLAM Roy
Born: Hemsworth, West Yorkshire, England, 13 January, 1943 — CD

League Club	Source	Date Signed	Seasons Played	Apps	Subs	Gls
Bradford C	Robin Hood Ath	05/61	61-65	149	0	12
Huddersfield T	Tr	01/66	66-71	206	0	8
Leeds U	Tr	08/72	72-73	9	2	0
Huddersfield T	Tr	07/74	74	18	0	2

ELLAMS Lloyd Ashley
Born: Chester, England, 11 January, 1991 — F

League Club	Source	Date Signed	Seasons Played	Apps	Subs	Gls
Chester C	Sch	08/09	08	2	2	1

ELLAWAY William John (Bill)
Born: Crediton, Devon, England, 12 October, 1932 — IF

League Club	Source	Date Signed	Seasons Played	Apps	Subs	Gls
Exeter C	Barnstaple T	11/54	53-55	31	-	9
Bournemouth	Tr	06/56	56-57	4	-	0

ELLEGAARD Kevin Stuhr
Born: Copenhagen, Denmark, 23 May, 1983 — G
Denmark: U21-20/Youth

League Club	Source	Date Signed	Seasons Played	Apps	Subs	Gls
Manchester C	Farum (DEN)	11/01	03	2	2	0
Blackpool	L	12/04	04	2	0	0

ELLENDER Paul
Born: Scunthorpe, North Lincolnshire, England, 21 October, 1974 — CD
England: Semi Pro-1

League Club	Source	Date Signed	Seasons Played	Apps	Subs	Gls
Scunthorpe U	YT	04/93				
Boston U	Scarborough	08/01	02-06	171	3	8
Chester C	L	02/06	05	5	0	0

ELLERINGTON William (Bill)
Born: Southampton, England, 30 June, 1923 — RB
Died: Baddesley, Hampshire, England, 4 April, 2015
England: 2/B-1/FLge-1/Schools

League Club	Source	Date Signed	Seasons Played	Apps	Subs	Gls
Southampton	Sunderland (Am)	09/40	46-55	227	-	10

ELLINGTON Lee Simon
Born: Bradford, England, 3 July, 1980 — F

League Club	Source	Date Signed	Seasons Played	Apps	Subs	Gls
Hull C	YT	07/98	96-98	7	8	2
Exeter C	Tr	03/00	99	0	1	0

ELLINGTON Nathan Levi Fontaine
Born: Bradford, England, 2 July, 1981 — F

League Club	Source	Date Signed	Seasons Played	Apps	Subs	Gls
Bristol Rov	Walton & Hersham	02/99	98-01	76	40	35
Wigan Ath	Tr	03/02	01-04	130	4	59
West Bromwich A	Tr	08/05	05-07	34	34	15
Watford	Tr	08/07	07-09	20	31	5
Derby Co	L	05/08	08	13	14	3
Preston NE	L	01/11	10	7	11	2
Ipswich T	Tr	07/11	11-12	1	16	0
Scunthorpe U	L	11/12	12	2	4	0
Crewe Alex	Tr	03/13	12	2	6	0

ELLIOT Robert (Rob)
Born: Greenwich, SE London, England, 30 April, 1986 — G
Republic of Ireland: 3/Youth

League Club	Source	Date Signed	Seasons Played	Apps	Subs	Gls
Charlton Ath	Sch	01/05	07-11	95	1	0
Notts Co	L	01/05	04	3	1	0
Accrington Stan	L	08/06	06	7	0	0
Newcastle U	Tr	08/11	12-14	14	1	0

ELLIOTT Andrew (Andy)
Born: Newcastle-upon-Tyne, England, 2 May, 1974 — M

League Club	Source	Date Signed	Seasons Played	Apps	Subs	Gls
Hartlepool U	Spennymoor U	02/97	96-97	2	6	0

ELLIOTT Andrew (Andy)
Born: Ashton-under-Lyne, Greater Manchester, England, 21 November, 1963 — M

League Club	Source	Date Signed	Seasons Played	Apps	Subs	Gls
Manchester C	App	11/81	81	1	0	0
Chester C	Sligo Rov (ROI)	09/83	83	24	8	3

ELLIOTT Anthony Robert (Tony)
Born: Nuneaton, Warwickshire, England, 30 November, 1969 — G
England: Youth/Schools

League Club	Source	Date Signed	Seasons Played	Apps	Subs	Gls
Birmingham C	App	12/86				
Hereford U	Tr	12/88	88-91	75	0	0
Huddersfield T	Tr	07/92	92	15	0	0
Carlisle U	Tr	06/93	93-95	21	1	0
Cardiff C	Tr	07/96	96-97	38	1	0
Scarborough	Tr	02/98	97-98	35	0	0

ELLIOTT Bernard Henry (Bryn)
Born: Beeston, Nottinghamshire, England, 3 May, 1925 — LH

League Club	Source	Date Signed	Seasons Played	Apps	Subs	Gls
Nottingham F	Beeston BC	10/42	47-48	10	-	0
Southampton	Boston U	10/49	49-57	235	-	2

ELLIOTT Charles Standish (Charlie)
Born: Bolsover, Derbyshire, England, 24 April, 1912 — FB
Died: Nottingham, England, 1 January, 2004

League Club	Source	Date Signed	Seasons Played	Apps	Subs	Gls
Chesterfield	Bolsover Colliery	11/30				
Coventry C	Tr	08/31	31-47	95	-	2

ELLIOTT David (Dave)
Born: Tantobie, County Durham, England, 10 February, 1945 — M

League Club	Source	Date Signed	Seasons Played	Apps	Subs	Gls
Sunderland	App	02/62	63-66	30	1	1
Newcastle U	Tr	12/66	66-70	78	2	4
Southend U	Tr	02/71	70-74	174	4	9
Newport Co	Tr	07/75	75	21	0	0
Newport Co	Bangor C	10/78	78	0	2	0

ELLIOTT Eamonn Gerard
Born: Belfast, Northern Ireland, 27 July, 1971 — M

League Club	Source	Date Signed	Seasons Played	Apps	Subs	Gls
Carlisle U	YT	07/90	90	3	1	0

ELLIOTT Edward (Ted)
Born: Carlisle, Cumbria, England, 24 May, 1919 — G
Died: Carlisle, Cumbria, England, September, 1984

League Club	Source	Date Signed	Seasons Played	Apps	Subs	Gls
Carlisle U		12/37	37-38	11	-	0
Wolverhampton W	Tr	02/39	46-47	7	-	0
Chester C	Tr	10/48	48-50	59	-	0
Halifax T	Tr	11/50	50-51	33	-	0

ELLIOTT Frederick Francis George (Frank)
Born: Lambeth, S London, England, 23 July, 1929 — G

League Club	Source	Date Signed	Seasons Played	Apps	Subs	Gls
Swansea C	Merthyr Tydfil	09/49				
Stoke C	Tr	12/52	52-53	22	-	0
Fulham	Tr	03/54	53-55	25	-	0
Mansfield T	Tr	07/56	56-57	63	-	0

ELLIOTT Harvey
Born: Middleton, Greater Manchester, England, 21 January, 1922 — IF
Died: Manchester, England, February, 1996

League Club	Source	Date Signed	Seasons Played	Apps	Subs	Gls
Hull C		12/46	46	4	-	0

ELLIOTT Ian
Born: Barrow, Cumbria, England, 16 December, 1953 — G

League Club	Source	Date Signed	Seasons Played	Apps	Subs	Gls
Barrow	Jnr	-	69	1	0	0

ELLIOTT John
Born: Penrith, Cumbria, England, 6 May, 1938 — IF

League Club	Source	Date Signed	Seasons Played	Apps	Subs	Gls
Carlisle U	Jnr	08/55	55-57	2	-	1

ELLIOTT John Walter
Born: Warkworth, Northumberland, England, 23 December, 1946 — LW

League Club	Source	Date Signed	Seasons Played	Apps	Subs	Gls
Notts Co	Ashington	08/67	67-68	61	3	7

ELLIOTT Kevan
Born: Chilton, County Durham, England, 5 September, 1958 — M

League Club	Source	Date Signed	Seasons Played	Apps	Subs	Gls
Hartlepool U	App	09/76	75-76	24	3	1

ELLIOTT Lee
Born: Ormskirk, Lancashire, England, 5 May, 1970 — F

League Club	Source	Date Signed	Seasons Played	Apps	Subs	Gls
Crewe Alex	Everton (YT)	06/88	88	1	0	0

ELLIOTT Marvin Conrad
Born: Wandsworth, SW London, England, 15 September, 1984 — M
Jamaica: 9

League Club	Source	Date Signed	Seasons Played	Apps	Subs	Gls
Millwall	Sch	02/02	02-06	119	25	3
Bristol C	Tr	07/07	07-13	216	26	25
Crawley T	Tr	09/14	14	22	5	6

ELLIOTT Matthew Stephen (Matt)
Born: Wandsworth, SW London, England, 1 November, 1968 — CD
Scotland: 18

League Club	Source	Date Signed	Seasons Played	Apps	Subs	Gls
Charlton Ath	Epsom & Ewell	09/88				
Torquay U	Tr	03/89	88-91	123	1	15
Scunthorpe U	Tr	03/92	91-93	61	0	8
Oxford U	Tr	11/93	93-96	148	0	21
Leicester C	Tr	01/97	96-04	239	6	27
Ipswich T	L	03/04	03	10	0	0

ELLIOTT Paul Marcellus
Born: Lewisham, SE London, England, 18 March, 1964 — CD
England: B-1/U21-3/Youth

League Club	Source	Date Signed	Seasons Played	Apps	Subs	Gls
Charlton Ath	App	03/81	81-82	61	2	1
Luton T	Tr	03/83	82-85	63	3	4
Aston Villa	Tr	12/85	85-86	56	1	7
Chelsea	Glasgow Celtic	07/91	91-92	42	0	3

ELLIOTT Raymond Charles (Ray)
Born: Eastleigh, Hampshire, England, 11 June, 1947 — F

League Club	Source	Date Signed	Seasons Played	Apps	Subs	Gls
Charlton Ath	App	06/65				
Exeter C	Tr	03/66	65-66	28	0	3

ELLIOTT Raymond John (Ray)
Born: Ystrad Rhondda, Rhondda Cynon Taff, Wales, 23 March, 1929 — CF
Died: Chandler's Ford, Hampshire, England, 22 May, 2006

League Club	Source	Date Signed	Seasons Played	Apps	Subs	Gls
Millwall	Woking	11/46	47-48	2	-	0

ELLIOTT Richard Mark (Mark)
Born: Ton Pentre, Rhondda Cynon Taff, Wales, 20 March, 1959 — W

League Club	Source	Date Signed	Seasons Played	Apps	Subs	Gls
Brighton & HA	Merthyr Tydfil	02/77	76	3	0	0
Cardiff C	Tr	09/79	79	6	1	0
Bournemouth	L	01/80	79	4	0	0
Wimbledon	Ton Pentre	02/82	81	7	4	1

ELLIOTT Robert James (Robbie)
Born: Gosforth, Tyne and Wear, England, 25 December, 1973 — LB
England: U21-2/Youth

League Club	Source	Date Signed	Seasons Played	Apps	Subs	Gls
Newcastle U	YT	04/91	90-96	71	8	9
Bolton W	Tr	07/97	97-00	71	15	5
Newcastle U	Tr	07/01	01-05	55	8	2
Sunderland	Tr	08/06	06	7	0	0
Leeds U	Tr	01/07	06	5	2	0
Hartlepool U	Tr	07/07	07	14	1	0

ELLIOTT Shaun
Born: Haydon Bridge, Northumberland, England, 26 January, 1957 — CD
England: B-3

League Club	Source	Date Signed	Seasons Played	Apps	Subs	Gls
Sunderland	App	01/75	76-85	316	5	12
Norwich C	Tr	08/86	86-87	29	2	2
Blackpool	Tr	08/88	88-89	66	1	0

ELLIOTT Simon John
Born: Wellington, New Zealand, 10 June, 1974 — M
New Zealand: 59

League Club	Source	Date Signed	Seasons Played	Apps	Subs	Gls
Fulham	Columbus Crew (USA)	01/06	05	12	0	0

ELLIOTT Stephen Blair (Steve)
Born: Haltwhistle, Northumberland, England, 15 September, 1958 — F

League Club	Source	Date Signed	Seasons Played	Apps	Subs	Gls
Nottingham F	App	09/76	78	4	0	0
Preston NE	Tr	03/79	78-83	202	6	70
Luton T	Tr	07/84	84	12	0	3
Walsall	Tr	12/84	84-85	68	1	21
Bolton W	Tr	07/86	86-88	57	3	10
Bury	Tr	09/88	88	31	0	11
Rochdale	Tr	10/89	89-90	46	6	9

ELLIOTT Stephen William
Born: Dublin, Republic of Ireland, 6 January, 1984 — F
Republic of Ireland: 9/U21-10/Youth

League Club	Source	Date Signed	Seasons Played	Apps	Subs	Gls
Manchester C	YT	01/01	03	0	2	0
Sunderland	Tr	08/04	04-06	55	26	22
Wolverhampton W	Tr	07/07	07	18	11	4
Preston NE	Tr	09/08	08-09	26	20	7
Norwich C	L	03/10	09	4	6	2
Coventry C	Heart of Midlothian	07/12	12	10	8	4
Carlisle U	Tr	08/14	14	4	11	1

ELLIOTT Steven William (Steve)
Born: Derby, England, 29 October, 1978 — CD
England: U21-2/U21-3

League Club	Source	Date Signed	Seasons Played	Apps	Subs	Gls
Derby Co	YT	03/97	97-03	58	15	1
Blackpool	Tr	11/03	03	28	0	0
Bristol Rov	Tr	07/04	04-09	217	1	16
Cheltenham T	Tr	07/10	10-14	172	2	9

ELLIOTT Stuart
Born: Belfast, Northern Ireland, 23 July, 1978 — LW
Northern Ireland: 39/B-1/U21-3

League Club	Source	Date Signed	Seasons Played	Apps	Subs	Gls
Hull C	Motherwell	07/02	02-07	156	37	65
Doncaster Rov	Tr	01/08	07-08	4	15	0
Grimsby T	L	01/09	08	9	2	2

ELLIOTT Stuart Thomas
Born: Hendon, N London, England, 27 August, 1977 — CD

League Club	Source	Date Signed	Seasons Played	Apps	Subs	Gls
Newcastle U	YT	08/95				
Hull C	L	02/97	96	3	0	0
Swindon T	L	02/98	97	1	1	0
Gillingham	L	10/98	98	4	1	0
Hartlepool U	L	01/99	98	5	0	0
Wrexham	L	03/99	98	8	1	0
Bournemouth	L	12/99	99	6	2	0
Stockport Co	L	02/00	99	4	1	0
Darlington	Tr	07/00	00	20	4	0
Plymouth Arg	Tr	03/01	00	11	1	0
Carlisle U	Tr	08/01	01	6	0	0
Exeter C	Tr	02/02	01	0	1	0

ELLIOTT Thomas Joshua (Tom)
Born: Leeds, England, 9 September, 1989 — F

League Club	Source	Date Signed	Seasons Played	Apps	Subs	Gls
Leeds U	Sch	08/08	06	0	3	0
Macclesfield T	L	01/09	08	4	2	0
Bury	L	09/09	09	7	9	1
Rotherham U	L	07/10	10	4	2	0
Cambridge U	Stockport Co	07/12	14	30	0	8

ELLIOTT Wade Patrick
Born: Eastleigh, Hampshire, England, 14 December, 1978 — RM
England: Schools

League Club	Source	Date Signed	Seasons Played	Apps	Subs	Gls
Bournemouth	Bashley	02/00	99-04	178	42	31
Burnley	Tr	07/05	05-11	222	30	19
Birmingham C	Tr	08/11	11-13	63	25	7
Bristol C	L	01/14	13-14	43	12	5

ELLIOTT William (Billy)
Born: Poole, Dorset, England, 23 October, 1961 — M

League Club	Source	Date Signed	Seasons Played	Apps	Subs	Gls
Plymouth Arg	App	03/79				
Bournemouth	Tr	05/80	80	6	5	1

ELLIOTT William Bethwaite (Billy)
Born: Harrington, Cumbria, England, 6 August, 1919 — RW
Died: Canary Isles, Spain, 24 November, 1966
England: War-2

League Club	Source	Date Signed	Seasons Played	Apps	Subs	Gls
Carlisle U	Jnr	11/36				
Wolverhampton W	Dudley T	07/37				
Bournemouth	Tr	05/38	38	10	-	1
West Bromwich A	Tr	12/38	38-50	170	-	39

ELLIOTT William Henry (Billy)
Born: Bradford, England, 20 March, 1925 — LW
Died: Sunderland, England, 21 January, 2008
England: 5/FLge-4

League Club	Source	Date Signed	Seasons Played	Apps	Subs	Gls
Bradford Park Ave	Jnr	04/42	46-50	176	-	21
Burnley	Tr	09/51	51-52	74	-	14
Sunderland	Tr	06/53	53-58	193	-	23

ELLIS Alan
Born: Alfreton, Derbyshire, England, 17 November, 1951 — M

League Club	Source	Date Signed	Seasons Played	Apps	Subs	Gls
Charlton Ath	App	11/69	70-72	9	5	0

ELLIS Anthony Joseph (Tony)
Born: Salford, England, 20 October, 1964 — F

League Club	Source	Date Signed	Seasons Played	Apps	Subs	Gls
Oldham Ath	Horwich RMI	08/86	86-87	5	3	0
Preston NE	Tr	10/87	87-89	80	6	26
Stoke C	Tr	12/89	89-91	66	11	19
Preston NE	Tr	08/92	92-93	70	2	48
Blackpool	Tr	07/94	94-97	140	6	54
Bury	Tr	12/97	97-98	24	14	8
Stockport Co	Tr	02/99	98-99	17	3	6
Rochdale	Tr	11/99	99-00	55	4	17
Burnley	Tr	07/01	01	0	11	1

ELLIS Clinton (Clint)
Born: Ealing, W London, England, 7 July, 1977 — F
England: Youth/Schools

League Club	Source	Date Signed	Seasons Played	Apps	Subs	Gls
Bristol Rov	Willesden Constantine	03/00	00	2	13	1

ELLIS Daniel James (Dan)
Born: Stockport, Greater Manchester, England, 18 November, 1988 — F

League Club	Source	Date Signed	Seasons Played	Apps	Subs	Gls
Stockport Co	Sch	11/06	05-06	0	5	0

ELLIS David (Dave)
Born: Wishaw, Lanarkshire, Scotland, 25 September, 1920 — W
Died: Bury, Greater Manchester, England, May, 2005

League Club	Source	Date Signed	Seasons Played	Apps	Subs	Gls
Bury	Pollok Jnrs	04/47				
Halifax T	Tr	01/48	47	2	-	0
Barrow	Tr	10/48	48	1	-	0

ELLIS Glenn Douglas
Born: Dagenham, E London, England, 31 October, 1957 — G
England: Schools

League Club	Source	Date Signed	Seasons Played	Apps	Subs	Gls
Ipswich T	App	10/75				
Colchester U	L	12/76	76	2	0	0

ELLIS Keith Duncan
Born: Sheffield, England, 6 November, 1935 — CF

League Club	Source	Date Signed	Seasons Played	Apps	Subs	Gls
Sheffield Wed	Jnr	04/55	54-63	102	-	52
Scunthorpe U	Tr	03/64	63	10	-	5
Cardiff C	Tr	09/64	64	22	-	9
Lincoln C	Tr	06/65	65	7	0	0

ELLIS Kenneth (Ken)
Born: Buckley, Flintshire, Wales, 22 January, 1928 — W
Died: Mold, Flintshire, Wales, 25 July, 2003

League Club	Source	Date Signed	Seasons Played	Apps	Subs	Gls
Chester C (Am)	Jnr	05/46	46	1	-	0
Wrexham (Am)		05/49	49	5	-	0

ELLIS Kenneth (Ken)
Born: Sunderland, England, 29 May, 1948 — F/M
Died: Darlington, County Durham, England, 4 February, 1992

League Club	Source	Date Signed	Seasons Played	Apps	Subs	Gls
Hartlepool U	Scarborough	07/71	71	32	2	4
Darlington	Verna (BEL)	07/79	79	21	0	0

ELLIS Kevin Edward
Born: Tiptree, Essex, England, 11 May, 1977 — FB

League Club	Source	Date Signed	Seasons Played	Apps	Subs	Gls
Ipswich T	YT	08/95	94	1	0	0

ELLIS Mark Edward
Born: Bradford, England, 6 January, 1962 — LW

League Club	Source	Date Signed	Seasons Played	Apps	Subs	Gls
Bradford C	Trinity Ath	08/80	80-89	190	28	30
Halifax T	Tr	10/90	90-91	33	4	4

ELLIS Mark Ian
Born: Kingsbridge, Devon, England, 30 September, 1988 — CD

League Club	Source	Date Signed	Seasons Played	Apps	Subs	Gls
Torquay U	Bolton W (Sch)	09/07	09-11	83	6	8
Crewe Alex	Tr	07/12	12-13	79	2	6
Shrewsbury T	Tr	05/14	14	32	0	2

ELLIS Neil James
Born: Bebington, Wirral, England, 30 April, 1969 — LW

League Club	Source	Date Signed	Seasons Played	Apps	Subs	Gls
Chester C	Bangor C	06/90	90	13	8	1
Maidstone U	Tr	07/91	91	22	6	0

ELLIS Peter James
Born: Portsmouth, England, 20 March, 1956 — D

League Club	Source	Date Signed	Seasons Played	Apps	Subs	Gls
Portsmouth	App	03/74	73-83	226	21	1
Southend U	Tr	09/84	84	12	0	1

ELLIS Samuel (Sam)
Born: Ashton-under-Lyne, Greater Manchester, England, 12 September, 1946 — CD
England: U23-3

League Club	Source	Date Signed	Seasons Played	Apps	Subs	Gls
Sheffield Wed	Smiths, Manchester	09/64	65-70	155	2	1
Mansfield T	Tr	01/72	71-72	64	0	7
Lincoln C	Tr	05/73	73-76	173	0	33
Watford	Tr	08/77	77-78	30	4	4

ELLIS Sydney Carey (Syd)
Born: Charlton, SE London, England, 16 August, 1931 — LB
Died: Greenwich, SE London, England, 26 March, 2001
England: U23-1

League Club	Source	Date Signed	Seasons Played	Apps	Subs	Gls
Charlton Ath	Crystal Palace (Am)	05/49	53-57	48	-	0
Brighton & HA	Tr	11/57	57-58	42	-	0

ELLISON Anthony Lee (Lee)
Born: Bishop Auckland, County Durham, England, 13 January, 1973 — F

League Club	Source	Date Signed	Seasons Played	Apps	Subs	Gls
Darlington	YT	11/90	90-93	54	18	17
Hartlepool U	L	03/93	92	3	1	1
Leicester C	Tr	08/94				
Crewe Alex	Tr	08/95	95-96	3	1	2
Hereford U	Halifax T	10/96	96	0	1	0
Darlington	Bishop Auckland	03/98	97-98	7	21	3

ELLISON James
Born: Liverpool, England, 25 October, 1991 — F

League Club	Source	Date Signed	Seasons Played	Apps	Subs	Gls
Liverpool	Sch	07/09				
Burton A	Tr	08/10	10	0	2	0

ELLISON Kevin
Born: Liverpool, England, 23 February, 1979 — LW

League Club	Source	Date Signed	Seasons Played	Apps	Subs	Gls
Leicester C	Altrincham	02/01	00	0	1	0
Stockport Co	Tr	11/01	01-03	33	15	2
Lincoln C	L	03/04	03	11	0	0
Chester C	Tr	08/04	04	24	0	9
Hull C	Tr	01/05	04-05	26	13	2
Tranmere Rov	Tr	07/06	06	26	8	4
Chester C	Tr	07/07	07-08	75	0	19
Rotherham U	Tr	05/09	09-10	56	6	11
Bradford C	L	02/11	10	6	1	1
Morecambe	Tr	07/11	11-14	137	22	47

ELLISON Norman
Born: Bebington, Wirral, England, 2 November, 1929 — RW
Died: Bebington, Wirral, England, 1 October, 1999

League Club	Source	Date Signed	Seasons Played	Apps	Subs	Gls
Tranmere Rov		10/49	49-50	2	-	0

ELLISON Raymond (Ray)
Born: Newcastle-upon-Tyne, England, 31 December, 1950 — FB/M

League Club	Source	Date Signed	Seasons Played	Apps	Subs	Gls
Newcastle U	App	10/68	71	5	0	0
Sunderland	Tr	03/73	72	2	0	0
Torquay U	Tr	07/74	74	11	5	0
Workington	Tr	07/75	75-76	57	0	3

ELLISON Samuel Walter (Walter)
Born: Leadgate, County Durham, England, 27 August, 1923 — RW
Died: Isle of Wight, England, December, 1994

League Club	Source	Date Signed	Seasons Played	Apps	Subs	Gls
Sunderland	Middlesbrough Crus'rs	10/45	46	3	-	0
Reading	Consett	06/49	49	4	-	0

ELLISON William Roy (Roy)
Born: Newbiggin, Northumberland, England, 5 July, 1948 — M

League Club	Source	Date Signed	Seasons Played	Apps	Subs	Gls
Newcastle U	App	06/66				
Barrow	Tr	02/68	67-70	76	10	7
Hartlepool U	L	10/70	70	5	0	0

ELLSON Peter Edward
Born: Audlem, Cheshire, England, 21 August, 1925 — G
Died: Cheshire, England, 14 April, 2014

League Club	Source	Date Signed	Seasons Played	Apps	Subs	Gls
Crewe Alex	Crewe Railway Police	05/49	48-55	219	-	0

ELM David
Born: Emmaboda, Sweden, 10 January, 1983 — F

League Club	Source	Date Signed	Seasons Played	Apps	Subs	Gls
Fulham	Kalmar (SWE)	09/09	09	3	7	1

ELMANDER Johan Erik Calvin
Born: Alingsaas, Sweden, 27 May, 1981 — F
Sweden: 85/U21-30

League Club	Source	Date Signed	Seasons Played	Apps	Subs	Gls
Bolton W	Toulouse (FRA)	07/08	08-10	82	10	18
Norwich C (L)	Galatasaray (TKY)	08/13	13	16	13	1

ELMES Timothy (Tim)
Born: Croydon, S London, England, 28 September, 1962 — M

League Club	Source	Date Signed	Seasons Played	Apps	Subs	Gls
Chelsea	App	07/80	80	2	2	0

EL MOHAMADY Ahmed Eissa
Born: Basyoun, Egypt, 9 September, 1987 — RB/M
Egypt: 69

League Club	Source	Date Signed	Seasons Played	Apps	Subs	Gls
Sunderland	ENPPI (EGY)	08/10	10-12	33	23	1
Hull C	L	08/12	12-12	23	0	1
Hull C	Tr	01/13	12-14	94	0	6

ELMS James Brian (Jimmy)
Born: Manchester, England, 16 September, 1940 — LW
England: Youth

League Club	Source	Date Signed	Seasons Played	Apps	Subs	Gls
Manchester U	Jnr	04/58				
Crewe Alex	Tr	10/60	60	1	-	0

ELOKOBI George Nganyuo
Born: Mogadishu, Somalia, 31 January, 1986 — LB

League Club	Source	Date Signed	Seasons Played	Apps	Subs	Gls
Colchester U	Dulwich Hamlet	07/04	05-07	35	4	2
Chester C	L	01/05	04	4	1	0
Wolverhampton W	Tr	01/08	07-13	63	22	2
Nottingham F	L	02/12	11	8	4	0
Bristol C	L	09/12	12	1	0	0
Oldham Ath	Tr	08/14	14	20	4	3

ELPHICK Gary
Born: Brighton, England, 17 October, 1985 — CD

League Club	Source	Date Signed	Seasons Played	Apps	Subs	Gls
Brighton & HA	Sch	06/05	05	1	1	0

ELPHICK Thomas (Tommy)
Born: Brighton, England, 7 September, 1987 — CD

League Club	Source	Date Signed	Seasons Played	Apps	Subs	Gls
Brighton & HA	Sch	06/06	05-10	144	9	7
Bournemouth	Tr	08/12	12-14	114	4	4

ELRICH Ahmad
Born: Sydney, Australia, 30 May, 1981 — W
Australia: 17

League Club	Source	Date Signed	Seasons Played	Apps	Subs	Gls
Fulham	Busan Icons (KOR)	07/05	05	2	4	0

ELSBY Ian Christopher
Born: Newcastle-under-Lyme, Potteries, England, 13 September, 1960 — M

League Club	Source	Date Signed	Seasons Played	Apps	Subs	Gls
Port Vale	Jnr	06/78	78-80	32	11	1

ELSBY James (Jim)
Born: Newcastle-under-Lyme, Potteries, England, 1 August, 1928 — FB
Died: Newcastle-under-Lyme, Potteries, England, 7 September, 1987

League Club	Source	Date Signed	Seasons Played	Apps	Subs	Gls
Port Vale		05/47	48-53	12	-	0

ELSE Frederick (Fred)
Born: Golborne, Greater Manchester, England, 31 March, 1933 — G
Died: Barrow in Furness, Cumbria, England, 20 July, 2015
England: B-1

League Club	Source	Date Signed	Seasons Played	Apps	Subs	Gls
Preston NE	Axwell Park CW	08/53	53-60	215	-	0
Blackburn Rov	Tr	08/61	61-65	187	0	0
Barrow	Tr	07/66	66-69	148	0	0

ELSEY Karl William
Born: Swansea, Wales, 20 November, 1958 — M

League Club	Source	Date Signed	Seasons Played	Apps	Subs	Gls
Queens Park Rgrs	Pembroke Bor	01/79	78-79	6	1	0
Newport Co	Tr	07/80	80-83	114	9	15
Cardiff C	Tr	09/83	83-84	59	0	5
Gillingham	Tr	08/85	85-87	126	2	13
Reading	Tr	08/88	88	41	3	3
Maidstone U	Tr	07/89	89-90	70	2	5
Gillingham	Tr	08/91	91	25	2	3

ELSTRUP Lars Dahl
Born: Randers, Denmark, 24 March, 1963 — F

League Club	Source	Date Signed	Seasons Played	Apps	Subs	Gls

Denmark: 34

Luton T	OB Odense (DEN)	08/89	89-90	50	10	19

ELSWORTHY John
Born: Nant-y-derry, Monmouthshire, Wales, 26 July, 1931 LH
Died: Ipswich, England, 3 May, 2009

Ipswich T	Newport Co (Am)	05/49	49-64	396	-	44

ELVINS Robert Mark (Rob)
Born: Alvechurch, Worcestershire, England, 17 September, 1986 F

West Bromwich A	Sch	07/05				
Cheltenham T	L	09/06	06	0	5	0
Aldershot T	Tr	07/07	08	7	8	1

ELVY Reginald (Reg)
Born: Leeds, England, 25 November, 1920 G
Died: Kingsthorpe, Northamptonshire, England, 13 July, 1991

Halifax T	Leeds U (Am)	03/44	46	22	-	0
Bolton W	Tr	03/47	47-49	31	-	0
Blackburn Rov	Tr	11/51	51-55	192	-	0
Northampton T	Tr	07/56	56-58	67	-	0

ELWELL Terence Thomas (Terry)
Born: Newport, Wales, 13 April, 1926 FB
Died: Newport, Wales, August, 2004

Swansea C	Barry T	08/48	48-51	62	-	0
Swindon T	Tr	07/52	52-53	61	-	0

ELWISS Michael Walter (Mike)
Born: Doncaster, South Yorkshire, England, 2 May, 1954 F

Doncaster Rov	Jnr	07/71	71-73	96	1	30
Preston NE	Tr	02/74	73-77	191	1	60
Crystal Palace	Tr	07/78	78	19	1	7
Preston NE	L	03/80	79	8	2	3

ELWOOD Joseph Patrick (Joe)
Born: Belfast, Northern Ireland, 26 October, 1939 LW
Northern Ireland: B-1/U23-1/Schools

Leyton Orient	Glenavon	04/58	58-65	101	2	25

EL ZHAR Nabil
Born: Ales, France, 27 August, 1986 W
France: Youth//Morocco: 24

Liverpool	Saint-Etienne (FRA)	08/06	06-09	2	19	0

EMANUEL Lewis James
Born: Bradford, England, 14 October, 1983 LB/M
England: Youth

Bradford C	YT	07/01	01-05	102	37	4
Luton T	Tr	07/06	06-08	71	6	5
Brentford	L	10/07	07	3	0	0

EMANUEL William John (John)
Born: Treherbert, Rhondda Cynon Taff, Wales, 5 April, 1948 M
Wales: 2/Amateur

Bristol C	Ferndale	05/71	71-75	124	4	10
Swindon T	L	01/76	75	6	0	0
Gillingham	L	02/76	75	4	0	0
Newport Co	Tr	06/76	76-77	79	0	4

EMANUELSON Urby Vitorrio Diego
Born: Amsterdam, Netherlands, 16 June, 1986 W
Netherlands: 17/U21-13

Fulham (L)	AC Milan (ITA)	01/13	12	5	8	1

EMBERSON Carl Wayne
Born: Epsom, Surrey, England, 13 July, 1973 G

Millwall	YT	05/91				
Colchester U	L	12/92	92	13	0	0
Colchester U	Tr	07/94	94-98	178	1	0
Walsall	Tr	06/99	99-00	6	2	0
Luton T	Tr	07/01	01-02	51	2	0
Southend U	Tr	07/03	03	6	0	0

EMBERY Benjamin James (Ben)
Born: Barking, E London, England, 10 October, 1944 RB

Tottenham H	App	06/62				
Exeter C	Tr	06/66	66-67	36	3	0

EMBLEN Neil Robert
Born: Bromley, SE London, England, 19 June, 1971 M/CD

Millwall	Sittingbourne	11/93	93	12	0	0
Wolverhampton W	Tr	07/94	94-96	80	8	9
Crystal Palace	Tr	08/97	97	8	5	0
Wolverhampton W	Tr	03/98	97-00	102	12	7
Norwich C	Tr	07/01	01-02	6	8	0
Walsall	L	01/03	02	2	2	0
Walsall	Tr	05/03	02-04	62	14	7

League Club	Source	Date Signed	Seasons Played	Apps	Subs	Gls

EMBLEN Paul David
Born: Bromley, SE London, England, 3 April, 1976 F/W

Charlton Ath	Tonbridge Angels	05/97	97	0	4	0
Brighton & HA	L	11/97	97	15	0	4
Wycombe W	Tr	08/98	98-01	45	18	3

EMBLETON Daniel Charles
Born: Liverpool, England, 27 March, 1975 G

Liverpool	YT	04/93				
Walsall	Bury (NC)	08/94	94	0	1	0

EMBLETON David
Born: Newcastle-upon-Tyne, England, 14 September, 1952 D

Newcastle U	App	08/71				
Bury	Tr	07/72	72	6	1	0
Hartlepool U	Tr	07/73	73-75	24	2	0

EMENALO Michael Ahamefula
Born: Aba, Nigeria, 14 July, 1965 FB
Nigeria: 14

Notts Co	Eintracht Trier (BEL)	08/94	94	7	0	0

[EMERSON] COSTA MOISES Emerson
Born: Rio de Janeiro, Brazil, 12 April, 1972 M

Middlesbrough	FC Porto (POR)	06/96	96-97	53	0	9

EMERSON Dean
Born: Salford, England, 27 December, 1962 M

Stockport Co	Jnr	02/82	81-84	156	0	7
Rotherham U	Tr	07/85	85-86	55	0	8
Coventry C	Tr	10/86	86-91	98	16	0
Hartlepool U	Tr	07/92	92-93	44	1	1
Stockport Co	Tr	11/93	93-94	8	3	0
Preston NE	Tr	11/94	94	1	1	0

EMERTON Brett Michael
Born: Sydney, Australia, 22 February, 1979 RB/M
Australia: 95/U23-25/Youth

Blackburn Rov	Feyenoord (NED)	07/03	03-11	206	41	13

EMERTON Daniel James (Danny)
Born: Beverley, East Riding of Yorkshire, England, 27 September, 1991 W

Hull C	Sch	07/10				
Northampton T	Tr	08/13	13	11	5	0

EMERY Anthony John (Tony)
Born: Lincoln, England, 4 November, 1927 CH
Died: Lincoln, England, 5 December, 2005

Lincoln C	Jnr	08/47	46-58	402	-	1
Mansfield T	Tr	06/59	59-60	26	-	0

EMERY Dennis
Born: Sandy, Bedfordshire, England, 4 October, 1933 IF
Died: Bedford, England, 1 May, 1986

Tottenham H	Eynesbury Rov	12/51				
Peterborough U	Eynesbury Rov	07/54	60-62	68	-	29

EMERY Donald Kenneth James (Don)
Born: Cardiff, Wales, 11 June, 1920 LB
Died: Aberdeen, Scotland, 19 November, 1993
Wales: Schools

Swindon T	Cardiff C (Am)	06/37	37-47	69	-	3

EMERY James (Jim)
Born: Lisburn, Belfast, Northern Ireland, 2 March, 1940 CF

Exeter C	Distillery	08/59				
Barrow	Tr	07/60	60	2	-	0

EMERY Joshua Stephen (Josh)
Born: Ledbury, Herefordshire, England, 30 September, 1990 M

Cheltenham T	Sch	07/10	08	0	1	0

EMERY Stephen Roger (Steve)
Born: Ledbury, Herefordshire, England, 7 February, 1956 M/RB

Hereford U	App	02/74	73-79	203	1	10
Derby Co	Tr	09/79	79-81	73	2	4
Newport Co	Tr	03/83				
Hereford U	Tr	06/83	83-84	72	3	2
Wrexham	Tr	08/85	85	8	1	0

EMERY Terence George (Terry)
Born: Bristol, England, 8 September, 1936 RH

Bristol C		02/57	56-57	11	-	0

EMMANUEL David Leonard (Len)
Born: Swansea, Wales, 3 September, 1917 LH
Died: Swansea, Wales, July, 2010
Wales: Schools

Swansea C		04/36	37-46	49	-	1
Newport Co	Tr	05/47	46-47	33	-	7

EMMANUEL John Gary (Gary)
Born: Swansea, Wales, 1 February, 1954 — M
Wales: U23-1

League Club	Source	Date Signed	Seasons Played	Apps	Subs	Gls
Birmingham C	App	07/71	74-78	61	10	6
Bristol Rov	Tr	12/78	78-80	59	6	2
Swindon T	Tr	07/81	81-83	109	2	8
Newport Co	Tr	07/84	84	12	0	0
Bristol C	Forest Green Rov	08/85	85	2	0	0
Swansea C	Tr	08/85	85-87	104	7	5

EMMANUEL-THOMAS Jay Aston
Born: Forest Gate, E London, England, 27 December, 1990 — F
England: Youth

League Club	Source	Date Signed	Seasons Played	Apps	Subs	Gls
Arsenal	Sch	07/08	10	0	1	0
Blackpool	L	08/09	09	6	5	1
Doncaster Rov	L	02/10	09	12	2	5
Cardiff C	L	01/11	10	7	7	2
Ipswich T	Tr	07/11	11-12	38	33	8
Bristol C	Tr	07/13	13-14	52	30	24

EMMERSON Mark
Born: Cuddington, Cheshire, England, 7 August, 1965 — M

League Club	Source	Date Signed	Seasons Played	Apps	Subs	Gls
Wrexham	Jnr	08/82	82	1	1	0

EMMERSON Morris
Born: Sunniside, Tyne and Wear, England, 23 October, 1942 — G
England: Schools

League Club	Source	Date Signed	Seasons Played	Apps	Subs	Gls
Middlesbrough	Jnr	10/59	62	10	-	0
Peterborough U	Tr	07/63	63	7	-	0
Luton T	Tr	03/65				

EMMERSON Scott
Born: Durham, England, 10 October, 1982 — F

League Club	Source	Date Signed	Seasons Played	Apps	Subs	Gls
York C	YT	-	00-01	3	11	1

EMMERSON Wayne Edward
Born: Ottawa, Canada, 2 November, 1947 — F

League Club	Source	Date Signed	Seasons Played	Apps	Subs	Gls
Manchester U	Jnr	09/65				
Crewe Alex	Tr	07/68	68	6	2	1

EMNES Marvin
Born: Rotterdam, Netherlands, 27 May, 1988 — F
Netherlands: U21-3/Youth

League Club	Source	Date Signed	Seasons Played	Apps	Subs	Gls
Middlesbrough	Sparta Rotterdam (NED)	07/08	08-13	103	39	24
Swansea C	L	10/10	10	3	1	2
Swansea C	Tr	01/14	13-14	5	19	1

EMPTAGE Albert Taylor
Born: Grimsby, North Lincolnshire, England, 26 December, 1917 — WH
Died: Stockport, Greater Manchester, England, December, 1997
England: FLge-1

League Club	Source	Date Signed	Seasons Played	Apps	Subs	Gls
Manchester C	Scunthorpe U	02/37	37-50	136	-	1
Stockport Co	Tr	01/51	50-52	36	-	1

[EMRE] BELOZOGLU Emre
Born: Istanbul, Turkey, 7 September, 1980 — M
Turkey: 94/U21-12/Youth

League Club	Source	Date Signed	Seasons Played	Apps	Subs	Gls
Newcastle U	Inter Milan (ITA)	07/05	05-07	46	12	5

EMSON Paul David
Born: Lincoln, England, 22 October, 1958 — W

League Club	Source	Date Signed	Seasons Played	Apps	Subs	Gls
Derby Co	Brigg T	09/78	78-82	112	15	13
Grimsby T	Tr	08/83	83-85	90	7	15
Wrexham	Tr	07/86	86-87	42	7	5
Darlington	Tr	08/88	88-90	39	9	5

ENCKELMAN Peter Mikael
Born: Turku, Finland, 10 March, 1977 — G
Finland: 12/U21-15

League Club	Source	Date Signed	Seasons Played	Apps	Subs	Gls
Aston Villa	TPS Turku (FIN)	02/99	99-02	51	1	0
Blackburn Rov	Tr	11/03	03	2	0	0
Cardiff C	Tr	01/08	07-09	29	3	0

ENDEAN Barry
Born: Chester-le-Street, County Durham, England, 22 March, 1946 — F

League Club	Source	Date Signed	Seasons Played	Apps	Subs	Gls
Watford	Pelton Fell	09/68	68-70	72	5	28
Charlton Ath	Tr	02/71	70-71	27	0	1
Blackburn Rov	Tr	10/71	71-74	65	14	18
Huddersfield T	Tr	03/75	74-75	8	4	1
Workington	L	10/75	75	8	0	2
Hartlepool U	Tr	03/76	75-76	24	1	5

ENDERSBY Scott Ian Glenn
Born: Lewisham, SE London, England, 20 February, 1962 — G
England: Youth

League Club	Source	Date Signed	Seasons Played	Apps	Subs	Gls
Ipswich T	App	03/79				
Tranmere Rov	Tr	07/81	81-82	79	0	0
Swindon T	Tr	08/83	83-85	85	0	0
Carlisle U	Tr	11/85	85-86	52	0	0
York C	Tr	07/87	87-88	35	0	0
Cardiff C	L	12/87	87	4	0	0

ENES Robert Manuel (Robbie)
Born: Sydney, Australia, 22 August, 1975 — M
Australia:

League Club	Source	Date Signed	Seasons Played	Apps	Subs	Gls
Portsmouth	Sydney U (AUS)	10/97	97	1	4	0

ENGLAND Frederick Watson (Fred)
Born: Holmfirth, West Yorkshire, England, 11 July, 1923 — IF
Died: East Yorkshire, England, August, 2002

League Club	Source	Date Signed	Seasons Played	Apps	Subs	Gls
Halifax T	Huddersfield T (Am)	05/46	46-47	18	-	1

ENGLAND Harold Michael (Mike)
Born: Holywell, Flintshire, Wales, 2 December, 1941 — CD
Wales: 44/U23-11

League Club	Source	Date Signed	Seasons Played	Apps	Subs	Gls
Blackburn Rov	Jnr	04/59	59-65	165	0	21
Tottenham H	Tr	08/66	66-74	300	0	14
Cardiff C	Seattle Sounders (USA)	08/75	75	40	0	1

ENGLAND Michael (Mike)
Born: Kingswood, Avon, England, 4 January, 1961 — CD

League Club	Source	Date Signed	Seasons Played	Apps	Subs	Gls
Bristol Rov	App	01/79	78	1	0	0
Bristol Rov	Forest Green Rov	09/85	85	17	0	0

ENGLEFIELD Grahame William Elwyn
Born: Eltham, SE London, England, 21 September, 1931 — LH
Died: Whitstable, Kent, England, 5 February, 2003

League Club	Source	Date Signed	Seasons Played	Apps	Subs	Gls
Charlton Ath	Jnr	01/49				
Norwich C	Tr	05/54	55-56	22	-	0

ENGLISH Anthony Karl (Tony)
Born: Luton, England, 19 October, 1966 — M/D
England: Youth

League Club	Source	Date Signed	Seasons Played	Apps	Subs	Gls
Colchester U	Coventry C (App)	12/84	84-95	345	6	40

ENGLISH John (Jack)
Born: South Shields, Tyne and Wear, England, 19 March, 1923 — RW
Died: Northallerton, North Yorkshire, England, 18 November, 1985

League Club	Source	Date Signed	Seasons Played	Apps	Subs	Gls
Northampton T	Bristol C (Am)	10/46	47-59	302	-	135

ENGLISH Robert Harold (Bobby)
Born: Stockport, Greater Manchester, England, 19 April, 1939 — RH

League Club	Source	Date Signed	Seasons Played	Apps	Subs	Gls
Manchester U	Jnr	03/57				
Southport	Tr	11/61	61-62	20	-	0

ENGLISH Thomas Steven (Tommy)
Born: Cirencester, Gloucestershire, England, 18 October, 1961 — F
England: Youth

League Club	Source	Date Signed	Seasons Played	Apps	Subs	Gls
Coventry C	App	06/79	79-81	62	4	17
Leicester C	Tr	09/82	82-83	29	17	3
Rochdale	Tr	09/84	84	3	0	1
Plymouth Arg	Tr	09/84	84	0	4	1
Colchester U	Canberra C (AUS)	11/85	85-86	34	13	19
Colchester U	Bishops Stortford	10/89	89	12	1	3

ENGONGA Vincente Mate
Born: Barcelona, Spain, 20 October, 1969 — M
Spain: 14

League Club	Source	Date Signed	Seasons Played	Apps	Subs	Gls
Coventry C (L)	Real Oviedo (SPN)	02/03	02	5	3	0

ENGWELL Michael Leonard (Micky)
Born: Grays, Essex, England, 27 September, 1966 — F

League Club	Source	Date Signed	Seasons Played	Apps	Subs	Gls
Southend U	Jnr	08/84	84-85	7	2	3
Crewe Alex	Tr	10/86	86	0	2	0

ENNIS Mark
Born: Bradford, England, 6 January, 1962 — FB

League Club	Source	Date Signed	Seasons Played	Apps	Subs	Gls
Rochdale	Rochdale Joiners	11/83	83	1	0	0

ENNIS Paul Davis
Born: Manchester, England, 1 February, 1990 — LW

League Club	Source	Date Signed	Seasons Played	Apps	Subs	Gls
Stockport Co	Sch	07/08	08	0	2	0

ENOH Eyong Tarkang
Born: Kumba, Cameroon, 23 March, 1986 — DM
Cameroon: 51

League Club	Source	Date Signed	Seasons Played	Apps	Subs	Gls
Fulham (L)	Ajax (NED)	01/13	12	8	1	0

ENTWISTLE Robert Peter (Bobby)
Born: Bury, Greater Manchester, England, 6 October, 1938 — CF
Died: New Forest, Hampshire, England, March, 2000

League Club	Source	Date Signed	Seasons Played	Apps	Subs	Gls
Rochdale (Am)	Macclesfield T	03/59	58	1	-	0
Accrington Stan	Tr	09/60	60	2	-	0
Hartlepool U	Llandudno	10/64	64	14	-	3

ENTWISTLE Wayne Peter
Born: Bury, Greater Manchester, England, 6 August, 1958 — F
England: Youth

League Club	Source	Date Signed	Seasons Played	Apps	Subs	Gls
Bury	App	08/76	76-77	25	6	7
Sunderland	Tr	11/77	77-79	43	2	12

League Club	Source	Date Signed	Seasons Played	Apps	Subs	Gls
Leeds U	Tr	10/79	79	7	4	2
Blackpool	Tr	11/80	80-81	27	5	6
Crewe Alex	Tr	03/82	81	11	0	0
Wimbledon	Tr	07/82	82	4	5	3
Bury	Grays Ath	08/83	83-84	80	3	32
Carlisle U	Tr	06/85	85	8	1	2
Bolton W	Tr	10/85	85	5	3	0
Burnley	L	08/86	86	6	2	2
Stockport Co	Tr	10/86	86-87	38	11	8
Bury	Tr	08/88	88	0	2	0
Wigan Ath	Tr	10/88	88	24	5	6
Hartlepool U	Altrincham	09/89	89	2	0	0

EPESSE-TITI Steeve Gaston
Born: Bordeaux, France, 5 September, 1979 — CD

League Club	Source	Date Signed	Seasons Played	Apps	Subs	Gls
Wolverhampton W	Bordeaux (FRA)	08/00				
Exeter C	Tr	03/01	00	5	1	0

EPHGRAVE George Arthur
Born: Reading, England, 29 April, 1918 — G
Died: Guernsey, Channel Islands, 9 December, 2004

League Club	Source	Date Signed	Seasons Played	Apps	Subs	Gls
Aston Villa	Northfleet	10/36				
Swindon T	Tr	03/39	38	1	-	0
Southampton	Tr	09/46	46-47	36	-	0
Norwich C	Tr	07/48	48-50	5	-	0
Watford	Tr	08/51	51	4	-	0

EPHRAIM Hogan Phillip
Born: Islington, N London, England, 31 March, 1988 — LW
England: Youth

League Club	Source	Date Signed	Seasons Played	Apps	Subs	Gls
West Ham U	Sch	04/05				
Colchester U	L	11/06	06	5	16	1
Queens Park Rgrs	Tr	08/07	07-11	71	37	7
Leeds U	L	11/09	09	1	2	0
Charlton Ath	L	11/11	11	4	1	1
Bristol C	L	03/12	11	3	2	1
Peterborough U	L	11/13	13	6	2	0
Wycombe W		10/14	14	5	9	1

ERANIO Stefano
Born: Genoa, Italy, 29 December, 1966 — RW
Italy: 20

League Club	Source	Date Signed	Seasons Played	Apps	Subs	Gls
Derby Co	AC Milan (ITA)	07/97	97-00	83	12	7

ERIBENNE Chukwunyeaka Osondu (Chukki)
Born: Westminster, Central London, England, 2 November, 1980 — F

League Club	Source	Date Signed	Seasons Played	Apps	Subs	Gls
Coventry C	YT	01/98				
Bournemouth	Tr	07/00	00-02	12	35	1

ERIKSEN Christian Dannemann
Born: Middelfart, Denmark, 14 February, 1992 — M
Denmark: 53/U21-3/Youth

League Club	Source	Date Signed	Seasons Played	Apps	Subs	Gls
Tottenham H	Ajax (NED)	08/13	13-14	60	3	17

ERIKSSON Jan Jonas Jakub
Born: Sundsvall, Sweden, 24 August, 1967 — CD
Sweden: 36

League Club	Source	Date Signed	Seasons Played	Apps	Subs	Gls
Sunderland	Helsingborgs (SWE)	01/97	96	1	0	0

ERSKINE Emmanuel Jacob Kenneth (Jacob)
Born: Lambeth, S London, England, 13 January, 1989 — F

League Club	Source	Date Signed	Seasons Played	Apps	Subs	Gls
Dagenham & Red	Jnr	11/07				
Gillingham	Tr	08/09	09	0	4	0

ERTL Johannes Bruno (Johnny)
Born: Graz, Austria, 13 November, 1982 — DM
Austria: 7

League Club	Source	Date Signed	Seasons Played	Apps	Subs	Gls
Crystal Palace	FK Austria Wien (AUT)	07/08	08-09	32	13	0
Sheffield U	Tr	06/10	10-11	27	8	0
Portsmouth	Tr	10/12	12-14	60	20	2

ESAJAS Etienne
Born: Amsterdam, Netherlands, 4 November, 1984 — LW

League Club	Source	Date Signed	Seasons Played	Apps	Subs	Gls
Sheffield Wed	Vitesse Arnhem (NED)	08/07	07-09	28	32	5
Swindon T	Helmond Sport (NED)	07/11	11	2	4	0
Scunthorpe U		07/13	13	8	5	2

ESDAILLE Darren
Born: Manchester, England, 4 November, 1974 — FB/M

League Club	Source	Date Signed	Seasons Played	Apps	Subs	Gls
Doncaster Rov	Hyde U	01/97	96-97	37	3	1

ESDAILLE David
Born: Manchester, England, 22 July, 1963 — M

League Club	Source	Date Signed	Seasons Played	Apps	Subs	Gls
Wrexham	Winsford U	08/92	92	4	0	0
Bury	Tr	01/93	92	1	5	0
Doncaster Rov	Droylsden	08/97	97	10	3	0

ESHELBY Paul
Born: Sheffield, England, 29 May, 1970 — W

League Club	Source	Date Signed	Seasons Played	Apps	Subs	Gls
Exeter C	Endcliffe U	12/89	89-90	10	9	1
Scarborough	Tr	03/91	90	2	1	0

ESPARTERO Mario
Born: Frejus, France, 17 January, 1978 — M

League Club	Source	Date Signed	Seasons Played	Apps	Subs	Gls
Bolton W (L)	FC Metz (FRA)	02/02	01	0	3	0

ESPINOZA Roger Anibal
Born: Puerto Cortes, Honduras, 25 October, 1986 — DM
Honduras: 42

League Club	Source	Date Signed	Seasons Played	Apps	Subs	Gls
Wigan Ath	Sport'g Kansas C (USA)	01/13	12-14	19	23	2

ESSAM Connor
Born: Sheerness, Kent, England, 9 July, 1992 — CD

League Club	Source	Date Signed	Seasons Played	Apps	Subs	Gls
Gillingham	Sch	07/10	11	17	1	0
Crawley T	Tr	01/13	12-13	8	3	1

ESSANDOH Roy Kabina
Born: Belfast, Northern Ireland, 17 February, 1976 — F
Northern Ireland: Youth

League Club	Source	Date Signed	Seasons Played	Apps	Subs	Gls
Wycombe W	Rushden & D	02/01	00	8	5	0

ESSER Edward David (David)
Born: Altrincham, Greater Manchester, England, 20 June, 1957 — M

League Club	Source	Date Signed	Seasons Played	Apps	Subs	Gls
Everton	App	05/75				
Rochdale	Tr	07/77	77-81	169	11	24

ESSERS Pierre
Born: Maastricht, Netherlands, 20 February, 1959 — F

League Club	Source	Date Signed	Seasons Played	Apps	Subs	Gls
Walsall	RSC Charleroi (BEL)	09/91	91	1	0	0

ESSIEN Michael Kojo
Born: Accra, Ghana, 3 December, 1982 — M
Ghana: 58

League Club	Source	Date Signed	Seasons Played	Apps	Subs	Gls
Chelsea	Olymp Lyonnais (FRA)	08/05	05-13	150	18	17

ESSON Ryan John
Born: Aberdeen, Scotland, 19 March, 1980 — G
Scotland: U21-7/Youth

League Club	Source	Date Signed	Seasons Played	Apps	Subs	Gls
Shrewsbury T	Aberdeen	07/06	06	6	0	0
Hereford U	Tr	02/08	07	1	0	0

ETHERIDGE Brian George
Born: Northampton, England, 4 March, 1944 — IF
Died: Moulton, Northamptonshire, England, 26 March, 2011
England: Youth

League Club	Source	Date Signed	Seasons Played	Apps	Subs	Gls
Northampton T	Jnr	07/62	61-64	17	-	1
Brentford	Tr	02/66	65-66	22	0	2

ETHERIDGE Neil Leonard Dula
Born: Enfield, N London, England, 7 February, 1990 — G
Philippines: 44

League Club	Source	Date Signed	Seasons Played	Apps	Subs	Gls
Fulham	Sch	03/09				
Bristol Rov	L	09/12	12	12	0	0
Crewe Alex	L	11/13	13	4	0	0
Oldham Ath		10/14	14			
Charlton Ath	Tr	11/14	14	4	0	0

ETHERIDGE Richard Keith (Keith)
Born: Ivybridge, Devon, England, 14 May, 1944 — F/M

League Club	Source	Date Signed	Seasons Played	Apps	Subs	Gls
Plymouth Arg	St Blazey	07/66	66-67	30	1	5

ETHERIDGE Robert James (Bobby)
Born: Gloucester, England, 21 March, 1934 — WH/IF
Died: Gloucester, England, 4 April, 1988

League Club	Source	Date Signed	Seasons Played	Apps	Subs	Gls
Bristol C	Gloucester C	09/56	56-63	259	-	42

ETHERINGTON Craig
Born: Basildon, England, 16 September, 1979 — W

League Club	Source	Date Signed	Seasons Played	Apps	Subs	Gls
West Ham U	YT	07/97				
Halifax T	L	02/99	98	4	0	0
Plymouth Arg	L	03/00	99	4	1	0

ETHERINGTON Matthew
Born: Falmouth, Cornwall, England, 14 August, 1981 — LW
England: U21-3/Youth

League Club	Source	Date Signed	Seasons Played	Apps	Subs	Gls
Peterborough U	YT	08/98	96-99	43	8	6
Tottenham H	Tr	01/00	99-02	20	25	1
Bradford C	L	10/01	01	12	1	1
West Ham U	Tr	08/03	03-08	151	14	16
Stoke C	Tr	01/09	08-13	131	21	13

ETO'O Samuel
Born: Douala, Cameroon, 10 March, 1981 — F
Cameroon: 118/U23-6

League Club	Source	Date Signed	Seasons Played	Apps	Subs	Gls
Chelsea	Anzhi Makhachk'a (RUS)	08/13	13	16	5	9
Everton	Tr	08/14	14	8	6	3

ETUHU Dickson Paul
Born: Kano, Nigeria, 8 June, 1982 — M
Nigeria: 20

League Club	Source	Date Signed	Seasons Played	Apps	Subs	Gls
Manchester C	YT	12/99	01	11	1	0
Preston NE	Tr	01/02	01-05	100	34	17

League Club	Source	Date Signed	Seasons Played	Apps	Subs	Gls
Norwich C	Tr	11/05	05-06	57	5	6
Sunderland	Tr	07/07	07	18	2	1
Fulham	Tr	09/08	08-11	65	26	3
Blackburn Rov	Tr	08/12	12-13	19	4	1

ETUHU Kelvin Peter
Born: Kano, Nigeria, 30 May, 1988 M
England: Youth

League Club	Source	Date Signed	Seasons Played	Apps	Subs	Gls
Manchester C	Sch	11/05	07-09	4	6	1
Rochdale	L	01/07	06	3	1	2
Leicester C	L	03/08	07	2	2	0
Cardiff C	L	08/09	09	7	9	0
Portsmouth	Kavala (GRE)	03/12	11	9	4	1
Barnsley	Tr	06/12	12-13	33	13	0
Bury	Tr	06/14	14	43	0	2

EUELL Jason Joseph
Born: Lambeth, S London, England, 6 February, 1977 F/M
England: U21-6/Youth//Jamaica: 3

League Club	Source	Date Signed	Seasons Played	Apps	Subs	Gls
Wimbledon	YT	06/95	95-00	118	23	41
Charlton Ath	Tr	07/01	01-05	102	37	34
Middlesbrough	Tr	08/06	06	9	8	0
Southampton	Tr	08/07	07-08	49	13	5
Blackpool	Tr	07/09	09-10	24	12	4
Doncaster Rov	L	02/11	10	7	5	3
Charlton Ath	Tr	08/11	11	0	11	0
AFC Wimbledon	L	01/12	11	8	1	0

EUSTACE John Mark
Born: Solihull, West Midlands, England, 3 November, 1979 M

League Club	Source	Date Signed	Seasons Played	Apps	Subs	Gls
Coventry C	YT	11/96	99-02	62	24	7
Middlesbrough	L	01/03	02	0	1	0
Stoke C	Tr	08/03	03-07	55	19	5
Hereford U	L	10/06	06	8	0	0
Watford	Tr	01/08	07-12	143	14	16
Derby Co	L	03/09	08	6	3	1
Derby Co	Tr	07/13	13-14	41	7	2

EUSTACE Peter
Born: Stocksbridge, South Yorkshire, England, 31 July, 1944 M

League Club	Source	Date Signed	Seasons Played	Apps	Subs	Gls
Sheffield Wed	App	06/62	62-69	189	3	21
West Ham U	Tr	01/70	69-71	41	2	6
Rotherham U	L	03/72	71	6	0	1
Sheffield Wed	Tr	08/72	72-74	48	8	4
Peterborough U	Tr	07/75	75	42	1	5

EUSTACE Scott Douglas
Born: Leicester, England, 13 June, 1975 CD

League Club	Source	Date Signed	Seasons Played	Apps	Subs	Gls
Leicester C	YT	07/93	93	0	1	0
Mansfield T	Tr	06/95	95-97	90	8	6
Chesterfield	Tr	08/98				
Cambridge U	Tr	01/99	98-99	49	3	1
Lincoln C	Tr	07/00	00	0	1	0

EVANS Alex
Born: Treharris, Merthyr Tydfil, Wales, 17 September, 1992 CD
Wales: Youth

League Club	Source	Date Signed	Seasons Played	Apps	Subs	Gls
Cardiff C	Sch	05/11				
Oxford U	Tr	08/12	12	0	1	0

EVANS Allan James
Born: Polbeth, West Lothian, Scotland, 12 October, 1956 CD
Scotland: 4

League Club	Source	Date Signed	Seasons Played	Apps	Subs	Gls
Aston Villa	Dunfermline Ath	05/77	77-88	374	6	51
Leicester C	Tr	08/89	89	14	0	0
Darlington	Brisbane U (AUS)	03/91	90	0	1	0

EVANS Alun John
Born: Pencader, Carmarthenshire, Wales, 1 December, 1922 WH
Died: Worcester, England, January, 2008

League Club	Source	Date Signed	Seasons Played	Apps	Subs	Gls
West Bromwich A	Wilden	01/43	47	18	-	0

EVANS Alun William
Born: Kidderminster, Worcestershire, England, 30 September, 1949 F/M
England: U23-4/Youth/Schools

League Club	Source	Date Signed	Seasons Played	Apps	Subs	Gls
Wolverhampton W	App	10/66	67-68	20	2	4
Liverpool	Tr	09/68	68-71	77	2	21
Aston Villa	Tr	06/72	72-73	53	7	11
Walsall	Tr	12/75	75-77	78	9	7

EVANS Andrew Clive (Clive)
Born: Heswall, Wirral, England, 1 May, 1957 M

League Club	Source	Date Signed	Seasons Played	Apps	Subs	Gls
Tranmere Rov	App	05/75	76-80	175	3	26
Wigan Ath	Tr	07/81	81	29	3	2
Crewe Alex	Tr	08/82	82	26	2	7
Stockport Co	Tr	08/83	83-87	158	2	23
Lincoln C	Tr	09/87	88	42	0	2

EVANS Andrew David Stanley
Born: Swansea, Wales, 3 October, 1957 LW
Wales: U21-1/Youth/Schools

League Club	Source	Date Signed	Seasons Played	Apps	Subs	Gls
Bristol Rov	App	09/75	75-77	34	8	2

EVANS Anthony (Tony)
Born: Liverpool, England, 11 January, 1954 F

League Club	Source	Date Signed	Seasons Played	Apps	Subs	Gls
Blackpool	Formby	06/73	74	4	2	0
Cardiff C	Tr	06/75	75-78	120	4	47
Birmingham C	Tr	07/79	79-82	62	4	28
Crystal Palace	Tr	08/83	83	19	2	7
Wolverhampton W	Tr	06/84	84	20	3	5
Bolton W	L	02/85	84	4	0	0
Swindon T	Tr	08/85	85	8	2	0

EVANS Anthony William (Tony)
Born: Colchester, Essex, England, 14 March, 1960 W

League Club	Source	Date Signed	Seasons Played	Apps	Subs	Gls
Colchester U	App	03/78	77-80	21	9	2

EVANS Arthur
Born: Urmston, Greater Manchester, England, 13 May, 1933 G
England: Youth/Schools

League Club	Source	Date Signed	Seasons Played	Apps	Subs	Gls
Bury	Jnr	06/50	50	2	-	0
Stockport Co	Tr	08/52				
Gillingham	Tr	09/53	53-54	14	-	0

EVANS Bernard
Born: Chester, England, 4 January, 1937 CF

League Club	Source	Date Signed	Seasons Played	Apps	Subs	Gls
Wrexham	Saltney Jnrs	08/54	54-60	114	-	47
Queens Park Rgrs	Tr	10/60	60-62	78	-	35
Oxford U	Tr	12/62	62-63	13	-	3
Tranmere Rov	Tr	10/63	63	12	-	5

EVANS Bernard Royden (Roy)
Born: Rotherhithe, SE London, England, 7 October, 1929 IF

League Club	Source	Date Signed	Seasons Played	Apps	Subs	Gls
Millwall		03/50				
Watford	Tr	08/51	51	2	-	1

EVANS Brian Clifford
Born: Brynmawr, Blaenau Gwent, Wales, 2 December, 1942 W
Died: Swansea, Wales, 26 February, 2003
Wales: 7/U23-2

League Club	Source	Date Signed	Seasons Played	Apps	Subs	Gls
Swansea C	Abergavenny Thursday	07/63	63-72	340	3	57
Hereford U	Tr	08/73	73-74	44	4	9

EVANS Ceri Lee
Born: Christchurch, New Zealand, 2 October, 1963 CD
New Zealand: 56

League Club	Source	Date Signed	Seasons Played	Apps	Subs	Gls
Oxford U	Christchurch U (NZL)	02/89	88-92	113	3	3

EVANS Charles James (Charlie)
Born: West Bromwich, West Midlands, England, 4 February, 1923 IF
Died: Bromsgrove, Worcestershire, England, February, 1998

League Club	Source	Date Signed	Seasons Played	Apps	Subs	Gls
West Bromwich A	Cordley Victoria	08/41	46	1	-	0

EVANS Chedwyn Michael (Ched)
Born: Rhyl, Denbighshire, Wales, 28 December, 1988 F
Wales: 13/U21-13/Youth

League Club	Source	Date Signed	Seasons Played	Apps	Subs	Gls
Manchester C	Sch	07/07	08	3	13	1
Norwich C	L	11/07	07	20	8	10
Sheffield U	Tr	07/09	09-11	77	26	42

EVANS Christopher Brian (Chris)
Born: Ystrad Rhondda, Rhondda Cynon Taff, Wales, 13 October, 1962 RB

League Club	Source	Date Signed	Seasons Played	Apps	Subs	Gls
Arsenal	App	06/80				
Stoke C	Tr	08/81				
York C	Tr	08/82	82-85	93	3	1
Darlington	Tr	10/85	85-86	58	0	1

EVANS Corry John
Born: Belfast, Northern Ireland, 30 July, 1990 DM
Northern Ireland: 30/U21-10

League Club	Source	Date Signed	Seasons Played	Apps	Subs	Gls
Manchester U	Sch	08/07				
Carlisle U	L	10/10	10	1	0	0
Hull C	L	01/11	10	17	1	3
Hull C	Tr	05/11	11-12	61	14	3
Blackburn Rov	Tr	08/13	13-14	54	5	2

EVANS Darren
Born: Wolverhampton, England, 30 September, 1974 RB

League Club	Source	Date Signed	Seasons Played	Apps	Subs	Gls
Aston Villa	YT	07/93				
Hereford U	Tr	09/95	95	24	0	0

EVANS David (Dai)
Born: Colwyn Bay, Conwy, Wales, 19 June, 1934 G

League Club	Source	Date Signed	Seasons Played	Apps	Subs	Gls
Crewe Alex	Llandudno	03/57	56-59	48	-	0

EVANS David
Born: Chester, England, 4 April, 1967 RB

League Club	Source	Date Signed	Seasons Played	Apps	Subs	Gls
Chester C	Jnr	05/84	83-84	15	1	1

EVANS David Andrew (Andy)
Born: Aberystwyth, Ceredigion, Wales, 25 November, 1975 F
Wales: Youth

League Club	Source	Date Signed	Seasons Played	Apps	Subs	Gls
Cardiff C	YT	12/94	93-95	5	10	0
Barnsley	Aberystwyth T	09/99				
Mansfield T	L	03/00	99	4	2	0

EVANS David Douglas (Doug)
Born: Ystradgynlais, Powys, Wales, 27 September, 1956 W

League Club	Source	Date Signed	Seasons Played	Apps	Subs	Gls
Norwich C	App	08/74	76-79	14	4	1
Cambridge U	Tr	03/80	79-80	11	1	2

EVANS David Gordon
Born: West Bromwich, West Midlands, England, 20 May, 1958 CD

League Club	Source	Date Signed	Seasons Played	Apps	Subs	Gls
Aston Villa	App	02/76	78	2	0	0
Halifax T	Tr	06/79	79-83	218	0	9
Bradford C	Tr	06/84	84-89	222	1	3
Halifax T	Tr	08/90	90-91	68	5	1

EVANS David Thom (Dave)
Born: Peterlee, County Durham, England, 6 April, 1959 F

League Club	Source	Date Signed	Seasons Played	Apps	Subs	Gls
Hartlepool U		07/78	78-79	2	2	0

EVANS Dennis
Born: Chester, England, 23 July, 1935 LB

League Club	Source	Date Signed	Seasons Played	Apps	Subs	Gls
Wrexham		03/55	55-57	11	-	0
Tranmere Rov	Tr	06/58	58-59	3	-	0

EVANS Dennis Joseph
Born: Liverpool, England, 18 May, 1930 LB
Died: Southgate, N London, England, 23 February, 2000

League Club	Source	Date Signed	Seasons Played	Apps	Subs	Gls
Arsenal	Ellesmere Port T	01/51	53-59	189	-	10

EVANS Denzil Ralph (Ralph)
Born: Hungerford, Berkshire, England, 9 October, 1915 IF
Died: Langley, Berkshire, England, 20 February, 1996

League Club	Source	Date Signed	Seasons Played	Apps	Subs	Gls
Bury	Yeovil & Petters U	07/35				
Halifax T	Tr	07/36	36	21	-	1
Watford	Tr	07/37	37-47	88	-	30

EVANS Duncan Wayne (Wayne)
Born: Abermule, Powys, Wales, 25 August, 1971 FB

League Club	Source	Date Signed	Seasons Played	Apps	Subs	Gls
Walsall	Welshpool T	08/93	93-98	173	10	1
Rochdale	Tr	07/99	99-04	259	0	3

EVANS Elfed Ellison
Born: Ferndale, Rhondda Cynon Taff, Wales, 28 August, 1926 IF
Died: Burton-on-Trent, Staffordshire, England, 13 May, 1988

League Club	Source	Date Signed	Seasons Played	Apps	Subs	Gls
Cardiff C	Treharris	05/49	49-51	44	-	16
Torquay U	L	03/51	50	12	-	6
West Bromwich A	Tr	06/52	52	17	-	3
Wrexham	Tr	06/55	55-56	34	-	16
Southport	Tr	12/56	56	13	-	0

EVANS Emrys Brian
Born: Tonypandy, Rhondda Cynon Taff, Wales, 16 September, 1930 IF

League Club	Source	Date Signed	Seasons Played	Apps	Subs	Gls
Newport Co	Tottenham H (Am)	08/52	52	18	-	5

EVANS Frederick John (Fred)
Born: Petersfield, Hampshire, England, 20 May, 1923 IF

League Club	Source	Date Signed	Seasons Played	Apps	Subs	Gls
Portsmouth	Army	01/45	46	9	-	2
Notts Co	Tr	07/47	47-50	39	-	14
Crystal Palace	Tr	03/51	50-52	52	-	11
Rochdale	Tr	06/53	53	12	-	0

EVANS Gareth Charles (Gary)
Born: Stockport, Greater Manchester, England, 26 April, 1988 W

League Club	Source	Date Signed	Seasons Played	Apps	Subs	Gls
Macclesfield T	Crewe Alex (Sch)	08/07	07-08	55	27	19
Bradford C	Tr	07/09	09-10	66	13	14
Rotherham U	Tr	07/11	11-12	38	7	9
Fleetwood T	Tr	01/13	12-14	75	18	10

EVANS Gareth David
Born: Wrexham, Wales, 10 January, 1987 CD

League Club	Source	Date Signed	Seasons Played	Apps	Subs	Gls
Wrexham	Sch	08/06	06-07	19	6	0

EVANS Gareth John
Born: Coventry, England, 14 January, 1967 F

League Club	Source	Date Signed	Seasons Played	Apps	Subs	Gls
Coventry C	App	01/85	85-86	5	2	0
Rotherham U	Tr	10/86	86-87	62	1	13
Stoke C (L)	Hibernian	10/90	90	5	0	1
Northampton T (L)	Hibernian	12/90	90	2	0	0

EVANS Gareth Joseph
Born: Leeds, England, 15 February, 1981 LB
England: Youth

League Club	Source	Date Signed	Seasons Played	Apps	Subs	Gls
Leeds U	YT	03/98	00	0	1	0
Huddersfield T	Tr	08/01	01	35	0	0
Blackpool	Tr	08/03	03-04	43	2	0

EVANS Gary Lee
Born: Doncaster, South Yorkshire, England, 13 September, 1982 FB

League Club	Source	Date Signed	Seasons Played	Apps	Subs	Gls
Bury	Sch	03/03	01	1	0	0

EVANS Gary Neil
Born: Doncaster, South Yorkshire, England, 20 December, 1968 F

League Club	Source	Date Signed	Seasons Played	Apps	Subs	Gls
Chesterfield	Thorne Colliery	08/91	91	1	4	0

EVANS George
Born: Cheadle, Greater Manchester, England, 13 December, 1994 M
England: Youth

League Club	Source	Date Signed	Seasons Played	Apps	Subs	Gls
Manchester C	Sch	07/12				
Crewe Alex	L	10/13	13	22	1	1
Scunthorpe U	L	01/15	14	9	7	1

EVANS George Albert
Born: Rhostyllen, Wrexham, Wales, 6 July, 1935 LH
Died: Wrexham, Wales, December, 2000

League Club	Source	Date Signed	Seasons Played	Apps	Subs	Gls
Wrexham	Oswestry T	07/57	57-62	175	-	9
Chester C	Tr	06/63	63-68	109	4	0

EVANS Gwilym Hugh (Hugh)
Born: Ynysybwl, Rhondda Cynon Taff, Wales, 12 December, 1919 IF
Died: Wickford, Essex, England, 3 February, 2010

League Club	Source	Date Signed	Seasons Played	Apps	Subs	Gls
Birmingham C	Redditch T	12/47	48-49	11	-	0
Bournemouth	Tr	06/50	50	22	-	8
Walsall	Tr	08/51	51	36	-	12
Watford	Tr	08/52	52	7	-	2

EVANS Gwyn
Born: Ton Pentre, Rhondda Cynon Taff, Wales, 24 December, 1935 CD

League Club	Source	Date Signed	Seasons Played	Apps	Subs	Gls
Crystal Palace	Treorchy	03/55	58-62	80	-	0

EVANS Henry Alfred (Harry)
Born: Lambeth, S London, England, 17 April, 1919 IF
Died: St Pancras, Central London, England, 22 December, 1962

League Club	Source	Date Signed	Seasons Played	Apps	Subs	Gls
Southampton	Woking	10/43	46	1	-	0
Exeter C	Tr	04/47	47-48	41	-	6
Aldershot	Tr	03/49	48-49	16	-	5

EVANS Hubert William Richard
Born: Swansea, Wales, 10 August, 1922 WH

League Club	Source	Date Signed	Seasons Played	Apps	Subs	Gls
Swansea C	Jnr	08/39				
Newport Co	Lovells Ath	04/51	50-51	14	-	1

EVANS Ian Peter
Born: Egham, Surrey, England, 30 January, 1952 CD
Wales: 13/U23-2

League Club	Source	Date Signed	Seasons Played	Apps	Subs	Gls
Queens Park Rgrs	App	01/70	70-73	39	0	2
Crystal Palace	Tr	09/74	74-77	137	0	14
Barnsley	Tr	12/79	79-82	102	0	3
Exeter C	L	08/83	83	4	0	0
Cambridge U	L	10/83	83	1	0	0

EVANS Ivor James
Born: Cardiff, Wales, 25 October, 1933 IF

League Club	Source	Date Signed	Seasons Played	Apps	Subs	Gls
Portsmouth	GKN Sankey	09/56	56	1	-	0

EVANS Jack Peter
Born: Gravesend, Kent, England, 19 March, 1993 RB

League Club	Source	Date Signed	Seasons Played	Apps	Subs	Gls
Gillingham	Sch	07/11	11	4	3	0

EVANS Jason Stuart
Born: Cambridge, England, 22 January, 1974 FB

League Club	Source	Date Signed	Seasons Played	Apps	Subs	Gls
Shrewsbury T	YT	07/92	92	0	1	0

EVANS John
Born: Hetton-le-Hole, Tyne and Wear, England, 21 October, 1932 IF
Died: Durham, England, February, 2009

League Club	Source	Date Signed	Seasons Played	Apps	Subs	Gls
Norwich C	Jnr	10/49				
Sunderland	Tr	08/54	54	1	-	0
Chesterfield	Tr	05/56				

EVANS John Alwyn
Born: Aberystwyth, Ceredigion, Wales, 22 October, 1922 FB
Died: South West Essex, Essex, England, 24 February, 1956

League Club	Source	Date Signed	Seasons Played	Apps	Subs	Gls
Millwall	Aberystwyth	09/43	46-49	73	-	2
Leyton Orient	Tr	06/50	50-53	149	-	0

EVANS John Charles
Born: Torquay, Devon, England, 24 March, 1947 RW

League Club	Source	Date Signed	Seasons Played	Apps	Subs	Gls
Torquay U	App	04/65	64-66	6	1	1

EVANS John David (Johnny)
Born: Liverpool, England, 13 March, 1938 IF
Died: Liverpool, England, 6 January, 2004

League Club	Source	Date Signed	Seasons Played	Apps	Subs	Gls
Liverpool		05/58				
Bournemouth	Tr	05/59				
Stockport Co	Salisbury	10/62	62-63	52	-	20
Carlisle U	Tr	02/64	63-65	77	0	37

League Club	Source	Date Signed	Seasons Played	Apps	Subs	Gls
Exeter C	Tr	03/66	65-66	11	1	2
Barnsley	Tr	11/66	66-70	165	5	54

EVANS John David
Born: Chester, England, 24 March, 1941 — FB

League Club	Source	Date Signed	Seasons Played	Apps	Subs	Gls
Chester C		08/61	61-64	40	-	0

EVANS John Joseph (Jack)
Born: Coventry, England, 11 March, 1926 — CF
Died: Coventry, England, 15 April, 2012

League Club	Source	Date Signed	Seasons Played	Apps	Subs	Gls
Coventry C	Modern Machine Tools	06/47	48-50	8	-	1

EVANS John Llewellyn
Born: Wattstown, Rhondda Cynon Taff, Wales, 4 October, 1937 — RH

League Club	Source	Date Signed	Seasons Played	Apps	Subs	Gls
Gillingham	Lovells Ath	04/56	57	7	-	0

EVANS John Royston (Royston)
Born: Lampeter, Ceredigion, Wales, 9 February, 1939 — RW

League Club	Source	Date Signed	Seasons Played	Apps	Subs	Gls
Wolverhampton W	Bangor C	08/56				
Wrexham	Tr	07/57				
Chester C	Tr	10/57	57-59	23	-	3
Halifax T	Sankey's	10/60	60	7	-	0

EVANS John William
Born: Tilbury, Essex, England, 28 August, 1929 — IF
Died: Brentwood, Essex, England, August, 1999
England: FLge-1

League Club	Source	Date Signed	Seasons Played	Apps	Subs	Gls
Charlton Ath	Tilbury	05/50	50-53	90	-	38
Liverpool	Tr	12/53	53-56	96	-	49
Colchester U	Tr	11/57	57-59	56	-	22

EVANS Jonathan Grant (Jonny)
Born: Belfast, Northern Ireland, 3 January, 1987 — CD
Northern Ireland: 41/U21-3/Youth/Schools

League Club	Source	Date Signed	Seasons Played	Apps	Subs	Gls
Manchester U	Sch	04/05	08-14	123	8	4
Sunderland	L	01/07	06	18	0	1
Sunderland	L	01/08	07	15	0	0

EVANS Keith
Born: Trealaw, Rhondda Cynon Taff, Wales, 15 September, 1953 — CD

League Club	Source	Date Signed	Seasons Played	Apps	Subs	Gls
Swansea C	App	08/71	70-72	12	0	0

EVANS Kenneth Philip (Ken)
Born: Swansea, Wales, 17 July, 1931 — G
Died: Swansea, Wales, May, 2000

League Club	Source	Date Signed	Seasons Played	Apps	Subs	Gls
Swansea C	South Wales Builders	06/50	54-56	14	-	0
Walsall	Tr	08/57	57	2	-	0

EVANS Kevin Aherne
Born: Carmarthen, Wales, 16 December, 1980 — M
Wales: U21-4/Youth

League Club	Source	Date Signed	Seasons Played	Apps	Subs	Gls
Leeds U	YT	01/98				
Swansea C	L	01/00	99	1	1	0
Cardiff C	Tr	08/00	00	24	6	3

EVANS Lee
Born: Newport, Wales, 24 July, 1994 — M
Wales: U21-7/Youth

League Club	Source	Date Signed	Seasons Played	Apps	Subs	Gls
Wolverhampton W	Newport Co	01/13	13-14	36	8	3

EVANS Leslie Norman
Born: Kingswinford, West Midlands, England, 13 October, 1929 — LW
Died: Cardiff, Wales, April, 2007

League Club	Source	Date Signed	Seasons Played	Apps	Subs	Gls
Cardiff C	Brierley Hill Alliance	10/50	50-51	3	-	1
Plymouth Arg	Tr	06/52				

EVANS Leslie Thomas (Les)
Born: Ystrad Rhondda, Rhondda Cynon Taff, Wales, 26 December, 1924 — CH
Died: Cardiff, Wales, 5 October, 2002

League Club	Source	Date Signed	Seasons Played	Apps	Subs	Gls
Cardiff C		09/45				
Torquay U	L	07/47	47	24	-	0

EVANS Mark
Born: Leeds, England, 24 August, 1970 — G

League Club	Source	Date Signed	Seasons Played	Apps	Subs	Gls
Bradford C	YT	07/88	88-91	12	0	0
Scarborough	Tr	08/92	92-93	46	0	0

EVANS Mark Graham
Born: Chester, England, 16 September, 1982 — FB

League Club	Source	Date Signed	Seasons Played	Apps	Subs	Gls
Wrexham	Sch	07/02	01-02	0	5	0

EVANS Maurice George
Born: Didcot, Oxfordshire, England, 22 September, 1936 — WH
Died: Reading, England, 18 August, 2000

League Club	Source	Date Signed	Seasons Played	Apps	Subs	Gls
Reading	Jnr	09/53	55-66	407	0	13

EVANS Medwyn John
Born: Brynteg, Anglesey, Wales, 8 November, 1964 — M
Wales: Schools

League Club	Source	Date Signed	Seasons Played	Apps	Subs	Gls
Wrexham	Jnr	08/83	82-83	13	4	0

EVANS Micah
Born: Manchester, England, 3 March, 1993 — RW

League Club	Source	Date Signed	Seasons Played	Apps	Subs	Gls
Blackburn Rov	Sch	07/11				
Accrington Stan	L	10/11	11	14	9	3
Chesterfield	L	09/12	12	1	3	0
Burnley	Tr	10/13				

EVANS Michael (Micky)
Born: West Bromwich, West Midlands, England, 3 August, 1946 — LB

League Club	Source	Date Signed	Seasons Played	Apps	Subs	Gls
Walsall	Vono Sports	05/64	65-72	229	2	7
Swansea C	Tr	12/72	72-74	92	0	6
Crewe Alex	Tr	07/75	75-76	62	0	4

EVANS Michael
Born: Venlo, Netherlands, 21 July, 1976 — F

League Club	Source	Date Signed	Seasons Played	Apps	Subs	Gls
York C	VVV Venlo (NED)	09/01	01	1	1	0

EVANS Michael Graham (Mickey)
Born: Llanidloes, Powys, Wales, 4 June, 1947 — D
Wales: U23-2/Schools

League Club	Source	Date Signed	Seasons Played	Apps	Subs	Gls
Wolverhampton W	App	07/64				
Wrexham	Tr	07/66	66-78	368	15	19

EVANS Michael James (Mickey)
Born: Plymouth, England, 1 January, 1973 — F
Republic of Ireland: 1

League Club	Source	Date Signed	Seasons Played	Apps	Subs	Gls
Plymouth Arg	YT	03/91	90-96	130	33	38
Southampton	Tr	03/97	96-97	14	8	4
West Bromwich A	Tr	10/97	97-99	35	28	6
Bristol Rov	Tr	08/00	00	19	2	4
Plymouth Arg	Tr	03/01	00-05	179	42	34
Torquay U	Tr	07/06	06	14	0	1

EVANS Nicholas (Nick)
Born: Trimdon, County Durham, England, 23 November, 1925 — W
Died: Hartlepool, Cleveland, England, December, 1992

League Club	Source	Date Signed	Seasons Played	Apps	Subs	Gls
New Brighton (Am)	Hesleden	03/47	46	1	-	0

EVANS Nicholas Andrew (Nicky)
Born: Carmarthen, Wales, 12 May, 1980 — M

League Club	Source	Date Signed	Seasons Played	Apps	Subs	Gls
Hartlepool U	YT	07/98	98	0	1	0

EVANS Nicholas John (Nicky)
Born: Bedford, England, 6 July, 1958 — F

League Club	Source	Date Signed	Seasons Played	Apps	Subs	Gls
Queens Park Rgrs	App	07/76				
Peterborough U	Tr	08/77				
Barnet	Wycombe W	01/91	91-93	16	23	8

EVANS Oswald Vernon
Born: Llanelli, Carmarthenshire, Wales, 2 September, 1916 — G
Died: Blackburn, Greater Manchester, England, May, 1986

League Club	Source	Date Signed	Seasons Played	Apps	Subs	Gls
Fulham	Milford Haven	02/46	46	1	-	0

EVANS Paul
Born: Kiveton Park, South Yorkshire, England, 24 February, 1949 — G

League Club	Source	Date Signed	Seasons Played	Apps	Subs	Gls
Sheffield Wed	Jnr	02/66				
Mansfield T	Boston U	10/75	75	6	0	0

EVANS Paul Alan
Born: Blackwood, Caerphilly, Wales, 14 September, 1964 — F

League Club	Source	Date Signed	Seasons Played	Apps	Subs	Gls
Cardiff C	Jnr	09/82	83	0	2	0
Newport Co	Brecon Corinthians	07/87	87	9	1	2

EVANS Paul Anthony
Born: Newcastle, South Africa, 28 December, 1973 — G
South Africa: U23-8

League Club	Source	Date Signed	Seasons Played	Apps	Subs	Gls
Leeds U	Wits Univ (RSA)	12/95				
Sheffield Wed	Jomo Cosmos (RSA)	08/02	02	7	0	0
Rushden & D	Tr	10/03	03	2	0	0

EVANS Paul Simon
Born: Oswestry, Shropshire, England, 1 September, 1974 — M
Wales: 2/U21-1/Youth

League Club	Source	Date Signed	Seasons Played	Apps	Subs	Gls
Shrewsbury T	YT	07/93	91-98	178	20	26
Brentford	Tr	03/99	98-01	130	0	31
Bradford C	Tr	08/02	02-03	36	6	5
Blackpool	L	01/03	02	10	0	1
Nottingham F	Tr	03/04	03-04	42	5	4
Rotherham U	L	11/05	05	4	0	0
Swindon T	Tr	08/06	06	11	4	3
Bradford C	Tr	08/07	07	19	6	0

EVANS Philip (Phil)
Born: Swansea, Wales, 14 May, 1957 — CD

League Club	Source	Date Signed	Seasons Played	Apps	Subs	Gls
Swansea C	Jnr	08/75	75	10	0	0

EVANS Raphale Mondale (Rapha)
Born: Manchester, England, 7 May, 1990 — CD

League Club	Source	Date Signed	Seasons Played	Apps	Subs	Gls
Rochdale	Sch	07/08	07	1	0	0

EVANS Raymond (Ray)
Born: Mansfield, Nottinghamshire, England, 27 November, 1927 — CF
Died: Mansfield, Nottinghamshire, England, 7 January, 2010

League Club	Source	Date Signed	Seasons Played	Apps	Subs	Gls
Coventry C		05/48				
Mansfield T	Stafford Rgrs	11/49	49-52	39	-	12

EVANS Raymond Frederick (Ray)
Born: Carlisle, Cumbria, England, 8 October, 1929 — G
Died: South Cheshire, England, 26 November, 2005

League Club	Source	Date Signed	Seasons Played	Apps	Subs	Gls
Crewe Alex	Hightown YC	10/48	48-50	20	-	0
Stoke C	Tr	04/54				
Crewe Alex	Tr	08/55				

EVANS Raymond Leslie (Ray)
Born: Edmonton, N London, England, 20 September, 1949 — RB
England: Youth

League Club	Source	Date Signed	Seasons Played	Apps	Subs	Gls
Tottenham H	App	06/67	68-74	130	4	2
Millwall	Tr	01/75	74-76	74	0	3
Fulham	Tr	03/77	76-78	86	0	6
Stoke C	Tr	08/79	79-81	94	0	1

EVANS Raymond Peter (Ray)
Born: Preston, Lancashire, England, 21 June, 1933 — IF
Died: Chorley, Lancashire, England, 26 June, 2009

League Club	Source	Date Signed	Seasons Played	Apps	Subs	Gls
Preston NE	Jnr	05/51	53-56	33	-	2
Bournemouth	Tr	06/59	59-60	36	-	9

EVANS Reginald (Reg)
Born: Consett, County Durham, England, 18 March, 1939 — LW

League Club	Source	Date Signed	Seasons Played	Apps	Subs	Gls
Newcastle U	Jnr	03/56	58	4	-	0
Charlton Ath	Tr	03/59	58-59	14	-	2

EVANS Reuben
Born: Dublin, Republic of Ireland, 19 March, 1941 — IF

League Club	Source	Date Signed	Seasons Played	Apps	Subs	Gls
Bradford Park Ave	Glasgow Rangers	06/63	63	13	-	5

EVANS Rhys Karl
Born: Swindon, England, 27 January, 1982 — G
England: U21-2/Youth/Schools

League Club	Source	Date Signed	Seasons Played	Apps	Subs	Gls
Chelsea	YT	02/99				
Bristol Rov	L	02/00	99	4	0	0
Queens Park Rgrs	L	11/01	01	11	0	0
Leyton Orient	L	08/02	02	7	0	0
Swindon T	Tr	07/03	03-05	118	0	0
Blackpool	Tr	07/06	06	32	0	0
Bradford C	L	10/07	07	4	0	0
Millwall	Tr	01/08	07	21	0	0
Bradford C	Tr	08/08	08	45	0	0
Bristol Rov	Tr	08/09	09	3	0	0
Southend U	Tr	08/10	10	13	0	0
Exeter C	Staines T	07/12	12	4	1	0

EVANS Richard Glyn
Born: Cardiff, Wales, 19 June, 1983 — W

League Club	Source	Date Signed	Seasons Played	Apps	Subs	Gls
Birmingham C	Sch	07/02				
Sheffield Wed	Tr	03/03	02-03	8	2	1
Shrewsbury T	Tr	01/06	05	2	4	0

EVANS Richard William
Born: Ebbw Vale, Blaenau Gwent, Wales, 12 April, 1968 — W

League Club	Source	Date Signed	Seasons Played	Apps	Subs	Gls
Bristol Rov	Weymouth	08/91	91-93	9	6	1
Exeter C	L	10/92	92	5	0	2

EVANS Robert (Bobby)
Born: Glasgow, Scotland, 16 July, 1927 — CH
Died: Airdrie, Lanarkshire, Scotland, 1 September, 2001
Scotland: 48/SLge-25

League Club	Source	Date Signed	Seasons Played	Apps	Subs	Gls
Chelsea	Glasgow Celtic	05/60	60	32	-	0
Newport Co	Tr	06/61	61	31	-	0

EVANS Ronald (Ron)
Born: St Helens, Merseyside, England, 21 February, 1929 — WH

League Club	Source	Date Signed	Seasons Played	Apps	Subs	Gls
Stockport Co	Bolton W (Am)	07/50	50-53	6	-	0

EVANS Roy Quintin Echlin
Born: Crosby, Merseyside, England, 4 October, 1948 — LB
England: Schools

League Club	Source	Date Signed	Seasons Played	Apps	Subs	Gls
Liverpool	App	10/65	69-73	9	0	0

EVANS Royston Sidney (Roy)
Born: Swansea, Wales, 5 July, 1943 — RB
Died: Blackwood, Caerphilly, Wales, July, 1969
Wales: 1/U23-3

League Club	Source	Date Signed	Seasons Played	Apps	Subs	Gls
Swansea C	Jnr	07/60	62-67	212	2	7

EVANS Stephen James (Steve)
Born: Blackwood, Caerphilly, Wales, 25 September, 1980 — M
Wales: U21-2/Youth

League Club	Source	Date Signed	Seasons Played	Apps	Subs	Gls
Crystal Palace	YT	10/98	98-00	0	6	0
Swansea C	L	11/01	01	4	0	0
Brentford	Tr	03/02	02-03	34	14	5

EVANS Steven James (Steve)
Born: Wrexham, Wales, 26 February, 1979 — CD
Wales: 7

League Club	Source	Date Signed	Seasons Played	Apps	Subs	Gls
Wrexham	The New Saints	08/06	06-07	64	2	5

EVANS Stewart John
Born: Maltby, South Yorkshire, England, 15 November, 1960 — F

League Club	Source	Date Signed	Seasons Played	Apps	Subs	Gls
Rotherham U	App	11/78				
Sheffield U	Gainsborough Trinity	11/80				
Wimbledon	Tr	03/82	81-85	165	10	50
West Bromwich A	Tr	08/86	86	13	1	1
Plymouth Arg	Tr	03/87	86-88	36	9	10
Rotherham U	Tr	11/88	88-90	45	20	14
Torquay U	L	03/91	90	15	0	5
Crewe Alex	Tr	09/91	91-93	74	9	12

EVANS Terence (Terry)
Born: Pontypridd, Rhondda Cynon Taff, Wales, 8 January, 1976 — D
Wales: U21-4

League Club	Source	Date Signed	Seasons Played	Apps	Subs	Gls
Cardiff C	YT	07/94	93-95	12	2	0
Swansea C	Barry T	10/01	01-02	41	2	0

EVANS Terence William (Terry)
Born: Hammersmith, W London, England, 12 April, 1965 — CD

League Club	Source	Date Signed	Seasons Played	Apps	Subs	Gls
Brentford	Hillingdon Bor	07/85	85-92	228	1	23
Wycombe W	Tr	08/93	93-96	128	8	15

EVANS Thomas Raymond (Tom)
Born: Doncaster, South Yorkshire, England, 31 December, 1976 — G
Northern Ireland: Youth

League Club	Source	Date Signed	Seasons Played	Apps	Subs	Gls
Sheffield U	YT	07/95				
Crystal Palace	Tr	06/96				
Scunthorpe U	Tr	08/97	97-05	244	1	0

EVANS William Emmanuel (Billy)
Born: Birmingham, England, 5 September, 1921 — IF
Died: Grimsby, North Lincolnshire, England, August, 1960

League Club	Source	Date Signed	Seasons Played	Apps	Subs	Gls
Aston Villa	Linread Works	09/46	46-48	7	-	3
Notts Co	Tr	06/49	49-52	96	-	14
Gillingham	Tr	07/53	53-54	89	-	12
Grimsby T	Tr	06/55	55-57	102	-	28

EVANS William George (Will)
Born: Cricklade, Gloucestershire, England, 19 October, 1991 — M

League Club	Source	Date Signed	Seasons Played	Apps	Subs	Gls
Swindon T	Sch	07/10				
Hereford U	L	08/11	11	3	1	0
Hereford U	Tr	01/12	11	18	3	5

EVANS Wyndham Edgar
Born: Llanelli, Carmarthenshire, Wales, 19 March, 1951 — RB

League Club	Source	Date Signed	Seasons Played	Apps	Subs	Gls
Swansea C	Stoke C (Am)	02/71	70-82	348	4	20
Swansea C	Llanelli	12/83	83-84	35	2	0

EVANSON John Michael
Born: Newcastle-under-Lyme, Potteries, England, 10 May, 1947 — M

League Club	Source	Date Signed	Seasons Played	Apps	Subs	Gls
Oxford U	Towcester	02/65	66-73	144	10	10
Blackpool	Tr	02/74	73-75	63	4	0
Fulham	Miami Toros (USA)	08/76	76-78	84	11	5
Bournemouth	Tr	07/79	79-80	52	1	2

EVATT Ian Ross
Born: Coventry, England, 19 November, 1981 — CD

League Club	Source	Date Signed	Seasons Played	Apps	Subs	Gls
Derby Co	YT	12/98	00-02	19	15	0
Northampton T	L	08/01	01	10	1	0
Chesterfield	Tr	08/03	03-04	84	0	9
Queens Park Rgrs	Tr	06/05	05	21	6	0
Blackpool	Tr	08/06	06-12	221	9	9
Chesterfield	Tr	07/13	13-14	73	1	2

EVE Angus
Born: Carenage, Trinidad, 23 February, 1972 — M
Trinidad And Tobago: 117

League Club	Source	Date Signed	Seasons Played	Apps	Subs	Gls
Chester C	Joe Public (TRD)	12/99	99	9	5	4

EVELEIGH Gordon Ernest
Born: Lymington, Hampshire, England, 26 July, 1922 — LW
Died: Southampton, England, May, 2008

League Club	Source	Date Signed	Seasons Played	Apps	Subs	Gls
Bristol C	Guildford C	05/48	48	2	-	0

EVERALL William Frederick (Bill)
Born: Nantwich, Cheshire, England, 18 July, 1928 — LB

League Club	Source	Date Signed	Seasons Played	Apps	Subs	Gls
Crewe Alex		08/53	53	1	-	0

EVERETT Harold
Born: Worksop, Nottinghamshire, England, 9 June, 1922 — LB
Died: Mansfield, Nottinghamshire, England, July, 2000

League Club	Source	Date Signed	Seasons Played	Apps	Subs	Gls
Notts Co	Rufford Colliery	04/43				
Mansfield T	Tr	09/46	46	15	-	0

League Club	Source	Date Signed	Seasons Played	Career Record Apps	Subs	Gls

EVERETT Harry
Born: Worksop, Nottinghamshire, England, 11 November, 1920 — WH
Died: Mansfield, Nottinghamshire, England, 29 August, 1998

Mansfield T	Warsop Main	08/45	46	3	-	0

EVERETT Michael (Mike)
Born: Mile End, E London, England, 21 March, 1958 — F

Leyton Orient	Crystal Palace (App)	03/76	75	0	1	0

EVERINGHAM Nicholas Peter (Nick)
Born: Hull, England, 1 November, 1973 — M

Oldham Ath	YT	07/92				
Halifax T	Tr	02/93	92	2	0	0

EVERITT Michael Dennis (Mike)
Born: Weeley, Essex, England, 16 January, 1941 — LB

Arsenal	Jnr	02/58	59-60	9	-	1
Northampton T	Tr	02/61	60-66	206	1	15
Plymouth Arg	Tr	03/67	66-67	29	0	0
Brighton & HA	Tr	07/68	68-69	24	3	1

EVERITT Richard Ewart
Born: Carlisle, Cumbria, England, 3 May, 1922 — W
Died: Rotherham, South Yorkshire, England, 18 May, 2012

Darlington	Sheffield Wed (Am)	07/45	46	1	-	0

EVERS Sean Anthony
Born: Hitchin, Hertfordshire, England, 10 October, 1977 — M

Luton T	YT	05/96	95-98	43	9	6
Reading	Tr	03/99	98-99	8	10	0
Plymouth Arg	Tr	03/01	00-01	5	9	0

EVERSHAM Paul Jonathan
Born: Hereford, England, 28 January, 1975 — M

Hereford U	YT	07/93	93-94	6	7	1

EVERSON Benjamin John (Ben)
Born: Middlesbrough, England, 11 February, 1987 — F

York C	Breidablik (ICE)	01/13	12	0	2	0

EVES John Robert
Born: Sunderland, England, 28 February, 1922 — FB
Died: Sunderland, England, November, 2007

Sunderland	Monks Central OB	11/41				
Darlington	Tr	09/46	46-51	176	-	1

EVES Melvyn James (Mel)
Born: Wednesbury, West Midlands, England, 10 September, 1956 — F
England: B-3/Schools

Wolverhampton W	Jnr	07/75	77-83	169	11	44
Huddersfield T	L	03/84	83	7	0	4
Sheffield U	Tr	12/84	84-85	25	1	10
Gillingham	Tr	08/86	86-87	19	8	9
Mansfield T	L	10/87	87	3	0	0

EVINA-SI David Cedric Yannick (Cedric)
Born: Cameroon, 16 November, 1991 — LB

Arsenal	Sch	07/09				
Oldham Ath	Tr	10/10	10	24	3	2
Charlton Ath	Tr	07/11	11-13	16	7	0
Doncaster Rov	Tr	07/14	14	17	2	0

EVRA Patrice Latyr
Born: Dakar, Senegal, 15 May, 1981 — LB
France: 66/U21-11

Manchester U	AS Monaco (FRA)	01/06	05-13	265	8	7

EVTIMOV Dimitar Ivanov
Born: Pleven, Bulgaria, 7 September, 1993 — G
Bulgaria: U21-4/Youth

Nottingham F	Sch	04/13	13	0	1	0
Mansfield T	L	08/14	14	10	0	0

EVTUSHOK Aleksandr (Alex)
Born: Kiev, Ukraine, 11 January, 1970 — D
Ukraine: 6

Coventry C	Karpaty Lviv (UKR)	02/97	96	3	0	0

EWING David (Dave)
Born: Logierait, Perthshire, Scotland, 10 May, 1929 — CH
Died: Manchester, England, July, 1999

Manchester C	Luncarty Jnrs	06/49	52-61	279	-	1
Crewe Alex	Tr	07/62	62-63	48	-	0

EWING Thomas (Tommy)
Born: Larkhall, Lanarkshire, Scotland, 2 May, 1937 — RW
Scotland: 2/SLge-1

Aston Villa	Partick Thistle	02/62	61-63	39	-	4

League Club	Source	Date Signed	Seasons Played	Career Record Apps	Subs	Gls

EWING Thomas McCall Halliday (Tommy)
Born: Musselburgh, East Lothian, Scotland, 8 August, 1934 — LH

Doncaster Rov	Dunfermline Ath	08/51	51-57	39	-	6

EXLEY William
Born: Bradford, England, 2 May, 1924 — G
Died: Bradford, England, 13 April, 1997

Bradford C (Am)	Goole T	08/52	52	2	-	0

EYDELIE Jean-Jacques
Born: Angouleme, France, 3 February, 1966 — M

Walsall (L)	Sion (FRA)	03/98	97	10	1	0

EYJOLFSSON Holmar Orn
Born: Saudarkrokur, Iceland, 6 August, 1990 — CD
Iceland: 1/U21-27/Youth

West Ham U	HK Kopavagur (ICE)	07/08				
Cheltenham T	L	10/09	09	4	0	0

EYJOLFSSON Sigurdur Ragnar (Siggi)
Born: Reykjavik, Iceland, 1 December, 1973 — F
Iceland: Youth

Walsall	IA Akranes (ICE)	01/99	98-99	1	22	2
Chester C	L	01/00	99	9	0	3

EYRE Ernest Leslie (Les)
Born: Ilkeston, Derbyshire, England, 7 January, 1922 — IF
Died: Norwich, England, 19 November, 1991

Norwich C	Cardiff C (Am)	07/46	46-51	185	-	58
Bournemouth	Tr	11/51	51-52	38	-	10

EYRE John Robert
Born: Hull, England, 9 October, 1974 — M/F

Oldham Ath	YT	07/93	93-94	4	6	1
Scunthorpe U	L	12/94	94	9	0	8
Scunthorpe U	Tr	07/95	95-98	151	13	43
Hull C	Tr	07/99	99-00	43	9	13
Oldham Ath	Tr	07/01	01-04	98	20	14

EYRE Richard Paul
Born: Poynton, Cheshire, England, 15 September, 1976 — M

Port Vale	YT	06/95	97-00	26	22	1
Macclesfield T	Tr	08/01	01	12	2	0

EYRE Stanley Frederick (Fred)
Born: Manchester, England, 3 February, 1944 — FB

Manchester C	App	07/61				
Lincoln C	Tr	07/63				
Crewe Alex	Tr	08/64				
Bradford Park Ave	Chadderton	12/69	69	1	0	0

EYRES David
Born: Liverpool, England, 26 February, 1964 — LW

Blackpool	Rhyl	08/89	89-92	147	11	38
Burnley	Tr	07/93	93-97	171	4	37
Preston NE	Tr	10/97	97-00	85	23	19
Oldham Ath	Tr	10/00	00-05	187	20	33

League Club	Source	Date Signed	Seasons Played	Apps	Subs	Gls
FABBRINI Diego						
Born: Pisa, Italy, 31 July, 1990						F/W
Italy: 1/U21-12						
Watford	Udinese (ITA)	07/13	13-14	10	13	1
Millwall	L	01/15	14	11	1	1
Birmingham C	L	03/15	14	5	0	0
FABIANO Nicolas						
Born: Paris, France, 8 February, 1981						M
France: Youth						
Swansea C (L)	Paris St-Germain (FRA)	02/01	00	12	4	1
FABIANSKI Lukasz						
Born: Kostrzyn, Poland, 18 April, 1985						G
Poland: 24						
Arsenal	Legia Warsaw (POL)	07/07	07-13	31	1	0
Swansea C	Tr	07/14	14	37	0	0
[FABIO] DA SILVA Fabio Pereira						
Born: Rio de Janeiro, Brazil, 9 July, 1990						FB
Brazil: 2/Youth						
Manchester U	Fluminense (BRA)	08/08	09-13	9	13	1
Queens Park Rgrs	L	08/12	12	13	8	0
Cardiff C	Tr	01/14	13-14	35	6	0
FABREGAS Francesco (Cesc)						
Born: Barcelona, Spain, 4 May, 1987						M
Spain: 97/U21/Youth						
Arsenal	Sch	09/04	04-10	190	22	35
Chelsea	Barcelona (SPN)	06/14	14	33	1	3
FACEY Delroy Michael						
Born: Huddersfield, West Yorkshire, England, 22 April, 1980						F
Grenada: 15						
Huddersfield T	YT	05/97	96-01	40	35	15
Bolton W	Tr	07/02	02-03	1	9	1
Bradford C	L	11/02	02	6	0	1
Burnley	L	09/03	03	12	2	5
West Bromwich A	Tr	01/04	03	2	7	0
Hull C	Tr	07/04	04	12	9	4
Huddersfield T	L	02/05	04	4	0	0
Oldham Ath	Tr	03/05	04	1	5	0
Tranmere Rov	Tr	08/05	05	30	7	8
Rotherham U	Tr	07/06	06	37	3	10
Gillingham	Tr	07/07	07	27	5	3
Wycombe W	L	03/08	07	4	2	1
Notts Co	Tr	08/08	08-09	51	12	11
Lincoln C	L	11/09	09	9	1	1
Lincoln C	Tr	07/10	10	26	6	3
Hereford U	Tr	07/11	11	32	8	6
FACEY Kenneth William (Ken)						
Born: Hackney, E London, England, 12 October, 1927						RH/IF
Died: Colchester, Essex, England, 25 July, 2008						
Leyton Orient	Leyton	06/52	52-60	301	-	74
FADIDA Aharon						
Born: Haifa, Israel, 20 September, 1961						F
Aldershot	Hapoel Haifa (ISR)	12/85	85-86	9	5	6
FADIGA Khalilou						
Born: Dakar, Senegal, 30 December, 1974						M
Senegal: 38						
Bolton W	Inter Milan (ITA)	10/04	04-05	5	8	1
Derby Co	L	09/05	05	2	2	0
Coventry C	Al-Wakrah (QAT)	02/07	06	1	5	0
FAE Emerse						
Born: Nantes, France, 24 January, 1984						M
Ivory Coast: 46//France: U21/Youth						
Reading	FC Nantes (FRA)	08/07	07	3	5	0
FAERBER Winston						
Born: Paramaribo, Suriname, 27 March, 1971						RB
Cardiff C	ADO Den Haag (NED)	08/99	99	31	2	1
FAGAN Bernard						
Born: Houghton-le-Spring, Tyne and Wear, England, 29 January, 1949						LW
Sunderland	App	02/66				
Northampton T	Tr	07/69	69	6	0	0
FAGAN Christopher James (Kit)						
Born: Manchester, England, 5 June, 1950						D
Liverpool	Jnr	07/70	70	1	0	0
Tranmere Rov	Tr	10/71	71-74	77	7	2
FAGAN Christopher Joseph (Christy)						
Born: Dublin, Republic of Ireland, 11 May, 1989						F
Republic of Ireland: U21-3/Youth						
Manchester U	Sch	07/06				
Lincoln C	Glenn Hoddle Academy	06/09	09	10	3	3
FAGAN Craig Anthony						
Born: Birmingham, England, 11 December, 1982						F/W
Birmingham C	YT	12/01	02	0	1	0
Bristol C	L	01/03	02	5	1	1
Colchester U	Tr	08/03	03-04	55	8	17
Hull C	Tr	02/05	04-06	67	13	15
Derby Co	Tr	01/07	06-07	29	10	1
Hull C	Tr	03/08	07-10	43	17	5
Bradford C	Tr	09/11	11	29	2	7
Bury		02/13	12	9	2	1
Gillingham		11/13	13	12	6	2
FAGAN Fionan Richard (Paddy)						
Born: Dublin, Republic of Ireland, 7 June, 1930						W
Died: Manchester, England, 19 November, 2014						
Republic of Ireland: 8/B-1						
Hull C	Transport (ROI)	03/51	51-53	26	-	2
Manchester C	Tr	12/53	53-59	153	-	34
Derby Co	Tr	03/60	59-60	24	-	6
FAGAN George						
Born: Dundee, Scotland, 27 September, 1934						LH/FB
Leeds U	Dundee St Joseph	11/53				
Halifax T	Tr	06/58	58-61	67	-	3
FAGAN Joseph (Joe)						
Born: Liverpool, England, 12 March, 1921						CH
Died: Liverpool, England, 1 July, 2001						
Manchester C	Earlestown Bohemians	10/38	46-50	148	-	2
Bradford Park Ave	Nelson	08/53	53	3	-	0
FAGAN Michael Jeffrey (Mike)						
Born: Newcastle-upon-Tyne, England, 22 June, 1960						CD
Hartlepool U	Carlisle U (NC)	08/79	79-82	36	1	1
FAGAN William (Willie)						
Born: Musselburgh, East Lothian, Scotland, 20 February, 1917						IF
Died: Wellingborough, Northamptonshire, England, 20 February, 1992						
Scotland: War-1						
Preston NE	Glasgow Celtic	10/36	36-37	35	-	6
Liverpool	Tr	10/37	37-51	158	-	47
FAHEY Keith Declan						
Born: Dublin, Republic of Ireland, 15 January, 1983						M
Republic of Ireland: 16/Youth						
Aston Villa	Arsenal (Sch)	04/00				
Birmingham C	St Patricks Ath (ROI)	01/09	08-12	91	30	9
FAHY Alan						
Born: Liverpool, England, 27 January, 1972						M
Doncaster Rov	Barrow	03/97	96	0	5	0
FAHY John Joseph						
Born: Paisley, Renfrewshire, Scotland, 13 May, 1943						CF
Oxford U	Bedford T	01/64	63-65	23	0	14
FAIRBROTHER Barrie Edward						
Born: Hackney, E London, England, 30 December, 1950						F
Leyton Orient	App	01/69	69-74	171	17	41
Millwall	Tr	06/74	75-76	12	3	1
FAIRBROTHER Ian Andrew						
Born: Bootle, Merseyside, England, 2 October, 1966						M
England: Schools						
Liverpool	App	07/84				
Bury	Tr	02/87	86-87	16	10	3
Wrexham	L	10/87	87	7	0	0
FAIRBROTHER John (Jack)						
Born: Burton-on-Trent, Staffordshire, England, 16 August, 1917						G
Died: Oundle, Northamptonshire, England, October, 1999						
England: FLge-1						
Preston NE	Burton T	03/37	46	41	-	0
Newcastle U	Tr	07/47	47-51	132	-	0

FAIRBROTHER John
Born: Cricklewood, NW London, England, 12 February, 1941 — CF

League Club	Source	Date Signed	Seasons Played	Apps	Subs	Gls
Watford	Bennetts End	08/59	60-62	40	-	19
Peterborough U	Worcester C	05/65	65-67	69	3	37
Northampton T	Tr	02/68	67-71	135	5	56
Mansfield T	Tr	09/71	71-72	83	2	38
Torquay U	Tr	06/73	73	15	0	3

FAIRCHILD Michael Peter (Mick)
Born: Brixworth, Northamptonshire, England, 24 November, 1942 — RW

League Club	Source	Date Signed	Seasons Played	Apps	Subs	Gls
Luton T	Lowestoft T	11/60	60-63	21	-	1
Reading	Tr	07/64	64-65	24	0	6

FAIRCLOUGH Benjamin Michael Stanley (Ben)
Born: Nottingham, England, 18 April, 1989 — F

League Club	Source	Date Signed	Seasons Played	Apps	Subs	Gls
Notts Co	Nottingham F (Sch)	08/08	08	2	6	0

FAIRCLOUGH Courtney Huw (Chris)
Born: Nottingham, England, 12 April, 1964 — CD
England: B-1/U21-7

League Club	Source	Date Signed	Seasons Played	Apps	Subs	Gls
Nottingham F	App	10/81	82-86	102	5	1
Tottenham H	Tr	07/87	87-88	60	0	5
Leeds U	Tr	03/89	88-94	187	6	21
Bolton W	Tr	07/95	95-97	89	1	8
Notts Co	Tr	07/98	98	16	0	1
York C	Tr	03/99	98-99	36	1	0

FAIRCLOUGH Cyril
Born: Radcliffe, Greater Manchester, England, 21 April, 1923 — RB
Died: Manchester, England, 20 February, 2008

League Club	Source	Date Signed	Seasons Played	Apps	Subs	Gls
Bury	Urmston	09/45	46-57	191	-	2

FAIRCLOUGH David
Born: Liverpool, England, 5 January, 1957 — F
England: B-1/U21-1

League Club	Source	Date Signed	Seasons Played	Apps	Subs	Gls
Liverpool	App	01/74	75-82	64	34	34
Norwich C	FC Luzern (SUI)	03/85	84	1	1	0
Oldham Ath	Tr	08/85	85	6	11	1
Tranmere Rov	SK Beveren (BEL)	08/89	89	3	11	1
Wigan Ath	Tr	08/90	90	4	3	1

FAIRCLOUGH Michael Joseph (Mick)
Born: Drogheda, Republic of Ireland, 22 October, 1952 — M
Republic of Ireland: 2/LoI-1

League Club	Source	Date Signed	Seasons Played	Apps	Subs	Gls
Huddersfield T	Drogheda (ROI)	08/71	71-74	25	10	2

FAIRCLOUGH Wayne Ricks
Born: Nottingham, England, 27 April, 1968 — D/M

League Club	Source	Date Signed	Seasons Played	Apps	Subs	Gls
Notts Co	App	04/86	85-89	39	32	0
Mansfield T	Tr	03/90	89-93	131	10	12
Chesterfield	Tr	06/94	94-95	12	3	0
Scarborough	L	03/96	95	7	0	0

FAIRFAX Raymond John (Ray)
Born: Smethwick, West Midlands, England, 13 November, 1941 — RB

League Club	Source	Date Signed	Seasons Played	Apps	Subs	Gls
West Bromwich A	Jnr	08/59	62-67	79	2	0
Northampton T	Tr	06/68	68-70	115	0	2

FAIRHURST John
Born: Bentley, South Yorkshire, England, 15 March, 1944 — RH/IF

League Club	Source	Date Signed	Seasons Played	Apps	Subs	Gls
Doncaster Rov	App	07/61	61-65	21	0	0

FAIRHURST Waide Simon
Born: Sheffield, England, 7 May, 1989 — F

League Club	Source	Date Signed	Seasons Played	Apps	Subs	Gls
Doncaster Rov	Sch	07/08	08-10	2	9	2
Shrewsbury T	L	10/09	09	10	0	4
Southend U	L	10/10	10	2	1	0
Hereford U	L	02/11	10	10	6	3
Macclesfield T	Tr	07/11	11	4	14	0

FAIRLEY Thomas (Tom)
Born: Houghton-le-Spring, Tyne and Wear, England, 12 October, 1932 — G

League Club	Source	Date Signed	Seasons Played	Apps	Subs	Gls
Sunderland	Bankhead Jnrs	10/51	52	2	-	0
Carlisle U	Tr	05/56	56-58	55	-	0

FAIRWEATHER Carlton
Born: Camberwell, S London, England, 22 September, 1961 — W

League Club	Source	Date Signed	Seasons Played	Apps	Subs	Gls
Wimbledon	Tooting & Mitcham U	12/84	84-91	118	20	26
Carlisle U	Tr	08/93	93	11	1	1

FAIRWEATHER John Wilson (Wilson)
Born: Dornoch, Highlands, Scotland, 12 August, 1924 — RH
Died: Bath, England, December, 1989

League Club	Source	Date Signed	Seasons Played	Apps	Subs	Gls
Blackburn Rov	Annan Ath	04/44				
Carlisle U	Cowdenbeath	11/48	49	1	-	0

FALANA Waid Robert
Born: Westminster, Central London, England, 7 January, 1970 — F

League Club	Source	Date Signed	Seasons Played	Apps	Subs	Gls
Doncaster Rov	Tooting & Mitcham U	10/92	92	2	2	0
Chesterfield	Scarborough (NC)	03/93	92	4	1	0

FALCAO Radamel
Born: Santa Marta, Colombia, 10 February, 1986 — F
Colombia: 61/Youth

League Club	Source	Date Signed	Seasons Played	Apps	Subs	Gls
Manchester U	AS Monaco (FRA)	09/14	14	14	12	4

FALCO Mark Peter
Born: Hackney, E London, England, 22 October, 1960 — F
England: Youth

League Club	Source	Date Signed	Seasons Played	Apps	Subs	Gls
Tottenham H	App	07/78	78-86	162	12	67
Chelsea	L	11/82	82	3	0	0
Watford	Tr	10/86	86	33	0	14
Queens Park Rgrs	Glasgow Rangers	12/87	87-90	65	22	27
Millwall	Tr	08/91	91	19	2	4

FALCONER Andrew Gordon (Andy)
Born: South Africa, 27 June, 1925 — IF

League Club	Source	Date Signed	Seasons Played	Apps	Subs	Gls
Blackpool	South Africa	09/49	49	4	-	0

FALCONER Henry (Harry)
Born: Newcastle-upon-Tyne, England, 22 December, 1954 — FB

League Club	Source	Date Signed	Seasons Played	Apps	Subs	Gls
Bournemouth	Burnley (App)	07/72	74	4	3	0

FALCONER William Henry (Willie)
Born: Aberdeen, Scotland, 5 April, 1966 — M
Scotland: Youth/Schools

League Club	Source	Date Signed	Seasons Played	Apps	Subs	Gls
Watford	Aberdeen	06/88	88-90	85	13	12
Middlesbrough	Tr	08/91	91-92	47	6	10
Sheffield U	Tr	08/93	93	21	2	3
Grimsby T	St Johnstone	03/02	01	1	1	0

FALDER David Edward James
Born: Liverpool, England, 21 October, 1922 — CH
Died: Birkenhead, Wirral, England, March, 2001

League Club	Source	Date Signed	Seasons Played	Apps	Subs	Gls
Everton	Wigan Ath	12/45	49-50	25	-	0

FALLON Henry (Harry)
Born: Paisley, Renfrewshire, Scotland, 28 April, 1942 — G

League Club	Source	Date Signed	Seasons Played	Apps	Subs	Gls
York C	St Johnstone	09/65	65-67	67	0	0

FALLON Kevin Barry
Born: Maltby, South Yorkshire, England, 3 December, 1948 — CD

League Club	Source	Date Signed	Seasons Played	Apps	Subs	Gls
Rotherham U	App	12/65				
Southend U	Sligo Rov (ROI)	07/70	70	4	0	0

FALLON Peadar Domnal (Peter)
Born: Dublin, Republic of Ireland, 19 October, 1922 — WH

League Club	Source	Date Signed	Seasons Played	Apps	Subs	Gls
Exeter C	Notts Co (Am)	06/47	47-52	110	-	8
Queens Park Rgrs	Tr	08/53	53	1	-	0

FALLON Rory Michael
Born: Gisbourne, New Zealand, 20 March, 1982 — F
England: Youth//New Zealand: 18

League Club	Source	Date Signed	Seasons Played	Apps	Subs	Gls
Barnsley	YT	03/99	00-03	33	19	11
Shrewsbury T	L	12/01	01	8	3	0
Swindon T	Tr	11/03	03-05	43	32	21
Yeovil T	L	02/05	04	2	4	1
Swansea C	Tr	01/06	05-06	34	7	12
Plymouth Arg	Tr	01/07	06-10	94	55	22
Ipswich T	L	11/10	10	4	2	1
Yeovil T	Tr	07/11	11	0	5	0
Crawley T	St Johnstone	02/14	13	3	5	0
Scunthorpe U	Tr	09/14	14	4	0	3

FALLON Shaun
Born: Widnes, Cheshire, England, 10 September, 1970 — LB

League Club	Source	Date Signed	Seasons Played	Apps	Subs	Gls
Wigan Ath	YT	07/89	88-89	2	1	0

FALLON Stephen Paul (Steve)
Born: Whittlesey, Cambridgeshire, England, 3 August, 1956 — CD

League Club	Source	Date Signed	Seasons Played	Apps	Subs	Gls
Cambridge U	Kettering T	12/74	74-86	405	5	27

FALLON William Joseph (Bill)
Born: Killarney, Republic of Ireland, 14 January, 1912 — LW
Died: Nottingham, England, March, 1989
Republic of Ireland: 9/LoI-6

League Club	Source	Date Signed	Seasons Played	Apps	Subs	Gls
Notts Co	Dolphin (ROI)	02/34	33-37	120	-	20
Sheffield Wed	Tr	03/38	37-38	44	-	12
Notts Co	Dundalk (ROI)	06/46	46	15	-	3
Exeter C	Tr	06/47	47	8	-	2

FALQUE Iago
Born: Vigo, Spain, 4 April, 1990 — LW
Spain: U21-1/Youth

League Club	Source	Date Signed	Seasons Played	Apps	Subs	Gls
Tottenham H	Juventus (ITA)	08/11	12	0	1	0
Southampton	L	01/12	11	1	0	0

FANCHONE Jean-Alain
Born: Mulhouse, France, 22 September, 1988 — LB
France: Youth

League Club	Source	Date Signed	Seasons Played	Apps	Subs	Gls
Watford (L)	Udinese (ITA)	08/12	12	1	0	0

FANGUEIRO Carlos Manuel
Born: Matosinhos, Portugal, 19 December, 1976 RW

League Club	Source	Date Signed	Seasons Played	Apps	Subs	Gls
Millwall	FC Maia (POR)	08/05	05	1	8	0
Walsall	Tr	08/06	06	2	3	1

FANIMO Matthias Olubori
Born: Lambeth, S London, England, 28 January, 1994 M
England: Youth

League Club	Source	Date Signed	Seasons Played	Apps	Subs	Gls
West Ham U	Sch	07/11				
Tranmere Rov	L	09/14	14	0	1	0

FANTHAM John
Born: Sheffield, England, 6 February, 1939 IF
Died: Sheffield, England, 25 June, 2014
England: 1/FLge-3/U23-1

League Club	Source	Date Signed	Seasons Played	Apps	Subs	Gls
Sheffield Wed	Jnr	10/56	57-69	381	7	147
Rotherham U	Tr	10/69	69-70	46	5	8

FAN ZHIYI (Fan)
Born: Shanghai, China, 22 January, 1970 CD
China: 106

League Club	Source	Date Signed	Seasons Played	Apps	Subs	Gls
Crystal Palace	Shanghai Shen (CHN)	09/98	98-01	87	1	4
Cardiff C	Dundee	11/02	02	6	0	0

FARAONI Marco Davide
Born: Bracciano, Italy, 25 October, 1991 FB
Italy: U21-6/Youth

League Club	Source	Date Signed	Seasons Played	Apps	Subs	Gls
Watford	Udinese (ITA)	07/13	13	26	12	2

FAREY John Albert
Born: Darlington, County Durham, England, 22 July, 1922 G
Died: Scotland, 1962

League Club	Source	Date Signed	Seasons Played	Apps	Subs	Gls
Sunderland		02/44				
Carlisle U		11/47	47	2	-	0

FARINA Frank
Born: Darwin, Australia, 5 September, 1964 F
Australia: 67/U23-5/Youth

League Club	Source	Date Signed	Seasons Played	Apps	Subs	Gls
Notts Co (L)	Bari (ITA)	03/92	91	1	2	0

FARLEY Adam John
Born: Liverpool, England, 12 January, 1980 FB

League Club	Source	Date Signed	Seasons Played	Apps	Subs	Gls
Everton	YT	02/98	98	0	1	0

FARLEY Alexander John (Alec)
Born: Finchley, N London, England, 11 May, 1925 LB
Died: Southampton, England, 23 February, 2010

League Club	Source	Date Signed	Seasons Played	Apps	Subs	Gls
Leyton Orient	Cromwell Ath	11/45	46-47	15	-	0
Bournemouth	Tr	06/48				

FARLEY Craig
Born: Oxford, England, 17 March, 1981 RB

League Club	Source	Date Signed	Seasons Played	Apps	Subs	Gls
Colchester U	Watford (YT)	07/99	99	8	6	0

FARLEY Henry Brian (Brian)
Born: Craven Arms, Shropshire, England, 1 January, 1927 CH
Died: Brentwood, Essex, England, 4 February, 1962

League Club	Source	Date Signed	Seasons Played	Apps	Subs	Gls
Tottenham H	Chelmsford C	07/49	51	1	-	0

FARLEY John Denis
Born: Middlesbrough, England, 21 September, 1951 LW

League Club	Source	Date Signed	Seasons Played	Apps	Subs	Gls
Watford	Stockton	07/69	70-73	97	8	8
Halifax T	L	09/71	71	6	0	3
Wolverhampton W	Tr	05/74	74-77	35	5	0
Blackpool	L	10/76	76	1	0	0
Hull C	Tr	05/78	78-79	59	1	5
Bury	Tr	08/80	80	17	1	2

FARM George Neil
Born: Edinburgh, Scotland, 13 July, 1924 G
Died: Edinburgh, Scotland, 14 July, 2004
Scotland: 10

League Club	Source	Date Signed	Seasons Played	Apps	Subs	Gls
Blackpool	Hibernian	09/48	48-59	461	-	1

FARMER Frederick Brian Webb (Brian)
Born: Rowley Regis, West Midlands, England, 29 July, 1933 RB
Died: Bournemouth, England, 1 January, 2014

League Club	Source	Date Signed	Seasons Played	Apps	Subs	Gls
Birmingham C	Stourbridge	07/54	56-61	118	-	0
Bournemouth	Tr	01/62	61-64	132	-	0

FARMER James Edward Colm (Ted)
Born: Rowley Regis, West Midlands, England, 21 January, 1940 CF
England: U23-2

League Club	Source	Date Signed	Seasons Played	Apps	Subs	Gls
Wolverhampton W	Jnr	08/57	60-63	57	-	44

FARMER John
Born: Biddulph, Staffordshire, England, 31 August, 1947 G
England: U23-1

League Club	Source	Date Signed	Seasons Played	Apps	Subs	Gls
Stoke C	Jnr	01/65	65-74	163	0	0
Leicester C	L	12/74	74	2	0	0

FARMER Kevin John
Born: Ramsgate, Kent, England, 24 January, 1960 CD/F

League Club	Source	Date Signed	Seasons Played	Apps	Subs	Gls
Leicester C	App	11/77	77	1	0	0
Northampton T	Tr	08/79	79-81	70	7	12

FARMER Michael Chester (Mick)
Born: Leicester, England, 22 November, 1944 LH

League Club	Source	Date Signed	Seasons Played	Apps	Subs	Gls
Birmingham C	App	04/62	63	1	-	1
Lincoln C	Tr	05/65	65	21	1	0

FARMER Ronald James (Ron)
Born: Guernsey, Channel Islands, 6 March, 1936 LH/IF

League Club	Source	Date Signed	Seasons Played	Apps	Subs	Gls
Nottingham F	Jnr	05/53	57	9	-	0
Coventry C	Tr	11/58	58-67	281	4	47
Notts Co	Tr	10/67	67-68	69	0	5

FARMER Terence (Terry)
Born: Maltby, South Yorkshire, England, 11 May, 1931 CF
Died: Rotherham, South Yorkshire, England, 9 May, 2014

League Club	Source	Date Signed	Seasons Played	Apps	Subs	Gls
Rotherham U	Gainsborough Trinity	07/52	52-57	61	-	24
York C	Tr	01/58	57-59	66	-	28

FARMER William Henry (Bill)
Born: Guernsey, Channel Islands, 24 November, 1927 G
Died: Corby, Northamptonshire, England, 12 July, 2014

League Club	Source	Date Signed	Seasons Played	Apps	Subs	Gls
Nottingham F	St Martin's, Guernsey	05/51	53-56	52	-	0
Oldham Ath	Brush Sports	07/57	57	5	-	0

FARNABY Craig
Born: Hartlepool, Cleveland, England, 8 August, 1967 M

League Club	Source	Date Signed	Seasons Played	Apps	Subs	Gls
Hartlepool U	Jnr	10/84	84	5	0	0
Middlesbrough	Easington Colliery	11/85				
Halifax T	Tr	09/86	86	7	3	1
Stockport Co	Shotton Comrades	09/87	87	17	5	1

FARNEN Austin Leslie (Les)
Born: St Helens, Merseyside, England, 17 September, 1919 CH
Died: Harrow, NW London, England, January, 1985

League Club	Source	Date Signed	Seasons Played	Apps	Subs	Gls
Watford		05/46	46-48	77	-	0
Bradford C	Tr	05/49	49	8	-	0

FARNSWORTH Peter Albert
Born: Barnsley, South Yorkshire, England, 17 May, 1946 WH

League Club	Source	Date Signed	Seasons Played	Apps	Subs	Gls
Barnsley	App	09/63	64	1	-	0

FARNWORTH Simon
Born: Chorley, Lancashire, England, 28 October, 1963 G
England: Schools

League Club	Source	Date Signed	Seasons Played	Apps	Subs	Gls
Bolton W	App	09/81	83-85	113	0	0
Stockport Co	L	09/86	86	10	0	0
Tranmere Rov	L	01/87	86	7	0	0
Bury	Tr	03/87	86-89	105	0	0
Preston NE	Tr	07/90	90-92	81	0	0
Wigan Ath	Tr	07/93	93-95	126	0	0

FARQUHAR Douglas Methven (Doug)
Born: Buckhaven, Fife, Scotland, 11 June, 1921 W
Died: New York, USA, 20 February, 2005

League Club	Source	Date Signed	Seasons Played	Apps	Subs	Gls
Arsenal	St Andrews U	05/44				
Reading	Tr	09/50	50-51	9	-	1

FARR Brian Sydney
Born: Swindon, England, 19 October, 1930 WH

League Club	Source	Date Signed	Seasons Played	Apps	Subs	Gls
Swindon T	Swindon Victoria	04/51	50-51	11	-	0

FARR Craig Jonathan
Born: Newbury, Berkshire, England, 27 June, 1984 G

League Club	Source	Date Signed	Seasons Played	Apps	Subs	Gls
Swindon T	Sch	08/02	02	2	0	0

FARR Ian
Born: Swindon, England, 13 February, 1958 F

League Club	Source	Date Signed	Seasons Played	Apps	Subs	Gls
Swindon T	App	-	75	0	1	0

FARR Thomas Francis (Chick)
Born: Bathgate, West Lothian, Scotland, 19 February, 1914 G
Died: Bradford, England, 15 June, 1980

League Club	Source	Date Signed	Seasons Played	Apps	Subs	Gls
Bradford Park Ave	Broxburn Ath	09/34	34-49	294	-	0

FARRALL Alec
Born: West Kirby, Wirral, England, 3 March, 1936 IF/LH
England: Schools

League Club	Source	Date Signed	Seasons Played	Apps	Subs	Gls
Everton	Jnr	03/53	52-56	5	-	0
Preston NE	Tr	05/57	57-59	27	-	9
Gillingham	Tr	07/60	60-64	202	-	19
Lincoln C	Tr	06/65	65	20	0	2
Watford	Tr	07/66	66-67	47	1	8

FARRAR John Norman
Born: St Helens, Merseyside, England, 6 May, 1928 RH
Died: Wigan, Greater Manchester, England, 4 December, 1988

League Club	Source	Date Signed	Seasons Played	Apps	Subs	Gls
Manchester C		03/48				
Crewe Alex	Tr	01/51	50	2	-	0

FARRELL Andrew (Andy)
Born: Easington, County Durham, England, 21 December, 1983 — F

League Club	Source	Date Signed	Seasons Played	Apps	Subs	Gls
Halifax T	YT	10/02	01	7	2	0

FARRELL Andrew James (Andy)
Born: Colchester, Essex, England, 7 October, 1965 — M/D

League Club	Source	Date Signed	Seasons Played	Apps	Subs	Gls
Colchester U	App	09/83	83-86	98	7	5
Burnley	Tr	08/87	87-93	237	20	20
Wigan Ath	Tr	09/94	94-95	51	3	1
Rochdale	Tr	07/96	96-98	113	5	6

FARRELL Arthur
Born: Huddersfield, West Yorkshire, England, 1 November, 1920 — LB
Died: Isle of Wight, England, September, 2000

League Club	Source	Date Signed	Seasons Played	Apps	Subs	Gls
Bradford Park Ave	Meltham Mills	05/40	46-50	156	-	4
Barnsley	Tr	05/51	51	18	-	0

FARRELL Craig Wayne
Born: Middlesbrough, England, 5 December, 1982 — F

League Club	Source	Date Signed	Seasons Played	Apps	Subs	Gls
Leeds U	YT	12/99				
Carlisle U	Tr	10/02	02-03	52	11	18

FARRELL David William (Dave)
Born: Birmingham, England, 11 November, 1971 — W

League Club	Source	Date Signed	Seasons Played	Apps	Subs	Gls
Aston Villa	Redditch U	01/92	92-93	5	1	0
Scunthorpe U	L	01/93	92	4	1	1
Wycombe W	Tr	09/95	95-96	44	16	8
Peterborough U	Tr	07/97	97-05	267	70	42
Boston U	Tr	07/06	06	23	16	1

FARRELL Gerard William (Gerry)
Born: Liverpool, England, 19 March, 1952 — LB

League Club	Source	Date Signed	Seasons Played	Apps	Subs	Gls
Wolverhampton W	App	03/70				
Watford	Tr	08/71				
Blackburn Rov	Tr	10/71	71-72	21	1	1

FARRELL Gregory James Philip (Greg)
Born: Motherwell, Lanarkshire, Scotland, 19 March, 1944 — RW

League Club	Source	Date Signed	Seasons Played	Apps	Subs	Gls
Birmingham C	App	03/61	62-63	4	-	0
Cardiff C	Tr	03/64	63-66	93	1	8
Bury	Tr	03/67	66-69	83	0	15

FARRELL John (Jackie)
Born: Clunie, Perthshire, Scotland, 22 June, 1933 — LW

League Club	Source	Date Signed	Seasons Played	Apps	Subs	Gls
Accrington Stan	Perth Celtic	08/54	54	2	-	0

FARRELL Kevin Michael (Mick)
Born: Ilkley, West Yorkshire, England, 13 March, 1959 — M

League Club	Source	Date Signed	Seasons Played	Apps	Subs	Gls
Scunthorpe U	App	03/77	75-77	5	4	1

FARRELL Paul Anthony
Born: Liverpool, England, 1 November, 1958 — F

League Club	Source	Date Signed	Seasons Played	Apps	Subs	Gls
Southport	App	-	75	0	2	0

FARRELL Peter Desmond
Born: Dublin, Republic of Ireland, 16 August, 1922 — WH
Died: Dublin, Republic of Ireland, March, 1999
Republic of Ireland: 28/LoI-7//Northern Ireland: 7

League Club	Source	Date Signed	Seasons Played	Apps	Subs	Gls
Everton	Shamrock Rov (ROI)	08/46	46-56	422	-	13
Tranmere Rov	Tr	10/57	57-59	114	-	1

FARRELL Peter John
Born: Liverpool, England, 10 January, 1957 — M

League Club	Source	Date Signed	Seasons Played	Apps	Subs	Gls
Bury	Ormskirk	09/75	75-78	49	5	9
Port Vale	Tr	11/78	78-81	85	4	10
Rochdale	Tr	08/82	82-84	71	2	17
Crewe Alex	Tr	09/84	84-85	26	2	2

FARRELL Raymond Leo (Ray)
Born: Cardiff, Wales, 31 May, 1933 — CF
Died: Cardiff, Wales, October, 1999

League Club	Source	Date Signed	Seasons Played	Apps	Subs	Gls
Crystal Palace	Treharris	05/57	57-58	5	-	0

FARRELL Sean Paul
Born: Watford, Hertfordshire, England, 28 February, 1969 — F

League Club	Source	Date Signed	Seasons Played	Apps	Subs	Gls
Luton T	App	03/87	89-91	14	11	1
Colchester U	L	03/88	87	4	5	1
Northampton T	L	09/91	91	4	0	1
Fulham	Tr	12/91	91-93	93	1	31
Peterborough U	Tr	08/94	94-96	49	17	20
Notts Co	Tr	10/96	96-00	58	30	22

FARRELL Stephen Edward (Steve)
Born: Kilwinning, Ayrshire, Scotland, 8 March, 1973 — M

League Club	Source	Date Signed	Seasons Played	Apps	Subs	Gls
Stoke C	YT	07/91	89	0	2	0

FARRELLY Gareth
Born: Dublin, Republic of Ireland, 28 August, 1975 — M
Republic of Ireland: 6/B-1/U21-11/Youth/Schools

League Club	Source	Date Signed	Seasons Played	Apps	Subs	Gls
Aston Villa	YT	01/92	95-96	2	6	0
Rotherham U	L	03/95	94	9	1	2
Everton	Tr	07/97	97-98	18	9	1
Bolton W	Tr	11/99	99-02	61	17	5
Rotherham U	L	03/03	02	6	0	0
Burnley	L	09/03	03	9	3	0
Bradford C	L	11/03	03	14	0	0
Wigan Ath	Tr	03/04	03	3	4	0
Blackpool	Bohemians (ROI)	11/06	06	0	1	0

FARRELLY Michael (Mike)
Born: Manchester, England, 1 November, 1962 — M
England: Semi Pro/Schools

League Club	Source	Date Signed	Seasons Played	Apps	Subs	Gls
Preston NE	Jnr	06/81	81-84	77	5	4

FARRELLY Stephen (Steve)
Born: Liverpool, England, 27 March, 1965 — G
England: Semi Pro

League Club	Source	Date Signed	Seasons Played	Apps	Subs	Gls
Chester C	Knowsley U	11/88				
Rotherham U	Macclesfield T	07/95	96	7	0	0

FARRIMOND Sydney (Syd)
Born: Hindley, Greater Manchester, England, 17 July, 1940 — LB
England: Youth

League Club	Source	Date Signed	Seasons Played	Apps	Subs	Gls
Bolton W	Moss Lane YC	01/58	58-70	364	1	1
Tranmere Rov	Tr	02/71	70-73	132	2	0
Halifax T	Tr	11/74				

FARRINGTON John Robert
Born: Lynemouth, Northumberland, England, 19 June, 1947 — RW

League Club	Source	Date Signed	Seasons Played	Apps	Subs	Gls
Wolverhampton W	App	06/65	66-69	31	3	2
Leicester C	Tr	10/69	69-73	115	3	19
Cardiff C	Tr	11/73	73-74	23	0	6
Northampton T	Tr	10/74	74-79	224	8	29

FARRINGTON Mark Anthony
Born: Liverpool, England, 15 June, 1965 — F

League Club	Source	Date Signed	Seasons Played	Apps	Subs	Gls
Norwich C	Everton (App)	05/83	83-84	11	3	2
Cambridge U	Tr	03/85	84	10	0	1
Cardiff C	Tr	07/85	85	24	7	3
Brighton & HA	Feyenoord (NED)	08/91	91-93	15	13	4
Hereford U	AIF (NOR)	10/94	94	0	1	0

FARRINGTON Roy Arthur
Born: Tonbridge, Kent, England, 6 June, 1925 — IF
Died: Tunbridge Wells, Kent, England, 17 March, 2006

League Club	Source	Date Signed	Seasons Played	Apps	Subs	Gls
Crystal Palace	High Brooms	11/47	47-48	3	-	0

FARROW Desmond Albert (Des)
Born: Peterborough, England, 11 February, 1926 — LH

League Club	Source	Date Signed	Seasons Played	Apps	Subs	Gls
Queens Park Rgrs	Leicester C (Am)	11/44	48-52	118	-	7
Stoke C	Tr	10/52	52-53	8	-	0

FARROW George Henry
Born: Whitburn, Tyne and Wear, England, 4 October, 1913 — WH
Died: Sunderland, England, 1980

League Club	Source	Date Signed	Seasons Played	Apps	Subs	Gls
Stockport Co	Whitburn	10/30	31	6	-	0
Wolverhampton W	Tr	01/32	32	11	-	0
Bournemouth	Tr	07/33	33-35	107	-	12
Blackpool	Tr	06/36	36-47	143	-	15
Sheffield U	Tr	01/48	47	1	-	0

FASCIONE Joseph Victor (Joe)
Born: Coatbridge, Lanarkshire, Scotland, 5 February, 1945 — W

League Club	Source	Date Signed	Seasons Played	Apps	Subs	Gls
Chelsea	Kirkintilloch Rob Roy	10/62	65-68	22	7	1

FASHANU John
Born: Kensington, Central London, England, 18 September, 1962 — F
England: 2

League Club	Source	Date Signed	Seasons Played	Apps	Subs	Gls
Norwich C	Cambridge U (Jnr)	10/79	81-82	6	1	1
Crystal Palace	L	08/83	83	1	0	0
Lincoln C	Tr	09/83	83-84	31	5	11
Millwall	Tr	11/84	84-85	50	0	12
Wimbledon	Tr	03/86	85-93	271	5	107
Aston Villa	Tr	08/94	94	11	2	3

FASHANU Justinus Soni (Justin)
Born: Hackney, E London, England, 19 February, 1961 — F
Died: Shoreditch, Central London, England, 2 May, 1998
England: B-1/U21-11/Youth

League Club	Source	Date Signed	Seasons Played	Apps	Subs	Gls
Norwich C	App	12/78	78-80	84	6	35
Nottingham F	Tr	08/81	81	31	1	3
Southampton	L	08/82	82	9	0	3
Notts Co	Tr	12/82	82-84	63	1	20
Brighton & HA	Tr	06/85	85	16	0	2
Manchester C	Edmonton Brick'n (CAN)	10/89	89	0	2	0
West Ham U	Tr	11/89	89	2	0	0
Leyton Orient	Tr	03/90	89	3	2	0

League Club	Source	Date Signed	Seasons Played	Apps	Subs	Gls
Newcastle U	Toronto Blizzard (CAN)	10/91				
Torquay U	Leatherhead	12/91	91-92	41	0	15

FATHI Ahmed
Born: Banha, Egypt, 11 October, 1984 — RB
Egypt: 101

League Club	Source	Date Signed	Seasons Played	Apps	Subs	Gls
Sheffield U	Ismailia (EGY)	01/07	06	2	1	0
Hull C (L)	Al Ahly (EGY)	01/13	12	1	6	0

FAUBERT Julien
Born: Le Havre, France, 1 August, 1983 — M/RB
France: 1/U21-17

League Club	Source	Date Signed	Seasons Played	Apps	Subs	Gls
West Ham U	Bordeaux (FRA)	07/07	07-11	86	17	2

FAULCONBRIDGE Craig Michael
Born: Nuneaton, Warwickshire, England, 20 April, 1978 — F

League Club	Source	Date Signed	Seasons Played	Apps	Subs	Gls
Coventry C	YT	07/96				
Hull C	L	12/98	98	4	6	0
Wrexham	Tr	08/99	99-01	92	19	31
Wycombe W	Tr	07/02	02-04	46	12	8

FAULKES Brian Keith
Born: Abingdon, Oxfordshire, England, 10 April, 1945 — FB

League Club	Source	Date Signed	Seasons Played	Apps	Subs	Gls
Reading	Jnr	09/63	63-66	23	1	0
Northampton T	Tr	07/67	67-68	51	1	2
Torquay U	Tr	07/69	69	6	0	0

FAULKNER David Peter
Born: Sheffield, England, 8 October, 1975 — CD
England: Youth/Schools

League Club	Source	Date Signed	Seasons Played	Apps	Subs	Gls
Sheffield Wed	YT	12/92				
Darlington	Tr	08/96	96	2	2	0

FAULKNER John Gilbert
Born: Orpington, SE London, England, 10 March, 1948 — CD

League Club	Source	Date Signed	Seasons Played	Apps	Subs	Gls
Leeds U	Sutton U	03/70	69	2	0	0
Luton T	Tr	03/72	72-77	209	0	6

FAULKNER Kenneth Gordon (Ken)
Born: Smethwick, West Midlands, England, 10 September, 1923 — W
Died: Birmingham, England, December, 2000
England: Schools

League Club	Source	Date Signed	Seasons Played	Apps	Subs	Gls
Birmingham C	Smethwick Highfield	09/44	46	2	-	0

FAULKNER Michael (Mike)
Born: Conisbrough, South Yorkshire, England, 3 January, 1950 — M

League Club	Source	Date Signed	Seasons Played	Apps	Subs	Gls
Sheffield U	App	12/67				
Oldham Ath	Tr	07/69	69	1	0	0

FAULKNER Raymond Arthur (Ray)
Born: Horncastle, Lincolnshire, England, 26 May, 1934 — RW

League Club	Source	Date Signed	Seasons Played	Apps	Subs	Gls
Grimsby T	Horncastle T	10/54	54	5	-	1

FAULKNER Roy Vincent
Born: Manchester, England, 28 June, 1935 — IF

League Club	Source	Date Signed	Seasons Played	Apps	Subs	Gls
Manchester C	Jnr	12/52	55	7	-	4
Walsall	Tr	03/58	57-60	100	-	44

FAULKNER Stephen Andrew (Steve)
Born: Sheffield, England, 18 December, 1954 — CD

League Club	Source	Date Signed	Seasons Played	Apps	Subs	Gls
Sheffield U	App	02/72	72-76	14	1	0
Stockport Co	L	03/78	77	3	1	0
York C	Tr	05/78	78-80	90	0	7

FAURLIN Alejandro Damian
Born: Rosario, Argentina, 9 August, 1986 — M
Argentina: Youth

League Club	Source	Date Signed	Seasons Played	Apps	Subs	Gls
Queens Park Rgrs	Inst Cordoba (ARG)	07/09	09-14	112	9	5

FAWCETT Brian
Born: Barnburgh, South Yorkshire, England, 14 February, 1932 — W
Died: Huddersfield, West Yorkshire, England, 20 June, 1991

League Club	Source	Date Signed	Seasons Played	Apps	Subs	Gls
Scunthorpe U	Bentley Colliery	02/55	54	1	-	0
Bradford Park Ave	Tr	07/56				

FAWCETT Roy
Born: Leeds, England, 20 January, 1938 — W

League Club	Source	Date Signed	Seasons Played	Apps	Subs	Gls
Blackpool	Jnr	03/55	55-59	4	-	0

FAWELL Derek Stuart
Born: Hartlepool, Cleveland, England, 22 March, 1944 — CF

League Club	Source	Date Signed	Seasons Played	Apps	Subs	Gls
Notts Co	Spennymoor U	10/64	64	1	-	0
Lincoln C	Tr	09/65	65	3	0	0

FAWLEY Ronald (Ron)
Born: Ashton-under-Lyne, Greater Manchester, England, 22 April, 1927 — LW/LB
Died: Tameside, Greater Manchester, England, 2 February, 1982

League Club	Source	Date Signed	Seasons Played	Apps	Subs	Gls
Oldham Ath	Ashton U	08/50	50-57	94	-	9

FAYADH Jassim Swadi
Born: Baghdad, Iraq, 1 July, 1975 — M
Iraq: 21

League Club	Source	Date Signed	Seasons Played	Apps	Subs	Gls
Macclesfield T	Al Jawiya (IRQ)	08/04	04	0	1	0

FAYE Abdoulaye Diagne
Born: Dakar, Senegal, 26 February, 1978 — CD
Senegal: 35

League Club	Source	Date Signed	Seasons Played	Apps	Subs	Gls
Bolton W	RC Lens (FRA)	08/05	05-07	53	7	3
Newcastle U	Tr	08/07	07	20	2	1
Stoke C	Tr	08/08	08-10	78	3	6
West Ham U	Tr	07/11	11	25	4	0
Hull C	Tr	07/12	12-13	31	3	4

FAYE Amdy Mustapha
Born: Dakar, Senegal, 12 March, 1977 — DM
Senegal: 31

League Club	Source	Date Signed	Seasons Played	Apps	Subs	Gls
Portsmouth	AJ Auxerre (FRA)	08/03	03-04	44	3	0
Newcastle U	Tr	01/05	04-05	22	9	0
Charlton Ath	Tr	08/06	06-07	25	4	1
Stoke C	Tr	08/08	08	18	3	0
Leeds U	Tr	09/10	10	6	2	0

FAZACKERLEY Derek William
Born: Preston, Lancashire, England, 5 November, 1951 — CD

League Club	Source	Date Signed	Seasons Played	Apps	Subs	Gls
Blackburn Rov	App	10/69	70-86	593	3	23
Chester C	Tr	01/87	86-87	66	0	0
York C	Tr	07/88	88	16	0	0
Bury	Tr	12/88	88	7	7	0

FAZACKERLEY Michael Alexander (Mick)
Born: Manchester, England, 8 April, 1932 — LB

League Club	Source	Date Signed	Seasons Played	Apps	Subs	Gls
Bradford Park Ave	Bradford C (Am)	08/55	55	2	-	0

FEALEY Nathan James
Born: Aldershot, Hampshire, England, 12 March, 1973 — M

League Club	Source	Date Signed	Seasons Played	Apps	Subs	Gls
Reading	YT	07/91	91	1	0	0

FEAR Keith William
Born: Bristol, England, 8 May, 1952 — F/M
England: Schools

League Club	Source	Date Signed	Seasons Played	Apps	Subs	Gls
Bristol C	Jnr	06/69	70-76	126	25	32
Hereford U	L	09/77	77	6	0	0
Blackburn Rov	L	12/77	77	5	0	2
Plymouth Arg	Tr	02/78	77-79	41	5	9
Brentford	L	11/79	79	7	1	2
Chester C	Tr	01/80	79-80	41	3	3

FEAR Peter Stanley
Born: Sutton, S London, England, 10 September, 1973 — M
England: U21-3

League Club	Source	Date Signed	Seasons Played	Apps	Subs	Gls
Wimbledon	YT	07/92	92-98	51	22	4
Oxford U	Tr	07/99	99-00	27	11	3

FEAR Vivien James
Born: Bristol, England, 24 October, 1955 — M

League Club	Source	Date Signed	Seasons Played	Apps	Subs	Gls
Hereford U	Bristol C (App)	07/74	74	2	1	0

FEARNLEY Gordon
Born: Bradford, England, 25 January, 1950 — F/W
Died: Florida, USA, 25 June, 2015
England: Schools

League Club	Source	Date Signed	Seasons Played	Apps	Subs	Gls
Sheffield Wed	Jnr	07/68				
Bristol Rov	Tr	07/70	70-76	95	27	21

FEARNLEY Harrison Lockhead (Harry)
Born: Morley, West Yorkshire, England, 27 May, 1923 — G
Died: Morley, West Yorkshire, England, 6 January, 2012

League Club	Source	Date Signed	Seasons Played	Apps	Subs	Gls
Leeds U	Bradford Park Ave (Am)	11/45	46-48	28	-	0
Halifax T	Tr	01/49	48	3	-	0
Newport Co	Tr	07/49	49-52	103	-	0
Rochdale	Selby T	07/55	55	1	-	0

FEARNLEY Henry (Harry)
Born: Penistone, South Yorkshire, England, 16 June, 1935 — G
Died: Poole, Dorset, England, 12 January, 2013

League Club	Source	Date Signed	Seasons Played	Apps	Subs	Gls
Huddersfield T	Jnr	12/52	55-62	90	-	0
Oxford U	Tr	10/63	63-65	90	0	0
Doncaster Rov	Tr	02/66	65-66	32	0	0

FEARON Ronald Thomas (Ron)
Born: Romford, E London, England, 19 November, 1960 — G

League Club	Source	Date Signed	Seasons Played	Apps	Subs	Gls
Reading	Dover	02/80	80-82	61	0	0
Ipswich T	Sutton U	09/87	87-88	28	0	0
Brighton & HA	L	09/88	88	7	0	0
Walsall	Sutton U	02/93	92	1	0	0
Southend U	Tr	10/93				
Leyton Orient	Barkingside	08/95	95	18	0	0

FEASEY Paul Cedric
Born: Hull, England, 4 May, 1933 — CH
Died: Cottingham, East Riding of Yorkshire, England, 12 January, 2012

League Club	Source	Date Signed	Seasons Played	Apps	Subs	Gls
Hull C	York RI	05/50	52-64	271	-	0

League Club	Source	Date Signed	Seasons Played	Career Record Apps	Subs	Gls

FEATHERSTONE James Lee (Jamie)
Born: Yeadon, West Yorkshire, England, 12 November, 1979 — F

League Club	Source	Date Signed	Seasons Played	Apps	Subs	Gls
Scunthorpe U	Blackburn Rov (YT)	03/98	97	0	1	0

FEATHERSTONE Keith
Born: Bradford, England, 30 August, 1935 — G
Died: Frome, Somerset, England, 21 March, 2006

League Club	Source	Date Signed	Seasons Played	Apps	Subs	Gls
Bradford Park Ave	Wyke Celtic	12/55	55	1	-	0

FEATHERSTONE Lee Paul
Born: Chesterfield, Derbyshire, England, 20 July, 1983 — W

League Club	Source	Date Signed	Seasons Played	Apps	Subs	Gls
Sheffield U	YT	07/01				
Scunthorpe U	Tr	10/02	02-04	17	15	0

FEATHERSTONE Nicky Lee
Born: Goole, East Riding of Yorkshire, England, 22 September, 1988 — M

League Club	Source	Date Signed	Seasons Played	Apps	Subs	Gls
Hull C	Sch	12/06	06-07	0	8	0
Grimsby T	L	11/09	09	7	1	0
Hereford U	Tr	11/10	10-11	56	9	1
Walsall	Tr	08/12	12-13	39	17	0
Hartlepool U	Harrogate T	10/14	14	22	3	0

FEDERICI Adam Jay
Born: Nowra, N.S.W., Australia, 31 January, 1985 — G
Australia: 10/U23-5/Youth

League Club	Source	Date Signed	Seasons Played	Apps	Subs	Gls
Reading	Sassari Torres (ITA)	09/05	06-14	206	3	1
Southend U	L	09/08	08	10	0	0

[FEDERICO] FAZIO Federico Julian
Born: Buenos Aires, Argentina, 17 March, 1987 — CD
Argentina: 3/U23-2/Youth

League Club	Source	Date Signed	Seasons Played	Apps	Subs	Gls
Tottenham H	Sevilla (SPN)	08/14	14	20	0	0

FEDERICO Jerome Joshua
Born: Watford, Hertfordshire, England, 14 May, 1992 — RW

League Club	Source	Date Signed	Seasons Played	Apps	Subs	Gls
Wycombe W	Sch	07/10	10	0	1	0

FEE Gregory Paul (Greg)
Born: Halifax, West Yorkshire, England, 24 June, 1964 — CD

League Club	Source	Date Signed	Seasons Played	Apps	Subs	Gls
Bradford C	App	05/83	82-83	6	1	0
Sheffield Wed	Boston U	08/87	87-89	16	10	0
Preston NE	L	09/90	90	10	0	0
Northampton T	L	11/90	90	1	0	0
Preston NE	L	01/91	90	5	0	0
Leyton Orient	L	03/91	90	4	1	0
Mansfield T	Tr	03/91	90-92	50	4	7
Chesterfield	L	12/92	92	10	0	0

FEEHAN John Ignatius (Sonny)
Born: Dublin, Republic of Ireland, 17 September, 1926 — G
Died: Republic of Ireland, 11 March, 1995

League Club	Source	Date Signed	Seasons Played	Apps	Subs	Gls
Manchester U	Waterford (ROI)	11/48	49	12	-	0
Northampton T	Tr	08/50	50-51	39	-	0
Brentford	Tr	08/54	54-58	30	-	0

FEELEY Andrew James (Andy)
Born: Hereford, England, 30 September, 1961 — RB/M

League Club	Source	Date Signed	Seasons Played	Apps	Subs	Gls
Hereford U	App	08/79	78-79	50	1	3
Leicester C	Trowbridge T	02/84	83-86	74	2	0
Brentford	Tr	08/87	87-88	57	10	0
Bury	Tr	07/89	89-90	46	11	2

FEELY Kevin Roderick
Born: Dublin, Republic of Ireland, 30 August, 1992 — D
Republic of Ireland: U21-1

League Club	Source	Date Signed	Seasons Played	Apps	Subs	Gls
Charlton Ath	Bohemians (ROI)	01/13				
Carlisle U	L	08/13	13	1	1	0
Newport Co	Tr	03/14	13-14	27	5	1

FEELY Peter John
Born: City of London, England, 3 January, 1950 — F
England: Amateur-2/Youth

League Club	Source	Date Signed	Seasons Played	Apps	Subs	Gls
Chelsea	Enfield	05/70	70-72	4	1	2
Bournemouth	Tr	02/73	72-73	8	1	2
Fulham	Tr	07/74				
Gillingham	Tr	10/74	74-75	41	0	22
Sheffield Wed	Tr	02/76	75-76	17	2	2
Stockport Co	L	01/77	76	2	0	0

FEENEY James McBurney (Jim)
Born: Belfast, Northern Ireland, 23 June, 1921 — LB
Died: Belfast, Northern Ireland, March, 1985
Northern Ireland: 2/NILge-3/War-2

League Club	Source	Date Signed	Seasons Played	Apps	Subs	Gls
Swansea C	Linfield	12/46	46-49	88	-	0
Ipswich T	Tr	03/50	49-55	214	-	0

FEENEY Joseph (Joe)
Born: Glasgow, Scotland, 21 July, 1926 — IF
Died: Glasgow, Scotland, 1 December, 1992

League Club	Source	Date Signed	Seasons Played	Apps	Subs	Gls
Sunderland	St Theresa's	07/47				
Chester C	Rhyl	09/51	51	5	-	0

FEENEY Liam Michael
Born: Hammersmith, W London, England, 21 January, 1987 — M

League Club	Source	Date Signed	Seasons Played	Apps	Subs	Gls
Southend U (L)	Salisbury C	11/08	08	0	1	0
Bournemouth	Salisbury C	02/09	08-11	99	10	12
Millwall	Tr	08/11	11-13	44	29	5
Bolton W	L	09/13	13	3	1	0
Blackburn Rov	L	03/14	13	1	5	0
Bolton W	Tr	07/14	14	35	6	3

FEENEY Mark Anthony
Born: Derry, Northern Ireland, 26 July, 1974 — M

League Club	Source	Date Signed	Seasons Played	Apps	Subs	Gls
Barnsley	YT	07/93	92	0	2	0

FEENEY Warren James
Born: Belfast, Northern Ireland, 17 January, 1981 — F
Northern Ireland: 46/U21-8/Youth/Schools

League Club	Source	Date Signed	Seasons Played	Apps	Subs	Gls
Leeds U	St Andrew's, Belfast	01/98				
Bournemouth	Tr	03/01	00-03	83	25	36
Stockport Co	Tr	07/04	04	31	0	15
Luton T	Tr	03/05	04-06	45	32	8
Cardiff C	Tr	03/07	06-09	6	14	0
Swansea C	L	08/07	07	7	3	5
Sheffield Wed	L	11/09	09	0	1	0
Oldham Ath	Tr	07/10	10	13	10	0
Plymouth Arg	Tr	08/11	11-12	37	12	5

FEILHABER Benny
Born: Rio de Janeiro, Brazil, 19 January, 1985 — M
USA: 41

League Club	Source	Date Signed	Seasons Played	Apps	Subs	Gls
Derby Co	Hamburger SV (GER)	08/07	07	1	9	0

FELGATE David Wynne
Born: Blaenau Ffestiniog, Gwynedd, Wales, 4 March, 1960 — G
Wales: 1/Schools

League Club	Source	Date Signed	Seasons Played	Apps	Subs	Gls
Bolton W	Blaenau Ffestiniog	08/78				
Rochdale	L	10/78	78	35	0	0
Crewe Alex	L	09/79	79	14	0	0
Rochdale	L	03/80	79	12	0	0
Lincoln C	Tr	09/80	80-84	198	0	0
Cardiff C	L	12/84	84	4	0	0
Grimsby T	L	02/85	84	12	0	0
Grimsby T	Tr	06/85	85-86	24	0	0
Bolton W	L	02/86	85	15	0	0
Bolton W	Tr	02/87	86-91	223	0	0
Bury	Tr	07/93				
Chester C	Wolverhampton W (NC)	10/93	93-94	71	1	0
Wigan Ath	Tr	07/95	95	3	0	0

FELIX Gary
Born: Manchester, England, 31 October, 1957 — M

League Club	Source	Date Signed	Seasons Played	Apps	Subs	Gls
Leeds U	App	11/75				
Chester C	Manchester C (NC)	01/79	78	8	0	0

FELL Geoffrey Mark (Geoff)
Born: Carlisle, Cumbria, England, 8 May, 1960 — F

League Club	Source	Date Signed	Seasons Played	Apps	Subs	Gls
Carlisle U	Jnr	06/77	77-79	0	3	0

FELL Gerald Charles (Gerry)
Born: Newark, Nottinghamshire, England, 1 March, 1951 — W

League Club	Source	Date Signed	Seasons Played	Apps	Subs	Gls
Brighton & HA	Long Eaton U	11/74	74-77	65	14	19
Southend U	Tr	11/77	77-79	43	2	10
Torquay U	Tr	07/80	80-81	50	0	12
York C	Tr	03/82	81	2	3	0

FELL James Irving (Jimmy)
Born: Cleethorpes, North Lincolnshire, England, 4 January, 1936 — LW
Died: Grimsby, North Lincolnshire, England, 2 February, 2011

League Club	Source	Date Signed	Seasons Played	Apps	Subs	Gls
Grimsby T	Waltham	04/54	56-60	166	-	35
Everton	Tr	03/61	60-61	27	-	4
Newcastle U	Tr	03/62	61-62	49	-	16
Walsall	Tr	07/63	63	21	-	4
Lincoln C	Tr	01/64	63-65	64	0	10

FELL Leslie James (Les)
Born: Leyton, NE London, England, 16 December, 1920 — W
Died: Rainham, Kent, England, 4 October, 2010

League Club	Source	Date Signed	Seasons Played	Apps	Subs	Gls
Charlton Ath	Gravesend U	12/45	46-51	13	-	2
Crystal Palace	Tr	10/52	52-53	65	-	6

FELLAINI Marouane
Born: Brussels, Belgium, 22 November, 1987 — M/F
Belgium: 63/U21-7/Youth

League Club	Source	Date Signed	Seasons Played	Apps	Subs	Gls
Everton	Standard Liege (BEL)	09/08	08-13	132	9	25
Manchester U	Tr	09/13	13-14	31	12	6

FELLOWES William James (Billy)
Born: Bradford, England, 15 March, 1910 — LH
Died: Plymouth, England, November, 1987

League Club	Source	Date Signed	Seasons Played	Apps	Subs	Gls
Plymouth Arg	Tavistock T	07/27	29-32	5	-	0

League Club	Source	Date Signed	Seasons Played	Apps	Subs	Gls
Leyton Orient	Tr	07/33	33-34	78	-	1
Luton T	Tr	05/35	35-37	110	-	3
Exeter C	Tr	06/38	38-46	56	-	1

FELLOWS Geoffrey Alan (Geoff)
Born: West Bromwich, West Midlands, England, 26 July, 1944 LB

League Club	Source	Date Signed	Seasons Played	Apps	Subs	Gls
Aston Villa	App	10/61				
Shrewsbury T	Tr	06/65	65-72	276	4	2

FELLOWS Gregory Frederick Arthur (Greg)
Born: Dudley, West Midlands, England, 10 October, 1953 F

League Club	Source	Date Signed	Seasons Played	Apps	Subs	Gls
Aston Villa	App	09/71				
Crewe Alex	L	02/73	72	3	0	1
Manchester U	Atlanta Apollos (USA)	08/73				

FELLOWS Stewart
Born: Stockton-on-Tees, Cleveland, England, 9 October, 1948 CD

League Club	Source	Date Signed	Seasons Played	Apps	Subs	Gls
Newcastle U	App	03/66				
York C	Tr	06/67	67	0	2	0

FELTON Graham MacLean
Born: Cambridge, England, 1 March, 1949 W
England: Youth

League Club	Source	Date Signed	Seasons Played	Apps	Subs	Gls
Northampton T	Cambridge U	09/66	66-75	243	10	25
Barnsley	L	02/76	75	12	0	2
Barnsley	Tr	07/76	76	24	0	3

FELTON Kenneth Carl (Ken)
Born: Blackhall, County Durham, England, 18 February, 1949 LB/F

League Club	Source	Date Signed	Seasons Played	Apps	Subs	Gls
Darlington	Jnr	04/67	67-69	50	2	7

FELTON Robert Francis Foster (Bobby)
Born: Gateshead, Tyne and Wear, England, 12 August, 1918 FB
Died: Aintree, Merseyside, England, 4 April, 1982

League Club	Source	Date Signed	Seasons Played	Apps	Subs	Gls
Liverpool	Hill Top U	08/35				
Everton	Tr	08/37				
Port Vale	Tr	06/38	38	10	-	0
Crystal Palace	Tr	09/46	46	1	-	0

FELTON Vivien Edward
Born: Southgate, N London, England, 13 August, 1929 LH
Died: Enfield, N London, England, 13 October, 2005

League Club	Source	Date Signed	Seasons Played	Apps	Subs	Gls
Crystal Palace	Barnet	08/54	54-55	2	-	0

FENCOTT Kenneth Sydney (Ken)
Born: Walsall, West Midlands, England, 27 December, 1943 F

League Club	Source	Date Signed	Seasons Played	Apps	Subs	Gls
Aston Villa	App	01/61	61-63	3	-	0
Lincoln C	Tr	06/64	64-66	67	6	13

FENELON (GOODWIN) Shamir Daniel Sanchez
Born: Crawley, West Sussex, England, 3 August, 1994 F
Republic of Ireland: U21-1

League Club	Source	Date Signed	Seasons Played	Apps	Subs	Gls
Brighton & HA	Sch	05/12	14	1	1	0
Torquay U	L	01/14	13	11	1	1
Rochdale	L	08/14	14	0	4	0
Tranmere Rov	L	11/14	14	9	1	2
Dagenham & Red	L	02/15	14	3	1	0

FENLON James Shaquelle Christopher (Jim)
Born: Lewisham, SE London, England, 3 March, 1994 M/FB

League Club	Source	Date Signed	Seasons Played	Apps	Subs	Gls
AFC Wimbledon	Sch	05/12	12-13	31	5	1

FENN Neale Michael Charles
Born: Edmonton, N London, England, 18 January, 1977 F
Republic of Ireland: B-1/U21-9/Youth

League Club	Source	Date Signed	Seasons Played	Apps	Subs	Gls
Tottenham H	YT	07/95	96-97	0	8	0
Leyton Orient	L	01/98	97	3	0	0
Norwich C	L	03/98	97	6	1	1
Swindon T	L	11/98	98	4	0	0
Lincoln C	L	12/98	98	0	4	0
Peterborough U	Tr	07/01	01-02	33	17	7

FENNEY Stanley (Stan)
Born: Barry, Vale of Glamorgan, Wales, 21 June, 1923 LB
Died: Bridgend, Wales, 21 October, 2003

League Club	Source	Date Signed	Seasons Played	Apps	Subs	Gls
Barrow	Stranraer	12/45	46	27	-	0

FENOUGHTY Thomas (Tom)
Born: Rotherham, South Yorkshire, England, 7 June, 1941 M

League Club	Source	Date Signed	Seasons Played	Apps	Subs	Gls
Sheffield U	Sheffield FC	11/63	63-68	47	3	4
Chesterfield	Tr	07/69	69-71	97	3	15

FENSOME Andrew Brian (Andy)
Born: Northampton, England, 18 February, 1969 RB

League Club	Source	Date Signed	Seasons Played	Apps	Subs	Gls
Norwich C	App	02/87				
Cambridge U	Bury T	11/89	89-93	122	4	1
Preston NE	Tr	10/93	93-95	93	0	1
Rochdale	Tr	06/96	96-97	80	2	0

FENTON Alexander Ewan (Ewan)
Born: Dundee, Scotland, 17 November, 1929 WH
Died: Limerick, Republic of Ireland, 3 April, 2006

League Club	Source	Date Signed	Seasons Played	Apps	Subs	Gls
Blackpool	Dundee North End	11/46	48-58	203	-	20
Wrexham	Tr	05/59	59	24	-	0

FENTON Anthony Brian (Tony)
Born: Preston, Lancashire, England, 23 November, 1979 CD
England: Youth

League Club	Source	Date Signed	Seasons Played	Apps	Subs	Gls
Manchester C	YT	11/96				
Portsmouth	Tr	03/99	99	0	1	0

FENTON Benjamin Robert Vincent (Benny)
Born: West Ham, E London, England, 28 October, 1918 RH/IF
Died: Poole, Dorset, England, July, 2000

League Club	Source	Date Signed	Seasons Played	Apps	Subs	Gls
West Ham U	Colchester T	10/35	37-38	21	-	9
Millwall	Tr	03/39	38-46	20	-	7
Charlton Ath	Tr	01/47	46-54	264	-	22
Colchester U	Tr	02/55	54-57	104	-	15

FENTON Graham Anthony
Born: Wallsend, Tyne and Wear, England, 22 May, 1974 F
England: U21-1

League Club	Source	Date Signed	Seasons Played	Apps	Subs	Gls
Aston Villa	YT	02/92	93-95	16	16	3
West Bromwich A	L	01/94	93	7	0	3
Blackburn Rov	Tr	11/95	95-96	9	18	7
Leicester C	Tr	08/97	97-99	13	21	3
Walsall	Tr	03/00	99	8	1	1
Stoke C	Tr	08/00	00	2	3	1
Blackpool	St Mirren	08/01	01	6	9	5
Darlington	L	09/02	02	4	2	1

FENTON Michael (Micky)
Born: Stockton-on-Tees, Cleveland, England, 30 October, 1913 CF
Died: Stockton-on-Tees, Cleveland, England, 5 February, 2003
England: 1/War-1

League Club	Source	Date Signed	Seasons Played	Apps	Subs	Gls
Middlesbrough	South Bank East End	03/33	32-49	240	-	147

FENTON Nicholas Leonard (Nicky)
Born: Preston, Lancashire, England, 23 November, 1979 CD
England: Youth

League Club	Source	Date Signed	Seasons Played	Apps	Subs	Gls
Manchester C	YT	11/96	98	15	0	0
Notts Co	L	10/99	99	13	0	1
Bournemouth	L	03/00	99	8	0	0
Bournemouth	L	08/00	00	4	1	0
Notts Co	Tr	09/00	00-03	153	2	9
Doncaster Rov	Tr	07/04	04-05	58	5	3
Grimsby T	Tr	08/06	06-07	77	3	6
Rotherham U	Tr	08/08	08-10	110	2	4
Morecambe	Tr	07/11	11-12	72	1	4

FENTON Ronald (Ronnie)
Born: South Shields, Tyne and Wear, England, 21 September, 1940 IF
Died: Beeston, Nottinghamshire, England, 25 September, 2013

League Club	Source	Date Signed	Seasons Played	Apps	Subs	Gls
Burnley	South Shields	09/57	60-61	11	-	1
West Bromwich A	Tr	11/62	62-64	59	-	16
Birmingham C	Tr	01/65	64-67	28	5	7
Brentford	Tr	01/68	67-69	87	4	19
Notts Co	Tr	07/70				

FENTON Stephen James (Steve)
Born: Hartlepool, Cleveland, England, 25 February, 1951 M
England: Youth

League Club	Source	Date Signed	Seasons Played	Apps	Subs	Gls
Middlesbrough	Jnr	08/69				
Bradford C	Tr	06/72	72	9	1	1

FENTON William Hartes (Billy)
Born: Hartlepool, Cleveland, England, 23 June, 1926 LW
Died: York, England, 19 April, 1973

League Club	Source	Date Signed	Seasons Played	Apps	Subs	Gls
Barnsley	Elwick Road	11/44				
Blackburn Rov	Horden CW	12/48	48-50	33	-	7
York C	Tr	05/51	51-57	257	-	118

FENWICK Paul Joseph
Born: Camden, N London, England, 25 August, 1969 CD
Canada: 34

League Club	Source	Date Signed	Seasons Played	Apps	Subs	Gls
Birmingham C	Winnipeg Fury (CAN)	11/92	92-93	9	10	0

FENWICK Scott James
Born: Gateshead, Tyne and Wear, England, 9 April, 1990 F

League Club	Source	Date Signed	Seasons Played	Apps	Subs	Gls
Hartlepool U	Dunston UTS	11/14	14	10	9	6

FENWICK Terence William (Terry)
Born: Seaham, County Durham, England, 17 November, 1959 CD
England: 20/U21-11/Youth

League Club	Source	Date Signed	Seasons Played	Apps	Subs	Gls
Crystal Palace	App	12/76	77-80	62	8	0
Queens Park Rgrs	Tr	12/80	80-87	256	0	33
Tottenham H	Tr	12/87	87-92	90	3	8
Leicester C	L	10/90	90	8	0	1
Swindon T	Tr	09/93	93-94	25	3	0

League Club	Source	Date Signed	Seasons Played	Apps	Subs	Gls

FER Leroy Johan
Born: Zoetermeer, Netherlands, 5 January, 1990 — M
Netherlands: 11/U21-31/Youth

League Club	Source	Date Signed	Seasons Played	Apps	Subs	Gls
Norwich C	FC Twente (NED)	07/13	13-14	28	2	3
Queens Park Rgrs	Tr	08/14	14	27	2	6

FERDINAND Anton Julian
Born: Peckham, SE London, England, 18 February, 1985 — CD
England: U21-17/Youth

League Club	Source	Date Signed	Seasons Played	Apps	Subs	Gls
West Ham U	Sch	08/02	03-07	118	20	5
Sunderland	Tr	08/08	08-11	76	9	0
Queens Park Rgrs	Tr	08/11	11-12	41	3	0
Reading	Antalyaspor (TKY)	08/14	14	1	1	0

FERDINAND Kane Ryan
Born: Newham, E London, England, 7 October, 1992 — M
Republic of Ireland: U21-2/Youth

League Club	Source	Date Signed	Seasons Played	Apps	Subs	Gls
Southend U	Sch	03/11	10-12	50	11	10
Peterborough U	Tr	08/12	12-14	17	29	1
Northampton T	L	10/13	13	4	0	0
Cheltenham T	L	11/14	14	15	1	0

FERDINAND Leslie (Les)
Born: Acton, W London, England, 8 December, 1966 — F
England: 17/B-1/Youth

League Club	Source	Date Signed	Seasons Played	Apps	Subs	Gls
Queens Park Rgrs	Hayes	03/87	86-94	152	11	80
Brentford	L	03/88	87	3	0	0
Newcastle U	Tr	06/95	95-96	67	1	41
Tottenham H	Tr	08/97	97-02	97	21	33
West Ham U	Tr	01/03	02	12	2	2
Leicester C	Tr	07/03	03	20	9	12
Bolton W	Tr	07/04	04	1	11	1
Reading	Tr	01/05	04	4	8	1

FERDINAND Rio Gavin
Born: Peckham, SE London, England, 7 November, 1978 — CD
England: 81/U21-5/Youth

League Club	Source	Date Signed	Seasons Played	Apps	Subs	Gls
West Ham U	YT	11/95	95-00	122	5	2
Bournemouth	L	11/96	96	10	0	0
Leeds U	Tr	11/00	00-01	54	0	2
Manchester U	Tr	07/02	02-13	305	7	7
Queens Park Rgrs	Tr	07/14	14	11	0	0

FEREBEE Stewart Raymond
Born: Carshalton, S London, England, 6 September, 1960 — F

League Club	Source	Date Signed	Seasons Played	Apps	Subs	Gls
York C	Harrogate T	07/79	79-80	7	6	0
Darlington	Harrogate T	03/87	86	8	0	0
Halifax T	Tr	07/87	87	6	6	0

FEREDAY Wayne
Born: Warley, West Midlands, England, 16 June, 1963 — FB/M
England: FLge/U21-5

League Club	Source	Date Signed	Seasons Played	Apps	Subs	Gls
Queens Park Rgrs	App	09/80	80-88	167	29	21
Newcastle U	Tr	06/89	89-90	27	6	0
Bournemouth	Tr	11/90	90-91	20	3	0
West Bromwich A	Tr	12/91	91-93	39	9	3
Cardiff C	Tr	03/94	93-94	43	1	2

FERENCZI Istvan
Born: Gyor, Hungary, 14 September, 1977 — F
Hungary: 9/U21-11/Youth

League Club	Source	Date Signed	Seasons Played	Apps	Subs	Gls
Barnsley	Zalaegerszegi (HUN)	01/07	06-07	39	14	11

FERGUSON Alexander Stirling Brown (Alex)
Born: Lochore, Fife, Scotland, 5 August, 1903 — G
Died: Swansea, Wales, 1974
Wales: WLge-2

League Club	Source	Date Signed	Seasons Played	Apps	Subs	Gls
Wigan Bor	Vale of Clyde	11/24	24	1	-	0
Gillingham	Tr	06/25	25-26	67	-	0
Swansea C	Tr	02/27	26-35	280	-	0
Bury	Tr	06/36	36-37	63	-	0
Newport Co	Tr	06/38	38	41	-	0
Bristol C	Tr	05/46	46	32	-	0
Swindon T	Tr	09/47	47	7	-	0

FERGUSON Archibald (Archie)
Born: Lochore, Fife, Scotland, 9 December, 1918 — G
Died: Dunfermline, Fife, Scotland, 19 March, 1998

League Club	Source	Date Signed	Seasons Played	Apps	Subs	Gls
Doncaster Rov	Raith Rov	12/41	46-47	61	-	0
Wrexham	Tr	07/48	48-52	126	-	0

FERGUSON Barry
Born: Dublin, Republic of Ireland, 7 September, 1979 — CD
Republic of Ireland: U21-6

League Club	Source	Date Signed	Seasons Played	Apps	Subs	Gls
Coventry C	Home Farm (ROI)	09/98				
Colchester U	L	03/00	99	5	1	0
Hartlepool U	L	07/00	00	4	0	0
Northampton T	L	12/00	00	1	2	0

FERGUSON Barry
Born: Hamilton, Lanarkshire, Scotland, 2 February, 1978 — DM
Scotland: 45/U21-12

League Club	Source	Date Signed	Seasons Played	Apps	Subs	Gls
Blackburn Rov	Glasgow Rangers	08/03	03-04	35	1	3
Birmingham C	Glasgow Rangers	07/09	09-10	72	0	0
Blackpool	Tr	07/11	11-13	77	3	1
Fleetwood T	L	11/12	12	6	0	0

FERGUSON Charles (Charlie)
Born: Glasgow, Scotland, 22 April, 1930 — D

League Club	Source	Date Signed	Seasons Played	Apps	Subs	Gls
Accrington Stan	Hamilton Academical	05/54	54	1	-	0
Rochdale	Tr	09/55	55-58	150	-	3
Oldham Ath	Tr	07/59	59-60	57	-	0

FERGUSON Darren
Born: Glasgow, Scotland, 9 February, 1972 — M
Scotland: U21-5/Youth

League Club	Source	Date Signed	Seasons Played	Apps	Subs	Gls
Manchester U	YT	07/90	90-93	20	7	0
Wolverhampton W	Tr	01/94	93-98	94	23	4
Wrexham	Sparta Rotterdam (NED)	09/99	99-06	292	5	24

FERGUSON David Dyer
Born: Bonnybridge, Falkirk, Scotland, 11 March, 1929 — LW

League Club	Source	Date Signed	Seasons Played	Apps	Subs	Gls
Coventry C	Alloa Ath	10/56	56	4	-	0

FERGUSON David Lee
Born: Sunderland, England, 7 June, 1994 — LB/M

League Club	Source	Date Signed	Seasons Played	Apps	Subs	Gls
Sunderland	Darlington (Sch)	07/12				
Blackpool	Tr	01/15	14	6	4	1

FERGUSON Derek
Born: Glasgow, Scotland, 31 July, 1967 — DM
Scotland: 2/U21-5/Youth/Schools

League Club	Source	Date Signed	Seasons Played	Apps	Subs	Gls
Sunderland	Heart of Midlothian	07/93	93-94	64	0	0

FERGUSON Donald (Don)
Born: Toronto, Canada, 2 January, 1963 — G
Canada: B

League Club	Source	Date Signed	Seasons Played	Apps	Subs	Gls
Wrexham	Toronto First (CAN)	01/86	85	20	0	0

FERGUSON Duncan Cowan
Born: Stirling, Scotland, 27 December, 1971 — F
Scotland: 7/U21-7/Youth/Schools

League Club	Source	Date Signed	Seasons Played	Apps	Subs	Gls
Everton	Glasgow Rangers	10/94	94-98	110	6	37
Newcastle U	Tr	11/98	98-99	24	6	8
Everton	Tr	08/00	00-05	52	71	23

FERGUSON Edward Brodie (Eddie)
Born: Whitburn, West Lothian, Scotland, 10 September, 1949 — M

League Club	Source	Date Signed	Seasons Played	Apps	Subs	Gls
Rotherham U	Dumbarton	02/71	70-73	64	3	5
Grimsby T	L	11/71	71	1	1	0

FERGUSON Hubert
Born: Belfast, Northern Ireland, 23 May, 1926 — FB
Died: Dewsbury, West Yorkshire, England, July, 1994

League Club	Source	Date Signed	Seasons Played	Apps	Subs	Gls
Bradford C	Ballymena U	07/48	48-52	132	-	0
Halifax T	Frickley Colliery	09/54	54-57	95	-	0

FERGUSON Iain John
Born: Newarthill, Lanarkshire, Scotland, 4 August, 1962 — F
Scotland: U21-4

League Club	Source	Date Signed	Seasons Played	Apps	Subs	Gls
Charlton Ath (L)	Heart of Midlothian	11/89	89	1	0	0
Bristol C (L)	Heart of Midlothian	03/90	89	8	3	2

FERGUSON James Brian (Brian)
Born: Irvine, Ayrshire, Scotland, 14 December, 1960 — M/RB

League Club	Source	Date Signed	Seasons Played	Apps	Subs	Gls
Newcastle U	Mansfield T (App)	01/79	79	4	1	1
Hull C	Tr	12/80	80-81	24	4	2
Southend U	Goole T	08/83	83-84	31	10	6
Chesterfield	Tr	10/84	84	30	1	0

FERGUSON James Cameron Mars (Jim)
Born: Glasgow, Scotland, 20 February, 1935 — G

League Club	Source	Date Signed	Seasons Played	Apps	Subs	Gls
Oldham Ath	Falkirk	05/59	59	36	-	0
Crewe Alex	Tr	08/60	60-61	27	-	0
Darlington	Tr	07/62	62	32	-	0

FERGUSON John (Jackie)
Born: Maybole, Ayrshire, Scotland, 29 August, 1939 — RW

League Club	Source	Date Signed	Seasons Played	Apps	Subs	Gls
Southend U	Airdrieonians	06/67	67	13	1	2

FERGUSON John Theodore Hever
Born: Edinburgh, Scotland, 14 June, 1939 — LW

League Club	Source	Date Signed	Seasons Played	Apps	Subs	Gls
Oldham Ath	St Andrew's U	11/56	56	1	-	0

FERGUSON Mark
Born: Liverpool, England, 6 November, 1960 — M

League Club	Source	Date Signed	Seasons Played	Apps	Subs	Gls
Tranmere Rov	Scarborough	08/81	81-84	72	16	13

FERGUSON Martin Murphy
Born: Glasgow, Scotland, 21 December, 1942 F/M

League Club	Source	Date Signed	Seasons Played	Apps	Subs	Gls
Barnsley	Greenock Morton	08/65	65	40	0	17
Doncaster Rov	Tr	07/66	66	3	0	0

FERGUSON Michael John (Mick)
Born: Newcastle-upon-Tyne, England, 3 October, 1954 F

League Club	Source	Date Signed	Seasons Played	Apps	Subs	Gls
Coventry C	App	12/71	74-80	121	6	51
Everton	Tr	08/81	81	7	1	4
Birmingham C	L	11/82	82	20	0	8
Birmingham C	Tr	06/83	84	2	0	1
Coventry C	L	03/84	83	7	0	3
Brighton & HA	Tr	09/84	84-85	17	0	6
Colchester U	Tr	03/86	85-86	25	1	11

FERGUSON Michael Kevin (Mike)
Born: Burnley, Lancashire, England, 9 March, 1943 M

League Club	Source	Date Signed	Seasons Played	Apps	Subs	Gls
Accrington Stan	Plymouth Arg (Am)	07/60	60	23	-	1
Blackburn Rov	Tr	03/62	62-67	220	0	29
Aston Villa	Tr	05/68	68-69	38	0	2
Queens Park Rgrs	Tr	11/69	69-72	67	1	2
Cambridge U	Tr	07/73	73	39	0	4
Rochdale	Tr	07/74	74-75	68	1	5
Halifax T	IA Akranes (ICE)	12/76	76	2	0	0

FERGUSON Robert (Bobby)
Born: Kilwinning, Ayrshire, Scotland, 1 March, 1945 G
Scotland: 7/SLge-2/U23-1

League Club	Source	Date Signed	Seasons Played	Apps	Subs	Gls
West Ham U	Kilmarnock	06/67	67-79	240	0	0
Sheffield Wed	L	02/74	73	5	0	0

FERGUSON Robert (Bob)
Born: Grangetown, Cleveland, England, 25 July, 1917 G
Died: Marlow, Buckinghamshire, England, 17 June, 2006

League Club	Source	Date Signed	Seasons Played	Apps	Subs	Gls
Middlesbrough	Hurworth Jnrs	08/35	36-37	10	-	0
York C	Tr	05/39	46	26	-	0

FERGUSON Robert Burnitt (Bobby)
Born: Dudley, Northumberland, England, 8 January, 1938 LB

League Club	Source	Date Signed	Seasons Played	Apps	Subs	Gls
Newcastle U	Dudley Welfare	05/55	55-62	11	-	0
Derby Co	Tr	10/62	62-65	121	0	0
Cardiff C	Tr	12/65	65-68	88	1	0
Newport Co	Barry T	07/69	69-70	71	0	2

FERGUSON Ronald Charles (Ron)
Born: Accrington, Lancashire, England, 9 February, 1957 F

League Club	Source	Date Signed	Seasons Played	Apps	Subs	Gls
Sheffield Wed	App	02/75	74	10	1	1
Scunthorpe U	L	12/75	75	3	0	0
Darlington	Tr	02/76	75-79	101	13	18

FERGUSON Shane Kevin
Born: Limavady, Derry, Northern Ireland, 12 July, 1991 LW
Northern Ireland: 18/B-1/U21-11/Youth

League Club	Source	Date Signed	Seasons Played	Apps	Subs	Gls
Newcastle U	Sch	07/09	10-12	7	16	0
Birmingham C	L	02/13	12	10	1	1
Birmingham C	L	07/13	13	9	9	0

FERN Rodney Alan
Born: Measham, Leicestershire, England, 13 December, 1948 F

League Club	Source	Date Signed	Seasons Played	Apps	Subs	Gls
Leicester C	Measham Social Welfare	12/66	67-71	133	16	31
Luton T	Tr	06/72	72-74	34	5	5
Chesterfield	Tr	06/75	75-78	150	2	54
Rotherham U	Tr	06/79	79-82	98	7	34

FERNANDES Fabrice
Born: Aubervilliers, France, 29 October, 1979 LW

League Club	Source	Date Signed	Seasons Played	Apps	Subs	Gls
Fulham (L)	Stade Rennais (FRA)	08/00	00	23	6	2
Southampton	Stade Rennais (FRA)	12/01	01-04	76	15	5
Bolton W	Tr	08/05	05	0	1	0

FERNANDES Gelson
Born: Praia, Cape Verde Islands, 2 September, 1986 DM
Switzerland: 51/U21-9

League Club	Source	Date Signed	Seasons Played	Apps	Subs	Gls
Manchester C	FC Sion (SUI)	07/07	07-08	24	19	3
Leicester C (L)	Saint-Etienne (FRA)	08/11	11	10	5	1

FERNANDES Manuel Henriques Tavares
Born: Lisbon, Portugal, 5 February, 1986 M
Portugal: 9/U21-22

League Club	Source	Date Signed	Seasons Played	Apps	Subs	Gls
Portsmouth (L)	Benfica (POR)	08/06	06	7	3	0
Everton (L)	Benfica (POR)	01/07	06	8	1	2
Everton (L)	Valencia (SPN)	01/08	07	9	3	0

FERNANDES Tamer Hasan
Born: Paddington, Central London, England, 7 December, 1974 G
England: Youth

League Club	Source	Date Signed	Seasons Played	Apps	Subs	Gls
Brentford	YT	07/93	93-96	10	2	0
Colchester U	Tr	01/98	98	8	0	0

FERNANDEZ Federico
Born: Carlos Tejedor, Argentina, 21 February, 1989 CD
Argentina: 31/Youth

League Club	Source	Date Signed	Seasons Played	Apps	Subs	Gls
Swansea C	Napoli (ITA)	08/14	14	27	1	0

FERNANDEZ Vincent Santiago Georges
Born: Marseille, France, 19 September, 1986 CD

League Club	Source	Date Signed	Seasons Played	Apps	Subs	Gls
Nottingham F	Sch	01/05	05	0	1	0
Wycombe W	L	08/06	06	1	0	0
Blackpool	L	11/06	06	0	1	0

[FERNANDINHO] FERNANDO Luiz Roza
Born: Londrina, Brazil, 4 May, 1985 M
Brazil: 20/Youth

League Club	Source	Date Signed	Seasons Played	Apps	Subs	Gls
Manchester C	Shakhtar Donetsk (UKR)	06/13	13-14	54	12	8

[FERNANDO] REGES Francisco
Born: Goias, Brazil, 25 July, 1987 DM
Brazil: Youth

League Club	Source	Date Signed	Seasons Played	Apps	Subs	Gls
Manchester C	FC Porto (POR)	06/14	14	22	3	2

FERNEY Martin John
Born: Lambeth, S London, England, 8 November, 1971 M

League Club	Source	Date Signed	Seasons Played	Apps	Subs	Gls
Fulham	YT	07/90	90-94	49	11	1

FERNIE James (Jim)
Born: Kirkcaldy, Fife, Scotland, 31 October, 1936 IF

League Club	Source	Date Signed	Seasons Played	Apps	Subs	Gls
Doncaster Rov	Arbroath	10/58	58-60	89	-	31

FERNIE William (Willie)
Born: Kinglassie, Fife, Scotland, 22 November, 1928 IF
Died: Glasgow, Scotland, 1 July, 2011
Scotland: 12/B/SLge-5

League Club	Source	Date Signed	Seasons Played	Apps	Subs	Gls
Middlesbrough	Glasgow Celtic	12/58	58-60	65	-	3

FERNS Philip (Phil)
Born: Liverpool, England, 14 November, 1937 WH
Died: Bournemouth, England, 25 August, 2007

League Club	Source	Date Signed	Seasons Played	Apps	Subs	Gls
Liverpool	Manchester C (Am)	09/57	62-64	27	-	1
Bournemouth	Tr	08/65	65	46	0	0
Mansfield T	Tr	08/66	66-67	55	1	1

FERNS Philip David (Phil)
Born: Liverpool, England, 12 September, 1961 LB

League Club	Source	Date Signed	Seasons Played	Apps	Subs	Gls
Bournemouth	App	02/79	78-80	94	1	6
Charlton Ath	Tr	08/81	81-82	35	3	1
Wimbledon	L	12/82	82	7	0	0
Blackpool	Tr	08/83	83-84	44	3	0
Aldershot	Tr	07/85	85	24	0	2

FERRARI Carlos Eduardo
Born: Londrina, Brazil, 19 February, 1979 M

League Club	Source	Date Signed	Seasons Played	Apps	Subs	Gls
Birmingham C (L)	Mirassol (BRA)	08/01	01	0	4	0

FERRARI Matteo
Born: Aflou, Algeria, 5 December, 1979 LB
Italy: 11/U21-27

League Club	Source	Date Signed	Seasons Played	Apps	Subs	Gls
Everton (L)	AS Roma (ITA)	08/05	05	6	2	0

FERREIRA Fabio Miguel Lourenco
Born: Lisbon, Portugal, 3 May, 1989 M
Portugal: Youth

League Club	Source	Date Signed	Seasons Played	Apps	Subs	Gls
Chelsea	Sch	07/06				
Oldham Ath	L	03/09	08	0	1	0

FERREIRA Paulo Renato Rebocho
Born: Cascais, Portugal, 18 January, 1979 RB
Portugal: 62

League Club	Source	Date Signed	Seasons Played	Apps	Subs	Gls
Chelsea	FC Porto (POR)	07/04	04-12	107	34	0

FERRELL Andrew Eric (Andy)
Born: Newcastle-upon-Tyne, England, 9 January, 1984 M

League Club	Source	Date Signed	Seasons Played	Apps	Subs	Gls
Newcastle U	Sch	12/02				
Watford	Tr	07/04				
Hereford U	Tr	08/05	06	15	6	0

FERRER Albert Llopes
Born: Barcelona, Spain, 6 June, 1970 RB
Spain: 36/U23-6/Youth

League Club	Source	Date Signed	Seasons Played	Apps	Subs	Gls
Chelsea	Barcelona (SPN)	08/98	98-02	71	5	0

FERRETT Christopher Andrew (Chris)
Born: Poole, Dorset, England, 10 February, 1977 M

League Club	Source	Date Signed	Seasons Played	Apps	Subs	Gls
Bournemouth	YT	-	94	0	1	0

FERRETTI Andrea
Born: Parma, Italy, 18 September, 1996 F

League Club	Source	Date Signed	Seasons Played	Apps	Subs	Gls
Cardiff C	Parma Jnrs (ITA)	08/05	05-06	0	5	0
Scunthorpe U	L	08/06	06	0	4	0

FERRI Jean-Michel
Born: Lyon, France, 7 February, 1969 — DM
France: 5

League Club	Source	Date Signed	Seasons Played	Apps	Subs	Gls
Liverpool	Istanbulspor (TKY)	12/98	98	0	2	0

FERRIDAY Leslie (Les)
Born: Manchester, England, 3 June, 1929 — WH
Died: West Cheshire, England, August, 2010

League Club	Source	Date Signed	Seasons Played	Apps	Subs	Gls
Walsall	Buxton	05/54	54	32	-	1

FERRIER Henry (Harry)
Born: Ratho, Edinburgh, Scotland, 20 May, 1920 — LB
Died: Earls Colne, Essex, England, 16 October, 2002

League Club	Source	Date Signed	Seasons Played	Apps	Subs	Gls
Barnsley	Ratho Amats	09/37				
Portsmouth	Tr	03/46	46-53	241	-	8

FERRIER John
Born: Edinburgh, Scotland, 6 October, 1927 — LB
Died: Chryston, Lanarkshire, Scotland, 25 September, 1998

League Club	Source	Date Signed	Seasons Played	Apps	Subs	Gls
Brighton & HA		10/46	46	1	-	1
Exeter C	Clyde	05/56	56	31	-	0

FERRIER Ronald Johnson (Ron)
Born: Cleethorpes, North Lincolnshire, England, 26 April, 1914 — IF
Died: Cleethorpes, North Lincolnshire, England, 11 October, 1991

League Club	Source	Date Signed	Seasons Played	Apps	Subs	Gls
Grimsby T	Grimsby W	05/33				
Manchester U	Tr	05/35	35-37	18	-	4
Oldham Ath	Tr	03/38	37-46	45	-	25
Lincoln C	Tr	08/47				

FERRIS John Owner
Born: Bristol, England, 4 September, 1939 — G

League Club	Source	Date Signed	Seasons Played	Apps	Subs	Gls
Torquay U	Minehead	09/58	58	3	-	0

FERRIS Paul James
Born: Lisburn, Belfast, Northern Ireland, 10 July, 1965 — W

League Club	Source	Date Signed	Seasons Played	Apps	Subs	Gls
Newcastle U	App	03/83	81-84	1	10	0

FERRIS Raymond Osborn (Ray)
Born: Newry, Armagh, Northern Ireland, 22 September, 1920 — LH
Died: Manchester, England, February, 1994
Northern Ireland: 3

League Club	Source	Date Signed	Seasons Played	Apps	Subs	Gls
Crewe Alex	Cambridge T	03/45	46-48	102	-	22
Birmingham C	Tr	03/49	48-52	93	-	3

FERRIS Samuel (Sam)
Born: Motherwell, Lanarkshire, Scotland, 14 March, 1951 — F

League Club	Source	Date Signed	Seasons Played	Apps	Subs	Gls
Chesterfield	Albion Rov	03/72	71-73	25	6	3
Workington	L	02/74	73	2	1	0

FERRY Gordon
Born: Sunderland, England, 22 December, 1943 — CH

League Club	Source	Date Signed	Seasons Played	Apps	Subs	Gls
Arsenal	App	01/61	64	11	-	0
Leyton Orient	Tr	05/65	65	42	0	0

FERRY Simon William
Born: Dundee, Scotland, 11 January, 1988 — M
Scotland: Youth

League Club	Source	Date Signed	Seasons Played	Apps	Subs	Gls
Swindon T	Glasgow Celtic	08/09	09-12	126	21	8
Portsmouth	Tr	07/13	13	19	1	1

FERRY William (Willie)
Born: Sunderland, England, 21 November, 1966 — F
England: Schools

League Club	Source	Date Signed	Seasons Played	Apps	Subs	Gls
Scunthorpe U	App	09/84	84-86	2	3	0
Barnsley	Tr	11/86	86	3	1	1

FERUZ Islam Salieh
Born: Kismayo, Somalia, 10 September, 1995 — F
Scotland: U21-4/Youth

League Club	Source	Date Signed	Seasons Played	Apps	Subs	Gls
Chelsea	Sch	09/12				
Blackpool	L	01/15	14	0	2	0

FESTA Gianluca
Born: Cagliari, Sardinia, Italy, 15 March, 1969 — D

League Club	Source	Date Signed	Seasons Played	Apps	Subs	Gls
Middlesbrough	Inter Milan (ITA)	01/97	96-01	132	6	10
Portsmouth	Tr	08/02	02	27	0	1

FETTIS Alan William
Born: Newtownards, Down, Northern Ireland, 1 February, 1971 — G
Northern Ireland: 25/B-3/Youth/Schools

League Club	Source	Date Signed	Seasons Played	Apps	Subs	Gls
Hull C	Ards	08/91	91-95	131	4	2
West Bromwich A	L	11/95	95	3	0	0
Nottingham F	Tr	01/96	96	4	0	0
Blackburn Rov	Tr	09/97	97-99	9	2	0
York C	Tr	03/00	99-02	125	0	0
Hull C	Tr	01/03	02-03	20	0	0
Sheffield U	L	12/03	03	2	1	0
Grimsby T	L	03/04	03	11	0	0
Macclesfield T	Tr	07/04	04-05	61	0	0
Bury	Tr	07/06	06	9	0	0

FEUER Anthony Ian (Ian)
Born: Las Vegas, Nevada, USA, 20 May, 1971 — G
USA: 1

League Club	Source	Date Signed	Seasons Played	Apps	Subs	Gls
West Ham U	Los Angeles Sals (USA)	03/94				
Peterborough U	L	02/95	94	16	0	0
Luton T	Tr	09/95	95-97	97	0	0
Cardiff C	Colorado Rapids (USA)	01/00				
West Ham U	Tr	02/00	99	3	0	0
Wimbledon	Tr	06/00	01	2	2	0
Derby Co	L	10/01	01	2	0	0
Tranmere Rov	Tr	08/02	02	2	0	0

FEWINGS Patrick John Henry (Pat)
Born: Barnstaple, Devon, England, 21 January, 1931 — RW
Died: Barnstaple, Devon, England, 4 June, 1997

League Club	Source	Date Signed	Seasons Played	Apps	Subs	Gls
Torquay U	Barnstaple T	11/53	53-54	8	-	0

FEWINGS Paul John
Born: Hull, England, 18 February, 1978 — F/M

League Club	Source	Date Signed	Seasons Played	Apps	Subs	Gls
Hull C	App	08/95	94-97	32	25	2

FICKLING Ashley Spencer
Born: Sheffield, England, 15 November, 1972 — CD
England: Schools

League Club	Source	Date Signed	Seasons Played	Apps	Subs	Gls
Sheffield U	Jnr	07/91				
Darlington	L	11/92	92	14	0	0
Darlington	L	08/93	93	1	0	0
Grimsby T	Tr	03/95	94-96	26	13	2
Darlington	L	03/98	97	8	0	0
Scunthorpe U	Tr	07/98	98-00	55	13	1

FIDLER Denis John
Born: Stockport, Greater Manchester, England, 22 June, 1938 — LW
Died: Italy, 2 June, 2015

League Club	Source	Date Signed	Seasons Played	Apps	Subs	Gls
Manchester C	Manchester U (Am)	01/57	57-58	5	-	1
Port Vale	Tr	06/60	60-61	38	-	12
Grimsby T	Tr	10/61	61	9	-	3
Halifax T	Tr	04/63	62-66	141	1	40
Darlington	Tr	10/66	66-67	32	2	3

FIDLER Frank
Born: Middleton, Greater Manchester, England, 16 August, 1924 — CF
Died: Farnborough, Hampshire, England, 21 November, 2009

League Club	Source	Date Signed	Seasons Played	Apps	Subs	Gls
Wrexham	Witton A	05/50	50-51	36	-	15
Leeds U	Tr	10/51	51-52	22	-	8
Bournemouth	Tr	12/52	52-54	61	-	31

FIDLER Richard Michael
Born: Sheffield, England, 26 October, 1976 — M
England: Schools

League Club	Source	Date Signed	Seasons Played	Apps	Subs	Gls
Leeds U	Jnr	07/95				
Hull C	Tr	12/95	95	0	1	0

FIDLER Thomas George (Tommy)
Born: Hounslow, SW London, England, 4 September, 1933 — CF
Died: South East Surrey, England, 7 March, 1992

League Club	Source	Date Signed	Seasons Played	Apps	Subs	Gls
Queens Park Rgrs	Hounslow	05/54	54	12	-	2

FIELD Anthony (Tony)
Born: Halifax, West Yorkshire, England, 6 July, 1946 — F

League Club	Source	Date Signed	Seasons Played	Apps	Subs	Gls
Halifax T	Illingworth U	07/63	63-65	20	0	3
Barrow	Tr	08/66	66-67	36	2	16
Southport	Tr	03/68	67-71	127	6	41
Blackburn Rov	Tr	10/71	71-73	104	2	45
Sheffield U	Tr	03/74	73-75	63	3	13

FIELD Anthony Frederick (Tony)
Born: Chester, England, 23 May, 1942 — CF

League Club	Source	Date Signed	Seasons Played	Apps	Subs	Gls
Chester C		08/61	60	2	-	0
Southport	Tr	07/62				

FIELD Norman
Born: Durham, England, 27 August, 1927 — WH
Died: Gateshead, Tyne and Wear, England, June, 1993

League Club	Source	Date Signed	Seasons Played	Apps	Subs	Gls
Portsmouth	Sherburn Jnrs	08/45				
Mansfield T	Tr	06/50	51-52	20	-	0

FIELDER Colin Michael Raynor
Born: Alton, Hampshire, England, 5 January, 1964 — M

League Club	Source	Date Signed	Seasons Played	Apps	Subs	Gls
Aldershot	App	01/82	81-86	56	12	8

FIELDING Alfred Walter (Wally)
Born: Edmonton, N London, England, 26 November, 1919 — IF
Died: Bude, Cornwall, England, 18 January, 2008

League Club	Source	Date Signed	Seasons Played	Apps	Subs	Gls
Everton	Walthamstow Ave	09/45	46-58	380	-	49
Southport	Tr	01/59	58-59	20	-	1

FIELDING Francis David (Frank)
Born: Blackburn, Greater Manchester, England, 4 April, 1988 — G
England: U21-12/Youth

League Club	Source	Date Signed	Seasons Played	Apps	Subs	Gls
Blackburn Rov	Sch	07/06				

League Club	Source	Date Signed	Seasons Played	Apps	Subs	Gls
Wycombe W	L	09/07	07	36	0	0
Northampton T	L	09/08	08	12	0	0
Rochdale	L	01/09	08	23	0	0
Rochdale	L	01/10	09	18	0	0
Derby Co	L	10/10	10	16	0	0
Derby Co	Tr	05/11	11-12	60	0	0
Bristol C	Tr	06/13	13-14	62	0	0
FIELDING John Arnold (Johnny)						
Born: Speke, Merseyside, England, 2 September, 1939						IF
Southport	Wigan Ath	03/61	60-62	76	-	21
Brentford	Tr	03/63	62-65	82	0	18
Grimsby T	Tr	12/65	65-66	29	1	8
FIELDING John Robert						
Born: Billingham, Cleveland, England, 7 April, 1982						CD
York C	YT	07/01	01	9	0	1
FIELDING Mark John						
Born: Bury, Greater Manchester, England, 10 November, 1956						RB
Preston NE	App	11/74	74	9	0	0
FIELDING Michael Anthony (Mike)						
Born: Liverpool, England, 3 December, 1965						D
Barnsley	Everton (App)	08/84				
Rochdale	L	10/84	84	6	0	0
FIELDING Paul Anthony						
Born: Oldham, Greater Manchester, England, 4 December, 1955						M
Rochdale	App	12/73	72-75	65	7	5
FIELDING William (Bill)						
Born: Broadbottom, Greater Manchester, England, 17 June, 1915						G
Died: Blackpool, Lancashire, England, May, 2006						
Cardiff C	Hurst	05/36	36-38	50	-	0
Bolton W	Tr	06/44				
Manchester U	Tr	01/47	46	6	-	0
FIELDS Alfred George (Alf)						
Born: Canning Town, E London, England, 15 November, 1918						CH
Died: Waltham Abbey, Essex, England, 13 November, 2011						
Arsenal	West Ham YC	05/37	38-50	19	-	0
FIELDS Maurice John Bernard (Mike)						
Born: Chester, England, 12 August, 1935						F
Died: Chester, England, 27 May, 2014						
Chester C	Christleton	08/55	55-57	22	-	1
FIELDWICK Lee Peter						
Born: Croydon, S London, England, 6 September, 1982						D
Brentford	YT	07/01	02-03	10	2	0
Swansea C	L	03/04	03	4	1	0
FIFE Adrian						
Born: Peterborough, England, 13 September, 1969						F
Peterborough U	YT	07/88	86-87	1	1	0
FIFIELD David						
Born: Plymouth, England, 10 December, 1966						M
Torquay U	App	-	83	0	1	0
FIGGINS Philip Eric (Phil)						
Born: Portsmouth, England, 20 August, 1955						G
England: Schools						
Portsmouth	Waterlooville	07/73	74-77	36	0	0
FIGUEROA Luciano Gabriel						
Born: Rosario, Argentina, 19 May, 1981						F
Argentina: 15/U23-1						
Birmingham C	Rosario Central (ARG)	08/03	03	0	1	0
FIGUEROA Maynor Alexis						
Born: La Ceiba, Honduras, 2 May, 1983						LB
Honduras: 113/U23-8/Youth						
Wigan Ath	Depo Olimpia (HON)	01/08	07-12	176	3	4
Hull C	Tr	06/13	13-14	33	2	0
Wigan Ath	L	10/14	14	6	0	0
FILAN John Richard						
Born: Sydney, Australia, 8 February, 1970						G
Australia: 2/U23-14						
Cambridge U	Wollongong (AUS)	03/93	92-94	68	0	0
Coventry C	Tr	03/95	94-96	15	1	0
Blackburn Rov	Tr	07/97	97-00	61	1	0
Wigan Ath	Tr	12/01	01-06	187	0	0
Doncaster Rov	L	10/06	06	3	0	0
FILBY Ian Frederick						
Born: Woodford, NE London, England, 9 October, 1954						W
Leyton Orient	App	10/72				
Brentford	L	09/74	74	1	2	0

League Club	Source	Date Signed	Seasons Played	Apps	Subs	Gls
[FILIPE LUIS] KASMIRSKI Filipe Luis						
Born: Jaragua do Sol, Brazil, 9 August, 1985						LB
Brazil: 10/Youth						
Chelsea	Atletico Madrid (SPN)	07/14	14	9	6	0
FILLERY Michael Christopher (Mike)						
Born: Mitcham, S London, England, 17 September, 1960						M
England: Youth/Schools						
Chelsea	App	08/78	78-82	156	5	32
Queens Park Rgrs	Tr	08/83	83-86	95	2	9
Portsmouth	Tr	07/87	87-90	62	5	6
Oldham Ath	Tr	10/90	90	1	1	0
Millwall	L	03/91	90	1	0	0
Torquay U	L	09/91	91	4	0	0
FILLO Martin						
Born: Plana, Czech Republic, 7 February, 1986						RW
Czech Republic: 3/U21-21/Youth						
Brentford (L)	Viktoria Plzen (CZE)	07/13	13	4	3	0
FILSON Robert Martin (Martin)						
Born: St Helens, Merseyside, England, 25 June, 1968						CD
Wrexham	Preston NE (NC)	02/89	88-89	0	2	0
FINAN Robert Joseph (Bobby)						
Born: Old Kilpatrick, Dunbartonshire, Scotland, 1 March, 1912						CF
Died: Old Kilpatrick, Dunbartonshire, Scotland, 25 July, 1983						
Scotland: War-1						
Blackpool	Yoker Ath	08/33	33-38	170	-	83
Crewe Alex	Tr	09/47	47-48	62	-	14
FINC Robert (Bobby)						
Born: Rochdale, Greater Manchester, England, 13 February, 1959						M
Rochdale	Milton	10/77	77	0	1	0
FINCH Derek						
Born: Arley, Warwickshire, England, 29 July, 1940						FB
West Bromwich A	Jnr	08/57				
Aldershot	Tr	06/60	60	3	-	0
FINCH Desmond Richard (Des)						
Born: Worksop, Nottinghamshire, England, 26 February, 1950						G
Mansfield T		03/69	68-70	4	0	0
FINCH Jack Matthew						
Born: Fenny Compton, Warwickshire, England, 6 August, 1996						M
Coventry C	Sch	07/14	14	8	8	0
FINCH John						
Born: Lambeth, S London, England, 5 July, 1966						CD
Fulham	Dorking	12/90	90-91	6	1	0
FINCH Keith John						
Born: Easington, County Durham, England, 6 May, 1982						G
Darlington	YT	07/01	01	11	1	0
FINCH Michael (Mike)						
Born: Stockton-on-Tees, Cleveland, England, 30 June, 1965						G
Hartlepool U		12/83	83-84	3	0	0
FINCH Robert (Bobby)						
Born: Camberwell, S London, England, 24 August, 1948						RB
Died: Beckenham, SE London, England, 18 September, 1978						
Queens Park Rgrs	App	08/66	67-68	5	0	0
FINCH Roy						
Born: Barry, Vale of Glamorgan, Wales, 7 April, 1922						W
Died: Lincoln, England, 14 August, 2007						
Swansea C	Barians	08/39				
West Bromwich A	Tr	06/44	46-48	15	-	1
Lincoln C	Tr	02/49	48-58	275	-	56
FINCHAM Gordon Richard						
Born: Peterborough, England, 8 January, 1935						CH
Died: Peterborough, England, June, 2012						
Leicester C	Phorpres Sports	11/52	52-57	50	-	0
Plymouth Arg	Tr	07/58	58-62	136	-	4
Luton T	Tr	07/63	63-64	64	-	0
FINDLAY John Williamson (Jake)						
Born: Blairgowrie, Perthshire, Scotland, 13 July, 1954						G
Aston Villa	App	06/72	73-76	14	0	0
Luton T	Tr	11/78	78-84	167	0	0
Barnsley	L	09/83	83	6	0	0
Derby Co	L	01/84	83	1	0	0
Swindon T	Tr	07/85	85	4	0	0
Coventry C	Tr	08/86				
FINDLEY Robert (Robbie)						
Born: Phoenix, Arizona, USA, 4 August, 1985						F

League Club	Source	Date Signed	Seasons Played	Apps	Subs	Gls

USA: 11/U23-5

League Club	Source	Date Signed	Seasons Played	Apps	Subs	Gls
Nottingham F	Real Salt Lake (USA)	01/11	10-11	10	15	3
Gillingham	L	09/12	12	3	4	0

FINLAY Allan Jackson
Born: Edinburgh, Scotland, 9 January, 1939 IF
Scotland: Schools

League Club	Source	Date Signed	Seasons Played	Apps	Subs	Gls
Newport Co	Heart of Midlothian	07/61	61	20	-	1

FINLAY Darren Jonathan
Born: Belfast, Northern Ireland, 19 December, 1973 LM
Northern Ireland: B/Youth

League Club	Source	Date Signed	Seasons Played	Apps	Subs	Gls
Queens Park Rgrs	YT	05/92				
Doncaster Rov	Tr	08/94	94	6	2	1

FINLAY John
Born: Birtley, Tyne and Wear, England, 16 February, 1919 IF
Died: Cleveland, England, 5 March, 1985

League Club	Source	Date Signed	Seasons Played	Apps	Subs	Gls
Sunderland	Ouston Jnrs	05/38	46	1	-	0

FINLAY John (Jock)
Born: Glasgow, Scotland, 1 July, 1925 RW

League Club	Source	Date Signed	Seasons Played	Apps	Subs	Gls
New Brighton	Clyde	03/51	50	15	-	2
Leeds U	Tr	06/51	51	1	-	0
Walsall	Yeovil T	08/53	53	11	-	0

FINLAY Kenneth (Ken)
Born: Pegswood, Northumberland, England, 24 March, 1926 D
Died: Northumberland, England, December, 2014

League Club	Source	Date Signed	Seasons Played	Apps	Subs	Gls
Aldershot	Aberdeen	08/50	50	7	-	0

FINLAY Matthew James (Matt)
Born: Salisbury, Wiltshire, England, 25 January, 1990 LB/M

League Club	Source	Date Signed	Seasons Played	Apps	Subs	Gls
Bournemouth	Jnr	08/07	07	0	1	0

FINLAY Patrick (Pat)
Born: Birkenhead, Wirral, England, 18 March, 1938 LW

League Club	Source	Date Signed	Seasons Played	Apps	Subs	Gls
Tranmere Rov		08/59	61	3	-	0

FINLAYSON Malcolm John
Born: Dumbarton, Dunbartonshire, Scotland, 14 June, 1930 G
Died: Dudley, West Midlands, England, 26 November, 2014

League Club	Source	Date Signed	Seasons Played	Apps	Subs	Gls
Millwall	Renfrew Jnrs	02/48	47-55	230	-	0
Wolverhampton W	Tr	08/56	56-63	179	-	0

FINLEY Alan James
Born: Liverpool, England, 10 December, 1967 CD

League Club	Source	Date Signed	Seasons Played	Apps	Subs	Gls
Shrewsbury T	Marine	06/88	88-89	60	3	2
Stockport Co	Tr	08/90	90-93	63	3	5
Carlisle U	L	12/92	92	1	0	0
Rochdale	L	12/93	93	1	0	0

FINLEY Gary
Born: Liverpool, England, 14 November, 1970 CD

League Club	Source	Date Signed	Seasons Played	Apps	Subs	Gls
Doncaster Rov	Netherfield	08/97	97	6	1	0

FINLEY Thomas (Tom)
Born: Frizington, Cumbria, England, 6 October, 1933 WH
Died: Whitehaven, Cumbria, England, April, 2008

League Club	Source	Date Signed	Seasons Played	Apps	Subs	Gls
Workington	Northside Jnrs	01/56	55-59	94	-	2
Southport	Tr	02/60	59	6	-	0

FINN Michael Gerard (Mike)
Born: Liverpool, England, 1 May, 1954 G

League Club	Source	Date Signed	Seasons Played	Apps	Subs	Gls
Burnley	App	12/71	73-74	4	0	0

FINN Neil Edward
Born: Barking, E London, England, 29 December, 1978 G

League Club	Source	Date Signed	Seasons Played	Apps	Subs	Gls
West Ham U	YT	-	95	1	0	0

FINNAN Stephen John (Steve)
Born: Limerick, Republic of Ireland, 20 April, 1976 RB
Republic of Ireland: 53/B-1/U21-8

League Club	Source	Date Signed	Seasons Played	Apps	Subs	Gls
Birmingham C	Welling U	06/95	95-96	9	6	1
Notts Co	L	03/96	95	14	3	2
Notts Co	Tr	10/96	96-98	71	9	5
Fulham	Tr	11/98	98-02	171	1	6
Liverpool	Tr	06/03	03-07	134	11	1
Portsmouth	RCD Espanyol (SPN)	08/09	09	20	1	0

FINNEY Alan
Born: Langwith, Derbyshire, England, 31 October, 1933 RW
England: B-1/U23-3

League Club	Source	Date Signed	Seasons Played	Apps	Subs	Gls
Sheffield Wed	Jnr	11/50	50-65	455	0	83
Doncaster Rov	Tr	01/66	65-66	30	0	3

FINNEY Charles William Thomas (Bill)
Born: Stoke-on-Trent, England, 5 September, 1931 IF

League Club	Source	Date Signed	Seasons Played	Apps	Subs	Gls
Stoke C	Crewe Alex (Am)	05/49	52-54	57	-	14
Birmingham C	Tr	11/55	55-56	14	-	0
Queens Park Rgrs	Tr	05/57	57	10	-	1
Crewe Alex	Tr	07/58	58	1	-	0
Rochdale	Tr	09/58	58	31	-	1

FINNEY John Richard (Richard)
Born: Rotherham, South Yorkshire, England, 14 March, 1956 RW
England: Youth

League Club	Source	Date Signed	Seasons Played	Apps	Subs	Gls
Rotherham U	Jnr	07/74	73-80	236	0	67

FINNEY Kevin
Born: Newcastle-under-Lyme, Potteries, England, 19 October, 1969 M

League Club	Source	Date Signed	Seasons Played	Apps	Subs	Gls
Port Vale	App	06/87	87-89	20	17	1
Lincoln C	Tr	07/91	91-92	31	6	2

FINNEY Richard Kenneth (Ken)
Born: St Helens, Merseyside, England, 10 March, 1929 RW

League Club	Source	Date Signed	Seasons Played	Apps	Subs	Gls
Stockport Co	St Helens	12/47	47-57	191	-	33
Tranmere Rov	Tr	03/58	57-62	180	-	27

FINNEY Shaun Barry
Born: Dinnington, South Yorkshire, England, 5 October, 1966 F

League Club	Source	Date Signed	Seasons Played	Apps	Subs	Gls
Scunthorpe U	Nottingham F (App)	10/84	84	1	1	0

FINNEY Stephen Kenneth (Steve)
Born: Hexham, Northumberland, England, 31 October, 1973 F

League Club	Source	Date Signed	Seasons Played	Apps	Subs	Gls
Preston NE	YT	05/92	91-92	1	5	1
Manchester C	Tr	02/93				
Swindon T	Tr	06/95	95-97	47	26	18
Cambridge U	L	10/97	97	4	3	2
Carlisle U	Tr	07/98	98	22	11	6
Leyton Orient	Tr	03/99	98	2	3	0
Chester C	Barrow	10/99	99	4	9	0

FINNEY Thomas (Tom)
Born: Belfast, Northern Ireland, 6 November, 1952 M
Northern Ireland: 14

League Club	Source	Date Signed	Seasons Played	Apps	Subs	Gls
Luton T	Crusaders	08/73	73	13	1	5
Sunderland	Tr	07/74	74-75	8	7	1
Cambridge U	Tr	08/76	76-83	259	9	56
Brentford	Tr	02/84	83-84	19	1	2
Cambridge U	Tr	12/84	84-85	64	0	5

FINNEY Thomas (Tom)
Born: Preston, Lancashire, England, 5 April, 1922 F
Died: Preston, Lancashire, England, 14 February, 2014
England: 76/FLge-17

League Club	Source	Date Signed	Seasons Played	Apps	Subs	Gls
Preston NE	Jnr	01/40	46-59	433	-	187

FINNIESTON Stephen James (Steve)
Born: Edinburgh, Scotland, 30 November, 1954 F
Scotland: Youth

League Club	Source	Date Signed	Seasons Played	Apps	Subs	Gls
Chelsea	App	12/71	74-77	78	2	34
Cardiff C	L	10/74	74	9	0	2
Sheffield U	Tr	06/78	78	23	0	4

FINNIGAN Anthony (Tony)
Born: Wimbledon, SW London, England, 17 October, 1962 M
England: Youth

League Club	Source	Date Signed	Seasons Played	Apps	Subs	Gls
Fulham	App	11/80				
Crystal Palace	Corinthian Casuals	02/85	84-87	94	11	10
Blackburn Rov	Tr	07/88	88-89	21	15	0
Hull C	Tr	09/90	90	15	3	1
Swindon T	Tr	03/91	90	2	1	0
Brentford	Sea Bee (HKG)	01/92	91	3	0	0
Barnet	Earnest Borel (HKG)	09/93	93	5	1	1
Fulham	Dulwich Hamlet	09/94	94-95	8	5	0

FINNIGAN Denis Vincent
Born: Sheffield, England, 23 March, 1940 CH
Died: Sheffield, England, 4 December, 1994

League Club	Source	Date Signed	Seasons Played	Apps	Subs	Gls
Sheffield U		04/59	59-66	14	0	0
Chesterfield	Tr	09/68	68-69	27	0	0

FINNIGAN John
Born: Glasgow, Scotland, 3 July, 1943 FB

League Club	Source	Date Signed	Seasons Played	Apps	Subs	Gls
Millwall	Clyde	06/63	63	6	-	0

FINNIGAN John Francis
Born: Wakefield, England, 29 March, 1976 M

League Club	Source	Date Signed	Seasons Played	Apps	Subs	Gls
Nottingham F	YT	05/93				
Lincoln C	Tr	03/98	97-01	139	4	3
Cheltenham T	Tr	03/02	01-08	210	10	20

FINNIGAN Raymond William (Ray)
Born: Wallsend, Tyne and Wear, England, 22 January, 1947 FB

League Club	Source	Date Signed	Seasons Played	Apps	Subs	Gls
Newcastle U	App	01/65				
Darlington	Tr	07/66	66-67	8	3	0

FINNIGAN Thomas Trevor (Trevor)
Born: Bedlington, Northumberland, England, 14 October, 1952 F
England: SemiPro - 2

League Club	Source	Date Signed	Seasons Played	Apps	Subs	Gls
Everton	New Brighton	05/71				
Blackpool	Runcorn	03/77	76-77	13	4	3
Bournemouth	Tr	01/78	77-78	23	2	5
FINNIS Harold Alexander						
Born: Liverpool, England, 21 October, 1920						LB
Died: Crosby, Merseyside, England, 9 February, 1991						
Everton		06/46	46	1	-	0
FIOCCA Paul						
Born: Italy, 13 January, 1955						M
Swindon T	App	01/73	73	1	0	0
FIORE Mark Joseph						
Born: Southwark, S London, England, 18 November, 1969						LW
Wimbledon	YT	07/88	88	1	0	0
Plymouth Arg	Tr	03/90	89-92	74	9	8
FIRM Neil John						
Born: Bradford, England, 23 January, 1958						CD
Leeds U	App	01/76	79-81	11	1	0
Oldham Ath	L	03/82	81	9	0	0
Peterborough U	Tr	08/82	82-84	71	1	3
FIRMAN Kenneth (Ken)						
Born: Felling, Tyne and Wear, England, 5 February, 1941						IF
Died: Gateshead, Tyne and Wear, England, November, 2000						
Gateshead	Jarrow Mercantile	02/59	58	1	-	0
FIRMANI Edward Ronald (Eddie)						
Born: Cape Town, South Africa, 7 August, 1933						CF
Charlton Ath	Clyde (RSA)	02/50	51-54	100	-	50
Charlton Ath	Genoa (ITA)	10/63	63-64	55	-	32
Southend U	Tr	06/65	65-66	55	0	24
Charlton Ath	Tr	03/67	66-67	10	0	6
FIRMANI Peter Walter						
Born: Cape Town, South Africa, 14 February, 1936						RB
Died: Johannesburg, South Africa, December, 2004						
Charlton Ath	Marist Brothers (RSA)	09/53	55-58	31	-	2
FIRTH Francis Martin (Franny)						
Born: Dewsbury, West Yorkshire, England, 27 May, 1956						RW
Huddersfield T	App	11/73	73-76	26	1	4
Halifax T	Tr	02/78	77-81	157	11	19
Bury	Tr	08/82	82	33	0	4
FISH Mark Anthony						
Born: Cape Town, South Africa, 14 March, 1974						CD
South Africa: 62						
Bolton W	SS Lazio (ITA)	09/97	97-00	102	1	3
Charlton Ath	Tr	11/00	00-04	101	1	2
Ipswich T	L	08/05	05	1	0	0
FISH Matthew (Matt)						
Born: Croydon, S London, England, 5 January, 1989						RB
Gillingham	Dover Ath	07/11	11-14	65	7	3
Portsmouth	L	11/14	14	3	0	0
FISHENDEN Paul						
Born: Hillingdon, W London, England, 2 August, 1963						F
Wimbledon	App	10/81	81-85	57	18	25
Fulham	L	12/85	85	3	0	0
Millwall	L	09/86	86	3	0	0
Leyton Orient	L	10/86	86	4	0	0
Crewe Alex	Tr	02/88	87-89	79	2	25
FISHER Alexander Anthony (Alex)						
Born: Westminster, Central London, England, 30 June, 1990						F
Mansfield T	Monza (ITA)	07/14	14	6	8	1
FISHER Alexander James (Alex)						
Born: Southampton, England, 30 January, 1973						RB
Aldershot	YT	07/91	90	2	0	0
FISHER Charles Kitchener (Charlie)						
Born: Pontypridd, Rhondda Cynon Taff, Wales, 4 January, 1915						LB
Died: Pontypridd, Rhondda Cynon Taff, Wales, 14 March, 1986						
Swansea C	Lovells Ath	08/39	46-47	65	-	0
FISHER Frederick (Freddie)						
Born: Hetton-le-Hole, Tyne and Wear, England, 28 November, 1924						RW
Died: New Forest, Hampshire, England, September, 2004						
Reading	Slough T	08/44	46-51	139	-	23
Shrewsbury T	Tr	07/52	52-53	64	-	9
Leyton Orient	Tr	07/54	54	2	-	1
FISHER Frederick Thomas (Fred)						
Born: Wednesbury, West Midlands, England, 12 January, 1920						RB
Died: Grimsby, North Lincolnshire, England, June, 1993						
Grimsby T	Fallings Heath	05/37	38-50	166	-	0
Rochdale	Tr	06/51	51	1	-	0

League Club	Source	Date Signed	Seasons Played	Apps	Subs	Gls
FISHER George Sidney						
Born: Bermondsey, SE London, England, 19 June, 1925						RB
Millwall	Bermondsey ATC	12/44	46-54	286	-	4
Fulham	Tr	11/54	54	8	-	0
Colchester U	Tr	09/55	55-59	164	-	6
FISHER Hugh Donnelly						
Born: Pollok, Glasgow, Scotland, 9 January, 1944						M
Blackpool	Gowanbank	08/62	63-66	51	3	1
Southampton	Tr	03/67	66-76	297	5	7
Southport	Tr	03/77	76-77	60	0	0
FISHER James (Jimmy)						
Born: Barrow, Cumbria, England, 12 June, 1934						IF
Barrow	Holker Central OB	10/55	52-57	10	-	1
FISHER James Bernard (Bernard)						
Born: York, England, 23 February, 1934						G
Hull C	Jnr	11/55	55-62	126	-	0
Bradford C	Tr	07/63	63-64	60	-	0
FISHER John Alfred (Jackie)						
Born: Bermondsey, SE London, England, 19 June, 1925						LB
Millwall	Royal Navy	05/46	47-48	3	-	0
Bournemouth	Tr	06/49	49-52	52	-	0
FISHER Kenneth Douglas Walter (Ken)						
Born: Southampton, England, 30 September, 1921						FB
Died: Watford, Hertfordshire, England, 29 April, 1989						
Southampton	Bitterne Nomads	09/46				
Watford	Tr	08/47	47-50	106	-	2
FISHER Leslie Barry (Les)						
Born: Southampton, England, 8 January, 1948						FB
Blackpool		12/67	68	1	0	0
FISHER Neil John						
Born: St Helens, Merseyside, England, 7 November, 1970						M
Bolton W	YT	07/89	91-94	17	7	1
Chester C	Tr	06/95	95-97	91	17	4
Chester C	Bangor C	03/99	98-99	41	8	1
FISHER Paul						
Born: Mansfield, Nottinghamshire, England, 19 January, 1951						LB
Huddersfield T		02/69				
Darlington	Tr	06/70	70	2	1	0
FISHER Peter McArthur						
Born: Edinburgh, Scotland, 17 February, 1920						FB
Died: Devon, England, December, 2010						
Northampton T		09/47	47	8	-	0
Shrewsbury T	Tr	08/50	50-51	39	-	0
Wrexham	Tr	10/51	51-53	85	-	0
FISHER Philip John (Phil)						
Born: Ammanford, Carmarthenshire, Wales, 10 January, 1958						W
Exeter C	Bridgend T	02/81	80-81	9	2	1
Swansea C	Merthyr Tydfil	03/85	84	2	0	0
FISHER Robert Paul (Bobby)						
Born: Wembley, NW London, England, 3 August, 1956						RB
Leyton Orient	App	08/73	73-82	308	6	4
Cambridge U	Tr	11/82	82-83	42	0	0
Brentford	Tr	02/84	83-84	44	1	0
FISHER Ronald (Ron)						
Born: Sheffield, England, 9 March, 1923						RB
Died: Sheffield, England, January, 1987						
Halifax T	Sheffield FC	08/50	50	4	-	0
FISHER Stanley (Stan)						
Born: Barnsley, South Yorkshire, England, 29 September, 1924						CF
Died: Doncaster, South Yorkshire, England, 21 October, 2003						
Barnsley	Rockingham Colliery	09/44	46	1	-	0
Halifax T	Tr	01/47	46-47	26	-	7
FISHER Thomas Michael (Tom)						
Born: Wythenshawe, Greater Manchester, England, 28 June, 1992						F
Stockport Co	Sch	07/10	08-10	6	22	1
Macclesfield T	Tr	07/11	11	0	1	0
FISHLOCK Murray Edward						
Born: Marlborough, Wiltshire, England, 23 September, 1973						LB
Hereford U	Trowbridge T	09/94	94-96	67	4	4
FISKEN Gary Stewart						
Born: Watford, Hertfordshire, England, 27 October, 1981						M
Watford	YT	02/00	01-03	15	7	1
Swansea C	Tr	07/04	04	1	4	0

FITCH Barry Edward
Born: Brighton, England, 19 November, 1943 — FB
Died: Durrington, West Sussex, England, 9 March, 2010

League Club	Source	Date Signed	Seasons Played	Apps	Subs	Gls
Brighton & HA	Jnr	11/61	63	1	-	0

FITTON John
Born: Royton, Greater Manchester, England, 12 January, 1951 — G

League Club	Source	Date Signed	Seasons Played	Apps	Subs	Gls
Oldham Ath	Jnr	10/68	69	3	0	0

FITZGERALD Alfred Michael (Alf)
Born: Conisbrough, South Yorkshire, England, 25 January, 1911 — IF/WH
Died: Brighton, England, 1981

League Club	Source	Date Signed	Seasons Played	Apps	Subs	Gls
Reading	Denaby U	08/34	34-35	6	-	1
Queens Park Rgrs	Tr	05/36	36-38	94	-	43
Aldershot	Tr	11/45	46-47	59	-	1

FITZGERALD Brian Maurice
Born: Perivale, W London, England, 23 October, 1983 — M
Republic of Ireland: Youth

League Club	Source	Date Signed	Seasons Played	Apps	Subs	Gls
Queens Park Rgrs	YT	10/00	01	0	1	0

FITZGERALD Gary Michael
Born: Hampstead, NW London, England, 27 October, 1976 — CD

League Club	Source	Date Signed	Seasons Played	Apps	Subs	Gls
Watford	YT	11/94	94	1	0	0

FITZGERALD John Desmond
Born: Dublin, Republic of Ireland, 10 February, 1984 — CD
Republic of Ireland: U21-14/Youth

League Club	Source	Date Signed	Seasons Played	Apps	Subs	Gls
Blackburn Rov	YT	02/01				
Bury	L	01/05	04-06	56	8	3

FITZGERALD Peter Joseph
Born: Waterford, Republic of Ireland, 17 June, 1937 — F
Died: Waterford, Republic of Ireland, 29 June, 2013
Republic of Ireland: 5/LoI-4

League Club	Source	Date Signed	Seasons Played	Apps	Subs	Gls
Leeds U	Sparta Rotterdam (NED)	08/60	60	8	-	0
Chester C	Tr	07/61	61-63	80	-	12

FITZGERALD Scott Brian
Born: Westminster, Central London, England, 13 August, 1969 — CD
Republic of Ireland: B-1/U21-4

League Club	Source	Date Signed	Seasons Played	Apps	Subs	Gls
Wimbledon	YT	07/89	89-95	95	11	1
Sheffield U	L	11/95	95	6	0	0
Millwall	L	10/96	96	7	0	0
Millwall	Tr	07/97	97-00	79	3	1
Colchester U	Tr	10/00	00-03	114	2	0
Brentford	Tr	03/04	03-04	21	0	0

FITZGERALD Scott Peter
Born: Hillingdon, W London, England, 18 November, 1979 — F

League Club	Source	Date Signed	Seasons Played	Apps	Subs	Gls
Watford	Northwood	03/03	02-04	29	26	11
Swansea C	L	09/04	04	0	3	0
Leyton Orient	L	01/05	04	1	0	0
Brentford	Tr	03/05	04-05	10	13	5
Oxford U	L	11/05	05	2	1	1
Walsall	L	02/06	05	1	4	0

FITZHENRY Neil
Born: Billinge, Merseyside, England, 24 September, 1978 — CD

League Club	Source	Date Signed	Seasons Played	Apps	Subs	Gls
Wigan Ath	YT	07/97	97-98	2	2	0

FITZPATRICK Anthony Charles (Tony)
Born: Glasgow, Scotland, 3 March, 1956 — M
Scotland: SLge-1/U21-5

League Club	Source	Date Signed	Seasons Played	Apps	Subs	Gls
Bristol C	St Mirren	08/79	79-80	75	0	1

FITZPATRICK David Hugh Aborlo
Born: Surbiton, SW London, England, 10 February, 1995 — W

League Club	Source	Date Signed	Seasons Played	Apps	Subs	Gls
Queens Park Rgrs	Sch	02/12				
AFC Wimbledon	Tr	09/14	14	0	3	0

FITZPATRICK Gary Gerard
Born: Birmingham, England, 5 August, 1971 — M
Republic of Ireland: Youth

League Club	Source	Date Signed	Seasons Played	Apps	Subs	Gls
Leicester C	YT	01/90	89	0	1	0

FITZPATRICK Ian Matthew
Born: Manchester, England, 22 September, 1980 — F
England: Youth/Schools

League Club	Source	Date Signed	Seasons Played	Apps	Subs	Gls
Manchester U	YT	07/98				
Halifax T	Tr	03/00	99-01	37	12	10

FITZPATRICK John Herbert Norton
Born: Aberdeen, Scotland, 18 August, 1946 — M

League Club	Source	Date Signed	Seasons Played	Apps	Subs	Gls
Manchester U	Jnr	09/63	64-72	111	6	8

FITZPATRICK Jordan Philip
Born: Stourbridge, West Midlands, England, 15 June, 1988 — M

League Club	Source	Date Signed	Seasons Played	Apps	Subs	Gls
Hereford U	Wolverhampton W (Sch)	08/06	06	0	1	0

FITZPATRICK Joseph (Joe)
Born: West Bromwich, West Midlands, England, 20 August, 1997 — M

League Club	Source	Date Signed	Seasons Played	Apps	Subs	Gls
Mansfield T	Sch	03/15	14	1	2	0

FITZPATRICK Lee Gareth
Born: Manchester, England, 31 October, 1978 — W

League Club	Source	Date Signed	Seasons Played	Apps	Subs	Gls
Blackburn Rov	YT	07/96				
Hartlepool U	Tr	09/99	99-00	28	19	6

FITZPATRICK Paul James
Born: Liverpool, England, 5 October, 1965 — CD/M

League Club	Source	Date Signed	Seasons Played	Apps	Subs	Gls
Bolton W	Preston NE (NC)	03/85	84-85	13	1	0
Bristol C	Tr	08/86	86-88	40	4	7
Carlisle U	Tr	10/88	88-90	106	3	4
Preston NE	L	12/88	88	2	0	0
Leicester C	Tr	07/91	91-92	21	6	4
Birmingham C	Tr	01/93	92	7	0	0
Bury	L	03/93	92	8	1	0
Northampton T	Hamilton Academical	02/94	93	1	1	1

FITZPATRICK Peter
Born: Bebington, Wirral, England, 27 April, 1929 — IF
Died: Wirral, England, September, 2013

League Club	Source	Date Signed	Seasons Played	Apps	Subs	Gls
New Brighton (Am)		01/50	49	1	-	0

FITZPATRICK Trevor Joseph James
Born: Frimley, Surrey, England, 19 February, 1980 — F
Republic of Ireland: Youth

League Club	Source	Date Signed	Seasons Played	Apps	Subs	Gls
Southend U	YT	07/98	97-00	17	36	8

FITZSIMMONS Eric James
Born: Oldham, Greater Manchester, England, 23 October, 1948 — F

League Club	Source	Date Signed	Seasons Played	Apps	Subs	Gls
Bradford Park Ave (Am)		02/70	69	1	0	0

FITZSIMONS Arthur Gerard
Born: Dublin, Republic of Ireland, 16 December, 1929 — IF
Republic of Ireland: 26/LoI-2

League Club	Source	Date Signed	Seasons Played	Apps	Subs	Gls
Middlesbrough	Shelbourne (ROI)	05/49	49-58	223	-	49
Lincoln C	Tr	03/59	58	7	-	0
Mansfield T	Tr	08/59	59-60	62	-	23

FJORTOFT Jan Aage
Born: Sande, Norway, 10 January, 1967 — F
Norway: 72

League Club	Source	Date Signed	Seasons Played	Apps	Subs	Gls
Swindon T	Rapid Vienna (AUT)	07/93	93-94	62	10	28
Middlesbrough	Tr	03/95	94-96	37	4	9
Sheffield U	Tr	01/97	96-97	30	4	19
Barnsley	Tr	01/98	97-98	21	13	9

FLACK Douglas Billy Halbert (Doug)
Born: Staines, Surrey, England, 24 October, 1920 — G
Died: Purley, S London, England, 18 October, 2005

League Club	Source	Date Signed	Seasons Played	Apps	Subs	Gls
Fulham	Jnr	12/38	48-52	54	-	0
Walsall	Tr	08/53	53	11	-	0

FLACK Steven Richard (Steve)
Born: Cambridge, England, 29 May, 1971 — F

League Club	Source	Date Signed	Seasons Played	Apps	Subs	Gls
Cardiff C	Cambridge C	11/95	95-96	6	5	1
Exeter C	Tr	09/96	96-02	213	55	63

FLACK William Leonard Wallace (Len)
Born: Cambridge, England, 1 June, 1916 — RB
Died: Bury St Edmunds, Suffolk, England, 29 March, 1995
England: Schools

League Club	Source	Date Signed	Seasons Played	Apps	Subs	Gls
Norwich C	Cambridge T	07/33	34-46	49	-	0

FLAHAVAN Aaron Adam
Born: Southampton, England, 15 December, 1975 — G
Died: Bournemouth, England, 4 August, 2001

League Club	Source	Date Signed	Seasons Played	Apps	Subs	Gls
Portsmouth	YT	02/94	96-00	93	0	0

FLAHAVAN Darryl James
Born: Southampton, England, 9 September, 1977 — G

League Club	Source	Date Signed	Seasons Played	Apps	Subs	Gls
Southampton	YT	05/96				
Southend U	Chesham U	10/00	00-07	289	2	0
Crystal Palace	Tr	07/08	08-09	2	0	0
Oldham Ath	L	11/09	09	18	0	0
Portsmouth	Tr	07/10				
Bournemouth	Tr	07/11	11-14	44	2	0

FLAMINI Mathieu
Born: Marseille, France, 7 March, 1984 — DM
France: 3/U21-8

League Club	Source	Date Signed	Seasons Played	Apps	Subs	Gls
Arsenal	Olymp Marseille (FRA)	07/04	04-07	67	35	7
Arsenal	AC Milan (ITA)	08/13	13-14	33	17	3

FLANAGAN Alan
Born: Drogheda, Republic of Ireland, 9 October, 1980 — G
Republic of Ireland: Youth

League Club	Source	Date Signed	Seasons Played	Apps	Subs	Gls
Swindon T	YT	07/99	99	0	1	0

FLANAGAN Daniel Christopher
Born: Dublin, Republic of Ireland, 24 November, 1924 — CF
Republic of Ireland: LoI-1

League Club	Source	Date Signed	Seasons Played	Apps	Subs	Gls
Notts Co (Am)	Dundalk (ROI)	12/46	46	2	-	2
Manchester C	Shelbourne (ROI)	02/47				
Bradford C	Tr	12/47	47	13	-	6

FLANAGAN Jonathan Patrick (Jon)
Born: Liverpool, England, 1 January, 1993 — FB
England: 1/U21-3/Youth

League Club	Source	Date Signed	Seasons Played	Apps	Subs	Gls
Liverpool	Sch	07/10	10-13	35	0	1

FLANAGAN Michael Anthony (Mike)
Born: Ilford, E London, England, 9 November, 1952 — F
England: B-3/Youth

League Club	Source	Date Signed	Seasons Played	Apps	Subs	Gls
Charlton Ath	Tottenham H (Jnr)	08/71	71-78	241	13	85
Crystal Palace	Tr	08/79	79-80	56	0	8
Queens Park Rgrs	Tr	12/80	80-83	71	7	20
Charlton Ath	Tr	01/84	83-85	89	4	24
Cambridge U	Tr	09/86	86	7	2	3

FLANAGAN Reece James
Born: Birmingham, England, 19 October, 1994 — M

League Club	Source	Date Signed	Seasons Played	Apps	Subs	Gls
Walsall	Sch	01/13	14	9	7	0

FLANAGAN Shaun
Born: Doncaster, South Yorkshire, England, 25 December, 1960 — M

League Club	Source	Date Signed	Seasons Played	Apps	Subs	Gls
Doncaster Rov	App	01/79	78-80	41	9	3

FLANAGAN Thomas Michael (Tom)
Born: Chalfont St Peter, Buckinghamshire, England, 21 October, 1991 — CD
Northern Ireland: U21-1

League Club	Source	Date Signed	Seasons Played	Apps	Subs	Gls
MK Dons	Sch	08/10	09-14	29	8	3
Gillingham	L	07/12	12	12	1	1
Barnet	L	03/13	12	8	1	0
Stevenage	L	03/14	13	1	1	0
Plymouth Arg	L	01/15	14	4	0	0

FLANNIGAN Raymond John (Ray)
Born: Margate, Kent, England, 15 March, 1949 — LB/M

League Club	Source	Date Signed	Seasons Played	Apps	Subs	Gls
Reading	Margate	02/70	70-71	36	4	0

FLASH Richard Garfield
Born: Birmingham, England, 8 April, 1976 — W/RB

League Club	Source	Date Signed	Seasons Played	Apps	Subs	Gls
Manchester U	YT	07/94				
Wolverhampton W	Tr	09/95				
Watford	Tr	07/96	96	0	1	0
Lincoln C	L	10/97	97	2	3	0
Plymouth Arg	Tr	08/98	98	4	1	0

FLATLEY Albert Austin (Bert)
Born: Bradford, England, 5 September, 1919 — IF
Died: Yeadon, West Yorkshire, England, 9 April, 1987

League Club	Source	Date Signed	Seasons Played	Apps	Subs	Gls
Wolverhampton W	Guiseley	07/38				
York C	Tr	02/39	38	4	-	0
Port Vale	Tr	06/39				
Bradford Park Ave	Tr	07/44				
Bury	Tr	12/46				
Workington	Alessandria (ITA)	11/51	51	8	-	0

FLATT Colin Harold
Born: Blythburgh, Suffolk, England, 30 January, 1940 — CF

League Club	Source	Date Signed	Seasons Played	Apps	Subs	Gls
Leyton Orient	Wisbech T	05/65	65	32	1	8
Southend U	Tr	06/66	66	20	2	8

FLATTS Mark Michael
Born: Islington, N London, England, 14 October, 1972 — W
England: Youth

League Club	Source	Date Signed	Seasons Played	Apps	Subs	Gls
Arsenal	YT	12/90	92-94	9	7	0
Cambridge U	L	10/93	93	5	0	1
Brighton & HA	L	12/93	93	9	1	1
Bristol C	L	03/95	94	4	2	0
Grimsby T	L	03/96	95	4	1	0

FLAVELL John Alfred (Jack)
Born: Kingswinford, West Midlands, England, 15 May, 1929 — FB
Died: Barmouth, Gwynedd, Wales, 25 February, 2004

League Club	Source	Date Signed	Seasons Played	Apps	Subs	Gls
West Bromwich A	Lye T	05/47				
Walsall	Tr	09/53	53	22	-	0

FLAVELL Robert William (Bobby)
Born: Berwick-on-Tweed, Northumberland, England, 7 March, 1956 — RB/M
Died: Dalkeith, Midlothian, Scotland, 11 December, 1995

League Club	Source	Date Signed	Seasons Played	Apps	Subs	Gls
Burnley	App	03/73				
Halifax T	Tr	02/76	75-77	91	0	7
Chesterfield	Tr	08/78	78	27	2	2
Barnsley	Tr	07/79	79	25	0	0
Halifax T	Tr	12/80	80	1	0	0

FLAY Stephen (Steve)
Born: Poole, Dorset, England, 2 October, 1954 — LB

League Club	Source	Date Signed	Seasons Played	Apps	Subs	Gls
Oxford U	App	10/72	73-74	3	0	0

FLECK John Alan
Born: Glasgow, Scotland, 24 August, 1991 — M
Scotland: U21-4/Youth

League Club	Source	Date Signed	Seasons Played	Apps	Subs	Gls
Blackpool (L)	Glasgow Rangers	01/12	11	4	3	0
Coventry C	Tr	08/12	12-14	106	16	4

FLECK Robert William
Born: Glasgow, Scotland, 11 August, 1965 — F
Scotland: 4/U21-6/Youth

League Club	Source	Date Signed	Seasons Played	Apps	Subs	Gls
Norwich C	Glasgow Rangers	12/87	87-91	130	13	40
Chelsea	Tr	08/92	92-93	35	5	3
Bolton W	L	12/93	93	6	1	1
Bristol C	L	01/95	94	10	0	1
Norwich C	Tr	08/95	95-97	93	11	16
Reading	Tr	03/98	97-98	5	4	1

FLEET Stephen (Steve)
Born: Urmston, Greater Manchester, England, 2 July, 1937 — G

League Club	Source	Date Signed	Seasons Played	Apps	Subs	Gls
Manchester C	Jnr	02/55	57-60	5	-	0
Wrexham	Tr	06/63	63-65	79	0	0
Stockport Co	Tr	01/66	65-67	36	0	0

FLEETING James Taylor (Jim)
Born: Glasgow, Scotland, 8 April, 1955 — CD

League Club	Source	Date Signed	Seasons Played	Apps	Subs	Gls
Norwich C	Kilbirnie Ladeside	04/75	76	0	1	0

FLEETWOOD Steven Robert
Born: Sheffield, England, 27 February, 1962 — M

League Club	Source	Date Signed	Seasons Played	Apps	Subs	Gls
Rotherham U	App	03/80				
Rotherham U	Rtd	02/87	86	0	1	0

FLEETWOOD Stuart Keith Wakley
Born: Chepstow, Monmouthshire, Wales, 23 April, 1986 — F
Wales: U21-5/Youth

League Club	Source	Date Signed	Seasons Played	Apps	Subs	Gls
Cardiff C	Sch	02/04	03-04	1	7	0
Hereford U	Tr	01/06	06	21	6	3
Accrington Stan	L	01/07	06	3	0	0
Charlton Ath	Forest Green Rov	07/08				
Cheltenham T	L	09/08	08	6	0	2
Brighton & HA	L	10/08	08	5	6	1
Exeter C	L	03/09	08	7	2	3
Exeter C	L	09/09	09	16	11	4
Hereford U	Tr	07/10	10-11	40	8	14

FLEMING Andrew Lee (Andy)
Born: Liverpool, England, 18 February, 1989 — M
England: Semi Pro-2

League Club	Source	Date Signed	Seasons Played	Apps	Subs	Gls
Wrexham	Sch	07/07	06-07	3	3	0
Morecambe	Tr	07/10	10-14	127	22	13

FLEMING Bernard James
Born: Middlesbrough, England, 8 January, 1937 — FB

League Club	Source	Date Signed	Seasons Played	Apps	Subs	Gls
Grimsby T	RAF Binbrook	04/57	57-60	22	-	0
Workington	Tr	07/61	61	20	-	0
Chester C	Tr	05/62	62-63	64	-	0

FLEMING Charles (Charlie)
Born: Culross, Fife, Scotland, 12 July, 1927 — CF
Died: Edinburgh, Scotland, 14 August, 1997
Scotland: 1

League Club	Source	Date Signed	Seasons Played	Apps	Subs	Gls
Sunderland	East Fife	01/55	54-57	107	-	62

FLEMING Craig
Born: Halifax, West Yorkshire, England, 6 October, 1971 — CD

League Club	Source	Date Signed	Seasons Played	Apps	Subs	Gls
Halifax T	YT	03/90	88-90	56	1	0
Oldham Ath	Tr	08/91	91-96	158	6	1
Norwich C	Tr	06/97	97-06	325	18	12
Wolverhampton W	L	01/07	06	1	0	0
Rotherham U	Tr	01/07	06	17	0	0

FLEMING Craig Matthew
Born: Stockport, Greater Manchester, England, 1 December, 1984 — F

League Club	Source	Date Signed	Seasons Played	Apps	Subs	Gls
Oldham Ath	Sch	-	03	0	1	0

FLEMING Curtis
Born: Manchester, England, 8 October, 1968 — RB
Republic of Ireland: 10/U23-2/U21-5/Youth

League Club	Source	Date Signed	Seasons Played	Apps	Subs	Gls
Middlesbrough	St Patrick's Ath (ROI)	08/91	91-01	248	18	3
Birmingham C	L	11/01	01	6	0	0
Crystal Palace	Tr	12/01	01-03	41	4	0
Darlington	Tr	08/04	04	24	3	0

FLEMING Francis Joseph (Frank)
Born: South Shields, Tyne and Wear, England, 21 December, 1945 — G

League Club	Source	Date Signed	Seasons Played	Apps	Subs	Gls
Darlington		07/64	64	2	-	0

FLEMING George Keith
Born: Gourock, Inverclyde, Scotland, 25 February, 1935 — IF
Died: Watford, Hertfordshire, England, March, 1999

League Club	Source	Date Signed	Seasons Played	Apps	Subs	Gls
Watford	Greenock Morton	06/58	58-59	27	-	10
Carlisle U	Tr	06/60	60	7	-	0
Barrow	Tr	09/60	60	17	-	3

FLEMING Greg William Edward
Born: Dunfermline, Fife, Scotland, 27 September, 1986 — G
Scotland: U21-1

League Club	Source	Date Signed	Seasons Played	Apps	Subs	Gls
Oldham Ath	Gretna	06/08	08	17	1	0
Chesterfield	Galway U (ROI)	08/11	11	9	1	0
Carlisle U	Grimsby T	08/13	13	4	0	0

FLEMING Hayden Valentine
Born: Islington, N London, England, 14 March, 1978 — RB

League Club	Source	Date Signed	Seasons Played	Apps	Subs	Gls
Cardiff C	YT	07/96	95-96	29	3	0

FLEMING James (Jimmy)
Born: Tannochside, Lanarkshire, Scotland, 4 November, 1952 — M

League Club	Source	Date Signed	Seasons Played	Apps	Subs	Gls
Carlisle U	Manchester U (App)	07/71				
Barrow	L	01/72	71	1	1	0

FLEMING James Freeburn
Born: Glasgow, Scotland, 7 January, 1929 — FB

League Club	Source	Date Signed	Seasons Played	Apps	Subs	Gls
Workington	Stirling A	05/54	54-57	88	-	1

FLEMING James Gary (Gary)
Born: Derry, Northern Ireland, 17 February, 1967 — D
Northern Ireland: 31/U23-1/Youth

League Club	Source	Date Signed	Seasons Played	Apps	Subs	Gls
Nottingham F	App	11/84	84-87	71	3	0
Manchester C	Tr	08/89	89	13	1	0
Notts Co	L	03/90	89	3	0	0
Barnsley	Tr	03/90	89-95	236	3	0

FLEMING James Paterson (Jim)
Born: Alloa, Stirlingshire, Scotland, 7 January, 1942 — LW

League Club	Source	Date Signed	Seasons Played	Apps	Subs	Gls
Luton T	Partick Thistle	11/60	60-62	66	-	9

FLEMING John Hares (Ian)
Born: Maybole, Ayrshire, Scotland, 15 January, 1953 — F

League Club	Source	Date Signed	Seasons Played	Apps	Subs	Gls
Sheffield Wed	Aberdeen	02/79	78-79	13	0	1

FLEMING John Joseph
Born: Nottingham, England, 1 July, 1953 — M

League Club	Source	Date Signed	Seasons Played	Apps	Subs	Gls
Oxford U	Jnr	09/70	71-74	67	8	2
Lincoln C	Tr	07/75	75-78	109	12	17
Port Vale	Tr	03/80	79	3	0	0

FLEMING Mark John
Born: Hammersmith, W London, England, 11 August, 1969 — LB

League Club	Source	Date Signed	Seasons Played	Apps	Subs	Gls
Queens Park Rgrs	YT	01/88	87-88	1	2	0
Brentford	Tr	07/89	89-90	33	2	1

FLEMING Michael Anthony (Mike)
Born: India, 23 February, 1928 — IF
Died: Rochdale, Greater Manchester, England, 10 July, 1994

League Club	Source	Date Signed	Seasons Played	Apps	Subs	Gls
Tranmere Rov		09/53	53-57	115	-	8

FLEMING Neil
Born: Felixstowe, Suffolk, England, 9 January, 1950 — CD

League Club	Source	Date Signed	Seasons Played	Apps	Subs	Gls
Lincoln C (Am)	Lincoln Claytons	07/73	73	1	0	0

FLEMING Paul
Born: Halifax, West Yorkshire, England, 6 September, 1967 — RB

League Club	Source	Date Signed	Seasons Played	Apps	Subs	Gls
Halifax T	App	09/85	85-90	135	4	1
Mansfield T	Tr	07/91	91-94	65	3	0

FLEMING Terence Maurice (Terry)
Born: Birmingham, England, 5 January, 1973 — M/RB

League Club	Source	Date Signed	Seasons Played	Apps	Subs	Gls
Coventry C	YT	07/91	90-92	8	5	0
Northampton T	Tr	08/93	93	26	5	1
Preston NE	Tr	07/94	94-95	25	7	2
Lincoln C	Tr	12/95	95-99	175	8	8
Plymouth Arg	Tr	07/00	00	15	2	0
Cambridge U	Tr	03/01	00-03	96	9	4
Grimsby T	Tr	07/04	04	43	0	2

FLETCHER Alan Frederick
Born: Salford, England, 28 October, 1917 — IF
Died: Hillingdon, W London, England, 1984

League Club	Source	Date Signed	Seasons Played	Apps	Subs	Gls
Blackpool		01/37				
Bournemouth	Tr	06/38	38	12	-	0
Bristol Rov	Tr	06/39				
Crewe Alex	Tr	09/47	47	1	-	0

FLETCHER Andrew Michael (Andy)
Born: Cleveland, England, 12 August, 1971 — F

League Club	Source	Date Signed	Seasons Played	Apps	Subs	Gls
Middlesbrough	YT	05/89				
Scarborough	Tr	02/91	90-91	15	12	6

FLETCHER Carl Neil
Born: Camberley, Surrey, England, 7 April, 1980 — M
Wales: 36

League Club	Source	Date Signed	Seasons Played	Apps	Subs	Gls
Bournemouth	YT	07/98	97-04	186	7	19
West Ham U	Tr	08/04	04-05	32	12	3
Watford	L	09/05	05	3	0	0
Crystal Palace	Tr	07/06	06-08	50	18	4
Nottingham F	L	10/08	08	4	1	0
Plymouth Arg	Tr	02/09	08-11	99	2	8

FLETCHER Christopher Columba (Chris)
Born: Buncrana, Co. Donegal, Republic of Ireland, 14 June, 1933 — IF

League Club	Source	Date Signed	Seasons Played	Apps	Subs	Gls
Brentford	Cheltenham T	12/57	57	3	-	0

FLETCHER Dan Calum
Born: Teversal, Nottinghamshire, England, 4 March, 1997 — F

League Club	Source	Date Signed	Seasons Played	Apps	Subs	Gls
Mansfield T	Sch	12/14	14	0	1	0

FLETCHER Darren Barr
Born: Dalkeith, Midlothian, Scotland, 1 February, 1984 — M
Scotland: 68/B-1/U21-2

League Club	Source	Date Signed	Seasons Played	Apps	Subs	Gls
Manchester U	YT	02/01	03-14	179	44	18
West Bromwich A	Tr	02/15	14	15	0	1

FLETCHER Douglas (Doug)
Born: Sheffield, England, 17 September, 1930 — CF/RW

League Club	Source	Date Signed	Seasons Played	Apps	Subs	Gls
Sheffield Wed	Hillsborough BC	01/48	48-49	4	-	0
Bury	Tr	05/51	51-55	67	-	17
Scunthorpe U	Tr	07/56	56-57	64	-	26
Darlington	Tr	07/58	58	43	-	13
Halifax T	Tr	06/59	59	20	-	4

FLETCHER Gavin
Born: Bellshill, Lanarkshire, Scotland, 30 October, 1941 — IF

League Club	Source	Date Signed	Seasons Played	Apps	Subs	Gls
Bradford C	Third Lanark	07/63	63	8	-	1

FLETCHER Hugh Malcolm
Born: Lochgilphead, Argyll & Bute, Scotland, 8 April, 1933 — FB/F

League Club	Source	Date Signed	Seasons Played	Apps	Subs	Gls
Carlisle U	Glasgow Celtic	05/56	56-60	124	-	18

FLETCHER James (Jimmy)
Born: Houghton-le-Spring, Tyne and Wear, England, 6 November, 1934 — CF

League Club	Source	Date Signed	Seasons Played	Apps	Subs	Gls
Doncaster Rov	Eppleton CW	01/58	57-59	45	-	15
Stockport Co	Tr	01/60	59-60	61	-	19

FLETCHER James Alfred (Jimmy)
Born: Wouldham, Kent, England, 10 November, 1931 — IF
England: Amateur-4

League Club	Source	Date Signed	Seasons Played	Apps	Subs	Gls
Gillingham	Maidstone U	07/57	57	23	-	8
Southend U	Tr	07/58				

FLETCHER James Robert
Born: Brewood, Staffordshire, England, 23 December, 1926 — W
Died: North Yorkshire, England, March, 2014

League Club	Source	Date Signed	Seasons Played	Apps	Subs	Gls
Birmingham C	Bilston	06/50				
Chester C	Tr	07/51	51	23	-	9

FLETCHER James Rodney (Rod)
Born: Preston, Lancashire, England, 23 September, 1945 — F

League Club	Source	Date Signed	Seasons Played	Apps	Subs	Gls
Leeds U	Colne	12/62				
Crewe Alex	Madeley College	03/67	66	1	0	0
Lincoln C	Tr	08/67	67-70	86	6	29
Scunthorpe U	Tr	06/71	71-73	97	1	30
Grimsby T	Tr	11/73	73-74	9	3	1

FLETCHER John
Born: Sheffield, England, 22 February, 1943 — FB
Died: Sheffield, England, May, 2013

League Club	Source	Date Signed	Seasons Played	Apps	Subs	Gls
Doncaster Rov		06/61	61	1	-	0

FLETCHER Joseph Michael (Joe)
Born: Manchester, England, 25 September, 1946 — F

League Club	Source	Date Signed	Seasons Played	Apps	Subs	Gls
Rochdale	Manchester C (Am)	01/67	66-68	55	2	21
Grimsby T	Tr	07/69	69	11	0	1
Barrow	Tr	10/69	69	7	1	1

FLETCHER Kenneth (Ken)
Born: Liverpool, England, 31 December, 1931 — RB
Died: New South Wales, Australia, 13 October, 2011

League Club	Source	Date Signed	Seasons Played	Apps	Subs	Gls
Everton	Jnr	08/49				
Chester C	Tr	07/53	53-55	34	-	0

FLETCHER Leonard Gerald George (Len)
Born: Hammersmith, W London, England, 28 April, 1929 — WH

League Club	Source	Date Signed	Seasons Played	Apps	Subs	Gls
Ipswich T	RAF Didcot	11/49	49-54	20	-	0

FLETCHER Mark Robert John
Born: Barnsley, South Yorkshire, England, 1 April, 1965 — RB

League Club	Source	Date Signed	Seasons Played	Apps	Subs	Gls
Barnsley	App	04/83	83	1	0	0
Bradford C	Tr	06/84	84	4	2	0

FLETCHER Paul John
Born: Bolton, Greater Manchester, England, 13 January, 1951 — F
England: U23-4

League Club	Source	Date Signed	Seasons Played	Apps	Subs	Gls
Bolton W	App	11/68	68-70	33	3	5
Burnley	Tr	03/71	70-79	291	2	71
Blackpool	Tr	02/80	79-81	19	1	8

FLETCHER Peter
Born: Manchester, England, 2 December, 1953 — F

League Club	Source	Date Signed	Seasons Played	Apps	Subs	Gls
Manchester U	App	12/70	72-73	2	5	0
Hull C	Tr	05/74	74-75	26	10	5
Stockport Co	Tr	05/76	76-77	43	8	13
Huddersfield T	Tr	07/78	78-81	83	16	36

FLETCHER Steven Kenneth
Born: Shrewsbury, Shropshire, England, 26 March, 1987 — F
Scotland: 21/B-1/U21-7/Youth

League Club	Source	Date Signed	Seasons Played	Apps	Subs	Gls
Burnley	Hibernian	07/09	09	35	0	8
Wolverhampton W	Tr	07/10	10-11	41	20	22
Sunderland	Tr	08/12	12-14	61	17	19

FLETCHER Steven Mark (Steve)
Born: Hartlepool, Cleveland, England, 26 June, 1972 — F

League Club	Source	Date Signed	Seasons Played	Apps	Subs	Gls
Hartlepool U	YT	08/90	90-91	19	13	4
Bournemouth	Tr	07/92	92-06	446	47	88
Chesterfield	Tr	07/07	07	23	15	5
Bournemouth	Crawley T	01/09	08-12	59	76	15
Plymouth Arg	L	03/12	11	2	4	0

FLETCHER Wesleigh James (Wes)
Born: Ormskirk, Lancashire, England, 28 February, 1991 — F

League Club	Source	Date Signed	Seasons Played	Apps	Subs	Gls
Burnley	Sch	07/09				
Grimsby T	L	01/10	09	1	5	1
Stockport Co	L	10/10	10	8	1	1
Accrington Stan	L	08/11	11	10	0	2
Crewe Alex	L	11/11	11	3	3	1
Yeovil T	L	02/13	12	0	1	0
York C	Tr	06/13	13-14	46	15	16

FLETT Alexander Edward (Alex)
Born: Grimsby, North Lincolnshire, England, 20 September, 1992 — M

League Club	Source	Date Signed	Seasons Played	Apps	Subs	Gls
Bradford C	Sch	07/11	10	0	1	0

FLEWIN Reginald (Reg)
Born: Portsmouth, England, 28 November, 1920 — CH
Died: Shanklin, Isle of Wight, England, 24 May, 2008
England: War-1

League Club	Source	Date Signed	Seasons Played	Apps	Subs	Gls
Portsmouth	Jnr	11/37	38-52	150	-	0

FLEXNEY Paul
Born: Glasgow, Scotland, 18 January, 1965 — CD

League Club	Source	Date Signed	Seasons Played	Apps	Subs	Gls
Northampton T	Clyde	08/88	88	12	0	0

FLINDERS Scott Liam
Born: Rotherham, South Yorkshire, England, 12 June, 1986 — G
England: Youth

League Club	Source	Date Signed	Seasons Played	Apps	Subs	Gls
Barnsley	Sch	04/05	04-05	14	0	0
Crystal Palace	Tr	07/06	06	7	1	0
Gillingham	L	09/06	06	9	0	0
Brighton & HA	L	02/07	06	12	0	0
Yeovil T	L	02/08	07	9	0	0
Hartlepool U	Tr	07/09	09-14	252	0	1

FLINT Aden
Born: Pinxton, Derbyshire, England, 11 July, 1989 — CD
England: Semi Pro-2

League Club	Source	Date Signed	Seasons Played	Apps	Subs	Gls
Swindon T	Alfreton T	01/11	10-12	58	6	4
Bristol C	Tr	06/13	13-14	78	2	17

FLINT Kenneth (Ken)
Born: Selston, Nottinghamshire, England, 12 November, 1923 — LW
Died: Barnet, N London, England, 21 May, 2010

League Club	Source	Date Signed	Seasons Played	Apps	Subs	Gls
Tottenham H	Bedford T	07/47	47	5	-	1
Aldershot	Tr	07/50	50-57	324	-	70
Leyton Orient	Tr	06/58	58	4	-	0

FLITCROFT David John (Dave)
Born: Bolton, Greater Manchester, England, 14 January, 1974 — M

League Club	Source	Date Signed	Seasons Played	Apps	Subs	Gls
Preston NE	YT	05/92	92	4	4	2
Lincoln C	L	09/93	93	2	0	0
Chester C	Tr	12/93	93-98	146	21	18
Rochdale	Tr	07/99	99-02	141	19	4
Macclesfield T	Tr	07/03	03	14	1	0
Bury	Tr	01/04	03-06	95	5	4
Rochdale	Hyde U	01/07	09	0	1	0

FLITCROFT Garry William
Born: Bolton, Greater Manchester, England, 6 November, 1972 — M
England: U21-10/Youth/Schools

League Club	Source	Date Signed	Seasons Played	Apps	Subs	Gls
Manchester C	YT	07/91	92-95	109	6	13
Bury	L	03/92	91	12	0	0
Blackburn Rov	Tr	03/96	95-05	231	15	14
Sheffield U	L	01/06	05	3	3	0

FLITNEY Ross Daniel
Born: Hitchin, Hertfordshire, England, 1 June, 1984 — G

League Club	Source	Date Signed	Seasons Played	Apps	Subs	Gls
Fulham	Sch	07/03				
Brighton & HA	L	08/03	03	3	0	0
Barnet	Tr	07/05	05-06	47	3	0
Gillingham	Dover Ath	07/11	11	27	0	0

FLO Havard
Born: Stryn, Norway, 4 April, 1970 — F
Norway: 26

League Club	Source	Date Signed	Seasons Played	Apps	Subs	Gls
Wolverhampton W	Werder Bremen (GER)	01/99	98-99	27	11	9

FLO Jostein
Born: Stryn, Norway, 3 October, 1964 — F
Norway: 53

League Club	Source	Date Signed	Seasons Played	Apps	Subs	Gls
Sheffield U	Stryn Sogndal (NOR)	08/93	93-95	74	10	19

FLO Tore Andre
Born: Stryn, Norway, 15 June, 1973 — F
Norway: 76/U21-28

League Club	Source	Date Signed	Seasons Played	Apps	Subs	Gls
Chelsea	SK Brann Bergen (NOR)	08/97	97-00	59	53	34
Sunderland	Glasgow Rangers	08/02	02	23	6	4
Leeds U	Valerenga (NOR)	01/07	06-07	5	18	4
MK Dons	Rtd	11/08	08	2	11	0

FLOCKETT Thomas William (Tommy)
Born: Ferryhill, County Durham, England, 17 July, 1927 — RB
Died: Chesterfield, Derbyshire, England, 12 July, 1997

League Club	Source	Date Signed	Seasons Played	Apps	Subs	Gls
Chesterfield	Spennymoor U	04/49	49-56	200	-	1
Bradford C	Tr	06/57	57-62	227	-	1

FLOOD Anthony
Born: Dublin, Republic of Ireland, 31 December, 1984 — F

League Club	Source	Date Signed	Seasons Played	Apps	Subs	Gls
Southend U	Bohemians (ROI)	01/12	11	0	1	0

FLOOD Edward David (Eddie)
Born: Liverpool, England, 19 November, 1952 — LB

League Club	Source	Date Signed	Seasons Played	Apps	Subs	Gls
Liverpool	App	11/69				
Tranmere Rov	Tr	07/72	72-80	313	2	6
York C	Tr	08/81	81	13	2	0

FLOOD John Ernest
Born: Southampton, England, 21 October, 1932 — RW
England: Schools

League Club	Source	Date Signed	Seasons Played	Apps	Subs	Gls
Southampton	Jnr	11/49	52-57	122	-	28
Bournemouth	Tr	06/58	58	17	-	3

FLOOD John Gerard
Born: Glasgow, Scotland, 25 December, 1960 — RW

League Club	Source	Date Signed	Seasons Played	Apps	Subs	Gls
Sheffield U	App	10/78	78-80	16	3	1

FLOOD Paul Anthony
Born: Dublin, Republic of Ireland, 29 June, 1948 — LW

League Club	Source	Date Signed	Seasons Played	Apps	Subs	Gls
Brighton & HA	Bohemians (ROI)	06/67	67-70	32	3	7

FLOOD William Robert (Willo)
Born: Dublin, Republic of Ireland, 10 April, 1985 — RW
Republic of Ireland: U21-11/Youth

League Club	Source	Date Signed	Seasons Played	Apps	Subs	Gls
Manchester C	Sch	04/02	04-05	5	9	1
Rochdale	L	03/04	03	6	0	0
Coventry C	L	08/05	05	7	1	1
Cardiff C	Tr	08/06	06	5	20	1
Middlesbrough	Glasgow Celtic	01/10	09-10	12	4	1

FLORES Jordan Michael
Born: Aspull, Greater Manchester, England, 4 October, 1995 — M

League Club	Source	Date Signed	Seasons Played	Apps	Subs	Gls
Wigan Ath	Sch	07/14	14	0	1	0

FLORO Rafael da Silva
Born: Faro, Portugal, 19 January, 1994 — LB

League Club	Source	Date Signed	Seasons Played	Apps	Subs	Gls
Sheffield Wed	FC Porto Jnrs (POR)	08/13	13	1	0	0

FLOUNDERS Andrew John (Andy)
Born: Hull, England, 13 December, 1963 — F

League Club	Source	Date Signed	Seasons Played	Apps	Subs	Gls
Hull C	App	12/81	80-86	126	33	54
Scunthorpe U	Tr	03/87	86-90	186	10	87
Rochdale	Tr	07/91	91-93	82	3	31
Rotherham U	L	02/93	92	6	0	2
Carlisle U	L	10/93	93	5	0	1
Carlisle U	L	02/94	93	1	2	0
Northampton T	Halifax T	12/94	94	2	0	0

FLOWER Anthony John (Tony)
Born: Carlton, Nottinghamshire, England, 2 January, 1945 — W

League Club	Source	Date Signed	Seasons Played	Apps	Subs	Gls
Notts Co	Jnr	01/62	61-66	127	2	17
Halifax T	Tr	07/67	67-69	78	1	11

FLOWER Johannes Graham (John)
Born: Northampton, England, 9 December, 1964 — CD

League Club	Source	Date Signed	Seasons Played	Apps	Subs	Gls
Sheffield U	Corby T	08/89				
Aldershot	Tr	10/90	90	30	2	2

FLOWERS John Edward
Born: Bedlington, Northumberland, England, 26 August, 1944 — WH

League Club	Source	Date Signed	Seasons Played	Apps	Subs	Gls
Stoke C	App	09/61	63-65	8	0	0
Doncaster Rov	Tr	08/66	66-70	162	2	4
Port Vale	Tr	08/71	71	34	0	0

FLOWERS Malcolm Thomas
Born: Mansfield, Nottinghamshire, England, 9 August, 1938 — CH

League Club	Source	Date Signed	Seasons Played	Apps	Subs	Gls
Mansfield T	Jnr	08/56	56	3	-	0

FLOWERS Paul Anthony
Born: Stepney, E London, England, 7 September, 1974 — CD

League Club	Source	Date Signed	Seasons Played	Apps	Subs	Gls
Colchester U	YT	08/93	92	2	1	0

FLOWERS Ronald (Ron)
Born: Bedlington, Northumberland, England, 28 July, 1934 — LH
England: 49/FLge-13/U23-2

League Club	Source	Date Signed	Seasons Played	Apps	Subs	Gls
Wolverhampton W	Jnr	08/51	52-66	467	0	33
Northampton T	Tr	09/67	67-68	61	1	4

FLOWERS Timothy David (Tim)
Born: Kenilworth, Warwickshire, England, 3 February, 1967 — G
England: 11/U21-3/Youth

League Club	Source	Date Signed	Seasons Played	Apps	Subs	Gls
Wolverhampton W	App	08/84	84-85	63	0	0
Southampton	Tr	06/86	86-93	192	0	0
Swindon T	L	03/87	86	2	0	0
Swindon T	L	11/87	87	5	0	0
Blackburn Rov	Tr	11/93	93-98	175	2	0
Leicester C	Tr	07/99	99-02	54	2	0
Stockport Co	L	10/01	01	4	0	0
Coventry C	L	02/02	01	5	0	0

FLOYD Ronald Charles (Ron)
Born: Coventry, England, 17 August, 1932 — G

League Club	Source	Date Signed	Seasons Played	Apps	Subs	Gls
West Bromwich A	Jnr	11/49				
Crewe Alex	Tr	07/53	53-54	39	-	0

FLYNN Brian
Born: Port Talbot, Wales, 12 October, 1955 — M
Wales: 66/U23-2/Schools

League Club	Source	Date Signed	Seasons Played	Apps	Subs	Gls
Burnley	App	10/72	73-77	115	5	8
Leeds U	Tr	11/77	77-82	152	2	11
Burnley	L	03/82	81	2	0	0
Burnley	Tr	11/82	82-84	76	4	10
Cardiff C	Tr	11/84	84-85	32	0	0
Doncaster Rov	Tr	11/85	85	27	0	0
Bury	Tr	07/86	86	19	0	0
Doncaster Rov	Limerick (ROI)	08/87	87	18	6	1
Wrexham	Tr	02/88	87-92	91	9	5

FLYNN Christopher Peter (Chris)
Born: Market Drayton, Shropshire, England, 5 November, 1987 — M

League Club	Source	Date Signed	Seasons Played	Apps	Subs	Gls
Crewe Alex	Sch	07/06	06	0	1	0

FLYNN John Edward
Born: Workington, Cumbria, England, 20 March, 1948 — CD

League Club	Source	Date Signed	Seasons Played	Apps	Subs	Gls
Workington	Cockermouth	09/67	66-68	35	3	0
Sheffield U	Tr	07/69	69-77	185	5	8
Rotherham U	Tr	07/78	78-79	30	1	1

FLYNN Jonathan Joseph (Jonny)
Born: Ballymena, Antrim, Northern Ireland, 18 November, 1989 — CD
Northern Ireland: U21-11/Youth

League Club	Source	Date Signed	Seasons Played	Apps	Subs	Gls
Blackburn Rov	Ballymena U	01/08				
Accrington Stan	L	11/09	09	6	2	0

FLYNN Lee David
Born: Hampstead, NW London, England, 4 September, 1973 — LB

League Club	Source	Date Signed	Seasons Played	Apps	Subs	Gls
Barnet	Hayes	01/01	00	17	0	0

FLYNN Matthew Edward (Matt)
Born: Preston, Lancashire, England, 10 May, 1989 — RB

League Club	Source	Date Signed	Seasons Played	Apps	Subs	Gls
Macclesfield T	Sch	07/07	08	23	5	0
Rochdale	Tr	08/09	09-10	7	4	0

FLYNN Michael Anthony (Mike)
Born: Oldham, Greater Manchester, England, 23 February, 1969 — CD

League Club	Source	Date Signed	Seasons Played	Apps	Subs	Gls
Oldham Ath	App	02/87	87-88	37	3	1
Norwich C	Tr	12/88				
Preston NE	Tr	12/89	89-92	134	2	7
Stockport Co	Tr	03/93	92-01	386	1	16
Stoke C	L	01/02	01	11	2	0
Barnsley	Tr	03/02	01-02	20	1	0
Blackpool	Tr	01/03	02-04	55	2	1

FLYNN Michael John (Mike)
Born: Newport, Wales, 17 October, 1980 — M

League Club	Source	Date Signed	Seasons Played	Apps	Subs	Gls
Wigan Ath	Barry T	06/02	02-04	5	33	2
Blackpool	L	08/04	04	6	0	0
Gillingham	Tr	02/05	04-06	90	7	19
Blackpool	Tr	07/07	07	20	8	3
Huddersfield T	Tr	07/08	08	18	7	4
Darlington	L	11/08	08	4	0	0
Bradford C	Tr	08/09	09-11	84	7	10
Newport Co	Tr	07/12	13-14	21	22	4

FLYNN Patrick James
Born: Dublin, Republic of Ireland, 13 January, 1985 — RB
Republic of Ireland: Youth

League Club	Source	Date Signed	Seasons Played	Apps	Subs	Gls
Wolverhampton W	Sch	07/02				
Torquay U	Tr	09/05	05	1	0	0

FLYNN Peter
Born: Glasgow, Scotland, 11 October, 1936 — WH

League Club	Source	Date Signed	Seasons Played	Apps	Subs	Gls
Leeds U	Petershill	10/53	53	1	-	0
Bradford Park Ave	Tr	06/57	58-65	130	1	9

FLYNN Ryan
Born: Falkirk, Scotland, 4 September, 1988 — RW
Scotland: Youth

League Club	Source	Date Signed	Seasons Played	Apps	Subs	Gls
Liverpool	Sch	07/06				
Sheffield U	Falkirk	07/11	11-14	94	32	11

FLYNN Sean Michael
Born: Birmingham, England, 13 March, 1968 — RM

League Club	Source	Date Signed	Seasons Played	Apps	Subs	Gls
Coventry C	Halesowen T	12/91	91-94	90	7	9
Derby Co	Tr	08/95	95-96	39	20	3
Stoke C	L	03/97	96	5	0	0
West Bromwich A	Tr	08/97	97-99	99	10	8
Tranmere Rov	Tr	07/00	00-01	65	1	6
Kidderminster Hrs	Tr	08/02	02-03	49	2	2

FLYNN William
Born: Kirkmaiden, Dumfries & Galloway, Scotland, 2 January, 1927 — LW
Died: Rotherham, South Yorkshire, England, 2 October, 2006

League Club	Source	Date Signed	Seasons Played	Apps	Subs	Gls
Rotherham U	Maybole Jnrs	07/49	49	6	-	0

FOAN Albert Thomas
Born: Rotherhithe, SE London, England, 30 October, 1923 — IF
Died: Norwich, England, 14 August, 2009

League Club	Source	Date Signed	Seasons Played	Apps	Subs	Gls
Norwich C	BAOR Germany	04/47	47-49	18	-	4
West Ham U	Tr	07/50	50-56	53	-	6

FODERINGHAM Wesley Andrew (Wes)
Born: Hammersmith, W London, England, 14 January, 1991 — G
England: Youth

League Club	Source	Date Signed	Seasons Played	Apps	Subs	Gls
Fulham	Sch	05/09				
Crystal Palace	Tr	08/10				
Swindon T	Tr	10/11	11-14	164	0	0

FOE Marc-Vivien
Born: Yaounde, Cameroon, 1 May, 1975 — M
Died: Lyon, France, 26 June, 2003
Cameroon: 64

League Club	Source	Date Signed	Seasons Played	Apps	Subs	Gls
West Ham U	RC Lens (FRA)	01/99	98-99	38	0	1
Manchester C (L)	Olymp Lyonnais (FRA)	07/02	02	35	0	9

FOFANA Aboubacar
Born: Paris, France, 4 October, 1982 — LW

League Club	Source	Date Signed	Seasons Played	Apps	Subs	Gls
Millwall	Juventus (ITA)	08/03	03	9	7	0

FOFANA Seko Mohamed
Born: Paris, France, 7 May, 1995 — M
France: Youth

League Club	Source	Date Signed	Seasons Played	Apps	Subs	Gls
Manchester C	Lorient (FRA)	03/13				
Fulham	L	11/14	14	13	8	1

FOGARTY Ambrose Gerald (Amby)
Born: Dublin, Republic of Ireland, 11 September, 1933 — IF
Republic of Ireland: 11

League Club	Source	Date Signed	Seasons Played	Apps	Subs	Gls
Sunderland	Glentoran	10/57	57-63	152	-	37
Hartlepool U	Tr	11/63	63-66	127	0	22

FOGARTY Kenneth Anthony (Ken)
Born: Manchester, England, 25 January, 1955 — CD

League Club	Source	Date Signed	Seasons Played	Apps	Subs	Gls
Stockport Co	App	11/72	71-79	265	4	6

FOGARTY William Francis (Bill)
Born: Dulwich, S London, England, 27 June, 1957 — M

League Club	Source	Date Signed	Seasons Played	Apps	Subs	Gls
Gillingham	App	07/75	74-76	25	4	0
Charlton Ath	Tr	12/76				

FOGDEN Wesley Keith (Wes)
Born: Brighton, England, 12 April, 1988 — W

League Club	Source	Date Signed	Seasons Played	Apps	Subs	Gls
Brighton & HA	Sch	06/06	07	1	2	0

League Club	Source	Date Signed	Seasons Played	Apps	Subs	Gls
Bournemouth	Havant & Waterlooville	10/11	11-12	32	21	4
Portsmouth	Tr	01/14	13-14	19	9	2

FOGG David
Born: Liverpool, England, 28 May, 1951 LB

League Club	Source	Date Signed	Seasons Played	Apps	Subs	Gls
Wrexham	English Elec	05/70	70-75	159	2	0
Oxford U	Tr	07/76	76-84	289	4	16

FOGG Ronald William James (Ron)
Born: Tilbury, Essex, England, 3 June, 1938 CF

League Club	Source	Date Signed	Seasons Played	Apps	Subs	Gls
Southend U (Am)	Tilbury	08/59	59	2	-	0
Aldershot	Weymouth	07/63	63-64	64	-	28

FOGGO Kenneth Taylor (Ken)
Born: Perth, Scotland, 7 November, 1943 RW
Scotland: Schools

League Club	Source	Date Signed	Seasons Played	Apps	Subs	Gls
West Bromwich A	Peebles YMCA	11/60	62-67	128	1	29
Norwich C	Tr	10/67	67-72	181	4	54
Portsmouth	Tr	01/73	72-74	47	13	3
Brentford	Tr	06/75				
Southend U	Tr	09/75	75	30	0	6

FOGGON Alan
Born: West Pelton, County Durham, England, 23 February, 1950 LW/F
England: Youth

League Club	Source	Date Signed	Seasons Played	Apps	Subs	Gls
Newcastle U	App	11/67	67-70	54	7	14
Cardiff C	Tr	08/71	71-72	14	3	1
Middlesbrough	Tr	10/72	72-75	105	10	45
Manchester U	Hartford B'ls (USA)	07/76	76	0	3	0
Sunderland	Tr	09/76	76	7	1	0
Southend U	Tr	06/77	77	22	0	0
Hartlepool U	L	02/78	77	18	0	2

FOJUT Jaroslaw
Born: Legionowo, Poland, 17 October, 1987 CD
Poland: Youth

League Club	Source	Date Signed	Seasons Played	Apps	Subs	Gls
Bolton W	Sch	07/06	05	0	1	0
Luton T	L	08/07	07	15	1	2
Stockport Co	L	10/08	08	3	0	0

FOLAN Anthony Stephen (Tony)
Born: Lewisham, SE London, England, 18 September, 1978 W
Republic of Ireland: U21-6

League Club	Source	Date Signed	Seasons Played	Apps	Subs	Gls
Crystal Palace	YT	09/95	97	0	1	0
Brentford	Tr	09/98	98-00	31	28	7

FOLAN Caleb Colman
Born: Leeds, England, 26 October, 1982 F
Republic of Ireland: 7

League Club	Source	Date Signed	Seasons Played	Apps	Subs	Gls
Leeds U	YT	11/99				
Rushden & D	L	10/01	01	1	5	0
Hull C	L	11/01	01	0	1	0
Chesterfield	Tr	02/03	02-06	57	45	15
Wigan Ath	Tr	01/07	06	9	6	2
Hull C	Tr	08/07	07-10	29	26	11
Middlesbrough	L	09/09	09	0	1	0
Bradford C	T-Team (MLY)	09/13	13	0	6	0

FOLDS Robert James (Bobby)
Born: Bedford, England, 18 April, 1949 LB

League Club	Source	Date Signed	Seasons Played	Apps	Subs	Gls
Gillingham	App	04/67	68-70	38	6	1
Northampton T	Tr	08/71	71	29	0	0

FOLETTI Patrick
Born: Lugano, Switzerland, 27 May, 1974 G

League Club	Source	Date Signed	Seasons Played	Apps	Subs	Gls
Derby Co (L)	Lucerne (SUI)	02/02	01	1	1	0

FOLEY Charles
Born: Salford, England, 7 January, 1952 M

League Club	Source	Date Signed	Seasons Played	Apps	Subs	Gls
Stockport Co	App	01/70	69-70	6	0	0

FOLEY David John
Born: South Shields, Tyne and Wear, England, 12 May, 1987 F

League Club	Source	Date Signed	Seasons Played	Apps	Subs	Gls
Hartlepool U	Sch	07/06	03-09	21	77	0

FOLEY Dominic Joseph
Born: Cork, Republic of Ireland, 7 July, 1976 F
Republic of Ireland: 6/U21-8

League Club	Source	Date Signed	Seasons Played	Apps	Subs	Gls
Wolverhampton W	St James' Gate (ROI)	08/95	95-98	4	16	3
Watford	L	02/98	97	2	6	1
Notts Co	L	12/98	98	2	0	0
Watford	Tr	06/99	99-02	12	21	5
Queens Park Rgrs	L	10/01	01	1	0	0
Swindon T	L	01/02	01	5	2	1
Queens Park Rgrs	L	03/02	01	2	2	1
Southend U	L	02/03	02	5	0	0
Oxford U	L	03/03	02	4	2	0

FOLEY Kevin Patrick
Born: Luton, England, 1 November, 1984 RB
Republic of Ireland: 8/B-1/U21-9

League Club	Source	Date Signed	Seasons Played	Apps	Subs	Gls
Luton T	Sch	03/04	02-06	143	8	3
Wolverhampton W	Tr	08/07	07-13	175	19	5
Blackpool	L	02/14	13	4	1	0
Blackpool	L	11/14	14	4	0	0

FOLEY Peter
Born: Bicester, Oxfordshire, England, 10 September, 1956 F
Republic of Ireland: Youth

League Club	Source	Date Signed	Seasons Played	Apps	Subs	Gls
Oxford U	App	09/74	74-82	262	15	71
Gillingham	L	02/83	82	5	0	0
Aldershot	Bulova (HKG)	08/84	84	6	3	2
Exeter C		03/87	86	1	0	0

FOLEY Peter Allan
Born: Edinburgh, Scotland, 28 June, 1944 W

League Club	Source	Date Signed	Seasons Played	Apps	Subs	Gls
Workington	Preston Ath	02/65	64-66	74	0	15
Scunthorpe U	Tr	07/67	67-68	15	2	3
Chesterfield	Tr	08/69	69	2	0	0

FOLEY Samuel Robert (Sam)
Born: Upton-on-Severn, Worcestershire, England, 17 October, 1986 F/M

League Club	Source	Date Signed	Seasons Played	Apps	Subs	Gls
Cheltenham T	Sch	07/06				
Yeovil T	Newport Co	07/12	12-14	78	10	7
Shrewsbury T	L	03/14	13	6	3	0

FOLEY Stephen Paul (Steve)
Born: Clacton, Essex, England, 21 June, 1953 M

League Club	Source	Date Signed	Seasons Played	Apps	Subs	Gls
Colchester U	App	09/71	71-81	273	10	54

FOLEY Steven (Steve)
Born: Bootle, Merseyside, England, 4 October, 1962 M

League Club	Source	Date Signed	Seasons Played	Apps	Subs	Gls
Liverpool	App	09/80				
Fulham	L	12/83	83	2	1	0
Grimsby T	Tr	08/84	84	31	0	2
Sheffield U	Tr	08/85	85-86	56	10	14
Swindon T	Tr	06/87	87-91	142	9	23
Stoke C	Tr	01/92	91-93	106	1	9
Lincoln C	Tr	07/94	94	15	1	0
Bradford C	Tr	08/95	95	0	1	0

FOLEY Terence (Terry)
Born: Portsmouth, England, 8 February, 1938 CF

League Club	Source	Date Signed	Seasons Played	Apps	Subs	Gls
Portsmouth	Ryde	05/59	59	7	-	0
Chesterfield	Tr	07/60	60	28	-	11

FOLEY Theodore Cornelius (Theo)
Born: Dublin, Republic of Ireland, 2 April, 1937 RB
Republic of Ireland: 9

League Club	Source	Date Signed	Seasons Played	Apps	Subs	Gls
Exeter C	Home Farm (ROI)	03/55	55-60	155	-	1
Northampton T	Tr	05/61	61-66	204	0	8
Charlton Ath	Tr	08/67	67	6	0	0

FOLEY William (Will)
Born: Bellshill, Lanarkshire, Scotland, 25 June, 1960 F

League Club	Source	Date Signed	Seasons Played	Apps	Subs	Gls
Swansea C	Frickley Ath	01/86	85	4	1	2
Cardiff C	Tr	03/86	85	5	2	1

FOLEY-SHERIDAN Steven
Born: Dublin, Republic of Ireland, 10 February, 1986 M
Republic of Ireland: Youth

League Club	Source	Date Signed	Seasons Played	Apps	Subs	Gls
Aston Villa	Sch	02/03				
Bournemouth	Tr	08/05	05-06	48	5	6

FOLLAN Edward Harvey (Eddie)
Born: Greenock, Inverclyde, Scotland, 3 October, 1929 IF
Died: Birmingham, England, 16 May, 1975

League Club	Source	Date Signed	Seasons Played	Apps	Subs	Gls
Aston Villa	Prescot Cables	06/52	54-55	34	-	7

FOLLAND Robert (Bobby)
Born: Hartlepool, Cleveland, England, 3 December, 1940 CF

League Club	Source	Date Signed	Seasons Played	Apps	Subs	Gls
Hartlepool U	Newcastle U (Am)	05/59	59-62	58	-	24

FOLLAND Robert William (Rob)
Born: Swansea, Wales, 16 September, 1979 M
Wales: U21-1/Youth

League Club	Source	Date Signed	Seasons Played	Apps	Subs	Gls
Oxford U	YT	07/98	97-01	18	22	2

FOLLY Yoann
Born: Paris, France, 6 June, 1985 DM
France: U21-10/Youth//Togo: 1

League Club	Source	Date Signed	Seasons Played	Apps	Subs	Gls
Southampton	Saint-Etienne (FRA)	07/03	03-05	12	2	0
Nottingham F	L	01/05	04	0	1	0
Preston NE	L	03/05	04	0	2	0
Sheffield Wed	Tr	01/06	05-07	41	12	0
Plymouth Arg	Tr	01/08	07-09	11	11	0
Dagenham & Red	L	02/10	09	5	2	0

FONTAINE Jean-Michel
Born: Saint-Pierre, Reunion, 28 August, 1988 F

Reunion: 16

League Club	Source	Date Signed	Seasons Played	Apps	Subs	Gls
Fleetwood T	JS St Pierroise (REU)	02/13	12	4	9	0

FONTAINE Liam Vaughan Henry
Born: Beckenham, SE London, England, 7 January, 1986 — CD

League Club	Source	Date Signed	Seasons Played	Apps	Subs	Gls
Fulham	Sch	03/04	04	0	1	0
Yeovil T	L	08/04	04	15	0	0
Yeovil T	L	08/05	05	10	0	0
Bristol C	Tr	01/06	05-13	240	22	6
Yeovil T	L	09/13	13	4	1	0

FONTE Jose Miguel da Rocha
Born: Penafiel, Portugal, 22 December, 1983 — CD
Portugal: 4/B-1/U21-3

League Club	Source	Date Signed	Seasons Played	Apps	Subs	Gls
Crystal Palace	Benfica (POR)	07/07	07-09	75	7	6
Southampton	Tr	01/10	09-14	203	3	13

FONTE Rui Pedro
Born: Lisbon, Portugal, 23 April, 1990 — W
Portugal: U21-20

League Club	Source	Date Signed	Seasons Played	Apps	Subs	Gls
Arsenal	Sch	07/07				
Crystal Palace	L	01/09	08	5	5	0

FOOT Daniel Francis (Danny)
Born: Edmonton, N London, England, 6 September, 1975 — FB

League Club	Source	Date Signed	Seasons Played	Apps	Subs	Gls
Southend U	Tottenham H (YT)	08/94	94	2	1	0

FOOTE Christopher Robert Thomas (Chris)
Born: Bournemouth, England, 19 November, 1950 — M

League Club	Source	Date Signed	Seasons Played	Apps	Subs	Gls
Bournemouth	App	08/68	68-69	44	1	2
Cambridge U	Tr	03/71	70-73	76	10	6

FOOTITT Donald (Don)
Born: Grantham, Lincolnshire, England, 24 May, 1929 — G
Died: Grantham, Lincolnshire, England, 10 June, 1995

League Club	Source	Date Signed	Seasons Played	Apps	Subs	Gls
Lincoln C	Grantham St John's	12/46	46	24	-	0
Crewe Alex	Tr	07/49	49	1	-	0

FORAN Mark James
Born: Aldershot, Hampshire, England, 30 October, 1973 — CD

League Club	Source	Date Signed	Seasons Played	Apps	Subs	Gls
Millwall	YT	11/90				
Sheffield U	Tr	08/93	94-95	10	1	1
Rotherham U	L	08/94	94	3	0	0
Wycombe W	L	08/95	95	5	0	0
Peterborough U	Tr	02/96	95-97	22	3	1
Lincoln C	L	01/97	96	1	1	0
Oldham Ath	L	03/97	96	0	1	0
Crewe Alex	Tr	12/97	97-99	25	6	1
Bristol Rov	Tr	08/00	00-01	39	4	2

FORAN Richard (Richie)
Born: Dublin, Republic of Ireland, 16 June, 1980 — F
Republic of Ireland: U21-2

League Club	Source	Date Signed	Seasons Played	Apps	Subs	Gls
Carlisle U	Shelbourne (ROI)	08/01	01-03	84	7	25
Oxford U	L	01/04	03	3	1	0
Southend U	Motherwell	01/07	06-07	9	12	1
Darlington	L	11/07	07	11	1	2
Darlington	L	10/08	08	7	2	3

FORBES Adrian Emmanuel
Born: Greenford, W London, England, 23 January, 1979 — RW
England: Youth

League Club	Source	Date Signed	Seasons Played	Apps	Subs	Gls
Norwich C	YT	01/97	96-00	66	46	8
Luton T	Tr	07/01	01-03	39	33	14
Swansea C	Tr	07/04	04-05	48	21	11
Blackpool	Tr	07/06	06-07	26	10	1
Millwall	Tr	01/08	07	6	7	0
Grimsby T	Tr	02/09	08-09	16	12	4

FORBES Alexander Rooney (Alex)
Born: Dundee, Scotland, 21 January, 1925 — RH
Died: Johannesburg, South Africa, 28 July, 2014
Scotland: 14

League Club	Source	Date Signed	Seasons Played	Apps	Subs	Gls
Sheffield U	Dundee North End	12/44	46-47	61	-	6
Arsenal	Tr	02/48	47-55	217	-	20
Leyton Orient	Tr	08/56	56	8	-	0
Fulham	Tr	11/57	57	4	-	0

FORBES Boniek Manuel Gomes
Born: Guinea-Bissau, 30 September, 1983 — M

League Club	Source	Date Signed	Seasons Played	Apps	Subs	Gls
Leyton Orient	Sch	08/03	02-03	0	13	0

FORBES Dudley Douglas
Born: Johannesburg, South Africa, 19 April, 1926 — WH
Died: Johannesburg, South Africa, 15 May, 2009

League Club	Source	Date Signed	Seasons Played	Apps	Subs	Gls
Charlton Ath	Marist Brothers (RSA)	12/47	48-50	57	-	1

FORBES Duncan Scott
Born: Edinburgh, Scotland, 19 June, 1941 — CD

League Club	Source	Date Signed	Seasons Played	Apps	Subs	Gls
Colchester U	Musselburgh Ath	09/61	61-68	270	0	3
Norwich C	Tr	09/68	68-80	289	6	10
Torquay U	L	10/76	76	7	0	0

FORBES George Parrott
Born: Dukinfield, Greater Manchester, England, 21 July, 1914 — CH
Died: Barrow, Cumbria, England, 28 November, 1964

League Club	Source	Date Signed	Seasons Played	Apps	Subs	Gls
Blackburn Rov	Hyde U	01/37	36	2	-	1
Barrow	Hurst	06/46	46-50	177	-	3

FORBES Graeme Scott Alexander
Born: Forfar, Angus, Scotland, 29 July, 1958 — CD

League Club	Source	Date Signed	Seasons Played	Apps	Subs	Gls
Walsall	Motherwell	09/86	86-89	173	0	9

FORBES Richard John (Dick)
Born: Ashford, Kent, England, 12 March, 1955 — M

League Club	Source	Date Signed	Seasons Played	Apps	Subs	Gls
Exeter C	Woking	04/78	77-80	55	4	5
Plymouth Arg	Bideford	08/83	83	3	0	0

FORBES Scott Hugh
Born: Canewdon, Essex, England, 3 December, 1976 — LM

League Club	Source	Date Signed	Seasons Played	Apps	Subs	Gls
Southend U	Saffron Walden T	08/00	00-01	30	17	3

FORBES Steven Dudley (Steve)
Born: Stoke Newington, N London, England, 24 December, 1975 — M

League Club	Source	Date Signed	Seasons Played	Apps	Subs	Gls
Millwall	Sittingbourne	07/94	94-95	0	5	0
Colchester U	Tr	03/97	96-99	34	19	4
Peterborough U	L	03/99	98	1	2	0

FORBES Terrell Dishan
Born: Southwark, S London, England, 17 August, 1981 — CD

League Club	Source	Date Signed	Seasons Played	Apps	Subs	Gls
West Ham U	YT	07/99				
Bournemouth	L	10/99	99	3	0	0
Queens Park Rgrs	Tr	07/01	01-04	113	1	0
Grimsby T	Tr	09/04	04	33	0	0
Oldham Ath	Tr	07/05	05	33	6	0
Yeovil T	Tr	07/06	06-09	160	3	1
Leyton Orient	Tr	07/10	10-11	70	3	2
Chesterfield	Tr	07/12	12	17	0	1
Aldershot T	Tr	01/13	12	10	0	0

FORBES William (Willie)
Born: Glasgow, Scotland, 25 May, 1922 — LH
Died: Chorley, Lancashire, England, February, 1999

League Club	Source	Date Signed	Seasons Played	Apps	Subs	Gls
Wolverhampton W	Dunfermline Ath	09/46	46-49	71	-	23
Preston NE	Tr	12/49	49-55	191	-	7
Carlisle U	Tr	07/56	56-57	26	-	0

FORBES-SWINDELLS Nathan
Born: Sheffield, England, 29 December, 1989 — F

League Club	Source	Date Signed	Seasons Played	Apps	Subs	Gls
Boston U	Sch	-	06	0	1	0

FORD Alan Lenane
Born: Ferndale, Rhondda Cynon Taff, Wales, 28 October, 1925 — G
Died: Uxbridge, W London, England, 1 October, 1963

League Club	Source	Date Signed	Seasons Played	Apps	Subs	Gls
Workington (Am)		07/51	51-53	39	-	0

FORD Andrew Carl (Andy)
Born: Minehead, Somerset, England, 4 May, 1954 — LB

League Club	Source	Date Signed	Seasons Played	Apps	Subs	Gls
Bournemouth	Minehead	07/71				
Southend U	Tr	05/73	73-76	135	3	3
Swindon T	Tr	08/77	77-79	92	6	0
Gillingham	Tr	07/80	80-81	62	0	3

FORD Anthony Michael (Tony)
Born: Thornbury, Avon, England, 26 November, 1944 — RB
England: Youth

League Club	Source	Date Signed	Seasons Played	Apps	Subs	Gls
Bristol C	App	11/61	61-69	170	1	10
Bristol Rov	Tr	12/69	69-70	28	0	1

FORD Clive
Born: West Bromwich, West Midlands, England, 10 April, 1945 — F

League Club	Source	Date Signed	Seasons Played	Apps	Subs	Gls
Wolverhampton W	App	10/62	64	2	-	0
Walsall	Tr	12/64	64-66	11	3	0
Lincoln C	Tr	02/67	66-67	48	1	16

FORD Colin
Born: Lewisham, SE London, England, 18 September, 1960 — FB

League Club	Source	Date Signed	Seasons Played	Apps	Subs	Gls
Gillingham	App	09/78	79	1	0	0

FORD David
Born: Sheffield, England, 2 March, 1945 — F/M
England: U23-2

League Club	Source	Date Signed	Seasons Played	Apps	Subs	Gls
Sheffield Wed	App	01/63	65-69	117	5	31
Newcastle U	Tr	12/69	69-70	24	2	3
Sheffield U	Tr	01/71	70-72	21	6	2
Halifax T	Tr	08/73	73-75	83	2	6

FORD Francis Martin
Born: Bridgend, Wales, 3 February, 1967 — FB

League Club	Source	Date Signed	Seasons Played	Apps	Subs	Gls
Cardiff C	Jnr	03/85	84	1	1	0

FORD Frederick George Luther (Fred)
Born: Dartford, Kent, England, 10 February, 1916 RH
Died: Kidlington, Oxfordshire, England, 16 October, 1981

League Club	Source	Date Signed	Seasons Played	Apps	Subs	Gls
Charlton Ath	Erith & Belvedere	03/36	36-37	22	-	0
Millwall	Tr	11/45	46	9	-	0
Carlisle U	Tr	07/47	47	28	-	0

FORD Gary
Born: York, England, 8 February, 1961 RW

League Club	Source	Date Signed	Seasons Played	Apps	Subs	Gls
York C	App	02/79	78-86	359	7	52
Leicester C	Tr	07/87	87	15	1	2
Port Vale	Tr	01/88	87-90	66	9	12
Walsall	L	03/90	89	13	0	2
Mansfield T	Tr	03/91	90-92	88	0	6
Hartlepool U	Harstad (NOR)	09/95	95	2	1	0

FORD James Anthony
Born: Portsmouth, England, 23 October, 1981 M

League Club	Source	Date Signed	Seasons Played	Apps	Subs	Gls
Bournemouth	YT	04/00	99-01	5	7	0

FORD Jonathan Steven (Jon)
Born: Stourbridge, West Midlands, England, 12 April, 1968 CD

League Club	Source	Date Signed	Seasons Played	Apps	Subs	Gls
Swansea C	Cradley T	08/91	91-94	145	15	7
Bradford C	Tr	07/95	95	18	1	0
Gillingham	Tr	08/96	96	2	2	0
Barnet	Tr	02/97	96-98	47	0	2

FORD Kenneth (Ken)
Born: Sheffield, England, 1 December, 1940 RW

League Club	Source	Date Signed	Seasons Played	Apps	Subs	Gls
Sheffield Wed	Jnr	03/60				
Oldham Ath	Tr	06/61	61	5	-	1

FORD Liam Anthony
Born: Dewsbury, West Yorkshire, England, 8 September, 1979 F

League Club	Source	Date Signed	Seasons Played	Apps	Subs	Gls
Plymouth Arg	YT	07/98	98	0	1	0

FORD Mark Stuart
Born: Pontefract, West Yorkshire, England, 10 October, 1975 M
England: U21-2/Youth

League Club	Source	Date Signed	Seasons Played	Apps	Subs	Gls
Leeds U	YT	03/93	93-96	27	2	1
Burnley	Tr	07/97	97-98	43	5	1
Torquay U	KFC Lommelse (BEL)	07/00	00	28	0	3
Darlington	Tr	02/01	00-02	55	2	9

FORD Michael Paul (Mike)
Born: Bristol, England, 9 February, 1966 D

League Club	Source	Date Signed	Seasons Played	Apps	Subs	Gls
Leicester C	App	02/84				
Cardiff C	Devizes T	09/84	84-87	144	1	13
Oxford U	Tr	06/88	88-97	273	16	18
Cardiff C	Tr	07/98	98-99	48	3	0
Oxford U	Tr	09/00	00	1	0	0

FORD Peter Leslie
Born: Hanley, Potteries, England, 10 August, 1933 CH

League Club	Source	Date Signed	Seasons Played	Apps	Subs	Gls
Stoke C	West Bromwich A (Am)	05/53	56-58	14	-	0
Port Vale	Tr	09/59	59-62	104	-	5

FORD Robert John (Bobby)
Born: Bristol, England, 22 September, 1974 M

League Club	Source	Date Signed	Seasons Played	Apps	Subs	Gls
Oxford U	YT	10/92	93-97	104	12	7
Sheffield U	Tr	11/97	97-01	138	17	6
Oxford U	Tr	08/02	02	31	6	1

FORD Robert Milroy
Born: Rutherglen, Glasgow, Scotland, 13 August, 1934 IF

League Club	Source	Date Signed	Seasons Played	Apps	Subs	Gls
Aldershot	Vale of Clyde	07/57	57	2	-	0

FORD Ryan
Born: Worksop, Nottinghamshire, England, 3 September, 1978 M

League Club	Source	Date Signed	Seasons Played	Apps	Subs	Gls
Manchester U	YT	07/97				
Notts Co	Tr	02/00	99	0	1	0

FORD Simon Gary
Born: West Ham, E London, England, 17 November, 1981 CD

League Club	Source	Date Signed	Seasons Played	Apps	Subs	Gls
Grimsby T	Charlton Ath (YT)	07/01	01-03	64	14	4
Bristol Rov	Tr	08/04				
Chesterfield	Kilmarnock	07/10	10-11	49	0	1

FORD Stephen Derek (Steve)
Born: Shoreham-by-Sea, West Sussex, England, 17 February, 1959 F
England: Schools

League Club	Source	Date Signed	Seasons Played	Apps	Subs	Gls
Stoke C	Lewes	07/81	81	1	1	0

FORD Stuart Trevor
Born: Sheffield, England, 20 July, 1971 G

League Club	Source	Date Signed	Seasons Played	Apps	Subs	Gls
Rotherham U	YT	07/89	89-91	5	0	0
Scarborough	L	03/92	91	6	0	0
Scarborough	Tr	08/92	92	22	0	0
Doncaster Rov	Tr	08/93	93	4	2	0
Scarborough	Tr	07/94	94	6	0	0

FORD Tony
Born: Grimsby, North Lincolnshire, England, 14 May, 1959 RW/M
England: B-2

League Club	Source	Date Signed	Seasons Played	Apps	Subs	Gls
Grimsby T	App	05/77	75-85	321	34	55
Sunderland	L	03/86	85	8	1	1
Stoke C	Tr	07/86	86-88	112	0	13
West Bromwich A	Tr	03/89	88-91	114	0	14
Grimsby T	Tr	11/91	91-93	59	9	3
Bradford C	L	09/93	93	5	0	0
Scunthorpe U	Tr	08/94	94-95	73	3	9
Mansfield T	Barrow	10/96	96-98	97	6	7
Rochdale	Tr	07/99	99-01	81	8	6

FORD Trevor
Born: Swansea, Wales, 1 October, 1923 CF
Died: Swansea, Wales, 29 May, 2003
Wales: 38/War-1

League Club	Source	Date Signed	Seasons Played	Apps	Subs	Gls
Swansea C	Tawe U	05/42	46	16	-	9
Aston Villa	Tr	01/47	46-50	120	-	60
Sunderland	Tr	10/50	50-53	108	-	67
Cardiff C	Tr	12/53	53-56	96	-	42
Newport Co	PSV Eindhoven (NED)	07/60	60	8	-	3

FORDE Anthony
Born: Limerick, Republic of Ireland, 16 November, 1993 W
Republic of Ireland: U21-11/Youth

League Club	Source	Date Signed	Seasons Played	Apps	Subs	Gls
Wolverhampton W	Sch	07/11	11-13	4	17	0
Scunthorpe U	L	03/13	12	7	1	0
Walsall	Tr	08/14	14	24	13	3

FORDE Clevere
Born: Hammersmith, W London, England, 14 November, 1958 W

League Club	Source	Date Signed	Seasons Played	Apps	Subs	Gls
Plymouth Arg	Hounslow	12/78	78	4	1	0

FORDE David
Born: Galway, Republic of Ireland, 20 December, 1979 G
Republic of Ireland: 23

League Club	Source	Date Signed	Seasons Played	Apps	Subs	Gls
West Ham U	Barry T	02/02				
Cardiff C	Derry C (ROI)	01/07	06	7	0	0
Luton T	L	08/07	07	5	0	0
Bournemouth	L	03/08	07	11	0	0
Millwall	Tr	07/08	08-14	291	0	0

FORDE Fabian Wesley
Born: Harrow, NW London, England, 26 October, 1981 F

League Club	Source	Date Signed	Seasons Played	Apps	Subs	Gls
Watford	YT	03/01	00	0	1	0

FORDE Stephen (Steve)
Born: South Kirkby, West Yorkshire, England, 29 August, 1914 LB
Died: South Kirkby, West Yorkshire, England, July, 1992

League Club	Source	Date Signed	Seasons Played	Apps	Subs	Gls
Sheffield Wed	South Elmsall	01/33				
Rotherham U	Tr	04/33	32-36	116	-	1
West Ham U	Tr	01/37	37-51	170	-	1

FORDYCE Daryl Thomas
Born: Belfast, Northern Ireland, 2 January, 1987 RW
Northern Ireland: U21-12/Youth

League Club	Source	Date Signed	Seasons Played	Apps	Subs	Gls
Portsmouth	Sch	07/05				
Bournemouth	L	02/06	05	3	0	0

FORECAST Tommy Steven
Born: Newham, E London, England, 15 October, 1986 G

League Club	Source	Date Signed	Seasons Played	Apps	Subs	Gls
Tottenham H	Sch	07/05				
Southampton	Tr	07/08				
Grimsby T	L	08/09	09	4	0	0
Gillingham	L	08/12	12	1	1	0

FOREMAN Alexander George (George)
Born: Walthamstow, NE London, England, 1 March, 1914 CF
Died: Waltham Forest, NE London, England, 19 June, 1969
England: Amateur

League Club	Source	Date Signed	Seasons Played	Apps	Subs	Gls
West Ham U	Walthamstow Ave	03/38	38	6	-	1
Tottenham H	Tr	02/46	46	36	-	14

FOREMAN Darren
Born: Southampton, England, 12 February, 1968 F
England: Schools

League Club	Source	Date Signed	Seasons Played	Apps	Subs	Gls
Barnsley	Fareham T	08/86	86-89	33	14	8
Crewe Alex	Tr	03/90	89-90	19	4	4
Scarborough	Tr	03/91	90-94	77	20	35

FOREMAN Denis Joseph
Born: Cape Town, South Africa, 1 February, 1933 IF

League Club	Source	Date Signed	Seasons Played	Apps	Subs	Gls
Brighton & HA	Hibernian (RSA)	03/52	52-60	211	-	63

FOREMAN Matthew (Matt)
Born: Gateshead, Tyne and Wear, England, 15 February, 1975 M

League Club	Source	Date Signed	Seasons Played	Apps	Subs	Gls
Sheffield U	YT	07/93				
Scarborough	Tr	03/96	95	1	3	0

League Club	Source	Date Signed	Seasons Played	Career Record Apps	Subs	Gls

FOREMAN William Ernest (Billy)
Born: Havant, Hampshire, England, 3 February, 1958 — M

League Club	Source	Date Signed	Seasons Played	Apps	Subs	Gls
Bristol Rov	Bournemouth (App)	05/76	76-77	0	2	0

FORESTIERI Fernando Martin
Born: Rosario, Argentina, 15 January, 1990 — F
Italy: U21-2/Youth

League Club	Source	Date Signed	Seasons Played	Apps	Subs	Gls
Watford	Udinese (ITA)	08/12	12-14	48	32	20

FORGAN Thomas Carr (Tommy)
Born: Middlesbrough, England, 12 October, 1929 — G

League Club	Source	Date Signed	Seasons Played	Apps	Subs	Gls
Hull C	Sutton Estates	05/49	53	10	-	0
York C	Tr	06/54	54-65	388	0	0

FORGE Nicolas
Born: Roanne, France, 13 May, 1971 — M

League Club	Source	Date Signed	Seasons Played	Apps	Subs	Gls
Leyton Orient	ASOA Valence (FRA)	03/01	00	1	0	0

FORINTON Howard Lee
Born: Boston, Lincolnshire, England, 18 September, 1975 — F

League Club	Source	Date Signed	Seasons Played	Apps	Subs	Gls
Birmingham C	Yeovil T	07/97	97-99	0	5	1
Plymouth Arg	L	12/98	98	8	1	3
Peterborough U	Tr	09/99	99-01	34	16	10
Torquay U	Tr	08/02	02	1	0	0

FORLAN Corazo Diego (Diego)
Born: Montevideo, Uruguay, 19 May, 1979 — F
Uruguay: 112

League Club	Source	Date Signed	Seasons Played	Apps	Subs	Gls
Manchester U	Independiente (UGY)	01/02	01-04	23	40	10

FORMAN Matthew Charles
Born: Evesham, Worcestershire, England, 8 September, 1967 — M

League Club	Source	Date Signed	Seasons Played	Apps	Subs	Gls
Aston Villa	App	09/85				
Wolverhampton W	Tr	08/86	86	24	1	4

FORMBY Kevin
Born: Ormskirk, Lancashire, England, 22 July, 1971 — LB

League Club	Source	Date Signed	Seasons Played	Apps	Subs	Gls
Rochdale	Burscough	03/94	93-96	59	8	1

FORMICA Mauro Abel
Born: Rosario, Argentina, 4 April, 1988 — M
Argentina: 1/Youth

League Club	Source	Date Signed	Seasons Played	Apps	Subs	Gls
Blackburn Rov	Newells Old Boys (ARG)	02/11	11-12	37	12	5

FORREST Craig Lorne
Born: Vancouver, Canada, 20 September, 1967 — G
Canada: 56

League Club	Source	Date Signed	Seasons Played	Apps	Subs	Gls
Ipswich T	App	08/85	88-96	263	0	0
Colchester U	L	03/88	87	11	0	0
Chelsea	L	03/97	96	2	1	0
West Ham U	Tr	07/97	97-00	26	4	0

FORREST Daniel Paul Halafihi (Danny)
Born: Keighley, West Yorkshire, England, 23 October, 1984 — M
England: Youth

League Club	Source	Date Signed	Seasons Played	Apps	Subs	Gls
Bradford C	Sch	07/03	02-04	16	34	5

FORREST Ernest (Ernie)
Born: Sunderland, England, 19 February, 1919 — RH
Died: Bolton, Greater Manchester, England, January, 1987

League Club	Source	Date Signed	Seasons Played	Apps	Subs	Gls
Bolton W	Usworth Colliery	01/38	38-47	69	-	1
Grimsby T	Tr	05/48	48	33	-	1
Millwall	Tr	06/49	49	37	-	4

FORREST Gerald (Gerry)
Born: Stockton-on-Tees, Cleveland, England, 21 January, 1957 — RB

League Club	Source	Date Signed	Seasons Played	Apps	Subs	Gls
Rotherham U	South Bank	02/77	77-85	357	0	7
Southampton	Tr	12/85	85-89	112	3	0
Rotherham U	Tr	08/90	90	32	2	0

FORREST James (Jimmy)
Born: Dalkeith, Midlothian, Scotland, 14 November, 1929 — IF

League Club	Source	Date Signed	Seasons Played	Apps	Subs	Gls
Leeds U	Musselburgh Ath	12/50				
Accrington Stan	Tr	11/51	51	5	-	2

FORREST James (Jim)
Born: Glasgow, Scotland, 22 September, 1944 — CF
Scotland: 5/U23-2/Schools

League Club	Source	Date Signed	Seasons Played	Apps	Subs	Gls
Preston NE	Glasgow Rangers	03/67	66-67	24	2	3

FORREST John Anthony
Born: Tottington, Greater Manchester, England, 9 October, 1947 — G

League Club	Source	Date Signed	Seasons Played	Apps	Subs	Gls
Bury	Jnr	03/66	67-80	430	0	0

FORREST John Robert (Bob)
Born: Rossington, South Yorkshire, England, 13 May, 1931 — IF
Died: Weymouth, Dorset, England, 3 May, 2005

League Club	Source	Date Signed	Seasons Played	Apps	Subs	Gls
Leeds U	Retford T	12/52	52-58	118	-	36
Notts Co	Tr	02/59	58-61	117	-	37

FORREST Keith
Born: Hartlepool, Cleveland, England, 18 February, 1951 — F

League Club	Source	Date Signed	Seasons Played	Apps	Subs	Gls
Hartlepool U (Am)	St James'	07/69	69-70	4	2	0

FORREST Martyn William
Born: Bury, Greater Manchester, England, 2 January, 1979 — M

League Club	Source	Date Signed	Seasons Played	Apps	Subs	Gls
Bury	YT	07/97	98-02	82	24	2

FORREST William
Born: Carriden, Falkirk, Scotland, 19 January, 1945 — WH

League Club	Source	Date Signed	Seasons Played	Apps	Subs	Gls
Carlisle U	Heart of Midlothian	07/62	62-63	10	-	0

FORRESTER Anthony Charles (Tony)
Born: Poole, Dorset, England, 14 January, 1940 — RW

League Club	Source	Date Signed	Seasons Played	Apps	Subs	Gls
West Bromwich A	Jnr	03/57	58	6	-	3
Southend U	Tr	04/59	59	10	-	1

FORRESTER Anton George
Born: Liverpool, England, 11 February, 1994 — F

League Club	Source	Date Signed	Seasons Played	Apps	Subs	Gls
Everton	Sch	02/11				
Blackburn Rov	Tr	01/13				
Bury	L	07/13	13	18	10	6

FORRESTER George Hogg
Born: Edinburgh, Scotland, 28 August, 1934 — RB
Died: Edinburgh, Scotland, 13 April, 2001

League Club	Source	Date Signed	Seasons Played	Apps	Subs	Gls
Sunderland	Raith Rov	03/53				
Accrington Stan	Eyemouth U	02/60	59-60	54	-	0

FORRESTER George Larmouth
Born: Cannock, Staffordshire, England, 8 June, 1927 — LH/LW
Died: Reading, England, 25 September, 1981

League Club	Source	Date Signed	Seasons Played	Apps	Subs	Gls
Gillingham	West Bromwich A (Am)	08/47	50-54	100	-	3
Reading	Tr	07/55	55	6	-	2

FORRESTER Harry Lee
Born: Milton Keynes, England, 2 January, 1991 — M
England: Youth

League Club	Source	Date Signed	Seasons Played	Apps	Subs	Gls
Aston Villa	Sch	01/08				
Brentford	Tr	08/11	11-12	32	23	8
Doncaster Rov	Tr	07/13	13-14	27	20	7

FORRESTER Jamie Mark
Born: Bradford, England, 1 November, 1974 — F
England: Youth/Schools

League Club	Source	Date Signed	Seasons Played	Apps	Subs	Gls
Leeds U	AJ Auxerre (FRA)	10/92	92-93	7	2	0
Southend U	L	09/94	94	3	2	0
Grimsby T	L	03/95	94	7	2	1
Grimsby T	Tr	10/95	95-96	27	14	6
Scunthorpe U	Tr	03/97	96-98	99	2	37
Walsall (L)	FC Utrecht (NED)	12/99	99	2	3	0
Northampton T	FC Utrecht (NED)	03/00	99-02	109	12	45
Hull C	Tr	01/03	02-03	17	15	7
Bristol Rov	Tr	07/04	04-05	23	29	9
Lincoln C	Tr	03/06	05-07	85	5	35
Notts Co	Tr	07/08	08	27	3	8

FORRESTER Mark
Born: Stockton-on-Tees, Cleveland, England, 15 April, 1981 — F

League Club	Source	Date Signed	Seasons Played	Apps	Subs	Gls
Torquay U	YT	-	98-99	1	5	0

FORRESTER Paul
Born: Edinburgh, Scotland, 3 November, 1972 — F

League Club	Source	Date Signed	Seasons Played	Apps	Subs	Gls
Middlesbrough	Musselburgh Windsor	03/93	93	0	1	0

FORSHAW Adam John
Born: Liverpool, England, 8 October, 1991 — M

League Club	Source	Date Signed	Seasons Played	Apps	Subs	Gls
Everton	Sch	01/10	10	0	1	0
Brentford	L	02/12	11	6	1	0
Brentford	Tr	07/12	12-13	73	9	11
Wigan Ath	Tr	09/14	14	13	3	1
Middlesbrough	Tr	01/15	14	6	12	0

FORSSELL Mikael Kaj
Born: Steinfurt, Germany, 15 March, 1981 — F
Finland: 86/U21-8/Youth

League Club	Source	Date Signed	Seasons Played	Apps	Subs	Gls
Chelsea	HJK Helsinki (FIN)	12/98	98-04	6	27	5
Crystal Palace	L	02/00	99	13	0	3
Crystal Palace	L	06/00	00	31	8	13
Birmingham C	L	08/03	03	32	0	17
Birmingham C	L	07/04	04	4	0	0
Birmingham C	Tr	07/05	05-07	34	31	13
Leeds U	Hannover 96 (GER)	09/11	11	1	14	0

FORSTER Derek
Born: Newcastle-upon-Tyne, England, 19 February, 1949 — G
England: Schools

League Club	Source	Date Signed	Seasons Played	Apps	Subs	Gls
Sunderland	App	02/66	64-71	18	0	0
Charlton Ath	Tr	07/73	73	9	0	0
Brighton & HA	Tr	07/74	74	3	0	0

FORSTER Fraser Gerard
Born: Hexham, Northumberland, England, 17 March, 1988 G
England: 3

League Club	Source	Date Signed	Seasons Played	Apps	Subs	Gls
Newcastle U	Sch	07/07				
Stockport Co	L	10/08	08	6	0	0
Bristol Rov	L	07/09	09	4	0	0
Norwich C	L	08/09	09	38	0	0
Southampton	Glasgow Celtic	08/14	14	30	0	0

FORSTER Geoffrey Patrick (Geoff)
Born: Middlesbrough, England, 3 August, 1954 F

League Club	Source	Date Signed	Seasons Played	Apps	Subs	Gls
Rochdale	South Bank	11/78	78	0	1	0
Hartlepool U	Whitby T	05/80	80	10	4	4

FORSTER Leslie James
Born: Byker, Tyne and Wear, England, 22 July, 1915 RW
Died: Newcastle-upon-Tyne, England, June, 1986

League Club	Source	Date Signed	Seasons Played	Apps	Subs	Gls
Blackpool	Walker Celtic	04/37	38	2	-	0
York C	Tr	09/46	46	10	-	2
Gateshead	Tr	02/47	46-47	14	-	3

FORSTER Mark Erwin
Born: Middlesbrough, England, 1 November, 1964 F

League Club	Source	Date Signed	Seasons Played	Apps	Subs	Gls
Leicester C	Guisborough T	06/83				
Darlington	Tr	03/84	83-85	31	7	13

FORSTER Martyn Gerald
Born: Kettering, Northamptonshire, England, 1 February, 1963 FB
England: Schools

League Club	Source	Date Signed	Seasons Played	Apps	Subs	Gls
Northampton T	Kettering T	08/83	83	41	1	0

FORSTER Nicholas Michael (Nicky)
Born: Caterham, Surrey, England, 8 September, 1973 F
England: U21-4

League Club	Source	Date Signed	Seasons Played	Apps	Subs	Gls
Gillingham	Horley T	05/92	92-93	54	13	24
Brentford	Tr	06/94	94-96	108	1	39
Birmingham C	Tr	01/97	96-98	24	44	11
Reading	Tr	06/99	99-04	157	30	60
Ipswich T	Tr	07/05	05-06	21	3	8
Hull C	Tr	08/06	06	26	9	5
Brighton & HA	Tr	06/07	07-09	88	10	40
Charlton Ath	L	03/10	09	8	0	2
Brentford	Tr	07/10	10	6	12	1

FORSTER Ronald (Ron)
Born: Stockton-on-Tees, Cleveland, England, 19 August, 1935 RW
Died: Stockton-on-Tees, Cleveland, England, January, 2002

League Club	Source	Date Signed	Seasons Played	Apps	Subs	Gls
Darlington	Shotton CW	05/56	56-59	57	-	4

FORSTER Stanley Gerard (Stan)
Born: Aylesham, Kent, England, 1 November, 1943 W

League Club	Source	Date Signed	Seasons Played	Apps	Subs	Gls
Crystal Palace	Margate	11/61	62	2	-	1

FORSTER-CASKEY Jake Dane
Born: Southend-on-Sea, England, 25 April, 1994 M
England: U21-10/Youth

League Club	Source	Date Signed	Seasons Played	Apps	Subs	Gls
Brighton & HA	Sch	04/11	09-14	50	15	5
Oxford U	L	07/12	12	13	3	3

FORSYTH Alexander (Alex)
Born: Swinton, Glasgow, Scotland, 5 February, 1952 LB
Scotland: 10/SLge-1/U23-1

League Club	Source	Date Signed	Seasons Played	Apps	Subs	Gls
Manchester U	Partick Thistle	12/72	72-77	99	2	4

FORSYTH Alexander Simpson Hutchinson (Alex)
Born: Falkirk, Scotland, 29 September, 1928 LW

League Club	Source	Date Signed	Seasons Played	Apps	Subs	Gls
Darlington	Falkirk	08/52	52	26	-	7

FORSYTH Craig
Born: Carnoustie, Angus, Scotland, 24 February, 1989 LB
Scotland: 1

League Club	Source	Date Signed	Seasons Played	Apps	Subs	Gls
Watford	Dundee	06/11	11-12	16	6	3
Bradford C	L	10/12	12	5	2	0
Derby Co	Tr	03/13	12-14	100	0	3

FORSYTH David
Born: Falkirk, Scotland, 5 May, 1945 FB
Died: Tavistock, Devon, England, October, 2008

League Club	Source	Date Signed	Seasons Played	Apps	Subs	Gls
Leyton Orient	Kirkintilloch Rob Roy	05/64	65-66	32	0	0

FORSYTH Michael Eric (Mike)
Born: Liverpool, England, 20 March, 1966 LB
England: B-1/U21-1/Youth

League Club	Source	Date Signed	Seasons Played	Apps	Subs	Gls
West Bromwich A	App	11/83	83-85	28	1	0
Derby Co	Tr	03/86	86-94	323	2	8
Notts Co	Tr	02/95	94	7	0	0
Hereford U	L	09/96	96	12	0	0
Wycombe W	Tr	12/96	96-98	51	1	2

FORSYTH Richard Michael
Born: Dudley, West Midlands, England, 3 October, 1970 M
England: Semi Pro-3

League Club	Source	Date Signed	Seasons Played	Apps	Subs	Gls
Birmingham C	Kidderminster Hrs	07/95	95	12	14	2
Stoke C	Tr	07/96	96-98	90	5	17
Blackpool	Tr	07/99	99	10	3	0
Peterborough U	Tr	07/00	00-02	61	9	2
Cheltenham T	Tr	10/02	02-03	28	11	4

FORSYTH Robert Campbell (Campbell)
Born: Plean, Stirlingshire, Scotland, 5 May, 1934 G
Scotland: 4/SLge-2

League Club	Source	Date Signed	Seasons Played	Apps	Subs	Gls
Southampton	Kilmarnock	12/65	65-67	48	0	0

FORSYTH William Alan (Bill)
Born: Cardenden, Fife, Scotland, 29 March, 1932 D
Died: Wigan, Greater Manchester, England, March, 2004

League Club	Source	Date Signed	Seasons Played	Apps	Subs	Gls
Blackburn Rov	Bowhill Rov	08/49				
Southport	Tr	07/52	52-56	55	-	5

FORSYTHE John Thomson
Born: Dalmuir, Dunbartonshire, Scotland, 20 December, 1918 LW
Died: Wallasey, Wirral, England, February, 1995

League Club	Source	Date Signed	Seasons Played	Apps	Subs	Gls
Luton T	Dumbarton	08/42				
New Brighton	Tr	07/46	46-47	64	-	4
Chester C	Tr	07/48	48	32	-	1

FORSYTHE Robert Haddon
Born: Belfast, Northern Ireland, 27 February, 1925 RW

League Club	Source	Date Signed	Seasons Played	Apps	Subs	Gls
Bradford C	Ballymoney U	07/48	48	1	-	0

FORT Samuel Marsh (Sam)
Born: Bentley, South Yorkshire, England, 27 April, 1929 FB
Died: Walsall, West Midlands, England, 1973

League Club	Source	Date Signed	Seasons Played	Apps	Subs	Gls
Walsall	Retford T	02/54	53-54	28	-	0

FORTE Jonathan Ronald James
Born: Sheffield, England, 25 July, 1986 F
Barbados: 2//England: Youth

League Club	Source	Date Signed	Seasons Played	Apps	Subs	Gls
Sheffield U	Sch	07/04	03-05	2	28	1
Doncaster Rov	L	08/05	05	6	2	4
Doncaster Rov	L	11/05	05	3	2	0
Rotherham U	L	01/06	05	8	3	4
Doncaster Rov	L	07/06	06	31	10	5
Scunthorpe U	Tr	07/07	07-10	43	55	9
Notts Co	L	11/08	08	4	0	4
Notts Co	L	02/09	08	11	3	4
Southampton	Tr	01/11	10-11	2	9	2
Preston NE	L	11/11	11	2	1	0
Notts Co	L	01/12	11	6	4	5
Crawley T	L	08/12	12	4	8	3
Sheffield U	L	01/13	12	7	5	1
Oldham Ath	Tr	08/14	14	32	2	15

FORTUNE Clayton Alexander
Born: Forest Gate, E London, England, 10 November, 1982 CD

League Club	Source	Date Signed	Seasons Played	Apps	Subs	Gls
Bristol C	Tottenham H (YT)	03/01	01-05	29	24	0
Port Vale	L	11/05	05	20	5	2
Leyton Orient	Tr	08/06	06-07	9	1	0
Port Vale	L	11/06	06	11	2	0
Darlington	Tr	07/08	08	3	4	0
Aldershot T	Weston-super-Mare	08/10	10	3	4	0

FORTUNE Jonathan Jay (Jon)
Born: Islington, N London, England, 23 August, 1980 CD

League Club	Source	Date Signed	Seasons Played	Apps	Subs	Gls
Charlton Ath	YT	07/98	01-08	140	26	7
Mansfield T	L	02/00	99	4	0	0
Mansfield T	L	08/00	00	14	0	0
Stoke C	L	01/07	06	4	0	0
Stoke C	L	03/07	06	10	0	1
Sheffield U	Tr	09/09	09	3	2	1
Charlton Ath	Tr	08/10	10	12	4	0
Exeter C		03/12	11	5	0	0
Barnet	Tr	07/12	12	4	2	0
Dagenham & Red	Chatham T	03/13	12	0	1	0

FORTUNE Marc-Antoine
Born: Cayenne, French Guiana, 2 July, 1981 F

League Club	Source	Date Signed	Seasons Played	Apps	Subs	Gls
West Bromwich A (L)	AS Nancy (FRA)	01/09	08	17	0	5
West Bromwich A	Glasgow Celtic	08/10	10-12	35	28	6
Doncaster Rov	L	11/11	11	5	0	1
Wigan Ath	Tr	07/13	13-14	43	28	5

FORTUNE Quinton
Born: Cape Town, South Africa, 21 May, 1977 LW
South Africa: 53/U23-18

League Club	Source	Date Signed	Seasons Played	Apps	Subs	Gls
Manchester U	Atletico Madrid (SPN)	08/99	99-04	53	23	5
Bolton W	Tr	07/06	06	5	1	0
Doncaster Rov	Tubize (BEL)	08/09	09	3	3	1

FORTUNE-WEST Leopold Paul Osborne (Leo)
Born: Stratford, E London, England, 9 April, 1971 — F

League Club	Source	Date Signed	Seasons Played	Apps	Subs	Gls
Gillingham	Stevenage Bor	07/95	95-97	48	19	18
Leyton Orient	L	03/97	96	1	4	0
Lincoln C	Tr	07/98	98	7	2	1
Rotherham U	L	10/98	98	5	0	4
Brentford	Tr	11/98	98	2	9	0
Rotherham U	Tr	02/99	98-00	59	0	26
Cardiff C	Tr	09/00	00-02	53	39	23
Doncaster Rov	Tr	07/03	03-05	60	30	19
Torquay U (L)	Rushden & D	09/06	06	2	3	0
Shrewsbury T (L)	Rushden & D	11/06	06	10	9	7

FOSS Sidney Lacy Richard (Dick)
Born: Barking, E London, England, 28 November, 1912 — LH
Died: Merton, S London, England, 3 August, 1995

League Club	Source	Date Signed	Seasons Played	Apps	Subs	Gls
Chelsea	Southall	05/36	36-47	41	-	3

FOSTER Adrian Michael
Born: Kidderminster, Worcestershire, England, 19 March, 1971 — F

League Club	Source	Date Signed	Seasons Played	Apps	Subs	Gls
West Bromwich A	YT	07/89	89-91	13	14	2
Torquay U	Tr	07/92	92-93	55	10	24
Gillingham	Tr	08/94	94-95	28	12	9
Exeter C	L	03/96	95	4	3	0
Hereford U	Tr	08/96	96	42	1	16

FOSTER Alan
Born: South Shields, Tyne and Wear, England, 20 November, 1934 — CF

League Club	Source	Date Signed	Seasons Played	Apps	Subs	Gls
Crewe Alex	Northwich Victoria	08/59	59-60	22	-	7

FOSTER Anthony Joseph (Tony)
Born: Dublin, Republic of Ireland, 13 February, 1949 — M

League Club	Source	Date Signed	Seasons Played	Apps	Subs	Gls
Arsenal	Bolton Ath (ROI)	02/66				
Oldham Ath	Tr	09/66	66-67	8	1	0

FOSTER Barry
Born: Worksop, Nottinghamshire, England, 21 September, 1951 — LB
England: Youth

League Club	Source	Date Signed	Seasons Played	Apps	Subs	Gls
Mansfield T	Jnr	07/70	71-81	282	5	0

FOSTER Benjamin Anthony (Ben)
Born: Leamington Spa, Warwickshire, England, 3 April, 1983 — G
England: 8

League Club	Source	Date Signed	Seasons Played	Apps	Subs	Gls
Stoke C	Racing Club Warwick	04/01				
Kidderminster Hrs	L	10/04	04	2	0	0
Wrexham	L	01/05	04	17	0	0
Manchester U	Tr	07/05	07-09	12	0	0
Watford	L	08/05	05	44	0	0
Watford	L	08/06	06	29	0	0
Birmingham C	Tr	06/10	10	38	0	0
West Bromwich A	L	07/11	11	37	0	0
West Bromwich A	Tr	06/12	12-14	82	0	0

FOSTER Colin
Born: Bulwell, Nottinghamshire, England, 26 December, 1952 — CD

League Club	Source	Date Signed	Seasons Played	Apps	Subs	Gls
Mansfield T	App	12/70	71-78	195	10	17
Peterborough U	Tr	06/79	79-80	71	0	5

FOSTER Colin John
Born: Chislehurst, SE London, England, 16 July, 1964 — CD

League Club	Source	Date Signed	Seasons Played	Apps	Subs	Gls
Leyton Orient	App	02/82	81-86	173	1	10
Nottingham F	Tr	03/87	86-89	68	4	5
West Ham U	Tr	09/89	89-93	88	5	5
Notts Co	L	01/94	93	9	0	0
Watford	Tr	03/94	93-95	66	0	8
Cambridge U	Tr	03/97	96-97	33	0	1

FOSTER Craig Andrew
Born: Melbourne, Australia, 15 April, 1969 — M
Australia: 29/Youth

League Club	Source	Date Signed	Seasons Played	Apps	Subs	Gls
Portsmouth	Marconi Fairf'ld (AUS)	09/97	97	13	3	2
Crystal Palace	Tr	10/98	98-99	47	5	3

FOSTER Daniel (Danny)
Born: Enfield, N London, England, 23 September, 1984 — RB
England: Semi Pro-3/Youth

League Club	Source	Date Signed	Seasons Played	Apps	Subs	Gls
Tottenham H	Sch	07/02				
Dagenham & Red	Tr	09/04	07-08	69	1	3
Brentford	Tr	07/09	09	32	4	0
Wycombe W	Tr	07/10	10-12	75	1	1

FOSTER Emanuel (Manny)
Born: Newcastle-under-Lyme, Potteries, England, 4 December, 1921 — G
Died: Stoke-on-Trent, England, December, 1965

League Club	Source	Date Signed	Seasons Played	Apps	Subs	Gls
Stoke C	Mow Cop	12/43	46	1	-	0

FOSTER George Clifford (Cliff)
Born: Shevington, Greater Manchester, England, 14 January, 1931 — IF
Died: Wigan, Greater Manchester, England, 12 October, 1998

League Club	Source	Date Signed	Seasons Played	Apps	Subs	Gls
Southport (Am)	Burscough	08/51	51-52	10	-	2

FOSTER George Walter
Born: Plymouth, England, 26 September, 1956 — CD

League Club	Source	Date Signed	Seasons Played	Apps	Subs	Gls
Plymouth Arg	App	09/74	73-81	201	11	6
Torquay U	L	10/76	76	6	0	3
Exeter C	L	12/81	81	28	0	0
Derby Co	Tr	06/82	82	30	0	0
Mansfield T	Tr	08/83	83-92	373	0	0

FOSTER James Ian (Ian)
Born: Liverpool, England, 11 November, 1976 — F
England: Semi Pro-1/Schools

League Club	Source	Date Signed	Seasons Played	Apps	Subs	Gls
Hereford U	Liverpool (Jnr)	07/96	96	4	15	0
Kidderminster Hrs	Barrow	08/99	00-02	37	35	11
Kidderminster Hrs	Chester C	02/04	03-04	25	13	9

FOSTER John Colin
Born: Blackley, Greater Manchester, England, 19 September, 1973 — RB
England: Schools

League Club	Source	Date Signed	Seasons Played	Apps	Subs	Gls
Manchester C	YT	07/92	93-96	17	2	0
Carlisle U	Tr	03/98	97	7	0	0
Bury	Tr	07/98	98	6	1	0

FOSTER Karl Adolphus
Born: Birmingham, England, 15 September, 1965 — F

League Club	Source	Date Signed	Seasons Played	Apps	Subs	Gls
Shrewsbury T	App	09/83	82	1	1	0

FOSTER Lee
Born: Bishop Auckland, County Durham, England, 21 October, 1977 — M

League Club	Source	Date Signed	Seasons Played	Apps	Subs	Gls
Hartlepool U	YT	-	95	0	1	0

FOSTER Liam Paul Kendrick
Born: Eccles, Greater Manchester, England, 4 September, 1987 — FB

League Club	Source	Date Signed	Seasons Played	Apps	Subs	Gls
Stockport Co	Sch	-	05	0	1	0

FOSTER Luke James
Born: Mexborough, South Yorkshire, England, 8 September, 1985 — CD
England: Semi Pro-1

League Club	Source	Date Signed	Seasons Played	Apps	Subs	Gls
Lincoln C	Sheffield Wed (Sch)	07/05	05	14	2	1
Stevenage	Mansfield T	06/10	10	16	7	1
Rotherham U	Tr	07/11	11	1	4	0
Preston NE	Matlock T	12/12	12	3	3	0

FOSTER Martin
Born: Sheffield, England, 29 October, 1977 — M

League Club	Source	Date Signed	Seasons Played	Apps	Subs	Gls
Leeds U	YT	06/96				
Blackpool	L	12/97	97	1	0	0

FOSTER Michael Sidney (Mike)
Born: Leicester, England, 3 February, 1939 — RW

League Club	Source	Date Signed	Seasons Played	Apps	Subs	Gls
Leicester C		08/59				
Colchester U	Tr	05/61	61	36	-	8
Norwich C	Tr	09/62				
Millwall	Tr	07/63	63	13	-	2

FOSTER Nigel
Born: Sutton-in-Ashfield, Nottinghamshire, England, 23 March, 1968 — FB

League Club	Source	Date Signed	Seasons Played	Apps	Subs	Gls
Mansfield T	App	08/85	84	1	0	0

FOSTER Richard Martyn (Ricky)
Born: Aberdeen, Scotland, 31 July, 1985 — RB
Scotland: U21-5

League Club	Source	Date Signed	Seasons Played	Apps	Subs	Gls
Bristol C	Aberdeen	01/12	11-12	47	3	0

FOSTER Robert John (Bobby)
Born: Sheffield, England, 19 July, 1929 — IF
Died: Chesterfield, Derbyshire, England, 28 February, 2006
England: B-1

League Club	Source	Date Signed	Seasons Played	Apps	Subs	Gls
Chesterfield	Jnr	08/47	48-50	4	-	0
Preston NE	Tr	07/51	51-56	101	-	41
Rotherham U	Tr	05/58	58	1	-	0

FOSTER Ronald Edmund (Ronnie)
Born: Islington, N London, England, 22 November, 1938 — IF

League Club	Source	Date Signed	Seasons Played	Apps	Subs	Gls
Leyton Orient	Clapton	03/57	59-62	72	-	17
Grimsby T	Tr	12/62	62-65	129	0	24
Reading	Tr	07/66	66-67	44	1	4
Brentford	Dallas Tornado (USA)	03/69	68	3	1	0

FOSTER Stephen (Steve)
Born: Mansfield, Nottinghamshire, England, 3 December, 1974 — CD

League Club	Source	Date Signed	Seasons Played	Apps	Subs	Gls
Mansfield T	YT	07/93	93	2	3	0
Bristol Rov	Woking	05/97	97-01	193	4	7
Doncaster Rov	Tr	08/02	03-05	95	0	2
Scunthorpe U	Tr	01/06	05-06	62	0	0
Darlington	Tr	07/07	07-09	91	1	2

FOSTER Stephen Brian (Steve)
Born: Portsmouth, England, 24 September, 1957 — CD
England: 3/U21-1

League Club	Source	Date Signed	Seasons Played	Apps	Subs	Gls
Portsmouth	App	10/75	75-78	101	8	6
Brighton & HA	Tr	07/79	79-83	171	1	6

League Club	Source	Date Signed	Seasons Played	Apps	Subs	Gls
Aston Villa	Tr	03/84	83-84	15	0	3
Luton T	Tr	11/84	84-88	163	0	11
Oxford U	Tr	07/89	89-91	95	0	9
Brighton & HA	Tr	08/92	92-95	115	0	7

FOSTER Stephen John (Steve)
Born: Warrington, Cheshire, England, 10 September, 1980 — CD
England: Schools

League Club	Source	Date Signed	Seasons Played	Apps	Subs	Gls
Crewe Alex	YT	09/98	98-05	200	18	15
Burnley	Tr	07/06	06	7	10	0
Barnsley	Tr	08/07	07-12	223	3	10
Tranmere Rov	Tr	06/13	13	4	0	0

FOSTER Trevor
Born: Walsall, West Midlands, England, 11 January, 1941 — F

League Club	Source	Date Signed	Seasons Played	Apps	Subs	Gls
Walsall	Jnr	07/59	59-64	63	-	12

FOSTER Wayne Paul
Born: Leigh, Greater Manchester, England, 11 September, 1963 — M
England: Youth

League Club	Source	Date Signed	Seasons Played	Apps	Subs	Gls
Bolton W	App	08/81	81-84	92	13	13
Preston NE	Tr	06/85	85	25	6	3
Hartlepool U (L)	Heart of Midlothian	10/94	94	4	0	1

FOSTER Winston Arthur
Born: Birmingham, England, 1 November, 1941 — CH

League Club	Source	Date Signed	Seasons Played	Apps	Subs	Gls
Birmingham C	Jnr	11/58	60-68	151	1	2
Crewe Alex	L	03/69	68	13	0	0
Plymouth Arg	Tr	06/69	69-70	33	0	0

FOSTERVOLD Knut Anders
Born: Molde, Norway, 4 October, 1971 — LB

League Club	Source	Date Signed	Seasons Played	Apps	Subs	Gls
Grimsby T (L)	Molde FK (NOR)	11/00	00	9	1	0

FOSU-HENRY Tarique Kumahl Malachi Akwesi
Born: Wandsworth, SW London, England, 5 November, 1995 — RW

League Club	Source	Date Signed	Seasons Played	Apps	Subs	Gls
Reading	Sch	11/12	14	0	1	0

FOTHERGILL Ashley Grove
Born: Harrogate, North Yorkshire, England, 3 October, 1969 — M

League Club	Source	Date Signed	Seasons Played	Apps	Subs	Gls
Rochdale	Middlesbrough (YT)	10/88	88	8	1	0

FOTHERINGHAM James Gibb (Jim)
Born: Hamilton, Lanarkshire, Scotland, 19 December, 1933 — CH
Died: Corby, Northamptonshire, England, 16 September, 1977

League Club	Source	Date Signed	Seasons Played	Apps	Subs	Gls
Arsenal	Jnr	03/51	54-58	72	-	0
Northampton T	Heart of Midlothian	08/59	59	11	-	0

FOTHERINGHAM Mark McKay
Born: Dundee, Scotland, 22 October, 1983 — M
Scotland: U21-3

League Club	Source	Date Signed	Seasons Played	Apps	Subs	Gls
Norwich C	FC Aarau (SUI)	02/07	06-08	55	14	3
Notts Co	Ross Co	07/13	13	23	5	1
Fulham	Tr	08/14	14	2	0	0

FOTIADIS Panos Andrew (Andrew)
Born: Hitchin, Hertfordshire, England, 6 September, 1977 — F
England: Schools

League Club	Source	Date Signed	Seasons Played	Apps	Subs	Gls
Luton T	Jnr	07/96	96-02	50	73	18
Peterborough U	Tr	02/03	02-03	6	13	2

FOULDS Albert (Bert)
Born: Salford, England, 8 August, 1919 — IF

League Club	Source	Date Signed	Seasons Played	Apps	Subs	Gls
Chester C	Altrincham	08/48	48	31	-	14
Rochdale	Yeovil T	09/50	50	6	-	1
Rochdale	Scarborough	10/51	51-52	56	-	23
Crystal Palace	Tr	07/53	53	17	-	4
Crewe Alex	Tr	01/54	53	14	-	2

FOULKES Reginald Ernest (Reg)
Born: Somerset, England, 23 February, 1923 — CH
Died: Shropshire, England, November, 2014
England: Schools

League Club	Source	Date Signed	Seasons Played	Apps	Subs	Gls
Walsall	Birmingham C (Am)	08/45	46-49	160	-	6
Norwich C	Tr	05/50	50-55	216	-	8

FOULKES William Anthony (Bill)
Born: St Helens, Merseyside, England, 5 January, 1932 — CH
Died: Manchester, England, 25 November, 2013
England: 1/FLge-2/U23-2

League Club	Source	Date Signed	Seasons Played	Apps	Subs	Gls
Manchester U	Whiston BC	08/51	52-69	563	3	7

FOULKES William Isaiah (Billy)
Born: Merthyr Tydfil, Wales, 29 May, 1926 — RW
Died: Chester, England, 7 February, 1979
Wales: 11

League Club	Source	Date Signed	Seasons Played	Apps	Subs	Gls
Cardiff C		02/45				
Chester C	Tr	05/48	48-51	118	-	14
Newcastle U	Tr	10/51	51-53	58	-	8
Southampton	Tr	08/54	54	23	-	1
Chester C	Winsford U	07/56	56-60	178	-	23

FOUNTAIN John (Jack)
Born: Leeds, England, 27 May, 1932 — WH
Died: Leeds, England, August, 2012

League Club	Source	Date Signed	Seasons Played	Apps	Subs	Gls
Sheffield U	Leeds Ashley Road	11/49	50-55	31	-	0
Swindon T	Tr	01/57	56-59	81	-	2
York C	Tr	08/60	60-63	130	-	3

FOWLER Derek William
Born: Torquay, Devon, England, 28 November, 1961 — D/M

League Club	Source	Date Signed	Seasons Played	Apps	Subs	Gls
Torquay U	STC Paignton	03/84	83-85	65	8	4

FOWLER Henry Norman (Norman)
Born: Stockton-on-Tees, Cleveland, England, 3 September, 1919 — FB
Died: Stockton-on-Tees, Cleveland, England, 17 December, 1990
England: Schools

League Club	Source	Date Signed	Seasons Played	Apps	Subs	Gls
Middlesbrough	South Bank	09/36	37-38	7	-	0
Hull C	Tr	09/46	46-49	52	-	0
Gateshead	Tr	11/49	49-51	64	-	0

FOWLER Jason Kenneth George
Born: Bristol, England, 20 August, 1974 — M

League Club	Source	Date Signed	Seasons Played	Apps	Subs	Gls
Bristol C	YT	07/93	92-95	16	9	0
Cardiff C	Tr	06/96	96-00	138	7	14
Torquay U	Tr	11/01	01-04	85	12	7

FOWLER John
Born: Leith, Edinburgh, Scotland, 17 October, 1933 — LB
Died: Colchester, Essex, England, 28 March, 1976

League Club	Source	Date Signed	Seasons Played	Apps	Subs	Gls
Colchester U	Bonnyrigg Rose	06/55	55-67	415	0	5

FOWLER John Anthony
Born: Preston, Lancashire, England, 27 October, 1974 — M

League Club	Source	Date Signed	Seasons Played	Apps	Subs	Gls
Cambridge U	YT	04/92	92-95	30	11	0
Preston NE	L	02/93	92	5	1	0

FOWLER John Berry (Jack)
Born: Rotherham, South Yorkshire, England, 13 April, 1935 — RW

League Club	Source	Date Signed	Seasons Played	Apps	Subs	Gls
Sheffield U		07/54				
Halifax T	Tr	06/56	56-58	19	-	3

FOWLER Jordan Michael
Born: Barking, E London, England, 1 October, 1984 — M

League Club	Source	Date Signed	Seasons Played	Apps	Subs	Gls
Arsenal	Sch	07/02				
Chesterfield	L	01/05	04	4	2	0

FOWLER Lee Anthony
Born: Cardiff, Wales, 10 June, 1983 — DM
Wales: U21-9/Youth

League Club	Source	Date Signed	Seasons Played	Apps	Subs	Gls
Coventry C	YT	07/00	01-02	6	8	0
Huddersfield T	Tr	08/03	03-04	35	14	0
Fleetwood T	Wrexham	01/12	12	10	0	0
Doncaster Rov	Tr	01/13	12	1	3	0
Burton A	L	03/13	12	2	1	0
Crawley T (L)	Nuneaton T	01/15	14	16	3	1

FOWLER Lee Edward
Born: Eastwood, Nottinghamshire, England, 26 January, 1969 — M/LB

League Club	Source	Date Signed	Seasons Played	Apps	Subs	Gls
Stoke C	YT	07/88	87-91	42	7	1
Preston NE	Tr	07/92	92	29	3	2
Doncaster Rov	Tr	12/93	93	7	4	0

FOWLER Martin
Born: York, England, 17 January, 1957 — M

League Club	Source	Date Signed	Seasons Played	Apps	Subs	Gls
Huddersfield T	App	01/74	73-77	62	11	2
Blackburn Rov	Tr	07/78	78-79	36	2	0
Hartlepool U	L	03/80	79	6	0	0
Stockport Co	Tr	08/80	80-81	74	1	6
Scunthorpe U	Tr	09/82	82	15	3	0

FOWLER Robert Bernard (Robbie)
Born: Liverpool, England, 9 April, 1975 — F
England: 26/B-1/U21-8/Youth

League Club	Source	Date Signed	Seasons Played	Apps	Subs	Gls
Liverpool	YT	04/92	93-01	210	26	120
Leeds U	Tr	11/01	01-02	24	6	14
Manchester C	Tr	01/03	02-05	63	17	21
Liverpool	Tr	01/06	05-06	15	15	8
Cardiff C	Tr	07/07	07	10	3	4
Blackburn Rov	Tr	09/08	08	1	2	0

FOWLER Thomas (Tommy)
Born: Prescot, Merseyside, England, 16 December, 1924 — LW
Died: Northampton, England, 3 May, 2009

League Club	Source	Date Signed	Seasons Played	Apps	Subs	Gls
Northampton T	Everton (Am)	03/45	46-61	521	-	84
Aldershot	Tr	12/61	61-62	14	-	0

FOWLER Tony
Born: Birmingham, England, 3 October, 1962 — G

League Club	Source	Date Signed	Seasons Played	Apps	Subs	Gls
Torquay U	Foxhole U	03/85	84-85	9	0	0

FOX Alan
Born: Holywell, Flintshire, Wales, 10 July, 1936 — CH
Republic of Ireland: LoI-1//Wales: U23-1

League Club	Source	Date Signed	Seasons Played	Apps	Subs	Gls
Wrexham	Carmel U (ROI)	04/54	53-63	350	-	3
Hartlepool U	Tr	06/64	64-65	58	0	0
Bradford C	Tr	10/65	65	33	0	0

FOX Christian Benjamin
Born: Laurencekirk, Aberdeenshire, Scotland, 11 April, 1981 — M

League Club	Source	Date Signed	Seasons Played	Apps	Subs	Gls
York C	YT	06/99	99-03	44	26	1

FOX Daniel (Danny)
Born: Winsford, Cheshire, England, 29 May, 1986 — LB
England: U21-1//Scotland: 4

League Club	Source	Date Signed	Seasons Played	Apps	Subs	Gls
Everton	Sch	07/04				
Walsall	Tr	07/05	05-07	98	1	6
Coventry C	Tr	01/08	07-08	57	0	6
Burnley	Glasgow Celtic	01/10	09-11	49	1	1
Southampton	Tr	08/11	11-13	54	10	1
Nottingham F	Tr	01/14	13-14	39	2	0

FOX David Lee
Born: Leek, Staffordshire, England, 13 December, 1983 — M
England: Youth

League Club	Source	Date Signed	Seasons Played	Apps	Subs	Gls
Manchester U	YT	12/00				
Shrewsbury T	L	10/04	04	2	2	1
Blackpool	Tr	01/06	05-08	68	26	6
Colchester U	Tr	07/09	09	15	3	3
Norwich C	Tr	06/10	10-12	53	9	1
Barnsley	L	09/13	13	7	0	0
Colchester U	Tr	10/14	14	29	1	2

FOX Geoffrey Roy (Geoff)
Born: Bristol, England, 19 January, 1925 — LB
Died: Worcester, England, 1 January, 1994

League Club	Source	Date Signed	Seasons Played	Apps	Subs	Gls
Ipswich T	Bristol C (Am)	08/45	46	11	-	1
Bristol Rov	Tr	06/47	47-54	276	-	2
Swindon T	Tr	10/55	55-56	48	-	0

FOX Kevin
Born: Sheffield, England, 22 September, 1960 — G

League Club	Source	Date Signed	Seasons Played	Apps	Subs	Gls
Lincoln C	Jnr	03/78	79	4	0	0

FOX Mark Stephen
Born: Basingstoke, Hampshire, England, 17 November, 1975 — M

League Club	Source	Date Signed	Seasons Played	Apps	Subs	Gls
Brighton & HA	YT	07/94	93-96	8	17	1

FOX Matthew Christopher
Born: Birmingham, England, 13 July, 1971 — CD

League Club	Source	Date Signed	Seasons Played	Apps	Subs	Gls
Birmingham C	YT	07/89	88-90	12	2	0
Northampton T		03/93	92	0	1	0

FOX Michael James Stephen Neil
Born: Mansfield, Nottinghamshire, England, 7 September, 1985 — M

League Club	Source	Date Signed	Seasons Played	Apps	Subs	Gls
Chesterfield	Sch	-	04	0	1	0

FOX Morgan Alexander
Born: South Woodham Ferrers, Essex, England, 21 September, 1993 — LB
Wales: U21-7

League Club	Source	Date Signed	Seasons Played	Apps	Subs	Gls
Charlton Ath	Sch	07/12	13-14	28	9	0
Notts Co	L	11/13	13	6	1	1

FOX Nathan James
Born: Leicester, England, 14 November, 1992 — LW

League Club	Source	Date Signed	Seasons Played	Apps	Subs	Gls
Notts Co	Sch	07/09	09	0	1	0

FOX Oscar
Born: Clowne, Derbyshire, England, 1 January, 1921 — WH/IF
Died: Sheffield, England, 15 January, 1990

League Club	Source	Date Signed	Seasons Played	Apps	Subs	Gls
Sheffield Wed		10/43	46-49	44	-	3
Mansfield T	Tr	06/50	50-56	248	-	30

FOX Peter David
Born: Scunthorpe, North Lincolnshire, England, 5 July, 1957 — G

League Club	Source	Date Signed	Seasons Played	Apps	Subs	Gls
Sheffield Wed	App	06/75	72-76	49	0	0
Barnsley	L	12/77	77	1	0	0
Stoke C	Tr	03/78	78-92	409	0	0
Exeter C	Tr	07/93	93-96	107	1	0

FOX Raymond (Ray)
Born: Manchester, England, 13 December, 1934 — W
Died: Manchester, England, May, 2008

League Club	Source	Date Signed	Seasons Played	Apps	Subs	Gls
Oldham Ath (Am)	Army	08/57	57	1	-	0

FOX Raymond Victor (Ray)
Born: Weston-super-Mare, Somerset, England, 28 January, 1921 — FB
Died: Weston-super-Mare, Somerset, England, 19 February, 2008

League Club	Source	Date Signed	Seasons Played	Apps	Subs	Gls
Bristol C	St Aldhelm's	10/46	46-48	23	-	0

FOX Reginald Alan (Reg)
Born: Tufnell Park, N London, England, 16 October, 1929 — FB
Died: Brighton, England, 19 April, 2010

League Club	Source	Date Signed	Seasons Played	Apps	Subs	Gls
Fulham	Tufnel Park	12/49				
Brighton & HA	Tr	10/52	52-55	20	-	0

FOX Ruel Adrian
Born: Ipswich, England, 14 January, 1968 — RW
England: B-2

League Club	Source	Date Signed	Seasons Played	Apps	Subs	Gls
Norwich C	App	01/86	86-93	148	24	22
Newcastle U	Tr	02/94	93-95	56	2	12
Tottenham H	Tr	10/95	95-99	95	11	13
West Bromwich A	Tr	08/00	00-01	38	20	2

FOX Simon Mark
Born: Basingstoke, Hampshire, England, 28 August, 1977 — F

League Club	Source	Date Signed	Seasons Played	Apps	Subs	Gls
Brighton & HA	YT	05/95	93-96	6	15	0

FOX Stephen Douglas (Steve)
Born: Tamworth, Staffordshire, England, 17 February, 1958 — W
Died: Tamworth, Staffordshire, England, 1 December, 2012

League Club	Source	Date Signed	Seasons Played	Apps	Subs	Gls
Birmingham C	App	02/76	76-78	26	3	1
Wrexham	Tr	12/78	78-82	136	6	10
Port Vale	Tr	10/82	82-83	71	3	6
Chester C	Tr	07/84	84-85	29	4	4

FOX Walter
Born: Bolsover, Derbyshire, England, 10 April, 1921 — RB
Died: Chesterfield, Derbyshire, England, 30 October, 2000

League Club	Source	Date Signed	Seasons Played	Apps	Subs	Gls
Mansfield T	Creswell Colliery	05/46	46-49	62	-	0

FOXE Hayden Vernon
Born: Canberra, Australia, 23 June, 1977 — CD
Australia: 14/U23-9/Youth

League Club	Source	Date Signed	Seasons Played	Apps	Subs	Gls
West Ham U	San. Hiroshima (JPN)	03/01	00-01	7	4	0
Portsmouth	Tr	06/02	02-03	38	4	2
Leeds U	Tr	08/06	06	12	6	1

FOXON David Neil (Neil)
Born: Nottingham, England, 10 July, 1948 — LW

League Club	Source	Date Signed	Seasons Played	Apps	Subs	Gls
Scunthorpe U	Notts Co (Am)	08/65	66-67	20	2	1

FOXTON David Graham (Graham)
Born: Harrogate, North Yorkshire, England, 2 October, 1949 — RB

League Club	Source	Date Signed	Seasons Played	Apps	Subs	Gls
Scunthorpe U	App	10/67	67-72	148	6	1

FOXTON John Dixon (Jack)
Born: Salford, England, 17 June, 1921 — WH

League Club	Source	Date Signed	Seasons Played	Apps	Subs	Gls
Portsmouth	Bolton W (Am)	05/45	46	1	-	0
Swindon T	Tr	09/48	48-50	49	-	0

FOY David Lee
Born: Coventry, England, 20 October, 1972 — M

League Club	Source	Date Signed	Seasons Played	Apps	Subs	Gls
Birmingham C	YT	07/91	92	3	0	0
Scunthorpe U	Tr	03/93	92	1	2	0

FOY John Joseph
Born: Huyton, Merseyside, England, 28 May, 1950 — LW

League Club	Source	Date Signed	Seasons Played	Apps	Subs	Gls
Southport (Am)	Ormskirk	08/74	74	1	0	0

FOY Keith Patrick
Born: Dublin, Republic of Ireland, 30 December, 1981 — LB
Republic of Ireland: U21-7/Youth

League Club	Source	Date Signed	Seasons Played	Apps	Subs	Gls
Nottingham F	YT	01/99	00-01	19	3	1

FOY Robert Andrew (Robbie)
Born: Edinburgh, Scotland, 29 October, 1985 — W
Scotland: U21-5

League Club	Source	Date Signed	Seasons Played	Apps	Subs	Gls
Liverpool	Sch	01/03				
Chester C	L	02/05	04	13	0	0
Wrexham	L	08/05	05	7	0	3
Scunthorpe U	Tr	08/06	06	1	4	0

FOYEWA Amos
Born: Nigeria, 26 December, 1981 — F

League Club	Source	Date Signed	Seasons Played	Apps	Subs	Gls
Bournemouth	West Ham U (YT)	07/01	01-02	1	8	0

FOYLE Ashley Peter
Born: Sheffield, England, 17 September, 1986 — D

League Club	Source	Date Signed	Seasons Played	Apps	Subs	Gls
Chesterfield	Sch	07/05	05	0	1	0
Accrington Stan	Tr	08/06				

FOYLE Martin John
Born: Salisbury, Wiltshire, England, 2 May, 1963 — F

League Club	Source	Date Signed	Seasons Played	Apps	Subs	Gls
Southampton	Jnr	08/80	82-83	7	6	1
Aldershot	Tr	08/84	84-86	98	0	35
Oxford U	Tr	03/87	86-90	120	6	36
Port Vale	Tr	06/91	91-99	226	70	83

FRADIN Karim
Born: Grenoble, France, 2 February, 1972 M

League Club	Source	Date Signed	Seasons Played	Apps	Subs	Gls
Stockport Co	OGC Nice (FRA)	11/99	99-02	72	9	9

FRAIL Stephen Charles
Born: Glasgow, Scotland, 10 August, 1969 RB

League Club	Source	Date Signed	Seasons Played	Apps	Subs	Gls
Tranmere Rov	Heart of Midlothian	01/98	97-99	10	4	0

FRAIN David
Born: Sheffield, England, 11 October, 1962 M

League Club	Source	Date Signed	Seasons Played	Apps	Subs	Gls
Sheffield U	Norton Woodseats	09/85	85-87	35	9	6
Rochdale	Tr	07/88	88	42	0	12
Stockport Co	Tr	07/89	89-94	176	11	12
Mansfield T	L	09/94	94	4	2	0

FRAIN John William
Born: Birmingham, England, 8 October, 1968 LB/M

League Club	Source	Date Signed	Seasons Played	Apps	Subs	Gls
Birmingham C	App	10/86	85-96	265	9	23
Northampton T	Tr	01/97	96-02	203	4	4

FRAIN Peter John Andrew
Born: Birmingham, England, 18 March, 1965 F

League Club	Source	Date Signed	Seasons Played	Apps	Subs	Gls
West Bromwich A	App	03/82				
Mansfield T	L	01/84	83	1	1	0

FRAME William James
Born: Castle Douglas, Lanarkshire, Scotland, 1 August, 1939 G
Died: Castle Douglas, Dumfries & Galloway, Scotland, 6 June, 2002

League Club	Source	Date Signed	Seasons Played	Apps	Subs	Gls
Workington	Dumfries	11/58	58	9	-	0

FRAME William Lammie (Billy)
Born: Carluke, Lanarkshire, Scotland, 7 May, 1912 FB
Died: Nottingham, England, January, 1993

League Club	Source	Date Signed	Seasons Played	Apps	Subs	Gls
Leicester C	Shawfield Jnrs	10/33	34-49	220	-	0

FRAMPTON Andrew James Kerr (Andy)
Born: Wimbledon, SW London, England, 3 September, 1979 D

League Club	Source	Date Signed	Seasons Played	Apps	Subs	Gls
Crystal Palace	YT	05/98	98-02	19	9	0
Brentford	Tr	10/02	02-06	121	13	4
Millwall	Tr	06/07	07-09	80	8	4
Leyton Orient	L	09/10	10	1	0	0
Swindon T	L	10/10	10	23	0	0
Gillingham	Tr	07/11	11-12	48	10	0
AFC Wimbledon	Tr	06/13	13-14	34	1	4

FRANCE Anthony (Tony)
Born: Sheffield, England, 11 April, 1939 IF

League Club	Source	Date Signed	Seasons Played	Apps	Subs	Gls
Huddersfield T	Atlas & Norfolk	04/56	57-59	9	-	2
Darlington	Tr	12/61	61-62	47	-	9
Stockport Co	Tr	07/63	63	30	-	8

FRANCE Darren Brian
Born: Hull, England, 8 August, 1967 F

League Club	Source	Date Signed	Seasons Played	Apps	Subs	Gls
Hull C	North Ferriby U	11/91	91-92	19	24	7
Doncaster Rov	Tr	08/93	93	0	1	0

FRANCE Gary
Born: Whitwell, Derbyshire, England, 18 June, 1955 F

League Club	Source	Date Signed	Seasons Played	Apps	Subs	Gls
Sheffield U	App	06/73	73-74	1	1	0

FRANCE Gary Lawton
Born: Stalybridge, Greater Manchester, England, 5 May, 1946 IF

League Club	Source	Date Signed	Seasons Played	Apps	Subs	Gls
Burnley	Stalybridge Celtic	04/66	66-67	1	2	0
Bury	Tr	07/68	68	0	1	0

FRANCE John (Jack)
Born: Stalybridge, Greater Manchester, England, 30 November, 1913 WH
Died: Stalybridge, Greater Manchester, England, December, 1995

League Club	Source	Date Signed	Seasons Played	Apps	Subs	Gls
Swindon T	Stalybridge Celtic	08/37	37	1	-	0
Halifax T	Bath C	06/39	46-47	51	-	1

FRANCE Michael Paul (Paul)
Born: Holmfirth, West Yorkshire, England, 10 September, 1968 CD

League Club	Source	Date Signed	Seasons Played	Apps	Subs	Gls
Huddersfield T	App	06/87	87-88	7	4	0
Bristol C	Tr	07/89				
Burnley	Tr	07/90	90-91	7	1	0

FRANCE Peter
Born: Huddersfield, West Yorkshire, England, 27 March, 1936 G

League Club	Source	Date Signed	Seasons Played	Apps	Subs	Gls
Huddersfield T		09/56				
Bradford Park Ave	Tr	05/57	57	16	-	0

FRANCE Ryan
Born: Sheffield, England, 13 December, 1980 RW

League Club	Source	Date Signed	Seasons Played	Apps	Subs	Gls
Hull C	Alfreton T	09/03	03-08	76	57	6
Sheffield U	Tr	07/09	09	3	6	0

FRANCIS Carlos Everton (Carl)
Born: West Ham, E London, England, 21 August, 1962 W

League Club	Source	Date Signed	Seasons Played	Apps	Subs	Gls
Birmingham C	App	08/80	82	2	3	0
Hereford U	L	12/83	83	5	0	0

FRANCIS Damien Jerome
Born: Wandsworth, SW London, England, 27 February, 1979 M
Jamaica: 1

League Club	Source	Date Signed	Seasons Played	Apps	Subs	Gls
Wimbledon	YT	03/97	97-02	80	17	15
Norwich C	Tr	07/03	03-04	71	2	14
Wigan Ath	Tr	08/05	05	16	4	1
Watford	Tr	07/06	06-08	34	13	5

FRANCIS Francino Rousseu (Fran)
Born: Kingston, Jamaica, 18 January, 1987 CD

League Club	Source	Date Signed	Seasons Played	Apps	Subs	Gls
Watford	Sch	-	05	0	1	0

FRANCIS George Edward
Born: Acton, W London, England, 4 February, 1934 CF
Died: Slough, Berkshire, England, 22 October, 2014

League Club	Source	Date Signed	Seasons Played	Apps	Subs	Gls
Brentford	Jnr	01/53	54-60	228	-	110
Queens Park Rgrs	Tr	05/61	61	2	-	1
Brentford	Tr	10/61	61	32	-	14
Gillingham	Tr	08/62	62-63	51	-	19

FRANCIS Gerald (Gerry)
Born: Johannesburg, South Africa, 6 December, 1933 RW

League Club	Source	Date Signed	Seasons Played	Apps	Subs	Gls
Leeds U	City & Suburban (RSA)	07/57	57-61	48	-	9
York C	Tr	10/61	61	16	-	4

FRANCIS Gerald Charles James (Gerry)
Born: Chiswick, W London, England, 6 December, 1951 M
England: 12/U23-6

League Club	Source	Date Signed	Seasons Played	Apps	Subs	Gls
Queens Park Rgrs	App	06/69	68-78	290	5	53
Crystal Palace	Tr	07/79	79-80	59	0	7
Queens Park Rgrs	Tr	02/81	80-81	17	0	4
Coventry C	Tr	02/82	81-82	50	0	2
Exeter C	Tr	08/83	83	28	0	3
Cardiff C	Tr	09/84	84	7	0	0
Swansea C	Tr	10/84	84	3	0	0
Portsmouth	Tr	11/84	84	3	0	0
Bristol Rov	Tr	09/85	85-86	32	0	0

FRANCIS John Andrew
Born: Dewsbury, West Yorkshire, England, 21 November, 1963 F

League Club	Source	Date Signed	Seasons Played	Apps	Subs	Gls
Halifax T	Emley	02/85	84	1	3	0
Sheffield U	Emley	09/88	88-89	14	28	6
Burnley	Tr	01/90	89-91	99	2	26
Cambridge U	Tr	08/92	92	15	14	3
Burnley	Tr	03/93	92-95	44	32	10
Scunthorpe U	Tr	08/96	96	1	4	0

FRANCIS Keith Roy
Born: Yeovil, Somerset, England, 22 July, 1929 WH

League Club	Source	Date Signed	Seasons Played	Apps	Subs	Gls
Leyton Orient	Yeovil T	06/50	50	3	-	0

FRANCIS Kevin Michael Derek
Born: Birmingham, England, 6 December, 1967 F
St Kitts & Nevis: 2

League Club	Source	Date Signed	Seasons Played	Apps	Subs	Gls
Derby Co	Mile Oak Rov	02/89	89-90	0	10	0
Stockport Co	Tr	02/91	90-94	147	5	88
Birmingham C	Tr	01/95	94-97	32	41	13
Oxford U	Tr	02/98	97-99	27	9	8
Stockport Co	Tr	03/00	99	4	0	0
Exeter C	Castleton Gabriels	11/00	00	3	4	1
Hull C	Tr	12/00	00	22	0	5

FRANCIS Lee Charles
Born: Walthamstow, NE London, England, 24 October, 1969 RB/M

League Club	Source	Date Signed	Seasons Played	Apps	Subs	Gls
Arsenal	YT	11/87				
Chesterfield	L	03/90	89	2	0	0
Chesterfield	Tr	06/90	90-91	63	5	2

FRANCIS Mark James
Born: Dorchester, Dorset, England, 12 December, 1994 M

League Club	Source	Date Signed	Seasons Played	Apps	Subs	Gls
Swindon T	Sch	07/13	12	0	2	0

FRANCIS Sean Robert
Born: Birmingham, England, 1 August, 1972 F

League Club	Source	Date Signed	Seasons Played	Apps	Subs	Gls
Birmingham C	Jnr	07/90	90-91	0	6	0
Northampton T	Telford U	08/93	93	0	1	0

FRANCIS Simon Charles
Born: Nottingham, England, 16 February, 1985 RB
England: Youth

League Club	Source	Date Signed	Seasons Played	Apps	Subs	Gls
Bradford C	Sch	05/03	02-03	49	6	1
Sheffield U	Tr	03/04	03-05	6	6	0
Grimsby T	L	09/05	05	5	0	0
Tranmere Rov	L	11/05	05	16	1	1
Southend U	Tr	06/06	06-09	138	19	4
Charlton Ath	Tr	07/10	10	32	2	0
Bournemouth	Tr	11/11	11-14	158	1	3

FRANCIS Stephen Stuart (Steve)
Born: Billericay, Essex, England, 29 May, 1964 — G
England: Youth

League Club	Source	Date Signed	Seasons Played	Apps	Subs	Gls
Chelsea	App	04/82	81-85	71	0	0
Reading	Tr	02/87	86-92	216	0	0
Huddersfield T	Tr	08/93	93-98	187	0	0
Northampton T	Tr	01/99	98	3	0	0

FRANCIS Terence (Terry)
Born: Hartlepool, Cleveland, England, 18 June, 1943 — IF

League Club	Source	Date Signed	Seasons Played	Apps	Subs	Gls
Hartlepool U	Billingham Synthonia	12/63	63-64	18	-	4

FRANCIS Thomas George (Tom)
Born: Bermondsey, SE London, England, 30 October, 1920 — G
Died: Lambeth, S London, England, April, 1996

League Club	Source	Date Signed	Seasons Played	Apps	Subs	Gls
Millwall	Cheltenham T	05/46	46	1	-	0

FRANCIS Trevor John
Born: Plymouth, England, 19 April, 1954 — F
England: 52/U23-5/Youth

League Club	Source	Date Signed	Seasons Played	Apps	Subs	Gls
Birmingham C	App	05/71	70-78	278	2	119
Nottingham F	Tr	02/79	78-81	69	1	28
Manchester C	Tr	09/81	81	26	0	12
Queens Park Rgrs	Glasgow Rangers	03/88	87-89	30	2	12
Sheffield Wed	Tr	02/91	89-93	29	47	5

FRANCIS Willis David
Born: Nottingham, England, 26 July, 1985 — M

League Club	Source	Date Signed	Seasons Played	Apps	Subs	Gls
Notts Co	Sch	-	02-03	2	11	0

FRANCO Guillermo Luis (Guille)
Born: Corrientes, Argentina, 3 November, 1976 — F
Mexico: 25

League Club	Source	Date Signed	Seasons Played	Apps	Subs	Gls
West Ham U	Villarreal (SPN)	09/09	09	16	7	5

FRANCOMB Georgie
Born: Hackney, E London, England, 8 September, 1991 — RB/M

League Club	Source	Date Signed	Seasons Played	Apps	Subs	Gls
Norwich C	Sch	07/10	09	2	0	0
Barnet	L	10/10	10	13	0	0
AFC Wimbledon	L	08/12	12	14	1	0
AFC Wimbledon	Tr	06/13	13-14	59	11	6

FRANCOMBE Peter
Born: Cardiff, Wales, 4 August, 1963 — FB

League Club	Source	Date Signed	Seasons Played	Apps	Subs	Gls
Cardiff C	Crystal Palace (App)	09/81	81	2	1	0

FRANDSEN Per
Born: Copenhagen, Denmark, 6 February, 1970 — M
Denmark: 23/U21-21/Youth

League Club	Source	Date Signed	Seasons Played	Apps	Subs	Gls
Bolton W	FC Copenhagen (DEN)	08/96	96-99	129	1	17
Blackburn Rov	Tr	09/99	99	26	5	5
Bolton W	Tr	07/00	00-03	116	19	13
Wigan Ath	Tr	07/04	04	9	0	1

FRANKLAND Anthony (Tony)
Born: Greenwich, SE London, England, 11 October, 1972 — W

League Club	Source	Date Signed	Seasons Played	Apps	Subs	Gls
Exeter C	YT	07/90	89-90	3	4	0

FRANKLIN Cornelius (Neil)
Born: Stoke-on-Trent, England, 24 January, 1922 — CH
Died: Stone, Staffordshire, England, 9 February, 1996
England: 27/FLge-5/War-10

League Club	Source	Date Signed	Seasons Played	Apps	Subs	Gls
Stoke C	Jnr	01/39	46-49	142	-	0
Hull C	Independiente (COL)	02/51	50-55	95	-	0
Crewe Alex	Tr	02/56	55-57	66	-	4
Stockport Co	Tr	10/57	57	20	-	0

FRANKLIN Graham Nigel
Born: Bicester, Oxfordshire, England, 25 January, 1957 — F

League Club	Source	Date Signed	Seasons Played	Apps	Subs	Gls
Southend U	Lowestoft T	12/77	77-79	1	5	1

FRANKLIN Jeffrey Terence (Jeff)
Born: Darlington, County Durham, England, 8 December, 1973 — W

League Club	Source	Date Signed	Seasons Played	Apps	Subs	Gls
Torquay U	YT	-	91	1	1	0

FRANKLIN John Leonard
Born: Stockton-on-Tees, Cleveland, England, 27 November, 1924 — RW
Died: Stockton-on-Tees, Cleveland, England, September, 2005

League Club	Source	Date Signed	Seasons Played	Apps	Subs	Gls
Middlesbrough		12/43				
Darlington	Bath C	08/47	47	8	-	3

FRANKLIN Neil John
Born: Lincoln, England, 10 March, 1969 — FB

League Club	Source	Date Signed	Seasons Played	Apps	Subs	Gls
Lincoln C	App	06/87	86	15	0	0
Lincoln C	Nykopings (SWE)	10/88	88	0	1	0

FRANKLIN Paul Leslie
Born: Hainault, NE London, England, 5 October, 1963 — CD

League Club	Source	Date Signed	Seasons Played	Apps	Subs	Gls
Watford	App	08/81	82-86	32	0	0
Shrewsbury T	L	10/86	86	6	0	0
Swindon T	L	11/86	86	5	0	1
Reading	Tr	06/87	87-88	17	3	0

FRANKLIN Stanley Thomas (Stan)
Born: Shrewsbury, Shropshire, England, 16 September, 1919 — CH
Died: South Cheshire, England, July, 2006

League Club	Source	Date Signed	Seasons Played	Apps	Subs	Gls
Blackpool	Kenwood Jnrs	05/38				
Crewe Alex	Tr	04/46	46-47	29	-	0

FRANKLIN William Michael (Mike)
Born: Tiverton, Devon, England, 3 March, 1955 — G

League Club	Source	Date Signed	Seasons Played	Apps	Subs	Gls
Charlton Ath	App	03/73	72-74	13	0	0

FRANKOWSKI Tomasz
Born: Bialystok, Poland, 16 August, 1974 — F
Poland: 20

League Club	Source	Date Signed	Seasons Played	Apps	Subs	Gls
Wolverhampton W	Elche (SPN)	01/06	05	12	4	0

FRANKS Albert John
Born: Boldon, Tyne and Wear, England, 13 April, 1936 — WH

League Club	Source	Date Signed	Seasons Played	Apps	Subs	Gls
Newcastle U	Boldon CW	12/53	56-59	72	-	4
Lincoln C	Greenock Morton	11/61	61-62	58	-	5

FRANKS Billy Robert
Born: Shoreham-by-Sea, West Sussex, England, 26 November, 1989 — CD

League Club	Source	Date Signed	Seasons Played	Apps	Subs	Gls
Bournemouth	Jnr	08/07	07	1	0	0

FRANKS Colin James
Born: Willesden, NW London, England, 16 April, 1951 — CD

League Club	Source	Date Signed	Seasons Played	Apps	Subs	Gls
Watford	Wealdstone	07/69	69-72	99	13	8
Sheffield U	Tr	07/73	73-78	139	11	7

FRANKS Fraser George
Born: Hammersmith, W London, England, 22 November, 1990 — CD

League Club	Source	Date Signed	Seasons Played	Apps	Subs	Gls
Brentford	Sch	07/09				
AFC Wimbledon	Tr	08/10	11	3	1	0
Luton T	Welling U	01/14	14	10	3	0

FRANKS Jonathan Ian
Born: Stockton-on-Tees, Cleveland, England, 8 April, 1990 — W
England: Youth

League Club	Source	Date Signed	Seasons Played	Apps	Subs	Gls
Middlesbrough	Sch	07/07	08-10	10	18	3
Oxford U	L	08/11	11	0	1	0
Yeovil T	L	02/12	11	13	1	3
Hartlepool U	Tr	07/12	12-14	104	25	11

FRANKS Kenneth (Ken)
Born: Motherwell, Lanarkshire, Scotland, 24 April, 1944 — LW

League Club	Source	Date Signed	Seasons Played	Apps	Subs	Gls
Brighton & HA	Blantyre Vic	06/62	62	1	-	0

FRANKS Leigh David
Born: Bridlington, East Riding of Yorkshire, England, 7 March, 1991 — CD

League Club	Source	Date Signed	Seasons Played	Apps	Subs	Gls
Huddersfield T	Sch	07/09				
Oxford U	L	07/10	10	4	1	0

FRASER Andrew McKnight (Andy)
Born: Newtongrange, Midlothian, Scotland, 29 August, 1940 — CH

League Club	Source	Date Signed	Seasons Played	Apps	Subs	Gls
Hartlepool U	Heart of Midlothian	10/61	61-63	82	-	2

FRASER David McLean
Born: Newtongrange, Midlothian, Scotland, 6 June, 1937 — LW

League Club	Source	Date Signed	Seasons Played	Apps	Subs	Gls
Hull C	Arniston Rgrs	07/54	55-57	11	-	7
Mansfield T	Tr	07/58	58	6	-	1

FRASER Douglas Michael (Doug)
Born: Busby, Renfrewshire, Scotland, 8 December, 1941 — FB/WH
Scotland: 2

League Club	Source	Date Signed	Seasons Played	Apps	Subs	Gls
West Bromwich A	Aberdeen	09/63	63-70	255	2	8
Nottingham F	Tr	01/71	70-72	85	0	3
Walsall	Tr	07/73	73	26	1	0

FRASER Gordon
Born: Elgin, Moray, Scotland, 27 November, 1943 — CF

League Club	Source	Date Signed	Seasons Played	Apps	Subs	Gls
Cardiff C	Forres Mechanics	01/61	62	4	-	0
Millwall	Tr	09/63	63	5	-	0
Newport Co	Barry T	08/66	66	11	1	2

FRASER James (Jimmy)
Born: Coatbridge, Lanarkshire, Scotland, 17 November, 1932 — RB

League Club	Source	Date Signed	Seasons Played	Apps	Subs	Gls
Barrow	Bellshill Ath	03/58	57-58	32	-	0

FRASER John
Born: Shepherds Bush, W London, England, 12 July, 1953 — RB

League Club	Source	Date Signed	Seasons Played	Apps	Subs	Gls
Fulham	App	06/71	71-75	55	1	1
Brentford	Tr	07/76	76-79	121	2	6

FRASER John Cameron (Cammie)
Born: Blackford, Perthshire, Scotland, 24 May, 1941 — RB
Scotland: U23-2

League Club	Source	Date Signed	Seasons Played	Apps	Subs	Gls
Aston Villa	Dunfermline Ath	10/62	62-63	33	-	1
Birmingham C	Tr	02/65	64-65	38	1	0

FRASER John Watson
Born: Belfast, Northern Ireland, 15 September, 1938 — RW
Died: Waterford, Republic of Ireland, 13 March, 2011

League Club	Source	Date Signed	Seasons Played	Apps	Subs	Gls
Sunderland	Glentoran	03/59	58-59	22	-	1
Portsmouth	Tr	06/60	60	1	-	0
Watford	Margate	07/62	62-63	24	-	3

FRASER Robert
Born: Glasgow, Scotland, 23 January, 1917 — CH
Died: Newcastle-upon-Tyne, England, April, 2003

League Club	Source	Date Signed	Seasons Played	Apps	Subs	Gls
Newcastle U	Hibernian	01/47	46-48	26	-	0

FRASER Ryan
Born: Aberdeen, Scotland, 24 February, 1994 — W
Scotland: U21-8/Youth

League Club	Source	Date Signed	Seasons Played	Apps	Subs	Gls
Bournemouth	Aberdeen	01/13	12-14	29	34	4

FRASER Stuart James
Born: Cheltenham, Gloucestershire, England, 1 August, 1978 — G

League Club	Source	Date Signed	Seasons Played	Apps	Subs	Gls
Stoke C	Cheltenham T	07/96	98	0	1	0
Exeter C	Tr	07/00	00-02	15	4	0

FRASER Stuart Thomas
Born: Edinburgh, Scotland, 9 January, 1980 — D
Scotland: U21-4

League Club	Source	Date Signed	Seasons Played	Apps	Subs	Gls
Luton T	YT	04/98	97-00	36	8	1

FRASER Thomas Francis Peter (Tom)
Born: Brighton, England, 5 December, 1987 — M

League Club	Source	Date Signed	Seasons Played	Apps	Subs	Gls
Brighton & HA	Sch	06/06	06-08	51	28	2
Port Vale	Tr	07/09	09-10	40	10	1
Barnet	Tr	01/11	10-11	12	8	0

FRASER William Alexander (Willie)
Born: Melbourne, Australia, 24 February, 1929 — G
Died: Kirkcaldy, Fife, Scotland, 7 March, 1996
Scotland: 2

League Club	Source	Date Signed	Seasons Played	Apps	Subs	Gls
Sunderland	Airdrieonians	03/54	53-58	127	-	0
Nottingham F	Tr	12/58	58	2	-	0

FRASER William Thomas
Born: Edinburgh, Scotland, 12 August, 1945 — LW

League Club	Source	Date Signed	Seasons Played	Apps	Subs	Gls
Huddersfield T	Dunfermline Ath	04/63	63-64	8	-	2

FRASER-ALLEN Kyle Alexander
Born: Wanstead, NE London, England, 12 February, 1990 — RW

League Club	Source	Date Signed	Seasons Played	Apps	Subs	Gls
Tottenham H	Sch	07/08				
Macclesfield T	L	02/09	08	0	2	0

FRAUGHAN Ryan Stephen
Born: Liverpool, England, 11 February, 1991 — M

League Club	Source	Date Signed	Seasons Played	Apps	Subs	Gls
Tranmere Rov	Sch	01/09	09-10	5	15	0

FREAR Brian
Born: Cleckheaton, West Yorkshire, England, 8 July, 1933 — IF
Died: Bradford, England, January, 1997

League Club	Source	Date Signed	Seasons Played	Apps	Subs	Gls
Huddersfield T	Liversedge	09/50	51-56	37	-	10
Chesterfield	Tr	02/57	56-63	281	-	84
Halifax T	Tr	07/64	64	36	-	7

FREAR Elliott Thomas
Born: Exeter, England, 11 September, 1990 — LW

League Club	Source	Date Signed	Seasons Played	Apps	Subs	Gls
Exeter C	Sch	07/09	11-12	5	7	0

FRECKLINGTON Lee Craig
Born: Lincoln, England, 8 September, 1985 — M
Republic of Ireland: B-1

League Club	Source	Date Signed	Seasons Played	Apps	Subs	Gls
Lincoln C	Sch	07/05	04-08	97	27	21
Peterborough U	Tr	02/09	08-12	70	23	8
Rotherham U	Tr	10/12	12-14	90	9	18

FREDERICKS Ryan Marlowe
Born: Hammersmith, W London, England, 10 October, 1992 — RB
England: Youth

League Club	Source	Date Signed	Seasons Played	Apps	Subs	Gls
Tottenham H	Sch	07/10				
Brentford	L	08/12	12	1	3	0
Millwall	L	01/14	13	11	3	1
Middlesbrough	L	08/14	14	16	1	0

FREDGAARD Carsten
Born: Hillerod, Denmark, 20 May, 1976 — LM
Denmark: 1/U21-10/Youth

League Club	Source	Date Signed	Seasons Played	Apps	Subs	Gls
Sunderland	Lyngby (NOR)	07/99	99	0	1	0
West Bromwich A	L	02/00	99	5	0	0
Bolton W	L	11/00	00	1	4	0

FREDRIKSEN Jon-Andre
Born: Moss, Norway, 5 April, 1982 — M

League Club	Source	Date Signed	Seasons Played	Apps	Subs	Gls
Hartlepool U	Sarpsborg (NOR)	08/09	09-10	4	9	0

FREEBURN William Openshaw
Born: Hamilton, Lanarkshire, Scotland, 7 April, 1930 — RB

League Club	Source	Date Signed	Seasons Played	Apps	Subs	Gls
Grimsby T	East Stirlingshire	08/51	51-54	34	-	0

FREEDMAN Douglas Alan (Dougie)
Born: Glasgow, Scotland, 21 January, 1974 — F
Scotland: 2/B-1/U21-8/Schools

League Club	Source	Date Signed	Seasons Played	Apps	Subs	Gls
Queens Park Rgrs	YT	05/92				
Barnet	Tr	07/94	94-95	47	0	27
Crystal Palace	Tr	09/95	95-97	72	18	31
Wolverhampton W	Tr	10/97	97	25	4	10
Nottingham F	Tr	08/98	98-00	50	20	18
Crystal Palace	Tr	10/00	00-07	141	96	64
Leeds U	L	03/08	07	9	2	5
Southend U	Tr	09/08	08-09	21	15	6

FREEMAN Alfred (Alf)
Born: Bethnal Green, E London, England, 2 January, 1920 — IF
Died: Camden, N London, England, 4 February, 2006

League Club	Source	Date Signed	Seasons Played	Apps	Subs	Gls
Southampton	Army	11/43	46	7	-	2
Crystal Palace	Tr	04/48	48	2	-	0
Reading	Tr	08/49				

FREEMAN Andrew James (Andy)
Born: Reading, England, 8 September, 1977 — M

League Club	Source	Date Signed	Seasons Played	Apps	Subs	Gls
Reading	YT	07/96	95	0	1	0

FREEMAN Anthony (Tony)
Born: Melton Mowbray, Leicestershire, England, 29 August, 1928 — RW
Died: Leicester, England, 7 December, 2004

League Club	Source	Date Signed	Seasons Played	Apps	Subs	Gls
Notts Co	Melton T	01/46	46-49	44	-	2

FREEMAN Clive Richard
Born: Leeds, England, 12 September, 1962 — M/LB

League Club	Source	Date Signed	Seasons Played	Apps	Subs	Gls
Swansea C	Bridlington T	08/90	90-91	10	4	0
Carlisle U	L	01/92	91	4	0	0
Doncaster Rov	Altrincham	08/93	93	23	2	2

FREEMAN Darren Barry Andduet
Born: Brighton, England, 22 August, 1973 — W

League Club	Source	Date Signed	Seasons Played	Apps	Subs	Gls
Gillingham	Horsham	01/95	94-95	4	8	0
Fulham	Tr	07/96	96-97	32	14	9
Brentford	Tr	07/98	98	16	6	6
Brighton & HA	Tr	07/99	99-00	41	13	12

FREEMAN David Barry
Born: Dublin, Republic of Ireland, 25 November, 1979 — F
Republic of Ireland: U21-1/Youth

League Club	Source	Date Signed	Seasons Played	Apps	Subs	Gls
Nottingham F	YT	12/96	99-00	2	6	0
Port Vale	L	09/00	00	2	1	0
Carlisle U	Tr	09/02	02	3	1	0

FREEMAN Donald Richard (Don)
Born: Dartford, Kent, England, 29 August, 1921 — WH

League Club	Source	Date Signed	Seasons Played	Apps	Subs	Gls
Charlton Ath	Dartford	03/46				
Bristol C	Tr	05/49	49	8	-	0
Southend U	Tr	08/50				
Watford	Tr	11/50				
Gillingham	Tr	06/51				

FREEMAN Henry George (Harry)
Born: Worcester, England, 4 November, 1918 — RB
Died: Kidlington, Oxfordshire, England, 19 March, 1997

League Club	Source	Date Signed	Seasons Played	Apps	Subs	Gls
Fulham	Woodstock T	10/37	38-51	179	-	6
Walsall	Tr	10/52	52	20	-	1

FREEMAN Kieron Samuel
Born: Arnold, Nottinghamshire, England, 21 March, 1992 — RB
Wales: U21-15/Youth

League Club	Source	Date Signed	Seasons Played	Apps	Subs	Gls
Nottingham F	Sch	07/10				
Notts Co	L	01/12	11	18	1	1
Derby Co	Tr	08/12	12-13	15	10	0
Notts Co	L	11/13	13	16	0	0
Sheffield U	L	03/14	13	10	2	0
Mansfield T	L	10/14	14	11	0	0
Sheffield U	Tr	01/15	14	13	6	1

FREEMAN Luke Anthony
Born: Dartford, Kent, England, 22 March, 1992 — LW
England: Youth

League Club	Source	Date Signed	Seasons Played	Apps	Subs	Gls
Gillingham	Jnr	-	07	0	1	0
Arsenal	Sch	04/09				
Yeovil T	L	07/10	10	5	8	2
Stevenage	Tr	11/11	11-13	93	17	15
Bristol C	Tr	06/14	14	44	2	7

FREEMAN Mark Wayne
Born: Walsall, West Midlands, England, 27 January, 1970 — CD

League Club	Source	Date Signed	Seasons Played	Apps	Subs	Gls
Wolverhampton W	Bilston T	10/87				
Cheltenham T	Gloucester C	03/96	99-00	61	4	2

FREEMAN Neil
Born: Northampton, England, 16 February, 1955 — G

League Club	Source	Date Signed	Seasons Played	Apps	Subs	Gls
Arsenal	Jnr	06/72				
Grimsby T	Tr	03/74	73-75	33	0	0
Southend U	Tr	07/76	76-77	69	0	0
Birmingham C	Tr	07/78	78-79	31	0	0
Walsall	L	08/80	80	8	0	0
Huddersfield T	L	01/81	80	18	0	0
Peterborough U	Tr	09/81	81	41	0	0
Northampton T	Tr	08/82	82	22	0	0

FREEMAN Neville Frank
Born: Brixworth, Northamptonshire, England, 25 January, 1925 — G
Died: Northampton, England, February, 1984

League Club	Source	Date Signed	Seasons Played	Apps	Subs	Gls
Northampton T	Pitsford	10/49	50	1	-	0

FREEMAN Ronald Peter Percy
Born: Newark, Nottinghamshire, England, 4 July, 1945 — F

League Club	Source	Date Signed	Seasons Played	Apps	Subs	Gls
West Bromwich A	Stourbridge	04/68	69	2	1	0
Lincoln C	Tr	06/70	70-72	76	4	30
Reading	Tr	01/73	72-74	53	7	13
Lincoln C	Tr	01/75	74-76	62	10	34

FREESTONE Christopher Mark (Chris)
Born: Nottingham, England, 4 September, 1971 — F

League Club	Source	Date Signed	Seasons Played	Apps	Subs	Gls
Middlesbrough	Arnold T	12/94	94-97	2	7	1
Carlisle U	L	03/97	96	3	2	2
Northampton T	Tr	12/97	97-98	40	17	13
Hartlepool U	Tr	03/99	98-99	24	13	7
Cheltenham T	L	02/00	99	5	0	2
Shrewsbury T	Tr	07/00	00-01	19	8	0

FREESTONE Roger
Born: Caerleon, Monmouthshire, Wales, 19 August, 1968 — G
Wales: 1/U21-1/Youth/Schools

League Club	Source	Date Signed	Seasons Played	Apps	Subs	Gls
Newport Co	App	04/86	86	11	0	0
Chelsea	Tr	03/87	86-88	42	0	0
Newport Co	L	03/87	86	2	0	0
Swansea C	L	09/89	89	14	0	0
Hereford U	L	03/90	89	8	0	0
Swansea C	Tr	09/91	91-03	549	3	3

FREESTONE Trevor
Born: Market Bosworth, Leicestershire, England, 16 February, 1954 — F

League Club	Source	Date Signed	Seasons Played	Apps	Subs	Gls
Peterborough U	Jnr	01/73	72	2	1	1

FREI Kerim
Born: Feldkirch, Austria, 19 November, 1993 — W
Switzerland: U21-2/Youth//Turkey: 4/U21-4

League Club	Source	Date Signed	Seasons Played	Apps	Subs	Gls
Fulham	Sch	11/10	11-12	8	15	0
Cardiff C	L	10/12	12	1	2	0

FREIMANIS Eduards (Eddie)
Born: Latvia, 22 February, 1920 — CF
Died: Nuneaton, Warwickshire, England, May, 1993
Latvia: 2

League Club	Source	Date Signed	Seasons Played	Apps	Subs	Gls
Northampton T	Peterborough U	05/48	48-49	19	-	4

FREITER Michael Thomas John
Born: Gillingham, Kent, England, 15 January, 1996 — DM

League Club	Source	Date Signed	Seasons Played	Apps	Subs	Gls
Gillingham	Sch	07/14	14	0	1	0

FRENCH Daniel John
Born: Peterborough, England, 25 November, 1979 — M

League Club	Source	Date Signed	Seasons Played	Apps	Subs	Gls
Peterborough U	YT	07/98	99-01	2	16	1

FRENCH George Noah
Born: Colchester, Essex, England, 10 November, 1926 — FB
Died: Colchester, Essex, England, 19 July, 2012

League Club	Source	Date Signed	Seasons Played	Apps	Subs	Gls
Colchester U (Am)		05/52	52-53	3	-	0

FRENCH (LAFITE) Graham Edward
Born: Wolverhampton, England, 6 April, 1945 — W
England: Youth

League Club	Source	Date Signed	Seasons Played	Apps	Subs	Gls
Shrewsbury T	App	11/62	61-62	27	-	1
Swindon T	Tr	08/63	63	5	-	0
Watford	Tr	08/64	64	4	-	0
Luton T	Wellington T	10/65	65-72	180	2	21
Reading	L	11/73	73	3	0	0
Southport	Boston Minutemen (USA)	03/76	75	2	0	0

FRENCH James Robert (Jim)
Born: Stockton-on-Tees, Cleveland, England, 27 November, 1926 — IF
Died: Stockport, Greater Manchester, England, February, 2004

League Club	Source	Date Signed	Seasons Played	Apps	Subs	Gls
Middlesbrough		08/45				
Southend U	Tr	08/49				
Northampton T		08/51	51	1	-	0
Darlington	Tr	08/53	53-54	52	-	8

FRENCH John William (Jackie)
Born: Stockton-on-Tees, Cleveland, England, 19 January, 1925 — WH/IF
Died: Ipswich, England, 9 March, 2002

League Club	Source	Date Signed	Seasons Played	Apps	Subs	Gls
Middlesbrough		10/43				
Southend U	Tr	02/47	46-52	182	-	19
Nottingham F	Tr	11/52	52-55	80	-	8
Southend U	Tr	07/56	56	5	-	0

FRENCH Jonathan Charles (Jon)
Born: Bristol, England, 25 September, 1976 — W

League Club	Source	Date Signed	Seasons Played	Apps	Subs	Gls
Bristol Rov	YT	07/95	95-97	8	9	1
Hull C	Tr	07/98	98	9	6	0

FRENCH Michael John (Mickey)
Born: Eastbourne, East Sussex, England, 7 May, 1955 — F
England: Youth

League Club	Source	Date Signed	Seasons Played	Apps	Subs	Gls
Queens Park Rgrs	App	05/73				
Brentford	Tr	02/75	74-76	56	9	16
Swindon T	Tr	02/77	76-77	5	5	1
Doncaster Rov	Tr	07/78	78	36	0	5
Aldershot	Tr	05/79	79-81	70	4	16
Rochdale	Tr	08/82	82	35	1	11

FRENCH Nigel Peter
Born: Swansea, Wales, 24 March, 1968 — M

League Club	Source	Date Signed	Seasons Played	Apps	Subs	Gls
Swansea C	App	03/86	85-86	13	13	3

FRENCH Raymond (Ray)
Born: Wigton, Cumbria, England, 16 December, 1946 — CD

League Club	Source	Date Signed	Seasons Played	Apps	Subs	Gls
Workington (Am)	Wigton	11/73	73	2	0	0

FRETWELL David
Born: Normanton, West Yorkshire, England, 18 February, 1952 — CD

League Club	Source	Date Signed	Seasons Played	Apps	Subs	Gls
Bradford C	App	07/70	70-77	247	6	5
Wigan Ath	Chicago Sting (USA)	10/78	78-80	111	1	0

FREUND Steffen
Born: Brandenburg, Germany, 19 January, 1970 — DM
Germany: 21/U21/Youth

League Club	Source	Date Signed	Seasons Played	Apps	Subs	Gls
Tottenham H	Bor Dortmund (GER)	12/98	98-02	92	10	0
Leicester C (L)	Kaiserslautern (GER)	01/04	03	13	1	0

FRIAR John Paul (Paul)
Born: Glasgow, Scotland, 6 June, 1963 — LB
Scotland: Youth

League Club	Source	Date Signed	Seasons Played	Apps	Subs	Gls
Leicester C	App	08/80	80-82	56	2	0
Rotherham U	Tr	02/83	82-83	20	0	0
Charlton Ath	Tr	07/84	84-85	36	0	0
Northampton T	L	03/86	85	14	0	0
Aldershot	Tr	08/86	86	29	0	1

FRIARS Emmet Charles
Born: Derry, Northern Ireland, 14 September, 1985 — D
Northern Ireland: U21-7/Youth

League Club	Source	Date Signed	Seasons Played	Apps	Subs	Gls
Notts Co	Sch	02/04	04-05	9	5	1

FRIARS Sean Martin
Born: Derry, Northern Ireland, 15 May, 1979 — W
Northern Ireland: U21-14

League Club	Source	Date Signed	Seasons Played	Apps	Subs	Gls
Liverpool	Jnr	05/96				
Ipswich T	Tr	07/98	99	0	1	0
Carlisle U	Newry T	11/01	01	0	1	0

FRIDAY Robin
Born: Acton, W London, England, 27 July, 1952 — F
Died: Ealing, W London, England, March, 1991

League Club	Source	Date Signed	Seasons Played	Apps	Subs	Gls
Reading	Hayes	02/74	73-76	121	0	46
Cardiff C	Tr	12/76	76-77	20	1	6

FRIDAY Terence John (Terry)
Born: Sittingbourne, Kent, England, 1 May, 1936 — G

League Club	Source	Date Signed	Seasons Played	Apps	Subs	Gls
Gillingham (Am)	Sheppey U	03/61	60	2	-	0

FRIDGE Leslie Francis (Les)
Born: Inverness, Scotland, 27 August, 1968 — G
Scotland: U21-1/Youth

League Club	Source	Date Signed	Seasons Played	Apps	Subs	Gls
Chelsea	App	09/85	85	1	0	0

FRIEDEL Bradley Howard (Brad)
Born: Cleveland, Ohio, USA, 18 May, 1971 — G
USA: 82

League Club	Source	Date Signed	Seasons Played	Apps	Subs	Gls
Liverpool	Columbus Crew (USA)	12/97	97-99	25	0	0
Blackburn Rov	Tr	11/00	00-07	288	0	1
Aston Villa	Tr	07/08	08-10	114	0	0
Tottenham H	Tr	07/11	11-13	50	0	0

FRIEL Bernard James (Benny)
Born: Glasgow, Scotland, 16 September, 1941 — IF
Died: Phoenix, Arizona, USA, 16 February, 2010

League Club	Source	Date Signed	Seasons Played	Apps	Subs	Gls
Southend U	Dumbarton	05/63	63-64	17	-	8

FRIEL George Patrick
Born: Reading, England, 11 October, 1970 W

League Club	Source	Date Signed	Seasons Played	Apps	Subs	Gls
Reading	YT	06/89	89-90	10	6	1

FRIEL John Patrick
Born: Glasgow, Scotland, 1 September, 1923 IF
Died: Birkenhead, Wirral, England, 30 October, 1998

League Club	Source	Date Signed	Seasons Played	Apps	Subs	Gls
New Brighton	Third Lanark	06/50	50	3	-	0
Torquay U	Queen of the South	10/52				

FRIEL Peter
Born: Wishaw, Lanarkshire, Scotland, 27 March, 1939 RW

League Club	Source	Date Signed	Seasons Played	Apps	Subs	Gls
Workington	Cambuslang Rgrs	08/61	61	4	-	0

FRIEND Barry Neil
Born: Wandsworth, SW London, England, 13 October, 1951 W
England: Amateur-6

League Club	Source	Date Signed	Seasons Played	Apps	Subs	Gls
Fulham	Leatherhead	10/73	73	2	1	0

FRIEND George Andrew Jordan
Born: Barnstaple, Devon, England, 19 October, 1987 LB

League Club	Source	Date Signed	Seasons Played	Apps	Subs	Gls
Exeter C	Sch	06/06	08	4	0	0
Wolverhampton W	Tr	09/08	08-09	5	2	0
Millwall	L	08/09	09	4	2	0
Southend U	L	09/09	09	5	1	1
Scunthorpe U	L	10/09	09	2	2	0
Exeter C	L	03/10	09	13	0	1
Doncaster Rov	Tr	07/10	10-11	54	5	1
Middlesbrough	Tr	07/12	12-14	115	2	4

FRIIO David
Born: Thionville, Lorraine, France, 17 February, 1973 M

League Club	Source	Date Signed	Seasons Played	Apps	Subs	Gls
Plymouth Arg	ASOA Valence (FRA)	11/00	00-04	158	9	39
Nottingham F	Tr	02/05	04-05	16	6	1

FRIMPONG Emmanuel Yaw
Born: Kumasi, Ghana, 10 January, 1992 M
England: Youth//Ghana: 1

League Club	Source	Date Signed	Seasons Played	Apps	Subs	Gls
Arsenal	Sch	01/09	11	3	3	0
Wolverhampton W	L	01/12	11	5	0	0
Charlton Ath	L	11/12	12	6	0	0
Fulham	L	01/13	12	2	4	0
Barnsley	Tr	01/14	13	6	3	0

FRITH David William Malcolm
Born: Liverpool, England, 17 March, 1929 FB
Died: Blackpool, Lancashire, England, 29 May, 2011

League Club	Source	Date Signed	Seasons Played	Apps	Subs	Gls
Blackpool	Jnr	05/49	52-56	32	-	0
Tranmere Rov	Tr	08/58	58-62	177	-	0

FRITH William (Billy)
Born: Sheffield, England, 9 June, 1912 WH
Died: Warwick, England, 6 July, 1996

League Club	Source	Date Signed	Seasons Played	Apps	Subs	Gls
Chesterfield	Mansfield T	05/31	31	9	-	3
Coventry C	Tr	05/32	32-38	162	-	4
Coventry C	Port Vale (Mgr)	10/46	46	7	-	0

FRIZZELL James Letson (Jimmy)
Born: Greenock, Inverclyde, Scotland, 16 February, 1937 IF/WH

League Club	Source	Date Signed	Seasons Played	Apps	Subs	Gls
Oldham Ath	Greenock Morton	05/60	60-69	308	9	56

FROGGATT John (Jack)
Born: Sheffield, England, 17 November, 1922 LW/CH
Died: Worthing, West Sussex, England, 17 February, 1993
England: 13/FLge-4

League Club	Source	Date Signed	Seasons Played	Apps	Subs	Gls
Portsmouth	Vospers	09/45	46-53	280	-	64
Leicester C	Tr	03/54	53-57	143	-	18

FROGGATT John Lawrence
Born: Stanton Hill, Nottinghamshire, England, 13 December, 1945 F

League Club	Source	Date Signed	Seasons Played	Apps	Subs	Gls
Notts Co	East Kirkby MW	06/64	63-64	4	-	0
Colchester U	Boston U	07/74	74-77	155	0	29
Port Vale	Tr	02/78	77-78	12	2	3
Northampton T	Tr	09/78	78	42	0	13

FROGGATT Redfern
Born: Sheffield, England, 23 August, 1924 IF
Died: Sheffield, England, 26 December, 2003
England: 4/B-1/FLge-1

League Club	Source	Date Signed	Seasons Played	Apps	Subs	Gls
Sheffield Wed	Sheffield YMCA	08/42	46-59	434	-	140

FROGGATT Stephen Junior (Steve)
Born: Lincoln, England, 9 March, 1973 LW
England: U21-2

League Club	Source	Date Signed	Seasons Played	Apps	Subs	Gls
Aston Villa	YT	01/91	91-93	30	5	2
Wolverhampton W	Tr	07/94	94-98	99	7	7
Coventry C	Tr	10/98	98-99	44	5	2

FRONTZECK Michael
Born: Moenchengladbach, Germany, 26 March, 1964 FB
Germany: 19/U21-6

League Club	Source	Date Signed	Seasons Played	Apps	Subs	Gls
Manchester C	Borussia M'bach (GER)	01/96	95-96	19	4	0

FROST Brian Philip
Born: Sheffield, England, 5 June, 1938 IF

League Club	Source	Date Signed	Seasons Played	Apps	Subs	Gls
Chesterfield	Oswestry T	05/59	59-64	103	-	20

FROST Desmond (Des)
Born: Congleton, Cheshire, England, 3 August, 1926 CF
Died: South Cheshire, England, June, 1993

League Club	Source	Date Signed	Seasons Played	Apps	Subs	Gls
Leeds U	Congleton T	04/49	49-50	10	-	2
Halifax T	Tr	01/51	50-53	116	-	54
Rochdale	Tr	11/53	53-54	16	-	6
Crewe Alex	Tr	09/54	54-55	45	-	12

FROST John (Jack)
Born: Wallsend, Tyne and Wear, England, 13 February, 1920 G
Died: York, England, 21 January, 1988

League Club	Source	Date Signed	Seasons Played	Apps	Subs	Gls
Grimsby T	North Shields	07/39				
York C	Tr	07/48	48-51	45	-	0

FROST Lee Adrian
Born: Wokingham, Berkshire, England, 4 December, 1957 F

League Club	Source	Date Signed	Seasons Played	Apps	Subs	Gls
Chelsea	App	07/76	77-79	11	3	5
Brentford	L	10/78	78	5	1	0
Brentford	Tr	12/80	80	15	0	3

FROST Ronald Albert
Born: Stockport, Greater Manchester, England, 16 January, 1947 W

League Club	Source	Date Signed	Seasons Played	Apps	Subs	Gls
Manchester C	App	05/64	63	2	-	1

FROST Stanleigh David (Stan)
Born: Northampton, England, 19 October, 1922 RW
Died: Northampton, England, May, 2006

League Club	Source	Date Signed	Seasons Played	Apps	Subs	Gls
Leicester C	Northampton T (Am)	03/41				
Northampton T	Tr	01/47	46	6	-	1

FROST Stefan (Stef)
Born: Nottingham, England, 3 July, 1989 W

League Club	Source	Date Signed	Seasons Played	Apps	Subs	Gls
Notts Co	Sch	07/06	05-07	0	6	0

FROWEN John
Born: Treharris, Merthyr Tydfil, Wales, 11 October, 1931 D
Died: Newport, Wales, August, 2011

League Club	Source	Date Signed	Seasons Played	Apps	Subs	Gls
Cardiff C	Nelson, Wales	05/51	52-57	35	-	0
Bristol Rov	Tr	08/58	58-62	84	-	0
Newport Co	Tr	03/63	62-65	67	1	0

FRUDE Roger Gordon
Born: Plymouth, England, 19 November, 1946 IF
Died: Plymouth, England, 14 June, 1996

League Club	Source	Date Signed	Seasons Played	Apps	Subs	Gls
Bristol Rov	App	12/64	63-67	38	3	8
Mansfield T	Tr	09/67	67-68	14	1	0
Brentford	Tr	07/69	69	1	1	0

FRUTOS Alexandre Marius Lucien (Alex)
Born: Vitry-le-Francois, France, 23 April, 1983 LM

League Club	Source	Date Signed	Seasons Played	Apps	Subs	Gls
Brighton & HA	FC Metz (FRA)	08/05	05-06	32	14	3

FRY Adam George
Born: Bedford, England, 9 February, 1985 W

League Club	Source	Date Signed	Seasons Played	Apps	Subs	Gls
Peterborough U	Sch	07/04	04	3	0	0

FRY Barry Francis
Born: Bedford, England, 7 April, 1945 IF
England: Schools

League Club	Source	Date Signed	Seasons Played	Apps	Subs	Gls
Manchester U	App	04/62				
Bolton W	Tr	05/64	64	3	-	1
Luton T	Tr	07/65	65	6	0	0
Leyton Orient	Gravesend & Northfleet	12/66	66	2	1	0
Leyton Orient	Bedford T	06/67	67	5	5	0

FRY Christopher David (Chris)
Born: Cardiff, Wales, 23 October, 1969 FB/W
Wales: Youth

League Club	Source	Date Signed	Seasons Played	Apps	Subs	Gls
Cardiff C	YT	08/88	88-90	22	33	1
Hereford U	Tr	08/91	91-93	76	14	10
Colchester U	Tr	10/93	93-96	102	28	16
Exeter C	Tr	07/97	97-98	43	17	3

FRY David Paul
Born: Bournemouth, England, 5 January, 1960 G

League Club	Source	Date Signed	Seasons Played	Apps	Subs	Gls
Crystal Palace	Weymouth	01/77	77-82	40	0	0
Gillingham	Tr	07/83	83-84	49	0	0
Torquay U	Millwall (NC)	10/85	85	30	0	0

FRY Keith Frederick
Born: Cardiff, Wales, 11 April, 1941 RW
Wales: Schools

League Club	Source	Date Signed	Seasons Played	Apps	Subs	Gls
Newport Co	Jnr	10/58	58-61	57	-	2

League Club	Source	Date Signed	Seasons Played	Apps	Subs	Gls
Notts Co	Tr	02/62	61-63	73	-	9
Chesterfield	Merthyr Tydfil	01/66	65	2	0	1

FRY Matthew Ronald (Matt)
Born: Longfield, Kent, England, 26 September, 1990 — LB

League Club	Source	Date Signed	Seasons Played	Apps	Subs	Gls
West Ham U	Sch	07/09				
Gillingham	L	10/09	09	11	0	0
Charlton Ath	L	08/10	10	20	5	1
Bradford C	Tr	02/12	11	5	1	0

FRY Robert Philip (Bob)
Born: Pontypridd, Rhondda Cynon Taff, Wales, 29 June, 1935 — G

League Club	Source	Date Signed	Seasons Played	Apps	Subs	Gls
Crystal Palace		04/56	55	6	-	0
Queens Park Rgrs	Bath C	08/57	57	1	-	0

FRY Roger Norman
Born: Southampton, England, 18 August, 1948 — LB

League Club	Source	Date Signed	Seasons Played	Apps	Subs	Gls
Southampton	Jnr	10/67	70-71	23	0	0
Walsall	Tr	07/73	73-76	120	0	1

FRY Russell Harok
Born: Hull, England, 4 December, 1985 — M
Wales: Youth

League Club	Source	Date Signed	Seasons Played	Apps	Subs	Gls
Hull C	Sch	12/02	04-05	1	1	0

FRYATT James Edward (Jim)
Born: Southampton, England, 2 September, 1940 — CF

League Club	Source	Date Signed	Seasons Played	Apps	Subs	Gls
Charlton Ath	Moor End United YC	10/57	59	5	-	3
Southend U	Tr	06/60	60-62	61	-	24
Bradford Park Ave	Tr	06/63	63-65	101	0	38
Southport	Tr	03/66	65-66	39	0	15
Torquay U	Tr	03/67	66-67	27	0	11
Stockport Co	Tr	10/67	67-68	45	0	28
Blackburn Rov	Tr	10/68	68-69	29	8	5
Oldham Ath	Tr	02/70	69-71	76	0	40
Southport	Tr	11/71	71-73	102	2	24
Stockport Co	Philadelphia A's (USA)	09/74	74	1	0	1
Torquay U	Tr	12/74	74	3	0	0

FRYATT Matthew Charles (Matty)
Born: Nuneaton, Warwickshire, England, 5 March, 1986 — F
England: Youth

League Club	Source	Date Signed	Seasons Played	Apps	Subs	Gls
Walsall	Sch	04/03	03-05	49	21	27
Carlisle U	L	12/03	03	9	1	1
Leicester C	Tr	01/06	05-10	137	31	51
Hull C	Tr	01/11	10-13	62	20	27
Sheffield Wed	L	09/13	13	7	2	4
Nottingham F	Tr	06/14	14	17	8	6

FRYE John Marr (Johnny)
Born: Ardrossan, Ayrshire, Scotland, 27 July, 1933 — IF
Died: Ardrossan, Ayrshire, Scotland, 21 March, 2005

League Club	Source	Date Signed	Seasons Played	Apps	Subs	Gls
Sheffield Wed	St Mirren	01/61				
Tranmere Rov	Tr	10/61	61	21	-	6

FRYER John Hilary (Jack)
Born: Manchester, England, 24 June, 1924 — CF
Died: Bury, Greater Manchester, England, March, 2004

League Club	Source	Date Signed	Seasons Played	Apps	Subs	Gls
Oldham Ath	Goslings	04/47	47	9	-	3

FRYERS Ezekiel David (Zeki)
Born: Manchester, England, 9 September, 1992 — CD
England: Youth

League Club	Source	Date Signed	Seasons Played	Apps	Subs	Gls
Manchester U	Sch	07/11	11	0	2	0
Tottenham H	Standard Liege (BEL)	01/13	13	3	4	0
Crystal Palace	Tr	09/14	14	0	1	0
Rotherham U	L	01/15	14	10	0	0
Ipswich T	L	03/15	14	2	1	0

FUCCILLO Pasquale (Lil)
Born: Bedford, England, 2 May, 1956 — M

League Club	Source	Date Signed	Seasons Played	Apps	Subs	Gls
Luton T	App	07/74	74-82	153	7	24
Southend U	Tulsa Roughnecks (USA)	12/83	83-84	40	5	4
Peterborough U	Tr	08/85	85-86	82	0	3
Cambridge U	Valetta (MLT)	01/88	87	18	1	2

FUCHS Uwe
Born: Kaiserslautern, Germany, 23 July, 1966 — F
West Germany: U21-1

League Club	Source	Date Signed	Seasons Played	Apps	Subs	Gls
Middlesbrough (L)	Kaiserslautern (GER)	01/95	94	13	2	9
Millwall	Kaiserslautern (GER)	07/95	95	21	11	5

FUDGE Michael Henry (Micky)
Born: Bristol, England, 5 December, 1945 — M

League Club	Source	Date Signed	Seasons Played	Apps	Subs	Gls
West Bromwich A	App	12/63	63-64	13	-	5
Exeter C	Wellington T	06/67	67	32	2	6

FUERTES Esteban Oscar
Born: Coronel Dorrego, Argentina, 26 December, 1976 — F
Argentina: 1

League Club	Source	Date Signed	Seasons Played	Apps	Subs	Gls
Derby Co	CD Santa Fe (ARG)	08/99	99	8	0	1

FUGLESTAD Erik
Born: Stavanger, Norway, 13 August, 1974 — LB
Norway: U21-1

League Club	Source	Date Signed	Seasons Played	Apps	Subs	Gls
Norwich C	Viking Stavanger (NOR)	11/97	97-99	71	3	2

FULBROOK Gary
Born: Bath, England, 4 May, 1966 — LB

League Club	Source	Date Signed	Seasons Played	Apps	Subs	Gls
Swindon T	App	09/84	84	0	1	0
Carlisle U	Bath C	09/87	87	6	0	0

FULLAM John Rowan (Johnny)
Born: Dublin, Republic of Ireland, 22 March, 1940 — RH/IF
Died: Dublin, Republic of Ireland, 10 June, 2015
Republic of Ireland: 11/B/LoI-12

League Club	Source	Date Signed	Seasons Played	Apps	Subs	Gls
Preston NE	Home Farm (ROI)	10/58	59-60	49	-	6

FULLARTON James (Jamie)
Born: Bellshill, Lanarkshire, Scotland, 20 July, 1974 — M
Scotland: U21-17

League Club	Source	Date Signed	Seasons Played	Apps	Subs	Gls
Crystal Palace	SC Bastia (FRA)	08/97	97-00	40	7	1
Bolton W	L	03/99	98	1	0	0
Brentford	Dundee U	08/02	02	22	5	1
Southend U	Tr	07/03	03	7	0	0
Chesterfield	Tr	03/04	03	0	1	0

FULLBROOK John Frederick Albert
Born: Grays, Essex, England, 15 July, 1918 — FB
Died: Grays, Essex, England, March, 1992

League Club	Source	Date Signed	Seasons Played	Apps	Subs	Gls
Leyton Orient	Plymouth Arg (Am)	04/46	46-47	36	-	1

FULLER Ashley John
Born: Bedford, England, 14 November, 1986 — M

League Club	Source	Date Signed	Seasons Played	Apps	Subs	Gls
Cambridge U	Sch	-	03-04	0	3	0

FULLER Barry Marc
Born: Ashford, Kent, England, 25 September, 1984 — RB
England: Semi Pro-1

League Club	Source	Date Signed	Seasons Played	Apps	Subs	Gls
Charlton Ath	Sch	07/04				
Barnet	L	01/06	05	15	0	1
Gillingham	Stevenage Bor	01/08	07-11	130	4	0
Barnet	Tr	08/12	12	39	0	0
AFC Wimbledon	Tr	06/13	13-14	90	0	1

FULLER Joshua Piers (Josh)
Born: Grimsby, North Lincolnshire, England, 9 February, 1992 — RM

League Club	Source	Date Signed	Seasons Played	Apps	Subs	Gls
Grimsby T	Sch	11/09	08-09	2	4	0

FULLER Ricardo Dwayne
Born: Kingston, Jamaica, 31 October, 1979 — F
Jamaica: 73

League Club	Source	Date Signed	Seasons Played	Apps	Subs	Gls
Crystal Palace (L)	Tivoli Gardens (JAM)	02/01	00	2	6	0
Preston NE	Heart of Midlothian	07/02	02-04	57	1	27
Portsmouth	Tr	08/04	04	13	18	1
Southampton	Tr	08/05	05-06	22	9	9
Ipswich T	L	02/06	05	3	0	2
Stoke C	Tr	08/06	06-11	123	59	43
Charlton Ath	Tr	08/12	12	20	11	5
Blackpool	Tr	08/13	13	22	5	6
Millwall	Tr	07/14	14	16	22	4

FULLER William James (Bill)
Born: Brixton, S London, England, 6 April, 1944 — FB

League Club	Source	Date Signed	Seasons Played	Apps	Subs	Gls
Crystal Palace	Jnr	01/63	62-64	3	-	0

FULLERTON George
Born: Ballymena, Antrim, Northern Ireland, 14 June, 1939 — G

League Club	Source	Date Signed	Seasons Played	Apps	Subs	Gls
Leeds U	Glentoran	05/58				
Barrow	Distillery	07/60	60	12	-	0

FULOP Marton
Born: Budapest, Hungary, 3 May, 1983 — G
Hungary: 24/U21-11

League Club	Source	Date Signed	Seasons Played	Apps	Subs	Gls
Tottenham H	MTK Budapest (HUN)	06/04				
Chesterfield	L	03/05	04	7	0	0
Coventry C	L	10/05	05	31	0	0
Sunderland	Tr	11/06	06-09	44	1	0
Leicester C	L	08/07	07	24	0	0
Manchester C	L	04/10	09	3	0	0
Ipswich T	Tr	08/10	10	35	0	0
West Bromwich A	Tr	08/11	11	1	0	0

FULTON Bryce
Born: Kilwinning, Ayrshire, Scotland, 7 August, 1935 — LB
Died: Barton, Cambridgeshire, England, 1976

League Club	Source	Date Signed	Seasons Played	Apps	Subs	Gls
Manchester U	Jnr	03/53				
Plymouth Arg	Tr	08/57	57-63	176	-	0
Exeter C	Tr	07/64	64-65	37	0	0

FULTON Jay
Born: Bolton, Greater Manchester, England, 4 April, 1994 — M

Scotland: U21-1/Youth

League Club	Source	Date Signed	Seasons Played	Apps	Subs	Gls
Swansea C	Falkirk	01/14	13-14	2	2	0

FULTON Raymond Hamilton (Ray)
Born: Hendon, N London, England, 24 September, 1953 FB

League Club	Source	Date Signed	Seasons Played	Apps	Subs	Gls
Leyton Orient	West Ham U (App)	08/72	72	1	0	0

FULTON Stephen (Steve)
Born: Greenock, Inverclyde, Scotland, 10 August, 1970 M
Scotland: U21-7

League Club	Source	Date Signed	Seasons Played	Apps	Subs	Gls
Bolton W	Glasgow Celtic	07/93	93	4	0	0
Peterborough U	L	12/93	93	3	0	0

[FUMACA] ANTUNES Jose Rodriguez Alves
Born: Belem, Brazil, 15 July, 1976 M

League Club	Source	Date Signed	Seasons Played	Apps	Subs	Gls
Colchester U	Catuense (BRA)	03/99	98	1	0	0
Barnsley	Tr	03/99				
Crystal Palace	Tr	09/99	99	2	1	0
Newcastle U	Tr	09/99	99	1	4	0

FUNNELL Anthony (Tony)
Born: Eastbourne, East Sussex, England, 20 August, 1957 F

League Club	Source	Date Signed	Seasons Played	Apps	Subs	Gls
Southampton	Eastbourne U	01/77	77-78	13	4	8
Gillingham	Tr	03/79	78-79	27	6	10
Brentford	Tr	03/80	79-80	29	3	8
Bournemouth	Tr	09/81	81-82	59	5	22

FUNNELL Simon Paul
Born: Shoreham-by-Sea, West Sussex, England, 8 August, 1974 F

League Club	Source	Date Signed	Seasons Played	Apps	Subs	Gls
Brighton & HA	YT	07/92	91-94	14	14	2

FURIE John Patrick Christopher
Born: Hammersmith, W London, England, 13 May, 1948 RB

League Club	Source	Date Signed	Seasons Played	Apps	Subs	Gls
Watford	App	05/66	66	0	1	0
Gillingham	Tr	07/67	67	17	0	0

FURLONG Carl David
Born: Liverpool, England, 18 October, 1976 F

League Club	Source	Date Signed	Seasons Played	Apps	Subs	Gls
Wigan Ath	YT	07/95	93-94	1	2	1

FURLONG Darnell Anthony
Born: Luton, England, 31 October, 1995 RB

League Club	Source	Date Signed	Seasons Played	Apps	Subs	Gls
Queens Park Rgrs	Sch	03/14	14	3	0	0

FURLONG Paul Anthony
Born: Wood Green, N London, England, 1 October, 1968 F
England: Semi Pro-6

League Club	Source	Date Signed	Seasons Played	Apps	Subs	Gls
Coventry C	Enfield	07/91	91	27	10	4
Watford	Tr	07/92	92-93	79	0	37
Chelsea	Tr	05/94	94-95	44	20	13
Birmingham C	Tr	07/96	96-01	104	27	50
Queens Park Rgrs	L	08/00	00	3	0	1
Sheffield U	L	02/02	01	4	0	2
Queens Park Rgrs	Tr	08/02	02-06	137	31	56
Luton T	Tr	07/07	07	24	8	8
Southend U	Tr	07/08	08	1	2	0
Barnet	Tr	01/09	08-09	52	7	14

FURMAN Dean
Born: Cape Town, South Africa, 22 June, 1988 M
South Africa: 25

League Club	Source	Date Signed	Seasons Played	Apps	Subs	Gls
Bradford C (L)	Glasgow Rangers	08/08	08	26	6	4
Oldham Ath	Glasgow Rangers	07/09	09-12	119	12	8
Doncaster Rov	Tr	03/13	12-14	63	11	3

FURNELL Andrew Paul (Andy)
Born: Peterborough, England, 13 February, 1977 F
England: Youth

League Club	Source	Date Signed	Seasons Played	Apps	Subs	Gls
Peterborough U	YT	12/94	93-95	9	10	1

FURNELL James (Jim)
Born: Clitheroe, Lancashire, England, 23 November, 1937 G

League Club	Source	Date Signed	Seasons Played	Apps	Subs	Gls
Burnley	Jnr	11/54	59-60	2	-	0
Liverpool	Tr	02/62	61-63	28	-	0
Arsenal	Tr	11/63	63-67	141	0	0
Rotherham U	Tr	09/68	68-69	76	0	0
Plymouth Arg	Tr	12/70	70-75	183	0	0

FURNESS William Isaac (Billy)
Born: Washington, Tyne and Wear, England, 8 June, 1909 IF
Died: Norwich, England, 29 August, 1980
England: 1

League Club	Source	Date Signed	Seasons Played	Apps	Subs	Gls
Leeds U	Usworth Colliery	08/28	29-36	243	-	62
Norwich C	Tr	06/37	37-46	93	-	21

FURNISS Frederick (Fred)
Born: Sheffield, England, 10 July, 1922 RB

League Club	Source	Date Signed	Seasons Played	Apps	Subs	Gls
Sheffield U	Hallam	01/43	46-54	279	-	14
Chesterfield	Tr	08/55				

FURPHY Keith
Born: Stockton-on-Tees, Cleveland, England, 30 July, 1958 W

League Club	Source	Date Signed	Seasons Played	Apps	Subs	Gls
Queens Park Rgrs	Sheffield U (App)	10/76				
Plymouth Arg	Atlanta Chiefs (USA)	08/87	87	6	0	1

FURPHY Kenneth (Ken)
Born: Stockton-on-Tees, Cleveland, England, 28 May, 1931 FB/WH
Died: Teignmouth, Devon, England, 17 January, 2015

League Club	Source	Date Signed	Seasons Played	Apps	Subs	Gls
Everton	Stockton West End	11/50				
Darlington	Runcorn	08/53	53-61	316	-	6
Workington	Tr	07/62	62-64	105	-	3
Watford	Tr	11/64	64-67	95	6	1

FURSDON Alan Harry
Born: Grantham, Lincolnshire, England, 16 October, 1947 FB

League Club	Source	Date Signed	Seasons Played	Apps	Subs	Gls
Swindon T		09/65				
Oxford U		05/67	68	0	1	0

FURY Paul
Born: Swansea, Wales, 16 March, 1955 RB
Wales: Schools

League Club	Source	Date Signed	Seasons Played	Apps	Subs	Gls
Swansea C	App	-	71-72	11	0	0

FUSCHILLO Paul Michael
Born: Islington, N London, England, 20 October, 1948 D
England: Amateur-1/Schools

League Club	Source	Date Signed	Seasons Played	Apps	Subs	Gls
Blackpool	Wycombe W	07/71	71-73	8	3	0
Brighton & HA	Tr	02/74	73-74	17	0	1

FUSEINI Ali
Born: Accra, Ghana, 7 December, 1988 M

League Club	Source	Date Signed	Seasons Played	Apps	Subs	Gls
Millwall	Sch	09/06	06-09	57	19	2
Lincoln C	Unattached	01/11	10	15	3	0

FUTACS Marko
Born: Budapest, Hungary, 22 February, 1990 F
Hungary: 3/U21-18/Youth

League Club	Source	Date Signed	Seasons Played	Apps	Subs	Gls
Portsmouth	Werder Bremen (GER)	08/11	11	12	17	5
Leicester C	Tr	07/12	12	0	9	1
Blackpool	L	03/13	12	0	4	0

FUTCHER Benjamin Paul (Ben)
Born: Manchester, England, 20 February, 1981 CD

League Club	Source	Date Signed	Seasons Played	Apps	Subs	Gls
Oldham Ath	YT	07/99	99-00	2	8	0
Lincoln C	Doncaster Rov	08/02	02-04	119	2	13
Boston U	Tr	07/05	05	13	1	0
Grimsby T	Tr	01/06	05-06	15	4	2
Peterborough U	Tr	08/06	06	22	3	3
Bury	Tr	07/07	07-10	108	9	3
Oxford U	L	11/10	10	6	0	0
Macclesfield T	L	02/12	11	10	0	0

FUTCHER Graham
Born: Chester, England, 15 June, 1953 F

League Club	Source	Date Signed	Seasons Played	Apps	Subs	Gls
Chester C	Jnr	08/71	71-72	5	5	0

FUTCHER Paul
Born: Chester, England, 25 September, 1956 CD
England: U21-11

League Club	Source	Date Signed	Seasons Played	Apps	Subs	Gls
Chester C	App	01/74	72-73	20	0	0
Luton T	Tr	06/74	74-77	131	0	1
Manchester C	Tr	06/78	78-79	36	1	0
Oldham Ath	Tr	08/80	80-82	98	0	1
Derby Co	Tr	01/83	82-83	35	0	0
Barnsley	Tr	03/84	83-89	229	1	0
Halifax T	Tr	07/90	90	15	0	0
Grimsby T	Tr	01/91	90-94	131	1	0

FUTCHER Ronald (Ron)
Born: Chester, England, 25 September, 1956 F

League Club	Source	Date Signed	Seasons Played	Apps	Subs	Gls
Chester C	App	01/74	73	4	0	0
Luton T	Tr	06/74	74-77	116	4	40
Manchester C	Tr	08/78	78	10	7	7
Barnsley	NAC Breda (NED)	12/84	84	18	1	5
Oldham Ath	Tr	07/85	85-86	65	0	30
Bradford C	Tr	03/87	86-87	35	7	18
Port Vale	Tr	08/88	88-89	46	6	20
Burnley	Tr	11/89	89-90	52	5	25
Crewe Alex	Tr	07/91	91	18	3	4

FUTRE Paulo Jorge
Born: Montijo, Portugal, 28 February, 1966 LW
Portugal: 41

League Club	Source	Date Signed	Seasons Played	Apps	Subs	Gls
West Ham U	AC Milan (ITA)	06/96	96	4	5	0

FYFE Graham
Born: Dundee, Scotland, 7 December, 1982 M

League Club	Source	Date Signed	Seasons Played	Apps	Subs	Gls
Cheltenham T	Glasgow Celtic	08/03	03-04	16	7	0

FYFE Tony

Born: Carlisle, Cumbria, England, 23 February, 1962 — F

League Club	Source	Date Signed	Seasons Played	Career Record Apps	Subs	Gls
Carlisle U	Penrith	09/87	87-89	28	20	12
Scarborough	L	12/89	89	6	0	1
Halifax T	Tr	01/90	89-90	13	3	0
Carlisle U	Tr	10/90	90-91	33	9	8

FYFIELD Jamal Nehemiah

Born: Leyton, NE London, England, 17 March, 1989 — FB

League Club	Source	Date Signed	Seasons Played	Career Record Apps	Subs	Gls
York C	Maidenhead U	09/10	12-13	30	5	0

FYVIE Fraser

Born: Aberdeen, Scotland, 27 March, 1993 — M

Scotland: U21-8/Youth

League Club	Source	Date Signed	Seasons Played	Career Record Apps	Subs	Gls
Wigan Ath	Aberdeen	07/12	12	0	1	0
Yeovil T	L	10/13	13	2	0	0
Shrewsbury T	L	01/14	13	4	0	0

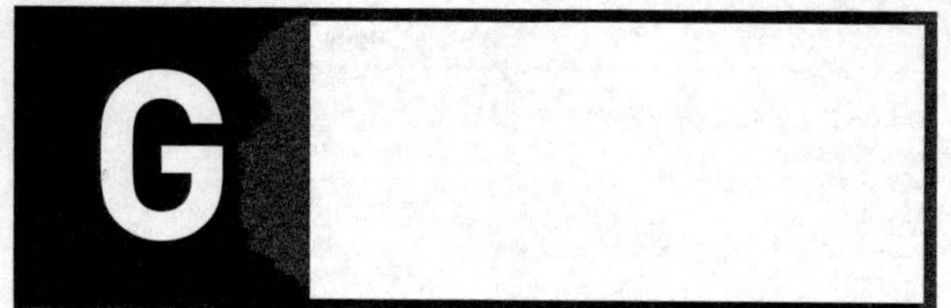

League Club	Source	Date Signed	Seasons Played	Career Record Apps	Subs	Gls

GAARDSOE Thomas
Born: Randers, Denmark, 23 November, 1979 CD
Denmark: 2/U21-10/Youth

League Club	Source	Date Signed	Seasons Played	Apps	Subs	Gls
Ipswich T	AAB Aalborg (DEN)	08/01	01-02	40	1	5
West Bromwich A	Tr	08/03	03-05	77	4	4

GABBIADINI Marco
Born: Nottingham, England, 20 January, 1968 F
England: B-1/FLge/U21-2

League Club	Source	Date Signed	Seasons Played	Apps	Subs	Gls
York C	App	09/85	84-87	42	18	14
Sunderland	Tr	09/87	87-91	155	2	74
Crystal Palace	Tr	10/91	91	15	0	5
Derby Co	Tr	01/92	91-96	163	25	50
Birmingham C	L	10/96	96	0	2	0
Oxford U	L	01/97	96	5	0	1
Stoke C	Panionios (GRE)	12/97	97	2	6	0
York C	Tr	02/98	97	5	2	1
Darlington	Tr	07/98	98-99	81	1	47
Northampton T	Tr	06/00	00-02	97	23	25
Hartlepool U	Tr	07/03	03	9	6	5

GABBIADINI Riccardo
Born: Newport, Wales, 11 March, 1970 F

League Club	Source	Date Signed	Seasons Played	Apps	Subs	Gls
York C	YT	-	87	0	1	0
Sunderland	Tr	06/88	89	0	1	0
Blackpool	L	09/89	89	5	0	3
Grimsby T	Tr	10/89	89	3	0	1
Brighton & HA	L	03/90	89	0	1	0
Crewe Alex	L	10/90	90	1	1	0
Hartlepool U	Tr	03/91	90-91	2	12	2
Scarborough	Tr	03/92	91	3	4	1
Carlisle U	Tr	08/92	92	18	6	3

GABBIDON Daniel Leon (Danny)
Born: Cwmbran, Torfaen, Wales, 8 August, 1979 CD
Wales: 49/U21-17/Youth

League Club	Source	Date Signed	Seasons Played	Apps	Subs	Gls
West Bromwich A	YT	07/98	98-99	20	0	0
Cardiff C	Tr	08/00	00-04	194	3	10
West Ham U	Tr	07/05	05-10	89	7	0
Queens Park Rgrs	Tr	07/11	11	15	2	0
Crystal Palace	Tr	09/12	12-13	30	3	2
Cardiff C	Tr	09/14	14	0	1	0

GABILONDO Lander
Born: San Sebastian, Spain, 8 August, 1979 W

League Club	Source	Date Signed	Seasons Played	Apps	Subs	Gls
Swindon T	CA Osasuna B (SPN)	08/11	11	4	6	0

GABRIEL James (Jimmy)
Born: Dundee, Scotland, 16 October, 1940 M
Scotland: 2/U23-6/Schools

League Club	Source	Date Signed	Seasons Played	Apps	Subs	Gls
Everton	Dundee	03/60	59-66	255	1	33
Southampton	Tr	07/67	67-71	190	1	25
Bournemouth	Tr	07/72	72-73	53	0	4
Swindon T	L	10/73	73	6	0	0
Brentford	Tr	03/74	73	9	0	0

GABRIELI Emanuele
Born: L'Aquila, Italy, 31 December, 1980 CD

League Club	Source	Date Signed	Seasons Played	Apps	Subs	Gls
Sheffield U	Cavese (ITA)	10/04	04	0	1	0
Boston U	L	02/05	04	4	0	0

[GABRIEL PAULISTA] DE ABREU Gabriel Armando
Born: Sao Paulo, Brazil, 26 November, 1990 CD

League Club	Source	Date Signed	Seasons Played	Apps	Subs	Gls
Arsenal	Villarreal (SPN)	01/15	14	4	2	0

GADDES Graham Robert (Robert)
Born: Byfleet, Surrey, England, 27 September, 1941 G
England: Youth

League Club	Source	Date Signed	Seasons Played	Apps	Subs	Gls
Portsmouth	Jnr	06/60	59	1	-	0

GADSBY Kenneth Joseph (Ken)
Born: Chesterfield, Derbyshire, England, 3 July, 1916 LB
Died: Downham Market, Norfolk, England, June, 2003

League Club	Source	Date Signed	Seasons Played	Apps	Subs	Gls
Leeds U	Scarborough	10/34	36-47	78	-	0

GADSBY Matthew John (Matt)
Born: Sutton Coldfield, West Midlands, England, 6 September, 1979 D
Died: Harrogate, North Yorkshire, England, 9 September, 2006

League Club	Source	Date Signed	Seasons Played	Apps	Subs	Gls
Walsall	YT	02/98	97-01	23	14	0
Mansfield T	Tr	11/02	02	13	7	0
Kidderminster Hrs	Tr	07/03	03	23	9	2

GADSBY Michael David (Mick)
Born: Oswestry, Shropshire, England, 1 August, 1947 G

League Club	Source	Date Signed	Seasons Played	Apps	Subs	Gls
Notts Co	Ashbourne	01/68	67	11	0	0
York C	Tr	07/69	69	13	0	0
Grimsby T	L	09/70	70	2	0	0
Bradford C	L	12/70	70	6	0	0
Hartlepool U	Tr	07/71	71	21	0	0

GADSTON Joseph Edward (Joe)
Born: Hanwell, W London, England, 13 September, 1945 F

League Club	Source	Date Signed	Seasons Played	Apps	Subs	Gls
Brentford	West Ham U (Am)	08/64				
Bristol Rov	Cheltenham T	06/68	68	10	1	5
Exeter C	Tr	11/69	69-71	85	0	30
Aldershot	Tr	07/72	72	2	2	0
Hartlepool U	L	02/73	72	1	0	0

GAFAITI Adel
Born: Nancy, France, 13 September, 1994 CD

League Club	Source	Date Signed	Seasons Played	Apps	Subs	Gls
Norwich C	AS Nancy (FRA)	08/12				
Oldham Ath	L	03/14	13	0	1	0

GAFFNEY Terence (Terry)
Born: Hartlepool, Cleveland, England, 15 February, 1952 M

League Club	Source	Date Signed	Seasons Played	Apps	Subs	Gls
Hartlepool U	Billingham Synthonia	07/77	77	10	3	1

GAGE Kevin William
Born: Chiswick, W London, England, 21 April, 1964 FB/M
England: Youth

League Club	Source	Date Signed	Seasons Played	Apps	Subs	Gls
Wimbledon	App	01/82	80-86	135	33	15
Aston Villa	Tr	07/87	87-90	113	2	8
Sheffield U	Tr	11/91	91-95	107	5	7
Preston NE	Tr	03/96	95-96	20	3	0
Hull C	Tr	09/97	97-98	10	3	0

GAGE Laurence Albert (Larry)
Born: Walthamstow, NE London, England, 10 September, 1922 G
Died: Norwich, England, May, 1996

League Club	Source	Date Signed	Seasons Played	Apps	Subs	Gls
Fulham	Walthamstow Ave	08/44				
Aldershot	Tr	07/46	46-47	38	-	0
Fulham	Canada	08/48	48	3	-	0
Gillingham	Tr	06/50	50	40	-	0

GAGE Wakeley Alexander John
Born: Northampton, England, 5 May, 1958 CD

League Club	Source	Date Signed	Seasons Played	Apps	Subs	Gls
Northampton T	Desborough T	10/79	79-84	215	3	17
Chester C	Tr	08/85	85	17	0	1
Peterborough U	Tr	11/85	85-86	73	0	1
Crewe Alex	Tr	06/87	87-88	45	9	1

GAGER Horace Edwin
Born: West Ham, E London, England, 25 January, 1917 CH
Died: Bingham, Nottinghamshire, England, March, 1984
Northern Ireland: NILge-2

League Club	Source	Date Signed	Seasons Played	Apps	Subs	Gls
Luton T	Vauxhall Motors	11/37	46-47	59	-	2
Nottingham F	Tr	02/48	47-54	258	-	11

GAIA Marcio
Born: Sao Mateus, Brazil, 8 September, 1978 CD
Brazil: Youth

League Club	Source	Date Signed	Seasons Played	Apps	Subs	Gls
Exeter C	Agremiacao SA (BRA)	07/02	02	33	0	1

GAILLARD Marcel Jean Elie
Born: Charleroi, Belgium, 15 January, 1927 LW
Died: Gaillard, France, June, 1976

League Club	Source	Date Signed	Seasons Played	Apps	Subs	Gls
Crystal Palace	OD Charleroi (BEL)	02/48	47-49	21	-	3
Portsmouth	Tonbridge	02/51	50-52	58	-	7

GAIN Peter Thomas
Born: Hammersmith, W London, England, 11 November, 1976 M
Republic of Ireland: U21-1/Youth

League Club	Source	Date Signed	Seasons Played	Apps	Subs	Gls
Tottenham H	YT	07/95				
Lincoln C	L	12/98	98	0	3	0
Lincoln C	Tr	03/99	98-04	195	29	21
Peterborough U	Tr	07/05	05-06	63	8	9
Dagenham & Red	Tr	01/08	07-11	142	7	4

GALBRAITH Daniel William (Danny)
Born: Galashiels, Borders, Scotland, 19 August, 1990 W

League Club	Source	Date Signed	Seasons Played	Apps	Subs	Gls
Manchester U	Sch	08/07				
Gillingham	Limerick (ROI)	12/14	14	3	4	0

GALBRAITH David James
Born: Luton, England, 20 December, 1983 M

League Club	Source	Date Signed	Seasons Played	Apps	Subs	Gls
Northampton T	Tottenham H (Sch)	01/04	04-05	10	19	1
Boston U	Tr	11/05	05-06	27	15	2

GALBRAITH Walter McMurray (Wally)
Born: Glasgow, Scotland, 26 May, 1918 LB
Died: Wallasey, Wirral, England, November, 1995

League Club	Source	Date Signed	Seasons Played	Apps	Subs	Gls
New Brighton	Clyde	09/48	48-50	109	-	1
Grimsby T	Tr	08/51	51-52	77	-	0
Accrington Stan	Tr	06/53	53	21	-	0

GALE Anthony Peter (Tony)
Born: Westminster, Central London, England, 19 November, 1959 CD
England: U21-1/Youth

League Club	Source	Date Signed	Seasons Played	Apps	Subs	Gls
Fulham	App	08/77	77-83	277	0	19
West Ham U	Tr	08/84	84-93	293	7	5
Blackburn Rov	Tr	08/94	94	15	0	0
Crystal Palace	Tr	09/95	95	2	0	0

GALE Colin Maurice
Born: Pontypridd, Rhondda Cynon Taff, Wales, 31 August, 1932 CH
Died: Rhydyfelin, Rhondda Cynon Taff, Wales, 27 October, 2008

League Club	Source	Date Signed	Seasons Played	Apps	Subs	Gls
Cardiff C	Jnr	07/50	53-55	13	-	0
Northampton T	Tr	03/56	55-60	211	-	0

GALE Darren
Born: Port Talbot, Wales, 25 October, 1963 F
Wales: U21-2

League Club	Source	Date Signed	Seasons Played	Apps	Subs	Gls
Swansea C	App	10/80	81-84	26	11	6
Exeter C	Tr	09/85	85-86	19	1	5

GALE Ian James
Born: Slough, Berkshire, England, 3 March, 1961 M

League Club	Source	Date Signed	Seasons Played	Apps	Subs	Gls
Millwall	App	03/78	78	4	1	0

GALE Shaun Michael
Born: Reading, England, 8 October, 1969 FB

League Club	Source	Date Signed	Seasons Played	Apps	Subs	Gls
Portsmouth	YT	07/88	90	2	1	0
Barnet	Tr	07/94	94-96	109	5	5
Exeter C	Tr	06/97	97-99	81	12	5

GALE Thomas (Tommy)
Born: Washington, Tyne and Wear, England, 4 November, 1920 CH
Died: Bath, England, 29 January, 1975

League Club	Source	Date Signed	Seasons Played	Apps	Subs	Gls
Sheffield Wed	Gateshead (Am)	04/45	46	6	-	0
York C	Tr	08/47	47-48	76	-	0

GALL Benny
Born: Copenhagen, Denmark, 14 March, 1971 G
Denmark: U21-1

League Club	Source	Date Signed	Seasons Played	Apps	Subs	Gls
Shrewsbury T	De Graafschap (NED)	08/96	96-97	34	0	0

GALL Kevin Alexander
Born: Merthyr Tydfil, Wales, 4 February, 1982 F/W
Wales: U21-8/Youth/Schools

League Club	Source	Date Signed	Seasons Played	Apps	Subs	Gls
Newcastle U	YT	04/99				
Bristol Rov	Tr	03/01	00-02	28	22	5
Yeovil T	Tr	02/03	03-05	80	43	13
Carlisle U	Tr	07/06	06-07	54	12	9
Darlington	L	01/08	07	7	1	0
Lincoln C	L	07/08	08	6	3	0
Port Vale	L	02/09	08	7	0	0
Darlington	Tr	08/09	09	9	1	2

GALL Mark Ian
Born: Brixton, S London, England, 14 May, 1963 F

League Club	Source	Date Signed	Seasons Played	Apps	Subs	Gls
Maidstone U	Greenwich Bor	02/88	89-91	69	16	31
Brighton & HA	Tr	10/91	91	30	1	13

GALL Norman Albert
Born: Wallsend, Tyne and Wear, England, 30 September, 1942 CD

League Club	Source	Date Signed	Seasons Played	Apps	Subs	Gls
Brighton & HA	Gateshead	03/62	62-73	427	13	4

GALLACHER Bernard
Born: Johnstone, Renfrewshire, Scotland, 22 March, 1967 LB
Died: Sutton Coldfield, West Midlands, England, 28 August, 2011

League Club	Source	Date Signed	Seasons Played	Apps	Subs	Gls
Aston Villa	App	03/85	86-90	55	2	0
Blackburn Rov	L	11/90	90	4	0	0
Doncaster Rov	Tr	09/91	91	2	0	0
Brighton & HA	Tr	10/91	91-92	45	0	1
Northampton T	Tr	01/94	93	5	0	0

GALLACHER Connor (Con)
Born: Nantyderry, Monmouthshire, Wales, 24 April, 1922 IF

League Club	Source	Date Signed	Seasons Played	Apps	Subs	Gls
Middlesbrough	Lochee Harp	01/47	46	1	-	0
Hull C	Tr	05/47	47	18	-	3
Rochdale	Tr	03/48	47	6	-	1

GALLACHER John Anthony
Born: Glasgow, Scotland, 26 January, 1969 W

League Club	Source	Date Signed	Seasons Played	Apps	Subs	Gls
Newcastle U	Falkirk	06/89	89-90	22	7	6
Hartlepool U	Tr	08/92	92-93	18	5	2

GALLACHER Kevin William
Born: Clydebank, Dunbartonshire, Scotland, 23 November, 1966 F/W
Scotland: 53/B-2/U21-7/Youth

League Club	Source	Date Signed	Seasons Played	Apps	Subs	Gls
Coventry C	Dundee U	01/90	89-92	99	1	28
Blackburn Rov	Tr	03/93	92-99	132	12	46
Newcastle U	Tr	10/99	99-00	27	12	4
Preston NE	Tr	08/01	01	1	4	1
Sheffield Wed	Tr	03/02	01	0	4	0
Huddersfield T	Tr	08/02	02	5	2	0

GALLACHER Patrick (Pat)
Born: Glasgow, Scotland, 9 January, 1913 IF
Died: Hastings, East Sussex, England, June, 1983

League Club	Source	Date Signed	Seasons Played	Apps	Subs	Gls
Millwall	Dunoon	11/33				
Blackburn Rov	Third Lanark	10/36	36-37	11	-	0
Bournemouth	Tr	06/38	38-47	35	-	3

GALLACHER Paul James
Born: Glasgow, Scotland, 16 August, 1979 G
Scotland: 8/U21-7

League Club	Source	Date Signed	Seasons Played	Apps	Subs	Gls
Norwich C	Dundee U	06/04	05-06	30	1	0
Gillingham	L	12/04	04	3	0	0
Sheffield Wed	L	03/05	04	8	0	0

GALLAGHER Barry Patrick
Born: Bradford, England, 7 April, 1961 M

League Club	Source	Date Signed	Seasons Played	Apps	Subs	Gls
Bradford C	App	04/79	77-82	66	5	22
Mansfield T	L	01/83	82	2	1	0
Halifax T	Tr	03/83	82-85	110	5	27

GALLAGHER Brian
Born: Oldham, Greater Manchester, England, 22 July, 1938 FB
Died: Los Angeles, California, USA, 7 February, 2011

League Club	Source	Date Signed	Seasons Played	Apps	Subs	Gls
Bury	Ashton U	10/56	57-64	131	-	1
Carlisle U	Tr	05/65	65-66	43	2	1
Stockport Co	Tr	07/67	67	13	0	0

GALLAGHER Daniel Lee (Dan)
Born: Epsom, Surrey, England, 20 June, 1997 M

League Club	Source	Date Signed	Seasons Played	Apps	Subs	Gls
AFC Wimbledon	Sch	02/15	14	0	1	0

GALLAGHER Ian
Born: Hartlepool, Cleveland, England, 30 May, 1978 M

League Club	Source	Date Signed	Seasons Played	Apps	Subs	Gls
Hartlepool U	YT	07/96	95	1	0	0

GALLAGHER James (Jimmy)
Born: Bury, Greater Manchester, England, 2 September, 1911 CH
Died: Southampton, England, 4 December, 1972

League Club	Source	Date Signed	Seasons Played	Apps	Subs	Gls
Bury	Grenadier Guards	01/36				
Notts Co	Lancaster T	08/37	37-38	23	-	2
Exeter C	Tr	06/39				
Exeter C	Notts Co (Coach)	09/48	48	1	-	0

GALLAGHER John Christopher (Jackie)
Born: Wisbech, Cambridgeshire, England, 6 April, 1958 F

League Club	Source	Date Signed	Seasons Played	Apps	Subs	Gls
Lincoln C	March T	02/76	76	1	0	0
Peterborough U	Wisbech T	04/80	79-80	11	2	1
Torquay U	Eastern AA (HKG)	08/82	82	38	4	7
Peterborough U	Wisbech T	08/85	85-86	78	4	20
Wolverhampton W	Tr	06/87	87-88	10	17	4

GALLAGHER Joseph Anthony (Joe)
Born: Liverpool, England, 11 January, 1955 CD
England: B-1

League Club	Source	Date Signed	Seasons Played	Apps	Subs	Gls
Birmingham C	App	01/72	73-80	281	5	17
Wolverhampton W	Tr	08/81	81-82	31	0	0
West Ham U	Tr	12/82	82	8	1	0
Burnley	Tr	08/83	83-86	46	1	3
Halifax T	L	10/83	83	4	0	0

GALLAGHER Michael (Mike)
Born: Cambuslang, Glasgow, Scotland, 16 January, 1932 LW
Died: Glasgow, Scotland, 1975

League Club	Source	Date Signed	Seasons Played	Apps	Subs	Gls
Bolton W	Benburb Jnrs	01/52				
West Bromwich A	Tr	12/52	52	1	-	0

GALLAGHER Nicholas (Nicky)
Born: Boston, Lincolnshire, England, 28 January, 1971 W
England: Schools

League Club	Source	Date Signed	Seasons Played	Apps	Subs	Gls
Doncaster Rov	Jnr	05/89	89	0	1	0

GALLAGHER Paul
Born: Glasgow, Scotland, 9 August, 1984 F
Scotland: 1/B-5/U21-11

League Club	Source	Date Signed	Seasons Played	Apps	Subs	Gls
Blackburn Rov	Sch	02/03	02-09	19	42	6
Stoke C	L	08/05	05	32	5	11
Preston NE	L	08/07	07	15	4	1
Stoke C	L	01/08	07	2	5	0
Plymouth Arg	L	08/08	08	36	4	13

League Club	Source	Date Signed	Seasons Played	Apps	Subs	Gls
Leicester C	Tr	08/09	09-12	81	37	25
Sheffield U	L	09/12	12	6	0	1
Preston NE	L	10/13	13	26	2	6
Preston NE	L	07/14	14	45	1	7

GALLAGHER Samuel James (Sam)
Born: Crediton, Devon, England, 15 September, 1995 F
England: Youth//Scotland: Youth

League Club	Source	Date Signed	Seasons Played	Apps	Subs	Gls
Southampton	Sch	09/12	13	3	15	1

GALLAGHER Thomas Duncan (Tommy)
Born: Nottingham, England, 25 August, 1974 RB/M

League Club	Source	Date Signed	Seasons Played	Apps	Subs	Gls
Notts Co	YT	06/92	93-96	42	1	2

GALLANT David
Born: Middlesbrough, England, 12 October, 1949 F

League Club	Source	Date Signed	Seasons Played	Apps	Subs	Gls
Leeds U	Jnr	12/66				
Darlington	L	01/68	67	1	0	0

GALLAS William Eric
Born: Paris, France, 17 August, 1977 CD
France: 84/U21-11/Youth

League Club	Source	Date Signed	Seasons Played	Apps	Subs	Gls
Chelsea	Olymp Marseille (FRA)	07/01	01-05	147	12	12
Arsenal	Tr	08/06	06-09	101	0	12
Tottenham H	Tr	07/10	10-12	57	4	1

GALLEGO Antonio (Tony)
Born: San Sebastian, Spain, 2 June, 1924 G
Died: Cambridge, England, 3 May, 2015

League Club	Source	Date Signed	Seasons Played	Apps	Subs	Gls
Norwich C	Abbey U	03/47	46	1	-	0

GALLEGO Jose Augustin
Born: San Sebastian, Spain, 8 April, 1923 W
Died: Cambridge, England, 17 September, 2006

League Club	Source	Date Signed	Seasons Played	Apps	Subs	Gls
Brentford	Abbey U	01/47	46-47	6	-	0
Southampton	Tr	05/48	48	1	-	0
Colchester U	Tr	08/49	50	4	-	0

GALLEN Joseph Martin (Joe)
Born: Hammersmith, W London, England, 2 September, 1972 F
Republic of Ireland: U21-6

League Club	Source	Date Signed	Seasons Played	Apps	Subs	Gls
Watford	YT	05/91				
Exeter C	L	12/92	92	6	0	0
Shrewsbury T	Tr	07/93	93	4	2	1

GALLEN Kevin Andrew
Born: Chiswick, W London, England, 21 September, 1975 F
England: U21-4/Youth/Schools

League Club	Source	Date Signed	Seasons Played	Apps	Subs	Gls
Queens Park Rgrs	YT	09/92	94-99	126	45	36
Huddersfield T	Tr	08/00	00	30	8	10
Barnsley	Tr	07/01	01	8	1	2
Queens Park Rgrs	Tr	11/01	01-06	183	11	54
Plymouth Arg	L	01/07	06	6	7	1
MK Dons	Tr	07/07	07-08	16	14	9
Luton T	Tr	11/08	08	26	3	3
Barnet	L	10/10	10	6	1	1

GALLEY Gordon Walter
Born: Worksop, Nottinghamshire, England, 4 February, 1930 LW

League Club	Source	Date Signed	Seasons Played	Apps	Subs	Gls
Sheffield Wed	Jnr	06/47				
Darlington	Tr	10/48	48-51	61	-	12

GALLEY John Edward
Born: Clowne, Derbyshire, England, 7 May, 1944 CF

League Club	Source	Date Signed	Seasons Played	Apps	Subs	Gls
Wolverhampton W	Jnr	05/61	62-64	5	-	2
Rotherham U	Tr	12/64	64-67	108	0	46
Bristol C	Tr	12/67	67-72	172	0	84
Nottingham F	Tr	12/72	72-74	31	6	6
Peterborough U	L	10/74	74	7	0	1
Hereford U	Tr	12/74	74-76	77	3	10

GALLEY Keith John
Born: Worksop, Nottinghamshire, England, 17 October, 1955 F

League Club	Source	Date Signed	Seasons Played	Apps	Subs	Gls
Southport	Morecambe	12/75	75-76	50	10	11

GALLEY Maurice
Born: Clowne, Derbyshire, England, 10 August, 1934 WH

League Club	Source	Date Signed	Seasons Played	Apps	Subs	Gls
Chesterfield	Jnr	07/52	54-58	55	-	5

GALLEY Thomas (Tom)
Born: Hednesford, Staffordshire, England, 4 August, 1915 WH/IF
Died: Cannock, Staffordshire, England, 12 July, 2000
England: 2/FLge-1

League Club	Source	Date Signed	Seasons Played	Apps	Subs	Gls
Wolverhampton W	Notts Co (Am)	04/34	34-47	183	-	41
Grimsby T	Tr	11/47	47-48	32	-	2

GALLI Filippo
Born: Monza, Italy, 19 May, 1963 CD
Italy: U21-7

League Club	Source	Date Signed	Seasons Played	Apps	Subs	Gls
Watford	Brescia (ITA)	07/01	01	27	1	1

GALLIER William Henry (Bill)
Born: Cannock, Staffordshire, England, 24 April, 1932 LB
Died: Tamworth, Staffordshire, England, 6 February, 2011

League Club	Source	Date Signed	Seasons Played	Apps	Subs	Gls
West Bromwich A	Beaudesert Sports	07/53				
Walsall	Tr	06/55	55	10	-	0

GALLIERS Steven (Steve)
Born: Preston, Lancashire, England, 21 August, 1957 M

League Club	Source	Date Signed	Seasons Played	Apps	Subs	Gls
Wimbledon	Chorley	06/77	77-81	148	7	10
Crystal Palace	Tr	10/81	81	8	5	0
Wimbledon	Tr	08/82	82-87	145	1	5
Bristol C	L	02/87	86	9	0	0
Bristol C	Tr	09/87	87-88	65	3	6
Maidstone U	Tr	07/89	89	7	1	0

GALLIMORE Anthony Mark (Tony)
Born: Nantwich, Cheshire, England, 21 February, 1972 LB

League Club	Source	Date Signed	Seasons Played	Apps	Subs	Gls
Stoke C	YT	07/90	89-91	6	5	0
Carlisle U	L	10/91	91	8	0	0
Carlisle U	L	02/92	91	8	0	0
Carlisle U	Tr	03/93	92-95	124	0	9
Grimsby T	Tr	03/96	95-02	263	10	4
Barnsley	Tr	08/03	03	20	0	0
Rochdale	Tr	08/04	04-05	64	4	0

GALLIMORE Leonard (Len)
Born: Northwich, Cheshire, England, 14 September, 1912 LB
Died: Stockport, Greater Manchester, England, 1978

League Club	Source	Date Signed	Seasons Played	Apps	Subs	Gls
Preston NE	Barnton Victoria	01/32	33-36	9		0
Watford	Tr	05/37	37-46	64	-	0

GALLINAGH Andrew Anthony (Andy)
Born: Sutton Coldfield, West Midlands, England, 16 March, 1985 D/M

League Club	Source	Date Signed	Seasons Played	Apps	Subs	Gls
Cheltenham T	Stratford T	07/04	05-10	110	20	4

GALLOGLY Charles (Charlie)
Born: Banbridge, Down, Northern Ireland, 16 June, 1925 RB
Died: New York, USA, 12 January, 1993
Northern Ireland: 2

League Club	Source	Date Signed	Seasons Played	Apps	Subs	Gls
Huddersfield T	Glenavon	12/49	49-51	76		0
Watford	Tr	08/52	52-53	47	-	0
Bournemouth	Tr	07/54				

GALLON John William (Jack)
Born: Burradon, Tyne and Wear, England, 12 February, 1914 IF
Died: Camberley, Surrey, England, July, 1993

League Club	Source	Date Signed	Seasons Played	Apps	Subs	Gls
Bradford C	Bedlington U	06/36	36-37	20	-	5
Bradford Park Ave	Tr	02/38	37-38	31	-	4
Swansea C	Tr	06/39				
Gateshead	Tr	03/46	46	20	-	2

GALLOWAY Brendon Joel Zibusiso
Born: Harare, Zimbabwe, 17 March, 1996 M/D
England: Youth

League Club	Source	Date Signed	Seasons Played	Apps	Subs	Gls
MK Dons	Sch	07/14	11-13	4	6	0
Everton	Tr	08/14	14	2	0	0

GALLOWAY John
Born: Bo'ness, Falkirk, Scotland, 29 October, 1918 IF

League Club	Source	Date Signed	Seasons Played	Apps	Subs	Gls
Chelsea	Glasgow Rangers	08/46	46-47	4	-	0

GALLOWAY Michael (Mick)
Born: Oswestry, Shropshire, England, 30 May, 1965 CD
Scotland: 1/U21-2/Youth

League Club	Source	Date Signed	Seasons Played	Apps	Subs	Gls
Mansfield T	Berwick Rgrs	09/83	83-85	39	15	3
Halifax T	Tr	02/86	85-87	79	0	5
Leicester C (L)	Glasgow Celtic	02/95	94	4	1	0

GALLOWAY Michael Anthony (Mick)
Born: Nottingham, England, 13 October, 1974 M

League Club	Source	Date Signed	Seasons Played	Apps	Subs	Gls
Notts Co	YT	06/93	94-96	17	4	0
Gillingham	Tr	03/97	96-99	58	17	5
Lincoln C	L	09/99	99	5	0	0
Chesterfield	Tr	11/99	99-00	18	2	1
Carlisle U	Tr	11/00	00-02	30	5	1

GALLOWAY Steven George (Steve)
Born: Hannover, Germany, 13 February, 1963 F

League Club	Source	Date Signed	Seasons Played	Apps	Subs	Gls
Crystal Palace	Sutton U	10/84	84-85	3	2	1
Cambridge U	L	03/86	85	0	1	0

GALVIN Anthony (Tony)
Born: Huddersfield, West Yorkshire, England, 12 July, 1956 LW
England: Schools//Republic of Ireland: 29

League Club	Source	Date Signed	Seasons Played	Apps	Subs	Gls
Tottenham H	Goole T	01/78	78-86	194	7	20
Sheffield Wed	Tr	08/87	87-88	21	15	1
Swindon T	Tr	08/89	89	6	5	0

GALVIN Christopher (Chris)
Born: Huddersfield, West Yorkshire, England, 24 November, 1951 M

England: Youth

League Club	Source	Date Signed	Seasons Played	Apps	Subs	Gls
Leeds U	App	11/68	69-72	6	1	0
Hull C	Tr	08/73	73-78	132	11	11
York C	L	12/76	76	22	0	6
Stockport Co	Tr	04/79	78-80	67	1	3

GALVIN David
Born: Denaby, South Yorkshire, England, 5 October, 1946 — CD

League Club	Source	Date Signed	Seasons Played	Apps	Subs	Gls
Wolverhampton W	Jnr	05/65	68	5	0	0
Gillingham	Tr	10/69	69-76	240	6	17
Wimbledon	Tr	08/77	77-78	73	0	7

GAMBARO Enzo
Born: Genoa, Italy, 23 February, 1966 — D

League Club	Source	Date Signed	Seasons Played	Apps	Subs	Gls
Bolton W	AC Milan (ITA)	01/96				
Grimsby T	Tr	03/96	95	0	1	0

GAMBIN Luke David
Born: Sutton, S London, England, 16 March, 1993 — LW

League Club	Source	Date Signed	Seasons Played	Apps	Subs	Gls
Barnet	Sch	07/12	11-12	5	6	2

GAMBLE Bradley David
Born: Southwark, S London, England, 4 February, 1975 — F

League Club	Source	Date Signed	Seasons Played	Apps	Subs	Gls
Leyton Orient	YT	07/93	93	1	0	0

GAMBLE Francis (Frank)
Born: Liverpool, England, 21 August, 1961 — LW

League Club	Source	Date Signed	Seasons Played	Apps	Subs	Gls
Derby Co	Burscough	05/81	81-82	5	1	2
Rochdale	Barrow	12/84	84-85	41	5	9

GAMBLE Joseph Finbar (Joe)
Born: Cork, Republic of Ireland, 14 January, 1982 — M
Republic of Ireland: 2/B-1/U21-8/Youth

League Club	Source	Date Signed	Seasons Played	Apps	Subs	Gls
Reading	Cork C (ROI)	08/00	00-01	2	5	0
Hartlepool U	Cork C (ROI)	01/10	09-10	47	5	3

GAMBLE Simon William (Willie)
Born: Cottam, Nottinghamshire, England, 5 March, 1968 — F

League Club	Source	Date Signed	Seasons Played	Apps	Subs	Gls
Lincoln C	App	01/86	85-88	44	20	15

GAMBLIN Derek
Born: Havant, Hampshire, England, 7 April, 1943 — FB
England: Amateur-29

League Club	Source	Date Signed	Seasons Played	Apps	Subs	Gls
Portsmouth (Am)	Sutton U	07/65	65	1	0	0

GAMBOA Cristian Esteban
Born: Liberia, Costa Rica, 24 October, 1989 — M/RB
Costa Rica: 30/Youth

League Club	Source	Date Signed	Seasons Played	Apps	Subs	Gls
West Bromwich A	Rosenborg (NOR)	08/14	14	1	9	0

GAMBRILL Brian Daniel
Born: Whitstable, Kent, England, 23 December, 1943 — G

League Club	Source	Date Signed	Seasons Played	Apps	Subs	Gls
Millwall	Whitstable	12/65	65	1	0	0

GAME Kirk Michael
Born: Leigh-on-Sea, Essex, England, 22 October, 1966 — CD

League Club	Source	Date Signed	Seasons Played	Apps	Subs	Gls
Colchester U	Southend U (App)	08/85	85-86	28	1	0

GAMMON Stephen George (Steve)
Born: Swansea, Wales, 24 September, 1939 — RH
Wales: U23-2

League Club	Source	Date Signed	Seasons Played	Apps	Subs	Gls
Cardiff C	Jnr	04/58	58-64	66	-	1

GANE Alan
Born: Chiswick, W London, England, 11 June, 1950 — M
England: Schools

League Club	Source	Date Signed	Seasons Played	Apps	Subs	Gls
Hereford U	Slough T	09/73	73	6	3	1

GANEA Ioan Viorel (Ionel)
Born: Fagaras, Romania, 10 August, 1973 — F
Romania: 45

League Club	Source	Date Signed	Seasons Played	Apps	Subs	Gls
Wolverhampton W	Bursaspor (TKY)	01/04	03-05	17	17	7

GANNON Edward (Eddie)
Born: Dublin, Republic of Ireland, 3 January, 1921 — WH
Died: Dublin, Republic of Ireland, 31 July, 1989
Republic of Ireland: 14/LoI-11

League Club	Source	Date Signed	Seasons Played	Apps	Subs	Gls
Notts Co	Shelbourne (ROI)	08/46	46-48	107	-	2
Sheffield Wed	Tr	03/49	48-54	204	-	4

GANNON James Paul (Jim)
Born: Southwark, S London, England, 7 September, 1968 — CD/M

League Club	Source	Date Signed	Seasons Played	Apps	Subs	Gls
Sheffield U	Dundalk (ROI)	04/89				
Halifax T	L	02/90	89	2	0	0
Stockport Co	Tr	03/90	89-99	350	33	52
Notts Co	L	01/94	93	2	0	0
Crewe Alex	Tr	12/00	00	5	2	0

GANNON John Spencer
Born: Wimbledon, SW London, England, 18 December, 1966 — M

League Club	Source	Date Signed	Seasons Played	Apps	Subs	Gls
Wimbledon	App	12/84	85-87	13	3	2
Crewe Alex	L	12/86	86	14	1	0
Sheffield U	Tr	02/89	88-95	162	12	6
Middlesbrough	L	11/93	93	6	1	0
Oldham Ath	Tr	03/96	95-96	6	0	0

GANNON Michael John (Mick)
Born: Liverpool, England, 2 February, 1943 — LH

League Club	Source	Date Signed	Seasons Played	Apps	Subs	Gls
Everton	Jnr	02/60	61	3	-	0
Scunthorpe U	Tr	05/62	62-63	15	-	0
Crewe Alex	Tr	10/64	64-69	205	3	2

GAPE Dominic Edward
Born: Bridport, Dorset, England, 9 September, 1994 — M

League Club	Source	Date Signed	Seasons Played	Apps	Subs	Gls
Southampton	Sch	02/13	14	0	1	0

GARBETT Terence Graham (Terry)
Born: Lanchester, County Durham, England, 9 September, 1945 — M

League Club	Source	Date Signed	Seasons Played	Apps	Subs	Gls
Middlesbrough	Stockton	08/63	65	7	0	1
Watford	Tr	08/66	66-71	196	4	46
Blackburn Rov	Tr	09/71	71-73	90	0	6
Sheffield U	Tr	02/74	73-75	26	5	0

GARBETT William Edward (Eddie)
Born: Dawley, Telford & Wrekin, England, 14 September, 1949 — RW

League Club	Source	Date Signed	Seasons Played	Apps	Subs	Gls
Shrewsbury T	App	09/67	67-68	7	4	2
Barrow	Tr	07/69	69-71	119	0	27
Stockport Co	Tr	07/72	72-73	63	7	11

GARBUTT Eric John Edward
Born: Scarborough, North Yorkshire, England, 27 March, 1920 — G
Died: Billingham, Cleveland, England, 6 January, 1997

League Club	Source	Date Signed	Seasons Played	Apps	Subs	Gls
Newcastle U	Billingham Synthonia	01/39	46-49	52	-	0

GARBUTT Luke Samuel
Born: Harrogate, North Yorkshire, England, 21 May, 1993 — LB
England: U21-11/Youth

League Club	Source	Date Signed	Seasons Played	Apps	Subs	Gls
Everton	Sch	07/10	13-14	3	2	0
Cheltenham T	L	09/11	11	34	0	2
Colchester U	L	09/13	13	19	0	2

GARBUTT Peter
Born: Corbridge, Northumberland, England, 24 December, 1939 — LH
Died: Devon, England, June, 2009
England: Amateur-1

League Club	Source	Date Signed	Seasons Played	Apps	Subs	Gls
Carlisle U	Crook T	08/64	64-70	134	2	13

GARBUTT Raymond Hardiman (Ray)
Born: Middlesbrough, England, 9 May, 1925 — CF
Died: Middleton, Derbyshire, England, 2 November, 1994

League Club	Source	Date Signed	Seasons Played	Apps	Subs	Gls
Manchester C	South Bank	09/47				
Watford	Spennymoor U	05/50	50	22	-	8
Brighton & HA	Tr	03/51	50-51	32	-	17
Workington	Tr	10/52	52	8	-	2

GARCIA Anthony (Tony)
Born: Pierrelatte, Rhone-Alpes, France, 18 March, 1972 — M

League Club	Source	Date Signed	Seasons Played	Apps	Subs	Gls
Notts Co	Lille OSC (FRA)	09/98	98	10	9	2

GARCIA Francisco Javier (Javi)
Born: Murcia, Spain, 8 February, 1987 — DM
Spain: 3/U21-9/Youth

League Club	Source	Date Signed	Seasons Played	Apps	Subs	Gls
Manchester C	Benfica (POR)	08/12	12-13	31	22	2

GARCIA Luis Javier
Born: Barcelona, Spain, 24 June, 1978 — W
Spain: 18

League Club	Source	Date Signed	Seasons Played	Apps	Subs	Gls
Liverpool	Barcelona (SPN)	08/04	04-06	52	25	18

GARCIA Omar
Born: Logrones, Spain, 9 July, 1983 — W

League Club	Source	Date Signed	Seasons Played	Apps	Subs	Gls
Rotherham U	CD Logrones (SPN)	08/08	08	2	0	0

GARCIA Richard
Born: Perth, Australia, 4 September, 1981 — W
Australia: 18/U23-2/Youth

League Club	Source	Date Signed	Seasons Played	Apps	Subs	Gls
West Ham U	YT	09/98	01-04	4	12	0
Leyton Orient	L	08/00	00	18	0	4
Colchester U	Tr	09/04	04-06	62	20	16
Hull C	Tr	07/07	07-11	84	30	8

GARDE Remi
Born: L'Arbresle, Lyon, France, 3 April, 1966 — DM
France: 6

League Club	Source	Date Signed	Seasons Played	Apps	Subs	Gls
Arsenal	Strasbourg (FRA)	08/96	96-98	19	12	0

GARDEN Stuart Robertson
Born: Dundee, Scotland, 10 February, 1972 — G

League Club	Source	Date Signed	Seasons Played	Apps	Subs	Gls
Notts Co	Forfar Ath	07/01	01-03	51	1	0

GARDINER Douglas (Doug)
Born: Douglas, Lanarkshire, Scotland, 29 March, 1917 — LH

League Club	Source	Date Signed	Seasons Played	Career Record Apps	Subs	Gls

Died: Bedford, England, March, 1980

Luton T	Auchinleck Talbot	05/38	46-50	121	-	1

GARDINER John
Born: Chester-le-Street, County Durham, England, 5 November, 1914 IF
Died: Chelmsford, England, June, 1997

Southend U (Am)	Holfords	05/46	46	1	-	0

GARDINER Mark Christopher
Born: Cirencester, Gloucestershire, England, 25 December, 1966 F/M

Swindon T	App	10/84	83-86	7	3	1
Torquay U	Tr	02/87	86-87	37	12	4
Crewe Alex	Tr	08/88	88-94	179	14	33
Chester C	L	03/95	94	2	1	0
Macclesfield T	Frederikstad (NOR)	10/95	97	7	0	2

GARDINER Matthew (Matt)
Born: Birmingham, England, 28 March, 1974 RB

Torquay U	YT	07/92	92	5	2	0

GARDINER William Silcock (Willie)
Born: Larbert, Falkirk, Scotland, 15 August, 1929 CF
Died: Stirling, Scotland, 5 January, 2007
Scotland: B

Leicester C	Glasgow Rangers	08/55	55-57	69	-	48
Reading	Tr	11/58	58-59	8	-	2

GARDNER Anthony Derek
Born: Stone, Staffordshire, England, 19 September, 1980 CD
England: 1/U21-1

Port Vale	YT	07/98	98-99	40	1	4
Tottenham H	Tr	01/00	00-07	94	20	2
Hull C	Tr	07/08	08-10	32	0	0
Crystal Palace	L	08/10	10	26	2	1
Crystal Palace	Tr	08/11	11	25	3	0
Sheffield Wed	Tr	07/12	12-13	42	0	0

GARDNER Charles Claridge (Charlie)
Born: Dundee, Scotland, 17 March, 1925 RH/IF

Aldershot	St Mirren	08/50	50	6	-	0

GARDNER Charles Donald (Don)
Born: Kingston, Jamaica, 30 August, 1955 M

Wolverhampton W	App	08/73	74	1	2	0

GARDNER Craig
Born: Solihull, West Midlands, England, 25 November, 1986 M/RB
England: U21-14

Aston Villa	Sch	02/05	05-09	32	27	5
Birmingham C	Tr	01/10	09-10	35	7	9
Sunderland	Tr	06/11	11-13	61	20	11
West Bromwich A	Tr	05/14	14	30	5	3

GARDNER Daniel Keith (Dan)
Born: Manchester, England, 1 May, 1990 M

Crewe Alex	Flixton	02/10	09	0	2	0
Chesterfield	FC Halifax T	01/14	13-14	19	14	4
Tranmere Rov	L	03/15	14	2	2	2

GARDNER Frederick Charles (Fred)
Born: Coventry, England, 4 June, 1922 IF
Died: Coventry, England, 12 January, 1979

Birmingham C		09/40				
Coventry C	Tr	05/46	46-48	13	-	3
Newport Co	Tr	05/49	49	4	-	2

GARDNER Gary
Born: Solihull, West Midlands, England, 29 June, 1992 M
England: U21-5/Youth

Aston Villa	Sch	10/09	11-12	5	11	0
Coventry C	L	11/11	11	4	0	1
Sheffield Wed	L	02/14	13	3	0	0
Brighton & HA	L	08/14	14	14	3	2
Nottingham F	L	01/15	14	16	2	4

GARDNER James Francis (Jimmy)
Born: Dunfermline, Fife, Scotland, 27 September, 1967 LW

Scarborough	St Mirren	08/95	95	5	1	1
Cardiff C	Tr	09/95	95-96	51	12	5
Exeter C	Tr	07/97	97-98	42	8	1

GARDNER Paul Anthony
Born: Southport, Merseyside, England, 22 September, 1957 RB

Blackpool	App	09/75	76-81	149	3	1
Bury	Tr	08/82	82-83	90	0	0
Swansea C	Tr	10/84	84	4	0	0
Wigan Ath	Preston NE (NC)	01/85	84	5	0	0

GARDNER Ricardo Wayne
Born: Kingston, Jamaica, 25 September, 1978 M/LB
Jamaica: 112

Bolton W	Harbour View (JAM)	08/98	98-11	281	61	20
Preston NE	L	03/11	10	4	0	0

GARDNER Robert Lee (Lee)
Born: Ayr, Scotland, 11 July, 1970 M

Oxford U (L)	Aberdeen	03/91	90	2	5	0

GARDNER Ross
Born: South Shields, Tyne and Wear, England, 15 December, 1985 M
England: Youth

Newcastle U	Sch	05/02				
Nottingham F	Tr	08/03	03-05	16	12	0
Port Vale	Tr	11/06	06	12	4	1

GARDNER Scott Andrew
Born: Luxembourg City, Luxembourg, 1 April, 1988 RW
England: Youth

Leeds U	Sch	04/06	07	1	0	0

GARDNER Stephen David (Steve)
Born: Hemsworth, West Yorkshire, England, 7 October, 1958 M
England: Schools

Ipswich T	App	10/75				
Oldham Ath	Tr	12/77	77-80	41	12	2

GARDNER Stephen George (Steve)
Born: Middlesbrough, England, 3 July, 1968 CD

Manchester U	App	07/86				
Burnley	Tr	07/87	87-89	93	2	0
Bradford C	Glossop North End	08/91	91	14	0	0
Bury		10/92	92	1	0	0

GARDNER Thomas
Born: Liverpool, England, 17 March, 1923 RW

Liverpool	South Liverpool	10/46				
Everton	Tr	06/47	47	1	-	0

GARDNER Thomas (Tommy)
Born: Huyton, Merseyside, England, 28 May, 1910 RH
Died: Chester, England, 1970
England: 2

Liverpool	Orrell	04/29	29	5	-	0
Grimsby T	Tr	06/31	31	13	-	0
Hull C	Tr	05/32	32-33	66	-	2
Aston Villa	Tr	02/34	33-37	77	-	1
Burnley	Tr	04/38	38	39	-	3
Wrexham	Tr	12/45	46	33	-	4

GARDOS Florin
Born: Satu Mare, Romania, 29 October, 1988 CD
Romania: 14/U21-9/Youth

Southampton	Steaua Bucharest (ROM)	08/14	14	5	6	0

GARGAN John
Born: York, England, 6 June, 1928 WH
Died: Keswick, Cumbria, England, 4 February, 2007

York C	Cliftonville, York	08/45	46	1	-	0

GARGAN Samuel Joseph (Sam)
Born: Brighton, England, 24 January, 1989 F

Brighton & HA	Sch	06/07	07	0	1	0

GARIANI Moshe
Born: Tiberias, Israel, 18 June, 1957 M
Israel: 11

Brighton & HA	Maccabi Netanya (ISR)	06/80	80	0	1	0

GARLAND Christopher Stephen (Chris)
Born: Bristol, England, 24 April, 1949 F
England: U23-1

Bristol C	App	05/66	66-71	142	1	31
Chelsea	Tr	09/71	71-74	89	3	22
Leicester C	Tr	02/75	74-76	52	3	15
Bristol C	Tr	12/76	76-82	53	11	11

GARLAND David
Born: Grimsby, North Lincolnshire, England, 18 June, 1948 CF

Grimsby T	Jnr	07/65	65	2	0	0
Scunthorpe U	Tr	07/67				

GARLAND Peter John
Born: Croydon, S London, England, 20 January, 1971 M
England: Youth

Tottenham H	YT	07/89	90	0	1	0
Newcastle U	Tr	03/92	91	0	2	0
Charlton Ath	Tr	12/92	92-95	40	13	2
Wycombe W	L	03/95	94	5	0	0
Leyton Orient	Tr	07/96	96	13	8	0

GARLAND Ronald (Ron)
Born: Middlesbrough, England, 28 July, 1931 — CF
Died: Oldham, Greater Manchester, England, 4 April, 1989

League Club	Source	Date Signed	Seasons Played	Apps	Subs	Gls
Oldham Ath	South Bank St Peter's	12/51	54-55	9	-	3

GARMSTON Bradley Jordan
Born: Chorley, Lancashire, England, 18 January, 1994 — LB
Republic of Ireland: U21-1/Youth

League Club	Source	Date Signed	Seasons Played	Apps	Subs	Gls
West Bromwich A	Sch	01/13				
Colchester U	L	02/13	12	10	3	0
Gillingham	L	01/15	14	7	1	1

GARNER Alan Henry
Born: Lambeth, S London, England, 2 February, 1951 — CD

League Club	Source	Date Signed	Seasons Played	Apps	Subs	Gls
Millwall	App	02/69	70	2	0	0
Luton T	Tr	07/71	71-74	88	0	3
Watford	Tr	02/75	74-79	200	0	15
Portsmouth	Tr	02/80	79-81	36	0	2

GARNER Andrew (Andy)
Born: Stonebroom, Derbyshire, England, 8 March, 1966 — F/M

League Club	Source	Date Signed	Seasons Played	Apps	Subs	Gls
Derby Co	App	12/83	83-87	48	23	17
Blackpool	Tr	08/88	88-92	151	8	37

GARNER Darren John
Born: Plymouth, England, 10 December, 1971 — M

League Club	Source	Date Signed	Seasons Played	Apps	Subs	Gls
Plymouth Arg	YT	03/89	88-92	22	5	1
Rotherham U	Dorchester T	06/95	95-04	248	16	23
Torquay U	Tr	03/05	04-06	56	4	3

GARNER Glyn
Born: Pontypool, Torfaen, Wales, 9 December, 1976 — G
Wales: 1

League Club	Source	Date Signed	Seasons Played	Apps	Subs	Gls
Bury	Llanelli	07/00	01-04	124	2	0
Leyton Orient	Tr	07/05	05-06	86	0	0
Shrewsbury T	Tr	07/07	07-08	45	0	0

GARNER Joseph Alan (Joe)
Born: Blackburn, Greater Manchester, England, 12 April, 1988 — F
England: Youth

League Club	Source	Date Signed	Seasons Played	Apps	Subs	Gls
Blackburn Rov	Sch	04/05				
Carlisle U	Tr	01/07	06-07	47	2	19
Nottingham F	Tr	07/08	08-11	34	14	9
Huddersfield T	L	07/10	10	10	6	0
Scunthorpe U	L	01/11	10	17	1	6
Watford	Tr	08/11	11-12	16	8	1
Carlisle U	L	09/12	12	15	1	7
Preston NE	Tr	01/13	12-14	72	14	43

GARNER Louis
Born: Manchester, England, 31 October, 1994 — M

League Club	Source	Date Signed	Seasons Played	Apps	Subs	Gls
Coventry C	Sch	07/13	13	0	3	0

GARNER Paul
Born: Edlington, South Yorkshire, England, 1 December, 1955 — LB
England: Youth

League Club	Source	Date Signed	Seasons Played	Apps	Subs	Gls
Huddersfield T	App	12/72	72-75	96	0	2
Sheffield U	Tr	11/75	75-83	248	3	7
Gillingham	L	09/83	83	5	0	0
Mansfield T	Tr	09/84	84-88	102	9	8

GARNER Simon
Born: Boston, Lincolnshire, England, 23 November, 1959 — F

League Club	Source	Date Signed	Seasons Played	Apps	Subs	Gls
Blackburn Rov	App	07/78	78-91	455	29	168
West Bromwich A	Tr	08/92	92-93	25	8	8
Wycombe W	Tr	02/94	93-95	53	13	15
Torquay U	L	01/96	95	10	1	1

GARNER Timothy (Tim)
Born: Hitchin, Hertfordshire, England, 30 March, 1961 — G

League Club	Source	Date Signed	Seasons Played	Apps	Subs	Gls
Northampton T	AP Leamington	03/86	85	2	0	0

GARNER William (Willie)
Born: Stirling, Scotland, 24 July, 1955 — CD

League Club	Source	Date Signed	Seasons Played	Apps	Subs	Gls
Rochdale (L)	Glasgow Celtic	10/82	82	4	0	0

GARNER William David (Bill)
Born: Leicester, England, 14 December, 1947 — F

League Club	Source	Date Signed	Seasons Played	Apps	Subs	Gls
Notts Co	Jnr	07/66	66	2	0	0
Southend U	Bedford T	11/69	69-72	101	1	41
Chelsea	Tr	09/72	72-78	94	11	31
Cambridge U	Tr	11/78	78-79	17	7	3
Brentford	Bedford T	08/83	83	2	1	1

GARNETT Malcolm John
Born: Wickersley, South Yorkshire, England, 8 September, 1943 — CH

League Club	Source	Date Signed	Seasons Played	Apps	Subs	Gls
Doncaster Rov	Jnr	07/61	61	1	-	0

GARNETT Shaun Maurice
Born: Wallasey, Wirral, England, 22 November, 1969 — CD

League Club	Source	Date Signed	Seasons Played	Apps	Subs	Gls
Tranmere Rov	YT	06/88	87-95	110	2	5
Chester C	L	10/92	92	9	0	0
Preston NE	L	12/92	92	10	0	2
Wigan Ath	L	02/93	92	13	0	1
Swansea C	Tr	03/96	95-96	15	0	0
Oldham Ath	Tr	09/96	96-01	165	8	9

GARNEYS Thomas Thurston (Tommy)
Born: Leyton, NE London, England, 25 August, 1923 — CF
Died: Basildon, England, March, 2007

League Club	Source	Date Signed	Seasons Played	Apps	Subs	Gls
Notts Co	Leytonstone	08/48				
Brentford	Chingford T	12/49	49-50	12	-	2
Ipswich T	Tr	05/51	51-58	248	-	123

GARNHAM Stuart Edward
Born: Selby, North Yorkshire, England, 30 November, 1955 — G

League Club	Source	Date Signed	Seasons Played	Apps	Subs	Gls
Wolverhampton W	App	12/73				
Northampton T	L	09/74	74	1	0	0
Peterborough U	Tr	03/77	76	2	0	0
Northampton T	L	08/77	77	11	0	0

GARRARD Luke Edward
Born: Barnet, N London, England, 22 September, 1985 — M/RB

League Club	Source	Date Signed	Seasons Played	Apps	Subs	Gls
Swindon T	Tottenham H (Jnr)	07/02	02-04	8	3	0

GARRATT Benjamin Jack (Ben)
Born: Market Drayton, Shropshire, England, 25 April, 1994 — G
England: Youth

League Club	Source	Date Signed	Seasons Played	Apps	Subs	Gls
Crewe Alex	Sch	07/11	12-14	57	0	0

GARRATT Geoffrey (Geoff)
Born: Whitehaven, Cumbria, England, 2 February, 1930 — LW
Died: Barrow, Cumbria, England, February, 1999

League Club	Source	Date Signed	Seasons Played	Apps	Subs	Gls
Barrow	Barrow Social	09/51	52	2	-	0
Workington	Tr	08/53	53	2	-	0

GARRATT Martin Blake George
Born: York, England, 22 February, 1980 — M
Died: Middlesbrough, England, 24 October, 2014

League Club	Source	Date Signed	Seasons Played	Apps	Subs	Gls
York C	YT	07/98	98-99	35	10	1
Mansfield T	Tr	03/00	99	4	2	0
Lincoln C	St Patrick's Ath (ROI)	12/00	00	2	0	0

GARRETT Archibald Campbell Elson (Archie)
Born: Lesmahagow, Lanarkshire, Scotland, 17 June, 1919 — CF
Died: Bristol, England, 10 April, 1994

League Club	Source	Date Signed	Seasons Played	Apps	Subs	Gls
Preston NE	Airdrieonians	12/37	37	2	-	2
Northampton T	Heart of Midlothian	09/46	46-47	51	-	35
Birmingham C	Tr	12/47	47-48	19	-	5
Northampton T	Tr	12/48	48-50	43	-	15

GARRETT James Edward (Jim)
Born: Dumfries, Scotland, 15 March, 1939 — W
Died: Rhyl, Denbighshire, Wales, 25 February, 2014

League Club	Source	Date Signed	Seasons Played	Apps	Subs	Gls
Carlisle U	Queen of the South	08/63	63	1	-	0

GARRETT Leonard George (Len)
Born: Hackney, E London, England, 14 May, 1936 — FB
England: Youth

League Club	Source	Date Signed	Seasons Played	Apps	Subs	Gls
Arsenal	Eton Manor	05/54				
Ipswich T	Tr	05/58	58	1	-	0

GARRETT Robert (Robbie)
Born: Belfast, Northern Ireland, 5 May, 1988 — W
Northern Ireland: 5/U21-14/Youth

League Club	Source	Date Signed	Seasons Played	Apps	Subs	Gls
Stoke C	Sch	06/06	05	0	2	0
Wrexham	L	01/07	06	10	0	0
Wrexham	L	09/07	07	9	3	0

GARRETT Scott
Born: Gateshead, Tyne and Wear, England, 9 January, 1974 — RB

League Club	Source	Date Signed	Seasons Played	Apps	Subs	Gls
Hartlepool U	YT	05/92	93-94	14	1	0

GARRETT Thomas (Tommy)
Born: South Shields, Tyne and Wear, England, 28 February, 1926 — FB
Died: Newcastle, N.S.W, Australia, 16 April, 2006
England: 3/FLge-3

League Club	Source	Date Signed	Seasons Played	Apps	Subs	Gls
Blackpool	Horden CW	10/44	47-60	305	-	3
Millwall	Tr	05/61	61	12	-	0

GARRIDO Javier
Born: Irun, Spain, 15 March, 1985 — LB
Spain: U21-9/Youth

League Club	Source	Date Signed	Seasons Played	Apps	Subs	Gls
Manchester C	Real Sociedad (SPN)	08/07	07-09	39	10	2
Norwich C	SS Lazio (ITA)	08/12	12-14	43	4	0

GARRITY Kenneth (Ken)
Born: Blackburn, Greater Manchester, England, 6 August, 1935 — F/FB

League Club	Source	Date Signed	Seasons Played	Apps	Subs	Gls
Accrington Stan		02/56	58-59	37	-	5

League Club	Source	Date Signed	Seasons Played	Apps	Subs	Gls

GARROCHO Carlos Miguel
Born: Benguela, Angola, 26 January, 1974 — LM

League Club	Source	Date Signed	Seasons Played	Apps	Subs	Gls
Walsall	Leca (POR)	08/01	01	2	2	0

GARROW Herbert Alexander (Bert)
Born: Elgin, Moray, Scotland, 24 January, 1942 — G

League Club	Source	Date Signed	Seasons Played	Apps	Subs	Gls
Newcastle U	Fochabers	02/60	60-62	4	-	0

GARRY Ryan Felix Mayne
Born: Hornchurch, E London, England, 29 September, 1983 — D
England: Youth

League Club	Source	Date Signed	Seasons Played	Apps	Subs	Gls
Arsenal	YT	07/01	02	1	0	0
Bournemouth	Tr	08/07	07-10	70	7	3

GARTH James Russell (Jimmy)
Born: Bridgeton, Glasgow, Scotland, 1 May, 1922 — IF
Died: Florida, USA, June, 1972

League Club	Source	Date Signed	Seasons Played	Apps	Subs	Gls
Preston NE	Greenock Morton	11/46	46-47	23	-	8

GARTLAND Paul
Born: Shipley, West Yorkshire, England, 8 February, 1959 — LB

League Club	Source	Date Signed	Seasons Played	Apps	Subs	Gls
Huddersfield T	App	02/77	76-78	8	0	0

GARTON William Francis (Billy)
Born: Salford, England, 15 March, 1965 — CD

League Club	Source	Date Signed	Seasons Played	Apps	Subs	Gls
Manchester U	App	03/83	84-88	39	2	0
Birmingham C	L	03/86	85	5	0	0

GARVAN Owen William
Born: Dublin, Republic of Ireland, 29 January, 1988 — M
Republic of Ireland: U21-16/Youth

League Club	Source	Date Signed	Seasons Played	Apps	Subs	Gls
Ipswich T	Sch	05/05	05-09	128	36	13
Crystal Palace	Tr	08/10	10-13	63	14	10
Millwall	L	02/14	13	13	0	0
Bolton W	L	09/14	14	3	0	0

GARVEY Brian
Born: Hull, England, 3 July, 1937 — D

League Club	Source	Date Signed	Seasons Played	Apps	Subs	Gls
Hull C	Jnr	01/58	57-64	232	-	3
Watford	Tr	07/65	65-69	179	1	2
Colchester U	Tr	06/70	70-71	75	2	1

GARVEY James (Jim)
Born: Motherwell, Lanarkshire, Scotland, 4 June, 1919 — WH
Died: South Derbyshire, England, January, 2009

League Club	Source	Date Signed	Seasons Played	Apps	Subs	Gls
Northampton T	Stewart & Lloyds	05/39				
Leicester C	Tr	06/46	46-48	15	-	0

GARVEY Stephen Hugh (Steve)
Born: Stalybridge, Greater Manchester, England, 22 November, 1973 — RW

League Club	Source	Date Signed	Seasons Played	Apps	Subs	Gls
Crewe Alex	YT	10/91	90-97	68	40	8
Chesterfield	L	10/97	97	2	1	0
Blackpool	Tr	07/98	98-99	7	10	1

GARVIE John (Johnny)
Born: Bellshill, Lanarkshire, Scotland, 16 October, 1927 — CF
Died: Corby, Northamptonshire, England, 3 January, 1996

League Club	Source	Date Signed	Seasons Played	Apps	Subs	Gls
Preston NE	Hibernian	08/49	49	5	-	0
Lincoln C	Tr	08/50	50-55	184	-	78
Carlisle U	Tr	05/56	56	25	-	6

GARWOOD Colin Arthur
Born: Heacham, Norfolk, England, 29 June, 1949 — F
England: Youth

League Club	Source	Date Signed	Seasons Played	Apps	Subs	Gls
Peterborough U	Jnr	07/67	67-70	58	8	30
Oldham Ath	Tr	07/71	71-74	84	9	35
Huddersfield T	Tr	12/74	74-75	22	6	8
Colchester U	Tr	02/76	75-77	83	4	25
Portsmouth	Tr	03/78	77-79	62	9	34
Aldershot	Tr	02/80	79-81	79	2	25

GARWOOD Jason
Born: Birmingham, England, 23 March, 1969 — LW

League Club	Source	Date Signed	Seasons Played	Apps	Subs	Gls
Leicester C	App	03/87				
Northampton T	L	09/88	88	5	1	0

GARWOOD Leonard Frank (Len)
Born: Ranikhet, India, 28 July, 1923 — WH
Died: Biggleswade, Bedfordshire, England, 16 July, 1979

League Club	Source	Date Signed	Seasons Played	Apps	Subs	Gls
Tottenham H	Hitchin T	05/46	48	2	-	0

GASCOIGNE Paul John
Born: Gateshead, Tyne and Wear, England, 27 May, 1967 — M
England: 57/B-4/U21-13/Youth

League Club	Source	Date Signed	Seasons Played	Apps	Subs	Gls
Newcastle U	App	05/85	84-87	83	9	21
Tottenham H	Tr	07/88	88-90	91	1	19
Middlesbrough	Glasgow Rangers	03/98	97-99	39	2	4
Everton	Tr	07/00	00-01	18	14	1
Burnley	Tr	03/02	01	3	3	0
Boston U	Gansu Tianma (CHN)	07/04	04	2	2	0

GASKELL Alexander (Alec)
Born: Leigh, Greater Manchester, England, 30 July, 1932 — CF
Died: Bolton, Greater Manchester, England, 14 March, 2014

League Club	Source	Date Signed	Seasons Played	Apps	Subs	Gls
Southport	Manchester U (Am)	11/52	51-53	44	-	18
Newcastle U	Tr	10/53	53	1	-	0
Mansfield T	Tr	06/54	54-55	42	-	17
Tranmere Rov	Grantham	06/57	57	6	-	6

GASKELL Edward (Ted)
Born: Bredbury, Greater Manchester, England, 19 December, 1916 — G
Died: Maidenhead, Berkshire, England, 10 February, 2009

League Club	Source	Date Signed	Seasons Played	Apps	Subs	Gls
Chesterfield	Stockport Co (Am)	06/36				
Brentford	Tr	05/38	47-51	34	-	0

GASKELL John David (David)
Born: Wigan, Greater Manchester, England, 5 October, 1940 — G
England: Youth/Schools

League Club	Source	Date Signed	Seasons Played	Apps	Subs	Gls
Manchester U	Jnr	10/57	57-66	96	0	0
Wrexham	Wigan Ath	06/69	69-71	95	0	0

GASKELL Ronald (Ronnie)
Born: Walkden, Greater Manchester, England, 1 March, 1926 — WH
Died: Salford, England, September, 2004

League Club	Source	Date Signed	Seasons Played	Apps	Subs	Gls
Southport	Walkden Yard	05/50	49-50	2	-	0

GASMI Romain
Born: Lyon, France, 15 February, 1987 — M

League Club	Source	Date Signed	Seasons Played	Apps	Subs	Gls
Southampton (L)	Strasbourg (FRA)	09/08	08	0	4	0

GASTON Raymond (Ray)
Born: Belfast, Northern Ireland, 22 December, 1946 — CF
Northern Ireland: 1/U23-1

League Club	Source	Date Signed	Seasons Played	Apps	Subs	Gls
Wolverhampton W	Coleraine	05/65				
Oxford U	Coleraine	09/68	68	12	0	2
Lincoln C	L	02/70	69	4	0	1

GATE Kenneth Bruce (Ken)
Born: Hartlepool, Cleveland, England, 26 October, 1948 — FB

League Club	Source	Date Signed	Seasons Played	Apps	Subs	Gls
Hartlepool U (Am)	St Joseph's	08/68	68	1	0	0

GATER Roy
Born: Chesterton, Potteries, England, 22 June, 1940 — CH

League Club	Source	Date Signed	Seasons Played	Apps	Subs	Gls
Port Vale	Jnr	04/60	60-61	5	-	0
Bournemouth	Tr	07/62	62-68	216	0	3
Crewe Alex	Tr	01/69	68-72	156	0	5

GATES Eric Lazenby
Born: Ferryhill, County Durham, England, 28 June, 1955 — F
England: 2

League Club	Source	Date Signed	Seasons Played	Apps	Subs	Gls
Ipswich T	App	10/72	73-84	267	29	73
Sunderland	Tr	08/85	85-89	163	18	43
Carlisle U	Tr	06/90	90	33	5	8

GATES William Lazenby (Bill)
Born: Ferryhill, County Durham, England, 8 May, 1944 — CD
England: Youth

League Club	Source	Date Signed	Seasons Played	Apps	Subs	Gls
Middlesbrough	Jnr	10/61	61-73	277	6	12

GATTING Joseph Stephen (Joe)
Born: Brighton, England, 25 November, 1987 — F

League Club	Source	Date Signed	Seasons Played	Apps	Subs	Gls
Brighton & HA	Sch	04/06	05-07	15	29	4

GATTING Stephen Paul (Steve)
Born: Willesden, NW London, England, 29 May, 1959 — CD/M

League Club	Source	Date Signed	Seasons Played	Apps	Subs	Gls
Arsenal	App	03/77	78-80	50	8	5
Brighton & HA	Tr	09/81	81-90	313	3	19
Charlton Ath	Tr	08/91	91-92	61	3	3

GAUDEN Allan
Born: Ashington, Northumberland, England, 20 November, 1944 — W/M

League Club	Source	Date Signed	Seasons Played	Apps	Subs	Gls
Sunderland	Langley Park Jnrs	03/62	65-67	40	3	6
Darlington	Tr	10/68	68-71	124	3	39
Grimsby T	Tr	02/72	71-72	54	1	12
Hartlepool U	Tr	08/73	73-74	63	0	15
Gillingham	Tr	12/74	74-75	41	0	3

GAUDINO Maurizio
Born: Mannheim, Germany, 12 December, 1966 — M
Germany: 5

League Club	Source	Date Signed	Seasons Played	Apps	Subs	Gls
Manchester C (L)	Eintracht F'furt (GER)	12/94	94	17	3	3

GAUGHAN Steven Edward (Steve)
Born: Doncaster, South Yorkshire, England, 14 April, 1970 — M

League Club	Source	Date Signed	Seasons Played	Apps	Subs	Gls
Doncaster Rov	Hatfield Main	01/88	87-89	42	25	3
Sunderland	Tr	07/90				
Darlington	Tr	01/92	91-95	159	12	15
Chesterfield	Tr	08/96	96-97	16	4	0
Darlington	Tr	11/97	97-98	35	12	3
Halifax T	Tr	07/99	99-00	35	12	1

GAULD James (Jimmy)
Born: Aberdeen, Scotland, 9 May, 1931 — IF
Died: Westminster, Central London, England, 9 December, 2004
Republic of Ireland: LoI-2

League Club	Source	Date Signed	Seasons Played	Apps	Subs	Gls
Charlton Ath	Waterford (ROI)	05/55	55-56	47	-	21
Everton	Tr	10/56	56	23	-	7
Plymouth Arg	Tr	10/57	57-58	64	-	25
Swindon T	Tr	08/59	59	40	-	14
Mansfield T	St Johnstone	11/60	60	4	-	3

GAVAN John Thomas
Born: Walsall, West Midlands, England, 8 December, 1939 — G

League Club	Source	Date Signed	Seasons Played	Apps	Subs	Gls
Aston Villa	Walsall Wood	11/62	62-65	9	0	0
Doncaster Rov	Tr	07/67	67-68	21	0	0

GAVILAN Zarate Diego Antonio (Diego)
Born: Ascuncion, Paraguay, 1 March, 1980 — M
Paraguay: 43

League Club	Source	Date Signed	Seasons Played	Apps	Subs	Gls
Newcastle U	Cerro Porteno (PAR)	02/00	99-00	2	5	1

GAVIN Jason Joseph
Born: Dublin, Republic of Ireland, 14 March, 1980 — CD
Republic of Ireland: U21-6/Youth

League Club	Source	Date Signed	Seasons Played	Apps	Subs	Gls
Middlesbrough	YT	03/97	98-01	19	12	0
Grimsby T	L	11/02	02	8	2	0
Huddersfield T	L	03/03	02	10	0	1
Bradford C	Tr	07/03	03-04	38	3	0

GAVIN John Thomas (Johnny)
Born: Limerick, Republic of Ireland, 20 April, 1928 — RW
Died: Cambridge, England, 18 September, 2007
Republic of Ireland: 7

League Club	Source	Date Signed	Seasons Played	Apps	Subs	Gls
Norwich C	Limerick (ROI)	08/48	48-54	203	-	76
Tottenham H	Tr	10/54	54-55	32	-	15
Norwich C	Tr	11/55	55-57	109	-	46
Watford	Tr	07/58	58	43	-	12
Crystal Palace	Tr	05/59	59-60	66	-	15

GAVIN Mark Wilson
Born: Baillieston, Glasgow, Scotland, 10 December, 1963 — W

League Club	Source	Date Signed	Seasons Played	Apps	Subs	Gls
Leeds U	App	12/81	82-84	20	10	3
Hartlepool U	L	03/85	84	7	0	1
Carlisle U	Tr	07/85	85	12	1	1
Bolton W	Tr	03/86	85-86	48	1	3
Rochdale	Tr	08/87	87	23	0	6
Bristol C	Heart of Midlothian	10/88	88-89	62	7	6
Watford	Tr	08/90	90	8	5	0
Bristol C	Tr	12/91	91-93	34	7	2
Exeter C	Tr	02/94	93-95	73	4	4
Scunthorpe U	Tr	08/96	96	10	1	0
Hartlepool U	Tr	09/97	97	0	3	0

GAVIN Patrick John (Pat)
Born: Hammersmith, W London, England, 5 June, 1967 — F

League Club	Source	Date Signed	Seasons Played	Apps	Subs	Gls
Gillingham	Hanwell T	03/89	88	13	0	7
Leicester C	Tr	06/89	90	1	2	0
Gillingham	L	09/89	89	18	16	1
Peterborough U	Tr	03/91	90-92	18	5	5
Northampton T	Barnet (NC)	02/93	92	13	1	4
Wigan Ath	Tr	07/93	93-94	37	5	8

GAVIN Patrick Joseph Edward (Paddy)
Born: Drogheda, Republic of Ireland, 6 June, 1929 — LB/WH
Died: Doncaster, South Yorkshire, England, 9 April, 2006
Republic of Ireland: B/LoI-2

League Club	Source	Date Signed	Seasons Played	Apps	Subs	Gls
Doncaster Rov	Dundalk (ROI)	06/53	53-59	147	-	5

GAWLER Ronald Victor (Ron)
Born: Canterbury, England, 10 July, 1924 — WH
Died: Canterbury, England, 9 March, 2011

League Club	Source	Date Signed	Seasons Played	Apps	Subs	Gls
Southend U	Canterbury C	06/49	49-50	8	-	1

GAY Daniel Karl (Danny)
Born: Kings Lynn, Norfolk, England, 5 August, 1982 — G

League Club	Source	Date Signed	Seasons Played	Apps	Subs	Gls
Southend U	Norwich C (YT)	07/01	01-02	10	1	0

GAY Geoffrey (Geoff)
Born: Romford, E London, England, 4 February, 1957 — M

League Club	Source	Date Signed	Seasons Played	Apps	Subs	Gls
Bolton W	App	01/75				
Exeter C	L	03/77	76	5	1	0
Southport	Tr	08/77	77	40	0	5
Wigan Ath	Tr	07/78	78	1	0	0

GAYLE Andrew Keith (Andy)
Born: Manchester, England, 17 September, 1970 — W

League Club	Source	Date Signed	Seasons Played	Apps	Subs	Gls
Oldham Ath	YT	07/89	88	0	1	0
Crewe Alex	Tr	02/90	89	0	1	0
Bury	Tr	08/90				

GAYLE Brian Wilbert
Born: Kingston-on-Thames, SW London, England, 6 March, 1965 — CD

League Club	Source	Date Signed	Seasons Played	Apps	Subs	Gls
Wimbledon	YT	10/84	84-87	76	7	3
Manchester C	Tr	07/88	88-89	55	0	3
Ipswich T	Tr	01/90	89-91	58	0	4
Sheffield U	Tr	09/91	91-95	115	2	9
Exeter C	Tr	08/96	96	10	0	0
Rotherham U	Tr	10/96	96	19	1	0
Bristol Rov	Tr	03/97	96-97	23	0	0
Shrewsbury T	Tr	12/97	97-98	66	0	1

GAYLE Cameron Gordon
Born: Birmingham, England, 22 November, 1992 — RB/M

League Club	Source	Date Signed	Seasons Played	Apps	Subs	Gls
West Bromwich A	Sch	07/10				
Shrewsbury T	L	11/12	12	18	0	1
Shrewsbury T	L	11/13	13	2	1	0
Shrewsbury T	Tr	07/14	14	27	1	0

GAYLE Dwight Devon Boyd
Born: Walthamstow, NE London, England, 20 October, 1990 — F

League Club	Source	Date Signed	Seasons Played	Apps	Subs	Gls
Dagenham & Red	Stansted	08/11	12	16	2	7
Peterborough U	Tr	11/12	12	28	1	13
Crystal Palace	Tr	07/13	13-14	19	29	12

GAYLE Howard Anthony
Born: Liverpool, England, 18 May, 1958 — RW
England: U21-3

League Club	Source	Date Signed	Seasons Played	Apps	Subs	Gls
Liverpool	Jnr	11/77	80	3	1	1
Fulham	L	01/80	79	14	0	0
Newcastle U	L	11/82	82	8	0	2
Birmingham C	Tr	01/83	82-83	45	1	9
Sunderland	Tr	08/84	84-85	39	9	4
Stoke C	Dallas Sidekicks (USA)	03/87	86	4	2	2
Blackburn Rov	Tr	07/87	87-91	97	24	29
Halifax T	Tr	08/92	92	2	3	0

GAYLE Ian George
Born: Welling, SE London, England, 23 October, 1992 — D

League Club	Source	Date Signed	Seasons Played	Apps	Subs	Gls
Dagenham & Red	Jnr	07/11	13-14	9	1	0

GAYLE John
Born: Bromsgrove, Worcestershire, England, 30 July, 1964 — F

League Club	Source	Date Signed	Seasons Played	Apps	Subs	Gls
Wimbledon	Burton A	03/89	88-90	17	3	2
Birmingham C	Tr	11/90	90-92	39	5	10
Walsall	L	08/93	93	4	0	1
Coventry C	Tr	09/93	93	3	0	0
Burnley	Tr	08/94	94	7	7	3
Stoke C	Tr	01/95	94-96	14	12	4
Gillingham	L	03/96	95	9	0	3
Northampton T	Tr	02/97	96-97	35	13	7
Scunthorpe U	Tr	07/98	98-99	38	11	4
Shrewsbury T	Tr	11/99	99-00	17	2	2
Torquay U	Tr	12/00	00	5	8	1

GAYLE Marcus Anthony
Born: Hammersmith, W London, England, 27 September, 1970 — F
England: Youth//Jamaica: 18

League Club	Source	Date Signed	Seasons Played	Apps	Subs	Gls
Brentford	YT	07/89	88-93	118	38	22
Wimbledon	Tr	03/94	93-00	198	38	37
Watford	Glasgow Rangers	08/01	01-04	90	12	5
Brentford	Tr	03/05	04-05	20	10	2

GAYLE Mark Samuel Roye
Born: Bromsgrove, Worcestershire, England, 21 October, 1969 — G

League Club	Source	Date Signed	Seasons Played	Apps	Subs	Gls
Leicester C	YT	07/88				
Blackpool	Tr	08/89				
Walsall	Worcester C	05/91	91-93	74	1	0
Crewe Alex	Tr	12/93	93-96	82	1	0
Chesterfield	L	10/97	97	5	0	0
Chesterfield	Rushden & D	08/99	99	29	1	0

GAYNOR James Michael (Jimmy)
Born: Dublin, Republic of Ireland, 22 August, 1928 — RW
Republic of Ireland: LoI-1

League Club	Source	Date Signed	Seasons Played	Apps	Subs	Gls
Ipswich T	Shamrock Rov (ROI)	03/52	51-52	47	-	3
Aldershot	Tr	09/53	53-57	165	-	39

GAYNOR Leonard Alfred (Len)
Born: Ollerton, Nottinghamshire, England, 22 September, 1925 — IF

League Club	Source	Date Signed	Seasons Played	Apps	Subs	Gls
Hull C	Eastwood Colliery	04/48	50	2	-	0
Bournemouth	Tr	06/51	51-53	51	-	12
Southampton	Tr	03/54	53	12	-	1
Aldershot	Tr	02/55	54-56	62	-	9
Oldham Ath	Tr	07/57	57	5	-	0

GAYNOR Ross Leon
Born: Brighton, England, 9 September, 1987 — M

League Club	Source	Date Signed	Seasons Played	Apps	Subs	Gls
Millwall	Sch	05/06	07	1	2	0

GAYNOR Thomas (Tommy)
Born: Limerick, Republic of Ireland, 29 January, 1963 F

League Club	Source	Date Signed	Seasons Played	Apps	Subs	Gls
Doncaster Rov	Limerick C (ROI)	12/86	86-87	28	5	7
Nottingham F	Tr	10/87	87-91	43	14	10
Newcastle U	L	11/90	90	4	0	1
Millwall	Tr	03/93	92	0	3	0

GAZZANIGA Paulo Dino
Born: Santa Fe, Argentina, 2 January, 1992 G

League Club	Source	Date Signed	Seasons Played	Apps	Subs	Gls
Gillingham	Valencia Jnrs (SPN)	08/11	11	19	1	0
Southampton	Tr	07/12	12-14	18	1	0

GAZZARD Gerald (Gerry)
Born: Cinderford, Gloucestershire, England, 15 March, 1925 IF
Died: Penzance, Cornwall, England, 29 September, 2006

League Club	Source	Date Signed	Seasons Played	Apps	Subs	Gls
West Ham U	Penzance	05/49	49-53	119	-	29
Brentford	Tr	01/54	53	13	-	6

GBARSSIN Marco Antoine
Born: Bordeaux, France, 11 December, 1984 DM

League Club	Source	Date Signed	Seasons Played	Apps	Subs	Gls
Carlisle U	Fredericia (DEN)	01/11				
Walsall	L	03/11	10	8	1	0

GEARD Leonard (Len)
Born: Hammersmith, W London, England, 12 February, 1934 WH

League Club	Source	Date Signed	Seasons Played	Apps	Subs	Gls
Fulham	Jnr	05/51				
Brentford	Tr	03/53	54-55	4	-	0

GEARY Derek Peter
Born: Dublin, Republic of Ireland, 19 June, 1980 RB

League Club	Source	Date Signed	Seasons Played	Apps	Subs	Gls
Sheffield Wed	Cherry Orchard (ROI)	11/97	00-03	95	9	0
Stockport Co	Tr	08/04	04	12	1	0
Sheffield U	Tr	10/04	04-09	82	12	1

GEBBIE Robert Brown Robertson (Bert)
Born: Cambuslang, Glasgow, Scotland, 18 November, 1934 G

League Club	Source	Date Signed	Seasons Played	Apps	Subs	Gls
Bradford Park Ave	Queen of the South	07/60	60-63	112	-	0

GECOV Marcel
Born: Prague, Czech Republic, 1 January, 1988 M
Czech Republic: 1/U21-18/Youth

League Club	Source	Date Signed	Seasons Played	Apps	Subs	Gls
Fulham	Slovan Liberec (CZE)	07/11	11	0	2	0

GEDDES Andrew (Andy)
Born: Motherwell, Lanarkshire, Scotland, 6 September, 1922 RH/IF
Died: New Cumnock, Ayrshire, Scotland, 2 February, 1958

League Club	Source	Date Signed	Seasons Played	Apps	Subs	Gls
Bradford C	St Cuthbert's W	06/49	49-50	30	-	4
Mansfield T	Tr	08/51	51	11	-	2
Halifax T	Tr	07/52	52-54	50	-	4

GEDDES Gavin John
Born: Hove, East Sussex, England, 7 October, 1972 F

League Club	Source	Date Signed	Seasons Played	Apps	Subs	Gls
Brighton & HA	Wick	07/93	93	7	5	1

GEDDES James George (Jim)
Born: Burntisland, Fife, Scotland, 25 May, 1942 WH

League Club	Source	Date Signed	Seasons Played	Apps	Subs	Gls
Bradford Park Ave	Third Lanark	08/65	65	1	0	0

GEDDES Paul
Born: Paisley, Renfrewshire, Scotland, 19 April, 1961 CD

League Club	Source	Date Signed	Seasons Played	Apps	Subs	Gls
Leicester C	Kilbirnie Ladeside	04/79				
Wimbledon	Hibernian	11/81	81	2	0	0

GEDDIS David
Born: Carlisle, Cumbria, England, 12 March, 1958 F
England: B-1/Youth

League Club	Source	Date Signed	Seasons Played	Apps	Subs	Gls
Ipswich T	App	08/75	76-78	26	17	5
Luton T	L	02/77	76	9	4	4
Aston Villa	Tr	09/79	79-82	43	4	12
Luton T	L	12/82	82	4	0	0
Barnsley	Tr	09/83	83-84	45	0	24
Birmingham C	Tr	12/84	84-86	45	1	18
Brentford	L	11/86	86	4	0	0
Shrewsbury T	Tr	02/87	86-88	36	3	10
Swindon T	Tr	10/88	88	8	2	3
Darlington	Tr	03/90	90	2	11	0

GEDNEY Christopher (Chris)
Born: Boston, Lincolnshire, England, 1 September, 1945 IF

League Club	Source	Date Signed	Seasons Played	Apps	Subs	Gls
Lincoln C (Am)	Holbeach U	05/62	62-65	9	0	1

[GEDO] NAGY Mohamed Afash
Born: Damanhur, Egypt, 30 October, 1984 F
Egypt: 37

League Club	Source	Date Signed	Seasons Played	Apps	Subs	Gls
Hull C (L)	Al Ahly (EGY)	01/13	12	10	2	5
Hull C (L)	Al Ahly (EGY)	09/13	13	0	2	0

GEE Alan
Born: Chesterfield, Derbyshire, England, 16 March, 1932 LW

League Club	Source	Date Signed	Seasons Played	Apps	Subs	Gls
Rotherham U (Am)	Worksop T	08/52	52	2	-	0

GEE James Percival (Jimmy)
Born: Plymouth, England, 6 June, 1933 G
Died: Tamerton Foliot, Devon, England, 21 April, 2008

League Club	Source	Date Signed	Seasons Played	Apps	Subs	Gls
Plymouth Arg (Am)	Launceston T	08/56	56	1	-	0

GEE Philip John (Phil)
Born: Pelsall, West Midlands, England, 19 December, 1964 F

League Club	Source	Date Signed	Seasons Played	Apps	Subs	Gls
Derby Co	Gresley Rov	09/85	85-91	107	17	26
Leicester C	Tr	03/92	91-95	35	18	9
Plymouth Arg	L	01/95	94	6	0	0

GEIDMINTIS Anthony Joseph (Tony)
Born: Stepney, E London, England, 30 July, 1949 D
Died: Halifax, West Yorkshire, England, 16 April, 1993

League Club	Source	Date Signed	Seasons Played	Apps	Subs	Gls
Workington	App	08/66	64-75	323	5	37
Watford	Tr	07/76	76-77	48	1	0
Northampton T	Tr	02/78	77-78	63	0	1
Halifax T	Tr	07/79	79	10	2	0

GEIJO Alexandre (Alex)
Born: Geneva, Switzerland, 11 March, 1982 F

League Club	Source	Date Signed	Seasons Played	Apps	Subs	Gls
Watford (L)	Udinese (ITA)	08/12	12	7	11	2

GEKAS Theofanis (Fanis)
Born: Larissa, Greece, 23 May, 1980 F
Greece: 76

League Club	Source	Date Signed	Seasons Played	Apps	Subs	Gls
Portsmouth (L)	Bayer Leverkusen (GER)	01/09	08	0	1	0

GELDARD Albert
Born: Bradford, England, 11 April, 1914 RW
Died: Bury, Greater Manchester, England, 9 October, 1989
England: 4/FLge-1/Schools

League Club	Source	Date Signed	Seasons Played	Apps	Subs	Gls
Bradford Park Ave	Jnr	04/30	29-32	34	-	6
Everton	Tr	11/32	32-37	167	-	31
Bolton W	Tr	06/38	38-46	29	-	1

GELSON Peter William John
Born: Hammersmith, W London, England, 18 October, 1941 CD

League Club	Source	Date Signed	Seasons Played	Apps	Subs	Gls
Brentford	Jnr	03/60	61-74	468	3	17

GEMMELL Andrew (Andy)
Born: Greenock, Inverclyde, Scotland, 27 July, 1945 LW

League Club	Source	Date Signed	Seasons Played	Apps	Subs	Gls
Bradford C	Greenock Morton	01/67	66	3	0	0

GEMMELL Eric
Born: Manchester, England, 7 April, 1921 CF
Died: Cambridge, England, 20 February, 2008

League Club	Source	Date Signed	Seasons Played	Apps	Subs	Gls
Manchester C	Manchester U (Am)	03/46				
Oldham Ath	Tr	06/47	47-53	195	-	109
Crewe Alex	Tr	02/54	53-54	14	-	5
Rochdale	Tr	09/54	54-55	65	-	32

GEMMELL James (Jimmy)
Born: Sunderland, England, 17 November, 1911 FB
Died: Birmingham, England, 11 May, 1992

League Club	Source	Date Signed	Seasons Played	Apps	Subs	Gls
Bury	West Stanley	03/30	30-38	255	-	0
Southport	Tr	08/45	46	25	-	0

GEMMELL Matthew (Matt)
Born: Glasgow, Scotland, 10 March, 1931 IF

League Club	Source	Date Signed	Seasons Played	Apps	Subs	Gls
Portsmouth	Shawfield Jnrs	09/51	53-54	3	-	0
Swindon T	Tr	10/54	54	8	-	2

GEMMELL Thomas (Tommy)
Born: Glasgow, Scotland, 16 October, 1943 FB
Scotland: 18/SLge-5

League Club	Source	Date Signed	Seasons Played	Apps	Subs	Gls
Nottingham F	Glasgow Celtic	12/71	71-72	39	0	6

GEMMILL Archibald (Archie)
Born: Paisley, Renfrewshire, Scotland, 24 March, 1947 M
Scotland: 43/U23-1

League Club	Source	Date Signed	Seasons Played	Apps	Subs	Gls
Preston NE	St Mirren	06/67	67-70	93	8	13
Derby Co	Tr	09/70	70-77	261	0	17
Nottingham F	Tr	09/77	77-78	56	3	4
Birmingham C	Tr	08/79	79-81	97	0	12
Wigan Ath	Jacksonville TM (USA)	09/82	82	11	0	0
Derby Co	Tr	11/82	82-83	63	0	8

GEMMILL Scot
Born: Paisley, Renfrewshire, Scotland, 2 January, 1971 M
Scotland: 26/B-2/U21-4

League Club	Source	Date Signed	Seasons Played	Apps	Subs	Gls
Nottingham F	YT	01/90	90-98	228	17	21
Everton	Tr	03/99	98-02	79	18	5
Preston NE	L	03/04	03	7	0	1
Leicester C	Tr	08/04	04	11	6	0
Oxford U	Tr	03/06	05	0	1	0

GENAUX Regis Herve
Born: Charleroi, Belgium, 31 August, 1973 RB
Died: Liege, Belgium, 8 November, 2008

League Club	Source	Date Signed	Seasons Played	Apps	Subs	Gls

Belgium: 22/U21-8/Youth

Coventry C	Standard Liege (BEL)	08/96	96	3	1	0

GENDALL Richard Martin (Richie)
Born: Wrexham, Wales, 25 September, 1960 — M

Chester C	App	09/78	80	4	1	0

GENNOE Terence William (Terry)
Born: Shrewsbury, Shropshire, England, 16 March, 1953 — G
England: Schools

Bury	Bricklayers Sports	04/73	72-73	3	0	0
Halifax T	Tr	05/75	75-77	78	0	0
Southampton	Tr	02/78	78-79	36	0	0
Crystal Palace	L	01/81	80	3	0	0
Blackburn Rov	Tr	08/81	81-90	289	0	0

GENOVESE Domenico
Born: Peterborough, England, 2 February, 1961 — F

Peterborough U	Cambridge C	03/88	87-88	8	8	1

GENTLE Justin David
Born: Enfield, N London, England, 6 June, 1974 — F

Luton T	Boreham Wood	07/93				
Colchester U	L	03/94	93	0	2	0

GEOHAGHON Exodus Isaac
Born: Birmingham, England, 27 February, 1985 — CD
England: Semi Pro-2

Peterborough U	Kettering T	11/09	09	17	2	1
Rotherham U	L	08/10	10	14	0	1
Shrewsbury T	L	11/10	10	2	0	0
Port Vale	L	01/11	10	11	1	0
Barnet	Tr	08/11	11	0	2	0
Dagenham & Red (L)	Darlington	11/11	11	1	1	0

GEORGE Ben William
Born: Birmingham, England, 14 November, 1993 — RB

Walsall	Sch	07/12	12	1	0	0

GEORGE Daniel Stephen (Danny)
Born: Lincoln, England, 22 October, 1978 — W

Nottingham F	YT	10/95				
Doncaster Rov	Tr	01/98	97	16	2	1

GEORGE Finidi
Born: Port Harcourt, Nigeria, 15 April, 1971 — F
Nigeria: 62

Ipswich T	RCD Mallorca (SPN)	08/01	01-02	24	11	7

GEORGE Frank Richard
Born: Stepney, E London, England, 20 November, 1933 — G
Died: Ramsgate, Kent, England, 9 July, 2007

Leyton Orient	Carshalton Ath	07/54	56-62	119	-	0
Watford	Tr	07/63	64	10	-	0

GEORGE Frederick Charles (Charlie)
Born: Islington, N London, England, 10 October, 1950 — F/M
England: 1/U23-5

Arsenal	App	03/68	69-74	113	20	31
Derby Co	Tr	07/75	75-78	106	0	34
Southampton	Minnesota Kicks (USA)	12/78	78-80	44	0	11
Nottingham F	L	01/80	79	2	0	0
Bournemouth	Bulova (HKG)	03/82	81	2	0	0
Derby Co	Tr	03/82	81	11	0	2

GEORGE Liam Brendan
Born: Luton, England, 2 February, 1979 — F
Republic of Ireland: U21-4/Youth

Luton T	YT	01/97	97-01	81	21	20
Bury	Stevenage Bor	08/02	02	3	5	1
Boston U	Tr	02/03	02	1	2	0
York C	St Patrick's Ath (ROI)	08/03	03	14	8	3

GEORGE Richard Stuart (Ricky)
Born: Barnet, N London, England, 28 June, 1946 — W

Tottenham H	App	10/63				
Watford	Tr	08/64	64	4	-	0
Bournemouth	Tr	05/65	65	2	1	0
Oxford U	Tr	07/66	66	6	0	0

GEORGE Ronald Anthony (Ron)
Born: Bristol, England, 14 August, 1922 — FB
Died: Colchester, Essex, England, October, 1989

Crystal Palace	BAC, Filton	02/47	48-53	122	-	2
Colchester U	Tr	07/54	54	6	-	0

GEORGESON Roderick Bruce (Roddie)
Born: Cairo, Egypt, 31 July, 1948 — CF

Port Vale	Bo'ness U	01/66	65-66	26	1	6

GEORGIADIS Georgios
Born: Kavala, Greece, 8 March, 1972 — RW
Greece: 63

Newcastle U	Panathinaikos (GRE)	08/98	98	7	3	0

GEORGIOU George Jordaris
Born: St Pancras, Central London, England, 19 August, 1972 — F

Fulham	Wembley	08/91	91	1	3	0

[GEOVANNI] DEIDERSON GOMEZ Geovanni Mauricio
Born: Belo Horizonte, Brazil, 11 January, 1980 — F/W
Brazil: 1/U23-6

Manchester C	Cruzeiro (BRA)	07/07	07	2	17	3
Hull C	Tr	07/08	08-09	48	12	11

GERA Zoltan
Born: Pecs, Hungary, 22 April, 1979 — M
Hungary: 81/U21-3

West Bromwich A	Ferencvaros (HUN)	08/04	04-07	104	32	21
Fulham	Tr	07/08	08-10	49	37	5
West Bromwich A	Tr	07/11	11-13	22	11	4

GERBA Ali Ngon
Born: Yaounde, Cameroon, 27 July, 1982 — F
Canada: 31/Youth

MK Dons	Ingolstadt (GER)	09/08	08	16	8	10

[GEREMI] N'JITAP FOTSO Geremi Sorele
Born: Bafoussam, Cameroon, 20 December, 1978 — RM
Cameroon: 118

Middlesbrough (L)	Real Madrid (SPN)	07/02	02	33	0	7
Chelsea	Real Madrid (SPN)	08/03	03-06	48	24	4
Newcastle U	Tr	07/07	07-09	38	11	1

GERHARDI Hugh
Born: Johannesburg, South Africa, 5 May, 1933 — IF

Liverpool	Thistle (RSA)	08/52	52	6	-	0

GERKEN Dean Jeffery
Born: Southend-on-Sea, England, 22 May, 1985 — G

Colchester U	Sch	07/04	03-08	107	2	0
Darlington	L	01/09	08	7	0	0
Bristol C	Tr	07/09	09-12	53	0	0
Ipswich T	Tr	07/13	13-14	57	0	0

GERMAIN Steven (Steve)
Born: Cannes, France, 22 June, 1981 — F

Colchester U	AS Cannes (FRA)	03/99	98-99	2	7	0

GERMAINE Gary Paul
Born: Birmingham, England, 2 August, 1976 — G
Scotland: U21-1

West Bromwich A	YT	07/94				
Scunthorpe U	L	03/96	95	11	0	0
Shrewsbury T	L	01/98	97	1	0	0

GERMAN Antonio Timothy
Born: Wembley, NW London, England, 6 February, 1986 — W

Queens Park Rgrs	Sch	07/09	08-10	5	13	2
Aldershot T	L	10/09	09	2	1	0
Southend U	L	11/10	10	3	1	0
Yeovil T	L	02/11	10	0	4	0
Brentford	Bromley	01/12	11-12	0	4	1
Gillingham	L	02/13	12	4	3	1
Gillingham	Tr	06/13	13-14	1	18	1
Northampton T	L	01/14	13	5	2	0

GERMAN David
Born: Sheffield, England, 16 October, 1973 — RB/M

Halifax T	YT	07/92	90-92	30	9	2

GERNON Frederick Anthony John (Irvin)
Born: Birmingham, England, 30 December, 1962 — D
England: U21-1/Youth/Schools

Ipswich T	App	01/80	81-86	76	0	0
Northampton T	L	11/86	86	9	0	0
Gillingham	Tr	03/87	86-87	33	2	1
Reading	Tr	09/88	88-89	21	4	0
Northampton T	Tr	10/89	89-91	47	1	1

GERRARD Anthony
Born: Huyton, Merseyside, England, 6 February, 1986 — CD

Everton	Sch	07/04				
Walsall	Tr	03/05	04-08	157	6	7
Cardiff C	Tr	07/09	09-11	57	2	3
Hull C	L	08/10	10	41	0	5
Huddersfield T	Tr	08/12	12-14	72	9	2
Oldham Ath	L	03/15	14	6	0	0

GERRARD Paul William
Born: Heywood, Greater Manchester, England, 22 January, 1973 G
England: U21-18

League Club	Source	Date Signed	Seasons Played	Apps	Subs	Gls
Oldham Ath	YT	11/91	92-95	118	1	0
Everton	Tr	07/96	96-02	89	1	0
Oxford U	L	12/98	98	16	0	0
Ipswich T	L	11/02	02	5	0	0
Sheffield U	L	08/03	03	16	0	0
Nottingham F	Tr	03/04	03-05	71	1	0
Sheffield U	Tr	09/06	06	2	0	0
Stockport Co	Rtd	08/09				
Oldham Ath	Tr	08/10	11	0	1	0

GERRARD Steven George
Born: Huyton, Merseyside, England, 30 May, 1980 M
England: 114/U21-4/Youth

League Club	Source	Date Signed	Seasons Played	Apps	Subs	Gls
Liverpool	YT	02/98	98-14	466	38	120

GERRBRAND Patrik Mikael
Born: Stockholm, Sweden, 27 April, 1981 CD
Sweden: U21-7

League Club	Source	Date Signed	Seasons Played	Apps	Subs	Gls
Leicester C	Hammarby IF (SWE)	07/05	05	14	3	0

GERRIE Sydney (Syd)
Born: Aberdeen, Scotland, 14 June, 1927 CF
Died: Inverurie, Aberdeenshire, Scotland, 9 May, 2005

League Club	Source	Date Signed	Seasons Played	Apps	Subs	Gls
Hull C	Dundee	11/50	50-56	146	-	59

GERULA Stanislaw Eugeniusz (Stan)
Born: Tarnobrzeg, Poland, 21 February, 1914 G
Died: Shepherd's Bush, W London, England, 29 August, 1979
Poland: Amateur

League Club	Source	Date Signed	Seasons Played	Apps	Subs	Gls
Leyton Orient (Am)	Carpathians (POL)	05/48	48-49	30	-	0

[GERVINHO] KOUASSI Gervais Yao
Born: Abidjan, Ivory Coast, 27 May, 1987 F/W
Ivory Coast: 71/U21

League Club	Source	Date Signed	Seasons Played	Apps	Subs	Gls
Arsenal	OSC Lille (FRA)	07/11	11-12	31	15	9

GESTEDE Rudolphe Phillipe Michel (Rudy)
Born: Nancy, France, 10 October, 1988 F
Benin: 6//France: Youth

League Club	Source	Date Signed	Seasons Played	Apps	Subs	Gls
Cardiff C	FC Metz (FRA)	07/11	11-13	10	45	7
Blackburn Rov	Tr	11/13	13-14	52	14	33

GHAICHEM James Jamal Finnigan (Jimmy)
Born: Sheffield, England, 11 April, 1984 W

League Club	Source	Date Signed	Seasons Played	Apps	Subs	Gls
Peterborough U	Handsworth FC	08/06	06	1	1	0

GHALY Hossam El Sayed
Born: Kafr El-Sheikh, Egypt, 15 December, 1981 M
Egypt: 64

League Club	Source	Date Signed	Seasons Played	Apps	Subs	Gls
Tottenham H	Feyenoord (NED)	01/06	06	17	4	1
Derby Co	L	01/08	07	13	2	0

GHAZGHAZI Sufyan Abdel-Ali Benlofti
Born: Honiton, Devon, England, 24 August, 1977 F
England: Youth/Schools

League Club	Source	Date Signed	Seasons Played	Apps	Subs	Gls
Exeter C	YT	07/96	96-97	2	13	0

GHENT Matthew Ian
Born: Burton-on-Trent, Staffordshire, England, 5 October, 1980 G
England: Youth/Schools

League Club	Source	Date Signed	Seasons Played	Apps	Subs	Gls
Aston Villa	YT	10/97				
Lincoln C	Tr	12/00	00	0	1	0
Barnsley	Forest Green Rov	08/01	01-02	8	0	0

GHILAS Kamel Fathi
Born: Marseille, France, 9 March, 1984 F
Algeria: 19

League Club	Source	Date Signed	Seasons Played	Apps	Subs	Gls
Hull C	Celta Vigo (SPN)	08/09	09	6	7	1

GHRAYIB Najwan
Born: Nazareth, Israel, 30 January, 1974 LB
Israel: 18

League Club	Source	Date Signed	Seasons Played	Apps	Subs	Gls
Aston Villa	Hapoel Haifa (ISR)	08/99	99	1	4	0

GIACCHERINI Emanuele
Born: Arezzo, Italy, 5 May, 1985 W
Italy: 21

League Club	Source	Date Signed	Seasons Played	Apps	Subs	Gls
Sunderland	Juventus (ITA)	07/13	13-14	18	14	4

GIALLANZA Gaetano
Born: Basel, Switzerland, 6 June, 1974 F

League Club	Source	Date Signed	Seasons Played	Apps	Subs	Gls
Bolton W (L)	FC Nantes (FRA)	03/98	97	0	3	0
Norwich C	Lugano (FRA)	03/00	99-00	7	7	2
Darlington	FC Aarau (SUI)	07/06	06	12	2	3

GIAMATTEI Aaron Pietro
Born: Reading, England, 11 October, 1973 M

League Club	Source	Date Signed	Seasons Played	Apps	Subs	Gls
Reading	YT	07/92	91	0	2	0

GIANNAKOPOULOS Stylianos (Stelios)
Born: Athens, Greece, 12 July, 1974 W
Greece: 77

League Club	Source	Date Signed	Seasons Played	Apps	Subs	Gls
Bolton W	Olympiakos (GRE)	07/03	03-07	86	51	20
Hull C	Tr	09/08	08	0	2	0

GIBB Alistair Stuart (Ally)
Born: Salisbury, Wiltshire, England, 17 February, 1976 RB

League Club	Source	Date Signed	Seasons Played	Apps	Subs	Gls
Norwich C	YT	07/94				
Northampton T	L	09/95	95	9	0	1
Northampton T	Tr	02/96	95-99	51	71	3
Stockport Co	Tr	02/00	99-03	157	8	1
Bristol Rov	Tr	03/04	03-05	45	19	1
Hartlepool U	Tr	08/06	06-07	16	15	0
Notts Co	L	01/08	07	9	0	0

GIBB Dean Alan
Born: Newcastle-upon-Tyne, England, 26 October, 1966 M

League Club	Source	Date Signed	Seasons Played	Apps	Subs	Gls
Hartlepool U	Brandon U	07/86	86-87	32	16	3

GIBB James Barry (Barry)
Born: Workington, Cumbria, England, 21 May, 1940 LH

League Club	Source	Date Signed	Seasons Played	Apps	Subs	Gls
Workington	Jnr	07/60	59-60	6	-	0

GIBB Thomas (Tommy)
Born: Bathgate, West Lothian, Scotland, 13 December, 1944 M
Scotland: U23-1

League Club	Source	Date Signed	Seasons Played	Apps	Subs	Gls
Newcastle U	Partick Thistle	08/68	68-74	190	9	12
Sunderland	Tr	06/75	75-76	7	3	1
Hartlepool U	Tr	07/77	77	40	0	4

GIBBENS Kevin
Born: Southampton, England, 4 November, 1979 M

League Club	Source	Date Signed	Seasons Played	Apps	Subs	Gls
Southampton	YT	01/98	97-00	5	4	0
Stockport Co	L	09/99	99	1	1	0

GIBBINS Edward (Eddie)
Born: Shoreditch, Central London, England, 24 March, 1926 CD
Died: Taunton, Somerset, England, August, 2011

League Club	Source	Date Signed	Seasons Played	Apps	Subs	Gls
Tottenham H	Finchley	09/46	52	1	-	0

GIBBINS Roger Graeme
Born: Enfield, N London, England, 6 September, 1955 M
England: Schools

League Club	Source	Date Signed	Seasons Played	Apps	Subs	Gls
Tottenham H	App	12/72				
Oxford U	Tr	08/75	75	16	3	2
Norwich C	Tr	06/76	76-77	47	1	12
Cambridge U	New England TM (USA)	09/79	79-81	97	3	12
Cardiff C	Tr	08/82	82-85	135	4	18
Swansea C	Tr	10/85	85	35	0	6
Newport Co	Tr	08/86	86-87	79	0	8
Torquay U	Tr	03/88	87-88	32	1	5
Cardiff C	Newport Co	03/89	88-92	132	10	7

GIBBON Arthur Thomas
Born: Greatham, County Durham, England, 24 May, 1937 LB
Died: Hartlepool, Cleveland, England, May, 1994

League Club	Source	Date Signed	Seasons Played	Apps	Subs	Gls
Hartlepool U		09/58	58	13	-	0

GIBBON Malcolm
Born: North Shields, Tyne and Wear, England, 24 October, 1950 M

League Club	Source	Date Signed	Seasons Played	Apps	Subs	Gls
Port Vale	App	-	66-67	4	1	0

GIBBONS Albert Henry (Jackie)
Born: Fulham, W London, England, 10 April, 1914 CF
England: Amateur/War-1

League Club	Source	Date Signed	Seasons Played	Apps	Subs	Gls
Tottenham H (Am)	Kingstonian	07/37	37	27	-	13
Brentford (Am)	Tr	08/38	38	11	-	1
Bradford Park Ave	Tottenham H (Am)	05/46	46	42	-	21
Brentford	Tr	08/47	47-48	56	-	16

GIBBONS David
Born: Belfast, Northern Ireland, 4 November, 1952 FB

League Club	Source	Date Signed	Seasons Played	Apps	Subs	Gls
Manchester C	App	08/70				
Stockport Co	L	02/72	71	1	0	0

GIBBONS Ian Kenneth
Born: Stoke-on-Trent, England, 8 February, 1970 W

League Club	Source	Date Signed	Seasons Played	Apps	Subs	Gls
Stoke C	YT	-	87	0	1	0

GIBBONS John Ronald (Johnny)
Born: Charlton, SE London, England, 8 April, 1925 CF

League Club	Source	Date Signed	Seasons Played	Apps	Subs	Gls
Queens Park Rgrs	Dartford	12/47	48	8	-	2
Ipswich T	Tr	05/49	49	11	-	3
Tottenham H	Tr	03/50				

GIBBONS Leonard (Len)
Born: Birkenhead, Wirral, England, 22 November, 1930 LB

League Club	Source	Date Signed	Seasons Played	Apps	Subs	Gls
Wolverhampton W	Jnr	02/48	51-53	25	-	0

GIBBONS Robert James (Robbie)
Born: Dublin, Republic of Ireland, 8 October, 1991 — M

League Club	Source	Date Signed	Seasons Played	Apps	Subs	Gls
Nottingham F	Jnr	10/08				
Scunthorpe U	Ermis Aradippou (CYP)	01/12	11-12	10	1	0

GIBBS Alan Martin
Born: Orpington, SE London, England, 7 February, 1934 — IF

League Club	Source	Date Signed	Seasons Played	Apps	Subs	Gls
Cardiff C		10/54				
Swindon T	Tr	05/56	56	16	-	5

GIBBS Brian Richard
Born: Gillingham, Dorset, England, 6 October, 1936 — IF
Died: 27 January, 2014

League Club	Source	Date Signed	Seasons Played	Apps	Subs	Gls
Bournemouth	Gosport Bor	10/57	57-62	58	-	15
Gillingham	Tr	10/62	62-68	259	0	101
Colchester U	Tr	09/68	68-71	153	3	38

GIBBS Derek William
Born: Fulham, W London, England, 22 December, 1934 — IF/WH
Died: Bridgend, Wales, November, 2009

League Club	Source	Date Signed	Seasons Played	Apps	Subs	Gls
Chelsea	Jnr	04/55	56-60	23	-	5
Leyton Orient	Tr	11/60	60-62	33	-	4
Queens Park Rgrs	Tr	08/63	63-64	27	-	0

GIBBS Kieran James Ricardo
Born: Lambeth, S London, England, 26 September, 1989 — LB
England: 8/U21-15/Youth

League Club	Source	Date Signed	Seasons Played	Apps	Subs	Gls
Arsenal	Sch	09/07	08-14	93	18	1
Norwich C	L	01/08	07	6	1	0

GIBBS Nigel James
Born: St Albans, Hertfordshire, England, 20 November, 1965 — RB
England: U21-5/Youth

League Club	Source	Date Signed	Seasons Played	Apps	Subs	Gls
Watford	App	11/83	83-01	385	23	5

GIBBS Paul Derek
Born: Gorleston, Norfolk, England, 26 October, 1972 — LB

League Club	Source	Date Signed	Seasons Played	Apps	Subs	Gls
Colchester U	Diss T	03/95	94-96	39	14	3
Torquay U	Tr	07/97	97	40	1	7
Plymouth Arg	Tr	07/98	98-99	30	4	3
Brentford	Tr	07/00	00-01	49	5	3
Barnsley	Tr	03/02	01-03	27	6	1

GIBBS Peter Leslie
Born: Chingola, Zambia, 24 August, 1956 — G

League Club	Source	Date Signed	Seasons Played	Apps	Subs	Gls
Watford	Tring T	07/75	75-76	4	0	0

GIBLIN Edmund John (John)
Born: Stoke-on-Trent, England, 29 June, 1923 — WH
Died: Newcastle-under-Lyme, Potteries, England, 28 January, 2000

League Club	Source	Date Signed	Seasons Played	Apps	Subs	Gls
Stoke C	Tunstall BC	04/43	47	1	-	0

GIBSON Aidan Michael
Born: Newcastle-under-Lyme, Potteries, England, 17 May, 1963 — M

League Club	Source	Date Signed	Seasons Played	Apps	Subs	Gls
Derby Co	App	05/81	80-81	0	2	0
Exeter C	Tr	07/82	82	17	1	1

GIBSON Alexander Jonathan (Alex)
Born: Plymouth, England, 12 August, 1982 — FB

League Club	Source	Date Signed	Seasons Played	Apps	Subs	Gls
Port Vale	Stoke C (YT)	07/01	01	1	0	0

GIBSON Alexander Pollock Stitt (Alex)
Born: Kirkconnel, Dumfries & Galloway, Scotland, 28 November, 1939 — CD
Died: Basford, Nottinghamshire, England, 22 November, 2003

League Club	Source	Date Signed	Seasons Played	Apps	Subs	Gls
Notts Co	Auchinleck Talbot	04/59	59-68	344	3	10

GIBSON Alexander Rose (Alex)
Born: Glasgow, Scotland, 25 January, 1925 — RB
Died: Clydebank, Dunbartonshire, Scotland, 21 April, 1993

League Club	Source	Date Signed	Seasons Played	Apps	Subs	Gls
Hull C	Clyde	03/50	49-50	21	-	0

GIBSON Alfred (Alf)
Born: Castleford, West Yorkshire, England, 9 September, 1919 — CH
Died: Rotherham, South Yorkshire, England, 13 February, 1988

League Club	Source	Date Signed	Seasons Played	Apps	Subs	Gls
Rotherham U	Army	10/45	46-53	152	-	0

GIBSON Archibald Boyle (Archie)
Born: Dailly, Ayrshire, Scotland, 30 December, 1933 — RH
Died: Scunthorpe, North Lincolnshire, England, 23 July, 2012

League Club	Source	Date Signed	Seasons Played	Apps	Subs	Gls
Leeds U	Coylton Juveniles	05/51	54-59	169	-	5
Scunthorpe U	Tr	07/60	60-63	138	-	5
Barnsley	Tr	09/64				

GIBSON Benjamin James (Ben)
Born: Middlesbrough, England, 15 January, 1993 — CD
England: U21-10/Youth

League Club	Source	Date Signed	Seasons Played	Apps	Subs	Gls
Middlesbrough	Sch	07/10	10-14	59	10	1
Plymouth Arg	L	08/11	11	12	1	0
Tranmere Rov	L	08/12	12	20	0	0
Tranmere Rov	L	03/13	12	8	0	1

GIBSON Brian
Born: Huddersfield, West Yorkshire, England, 22 February, 1928 — FB
Died: Dewsbury, West Yorkshire, England, 11 May, 2010

League Club	Source	Date Signed	Seasons Played	Apps	Subs	Gls
Huddersfield T	Paddock Ath	05/51	51-60	157	-	1

GIBSON Charles
Born: Dumbarton, Dunbartonshire, Scotland, 12 June, 1961 — M

League Club	Source	Date Signed	Seasons Played	Apps	Subs	Gls
Shrewsbury T	St Anthony's	03/81	81	2	4	0

GIBSON Colin Hayward
Born: Normanby, Cleveland, England, 16 September, 1923 — RW
Died: Stourbridge, West Midlands, England, 27 March, 1992
England: B-1/FLge-1

League Club	Source	Date Signed	Seasons Played	Apps	Subs	Gls
Cardiff C	Penarth Pontoons	04/44	46-47	71	-	16
Newcastle U	Tr	07/48	48	23	-	5
Aston Villa	Tr	02/49	48-55	158	-	24
Lincoln C	Tr	01/56	55-56	36	-	12

GIBSON Colin John
Born: Bridport, Dorset, England, 6 April, 1960 — LB/M
England: B-1/U21-1/Schools

League Club	Source	Date Signed	Seasons Played	Apps	Subs	Gls
Aston Villa	App	04/78	78-85	181	4	10
Manchester U	Tr	11/85	85-89	74	5	9
Port Vale	L	09/90	90	5	1	2
Leicester C	Tr	12/90	90-93	50	9	4
Blackpool	Tr	08/94	94	1	1	0
Walsall	Tr	09/94	94	31	2	0

GIBSON Darron Thomas Daniel
Born: Derry, Northern Ireland, 23 October, 1987 — M
Republic of Ireland: 25/U21-1/Youth

League Club	Source	Date Signed	Seasons Played	Apps	Subs	Gls
Manchester U	Sch	08/05	08-11	14	17	3
Wolverhampton W	L	11/07	07	15	6	1
Everton	Tr	01/12	11-14	36	8	2

GIBSON David
Born: Seaham, County Durham, England, 14 February, 1958 — M

League Club	Source	Date Signed	Seasons Played	Apps	Subs	Gls
Hull C	App	12/75	75-77	19	5	0
Scunthorpe U	Tr	07/78	78-79	16	6	1

GIBSON David James (Dave)
Born: Runcorn, Cheshire, England, 18 March, 1931 — RW

League Club	Source	Date Signed	Seasons Played	Apps	Subs	Gls
Everton	Jnr	08/50	50-51	3	-	0
Swindon T	Tr	11/54	54-56	70	-	6

GIBSON David Wedderburn
Born: Winchburgh, West Lothian, Scotland, 23 September, 1938 — M
Scotland: 7

League Club	Source	Date Signed	Seasons Played	Apps	Subs	Gls
Leicester C	Hibernian	01/62	61-69	274	6	41
Aston Villa	Tr	09/70	70-71	16	3	1
Exeter C	Tr	01/72	71-73	69	2	3

GIBSON Frank Alec
Born: Croxley Green, Hertfordshire, England, 7 June, 1914 — RW
Died: Watford, Hertfordshire, England, October, 2005

League Club	Source	Date Signed	Seasons Played	Apps	Subs	Gls
Watford (Am)	Rickmansworth	05/46	46	1	-	0

GIBSON Henry (Harry)
Born: Newcastle-upon-Tyne, England, 17 April, 1930 — CH
Died: New Romney, Kent, England, 20 November, 1993

League Club	Source	Date Signed	Seasons Played	Apps	Subs	Gls
Fulham	Spennymoor U	11/52	54	1	-	0
Aldershot	King's Lynn	08/56	56	3	-	0

GIBSON Ian Stewart
Born: Newton Stewart, Dumfries & Galloway, Scotland, 30 March, 1943 — M
Scotland: U23-2/Schools

League Club	Source	Date Signed	Seasons Played	Apps	Subs	Gls
Accrington Stan (Am)	Jnr	07/58	58	9	-	3
Bradford Park Ave	Tr	04/60	59-61	88	-	18
Middlesbrough	Tr	03/62	61-65	168	0	44
Coventry C	Tr	07/66	66-69	90	3	13
Cardiff C	Tr	07/70	70-72	89	1	11
Bournemouth	Tr	10/72	72-73	17	3	0

GIBSON James (Jimmy)
Born: Belfast, Northern Ireland, 4 September, 1940 — RH

League Club	Source	Date Signed	Seasons Played	Apps	Subs	Gls
Newcastle U	Linfield	01/59	58-60	2	-	1
Luton T	Cambridge U	02/65	64-65	31	1	0

GIBSON John Stephen (Steve)
Born: Huddersfield, West Yorkshire, England, 2 May, 1949 — D

League Club	Source	Date Signed	Seasons Played	Apps	Subs	Gls
Bradford Park Ave	Huddersfield T (Am)	12/67	67-68	28	4	0

GIBSON Joseph (Joe)
Born: Banknock, Falkirk, Scotland, 20 March, 1926 — IF
Died: Gipping, Suffolk, England, October, 2008

League Club	Source	Date Signed	Seasons Played	Apps	Subs	Gls
Ipswich T	Polkemmet Jnrs	09/47	48	1	-	0
West Ham U	Tr	07/49				

GIBSON Michael James (Mike)
Born: Derby, England, 15 July, 1939 — G

England: Youth

League Club	Source	Date Signed	Seasons Played	Apps	Subs	Gls
Shrewsbury T	Nuneaton Bor	03/60	60-62	76	-	0
Bristol C	Tr	04/63	62-71	331	0	0
Gillingham	Tr	07/72	72-73	80	0	0

GIBSON Neil David
Born: Prestatyn, Denbighshire, Wales, 10 October, 1979 — M
Wales: U21-3

League Club	Source	Date Signed	Seasons Played	Apps	Subs	Gls
Tranmere Rov	YT	11/97	98	0	1	0
Sheffield Wed	Rhyl	01/01				

GIBSON Paul Richard
Born: Sheffield, England, 1 November, 1976 — G

League Club	Source	Date Signed	Seasons Played	Apps	Subs	Gls
Manchester U	YT	07/95				
Mansfield T	L	10/97	97	13	0	0
Hull C	L	11/98	98	4	0	0
Notts Co	Tr	03/99	98-00	11	0	0
Rochdale	L	02/00	99	5	0	0

GIBSON Reginald (Reg)
Born: Tideswell, Derbyshire, England, 15 May, 1919 — CH
Died: Hatfield, Hertfordshire, England, January, 1991

League Club	Source	Date Signed	Seasons Played	Apps	Subs	Gls
Manchester U	Buxton	09/38				
Plymouth Arg	Tr	02/46	46	6	-	0
Exeter C	Tr	06/47	47-48	40	-	0

GIBSON Robert (Bob)
Born: Washington, Tyne and Wear, England, 29 December, 1916 — IF
Died: Chelmsford, England, December, 1995

League Club	Source	Date Signed	Seasons Played	Apps	Subs	Gls
Portsmouth		11/35				
Southend U	Hoffmann Ath	06/45	46	2	-	0

GIBSON Robert Henry (Bob)
Born: Ashington, Northumberland, England, 5 August, 1927 — CF
Died: Ashington, Northumberland, England, March, 1989

League Club	Source	Date Signed	Seasons Played	Apps	Subs	Gls
Hull C	Aberdeen	10/49	49	12	-	5
Lincoln C	Ashington	05/51	51-54	43	-	20
Gateshead	Peterborough U	03/57	56-58	49	-	22

GIBSON Robin John
Born: Crewe, Cheshire, England, 15 November, 1979 — RW

League Club	Source	Date Signed	Seasons Played	Apps	Subs	Gls
Wrexham	YT	07/98	98-01	49	28	3

GIBSON Simon John
Born: Nottingham, England, 10 December, 1964 — CD

League Club	Source	Date Signed	Seasons Played	Apps	Subs	Gls
Chelsea	App	12/82				
Swindon T	Tr	11/83	83-84	29	2	3
Preston NE	Tr	12/84	84-85	42	0	5
Rochdale	Tr	08/86	86	3	2	0

GIBSON Terence Bradley (Terry)
Born: Walthamstow, NE London, England, 23 December, 1962 — F
England: Youth/Schools

League Club	Source	Date Signed	Seasons Played	Apps	Subs	Gls
Tottenham H	App	01/80	79-82	16	2	4
Coventry C	Tr	08/83	83-85	97	1	43
Manchester U	Tr	01/86	85-86	14	9	1
Wimbledon	Tr	08/87	87-92	80	6	22
Swindon T	L	03/92	91	8	1	1
Peterborough U	Tr	12/93	93	1	0	0
Barnet	Tr	02/94	93-94	24	8	5

GIBSON Thomas Richard Donald (Don)
Born: Manchester, England, 12 May, 1929 — WH

League Club	Source	Date Signed	Seasons Played	Apps	Subs	Gls
Manchester U	Jnr	08/47	50-54	108	-	0
Sheffield Wed	Tr	06/55	55-59	80	-	2
Leyton Orient	Tr	06/60	60	8	-	0

GIBSON William (Billy)
Born: Lanark, Scotland, 24 June, 1959 — LB

League Club	Source	Date Signed	Seasons Played	Apps	Subs	Gls
Leicester C	Easthouses BC	07/79	80-81	28	0	0

GIBSON William James McNab (Bill)
Born: Glasgow, Scotland, 17 September, 1926 — RB
Died: Westminster, Central London, England, 31 January, 1995

League Club	Source	Date Signed	Seasons Played	Apps	Subs	Gls
Brentford	Arsenal (Am)	01/47				
Tranmere Rov	Tr	06/51	51-53	72	-	1

GIBSON William Michael Hubert (Billy)
Born: Harrow, NW London, England, 30 September, 1990 — LM

League Club	Source	Date Signed	Seasons Played	Apps	Subs	Gls
Watford	Sch	09/08				
Yeovil T	Tr	08/10	10-11	1	8	0

GIDDINGS Stuart James
Born: Coventry, England, 27 March, 1986 — LB
England: Youth

League Club	Source	Date Signed	Seasons Played	Apps	Subs	Gls
Coventry C	Sch	06/04	03-06	12	4	0
Oldham Ath	L	08/07	07	2	0	0
Darlington	Hinckley U	11/09	09	22	0	0

GIDMAN John
Born: Liverpool, England, 10 January, 1954 — RB
England: 1/B-2/U23-4/Youth

League Club	Source	Date Signed	Seasons Played	Apps	Subs	Gls
Aston Villa	Liverpool (App)	08/71	72-79	196	1	9
Everton	Tr	10/79	79-80	64	0	2
Manchester U	Tr	08/81	81-85	94	1	4
Manchester C	Tr	10/86	86-87	52	1	1
Stoke C	Tr	08/88	88	7	3	0
Darlington	Tr	02/89	88	13	0	1

GIER Robert James Dazo (Rob)
Born: Bracknell, Berkshire, England, 6 January, 1980 — CD
Philippines: 54

League Club	Source	Date Signed	Seasons Played	Apps	Subs	Gls
Wimbledon	YT	05/99	00-03	67	4	0
Rushden & D	Tr	07/04	04-05	64	3	2

GIGGS Ryan Joseph
Born: Cardiff, Wales, 29 November, 1973 — W/M
England: Schools//Wales: 64/U21-1/Youth

League Club	Source	Date Signed	Seasons Played	Apps	Subs	Gls
Manchester U	YT	12/90	90-13	555	117	114

GIJSBRECHTS David (Davy)
Born: Ghent, Belgium, 20 September, 1972 — CD

League Club	Source	Date Signed	Seasons Played	Apps	Subs	Gls
Sheffield U	KSC Lokeren (BEL)	08/99	99	9	8	0

GIL Carles
Born: Valencia, Spain, 22 November, 1992 — W
Spain: U21-1

League Club	Source	Date Signed	Seasons Played	Apps	Subs	Gls
Aston Villa	Valencia (SPN)	01/15	14	4	1	0

GILBERG Harold (Harry)
Born: Tottenham, N London, England, 27 June, 1923 — IF/WH
Died: Torquay, Devon, England, 16 September, 1994

League Club	Source	Date Signed	Seasons Played	Apps	Subs	Gls
Tottenham H	Jnr	09/44	46-47	2	-	0
Queens Park Rgrs	Tr	08/51	51-52	66	-	12
Brighton & HA	Tr	12/52	52-55	67	-	3

GILBERT Carl Graham
Born: Folkestone, Kent, England, 20 March, 1948 — F

League Club	Source	Date Signed	Seasons Played	Apps	Subs	Gls
Gillingham	Jnr	10/65	67-69	28	2	11
Bristol Rov	Tr	12/69	69-70	39	5	15
Rotherham U	Tr	03/71	70-73	78	16	37

GILBERT David George
Born: Smethwick, West Midlands, England, 5 August, 1940 — RW

League Club	Source	Date Signed	Seasons Played	Apps	Subs	Gls
Chesterfield	Redditch U	05/60	60	22	-	2

GILBERT David James
Born: Lincoln, England, 22 June, 1963 — M

League Club	Source	Date Signed	Seasons Played	Apps	Subs	Gls
Lincoln C	App	06/81	80-81	15	15	1
Scunthorpe U	Tr	08/82	82	1	0	0
Northampton T	Boston U	06/86	86-88	120	0	21
Grimsby T	Tr	03/89	88-94	259	0	41
West Bromwich A	Tr	08/95	95-97	46	16	6
York C	L	03/97	96	9	0	1
Grimsby T	L	08/97	97	5	0	0

GILBERT Eric Peter (Peter)
Born: Newcastle-upon-Tyne, England, 31 July, 1983 — LB
Wales: U21-12

League Club	Source	Date Signed	Seasons Played	Apps	Subs	Gls
Birmingham C	Sch	07/02				
Plymouth Arg	Tr	07/03	03-04	78	0	1
Leicester C	Tr	07/05	05	4	1	0
Sheffield Wed	Tr	11/05	05-08	39	2	0
Doncaster Rov	L	01/07	06	4	0	0
Oldham Ath	L	08/09	09	5	0	0
Northampton T	Tr	11/09	09	30	0	0
Southend U	Tr	08/10	10-11	55	2	3

GILBERT Kenneth Robert (Kenny)
Born: Aberdeen, Scotland, 8 March, 1975 — M
Scotland: Youth/Schools

League Club	Source	Date Signed	Seasons Played	Apps	Subs	Gls
Hull C	Aberdeen	01/96	95-96	21	11	1

GILBERT Kerrea Kuche
Born: Willesden, NW London, England, 28 February, 1987 — RB
England: Youth

League Club	Source	Date Signed	Seasons Played	Apps	Subs	Gls
Arsenal	Sch	07/05	05	2	0	0
Cardiff C	L	07/06	06	21	3	0
Southend U	L	08/07	07	5	0	0
Leicester C	L	07/08	08	33	1	1
Peterborough U	L	01/10	09	7	3	0
Yeovil T	MK Dons (NC)	08/11	11	3	5	0

GILBERT Noel Albert
Born: North Walsham, Norfolk, England, 25 December, 1931 — RW

League Club	Source	Date Signed	Seasons Played	Apps	Subs	Gls
Norwich C	North Walsham	08/55	55	1	-	0

GILBERT Philip Leonard (Phil)
Born: Sandwich, Kent, England, 11 September, 1944 — IF

League Club	Source	Date Signed	Seasons Played	Apps	Subs	Gls
Brighton & HA	Ramsgate Ath	01/62	61-63	6	-	3

GILBERT Timothy Hew (Tim)
Born: South Shields, Tyne and Wear, England, 28 August, 1958 LB/M
Died: Cleadon, Tyne and Wear, England, 25 May, 1995

League Club	Source	Date Signed	Seasons Played	Apps	Subs	Gls
Sunderland	App	08/76	76-79	34	2	3
Cardiff C	Tr	02/81	80-81	33	0	1
Darlington	Tr	08/82	82-83	62	3	3

GILBERT William Albert (Billy)
Born: Lewisham, SE London, England, 10 November, 1959 CD
England: U21-11/Youth/Schools

League Club	Source	Date Signed	Seasons Played	Apps	Subs	Gls
Crystal Palace	App	12/76	77-83	235	2	3
Portsmouth	Tr	06/84	84-88	133	7	0
Colchester U		10/89	89	26	1	0
Maidstone U	Tr	10/90	90	2	2	0

GILBERT William Arthur (Billy)
Born: Newcastle-upon-Tyne, England, 7 November, 1925 G
Died: Coventry, England, 22 July, 1998

League Club	Source	Date Signed	Seasons Played	Apps	Subs	Gls
Coventry C	Murton CW	09/48	51-52	14	-	0
Stockport Co	Snowdown CW	07/54	54	33	-	0

[GILBERTO] DA SILVA MELO Gilberto
Born: Rio de Janeiro, Brazil, 25 April, 1976 LB/M
Brazil: 32

League Club	Source	Date Signed	Seasons Played	Apps	Subs	Gls
Tottenham H	Hertha Berlin (GER)	01/08	07-08	4	3	1

[GILBERTO SILVA] SILVA Gilberto
Born: Lagoa da Prata, Brazil, 7 October, 1976 M
Brazil: 93

League Club	Source	Date Signed	Seasons Played	Apps	Subs	Gls
Arsenal	Atletico Mineiro (BRA)	08/02	02-07	153	17	17

GILBEY Alexander Scott (Alex)
Born: Dagenham, E London, England, 9 December, 1994 M

League Club	Source	Date Signed	Seasons Played	Apps	Subs	Gls
Colchester U	Sch	02/12	12-14	60	13	2

GILCHRIST Alexander (Alex)
Born: Holytown, Lanarkshire, Scotland, 28 September, 1923 RW
Died: Bellshill, Lanarkshire, Scotland, 27 June, 1989

League Club	Source	Date Signed	Seasons Played	Apps	Subs	Gls
Cardiff C	Holytown	05/48	48	1	-	0

GILCHRIST Jason Lee
Born: St Helens, Merseyside, England, 17 December, 1994 F

League Club	Source	Date Signed	Seasons Played	Apps	Subs	Gls
Burnley	Sch	04/13				
Accrington Stan	L	03/15	14	1	4	0

GILCHRIST John Skidmore
Born: Wishaw, Lanarkshire, Scotland, 5 September, 1939 RB
Died: Westminster, Central London, England, 13 August, 1991
Scotland: Schools

League Club	Source	Date Signed	Seasons Played	Apps	Subs	Gls
Millwall	Airdrieonians	03/61	60-68	279	0	10
Fulham	Tr	07/69	69	20	3	1
Colchester U	Tr	07/70	70-71	41	0	2

GILCHRIST Paul Anthony
Born: Dartford, Kent, England, 5 January, 1951 F

League Club	Source	Date Signed	Seasons Played	Apps	Subs	Gls
Charlton Ath	App	03/68	69	5	2	0
Doncaster Rov	Tr	07/71	71	22	0	8
Southampton	Tr	03/72	71-76	96	11	17
Portsmouth	Tr	03/77	76-77	38	1	3
Swindon T	Tr	08/78	78-79	10	7	6
Hereford U	Tr	03/80	79	11	0	1

GILCHRIST Philip Alexander (Phil)
Born: Stockton-on-Tees, Cleveland, England, 25 August, 1973 CD

League Club	Source	Date Signed	Seasons Played	Apps	Subs	Gls
Nottingham F	YT	12/90				
Middlesbrough	Tr	01/92				
Hartlepool U	Tr	11/92	92-94	77	5	0
Oxford U	Tr	02/95	94-99	173	4	10
Leicester C	Tr	08/99	99-00	23	16	1
West Bromwich A	Tr	03/01	00-03	89	1	0
Rotherham U	Tr	03/04	03-05	40	5	1

GILCHRIST Robert Cook (Bob)
Born: Bellshill, Lanarkshire, Scotland, 17 August, 1932 FB

League Club	Source	Date Signed	Seasons Played	Apps	Subs	Gls
Aldershot	Dunfermline Ath	06/52	52-56	47	-	0

GILDER Carlton Eric (Carl)
Born: Chelmsford, England, 25 July, 1957 F

League Club	Source	Date Signed	Seasons Played	Apps	Subs	Gls
Cambridge U	Jnr	01/75	74-75	0	2	0

GILES Albert Edgar
Born: Swansea, Wales, 4 May, 1924 WH

League Club	Source	Date Signed	Seasons Played	Apps	Subs	Gls
Bristol Rov	Jnr	05/41	46	1	-	0

GILES Christopher (Chris)
Born: Milborne Port, Somerset, England, 16 April, 1982 CD

League Club	Source	Date Signed	Seasons Played	Apps	Subs	Gls
Yeovil T	Sherborne	06/00	03	0	1	0

GILES Christopher Joseph (Chris)
Born: Dublin, Republic of Ireland, 17 July, 1928 RW
Republic of Ireland: 1

League Club	Source	Date Signed	Seasons Played	Apps	Subs	Gls
Doncaster Rov	Drumcondra (ROI)	06/50	50-51	27	-	4
Aldershot	Tr	08/53				

GILES David Charles
Born: Cardiff, Wales, 21 September, 1956 W/M
Wales: 12/U21-4/Schools

League Club	Source	Date Signed	Seasons Played	Apps	Subs	Gls
Cardiff C	App	09/74	74-78	51	8	3
Wrexham	Tr	12/78	78-79	38	0	3
Swansea C	Tr	11/79	79-81	49	5	13
Leyton Orient	L	11/81	81	3	0	2
Crystal Palace	Tr	03/82	81-83	83	5	6
Birmingham C	Tr	08/84				
Newport Co	Tr	10/84	84	28	4	1
Cardiff C	Tr	09/85	85-86	50	0	0

GILES James Archer (Jimmy)
Born: Kidlington, Oxfordshire, England, 21 April, 1946 CD

League Club	Source	Date Signed	Seasons Played	Apps	Subs	Gls
Swindon T	Kidlington	03/65	65-67	12	1	0
Aldershot	Tr	10/68	68-70	81	1	3
Exeter C	Tr	03/71	70-74	183	0	8
Charlton Ath	Tr	06/75	75-77	92	1	6
Exeter C	Tr	12/77	77-80	130	0	5

GILES John Edgar
Born: Bristol, England, 7 November, 1947 M

League Club	Source	Date Signed	Seasons Played	Apps	Subs	Gls
Bristol C	App	06/65	66	3	0	1
Bradford Park Ave	L	03/68	67	9	0	0
Exeter C	Tr	05/69	69-71	55	5	2

GILES Martin William
Born: Shrewsbury, Shropshire, England, 1 January, 1979 LB

League Club	Source	Date Signed	Seasons Played	Apps	Subs	Gls
Chester C	YT	07/97	97	8	2	0

GILES Martyn
Born: Cardiff, Wales, 10 April, 1983 LW
Wales: Youth

League Club	Source	Date Signed	Seasons Played	Apps	Subs	Gls
Cardiff C	YT	03/01	00	1	4	0
Hereford U	Carmarthen T	08/06	06	11	2	0

GILES Michael John (Johnny)
Born: Dublin, Republic of Ireland, 6 January, 1940 M
Republic of Ireland: 59

League Club	Source	Date Signed	Seasons Played	Apps	Subs	Gls
Manchester U	Home Farm (ROI)	11/57	59-62	99	-	10
Leeds U	Tr	08/63	63-74	380	3	88
West Bromwich A	Tr	06/75	75-76	74	1	3

GILES Paul Anthony
Born: Cardiff, Wales, 21 February, 1961 W
Wales: U21-3

League Club	Source	Date Signed	Seasons Played	Apps	Subs	Gls
Cardiff C	Jnr	06/79	80-82	17	7	1
Exeter C	L	03/82	81	9	0	1
Newport Co	SVV Dordrecht (NED)	12/84	84	0	1	0
Newport Co	Merthyr Tydfil	03/87	86-87	28	1	2

GILES Philip Richard (Phil)
Born: Walsall, West Midlands, England, 8 October, 1929 LW
Died: Birmingham, England, 3 September, 1999
England: Youth

League Club	Source	Date Signed	Seasons Played	Apps	Subs	Gls
Walsall	Jnr	05/48	48-52	68	-	14

GILES Terence (Terry)
Born: Halifax, West Yorkshire, England, 25 March, 1943 LW

League Club	Source	Date Signed	Seasons Played	Apps	Subs	Gls
Halifax T (Am)		09/61	61-62	3	-	1

GILFILLAN Robert (Bobby)
Born: Dunfermline, Fife, Scotland, 14 March, 1926 IF

League Club	Source	Date Signed	Seasons Played	Apps	Subs	Gls
Blackpool	Jeanfield Swifts	07/47				
Rochdale	Cowdenbeath	06/51	51-53	62	-	11

GILFILLAN Robert Inglis (Bob)
Born: Cowdenbeath, Fife, Scotland, 29 June, 1938 F
Died: Perth, Scotland, 8 November, 2012

League Club	Source	Date Signed	Seasons Played	Apps	Subs	Gls
Newcastle U	Cowdenbeath	10/59	59-60	7	-	2
Southend U	Raith Rov	06/63	63-65	65	1	33
Doncaster Rov	Tr	11/65	65-70	178	7	34

GILKES Michael Earl Glenis McDonald
Born: Hackney, E London, England, 20 July, 1965 LW
Barbados: 6

League Club	Source	Date Signed	Seasons Played	Apps	Subs	Gls
Reading	Leicester C (Jnr)	07/84	84-96	348	45	43
Chelsea	L	01/92	91	0	1	0
Southampton	L	03/92	91	4	2	0
Wolverhampton W	Tr	03/97	96-98	33	5	1
Millwall	Tr	07/99	99-00	28	4	2

GILKS Matthew (Matty)
Born: Oldham, Greater Manchester, England, 4 June, 1982 G
Scotland: 3

League Club	Source	Date Signed	Seasons Played	Apps	Subs	Gls
Rochdale	YT	07/01	00-06	174	2	0

League Club	Source	Date Signed	Seasons Played	Apps	Subs	Gls
Norwich C	Tr	07/07				
Blackpool	Tr	07/08	08-13	181	1	0
Shrewsbury T	L	11/08	08	4	0	0
Burnley	Tr	07/14				

GILL Anthony Dean (Tony)
Born: Bradford, England, 6 March, 1968 — FB/M

League Club	Source	Date Signed	Seasons Played	Apps	Subs	Gls
Manchester U	App	03/86	86-88	5	5	1

GILL Benjamin David (Ben)
Born: Harrow, NW London, England, 9 October, 1987 — M

League Club	Source	Date Signed	Seasons Played	Apps	Subs	Gls
Watford	Arsenal (Sch)	03/06				
Cheltenham T	Tr	07/07	07-08	0	7	1

GILL Colin John Peter
Born: Swindon, England, 20 January, 1933 — G

League Club	Source	Date Signed	Seasons Played	Apps	Subs	Gls
Swindon T	Garrards Ath	10/55	55	1	-	0

GILL Eric Norman
Born: St Pancras, Central London, England, 3 November, 1930 — G

League Club	Source	Date Signed	Seasons Played	Apps	Subs	Gls
Charlton Ath	Tonbridge	04/48	51	1	-	0
Brighton & HA	Tr	06/52	52-59	280	-	0

GILL Frank
Born: Manchester, England, 5 December, 1948 — LW

League Club	Source	Date Signed	Seasons Played	Apps	Subs	Gls
Manchester U	App	12/65				
Tranmere Rov	Tr	07/68	68-70	69	4	8

GILL Gary
Born: Middlesbrough, England, 28 November, 1964 — M

League Club	Source	Date Signed	Seasons Played	Apps	Subs	Gls
Middlesbrough	App	11/82	83-89	69	8	2
Hull C	L	12/83	83	0	1	0
Darlington	Tr	12/89	90-91	55	1	9
Cardiff C	Tr	03/92	91	3	3	1

GILL Jeremy Morley (Jerry)
Born: Clevedon, Somerset, England, 8 September, 1970 — RB
England: Semi Pro-1

League Club	Source	Date Signed	Seasons Played	Apps	Subs	Gls
Leyton Orient	Trowbridge T	12/88				
Birmingham C	Yeovil T	07/97	97-01	43	17	0
Northampton T	Tr	08/02	02	41	0	0
Cheltenham T	Tr	02/04	03-08	176	5	0

GILL John Barry Anthony (Johnny)
Born: Wednesbury, West Midlands, England, 3 February, 1941 — CH

League Club	Source	Date Signed	Seasons Played	Apps	Subs	Gls
Nottingham F	Jnr	03/58				
Mansfield T	Tr	07/61	61-65	138	1	0
Hartlepool U	Tr	02/66	65-70	201	3	1

GILL Joseph (Joe)
Born: Sunderland, England, 10 November, 1945 — G

League Club	Source	Date Signed	Seasons Played	Apps	Subs	Gls
Hartlepool U (Am)	Ashington	01/69	68	4	0	0

GILL Kenneth (Kenny)
Born: Swindon, England, 5 November, 1955 — RW

League Club	Source	Date Signed	Seasons Played	Apps	Subs	Gls
Newport Co	Forest Green Rov	09/85	85	13	6	1

GILL Matthew James
Born: Cambridge, England, 8 November, 1980 — M

League Club	Source	Date Signed	Seasons Played	Apps	Subs	Gls
Peterborough U	YT	03/98	97-03	121	30	4
Notts Co	Tr	06/04	04-05	45	12	0
Exeter C	Tr	01/06	08	43	0	9
Norwich C	Tr	07/09	09-10	5	7	0
Peterborough U	L	09/10	10	4	0	0
Walsall	L	01/11	10	8	0	2
Bristol Rov	Tr	07/11	11-13	42	3	0
Exeter C	Tr	10/13	13	19	5	0
Tranmere Rov	Tr	05/14	14	8	0	0

GILL Mervyn John
Born: Exeter, England, 13 April, 1931 — G
Died: Bridport, Dorset, England, September, 2007

League Club	Source	Date Signed	Seasons Played	Apps	Subs	Gls
Portsmouth (Am)	Bideford	08/53	53	6	-	0
Southampton	Woking	04/56	55	1	-	0
Torquay U	Tr	09/56	56-61	157	-	0

GILL Oliver David
Born: Frimley, Surrey, England, 15 September, 1990 — D

League Club	Source	Date Signed	Seasons Played	Apps	Subs	Gls
Manchester U	Sch	07/09				
Bradford C	L	09/10	10	4	0	0

GILL Raymond (Ray)
Born: Manchester, England, 8 December, 1924 — LB
Died: Rochdale, Greater Manchester, England, 17 September, 2001

League Club	Source	Date Signed	Seasons Played	Apps	Subs	Gls
Manchester C	Jnr	09/47	48-49	8	-	0
Chester C	Tr	06/51	51-61	406	-	3

GILL Robert
Born: Nottingham, England, 10 February, 1982 — F

League Club	Source	Date Signed	Seasons Played	Apps	Subs	Gls
Doncaster Rov	Nottingham F (YT)	08/00	03	0	1	0

GILL Wayne John
Born: Chorley, Lancashire, England, 28 November, 1975 — M

League Club	Source	Date Signed	Seasons Played	Apps	Subs	Gls
Blackburn Rov	YT	07/94				
Blackpool	Tr	03/00	99	12	0	7
Tranmere Rov	Tr	07/00	00	7	9	2
Oldham Ath	Tr	10/01	01	3	0	0

GILLARD Ian Terry
Born: Kensington, Central London, England, 9 October, 1950 — LB
England: 3/U23-5

League Club	Source	Date Signed	Seasons Played	Apps	Subs	Gls
Queens Park Rgrs	App	10/68	68-81	403	5	9
Aldershot	Tr	07/82	82-85	83	0	2

GILLARD Kenneth Joseph (Ken)
Born: Dublin, Republic of Ireland, 30 April, 1972 — LB
Republic of Ireland: U21-1

League Club	Source	Date Signed	Seasons Played	Apps	Subs	Gls
Luton T	YT	05/89				
Northampton T	Tr	03/93	92-93	22	1	0

GILLESPIE Gary Thompson
Born: Bonnybridge, Falkirk, Scotland, 5 July, 1960 — CD
Scotland: 13/U21-8

League Club	Source	Date Signed	Seasons Played	Apps	Subs	Gls
Coventry C	Falkirk	03/78	78-82	171	1	6
Liverpool	Tr	07/83	84-90	152	4	14
Coventry C	Glasgow Celtic	08/94	94	2	1	0

GILLESPIE Ian Colin
Born: Plymouth, England, 6 May, 1913 — IF
Died: Ipswich, England, March, 1988

League Club	Source	Date Signed	Seasons Played	Apps	Subs	Gls
Crystal Palace	Harwich & Parkeston	02/37	36-38	21	-	4
Ipswich T	Tr	04/46	46	6	-	1

GILLESPIE Keith Robert
Born: Larne, Antrim, Northern Ireland, 18 February, 1975 — RW
Northern Ireland: 86/U21-1/Youth/Schools

League Club	Source	Date Signed	Seasons Played	Apps	Subs	Gls
Manchester U	YT	02/93	94	3	6	1
Wigan Ath	L	09/93	93	8	0	4
Newcastle U	Tr	01/95	94-98	94	19	11
Blackburn Rov	Tr	12/98	98-02	67	46	5
Wigan Ath	L	12/00	00	4	1	0
Leicester C	Tr	07/03	03-04	26	16	2
Sheffield U	Tr	08/05	05-08	58	39	4
Charlton Ath	L	11/08	08	4	2	0
Bradford C	L	03/09	08	2	1	0

GILLESPIE Mark Joseph
Born: Newcastle-upon-Tyne, England, 27 March, 1992 — G

League Club	Source	Date Signed	Seasons Played	Apps	Subs	Gls
Carlisle U	Sch	07/10	09-14	69	1	0

GILLESPIE Norman (Norrie)
Born: Edinburgh, Scotland, 20 April, 1940 — IF

League Club	Source	Date Signed	Seasons Played	Apps	Subs	Gls
Wrexham	Falkirk	12/63	63	3	-	0

GILLESPIE Patrick (Pat)
Born: Bellshill, Lanarkshire, Scotland, 22 September, 1922 — G

League Club	Source	Date Signed	Seasons Played	Apps	Subs	Gls
Watford	Partick Thistle	07/45	46	6	-	0
Northampton T	Tr	08/47	47	1	-	0
Doncaster Rov	Tr	11/47	47-48	8	-	1

GILLESPIE Steven
Born: Liverpool, England, 4 June, 1984 — F

League Club	Source	Date Signed	Seasons Played	Apps	Subs	Gls
Bristol C	Liverpool (Sch)	08/04	04-05	4	8	1
Cheltenham T	L	01/05	04	10	2	5
Cheltenham T	Tr	11/05	05-07	52	22	24
Colchester U	Tr	07/08	08-11	46	52	25
Fleetwood T	Tr	06/12	12	9	13	4
Cheltenham T	L	08/13	13	3	1	0
Bristol Rov	Tr	02/14	13	3	10	1

GILLET Kenny Lego
Born: Bordeaux, France, 3 January, 1986 — LB

League Club	Source	Date Signed	Seasons Played	Apps	Subs	Gls
Barnet	SM Caen (FRA)	08/07	07-09	89	11	0

GILLET Stephane
Born: Luxembourg City, Luxembourg, 20 August, 1977 — G
Luxembourg: 20

League Club	Source	Date Signed	Seasons Played	Apps	Subs	Gls
Chester C (L)	RU Letzebuerg (LUX)	01/06	05	8	0	0

GILLETT David John (Dave)
Born: Edinburgh, Scotland, 2 April, 1951 — D

League Club	Source	Date Signed	Seasons Played	Apps	Subs	Gls
Crewe Alex	Hibernian	08/72	72-74	64	5	2

GILLETT Simon James
Born: Oxford, England, 6 January, 1985 — M

League Club	Source	Date Signed	Seasons Played	Apps	Subs	Gls
Southampton	Sch	11/03	07-09	23	8	0
Walsall	L	09/05	05	2	0	0
Blackpool	L	08/06	06	13	1	1
Bournemouth	L	11/06	06	7	0	1
Blackpool	L	01/07	06	7	10	0
Yeovil T	L	09/07	07	3	1	0

League Club	Source	Date Signed	Seasons Played	Apps	Subs	Gls
Doncaster Rov	L	10/09	09	10	1	0
Doncaster Rov	Tr	07/10	10-11	64	4	4
Nottingham F	Tr	08/12	12	24	1	0
Bristol C	L	10/13	13	21	2	2
Yeovil T	Tr	08/14	14	14	3	1

GILLIAM Reginald Charles (Reg)
Born: Farnham, Surrey, England, 19 February, 1931 — G
Died: Fleet, Hampshire, England, 11 March, 2004

League Club	Source	Date Signed	Seasons Played	Apps	Subs	Gls
Aldershot	Farnham T	02/56	56	1	-	0

GILLIBRAND Ian Victor
Born: Blackburn, Greater Manchester, England, 24 November, 1948 — CD

League Club	Source	Date Signed	Seasons Played	Apps	Subs	Gls
Arsenal	App	12/65				
Wigan Ath	Tr	07/68	78	7	0	0

GILLIES Donald George (Don)
Born: Glencoe, Highlands, Scotland, 20 June, 1951 — FB/M
Scotland: U23-1

League Club	Source	Date Signed	Seasons Played	Apps	Subs	Gls
Bristol C	Greenock Morton	03/73	72-79	183	17	26
Bristol Rov	Tr	06/80	80-81	56	3	0

GILLIES John Crawford
Born: Glasgow, Scotland, 22 October, 1918 — LW
Died: Glasgow, Scotland, 4 November, 1991

League Club	Source	Date Signed	Seasons Played	Apps	Subs	Gls
Brentford	St Mirren	05/46	46	5	-	0

GILLIES Joshua James (Josh)
Born: Sunderland, England, 12 June, 1990 — LW
England: Semi Pro-2

League Club	Source	Date Signed	Seasons Played	Apps	Subs	Gls
Carlisle U	Gateshead	07/13	13-14	6	6	1

GILLIES Matthew Muirhead (Matt)
Born: Loganlea, West Lothian, Scotland, 12 August, 1921 — CH
Died: Nottingham, England, 24 December, 1998

League Club	Source	Date Signed	Seasons Played	Apps	Subs	Gls
Bolton W	RAF Weeton	10/42	46-51	145	-	1
Leicester C	Tr	01/52	51-54	103	-	0

GILLIGAN Augustus Anthony (Gus)
Born: Abingdon, Oxfordshire, England, 19 August, 1959 — F

League Club	Source	Date Signed	Seasons Played	Apps	Subs	Gls
Swindon T	App	08/77	77	3	1	0
Doncaster Rov	L	09/78	78	1	0	0

GILLIGAN James Martin (Jimmy)
Born: Hammersmith, W London, England, 24 January, 1964 — F
England: Youth

League Club	Source	Date Signed	Seasons Played	Apps	Subs	Gls
Watford	App	08/81	81-84	18	9	6
Lincoln C	L	10/82	82	0	3	0
Grimsby T	Tr	08/85	85	19	5	4
Swindon T	Tr	06/86	86	13	4	5
Newport Co	L	02/87	86	4	1	1
Lincoln C	Tr	03/87	86	11	0	1
Cardiff C	Tr	07/87	87-89	99	0	35
Portsmouth	Tr	10/89	89	24	8	5
Swansea C	Tr	08/90	90-91	60	2	23

GILLIGAN John
Born: Abingdon, Oxfordshire, England, 2 May, 1957 — M

League Club	Source	Date Signed	Seasons Played	Apps	Subs	Gls
Swindon T	App	10/75	75-76	2	4	0
Huddersfield T	L	09/76	76	0	1	0
Northampton T	L	01/77	76	5	0	1

GILLIGAN Malcolm
Born: Cardiff, Wales, 11 October, 1942 — RW

League Club	Source	Date Signed	Seasons Played	Apps	Subs	Gls
Swansea C	Llanelli	05/62	62	3	-	0

GILLIGAN Ryan James
Born: Swindon, England, 18 January, 1987 — RW

League Club	Source	Date Signed	Seasons Played	Apps	Subs	Gls
Northampton T	Watford (Sch)	08/05	05-11	130	52	20
Torquay U	L	02/11	10	0	5	0

GILLIVER Allan Henry
Born: Swallownest, South Yorkshire, England, 3 August, 1944 — CF

League Club	Source	Date Signed	Seasons Played	Apps	Subs	Gls
Huddersfield T	Jnr	08/61	62-65	45	0	22
Blackburn Rov	Tr	06/66	66-67	32	2	9
Rotherham U	Tr	05/68	68	24	2	2
Brighton & HA	Tr	07/69	69-70	54	3	19
Lincoln C	Tr	02/71	70-71	33	4	8
Bradford C	Tr	06/72	72-73	68	2	30
Stockport Co	Tr	06/74	74	22	3	5
Bradford C	Boston U	08/78	78	1	1	0

GILLOTT Peter
Born: Barnsley, South Yorkshire, England, 20 July, 1935 — LB
England: Youth

League Club	Source	Date Signed	Seasons Played	Apps	Subs	Gls
Barnsley	Worsbrough Common U	05/53	55-58	5	-	0

GILMARTIN Rene Patrick
Born: Dublin, Republic of Ireland, 31 May, 1987 — G
Republic of Ireland: U21-1/Youth

League Club	Source	Date Signed	Seasons Played	Apps	Subs	Gls
Walsall	St Kevins BC (ROI)	08/05	05-09	34	1	0
Watford	Tr	07/10	11	2	0	0
Yeovil T	L	11/11	11	8	0	0
Crawley T	L	02/12	11	6	0	0
Plymouth Arg	Tr	07/12	12	13	0	0
Watford	St Patricks Ath (ROI)	08/14				

GILMOUR Brian Thomas
Born: Irvine, Ayrshire, Scotland, 8 May, 1987 — M
Scotland: Youth

League Club	Source	Date Signed	Seasons Played	Apps	Subs	Gls
Lincoln C	FC Haka (FIN)	11/09	09	14	2	2

GILMOUR George Reynolds
Born: Barrhead, Renfrewshire, Scotland, 7 May, 1919 — RH
Died: Barrhead, Renfrewshire, Scotland, 3 May, 1987

League Club	Source	Date Signed	Seasons Played	Apps	Subs	Gls
Halifax T	Edinburgh C	09/48	48-49	36	-	2

GILMOUR Ronald (Ron)
Born: Workington, Cumbria, England, 28 February, 1935 — LW
Died: Whitehaven, Cumbria, England, January, 2002

League Club	Source	Date Signed	Seasons Played	Apps	Subs	Gls
Workington	Jnr	12/52	53	2	-	0

GILPIN James (Jim)
Born: Edinburgh, Scotland, 12 June, 1945 — LW

League Club	Source	Date Signed	Seasons Played	Apps	Subs	Gls
Bradford Park Ave	Raith Rov	08/65	65	10	1	1

GILROY David Miles
Born: Yeovil, Somerset, England, 23 December, 1982 — F

League Club	Source	Date Signed	Seasons Played	Apps	Subs	Gls
Bristol Rov	Sch	07/02	01-03	6	13	0

GILROY Joseph (Joe)
Born: Glasgow, Scotland, 19 October, 1941 — CF

League Club	Source	Date Signed	Seasons Played	Apps	Subs	Gls
Fulham	Clyde	10/67	67-68	23	1	8

GILROY Keith
Born: Sligo, Republic of Ireland, 8 July, 1983 — LW
Republic of Ireland: U21-3/Youth

League Club	Source	Date Signed	Seasons Played	Apps	Subs	Gls
Middlesbrough	Sligo Rov (ROI)	09/00				
Darlington	Scarborough	02/05	04	1	1	0
Burton A	Tr	08/05	09-10	4	5	0

GILZEAN Alan John
Born: Coupar Angus, Perthshire, Scotland, 22 October, 1938 — F
Scotland: 22/SLge-3/U23-3

League Club	Source	Date Signed	Seasons Played	Apps	Subs	Gls
Tottenham H	Dundee	12/64	64-73	335	8	93

GILZEAN Ian Roger
Born: Enfield, N London, England, 10 December, 1969 — F

League Club	Source	Date Signed	Seasons Played	Apps	Subs	Gls
Tottenham H	YT	07/88				
Doncaster Rov (L)	Dundee	02/93	92	3	0	0
Northampton T	Dundee	08/93	93	29	4	10

GINNELLY Joshua Lloyd (Josh)
Born: Coventry, England, 24 March, 1997 — M

League Club	Source	Date Signed	Seasons Played	Apps	Subs	Gls
Shrewsbury T	Sch	-	14	0	3	0

GINOLA David Desire Marc
Born: Saint Tropez, France, 25 January, 1967 — LW
France: 17/B-2/U21

League Club	Source	Date Signed	Seasons Played	Apps	Subs	Gls
Newcastle U	Paris St-Germain (FRA)	07/95	95-96	54	4	6
Tottenham H	Tr	07/97	97-99	100	0	12
Aston Villa	Tr	08/00	00-01	14	18	3
Everton	Tr	02/02	01	2	3	0

GINTER Anthony Paul (Tony)
Born: Plymouth, England, 6 November, 1974 — M

League Club	Source	Date Signed	Seasons Played	Apps	Subs	Gls
Torquay U	YT	-	92	1	0	0

GINTY Rory Vincent
Born: Galway, Republic of Ireland, 23 January, 1977 — W

League Club	Source	Date Signed	Seasons Played	Apps	Subs	Gls
Crystal Palace	YT	11/94	97	2	3	0

GIOACCHINI Stefano
Born: Rome, Italy, 25 November, 1976 — W

League Club	Source	Date Signed	Seasons Played	Apps	Subs	Gls
Coventry C (L)	Venezia (ITA)	01/99	98	0	3	0

[GIOVANI] DOS SANTOS Giovani Alex
Born: Monterey, Mexico, 11 May, 1989 — F
Mexico: 87/U23-9/Youth

League Club	Source	Date Signed	Seasons Played	Apps	Subs	Gls
Tottenham H	Barcelona (SPN)	08/08	08-11	2	15	0
Ipswich T	L	03/09	08	6	2	4

GIPP David Thomas
Born: Forest Gate, E London, England, 13 July, 1969 — F

League Club	Source	Date Signed	Seasons Played	Apps	Subs	Gls
Brighton & HA	App	07/86	86-87	1	4	0

GIRLING Howard Milton (Dickie)
Born: Birmingham, England, 24 May, 1922 — LW
Died: Camden, N London, England, 7 January, 1992

League Club	Source	Date Signed	Seasons Played	Apps	Subs	Gls
Crystal Palace	Army	10/43	46	26	-	6
Brentford	Tr	02/47	46-49	86	-	9
Bournemouth	Tr	07/51	51	4	-	0

GIROUD Olivier
Born: Chambery, France, 30 September, 1986 — F
France: 38

League Club	Source	Date Signed	Seasons Played	Apps	Subs	Gls
Arsenal	Montpellier (FRA)	06/12	12-14	81	16	41

GISBOURNE Charles Joseph (Charlie)
Born: Bury, Greater Manchester, England, 7 October, 1952 — RB/M

League Club	Source	Date Signed	Seasons Played	Apps	Subs	Gls
Bury	App	10/70	72-74	13	3	1
Crewe Alex	Tr	10/74	74	5	1	0

GISLASON Sigursteinn (Siggi)
Born: Akranes, Iceland, 25 June, 1968 — LB
Died: Reykjavik, Iceland, 16 January, 2012
Iceland: 22

League Club	Source	Date Signed	Seasons Played	Apps	Subs	Gls
Stoke C (L)	KR Reykjavik (ICE)	11/99	99	4	4	0

GISLASON Valur Fannar
Born: Reykjavik, Iceland, 8 September, 1977 — LM
Iceland: 5/U21-15/Youth

League Club	Source	Date Signed	Seasons Played	Apps	Subs	Gls
Arsenal	Fram (ICE)	07/96				
Brighton & HA	L	10/97	97	7	0	0

GISSING John William Dennis
Born: Stapleford, Nottinghamshire, England, 24 November, 1938 — RW
Died: Nottingham, England, 6 August, 2009

League Club	Source	Date Signed	Seasons Played	Apps	Subs	Gls
Notts Co	Stapleford BC	07/56	57-60	22	-	1
Chesterfield	Tr	07/61	61	2	-	0

GITSHAM James William (Jimmy)
Born: Hammersmith, W London, England, 12 May, 1942 — LB

League Club	Source	Date Signed	Seasons Played	Apps	Subs	Gls
Brentford	Jnr	07/59	60-62	54	-	0

GITTENS Jonathan Antoni (Jon)
Born: Birmingham, England, 22 January, 1964 — CD

League Club	Source	Date Signed	Seasons Played	Apps	Subs	Gls
Southampton	Paget Rgrs	10/85	85-86	18	0	0
Swindon T	Tr	07/87	87-90	124	2	6
Southampton	Tr	03/91	90-91	16	3	0
Middlesbrough	L	02/92	91	9	3	1
Middlesbrough	Tr	07/92	92	13	0	0
Portsmouth	Tr	08/93	93-95	81	2	2
Torquay U	Tr	08/96	96-97	78	0	9
Exeter C	Tr	07/98	98-99	82	0	4

GIUMARRA William Giorgio (Willy)
Born: Ontario, Canada, 26 August, 1971 — M

League Club	Source	Date Signed	Seasons Played	Apps	Subs	Gls
Darlington	Montreal Impact (CAN)	08/97	97	0	4	0

GIVEN Seamus John James (Shay)
Born: Lifford, Republic of Ireland, 20 April, 1976 — G
Republic of Ireland: 125/U21-5/Youth

League Club	Source	Date Signed	Seasons Played	Apps	Subs	Gls
Blackburn Rov	Glasgow Celtic (Jnr)	08/94	96	2	0	0
Swindon T	L	08/95	95	5	0	0
Sunderland	L	01/96	95	17	0	0
Newcastle U	Tr	07/97	97-08	354	0	0
Manchester C	Tr	02/09	08-09	50	0	0
Aston Villa	Tr	07/11	11-14	37	0	0
Middlesbrough	L	11/13	13	16	0	0

GIVENS Daniel Joseph (Don)
Born: Limerick, Republic of Ireland, 9 August, 1949 — F
Republic of Ireland: 56

League Club	Source	Date Signed	Seasons Played	Apps	Subs	Gls
Manchester U	App	12/66	69	4	4	1
Luton T	Tr	04/70	70-71	80	3	19
Queens Park Rgrs	Tr	07/72	72-77	242	0	77
Birmingham C	Tr	08/78	78-80	49	10	10
Bournemouth	L	03/80	79	5	0	4
Sheffield U	Tr	03/81	80	11	0	3

GIVET Gael
Born: Arles, France, 9 October, 1981 — CD
France: 12

League Club	Source	Date Signed	Seasons Played	Apps	Subs	Gls
Blackburn Rov	Olymp Marseille (FRA)	01/09	08-12	112	3	3

GJOKAJ Valentin
Born: Lucerne, Switzerland, 23 August, 1993 — D
Albania: U21-9

League Club	Source	Date Signed	Seasons Played	Apps	Subs	Gls
Derby Co	FC Luzern (SUI)	08/12	12	2	4	0

GLADWIN Ben Thomas
Born: Reading, England, 8 June, 1992 — M

League Club	Source	Date Signed	Seasons Played	Apps	Subs	Gls
Swindon T	Marlow	11/13	13-14	34	13	8

GLADWIN Robin
Born: Harlow, Essex, England, 12 August, 1940 — LB

League Club	Source	Date Signed	Seasons Played	Apps	Subs	Gls
Norwich C	Chelmsford C	01/66	65-67	16	0	0
Oxford U	Tr	07/68	68-69	44	0	0

GLAISTER George
Born: Prudhoe, Northumberland, England, 18 May, 1918 — LW
Died: Lancashire, England, 1966

League Club	Source	Date Signed	Seasons Played	Apps	Subs	Gls
Blackburn Rov	North Shields	05/37	46	8	-	1
Stockport Co	Tr	04/47	46-49	92	-	21
Halifax T	Tr	08/50	50	34	-	7
Accrington Stan	Tr	09/51	51	24	-	1

GLASBY Herbert
Born: Bradford, England, 21 September, 1919 — RW
Died: Bradford, England, 1969

League Club	Source	Date Signed	Seasons Played	Apps	Subs	Gls
Bradford Park Ave	Aldershot (Am)	05/46	46-48	11	-	1

GLASGOW Byron Fitzgerald
Born: Tooting, SW London, England, 18 February, 1979 — M

League Club	Source	Date Signed	Seasons Played	Apps	Subs	Gls
Reading	YT	08/96	96-98	31	8	1

GLASS James Robert (Jimmy)
Born: Epsom, Surrey, England, 1 August, 1973 — G

League Club	Source	Date Signed	Seasons Played	Apps	Subs	Gls
Crystal Palace	YT	07/91				
Portsmouth	L	02/95	94	3	0	0
Bournemouth	Tr	03/96	95-97	94	0	0
Swindon T	Tr	06/98	98-99	11	0	0
Carlisle U	L	04/99	98	3	0	1
Brentford	Cambridge U (NC)	03/00	99	1	1	0
Oxford U	Tr	08/00	00	1	0	0

GLASS Stephen
Born: Dundee, Scotland, 23 May, 1976 — LW
Scotland: 1/B-2/U21-11/Schools

League Club	Source	Date Signed	Seasons Played	Apps	Subs	Gls
Newcastle U	Aberdeen	07/98	98-00	24	19	7
Watford	Tr	07/01	01-02	55	9	4

[GLAUBER] BERTI GLAUBER Leandro Honorato
Born: Belo Horizonte, Brazil, 5 August, 1983 — CD
Brazil: 1

League Club	Source	Date Signed	Seasons Played	Apps	Subs	Gls
Manchester C	FC Nurnberg (GER)	08/08	08	0	1	0

GLAVIN Ronald Michael (Ronnie)
Born: Glasgow, Scotland, 27 March, 1951 — M
Scotland: 1

League Club	Source	Date Signed	Seasons Played	Apps	Subs	Gls
Barnsley	Glasgow Celtic	06/79	79-83	171	5	73
Barnsley	Belenenses (POR)	08/85	85	5	1	0
Stockport Co	Tr	08/86	86	5	5	1

GLAZIER William James (Bill)
Born: Nottingham, England, 2 August, 1943 — G
England: FLge-1/U23-3

League Club	Source	Date Signed	Seasons Played	Apps	Subs	Gls
Crystal Palace	Torquay U (Am)	10/61	61-64	106	-	0
Coventry C	Tr	10/64	64-74	346	0	0
Brentford	Tr	06/75	75	9	0	0

GLAZZARD James (Jimmy)
Born: Normanton, West Yorkshire, England, 23 April, 1923 — CF
Died: Huddersfield, West Yorkshire, England, August, 1996

League Club	Source	Date Signed	Seasons Played	Apps	Subs	Gls
Huddersfield T	Altofts Colliery	10/43	46-55	299	-	141
Everton	Tr	09/56	56	3	-	0
Mansfield T	Tr	12/56	56-57	21	-	10

GLAZZARD Malcolm
Born: Eastham, Wirral, England, 1 July, 1931 — LW
Died: Rhode Island, USA, 26 June, 2012

League Club	Source	Date Signed	Seasons Played	Apps	Subs	Gls
Liverpool	Jnr	05/49				
Accrington Stan	Tr	08/51	51	1	-	0

GLEADALL Dennis
Born: Sheffield, England, 15 February, 1934 — CH
Died: Leeds, England, December, 2014

League Club	Source	Date Signed	Seasons Played	Apps	Subs	Gls
Bury	Boynton Sports	08/54				
Bradford Park Ave	Tr	07/56	56-57	34	-	0

GLEADALL Edward (Eddie)
Born: Sheffield, England, 21 August, 1931 — W
Died: Salford, England, May, 1993

League Club	Source	Date Signed	Seasons Played	Apps	Subs	Gls
Bury	Boynton Sports	01/52	51-56	74	-	18
Scunthorpe U	Tr	03/57	56-57	6	-	2

GLEASURE Peter Francis
Born: Luton, England, 8 October, 1960 — G

League Club	Source	Date Signed	Seasons Played	Apps	Subs	Gls
Millwall	App	08/78	80-82	55	0	0
Northampton T	Tr	03/83	82-90	344	0	0
Gillingham	L	03/91	90	3	0	0

GLEAVE Colin
Born: Stockport, Greater Manchester, England, 6 April, 1919 — CH
Died: Stockport, Greater Manchester, England, 15 May, 2004

League Club	Source	Date Signed	Seasons Played	Apps	Subs	Gls
Stockport Co		02/38	46-47	57	-	1

GLEDHILL Lee Cameron
Born: Bury, Greater Manchester, England, 7 November, 1980 — RB

League Club	Source	Date Signed	Seasons Played	Apps	Subs	Gls
Barnet	YT	07/99	98-00	9	7	0

GLEDHILL Samuel (Sammy)
Born: Castleford, West Yorkshire, England, 7 July, 1913 — WH
Died: Leeds, England, January, 1995

League Club	Source	Date Signed	Seasons Played	Apps	Subs	Gls
York C	Altofts	09/36	36-48	123	-	6

GLEDSTONE Peter Hayward
Born: Ferndown, Hampshire, England, 4 May, 1934 — LB
Died: 30 December, 2014

League Club	Source	Date Signed	Seasons Played	Apps	Subs	Gls
Bournemouth	Bournemouth Gasworks	11/55	57-63	131	-	2

GLEESON Daniel Edward (Dan)
Born: Cambridge, England, 17 February, 1985 — RB
England: Semi Pro-7

League Club	Source	Date Signed	Seasons Played	Apps	Subs	Gls
Cambridge U	Welling U	02/04	03-04	24	13	0
Notts Co	Tr	07/06	06	16	1	0

GLEESON Jamie Bradley
Born: Poole, Dorset, England, 15 January, 1985 — F

League Club	Source	Date Signed	Seasons Played	Apps	Subs	Gls
Southampton	Sch	07/02				
Kidderminster Hrs	Tr	08/04	04	2	5	0

GLEESON Percy
Born: Acton, W London, England, 18 July, 1921 — IF

League Club	Source	Date Signed	Seasons Played	Apps	Subs	Gls
Brentford	Hounslow T	03/47	47	9	-	1

GLEESON Stephen Michael
Born: Dublin, Republic of Ireland, 3 August, 1988 — M
Republic of Ireland: 2/U21-10/Youth

League Club	Source	Date Signed	Seasons Played	Apps	Subs	Gls
Wolverhampton W	Sch	05/06	06	0	3	0
Stockport Co	L	11/06	06	14	0	2
Hereford U	L	02/08	07	3	1	0
Stockport Co	L	03/08	07	4	2	0
Stockport Co	L	08/08	08	17	4	2
MK Dons	Tr	03/09	08-13	167	7	16
Birmingham C	Tr	06/14	14	34	5	0

GLEGHORN Nigel William
Born: Seaham, County Durham, England, 12 August, 1962 — M/W

League Club	Source	Date Signed	Seasons Played	Apps	Subs	Gls
Ipswich T	Seaham Red Star	08/85	85-87	54	12	11
Manchester C	Tr	08/88	88-89	27	7	7
Birmingham C	Tr	09/89	89-92	142	0	33
Stoke C	Tr	10/92	92-95	162	4	26
Burnley	Tr	07/96	96-97	33	1	4
Brentford	L	11/97	97	11	0	1
Northampton T	L	02/98	97	3	5	1

GLENDINNING Brian
Born: Newcastle-upon-Tyne, England, 26 December, 1934 — W

League Club	Source	Date Signed	Seasons Played	Apps	Subs	Gls
Darlington	Felham BC	05/55	55	12	-	2

GLENDINNING Kevin
Born: Corbridge, Northumberland, England, 23 January, 1962 — LB

League Club	Source	Date Signed	Seasons Played	Apps	Subs	Gls
Darlington	Jnr	08/80	80	4	0	0

GLENDON Kevin William
Born: Manchester, England, 21 June, 1961 — M

League Club	Source	Date Signed	Seasons Played	Apps	Subs	Gls
Manchester C	App	06/79				
Crewe Alex	Tr	08/80	80	3	1	0
Burnley	Hyde U	12/83	83	4	0	0

GLENN David Anthony
Born: Wigan, Greater Manchester, England, 30 November, 1962 — RB

League Club	Source	Date Signed	Seasons Played	Apps	Subs	Gls
Wigan Ath	App	11/80	80-82	68	4	4
Blackburn Rov	Tr	08/83	83-84	23	1	0
Chester C	Tr	07/85	85-88	70	3	1

GLENNON Christopher David (Chris)
Born: Manchester, England, 29 October, 1949 — F

League Club	Source	Date Signed	Seasons Played	Apps	Subs	Gls
Manchester C	App	11/67	68-69	3	1	0
Tranmere Rov	L	01/71	70	2	0	0

GLENNON Matthew William (Matty)
Born: Stockport, Greater Manchester, England, 8 October, 1978 — G
England: Semi Pro-2

League Club	Source	Date Signed	Seasons Played	Apps	Subs	Gls
Bolton W	YT	07/97				
Bristol Rov	L	09/00	00	1	0	0
Carlisle U	L	11/00	00	29	0	0
Hull C	Tr	06/01	01-02	35	0	0
Carlisle U	Tr	10/02	02-03	76	0	0
Huddersfield T	Falkirk	07/06	06-08	109	0	0
Bradford C	Tr	01/10	09	17	0	0
Stockport Co	Tr	09/10	10	36	0	0

GLIDDEN Gilbert Swinburne
Born: Sunderland, England, 15 December, 1915 — IF/WH
Died: Staffordshire, England, October, 1988
England: Schools

League Club	Source	Date Signed	Seasons Played	Apps	Subs	Gls
Sunderland	Jnr	02/32				
Port Vale	Tr	05/35	35	5	-	1
Reading	Tr	05/36	36-49	111	-	24
Leyton Orient	Tr	11/50	50	1	-	0

GLOMBARD Luigi
Born: Paris, France, 21 August, 1984 — F
France: Youth

League Club	Source	Date Signed	Seasons Played	Apps	Subs	Gls
Cardiff C	FC Nantes (FRA)	07/06	06	1	5	0
Leicester C	L	01/07	06	0	1	0
Oldham Ath	L	03/07	06	3	5	1

GLOSSOP Terence (Terry)
Born: Sheffield, England, 10 May, 1940 — RW

League Club	Source	Date Signed	Seasons Played	Apps	Subs	Gls
Chesterfield	Sheffield Wed (Am)	05/59	59	7	-	1

GLOVER Alexander (Alec)
Born: Glasgow, Scotland, 28 February, 1922 — RW
Died: Ulverston, Cumbria, England, July, 2000

League Club	Source	Date Signed	Seasons Played	Apps	Subs	Gls
Bradford Park Ave	Partick Thistle	03/48	47-49	48	-	5
Luton T	Tr	09/49	49-50	56	-	6
Blackburn Rov	Tr	09/51	51-53	64	-	4
Barrow	Tr	08/54	54-57	85	-	7

GLOVER Allan Richard
Born: Staines, Surrey, England, 21 October, 1950 — M

League Club	Source	Date Signed	Seasons Played	Apps	Subs	Gls
Queens Park Rgrs	App	03/68	68	5	1	0
West Bromwich A	Tr	06/69	69-76	84	8	9
Southend U	L	01/76	75	0	1	0
Brentford	L	10/76	76	6	0	0
Leyton Orient	Tr	03/77	76-77	37	0	5
Brentford	Tr	11/78	78-79	21	2	2

GLOVER Arthur
Born: Barnsley, South Yorkshire, England, 27 March, 1918 — D
Died: Barnsley, South Yorkshire, England, September, 1998

League Club	Source	Date Signed	Seasons Played	Apps	Subs	Gls
Barnsley	Regent Street Congs	03/35	37-52	186	-	5

GLOVER Benjamin David (Benny)
Born: Birmingham, England, 30 November, 1946 — WH

League Club	Source	Date Signed	Seasons Played	Apps	Subs	Gls
Coventry C		10/66	66	0	1	0

GLOVER Bevil Arthur (Bev)
Born: Salford, England, 25 March, 1926 — CH
Died: Tameside, Greater Manchester, England, February, 2000

League Club	Source	Date Signed	Seasons Played	Apps	Subs	Gls
Stockport Co	Cheadle	01/48	47-53	137	-	1
Rochdale	Tr	03/54	53-58	169	-	1

GLOVER Daniel (Danny)
Born: Crewe, Cheshire, England, 24 October, 1989 — F

League Club	Source	Date Signed	Seasons Played	Apps	Subs	Gls
Port Vale	Sch	07/07	07-09	20	21	4
Rochdale	L	11/09	09	0	2	0

GLOVER Dean Victor
Born: West Bromwich, West Midlands, England, 29 December, 1963 — CD

League Club	Source	Date Signed	Seasons Played	Apps	Subs	Gls
Aston Villa	App	12/81	84-86	25	3	0
Sheffield U	L	10/86	86	5	0	0
Middlesbrough	Tr	06/87	87-88	44	6	5
Port Vale	Tr	02/89	88-97	354	9	15

GLOVER Edward Lee (Lee)
Born: Kettering, Northamptonshire, England, 24 April, 1970 — F
Scotland: U21-3/Youth

League Club	Source	Date Signed	Seasons Played	Apps	Subs	Gls
Nottingham F	App	05/87	87-93	61	15	9
Leicester C	L	09/89	89	3	2	1
Barnsley	L	01/90	89	8	0	0
Luton T	L	09/91	91	1	0	0
Port Vale	Tr	08/94	94-95	38	14	7
Rotherham U	Tr	08/96	96-99	70	15	29
Huddersfield T	L	03/97	96	11	0	0
Macclesfield T	Tr	07/00	00-02	72	13	18
Mansfield T	Tr	09/02	02	0	2	0

GLOVER Gerard John (Gerry)
Born: Liverpool, England, 27 September, 1946 — M
England: Youth/Schools

League Club	Source	Date Signed	Seasons Played	Apps	Subs	Gls
Everton	App	08/64	64-65	2	1	0
Mansfield T	Tr	09/67	67	18	1	0

GLOVER John James
Born: Workington, Cumbria, England, 6 February, 1935 — IF
Died: Whitehaven, Cumbria, England, 19 November, 2011

League Club	Source	Date Signed	Seasons Played	Apps	Subs	Gls
Workington	Marsh BC	10/54	54	2	-	0

GLOVER Leonard (Len)
Born: Kennington, S London, England, 31 January, 1944 — LW

League Club	Source	Date Signed	Seasons Played	Apps	Subs	Gls
Charlton Ath	Jnr	05/62	62-67	177	0	20
Leicester C	Tr	11/67	67-75	245	7	38

GLOVER Peter
Born: Bradford, England, 16 October, 1936 — WH

League Club	Source	Date Signed	Seasons Played	Apps	Subs	Gls
Bradford C		11/57	57	1	-	0

GLOZIER Robert (Bob)
Born: East Ham, E London, England, 20 November, 1948 — FB

England: Schools

League Club	Source	Date Signed	Seasons Played	Apps	Subs	Gls
West Ham U	App	05/66				
Torquay U	Tr	08/69	69-71	57	0	1

GLYNN Terence Robert (Terry)
Born: Hackney, E London, England, 17 December, 1958 — F

League Club	Source	Date Signed	Seasons Played	Apps	Subs	Gls
Leyton Orient	App	12/76	76	1	1	0

GNABRY Serge
Born: Stuttgart, Germany, 14 July, 1995 — W
Germany: U21-2/Youth

League Club	Source	Date Signed	Seasons Played	Apps	Subs	Gls
Arsenal	Sch	07/12	12-13	5	5	1

GNANDUILLET Armand Erwan
Born: Angers, France, 13 February, 1992 — F
Ivory Coast: Youth

League Club	Source	Date Signed	Seasons Played	Apps	Subs	Gls
Chesterfield	Poissy (FRA)	01/13	12-14	26	47	10
Tranmere Rov	L	10/14	14	4	0	2
Oxford U	L	03/15	14	0	4	0

GNAPKA Claude
Born: Marseille, France, 9 June, 1983 — LW

League Club	Source	Date Signed	Seasons Played	Apps	Subs	Gls
Peterborough U	FC Vaduz (SUI)	07/07	07	25	3	0
Luton T	Tr	08/08	08	19	8	1
Walsall	Tr	07/11	11	8	12	1

GNOHERE David Arthur (Arthur)
Born: Yamoussoukro, Ivory Coast, 20 November, 1978 — CD

League Club	Source	Date Signed	Seasons Played	Apps	Subs	Gls
Burnley	SM Caen (FRA)	08/01	01-03	74	7	6
Queens Park Rgrs	L	09/03	03	6	0	0
Queens Park Rgrs	Tr	02/04	03-04	14	1	0

GOAD Alan Michael
Born: Hailsham, East Sussex, England, 8 August, 1948 — CD

League Club	Source	Date Signed	Seasons Played	Apps	Subs	Gls
Exeter C	Jnr	12/65				
Hartlepool U	Tr	07/67	67-77	366	9	11

GOALEN Harold Keith (Keith)
Born: Hindley, Greater Manchester, England, 24 May, 1933 — LW

League Club	Source	Date Signed	Seasons Played	Apps	Subs	Gls
Stockport Co	Jnr	04/53	50-55	18	-	2

GOATER Leonard Shaun (Shaun)
Born: Hamilton, Bermuda, 25 February, 1970 — F
Bermuda: 36/Youth

League Club	Source	Date Signed	Seasons Played	Apps	Subs	Gls
Manchester U	North Village (BER)	05/89				
Rotherham U	Tr	10/89	89-95	169	40	70
Notts Co	L	11/93	93	1	0	0
Bristol C	Tr	07/96	96-97	67	8	40
Manchester C	Tr	03/98	97-02	164	20	84
Reading	Tr	08/03	03-04	32	11	12
Coventry C	L	03/05	04	4	2	0
Southend U	Tr	08/05	05	28	6	11

GOBERN Lewis Thomas
Born: Birmingham, England, 28 January, 1985 — RW

League Club	Source	Date Signed	Seasons Played	Apps	Subs	Gls
Wolverhampton W	Sch	03/04	05-06	6	7	2
Hartlepool U	L	11/04	04	1	0	0
Blackpool	L	11/05	05	4	4	1
Bury	L	03/06	05	7	0	1
Colchester U	L	01/09	08	5	7	0
MK Dons	Tr	07/09	09	7	13	0
Notts Co	Grimsby T	01/11	10	0	5	0

GOBERN Oscar Lee
Born: Birmingham, England, 26 January, 1991 — M
England: Youth

League Club	Source	Date Signed	Seasons Played	Apps	Subs	Gls
Southampton	Sch	09/08	08-10	5	16	1
MK Dons	L	09/09	09	0	2	0
Huddersfield T	Tr	07/11	11-14	51	20	3
Chesterfield	L	10/14	14	3	0	0

GOBLE Stephen Richard (Steve)
Born: Erpingham, Norfolk, England, 5 September, 1960 — LW

League Club	Source	Date Signed	Seasons Played	Apps	Subs	Gls
Norwich C	App	09/78	79-80	30	0	2
Norwich C	Groningen (NED)	08/84	84	0	1	0
Cambridge U	Heracles Almelo (NED)	02/88	87	1	1	0

GODBOLD Daryl Martin
Born: Ipswich, England, 5 September, 1964 — FB

League Club	Source	Date Signed	Seasons Played	Apps	Subs	Gls
Norwich C	App	09/82	83	0	2	0
Colchester U	Tr	08/84	84	4	2	1

GODBOLD Harold (Harry)
Born: Springwell, Tyne and Wear, England, 31 January, 1939 — LW

League Club	Source	Date Signed	Seasons Played	Apps	Subs	Gls
Sunderland	Usworth Colliery	05/56	57-59	12	-	1
Hartlepool U	Tr	01/61	60-62	65	-	8
Lincoln C	Boston U	03/66	65-66	22	1	3

GODDARD Howard John
Born: Over Wallop, Wiltshire, England, 10 May, 1957 — F

League Club	Source	Date Signed	Seasons Played	Apps	Subs	Gls
Bournemouth	App	07/74	72-75	62	2	18
Swindon T	Tr	06/76	76	10	2	0
Newport Co	Tr	08/77	77-81	101	4	42
Blackpool	L	09/81	81	4	0	2
Bournemouth	Tr	12/81	81	6	3	2
Aldershot	Tr	08/82	82	26	2	9

GODDARD Karl Eric
Born: Leeds, England, 29 December, 1967 — LB/M
England: Schools

League Club	Source	Date Signed	Seasons Played	Apps	Subs	Gls
Manchester U	App	12/85				
Bradford C	Tr	06/86	86-89	67	6	0
Exeter C	L	12/89	89	0	1	0
Colchester U	L	01/90	89	16	0	1
Hereford U	Tr	09/90	90-91	8	1	1

GODDARD Paul
Born: Harlington, W London, England, 12 October, 1959 — F
England: 1/B-1/U21-8

League Club	Source	Date Signed	Seasons Played	Apps	Subs	Gls
Queens Park Rgrs	App	07/77	77-79	63	7	23
West Ham U	Tr	08/80	80-86	159	11	54
Newcastle U	Tr	11/86	86-87	61	0	19
Derby Co	Tr	08/88	88-89	49	0	15
Millwall	Tr	12/89	89-90	17	3	1
Ipswich T	Tr	01/91	90-93	59	13	13

GODDARD Raymond (Ray)
Born: Ecclesfield, South Yorkshire, England, 17 October, 1920 — CD
Died: Gornal, West Midlands, England, 1 February, 1974

League Club	Source	Date Signed	Seasons Played	Apps	Subs	Gls
Wolverhampton W	Red Rov	09/38	38	4	-	0
Chelsea	Tr	09/46	46-47	14	-	1
Plymouth Arg	Tr	07/48	48-49	43	-	1
Exeter C	Tr	12/49	49-53	130	-	2

GODDARD Raymond (Ray)
Born: Fulham, W London, England, 13 February, 1949 — G
Died: Spain, 11 December, 2007

League Club	Source	Date Signed	Seasons Played	Apps	Subs	Gls
Leyton Orient	Fulham (App)	02/67	66-73	278	0	0
Millwall	Tr	11/74	75-77	80	0	0
Wimbledon	Tr	02/78	77-80	119	0	1

GODDARD-CRAWLEY Richard Lewis
Born: Edgware, NW London, England, 31 March, 1978 — CD

League Club	Source	Date Signed	Seasons Played	Apps	Subs	Gls
Brentford	Arsenal (YT)	07/96	96	0	1	0

GODDEN Anthony Leonard (Tony)
Born: Gillingham, Kent, England, 2 August, 1955 — G

League Club	Source	Date Signed	Seasons Played	Apps	Subs	Gls
West Bromwich A	Ashford T, Kent	08/75	76-85	267	0	0
Luton T	L	03/83	82	12	0	0
Walsall	L	10/83	83	19	0	0
Chelsea	Tr	03/86	85-86	34	0	0
Birmingham C	Tr	07/87	87-88	29	0	0
Bury	L	12/88	88	1	0	0
Peterborough U	Tr	07/89	89	24	0	0

GODDEN Matthew James
Born: Canterbury, England, 29 July, 1991 — F

League Club	Source	Date Signed	Seasons Played	Apps	Subs	Gls
Scunthorpe U	Sch	07/09	10-13	5	13	0

GODDERIDGE Alan Edward
Born: Tamworth, Staffordshire, England, 23 May, 1928 — WH

League Club	Source	Date Signed	Seasons Played	Apps	Subs	Gls
Swansea C	Tamworth	10/50	51	1	-	0
Walsall	Tr	07/52	52	3	-	0

GODDING Earl George
Born: Hawarden, Flintshire, Wales, 6 January, 1934 — G

League Club	Source	Date Signed	Seasons Played	Apps	Subs	Gls
Wrexham	Caergwrle	04/54	52-58	21	-	0
Workington	Tr	08/59	59	10	-	0

GODFREY Anthony William (Tony)
Born: Wokingham, Berkshire, England, 30 April, 1939 — G

League Club	Source	Date Signed	Seasons Played	Apps	Subs	Gls
Southampton	Basingstoke T	04/58	58-65	141	0	0
Aldershot	Tr	12/65	65-69	171	0	0
Rochdale	Tr	07/70	70-71	71	0	0
Aldershot	Tr	07/72	72-75	68	0	0

GODFREY Brian Cameron
Born: Flint, Wales, 1 May, 1940 — IF
Died: Nicosia, Cyprus, 11 February, 2010
Wales: 3/U23-1

League Club	Source	Date Signed	Seasons Played	Apps	Subs	Gls
Everton	Flint Town U	05/58	59	1	-	0
Scunthorpe U	Tr	06/60	60-63	87	-	24
Preston NE	Tr	10/63	63-67	126	1	52
Aston Villa	Tr	09/67	67-70	139	4	22
Bristol Rov	Tr	05/71	71-72	79	2	16
Newport Co	Tr	06/73	73-75	117	1	14

GODFREY Elliott James
Born: Toronto, Canada, 22 February, 1983 — F

League Club	Source	Date Signed	Seasons Played	Apps	Subs	Gls
Watford	YT	03/01	02	0	1	0

League Club	Source	Date Signed	Seasons Played	Career Record Apps	Subs	Gls

GODFREY Kevin
Born: Kennington, S London, England, 24 February, 1960 RW/F

League Club	Source	Date Signed	Seasons Played	Apps	Subs	Gls
Leyton Orient	App	03/77	77-87	255	30	62
Plymouth Arg	L	02/86	85	7	0	1
Brentford	Maidenhead U	10/88	88-92	101	39	17

GODFREY Paul
Born: Derby, England, 27 September, 1972 M

League Club	Source	Date Signed	Seasons Played	Apps	Subs	Gls
Chesterfield	YT	-	90	2	0	0

GODFREY Peter Ronald
Born: Woolwich, SE London, England, 15 March, 1938 RW

League Club	Source	Date Signed	Seasons Played	Apps	Subs	Gls
Charlton Ath	Jnr	11/55	60	1	-	0
Gillingham	Tr	07/61	61-64	66	-	9
Chesterfield	Tr	07/65	65	27	0	2
Exeter C	Tr	06/66	66	42	0	4

GODFREY Warren Paul Thomas
Born: Liverpool, England, 31 March, 1973 M

League Club	Source	Date Signed	Seasons Played	Apps	Subs	Gls
Liverpool	YT	05/91				
Barnsley	Tr	07/92	92	1	7	0

GODSELL John Dryburgh (Jack)
Born: Lassodie, Fife, Scotland, 13 September, 1924 LB

League Club	Source	Date Signed	Seasons Played	Apps	Subs	Gls
Huddersfield T	Forfar Ath	06/46				
Bradford C	Tr	09/48	49	9	-	0
Southport	Tr	08/51	51	3	-	0

GODSMARK Jonathan (Jonny)
Born: Choppington, Northumberland, England, 3 September, 1989 W

League Club	Source	Date Signed	Seasons Played	Apps	Subs	Gls
Newcastle U	Sch	07/08				
Hereford U	L	08/09	09	7	1	1

GODWIN Donald John (Don)
Born: Aberbargoed, Caerphilly, Wales, 15 July, 1932 LW
Died: Caerphilly, Wales, March, 2002

League Club	Source	Date Signed	Seasons Played	Apps	Subs	Gls
Cardiff C	Bargoed	12/53	56	2	-	0

GODWIN Robert Geoffrey
Born: Wootton Bassett, Wiltshire, England, 3 February, 1928 IF

League Club	Source	Date Signed	Seasons Played	Apps	Subs	Gls
Swindon T	Old Headlandians	09/51	51	2	-	0

GODWIN Thomas Fergus (Tommy)
Born: Dublin, Republic of Ireland, 20 August, 1927 G
Died: Bournemouth, England, 27 August, 1996
Republic of Ireland: 13/LoI-1

League Club	Source	Date Signed	Seasons Played	Apps	Subs	Gls
Leicester C	Shamrock Rov (ROI)	10/49	49-51	45	-	0
Bournemouth	Tr	06/52	52-61	357	-	0

GODWIN Verdi
Born: Blackburn, Greater Manchester, England, 11 February, 1926 CF
Died: Southport, Merseyside, England, 1 December, 2013

League Club	Source	Date Signed	Seasons Played	Apps	Subs	Gls
Blackburn Rov	Jnr	03/46	46-47	27	-	6
Manchester C	Tr	06/48	48	8	-	3
Stoke C	Tr	06/49	49	22	-	2
Mansfield T	Tr	01/50	49-50	31	-	9
Middlesbrough	Tr	11/51				
Grimsby T	Tr	01/52	51	1	-	0
Brentford	Tr	03/52	51-52	7	-	1
Southport	Tr	07/54	54	17	-	2
Barrow	Tr	08/55	55	15	-	3
Tranmere Rov	Tr	08/56	56	14	-	2

GOFF Shaun John
Born: Tiverton, Devon, England, 13 April, 1984 LB

League Club	Source	Date Signed	Seasons Played	Apps	Subs	Gls
Exeter C	Sch	08/02	01	2	0	0

GOFFIN William Charles (Billy)
Born: Tamworth, Staffordshire, England, 12 February, 1920 W
Died: Tamworth, Staffordshire, England, 15 September, 1987

League Club	Source	Date Signed	Seasons Played	Apps	Subs	Gls
Aston Villa	Tamworth	12/37	46-53	156	-	36
Walsall	Tr	08/54	54	8	-	1

GOHOURI Lohore Steve Ulrich (Steve)
Born: Abidjan, Ivory Coast, 8 February, 1981 D
Ivory Coast: 13

League Club	Source	Date Signed	Seasons Played	Apps	Subs	Gls
Wigan Ath	Borussia M'bach (GER)	01/10	09-11	38	4	2

GOLAC Ivan
Born: Koprivnica, Croatia, 15 June, 1950 RB
Yugoslavia: 1

League Club	Source	Date Signed	Seasons Played	Apps	Subs	Gls
Southampton	Part'n Belgrade (YUG)	11/78	78-81	143	1	4
Bournemouth	Tr	11/82	82	9	0	0
Manchester C	Tr	03/83	82	2	0	0
Southampton	Belasica (MCD)	03/84	83-85	24	0	0
Portsmouth	L	01/85	84	8	0	0

GOLBOURNE Scott Julian
Born: Bristol, England, 29 February, 1988 LB
England: Youth

League Club	Source	Date Signed	Seasons Played	Apps	Subs	Gls
Bristol C	Sch	03/05	04-05	11	3	0
Reading	Tr	01/06	05-07	1	1	0
Wycombe W	L	08/06	06	13	2	1
Wycombe W	L	01/07	06	18	1	0
Bournemouth	L	11/07	07	5	0	0
Oldham Ath	L	01/09	08	7	1	0
Exeter C	Tr	07/09	09-11	98	6	2
Barnsley	Tr	01/12	11-13	45	2	2
Wolverhampton W	Tr	08/13	13-14	62	5	1

GOLDBAEK Bjarne
Born: Nykobing Falster, Denmark, 6 October, 1968 RM
Denmark: 28/B-1/U21-5/Youth

League Club	Source	Date Signed	Seasons Played	Apps	Subs	Gls
Chelsea	FC Copenhagen (DEN)	11/98	98-99	15	14	5
Fulham	Tr	01/00	99-02	73	12	6

GOLDBERG Bradley Jack
Born: Bromley, SE London, England, 20 October, 1993 F

League Club	Source	Date Signed	Seasons Played	Apps	Subs	Gls
Dagenham & Red	Hastings U	08/13	14	0	5	0

GOLDBERG (GAUNT) Leslie (Les)
Born: Leeds, England, 3 January, 1918 RB
England: Schools

League Club	Source	Date Signed	Seasons Played	Apps	Subs	Gls
Leeds U	Jnr	05/35	37-46	31	-	0
Reading	Tr	03/47	46-49	71	-	0

GOLDER James (Jimmy)
Born: Manchester, England, 28 March, 1955 M
Died: Stockport, Greater Manchester, England, 5 April, 2000

League Club	Source	Date Signed	Seasons Played	Apps	Subs	Gls
Stockport Co	App	-	71	0	1	0

GOLDIE James (Jim)
Born: Denny, Falkirk, Scotland, 29 June, 1940 CF

League Club	Source	Date Signed	Seasons Played	Apps	Subs	Gls
Luton T	Kilsyth Rgrs	04/62	62	7	-	2
York C	Tr	06/63	63	22	-	7

GOLDIE Peter
Born: Dumbarton, Dunbartonshire, Scotland, 7 June, 1934 LB

League Club	Source	Date Signed	Seasons Played	Apps	Subs	Gls
Aldershot	Glasgow Celtic	06/58	58	5	-	0

GOLDING Norman John William (John)
Born: Southwark, S London, England, 23 January, 1937 RW

League Club	Source	Date Signed	Seasons Played	Apps	Subs	Gls
Queens Park Rgrs	Tonbridge	08/59	59-60	30	-	6

GOLDRING Mark
Born: Havant, Hampshire, England, 17 September, 1972 G

League Club	Source	Date Signed	Seasons Played	Apps	Subs	Gls
Chesterfield	YT	07/91	91	7	0	0

GOLDSMITH Craig Stephen William
Born: Peterborough, England, 27 August, 1963 LW

League Club	Source	Date Signed	Seasons Played	Apps	Subs	Gls
Peterborough U	Mirlees Blackstone	08/88	88-89	39	7	6
Carlisle U	Tr	12/89	89-90	21	9	1

GOLDSMITH Martin Sidney
Born: Carmarthen, Wales, 25 May, 1962 F

League Club	Source	Date Signed	Seasons Played	Apps	Subs	Gls
Cambridge U	Carmarthen T	05/80	80-83	28	7	5
Cardiff C	Tr	01/84	83	3	6	2

GOLDSMITH Martyn
Born: Walsall, West Midlands, England, 4 November, 1969 F

League Club	Source	Date Signed	Seasons Played	Apps	Subs	Gls
Walsall	YT	08/88	88-90	2	5	2

GOLDSON Conor Lambert
Born: York, England, 18 December, 1992 D

League Club	Source	Date Signed	Seasons Played	Apps	Subs	Gls
Shrewsbury T	Sch	08/10	10-14	91	13	8
Cheltenham T	L	11/13	13	3	1	0

GOLDTHORPE Robert James (Bobby)
Born: Osterley, W London, England, 6 December, 1950 CD

League Club	Source	Date Signed	Seasons Played	Apps	Subs	Gls
Crystal Palace	Jnr	07/68	71	1	0	0
Charlton Ath	Tr	12/72	72-75	70	9	6
Aldershot	L	02/76	75	16	0	0
Brentford	Tr	07/76	76	19	0	2

GOLDTHORPE Wayne
Born: Staincross, South Yorkshire, England, 19 September, 1957 F/M

League Club	Source	Date Signed	Seasons Played	Apps	Subs	Gls
Huddersfield T	App	09/75	75-77	19	7	7
Hartlepool U	L	12/76	76	6	1	1
Hartlepool U	Tr	08/78	78-79	43	4	8
Crewe Alex	Tr	10/79	79	0	1	0

GOLLEY Mark Anthony
Born: Beckenham, SE London, England, 28 October, 1962 CD

League Club	Source	Date Signed	Seasons Played	Apps	Subs	Gls
Maidstone U	Sutton U	07/88	89-90	77	4	3

GOLLOGLY John
Born: Bridlington, East Riding of Yorkshire, England, 4 July, 1962 M

League Club	Source	Date Signed	Seasons Played	Apps	Subs	Gls
Hartlepool U	Whitby T	03/85	84-86	29	2	5

GOLOBART Roman
Born: Barcelona, Spain, 21 March, 1992 CD

League Club	Source	Date Signed	Seasons Played	Apps	Subs	Gls
Wigan Ath	RCD Espanyol (SPN)	08/09	12	2	1	0
Tranmere Rov	L	08/12	12	1	0	0

GOMA Alain
Born: Vaucluse, Provence, France, 5 October, 1972 — CD
France: 2/B-1/U21/Youth

League Club	Source	Date Signed	Seasons Played	Apps	Subs	Gls
Newcastle U	Paris St-Germain (FRA)	07/99	99-00	32	1	1
Fulham	Tr	03/01	00-05	115	2	0

GOMERSALL Victor (Vic)
Born: Manchester, England, 17 June, 1942 — LB

League Club	Source	Date Signed	Seasons Played	Apps	Subs	Gls
Manchester C	Jnr	07/60	61-65	39	0	0
Swansea C	Tr	08/66	66-70	178	0	6

GOMES Heurelho
Born: Minas Gerais, Brazil, 15 February, 1981 — G
Brazil: 11/U23-14

League Club	Source	Date Signed	Seasons Played	Apps	Subs	Gls
Tottenham H	PSV Eindhoven (NED)	07/08	08-10	95	0	0
Watford	Tr	05/14	14	44	0	0

GOMES Tiago Felipe Figueiras
Born: VilaFranca de Xira, Portugal, 18 August, 1985 — M
Portugal: U21-2

League Club	Source	Date Signed	Seasons Played	Apps	Subs	Gls
Blackpool	Hercul Alicante (SPN)	07/12	12	21	4	0

GOMEZ Fernando Colomer
Born: Valencia, Spain, 11 September, 1965 — M
Spain: 8/U21-9/Youth

League Club	Source	Date Signed	Seasons Played	Apps	Subs	Gls
Wolverhampton W	Valencia (SPN)	08/98	98	17	2	2

GOMEZ Joseph Dave (Joe)
Born: Catford, SE London, England, 23 May, 1997 — CD
England: Youth

League Club	Source	Date Signed	Seasons Played	Apps	Subs	Gls
Charlton Ath	Sch	05/14	14	16	5	0

GOMIS Bafetimbi
Born: Toulon, France, 6 August, 1985 — F
France: 12/Youth

League Club	Source	Date Signed	Seasons Played	Apps	Subs	Gls
Swansea C	Olymp Lyonnais (FRA)	06/14	14	18	13	7

GOMIS Bedsente
Born: Mont Saint Aignon, France, 14 April, 1988 — M

League Club	Source	Date Signed	Seasons Played	Apps	Subs	Gls
Southend U	UD Almeria (SPN)	01/14	13	0	2	0

GOMIS Kevin Mickail Junior
Born: Paris, France, 20 January, 1989 — CD

League Club	Source	Date Signed	Seasons Played	Apps	Subs	Gls
Nottingham F (L)	OGC Nice (FRA)	01/14	13	1	0	0

GOMIS Morgaro Lima
Born: Paris, France, 14 July, 1985 — DM
Senegal: 2

League Club	Source	Date Signed	Seasons Played	Apps	Subs	Gls
Birmingham C	Dundee U	06/11	11-12	22	9	0

GONZAGUE Michael Alexander Granville
Born: Canning Town, E London, England, 27 March, 1975 — FB

League Club	Source	Date Signed	Seasons Played	Apps	Subs	Gls
Southend U	YT	07/93				
Hereford U	Tr	08/94	94	2	1	0

GONZALEZ David
Born: Medellin, Colombia, 20 July, 1982 — G
Colombia: 2

League Club	Source	Date Signed	Seasons Played	Apps	Subs	Gls
Manchester C	Huracan (ARG)	01/10				
Brighton & HA	Tr	01/12	11	2	0	0
Barnsley	Tr	08/12	12	3	0	0

GONZALEZ Ignacio Maria (Nacho)
Born: Montevideo, Uruguay, 14 May, 1982 — M
Uruguay: 18

League Club	Source	Date Signed	Seasons Played	Apps	Subs	Gls
Newcastle U (L)	Valencia (SPN)	09/08	08	0	2	0

GONZALEZ Mark Dennis
Born: Durban, South Africa, 10 July, 1984 — LW
Chile: 48

League Club	Source	Date Signed	Seasons Played	Apps	Subs	Gls
Liverpool	Catolica Univ (CHL)	06/04	06	14	11	2

GOOCH James Arthur George (Jimmy)
Born: West Ham, E London, England, 11 July, 1921 — G
Died: Southport, Merseyside, England, 18 November, 2001

League Club	Source	Date Signed	Seasons Played	Apps	Subs	Gls
Preston NE	Becontree	05/42	46-51	135	-	0
Bradford C	Tr	07/53	53	22	-	0
Watford	Tr	07/54	55-56	43	-	0

GOOD Curtis Edward
Born: Melbourne, Australia, 23 March, 1993 — CD
Australia: 1/Youth

League Club	Source	Date Signed	Seasons Played	Apps	Subs	Gls
Newcastle U	Melbourne Heart (AUS)	08/12				
Bradford C	L	11/12	12	2	1	0

GOOD John Russell
Born: Portsmouth, England, 29 January, 1933 — LW
Died: Great Budworth, Cheshire, England, 23 March, 2005

League Club	Source	Date Signed	Seasons Played	Apps	Subs	Gls
Nottingham F		06/53				
Bury	Tr	06/54				
Tranmere Rov	Buxton	07/55	55	5	-	0

GOODACRE Samuel David (Sam)
Born: Chesterfield, Derbyshire, England, 1 December, 1970 — F
England: Schools

League Club	Source	Date Signed	Seasons Played	Apps	Subs	Gls
Sheffield Wed	Jnr	07/89				
Scunthorpe U	Tr	07/91	92-94	24	20	12

GOODALL Alan Jeffrey
Born: Birkenhead, Wirral, England, 2 December, 1981 — LB

League Club	Source	Date Signed	Seasons Played	Apps	Subs	Gls
Rochdale	Bangor C	07/04	04-06	110	10	8
Luton T	Tr	07/07	07	25	4	1
Chesterfield	Tr	08/08	08-09	38	7	3
Rochdale	Tr	07/10	10	3	2	0
Stockport Co	Tr	02/11	10	13	0	0
Fleetwood T	Tr	07/11	12-13	46	2	4
Morecambe	Tr	07/14	14	22	6	0

GOODALL Bernard
Born: Islington, N London, England, 4 October, 1937 — RB
Died: Warborough, Oxfordshire, England, 9 January, 2005

League Club	Source	Date Signed	Seasons Played	Apps	Subs	Gls
Reading		07/59	59-61	98	-	0
Carlisle U	Tr	07/63	63	1	-	0
Halifax T	Tr	11/64	64	23	-	0

GOODALL David George (Dave)
Born: Madeley, Telford & Wrekin, England, 18 May, 1943 — CH

League Club	Source	Date Signed	Seasons Played	Apps	Subs	Gls
Shrewsbury T	Jnr	05/61	61	1	-	0

GOODCHILD Gary Dean
Born: Chelmsford, England, 27 January, 1958 — F
England: Schools

League Club	Source	Date Signed	Seasons Played	Apps	Subs	Gls
Arsenal	App	01/75				
Hereford U	Tr	06/76	76	1	3	0
Reading	Tr	09/77	77	0	1	0
Crystal Palace	Kramfors (SWE)	12/79	79-80	0	2	0

GOODCHILD John (Johnny)
Born: Gateshead, Tyne and Wear, England, 2 January, 1939 — LW/IF
Died: Durham, England, 25 August, 2011

League Club	Source	Date Signed	Seasons Played	Apps	Subs	Gls
Sunderland	Ludworth Jnrs	09/56	57-60	44	-	21
Brighton & HA	Tr	05/61	61-65	162	1	44
York C	Tr	06/66	66	29	0	6
Darlington	Tr	07/67	67	2	0	0

GOODE Terence Joseph (Terry)
Born: Islington, N London, England, 29 October, 1961 — F

League Club	Source	Date Signed	Seasons Played	Apps	Subs	Gls
Birmingham C	App	09/79	80	0	2	0

GOODEN Ty Michael
Born: Canvey Island, Essex, England, 23 October, 1972 — LW

League Club	Source	Date Signed	Seasons Played	Apps	Subs	Gls
Swindon T	Wycombe W	09/93	93-99	118	28	9
Gillingham	Tr	01/00	99-01	52	7	5

GOODEVE Kenneth George Alfred (Ken)
Born: Manchester, England, 3 September, 1950 — D

League Club	Source	Date Signed	Seasons Played	Apps	Subs	Gls
Manchester U	App	09/67				
Luton T	Tr	04/70	70-72	9	6	0
Brighton & HA	Tr	12/73	73	5	1	0
Watford	Tr	06/74	74-75	67	0	4

GOODFELLOW Derrick Ormond
Born: Shilbottle, Northumberland, England, 26 June, 1914 — G
Died: Northumberland, England, December, 2001

League Club	Source	Date Signed	Seasons Played	Apps	Subs	Gls
Gateshead	Jnr	03/35	34-35	29	-	0
Sheffield Wed	Tr	05/36	36-46	69	-	0
Middlesbrough	Tr	06/47	47	36	-	0

GOODFELLOW James (Jimmy)
Born: Sunderland, England, 16 September, 1943 — M

League Club	Source	Date Signed	Seasons Played	Apps	Subs	Gls
Port Vale	Bishop Auckland	06/66	66-68	76	9	10
Workington	Tr	07/69	69-73	199	0	15
Rotherham U	Tr	01/74	73-77	192	0	8
Stockport Co	Tr	08/78	78	2	1	0

GOODFELLOW James Boyd (Jimmy)
Born: Edinburgh, Scotland, 30 July, 1938 — M
Died: Buckinghamshire, England, 1 April, 2011

League Club	Source	Date Signed	Seasons Played	Apps	Subs	Gls
Leicester C	Third Lanark	05/63	63-67	96	2	26
Mansfield T	Tr	03/68	67-70	96	4	14

GOODFELLOW Marc David
Born: Swadlincote, Derbyshire, England, 20 September, 1981 — W

League Club	Source	Date Signed	Seasons Played	Apps	Subs	Gls
Stoke C	Jnr	01/99	00-03	17	37	6
Bristol C	Tr	01/04	03-04	8	12	4
Port Vale	L	10/04	04	4	1	0
Swansea C	L	11/04	04	6	0	3
Colchester U	L	03/05	04	4	1	1
Swansea C	Tr	07/05	05	5	6	0
Grimsby T	Tr	01/06	05	8	2	1
Bury	Tr	07/06	06	2	2	0
Burton A	Tr	01/07	09	0	3	0

GOODFELLOW Sydney (Syd)
Born: Wolstanton, Potteries, England, 6 July, 1915 — RH
Died: Melbourne, Australia, 27 November, 1998

League Club	Source	Date Signed	Seasons Played	Apps	Subs	Gls
Port Vale	Hanley	11/36	36	16	-	1
Rochdale	Glentoran	05/38	38	41	-	2
Chesterfield	Tr	04/39	46-47	80	-	0
Doncaster Rov	Tr	05/48	48-49	66	-	2
Oldham Ath	Tr	09/50	50-51	72	-	2
Accrington Stan	Tr	06/52	52	28	-	3

GOODGAME Anthony Alan (Tony)
Born: Hammersmith, W London, England, 19 February, 1946 — FB

League Club	Source	Date Signed	Seasons Played	Apps	Subs	Gls
Fulham	App	02/64				
Leyton Orient	Tr	08/66	66	7	1	0

GOODHIND Warren Ernest
Born: Johannesburg, South Africa, 16 August, 1977 — D

League Club	Source	Date Signed	Seasons Played	Apps	Subs	Gls
Barnet	YT	07/96	96-00	73	20	3
Cambridge U	Tr	09/01	01-04	95	8	0
Rochdale	Tr	09/05	05	10	0	0
Oxford U	L	02/06	05	4	2	0

GOODING Michael Charles (Mick)
Born: Newcastle-upon-Tyne, England, 12 April, 1959 — M

League Club	Source	Date Signed	Seasons Played	Apps	Subs	Gls
Rotherham U	Bishop Auckland	07/79	79-82	90	12	9
Chesterfield	Tr	12/82	82	12	0	0
Rotherham U	Tr	09/83	83-86	149	7	32
Peterborough U	Tr	08/87	87-88	47	0	21
Wolverhampton W	Tr	09/88	88-89	43	1	4
Reading	Tr	12/89	89-96	303	11	26
Southend U	Plymouth Arg (Coach)	07/98	98-99	19	6	0

GOODING Raymond (Ray)
Born: Hartlepool, Cleveland, England, 16 February, 1959 — M

League Club	Source	Date Signed	Seasons Played	Apps	Subs	Gls
Coventry C	App	06/76	76-81	46	3	5
Bristol C	L	03/82	81	3	0	0
Plymouth Arg	Tr	08/82	82	7	0	1

GOODING Scott Osmond
Born: Croydon, S London, England, 2 January, 1982 — M

League Club	Source	Date Signed	Seasons Played	Apps	Subs	Gls
Crystal Palace	YT	07/01	01	0	1	0

GOODISON Christopher Wayne (Wayne)
Born: Wakefield, England, 23 September, 1964 — RB/M

League Club	Source	Date Signed	Seasons Played	Apps	Subs	Gls
Barnsley	App	09/82	82-85	31	5	0
Crewe Alex	Tr	09/86	86-88	90	4	1
Rochdale	Tr	07/89	89-90	78	1	4

GOODISON Ian de Souza
Born: Montego Bay, Jamaica, 21 November, 1972 — CD
Jamaica: 120

League Club	Source	Date Signed	Seasons Played	Apps	Subs	Gls
Hull C	Olympic Gardens (JAM)	10/99	99-01	67	3	1
Tranmere Rov	Seba U (JAM)	02/04	03-13	351	13	11

GOODLAD Mark
Born: Barnsley, South Yorkshire, England, 9 September, 1979 — G

League Club	Source	Date Signed	Seasons Played	Apps	Subs	Gls
Nottingham F	YT	10/96				
Scarborough	L	02/99	98	3	0	0
Port Vale	Tr	03/00	99-06	210	2	0

GOODLASS Ronald (Ronnie)
Born: Liverpool, England, 6 September, 1953 — LW
England: Schools

League Club	Source	Date Signed	Seasons Played	Apps	Subs	Gls
Everton	App	07/71	75-77	31	4	2
Fulham	Den Haag (NED)	09/80	80	21	1	2
Scunthorpe U	Tr	03/82	81	9	0	0
Tranmere Rov	Seiko Sports Ass (HKG)	12/83	83-84	19	2	0

GOODMAN Donald Ralph (Don)
Born: Leeds, England, 9 May, 1966 — F

League Club	Source	Date Signed	Seasons Played	Apps	Subs	Gls
Bradford C	Hunslet FC	03/84	83-86	65	5	14
West Bromwich A	Tr	03/87	86-91	140	18	60
Sunderland	Tr	12/91	91-94	112	4	40
Wolverhampton W	Tr	12/94	94-97	115	10	33
Barnsley (L)	Kashima Antlers (JPN)	12/98	98	5	3	0
Walsall	Motherwell	03/01	00-01	15	10	3
Exeter C	Tr	08/02	02	11	2	1

GOODMAN Jake Phillip
Born: Bexley, SE London, England, 5 August, 1993 — CD

League Club	Source	Date Signed	Seasons Played	Apps	Subs	Gls
Millwall	Sch	06/12				
AFC Wimbledon	L	11/14	14	13	2	1

GOODMAN John
Born: King's Lynn, Norfolk, England, 8 September, 1935 — G

League Club	Source	Date Signed	Seasons Played	Apps	Subs	Gls
Crewe Alex		10/58	58	1	-	0

GOODMAN Jonathan (Jon)
Born: Walthamstow, NE London, England, 2 June, 1971 — F
Republic of Ireland: 4

League Club	Source	Date Signed	Seasons Played	Apps	Subs	Gls
Millwall	Bromley	08/90	90-94	97	12	35
Wimbledon	Tr	11/94	94-98	28	32	11

GOODMAN Malcolm John
Born: Solihull, West Midlands, England, 6 May, 1961 — D

League Club	Source	Date Signed	Seasons Played	Apps	Subs	Gls
Halifax T	Bromsgrove Rov	09/79	79-82	70	16	1

GOODRIDGE Gregory Ronald St Clair (Greg)
Born: Barbados, 10 July, 1971 — LW
Barbados: 63

League Club	Source	Date Signed	Seasons Played	Apps	Subs	Gls
Torquay U	Lambada (SVG)	03/94	93-94	32	6	4
Queens Park Rgrs	Tr	08/95	95	0	7	1
Bristol C	Tr	08/96	96-01	76	43	14
Cheltenham T	L	02/01	00	10	1	1
Torquay U	Tr	11/01	01	9	8	1

GOODWILLIE David
Born: Stirling, Scotland, 23 March, 1989 — F/W
Scotland: 3/U21-9/Youth

League Club	Source	Date Signed	Seasons Played	Apps	Subs	Gls
Blackburn Rov	Dundee U	08/11	11-12	6	22	2
Crystal Palace	L	08/12	12	0	1	0
Blackpool	L	01/14	13	8	5	3

GOODWIN Craig
Born: Wrexham, Wales, 12 February, 1974 — D

League Club	Source	Date Signed	Seasons Played	Apps	Subs	Gls
Chester C	Aston Villa (YT)	08/92	92	3	2	0

GOODWIN David (Dave)
Born: Nantwich, Cheshire, England, 15 October, 1954 — F

League Club	Source	Date Signed	Seasons Played	Apps	Subs	Gls
Stoke C	App	06/72	73-77	22	4	3
Workington	L	10/76	76	7	0	0
Mansfield T	Tr	11/77	77-79	42	4	5
Bury	Tr	09/80	80	2	2	0
Rochdale	Tr	08/81	81	34	5	6
Crewe Alex	Tr	08/82	82	4	3	0

GOODWIN Eric
Born: Chesterfield, Derbyshire, England, 6 March, 1929 — CH
Died: Nottinghamshire, England, November, 2012

League Club	Source	Date Signed	Seasons Played	Apps	Subs	Gls
Mansfield T	St Aidan Stags	09/53	53-54	9	-	0

GOODWIN Frederick (Freddie)
Born: Heywood, Greater Manchester, England, 28 June, 1933 — WH

League Club	Source	Date Signed	Seasons Played	Apps	Subs	Gls
Manchester U		10/53	54-59	95	-	7
Leeds U	Tr	03/60	59-63	107	-	2
Scunthorpe U	Tr	12/64	65	5	1	1

GOODWIN Frederick James (Freddie)
Born: Stockport, Greater Manchester, England, 4 January, 1944 — M

League Club	Source	Date Signed	Seasons Played	Apps	Subs	Gls
Wolverhampton W	Jnr	01/61	61-65	44	1	0
Stockport Co	Tr	01/66	65-69	171	5	20
Blackburn Rov	Tr	03/70	69-71	63	1	4
Southport	Tr	10/71	71	10	2	0
Port Vale	Tr	08/72	72	27	0	2
Stockport Co	Macclesfield T	08/74	74	29	0	1

GOODWIN Ian David
Born: Irlam, Greater Manchester, England, 14 November, 1950 — CD

League Club	Source	Date Signed	Seasons Played	Apps	Subs	Gls
Coventry C	Oldham Ath (App)	12/68	70	4	0	0
Brighton & HA	Tr	10/70	70-73	52	4	0

GOODWIN James Michael (Jim)
Born: Waterford, Republic of Ireland, 20 November, 1981 — CD/M
Republic of Ireland: 1/B-1/U21-14

League Club	Source	Date Signed	Seasons Played	Apps	Subs	Gls
Stockport Co	Glasgow Celtic	06/02	02-04	81	22	7
Scunthorpe U	Tr	07/05	05-07	74	10	6
Huddersfield T	Tr	07/08	08-09	38	4	1
Oldham Ath	L	01/10	09	8	0	0

GOODWIN John William (Jackie)
Born: Worcester, England, 29 September, 1920 — RW
Died: Worcester, England, 7 May, 1995

League Club	Source	Date Signed	Seasons Played	Apps	Subs	Gls
Birmingham C	Worcester C	05/46	46-48	32	-	8
Brentford	Tr	04/49	49-53	131	-	22

GOODWIN Lee Jon
Born: Basildon, England, 5 September, 1978 — RB

League Club	Source	Date Signed	Seasons Played	Apps	Subs	Gls
West Ham U	YT	07/97				
Dagenham & Red	Tr	08/98	07	0	1	0

GOODWIN Leslie (Les)
Born: Manchester, England, 30 April, 1924 — W
Died: Workington, Cumbria, England, 20 December, 2002

League Club	Source	Date Signed	Seasons Played	Apps	Subs	Gls
Oldham Ath	Blackpool (Am)	08/44	46	7	-	0
Southport	Tr	07/47	47-48	16	-	2

GOODWIN Mark Adrian
Born: Sheffield, England, 23 February, 1960 — M

League Club	Source	Date Signed	Seasons Played	Apps	Subs	Gls
Leicester C	App	11/77	77-80	69	22	8
Notts Co	Tr	03/81	80-86	226	11	24
Walsall	Tr	07/87	87-89	81	11	2

GOODWIN Samuel Gourlay (Sam)
Born: Tarbolton, Ayrshire, Scotland, 14 March, 1943 — M/LB
Died: Coatbridge, Lanarkshire, Scotland, 9 March, 2005

League Club	Source	Date Signed	Seasons Played	Apps	Subs	Gls
Crystal Palace	Airdrieonians	09/71	71	18	7	0

GOODWIN Shaun Lee
Born: Rotherham, South Yorkshire, England, 14 June, 1969 — M

League Club	Source	Date Signed	Seasons Played	Apps	Subs	Gls
Rotherham U	YT	07/87	87-97	258	22	39

GOODWIN Stephen Alan (Steve)
Born: Chadderton, Greater Manchester, England, 23 February, 1954 — M

League Club	Source	Date Signed	Seasons Played	Apps	Subs	Gls
Norwich C	App	02/72	70-74	2	1	0
Scunthorpe U	L	09/73	73	2	0	0
Southend U	Tr	06/75	75-78	68	7	10

GOODWIN Thomas Neil (Tommy)
Born: Leicester, England, 8 November, 1979 — CD

League Club	Source	Date Signed	Seasons Played	Apps	Subs	Gls
Leicester C	YT	07/98	99	1	0	0

GOODYEAR Clive
Born: Lincoln, England, 15 January, 1961 — CD

League Club	Source	Date Signed	Seasons Played	Apps	Subs	Gls
Luton T	Lincoln U	10/78	79-83	85	5	4
Plymouth Arg	Tr	08/84	84-86	99	7	5
Wimbledon	Tr	07/87	87-89	25	1	0
Brentford	Tr	03/91	90	10	0	0

GOODYEAR George William
Born: Luton, England, 5 July, 1916 — WH
Died: Bedford, England, 16 July, 2001

League Club	Source	Date Signed	Seasons Played	Apps	Subs	Gls
Luton T	Hitchin T	10/38	46	10	-	0
Southend U	Tr	07/47	47-48	59	-	1
Crystal Palace	Tr	06/49				

GOPE-FENEPEJ John
Born: Noumea, New Caledonia, 16 November, 1978 — CD

League Club	Source	Date Signed	Seasons Played	Apps	Subs	Gls
Bolton W (L)	FC Nantes (FRA)	09/00	00	0	2	0

GORAM Andrew Lewis (Andy)
Born: Bury, Greater Manchester, England, 13 April, 1964 — G
Scotland: 43/U21-1

League Club	Source	Date Signed	Seasons Played	Apps	Subs	Gls
Oldham Ath	West Bromwich A (App)	08/81	81-87	195	0	0
Notts Co	Glasgow Rangers	09/98	98	1	0	0
Sheffield U	Tr	09/98	98	7	0	0
Manchester U	Motherwell	03/01	00	2	0	0
Coventry C	Tr	08/01	01	6	1	0
Oldham Ath	Tr	03/02	01	4	0	0

GORAM Lewis Albert
Born: Edinburgh, Scotland, 2 July, 1926 — G
Died: Bury, Greater Manchester, England, January, 1989

League Club	Source	Date Signed	Seasons Played	Apps	Subs	Gls
Bury	Third Lanark	06/50	50-56	114	-	0

GORDINE Barry
Born: Bethnal Green, E London, England, 1 September, 1948 — G

League Club	Source	Date Signed	Seasons Played	Apps	Subs	Gls
Sheffield U	Gravesend & Northfleet	06/68				
Oldham Ath	Tr	12/68	68-70	83	0	0
Southend U	Tr	08/71				
Brentford		10/74				

GORDON Andrew (Andy)
Born: Bathgate, West Lothian, Scotland, 6 July, 1944 — F

League Club	Source	Date Signed	Seasons Played	Apps	Subs	Gls
Darlington (Am)	West Auckland T	08/69	69	2	2	0

GORDON Benjamin Lawrence (Ben)
Born: Bradford, England, 2 March, 1991 — LB
England: Youth

League Club	Source	Date Signed	Seasons Played	Apps	Subs	Gls
Chelsea	Sch	07/08				
Tranmere Rov	L	03/10	09	4	0	0
Scunthorpe U	L	01/11	10	13	1	0
Peterborough U	L	08/11	11	0	1	0
Birmingham C	L	08/12	12	1	0	0
Yeovil T	L	03/13	12	1	2	0
Colchester U	Ross Co	07/14	14	16	2	0

GORDON Colin Kenneth
Born: Stourbridge, West Midlands, England, 17 January, 1963 — F

League Club	Source	Date Signed	Seasons Played	Apps	Subs	Gls
Swindon T	Oldbury U	10/84	84-85	70	2	34
Wimbledon	Tr	06/86	86	2	1	0
Gillingham	L	02/87	86	4	0	2
Reading	Tr	07/87	87-88	23	1	9
Bristol C	L	03/88	87	8	0	4
Fulham	Tr	10/88	88	12	5	2
Birmingham C	Tr	06/89	89-90	17	9	3
Hereford U	L	09/90	90	6	0	0
Walsall	L	12/90	90	6	0	1
Bristol Rov	L	01/91	90	1	3	0
Leicester C	Tr	07/91	91-92	18	6	5

GORDON Craig Anthony
Born: Edinburgh, Scotland, 31 December, 1982 — G
Scotland: 43/B-2/U21-5

League Club	Source	Date Signed	Seasons Played	Apps	Subs	Gls
Sunderland	Heart of Midlothian	08/07	07-11	88	0	0

GORDON Dale Andrew
Born: Caister-On-Sea, Norfolk, England, 9 January, 1967 — W
England: B-2/U21-4/Youth/Schools

League Club	Source	Date Signed	Seasons Played	Apps	Subs	Gls
Norwich C	App	01/84	84-91	194	12	31
West Ham U	Glasgow Rangers	07/93	93-95	8	1	1
Peterborough U	L	03/95	94	6	0	1
Millwall	L	03/96	95	6	0	0
Bournemouth	Tr	08/96	96	14	2	0

GORDON Dean Dwight Joshua
Born: Thornton Heath, S London, England, 10 February, 1973 — LB
England: U21-13

League Club	Source	Date Signed	Seasons Played	Apps	Subs	Gls
Crystal Palace	YT	07/91	91-97	181	20	20
Middlesbrough	Tr	07/98	98-01	53	10	4
Cardiff C	L	11/01	01	7	0	2
Coventry C	Tr	08/02	02-03	33	2	1
Reading	L	03/04	03	0	3	0
Grimsby T	Tr	08/04	04	20	0	2
Blackpool	Apoel Nicosia (CYP)	01/06	05	1	0	0
Torquay U	Lewes	02/07	06	8	0	0

GORDON Denis William
Born: Bilston, West Midlands, England, 7 June, 1924 — RW
Died: Jersey, Channel Islands, May, 1998

League Club	Source	Date Signed	Seasons Played	Apps	Subs	Gls
West Bromwich A	Oxford C	09/47	47-51	27	-	2
Brighton & HA	Tr	07/52	52-60	277	-	62

GORDON Henry (Harry)
Born: Glasgow, Scotland, 10 December, 1931 — WH
Died: 29 July, 2014

League Club	Source	Date Signed	Seasons Played	Apps	Subs	Gls
Bury	Strathclyde	06/51	52-56	21	-	0

GORDON Henry Alexander (Alec)
Born: Livingston, West Lothian, Scotland, 25 July, 1940 — WH
Died: Moffat, Dumfries & Galloway, Scotland, 18 February, 1996

League Club	Source	Date Signed	Seasons Played	Apps	Subs	Gls
Bradford Park Ave	Dundee U	08/65	65-66	61	0	2

GORDON James (Jimmy)
Born: Fauldhouse, West Lothian, Scotland, 23 October, 1915 — WH
Died: Derby, England, 22 August, 1996

League Club	Source	Date Signed	Seasons Played	Apps	Subs	Gls
Newcastle U	Wishaw Jnrs	04/35	34-38	132	-	2
Middlesbrough	Tr	11/45	46-53	231	-	3

GORDON James Stephen (Jimmy)
Born: Birmingham, England, 3 October, 1955 — G
England: Schools

League Club	Source	Date Signed	Seasons Played	Apps	Subs	Gls
Luton T	Blackpool (App)	09/73				
Lincoln C	Tr	07/74	76-77	4	0	0
Scunthorpe U	Reading (NC)	09/78	79-80	34	0	0

GORDON John Duncan Sinclair (Johnny)
Born: Portsmouth, England, 11 September, 1931 — IF
Died: Portsmouth, England, 26 May, 2001

League Club	Source	Date Signed	Seasons Played	Apps	Subs	Gls
Portsmouth	Carnoustie Panmure	01/49	51-58	209	-	69
Birmingham C	Tr	09/58	58-60	96	-	32
Portsmouth	Tr	03/61	60-66	234	0	37

GORDON Kenyatta Gavin (Gavin)
Born: Manchester, England, 24 June, 1979 — F

League Club	Source	Date Signed	Seasons Played	Apps	Subs	Gls
Hull C	YT	07/96	95-97	22	16	9
Lincoln C	Tr	11/97	97-00	87	12	28
Cardiff C	Tr	12/00	00-03	26	24	5
Oxford U	L	09/02	02	3	3	1
Notts Co	Tr	07/04	04-05	27	6	5

GORDON Michael Alexander
Born: Tooting, SW London, England, 11 October, 1984 — W

League Club	Source	Date Signed	Seasons Played	Apps	Subs	Gls
Wimbledon	Arsenal (YT)	03/03	02-03	8	11	0
Lincoln C	Merstham	11/09	09	4	1	0

GORDON Neville Spencer Damian
Born: Greenwich, SE London, England, 15 November, 1975 — F

League Club	Source	Date Signed	Seasons Played	Apps	Subs	Gls
Millwall	YT	05/94				
Reading	Tr	08/95	95	0	1	0

GORDON Peter John
Born: Northampton, England, 21 May, 1932 — IF/W
Died: Claydon, Suffolk, England, 22 May, 1990

League Club	Source	Date Signed	Seasons Played	Apps	Subs	Gls
Norwich C	Northampton Amats	12/49	53-57	160	-	34
Watford	Tr	07/58	58-59	43	-	13
Exeter C	Tr	07/60	60-61	67	-	12
Newport Co	Tr	07/62	62	8	-	1

GORDON Robert Baxter
Born: Ormiston, East Lothian, Scotland, 5 September, 1923 — IF
Died: Edinburgh, Scotland, 20 October, 2001

League Club	Source	Date Signed	Seasons Played	Apps	Subs	Gls
Millwall	Annandale Jnrs	01/45	46-47	5	-	0

GORDON Rohdell Antonio
Born: Wandsworth, SW London, England, 28 March, 1996 — W

League Club	Source	Date Signed	Seasons Played	Apps	Subs	Gls
Stevenage	Sch	07/14	13	1	2	0

GORDON William James Woodhouse (Billy)
Born: Carlisle, Cumbria, England, 22 November, 1926 — CF
Died: Barrow, Cumbria, England, 11 October, 1983

League Club	Source	Date Signed	Seasons Played	Apps	Subs	Gls
Carlisle U		08/48	47-48	16	-	3
Barrow	Tr	07/50	49-57	302	-	145
Workington	Tr	03/58	57-58	33	-	7
Barrow	Tr	10/59				

GORDON-HUTTON Jaanai Dereece
Born: Northampton, England, 7 December, 1995 — F

League Club	Source	Date Signed	Seasons Played	Apps	Subs	Gls
Peterborough U	Sch	12/12	12-13	1	3	0
West Ham U	Tr	01/14				

GORE Ian George
Born: Prescot, Merseyside, England, 10 January, 1968 — CD

League Club	Source	Date Signed	Seasons Played	Apps	Subs	Gls
Birmingham C	App	01/86				
Blackpool	Southport	01/88	88-94	196	4	0
Torquay U	Tr	08/95	95	25	0	2
Doncaster Rov	Tr	03/96	95-97	65	1	1

GORE Shane Stephen
Born: Ashford, Kent, England, 28 October, 1981 — G

League Club	Source	Date Signed	Seasons Played	Apps	Subs	Gls
Wimbledon	YT	06/01	01	0	1	0

GORE Shaun Michael
Born: West Ham, E London, England, 21 September, 1968 — CD

League Club	Source	Date Signed	Seasons Played	Apps	Subs	Gls
Fulham	App	06/86	85-88	25	1	0
Halifax T	L	02/91	90	15	0	0

GORE Thomas John (Tommy)
Born: Liverpool, England, 26 November, 1953 — M

League Club	Source	Date Signed	Seasons Played	Apps	Subs	Gls
Tranmere Rov	Liverpool (Jnr)	08/72				
Wigan Ath	Tr	01/74	78-80	102	0	14
Bury	Tr	10/80	80-82	118	1	16
Port Vale	Tr	07/83	83	33	3	2

GORIN Edward Rosser (Ted)
Born: Cardiff, Wales, 2 March, 1924 — CF
Died: Cardiff, Wales, 30 May, 2013

League Club	Source	Date Signed	Seasons Played	Apps	Subs	Gls
Cardiff C	Grange Ath	10/48	48-49	6	-	2
Scunthorpe U	Tr	07/50	50	26	-	12
Shrewsbury T	Tr	01/51	50-51	18	-	3

GORING Harry (Peter)
Born: Bishop's Cleeve, Gloucestershire, England, 2 January, 1927 — WH/CF
Died: Bishop's Cleeve, Gloucestershire, England, December, 1994

League Club	Source	Date Signed	Seasons Played	Apps	Subs	Gls
Arsenal	Cheltenham T	01/48	49-58	220	-	51

GORKSS Kaspars
Born: Riga, Latvia, 6 November, 1981 — CD
Latvia: 69/U21-12

League Club	Source	Date Signed	Seasons Played	Apps	Subs	Gls
Blackpool	Ventspils (LAT)	01/07	06-07	47	3	5
Queens Park Rgrs	Tr	08/08	08-10	112	2	6
Reading	Tr	08/11	11-13	80	1	7
Wolverhampton W	L	02/13	12	15	0	0
Colchester U		12/14	14	7	0	1

GORMAN Andrew David (Andy)
Born: Cardiff, Wales, 13 September, 1974 — RB

League Club	Source	Date Signed	Seasons Played	Apps	Subs	Gls
Cardiff C	YT	-	91-92	8	4	1

GORMAN John (Johnny)
Born: Winchburgh, West Lothian, Scotland, 16 August, 1949 — LB
Northern Ireland: U21-4

League Club	Source	Date Signed	Seasons Played	Apps	Subs	Gls
Carlisle U	Glasgow Celtic	09/70	70-76	228	1	5
Tottenham H	Tr	11/76	76-78	30	0	0

GORMAN Keith
Born: Bishop Auckland, County Durham, England, 13 October, 1966 — LW

League Club	Source	Date Signed	Seasons Played	Apps	Subs	Gls
Ipswich T	App	01/84				
Colchester U	L	09/86	86	0	1	0
Darlington	Tr	01/87	86	4	3	2

GORMAN Paul Anthony
Born: Dublin, Republic of Ireland, 6 August, 1963 — M/FB
Republic of Ireland: U21-1/Youth

League Club	Source	Date Signed	Seasons Played	Apps	Subs	Gls
Arsenal	App	10/80	81-83	5	1	0
Birmingham C	Tr	06/84	84	6	0	0
Carlisle U	Tr	03/85	84-89	137	11	7
Shrewsbury T	Tr	11/89	89-91	58	6	1
Carlisle U	Tr	12/91	91	5	0	0

GORMAN Paul Michael
Born: Macclesfield, Cheshire, England, 18 September, 1968 — F

League Club	Source	Date Signed	Seasons Played	Apps	Subs	Gls
Doncaster Rov	YT	07/87	87-88	1	15	2
Charlton Ath	Fisher Ath	03/91	90-93	19	21	8

GORMAN Rory John McCaughan (Johnny)
Born: Sheffield, England, 26 October, 1992 — W
Northern Ireland: 9/U21-4/Youth

League Club	Source	Date Signed	Seasons Played	Apps	Subs	Gls
Wolverhampton W	Sch	12/10	11	0	1	0
Plymouth Arg	L	08/12	12	1	1	0
Leyton Orient	Tr	08/13	13	0	2	0

GORMAN William Charles (Bill)
Born: Sligo, Republic of Ireland, 13 July, 1911 — FB
Died: Bury, Greater Manchester, England, December, 1978
Republic of Ireland: 13//Northern Ireland: 4

League Club	Source	Date Signed	Seasons Played	Apps	Subs	Gls
Bury	Shettleston Jnrs	09/34	36-38	52	-	0
Brentford	Tr	12/38	38-49	125	-	0

GORMLEY Edward Joseph (Eddie)
Born: Dublin, Republic of Ireland, 23 October, 1968 — M
Republic of Ireland: U21-3

League Club	Source	Date Signed	Seasons Played	Apps	Subs	Gls
Tottenham H	Bray W (ROI)	11/87				
Chesterfield	L	11/88	88	4	0	0
Doncaster Rov	Tr	07/90	90-92	110	8	16

GORMLEY Philip (Phil)
Born: Greenock, Inverclyde, Scotland, 13 October, 1924 — CF/WH
Died: Greenock, Inverclyde, Scotland, 24 January, 1988

League Club	Source	Date Signed	Seasons Played	Apps	Subs	Gls
Aldershot	Glasgow Celtic	08/50	50-52	65	-	9

GORNALL John (Jack)
Born: Preston, Lancashire, England, 28 March, 1941 — CH

League Club	Source	Date Signed	Seasons Played	Apps	Subs	Gls
Preston NE	Jnr	07/60	61-62	4	-	0

GORNELL Terence Michael (Terry)
Born: Liverpool, England, 16 December, 1989 — F

League Club	Source	Date Signed	Seasons Played	Apps	Subs	Gls
Tranmere Rov	Sch	07/08	08-10	25	15	3
Accrington Stan	L	09/08	08	10	1	4
Accrington Stan	Tr	08/10	10	40	0	13
Shrewsbury T	Tr	07/11	11-12	37	16	9
Rochdale	Tr	11/12	12	16	3	5
Cheltenham T	Tr	07/13	13-14	39	20	6
Accrington Stan	Tr	01/15	14	14	1	4

GORRE Dean
Born: Paramaribo, Suriname, 10 September, 1970 — M

League Club	Source	Date Signed	Seasons Played	Apps	Subs	Gls
Huddersfield T	Ajax (NED)	09/99	99-00	49	13	6
Barnsley	Tr	07/01	01-03	48	17	9
Blackpool	Tr	08/04	04	0	1	0

GORRE Kenji Joel
Born: Rotterdam, Netherlands, 29 September, 1994 — W

League Club	Source	Date Signed	Seasons Played	Apps	Subs	Gls
Swansea C	Manchester U (Sch)	04/13	14	0	1	0

GORRIE David Alexander
Born: Liverpool, England, 21 January, 1943 — RH

League Club	Source	Date Signed	Seasons Played	Apps	Subs	Gls
Everton	Jnr	05/60				
Stockport Co	Tr	07/62	62	18	-	0

GORRY Martin Christopher
Born: Derby, England, 29 December, 1954 — LB

League Club	Source	Date Signed	Seasons Played	Apps	Subs	Gls
Barnsley	App	12/72	75-76	34	0	3
Newcastle U	Tr	10/76	77	0	1	0
Hartlepool U	Tr	07/78	78-79	59	0	0

GORTON Andrew William (Andy)
Born: Salford, England, 23 September, 1966 — G

League Club	Source	Date Signed	Seasons Played	Apps	Subs	Gls
Oldham Ath	App	07/84	85-87	26	0	0
Stockport Co	L	12/86	86	14	0	0
Tranmere Rov	L	05/88	87	1	0	0
Stockport Co	Tr	08/88	88	34	0	0
Lincoln C	Tr	08/89	89	20	0	0
Oldham Ath	Glossop NE	02/91				
Crewe Alex	Tr	03/91	90	3	0	0

GOSLIN Richard William
Born: Bovey Tracey, Devon, England, 31 October, 1956 — F

League Club	Source	Date Signed	Seasons Played	Apps	Subs	Gls
Torquay U	Nottingham F (App)	04/74	73-75	14	5	2

GOSLING Daniel (Dan)
Born: Brixham, Devon, England, 2 February, 1990 — M
England: U21-3/Youth

League Club	Source	Date Signed	Seasons Played	Apps	Subs	Gls
Plymouth Arg	Sch	02/07	06-07	13	9	2
Everton	Tr	01/08	08-09	9	13	4
Newcastle U	Tr	07/10	10-13	5	19	1
Blackpool	L	10/13	13	13	1	2
Bournemouth	Tr	05/14	14	1	17	0

GOSLING Jake
Born: Newquay, Cornwall, England, 11 August, 1993 — W
Gibraltar: 6

League Club	Source	Date Signed	Seasons Played	Apps	Subs	Gls
Exeter C	Sch	07/11	12-13	6	9	1

GOSLING Jamie John
Born: Bath, England, 21 March, 1982 — M

League Club	Source	Date Signed	Seasons Played	Apps	Subs	Gls
Yeovil T	Bath C	07/03	03	4	8	1
Torquay U	Team Bath	12/04	04	6	1	1

GOSNEY Andrew Robert (Andy)
Born: Southampton, England, 8 November, 1963 — G
England: Youth

League Club	Source	Date Signed	Seasons Played	Apps	Subs	Gls
Portsmouth	App	11/81	81-91	48	0	0
York C	L	10/91	91	5	0	0
Birmingham C	Tr	07/92	92	21	0	0
Exeter C	Tr	10/93	93	1	0	0

GOSS Jeremy (Jerry)
Born: Dhekelia, Cyprus, 11 May, 1965 — M
England: Schools//Wales: 9

League Club	Source	Date Signed	Seasons Played	Apps	Subs	Gls
Norwich C	Jnr	03/83	83-95	155	33	14

GOSSET Daniel Sion (Danny)
Born: Bangor, Gwynedd, Wales, 30 September, 1994 — M

League Club	Source	Date Signed	Seasons Played	Apps	Subs	Gls
Oldham Ath	Sch	07/13	12	1	1	0

GOTSMANOV Sergei Anaiolyenich
Born: Minsk, Belarus, 17 March, 1959 — F
Belarus: 3//Soviet Union: 31/U23-6

League Club	Source	Date Signed	Seasons Played	Apps	Subs	Gls
Brighton & HA	Dynamo Minsk (BLR)	02/90	89	14	2	4
Southampton	Dynamo Minsk (BLR)	08/90	90	2	6	0

GOTTS James Atkinson (Jim)
Born: Seaton Delaval, Northumberland, England, 17 January, 1917 — RW
Died: Ealing, W London, England, December, 1998

League Club	Source	Date Signed	Seasons Played	Apps	Subs	Gls
Brentford	Ashington	01/46				
Brighton & HA	Tr	07/46	46	2	-	0

GOTTSKALKSSON Olafur (Ole)
Born: Keflavik, Iceland, 12 March, 1968 — G
Iceland: 10/U21-6/Youth

League Club	Source	Date Signed	Seasons Played	Apps	Subs	Gls
Brentford	Hibernian	07/00	00-01	73	0	0
Torquay U	Tr	09/04	04	15	0	0

GOUCK Andrew Scott (Andy)
Born: Blackpool, Lancashire, England, 8 June, 1972 — M

League Club	Source	Date Signed	Seasons Played	Apps	Subs	Gls
Blackpool	YT	07/90	89-95	121	27	12
Rochdale	Tr	07/96	96-97	58	8	8

GOUFFRAN Yoan
Born: Paris, France, 25 May, 1986 — W
France: U21-22

League Club	Source	Date Signed	Seasons Played	Apps	Subs	Gls
Newcastle U	Bordeaux (FRA)	01/13	12-14	69	12	11

GOUGH Alan Thomas
Born: Watford, Hertfordshire, England, 10 March, 1971 — G
Republic of Ireland: U21-5/Youth

League Club	Source	Date Signed	Seasons Played	Apps	Subs	Gls
Portsmouth	Shelbourne (ROI)	07/89				
Fulham	Tr	06/92	92	3	0	0

GOUGH Anthony Michael (Tony)
Born: Bath, England, 18 March, 1940 — M

League Club	Source	Date Signed	Seasons Played	Apps	Subs	Gls
Bristol Rov	Bath C	05/58	58	1	-	0
Swindon T	Bath C	07/70	70	25	1	2
Torquay U	Hereford U	07/72	72	2	0	0

GOUGH Charles Richard (Richard)
Born: Stockholm, Sweden, 5 April, 1962 — CD
Scotland: 61/U21-5

League Club	Source	Date Signed	Seasons Played	Apps	Subs	Gls
Tottenham H	Dundee U	08/86	86-87	49	0	2
Nottingham F (L)	San Jose Clash (USA)	03/99	98	7	0	0
Everton	San Jose Clash (USA)	06/99	99-00	38	0	1

GOUGH Charles Storrar (Charlie)
Born: Glasgow, Scotland, 21 May, 1939 — LH
Died: Cape Town, South Africa, 3 April, 2015

League Club	Source	Date Signed	Seasons Played	Apps	Subs	Gls
Charlton Ath	Alton T	06/63	64	4	-	0

GOUGH Conor John Joseph
Born: Ilford, E London, England, 9 August, 1993 — G

League Club	Source	Date Signed	Seasons Played	Apps	Subs	Gls
Charlton Ath	Sch	07/11				
Bristol Rov	Tr	05/12	11-12	2	0	0

GOUGH Keith
Born: Willenhall, West Midlands, England, 4 February, 1953 — M/RW
England: Schools

League Club	Source	Date Signed	Seasons Played	Apps	Subs	Gls
Walsall	App	02/71	69-71	11	4	0
Oxford U	Tr	07/72	72-74	32	7	5

GOUGH Matthew Michael (Mike)
Born: Beeston, Nottinghamshire, England, 29 December, 1935 — LH
Died: Basford, Nottinghamshire, England, November, 1998

League Club	Source	Date Signed	Seasons Played	Apps	Subs	Gls
Aldershot	Aldershot Garrison	05/56	56-58	20	-	1

GOUGH Neil
Born: Harlow, Essex, England, 1 September, 1981 — F

League Club	Source	Date Signed	Seasons Played	Apps	Subs	Gls
Leyton Orient	YT	07/00	99-01	2	13	1

GOUGH Raymond John (Ray)
Born: Belfast, Northern Ireland, 8 February, 1938 — LH

League Club	Source	Date Signed	Seasons Played	Apps	Subs	Gls
Exeter C	Linfield	10/63				
Millwall	Tr	10/64	64	13	-	0

GOUGH Robert George (Bobby)
Born: Birmingham, England, 20 July, 1949 — F/M

League Club	Source	Date Signed	Seasons Played	Apps	Subs	Gls
Walsall	App	07/67	66	1	0	0
Port Vale	Tr	07/68	68-73	189	21	33
Stockport Co	L	02/73	73	6	0	0
Southport	Tr	07/74	74-75	61	0	16
Colchester U	Tr	01/76	75-80	195	1	65

GOULD Geoffrey (Geoff)
Born: Blackburn, Greater Manchester, England, 7 January, 1945 — LW

League Club	Source	Date Signed	Seasons Played	Apps	Subs	Gls
Bradford Park Ave	App	01/62	62-68	129	2	18
Lincoln C	L	02/68	67	1	0	0
Notts Co	Tr	07/69	69	1	0	0

GOULD Henry (Harry)
Born: Birkenhead, Wirral, England, 5 January, 1925 — IF
Died: Preston, Lancashire, England, 20 May, 2010

League Club	Source	Date Signed	Seasons Played	Apps	Subs	Gls
Tranmere Rov	Liverpool (Am)	09/46	46-48	5	-	2
Southport	Northwich Victoria	09/50	50	16	-	2
Tranmere Rov	Tr	07/51				

GOULD James Robert (Jamie)
Born: Rushden, Northamptonshire, England, 15 January, 1982 — M

League Club	Source	Date Signed	Seasons Played	Apps	Subs	Gls
Northampton T	YT	07/00	00	0	1	0
Boston U	Tr	07/01	02	10	10	2

GOULD John Barrie (Barrie)
Born: Ammanford, Carmarthenshire, Wales, 18 January, 1944 — CF/RH

League Club	Source	Date Signed	Seasons Played	Apps	Subs	Gls
Arsenal	App	11/61				
Chelsea	Tr	02/64				
Peterborough U	Tr	07/65	65	18	0	3

GOULD Jonathan Alan
Born: Paddington, Central London, England, 18 July, 1968 — G
Scotland: 2/B-1

League Club	Source	Date Signed	Seasons Played	Apps	Subs	Gls
Halifax T	Clevedon T	07/90	90-91	32	0	0
West Bromwich A	Tr	01/92				
Coventry C	Tr	07/92	92-94	25	0	0
Bradford C	Tr	03/96	95-96	18	0	0
Gillingham	L	10/96	96	3	0	0
Preston NE	Glasgow Celtic	01/03	02-04	54	1	0

GOULD Robert Alfred (Bobby)
Born: Coventry, England, 12 June, 1946 — F

League Club	Source	Date Signed	Seasons Played	Apps	Subs	Gls
Coventry C	App	06/64	63-67	78	4	40
Arsenal	Tr	02/68	67-69	57	8	16
Wolverhampton W	Tr	06/70	70-71	39	1	18
West Bromwich A	Tr	09/71	71-72	52	0	18
Bristol C	Tr	12/72	72-73	35	0	15
West Ham U	Tr	11/73	73-75	46	5	15
Wolverhampton W	Tr	12/75	75-76	24	10	13
Bristol Rov	Tr	10/77	77-78	35	1	12
Hereford U	Tr	09/78	78-79	42	3	13

GOULD Ronald Donald (Ronnie)
Born: Bethnal Green, E London, England, 27 September, 1982 — M

League Club	Source	Date Signed	Seasons Played	Apps	Subs	Gls
Leyton Orient	YT	10/00	99	0	2	0

GOULD Trevor Roy
Born: Coventry, England, 5 March, 1950 — RB/M
England: Schools

League Club	Source	Date Signed	Seasons Played	Apps	Subs	Gls
Coventry C	Jnr	07/67	69	9	0	0
Northampton T	Tr	10/70	70-72	102	3	6

GOULD Walter (Wally)
Born: Thrybergh, South Yorkshire, England, 25 September, 1938 — RW

League Club	Source	Date Signed	Seasons Played	Apps	Subs	Gls
Sheffield U	Rawmarsh Welfare	02/58	58	5	-	1
York C	Tr	02/61	60-63	120	-	25
Brighton & HA	Tr	01/64	63-67	166	2	45

GOULDEN Albert Edward
Born: Salford, England, 5 February, 1945 — LB

League Club	Source	Date Signed	Seasons Played	Apps	Subs	Gls
Bolton W	Jnr	02/62	62	1	-	0

GOULDEN Leonard Arthur (Len)
Born: Hackney, E London, England, 9 July, 1912 — IF
Died: Plaistow, E London, England, 14 February, 1995
England: 14/FLge-2/Schools/War-6

League Club	Source	Date Signed	Seasons Played	Apps	Subs	Gls
West Ham U	Leyton	04/33	32-38	239	-	54
Chelsea	Tr	08/45	46-49	99	-	17

GOULDEN Roy Leonard
Born: Ilford, E London, England, 22 September, 1937 IF
England: Schools

League Club	Source	Date Signed	Seasons Played	Apps	Subs	Gls
Arsenal	Jnr	09/54	58	1	-	0
Southend U	Tr	05/61	61	9	-	2
Ipswich T	Tr	07/62				

GOULDING Eric
Born: Winsford, Cheshire, England, 22 November, 1924 RB

League Club	Source	Date Signed	Seasons Played	Apps	Subs	Gls
Everton	Over Ath	10/45				
Crewe Alex	Tr	10/46	46	1	-	0

GOULDING Jeffrey Colin (Jeff)
Born: Sutton, S London, England, 13 May, 1984 F
England: Semi Pro-1

League Club	Source	Date Signed	Seasons Played	Apps	Subs	Gls
Bournemouth	Fisher Ath	09/08	08-09	17	27	4
Cheltenham T	Tr	07/10	10-12	55	38	18
Aldershot T	Tr	02/13	12	5	5	1

GOULDING Stephen (Steve)
Born: Mexborough, South Yorkshire, England, 21 January, 1954 RB
Died: Doncaster, South Yorkshire, England, April, 1985

League Club	Source	Date Signed	Seasons Played	Apps	Subs	Gls
Sheffield U	App	05/71	71-75	28	0	0

GOULET Brent
Born: North Dakota, USA, 19 June, 1964 F
USA: 8

League Club	Source	Date Signed	Seasons Played	Apps	Subs	Gls
Bournemouth	FC Portland (USA)	11/87	87	2	4	0
Crewe Alex	L	01/88	87	2	1	3

GOULON Darryl Herold (Herold)
Born: Paris, France, 12 June, 1988 M
France: U21-3

League Club	Source	Date Signed	Seasons Played	Apps	Subs	Gls
Middlesbrough	Olymp Lyonnais (FRA)	07/06				
Blackburn Rov	UC Le Mans (FRA)	10/10	10	1	3	0
Doncaster Rov	L	11/11	11	5	1	0

GOULOOZE Richard
Born: Alkmaar, Netherlands, 16 November, 1967 M
Netherlands: Youth

League Club	Source	Date Signed	Seasons Played	Apps	Subs	Gls
Derby Co	Heerenveen (NED)	09/92	92	7	5	0

GOUNDRY William (Bill)
Born: Middlesbrough, England, 28 March, 1934 WH/IF
Died: Cleveland, England, February, 2012

League Club	Source	Date Signed	Seasons Played	Apps	Subs	Gls
Brentford	Huddersfield T (Am)	05/55	55-60	141	-	12

GOURLAY Archibald Murdoch (Archie)
Born: Greenock, Inverclyde, Scotland, 29 June, 1969 M

League Club	Source	Date Signed	Seasons Played	Apps	Subs	Gls
Newcastle U	Greenock Morton	03/88	88-90	2	1	0
Hartlepool U	Motherwell	09/94	94	0	1	0

GOVAN Alexander (Alex)
Born: Glasgow, Scotland, 16 June, 1929 W

League Club	Source	Date Signed	Seasons Played	Apps	Subs	Gls
Plymouth Arg	Bridgeton Cross BC	09/46	46-52	110	-	28
Birmingham C	Tr	06/53	53-57	165	-	53
Portsmouth	Tr	03/58	57-58	11	-	2
Plymouth Arg	Tr	09/58	58-59	32	-	8

GOVAN Charles Pearson
Born: Belfast, Northern Ireland, 12 January, 1943 IF
Northern Ireland: Schools

League Club	Source	Date Signed	Seasons Played	Apps	Subs	Gls
Burnley	Jnr	01/60				
Mansfield T	Tr	06/63	63-64	11	-	0

GOVIER Stephen (Steve)
Born: Watford, Hertfordshire, England, 6 April, 1952 CD

League Club	Source	Date Signed	Seasons Played	Apps	Subs	Gls
Norwich C	App	07/69	70-73	22	0	1
Brighton & HA	Tr	04/74	74	12	0	1
Grimsby T	Tr	12/74	74-76	23	1	0

GOW Alan
Born: Clydebank, Dunbartonshire, Scotland, 9 October, 1982 F
Scotland: B-1

League Club	Source	Date Signed	Seasons Played	Apps	Subs	Gls
Blackpool (L)	Glasgow Rangers	09/08	08	10	7	5
Norwich C (L)	Glasgow Rangers	02/09	08	8	5	0
Plymouth Arg	Glasgow Rangers	08/09	09	8	6	2
Notts Co (L)	Motherwell	01/11	10	12	4	1
Exeter C	K'fisher Bengal (IND)	03/12	11-13	45	13	14
Bristol Rov	L	02/14	13	4	0	0

GOW Gerald (Gerry)
Born: Glasgow, Scotland, 29 May, 1952 M
Scotland: U23-1

League Club	Source	Date Signed	Seasons Played	Apps	Subs	Gls
Bristol C	Jnr	06/69	69-80	368	7	48
Manchester C	Tr	10/80	80-81	26	0	5
Rotherham U	Tr	01/82	81-82	58	0	4
Burnley	Tr	08/83	83	8	1	0

GOWANS Peter Taylor
Born: Dundee, Scotland, 25 May, 1944 W
Died: Crewe, Cheshire, England, November, 2009

League Club	Source	Date Signed	Seasons Played	Apps	Subs	Gls
Crewe Alex	Glasgow Celtic	07/63	63-66	141	0	45
Aldershot	Tr	07/67	67-69	111	2	27
Rochdale	Tr	07/70	70-73	137	8	21
Southport	Tr	07/74	74	3	1	0

GOWARD Ryan Lee
Born: Mansfield, Nottinghamshire, England, 1 November, 1989 LW

League Club	Source	Date Signed	Seasons Played	Apps	Subs	Gls
Mansfield T	Sch	-	07	0	2	0

GOWER Mark
Born: Edmonton, N London, England, 5 October, 1978 M
England: Semi Pro-4/Youth/Schools

League Club	Source	Date Signed	Seasons Played	Apps	Subs	Gls
Tottenham H	YT	04/97				
Barnet	Tr	01/01	00	10	4	1
Southend U	Tr	07/03	03-07	189	14	35
Swansea C	Tr	08/08	08-12	108	20	3
Charlton Ath	Tr	03/13	12-13	8	5	0

GOWLING Alan Edwin
Born: Stockport, Greater Manchester, England, 16 March, 1949 F/M
England: U23-1/Amateur/Schools

League Club	Source	Date Signed	Seasons Played	Apps	Subs	Gls
Manchester U	Manchester Univ	04/67	67-71	64	7	18
Huddersfield T	Tr	06/72	72-74	128	0	58
Newcastle U	Tr	08/75	75-77	91	1	30
Bolton W	Tr	03/78	77-81	147	2	28
Preston NE	Tr	09/82	82	37	3	5

GOWLING Joshua Anthony Izaac (Josh)
Born: Coventry, England, 29 November, 1983 CD

League Club	Source	Date Signed	Seasons Played	Apps	Subs	Gls
Bournemouth	Herfolge (DEN)	08/05	05-07	72	11	1
Carlisle U	Tr	07/08	08	3	1	0
Hereford U	L	11/08	08	13	0	0
Gillingham	Tr	07/09	09-10	50	2	4
Lincoln C	L	10/10	10	4	0	0

GOY Peter John
Born: Beverley, East Riding of Yorkshire, England, 8 June, 1938 G

League Club	Source	Date Signed	Seasons Played	Apps	Subs	Gls
Arsenal	Jnr	06/55	58	2	-	0
Southend U	Tr	10/60	60-63	118	-	0
Watford	Tr	07/64	64	27	-	0
Huddersfield T	Tr	07/65	66	4	0	0

GRABBAN Lewis James
Born: Croydon, S London, England, 12 January, 1988 F

League Club	Source	Date Signed	Seasons Played	Apps	Subs	Gls
Crystal Palace	Sch	07/06	06-07	0	10	1
Oldham Ath	L	08/06	06	1	8	0
Millwall	Tr	01/08	07-10	45	11	9
Brentford	L	03/10	09	7	0	2
Brentford	L	10/10	10	1	3	1
Brentford	Tr	01/11	10	12	6	4
Rotherham U	Tr	07/11	11	39	4	18
Bournemouth	Tr	06/12	12-13	82	4	35
Norwich C	Tr	06/14	14	23	12	12

GRABBI Corrado
Born: Turin, Italy, 29 July, 1975 F

League Club	Source	Date Signed	Seasons Played	Apps	Subs	Gls
Blackburn Rov	Ternana (ITA)	07/01	01-03	11	19	2

GRABOVAC Zarko
Born: Ruma, Yugoslavia, 16 March, 1983 F

League Club	Source	Date Signed	Seasons Played	Apps	Subs	Gls
Blackpool	Geldrop AEK (NED)	01/05	04	1	2	0

GRACCO Gianluca
Born: Naples, Italy, 19 June, 1990 F

League Club	Source	Date Signed	Seasons Played	Apps	Subs	Gls
Dagenham & Red	Citta de Pompeii (ITA)	01/13	12	0	1	0

GRACE Derek George
Born: Chiswick, W London, England, 29 December, 1944 IF

League Club	Source	Date Signed	Seasons Played	Apps	Subs	Gls
Exeter C	Queens Park Rgrs (App)	05/62	62-64	40	-	4
Gillingham	Tr	07/65	65	4	0	0

GRACE John Michael
Born: Dublin, Republic of Ireland, 16 February, 1964 G

League Club	Source	Date Signed	Seasons Played	Apps	Subs	Gls
Colchester U	Tolka Rov (ROI)	07/89	89	19	0	0

GRADEL Max-Alain
Born: Abidjan, Ivory Coast, 30 September, 1987 LW
Ivory Coast: 41

League Club	Source	Date Signed	Seasons Played	Apps	Subs	Gls
Leicester C	Jnr	09/05	08	16	11	1
Bournemouth	L	08/07	07	31	3	9
Leeds U	Tr	10/09	09-11	53	24	25

GRAFTON Stanley Thomas (Stan)
Born: Wolverhampton, England, 2 April, 1923 WH
Died: Wolverhampton, England, 27 June, 1953

League Club	Source	Date Signed	Seasons Played	Apps	Subs	Gls
Aldershot	Bilston T	08/47	47-48	2	-	0

League Club	Source	Date Signed	Seasons Played	Career Record Apps	Subs	Gls

GRAHAM Allan
Born: Ryhope, Tyne and Wear, England, 23 October, 1937 — RB

League Club	Source	Date Signed	Seasons Played	Apps	Subs	Gls
Sunderland	Silksworth Jnrs	05/55	57	3	-	0

GRAHAM Arthur
Born: Glasgow, Scotland, 26 October, 1952 — LW
Scotland: 11/SLge-1/U23-3

League Club	Source	Date Signed	Seasons Played	Apps	Subs	Gls
Leeds U	Aberdeen	07/77	77-82	222	1	37
Manchester U	Tr	08/83	83	33	4	5
Bradford C	Tr	06/85	85-86	28	3	2

GRAHAM Bagasan Assigi
Born: Plaistow, E London, England, 6 October, 1992 — W

League Club	Source	Date Signed	Seasons Played	Apps	Subs	Gls
Cheltenham T	Queens Park Rgrs (Sch)	07/11	11-12	1	7	0

GRAHAM Benjamin (Ben)
Born: Pontypool, Torfaen, Wales, 23 September, 1975 — FB

League Club	Source	Date Signed	Seasons Played	Apps	Subs	Gls
Cardiff C	YT	07/94	93	0	1	0

GRAHAM Daniel Anthony William (Danny)
Born: Gateshead, Tyne and Wear, England, 12 August, 1985 — F
England: Youth

League Club	Source	Date Signed	Seasons Played	Apps	Subs	Gls
Middlesbrough	Sch	03/04	04-06	1	14	1
Darlington	L	03/04	03	7	2	2
Derby Co	L	11/05	05	11	3	0
Leeds U	L	03/06	05	1	2	0
Blackpool	L	08/06	06	1	3	1
Carlisle U	Tr	01/07	06-08	89	11	36
Watford	Tr	07/09	09-10	82	9	37
Swansea C	Tr	07/11	11-12	42	12	15
Sunderland	Tr	01/13	12-14	18	9	1
Hull C	L	07/13	13	12	6	1
Middlesbrough	L	01/14	13	17	1	6
Wolverhampton W	L	11/14	14	5	0	1

GRAHAM David Baillie
Born: Edinburgh, Scotland, 6 October, 1978 — F
Scotland: U21-8

League Club	Source	Date Signed	Seasons Played	Apps	Subs	Gls
Torquay U	Dunfermline Ath	03/01	00-03	103	17	47
Wigan Ath	Tr	07/04	04	13	17	1
Sheffield Wed	Tr	08/05	05-06	19	9	2
Huddersfield T	L	01/06	05	15	1	9
Bradford C	L	07/06	06	17	5	3
Torquay U	L	03/07	06	7	0	0
Gillingham	Tr	08/07	07	7	9	3
Lincoln C	Tr	07/08	08	2	7	0

GRAHAM Deiniol William Thomas
Born: Cannock, Staffordshire, England, 4 October, 1969 — F
Wales: U21-1/Youth

League Club	Source	Date Signed	Seasons Played	Apps	Subs	Gls
Manchester U	YT	10/87	87-89	1	1	0
Barnsley	Tr	08/91	91-93	18	20	2
Preston NE	L	10/92	92	8	0	0
Carlisle U	L	11/93	93	2	0	1
Stockport Co	Tr	06/94	94	5	6	2
Scunthorpe U	Tr	08/95	95	1	2	1

GRAHAM Donald (Don)
Born: Oldham, Greater Manchester, England, 2 April, 1953 — LB

League Club	Source	Date Signed	Seasons Played	Apps	Subs	Gls
Bury	Hyde U	10/79	79-80	3	4	0

GRAHAM Douglas (Doug)
Born: Morpeth, Northumberland, England, 15 July, 1921 — RB
Died: Newcastle-upon-Tyne, England, 10 November, 1993

League Club	Source	Date Signed	Seasons Played	Apps	Subs	Gls
Newcastle U	Barrington U	08/40	46-50	71	-	0
Preston NE	Tr	11/50				
Lincoln C	Tr	12/51	51-56	182	-	0

GRAHAM Douglas Richard (Dick)
Born: Corby, Northamptonshire, England, 6 May, 1922 — G
Died: Colchester, Essex, England, 7 March, 2013

League Club	Source	Date Signed	Seasons Played	Apps	Subs	Gls
Leicester C	Northampton T (Am)	11/44				
Crystal Palace	Tr	12/45	46-50	155	-	0

GRAHAM Gareth Lee
Born: Belfast, Northern Ireland, 6 December, 1978 — M
Northern Ireland: U21-5

League Club	Source	Date Signed	Seasons Played	Apps	Subs	Gls
Crystal Palace	YT	03/97	98	0	1	0
Brentford	Tr	09/99	99-00	5	9	0

GRAHAM George
Born: Bargeddie, Lanarkshire, Scotland, 30 November, 1944 — F/M
Scotland: 12/U23-2/Schools

League Club	Source	Date Signed	Seasons Played	Apps	Subs	Gls
Aston Villa	App	12/61	62-63	8	-	2
Chelsea	Tr	07/64	64-66	72	0	35
Arsenal	Tr	09/66	66-72	219	8	59
Manchester U	Tr	12/72	72-74	41	2	2
Portsmouth	Tr	11/74	74-76	61	0	5
Crystal Palace	Tr	11/76	76-77	43	1	2

GRAHAM Gerald Wilson (Gerry)
Born: Aspatria, Cumbria, England, 31 January, 1941 — WH/CF

League Club	Source	Date Signed	Seasons Played	Apps	Subs	Gls
Blackpool	Jnr	08/59				
Peterborough U	Tr	07/60	60-63	17	-	1
Mansfield T	Cambridge U	06/64	64	18	-	3
Workington	Worcester C	07/68	68	6	0	0

GRAHAM James (Jimmy)
Born: Glasgow, Scotland, 5 November, 1969 — LB

League Club	Source	Date Signed	Seasons Played	Apps	Subs	Gls
Bradford C	YT	09/88	88-89	6	1	0
Rochdale	L	11/89	89	11	0	0
Rochdale	Tr	07/90	90-93	120	6	1
Hull C	Tr	08/94	94-95	63	0	1

GRAHAM John
Born: Leyland, Lancashire, England, 26 April, 1926 — IF

League Club	Source	Date Signed	Seasons Played	Apps	Subs	Gls
Aston Villa	Leyland Motors	11/46	46-48	10	-	3
Wrexham	Tr	06/49	49-51	45	-	7
Rochdale	Wigan Ath	02/53	52	10	-	1
Bradford C	Tr	07/53	53	18	-	1

GRAHAM John Joseph (Jackie)
Born: Glasgow, Scotland, 16 July, 1946 — M

League Club	Source	Date Signed	Seasons Played	Apps	Subs	Gls
Brentford	Guildford C	07/70	70-79	371	3	38

GRAHAM Jordan Tyler
Born: Coventry, England, 5 March, 1995 — M
England: Youth

League Club	Source	Date Signed	Seasons Played	Apps	Subs	Gls
Aston Villa	Sch	03/12				
Ipswich T	L	11/13	13	0	2	0
Bradford C	L	01/14	13	0	1	0
Wolverhampton W	Tr	11/14				

GRAHAM Leslie (Les)
Born: Flixton, Greater Manchester, England, 14 May, 1924 — IF
Died: Cwmbran, Torfaen, Wales, 18 January, 1998

League Club	Source	Date Signed	Seasons Played	Apps	Subs	Gls
Blackburn Rov	Flixton	04/47	47-52	150	-	42
Newport Co	Tr	02/53	52-54	96	-	39
Watford	Tr	07/55	55-57	90	-	26
Newport Co	Tr	09/57	57-58	64	-	15

GRAHAM Malcolm
Born: Crigglestone, West Yorkshire, England, 26 January, 1934 — IF
Died: Barnsley, South Yorkshire, England, 12 September, 2015

League Club	Source	Date Signed	Seasons Played	Apps	Subs	Gls
Barnsley	Hall Green	04/53	54-58	109	-	35
Bristol C	Tr	05/59	59	14	-	8
Leyton Orient	Tr	06/60	60-62	75	-	29
Queens Park Rgrs	Tr	07/63	63	21	-	7
Barnsley	Tr	07/64	64	20	-	5

GRAHAM Mark Roland
Born: Newry, Armagh, Northern Ireland, 24 October, 1974 — M/RB
Northern Ireland: B-4/Youth/Schools

League Club	Source	Date Signed	Seasons Played	Apps	Subs	Gls
Queens Park Rgrs	YT	05/93	96	16	2	0
Cambridge U	Tr	08/99	99	0	1	0

GRAHAM Michael Anthony (Mike)
Born: Lancaster, England, 24 February, 1959 — FB

League Club	Source	Date Signed	Seasons Played	Apps	Subs	Gls
Bolton W	App	02/77	77-80	43	3	0
Swindon T	Tr	07/81	81-84	141	0	1
Mansfield T	Tr	07/85	85-88	132	1	1
Carlisle U	Tr	09/88	88-91	137	1	3

GRAHAM Milton Mackay
Born: Hackney, E London, England, 2 November, 1962 — M

League Club	Source	Date Signed	Seasons Played	Apps	Subs	Gls
Bournemouth	Jnr	05/81	81-84	54	19	12
Chester C	Tr	08/85	85-88	123	6	11
Peterborough U	Tr	07/89	89	10	4	2

GRAHAM Peter
Born: Barnsley, South Yorkshire, England, 19 April, 1947 — F

League Club	Source	Date Signed	Seasons Played	Apps	Subs	Gls
Barnsley	Worsbrough Bridge Ath	01/67	66-69	16	3	1
Halifax T	L	03/70	69	6	0	0
Darlington	Tr	06/70	70-73	118	1	44
Lincoln C	Tr	09/73	73-77	142	16	47
Cambridge U	Tr	06/78	78-79	35	3	0

GRAHAM Ralph Cowell
Born: Durham, England, 29 December, 1929 — W
Died: Vancouver, Canada, 20 March, 2009

League Club	Source	Date Signed	Seasons Played	Apps	Subs	Gls
Doncaster Rov	Broadway Ath	05/47	48-49	5	-	0
Southport	Tr	07/50	50-51	29	-	9

GRAHAM Richard Ean
Born: Dewsbury, West Yorkshire, England, 28 November, 1974 — CD
Republic of Ireland: U21-2

League Club	Source	Date Signed	Seasons Played	Apps	Subs	Gls
Oldham Ath	YT	07/93	93-99	139	11	14

GRAHAM Richard Stephen
Born: Newry, Armagh, Northern Ireland, 5 August, 1979 — M

League Club	Source	Date Signed	Seasons Played	Apps	Subs	Gls

Northern Ireland: U21-15/Youth

League Club	Source	Date Signed	Seasons Played	Apps	Subs	Gls
Queens Park Rgrs	YT	08/96	98	0	2	0
Barnet	Kettering T	07/04	05-06	35	14	3
Dagenham & Red	Tr	07/07	07-08	7	5	0

GRAHAM Robert (Bobby)
Born: Motherwell, Lanarkshire, Scotland, 22 November, 1944 — F

League Club	Source	Date Signed	Seasons Played	Apps	Subs	Gls
Liverpool	App	11/61	64-71	96	5	31
Coventry C	Tr	03/72	71-72	19	0	3
Tranmere Rov	L	01/73	72	10	0	3

GRAHAM Thomas (Tommy)
Born: Glasgow, Scotland, 31 March, 1958 — M

League Club	Source	Date Signed	Seasons Played	Apps	Subs	Gls
Aston Villa	Arthurlie	04/78				
Barnsley	Tr	12/78	78-79	36	2	13
Halifax T	Tr	10/80	80-81	68	3	17
Doncaster Rov	Tr	08/82	82	9	2	2
Scunthorpe U	Tr	03/83	82-85	102	7	21
Scarborough	Tr	08/86	87-89	104	7	11
Halifax T	Tr	01/90	89-91	56	2	4

GRAHAM William George Leonard (Len)
Born: Belfast, Northern Ireland, 17 October, 1925 — LB
Died: Blackpool, Lancashire, England, 30 September, 2007
Northern Ireland: 14

League Club	Source	Date Signed	Seasons Played	Apps	Subs	Gls
Doncaster Rov	Brantwood	10/49	49-58	312	-	3
Torquay U	Tr	11/58	58	20	-	0

GRAHAM William Reynolds (Billy)
Born: Carlisle, Cumbria, England, 8 May, 1929 — LH

League Club	Source	Date Signed	Seasons Played	Apps	Subs	Gls
Workington		07/51				
Carlisle U	Consett	01/54	53-60	35	-	2

GRAHAM William Valentine (Willie)
Born: Armagh, Northern Ireland, 14 February, 1959 — M

League Club	Source	Date Signed	Seasons Played	Apps	Subs	Gls
Brentford	Northampton T (App)	08/77	77-80	42	6	3

GRAINGER Colin
Born: Hemsworth, West Yorkshire, England, 10 June, 1933 — LW
England: 7/FLge-3

League Club	Source	Date Signed	Seasons Played	Apps	Subs	Gls
Wrexham	South Elmsall	10/50	50-52	5	-	0
Sheffield U	Tr	07/53	53-56	88	-	26
Sunderland	Tr	02/57	56-59	120	-	14
Leeds U	Tr	07/60	60	33	-	5
Port Vale	Tr	10/61	61-63	39	-	6
Doncaster Rov	Tr	08/64	64-65	40	0	3

GRAINGER Daniel John (Danny)
Born: Thrapston, Northamptonshire, England, 15 October, 1986 — M/RB

League Club	Source	Date Signed	Seasons Played	Apps	Subs	Gls
Rushden & D	Sch	07/05	05	2	12	1

GRAINGER Daniel Leslie (Danny)
Born: Penrith, Cumbria, England, 28 July, 1986 — LB

League Club	Source	Date Signed	Seasons Played	Apps	Subs	Gls
Carlisle U	Dunfermline Ath	06/14	14	41	0	3

GRAINGER Dennis
Born: Royston, South Yorkshire, England, 5 March, 1920 — LW
Died: Chesterfield, Derbyshire, England, 6 June, 1986

League Club	Source	Date Signed	Seasons Played	Apps	Subs	Gls
Southport	South Kirkby Colliery	10/38				
Leeds U	Tr	10/45	46-47	37	-	5
Wrexham	Tr	12/47	47-50	98	-	12
Oldham Ath	Tr	06/51	51	3	-	0

GRAINGER John (Jack)
Born: Royston, South Yorkshire, England, 17 July, 1912 — FB
Died: Southport, Merseyside, England, 18 January, 1976

League Club	Source	Date Signed	Seasons Played	Apps	Subs	Gls
Barnsley	Royston Ath	08/32	32	1	-	0
Southport	Tr	08/33	33-46	222	-	0

GRAINGER John (Jack)
Born: Darton, South Yorkshire, England, 3 April, 1924 — RW
Died: Pontefract, West Yorkshire, England, 10 January, 1983
England: B-1

League Club	Source	Date Signed	Seasons Played	Apps	Subs	Gls
Rotherham U	Frickley Colliery	11/45	47-56	352	-	112
Lincoln C	Tr	06/57	57-58	42	-	14

GRAINGER Martin Robert
Born: Enfield, N London, England, 23 August, 1972 — LB

League Club	Source	Date Signed	Seasons Played	Apps	Subs	Gls
Colchester U	YT	07/90	89-93	37	9	7
Brentford	Tr	10/93	93-95	100	1	12
Birmingham C	Tr	03/96	95-03	205	21	25
Coventry C	L	02/04	03	7	0	0

GRAND Simon
Born: Chorley, Lancashire, England, 23 February, 1984 — CD
England: Semi Pro-1

League Club	Source	Date Signed	Seasons Played	Apps	Subs	Gls
Rochdale	Sch	07/02	02-03	33	7	2
Carlisle U	Tr	08/04	05-06	3	9	2
Grimsby T	Tr	01/07	06	4	3	0
Morecambe	Tr	08/07	07	4	2	1
Aldershot T (L)	Fleetwood T	01/11	10	6	0	0

GRANDIN Elliot
Born: Caen, France, 17 October, 1987 — M
France: U21-3

League Club	Source	Date Signed	Seasons Played	Apps	Subs	Gls
Blackpool	CSKA Sofia (BUL)	08/10	10-12	31	11	6
Crystal Palace	Tr	07/13				
Blackpool	Tr	02/14	13	3	4	1

GRANDISON Jermaine Mickel
Born: Birmingham, England, 15 December, 1990 — RB

League Club	Source	Date Signed	Seasons Played	Apps	Subs	Gls
Coventry C	Sch	06/09	08-09	1	4	0
Tranmere Rov	L	08/10	10	6	2	0
Shrewsbury T	Tr	01/11	10-14	117	14	5

GRANERO Esteban Felix
Born: Madrid, Spain, 2 July, 1989 — M
Spain: U21-10/Youth

League Club	Source	Date Signed	Seasons Played	Apps	Subs	Gls
Queens Park Rgrs	Real Madrid (SPN)	08/12	12-13	20	5	1

GRANGER Keith William
Born: Southampton, England, 5 October, 1968 — G

League Club	Source	Date Signed	Seasons Played	Apps	Subs	Gls
Southampton	App	10/86	85	2	0	0
Darlington	Tr	12/87	87	23	0	0

GRANGER Michael (Mick)
Born: Leeds, England, 7 October, 1931 — G

League Club	Source	Date Signed	Seasons Played	Apps	Subs	Gls
York C	Cliftonville, York	12/51	54-61	71	-	0
Hull C	Tr	07/62	62	2	-	0
Halifax T	Tr	07/63	63-64	2	-	0

GRANQVIST Andreas
Born: Helsingborg, Sweden, 16 April, 1985 — CD
Sweden: 42/U21-26

League Club	Source	Date Signed	Seasons Played	Apps	Subs	Gls
Wigan Ath	Helsingborgs (SWE)	01/07	07	13	1	0

GRANT Alan James
Born: Havant, Hampshire, England, 6 January, 1935 — WH

League Club	Source	Date Signed	Seasons Played	Apps	Subs	Gls
Brighton & HA	Gosport Bor	04/56	56	1	-	0
Exeter C	Tr	06/60	60	4	-	0

GRANT Alexander Frank (Alick)
Born: Peasedown St John, Somerset, England, 11 August, 1916 — G
Died: Taunton, Somerset, England, 3 September, 2008

League Club	Source	Date Signed	Seasons Played	Apps	Subs	Gls
Bury	Sheffield U (Am)	08/37				
Aldershot	Tr	05/38	38	5	-	0
Leicester C	Tr	12/41	46	2	-	0
Derby Co	Tr	11/46	46-47	12	-	0
Newport Co	Tr	11/48	48	20	-	0
Leeds U	Tr	08/49				
York C	Tr	03/50	49	3	-	0

GRANT Anthony (Tony)
Born: Drogheda, Republic of Ireland, 20 August, 1976 — F
Republic of Ireland: Youth/Schools

League Club	Source	Date Signed	Seasons Played	Apps	Subs	Gls
Leeds U	YT	08/94				
Preston NE	Tr	11/95	95	0	1	0

GRANT Anthony James (Tony)
Born: Liverpool, England, 14 November, 1974 — DM
England: U21-1

League Club	Source	Date Signed	Seasons Played	Apps	Subs	Gls
Everton	YT	07/93	94-99	43	18	2
Swindon T	L	01/96	95	3	0	1
Tranmere Rov	L	09/99	99	8	1	0
Manchester C	Tr	12/99	99-01	11	10	0
West Bromwich A	L	12/00	00	3	2	0
Burnley	Tr	10/01	01-04	121	20	3
Bristol C	Tr	08/05				
Crewe Alex	Tr	01/06	05-06	13	1	0
Accrington Stan	Tr	01/07	06	6	0	0
Chester C	Tr	07/07	07	15	4	1

GRANT Anthony Paul Shaun Andrew
Born: Lambeth, S London, England, 4 June, 1987 — DM

League Club	Source	Date Signed	Seasons Played	Apps	Subs	Gls
Chelsea	Sch	07/04	04	0	1	0
Oldham Ath	L	01/06	05	2	0	0
Wycombe W	L	07/06	06	39	1	0
Luton T	L	11/07	07	1	3	0
Southend U	Tr	01/08	07-11	127	32	10
Stevenage	Tr	07/12	12	34	7	0
Crewe Alex	Tr	07/13	13-14	76	5	4

GRANT Bernard
Born: Airdrie, Lanarkshire, Scotland, 23 May, 1920 — IF
Died: Exeter, England, October, 1984

League Club	Source	Date Signed	Seasons Played	Apps	Subs	Gls
Exeter C	Third Lanark	07/47	48	2	-	0

GRANT Brian Patrick
Born: Coatbridge, Lanarkshire, Scotland, 10 May, 1943 — FB

League Club	Source	Date Signed	Seasons Played	Apps	Subs	Gls
Nottingham F	Bellshill Ath	05/60	60-64	18	-	0
Hartlepool U	Tr	01/66	65-66	35	0	0
Cambridge U	Bradford C (NC)	01/68	70	14	0	0

GRANT Cyril
Born: Wath-on-Dearne, South Yorkshire, England, 10 July, 1920 — CF
Died: Lewisham, SE London, England, 10 February, 2002

League Club	Source	Date Signed	Seasons Played	Apps	Subs	Gls
Lincoln C	Mexborough	06/39				
Arsenal	Tr	07/46	46	2	-	0
Fulham	Tr	12/46	46-47	14	-	4
Southend U	Tr	03/48	47-54	175	-	63

GRANT David
Born: Sheffield, England, 2 June, 1960 — LB

League Club	Source	Date Signed	Seasons Played	Apps	Subs	Gls
Sheffield Wed	App	02/78	77-81	132	1	4
Oxford U	Tr	07/82	82-83	24	0	1
Chesterfield	L	09/83	83	7	0	0
Crystal Palace	Tr	01/84				
Cardiff C	Tr	03/84	83-84	25	0	0
Rochdale	Tr	03/85	84-86	97	0	2

GRANT David Bell
Born: Edinburgh, Scotland, 31 July, 1943 — F
Died: Edinburgh, Scotland, 30 April, 2008

League Club	Source	Date Signed	Seasons Played	Apps	Subs	Gls
Reading	Third Lanark	05/63	63-64	17	-	3

GRANT David John
Born: Liverpool, England, 18 December, 1947 — LH
England: Schools

League Club	Source	Date Signed	Seasons Played	Apps	Subs	Gls
Everton	App	12/65				
Wrexham	Tr	09/66	66	6	5	0

GRANT Edward Anthony (Eddie)
Born: Greenock, Inverclyde, Scotland, 1 October, 1928 — IF
Died: Greenock, Inverclyde, Scotland, 30 June, 1979

League Club	Source	Date Signed	Seasons Played	Apps	Subs	Gls
Sheffield U	Weymouth	05/50	50	4	-	0
Grimsby T	Kilmarnock	07/52	52-53	15	-	5

GRANT Gareth Michael
Born: Leeds, England, 6 September, 1980 — F

League Club	Source	Date Signed	Seasons Played	Apps	Subs	Gls
Bradford C	YT	04/98	97-01	6	18	1
Halifax T	L	02/99	98	0	3	0
Lincoln C	L	02/01	00	3	0	0

GRANT Gavin Renaldo
Born: Harlesden, NW London, England, 27 March, 1984 — F/W

League Club	Source	Date Signed	Seasons Played	Apps	Subs	Gls
Gillingham	Tooting & Mitcham U	12/05	05	1	9	1
Millwall	Tr	05/06	06	1	3	0
Wycombe W	Tr	07/08	08	9	1	0
Bradford C	Tr	02/10	09	7	4	0

GRANT Harry Edward
Born: Reading, England, 31 December, 1993 — M

League Club	Source	Date Signed	Seasons Played	Apps	Subs	Gls
Sheffield Wed	Swindon T (Sch)	07/12				
Gillingham	Tr	03/13	12	1	0	0

GRANT James (Jim)
Born: Chapelhall, Lanarkshire, Scotland, 10 June, 1940 — W

League Club	Source	Date Signed	Seasons Played	Apps	Subs	Gls
Scunthorpe U	Larkhall Thistle	11/58	58	1	-	0

GRANT James (Jim)
Born: Scotland — RW

League Club	Source	Date Signed	Seasons Played	Apps	Subs	Gls
Brighton & HA (Am)	RAF	12/46	46	1	-	0

GRANT Joel Valentino
Born: Acton, W London, England, 27 August, 1987 — LW

League Club	Source	Date Signed	Seasons Played	Apps	Subs	Gls
Watford	Sch	03/06	05	2	5	0
Crewe Alex	Aldershot T	07/08	08-10	76	20	16
Wycombe W	Tr	07/11	11-12	62	9	14
Yeovil T	Tr	06/13	13-14	42	13	6

GRANT John Albert (Jackie)
Born: High Spen, Tyne and Wear, England, 8 September, 1924 — RH
Died: Liverpool, England, 16 August, 1999

League Club	Source	Date Signed	Seasons Played	Apps	Subs	Gls
Everton	High Spen Ath	12/42	46-54	121	-	10
Rochdale	Tr	05/56	56-58	102	-	3
Southport	Tr	01/59	58-59	40	-	0

GRANT John Anthony Carlton
Born: Manchester, England, 9 August, 1981 — F
England: Semi Pro-4

League Club	Source	Date Signed	Seasons Played	Apps	Subs	Gls
Crewe Alex	YT	07/99	99-01	2	5	0
Shrewsbury T	Telford U	08/04	04	10	9	2
Aldershot T	Halifax T	07/06	08-09	33	19	8
Macclesfield T	Barrow	08/11	11	0	4	0

GRANT Jorge Edward
Born: Banbury, Oxfordshire, England, 19 December, 1994 — M

League Club	Source	Date Signed	Seasons Played	Apps	Subs	Gls
Nottingham F	Reading (Sch)	04/13	14	0	1	0

GRANT Kenneth (Ken)
Born: High Spen, Tyne and Wear, England, 13 November, 1938 — RW

League Club	Source	Date Signed	Seasons Played	Apps	Subs	Gls
Gateshead (Am)	Crook T	12/58	58	6	-	0

GRANT Kimberley Tyrone (Kim)
Born: Sekondi-Takaradi, Ghana, 25 September, 1972 — F
Ghana: 7

League Club	Source	Date Signed	Seasons Played	Apps	Subs	Gls
Charlton Ath	YT	03/91	90-95	74	49	18
Luton T	Tr	03/96	95-96	18	17	5
Millwall	Tr	08/97	97-98	35	20	11
Notts Co	L	12/98	98	6	0	1
Scunthorpe U	FC Marco (POR)	08/01	01	3	1	1

GRANT Lee Anderson
Born: Hemel Hempstead, Hertfordshire, England, 27 January, 1983 — G
England: U21-4/Youth

League Club	Source	Date Signed	Seasons Played	Apps	Subs	Gls
Derby Co	YT	02/01	02-06	69	5	0
Burnley	L	11/05	05	1	0	0
Oldham Ath	L	01/06	05	16	0	0
Sheffield Wed	Tr	07/07	07-09	136	0	0
Burnley	Tr	07/10	10-12	113	1	0
Derby Co	Tr	07/13	13-14	86	0	0

GRANT Lee Mark
Born: York, England, 31 December, 1985 — M

League Club	Source	Date Signed	Seasons Played	Apps	Subs	Gls
York C	Jnr	-	01	0	1	0
Aston Villa	Tr	05/03				

GRANT Peter
Born: Coatbridge, Lanarkshire, Scotland, 30 August, 1965 — M
Scotland: 2/B-2/U21-10/Youth/Schools

League Club	Source	Date Signed	Seasons Played	Apps	Subs	Gls
Norwich C	Glasgow Celtic	08/97	97-98	64	4	3
Reading	Tr	08/99	99	27	2	1
Bournemouth	Tr	08/00	00	14	1	0

GRANT Peter John
Born: Glasgow, Scotland, 11 April, 1968 — FB

League Club	Source	Date Signed	Seasons Played	Apps	Subs	Gls
Stockport Co	Ipswich T (App)	07/86	86	1	0	0

GRANT Robert
Born: Edinburgh, Scotland, 25 September, 1940 — IF

League Club	Source	Date Signed	Seasons Played	Apps	Subs	Gls
Carlisle U	St Johnstone	07/62	62	2	-	1
Leyton Orient	Tr	12/62				

GRANT Robert (Bobby)
Born: Litherland, Merseyside, England, 1 July, 1990 — F/M

League Club	Source	Date Signed	Seasons Played	Apps	Subs	Gls
Accrington Stan	Sch	02/08	06-09	53	12	15
Scunthorpe U	Tr	07/10	10-12	29	30	7
Rochdale	L	11/10	10	5	1	2
Accrington Stan	L	03/12	11	8	0	3
Rochdale	Tr	08/12	12	35	1	15
Blackpool	Tr	07/13	13	5	1	0
Fleetwood T	L	02/14	13	1	0	0
Shrewsbury T	L	10/14	14	28	5	6

GRANT Stephen Hubert
Born: Birr, Offaly, Republic of Ireland, 14 April, 1977 — F
Republic of Ireland: U21-4/Schools

League Club	Source	Date Signed	Seasons Played	Apps	Subs	Gls
Sunderland	Athlone T (ROI)	08/95				
Stockport Co	Shamrock Rov (ROI)	09/97	97-98	10	19	4

GRANT Wilfred (Wilf)
Born: Ashington, Northumberland, England, 3 August, 1920 — CF
Died: Worcester, England, 17 September, 1990
England: B-1//Wales: WLge-1

League Club	Source	Date Signed	Seasons Played	Apps	Subs	Gls
Manchester C	Morpeth T	02/43				
Southampton	Tr	10/46	46-49	61	-	12
Cardiff C	Tr	03/50	49-54	154	-	65
Ipswich T	Tr	10/54	54-56	75	-	22

GRANT William Fraser
Born: Spittalfield, Perth, Perthshire, Scotland, 7 October, 1933 — WH

League Club	Source	Date Signed	Seasons Played	Apps	Subs	Gls
Gillingham	Brechin C	08/56	56	1	-	0

GRANVILLE Anthony Ralph (Ralph)
Born: Glasgow, Scotland, 23 April, 1931 — WH

League Club	Source	Date Signed	Seasons Played	Apps	Subs	Gls
Nottingham F	Clyde	08/57				
Gateshead	Tr	10/57	57	2	-	0

GRANVILLE Daniel Patrick (Danny)
Born: Islington, N London, England, 19 January, 1975 — LB
England: U21-3

League Club	Source	Date Signed	Seasons Played	Apps	Subs	Gls
Cambridge U	YT	05/93	93-96	89	10	7
Chelsea	Tr	03/97	96-97	12	6	0
Leeds U	Tr	07/98	98	7	2	0
Manchester C	Tr	08/99	99-01	56	14	3
Norwich C	L	10/00	00	6	0	0
Crystal Palace	Tr	12/01	01-06	117	5	9
Colchester U	Tr	07/07	07	14	5	0
Leyton Orient	Tr	07/08	08	12	0	0

GRANVILLE John Hubert
Born: Scarborough, Trinidad, 6 May, 1956 — G
Trinidad & Tobago:

League Club	Source	Date Signed	Seasons Played	Apps	Subs	Gls
Millwall	Slough T	10/85	85	6	0	0

GRANVILLE Norman Trevor (Trevor)
Born: Newport, Wales, 25 November, 1919 — W

Died: Cardiff, Wales, 16 December, 1992

League Club	Source	Date Signed	Seasons Played	Apps	Subs	Gls
Newport Co	Cliftonville	01/46	46	1	-	0
Exeter C	Tr	10/46	46-47	20	-	1

GRANYCOMBE Neal
Born: Middlesbrough, England, 23 October, 1958 — F

League Club	Source	Date Signed	Seasons Played	Apps	Subs	Gls
Hartlepool U	South Bank	02/81	80	1	0	0

GRAPES Stephen Philip (Steve)
Born: Norwich, England, 25 February, 1953 — M/W

League Club	Source	Date Signed	Seasons Played	Apps	Subs	Gls
Norwich C	App	07/70	70-76	34	7	3
Bournemouth	L	03/76	75	7	0	1
Cardiff C	Tr	10/76	76-81	138	9	6
Torquay U	Tr	08/82	82	31	0	0

GRATRIX Roy
Born: Salford, England, 9 February, 1932 — CH
Died: Blackpool, Lancashire, England, 20 April, 2002
England: B-1/FLge-1

League Club	Source	Date Signed	Seasons Played	Apps	Subs	Gls
Blackpool	Taylor Brothers	03/53	53-64	400	-	0
Manchester C	Tr	09/64	64	15	-	0

GRATTAN James (Jimmy)
Born: Belfast, Northern Ireland, 30 November, 1958 — F

League Club	Source	Date Signed	Seasons Played	Apps	Subs	Gls
Sunderland	App	10/76				
Mansfield T	L	11/78	78	1	0	0

GRATTON Dennis
Born: Rotherham, South Yorkshire, England, 21 April, 1934 — CH

League Club	Source	Date Signed	Seasons Played	Apps	Subs	Gls
Sheffield U	Worksop T	10/52	55-58	6	-	0
Lincoln C	Tr	09/59	59-60	45	-	0

GRAVELAINE Xavier
Born: Tours, France, 5 October, 1968 — F
France: 4

League Club	Source	Date Signed	Seasons Played	Apps	Subs	Gls
Watford (L)	Paris St-Germain (FRA)	11/99	99	7	0	2

GRAVER Andrew Martin (Andy)
Born: Craghead, County Durham, England, 12 September, 1927 — CF
Died: York, England, 8 January, 2014

League Club	Source	Date Signed	Seasons Played	Apps	Subs	Gls
Newcastle U	Annfield Plain	09/47	49	1	-	0
Lincoln C	Tr	09/50	50-54	170	-	106
Leicester C	Tr	12/54	54	11	-	3
Lincoln C	Tr	07/55	55	15	-	4
Stoke C	Tr	11/55	55-56	37	-	12
Lincoln C	Boston U	10/58	58-60	89	-	33

GRAVES Mark Terence
Born: Isleworth, W London, England, 14 December, 1960 — F

League Club	Source	Date Signed	Seasons Played	Apps	Subs	Gls
Plymouth Arg	App	09/78	77-80	25	9	3

GRAVES Robert Edward (Bob)
Born: Marylebone, Central London, England, 7 November, 1942 — G

League Club	Source	Date Signed	Seasons Played	Apps	Subs	Gls
Lincoln C	Kirton	04/60	59-64	79	-	0

GRAVES Wayne Alan
Born: Scunthorpe, North Lincolnshire, England, 18 September, 1980 — M/RB

League Club	Source	Date Signed	Seasons Played	Apps	Subs	Gls
Scunthorpe U	YT	03/99	97-03	97	38	6

GRAVESEN Thomas
Born: Vejle, Denmark, 11 March, 1976 — DM
Denmark: 66/U21-11/Youth

League Club	Source	Date Signed	Seasons Played	Apps	Subs	Gls
Everton	SV Hamburg (GER)	08/00	00-04	131	10	11
Everton (L)	Glasgow Celtic	08/07	07	1	7	0

GRAVETTE Warren
Born: Thetford, Norfolk, England, 13 September, 1968 — M

League Club	Source	Date Signed	Seasons Played	Apps	Subs	Gls
Tottenham H	App	08/86				
Brentford	Tr	07/87	87	1	4	0

GRAY Alan Muir
Born: Carlisle, Cumbria, England, 2 May, 1974 — RB

League Club	Source	Date Signed	Seasons Played	Apps	Subs	Gls
Doncaster Rov	Richmond Univ (USA)	08/96	96	1	0	0
Darlington	Bishop Auckland	08/97	97	6	0	0
Carlisle U	Tr	02/98	97	0	1	0

GRAY Alexander David (Alick)
Born: Arbroath, Angus, Scotland, 7 November, 1936 — LB

League Club	Source	Date Signed	Seasons Played	Apps	Subs	Gls
Burnley	Dundee Violet	06/54				
Cardiff C	Arbroath	03/57	58	2	-	0

GRAY Andre Anthony
Born: Wolverhampton, England, 26 June, 1991 — F
England: Semi Pro-6

League Club	Source	Date Signed	Seasons Played	Apps	Subs	Gls
Shrewsbury T	Sch	07/09	09	0	4	0
Brentford	Luton T	06/14	14	43	2	16

GRAY Andrew (Andy)
Born: Southampton, England, 25 October, 1973 — F

League Club	Source	Date Signed	Seasons Played	Apps	Subs	Gls
Reading	YT	07/92	91-93	8	9	3
Leyton Orient	Tr	07/94	94-95	16	16	3

GRAY Andrew Arthur (Andy)
Born: Lambeth, S London, England, 22 February, 1964 — M
England: 1/U21-2

League Club	Source	Date Signed	Seasons Played	Apps	Subs	Gls
Crystal Palace	Dulwich Hamlet	11/84	84-87	91	7	27
Aston Villa	Tr	11/87	87-88	34	3	4
Queens Park Rgrs	Tr	02/89	88	11	0	2
Crystal Palace	Tr	08/89	89-91	87	3	12
Tottenham H	Tr	02/92	91-93	23	10	3
Swindon T	L	12/92	92	3	0	0
Bury	Falkirk	07/97	97	21	0	1
Millwall	Tr	01/98	97	12	0	1

GRAY Andrew David (Andy)
Born: Harrogate, North Yorkshire, England, 15 November, 1977 — LW/F
Scotland: 2/B-3/Youth

League Club	Source	Date Signed	Seasons Played	Apps	Subs	Gls
Leeds U	YT	07/95	95-96	13	9	0
Bury	L	12/97	97	4	2	1
Nottingham F	Tr	09/98	98-01	34	30	1
Preston NE	L	02/99	98	5	0	0
Oldham Ath	L	03/99	98	4	0	0
Bradford C	Tr	08/02	02-03	77	0	20
Sheffield U	Tr	02/04	03-05	56	2	25
Sunderland	Tr	08/05	05	13	8	1
Burnley	Tr	03/06	05-07	68	1	28
Charlton Ath	Tr	01/08	07-09	31	14	9
Barnsley	Tr	08/09	09-11	68	28	21
Leeds U	Tr	08/12	12	0	8	1
Bradford C	Tr	01/13	12-13	8	7	1

GRAY Andrew Mullen (Andy)
Born: Glasgow, Scotland, 30 November, 1955 — F
Scotland: 20/U23-4

League Club	Source	Date Signed	Seasons Played	Apps	Subs	Gls
Aston Villa	Dundee U	10/75	75-78	112	1	54
Wolverhampton W	Tr	09/79	79-83	130	3	38
Everton	Tr	11/83	83-84	44	5	14
Aston Villa	Tr	07/85	85-86	53	1	5
Notts Co	L	08/87	87	3	1	0
West Bromwich A	Tr	09/87	87-88	32	3	10

GRAY Daniel Edward (Dan)
Born: Mansfield, Nottinghamshire, England, 23 November, 1989 — FB/M

League Club	Source	Date Signed	Seasons Played	Apps	Subs	Gls
Chesterfield	Sch	07/08	08-10	37	9	0
Macclesfield T	L	01/11	10	18	3	1
Macclesfield T	L	11/11	11	2	0	0

GRAY David (Davie)
Born: Coupar Angus, Perthshire, Scotland, 8 February, 1922 — RB
Died: Dundee, Scotland, 17 May, 2008

League Club	Source	Date Signed	Seasons Played	Apps	Subs	Gls
Preston NE	Glasgow Rangers	05/47	47	36	-	0
Blackburn Rov	Tr	08/48	48-52	107	-	5

GRAY David
Born: Rossendale, Lancashire, England, 19 January, 1980 — F

League Club	Source	Date Signed	Seasons Played	Apps	Subs	Gls
Rochdale	YT	07/98	98	0	3	0

GRAY David Downie
Born: Clydebank, Dunbartonshire, Scotland, 13 April, 1923 — RH

League Club	Source	Date Signed	Seasons Played	Apps	Subs	Gls
Bradford C	Queensbury	09/48	48-55	242	-	13

GRAY David Peter
Born: Edinburgh, Scotland, 4 May, 1988 — RB
Scotland: U21-2/Youth

League Club	Source	Date Signed	Seasons Played	Apps	Subs	Gls
Manchester U	Sch	08/05				
Crewe Alex	L	11/07	07	1	0	0
Plymouth Arg	L	01/09	08	14	0	0
Plymouth Arg	L	09/09	09	12	0	0
Preston NE	Tr	07/10	10-11	30	15	0
Stevenage	Tr	07/12	12-13	51	2	0
Burton A	Tr	01/14	13	7	5	0

GRAY Demarai Ramelle
Born: Birmingham, England, 28 June, 1996 — W
England: Youth

League Club	Source	Date Signed	Seasons Played	Apps	Subs	Gls
Birmingham C	Sch	12/13	13-14	29	19	7

GRAY Edward (Eddie)
Born: Bellshill, Lanarkshire, Scotland, 19 October, 1934 — IF
Scotland: Schools

League Club	Source	Date Signed	Seasons Played	Apps	Subs	Gls
Barrow	Yeovil T	12/57	57-58	17	-	4
Accrington Stan	Tr	07/59	59	6	-	0

GRAY Edwin (Eddie)
Born: Glasgow, Scotland, 17 November, 1948 — LW
Scotland: 12/U23-2/Schools

League Club	Source	Date Signed	Seasons Played	Apps	Subs	Gls
Leeds U	Jnr	01/65	65-83	441	13	52

GRAY Francis Tierney (Frank)
Born: Glasgow, Scotland, 27 October, 1954 — LB
Scotland: 32/U23-5/Schools

League Club	Source	Date Signed	Seasons Played	Apps	Subs	Gls
Leeds U	App	11/71	72-78	188	5	17

League Club	Source	Date Signed	Seasons Played	Apps	Subs	Gls
Nottingham F	Tr	08/79	79-80	81	0	5
Leeds U	Tr	05/81	81-84	139	0	10
Sunderland	Tr	07/85	85-88	118	28	8
Darlington	Tr	07/89	90-91	49	0	7

GRAY Gareth
Born: Longridge, Lancashire, England, 24 February, 1970 — G

League Club	Source	Date Signed	Seasons Played	Apps	Subs	Gls
Bolton W	Darwen	02/88				
Rochdale	Tr	07/90	91	6	0	0

GRAY George
Born: Glasgow, Scotland, 6 October, 1929 — RW
Died: Paisley, Renfrewshire, Scotland, 17 November, 1984

League Club	Source	Date Signed	Seasons Played	Apps	Subs	Gls
Carlisle U	Vale of Clyde	11/47	47	1	-	1
Scunthorpe U	Sligo Rov (ROI)	08/51	51	9	-	3

GRAY George James Pope
Born: Sunderland, England, 7 July, 1925 — WH
Died: Kettering, Northamptonshire, England, 7 April, 1995

League Club	Source	Date Signed	Seasons Played	Apps	Subs	Gls
Grimsby T	Derby Co (Am)	01/47	50	3	-	0
Swindon T	Tr	07/51	51-52	45	-	0
Darlington	Tr	07/53	53	6	-	0

GRAY George Walter
Born: Canning Town, E London, England, 30 November, 1922 — CF
Died: Westcliff-on-Sea, Essex, England, 10 December, 2007

League Club	Source	Date Signed	Seasons Played	Apps	Subs	Gls
Aldershot	West Ham U (Am)	02/47	46-47	9	-	0

GRAY Harry
Born: Hemsworth, West Yorkshire, England, 26 October, 1918 — IF
Died: Sheffield, England, January, 1989

League Club	Source	Date Signed	Seasons Played	Apps	Subs	Gls
Barnsley	Grimethorpe Rov	02/38	46	7	-	1
Bournemouth	Tr	12/46	46-47	30	-	7
Southend U	Tr	06/48	48-49	19	-	0

GRAY Ian James
Born: Manchester, England, 25 February, 1975 — G

League Club	Source	Date Signed	Seasons Played	Apps	Subs	Gls
Oldham Ath	YT	07/93				
Rochdale	L	11/94	94	12	0	0
Rochdale	Tr	07/95	95-96	66	0	0
Stockport Co	Tr	07/97	97-99	14	2	0
Rotherham U	Tr	07/00	00-02	38	2	0
Huddersfield T	Tr	08/03	03-04	29	0	0

GRAY Irvine William
Born: Hoyland, South Yorkshire, England, 27 February, 1933 — LW

League Club	Source	Date Signed	Seasons Played	Apps	Subs	Gls
Barnsley	Thorncliffe Rec	09/52				
Gillingham	Tr	08/56	56	9	-	0

GRAY Jake Stephen
Born: Aylesbury, Buckinghamshire, England, 25 December, 1995 — M

League Club	Source	Date Signed	Seasons Played	Apps	Subs	Gls
Crystal Palace	Sch	01/13				
Cheltenham T	L	01/15	14	3	1	0

GRAY James Philip
Born: Yarm, Cleveland, England, 26 June, 1992 — F
Northern Ireland: U21-12/Youth

League Club	Source	Date Signed	Seasons Played	Apps	Subs	Gls
Accrington Stan	Kettering T	08/12	12-14	39	29	13
Northampton T	L	03/15	14	7	1	3

GRAY Joshua Ian (Josh)
Born: South Shields, Tyne and Wear, England, 22 July, 1991 — LW

League Club	Source	Date Signed	Seasons Played	Apps	Subs	Gls
Darlington	Sch	04/09	08-09	11	21	1

GRAY Julian Raymond Marvin
Born: Lewisham, SE London, England, 21 September, 1979 — LW

League Club	Source	Date Signed	Seasons Played	Apps	Subs	Gls
Arsenal	YT	07/98	99	0	1	0
Crystal Palace	Tr	07/00	00-03	100	25	10
Cardiff C	L	10/03	03	5	4	0
Birmingham C	Tr	06/04	04-06	38	22	3
Coventry C	Tr	07/07	07-08	23	6	4
Fulham	Tr	09/08	08	0	1	0
Barnsley	Tr	09/09	09	1	4	0
Walsall	Tr	02/10	09-10	59	2	14
Walsall	Nea Salamis (CYP)	09/13	13	0	12	1

GRAY Kevin John
Born: Sheffield, England, 7 January, 1972 — CD

League Club	Source	Date Signed	Seasons Played	Apps	Subs	Gls
Mansfield T	YT	07/90	88-93	129	12	3
Huddersfield T	Tr	07/94	94-01	214	16	6
Stockport Co	L	08/00	00	1	0	0
Tranmere Rov	Tr	07/02	02-03	11	1	1
Carlisle U	Tr	11/03	03-06	96	4	9
Chesterfield	Tr	07/07	07	10	5	0

GRAY Mark Stuart
Born: Tenby, Pembrokeshire, Wales, 24 November, 1959 — F
Wales: Youth

League Club	Source	Date Signed	Seasons Played	Apps	Subs	Gls
Swansea C	App	09/77	77	1	1	0
Fulham	Tr	01/78				
Leyton Orient	Tr	02/79	78	1	1	0

GRAY Martin David
Born: Stockton-on-Tees, Cleveland, England, 17 August, 1971 — M

League Club	Source	Date Signed	Seasons Played	Apps	Subs	Gls
Sunderland	YT	02/90	91-95	46	18	1
Aldershot	L	01/91	90	3	2	0
Fulham	L	10/95	95	6	0	0
Oxford U	Tr	03/96	95-98	115	6	4
Darlington	Tr	06/99	99-00	65	1	0

GRAY Matthew (Matt)
Born: Renfrew, Renfrewshire, Scotland, 11 July, 1936 — IF

League Club	Source	Date Signed	Seasons Played	Apps	Subs	Gls
Manchester C	Third Lanark	03/63	62-66	87	4	21

GRAY Michael (Micky)
Born: United Kingdom — IF

League Club	Source	Date Signed	Seasons Played	Apps	Subs	Gls
Aldershot	Glenavon	09/46	46	7	-	1
Watford	Tr	06/47	47	10	-	3

GRAY Michael
Born: Sunderland, England, 3 August, 1974 — LB
England: 3

League Club	Source	Date Signed	Seasons Played	Apps	Subs	Gls
Sunderland	YT	07/92	92-03	341	22	16
Blackburn Rov	Tr	01/04	03-06	63	1	0
Leeds U	L	02/05	04	10	0	0
Leeds U	L	03/07	06	6	0	0
Wolverhampton W	Tr	07/07	07-08	33	8	4
Sheffield Wed	Tr	01/09	08-09	40	3	2

GRAY Nigel Robert
Born: Fulham, W London, England, 2 November, 1956 — CD

League Club	Source	Date Signed	Seasons Played	Apps	Subs	Gls
Leyton Orient	App	07/74	74-82	233	0	4
Charlton Ath	L	12/82	82	3	0	0
Swindon T	Tr	07/83	83-84	33	0	0
Brentford	L	03/84	83	16	0	1
Aldershot	L	09/84	84	4	0	0

GRAY Philip (Phil)
Born: Belfast, Northern Ireland, 2 October, 1968 — F
Northern Ireland: 26/U23-1/U21-1/Youth/Schools

League Club	Source	Date Signed	Seasons Played	Apps	Subs	Gls
Tottenham H	App	08/86	86-90	4	5	0
Barnsley	L	01/90	89	3	0	0
Fulham	L	11/90	90	3	0	0
Luton T	Tr	08/91	91-92	54	5	22
Sunderland	Tr	07/93	93-95	108	7	34
Luton T	Fortuna Sittard (NED)	09/97	97-99	74	7	21
Burnley	Tr	07/00	00	5	0	1
Oxford U	Tr	11/00	00-01	35	9	11

GRAY Reece Anthony
Born: Oldham, Greater Manchester, England, 1 September, 1992 — F

League Club	Source	Date Signed	Seasons Played	Apps	Subs	Gls
Rochdale	Sch	07/11	09-13	2	11	2

GRAY Robert
Born: Glasgow, Scotland, 8 June, 1953 — M
Scotland: Schools

League Club	Source	Date Signed	Seasons Played	Apps	Subs	Gls
Workington	Nottingham F (App)	08/72	72	0	1	0

GRAY Robert (Bobby)
Born: Cambuslang, Glasgow, Scotland, 18 June, 1927 — W

League Club	Source	Date Signed	Seasons Played	Apps	Subs	Gls
Lincoln C	Wishaw Jnrs	10/49	49	2	-	0

GRAY Robert (Bob)
Born: Newcastle-upon-Tyne, England, 14 December, 1923 — G

League Club	Source	Date Signed	Seasons Played	Apps	Subs	Gls
Gateshead	Newcastle U (Am)	03/44	47-58	432	-	0

GRAY Robert Henry William
Born: Aberdeen, Scotland, 21 January, 1951 — G

League Club	Source	Date Signed	Seasons Played	Apps	Subs	Gls
Torquay U (Am)	Inverurie Loco	11/69	69	2	0	0

GRAY Robert Paul (Paul)
Born: Portsmouth, England, 28 January, 1970 — F

League Club	Source	Date Signed	Seasons Played	Apps	Subs	Gls
Luton T	YT	06/88	89	2	5	1
Wigan Ath	Tr	05/91	91	2	3	0

GRAY Roland (Ron)
Born: North Shields, Tyne and Wear, England, 25 June, 1920 — WH
Died: Ipswich, England, 11 October, 2002

League Club	Source	Date Signed	Seasons Played	Apps	Subs	Gls
Sheffield U	Boldon CW	05/38				
Lincoln C	Tr	05/39				
Watford	Tr	08/45	46	16	-	0

GRAY Stewart Alexander
Born: Doncaster, South Yorkshire, England, 16 October, 1950 — CD

League Club	Source	Date Signed	Seasons Played	Apps	Subs	Gls
Doncaster Rov	App	09/68	67-70	53	4	0
Grimsby T	Tr	09/70	70-76	263	1	2
Doncaster Rov	Frickley Ath	03/78	77	6	0	0

GRAY Stuart
Born: Withernsea, East Riding of Yorkshire, England, 19 April, 1960 — LB/M

League Club	Source	Date Signed	Seasons Played	Apps	Subs	Gls
Nottingham F	Withernsea YC	12/80	80-82	48	1	3
Bolton W	L	03/83	82	10	0	0

League Club	Source	Date Signed	Seasons Played	Apps	Subs	Gls
Barnsley	Tr	08/83	83-87	117	3	23
Aston Villa	Tr	11/87	87-90	102	4	9
Southampton	Tr	09/91	91	10	2	0

GRAY Stuart Edward
Born: Harrogate, North Yorkshire, England, 18 December, 1973 M
Scotland: U21-7

League Club	Source	Date Signed	Seasons Played	Apps	Subs	Gls
Reading	Glasgow Celtic	03/98	97-00	46	6	2
Rushden & D	Tr	03/01	01-04	116	7	13
Oxford U	Tr	07/05	05	10	0	0

GRAY Terence Ian (Terry)
Born: Bradford, England, 3 June, 1954 W
England: Youth/Schools

League Club	Source	Date Signed	Seasons Played	Apps	Subs	Gls
Huddersfield T	Leeds Ashley Road	08/72	73-78	146	17	36
Southend U	Tr	07/79	79-81	106	4	28
Bradford C	Tr	08/82	82-84	72	4	15
Preston NE	Tr	10/84	84-85	40	0	1

GRAY Wayne William
Born: Camberwell, S London, England, 7 November, 1980 F

League Club	Source	Date Signed	Seasons Played	Apps	Subs	Gls
Wimbledon	YT	02/99	99-03	33	42	6
Swindon T	L	03/00	99	8	4	2
Port Vale	L	10/00	00	2	1	0
Leyton Orient	L	11/01	01	13	2	5
Brighton & HA	L	03/02	01	3	1	1
Southend U	Tr	07/04	04-05	56	27	20
Yeovil T	Tr	07/06	06	24	22	11
Leyton Orient	Tr	07/07	07-08	36	18	8

GRAY William Mair (Billy)
Born: Coventry, England, 3 December, 1931 WH
Died: Bellingham, Northumberland, England, 18 July, 2014

League Club	Source	Date Signed	Seasons Played	Apps	Subs	Gls
Coventry C	Jnr	12/48	51	2	-	0

GRAY William Patrick (Billy)
Born: Ashington, Northumberland, England, 24 May, 1927 W/LB
Died: Nottingham, England, 11 April, 2011
England: B-1

League Club	Source	Date Signed	Seasons Played	Apps	Subs	Gls
Leyton Orient	Dinnington Colliery	05/47	47-48	19	-	1
Chelsea	Tr	03/49	48-52	146	-	12
Burnley	Tr	08/53	53-56	120	-	30
Nottingham F	Tr	06/57	57-62	201	-	29
Millwall	Tr	12/63	63-64	20	-	1

GRAYDON Keith
Born: Dublin, Republic of Ireland, 10 February, 1983 F
Republic of Ireland: Youth

League Club	Source	Date Signed	Seasons Played	Apps	Subs	Gls
Sunderland	YT	02/00				
York C	L	03/03	02	4	3	1

GRAYDON Raymond Jack (Ray)
Born: Bristol, England, 21 July, 1947 RW
England: Youth

League Club	Source	Date Signed	Seasons Played	Apps	Subs	Gls
Bristol Rov	App	09/65	65-70	131	2	33
Aston Villa	Tr	06/71	71-76	189	4	68
Coventry C	Tr	07/77	77	17	3	5
Oxford U	Washington Dip's (USA)	11/78	78-80	36	6	10

GRAYSON Barry John
Born: Manchester, England, 12 October, 1944 IF

League Club	Source	Date Signed	Seasons Played	Apps	Subs	Gls
Manchester U	App	11/61				
Bury	Tr	01/65	64	1	-	0

GRAYSON Neil
Born: York, England, 1 November, 1964 F
England: Semi Pro-4

League Club	Source	Date Signed	Seasons Played	Apps	Subs	Gls
Doncaster Rov	Rowntree-Mack'sh	03/90	89-90	21	8	6
York C	Tr	03/91	90	0	1	0
Chesterfield	Tr	08/91	91	9	6	0
Northampton T	Boston U	06/94	94-96	103	17	31
Cheltenham T	Hereford U	03/98	99-01	75	33	24

GRAYSON Simon Darrell
Born: Sheffield, England, 21 October, 1968 F

League Club	Source	Date Signed	Seasons Played	Apps	Subs	Gls
Sheffield U	App	10/86				
Chesterfield	L	11/87	87	7	1	0
Hartlepool U	Tr	04/88	87-89	39	5	13

GRAYSON Simon Nicholas
Born: Ripon, North Yorkshire, England, 16 December, 1969 RB

League Club	Source	Date Signed	Seasons Played	Apps	Subs	Gls
Leeds U	YT	06/88	87	2	0	0
Leicester C	Tr	03/92	91-96	175	13	4
Aston Villa	Tr	07/97	97-98	32	16	0
Blackburn Rov	Tr	07/99	99	31	3	0
Sheffield Wed	L	08/00	00	5	0	0
Stockport Co	L	01/01	00	13	0	0
Notts Co	L	09/01	01	10	0	1
Bradford C	L	02/02	01	7	0	0
Blackpool	Tr	08/02	02-05	112	14	6

GRAYSTON Neil James
Born: Keighley, West Yorkshire, England, 25 November, 1975 LB

League Club	Source	Date Signed	Seasons Played	Apps	Subs	Gls
Bradford C	YT	05/94	93-95	7	0	0

GRAZIOLI Giuliano Stefano Luigi
Born: Marylebone, Central London, England, 23 March, 1975 F

League Club	Source	Date Signed	Seasons Played	Apps	Subs	Gls
Peterborough U	Wembley	10/95	95-98	23	18	16
Swindon T	Tr	07/99	99-01	45	33	18
Bristol Rov	Tr	07/02	02	28	6	11
Barnet	Tr	07/03	05-07	36	21	9

GREALISH Anthony Patrick (Tony)
Born: Paddington, Central London, England, 21 September, 1956 M
Died: Ilfracombe, Devon, England, 23 April, 2013
Republic of Ireland: 45/Youth

League Club	Source	Date Signed	Seasons Played	Apps	Subs	Gls
Leyton Orient	App	07/74	74-78	169	2	10
Luton T	Tr	08/79	79-80	78	0	2
Brighton & HA	Tr	07/81	81-83	95	5	6
West Bromwich A	Tr	03/84	83-85	55	10	5
Manchester C	Tr	10/86	86	11	0	0
Rotherham U	Tr	08/87	87-89	105	5	6
Walsall	Tr	08/90	90-91	32	4	1

GREALISH Jack
Born: Birmingham, England, 10 September, 1995 LW
Republic of Ireland: U21-6/Youth

League Club	Source	Date Signed	Seasons Played	Apps	Subs	Gls
Aston Villa	Sch	09/12	13-14	7	11	0
Notts Co	L	09/13	13	32	5	5

GREATREX Edward John (John)
Born: Nuneaton, Warwickshire, England, 18 November, 1936 G

League Club	Source	Date Signed	Seasons Played	Apps	Subs	Gls
Norwich C	Jnr	06/54	57	1	-	0

GREAVES Daniel Thomas (Danny)
Born: Upminster, E London, England, 31 January, 1963 F

League Club	Source	Date Signed	Seasons Played	Apps	Subs	Gls
Southend U	Tottenham H (Jnr)	01/81	81-83	30	19	14
Cambridge U	Maldon T	09/84	84	2	2	1

GREAVES Ian Denzil
Born: Shaw, Greater Manchester, England, 26 May, 1932 FB
Died: Ainsworth, Greater Manchester, England, 2 January, 2009

League Club	Source	Date Signed	Seasons Played	Apps	Subs	Gls
Manchester U	Buxton	05/53	54-59	67	-	0
Lincoln C	Tr	12/60	60	11	-	0
Oldham Ath	Tr	05/61	61-62	22	-	0

GREAVES James Peter (Jimmy)
Born: East Ham, E London, England, 20 February, 1940 F
England: 57/FLge-10/U23-12/Youth

League Club	Source	Date Signed	Seasons Played	Apps	Subs	Gls
Chelsea	Jnr	05/57	57-60	157	-	124
Tottenham H	AC Milan (ITA)	12/61	61-69	321	0	220
West Ham U	Tr	03/70	69-70	36	2	13

GREAVES Mark Andrew
Born: Hull, England, 22 January, 1975 CD

League Club	Source	Date Signed	Seasons Played	Apps	Subs	Gls
Hull C	Brigg T	06/96	96-02	152	25	10
Boston U	Tr	08/02	02-06	148	10	5

GREAVES Philip (Phil)
Born: Chesterfield, Derbyshire, England, 5 September, 1961 LW

League Club	Source	Date Signed	Seasons Played	Apps	Subs	Gls
Chesterfield	Alfreton T	10/86	86	5	0	0

GREAVES Roy
Born: Farnworth, Greater Manchester, England, 4 April, 1947 M

League Club	Source	Date Signed	Seasons Played	Apps	Subs	Gls
Bolton W	Jnr	01/65	65-79	487	8	66
Rochdale	Seattle Sounders (USA)	11/82	82	19	2	0

GREAVES Steven Ronald (Steve)
Born: Chelsea, W London, England, 17 January, 1970 CD

League Club	Source	Date Signed	Seasons Played	Apps	Subs	Gls
Fulham	YT	07/88	87	0	1	0
Preston NE	Tr	08/90	90	2	0	0
Ipswich T	Tr	01/91				
Scunthorpe U	Tr	08/92	92	9	6	0

GREEN Adam
Born: Hillingdon, W London, England, 12 January, 1984 LB

League Club	Source	Date Signed	Seasons Played	Apps	Subs	Gls
Fulham	Sch	07/03	03-04	8	0	0
Sheffield Wed	L	01/05	04	3	0	0
Bournemouth	L	03/05	04	3	0	0
Bristol C	L	01/06	05	1	1	0

GREEN Adrian (Adie)
Born: Leicester, England, 22 October, 1957 M

League Club	Source	Date Signed	Seasons Played	Apps	Subs	Gls
Leicester C	App	10/75				
Rochdale	L	12/77	77	7	0	0
Aldershot	Tr	07/78	78-79	7	14	0

GREEN Alan Paul
Born: Worcester, England, 1 January, 1954 F
England: Youth

League Club	Source	Date Signed	Seasons Played	Apps	Subs	Gls
Coventry C	App	01/71	71-78	98	19	30

GREEN Alan Peter Charles
Born: Fordingbridge, Hampshire, England, 19 April, 1951 — F

League Club	Source	Date Signed	Seasons Played	Apps	Subs	Gls
Bournemouth	Jnr	07/69				
Mansfield T	Tr	07/72	72	1	0	0

GREEN Allan
Born: Darfield, South Yorkshire, England, 14 December, 1939 — LB

League Club	Source	Date Signed	Seasons Played	Apps	Subs	Gls
Barnsley	Dodworth MW	01/59	60-61	19	-	0
York C	Tr	07/62				

GREEN Anthony (Tony)
Born: Glasgow, Scotland, 3 October, 1946 — M
Scotland: 6

League Club	Source	Date Signed	Seasons Played	Apps	Subs	Gls
Blackpool	Albion Rov	05/67	66-71	121	1	13
Newcastle U	Tr	10/71	71-72	33	0	3

GREEN Arthur
Born: Liverpool, England, 28 April, 1928 — FB
Died: Liverpool, England, 12 February, 1992

League Club	Source	Date Signed	Seasons Played	Apps	Subs	Gls
Huddersfield T	Burscough	02/51	51	3	-	0

GREEN Brian Geoffrey
Born: Droylsden, Greater Manchester, England, 5 June, 1935 — CF
Died: Rochdale, Greater Manchester, England, 14 August, 2012

League Club	Source	Date Signed	Seasons Played	Apps	Subs	Gls
Rochdale	Haggate Lads	08/55	54-58	46	-	8
Southport	Tr	03/59	58-59	20	-	7
Bury	Tr	07/60				
Barrow	Colwyn Bay	09/60	60	3	-	0
Exeter C	Altrincham	08/62	62	9	-	1
Chesterfield	Tr	02/63	62	2	-	0

GREEN Clive Peter
Born: Portsmouth, England, 6 December, 1959 — F
England: Schools

League Club	Source	Date Signed	Seasons Played	Apps	Subs	Gls
Portsmouth	Jnr	07/76	76-77	34	6	4

GREEN Colin Robert
Born: Wrexham, Wales, 10 February, 1942 — FB
Wales: 15/U23-7

League Club	Source	Date Signed	Seasons Played	Apps	Subs	Gls
Everton	Jnr	02/59	60-61	15	-	1
Birmingham C	Tr	12/62	62-70	183	0	1
Wrexham	L	01/71	70	3	0	0

GREEN Daniel James (Danny)
Born: Harlow, Essex, England, 4 August, 1990 — W

League Club	Source	Date Signed	Seasons Played	Apps	Subs	Gls
Dagenham & Red	Billericay T	07/10	10-12	4	13	1

GREEN Daniel Richard (Danny)
Born: Harlow, Essex, England, 9 July, 1988 — RW

League Club	Source	Date Signed	Seasons Played	Apps	Subs	Gls
Northampton T	Sch	07/06				
Nottingham F	Tr	07/07				
Dagenham & Red	Bishops Stortford	07/09	09-10	86	1	24
Charlton Ath	Tr	06/11	11-13	37	25	4
MK Dons	L	09/13	13	5	0	0
MK Dons	Tr	05/14	14	4	10	1

GREEN Dominic Ashley
Born: Newham, E London, England, 5 July, 1989 — W

League Club	Source	Date Signed	Seasons Played	Apps	Subs	Gls
Dagenham & Red	Jnr	07/07	07-08	4	10	1
Peterborough U	Tr	08/08	08-09	9	18	2
Chesterfield	L	01/10	09	10	0	2
Dagenham & Red	Tr	09/11	11-12	9	17	1

GREEN Donald (Don)
Born: Blackburn, Greater Manchester, England, 13 May, 1932 — LB
Died: Garstang, Lancashire, England, December, 1992

League Club	Source	Date Signed	Seasons Played	Apps	Subs	Gls
Accrington Stan (Am)	Blackburn Rov (Am)	05/52	52	12	-	0

GREEN Donald (Don)
Born: Needham Market, Suffolk, England, 30 November, 1924 — CH
Died: Ipswich, England, May, 1996

League Club	Source	Date Signed	Seasons Played	Apps	Subs	Gls
Ipswich T	Bramford	03/47	46-51	52	-	0

GREEN Francis James
Born: Nottingham, England, 25 April, 1980 — F

League Club	Source	Date Signed	Seasons Played	Apps	Subs	Gls
Peterborough U	Ilkeston T	03/98	97-03	51	57	14
Lincoln C	Tr	09/03	03-05	79	21	18
Boston U	L	11/05	05	5	1	1
Boston U	Tr	07/06	06	35	4	4
Macclesfield T	Tr	07/07	07-08	44	21	14

GREEN Frederick Zeanes (Freddie)
Born: Sheffield, England, 9 September, 1916 — RB
Died: Torquay, Devon, England, 10 September, 1998

League Club	Source	Date Signed	Seasons Played	Apps	Subs	Gls
Torquay U	Mosborough Trinity	06/35	35-37	86	-	0
Brighton & HA	Tr	06/38	38-47	26	-	0

GREEN George Frederick
Born: Northowram, West Yorkshire, England, 21 December, 1914 — WH
Died: Northowram, West Yorkshire, England, June, 1995

League Club	Source	Date Signed	Seasons Played	Apps	Subs	Gls
Bradford Park Ave	Jnr	05/36	36	2	-	0
Huddersfield T	Tr	10/44	46-47	9	-	1
Reading	Tr	10/47	47-48	44	-	6

GREEN George William
Born: Dewsbury, West Yorkshire, England, 2 January, 1996 — M

League Club	Source	Date Signed	Seasons Played	Apps	Subs	Gls
Everton	Sch	01/13				
Tranmere Rov	L	03/15	14	5	1	1

GREEN Harry Rodney (Rodney)
Born: Halifax, West Yorkshire, England, 24 June, 1939 — F

League Club	Source	Date Signed	Seasons Played	Apps	Subs	Gls
Halifax T	Elland U	08/60	60-61	9	-	2
Bradford Park Ave	Tr	06/62	62	19	-	6
Bradford C	Tr	01/63	62-63	66	-	39
Gillingham	Tr	07/64	64	33	-	17
Grimsby T	Tr	08/65	65-66	65	0	20
Charlton Ath	Tr	02/67	66	3	1	1
Luton T	Tr	08/67	67	9	2	3
Watford	Tr	08/68	68-69	19	11	8

GREEN Horace
Born: Barnsley, South Yorkshire, England, 23 April, 1918 — LB/RH
Died: Barnsley, South Yorkshire, England, July, 2000

League Club	Source	Date Signed	Seasons Played	Apps	Subs	Gls
Halifax T	Worsbrough Bridge OB	11/36	37-48	155	-	5
Lincoln C	Tr	02/49	48-54	212	-	14

GREEN Ivan David
Born: Bexhill on Sea, East Sussex, England, 29 July, 1933 — IF

League Club	Source	Date Signed	Seasons Played	Apps	Subs	Gls
Millwall		09/53	54	1	-	0

GREEN Jamie Paul
Born: Rossington, South Yorkshire, England, 18 August, 1989 — LB

League Club	Source	Date Signed	Seasons Played	Apps	Subs	Gls
Rotherham U	Sch	06/07	07-10	54	12	2

GREEN John
Born: Warrington, Cheshire, England, 22 May, 1939 — LH/IF
Died: Warrington, Cheshire, England, 14 August, 2010

League Club	Source	Date Signed	Seasons Played	Apps	Subs	Gls
Tranmere Rov	Stockton Heath	02/58	58	17	-	5
Blackpool	Tr	03/59	59-66	135	0	9
Port Vale	Tr	09/67	67	11	0	0
Port Vale	Vancouver Royals (CAN)	11/68	68-70	81	2	7

GREEN John Richard
Born: Rotherham, South Yorkshire, England, 7 March, 1958 — CD

League Club	Source	Date Signed	Seasons Played	Apps	Subs	Gls
Rotherham U	App	03/76	75-83	247	1	8
Scunthorpe U	Tr	09/83	83-85	100	0	4
Darlington	Tr	10/85	85-86	45	0	2
Rotherham U	Tr	12/86	86-88	84	1	3

GREEN Kenneth (Ken)
Born: Hull, England, 20 November, 1929 — CF
Died: Leeds, England, March, 2012

League Club	Source	Date Signed	Seasons Played	Apps	Subs	Gls
Grimsby T	Selby T	04/51	51	1	-	0

GREEN Kenneth (Ken)
Born: Plaistow, E London, England, 27 April, 1924 — LB
Died: Sutton Coldfield, West Midlands, England, 7 June, 2001
England: B-2/FLge-2

League Club	Source	Date Signed	Seasons Played	Apps	Subs	Gls
Birmingham C	Millwall (Am)	11/43	47-58	401	-	3

GREEN Kieran Thomas
Born: Stockton-on-Tees, Cleveland, England, 30 June, 1997 — M

League Club	Source	Date Signed	Seasons Played	Apps	Subs	Gls
Hartlepool U	Sch	05/15	14	0	1	0

GREEN Leonard Hope (Len)
Born: Bishop Auckland, County Durham, England, 2 October, 1936 — RB

League Club	Source	Date Signed	Seasons Played	Apps	Subs	Gls
Darlington	Lingfield Lane	10/55	55-60	50	-	0

GREEN Leslie (Les)
Born: Atherstone, Warwickshire, England, 17 October, 1941 — G
Died: Leicester, England, 30 July, 2012

League Club	Source	Date Signed	Seasons Played	Apps	Subs	Gls
Hull C	Atherstone T	08/60	61	4	-	0
Hartlepool U	Burton A	11/65	65-66	34	0	0
Rochdale	Tr	04/67	67	44	0	0
Derby Co	Tr	05/68	68-70	107	0	0

GREEN Liam Thomas
Born: Grimsby, North Lincolnshire, England, 17 March, 1988 — LB/M

League Club	Source	Date Signed	Seasons Played	Apps	Subs	Gls
Doncaster Rov	Sch	08/06	06	0	2	0

GREEN Matthew James (Matty)
Born: Bath, England, 2 January, 1987 — F
England: Semi Pro-1

League Club	Source	Date Signed	Seasons Played	Apps	Subs	Gls
Cardiff C	Newport Co	01/07	06	0	6	0
Darlington	L	10/07	07	3	1	0
Oxford U	Torquay U	07/10	10	9	8	1
Cheltenham T	L	01/11	10	10	9	0
Birmingham C	Mansfield T	07/13	13	7	3	1

GREEN Melvyn (Mel)
Born: Hull, England, 20 October, 1951 — CD

League Club	Source	Date Signed	Seasons Played	Apps	Subs	Gls
Hull C	App	10/69	71-72	10	0	0
Cambridge U	Tr	07/74	74	3	0	0

GREEN Michael Clive (Mike)
Born: Carlisle, Cumbria, England, 8 September, 1946 — CD/F

League Club	Source	Date Signed	Seasons Played	Apps	Subs	Gls
Carlisle U	App	09/64	65	2	0	0
Gillingham	Tr	07/68	68-70	131	1	24
Bristol Rov	Tr	07/71	71-73	74	3	2
Plymouth Arg	Tr	07/74	74-76	108	0	8
Torquay U	Tr	03/77	76-78	88	0	7

GREEN Michael James (Mike)
Born: Southampton, England, 12 May, 1989 — LB

League Club	Source	Date Signed	Seasons Played	Apps	Subs	Gls
Port Vale	AFC Totton	07/11	11	4	0	0

GREEN Michael John (Mike)
Born: Southend-on-Sea, England, 20 November, 1957 — FB
Died: Kensington, Central London, England, 7 February, 2009

League Club	Source	Date Signed	Seasons Played	Apps	Subs	Gls
Exeter C	App	11/75	76	0	1	0

GREEN Michael John (Mike)
Born: Bristol, England, 23 July, 1989 — G

League Club	Source	Date Signed	Seasons Played	Apps	Subs	Gls
Bristol Rov	Jnr	07/06	10	2	0	0

GREEN Nathan
Born: Bermondsey, SE London, England, 8 June, 1992 — LB

League Club	Source	Date Signed	Seasons Played	Apps	Subs	Gls
Dagenham & Red	Tonbridge Angels	06/14	14	6	1	0

GREEN Norman Russell (Russell)
Born: Donington, Lincolnshire, England, 13 August, 1933 — FB/WH
Died: Gainsborough, Lincolnshire, England, 21 April, 2012

League Club	Source	Date Signed	Seasons Played	Apps	Subs	Gls
Lincoln C	Quadring	08/51				
Lincoln C	Corby T	05/57	57-63	125	-	8

GREEN Paul Jason
Born: Sheffield, England, 10 April, 1983 — RM
Republic of Ireland: 22

League Club	Source	Date Signed	Seasons Played	Apps	Subs	Gls
Doncaster Rov	YT	10/00	03-07	161	37	25
Derby Co	Tr	06/08	08-11	121	4	8
Leeds U	Tr	07/12	12-13	37	4	4
Ipswich T	L	02/14	13	6	8	2
Rotherham U	Tr	06/14	14	34	3	3

GREEN Paul Michael
Born: Birmingham, England, 15 April, 1987 — D

League Club	Source	Date Signed	Seasons Played	Apps	Subs	Gls
Aston Villa	Sch	04/05				
Lincoln C	Tr	01/07	06-10	107	10	4

GREEN Philip (Phil)
Born: Cardiff, Wales, 30 October, 1957 — F

League Club	Source	Date Signed	Seasons Played	Apps	Subs	Gls
Newport Co	Barry T	03/84	83-84	11	5	2

GREEN Richard (Rick)
Born: Scunthorpe, North Lincolnshire, England, 23 November, 1952 — F

League Club	Source	Date Signed	Seasons Played	Apps	Subs	Gls
Scunthorpe U	Appleby Frodingham	09/75	75-76	66	0	19
Chesterfield	Tr	02/77	76-77	45	3	13
Notts Co	Tr	06/78	78	6	3	0
Scunthorpe U	Tr	08/79	79-81	66	5	19

GREEN Richard Edward
Born: Wolverhampton, England, 22 November, 1967 — CD

League Club	Source	Date Signed	Seasons Played	Apps	Subs	Gls
Shrewsbury T	App	07/86	86-89	120	5	5
Swindon T	Tr	10/90				
Gillingham	Tr	03/92	91-97	206	10	16
Walsall	Tr	08/98	98	22	8	1
Rochdale	L	09/99	99	6	0	0
Northampton T	Tr	01/00	99-00	55	4	2
Rochdale	Tr	07/01				

GREEN Robert Paul (Rob)
Born: Chertsey, Surrey, England, 18 January, 1980 — G
England: 12/Youth

League Club	Source	Date Signed	Seasons Played	Apps	Subs	Gls
Norwich C	YT	07/97	98-05	222	1	0
West Ham U	Tr	08/06	06-11	219	0	0
Queens Park Rgrs	Tr	07/12	12-14	95	2	0

GREEN Roger
Born: Cardiff, Wales, 20 September, 1944 — CD

League Club	Source	Date Signed	Seasons Played	Apps	Subs	Gls
Newport Co	Barry T	01/72	71	1	0	0

GREEN Ronald Rex (Ron)
Born: Birmingham, England, 3 October, 1956 — G

League Club	Source	Date Signed	Seasons Played	Apps	Subs	Gls
Walsall	Alvechurch	06/77	77-83	163	0	0
Shrewsbury T	Tr	06/84	84	19	0	0
Bristol Rov	Tr	02/85	84-85	56	0	0
Scunthorpe U	Tr	08/86	86-87	78	0	0
Wimbledon	Tr	08/88	88	4	0	0
Shrewsbury T	L	09/88	88	17	0	0
Walsall	Tr	03/89	88-90	67	0	0
Colchester U	Kidderminster Hrs	11/92	92	4	0	0

GREEN Roy Francis
Born: Loughborough, Leicestershire, England, 8 June, 1931 — IF
Died: Reading, England, January, 2007

League Club	Source	Date Signed	Seasons Played	Apps	Subs	Gls
Reading	Bloxwich Strollers	12/52	55-56	14	-	3

GREEN Ryan Michael
Born: Cardiff, Wales, 20 October, 1980 — RB
Wales: 2/U21-16/Youth

League Club	Source	Date Signed	Seasons Played	Apps	Subs	Gls
Wolverhampton W	YT	10/97	98-00	6	2	0
Torquay U	L	03/01	00	10	0	0
Millwall	Tr	10/01	01	12	1	0
Cardiff C	Tr	08/02				
Sheffield Wed	Tr	11/02	02	4	0	0
Bristol Rov	Hereford U	06/06	06-08	64	7	0
Hereford U	Tr	07/09	09-11	97	3	2

GREEN Scott Paul
Born: Willenhall, West Midlands, England, 15 January, 1970 — RB/M

League Club	Source	Date Signed	Seasons Played	Apps	Subs	Gls
Derby Co	YT	07/88				
Bolton W	Tr	03/90	89-96	166	54	25
Wigan Ath	Tr	06/97	97-02	177	22	10
Wrexham	Tr	02/03	02	12	3	3
Wrexham	Telford U	11/04	04	5	7	0

GREEN Stanley (Stan)
Born: West Bromwich, West Midlands, England, 6 September, 1928 — CD
Died: West Bromwich, West Midlands, United Kingdom, 23 February, 2006

League Club	Source	Date Signed	Seasons Played	Apps	Subs	Gls
Bristol Rov	Accles & Pollock	03/52	51	1	-	0

GREEN Stuart
Born: Whitehaven, Cumbria, England, 15 June, 1981 — M

League Club	Source	Date Signed	Seasons Played	Apps	Subs	Gls
Newcastle U	YT	07/99				
Carlisle U	L	12/01	01	16	0	3
Hull C	Tr	07/02	02-05	111	26	24
Carlisle U	L	02/03	02	9	1	2
Crystal Palace	Tr	08/06	06-07	12	12	4
Blackpool	Tr	01/08	07	1	5	0
Crewe Alex	L	11/08	08	2	0	0
Wycombe W	Tr	07/09	09	10	3	0

GREEN Thomas (Tommy)
Born: Birkenhead, Wirral, England, 18 September, 1926 — RH
Died: Indonesia, 4 August, 1952

League Club	Source	Date Signed	Seasons Played	Apps	Subs	Gls
Southport	West Lancashire ATC	05/46	46	4	-	0

GREEN William (Bill)
Born: Newcastle-upon-Tyne, England, 22 December, 1950 — CD

League Club	Source	Date Signed	Seasons Played	Apps	Subs	Gls
Hartlepool U	Jnr	06/69	69-72	128	3	9
Carlisle U	Tr	07/73	73-75	119	0	4
West Ham U	Tr	06/76	76-77	35	0	1
Peterborough U	Tr	07/78	78	30	0	0
Chesterfield	Tr	06/79	79-82	160	0	5
Doncaster Rov	Tr	06/83	83	10	1	1

GREEN William Charles (Billy)
Born: Hull, England, 9 October, 1927 — D
Died: Northampton, England, March, 1996

League Club	Source	Date Signed	Seasons Played	Apps	Subs	Gls
Wolverhampton W	Jnr	09/45				
Leeds U	Tr	08/49				
Walsall	Tr	09/49	49-53	180	-	8
Wrexham	Tr	06/54	54-56	60	-	2

GREENACRE Christopher Mark (Chris)
Born: Halifax, West Yorkshire, England, 23 December, 1977 — F

League Club	Source	Date Signed	Seasons Played	Apps	Subs	Gls
Manchester C	YT	07/95	96-98	3	5	1
Cardiff C	L	08/97	97	11	0	2
Blackpool	L	03/98	97	2	2	0
Scarborough	L	12/98	98	10	2	2
Mansfield T	Tr	11/99	99-01	120	1	49
Stoke C	Tr	07/02	02-04	44	31	7
Tranmere Rov	Tr	07/05	05-08	126	16	46

GREENALL Colin Anthony
Born: Billinge, Merseyside, England, 30 December, 1963 — CD
England: Youth

League Club	Source	Date Signed	Seasons Played	Apps	Subs	Gls
Blackpool	App	01/81	80-86	179	4	9
Gillingham	Tr	09/86	86-87	62	0	5
Oxford U	Tr	02/88	87-89	67	0	2
Bury	L	01/90	89	3	0	0
Bury	Tr	07/90	90-91	66	2	5
Preston NE	Tr	03/92	91-92	29	0	1
Chester C	Tr	08/93	93	42	0	1
Lincoln C	Tr	07/94	94-95	43	0	3
Wigan Ath	Tr	09/95	95-98	162	0	14

GREENALL George Edward
Born: Liverpool, England, 5 November, 1937 — CH

League Club	Source	Date Signed	Seasons Played	Apps	Subs	Gls
Manchester C	Andover	11/58				
Oldham Ath	Tr	09/60	60	25	-	0

GREENAWAY Arthur Robert
Born: Swindon, England, 5 April, 1928 — IF
Died: Swindon, England, 29 September, 2004

League Club	Source	Date Signed	Seasons Played	Apps	Subs	Gls
Plymouth Arg	Tavistock Rgrs	08/47				
Exeter C	Tr	05/50	50	1	-	0
Swansea C	Tr	10/51				

GREENAWAY Brian Joseph
Born: Hammersmith, W London, England, 26 September, 1957 — W

League Club	Source	Date Signed	Seasons Played	Apps	Subs	Gls
Fulham	App	06/75	76-80	68	17	8

GREENE David Michael
Born: Luton, England, 26 October, 1973 — CD
Republic of Ireland: U21-14

League Club	Source	Date Signed	Seasons Played	Apps	Subs	Gls
Luton T	Jnr	09/91	92-94	18	1	0
Colchester U	L	11/95	95	14	0	1
Brentford	L	03/96	95	11	0	0
Colchester U	Tr	06/96	96-99	153	0	15
Cardiff C	Tr	07/00	00	10	0	0
Cambridge U	Tr	03/01	00	1	0	0

GREENER Ronald (Ron)
Born: Easington, County Durham, England, 31 January, 1934 — CH

League Club	Source	Date Signed	Seasons Played	Apps	Subs	Gls
Newcastle U	Easington CW	05/51	53	3	-	0
Darlington	Tr	08/55	55-66	439	0	5

GREENHALGH Brian Arthur
Born: Chesterfield, Derbyshire, England, 20 February, 1947 — F

League Club	Source	Date Signed	Seasons Played	Apps	Subs	Gls
Preston NE	App	02/65	65-67	19	0	9
Aston Villa	Tr	09/67	67-68	37	3	12
Leicester C	Tr	02/69	68	2	2	0
Huddersfield T	Tr	06/69	69-70	15	0	0
Cambridge U	Tr	07/71	71-73	116	0	47
Bournemouth	Tr	02/74	73-74	23	1	7
Torquay U	L	06/74	74	9	0	1
Watford	Tr	03/75	74-75	17	1	1

GREENHALGH James Radcliffe (Jimmy)
Born: Manchester, England, 25 August, 1923 — WH
Died: Darlington, County Durham, England, 31 August, 2013

League Club	Source	Date Signed	Seasons Played	Apps	Subs	Gls
Hull C	Newton Heath Loco	08/46	46-50	148	-	5
Bury	Tr	12/50	50-54	122	-	1
Gillingham	Wigan Ath	07/56	56	16	-	1

GREENHALGH Laurence Lee (Loz)
Born: Salford, England, 2 April, 1974 — LB

League Club	Source	Date Signed	Seasons Played	Apps	Subs	Gls
Bury	YT	07/92	92	2	0	0

GREENHALGH Norman
Born: Bolton, Greater Manchester, England, 10 August, 1914 — LB
Died: Birkenhead, Wirral, England, January, 1995
England: FLge-1/War-1

League Club	Source	Date Signed	Seasons Played	Apps	Subs	Gls
Bolton W		09/33				
New Brighton	Tr	10/35	35-37	77	-	8
Everton	Tr	01/38	37-48	106	-	1

GREENHOFF Brian
Born: Barnsley, South Yorkshire, England, 28 April, 1953 — CD/M
Died: Rochdale, Greater Manchester, England, 22 May, 2013
England: 18/B-1/U23-4

League Club	Source	Date Signed	Seasons Played	Apps	Subs	Gls
Manchester U	App	06/70	73-78	218	3	13
Leeds U	Tr	08/79	79-81	68	4	1
Rochdale	RoPs Rovaniemi (FIN)	03/83	82-83	15	1	0

GREENHOFF Frank
Born: Barnsley, South Yorkshire, England, 3 March, 1924 — LW
Died: Surrey South East, Surrey, England, February, 1999

League Club	Source	Date Signed	Seasons Played	Apps	Subs	Gls
Barnsley	Manchester C (Am)	09/47				
Bradford C	Tr	10/48	48-51	81	-	11

GREENHOFF James (Jimmy)
Born: Barnsley, South Yorkshire, England, 19 June, 1946 — F
England: FLge-1/U23-5

League Club	Source	Date Signed	Seasons Played	Apps	Subs	Gls
Leeds U	App	08/63	62-68	88	6	21
Birmingham C	Tr	08/68	68	31	0	14
Stoke C	Tr	08/69	69-76	274	0	76
Manchester U	Tr	11/76	76-80	94	3	26
Crewe Alex	Tr	12/80	80	11	0	4
Port Vale	Toronto Blizzard (CAN)	08/81	81-82	44	4	5
Rochdale	Tr	03/83	82-83	16	0	0

GREENING Jonathan
Born: Scarborough, North Yorkshire, England, 2 January, 1979 — DM
England: U21-18/Youth

League Club	Source	Date Signed	Seasons Played	Apps	Subs	Gls
York C	YT	12/96	96-97	5	20	2
Manchester U	Tr	03/98	98-00	4	10	0
Middlesbrough	Tr	08/01	01-03	91	8	4
West Bromwich A	Tr	07/04	04-09	190	6	7
Fulham	L	08/09	09	15	8	1
Fulham	Tr	07/10	10	6	4	0
Nottingham F	Tr	07/11	11-13	31	18	0
Barnsley	L	11/12	12	6	0	1

GREENMAN Christopher (Chris)
Born: Bristol, England, 22 December, 1968 — CD
England: Schools

League Club	Source	Date Signed	Seasons Played	Apps	Subs	Gls
Coventry C	Jnr	07/88	91-92	5	1	0
Peterborough U	Tr	03/93	92-93	32	2	0

GREENOUGH Richard Anthony (Ricky)
Born: Mexborough, South Yorkshire, England, 30 May, 1961 — CD/F

League Club	Source	Date Signed	Seasons Played	Apps	Subs	Gls
Chester C	Alfreton T	01/85	84-87	123	9	16
Scarborough	Tr	07/88				
York C	Tr	11/88	88-89	28	1	1

GREENSMITH Ronald (Ron)
Born: Sheffield, England, 22 January, 1933 — LW

League Club	Source	Date Signed	Seasons Played	Apps	Subs	Gls
Sheffield Wed	Shiregreen WMC	01/54	54-57	5	-	0
York C	Tr	01/58	57-59	42	-	1

GREENWAY Mark
Born: Halifax, West Yorkshire, England, 19 April, 1966 — LB

League Club	Source	Date Signed	Seasons Played	Apps	Subs	Gls
Halifax T	App	04/84	83-84	15	1	1

GREENWELL Donald (Don)
Born: Chester-le-Street, County Durham, England, 4 January, 1924 — WH
Died: Sunderland, England, December, 2002

League Club	Source	Date Signed	Seasons Played	Apps	Subs	Gls
York C		12/46	46	1	-	0

GREENWOOD Alexander John (Alex)
Born: Fulham, W London, England, 17 June, 1933 — FB
Died: Durham, England, January, 2006

League Club	Source	Date Signed	Seasons Played	Apps	Subs	Gls
Chelsea	Ferryhill Ath	09/53				
Crystal Palace	Tr	05/54	54	2	-	0
Darlington	Scarborough	06/55	55	8	-	0

GREENWOOD John Jones
Born: Manchester, England, 22 January, 1921 — WH
Died: Manchester, England, 25 November, 1994

League Club	Source	Date Signed	Seasons Played	Apps	Subs	Gls
Manchester C		09/46	48	1	-	0
Exeter C	Tr	06/49	49	31	-	2
Aldershot	Tr	03/51	50	12	-	0
Halifax T	Tr	11/51				

GREENWOOD Nigel Patrick
Born: Preston, Lancashire, England, 27 November, 1966 — F

League Club	Source	Date Signed	Seasons Played	Apps	Subs	Gls
Preston NE	App	09/84	84-85	36	9	14
Bury	Tr	08/86	86-89	78	32	25
Preston NE	Tr	02/90	89-91	24	6	4
Halifax T	Tr	07/92	92	21	4	5

GREENWOOD Patrick George (Paddy)
Born: Hull, England, 17 October, 1946 — M/D

League Club	Source	Date Signed	Seasons Played	Apps	Subs	Gls
Hull C	Jnr	11/64	65-71	137	12	3
Barnsley	Tr	11/71	71-73	110	1	6
Nottingham F	Boston Minutemen (USA)	10/74	74	15	0	0

GREENWOOD Peter
Born: Todmorden, West Yorkshire, England, 11 September, 1924 — WH

League Club	Source	Date Signed	Seasons Played	Apps	Subs	Gls
Burnley	Todmorden	10/46				
Chester C	Tr	07/48	48-51	62	-	3

GREENWOOD Peter
Born: Rawtenstall, Lancashire, England, 30 April, 1938 — CF

League Club	Source	Date Signed	Seasons Played	Apps	Subs	Gls
Bury	Bolton W (Am)	10/56	56	1	-	0

GREENWOOD Ronald (Ron)
Born: Burnley, Lancashire, England, 11 November, 1921 — CH
Died: Bury St Edmunds, Suffolk, England, 9 February, 2006
England: B-1

League Club	Source	Date Signed	Seasons Played	Apps	Subs	Gls
Chelsea	Belfast Celtic	10/43				
Bradford Park Ave	Tr	12/45	46-47	59	-	0
Brentford	Tr	03/49	48-52	142	-	1
Chelsea	Tr	10/52	52-54	65	-	0
Fulham	Tr	02/55	54-55	42	-	0

GREENWOOD Ross Michael
Born: York, England, 1 November, 1985 — RB

League Club	Source	Date Signed	Seasons Played	Apps	Subs	Gls
Sheffield Wed	Sch	-	04	0	2	0
Stockport Co	Tr	07/05	05	17	5	0

GREENWOOD Roy Thornton
Born: Leeds, England, 26 September, 1952 — LW

League Club	Source	Date Signed	Seasons Played	Apps	Subs	Gls
Hull C	App	10/70	71-75	118	8	24
Sunderland	Tr	01/76	75-78	45	11	9
Derby Co	Tr	01/79	78-79	26	5	1
Swindon T	Tr	02/80	79-81	49	4	7
Huddersfield T	Tr	08/82	82-83	5	3	0
Tranmere Rov	L	11/83	83	3	0	0

League Club	Source	Date Signed	Seasons Played	Apps	Subs	Gls

GREENWOOD Roy Tony
Born: Croydon, S London, England, 22 May, 1931 — LB
Died: Caterham, Surrey, England, 31 December, 2011

League Club	Source	Date Signed	Seasons Played	Apps	Subs	Gls
Crystal Palace	Beckenham T	11/54	54-58	111	-	0

GREER Gordon
Born: Glasgow, Scotland, 14 December, 1980 — CD
Scotland: 8/B-2

League Club	Source	Date Signed	Seasons Played	Apps	Subs	Gls
Blackburn Rov	Clyde	05/01				
Stockport Co	L	03/03	02	4	1	1
Doncaster Rov	Kilmarnock	07/07	07-08	10	2	1
Swindon T	L	01/09	08	19	0	1
Swindon T	Tr	07/09	09	43	1	1
Brighton & HA	Tr	07/10	10-14	188	1	5

GREER Ross
Born: Perth, Australia, 23 September, 1967 — F
Hong Kong: 3

League Club	Source	Date Signed	Seasons Played	Apps	Subs	Gls
Chester C	Floreat Athena (AUS)	11/89	89	2	0	0

GREETHAM Harold
Born: Grimsby, North Lincolnshire, England, 7 March, 1930 — FB

League Club	Source	Date Signed	Seasons Played	Apps	Subs	Gls
Grimsby T	Jnr	06/50	50	4	-	0

GREGAN Sean Matthew
Born: Guisborough, Cleveland, England, 29 March, 1974 — M/CD

League Club	Source	Date Signed	Seasons Played	Apps	Subs	Gls
Darlington	YT	01/91	91-96	129	7	4
Preston NE	Tr	11/96	96-01	206	6	12
West Bromwich A	Tr	08/02	02-03	76	3	2
Leeds U	Tr	09/04	04-06	63	1	0
Oldham Ath	Tr	11/06	06-10	126	3	1

GREGG Frank
Born: Stourbridge, West Midlands, England, 9 October, 1942 — FB

League Club	Source	Date Signed	Seasons Played	Apps	Subs	Gls
Walsall	Jnr	10/59	60-72	389	4	3

GREGG Henry (Harry)
Born: Derry, Northern Ireland, 25 October, 1932 — G
Northern Ireland: 25/NILge-1/Amateur/Schools

League Club	Source	Date Signed	Seasons Played	Apps	Subs	Gls
Doncaster Rov	Coleraine	10/52	52-57	94	-	0
Manchester U	Tr	12/57	57-66	210	0	0
Stoke C	Tr	12/66	66	2	0	0

GREGG Matthew Stephen (Matt)
Born: Cheltenham, Gloucestershire, England, 30 November, 1978 — G

League Club	Source	Date Signed	Seasons Played	Apps	Subs	Gls
Torquay U	YT	07/97	95-98	32	0	0
Crystal Palace	Tr	10/98	99-00	7	0	0
Swansea C	L	02/99	98	5	0	0
Exeter C	L	09/01	01	2	0	0

GREGO-COX Reece Randall
Born: Hammersmith, W London, England, 12 November, 1996 — F
Republic of Ireland: Youth

League Club	Source	Date Signed	Seasons Played	Apps	Subs	Gls
Queens Park Rgrs	Sch	12/14	14	1	3	0

GREGOIRE Roland Barry (Roly)
Born: Liverpool, England, 23 November, 1958 — F

League Club	Source	Date Signed	Seasons Played	Apps	Subs	Gls
Halifax T	Jnr	08/76	77	5	0	0
Sunderland	Tr	11/77	77-78	6	3	1

GREGORIO Adolfo Sousa
Born: Turlock, California, USA, 1 October, 1982 — M
USA: U23-2/Youth

League Club	Source	Date Signed	Seasons Played	Apps	Subs	Gls
Darlington	Orange County BS (USA)	09/04	04	19	5	2

GREGORY Andrew (Andy)
Born: Barnsley, South Yorkshire, England, 8 October, 1976 — M

League Club	Source	Date Signed	Seasons Played	Apps	Subs	Gls
Barnsley	YT	07/95				
Carlisle U	L	09/99	99	6	1	1

GREGORY Anthony Charles (Tony)
Born: Luton, England, 16 May, 1937 — LH/LW
England: Youth

League Club	Source	Date Signed	Seasons Played	Apps	Subs	Gls
Luton T	Vauxhall Motors	05/55	55-59	59	-	17
Watford	Tr	03/60	59-63	107	-	14

GREGORY Anthony Gerard (Tony)
Born: Doncaster, South Yorkshire, England, 21 March, 1968 — M
England: Youth/Schools

League Club	Source	Date Signed	Seasons Played	Apps	Subs	Gls
Sheffield Wed	App	01/86	85-88	14	4	1
Halifax T	Tr	08/90	90-91	16	1	1

GREGORY Anthony Thomas (Tony)
Born: Dawley, Telford & Wrekin, England, 10 March, 1947 — RB

League Club	Source	Date Signed	Seasons Played	Apps	Subs	Gls
Shrewsbury T	App	03/65	64-75	286	8	0

GREGORY Brian
Born: Belfast, Northern Ireland, 11 January, 1955 — F

League Club	Source	Date Signed	Seasons Played	Apps	Subs	Gls
Gillingham	Jnr	08/74	74	1	1	0
Luton T	Margate	06/76				

GREGORY Charles Frederick (Fred)
Born: Doncaster, South Yorkshire, England, 24 October, 1911 — FB
Died: Doncaster, South Yorkshire, England, January, 2010

League Club	Source	Date Signed	Seasons Played	Apps	Subs	Gls
Doncaster Rov	Brodsworth Main	10/28	29	13	-	3
Manchester C	Tr	03/30	31-33	21	-	2
Reading	Tr	03/34	33-37	129	-	6
Crystal Palace	Tr	12/37	37-38	43	-	9
Hartlepool U	Tr	06/46	46	21	-	0
Rotherham U	Tr	02/47	46	1	-	0

GREGORY David Harry
Born: Peterborough, England, 6 October, 1951 — F

League Club	Source	Date Signed	Seasons Played	Apps	Subs	Gls
Peterborough U	Chatteris T	08/73	73-76	125	17	32
Stoke C	Tr	06/77	77	22	1	3
Blackburn Rov	Tr	07/78	78	5	0	3
Bury	Tr	09/78	78-79	50	2	13
Portsmouth	Tr	12/79	79-81	64	10	18
Wrexham	Tr	08/82	82-85	145	8	31
Peterborough U	Tr	08/86	86	16	15	8

GREGORY David Peter
Born: Camden, N London, England, 19 February, 1960 — LB

League Club	Source	Date Signed	Seasons Played	Apps	Subs	Gls
Millwall	Crystal Palace (Jnr)	08/78	78-80	52	0	2

GREGORY David Spencer
Born: Sudbury, Suffolk, England, 23 January, 1970 — M

League Club	Source	Date Signed	Seasons Played	Apps	Subs	Gls
Ipswich T	App	03/87	88-94	16	16	2
Hereford U	L	01/95	94	2	0	0
Peterborough U	Tr	07/95	95	0	3	0
Colchester U	Tr	12/95	95-01	211	14	20

GREGORY Ernest (Ernie)
Born: Stratford, E London, England, 10 November, 1921 — G
Died: Basildon, England, 21 January, 2012
England: B-1

League Club	Source	Date Signed	Seasons Played	Apps	Subs	Gls
West Ham U	Leytonstone	05/39	46-59	382	-	0

GREGORY Gordon (Harry)
Born: Hackney, E London, England, 24 October, 1943 — M
England: Youth

League Club	Source	Date Signed	Seasons Played	Apps	Subs	Gls
Leyton Orient	Jnr	10/61	62-65	79	0	12
Charlton Ath	Tr	08/66	66-70	146	3	24
Aston Villa	Tr	10/70	70-71	18	6	2
Hereford U	Tr	08/72	72-74	71	2	6

GREGORY John Charles
Born: Scunthorpe, North Lincolnshire, England, 11 May, 1954 — M
England: 6

League Club	Source	Date Signed	Seasons Played	Apps	Subs	Gls
Northampton T	App	05/72	72-76	187	0	8
Aston Villa	Tr	06/77	77-78	59	6	10
Brighton & HA	Tr	07/79	79-80	72	0	7
Queens Park Rgrs	Tr	06/81	81-85	159	2	36
Derby Co	Tr	11/85	85-87	103	0	22
Plymouth Arg	Rtd	01/90	89	3	0	0
Bolton W	Tr	03/90	89	2	5	0

GREGORY John Ernest (Jack)
Born: Shoreditch, Central London, England, 24 September, 1926 — IF
Died: Horsham, West Sussex, England, 10 October, 1995

League Club	Source	Date Signed	Seasons Played	Apps	Subs	Gls
West Ham U	Bromley	06/51	51-52	24	-	6
Scunthorpe U	Tr	06/53	53-56	147	-	63
Aldershot	Tr	06/57	57	6	-	2

GREGORY John Graham
Born: Hounslow, SW London, England, 16 May, 1977 — G

League Club	Source	Date Signed	Seasons Played	Apps	Subs	Gls
Fulham	YT	-	94	0	1	0

GREGORY John Leslie (Jack)
Born: Southampton, England, 25 January, 1925 — FB
Died: Southampton, England, 17 March, 2008

League Club	Source	Date Signed	Seasons Played	Apps	Subs	Gls
Southampton	Woolston	12/44	46-53	66	-	0
Leyton Orient	Tr	07/55	55-58	91	-	0
Bournemouth	Tr	07/59	59	17	-	0

GREGORY Lee Andrew
Born: Sheffield, England, 26 August, 1988 — F

League Club	Source	Date Signed	Seasons Played	Apps	Subs	Gls
Millwall	FC Halifax T	06/14	14	28	11	9

GREGORY Neil Richard
Born: Ndola, Zambia, 7 October, 1972 — F

League Club	Source	Date Signed	Seasons Played	Apps	Subs	Gls
Ipswich T	YT	02/92	94-97	18	27	9
Chesterfield	L	02/94	93	2	1	1
Scunthorpe U	L	03/95	94	10	0	7
Torquay U	L	11/96	96	5	0	0
Peterborough U	L	11/97	97	2	1	1
Colchester U	Tr	01/98	97-98	41	12	11

GREGORY Paul Gordon
Born: Sheffield, England, 26 July, 1961 — G

League Club	Source	Date Signed	Seasons Played	Apps	Subs	Gls
Chesterfield	App	07/79	80-83	23	0	0
Doncaster Rov	Tr	03/84	84	1	0	0
Scunthorpe U	Tr	10/84	84-86	69	0	0
Halifax T	L	09/86	86	6	0	0

GREGORY Peter
Born: Eastbourne, East Sussex, England, 25 July, 1992 — DM

League Club	Source	Date Signed	Seasons Played	Apps	Subs	Gls
Portsmouth	Sch	07/10	10	0	1	0
Nottingham F	Lewes	09/12				

GREGORY Steven Michael
Born: Haddenham, Buckinghamshire, England, 19 March, 1987 — DM
England: Semi Pro-4

League Club	Source	Date Signed	Seasons Played	Apps	Subs	Gls
Wycombe W	Sch	06/06	05-06	0	4	0
Bournemouth	AFC Wimbledon	07/11	11	23	5	2
AFC Wimbledon	L	09/12	12	15	0	0
Gillingham	Tr	01/13	12-13	48	8	0

GREGSON Colin
Born: Newcastle-upon-Tyne, England, 19 January, 1958 — M

League Club	Source	Date Signed	Seasons Played	Apps	Subs	Gls
West Bromwich A	App	01/76				
Sheffield Wed	Tr	07/77	77	1	1	0

GREGSON John
Born: Skelmersdale, Lancashire, England, 17 May, 1939 — RW

League Club	Source	Date Signed	Seasons Played	Apps	Subs	Gls
Blackpool	Skelmersdale U	05/57	57-58	3	-	1
Chester C	Tr	05/62	62	32	-	5
Shrewsbury T	Tr	03/63	62-64	56	-	6
Mansfield T	Tr	11/64	64-66	75	1	5
Lincoln C	Tr	06/67	67	31	5	3
Cambridge U	Tr	07/68	70	32	0	1

GREGSON Peter George
Born: Blackpool, Lancashire, England, 12 May, 1953 — G

League Club	Source	Date Signed	Seasons Played	Apps	Subs	Gls
Southport	Blackpool (App)	07/71	71-72	35	0	0

GREIG John Robert (Bobby)
Born: Sunderland, England, 13 September, 1949 — RW

League Club	Source	Date Signed	Seasons Played	Apps	Subs	Gls
Leicester C	App	01/67				
Workington	Tr	02/68	67	4	1	0

GRELLA Michele (Mike)
Born: New York, USA, 23 January, 1987 — F
USA: Youth

League Club	Source	Date Signed	Seasons Played	Apps	Subs	Gls
Leeds U	Duke Univ (USA)	02/09	08-10	3	26	1
Carlisle U	L	10/10	10	7	3	3
Swindon T	L	02/11	10	6	1	1
Brentford	Tr	08/11	11	1	10	0
Bury	Tr	02/12	11	8	2	4
Scunthorpe U	Tr	07/12	12	10	15	1

GRELLA Vincenzo (Vince)
Born: Melbourne, Australia, 5 October, 1979 — DM
Australia: 46/U23-17/Youth

League Club	Source	Date Signed	Seasons Played	Apps	Subs	Gls
Blackburn Rov	Torino (ITA)	08/08	08-11	29	9	0

GRENET Francois
Born: Bordeaux, France, 8 March, 1975 — RB

League Club	Source	Date Signed	Seasons Played	Apps	Subs	Gls
Derby Co	Bordeaux (FRA)	11/01	01-02	14	4	0

GRENFELL Stephen John (Steve)
Born: Enfield, N London, England, 27 October, 1966 — LB/M

League Club	Source	Date Signed	Seasons Played	Apps	Subs	Gls
Tottenham H	App	08/84				
Colchester U	Tr	10/86	86-88	67	3	1

GRESKO Vratislav
Born: Banska Bystrica, Slovakia, 24 July, 1977 — LB
Slovakia: 29

League Club	Source	Date Signed	Seasons Played	Apps	Subs	Gls
Blackburn Rov	Parma (ITA)	01/03	02-05	35	5	1

GRESTY Philip (Phil)
Born: Tarporley, Cheshire, England, 2 June, 1953 — W

League Club	Source	Date Signed	Seasons Played	Apps	Subs	Gls
Crewe Alex (Am)	Jnr	07/71	74	3	1	0

GREULICH Corey Patrick Wilhelm (Billy)
Born: Hendon, N London, England, 24 April, 1991 — F

League Club	Source	Date Signed	Seasons Played	Apps	Subs	Gls
Hartlepool U	Brandon U	08/09	09	0	4	0

GREW Mark Stuart
Born: Bilston, West Midlands, England, 15 February, 1958 — G

League Club	Source	Date Signed	Seasons Played	Apps	Subs	Gls
West Bromwich A	Jnr	06/76	81-82	33	0	0
Wigan Ath	L	12/78	78	4	0	0
Leicester C	Tr	07/83	83	5	0	0
Oldham Ath	L	10/83	83	5	0	0
Ipswich T	Tr	03/84	84	6	0	0
Fulham	L	09/85	85	4	0	0
West Bromwich A	L	01/86	85	1	0	0
Port Vale	Tr	06/86	86-91	184	0	0
Blackburn Rov	L	10/90	90	13	0	0
Cardiff C	Tr	08/92	92-93	21	0	0

GREWCOCK Neil
Born: Leicester, England, 26 April, 1962 — RW

League Club	Source	Date Signed	Seasons Played	Apps	Subs	Gls
Leicester C	App	07/79	78-80	7	1	1
Gillingham	Tr	03/82	81-82	30	4	4
Burnley	Shepshed Charterhouse	06/84	84-90	180	22	26

GREY William Brian (Brian)
Born: Swansea, Wales, 7 September, 1948 — M

League Club	Source	Date Signed	Seasons Played	Apps	Subs	Gls
Swansea C	App	09/66	67-69	27	3	8

GREYGOOSE Dean
Born: Thetford, Norfolk, England, 18 December, 1964 — G
England: Youth

League Club	Source	Date Signed	Seasons Played	Apps	Subs	Gls
Cambridge U	App	11/82	83-84	26	0	0
Lincoln C	L	09/85	85	6	0	0
Leyton Orient	Tr	12/85	85	1	0	0
Crystal Palace	Tr	08/86				
Crewe Alex	Tr	08/87	87-92	205	0	0

GREYLING Anton
Born: Pretoria, South Africa, 5 November, 1977 — M
South Africa: U23-11

League Club	Source	Date Signed	Seasons Played	Apps	Subs	Gls
Torquay U	Supersport U (RSA)	08/01	01	0	2	0

GRIBBIN Brian Thomas
Born: Newcastle-upon-Tyne, England, 2 June, 1954 — FB

League Club	Source	Date Signed	Seasons Played	Apps	Subs	Gls
Hartlepool U	Jnr	07/73	72	1	0	0

GRICE Michael John (Mike)
Born: Woking, Surrey, England, 3 November, 1931 — RW
Died: Lowestoft, Suffolk, England, 22 August, 2002

League Club	Source	Date Signed	Seasons Played	Apps	Subs	Gls
Colchester U	Lowestoft T	06/52	52-55	106	-	15
West Ham U	Tr	03/56	55-60	142	-	18
Coventry C	Tr	08/61	61	37	-	6
Colchester U	Tr	06/62	62-65	138	1	13

GRIDELET Philip Raymond (Phil)
Born: Edgware, NW London, England, 30 April, 1967 — M
England: Semi Pro-5

League Club	Source	Date Signed	Seasons Played	Apps	Subs	Gls
Barnsley	Barnet	01/90	90-92	3	3	0
Rotherham U	L	03/93	92	9	0	0
Southend U	Tr	09/93	93-97	149	27	10

GRIEMINK Bart
Born: Groningen, Netherlands, 29 March, 1972 — G

League Club	Source	Date Signed	Seasons Played	Apps	Subs	Gls
Birmingham C	WK Emmen (NED)	11/95	95	20	0	0
Peterborough U	Tr	10/96	96-99	58	0	0
Swindon T	L	02/00	99	4	0	0
Swindon T	Tr	07/00	00-03	118	2	0
Southend U	Tr	07/04	04-05	22	0	0

GRIERSON Darrell Philip
Born: Blackpool, Lancashire, England, 13 October, 1968 — G

League Club	Source	Date Signed	Seasons Played	Apps	Subs	Gls
Tranmere Rov	App	10/86	86	4	0	0

GRIEVE David
Born: Selkirk, Borders, Scotland, 15 February, 1929 — RW
Died: Worcester, England, July, 2004

League Club	Source	Date Signed	Seasons Played	Apps	Subs	Gls
Reading	Dalry Thistle	02/52	51-53	19	-	1
Crystal Palace	Tr	04/54	54	22	-	3

GRIEVE Matthew Andrias
Born: Ashington, Northumberland, England, 8 November, 1990 — CD

League Club	Source	Date Signed	Seasons Played	Apps	Subs	Gls
Newcastle U	Sch	07/10				
Stockport Co	L	01/11	10	3	0	0

GRIEVE Richard Maxwell
Born: Aberdeen, Scotland, 29 June, 1924 — IF
Died: Aberdeen, Scotland, 12 February, 1997

League Club	Source	Date Signed	Seasons Played	Apps	Subs	Gls
Rochdale	Montrose	05/50				
Wrexham	Tr	09/50	50	1	-	0

GRIEVES Kenneth James (Ken)
Born: Sydney, Australia, 27 August, 1925 — G
Died: Whitefield, Greater Manchester, England, 3 January, 1992

League Club	Source	Date Signed	Seasons Played	Apps	Subs	Gls
Bury	Wigan Ath	04/47	47-49	59	-	0
Bolton W	Tr	12/51	51-55	49	-	0
Stockport Co	Tr	07/57	57	39	-	0

GRIEVESON Henry (Harry)
Born: Easington, County Durham, England, 10 April, 1941 — WH
Died: Sunderland, England, July, 2012

League Club	Source	Date Signed	Seasons Played	Apps	Subs	Gls
Sunderland	Jnr	04/58				
Southend U	Tr	07/61	61	24	-	1

GRIFFIN Adam
Born: Salford, England, 26 August, 1984 — M/LB

League Club	Source	Date Signed	Seasons Played	Apps	Subs	Gls
Oldham Ath	Sch	08/03	01-04	58	4	3
Oxford U	L	11/05	05	8	1	0
Stockport Co	Tr	01/06	05-07	68	23	6
Darlington	Tr	07/08	08	9	8	0
Stockport Co	Tr	08/09	09-10	51	12	1

GRIFFIN Andrew (Andy)
Born: Billinge, Merseyside, England, 7 March, 1979 — RB
England: U21-3/Youth

League Club	Source	Date Signed	Seasons Played	Apps	Subs	Gls
Stoke C	YT	09/96	96-97	52	5	2
Newcastle U	Tr	01/98	97-03	63	13	2
Portsmouth	Tr	07/04	04-05	38	6	0
Stoke C	L	09/06	06	32	1	2
Derby Co	Tr	08/07	07	13	2	0
Stoke C	Tr	01/08	07-08	32	3	0
Reading	Tr	01/10	09-11	63	0	0
Doncaster Rov	Tr	10/12	12	8	8	0

GRIFFIN Anthony Richard (Tony)
Born: Bournemouth, England, 22 March, 1979 — RB

League Club	Source	Date Signed	Seasons Played	Apps	Subs	Gls
Bournemouth	YT	07/97	98	1	5	0
Cheltenham T	Tr	07/99	99-03	67	29	1

GRIFFIN Charles John (Charlie)
Born: Bath, England, 25 June, 1979 — F

League Club	Source	Date Signed	Seasons Played	Apps	Subs	Gls
Swindon T	Chippenham T	01/99	98-00	8	20	2
Wycombe W	Forest Green Rov	05/05	05	13	9	3
Stevenage	Salisbury C	05/09	10	13	2	3

GRIFFIN Colin Raymond
Born: Dudley, West Midlands, England, 8 January, 1956 — CD

League Club	Source	Date Signed	Seasons Played	Apps	Subs	Gls
Derby Co	App	01/74				
Shrewsbury T	Tr	01/76	75-88	402	4	7

GRIFFIN Daniel Joseph (Danny)
Born: Belfast, Northern Ireland, 19 August, 1977 — CD
Northern Ireland: 29/U21-10

League Club	Source	Date Signed	Seasons Played	Apps	Subs	Gls
Stockport Co	Dundee U	01/04	03-05	35	0	1

GRIFFIN Frank Albert
Born: Pendlebury, Greater Manchester, England, 28 March, 1928 — RW
Died: Shrewsbury, Shropshire, England, 4 June, 2007

League Club	Source	Date Signed	Seasons Played	Apps	Subs	Gls
Shrewsbury T	Eccles T	08/49	50	37	-	5
West Bromwich A	Tr	04/51	50-58	240	-	47
Northampton T	Tr	07/59	59	16	-	0

GRIFFIN Kevin Russell
Born: Plymouth, England, 5 October, 1953 — F

League Club	Source	Date Signed	Seasons Played	Apps	Subs	Gls
Bristol C	App	09/71	71-74	5	3	0
Mansfield T	L	03/75	74	4	0	2
Cambridge U	L	09/75	75	7	1	1

GRIFFIN William (Billy)
Born: Bircotes, Nottinghamshire, England, 24 September, 1940 — IF

League Club	Source	Date Signed	Seasons Played	Apps	Subs	Gls
Sheffield Wed	Jnr	09/57	58-62	35	-	20
Bury	Tr	12/62	62-65	84	4	22
Workington	Tr	02/66	65-68	82	0	18
Rotherham U	Tr	01/69	68-69	14	3	1

GRIFFIT Leandre
Born: Maubeuge, France, 21 May, 1984 — M

League Club	Source	Date Signed	Seasons Played	Apps	Subs	Gls
Southampton	Amiens SC (FRA)	07/03	03-04	2	5	2
Leeds U	L	01/05	04	0	1	0
Rotherham U	L	03/05	04	1	1	0
Crystal Palace	Elfsborg (SWE)	08/08	08	2	3	0

GRIFFITH Anthony James
Born: Huddersfield, West Yorkshire, England, 28 October, 1986 — DM
Montserrat: 4

League Club	Source	Date Signed	Seasons Played	Apps	Subs	Gls
Doncaster Rov	Glasshoughton Welfare	09/05	05-06	6	0	0
Darlington	L	11/06	06	2	2	0
Port Vale	Tr	05/08	08-11	154	7	2
Leyton Orient	Tr	07/12	12	16	5	0
Port Vale	Tr	03/13	12-13	44	4	0
Shrewsbury T	Harrogate T	08/14	14	1	4	0
Carlisle U	Tr	01/15	14	10	1	0

GRIFFITH Cohen
Born: Georgetown, Guyana, 26 December, 1962 — W
Wales: U21-1

League Club	Source	Date Signed	Seasons Played	Apps	Subs	Gls
Cardiff C	Kettering T	10/89	89-94	205	29	39

GRIFFITHS Adam David
Born: Sydney, Australia, 21 August, 1979 — DM
Australia: 2

League Club	Source	Date Signed	Seasons Played	Apps	Subs	Gls
Watford	KV Oostende (BEL)	07/05				
Bournemouth	Tr	01/06	05	6	1	1
Brentford	Tr	07/06	06	32	5	1

GRIFFITHS Arfon Trevor
Born: Wrexham, Wales, 23 August, 1941 — M
Wales: 17/U23-3

League Club	Source	Date Signed	Seasons Played	Apps	Subs	Gls
Wrexham	Jnr	05/59	59-60	41	-	8
Arsenal	Tr	01/61	60-61	15	-	2
Wrexham	Tr	09/62	62-78	545	6	112

GRIFFITHS Ashley Russell
Born: Barry, Vale of Glamorgan, Wales, 5 January, 1961 — M
Wales: Youth/Schools

League Club	Source	Date Signed	Seasons Played	Apps	Subs	Gls
Bristol Rov	App	01/79	79-80	6	1	0
Torquay U	Tr	08/81				

GRIFFITHS Barry
Born: Manchester, England, 21 November, 1940 — G
Died: Oldham, Greater Manchester, England, 4 April, 1997

League Club	Source	Date Signed	Seasons Played	Apps	Subs	Gls
Blackburn Rov	Sheffield Wed (Am)	04/60	59-62	2	-	0

GRIFFITHS Brian
Born: Penycae, Wrexham, Wales, 21 November, 1933 — IF

League Club	Source	Date Signed	Seasons Played	Apps	Subs	Gls
Wrexham	Blackpool (Am)	05/52	51-57	23	-	11
Chester C	Tr	07/58	58	2	-	1

GRIFFITHS Bryan
Born: Litherland, Merseyside, England, 21 November, 1938 — LB

League Club	Source	Date Signed	Seasons Played	Apps	Subs	Gls
Everton	Jnr	03/56	58	2	-	0
Southport	Tr	06/60	60-62	117	-	1

GRIFFITHS Bryan Kenneth
Born: Prescot, Merseyside, England, 26 January, 1965 — LW

League Club	Source	Date Signed	Seasons Played	Apps	Subs	Gls
Wigan Ath	St Helens T	11/88	88-92	176	13	44
Blackpool	Tr	07/93	93-94	54	3	17
Scarborough	L	12/94	94	5	0	1

GRIFFITHS Carl Brian
Born: Welshpool, Powys, Wales, 15 July, 1971 — F
Wales: B-1/U21-1/Youth

League Club	Source	Date Signed	Seasons Played	Apps	Subs	Gls
Shrewsbury T	YT	09/88	88-93	110	33	54
Manchester C	Tr	10/93	93-94	11	7	4
Portsmouth	Tr	08/95	95	2	12	2
Peterborough U	Tr	03/96	95-96	6	10	2
Leyton Orient	L	10/96	96	5	0	3
Leyton Orient	Tr	03/97	96-98	60	5	29
Wrexham	L	01/99	98	4	0	3
Port Vale	Tr	03/99	98-99	3	5	1
Leyton Orient	Tr	12/99	99-00	46	2	18
Luton T	Tr	07/01	01-02	13	0	8

GRIFFITHS Clive Leslie
Born: Pontypridd, Rhondda Cynon Taff, Wales, 22 January, 1955 — CD
Wales: U23-2/Schools

League Club	Source	Date Signed	Seasons Played	Apps	Subs	Gls
Manchester U	App	01/72	73	7	0	0
Plymouth Arg	L	07/74	74	10	1	0
Tranmere Rov	Tr	11/75	75-76	59	0	0

GRIFFITHS David (Dave)
Born: Woking, Surrey, England, 13 December, 1937 — WH

League Club	Source	Date Signed	Seasons Played	Apps	Subs	Gls
Portsmouth		03/56				
Aldershot	Tr	08/57	58-59	5	-	0

GRIFFITHS David
Born: Newport, Wales, 20 May, 1962 — CD

League Club	Source	Date Signed	Seasons Played	Apps	Subs	Gls
Newport Co	Cwmbran T	03/88	87	0	1	0

GRIFFITHS David Bernard
Born: Liverpool, England, 25 May, 1951 — RB

League Club	Source	Date Signed	Seasons Played	Apps	Subs	Gls
Tranmere Rov	Jnr	02/70	69	6	0	0

GRIFFITHS Dennis
Born: Ruabon, Wrexham, Wales, 12 August, 1935 — RH
Died: Wrexham, Wales, 13 August, 2005

League Club	Source	Date Signed	Seasons Played	Apps	Subs	Gls
Wrexham	Jnr	08/52	53-57	67	-	3

GRIFFITHS Douglas James (Doug)
Born: Birmingham, England, 23 October, 1948 — CD

League Club	Source	Date Signed	Seasons Played	Apps	Subs	Gls
Wolverhampton W	App	10/66				
Stockport Co	Tr	07/68	68-69	20	1	0

GRIFFITHS Estyn
Born: Mold, Flintshire, Wales, 22 July, 1927 — CH
Wales: Amateur

League Club	Source	Date Signed	Seasons Played	Apps	Subs	Gls
Wrexham	Llay U	04/50	50-51	10	-	0

GRIFFITHS Evan Gareth (Gary)
Born: Aylesham, Kent, England, 19 April, 1943 — W

League Club	Source	Date Signed	Seasons Played	Apps	Subs	Gls
Gillingham		07/61	60	1	-	0

GRIFFITHS Gareth John
Born: Winsford, Cheshire, England, 10 April, 1970 — CD

League Club	Source	Date Signed	Seasons Played	Apps	Subs	Gls
Port Vale	Rhyl	02/93	93-97	90	4	4
Shrewsbury T	L	10/97	97	6	0	0
Wigan Ath	Tr	07/98	98-00	44	9	2
Rochdale	Tr	07/01	01-05	176	8	14

GRIFFITHS George
Born: Earlestown, Merseyside, England, 23 June, 1924 — RB
Died: St Helens, Merseyside, England, 8 January, 2004

League Club	Source	Date Signed	Seasons Played	Apps	Subs	Gls
Bury	Earlestown	03/42	46-53	239	-	7
Halifax T	Tr	06/54	54-57	166	-	14

League Club	Source	Date Signed	Seasons Played	Apps	Subs	Gls

GRIFFITHS George Keith (Keith)
Born: Chester, England, 30 December, 1927 — G

League Club	Source	Date Signed	Seasons Played	Apps	Subs	Gls
Chester C	Rhyl	07/55	55-58	54	-	0

GRIFFITHS Gerald Leslie (Gerry)
Born: Swansea, Wales, 15 December, 1934 — WH
Wales: Schools

League Club	Source	Date Signed	Seasons Played	Apps	Subs	Gls
Swansea C	Jnr	06/52				
Crewe Alex	Tr	06/56	56	21	-	3

GRIFFITHS Harry Stanley
Born: Liverpool, England, 17 November, 1912 — CH
Died: Stoke-on-Trent, England, 11 June, 1981

League Club	Source	Date Signed	Seasons Played	Apps	Subs	Gls
Everton		08/32				
Port Vale	Tr	05/35	35-46	103	-	3

GRIFFITHS Ian James
Born: Birkenhead, Wirral, England, 17 April, 1960 — LW

League Club	Source	Date Signed	Seasons Played	Apps	Subs	Gls
Tranmere Rov	Jnr	02/79	78-82	110	6	5
Rochdale	Tr	08/83	83-84	40	1	5
Port Vale	Tr	09/84	84	9	3	0
Wigan Ath	Tr	07/85	85-87	73	9	7
Wigan Ath	Mazda Hiroshima (JPN)	08/90	90	6	5	0
Wrexham	Tr	03/91	90-91	14	0	0

GRIFFITHS Ivor
Born: Port Talbot, Wales, 19 June, 1918 — W
Died: Shrewsbury, Shropshire, England, October, 1993

League Club	Source	Date Signed	Seasons Played	Apps	Subs	Gls
Chester C		09/46	46	1	-	0

GRIFFITHS James Henry (Harry)
Born: Swansea, Wales, 4 January, 1931 — LB/IF
Died: Swansea, Wales, 25 April, 1978
Wales: 1/WLge-1

League Club	Source	Date Signed	Seasons Played	Apps	Subs	Gls
Swansea C	Jnr	06/49	49-63	422	-	72

GRIFFITHS James Stephen (Steve)
Born: Barnsley, South Yorkshire, England, 23 February, 1914 — IF
Died: Barnsley, South Yorkshire, England, 10 June, 1998

League Club	Source	Date Signed	Seasons Played	Apps	Subs	Gls
Chesterfield	Thurnscoe Victoria	10/34				
Halifax T	Tr	07/37	37-38	75	-	14
Portsmouth	Tr	06/39				
Aldershot	Tr	06/46	46	42	-	9
Barnsley	Tr	07/47	47-50	65	-	29
York C	Tr	06/51	51-52	74	-	12

GRIFFITHS James Thomas
Born: Gowerton, Swansea, Wales, 5 October, 1941 — CF
Died: Wolverhampton, England, December, 2012

League Club	Source	Date Signed	Seasons Played	Apps	Subs	Gls
Stockport Co		03/63	62	3	-	0

GRIFFITHS Jamie
Born: Sudbury, Suffolk, England, 4 January, 1992 — M

League Club	Source	Date Signed	Seasons Played	Apps	Subs	Gls
Ipswich T	Sch	07/10				
Plymouth Arg	L	08/11	11	4	5	0

GRIFFITHS Jeffrey Kenneth (Jeff)
Born: Swansea, Wales, 19 March, 1957 — F

League Club	Source	Date Signed	Seasons Played	Apps	Subs	Gls
Swansea C	Sketty Park BC	04/76	75-77	7	7	1

GRIFFITHS Joel Michael
Born: Sydney, Australia, 21 August, 1979 — RM
Australia: 3/Youth

League Club	Source	Date Signed	Seasons Played	Apps	Subs	Gls
Leeds U	Neuchatel Xamax (SUI)	01/06	05	0	2	0

GRIFFITHS John
Born: Oldbury, West Midlands, England, 16 June, 1951 — M

League Club	Source	Date Signed	Seasons Played	Apps	Subs	Gls
Aston Villa	App	11/68	68-69	1	2	0
Stockport Co	Tr	05/70	70-74	167	15	31

GRIFFITHS Kenneth George (Kenny)
Born: Cardiff, Wales, 11 November, 1925 — IF
Died: Surrey, England, 17 February, 1985

League Club	Source	Date Signed	Seasons Played	Apps	Subs	Gls
Cardiff C	Jnr	06/43				
Torquay U	L	01/48	47	6	-	1
Torquay U	L	08/48	48	5	-	0
Newport Co	Distillery	09/49	49	14	-	6

GRIFFITHS Kenneth James (Ken)
Born: Stoke-on-Trent, England, 2 April, 1930 — IF
Died: Stoke-on-Trent, England, 10 August, 2008

League Club	Source	Date Signed	Seasons Played	Apps	Subs	Gls
Port Vale	Northwood Mission	03/50	49-57	179	-	52
Mansfield T	Tr	01/58	57-58	42	-	7

GRIFFITHS Leigh
Born: Leith, Edinburgh, Scotland, 20 August, 1990 — F
Scotland: 4/B-1/U21-11/Youth

League Club	Source	Date Signed	Seasons Played	Apps	Subs	Gls
Wolverhampton W	Dundee	01/11	13	18	8	12

GRIFFITHS Leroy Henerica Septon
Born: Lambeth, S London, England, 30 December, 1976 — F

League Club	Source	Date Signed	Seasons Played	Apps	Subs	Gls
Queens Park Rgrs	Hampton & Richmond Bor	05/01	01-02	26	10	3
Gillingham	Lewes	11/07	07	4	20	2

GRIFFITHS Michael Antony
Born: Birmingham, England, 14 March, 1970 — F

League Club	Source	Date Signed	Seasons Played	Apps	Subs	Gls
Torquay U	Worcester C	10/99	99	8	14	3

GRIFFITHS Neil
Born: Newcastle-under-Lyme, Potteries, England, 12 October, 1951 — LB

League Club	Source	Date Signed	Seasons Played	Apps	Subs	Gls
Chester C	St Lukes YC	11/70	70-73	89	1	5
Port Vale	Tr	12/73	73-80	214	4	13
Crewe Alex	Tr	08/81	81	32	2	1

GRIFFITHS Neil
Born: Halifax, West Yorkshire, England, 4 September, 1972 — CD

League Club	Source	Date Signed	Seasons Played	Apps	Subs	Gls
Halifax T	YT	07/91	90-92	2	2	0

GRIFFITHS Peter
Born: St Helens, Merseyside, England, 13 March, 1980 — RW

League Club	Source	Date Signed	Seasons Played	Apps	Subs	Gls
Macclesfield T	Ashton U	07/98	98	4	0	1

GRIFFITHS Peter James
Born: Barnstaple, Devon, England, 14 August, 1957 — RW

League Club	Source	Date Signed	Seasons Played	Apps	Subs	Gls
Stoke C	Bideford	11/80	80-83	46	14	5
Bradford C	L	03/84	83	2	0	0
Port Vale	Tr	07/84	84-85	32	4	4

GRIFFITHS Raymond (Ray)
Born: Llanelli, Carmarthenshire, Wales, 26 September, 1931 — LH

League Club	Source	Date Signed	Seasons Played	Apps	Subs	Gls
Chester C	Stockton Heath	09/55	55-59	18	-	0

GRIFFITHS Rhys Tomas
Born: Cardiff, Wales, 1 March, 1980 — F

League Club	Source	Date Signed	Seasons Played	Apps	Subs	Gls
Plymouth Arg	Llanelli	08/12	12	6	8	3

GRIFFITHS Richard David (Richie)
Born: Earls Colne, Essex, England, 21 March, 1942 — RB

League Club	Source	Date Signed	Seasons Played	Apps	Subs	Gls
Colchester U	Jnr	06/61	61-64	48	-	0

GRIFFITHS Robert William (Bob)
Born: Aldridge, West Midlands, England, 15 September, 1942 — WH

League Club	Source	Date Signed	Seasons Played	Apps	Subs	Gls
Stoke C	Rhyl	09/60				
Chester C	Tr	07/62	62	2	-	0

GRIFFITHS Roger David Norman
Born: Hereford, England, 20 February, 1945 — RB
Died: Hereford, England, 19 July, 2006

League Club	Source	Date Signed	Seasons Played	Apps	Subs	Gls
Hereford U	Worcester C	07/70	72	7	2	0

GRIFFITHS Rostyn John
Born: Stoke-on-Trent, England, 10 March, 1988 — CD
Australia: Youth

League Club	Source	Date Signed	Seasons Played	Apps	Subs	Gls
Blackburn Rov	Sch	11/05				
Accrington Stan	L	09/08	08	13	0	1

GRIFFITHS Scott Robert
Born: Westminster, Central London, England, 27 November, 1985 — LB
England: Semi Pro-2

League Club	Source	Date Signed	Seasons Played	Apps	Subs	Gls
Dagenham & Red	Aveley	08/04	07-09	97	1	0
Peterborough U	Tr	10/09	09	20	0	0
Chesterfield	L	08/10	10	28	1	0
Crawley T	L	09/11	11	6	0	0
Chesterfield	L	11/11	11	3	0	0
Rotherham U	L	01/12	11	8	0	0
Plymouth Arg	L	10/12	12	4	0	0
Luton T	Tr	03/13	14	35	0	2

GRIFFITHS Stephen (Steve)
Born: Billingham, Cleveland, England, 28 November, 1957 — F

League Club	Source	Date Signed	Seasons Played	Apps	Subs	Gls
Hartlepool U	App	-	74	0	1	0

GRIFFITHS Vernon
Born: Birmingham, England, 14 June, 1936 — WH
Died: Birmingham, England, 27 April, 2011

League Club	Source	Date Signed	Seasons Played	Apps	Subs	Gls
Coventry C	Sheldon T	02/57	57-58	15	-	1

GRIFFITHS William (Bill)
Born: Earlestown, Merseyside, England, 13 January, 1921 — D
Died: Hastings, East Sussex, England, 1964

League Club	Source	Date Signed	Seasons Played	Apps	Subs	Gls
Bury	Earlestown	05/39	46-51	193	-	11

GRIFFITHS William Edward (Billy)
Born: Warrington, Cheshire, England, 23 May, 1944 — W

League Club	Source	Date Signed	Seasons Played	Apps	Subs	Gls
Torquay U	App	05/62	62	1	-	0

GRIFFITHS William Malwyn (Mal)
Born: Merthyr Tydfil, Wales, 8 March, 1919 — RW
Died: Wigston, Leicestershire, England, 5 April, 1969
Wales: 11

League Club	Source	Date Signed	Seasons Played	Apps	Subs	Gls
Arsenal	Merthyr Thursday	02/37	37	9	-	5
Leicester C	Tr	09/38	38-55	373	-	66

GRIFFITHS Wyn Rhys
Born: Blaengwynfi, Neath Port Talbot, Wales, 17 October, 1919 G
Died: Newport, Wales, 29 May, 2006

League Club	Source	Date Signed	Seasons Played	Apps	Subs	Gls
Cardiff C (Am)	Derby Co (Am)	08/47	47	1	-	0
Newport Co (Am)	Tr	01/52	51	3	-	0

GRIGG William Donald (Will)
Born: Solihull, West Midlands, England, 3 July, 1991 F
Northern Ireland: 6/U21-10/Youth

League Club	Source	Date Signed	Seasons Played	Apps	Subs	Gls
Walsall	Stratford T	07/09	08-12	63	36	27
Brentford	Tr	07/13	13	16	18	4
MK Dons	L	07/14	14	31	13	20

GRIGGS Robert (Bobby)
Born: Petersfield, Hampshire, England, 12 December, 1952 M

League Club	Source	Date Signed	Seasons Played	Apps	Subs	Gls
Aldershot	App	07/70	68-69	3	1	0

GRIMALDI Sebastien
Born: Givors, France, 10 September, 1979 CD

League Club	Source	Date Signed	Seasons Played	Apps	Subs	Gls
Chesterfield	Excel'r Mouscron (FRA)	01/07	06	8	0	0

GRIMANDI Gilles
Born: Gap, Hautes-Alpes, France, 11 November, 1970 CD/M

League Club	Source	Date Signed	Seasons Played	Apps	Subs	Gls
Arsenal	AS Monaco (FRA)	06/97	97-01	85	29	4

GRIMES Ashley James
Born: Swinton, Greater Manchester, England, 9 December, 1986 F

League Club	Source	Date Signed	Seasons Played	Apps	Subs	Gls
Manchester C	Sch	07/06				
Swindon T	L	03/07	06	0	4	0
Millwall	Tr	07/08	08-09	6	15	2
Lincoln C	L	10/10	10	24	3	15
Rochdale	Tr	07/11	11-12	54	20	18
Bury	Tr	06/13	13	6	9	0
Walsall	Tr	07/14	14	11	16	2

GRIMES Augustine Ashley (Ashley)
Born: Dublin, Republic of Ireland, 2 August, 1957 LB/M
Republic of Ireland: 18/U21-6

League Club	Source	Date Signed	Seasons Played	Apps	Subs	Gls
Manchester U	Bohemians (ROI)	03/77	77-82	62	28	10
Coventry C	Tr	08/83	83	29	3	1
Luton T	Tr	08/84	84-88	85	2	3
Stoke C	CA Osasuna (SPN)	01/92	91	4	6	1

GRIMES Matthew Jacob (Matt)
Born: Exeter, England, 15 July, 1995 M
England: Youth

League Club	Source	Date Signed	Seasons Played	Apps	Subs	Gls
Exeter C	Sch	07/13	13-14	45	13	5
Swansea C	Tr	01/15	14	0	3	0

GRIMES Vincent (Vince)
Born: Scunthorpe, North Lincolnshire, England, 13 May, 1954 M

League Club	Source	Date Signed	Seasons Played	Apps	Subs	Gls
Hull C	App	05/72	73-77	84	5	9
Bradford C	L	12/77	77	7	0	1
Scunthorpe U	Tr	01/78	77-81	143	0	12

GRIMLEY Thomas William (Tom)
Born: Dinnington, South Yorkshire, England, 1 November, 1920 G
Died: Birmingham, England, 4 November, 1976

League Club	Source	Date Signed	Seasons Played	Apps	Subs	Gls
West Bromwich A	Swallownest	04/39	46-47	30	-	0
New Brighton	Tr	08/48	48-50	94	-	0

GRIMMER Jack
Born: Aberdeen, Scotland, 25 January, 1994 RB
Scotland: U21-1/Youth

League Club	Source	Date Signed	Seasons Played	Apps	Subs	Gls
Fulham	Aberdeen	01/12	14	13	0	0
Port Vale	L	01/14	13	13	0	1
Shrewsbury T	L	10/14	14	6	0	0

GRIMSDITCH Samuel Walker (Walker)
Born: Bolton, Greater Manchester, England, 10 August, 1920 G
Died: Oldham, Greater Manchester, England, 19 June, 1996

League Club	Source	Date Signed	Seasons Played	Apps	Subs	Gls
Southport	Rossendale U	11/45	46	10	-	0

GRIMSHAW Anthony (Tony)
Born: Manchester, England, 8 December, 1957 M

League Club	Source	Date Signed	Seasons Played	Apps	Subs	Gls
Manchester U	App	12/74	75	0	1	0

GRIMSHAW Christopher Anthony (Chris)
Born: Accrington, Lancashire, England, 1 October, 1965 M

League Club	Source	Date Signed	Seasons Played	Apps	Subs	Gls
Burnley	App	10/83				
Crewe Alex	Tr	03/84	83	1	2	0
Bury	Tr	08/84	84-85	1	2	0

GRIMSHAW Colin George
Born: Betchworth, Surrey, England, 16 September, 1925 WH
Died: Redhill, Surrey, England, December, 1995

League Club	Source	Date Signed	Seasons Played	Apps	Subs	Gls
Arsenal	Redhill	06/48				
Crystal Palace	Tr	10/52	52	32	-	3

GRINNEY Ian George
Born: Crediton, Devon, England, 8 March, 1936 RW

League Club	Source	Date Signed	Seasons Played	Apps	Subs	Gls
Exeter C	Crediton	09/54	55	2	-	0

GRIPTON Ernest William (Billy)
Born: Tipton, West Midlands, England, 2 July, 1920 CH
Died: Tipton, West Midlands, England, 1981

League Club	Source	Date Signed	Seasons Played	Apps	Subs	Gls
West Bromwich A	Toll End Wesley	11/37	38-47	13	-	0
Luton T	Tr	06/48	48	3	-	0
Bournemouth	Tr	07/50	50-51	79	-	0

GRITT Stephen John (Steve)
Born: Bournemouth, England, 31 October, 1957 M

League Club	Source	Date Signed	Seasons Played	Apps	Subs	Gls
Bournemouth	App	10/75	76	4	2	3
Charlton Ath	Tr	07/77	77-88	320	27	24
Walsall	Tr	07/89	89	20	0	1
Charlton Ath	Tr	02/90	89-92	15	18	1

GRITTON Martin Francis
Born: Glasgow, Scotland, 1 June, 1978 F

League Club	Source	Date Signed	Seasons Played	Apps	Subs	Gls
Plymouth Arg	Porthleven	08/98	98-01	15	29	7
Torquay U	Tr	08/02	02-04	72	21	23
Grimsby T	Tr	12/04	04-05	29	20	6
Lincoln C	Tr	01/06	05-06	9	18	3
Mansfield T	L	01/07	06	14	5	6
Macclesfield T	Tr	07/07	07-08	40	12	13
Chesterfield	Tr	01/09	08-09	21	8	5
Torquay U	L	07/10	10	3	9	0
Yeovil T	Chester FC	03/11	10	0	2	0

GROBBELAAR Bruce David
Born: Durban, South Africa, 6 October, 1957 G
England: FLge//Zimbabwe: 33

League Club	Source	Date Signed	Seasons Played	Apps	Subs	Gls
Crewe Alex (L)	Vancouver W'caps (CAN)	12/79	79	24	0	1
Liverpool	Vancouver W'caps (CAN)	03/81	81-93	440	0	0
Stoke C	L	03/93	92	4	0	0
Southampton	Tr	08/94	94-95	32	0	0
Plymouth Arg	Tr	08/96	96	36	0	0
Oldham Ath	Sheffield Wed (NC)	12/97	97	4	0	0
Bury	Chesham U	09/98	98	1	0	0
Lincoln C	Chesham U	12/98	98	2	0	0

GROCOCK Christopher Richard (Chris)
Born: Grimsby, North Lincolnshire, England, 30 October, 1968 LW
England: Schools

League Club	Source	Date Signed	Seasons Played	Apps	Subs	Gls
Grimsby T	Jnr	06/87	85-88	18	25	1

GROCOTT Kevin James
Born: Derby, England, 31 July, 1992 RB

League Club	Source	Date Signed	Seasons Played	Apps	Subs	Gls
Burton A	Notts Co (Jnr)	08/10	10	0	2	0

GRODAS Frode
Born: Sogndal, Norway, 24 October, 1964 G
Norway: 50/U21-5/Youth

League Club	Source	Date Signed	Seasons Played	Apps	Subs	Gls
Chelsea	Lillestrom (NOR)	09/96	96	20	1	0

GROENENDIJK Alfons
Born: Leiden, Netherlands, 17 May, 1964 M

League Club	Source	Date Signed	Seasons Played	Apps	Subs	Gls
Manchester C	Ajax (NED)	07/93	93	9	0	0

GROF David Attila
Born: Budapest, Hungary, 17 April, 1989 G

League Club	Source	Date Signed	Seasons Played	Apps	Subs	Gls
Notts Co	Hibernian	07/10				
Walsall	Tr	07/11	11-12	32	1	0

GROGAN John (Johnny)
Born: Paisley, Renfrewshire, Scotland, 30 October, 1915 CH
Died: Leicester, England, 2 April, 1976

League Club	Source	Date Signed	Seasons Played	Apps	Subs	Gls
Leicester C	Shawfield Jnrs	10/33	35-46	46	-	0
Mansfield T	Tr	09/47	47-51	201	-	0

GRONDIN David
Born: Paris, France, 8 May, 1980 LB
France: Youth

League Club	Source	Date Signed	Seasons Played	Apps	Subs	Gls
Arsenal	Saint-Etienne (FRA)	07/98	98	1	0	0

GRONKJAER Jesper
Born: Nuuk, Greenland, 12 August, 1977 W
Denmark: 80/U21-24/Youth

League Club	Source	Date Signed	Seasons Played	Apps	Subs	Gls
Chelsea	Ajax (NED)	12/00	00-03	56	32	7
Birmingham C	Tr	07/04	04	13	3	0

GROOMBRIDGE David Henry (Dave)
Born: Norbury, S London, England, 13 April, 1930 G
Died: Camberley, Surrey, England, 15 January, 2015

League Club	Source	Date Signed	Seasons Played	Apps	Subs	Gls
Leyton Orient	Hayes	06/51	51-59	133	-	0

GROOME Patrick Bernard (Pat)
Born: Nottingham, England, 16 March, 1934 LB

League Club	Source	Date Signed	Seasons Played	Apps	Subs	Gls
Notts Co	Jnr	11/51	52-57	40	-	0

League Club	Source	Date Signed	Seasons Played	Apps	Subs	Gls

GROS William Joseph
Born: Saint-Pierre, Reunion, 31 March, 1992 F

League Club	Source	Date Signed	Seasons Played	Apps	Subs	Gls
Oldham Ath	Kilmarnock	07/14	14	0	1	0

GROSS Adam Charles
Born: Thamesmead, SE London, England, 16 February, 1986 LB

League Club	Source	Date Signed	Seasons Played	Apps	Subs	Gls
Barnet	Charlton Ath (Sch)	08/05	05-06	45	2	1

GROSS Marcus John
Born: Barnstaple, Devon, England, 15 December, 1982 RB

League Club	Source	Date Signed	Seasons Played	Apps	Subs	Gls
Exeter C	YT	-	01	1	0	0

GROTIER Peter David
Born: Stratford, E London, England, 18 October, 1950 G

League Club	Source	Date Signed	Seasons Played	Apps	Subs	Gls
West Ham U	App	03/68	68-72	50	0	0
Cardiff C	L	11/73	73	2	0	0
Lincoln C	Tr	08/74	74-79	233	0	0
Cardiff C	Tr	12/79	79-81	38	0	0
Grimsby T	Tr	03/82	82-84	10	0	0

GROUNDS Jonathan Martin
Born: Thornaby, Cleveland, England, 2 February, 1988 LB

League Club	Source	Date Signed	Seasons Played	Apps	Subs	Gls
Middlesbrough	Sch	07/07	07-10	28	5	1
Norwich C	L	09/08	08	3	2	0
Norwich C	L	01/09	08	11	0	3
Chesterfield	L	08/11	11	13	0	0
Yeovil T	L	02/12	11	13	1	0
Oldham Ath	Tr	07/12	12-13	89	0	4
Birmingham C	Tr	06/14	14	45	0	1

GROVES Alan James
Born: Ainsdale, Merseyside, England, 24 October, 1948 LW
Died: Royton, Greater Manchester, England, 15 June, 1978

League Club	Source	Date Signed	Seasons Played	Apps	Subs	Gls
Southport	Blowick	12/68	68-69	10	4	2
Chester C	Tr	07/70	70	21	1	3
Shrewsbury T	Tr	02/71	70-72	76	0	11
Bournemouth	Tr	10/72	72-73	31	5	4
Oldham Ath	Tr	02/74	73-77	136	4	12
Blackpool	Tr	11/77	77	11	4	1

GROVES Daniel Charles (Danny)
Born: Middlesbrough, England, 10 December, 1990 M

League Club	Source	Date Signed	Seasons Played	Apps	Subs	Gls
Darlington	Sch	06/09	08-09	8	9	0

GROVES Edward Gwynfryn (Gwyn)
Born: Merthyr Tydfil, Wales, 24 July, 1930 G
Died: Merthyr Tydfil, Wales, 24 March, 1997
Wales: Amateur

League Club	Source	Date Signed	Seasons Played	Apps	Subs	Gls
Swansea C	Troedyrhiw	06/52	52-53	34	-	0

GROVES John
Born: Derby, England, 16 September, 1933 WH/IF

League Club	Source	Date Signed	Seasons Played	Apps	Subs	Gls
Luton T	Jnr	10/50	53-62	218	-	16
Bournemouth	Tr	09/63	63-64	54	-	0

GROVES Kenneth Ernest Leonard (Ken)
Born: Eton, Berkshire, England, 9 October, 1921 G
Died: Windsor, Berkshire, England, May, 2002

League Club	Source	Date Signed	Seasons Played	Apps	Subs	Gls
Preston NE	Windsor & Eton	03/39				
Reading	Tr	08/46	46	4	-	0

GROVES Matthew (Matt)
Born: Bristol, England, 11 December, 1988 F

League Club	Source	Date Signed	Seasons Played	Apps	Subs	Gls
Bristol Rov	Jnr	06/07	07	0	1	0

GROVES Paul
Born: Derby, England, 28 February, 1966 M

League Club	Source	Date Signed	Seasons Played	Apps	Subs	Gls
Leicester C	Burton A	04/88	87-88	7	9	1
Lincoln C	L	08/89	89	8	0	1
Blackpool	Tr	01/90	89-91	106	1	21
Grimsby T	Tr	08/92	92-95	183	1	38
West Bromwich A	Tr	07/96	96	27	2	4
Grimsby T	Tr	07/97	97-03	262	8	33
Scunthorpe U	Tr	02/04	03	13	0	3

GROVES Perry
Born: Bow, E London, England, 19 April, 1965 LW/F

League Club	Source	Date Signed	Seasons Played	Apps	Subs	Gls
Colchester U	App	06/82	81-86	142	14	26
Arsenal	Tr	09/86	86-92	91	65	21
Southampton	Tr	08/92	92	13	2	2

GROVES Victor George (Vic)
Born: Stepney, E London, England, 5 November, 1932 LH/IF
Died: January, 2015
England: B-1/U23-1/Amateur-4/Youth

League Club	Source	Date Signed	Seasons Played	Apps	Subs	Gls
Tottenham H (Am)	Leytonstone	06/52	52-53	4	-	3
Leyton Orient	Walthamstow Ave	10/54	54-55	42	-	24
Arsenal	Tr	11/55	55-63	185	-	31

GROZIER William (Bill)
Born: Cumnock, Ayrshire, Scotland, 24 August, 1956 FB

League Club	Source	Date Signed	Seasons Played	Apps	Subs	Gls
Mansfield T	App	08/74	73	1	0	0

GRUBB Alan Johnstone
Born: Leven, Fife, Scotland, 5 February, 1928 RW

League Club	Source	Date Signed	Seasons Played	Apps	Subs	Gls
Tottenham H	Gloucester C	03/52	52	2	-	0
Walsall	Tr	08/53	53	15	-	0

GRUMMETT James (Jimmy)
Born: Maltby, South Yorkshire, England, 11 July, 1945 CD
England: Youth

League Club	Source	Date Signed	Seasons Played	Apps	Subs	Gls
Lincoln C	Ruston-Bucyrus	06/63	63-70	246	5	19
Aldershot	Tr	07/71	71-72	81	0	6
Chester C	Tr	06/73	73	15	1	0
Rochdale	Tr	12/73	73-74	32	2	2

GRUMMETT James (Jim)
Born: Birdwell, South Yorkshire, England, 3 July, 1918 WH
Died: Lincoln, England, 11 May, 1996

League Club	Source	Date Signed	Seasons Played	Apps	Subs	Gls
Lincoln C	Rustons Sports	09/43	46-51	165	-	12
Accrington Stan	Tr	09/52	52	40	-	1

GRUMMITT Peter Malcolm
Born: Bourne, Lincolnshire, England, 19 August, 1942 G
England: FLge-1/U23-3

League Club	Source	Date Signed	Seasons Played	Apps	Subs	Gls
Nottingham F	Bourne T	05/60	60-69	313	0	0
Sheffield Wed	Tr	01/70	69-72	121	0	0
Brighton & HA	Tr	12/73	73-76	136	0	0

GRUNDY Aaron Philip
Born: Bolton, Greater Manchester, England, 21 January, 1988 G

League Club	Source	Date Signed	Seasons Played	Apps	Subs	Gls
Bury	Sch	06/06	05-06	0	2	0

GRUNDY Brian
Born: Atherton, Greater Manchester, England, 9 May, 1945 LW

League Club	Source	Date Signed	Seasons Played	Apps	Subs	Gls
Bury	Wigan Ath	11/67	67-70	92	7	10

GRYBA John Raymond (Ray)
Born: Liverpool, England, 19 August, 1935 WH/IF
Died: New Brighton, Wirral, England, 23 May, 1999

League Club	Source	Date Signed	Seasons Played	Apps	Subs	Gls
Liverpool	Jnr	08/52				
Blackpool	Tr	08/53				
Southport	RAOC Feltham	10/55	55-57	72	-	14

GRYGERA Zdenek
Born: Zlin, Czech Republic, 14 May, 1980 D
Czech Republic: 65

League Club	Source	Date Signed	Seasons Played	Apps	Subs	Gls
Fulham	Juventus (ITA)	08/11	11	5	0	0

GUARD Anthony Francis (Tony)
Born: Swansea, Wales, 19 April, 1964 M

League Club	Source	Date Signed	Seasons Played	Apps	Subs	Gls
Swansea C	App	04/82	83	1	0	0

GUATELLI Andrea
Born: Parma, Italy, 5 May, 1984 G

League Club	Source	Date Signed	Seasons Played	Apps	Subs	Gls
Portsmouth	Parma Jnrs (ITA)	07/04				
Oxford U	L	03/06	05	4	0	0

GUBBINS Ralph Grayham
Born: Ellesmere Port, Cheshire, England, 31 January, 1932 F/LH
Died: Bolton, Greater Manchester, England, 17 September, 2011

League Club	Source	Date Signed	Seasons Played	Apps	Subs	Gls
Bolton W	Ellesmere Port	10/52	52-59	97	-	15
Hull C	Tr	10/59	59-60	45	-	10
Tranmere Rov	Tr	03/61	60-63	107	-	36

GUDJOHNSEN Eidur Smari
Born: Reykjavik, Iceland, 15 September, 1978 F
Iceland: 79/U21-11/Youth

League Club	Source	Date Signed	Seasons Played	Apps	Subs	Gls
Bolton W	KR Reykjavik (ICE)	08/98	98-99	48	7	18
Chelsea	Tr	07/00	00-05	126	60	54
Tottenham H (L)	AS Monaco (FRA)	01/10	09	3	8	1
Stoke C	AS Monaco (FRA)	08/10	10	0	4	0
Fulham	L	01/11	10	4	6	0
Bolton W	Club Brugge (BEL)	01/15	14	12	9	5

GUDJONSSON Bjarni Eggerts
Born: Akranes, Iceland, 26 February, 1979 M
Iceland: 23/U21-20/Youth

League Club	Source	Date Signed	Seasons Played	Apps	Subs	Gls
Newcastle U	IA Akranes (ICE)	07/97				
Stoke C	KRC Genk (BEL)	03/00	99-02	119	13	11
Coventry C	VfL Bochum (GER)	01/04	03-04	20	8	3
Plymouth Arg	Tr	12/04	04-05	18	7	0

GUDJONSSON Johannes Karl (Joey)
Born: Akranes, Iceland, 25 May, 1980 M
Iceland: 34/U21-10/Youth

League Club	Source	Date Signed	Seasons Played	Apps	Subs	Gls
Aston Villa (L)	Real Betis (SPN)	01/03	02	9	2	2
Wolverhampton W (L)	Real Betis (SPN)	08/03	03	5	6	0
Leicester C	Real Betis (SPN)	08/04	04-05	66	11	10

League Club	Source	Date Signed	Seasons Played	Apps	Subs	Gls
Burnley	AZ Alkmaar (NED)	01/07	06-09	43	45	7
Huddersfield T	Tr	06/10	10-11	35	10	2

GUDJONSSON Thordur
Born: Akranes, Iceland, 14 October, 1973 — M
Iceland: 58/U21-10/Youth

League Club	Source	Date Signed	Seasons Played	Apps	Subs	Gls
Derby Co (L)	Las Palmas (SPN)	03/01	00	2	8	1
Preston NE (L)	Las Palmas (SPN)	02/02	01	4	3	0
Stoke C	VfL Bochum (GER)	01/05	04	0	2	0

GUDMUNDSSON Albert Sigurdur
Born: Reykjavik, Iceland, 5 October, 1923 — IF
Died: Iceland, May, 1994
Iceland:

League Club	Source	Date Signed	Seasons Played	Apps	Subs	Gls
Arsenal (Am)	Glasgow Rangers	09/46	46	2	-	0

GUDMUNDSSON Johann Berg
Born: Reykjavik, Iceland, 27 October, 1990 — LW
Iceland: 37/U21-14/Youth

League Club	Source	Date Signed	Seasons Played	Apps	Subs	Gls
Charlton Ath	AZ Alkmaar (NED)	07/14	14	38	3	10

GUDMUNDSSON Johann Birnir
Born: Reykjavik, Iceland, 5 December, 1977 — M
Iceland: 8/U21-11/Youth

League Club	Source	Date Signed	Seasons Played	Apps	Subs	Gls
Watford	Keflavik (ICE)	03/98	98-99	7	15	2
Cambridge U	L	11/00	00	3	0	0

GUDMUNDSSON Niklas
Born: Halmstad, Sweden, 29 February, 1972 — F
Sweden: 7

League Club	Source	Date Signed	Seasons Played	Apps	Subs	Gls
Blackburn Rov	Halmstad (SWE)	12/95	95-96	1	5	0
Ipswich T	L	03/97	96	2	6	2

GUEDIOURA Adlene
Born: La Roche-sur-Yon, France, 12 November, 1985 — DM
Algeria: 32

League Club	Source	Date Signed	Seasons Played	Apps	Subs	Gls
Wolverhampton W	RSC Charleroi (BEL)	01/10	09-11	13	21	2
Nottingham F	Tr	01/12	11-13	54	5	4
Crystal Palace	Tr	09/13	13-14	4	11	0
Watford	L	11/14	14	2	4	2
Watford	L	02/15	14	11	0	1

GUENTCHEV Boncho Lyubomirov
Born: Dobrich, Bulgaria, 7 July, 1964 — W
Bulgaria: 12

League Club	Source	Date Signed	Seasons Played	Apps	Subs	Gls
Ipswich T	Sporting Lisbon (POR)	12/92	92-94	39	22	6
Luton T	Tr	08/95	95-96	40	22	10

GUERET Willy July
Born: St Claude, Guadeloupe, 3 August, 1973 — G

League Club	Source	Date Signed	Seasons Played	Apps	Subs	Gls
Millwall	Le Mans (FRA)	07/00	00-03	13	1	0
Swansea C	Tr	08/04	04-06	132	0	0
MK Dons	Tr	08/07	07-09	133	0	0

GUERRA Javier (Javi)
Born: Velez-Malaga, Spain, 15 March, 1982 — F

League Club	Source	Date Signed	Seasons Played	Apps	Subs	Gls
Cardiff C	Real Valladolid (SPN)	05/14	14	0	3	0

GUERRERO Fernando Alexander
Born: Quito, Ecuador, 30 September, 1989 — M
Ecuador: 3

League Club	Source	Date Signed	Seasons Played	Apps	Subs	Gls
Burnley (L)	Independiente (ECU)	08/09	09	0	7	0

GUERRERO Mario Ivan (Ivan)
Born: Comayagua, Honduras, 30 November, 1977 — FB
Honduras: 84/U23-3

League Club	Source	Date Signed	Seasons Played	Apps	Subs	Gls
Coventry C	Motagua (HON)	10/00	00-01	6	1	0

GUEST Brendan John
Born: Barnsley, South Yorkshire, England, 19 December, 1958 — RB
England: Youth

League Club	Source	Date Signed	Seasons Played	Apps	Subs	Gls
Lincoln C	App	12/76	76-79	99	5	2
Swindon T	Tr	07/80				

GUEST Gladstone
Born: Rotherham, South Yorkshire, England, 26 June, 1917 — IF
Died: Rotherham, South Yorkshire, England, July, 1998

League Club	Source	Date Signed	Seasons Played	Apps	Subs	Gls
Rotherham U	Rawmarsh Welfare	12/39	46-55	358	-	130

GUEST William Francis (Billy)
Born: Brierley Hill, West Midlands, England, 8 February, 1914 — LW
Died: Darwen, Lancashire, England, 15 September, 1994

League Club	Source	Date Signed	Seasons Played	Apps	Subs	Gls
Birmingham C	Bromley Jnrs	02/32	33-36	76	-	15
Blackburn Rov	Tr	01/37	36-46	88	-	30
Walsall	Tr	08/47	47	5	-	0

GUEYE Magaye Serigne Falilou Dit Nelson
Born: Paris, France, 6 July, 1990 — W
France: U21-8/Youth//Senegal: U23-3

League Club	Source	Date Signed	Seasons Played	Apps	Subs	Gls
Everton	Strasbourg (FRA)	07/10	10-12	5	19	1
Millwall	Tr	07/14	14	9	23	5

GUIDETTI John Alberto Fernando Andres Luigi Olof
Born: Stockholm, Sweden, 15 April, 1992 — F
Sweden: 2/U21-17/Youth

League Club	Source	Date Signed	Seasons Played	Apps	Subs	Gls
Manchester C	Sch	08/09				
Burnley	L	11/10	10	2	3	1
Stoke C	L	01/14	13	0	6	0

GUILD Alan Nicoll
Born: Forfar, Angus, Scotland, 27 March, 1947 — CD
Scotland: Amateur

League Club	Source	Date Signed	Seasons Played	Apps	Subs	Gls
Luton T	East Fife	07/69	70	1	0	0
Cambridge U	Tr	05/71	71-73	117	10	1

GUILD James (Jimmy)
Born: Glasgow, Scotland, 10 December, 1928 — WH

League Club	Source	Date Signed	Seasons Played	Apps	Subs	Gls
New Brighton	Dunoon Ath	09/50	50	2	-	0

GUINAN Stephen Anthony (Steve)
Born: Birmingham, England, 24 December, 1975 — F
England: Semi Pro-4

League Club	Source	Date Signed	Seasons Played	Apps	Subs	Gls
Nottingham F	YT	01/93	95-99	2	5	0
Darlington	L	12/95	95	3	0	1
Burnley	L	03/97	96	0	6	0
Crewe Alex	L	03/98	97	3	0	0
Halifax T	L	10/98	98	12	0	2
Plymouth Arg	L	03/99	98	11	0	7
Scunthorpe U	L	09/99	99	2	1	1
Cambridge U	Tr	12/99	99	4	2	0
Plymouth Arg	Tr	03/00	99-00	15	15	3
Shrewsbury T	Tr	03/02	01	4	1	0
Cheltenham T	Hereford U	05/04	04-06	79	13	13
Hereford U	Tr	01/07	06-08	76	11	25
Northampton T	Tr	07/09	09-10	24	15	5

GUIVARC'H Stephane
Born: Concarneau, Brittany, France, 6 September, 1970 — F
France: 14

League Club	Source	Date Signed	Seasons Played	Apps	Subs	Gls
Newcastle U	AJ Auxerre (FRA)	07/98	98	2	2	1

GULACSI Peter
Born: Budapest, Hungary, 6 May, 1990 — G
Hungary: 2/U21-26/Youth

League Club	Source	Date Signed	Seasons Played	Apps	Subs	Gls
Liverpool	MTK Budapest (HUN)	08/07				
Hereford U	L	02/09	08	18	0	0
Tranmere Rov	L	04/10	09	5	0	0
Tranmere Rov	L	09/10	10	12	0	0
Hull C	L	07/11	11	13	2	0

GULLAN Stanley Knox (Stan)
Born: Edinburgh, Scotland, 26 January, 1926 — G
Died: Peterculter, Aberdeenshire, Scotland, 29 June, 1999

League Club	Source	Date Signed	Seasons Played	Apps	Subs	Gls
Queens Park Rgrs	Clyde	07/49	50-54	48	-	0

GULLIT Ruud
Born: Amsterdam, Netherlands, 1 September, 1962 — M
Netherlands: 65/U21-4/Youth

League Club	Source	Date Signed	Seasons Played	Apps	Subs	Gls
Chelsea	Sampdoria (ITA)	07/95	95-97	37	12	4

GULLIVER Joffre (Jeff)
Born: Merthyr Tydfil, Wales, 2 August, 1915 — LB
Died: Wokingham, Berkshire, England, 1 August, 1999

League Club	Source	Date Signed	Seasons Played	Apps	Subs	Gls
Southend U		08/34				
Leeds U	Bangor C	03/38				
Reading	Tr	06/39	46-50	159	-	0
Swindon T	Tr	08/51	51	11	-	0

GULLIVER Philip Stephen (Phil)
Born: Bishop Auckland, County Durham, England, 12 September, 1982 — CD

League Club	Source	Date Signed	Seasons Played	Apps	Subs	Gls
Middlesbrough	YT	07/00				
Blackpool	L	11/02	02	2	1	0
Carlisle U	L	12/02	02	1	0	0
Bournemouth	L	03/03	02	4	2	0
Bury	L	10/03	03	10	0	0
Scunthorpe U	L	01/04	03	2	0	0
Rushden & D	Tr	08/04	04-05	69	3	4
Hereford U	Tr	08/06	06	24	2	0

GULLIVER Terence Reginald (Terry)
Born: Shaftesbury, Dorset, England, 30 September, 1944 — FB

League Club	Source	Date Signed	Seasons Played	Apps	Subs	Gls
Bournemouth	Weymouth	08/66	66-71	162	2	2

GUMBS Evan
Born: Runcorn, Cheshire, England, 21 July, 1997 — RB

League Club	Source	Date Signed	Seasons Played	Apps	Subs	Gls
Tranmere Rov	Sch	06/15	14	0	1	0

GUMMER Jason Craig
Born: Tredegar, Blaenau Gwent, Wales, 27 October, 1967 — M
Wales: Youth

League Club	Source	Date Signed	Seasons Played	Apps	Subs	Gls
Cardiff C	App	07/85	85-89	28	6	5
Torquay U	L	03/89	88	7	0	1

GUNBY Peter
Born: Leeds, England, 20 November, 1934 RH

League Club	Source	Date Signed	Seasons Played	Apps	Subs	Gls
Leeds U	Leeds UYMI	09/55				
Bradford C	Tr	07/56	56	3	-	0

GUNBY Stephen Robert (Steve)
Born: Boston, Lincolnshire, England, 14 April, 1984 M

League Club	Source	Date Signed	Seasons Played	Apps	Subs	Gls
Bury	Sch	11/02	01-03	1	5	0

GUNN Alfred Herman (Alf)
Born: Essen, Germany, 11 July, 1924 CF
Died: Brighton, England, March, 1982

League Club	Source	Date Signed	Seasons Played	Apps	Subs	Gls
Nottingham F	Brighton & HA (Am)	02/47	46	2	-	0

GUNN Alistair Robert
Born: Broughty Ferry, Angus, Scotland, 2 November, 1924 RW
Died: Dundee, Scotland, 3 April, 2010

League Club	Source	Date Signed	Seasons Played	Apps	Subs	Gls
Huddersfield T	Dundee	01/51	50-53	83	-	11
Bournemouth	Tr	06/54	54	27	-	2

GUNN Andrew Charles (Andy)
Born: Barking, E London, England, 2 February, 1971 LW

League Club	Source	Date Signed	Seasons Played	Apps	Subs	Gls
Watford	YT	03/89				
Crewe Alex	Tr	02/90	89-90	2	2	0

GUNN Bryan James
Born: Thurso, Highlands, Scotland, 22 December, 1963 G
Scotland: 6/B/U21-9/Youth/Schools

League Club	Source	Date Signed	Seasons Played	Apps	Subs	Gls
Norwich C	Aberdeen	10/86	86-97	390	0	0

GUNN Brynley Charles (Bryn)
Born: Kettering, Northamptonshire, England, 21 August, 1958 D

League Club	Source	Date Signed	Seasons Played	Apps	Subs	Gls
Nottingham F	App	08/75	75-84	129	2	1
Shrewsbury T	L	11/85	85	9	0	0
Walsall	L	01/86	85	6	0	0
Mansfield T	L	03/86	85	5	0	0
Peterborough U	Tr	08/86	86-88	130	1	14
Chesterfield	Tr	07/89	89-91	89	2	10

GUNNARSSON Aron Einar Malmquist
Born: Akureyri, Iceland, 22 April, 1989 M
Iceland: 51/U21-11/Youth

League Club	Source	Date Signed	Seasons Played	Apps	Subs	Gls
Coventry C	AZ Alkmaar (NED)	07/08	08-10	109	13	6
Cardiff C	Tr	07/11	11-14	136	19	18

GUNNARSSON Brynjar Bjorn
Born: Reykjavik, Iceland, 16 October, 1975 M
Iceland: 74/U21-8/Youth

League Club	Source	Date Signed	Seasons Played	Apps	Subs	Gls
Stoke C	Orgryte IS (SWE)	01/00	99-02	128	3	16
Nottingham F	Tr	08/03	03	9	4	0
Stoke C	Tr	03/04	03	1	2	0
Watford	Tr	07/04	04	34	2	3
Reading	Tr	07/05	05-11	89	53	9

GUNNING Gavin Jude
Born: Dublin, Republic of Ireland, 26 January, 1991 CD
Republic of Ireland: U21-7/Youth

League Club	Source	Date Signed	Seasons Played	Apps	Subs	Gls
Blackburn Rov	Sch	01/08				
Tranmere Rov	L	08/09	09	6	0	0
Rotherham U	L	01/10	09	21	0	0
Bury	L	11/10	10	2	0	0
Birmingham C	Dundee U	06/14				

GUNNING Henry (Harry)
Born: Leigh, Greater Manchester, England, 8 February, 1932 LW
Died: Islington, N London, England, July, 2005

League Club	Source	Date Signed	Seasons Played	Apps	Subs	Gls
West Ham U	Gravesend & Northfleet	06/52	52	1	-	0
Crystal Palace	Tr	05/54	54-56	62	-	4
Reading	Tr	05/57	57	12	-	1

GUNNING James Michael (Jimmy)
Born: Helensburgh, Argyll & Bute, Scotland, 25 June, 1929 RW
Died: Dublin, Republic of Ireland, 27 August, 1993

League Club	Source	Date Signed	Seasons Played	Apps	Subs	Gls
Manchester C	Hibernian	11/50	50-52	13	-	0
Barrow	Weymouth	07/54	54	10	-	1

GUNNLAUGSSON Arnar Bergmann (Arnie)
Born: Akranes, Iceland, 6 March, 1973 F
Iceland: 32/U21-6/Youth

League Club	Source	Date Signed	Seasons Played	Apps	Subs	Gls
Bolton W	IA Akranes (ICE)	08/97	97-98	24	18	13
Leicester C	Tr	02/99	98-01	10	20	3
Stoke C	L	03/00	99	10	3	2
Stoke C	Tr	02/02	01	9	0	3

GUNNLAUGSSON Bjarke Bergmann
Born: Akranes, Iceland, 6 March, 1973 F
Iceland: 27/U21-4/Youth

League Club	Source	Date Signed	Seasons Played	Apps	Subs	Gls
Preston NE	KR Reykjavik (ICE)	09/99	99-00	17	28	2

GUNTER Christopher Ross (Chris)
Born: Newport, Wales, 21 July, 1989 RB
Wales: 59/U21-8/Youth

League Club	Source	Date Signed	Seasons Played	Apps	Subs	Gls
Cardiff C	Sch	10/06	06-07	20	8	0
Tottenham H	Tr	01/08	07-08	3	2	0
Nottingham F	Tr	03/09	08-11	136	5	2
Reading	Tr	07/12	12-14	102	0	0

GUNTER David Reginald
Born: Portsmouth, England, 4 March, 1933 LB
Died: Droxford, Hampshire, England, 6 January, 2005

League Club	Source	Date Signed	Seasons Played	Apps	Subs	Gls
Southampton	Portsmouth (Am)	05/55	55	7	-	0

GUNTER Philip Edward (Phil)
Born: Portsmouth, England, 6 January, 1932 D
Died: Australia, 10 July, 2007
England: B-1/U23-1

League Club	Source	Date Signed	Seasons Played	Apps	Subs	Gls
Portsmouth	Jnr	08/49	51-63	321	-	2
Aldershot	Tr	07/64	64-65	78	0	8

GUNTHORPE Kenneth (Ken)
Born: Sheffield, England, 14 November, 1938 CD

League Club	Source	Date Signed	Seasons Played	Apps	Subs	Gls
Rotherham U		05/58	58	2	-	0
Accrington Stan	Scarborough	02/60				

GUPPY Stephen Andrew (Steve)
Born: Winchester, Hampshire, England, 29 March, 1969 LW
England: 1/B-1/U21-1/Semi Pro-1

League Club	Source	Date Signed	Seasons Played	Apps	Subs	Gls
Wycombe W	Colden Common	09/89	93	41	0	8
Newcastle U	Tr	08/94				
Port Vale	Tr	11/94	94-96	102	3	12
Leicester C	Tr	02/97	96-00	133	13	9
Leicester C	Glasgow Celtic	01/04	03	9	6	0
Leeds U	Tr	08/04	04	1	2	1
Stoke C	Tr	09/04	04	0	4	0
Wycombe W	Tr	11/04	04	12	2	1

GURINOVICH Igor Nikolaivich
Born: Minsk, Belarus, 5 March, 1960 F
Belarus: 3//Soviet Union: 1

League Club	Source	Date Signed	Seasons Played	Apps	Subs	Gls
Brighton & HA	Dynamo Minsk (BLR)	11/90	90	3	1	1

GURNEY Andrew Robert (Andy)
Born: Bristol, England, 25 January, 1974 RB/M

League Club	Source	Date Signed	Seasons Played	Apps	Subs	Gls
Bristol Rov	YT	07/92	93-96	100	8	9
Torquay U	Tr	07/97	97-98	64	0	10
Reading	Tr	01/99	98-00	55	12	3
Swindon T	Tr	07/01	01-04	132	0	20
Swansea C	Tr	09/04	04	25	3	1
Swindon T	Tr	08/05	05	24	4	1

GURR Gerald Robert (Gerry)
Born: Brighton, England, 20 October, 1946 G

League Club	Source	Date Signed	Seasons Played	Apps	Subs	Gls
Southampton	Guildford C	03/64	66-69	42	0	0
Aldershot	Tr	03/71	70-71	55	0	0

GURRIERI Andres
Born: Winterthur, Switzerland, 3 July, 1989 W

League Club	Source	Date Signed	Seasons Played	Apps	Subs	Gls
Burton A	Sud America (UGY)	11/11	11	6	7	0
Plymouth Arg	Tr	08/12	12-13	41	19	2

GUSCOTT Lindon
Born: Lambeth, S London, England, 29 March, 1972 F

League Club	Source	Date Signed	Seasons Played	Apps	Subs	Gls
Gillingham	YT	07/89	88	0	2	0

GUSCOTT Raymond Melvin (Ray)
Born: Newport, Wales, 18 November, 1957 M
Wales: Schools

League Club	Source	Date Signed	Seasons Played	Apps	Subs	Gls
Bristol Rov	App	11/75	76	1	0	0
Newport Co	Minehead	10/77	77	12	5	1

GUSTAFSSON (ANTONELIUS) Tomas Emil Rune
Born: Stockholm, Sweden, 7 May, 1973 RB
Sweden: 6

League Club	Source	Date Signed	Seasons Played	Apps	Subs	Gls
Coventry C	AIK Solna (SWE)	12/99	99-01	10	5	0

GUTHRIE Christopher William (Chris)
Born: Hexham, Northumberland, England, 7 September, 1953 F
England: Schools

League Club	Source	Date Signed	Seasons Played	Apps	Subs	Gls
Newcastle U	App	01/71	71	3	0	0
Southend U	Tr	11/72	72-74	107	1	35
Sheffield U	Tr	05/75	75-76	58	2	15
Swindon T	Tr	07/77	77-78	44	1	12
Fulham	Tr	09/78	78-79	49	1	15
Millwall	Tr	03/80	79	7	0	1

GUTHRIE Daniel Sean (Danny)
Born: Shrewsbury, Shropshire, England, 18 April, 1987 M
England: Youth

League Club	Source	Date Signed	Seasons Played	Apps	Subs	Gls
Liverpool	Sch	12/04	06	0	3	0
Southampton	L	03/07	06	8	2	0
Bolton W	L	07/07	07	21	4	0

League Club	Source	Date Signed	Seasons Played	Apps	Subs	Gls
Newcastle U	Tr	07/08	08-11	81	11	7
Reading	Tr	07/12	12-14	50	12	5
Fulham	L	03/15	14	6	0	0

GUTHRIE James Eric (Jimmy)
Born: Luncarty, Perthshire, Scotland, 13 June, 1913 — WH
Died: Lambeth, S London, England, 10 September, 1981

League Club	Source	Date Signed	Seasons Played	Apps	Subs	Gls
Portsmouth	Dundee	08/37	37-38	76	-	1
Crystal Palace	Tr	10/46	46	5	-	0

GUTHRIE Jonathan Neil (Jon)
Born: Devizes, Wiltshire, England, 1 February, 1993 — LB

League Club	Source	Date Signed	Seasons Played	Apps	Subs	Gls
Crewe Alex	Pewsey Vale	02/12	12-14	45	5	0

GUTHRIE Kurtis Owen
Born: Jersey, Channel Islands, 21 April, 1993 — F

League Club	Source	Date Signed	Seasons Played	Apps	Subs	Gls
Accrington Stan	Trinity FC, Jersey	07/11	11	6	7	0

GUTHRIE Peter John
Born: Newcastle-upon-Tyne, England, 10 October, 1961 — G

League Club	Source	Date Signed	Seasons Played	Apps	Subs	Gls
Tottenham H	Weymouth	01/88				
Swansea C	L	02/88	87	14	0	0
Bournemouth	Barnet	08/90	90	10	0	0

GUTHRIE Ralph
Born: West Hartlepool, County Durham, England, 13 September, 1932 — G
Died: Hartlepool, Cleveland, England, September, 1996

League Club	Source	Date Signed	Seasons Played	Apps	Subs	Gls
Arsenal	Tow Law T	05/53	54	2	-	0
Hartlepool U	Tr	07/56	56-57	78	-	0

GUTHRIE Ronald George (Ron)
Born: Burradon, Tyne and Wear, England, 19 April, 1944 — LB

League Club	Source	Date Signed	Seasons Played	Apps	Subs	Gls
Newcastle U	Jnr	07/63	66-72	52	3	2
Sunderland	Tr	01/73	72-74	66	0	1

GUTIERREZ Jonas Manuel
Born: Buenos Aires, Argentina, 5 July, 1983 — LW
Argentina: 22

League Club	Source	Date Signed	Seasons Played	Apps	Subs	Gls
Newcastle U	RCD Mallorca (SPN)	08/08	08-14	169	18	11
Norwich C	L	01/14	13	2	2	0

GUTTRIDGE Luke Horace
Born: Barnstaple, Devon, England, 27 March, 1982 — M

League Club	Source	Date Signed	Seasons Played	Apps	Subs	Gls
Torquay U	YT	-	99	0	1	0
Cambridge U	Tr	08/00	00-04	127	9	17
Southend U	Tr	03/05	04-06	59	4	5
Leyton Orient	L	11/06	06	7	0	1
Leyton Orient	Tr	01/07	06	8	2	0
Colchester U	Tr	07/07	07	5	9	0
Northampton T	Tr	08/08	08-09	47	9	6
Aldershot T	Tr	07/10	10-11	60	6	12
Northampton T	Tr	01/12	11-12	39	5	4
Luton T	Tr	07/13	14	17	10	3

GUTTRIDGE Ronald (Ron)
Born: Widnes, Cheshire, England, 28 April, 1916 — LB
Died: Preston, Lancashire, England, June, 1981

League Club	Source	Date Signed	Seasons Played	Apps	Subs	Gls
Aston Villa	Prescot Cables	03/37	46-47	15	-	0
Brighton & HA	Tr	06/48	48-49	17	-	0

GUTTRIDGE William Henry (Bill)
Born: Darlaston, West Midlands, England, 4 March, 1931 — LB
Died: Walsall, West Midlands, England, 6 April, 2013

League Club	Source	Date Signed	Seasons Played	Apps	Subs	Gls
Wolverhampton W	Metroshaft Works	03/48	51-53	6	-	0
Walsall	Tr	11/54	54-61	198	-	0

GUTZMORE Leon Johnson Fitzgerald
Born: St Pancras, Central London, England, 30 October, 1976 — F

League Club	Source	Date Signed	Seasons Played	Apps	Subs	Gls
Cambridge U	YT	09/95	95	0	2	0

GUY Alan
Born: Jarrow, Tyne and Wear, England, 8 September, 1957 — M

League Club	Source	Date Signed	Seasons Played	Apps	Subs	Gls
Newcastle U	App	09/75	76-78	3	1	0
Peterborough U	Tr	03/79	78-80	42	11	4

GUY Edward Frederick (Eddie)
Born: Seaham, County Durham, England, 6 February, 1956 — G

League Club	Source	Date Signed	Seasons Played	Apps	Subs	Gls
Hartlepool U	App	02/74	74	1	0	0

GUY Harold George
Born: Wolverhampton, England, 1 January, 1932 — FB
Died: Wolverhampton, England, 30 January, 2013

League Club	Source	Date Signed	Seasons Played	Apps	Subs	Gls
West Bromwich A	Springfield OB	03/50	50	1	-	0

GUY Ivor
Born: Chipping Sodbury, Avon, England, 27 February, 1926 — RB
Died: Bristol, England, 1 September, 1986

League Club	Source	Date Signed	Seasons Played	Apps	Subs	Gls
Bristol C	Hambrook Villa	10/44	46-56	404	-	2

GUY Jamie Lesley
Born: Barking, E London, England, 1 August, 1987 — F

League Club	Source	Date Signed	Seasons Played	Apps	Subs	Gls
Colchester U	Sch	07/06	04-09	2	50	3
Dagenham & Red	L	03/09	08	5	4	1
Port Vale	L	10/09	09	0	3	0

GUY Keith
Born: Seaham, County Durham, England, 19 May, 1959 — M

League Club	Source	Date Signed	Seasons Played	Apps	Subs	Gls
Newcastle U	App	06/77				
Hartlepool U	Tr	06/78	78	7	3	0

GUY Lewis Brett
Born: Penrith, Cumbria, England, 27 August, 1985 — F
England: Youth

League Club	Source	Date Signed	Seasons Played	Apps	Subs	Gls
Newcastle U	Sch	08/02				
Doncaster Rov	Tr	03/05	04-09	74	73	18
Hartlepool U	L	02/09	08	4	0	0
Oldham Ath	L	03/10	09	12	0	3
MK Dons	Tr	07/10	10-11	20	15	2
Oxford U	L	08/11	11	6	0	1
Oxford U	L	11/11	11	2	0	0
Carlisle U	St Mirren	07/13	13	13	10	1

GUY Michael James (Mike)
Born: Limavady, Derry, Northern Ireland, 4 February, 1953 — M

League Club	Source	Date Signed	Seasons Played	Apps	Subs	Gls
Sheffield U	Coleraine	03/78	77-78	12	6	2
Crewe Alex	Tr	09/79	79-80	54	1	7

GUY Richard (Dickie)
Born: Greenwich, SE London, England, 6 January, 1949 — G

League Club	Source	Date Signed	Seasons Played	Apps	Subs	Gls
Wimbledon	Tooting & Mitcham U	01/68	77	13	0	0

GUY Richard James (Jimmy)
Born: Swansea, Wales, 29 January, 1921 — WH
Died: Great Yarmouth, Norfolk, England, 22 November, 1990

League Club	Source	Date Signed	Seasons Played	Apps	Subs	Gls
Norwich C	RAF St Athan	08/46	46-47	12	-	1

GUY Ronald (Ron)
Born: Salford, England, 25 April, 1936 — CF

League Club	Source	Date Signed	Seasons Played	Apps	Subs	Gls
Stockport Co		09/58	58-59	9	-	2

GUYETT Scott Barry
Born: Ascot, Berkshire, England, 20 January, 1976 — CD
England: Semi Pro-5

League Club	Source	Date Signed	Seasons Played	Apps	Subs	Gls
Oxford U	Southport	07/01	01	20	2	0
Yeovil T	Chester C	07/04	04-07	73	16	2
Bournemouth	Tr	08/08	08-09	27	7	0

GUZAN Bradley Edwin (Brad)
Born: Chicago, Illinois, USA, 9 September, 1984 — G
USA: 31

League Club	Source	Date Signed	Seasons Played	Apps	Subs	Gls
Aston Villa	Chivas (USA)	08/08	08-14	114	2	0
Hull C	L	12/10	10	16	0	0

GWATKIN Philip Arthur (Arthur)
Born: Harrow, NW London, England, 5 August, 1929 — W
Died: Wallasey, Wirral, England, 9 July, 2006

League Club	Source	Date Signed	Seasons Played	Apps	Subs	Gls
Wrexham		10/52	53-55	56	-	8
Tranmere Rov	Tr	06/56	56	21	-	6

GWILLIM Gareth Stuart
Born: Bromley, SE London, England, 9 February, 1983 — LB

League Club	Source	Date Signed	Seasons Played	Apps	Subs	Gls
Crystal Palace	Welling U (Jnr)	08/00				
Dagenham & Red	Histon	06/10	10	0	2	0
AFC Wimbledon	Tr	07/11	11	27	0	1

GWINNETT Melvyn Lawrence (Mel)
Born: Worcester, England, 14 May, 1963 — G

League Club	Source	Date Signed	Seasons Played	Apps	Subs	Gls
Peterborough U	Stourbridge	05/81				
Hereford U	Tr	09/82	82	1	0	0
Bradford C	Gloucester C	06/84				
Exeter C	Tr	08/85	85-88	46	0	0

GWYNNE Samuel Luke (Sam)
Born: Hereford, England, 17 December, 1987 — RM

League Club	Source	Date Signed	Seasons Played	Apps	Subs	Gls
Hereford U	Jnr	02/05	07-10	50	18	1

GWYTHER David Jeffrey Andrew (Dave)
Born: Birmingham, England, 6 December, 1948 — F
Wales: U23-2

League Club	Source	Date Signed	Seasons Played	Apps	Subs	Gls
Swansea C	South Gower	03/66	65-72	212	4	60
Halifax T	Tr	08/73	73-75	104	0	26
Rotherham U	Tr	02/76	75-79	162	0	45
Newport Co	Tr	12/79	79-82	84	21	28
Crewe Alex	L	01/82	81	7	0	1
Newport Co	Port Talbot Ath	03/85	84	1	1	0

GYAN Asamoah
Born: Accra, Ghana, 22 November, 1985 — F
Ghana: 90

League Club	Source	Date Signed	Seasons Played	Apps	Subs	Gls
Sunderland	Stade Rennais (FRA)	08/10	10-11	23	11	10

League Club	Source	Date Signed	Seasons Played	Apps	Subs	Gls
GYEPES Gabor						
Born: Budapest, Hungary, 26 June, 1981						CD
Hungary: 26						
Wolverhampton W	Ferencvaros (HUN)	08/05	05	19	1	0
Northampton T	Queens Park Rgrs (NC)	01/08	07	15	0	0
Cardiff C	Tr	08/08	08-10	57	7	4
Portsmouth	Vasas SC (HUN)	09/12	12	34	1	4
GYMER John Paul						
Born: Romford, E London, England, 11 November, 1966						W
Southend U	App	08/84	83-86	30	25	12
Crewe Alex	Tr	07/87	87	10	5	5
GYNN Michael (Micky)						
Born: Peterborough, England, 19 August, 1961						M
Peterborough U	App	04/79	78-82	152	4	33
Coventry C	Tr	08/83	83-92	206	35	32
Stoke C	Tr	08/93	93	14	7	0
GYORIO Mozesh (Mozzi)						
Born: Subotica, Yugoslavia, 1 August, 1989						M
Fleetwood T	Tampa Bay R's (USA)	01/13	12	0	1	0

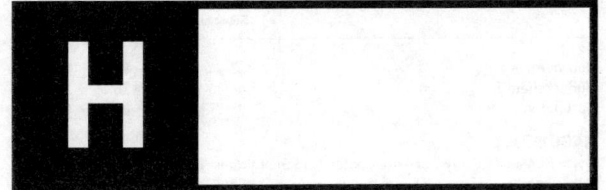

HAAG Kelly Jason
Born: Enfield, N London, England, 6 October, 1970 — F

League Club	Source	Date Signed	Seasons Played	Apps	Subs	Gls
Brentford	YT	07/89	89	1	4	0
Fulham	Tr	08/90	90-92	35	32	9
Barnet	Tr	08/93	93	31	7	8

HAALAND Alf-Inge Rasdal
Born: Stavanger, Norway, 23 November, 1972 — RB/M
Norway: 34/U21-29/Youth

League Club	Source	Date Signed	Seasons Played	Apps	Subs	Gls
Nottingham F	Bryne (NOR)	01/94	93-96	66	9	7
Leeds U	Tr	07/97	97-99	57	17	8
Manchester C	Tr	06/00	00-01	35	3	3

HAARHOFF James Phiri (Jimmy)
Born: Lusaka, Zambia, 27 May, 1981 — M

League Club	Source	Date Signed	Seasons Played	Apps	Subs	Gls
Birmingham C	YT	06/98	99	0	1	0

HAAS Bernt
Born: Vienna, Austria, 8 April, 1978 — RB
Switzerland: 36

League Club	Source	Date Signed	Seasons Played	Apps	Subs	Gls
Sunderland	G'hopper Zurich (SUI)	08/01	01	27	0	0
West Bromwich A	Tr	08/03	03-04	45	1	1

HAAS Maximilian
Born: Freising, Germany, 7 December, 1985 — DM

League Club	Source	Date Signed	Seasons Played	Apps	Subs	Gls
Middlesbrough	Bayern Munich B (GER)	01/11	10	1	1	0

HAASZ John (Johnny)
Born: Budapest, Hungary, 7 July, 1937 — IF/RH

League Club	Source	Date Signed	Seasons Played	Apps	Subs	Gls
Swansea C	Gainsborough Trinity	09/60	60	1	-	0
Workington	Tr	07/61	61-62	50	-	13

HABBIN Richard Leonard (Dick)
Born: Cambridge, England, 6 January, 1949 — F

League Club	Source	Date Signed	Seasons Played	Apps	Subs	Gls
Reading	Cambridge U	03/69	69-74	204	15	42
Rotherham U	Tr	01/75	74-77	79	5	19
Doncaster Rov	Tr	09/77	77-78	57	3	12

HABER Marcus Warren
Born: Vancouver, Canada, 11 January, 1989 — F
Canada: 15/U23-6/Youth

League Club	Source	Date Signed	Seasons Played	Apps	Subs	Gls
West Bromwich A	Vancouver W'caps (CAN)	01/10				
Exeter C	L	02/10	09	3	2	0
Stevenage	St Johnstone	08/12	12-13	34	11	7
Notts Co	L	09/13	13	5	6	2
Crewe Alex	Tr	07/14	14	25	11	7

HABIBOU Mouhamadou Habib
Born: Bria, Central African Republic, 16 April, 1987 — F

League Club	Source	Date Signed	Seasons Played	Apps	Subs	Gls
Leeds U (L)	Zulte-Waregem (BEL)	02/13	12	1	3	0

HACKETT Bernard Edward Keith
Born: Ramsbottom, Greater Manchester, England, 7 September, 1933 — CF

League Club	Source	Date Signed	Seasons Played	Apps	Subs	Gls
Aston Villa	Birmingham C (Am)	11/53				
Chester C	Tr	07/55	55-56	21	-	4

HACKETT Christopher James (Chris)
Born: Oxford, England, 1 March, 1983 — W

League Club	Source	Date Signed	Seasons Played	Apps	Subs	Gls
Oxford U	YT	04/00	99-05	72	53	9
Millwall	Heart of Midlothian	08/06	06-11	78	42	5
Exeter C	L	11/11	11	5	0	0
Wycombe W	L	02/12	11	6	2	0
Northampton T	Tr	07/12	12-14	94	22	11

HACKETT Gary Stuart
Born: Stourbridge, West Midlands, England, 11 October, 1962 — W/M

League Club	Source	Date Signed	Seasons Played	Apps	Subs	Gls
Shrewsbury T	Bromsgrove Rov	07/83	83-86	142	8	17
Stoke C	Aberdeen	03/88	87-89	64	9	7
West Bromwich A	Tr	03/90	89-92	26	18	3
Peterborough U	Tr	09/93	93	18	4	1
Chester C	Tr	09/94	94	30	5	5

HACKETT Warren James
Born: Plaistow, E London, England, 16 December, 1971 — LB
Saint Lucia: 21

League Club	Source	Date Signed	Seasons Played	Apps	Subs	Gls
Leyton Orient	Tottenham H (YT)	07/90	90-93	74	2	3
Doncaster Rov	Tr	07/94	94-95	46	0	2
Mansfield T	Tr	10/95	95-98	114	3	5
Barnet	Tr	03/99	98-99	37	4	1

HACKING John (Jack)
Born: Blackpool, Lancashire, England, 24 August, 1925 — G

League Club	Source	Date Signed	Seasons Played	Apps	Subs	Gls
Accrington Stan	Blackburn Rov (Am)	09/45	46	8	-	0
Stockport Co	Tr	11/46	46-49	4	-	0

HACKING Robert Edward (Bob)
Born: Blackburn, Greater Manchester, England, 30 March, 1918 — LH
Died: Preston, Lancashire, England, 29 March, 2001

League Club	Source	Date Signed	Seasons Played	Apps	Subs	Gls
Luton T	Blackburn Rov (Am)	04/45	46	1	-	0
Brighton & HA	Tr	08/47	47	17	-	2
Southport	Tr	08/48	48-53	181	-	6

HACKNEY Simon John
Born: Stockport, Greater Manchester, England, 5 February, 1984 — LW

League Club	Source	Date Signed	Seasons Played	Apps	Subs	Gls
Carlisle U	Woodley Sports	02/05	05-08	78	35	17
Colchester U	Tr	01/09	08-10	20	15	1
Morecambe	L	03/10	09	8	0	1
Oxford U	L	01/11	10	2	11	0
Rochdale	Tr	07/11	11	1	1	0

HACKWORTH Anthony (Tony)
Born: Durham, England, 19 May, 1980 — F
England: Youth

League Club	Source	Date Signed	Seasons Played	Apps	Subs	Gls
Leeds U	YT	05/97				
Notts Co	Tr	07/01	01-03	17	37	1

HADDAOUI Karim Ben (Raffi)
Born: Copenhagen, Denmark, 24 March, 1971 — M

League Club	Source	Date Signed	Seasons Played	Apps	Subs	Gls
Torquay U (L)	B93 Copenhagen (DEN)	03/96	95	0	2	0

HADDINGTON Harold (Harry)
Born: Scarborough, North Yorkshire, England, 7 August, 1931 — RB
Died: Bradford, England, January, 2010

League Club	Source	Date Signed	Seasons Played	Apps	Subs	Gls
Bradford Park Ave	Scarborough	02/49	52	2	-	0
West Bromwich A	Tr	05/53				
Walsall	Tr	07/55	55-60	226	-	0

HADDINGTON William Raymond (Ray)
Born: Scarborough, North Yorkshire, England, 18 November, 1923 — IF
Died: Adelaide, Australia, 26 July, 1994

League Club	Source	Date Signed	Seasons Played	Apps	Subs	Gls
Bradford C	Bradford Park Ave (Am)	09/46				
Oldham Ath	Tr	08/47	47-50	117	-	63
Manchester C	Tr	11/50	50	6	-	4
Stockport Co	Tr	12/51	51	11	-	4
Bournemouth	Tr	07/52	52	2	-	0
Rochdale	Tr	10/52	52-53	38	-	12
Halifax T	Tr	11/53	53	8	-	1

HADDOCK Andrew Edward Robinson (Andy)
Born: Edinburgh, Scotland, 5 May, 1946 — RW

League Club	Source	Date Signed	Seasons Played	Apps	Subs	Gls
Chester C	Jnr	08/63	63	12	-	0
Crewe Alex	Tr	08/64	64	4	-	0
Rotherham U	Falkirk	12/66	66	4	0	0
Bradford Park Ave	Chelmsford C	12/67	67	5	0	0
Chester C	Tr	03/68	67	10	0	1

HADDOCK Henry (Harry)
Born: Glasgow, Scotland, 26 July, 1925 — FB
Died: Rutherglen, Glasgow, Scotland, 18 December, 1998
Scotland: 6/SLge-7

League Club	Source	Date Signed	Seasons Played	Apps	Subs	Gls
Exeter C (Am)	Renfrew Jnrs	05/46	46	1	-	0

HADDOCK Peter Murray
Born: Newcastle-upon-Tyne, England, 9 December, 1961 — D

League Club	Source	Date Signed	Seasons Played	Apps	Subs	Gls
Newcastle U	App	12/79	81-85	53	4	0
Burnley	L	03/86	85	7	0	0
Leeds U	Tr	07/86	86-90	106	12	1

HADDON Henry Llewellyn (Harry)
Born: Cardiff, Wales, 8 April, 1923 — IF
Died: Bradford-on-Avon, Wiltshire, England, 10 August, 2013

League Club	Source	Date Signed	Seasons Played	Apps	Subs	Gls
Cardiff C	Royal Navy	04/46				
Newport Co	Bangor C	02/47	46-48	10	-	1
Bristol Rov	Tr	11/48	48	2	-	0

HADDOW Alexander (Alex)
Born: Fleet, Hampshire, England, 8 January, 1982 — M

League Club	Source	Date Signed	Seasons Played	Apps	Subs	Gls
Reading	YT	03/00	99-00	1	2	0
Carlisle U	Tr	08/01	01	4	0	0

HADDOW Paul Andrew
Born: Fleetwood, Lancashire, England, 11 October, 1978 — M

League Club	Source	Date Signed	Seasons Played	Apps	Subs	Gls
Blackpool	YT	07/97	97	0	1	0

HADDRELL Matthew Charles (Matt)
Born: Stoke-on-Trent, England, 19 March, 1981 — CD

League Club	Source	Date Signed	Seasons Played	Apps	Subs	Gls
Macclesfield T	Vauxhall Motors	03/03	02-03	6	8	1

HADDRICK Robert (Bobby)
Born: West Ham, E London, England, 1 May, 1950 — CH

League Club	Source	Date Signed	Seasons Played	Apps	Subs	Gls
Southend U	App	-	66	2	0	0

HADFIELD Jordan Michael

Born: Swinton, Greater Manchester, England, 12 August, 1987 — M

League Club	Source	Date Signed	Seasons Played	Apps	Subs	Gls
Stockport Co	Sch	07/03	04	1	0	0
Macclesfield T	Tr	07/06	06-08	44	11	1
MK Dons	L	11/07	07	6	7	0

HADJI Mustapha

Born: Ifrane, Morocco, 16 November, 1971 — M
Morocco: 63

League Club	Source	Date Signed	Seasons Played	Apps	Subs	Gls
Coventry C	Depo la Coruna (SPN)	08/99	99-00	61	1	12
Aston Villa	Tr	07/01	01-03	24	11	2

HADLAND Philip Jonathan (Phil)

Born: Warrington, Cheshire, England, 20 October, 1980 — W

League Club	Source	Date Signed	Seasons Played	Apps	Subs	Gls
Reading	YT	06/99				
Rochdale	Tr	08/00	00	12	20	2
Leyton Orient	Tr	07/01	01	0	5	1
Carlisle U	L	11/01	01	4	0	1
Brighton & HA	Tr	03/02	01	0	2	0
Darlington	Tr	08/02	02	4	2	0
Colchester U	Tr	08/03	03	0	1	0

HADLEY Anthony Paul Frederick (Tony)

Born: Upminster, E London, England, 5 July, 1955 — CD

League Club	Source	Date Signed	Seasons Played	Apps	Subs	Gls
Southend U	Basildon U	07/74	74-82	241	21	16
Colchester U	Tr	08/83	83	44	1	0
Southend U	Tr	08/84	84	31	1	3

HADLEY Shaun Leon

Born: Birmingham, England, 6 February, 1980 — M

League Club	Source	Date Signed	Seasons Played	Apps	Subs	Gls
Torquay U	YT	06/98	98	0	2	0

HADLEY Stewart Anson

Born: Dudley, West Midlands, England, 30 December, 1973 — F

League Club	Source	Date Signed	Seasons Played	Apps	Subs	Gls
Derby Co	Halesowen T	07/92				
Mansfield T	Tr	02/94	93-97	100	24	31
Kidderminster Hrs	Tr	06/98	00-01	23	20	6

HADLINGTON John (Jack)

Born: Brierley Hill, West Midlands, England, 16 August, 1933 — LW

League Club	Source	Date Signed	Seasons Played	Apps	Subs	Gls
Walsall	Cradley Heath	02/54	53	1	-	0

HADZIABDIC Dzemal

Born: Mostar, Yugoslavia, 25 July, 1953 — LB
Yugoslavia: 20

League Club	Source	Date Signed	Seasons Played	Apps	Subs	Gls
Swansea C	Velez Mostar (YUG)	08/80	80-82	87	2	1

HAESTAD Kristofer

Born: Kristiansand, Norway, 9 December, 1983 — M
Norway: 28

League Club	Source	Date Signed	Seasons Played	Apps	Subs	Gls
Wigan Ath (L)	IK Start (NOR)	01/07	06	1	1	0

HAFFEY Francis (Frank)

Born: Glasgow, Scotland, 28 November, 1938 — G
Scotland: 2

League Club	Source	Date Signed	Seasons Played	Apps	Subs	Gls
Swindon T	Glasgow Celtic	10/64	64	4	-	0

HAGAN James (Jim)

Born: Monkstown, Northern Ireland, 10 August, 1956 — CD

League Club	Source	Date Signed	Seasons Played	Apps	Subs	Gls
Coventry C	Larne T	11/77	78	12	1	0
Torquay U	L	09/79	79	7	0	0
Coventry C	Seiko Sports Ass (HKG)	07/81	81	3	0	0
Birmingham C	Tr	05/82	82-86	124	13	0
Colchester U	Celta Vigo (SPN)	11/89	89	2	0	0

HAGAN James (Jimmy)

Born: Washington, Tyne and Wear, England, 21 January, 1918 — IF
Died: Sheffield, England, 27 February, 1998
England: 1/FLge-3/Schools/War-16

League Club	Source	Date Signed	Seasons Played	Apps	Subs	Gls
Derby Co	Liverpool (Am)	01/35	35-38	30	-	7
Sheffield U	Tr	11/38	38-57	361	-	117

HAGEN Erik Bjornstad

Born: Honefoss, Norway, 20 July, 1975 — CD
Norway: 28

League Club	Source	Date Signed	Seasons Played	Apps	Subs	Gls
Wigan Ath (L)	Zenit St P'burg (RUS)	01/08	07	1	0	0

HAGGERTY David Patrick

Born: Sheffield, England, 28 March, 1991 — CD

League Club	Source	Date Signed	Seasons Played	Apps	Subs	Gls
Rotherham U	Sch	05/09	07	0	1	0

HAGUE Keith

Born: Hull, England, 25 May, 1946 — CD

League Club	Source	Date Signed	Seasons Played	Apps	Subs	Gls
York C	Goole T	10/65	65	0	1	0

HAGUE Neil

Born: Thurcroft, South Yorkshire, England, 1 December, 1949 — CD/M
England: Youth

League Club	Source	Date Signed	Seasons Played	Apps	Subs	Gls
Rotherham U	App	12/66	67-71	135	9	23
Plymouth Arg	Tr	11/71	71-73	98	0	15
Bournemouth	Tr	07/74	74-75	89	0	7
Huddersfield T	Tr	06/76	76	25	0	2
Darlington	Tr	05/77	77-78	80	0	4

HAGUE Paul

Born: Consett, County Durham, England, 16 September, 1972 — CD

League Club	Source	Date Signed	Seasons Played	Apps	Subs	Gls
Gillingham	YT	05/91	90-93	8	1	0
Leyton Orient	Tr	09/94	94	17	1	1

HAHNEMANN Marcus Stephen

Born: Seattle, Washington, USA, 15 June, 1972 — G
USA: 9

League Club	Source	Date Signed	Seasons Played	Apps	Subs	Gls
Fulham	Colorado Rapids (USA)	07/99	00	2	0	0
Rochdale	L	10/01	01	5	0	0
Reading	L	12/01	01	6	0	0
Reading	Tr	08/02	02-08	276	0	0
Wolverhampton W	Tr	07/09	09-10	39	0	0
Everton	Tr	09/11				

HAIDARA Massadio

Born: Paris, France, 2 December, 1992 — LB
France: U21-2/Youth

League Club	Source	Date Signed	Seasons Played	Apps	Subs	Gls
Newcastle U	AS Nancy (FRA)	01/13	12-14	17	13	0

HAIG Richard Neil

Born: Pontypridd, Rhondda Cynon Taff, Wales, 29 December, 1970 — F

League Club	Source	Date Signed	Seasons Played	Apps	Subs	Gls
Cardiff C	YT	07/89	88-89	1	4	0

HAIGH Gordon

Born: Barnsley, South Yorkshire, England, 18 August, 1921 — IF
Died: Nelson, Lancashire, England, 22 August, 2011

League Club	Source	Date Signed	Seasons Played	Apps	Subs	Gls
Burnley	Ransome & Marles	11/45	46-49	18	-	3
Bournemouth	Tr	04/50	49-50	17	-	3
Watford	Tr	08/51	51	29	-	5

HAIGH Graham

Born: Huddersfield, West Yorkshire, England, 16 September, 1946 — WH

League Club	Source	Date Signed	Seasons Played	Apps	Subs	Gls
Halifax T	App	-	64	1	-	0

HAIGH John (Jack)

Born: Rotherham, South Yorkshire, England, 10 September, 1928 — IF/RH
Died: Balby, Yorkshire, England, 17 September, 2007

League Club	Source	Date Signed	Seasons Played	Apps	Subs	Gls
Liverpool	Gainsborough Trinity	10/49	50-51	11	-	3
Scunthorpe U	Tr	08/52	52-59	329	-	66
Doncaster Rov	Tr	07/60	60-61	72	-	6

HAIGH Paul

Born: Scarborough, North Yorkshire, England, 4 May, 1958 — CD
England: U21-1

League Club	Source	Date Signed	Seasons Played	Apps	Subs	Gls
Hull C	App	06/75	74-80	179	1	8
Carlisle U	Tr	11/80	80-86	228	5	4
Hartlepool U	Tr	07/87	87-88	49	1	0

HAILS Julian

Born: Lincoln, England, 20 November, 1967 — W/RB

League Club	Source	Date Signed	Seasons Played	Apps	Subs	Gls
Fulham	Hemel Hempstead	08/90	91-94	99	10	12
Southend U	Tr	12/94	94-99	143	18	7

HAILS William (Billy)

Born: Nettlesworth, County Durham, England, 19 February, 1935 — RW

League Club	Source	Date Signed	Seasons Played	Apps	Subs	Gls
Lincoln C	Kimblesworth Jnrs	03/53	53-54	9	-	0
Peterborough U	Tr	07/55	60-62	94	-	28
Northampton T	Tr	11/62	62-63	59	-	13
Luton T	Tr	06/64	64	3	-	0

HAILWOOD David John (Dave)

Born: Blackpool, Lancashire, England, 17 October, 1954 — W

League Club	Source	Date Signed	Seasons Played	Apps	Subs	Gls
Mansfield T	Long Eaton U	07/73	74	1	0	0

HAINES Donald Noah (Don)

Born: Ynysybwl, Rhondda Cynon Taff, Wales, 23 September, 1925 — RB
Died: Cynon-Taff, Rhondda Cynon Taff, Wales, August, 2000

League Club	Source	Date Signed	Seasons Played	Apps	Subs	Gls
Bournemouth	Tynte Rov	10/48				
Newport Co	Yeovil T	12/51	50-53	77	-	1

HAINES Ivan Gerald

Born: Chatham, Kent, England, 14 September, 1968 — CD

League Club	Source	Date Signed	Seasons Played	Apps	Subs	Gls
Gillingham	App	06/87	87-90	45	6	0

HAINES John Thomas William (Jack)

Born: Evesham, Worcestershire, England, 24 April, 1920 — IF
Died: Worcester, England, 19 March, 1987
England: 1

League Club	Source	Date Signed	Seasons Played	Apps	Subs	Gls
Liverpool	Cheltenham T	11/37				
Swansea C	Tr	06/39	46	29	-	7
Leicester C	Tr	06/47	47	12	-	3
West Bromwich A	Tr	03/48	47-49	59	-	23
Bradford Park Ave	Tr	12/49	49-53	136	-	34
Rochdale	Tr	10/53	53-54	60	-	16
Chester C	Tr	07/55	55-56	46	-	8

HAINES Keith Harry
Born: Wigston, Leicestershire, England, 19 December, 1937 — CH
England: Youth

League Club	Source	Date Signed	Seasons Played	Apps	Subs	Gls
Leeds U	Matlock T	05/59				
Lincoln C	Tr	07/60	60-62	13	-	0

HAINES Mervyn John
Born: Mountain Ash, Rhondda Cynon Taff, Wales, 2 May, 1923 — W
Died: Rhondda, Rhondda Cynon Taff, Wales, May, 2005

League Club	Source	Date Signed	Seasons Played	Apps	Subs	Gls
Bournemouth	Swansea C (Am)	10/48				
Newport Co	Yeovil T	05/50	50	14	-	2

HAINING William Wallace (Will)
Born: Glasgow, Scotland, 2 October, 1982 — CD

League Club	Source	Date Signed	Seasons Played	Apps	Subs	Gls
Oldham Ath	YT	10/01	01-06	147	8	11
Morecambe	St Mirren	08/09	09-12	109	11	2

HAINSWORTH Leonard (Len)
Born: Rotherham, South Yorkshire, England, 25 January, 1918 — D
Died: Rotherham, South Yorkshire, England, 22 September, 1990

League Club	Source	Date Signed	Seasons Played	Apps	Subs	Gls
Rotherham U		03/39	38-47	33	-	7
Doncaster Rov	Tr	07/48	48-50	67	-	0
Workington	Tr	07/51	51-52	75	-	0

HAIR George
Born: Ryton-on-Tyne, Tyne and Wear, England, 28 April, 1925 — LW
Died: Peterborough, England, 24 October, 1994

League Club	Source	Date Signed	Seasons Played	Apps	Subs	Gls
Newcastle U	Spen Jnrs	05/43	46-48	23	-	7
Grimsby T	Tr	02/49	48-50	68	-	8

HAIR Kenneth Grenville Arthur (Grenville)
Born: Burton-on-Trent, Staffordshire, England, 16 November, 1931 — FB
Died: Bradford, England, 7 March, 1968

League Club	Source	Date Signed	Seasons Played	Apps	Subs	Gls
Leeds U	Newhall U	11/48	50-63	443	-	1

HAIRE Garry
Born: Sedgefield, County Durham, England, 24 July, 1963 — RW

League Club	Source	Date Signed	Seasons Played	Apps	Subs	Gls
Oxford U	App	07/81				
Bradford C	Whitley Bay	06/83	83-84	43	6	13
Darlington	Tr	02/85	84-85	16	9	2
Rochdale	L	10/85	85	3	0	0

HAJROVIC Sead
Born: Brugg, Switzerland, 4 June, 1993 — DM
Bosnia & Herzegovina: U21-2//Switzerland: Youth

League Club	Source	Date Signed	Seasons Played	Apps	Subs	Gls
Arsenal	Sch	07/10				
Barnet	L	01/12	11	7	3	0

HAJTO Tomasz
Born: Karpat, Poland, 16 October, 1972 — CD
Poland: 62

League Club	Source	Date Signed	Seasons Played	Apps	Subs	Gls
Southampton	FC Nurnberg (GER)	07/05	05	15	5	0
Derby Co	Tr	01/06	05	5	0	0

HALBERT Paul John
Born: St Albans, Hertfordshire, England, 28 October, 1973 — F

League Club	Source	Date Signed	Seasons Played	Apps	Subs	Gls
Aldershot	YT	-	90	0	3	0

HALDANE Lewis Oliver
Born: Trowbridge, Wiltshire, England, 13 March, 1985 — LW
Wales: U21-1

League Club	Source	Date Signed	Seasons Played	Apps	Subs	Gls
Bristol Rov	Sch	10/03	03-08	90	57	15
Port Vale	Tr	09/09	09-11	43	20	3

HALE Alfred (Alfie)
Born: Waterford, Republic of Ireland, 28 August, 1939 — IF
Republic of Ireland: 13/LoI-11/Amateur

League Club	Source	Date Signed	Seasons Played	Apps	Subs	Gls
Aston Villa	Waterford (ROI)	06/60	60-61	5	-	1
Doncaster Rov	Tr	07/62	62-64	119	-	42
Newport Co	Tr	08/65	65	34	0	21

HALE Denzil William (Paddy)
Born: Clevedon, Somerset, England, 9 April, 1928 — CH
Died: Weston-super-Mare, Somerset, England, 15 July, 2004

League Club	Source	Date Signed	Seasons Played	Apps	Subs	Gls
Bristol Rov	Clevedon T	02/52	53-58	120	-	12

HALE Joseph Richard (Dixie)
Born: Waterford, Republic of Ireland, 29 May, 1935 — WH
Republic of Ireland: LoI-3

League Club	Source	Date Signed	Seasons Played	Apps	Subs	Gls
Swansea C	Waterford (ROI)	10/59	59-60	34	-	3
Barrow	Tr	07/61	61-63	118	-	16
Workington	Tr	08/64	64-66	131	0	10
Watford	Tr	07/67	67-69	95	3	7

HALE Kenneth Oliver (Ken)
Born: Blyth, Northumberland, England, 18 September, 1939 — IF
Died: 5 January, 2015

League Club	Source	Date Signed	Seasons Played	Apps	Subs	Gls
Newcastle U	Jnr	10/56	57-62	30	-	15
Coventry C	Tr	12/62	62-65	98	1	27
Oxford U	Tr	03/66	65-67	64	2	13
Darlington	Tr	05/68	68-71	173	0	25
Halifax T	Tr	07/72	72-73	52	0	4

HALES Derek David
Born: Lower Halstow, Kent, England, 15 December, 1951 — F

League Club	Source	Date Signed	Seasons Played	Apps	Subs	Gls
Luton T	Dartford	03/72	72	5	2	1
Charlton Ath	Tr	10/73	73-76	126	3	73
Derby Co	Tr	12/76	76-77	22	1	4
West Ham U	Tr	09/77	77	23	1	10
Charlton Ath	Tr	07/78	78-84	186	5	76
Gillingham	Tr	03/85	84-85	31	9	9

HALES John McKendrick
Born: Glasgow, Scotland, 15 May, 1940 — W

League Club	Source	Date Signed	Seasons Played	Apps	Subs	Gls
Brentford	St Roch's	09/58	58-63	62	-	7

HALES Kevin Peter
Born: Dartford, Kent, England, 13 January, 1961 — M

League Club	Source	Date Signed	Seasons Played	Apps	Subs	Gls
Chelsea	App	01/79	79-82	18	2	2
Leyton Orient	Tr	08/83	83-92	285	15	23

HALES Richard Joseph (Dick)
Born: Gillingham, Kent, England, 24 August, 1925 — RB
Died: Sittingbourne, Kent, England, 21 February, 2009

League Club	Source	Date Signed	Seasons Played	Apps	Subs	Gls
Gillingham (Am)	Sittingbourne	08/51	51	5	-	0

HALES William Henry (Bill)
Born: Gillingham, Kent, England, 6 January, 1920 — CF
Died: Rainham, Kent, England, 1 October, 1984

League Club	Source	Date Signed	Seasons Played	Apps	Subs	Gls
Gillingham (Am)	Sittingbourne	09/49	50-51	15	-	9

HALEY Grant Richard
Born: Bristol, England, 20 September, 1979 — FB

League Club	Source	Date Signed	Seasons Played	Apps	Subs	Gls
Peterborough U	YT	07/98	99	1	0	0

HALEY John
Born: Sunderland, England, 24 April, 1932 — WH
Died: Newcastle-upon-Tyne, England, 1956

League Club	Source	Date Signed	Seasons Played	Apps	Subs	Gls
Gateshead	Middlesbrough (Am)	09/53	53-56	38	-	2

HALFORD Carl
Born: Ashton-under-Lyne, Greater Manchester, England, 27 November, 1958 — M

League Club	Source	Date Signed	Seasons Played	Apps	Subs	Gls
Manchester C	App	08/76				
Stockport Co	Tr	07/77	77-78	65	9	5
Bury	Tr	08/79	79-80	31	0	2

HALFORD Gregory (Greg)
Born: Chelmsford, England, 8 December, 1984 — M/D
England: Youth

League Club	Source	Date Signed	Seasons Played	Apps	Subs	Gls
Colchester U	Sch	08/03	02-06	132	4	18
Reading	Tr	01/07	06	2	1	0
Sunderland	Tr	06/07	07	8	0	0
Charlton Ath	L	01/08	07	16	0	2
Sheffield U	L	07/08	08	31	10	4
Wolverhampton W	Tr	07/09	09-10	12	5	0
Portsmouth	L	10/10	10	33	0	5
Portsmouth	Tr	07/11	11	42	0	7
Nottingham F	Tr	07/12	12-13	62	11	7
Brighton & HA	L	11/14	14	14	5	0

HALFORD Stephen Paul (Steve)
Born: Bury, Greater Manchester, England, 21 September, 1980 — CD

League Club	Source	Date Signed	Seasons Played	Apps	Subs	Gls
Bury	YT	07/99	99-00	3	2	0

HALL Albert Edwards Benjamin
Born: Barry, Vale of Glamorgan, Wales, 3 September, 1918 — RW
Died: Shrewsbury, Shropshire, England, 3 February, 1998
Wales: Schools

League Club	Source	Date Signed	Seasons Played	Apps	Subs	Gls
Tottenham H	Jnr	10/35	35-46	40	-	10
Plymouth Arg	Tr	07/47	47	9	-	0

HALL Alexander Frank (Alec)
Born: Grimsby, North Lincolnshire, England, 17 September, 1909 — RH
Died: Grimsby, North Lincolnshire, England, 28 April, 1992

League Club	Source	Date Signed	Seasons Played	Apps	Subs	Gls
Grimsby T	Cleethorpes T	05/29	29-47	358	-	4

HALL Allan Samuel
Born: Urmston, Greater Manchester, England, 26 May, 1938 — WH/IF
England: Youth

League Club	Source	Date Signed	Seasons Played	Apps	Subs	Gls
Oldham Ath	Manchester U (Am)	11/57	57-60	74	-	5

HALL Almeric George (Almer)
Born: Hove, East Sussex, England, 12 November, 1912 — IF
Died: Margate, Kent, England, 7 November, 1994

League Club	Source	Date Signed	Seasons Played	Apps	Subs	Gls
Brighton & HA	Southwick	02/31				
Tottenham H	Tr	09/33	34-35	16	-	3
Southend U	Tr	05/37	37-38	37	-	10
Bradford C	Tr	06/39				
West Ham U	Tr	12/45	46-48	50	-	11

HALL Anthony David (Tony)
Born: Billingham, Cleveland, England, 17 January, 1969 — CD

League Club	Source	Date Signed	Seasons Played	Apps	Subs	Gls
Tranmere Rov	Billingham T	08/87	87	0	1	0
Hartlepool U	Tr	10/87	87	0	1	0

HALL Arthur
Born: Sheffield, England, 23 November, 1925 — RW/IF
Died: Durham, England, June, 2007

League Club	Source	Date Signed	Seasons Played	Apps	Subs	Gls
Chesterfield	Gainsborough Trinity	07/47	47-48	23	-	4
Scunthorpe U	Goole T	08/51	51	15	-	5

HALL Arthur Brian
Born: Keynsham, Avon, England, 24 March, 1937 — FB

League Club	Source	Date Signed	Seasons Played	Apps	Subs	Gls
Bristol Rov	Witney T	07/59	60-61	2	-	0

HALL Asa Philip
Born: Dudley, West Midlands, England, 29 November, 1986 — M
England: Youth

League Club	Source	Date Signed	Seasons Played	Apps	Subs	Gls
Birmingham C	Sch	11/04				
Boston U	L	01/06	05	5	7	0
Shrewsbury T	L	01/08	07	13	2	3
Luton T	Tr	08/08	08	35	7	10
Oxford U	Tr	05/10	10-11	58	17	11
Shrewsbury T	Tr	07/12	12-13	18	14	2
Aldershot T	L	01/13	12	12	4	0
Oxford U	L	07/13	13	15	4	3
Cheltenham T	Tr	05/14	14	1	0	0

HALL Bernard Roy
Born: Bath, England, 8 July, 1942 — G

League Club	Source	Date Signed	Seasons Played	Apps	Subs	Gls
Bristol Rov	Jnr	09/59	61-66	163	0	0

HALL Brian Samuel
Born: Buxton, Derbyshire, England, 9 March, 1939 — LB/W
Died: Colchester, Essex, England, September, 2002

League Club	Source	Date Signed	Seasons Played	Apps	Subs	Gls
Mansfield T	Belper T	04/59	58-64	72	-	19
Colchester U	Tr	03/65	64-72	324	4	27

HALL Brian William
Born: Glasgow, Scotland, 22 January, 1946 — M
Died: 16 July, 2015

League Club	Source	Date Signed	Seasons Played	Apps	Subs	Gls
Liverpool	Manchester Univ	07/68	68-75	140	13	15
Plymouth Arg	Tr	07/76	76-77	49	2	16
Burnley	Tr	11/77	77-79	39	4	3

HALL Christopher Michael (Chris)
Born: Manchester, England, 27 November, 1986 — F

League Club	Source	Date Signed	Seasons Played	Apps	Subs	Gls
Oldham Ath	Sch	10/05	03-06	7	36	1

HALL Colin Thomas
Born: Wolverhampton, England, 2 February, 1948 — W/CF
England: Youth

League Club	Source	Date Signed	Seasons Played	Apps	Subs	Gls
Nottingham F	Jnr	03/66	67-69	27	9	2
Bradford C	Tr	06/70	70-71	65	1	7
Bristol C	Tr	07/72	72	0	1	0
Hereford U	L	09/72	72	5	0	0

HALL Daniel Andrew (Danny)
Born: Ashton-under-Lyne, Greater Manchester, England, 14 November, 1983 — CD

League Club	Source	Date Signed	Seasons Played	Apps	Subs	Gls
Oldham Ath	Sch	08/03	02-05	57	7	1
Shrewsbury T	Tr	07/06	06-07	28	14	0
Chesterfield	Gretna	07/08	08-09	30	2	2
Darlington	L	11/09	09	3	0	0

HALL David
Born: Doncaster, South Yorkshire, England, 26 September, 1960 — CD

League Club	Source	Date Signed	Seasons Played	Apps	Subs	Gls
Scunthorpe U	App	09/78	78-79	16	1	0

HALL David Henry
Born: Sheffield, England, 16 March, 1954 — M

League Club	Source	Date Signed	Seasons Played	Apps	Subs	Gls
Sheffield Wed	App	03/72				
Bradford C	Tr	07/75	75-76	51	3	3

HALL Derek Robert
Born: Ashton-under-Lyne, Greater Manchester, England, 5 January, 1965 — M/W

League Club	Source	Date Signed	Seasons Played	Apps	Subs	Gls
Coventry C	App	10/82	82	1	0	0
Torquay U	Tr	03/84	83-84	55	0	6
Swindon T	Tr	07/85	85	9	1	0
Southend U	Tr	08/86	86-88	122	3	15
Halifax T	Tr	07/89	89-90	48	1	4
Hereford U	Tr	07/91	91-93	98	5	18
Rochdale	Tr	08/94	94-95	14	9	2

HALL Fitz Benjamin
Born: Leytonstone, NE London, England, 20 December, 1980 — CD

League Club	Source	Date Signed	Seasons Played	Apps	Subs	Gls
Oldham Ath	Chesham U	03/02	01-02	44	0	5
Southampton	Tr	07/03	03	7	4	0
Crystal Palace	Tr	08/04	04-05	75	0	3
Wigan Ath	Tr	06/06	06-07	22	3	0
Queens Park Rgrs	Tr	01/08	07-11	67	18	3
Newcastle U	L	01/10	09	7	0	0
Watford	Tr	07/12	12-13	22	4	0

HALL Frederick (Fred)
Born: Worksop, Nottinghamshire, England, 24 November, 1924 — CF
Died: Huntingdon, Cambridgeshire, England, May, 2006

League Club	Source	Date Signed	Seasons Played	Apps	Subs	Gls
Birmingham C	Whitwell OB	03/47	46-48	5	-	2

HALL Frederick (Fred)
Born: Drayton, Norfolk, England, 20 October, 1914 — G
Died: South Africa, 25 February, 2003

League Club	Source	Date Signed	Seasons Played	Apps	Subs	Gls
Norwich C	Hellesdon Hospital	09/34	35-46	90	-	0

HALL Frederick Michael George (Freddy)
Born: St Georges, Bermuda, 3 March, 1985 — G

League Club	Source	Date Signed	Seasons Played	Apps	Subs	Gls
Northampton T	Bermuda Hogges (BER)	07/11	11	2	1	0

HALL Frederick Wilkinson (Fred)
Born: Chester-le-Street, County Durham, England, 18 November, 1917 — CH
Died: Stanley, County Durham, England, 8 January, 1989

League Club	Source	Date Signed	Seasons Played	Apps	Subs	Gls
Blackburn Rov	Ouston Jnrs	11/35	36-38	29	-	0
Sunderland	Tr	08/46	46-54	215	-	1
Barrow	Tr	09/55	55	16	-	1

HALL Gareth David
Born: Croydon, S London, England, 12 March, 1969 — RB
England: Schools//Wales: 9/U21-1

League Club	Source	Date Signed	Seasons Played	Apps	Subs	Gls
Chelsea	App	04/86	86-95	120	18	4
Sunderland	Tr	12/95	95-97	41	7	0
Brentford	L	10/97	97	6	0	0
Swindon T	Tr	05/98	98-00	80	7	3

HALL Grant Terry
Born: Brighton, England, 29 October, 1991 — CD

League Club	Source	Date Signed	Seasons Played	Apps	Subs	Gls
Brighton & HA	Lewes	10/09	11	0	1	0
Tottenham H	Tr	07/12				
Swindon T	L	07/13	13	26	1	0
Birmingham C	L	07/14	14	7	0	0
Blackpool	L	01/15	14	11	1	1

HALL Ian
Born: Egremont, Cumbria, England, 28 November, 1950 — RB/M

League Club	Source	Date Signed	Seasons Played	Apps	Subs	Gls
Workington	Egremont T	07/72	71-73	25	11	1
Southport	Tr	07/74	74	0	1	0

HALL Ian William
Born: Sutton Scarsdale, Derbyshire, England, 27 December, 1939 — RH/IF
England: Youth/Schools

League Club	Source	Date Signed	Seasons Played	Apps	Subs	Gls
Derby Co	Wolverhampton W (Am)	09/59	59-61	44	-	13
Mansfield T	Tr	09/62	62-67	145	0	10

HALL James (Jimmy)
Born: Bootle, Merseyside, England, 5 October, 1959 — M

League Club	Source	Date Signed	Seasons Played	Apps	Subs	Gls
Blackpool	App	10/77	78	1	0	0
Blackburn Rov	Tr	07/80				

HALL James Franklin (Jimmy)
Born: Manchester, England, 7 May, 1945 — FB

League Club	Source	Date Signed	Seasons Played	Apps	Subs	Gls
Oldham Ath	Mather & Platt	04/66	65	2	0	0

HALL James Leonard (Jim)
Born: Northampton, England, 21 March, 1945 — F
England: Youth

League Club	Source	Date Signed	Seasons Played	Apps	Subs	Gls
Northampton T	Jnr	07/63	63-67	54	1	7
Peterborough U	Tr	12/67	67-74	298	4	122
Northampton T	Tr	01/75	74-77	69	0	28
Cambridge U	L	12/76	76	24	0	15

HALL Jeffrey James (Jeff)
Born: Scunthorpe, North Lincolnshire, England, 7 September, 1929 — RB
Died: Birmingham, England, 4 April, 1959
England: 17/B-1/FLge-4

League Club	Source	Date Signed	Seasons Played	Apps	Subs	Gls
Birmingham C	Bradford Park Ave (Am)	05/50	50-58	227	-	1

HALL John (Jack)
Born: Doncaster, South Yorkshire, England, 19 November, 1931 — CF
Died: Sheffield, England, 26 February, 1992

League Club	Source	Date Signed	Seasons Played	Apps	Subs	Gls
Doncaster Rov		08/51	51	2	-	0
Halifax T	Goole T	08/55				

HALL John Franklin
Born: Bramley, Leeds, England, 18 April, 1944 — RW

League Club	Source	Date Signed	Seasons Played	Apps	Subs	Gls
Bradford C	Jnr	05/62	62-73	417	13	63

HALL Joseph Edgar
Born: Sherburn, County Durham, England, 10 April, 1934 — IF

League Club	Source	Date Signed	Seasons Played	Apps	Subs	Gls
Fulham	Newcastle U (Am)	10/51	55	1	-	0

HALL Kenneth Dennis (Dennis)
Born: Southwell, Nottinghamshire, England, 24 December, 1930 — RB
Died: Droxford, Hampshire, England, 19 October, 2004

League Club	Source	Date Signed	Seasons Played	Apps	Subs	Gls
Portsmouth	Bilsthorpe	09/48	52-53	10	-	0
Reading	Tr	08/54	54	13	-	0
Bournemouth	Tr	07/55				

HALL Lancelot (Lance)
Born: Darlington, County Durham, England, 23 January, 1915 LB/CH
Died: Barrow, Cumbria, England, 26 February, 1985

League Club	Source	Date Signed	Seasons Played	Apps	Subs	Gls
Luton T	Cockfield	01/37				
Barrow	Tr	07/38	38-48	108	-	1

HALL Leigh
Born: Hereford, England, 10 June, 1975 M

League Club	Source	Date Signed	Seasons Played	Apps	Subs	Gls
Hereford U	Ledbury T	03/95	94-95	0	2	0

HALL Leslie Frederick (Les)
Born: St Albans, Hertfordshire, England, 1 October, 1921 CH
Died: St Albans, Hertfordshire, England, 20 March, 2010

League Club	Source	Date Signed	Seasons Played	Apps	Subs	Gls
Luton T	St Albans C	08/43	47-54	79	-	0

HALL Marcus Thomas Jackson
Born: Coventry, England, 24 March, 1976 LB
England: B-1/U21-8

League Club	Source	Date Signed	Seasons Played	Apps	Subs	Gls
Coventry C	YT	07/94	94-01	113	19	2
Nottingham F	Tr	08/02	02	1	0	0
Southampton	Tr	08/02				
Stoke C	Tr	12/02	02-04	76	3	1
Coventry C	Tr	02/05	04-09	125	13	0
Northampton T	Tr	07/10	10	21	3	0

HALL Mark
Born: Doncaster, South Yorkshire, England, 11 May, 1970 RB

League Club	Source	Date Signed	Seasons Played	Apps	Subs	Gls
Doncaster Rov	YT	06/88	87-88	1	1	0

HALL Mark Anthony
Born: Islington, N London, England, 13 January, 1973 W

League Club	Source	Date Signed	Seasons Played	Apps	Subs	Gls
Southend U	Tottenham H (YT)	08/91	91-92	4	8	0
Barnet	L	09/93	93	3	0	0
Torquay U	Tr	07/95	95	22	7	0

HALL Paul Anthony
Born: Manchester, England, 3 July, 1972 RW
Jamaica: 41

League Club	Source	Date Signed	Seasons Played	Apps	Subs	Gls
Torquay U	YT	07/90	89-92	77	16	1
Portsmouth	Tr	03/93	93-97	148	40	37
Coventry C	Tr	08/98	98-99	2	8	0
Bury	L	02/99	98	7	0	0
Sheffield U	L	12/99	99	1	3	1
West Bromwich A	L	02/00	99	4	0	0
Walsall	Tr	03/00	99-00	46	6	10
Rushden & D	Tr	10/01	01-03	106	6	26
Tranmere Rov	Tr	03/04	03-04	49	6	13
Chesterfield	Tr	07/05	05-06	84	7	20
Walsall	Tr	07/07	07	7	12	1
Wrexham	L	01/08	07	7	4	1

HALL Peter
Born: Stoke-on-Trent, England, 29 September, 1939 RW

League Club	Source	Date Signed	Seasons Played	Apps	Subs	Gls
Port Vale	Stoke C (Am)	05/58	58-60	16	-	4
Bournemouth	Tr	07/61				
Gillingham	Bedford T	11/67	67	9	0	1

HALL Richard Anthony
Born: Ipswich, England, 14 March, 1972 CD
England: U21-11/Youth

League Club	Source	Date Signed	Seasons Played	Apps	Subs	Gls
Scunthorpe U	YT	03/90	89-90	22	0	3
Southampton	Tr	02/91	90-95	119	7	12
West Ham U	Tr	07/96	96	7	0	0

HALL Richard Frank
Born: Weymouth, Dorset, England, 3 July, 1945 M

League Club	Source	Date Signed	Seasons Played	Apps	Subs	Gls
Bournemouth	Weymouth	06/67	67	8	3	0

HALL Robert Kieran Dennis (Rob)
Born: Aylesbury, Buckinghamshire, England, 20 October, 1993 F
England: Youth

League Club	Source	Date Signed	Seasons Played	Apps	Subs	Gls
West Ham U	Sch	10/10	11-12	0	4	0
Oxford U	L	09/11	11	11	2	5
MK Dons	L	03/12	11	0	2	0
Birmingham C	L	11/12	12	11	2	0
Bolton W	Tr	03/13	12-14	14	18	1
MK Dons	L	03/15	14	5	2	3

HALL Ronald (Ron)
Born: Dudley, West Midlands, England, 8 February, 1933 WH

League Club	Source	Date Signed	Seasons Played	Apps	Subs	Gls
Walsall	Cradley Heath	06/54	54-55	2	-	0

HALL Ryan Marcus Leon
Born: Dulwich, S London, England, 4 January, 1988 LW
England: Semi Pro-1

League Club	Source	Date Signed	Seasons Played	Apps	Subs	Gls
Crystal Palace	Sch	08/05	07	0	1	0
Dagenham & Red	L	01/08	07	2	6	2
Southend U	Bromley	08/10	10-12	72	14	19
Leeds U	Tr	10/12	12	2	6	0
Sheffield U	L	09/13	13	3	1	0
MK Dons	Bromley	02/14	13	4	7	1
Rotherham U	Tr	06/14	14	2	1	1
Notts Co	L	11/14	14	2	2	0
Luton T	Tr	01/15	14	4	3	0

HALL Stanley Arthur (Stan)
Born: Southgate, N London, England, 18 February, 1917 G
Died: Enfield, N London, England, September, 1999

League Club	Source	Date Signed	Seasons Played	Apps	Subs	Gls
Leyton Orient	Finchley	03/38	38-46	26	-	0

HALL Wayne
Born: Rotherham, South Yorkshire, England, 25 October, 1968 LB

League Club	Source	Date Signed	Seasons Played	Apps	Subs	Gls
York C	Hatfield Main	03/89	88-00	353	20	9

HALL Wilfred (Wilf)
Born: Haydock, Merseyside, England, 14 October, 1934 G
Died: Macclesfield, Cheshire, England, 6 August, 2007

League Club	Source	Date Signed	Seasons Played	Apps	Subs	Gls
Stoke C	Earlestown	10/53	54-59	45	-	0
Ipswich T	Tr	06/60	60-62	16	-	0

HALL William (Billy)
Born: Gosport, Hampshire, England, 24 August, 1930 CF
Died: South Hampshire, England, June, 2011

League Club	Source	Date Signed	Seasons Played	Apps	Subs	Gls
Gillingham	Gosport Bor	09/52	52	9	-	0

HALL William Furness (Willie)
Born: Bamber Bridge, Lancashire, England, 6 February, 1926 G
Died: Preston, Lancashire, England, 23 January, 1986

League Club	Source	Date Signed	Seasons Played	Apps	Subs	Gls
Preston NE	Jnr	02/48	47	7	-	0
Blackpool	Tr	07/49	52	3	-	0
Reading	Tr	07/53	53	16	-	0

HALL William Wilson (Billy)
Born: Liverpool, England, 3 June, 1917 W
Died: Knowsley, Merseyside, England, 6 May, 2005

League Club	Source	Date Signed	Seasons Played	Apps	Subs	Gls
Liverpool	Thorndale	11/43				
Southport	Tr	06/46	46	16	-	1

HALLAM Anthony Kenneth (Tony)
Born: Chesterfield, Derbyshire, England, 9 October, 1946 FB

League Club	Source	Date Signed	Seasons Played	Apps	Subs	Gls
Chesterfield	App	10/64	65-66	5	1	0

HALLAM Norman Henry
Born: Stoke-on-Trent, England, 23 October, 1920 WH
Died: Epping, Essex, England, November, 1997

League Club	Source	Date Signed	Seasons Played	Apps	Subs	Gls
Port Vale	Chelsea (Am)	05/46	46-52	63	-	4
Barnsley	Tr	09/53				
Halifax T	Tr	10/53	53	3	-	0

HALLARD William (Billy)
Born: St Helens, Merseyside, England, 28 August, 1913 WH
Died: Rochdale, Greater Manchester, England, 21 January, 1980

League Club	Source	Date Signed	Seasons Played	Apps	Subs	Gls
Bury	Runcorn	08/35	35	1	-	0
Bradford Park Ave	Tr	06/37	37-38	69	-	5
Rochdale	Tr	06/46	46	17	-	2
Accrington Stan	Tr	03/47	46	3	-	0

HALLAS Geoffrey (Geoff)
Born: Oldham, Greater Manchester, England, 8 December, 1930 FB
Died: Oldham, Greater Manchester, England, 6 June, 1982

League Club	Source	Date Signed	Seasons Played	Apps	Subs	Gls
West Ham U	Warminster	03/54	54	3	-	0

HALLE Gunnar
Born: Larvik, Norway, 11 August, 1965 RB
Norway: 64/U21-23/Youth

League Club	Source	Date Signed	Seasons Played	Apps	Subs	Gls
Oldham Ath	Lillestrom (NOR)	02/91	90-96	185	3	17
Leeds U	Tr	12/96	96-98	65	5	4
Bradford C	Tr	06/99	99-01	78	5	1
Wolverhampton W	L	03/02	01	4	1	0

HALLETT Thomas Reginald (Tom)
Born: Glyn Neath, Neath Port Talbot, Wales, 10 April, 1939 CH
Wales: Schools

League Club	Source	Date Signed	Seasons Played	Apps	Subs	Gls
Leeds U	Jnr	04/56				
Swindon T	Tr	07/63	63-65	26	0	0
Bradford C	Tr	06/66	66-70	177	2	2

HALLFREDSSON Emil
Born: Hornafjordur, Iceland, 29 June, 1984 LW
Iceland: 42/U21-14/Youth

League Club	Source	Date Signed	Seasons Played	Apps	Subs	Gls
Tottenham H	Hafnar Fjordur (ICE)	12/04				
Barnsley (L)	Reggina (ITA)	08/09	09	22	5	3

HALLICHE Rafik
Born: Algiers, Algeria, 2 September, 1986 CD
Algeria: 37/U23-6

League Club	Source	Date Signed	Seasons Played	Apps	Subs	Gls
Fulham	Benfica (POR)	08/10	10	0	1	0

League Club	Source	Date Signed	Seasons Played	Apps	Subs	Gls
HALLIDAY Andrew William (Andy)						
Born: Glasgow, Scotland, 11 October, 1991						M/W
Middlesbrough	Livingston	07/10	10-13	18	18	1
Walsall	L	11/11	11	2	5	0
Blackpool	L	01/14	13	12	6	1
Bradford C	Tr	10/14	14	20	5	1
HALLIDAY Bradley (Brad)						
Born: Redcar, Cleveland, England, 10 July, 1995						RB/M
Middlesbrough	Redcar T	07/13				
York C	L	11/14	14	24	0	1
HALLIDAY Brian						
Born: Farnworth, Greater Manchester, England, 19 January, 1938						RW
Died: Rochdale, Greater Manchester, England, 16 January, 2009						
Stockport Co	Bolton W (Am)	10/58	58	1	-	0
HALLIDAY Brian Joseph						
Born: Liverpool, England, 30 December, 1944						W
Liverpool	Jnr	05/63				
Tranmere Rov	Tr	07/65				
Crewe Alex	Tr	10/65	65	1	0	0
HALLIDAY Bruce						
Born: Sunderland, England, 3 January, 1961						CD
Newcastle U	App	01/79	80-81	32	0	1
Darlington	L	09/82	82	7	0	0
Bury	Tr	11/82	82	29	0	0
Bristol C	Tr	08/83	83-84	52	1	0
Hereford U	Tr	06/85	85-86	61	1	6
HALLIDAY Gary						
Born: Bradford, England, 9 May, 1951						F
Bradford Park Ave	Jnr	08/68	68	0	1	0
HALLIDAY Matthew Richard						
Born: Norwich, England, 23 January, 1987						CD
Norwich C	Sch	07/06				
Torquay U	L	01/07	06	3	0	0
HALLIDAY Stephen William (Steve)						
Born: Sunderland, England, 3 May, 1976						F
Hartlepool U	YT	07/94	93-97	111	29	25
Carlisle U (L)	Motherwell	02/00	99	16	0	7
Carlisle U	Doncaster Rov	10/00	00-01	31	36	8
HALLIDAY Thomas (Tommy)						
Born: Ardrossan, Ayrshire, Scotland, 28 April, 1940						CF
Cardiff C	Dumbarton	10/63	63-64	16	-	2
HALLOWS Paul Charles Richard						
Born: Chester, England, 22 June, 1950						RB
Bolton W	App	10/67	68-73	44	2	0
Rochdale	Tr	05/74	74-79	197	0	2
HALLS Andrew Thomas (Andy)						
Born: Urmston, Greater Manchester, England, 20 April, 1992						RB
Stockport Co	Sch	07/09	08-10	29	6	0
HALLS John						
Born: Islington, N London, England, 14 February, 1982						D
England: Youth						
Arsenal	YT	07/00				
Colchester U	L	01/02	01	6	0	0
Stoke C	Tr	10/03	03-05	67	2	2
Reading	Tr	01/06	05-07	1	1	1
Preston NE	L	11/07	07	4	0	0
Crystal Palace	L	01/08	07	5	0	0
Sheffield U	L	03/08	07	5	1	0
Brentford	Tr	09/08	08	22	1	0
Aldershot T	Tr	07/09	09-10	26	13	1
Wycombe W	Tr	06/11	11	5	2	0
HALLWORTH Jonathan Geoffrey (Jon)						
Born: Stockport, Greater Manchester, England, 26 October, 1965						G
Ipswich T	App	05/83	85-87	45	0	0
Bristol Rov	L	01/85	84	2	0	0
Oldham Ath	Tr	02/89	88-96	171	3	0
Cardiff C	Tr	08/97	97-99	123	0	0
HALLYBONE James Michael (Jimmy)						
Born: Leytonstone, NE London, England, 15 March, 1962						W
Leyton Orient	App	05/80	81	5	3	0
Halifax T	Tr	07/82	82	11	5	0
HALMOSI Peter						
Born: Szombathely, Hungary, 25 September, 1979						LW
Hungary: 35/U21-2						
Plymouth Arg	Debrecen (HUN)	01/07	06-07	55	4	12
Hull C	Tr	07/08	08	4	14	0
HALOM Victor Lewis (Vic)						
Born: Linton, Derbyshire, England, 3 October, 1948						F
Charlton Ath	App	01/66	65-67	9	3	0
Leyton Orient	Tr	08/67	67-68	53	0	12
Fulham	Tr	11/68	68-71	66	6	22
Luton T	Tr	09/71	71-72	57	2	17
Sunderland	Tr	02/73	72-75	110	3	35
Oldham Ath	Tr	07/76	76-79	121	2	43
Rotherham U	Tr	02/80	79-80	19	1	2
HALPIN John Thomas (Tommy)						
Born: Manchester, England, 5 June, 1927						RB
Died: Chester, England, August, 2001						
Bury		11/48	48	2	-	0
Shrewsbury T	Tr	08/51	51-52	42	-	0
HALPIN John William						
Born: Broxburn, West Lothian, Scotland, 15 November, 1961						LW
Scotland: Youth						
Carlisle U	Glasgow Celtic	10/84	84-90	148	5	17
Rochdale	Tr	07/91	91	22	9	1
HALPIN Michael Saul (Saul)						
Born: Bodmin, Cornwall, England, 31 May, 1991						W
Torquay U	Jnr	11/09	10-12	0	7	0
HALSALL Alan						
Born: Menai Bridge, Anglesey, Wales, 17 November, 1940						G
Blackpool	Skelmersdale U	04/62	61	2	-	0
Oldham Ath	Tr	07/63	63	2	-	0
HALSALL Michael (Mick)						
Born: Bootle, Merseyside, England, 21 July, 1961						M
Liverpool	App	05/79				
Birmingham C	Tr	03/83	82-84	35	1	3
Carlisle U	Tr	10/84	84-86	92	0	11
Grimsby T	Tr	02/87	86	12	0	0
Peterborough U	Tr	07/87	87-93	248	1	28
HALSEY Mark Alan						
Born: Romford, E London, England, 1 December, 1959						M
Norwich C	App	12/77	77-79	3	0	0
HALSTEAD Mark James						
Born: Blackpool, Lancashire, England, 1 September, 1990						G
Blackpool	Sch	05/09	10-12	1	2	0
Shrewsbury T	Tr	06/14	14	0	1	0
HALSTEAD Roy						
Born: Whitworth, Lancashire, England, 26 July, 1931						IF
Died: Whitworth, Lancashire, England, 6 August, 1997						
Burnley	Jnr	06/53				
Chester C	Tr	06/54	54	21	-	4
HALTON Reginald Lloyd (Reg)						
Born: Leek, Staffordshire, England, 11 July, 1916						LH
Died: Leek, Staffordshire, England, 17 March, 1988						
Manchester U	Buxton	10/36	36	4	-	1
Notts Co	Tr	06/37	37	6	-	0
Bury	Tr	11/37	37-48	114	-	19
Chesterfield	Tr	12/48	48-50	61	-	10
Leicester C	Tr	09/50	50-51	64	-	3
HAM Michael Thomas (Mike)						
Born: Plymouth, England, 6 December, 1963						CD
Plymouth Arg	App	12/81	81-84	16	1	0
HAM Robert Stanley (Bobby)						
Born: Bradford, England, 29 March, 1942						F
Bradford Park Ave	Jnr	10/61	61-62	25	-	6
Grimsby T	Gainsborough Trinity	02/64	63	2	-	1
Bradford Park Ave	Tr	08/64	64-67	134	0	47
Bradford C	Tr	02/68	67-70	115	0	40
Preston NE	Tr	10/70	70-71	43	0	14
Rotherham U	Tr	10/71	71-72	67	1	24
Bradford C	Tr	07/73	73-74	72	1	24
HAMANN Dietmar Johann Wolfgang (Didi)						
Born: Waldsassen, Bavaria, Germany, 27 August, 1973						DM
Germany: 59/U21-10/Youth						
Newcastle U	Bayern Munich (GER)	08/98	98	22	1	4
Liverpool	Tr	07/99	99-05	174	17	8
Manchester C	Tr	07/06	06-08	43	11	0
MK Dons	Rtd	07/10	10	12	0	0
HAMER Benjamin John (Ben)						
Born: Chard, Somerset, England, 20 November, 1987						G
Reading	Sch	07/06				
Brentford	L	08/07	07	6	0	0
Brentford	L	01/08	07	14	0	0

League Club	Source	Date Signed	Seasons Played	Apps	Subs	Gls
Brentford	L	07/08	08	45	0	0
Brentford	L	08/10	10	10	0	0
Exeter C	L	01/11	10	18	0	0
Charlton Ath	Tr	08/11	11-13	114	0	0
Leicester C	Tr	05/14	14	8	0	0

HAMER John
Born: Bradford, England, 5 April, 1944 — FB

League Club	Source	Date Signed	Seasons Played	Apps	Subs	Gls
Bradford C (Am)	Harrogate Railway Ath	04/64	64	1	-	0

HAMER Kevin John
Born: Merthyr Tydfil, Wales, 2 February, 1969 — CD

League Club	Source	Date Signed	Seasons Played	Apps	Subs	Gls
Newport Co	YT	07/87	85-87	15	2	1

HAMILL Joseph Patrick (Joe)
Born: Airdrie, Lanarkshire, Scotland, 25 February, 1984 — M

League Club	Source	Date Signed	Seasons Played	Apps	Subs	Gls
Leicester C	Heart of Midlothian	08/05	05	7	5	0

HAMILL Rory
Born: Coleraine, Derry, Northern Ireland, 4 May, 1976 — LW
Northern Ireland: Youth/Schools

League Club	Source	Date Signed	Seasons Played	Apps	Subs	Gls
Fulham	Portstewart	11/94	94-95	24	24	7

HAMILL Stewart Peter
Born: Glasgow, Scotland, 22 January, 1960 — RW

League Club	Source	Date Signed	Seasons Played	Apps	Subs	Gls
Leicester C	Pollok Jnrs	09/80	80-81	10	0	2
Scunthorpe U	L	03/82	81	4	0	0
Northampton T	Nuneaton Bor	03/86	85	3	0	1
Scarborough	Altrincham	07/87	87	19	9	3

HAMILTON Alexander McGregor (Alex)
Born: Kirkcolm, Dumfries & Galloway, Scotland, 21 November, 1937 — WH
Died: Accrington, Lancashire, England, 3 November, 2009

League Club	Source	Date Signed	Seasons Played	Apps	Subs	Gls
Accrington Stan	Drumore Jnrs	08/57	58-60	82	-	0
York C	Tr	03/62	61	11	-	0

HAMILTON Bradley Darren
Born: Newham, E London, England, 30 August, 1992 — RB

League Club	Source	Date Signed	Seasons Played	Apps	Subs	Gls
Colchester U	Sch	07/11	11	0	1	0

HAMILTON Bryan
Born: Belfast, Northern Ireland, 21 December, 1946 — M
Northern Ireland: 50/NILge-3/U23-2

League Club	Source	Date Signed	Seasons Played	Apps	Subs	Gls
Ipswich T	Linfield	08/71	71-75	142	11	43
Everton	Tr	11/75	75-76	38	3	5
Millwall	Tr	07/77	77-78	48	1	6
Swindon T	Tr	11/78	78-80	19	5	1
Tranmere Rov	Tr	10/80	80-84	95	14	6

HAMILTON Charles McDermott
Born: Glasgow, Scotland, 16 June, 1933 — W
Died: Annan, Dumfries & Galloway, Scotland, 2013

League Club	Source	Date Signed	Seasons Played	Apps	Subs	Gls
Plymouth Arg	Jnr	07/50				
Stockport Co	Tr	11/55	55	7	-	1

HAMILTON David
Born: South Shields, Tyne and Wear, England, 7 November, 1960 — M
England: Youth

League Club	Source	Date Signed	Seasons Played	Apps	Subs	Gls
Sunderland	App	09/78				
Blackburn Rov	Tr	01/81	80-85	104	10	7
Cardiff C	L	03/85	84	10	0	0
Wigan Ath	Tr	07/86	86-88	97	6	7
Chester C	Tr	08/89	89	26	4	0
Burnley	Tr	08/90	90-91	11	4	0

HAMILTON David Stewart
Born: Carlisle, Cumbria, England, 8 February, 1919 — IF

League Club	Source	Date Signed	Seasons Played	Apps	Subs	Gls
Newcastle U	Shawfield Jnrs	05/39				
Southend U	Tr	05/46	46	4	-	0

HAMILTON Derrick Vivian (Des)
Born: Bradford, England, 15 August, 1976 — M
England: U21-1

League Club	Source	Date Signed	Seasons Played	Apps	Subs	Gls
Bradford C	YT	06/94	93-96	67	21	5
Newcastle U	Tr	03/97	97	7	5	0
Sheffield U	L	10/98	98	6	0	0
Huddersfield T	L	02/99	98	10	0	1
Norwich C	L	03/00	99	7	0	0
Tranmere Rov	L	10/00	00	2	0	0
Tranmere Rov	L	01/01	00	3	1	0
Cardiff C	Tr	07/01	01-02	16	9	0
Grimsby T	Tr	07/03	03	20	7	0

HAMILTON Edward (Eddie)
Born: Glasgow, Scotland, 17 January, 1927 — IF
Died: Barnsley, South Yorkshire, England, September, 2007
Republic of Ireland: LoI-1

League Club	Source	Date Signed	Seasons Played	Apps	Subs	Gls
Barnsley	Dundalk (ROI)	04/49	49	1	-	0
Rotherham U	St Patricks Ath (ROI)	04/53				

HAMILTON Gary Ian
Born: Banbridge, Down, Northern Ireland, 6 October, 1980 — F
Northern Ireland: U21-12/Youth/Schools

League Club	Source	Date Signed	Seasons Played	Apps	Subs	Gls
Blackburn Rov	YT	10/97				
Rochdale	L	10/98	00	0	3	0

HAMILTON Gary James
Born: Glasgow, Scotland, 27 December, 1965 — M
Scotland: Youth

League Club	Source	Date Signed	Seasons Played	Apps	Subs	Gls
Middlesbrough	App	06/83	82-88	217	12	25
Darlington	L	09/91	91	11	0	2

HAMILTON Hugh Hare (Hughie)
Born: Newton Mearns, Renfrewshire, Scotland, 16 June, 1942 — RW

League Club	Source	Date Signed	Seasons Played	Apps	Subs	Gls
Hartlepool U	Falkirk	07/63	63-65	38	1	7

HAMILTON Ian
Born: Thornbury, Avon, England, 12 September, 1940 — IF

League Club	Source	Date Signed	Seasons Played	Apps	Subs	Gls
Bristol Rov	Thornbury T	01/58	58-67	149	0	61
Exeter C	L	10/67	67	4	0	1
Newport Co	Tr	07/68	68	11	2	2

HAMILTON Ian Michael (Chico)
Born: Streatham, S London, England, 31 October, 1950 — M
England: Youth

League Club	Source	Date Signed	Seasons Played	Apps	Subs	Gls
Chelsea	App	01/68	66	3	2	2
Southend U	Tr	09/68	68	34	2	11
Aston Villa	Tr	06/69	69-75	189	19	40
Sheffield U	Tr	07/76	76-77	55	5	13

HAMILTON Ian Richard
Born: Stevenage, Hertfordshire, England, 14 December, 1967 — M

League Club	Source	Date Signed	Seasons Played	Apps	Subs	Gls
Southampton	App	12/85				
Cambridge U	Tr	03/88	87-88	23	1	1
Scunthorpe U	Tr	12/88	88-91	139	6	18
West Bromwich A	Tr	06/92	92-97	229	11	23
Sheffield U	Tr	03/98	97-99	38	7	3
Grimsby T	L	11/99	99	6	0	1
Notts Co	Tr	08/00	00-01	29	5	0
Lincoln C	Tr	11/01	01	26	0	0

HAMILTON Ian Walter
Born: South Shields, Tyne and Wear, England, 21 July, 1956 — M

League Club	Source	Date Signed	Seasons Played	Apps	Subs	Gls
Darlington	Boldon CW	11/79	79-81	99	4	19

HAMILTON James (Jimmy)
Born: Baillieston, Glasgow, Scotland, 14 June, 1955 — M

League Club	Source	Date Signed	Seasons Played	Apps	Subs	Gls
Sunderland	App	06/72	71-73	9	8	2
Plymouth Arg	Tr	11/75	76	6	2	0
Bristol Rov	Tr	12/76	76-77	16	4	1
Carlisle U	Tr	09/77	77-81	150	4	12
Hartlepool U	Gretna	11/82	82	2	1	0

HAMILTON John
Born: Larkhall, Lanarkshire, Scotland, 22 January, 1935 — W
Died: Edinburgh, Scotland, 13 August, 2013
Scotland: SLge-1/U23-2

League Club	Source	Date Signed	Seasons Played	Apps	Subs	Gls
Watford	Heart of Midlothian	05/67	67	7	1	2

HAMILTON John Turner
Born: Glasgow, Scotland, 10 July, 1949 — F

League Club	Source	Date Signed	Seasons Played	Apps	Subs	Gls
Millwall	Glasgow Rangers	06/78	78	1	1	0

HAMILTON Lewis Emmanuel
Born: Derby, England, 21 November, 1984 — FB

League Club	Source	Date Signed	Seasons Played	Apps	Subs	Gls
Queens Park Rgrs	Derby Co (Sch)	08/04	04	0	1	0

HAMILTON Marvin Dolapo Ananda Daniel
Born: Leytonstone, NE London, England, 8 October, 1988 — LB

League Club	Source	Date Signed	Seasons Played	Apps	Subs	Gls
Gillingham	Sch	08/07	07	3	2	0

HAMILTON Neville Roy
Born: Leicester, England, 19 April, 1960 — M
Died: Leicester, England, 9 February, 2009

League Club	Source	Date Signed	Seasons Played	Apps	Subs	Gls
Leicester C	App	11/77	77	4	0	0
Mansfield T	Tr	01/79	78-80	84	5	4
Rochdale	Tr	08/81	81-83	72	2	5

HAMILTON Robert Menzies (Bobby)
Born: Edinburgh, Scotland, 25 April, 1924 — RW
Died: Yeovil, Somerset, England, November, 1999

League Club	Source	Date Signed	Seasons Played	Apps	Subs	Gls
Chester C	Heart of Midlothian	11/45	46-47	68	-	10

HAMILTON William (Willie)
Born: Hamilton, Lanarkshire, Scotland, 1 September, 1918 — LH
Died: British Columbia, Canada, 4 December, 2009

League Club	Source	Date Signed	Seasons Played	Apps	Subs	Gls
Preston NE	Blantyre Victoria	09/37	46	37	-	0

HAMILTON William Murdoch (Willie)
Born: Chapelhall, Lanarkshire, Scotland, 16 February, 1938 — IF

League Club	Source	Date Signed	Seasons Played	Apps	Subs	Gls

Died: Calgary, Canada, 22 October, 1976
Scotland: 1/SLge-2

League Club	Source	Date Signed	Seasons Played	Apps	Subs	Gls
Sheffield U	Drumpellier Amats	02/56	56-60	79	-	21
Middlesbrough	Tr	02/61	60-61	10	-	1
Aston Villa	Hibernian	08/65	65-66	49	0	9

HAMILTON William Robert (Billy)
Born: Belfast, Northern Ireland, 9 May, 1957 — F
Northern Ireland: 41/U21-1

League Club	Source	Date Signed	Seasons Played	Apps	Subs	Gls
Queens Park Rgrs	Linfield	04/78	78-79	9	3	2
Burnley	Tr	11/79	79-83	200	0	58
Oxford U	Tr	08/84	84-86	32	0	12

HAMLET Alan Graham
Born: Watford, Hertfordshire, England, 30 September, 1977 — RB

League Club	Source	Date Signed	Seasons Played	Apps	Subs	Gls
Barnet	YT	07/96	94	3	0	0

HAMLETT Thomas Lawrence (Lol)
Born: Stoke-on-Trent, England, 24 January, 1917 — RB
Died: Stoke-on-Trent, England, 22 May, 1986

League Club	Source	Date Signed	Seasons Played	Apps	Subs	Gls
Bolton W	Congleton T	05/38	46-48	72	-	9
Port Vale	Tr	05/49	49-51	109	-	0

HAMMELL Connor Rhys
Born: Whitehaven, Cumbria, England, 27 September, 1996 — M

League Club	Source	Date Signed	Seasons Played	Apps	Subs	Gls
Carlisle U	Sch	05/15	14	0	3	0

HAMMELL Steven (Steve)
Born: Rutherglen, Glasgow, Scotland, 18 February, 1982 — LB
Scotland: 1/B-2/U21-11

League Club	Source	Date Signed	Seasons Played	Apps	Subs	Gls
Southend U	Motherwell	07/06	06-07	54	1	3

HAMMILL Adam James
Born: Liverpool, England, 25 January, 1988 — LB/LW
England: U21-1/Youth

League Club	Source	Date Signed	Seasons Played	Apps	Subs	Gls
Liverpool	Sch	01/06				
Southampton	L	07/07	07	12	13	0
Blackpool	L	07/08	08	14	8	1
Barnsley	L	02/09	08-10	65	13	13
Wolverhampton W	Tr	01/11	10-12	10	13	0
Middlesbrough	L	03/12	11	8	2	0
Huddersfield T	L	08/12	12	6	10	2
Huddersfield T	Tr	06/13	13-14	43	6	4
Rotherham U	L	01/15	14	4	10	0

HAMMILL John (Jack)
Born: Irvine, Ayrshire, Scotland, 8 January, 1924 — RH
Died: Irvine, Ayrshire, Scotland, 18 March, 1999

League Club	Source	Date Signed	Seasons Played	Apps	Subs	Gls
Newport Co	Arbroath	04/47	46-47	12	-	0

HAMMOND Albert William Arthur
Born: Hanwell, W London, England, 5 February, 1924 — IF
Died: Gravesend, Kent, England, 14 February, 1989

League Club	Source	Date Signed	Seasons Played	Apps	Subs	Gls
Brentford	Queens Park Rgrs (Am)	01/46				
Exeter C	Tr	06/46	46	2	-	0

HAMMOND Andrew Bendall (Andy)
Born: Rotherham, South Yorkshire, England, 21 November, 1978 — F

League Club	Source	Date Signed	Seasons Played	Apps	Subs	Gls
Doncaster Rov	YT	-	97	1	0	0

HAMMOND Cyril Samuel
Born: Woolwich, SE London, England, 10 February, 1927 — LH

League Club	Source	Date Signed	Seasons Played	Apps	Subs	Gls
Charlton Ath	Erith & Belvedere	04/46	50-57	201	-	2
Colchester U	Tr	07/58	58-60	95	-	5

HAMMOND Dean John
Born: Hastings, East Sussex, England, 7 March, 1983 — M

League Club	Source	Date Signed	Seasons Played	Apps	Subs	Gls
Brighton & HA	Sch	06/02	02-07	122	14	21
Leyton Orient	L	10/03	03	6	2	0
Colchester U	Tr	01/08	07-09	51	5	5
Southampton	Tr	08/09	09-11	111	13	10
Brighton & HA	L	08/12	12	31	6	2
Leicester C	Tr	08/13	13-14	16	25	1

HAMMOND Elvis Zark
Born: Accra, Ghana, 6 October, 1980 — F
Ghana: 1

League Club	Source	Date Signed	Seasons Played	Apps	Subs	Gls
Fulham	YT	07/99	02-04	3	8	0
Bristol Rov	L	08/01	01	3	4	0
Norwich C	L	08/03	03	0	4	0
Leicester C	Tr	08/05	05-06	32	32	8
Cheltenham T		11/08	08-09	31	15	9

HAMMOND Geoffrey (Geoff)
Born: Sudbury, Suffolk, England, 24 March, 1950 — RB

League Club	Source	Date Signed	Seasons Played	Apps	Subs	Gls
Ipswich T	Jnr	07/68	70-73	52	3	2
Manchester C	Tr	09/74	74-75	33	1	2
Charlton Ath	Tr	07/76	76	15	1	0

HAMMOND Nicholas David (Nicky)
Born: Hornchurch, E London, England, 7 September, 1967 — G

League Club	Source	Date Signed	Seasons Played	Apps	Subs	Gls
Arsenal	App	07/85				
Bristol Rov	L	08/86	86	3	0	0
Swindon T	Tr	07/87	87-94	65	2	0
Plymouth Arg	Tr	08/95	95	4	0	0
Reading	Tr	02/96	95-98	25	0	0

HAMMOND Paul Anthony
Born: Nottingham, England, 26 July, 1953 — G

League Club	Source	Date Signed	Seasons Played	Apps	Subs	Gls
Crystal Palace	App	07/71	72-76	117	0	0

HAMON Christopher Anthony (Chris)
Born: Jersey, Channel Islands, 27 April, 1970 — F

League Club	Source	Date Signed	Seasons Played	Apps	Subs	Gls
Swindon T	St Peter's, Jersey	07/92	92-94	3	5	1

HAMON James Charles
Born: Guernsey, Channel Islands, 1 July, 1995 — G

League Club	Source	Date Signed	Seasons Played	Apps	Subs	Gls
Exeter C	Guernsey FC	07/14	14	21	0	0

HAMPSHIRE Paul
Born: Guildford, Surrey, England, 10 October, 1961 — F

League Club	Source	Date Signed	Seasons Played	Apps	Subs	Gls
Aldershot	Jnr	06/79	80-81	4	1	2

HAMPSON Alan
Born: Prescot, Merseyside, England, 31 December, 1927 — IF
Died: Knowsley, Merseyside, England, August, 1989

League Club	Source	Date Signed	Seasons Played	Apps	Subs	Gls
Everton		08/49	50	1	-	0
Halifax T	Tr	11/52	52-55	121	-	32
Bradford C	Tr	07/56	56	6	-	4

HAMPSON Eric
Born: Hanley, Potteries, England, 11 November, 1921 — WH

League Club	Source	Date Signed	Seasons Played	Apps	Subs	Gls
Stoke C	Stafford Rgrs	05/39	48-51	8	-	0

HAMPSON Raymond Geoffrey (Ray)
Born: Manchester, England, 27 July, 1932 — RW

League Club	Source	Date Signed	Seasons Played	Apps	Subs	Gls
Manchester U	Jnr	04/51				
Reading	Tr	04/53				
Aldershot	Tr	07/55	55-56	21	-	2
Bournemouth	Tr	07/57	57-58	15	-	2

HAMPTON Derek
Born: Loftus, Cleveland, England, 25 April, 1952 — LW

League Club	Source	Date Signed	Seasons Played	Apps	Subs	Gls
Hartlepool U	Whitby T	11/79	79-81	66	8	18

HAMPTON Ivan Keith
Born: Kimberley, Nottinghamshire, England, 15 October, 1942 — RB

League Club	Source	Date Signed	Seasons Played	Apps	Subs	Gls
Notts Co	Rotherham U (Am)	03/61	60-66	139	2	1
Halifax T	Tr	07/67	67-68	57	2	2
Peterborough U	Tr	07/69	69	3	1	0

HAMPTON Peter John
Born: Oldham, Greater Manchester, England, 12 September, 1954 — LB
England: Youth

League Club	Source	Date Signed	Seasons Played	Apps	Subs	Gls
Leeds U	App	09/71	72-79	63	5	2
Stoke C	Tr	08/80	80-83	134	4	4
Burnley	Tr	08/84	84-86	116	2	2
Rochdale	Tr	08/87	87	19	0	1
Carlisle U	Tr	12/87	87	12	0	0

HAMSHAW Matthew Thomas (Matt)
Born: Rotherham, South Yorkshire, England, 1 January, 1982 — RW
England: Youth/Schools

League Club	Source	Date Signed	Seasons Played	Apps	Subs	Gls
Sheffield Wed	YT	01/99	00-04	35	39	2
Stockport Co	Tr	07/05	05	35	4	5
Mansfield T	Tr	07/06	06-07	83	2	6
Notts Co	Tr	07/08	08-09	41	20	3
Macclesfield T	Tr	07/10	10-11	48	18	4

HAMSHER John James
Born: Lambeth, S London, England, 14 January, 1978 — RB

League Club	Source	Date Signed	Seasons Played	Apps	Subs	Gls
Fulham	YT	07/96	95	0	3	0

HAMSON Gary
Born: Stapleford, Nottinghamshire, England, 24 August, 1959 — M

League Club	Source	Date Signed	Seasons Played	Apps	Subs	Gls
Sheffield U	App	11/76	76-78	107	1	8
Leeds U	Tr	07/79	79-85	126	8	3
Bristol C	Tr	07/86	86	12	0	2
Port Vale	Tr	12/86	86-87	36	2	3

HAMSTEAD George William
Born: Rotherham, South Yorkshire, England, 24 January, 1946 — LW

League Club	Source	Date Signed	Seasons Played	Apps	Subs	Gls
York C	Rotherham U (Am)	09/64	64-65	32	3	1
Barnsley	Tr	07/66	66-70	147	2	22
Bury	Tr	07/71	71-78	189	7	29
Rochdale	L	01/77	76	3	1	0

HANBY Robert James
Born: Pontefract, West Yorkshire, England, 24 December, 1974 — FB

League Club	Source	Date Signed	Seasons Played	Apps	Subs	Gls
Barnsley	YT	07/93				
Scarborough	Tr	08/96	96	1	3	0

HANCOCK Anthony Eric (Tony)
Born: Manchester, England, 31 January, 1967 F

League Club	Source	Date Signed	Seasons Played	Apps	Subs	Gls
Stockport Co	Stockport Georgians	12/88	88	12	10	5
Burnley	Tr	06/89	89	9	8	0
Preston NE	Tr	01/90				

HANCOCK Barry John
Born: Stoke-on-Trent, England, 30 December, 1938 IF
Died: Sneyd Green, Hanley, Potteries, England, 10 September, 2013

League Club	Source	Date Signed	Seasons Played	Apps	Subs	Gls
Port Vale	Birches Head	07/57	60-63	21	-	1
Crewe Alex	Tr	08/64	64	3	-	0

HANCOCK Charles Raymond
Born: Stoke-on-Trent, England, 16 February, 1925 G
Died: Stafford, England, April, 2007

League Club	Source	Date Signed	Seasons Played	Apps	Subs	Gls
Port Vale	Birches Head	05/48	48-55	50	-	0

HANCOCK David Jeffrey
Born: Exeter, England, 24 July, 1938 WH
Died: South Africa, July, 2007

League Club	Source	Date Signed	Seasons Played	Apps	Subs	Gls
Plymouth Arg	Jnr	09/55	56	2	-	0
Torquay U	Tr	01/59	58-63	177	-	11
Exeter C	Tr	03/64	63-64	40	-	3

HANCOCK Glynn Roy
Born: Biddulph, Staffordshire, England, 24 May, 1982 M

League Club	Source	Date Signed	Seasons Played	Apps	Subs	Gls
Stockport Co	YT	08/99	00-01	1	2	0

HANCOCK Kenneth Paul (Ken)
Born: Hanley, Potteries, England, 25 November, 1937 G

League Club	Source	Date Signed	Seasons Played	Apps	Subs	Gls
Port Vale	Stoke C (Am)	12/58	58-64	241	-	0
Ipswich T	Tr	12/64	64-68	163	0	0
Tottenham H	Tr	03/69	69-70	3	0	0
Bury	Tr	07/71	71-72	35	0	0

HANCOCK Michael (Mike)
Born: Newport, Wales, 17 February, 1954 CD
Wales: Schools

League Club	Source	Date Signed	Seasons Played	Apps	Subs	Gls
Newport Co	Cardiff College	01/72	71-75	51	9	1

HANCOCKS John (Johnny)
Born: Oakengates, Telford & Wrekin, England, 30 April, 1919 W
Died: Telford, England, 19 February, 1994
England: 3/FLge-2

League Club	Source	Date Signed	Seasons Played	Apps	Subs	Gls
Walsall	Oakengates T	08/38	38	30	-	9
Wolverhampton W	Tr	05/46	46-55	343	-	158

HANCOX David Thomas
Born: Conisbrough, South Yorkshire, England, 2 October, 1947 CF

League Club	Source	Date Signed	Seasons Played	Apps	Subs	Gls
Sheffield U	App	09/65				
Chester C	Tr	07/67	67	17	2	4

HANCOX Mitchell John (Mitch)
Born: Solihull, West Midlands, England, 9 November, 1993 LB

League Club	Source	Date Signed	Seasons Played	Apps	Subs	Gls
Birmingham C	Sch	07/12	12-13	25	8	0

HANCOX Paul Anthony
Born: Manchester, England, 22 July, 1970 M

League Club	Source	Date Signed	Seasons Played	Apps	Subs	Gls
Rochdale	YT	-	87	0	2	0

HANCOX Raymond (Ray)
Born: Mansfield, Nottinghamshire, England, 1 May, 1929 IF

League Club	Source	Date Signed	Seasons Played	Apps	Subs	Gls
Crystal Palace	Sutton U	08/50	50-52	20	-	3
Southend U	Tr	06/53				

HANCOX Richard James
Born: Wolverhampton, England, 4 October, 1970 F/W

League Club	Source	Date Signed	Seasons Played	Apps	Subs	Gls
Torquay U	Stourport Swifts	03/93	92-96	56	26	10
Torquay U	Taunton T	07/05	05	0	1	0

HAND Eoin Kevin Joseph Colin
Born: Dublin, Republic of Ireland, 30 March, 1946 CD
Republic of Ireland: 20/LoI-1

League Club	Source	Date Signed	Seasons Played	Apps	Subs	Gls
Swindon T	Drumcondra (ROI)	06/64				
Portsmouth	Drumcondra (ROI)	10/68	68-75	259	1	12
Portsmouth	Shamrock Rov (ROI)	12/77	77-78	15	2	2

HAND James Francis
Born: Monaghan, Republic of Ireland, 22 October, 1986 LW
Republic of Ireland: U21-5/Youth

League Club	Source	Date Signed	Seasons Played	Apps	Subs	Gls
Huddersfield T	Sch	07/06	06	0	1	0

HAND Jamie
Born: Uxbridge, W London, England, 7 February, 1984 M
England: Youth

League Club	Source	Date Signed	Seasons Played	Apps	Subs	Gls
Watford	Sch	04/02	01-03	40	15	0
Oxford U	L	08/04	04	11	0	0
Peterborough U	L	09/05	05	9	0	0
Northampton T	Tr	02/06	05	8	3	0
Chester C	Tr	07/06	06-07	43	1	2
Lincoln C	Tr	08/07	07	19	6	0

HANDFORD Philip Michael (Phil)
Born: Chatham, Kent, England, 18 July, 1964 M

League Club	Source	Date Signed	Seasons Played	Apps	Subs	Gls
Gillingham	App	07/82	82-83	29	3	1
Wimbledon	Tr	08/84	84	7	0	0
Crewe Alex	L	01/86	85	9	0	0

HANDLEY Brian
Born: Wakefield, England, 21 June, 1936 CF
Died: Hemsworth, West Yorkshire, England, 5 March, 1982

League Club	Source	Date Signed	Seasons Played	Apps	Subs	Gls
Aston Villa	Goole T	09/57	59	3	-	0
Torquay U	Tr	09/60	60-63	80	-	32
Rochdale	Bridgwater T	02/66	65	3	0	0

HANDSCOMBE Malcolm (Mal)
Born: Normanton, West Yorkshire, England, 29 June, 1934 CH

League Club	Source	Date Signed	Seasons Played	Apps	Subs	Gls
Chester C (Am)		05/57	57	4	-	0

HANDYSIDE Peter David
Born: Dumfries, Scotland, 31 July, 1974 CD
Scotland: U21-7

League Club	Source	Date Signed	Seasons Played	Apps	Subs	Gls
Grimsby T	YT	11/92	92-00	181	9	4
Stoke C	Tr	07/01	01-02	78	0	0
Barnsley	Tr	08/03	03	28	0	0

HANDYSIDES Ian Robert
Born: Jarrow, Tyne and Wear, England, 14 December, 1962 W/M
Died: Solihull, West Midlands, England, 17 August, 1990
England: Youth

League Club	Source	Date Signed	Seasons Played	Apps	Subs	Gls
Birmingham C	App	01/80	80-83	44	18	2
Walsall	Tr	01/84	83-85	58	8	11
Birmingham C	Tr	03/86	85-87	53	3	4
Wolverhampton W	L	09/86	86	11	0	2

HANFORD Daniel James
Born: Swansea, Wales, 6 March, 1991 G

League Club	Source	Date Signed	Seasons Played	Apps	Subs	Gls
Carlisle U	Floriana (MLT)	07/14	14	25	0	0

HANFORD Harold (Harry)
Born: Blaengwynfi, Neath Port Talbot, Wales, 9 October, 1907 CH
Died: Melbourne, Australia, 26 November, 1995
Wales: 7/WLge-1/Schools

League Club	Source	Date Signed	Seasons Played	Apps	Subs	Gls
Swansea C	Blaengwynfi Jnrs	05/26	27-35	201	-	0
Sheffield Wed	Tr	02/36	35-38	85	-	1
Exeter C	Tr	05/46	46	36	-	0

HANGELAND Brede Paulsen
Born: Houston, Texas, USA, 20 June, 1981 CD
Norway: 91/U21-12

League Club	Source	Date Signed	Seasons Played	Apps	Subs	Gls
Fulham	FC Copenhagen (DEN)	01/08	07-13	217	0	8
Crystal Palace	Tr	08/14	14	12	2	2

HANKEY Albert Edward (Ted)
Born: Stoke-on-Trent, England, 24 May, 1914 G
Died: Portsmouth, England, September, 1998

League Club	Source	Date Signed	Seasons Played	Apps	Subs	Gls
Southend U	Royal Artillery	10/37	37-49	125	-	0

HANKEY Dean Anthony
Born: Sutton-in-Ashfield, Nottinghamshire, England, 23 August, 1986 M

League Club	Source	Date Signed	Seasons Played	Apps	Subs	Gls
Mansfield T	Sch	-	02	0	1	0

HANKIN Raymond (Ray)
Born: Wallsend, Tyne and Wear, England, 21 February, 1956 F
England: U23-3/Youth

League Club	Source	Date Signed	Seasons Played	Apps	Subs	Gls
Burnley	App	02/73	72-76	110	2	37
Leeds U	Tr	09/76	76-79	82	1	32
Arsenal	Vancouver W'caps (CAN)	11/81				
Middlesbrough	Vancouver W'caps (CAN)	09/82	82	19	2	1
Peterborough U	Tr	09/83	83-84	31	2	8
Wolverhampton W	Tr	03/85	84	9	1	1

HANKIN Sean Anthony
Born: Camberley, Surrey, England, 28 February, 1981 LB

League Club	Source	Date Signed	Seasons Played	Apps	Subs	Gls
Crystal Palace	YT	06/99	99	0	1	0
Torquay U	Tr	10/01	01-03	45	2	1

HANKINSON James (Jim)
Born: Preston, Lancashire, England, 1 July, 1928 IF

League Club	Source	Date Signed	Seasons Played	Apps	Subs	Gls
Preston NE	Lancaster C	09/47				
Chester C	Tr	06/50	50	15	-	1

HANKS Joseph Peter (Joe)
Born: Churchdown, Gloucestershire, England, 2 March, 1995 M

League Club	Source	Date Signed	Seasons Played	Apps	Subs	Gls
Cheltenham T	Sch	07/13	12-14	17	19	2

HANLEY Grant Campbell
Born: Dumfries, Scotland, 20 November, 1991 CD

Scotland: 17/U21-1/Youth

League Club	Source	Date Signed	Seasons Played	Apps	Subs	Gls
Blackburn Rov	Sch	11/08	09-14	129	10	5

HANLON John James (Jimmy)
Born: Manchester, England, 12 October, 1917 — IF
Died: Trafford, Greater Manchester, England, January, 2002

League Club	Source	Date Signed	Seasons Played	Apps	Subs	Gls
Manchester U	St Wilfrid's, Hulme	11/35	38-48	63	-	20
Bury	Tr	10/48	48-49	31	-	1

HANLON Richard Kenneth (Richie)
Born: Kenton, NW London, England, 26 May, 1978 — M

League Club	Source	Date Signed	Seasons Played	Apps	Subs	Gls
Southend U	Chelsea (YT)	07/96	96	1	1	0
Peterborough U	Rushden & D	12/98	98	0	4	1
Peterborough U	Welling U	12/99	99-01	30	13	2
Rushden & D	Tr	09/01	01-03	51	11	7
Lincoln C	Stevenage Bor	12/04	04	6	6	1

HANLON Stephen Henry (Steve)
Born: Chester, England, 18 July, 1963 — M

League Club	Source	Date Signed	Seasons Played	Apps	Subs	Gls
Crewe Alex	App	07/81	80-82	23	4	0

HANLON Walter Andrew (Wally)
Born: Glasgow, Scotland, 23 September, 1919 — LW
Died: Poole, Dorset, England, 23 April, 1999

League Club	Source	Date Signed	Seasons Played	Apps	Subs	Gls
Brighton & HA	Clyde	08/46	46-47	72	-	4
Bournemouth	Tr	05/48	48	19	-	3
Crystal Palace	Tr	07/48	49-54	126	-	8

HANMER Gareth Craig (Gary)
Born: Shrewsbury, Shropshire, England, 12 October, 1973 — LB

League Club	Source	Date Signed	Seasons Played	Apps	Subs	Gls
West Bromwich A	Newtown	06/96				
Shrewsbury T	Tr	07/97	97-00	134	6	1

HANN Matthew
Born: Saffron Walden, Essex, England, 6 September, 1980 — W

League Club	Source	Date Signed	Seasons Played	Apps	Subs	Gls
Peterborough U	YT	01/99	98	0	4	0

HANN Ralph
Born: Whitburn, Tyne and Wear, England, 4 July, 1911 — CH
Died: Littleover, Derbyshire, England, 17 July, 1990

League Club	Source	Date Signed	Seasons Played	Apps	Subs	Gls
Sunderland	Whitburn St Mary's	12/29				
Newcastle U	Tr	08/30				
Derby Co	Tr	03/32	32-38	115	-	0
Crystal Palace	Tr	04/47	46	1	-	0

HANNABY Cyril
Born: Doncaster, South Yorkshire, England, 11 October, 1923 — G
Died: Maryland, USA, 26 February, 2010

League Club	Source	Date Signed	Seasons Played	Apps	Subs	Gls
Wolverhampton W	Wath W	03/44				
Hull C	Tr	08/46	46-47	17	-	0
Halifax T	Tr	02/48	47	2	-	0

HANNAH David
Born: Coatbridge, Lanarkshire, Scotland, 4 August, 1974 — M
Scotland: U21-16

League Club	Source	Date Signed	Seasons Played	Apps	Subs	Gls
Bury (L)	St Johnstone	02/06	05	1	1	0

HANNAH George
Born: Liverpool, England, 11 December, 1928 — IF
Died: Manchester, England, 5 May, 1990
Northern Ireland: NILge-1

League Club	Source	Date Signed	Seasons Played	Apps	Subs	Gls
Newcastle U	Linfield	09/49	49-56	167	-	41
Lincoln C	Tr	09/57	57-58	38	-	4
Manchester C	Tr	09/58	58-63	114	-	15
Notts Co	Tr	07/64	64-65	25	0	1
Bradford C	Tr	10/65	65	29	1	2

HANNAH John
Born: Wakefield, England, 25 October, 1962 — F

League Club	Source	Date Signed	Seasons Played	Apps	Subs	Gls
Darlington	Fryston CW	10/83	83-84	15	7	8

HANNAH Ross
Born: Sheffield, England, 14 May, 1986 — F

League Club	Source	Date Signed	Seasons Played	Apps	Subs	Gls
Bradford C	Matlock T	05/11	11-12	4	15	2

HANNAH William King (Willie)
Born: Shotts, Lanarkshire, Scotland, 6 August, 1921 — LW
Died: Preston, Lancashire, England, September, 1978

League Club	Source	Date Signed	Seasons Played	Apps	Subs	Gls
Preston NE	Albion Rov	12/47	47-49	15	-	4
Barrow	Tr	02/51	50-53	106	-	16

HANNAM David Vincent
Born: Islington, N London, England, 10 May, 1944 — RW

League Club	Source	Date Signed	Seasons Played	Apps	Subs	Gls
Brighton & HA	Jnr	06/61	62	5	-	2

HANNAWAY Jack
Born: Bootle, Merseyside, England, 22 October, 1927 — FB/WH
Died: Liverpool, England, 2 July, 2007

League Club	Source	Date Signed	Seasons Played	Apps	Subs	Gls
Manchester C	Seaforth Fellowship	04/50	51-56	64	-	0
Gillingham	Tr	06/57	57-59	126	-	4
Southport	Tr	06/60	60-61	73	-	2

HANNIGAN Al James
Born: Islington, N London, England, 26 January, 1971 — CD

League Club	Source	Date Signed	Seasons Played	Apps	Subs	Gls
Arsenal	YT	03/89				
Torquay U	L	03/90	89	5	2	0

HANNIGAN Brendan
Born: Dublin, Republic of Ireland, 3 September, 1943 — IF
Republic of Ireland: LoI-2

League Club	Source	Date Signed	Seasons Played	Apps	Subs	Gls
Wrexham	Shelbourne (ROI)	12/65	65	7	0	2

HANNIGAN Ernest (Ernie)
Born: Glasgow, Scotland, 23 January, 1943 — RW
Died: Perth, Australia, 21 May, 2015

League Club	Source	Date Signed	Seasons Played	Apps	Subs	Gls
Preston NE	Queen of the South	08/64	64-67	97	0	28
Coventry C	Tr	11/67	67-69	43	4	6
Torquay U	L	12/69	69	2	0	0

HANNIGAN John Leckie (Johnny)
Born: Barrhead, Renfrewshire, Scotland, 17 February, 1933 — W/F

League Club	Source	Date Signed	Seasons Played	Apps	Subs	Gls
Sunderland	Greenock Morton	07/55	55-57	33	-	8
Derby Co	Tr	05/58	58-60	72	-	19
Bradford Park Ave	Tr	06/61	61-63	96	-	26

HANNON Kevin Michael
Born: Prescot, Merseyside, England, 4 May, 1980 — CD

League Club	Source	Date Signed	Seasons Played	Apps	Subs	Gls
Wrexham	YT	05/99	99	0	1	0

HANSBURY Roger
Born: Barnsley, South Yorkshire, England, 26 January, 1955 — G

League Club	Source	Date Signed	Seasons Played	Apps	Subs	Gls
Norwich C	App	01/73	74-80	78	0	0
Cambridge U	L	11/77	77	11	0	0
Burnley	Eastern AA (HKG)	08/83	83-84	83	0	0
Cambridge U	Tr	07/85	85	37	0	0
Birmingham C	Tr	03/86	86-89	57	0	0
Sheffield U	L	10/87	87	5	0	0
Wolverhampton W	L	03/89	88	3	0	0
Colchester U	L	08/89	89	4	0	0
Cardiff C	Tr	10/89	89-91	99	0	0

HANSELL Ronald Arthur Robert (Ron)
Born: Norwich, England, 3 October, 1930 — IF
Died: Caistor, Norfolk, England, 8 February, 2013

League Club	Source	Date Signed	Seasons Played	Apps	Subs	Gls
Norwich C	Norwich St Barnabas	06/50	53-55	29	-	7
Chester C	Tr	06/56	56	36	-	9

HANSEN Alan David
Born: Alloa, Stirlingshire, Scotland, 13 June, 1955 — CD
Scotland: 26/U23-3

League Club	Source	Date Signed	Seasons Played	Apps	Subs	Gls
Liverpool	Partick Thistle	04/77	77-89	434	0	8

HANSEN Bo Jannik Nyby
Born: Holstebro, Denmark, 16 June, 1972 — F
Denmark: 22

League Club	Source	Date Signed	Seasons Played	Apps	Subs	Gls
Bolton W	Brondby (DEN)	02/99	98-01	64	32	15

HANSEN Edwin
Born: Koge, Denmark, 21 January, 1920 — IF

League Club	Source	Date Signed	Seasons Played	Apps	Subs	Gls
Grimsby T (Am)	Koge KB (DEN)	12/46	46	1	-	0

HANSEN John Schnabel
Born: Mannheim, Germany, 14 September, 1973 — M

League Club	Source	Date Signed	Seasons Played	Apps	Subs	Gls
Cambridge U	Esbjerg (DEN)	02/00	99-00	19	9	3

HANSEN Karl Aage
Born: Copenhagen, Denmark, 4 July, 1921 — IF
Died: Denmark, 23 November, 1990

League Club	Source	Date Signed	Seasons Played	Apps	Subs	Gls
Huddersfield T (Am)	Akademisk BK (DEN)	01/49	48	15	-	2

HANSEN Martin
Born: Glostrup, Denmark, 15 June, 1990 — G
Denmark: U21-1/Youth

League Club	Source	Date Signed	Seasons Played	Apps	Subs	Gls
Liverpool	Sch	07/07				
Bradford C	L	07/11	11	4	0	0

HANSEN Vegard
Born: Drammen, Norway, 8 August, 1969 — RB

League Club	Source	Date Signed	Seasons Played	Apps	Subs	Gls
Bristol C	Stromgodset (NOR)	11/94	94-95	36	1	0

HANSON Christian
Born: Middlesbrough, England, 3 August, 1981 — CD
England: Youth/Schools

League Club	Source	Date Signed	Seasons Played	Apps	Subs	Gls
Middlesbrough	YT	08/98				
Cambridge U	L	03/01	00	8	0	0
Torquay U	L	11/01	01	6	0	0
Port Vale	Spennymoor U	12/04	04	3	2	0
Leyton Orient	Billingham Synthonia	10/05	05	0	2	0

HANSON David Paul (Dave)
Born: Huddersfield, West Yorkshire, England, 19 November, 1968 — F

League Club	Source	Date Signed	Seasons Played	Apps	Subs	Gls
Bury	Farsley Celtic	07/93	93	1	0	0

League Club	Source	Date Signed	Seasons Played	Apps	Subs	Gls
Leyton Orient	Hednesford T	10/95	95-97	26	22	5
Chesterfield	L	03/97	96	3	0	1
Halifax T	Tr	01/98	98	19	12	2

HANSON Frederick (Fred)
Born: Sheffield, England, 23 May, 1915 — LW
Died: Rotherham, South Yorkshire, England, 1967

League Club	Source	Date Signed	Seasons Played	Apps	Subs	Gls
Sheffield U	Indus Sports	05/33				
Bradford C	Tr	05/34				
Wolverhampton W	Tr	01/35				
Crystal Palace	Tr	05/35	35	1	-	0
Rotherham U	Tr	03/36	36-46	106	-	29

HANSON James Robert
Born: Bradford, England, 9 November, 1987 — F

League Club	Source	Date Signed	Seasons Played	Apps	Subs	Gls
Bradford C	Guiseley	08/09	09-14	204	21	62

HANSON James William (Jamie)
Born: Burton on Trent, Staffordshire, England, 10 November, 1995 — DM

League Club	Source	Date Signed	Seasons Played	Apps	Subs	Gls
Derby Co	Sch	03/13	14	2	0	0

HANSON John
Born: Bradford, England, 3 December, 1962 — F

League Club	Source	Date Signed	Seasons Played	Apps	Subs	Gls
Bradford C	App	12/80	80	1	0	0

HANSON Mitchell Gene Ben
Born: Derby, England, 2 September, 1988 — RB

League Club	Source	Date Signed	Seasons Played	Apps	Subs	Gls
Derby Co	Sch	07/07				
Notts Co	L	11/08	08	5	0	0
Oxford U	Tr	02/11	10	0	2	0

HANSON Neil
Born: Blackburn, Greater Manchester, England, 16 June, 1964 — F

League Club	Source	Date Signed	Seasons Played	Apps	Subs	Gls
Preston NE	App	09/81				
Halifax T	Tr	08/83	83	1	1	0

HANSON Stanley (Stan)
Born: Bootle, Merseyside, England, 27 December, 1915 — G
Died: Bolton, Greater Manchester, England, 24 November, 1987

League Club	Source	Date Signed	Seasons Played	Apps	Subs	Gls
Bolton W	Litherland	10/35	36-55	384	-	0

HANSSON Mikael
Born: Norrkoping, Sweden, 15 March, 1968 — RB
Sweden: 1

League Club	Source	Date Signed	Seasons Played	Apps	Subs	Gls
Stoke C	Norrkoping (SWE)	12/99	99-00	60	5	2

HANVEY Keith
Born: Manchester, England, 18 January, 1952 — D

League Club	Source	Date Signed	Seasons Played	Apps	Subs	Gls
Manchester C	Jnr	08/71				
Swansea C	Tr	07/72	72	11	0	0
Rochdale	Tr	07/73	73-76	121	0	10
Grimsby T	Tr	02/77	76-77	54	0	2
Huddersfield T	Tr	07/78	78-83	205	0	14
Rochdale	Tr	07/84	84	15	0	0

HAPGOOD Edris Anthony (Tony)
Born: Kettering, Northamptonshire, England, 13 June, 1930 — RW
Died: Blackburn, Greater Manchester, England, 1 September, 2011

League Club	Source	Date Signed	Seasons Played	Apps	Subs	Gls
Burnley	Jnr	03/48	51	7	-	2
Watford	Tr	07/53	53	1	-	0

HAPGOOD Leon Duane
Born: Torquay, Devon, England, 7 August, 1979 — M

League Club	Source	Date Signed	Seasons Played	Apps	Subs	Gls
Torquay U	YT	05/98	96-98	26	14	3
Torquay U	Clevedon T	01/07	06	0	1	0

HARBACH Peter Colin
Born: Carlisle, Cumbria, England, 30 April, 1967 — F

League Club	Source	Date Signed	Seasons Played	Apps	Subs	Gls
Newcastle U	App	04/85				
Carlisle U	Tr	08/87	87	0	7	0

HARBAN Thomas John (Tom)
Born: Barnsley, South Yorkshire, England, 12 November, 1985 — RB
England: Youth

League Club	Source	Date Signed	Seasons Played	Apps	Subs	Gls
Barnsley	Sch	07/05				
Bradford C	L	07/07	07	6	0	0

HARBER William Hudson (Billy)
Born: Hitchin, Hertfordshire, England, 3 December, 1944 — W

League Club	Source	Date Signed	Seasons Played	Apps	Subs	Gls
Swindon T	App	12/61	62	2	-	0
Luton T	Tr	09/64	64-65	28	0	3

HARBERTSON Ronald (Ron)
Born: Redcar, Cleveland, England, 23 December, 1929 — IF

League Club	Source	Date Signed	Seasons Played	Apps	Subs	Gls
Newcastle U	North Shields	01/49				
Bradford C	Tr	08/50	50	16	-	1
Brighton & HA	Tr	10/51				
Bradford C	Tr	05/52	53	13	-	3
Grimsby T	Tr	07/54	54	26	-	6
Darlington	Ashington	01/57	56-57	49	-	21
Lincoln C	Tr	03/58	57-59	57	-	22
Wrexham	Tr	03/60	59-60	28	-	13
Darlington	Tr	01/61	60	14	-	2
Lincoln C	Tr	07/61	61	29	-	3

HARBEY Graham Keith
Born: Chesterfield, Derbyshire, England, 29 August, 1964 — LB

League Club	Source	Date Signed	Seasons Played	Apps	Subs	Gls
Derby Co	App	08/82	83-86	35	5	1
Ipswich T	Tr	07/87	87-89	53	6	1
West Bromwich A	Tr	11/89	89-91	97	0	2
Stoke C	Tr	07/92	92-93	18	1	0

HARBOTTLE Mark Stuart
Born: Nottingham, England, 26 September, 1968 — F
England: Youth

League Club	Source	Date Signed	Seasons Played	Apps	Subs	Gls
Notts Co	App	09/86	85	1	3	1
Doncaster Rov	L	01/88	87	4	0	0

HARBURN Peter Arthur Patrick
Born: Shoreditch, Central London, England, 18 June, 1931 — CF
Died: Great Baddow, Essex, England, 13 March, 2010

League Club	Source	Date Signed	Seasons Played	Apps	Subs	Gls
Brighton & HA	Royal Navy	07/54	54-57	126	-	61
Everton	Tr	08/58	58	4	-	1
Scunthorpe U	Tr	01/59	58-59	20	-	8
Workington	Tr	10/59	59-60	67	-	23

HARBURN William Nicholson
Born: Stockton-on-Tees, Cleveland, England, 19 November, 1923 — CF
Died: Melbourne, Australia, October, 1970

League Club	Source	Date Signed	Seasons Played	Apps	Subs	Gls
Darlington (Am)	South Bank	06/47	47	1	-	0

HARBY Michael John (Mick)
Born: Nottingham, England, 7 November, 1948 — G

League Club	Source	Date Signed	Seasons Played	Apps	Subs	Gls
Nottingham F	Jnr	07/66	67	3	0	0

HARDCASTLE Cyril
Born: Halifax, West Yorkshire, England, 22 November, 1919 — CF
Died: Halifax, West Yorkshire, England, 13 July, 1982

League Club	Source	Date Signed	Seasons Played	Apps	Subs	Gls
Bradford C (Am)		09/48	48	4	-	1

HARDCASTLE Peter David
Born: Leeds, England, 27 January, 1949 — RB/M
England: Amateur-4/Schools

League Club	Source	Date Signed	Seasons Played	Apps	Subs	Gls
Blackpool	Skelmersdale U	07/71	71-73	29	7	0
Plymouth Arg	Tr	07/74	74-75	12	2	1
Bradford C	Tr	07/76	76-77	62	0	1

HARDEN Leo
Born: Hartlepool, Cleveland, England, 7 May, 1923 — LW
Died: Hartlepool, Cleveland, England, 5 December, 1999

League Club	Source	Date Signed	Seasons Played	Apps	Subs	Gls
Hartlepool U	Railway Ath	05/46	46-55	169	-	47

HARDIE John Clarke
Born: Edinburgh, Scotland, 7 February, 1938 — G

League Club	Source	Date Signed	Seasons Played	Apps	Subs	Gls
Oldham Ath	Falkirk	07/60	60	17	-	0
Chester C	Tr	07/61	61-62	84	-	0
Bradford Park Ave	Tr	12/63	63-69	265	0	0
Crystal Palace	Tr	08/70				

HARDIKER John David
Born: Preston, Lancashire, England, 17 July, 1982 — D/M

League Club	Source	Date Signed	Seasons Played	Apps	Subs	Gls
Stockport Co	Morecambe	01/02	01-04	94	9	3
Bury	Tr	07/05	05	11	0	0

HARDING Alan
Born: Sunderland, England, 14 May, 1948 — LW/M

League Club	Source	Date Signed	Seasons Played	Apps	Subs	Gls
Darlington	Spennymoor U	01/70	69-72	125	4	37
Lincoln C	Tr	03/73	72-78	203	6	38
Hartlepool U	Tr	03/79	78-82	79	5	8

HARDING Benjamin Scott (Ben)
Born: Carshalton, S London, England, 6 September, 1984 — M
England: Semi Pro-3/Youth

League Club	Source	Date Signed	Seasons Played	Apps	Subs	Gls
Wimbledon	YT	10/01	03	10	5	0
MK Dons	Wimbledon relocation	07/04	04-05	29	7	6
Aldershot T	Tr	08/07	08-10	86	11	6
Wycombe W	Tr	07/11	11	3	4	0
Northampton T	Tr	01/12	11-12	54	0	2
Torquay U	Tr	07/13	13	16	1	0

HARDING Daniel Andrew (Dan)
Born: Gloucester, England, 23 December, 1983 — LB
England: U21-4

League Club	Source	Date Signed	Seasons Played	Apps	Subs	Gls
Brighton & HA	Sch	07/03	02-04	56	11	1
Leeds U	Tr	07/05	05	20	0	0
Ipswich T	Tr	08/06	06-08	70	3	1
Southend U	L	08/08	08	19	0	1
Reading	L	01/09	08	3	0	0
Southampton	Tr	07/09	09-11	89	9	4
Nottingham F	Tr	07/12	12-14	45	9	0
Millwall	L	01/15	14	20	0	0

League Club	Source	Date Signed	Seasons Played	Apps	Subs	Gls
HARDING David						
Born: Liverpool, England, 14 August, 1946						F
Australia: 45						
Wrexham		09/65	65	9	1	0
HARDING Edward James (Ted)						
Born: Croydon, S London, England, 5 April, 1925						RB
Crystal Palace	Coalville	11/44	46-52	151	-	0
HARDING Kevin						
Born: Isleworth, W London, England, 19 March, 1957						M/RB
Brentford	App	-	73-74	8	0	0
HARDING Mitchell Peter (Mitch)						
Born: Weston-super-Mare, Somerset, England, 27 January, 1994						W
Bristol Rov	Sch	06/12	11-13	5	12	0
HARDING Paul John						
Born: Mitcham, S London, England, 6 March, 1964						M
Notts Co	Barnet	09/90	90-92	45	9	1
Southend U	L	08/93	93	2	3	0
Watford	L	11/93	93	1	1	0
Birmingham C	Tr	12/93	93-94	19	3	0
Cardiff C	Tr	08/95	95	36	0	0
HARDING Stephen John (Steve)						
Born: Bristol, England, 23 July, 1956						CD
Bristol C	App	07/74	75	2	0	0
Southend U	L	01/76	75	2	0	0
Grimsby T	L	09/76	76	8	0	0
Bristol Rov	Tr	06/77	77-79	37	1	1
Brentford	L	01/80	79	3	1	0
HARDING William (Billy)						
Born: Carshalton, S London, England, 20 January, 1985						F
Wycombe W	Sch	-	03	0	2	0
HARDISTY John Roderick Elliott (Bob)						
Born: Chester-le-Street, County Durham, England, 1 February, 1921						IF
Died: Bishop Auckland, County Durham, England, 31 October, 1986						
England: Amateur-16						
Darlington (Am)	Bishop Auckland	12/46	46-48	6	-	0
HARDMAN Colin Arthur						
Born: Altrincham, Greater Manchester, England, 13 November, 1955						W
Stockport Co		03/76	75-76	6	3	1
HARDMAN John Alan						
Born: Bury, Greater Manchester, England, 17 December, 1940						D
Died: Bury, Greater Manchester, England, March, 1998						
Rochdale	Bess's Boys	08/60	60-66	40	0	2
HARDMAN Lewis Terence						
Born: Middlesbrough, England, 25 March, 1989						RB
Darlington	Sch	07/07	06	0	1	0
HARDS Neil Andrew						
Born: Portsmouth, England, 28 January, 1962						G
Plymouth Arg	App	01/80	79-82	6	0	0
HARDSTAFF Cecil						
Born: Crewe, Cheshire, England, 14 November, 1931						RB
Crewe Alex	Wolverhampton W (Am)	06/49	49	1	-	0
HARDWICK George Francis Moutry						
Born: Saltburn, Cleveland, England, 2 February, 1920						LB
Died: Stockton-on-Tees, Cleveland, England, 19 April, 2004						
England: 13/FLge-3/War-17						
Middlesbrough	South Bank East End	04/37	37-50	143	-	5
Oldham Ath	Tr	11/50	50-55	190	-	14
HARDWICK Kenneth (Ken)						
Born: West Auckland, County Durham, England, 27 January, 1924						G
Died: Doncaster, South Yorkshire, England, 1983						
Doncaster Rov	Rossington Main	04/45	47-56	307	-	0
Scunthorpe U	Tr	04/57	56-59	96	-	0
Barrow	Tr	12/59	59	12	-	0
HARDWICK Steven (Steve)						
Born: Mansfield, Nottinghamshire, England, 6 September, 1956						G
England: Youth						
Chesterfield	Jnr	07/74	74-76	38	0	0
Newcastle U	Tr	12/76	77-82	92	0	0
Oxford U	Tr	02/83	82-87	156	0	0
Crystal Palace	L	03/86	85	3	0	0
Sunderland	L	08/87	87	6	0	0
Huddersfield T	Tr	07/88	88-90	109	0	0
HARDY Aaron						
Born: South Elmsall, West Yorkshire, England, 26 May, 1986						RB
Huddersfield T	Sch	07/05	06-07	10	5	0

League Club	Source	Date Signed	Seasons Played	Apps	Subs	Gls
HARDY Edwin Malcolm						
Born: Chesterfield, Derbyshire, England, 16 October, 1953						G
Chesterfield	Jnr	08/71	72	6	0	0
HARDY Gordon Douglas (Bob)						
Born: Kingston-on-Thames, SW London, England, 23 May, 1923						CH
Died: East Dorset, England, November, 2003						
Millwall	Brodsworth Main	08/45	46	3	-	0
Southport	Tr	07/48	48-49	16	-	0
Bournemouth	Tr	06/50	51-53	76	-	0
HARDY Herbert Thomas						
Born: Barrow, Cumbria, England, 6 December, 1929						CF
Died: North Yorkshire, England, August, 2014						
Barrow		03/52	51	2	-	1
HARDY Jason Paul						
Born: Burnley, Lancashire, England, 14 December, 1969						LB
Burnley	YT	07/88	86-91	38	5	1
Halifax T	L	01/92	91	0	4	0
Halifax T	Tr	07/92	92	20	2	2
Rochdale	Prestwich Heys	08/95	95	5	2	0
HARDY John Henry (Jack)						
Born: Chesterfield, Derbyshire, England, 15 June, 1910						LH
Died: Lincoln, England, 1978						
Chesterfield	Unstone	12/34	34-36	48	-	1
Hull C	Tr	07/37	37-38	65	-	0
Lincoln C	Tr	05/39	46	18	-	0
HARDY Lee						
Born: Blackpool, Lancashire, England, 26 November, 1981						M
Blackburn Rov	YT	07/00				
Oldham Ath	Tr	07/01	01	0	1	0
Macclesfield T	Tr	07/02	02	8	8	0
HARDY Neil John Paul						
Born: Bury, Greater Manchester, England, 29 December, 1973						F
Stockport Co	Radcliffe Bor	06/01	01	4	6	2
HARDY Paul Alan						
Born: Plymouth, England, 29 August, 1975						M
Torquay U	YT	08/93	93	0	1	0
HARDY Philip (Phil)						
Born: Ellesmere Port, Cheshire, England, 9 April, 1973						LB
Republic of Ireland: U21-9						
Wrexham	YT	11/90	89-00	346	3	1
Port Vale	Tr	07/01	01	8	0	1
HARDY Robin						
Born: Worksop, Nottinghamshire, England, 18 January, 1941						WH
Sheffield Wed	Jnr	02/58	61-63	30	-	1
Rotherham U	Tr	02/65	64-65	42	0	2
Cambridge U	Tr	08/67	70	15	1	1
HARDY William						
Born: Whitehaven, Cumbria, England, 23 August, 1929						WH
Died: Whitehaven, Cumbria, England, April, 2003						
Workington	Queen of the South	10/51	51-53	55	-	2
HARDYMAN Paul George						
Born: Portsmouth, England, 11 March, 1964						LB
England: U21-2						
Portsmouth	Waterlooville	07/83	83-88	113	4	3
Sunderland	Tr	07/89	89-91	101	5	9
Bristol Rov	Tr	08/92	92-94	54	13	5
Wycombe W	Tr	08/95	95	12	3	0
Barnet	Tr	08/96	96	13	3	2
HARE Joshua Darren (Josh)						
Born: Canterbury, England, 12 August, 1994						CD
Gillingham	Sch	11/12	14	2	0	0
HARE Mathew (Matt)						
Born: Barnstaple, Devon, England, 26 December, 1976						M/D
Exeter C	YT	08/95	95-97	31	14	1
HARE Thomas (Tommy)						
Born: Motherwell, Lanarkshire, Scotland, 1 April, 1944						RB
Southampton	Fauldhouse U	04/63	65	13	0	0
Luton T	Tr	07/67	67	12	0	0
HAREIDE Aage Fridtjof						
Born: Hareid, Norway, 23 September, 1953						M/D
Norway: 50						
Manchester C	Molde FK (NOR)	10/81	81-82	17	7	0
Norwich C	L	11/82	82	12	0	0
Norwich C	Tr	09/83	83	26	2	2

League Club	Source	Date Signed	Seasons Played	Apps	Subs	Gls

HAREWOOD Marlon Anderson
Born: Hampstead, NW London, England, 25 August, 1979 — F

League Club	Source	Date Signed	Seasons Played	Apps	Subs	Gls
Nottingham F	YT	09/96	97-03	124	58	51
Ipswich T	L	01/99	98	5	1	1
West Ham U	Tr	11/03	03-06	123	19	47
Aston Villa	Tr	07/07	07-08	1	28	5
Wolverhampton W	L	03/09	08	2	3	0
Newcastle U	L	09/09	09	9	6	5
Blackpool	Tr	08/10	10	7	9	5
Barnsley	L	02/11	10	9	1	4
Nottingham F	Guangzhou (CHN)	01/12	11	4	0	0
Barnsley	Tr	08/12	12	17	15	2
Bristol C	Tr	08/13	13	0	12	1
Hartlepool U	Tr	01/14	13-14	33	20	6

HARFIELD Leslie Philip (Les)
Born: Southampton, England, 22 November, 1952 — W
England: Youth/Schools

League Club	Source	Date Signed	Seasons Played	Apps	Subs	Gls
Southampton	App	11/69	70	2	0	1
Luton T	Tr	09/72	72	0	1	0

HARFORD Michael Gordon (Mick)
Born: Sunderland, England, 12 February, 1959 — F
England: 2/B-1

League Club	Source	Date Signed	Seasons Played	Apps	Subs	Gls
Lincoln C	Lambton Street BC	07/77	77-80	109	6	41
Newcastle U	Tr	12/80	80	18	1	4
Bristol C	Tr	08/81	81	30	0	11
Birmingham C	Tr	03/82	81-84	92	0	25
Luton T	Tr	12/84	84-89	135	4	58
Derby Co	Tr	01/90	89-91	58	0	15
Luton T	Tr	09/91	91	29	0	12
Chelsea	Tr	08/92	92	27	1	9
Sunderland	Tr	03/93	92	10	1	2
Coventry C	Tr	07/93	93	0	1	1
Wimbledon	Tr	08/94	94-96	37	24	9

HARFORD Paul Raymond Thomas
Born: Chelmsford, England, 21 October, 1974 — M

League Club	Source	Date Signed	Seasons Played	Apps	Subs	Gls
Blackburn Rov	Arsenal (YT)	08/93				
Wigan Ath	L	09/94	94	3	0	0
Shrewsbury T	L	12/94	94	3	3	0

HARFORD Raymond Thomas (Ray)
Born: Halifax, West Yorkshire, England, 1 June, 1945 — CD
Died: Banstead, Surrey, England, 9 August, 2003

League Club	Source	Date Signed	Seasons Played	Apps	Subs	Gls
Charlton Ath	Jnr	05/64	65	3	0	0
Exeter C	Tr	01/66	65-66	55	0	1
Lincoln C	Tr	07/67	67-70	161	0	10
Mansfield T	Tr	06/71	71	7	0	0
Port Vale	Tr	12/71	71-72	20	0	1
Colchester U	Tr	01/73	72-74	107	1	4

HARGREAVES Allan
Born: Dewsbury, West Yorkshire, England, 29 March, 1931 — CF
Died: Kirklees, West Yorkshire, England, February, 2013

League Club	Source	Date Signed	Seasons Played	Apps	Subs	Gls
Bradford C		07/54	54-55	4	-	1

HARGREAVES Christian (Chris)
Born: Cleethorpes, North Lincolnshire, England, 12 May, 1972 — M

League Club	Source	Date Signed	Seasons Played	Apps	Subs	Gls
Grimsby T	YT	12/89	89-92	15	36	5
Scarborough	L	03/93	92	2	1	0
Hull C	Tr	07/93	93-94	34	15	0
West Bromwich A	Tr	07/95	95	0	1	0
Hereford U	Tr	02/96	95-96	57	4	6
Plymouth Arg	Tr	07/98	98-99	74	2	5
Northampton T	Tr	07/00	00-03	144	7	6
Brentford	Tr	07/04	04	30	0	2
Oxford U	Tr	07/05	05	34	1	1
Torquay U	Tr	06/07	09	21	2	3

HARGREAVES David
Born: Accrington, Lancashire, England, 27 August, 1954 — F

League Club	Source	Date Signed	Seasons Played	Apps	Subs	Gls
Blackburn Rov	Accrington Stan	12/77	77	2	0	0

HARGREAVES John (Jackie)
Born: Rotherham, South Yorkshire, England, 1 May, 1915 — LW
Died: Bristol, England, 22 December, 1978

League Club	Source	Date Signed	Seasons Played	Apps	Subs	Gls
Leeds U		08/34	35-38	45	-	10
Bristol C	Tr	08/45	46	26	-	9
Reading	Tr	04/47	46-47	15	-	1

HARGREAVES Joseph Albert (Joe)
Born: Accrington, Lancashire, England, 30 October, 1915 — CF
Died: Blackburn, Greater Manchester, England, July, 1992

League Club	Source	Date Signed	Seasons Played	Apps	Subs	Gls
Rochdale	Rossendale U	10/45	46-47	35	-	24

HARGREAVES Owen Lee
Born: Calgary, Canada, 20 January, 1981 — DM
England: 42/B-1/U21-3

League Club	Source	Date Signed	Seasons Played	Apps	Subs	Gls
Manchester U	Bayern Munich (GER)	07/07	07-10	18	9	2
Manchester C	Tr	08/11	11	0	1	0

HARGREAVES Thomas (Tom)
Born: Blackburn, Greater Manchester, England, 29 October, 1917 — CH
Died: Blackburn, Greater Manchester, England, 27 March, 1997

League Club	Source	Date Signed	Seasons Played	Apps	Subs	Gls
Blackburn Rov	Crosshill	10/36	37	4	-	2
Rochdale	Tr	05/46	46	7	-	0

HARGREAVES Wilfred Oscar (Wilf)
Born: Rawmarsh, South Yorkshire, England, 15 December, 1921 — WH
Died: Rotherham, South Yorkshire, England, 9 April, 1993

League Club	Source	Date Signed	Seasons Played	Apps	Subs	Gls
Rotherham U	Rawmarsh Welfare	03/45	46-47	3	-	0

HARKER Christopher Joseph (Chris)
Born: Shiremoor, Tyne and Wear, England, 29 June, 1937 — G
Died: Darlington, County Durham, England, 5 September, 2014

League Club	Source	Date Signed	Seasons Played	Apps	Subs	Gls
Newcastle U	West Allotment Celtic	03/55	57	1	-	0
Bury	Aberdeen	12/61	61-66	178	0	0
Grimsby T	Tr	06/67	67	10	0	0
Rochdale	Tr	07/68	68-69	92	0	0

HARKES John Andrew
Born: Newark, New Jersey, USA, 8 March, 1967 — M/RB
USA: 90

League Club	Source	Date Signed	Seasons Played	Apps	Subs	Gls
Sheffield Wed	N Carolina Univ (USA)	10/90	90-92	59	22	7
Derby Co	Tr	08/93	93-95	67	7	2
West Ham U	L	10/95	95	6	5	0
Nottingham F (L)	Washington DC U (USA)	01/99	98	3	0	0

HARKIN James (Jim)
Born: Brinsworth, South Yorkshire, England, 8 August, 1913 — IF
Died: Doncaster, South Yorkshire, England, December, 1988

League Club	Source	Date Signed	Seasons Played	Apps	Subs	Gls
Doncaster Rov	Denaby U	08/34	34	1	-	0
Mansfield T	Shrewsbury T	02/39	38-46	23	-	5

HARKIN John Terence (Terry)
Born: Derry, Northern Ireland, 14 September, 1941 — CF
Republic of Ireland: LoI-2//Northern Ireland: 5/U23-1

League Club	Source	Date Signed	Seasons Played	Apps	Subs	Gls
Port Vale	Coleraine	09/62	62-63	27	-	11
Crewe Alex	Tr	06/64	64	42	-	34
Cardiff C	Tr	08/65	65	19	1	10
Notts Co	Tr	09/66	66	27	1	10
Southport	Tr	07/67	67-68	63	1	31
Shrewsbury T	Tr	03/69	68-70	79	0	29

HARKIN Maurice Presley (Mo)
Born: Derry, Northern Ireland, 16 August, 1979 — M
Northern Ireland: U21-9/Youth

League Club	Source	Date Signed	Seasons Played	Apps	Subs	Gls
Wycombe W	YT	02/97	96-00	26	47	2
Carlisle U	Tr	08/01	01	2	2	0

HARKINS Gary
Born: Greenock, Inverclyde, Scotland, 2 January, 1985 — LM

League Club	Source	Date Signed	Seasons Played	Apps	Subs	Gls
Blackburn Rov	Sch	01/04				
Huddersfield T	L	03/04	03	1	2	0
Bury	L	02/05	04	4	1	0
Blackpool	L	11/05	05	4	0	1
Grimsby T	Tr	07/06	06	11	6	0
Oldham Ath (L)	St Mirren	01/14	13	22	1	5

HARKNESS James (Jim)
Born: Edinburgh, Scotland, 19 May, 1940 — G
Died: Lockerbie, Dumfries & Galloway, Scotland, 11 July, 2012

League Club	Source	Date Signed	Seasons Played	Apps	Subs	Gls
Carlisle U	Hamilton Academical	08/61	61-62	16	-	0

HARKNESS Jonathan (Jon)
Born: Antrim, Northern Ireland, 18 November, 1985 — LB

League Club	Source	Date Signed	Seasons Played	Apps	Subs	Gls
Walsall	Sch	07/05	04-05	2	0	0

HARKNESS Steven (Steve)
Born: Carlisle, Cumbria, England, 27 August, 1971 — LB
England: Youth

League Club	Source	Date Signed	Seasons Played	Apps	Subs	Gls
Carlisle U	YT	03/89	88	12	1	0
Liverpool	Tr	07/89	91-98	90	12	3
Huddersfield T	L	09/93	93	5	0	0
Southend U	L	02/95	94	6	0	0
Blackburn Rov	Benfica (POR)	09/99	99	17	0	0
Sheffield Wed	Tr	02/00	00	28	2	1

HARKNESS William Jardine (Willie)
Born: Glasgow, Scotland, 21 July, 1918 — IF
Died: Dumfries, Scotland, 14 January, 1995

League Club	Source	Date Signed	Seasons Played	Apps	Subs	Gls
Carlisle U	Stirling A	10/47				
Workington	South Shields	07/49	51	7	-	1

HARKOUK Rachid Peter
Born: Chelsea, W London, England, 19 May, 1956 — LW/M
Algeria: 4

League Club	Source	Date Signed	Seasons Played	Apps	Subs	Gls
Crystal Palace	Feltham	06/76	76-77	51	3	20

League Club	Source	Date Signed	Seasons Played	Apps	Subs	Gls
Queens Park Rgrs	Tr	06/78	78-79	15	5	3
Notts Co	Tr	06/80	80-85	124	20	39

HARLAND Stanley Clarence (Stan)
Born: Liverpool, England, 19 June, 1940 — LH
Died: Yeovil, Somerset, England, 30 August, 2001

League Club	Source	Date Signed	Seasons Played	Apps	Subs	Gls
Everton	New Brighton	02/59				
Bradford C	Tr	07/61	61-63	120	-	20
Carlisle U	Tr	06/64	64-65	77	0	7
Swindon T	Tr	08/66	66-71	237	0	6
Birmingham C	Tr	12/71	71-72	37	1	0

HARLE David
Born: Denaby, South Yorkshire, England, 15 August, 1963 — M
England: Youth

League Club	Source	Date Signed	Seasons Played	Apps	Subs	Gls
Doncaster Rov	App	11/80	79-81	48	13	3
Exeter C	Tr	07/82	82-83	42	1	6
Doncaster Rov	Tr	09/83	83-85	80	3	17
Leeds U	Tr	12/85	85	3	0	0
Bristol C	Tr	03/86	85-86	23	0	2
Scunthorpe U	Tr	11/86	86-88	88	1	10
Peterborough U	Tr	03/89	88-89	21	1	2
Doncaster Rov	Tr	03/90	89-91	39	6	3

HARLE Michael James Lee (Mike)
Born: Lewisham, SE London, England, 31 October, 1972 — LB/M

League Club	Source	Date Signed	Seasons Played	Apps	Subs	Gls
Gillingham	YT	-	90	1	1	0
Millwall	Sittingbourne	11/93	96	12	9	1
Bury	L	12/95	95	0	1	0
Barnet	Tr	07/97	97-98	53	1	2

HARLEY Albert George
Born: Chester, England, 17 April, 1940 — WH
Died: Chester, England, June, 1993

League Club	Source	Date Signed	Seasons Played	Apps	Subs	Gls
Shrewsbury T	Jnr	04/57	56-64	220	-	14
Swansea C	Tr	09/64	64-65	25	1	0
Crewe Alex	Guildford C	07/66	66	22	0	5
Stockport Co	Tr	02/67	66-68	77	3	11
Chester C	Tr	06/69	69	3	0	1

HARLEY Alexander (Alex)
Born: Glasgow, Scotland, 20 April, 1936 — CF
Died: Birmingham, England, 24 June, 1969

League Club	Source	Date Signed	Seasons Played	Apps	Subs	Gls
Manchester C	Third Lanark	08/62	62	40	-	23
Birmingham C	Tr	08/63	63-64	28	-	9
Leicester C	Dundee	05/65				

HARLEY James (Jim)
Born: Methil, Fife, Scotland, 2 February, 1917 — FB
Died: Kirkcaldy, Fife, Scotland, 7 September, 1989
Scotland: War-2

League Club	Source	Date Signed	Seasons Played	Apps	Subs	Gls
Liverpool	Hearts o' Beath	04/34	35-47	114	-	0

HARLEY Jonathan (Jon)
Born: Maidstone, Kent, England, 26 September, 1979 — LB
England: U21-3/Youth

League Club	Source	Date Signed	Seasons Played	Apps	Subs	Gls
Chelsea	YT	03/97	97-00	22	8	2
Wimbledon	L	10/00	00	6	0	2
Fulham	Tr	08/01	01-03	19	6	1
Sheffield U	L	10/02	02	8	1	1
Sheffield U	L	09/03	03	5	0	0
West Ham U	L	01/04	03	15	0	1
Sheffield U	Tr	08/04	04	44	0	2
Burnley	Tr	08/05	05-07	116	3	3
Watford	Tr	07/08	08-09	52	23	2
Notts Co	Tr	07/10	10-11	50	3	0
Rotherham U	L	10/11	11	11	1	0
Portsmouth	Tr	08/12	12	23	0	1

HARLEY Lee
Born: Crewe, Cheshire, England, 7 July, 1967 — F

League Club	Source	Date Signed	Seasons Played	Apps	Subs	Gls
Chester C	App	-	85	0	1	0

HARLEY Leslie (Les)
Born: Chester, England, 26 September, 1946 — RW

League Club	Source	Date Signed	Seasons Played	Apps	Subs	Gls
Chester C	Jnr	09/64	64-66	22	3	3
Blackpool	Tr	07/67				
Rochdale	L	02/68	67	5	0	0

HARLEY Richard John (John)
Born: March, Cambridgeshire, England, 22 April, 1949 — D/M

League Club	Source	Date Signed	Seasons Played	Apps	Subs	Gls
Reading	Stevenage Ath	09/69	69-72	64	10	6
Aldershot	Tr	07/73	73-74	16	12	0
Hartlepool U	Wokingham T	09/76	76	4	0	1

HARLEY Ryan Bernard
Born: Bristol, England, 22 January, 1985 — M

League Club	Source	Date Signed	Seasons Played	Apps	Subs	Gls
Bristol C	Sch	07/04	04	1	1	0
Exeter C	Weston-super-Mare	12/07	08-10	87	9	20
Swansea C	Tr	01/11				
Exeter C	L	02/11	10	21	0	4
Brighton & HA	Tr	08/11	11-12	13	5	2
MK Dons	L	01/13	12	8	0	0
Swindon T	Tr	07/13	13	16	5	1
Exeter C	Tr	11/14	14	22	3	4

HARLOCK Desmond Southern (Des)
Born: Blaenau Ffestiniog, Gwynedd, Wales, 20 December, 1922 — RW
Died: Liverpool, England, 6 April, 1981

League Club	Source	Date Signed	Seasons Played	Apps	Subs	Gls
Tranmere Rov	Ellesmere Port T	03/42	46-53	150	-	17

HARMAN Peter Robert
Born: Guildford, Surrey, England, 11 October, 1950 — F

League Club	Source	Date Signed	Seasons Played	Apps	Subs	Gls
Bournemouth	App	08/68	69	1	0	0
Reading	Tr	08/70	71-72	34	2	9

HARMER Thomas Charles (Tommy)
Born: Hackney, E London, England, 2 February, 1928 — IF
Died: Edmonton, N London, England, 24 October, 2007
England: B-1

League Club	Source	Date Signed	Seasons Played	Apps	Subs	Gls
Tottenham H	Finchley	08/48	51-59	205	-	47
Watford	Tr	10/60	60-61	63	-	6
Chelsea	Tr	09/62	62-63	8	-	1

HARMON Darren John
Born: Northampton, England, 30 January, 1973 — M

League Club	Source	Date Signed	Seasons Played	Apps	Subs	Gls
Notts Co	YT	07/91				
Shrewsbury T	Tr	02/92	91-92	1	5	2
Northampton T	Tr	10/92	92-94	76	13	12

HARMSTON Michael James (Mick)
Born: Sheffield, England, 7 April, 1950 — LB

League Club	Source	Date Signed	Seasons Played	Apps	Subs	Gls
Sheffield U	App	05/67	68	5	0	0
Southend U	L	12/70	70	1	0	0

HARMSWORTH Lee Anthony
Born: Southwark, S London, England, 27 October, 1967 — G

League Club	Source	Date Signed	Seasons Played	Apps	Subs	Gls
Charlton Ath	App	10/85	84	3	0	0

HARNBY Donald Reed (Don)
Born: Hurworth, County Durham, England, 20 July, 1923 — FB
Died: Stockton-on-Tees, Cleveland, England, 24 October, 2009

League Club	Source	Date Signed	Seasons Played	Apps	Subs	Gls
Newcastle U	Spennymoor U	05/45				
York C	Tr	08/47	47	1	-	0
Grimsby T	Spennymoor U	09/49	49-51	34	-	0

HARNESS Marcus Anthony
Born: Coventry, England, 24 February, 1996 — M

League Club	Source	Date Signed	Seasons Played	Apps	Subs	Gls
Burton A	Sch	07/14	13-14	2	19	0

HARNEY David
Born: Jarrow, Tyne and Wear, England, 2 March, 1947 — CF

League Club	Source	Date Signed	Seasons Played	Apps	Subs	Gls
Grimsby T	Jnr	11/64				
Scunthorpe U	Tr	07/67	67-68	20	5	1
Brentford	Tr	10/69	69	0	1	0

HARNEY James Joseph (Jamie)
Born: Strabane, Tyrone, Northern Ireland, 4 March, 1996 — CD
Northern Ireland: U21-1/Schools

League Club	Source	Date Signed	Seasons Played	Apps	Subs	Gls
West Ham U	Sch	07/14				
Colchester U	Tr	11/14	14	0	1	0

HARNEY Stephen Graham (Steve)
Born: Bradford, England, 18 February, 1951 — RB

League Club	Source	Date Signed	Seasons Played	Apps	Subs	Gls
Bradford C (Am)	Drum Rov	07/68	68-70	13	1	0

HARNWELL Jamie
Born: Perth, Australia, 21 January, 1977 — CD

League Club	Source	Date Signed	Seasons Played	Apps	Subs	Gls
Leyton Orient	Perth Glory (AUS)	08/03	03	1	2	0

HAROLD Michael Lloyd (Mike)
Born: Stockport, Greater Manchester, England, 22 September, 1943 — RB

League Club	Source	Date Signed	Seasons Played	Apps	Subs	Gls
Stockport Co	Manchester C (Am)	08/64	64	4	-	0

HAROUN Faris Dominguere Jenny
Born: Brussels, Belgium, 22 September, 1985 — M
Belgium: 6/U21-25

League Club	Source	Date Signed	Seasons Played	Apps	Subs	Gls
Middlesbrough	Germ'l Beerschot (BEL)	08/11	11-13	43	13	6
Blackpool	Tr	01/14	13	5	4	0

HARPER Alan
Born: Liverpool, England, 1 November, 1960 — D/M
England: Youth

League Club	Source	Date Signed	Seasons Played	Apps	Subs	Gls
Liverpool	App	04/78				
Everton	Tr	06/83	83-87	103	23	4
Sheffield Wed	Tr	07/88	88-89	32	3	0
Manchester C	Tr	12/89	89-90	46	4	1
Everton	Tr	08/91	91-92	45	6	0
Luton T	Tr	09/93	93	40	1	1

League Club	Source	Date Signed	Seasons Played	Apps	Subs	Gls
Burnley	Tr	08/94	94-95	30	1	0
Cardiff C	L	11/95	95	5	0	0

HARPER Antony Frederick (Tony)
Born: Oxford, England, 26 May, 1925 WH
Died: Bullingdon, Oxfordshire, England, 28 June, 1982

League Club	Source	Date Signed	Seasons Played	Apps	Subs	Gls
Brentford	Headington U	04/48	48-54	173	-	6

HARPER Colin George
Born: Ipswich, England, 25 July, 1946 LB

League Club	Source	Date Signed	Seasons Played	Apps	Subs	Gls
Ipswich T	Jnr	08/64	65-74	144	4	5
Grimsby T	L	12/76	76	3	0	0
Cambridge U	L	02/77	76	15	0	0
Port Vale	Tr	08/77	77	4	0	0

HARPER David (Dave)
Born: Peckham, SE London, England, 29 September, 1938 WH
Died: Eastbourne, East Sussex, England, 24 January, 2013
England: Youth

League Club	Source	Date Signed	Seasons Played	Apps	Subs	Gls
Millwall	Jnr	05/57	57-64	165	-	4
Ipswich T	Tr	03/65	64-66	70	2	2
Swindon T	Tr	07/67	67	4	0	0
Leyton Orient	Tr	10/67	67-70	82	3	4

HARPER Dennis
Born: Tipton, West Midlands, England, 12 October, 1936 IF

League Club	Source	Date Signed	Seasons Played	Apps	Subs	Gls
Birmingham C	Darlaston	08/56	56	1	-	0

HARPER Donald (Don)
Born: Blackwell, Derbyshire, England, 26 October, 1921 RW
Died: Chesterfield, Derbyshire, England, November, 1990

League Club	Source	Date Signed	Seasons Played	Apps	Subs	Gls
Chesterfield	Blackwell Colliery	12/43				
Mansfield T	Tr	07/46	46	21	-	1

HARPER Ian Thomas
Born: Scunthorpe, North Lincolnshire, England, 23 November, 1944 RB

League Club	Source	Date Signed	Seasons Played	Apps	Subs	Gls
Scunthorpe U	Jnr	07/62	63-64	21	-	0

HARPER Ivor Roy
Born: Watford, Hertfordshire, England, 23 June, 1933 IF

League Club	Source	Date Signed	Seasons Played	Apps	Subs	Gls
Watford (Am)	Hemel Hempstead	10/51	51	3	-	0

HARPER James Alan John
Born: Chelmsford, England, 9 November, 1980 M

League Club	Source	Date Signed	Seasons Played	Apps	Subs	Gls
Arsenal	YT	07/99				
Cardiff C	L	12/00	00	3	0	0
Reading	Tr	02/01	00-09	282	30	25
Sheffield U	Tr	09/09	09	31	3	4
Hull C	Tr	07/10	10-11	27	2	1
Wycombe W	L	01/12	11	5	0	0
Doncaster Rov	Tr	08/12	12	19	8	0

HARPER Joseph John (Joe)
Born: Muirhead, Lanarkshire, Scotland, 12 January, 1920 FB
Died: Watford, Hertfordshire, England, 5 March, 1987

League Club	Source	Date Signed	Seasons Played	Apps	Subs	Gls
Watford	Twechar U	05/37	46-51	159	-	1

HARPER Joseph Montgomerie (Joe)
Born: Greenock, Inverclyde, Scotland, 11 January, 1948 F
Scotland: 4/SLge-1/U23-2

League Club	Source	Date Signed	Seasons Played	Apps	Subs	Gls
Huddersfield T	Greenock Morton	03/67	66-67	26	2	4
Everton	Aberdeen	12/72	72-73	40	3	12

HARPER Kenneth (Ken)
Born: Farnworth, Greater Manchester, England, 27 April, 1924 WH
Died: Greater Manchester, England, December, 2010

League Club	Source	Date Signed	Seasons Played	Apps	Subs	Gls
Blackpool		12/45				
Rochdale		12/47				
Shrewsbury T	Hindsford	08/49	50	1	-	0

HARPER Kenneth (Ken)
Born: Barnsley, South Yorkshire, England, 15 April, 1917 FB
Died: Doncaster, South Yorkshire, England, February, 1994

League Club	Source	Date Signed	Seasons Played	Apps	Subs	Gls
Walsall		03/35	37-38	22	-	2
Bradford C	Tr	01/46	46-48	50	-	0

HARPER Kevin Patrick
Born: Oldham, Greater Manchester, England, 15 January, 1976 RW
Scotland: B-1/U21-7/Schools

League Club	Source	Date Signed	Seasons Played	Apps	Subs	Gls
Derby Co	Hibernian	09/98	98-99	6	26	1
Walsall	L	12/99	99	8	1	1
Portsmouth	Tr	03/00	99-03	85	34	9
Norwich C	L	09/03	03	9	0	0
Leicester C	L	09/04	04	2	0	0
Stoke C	Tr	02/05	04-06	13	13	1
Carlisle U	L	10/06	06	7	0	0
Walsall	L	02/07	06	10	0	4

HARPER Lee Charles Philip
Born: Chelsea, W London, England, 30 October, 1971 G

League Club	Source	Date Signed	Seasons Played	Apps	Subs	Gls
Arsenal	Sittingbourne	06/94	96	1	0	0
Queens Park Rgrs	Tr	07/97	97-00	117	1	0
Walsall	Tr	07/01	01	3	0	0
Northampton T	Tr	07/02	02-06	156	0	0
MK Dons	Tr	10/06	06	22	0	0

HARPER Lee James
Born: Bridlington, East Riding of Yorkshire, England, 24 March, 1975 FB

League Club	Source	Date Signed	Seasons Played	Apps	Subs	Gls
Scarborough	YT	03/94	93	0	2	0

HARPER Robert (Bobby)
Born: Glasgow, Scotland, 6 June, 1920 LW
Died: New Cumnock, Ayrshire, Scotland, 18 December, 1978

League Club	Source	Date Signed	Seasons Played	Apps	Subs	Gls
Huddersfield T	Ayr U	06/46				
Newport Co	Tr	11/46	46-49	114	-	12
Southend U	Tr	07/50	50	6	-	0

HARPER Stephen Alan (Steve)
Born: Seaham, County Durham, England, 14 March, 1975 G

League Club	Source	Date Signed	Seasons Played	Apps	Subs	Gls
Newcastle U	Seaham Red Star	07/93	98-12	149	8	0
Bradford C	L	09/95	95	1	0	0
Hartlepool U	L	08/97	97	15	0	0
Huddersfield T	L	12/97	97	24	0	0
Brighton & HA	L	10/11	11	5	0	0
Hull C	Tr	07/13	13-14	21	2	0

HARPER Steven James (Steve)
Born: Newcastle-under-Lyme, Potteries, England, 3 February, 1969 W

League Club	Source	Date Signed	Seasons Played	Apps	Subs	Gls
Port Vale	App	06/87	87-88	16	12	2
Preston NE	Tr	03/89	88-90	57	20	10
Burnley	Tr	07/91	91-92	64	5	8
Doncaster Rov	Tr	08/93	93-95	56	9	11
Mansfield T	Tr	09/95	95-98	157	3	18
Hull C	Tr	07/99	99-00	63	2	4
Darlington	Tr	02/01	00-01	32	8	1

HARPER-PENMAN Jed Ethan Patrick
Born: Bideford, Devon, England, 2 February, 1994 RW

League Club	Source	Date Signed	Seasons Played	Apps	Subs	Gls
Plymouth Arg	Sch	07/12	10-11	0	2	0

HARRAD Shaun Nicholas
Born: Nottingham, England, 11 December, 1984 F
England: Semi Pro-8

League Club	Source	Date Signed	Seasons Played	Apps	Subs	Gls
Notts Co	Sch	04/04	02-04	4	25	1
Burton A	Tr	08/05	09-10	51	11	31
Northampton T	Tr	01/11	10	18	0	6
Bury	Tr	08/11	11-13	24	20	2
Rotherham U	L	02/12	11	6	2	3
Cheltenham T	L	08/12	12	20	11	8
Notts Co	Alfreton T	08/14	14	4	8	1
Cheltenham T	L	02/15	14	10	2	1

HARRIES Paul Graham
Born: Sydney, Australia, 19 November, 1977 F

League Club	Source	Date Signed	Seasons Played	Apps	Subs	Gls
Portsmouth	NSW Soccer Acad (AUS)	09/97	97	0	1	0
Crystal Palace	Tr	09/98				
Torquay U	L	02/99	98	5	0	0
Carlisle U	Tr	07/99	99	6	14	2
Macclesfield T	Wollongong Wolv (AUS)	02/01				
Exeter C	Merthyr Tydfil	09/02	02	0	1	0

HARRIGAN Duncan
Born: Paisley, Renfrewshire, Scotland, 26 June, 1921 CF
Died: Paisley, Renfrewshire, Scotland, 16 February, 2005

League Club	Source	Date Signed	Seasons Played	Apps	Subs	Gls
Crewe Alex	St Mirren	08/46	46-47	57	-	23
Aston Villa	Tr	04/48				
Chester C	Tr	10/48	48	20	-	4

HARRIMAN Michael Grant
Born: Chichester, West Sussex, England, 23 October, 1992 RB
Republic of Ireland: U21-4/Youth

League Club	Source	Date Signed	Seasons Played	Apps	Subs	Gls
Queens Park Rgrs	Sch	03/11	11-12	1	1	0
Wycombe W	L	01/13	12	19	1	0
Gillingham	L	08/13	13	33	1	1
Luton T	L	10/14	14	35	0	1

HARRINGTON Alan Charles
Born: Penarth, Vale of Glamorgan, Wales, 17 November, 1933 RB/WH
Wales: 11/WLge-1

League Club	Source	Date Signed	Seasons Played	Apps	Subs	Gls
Cardiff C	Cardiff Nomads	10/51	52-65	348	0	6

HARRINGTON Colin Andrew
Born: Bicester, Oxfordshire, England, 3 April, 1943 LW

League Club	Source	Date Signed	Seasons Played	Apps	Subs	Gls
Oxford U	Wolverhampton W (Am)	10/62	62-70	230	4	30
Mansfield T	Tr	06/71	71	7	6	0

HARRINGTON Justin David
Born: Truro, Cornwall, England, 18 September, 1975 M

League Club	Source	Date Signed	Seasons Played	Apps	Subs	Gls
Norwich C	YT	07/94				
Leicester C	Tr	08/96				
Bournemouth	Tr	07/97	97	4	4	0

League Club	Source	Date Signed	Seasons Played	Apps	Subs	Gls

HARRINGTON Paul
Born: Hartlepool, Cleveland, England, 26 September, 1964 — M

League Club	Source	Date Signed	Seasons Played	Apps	Subs	Gls
Hartlepool U		04/83	83	0	2	0

HARRINGTON Philip (Phil)
Born: Bangor, Gwynedd, Wales, 20 November, 1963 — G
Wales: Youth

League Club	Source	Date Signed	Seasons Played	Apps	Subs	Gls
Chester C	App	11/81	81-84	76	0	0
Blackpool	Tr	03/85				
Burnley	L	11/85	85	2	0	0
Preston NE	L	02/86	85	2	0	0

HARRIOTT Callum Kyle
Born: Norbury, S London, England, 4 March, 1994 — LW
England: Youth

League Club	Source	Date Signed	Seasons Played	Apps	Subs	Gls
Charlton Ath	Sch	07/11	10-14	40	26	8

HARRIOTT Marvin Lee
Born: Dulwich, S London, England, 20 April, 1974 — RB
England: Youth/Schools

League Club	Source	Date Signed	Seasons Played	Apps	Subs	Gls
Oldham Ath	West Ham U (YT)	04/92				
Barnsley	Tr	04/93				
Leyton Orient	L	10/93	93	8	0	0
Bristol C	Tr	12/93	93-94	36	0	0

HARRIOTT Matthew Anthony (Matty)
Born: Luton, England, 23 September, 1992 — M

League Club	Source	Date Signed	Seasons Played	Apps	Subs	Gls
Sheffield U	Luton T (Sch)	08/10	10	0	2	0
Burton A	L	03/12	11	3	1	0
Northampton T	Tr	08/13	13	2	3	0

HARRIS Albert Edward (Bert)
Born: Bootle, Merseyside, England, 21 November, 1931 — G

League Club	Source	Date Signed	Seasons Played	Apps	Subs	Gls
Everton	Maghull	01/55	55	5	-	0
Tranmere Rov	Tr	05/57	57-59	33	-	0
Southport	Tr	07/60	60-64	159	-	0

HARRIS Alexander (Sandy)
Born: Hong Kong, 22 October, 1934 — RW
Died: Blackburn, Greater Manchester, England, December, 2014

League Club	Source	Date Signed	Seasons Played	Apps	Subs	Gls
Blackpool	Jnr	11/51	52-57	21	-	4

HARRIS Allan John
Born: Northampton, England, 28 December, 1942 — LB
England: Youth/Schools

League Club	Source	Date Signed	Seasons Played	Apps	Subs	Gls
Chelsea	Jnr	06/60	60-64	70	-	0
Coventry C	Tr	11/64	64-65	60	0	0
Chelsea	Tr	05/66	66	12	2	0
Queens Park Rgrs	Tr	07/67	67-70	90	4	0
Plymouth Arg	Tr	03/71	70-72	64	0	0
Cambridge U	Tr	07/73	73	6	0	0

HARRIS Andrew (Andy)
Born: Birmingham, England, 17 November, 1970 — M

League Club	Source	Date Signed	Seasons Played	Apps	Subs	Gls
Birmingham C	YT	07/89	89	0	1	0
Oxford U	L	10/91	91	1	0	0
Exeter C	Tr	11/91	91-93	32	6	1

HARRIS Andrew David Douglas (Andy)
Born: Springs, South Africa, 26 February, 1977 — M/D

League Club	Source	Date Signed	Seasons Played	Apps	Subs	Gls
Liverpool	YT	03/94				
Southend U	Tr	07/96	96-98	70	2	0
Leyton Orient	Tr	07/99	99-02	143	6	2
Chester C	Tr	07/03	04	9	10	0

HARRIS Anthony Thomas (Tony)
Born: Berrington, Shropshire, England, 20 December, 1945 — CH

League Club	Source	Date Signed	Seasons Played	Apps	Subs	Gls
Shrewsbury T	App	07/63	63-66	54	1	4
Bradford Park Ave	Tr	07/68	68	10	0	0

HARRIS Arthur
Born: Coventry, England, 28 July, 1914 — RH
Died: Nuneaton, Warwickshire, England, September, 1973

League Club	Source	Date Signed	Seasons Played	Apps	Subs	Gls
Southend U	Nuneaton T	07/36	36-46	114	-	1

HARRIS Ashley Grant
Born: Waterlooville, Hampshire, England, 9 December, 1993 — W

League Club	Source	Date Signed	Seasons Played	Apps	Subs	Gls
Portsmouth	Sch	07/12	11-13	9	23	3

HARRIS Brian
Born: Bebington, Wirral, England, 16 May, 1935 — LH/W
Died: Chepstow, Monmouthshire, Wales, 17 February, 2008
England: Youth

League Club	Source	Date Signed	Seasons Played	Apps	Subs	Gls
Everton	Port Sunlight	01/54	55-66	310	0	23
Cardiff C	Tr	10/66	66-70	146	3	0
Newport Co	Tr	07/71	71-73	85	0	0

HARRIS Christopher Robert (Chris)
Born: Hastings, East Sussex, England, 23 January, 1957 — F

League Club	Source	Date Signed	Seasons Played	Apps	Subs	Gls
Millwall	Bexhill U	10/76	76	3	0	0

HARRIS David (Dave)
Born: Stoke-on-Trent, England, 19 November, 1953 — CD

League Club	Source	Date Signed	Seasons Played	Apps	Subs	Gls
Port Vale		08/73	73-78	175	1	8
Halifax T	Tr	07/79	79-80	69	2	3

HARRIS David John (Johnny)
Born: Gornal, West Midlands, England, 3 April, 1939 — LB

League Club	Source	Date Signed	Seasons Played	Apps	Subs	Gls
Wolverhampton W	Sedgley Rov	05/58	61-62	3	-	0
Walsall	Tr	01/65	64-68	74	0	2

HARRIS Derek Harold (Harry)
Born: Magor, Monmouthshire, Wales, 2 November, 1933 — WH/IF
Died: Leeds, England, 9 June, 2004

League Club	Source	Date Signed	Seasons Played	Apps	Subs	Gls
Newport Co	Undy U	09/54	54-57	156	-	57
Portsmouth	Tr	07/58	58-70	378	2	48
Newport Co	L	10/70	70	16	0	2

HARRIS Frederick (Fred)
Born: Birmingham, England, 2 July, 1912 — IF/WH
Died: Solihull, West Midlands, England, 11 October, 1998
England: FLge-1

League Club	Source	Date Signed	Seasons Played	Apps	Subs	Gls
Birmingham C	Osborne Ath	04/33	34-49	280	-	61

HARRIS Gary Wayne
Born: Birmingham, England, 31 May, 1959 — LW

League Club	Source	Date Signed	Seasons Played	Apps	Subs	Gls
Cardiff C	App	05/77	78-79	4	0	0

HARRIS Geoffrey Robert (Geoff)
Born: Heywood, Greater Manchester, England, 1 February, 1956 — F

League Club	Source	Date Signed	Seasons Played	Apps	Subs	Gls
Oldham Ath	App	02/74				
Halifax T	Tr	07/75	75-76	10	5	1

HARRIS George
Born: Stanley, County Durham, England, 24 August, 1936 — W

League Club	Source	Date Signed	Seasons Played	Apps	Subs	Gls
Preston NE	Craghead	08/57				
Southport	Tr	07/59	59	1	-	0

HARRIS George Alfred
Born: Lambeth, S London, England, 10 June, 1940 — W

League Club	Source	Date Signed	Seasons Played	Apps	Subs	Gls
Newport Co	Woking	07/61	61	31	-	7
Watford	Tr	04/62	61-65	162	1	55
Reading	Tr	07/66	66-69	134	2	57
Cambridge U	Tr	07/70	70-71	33	2	11

HARRIS Gerald William (Gerry)
Born: Claverley, Shropshire, England, 8 October, 1935 — LB
England: U23-4

League Club	Source	Date Signed	Seasons Played	Apps	Subs	Gls
Wolverhampton W	Bebington	01/54	56-65	235	0	2
Walsall	Tr	04/66	65-67	13	2	0

HARRIS Gordon
Born: Worksop, Nottinghamshire, England, 2 June, 1940 — M/LW
Died: Langold, Nottinghamshire, England, 10 February, 2014
England: 1/FLge-2/U23-2

League Club	Source	Date Signed	Seasons Played	Apps	Subs	Gls
Burnley	Firbeck Colliery	01/58	58-67	258	0	69
Sunderland	Tr	01/68	67-71	124	1	16

HARRIS Gordon William
Born: Coupar Angus, Perthshire, Scotland, 19 February, 1943 — LB

League Club	Source	Date Signed	Seasons Played	Apps	Subs	Gls
Cardiff C	Forfar Ath	03/65	64	5	-	0

HARRIS James (Jimmy)
Born: Birkenhead, Wirral, England, 18 August, 1933 — CF
England: FLge-1/U23-1

League Club	Source	Date Signed	Seasons Played	Apps	Subs	Gls
Everton	Jnr	09/51	55-60	191	-	65
Birmingham C	Tr	12/60	60-63	93	-	37
Oldham Ath	Tr	07/64	64-65	28	1	9
Tranmere Rov	Tr	08/66				

HARRIS James Christopher (Jamie)
Born: Swansea, Wales, 28 June, 1979 — F

League Club	Source	Date Signed	Seasons Played	Apps	Subs	Gls
Swansea C	Mumbles Rgrs	07/97	97	0	6	0

HARRIS James William (Jay)
Born: Liverpool, England, 15 April, 1986 — M

League Club	Source	Date Signed	Seasons Played	Apps	Subs	Gls
Everton	Sch	07/05				
Accrington Stan	Tr	08/06	06-07	64	9	2
Chester C	Tr	07/08	08	24	7	0

HARRIS Jamie
Born: Exeter, England, 4 February, 1969 — F

League Club	Source	Date Signed	Seasons Played	Apps	Subs	Gls
Exeter C	App	08/86	87-88	6	8	1

HARRIS Jason Andre Sebastian
Born: Sutton, S London, England, 24 November, 1976 — F

League Club	Source	Date Signed	Seasons Played	Apps	Subs	Gls
Crystal Palace	YT	07/95	96	0	2	0
Bristol Rov	L	11/96	96	5	1	2
Lincoln C	L	08/97	97	0	1	0
Leyton Orient	Tr	09/97	97-98	22	15	7
Preston NE	Tr	08/98	98	9	25	6

League Club	Source	Date Signed	Seasons Played	Apps	Subs	Gls
Hull C	Tr	07/99	99-00	19	19	4
Shrewsbury T	L	03/01	00	1	3	0
Southend U	Tr	07/01	01	2	3	0
HARRIS Jason Mark						
Born: Rochdale, Greater Manchester, England, 26 December, 1969						M
Burnley	YT	07/88	86	4	0	0
HARRIS Jeffrey Bruce (Jeff)						
Born: Stepney, E London, England, 11 June, 1942						LH
England: Amateur-5						
Leyton Orient	Enfield	05/64	64	14	-	0
HARRIS John						
Born: Glasgow, Scotland, 30 June, 1917						CH
Died: Sheffield, England, 15 July, 1988						
Scotland: War-1						
Swansea C	Swindon T (Am)	08/34	36-38	28	-	4
Tottenham H	Tr	02/39				
Wolverhampton W	Tr	05/39				
Chelsea	Tr	08/45	46-55	326	-	14
Chester C	Tr	07/56	56	27	-	1
HARRIS John Patrick						
Born: London, England, 16 September, 1937						IF
Millwall (Am)		06/56	56	1	-	0
HARRIS Joseph (Joe)						
Born: Belfast, Northern Ireland, 8 April, 1929						CF
Blackburn Rov	Larne	01/51	50-51	35	-	15
Oldham Ath	Tr	03/53	52-53	27	-	4
HARRIS Joseph Anthony (Joe)						
Born: Liverpool, England, 20 September, 1926						RW
Died: Liverpool, England, May, 2005						
Everton		07/50	50-52	14	-	4
HARRIS Kadeem Raymond Maturin						
Born: Westminster, Central London, England, 8 June, 1993						RM
Wycombe W	Sch	07/11	09-11	10	9	0
Cardiff C	Tr	01/12	14	3	11	1
Brentford	L	10/13	13	9	1	1
HARRIS Leonard James (Len)						
Born: Nuneaton, Warwickshire, England, 29 May, 1949						RB
Nottingham F	Jnr	06/66	68-69	2	0	0
Doncaster Rov	L	09/70	70	4	0	0
HARRIS Leslie (Les)						
Born: Treorchy, Rhondda Cynon Taff, Wales, 1 November, 1941						LW
Swansea C	Aberystwyth Univ	08/63	63-64	4	-	0
HARRIS Leslie Henry (Les)						
Born: Stocksbridge, South Yorkshire, England, 29 May, 1955						F
Barnsley	Jnr	05/74	75-76	11	15	2
HARRIS Louis David						
Born: Sutton Coldfield, West Midlands, England, 7 December, 1992						M
Wolverhampton W	Sch	06/11				
Notts Co	L	03/12	11	1	1	0
AFC Wimbledon	Tr	07/12	12	6	1	0
HARRIS Mark Andrew						
Born: Reading, England, 15 July, 1963						CD
Crystal Palace	Wokingham T	02/88	88	0	2	0
Burnley	L	08/89	89	4	0	0
Swansea C	Tr	09/89	89-94	228	0	14
Gillingham	Tr	08/95	95-96	63	2	3
Cardiff C	Tr	08/97	97	38	0	1
HARRIS Martin						
Born: Doncaster, South Yorkshire, England, 22 December, 1955						RW
Workington	Grimsby T (App)	07/74	74-76	97	9	13
Hartlepool U	Tr	12/77	77	0	1	0
HARRIS Neil						
Born: Thurrock, Essex, England, 12 July, 1977						F
Millwall	Cambridge C	03/98	97-04	186	47	93
Cardiff C	L	12/04	04	1	2	1
Nottingham F	Tr	12/04	04-06	16	17	1
Gillingham	L	08/05	05	28	8	6
Millwall	Tr	01/07	06-10	88	53	31
Southend U	Tr	07/11	11-12	21	19	8
HARRIS Neil						
Born: Glasgow, Scotland, 9 February, 1920						CF
Southampton	Swindon T (Am)	02/41				
Queens Park Rgrs		09/46	46	1	-	1
HARRIS Neil John						
Born: Manchester, England, 7 November, 1969						M
Crewe Alex	YT	07/88	87	3	0	0

League Club	Source	Date Signed	Seasons Played	Apps	Subs	Gls
HARRIS Paul Edwin						
Born: Hackney, E London, England, 19 May, 1953						CD
Leyton Orient	App	07/70	70-74	96	0	4
Swansea C	Tr	07/75	75-76	47	2	2
HARRIS Peter						
Born: Neath, Wales, 9 August, 1953						M
Newport Co	App	08/71	70-72	21	10	1
HARRIS Peter Philip						
Born: Portsmouth, England, 19 December, 1925						RW
Died: Hayling Island, Hampshire, England, 5 January, 2003						
England: 2/FLge-5						
Portsmouth	Gosport Bor	11/44	46-59	479	-	193
HARRIS Philip (Phil)						
Born: Swindon, England, 18 December, 1958						M
Swindon T	App	-	76	0	1	0
HARRIS Richard Lewis Scott						
Born: Croydon, S London, England, 23 October, 1980						F
Crystal Palace	YT	12/97	98-00	2	7	0
Mansfield T	L	09/01	01	0	6	0
Wycombe W	Tr	03/02	01-03	13	22	5
HARRIS Robert (Bob)						
Born: Glasgow, Scotland, 28 August, 1987						LB
Blackpool	Queen of the South	08/11	11-13	9	4	0
Rotherham U	L	09/12	12	5	0	1
Sheffield U	Tr	01/14	13-14	44	7	3
HARRIS Ronald Edward (Ron)						
Born: Hackney, E London, England, 13 November, 1944						D
England: U23-4/Youth/Schools						
Chelsea	Jnr	11/61	61-79	646	9	13
Brentford	Tr	05/80	80-83	60	1	0
HARRIS Sebastian James (Seb)						
Born: Rochester, Michigan, USA, 5 August, 1987						CD
Northampton T	Michigan Bucks (USA)	08/09	09-10	1	12	1
HARRIS Stephen Carl (Carl)						
Born: Neath, Wales, 3 November, 1956						RW
Wales: 24/U23-1/Schools						
Leeds U	App	11/73	74-81	123	30	26
Charlton Ath	Tr	07/82	82-84	73	3	8
Bury	Leeds U (NC)	12/85	85-86	33	5	4
Rochdale	Cardiff C (NC)	01/88	87-88	24	1	3
Exeter C	Tr	12/88	88	11	5	1
HARRIS Thomas Alfred (Tommy)						
Born: Chelsea, W London, England, 8 November, 1924						IF
Died: Kensington, Central London, England, 11 October, 2001						
Fulham		09/47				
Leyton Orient	Tr	09/51	51-52	31	-	11
Colchester U	Tr	06/53	53	3	-	0
HARRIS Thomas James George (George)						
Born: Ogmore Vale, Bridgend, Wales, 15 February, 1916						G
Died: Caerphilly, Wales, 26 January, 1998						
Charlton Ath	Bexleyheath & Welling	08/39				
Plymouth Arg	Aberaman Ath	05/48	48	3	-	0
HARRIS Thomas John (John)						
Born: Swansea, Wales, 18 May, 1934						CH
Died: Swansea, Wales, September, 2006						
Leeds U		11/51				
Halifax T	Tr	10/55	55-56	9	-	0
HARRIS Thomas Kevin (Kevin)						
Born: Dublin, Republic of Ireland, 20 February, 1918						IF
Died: Republic of Ireland, 1984						
Notts Co	Irish Guards	09/45				
Brentford	Limerick (ROI)	08/48	48	4	-	0
HARRIS Trevor John						
Born: Colchester, Essex, England, 6 February, 1936						WH
Colchester U	Wilson MS	07/54	54-62	99	-	6
HARRIS William (Bill)						
Born: Dudley, West Midlands, England, 1 December, 1918						G
Died: Dudley, West Midlands, England, 20 February, 1996						
West Bromwich A	Whiteheath	02/37	37	2	-	0
Oldham Ath	Tr	06/46	46	32	-	0
Accrington Stan	Tr	08/47	47-49	99	-	0
HARRIS William Charles (Bill)						
Born: Swansea, Wales, 31 October, 1928						WH/IF
Died: Middlesbrough, England, December, 1989						
Wales: 6						

League Club	Source	Date Signed	Seasons Played	Apps	Subs	Gls
Hull C	Llanelli	03/50	49-53	131	-	6
Middlesbrough	Tr	03/54	53-64	360	-	69
Bradford C	Tr	03/65	64-65	9	0	1

HARRIS William Thomas (Tommy)
Born: Aberbargoed, Caerphilly, Wales, 30 June, 1913 — FB/W
Died: Sittingbourne, Kent, England, January, 1997

League Club	Source	Date Signed	Seasons Played	Apps	Subs	Gls
Watford	New Tredegar	04/33	35-48	94	-	6

HARRISON Andrew Frank (Andy)
Born: Long Eaton, Derbyshire, England, 13 September, 1957 — RB

League Club	Source	Date Signed	Seasons Played	Apps	Subs	Gls
Scarborough	Kettering T	07/86	87	3	1	0

HARRISON Anthony Leslie (Tony)
Born: Gateshead, Tyne and Wear, England, 9 January, 1954 — G

League Club	Source	Date Signed	Seasons Played	Apps	Subs	Gls
Southport	Whitley Bay	02/77	76-77	48	0	0
Carlisle U	Tr	06/78	80	8	0	0

HARRISON Ben Nicholas
Born: Richmond, SW London, England, 2 March, 1997 — LB

League Club	Source	Date Signed	Seasons Played	Apps	Subs	Gls
AFC Wimbledon	Sch	09/14	14	5	2	0

HARRISON Bernard Reginald Stanhope (Bernie)
Born: Worcester, England, 28 September, 1934 — W
Died: Andover, Hampshire, England, 10 March, 2006

League Club	Source	Date Signed	Seasons Played	Apps	Subs	Gls
Crystal Palace	Portsmouth (Am)	10/55	55-58	92	-	12
Southampton	Tr	08/59	59	3	-	0
Exeter C	Tr	07/60	60	18	-	4

HARRISON Byron Junior
Born: Wandsworth, SW London, England, 15 June, 1987 — F

League Club	Source	Date Signed	Seasons Played	Apps	Subs	Gls
Stevenage	Carshalton Ath	01/11	10-11	21	17	10
AFC Wimbledon	Tr	01/12	11-12	27	13	10
Cheltenham T	Tr	01/13	12-14	60	26	18
Chesterfield	Tr	01/15	14	4	8	1

HARRISON Christopher Colin (Chris)
Born: Launceston, Cornwall, England, 17 October, 1956 — D

League Club	Source	Date Signed	Seasons Played	Apps	Subs	Gls
Plymouth Arg	App	10/74	75-84	314	9	7
Swansea C	Tr	09/85	85-87	114	3	14

HARRISON Colin George
Born: Pelsall, West Midlands, England, 18 March, 1946 — D/M

League Club	Source	Date Signed	Seasons Played	Apps	Subs	Gls
Walsall	Jnr	11/63	64-81	453	20	33

HARRISON Craig
Born: Gateshead, Tyne and Wear, England, 10 November, 1977 — LB

League Club	Source	Date Signed	Seasons Played	Apps	Subs	Gls
Middlesbrough	YT	07/96	97-98	19	5	0
Preston NE	L	01/99	98	6	0	0
Crystal Palace	Tr	08/00	00-01	34	4	0

HARRISON Daniel Robert (Danny)
Born: Liverpool, England, 4 November, 1982 — M

League Club	Source	Date Signed	Seasons Played	Apps	Subs	Gls
Tranmere Rov	Sch	05/02	01-06	89	35	5
Rotherham U	Tr	06/07	07-11	161	24	15
Tranmere Rov	Tr	07/12	12	4	9	0

HARRISON Derek
Born: Narborough, Leicestershire, England, 9 February, 1950 — CD

League Club	Source	Date Signed	Seasons Played	Apps	Subs	Gls
Leicester C	App	02/67				
Torquay U	Tr	01/71	70-74	124	3	4
Colchester U	Tr	06/75	75	5	2	0

HARRISON Ellis Wade
Born: Newport, Wales, 1 February, 1994 — F
Wales: U21-5

League Club	Source	Date Signed	Seasons Played	Apps	Subs	Gls
Bristol Rov	Sch	06/12	10-13	19	20	4

HARRISON Eric George
Born: Mytholmroyd, West Yorkshire, England, 5 February, 1938 — WH

League Club	Source	Date Signed	Seasons Played	Apps	Subs	Gls
Halifax T	Mytholmroyd	07/57	57-63	199	-	10
Hartlepool U	Tr	08/64	64-65	81	0	4
Barrow	Tr	07/66	66-68	127	3	1
Southport	Tr	06/69	69-70	75	0	0
Barrow	Tr	07/71	71	31	1	1

HARRISON Francis John (Frank)
Born: Gateshead, Tyne and Wear, England, 12 November, 1931 — RB
Died: York, England, November, 1981
England: Youth

League Club	Source	Date Signed	Seasons Played	Apps	Subs	Gls
Hull C	Ainthorpe Grove YC	05/49	52-59	199	-	0

HARRISON Francis Nicholas (Frankie)
Born: Eston, Cleveland, England, 19 September, 1963 — LB

League Club	Source	Date Signed	Seasons Played	Apps	Subs	Gls
Middlesbrough	Guisborough T	09/82				
Lincoln C	Carnegie College	11/85	85	0	1	0
Halifax T	Guiseley	03/87	86-89	48	6	0

HARRISON Gary Mark
Born: Northampton, England, 12 March, 1975 — M

League Club	Source	Date Signed	Seasons Played	Apps	Subs	Gls
Northampton T	Aston Villa (YT)	12/93	93-94	7	0	0

HARRISON Gerald Randall (Gerry)
Born: Lambeth, S London, England, 15 April, 1972 — M/D
England: Schools

League Club	Source	Date Signed	Seasons Played	Apps	Subs	Gls
Watford	YT	12/89	89-90	6	3	0
Bristol C	Tr	07/91	91-93	25	13	1
Cardiff C	L	01/92	91	10	0	1
Hereford U	L	11/93	93	6	0	0
Huddersfield T	Tr	03/94				
Burnley	Tr	08/94	94-97	116	8	3
Sunderland	Tr	07/98				
Luton T	L	12/98	98	14	0	0
Hull C	L	03/99	98	8	0	0
Hull C	L	10/99	99	3	0	0
Halifax T	Tr	08/00	00	7	2	1

HARRISON Harry
Born: Sunderland, England, 26 June, 1917 — FB
Died: Adelaide, Australia, 6 April, 2000

League Club	Source	Date Signed	Seasons Played	Apps	Subs	Gls
Chesterfield	Hartlepool U (Am)	06/37				
Southport	Tr	07/39	46-50	135	-	1

HARRISON Herbert
Born: Burnley, Lancashire, England, 23 January, 1916 — RW

League Club	Source	Date Signed	Seasons Played	Apps	Subs	Gls
Accrington Stan (Am)	Morecambe	10/47	47	3	-	0

HARRISON James Charles (Jimmy)
Born: Leicester, England, 12 February, 1921 — LB
Died: Leicester, England, 19 July, 2004

League Club	Source	Date Signed	Seasons Played	Apps	Subs	Gls
Leicester C	Wellington Victoria	12/41	46-48	81	-	1
Aston Villa	Tr	07/49	49	8	-	1
Coventry C	Tr	07/51	51-52	20	-	2

HARRISON James Herbert (Jim)
Born: Hammersmith, W London, England, 31 July, 1928 — CF
Died: Hillingdon, W London, England, April, 2010

League Club	Source	Date Signed	Seasons Played	Apps	Subs	Gls
Queens Park Rgrs	Willesden T	02/52	52	6	-	1

HARRISON John
Born: Swansea, Wales, 30 September, 1932 — G

League Club	Source	Date Signed	Seasons Played	Apps	Subs	Gls
Crewe Alex		08/56	56	2	-	0

HARRISON John Gilbert
Born: Worksop, Nottinghamshire, England, 18 May, 1946 — W

League Club	Source	Date Signed	Seasons Played	Apps	Subs	Gls
Sheffield U	Worksop T	01/67				
Lincoln C	Tr	07/68	68	4	0	0

HARRISON John James
Born: York, England, 7 June, 1961 — LB

League Club	Source	Date Signed	Seasons Played	Apps	Subs	Gls
York C	App	06/79	79	8	0	0

HARRISON John Michael
Born: Stepney, E London, England, 16 January, 1958 — W

League Club	Source	Date Signed	Seasons Played	Apps	Subs	Gls
Charlton Ath	App	01/76	75	5	0	2

HARRISON John Robert (Robert)
Born: Manchester, England, 23 December, 1930 — RW

League Club	Source	Date Signed	Seasons Played	Apps	Subs	Gls
Carlisle U	Army	02/53	52-54	67	-	16
Stockport Co	Mossley	07/56				

HARRISON John Walter
Born: Leicester, England, 27 September, 1927 — RB

League Club	Source	Date Signed	Seasons Played	Apps	Subs	Gls
Aston Villa		08/48				
Colchester U	Tr	07/50	50-56	237	-	1

HARRISON Kenneth (Ken)
Born: Stockton-on-Tees, Cleveland, England, 20 January, 1926 — W
Died: Hull, England, November, 2010

League Club	Source	Date Signed	Seasons Played	Apps	Subs	Gls
Hull C	Billingham Synthonia	04/47	46-54	238	-	47
Derby Co	Tr	07/54	54-55	15	-	3

HARRISON Lee David
Born: Billericay, Essex, England, 12 September, 1971 — G

League Club	Source	Date Signed	Seasons Played	Apps	Subs	Gls
Charlton Ath	YT	07/90				
Gillingham	L	03/92	91	2	0	0
Fulham	Tr	12/92	94-95	11	1	0
Barnet	Tr	07/96	96-00	183	0	0
Peterborough U	L	12/02	02	12	0	0
Leyton Orient	Tr	03/03	02-04	59	1	0
Peterborough U	Tr	08/05	05	6	0	0
Barnet	Tr	08/06	06-08	85	2	0

HARRISON Mark Simon
Born: Derby, England, 11 December, 1960 — G

League Club	Source	Date Signed	Seasons Played	Apps	Subs	Gls
Southampton	App	12/78				
Port Vale	Tr	02/80	80-81	70	0	0
Stoke C	Tr	08/82	82	7	0	0

HARRISON Michael (Mike)
Born: Leicester, England, 21 December, 1952 — CD

League Club	Source	Date Signed	Seasons Played	Apps	Subs	Gls
Birmingham C	App	02/70	70-71	3	0	0
Southend U	Tr	07/72	72	16	0	0

League Club	Source	Date Signed	Seasons Played	Career Record Apps	Subs	Gls

HARRISON Michael John (Mike)
Born: Ilford, E London, England, 18 April, 1940 — LW
England: U23-3/Schools

League Club	Source	Date Signed	Seasons Played	Apps	Subs	Gls
Chelsea	Jnr	04/57	56-62	61	-	8
Blackburn Rov	Tr	09/62	62-67	160	0	40
Plymouth Arg	Tr	09/67	67	15	0	3
Luton T	Tr	06/68	68-69	28	3	6

HARRISON Paul Anthony
Born: Liverpool, England, 18 December, 1984 — G

League Club	Source	Date Signed	Seasons Played	Apps	Subs	Gls
Liverpool	Sch	05/04				
Wolverhampton W	Prescot Cables	11/05				
Chester C	Tr	02/06	05	4	0	0
Hereford U	Tr	08/06	06	0	1	0

HARRISON Peter
Born: Sleaford, Lincolnshire, England, 25 October, 1927 — W
Died: Penarth, Vale of Glamorgan, Wales, 25 July, 2006

League Club	Source	Date Signed	Seasons Played	Apps	Subs	Gls
Leeds U	Peterborough U	01/49	49-51	65	-	9
Bournemouth	Tr	08/52	52-56	173	-	34
Reading	Tr	06/57	57-58	40	-	5
Southport	Tr	07/59	59-61	126	-	22

HARRISON Ralph
Born: Clayton-Le-Moors, Lancashire, England, 18 December, 1926 — LW

League Club	Source	Date Signed	Seasons Played	Apps	Subs	Gls
Leeds U	Great Harwood	01/49	49	2	-	0

HARRISON Raymond William (Ray)
Born: Boston, Lincolnshire, England, 21 June, 1921 — CF
Died: Doncaster, South Yorkshire, England, June, 2000

League Club	Source	Date Signed	Seasons Played	Apps	Subs	Gls
Burnley	Boston U	04/46	46-49	60	-	19
Doncaster Rov	Tr	01/50	49-53	126	-	47
Grimsby T	Tr	07/54	54	38	-	7

HARRISON Reginald Frederick (Reg)
Born: Derby, England, 22 May, 1923 — RW

League Club	Source	Date Signed	Seasons Played	Apps	Subs	Gls
Derby Co	Derby Corinthians	03/44	46-54	254	-	52

HARRISON Robert Alan
Born: Chatham, Kent, England, 25 December, 1947 — CF

League Club	Source	Date Signed	Seasons Played	Apps	Subs	Gls
Gillingham	Jnr	06/67	66	1	0	0

HARRISON Ronald (Ron)
Born: Hebburn, Tyne and Wear, England, 15 May, 1923 — IF
Died: Northumberland, England, July, 2004

League Club	Source	Date Signed	Seasons Played	Apps	Subs	Gls
Darlington	Gateshead (Am)	08/45	46	8	-	3
Gateshead	Tr	07/47	47	6	-	1

HARRISON Ryan Andrew
Born: Sherburn-in-Elmet, North Yorkshire, England, 13 October, 1991 — LB/M

League Club	Source	Date Signed	Seasons Played	Apps	Subs	Gls
Bradford C	Sch	07/10	09	0	1	0

HARRISON Scott Nathan
Born: Middlesbrough, England, 3 September, 1993 — CD

League Club	Source	Date Signed	Seasons Played	Apps	Subs	Gls
Sunderland	Darlington (Sch)	10/12				
Bury	L	11/13	13	0	1	0
Hartlepool U	Tr	03/14	13-14	41	1	1

HARRISON Steven John (Steve)
Born: Blackpool, Lancashire, England, 26 December, 1952 — LB

League Club	Source	Date Signed	Seasons Played	Apps	Subs	Gls
Blackpool	App	12/70	71-77	141	5	0
Watford	Vancouver W'caps (CAN)	09/78	78-80	82	1	0
Charlton Ath	Tr	07/81	81	3	0	0

HARRISON Terence John (Terry)
Born: Thornaby, Cleveland, England, 12 September, 1950 — F

League Club	Source	Date Signed	Seasons Played	Apps	Subs	Gls
Newcastle U	Stockton	11/67				
Barrow	Tr	07/70	70	4	0	0

HARRISON Thomas Edward (Tommy)
Born: Edinburgh, Scotland, 22 January, 1974 — M
Scotland: Youth/Schools

League Club	Source	Date Signed	Seasons Played	Apps	Subs	Gls
York C	Clyde	01/97	96	0	1	0
Carlisle U	Tr	08/97	97	6	4	0

HARRISON Walter Edward
Born: Coalville, Leicestershire, England, 16 January, 1923 — WH
Died: Leicester, England, 27 June, 1979
England: B-2

League Club	Source	Date Signed	Seasons Played	Apps	Subs	Gls
Leicester C	Coalville T	08/45	46-50	125	-	3
Chesterfield	Tr	12/50	50-52	74	-	12

HARRISON Wayne
Born: Stockport, Greater Manchester, England, 15 November, 1967 — F
Died: Stockport, Greater Manchester, England, 25 December, 2013

League Club	Source	Date Signed	Seasons Played	Apps	Subs	Gls
Oldham Ath	App	12/84	84	4	1	1
Liverpool	Tr	03/85				
Oldham Ath	L	03/85	84	1	0	0
Crewe Alex	L	12/88	88	3	0	1

HARRISON Wayne Moffat
Born: Whitehaven, Cumbria, England, 16 October, 1957 — M

League Club	Source	Date Signed	Seasons Played	Apps	Subs	Gls
Workington	Everton (App)	08/75	75	1	3	0
Blackpool	Sheffield Wed (NC)	09/79	79-81	81	5	6
Carlisle U	Workington	08/87	87	1	1	0

HARRITY Michael David (Mick)
Born: Sheffield, England, 5 October, 1946 — FB

League Club	Source	Date Signed	Seasons Played	Apps	Subs	Gls
Rotherham U		10/65	65-68	36	5	0
Doncaster Rov	Tr	09/68	68	2	0	0

HARROLD Mark Anthony
Born: Halifax, West Yorkshire, England, 29 January, 1957 — M

League Club	Source	Date Signed	Seasons Played	Apps	Subs	Gls
Halifax T	Jnr	08/74	74-75	8	5	1

HARROLD Matthew James (Matt)
Born: Leyton, NE London, England, 25 July, 1984 — F

League Club	Source	Date Signed	Seasons Played	Apps	Subs	Gls
Brentford	Harlow T	08/03	03-04	11	21	2
Grimsby T	L	03/05	04	6	0	2
Yeovil T	Tr	07/05	05-06	30	17	9
Southend U	Tr	08/06	06-07	25	27	3
Wycombe W	Tr	09/08	08-09	57	16	17
Shrewsbury T	Tr	08/10	10	28	13	8
Bristol Rov	Tr	06/11	11-13	62	14	24
Crawley T	Tr	06/14	14	4	16	1
Cambridge U	L	02/15	14	6	1	1

HARROP Jack
Born: Manchester, England, 25 June, 1929 — LB
Died: Hemel Hempstead, Hertfordshire, England, 18 February, 1977

League Club	Source	Date Signed	Seasons Played	Apps	Subs	Gls
Swansea C	Charlton Ath (Am)	08/52	52-53	10	-	0
Watford	Tr	07/56	56-59	111	-	0

HARROP Max
Born: Oldham, Greater Manchester, England, 30 June, 1993 — LB/M

League Club	Source	Date Signed	Seasons Played	Apps	Subs	Gls
Bury	Sch	07/11	10-11	0	8	0

HARROP Robert (Bobby)
Born: Manchester, England, 25 August, 1936 — WH
Died: Margate, Kent, England, 8 November, 2007

League Club	Source	Date Signed	Seasons Played	Apps	Subs	Gls
Manchester U	Benchill YC	05/54	57-58	10	-	0
Tranmere Rov	Tr	11/59	59-60	41	-	2

HARROW Andrew (Andy)
Born: Kirkcaldy, Fife, Scotland, 6 November, 1956 — F

League Club	Source	Date Signed	Seasons Played	Apps	Subs	Gls
Luton T	Raith Rov	09/80	80	3	1	0

HARROWER James (Jimmy)
Born: Alva, Stirlingshire, Scotland, 18 August, 1935 — IF
Died: Stirling, Scotland, 28 November, 2006
Scotland: U23-1

League Club	Source	Date Signed	Seasons Played	Apps	Subs	Gls
Liverpool	Hibernian	01/58	57-60	96	-	21
Newcastle U	Tr	03/61	60-61	5	-	0

HARROWER James Swanson (Jimmy)
Born: Crossgates, Fife, Scotland, 19 June, 1924 — D
Died: Blackburn, Greater Manchester, England, February, 1992

League Club	Source	Date Signed	Seasons Played	Apps	Subs	Gls
Accrington Stan	Third Lanark	12/54	54-60	246	-	2

HARROWER Steven Gordon (Steve)
Born: Exeter, England, 9 October, 1961 — M/RB

League Club	Source	Date Signed	Seasons Played	Apps	Subs	Gls
Exeter C	Dawlish T	01/84	83-89	165	22	10

HARROWER William (Bill)
Born: Dunfermline, Fife, Scotland, 13 April, 1922 — WH/IF
Died: Exeter, England, 29 May, 2003

League Club	Source	Date Signed	Seasons Played	Apps	Subs	Gls
Torquay U	Third Lanark	05/46	46-47	16	-	3
Exeter C	Tr	07/48	48-51	85	-	11

HARSLEY Paul
Born: Scunthorpe, North Lincolnshire, England, 29 May, 1978 — M

League Club	Source	Date Signed	Seasons Played	Apps	Subs	Gls
Grimsby T	YT	07/96				
Scunthorpe U	Tr	07/97	97-00	110	18	5
Halifax T	Tr	07/01	01	45	0	11
Northampton T	Tr	07/02	02-03	46	13	2
Macclesfield T	Tr	02/04	03-05	105	2	11
Port Vale	Tr	07/06	06-07	68	5	6
Chesterfield	Tr	07/08	08-09	7	13	1
Darlington	L	11/09	09	3	0	0

HARSTON John Charles (Jack)
Born: Barnsley, South Yorkshire, England, 7 October, 1920 — RB
Died: Barnsley, South Yorkshire, England, 25 June, 2013

League Club	Source	Date Signed	Seasons Played	Apps	Subs	Gls
Wolverhampton W	Ardsley Ath	10/37				
Barnsley	Tr	09/38	46-48	20	-	1
Bradford C	Tr	06/49	49	24	-	1

HART Alan Michael
Born: Woolwich, SE London, England, 21 February, 1956 — M

League Club	Source	Date Signed	Seasons Played	Apps	Subs	Gls
Charlton Ath	App	02/74	74	3	0	2
Millwall	Tr	06/75	75	13	3	0

HART Andrew (Andy)
Born: Great Yarmouth, Norfolk, England, 14 January, 1963 FB

League Club	Source	Date Signed	Seasons Played	Apps	Subs	Gls
Norwich C	App	01/81	81	0	1	0

HART Brian Patrick
Born: Farnworth, Greater Manchester, England, 14 July, 1959 D

League Club	Source	Date Signed	Seasons Played	Apps	Subs	Gls
Rochdale	Bolton W (App)	12/77	77-79	73	5	0

HART Callum Louis
Born: Cardiff, Wales, 21 December, 1985 LB

League Club	Source	Date Signed	Seasons Played	Apps	Subs	Gls
Bournemouth	Bristol C (Sch)	08/05	05-06	40	7	0

HART Charles Joseph John (Joe)
Born: Shrewsbury, Shropshire, England, 19 April, 1987 G
England: 52/U21-21/Youth

League Club	Source	Date Signed	Seasons Played	Apps	Subs	Gls
Shrewsbury T	Sch	08/04	04-05	52	0	0
Manchester C	Tr	05/06	06-14	231	0	0
Tranmere Rov	L	01/07	06	6	0	0
Blackpool	L	04/07	06	5	0	0
Birmingham C	L	07/09	09	36	0	0

HART Danny Gary
Born: Barnet, N London, England, 26 April, 1989 W

League Club	Source	Date Signed	Seasons Played	Apps	Subs	Gls
Barnet	Boreham Wood	09/07	07-09	2	4	1

HART Gary John
Born: Harlow, Essex, England, 21 September, 1976 F/M

League Club	Source	Date Signed	Seasons Played	Apps	Subs	Gls
Brighton & HA	Stansted	06/98	98-10	298	75	44

HART Harold (Harry)
Born: Sheffield, England, 29 September, 1926 IF
Died: Morecambe, Lancashire, England, 11 February, 2012

League Club	Source	Date Signed	Seasons Played	Apps	Subs	Gls
Rotherham U	Woodthorpe YC	12/45	49	10	-	4
Coventry C	Tr	06/50	50-51	10	-	1
Grimsby T	Tr	12/52	52	13	-	3

HART John Leslie (Les)
Born: Ashton-under-Lyne, Greater Manchester, England, 28 February, 1917 CH
Died: Bury, Greater Manchester, England, August, 1996

League Club	Source	Date Signed	Seasons Played	Apps	Subs	Gls
Bury	Earlestown White Star	12/36	38-53	280	-	2

HART John Paul (Johnny)
Born: Golborne, Greater Manchester, England, 8 June, 1928 IF

League Club	Source	Date Signed	Seasons Played	Apps	Subs	Gls
Manchester C	Loughton YC	06/45	47-60	169	-	67

HART Marvin Stuart (Stuart)
Born: Long Eaton, Derbyshire, England, 15 January, 1941 W

League Club	Source	Date Signed	Seasons Played	Apps	Subs	Gls
Exeter C	Long Eaton U	08/67	67	20	2	1

HART Michael
Born: Airdrie, Lanarkshire, Scotland, 10 February, 1980 RB

League Club	Source	Date Signed	Seasons Played	Apps	Subs	Gls
Preston NE	Aberdeen	01/08	07-09	17	2	0

HART Nigel
Born: Golborne, Greater Manchester, England, 1 October, 1958 CD

League Club	Source	Date Signed	Seasons Played	Apps	Subs	Gls
Wigan Ath	Stockport Co (NC)	08/78	79	1	0	0
Leicester C	Tr	10/79				
Blackpool	Tr	08/81	81-82	36	1	0
Crewe Alex	Tr	11/82	82-86	139	3	10
Bury	Tr	02/87	86-87	33	12	2
Stockport Co	Tr	07/88	88-89	38	1	2
Chesterfield	Tr	08/89	89-90	45	1	2
York C	Tr	02/91	90	1	0	0

HART Paul Anthony
Born: Golborne, Greater Manchester, England, 4 May, 1953 CD

League Club	Source	Date Signed	Seasons Played	Apps	Subs	Gls
Stockport Co	Jnr	09/70	70-72	87	0	5
Blackpool	Tr	06/73	73-77	143	0	15
Leeds U	Tr	03/78	77-82	191	0	16
Nottingham F	Tr	05/83	83-84	70	0	1
Sheffield Wed	Tr	08/85	85-86	52	0	2
Birmingham C	Tr	12/86	86	1	0	0
Notts Co	Tr	06/87	87	23	0	0

HART Peter
Born: Wickersley, South Yorkshire, England, 6 September, 1949 RB
England: Schools

League Club	Source	Date Signed	Seasons Played	Apps	Subs	Gls
Bradford Park Ave	Rotherham U (App)	03/68	67	3	0	0

HART Peter Osborne
Born: Mexborough, South Yorkshire, England, 14 August, 1957 CD

League Club	Source	Date Signed	Seasons Played	Apps	Subs	Gls
Huddersfield T	App	08/74	73-79	208	2	7
Walsall	Tr	08/80	80-89	389	1	12

HART Roy Ernest
Born: Acton, W London, England, 30 May, 1933 CH
Died: West Sussex, England, June, 2014
England: Schools

League Club	Source	Date Signed	Seasons Played	Apps	Subs	Gls
Brentford	Jnr	06/50	54	2	-	0

HART William Robert (Bill)
Born: North Shields, Tyne and Wear, England, 1 April, 1923 RH
Died: North Shields, Tyne and Wear, England, March, 1990

League Club	Source	Date Signed	Seasons Played	Apps	Subs	Gls
Newcastle U	Willington Quay	09/40				
Chesterfield	North Shields	03/45	46	1	-	0
Bradford C	Tr	05/47	46-48	25	-	0

HARTBURN John (Johnny)
Born: Houghton-le-Spring, Tyne and Wear, England, 20 December, 1920 LW
Died: Bournemouth, England, 21 January, 2001

League Club	Source	Date Signed	Seasons Played	Apps	Subs	Gls
Queens Park Rgrs	Yeovil T	03/47	47-48	58	-	11
Watford	Tr	09/49	49-50	66	-	19
Millwall	Tr	03/51	50-53	104	-	29
Leyton Orient	Tr	06/54	54-57	112	-	36

HARTE Ian Patrick
Born: Drogheda, Republic of Ireland, 31 August, 1977 LB/M
Republic of Ireland: 64/U21-6

League Club	Source	Date Signed	Seasons Played	Apps	Subs	Gls
Leeds U	YT	12/95	95-03	199	14	28
Sunderland	Levante (SPN)	08/07	07	3	5	0
Blackpool	Charlton Ath (NC)	12/08	08	4	0	0
Carlisle U	Tr	03/09	08-10	52	0	19
Reading	Tr	08/10	10-12	85	3	15
Bournemouth	Tr	07/13	13-14	26	2	1

HARTENBERGER Uwe
Born: Lauterecken, Germany, 1 February, 1968 F

League Club	Source	Date Signed	Seasons Played	Apps	Subs	Gls
Reading	Bayer Uerdingen (GER)	09/93	93-94	8	16	4

HARTERY John
Born: Waterford, Republic of Ireland, 25 November, 1920 RB
Republic of Ireland: LoI-7

League Club	Source	Date Signed	Seasons Played	Apps	Subs	Gls
Plymouth Arg	Limerick (ROI)	06/48	49	1	-	0

HARTFIELD Charles Joseph (Charlie)
Born: Lambeth, S London, England, 4 September, 1971 M/FB
England: Youth

League Club	Source	Date Signed	Seasons Played	Apps	Subs	Gls
Arsenal	YT	09/89				
Sheffield U	Tr	08/91	91-96	45	11	1
Fulham	L	02/97	96	1	1	0
Swansea C	Tr	11/97	97	22	0	2
Lincoln C	L	09/98	98	3	0	1

HARTFORD Richard Asa (Asa)
Born: Clydebank, Dunbartonshire, Scotland, 24 October, 1950 M
Scotland: 50/U23-5/U21-1

League Club	Source	Date Signed	Seasons Played	Apps	Subs	Gls
West Bromwich A	Drumchapel Amats	11/67	67-73	206	8	18
Manchester C	Tr	08/74	74-78	184	1	22
Nottingham F	Tr	07/79	79	3	0	0
Everton	Tr	08/79	79-81	81	0	6
Manchester C	Tr	10/81	81-83	75	0	7
Norwich C	Tr	10/84	84	28	0	2
Bolton W	Ft Laud'ale Suns (USA)	07/85	85-86	81	0	8
Stockport Co	Tr	06/87	87-88	42	3	0
Oldham Ath	Tr	03/89	88	3	4	0
Shrewsbury T	Tr	08/89	89-90	22	3	0

HARTLAND Michael Leo (Mick)
Born: Dunfermline, Fife, Scotland, 7 January, 1944 M

League Club	Source	Date Signed	Seasons Played	Apps	Subs	Gls
Oxford U	Nuneaton Bor	06/63	63-64	19	-	6
Barrow	Tr	07/65	65-70	168	9	19
Crewe Alex	Tr	12/70	70	3	0	1
Southport	Tr	07/71	71-72	32	5	4

HARTLE Barry
Born: Salford, England, 8 August, 1939 LW/LB

League Club	Source	Date Signed	Seasons Played	Apps	Subs	Gls
Watford	Jnr	08/56	58-59	39	-	7
Sheffield U	Tr	06/60	60-65	101	0	16
Carlisle U	Tr	07/66	66-67	28	1	1
Stockport Co	Tr	09/67	67-69	88	0	1
Oldham Ath	Tr	06/70	70	8	1	2
Southport	Tr	07/71	71	37	4	6

HARTLE Leslie Roy (Roy)
Born: Catshill, Worcestershire, England, 4 October, 1931 RB
Died: Bolton, Greater Manchester, England, 5 November, 2014
England: FLge-1

League Club	Source	Date Signed	Seasons Played	Apps	Subs	Gls
Bolton W	Bromsgrove Rov	02/51	52-65	446	1	11

HARTLEY Edmund (Eddie)
Born: Burnley, Lancashire, England, 5 May, 1932 W
Died: Blackburn, Greater Manchester, England, May, 2013

League Club	Source	Date Signed	Seasons Played	Apps	Subs	Gls
Burnley	Jnr	11/50				
Oldham Ath	Rossendale U	07/56	56	1	-	0

HARTLEY Paul James
Born: Hamilton, Lanarkshire, Scotland, 19 October, 1976 M/W
Scotland: 25/U21-1

League Club	Source	Date Signed	Seasons Played	Apps	Subs	Gls
Millwall	Hamilton Academical	07/96	96	35	9	4
Bristol C	Glasgow Celtic	07/09	09	36	4	5

League Club	Source	Date Signed	Seasons Played	Career Record Apps	Subs	Gls

HARTLEY Peter
Born: Hartlepool, Cleveland, England, 3 April, 1988 — CD

League Club	Source	Date Signed	Seasons Played	Apps	Subs	Gls
Sunderland	Sch	07/06	06	0	1	0
Chesterfield	L	02/08	07	12	0	0
Hartlepool U	Tr	07/09	09-13	164	2	10
Stevenage	Tr	08/13	13	29	2	2
Plymouth Arg	Tr	07/14	14	38	1	4

HARTLEY Thomas William (Tom)
Born: Gateshead, Tyne and Wear, England, 7 May, 1917 — IF
Died: Chesterfield, Derbyshire, England, January, 1984

League Club	Source	Date Signed	Seasons Played	Apps	Subs	Gls
Gateshead	Birtley BC	02/36	35-36	5	-	1
Bury	Tr	05/38				
Chesterfield	Tr	05/39				
Leicester C	Stockton	01/48				
Watford	Tr	02/48	47	6	-	1

HARTLEY Trevor John
Born: Doncaster, South Yorkshire, England, 16 March, 1947 — RW

League Club	Source	Date Signed	Seasons Played	Apps	Subs	Gls
West Ham U	Jnr	07/64	66-68	4	1	0
Bournemouth	Tr	07/69	69-70	35	8	2

HARTNETT James Benedict (Jimmy)
Born: Dublin, Republic of Ireland, 21 March, 1927 — LW
Died: Middlesbrough, England, December, 1988
Republic of Ireland: 2/LoI-1

League Club	Source	Date Signed	Seasons Played	Apps	Subs	Gls
Middlesbrough	Dundalk (ROI)	06/48	48-54	48	-	8
Hartlepool U	Barry T	09/57	57	7	-	1
York C	Tr	08/58	58	2	-	1

HARTSON John
Born: Neath, Wales, 5 April, 1975 — F
Wales: 51/U21-9/Youth

League Club	Source	Date Signed	Seasons Played	Apps	Subs	Gls
Luton T	YT	12/92	93-94	32	22	11
Arsenal	Tr	01/95	94-96	43	10	14
West Ham U	Tr	02/97	96-98	59	1	24
Wimbledon	Tr	01/99	98-00	46	3	19
Coventry C	Tr	02/01	00	12	0	6
West Bromwich A	Glasgow Rangers	07/06	06	14	7	5
Norwich C	L	10/07	07	2	2	0

HARTY Ian McGuinness
Born: Airdrie, Lanarkshire, Scotland, 8 April, 1978 — F

League Club	Source	Date Signed	Seasons Played	Apps	Subs	Gls
Darlington	Airdrieonians	07/07	07	0	1	0

HARVEY Alexander (Alex)
Born: Kirkconnel, Dumfries & Galloway, Scotland, 25 August, 1925 — LH
Died: Penicuik, Midlothian, Scotland, 15 April, 2002

League Club	Source	Date Signed	Seasons Played	Apps	Subs	Gls
Carlisle U	Queen of the South	08/46	46	1	-	0

HARVEY Alexander (Alex)
Born: Ayr, Scotland, 28 September, 1928 — IF
Died: Chesterfield, Derbyshire, England, 21 May, 1998

League Club	Source	Date Signed	Seasons Played	Apps	Subs	Gls
Chesterfield	Saltcoats Victoria	11/50	50-52	27	-	9

HARVEY Brian
Born: Liverpool, England, 12 January, 1947 — WH

League Club	Source	Date Signed	Seasons Played	Apps	Subs	Gls
Chester C	Sheffield Wed (Am)	09/64	64	1	-	0

HARVEY Bryan Robert
Born: Stepney, E London, England, 26 August, 1938 — G
Died: Northampton, England, 31 March, 2006

League Club	Source	Date Signed	Seasons Played	Apps	Subs	Gls
Newcastle U	Wisbech T	09/58	58-60	86	-	0
Blackpool	Cambridge C	02/62	61-63	11	-	0
Northampton T	Tr	10/63	63-67	165	0	0

HARVEY David
Born: Leeds, England, 7 February, 1948 — G
Scotland: 16

League Club	Source	Date Signed	Seasons Played	Apps	Subs	Gls
Leeds U	Jnr	02/65	65-79	277	0	0
Leeds U	Vancouver W'caps (CAN)	09/82	82-84	73	0	0
Bradford C	Tr	02/85	84	6	0	0

HARVEY David
Born: Hetton-le-Hole, Tyne and Wear, England, 15 February, 1954 — W

League Club	Source	Date Signed	Seasons Played	Apps	Subs	Gls
Hartlepool U	App	-	70	3	2	0

HARVEY Gary
Born: Colchester, Essex, England, 19 November, 1961 — F

League Club	Source	Date Signed	Seasons Played	Apps	Subs	Gls
Colchester U	App	11/79	79-80	6	0	2

HARVEY James (Jimmy)
Born: Lurgan, Armagh, Northern Ireland, 2 May, 1958 — M
Northern Ireland: U23-1

League Club	Source	Date Signed	Seasons Played	Apps	Subs	Gls
Arsenal	Glenavon	08/77	77-78	2	1	0
Hereford U	Tr	03/80	79-86	276	2	38
Bristol C	Tr	03/87	86-87	2	1	0
Wrexham	L	09/87	87	6	0	0
Tranmere Rov	Tr	10/87	87-91	174	10	18
Crewe Alex	Tr	07/92	92	16	1	0

HARVEY James Colin (Colin)
Born: Liverpool, England, 16 November, 1944 — M
England: 1/FLge-3/U23-5

League Club	Source	Date Signed	Seasons Played	Apps	Subs	Gls
Everton	App	10/62	63-74	317	3	18
Sheffield Wed	Tr	09/74	74-75	45	0	2

HARVEY Joseph (Joe)
Born: Bedlington, Northumberland, England, 11 June, 1918 — RH
Died: Newcastle-upon-Tyne, England, 24 February, 1989
England: FLge-3

League Club	Source	Date Signed	Seasons Played	Apps	Subs	Gls
Bradford Park Ave	Edlington Rgrs	05/36				
Wolverhampton W	Tr	11/36				
Bournemouth	Tr	05/37	37	1	-	0
Bradford C	Tr	07/38				
Newcastle U	Tr	10/45	46-52	224	-	12

HARVEY Lawrence (Lol)
Born: Heanor, Derbyshire, England, 25 July, 1934 — FB/WH

League Club	Source	Date Signed	Seasons Played	Apps	Subs	Gls
Coventry C	Jnr	07/51	51-60	140	-	1

HARVEY Lee Derek
Born: Harlow, Essex, England, 21 December, 1966 — M
England: Youth

League Club	Source	Date Signed	Seasons Played	Apps	Subs	Gls
Leyton Orient	App	12/84	83-92	135	49	23
Nottingham F	Tr	08/93	93	0	2	0
Brentford	Tr	11/93	93-96	87	18	6

HARVEY Leighton
Born: Neath, Wales, 27 August, 1959 — W

League Club	Source	Date Signed	Seasons Played	Apps	Subs	Gls
Swansea C	App	-	75-76	1	1	0

HARVEY Martin
Born: Belfast, Northern Ireland, 19 September, 1941 — RH/FB
Northern Ireland: 34/B/U23-3/Schools

League Club	Source	Date Signed	Seasons Played	Apps	Subs	Gls
Sunderland	Jnr	09/58	59-71	311	5	5

HARVEY Neil Anthony Cory
Born: Westminster, Central London, England, 6 August, 1983 — F
Barbados: 4

League Club	Source	Date Signed	Seasons Played	Apps	Subs	Gls
Macclesfield T	Retford U	07/08	08	0	5	0

HARVEY Richard George
Born: Letchworth, Hertfordshire, England, 17 April, 1969 — LB
England: Youth/Schools

League Club	Source	Date Signed	Seasons Played	Apps	Subs	Gls
Luton T	App	01/87	86-97	134	27	4
Blackpool	L	10/92	92	4	1	0

HARVEY Tyler Marshall
Born: Plymouth, England, 29 June, 1995 — F

League Club	Source	Date Signed	Seasons Played	Apps	Subs	Gls
Plymouth Arg	Sch	06/13	12-14	8	36	3

HARVEY William Derek (Bill)
Born: Doncaster, South Yorkshire, England, 30 September, 1934 — FB

League Club	Source	Date Signed	Seasons Played	Apps	Subs	Gls
Doncaster Rov	Jnr	11/51	52	2	-	0

HARVEY William James
Born: Clydebank, Dunbartonshire, Scotland, 23 November, 1929 — IF
Died: June, 2014

League Club	Source	Date Signed	Seasons Played	Apps	Subs	Gls
Bradford Park Ave	Dunfermline Ath	01/59	58-59	26	-	1

HARVEY William Keith (Keith)
Born: Crediton, Devon, England, 25 December, 1934 — CH

League Club	Source	Date Signed	Seasons Played	Apps	Subs	Gls
Exeter C	Crediton	08/52	52-68	483	0	28

HARWOOD Lee
Born: Southall, W London, England, 4 October, 1960 — CD

League Club	Source	Date Signed	Seasons Played	Apps	Subs	Gls
Southampton	App	10/78				
Wimbledon	Tr	01/79	78	1	0	0
Port Vale	Leatherhead	02/80	79-80	19	0	1

HARWOOD Richard Andrew
Born: Sheffield, England, 13 September, 1960 — M

League Club	Source	Date Signed	Seasons Played	Apps	Subs	Gls
Sheffield U	App	07/78	78	2	1	0

HASELDEN John James
Born: Doncaster, South Yorkshire, England, 3 August, 1943 — CD

League Club	Source	Date Signed	Seasons Played	Apps	Subs	Gls
Rotherham U	Denaby U	02/62	61-68	98	1	0
Doncaster Rov	Tr	09/68	68-73	168	4	20
Mansfield T	L	02/72	71	4	0	0

HASFORD Jason Miles
Born: Manchester, England, 1 April, 1971 — F

League Club	Source	Date Signed	Seasons Played	Apps	Subs	Gls
Rochdale	Manchester C (YT)	07/89	89	0	1	0

HASKINS Anthony John
Born: Northampton, England, 26 July, 1935 — LB

League Club	Source	Date Signed	Seasons Played	Apps	Subs	Gls
Northampton T		01/59	59-61	8	-	0

HASLAM Graham
Born: Doncaster, South Yorkshire, England, 29 April, 1956 — G

League Club	Source	Date Signed	Seasons Played	Apps	Subs	Gls
Rotherham U	App	04/74	75	2	0	0

HASLAM Harry
Born: Manchester, England, 30 July, 1921 FB
Died: Biggleswade, Bedfordshire, England, 11 September, 1986

League Club	Source	Date Signed	Seasons Played	Apps	Subs	Gls
Oldham Ath	Rochdale (Am)	05/46	46	2	-	0
Brighton & HA	Tr	09/47				
Leyton Orient	Tr	07/48	48	7	-	0

HASLAM Steven Robert (Steve)
Born: Sheffield, England, 6 September, 1979 RB
England: Semi Pro-3/Youth/Schools

League Club	Source	Date Signed	Seasons Played	Apps	Subs	Gls
Sheffield Wed	YT	09/96	98-03	115	29	2
Northampton T	Halifax T	08/04	04	2	1	0
Bury	Halifax T	07/07	07-08	50	0	1
Hartlepool U	Tr	08/09	09-11	40	14	0

HASLEGRAVE Sean Matthew
Born: Stoke-on-Trent, England, 7 June, 1951 M

League Club	Source	Date Signed	Seasons Played	Apps	Subs	Gls
Stoke C	Jnr	11/68	70-75	106	7	5
Nottingham F	Tr	07/76	76	5	2	1
Preston NE	Tr	09/77	77-80	111	2	2
Crewe Alex	Tr	08/81	81-82	78	4	1
York C	Tr	07/83	83-86	137	5	0
Torquay U	Tr	08/87	87-88	32	4	1

HASPELL Alan
Born: Northwich, Cheshire, England, 23 January, 1943 IF

League Club	Source	Date Signed	Seasons Played	Apps	Subs	Gls
Burnley	Jnr	01/60				
Doncaster Rov	Tr	07/63	63	1	-	0

HASSALL Harold William
Born: Tyldesley, Greater Manchester, England, 4 March, 1929 IF
Died: Bolton, Greater Manchester, England, 30 January, 2015
England: 5/FLge-3

League Club	Source	Date Signed	Seasons Played	Apps	Subs	Gls
Huddersfield T	Mossley Common	09/46	48-51	74	-	26
Bolton W	Tr	01/52	51-54	102	-	34

HASSALL Wilfred (Wilf)
Born: Prestwich, Greater Manchester, England, 23 September, 1923 FB
Died: Hull, England, 25 June, 1998

League Club	Source	Date Signed	Seasons Played	Apps	Subs	Gls
Hull C	RM Alsager	09/46	46-52	141	-	3

HASSAN Emmanuel Oluwaseun (Callum)
Born: Southwark, S London, England, 23 January, 1993 F

League Club	Source	Date Signed	Seasons Played	Apps	Subs	Gls
Hartlepool U	Sch	07/11	11	0	1	0

HASSELBAINK Jerrel (Jimmy Floyd)
Born: Paramaribo, Suriname, 27 March, 1972 F
Netherlands: 23

League Club	Source	Date Signed	Seasons Played	Apps	Subs	Gls
Leeds U	Boavista (POR)	07/97	97-98	66	3	34
Chelsea	Atletico Madrid (SPN)	07/00	00-03	119	17	69
Middlesbrough	Tr	07/04	04-05	48	10	22
Charlton Ath	Tr	07/06	06	11	14	2
Cardiff C	Tr	08/07	07	33	3	7

HASSELL Richard (Ricky)
Born: Coatbridge, Lanarkshire, Scotland, 12 January, 1951 WH

League Club	Source	Date Signed	Seasons Played	Apps	Subs	Gls
Carlisle U	Jnr	01/69	68-69	2	3	0

HASSELL Robert John Francis (Bobby)
Born: Derby, England, 4 June, 1980 RB

League Club	Source	Date Signed	Seasons Played	Apps	Subs	Gls
Mansfield T	YT	07/98	97-03	151	9	3
Barnsley	Tr	07/04	04-13	236	31	7

HASSELL Thomas William (Tommy)
Born: Eastleigh, Hampshire, England, 5 April, 1919 W
Died: Hove, East Sussex, England, April, 1984

League Club	Source	Date Signed	Seasons Played	Apps	Subs	Gls
Southampton	Romsey T	02/40				
Aldershot	Tr	05/46	46-49	114	-	16
Brighton & HA	Tr	08/50	50	11	-	4

HASTIE John Kenneth George (Ken)
Born: Cape Town, South Africa, 6 September, 1928 CF

League Club	Source	Date Signed	Seasons Played	Apps	Subs	Gls
Leeds U	Clyde Ath (RSA)	08/52	52	4	-	2

HASTINGS John Joseph David
Born: Lambeth, S London, England, 26 September, 1983 F

League Club	Source	Date Signed	Seasons Played	Apps	Subs	Gls
MK Dons	Tooting & Mitcham U	07/06	06	0	7	0

HASTY Patrick Joseph (Paddy)
Born: Belfast, Northern Ireland, 17 March, 1932 CF
Died: Northern Ireland, August, 2000
Northern Ireland: Amateur

League Club	Source	Date Signed	Seasons Played	Apps	Subs	Gls
Leyton Orient (Am)	Tooting & Mitcham U	07/58	58	2	-	2
Queens Park Rgrs (Am)	Tooting & Mitcham U	10/59	59	1	-	0
Aldershot	Tooting & Mitcham U	03/61	60-62	35	-	14

HATCH Liam Morris Adam
Born: Hitchin, Hertfordshire, England, 3 April, 1982 F
England: Semi Pro-6

League Club	Source	Date Signed	Seasons Played	Apps	Subs	Gls
Barnet	Gravesend & Northfleet	07/03	05-07	49	38	11
Peterborough U	Tr	01/08	07-08	1	11	2
Darlington	L	08/08	08	23	3	8

HATCH Peter Derek
Born: Wargrave, Berkshire, England, 22 October, 1949 LB/M

League Club	Source	Date Signed	Seasons Played	Apps	Subs	Gls
Oxford U	App	10/66	67-72	15	4	2
Exeter C	Tr	12/73	73-81	343	3	18

HATCHER Clifford Henry (Cliff)
Born: Keynsham, Avon, England, 27 June, 1925 G
Died: Bath, England, 2 December, 1978

League Club	Source	Date Signed	Seasons Played	Apps	Subs	Gls
Reading	JS Fry & Sons	06/46	47-48	2	-	0

HATCHER Daniel Ian (Danny)
Born: Newport, Isle of Wight, England, 24 December, 1983 F

League Club	Source	Date Signed	Seasons Played	Apps	Subs	Gls
Leyton Orient	YT	-	00-02	3	13	0

HATCHER Douglas Terence (Doug)
Born: Carshalton, S London, England, 6 March, 1962 G

League Club	Source	Date Signed	Seasons Played	Apps	Subs	Gls
Fulham	App	03/80				
Aldershot	Wokingham T	08/83	83	1	0	0

HATELEY Anthony (Tony)
Born: Derby, England, 13 June, 1941 CF
Died: Preston, Lancashire, England, 1 February, 2014

League Club	Source	Date Signed	Seasons Played	Apps	Subs	Gls
Notts Co	Jnr	06/58	58-62	131	-	77
Aston Villa	Tr	08/63	63-66	127	0	68
Chelsea	Tr	10/66	66	26	1	6
Liverpool	Tr	07/67	67-68	42	0	17
Coventry C	Tr	09/68	68	17	0	4
Birmingham C	Tr	08/69	69-70	28	0	6
Notts Co	Tr	11/70	70-71	57	0	32
Oldham Ath	Tr	07/72	73	1	4	1

HATELEY Mark Wayne
Born: Derby, England, 7 November, 1961 F
England: 32/U21-10/Youth

League Club	Source	Date Signed	Seasons Played	Apps	Subs	Gls
Coventry C	App	12/78	78-82	86	6	25
Portsmouth	Tr	06/83	83	38	0	22
Queens Park Rgrs	Glasgow Rangers	11/95	95-96	18	9	3
Leeds U	L	08/96	96	5	1	0
Hull C	Glasgow Rangers	08/97	97-98	12	9	3

HATELEY Thomas Nathan (Tom)
Born: Monte Carlo, Monaco, 12 September, 1989 RB/M

League Club	Source	Date Signed	Seasons Played	Apps	Subs	Gls
Reading	Sch	07/08				
Tranmere Rov	Motherwell	09/13	13	8	0	0

HATFIELD William Henry (Will)
Born: Liversedge, West Yorkshire, England, 10 October, 1991 W

League Club	Source	Date Signed	Seasons Played	Apps	Subs	Gls
Leeds U	Sch	07/09				
Accrington Stan	L	10/11	11	2	2	0
Accrington Stan	FC Halifax T	02/12	11-14	44	39	5

HATHAWAY Ian Ashley
Born: Dudley, West Midlands, England, 22 August, 1968 LW/M

League Club	Source	Date Signed	Seasons Played	Apps	Subs	Gls
Mansfield T	Bedworth U	02/89	88-90	21	23	2
Rotherham U	Tr	03/91	90-91	5	8	1
Torquay U	Tr	07/93	93-96	114	26	14
Colchester U	Tr	06/97	97	5	7	0

HATSELL Dennis
Born: Preston, Lancashire, England, 9 June, 1930 CF
Died: Basildon, England, 1 January, 1998

League Club	Source	Date Signed	Seasons Played	Apps	Subs	Gls
Preston NE	Jnr	06/48	53-59	115	-	54

HATSWELL Wayne Mervin
Born: Swindon, England, 8 February, 1975 CD
England: Semi Pro-6

League Club	Source	Date Signed	Seasons Played	Apps	Subs	Gls
Oxford U	Forest Green Rov	12/00	00-01	47	1	0
Kidderminster Hrs	Chester C	10/03	03-04	70	2	3
Rushden & D	Tr	01/06	05	17	0	1

HATTER Stephen John (Steve)
Born: East Ham, E London, England, 21 October, 1958 CD

League Club	Source	Date Signed	Seasons Played	Apps	Subs	Gls
Fulham	App	05/76	77-80	25	1	1
Exeter C	L	09/82	82	11	0	1
Wimbledon	Tr	11/82	82-84	82	2	4
Southend U	Tr	03/85	84-85	61	0	2

HATTON Cyril
Born: Grantham, Lincolnshire, England, 14 September, 1918 IF
Died: Grantham, Lincolnshire, England, 3 July, 1987

League Club	Source	Date Signed	Seasons Played	Apps	Subs	Gls
Notts Co	Grantham Co-operative	12/36	36-38	62	-	15
Queens Park Rgrs	Tr	04/46	46-52	162	-	64
Chesterfield	Tr	06/53	53	36	-	10

HATTON David Howcroft (Dave)
Born: Farnworth, Greater Manchester, England, 30 October, 1943 CD

League Club	Source	Date Signed	Seasons Played	Apps	Subs	Gls
Bolton W	Jnr	11/60	61-69	231	0	8
Blackpool	Tr	09/69	69-75	250	1	7
Bury	Tr	08/76	76-78	96	1	2

League Club	Source	Date Signed	Seasons Played	Career Record Apps	Subs	Gls

HATTON Robert James (Bob)
Born: Hull, England, 10 April, 1947 — F

League Club	Source	Date Signed	Seasons Played	Apps	Subs	Gls
Wolverhampton W	Jnr	11/64	66	10	0	7
Bolton W	Tr	03/67	66-67	23	1	2
Northampton T	Tr	10/68	68	29	4	7
Carlisle U	Tr	07/69	69-71	93	0	38
Birmingham C	Tr	10/71	71-75	170	5	58
Blackpool	Tr	07/76	76-77	75	0	32
Luton T	Tr	07/78	78-79	81	1	29
Sheffield U	Tr	07/80	80-82	92	3	34
Cardiff C	Tr	12/82	82	29	1	9

HATTON Samuel William (Sam)
Born: St Albans, Hertfordshire, England, 7 February, 1988 — RB
England: Semi Pro-3

League Club	Source	Date Signed	Seasons Played	Apps	Subs	Gls
AFC Wimbledon	Stevenage Bor	08/07	11	41	3	1

HAUGHEY Frederick (Fred)
Born: Conisbrough, South Yorkshire, England, 12 May, 1921 — LB

League Club	Source	Date Signed	Seasons Played	Apps	Subs	Gls
Bradford C (Am)	Halifax T (Am)	08/46	46	3	-	0

HAUGHEY William
Born: Glasgow, Scotland, 20 December, 1932 — IF
Died: Rutherglen, Glasgow, Scotland, 15 February, 2012

League Club	Source	Date Signed	Seasons Played	Apps	Subs	Gls
Everton	Larkhall Thistle	06/56	56-57	4	-	1

HAUGHTON Nicholas George (Nick)
Born: Manchester, England, 20 September, 1994 — M

League Club	Source	Date Signed	Seasons Played	Apps	Subs	Gls
Fleetwood T	Runcorn T	02/14	14	11	11	1

HAUSE Kortney Paul Duncan
Born: Ilford, E London, England, 16 July, 1995 — CD
England: Youth

League Club	Source	Date Signed	Seasons Played	Apps	Subs	Gls
Wycombe W	Birmingham C (Sch)	07/12	12-13	21	2	2
Wolverhampton W	Tr	01/14	14	15	2	0
Gillingham	L	07/14	14	14	0	1

HAUSER Peter Benjamin
Born: Kimberley, South Africa, 20 April, 1934 — RH/IF

League Club	Source	Date Signed	Seasons Played	Apps	Subs	Gls
Blackpool	Kimberley Ath (RSA)	11/55	57-61	83	-	10
Chester C	Cheltenham T	08/63	63-66	117	4	3

HAUSER Thomas
Born: Schopfheim, Germany, 10 April, 1965 — F

League Club	Source	Date Signed	Seasons Played	Apps	Subs	Gls
Sunderland	Basle OB (SUI)	02/89	88-91	22	31	9

HAVENGA William Stephanus (Willie)
Born: Bloemfontein, South Africa, 6 November, 1924 — W
Died: South Africa, 12 December, 2008

League Club	Source	Date Signed	Seasons Played	Apps	Subs	Gls
Birmingham C	Bremner OB (RSA)	07/48	49	1	-	0
Luton T	Tr	05/50	50-51	18	-	6
Ipswich T	Tr	01/52	51-52	19	-	3

HAVENHAND Keith
Born: Dronfield, Derbyshire, England, 11 September, 1937 — IF
England: Youth

League Club	Source	Date Signed	Seasons Played	Apps	Subs	Gls
Chesterfield	Jnr	09/54	53-61	176	-	58
Derby Co	Tr	10/61	61	26	-	14
Oxford U	Tr	12/63	63-64	12	-	3

HAVERN Gianluca
Born: Manchester, England, 24 September, 1988 — CD

League Club	Source	Date Signed	Seasons Played	Apps	Subs	Gls
Stockport Co	Sch	04/07	07	1	0	1
Stockport Co	Mansfield T	08/09	09	7	0	0

HAVERSON Paul Timothy
Born: Chigwell, Essex, England, 19 February, 1959 — FB/M
England: Schools

League Club	Source	Date Signed	Seasons Played	Apps	Subs	Gls
Queens Park Rgrs	App	08/76				
Wimbledon	Tr	10/78	78-79	27	1	2

HAVERTY Joseph (Joe)
Born: Dublin, Republic of Ireland, 17 February, 1936 — LW
Died: Dublin, Republic of Ireland, 7 February, 2009
Republic of Ireland: 32

League Club	Source	Date Signed	Seasons Played	Apps	Subs	Gls
Arsenal	St Patrick's Ath (ROI)	07/54	54-60	114	-	25
Blackburn Rov	Tr	08/61	61-62	27	-	1
Millwall	Tr	09/62	62-63	68	-	8
Bristol Rov	Glasgow Celtic	12/64	64	13	-	1

HAW Robert Andrew (Rob)
Born: York, England, 10 October, 1986 — F

League Club	Source	Date Signed	Seasons Played	Apps	Subs	Gls
York C	Sch	-	03	0	1	0

HAWDEN Kenneth
Born: Huddersfield, West Yorkshire, England, 16 September, 1931 — CF
Died: Derby, England, 13 June, 2008

League Club	Source	Date Signed	Seasons Played	Apps	Subs	Gls
Derby Co	Ashenhurst SC	04/53	53	2	-	0

HAWE Steven John (Steve)
Born: Magherafelt, Derry, Northern Ireland, 23 December, 1980 — CD
Northern Ireland: U21-2/Youth/Schools

League Club	Source	Date Signed	Seasons Played	Apps	Subs	Gls
Blackburn Rov	YT	12/97				
Blackpool	L	08/00	00	2	0	0
Halifax T	L	11/00	00	6	2	0

HAWES Steven Robert (Steve)
Born: High Wycombe, Buckinghamshire, England, 17 July, 1978 — M

League Club	Source	Date Signed	Seasons Played	Apps	Subs	Gls
Sheffield U	YT	03/96	95-96	1	3	0
Doncaster Rov	L	09/97	97	8	3	0
Hull C	Tr	07/98	98	18	1	0

HAWKE Warren Robert
Born: Durham, England, 20 September, 1970 — F

League Club	Source	Date Signed	Seasons Played	Apps	Subs	Gls
Sunderland	YT	11/88	88-92	7	18	1
Chesterfield	L	09/91	91	7	0	1
Carlisle U	L	10/92	92	8	0	2
Northampton T	L	03/93	92	7	0	1
Scarborough	Raith Rov	12/93	93	0	1	0

HAWKER David
Born: Hull, England, 29 November, 1958 — RM

League Club	Source	Date Signed	Seasons Played	Apps	Subs	Gls
Hull C	App	08/76	77-79	33	2	2
Darlington	Tr	03/80	79-82	84	4	2
Darlington	Bishop Auckland	08/84	84	4	3	0

HAWKER Philip Nigel (Phil)
Born: Solihull, West Midlands, England, 7 December, 1962 — CD
England: Youth

League Club	Source	Date Signed	Seasons Played	Apps	Subs	Gls
Birmingham C	App	06/80	80-82	34	1	1
Walsall	Tr	12/82	82-89	159	18	10
West Bromwich A	Tr	09/90	90	1	0	0

HAWKES Barry
Born: Shotton Colliery, County Durham, England, 21 March, 1938 — W/IF

League Club	Source	Date Signed	Seasons Played	Apps	Subs	Gls
Luton T	Shotton CW	11/55	58-59	8	-	0
Darlington	Tr	06/60	60	11	-	3
Hartlepool U	Tr	07/61	61	9	-	0

HAWKES Kenneth Kilby (Ken)
Born: Shotton Colliery, County Durham, England, 6 May, 1933 — LB
Died: 2 February, 2015

League Club	Source	Date Signed	Seasons Played	Apps	Subs	Gls
Luton T	Shotton CW	10/51	57-60	90	-	1
Peterborough U	Tr	06/61	61	1	-	0

HAWKINGS Barry
Born: Birmingham, England, 7 November, 1931 — CF
Died: Hereford, England, 9 May, 2010

League Club	Source	Date Signed	Seasons Played	Apps	Subs	Gls
Coventry C	Rugby T	01/49	53-55	34	-	12
Lincoln C	Tr	03/56	55-56	15	-	6
Northampton T	Tr	06/57	57-58	65	-	25

HAWKINS Bertram William (Bert)
Born: Bristol, England, 29 September, 1923 — CF
Died: Bristol, England, 21 June, 2002

League Club	Source	Date Signed	Seasons Played	Apps	Subs	Gls
Bristol Rov	De Veys	08/47				
Bristol C	Tr	05/49	49	8	-	4
West Ham U	Bath C	09/51	51-52	34	-	16
Queens Park Rgrs	Tr	06/53	53	8	-	3

HAWKINS Colin Joseph
Born: Galway, Republic of Ireland, 17 August, 1977 — CD
Republic of Ireland: U21-9/Youth

League Club	Source	Date Signed	Seasons Played	Apps	Subs	Gls
Coventry C	Salthill Devon (ROI)	11/95				
Coventry C	Shelbourne (ROI)	01/07	06	13	0	0
Chesterfield	L	03/08	07	5	0	0
Brighton & HA	Tr	07/08	08-09	17	1	0

HAWKINS David John
Born: Kingston-on-Thames, SW London, England, 11 August, 1931 — CF

League Club	Source	Date Signed	Seasons Played	Apps	Subs	Gls
Gillingham (Am)	Sheppey U	01/56	55	14	-	8

HAWKINS Dennis Ronald
Born: Swansea, Wales, 22 October, 1947 — M
Wales: U23-6/Schools

League Club	Source	Date Signed	Seasons Played	Apps	Subs	Gls
Leeds U	App	10/64	66-67	2	0	0
Shrewsbury T	Tr	10/68	68-69	50	6	10
Chester C	L	09/70	70	6	1	1
Workington	L	03/72	71	6	0	1
Newport Co	Tr	05/72	72	9	0	1

HAWKINS George Harry (Harry)
Born: Middlesbrough, England, 24 November, 1915 — IF
Died: Middlesbrough, England, 14 March, 1992

League Club	Source	Date Signed	Seasons Played	Apps	Subs	Gls
Middlesbrough	South Bank East End	02/35	35	1	-	0
Watford	Tr	06/37	37	5	-	0
Southport	Tr	07/38	38-46	79	-	30
Gateshead	Tr	06/47	47	27	-	12
Hartlepool U	Tr	03/48	47-48	30	-	4

HAWKINS Graham Norman
Born: Darlaston, West Midlands, England, 5 March, 1946 CD

League Club	Source	Date Signed	Seasons Played	Apps	Subs	Gls
Wolverhampton W	App	06/63	64-67	28	6	0
Preston NE	Tr	01/68	67-73	241	4	3
Blackburn Rov	Tr	06/74	74-77	108	1	4
Port Vale	Tr	01/78	77-79	61	1	3

HAWKINS Herbert Henry (Bert)
Born: Lambeth, S London, England, 15 July, 1923 CF
Died: Basingstoke, Hampshire, England, March, 1982

League Club	Source	Date Signed	Seasons Played	Apps	Subs	Gls
Leyton Orient	Gravesend & Northfleet	06/51	51-52	5	-	0

HAWKINS Lewis Henry
Born: Middlesbrough, England, 15 June, 1993 M

League Club	Source	Date Signed	Seasons Played	Apps	Subs	Gls
Hartlepool U	Sch	07/12	11-14	5	14	0

HAWKINS Nigel Sean
Born: Bristol, England, 7 September, 1968 F

League Club	Source	Date Signed	Seasons Played	Apps	Subs	Gls
Bristol C	YT	02/87	87-88	8	10	2
Blackpool	Tr	10/89	89	4	3	0

HAWKINS Peter Michael
Born: Swansea, Wales, 18 December, 1951 LW
Wales: Schools

League Club	Source	Date Signed	Seasons Played	Apps	Subs	Gls
Northampton T	App	12/68	68-73	49	9	10

HAWKINS Peter Steven
Born: Maidstone, Kent, England, 19 September, 1978 LB

League Club	Source	Date Signed	Seasons Played	Apps	Subs	Gls
Wimbledon	YT	03/97	00-03	113	7	0
York C	L	02/00	99	14	0	0
Rushden & D	Tr	07/04	04-05	61	1	1

HAWKRIDGE Terry Paul
Born: Nottingham, England, 23 February, 1990 RM

League Club	Source	Date Signed	Seasons Played	Apps	Subs	Gls
Scunthorpe U	Gainsborough Trinity	06/13	13-14	47	9	1
Mansfield T	L	03/15	14	4	1	0

HAWKSBY John Frederick
Born: York, England, 12 June, 1942 IF/LW
England: Youth

League Club	Source	Date Signed	Seasons Played	Apps	Subs	Gls
Leeds U	Jnr	06/59	60-62	37	-	2
Lincoln C	Tr	08/64	64-65	64	1	4
York C	Tr	03/66	65-67	72	2	7

HAWKSFORD Edward (Eddie)
Born: Liverpool, England, 7 November, 1931 RW
Died: Kendal, Cumbria, England, 7 November, 1985

League Club	Source	Date Signed	Seasons Played	Apps	Subs	Gls
Mansfield T	RAOC Chilwell	03/52	52	1	-	0

HAWKSWORTH Anthony
Born: Sheffield, England, 15 January, 1938 G
England: Youth/Schools

League Club	Source	Date Signed	Seasons Played	Apps	Subs	Gls
Manchester U	Jnr	04/55	56	1	-	0

HAWKSWORTH Derek Marshall
Born: Bradford, England, 16 July, 1927 LW
England: B-1

League Club	Source	Date Signed	Seasons Played	Apps	Subs	Gls
Bradford C	Huddersfield T (Am)	10/48	48-50	75	-	20
Sheffield U	Tr	12/50	50-57	255	-	88
Huddersfield T	Tr	05/58	58-59	55	-	14
Lincoln C	Tr	02/60	59-60	36	-	14
Bradford C	Tr	01/61	60-61	44	-	8

HAWLEY Alan James
Born: Wokingham, Berkshire, England, 7 June, 1946 RB

League Club	Source	Date Signed	Seasons Played	Apps	Subs	Gls
Brentford	App	06/63	62-73	315	2	4

HAWLEY John East
Born: Patrington, East Riding of Yorkshire, England, 8 May, 1954 F

League Club	Source	Date Signed	Seasons Played	Apps	Subs	Gls
Hull C	Jnr	04/72	72-77	101	13	22
Leeds U	Tr	04/78	78-79	30	3	16
Sunderland	Tr	10/79	79-80	25	0	11
Arsenal	Tr	09/81	81-82	14	6	3
Leyton Orient	L	10/82	82	4	0	1
Hull C	L	12/82	82	3	0	1
Bradford C	Happy Valley (HKG)	09/83	83-84	61	6	28
Scunthorpe U	Tr	07/85	85	18	3	7

HAWLEY Karl Leon
Born: Walsall, West Midlands, England, 6 December, 1981 F
England: Semi Pro-2

League Club	Source	Date Signed	Seasons Played	Apps	Subs	Gls
Walsall	YT	01/01	01	0	1	0
Carlisle U	Tr	08/04	05-06	76	2	34
Preston NE	Tr	07/07	07-08	20	10	3
Northampton T	L	09/08	08	11	0	2
Colchester U	L	03/09	08	4	0	0
Notts Co	Tr	08/09	09-11	41	40	5
Crawley T	L	01/12	11	1	3	0
Scunthorpe U	Tr	09/12	12	37	2	11
Torquay U	Tr	08/13	13	22	5	3

HAWORTH Andrew Alan David (Andy)
Born: Lancaster, England, 28 November, 1988 W

League Club	Source	Date Signed	Seasons Played	Apps	Subs	Gls
Blackburn Rov	Sch	07/07				
Rochdale	L	01/10	09	3	4	0
Bury	Tr	07/10	10-11	20	26	3
Oxford U	L	10/11	11	2	2	0
Bradford C	L	01/12	11	2	1	0
Rochdale	Falkirk	01/13	12	3	4	0
Notts Co	Tr	07/13	13	0	2	0
Cheltenham T	Tr	06/14	14	0	5	0

HAWORTH Gary
Born: Bury, Greater Manchester, England, 25 April, 1959 F

League Club	Source	Date Signed	Seasons Played	Apps	Subs	Gls
Rochdale	Radcliffe Bor	08/84	84	1	0	0

HAWORTH Herbert
Born: Accrington, Lancashire, England, 5 May, 1920 IF
Died: Accrington, Lancashire, England, 28 September, 1993

League Club	Source	Date Signed	Seasons Played	Apps	Subs	Gls
Accrington Stan (Am)	Woodcock Amats	10/46	46	2	-	0

HAWORTH Robert John (Rob)
Born: Edgware, NW London, England, 21 November, 1975 F

League Club	Source	Date Signed	Seasons Played	Apps	Subs	Gls
Fulham	YT	07/93	93-94	7	14	1

HAWORTH Simon Owen
Born: Cardiff, Wales, 30 March, 1977 F
Wales: 5/B-1/U21-12/Youth

League Club	Source	Date Signed	Seasons Played	Apps	Subs	Gls
Cardiff C	YT	08/95	95-96	27	10	9
Coventry C	Tr	06/97	97-98	5	6	0
Wigan Ath	Tr	10/98	98-01	99	18	44
Tranmere Rov	Tr	02/02	01-04	77	2	31

HAWSON Alexander (Alex)
Born: Auchinairn, Glasgow, Scotland, 23 October, 1923 RH
Died: Lenzie, Dunbartonshire, Scotland, 27 January, 1997

League Club	Source	Date Signed	Seasons Played	Apps	Subs	Gls
Rochdale	Aberdeen	12/48	48	1	-	0

HAWTHORNE Mark
Born: Sunderland, England, 21 August, 1979 CD

League Club	Source	Date Signed	Seasons Played	Apps	Subs	Gls
Doncaster Rov	YT	12/96	97	7	1	0

HAWTHORNE Mark David
Born: Glasgow, Scotland, 31 October, 1973 M

League Club	Source	Date Signed	Seasons Played	Apps	Subs	Gls
Crystal Palace	Jnr	06/92				
Sheffield U	Tr	08/94				
Torquay U	Walsall (NC)	03/95	94-96	43	15	2

HAWTIN Aidan James
Born: Bicester, Oxfordshire, England, 13 June, 1995 RM

League Club	Source	Date Signed	Seasons Played	Apps	Subs	Gls
Oxford U	Sch	07/14	14	0	1	0

HAWTIN Craig Scott
Born: Buxton, Derbyshire, England, 29 March, 1970 RB

League Club	Source	Date Signed	Seasons Played	Apps	Subs	Gls
Chester C	Port Vale (YT)	09/88	87-88	6	1	1

HAY Alan Browning
Born: Dunfermline, Fife, Scotland, 28 November, 1958 LB

League Club	Source	Date Signed	Seasons Played	Apps	Subs	Gls
Bolton W	Dundee	03/77				
Bristol C	Tr	07/78	79-81	72	2	1
York C	Tr	08/82	82-85	147	3	3
Tranmere Rov	Tr	08/86	86	27	1	0
York C	Hill o' Beath	12/88	88	1	0	0
Sunderland	Tr	02/89	88	1	0	0
Torquay U	Tr	09/89	89-90	10	0	0

HAY Alexander Neil (Alex)
Born: Birkenhead, Wirral, England, 14 October, 1981 F

League Club	Source	Date Signed	Seasons Played	Apps	Subs	Gls
Tranmere Rov	YT	03/00	01-03	16	25	3
Rushden & D	Tr	07/04	04	29	13	3

HAY Christopher Drummond (Chris)
Born: Glasgow, Scotland, 28 August, 1974 F

League Club	Source	Date Signed	Seasons Played	Apps	Subs	Gls
Swindon T	Glasgow Celtic	08/97	97-99	73	21	30
Huddersfield T	Tr	03/00	99-01	21	21	5

HAY Daniel John (Danny)
Born: Auckland, New Zealand, 15 May, 1975 CD
New Zealand: 31

League Club	Source	Date Signed	Seasons Played	Apps	Subs	Gls
Leeds U	Perth Glory (AUS)	08/99	00	2	2	0
Walsall	Tr	08/02	02-03	40	5	0

HAY Darran Andrew
Born: Hitchin, Hertfordshire, England, 17 December, 1969 F

League Club	Source	Date Signed	Seasons Played	Apps	Subs	Gls
Cambridge U	Biggleswade T	03/94	93-94	7	22	3
Cambridge U (L)	Woking	10/96	96	0	4	0

HAY David
Born: Paisley, Renfrewshire, Scotland, 29 January, 1948 CD/M
Scotland: 27/SLge-4/U23-3

League Club	Source	Date Signed	Seasons Played	Apps	Subs	Gls
Chelsea	Glasgow Celtic	08/74	74-78	107	1	2

HAYCOCK Frederick Joseph (Freddie)
Born: Liverpool, England, 19 April, 1912 IF
Died: Birmingham, England, 10 April, 1989

League Club	Source	Date Signed	Seasons Played	Apps	Subs	Gls
Aston Villa	Prescot Cables	02/34	36-38	99	-	28
Wrexham	Tr	12/45	46	6	-	1

HAYCOCK Thomas Paul (Paul)
Born: Sheffield, England, 8 July, 1962 F

League Club	Source	Date Signed	Seasons Played	Apps	Subs	Gls
Rotherham U	Burton A	08/86	86-89	77	20	22

HAYDE Michael Patrick (Mick)
Born: St Helens, Merseyside, England, 20 June, 1971 FB

League Club	Source	Date Signed	Seasons Played	Apps	Subs	Gls
Chester C	Liverpool (YT)	08/89	89	0	1	0

HAYDOCK Frank
Born: Eccles, Greater Manchester, England, 29 November, 1940 CH

League Club	Source	Date Signed	Seasons Played	Apps	Subs	Gls
Manchester U	Jnr	12/58	60-62	6	-	0
Charlton Ath	Tr	08/63	63-65	84	0	4
Portsmouth	Tr	12/65	65-68	71	0	1
Southend U	Tr	01/69	68-69	28	3	4

HAYDOCK William Edward (Billy)
Born: Salford, England, 19 January, 1936 RB/M

League Club	Source	Date Signed	Seasons Played	Apps	Subs	Gls
Manchester C	Buxton	03/59	59-60	3	-	1
Crewe Alex	Tr	03/61	60-64	142	-	31
Grimsby T	Tr	11/64	64	21	-	4
Stockport Co	Tr	08/65	65-70	257	4	4
Southport	Port Elizabeth C (RSA)	11/71	71	7	0	0

HAYDON Nicholas (Nicky)
Born: Barking, E London, England, 10 August, 1978 RB

League Club	Source	Date Signed	Seasons Played	Apps	Subs	Gls
Colchester U	YT	08/95	96-98	16	15	2

HAYES Adrian Michael (Adie)
Born: Norwich, England, 22 May, 1978 W
Died: 18 August, 2014

League Club	Source	Date Signed	Seasons Played	Apps	Subs	Gls
Cambridge U	YT	07/96	95-97	25	9	0

HAYES Austin William Patrick
Born: Hammersmith, W London, England, 15 July, 1958 LM
Died: Hammersmith, W London, England, 3 December, 1986
Republic of Ireland: 1/U21-1

League Club	Source	Date Signed	Seasons Played	Apps	Subs	Gls
Southampton	App	07/76	76-79	22	9	5
Millwall	Tr	02/81	80-82	40	7	5
Northampton T	Tr	08/83	83-84	60	4	14

HAYES Hugh
Born: Bangor, Down, Northern Ireland, 23 June, 1925 WH

League Club	Source	Date Signed	Seasons Played	Apps	Subs	Gls
Ipswich T	Bangor	06/46	48-49	9	-	0

HAYES Jonathan (Jonny)
Born: Dublin, Republic of Ireland, 9 July, 1987 W
Republic of Ireland: U21-3

League Club	Source	Date Signed	Seasons Played	Apps	Subs	Gls
Reading	Sch	07/04				
MK Dons	L	01/07	06	0	11	0
Leicester C	Tr	07/07	07	1	6	0
Northampton T	L	01/08	07	5	6	0
Cheltenham T	L	10/08	08	3	3	0

HAYES Joseph (Joe)
Born: Kearsley, Greater Manchester, England, 20 January, 1936 IF
Died: Bolton, Greater Manchester, England, 1 February, 1999
England: U23-2

League Club	Source	Date Signed	Seasons Played	Apps	Subs	Gls
Manchester C	Jnr	08/53	53-64	331	-	142
Barnsley	Tr	07/65	65	26	0	3

HAYES Martin
Born: Walthamstow, NE London, England, 21 March, 1966 LW
England: U21-3

League Club	Source	Date Signed	Seasons Played	Apps	Subs	Gls
Arsenal	App	11/83	85-89	70	32	26
Wimbledon (L)	Glasgow Celtic	02/92	91	1	1	0
Swansea C	Glasgow Celtic	01/93	92-94	44	17	8

HAYES Michael (Mike)
Born: Newport, Wales, 11 September, 1954 CD

League Club	Source	Date Signed	Seasons Played	Apps	Subs	Gls
Newport Co	Dairy U	01/76	75	4	1	0

HAYES Michael Charles (Mike)
Born: Aberdare, Rhondda Cynon Taff, Wales, 24 April, 1944 RH

League Club	Source	Date Signed	Seasons Played	Apps	Subs	Gls
Swansea C	Jnr	06/61	62	3	-	0

HAYES Paul Edward
Born: Dagenham, E London, England, 20 September, 1983 F

League Club	Source	Date Signed	Seasons Played	Apps	Subs	Gls
Scunthorpe U	Norwich C (Sch)	03/03	02-04	68	31	28
Barnsley	Tr	07/05	05-06	63	12	11
Huddersfield T	L	02/07	06	4	0	1
Scunthorpe U	Tr	07/07	07-09	116	13	34
Preston NE	Tr	05/10	10	11	12	2
Barnsley	L	10/10	10	2	5	0
Charlton Ath	Tr	07/11	11	12	7	3
Wycombe W	L	02/12	11	6	0	6
Brentford	Tr	08/12	12	10	13	4
Crawley T	L	03/13	12	9	2	2
Plymouth Arg	L	10/13	13	4	2	0
Scunthorpe U	Tr	12/13	13	5	11	4
Wycombe W	Tr	05/14	14	38	1	12

HAYES Philip Henry (Phil)
Born: Chiswick, W London, England, 23 December, 1935 W

League Club	Source	Date Signed	Seasons Played	Apps	Subs	Gls
Millwall	Slough T	12/56	56-58	16	-	1

HAYES Samuel (Sam)
Born: Accrington, Lancashire, England, 21 June, 1920 G
Died: Burnley, Lancashire, England, 3 January, 1959

League Club	Source	Date Signed	Seasons Played	Apps	Subs	Gls
Accrington Stan	Blackburn Rov (Am)	10/46	46	13	-	0

HAYES Stephen Charles (Steve)
Born: Smethwick, West Midlands, England, 28 January, 1952 CD

League Club	Source	Date Signed	Seasons Played	Apps	Subs	Gls
Shrewsbury T	Warley Bor	02/74	74-79	69	3	0
Torquay U	L	09/75	75	1	0	0
Torquay U	Tr	07/80	80	25	0	0

HAYES William (Bill)
Born: Runcorn, Cheshire, England, 8 June, 1919 CH
Died: Cheshire, England, September, 2002

League Club	Source	Date Signed	Seasons Played	Apps	Subs	Gls
Oldham Ath	Halton Jnrs	01/37	38-50	126	-	3

HAYES William (Billy)
Born: Newcastle-under-Lyme, Potteries, England, 2 March, 1918 CH
Died: Newcastle-under-Lyme, Potteries, England, January, 1996

League Club	Source	Date Signed	Seasons Played	Apps	Subs	Gls
Crewe Alex	ROF Radway Green	09/46	46	29	-	0

HAYES William Edward (Bill)
Born: Cork, Republic of Ireland, 7 November, 1915 RB
Died: Blackburn, Greater Manchester, England, 22 April, 1987
Republic of Ireland: 2/LoI-2//Northern Ireland: 4

League Club	Source	Date Signed	Seasons Played	Apps	Subs	Gls
Huddersfield T	St Vincent's (ROI)	04/33	34-38	69	-	5
Huddersfield T	Cork U (ROI)	09/46	46-49	112	-	0
Burnley	Tr	02/50	49-50	12	-	0

HAYES William John (Billy)
Born: Limerick, Republic of Ireland, 30 March, 1928 G
Died: Torbay, Devon, England, August, 2014
Republic of Ireland: 1/LoI-1/Amateur

League Club	Source	Date Signed	Seasons Played	Apps	Subs	Gls
Wrexham	Limerick (ROI)	07/50	50	14	-	0
Torquay U	Ellesmere Port	08/52	52-55	54	-	0

HAYFIELD Matthew Anthony (Matt)
Born: Bristol, England, 8 August, 1975 M

League Club	Source	Date Signed	Seasons Played	Apps	Subs	Gls
Bristol Rov	YT	07/94	95-97	24	17	0
Shrewsbury T	Tr	08/98	98	1	1	0

HAYHURST Stanley Henry (Stan)
Born: Leyland, Lancashire, England, 13 May, 1925 G
Died: Chorley, Lancashire, England, November, 1998

League Club	Source	Date Signed	Seasons Played	Apps	Subs	Gls
Blackburn Rov	Leyland Motors	01/43	46-48	27	-	0
Tottenham H	Tr	10/48				
Barrow	Tr	06/50	50	26	-	0
Grimsby T	Tr	01/51	50-52	62	-	0

HAYHURST William (Will)
Born: Longridge, Lancashire, England, 24 February, 1994 LW
Republic of Ireland: U21-2/Youth

League Club	Source	Date Signed	Seasons Played	Apps	Subs	Gls
Preston NE	Sch	07/12	11-14	23	13	4
York C	L	01/14	13	14	4	2
Notts Co	Tr	01/15	14	8	4	0

HAYLES Barrington Edward (Barry)
Born: Lambeth, S London, England, 17 May, 1972 F
England: Semi Pro-2//Jamaica: 10

League Club	Source	Date Signed	Seasons Played	Apps	Subs	Gls
Bristol Rov	Stevenage Bor	06/97	97-98	62	0	32
Fulham	Tr	11/98	98-03	116	59	44
Sheffield U	Tr	06/04	04	4	0	0
Millwall	Tr	09/04	04-05	49	6	16
Plymouth Arg	Tr	07/06	06-07	58	4	15
Leicester C	Tr	01/08	07-08	10	18	2
Cheltenham T	L	08/08	08	6	1	3
Cheltenham T	L	11/08	08	5	0	1
Cheltenham T	Tr	08/09	09	23	16	7

HAYLOCK Gary Andrew
Born: Bradford, England, 31 December, 1970 F

League Club	Source	Date Signed	Seasons Played	Apps	Subs	Gls
Huddersfield T	YT	07/89	90-91	10	3	4

HAYLOCK Paul
Born: Lowestoft, Suffolk, England, 24 March, 1963 RB

League Club	Source	Date Signed	Seasons Played	Apps	Subs	Gls
Norwich C	App	01/81	81-85	154	1	3
Gillingham	Tr	08/86	86-89	149	3	0
Maidstone U	Tr	03/91	90-91	47	1	1
Shrewsbury T	Tr	09/92	92	16	2	1
Barnet	Woking	10/93	93	18	2	0

HAYMAN James (Jim)
Born: Ramsbottom, Greater Manchester, England, 19 February, 1928 FB

League Club	Source	Date Signed	Seasons Played	Apps	Subs	Gls
Bury	Radcliffe Bor	11/50	50	5	-	0

HAYNES Arthur Edwin Thomas
Born: Birmingham, England, 23 May, 1924 RW
Died: Walsall, West Midlands, England, 4 July, 1990

League Club	Source	Date Signed	Seasons Played	Apps	Subs	Gls
Aston Villa	Paget Rgrs	01/46	46	4	-	0
Walsall	Tr	05/48	48	2	-	0

HAYNES Daniel Lewis (Danny)
Born: Peckham, SE London, England, 19 January, 1988 W
England: Youth

League Club	Source	Date Signed	Seasons Played	Apps	Subs	Gls
Ipswich T	Sch	01/06	05-08	36	78	17
Millwall	L	09/06	06	5	0	2
Bristol C	Tr	07/09	09-10	39	12	8
Barnsley	Tr	01/11	10-11	24	8	6
Charlton Ath	Tr	01/12	11-12	15	19	9
Notts Co	Tr	07/13	13-14	16	7	3
Crewe Alex	L	10/14	14	2	1	0
Cheltenham T	Tr	03/15	14	5	3	1

HAYNES Eric
Born: Sheffield, England, 18 June, 1936 IF

League Club	Source	Date Signed	Seasons Played	Apps	Subs	Gls
Rotherham U	Thorncliffe	04/56	55	1	-	0

HAYNES John Norman (Johnny)
Born: Edmonton, N London, England, 17 October, 1934 IF
Died: Edinburgh, Scotland, 18 October, 2005
England: 56/B/FLge-13/U23-8/Youth/Schools

League Club	Source	Date Signed	Seasons Played	Apps	Subs	Gls
Fulham	Jnr	05/52	52-69	594	0	147

HAYNES Junior Lloyd
Born: Croydon, S London, England, 6 April, 1976 F

League Club	Source	Date Signed	Seasons Played	Apps	Subs	Gls
Barnet	Tottenham H (YT)	08/94	94	2	4	0

HAYNES Kyle John
Born: Wolverhampton, England, 29 December, 1991 RB

League Club	Source	Date Signed	Seasons Played	Apps	Subs	Gls
Cheltenham T	Sch	07/10	08-10	9	9	0

HAYNES Ryan Matthew
Born: Long Buckby, Northamptonshire, England, 27 September, 1995 LB

League Club	Source	Date Signed	Seasons Played	Apps	Subs	Gls
Coventry C	Sch	11/13	12-14	22	7	1

HAYNES-BROWN Curtis Levi
Born: Ipswich, England, 15 April, 1989 LB

League Club	Source	Date Signed	Seasons Played	Apps	Subs	Gls
Yeovil T	Lowestoft T	07/11	11	1	9	0
AFC Wimbledon	L	08/12	12	3	3	0

HAYRETTIN Hakan
Born: Enfield, N London, England, 4 February, 1970 M

League Club	Source	Date Signed	Seasons Played	Apps	Subs	Gls
Leyton Orient	YT	07/88				
Barnet	Tr	08/89	91-92	0	6	0
Torquay U	L	01/93	92	3	1	0
Wycombe W	Tr	07/93	93	15	4	1
Cambridge U	Tr	08/94	94	15	2	0

HAYS Christopher John (Jack)
Born: Ashington, Northumberland, England, 12 December, 1918 LW
Died: Gazeley, Suffolk, England, 23 February, 1983

League Club	Source	Date Signed	Seasons Played	Apps	Subs	Gls
Bradford Park Ave	Ipswich T	08/38	38	17	-	0
Burnley	Tr	05/39	46-50	146	-	12
Bury	Tr	09/51	51-52	27	-	2

HAYSMAN Kane Cruz
Born: Stepney, E London, England, 29 December, 1994 M

League Club	Source	Date Signed	Seasons Played	Apps	Subs	Gls
Gillingham	Sch	-	12	0	1	0

HAYTER James Edward
Born: Sandown, Isle of Wight, England, 9 April, 1979 F

League Club	Source	Date Signed	Seasons Played	Apps	Subs	Gls
Bournemouth	YT	07/97	96-06	305	53	94
Doncaster Rov	Tr	06/07	07-11	109	53	33
Yeovil T	Tr	07/12	12-14	89	30	25

HAYTON Eric
Born: Carlisle, Cumbria, England, 14 January, 1922 WH
Died: Carlisle, Cumbria, England, 29 December, 2006

League Club	Source	Date Signed	Seasons Played	Apps	Subs	Gls
Carlisle U	Jnr	08/45	46-50	49	-	5
Rochdale	Tr	05/51	51	12	-	0
Workington	Tr	10/52	52	19	-	0

HAYWARD Andrew William (Andy)
Born: Barnsley, South Yorkshire, England, 21 June, 1970 M/F

League Club	Source	Date Signed	Seasons Played	Apps	Subs	Gls
Rotherham U	Frickley Ath	08/94	94-97	93	27	15

HAYWARD Carl Basil (Basil)
Born: Leek, Staffordshire, England, 7 April, 1928 CH/CF
Died: Stoke-on-Trent, England, 9 December, 1989

League Club	Source	Date Signed	Seasons Played	Apps	Subs	Gls
Port Vale	Northwood Heath	05/46	46-57	349	-	55
Portsmouth	Tr	07/58	58-59	44	-	4

HAYWARD Douglas Stanworth (Dougie)
Born: Oakengates, Telford & Wrekin, England, 23 August, 1920 LB
Died: Weston-super-Mare, Somerset, England, 31 August, 2008

League Club	Source	Date Signed	Seasons Played	Apps	Subs	Gls
Huddersfield T	Jnr	05/39				
Bristol Rov	Barry T	09/46	46	1	-	0
Newport Co	Tr	11/46	46-55	260	-	11

HAYWARD Keith William
Born: Hove, East Sussex, England, 21 November, 1951 G

League Club	Source	Date Signed	Seasons Played	Apps	Subs	Gls
Charlton Ath	App	-	68	1	0	0

HAYWARD Lionel Eric (Eric)
Born: Newcastle-under-Lyme, Potteries, England, 2 August, 1917 CH
Died: Blackpool, Lancashire, England, 1976

League Club	Source	Date Signed	Seasons Played	Apps	Subs	Gls
Port Vale	Wardles	08/34	34-36	35	-	0
Blackpool	Tr	07/37	37-51	270	-	0

HAYWARD Steven Lee (Steve)
Born: Pelsall, West Midlands, England, 8 September, 1971 M
England: Youth

League Club	Source	Date Signed	Seasons Played	Apps	Subs	Gls
Derby Co	Jnr	09/88	89-94	15	11	1
Carlisle U	Tr	03/95	94-96	88	2	13
Fulham	Tr	06/97	97-00	108	7	7
Barnsley	Tr	01/01	00-03	40	8	2

HAYWOOD Clive
Born: Ramsgate, Kent, England, 1 November, 1960 F

League Club	Source	Date Signed	Seasons Played	Apps	Subs	Gls
Coventry C	App	08/78	80	1	0	0

HAYWOOD Raymond (Ray)
Born: Dudley, West Midlands, England, 12 January, 1949 F

League Club	Source	Date Signed	Seasons Played	Apps	Subs	Gls
Shrewsbury T	Stourbridge	05/74	74-76	75	12	27
Northampton T	Tr	03/77	76-77	14	2	2

HAZAN Alon
Born: Ashdod, Israel, 14 September, 1967 M
Israel: 72

League Club	Source	Date Signed	Seasons Played	Apps	Subs	Gls
Watford	Ironi Ashdod (ISR)	01/98	97-98	15	18	2

HAZARD Eden Michael
Born: La Louviere, Belgium, 7 January, 1991 M
Belgium: 57/Youth

League Club	Source	Date Signed	Seasons Played	Apps	Subs	Gls
Chelsea	OSC Lille (FRA)	06/12	12-14	101	6	37

HAZARD Michael (Micky)
Born: Sunderland, England, 5 February, 1960 M

League Club	Source	Date Signed	Seasons Played	Apps	Subs	Gls
Tottenham H	App	02/78	79-85	73	18	13
Chelsea	Tr	09/85	85-89	78	3	9
Portsmouth	Tr	01/90	89	8	0	1
Swindon T	Tr	09/90	90-93	112	7	17
Tottenham H	Tr	11/93	93-94	15	13	2

HAZEL Clifford (Cliff)
Born: Woolwich, SE London, England, 14 September, 1937 RW

League Club	Source	Date Signed	Seasons Played	Apps	Subs	Gls
Gillingham	Hastings U	07/55	57	2	-	0
Millwall	Tr	07/58				

HAZEL Desmond St Lloyd (Des)
Born: Bradford, England, 15 July, 1967 W
St Kitts & Nevis: 4

League Club	Source	Date Signed	Seasons Played	Apps	Subs	Gls
Sheffield Wed	App	07/85	87	5	1	0
Grimsby T	L	10/86	86	9	0	2
Rotherham U	Tr	07/88	88-94	204	34	30
Chesterfield	Tr	03/95	95	16	5	0

HAZEL Ian
Born: Merton, SW London, England, 1 December, 1967 M

League Club	Source	Date Signed	Seasons Played	Apps	Subs	Gls
Wimbledon	App	12/85	87-88	4	3	0
Bristol Rov	L	02/89	88	3	0	0
Bristol Rov	Tr	07/89	89-90	4	10	0
Maidstone U	Tr	03/92	91	6	2	0

HAZEL Jacob Louis
Born: Bradford, England, 15 April, 1994 LW

League Club	Source	Date Signed	Seasons Played	Apps	Subs	Gls
Chesterfield	Sch	07/12	12	1	1	0

HAZEL Julian
Born: Luton, England, 25 September, 1973 F

League Club	Source	Date Signed	Seasons Played	Apps	Subs	Gls
Colchester U	YT	08/92	92	2	0	0

HAZELDEN Walter
Born: Ashton-in-Makerfield, Greater Manchester, England, 13 February, 1941 IF
England: Youth

League Club	Source	Date Signed	Seasons Played	Apps	Subs	Gls
Aston Villa	Jnr	02/58	57-58	17	-	5

HAZELDINE Max Cameron
Born: Stockport, Greater Manchester, England, 13 February, 1997 F

League Club	Source	Date Signed	Seasons Played	Apps	Subs	Gls
Accrington Stan	Sch	04/15	14	0	1	0

League Club	Source	Date Signed	Seasons Played	Career Record Apps	Subs	Gls

HAZELL Anthony Philip (Tony)
Born: High Wycombe, Buckinghamshire, England, 19 September, 1947 — CD
England: Youth

League Club	Source	Date Signed	Seasons Played	Apps	Subs	Gls
Queens Park Rgrs	Jnr	10/64	64-74	362	7	4
Millwall	Tr	12/74	74-78	153	0	6
Crystal Palace	Tr	11/78	78	5	0	0
Charlton Ath	Tr	09/79	79-80	37	0	0

HAZELL Reuben
Born: Birmingham, England, 24 April, 1979 — CD

League Club	Source	Date Signed	Seasons Played	Apps	Subs	Gls
Aston Villa	YT	03/97				
Tranmere Rov	Tr	08/99	99-01	38	4	1
Torquay U	Tr	01/02	01-03	77	7	2
Kidderminster Hrs	Tr	07/04				
Chesterfield	Tr	08/05	05-06	69	3	2
Oldham Ath	Tr	09/07	07-10	149	2	7
Shrewsbury T	Tr	07/11	11-12	8	2	0

HAZELL Robert Joseph (Bob)
Born: Kingston, Jamaica, 14 June, 1959 — CD
England: B-1/U21-1/Youth

League Club	Source	Date Signed	Seasons Played	Apps	Subs	Gls
Wolverhampton W	App	05/77	77-78	32	1	1
Queens Park Rgrs	Tr	09/79	79-83	100	6	8
Leicester C	Tr	09/83	83-84	41	0	2
Wolverhampton W	L	09/85	85	1	0	0
Reading	Luton T (NC)	11/86	86	4	0	1
Port Vale	Tr	12/86	86-88	81	0	1

HAZLEDINE Albert Victor
Born: Royton, Greater Manchester, England, 28 July, 1918 — LW
Died: Oldham, Greater Manchester, England, April, 2007

League Club	Source	Date Signed	Seasons Played	Apps	Subs	Gls
Halifax T	West Ham U (Am)	11/45	46	10	-	2

HAZLEDINE Donald (Don)
Born: Arnold, Nottinghamshire, England, 10 July, 1929 — IF

League Club	Source	Date Signed	Seasons Played	Apps	Subs	Gls
Derby Co	Notts Regent	08/51	52-53	26	-	6
Northampton T	Tr	06/54	54	22	-	4

HAZLEDINE Geoffrey (Geoff)
Born: Arnold, Nottinghamshire, England, 27 February, 1932 — LH
Died: Sutton-in-Ashfield, Nottinghamshire, England, 21 December, 2002

League Club	Source	Date Signed	Seasons Played	Apps	Subs	Gls
Derby Co	Notts Regent	07/52	53	1	-	0
Southport	Boston U	07/57	57	29	-	5

HAZLETT George
Born: Glasgow, Scotland, 10 March, 1923 — RW
Died: Bromley, SE London, England, 21 December, 2012

League Club	Source	Date Signed	Seasons Played	Apps	Subs	Gls
Bury	Belfast Celtic	08/49	49-51	100	-	10
Cardiff C	Tr	08/52	52	7	-	1
Millwall	Tr	05/53	53-57	131	-	10

HAZLEY Matthew
Born: Banbridge, Down, Northern Ireland, 30 December, 1987 — LB/M
Northern Ireland: U21-3/Youth

League Club	Source	Date Signed	Seasons Played	Apps	Subs	Gls
Stoke C	Sch	07/06	05	0	1	0

HAZZLETON James (Jim)
Born: Bolton, Greater Manchester, England, 29 September, 1930 — IF
Died: Blackpool, Lancashire, England, 31 August, 1991

League Club	Source	Date Signed	Seasons Played	Apps	Subs	Gls
Bury	Atherton Collieries	05/50				
Rochdale	Tr	08/51	51	11	-	1
Accrington Stan	Tr	07/52	52	4	-	0

HEAD Bertram James (Bert)
Born: Midsomer Norton, Somerset, England, 8 June, 1916 — D
Died: Reading, England, 4 February, 2002

League Club	Source	Date Signed	Seasons Played	Apps	Subs	Gls
Torquay U	Welton Rov	10/36	36-50	222	-	6
Bury	Tr	02/52	51-52	22	-	0

HEAD David George
Born: Midsomer Norton, Somerset, England, 11 August, 1940 — CF/RH

League Club	Source	Date Signed	Seasons Played	Apps	Subs	Gls
Swindon T	Jnr	08/58				
Arsenal	Tr	03/59				
Reading	Tr	07/60	60	12	-	0
Bristol Rov	Tr	07/61				

HEAD Michael (Mike)
Born: Hull, England, 13 April, 1933 — RW

League Club	Source	Date Signed	Seasons Played	Apps	Subs	Gls
Hull C	Bridlington Central U	12/53	54	3	-	0

HEALD Gregory James (Greg)
Born: Enfield, N London, England, 26 September, 1971 — CD
England: Semi Pro-1/Schools

League Club	Source	Date Signed	Seasons Played	Apps	Subs	Gls
Peterborough U	Enfield	07/94	94-96	101	4	6
Barnet	Tr	08/97	97-00	141	0	13
Leyton Orient	Tr	03/03	02-03	9	0	1
Rochdale	Tr	03/04	03-04	39	0	3

HEALD Oliver Richard
Born: Vancouver, Canada, 13 March, 1975 — F
Canada: U23-14/Youth

League Club	Source	Date Signed	Seasons Played	Apps	Subs	Gls
Port Vale	Norvan (CAN)	10/93				
Scarborough	Tr	08/95	95	1	8	1

HEALD Paul Andrew
Born: Wath-on-Dearne, South Yorkshire, England, 20 September, 1968 — G

League Club	Source	Date Signed	Seasons Played	Apps	Subs	Gls
Sheffield U	App	06/87				
Leyton Orient	Tr	12/88	88-94	176	0	0
Coventry C	L	03/92	91	2	0	0
Swindon T	L	03/94	93	1	1	0
Wimbledon	Tr	07/95	95-03	36	2	0
Sheffield Wed	L	01/02	01	5	0	0

HEALE Gary John
Born: Canvey Island, Essex, England, 15 July, 1958 — F

League Club	Source	Date Signed	Seasons Played	Apps	Subs	Gls
Luton T	Canvey Island	12/76	77	7	0	1
Exeter C	L	12/77	77	3	1	0
Reading	Tr	08/79	79-81	68	8	20

HEALER Ernest (Ernie)
Born: Birtley, Tyne and Wear, England, 13 November, 1941 — IF

League Club	Source	Date Signed	Seasons Played	Apps	Subs	Gls
Darlington		08/61				
Brighton & HA	Berwick Rgrs	10/63	63	3	-	1

HEALEY Daniel Kevin
Born: Manchester, England, 22 October, 1953 — LW
Died: Manchester, England, July, 2010

League Club	Source	Date Signed	Seasons Played	Apps	Subs	Gls
Manchester U	App	01/71				
Bolton W	Tr	05/73				
Workington	Tr	07/74	74	13	4	2

HEALEY Jonathan Peter (Jon)
Born: Morecambe, Lancashire, England, 30 December, 1966 — M

League Club	Source	Date Signed	Seasons Played	Apps	Subs	Gls
Oldham Ath	App	06/85				
Crewe Alex	Alsager College	12/87	87	7	3	2

HEALEY Rhys James Evitt
Born: Manchester, England, 6 December, 1994 — F

League Club	Source	Date Signed	Seasons Played	Apps	Subs	Gls
Cardiff C	GAP Connahs Quay	01/13	13	0	1	0
Colchester U	L	09/14	14	7	14	4

HEALEY Ronald (Ron)
Born: Manchester, England, 30 August, 1952 — G
Republic of Ireland: 2

League Club	Source	Date Signed	Seasons Played	Apps	Subs	Gls
Manchester C	App	10/69	70-73	30	0	0
Coventry C	L	12/71	71	3	0	0
Preston NE	L	12/73	73	6	0	0
Cardiff C	Tr	03/74	73-81	216	0	0

HEALEY William Richard Ernest (Bill)
Born: Liverpool, England, 22 May, 1926 — WH

League Club	Source	Date Signed	Seasons Played	Apps	Subs	Gls
Arsenal	Chorley	05/49				
Fulham	Tr	12/52	52	1	-	0
Hartlepool U	Tr	08/55	55	6	-	0

HEALY Brian
Born: Glasgow, Scotland, 27 December, 1968 — M
England: Semi Pro-1

League Club	Source	Date Signed	Seasons Played	Apps	Subs	Gls
Torquay U	Morecambe	12/98	98-01	55	4	11
Darlington	Tr	11/01	01	1	1	1

HEALY Colin
Born: Cork, Republic of Ireland, 14 March, 1980 — M
Republic of Ireland: 13/U21-10

League Club	Source	Date Signed	Seasons Played	Apps	Subs	Gls
Coventry C (L)	Glasgow Celtic	01/02	01	17	0	2
Sunderland	Glasgow Celtic	08/03	03	16	4	0
Barnsley	Livingston	08/06	06	0	8	0
Bradford C	L	11/06	06	2	0	0
Ipswich T	Cork C (ROI)	07/09	09-11	11	9	2

HEALY David Jonathan
Born: Downpatrick, Northern Ireland, 5 August, 1979 — F
Northern Ireland: 93/B-1/U21-8/Youth/Schools

League Club	Source	Date Signed	Seasons Played	Apps	Subs	Gls
Manchester U	YT	11/97	00	0	1	0
Port Vale	L	02/00	99	15	1	3
Preston NE	Tr	12/00	00-04	104	35	44
Norwich C	L	01/03	02	5	0	1
Norwich C	L	03/03	02	5	3	1
Leeds U	Tr	10/04	04-06	82	29	29
Fulham	Tr	07/07	07	15	15	4
Sunderland	Tr	08/08	08-09	0	13	1
Ipswich T	L	02/10	09	5	7	1
Doncaster Rov	L	11/10	10	6	2	2
Bury	Glasgow Rangers	08/12	12	8	8	1

HEALY Joseph Benjamin (Joe)
Born: Sidcup, SE London, England, 26 December, 1986 — W

League Club	Source	Date Signed	Seasons Played	Apps	Subs	Gls
Millwall	Jnr	04/04	04-05	0	3	0

HEALY Patrick Joseph (Felix)
Born: Derry, Northern Ireland, 27 September, 1955 — M

League Club	Source	Date Signed	Seasons Played	Apps	Subs	Gls

Northern Ireland: 4/NILge-1

League Club	Source	Date Signed	Seasons Played	Apps	Subs	Gls
Port Vale	Finn Harps (ROI)	10/78	78-79	40	1	2

HEANEY Anthony James (Tony)
Born: Plymouth, England, 9 May, 1940 — FB
England: Youth

League Club	Source	Date Signed	Seasons Played	Apps	Subs	Gls
Southampton	Jnr	06/58	60	1	-	0

HEANEY Neil Andrew
Born: Middlesbrough, England, 3 November, 1971 — LW
England: U21-6/Youth

League Club	Source	Date Signed	Seasons Played	Apps	Subs	Gls
Arsenal	YT	11/89	91-93	4	3	0
Hartlepool U	L	01/91	90	2	1	0
Cambridge U	L	01/92	91	9	4	2
Southampton	Tr	03/94	93-96	42	19	5
Manchester C	Tr	11/96	96-97	13	5	1
Charlton Ath	L	03/98	97	4	2	0
Bristol C	L	03/99	98	2	1	0
Darlington	Tr	08/99	99	33	3	5
Plymouth Arg	Dundee U	12/01	01	1	7	0

HEAP Stuart
Born: Nelson, Lancashire, England, 7 February, 1965 — M

League Club	Source	Date Signed	Seasons Played	Apps	Subs	Gls
Tranmere Rov	Clitheroe	03/85	84	0	3	0

HEARD Timothy Patrick (Pat)
Born: Hull, England, 17 March, 1960 — M/LB
England: Youth

League Club	Source	Date Signed	Seasons Played	Apps	Subs	Gls
Everton	App	03/78	78-79	10	1	0
Aston Villa	Tr	10/79	79-82	20	5	2
Sheffield Wed	Tr	01/83	82-84	22	3	3
Newcastle U	Tr	09/84	84	34	0	2
Middlesbrough	Tr	08/85	85	25	0	2
Hull C	Tr	03/86	85-87	79	1	5
Rotherham U	Tr	07/88	88-89	41	3	7
Cardiff C	Tr	08/90	90-91	45	1	4
Hull C	Hall Road Rgrs	08/92	92	3	1	0

HEARN Charles Richard (Charley)
Born: Ashford, Kent, England, 5 November, 1983 — M

League Club	Source	Date Signed	Seasons Played	Apps	Subs	Gls
Millwall	YT	04/01	01-03	9	9	0
Northampton T	L	12/04	04	21	3	1

HEARN Frank Guy
Born: St Pancras, Central London, England, 5 November, 1929 — IF

League Club	Source	Date Signed	Seasons Played	Apps	Subs	Gls
Torquay U	Edgware T	08/50				
Hull C	Tr	08/51				
Northampton T	Tr	10/51				
Crystal Palace	Tr	06/54	54	8	-	1

HEARN Liam
Born: Nottingham, England, 27 August, 1985 — F
England: Semi Pro-1

League Club	Source	Date Signed	Seasons Played	Apps	Subs	Gls
Mansfield T	Grimsby T	05/14	14	0	3	0

HEARY Thomas Mark
Born: Dublin, Republic of Ireland, 14 February, 1978 — FB/M
Republic of Ireland: U21-4/Youth/Schools

League Club	Source	Date Signed	Seasons Played	Apps	Subs	Gls
Huddersfield T	YT	02/96	96-02	68	24	0

HEASELGRAVE Samuel Ernest (Sammy)
Born: Smethwick, West Midlands, England, 1 October, 1916 — IF
Died: Harborne, West Midlands, England, 22 April, 1975

League Club	Source	Date Signed	Seasons Played	Apps	Subs	Gls
West Bromwich A	Brierley Hill Alliance	10/34	36-38	49	-	16
Northampton T	Tr	10/45	46-47	42	-	4

HEATH Adrian Paul
Born: Stoke-on-Trent, England, 11 January, 1961 — F/M
England: B-1/U21-8

League Club	Source	Date Signed	Seasons Played	Apps	Subs	Gls
Stoke C	App	01/79	78-81	94	1	16
Everton	Tr	01/82	81-88	206	20	71
Aston Villa	RCD Espanyol (SPN)	08/89	89	8	1	0
Manchester C	Tr	02/90	89-91	58	17	4
Stoke C	Tr	03/92	91	5	1	0
Burnley	Tr	08/92	92-95	109	6	28
Sheffield U	Tr	12/95	95	0	4	0
Burnley	Tr	03/96	95-96	1	4	0

HEATH Colin
Born: Matlock, Derbyshire, England, 31 December, 1983 — W

League Club	Source	Date Signed	Seasons Played	Apps	Subs	Gls
Manchester U	YT	01/01				
Cambridge U	L	12/04	04	5	1	0
Swindon T	L	08/05	05	8	3	1
Chesterfield	Tr	01/06	05	1	3	0
Macclesfield T	Tr	07/06	06	16	9	4

HEATH Dennis John
Born: Chiswick, W London, England, 28 September, 1934 — RW
Died: Hounslow, SW London, England, 28 September, 2006

League Club	Source	Date Signed	Seasons Played	Apps	Subs	Gls
Brentford	Jnr	09/52	54-60	123	-	20

HEATH Donald (Don)
Born: Stockton-on-Tees, Cleveland, England, 26 December, 1944 — RW

League Club	Source	Date Signed	Seasons Played	Apps	Subs	Gls
Middlesbrough	App	12/62				
Norwich C	Tr	07/64	64-67	79	3	15
Swindon T	Tr	09/67	67-69	82	6	2
Oldham Ath	Tr	07/70	70-71	43	2	1
Peterborough U	Tr	07/72	72	43	1	4
Hartlepool U	Tr	07/73	73-74	36	1	2

HEATH Duncan Nigel
Born: Stoke-on-Trent, England, 23 October, 1961 — D

League Club	Source	Date Signed	Seasons Played	Apps	Subs	Gls
Aston Villa	App	07/79				
Crewe Alex	Tr	11/80	81	17	6	0

HEATH Herbert George
Born: Wolverhampton, England, 29 March, 1970 — CD

League Club	Source	Date Signed	Seasons Played	Apps	Subs	Gls
Exeter C	Darlaston	02/89	88	3	2	0

HEATH John
Born: Heywood, Greater Manchester, England, 5 June, 1936 — G

League Club	Source	Date Signed	Seasons Played	Apps	Subs	Gls
Bury	Blackburn Rov (Am)	09/56	56-61	8	-	0
Tranmere Rov	Tr	01/62	61-63	58	-	0
Rochdale	Wigan Ath	02/66	65	6	0	0

HEATH Joseph (Joe)
Born: Birkenhead, Wirral, England, 4 October, 1988 — LB

League Club	Source	Date Signed	Seasons Played	Apps	Subs	Gls
Nottingham F	Sch	11/05	08	9	1	0
Lincoln C	L	07/09	09	3	1	0
Exeter C	Tr	03/10				
Hereford U	Tr	11/10	10-11	41	2	0

HEATH Matthew Philip (Matt)
Born: Leicester, England, 1 November, 1981 — CD

League Club	Source	Date Signed	Seasons Played	Apps	Subs	Gls
Leicester C	YT	02/01	01-04	42	9	6
Stockport Co	L	10/03	03	8	0	0
Coventry C	Tr	07/05	05-06	30	2	1
Leeds U	Tr	11/06	06-07	51	1	4
Colchester U	Tr	03/08	07-12	83	13	4
Brighton & HA	L	03/09	08	6	0	1
Southend U	L	07/09	09	4	0	0
Northampton T	Tr	08/13	13	5	0	0

HEATH Michael
Born: Hull, England, 7 February, 1974 — G

League Club	Source	Date Signed	Seasons Played	Apps	Subs	Gls
Tottenham H	YT	05/92				
Scunthorpe U	Tr	12/93	93	1	1	0

HEATH Michael (Mick)
Born: Hillingdon, W London, England, 9 January, 1953 — F

League Club	Source	Date Signed	Seasons Played	Apps	Subs	Gls
Brentford (Am)	Walton & Hersham	04/71	70	1	0	0

HEATH Nicholas Alan (Nick)
Born: Sutton Coldfield, West Midlands, England, 2 January, 1985 — M

League Club	Source	Date Signed	Seasons Played	Apps	Subs	Gls
Kidderminster Hrs	Marconi, Coventry	03/03	02	0	1	0

HEATH Norman Harry
Born: Wolverhampton, England, 31 January, 1924 — G
Died: Great Barr, West Midlands, England, 22 November, 1983

League Club	Source	Date Signed	Seasons Played	Apps	Subs	Gls
West Bromwich A	Henry Meadows BC	10/43	47-53	121	-	0

HEATH Philip Adrian (Phil)
Born: Stoke-on-Trent, England, 24 November, 1964 — LW

League Club	Source	Date Signed	Seasons Played	Apps	Subs	Gls
Stoke C	App	10/82	82-87	144	12	16
Oxford U	Tr	06/88	88-89	24	13	1
Cardiff C	Tr	03/91	90	11	0	1

HEATH Richard Terence (Terry)
Born: Leicester, England, 17 November, 1943 — F/M
Died: Rajales, Spain, 25 January, 2011

League Club	Source	Date Signed	Seasons Played	Apps	Subs	Gls
Leicester C	App	11/61	62-63	8	-	2
Hull C	Tr	05/64	64-67	27	6	1
Scunthorpe U	Tr	03/68	67-72	174	2	50
Lincoln C	Tr	02/73	72-73	17	0	1

HEATH Robert
Born: Newcastle-under-Lyme, Potteries, England, 31 August, 1978 — FB

League Club	Source	Date Signed	Seasons Played	Apps	Subs	Gls
Stoke C	YT	07/96	97-99	11	8	0

HEATH Seamus Martin James Paul
Born: Belfast, Northern Ireland, 6 December, 1961 — M/D

League Club	Source	Date Signed	Seasons Played	Apps	Subs	Gls
Luton T	Jnr	04/79				
Lincoln C	L	08/82	82	6	1	0
Wrexham	Tr	08/83	83	32	0	1
Tranmere Rov	Tr	08/84	84	6	11	0

HEATH Stephen Dennis (Steve)
Born: Hull, England, 15 November, 1977 — CD
England: Youth

League Club	Source	Date Signed	Seasons Played	Apps	Subs	Gls
Leeds U	YT	11/94				
Carlisle U	Tr	07/96	96	0	1	0

League Club	Source	Date Signed	Seasons Played	Apps	Subs	Gls

HEATH William Henry Mansell (Bill)
Born: Bournemouth, England, 15 April, 1934 — G

League Club	Source	Date Signed	Seasons Played	Apps	Subs	Gls
Bournemouth	Jnr	12/51	56-57	34	-	0
Lincoln C	Tr	11/58	58-61	84	-	0

HEATH William John (Bill)
Born: Stepney, E London, England, 26 June, 1920 — FB
Died: Hackney, E London, England, December, 1994

League Club	Source	Date Signed	Seasons Played	Apps	Subs	Gls
Queens Park Rgrs		09/45	46-52	96	-	3

HEATHCOCK Adrian Neil
Born: Dudley, West Midlands, England, 26 January, 1975 — W

League Club	Source	Date Signed	Seasons Played	Apps	Subs	Gls
Hereford U	YT	-	92	1	1	0

HEATHCOTE Jonathan
Born: Frimley, Surrey, England, 10 November, 1983 — LB

League Club	Source	Date Signed	Seasons Played	Apps	Subs	Gls
Cambridge U	Sch	04/03	02	2	0	0

HEATHCOTE Michael (Mick)
Born: Kelloe, County Durham, England, 10 September, 1965 — CD

League Club	Source	Date Signed	Seasons Played	Apps	Subs	Gls
Sunderland	Spennymoor U	08/87	87-89	6	3	0
Halifax T	L	12/87	87	7	0	1
York C	L	01/90	89	3	0	0
Shrewsbury T	Tr	07/90	90-91	43	1	6
Cambridge U	Tr	09/91	91-94	123	5	13
Plymouth Arg	Tr	07/95	95-00	195	4	13
Shrewsbury T	Tr	08/01	01-02	39	1	2

HEATHCOTE Peter George Samuel
Born: Leicester, England, 13 November, 1932 — G

League Club	Source	Date Signed	Seasons Played	Apps	Subs	Gls
Southend U	Jnr	11/51	51	2	-	0

HEATHCOTE Wilfred (Wilf)
Born: Hemsworth, West Yorkshire, England, 29 June, 1911 — CF
Died: Lambeth, S London, England, 15 June, 1991

League Club	Source	Date Signed	Seasons Played	Apps	Subs	Gls
Queens Park Rgrs	Millwall (Am)	10/43	46	5	-	1
Millwall	Tr	12/46	46	8	-	2

HEATHER Leslie John (John)
Born: Winchcombe, Gloucestershire, England, 25 April, 1933 — IF
Died: Long Eaton, Derbyshire, England, 27 January, 2008

League Club	Source	Date Signed	Seasons Played	Apps	Subs	Gls
Mansfield T	Belper T	08/52	53	1	-	0

HEATON James Michael (Mick)
Born: Sheffield, England, 15 January, 1947 — FB
Died: Oswaldtwistle, Lancashire, England, 1 April, 1995

League Club	Source	Date Signed	Seasons Played	Apps	Subs	Gls
Sheffield U	App	11/64	66-70	31	3	0
Blackburn Rov	Tr	10/71	71-75	169	2	1

HEATON Paul John
Born: Hyde, Greater Manchester, England, 24 January, 1961 — M

League Club	Source	Date Signed	Seasons Played	Apps	Subs	Gls
Oldham Ath	App	01/79	77-83	124	12	28
Rochdale	Tr	03/84	83-85	85	4	9

HEATON Thomas David (Tom)
Born: Chester, England, 15 April, 1986 — G
England: U21-3/Youth

League Club	Source	Date Signed	Seasons Played	Apps	Subs	Gls
Manchester U	Sch	07/03				
Swindon T	L	08/05	05	14	0	0
Cardiff C	L	07/08	08	21	0	0
Rochdale	L	11/09	09	12	0	0
Wycombe W	L	02/10	09	16	0	0
Cardiff C	Tr	08/10	10-11	28	1	0
Bristol C	Tr	08/12	12	43	0	0
Burnley	Tr	05/13	13-14	84	0	0

HEATON William Henry (Billy)
Born: Leeds, England, 26 August, 1918 — LW
Died: Leeds, England, 16 January, 1990

League Club	Source	Date Signed	Seasons Played	Apps	Subs	Gls
Leeds U	Whitkirk	12/37	46-48	59	-	6
Southampton	Tr	02/49	48	15	-	0
Rochdale	Stalybridge Celtic	11/50	50	5	-	0

HEAVISIDE John
Born: Ferryhill, County Durham, England, 7 October, 1943 — LB

League Club	Source	Date Signed	Seasons Played	Apps	Subs	Gls
Darlington (Am)	Bishops Middleham	08/63	63	2	-	0

HEBBERD Trevor Neal
Born: New Alresford, Hampshire, England, 19 June, 1958 — M

League Club	Source	Date Signed	Seasons Played	Apps	Subs	Gls
Southampton	App	06/76	76-81	69	28	7
Bolton W	L	09/81	81	6	0	0
Leicester C	L	11/81	81	4	0	1
Oxford U	Tr	03/82	81-87	260	0	37
Derby Co	Tr	08/88	88-90	70	11	10
Portsmouth	Tr	10/91	91	1	3	0
Chesterfield	Tr	11/91	91-93	67	7	1
Lincoln C	Tr	07/94	94	20	5	0

HEBDITCH Alan
Born: Wigan, Greater Manchester, England, 11 October, 1961 — FB

League Club	Source	Date Signed	Seasons Played	Apps	Subs	Gls
Bradford C	Leeds U (Jnr)	02/81	80	2	0	0

HEBEL Dirk Josef
Born: Cologne, Germany, 24 November, 1972 — M

League Club	Source	Date Signed	Seasons Played	Apps	Subs	Gls
Tranmere Rov	Bursaspor (TKY)	09/97				
Brentford	Tr	08/98	98	6	9	0

HECKINGBOTTOM Paul
Born: Royston, South Yorkshire, England, 17 July, 1977 — LB

League Club	Source	Date Signed	Seasons Played	Apps	Subs	Gls
Sunderland	Manchester U (YT)	07/95				
Scarborough	L	10/97	97	28	1	0
Hartlepool U	L	09/98	98	5	0	1
Darlington	Tr	03/99	98-01	111	4	5
Norwich C	Tr	07/02	02	7	8	0
Bradford C	Tr	07/03	03	43	0	0
Sheffield Wed	Tr	07/04	04-05	41	1	4
Barnsley	Tr	01/06	05-06	45	4	1
Bradford C	Tr	07/07	07-08	53	0	0

HECKMAN Ronald Ernest (Ron)
Born: Peckham, SE London, England, 23 November, 1929 — IF/LW
Died: Bracknell, Berkshire, England, 26 November, 1990
England: Amateur-5

League Club	Source	Date Signed	Seasons Played	Apps	Subs	Gls
Leyton Orient	Bromley	07/55	55-57	87	-	38
Millwall	Tr	11/57	57-59	92	-	21
Crystal Palace	Tr	07/60	60-62	84	-	25

HECTOR Kevin James
Born: Leeds, England, 2 November, 1944 — F
England: 2/FLge-3

League Club	Source	Date Signed	Seasons Played	Apps	Subs	Gls
Bradford Park Ave	Middleton Parkside	07/62	62-66	176	0	113
Derby Co	Tr	09/66	66-77	426	4	147
Derby Co	Burton A	10/80	80-81	52	4	8

HECTOR Michael Anthony James
Born: East Ham, E London, England, 19 July, 1992 — CD

League Club	Source	Date Signed	Seasons Played	Apps	Subs	Gls
Reading	Jnr	10/09	13-14	44	6	3
Barnet	L	11/11	11	26	1	2
Shrewsbury T	L	07/12	12	8	0	0
Aldershot T	L	11/12	12	8	0	1
Cheltenham T	L	01/13	12	18	0	1

HEDGES Ryan Peter
Born: Hawarden, Flintshire, Wales, 7 September, 1995 — RW
Wales: U21-3/Youth

League Club	Source	Date Signed	Seasons Played	Apps	Subs	Gls
Swansea C	Flint Town U	07/13				
Leyton Orient	L	01/15	14	11	6	2

HEDLEY Graeme
Born: Easington, County Durham, England, 1 March, 1957 — M

League Club	Source	Date Signed	Seasons Played	Apps	Subs	Gls
Middlesbrough	App	03/75	76-81	36	14	6
Sheffield Wed	L	02/78	77	6	0	1
Darlington	L	03/79	78	14	0	1
York C	L	10/81	81	5	0	1
Hartlepool U	Horden CW	08/84	84	32	0	9

HEDLEY John Robert (Jack)
Born: Willington Quay, Tyne and Wear, England, 11 December, 1923 — RB
Died: North Tyneside, Tyne and Wear, England, 2 June, 1985

League Club	Source	Date Signed	Seasons Played	Apps	Subs	Gls
Everton	North Shields	04/45	47-49	54	-	0
Sunderland	Tr	08/50	50-58	269	-	0
Gateshead	Tr	07/59	59	11	-	0

HEDMAN Magnus Carl
Born: Stockholm, Sweden, 19 March, 1973 — G
Sweden: 49/B-1/U21-28/Youth

League Club	Source	Date Signed	Seasons Played	Apps	Subs	Gls
Coventry C	AIK Solna (SWE)	07/97	97-01	134	0	0

HEDMAN Rudolph Gideon (Rudi)
Born: Lambeth, S London, England, 16 November, 1964 — D

League Club	Source	Date Signed	Seasons Played	Apps	Subs	Gls
Colchester U		02/84	83-88	166	10	10
Crystal Palace	Tr	12/88	88-91	10	11	0
Leyton Orient	L	12/89	89	5	0	0

HEDWORTH Christopher (Chris)
Born: Wallsend, Tyne and Wear, England, 5 January, 1964 — D

League Club	Source	Date Signed	Seasons Played	Apps	Subs	Gls
Newcastle U	App	01/82	82-85	8	1	0
Barnsley	Tr	08/86	86-87	19	6	0
Halifax T	Tr	08/88	88-89	38	0	0
Blackpool	Tr	09/90	90-91	24	0	0

HEELEY David Mark (Mark)
Born: Peterborough, England, 8 September, 1959 — M

League Club	Source	Date Signed	Seasons Played	Apps	Subs	Gls
Peterborough U	App	11/76	75-76	12	5	3
Arsenal	Tr	09/77	77-78	9	6	1
Northampton T	Tr	03/80	79-82	84	8	5

HEENAN Thomas (Tommy)
Born: Glasgow, Scotland, 16 June, 1932 — RW

League Club	Source	Date Signed	Seasons Played	Apps	Subs	Gls
Bradford Park Ave	Raith Rov	05/58	58	5	-	1

League Club	Source	Date Signed	Seasons Played	Career Record Apps	Subs	Gls
HEEPS James Andrew (Jimmy)						
Born: Luton, England, 16 May, 1971						G
Swansea C	YT	07/89	89	1	0	0
HEEROO Gavin Harry						
Born: Tottenham, N London, England, 2 September, 1984						M
Mauritius: 1						
Crystal Palace	Jnr	09/01	03	0	1	0
HEESOM Darren Lea						
Born: Warrington, Cheshire, England, 8 May, 1968						LB
Burnley	App	12/85	85-86	36	2	1
HEFFER Paul Victor						
Born: West Ham, E London, England, 21 December, 1947						CH
West Ham U	Jnr	08/65	66-71	11	4	0
HEFFER Robert William (Bob)						
Born: Eriswell, Suffolk, England, 9 November, 1935						LW
Norwich C	RAF St Faiths	04/56	56	2	-	1
HEFFERNAN Dean James						
Born: Sydney, Australia, 19 May, 1980						LB
Australia: 2						
Huddersfield T	Central Coast M (AUS)	01/10	09	15	0	0
HEFFERNAN Paul						
Born: Dublin, Republic of Ireland, 29 December, 1981						F
Republic of Ireland: U21-3						
Notts Co	Newtown (ROI)	10/99	99-03	74	26	36
Bristol C	Tr	07/04	04	10	17	5
Doncaster Rov	Tr	06/05	05-09	88	39	36
Oldham Ath	L	11/09	09	4	0	0
Bristol Rov	L	02/10	09	11	0	4
Sheffield Wed	Tr	07/10	10	3	14	3
HEFFERNAN Thomas Patrick (Tom)						
Born: Dublin, Republic of Ireland, 30 April, 1955						RB
Tottenham H	Dunleary Celtic (ROI)	10/77				
Bournemouth	Tr	05/79	79-82	152	2	21
Sheffield U	Tr	08/83	83-84	82	0	5
Bournemouth	Tr	06/85	85-87	58	5	6
HEFFRON Charles Alphonsus (Charlie)						
Born: Belfast, Northern Ireland, 13 August, 1927						G
Northern Ireland: NILge-1						
Bradford Park Ave	Belfast Celtic	06/49	51-52	25	-	0
HEGAN Daniel (Danny)						
Born: Coatbridge, Lanarkshire, Scotland, 14 June, 1943						M
Died: Birmingham, England, 6 August, 2015						
Northern Ireland: 7						
Sunderland	Albion Rov	09/61				
Ipswich T	Tr	07/63	63-68	207	0	34
West Bromwich A	Tr	05/69	69	13	1	2
Wolverhampton W	Tr	05/70	70-73	49	4	6
Sunderland	Tr	11/73	73	3	3	0
HEGARTY Kevin Michael						
Born: Edinburgh, Scotland, 30 July, 1950						F
Carlisle U	Heart of Midlothian	09/71	71	1	6	0
HEGARTY Nicholas Ian (Nick)						
Born: Hemsworth, West Yorkshire, England, 25 August, 1986						LW
Grimsby T	Sch	01/06	04-09	73	19	8
HEGGARTY James Patrick (Jim)						
Born: Killarney, Republic of Ireland, 4 August, 1965						CD
Brighton & HA	Larne T	09/84				
Burnley	Tr	08/85	85	33	3	1
HEGGEM Vegard						
Born: Trondheim, Norway, 13 July, 1975						RB
Norway: 22/U21						
Liverpool	Rosenborg (NOR)	07/98	98-00	38	16	3
HEGGIE William Campbell (Bill)						
Born: Scone, Perthshire, Scotland, 7 June, 1927						CF
Died: Birkenhead, Wirral, England, 7 November, 1977						
New Brighton	Jeanfield Swifts	02/51	50	10	-	5
Leeds U	Tr	06/51				
Wrexham	Tr	08/52	52-54	33	-	13
Accrington Stan	Winsford U	02/55	54	1	-	0
HEGGS Carl Sydney						
Born: Leicester, England, 11 October, 1970						F
West Bromwich A	Leicester U	08/91	91-94	13	27	3
Bristol Rov	L	01/95	94	2	3	1
Swansea C	Tr	07/95	95-96	33	13	7
Northampton T	Tr	07/97	97-98	29	17	5

League Club	Source	Date Signed	Seasons Played	Career Record Apps	Subs	Gls
Chester C (L)	Rushden & D	03/00	99	11	0	2
Carlisle U	Rushden & D	08/00	00	16	14	5
HEGINBOTHAM Brian						
Born: Hyde, Greater Manchester, England, 3 October, 1937						FB
Died: Whaley Bridge, Derbyshire, England, 21 September, 2014						
Stockport Co	Jnr	10/54	58-59	11	-	0
HEIDENSTROM Bjorn						
Born: Porsgrunn, Norway, 15 January, 1968						M
Norway: U21-10						
Leyton Orient	Odd Grenland (NOR)	12/96	96	3	1	0
HEIGHWAY Stephen Derek (Steve)						
Born: Dublin, Republic of Ireland, 25 November, 1947						LW
England: Schools//Republic of Ireland: 34						
Liverpool	Skelmersdale U	05/70	70-80	312	17	50
HEIKKINEN Markus						
Born: Katrineholm, Finland, 13 October, 1978						CD
Finland: 61/U21-3/Youth						
Portsmouth (L)	HJK Helsinki (FIN)	01/03	02	0	2	0
Luton T	Aberdeen	07/05	05-06	75	1	3
HEINEMANN Nicholas (Nicky)						
Born: Bradford, England, 4 January, 1985						D
Halifax T	YT	-	01	3	0	0
HEINOLA Antti Juhani						
Born: Helsinki, Finland, 20 March, 1973						RB
Finland: 12/U21						
Queens Park Rgrs	Heracles (NED)	01/98	97-00	23	11	0
HEINZE Gabriel Ivan						
Born: Crespo, Entre Rios, Argentina, 19 April, 1978						LB
Argentina: 72						
Manchester U	Paris St-Germain (FRA)	07/04	04-06	45	7	1
HEISELBERG Kim						
Born: Tarm, Denmark, 21 September, 1977						LB
Denmark: U21/Youth						
Sunderland	Esbjerg (DEN)	03/97				
Swindon T	Midtjylland (DEN)	08/00	00	1	0	0
HEITINGA John Gijsbert Alan (Johnny)						
Born: Alphen, Netherlands, 15 November, 1983						CD
Netherlands: 87/Youth						
Everton	Atletico Madrid (SPN)	08/09	09-13	98	17	2
Fulham	Tr	01/14	13	14	0	1
HELAN Jeremy						
Born: Paris, France, 9 May, 1992						LB/M
France: Youth						
Manchester C	Stade Rennais (FRA)	07/09				
Carlisle U	L	10/11	11	0	2	0
Shrewsbury T	L	10/12	12	3	0	0
Sheffield Wed	Tr	11/12	12-14	85	24	4
[HELDER] RODRIGUEZ Christovao						
Born: Luanda, Angola, 21 March, 1971						CD
Portugal: 35/U21-6						
Newcastle U (L)	Depo la Coruna (SPN)	11/99	99	8	0	1
HELDER Glenn						
Born: Leiden, Netherlands, 28 October, 1968						LW
Netherlands: 4						
Arsenal	Vitesse Arnhem (NED)	02/95	94-96	27	12	1
HELENIUS Nicklas						
Born: Aalborg, Denmark, 8 May, 1991						F
Denmark: 2/U21-11/Youth						
Aston Villa	Aalborg BK (DEN)	06/13	13	0	3	0
HELGUSON Heidar						
Born: Akureyri, Iceland, 22 August, 1977						F
Iceland: 55/U21-6/Youth						
Watford	Lillestrom (NOR)	01/00	99-04	132	42	55
Fulham	Tr	07/05	05-06	31	26	12
Bolton W	Tr	07/07	07-08	3	4	2
Queens Park Rgrs	Tr	11/08	08-11	63	12	27
Watford	L	09/09	09	26	3	11
Cardiff C	Tr	08/12	12	27	11	8
HELIN Petri Juhani						
Born: Helsinki, Finland, 13 December, 1969						RB/M
Finland: 28						
Luton T	FC Jokerit (FIN)	11/00	00	23	0	1
Stockport Co	Tr	07/01	01	10	3	0
HELLAWELL John Rodney						
Born: Keighley, West Yorkshire, England, 20 December, 1943						IF

League Club	Source	Date Signed	Seasons Played	Apps	Subs	Gls
Bradford C	Salts	06/63	62-64	48	-	13
Rotherham U	Tr	01/65	64-65	9	1	3
Darlington	Tr	07/66	66	7	1	1
Bradford Park Ave	Tr	10/68	68	1	0	0

HELLAWELL Michael Stephen (Mike)
Born: Keighley, West Yorkshire, England, 30 June, 1938 — RW
England: 2

League Club	Source	Date Signed	Seasons Played	Apps	Subs	Gls
Queens Park Rgrs	Salts	08/55	55-56	45	-	7
Birmingham C	Tr	05/57	57-64	178	-	30
Sunderland	Tr	01/65	64-66	43	1	2
Huddersfield T	Tr	09/66	66-67	45	1	1
Peterborough U	Tr	12/68	68	9	0	0

HELLEWELL Keith
Born: Barnsley, South Yorkshire, England, 1 April, 1944 — G
Died: Retford, Nottinghamshire, England, 18 January, 2005

League Club	Source	Date Signed	Seasons Played	Apps	Subs	Gls
Doncaster Rov	Jnr	05/61	62-63	12	-	0

HELLIN Anthony (Tony)
Born: Merthyr Tydfil, Wales, 26 September, 1944 — LB
Wales: Schools

League Club	Source	Date Signed	Seasons Played	Apps	Subs	Gls
Swindon T	App	06/62				
Torquay U	Tr	07/64	64-65	29	0	1

HELLIN Matthew Karl
Born: Merthyr Tydfil, Wales, 12 September, 1966 — CD

League Club	Source	Date Signed	Seasons Played	Apps	Subs	Gls
Aston Villa	App	09/84				
Wolverhampton W	Tr	08/86	86	1	0	0

HELLINGS Dennis Raymond (Dan)
Born: Lincoln, England, 9 December, 1923 — IF
Died: Leicester, England, 19 May, 1996

League Club	Source	Date Signed	Seasons Played	Apps	Subs	Gls
Lincoln C	Ransome & Marles	12/45	46	3	-	0

HELLIWELL David
Born: Blackburn, Greater Manchester, England, 28 March, 1948 — W
Died: Blackburn, Greater Manchester, England, 22 March, 2003

League Club	Source	Date Signed	Seasons Played	Apps	Subs	Gls
Blackburn Rov	App	05/66	66-68	15	0	1
Lincoln C	Tr	05/69	69	11	2	1
Workington	Tr	07/70	70-75	184	14	20
Rochdale	Tr	07/76	76	20	11	3

HELLIWELL Ian
Born: Rotherham, South Yorkshire, England, 7 November, 1962 — F

League Club	Source	Date Signed	Seasons Played	Apps	Subs	Gls
York C	Matlock T	10/87	87-90	158	2	40
Scunthorpe U	Tr	08/91	91-92	78	2	22
Rotherham U	Tr	08/93	93-94	47	5	4
Stockport Co	Tr	01/95	94-95	35	4	13
Burnley	Tr	02/96	95	3	1	0
Mansfield T	L	09/96	96	4	1	1
Chester C	L	10/96	96	8	1	1
Doncaster Rov	L	11/97	97	8	0	1

HELMER Thomas
Born: Herford, Germany, 21 April, 1965 — CD
Germany: 68

League Club	Source	Date Signed	Seasons Played	Apps	Subs	Gls
Sunderland	Bayern Munich (GER)	07/99	99	1	1	0

HELVEG Thomas Lund
Born: Odense, Denmark, 24 June, 1971 — RB
Denmark: 108/U21-3

League Club	Source	Date Signed	Seasons Played	Apps	Subs	Gls
Norwich C	Inter Milan (ITA)	08/04	04	16	4	0

HEMMERMAN Jeffrey Lawrence (Jeff)
Born: Hull, England, 25 February, 1955 — F

League Club	Source	Date Signed	Seasons Played	Apps	Subs	Gls
Hull C	App	03/73	73-76	45	14	10
Scunthorpe U	L	09/75	75	4	1	1
Port Vale	Tr	06/77	77	13	2	5
Portsmouth	Tr	07/78	78-81	114	9	39
Cardiff C	Tr	07/82	82-83	54	1	22

HEMMING Christopher Anthony John (Chris)
Born: Newcastle-under-Lyme, Potteries, England, 13 April, 1966 — CD

League Club	Source	Date Signed	Seasons Played	Apps	Subs	Gls
Stoke C	Jnr	04/84	83-88	85	8	2
Wigan Ath	L	01/89	88	4	0	0
Hereford U	Tr	08/89	89-90	39	2	3

HEMMINGS Anthony George (Tony)
Born: Burton-on-Trent, Staffordshire, England, 21 September, 1967 — LW
England: Semi Pro-1

League Club	Source	Date Signed	Seasons Played	Apps	Subs	Gls
Wycombe W	Northwich Victoria	09/93	93-95	28	21	12
Chester C	Ilkeston T	01/00	99	19	0	2
Carlisle U	Tr	08/00	00	16	6	0

HEMMINGS Ashley Josiah
Born: Lewisham, SE London, England, 3 March, 1991 — LW
England: Youth

League Club	Source	Date Signed	Seasons Played	Apps	Subs	Gls
Wolverhampton W	Sch	01/09	08	0	2	0
Cheltenham T	L	02/09	08	0	1	0
Torquay U	L	10/10	10	4	5	0
Plymouth Arg	L	11/11	11	18	5	2
Walsall	Tr	07/12	12-13	24	31	3
Burton A	L	03/14	13	2	3	0
Dagenham & Red	Tr	07/14	14	36	5	5

HEMMINGS Kane
Born: Burton on Trent, Staffordshire, England, 8 April, 1992 — F

League Club	Source	Date Signed	Seasons Played	Apps	Subs	Gls
Barnsley	Cowdenbeath	06/14	14	11	12	3

HEMSLEY Edward John Orton (Ted)
Born: Stoke-on-Trent, England, 1 September, 1943 — LB/RH

League Club	Source	Date Signed	Seasons Played	Apps	Subs	Gls
Shrewsbury T	Jnr	07/61	60-68	234	1	22
Sheffield U	Tr	08/68	68-76	247	0	7
Doncaster Rov	Tr	07/77	77-78	32	0	1

HEMSTEAD Derek William
Born: Scunthorpe, North Lincolnshire, England, 22 May, 1943 — FB

League Club	Source	Date Signed	Seasons Played	Apps	Subs	Gls
Scunthorpe U	Jnr	05/60	60-68	248	0	2
Carlisle U	Tr	07/69	69-72	97	1	1

HEMSTOCK Brian
Born: Goldthorpe, South Yorkshire, England, 9 February, 1949 — IF

League Club	Source	Date Signed	Seasons Played	Apps	Subs	Gls
Barnsley	Jnr	12/66	66	1	0	0
Bradford Park Ave	Tr	07/68	68	4	0	0

HENCHER Kenneth Ernest Edward (Ken)
Born: Romford, E London, England, 2 February, 1928 — CH
Died: Rochford, Essex, England, 1 August, 2010

League Club	Source	Date Signed	Seasons Played	Apps	Subs	Gls
Millwall	Dagenham	12/49	49-55	48	-	0

HENCHER Nicholas (Nick)
Born: Wrexham, Wales, 24 August, 1961 — W

League Club	Source	Date Signed	Seasons Played	Apps	Subs	Gls
Wrexham	Lex X1	08/85	85-87	26	6	5

HENCHOZ Stephane
Born: Romont, Switzerland, 7 September, 1974 — CD
Switzerland: 72/Youth

League Club	Source	Date Signed	Seasons Played	Apps	Subs	Gls
Blackburn Rov	Hamburger SV (GER)	07/97	97-98	70	0	0
Liverpool	Tr	07/99	99-03	132	3	0
Wigan Ath	Tr	07/05	05	26	0	0
Blackburn Rov	Tr	09/06	06	10	2	0

HENDERSON Anthony Joseph (Tony)
Born: Newcastle-upon-Tyne, England, 14 January, 1954 — CD

League Club	Source	Date Signed	Seasons Played	Apps	Subs	Gls
Rotherham U	App	01/72	73	5	1	0

HENDERSON Brian Charles
Born: Allendale, Northumberland, England, 12 June, 1930 — FB
Died: Darlington, County Durham, England, 7 November, 2001

League Club	Source	Date Signed	Seasons Played	Apps	Subs	Gls
Carlisle U		05/50				
Darlington	Tr	07/52	52-63	423	-	3

HENDERSON Conor Alan
Born: Sidcup, SE London, England, 8 September, 1991 — M
England: Youth//Republic of Ireland: U21-3/Youth

League Club	Source	Date Signed	Seasons Played	Apps	Subs	Gls
Arsenal	Sch	01/09				
Coventry C	L	09/12	12	1	1	0
Hull C	Tr	09/13				
Stevenage	L	03/14	13	3	0	0
Crawley T	Tr	06/14	14	13	4	2

HENDERSON Damian Michael
Born: Leeds, England, 12 May, 1973 — F/CD

League Club	Source	Date Signed	Seasons Played	Apps	Subs	Gls
Leeds U	YT	07/91				
Scarborough	Tr	08/93	93	17	0	5
Scunthorpe U	Tr	12/93	93-94	31	6	4
Hereford U	L	01/95	94	5	0	0
Hartlepool U	Tr	03/95	94-95	45	3	6

HENDERSON Darius Alexis
Born: Sutton, S London, England, 7 September, 1981 — F

League Club	Source	Date Signed	Seasons Played	Apps	Subs	Gls
Reading	YT	12/99	99-03	5	66	11
Brighton & HA	L	08/03	03	10	0	2
Gillingham	Tr	01/04	03-04	31	5	9
Swindon T	L	08/04	04	6	0	5
Watford	Tr	08/05	05-07	85	20	29
Sheffield U	Tr	07/08	08-10	61	11	20
Millwall	Tr	07/11	11-12	41	10	22
Nottingham F	Tr	01/13	12-13	16	29	10
Leyton Orient	Tr	07/14	14	16	7	8

HENDERSON George
Born: Hartlepool, Cleveland, England, 7 March, 1946 — F
Died: Hartlepool, Cleveland, England, 25 August, 1991

League Club	Source	Date Signed	Seasons Played	Apps	Subs	Gls
Hartlepool U (Am)	Bishop Auckland	11/70	70	1	0	0

HENDERSON Ian
Born: Thetford, Norfolk, England, 24 January, 1985 — F
England: Youth

League Club	Source	Date Signed	Seasons Played	Apps	Subs	Gls
Norwich C	Sch	02/03	02-06	26	42	6

League Club	Source	Date Signed	Seasons Played	Apps	Subs	Gls
Rotherham U	L	01/07	06	18	0	1
Northampton T	Tr	07/07	07-08	9	17	0
Luton T	Tr	01/09	08	14	5	1
Colchester U	Ankaragucu (TKY)	01/10	09-12	89	28	24
Rochdale	Tr	02/13	12-14	101	0	36

HENDERSON James Stewart (Stewart)
Born: Bridge of Allan, Stirlingshire, Scotland, 5 June, 1947 FB
Scotland: Schools

League Club	Source	Date Signed	Seasons Played	Apps	Subs	Gls
Chelsea	Jnr	07/64				
Brighton & HA	Tr	07/65	65-72	198	0	1
Reading	Tr	06/73	73-82	159	7	6

HENDERSON John
Born: Johnshaven, Aberdeenshire, Scotland, 22 September, 1941 IF

League Club	Source	Date Signed	Seasons Played	Apps	Subs	Gls
Charlton Ath	Montrose Victoria	06/59	62	4	-	1
Exeter C	Tr	11/62	62-63	46	-	14
Doncaster Rov	Tr	07/64	64	10	-	0
Chesterfield	Tr	07/65	65	28	0	3

HENDERSON John Gillespie (Jackie)
Born: Bishopbriggs, Glasgow, Scotland, 17 January, 1932 CF/W
Died: Poole, Dorset, England, 26 January, 2005
Scotland: 7/B

League Club	Source	Date Signed	Seasons Played	Apps	Subs	Gls
Portsmouth	Kirkintilloch BC	01/49	51-57	217	-	69
Wolverhampton W	Tr	03/58	57-58	9	-	3
Arsenal	Tr	10/58	58-61	103	-	29
Fulham	Tr	01/62	61-63	45	-	7

HENDERSON John Swinton Pryde (Jock)
Born: Glasgow, Scotland, 13 October, 1923 IF
Died: Trowbridge, Wiltshire, England, 4 July, 2012

League Club	Source	Date Signed	Seasons Played	Apps	Subs	Gls
Rotherham U	Third Lanark	11/53	53-54	47	-	7
Leeds U	Tr	03/55	54-55	15	-	4

HENDERSON Jordan Brian
Born: Sunderland, England, 17 June, 1990 M
England: 22/U21-27/Youth

League Club	Source	Date Signed	Seasons Played	Apps	Subs	Gls
Sunderland	Sch	07/08	08-10	60	11	4
Coventry C	L	01/09	08	9	1	1
Liverpool	Tr	06/11	11-14	118	21	17

HENDERSON Joseph (Joe)
Born: Cleland, Lanarkshire, Scotland, 21 December, 1924 G
Died: Cleland, Lanarkshire, Scotland, 15 February, 1984

League Club	Source	Date Signed	Seasons Played	Apps	Subs	Gls
Northampton T	Albion Rov	05/49				
Accrington Stan	Stenhousemuir	07/53	53	14	-	0

HENDERSON Joseph James (Joe)
Born: Banbury, Oxfordshire, England, 2 November, 1993 D

League Club	Source	Date Signed	Seasons Played	Apps	Subs	Gls
Coventry C	Sch	06/12	11	0	1	0

HENDERSON Kevin Malcolm
Born: Ashington, Northumberland, England, 8 June, 1974 F

League Club	Source	Date Signed	Seasons Played	Apps	Subs	Gls
Burnley	Morpeth T	12/97	97-98	0	14	1
Hartlepool U	Tr	07/99	99-03	82	49	29
Carlisle U	Tr	09/03	03	10	9	2

HENDERSON Liam Marc
Born: Gateshead, Tyne and Wear, England, 28 December, 1989 F

League Club	Source	Date Signed	Seasons Played	Apps	Subs	Gls
Watford	Sch	07/08	08-09	0	18	0
Hartlepool U	L	01/09	08	2	6	0
Colchester U	L	09/10	10	0	8	0
Aldershot T	L	01/11	10	1	0	0
Rotherham U	L	02/11	10	5	6	0

HENDERSON Michael Robert (Mick)
Born: Gosforth, Tyne and Wear, England, 31 March, 1956 RB/M

League Club	Source	Date Signed	Seasons Played	Apps	Subs	Gls
Sunderland	App	03/74	75-78	81	3	2
Watford	Tr	11/79	79-81	50	1	0
Cardiff C	Tr	03/82	81	11	0	0
Sheffield U	Tr	08/82	82-84	65	2	0
Chesterfield	Tr	01/85	84-88	135	1	10

HENDERSON Paul John
Born: Sydney, Australia, 22 April, 1976 G

League Club	Source	Date Signed	Seasons Played	Apps	Subs	Gls
Bradford C	Northern Spirit (AUS)	08/04	04	40	0	0
Leicester C	Tr	07/05	05-08	62	1	0

HENDERSON Peter
Born: Berwick-on-Tweed, Northumberland, England, 29 September, 1952 LW

League Club	Source	Date Signed	Seasons Played	Apps	Subs	Gls
Chester C	Witton A	12/78	78-79	59	5	10
Gillingham	Tr	07/80	80	6	1	3
Crewe Alex	L	09/81	81	6	1	0
Chester C	Tr	12/81	81	28	0	5

HENDERSON Raymond (Ray)
Born: Wallsend, Tyne and Wear, England, 31 March, 1937 IF/RW

League Club	Source	Date Signed	Seasons Played	Apps	Subs	Gls
Middlesbrough	Ashington	05/57	57-60	9	-	5
Hull C	Tr	06/61	61-67	226	3	54
Reading	Tr	10/68	68	5	0	0

HENDERSON Stanley (Stan)
Born: Barrow, Cumbria, England, 15 October, 1925 RW
Died: Barrow, Cumbria, England, 1980

League Club	Source	Date Signed	Seasons Played	Apps	Subs	Gls
Barrow	Holker Central OB	06/46	46-47	25	-	3

HENDERSON Stephen
Born: Cork, Republic of Ireland, 5 February, 1988 G
Republic of Ireland: U21-8

League Club	Source	Date Signed	Seasons Played	Apps	Subs	Gls
Aston Villa	Sch	05/06				
Bristol C	Tr	07/07	07-09	3	2	0
Aldershot T	L	02/10	09	8	0	0
Yeovil T	L	09/10	10	33	0	0
Portsmouth	Tr	07/11	11	25	0	0
West Ham U	Tr	03/12				
Ipswich T	L	10/12	12	24	0	0
Bournemouth	L	10/13	13	2	0	0
Charlton Ath	Tr	07/14	14	31	0	0

HENDERSON Thomas (Tommy)
Born: Consett, County Durham, England, 6 April, 1949 RW

League Club	Source	Date Signed	Seasons Played	Apps	Subs	Gls
Bradford Park Ave	Tow Law T	02/69	68-69	22	0	3
York C	Tr	10/70	70-71	63	1	7

HENDERSON Thomas (Tom)
Born: Burnley, Lancashire, England, 1 October, 1927 RW
Died: 31 May, 2013

League Club	Source	Date Signed	Seasons Played	Apps	Subs	Gls
Burnley	Jnr	08/45	49	2	-	0

HENDERSON Thomas Wedlock (Tommy)
Born: Larkhall, Lanarkshire, Scotland, 25 July, 1943 RW

League Club	Source	Date Signed	Seasons Played	Apps	Subs	Gls
Leeds U	St Mirren	11/62	62-64	24	-	2
Bury	Tr	06/65	65	7	0	1
Swindon T	Tr	01/66	65	11	0	3
Stockport Co	Tr	07/66	66	17	2	4

HENDERSON Wayne Christopher
Born: Dublin, Republic of Ireland, 16 September, 1983 G
Republic of Ireland: 6/U21-13/Youth

League Club	Source	Date Signed	Seasons Played	Apps	Subs	Gls
Aston Villa	YT	09/00				
Wycombe W	L	04/04	03	3	0	0
Notts Co	L	08/04	04	9	0	0
Notts Co	L	12/04	04	2	0	0
Brighton & HA	Tr	08/05	05-06	52	0	0
Preston NE	Tr	01/07	06-09	8	1	0
Grimsby T	L	02/09	08	14	0	0

HENDERSON William (Willie)
Born: Caldercruix, Lanarkshire, Scotland, 24 January, 1944 RW
Scotland: 29/SLge-6/U23-2/Schools

League Club	Source	Date Signed	Seasons Played	Apps	Subs	Gls
Sheffield Wed	Glasgow Rangers	07/72	72-73	42	6	5

HENDERSON William John (Bill)
Born: Closeburn, Dumfries & Galloway, Scotland, 21 February, 1920 G
Died: Macclesfield, Cheshire, England, 25 October, 1965

League Club	Source	Date Signed	Seasons Played	Apps	Subs	Gls
Rochdale	Queen of the South	07/46	46	17	-	0
Southport	Tr	06/47	47	20	-	0

HENDERSON William Martin Melville (Martin)
Born: Kirkcaldy, Fife, Scotland, 3 May, 1956 F

League Club	Source	Date Signed	Seasons Played	Apps	Subs	Gls
Leicester C	Philadelphia F'y (USA)	10/78	78-80	79	12	12
Chesterfield	Tr	09/81	81-83	87	0	23
Port Vale	Tr	10/83	83	27	0	7

HENDON Ian Michael
Born: Ilford, E London, England, 5 December, 1971 D
England: U21-7/Youth

League Club	Source	Date Signed	Seasons Played	Apps	Subs	Gls
Tottenham H	YT	12/89	90-91	0	4	0
Portsmouth	L	01/92	91	1	3	0
Leyton Orient	L	03/92	91	5	1	0
Barnsley	L	03/93	92	6	0	0
Leyton Orient	Tr	08/93	93-96	130	1	5
Birmingham C	L	03/95	94	4	0	0
Notts Co	Tr	02/97	96-98	82	0	6
Northampton T	Tr	03/99	98-00	60	0	3
Sheffield Wed	Tr	10/00	00-02	49	0	2
Peterborough U	Tr	01/03	02	7	0	1
Barnet	Tr	05/03	05-07	61	4	8

HENDRICK Jeffrey Patrick (Jeff)
Born: Dublin, Republic of Ireland, 31 January, 1992 M
Republic of Ireland: 14/U21-7/Youth

League Club	Source	Date Signed	Seasons Played	Apps	Subs	Gls
Derby Co	Sch	07/10	10-14	133	29	20

HENDRIE John Grattan
Born: Lennoxtown, Dunbartonshire, Scotland, 24 October, 1963 RW
Scotland: Youth

League Club	Source	Date Signed	Seasons Played	Apps	Subs	Gls
Coventry C	App	05/81	81-83	15	6	2
Hereford U	L	01/84	83	6	0	0
Bradford C	Tr	07/84	84-87	173	0	46
Newcastle U	Tr	06/88	88	34	0	4

League Club	Source	Date Signed	Seasons Played	Apps	Subs	Gls
Leeds U	Tr	06/89	89	22	5	5
Middlesbrough	Tr	07/90	90-95	181	11	44
Barnsley	Tr	10/96	96-98	49	16	17

HENDRIE Lee Andrew
Born: Birmingham, England, 18 May, 1977 M
England: 1/B-1/U21-13/Youth

League Club	Source	Date Signed	Seasons Played	Apps	Subs	Gls
Aston Villa	YT	05/94	95-06	202	49	27
Stoke C	L	09/06	06	26	2	3
Sheffield U	Tr	07/07	07-08	7	10	1
Leicester C	L	02/08	07	9	0	1
Blackpool	L	11/08	08	5	1	0
Derby Co	Tr	09/09	09	4	5	0
Brighton & HA	L	03/10	09	6	2	0
Bradford C	Tr	09/10	10	8	4	2

HENDRIE Paul
Born: Glasgow, Scotland, 27 March, 1954 M

League Club	Source	Date Signed	Seasons Played	Apps	Subs	Gls
Birmingham C	Kirkintilloch Rob Roy	03/72	72-75	19	3	1
Bristol Rov	Tr	09/77	77-78	17	13	1
Halifax T	Tr	07/79	79-83	187	0	11
Stockport Co	Tr	08/84	84-88	114	7	6

HENDRIE Stuart Scott
Born: Solihull, West Midlands, England, 1 November, 1989 W

League Club	Source	Date Signed	Seasons Played	Apps	Subs	Gls
Morecambe	Atherstone T	08/10	10	1	6	0

HENDRY Edward Colin James (Colin)
Born: Dalkeith, Midlothian, Scotland, 7 December, 1965 CD
Scotland: 51/B-1

League Club	Source	Date Signed	Seasons Played	Apps	Subs	Gls
Blackburn Rov	Dundee	03/87	86-89	99	3	22
Manchester C	Tr	11/89	89-91	57	6	5
Blackburn Rov	Tr	11/91	91-97	229	5	12
Coventry C	Glasgow Rangers	03/00	99-00	10	1	0
Bolton W	Tr	12/00	00-01	25	0	3
Preston NE	L	02/02	01	2	0	0
Blackpool	L	12/02	02	14	0	0

HENDRY Ian
Born: Glasgow, Scotland, 19 October, 1959 M

League Club	Source	Date Signed	Seasons Played	Apps	Subs	Gls
Aston Villa	App	09/77				
Hereford U	Tr	02/79	78-79	21	0	0

HENDRY John Michael
Born: Glasgow, Scotland, 6 January, 1970 F
Scotland: U21-1

League Club	Source	Date Signed	Seasons Played	Apps	Subs	Gls
Tottenham H	Dundee	07/90	90-93	5	12	5
Charlton Ath	L	02/92	91	1	4	1
Swansea C	L	10/94	94	8	0	2

HENDRY William Michael (Will)
Born: Slough, Berkshire, England, 10 November, 1986 M

League Club	Source	Date Signed	Seasons Played	Apps	Subs	Gls
Millwall	Sch	10/05	05	2	1	0

HENLEY Adam David
Born: Knoxville, Tennessee, USA, 14 June, 1994 RB
Wales: U21-3/Youth

League Club	Source	Date Signed	Seasons Played	Apps	Subs	Gls
Blackburn Rov	Sch	12/11	11-14	45	9	1

HENLEY Leslie Donald (Les)
Born: Lambeth, S London, England, 26 September, 1922 WH/IF
Died: Taunton, Somerset, England, 1 May, 1996
England: Schools

League Club	Source	Date Signed	Seasons Played	Apps	Subs	Gls
Arsenal	Jnr	09/40				
Reading	Tr	12/46	46-52	181	-	29

HENNESSEY Wayne Robert
Born: Beaumaris, Anglesey, Wales, 24 January, 1987 G
Wales: 49/U21-6

League Club	Source	Date Signed	Seasons Played	Apps	Subs	Gls
Wolverhampton W	Sch	04/05	07-11	151	1	0
Stockport Co	L	01/07	06	15	0	0
Yeovil T	L	08/13	13	12	0	0
Crystal Palace	Tr	01/14	13-14	3	1	0

HENNESSEY William Terence (Terry)
Born: Llay, Wrexham, Wales, 1 September, 1942 CD
Wales: 39/U23-6/Schools

League Club	Source	Date Signed	Seasons Played	Apps	Subs	Gls
Birmingham C	Jnr	09/59	60-65	178	0	3
Nottingham F	Tr	11/65	65-69	159	0	5
Derby Co	Tr	02/70	69-72	62	1	4

HENNIGAN Michael (Mike)
Born: Rotherham, South Yorkshire, England, 20 December, 1942 CH

League Club	Source	Date Signed	Seasons Played	Apps	Subs	Gls
Sheffield Wed	Rotherham U (Am)	03/61				
Southampton	Tr	06/62	63	3	-	0
Brighton & HA	Tr	07/64	64	4	-	0

HENNIN Derek
Born: Prescot, Merseyside, England, 28 December, 1931 RH
Died: Knowsley, Merseyside, England, 15 January, 1989
England: Youth

League Club	Source	Date Signed	Seasons Played	Apps	Subs	Gls
Bolton W	Prescot Cables	06/49	53-60	164	-	8
Chester C	Tr	02/61	60-61	54	-	4

HENNINGS Robert Iva (Bobby)
Born: Glyncorrwg, Neath Port Talbot, Wales, 30 December, 1931 RH

League Club	Source	Date Signed	Seasons Played	Apps	Subs	Gls
Swansea C	Jnr	01/49	55-56	10	-	1

HENRIKSEN Bo
Born: Roskilde, Denmark, 7 February, 1975 F

League Club	Source	Date Signed	Seasons Played	Apps	Subs	Gls
Kidderminster Hrs	Herfolge (DEN)	11/01	01-03	74	10	30
Bristol Rov	Tr	03/04	03	1	3	0

HENRIQUEZ Angelo Jose
Born: Santiago, Chile, 13 April, 1994 F
Chile: 8/Youth

League Club	Source	Date Signed	Seasons Played	Apps	Subs	Gls
Manchester U	Univ de Chile (CHL)	08/12				
Wigan Ath	L	01/13	12	0	4	1

HENRY Anthony (Tony)
Born: Houghton-le-Spring, Tyne and Wear, England, 26 November, 1957 M

League Club	Source	Date Signed	Seasons Played	Apps	Subs	Gls
Manchester C	App	12/74	76-81	68	11	6
Bolton W	Tr	09/81	81-82	70	0	22
Oldham Ath	Tr	03/83	82-87	185	5	25
Stoke C	Tr	11/87	87-88	59	3	11
Shrewsbury T	Mazda Hiroshima (JPN)	08/91	91	39	1	7

HENRY Anthony Francis
Born: Stepney, E London, England, 13 September, 1979 CD

League Club	Source	Date Signed	Seasons Played	Apps	Subs	Gls
West Ham U	YT	06/97				
Lincoln C	Tr	08/99	99-00	15	3	1

HENRY Charles (Charlie)
Born: Stevenage, Hertfordshire, England, 28 September, 1986 LW
England: Semi Pro-2

League Club	Source	Date Signed	Seasons Played	Apps	Subs	Gls
Aldershot T (L)	Luton T	11/11	11	3	4	0

HENRY Charles Anthony (Charlie)
Born: Acton, W London, England, 13 February, 1962 M

League Club	Source	Date Signed	Seasons Played	Apps	Subs	Gls
Swindon T	App	02/80	80-88	200	23	26
Torquay U	L	02/87	86	6	0	1
Northampton T	L	03/87	86	4	0	1
Aldershot	Tr	08/89	89-90	81	0	18

HENRY Doneil Jor-Dee Ashley
Born: Toronto, Canada, 20 April, 1993 CD
Canada: 14/U23-3/Youth

League Club	Source	Date Signed	Seasons Played	Apps	Subs	Gls
West Ham U	Toronto FC (CAN)	01/15				
Blackburn Rov	L	03/15	14	3	0	0

HENRY Gerald Robert (Gerry)
Born: Hemsworth, West Yorkshire, England, 5 October, 1920 IF
Died: Derby, England, September, 1979

League Club	Source	Date Signed	Seasons Played	Apps	Subs	Gls
Leeds U	Outwood Stormcocks	10/37	38-47	44	-	4
Bradford Park Ave	Tr	11/47	47-49	79	-	31
Sheffield Wed	Tr	02/50	49-51	40	-	7
Halifax T	Tr	12/51	51-52	24	-	3

HENRY Gordon
Born: Troon, Ayrshire, Scotland, 9 October, 1930 CH/CF
Died: Aldershot, Hampshire, England, 23 December, 2007

League Club	Source	Date Signed	Seasons Played	Apps	Subs	Gls
Aldershot	St Mirren	06/56	56-63	175	-	15

HENRY James
Born: Reading, England, 10 June, 1989 RW
England: Youth

League Club	Source	Date Signed	Seasons Played	Apps	Subs	Gls
Reading	Sch	06/06	08-09	4	6	0
Nottingham F	L	03/07	06	0	1	0
Bournemouth	L	11/07	07	8	3	4
Norwich C	L	01/08	07	1	2	0
Millwall	L	02/09	08	15	1	3
Millwall	L	09/09	09	6	3	5
Millwall	Tr	07/10	10-13	100	21	10
Wolverhampton W	Tr	10/13	13-14	49	20	15

HENRY Karl Levi Daniel
Born: Wolverhampton, England, 26 November, 1982 DM
England: Youth

League Club	Source	Date Signed	Seasons Played	Apps	Subs	Gls
Stoke C	YT	11/99	01-05	63	57	1
Cheltenham T	L	01/04	03	8	1	1
Wolverhampton W	Tr	08/06	06-12	242	8	6
Queens Park Rgrs	Tr	07/13	13-14	44	16	1

HENRY Liburd Algernon
Born: Roseau, Dominica, 29 August, 1967 F

League Club	Source	Date Signed	Seasons Played	Apps	Subs	Gls
Watford	Leytonstone & Ilford	11/87	88-89	8	2	1
Halifax T	L	09/88	88	1	4	0
Maidstone U	Tr	06/90	90-91	61	6	9
Gillingham	Tr	06/92	92-93	37	5	2
Peterborough U	Tr	08/94	94	22	10	7

HENRY Nicholas Ian (Nick)
Born: Liverpool, England, 21 February, 1969 — M

League Club	Source	Date Signed	Seasons Played	Apps	Subs	Gls
Oldham Ath	YT	07/87	87-96	264	9	19
Sheffield U	Tr	02/97	96-98	13	3	0
Walsall	Tr	03/99	98	8	0	0
Tranmere Rov	Tr	07/99	99-01	84	5	2

HENRY Paul Nicholas
Born: Liverpool, England, 28 January, 1988 — M

League Club	Source	Date Signed	Seasons Played	Apps	Subs	Gls
Tranmere Rov	Sch	05/06	07-08	2	1	0

HENRY Rico Antonio
Born: Birmingham, England, 8 July, 1997 — LB

League Club	Source	Date Signed	Seasons Played	Apps	Subs	Gls
Walsall	Sch	07/14	14	4	5	0

HENRY Ronald Patrick (Ron)
Born: Shoreditch, Central London, England, 17 August, 1934 — LB
Died: Harpenden, Hertfordshire, England, 27 December, 2014
England: 1

League Club	Source	Date Signed	Seasons Played	Apps	Subs	Gls
Tottenham H	Redbourne	03/52	54-65	247	0	1

HENRY Ronnie Stephen
Born: Hemel Hempstead, Hertfordshire, England, 2 January, 1984 — D
England: Semi Pro-4

League Club	Source	Date Signed	Seasons Played	Apps	Subs	Gls
Tottenham H	Sch	07/02				
Southend U	L	03/03	02	3	0	0
Stevenage	Dublin C (ROI)	01/05	10-11	74	0	0
Stevenage	Luton T	07/14	14	34	0	0

HENRY Thierry Daniel
Born: Paris, France, 17 August, 1977 — F
France: 123/Youth

League Club	Source	Date Signed	Seasons Played	Apps	Subs	Gls
Arsenal	Juventus (ITA)	08/99	99-06	235	19	174
Arsenal (L)	New York R Bulls (USA)	01/12	11	0	4	1

HENSHALL Alex Charles
Born: Swindon, England, 15 February, 1994 — LW
England: Youth

League Club	Source	Date Signed	Seasons Played	Apps	Subs	Gls
Manchester C	Sch	02/11				
Chesterfield	L	02/13	12	1	6	0
Bristol Rov	L	10/13	13	1	1	1
Ipswich T	Tr	07/14	14	0	4	0
Blackpool	L	01/15	14	0	2	0

HENSHAW Gary
Born: Leeds, England, 18 February, 1965 — RW

League Club	Source	Date Signed	Seasons Played	Apps	Subs	Gls
Grimsby T	App	02/83	83-86	46	4	9
Bolton W	Tr	06/87	87-90	49	21	4
Rochdale	L	03/90	89	8	1	1

HENSON Anthony Harold (Tony)
Born: Dronfield, Derbyshire, England, 15 October, 1960 — M

League Club	Source	Date Signed	Seasons Played	Apps	Subs	Gls
Chesterfield	Alfreton T	11/81	81-82	26	2	0

HENSON Leonard (Len)
Born: Hull, England, 6 August, 1921 — WH
Died: Flatford, Suffolk, England, 8 May, 2008

League Club	Source	Date Signed	Seasons Played	Apps	Subs	Gls
Gillingham	RAF	09/44	50-51	8	-	0

HENSON Philip Michael (Phil)
Born: Manchester, England, 30 March, 1953 — M

League Club	Source	Date Signed	Seasons Played	Apps	Subs	Gls
Manchester C	App	07/70	71-74	12	4	0
Swansea C	L	07/72	72	1	0	0
Sheffield Wed	Tr	02/75	74-76	65	8	9
Stockport Co	Sparta Rotterdam (NED)	09/78	78-79	65	2	13
Rotherham U	Tr	02/80	79-83	87	5	7

HENWOOD Rodney Charles (Rod)
Born: Portsmouth, England, 27 November, 1931 — LW
Died: Portsmouth, England, 4 September, 2010

League Club	Source	Date Signed	Seasons Played	Apps	Subs	Gls
Portsmouth	Kingston BC	05/50	53	2	-	0

HEPBURN John Slaven
Born: Paisley, Renfrewshire, Scotland, 10 March, 1921 — RW
Died: Paisley, Renfrewshire, Scotland, 31 May, 1994

League Club	Source	Date Signed	Seasons Played	Apps	Subs	Gls
Workington	Alloa Ath	08/51	51	1	-	0

HEPBURN-MURPHY Rushian Marcus
Born: Birmingham, England, 19 September, 1998 — F
England: Youth

League Club	Source	Date Signed	Seasons Played	Apps	Subs	Gls
Aston Villa	Sch	-	14	0	1	0

HEPPELL George
Born: West Hartlepool, County Durham, England, 2 September, 1916 — G
Died: Stoke-on-Trent, England, 20 July, 1993

League Club	Source	Date Signed	Seasons Played	Apps	Subs	Gls
Wolverhampton W	Murton CW	09/36				
Port Vale	Tr	05/37	37-51	193	-	0

HEPPLE Gordon
Born: Sunderland, England, 16 September, 1925 — FB
Died: Bedford, England, 25 April, 1980

League Club	Source	Date Signed	Seasons Played	Apps	Subs	Gls
Middlesbrough	Sunderland (Am)	07/45	46-53	41	-	0
Norwich C	Tr	06/54	54	5	-	0

HEPPLE John Andrew
Born: Middlesbrough, England, 12 March, 1970 — F
Died: South Bank, Cleveland, England, 10 March, 2008

League Club	Source	Date Signed	Seasons Played	Apps	Subs	Gls
Sunderland	YT	07/87				
Hartlepool U	L	03/89	88	1	1	0

HEPPLEWHITE George
Born: Edmondsley, County Durham, England, 5 September, 1919 — CH
Died: Sunderland, England, August, 1989

League Club	Source	Date Signed	Seasons Played	Apps	Subs	Gls
Huddersfield T	Horden CW	05/39	46-50	156	-	3
Preston NE	Tr	03/51				
Bradford C	Tr	07/53	53-54	57	-	2

HEPPLEWHITE Wilson
Born: Washington, Tyne and Wear, England, 11 June, 1946 — LH/LW
Died: Johannesburg, South Africa, 23 March, 2003

League Club	Source	Date Signed	Seasons Played	Apps	Subs	Gls
Carlisle U	Crook T	03/65	65	2	0	0
Hartlepool U	Tr	07/67	67-68	50	2	2

HEPPOLETTE Richard Alfred William (Ricky)
Born: Bhusawal, India, 8 April, 1949 — M

League Club	Source	Date Signed	Seasons Played	Apps	Subs	Gls
Preston NE	App	03/67	67-72	149	5	13
Leyton Orient	Tr	12/72	72-76	113	0	10
Crystal Palace	Tr	10/76	76	13	2	0
Chesterfield	Tr	02/77	76-78	46	1	3
Peterborough U	Tr	08/79	79	5	0	0

HEPTON Stanley (Stan)
Born: Leeds, England, 3 December, 1932 — IF/RH

League Club	Source	Date Signed	Seasons Played	Apps	Subs	Gls
Blackpool	Leeds Ashley Road	03/50	52-56	7	-	3
Huddersfield T	Tr	08/57	57-58	6	-	1
Bury	Tr	06/59	59	15	-	3
Rochdale	Tr	07/60	60-63	149	-	21
Southport	Tr	07/64	64	22	-	2

HEPWORTH Maurice
Born: Hexham, Northumberland, England, 6 September, 1953 — FB

League Club	Source	Date Signed	Seasons Played	Apps	Subs	Gls
Sunderland	App	09/70	70	2	0	0
Darlington	L	01/75	74	4	0	0

HEPWORTH Ronald (Ronnie)
Born: Barnsley, South Yorkshire, England, 25 January, 1919 — FB
Died: Harrogate, North Yorkshire, England, 26 April, 2006

League Club	Source	Date Signed	Seasons Played	Apps	Subs	Gls
Chesterfield	Jnr	05/36				
Bradford Park Ave	Tr	05/39	46-50	101	-	0

HERBERT Courtney Anthony
Born: Northampton, England, 25 October, 1988 — F

League Club	Source	Date Signed	Seasons Played	Apps	Subs	Gls
Northampton T	Long Buckby	09/09	09-10	9	29	2

HERBERT Craig Justin
Born: Coventry, England, 9 November, 1975 — CD

League Club	Source	Date Signed	Seasons Played	Apps	Subs	Gls
West Bromwich A	Torquay U (YT)	03/94	94	8	0	0
Shrewsbury T	Tr	07/97	97-99	30	4	0

HERBERT David Ronald
Born: Sheffield, England, 23 January, 1956 — F

League Club	Source	Date Signed	Seasons Played	Apps	Subs	Gls
Sheffield Wed	App	01/74	74-75	12	5	5
Chesterfield	Tr	07/76				

HERBERT Frank
Born: Stocksbridge, South Yorkshire, England, 29 June, 1916 — RH
Died: Stocksbridge, South Yorkshire, England, 1972

League Club	Source	Date Signed	Seasons Played	Apps	Subs	Gls
Sheffield Wed	Oughtibridge	05/38				
Bury	Tr	10/45				
Oldham Ath	Tr	06/46	46	4	-	0

HERBERT Rikki Lloyd
Born: Auckland, New Zealand, 10 April, 1961 — CD
New Zealand: 61

League Club	Source	Date Signed	Seasons Played	Apps	Subs	Gls
Wolverhampton W	Sydney Olympic (AUS)	10/84	84-85	44	1	0

HERBERT Robert
Born: Durham, England, 29 August, 1983 — LH
Died: Kirkintilloch, Dunbartonshire, Scotland, 31 December, 2006

League Club	Source	Date Signed	Seasons Played	Apps	Subs	Gls
Halifax T	YT	10/00	99-01	15	10	0

HERBERT Robert (Bobby)
Born: Glasgow, Scotland, 21 November, 1925 — WH

League Club	Source	Date Signed	Seasons Played	Apps	Subs	Gls
Doncaster Rov	Blantyre Victoria	06/50	50-55	108	-	15

HERBERT Trevor Ernest
Born: Reading, England, 3 June, 1929 — CF
Died: Reading, England, June, 1981

League Club	Source	Date Signed	Seasons Played	Apps	Subs	Gls
Leyton Orient		08/49				
Crystal Palace	Tr	07/50	50	8	-	2

League Club	Source	Date Signed	Seasons Played	Apps	Subs	Gls

HERBERT William Stanley (Stan)
Born: Whitehaven, Cumbria, England, 29 August, 1946 — IF

League Club	Source	Date Signed	Seasons Played	Apps	Subs	Gls
Workington (Am)	Jnr	09/66	66	1	0	0

HERD Alexander (Alex)
Born: Selkirk, Borders, Scotland, 8 November, 1911 — IF
Died: Dumfries, Scotland, 21 August, 1982
Scotland: War-1

League Club	Source	Date Signed	Seasons Played	Apps	Subs	Gls
Manchester C	Hamilton Academical	02/33	32-47	257	-	107
Stockport Co	Tr	03/48	47-51	111	-	35

HERD Benjamin Alexander (Ben)
Born: Welwyn Garden City, Hertfordshire, England, 21 June, 1985 — RB

League Club	Source	Date Signed	Seasons Played	Apps	Subs	Gls
Watford	Sch	05/03				
Shrewsbury T	Tr	07/05	05-08	136	7	3
Aldershot T	Tr	08/09	09-12	164	1	1

HERD Christopher (Chris)
Born: Perth, Australia, 4 April, 1989 — RM
Australia: 3/Youth

League Club	Source	Date Signed	Seasons Played	Apps	Subs	Gls
Aston Villa	Sch	07/07	10-13	31	5	1
Port Vale	L	01/08	07	11	0	2
Wycombe W	L	03/08	07	3	1	0
Lincoln C	L	11/09	09	20	0	4
Bolton W	L	09/14	14	2	0	0
Wigan Ath	L	01/15	14	3	0	0

HERD David George
Born: Hamilton, Lanarkshire, Scotland, 15 April, 1934 — CF
Scotland: 5

League Club	Source	Date Signed	Seasons Played	Apps	Subs	Gls
Stockport Co	Jnr	04/51	50-53	15	-	6
Arsenal	Tr	08/54	54-60	166	-	97
Manchester U	Tr	07/61	61-67	201	1	114
Stoke C	Tr	07/68	68-69	39	5	11

HERD George
Born: Gartcosh, Lanarkshire, Scotland, 6 May, 1936 — IF
Scotland: 5/SLge-3/U23-2

League Club	Source	Date Signed	Seasons Played	Apps	Subs	Gls
Sunderland	Clyde	04/61	60-68	275	2	47
Hartlepool U	Tr	06/70	70	10	5	0

HERD Jonathan James (Jonny)
Born: Huntingdon, Cambridgeshire, England, 3 October, 1989 — LB

League Club	Source	Date Signed	Seasons Played	Apps	Subs	Gls
Southend U	Sch	07/08	08-10	28	7	0

HERD Stuart Alexander Laws
Born: Barlaston, Staffordshire, England, 25 February, 1974 — M

League Club	Source	Date Signed	Seasons Played	Apps	Subs	Gls
Torquay U	Rossington Main	10/92	92	5	2	0

HERITAGE Peter Mark
Born: Bexhill on Sea, East Sussex, England, 8 November, 1960 — F

League Club	Source	Date Signed	Seasons Played	Apps	Subs	Gls
Gillingham	Hythe T	08/89	89-90	42	15	11
Hereford U	Tr	02/91	90-91	55	2	9
Doncaster Rov	Tr	07/92	92	25	6	2

HERIVELTO Moreira
Born: Tres Rios, Brazil, 23 August, 1975 — M

League Club	Source	Date Signed	Seasons Played	Apps	Subs	Gls
Walsall	Cruizero (BRA)	08/01	01-02	11	17	5
Walsall	Ionikos (GRE)	12/04	04	0	1	0

HERNANDEZ Abel Mathias
Born: Pando, Uruguay, 8 August, 1990 — F
Uruguay: 18/U23-3

League Club	Source	Date Signed	Seasons Played	Apps	Subs	Gls
Hull C	US Palermo (ITA)	09/14	14	15	10	4

HERNANDEZ Javier (Chicharito)
Born: Guadalajara, Mexico, 1 June, 1988 — F
Mexico: 74

League Club	Source	Date Signed	Seasons Played	Apps	Subs	Gls
Manchester U	Guadalajara (MEX)	06/10	10-14	49	53	37

HERNANDEZ Pablo
Born: Castellon, Spain, 11 April, 1985 — LW
Spain: 4

League Club	Source	Date Signed	Seasons Played	Apps	Subs	Gls
Swansea C	Valencia (SPN)	08/12	12-13	44	13	5

HERNON James (Jimmy)
Born: Cleland, Lanarkshire, Scotland, 6 December, 1924 — IF
Died: Hastings, East Sussex, England, 7 March, 2009

League Club	Source	Date Signed	Seasons Played	Apps	Subs	Gls
Leicester C	Mossvale YMCA	04/42	46-47	31	-	7
Bolton W	Tr	09/48	48-50	43	-	2
Grimsby T	Tr	08/51	51-53	91	-	23
Watford	Tr	07/54	54-55	43	-	10

HEROD Dennis John
Born: Stoke-on-Trent, England, 27 October, 1923 — G
Died: Madeley, Staffordshire, England, 16 December, 2009

League Club	Source	Date Signed	Seasons Played	Apps	Subs	Gls
Stoke C	Trent Vale U	01/41	46-52	191	-	1
Stockport Co	Tr	07/53	53	33	-	0

HERON Brian
Born: Dumbarton, Dunbartonshire, Scotland, 19 June, 1948 — LW

League Club	Source	Date Signed	Seasons Played	Apps	Subs	Gls
Oxford U	Dumbarton	07/74	74-76	40	3	8
Scunthorpe U	Tr	07/77	77	20	5	1

HERON Daniel Craig (Danny)
Born: Cambridge, England, 9 October, 1986 — M

League Club	Source	Date Signed	Seasons Played	Apps	Subs	Gls
Mansfield T	Sch	-	04	1	2	0

HERON Thomas Russell Ferrie (Tommy)
Born: Irvine, Ayrshire, Scotland, 31 March, 1936 — LB/LW

League Club	Source	Date Signed	Seasons Played	Apps	Subs	Gls
Manchester U	Portadown	03/58	57-60	3	-	0
York C	Tr	05/61	61-65	192	0	6

HERON William Bolton
Born: Washington, Tyne and Wear, England, 29 March, 1932 — RW

League Club	Source	Date Signed	Seasons Played	Apps	Subs	Gls
Gateshead		02/55	54-56	22	-	1

HERRERA Ander
Born: Bilbao, Spain, 14 August, 1989 — M
Spain: U23-5/U21-15/Youth

League Club	Source	Date Signed	Seasons Played	Apps	Subs	Gls
Manchester U	Atletico Bilbao (SPN)	07/14	14	19	7	6

HERRERA Horacio Martin (Martin)
Born: Rio Cuarto, Cordoba, Argentina, 13 September, 1970 — G

League Club	Source	Date Signed	Seasons Played	Apps	Subs	Gls
Fulham	Dep Alaves (SPN)	07/02	02	1	1	0

HERRERA Roberto (Robbie)
Born: Torquay, Devon, England, 12 June, 1970 — LB

League Club	Source	Date Signed	Seasons Played	Apps	Subs	Gls
Queens Park Rgrs	YT	03/88	88-90	4	2	0
Torquay U	L	03/92	91	11	0	0
Torquay U	L	10/92	92	5	0	0
Fulham	Tr	10/93	93-97	143	2	1
Torquay U	Tr	08/98	98-01	104	3	1
Leyton Orient	Tr	10/01	01	2	0	0

HERRING David Harry (Harry)
Born: Hartlepool, Cleveland, England, 4 January, 1939 — RW

League Club	Source	Date Signed	Seasons Played	Apps	Subs	Gls
Hartlepool U	Caledonians	08/58	58	2	-	0

HERRING Ian
Born: Swindon, England, 14 February, 1984 — M

League Club	Source	Date Signed	Seasons Played	Apps	Subs	Gls
Swindon T	Sch	07/03	01-03	3	3	0

HERRING Paul John
Born: Hyde, Greater Manchester, England, 1 July, 1973 — M

League Club	Source	Date Signed	Seasons Played	Apps	Subs	Gls
Rochdale	YT	07/91	90	0	1	0

HERRINGTON Eric
Born: Rotherham, South Yorkshire, England, 30 October, 1943 — CH

League Club	Source	Date Signed	Seasons Played	Apps	Subs	Gls
Doncaster Rov	Jnr	01/61	61	1	-	0

HERRIOT James (Jim)
Born: Airdrie, Lanarkshire, Scotland, 20 December, 1939 — G
Scotland: 8/SLge-2

League Club	Source	Date Signed	Seasons Played	Apps	Subs	Gls
Birmingham C	Dunfermline Ath	05/65	65-69	181	0	0
Mansfield T	L	11/70	70	5	0	0

HERRITY Alan Michael
Born: Newport, Wales, 24 October, 1941 — LB
Wales: Schools

League Club	Source	Date Signed	Seasons Played	Apps	Subs	Gls
Newport Co	Jnr	12/58	59-61	28	-	0

HERRITY William Raymond (Billy)
Born: Newport, Wales, 2 September, 1938 — IF

League Club	Source	Date Signed	Seasons Played	Apps	Subs	Gls
Newport Co	Jnr	05/57	56-62	62	-	11

HERRON Alan
Born: Washington, Tyne and Wear, England, 6 October, 1932 — CH

League Club	Source	Date Signed	Seasons Played	Apps	Subs	Gls
Blackburn Rov	Newcastle U (Am)	08/50	55-56	4	-	0

HERRON John
Born: Widdrington, Northumberland, England, 2 March, 1938 — WH

League Club	Source	Date Signed	Seasons Played	Apps	Subs	Gls
Leeds U		10/56				
Gateshead	Tr	06/57	57-58	8	-	0

HERVE Laurent
Born: Quimper, Brittany, France, 19 June, 1976 — M

League Club	Source	Date Signed	Seasons Played	Apps	Subs	Gls
MK Dons	EA Guingamp (FRA)	08/04	04	15	5	0

HERY Bastien Charles Patrick
Born: Paris, France, 23 March, 1992 — M

League Club	Source	Date Signed	Seasons Played	Apps	Subs	Gls
Sheffield Wed	Paris St-Germain (FRA)	08/12				
Rochdale	Tr	05/13	13-14	16	17	2

HERZIG Nico
Born: Possneck, Thuringia, Germany, 10 December, 1983 — CD

League Club	Source	Date Signed	Seasons Played	Apps	Subs	Gls
Wimbledon	Carl Zeiss Jena (GER)	10/01	03	18	1	0

HESELTINE George Victor
Born: Wolverhampton, England, 25 March, 1926 — IF
Died: Stoke-on-Trent, England, June, 2012

League Club	Source	Date Signed	Seasons Played	Apps	Subs	Gls
Walsall	Hednesford T	02/49	48-49	8	-	0

HESELTINE Wayne Alan
Born: Bradford, England, 3 December, 1969 — FB

League Club	Source	Date Signed	Seasons Played	Apps	Subs	Gls
Manchester U	YT	12/87				
Oldham Ath	Tr	12/89	89	1	0	0
Bradford C	Tr	08/92	92-93	51	3	1

HESFORD Iain
Born: Ndola, Zambia, 4 March, 1960 — G
Died: Lytham, Lancashire, England, 20 November, 2014
England: U21-7/Youth

League Club	Source	Date Signed	Seasons Played	Apps	Subs	Gls
Blackpool	App	08/77	77-82	202	0	0
Sheffield Wed	Tr	08/83				
Fulham	L	01/85	84	3	0	0
Notts Co	L	11/85	85	10	0	0
Sunderland	Tr	08/86	86-88	97	0	0
Hull C	Tr	12/88	88-90	91	0	0
Maidstone U	Tr	08/91	91	42	0	1

HESFORD Robert Taylor (Bob)
Born: Bolton, Greater Manchester, England, 13 April, 1916 — G
Died: Blackpool, Lancashire, England, 13 June, 1982

League Club	Source	Date Signed	Seasons Played	Apps	Subs	Gls
Huddersfield T	South Shore	09/33	34-49	203	-	0

HESKETH Jake Alexander
Born: Stockport, Greater Manchester, England, 27 March, 1996 — M

League Club	Source	Date Signed	Seasons Played	Apps	Subs	Gls
Southampton	Sch	05/14	14	1	1	0

HESKEY Emile William Ivanhoe
Born: Leicester, England, 11 January, 1978 — F
England: 62/B-1/U21-16/Youth

League Club	Source	Date Signed	Seasons Played	Apps	Subs	Gls
Leicester C	YT	10/95	94-99	143	11	40
Liverpool	Tr	03/00	99-03	118	32	39
Birmingham C	Tr	07/04	04-05	68	0	14
Wigan Ath	Tr	06/06	06-08	80	2	15
Aston Villa	Tr	01/09	08-11	56	36	9
Bolton W	Newcastle Jets (AUS)	12/14	14	11	5	1

HESLOP Brian
Born: Carlisle, Cumbria, England, 4 August, 1947 — D/M

League Club	Source	Date Signed	Seasons Played	Apps	Subs	Gls
Carlisle U	App	08/65	65-66	4	0	0
Sunderland	Tr	05/67	67-70	57	1	0
Northampton T	Tr	03/71	70-71	49	1	0
Workington	Tr	09/72	72-75	139	1	5

HESLOP George Wilson
Born: Wallsend, Tyne and Wear, England, 1 July, 1940 — CH
Died: Lytham St Annes, Lancashire, England, 16 September, 2006

League Club	Source	Date Signed	Seasons Played	Apps	Subs	Gls
Newcastle U	Dudley Welfare	02/59	59-61	27	-	0
Everton	Tr	03/62	62-65	10	0	0
Manchester C	Tr	09/65	65-71	159	3	1
Bury	Tr	08/72	72	37	0	0

HESLOP Norman
Born: Bolton, Greater Manchester, England, 2 August, 1920 — IF
Died: Bolton, Greater Manchester, England, 27 February, 2007

League Club	Source	Date Signed	Seasons Played	Apps	Subs	Gls
Southport	Bolton W (Am)	10/46	46-47	30	-	4

HESLOP Simon James
Born: York, England, 1 May, 1987 — M

League Club	Source	Date Signed	Seasons Played	Apps	Subs	Gls
Barnsley	Sch	07/06	06	0	1	0
Grimsby T	L	08/08	08	5	3	0
Oxford U	Tr	07/10	10-12	70	21	7
Stevenage	Tr	07/13	13	23	4	1
Mansfield T	Tr	07/14	14	21	4	2

HESSENTHALER Andrew (Andy)
Born: Gravesend, Kent, England, 17 August, 1965 — M
England: Semi Pro-1

League Club	Source	Date Signed	Seasons Played	Apps	Subs	Gls
Watford	Redbridge Forest	09/91	91-95	195	0	12
Gillingham	Tr	08/96	96-05	273	30	20
Hull C	L	01/05	04	6	4	0
Barnet	Tr	01/06	05-06	35	5	2

HESSENTHALER Jakob Andrew (Jake)
Born: Gravesend, Kent, England, 20 April, 1994 — M

League Club	Source	Date Signed	Seasons Played	Apps	Subs	Gls
Gillingham	Sch	07/13	13-14	53	3	2

HESSEY Sean Peter
Born: Prescot, Merseyside, England, 19 September, 1978 — CD

League Club	Source	Date Signed	Seasons Played	Apps	Subs	Gls
Leeds U	Liverpool (YT)	09/97				
Wigan Ath	Tr	12/97				
Huddersfield T	Tr	03/98	97-98	7	4	0
Blackpool	Kilmarnock	02/04	03	4	2	0
Chester C	Tr	07/04	04-06	70	9	1
Macclesfield T	Tr	11/07	07-09	82	4	0
Accrington Stan	Tr	08/10	10-11	57	1	3

HETHERINGTON Henry (Harry)
Born: Chester-le-Street, County Durham, England, 7 November, 1928 — RW
Died: Westhoughton, Greater Manchester, England, October, 1987

League Club	Source	Date Signed	Seasons Played	Apps	Subs	Gls
Sunderland	Shiney Row St Oswalds	05/46	47	2	-	0
Gateshead	Tr	01/49	48	2	-	1

HETHERINGTON Robert Brent (Brent)
Born: Carlisle, Cumbria, England, 6 December, 1961 — F

League Club	Source	Date Signed	Seasons Played	Apps	Subs	Gls
Carlisle U	Workington	08/87	87-89	61	27	23

HETHERINGTON Thomas Burns (Tom)
Born: Walker, Tyne and Wear, England, 22 January, 1911 — G
Died: Newcastle-upon-Tyne, England, December, 1968

League Club	Source	Date Signed	Seasons Played	Apps	Subs	Gls
Burnley	Walker Celtic	12/33	33-37	67	-	0
Barnsley	Jarrow	02/39				
Gateshead	Tr	10/46	46	1	-	0

HETHERSTON Peter
Born: Coatbridge, Lanarkshire, Scotland, 6 November, 1964 — RW

League Club	Source	Date Signed	Seasons Played	Apps	Subs	Gls
Watford	Falkirk	07/87	87	2	3	0
Sheffield U	Tr	02/88	87	11	0	0

HETZKE Stephen Edward Richard (Steve)
Born: Marlborough, Wiltshire, England, 3 June, 1955 — CD

League Club	Source	Date Signed	Seasons Played	Apps	Subs	Gls
Reading	App	06/73	71-81	254	7	23
Blackpool	Tr	07/82	82-85	140	0	18
Sunderland	Tr	03/86	85-86	31	0	0
Chester C	Tr	06/87	87	14	0	0
Colchester U	Tr	03/88	87-88	27	2	2

HEVICON Ryan
Born: Manchester, England, 3 December, 1982 — M

League Club	Source	Date Signed	Seasons Played	Apps	Subs	Gls
Blackburn Rov	YT	07/01				
Carlisle U	Tr	08/02	02	0	1	0

HEWARD Brian John
Born: Lincoln, England, 17 July, 1935 — CH
Died: South Hykeham, Lincolnshire, England, 21 April, 2012

League Club	Source	Date Signed	Seasons Played	Apps	Subs	Gls
Scunthorpe U	Jnr	03/54	53-60	137	-	0
Lincoln C	Tr	07/61	61-63	72	-	2
Lincoln C	Bankstown (AUS)	11/64	64-65	25	0	0

HEWARD Graham Keith
Born: Newcastle-upon-Tyne, England, 13 October, 1965 — W

League Club	Source	Date Signed	Seasons Played	Apps	Subs	Gls
Cambridge U	App	10/83	83	1	0	0

HEWIE John Davison
Born: Pretoria, South Africa, 13 December, 1927 — RH/FB
Died: Boston, Lincolnshire, England, 11 May, 2015
Scotland: 19/B/U23-1

League Club	Source	Date Signed	Seasons Played	Apps	Subs	Gls
Charlton Ath	Arcadia Shep's (RSA)	10/49	51-65	495	0	37

HEWITT Daren Peter
Born: Chichester, West Sussex, England, 1 September, 1969 — M

League Club	Source	Date Signed	Seasons Played	Apps	Subs	Gls
Aldershot	YT	08/88	88	0	2	0

HEWITT Elliott Jack
Born: Rhyl, Denbighshire, Wales, 30 May, 1994 — RB/M
Wales: U21-10/Youth

League Club	Source	Date Signed	Seasons Played	Apps	Subs	Gls
Macclesfield T	Sch	05/11	10-11	18	4	0
Ipswich T	Tr	05/12	12-14	8	6	0
Gillingham	L	11/13	13	20	0	0
Colchester U	L	10/14	14	21	0	1

HEWITT Gerald (Gerry)
Born: Sheffield, England, 28 January, 1935 — RH
Died: Sheffield, England, August, 2007

League Club	Source	Date Signed	Seasons Played	Apps	Subs	Gls
Sheffield U	Jnr	07/54	56	2	-	0
Workington	Tr	06/58				

HEWITT Harold
Born: Chesterfield, Derbyshire, England, 24 June, 1919 — RW
Died: Buxton, Derbyshire, England, 25 March, 2011

League Club	Source	Date Signed	Seasons Played	Apps	Subs	Gls
Mansfield T	Chesterfield (Am)	11/45	46	1	-	0

HEWITT James Robert (Jamie)
Born: Chesterfield, Derbyshire, England, 17 May, 1968 — RB/M

League Club	Source	Date Signed	Seasons Played	Apps	Subs	Gls
Chesterfield	App	04/86	85-91	240	9	14
Doncaster Rov	Tr	08/92	92-93	32	1	0
Chesterfield	Tr	10/93	93-01	248	9	12

HEWITT John
Born: Aberdeen, Scotland, 9 February, 1963 — M
Scotland: U21-6/Youth/Schools

League Club	Source	Date Signed	Seasons Played	Apps	Subs	Gls
Middlesbrough (L)	Glasgow Celtic	09/91	91	0	2	0

HEWITT Leonard (Len)
Born: Wrexham, Wales, 20 March, 1920 — CF
Died: Rhostyllen, Wrexham, Wales, 24 May, 1979

League Club	Source	Date Signed	Seasons Played	Apps	Subs	Gls
Wrexham	Army	05/46	46	5	-	2

HEWITT Martin (Marty)
Born: Hartlepool, Cleveland, England, 24 July, 1965 — M

League Club	Source	Date Signed	Seasons Played	Apps	Subs	Gls
Hartlepool U	St James'	08/84	85-86	11	3	2

HEWITT Richard (Dick)
Born: South Kirkby, West Yorkshire, England, 25 May, 1943 — IF/LW

League Club	Source	Date Signed	Seasons Played	Apps	Subs	Gls
Huddersfield T	Moorthorpe St J'phs OB	05/61				
Bradford C	Tr	07/64	64	20	-	7
Barnsley	Tr	07/65	65-68	97	2	20
York C	Tr	03/69	68-71	87	4	7

HEWITT Ronald (Ron)
Born: Chesterfield, Derbyshire, England, 25 January, 1924 — G
Died: Chesterfield, Derbyshire, England, May, 2011

League Club	Source	Date Signed	Seasons Played	Apps	Subs	Gls
Sheffield U	Youlgreave	11/44				
Lincoln C	Tr	08/46	48	3	-	0

HEWITT Ronald (Ron)
Born: Flint, Wales, 21 June, 1928 — IF
Died: Wrexham, Wales, 23 September, 2001
Wales: 5

League Club	Source	Date Signed	Seasons Played	Apps	Subs	Gls
Wolverhampton W	Chester C (Am)	07/48				
Walsall	Tr	10/49	49	8	-	2
Darlington	Tr	06/50	50	36	-	3
Wrexham	Tr	07/51	51-56	204	-	83
Cardiff C	Tr	06/57	57-58	65	-	27
Wrexham	Tr	07/59	59	27	-	11
Coventry C	Tr	03/60	59-61	59	-	23
Chester C	Tr	03/62	61-62	29	-	6

HEWITT Stephen (Steve)
Born: Hull, England, 17 April, 1973 — G

League Club	Source	Date Signed	Seasons Played	Apps	Subs	Gls
Scarborough	YT	01/92	91	2	0	0

HEWITT Steven Daniel
Born: Manchester, England, 5 December, 1993 — M

League Club	Source	Date Signed	Seasons Played	Apps	Subs	Gls
Burnley	Sch	10/11	11-13	0	2	0

HEWITT Troy Roger
Born: Newham, E London, England, 10 February, 1990 — F

League Club	Source	Date Signed	Seasons Played	Apps	Subs	Gls
Queens Park Rgrs	Harrow Bor	02/11				
Dagenham & Red	L	09/11	11	3	3	0
Bury	L	10/12	12	5	3	2
Colchester U	L	03/13	12	0	1	0
Walsall	Tr	07/13	13	8	19	0

HEWKINS Kenneth John Robert (Ken)
Born: Pretoria, South Africa, 30 October, 1929 — G

League Club	Source	Date Signed	Seasons Played	Apps	Subs	Gls
Fulham	Clyde	11/55	55-61	38	-	0

HEWLETT Matthew Paul (Matt)
Born: Bristol, England, 25 February, 1976 — M
England: Youth

League Club	Source	Date Signed	Seasons Played	Apps	Subs	Gls
Bristol C	YT	08/93	93-99	111	16	9
Burnley	L	11/98	98	2	0	0
Swindon T	Tr	07/00	00-04	175	4	6
Torquay U	Tr	07/05	05	18	6	1

HEWS Chay
Born: Norrkoping, Sweden, 30 September, 1976 — F

League Club	Source	Date Signed	Seasons Played	Apps	Subs	Gls
Carlisle U	IF Sylvia (SWE)	09/01	01	4	1	2

HEWSON Patrick Carroll (Pat)
Born: Gateshead, Tyne and Wear, England, 2 June, 1926 — RB

League Club	Source	Date Signed	Seasons Played	Apps	Subs	Gls
West Bromwich A	Crook T	11/50				
Gateshead	Tr	07/53	53-57	131	-	0

HEWSON Sam
Born: Bolton, Greater Manchester, England, 28 November, 1988 — M

League Club	Source	Date Signed	Seasons Played	Apps	Subs	Gls
Manchester U	Sch	07/07				
Hereford U	L	01/09	08	9	1	3
Bury	L	02/10	09	1	6	0

HEY Antoine (Tony)
Born: Berlin, Germany, 19 September, 1970 — M

League Club	Source	Date Signed	Seasons Played	Apps	Subs	Gls
Birmingham C	Fortuna Cologne (GER)	06/97	97	8	1	0

HEYDON Cecil
Born: Birkenhead, Wirral, England, 24 May, 1919 — WH
Died: Brent, NW London, England, August, 2007

League Club	Source	Date Signed	Seasons Played	Apps	Subs	Gls
New Brighton	Victory Social	02/39	38	1	-	0
Derby Co	Tr	06/39				
Doncaster Rov	Tr	10/45	46-47	6	-	0
Rochdale	Tr	07/48	48	1	-	0

HEYDON John (Jackie)
Born: Birkenhead, Wirral, England, 19 October, 1928 — RH
Died: Wirral, England, September, 2012

League Club	Source	Date Signed	Seasons Played	Apps	Subs	Gls
Liverpool	Everton (Am)	01/49	50-52	63	-	0
Millwall	Tr	05/53	53-55	75	-	1
Tranmere Rov	Tr	07/56	56-60	76	-	1

HEYES Darren Lee
Born: Swansea, Wales, 11 January, 1967 — G
England: Youth/Schools

League Club	Source	Date Signed	Seasons Played	Apps	Subs	Gls
Nottingham F	Jnr	01/84				
Wrexham	L	01/87	86	2	0	0
Scunthorpe U	Tr	07/87	87	3	0	0

HEYES George
Born: Bolton, Greater Manchester, England, 16 November, 1937 — G

League Club	Source	Date Signed	Seasons Played	Apps	Subs	Gls
Rochdale	Jnr	04/56	58-59	24	-	0
Leicester C	Tr	07/60	60-65	25	0	0
Swansea C	Tr	09/65	65-68	99	0	0
Barrow	Tr	07/69	69	26	0	0

HEYES Kenneth (Ken)
Born: Haydock, Merseyside, England, 4 January, 1936 — RB
England: Youth/Schools

League Club	Source	Date Signed	Seasons Played	Apps	Subs	Gls
Everton	Jnr	02/53				
Preston NE	Tr	05/57	59	3	-	0

HEYS Michael (Mike)
Born: Preston, Lancashire, England, 23 June, 1938 — G

League Club	Source	Date Signed	Seasons Played	Apps	Subs	Gls
Preston NE	Jnr	05/57				
Barrow	Tr	03/59	58-61	70	-	0
Workington	Tr	08/62				
Halifax T		11/63	63	1	-	0

HEYWOOD Albert Edwards
Born: Hartlepool, Cleveland, England, 12 May, 1913 — G
Died: Hartlepool, Cleveland, England, May, 1989

League Club	Source	Date Signed	Seasons Played	Apps	Subs	Gls
Sunderland	Spennymoor U	03/37	38	4	-	0
Hartlepool U	Tr	05/46	46	39	-	0

HEYWOOD David Ian
Born: Wolverhampton, England, 25 July, 1967 — LB

League Club	Source	Date Signed	Seasons Played	Apps	Subs	Gls
Wolverhampton W	App	11/84	84	7	0	0

HEYWOOD Matthew Stephen (Matt)
Born: Chatham, Kent, England, 26 August, 1979 — CD

League Club	Source	Date Signed	Seasons Played	Apps	Subs	Gls
Burnley	YT	07/98	98	11	2	0
Swindon T	Tr	01/01	00-04	176	7	8
Bristol C	Tr	07/05	05	22	2	2
Brentford	Tr	08/06	06-07	55	5	2
Grimsby T	Tr	07/08	08-09	17	2	0

HIBBARD Mark Andrew
Born: Hereford, England, 12 August, 1977 — LB

League Club	Source	Date Signed	Seasons Played	Apps	Subs	Gls
Hereford U	YT	07/96	96	5	2	1

HIBBERD Stuart
Born: Sheffield, England, 11 October, 1961 — W

League Club	Source	Date Signed	Seasons Played	Apps	Subs	Gls
Lincoln C	App	10/79	80-82	36	6	3

HIBBERT Anthony James (Tony)
Born: Liverpool, England, 20 February, 1981 — RB

League Club	Source	Date Signed	Seasons Played	Apps	Subs	Gls
Everton	YT	07/98	00-14	242	22	0

HIBBERT David John (Dave)
Born: Eccleshall, Staffordshire, England, 28 January, 1986 — F

League Club	Source	Date Signed	Seasons Played	Apps	Subs	Gls
Port Vale	Sch	06/02	04	2	7	2
Preston NE	Tr	07/05	05	0	10	0
Rotherham U	L	08/06	06	12	9	2
Bradford C	L	01/07	06	4	4	0
Shrewsbury T	Tr	06/07	07-09	82	23	29
Peterborough U	Tr	08/10	10	0	7	1

HIBBITT Kenneth (Kenny)
Born: Bradford, England, 3 January, 1951 — M
England: U23-1

League Club	Source	Date Signed	Seasons Played	Apps	Subs	Gls
Bradford Park Ave	App	11/68	67-68	13	2	0
Wolverhampton W	Tr	11/68	68-83	447	19	89
Coventry C	Tr	08/84	84-85	42	5	4
Bristol Rov	Tr	08/86	86-88	51	2	5

HIBBITT Terence Arthur (Terry)
Born: Bradford, England, 1 December, 1947 — LW/M
Died: Newcastle-upon-Tyne, England, 5 August, 1994

League Club	Source	Date Signed	Seasons Played	Apps	Subs	Gls
Leeds U	Jnr	12/64	65-70	32	15	9
Newcastle U	Tr	08/71	71-75	138	0	7
Birmingham C	Tr	08/75	75-77	110	0	11
Newcastle U	Tr	05/78	78-80	89	1	5

HIBBS Gary Thomas
Born: Hammersmith, W London, England, 26 January, 1957 — M

League Club	Source	Date Signed	Seasons Played	Apps	Subs	Gls
Leyton Orient	App	07/74	75	1	0	0
Aldershot	L	02/77	76	4	2	0

HIBBURT James Anthony (Jimmy)
Born: Ashford, Surrey, England, 30 October, 1979 — M
England: Schools

League Club	Source	Date Signed	Seasons Played	Apps	Subs	Gls
Crystal Palace	YT	11/96	98-99	1	5	0

HICK Leslie David (Les)
Born: York, England, 23 April, 1927 RW
Died: Warminster, Wiltshire, England, 1971

League Club	Source	Date Signed	Seasons Played	Apps	Subs	Gls
Bradford C		04/49	48	1	-	0

HICKIE George Noel Ellerton
Born: Hawarden, Flintshire, Wales, 25 December, 1922 FB
Died: Carlisle, Cumbria, England, 2 November, 1994

League Club	Source	Date Signed	Seasons Played	Apps	Subs	Gls
Barnsley		05/46				
Carlisle U	Tr	09/46	46	1	-	0

HICKLIN Albert William (Bill)
Born: Dudley, West Midlands, England, 20 September, 1924 WH
Died: Walsall, West Midlands, England, 29 May, 2007

League Club	Source	Date Signed	Seasons Played	Apps	Subs	Gls
Birmingham C	West Bromwich A (Am)	03/45				
Watford	Tr	06/47	47	21	-	5
West Bromwich A	Tr	05/48				

HICKMAN Geoffrey Brian (Geoff)
Born: West Bromwich, West Midlands, England, 7 January, 1950 G

League Club	Source	Date Signed	Seasons Played	Apps	Subs	Gls
West Bromwich A	App	01/68				
Bradford Park Ave	Tr	06/69	69	9	0	0

HICKMAN Michael Frederick Thomas (Mike)
Born: Elstead, Surrey, England, 2 October, 1946 CF/M

League Club	Source	Date Signed	Seasons Played	Apps	Subs	Gls
Brighton & HA	Jnr	06/65	65-67	12	3	0
Grimsby T	Tr	06/68	68-74	247	7	48
Blackburn Rov	Tr	02/75	74-75	23	3	8
Torquay U	Tr	10/75	75-76	17	0	1

HICKS Anthony John (Tony)
Born: Swindon, England, 20 August, 1945 G

League Club	Source	Date Signed	Seasons Played	Apps	Subs	Gls
Swindon T	App	10/62	64-66	51	0	0

HICKS David Christopher
Born: Enfield, N London, England, 13 November, 1985 M

League Club	Source	Date Signed	Seasons Played	Apps	Subs	Gls
Northampton T	Tottenham H (Sch)	02/04	04	1	2	0

HICKS Graham
Born: Oldham, Greater Manchester, England, 17 February, 1981 FB

League Club	Source	Date Signed	Seasons Played	Apps	Subs	Gls
Rochdale	YT	01/99	98	1	0	0

HICKS James Michael (Jim)
Born: Ipswich, England, 16 September, 1960 CD

League Club	Source	Date Signed	Seasons Played	Apps	Subs	Gls
Exeter C	Warwick Univ	09/83	83	3	0	0
Oxford U	Tr	08/84				
Fulham	Tr	08/85	85-87	39	1	1

HICKS Keith
Born: Oldham, Greater Manchester, England, 9 August, 1954 CD
England: Youth

League Club	Source	Date Signed	Seasons Played	Apps	Subs	Gls
Oldham Ath	App	08/72	71-79	240	2	11
Hereford U	Tr	09/80	80-84	201	0	2
Rochdale	Tr	07/85	85-86	32	0	1

HICKS Mark
Born: Belfast, Northern Ireland, 24 July, 1981 F

League Club	Source	Date Signed	Seasons Played	Apps	Subs	Gls
Millwall	Jnr	07/98	98	0	1	0

HICKS Martin
Born: Stratford-on-Avon, Warwickshire, England, 27 February, 1957 CD

League Club	Source	Date Signed	Seasons Played	Apps	Subs	Gls
Charlton Ath	Stratford T	02/77				
Reading	Tr	02/78	77-90	499	1	23
Birmingham C	Tr	08/91	91-92	57	3	1

HICKS Stuart Jason
Born: Peterborough, England, 30 May, 1967 CD

League Club	Source	Date Signed	Seasons Played	Apps	Subs	Gls
Peterborough U	App	08/84				
Colchester U	Wisbech T	03/88	87-89	57	7	0
Scunthorpe U	Tr	08/90	90-91	67	0	1
Doncaster Rov	Tr	08/92	92	36	0	0
Huddersfield T	Tr	08/93	93	20	2	1
Preston NE	Tr	03/94	93-94	11	1	0
Scarborough	Tr	02/95	94-96	81	4	2
Leyton Orient	Tr	08/97	97-99	77	1	1
Chester C	Tr	02/00	99	13	0	0
Mansfield T	Tr	07/00	00	25	0	0

HICKSON David (Dave)
Born: Salford, England, 30 October, 1929 CF
Died: Liverpool, England, 8 July, 2013

League Club	Source	Date Signed	Seasons Played	Apps	Subs	Gls
Everton	Ellesmere Port T	05/48	51-55	139	-	63
Aston Villa	Tr	09/55	55	12	-	1
Huddersfield T	Tr	11/55	55-56	54	-	28
Everton	Tr	08/57	57-59	86	-	32
Liverpool	Tr	11/59	59-60	60	-	37
Bury	Cambridge C	01/62	61	8	-	0
Tranmere Rov	Tr	08/62	62-63	45	-	21

HICKSON George Geoffrey (Geoff)
Born: Crewe, Cheshire, England, 26 September, 1939 G

League Club	Source	Date Signed	Seasons Played	Apps	Subs	Gls
Stoke C	Blackburn Rov (Am)	08/57	59-60	11	-	0
Crewe Alex	Tr	07/62	62-66	104	0	0
Port Vale	L	08/68	68	17	0	0
Southport	Tr	12/68	68	3	0	0

HICKTON John
Born: Brimington, Derbyshire, England, 24 September, 1944 F/RB

League Club	Source	Date Signed	Seasons Played	Apps	Subs	Gls
Sheffield Wed	Jnr	01/62	63-65	52	1	21
Middlesbrough	Tr	09/66	66-77	395	20	159
Hull C	L	01/77	76	6	0	1

HICKTON Roy
Born: Chesterfield, Derbyshire, England, 19 September, 1948 FB

League Club	Source	Date Signed	Seasons Played	Apps	Subs	Gls
Chesterfield	App	11/65	68-70	47	2	1

HIDEN Martin
Born: Stainz, Styria, Austria, 11 March, 1973 CD
Austria: 50

League Club	Source	Date Signed	Seasons Played	Apps	Subs	Gls
Leeds U	Rapid Vienna (AUT)	02/98	97-99	25	1	0

HIERRO Fernando Ruiz
Born: Velez-Malaga, Spain, 23 March, 1968 CD
Spain: 89

League Club	Source	Date Signed	Seasons Played	Apps	Subs	Gls
Bolton W	Al Rayyan (QAT)	07/04	04	15	14	1

HIGDON Michael
Born: Liverpool, England, 2 September, 1983 F

League Club	Source	Date Signed	Seasons Played	Apps	Subs	Gls
Crewe Alex	YT	02/01	03-06	36	45	10
Sheffield U	NEC Nijmegen (NED)	08/14	14	9	4	2

HIGGINBOTHAM Daniel John (Danny)
Born: Manchester, England, 29 December, 1978 D

League Club	Source	Date Signed	Seasons Played	Apps	Subs	Gls
Manchester U	YT	07/97	97-99	2	2	0
Derby Co	Tr	07/00	00-02	82	4	3
Southampton	Tr	01/03	02-05	84	10	4
Stoke C	Tr	08/06	06-07	45	0	7
Sunderland	Tr	08/07	07-08	22	0	3
Stoke C	Tr	09/08	08-11	61	3	4
Nottingham F	L	01/12	11	5	1	1
Ipswich T	L	09/12	12	11	1	0
Sheffield U	Tr	01/13	12	13	2	0

HIGGINBOTHAM Kallum Michael
Born: Salford, England, 15 June, 1989 W

League Club	Source	Date Signed	Seasons Played	Apps	Subs	Gls
Rochdale	Oldham Ath (Sch)	06/07	07-09	31	38	7
Accrington Stan	L	10/08	08	1	4	0
Accrington Stan	L	01/09	08	4	3	0
Huddersfield T	Falkirk	01/12	11	3	1	0
Barnsley	L	03/12	11	2	3	0
Carlisle U	L	09/12	12	7	3	0

HIGGINBOTTOM Andrew John (Andy)
Born: Chesterfield, Derbyshire, England, 22 October, 1964 LW

League Club	Source	Date Signed	Seasons Played	Apps	Subs	Gls
Chesterfield	App	10/82	82	1	2	0
Everton	Tr	07/83				
Cambridge U	Tr	08/84	84	1	0	0
Crystal Palace		09/85	85-86	16	7	2

HIGGINBOTTOM Michael (Mike)
Born: Sheffield, England, 13 October, 1962 M

League Club	Source	Date Signed	Seasons Played	Apps	Subs	Gls
Chesterfield	Burton A	08/83	83	3	1	0

HIGGINS Alexander John (Alex)
Born: Sheffield, England, 22 July, 1981 M
England: Youth/Schools

League Club	Source	Date Signed	Seasons Played	Apps	Subs	Gls
Sheffield Wed	YT	11/98				
Queens Park Rgrs	Tr	03/01	00	0	1	0
Boston U	Stalybridge Celtic	10/02	02	13	0	0

HIGGINS Andrew Martin (Andy)
Born: Bolsover, Derbyshire, England, 12 February, 1960 CD

League Club	Source	Date Signed	Seasons Played	Apps	Subs	Gls
Chesterfield	App	02/78	78	1	0	0
Port Vale	Tr	02/81	80-81	11	3	0
Hartlepool U	King's Lynn	09/82	82	3	1	1
Rochdale	King's Lynn	03/83	82-83	31	2	6
Chester C	Tr	07/84	84	16	3	1

HIGGINS Augustine Robert (Ossie)
Born: Dublin, Republic of Ireland, 19 January, 1931 CF
Died: Newport, Wales, December, 2000

League Club	Source	Date Signed	Seasons Played	Apps	Subs	Gls
Aston Villa	Shamrock Rov (ROI)	11/49				
Ipswich T	Tr	07/52	52	2	-	0

HIGGINS Charles
Born: Bellshill, Lanarkshire, Scotland, 12 May, 1921 LB
Died: Lenzie, Dunbartonshire, Scotland, 30 January, 1997

League Club	Source	Date Signed	Seasons Played	Apps	Subs	Gls
Chester C	Arbroath	08/46	46	11	-	0

HIGGINS David Anthony (Dave)
Born: Liverpool, England, 19 August, 1961 RB

League Club	Source	Date Signed	Seasons Played	Apps	Subs	Gls
Tranmere Rov	Eagle	08/83	83-84	27	1	0
Tranmere Rov	Caernarfon T	07/87	87-96	315	4	12

HIGGINS Frederick Thomas (Fred)
Born: Hackney, E London, England, 21 January, 1930 — CH

League Club	Source	Date Signed	Seasons Played	Apps	Subs	Gls
Crystal Palace	Wood Green	03/52	52-53	11	-	0

HIGGINS George
Born: Batley, West Yorkshire, England, 12 September, 1932 — RB

League Club	Source	Date Signed	Seasons Played	Apps	Subs	Gls
Huddersfield T	Jnr	12/49				
Halifax T	Tr	07/57	57	5	-	0

HIGGINS George
Born: Dundee, Scotland, 16 June, 1925 — LB
Died: Grimsby, North Lincolnshire, England, 13 April, 1993

League Club	Source	Date Signed	Seasons Played	Apps	Subs	Gls
Blackburn Rov	Lochee Harp	10/46	46-50	53	-	0
Bolton W	Tr	07/51	51-53	69	-	0
Grimsby T	Tr	05/54	54-56	47	-	0

HIGGINS James (Jimmy)
Born: Dublin, Republic of Ireland, 3 February, 1926 — IF
Republic of Ireland: 1

League Club	Source	Date Signed	Seasons Played	Apps	Subs	Gls
Birmingham C	Dundalk (ROI)	11/49	49-52	50	-	12

HIGGINS John Oldfield
Born: Bakewell, Derbyshire, England, 15 November, 1932 — CH
Died: Macclesfield, Cheshire, England, 22 April, 2005

League Club	Source	Date Signed	Seasons Played	Apps	Subs	Gls
Bolton W	Buxton	10/50	52-60	183	-	0

HIGGINS John Wilson
Born: Kilmarnock, Ayrshire, Scotland, 27 January, 1933 — RB

League Club	Source	Date Signed	Seasons Played	Apps	Subs	Gls
Swindon T	St Mirren	05/59	59-60	28	-	0

HIGGINS Mark Nicholas
Born: Buxton, Derbyshire, England, 29 September, 1958 — CD
England: Youth/Schools

League Club	Source	Date Signed	Seasons Played	Apps	Subs	Gls
Everton	App	08/76	76-83	150	1	6
Manchester U	Rtd	12/85	85	6	0	0
Bury	Tr	01/87	86-88	67	1	0
Stoke C	Tr	09/88	88-89	37	2	1

HIGGINS Michael (Mick)
Born: Haslingden, Lancashire, England, 5 September, 1956 — LW

League Club	Source	Date Signed	Seasons Played	Apps	Subs	Gls
Blackburn Rov	App	12/73				
Workington	Tr	07/76	76	11	4	1

HIGGINS Peter
Born: Blidworth, Nottinghamshire, England, 1 August, 1944 — CD

League Club	Source	Date Signed	Seasons Played	Apps	Subs	Gls
Oxford U	Blidworth YC	07/62	62-68	35	5	0
Crewe Alex	Tr	06/69	69-71	56	1	0

HIGGINS Peter Clive
Born: Cardiff, Wales, 12 November, 1950 — LW

League Club	Source	Date Signed	Seasons Played	Apps	Subs	Gls
Bristol Rov	App	02/69	68-72	36	0	5
Doncaster Rov	Tr	07/73	73-75	63	5	10
Torquay U	L	03/76	75	3	1	1

HIGGINS Robert James (Bob)
Born: Bolsover, Derbyshire, England, 23 December, 1958 — CD
England: Schools

League Club	Source	Date Signed	Seasons Played	Apps	Subs	Gls
Burnley	App	07/76	77	3	0	0
Hartlepool U	L	11/79	79	2	0	0
Rochdale	Tr	10/80	80	4	1	0

HIGGINS Ronald Valentine (Ronnie)
Born: Silvertown, E London, England, 14 February, 1923 — CF

League Club	Source	Date Signed	Seasons Played	Apps	Subs	Gls
Leyton Orient (Am)	Green & Siley Weir	12/49	49	2	-	0
Brighton & HA	Tonbridge	01/52	51	8	-	0
Queens Park Rgrs	Tr	01/53	52	3	-	1

HIGGINS William Charles
Born: Birkenhead, Wirral, England, 26 February, 1924 — W
Died: Canterbury, England, 1981

League Club	Source	Date Signed	Seasons Played	Apps	Subs	Gls
Everton	Tranmere Rov (Am)	03/46	46-49	48	-	8

HIGGINSON Thomas (Tom)
Born: Newtongrange, Midlothian, Scotland, 6 January, 1937 — WH
Died: Hounslow, SW London, England, 22 July, 2012

League Club	Source	Date Signed	Seasons Played	Apps	Subs	Gls
Brentford	Kilmarnock	06/59	59-69	383	4	15

HIGGS Shane Peter
Born: Oxford, England, 13 May, 1977 — G

League Club	Source	Date Signed	Seasons Played	Apps	Subs	Gls
Bristol Rov	YT	07/95	96-97	10	0	0
Cheltenham T	Worcester C	06/99	00-08	235	2	0
Leeds U	Tr	07/09	09-10	25	0	0
Northampton T		12/11	11	3	0	0

HIGH David Henry
Born: Reading, England, 22 February, 1941 — LB
England: Youth

League Club	Source	Date Signed	Seasons Played	Apps	Subs	Gls
Reading	Jnr	02/58	59-63	72	-	2

HIGH Sidney William (Sid)
Born: Waterbeach, Cambridgeshire, England, 30 September, 1922 — RW

League Club	Source	Date Signed	Seasons Played	Apps	Subs	Gls
Luton T	Abbey U	10/46				
Watford	Tr	08/48	48	7	-	3

HIGHAM John Peter
Born: West Derby, Merseyside, England, 22 November, 1954 — CD

League Club	Source	Date Signed	Seasons Played	Apps	Subs	Gls
Liverpool	App	05/74				
Southport	Tr	01/76	75-77	96	0	1

HIGHAM Peter
Born: Wigan, Greater Manchester, England, 8 November, 1930 — CF

League Club	Source	Date Signed	Seasons Played	Apps	Subs	Gls
Portsmouth (Am)	Wigan Ath	11/49	49	1	-	0
Bolton W	Tr	11/50				
Preston NE	Tr	05/52	53-54	15	-	10
Nottingham F	Tr	08/55	55-57	61	-	20
Doncaster Rov	Tr	03/58	57-58	22	-	6

HIGNETT Alan James
Born: Liverpool, England, 1 November, 1946 — LB
England: Schools

League Club	Source	Date Signed	Seasons Played	Apps	Subs	Gls
Liverpool	App	11/63	64	1	-	0
Chester C	Tr	08/66	66	6	0	0

HIGNETT Craig John
Born: Prescot, Merseyside, England, 12 January, 1970 — W

League Club	Source	Date Signed	Seasons Played	Apps	Subs	Gls
Crewe Alex	Liverpool (YT)	05/88	88-92	108	13	42
Middlesbrough	Tr	11/92	92-97	126	30	33
Barnsley	Aberdeen	11/98	98-99	62	4	28
Blackburn Rov	Tr	07/00	00-02	20	33	8
Coventry C	L	11/02	02	7	1	2
Leicester C	Tr	07/03	03	3	10	1
Crewe Alex	L	02/04	03	11	4	0
Leeds U	Tr	08/04				
Darlington	Tr	09/04	04	17	2	9
Hartlepool U	Spennymoor T	03/07	06	0	2	0

HILAIRE Vince Mark
Born: Forest Hill, S London, England, 10 October, 1959 — LW
England: B-1/U21-9/Youth

League Club	Source	Date Signed	Seasons Played	Apps	Subs	Gls
Crystal Palace	App	10/76	76-83	239	16	29
Luton T	Tr	07/84	84	5	1	0
Portsmouth	Tr	11/84	84-87	144	2	25
Leeds U	Tr	07/88	88-89	42	2	6
Stoke C	L	11/89	89	5	0	1
Stoke C	Tr	11/90	90	10	0	2
Exeter C	Tr	09/91	91	24	9	4

[HILARIO] SAMPAIO Henrique Hilario Alves
Born: Porto, Portugal, 21 October, 1975 — G
Portugal: 1/U21-8

League Club	Source	Date Signed	Seasons Played	Apps	Subs	Gls
Chelsea	CD Nacional (POR)	07/06	06-11	18	2	0

HILDERSLEY Ronald (Ronnie)
Born: Kirkcaldy, Fife, Scotland, 6 April, 1965 — M

League Club	Source	Date Signed	Seasons Played	Apps	Subs	Gls
Manchester C	App	04/83	82	1	0	0
Chester C	L	01/84	83	9	0	0
Chester C	Tr	07/84	84	5	4	0
Rochdale	Tr	08/85	85	12	4	0
Preston NE	Tr	06/86	86-87	54	4	3
Cambridge U	L	02/88	87	9	0	3
Blackburn Rov	Tr	07/88	88-89	25	5	4
Wigan Ath	Tr	08/90	90	4	0	0
Halifax T	Tr	11/91	91-92	21	10	2

HILDITCH Mark
Born: Royton, Greater Manchester, England, 20 August, 1960 — F

League Club	Source	Date Signed	Seasons Played	Apps	Subs	Gls
Rochdale	Heyside	11/77	77-82	184	13	40
Tranmere Rov	Tr	08/83	83-85	47	2	12
Wigan Ath	Altrincham	09/86	86-89	89	14	26
Rochdale	Tr	08/90	90-91	12	4	2

HILDRETH Lee Mark
Born: Nuneaton, Warwickshire, England, 22 November, 1988 — M

League Club	Source	Date Signed	Seasons Played	Apps	Subs	Gls
Coventry C	Sch	07/07	06	0	1	0

HILEY Scott Patrick
Born: Plymouth, England, 27 September, 1968 — RB

League Club	Source	Date Signed	Seasons Played	Apps	Subs	Gls
Exeter C	App	08/86	87-92	205	5	12
Birmingham C	Tr	03/93	92-95	49	0	0
Manchester C	Tr	02/96	95-96	4	5	0
Southampton	Tr	08/98	98-99	30	2	0
Portsmouth	Tr	12/99	99-01	66	9	0
Exeter C	Tr	09/02	02	37	0	0

HILL Alan
Born: Barnsley, South Yorkshire, England, 3 November, 1943 — G

League Club	Source	Date Signed	Seasons Played	Apps	Subs	Gls
Barnsley	Jnr	04/61	60-65	133	0	0
Rotherham U	Tr	06/66	66-68	81	0	0
Nottingham F	Tr	03/69	68-69	41	0	0

League Club	Source	Date Signed	Seasons Played	Apps	Subs	Gls
HILL Alan George						
Born: Chester, England, 22 June, 1955						RB
Wrexham	Jnr	07/73	74-82	173	26	7
HILL Alastair Greenwood						
Born: Glasgow, Scotland, 25 April, 1934						RW
Bristol C	Dundee	11/59	59	3	-	0
HILL Andrew Robert (Andy)						
Born: Ilkeston, Derbyshire, England, 10 November, 1960						F
Derby Co	Kimberley T	06/81	81-83	19	3	2
Carlisle U	Tr	09/83	83-85	73	12	15
HILL Andrew Rowland (Andy)						
Born: Maltby, South Yorkshire, England, 20 January, 1965						RB
England: Youth						
Manchester U	App	01/83				
Bury	Tr	07/84	84-90	264	0	10
Manchester C	Tr	12/90	90-94	91	7	6
Port Vale	Tr	08/95	95-97	96	4	1
HILL Arthur (Archie)						
Born: Chesterfield, Derbyshire, England, 12 November, 1921						RW
Died: Chesterfield, Derbyshire, England, 7 September, 1999						
Chesterfield		09/46	47	1	-	0
HILL Bert (Bertie)						
Born: West Ham, E London, England, 8 March, 1930						WH
Chelsea	Jnr	05/50				
Colchester U	Tr	10/52	52-57	105	-	3
HILL Brian						
Born: Mansfield, Nottinghamshire, England, 15 December, 1942						LW
Grimsby T	Ollerton Colliery	08/60	60-66	180	0	26
Huddersfield T	Tr	11/66	66-68	85	3	6
Blackburn Rov	Tr	09/69	69-70	34	3	4
Torquay U	Tr	07/71	71	6	1	0
HILL Brian						
Born: Sheffield, England, 6 October, 1937						RB/LH
Died: Sheffield, England, 5 April, 1968						
Sheffield Wed	Jnr	04/55	56-65	116	1	1
HILL Brian William						
Born: Bedworth, Warwickshire, England, 31 July, 1941						D/W
Coventry C	Jnr	08/58	57-70	240	4	7
Bristol C	L	03/71	70	7	0	0
Torquay U	Tr	10/71	71-72	49	0	2
HILL Charles John (Charlie)						
Born: Cardiff, Wales, 6 September, 1918						IF
Died: Cardiff, Wales, December, 1998						
Cardiff C		06/38	38-46	19	-	3
Torquay U	Tr	07/47	47-48	63	-	15
Queens Park Rgrs	Tr	03/49	48-49	21	-	1
Swindon T	Tr	09/50	50	4	-	0
HILL Clinton Scott (Clint)						
Born: Huyton, Merseyside, England, 19 October, 1978						D
Tranmere Rov	YT	07/97	97-01	138	2	16
Oldham Ath	Tr	07/02	02	17	0	1
Stoke C	Tr	07/03	03-07	71	9	3
Crystal Palace	Tr	11/07	07-09	114	0	5
Queens Park Rgrs	Tr	07/10	10-14	149	7	5
Nottingham F	L	09/11	11	5	0	0
HILL Colin Frederick						
Born: Uxbridge, W London, England, 12 November, 1963						CD
Northern Ireland: 27						
Arsenal	App	08/81	82-84	46	0	1
Colchester U	CS Maritimo (POR)	10/87	87-88	64	5	0
Sheffield U	Tr	08/89	89-91	77	5	1
Leicester C	Tr	03/92	91-96	140	5	0
Northampton T	Trelleborgs (SWE)	11/97	97-98	49	5	0
HILL Daniel Ronald (Danny)						
Born: Enfield, N London, England, 1 October, 1974						M
England: U21-4/Youth						
Tottenham H	YT	09/92	92-94	4	6	0
Birmingham C	L	11/95	95	5	0	0
Watford	L	02/96	95	1	0	0
Cardiff C	L	02/98	97	7	0	0
Oxford U	Tr	07/98	98	1	8	0
Cardiff C	Tr	11/98	98-00	33	25	4
HILL David						
Born: Kettering, Northamptonshire, England, 28 September, 1953						G
Northampton T	App	09/71	70	1	0	0

League Club	Source	Date Signed	Seasons Played	Apps	Subs	Gls
HILL David						
Born: Bradford, England, 25 May, 1965						F
Bradford C	YT	08/82	82-83	2	3	1
HILL David Michael						
Born: Nottingham, England, 6 June, 1966						M
Scunthorpe U	YT	02/85	83-87	139	1	10
Ipswich T	Tr	07/88	88-90	54	7	0
Scunthorpe U	L	03/91	90	8	1	1
Scunthorpe U	Tr	09/91	91-92	55	1	5
Lincoln C	Tr	07/93	93-94	52	6	6
Chesterfield	L	08/94	94	3	0	0
HILL Dennis						
Born: Willenhall, West Midlands, England, 16 August, 1929						LW
Birmingham C	Darlaston	06/51	53-55	4	-	0
HILL Dilwyn						
Born: Porth, Rhondda Cynon Taff, Wales, 1 April, 1937						IF
Died: Salisbury, Wiltshire, England, 1963						
Exeter C	Pontypridd	06/55	57-59	14	-	3
HILL Ernest Alan (Alan)						
Born: Bromborough, Wirral, England, 1 July, 1933						LW
Died: Birkenhead, Wirral, England, July, 2010						
Tranmere Rov (Am)	Bebington	11/56	56	6	-	1
HILL Frank Robert						
Born: Forfar, Angus, Scotland, 21 May, 1906						RH
Died: California, USA, 26 August, 1993						
Scotland: 3/SLge-1						
Arsenal	Aberdeen	05/32	32-35	76	-	4
Blackpool	Tr	06/36	36-37	45	-	8
Southampton	Tr	09/37	37-38	51	-	3
Wrexham	Preston NE (Coach)	08/42				
Crewe Alex	Tr	07/44	46-47	20	-	0
HILL Frederick (Freddie)						
Born: Sheffield, England, 17 January, 1940						M
England: 2/FLge-2/U23-10						
Bolton W	Jnr	03/57	57-68	373	2	74
Halifax T	Tr	07/69	69	25	0	3
Manchester C	Tr	05/70	70-72	28	7	3
Peterborough U	Tr	08/73	73-74	73	2	7
HILL Geoffrey Raymond (Geoff)						
Born: Carlisle, Cumbria, England, 31 August, 1929						D
Carlisle U		10/49	49-57	190	-	0
HILL Gordon Alec						
Born: Sunbury, Surrey, England, 1 April, 1954						LW
England: 6/B-6/U23-1						
Millwall	Southall	01/73	72-75	79	7	20
Manchester U	Tr	11/75	75-77	100	1	39
Derby Co	Tr	04/78	77-79	22	2	5
Queens Park Rgrs	Tr	11/79	79-80	10	4	1
HILL Henry Alec						
Born: Lambeth, S London, England, 19 September, 1947						M
Fulham	App	10/64				
Ipswich T	San Diego Toros (USA)	03/69				
Gillingham	Jo'burg Rgrs (RSA)	07/71	71	1	1	0
Hereford U	Molesey	11/78	78	0	1	0
HILL James (Jimmy)						
Born: Wishaw, Lanarkshire, Scotland, 19 August, 1931						LW
Died: Coventry, England, January, 1993						
Coventry C	Jnr	08/48	49-55	67	-	8
Millwall	Tr	07/56	56	1	-	0
Shrewsbury T	Tr	07/57	57	8	-	0
HILL James William Thomas (Jimmy)						
Born: Balham, S London, England, 22 July, 1928						IF
Brentford	Reading (Am)	05/49	49-51	83	-	10
Fulham	Tr	03/52	51-60	276	-	41
HILL John Ernest						
Born: Yeovil, Somerset, England, 29 November, 1948						RB
Bournemouth	App	08/66	67	3	1	0
HILL Jonathan William (Jon)						
Born: Wigan, Greater Manchester, England, 20 August, 1970						LM
Rochdale	Crewe Alex (YT)	07/89	89-90	25	11	1
HILL Keith John						
Born: Bolton, Greater Manchester, England, 17 May, 1969						CD
Blackburn Rov	Jnr	05/87	87-92	89	7	3
Plymouth Arg	Tr	09/92	92-95	117	6	2
Rochdale	Tr	07/96	96-00	171	5	6
Cheltenham T	Tr	06/01	01	2	3	0
Wrexham	L	10/01	01	12	0	1

HILL Kenneth (Ken)
Born: Walsall, West Midlands, England, 28 April, 1938 — WH

League Club	Source	Date Signed	Seasons Played	Apps	Subs	Gls
Walsall	Bescot U	11/56	58-62	115	-	1
Norwich C	Tr	07/63	63-65	44	0	0
Walsall	Tr	10/66	66	15	0	0

HILL Kenneth George (Kenny)
Born: Canterbury, England, 7 March, 1953 — CD
England: Semi Pro-3

League Club	Source	Date Signed	Seasons Played	Apps	Subs	Gls
Gillingham	App	03/71	71-76	120	5	7
Lincoln C	L	12/74	74	1	0	0

HILL Kevin
Born: Exeter, England, 6 March, 1976 — M/LB

League Club	Source	Date Signed	Seasons Played	Apps	Subs	Gls
Torquay U	Torrington	08/97	97-06	355	49	49

HILL Leonard Winston (Len)
Born: Caerleon, Monmouthshire, Wales, 14 April, 1941 — M
Died: Newport, Wales, 10 April, 2007
Wales: Youth

League Club	Source	Date Signed	Seasons Played	Apps	Subs	Gls
Newport Co	Lovells Ath	11/62	62-69	267	2	51
Swansea C	Tr	07/70	70	12	0	1
Newport Co	Tr	01/72	71-73	93	4	13

HILL Mark Stephen
Born: Perivale, W London, England, 21 January, 1961 — LB

League Club	Source	Date Signed	Seasons Played	Apps	Subs	Gls
Queens Park Rgrs	App	07/79				
Brentford	Tr	07/80	80-81	54	2	3

HILL Matthew Clayton (Matt)
Born: Bristol, England, 26 March, 1981 — LB

League Club	Source	Date Signed	Seasons Played	Apps	Subs	Gls
Bristol C	YT	02/99	98-04	182	16	6
Preston NE	Tr	01/05	04-08	94	11	0
Wolverhampton W	Tr	09/08	08-09	15	0	0
Queens Park Rgrs	L	01/10	09	15	1	0
Barnsley	Tr	10/10	10	23	0	2
Blackpool	Tr	07/11	11	4	0	0
Sheffield U	Tr	03/12	11-13	69	9	0
Tranmere Rov	Tr	08/14	14	9	2	0

HILL Matthew James (Jimmy)
Born: Carrickfergus, Antrim, Northern Ireland, 31 October, 1935 — IF
Northern Ireland: 7/B/NILge-6/Amateur

League Club	Source	Date Signed	Seasons Played	Apps	Subs	Gls
Newcastle U	Linfield	07/57	57	11	-	2
Norwich C	Tr	07/58	58-62	161	-	55
Everton	Tr	08/63	63	7	-	1
Port Vale	Tr	10/65	65-67	63	0	8

HILL Maurice
Born: Halifax, West Yorkshire, England, 2 May, 1920 — CH
Died: Ormskirk, Lancashire, England, 1966

League Club	Source	Date Signed	Seasons Played	Apps	Subs	Gls
Everton	Park Side	05/39				
New Brighton	Tr	07/46	46-47	73	-	0

HILL Michael Richard (Mick)
Born: Hereford, England, 3 December, 1947 — F
Died: Hereford, England, 23 June, 2008
Wales: 2

League Club	Source	Date Signed	Seasons Played	Apps	Subs	Gls
Sheffield U	Bethesda Ath	09/65	66-69	35	2	9
Ipswich T	Tr	10/69	69-72	63	3	18
Crystal Palace	Tr	12/73	73-75	43	2	6

HILL Nicholas Damien (Nicky)
Born: Accrington, Lancashire, England, 26 February, 1981 — D/M

League Club	Source	Date Signed	Seasons Played	Apps	Subs	Gls
Bury	YT	07/99	99-02	16	6	0

HILL Paul James
Born: Nottingham, England, 28 January, 1973 — FB

League Club	Source	Date Signed	Seasons Played	Apps	Subs	Gls
Peterborough U	YT	07/89	90	1	0	0

HILL Peter
Born: Heanor, Derbyshire, England, 8 August, 1931 — IF
Died: 8 January, 2015

League Club	Source	Date Signed	Seasons Played	Apps	Subs	Gls
Coventry C	Rutland U	08/48	48-61	285	-	74

HILL Raymond William (Ray)
Born: Stourbridge, West Midlands, England, 15 February, 1936 — IF

League Club	Source	Date Signed	Seasons Played	Apps	Subs	Gls
Coventry C	Redditch U	11/57	57-58	14	-	5

HILL Richard Wilfred
Born: Hinckley, Leicestershire, England, 20 September, 1963 — LM

League Club	Source	Date Signed	Seasons Played	Apps	Subs	Gls
Leicester C	Jnr	11/81				
Northampton T	Nuneaton Bor	06/85	85-86	86	0	46
Watford	Tr	05/87	87	2	2	0
Oxford U	Tr	09/87	87-88	48	15	13

HILL Ricky Anthony
Born: Paddington, Central London, England, 5 March, 1959 — M
England: 3/Youth

League Club	Source	Date Signed	Seasons Played	Apps	Subs	Gls
Luton T	App	05/76	75-88	429	7	54
Leicester C	Le Havre (FRA)	08/90	90	19	7	0

HILL Robert (Bobby)
Born: Edinburgh, Scotland, 9 June, 1938 — IF

League Club	Source	Date Signed	Seasons Played	Apps	Subs	Gls
Colchester U	Easthouses Lily MW	06/55	55-64	238	-	21

HILL Stephen Bryan
Born: Prescot, Merseyside, England, 12 November, 1982 — LB

League Club	Source	Date Signed	Seasons Played	Apps	Subs	Gls
Rochdale	Sch	07/02	02-03	10	1	0

HILL Stephen Thomas (Mandy)
Born: Blackpool, Lancashire, England, 15 February, 1940 — RW
Died: Blackpool, Lancashire, England, 27 November, 2010
England: U23-4

League Club	Source	Date Signed	Seasons Played	Apps	Subs	Gls
Blackpool	Jnr	05/59	59-63	71	-	1
Tranmere Rov	Tr	09/64	64-67	130	1	10

HILL William
Born: Sheffield, England, 6 January, 1936 — RW/CF

League Club	Source	Date Signed	Seasons Played	Apps	Subs	Gls
York C	Rawmarsh Welfare	02/54	56-59	29	-	3

HILL William Henry
Born: Skegby, Nottinghamshire, England, 15 March, 1920 — IF
Died: Mansfield, Nottinghamshire, England, October, 1999

League Club	Source	Date Signed	Seasons Played	Apps	Subs	Gls
Mansfield T	Skegby MW	11/47	47	2	-	0

HILL William Leslie
Born: Uxbridge, W London, England, 9 June, 1930 — RW/IF
Died: High Wycombe, Buckinghamshire, England, 19 September, 2009

League Club	Source	Date Signed	Seasons Played	Apps	Subs	Gls
Queens Park Rgrs	Uxbridge T	04/51	51	10	-	1

HILLARD Douglas Alfred (Doug)
Born: Bristol, England, 10 August, 1935 — RB
Died: Bristol, England, January, 1997

League Club	Source	Date Signed	Seasons Played	Apps	Subs	Gls
Bristol Rov	Bristol MH	05/57	58-67	313	5	12

HILLARD John Gordon (Jock)
Born: Aberdeen, Scotland, 3 September, 1916 — RW
Died: Mablethorpe, Lincolnshire, England, 12 December, 2002

League Club	Source	Date Signed	Seasons Played	Apps	Subs	Gls
Leicester C	Coalville T	11/37				
Grimsby T	Tr	10/38				
Torquay U		09/46	46	6	-	0

HILLEY David (Dave)
Born: Glasgow, Scotland, 20 December, 1938 — F
Scotland: SLge-1/U23-1

League Club	Source	Date Signed	Seasons Played	Apps	Subs	Gls
Newcastle U	Third Lanark	08/62	62-67	194	0	31
Nottingham F	Tr	12/67	67-70	72	16	14

HILLIER Barry Guy
Born: Redcar, Cleveland, England, 8 April, 1936 — LB

League Club	Source	Date Signed	Seasons Played	Apps	Subs	Gls
Southampton	Jnr	04/53	57-58	9	-	0

HILLIER David
Born: Blackheath, SE London, England, 19 December, 1969 — M
England: U21-1

League Club	Source	Date Signed	Seasons Played	Apps	Subs	Gls
Arsenal	YT	02/88	90-96	82	22	2
Portsmouth	Tr	11/96	96-98	62	5	4
Bristol Rov	Tr	02/99	98-01	82	1	1

HILLIER Ian Michael
Born: Neath, Wales, 26 December, 1979 — FB
Wales: U21-5/Youth/Schools

League Club	Source	Date Signed	Seasons Played	Apps	Subs	Gls
Tottenham H	YT	07/98				
Luton T	Tr	08/01	01-03	31	25	1
Chester C	L	12/04	04	7	1	0

HILLIER John Kenneth (Jack)
Born: Halsall, Lancashire, England, 10 September, 1933 — G
Died: Lancashire, England, 9 May, 2006

League Club	Source	Date Signed	Seasons Played	Apps	Subs	Gls
Chester C (Am)	Bootle	11/54	54	6	-	0

HILLMAN Dennis Victor
Born: Southend-on-Sea, England, 27 November, 1918 — RW
Died: Colchester, Essex, England, 22 December, 1994

League Club	Source	Date Signed	Seasons Played	Apps	Subs	Gls
Brighton & HA	Barking	11/44				
Colchester U	Tr	08/46	50	4	-	0
Gillingham	Tr	08/51	51	21	-	0

HILLS John David
Born: St Annes, Lancashire, England, 21 April, 1978 — LB

League Club	Source	Date Signed	Seasons Played	Apps	Subs	Gls
Blackpool	YT	10/95				
Everton	Tr	11/95	96	1	2	0
Swansea C	L	01/97	96	11	0	0
Swansea C	L	08/97	97	7	0	1
Blackpool	Tr	01/98	97-02	146	16	16
Gillingham	Tr	08/03	03-04	47	5	2
Sheffield Wed	Tr	07/05	05-06	41	2	0
Blackpool	Tr	07/07	07	1	3	0

HILLS John Raymond (Johnny)
Born: Northfleet, Kent, England, 24 February, 1934 — RB

League Club	Source	Date Signed	Seasons Played	Apps	Subs	Gls
Tottenham H	Gravesend & Northfleet	08/53	57-59	29	-	0
Bristol Rov	Tr	07/61	61	7	-	0
HILLS Lee Mark						
Born: Croydon, S London, England, 13 April, 1990						LB
England: Youth						
Crystal Palace	Sch	01/08	07-09	24	21	1
Colchester U	L	11/08	08	1	1	0
Oldham Ath	L	11/09	09	3	0	0
Southend U	L	03/12	11	5	2	0
Stevenage	Tr	07/12	12-13	12	3	0
HILLYARD Ronald William (Ron)						
Born: Brinsworth, South Yorkshire, England, 31 March, 1952						G
York C	Jnr	12/69	69-73	61	0	0
Hartlepool U	L	01/72	71	23	0	0
Gillingham	Tr	07/74	74-90	563	0	0
HILTON Damien Alan						
Born: Norwich, England, 6 September, 1977						F
Norwich C	YT	07/96				
Brighton & HA	Tr	03/98	97	4	1	0
HILTON David						
Born: Barnsley, South Yorkshire, England, 10 November, 1977						FB
England: Youth/Schools						
Manchester U	YT	12/94				
Darlington	Tr	08/97	97	0	1	0
HILTON Gary						
Born: Manchester, England, 4 March, 1961						G
Bury	Ramsbottom U	08/83	83	1	0	0
HILTON John (Jack)						
Born: Rochdale, Greater Manchester, England, 20 February, 1925						CF
Wrexham	Hyde U	07/50	50	3	-	0
HILTON Joseph (Joe)						
Born: Bromborough, Wirral, England, 20 July, 1931						IF/LH
Died: Sheffield, England, June, 1995						
Leeds U	Jnr	09/48	49	1	-	0
Chester C	Tr	08/50	50-53	61	-	9
HILTON Kirk						
Born: Flixton, Greater Manchester, England, 2 April, 1981						LB
Manchester U	YT	07/99				
Blackpool	Tr	07/03	03	12	2	1
HILTON Mark Gerard						
Born: Middleton, Greater Manchester, England, 15 January, 1960						M
Oldham Ath	App	01/78	77-80	48	2	2
Bury	Tr	08/81	81-82	29	3	3
HILTON Maurice						
Born: Stockton-on-Tees, Cleveland, England, 14 March, 1979						LB
Doncaster Rov	YT	-	97	9	1	0
HILTON Patrick Carr (Pat)						
Born: Aylesham, Kent, England, 1 May, 1954						M
Brighton & HA	Canterbury C	02/73	72-73	18	2	1
Blackburn Rov	Tr	05/74	74	16	0	2
Gillingham	Tr	09/75	75-76	16	10	1
Aldershot	L	03/77	76	12	1	0
Southport	Tr	07/77	77	22	5	5
HILTON Paul						
Born: Oldham, Greater Manchester, England, 8 October, 1959						CD/F
England: Schools						
Bury	Chadderton	07/78	78-83	136	12	39
West Ham U	Tr	02/84	83-88	47	13	7
HILTON Peter Bowes						
Born: Tamworth, Staffordshire, England, 20 March, 1929						LB
Died: Swindon, England, 12 September, 1968						
West Bromwich A	Tamworth	07/49				
Swindon T	Tr	07/53	53-55	50	-	0
HIMSWORTH Gary Paul						
Born: Appleton-le-Moors, North Yorkshire, England, 19 December, 1969						M/W
York C	YT	01/88	87-90	74	14	8
Scarborough	Tr	12/90	90-92	83	9	6
Darlington	Tr	07/93	93-95	86	8	8
York C	Tr	02/96	95-98	60	9	3
Darlington	Tr	03/99	98-00	41	7	1
HINCE Paul Frank						
Born: Manchester, England, 2 March, 1945						RW
Manchester C	Pinnington Celtic	10/66	66-67	7	0	4
Charlton Ath	Tr	02/68	67-68	23	0	2
Bury	Tr	12/68	68-69	39	0	3
Crewe Alex	Tr	07/70	70	23	3	2
HINCH James Andrew (Jim)						
Born: Sheffield, England, 8 November, 1947						F
Tranmere Rov	Portmadoc	03/70	69-70	36	3	10
Plymouth Arg	Tr	02/71	70-73	102	5	28
Hereford U	Tr	10/73	73	22	5	7
York C	Tr	07/74	74-76	56	12	12
Southport	L	03/75	74	7	0	2
Sheffield Wed	Los Angeles Sk's (USA)	10/77	77	0	1	0
Barnsley	Tr	12/77	77	9	3	4
HINCHCLIFFE Alan Arthur						
Born: Chesterfield, Derbyshire, England, 8 December, 1936						G
Sheffield Wed	Jnr	12/53	56	2	-	0
Chesterfield	Tr	07/59				
HINCHCLIFFE Andrew George (Andy)						
Born: Manchester, England, 5 February, 1969						LB
England: 7/U21-1/Youth						
Manchester C	App	02/86	87-89	107	5	8
Everton	Tr	07/90	90-97	170	12	7
Sheffield Wed	Tr	01/98	97-01	86	0	7
HINCHCLIFFE Thomas (Tom)						
Born: Denaby, South Yorkshire, England, 6 December, 1913						IF
Died: West Bridgford, Nottinghamshire, England, 1978						
Grimsby T	Denaby U	10/33	36-37	27	-	5
Huddersfield T	Tr	02/38	37-38	13	-	4
Derby Co	Tr	11/38	38	6	-	1
Nottingham F	Tr	05/46	46	1	-	0
HINCHLEY Gary						
Born: Guisborough, Cleveland, England, 14 November, 1968						RB
Darlington	Jnr	08/86	86-87	13	1	0
Darlington	Guisborough T	02/92	91-92	13	0	1
HINCHLIFFE Ben						
Born: Preston, Lancashire, England, 9 October, 1988						G
Preston NE	Sch	05/06				
Tranmere Rov	L	02/07	06	1	1	0
Derby Co	Tr	07/07				
HINCHLIFFE John (Jackie)						
Born: Tillicoultry, Stirlingshire, Scotland, 4 June, 1938						RH
Scotland: Schools						
Aston Villa	L Pieter's BC	09/56	57	2	-	0
Workington	Tr	06/58	58-61	116	-	4
Hartlepool U	Tr	10/61	61-63	88	-	8
HINDLE Frank Johnston						
Born: Blackburn, Greater Manchester, England, 22 June, 1925						CH
Blackburn Rov		01/43				
Chester C	Tr	06/49	49-50	81	-	0
Bradford Park Ave	Tr	04/51	50-56	204	-	0
HINDLE John (Jack)						
Born: Preston, Lancashire, England, 10 November, 1921						G
Died: Barrow, Cumbria, England, 21 January, 1987						
Preston NE	Clifton BC	11/46	47	1	-	0
Barrow	Tr	05/48	48-49	84	-	0
Aston Villa	Tr	06/50	50	15	-	0
Barrow	Tr	08/51	51-55	182	-	0
HINDLE Thomas (Tom)						
Born: Keighley, West Yorkshire, England, 22 February, 1921						W/IF
Died: Keighley, West Yorkshire, England, 15 August, 2011						
Leeds U	Keighley T	09/43	46-48	43	-	2
York C	Tr	02/49	48-49	19	-	3
Halifax T	Tr	09/49	49-51	85	-	17
Rochdale	Tr	03/52	51	6	-	1
HINDLEY Frank Charles						
Born: Worksop, Nottinghamshire, England, 2 November, 1915						CF
Died: Worksop, Nottinghamshire, England, March, 2003						
Nottingham F	Netherton U	12/37	38	6	-	3
Brighton & HA	Tr	05/39	46	10	-	4
HINDLEY Peter						
Born: Worksop, Nottinghamshire, England, 19 May, 1944						RB
England: U23-1						
Nottingham F	Jnr	06/61	62-73	366	0	10
Coventry C	Tr	01/74	73-75	33	0	0
Peterborough U	Tr	07/76	76-78	112	0	1
HINDMARCH Robert (Rob)						
Born: Stannington, Northumberland, England, 27 April, 1961						CD
Died: Philadelphia, Pennsylvania, USA, 5 November, 2002						
England: Youth						
Sunderland	App	04/78	77-83	114	1	2
Portsmouth	L	12/83	83	2	0	0

League Club	Source	Date Signed	Seasons Played	Apps	Subs	Gls
Derby Co	Tr	07/84	84-89	164	0	9
Wolverhampton W	Tr	06/90	90	40	0	2

HINDMARCH Stephen David (Steve)
Born: Keswick, Cumbria, England, 16 November, 1989 — F

League Club	Source	Date Signed	Seasons Played	Apps	Subs	Gls
Carlisle U	Sch	-	06	0	7	0
Shrewsbury T	Tr	07/08	08	0	3	0

HINDMARSH Edward (Eddie)
Born: Sunderland, England, 7 September, 1922 — WH
Died: Durham, England, August, 1997

League Club	Source	Date Signed	Seasons Played	Apps	Subs	Gls
Sunderland	Hylton CW	10/43				
Carlisle U	Tr	07/45	46	15	-	0

HINDMARSH John William (Billy)
Born: Crook, County Durham, England, 26 December, 1919 — RB
Died: Spennymoor, County Durham, England, 28 November, 1994

League Club	Source	Date Signed	Seasons Played	Apps	Subs	Gls
Portsmouth	Willington	04/39	46-50	55	-	0
Swindon T	Tr	07/51	51	11	-	0

HINDS Richard Paul
Born: Sheffield, England, 22 August, 1980 — CD/M

League Club	Source	Date Signed	Seasons Played	Apps	Subs	Gls
Tranmere Rov	Jnr	07/98	98-02	42	13	0
Hull C	Tr	07/03	03-04	40	5	1
Scunthorpe U	L	03/05	04-06	85	8	8
Sheffield Wed	Tr	07/07	07-10	54	13	2
Yeovil T	Lincoln C	02/12	11-12	30	5	2
Bury	Tr	07/13	13	8	2	1

HINDSON Gordon
Born: Flint Hill, County Durham, England, 8 January, 1950 — W

League Club	Source	Date Signed	Seasons Played	Apps	Subs	Gls
Newcastle U	Jnr	08/68	68-71	7	0	1
Luton T	Tr	10/71	71-74	62	6	3
Carlisle U	L	09/75	75	1	2	0
Blackburn Rov	Tr	10/75	75	10	0	0

HINE Mark
Born: Middlesbrough, England, 18 May, 1964 — M

League Club	Source	Date Signed	Seasons Played	Apps	Subs	Gls
Grimsby T	Whitby T	10/83	84-85	20	2	1
Darlington	Tr	06/86	86-88	126	2	8
Peterborough U	Tr	01/90	89-90	55	0	7
Scunthorpe U	Tr	03/91	90-91	19	3	2
Doncaster Rov	Tr	06/92	92	18	7	1

HINES Derek Jabez
Born: Swadlincote, Derbyshire, England, 18 February, 1931 — CF
Died: Blackfordby, Leicestershire, England, 24 August, 2001
England: Youth

League Club	Source	Date Signed	Seasons Played	Apps	Subs	Gls
Leicester C	Moira U	03/48	47-60	299	-	116
Shrewsbury T	Tr	11/61	61-62	16	-	5

HINES Sebastian Tony (Seb)
Born: Wetherby, West Yorkshire, England, 29 May, 1988 — CD
England: Youth

League Club	Source	Date Signed	Seasons Played	Apps	Subs	Gls
Middlesbrough	Sch	07/05	07-14	59	10	3
Oldham Ath	L	02/09	08	4	0	0
Coventry C	L	09/14	14	6	3	0

HINES Zavon
Born: Kingston, Jamaica, 27 December, 1988 — W
England: U21-2

League Club	Source	Date Signed	Seasons Played	Apps	Subs	Gls
West Ham U	Sch	07/07	09-10	9	13	1
Coventry C	L	03/08	07	0	7	1
Burnley	Tr	08/11	11	0	13	0
Bournemouth	L	03/12	11	7	1	1
Bradford C	Tr	08/12	12	19	13	2
Dagenham & Red	Tr	08/13	13	26	1	6

HINNIGAN Joseph Peter (Joe)
Born: Liverpool, England, 3 December, 1955 — FB

League Club	Source	Date Signed	Seasons Played	Apps	Subs	Gls
Wigan Ath	South Liverpool	08/75	78-79	66	0	10
Sunderland	Tr	02/80	79-82	63	0	4
Preston NE	Tr	12/82	82-83	51	1	8
Gillingham	Tr	08/84	84-86	99	4	7
Wrexham	Tr	07/87	87	28	1	1
Chester C	Tr	08/88	88-89	52	2	2

HINSHELWOOD Adam
Born: Oxford, England, 8 January, 1984 — D

League Club	Source	Date Signed	Seasons Played	Apps	Subs	Gls
Brighton & HA	Sch	07/03	02-08	88	11	2
Aldershot T	Tr	08/09	09	13	2	0
Wycombe W	Tr	01/10	09	13	0	1

HINSHELWOOD Daniel Martin (Danny)
Born: Bromley, SE London, England, 12 December, 1975 — RB
England: Youth

League Club	Source	Date Signed	Seasons Played	Apps	Subs	Gls
Nottingham F	YT	12/92				
Portsmouth	Tr	02/96	95	5	0	0
Torquay U	L	03/97	96	7	2	0
Brighton & HA	Tr	08/98	98	3	1	0

HINSHELWOOD Martin Alan
Born: Reading, England, 16 June, 1953 — M

League Club	Source	Date Signed	Seasons Played	Apps	Subs	Gls
Crystal Palace	App	08/70	72-77	66	3	4

HINSHELWOOD Paul Alexander
Born: Bristol, England, 14 August, 1956 — RB
England: U21-2

League Club	Source	Date Signed	Seasons Played	Apps	Subs	Gls
Crystal Palace	App	08/73	73-82	271	5	22
Oxford U	Tr	08/83	83-84	45	0	0
Millwall	Tr	01/85	84-86	59	2	2
Colchester U	Tr	09/86	86-87	81	0	6

HINSHELWOOD Walter Alexander Alan (Wally)
Born: Battersea, SW London, England, 27 October, 1929 — RW

League Club	Source	Date Signed	Seasons Played	Apps	Subs	Gls
Fulham	Jnr	10/46	46-50	17	-	1
Chelsea	Tr	01/51	50	12	-	1
Fulham	Tr	05/51	51	2	-	0
Reading	Tr	12/52	52-55	135	-	31
Bristol C	Tr	02/56	55-59	148	-	16
Millwall	Tr	06/60	60	19	-	1
Newport Co	Canada	11/61	61	3	-	0

HINSHELWOOD William Douglas (Willie)
Born: Chapelhall, Lanarkshire, Scotland, 11 May, 1935 — LH

League Club	Source	Date Signed	Seasons Played	Apps	Subs	Gls
Hartlepool U	Tonbridge	07/63	63	17	-	3

HINSLEY George
Born: Sheffield, England, 19 July, 1914 — RH
Died: Keighley, West Yorkshire, England, 20 March, 1989

League Club	Source	Date Signed	Seasons Played	Apps	Subs	Gls
Barnsley	Denaby U	09/35	35-38	9	-	0
Bradford C	Tr	10/38	38-48	114	-	17
Halifax T	Tr	07/49	49	32	-	0

HINTON Alan Thomas
Born: Wednesbury, West Midlands, England, 6 October, 1942 — LW
England: 3/U23-7/Youth

League Club	Source	Date Signed	Seasons Played	Apps	Subs	Gls
Wolverhampton W	Jnr	10/59	61-63	75	-	29
Nottingham F	Tr	01/64	63-67	108	4	24
Derby Co	Tr	09/67	67-75	240	13	64

HINTON Craig
Born: Wolverhampton, England, 26 November, 1977 — CD

League Club	Source	Date Signed	Seasons Played	Apps	Subs	Gls
Birmingham C	YT	07/96				
Kidderminster Hrs	Tr	08/98	00-03	172	1	3
Bristol Rov	Tr	07/04	04-08	135	18	3
Northampton T	Tr	07/09	09	38	2	0

HINTON Edward (Ted)
Born: Belfast, Northern Ireland, 20 May, 1922 — G
Died: Belfast, Northern Ireland, 11 October, 1988
Northern Ireland: 7/NILge-1

League Club	Source	Date Signed	Seasons Played	Apps	Subs	Gls
Fulham	Distillery	08/46	46-48	82	-	0
Millwall	Tr	07/49	49-51	91	-	0

HINTON Marvin
Born: Norwood, S London, England, 2 February, 1940 — CD
England: U23-3

League Club	Source	Date Signed	Seasons Played	Apps	Subs	Gls
Charlton Ath	Jnr	04/57	57-63	131	-	2
Chelsea	Tr	08/63	63-74	257	8	3

HINTON Ronald (Ron)
Born: Keighley, West Yorkshire, England, 27 November, 1943 — CH
Died: Doncaster, South Yorkshire, England, 26 September, 1986

League Club	Source	Date Signed	Seasons Played	Apps	Subs	Gls
Doncaster Rov	App	07/61				
Chesterfield	Tr	07/63	63	1	-	0

HIPKIN Reginald Willmont (Reg)
Born: Syderstone, Norfolk, England, 31 December, 1921 — RH

League Club	Source	Date Signed	Seasons Played	Apps	Subs	Gls
Wolverhampton W	Norwich C (Am)	07/39				
Charlton Ath	Tr	09/46	47	2	-	0
Brighton & HA	Tr	02/48	47-48	15	-	1

HIRD Adrian Samuel (Sam)
Born: Askern, South Yorkshire, England, 7 September, 1987 — CD

League Club	Source	Date Signed	Seasons Played	Apps	Subs	Gls
Leeds U	Sch	09/05				
Doncaster Rov	Tr	02/07	06-11	100	45	1
Grimsby T	L	11/07	07	17	0	0
Chesterfield	Tr	07/12	12-14	91	13	7

HIRD Kevin
Born: Colne, Lancashire, England, 11 February, 1955 — RB/M

League Club	Source	Date Signed	Seasons Played	Apps	Subs	Gls
Blackburn Rov	App	02/73	73-78	129	3	20
Leeds U	Tr	03/79	78-83	165	16	19
Burnley	Tr	08/84	84-85	83	0	23

HIRD Robert Keith Bryan (Keith)
Born: Annfield Plain, County Durham, England, 25 November, 1939 — G
Died: Newcastle-upon-Tyne, England, 1967

League Club	Source	Date Signed	Seasons Played	Apps	Subs	Gls
Sunderland	Annfield Plain	09/57	60	1	-	0
Darlington	Tr	07/63	63	17	-	0

HIRON Raymond Michael Charles (Ray)
Born: Gosport, Hampshire, England, 22 July, 1943 — F

League Club	Source	Date Signed	Seasons Played	Apps	Subs	Gls
Portsmouth	Fareham T	05/64	64-74	323	7	110
Reading	Tr	07/75	75-77	88	4	14

HIRONS Paul Terence
Born: Bath, England, 6 March, 1971 — M

League Club	Source	Date Signed	Seasons Played	Apps	Subs	Gls
Torquay U	Bristol C (YT)	01/89	88-89	10	11	0

HIRSCHFELD Lars Justin
Born: Edmonton, Canada, 17 October, 1978 — G
Canada: 48/U23-4

League Club	Source	Date Signed	Seasons Played	Apps	Subs	Gls
Tottenham H	Calgary Storm (CAN)	08/02				
Luton T	L	02/03	02	5	0	0
Gillingham	L	02/04	03	2	0	0
Leicester C	Dundee U	01/05	04	1	0	0

HIRST Benjamin Matthew (Ben)
Born: York, England, 21 October, 1997 — F

League Club	Source	Date Signed	Seasons Played	Apps	Subs	Gls
York C	Sch	10/14	14	0	3	0

HIRST David Eric
Born: Cudworth, South Yorkshire, England, 7 December, 1967 — F
England: 3/B-3/U21-7/Youth

League Club	Source	Date Signed	Seasons Played	Apps	Subs	Gls
Barnsley	App	11/85	85	26	2	9
Sheffield Wed	Tr	08/86	86-97	261	33	106
Southampton	Tr	10/97	97-98	28	2	9

HIRST Keith Richard Halliwell
Born: Bradford, England, 15 October, 1932 — RW

League Club	Source	Date Signed	Seasons Played	Apps	Subs	Gls
Bradford Park Ave	Low Moor Celtic	01/54	53	1	-	0

HIRST Lee William
Born: Sheffield, England, 26 January, 1969 — CD

League Club	Source	Date Signed	Seasons Played	Apps	Subs	Gls
Scarborough	Sheffield Parks	02/90	89-92	107	1	6
Coventry C	Tr	07/93				
Lincoln C	L	12/93	93	7	0	0

HIRST Malcolm William
Born: Cudworth, South Yorkshire, England, 28 December, 1937 — CF

League Club	Source	Date Signed	Seasons Played	Apps	Subs	Gls
Barnsley	Darfield Road Jnrs	05/56	56	1	-	0

HIRST Martyn Paul
Born: Batley, West Yorkshire, England, 26 October, 1961 — M
England: Schools

League Club	Source	Date Signed	Seasons Played	Apps	Subs	Gls
Bristol C	Bath Univ	10/83	83-85	36	5	1
Torquay U	L	09/85	85	4	0	0

HISLOP Matthew Henry
Born: Wolverhampton, England, 31 January, 1987 — LB

League Club	Source	Date Signed	Seasons Played	Apps	Subs	Gls
Queens Park Rgrs	Arsenal (Sch)	03/05	05	1	0	0

HISLOP Neil Shaka (Shaka)
Born: Hackney, E London, England, 22 February, 1969 — G
England: U21-1//Trinidad & Tobago: 26

League Club	Source	Date Signed	Seasons Played	Apps	Subs	Gls
Reading	Howard Univ (USA)	09/92	92-94	104	0	0
Newcastle U	Tr	08/95	95-97	53	0	0
West Ham U	Tr	07/98	98-01	105	0	0
Portsmouth	Tr	07/02	02-04	93	0	0
West Ham U	Tr	07/05	05	16	0	0

HISLOP Steven James (Steve)
Born: Dalkeith, Midlothian, Scotland, 14 June, 1978 — F

League Club	Source	Date Signed	Seasons Played	Apps	Subs	Gls
Gillingham	Inverness CT	08/05	05	2	6	0

HISLOP Terence Kona (Kona)
Born: Hackney, E London, England, 21 December, 1970 — LW

League Club	Source	Date Signed	Seasons Played	Apps	Subs	Gls
Hartlepool U	Livingston	09/96	96	23	4	0

HITCHCOCK Alan Peter
Born: Bracknell, Berkshire, England, 5 October, 1949 — D

League Club	Source	Date Signed	Seasons Played	Apps	Subs	Gls
Reading	App	10/67	68-69	4	0	0

HITCHCOCK Kevin Joseph
Born: Canning Town, E London, England, 5 October, 1962 — G

League Club	Source	Date Signed	Seasons Played	Apps	Subs	Gls
Nottingham F	Barking	08/83				
Mansfield T	L	02/84	83	14	0	0
Mansfield T	Tr	06/84	84-87	168	0	0
Chelsea	Tr	03/88	87-98	92	4	0
Northampton T	L	12/90	90	17	0	0

HITCHCOCK Thomas Joseph (Tom)
Born: Hemel Hempstead, Hertfordshire, England, 1 October, 1992 — F

League Club	Source	Date Signed	Seasons Played	Apps	Subs	Gls
Blackburn Rov	Sch	10/09				
Plymouth Arg	L	07/11	11	3	5	0
Queens Park Rgrs	Tr	03/12	13	0	1	1
Bristol Rov	L	01/13	12	7	10	3
Crewe Alex	L	11/13	13	6	0	3
Rotherham U	L	01/14	13	4	7	5
MK Dons	Tr	07/14	14	1	11	0
Fleetwood T	L	10/14	14	4	2	1

HITCHEN Henry (Harry)
Born: Liverpool, England, 22 October, 1922 — RH
Died: Liverpool, England, 9 April, 1993

League Club	Source	Date Signed	Seasons Played	Apps	Subs	Gls
New Brighton	Formby	09/46	46-47	70	-	2
Sheffield U	Tr	05/48	48-52	154	-	15
Bury	Tr	05/53	53	2	-	0

HITCHEN Steven James (Steve)
Born: Salford, England, 28 November, 1976 — RB

League Club	Source	Date Signed	Seasons Played	Apps	Subs	Gls
Blackburn Rov	YT	07/95				
Macclesfield T	Tr	07/97	97-03	143	8	1

HITCHEN Trevor
Born: Sowerby Bridge, West Yorkshire, England, 25 September, 1926 — WH/IF

League Club	Source	Date Signed	Seasons Played	Apps	Subs	Gls
Notts Co	Halifax T (Am)	05/45				
Southport	Wellington T	01/49	48-55	242	-	34
Oldham Ath	Tr	08/56	56	3	-	0
Southport	Wigan Ath	08/58	58	5	-	0

HITCHENS Gerald Archibald (Gerry)
Born: Cannock, Staffordshire, England, 8 October, 1934 — CF
Died: Wrexham, Wales, 13 April, 1983
England: 7/FLge-1/U23-1//Italy: ILge-2

League Club	Source	Date Signed	Seasons Played	Apps	Subs	Gls
Cardiff C	Kidderminster Hrs	01/55	54-57	95	-	40
Aston Villa	Tr	12/57	57-60	132	-	78

HITCHON John
Born: Carlisle, Cumbria, England, 30 August, 1919 — G
Died: Carlisle, Cumbria, England, 22 December, 1985

League Club	Source	Date Signed	Seasons Played	Apps	Subs	Gls
Carlisle U	Lancaster C	04/47	46-49	5	-	0

HITZLSPERGER Thomas
Born: Munich, Germany, 5 April, 1982 — M
Germany: 52/U21-20/Youth

League Club	Source	Date Signed	Seasons Played	Apps	Subs	Gls
Aston Villa	Bayern Munich (GER)	08/00	00-04	74	25	8
Chesterfield	L	10/01	01	5	0	0
West Ham U	VfB Stuttgart (GER)	07/10	10	11	0	2
Everton	VfL Wolfsburg (GER)	10/12	12	4	3	0

HIWULA-MAYIFUILA Jordy
Born: Stretford, Greater Manchester, England, 21 September, 1994 — F
England: Youth

League Club	Source	Date Signed	Seasons Played	Apps	Subs	Gls
Manchester C	Sch	09/12				
Yeovil T	L	10/14	14	7	1	0
Walsall	L	02/15	14	17	2	9

HJELDE Jon Olav
Born: Levanger, Norway, 30 July, 1972 — CD

League Club	Source	Date Signed	Seasons Played	Apps	Subs	Gls
Nottingham F	Rosenborg (NOR)	08/97	97-02	136	21	4
Nottingham F	Busan Icons (KOR)	08/04	04	13	1	0
Mansfield T	Tr	08/05	05-06	55	4	2

HJORTH Jesper
Born: Odense, Denmark, 3 April, 1975 — F
Denmark: U21-10/Youth

League Club	Source	Date Signed	Seasons Played	Apps	Subs	Gls
Darlington	OB Odense (DEN)	11/99	99-00	16	29	7

HLEB Aleksandr Paulavich
Born: Minsk, Belarus, 1 May, 1981 — M
Belarus: 69

League Club	Source	Date Signed	Seasons Played	Apps	Subs	Gls
Arsenal	VfB Stuttgart (GER)	08/05	05-07	73	16	7
Birmingham C (L)	Barcelona (SPN)	08/10	10	13	6	1

HOADLEY Philip Frederick William (Phil)
Born: Battersea, SW London, England, 6 January, 1952 — CD
England: Youth

League Club	Source	Date Signed	Seasons Played	Apps	Subs	Gls
Crystal Palace	App	01/69	67-71	62	11	1
Leyton Orient	Tr	10/71	71-77	255	0	9
Norwich C	Tr	08/78	78-81	74	3	0

HOBAN Patrick Jefferson (Pat)
Born: Galway, Republic of Ireland, 28 July, 1991 — F

League Club	Source	Date Signed	Seasons Played	Apps	Subs	Gls
Bristol C	Mervue U (ROI)	09/10				
Oxford U	Dundalk (ROI)	11/14	14	15	5	1

HOBAN Thomas Michael (Tommie)
Born: Walthamstow, NE London, England, 24 January, 1994 — CD
Republic of Ireland: U21-5/Youth

League Club	Source	Date Signed	Seasons Played	Apps	Subs	Gls
Watford	Sch	07/11	10-14	44	10	2

HOBBINS Sydney George (Syd)
Born: Plumstead, SE London, England, 6 May, 1916 — G
Died: Shooters Hill, SE London, England, 16 March, 1984

League Club	Source	Date Signed	Seasons Played	Apps	Subs	Gls
Charlton Ath	Bromley	05/34	37-46	2	-	0
Millwall	Tr	05/48	48	15	-	0
Leyton Orient	Tr	12/49	49	11	-	0

HOBBIS Harold Henry Frederick
Born: Dartford, Kent, England, 9 March, 1913 — LW

Died: Eastbourne, East Sussex, England, 17 May, 1991
England: 2

League Club	Source	Date Signed	Seasons Played	Apps	Subs	Gls
Charlton Ath	Bromley	03/31	31-47	248	-	76

HOBBS Jack
Born: Portsmouth, England, 18 August, 1988 — CD

League Club	Source	Date Signed	Seasons Played	Apps	Subs	Gls
Lincoln C	Sch	07/04	04	0	1	0
Liverpool	Tr	08/05	07	1	1	0
Scunthorpe U	L	01/08	07	7	2	1
Leicester C	Tr	07/08	08-10	106	8	1
Hull C	L	02/11	10	9	4	0
Hull C	Tr	06/11	11-12	60	2	1
Nottingham F	Tr	07/13	13-14	44	0	1

HOBBS John Eric (Jack)
Born: Swanage, Dorset, England, 17 April, 1930 — CF

League Club	Source	Date Signed	Seasons Played	Apps	Subs	Gls
Bournemouth	Swanage	10/52	53-54	6	-	1

HOBBS Ronald George (Ronnie)
Born: Aldershot, Hampshire, England, 23 August, 1921 — RW
Died: West Surrey, England, 8 January, 2007

League Club	Source	Date Signed	Seasons Played	Apps	Subs	Gls
Aldershot	Woking	11/44	46-53	169	-	14

HOBBS Shane Michael
Born: Bristol, England, 30 April, 1985 — W

League Club	Source	Date Signed	Seasons Played	Apps	Subs	Gls
Bristol Rov	Sch	-	03	0	2	0

HOBSON Albert
Born: Glossop, Derbyshire, England, 7 April, 1925 — RW

League Club	Source	Date Signed	Seasons Played	Apps	Subs	Gls
Blackpool	Glossop	08/45	47-53	62	-	3
Huddersfield T	Tr	07/54	54-55	9	-	0
York C	Tr	03/56	55-56	22	-	1

HOBSON Gary
Born: North Ferriby, East Riding of Yorkshire, England, 12 November, 1972 — CD

League Club	Source	Date Signed	Seasons Played	Apps	Subs	Gls
Hull C	YT	07/91	90-95	135	7	0
Brighton & HA	Tr	03/96	95-99	92	6	1
Chester C	Tr	01/00	99	20	0	0
York C	Tr	07/00	00-02	46	9	0

HOBSON Gordon
Born: Sheffield, England, 27 November, 1957 — F

League Club	Source	Date Signed	Seasons Played	Apps	Subs	Gls
Lincoln C	Sheffield Rgrs	12/77	77-84	260	12	73
Grimsby T	Tr	06/85	85-86	50	2	18
Southampton	Tr	11/86	86-87	32	1	8
Lincoln C	Tr	09/88	88-89	61	0	23
Exeter C	Tr	08/90	90-91	37	1	7
Walsall	Salisbury C	09/91	91	3	0	0

HOBSON John
Born: Barnsley, South Yorkshire, England, 1 June, 1946 — W/IF

League Club	Source	Date Signed	Seasons Played	Apps	Subs	Gls
Blackpool	Jnr	09/63				
Barnsley	Tr	07/65	65-68	30	7	7
Notts Co	Tr	05/69	69-70	46	3	6

HOBSON Norman
Born: Shrewsbury, Shropshire, England, 22 August, 1933 — FB

League Club	Source	Date Signed	Seasons Played	Apps	Subs	Gls
Shrewsbury T	Oswestry T	10/54	55-60	212	-	5

HOBSON Wilfred (Wilf)
Born: Consett, County Durham, England, 26 January, 1932 — RH
Died: Durham, England, October, 2008

League Club	Source	Date Signed	Seasons Played	Apps	Subs	Gls
Oldham Ath	West Stanley	01/53	54-58	170	-	1
Gateshead	Tr	06/59	59	31	-	1

HOCKADAY David
Born: Sedgefield, County Durham, England, 9 November, 1957 — FB/W

League Club	Source	Date Signed	Seasons Played	Apps	Subs	Gls
Blackpool	Billingham Synthonia	06/75	76-82	131	16	24
Swindon T	Tr	08/83	83-90	227	18	7
Hull C	Tr	09/90	90-92	72	0	2
Stoke C	L	03/93	92	7	0	0
Shrewsbury T	Tr	08/93	93-94	46	2	0

HOCKENHULL Darren
Born: St Helens, Merseyside, England, 5 September, 1982 — RB

League Club	Source	Date Signed	Seasons Played	Apps	Subs	Gls
Blackburn Rov	Sch	07/02				
Rochdale	L	03/03	02	6	1	1

HOCKEY Trevor
Born: Keighley, West Yorkshire, England, 1 May, 1943 — W/M
Died: Keighley, West Yorkshire, England, 1 April, 1987
Wales: 9

League Club	Source	Date Signed	Seasons Played	Apps	Subs	Gls
Bradford C	Jnr	05/60	59-61	53	-	5
Nottingham F	Tr	11/61	61-63	73	-	6
Newcastle U	Tr	11/63	63-65	52	0	3
Birmingham C	Tr	11/65	65-70	195	1	8
Sheffield U	Tr	01/71	70-72	68	0	4
Norwich C	Tr	02/73	72	13	0	0
Aston Villa	Tr	06/73	73	24	0	1
Bradford C	Tr	06/74	74-75	43	1	1

HOCKING Matthew James (Matt)
Born: Boston, Lincolnshire, England, 30 January, 1978 — CD

League Club	Source	Date Signed	Seasons Played	Apps	Subs	Gls
Sheffield U	YT	05/96				
Hull C	Tr	09/97	97-98	55	2	2
York C	Tr	03/99	98-01	83	14	2
Boston U	Tr	08/02	02-03	60	7	1

HOCKLESS Graham
Born: Hull, England, 20 October, 1982 — M

League Club	Source	Date Signed	Seasons Played	Apps	Subs	Gls
Grimsby T	Hull C (Jnr)	07/01	02-04	8	12	2

HOCKLEY Matthew (Matt)
Born: Paignton, Devon, England, 5 June, 1982 — RB/M

League Club	Source	Date Signed	Seasons Played	Apps	Subs	Gls
Torquay U	YT	07/00	00-06	155	55	9

HOCKLEY Wayne
Born: Torquay, Devon, England, 6 September, 1978 — F

League Club	Source	Date Signed	Seasons Played	Apps	Subs	Gls
Torquay U	YT	08/97	96	0	2	0

HOCKTON Daniel John (Danny)
Born: Barking, E London, England, 7 February, 1979 — F

League Club	Source	Date Signed	Seasons Played	Apps	Subs	Gls
Millwall	YT	03/97	96-98	11	25	4
Leyton Orient	L	09/99	99	1	4	0

HODDER Kenneth (Ken)
Born: Stockport, Greater Manchester, England, 20 August, 1930 — CH
Died: 3 March, 2015

League Club	Source	Date Signed	Seasons Played	Apps	Subs	Gls
Stockport Co	Jnr	03/49	51-63	258	-	1

HODDER Stephen John (Steve)
Born: Sheffield, England, 18 October, 1971 — LB

League Club	Source	Date Signed	Seasons Played	Apps	Subs	Gls
Nottingham F	YT	07/90				
Notts Co	Tr	03/91				
Doncaster Rov	Tr	07/92	92	1	1	0

HODDLE Carl
Born: Harlow, Essex, England, 8 March, 1967 — M
Died: Sawbridgeworth, Hertfordshire, England, 2 March, 2008

League Club	Source	Date Signed	Seasons Played	Apps	Subs	Gls
Tottenham H	App	07/84				
Leyton Orient	Bishops Stortford	07/89	89-90	19	9	2
Barnet	Tr	07/91	91-94	80	12	3

HODDLE Glenn
Born: Hayes, W London, England, 27 October, 1957 — M
England: 53/B-2/U21-12/Youth

League Club	Source	Date Signed	Seasons Played	Apps	Subs	Gls
Tottenham H	App	04/75	75-86	371	7	88
Swindon T	AS Monaco (FRA)	08/91	91-92	63	1	1
Chelsea	Tr	06/93	93-94	19	12	1

HODDY Kevin Raymond
Born: Romford, E London, England, 6 January, 1968 — M

League Club	Source	Date Signed	Seasons Played	Apps	Subs	Gls
Fulham	App	01/86	86-88	13	9	1

HODGE Bryan Johnstone
Born: Hamilton, Lanarkshire, Scotland, 23 September, 1987 — M
Scotland: Youth

League Club	Source	Date Signed	Seasons Played	Apps	Subs	Gls
Blackburn Rov	Sch	11/04				
Mansfield T	L	02/07	06	9	0	0
Millwall	L	11/07	07	10	0	0
Darlington	L	02/08	07	7	0	0

HODGE Eric
Born: Edmonton, N London, England, 1 June, 1928 — G
Died: Edmonton, N London, England, 31 August, 1963

League Club	Source	Date Signed	Seasons Played	Apps	Subs	Gls
Tottenham H		08/48				
Newport Co	Tr	08/49	49	7	-	0

HODGE Eric Richard Carew
Born: Cape Town, South Africa, 3 April, 1933 — CH

League Club	Source	Date Signed	Seasons Played	Apps	Subs	Gls
Brighton & HA	South Africa	10/56	57	4	-	0
Aldershot	Tr	07/59	59	17	-	0

HODGE James Oswald (Jimmy)
Born: Perth, Scotland, 23 October, 1926 — LB

League Club	Source	Date Signed	Seasons Played	Apps	Subs	Gls
Newport Co	York C (Am)	08/46	46	1	-	0

HODGE John
Born: Ormskirk, Lancashire, England, 1 April, 1969 — W

League Club	Source	Date Signed	Seasons Played	Apps	Subs	Gls
Exeter C	Falmouth	09/91	91-92	57	8	10
Swansea C	Tr	07/93	93-95	87	25	10
Walsall	Tr	09/96	96-97	67	9	12
Gillingham	Tr	07/98	98-99	8	41	1
Northampton T	Tr	03/00	99-01	33	27	2

HODGE Martin John
Born: Southport, Merseyside, England, 4 February, 1959 — G

League Club	Source	Date Signed	Seasons Played	Apps	Subs	Gls
Plymouth Arg	App	02/77	77-78	43	0	0
Everton	Tr	07/79	79-80	25	0	0
Preston NE	L	12/81	81	28	0	0
Oldham Ath	L	07/82	82	4	0	0

League Club	Source	Date Signed	Seasons Played	Apps	Subs	Gls
Gillingham	L	01/83	82	4	0	0
Preston NE	L	02/83	82	16	0	0
Sheffield Wed	Tr	08/83	83-87	197	0	0
Leicester C	Tr	08/88	88-90	75	0	0
Hartlepool U	Tr	08/91	91-92	69	0	0
Rochdale	Tr	07/93	93	42	0	0
Plymouth Arg	Tr	08/94	94	17	0	0

HODGE Robert William (Bobby)
Born: Exeter, England, 30 April, 1954 — RW

League Club	Source	Date Signed	Seasons Played	Apps	Subs	Gls
Exeter C		07/74	74-78	120	8	18
Colchester U	Tr	09/78	78-80	87	5	14
Torquay U	Tr	08/81	81	3	1	1

HODGE Stephen Brian (Steve)
Born: Nottingham, England, 25 October, 1962 — M
England: 24/B-2/U21-8

League Club	Source	Date Signed	Seasons Played	Apps	Subs	Gls
Nottingham F	App	10/80	81-85	122	1	30
Aston Villa	Tr	08/85	85-86	53	0	12
Tottenham H	Tr	12/86	86-87	44	1	7
Nottingham F	Tr	08/88	88-90	79	3	20
Leeds U	Tr	07/91	91-93	28	26	10
Derby Co	L	08/94	94	10	0	2
Queens Park Rgrs	Tr	10/94	94	15	0	0
Watford	Tr	12/95	95	2	0	0
Leyton Orient	Hong Kong	08/97	97	1	0	0

HODGES Cyril Leslie
Born: Hackney, E London, England, 18 September, 1919 — CF
Died: Brighton, England, 1979

League Club	Source	Date Signed	Seasons Played	Apps	Subs	Gls
Arsenal	Eton Manor	04/45	46	2	-	0
Brighton & HA	Tr	10/46	46	9	-	3

HODGES David
Born: Ross-on-Wye, Herefordshire, England, 17 January, 1970 — M

League Club	Source	Date Signed	Seasons Played	Apps	Subs	Gls
Mansfield T	Jnr	08/87	86-90	67	18	7
Torquay U	Tr	01/91	90-91	8	8	0
Shrewsbury T	Bolton W (NC)	08/92	92	1	0	0

HODGES Glyn Peter
Born: Streatham, S London, England, 30 April, 1963 — LM
Wales: 18/B-1/U21-5/Youth

League Club	Source	Date Signed	Seasons Played	Apps	Subs	Gls
Wimbledon	App	02/81	80-86	200	32	49
Newcastle U	Tr	07/87	87	7	0	0
Watford	Tr	10/87	87-89	82	4	15
Crystal Palace	Tr	07/90	90	5	2	0
Sheffield U	Tr	01/91	90-95	116	31	19
Derby Co	Tr	02/96	95	1	8	0
Hull C	Sing Tao (HKG)	08/97	97	13	5	4
Nottingham F	Tr	02/98	98	3	2	0
Scarborough	Tr	01/99	98	1	0	0

HODGES John Kenneth
Born: Leicester, England, 22 January, 1980 — G

League Club	Source	Date Signed	Seasons Played	Apps	Subs	Gls
Leicester C	YT	07/98				
Plymouth Arg	Tr	07/00	00	2	0	0

HODGES Kevin
Born: Bridport, Dorset, England, 12 June, 1960 — RM/FB

League Club	Source	Date Signed	Seasons Played	Apps	Subs	Gls
Plymouth Arg	App	03/78	78-92	502	28	81
Torquay U	L	01/92	91	3	0	0
Torquay U	Tr	12/92	92-96	49	19	4

HODGES Lee Leslie
Born: Epping, Essex, England, 4 September, 1973 — M
England: Youth

League Club	Source	Date Signed	Seasons Played	Apps	Subs	Gls
Tottenham H	YT	02/92	92	0	4	0
Plymouth Arg	L	02/93	92	6	1	2
Wycombe W	L	12/93	93	2	2	0
Barnet	Tr	05/94	94-96	94	11	26
Reading	Tr	07/97	97-00	58	21	10
Plymouth Arg	Tr	08/01	01-07	162	33	11
Torquay U	Tr	08/08	09	2	3	0

HODGES Lee Leslie
Born: Plaistow, E London, England, 2 March, 1978 — W
England: Schools

League Club	Source	Date Signed	Seasons Played	Apps	Subs	Gls
West Ham U	YT	03/95	97-98	0	3	0
Exeter C	L	09/96	96	16	1	0
Leyton Orient	L	02/97	96	3	0	0
Plymouth Arg	L	11/97	97	9	0	0
Ipswich T	L	11/98	98	0	4	0
Southend U	L	03/99	98	10	0	1
Scunthorpe U	Tr	07/99	99-01	97	16	20
Rochdale	Tr	08/02	02	3	4	0
Bristol Rov	Tr	03/03	02-03	12	9	2

HODGES Leonard Herbert (Len)
Born: Bristol, England, 17 February, 1920 — IF
Died: Bristol, England, 5 August, 1959

League Club	Source	Date Signed	Seasons Played	Apps	Subs	Gls
Bristol Rov	Soundwell	08/46	46-49	118	-	20
Swansea C	Tr	08/50	50	3	-	0
Reading	Tr	08/51	51-52	6	-	2

HODGES Mark
Born: Sheffield, England, 24 October, 1971 — CD

League Club	Source	Date Signed	Seasons Played	Apps	Subs	Gls
Rotherham U	YT	07/90	90	3	1	0

HODGETTS Frank
Born: Dudley, West Midlands, England, 30 September, 1924 — LW

League Club	Source	Date Signed	Seasons Played	Apps	Subs	Gls
West Bromwich A	Accles & Pollock	10/42	46-48	67	-	11
Millwall	Tr	08/49	49-52	34	-	6

HODGKINS Jeffrey (Jeff)
Born: Portsmouth, England, 8 October, 1942 — CF

League Club	Source	Date Signed	Seasons Played	Apps	Subs	Gls
Portsmouth	Jnr	06/60	60	3	-	0

HODGKINSON Alan
Born: Laughton, South Yorkshire, England, 16 August, 1936 — G
England: 5/FLge-1/U23-7

League Club	Source	Date Signed	Seasons Played	Apps	Subs	Gls
Sheffield U	Worksop T	08/53	54-70	576	0	0

HODGKINSON Derek John
Born: Banwell, Somerset, England, 30 April, 1944 — IF

League Club	Source	Date Signed	Seasons Played	Apps	Subs	Gls
Manchester C	Margate	08/61	63	1	-	1
Stockport Co	Tr	06/64	64-65	46	0	9

HODGKINSON Edwin Slack (Eddie)
Born: Ilkeston, Derbyshire, England, 27 November, 1920 — IF/WH
Died: Mansfield, Nottinghamshire, England, 2 October, 2004

League Club	Source	Date Signed	Seasons Played	Apps	Subs	Gls
Leeds U	RAMC Beckett's Park	12/46	46-47	2	-	0
Halifax T	Tr	07/48	48-49	13	-	2

HODGKISS Jared
Born: Stafford, England, 15 November, 1986 — RB

League Club	Source	Date Signed	Seasons Played	Apps	Subs	Gls
West Bromwich A	Sch	01/06	05-07	3	7	0
Northampton T	L	03/09	08	4	1	0

HODGKISS Robert (Bob)
Born: Little Hulton, Greater Manchester, England, 22 March, 1918 — RB
Died: Worsley, Greater Manchester, England, 3 December, 2003

League Club	Source	Date Signed	Seasons Played	Apps	Subs	Gls
Southport	Walkden Meth's	11/38	38	10	-	0
Everton	Tr	08/46				
Southport	Tr	07/47	47-48	20	-	0

HODGKISSON William Kenneth (Ken)
Born: West Bromwich, West Midlands, England, 12 March, 1933 — IF

League Club	Source	Date Signed	Seasons Played	Apps	Subs	Gls
West Bromwich A	Jnr	04/50	52-55	21	-	4
Walsall	Tr	01/56	55-65	335	1	59

HODGSON Brian George
Born: Cleethorpes, North Lincolnshire, England, 29 January, 1936 — CF

League Club	Source	Date Signed	Seasons Played	Apps	Subs	Gls
Grimsby T	Askern WMC	09/56	56	7	-	1
Workington	Tr	10/59	59	1	-	0

HODGSON David James
Born: Gateshead, Tyne and Wear, England, 6 August, 1960 — F
England: U21-6

League Club	Source	Date Signed	Seasons Played	Apps	Subs	Gls
Middlesbrough	Redheugh BC	08/78	78-81	116	9	16
Liverpool	Tr	08/82	82-83	21	7	4
Sunderland	Tr	08/84	84-85	32	8	5
Norwich C	Tr	07/86	86	3	3	1
Middlesbrough	L	02/87	86	2	0	0
Sheffield Wed	Jerez (SPN)	08/88	88	6	5	1
Swansea C	FC Metz (FRA)	03/92	91	1	2	0

HODGSON Donald (Don)
Born: Liversedge, West Yorkshire, England, 22 December, 1922 — IF
Died: Dewsbury, West Yorkshire, England, 14 December, 1995

League Club	Source	Date Signed	Seasons Played	Apps	Subs	Gls
Bradford Park Ave	Bradford U	04/48	48-51	41	-	7
York C	Tr	08/52				

HODGSON Douglas John (Doug)
Born: Melbourne, Australia, 27 February, 1969 — CD

League Club	Source	Date Signed	Seasons Played	Apps	Subs	Gls
Sheffield U	Heidelberg U (AUS)	07/94	94-96	24	6	0
Plymouth Arg	L	08/95	95	3	2	0
Burnley	L	10/96	96	1	0	0
Oldham Ath	Tr	02/97	96-98	33	8	4
Northampton T	Tr	10/98	98	7	1	1

HODGSON Gordon Henry
Born: Newcastle-upon-Tyne, England, 13 October, 1952 — M
Died: Peterborough, England, April, 1999
England: Youth/Schools

League Club	Source	Date Signed	Seasons Played	Apps	Subs	Gls
Newcastle U	Jnr	06/71	71-73	8	1	0
Mansfield T	Tr	05/74	74-78	184	0	23
Oxford U	Tr	09/78	78-79	66	1	3
Peterborough U	Tr	08/80	80-81	82	1	5

HODGSON John Percival
Born: Seaham, County Durham, England, 10 May, 1922 — G
Died: Seaham, County Durham, England, 1973

League Club	Source	Date Signed	Seasons Played	Apps	Subs	Gls
Leeds U	Murton CW	11/43	46-47	20	-	0
Middlesbrough	Tr	03/48	47-54	13	-	0

HODGSON John Venner (Jack)
Born: Seaham, County Durham, England, 30 September, 1913 — LB
Died: Cleethorpes, North Lincolnshire, England, 20 June, 1970

League Club	Source	Date Signed	Seasons Played	Apps	Subs	Gls
Grimsby T	Seaham CW	01/32	32-47	212	-	2
Doncaster Rov	Tr	01/48	47-51	95	-	2

HODGSON Kenneth (Ken)
Born: Newcastle-upon-Tyne, England, 19 January, 1942 — F
Died: Cheshire, England, 23 October, 2007

League Club	Source	Date Signed	Seasons Played	Apps	Subs	Gls
Newcastle U	Montagu & North Fenham	05/59	60	6	-	0
Scunthorpe U	Tr	12/61	61-63	88	-	30
Bournemouth	Tr	06/64	64-65	77	1	24
Colchester U	Tr	07/66	66-68	56	1	19

HODGSON Lawrence (Laurie)
Born: Birkenhead, Wirral, England, 19 January, 1917 — FB
Died: Birkenhead, Wirral, England, 18 February, 1980

League Club	Source	Date Signed	Seasons Played	Apps	Subs	Gls
Tranmere Rov	Silver Green	01/39	46-50	78	-	0

HODGSON Michael (Mike)
Born: Newcastle-upon-Tyne, England, 6 July, 1945 — W

League Club	Source	Date Signed	Seasons Played	Apps	Subs	Gls
Hartlepool U (Am)	Billingham Synthonia	08/64	64	1	-	0

HODGSON Noel
Born: Workington, Cumbria, England, 25 December, 1938 — RW

League Club	Source	Date Signed	Seasons Played	Apps	Subs	Gls
Workington	Jnr	08/57	57-62	51	-	12

HODGSON Richard James
Born: Sunderland, England, 1 October, 1979 — LW

League Club	Source	Date Signed	Seasons Played	Apps	Subs	Gls
Nottingham F	YT	10/96				
Scunthorpe U	Tr	03/00	99	1	0	0
Darlington	Tr	08/00	00-02	66	32	6
Cambridge U	Crawley T	10/04	04	9	1	2

HODGSON Ronald (Ronnie)
Born: Birkenhead, Wirral, England, 2 November, 1922 — CH
Died: Birkenhead, Wirral, England, 26 August, 2009

League Club	Source	Date Signed	Seasons Played	Apps	Subs	Gls
Tranmere Rov	Jnr	02/41				
Manchester C	Tr	10/44	46	1	-	0
Southport	Tr	06/47	47-48	42	-	1
Crewe Alex	Tr	02/49	48-49	32	-	0

HODGSON Samuel (Sam)
Born: Seaham, County Durham, England, 21 January, 1919 — WH
Died: Middlesbrough, England, June, 2000

League Club	Source	Date Signed	Seasons Played	Apps	Subs	Gls
Grimsby T	Seaham CW	01/36	46-47	21	-	0
Mansfield T	Tr	07/48	48	2	-	0

HODGSON William (Billy)
Born: Glasgow, Scotland, 9 July, 1935 — W/IF

League Club	Source	Date Signed	Seasons Played	Apps	Subs	Gls
Sheffield U	St Johnstone	05/57	57-63	152	-	32
Leicester C	Tr	09/63	63-64	46	-	10
Derby Co	Tr	06/65	65-67	78	0	17
Rotherham U	Tr	09/67	67	9	0	0
York C	Tr	12/67	67-69	98	0	3

HODKINSON Andrew James (Andy)
Born: Ashton-under-Lyne, Greater Manchester, England, 4 November, 1965 — RW
England: Schools

League Club	Source	Date Signed	Seasons Played	Apps	Subs	Gls
Oldham Ath	Bolton W (App)	08/83	83-84	4	1	1
Stockport Co	Tr	08/85	85-87	114	4	18
Scunthorpe U	Tr	08/88	88-89	59	3	8

HODKINSON David
Born: Lancaster, England, 18 January, 1945 — LW

League Club	Source	Date Signed	Seasons Played	Apps	Subs	Gls
Oldham Ath	App	02/63	61	2	-	0

HODOUTO Kwami
Born: Lome, Togo, 31 October, 1974 — FB

League Club	Source	Date Signed	Seasons Played	Apps	Subs	Gls
Huddersfield T	AJ Auxerre (FRA)	09/99	99	1	1	0

HODSON Lee James Stephen
Born: Borehamwood, Hertfordshire, England, 2 October, 1991 — RB
Northern Ireland: 15/U21-10/Youth

League Club	Source	Date Signed	Seasons Played	Apps	Subs	Gls
Watford	Sch	11/08	08-12	76	7	1
Brentford	L	11/12	12	7	6	0
MK Dons	Tr	07/13	13-14	35	2	2

HODSON Simeon Paul
Born: Lincoln, England, 5 March, 1966 — RB
England: Semi Pro-3

League Club	Source	Date Signed	Seasons Played	Apps	Subs	Gls
Notts Co	App	03/84	83-84	27	0	0
Charlton Ath	Tr	03/85	84	5	0	0
Lincoln C	Lincoln U	01/86	85-86	54	2	0
Newport Co	Tr	08/87	87	34	0	1
West Bromwich A	Tr	03/88	87-92	78	5	0
Doncaster Rov	Tr	09/92	92	15	0	0
Mansfield T	Kidderminster Hrs	02/93	92	17	0	0

HODSON Stuart William
Born: Peterborough, England, 5 November, 1950 — D/M

League Club	Source	Date Signed	Seasons Played	Apps	Subs	Gls
Peterborough U	Ely C	11/74	74-76	24	10	0

HOEFKENS Carl
Born: Lier, Belgium, 6 October, 1978 — RB
Belgium: 22/U21-16/Youth

League Club	Source	Date Signed	Seasons Played	Apps	Subs	Gls
Stoke C	Germ'l Beerschot (BEL)	07/05	05-06	86	3	5
West Bromwich A	Tr	08/07	07-08	48	4	0

HOEKMAN Daniel (Danny)
Born: Nijmegen, Netherlands, 21 September, 1964 — M

League Club	Source	Date Signed	Seasons Played	Apps	Subs	Gls
Manchester C	Den Haag (NED)	10/91	91	0	1	0

HOEKSTRA Peter Martin
Born: Assen, Netherlands, 4 April, 1973 — M
Netherlands: 5

League Club	Source	Date Signed	Seasons Played	Apps	Subs	Gls
Stoke C	Ajax (NED)	07/01	01-03	66	12	11

HOGAN Charles (Charlie)
Born: Bury, Greater Manchester, England, 23 April, 1926 — W
Died: Arnhem, Netherlands, 25 October, 1992

League Club	Source	Date Signed	Seasons Played	Apps	Subs	Gls
Bury	Spartan Ath	06/47	47	1	-	0
Accrington Stan	Tr	08/49	49-50	56	-	4
Southport	Tr	08/51	51	9	-	1
Rochdale	Tr	08/52	52	3	-	0

HOGAN David Michael (Dave)
Born: Harlow, Essex, England, 31 May, 1989 — G

League Club	Source	Date Signed	Seasons Played	Apps	Subs	Gls
Dagenham & Red	Jnr	07/07	08-11	0	2	0

HOGAN John Terence (Terry)
Born: Hartlepool, Cleveland, England, 3 June, 1933 — IF

League Club	Source	Date Signed	Seasons Played	Apps	Subs	Gls
Hartlepool U		08/57	57	9	-	1

HOGAN Liam Anthony
Born: Salford, England, 8 February, 1989 — CD

League Club	Source	Date Signed	Seasons Played	Apps	Subs	Gls
Fleetwood T	FC Halifax T	07/13	13-14	18	2	0

HOGAN Roy David
Born: Hartlepool, Cleveland, England, 24 September, 1960 — M

League Club	Source	Date Signed	Seasons Played	Apps	Subs	Gls
Hartlepool U	App	09/78	77-82	133	10	15
Hartlepool U	Crook T	12/83	83-86	138	3	17

HOGAN Scott Andrew
Born: Salford, England, 13 April, 1992 — W

League Club	Source	Date Signed	Seasons Played	Apps	Subs	Gls
Rochdale	Hyde FC	07/13	13	29	4	17
Brentford	Tr	07/14	14	0	1	0

HOGAN Thomas Eric (Eric)
Born: Cork, Republic of Ireland, 17 December, 1971 — M

League Club	Source	Date Signed	Seasons Played	Apps	Subs	Gls
Birmingham C	Cobh Ramblers (ROI)	08/91	91	0	1	0

HOGAN William James Joseph (Billy)
Born: Salford, England, 9 January, 1924 — RW
Died: Cornwall, England, 6 June, 2007

League Club	Source	Date Signed	Seasons Played	Apps	Subs	Gls
Manchester C		05/42	48	3	-	0
Carlisle U	Tr	09/49	49-55	190	-	25

HOGANSON Michael George
Born: Newcastle-upon-Tyne, England, 3 December, 1993 — LB

League Club	Source	Date Signed	Seasons Played	Apps	Subs	Gls
Derby Co	Newcastle U (Sch)	08/12	12	3	1	0

HOGARTH Gordon
Born: Sunderland, England, 18 November, 1936 — RH

League Club	Source	Date Signed	Seasons Played	Apps	Subs	Gls
Gateshead	Throckley Welfare	06/57	57-58	12	-	0

HOGG Adam
Born: Airdrie, Lanarkshire, Scotland, 26 April, 1934 — FB

League Club	Source	Date Signed	Seasons Played	Apps	Subs	Gls
Swindon T	Airdrieonians	06/56	56	1	-	0

HOGG Anthony Raymond (Ray)
Born: Lowick, Northumberland, England, 11 December, 1929 — RB
Died: Newcastle-upon-Tyne, England, 10 March, 2013

League Club	Source	Date Signed	Seasons Played	Apps	Subs	Gls
Aston Villa	Berwick Rgrs	03/55	54-56	21	-	0
Mansfield T	Tr	07/58	58-59	11	-	0
Peterborough U	Tr	08/60	60	2	-	0

HOGG Christopher Francis (Chris)
Born: Middlesbrough, England, 12 March, 1985 — RB
England: Youth

League Club	Source	Date Signed	Seasons Played	Apps	Subs	Gls
Ipswich T	Sch	08/02				
Boston U	L	10/03	03	10	0	0

HOGG Derek
Born: Stockton-on-Tees, Cleveland, England, 4 November, 1930 — LW

League Club	Source	Date Signed	Seasons Played	Apps	Subs	Gls
Died: Lincolnshire, England, 4 November, 2014						
England: FLge-1						
Leicester C	Chorley	10/52	52-57	161	-	26
West Bromwich A	Tr	04/58	58-60	81	-	11
Cardiff C	Tr	10/60	60-61	41	-	7
HOGG Frederick William (Fred)						
Born: Bishop Auckland, County Durham, England, 24 April, 1918						IF/WH
Luton T	West Auckland T	12/36	37	4	-	0
Mansfield T	Tr	04/38	46-47	45	-	8
Halifax T	Tr	10/47	47-49	49	-	3
HOGG Graeme James						
Born: Aberdeen, Scotland, 17 June, 1964						CD
Scotland: U21-4/Youth						
Manchester U	App	06/82	83-87	82	1	1
West Bromwich A	L	11/87	87	7	0	0
Portsmouth	Tr	08/88	88-90	97	3	2
Notts Co	Heart of Midlothian	01/95	94-97	66	0	0
Brentford	Tr	01/98	97	17	0	2
HOGG Graham Stuart						
Born: Neath, Wales, 15 January, 1922						RW
Died: Cardiff, Wales, 17 October, 1999						
Wales: Amateur						
Cardiff C	Cardiff Corinthians	06/48	48	1	-	0
HOGG John (Jack)						
Born: Blyth, Northumberland, England, 7 October, 1931						LW/CF
Died: Blyth, Northumberland, England, 31 March, 2001						
Sunderland	Newbiggin CW	12/49				
Portsmouth	Blyth Spartans	12/54				
Gateshead	Peterborough U	07/57	57-59	80	-	21
HOGG Jonathan Lee						
Born: Middlesbrough, England, 6 December, 1988						DM
Aston Villa	Sch	07/07				
Darlington	L	11/09	09	5	0	1
Portsmouth	L	01/11	10	19	0	0
Watford	Tr	08/11	11-12	71	7	0
Huddersfield T	Tr	07/13	13-14	57	3	0
HOGG Lewis James						
Born: Bristol, England, 13 September, 1982						M
England: Semi Pro-1						
Bristol Rov	YT	09/99	00-02	61	13	3
HOGG Steven Roy (Steve)						
Born: Bury, Greater Manchester, England, 1 October, 1985						M
Shrewsbury T	Manchester U (Sch)	07/05	05-06	7	6	0
HOGGAN David Matthew						
Born: Falkirk, Scotland, 10 August, 1961						M
Bolton W	App	08/79	79-82	83	10	11
HOGGART Dennis Joseph						
Born: Glasgow, Scotland, 2 January, 1939						W
Leeds U	Ferndale Thistle	02/57				
York C	Tr	08/60	60-63	45	-	11
Stockport Co	Tr	08/64	64-65	30	0	6
HOGGETH Gary Denis						
Born: South Shields, Tyne and Wear, England, 7 October, 1979						G
Doncaster Rov	YT	-	97	8	0	0
HOGH Jes						
Born: Aalborg, Denmark, 7 May, 1966						CD
Denmark: 57						
Chelsea	Fenerbahce (TKY)	07/99	99	6	3	0
HOILETT David Wayne (Junior)						
Born: Brampton, Ontario, Canada, 5 June, 1990						LW
Blackburn Rov	Sch	08/08	09-11	59	22	12
Queens Park Rgrs	Tr	07/12	12-14	47	36	5
HOLAH Eric Tansley						
Born: Hull, England, 3 August, 1937						CF
Hull C (Am)	Malet Lambert OB	06/60	60	1	-	1
Bradford C	Tr	08/61	61	4	-	2
HOLBROOK Ian Clifford						
Born: Knutsford, Cheshire, England, 24 November, 1955						G
Bolton W	Jnr	07/74				
Stockport Co	Tr	07/76	76	37	0	0
HOLBROOK Leigh William						
Born: Belper, Derbyshire, England, 6 August, 1979						CD
Mansfield T	YT	07/97	96	0	1	0
HOLBROOK Stephen (Steve)						
Born: Richmond, North Yorkshire, England, 16 September, 1952						RW/M

League Club	Source	Date Signed	Seasons Played	Apps	Subs	Gls
England: Schools						
Hull C	App	09/70	70-71	2	1	0
Darlington	Tr	06/72	72-76	104	12	12
HOLBUTT Barry Lewis						
Born: Birmingham, England, 11 February, 1943						CF
Aston Villa	Jnr	10/60				
Walsall	Nuneaton Bor	03/65	65	0	1	0
HOLCROFT Peter Ian						
Born: Liverpool, England, 3 January, 1976						M
Everton	YT	07/94				
Swindon T	Tr	11/96	96	2	1	0
Exeter C	L	08/97	97	3	3	0
HOLD John David						
Born: Southampton, England, 28 March, 1948						F
Bournemouth	App	11/64	65-70	80	5	24
Crewe Alex	L	01/69	68	0	2	0
Northampton T	Tr	08/71	71-72	42	2	11
HOLD Oscar						
Born: Royston, South Yorkshire, England, 19 October, 1918						IF
Died: Sunderland, England, 11 October, 2005						
Barnsley	Denaby U	08/37				
Aldershot	Tr	04/39	46	14	-	4
Norwich C	Tr	03/47	46-48	44	-	18
Notts Co	Tr	10/48	48	19	-	9
Everton	Chelmsford C	02/50	49-50	22	-	5
Queens Park Rgrs	Tr	02/52	51-52	5	-	1
HOLDEN Alan						
Born: Haslingden, Lancashire, England, 12 October, 1941						WH
Blackburn Rov	Jnr	01/62	63	1	-	0
Stockport Co	Tr	07/66	66	1	0	0
HOLDEN Albert Douglas (Doug)						
Born: Manchester, England, 28 September, 1930						RW
England: 5/FLge-1/Youth						
Bolton W	Manchester YMCA	01/50	51-62	419	-	40
Preston NE	Tr	11/62	62-64	90	-	13
HOLDEN Andrew Ian (Andy)						
Born: Flint, Wales, 14 September, 1962						CD
Wales: 1/U21-1						
Chester C	Rhyl	08/83	83-86	100	0	16
Wigan Ath	Tr	10/86	86-88	48	1	4
Oldham Ath	Tr	01/89	88-94	22	0	4
HOLDEN Darren						
Born: Krugersdorp, South Africa, 27 August, 1993						LB
Hartlepool U	Sch	07/12	10-14	45	12	0
HOLDEN Dean Thomas John						
Born: Swinton, Greater Manchester, England, 15 September, 1979						RB
England: Youth						
Bolton W	YT	12/97	99-00	7	6	1
Oldham Ath	Tr	10/01	01-04	98	10	10
Peterborough U	Tr	07/05	05-06	54	2	4
Shrewsbury T	Falkirk	07/09	09-10	48	2	0
Rotherham U	L	08/10	10	4	2	0
Chesterfield	Tr	02/11	10-11	26	5	3
Rochdale	Tr	11/11	11	20	1	0
Walsall	Tr	07/12	12-14	26	3	2
HOLDEN Euan						
Born: Aberdeen, Scotland, 2 February, 1988						LB/M
Bury	Stockport Co	02/13	12-13	3	0	0
HOLDEN James Stewart (Stewart)						
Born: Grange Moor, West Yorkshire, England, 21 April, 1942						FB/WH
Died: Royton, Greater Manchester, England, 29 March, 2004						
Huddersfield T	Jnr	04/59	60-64	28	-	2
Oldham Ath	Tr	07/65	65-66	39	3	5
Rochdale	Tr	01/67	66	21	0	0
HOLDEN Melville George (Mel)						
Born: Dundee, Scotland, 25 August, 1954						F
Died: Preston, Lancashire, England, 31 January, 1981						
Preston NE	App	09/72	72-74	69	3	22
Sunderland	Tr	05/75	75-77	66	7	23
Blackpool	Tr	07/78	78	2	1	0
HOLDEN Richard William (Rick)						
Born: Skipton, North Yorkshire, England, 9 September, 1964						W
Burnley	Leeds Carnegie College	03/86	85	0	1	0
Halifax T	Tr	09/86	86-87	66	1	12
Watford	Tr	03/88	87-88	42	0	8
Oldham Ath	Tr	08/89	89-91	125	4	19
Manchester C	Tr	07/92	92-93	49	1	3
Oldham Ath	Tr	10/93	93-94	46	14	9
Blackpool	Tr	09/95	95	19	3	2

HOLDEN Robert (Robbie)
Born: Sunderland, England, 28 October, 1965 — F

League Club	Source	Date Signed	Seasons Played	Apps	Subs	Gls
Scunthorpe U	Sunderland (App)	09/83	83	6	1	1

HOLDEN Simon John
Born: Littleborough, Greater Manchester, England, 9 March, 1968 — M

League Club	Source	Date Signed	Seasons Played	Apps	Subs	Gls
Rochdale	Jnr	07/85				
Rochdale	Wheatsheaf	01/87	86-87	35	14	4

HOLDEN Stephen Anthony (Steve)
Born: Luton, England, 4 September, 1972 — CD
England: Semi Pro-5/Schools

League Club	Source	Date Signed	Seasons Played	Apps	Subs	Gls
Leicester C	YT	03/91	91	1	0	0
Carlisle U	Tr	10/92	92-93	22	0	1

HOLDEN Stuart Alistair
Born: Aberdeen, Scotland, 1 August, 1985 — M
USA: 25

League Club	Source	Date Signed	Seasons Played	Apps	Subs	Gls
Bolton W	Houston Dynamo (USA)	01/10	09-12	27	3	2
Sheffield Wed	L	03/13	12	4	0	0

HOLDEN William (Bill)
Born: Bolton, Greater Manchester, England, 1 April, 1928 — CF
Died: Morecambe, Lancashire, England, 26 January, 2011
England: B-1

League Club	Source	Date Signed	Seasons Played	Apps	Subs	Gls
Burnley	Everton (Am)	11/49	50-55	187	-	75
Sunderland	Tr	12/55	55	19	-	5
Stockport Co	Tr	10/56	56-58	87	-	37
Bury	Tr	03/59	58-61	100	-	33
Halifax T	Tr	06/62	62	37	-	10

HOLDER Alan Maurice
Born: Oxford, England, 10 December, 1931 — IF
Died: Oxfordshire, England, June, 2013

League Club	Source	Date Signed	Seasons Played	Apps	Subs	Gls
Nottingham F	RAOC Chilwell	04/52	54	3	-	0
Lincoln C	Tr	07/55	55	1	-	0
Tranmere Rov	Tr	12/56	56	13	-	1

HOLDER Colin Walter
Born: Cheltenham, Gloucestershire, England, 6 January, 1944 — CF

League Club	Source	Date Signed	Seasons Played	Apps	Subs	Gls
Coventry C	App	05/61	60-61	9	-	4

HOLDER David James (Dave)
Born: Cheltenham, Gloucestershire, England, 15 December, 1943 — CH
Died: Cheltenham, Gloucestershire, England, 26 April, 2002

League Club	Source	Date Signed	Seasons Played	Apps	Subs	Gls
Notts Co	Cardiff C (Am)	10/62	63	8	-	0
Barrow	Tr	07/64	64	29	-	0

HOLDER Jorden Andrew
Born: Oxford, England, 22 October, 1982 — M

League Club	Source	Date Signed	Seasons Played	Apps	Subs	Gls
Oxford U	YT	-	00	0	2	0

HOLDER Philip (Phil)
Born: Kilburn, NW London, England, 19 January, 1952 — M
England: Youth

League Club	Source	Date Signed	Seasons Played	Apps	Subs	Gls
Tottenham H	App	02/69	71-73	9	4	1
Crystal Palace	Tr	02/75	74-77	93	2	5
Bournemouth	Memphis Rogues (USA)	03/79	78-79	58	0	4

HOLDER Stephen William (Steve)
Born: Nottingham, England, 21 April, 1952 — W

League Club	Source	Date Signed	Seasons Played	Apps	Subs	Gls
Notts Co	App	04/70	69	0	1	0

HOLDING Edwin John (Eddie)
Born: Wolverhampton, England, 15 October, 1930 — RB/CF
Died: Walsall, West Midlands, England, 9 February, 2014

League Club	Source	Date Signed	Seasons Played	Apps	Subs	Gls
Walsall	Wolverhampton W (Am)	01/49	50-51	26	-	3
Derby Co	Tr	07/52				
Walsall	Tr	08/53	53	13	-	3
Barrow	Tr	07/54	54	5	-	5
Northampton T	Tr	10/54				

HOLDING Robert Samuel (Rob)
Born: Stalybridge, Greater Manchester, England, 20 September, 1995 — CD

League Club	Source	Date Signed	Seasons Played	Apps	Subs	Gls
Bolton W	Sch	07/13				
Bury	L	03/15	14	0	1	0

HOLDSWORTH Andrew (Andy)
Born: Pontefract, West Yorkshire, England, 29 January, 1984 — M/RB

League Club	Source	Date Signed	Seasons Played	Apps	Subs	Gls
Huddersfield T	Sch	12/03	03-08	214	17	6
Oldham Ath	Tr	07/09	09	11	1	0
Morecambe	Tr	01/11	10	12	3	1

HOLDSWORTH David Gary
Born: Walthamstow, NE London, England, 8 November, 1968 — CD
England: U21-1/Youth

League Club	Source	Date Signed	Seasons Played	Apps	Subs	Gls
Watford	App	11/86	88-95	249	9	10
Sheffield U	Tr	10/96	96-98	93	0	4
Birmingham C	Tr	03/99	98-01	78	7	7
Walsall	L	01/02	01	9	0	1

HOLDSWORTH Dean Christopher
Born: Walthamstow, NE London, England, 8 November, 1968 — F
England: B-1

League Club	Source	Date Signed	Seasons Played	Apps	Subs	Gls
Watford	App	11/86	87-89	2	14	3
Carlisle U	L	02/88	87	4	0	1
Port Vale	L	03/88	87	6	0	2
Swansea C	L	08/88	88	4	1	1
Brentford	L	10/88	88	2	5	1
Brentford	Tr	09/89	89-91	106	4	53
Wimbledon	Tr	07/92	92-97	148	21	58
Bolton W	Tr	10/97	97-02	97	61	39
Coventry C	Tr	11/02	02	13	4	0
Rushden & D	Tr	03/03	02	4	3	2
Wimbledon	Tr	07/03	03	14	14	3
Derby Co	Havant & Waterlooville	08/05	05	0	3	0

HOLE Alan Vincent
Born: Swansea, Wales, 26 December, 1930 — CH
Died: Llanrhidian, Gower, Swansea, Wales, 15 April, 2014

League Club	Source	Date Signed	Seasons Played	Apps	Subs	Gls
Swansea C	RAF	07/53	53	21	-	0

HOLE Barrington Gerard (Barrie)
Born: Swansea, Wales, 16 September, 1942 — WH
Wales: 30/U23-5/Schools

League Club	Source	Date Signed	Seasons Played	Apps	Subs	Gls
Cardiff C	Jnr	09/59	59-65	208	0	16
Blackburn Rov	Tr	07/66	66-68	79	0	13
Aston Villa	Tr	09/68	68-69	47	0	6
Swansea C	Tr	07/70	70-71	78	0	3

HOLE Stuart Mark
Born: Oxford, England, 17 July, 1985 — CD

League Club	Source	Date Signed	Seasons Played	Apps	Subs	Gls
Wycombe W	Sch	-	03	0	1	0

HOLGATE Ashan Bayyan Sellasse
Born: Swindon, England, 9 November, 1986 — F

League Club	Source	Date Signed	Seasons Played	Apps	Subs	Gls
Swindon T	Sch	07/06	04-06	2	7	0
Macclesfield T	L	01/07	06	2	4	1

HOLGATE Mason Anthony
Born: Doncaster, South Yorkshire, England, 22 October, 1996 — M

League Club	Source	Date Signed	Seasons Played	Apps	Subs	Gls
Barnsley	Sch	09/14	14	18	2	1

HOLGERSSON Sven Markus (Markus)
Born: Landskrona, Sweden, 16 April, 1985 — RB
Sweden: 1

League Club	Source	Date Signed	Seasons Played	Apps	Subs	Gls
Wigan Ath	New York R Bulls (USA)	02/14	13	0	1	0

HOLLA Danny
Born: Almere, Netherlands, 31 December, 1987 — DM
Netherlands: Youth

League Club	Source	Date Signed	Seasons Played	Apps	Subs	Gls
Brighton & HA	ADO Den Haag (NED)	08/14	14	23	1	1

HOLLAND Christopher James (Chris)
Born: Clitheroe, Lancashire, England, 11 September, 1975 — DM
England: U21-10/Youth

League Club	Source	Date Signed	Seasons Played	Apps	Subs	Gls
Preston NE	YT	-	93	0	1	0
Newcastle U	Tr	01/94	93	2	1	0
Birmingham C	Tr	09/96	96-99	39	31	0
Huddersfield T	Tr	02/00	99-03	113	7	2
Boston U	Tr	03/04	03-06	74	11	0

HOLLAND David William
Born: Chorley, Lancashire, England, 6 March, 1935 — IF/WH
Died: Chorley, Lancashire, England, May, 2005

League Club	Source	Date Signed	Seasons Played	Apps	Subs	Gls
Stockport Co	Horwich RMI	06/59	59-60	25	-	4

HOLLAND Eric Reginald (Reg)
Born: Sutton-in-Ashfield, Nottinghamshire, England, 23 January, 1940 — FB
England: Youth/Schools

League Club	Source	Date Signed	Seasons Played	Apps	Subs	Gls
Manchester U	Jnr	05/57				
Wrexham	Tr	03/60	59-65	118	0	0
Chester C	Tr	03/66	65-66	5	1	0

HOLLAND Kenneth (Ken)
Born: Doncaster, South Yorkshire, England, 18 April, 1922 — IF
Died: Basford, Nottinghamshire, England, December, 1972

League Club	Source	Date Signed	Seasons Played	Apps	Subs	Gls
Bury	Wolverhampton W (Am)	09/44				
Bournemouth	Tr	09/48	48	3	-	0

HOLLAND Matthew Rhys (Matt)
Born: Bury, Greater Manchester, England, 11 April, 1974 — M
Republic of Ireland: 49/B-1

League Club	Source	Date Signed	Seasons Played	Apps	Subs	Gls
West Ham U	YT	07/92				
Bournemouth	Tr	01/95	94-96	97	7	18
Ipswich T	Tr	07/97	97-02	259	0	38
Charlton Ath	Tr	06/03	03-08	162	29	13

HOLLAND Patrick George (Pat)
Born: Poplar, E London, England, 13 September, 1950 — W/M

League Club	Source	Date Signed	Seasons Played	Apps	Subs	Gls
West Ham U	App	09/68	68-80	227	18	23
Bournemouth	L	03/71	70	10	0	0

HOLLAND Paul
Born: Lincoln, England, 8 July, 1973 — M
England: U21-4/Youth/Schools

League Club	Source	Date Signed	Seasons Played	Apps	Subs	Gls
Mansfield T	Jnr	07/91	90-94	149	0	25
Sheffield U	Tr	06/95	95	11	7	1
Chesterfield	Tr	01/96	95-99	108	6	11
Bristol C	Tr	09/99	99-00	27	5	1

HOLLAND Robert James
Born: Willesden, NW London, England, 18 August, 1965 — LB

League Club	Source	Date Signed	Seasons Played	Apps	Subs	Gls
Crewe Alex	Harrow Bor	09/85	85	7	0	0

HOLLAND Simon Luke David
Born: Sunderland, England, 26 March, 1973 — F

League Club	Source	Date Signed	Seasons Played	Apps	Subs	Gls
Doncaster Rov	YT	01/91	90	1	0	0

HOLLANDS Daniel Timothy (Danny)
Born: Ashford, Surrey, England, 6 November, 1985 — M

League Club	Source	Date Signed	Seasons Played	Apps	Subs	Gls
Chelsea	Sch	11/03				
Torquay U	L	03/06	05	10	0	1
Bournemouth	Tr	07/06	06-10	158	35	24
Charlton Ath	Tr	07/11	11-12	54	3	7
Swindon T	L	11/12	12	8	2	2
Gillingham	L	08/13	13	16	1	1
Portsmouth	Tr	03/14	13-14	45	6	7

HOLLETT Ivan Ronald
Born: Pinxton, Derbyshire, England, 22 April, 1940 — CF

League Club	Source	Date Signed	Seasons Played	Apps	Subs	Gls
Mansfield T	Sutton T	08/58	58-64	98	-	40
Chesterfield	Tr	12/64	64-68	157	0	62
Crewe Alex	Tr	11/68	68-70	55	3	19
Cambridge U	Tr	11/70	70-71	37	1	13
Hereford U	Tr	01/72	72	11	0	2

HOLLEY Thomas (Tom)
Born: Sunderland, England, 15 November, 1913 — CH
Died: Leeds, England, 17 October, 1992

League Club	Source	Date Signed	Seasons Played	Apps	Subs	Gls
Barnsley	Wolverhampton W (Am)	09/33	33-35	72	-	4
Leeds U	Tr	07/36	36-48	162	-	1

HOLLIDAY Edwin (Eddie)
Born: Barnsley, South Yorkshire, England, 7 June, 1939 — LW
England: 3/FLge-1/U23-5

League Club	Source	Date Signed	Seasons Played	Apps	Subs	Gls
Middlesbrough	Jnr	08/56	57-61	134	-	18
Sheffield Wed	Tr	03/62	61-63	55	-	12
Middlesbrough	Tr	06/65	65	23	0	4
Workington	Hereford U	02/68	67-68	56	0	4
Peterborough U	Tr	07/69	69	12	4	1

HOLLIDAY John Richard
Born: Penrith, Cumbria, England, 13 March, 1970 — CD

League Club	Source	Date Signed	Seasons Played	Apps	Subs	Gls
Carlisle U	Newcastle Univ	09/89	90-92	19	0	0

HOLLIDAY Kenneth Joseph (Ken)
Born: Darwen, Lancashire, England, 19 August, 1925 — D
Died: Nelson, Lancashire, England, 1 February, 1999

League Club	Source	Date Signed	Seasons Played	Apps	Subs	Gls
Blackburn Rov	Darwen Jnrs	10/46	47-51	29	-	0
Accrington Stan	Tr	07/52	52-54	96	-	5
Barrow	Tr	09/55	55	5	-	0

HOLLIFIELD Michael (Mike)
Born: Middlesbrough, England, 2 May, 1961 — LB

League Club	Source	Date Signed	Seasons Played	Apps	Subs	Gls
Wolverhampton W	App	04/79	80-81	21	0	0
Hull C	Tr	08/83	83-84	45	0	1
Tranmere Rov	Tr	07/85	85	0	1	0

HOLLIGAN Gavin Victor
Born: Lambeth, S London, England, 13 June, 1980 — F

League Club	Source	Date Signed	Seasons Played	Apps	Subs	Gls
West Ham U	Kingstonian	11/98	98	0	1	0
Leyton Orient	L	09/99	99	1	0	0
Exeter C	L	10/00	00	3	0	0
Wycombe W	Tr	08/01	01-03	20	23	8

HOLLINS David Michael (Dave)
Born: Bangor, Gwynedd, Wales, 4 February, 1938 — G
Wales: 11/U23-2

League Club	Source	Date Signed	Seasons Played	Apps	Subs	Gls
Brighton & HA	Merrow	11/55	57-60	66	-	0
Newcastle U	Tr	03/61	60-66	112	0	0
Mansfield T	Tr	02/67	66-69	111	0	0
Nottingham F	L	03/70	69	9	0	0
Aldershot	Tr	07/70	70	16	0	0

HOLLINS John William
Born: Guildford, Surrey, England, 16 July, 1946 — M/D
England: 1/B-5/FLge-3/U23-12/Youth

League Club	Source	Date Signed	Seasons Played	Apps	Subs	Gls
Chelsea	App	07/63	63-74	436	0	47
Queens Park Rgrs	Tr	06/75	75-78	148	3	6
Arsenal	Tr	07/79	79-82	123	4	9
Chelsea	Tr	06/83	83	29	0	1

HOLLINSHEAD Shaun
Born: Sandbach, Cheshire, England, 21 February, 1961 — M

League Club	Source	Date Signed	Seasons Played	Apps	Subs	Gls
Crewe Alex	App	-	77	2	3	0

HOLLIS Andrew
Born: Huntingdon, Cambridgeshire, England, 16 September, 1963 — F

League Club	Source	Date Signed	Seasons Played	Apps	Subs	Gls
Cambridge U	Ramsey T	04/87	86-87	3	1	0

HOLLIS Harold (Harry)
Born: Deeside, Flintshire, Wales, 12 December, 1913 — FB
Died: Shotton, Flintshire, Wales, 18 August, 1982

League Club	Source	Date Signed	Seasons Played	Apps	Subs	Gls
Chester C		09/40				
Wrexham	Connah's Quay	08/46	46	1	-	0

HOLLIS Haydn Joseph
Born: Selston, Nottinghamshire, England, 14 October, 1992 — CD

League Club	Source	Date Signed	Seasons Played	Apps	Subs	Gls
Notts Co	Sch	07/11	11-14	56	2	4

HOLLIS Jermain Phydell
Born: Nottingham, England, 7 October, 1986 — RW
Jamaica: Youth

League Club	Source	Date Signed	Seasons Played	Apps	Subs	Gls
Kidderminster Hrs	Eastwood T	11/04	04	0	1	0

HOLLIS Kenneth Michael (Mick)
Born: Loughborough, Leicestershire, England, 14 November, 1949 — F/W

League Club	Source	Date Signed	Seasons Played	Apps	Subs	Gls
Leicester C	App	11/66				
Barrow	Tr	07/69	69-71	88	3	13
Chester C	Tr	07/72	72	34	3	8
Stockport Co	Tr	07/73	73-75	106	6	33
Reading	Tr	03/76	75-76	18	7	6

HOLLIS Roy Walter
Born: Great Yarmouth, Norfolk, England, 24 December, 1925 — CF
Died: Great Yarmouth, Norfolk, England, 12 November, 1998

League Club	Source	Date Signed	Seasons Played	Apps	Subs	Gls
Norwich C	Yarmouth T	05/47	47-51	96	-	52
Tottenham H	Tr	12/52	52	3	-	1
Southend U	Tr	02/54	53-59	240	-	120

HOLLIS Stephen John (Steve)
Born: Liverpool, England, 22 August, 1972 — FB

League Club	Source	Date Signed	Seasons Played	Apps	Subs	Gls
Liverpool	YT	05/90				
Wigan Ath	Knowsley U	08/93	93	0	1	0

HOLLOW Michael John (Mike)
Born: Lower Nazeing, Hertfordshire, England, 5 September, 1943 — FB
Died: Hoddesdon, Hertfordshire, England, 2 March, 2003

League Club	Source	Date Signed	Seasons Played	Apps	Subs	Gls
Leyton Orient	Bishops Stortford	08/62	63-64	34	-	0
Peterborough U	Tr	07/65	65	14	0	1

HOLLOWAY Aaron Joshua Amadi
Born: Cardiff, Wales, 21 February, 1993 — F/W
Wales: Youth

League Club	Source	Date Signed	Seasons Played	Apps	Subs	Gls
Bristol C	Sch	07/11				
Newport Co	Tr	02/14	13	0	4	0
Wycombe W	Tr	08/14	14	12	17	3

HOLLOWAY Christopher David (Chris)
Born: Swansea, Wales, 5 February, 1980 — M
Wales: U21-2

League Club	Source	Date Signed	Seasons Played	Apps	Subs	Gls
Exeter C	YT	07/98	97-00	51	17	2

HOLLOWAY Darren
Born: Crook, County Durham, England, 3 October, 1977 — RB
England: U21-1

League Club	Source	Date Signed	Seasons Played	Apps	Subs	Gls
Sunderland	YT	10/95	97-00	46	12	0
Carlisle U	L	08/97	97	5	0	0
Bolton W	L	12/99	99	3	1	0
Wimbledon	Tr	10/00	00-03	84	8	0
Scunthorpe U	L	02/04	03	5	0	1
Bradford C	Tr	08/04	04-05	54	3	1
Darlington	Tr	08/06	06	14	7	1

HOLLOWAY Ian Scott
Born: Kingswood, Avon, England, 12 March, 1963 — RW

League Club	Source	Date Signed	Seasons Played	Apps	Subs	Gls
Bristol Rov	App	03/81	80-84	104	7	14
Wimbledon	Tr	07/85	85	19	0	2
Brentford	L	03/86	85	13	0	2
Brentford	Tr	07/86	86-87	14	3	0
Torquay U	L	01/87	86	5	0	0
Bristol Rov	Tr	08/87	87-90	179	0	26
Queens Park Rgrs	Tr	08/91	91-95	130	17	4
Bristol Rov	Tr	07/96	96-98	96	11	1

HOLLOWBREAD John Frederick
Born: Enfield, N London, England, 2 January, 1934 — G
Died: Torrevieja, Spain, 7 December, 2007

League Club	Source	Date Signed	Seasons Played	Apps	Subs	Gls
Tottenham H	Enfield	01/52	58-63	67	-	0
Southampton	Tr	05/64	64-65	36	0	0

HOLLUND Martin
Born: Stord, Norway, 11 August, 1974 — G
Norway: U21

League Club	Source	Date Signed	Seasons Played	Apps	Subs	Gls
Hartlepool U	SK Brann Bergen (NOR)	11/97	97-01	117	0	0

HOLLYMAN Kenneth Charles (Ken)
Born: Cardiff, Wales, 18 November, 1922 — RH/FB
Died: Cardiff, Wales, 14 May, 2009
Wales: WLge-1

League Club	Source	Date Signed	Seasons Played	Apps	Subs	Gls
Cardiff C	Cardiff Nomads	04/42	46-53	189	-	8
Newport Co	Tr	11/53	53-59	229	-	4

HOLLYWOOD Denis Fallan
Born: Govan, Glasgow, Scotland, 3 November, 1944 — LB
Scotland: U23-1

League Club	Source	Date Signed	Seasons Played	Apps	Subs	Gls
Southampton	App	12/61	62-71	234	0	4

HOLMAN Brett Trevor
Born: Sydney, Australia, 27 March, 1984 — W
Australia: 63/U23-16/Youth

League Club	Source	Date Signed	Seasons Played	Apps	Subs	Gls
Aston Villa	AZ Alkmaar (NED)	07/12	12	16	11	1

HOLMAN Daniel George (Dan)
Born: Northampton, England, 5 June, 1990 — F

League Club	Source	Date Signed	Seasons Played	Apps	Subs	Gls
Colchester U	Braintree T	07/14	14	0	4	0

HOLMAN Harold Western (Harry)
Born: Exeter, England, 25 September, 1920 — CF
Died: Exeter, England, 13 July, 1977

League Club	Source	Date Signed	Seasons Played	Apps	Subs	Gls
Exeter C	Budleigh Salterton	12/46	46	4	-	2

HOLMAN Harold William (Harry)
Born: Exeter, England, 16 November, 1957 — F
England: Schools

League Club	Source	Date Signed	Seasons Played	Apps	Subs	Gls
Exeter C	Chelsea (App)	07/76	76-78	47	5	9
Peterborough U	Tr	12/78	78	9	0	1

HOLME Philip Charles (Phil)
Born: Briton Ferry, Neath Port Talbot, Wales, 21 June, 1947 — F

League Club	Source	Date Signed	Seasons Played	Apps	Subs	Gls
Swansea C	Bridgend T	03/71	70-71	19	4	5
Hull C	Tr	07/72	72-73	29	9	11

HOLMES Albert Colin (Colin)
Born: Winchester, Hampshire, England, 28 March, 1939 — CH
Died: Southampton, England, 3 December, 2009
England: Youth

League Club	Source	Date Signed	Seasons Played	Apps	Subs	Gls
Southampton	Jnr	02/57	59	1	-	0

HOLMES Albert Valentine
Born: Ecclesfield, South Yorkshire, England, 14 February, 1942 — RB

League Club	Source	Date Signed	Seasons Played	Apps	Subs	Gls
Chesterfield	East Midland Gas	06/61	61-75	468	3	10

HOLMES Andrew John (Andy)
Born: Stoke-on-Trent, England, 7 January, 1969 — CD

League Club	Source	Date Signed	Seasons Played	Apps	Subs	Gls
Stoke C	App	01/87	87-89	6	2	0
Doncaster Rov	Tr	07/90	90	10	1	0

HOLMES Barry
Born: Bradford, England, 4 October, 1942 — W

League Club	Source	Date Signed	Seasons Played	Apps	Subs	Gls
Halifax T	Ossett A	09/66	66-72	82	8	8

HOLMES Bert Harold Frank
Born: Norwich, England, 27 September, 1924 — CH
Died: Norwich, England, November, 2003

League Club	Source	Date Signed	Seasons Played	Apps	Subs	Gls
Norwich C	Gothic FC	08/47	48-54	58	-	1

HOLMES Daniel (Danny)
Born: Birkenhead, Wirral, England, 6 January, 1989 — RB

League Club	Source	Date Signed	Seasons Played	Apps	Subs	Gls
Tranmere Rov	Sch	07/07	08	1	0	0
Tranmere Rov	The New Saints	07/11	11-14	126	7	4

HOLMES Daniel Gavin Charles (Danny)
Born: Clophill, Bedfordshire, England, 13 June, 1972 — M

League Club	Source	Date Signed	Seasons Played	Apps	Subs	Gls
Middlesbrough	YT	01/90				
Bournemouth	Tr	07/91	92	0	1	0

HOLMES David James
Born: Derby, England, 22 November, 1971 — F

League Club	Source	Date Signed	Seasons Played	Apps	Subs	Gls
Scarborough	YT	07/91	89-91	4	7	1

HOLMES Derek
Born: Lanark, Scotland, 18 October, 1978 — F

League Club	Source	Date Signed	Seasons Played	Apps	Subs	Gls
Bournemouth	Ross Co	09/01	01-04	63	52	16
Carlisle U	Tr	02/05	05-06	38	38	10
Rotherham U	Tr	07/07	07	33	4	11

HOLMES Duane Octavius
Born: Columbus, Ohio, USA, 6 November, 1994 — RM

League Club	Source	Date Signed	Seasons Played	Apps	Subs	Gls
Huddersfield T	Sch	07/13	13	2	14	0
Yeovil T	L	02/14	13	5	0	0
Bury	L	08/14	14	0	6	0

HOLMES Ian David
Born: Ellesmere Port, Cheshire, England, 27 June, 1985 — F

League Club	Source	Date Signed	Seasons Played	Apps	Subs	Gls
Mansfield T	Matlock T	08/07	07	4	12	1

HOLMES Ian Michael
Born: Wombwell, South Yorkshire, England, 8 December, 1950 — M

League Club	Source	Date Signed	Seasons Played	Apps	Subs	Gls
Sheffield U	Jnr	01/68	71-72	4	2	0
York C	Tr	07/73	73-77	152	7	30
Huddersfield T	Tr	10/77	77-79	65	8	21

HOLMES James Paul (Jimmy)
Born: Dublin, Republic of Ireland, 11 November, 1953 — LB
Republic of Ireland: 30

League Club	Source	Date Signed	Seasons Played	Apps	Subs	Gls
Coventry C	App	11/70	71-76	122	6	6
Tottenham H	Tr	03/77	76-78	81	0	2
Leicester C	Vancouver W'caps (CAN)	10/82	82	2	0	0
Brentford	Tr	02/83	82	4	0	0
Torquay U	Tr	03/83	82-83	25	0	3
Peterborough U	Tr	11/83	83-85	48	1	7

HOLMES Joseph
Born: Clay Cross, Derbyshire, England, 10 February, 1926 — WH

League Club	Source	Date Signed	Seasons Played	Apps	Subs	Gls
Chesterfield	Parkhouse Colliery	09/46	47-51	29	-	3

HOLMES Kyle Jonathon
Born: Abergavenny, Monmouthshire, Wales, 25 September, 1959 — M

League Club	Source	Date Signed	Seasons Played	Apps	Subs	Gls
Hereford U	App	10/77	77-79	25	3	3

HOLMES Lee Daniel
Born: Mansfield, Nottinghamshire, England, 2 April, 1987 — W
England: Youth

League Club	Source	Date Signed	Seasons Played	Apps	Subs	Gls
Derby Co	Sch	05/04	02-06	26	20	2
Swindon T	L	12/04	04	14	1	1
Bradford C	L	08/06	06	16	0	0
Walsall	L	01/08	07	19	0	4
Southampton	Tr	06/08	08-11	13	16	1
Oxford U	L	02/12	11	5	2	2
Swindon T	L	03/12	11	7	3	1
Preston NE	Tr	07/12	12-13	40	20	6
Portsmouth	L	11/14	14	3	2	0
Exeter C	L	03/15	14	6	2	0

HOLMES Lee John
Born: Aveley, Essex, England, 28 September, 1955 — F

League Club	Source	Date Signed	Seasons Played	Apps	Subs	Gls
Brentford	Haringey Bor	06/79	79	26	2	6

HOLMES Matthew Jason (Matt)
Born: Luton, England, 1 August, 1969 — LM

League Club	Source	Date Signed	Seasons Played	Apps	Subs	Gls
Bournemouth	YT	08/88	88-91	105	9	8
Cardiff C	L	03/89	88	0	1	0
West Ham U	Tr	08/92	92-94	63	13	4
Blackburn Rov	Tr	08/95	95	8	1	1
Charlton Ath	Tr	07/97	97	10	6	1

HOLMES Michael Arthur (Micky)
Born: Blackpool, Lancashire, England, 9 September, 1965 — M

League Club	Source	Date Signed	Seasons Played	Apps	Subs	Gls
Bradford C	Yeadon Celtic	07/84	84	0	5	0
Wolverhampton W	Burnley (NC)	11/85	85-87	74	9	13
Huddersfield T	Tr	07/88	88	3	4	0
Cambridge U	Tr	02/89	88	7	4	0
Rochdale	Tr	07/89	89-90	47	7	7
Torquay U	Tr	12/90	90-91	34	6	3
Carlisle U	Tr	02/92	91-92	33	1	4
Northampton T	Tr	03/93	92	6	0	0

HOLMES Nicholas Charles (Nick)
Born: Southampton, England, 11 November, 1954 — M/LB

League Club	Source	Date Signed	Seasons Played	Apps	Subs	Gls
Southampton	App	11/72	73-86	437	7	56

HOLMES Paul
Born: Stocksbridge, South Yorkshire, England, 18 February, 1968 — RB

League Club	Source	Date Signed	Seasons Played	Apps	Subs	Gls
Doncaster Rov	App	02/86	85-87	42	5	1
Torquay U	Tr	08/88	88-91	127	12	4
Birmingham C	Tr	06/92	92	12	0	0
Everton	Tr	03/93	92-95	21	0	0
West Bromwich A	Tr	01/96	95-98	102	1	1
Torquay U	Tr	11/99	99-02	82	5	2

HOLMES Peter James
Born: Bishop Auckland, County Durham, England, 18 November, 1980 — M
England: Youth/Schools

League Club	Source	Date Signed	Seasons Played	Apps	Subs	Gls
Sheffield Wed	YT	12/97				
Luton T	Tr	08/00	00-06	67	38	11
Chesterfield	L	01/07	06	10	0	1
Lincoln C	L	03/07	06	5	0	0
Rotherham U	Tr	07/07	07-08	21	6	2

HOLMES Richard
Born: Leicestershire, England, 7 November, 1980 — RB

League Club	Source	Date Signed	Seasons Played	Apps	Subs	Gls
Notts Co	YT	03/99	98-02	47	12	0

HOLMES Ricky Lee
Born: Southend-on-Sea, England, 19 June, 1987 LW
England: Semi Pro-1

League Club	Source	Date Signed	Seasons Played	Apps	Subs	Gls
Barnet	Chelmsford C	06/10	10-12	72	19	15
Portsmouth	Tr	06/13	13-14	40	13	2
Northampton T	Tr	01/15	14	21	0	5

HOLMES Roger William
Born: Scunthorpe, North Lincolnshire, England, 9 September, 1942 M

League Club	Source	Date Signed	Seasons Played	Apps	Subs	Gls
Lincoln C	Jnr	09/59	59-71	276	2	36

HOLMES Shaun Paul
Born: Derry, Northern Ireland, 27 December, 1980 LB
Northern Ireland: 1/U21-13/Youth/Schools

League Club	Source	Date Signed	Seasons Played	Apps	Subs	Gls
Manchester C	YT	01/98				
Wrexham	Tr	08/01	01-03	55	28	2

HOLMES Stanley (Stan)
Born: Easington, County Durham, England, 27 November, 1920 RB
Died: Hartlepool, Cleveland, England, November, 1994

League Club	Source	Date Signed	Seasons Played	Apps	Subs	Gls
Hartlepool U	Deaf Hill	07/47	49	1	-	0

HOLMES Steven Peter (Steve)
Born: Middlesbrough, England, 13 January, 1971 CD

League Club	Source	Date Signed	Seasons Played	Apps	Subs	Gls
Lincoln C	YT	07/89				
Preston NE	Guisborough T	03/94	94-95	13	0	1
Hartlepool U	L	03/95	94	5	0	2
Lincoln C	L	10/95	95	12	0	1
Lincoln C	Tr	03/96	95-01	185	4	32

HOLMES Thomas (Tommy)
Born: Hemsworth, West Yorkshire, England, 14 December, 1934 IF

League Club	Source	Date Signed	Seasons Played	Apps	Subs	Gls
Barnsley	Hemsworth YC	03/53	54-58	35	-	7
Halifax T	Tr	07/59	59-60	50	-	16
Chesterfield	Tr	07/61	61	20	-	3

HOLMES William (Bill)
Born: Leeds, England, 29 October, 1926 CF
England: Amateur-4

League Club	Source	Date Signed	Seasons Played	Apps	Subs	Gls
Doncaster Rov (Am)	Wolverhampton W (Am)	10/50	50	2	-	0
Blackburn Rov (Am)	Morecambe	01/52	51-52	21	-	16
Bradford C	Morecambe	09/53	53	22	-	5
Southport	Tr	07/54	54-55	56	-	21

HOLMES William Gerald (Billy)
Born: Balham, S London, England, 4 February, 1951 F
Died: Daventry, Northamptonshire, England, March, 1988

League Club	Source	Date Signed	Seasons Played	Apps	Subs	Gls
Millwall	Woking	07/70	70	0	1	0
Luton T	Tr	07/73	73	0	1	0
Wimbledon	Barnet	07/75	77	15	0	5
Hereford U	Tr	11/77	77-78	21	10	5
Brentford	Tr	08/79	79	8	7	2

HOLMES-DENNIS Tareiq Marcus
Born: Bromley, SE London, England, 31 October, 1995 LB/M
England: Youth

League Club	Source	Date Signed	Seasons Played	Apps	Subs	Gls
Charlton Ath	Sch	10/12				
Oxford U	L	10/14	14	14	0	0
Plymouth Arg	L	02/15	14	17	0	1

HOLNESS Dean Thomas
Born: Lewisham, SE London, England, 25 July, 1976 M

League Club	Source	Date Signed	Seasons Played	Apps	Subs	Gls
Southend U	Dulwich Hamlet	08/01	01	1	1	0

HOLNESS Marcus Lewis
Born: Swinton, Greater Manchester, England, 8 December, 1988 CD

League Club	Source	Date Signed	Seasons Played	Apps	Subs	Gls
Oldham Ath	Sch	07/07				
Rochdale	Tr	10/07	07-11	93	15	4
Burton A	Tr	07/12	12-13	32	7	1
Tranmere Rov	Tr	07/14	14	15	2	0

HOLROYD Christopher (Chris)
Born: Macclesfield, Cheshire, England, 24 October, 1986 F
England: Semi Pro-2

League Club	Source	Date Signed	Seasons Played	Apps	Subs	Gls
Chester C	Crewe Alex (Sch)	04/06	06-07	21	26	4
Brighton & HA	Cambridge U	01/10	09-10	5	11	0
Stevenage	L	08/10	10	12	0	6
Bury	L	03/11	10	3	1	1
Rotherham U	Tr	07/11	11	5	10	1
Preston NE	Tr	01/12	11	14	6	1
Morecambe	Tr	01/13	12	8	8	1

HOLSGROVE John William
Born: Southwark, S London, England, 27 September, 1945 CD
England: Youth

League Club	Source	Date Signed	Seasons Played	Apps	Subs	Gls
Crystal Palace	Tottenham H (Am)	02/64	64	18	-	2
Wolverhampton W	Tr	05/65	65-70	178	2	7
Sheffield Wed	Tr	06/71	71-74	103	1	5
Stockport Co	Tr	08/75	75	9	0	0

HOLSGROVE Lee
Born: Wendover, Buckinghamshire, England, 13 December, 1979 M

League Club	Source	Date Signed	Seasons Played	Apps	Subs	Gls
Millwall	Jnr	07/96				
Wycombe W	Tr	03/98	98-99	5	5	0

HOLSGROVE Paul
Born: Wellington, Telford & Wrekin, England, 26 August, 1969 M

League Club	Source	Date Signed	Seasons Played	Apps	Subs	Gls
Aldershot	YT	02/87	87-88	0	3	0
Luton T	Wokingham T	01/91	90-91	1	1	0
Millwall	Heracles Almelo (NED)	08/92	92	3	8	0
Reading	Tr	08/94	94-97	63	7	6
Grimsby T	L	09/97	97	3	7	0
Crewe Alex	Tr	11/97	97	7	1	1
Stoke C	Tr	01/98	97	11	1	1
Brighton & HA	Tr	07/98				
Darlington	Hibernian	03/00	99	1	2	0

HOLSTER Marco
Born: Weesp, Netherlands, 4 December, 1971 W

League Club	Source	Date Signed	Seasons Played	Apps	Subs	Gls
Ipswich T	Heracles Almelo (NED)	07/98	98	1	9	0

HOLT Andrew (Andy)
Born: Stockport, Greater Manchester, England, 21 May, 1978 LB/M

League Club	Source	Date Signed	Seasons Played	Apps	Subs	Gls
Oldham Ath	YT	07/96	96-00	104	20	10
Hull C	Tr	03/01	00-03	45	26	3
Barnsley	L	08/02	02	4	3	0
Shrewsbury T	L	03/03	02	9	0	0
Wrexham	Tr	08/04	04-05	80	1	9
Northampton T	Tr	07/06	06-11	158	33	15

HOLT David
Born: Padiham, Lancashire, England, 26 February, 1952 D
Died: Wellington, New Zealand, 15 June, 2003

League Club	Source	Date Signed	Seasons Played	Apps	Subs	Gls
Bury	App	10/69	69-74	174	5	9
Oldham Ath	Tr	12/74	74-79	141	1	1
Burnley	Tr	07/80	80-82	84	0	1

HOLT David Arthur
Born: Manchester, England, 18 November, 1984 F

League Club	Source	Date Signed	Seasons Played	Apps	Subs	Gls
Stockport Co	Sch	10/02	01	0	1	0

HOLT David Ephraim
Born: Sunniside, Tyne and Wear, England, 7 January, 1945 CD

League Club	Source	Date Signed	Seasons Played	Apps	Subs	Gls
Blackburn Rov	Jnr	04/63	65-66	10	0	0

HOLT Gary James
Born: Irvine, Ayrshire, Scotland, 9 March, 1973 M/RB
Scotland: 10

League Club	Source	Date Signed	Seasons Played	Apps	Subs	Gls
Stoke C	Glasgow Celtic	10/94				
Norwich C	Kilmarnock	03/01	00-04	161	7	3
Nottingham F	Tr	07/05	05-06	53	12	1
Wycombe W	Tr	07/07	07-08	75	1	3

HOLT George
Born: Halifax, West Yorkshire, England, 28 February, 1927 IF

League Club	Source	Date Signed	Seasons Played	Apps	Subs	Gls
Halifax T		07/47	47-53	57	-	12

HOLT Grant
Born: Carlisle, Cumbria, England, 12 April, 1981 F

League Club	Source	Date Signed	Seasons Played	Apps	Subs	Gls
Halifax T	Workington	09/99	99-00	0	6	0
Sheffield Wed	Barrow	03/03	02-03	12	12	3
Rochdale	Tr	01/04	03-05	75	0	35
Nottingham F	Tr	01/06	05-07	74	22	21
Blackpool	L	03/08	07	0	4	0
Shrewsbury T	Tr	07/08	08	43	0	20
Norwich C	Tr	07/09	09-12	135	19	68
Wigan Ath	Tr	07/13	13	9	7	2
Aston Villa	L	01/14	13	3	7	1
Huddersfield T	L	09/14	14	14	1	2

HOLT Jason Derek
Born: Musselburgh, East Lothian, Scotland, 19 February, 1993 M
Scotland: U21-7/Youth

League Club	Source	Date Signed	Seasons Played	Apps	Subs	Gls
Sheffield U (L)	Heart of Midlothian	01/15	14	11	5	5

HOLT Jordan Rhys
Born: York, England, 4 May, 1994 CD

League Club	Source	Date Signed	Seasons Played	Apps	Subs	Gls
Notts Co	St Mirren	08/13	13	2	0	0

HOLT Michael Andrew
Born: Barnoldswick, Lancashire, England, 28 July, 1977 F

League Club	Source	Date Signed	Seasons Played	Apps	Subs	Gls
Blackburn Rov	YT	07/95				
Preston NE	Tr	08/96	96-98	12	24	5
Macclesfield T	L	09/98	98	3	1	1
Rochdale	Tr	11/98	98-99	25	13	7

HOLT Raymond (Ray)
Born: Thorne, South Yorkshire, England, 29 October, 1939 CH

League Club	Source	Date Signed	Seasons Played	Apps	Subs	Gls
Huddersfield T	Moor Ends Ath	08/58	61-63	16	-	0

League Club	Source	Date Signed	Seasons Played	Apps	Subs	Gls
Oldham Ath	Tr	07/65	65	14	1	0
Halifax T	Tr	07/66	66-67	86	0	0
Scunthorpe U	Tr	07/68	68-69	50	0	0
HOLT William Kenneth (Billy)						
Born: Boldon, Tyne and Wear, England, 31 March, 1926						CH
Died: Blackburn, Greater Manchester, England, 23 March, 2013						
Blackburn Rov	Boldon CW	01/49	48-52	78	-	0
Barrow	Weymouth	06/54	54-56	74	-	0
HOLTBY Lewis Harry						
Born: Erkelenz, Germany, 18 September, 1990						M
Germany: 3/U21-24/Youth						
Tottenham H	Schalke 04 (GER)	01/13	12-14	10	15	1
Fulham	L	01/14	13	11	2	1
HOLTHAM Dean Mark						
Born: Pontypridd, Rhondda Cynon Taff, Wales, 30 September, 1963						LB/M
Cardiff C	App	09/81				
Swansea C	Tr	08/82	83	6	0	0
Newport Co	Ebbw Vale	09/87	87	4	2	0
HOLTON Clifford Charles (Cliff)						
Born: Oxford, England, 29 April, 1929						F
Died: Almeria, Spain, 30 May, 1996						
Arsenal	Oxford C	11/47	50-58	198	-	83
Watford	Tr	10/58	58-61	120	-	84
Northampton T	Tr	09/61	61-62	62	-	50
Crystal Palace	Tr	12/62	62-64	101	-	40
Watford	Tr	05/65	65	24	0	12
Charlton Ath	Tr	02/66	65	18	0	7
Leyton Orient	Tr	07/66	66-67	47	0	17
HOLTON James Allan (Jim)						
Born: Lesmahagow, Lanarkshire, Scotland, 11 April, 1951						CD
Died: Mill Hill, NW London, England, January, 1993Oct						
Scotland: 15/U23-1						
West Bromwich A	Jnr	04/68				
Shrewsbury T	Tr	06/71	71-72	67	0	4
Manchester U	Tr	01/73	72-74	63	0	5
Sunderland	Miami Toros (USA)	09/76	76	15	0	0
Coventry C	Tr	03/77	76-79	91	0	0
Sheffield Wed	Detroit Express (USA)	08/81				
HOLTON Patrick Carr (Pat)						
Born: Hamilton, Lanarkshire, Scotland, 23 December, 1935						LB
Died: 19 December, 2014						
Chelsea	Motherwell	03/59	58	1	-	0
Southend U	Tr	08/60	60	11	-	0
HOLWIJN Melvin						
Born: Amsterdam, Netherlands, 2 January, 1980						W
Barnet	Telstar (NED)	11/12	12	0	1	0
HOLWYN Jermaine Titano Benito						
Born: Amsterdam, Netherlands, 16 April, 1973						D
Port Vale	Ajax (NED)	07/95	96	5	2	0
HOLYOAK Daniel (Danny)						
Born: Walthamstow, NE London, England, 27 November, 1983						CD
Mansfield T	Sch	-	02	0	2	0
HOLYOAK Philip (Phil)						
Born: Sunderland, England, 22 May, 1959						D
Tottenham H	App	05/77				
Scunthorpe U	L	02/78	77	1	0	0
HOLZMAN Mark Robin						
Born: Bracknell, Berkshire, England, 22 February, 1973						RB/M
Reading	YT	07/91	91-92	23	9	1
HOMER Christopher (Chris)						
Born: Stockton-on-Tees, Cleveland, England, 16 April, 1977						M
Hartlepool U	YT	07/95	94-96	2	5	0
HONE Daniel Joseph						
Born: Croydon, S London, England, 15 September, 1989						CD
Lincoln C	Sch	12/07	07-10	78	7	3
HONE Mark Joseph						
Born: Croydon, S London, England, 31 March, 1968						RB
England: Semi Pro-5						
Crystal Palace	Jnr	07/85	87-88	4	0	0
Southend U	Welling U	08/94	94-95	50	6	0
Lincoln C	Tr	07/96	96-97	48	5	2
HONEYWOOD Brian Roy						
Born: Chelmsford, England, 8 May, 1949						CD
Ipswich T	App	05/67				
Colchester U	Tr	06/68	68	11	6	0

League Club	Source	Date Signed	Seasons Played	Apps	Subs	Gls
HONOR Christian Robert (Chris)						
Born: Bristol, England, 5 June, 1968						RB
Bristol C	App	06/86	85-89	44	16	1
Torquay U	L	11/86	86	3	0	0
Hereford U	L	12/89	89	2	1	0
Swansea C	L	01/91	90	2	0	0
Cardiff C (L)	Airdrieonians	02/95	94	10	0	0
HONOUR Brian						
Born: Horden, County Durham, England, 16 February, 1964						M
Darlington	App	02/82	81-83	59	15	4
Hartlepool U	Peterlee Newtown	02/85	84-94	301	18	26
HONOUR John						
Born: Horden, County Durham, England, 1 November, 1953						M
West Bromwich A	App	05/71				
Hartlepool U	Tr	07/72	72-75	107	5	6
Workington	Tr	03/76	75-76	38	1	1
HOOD Derek						
Born: Washington, Tyne and Wear, England, 17 December, 1958						FB/M
West Bromwich A	App	12/76				
Hull C	Tr	08/77	77-79	20	4	0
York C	Tr	02/80	79-87	287	13	32
Lincoln C	L	03/87	86	9	0	0
HOOD George William						
Born: Houghton-le-Spring, Tyne and Wear, England, 27 November, 1920						LB
Died: Southwell, Nottinghamshire, England, 1973						
Gateshead	Houghton Main	10/47	47-48	30	-	0
HOOD Henry Anthony (Harry)						
Born: Glasgow, Scotland, 3 October, 1944						CF
Scotland: SLge-1/U23-1						
Sunderland	Clyde	11/64	64-66	31	0	9
HOOD John O'Dorman (Jackie)						
Born: Glasgow, Scotland, 8 January, 1938						IF
Everton	Shettleston	10/56				
Tranmere Rov	Tr	12/59	59	3	-	2
HOOD Melvyn Arthur (Mel)						
Born: Reading, England, 5 October, 1939						LW
Reading	Jnr	10/56	56-57	10	-	0
HOOD Owen Glyn (Glyn)						
Born: Abersychan, Torfaen, Wales, 12 March, 1925						LH
Died: Nuneaton, Warwickshire, England, 28 September, 2004						
West Bromwich A	Nuffield Works	09/45	46-49	69	-	0
HOOD Ronald (Ronnie)						
Born: Cowdenbeath, Fife, Scotland, 18 November, 1922						IF
Died: Glenrothes, Fife, Scotland, 7 May, 1999						
Aldershot	Hamilton Academical	08/47	47	14	-	8
Rochdale	Tr	11/48	48	9	-	1
HOOGLAND Tim Klaus						
Born: Marl, Germany, 11 June, 1985						RB
Germany: Youth						
Fulham	Schalke 04 (GER)	06/14	14	22	3	4
HOOIVELD Jos						
Born: Assen, Netherlands, 22 April, 1983						CD
Netherlands: Youth						
Southampton	Glasgow Celtic	08/11	11-13	65	2	7
Norwich C	L	09/14	14	6	0	0
Millwall	L	01/15	14	15	0	1
HOOKER Allan Thomas						
Born: Exeter, England, 23 June, 1956						LB
Exeter C	Jnr	07/74	74-76	46	4	0
HOOKER Jonathan William (Jon)						
Born: City of London, England, 31 March, 1972						M
Gillingham	Hertford T	10/94				
Brentford	Tr	11/94	94-95	4	1	0
HOOKER Keith William						
Born: Fleet, Hampshire, England, 31 January, 1950						M
Brentford	App	02/68	66-68	24	8	2
HOOKS Paul						
Born: Wallsend, Tyne and Wear, England, 30 May, 1959						M
Notts Co	App	06/77	76-82	144	29	30
Derby Co	Tr	03/83	82-84	46	2	4
HOOKS Victor Ronald (Vic)						
Born: Belfast, Northern Ireland, 4 July, 1955						F
Grimsby T	Manchester U (App)	10/72	72	0	1	0
HOOLAHAN Wesley (Wes)						
Born: Dublin, Republic of Ireland, 10 August, 1983						LW/M
Republic of Ireland: 20/B-1/U21-12						
Blackpool	Livingston	07/06	06-07	80	7	13
Norwich C	Tr	06/08	08-14	189	39	35

HOOLE David John
Born: Chesterfield, Derbyshire, England, 16 October, 1970 RB

League Club	Source	Date Signed	Seasons Played	Apps	Subs	Gls
Chesterfield	YT	07/89	88-89	6	8	0

HOOLEY Joseph Winston (Joe)
Born: Hoyland, South Yorkshire, England, 26 December, 1938 IF/W

League Club	Source	Date Signed	Seasons Played	Apps	Subs	Gls
Barnsley	Jnr	04/56	56	1	-	0
Sheffield U	Tr	12/57				
Workington	Tr	06/58	58	6	-	2
Bradford Park Ave	Holbeach U	11/59	59-60	13	-	4

HOOLICKIN Garry John
Born: Middleton, Greater Manchester, England, 29 October, 1957 D

League Club	Source	Date Signed	Seasons Played	Apps	Subs	Gls
Oldham Ath	App	07/75	76-86	209	2	2

HOOLICKIN Stephen (Steve)
Born: Moston, Greater Manchester, England, 13 December, 1951 RB

League Club	Source	Date Signed	Seasons Played	Apps	Subs	Gls
Oldham Ath	App	12/69	69-72	8	0	0
Bury	Tr	08/73	73-76	140	0	5
Carlisle U	Tr	10/76	76-80	143	0	2
Hull C	Tr	12/80	80-81	31	0	0

HOOMAN Harry James
Born: Worcester, England, 27 April, 1991 CD

League Club	Source	Date Signed	Seasons Played	Apps	Subs	Gls
Shrewsbury T	Sch	07/09	09	1	1	0
Cheltenham T	Tr	07/11	11-12	5	1	0

HOOPER Dean Raymond
Born: Harefield, NW London, England, 13 April, 1971 RB
England: Semi Pro-1

League Club	Source	Date Signed	Seasons Played	Apps	Subs	Gls
Swindon T	Hayes	03/95	94	0	4	0
Peterborough U	L	12/95	95	4	0	0
Peterborough U	Kingstonian	08/98	98-01	99	14	2

HOOPER Gary
Born: Loughton, Essex, England, 26 January, 1988 F

League Club	Source	Date Signed	Seasons Played	Apps	Subs	Gls
Southend U	Grays Ath	08/06	06-07	12	20	2
Leyton Orient	L	03/07	06	2	2	2
Hereford U	L	01/08	07	19	0	11
Scunthorpe U	Tr	07/08	08-09	76	4	43
Norwich C	Glasgow Celtic	07/13	13-14	38	24	18

HOOPER Harry
Born: Pittington, County Durham, England, 14 June, 1933 RW
England: B-6/FLge-5/U23-2

League Club	Source	Date Signed	Seasons Played	Apps	Subs	Gls
West Ham U	Hylton CW	11/50	50-55	119	-	39
Wolverhampton W	Tr	03/56	56	39	-	19
Birmingham C	Tr	12/57	57-60	105	-	34
Sunderland	Tr	09/60	60-62	65	-	16

HOOPER Harry Reed
Born: Burnley, Lancashire, England, 16 December, 1910 FB
Died: Halifax, West Yorkshire, England, 24 March, 1970

League Club	Source	Date Signed	Seasons Played	Apps	Subs	Gls
Nelson	Nelson Tradesmen	11/28	28-29	21	-	0
Sheffield U	Tr	02/30	30-38	269	-	10
Hartlepool U	Tr	07/47	47-49	66	-	4

HOOPER Jonathan James (JJ)
Born: Greenwich, SE London, England, 9 October, 1993 F

League Club	Source	Date Signed	Seasons Played	Apps	Subs	Gls
Northampton T	Newcastle U (Sch)	07/13	13	0	3	0

HOOPER Lyndon Fitzgerald
Born: Georgetown, Guyana, 30 May, 1966 M
Canada: 67

League Club	Source	Date Signed	Seasons Played	Apps	Subs	Gls
Birmingham C	Toronto Blizzard (CAN)	09/93	93	1	4	0

HOOPER Michael Dudley (Mike)
Born: Bristol, England, 10 February, 1964 G
England: Schools

League Club	Source	Date Signed	Seasons Played	Apps	Subs	Gls
Bristol C	Mangotsfield U	11/83	84	1	0	0
Wrexham	Tr	02/85	84-85	34	0	0
Liverpool	Tr	10/85	86-92	50	1	0
Leicester C	L	09/90	90	14	0	0
Newcastle U	Tr	09/93	93-94	23	2	0

HOOPER Percy William George
Born: Lambeth, S London, England, 17 December, 1914 G
Died: Kings Lynn, Norfolk, England, 3 July, 1997

League Club	Source	Date Signed	Seasons Played	Apps	Subs	Gls
Tottenham H	Islington Corinthians	01/35	34-38	97	-	0
Swansea C	Tr	03/47	46-47	12	-	0

HOOPER Peter John
Born: Teignmouth, Devon, England, 2 February, 1933 LW
Died: Barnstaple, Devon, England, 13 August, 2011
England: FLge-1

League Club	Source	Date Signed	Seasons Played	Apps	Subs	Gls
Bristol Rov	Dawlish T	05/53	53-61	297	-	101
Cardiff C	Tr	07/62	62	40	-	22
Bristol C	Tr	07/63	63-65	54	0	14

HOOPER Stuart Robert John
Born: St Annes, Lancashire, England, 16 June, 1970 F

League Club	Source	Date Signed	Seasons Played	Apps	Subs	Gls
Burnley	Jnr	07/88	88	0	1	0

HOOPER Wynne
Born: Seven Sisters, Neath Port Talbot, Wales, 5 June, 1952 W
Wales: Youth

League Club	Source	Date Signed	Seasons Played	Apps	Subs	Gls
Newport Co	App	06/70	68-76	164	14	21
Swindon T	Tr	12/76	76	4	2	0
Aldershot	Tr	07/77	77-78	21	19	1

HOPE Alexander John Henry (Alex)
Born: Musselburgh, East Lothian, Scotland, 22 June, 1924 LW

League Club	Source	Date Signed	Seasons Played	Apps	Subs	Gls
Swindon T	Greenock Morton	06/54	54	11	-	1

HOPE Christopher Jonathan (Chris)
Born: Sheffield, England, 14 November, 1972 CD

League Club	Source	Date Signed	Seasons Played	Apps	Subs	Gls
Nottingham F	Darlington (Jnr)	08/90				
Scunthorpe U	Tr	07/93	93-99	278	9	19
Gillingham	Tr	07/00	00-05	230	6	13

HOPE Darren
Born: Stoke-on-Trent, England, 3 April, 1971 W

League Club	Source	Date Signed	Seasons Played	Apps	Subs	Gls
Stoke C	YT	07/89				
Stockport Co	Tr	03/90	89	4	0	0

HOPE Eric
Born: Oakengates, Telford & Wrekin, England, 2 December, 1927 IF
Died: Telford, England, 11 August, 2009

League Club	Source	Date Signed	Seasons Played	Apps	Subs	Gls
Manchester C		01/46				
Shrewsbury T	Tr	08/50	50-51	27	-	3
Wrexham	Tr	10/51	51-53	37	-	9

HOPE George
Born: Haltwhistle, Northumberland, England, 4 April, 1954 F

League Club	Source	Date Signed	Seasons Played	Apps	Subs	Gls
Newcastle U	App	04/72	73	6	0	1
Charlton Ath	Tr	06/75	75-76	13	0	2
York C	Tr	11/76	76-77	34	8	8

HOPE Hallam Robert
Born: Manchester, England, 17 March, 1994 F
England: Youth

League Club	Source	Date Signed	Seasons Played	Apps	Subs	Gls
Everton	Sch	03/11				
Northampton T	L	01/14	13	3	0	1
Bury	L	03/14	13	8	0	5
Sheffield Wed	L	08/14	14	1	3	0
Bury	Tr	11/14	14	10	9	0

HOPE James Gibson
Born: Glasgow, Scotland, 11 September, 1919 LW
Died: Hawick, Borders, Scotland, 20 January, 1979

League Club	Source	Date Signed	Seasons Played	Apps	Subs	Gls
Manchester C	Ardeer Rec	02/39	46	7	-	0

HOPE James Greatrix (Jimmy)
Born: East Wemyss, Fife, Scotland, 4 October, 1919 CH
Died: Birkenhead, Wirral, England, November, 1993

League Club	Source	Date Signed	Seasons Played	Apps	Subs	Gls
New Brighton	East Fife	08/47	47-49	43	-	0

HOPE John William March
Born: Shildon, County Durham, England, 30 March, 1949 G

League Club	Source	Date Signed	Seasons Played	Apps	Subs	Gls
Darlington	App	05/67	64-68	14	0	0
Newcastle U	Tr	03/69	68	1	0	0
Sheffield U	Tr	01/71	70-73	63	0	0
Hartlepool U	Tr	07/75	75	23	0	0

HOPE Mark Bryan
Born: Isleworth, W London, England, 13 June, 1970 CD

League Club	Source	Date Signed	Seasons Played	Apps	Subs	Gls
Darlington	Porthleven	01/97	96	1	0	0

HOPE Richard Paul
Born: Stockton-on-Tees, Cleveland, England, 22 June, 1978 CD

League Club	Source	Date Signed	Seasons Played	Apps	Subs	Gls
Blackburn Rov	YT	08/95				
Darlington	Tr	01/97	96-98	62	1	1
Northampton T	Tr	12/98	98-02	113	22	7
York C	Tr	08/03	03	36	0	2
Chester C	Tr	07/04	04	26	2	0
Shrewsbury T	Tr	08/05	05-06	75	0	2
Wrexham	Tr	07/07	07	33	0	0
Grimsby T	Tr	07/08	08	6	0	0

HOPE Robert (Bobby)
Born: Bridge of Allan, Stirlingshire, Scotland, 28 September, 1943 M
Scotland: 2/U23-1/Schools

League Club	Source	Date Signed	Seasons Played	Apps	Subs	Gls
West Bromwich A	Jnr	09/60	59-71	331	5	33
Birmingham C	Tr	06/72	72-75	33	1	5
Sheffield Wed	Tr	09/76	76-77	39	3	7

HOPGOOD Ronald Frederick (Ron)
Born: Battersea, SW London, England, 24 November, 1934 G
Died: Ashford, Kent, England, April, 1990

League Club	Source	Date Signed	Seasons Played	Apps	Subs	Gls
Crystal Palace	Spicers Ath	05/57	57-59	14	-	0

HOPKIN David Isaac
Born: Greenock, Inverclyde, Scotland, 21 August, 1970 — M
Scotland: 7/B-1

League Club	Source	Date Signed	Seasons Played	Apps	Subs	Gls
Chelsea	Greenock Morton	09/92	92-94	21	19	1
Crystal Palace	Tr	07/95	95-96	79	4	21
Leeds U	Tr	07/97	97-99	64	9	6
Bradford C	Tr	07/00	00	8	3	0
Crystal Palace	Tr	03/01	00-01	21	8	4

HOPKINS Anthony (Tony)
Born: Cwmbran, Torfaen, Wales, 17 February, 1971 — W/LB

League Club	Source	Date Signed	Seasons Played	Apps	Subs	Gls
Newport Co	YT	-	87	2	4	0
Bristol C	Chelsea (YT)	10/89				
Aldershot	Ebbw Vale	02/91	90	9	1	0

HOPKINS Brian
Born: Derby, England, 15 March, 1933 — RW

League Club	Source	Date Signed	Seasons Played	Apps	Subs	Gls
Port Vale (Am)	Keele Univ	08/57	57	2	-	0

HOPKINS Gareth
Born: Cheltenham, Gloucestershire, England, 14 June, 1980 — F

League Club	Source	Date Signed	Seasons Played	Apps	Subs	Gls
Cheltenham T	YT	07/98	99-01	1	7	0

HOPKINS Gareth Gersom
Born: Swansea, Wales, 12 April, 1923 — W
Died: Morriston, Swansea, Wales, 2 July, 2006

League Club	Source	Date Signed	Seasons Played	Apps	Subs	Gls
Swansea C	RAF	11/46	47	2	-	0

HOPKINS Idris Morgan (Dai)
Born: Merthyr Tydfil, Wales, 11 October, 1910 — RW
Died: High Wycombe, Buckinghamshire, England, 9 October, 1994
Wales: 12/War-9

League Club	Source	Date Signed	Seasons Played	Apps	Subs	Gls
Crystal Palace	Ramsgate Press	05/32	32	4	-	0
Brentford	Tr	11/32	32-46	290	-	77
Bristol C	Tr	05/47	47	24	-	0

HOPKINS Jeffrey (Jeff)
Born: Swansea, Wales, 14 April, 1964 — CD
Wales: 16/U21-5/Youth

League Club	Source	Date Signed	Seasons Played	Apps	Subs	Gls
Fulham	App	09/81	80-87	213	6	4
Crystal Palace	Tr	08/88	88-89	70	0	2
Plymouth Arg	L	10/91	91	8	0	0
Bristol Rov	Tr	03/92	91	4	2	0
Reading	Tr	07/92	92-96	127	4	3

HOPKINS Kelvin Robert
Born: Perivale, W London, England, 26 July, 1953 — G

League Club	Source	Date Signed	Seasons Played	Apps	Subs	Gls
Aldershot	App	07/71	70-71	2	0	0

HOPKINS Melvyn (Mel)
Born: Ystrad Rhondda, Rhondda Cynon Taff, Wales, 7 November, 1934 — LB
Died: Worthing, West Sussex, England, 18 October, 2010
Wales: 34/U23-1

League Club	Source	Date Signed	Seasons Played	Apps	Subs	Gls
Tottenham H	Ystrad BC	05/52	52-63	219	-	0
Brighton & HA	Tr	10/64	64-66	57	1	2
Bradford Park Ave	Canterbury C	01/69	68-69	29	1	0

HOPKINS Oliver Thomas (Ollie)
Born: South Kirkby, West Yorkshire, England, 15 November, 1935 — CH
Died: Chelmsford, England, 14 April, 2014

League Club	Source	Date Signed	Seasons Played	Apps	Subs	Gls
Barnsley	Burntwood YC	03/54	57-60	50	-	10
Peterborough U	Tr	07/61	61-64	104	-	0

HOPKINS Paul David
Born: Liverpool, England, 29 November, 1986 — F
England: Youth

League Club	Source	Date Signed	Seasons Played	Apps	Subs	Gls
Everton	Sch	02/05				
Darlington	L	01/06	05	3	2	1

HOPKINS Robert Arthur
Born: Birmingham, England, 25 October, 1961 — W

League Club	Source	Date Signed	Seasons Played	Apps	Subs	Gls
Aston Villa	App	07/79	79-82	1	2	1
Birmingham C	Tr	03/83	82-86	123	0	21
Manchester C	Tr	08/86	86	7	0	1
West Bromwich A	Tr	10/86	86-88	81	2	11
Birmingham C	Tr	03/89	88-90	43	7	9
Shrewsbury T	Tr	06/91	91	18	9	3
Colchester U	Instant Dict (HKG)	02/93	92	13	1	1

HOPKINSON Alan
Born: Chapeltown, South Yorkshire, England, 15 April, 1953 — F

League Club	Source	Date Signed	Seasons Played	Apps	Subs	Gls
Barnsley	App	04/71	70-73	24	3	5

HOPKINSON Bobby Thomas
Born: Plymouth, England, 3 July, 1990 — M

League Club	Source	Date Signed	Seasons Played	Apps	Subs	Gls
Aldershot T	Tiverton T	08/09	09	0	1	0

HOPKINSON Edward (Eddie)
Born: Wheatley Hill, County Durham, England, 29 October, 1935 — G
Died: Royton, Greater Manchester, England, 25 April, 2004
England: 14/FLge-2/U23-6

League Club	Source	Date Signed	Seasons Played	Apps	Subs	Gls
Oldham Ath	Jnr	06/51	51	3	-	0
Bolton W	Tr	11/52	56-69	519	0	0

HOPKINSON Gordon
Born: Sheffield, England, 19 June, 1933 — RB

League Club	Source	Date Signed	Seasons Played	Apps	Subs	Gls
Doncaster Rov	Beighton MW	06/57	57	10	-	0
Bristol C	Tr	07/58	58-60	67	-	1

HOPKINSON Ian John
Born: Newcastle-upon-Tyne, England, 19 October, 1950 — F

League Club	Source	Date Signed	Seasons Played	Apps	Subs	Gls
Barrow	Newcastle U (App)	01/69	68-70	17	4	1
Workington	Tr	07/71	71	13	6	7
Darlington	Berwick Rgrs	12/72	72	7	2	1

HOPKINSON Michael Edward (Mick)
Born: Ambergate, Derbyshire, England, 24 February, 1942 — LH/LB

League Club	Source	Date Signed	Seasons Played	Apps	Subs	Gls
Derby Co	West End BC	07/59	60-67	112	3	4
Mansfield T	Tr	07/68	68-69	46	0	1
Port Vale	Tr	07/70	70	12	1	0

HOPKINSON Paul Edward
Born: Royton, Greater Manchester, England, 17 January, 1958 — G

League Club	Source	Date Signed	Seasons Played	Apps	Subs	Gls
Stockport Co	Manchester C (App)	10/75	75-76	39	0	0

HOPKINSON Stanley (Stan)
Born: Kiveton Park, South Yorkshire, England, 15 March, 1922 — G
Died: Hemel Hempstead, Hertfordshire, England, October, 2003

League Club	Source	Date Signed	Seasons Played	Apps	Subs	Gls
Watford (Am)	Hemel Hempstead	05/47	46	1	-	0

HOPPER Alan
Born: Newcastle-upon-Tyne, England, 17 July, 1937 — RB

League Club	Source	Date Signed	Seasons Played	Apps	Subs	Gls
Newcastle U		10/59				
Barnsley	South Shields	03/61	61-64	135	-	4
Bradford C	Tr	07/65	65	8	0	0

HOPPER Ryan
Born: Droylsden, Greater Manchester, England, 13 November, 1993 — RB

League Club	Source	Date Signed	Seasons Played	Apps	Subs	Gls
Accrington Stan	Sch	07/12	11	1	3	0

HOPPER Thomas Edward (Tom)
Born: Boston, Lincolnshire, England, 14 December, 1993 — F
England: Youth

League Club	Source	Date Signed	Seasons Played	Apps	Subs	Gls
Leicester C	Sch	10/11				
Bury	L	09/12	12	22	0	3
Scunthorpe U	L	01/15	14	12	0	4

HOPPER Tony
Born: Carlisle, Cumbria, England, 31 May, 1976 — M

League Club	Source	Date Signed	Seasons Played	Apps	Subs	Gls
Carlisle U	YT	07/94	92-99	75	25	1
Carlisle U	Bohemians (ROI)	02/01	00-01	24	14	1

HOPPER William (Bill)
Born: Bishop Auckland, County Durham, England, 20 February, 1938 — CF

League Club	Source	Date Signed	Seasons Played	Apps	Subs	Gls
Halifax T	West Auckland T	12/61	61-62	35	-	9
Workington	Tr	07/63	63-64	46	-	14
Darlington	Tr	07/65	65	6	0	0

HORACE Alain
Born: Tananarive, Madagascar, 4 December, 1971 — M

League Club	Source	Date Signed	Seasons Played	Apps	Subs	Gls
Hartlepool U	Mulhouse (FRA)	10/96	96	0	1	0

HORE John Stephen
Born: Liverpool, England, 18 August, 1982 — M

League Club	Source	Date Signed	Seasons Played	Apps	Subs	Gls
Carlisle U	YT	06/00	99-01	2	3	0

HORE Kenneth John (John)
Born: St Austell, Cornwall, England, 10 February, 1947 — D

League Club	Source	Date Signed	Seasons Played	Apps	Subs	Gls
Plymouth Arg	App	12/64	64-75	393	7	17
Exeter C	Tr	03/76	75-79	193	0	0

HORLAVILLE Christophe
Born: Rouen, France, 1 March, 1969 — F

League Club	Source	Date Signed	Seasons Played	Apps	Subs	Gls
Port Vale (L)	Le Havre (FRA)	11/98	98	1	1	0

HORLOCK Kevin
Born: Erith, SE London, England, 1 November, 1972 — M
Northern Ireland: 32/B-2

League Club	Source	Date Signed	Seasons Played	Apps	Subs	Gls
West Ham U	YT	07/91				
Swindon T	Tr	08/92	92-96	151	12	22
Manchester C	Tr	01/97	96-02	184	20	37
West Ham U	Tr	08/03	03	23	4	1
Ipswich T	Tr	07/04	04-05	46	12	0
Doncaster Rov	Tr	02/06	05-06	15	0	1
Scunthorpe U	Tr	01/08				
Mansfield T	L	03/08	07	0	5	0

HORMANTSCHUK Peter Anthony
Born: Coventry, England, 11 September, 1962 — RB

League Club	Source	Date Signed	Seasons Played	Apps	Subs	Gls
Coventry C	App	09/80	81-83	18	6	1

League Club	Source	Date Signed	Seasons Played	Apps	Subs	Gls

HORN Graham Roy
Born: Westminster, Central London, England, 23 August, 1954 — G
Died: Torbay, Devon, England, 29 June, 2012

League Club	Source	Date Signed	Seasons Played	Apps	Subs	Gls
Arsenal	App	04/72				
Portsmouth	L	06/72	72	22	0	0
Luton T	Tr	02/73	72-74	58	0	0
Brentford	L	11/75	75	3	0	0
Charlton Ath	Los Angeles Azt (USA)	12/76				
Southend U	Kettering T	12/77	77-78	9	0	0
Aldershot	Tr	01/80	79-81	9	0	0
Torquay U	Tr	08/82	82-83	47	0	0

HORN Robert Ian (Bobby)
Born: Westminster, Central London, England, 15 December, 1961 — G
England: Youth

League Club	Source	Date Signed	Seasons Played	Apps	Subs	Gls
Crystal Palace	App	04/79				
Barnsley	Tr	11/80	81-83	67	0	0
Cambridge U	L	11/83	83	8	0	0
Crystal Palace	Tr	07/84				

HORN William
Born: Glasgow, Scotland, 13 May, 1938 — LW

League Club	Source	Date Signed	Seasons Played	Apps	Subs	Gls
Brentford	Kilmarnock	10/58	58	1	-	0

HORNBY Eric
Born: Birkenhead, Wirral, England, 31 March, 1923 — LB

League Club	Source	Date Signed	Seasons Played	Apps	Subs	Gls
Tranmere Rov	Jnr	11/44	47-48	32	-	0
Crewe Alex	Tr	08/49	49-50	3	-	0

HORNBY Lewis Paul Ingham
Born: Northampton, England, 25 April, 1995 — M

League Club	Source	Date Signed	Seasons Played	Apps	Subs	Gls
Northampton T	Sch	01/13	12	19	6	0

HORNBY Ronald (Ron)
Born: Rochdale, Greater Manchester, England, 13 April, 1914 — LW
Died: Manchester, England, 13 July, 1962

League Club	Source	Date Signed	Seasons Played	Apps	Subs	Gls
Rochdale (Am)	Rochdale St Clement	02/32	31	2	-	0
Oldham Ath	Tr	07/33				
Burnley	Stalybridge Celtic	05/34	34-47	123	-	16

HORNBY-FORBES Tyler Cecil
Born: Preston, Lancashire, England, 8 March, 1996 — M/RB

League Club	Source	Date Signed	Seasons Played	Apps	Subs	Gls
Fleetwood T	Preston NE (Sch)	07/14	14	11	6	0

HORNE Alfred (Alf)
Born: Brixworth, Northamptonshire, England, 6 September, 1926 — LW

League Club	Source	Date Signed	Seasons Played	Apps	Subs	Gls
Northampton T		09/44	48	1	-	0

HORNE Barry
Born: Flint, Wales, 18 May, 1962 — M
Wales: 59

League Club	Source	Date Signed	Seasons Played	Apps	Subs	Gls
Wrexham	Rhyl	06/84	84-86	136	0	16
Portsmouth	Tr	07/87	87-88	66	4	7
Southampton	Tr	03/89	88-91	111	1	6
Everton	Tr	07/92	92-95	118	5	3
Birmingham C	Tr	06/96	96	33	0	0
Huddersfield T	Tr	10/97	97-99	55	9	1
Sheffield Wed	Tr	03/00	99	7	0	0
Kidderminster Hrs	Tr	08/00	00	21	6	1
Walsall	Tr	03/01	00	1	2	0

HORNE Brian Simon
Born: Billericay, Essex, England, 5 October, 1967 — G
England: U21-5/Youth

League Club	Source	Date Signed	Seasons Played	Apps	Subs	Gls
Millwall	App	10/85	86-90	163	0	0
Middlesbrough	L	08/92	92	3	1	0
Stoke C	L	10/92	92	1	0	0
Portsmouth	Tr	12/92	93	3	0	0
Hartlepool U	Tr	08/94	94-95	73	0	0

HORNE Desmond Tolton (Des)
Born: Johannesburg, South Africa, 12 December, 1939 — LW
Died: South Africa, 21 July, 2015

League Club	Source	Date Signed	Seasons Played	Apps	Subs	Gls
Wolverhampton W	Jnr	12/56	58-60	40	-	16
Blackpool	Tr	03/61	60-65	117	1	17

HORNE George
Born: Glasgow, Scotland, 23 November, 1933 — LW

League Club	Source	Date Signed	Seasons Played	Apps	Subs	Gls
Carlisle U	Maryhill Jnrs	08/57	57	4	-	2

HORNE Henry Leslie (Les)
Born: Dudley, West Midlands, England, 2 May, 1923 — CH
Died: Dudley, West Midlands, England, February, 1986

League Club	Source	Date Signed	Seasons Played	Apps	Subs	Gls
West Bromwich A	Netherton W	04/48	49-51	13	-	0
Plymouth Arg	Tr	07/52				
Walsall	Tr	11/52	52-53	52	-	1

HORNE John Robert
Born: Dudley, West Midlands, England, 4 November, 1961 — D

League Club	Source	Date Signed	Seasons Played	Apps	Subs	Gls
Walsall	App	11/79	79-81	10	6	1

HORNE Kenneth William (Ken)
Born: Burton-on-Trent, Staffordshire, England, 25 June, 1926 — FB
Died: September, 2015

League Club	Source	Date Signed	Seasons Played	Apps	Subs	Gls
Blackpool	Wolverhampton W (Am)	06/49				
Brentford	Tr	05/50	50-59	223	-	1

HORNE Louis Peter
Born: Bradford, England, 28 May, 1991 — LB

League Club	Source	Date Signed	Seasons Played	Apps	Subs	Gls
Bradford C	Sch	07/09	09	0	1	0

HORNE Stanley Frederick (Stan)
Born: Clanfield, Oxfordshire, England, 17 December, 1944 — M

League Club	Source	Date Signed	Seasons Played	Apps	Subs	Gls
Aston Villa	App	12/61	63	6	-	0
Manchester C	Tr	09/65	65-67	48	2	0
Fulham	Tr	02/69	68-72	73	6	0
Chester C	Tr	08/73	73	17	1	0
Rochdale	Tr	12/73	73-74	48	0	5

HORNER Philip Matthew (Phil)
Born: Leeds, England, 10 November, 1966 — CD
England: Youth

League Club	Source	Date Signed	Seasons Played	Apps	Subs	Gls
Leicester C	App	11/84	86-87	7	3	0
Rotherham U	L	03/86	85	3	1	0
Halifax T	Tr	08/88	88-89	70	2	4
Blackpool	Tr	09/90	90-94	184	3	22

HORNER William (Billy)
Born: Cassop, County Durham, England, 7 September, 1942 — D/M

League Club	Source	Date Signed	Seasons Played	Apps	Subs	Gls
Middlesbrough	Jnr	09/59	60-68	184	3	11
Darlington	Tr	06/69	69-74	211	7	5

HORNSBY Brian Geoffrey
Born: Great Shelford, Cambridgeshire, England, 10 September, 1954 — M/F
England: Youth/Schools

League Club	Source	Date Signed	Seasons Played	Apps	Subs	Gls
Arsenal	App	07/72	72-75	23	3	6
Shrewsbury T	Tr	06/76	76-77	75	0	16
Sheffield Wed	Tr	03/78	77-81	102	4	25
Chester C	L	11/81	81	4	0	0
Carlisle U	Edmonton Drill's (CAN)	08/82	82-83	9	1	1
Chesterfield	L	12/83	83	1	0	0

HORNSBY John
Born: Ferryhill, County Durham, England, 3 August, 1945 — LW

League Club	Source	Date Signed	Seasons Played	Apps	Subs	Gls
Colchester U	Evenwood T	10/64	65	11	0	1

HORNUSS Julien
Born: Paris, France, 12 June, 1986 — F

League Club	Source	Date Signed	Seasons Played	Apps	Subs	Gls
MK Dons	AJ Auxerre Jnrs (FRA)	07/04	04	0	3	0

HOROBIN Roy
Born: Brownhills, West Midlands, England, 10 March, 1935 — IF
Died: Walsall, West Midlands, England, 30 August, 2012

League Club	Source	Date Signed	Seasons Played	Apps	Subs	Gls
West Bromwich A	Walsall Wood	10/52	55-57	54	-	6
Notts Co	Tr	11/58	58-61	123	-	37
Peterborough U	Tr	06/62	62-63	80	-	20
Crystal Palace	Tr	07/64	64	4	-	0

HORREY Rowland George
Born: Bishop Auckland, County Durham, England, 7 March, 1943 — RW

League Club	Source	Date Signed	Seasons Played	Apps	Subs	Gls
Blackburn Rov	Ferryhill Ath	12/63	64-65	3	0	0
York C	Tr	07/66	66-67	74	0	9
Cambridge U	Tr	07/68	70-71	37	1	4

HORRIDGE Peter
Born: Manchester, England, 31 May, 1934 — LB
Died: Newton Heath, Greater Manchester, England, 26 November, 2008

League Club	Source	Date Signed	Seasons Played	Apps	Subs	Gls
Manchester C	Newton Heath PC	11/52	58	3	-	0
Crewe Alex	Tr	06/59				

HORRIGAN Darren
Born: Middlesbrough, England, 2 June, 1983 — G

League Club	Source	Date Signed	Seasons Played	Apps	Subs	Gls
Lincoln C	YT	10/01	01	0	1	0

HORRIGAN Kenneth Patrick (Ken)
Born: Gravesend, Kent, England, 7 December, 1919 — WH
Died: Gravesend, Kent, England, May, 1989

League Club	Source	Date Signed	Seasons Played	Apps	Subs	Gls
Carlisle U	Imperial Paper Mill	08/46	46	16	-	1

HORRIX Dean Victor
Born: Burnham, Buckinghamshire, England, 21 November, 1961 — F
Died: Kingsclere, Hampshire, England, 11 March, 1990

League Club	Source	Date Signed	Seasons Played	Apps	Subs	Gls
Millwall	App	04/79	80-82	65	7	19
Gillingham	Tr	03/83	82	7	7	0
Reading	Tr	08/83	83-87	135	23	35
Cardiff C	L	02/87	86	9	0	3
Millwall	Tr	03/88	87-89	5	6	1
Bristol C	Tr	03/90	89	3	0	0

HORROBIN Thomas (Tom)
Born: Askern, South Yorkshire, England, 8 August, 1943 — RB

League Club	Source	Date Signed	Seasons Played	Apps	Subs	Gls
Sheffield Wed	Jnr	08/60	62	3	-	0

League Club	Source	Date Signed	Seasons Played	Career Record Apps	Subs	Gls

HORSBURGH John James
Born: Edinburgh, Scotland, 17 November, 1936 — G

League Club	Source	Date Signed	Seasons Played	Apps	Subs	Gls
Oldham Ath	Dundee	08/61	61	1	-	0

HORSCROFT Grant
Born: Fletching, East Sussex, England, 30 July, 1961 — CD

League Club	Source	Date Signed	Seasons Played	Apps	Subs	Gls
Brighton & HA	Lewes	03/87	87	2	0	0

HORSELL Martin
Born: Totnes, Devon, England, 10 December, 1986 — G

League Club	Source	Date Signed	Seasons Played	Apps	Subs	Gls
Bristol Rov	Jnr	08/05				
Torquay U	Tr	07/06	06	5	1	0

HORSFALL Frank George (George)
Born: Perth, Australia, 19 September, 1924 — WH
Died: Southampton, England, 29 August, 1992

League Club	Source	Date Signed	Seasons Played	Apps	Subs	Gls
Southampton	Guildford C	05/47	46	2	-	0
Southend U	Tr	07/49	49	1	-	0

HORSFALL Thomas William (Tommy)
Born: Hamilton, Lanarkshire, Scotland, 7 January, 1951 — W/F

League Club	Source	Date Signed	Seasons Played	Apps	Subs	Gls
Southend U	Dover	11/72	72-73	11	5	1
Bury	L	11/73	73	0	1	0
Scunthorpe U	L	11/73	73	5	0	2
Cambridge U	Tr	12/74	74-76	79	4	28
Halifax T	Tr	07/77	77	15	1	3

HORSFIELD Alec
Born: Selby, North Yorkshire, England, 4 August, 1921 — IF
Died: York, England, 21 January, 1991

League Club	Source	Date Signed	Seasons Played	Apps	Subs	Gls
Arsenal	Selby T	11/46				
Bradford Park Ave	Tr	12/50	50	4	-	2

HORSFIELD Arthur
Born: Newcastle-upon-Tyne, England, 5 July, 1946 — F
England: Youth

League Club	Source	Date Signed	Seasons Played	Apps	Subs	Gls
Middlesbrough	App	07/63	63-68	107	4	51
Newcastle U	Tr	01/69	68	7	2	3
Swindon T	Tr	06/69	69-71	107	1	42
Charlton Ath	Tr	06/72	72-75	139	0	53
Watford	Tr	09/75	75-76	78	0	16

HORSFIELD Geoffrey Malcolm (Geoff)
Born: Barnsley, South Yorkshire, England, 1 November, 1973 — F

League Club	Source	Date Signed	Seasons Played	Apps	Subs	Gls
Scarborough	Worsbrough Bridge	07/92	92-93	12	0	1
Halifax T	Witton A	10/96	98	10	0	7
Fulham	Tr	10/98	98-99	54	5	22
Birmingham C	Tr	07/00	00-03	75	33	23
Wigan Ath	Tr	09/03	03	16	0	7
West Bromwich A	Tr	12/03	03-05	48	19	14
Sheffield U	L	02/06	05	1	2	0
Sheffield U	Tr	07/06				
Leeds U	L	08/06	06	11	3	2
Leicester C	L	01/07	06	9	4	2
Scunthorpe U	L	01/08	07	11	1	0
Lincoln C	Rtd	01/09	08	14	3	1
Port Vale	Tr	08/09	09	1	8	0

HORSMAN Leslie (Les)
Born: Burley-in-Wharfedale, West Yorkshire, England, 26 May, 1920 — CF/CH
Died: Leeds, England, December, 1996

League Club	Source	Date Signed	Seasons Played	Apps	Subs	Gls
Bradford Park Ave	Guiseley	06/45	46-52	239	-	18
Halifax T	Tr	08/53	53-56	120	-	8

HORSTEAD John Barry (Barry)
Born: Brigg, North Lincolnshire, England, 8 May, 1935 — D

League Club	Source	Date Signed	Seasons Played	Apps	Subs	Gls
Scunthorpe U	Jnr	05/56	56-67	316	4	3

HORSTED Liam Anthony
Born: Portsmouth, England, 28 October, 1985 — W

League Club	Source	Date Signed	Seasons Played	Apps	Subs	Gls
Portsmouth	Sch	03/05				
Oxford U	L	03/06	05	1	3	0

HORSWILL Michael Frederick (Micky)
Born: Annfield Plain, County Durham, England, 6 March, 1953 — M/D

League Club	Source	Date Signed	Seasons Played	Apps	Subs	Gls
Sunderland	App	03/70	71-73	68	1	3
Manchester C	Tr	03/74	73-74	11	3	0
Plymouth Arg	Tr	06/75	75-77	98	4	3
Hull C	Tr	07/78	78-81	82	2	6
Carlisle U	Barrow	08/83	83	1	0	0

HORTON Brian
Born: Hednesford, Staffordshire, England, 4 February, 1949 — M

League Club	Source	Date Signed	Seasons Played	Apps	Subs	Gls
Port Vale	Hednesford T	07/70	70-75	232	4	33
Brighton & HA	Tr	02/76	75-80	217	1	33
Luton T	Tr	08/81	81-83	118	0	8
Hull C	Tr	07/84	84-86	38	0	0

HORTON Duncan
Born: Maidstone, Kent, England, 18 February, 1967 — M/LB

League Club	Source	Date Signed	Seasons Played	Apps	Subs	Gls
Charlton Ath	App	02/85	84	1	0	0
Barnet	Welling U	03/91	91-92	52	5	3
Wycombe W	Tr	08/93	93	15	0	0

HORTON Henry
Born: Malvern, Worcestershire, England, 18 April, 1923 — WH
Died: Colwall, Herefordshire, England, 2 November, 1998

League Club	Source	Date Signed	Seasons Played	Apps	Subs	Gls
Blackburn Rov	Worcester C	01/47	46-50	92	-	5
Southampton	Tr	06/51	51-53	75	-	12
Bradford Park Ave	Tr	05/54	54	26	-	0

HORTON Joseph Kenneth (Ken)
Born: Preston, Lancashire, England, 26 August, 1922 — IF
Died: Preston, Lancashire, England, 10 February, 2000

League Club	Source	Date Signed	Seasons Played	Apps	Subs	Gls
Preston NE	Jnr	10/45	46-52	166	-	36
Hull C	Tr	10/52	52-54	76	-	16
Barrow	Tr	08/55	55	22	-	4

HORTON Leonard (Len)
Born: Darlaston, West Midlands, England, 17 September, 1923 — CH
Died: Blackpool, Lancashire, England, January, 1987

League Club	Source	Date Signed	Seasons Played	Apps	Subs	Gls
Walsall	Darlaston	06/47	46	1	-	0

HORTON Leslie (Les)
Born: Salford, England, 12 July, 1921 — WH
Died: Wigan, Greater Manchester, England, January, 2008

League Club	Source	Date Signed	Seasons Played	Apps	Subs	Gls
Rochdale	Tydesley U	04/41				
Oldham Ath	Tr	01/43	46-47	79	-	2
Carlisle U	Tr	08/48	48-49	66	-	0
Rochdale	Tr	04/50				
York C	Tr	07/50	50	21	-	0
Halifax T	Tr	03/51	50-51	35	-	1

HORTON William George (Billy)
Born: Aldershot, Hampshire, England, 27 August, 1942 — IF

League Club	Source	Date Signed	Seasons Played	Apps	Subs	Gls
Aldershot	Chelsea (Jnr)	11/61	62-64	9	-	1

HORWOOD Evan David
Born: Billingham, Cleveland, England, 10 March, 1986 — LB

League Club	Source	Date Signed	Seasons Played	Apps	Subs	Gls
Sheffield U	Sch	11/04				
Stockport Co	L	03/05	04	10	0	0
Chester C	L	01/06	05	1	0	0
Darlington	L	10/06	06	2	0	0
Darlington	L	01/07	06	18	0	0
Carlisle U	Tr	01/08	07-09	72	3	0
Hartlepool U	Tr	08/10	10-12	115	8	5
Tranmere Rov	Tr	07/13	13	12	6	0
Northampton T	Tr	03/14	13-14	30	3	0

HORWOOD Neil Kenneth
Born: Peterhead, Aberdeenshire, Scotland, 4 August, 1964 — F

League Club	Source	Date Signed	Seasons Played	Apps	Subs	Gls
Grimsby T	King's Lynn	08/86	86	0	1	0
Halifax T	L	12/86	86	3	0	0
Tranmere Rov	L	03/87	86	4	0	1
Cambridge U	Tr	08/87	87	4	10	2

HOSIE James England (Jim)
Born: Aberdeen, Scotland, 3 April, 1940 — W

League Club	Source	Date Signed	Seasons Played	Apps	Subs	Gls
Barnsley	Aberdeen	07/62	62	37	-	0

HOSKER Robert Charles (Bobby)
Born: Cannock, Staffordshire, England, 27 February, 1955 — W

League Club	Source	Date Signed	Seasons Played	Apps	Subs	Gls
Middlesbrough	App	03/72				
York C	Tr	08/73	75-76	16	9	1

HOSKIN James Ashley (Ashley)
Born: Accrington, Lancashire, England, 27 March, 1968 — LW

League Club	Source	Date Signed	Seasons Played	Apps	Subs	Gls
Burnley	App	12/85	85-88	72	16	11

HOSKIN Michael Andrew (Mick)
Born: Chesterfield, Derbyshire, England, 3 November, 1966 — FB

League Club	Source	Date Signed	Seasons Played	Apps	Subs	Gls
Chesterfield	YT	08/84	83-84	1	1	0

HOSKINS John Frederick
Born: Southampton, England, 10 May, 1931 — LW
Died: Southampton, England, 18 September, 2006

League Club	Source	Date Signed	Seasons Played	Apps	Subs	Gls
Southampton	Winchester C	07/52	52-58	220	-	64
Swindon T	Tr	07/59	59	10	-	3

HOSKINS Samuel Tobias (Sam)
Born: Dorchester, Dorset, England, 4 February, 1993 — F

League Club	Source	Date Signed	Seasons Played	Apps	Subs	Gls
Southampton	Sch	07/11				
Rotherham U	L	03/12	11	2	6	2
Stevenage	L	01/13	12	6	8	1
Yeovil T	Tr	07/13	13-14	8	23	1

HOSKINS William Richard (Will)
Born: Nottingham, England, 6 May, 1986 — F
England: Youth

League Club	Source	Date Signed	Seasons Played	Apps	Subs	Gls
Rotherham U	Sch	02/05	03-06	35	38	23
Watford	Tr	01/07	06-09	25	35	7
Millwall	L	09/07	07	9	1	2
Nottingham F	L	02/08	07	2	0	0
Bristol Rov	Tr	07/10	10	41	2	17
Brighton & HA	Tr	05/11	11-12	6	12	1
Sheffield U	L	01/12	11	4	8	2
Oxford U	Tr	08/14	14	2	2	0

HOTTE Mark Stephen
Born: Bradford, England, 27 September, 1978 — M

League Club	Source	Date Signed	Seasons Played	Apps	Subs	Gls
Oldham Ath	YT	07/97	97-00	59	6	0

HOTTE Timothy Alwin (Tim)
Born: Bradford, England, 4 October, 1963 — F

League Club	Source	Date Signed	Seasons Played	Apps	Subs	Gls
Huddersfield T	Arsenal (App)	09/81	81-82	14	2	4
Halifax T	Harrogate T	08/85	85	2	2	0
Hull C	North Ferriby U	10/87	87-88	1	4	0
York C	L	09/88	88	1	1	0

HOTTIGER Marc
Born: Lausanne, Switzerland, 7 November, 1967 — RB
Switzerland: 64

League Club	Source	Date Signed	Seasons Played	Apps	Subs	Gls
Newcastle U	Sion (FRA)	08/94	94-95	38	1	1
Everton	Tr	03/96	95-96	13	4	1

HOUCHEN Keith Morton
Born: Middlesbrough, England, 25 July, 1960 — F

League Club	Source	Date Signed	Seasons Played	Apps	Subs	Gls
Hartlepool U	Chesterfield (Jnr)	02/78	77-81	160	10	65
Leyton Orient	Tr	03/82	81-83	74	2	20
York C	Tr	03/84	83-85	56	11	20
Scunthorpe U	Tr	03/86	85	9	0	2
Coventry C	Tr	07/86	86-88	43	11	7
Port Vale	Hibernian	08/91	91-92	44	5	10
Hartlepool U	Tr	08/93	93-96	104	5	27

HOUGH David John
Born: Crewe, Cheshire, England, 20 February, 1966 — D/M
Wales: Youth

League Club	Source	Date Signed	Seasons Played	Apps	Subs	Gls
Swansea C	App	02/84	83-91	202	25	9

HOUGH Frederick Alan (Fred)
Born: Stoke-on-Trent, England, 23 December, 1935 — RW

League Club	Source	Date Signed	Seasons Played	Apps	Subs	Gls
Port Vale		06/55	57	4	-	0

HOUGH Harry
Born: Chapeltown, South Yorkshire, England, 26 September, 1924 — G

League Club	Source	Date Signed	Seasons Played	Apps	Subs	Gls
Barnsley	Thorncliffe Welfare	09/47	47-58	346	-	0
Bradford Park Ave	Tr	06/59	59-60	57	-	0

HOUGH John
Born: Halifax, West Yorkshire, England, 9 June, 1954 — G
Died: Halifax, West Yorkshire, England, July, 2009

League Club	Source	Date Signed	Seasons Played	Apps	Subs	Gls
Halifax T	Irish Dem's	09/79	79	1	0	0

HOUGH Thomas (Tommy)
Born: Preston, Lancashire, England, 17 January, 1922 — IF
Died: Preston, Lancashire, England, 2 July, 2001

League Club	Source	Date Signed	Seasons Played	Apps	Subs	Gls
Preston NE	Jnr	05/39				
Barrow	Tr	10/46	46	3	-	0

HOUGHTON Frank Calvert
Born: Preston, Lancashire, England, 15 February, 1926 — WH/IF
Died: Exeter, England, 19 August, 1994

League Club	Source	Date Signed	Seasons Played	Apps	Subs	Gls
Newcastle U	Ballymena U	12/47	47-50	55	-	10
Exeter C	Tr	08/54	54-56	27	-	10

HOUGHTON Harry Brian (Bud)
Born: Madras, India, 1 September, 1936 — CF
Died: Bromsgrove, Worcestershire, England, May, 1994

League Club	Source	Date Signed	Seasons Played	Apps	Subs	Gls
Bradford Park Ave	St Wilfred's YC	10/55	55-57	28	-	7
Birmingham C	Tr	10/57	57-58	4	-	1
Southend U	Tr	10/58	58-60	68	-	32
Oxford U	Tr	03/61	62-63	53	-	17
Lincoln C	Tr	10/63	63-64	54	-	22

HOUGHTON Keith
Born: Backworth, Tyne and Wear, England, 10 March, 1954 — CD
England: Semi Pro-1

League Club	Source	Date Signed	Seasons Played	Apps	Subs	Gls
Carlisle U	Blyth Spartans	01/80	79-82	82	5	2
Lincoln C	Tr	08/83	83	26	0	0

HOUGHTON Kenneth (Ken)
Born: Rotherham, South Yorkshire, England, 18 October, 1939 — IF

League Club	Source	Date Signed	Seasons Played	Apps	Subs	Gls
Rotherham U	Silverwood Colliery	05/60	60-64	149	-	56
Hull C	Tr	01/65	64-72	253	11	79
Scunthorpe U	Tr	06/73	73	33	0	5

HOUGHTON Peter
Born: Liverpool, England, 30 November, 1954 — F

League Club	Source	Date Signed	Seasons Played	Apps	Subs	Gls
Wigan Ath	South Liverpool	02/78	78-83	169	16	62
Preston NE	Tr	10/83	83-84	52	4	16
Wrexham	L	11/84	84	5	0	2
Chester C	Tr	08/85	85-87	78	7	13

HOUGHTON Raymond James (Ray)
Born: Glasgow, Scotland, 9 January, 1962 — M
Republic of Ireland: 73

League Club	Source	Date Signed	Seasons Played	Apps	Subs	Gls
West Ham U	Jnr	07/79	81	0	1	0
Fulham	Tr	07/82	82-85	129	0	16
Oxford U	Tr	09/85	85-87	83	0	10
Liverpool	Tr	10/87	87-91	147	6	28
Aston Villa	Tr	07/92	92-94	83	12	6
Crystal Palace	Tr	03/95	94-96	69	3	7
Reading	Tr	07/97	97-98	33	10	1

HOUGHTON Scott Aaron
Born: Hitchin, Hertfordshire, England, 22 October, 1971 — LW
England: Youth/Schools

League Club	Source	Date Signed	Seasons Played	Apps	Subs	Gls
Tottenham H	YT	08/90	91	0	10	2
Ipswich T	L	03/91	90	7	1	1
Gillingham	L	12/92	92	3	0	0
Charlton Ath	L	02/93	92	6	0	0
Luton T	Tr	08/93	93-94	7	9	1
Walsall	Tr	09/94	94-95	76	2	14
Peterborough U	Tr	07/96	96-98	57	13	13
Southend U	Tr	11/98	98-00	75	4	9
Leyton Orient	Tr	10/00	00-01	27	15	6
Halifax T	Tr	02/02	01	7	0	0

HOUGHTON William Eric (Eric)
Born: Billingborough, Lincolnshire, England, 29 June, 1910 — LW
Died: Sutton Coldfield, West Midlands, England, 1 May, 1996
England: 7/FLge-4

League Club	Source	Date Signed	Seasons Played	Apps	Subs	Gls
Aston Villa	Bourne T	08/27	29-46	361	-	160
Notts Co	Tr	12/46	46-48	55	-	10

HOUGHTON William Gascoigne (Billy)
Born: Hemsworth, West Yorkshire, England, 20 February, 1939 — LB/LH
England: Youth

League Club	Source	Date Signed	Seasons Played	Apps	Subs	Gls
Barnsley	Jnr	08/57	57-63	206	-	10
Watford	Tr	07/64	64-65	48	0	2
Ipswich T	Tr	06/66	66-68	107	0	3
Leicester C	Tr	07/69	69	6	2	0
Rotherham U	Tr	01/70	69-73	139	0	1

HOULAHAN Harold (Harry)
Born: Coundon, County Durham, England, 14 February, 1930 — IF

League Club	Source	Date Signed	Seasons Played	Apps	Subs	Gls
Newcastle U	Durham C	02/51				
Oldham Ath	Tr	05/52	52-53	6	-	3
Darlington	Tr	01/54	53-54	23	-	8

HOULT Alan John
Born: Hinckley, Leicestershire, England, 7 October, 1957 — F
England: Schools

League Club	Source	Date Signed	Seasons Played	Apps	Subs	Gls
Leicester C	Jnr	09/75				
Hull C	L	01/78	77	3	0	1
Lincoln C	L	03/78	77	2	2	1
Bristol Rov	Tr	07/78				

HOULT Russell
Born: Ashby-de-la-Zouch, Leicestershire, England, 22 November, 1972 — G

League Club	Source	Date Signed	Seasons Played	Apps	Subs	Gls
Leicester C	YT	03/91	92	10	0	0
Lincoln C	L	08/91	91	2	0	0
Bolton W	L	11/93	93	3	1	0
Lincoln C	L	08/94	94	15	0	0
Derby Co	Tr	02/95	94-99	121	2	0
Portsmouth	Tr	01/00	99-00	40	0	0
West Bromwich A	Tr	01/01	00-06	189	1	0
Nottingham F	L	07/05	05	8	0	0
Stoke C	Tr	01/07	06	1	0	0
Notts Co	L	02/08	07	14	0	0
Notts Co	Tr	07/08	08-09	19	1	0
Darlington	L	09/09	09	6	0	0
Hereford U	Rtd	02/11	11	2	0	0

HOUNSLEA William Hudson (Bill)
Born: Liverpool, England, 15 August, 1926 — RB
Died: Liverpool, England, March, 2013

League Club	Source	Date Signed	Seasons Played	Apps	Subs	Gls
New Brighton	Unity BC	12/47	47	16	-	0
Chester C	Tr	08/48	48	1	-	0

HOURIHANE Conor
Born: Cork, Republic of Ireland, 2 February, 1991 — M
Republic of Ireland: U21-8/Youth

League Club	Source	Date Signed	Seasons Played	Apps	Subs	Gls
Sunderland	Sch	07/08				
Ipswich T	Tr	07/10				
Plymouth Arg	Tr	07/11	11-13	119	6	15
Barnsley	Tr	06/14	14	45	1	13

HOUSAM Arthur
Born: Sunderland, England, 1 October, 1917 — WH
Died: Sunderland, England, 31 December, 1975

League Club	Source	Date Signed	Seasons Played	Apps	Subs	Gls
Sunderland	Hylton CW	05/37	37-47	55	-	2

HOUSDEN Denis
Born: Islington, N London, England, 15 March, 1953 — F

League Club	Source	Date Signed	Seasons Played	Apps	Subs	Gls
Gillingham	App	08/71	71-72	12	4	1

HOUSEMAN Peter
Born: Battersea, SW London, England, 24 December, 1945 — W
Died: Bicester, Oxfordshire, England, 19 March, 1977

League Club	Source	Date Signed	Seasons Played	Apps	Subs	Gls
Chelsea	App	12/62	63-74	252	17	20
Oxford U	Tr	05/75	75-76	65	0	2

HOUSHAM Steven James (Steve)
Born: Gainsborough, Lincolnshire, England, 24 February, 1976 — M/RB

League Club	Source	Date Signed	Seasons Played	Apps	Subs	Gls
Scunthorpe U	YT	12/93	94-99	90	25	4

HOUSLEY Stuart
Born: Doncaster, South Yorkshire, England, 15 September, 1948 — RW

League Club	Source	Date Signed	Seasons Played	Apps	Subs	Gls
Grimsby T	App	07/66	66-68	34	0	3

HOUSTON David
Born: Glasgow, Scotland, 7 July, 1948 — LH

League Club	Source	Date Signed	Seasons Played	Apps	Subs	Gls
Cardiff C	Jnr	07/65	65-66	17	1	0
Crystal Palace	Tr	01/67				

HOUSTON Graham Robert
Born: Gibraltar, 24 February, 1960 — LW

League Club	Source	Date Signed	Seasons Played	Apps	Subs	Gls
Preston NE	Jnr	03/78	79-84	90	38	11
Burnley	Tr	09/85				
Wigan Ath	Tr	06/86	86	16	1	4
Carlisle U	Northwich Victoria	10/87	87	8	8	1

HOUSTON Joseph (Joe)
Born: Wishaw, Lanarkshire, Scotland, 27 February, 1926 — G

League Club	Source	Date Signed	Seasons Played	Apps	Subs	Gls
Aldershot	Dunfermline Ath	07/51	51-52	47	-	0

HOUSTON Stewart Mackie
Born: Dunoon, Argyll & Bute, Scotland, 20 August, 1949 — D
Scotland: 1/U23-1

League Club	Source	Date Signed	Seasons Played	Apps	Subs	Gls
Chelsea	Port Glasgow Rgrs	08/67	67-69	6	3	0
Brentford	Tr	03/72	71-73	77	0	9
Manchester U	Tr	12/73	73-79	204	1	13
Sheffield U	Tr	07/80	80-82	93	1	1
Colchester U	Tr	08/83	83-85	106	1	5

HOVI Thomas Henning (Tom)
Born: Gjovik, Norway, 15 January, 1972 — LB

League Club	Source	Date Signed	Seasons Played	Apps	Subs	Gls
Charlton Ath (L)	Ham-Kam (NOR)	01/95	94	0	2	0

HOW Trevor Anthony
Born: Amersham, Buckinghamshire, England, 8 August, 1957 — RB

League Club	Source	Date Signed	Seasons Played	Apps	Subs	Gls
Watford	App	03/75	74-79	90	1	2

HOWARD Andrew Paul (Andy)
Born: Southport, Merseyside, England, 15 March, 1973 — F

League Club	Source	Date Signed	Seasons Played	Apps	Subs	Gls
Blackpool	Liverpool (YT)	09/91				
Rochdale	Fleetwood T	07/92	92-93	4	16	3

HOWARD Barry Peter
Born: Ashton-under-Lyne, Greater Manchester, England, 19 February, 1950 — F
England: Semi Pro-7

League Club	Source	Date Signed	Seasons Played	Apps	Subs	Gls
Stockport Co	Runcorn	02/78	77	12	1	1

HOWARD Brian Richard William
Born: Winchester, Hampshire, England, 23 January, 1983 — M
England: Youth

League Club	Source	Date Signed	Seasons Played	Apps	Subs	Gls
Southampton	YT	01/00				
Swindon T	Tr	08/03	03-04	49	21	9
Barnsley	Tr	07/05	05-08	115	6	27
Sheffield U	Tr	10/08	08-09	25	5	2
Reading	Tr	09/09	09-11	49	10	2
Millwall	L	09/11	11	11	1	0
Portsmouth	Tr	08/12	12	23	0	0
Bristol C	Tr	02/13	12	0	6	0
Birmingham C	CSKA Sofia (BUL)	01/14	13	4	1	1
Oxford U	Tr	09/14	14	7	0	0

HOWARD Charlie Sydney
Born: Southwark, S London, England, 26 November, 1989 — M

League Club	Source	Date Signed	Seasons Played	Apps	Subs	Gls
Gillingham	Sch	12/07	07	1	0	0

HOWARD David Frederick
Born: Hartlepool, Cleveland, England, 3 June, 1962 — F

League Club	Source	Date Signed	Seasons Played	Apps	Subs	Gls
Newcastle U	Jnr	07/79				
Hartlepool U	Tr	03/81	80-81	6	3	4

HOWARD Francis Henry (Frankie)
Born: Acton, W London, England, 30 January, 1931 — LW
Died: Brighton, England, 11 October, 2007

League Club	Source	Date Signed	Seasons Played	Apps	Subs	Gls
Brighton & HA	Guildford C	05/50	50-58	200	-	26

HOWARD Jonathan (Jon)
Born: Sheffield, England, 7 October, 1971 — F/W

League Club	Source	Date Signed	Seasons Played	Apps	Subs	Gls
Rotherham U	YT	07/90	90-93	25	11	5
Chesterfield	Buxton	12/94	94-02	152	84	39

HOWARD Lee
Born: Worksop, Nottinghamshire, England, 6 February, 1967 — W

League Club	Source	Date Signed	Seasons Played	Apps	Subs	Gls
Mansfield T	App	-	84	0	1	0

HOWARD Mark Edward
Born: King's Lynn, Norfolk, England, 21 October, 1964 — LW

League Club	Source	Date Signed	Seasons Played	Apps	Subs	Gls
Stockport Co	King's Lynn	04/88	87-89	13	6	2
Cambridge U	L	03/89	88	0	2	0

HOWARD Mark Stephen
Born: Southwark, S London, England, 21 September, 1986 — G
England: Youth

League Club	Source	Date Signed	Seasons Played	Apps	Subs	Gls
Arsenal	Sch	10/04				
Cardiff C	Tr	08/06				
Blackpool	Aberdeen	09/11	11	4	0	0
Sheffield U	Tr	02/12	12-14	65	0	0

HOWARD Matthew Jones
Born: Watford, Hertfordshire, England, 5 December, 1970 — CD

League Club	Source	Date Signed	Seasons Played	Apps	Subs	Gls
Brentford	YT	-	87	0	1	0

HOWARD Michael Anthony (Mike)
Born: Birkenhead, Wirral, England, 2 December, 1978 — LB

League Club	Source	Date Signed	Seasons Played	Apps	Subs	Gls
Tranmere Rov	YT	07/97				
Swansea C	Tr	02/98	97-03	221	7	2
Morecambe	Tr	07/04	07	2	2	0

HOWARD Patrick (Pat)
Born: Dodworth, South Yorkshire, England, 7 October, 1947 — CD

League Club	Source	Date Signed	Seasons Played	Apps	Subs	Gls
Barnsley	Jnr	10/65	65-71	176	1	6
Newcastle U	Tr	09/71	71-76	182	2	7
Arsenal	Tr	09/76	76	15	1	0
Birmingham C	Tr	08/77	77-78	40	0	0
Bury	Tr	07/79	79-81	117	1	5

HOWARD Richard James (Dick)
Born: Birkenhead, Wirral, England, 10 June, 1943 — G
Canada:

League Club	Source	Date Signed	Seasons Played	Apps	Subs	Gls
Chester C	Chester Tech College	09/65	65	1	0	0

HOWARD Stanley (Stan)
Born: Chorley, Lancashire, England, 1 July, 1934 — CF/W
Died: Preston, Lancashire, England, 19 June, 2004

League Club	Source	Date Signed	Seasons Played	Apps	Subs	Gls
Huddersfield T	Chisnall Rov	07/52	57-59	62	-	13
Bradford C	Tr	06/60	60	18	-	6
Barrow	Tr	01/61	60-63	86	-	22
Halifax T	Tr	07/64	64	21	-	1

HOWARD Steven John (Steve)
Born: Durham, England, 10 May, 1976 — F
Scotland: B-1

League Club	Source	Date Signed	Seasons Played	Apps	Subs	Gls
Hartlepool U	Tow Law T	08/95	95-98	117	25	26
Northampton T	Tr	02/99	98-00	67	19	18
Luton T	Tr	03/01	00-05	209	3	95
Derby Co	Tr	07/06	06-07	57	6	17
Leicester C	Tr	01/08	07-11	91	56	28
Hartlepool U	Tr	07/12	12-13	31	11	3
Sheffield Wed	L	03/13	12	5	3	1

HOWARD Terence (Terry)
Born: Stepney, E London, England, 26 February, 1966 — D
England: Youth

League Club	Source	Date Signed	Seasons Played	Apps	Subs	Gls
Chelsea	App	03/84	84-86	6	0	0
Crystal Palace	L	01/86	85	4	0	0
Chester C	L	01/87	86	2	0	0
Leyton Orient	Tr	03/87	86-94	323	5	31
Wycombe W	Tr	02/95	94-95	56	3	2

HOWARD Timothy Matthew (Tim)
Born: Brunswick, New Jersey, USA, 6 March, 1979 — G
USA: 104

League Club	Source	Date Signed	Seasons Played	Apps	Subs	Gls
Manchester U	New York M'stars (USA)	07/03	03-05	44	1	0
Everton	Tr	07/06	06-14	329	0	1

HOWARD Trevor Edward
Born: King's Lynn, Norfolk, England, 2 June, 1949 — M/RB

League Club	Source	Date Signed	Seasons Played	Apps	Subs	Gls
Norwich C	App	07/67	67-73	81	42	13
Bournemouth	Tr	08/74	74-75	86	0	11
Cambridge U	Tr	07/76	76-78	105	0	5

League Club	Source	Date Signed	Seasons Played	Apps	Subs	Gls
HOWARTH Christopher (Chris)						
Born: Bolton, Greater Manchester, England, 23 May, 1986						G
England: Youth						
Bolton W	Sch	07/05				
Oldham Ath	L	08/06	06	2	1	0
Carlisle U	Tr	03/07				
HOWARTH Frank						
Born: Budleigh Salterton, Devon, England, 17 November, 1964						RB/F
Exeter C	App	11/82	81-84	21	17	1
HOWARTH Jack						
Born: Stanley, County Durham, England, 27 February, 1945						CF
Chelsea	Stanley U	10/63				
Swindon T	Tr	10/64	64	2	-	0
Aldershot	Tr	07/65	65-71	258	1	114
Rochdale	Tr	01/72	71-72	40	0	12
Aldershot	Tr	11/72	72-76	163	0	59
Bournemouth	Tr	01/77	76-77	39	3	6
Southport	Dorchester T	03/78	77	9	0	1
HOWARTH Lee						
Born: Bolton, Greater Manchester, England, 3 January, 1968						CD
Peterborough U	Chorley	08/91	91-93	56	6	0
Mansfield T	Tr	08/94	94-95	56	1	2
Barnet	Tr	01/96	95-97	101	1	5
HOWARTH Neil						
Born: Farnworth, Greater Manchester, England, 15 November, 1971						CD
England: Semi Pro-2						
Burnley	YT	07/90	89	0	1	0
Macclesfield T	Tr	02/94	97-98	49	11	3
Cheltenham T	Tr	02/99	99-02	106	14	7
HOWARTH Russell Michael						
Born: York, England, 27 March, 1982						G
England: Youth						
York C	YT	08/99	99-01	6	2	0
Tranmere Rov	Tr	11/02	02-04	10	2	0
Bradford C	Tr	06/05	05	10	1	0
HOWARTH Sydney (Syd)						
Born: Bristol, England, 28 June, 1923						CF
Died: Cardiff, Wales, 11 January, 2004						
Aston Villa	Merthyr Tydfil	06/48	48-49	8	-	2
Swansea C	Tr	09/50	50-51	40	-	7
Walsall	Tr	09/52	52	6	-	0
HOWAT Ian Stuart						
Born: Wrexham, Wales, 29 July, 1958						F
Chester C	App	07/76	76-81	48	9	10
Crewe Alex	Tr	02/82	81	16	1	1
HOWCROFT Brian						
Born: Farnworth, Greater Manchester, England, 20 June, 1938						RB
Bury	Jnr	09/56	57-58	20	-	0
HOWDON Stephen (Steve)						
Born: Prudhoe, Northumberland, England, 1 February, 1922						LW
Died: Prudhoe, Northumberland, England, September, 1998						
Newcastle U	Hexham Hearts	08/41				
Gateshead	Tr	11/44	46	2	-	1
HOWE Albert Richard Henry (Bert)						
Born: Charlton, SE London, England, 16 November, 1938						FB
Crystal Palace	Faversham T	12/58	58-66	192	1	0
Leyton Orient	Tr	01/67	66-68	91	0	0
Colchester U	Tr	07/69	69	29	0	1
HOWE Anthony Valentine (Tony)						
Born: Colchester, Essex, England, 14 February, 1939						LW
Colchester U	Colchester Casuals	03/60	60	10	-	2
Southend U	Haverhill Rov	07/64	64	2	-	0
HOWE Denis Cecil						
Born: West Ham, E London, England, 14 September, 1928						CH
West Ham U		05/49				
Darlington	Tr	08/51	51-53	88	-	1
Southend U	Tr	08/54	54-57	101	-	0
Aldershot	Tr	07/58	58	33	-	0
HOWE Donald (Don)						
Born: Wolverhampton, England, 12 October, 1935						RB
England: 23/B/FLge-6/U23-6						
West Bromwich A	Jnr	11/52	55-63	342	-	17
Arsenal	Tr	04/64	64-66	70	0	1
HOWE Donald (Don)						
Born: Outwood, West Yorkshire, England, 26 November, 1917						WH/F
Died: Farnworth, Greater Manchester, England, 23 August, 1978						
Bolton W	Whitehall Printeries	11/34	36-51	266	-	35

League Club	Source	Date Signed	Seasons Played	Apps	Subs	Gls
HOWE Edward John Frank (Eddie)						
Born: Amersham, Buckinghamshire, England, 29 November, 1977						CD
England: U21-2						
Bournemouth	YT	07/96	95-01	183	17	10
Portsmouth	Tr	03/02	01-02	2	0	0
Bournemouth	Tr	08/04	04-06	63	7	2
HOWE Ernest James (Ernie)						
Born: Chiswick, W London, England, 15 February, 1953						CD
Fulham	Hounslow T	10/73	73-77	68	2	10
Queens Park Rgrs	Tr	12/77	77-81	89	0	3
Portsmouth	Tr	08/82	82-83	35	0	4
HOWE Frederick (Fred)						
Born: Bredbury, Greater Manchester, England, 24 September, 1912						CF
Died: Stockport, Greater Manchester, England, October, 1984						
Stockport Co	Wilmslow	09/31	31-32	2	-	0
Liverpool	Hyde U	03/35	34-37	89	-	36
Manchester C	Tr	06/38	38	6	-	5
Grimsby T	Tr	10/38	38	29	-	15
Oldham Ath	Tr	07/46	46	30	-	20
HOWE George						
Born: Wakefield, England, 10 January, 1924						LB
Died: Wakefield, England, 10 November, 1971						
Huddersfield T	Carlton U	05/42	46-53	40	-	0
York C	Tr	06/54	54-60	307	-	0
HOWE Herbert Alexander (Bert)						
Born: Rugby, Warwickshire, England, 1 April, 1916						LB
Died: Rugby, Warwickshire, England, 14 June, 1972						
Leicester C	Leicester Nomads	02/37	38-46	28	-	0
Notts Co	Tr	07/47	47-48	52	-	0
HOWE Jeremy Raymond						
Born: Dewsbury, West Yorkshire, England, 5 September, 1973						M
England: Youth						
Bradford C	YT	07/92	91	3	0	0
HOWE Jermaine Renee (Rene)						
Born: Bedford, England, 22 October, 1986						F
Peterborough U	Kettering T	07/07	07	2	13	1
Rochdale	L	01/08	07	19	1	9
Morecambe	L	07/08	08	35	2	10
Lincoln C	L	08/09	09	14	3	5
Gillingham	L	01/10	09	18	0	2
Bristol Rov	L	01/11	10	8	4	1
Torquay U	Tr	07/11	11-12	78	3	28
Burton A	Tr	07/13	13	7	8	1
Newport Co	Tr	01/14	13-14	17	12	3
HOWE John Robert (Jack)						
Born: West Hartlepool, County Durham, England, 7 October, 1915						LB
Died: Hartlepool, Cleveland, England, 5 April, 1987						
England: 3						
Hartlepool U	Wingate U	06/34	34-35	24	-	0
Derby Co	Tr	03/36	35-49	223	-	2
Huddersfield T	Tr	10/49	49-50	29	-	1
HOWE Robert John (Bobby)						
Born: Chadwell St Mary, Essex, England, 22 December, 1945						LB/M
West Ham U	App	01/63	66-71	68	7	4
Bournemouth	Tr	01/72	71-73	100	0	6
HOWE Stephen Robert (Bobby)						
Born: Annitsford, Tyne and Wear, England, 6 November, 1973						M
England: Youth						
Nottingham F	YT	12/90	93-96	6	8	2
Ipswich T	L	01/97	96	2	1	0
Swindon T	Tr	01/98	97-01	103	19	6
HOWELL Anthony Nikille Richard						
Born: Nottingham, England, 27 May, 1986						LW
Mansfield T	Alfreton T	07/11	13	30	3	3
HOWELL David Christopher						
Born: Hammersmith, W London, England, 10 October, 1958						CD
England: Semi Pro-14						
Barnet	Enfield	07/90	91-92	57	0	3
Southend U	Tr	07/93	93	6	0	0
Birmingham C	Rtd	10/94	94	2	0	0
HOWELL Dean George						
Born: Burton-on-Trent, Staffordshire, England, 29 November, 1980						LB
Notts Co	YT	07/99	99	0	1	0
Crewe Alex	Tr	07/00	00	0	1	0
Rochdale	L	03/01	00	2	1	0
Colchester U	Halifax T	08/05	05	1	3	0
Aldershot T	Rushden & D	06/08	08-09	14	3	1

League Club	Source	Date Signed	Seasons Played	Apps	Subs	Gls
Bury	L	11/08	08	0	3	0
Crawley T	Tr	07/10	11	36	1	3
Fleetwood T	Tr	07/12	12-13	36	2	1
Bury	L	11/13	13	8	0	0

HOWELL Graham Frank
Born: Urmston, Greater Manchester, England, 18 February, 1951 — RB

League Club	Source	Date Signed	Seasons Played	Apps	Subs	Gls
Manchester C	App	10/68				
Bradford C	Tr	06/71	71-72	45	0	0
Brighton & HA	Tr	08/72	72-73	40	4	0
Cambridge U	Tr	07/74	74-75	68	3	3

HOWELL James Alexander (Jamie)
Born: Littlehampton, West Sussex, England, 19 February, 1977 — M
England: Youth/Schools

League Club	Source	Date Signed	Seasons Played	Apps	Subs	Gls
Arsenal	YT	07/95				
Portsmouth	Tr	08/96				
Torquay U	Tr	03/97	96	2	2	0

HOWELL Luke Alexander
Born: Heathfield, East Sussex, England, 5 January, 1987 — M/RB

League Club	Source	Date Signed	Seasons Played	Apps	Subs	Gls
Gillingham	Sch	07/06	06	0	1	0
MK Dons	Tr	08/07	07-10	34	19	1
Lincoln C	Tr	10/10	10	23	2	1
Dagenham & Red	Tr	07/11	11-14	121	6	18

HOWELL Reginald William (Reg)
Born: Wolverhampton, England, 12 August, 1938 — G
Died: Wolverhampton, England, 2 January, 2004

League Club	Source	Date Signed	Seasons Played	Apps	Subs	Gls
Plymouth Arg	Army	11/56	56	1	-	0
Aston Villa	Tr	02/58				

HOWELL Ronald Roger (Ron)
Born: Tottenham, N London, England, 22 May, 1949 — M

League Club	Source	Date Signed	Seasons Played	Apps	Subs	Gls
Millwall	App	03/67	66-69	7	7	0
Cambridge U	Tr	09/70	70	10	2	1
Swindon T	Kettering T	07/72	72	22	3	1
Brighton & HA	Tr	07/73	73	26	1	9

HOWELLS David
Born: Guildford, Surrey, England, 15 December, 1967 — M
England: Youth

League Club	Source	Date Signed	Seasons Played	Apps	Subs	Gls
Tottenham H	App	01/85	85-97	238	39	22
Southampton	Tr	07/98	98	8	1	1
Bristol C	L	03/99	98	8	0	1

HOWELLS Gareth Jonathan
Born: Guildford, Surrey, England, 13 June, 1970 — G

League Club	Source	Date Signed	Seasons Played	Apps	Subs	Gls
Tottenham H	YT	07/88				
Torquay U	Tr	08/90	90-91	83	0	0

HOWELLS Jake Thomas
Born: St Albans, Hertfordshire, England, 18 April, 1991 — LM
England: Semi Pro-4//Wales: U21-5

League Club	Source	Date Signed	Seasons Played	Apps	Subs	Gls
Luton T	Sch	07/09	07-14	42	23	4

HOWELLS Jeffrey Denis (Jeff)
Born: Shoreham-by-Sea, West Sussex, England, 26 September, 1940 — WH

League Club	Source	Date Signed	Seasons Played	Apps	Subs	Gls
Millwall	Fulham (Am)	10/57	58-60	55	-	3

HOWELLS Lee David
Born: Fremantle, Australia, 14 October, 1968 — RM
England: Semi Pro-2

League Club	Source	Date Signed	Seasons Played	Apps	Subs	Gls
Bristol Rov	App	10/86				
Cheltenham T	Brisbane Lions (AUS)	12/91	99-03	119	2	6

HOWELLS Peter
Born: Middlesbrough, England, 23 September, 1932 — LW
Died: Middlesbrough, England, 16 January, 1993

League Club	Source	Date Signed	Seasons Played	Apps	Subs	Gls
Sheffield Wed		10/53	54-55	3	-	1
Hartlepool U	Tr	11/56	56	1	-	0

HOWELLS Raymond (Ray)
Born: Ystrad Rhondda, Rhondda Cynon Taff, Wales, 27 June, 1926 — LW

League Club	Source	Date Signed	Seasons Played	Apps	Subs	Gls
Crystal Palace	Mid-Rhondda U	06/47	46-49	25	-	5
Exeter C	Tr	07/51	51-52	15	-	3

HOWELLS Roger William
Born: Swansea, Wales, 18 September, 1931 — CF
Died: Llanelli, Carmarthenshire, Wales, 1975

League Club	Source	Date Signed	Seasons Played	Apps	Subs	Gls
Swansea C	Llanelli	03/50				
Darlington	Tr	02/53	52-53	2	-	0
Swansea C	Tr	07/54				

HOWELLS Ronald (Ron)
Born: Ferndale, Rhondda Cynon Taff, Wales, 3 August, 1935 — WH

League Club	Source	Date Signed	Seasons Played	Apps	Subs	Gls
Wolverhampton W	Nuneaton Bor	11/52	55-57	9	-	0
Portsmouth	Tr	03/59	58-60	65	-	2
Scunthorpe U	Tr	06/61	61-62	69	-	4
Walsall	Tr	07/63	63	13	-	0

HOWELLS Ronald Gilbert (Ron)
Born: Pont-henri, Carmarthenshire, Wales, 12 January, 1927 — G
Died: Pont-henri, Carmarthenshire, Wales, 29 December, 2011
Wales: 2/WLge-1

League Club	Source	Date Signed	Seasons Played	Apps	Subs	Gls
Swansea C	Pont-henri	04/48	47	9	-	0
Cardiff C	Barry T	07/50	51-56	155	-	0
Chester C	Worcester C	09/58	58-59	80	-	0

HOWELLS William Mansel (Billy)
Born: Grimsby, North Lincolnshire, England, 20 March, 1943 — CH

League Club	Source	Date Signed	Seasons Played	Apps	Subs	Gls
Grimsby T	Jnr	10/61	63	6	-	0

HOWES Shaun Colin
Born: Norwich, England, 7 November, 1977 — LB

League Club	Source	Date Signed	Seasons Played	Apps	Subs	Gls
Cambridge U	YT	07/96	95	0	1	0
Leyton Orient	Tr	11/96	96	3	2	0

HOWEY Lee Matthew
Born: Sunderland, England, 1 April, 1969 — CD

League Club	Source	Date Signed	Seasons Played	Apps	Subs	Gls
Ipswich T	App	10/86				
Sunderland	Bishop Auckland	03/93	92-96	39	30	8
Burnley	Tr	08/97	97-98	24	2	0
Northampton T	Tr	11/98	98-00	47	1	6

HOWEY Peter
Born: Kinsley, West Yorkshire, England, 23 January, 1958 — W

League Club	Source	Date Signed	Seasons Played	Apps	Subs	Gls
Huddersfield T	App	01/76	76-78	20	2	3

HOWEY Stephen Norman (Steve)
Born: Sunderland, England, 26 October, 1971 — CD
England: 4

League Club	Source	Date Signed	Seasons Played	Apps	Subs	Gls
Newcastle U	YT	12/89	88-99	167	24	6
Manchester C	Tr	08/00	00-02	94	0	11
Leicester C	Tr	07/03	03	13	0	1
Bolton W	Tr	01/04	03	2	1	0
Hartlepool U	New England Rev (USA)	03/05	04	0	1	0

HOWFIELD Robert Michael (Bobby)
Born: Watford, Hertfordshire, England, 3 December, 1936 — W/F

League Club	Source	Date Signed	Seasons Played	Apps	Subs	Gls
Watford	Bushey U	09/57	57-58	47	-	9
Crewe Alex	Tr	07/59	59	5	-	0
Aldershot	Tr	10/59	59-61	76	-	44
Watford	Tr	07/62	62-63	45	-	13
Fulham	Tr	11/63	63-64	26	-	9
Aldershot	Tr	08/65	65-66	33	1	10

HOWIE Scott
Born: Motherwell, Lanarkshire, Scotland, 4 January, 1972 — G
Scotland: U21-5

League Club	Source	Date Signed	Seasons Played	Apps	Subs	Gls
Norwich C	Clyde	08/93	93	1	1	0
Reading	Motherwell	03/98	97-99	84	1	0
Bristol Rov	Tr	08/01	01-02	90	0	0
Shrewsbury T	Tr	08/03	04	40	0	0

HOWIESON Cameron Drew Neru
Born: Dunedin, New Zealand, 22 December, 1994 — M
New Zealand: 9/U23-6/Youth

League Club	Source	Date Signed	Seasons Played	Apps	Subs	Gls
Burnley	Sch	03/12	11	0	2	0

HOWITT David John
Born: Birmingham, England, 4 August, 1952 — RB/M

League Club	Source	Date Signed	Seasons Played	Apps	Subs	Gls
Birmingham C	App	08/69	72	2	0	0
Bury	Tr	08/73	73	11	9	4
Workington	Tr	07/74	74	30	5	1
Aldershot	Tr	06/75	75-79	126	11	2

HOWITT Robert Gibb (Bobby)
Born: Glasgow, Scotland, 15 July, 1929 — IF/WH
Died: Carluke, Lanarkshire, Scotland, 31 January, 2005
Scotland: SLge-1

League Club	Source	Date Signed	Seasons Played	Apps	Subs	Gls
Sheffield U	Partick Thistle	07/55	55-57	89	-	31
Stoke C	Tr	04/58	58-62	133	-	14

HOWLAND David
Born: Ballynahinch, Down, Northern Ireland, 17 September, 1986 — M
Northern Ireland: U21-4

League Club	Source	Date Signed	Seasons Played	Apps	Subs	Gls
Birmingham C	Sch	11/04				
Port Vale	L	01/08	07	17	0	1
Port Vale	Tr	08/08	08-09	35	9	2

HOWLETT Gary Patrick
Born: Dublin, Republic of Ireland, 2 April, 1963 — M
Republic of Ireland: 1/U21-4/Youth

League Club	Source	Date Signed	Seasons Played	Apps	Subs	Gls
Coventry C	Home Farm (ROI)	11/80				
Brighton & HA	Tr	08/82	82-84	30	2	2
Bournemouth	Tr	12/84	84-86	56	4	7
Aldershot	L	08/87	87	1	0	0
Chester C	L	12/87	87	6	0	1
York C	Tr	01/88	87-90	94	7	13

HOWLETT Robert Victor (Bobby)
Born: West Ham, E London, England, 12 December, 1948 — CD

League Club	Source	Date Signed	Seasons Played	Apps	Subs	Gls
Chelsea	App	12/65				
Southend U	Tr	09/67	67-68	4	2	0
Colchester U	Tr	07/69	69	10	6	0

HOWSAM Alfred Dennis (Dennis)
Born: Sheffield, England, 21 October, 1922 — CF
Died: Sheffield, England, March, 1981

League Club	Source	Date Signed	Seasons Played	Apps	Subs	Gls
Sheffield Wed	Jnr	11/45				
Chesterfield	Tr	03/47	46-47	12	-	4
Halifax T	Tr	06/48	48	20	-	4

HOWSHALL Gerald Thomas (Gerry)
Born: Stoke-on-Trent, England, 27 October, 1944 — WH

League Club	Source	Date Signed	Seasons Played	Apps	Subs	Gls
West Bromwich A	App	05/62	63-67	43	2	3
Norwich C	Tr	11/67	67-70	36	4	0

HOWSON Jonathan Mark (Jonny)
Born: Morley, West Yorkshire, England, 21 May, 1988 — M
England: U21-1

League Club	Source	Date Signed	Seasons Played	Apps	Subs	Gls
Leeds U	Sch	07/06	06-11	157	28	23
Norwich C	Tr	01/12	11-14	88	14	13

HOWSON Stuart Leigh
Born: Chorley, Lancashire, England, 30 September, 1981 — M

League Club	Source	Date Signed	Seasons Played	Apps	Subs	Gls
Blackburn Rov	YT	07/99				
Chesterfield	Tr	02/02	01-03	51	4	3

HOY Kristian
Born: Doncaster, South Yorkshire, England, 27 April, 1976 — F

League Club	Source	Date Signed	Seasons Played	Apps	Subs	Gls
Doncaster Rov	Jnr	07/94	94	0	1	0

HOY Robert (Bobby)
Born: Halifax, West Yorkshire, England, 10 January, 1950 — W
England: Youth

League Club	Source	Date Signed	Seasons Played	Apps	Subs	Gls
Huddersfield T	App	11/67	66-74	140	4	18
Blackburn Rov	Tr	03/75	74-75	13	6	0
Halifax T	Tr	06/76	76	30	0	7
York C	Tr	08/77	77	10	4	1
Rochdale	Tr	12/77	77-80	61	5	12

HOY Roger Ernest
Born: Poplar, E London, England, 6 December, 1946 — M/D

League Club	Source	Date Signed	Seasons Played	Apps	Subs	Gls
Tottenham H	Jnr	05/64	65-67	10	0	0
Crystal Palace	Tr	09/68	68-69	54	0	6
Luton T	Tr	06/70	70	32	0	0
Cardiff C	Tr	08/71	71-72	14	2	0

HOYLAND Jamie William
Born: Sheffield, England, 23 January, 1966 — M
England: Youth

League Club	Source	Date Signed	Seasons Played	Apps	Subs	Gls
Manchester C	App	11/83	83-84	2	0	0
Bury	Tr	07/86	86-89	169	3	35
Sheffield U	Tr	07/90	90-94	72	17	6
Bristol C	L	03/94	93	6	0	0
Burnley	Tr	10/94	94-97	77	10	3
Carlisle U	L	11/97	97	5	0	0
Scarborough	Tr	08/98	98	44	0	3

HOYLAND Thomas (Tommy)
Born: Sheffield, England, 14 June, 1932 — RH/IF

League Club	Source	Date Signed	Seasons Played	Apps	Subs	Gls
Sheffield U	Jnr	10/49	49-60	181	-	18
Bradford C	Tr	10/61	61-62	27	-	6

HOYLE Colin Roy
Born: Wirksworth, Derbyshire, England, 15 January, 1972 — CD

League Club	Source	Date Signed	Seasons Played	Apps	Subs	Gls
Arsenal	YT	01/90				
Chesterfield	L	02/90	89	3	0	0
Barnsley	Tr	07/90				
Bradford C	Tr	08/92	92-93	55	7	1
Notts Co	Tr	08/94	94-95	5	0	0
Mansfield T	L	10/94	94	4	1	0

HOYLE Herbert (Bert)
Born: Baildon, West Yorkshire, England, 22 April, 1920 — G
Died: Torbay, Devon, England, July, 2003

League Club	Source	Date Signed	Seasons Played	Apps	Subs	Gls
Wolverhampton W	Army	05/46				
Exeter C	Tr	08/46	46-49	82	-	0
Bristol Rov	Tr	05/50	50-52	105	-	0

HOYTE Gavin Andrew
Born: Walthamstow, NE London, England, 6 June, 1990 — RB
England: Youth

League Club	Source	Date Signed	Seasons Played	Apps	Subs	Gls
Arsenal	Sch	09/07	08	1	0	0
Watford	L	01/09	08	6	1	0
Brighton & HA	L	10/09	09	16	2	0
Lincoln C	L	10/10	10	11	1	0
AFC Wimbledon	L	01/12	11	2	1	0
Dagenham & Red	Tr	07/12	12-13	65	3	0
Gillingham	Tr	08/14	14	26	4	0

HOYTE Justin Raymond
Born: Leytonstone, NE London, England, 20 November, 1984 — RB
England: U21-18/Youth

League Club	Source	Date Signed	Seasons Played	Apps	Subs	Gls
Arsenal	Sch	07/02	02-07	24	10	1
Sunderland	L	08/05	05	27	0	1
Middlesbrough	Tr	08/08	08-13	123	19	2
Millwall	Tr	11/13	13-14	5	2	0

HREIDARSSON Hermann
Born: Reykjavik, Iceland, 11 July, 1974 — CD
Iceland: 89/U21-6

League Club	Source	Date Signed	Seasons Played	Apps	Subs	Gls
Crystal Palace	IBV (ICE)	08/97	97-98	32	5	2
Brentford	Tr	09/98	98-99	41	0	6
Wimbledon	Tr	10/99	99-00	25	0	1
Ipswich T	Tr	08/00	00-02	101	1	2
Charlton Ath	Tr	03/03	03-06	130	2	3
Portsmouth	Tr	06/07	07-11	88	14	7
Coventry C	Tr	01/12	11	2	0	0

HRISTOV Gjorgi
Born: Bitola, Macedonia, 30 January, 1976 — F
Macedonia: 48/U21

League Club	Source	Date Signed	Seasons Played	Apps	Subs	Gls
Barnsley	Part'n Belgrade (YUG)	07/97	97-99	18	26	8

HUBBARD John (Jack)
Born: Wath-on-Dearne, South Yorkshire, England, 24 March, 1925 — RB/WH
Died: Wath on Dearne, South Yorkshire, England, 10 June, 2002

League Club	Source	Date Signed	Seasons Played	Apps	Subs	Gls
Notts Co		02/45	46	13	-	2
Scunthorpe U	Scarborough	08/50	50-59	359	-	12

HUBBARD John Gaulton (Johnny)
Born: Pretoria, South Africa, 16 December, 1930 — LW
Scotland: SLge-4

League Club	Source	Date Signed	Seasons Played	Apps	Subs	Gls
Bury	Glasgow Rangers	04/59	59-61	109	-	29

HUBBARD Philip John (Phil)
Born: Lincoln, England, 25 January, 1949 — M

League Club	Source	Date Signed	Seasons Played	Apps	Subs	Gls
Lincoln C	App	07/66	65-71	150	2	41
Norwich C	Tr	12/71	71-72	6	4	1
Grimsby T	Tr	10/72	72-75	144	2	37
Lincoln C	Tr	08/76	76-79	100	9	11

HUBBARD Terence John (Terry)
Born: Sebastopol, Torfaen, Wales, 6 November, 1950 — M
Wales: U23-2/Schools

League Club	Source	Date Signed	Seasons Played	Apps	Subs	Gls
Swindon T	App	11/68	70-75	81	1	3

HUBBICK David (Dave)
Born: South Shields, Tyne and Wear, England, 16 March, 1960 — F

League Club	Source	Date Signed	Seasons Played	Apps	Subs	Gls
Ipswich T	App	01/78				
Wimbledon	Tr	09/80	80-81	22	4	6
Colchester U	Dagenham	10/83	83-84	4	11	1

HUBBICK Henry Edward (Harry)
Born: Jarrow, Tyne and Wear, England, 12 November, 1910 — LB
Died: Preston, Lancashire, England, 18 March, 1992

League Club	Source	Date Signed	Seasons Played	Apps	Subs	Gls
Burnley	Spennymoor U	03/35	35-36	58	-	1
Bolton W	Tr	02/37	36-46	128	-	0
Port Vale	Tr	10/47	47-48	50	-	1
Rochdale	Tr	01/49	48-50	90	-	0

HUBBLE Conor Stephen James
Born: Chelmsford, England, 29 November, 1994 — W

League Club	Source	Date Signed	Seasons Played	Apps	Subs	Gls
Colchester U	Queens Park Rgrs (Sch)	07/13	13	0	1	0

HUBERTZ Poul
Born: Roskilde, Denmark, 21 September, 1976 — F

League Club	Source	Date Signed	Seasons Played	Apps	Subs	Gls
Millwall	AAB Aalborg (DEN)	08/06	06	14	20	9
Northampton T	Tr	08/07	07	33	7	13

HUCK William Roger Fernend (Willie)
Born: Paris, France, 17 March, 1979 — M

League Club	Source	Date Signed	Seasons Played	Apps	Subs	Gls
Arsenal	AS Monaco (FRA)	11/98				
Bournemouth	Tr	03/99	98-01	11	29	0

HUCKER Ian Peter (Peter)
Born: Hampstead, NW London, England, 28 October, 1959 — G
England: U21-2

League Club	Source	Date Signed	Seasons Played	Apps	Subs	Gls
Queens Park Rgrs	App	07/77	80-85	160	0	0
Oxford U	Tr	02/87	86-89	66	0	0
West Bromwich A	L	01/88	87	7	0	0
Millwall	Tr	11/89				
Aldershot	Tr	11/90	90	27	0	0

HUCKERBY Darren Carl
Born: Nottingham, England, 23 April, 1976 — F
England: B-1/U21-4

League Club	Source	Date Signed	Seasons Played	Apps	Subs	Gls
Lincoln C	YT	07/93	93-95	20	8	5
Newcastle U	Tr	11/95	95	0	1	0
Millwall	L	09/96	96	6	0	3
Coventry C	Tr	11/96	96-99	85	9	28
Leeds U	Tr	08/99	99-00	11	29	2
Manchester C	Tr	12/00	00-02	44	25	22
Nottingham F	L	02/03	02	9	0	5
Norwich C	Tr	09/03	03-07	177	13	41

HUDD David Clive
Born: Bristol, England, 9 July, 1944 — IF

League Club	Source	Date Signed	Seasons Played	Apps	Subs	Gls
Bristol Rov	Old Georgians	07/63	64	5	-	1

HUDDART David Joseph (Dave)
Born: Maryport, Cumbria, England, 18 November, 1937 — G

League Club	Source	Date Signed	Seasons Played	Apps	Subs	Gls
Aldershot		06/61				
Gillingham	Tr	07/62	62-64	10	-	0

HUDDLESTONE Edward Thomas
Born: Nottingham, England, 29 September, 1935 — CF

League Club	Source	Date Signed	Seasons Played	Apps	Subs	Gls
Nottingham F	Blackpool (Am)	12/56	56	1	-	0

HUDDLESTONE Thomas Andrew (Tom)
Born: Nottingham, England, 28 December, 1986 — DM
England: 4/U21-32/Youth

League Club	Source	Date Signed	Seasons Played	Apps	Subs	Gls
Derby Co	Sch	02/04	03-04	84	4	0
Tottenham H	Tr	07/05	05-12	104	40	8
Wolverhampton W	L	10/05	05	12	1	1
Hull C	Tr	08/13	13-14	65	2	3

HUDGELL Arthur John
Born: Hackney, E London, England, 28 December, 1920 — LB
Died: Enfield, N London, England, 13 October, 2000

League Club	Source	Date Signed	Seasons Played	Apps	Subs	Gls
Crystal Palace	Eton Manor	12/37	46	25	-	1
Sunderland	Tr	01/47	46-56	260	-	0

HUDSON Alan Anthony
Born: Chelsea, W London, England, 21 June, 1951 — M
England: 2/U23-10

League Club	Source	Date Signed	Seasons Played	Apps	Subs	Gls
Chelsea	App	06/68	68-73	144	1	10
Stoke C	Tr	01/74	73-76	105	0	9
Arsenal	Tr	12/76	76-77	36	0	0
Chelsea	Seattle Sounders (USA)	08/83				
Stoke C	Tr	01/84	83-85	38	1	0

HUDSON Albert George
Born: Swansea, Wales, 17 June, 1920 — IF
Died: Swansea, Wales, June, 2001
Wales: Schools

League Club	Source	Date Signed	Seasons Played	Apps	Subs	Gls
Fulham	Caerau	08/37	46	1	-	0

HUDSON Carl Bernard
Born: Bradford, England, 10 October, 1966 — CD

League Club	Source	Date Signed	Seasons Played	Apps	Subs	Gls
Rochdale	Bradford C (App)	08/86	86	13	2	1

HUDSON Charles Arthur (Charlie)
Born: Castle Bytham, Lincolnshire, England, 3 April, 1920 — CF
Died: Barnoldswick, Lancashire, England, 14 November, 2008

League Club	Source	Date Signed	Seasons Played	Apps	Subs	Gls
Accrington Stan (Am)	Guiseley	06/46	46	11	-	3

HUDSON Christopher Ben (Chris)
Born: Rotherham, South Yorkshire, England, 13 March, 1951 — RB

League Club	Source	Date Signed	Seasons Played	Apps	Subs	Gls
Rotherham U	App	03/68	68-71	52	7	1

HUDSON Christopher John (John)
Born: Middleton, Greater Manchester, England, 25 November, 1964 — LW

League Club	Source	Date Signed	Seasons Played	Apps	Subs	Gls
Oldham Ath	Manchester C (App)	09/82	82-83	16	4	0
Rochdale	Kramfors (SWE)	02/87	86	18	1	1

HUDSON Colin Arthur Richard
Born: Undy, Monmouthshire, Wales, 5 October, 1935 — W
Died: Monmouth, Wales, October, 2005

League Club	Source	Date Signed	Seasons Played	Apps	Subs	Gls
Newport Co	Undy U	04/54	53-56	82	-	20
Cardiff C	Tr	07/57	57-60	60	-	9
Brighton & HA	Tr	06/61	61	1	-	0
Newport Co	Tr	06/62	62	30	-	1

HUDSON Daniel Robert (Danny)
Born: Mexborough, South Yorkshire, England, 25 June, 1979 — M

League Club	Source	Date Signed	Seasons Played	Apps	Subs	Gls
Rotherham U	YT	06/97	97-00	29	19	5

HUDSON Gary
Born: West Auckland, County Durham, England, 1 November, 1955 — G

League Club	Source	Date Signed	Seasons Played	Apps	Subs	Gls
Preston NE (Am)		08/73	73	1	0	0

HUDSON Gary Paul
Born: Bradford, England, 25 February, 1951 — FB

League Club	Source	Date Signed	Seasons Played	Apps	Subs	Gls
Bradford Park Ave	Jnr	07/68	67-69	38	1	0

HUDSON Geoffrey Alan (Geoff)
Born: Leeds, England, 14 October, 1931 — FB

League Club	Source	Date Signed	Seasons Played	Apps	Subs	Gls
Bradford Park Ave	Jnr	12/49	50-56	95	-	0
Bradford C	Tr	02/57	56-58	34	-	0
Halifax T	Tr	08/59	59-60	52	-	0
Exeter C	Tr	07/61	61	41	-	0
Crewe Alex	Tr	07/62	62	1	-	0
Gillingham	Tr	07/63	63-64	81	-	1
Lincoln C	Tr	05/65	65	33	0	0
Rotherham U	Tr	06/66				

HUDSON George Anthony
Born: Manchester, England, 14 March, 1937 — CF

League Club	Source	Date Signed	Seasons Played	Apps	Subs	Gls
Blackburn Rov		01/58	58	4	-	1
Accrington Stan	Tr	07/60	60	44	-	35
Peterborough U	Tr	10/61	61-62	65	-	38
Coventry C	Tr	04/63	62-65	113	0	62
Northampton T	Tr	03/66	65-66	18	0	6
Tranmere Rov	Tr	01/67	66-68	54	1	18

HUDSON George William (Garth)
Born: Havant, Hampshire, England, 26 October, 1923 — CH
Died: Portsmouth, England, August, 2014

League Club	Source	Date Signed	Seasons Played	Apps	Subs	Gls
Portsmouth	Havant Rov	08/45	47	1	-	0
Swindon T	Tr	09/48	48-59	401	-	11

HUDSON John (Jackie)
Born: Blaydon, Tyne and Wear, England, 5 October, 1921 — CF/RW
Died: Chesterfield, Derbyshire, England, January, 2008

League Club	Source	Date Signed	Seasons Played	Apps	Subs	Gls
Newcastle U		08/40				
Chesterfield	West Stanley	10/46	46-51	169	-	33
Shrewsbury T	Bangor C	09/53	53-54	48	-	20

HUDSON Kirk
Born: Southend-on-Sea, England, 12 December, 1986 — W

League Club	Source	Date Signed	Seasons Played	Apps	Subs	Gls
Bournemouth	Glasgow Celtic (Jnr)	08/05	05	0	1	0
Aldershot T	Tr	01/06	08-09	59	18	15
Brentford	Tr	07/10	10	0	2	0

HUDSON Mark
Born: Bishop Auckland, County Durham, England, 24 October, 1980 — M

League Club	Source	Date Signed	Seasons Played	Apps	Subs	Gls
Middlesbrough	YT	07/99	00-01	0	5	0
Chesterfield	L	08/02	02	15	1	1
Carlisle U	L	12/02	02	14	1	1
Chesterfield	Tr	03/03	02-04	72	5	8
Huddersfield T	Tr	07/05	05-06	55	6	6
Rotherham U	Tr	07/07	07-08	65	8	14
Blackpool	Tr	08/09				
Grimsby T	Gainsborough Trinity	11/09	09	11	5	2

HUDSON Mark Alexander
Born: Guildford, Surrey, England, 30 March, 1982 — CD

League Club	Source	Date Signed	Seasons Played	Apps	Subs	Gls
Fulham	YT	04/99				
Oldham Ath	L	08/03	03	15	0	0
Crystal Palace	Tr	01/04	03-07	112	8	7
Charlton Ath	Tr	07/08	08	43	0	3
Cardiff C	Tr	07/09	09-14	141	3	11
Huddersfield T	Tr	09/14	14	41	0	2

HUDSON Morris
Born: Barnsley, South Yorkshire, England, 12 September, 1930 — LB

League Club	Source	Date Signed	Seasons Played	Apps	Subs	Gls
Barnsley	Jnr	01/49	50-53	36	-	0
Bradford C	Tr	07/55	55	4	-	0

HUDSON Raymond James (Ray)
Born: Slough, Berkshire, England, 21 November, 1937 — RB

League Club	Source	Date Signed	Seasons Played	Apps	Subs	Gls
Reading	Jnr	11/54	55-58	11	-	0

HUDSON Raymond Wilfred (Ray)
Born: Gateshead, Tyne and Wear, England, 24 March, 1955 — M

League Club	Source	Date Signed	Seasons Played	Apps	Subs	Gls
Newcastle U	App	03/73	73-77	16	4	1

HUDSON Stanley Robert (Stan)
Born: Fulham, W London, England, 10 February, 1923 — LW
Died: Fulham, W London, England, 21 June, 1951

League Club	Source	Date Signed	Seasons Played	Apps	Subs	Gls
Queens Park Rgrs	West Ham U (Am)	09/48	48-49	22	-	7

HUDSON William Albert (Billy)
Born: Swansea, Wales, 10 March, 1928 — W
Died: Swansea, Wales, February, 2014
Wales: Amateur

League Club	Source	Date Signed	Seasons Played	Apps	Subs	Gls
Leeds U	Pembroke Dock	05/51	51	4	-	0
Sheffield U	Tr	05/52	53	1	-	0
Mansfield T	Tr	05/54	54	8	-	1

HUDSON-ODOI Bradley
Born: Accra, Ghana, 29 November, 1988 — F

League Club	Source	Date Signed	Seasons Played	Apps	Subs	Gls
Hereford U	Fulham (Sch)	07/08	08	10	6	3

HUFFER Philip (Phil)
Born: Bedworth, Warwickshire, England, 23 January, 1932 — CH

Died: Coventry, England, August, 1995

League Club	Source	Date Signed	Seasons Played	Apps	Subs	Gls
Derby Co	Bedworth T	10/53				
Northampton T	Tr	05/54	54	1	-	0

HUGGINS John Edward Minden (Joe)
Born: India, 24 February, 1930 — IF

League Club	Source	Date Signed	Seasons Played	Apps	Subs	Gls
Aldershot	Alton T	12/55	55	6	-	5

HUGHES Aaron William
Born: Cookstown, Tyrone, Northern Ireland, 8 November, 1979 — CD
Northern Ireland: 96/B-2/Youth

League Club	Source	Date Signed	Seasons Played	Apps	Subs	Gls
Newcastle U	YT	03/97	97-04	193	12	4
Aston Villa	Tr	08/05	05-06	50	4	0
Fulham	Tr	07/07	07-13	191	5	1
Queens Park Rgrs	Tr	01/14	13	11	0	0
Brighton & HA	Tr	07/14	14	7	3	0

HUGHES Adam
Born: Wollongong, NSW, Australia, 14 July, 1982 — M

League Club	Source	Date Signed	Seasons Played	Apps	Subs	Gls
Doncaster Rov	Wollongong Wolv (AUS)	08/05	05	4	2	0

HUGHES Adrian Francis
Born: Billinge, Merseyside, England, 19 December, 1970 — CD

League Club	Source	Date Signed	Seasons Played	Apps	Subs	Gls
Preston NE	YT	03/89	87-91	91	9	3

HUGHES Alan
Born: Wallasey, Wirral, England, 5 October, 1948 — CF

League Club	Source	Date Signed	Seasons Played	Apps	Subs	Gls
Liverpool	Jnr	09/66				
Chester C	L	11/67	67	9	0	2

HUGHES Allan Leslie
Born: Swansea, Wales, 11 March, 1951 — FB

League Club	Source	Date Signed	Seasons Played	Apps	Subs	Gls
Swansea C	App	03/69	68	1	0	0

HUGHES Andrew John (Andy)
Born: Manchester, England, 2 January, 1978 — M

League Club	Source	Date Signed	Seasons Played	Apps	Subs	Gls
Oldham Ath	YT	01/96	95-97	18	15	1
Notts Co	Tr	01/98	97-00	85	25	17
Reading	Tr	07/01	01-04	157	9	18
Norwich C	Tr	07/05	05-06	63	9	2
Leeds U	Tr	08/07	07-10	93	23	1
Scunthorpe U	Tr	01/11	10	18	1	0
Charlton Ath	Tr	07/11	11-13	12	16	0

HUGHES Andrew Martyn
Born: Cardiff, Wales, 5 June, 1992 — LB

League Club	Source	Date Signed	Seasons Played	Apps	Subs	Gls
Newport Co	Cardiff C (Jnr)	07/10	13-14	39	3	3

HUGHES Anthony
Born: Liverpool, England, 3 October, 1973 — CD
England: Youth

League Club	Source	Date Signed	Seasons Played	Apps	Subs	Gls
Crewe Alex	YT	06/92	92-93	18	5	1

HUGHES Arthur
Born: Linlithgow, West Lothian, Scotland, 23 November, 1927 — IF

League Club	Source	Date Signed	Seasons Played	Apps	Subs	Gls
Notts Co	Jeanfield Swifts	07/49				
Nottingham F	Tr	05/51				
Grimsby T	Canterbury C	06/54	54	25	-	11
Gillingham	Tr	05/55	55	5	-	1

HUGHES Brian
Born: Skewen, Neath Port Talbot, Wales, 22 November, 1937 — FB/WH
Wales: U23-2/Schools

League Club	Source	Date Signed	Seasons Played	Apps	Subs	Gls
Swansea C	Jnr	07/56	58-66	219	0	7
Swansea C	Merthyr Tydfil	01/69	68	12	0	0

HUGHES Brian David
Born: Ludgershall, Wiltshire, England, 20 August, 1962 — M

League Club	Source	Date Signed	Seasons Played	Apps	Subs	Gls
Swindon T	App	07/80	80-82	67	3	5
Torquay U	Tr	08/83	83	33	5	6

HUGHES Bryan
Born: Liverpool, England, 19 June, 1976 — M

League Club	Source	Date Signed	Seasons Played	Apps	Subs	Gls
Wrexham	YT	07/94	93-96	71	23	12
Birmingham C	Tr	03/97	96-03	197	51	34
Charlton Ath	Tr	07/04	04-06	47	27	5
Hull C	Tr	07/07	07-08	27	14	1
Derby Co	L	10/09	09	3	0	0
Burton A	Tr	12/10	10	1	0	0
Accrington Stan	IBV (ICE)	10/11	11	15	6	3

HUGHES Byron Wayne (Wayne)
Born: Port Talbot, Wales, 8 March, 1958 — M
Wales: U21-3/Schools

League Club	Source	Date Signed	Seasons Played	Apps	Subs	Gls
West Bromwich A	App	03/76	76-77	3	3	2
Cardiff C	Tulsa Roughnecks (USA)	10/79	79-81	42	4	1

HUGHES Caspar Dennis Shankly
Born: Crewe, Cheshire, England, 9 June, 1993 — M

League Club	Source	Date Signed	Seasons Played	Apps	Subs	Gls
Crewe Alex	Sch	07/11	10-11	0	5	0

HUGHES Ceri Morgan
Born: Llwynypia, Rhondda Cynon Taff, Wales, 26 February, 1971 — M
Wales: 8/B-2/Youth

League Club	Source	Date Signed	Seasons Played	Apps	Subs	Gls
Luton T	YT	07/89	89-96	157	18	17
Wimbledon	Tr	07/97	97-98	21	10	1
Portsmouth	Tr	01/00	99-00	31	3	2

HUGHES Charles (Charlie)
Born: Manchester, England, 17 September, 1927 — LW/LB

League Club	Source	Date Signed	Seasons Played	Apps	Subs	Gls
Manchester U	Jnr	09/46				
Leeds U	Altrincham	09/50	50-51	21	-	2

HUGHES Charles James
Born: Blackpool, Lancashire, England, 7 September, 1939 — G

League Club	Source	Date Signed	Seasons Played	Apps	Subs	Gls
Wrexham		10/58	59-60	35	-	0

HUGHES Christopher (Chris)
Born: Sunderland, England, 5 March, 1984 — M

League Club	Source	Date Signed	Seasons Played	Apps	Subs	Gls
Darlington	Sch	07/03	03-04	29	16	2

HUGHES Connor Niall
Born: Bolton, Greater Manchester, England, 6 May, 1993 — W

League Club	Source	Date Signed	Seasons Played	Apps	Subs	Gls
Oldham Ath	Sch	07/11	11-12	0	8	0

HUGHES Daniel Paul (Danny)
Born: Bangor, Gwynedd, Wales, 13 February, 1980 — M

League Club	Source	Date Signed	Seasons Played	Apps	Subs	Gls
Wolverhampton W	YT	07/98				
Hartlepool U	Tr	03/99	98	6	2	0

HUGHES Darren John
Born: Prescot, Merseyside, England, 6 October, 1965 — LB/M

League Club	Source	Date Signed	Seasons Played	Apps	Subs	Gls
Everton	App	10/83	83-84	3	0	0
Shrewsbury T	Tr	06/85	85-86	34	3	1
Brighton & HA	Tr	09/86	86	26	0	2
Port Vale	Tr	09/87	87-91	183	1	4
Northampton T	Rtd	01/95	94-95	19	2	0
Exeter C	Tr	11/95	95-96	58	4	1

HUGHES David James
Born: Connah's Quay, Flintshire, Wales, 27 April, 1943 — RW

League Club	Source	Date Signed	Seasons Played	Apps	Subs	Gls
Wrexham	Jnr	05/61				
Tranmere Rov	Tr	07/62	62	2	-	0

HUGHES David John
Born: Liverpool, England, 23 September, 1951 — RW

League Club	Source	Date Signed	Seasons Played	Apps	Subs	Gls
Wrexham (Am)	Everton (Jnr)	05/70	70	1	0	0

HUGHES David Robert
Born: St Albans, Hertfordshire, England, 30 December, 1972 — M
England: Schools//Wales: U21-1

League Club	Source	Date Signed	Seasons Played	Apps	Subs	Gls
Southampton	Weymouth	07/91	93-98	21	33	3

HUGHES David Robert
Born: Blackburn, Greater Manchester, England, 7 September, 1948 — D/M

League Club	Source	Date Signed	Seasons Played	Apps	Subs	Gls
Preston NE	Blackburn YMCA	09/65	66-71	22	8	0
Southport	Tr	07/72	72	40	0	1
Bury	Tr	08/73	73	12	0	4
Southport	Tr	11/73	73-76	109	4	4
Crewe Alex		08/78	78	12	1	0

HUGHES David Thomas
Born: Birmingham, England, 19 March, 1958 — M/FB

League Club	Source	Date Signed	Seasons Played	Apps	Subs	Gls
Aston Villa	App	02/76	76	3	1	1
Lincoln C	Tr	04/77	77-80	61	1	1
Scunthorpe U	Tr	06/81	81	17	4	0

HUGHES Denis
Born: Stoke-on-Trent, England, 9 April, 1931 — RW
Died: Stoke-on-Trent, England, October, 1990

League Club	Source	Date Signed	Seasons Played	Apps	Subs	Gls
Stoke C	Jnr	09/48	50	1	-	0

HUGHES Derek
Born: Wrexham, Wales, 22 November, 1940 — RW

League Club	Source	Date Signed	Seasons Played	Apps	Subs	Gls
Wrexham (Am)	Druids U	07/61	61	1	-	0

HUGHES Edward Michael (Mike)
Born: Llanidloes, Powys, Wales, 3 September, 1940 — WH/IF

League Club	Source	Date Signed	Seasons Played	Apps	Subs	Gls
Cardiff C	Jnr	12/58	58	1	-	0
Exeter C	Tr	07/61	61-62	36	-	0
Chesterfield	Tr	07/63	63-68	208	2	9

HUGHES Emlyn Walter
Born: Barrow, Cumbria, England, 28 August, 1947 — CD/M
Died: Sheffield, England, 9 November, 2004
England: 62/FLge-9/U23-8

League Club	Source	Date Signed	Seasons Played	Apps	Subs	Gls
Blackpool	Jnr	09/64	65-66	27	1	0
Liverpool	Tr	03/67	66-78	474	0	35
Wolverhampton W	Tr	08/79	79-80	56	2	2
Rotherham U	Tr	09/81	81-82	55	1	6

League Club	Source	Date Signed	Seasons Played	Apps	Subs	Gls
Hull C	Tr	03/83	82	9	0	0
Swansea C	Mansfield T (NC)	09/83	83	7	0	0

HUGHES Garry
Born: Birmingham, England, 19 November, 1979 — D

League Club	Source	Date Signed	Seasons Played	Apps	Subs	Gls
Northampton T	YT	07/98	99-00	13	5	1

HUGHES Gordon
Born: Washington, Tyne and Wear, England, 19 June, 1936 — RW

League Club	Source	Date Signed	Seasons Played	Apps	Subs	Gls
Newcastle U	Tow Law T	08/56	56-62	133	-	18
Derby Co	Tr	08/63	63-67	184	0	22
Lincoln C	Tr	03/68	67-70	117	0	9

HUGHES Harold Anthony (Harry)
Born: Thurcroft, South Yorkshire, England, 12 August, 1937 — FB
Died: Rotherham, South Yorkshire, England, March, 2001

League Club	Source	Date Signed	Seasons Played	Apps	Subs	Gls
Rotherham U		06/59	59	1	-	0

HUGHES Harold James (Harry)
Born: Nuneaton, Warwickshire, England, 8 October, 1929 — CD
Died: Weymouth, Dorset, England, 15 October, 2013

League Club	Source	Date Signed	Seasons Played	Apps	Subs	Gls
Southport	Symingtons	08/50				
Chelsea	Tr	02/51	51	1	-	0
Bournemouth	Tr	06/52	52-57	77	-	2
Gillingham	Tr	07/58	58-62	205	-	14

HUGHES Ian
Born: Bangor, Gwynedd, Wales, 2 August, 1974 — CD/M
Wales: U21-12/Youth

League Club	Source	Date Signed	Seasons Played	Apps	Subs	Gls
Bury	YT	11/91	91-97	137	24	1
Blackpool	Tr	12/97	97-02	139	21	3
Huddersfield T	Tr	08/03	03	12	1	1

HUGHES Ian James
Born: Sunderland, England, 24 August, 1961 — CD
Wales: U21-1

League Club	Source	Date Signed	Seasons Played	Apps	Subs	Gls
Sunderland	App	08/79	79	1	0	0
Barnsley	Tr	07/81				

HUGHES Iorwerth (Iorrie)
Born: Abergele, Conwy, Wales, 26 May, 1925 — G
Died: Luton, England, 20 August, 1993
Wales: 4/Amateur

League Club	Source	Date Signed	Seasons Played	Apps	Subs	Gls
Luton T	Llandudno	04/49	49-50	36	-	0
Cardiff C	Tr	08/51	51	26	-	0
Newport Co	Worcester C	08/53	53-57	106	-	0

HUGHES James Horace (Jimmy)
Born: Leeds, England, 28 August, 1918 — WH/LB
Died: Ferndown, Dorset, England, 10 November, 1979

League Club	Source	Date Signed	Seasons Played	Apps	Subs	Gls
Fulham		09/46	46	1	-	0

HUGHES Jamie Joseph
Born: Liverpool, England, 5 April, 1977 — F

League Club	Source	Date Signed	Seasons Played	Apps	Subs	Gls
Tranmere Rov	YT	08/95				
Cardiff C	Connah's Quay Nomads	07/99	99	0	2	1

HUGHES Jeffrey Edward (Jeff)
Born: Larne, Antrim, Northern Ireland, 29 May, 1985 — LW
Northern Ireland: 2/U21-7

League Club	Source	Date Signed	Seasons Played	Apps	Subs	Gls
Lincoln C	Larne	08/05	05-06	55	8	8
Crystal Palace	Tr	07/07	07	4	6	0
Peterborough U	L	11/07	07	2	5	1
Bristol Rov	Tr	06/08	08-10	127	2	28
Notts Co	Tr	07/11	11-12	83	6	20
Fleetwood T	Tr	05/13	13-14	45	2	4

HUGHES Jerahl
Born: Brighton, England, 10 August, 1989 — W

League Club	Source	Date Signed	Seasons Played	Apps	Subs	Gls
Yeovil T	Crystal Palace (Sch)	07/07	07	0	1	0

HUGHES John
Born: Edinburgh, Scotland, 19 September, 1964 — F

League Club	Source	Date Signed	Seasons Played	Apps	Subs	Gls
Swansea C	Berwick Rgrs	11/89	89	16	8	4

HUGHES John
Born: Coatbridge, Lanarkshire, Scotland, 3 April, 1943 — F
Scotland: 8/SLge-6/U23-4

League Club	Source	Date Signed	Seasons Played	Apps	Subs	Gls
Crystal Palace	Glasgow Celtic	10/71	71-72	20	0	4
Sunderland	Tr	01/73	72	1	0	0

HUGHES John
Born: West Bromwich, West Midlands, England, 13 September, 1929 — IF
Died: 23 February, 2015

League Club	Source	Date Signed	Seasons Played	Apps	Subs	Gls
Walsall	Golden Lion	05/50	50-52	44	-	10

HUGHES John Gareth
Born: Prestatyn, Denbighshire, Wales, 18 February, 1942 — CF

League Club	Source	Date Signed	Seasons Played	Apps	Subs	Gls
Chester C	Rhyl	07/62	62	2	-	0

HUGHES John Ifor
Born: Bangor, Gwynedd, Wales, 4 May, 1951 — W

League Club	Source	Date Signed	Seasons Played	Apps	Subs	Gls
Blackpool	Bangor C	07/69	69-70	5	3	0
Southport	L	03/71	70	7	1	1
Stockport Co	Altrincham	01/76	75	11	1	3

HUGHES John Michael
Born: Manchester, England, 29 November, 1962 — M

League Club	Source	Date Signed	Seasons Played	Apps	Subs	Gls
Bury	Winsford U	11/80	81-82	1	1	0

HUGHES John Norman
Born: Tamworth, Staffordshire, England, 10 July, 1921 — W
Died: Lichfield, Staffordshire, England, 31 August, 2003

League Club	Source	Date Signed	Seasons Played	Apps	Subs	Gls
Birmingham C	Tamworth Castle	06/47	47-48	6	-	0

HUGHES John Paul (Paul)
Born: Hammersmith, W London, England, 19 April, 1976 — M
England: Schools

League Club	Source	Date Signed	Seasons Played	Apps	Subs	Gls
Chelsea	YT	07/94	96-97	13	8	2
Stockport Co	L	12/98	98	7	0	0
Norwich C	L	03/99	98	2	2	1
Southampton	Tr	03/00				
Luton T	Tr	08/01	01-03	62	17	6

HUGHES Kenneth David (Ken)
Born: Barmouth, Gwynedd, Wales, 9 January, 1966 — G

League Club	Source	Date Signed	Seasons Played	Apps	Subs	Gls
Crystal Palace	Jnr	08/85				
Shrewsbury T	Tr	07/86	86-91	74	0	0
Wrexham	Tr	08/92	92	8	0	0

HUGHES Lawrence (Laurie)
Born: Crosby, Merseyside, England, 2 March, 1924 — CH
Died: Liverpool, England, 9 September, 2011
England: 3/B-1

League Club	Source	Date Signed	Seasons Played	Apps	Subs	Gls
Liverpool	Tranmere Rov (Am)	02/43	46-57	303	-	1

HUGHES Lee
Born: Smethwick, West Midlands, England, 22 May, 1976 — F
England: Semi Pro-4

League Club	Source	Date Signed	Seasons Played	Apps	Subs	Gls
West Bromwich A	Kidderminster Hrs	05/97	97-00	137	19	78
Coventry C	Tr	08/01	01-02	38	4	15
West Bromwich A	Tr	08/02	02-03	35	20	11
Oldham Ath	Unattached	07/07	07-08	51	4	25
Blackpool	L	03/09	08	2	1	1
Notts Co	Tr	07/09	09-12	98	30	59
Port Vale	Tr	01/13	12-13	19	12	13

HUGHES Leslie Mark (Mark)
Born: Ruabon, Wrexham, Wales, 1 November, 1963 — F
Wales: 72/U21-5/Youth/Schools

League Club	Source	Date Signed	Seasons Played	Apps	Subs	Gls
Manchester U	App	11/80	83-85	85	4	37
Manchester U	Barcelona (SPN)	07/88	88-94	251	5	82
Chelsea	Tr	07/95	95-97	88	7	25
Southampton	Tr	07/98	98-99	50	2	2
Everton	Tr	03/00	99-00	15	3	1
Blackburn Rov	Tr	10/00	00-01	25	25	6

HUGHES Liam John
Born: Dudley, West Midlands, England, 11 September, 1988 — F

League Club	Source	Date Signed	Seasons Played	Apps	Subs	Gls
Wolverhampton W	Sch	03/07				
Bury	L	11/07	07	1	3	0

HUGHES Liam Michael
Born: Rotherham, South Yorkshire, England, 10 August, 1992 — M

League Club	Source	Date Signed	Seasons Played	Apps	Subs	Gls
Cambridge U	Jnr	10/10	14	26	4	3

HUGHES Lyndon James
Born: Smethwick, West Midlands, England, 16 September, 1950 — M/FB
England: Youth/Schools

League Club	Source	Date Signed	Seasons Played	Apps	Subs	Gls
West Bromwich A	App	01/68	68-74	89	9	3
Peterborough U	Tr	07/75	75-77	75	2	5

HUGHES Mark
Born: Port Talbot, Wales, 3 February, 1962 — CD
Wales: Schools

League Club	Source	Date Signed	Seasons Played	Apps	Subs	Gls
Bristol Rov	App	02/80	79-83	73	1	3
Torquay U	L	12/82	82	9	0	1
Swansea C	Tr	07/84	84	12	0	0
Bristol C	Tr	02/85	84-85	21	1	0
Tranmere Rov	Tr	09/85	85-93	258	8	9
Shrewsbury T	Tr	07/94	94-95	20	2	0

HUGHES Mark Anthony
Born: Kirkby, Merseyside, England, 9 December, 1986 — CD

League Club	Source	Date Signed	Seasons Played	Apps	Subs	Gls
Everton	Sch	12/04	06	0	1	0
Stockport Co	L	02/06	05	3	0	1
Northampton T	Tr	01/07	06-08	92	1	4
Walsall	Tr	07/09	09	24	2	1

League Club	Source	Date Signed	Seasons Played	Apps	Subs	Gls
Bury	N Queensland F'y (AUS)	06/11	11-12	46	6	0
Accrington Stan	L	01/13	12	5	0	0
Morecambe	Tr	07/13	13-14	83	1	8

HUGHES Mark Anthony
Born: Dungannon, Tyrone, Northern Ireland, 16 September, 1983 — M
Northern Ireland: 2/U23-1/U21-12/Youth/Schools

League Club	Source	Date Signed	Seasons Played	Apps	Subs	Gls
Tottenham H	YT	07/01				
Northampton T	L	08/04	04	3	0	0
Oldham Ath	Tr	11/04	04-05	55	5	1
Chesterfield	Tr	11/06	06	2	0	1
Chester C	Stevenage Bor	08/07	07-08	64	5	4
Barnet	Tr	10/09	08-11	123	5	7

HUGHES Mark Christopher
Born: Swindon, England, 17 July, 1967 — M
Wales: Youth

League Club	Source	Date Signed	Seasons Played	Apps	Subs	Gls
Swindon T	App	-	83	0	1	0

HUGHES Matthew Leonard (Matty)
Born: Golborne, Greater Manchester, England, 1 April, 1992 — F

League Club	Source	Date Signed	Seasons Played	Apps	Subs	Gls
Fleetwood T	Skelmersdale U	01/14	13-14	3	8	0

HUGHES Michael Eamonn
Born: Larne, Antrim, Northern Ireland, 2 August, 1971 — LW
Northern Ireland: 71/U23-2/U21-1/Youth/Schools

League Club	Source	Date Signed	Seasons Played	Apps	Subs	Gls
Manchester C	Carrick Rgrs	08/88	88-91	25	1	1
West Ham U (L)	RC Strasbourg (FRA)	11/94	94	15	2	2
West Ham U (L)	RC Strasbourg (FRA)	10/95	95	28	0	0
West Ham U	RC Strasbourg (FRA)	08/96	96-97	33	5	3
Wimbledon	Tr	09/97	97-01	99	16	13
Birmingham C	L	03/02	01	3	0	0
Crystal Palace	Tr	08/03	03-06	110	16	7
Coventry C	Tr	07/07	07	16	2	0

HUGHES Michael Richard (Mike)
Born: Bridgend, Wales, 19 August, 1964 — G
Wales: Youth

League Club	Source	Date Signed	Seasons Played	Apps	Subs	Gls
Swansea C	App	08/82	83-87	139	0	0

HUGHES Patrick Joseph (Pat)
Born: Coatbridge, Lanarkshire, Scotland, 28 February, 1945 — LW
Died: Coatbridge, Lanarkshire, Scotland, 25 February, 2010

League Club	Source	Date Signed	Seasons Played	Apps	Subs	Gls
Darlington	St Mirren	08/65	65	3	0	0

HUGHES Paul
Born: Manchester, England, 19 December, 1968 — RB

League Club	Source	Date Signed	Seasons Played	Apps	Subs	Gls
Bolton W	YT	07/87	87-89	12	1	0

HUGHES Philip Anthony (Phil)
Born: Belfast, Northern Ireland, 19 November, 1964 — G
Northern Ireland: 3/Youth

League Club	Source	Date Signed	Seasons Played	Apps	Subs	Gls
Leeds U	Manchester U (App)	01/83	83-84	6	0	0
Bury	Tr	07/85	85-87	80	0	0
Wigan Ath	Tr	11/87	87-90	99	0	0
Scarborough	Rochdale (NC)	10/91	91	17	0	0

HUGHES Richard (Ricky)
Born: Barrow, Cumbria, England, 27 December, 1950 — F

League Club	Source	Date Signed	Seasons Played	Apps	Subs	Gls
Barrow (Am)	Jnr	08/70	71	0	2	0

HUGHES Richard Daniel
Born: Glasgow, Scotland, 25 June, 1979 — DM
Scotland: 5/U21-9/Youth

League Club	Source	Date Signed	Seasons Played	Apps	Subs	Gls
Arsenal	Atalanta (ITA)	08/97				
Bournemouth	Tr	08/98	98-01	123	8	14
Portsmouth	Tr	06/02	02-10	96	35	0
Grimsby T	L	02/03	02	12	0	1
Bournemouth	Rtd	08/12	12-13	8	18	1

HUGHES Robert (Robbie)
Born: Carshalton, S London, England, 6 September, 1980 — M

League Club	Source	Date Signed	Seasons Played	Apps	Subs	Gls
Oxford U	Yeading	07/05	05	0	3	0

HUGHES Robert David
Born: Wrexham, Wales, 1 February, 1978 — CD
Wales: B-2/U21-13/Youth

League Club	Source	Date Signed	Seasons Played	Apps	Subs	Gls
Aston Villa	YT	07/96	96	4	3	0
Carlisle U	L	03/98	97	1	0	0
Shrewsbury T	Tr	09/99	99-00	42	4	3
Cardiff C	Tr	02/01	00-01	12	2	0

HUGHES Robert Ian
Born: Peterborough, England, 1 October, 1986 — M

League Club	Source	Date Signed	Seasons Played	Apps	Subs	Gls
Nottingham F	Sch	07/06	06	0	2	0

HUGHES Robert Ian (Ian)
Born: Cefn Mawr, Wrexham, Wales, 17 March, 1946 — RW

League Club	Source	Date Signed	Seasons Played	Apps	Subs	Gls
Wrexham	Oswestry T	02/66	65	9	0	3
Bradford Park Ave	Tr	07/67	67	13	0	0

HUGHES Ronald (Ron)
Born: Mold, Flintshire, Wales, 1 July, 1930 — RB/WH

League Club	Source	Date Signed	Seasons Played	Apps	Subs	Gls
Chester C	Mold Alex	09/50	51-61	399	-	21

HUGHES Ronald Hardwick (Ron)
Born: Workington, Cumbria, England, 17 August, 1955 — G

League Club	Source	Date Signed	Seasons Played	Apps	Subs	Gls
Workington	RNAD Broughton Moor	12/75	75	15	0	0

HUGHES Roy
Born: Manchester, England, 13 August, 1949 — M/D

League Club	Source	Date Signed	Seasons Played	Apps	Subs	Gls
Bury	App	09/66	67-71	45	4	2

HUGHES Stephen David
Born: Motherwell, Lanarkshire, Scotland, 14 November, 1982 — M
Scotland: 1/B-1/U21-12/Youth

League Club	Source	Date Signed	Seasons Played	Apps	Subs	Gls
Leicester C	Glasgow Rangers	01/05	04-06	75	16	7
Norwich C	Motherwell	07/09	09-10	12	18	3
MK Dons	L	02/11	10	2	4	0

HUGHES Stephen John
Born: Reading, England, 18 September, 1976 — M
England: U21-8/Youth/Schools

League Club	Source	Date Signed	Seasons Played	Apps	Subs	Gls
Arsenal	YT	07/95	94-99	22	27	4
Fulham	L	07/99	99	3	0	0
Everton	Tr	03/00	99-00	27	2	1
Watford	Tr	07/01	01	11	4	0
Charlton Ath	Tr	08/03				
Coventry C	Tr	07/04	04-07	125	8	6
Walsall	Tr	08/08	08	32	0	2

HUGHES Stephen John (Billy)
Born: Folkestone, Kent, England, 29 July, 1960 — M

League Club	Source	Date Signed	Seasons Played	Apps	Subs	Gls
Gillingham	Jnr	07/77	75-80	110	16	8
Crystal Palace	Tr	07/81	81	3	4	0
Wimbledon	Tr	03/82	81	2	0	0

HUGHES Stephen John (Steve)
Born: Warrington, Cheshire, England, 4 January, 1958 — F

League Club	Source	Date Signed	Seasons Played	Apps	Subs	Gls
Crewe Alex	Manchester C (App)	03/76	75	0	2	0

HUGHES Stephen Thomas
Born: High Wycombe, Buckinghamshire, England, 26 January, 1984 — F

League Club	Source	Date Signed	Seasons Played	Apps	Subs	Gls
Brentford	Sch	07/02	02-03	3	9	0

HUGHES Terence Philip (Terry)
Born: Llanidloes, Powys, Wales, 10 March, 1953 — F

League Club	Source	Date Signed	Seasons Played	Apps	Subs	Gls
Shrewsbury T	App	03/71	69-73	66	5	22

HUGHES Thomas Alexander (Tommy)
Born: Dalmuir, Dunbartonshire, Scotland, 11 July, 1947 — G
Scotland: U23-2

League Club	Source	Date Signed	Seasons Played	Apps	Subs	Gls
Chelsea	Clydebank Jnrs	07/65	66-69	11	0	0
Aston Villa	Tr	06/71	71	16	0	0
Brighton & HA	L	02/73	72	3	0	0
Hereford U	Tr	08/73	73-81	240	0	0

HUGHES Thomas Glynfor (Glyn)
Born: Coedpoeth, Wrexham, Wales, 29 November, 1931 — RW
Died: Southsea, Hampshire, England, 19 August, 1995

League Club	Source	Date Signed	Seasons Played	Apps	Subs	Gls
Sheffield Wed	Llay Welfare	01/51				
Wrexham	Tr	08/52	52-54	92	-	20
Newport Co	Tr	07/55	55	4	-	0

HUGHES Thomas Gwynfor (Gwyn)
Born: Blaenau Ffestiniog, Gwynedd, Wales, 7 May, 1922 — WH/IF
Died: Northampton, England, 14 March, 1999

League Club	Source	Date Signed	Seasons Played	Apps	Subs	Gls
Northampton T	Blaenau Ffestiniog	12/45	46-55	225	-	15

HUGHES Walter Cyril Joseph (Wally)
Born: Dingle, Merseyside, England, 15 March, 1934 — RW
Died: Auckland, New Zealand, 21 January, 2011

League Club	Source	Date Signed	Seasons Played	Apps	Subs	Gls
Liverpool	Bolton W (Am)	10/54				
Stockport Co	Tr	07/55				
Sheffield U	Winsford U	01/56	55	2	-	0
Bradford Park Ave	Wisbech T	04/57	56-57	20	-	0
Southport	Tr	02/58	57	11	-	0

HUGHES William (Billy)
Born: Ballymena, Antrim, Northern Ireland, 9 May, 1929 — RW
Died: Salford, England, June, 2005
Northern Ireland: 1

League Club	Source	Date Signed	Seasons Played	Apps	Subs	Gls
Bolton W	Larne T	08/48	48-52	47	-	2
Bournemouth	Tr	06/53	53	16	-	1

HUGHES William (Billy)
Born: Glasgow, Scotland, 3 March, 1929 — RW
Died: Malton, North Yorkshire, England, 17 October, 2003

League Club	Source	Date Signed	Seasons Played	Apps	Subs	Gls
York C	Newcastle U (Am)	05/51	51-61	349	-	55

HUGHES William (Billy)
Born: Coatbridge, Lanarkshire, Scotland, 30 December, 1948 — F

Scotland: 1

League Club	Source	Date Signed	Seasons Played	Apps	Subs	Gls
Sunderland	Jnr	02/66	66-76	264	24	74
Derby Co	Tr	08/77	77	17	2	8
Leicester C	Tr	12/77	77-78	36	1	5
Carlisle U	L	09/79	79	5	0	0

HUGHES William Arthur (Archie)
Born: Colwyn Bay, Conwy, Wales, 2 February, 1919 G
Died: Colwyn Bay, Conwy, Wales, 11 March, 1992
Wales: 5

League Club	Source	Date Signed	Seasons Played	Apps	Subs	Gls
Huddersfield T	Newry T	05/39				
Tottenham H	Tr	12/45	46-47	2	-	0
Blackburn Rov	Tr	10/48	48-49	27	-	0
Rochdale	Nelson	09/50	50	9	-	0
Crystal Palace	Tr	02/51	50-51	18	-	0

HUGHES William Henry (Billy)
Born: Cardiff, Wales, 2 October, 1920 CH
Died: Hartlepool, Cleveland, England, 30 March, 1995
Wales: Schools

League Club	Source	Date Signed	Seasons Played	Apps	Subs	Gls
Hartlepool U	Newcastle U (Am)	05/46	46-49	124	-	2

HUGHES William James (Will)
Born: Weybridge, Surrey, England, 7 April, 1995 M
England: U21-17/Youth

League Club	Source	Date Signed	Seasons Played	Apps	Subs	Gls
Derby Co	Sch	07/12	11-14	108	13	7

HUGHES William Marshall (Billy)
Born: Llanelli, Carmarthenshire, Wales, 6 March, 1918 LB
Died: Birmingham, England, 16 June, 1981
Wales: 10/War-14

League Club	Source	Date Signed	Seasons Played	Apps	Subs	Gls
Birmingham C	Llanelli	05/35	35-46	104	-	0
Luton T	Tr	07/47	47	31	-	0
Chelsea	Tr	03/48	47-50	93	-	0

HUGHES Zacari David
Born: Perth, Australia, 6 June, 1971 CD

League Club	Source	Date Signed	Seasons Played	Apps	Subs	Gls
Rochdale	YT	08/89	87	2	0	0

HUGHES-MASON Kiernan Peter
Born: Hackney, E London, England, 22 October, 1991 F

League Club	Source	Date Signed	Seasons Played	Apps	Subs	Gls
Millwall	Sch	08/09	09-10	0	2	0

HUGHTON Christopher William Gerard (Chris)
Born: Stratford, E London, England, 11 December, 1958 FB
Republic of Ireland: 53

League Club	Source	Date Signed	Seasons Played	Apps	Subs	Gls
Tottenham H	Jnr	06/77	79-89	293	4	12
West Ham U	Tr	11/90	90-91	32	1	0
Brentford	Tr	03/92	91-92	32	0	0

HUGHTON Cian James
Born: Broxbourne, Hertfordshire, England, 25 January, 1989 RB
Republic of Ireland: U21-2

League Club	Source	Date Signed	Seasons Played	Apps	Subs	Gls
Tottenham H	Sch	07/07				
Lincoln C	Tr	07/09	09-10	58	5	6
Birmingham C	Tr	02/12				

HUGHTON Henry Timothy
Born: Stratford, E London, England, 18 November, 1959 FB/M
Republic of Ireland: U21-1

League Club	Source	Date Signed	Seasons Played	Apps	Subs	Gls
Leyton Orient	App	12/76	78-81	104	7	2
Crystal Palace	Tr	07/82	82-85	113	5	1
Brentford	Tr	09/86	86	5	3	0
Leyton Orient	Tr	12/86	86-87	16	2	0

HUGILL Jordan Thomas
Born: Middlesbrough, England, 4 June, 1992 F

League Club	Source	Date Signed	Seasons Played	Apps	Subs	Gls
Port Vale	Marske U	07/13	13	7	13	4
Preston NE	Tr	06/14	14	0	3	0
Tranmere Rov	L	02/15	14	4	2	1
Hartlepool U	L	03/15	14	8	0	4

HUGO Roger Victor
Born: Woking, Surrey, England, 6 September, 1942 IF

League Club	Source	Date Signed	Seasons Played	Apps	Subs	Gls
West Ham U	Jnr	10/60	63	3	-	2
Watford	Tr	05/65	65	24	1	6

HUKE Shane
Born: Reading, England, 2 October, 1985 M

League Club	Source	Date Signed	Seasons Played	Apps	Subs	Gls
Peterborough U	Sch	10/03	04-06	18	11	1
Dagenham & Red	Tr	07/07	07-08	31	6	2

HUKIN Arthur
Born: Sheffield, England, 22 October, 1937 CF
Died: Bedford, England, 21 November, 1983

League Club	Source	Date Signed	Seasons Played	Apps	Subs	Gls
Sheffield Wed	Jnr	10/54	54	6	-	3

HULBERT Robin James
Born: Plymouth, England, 14 March, 1980 M
England: Youth/Schools

League Club	Source	Date Signed	Seasons Played	Apps	Subs	Gls
Swindon T	YT	09/97	97-99	12	17	0
Bristol C	Tr	03/00	99-02	21	18	0
Shrewsbury T	L	03/03	02	4	3	0
Port Vale	Telford U	07/04	04-07	54	13	1
Darlington	Tr	08/08	08	9	18	2

HULL Alan Edward
Born: Southend-on-Sea, England, 4 September, 1962 F

League Club	Source	Date Signed	Seasons Played	Apps	Subs	Gls
Leyton Orient	Barking	05/87	87-90	54	25	16

HULL Gary
Born: Sheffield, England, 21 June, 1956 RB

League Club	Source	Date Signed	Seasons Played	Apps	Subs	Gls
Sheffield Wed	App	06/74	75	6	2	0

HULL Jeffrey (Jeff)
Born: Southend-on-Sea, England, 25 August, 1960 LW

League Club	Source	Date Signed	Seasons Played	Apps	Subs	Gls
Southend U	App	08/78	78-80	10	5	1
Colchester U	Basildon U	12/82	82-85	82	1	10

HULLETT William Alexander (Bill)
Born: Liverpool, England, 19 November, 1915 CF
Died: Cardiff, Wales, 6 September, 1982

League Club	Source	Date Signed	Seasons Played	Apps	Subs	Gls
Everton		12/35				
New Brighton	L	01/37	36	13	-	8
Plymouth Arg	Tr	10/37	37-38	29	-	20
Manchester U	Tr	03/39				
Cardiff C	Merthyr Tydfil	02/48	47-48	27	-	15
Nottingham F	Tr	11/48	48	13	-	2

HULLIGAN Michael John (Mick)
Born: Liverpool, England, 28 February, 1923 RW
Died: Stoke-on-Trent, England, 12 September, 1978

League Club	Source	Date Signed	Seasons Played	Apps	Subs	Gls
Liverpool		12/42				
Port Vale	Tr	07/48	48-54	197	-	22

HULME Eric Martin
Born: Houghton-le-Spring, Tyne and Wear, England, 14 January, 1949 G

League Club	Source	Date Signed	Seasons Played	Apps	Subs	Gls
Nottingham F	Spennymoor U	03/70	71	5	0	0
Lincoln C	Tr	09/72	72-73	23	0	0

HULME John
Born: Mobberley, Cheshire, England, 6 February, 1945 CD
Died: Manchester, England, 26 May, 2008

League Club	Source	Date Signed	Seasons Played	Apps	Subs	Gls
Bolton W	Jnr	02/62	62-71	186	2	7
Notts Co	L	03/72	71	8	0	0
Reading	Tr	07/72	72-73	86	1	0
Bury	Tr	07/74	74-75	86	0	5

HULME Kevin
Born: Farnworth, Greater Manchester, England, 2 December, 1967 M/F

League Club	Source	Date Signed	Seasons Played	Apps	Subs	Gls
Bury	Radcliffe Bor	03/89	88-92	82	28	21
Chester C	L	10/89	89	4	0	0
Doncaster Rov	Tr	07/93	93	33	1	8
Bury	Tr	08/94	94-95	24	5	0
Lincoln C	Tr	09/95	95	4	1	0
Halifax T	Macclesfield T	10/96	98-99	32	1	4
York C	Tr	09/99	99-00	34	4	7

HULMES Gary Anthony
Born: Manchester, England, 28 February, 1957 F

League Club	Source	Date Signed	Seasons Played	Apps	Subs	Gls
Rochdale	Manchester C (App)	12/74	74-75	4	5	1

HULSE Robert Arthur
Born: Crewe, Cheshire, England, 5 November, 1948 F
England: Youth

League Club	Source	Date Signed	Seasons Played	Apps	Subs	Gls
Stoke C	Nantwich T	04/67	67	2	0	0

HULSE Robert James
Born: Gateshead, Tyne and Wear, England, 5 January, 1957 M

League Club	Source	Date Signed	Seasons Played	Apps	Subs	Gls
Darlington	Stade Quimper (FRA)	09/83	83	3	1	0

HULSE Robert William (Rob)
Born: Crewe, Cheshire, England, 25 October, 1979 F

League Club	Source	Date Signed	Seasons Played	Apps	Subs	Gls
Crewe Alex	YT	06/98	99-02	97	19	46
West Bromwich A	Tr	08/03	03-04	29	9	10
Leeds U	L	02/05	04-05	45	7	18
Sheffield U	Tr	07/06	06-07	38	12	8
Derby Co	Tr	07/08	08-10	73	9	28
Queens Park Rgrs	Tr	08/10	10-11	13	10	2
Charlton Ath	L	10/12	12	10	5	3
Millwall	L	01/13	12	7	4	0

HUMBLE Douglas (Dougie)
Born: Wolsingham, County Durham, England, 16 February, 1920 CF
Died: County Durham, England, 13 January, 1989

League Club	Source	Date Signed	Seasons Played	Apps	Subs	Gls
Sunderland	Bishop Auckland	05/45				
Southport	Tr	06/47	47	11	-	4

HUMBLE James Wilfred (Wilf)
Born: Ashington, Northumberland, England, 10 May, 1936 FB

League Club	Source	Date Signed	Seasons Played	Apps	Subs	Gls

Died: Mansfield, Nottinghamshire, England, 14 March, 1985

League Club	Source	Date Signed	Seasons Played	Apps	Subs	Gls
Mansfield T	Ashington	05/59	59-65	198	0	1

HUME Iain Edward
Born: Edinburgh, Scotland, 31 October, 1983 — F
Canada: 41/Youth

League Club	Source	Date Signed	Seasons Played	Apps	Subs	Gls
Tranmere Rov	Jnr	11/00	99-05	100	50	32
Leicester C	Tr	08/05	05-07	101	21	33
Barnsley	Tr	06/08	08-10	32	19	9
Preston NE	Tr	09/10	10-13	58	17	23
Doncaster Rov	L	08/12	12	24	9	6
Fleetwood T	L	03/14	13	7	1	1
Tranmere Rov	Kerala Blasters (IND)	01/15	14	3	9	0

HUME Robert William (Bobby)
Born: Kirkintilloch, Dunbartonshire, Scotland, 18 March, 1941 — W
Died: Johannesburg, South Africa, 23 December, 2007

League Club	Source	Date Signed	Seasons Played	Apps	Subs	Gls
Middlesbrough	Glasgow Rangers	09/62	62	19	-	5

HUME William Sanderson (Billy)
Born: Armadale, West Lothian, Scotland, 18 December, 1935 — IF
Died: Livingston, West Lothian, Scotland, 15 August, 1990

League Club	Source	Date Signed	Seasons Played	Apps	Subs	Gls
Birmingham C	Dunfermline Ath	02/58	58-59	10	-	2

HUMES Anthony (Tony)
Born: Blyth, Northumberland, England, 19 March, 1966 — CD

League Club	Source	Date Signed	Seasons Played	Apps	Subs	Gls
Ipswich T	App	05/83	86-91	107	13	10
Wrexham	Tr	03/92	91-98	191	8	8

HUMES James (Jimmy)
Born: Carlisle, Cumbria, England, 6 August, 1942 — RW

League Club	Source	Date Signed	Seasons Played	Apps	Subs	Gls
Preston NE	Jnr	09/59	59-61	18	-	1
Bristol Rov	Tr	06/62	62	2	-	0
Chester C	Tr	07/63	63-66	124	0	31
Barnsley	Tr	07/67	67	7	0	1

HUMPHREY Christopher Charles (Chris)
Born: Shrewsbury, Shropshire, England, 19 September, 1987 — RW
Jamaica: 7

League Club	Source	Date Signed	Seasons Played	Apps	Subs	Gls
Shrewsbury T	West Bromwich A (Sch)	09/06	06-08	31	43	2
Preston NE	Motherwell	06/13	13-14	62	24	7

HUMPHREY John
Born: Paddington, Central London, England, 31 January, 1961 — RB

League Club	Source	Date Signed	Seasons Played	Apps	Subs	Gls
Wolverhampton W	App	02/79	79-84	149	0	3
Charlton Ath	Tr	07/85	85-89	194	0	3
Crystal Palace	Tr	08/90	90-94	153	7	2
Reading	L	12/93	93	8	0	0
Charlton Ath	Tr	07/95	95	28	0	0
Gillingham	Tr	06/96	96	9	0	0
Brighton & HA	Tr	01/97	96-97	22	0	0

HUMPHREY John Mark
Born: Godalming, Surrey, England, 2 July, 1969 — F

League Club	Source	Date Signed	Seasons Played	Apps	Subs	Gls
Millwall	Leatherhead	02/91				
Exeter C	L	12/91	91	2	0	0

HUMPHREY Thomas Robson (Tommy)
Born: Houghton-le-Spring, Tyne and Wear, England, 27 October, 1937 — RW

League Club	Source	Date Signed	Seasons Played	Apps	Subs	Gls
Aldershot	Aldershot Garrison	03/59	58-60	22	-	3

HUMPHREYS Alan
Born: Chester, England, 18 October, 1939 — G

League Club	Source	Date Signed	Seasons Played	Apps	Subs	Gls
Shrewsbury T	Lache YC	10/56	56-59	32	-	0
Leeds U	Tr	02/60	59-61	40	-	0
Mansfield T	Gravesend & Northfleet	01/64	64-67	58	0	0
Chesterfield	Tr	07/68	68-69	51	0	0

HUMPHREYS Derek John Beattie
Born: Belfast, Northern Ireland, 5 October, 1949 — G

League Club	Source	Date Signed	Seasons Played	Apps	Subs	Gls
Arsenal	Jnr	10/66				
Sunderland	Crusaders	11/67				
Hartlepool U	L	10/69	69	4	0	0

HUMPHREYS Gerald (Gerry)
Born: Llandudno, Conwy, Wales, 14 January, 1946 — W
Wales: U23-5/Schools

League Club	Source	Date Signed	Seasons Played	Apps	Subs	Gls
Everton	App	09/63	65-69	12	0	2
Crystal Palace	Tr	06/70	70	4	7	0
Crewe Alex	Tr	01/72	71-76	184	9	30

HUMPHREYS John Stephen
Born: Farnworth, Greater Manchester, England, 18 July, 1964 — F

League Club	Source	Date Signed	Seasons Played	Apps	Subs	Gls
Oldham Ath	App	07/82	82-83	7	6	0
Rochdale	L	03/84	83	6	0	0

HUMPHREYS John Vaughan
Born: Llandudno, Conwy, Wales, 13 January, 1920 — CH
Died: Caernarvon, Gwynedd, Wales, 14 September, 1954
Wales: 1

League Club	Source	Date Signed	Seasons Played	Apps	Subs	Gls
Everton	Llandudno T	04/43	46-50	53	-	0

HUMPHREYS Percy Ronald
Born: Bradford, England, 28 October, 1924 — RW
Died: Halifax, West Yorkshire, England, September, 1999

League Club	Source	Date Signed	Seasons Played	Apps	Subs	Gls
Halifax T	Boothtown	11/43	46	3	-	1

HUMPHREYS Ritchie John
Born: Sheffield, England, 30 November, 1977 — LB/M
England: U21-3/Youth

League Club	Source	Date Signed	Seasons Played	Apps	Subs	Gls
Sheffield Wed	YT	02/96	95-00	34	33	4
Scunthorpe U	L	08/99	99	6	0	2
Cardiff C	L	11/99	99	8	1	2
Cambridge U	Tr	02/01	00	7	0	3
Hartlepool U	Tr	07/01	01-12	440	41	34
Port Vale	L	09/06	06	5	2	0
Chesterfield	Tr	07/13	13-14	47	14	2

HUMPHREYS Ronald Henry (Ron)
Born: Tonypandy, Rhondda Cynon Taff, Wales, 4 April, 1925 — FB
Died: Kent, England, April, 2014

League Club	Source	Date Signed	Seasons Played	Apps	Subs	Gls
Southend U	Snowdown CW	05/45	46	3	-	0

HUMPHREYS Samuel Aston (Sam)
Born: Chipping Norton, Oxfordshire, England, 3 November, 1995 — W

League Club	Source	Date Signed	Seasons Played	Apps	Subs	Gls
Oxford U	Sch	06/14	14	0	1	0

HUMPHRIES Charles William (Charlie)
Born: Birmingham, England, 19 March, 1922 — FB
Died: Lichfield, Staffordshire, England, April, 1995

League Club	Source	Date Signed	Seasons Played	Apps	Subs	Gls
Walsall	Paget Rgrs	09/46	47	6	-	0

HUMPHRIES David William (Dave)
Born: Wolverhampton, England, 10 August, 1939 — CH

League Club	Source	Date Signed	Seasons Played	Apps	Subs	Gls
Shrewsbury T		03/60	60	3	-	0

HUMPHRIES Glenn
Born: Hull, England, 11 August, 1964 — CD
England: Youth

League Club	Source	Date Signed	Seasons Played	Apps	Subs	Gls
Doncaster Rov	YT	08/82	80-87	174	6	8
Lincoln C	L	03/87	86	9	0	0
Bristol C	Tr	10/87	87-90	81	4	0
Scunthorpe U	Tr	03/91	90-92	71	1	5
Hull C	Golden (HKG)	08/95	95	9	3	0

HUMPHRIES Mark
Born: Glasgow, Scotland, 23 December, 1971 — LB

League Club	Source	Date Signed	Seasons Played	Apps	Subs	Gls
Leeds U	Aberdeen	06/93				
Bristol C	Tr	10/94	94	4	0	0

HUMPHRIES Robert (Bob)
Born: Hindhead, Surrey, England, 4 July, 1933 — RH/IF
Died: Spain, 1988

League Club	Source	Date Signed	Seasons Played	Apps	Subs	Gls
Sheffield U	Tottenham H (Am)	12/55				
Brighton & HA	Tr	11/56	56	10	-	2
Millwall	Tr	08/57	57-59	47	-	4

HUMPHRIES Stephen Rodney (Steve)
Born: Hull, England, 29 May, 1961 — G
England: Semi Pro-1

League Club	Source	Date Signed	Seasons Played	Apps	Subs	Gls
Leicester C	App	09/78				
Doncaster Rov	Tr	06/81	81	13	0	0
Cardiff C	Tr	08/82	82	1	0	0
Wrexham	Tr	09/82	82	2	0	0

HUMPHRIES William McCauley (Billy)
Born: Belfast, Northern Ireland, 8 June, 1936 — W
Northern Ireland: 14/NILge-12

League Club	Source	Date Signed	Seasons Played	Apps	Subs	Gls
Leeds U	Ards	09/58	58-59	25	-	2
Coventry C	Ards	04/62	61-64	109	-	23
Swansea C	Tr	03/65	64-67	143	0	22

HUMPSTON Ronald (Ron)
Born: Derby, England, 14 December, 1923 — G
Died: Cheltenham, Gloucestershire, England, 4 January, 2012

League Club	Source	Date Signed	Seasons Played	Apps	Subs	Gls
Portsmouth	Royal Navy	01/46	47-50	9	-	0
Huddersfield T	Tr	11/51	51	5	-	0

HUNT Andrew (Andy)
Born: West Thurrock, Essex, England, 9 June, 1970 — F

League Club	Source	Date Signed	Seasons Played	Apps	Subs	Gls
Newcastle U	Kettering T	01/91	90-91	34	9	11
West Bromwich A	Tr	03/93	92-97	201	11	76
Charlton Ath	Tr	07/98	98-00	83	3	35

HUNT Benjamin Murray (Ben)
Born: Catford, SE London, England, 23 January, 1990 — F

League Club	Source	Date Signed	Seasons Played	Apps	Subs	Gls
Bristol Rov	West Ham U (Sch)	07/08	08-09	0	14	0

HUNT David
Born: Leicester, England, 17 April, 1959 — M

League Club	Source	Date Signed	Seasons Played	Apps	Subs	Gls
Derby Co	App	04/77	77	5	0	0
Notts Co	Tr	03/78	77-86	331	5	28

League Club	Source	Date Signed	Seasons Played	Apps	Subs	Gls
Aston Villa	Tr	06/87	87-88	12	1	0
Mansfield T	Tr	06/89	89	21	1	0

HUNT David
Born: Durham, England, 5 March, 1980 — LB

League Club	Source	Date Signed	Seasons Played	Apps	Subs	Gls
Darlington	YT	07/98	96	0	1	0

HUNT David John
Born: Dulwich, S London, England, 10 September, 1982 — RB/M

League Club	Source	Date Signed	Seasons Played	Apps	Subs	Gls
Crystal Palace	Sch	07/02	02	2	0	0
Leyton Orient	Tr	07/03	03-04	57	8	1
Northampton T	Tr	03/05	04-06	57	16	3
Shrewsbury T	Tr	07/07	07-08	22	7	2
Brentford	Tr	01/09	08-10	28	19	5
Crawley T	Tr	12/10	11-12	45	5	0
Oxford U	Tr	06/13	13-14	48	1	0

HUNT Dennis Perrior
Born: Portsmouth, England, 8 September, 1937 — LB

League Club	Source	Date Signed	Seasons Played	Apps	Subs	Gls
Gillingham	Army	09/58	58-67	319	2	6
Brentford	Tr	06/68	68	12	0	0

HUNT Douglas Arthur (Doug)
Born: Shipton Bellinger, Wiltshire, England, 19 May, 1914 — CF
Died: Yeovil, Somerset, England, May, 1989

League Club	Source	Date Signed	Seasons Played	Apps	Subs	Gls
Tottenham H	Winchester C	03/34	34-36	17	-	6
Barnsley	Tr	03/37	36-37	36	-	18
Sheffield Wed	Tr	03/38	37-38	42	-	30
Leyton Orient	Tr	04/46	46-47	61	-	16

HUNT George Harold
Born: Bethnal Green, E London, England, 5 March, 1917 — CH
Died: Barnstaple, Devon, England, August, 1990

League Club	Source	Date Signed	Seasons Played	Apps	Subs	Gls
Charlton Ath	Bexleyheath	05/37				
Barnsley	Tr	05/38				
Watford	Tr	06/46	47-49	35	-	0

HUNT George Samuel
Born: Barnsley, South Yorkshire, England, 22 February, 1910 — CF
Died: Bolton, Greater Manchester, England, 19 September, 1996
England: 3

League Club	Source	Date Signed	Seasons Played	Apps	Subs	Gls
Chesterfield	Regent Street Congs	09/29	29	14	-	9
Tottenham H	Tr	06/30	30-36	185	-	125
Arsenal	Tr	10/37	37	18	-	3
Bolton W	Tr	02/38	37-46	45	-	24
Sheffield Wed	Tr	11/46	46-47	32	-	8

HUNT Jack Paul
Born: Rothwell, West Yorkshire, England, 6 December, 1990 — RB

League Club	Source	Date Signed	Seasons Played	Apps	Subs	Gls
Huddersfield T	Sch	07/09	10-13	97	7	2
Chesterfield	L	08/10	10	18	2	0
Crystal Palace	Tr	09/13				
Barnsley	L	01/14	13	9	2	0
Nottingham F	L	07/14	14	15	2	0
Rotherham U	L	01/15	14	14	2	0

HUNT James Malcolm
Born: Derby, England, 17 December, 1976 — M

League Club	Source	Date Signed	Seasons Played	Apps	Subs	Gls
Notts Co	YT	07/94	95-96	15	4	1
Northampton T	Tr	08/97	97-01	150	22	8
Oxford U	Tr	07/02	02-03	75	5	3
Bristol Rov	Tr	07/04	04-06	93	2	6
Grimsby T	Tr	01/07	06-08	68	6	2

HUNT John James (Johnny)
Born: Liverpool, England, 28 March, 1990 — LB/M
England: Semi Pro-1

League Club	Source	Date Signed	Seasons Played	Apps	Subs	Gls
Cambridge U	Wrexham	06/14	14	4	5	1

HUNT Jonathan Martin (Jon)
Born: Leeds, England, 11 September, 1984 — M

League Club	Source	Date Signed	Seasons Played	Apps	Subs	Gls
Scunthorpe U	Sch	08/04	03	0	1	0

HUNT Jonathan Richard
Born: Camden, N London, England, 2 November, 1971 — M

League Club	Source	Date Signed	Seasons Played	Apps	Subs	Gls
Barnet	Jnr	01/90	91-92	12	21	0
Southend U	Tr	07/93	93-94	41	8	6
Birmingham C	Tr	09/94	94-96	67	10	18
Derby Co	Tr	05/97	97-98	7	18	2
Sheffield U	L	08/98	98	5	1	1
Ipswich T	L	10/98	98	2	4	0
Sheffield U	Tr	03/99	98-99	15	6	1
Cambridge U	L	03/00	99	3	4	1
Wimbledon	Tr	09/00	00	8	4	0

HUNT Lewis James
Born: Solihull, West Midlands, England, 25 August, 1982 — RB

League Club	Source	Date Signed	Seasons Played	Apps	Subs	Gls
Derby Co	YT	02/01	02-03	8	3	0
Southend U	Tr	10/03	03-07	126	20	2
Wycombe W	Tr	08/08	08-09	46	1	1
Bradford C	Tr	08/10	10-11	24	1	1

HUNT Mark Geoffrey
Born: Farnworth, Greater Manchester, England, 5 October, 1969 — F

League Club	Source	Date Signed	Seasons Played	Apps	Subs	Gls
Rochdale	App	-	86-87	1	1	1

HUNT Morgan Marshall
Born: Bridgend, Wales, 5 March, 1931 — RH
Died: Doncaster, South Yorkshire, England, February, 2012

League Club	Source	Date Signed	Seasons Played	Apps	Subs	Gls
Doncaster Rov	Askern Welfare	02/52	53-57	50	-	2
Norwich C	Tr	07/58	58	7	-	0
Port Vale	Tr	08/59	59	2	-	0

HUNT Nicholas Brett (Nicky)
Born: Westhoughton, Greater Manchester, England, 3 September, 1983 — RB
England: U21-10

League Club	Source	Date Signed	Seasons Played	Apps	Subs	Gls
Bolton W	YT	07/01	00-08	113	15	1
Birmingham C	L	11/08	08	9	2	0
Derby Co	L	01/10	09	20	1	0
Bristol C	Tr	08/10	10	6	1	0
Preston NE	Tr	02/12	11	15	2	1
Rotherham U	Tr	07/12	12	6	3	0
Accrington Stan	Tr	01/13	12-14	75	2	0

HUNT Noel
Born: Waterford, Republic of Ireland, 26 December, 1982 — F
Republic of Ireland: 3/B-1/U21-3

League Club	Source	Date Signed	Seasons Played	Apps	Subs	Gls
Reading	Dundee U	07/08	08-12	94	51	33
Leeds U	Tr	07/13	13-14	14	6	0
Ipswich T	Tr	11/14	14	3	8	3

HUNT Paul Craig
Born: Swindon, England, 8 October, 1970 — F

League Club	Source	Date Signed	Seasons Played	Apps	Subs	Gls
Swindon T	YT	07/89	89-92	5	6	0

HUNT Paul Leslie
Born: Hereford, England, 7 March, 1959 — D/M

League Club	Source	Date Signed	Seasons Played	Apps	Subs	Gls
Hereford U	Coventry C (App)	11/77	78-80	41	10	4

HUNT Peter John
Born: Stepney, E London, England, 2 July, 1952 — M
England: Youth

League Club	Source	Date Signed	Seasons Played	Apps	Subs	Gls
Southend U	App	09/69	68-71	50	6	1
Charlton Ath	Tr	12/72	72-76	138	20	6
Gillingham	Tr	08/77	77	23	0	0

HUNT Ralph Robert Arthur
Born: Portsmouth, England, 14 August, 1933 — CF
Died: Grantham, Lincolnshire, England, 17 December, 1964

League Club	Source	Date Signed	Seasons Played	Apps	Subs	Gls
Portsmouth	Gloucester C	08/50	52-53	5	-	0
Bournemouth	Tr	02/54	53-54	33	-	7
Norwich C	Tr	07/55	55-57	124	-	67
Derby Co	Tr	08/58	58	24	-	10
Grimsby T	Tr	08/59	59-60	53	-	39
Swindon T	Tr	07/61	61	21	-	13
Port Vale	Tr	12/61	61	14	-	6
Newport Co	Tr	07/62	62-63	83	-	38
Chesterfield	Tr	07/64	64	17	-	5

HUNT Reginald George Albert (George)
Born: Swindon, England, 27 February, 1922 — RB
Died: Swindon, England, August, 1987

League Club	Source	Date Signed	Seasons Played	Apps	Subs	Gls
Swindon T	Ferndale Ath	01/47	48-57	304	-	0

HUNT Richard Anthony
Born: Reading, England, 5 January, 1971 — CD

League Club	Source	Date Signed	Seasons Played	Apps	Subs	Gls
Aldershot	Queens Park Rgrs (YT)	07/89	89	1	1	0

HUNT Robert
Born: Newcastle-upon-Tyne, England, 20 September, 1966 — RH

League Club	Source	Date Signed	Seasons Played	Apps	Subs	Gls
Halifax T	Barnsley (YT)	01/85	84	3	0	0

HUNT Robert (Bobby)
Born: Liverpool, England, 4 September, 1934 — WH

League Club	Source	Date Signed	Seasons Played	Apps	Subs	Gls
Wrexham	Saltney Jnrs	07/56				
Chester C	Tr	05/58	58-60	84	-	2

HUNT Robert Rex (Bobby)
Born: Colchester, Essex, England, 1 October, 1942 — F

League Club	Source	Date Signed	Seasons Played	Apps	Subs	Gls
Colchester U	Jnr	11/59	59-63	149	-	83
Northampton T	Tr	03/64	63-65	40	0	10
Millwall	Tr	09/66	66-67	43	0	13
Ipswich T	Tr	11/67	67-70	16	10	4
Charlton Ath	Tr	09/70	70-72	34	2	11
Northampton T	L	11/72	72	5	0	3
Reading	Tr	01/73	72-73	15	1	3

HUNT Roger
Born: Golborne, Greater Manchester, England, 20 July, 1938 — F
England: 34/FLge-5

League Club	Source	Date Signed	Seasons Played	Apps	Subs	Gls
Liverpool	Stockton Heath	05/59	59-69	401	3	245
Bolton W	Tr	12/69	69-71	72	4	24

HUNT Roger Patrick (Ernie)
Born: Swindon, England, 17 March, 1943 — F
England: U23-3

League Club	Source	Date Signed	Seasons Played	Apps	Subs	Gls
Swindon T	Jnr	03/60	59-65	214	0	82
Wolverhampton W	Tr	09/65	65-67	74	0	32
Everton	Tr	09/67	67	12	2	3
Coventry C	Tr	03/68	67-73	140	6	45
Doncaster Rov	L	01/73	72	9	0	1
Bristol C	Tr	12/73	73-74	9	3	2

HUNT Ronald Geoffrey (Ron)
Born: Paddington, Central London, England, 19 December, 1945 — CH

League Club	Source	Date Signed	Seasons Played	Apps	Subs	Gls
Queens Park Rgrs	App	03/63	64-72	214	5	1

HUNT Ronald Malcolm (Ron)
Born: Colchester, Essex, England, 26 September, 1933 — LH
Died: Colchester, Essex, England, April, 1999

League Club	Source	Date Signed	Seasons Played	Apps	Subs	Gls
Colchester U	Jnr	10/51	51-63	177	-	3

HUNT Simon
Born: Chester, England, 17 November, 1962 — M

League Club	Source	Date Signed	Seasons Played	Apps	Subs	Gls
Wrexham	Jnr	08/81	81-83	102	6	18

HUNT Stephen James
Born: Southampton, England, 11 November, 1984 — LB

League Club	Source	Date Signed	Seasons Played	Apps	Subs	Gls
Colchester U	Southampton (Sch)	07/04	04-05	16	6	1
Notts Co	Tr	07/06	06-10	103	13	4
Lincoln C	L	01/11	10	14	0	2

HUNT Stephen Kenneth (Steve)
Born: Birmingham, England, 4 August, 1956 — LW/M
England: 2

League Club	Source	Date Signed	Seasons Played	Apps	Subs	Gls
Aston Villa	App	01/74	74-76	4	3	1
Coventry C	New York Cosmos (USA)	08/78	78-83	178	7	27
West Bromwich A	Tr	03/84	83-85	68	0	15
Aston Villa	Tr	03/86	85-87	61	1	6

HUNT Stephen Patrick (Steve)
Born: Port Laoise, Republic of Ireland, 1 August, 1980 — LM
Republic of Ireland: 39/U21-1

League Club	Source	Date Signed	Seasons Played	Apps	Subs	Gls
Crystal Palace	YT	06/99	99	0	3	0
Brentford	Tr	08/01	01-04	126	10	25
Reading	Tr	06/05	05-08	109	47	17
Hull C	Tr	08/09	09	27	0	6
Wolverhampton W	Tr	06/10	10-12	38	18	7
Ipswich T		11/13	13-14	25	15	0

HUNT Warren David
Born: Portsmouth, England, 2 March, 1984 — M

League Club	Source	Date Signed	Seasons Played	Apps	Subs	Gls
Portsmouth	YT	11/01				
Leyton Orient	L	03/04	03	6	0	0

HUNT William Edmund (Billy)
Born: Colchester, Essex, England, 25 November, 1934 — CH

League Club	Source	Date Signed	Seasons Played	Apps	Subs	Gls
Colchester U	Jnr	08/53	55	1	-	0

HUNT-BROWN Peter Barry
Born: Halifax, West Yorkshire, England, 19 February, 1937 — CF

League Club	Source	Date Signed	Seasons Played	Apps	Subs	Gls
Halifax T	Elland U	12/58	58	1	-	0

HUNTER Allan
Born: Sion Mills, Tyrone, Northern Ireland, 30 June, 1946 — CD
Northern Ireland: 53/U23-1/Amateur

League Club	Source	Date Signed	Seasons Played	Apps	Subs	Gls
Oldham Ath	Coleraine	01/67	66-68	83	0	1
Blackburn Rov	Tr	06/69	69-71	84	0	1
Ipswich T	Tr	09/71	71-80	280	0	8
Colchester U	Tr	05/82	81-82	18	1	0

HUNTER Alvin Junior (Junior)
Born: Lambeth, S London, England, 1 February, 1975 — M/RB

League Club	Source	Date Signed	Seasons Played	Apps	Subs	Gls
Cambridge U	YT	05/93	93-94	26	14	0

HUNTER Ashley Matthew
Born: Derby, England, 29 September, 1995 — F

League Club	Source	Date Signed	Seasons Played	Apps	Subs	Gls
Fleetwood T	Ilkeston	01/15	14	3	9	1

HUNTER Barry Victor
Born: Coleraine, Derry, Northern Ireland, 18 November, 1968 — CD
Northern Ireland: 15/B-2/Youth

League Club	Source	Date Signed	Seasons Played	Apps	Subs	Gls
Newcastle U	Coleraine	11/87				
Wrexham	Crusaders	08/93	93-95	88	3	4
Reading	Tr	07/96	96-00	76	8	4
Southend U	L	02/99	98	5	0	2
Rushden & D	Tr	09/01	01-05	106	6	6

HUNTER Christopher Paul (Chris)
Born: Hong Kong, 18 January, 1964 — F

League Club	Source	Date Signed	Seasons Played	Apps	Subs	Gls
Preston NE	App	09/81	82	0	1	0
Preston NE	Chorley	09/84	84	3	3	0

HUNTER Donald (Don)
Born: Thorne, South Yorkshire, England, 10 March, 1927 — WH
Died: Southport, Merseyside, England, March, 2008

League Club	Source	Date Signed	Seasons Played	Apps	Subs	Gls
Huddersfield T	Luddenden Foot	03/44	48-50	26	-	1
Halifax T	Tr	08/51	51	11	-	0
Southport	Tr	08/52	52-56	174	-	1

HUNTER Edward (Eddie)
Born: Tillicoultry, Stirlingshire, Scotland, 7 March, 1928 — RH
Died: Burnley, Lancashire, England, August, 2002

League Club	Source	Date Signed	Seasons Played	Apps	Subs	Gls
Accrington Stan	Falkirk	08/54	54-58	169	-	4

HUNTER Garry Paul
Born: Morecambe, Lancashire, England, 1 January, 1985 — M

League Club	Source	Date Signed	Seasons Played	Apps	Subs	Gls
Morecambe	Jnr	05/03	07-11	125	43	6

HUNTER Geoffrey (Geoff)
Born: Hull, England, 27 October, 1959 — M

League Club	Source	Date Signed	Seasons Played	Apps	Subs	Gls
Manchester U	App	11/76				
Crewe Alex	Tr	08/79	79-80	86	1	8
Port Vale	Tr	08/81	81-86	218	3	15
Wrexham	Tr	08/87	87-90	116	6	14

HUNTER George Irvine
Born: Troon, Ayrshire, Scotland, 29 August, 1930 — G
Died: Nottingham, England, 10 May, 1990

League Club	Source	Date Signed	Seasons Played	Apps	Subs	Gls
Derby Co	Glasgow Celtic	06/54	54	19	-	0
Exeter C	Tr	08/55	55-58	147	-	0
Darlington	Yiewsley	06/61	61	20	-	0
Lincoln C	Burton A	09/65	65	1	0	0

HUNTER Gordon Greig
Born: Lyneham, Wiltshire, England, 8 November, 1954 — D/M

League Club	Source	Date Signed	Seasons Played	Apps	Subs	Gls
York C	Shrewsbury T (Am)	07/73	73-77	70	7	1

HUNTER John Dixon
Born: Backworth, Tyne and Wear, England, 20 September, 1934 — G
Died: North Shields, Tyne and Wear, England, 19 April, 2012

League Club	Source	Date Signed	Seasons Played	Apps	Subs	Gls
Gateshead		08/54	55	4	-	0

HUNTER John Smith
Born: Coalburn, Lanarkshire, Scotland, 26 May, 1934 — LW
Died: Kirkmuirhill, Lanarkshire, Scotland, 5 January, 2007

League Club	Source	Date Signed	Seasons Played	Apps	Subs	Gls
Rotherham U	Coltness U	06/56	56	5	-	1
Carlisle U	Tr	07/57	57	1	-	0
Barrow	King's Lynn	07/59	59-60	24	-	0

HUNTER Lee
Born: Oldham, Greater Manchester, England, 5 October, 1969 — M

League Club	Source	Date Signed	Seasons Played	Apps	Subs	Gls
Colchester U	YT	06/88	87-88	5	4	0

HUNTER Leslie (Les)
Born: Middlesbrough, England, 5 January, 1958 — CD

League Club	Source	Date Signed	Seasons Played	Apps	Subs	Gls
Chesterfield	App	08/75	75-81	156	9	8
Scunthorpe U	Tr	07/82	82-83	61	0	8
Chesterfield	Tr	01/84	83-85	99	0	9
Scunthorpe U	Tr	03/86	85-86	49	0	5
Chesterfield	Lincoln C	12/87	87-88	31	0	3

HUNTER Michael (Mick)
Born: Hexham, Northumberland, England, 27 May, 1948 — M

League Club	Source	Date Signed	Seasons Played	Apps	Subs	Gls
Blackpool		01/66				
Darlington	Tr	07/67	67	2	1	0

HUNTER Norman
Born: Gateshead, Tyne and Wear, England, 29 October, 1943 — CD
England: 28/FLge-6/U23-3

League Club	Source	Date Signed	Seasons Played	Apps	Subs	Gls
Leeds U	Jnr	04/61	62-76	540	0	18
Bristol C	Tr	10/76	76-78	108	0	4
Barnsley	Tr	06/79	79-82	28	3	0

HUNTER Paul
Born: Kirkcaldy, Fife, Scotland, 30 August, 1968 — F
Scotland: U21-3

League Club	Source	Date Signed	Seasons Played	Apps	Subs	Gls
Hull C	East Fife	03/90	89-92	37	31	11

HUNTER Philip (Phil)
Born: Hartlepool, Cleveland, England, 28 September, 1950 — RW

League Club	Source	Date Signed	Seasons Played	Apps	Subs	Gls
Hartlepool U (Am)	Jnr	08/69	69	1	0	0

HUNTER Reginald John (Reg)
Born: Colwyn Bay, Conwy, Wales, 25 October, 1938 — LW

League Club	Source	Date Signed	Seasons Played	Apps	Subs	Gls
Manchester U	Colwyn Bay	11/56	58	1	-	0
Wrexham	Tr	02/60	59-61	34	-	3

HUNTER Robert (Bob)
Born: Gateshead, Tyne and Wear, England, 25 March, 1951 — W

League Club	Source	Date Signed	Seasons Played	Apps	Subs	Gls
Hartlepool U		02/71	70	1	0	0

HUNTER Robert Russell (Bobby)
Born: Shotts, Lanarkshire, Scotland, 12 March, 1931 — W

League Club	Source	Date Signed	Seasons Played	Apps	Subs	Gls

Died: Wilmslow, Cheshire, England, 8 July, 2002

League Club	Source	Date Signed	Seasons Played	Apps	Subs	Gls
Swindon T	Motherwell	08/54	54	16	-	3

HUNTER Roy Ian
Born: Cleveland, England, 29 October, 1973 — M

League Club	Source	Date Signed	Seasons Played	Apps	Subs	Gls
West Bromwich A	YT	03/92	91-93	3	6	1
Northampton T	Tr	08/95	95-01	149	28	17
Oxford U	Nuneaton Bor	10/02	02	12	5	1

HUNTER Shaquille Junior Anthony
Born: Birmingham, England, 29 August, 1995 — W

League Club	Source	Date Signed	Seasons Played	Apps	Subs	Gls
Bristol Rov	Sch	08/12	13	0	3	0

HUNTER William Nibb (Willie)
Born: Cambuslang, Glasgow, Scotland, 7 April, 1942 — IF

League Club	Source	Date Signed	Seasons Played	Apps	Subs	Gls
Bradford Park Ave	Glasgow Rangers	07/64	64	14	-	0

HUNTINGTON Paul David
Born: Carlisle, Cumbria, England, 17 September, 1987 — CD
England: Youth

League Club	Source	Date Signed	Seasons Played	Apps	Subs	Gls
Newcastle U	Sch	06/05	06	10	1	1
Leeds U	Tr	08/07	07-08	16	5	2
Stockport Co	L	09/09	09	9	0	0
Stockport Co	Tr	02/10	09	17	0	0
Yeovil T	Tr	07/10	10-11	77	0	7
Preston NE	Tr	07/12	12-14	85	7	10

HUNTLEY John
Born: Great Lumley, County Durham, England, 5 November, 1967 — CD

League Club	Source	Date Signed	Seasons Played	Apps	Subs	Gls
Darlington	Chester-le-Street T	10/85	85	5	1	0

HUNTLEY Keith Stanley Murray
Born: Swansea, Wales, 12 February, 1931 — LW
Died: Swansea, Wales, December, 1995
Wales: Amateur

League Club	Source	Date Signed	Seasons Played	Apps	Subs	Gls
Swansea C	St Jude's	08/50	50	2	-	0

HUNTLEY Richard Bernard
Born: Sunderland, England, 5 January, 1949 — CD

League Club	Source	Date Signed	Seasons Played	Apps	Subs	Gls
Sunderland	Jnr	08/67	68	1	0	0

HUNTON Keith
Born: Wellington, Telford & Wrekin, England, 18 July, 1961 — G

League Club	Source	Date Signed	Seasons Played	Apps	Subs	Gls
Carlisle U	Workington	02/87	86	3	0	0

HURDLE Augustus Athel (Gus)
Born: Kensington, Central London, England, 14 October, 1973 — FB
Barbados:

League Club	Source	Date Signed	Seasons Played	Apps	Subs	Gls
Fulham	YT	07/92				
Brentford		07/94	94-97	63	8	0

HURFORD David George
Born: Chipping Sodbury, Avon, England, 17 January, 1945 — W

League Club	Source	Date Signed	Seasons Played	Apps	Subs	Gls
Bristol Rov	App	01/63	62-64	6	-	0

HURLEY Charles John (Charlie)
Born: Cork, Republic of Ireland, 4 October, 1936 — CH
Republic of Ireland: 40

League Club	Source	Date Signed	Seasons Played	Apps	Subs	Gls
Millwall	Jnr	10/53	53-57	105	-	2
Sunderland	Tr	09/57	57-68	357	1	23
Bolton W	Tr	06/69	69-70	42	1	3

HURLEY Christopher Joseph (Chris)
Born: Hornchurch, E London, England, 20 November, 1943 — CF

League Club	Source	Date Signed	Seasons Played	Apps	Subs	Gls
Millwall	Rainham T	03/64	63-64	4	-	2

HURLEY William Henry (Billy)
Born: Leytonstone, NE London, England, 11 December, 1959 — F
England: Schools

League Club	Source	Date Signed	Seasons Played	Apps	Subs	Gls
Leyton Orient	App	01/77	76	1	1	0

HURLOCK Terence Alan (Terry)
Born: Hackney, E London, England, 22 September, 1958 — M
England: B-3

League Club	Source	Date Signed	Seasons Played	Apps	Subs	Gls
Brentford	Leytonstone & Ilford	08/80	80-85	220	0	18
Reading	Tr	02/86	85-86	29	0	0
Millwall	Tr	02/87	86-89	103	1	8
Southampton	Glasgow Rangers	09/91	91-93	59	2	0
Millwall	Tr	03/94	93	13	0	0
Fulham	Tr	07/94	94	27	0	1

HURLSTONE Gary
Born: Mexborough, South Yorkshire, England, 25 April, 1963 — F

League Club	Source	Date Signed	Seasons Played	Apps	Subs	Gls
York C	Hatfield Main	03/89	88	1	1	0

HURRELL William (Billy)
Born: Newcastle-upon-Tyne, England, 15 September, 1955 — CD

League Club	Source	Date Signed	Seasons Played	Apps	Subs	Gls
Northampton T	App	09/73	72	5	0	0

HURRELL William Provan (Willie)
Born: Dundee, Scotland, 28 January, 1920 — IF
Died: Lewisham, SE London, England, 24 December, 1999

League Club	Source	Date Signed	Seasons Played	Apps	Subs	Gls
Millwall	Raith Rov	01/46	46-52	121	-	32
Queens Park Rgrs	Tr	07/53	53	6	-	1

HURST Charles (Charlie)
Born: Manchester, England, 25 January, 1919 — RH
Died: Chelmsford, England, January, 1999

League Club	Source	Date Signed	Seasons Played	Apps	Subs	Gls
Bristol Rov	Hyde U	09/38				
Oldham Ath	Tr	01/43				
Rochdale	Tr	06/46	46	4	-	1

HURST Christopher Mark (Chris)
Born: Barnsley, South Yorkshire, England, 3 October, 1973 — M

League Club	Source	Date Signed	Seasons Played	Apps	Subs	Gls
Huddersfield T	Emley	07/97	97	1	2	0

HURST Geoffrey Charles (Geoff)
Born: Ashton-under-Lyne, Greater Manchester, England, 8 December, 1941 — F
England: 49/FLge-7/U23-4/Youth

League Club	Source	Date Signed	Seasons Played	Apps	Subs	Gls
West Ham U	Jnr	04/59	59-71	410	1	180
Stoke C	Tr	08/72	72-74	103	5	30
West Bromwich A	Tr	08/75	75	10	0	2

HURST George John (Jack)
Born: Darcy Lever, Greater Manchester, England, 27 October, 1914 — CH
Died: Harrow, NW London, England, February, 2002

League Club	Source	Date Signed	Seasons Played	Apps	Subs	Gls
Bolton W	Lever Bridge Jnrs	05/33	34-46	60	-	2
Oldham Ath	Tr	02/47	46-50	98	-	2

HURST Glynn
Born: Barnsley, South Yorkshire, England, 17 January, 1976 — F

League Club	Source	Date Signed	Seasons Played	Apps	Subs	Gls
Barnsley	Tottenham H (YT)	07/94	94-96	0	8	0
Swansea C	L	12/95	95	2	0	1
Mansfield T	L	11/96	96	5	1	0
Stockport Co	Ayr U	02/01	00-01	22	4	4
Chesterfield	Tr	12/01	01-03	77	7	29
Notts Co	Tr	07/04	04-05	51	8	23
Shrewsbury T	Tr	01/06	05	15	1	3
Bury	Tr	09/06	06-08	77	37	25

HURST Gordon
Born: Oldham, Greater Manchester, England, 9 October, 1924 — RW
Died: Southwark, S London, England, 11 June, 1980
England: FLge-1

League Club	Source	Date Signed	Seasons Played	Apps	Subs	Gls
Charlton Ath	Ramsgate Ath	05/46	46-57	369	-	75

HURST Graham John
Born: Oldham, Greater Manchester, England, 23 November, 1967 — M

League Club	Source	Date Signed	Seasons Played	Apps	Subs	Gls
Rochdale	App	07/85	84	0	1	0

HURST James
Born: Sutton Coldfield, West Midlands, England, 31 January, 1992 — LB
England: Youth

League Club	Source	Date Signed	Seasons Played	Apps	Subs	Gls
Portsmouth	Sch	02/09				
West Bromwich A	Tr	08/10	10	1	0	0
Blackpool	L	08/11	11	0	2	0
Shrewsbury T	L	11/11	11	7	0	0
Chesterfield	L	01/12	11	10	0	0
Birmingham C	L	10/12	12	2	1	0
Shrewsbury T	L	03/13	12	4	0	0
Crawley T	Tr	07/13	13	11	7	0
Northampton T	L	01/14	13	1	0	0

HURST John
Born: Blackpool, Lancashire, England, 6 February, 1947 — CD
England: U23-9/Schools

League Club	Source	Date Signed	Seasons Played	Apps	Subs	Gls
Everton	App	10/64	65-75	336	11	29
Oldham Ath	Tr	06/76	76-80	169	1	2

HURST Kevan James
Born: Chesterfield, Derbyshire, England, 27 August, 1985 — W/M

League Club	Source	Date Signed	Seasons Played	Apps	Subs	Gls
Sheffield U	Sch	03/04	04	0	1	0
Boston U	L	03/04	03	3	4	1
Stockport Co	L	02/05	04	14	0	1
Chesterfield	L	08/05	05	30	7	4
Chesterfield	L	07/06	06	25	0	3
Scunthorpe U	Tr	01/07	06-08	55	11	3
Carlisle U	Tr	08/09	09-10	30	5	2
Morecambe	L	01/11	10	21	0	2
Walsall	Tr	07/11	11	30	4	2
Southend U	Tr	08/12	12-14	99	15	17

HURST Lee Jason
Born: Nuneaton, Warwickshire, England, 21 September, 1970 — M

League Club	Source	Date Signed	Seasons Played	Apps	Subs	Gls
Coventry C	YT	05/89	90-92	46	3	2

HURST Liam Karl
Born: Leicester, England, 2 September, 1994 — F

League Club	Source	Date Signed	Seasons Played	Apps	Subs	Gls
Cambridge U	Ibstock U	02/13	14	0	4	0

HURST Mark Patrick
Born: Mansfield, Nottinghamshire, England, 18 February, 1985 — FB

League Club	Source	Date Signed	Seasons Played	Apps	Subs	Gls
Mansfield T	Sch	-	02	1	0	0

HURST Paul Michael
Born: Sheffield, England, 25 September, 1974 — LB

League Club	Source	Date Signed	Seasons Played	Apps	Subs	Gls
Rotherham U	YT	08/93	93-07	382	51	13

HURST Thomas William (Tom)
Born: Leicester, England, 23 September, 1987 — CD

League Club	Source	Date Signed	Seasons Played	Apps	Subs	Gls
Boston U	Sch	-	04	0	1	0

HURST William Robert (Bill)
Born: Brierfield, Lancashire, England, 4 March, 1921 — W
Died: East Lancashire, England, September, 2005

League Club	Source	Date Signed	Seasons Played	Apps	Subs	Gls
Burnley	Jnr	03/38				
Plymouth Arg	Tr	06/39	46	4	-	0
Bury	Nelson	09/47	47	1	-	0
Accrington Stan	Northwich Victoria	10/48	48	1	-	0

HUSBAND James (Jimmy)
Born: Newcastle-upon-Tyne, England, 15 October, 1947 — RW/F
England: U23-5/Youth/Schools

League Club	Source	Date Signed	Seasons Played	Apps	Subs	Gls
Everton	App	10/64	64-73	158	7	44
Luton T	Tr	11/73	73-77	138	5	44

HUSBAND James Andrew
Born: Leeds, England, 3 January, 1994 — LB

League Club	Source	Date Signed	Seasons Played	Apps	Subs	Gls
Doncaster Rov	Sch	11/11	11-13	54	10	4
Middlesbrough	Tr	07/14	14	2	1	0
Fulham	L	03/15	14	5	0	0

HUSBAND Stephen
Born: Kelty, Fife, Scotland, 29 October, 1990 — M

League Club	Source	Date Signed	Seasons Played	Apps	Subs	Gls
Blackpool	Heart of Midlothian	02/10	09	1	2	0
Stockport Co	L	01/11	10	5	0	2

HUSBANDS Michael Paul
Born: Birmingham, England, 13 November, 1983 — F

League Club	Source	Date Signed	Seasons Played	Apps	Subs	Gls
Aston Villa	Sch	04/02				
Southend U	Tr	07/03	03-04	3	8	0
Walsall	Bristol Rov (NC)	09/05	05	1	3	0
Port Vale	Tr	10/05	05-06	9	38	5
Macclesfield T	Tr	07/07	07	2	0	0

HUSEKLEPP Erik Andre
Born: Sandvika, Norway, 5 September, 1984 — F/W
Norway: 34/U21-8

League Club	Source	Date Signed	Seasons Played	Apps	Subs	Gls
Portsmouth	Bari (ITA)	08/11	11	21	6	6
Birmingham C	L	02/12	11	4	7	2

HUSSEY Christopher Ian (Chris)
Born: Hammersmith, W London, England, 2 January, 1989 — LB

League Club	Source	Date Signed	Seasons Played	Apps	Subs	Gls
Coventry C	AFC Wimbledon	10/09	09-12	45	13	0
AFC Wimbledon	Tr	01/13	12	18	1	0
Burton A	Tr	07/13	13	22	5	1
Bury	L	03/14	13	10	1	2
Bury	Tr	05/14	14	30	8	0

HUSSEY Malcolm Frederick
Born: Darfield, South Yorkshire, England, 11 September, 1933 — CH

League Club	Source	Date Signed	Seasons Played	Apps	Subs	Gls
Rotherham U	Jnr	04/52	52-55	24	-	0
Scunthorpe U	Tr	08/56	56-57	23	-	0
Rochdale	Tr	03/59	58	1	-	0

HUTCHINGS Carl Emil
Born: Hammersmith, W London, England, 24 September, 1974 — M/RB

League Club	Source	Date Signed	Seasons Played	Apps	Subs	Gls
Brentford	YT	07/93	93-97	144	18	7
Bristol C	Tr	06/98	98-99	33	9	3
Brentford	L	02/00	99	7	1	0
Exeter C	L	11/00	00	2	0	0
Southend U	Tr	12/00	00-01	42	1	4
Leyton Orient	Tr	02/02	01-02	30	8	2

HUTCHINGS Christopher (Chris)
Born: Winchester, Hampshire, England, 5 July, 1957 — LB/M

League Club	Source	Date Signed	Seasons Played	Apps	Subs	Gls
Chelsea	Harrow Bor	07/80	80-83	83	4	3
Brighton & HA	Tr	11/83	83-87	153	0	4
Huddersfield T	Tr	12/87	87-89	110	0	10
Walsall	Tr	08/90	90	40	0	0
Rotherham U	Tr	07/91	91-93	76	2	4

HUTCHINGS Denis George
Born: Axminster, Devon, England, 1 December, 1924 — RW
Died: Honiton, Devon, England, 22 December, 1990

League Club	Source	Date Signed	Seasons Played	Apps	Subs	Gls
Exeter C	Axminster	04/47	46-51	82	-	13

HUTCHINGS Stephen Henry (Steve)
Born: Portsmouth, England, 13 December, 1990 — F

League Club	Source	Date Signed	Seasons Played	Apps	Subs	Gls
Bournemouth	Jnr	03/08	07	0	1	0

HUTCHINS Daniel Sean (Danny)
Born: Northolt, W London, England, 23 September, 1989 — RB

League Club	Source	Date Signed	Seasons Played	Apps	Subs	Gls
Tottenham H	Sch	07/07				
Yeovil T	Tr	03/09	08-09	12	4	0

HUTCHINS Donald (Don)
Born: Middlesbrough, England, 8 May, 1948 — LW

League Club	Source	Date Signed	Seasons Played	Apps	Subs	Gls
Leicester C	Stockton	02/66	67-68	4	0	0
Plymouth Arg	Tr	07/69	69-71	94	1	23
Blackburn Rov	Tr	07/72	72-73	37	3	6
Bradford C	Tr	06/74	74-80	252	4	44

HUTCHINSON Andrew Leslie (Andy)
Born: Lincoln, England, 10 March, 1992 — F

League Club	Source	Date Signed	Seasons Played	Apps	Subs	Gls
Lincoln C	Sch	07/10	08-10	3	16	1

HUTCHINSON Benjamin Lloyd Phillip (Ben)
Born: Nottingham, England, 27 November, 1987 — F

League Club	Source	Date Signed	Seasons Played	Apps	Subs	Gls
Middlesbrough	Arnold T	01/06	07	0	8	1
Swindon T (L)	Glasgow Celtic	08/09	09	6	4	1
Lincoln C (L)	Glasgow Celtic	08/10	10	26	10	4
Mansfield T	Kilmarnock	01/12	13	11	5	2

HUTCHINSON Colin
Born: Lanchester, County Durham, England, 20 October, 1936 — IF

League Club	Source	Date Signed	Seasons Played	Apps	Subs	Gls
Stoke C	Crook Hall	11/53	54-57	9	-	0

HUTCHINSON Colin Mark (Mark)
Born: Stoke-on-Trent, England, 2 November, 1963 — M

League Club	Source	Date Signed	Seasons Played	Apps	Subs	Gls
Aston Villa	App	11/81				
Leicester C	Tr	08/83				
Carlisle U	L	08/84	84	6	0	0
Northampton T	Tr	02/85	84	1	1	0

HUTCHINSON David Norman
Born: Grimsby, North Lincolnshire, England, 25 September, 1941 — F

League Club	Source	Date Signed	Seasons Played	Apps	Subs	Gls
Scunthorpe U	Brigg T	07/71	71	5	4	0

HUTCHINSON Douglas (Doug)
Born: Gateshead, Tyne and Wear, England, 3 May, 1922 — RW
Died: Newcastle-upon-Tyne, England, 30 May, 2009

League Club	Source	Date Signed	Seasons Played	Apps	Subs	Gls
Gateshead	Stirling A	08/46	46	3	-	0

HUTCHINSON Edward Stephen (Eddie)
Born: Kingston-on-Thames, SW London, England, 23 February, 1982 — M

League Club	Source	Date Signed	Seasons Played	Apps	Subs	Gls
Brentford	Sutton U	07/00	00-05	95	22	8

HUTCHINSON George Henry
Born: Allerton Bywater, West Yorkshire, England, 31 October, 1929 — RW
Died: Sheffield, England, 30 July, 1996

League Club	Source	Date Signed	Seasons Played	Apps	Subs	Gls
Huddersfield T	Jnr	01/47	47	1	-	0
Sheffield U	Tr	03/48	48-52	73	-	10
Tottenham H	Tr	06/53	53	5	-	1
Leeds U	Guildford C	08/55	55	11	-	5
Halifax T	Tr	07/56	56-57	44	-	11

HUTCHINSON Ian
Born: Derby, England, 4 August, 1948 — F
Died: Islington, N London, England, 19 September, 2002
England: U23-2

League Club	Source	Date Signed	Seasons Played	Apps	Subs	Gls
Chelsea	Cambridge U	07/68	68-75	112	7	44

HUTCHINSON Ian Nicholas
Born: Stockton-on-Tees, Cleveland, England, 7 November, 1972 — LB

League Club	Source	Date Signed	Seasons Played	Apps	Subs	Gls
Halifax T	YT	07/92	90-91	7	1	1
Gillingham	Cork C (ROI)	09/94	94	1	4	0

HUTCHINSON James Arthur (Jimmy)
Born: Sheffield, England, 28 December, 1915 — IF
Died: Sheffield, England, November, 1997

League Club	Source	Date Signed	Seasons Played	Apps	Subs	Gls
Sheffield U	Aqueduct	11/37				
Bournemouth	Tr	06/46	46	8	-	3
Lincoln C	Tr	11/46	46-48	85	-	55
Oldham Ath	Tr	02/49	48-49	14	-	3

HUTCHINSON James Barry (Barry)
Born: Sheffield, England, 27 January, 1936 — IF
Died: Rotherham, South Yorkshire, England, 12 June, 2005

League Club	Source	Date Signed	Seasons Played	Apps	Subs	Gls
Chesterfield	Bolton W (Am)	04/53	54-59	154	-	16
Derby Co	Tr	07/60	60-63	107	-	51
Lincoln C	Weymouth	07/65	65	24	0	18
Darlington	Tr	02/66	65-66	28	2	14
Halifax T	Tr	11/66	66	25	0	14
Rochdale	Tr	07/67	67	27	0	3

HUTCHINSON John Arthur (Jack)
Born: Codnor, Derbyshire, England, 1 June, 1921 — FB
Died: Loscoe, Derbyshire, England, 27 November, 2004

League Club	Source	Date Signed	Seasons Played	Apps	Subs	Gls
Nottingham F	Jnr	08/43	46-58	241	-	0

HUTCHINSON Jonathan (Joey)
Born: Middlesbrough, England, 2 April, 1982 — CD

League Club	Source	Date Signed	Seasons Played	Apps	Subs	Gls
Birmingham C	YT	07/00	01-02	1	3	0
Darlington	Tr	08/03	03-06	78	1	0

HUTCHINSON Keith Graham
Born: South Shields, Tyne and Wear, England, 7 September, 1920 — LB
Died: Southport, Merseyside, England, April, 1986

League Club	Source	Date Signed	Seasons Played	Apps	Subs	Gls
Darlington	Newcastle U (Am)	05/46	46-48	31	-	0

HUTCHINSON Paul
Born: Eaglescliffe, Cleveland, England, 20 February, 1953 — LB

League Club	Source	Date Signed	Seasons Played	Apps	Subs	Gls
Darlington	Jnr	09/71	71-72	8	2	0

HUTCHINSON Robert (Bobby)
Born: Glasgow, Scotland, 19 June, 1953 — M

League Club	Source	Date Signed	Seasons Played	Apps	Subs	Gls
Wigan Ath	Hibernian	07/80	80	34	1	3
Tranmere Rov	Tr	08/81	81-82	32	3	6
Mansfield T	Tr	10/82	82-83	35	0	3
Tranmere Rov	Tr	01/84	83	21	0	4
Bristol C	Tr	07/84	84-86	89	3	10
Walsall	Tr	02/87	86-87	8	8	0
Blackpool	L	09/87	87	3	3	0
Carlisle U	L	01/88	87	12	1	2

HUTCHINSON Robert Wayne (Bob)
Born: Bolton, Greater Manchester, England, 9 May, 1955 — F

League Club	Source	Date Signed	Seasons Played	Apps	Subs	Gls
Rochdale	Radcliffe Bor	12/74	74	2	0	1

HUTCHINSON Samuel Edward (Sam)
Born: Windsor, Berkshire, England, 3 August, 1989 — RB
England: Youth

League Club	Source	Date Signed	Seasons Played	Apps	Subs	Gls
Chelsea	Sch	08/06	06-11	1	4	0
Nottingham F	L	08/12	12	6	3	1
Sheffield Wed	Tr	02/14	13-14	24	6	1

HUTCHINSON Shaun Matthew
Born: Newcastle-on-Tyne, England, 23 November, 1990 — CD

League Club	Source	Date Signed	Seasons Played	Apps	Subs	Gls
Fulham	Motherwell	06/14	14	25	0	2

HUTCHINSON Simon
Born: Sheffield, England, 24 September, 1969 — M
England: Schools

League Club	Source	Date Signed	Seasons Played	Apps	Subs	Gls
Manchester U	YT	09/87				
Wycombe W	Eastwood T	09/90	93-94	2	10	0

HUTCHISON Donald (Don)
Born: Gateshead, Tyne and Wear, England, 9 May, 1971 — M
Scotland: 26/B-2

League Club	Source	Date Signed	Seasons Played	Apps	Subs	Gls
Hartlepool U	YT	03/90	89-90	19	5	2
Liverpool	Tr	11/90	91-93	33	12	7
West Ham U	Tr	08/94	94-95	30	5	11
Sheffield U	Tr	01/96	95-97	70	8	5
Everton	Tr	02/98	97-99	68	7	10
Sunderland	Tr	07/00	00-01	32	2	8
West Ham U	Tr	08/01	01-04	36	27	5
Millwall	Tr	08/05	05	7	4	2
Coventry C	Tr	11/05	05-06	13	25	4
Luton T	Tr	07/07	07	15	6	0

HUTCHISON Thomas (Tommy)
Born: Cardenden, Fife, Scotland, 22 September, 1947 — LW/M
Scotland: 17/U23-1

League Club	Source	Date Signed	Seasons Played	Apps	Subs	Gls
Blackpool	Alloa Ath	02/68	67-72	162	2	10
Coventry C	Tr	10/72	72-80	312	2	24
Manchester C	Tr	10/80	80-81	44	2	4
Burnley	Bulova (HKG)	08/83	83-84	92	0	4
Swansea C	Tr	07/85	85-90	163	15	9

HUTH Robert
Born: Berlin, Germany, 18 August, 1984 — CD
Germany: 19/U21-4/Youth

League Club	Source	Date Signed	Seasons Played	Apps	Subs	Gls
Chelsea	YT	08/01	01-05	23	19	0
Middlesbrough	Tr	08/06	06-09	44	9	2
Stoke C	Tr	08/09	09-14	143	6	13
Leicester C	L	01/15	14	14	0	1

HUTT Geoffrey (Geoff)
Born: Castleford, West Yorkshire, England, 28 September, 1949 — FB

League Club	Source	Date Signed	Seasons Played	Apps	Subs	Gls
Huddersfield T	App	09/67	68-75	245	0	4
Blackburn Rov	L	09/75	75	10	0	1
York C	Haarlem (NED)	02/77	76-77	63	0	1
Halifax T	Tr	04/78	78-79	75	1	0

HUTT Stephen Graham (Steve)
Born: Middlesbrough, England, 19 February, 1979 — M

League Club	Source	Date Signed	Seasons Played	Apps	Subs	Gls
Hartlepool U	YT	07/97	95-98	6	3	0

HUTTON Alan
Born: Glasgow, Scotland, 30 November, 1984 — RB
Scotland: 45/U21-7

League Club	Source	Date Signed	Seasons Played	Apps	Subs	Gls
Tottenham H	Glasgow Rangers	01/08	07-10	39	12	2
Sunderland	L	02/10	09	11	0	0
Aston Villa	Tr	08/11	11-14	56	5	1
Nottingham F	L	11/12	12	7	0	0
Bolton W	L	02/14	13	9	0	0

HUTTON Alexander Shaw (Alec)
Born: Edinburgh, Scotland, 10 October, 1941 — FB

League Club	Source	Date Signed	Seasons Played	Apps	Subs	Gls
Southend U	Tulliallan Thistle	08/63	64	1	-	0

HUTTON David Edward
Born: Enfield, N London, England, 4 December, 1989 — W

League Club	Source	Date Signed	Seasons Played	Apps	Subs	Gls
Tottenham H	Sch	07/08				
Cheltenham T	Tr	03/09	08-09	19	13	1

HUTTON John (Jackie)
Born: Bellshill, Lanarkshire, Scotland, 23 April, 1944 — RW
Died: Belfast, Northern Ireland, 20 May, 2015

League Club	Source	Date Signed	Seasons Played	Apps	Subs	Gls
Scunthorpe U	Hamilton Academical	06/63	63-65	53	1	7

HUTTON Joseph (Joe)
Born: Dundee, Scotland, 18 November, 1927 — IF
Died: Wallingford, Oxfordshire, England, April, 1999

League Club	Source	Date Signed	Seasons Played	Apps	Subs	Gls
Reading	Albion Rov	10/50	49-50	8	-	0
Stoke C	Ayr U	12/53	53-56	34	-	7
Gillingham	Tr	08/57	57	36	-	6
Millwall	Tr	08/58	58-59	24	-	9

HUTTON Rory Neil
Born: Ely, Cambridgeshire, England, 3 May, 1985 — FB
Republic of Ireland: Youth

League Club	Source	Date Signed	Seasons Played	Apps	Subs	Gls
Peterborough U	Sch	03/04				
Cambridge U	Tr	08/04	04	0	2	0

HUTTON Thomas Osborne (Tom)
Born: Gateshead, Tyne and Wear, England, 10 September, 1922 — FB
Died: Blackburn, Greater Manchester, England, December, 2004

League Club	Source	Date Signed	Seasons Played	Apps	Subs	Gls
Accrington Stan	Red Rose	05/45	46	18	-	0
Carlisle U	Tr	08/47	47-48	44	-	0
Rochdale	Tr	08/49				
Tranmere Rov	Nelson	08/50				

HUWS Emyr Wyn
Born: Llanelli, Carmarthenshire, Wales, 30 September, 1993 — DM
Wales: 4/U21-6/Youth

League Club	Source	Date Signed	Seasons Played	Apps	Subs	Gls
Manchester C	Sch	10/10				
Northampton T	L	10/12	12	9	1	0
Birmingham C	L	01/14	13	17	0	2
Wigan Ath	Tr	08/14	14	15	1	0

HUXFORD Clifford George (Cliff)
Born: Stroud, Gloucestershire, England, 8 June, 1937 — LH

League Club	Source	Date Signed	Seasons Played	Apps	Subs	Gls
Chelsea	Jnr	02/55	58	6	-	0
Southampton	Tr	05/59	59-66	276	2	4
Exeter C	Tr	06/67	67	40	1	1

HUXFORD Colin John
Born: Stroud, Gloucestershire, England, 26 May, 1944 — RB
England: Youth

League Club	Source	Date Signed	Seasons Played	Apps	Subs	Gls
Chelsea	App	10/61				
Swindon T	Tr	11/62	62	1	-	0

HUXFORD Richard John
Born: Scunthorpe, North Lincolnshire, England, 25 July, 1969 — M/RB

League Club	Source	Date Signed	Seasons Played	Apps	Subs	Gls
Barnet	Kettering T	08/92	92	33	0	1
Millwall	Tr	07/93	93-94	25	7	0
Birmingham C	L	02/94	93	5	0	0
Bradford C	Tr	10/94	94-96	55	6	2
Peterborough U	L	10/96	96	7	0	0
Burnley	Tr	01/97	96-97	6	7	0

HYAM Luke Thomas
Born: Ipswich, England, 24 October, 1991 — M

League Club	Source	Date Signed	Seasons Played	Apps	Subs	Gls
Ipswich T	Sch	07/10	10-14	88	11	3

HYATT John William
Born: Feltham, SW London, England, 20 December, 1932 — CF

League Club	Source	Date Signed	Seasons Played	Apps	Subs	Gls
Crystal Palace	Feltham	08/54	54	1	-	0

HYDE Frank Lomas
Born: Wath-on-Dearne, South Yorkshire, England, 11 January, 1927 — G
Died: Barnsley, South Yorkshire, England, December, 2004

League Club	Source	Date Signed	Seasons Played	Apps	Subs	Gls
Bradford C	Wath W	12/48	48-51	34	-	0

HYDE Gary Stuart
Born: Wolverhampton, England, 28 December, 1969 — M

League Club	Source	Date Signed	Seasons Played	Apps	Subs	Gls
Darlington	YT	07/88	87-88	32	7	3
Leicester C	Tr	04/90				
Scunthorpe U	Tr	08/91	91	1	7	0

HYDE Graham
Born: Doncaster, South Yorkshire, England, 10 November, 1970 — M

League Club	Source	Date Signed	Seasons Played	Apps	Subs	Gls
Sheffield Wed	YT	05/88	91-98	126	46	11

League Club	Source	Date Signed	Seasons Played	Career Record Apps	Subs	Gls
Birmingham C	Tr	02/99	98-01	35	17	1
Chesterfield	L	08/01	01	8	1	1
Peterborough U	L	09/02	02	8	1	0
Bristol Rov	Tr	11/02	02-03	54	4	3

HYDE Jake Matthew
Born: Maidenhead, Berkshire, England, 1 July, 1990 F

League Club	Source	Date Signed	Seasons Played	Apps	Subs	Gls
Swindon T	Sch	02/08				
Barnet	Tr	07/09	09	17	17	6
Barnet	Dundee	08/12	12	31	9	14
York C	Tr	06/14	14	32	7	8

HYDE Micah Anthony
Born: West Ham, E London, England, 10 November, 1974 M
Jamaica: 17

League Club	Source	Date Signed	Seasons Played	Apps	Subs	Gls
Cambridge U	YT	05/93	93-96	89	18	13
Watford	Tr	07/97	97-03	235	18	24
Burnley	Tr	07/04	04-06	95	7	1
Peterborough U	Tr	01/07	06-08	56	8	0
Barnet	Woking	08/09	09	41	0	1

HYDE Paul David
Born: Hayes, W London, England, 7 April, 1963 G

League Club	Source	Date Signed	Seasons Played	Apps	Subs	Gls
Wycombe W	Hillingdon Bor	07/93	93-95	105	0	0
Leyton Orient	Tr	02/97	96-97	41	0	0

HYDE Stephen Leslie (Steve)
Born: High Wycombe, Buckinghamshire, England, 18 December, 1943 W

League Club	Source	Date Signed	Seasons Played	Apps	Subs	Gls
Oxford U	Wycombe W	01/65	64-65	9	0	0

HYDES Arthur
Born: Barnsley, South Yorkshire, England, 24 November, 1910 CF
Died: Barnsley, South Yorkshire, England, June, 1990

League Club	Source	Date Signed	Seasons Played	Apps	Subs	Gls
Leeds U	Ardsley Ath	05/30	30-36	127	-	74
Newport Co	Scunthorpe U	05/38	38	27	-	13
Exeter C	Tr	02/46	46	4	-	0

HYLDGAARD Morten Lauridsen
Born: Herning, Denmark, 26 January, 1978 G
Denmark: U21-3/Youth

League Club	Source	Date Signed	Seasons Played	Apps	Subs	Gls
Coventry C	Ikast (DEN)	07/99	02	27	0	0
Scunthorpe U	L	01/00	99	5	0	0
Luton T	Hibernian	01/04	03	18	0	0

HYLTON Daniel Thomas (Danny)
Born: Camden, N London, England, 25 February, 1989 F

League Club	Source	Date Signed	Seasons Played	Apps	Subs	Gls
Aldershot T	Jnr	05/07	08-12	113	41	30
Rotherham U	Tr	07/13	13	0	1	0
Bury	L	10/13	13	7	0	2
AFC Wimbledon	L	01/14	13	10	7	3
Oxford U	Tr	06/14	14	41	3	14

HYLTON Jermaine
Born: Birmingham, England, 28 June, 1993 F

League Club	Source	Date Signed	Seasons Played	Apps	Subs	Gls
Swindon T	Redditch U	01/15	14	1	10	1

HYLTON Leon David
Born: Birmingham, England, 27 January, 1983 LB
England: Youth

League Club	Source	Date Signed	Seasons Played	Apps	Subs	Gls
Aston Villa	YT	02/00				
Swansea C	Tr	02/03	02-03	17	2	0

HYMERS Thomas (Tom)
Born: Thorne, South Yorkshire, England, 29 April, 1935 LB
Died: Sheffield, England, May, 1987

League Club	Source	Date Signed	Seasons Played	Apps	Subs	Gls
Doncaster Rov	Frickley Colliery	11/58	59-60	23	-	0

HYND John Roger Shankly (Roger)
Born: Falkirk, Scotland, 2 February, 1942 CD

League Club	Source	Date Signed	Seasons Played	Apps	Subs	Gls
Crystal Palace	Glasgow Rangers	07/69	69	29	1	0
Birmingham C	Tr	07/70	70-75	162	9	4
Oxford U	L	10/75	75	5	0	0
Walsall	Tr	12/75	75-77	89	0	1

HYNDMAN Emerson Schellas
Born: Dallas, Texas, USA, 9 April, 1996 M
USA: 1/U23-1/Youth

League Club	Source	Date Signed	Seasons Played	Apps	Subs	Gls
Fulham	Sch	04/13	14	9	0	0

HYNES Peter Joseph
Born: Dublin, Republic of Ireland, 28 November, 1983 F

League Club	Source	Date Signed	Seasons Played	Apps	Subs	Gls
Aston Villa	YT	11/00				
Doncaster Rov	L	12/03	03	0	5	1
Cheltenham T	L	01/04	03	2	2	0

HYSEN Glenn Tobias
Born: Gothenburg, Sweden, 30 October, 1959 CD
Sweden: 68/U21-13/Youth

League Club	Source	Date Signed	Seasons Played	Apps	Subs	Gls
Liverpool	Fiorentina (ITA)	07/89	89-91	70	2	2

HYSEN Tobias
Born: Gothenburg, Sweden, 9 March, 1982 LW
Sweden: 34/U21-13

League Club	Source	Date Signed	Seasons Played	Apps	Subs	Gls
Sunderland	Djurgaarden (SWE)	08/06	06	15	11	4

HYSLOP Christian Terence (Chris)
Born: Watford, Hertfordshire, England, 14 June, 1972 LB

League Club	Source	Date Signed	Seasons Played	Apps	Subs	Gls
Southend U	YT	04/90	90-92	16	3	0
Northampton T	L	12/93	93	8	0	0
Colchester U	Tr	02/94	93	8	0	0

HYSON Matthew Alexander (Matty)
Born: Stockton-on-Tees, Cleveland, England, 2 May, 1976 M

League Club	Source	Date Signed	Seasons Played	Apps	Subs	Gls
Hartlepool U	YT	07/94	94	1	4	0

HYYPIA Sami Tuomas
Born: Porvoo, Finland, 7 October, 1973 CD
Finland: 105/U21-27/Youth

League Club	Source	Date Signed	Seasons Played	Apps	Subs	Gls
Liverpool	Willem II (NED)	07/99	99-08	310	8	22

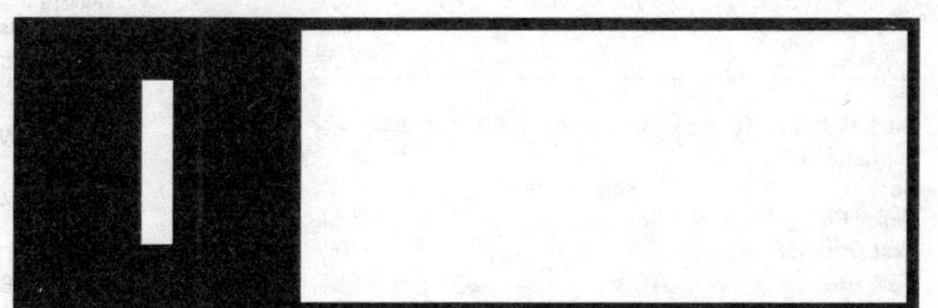

I'ANSON Paul
Born: Shipley, West Yorkshire, England, 31 May, 1946 — LH

League Club	Source	Date Signed	Seasons Played	Apps	Subs	Gls
Bradford Park Ave	App	06/64	63-67	49	1	2

IBANEZ Pablo
Born: Albacete, Spain, 3 August, 1981 — CD
Spain: 23/U21-10

League Club	Source	Date Signed	Seasons Played	Apps	Subs	Gls
West Bromwich A	Atletico Madrid (SPN)	07/10	10	8	2	1
Birmingham C	Tr	08/11	11-12	13	6	0

IBBOTSON Daniel (Danny)
Born: Morecambe, Lancashire, England, 5 October, 1968 — W

League Club	Source	Date Signed	Seasons Played	Apps	Subs	Gls
Preston NE	App	-	85	1	0	0

IBBOTSON Dennis
Born: Rotherham, South Yorkshire, England, 4 December, 1920 — FB
Died: Rotherham, South Yorkshire, England, 6 August, 2002
England: Schools

League Club	Source	Date Signed	Seasons Played	Apps	Subs	Gls
Rotherham U (Am)	Rotherham YMCA	11/46	46	4	-	0

IBBOTSON Wilfred (Wilf)
Born: Sheffield, England, 1 October, 1926 — IF
Died: Sheffield, England, January, 2014

League Club	Source	Date Signed	Seasons Played	Apps	Subs	Gls
Sheffield Wed	Jnr	04/44	47	1	-	0
Mansfield T	Tr	08/48	48	2	-	0

IBE Jordan Ashley Femi
Born: Bermondsey, SE London, England, 8 December, 1995 — W
England: Youth

League Club	Source	Date Signed	Seasons Played	Apps	Subs	Gls
Wycombe W	Sch	-	11	2	5	1
Liverpool	Sch	12/12	12-14	8	6	0
Birmingham C	L	02/14	13	4	7	1
Derby Co	L	08/14	14	13	7	5

IBE Okezie Enyeribenyam (Kezie)
Born: Camden, N London, England, 6 December, 1982 — F

League Club	Source	Date Signed	Seasons Played	Apps	Subs	Gls
Yeovil T	Staines T	08/04	04	0	3	0

IBEHRE Jabo Oshevire Michael
Born: Islington, N London, England, 28 January, 1983 — F

League Club	Source	Date Signed	Seasons Played	Apps	Subs	Gls
Leyton Orient	YT	07/01	99-07	112	97	36
Walsall	Tr	07/08	08	35	4	10
MK Dons	Tr	07/09	09-12	45	49	12
Southend U	L	11/09	09	4	0	0
Stockport Co	L	01/10	09	20	0	5
Colchester U	Tr	09/12	12-14	67	5	16
Oldham Ath	L	10/14	14	8	3	2
Barnsley	L	03/15	14	4	5	2

IBENFELDT Mads Max
Born: Birkerod, Denmark, 26 January, 1985 — CD

League Club	Source	Date Signed	Seasons Played	Apps	Subs	Gls
Southend U	AB Copenhagen (DEN)	08/14	14	0	1	0

IBRAHIM Abdisalam (Abdi)
Born: Mogadishu, Somalia, 4 May, 1991 — M
Norway: 2/U23-2/U21-12/Youth

League Club	Source	Date Signed	Seasons Played	Apps	Subs	Gls
Manchester C	Sch	07/08	09	0	1	0
Scunthorpe U	L	01/11	10	4	7	0

ICETON Osborne Lloyd (Lloyd)
Born: Workington, Cumbria, England, 30 March, 1920 — LW
Died: Birkenhead, Wirral, England, 12 August, 1994

League Club	Source	Date Signed	Seasons Played	Apps	Subs	Gls
Preston NE	Jnr	05/38				
Carlisle U	Tr	10/46	46-49	77	-	18
Tranmere Rov	Tr	06/50	50-54	140	-	18

ICKE David Vaughan
Born: Leicester, England, 29 May, 1952 — G

League Club	Source	Date Signed	Seasons Played	Apps	Subs	Gls
Coventry C	App	09/69				
Hereford U	Tr	08/71	72	37	0	0

IDDON Harold (Harry)
Born: Preston, Lancashire, England, 20 February, 1921 — W
Died: Preston, Lancashire, England, 13 March, 2005

League Club	Source	Date Signed	Seasons Played	Apps	Subs	Gls
Preston NE	Fulwood	02/43				
Barrow	Tr	10/46	46	25	-	6
Southport	Tr	06/47	47-48	42	-	3

IDE Charlie Joe
Born: Sunbury, Surrey, England, 10 May, 1988 — F

League Club	Source	Date Signed	Seasons Played	Apps	Subs	Gls
Brentford	Sch	07/06	04-07	40	6	7

IDEYE Aide Brown (Brown)
Born: Yenagoa, Nigeria, 10 October, 1988 — F
Nigeria: 24/Youth

League Club	Source	Date Signed	Seasons Played	Apps	Subs	Gls
West Bromwich A	Dynamo Kiev (UKR)	07/14	14	13	11	4

IDIAKEZ Inigo
Born: San Sebastian, Spain, 8 November, 1973 — W
Spain: U23-3/U21-6

League Club	Source	Date Signed	Seasons Played	Apps	Subs	Gls
Derby Co	Rayo Vallecano (SPN)	07/04	04-06	86	2	20
Southampton	Tr	08/06	06-07	26	9	2
Queens Park Rgrs	L	03/07	06	4	1	1

IDRAZAJ Besian
Born: Vienna, Austria, 12 October, 1987 — M
Died: Linz, Austria, 15 May, 2010
Austria: U21-12

League Club	Source	Date Signed	Seasons Played	Apps	Subs	Gls
Liverpool	Linzer ASK (AUT)	08/05				
Luton T	L	03/07	06	3	4	1
Crystal Palace	L	08/07	07	3	4	0
Swansea C	Eilenburg (GER)	08/09	09	1	3	0

IFEJIAGWA Chukwuemeka (Emeka)
Born: Aba, Nigeria, 30 October, 1977 — CD
Nigeria: 12

League Club	Source	Date Signed	Seasons Played	Apps	Subs	Gls
Charlton Ath	Udaji U (NIG)	08/98				
Brighton & HA	L	10/98	98	2	0	1

IFIL Jerel Christopher
Born: Willesden, NW London, England, 27 June, 1982 — CD

League Club	Source	Date Signed	Seasons Played	Apps	Subs	Gls
Watford	YT	02/00	02-03	10	1	0
Huddersfield T	L	03/02	01	1	1	0
Swindon T	L	01/03	02	5	4	0
Swindon T	L	09/03	03	6	0	0
Swindon T	L	11/03	03	10	0	0
Swindon T	Tr	07/04	04-08	172	9	3
Bristol Rov (L)	Aberdeen	02/11	10	3	0	0

IFIL Philip Nathan
Born: Willesden, NW London, England, 18 November, 1986 — RB
England: Youth

League Club	Source	Date Signed	Seasons Played	Apps	Subs	Gls
Tottenham H	Sch	11/04	04-06	3	0	0
Millwall	L	09/05	05	13	0	0
Millwall	L	01/06	05	3	0	0
Southampton	L	09/07	07	11	1	0
Colchester U	Tr	01/08	07-09	40	13	2
Dagenham & Red	Tr	09/10	10	13	1	0

IFILL Paul Everton
Born: Brighton, England, 20 October, 1979 — RW
Barbados: 10

League Club	Source	Date Signed	Seasons Played	Apps	Subs	Gls
Millwall	YT	06/98	98-04	188	42	40
Sheffield U	Tr	05/05	05-06	31	11	9
Crystal Palace	Tr	01/07	06-08	38	21	8

IGA Andrew Steven
Born: Kampala, Uganda, 9 December, 1977 — G

League Club	Source	Date Signed	Seasons Played	Apps	Subs	Gls
Millwall	Jnr	06/95	96	0	1	0

IGGLEDEN Horatio (Ray)
Born: Hull, England, 17 March, 1925 — IF
Died: Hull, England, 21 December, 2003

League Club	Source	Date Signed	Seasons Played	Apps	Subs	Gls
Leicester C	Constable Street OB	03/42	46-47	11	-	2
Leeds U	Tr	01/49	48-54	169	-	47
Exeter C	Tr	07/55	55	27	-	8

IGHALO Odion Jude
Born: Lagos, Nigeria, 16 June, 1989 — F
Nigeria: 3/Youth

League Club	Source	Date Signed	Seasons Played	Apps	Subs	Gls
Watford (L)	Udinese (ITA)	07/14	14	22	13	20

IGOE Samuel Gary (Sammy)
Born: Staines, Surrey, England, 30 September, 1975 — RM

League Club	Source	Date Signed	Seasons Played	Apps	Subs	Gls
Portsmouth	YT	02/94	94-99	100	60	11
Reading	Tr	03/00	99-02	53	34	7
Luton T	L	03/03	02	2	0	0
Swindon T	Tr	07/03	03-04	75	4	9
Millwall	Tr	08/05	05	3	2	0
Bristol Rov	L	01/06	05	10	1	1
Bristol Rov	Tr	08/06	06-07	44	17	1
Hereford U	L	03/08	07	4	0	0
Bournemouth	Tr	08/08	08-09	37	12	3

IHIEKWE Michael Uzoukwu Absolom
Born: Liverpool, England, 20 November, 1992 — CD

League Club	Source	Date Signed	Seasons Played	Apps	Subs	Gls
Wolverhampton W	Sch	06/11				

League Club	Source	Date Signed	Seasons Played	Apps	Subs	Gls
Cheltenham T	L	01/14	13	13	0	0
Tranmere Rov	Tr	06/14	14	37	1	1

IKEME Carl Onora

Born: Sutton Coldfield, West Midlands, England, 8 June, 1986 — G

League Club	Source	Date Signed	Seasons Played	Apps	Subs	Gls
Wolverhampton W	Sch	09/04	06-14	124	2	0
Stockport Co	L	08/05	05	9	0	0
Charlton Ath	L	10/09	09	4	0	0
Sheffield U	L	11/09	09	2	0	0
Queens Park Rgrs	L	01/10	09	17	0	0
Leicester C	L	08/10	10	5	0	0
Middlesbrough	L	08/11	11	10	0	0
Doncaster Rov	L	11/11	11	15	0	0

IKIN David

Born: Stoke-on-Trent, England, 18 February, 1946 — G

League Club	Source	Date Signed	Seasons Played	Apps	Subs	Gls
Port Vale		08/65	65	2	0	0

IKPEAZU Karl Anthony Uchechukwu (Uche)

Born: Harrow, NW London, England, 28 February, 1995 — F

League Club	Source	Date Signed	Seasons Played	Apps	Subs	Gls
Watford	Reading (Sch)	07/13				
Crewe Alex	L	01/14	13	10	5	4
Crewe Alex	L	11/14	14	7	1	2
Doncaster Rov	L	01/15	14	3	4	0
Crewe Alex	L	03/15	14	4	5	0

[ILAN] DALL'IGNA Ilan Araujo

Born: Curitiba, Brazil, 18 September, 1980 — F
Brazil: 3

League Club	Source	Date Signed	Seasons Played	Apps	Subs	Gls
West Ham U	Saint-Etienne (FRA)	02/10	09	6	5	4

ILES Richard

Born: Bristol, England, 21 May, 1967 — CD

League Club	Source	Date Signed	Seasons Played	Apps	Subs	Gls
Bristol Rov	Longwell Green	03/86	85	1	0	0

ILES Robert John (Bob)

Born: Leicester, England, 2 September, 1955 — G

League Club	Source	Date Signed	Seasons Played	Apps	Subs	Gls
Bournemouth	App	02/73				
Chelsea	Weymouth	06/78	78-82	14	0	0

ILESANMI Oluwafemi Abayomi (Femi)

Born: Southwark, S London, England, 18 April, 1981 — LB

League Club	Source	Date Signed	Seasons Played	Apps	Subs	Gls
Dagenham & Red	Queens Park Rgrs (Sch)	07/10	10-13	110	7	1
York C	Tr	05/14	14	29	4	0

ILEY James (Jim)

Born: South Kirkby, West Yorkshire, England, 15 December, 1935 — LH
England: FLge-2/U23-1

League Club	Source	Date Signed	Seasons Played	Apps	Subs	Gls
Sheffield U	Pontefract	06/53	54-57	99	-	7
Tottenham H	Tr	08/57	57-58	53	-	1
Nottingham F	Tr	07/59	59-62	93	-	4
Newcastle U	Tr	09/62	62-68	227	5	15
Peterborough U	Tr	01/69	68-72	64	4	4

ILIC Sasa

Born: Melbourne, Australia, 18 July, 1972 — G
Yugoslavia: 2

League Club	Source	Date Signed	Seasons Played	Apps	Subs	Gls
Charlton Ath	St Leonards Stamcroft	10/97	97-00	51	0	0
West Ham U	L	02/00	99	1	0	0
Portsmouth	L	09/01	01	7	0	0
Portsmouth	Zalaegerszegi (HUN)	02/03				
Barnsley	Tr	08/03	03	25	0	0
Sheffield U	Tr	02/04				
Blackpool	Tr	08/04	04	3	0	0

ILIEV Georg Georgiev

Born: Sofia, Bulgaria, 23 October, 1994 — F
Bulgaria: Youth

League Club	Source	Date Signed	Seasons Played	Apps	Subs	Gls
Bolton W	Sch	01/14				
Carlisle U	L	10/14	14	4	0	0

ILLINGWORTH Jeremy Marcus

Born: Huddersfield, West Yorkshire, England, 20 May, 1977 — M

League Club	Source	Date Signed	Seasons Played	Apps	Subs	Gls
Huddersfield T	YT	06/95	96	2	1	0

ILLMAN Neil David

Born: Doncaster, South Yorkshire, England, 29 April, 1975 — F

League Club	Source	Date Signed	Seasons Played	Apps	Subs	Gls
Middlesbrough	YT	03/93	93	0	1	0
Plymouth Arg	Eastwood T	03/96	96-97	13	18	4
Cambridge U	L	03/96	95	1	4	0
Exeter C	Tr	12/97	97	6	2	2

ILUNGA Herita N'Kongolo

Born: Kinshasa, DR Congo, 25 February, 1982 — LB
DR Congo: 32

League Club	Source	Date Signed	Seasons Played	Apps	Subs	Gls
West Ham U	Toulouse (FRA)	09/08	08-11	65	1	0
Doncaster Rov	Tr	10/11	11	19	0	0

IMLACH James John Stewart (Stewart)

Born: Lossiemouth, Moray, Scotland, 6 January, 1932 — LW
Died: Formby, Merseyside, England, 3 October, 2001
Scotland: 4

League Club	Source	Date Signed	Seasons Played	Apps	Subs	Gls
Bury	Lossiemouth	10/52	52-53	71	-	14
Derby Co	Tr	05/54	54	36	-	2
Nottingham F	Tr	07/55	55-59	184	-	43
Luton T	Tr	06/60	60	8	-	0
Coventry C	Tr	10/60	60-61	73	-	11
Crystal Palace	Tr	07/62	62-64	35	-	2
Crystal Palace	Chelmsford C	02/66	65-66	16	0	1

IMLACH Michael Thomas (Mike)

Born: Croydon, S London, England, 19 September, 1962 — FB

League Club	Source	Date Signed	Seasons Played	Apps	Subs	Gls
Preston NE	Everton (App)	08/80				
Leeds U	Tr	11/81				
Peterborough U	Tr	08/82	82-83	37	5	1
Tranmere Rov	Tr	08/84	84	4	0	0

IMMEL Eike

Born: Stadtallendorf, Hesse, Germany, 27 November, 1960 — G
West Germany: 19/U21-14/Youth

League Club	Source	Date Signed	Seasons Played	Apps	Subs	Gls
Manchester C	VfB Stuttgart (GER)	08/95	95-96	42	0	0

IMPEY Andrew Rodney (Andy)

Born: Hammersmith, W London, England, 30 September, 1971 — RB/M
England: U21-1

League Club	Source	Date Signed	Seasons Played	Apps	Subs	Gls
Queens Park Rgrs	Yeading	06/90	91-96	177	10	13
West Ham U	Tr	09/97	97-98	25	2	0
Leicester C	Tr	11/98	98-03	132	20	1
Nottingham F	Tr	02/04	03-04	33	3	1
Millwall	L	03/05	04	0	5	0
Coventry C	Tr	09/05	05	4	12	0

IMPEY John Edward

Born: Exeter, England, 11 August, 1954 — CD
England: Youth/Schools

League Club	Source	Date Signed	Seasons Played	Apps	Subs	Gls
Cardiff C	App	08/72	72-74	13	8	0
Bournemouth	Tr	07/75	75-82	280	4	7
Torquay U	Tr	08/83	83-84	72	0	0
Exeter C	Tr	08/85	85	26	0	0
Torquay U	Tr	07/86	86-87	58	0	2

IMRIE Adam Lyle

Born: Annan, Dumfries & Galloway, Scotland, 1 October, 1933 — RW
Died: Kirkcudbright, Dumfries & Galloway, Scotland, 20 July, 2005

League Club	Source	Date Signed	Seasons Played	Apps	Subs	Gls
Carlisle U	Kilmarnock	05/57	57	10	-	5

INAMOTO Junichi

Born: Kagoshima, Japan, 18 September, 1979 — M
Japan: 83/U23-15/Youth

League Club	Source	Date Signed	Seasons Played	Apps	Subs	Gls
Fulham (L)	Gamba Osaka (JPN)	07/02	02	9	10	2
Fulham (L)	Gamba Osaka (JPN)	07/03	03	15	7	2
West Bromwich A	Gamba Osaka (JPN)	08/04	04-06	16	12	0
Cardiff C	L	12/04	04	13	1	0

INCE Clayton

Born: Arima, Trinidad, 13 July, 1972 — G
Trinidad & Tobago: 79

League Club	Source	Date Signed	Seasons Played	Apps	Subs	Gls
Crewe Alex	Defence Force (TRD)	09/99	99-04	120	3	0
Coventry C	Tr	07/05	05	1	0	0
Walsall	Tr	07/06	06-09	151	1	0

INCE Paul Emerson Carlyle

Born: Ilford, E London, England, 21 October, 1967 — M
England: 53/B-1/U21-2/Youth

League Club	Source	Date Signed	Seasons Played	Apps	Subs	Gls
West Ham U	App	07/85	86-89	66	6	7
Manchester U	Tr	09/89	89-94	203	3	25
Liverpool	Inter Milan (ITA)	07/97	97-98	65	0	14
Middlesbrough	Tr	08/99	99-01	93	0	7
Wolverhampton W	Tr	08/02	02-05	107	8	10
Swindon T	Tr	08/06	06	2	1	0
Macclesfield T	Tr	12/06	06	0	1	0

INCE Rohan Greg

Born: Whitechapel, Central London, England, 8 November, 1992 — DM

League Club	Source	Date Signed	Seasons Played	Apps	Subs	Gls
Chelsea	Sch	07/10				
Yeovil T	L	07/12	12	1	1	0
Brighton & HA	Tr	02/13	13-14	49	11	1

INCE Thomas Christopher (Tom)

Born: Stockport, Greater Manchester, England, 30 January, 1992 — W
England: U21-18/Youth

League Club	Source	Date Signed	Seasons Played	Apps	Subs	Gls
Liverpool	Sch	07/09				
Notts Co	L	11/10	10	3	3	2
Blackpool	Tr	07/11	11-13	86	14	31
Crystal Palace	L	01/14	13	5	3	1
Hull C	Tr	07/14	14	3	4	0
Nottingham F	L	10/14	14	4	2	0
Derby Co	L	02/15	14	18	0	11

INGEBRIGTSEN Kaare Hedley
Born: Trondheim, Norway, 11 November, 1965 — M
Norway: 23

League Club	Source	Date Signed	Seasons Played	Apps	Subs	Gls
Manchester C	Rosenborg (NOR)	01/93	92-93	4	11	0

INGER James (Jimmy)
Born: Nottingham, England, 10 August, 1953 — G

League Club	Source	Date Signed	Seasons Played	Apps	Subs	Gls
Walsall (Am)	Long Eaton U	03/73	72	2	0	0

INGESSON Klas Inge
Born: Odeshog, Sweden, 20 August, 1968 — M
Died: Odeshog, Sweden, 29 October, 2014
Sweden: 58

League Club	Source	Date Signed	Seasons Played	Apps	Subs	Gls
Sheffield Wed	PSV Eindhoven (NED)	09/94	94-95	12	6	2

INGHAM Anthony (Tony)
Born: Harrogate, North Yorkshire, England, 18 February, 1925 — LB
Died: Harrow, NW London, England, 21 April, 2010

League Club	Source	Date Signed	Seasons Played	Apps	Subs	Gls
Leeds U	Harrogate T	04/47	47-49	3	-	0
Queens Park Rgrs	Tr	06/50	50-62	514	-	3

INGHAM Frederick Roy (Fred)
Born: Manchester, England, 3 April, 1954 — F

League Club	Source	Date Signed	Seasons Played	Apps	Subs	Gls
Stockport Co	App	04/72	71-72	12	7	1
Blackburn Rov	Tr	08/73				
Exeter C	Falmouth	03/78	77-78	4	4	1

INGHAM Gary
Born: Rotherham, South Yorkshire, England, 9 October, 1964 — G
Died: Rotherham, South Yorkshire, England, 20 November, 2012

League Club	Source	Date Signed	Seasons Played	Apps	Subs	Gls
Rotherham U	Bridlington T	03/93				
Doncaster Rov	Tr	03/94	93	1	0	0
Doncaster Rov	Gainsborough Trinity	08/97	97	10	0	0

INGHAM Michael Gerard
Born: Preston, Lancashire, England, 7 September, 1980 — G
Northern Ireland: 3/U21-4/Youth

League Club	Source	Date Signed	Seasons Played	Apps	Subs	Gls
Sunderland	Cliftonville	07/99	04	1	1	0
Carlisle U	L	10/99	99	7	0	0
Darlington	L	11/02	02	3	0	0
York C	L	01/03	02	17	0	0
Wrexham	L	03/04	03	11	0	0
Doncaster Rov	L	11/04	04	1	0	0
Wrexham	Tr	07/05	05-06	71	0	0
Hereford U	Tr	08/07				
York C	Tr	07/08	12-14	82	2	0

INGHAM Robert John (John)
Born: Hebburn, Tyne and Wear, England, 18 October, 1924 — W
Died: Newcastle-upon-Tyne, England, 6 May, 2000

League Club	Source	Date Signed	Seasons Played	Apps	Subs	Gls
Gateshead	Newburn	08/47	47-57	430	-	109

INGHAM William Charles (Billy)
Born: Stakeford, Northumberland, England, 22 October, 1952 — M
Died: Blackburn, Greater Manchester, England, 7 November, 2009

League Club	Source	Date Signed	Seasons Played	Apps	Subs	Gls
Burnley	App	11/69	71-79	181	30	22
Bradford C	Tr	08/80	80-81	78	0	4

INGIMARSSON Ivar
Born: Reykjavik, Iceland, 20 August, 1977 — M/CD
Iceland: 30/U21-14/Youth

League Club	Source	Date Signed	Seasons Played	Apps	Subs	Gls
Torquay U (L)	IBV (ICE)	10/99	99	4	0	1
Brentford	IBV (ICE)	11/99	99-01	109	4	10
Wolverhampton W	Tr	07/02	02	10	3	2
Brighton & HA	L	02/03	02	15	0	0
Reading	Tr	10/03	03-10	247	4	11
Ipswich T	Tr	07/11	11	6	2	0

INGLE Stephen Paul (Steve)
Born: Bradford, England, 22 October, 1946 — RB/CF

League Club	Source	Date Signed	Seasons Played	Apps	Subs	Gls
Bradford C	App	08/64	64-66	89	1	15
Southend U	Tr	01/67	66	14	1	3
Wrexham	Tr	07/67	67-71	145	4	5
Stockport Co	Tr	07/72	72	29	0	0
Southport	Tr	07/73	73	2	0	0
Darlington	Tr	10/73	73	8	0	0

INGLEDOW Jamie Graeme
Born: Barnsley, South Yorkshire, England, 23 August, 1980 — M/RB

League Club	Source	Date Signed	Seasons Played	Apps	Subs	Gls
Rotherham U	YT	07/98	98-99	17	8	2
Chesterfield	Tr	07/00	00-01	26	15	3

INGLETHORPE Alexander Matthew (Alex)
Born: Epsom, Surrey, England, 14 November, 1971 — F

League Club	Source	Date Signed	Seasons Played	Apps	Subs	Gls
Watford	Jnr	07/90	90-93	2	10	2
Barnet	L	03/95	94	5	1	3
Leyton Orient	Tr	05/95	95-99	105	18	32
Exeter C	L	02/00	99	0	1	0
Exeter C	Tr	07/00	00	11	7	2

INGLIS James McDougal (Jimmy)
Born: Glasgow, Scotland, 14 February, 1924 — CF
Died: Glasgow, Scotland, 20 June, 1999

League Club	Source	Date Signed	Seasons Played	Apps	Subs	Gls
Bury	Stirling A	05/50	50	2	-	0

INGLIS John
Born: Gateshead, Tyne and Wear, England, 5 August, 1933 — G

League Club	Source	Date Signed	Seasons Played	Apps	Subs	Gls
Gateshead (Am)	Blyth Spartans	06/57	57	2	-	0

INGLIS John
Born: Edinburgh, Scotland, 16 October, 1966 — CD

League Club	Source	Date Signed	Seasons Played	Apps	Subs	Gls
Carlisle U	Levski Sofia (BUL)	09/00	00	8	0	0

INGLIS John Francis
Born: Leven, Fife, Scotland, 19 May, 1947 — F

League Club	Source	Date Signed	Seasons Played	Apps	Subs	Gls
Aston Villa	Glenrothes	09/65	67	1	1	0
Crewe Alex	Tr	07/68	68-69	46	2	10

INGRAM Alexander David (Alex)
Born: Edinburgh, Scotland, 2 January, 1945 — F
Scotland: SLge-1/Amateur

League Club	Source	Date Signed	Seasons Played	Apps	Subs	Gls
Nottingham F	Ayr U	12/69	69-70	28	0	3

INGRAM Christopher David (Chris)
Born: Cardiff, Wales, 5 December, 1976 — RW

League Club	Source	Date Signed	Seasons Played	Apps	Subs	Gls
Cardiff C	YT	08/95	95	4	4	1

INGRAM Gerald (Gerry)
Born: Merthyr Tydfil, Wales, 28 January, 1951 — M
Wales: Schools

League Club	Source	Date Signed	Seasons Played	Apps	Subs	Gls
Swansea C	Cardiff College	08/70	70-72	36	2	1

INGRAM Gerald (Gerry)
Born: Beverley, East Riding of Yorkshire, England, 19 August, 1947 — F

League Club	Source	Date Signed	Seasons Played	Apps	Subs	Gls
Blackpool	Hull Brunswick	03/67	66-67	33	1	17
Preston NE	Tr	09/68	68-71	107	2	40
Bradford C	Tr	03/72	71-76	171	3	60

INGRAM Godfrey Patrick
Born: Luton, England, 26 October, 1959 — F
England: Youth/Schools

League Club	Source	Date Signed	Seasons Played	Apps	Subs	Gls
Luton T	App	10/77	77-81	22	5	6
Northampton T	L	03/80	79	10	0	4
Cardiff C	San Jose E'quake (USA)	09/82	82	7	4	2
Peterborough U	St Louis Storm (USA)	08/92	92	0	1	0

INGRAM Matthew Robert (Matt)
Born: High Wycombe, Buckinghamshire, England, 18 December, 1993 — G

League Club	Source	Date Signed	Seasons Played	Apps	Subs	Gls
Wycombe W	Sch	05/12	12-14	100	0	0

INGRAM Rae
Born: Manchester, England, 6 December, 1974 — D

League Club	Source	Date Signed	Seasons Played	Apps	Subs	Gls
Manchester C	YT	07/93	95-96	18	5	0
Macclesfield T	Tr	03/98	97-00	95	8	1
Port Vale	Tr	07/01	01-02	25	3	0

INGRAM Stuart Denevan (Denny)
Born: Sunderland, England, 27 June, 1976 — RB/M

League Club	Source	Date Signed	Seasons Played	Apps	Subs	Gls
Hartlepool U	YT	07/94	93-99	192	7	10

INGS Daniel William John (Danny)
Born: Netley, Hampshire, England, 16 March, 1992 — F
England: U21-13

League Club	Source	Date Signed	Seasons Played	Apps	Subs	Gls
Bournemouth	Jnr	08/10	10-11	22	5	7
Burnley	Tr	08/11	11-14	99	23	38

INKANGO Bruce Pascal
Born: Poitiers, France, 18 May, 1984 — W

League Club	Source	Date Signed	Seasons Played	Apps	Subs	Gls
Gillingham	Paris Red Star (FRA)	09/10	10	1	4	0

INMAN Bradden (Brad)
Born: Adelaide, Australia, 10 December, 1991 — W
Scotland: U21-2/Youth

League Club	Source	Date Signed	Seasons Played	Apps	Subs	Gls
Newcastle U	Sch	07/09				
Crewe Alex	L	11/12	12	17	4	5
Crewe Alex	Tr	08/13	13-14	40	17	5

INMAN Niall Edward
Born: Wakefield, England, 6 February, 1978 — M
Republic of Ireland: U21-8/Youth

League Club	Source	Date Signed	Seasons Played	Apps	Subs	Gls
Peterborough U	YT	07/96	95-99	6	6	2

INNES Gary John
Born: Consett, County Durham, England, 7 October, 1977 — F
England: Youth/Schools

League Club	Source	Date Signed	Seasons Played	Apps	Subs	Gls
Darlington	Esh Winning	07/96	96	1	14	0

INNES Mark
Born: Airdrie, Lanarkshire, Scotland, 27 September, 1978 — LW

League Club	Source	Date Signed	Seasons Played	Apps	Subs	Gls
Oldham Ath	YT	10/95	97-01	52	21	1
Chesterfield	Tr	12/01	01-04	62	14	2
Port Vale	Tr	03/05	04-05	19	9	0

INNISS Ryan Stuart Clayton
Born: Bromley, SE London, England, 5 June, 1995 — CD
England: Youth

League Club	Source	Date Signed	Seasons Played	Apps	Subs	Gls
Crystal Palace	Sch	07/12				
Cheltenham T	L	08/13	13	2	0	0
Gillingham	L	02/14	13	3	0	0
Yeovil T	L	10/14	14	4	2	0
Port Vale	L	02/15	14	5	0	0

INSKIP Frederick Clive (Fred)
Born: Cheadle, Staffordshire, England, 20 October, 1924 — RW
Died: Stoke-on-Trent, England, January, 2000

League Club	Source	Date Signed	Seasons Played	Apps	Subs	Gls
Nottingham F	Crewe Alex (Am)	12/44				
Crewe Alex	Tr	04/48	47-48	26	-	5

INSUA Emiliano Adrian
Born: Buenos Aires, Argentina, 7 January, 1989 — LB
Argentina: 4/U23-1

League Club	Source	Date Signed	Seasons Played	Apps	Subs	Gls
Liverpool	Boca Juniors (ARG)	01/07	06-09	43	3	0

INVINCIBILE Daniel (Danny)
Born: Brisbane, Australia, 31 March, 1979 — W
Australia: Youth/Schools

League Club	Source	Date Signed	Seasons Played	Apps	Subs	Gls
Swindon T	Marconi Stall'ns (AUS)	08/00	00-02	109	19	22

INWOOD Gordon Frederick
Born: Kislingbury, Northamptonshire, England, 18 June, 1928 — LW

League Club	Source	Date Signed	Seasons Played	Apps	Subs	Gls
West Bromwich A	Rushden T	01/49	49	10	-	0
Hull C	Tr	05/50	50	3	-	0

IOANNOU Nicky
Born: Camden, N London, England, 3 September, 1987 — RB

League Club	Source	Date Signed	Seasons Played	Apps	Subs	Gls
Barnet	Rushden & D (Jnr)	08/06	06	1	1	0

IORFA Dominic
Born: Gboko, Nigeria, 1 October, 1968 — F
Nigeria: 4

League Club	Source	Date Signed	Seasons Played	Apps	Subs	Gls
Queens Park Rgrs	Royal Antwerp (BEL)	03/90	89-91	1	7	0
Peterborough U	Galatasaray (TKY)	10/92	92-93	27	33	9
Southend U	Tr	08/94	94-95	5	5	1
Southend U	Billericay T	12/98	98	0	2	0

IORFA Dominic
Born: Southend-on-Sea, England, 8 July, 1995 — RB
England: Youth

League Club	Source	Date Signed	Seasons Played	Apps	Subs	Gls
Wolverhampton W	Sch	07/12	14	20	0	0
Shrewsbury T	L	03/14	13	6	1	0

IOVAN Stefan
Born: Bucharest, Romania, 23 August, 1960 — FB
Romania: 35/U21-12

League Club	Source	Date Signed	Seasons Played	Apps	Subs	Gls
Brighton & HA	Steaua Bucharest (ROM)	03/91	90-91	4	2	0

IPOUA Guy
Born: Douala, Cameroon, 14 January, 1976 — F

League Club	Source	Date Signed	Seasons Played	Apps	Subs	Gls
Bristol Rov	Alicante CF (SPN)	08/98	98	15	9	3
Scunthorpe U	Tr	08/99	99-00	50	15	23
Gillingham	Tr	03/01	00-02	42	40	13
Doncaster Rov	Al Shaab (UAE)	08/04	04	1	8	0
Mansfield T	L	10/04	04	4	1	0
Lincoln C	L	02/05	04	0	6	0

IPPOLITO Mario
Born: Peterborough, England, 16 April, 1964 — LW

League Club	Source	Date Signed	Seasons Played	Apps	Subs	Gls
Peterborough U	Jnr	04/83	82	8	0	3

IRELAND Craig Robert
Born: Dundee, Scotland, 29 November, 1975 — CD

League Club	Source	Date Signed	Seasons Played	Apps	Subs	Gls
Notts Co	Dundee	02/01	00-02	77	3	2
Barnsley	Tr	08/03	03	43	0	3
Peterborough U	Tr	08/04	04	22	1	0
Bristol C	L	01/05	04	5	0	0

IRELAND Daniel Anthony (Danny)
Born: Sydney, Australia, 30 September, 1990 — G
Australia: Youth

League Club	Source	Date Signed	Seasons Played	Apps	Subs	Gls
Coventry C	Sch	09/07	10	0	1	0

IRELAND Jeffrey John Charles (Jeff)
Born: Paddington, Central London, England, 1 December, 1935 — RW
Died: Eltham, SE London, England, 25 December, 2010

League Club	Source	Date Signed	Seasons Played	Apps	Subs	Gls
Tottenham H	Finchley	11/57	57-58	3	-	0
Shrewsbury T	Tr	06/59	59	38	-	4

IRELAND Jeremy (Jerry)
Born: Chester, England, 14 September, 1938 — IF/RH

League Club	Source	Date Signed	Seasons Played	Apps	Subs	Gls
Chester C		09/57	57-61	40	-	8

IRELAND Roy Peter
Born: Exeter, England, 3 February, 1961 — M/RB

League Club	Source	Date Signed	Seasons Played	Apps	Subs	Gls
Exeter C	App	02/79	78-80	17	4	0

IRELAND Simon Piers
Born: Barnstaple, Devon, England, 23 November, 1971 — W
England: Schools

League Club	Source	Date Signed	Seasons Played	Apps	Subs	Gls
Huddersfield T	Jnr	07/90	90-92	10	9	0
Wrexham	L	03/92	91	2	3	0
Blackburn Rov	Tr	11/92	92	0	1	0
Mansfield T	Tr	03/94	93-96	89	5	11
Doncaster Rov	L	10/96	96	9	0	1
Doncaster Rov	Tr	01/97	96-97	52	0	1

IRELAND Stephen James
Born: Cobh, Republic of Ireland, 22 August, 1986 — M
Republic of Ireland: 6/U21-1/Youth

League Club	Source	Date Signed	Seasons Played	Apps	Subs	Gls
Manchester C	Sch	09/04	05-09	109	29	16
Aston Villa	Tr	08/10	10-12	34	13	1
Newcastle U	L	01/11	10	0	2	0
Stoke C	Tr	09/13	13-14	25	18	2

IRIEKPEN Ezomo (Izzy)
Born: West Ham, E London, England, 14 May, 1982 — CD
England: Youth

League Club	Source	Date Signed	Seasons Played	Apps	Subs	Gls
West Ham U	YT	05/99				
Leyton Orient	L	10/02	02	5	0	1
Cambridge U	L	02/03	02	13	0	1
Swansea C	Tr	08/03	03-06	121	2	7
Scunthorpe U	Tr	07/07	07-08	26	7	5
Bristol C	Tr	01/09	08	4	5	0

[IRINEY] DA SILVA Santos Iriney
Born: Amazonas, Brazil, 23 April, 1981 — DM

League Club	Source	Date Signed	Seasons Played	Apps	Subs	Gls
Watford	Granada (SPN)	07/13	13	12	3	0

IRO Andrew (Andy)
Born: Liverpool, England, 26 November, 1984 — CD

League Club	Source	Date Signed	Seasons Played	Apps	Subs	Gls
Stevenage	Toronto FC (CAN)	09/12				
Barnet	L	11/12	12	9	0	1

IROHA Benedict (Ben)
Born: Aba, Nigeria, 29 November, 1969 — LB
Nigeria: 50

League Club	Source	Date Signed	Seasons Played	Apps	Subs	Gls
Watford	Elche (SPN)	12/98	98	8	2	0

IRONS Kenneth (Kenny)
Born: Liverpool, England, 4 November, 1970 — M

League Club	Source	Date Signed	Seasons Played	Apps	Subs	Gls
Tranmere Rov	YT	11/89	89-98	313	38	54
Huddersfield T	Tr	06/99	99-02	120	29	11

IRONSIDE Ian
Born: Sheffield, England, 8 March, 1964 — G

League Club	Source	Date Signed	Seasons Played	Apps	Subs	Gls
Barnsley	Jnr	09/82				
Scarborough	North Ferriby U	03/88	87-90	88	0	0
Middlesbrough	Tr	08/91	91-92	12	1	0
Scarborough	L	03/92	91	7	0	0
Stockport Co	Tr	09/93	93-94	17	2	0
Scarborough	Tr	03/95	94-96	88	0	0

IRONSIDE Joe Samuel
Born: Middlesbrough, England, 16 October, 1993 — F

League Club	Source	Date Signed	Seasons Played	Apps	Subs	Gls
Sheffield U	Sch	03/13	12-13	2	14	0
Hartlepool U	L	11/14	14	3	1	1

IRONSIDE Roy
Born: Sheffield, England, 28 May, 1935 — G

League Club	Source	Date Signed	Seasons Played	Apps	Subs	Gls
Rotherham U	Atlas & Norfolk	07/54	56-64	220	-	0
Barnsley	Tr	07/65	65-68	113	0	0

IRVIN Derek Vincent
Born: Stockton-on-Tees, Cleveland, England, 23 August, 1943 — W

League Club	Source	Date Signed	Seasons Played	Apps	Subs	Gls
Middlesbrough	Broomhall	09/61				
Watford	Brechin C	06/67	67	0	2	1

IRVINE Alan James
Born: Broxburn, West Lothian, Scotland, 20 November, 1962 — RW

League Club	Source	Date Signed	Seasons Played	Apps	Subs	Gls
Liverpool	Falkirk	11/86	86	0	2	0
Shrewsbury T	Dundee U	02/88	87-88	32	5	6

IRVINE Archibald (Archie)
Born: Coatbridge, Lanarkshire, Scotland, 25 June, 1946 — M/RW

League Club	Source	Date Signed	Seasons Played	Apps	Subs	Gls
Sheffield Wed	Airdrieonians	09/68	68-69	25	4	1
Doncaster Rov	Tr	12/69	69-74	220	8	16
Scunthorpe U	Tr	07/75	75	22	1	1

IRVINE James (Jim)
Born: Whitburn, West Lothian, Scotland, 17 August, 1940 — CF
Scotland: Schools

League Club	Source	Date Signed	Seasons Played	Apps	Subs	Gls
Middlesbrough	Dundee U	05/64	64-66	90	1	37
Barrow	Heart of Midlothian	07/70	70-71	67	0	17

IRVINE James Alan (Alan)
Born: Glasgow, Scotland, 12 July, 1958 — W

League Club	Source	Date Signed	Seasons Played	Apps	Subs	Gls
Everton	Queen's Park	05/81	81-83	51	9	4
Crystal Palace	Tr	08/84	84-86	108	1	12
Blackburn Rov	Dundee U	10/89	89-91	40	18	3

IRVINE Robert James (Bobby)
Born: Carrickfergus, Antrim, Northern Ireland, 17 January, 1942 — G
Northern Ireland: 8/NILge-5/U23-1/Schools

League Club	Source	Date Signed	Seasons Played	Apps	Subs	Gls
Stoke C	Linfield	06/63	63-65	25	0	0

IRVINE Samuel (Sammy)
Born: Glasgow, Scotland, 7 January, 1956 — M

League Club	Source	Date Signed	Seasons Played	Apps	Subs	Gls
Shrewsbury T	App	01/74	72-77	198	9	18
Stoke C	Tr	06/78	78-79	67	0	10

IRVINE Stuart Christopher
Born: Hartlepool, Cleveland, England, 1 March, 1979 — F

League Club	Source	Date Signed	Seasons Played	Apps	Subs	Gls
Hartlepool U	YT	07/97	96-98	13	18	2

IRVINE William John (Willie)
Born: Carrickfergus, Antrim, Northern Ireland, 18 June, 1943 — CF
Northern Ireland: 23/U23-3/Schools

League Club	Source	Date Signed	Seasons Played	Apps	Subs	Gls
Burnley	Jnr	06/60	62-67	124	2	78
Preston NE	Tr	03/68	67-70	77	4	27
Brighton & HA	Tr	03/71	70-72	66	3	27
Halifax T	Tr	12/72	72	9	1	1

IRVING David
Born: Cockermouth, Cumbria, England, 10 September, 1951 — F
England: Youth

League Club	Source	Date Signed	Seasons Played	Apps	Subs	Gls
Workington	Aspatria	05/70	70-72	57	8	16
Everton	Tr	01/73	73-75	4	2	0
Sheffield U	L	09/75	75	0	2	0
Oldham Ath	Tr	06/76	76-77	18	3	7

IRVING Gerald (Gerry)
Born: Maryport, Cumbria, England, 19 September, 1937 — W

League Club	Source	Date Signed	Seasons Played	Apps	Subs	Gls
Workington		08/56	56	1	-	0

IRVING Richard James
Born: Halifax, West Yorkshire, England, 10 September, 1975 — F
England: Youth/Schools

League Club	Source	Date Signed	Seasons Played	Apps	Subs	Gls
Manchester U	YT	10/92				
Nottingham F	Tr	07/95	95	0	1	0
Macclesfield T	Tr	10/97	97	6	3	0

IRVING Russell
Born: Wallsend, Tyne and Wear, England, 4 January, 1964 — F

League Club	Source	Date Signed	Seasons Played	Apps	Subs	Gls
Ipswich T	App	05/81				
Colchester U	Tr	08/84	84-85	36	14	9

IRWIN Cecil (Cec)
Born: Ellington, Northumberland, England, 8 April, 1942 — RB
England: Youth

League Club	Source	Date Signed	Seasons Played	Apps	Subs	Gls
Sunderland	Jnr	04/59	58-71	311	3	1

IRWIN Colin Thomas
Born: Liverpool, England, 9 February, 1957 — CD

League Club	Source	Date Signed	Seasons Played	Apps	Subs	Gls
Liverpool	Jnr	12/74	79-80	26	3	3
Swansea C	Tr	08/81	81-83	48	0	0

IRWIN Joseph Denis (Denis)
Born: Cork, Republic of Ireland, 31 October, 1965 — RB
Republic of Ireland: 56/B-1/U23-1/U21-3/Youth/Schools

League Club	Source	Date Signed	Seasons Played	Apps	Subs	Gls
Leeds U	App	11/83	83-85	72	0	1
Oldham Ath	Tr	05/86	86-89	166	1	4
Manchester U	Tr	06/90	90-01	356	12	22
Wolverhampton W	Tr	07/02	02-03	73	2	2

IRWIN William (Bill)
Born: Newtownards, Down, Northern Ireland, 23 July, 1951 — G
Northern Ireland: Amateur

League Club	Source	Date Signed	Seasons Played	Apps	Subs	Gls
Cardiff C	Bangor	10/71	71-77	180	0	0

ISAAC James (Jimmy)
Born: Cramlington, Northumberland, England, 23 October, 1916 — IF
Died: Huddersfield, West Yorkshire, England, 19 December, 1993

League Club	Source	Date Signed	Seasons Played	Apps	Subs	Gls
Huddersfield T	Cramlington	11/34	36-38	33	-	8
Bradford C	Tr	04/45	46	24	-	3
Hartlepool U	Tr	07/47	47-48	56	-	9

ISAAC Robert Charles (Bobby)
Born: Hackney, E London, England, 30 November, 1965 — CD
England: Youth

League Club	Source	Date Signed	Seasons Played	Apps	Subs	Gls
Chelsea	App	11/83	84-86	9	0	0
Brighton & HA	Tr	02/87	86-88	30	0	0

ISAAC William Henry (Peter)
Born: Pontypridd, Rhondda Cynon Taff, Wales, 16 May, 1935 — G

League Club	Source	Date Signed	Seasons Played	Apps	Subs	Gls
Stoke C		03/53				
Northampton T	Barry T	07/58	59	8	-	0

ISAACS Anthony Brian (Tony)
Born: Middlesbrough, England, 8 April, 1973 — M

League Club	Source	Date Signed	Seasons Played	Apps	Subs	Gls
Darlington	YT	07/91	91-93	37	14	2

ISAIAS Marques Soares
Born: Rio de Janeiro, Brazil, 17 November, 1963 — F

League Club	Source	Date Signed	Seasons Played	Apps	Subs	Gls
Coventry C	Benfica (POR)	08/95	95-96	9	3	2

ISAKSSON Andreas
Born: Trelleborg, Sweden, 3 October, 1981 — G
Sweden: 121/U21-23/Youth

League Club	Source	Date Signed	Seasons Played	Apps	Subs	Gls
Manchester C	Stade Rennais (FRA)	08/06	06-07	17	2	0

ISGROVE Lloyd Jeffrey
Born: Yeovil, Somerset, England, 12 January, 1993 — RW
Wales: U21-6

League Club	Source	Date Signed	Seasons Played	Apps	Subs	Gls
Southampton	Sch	07/11	14	0	1	0
Peterborough U	L	03/14	13	3	5	1
Sheffield Wed	L	03/15	14	7	1	0

ISHERWOOD Dennis
Born: Northwich, Cheshire, England, 9 January, 1924 — W
Died: Stoke-on-Trent, England, February, 1974

League Club	Source	Date Signed	Seasons Played	Apps	Subs	Gls
Wrexham	Rochdale (Am)	08/44				
Chester C	Tr	04/46	46	3	-	0

ISHERWOOD Dennis
Born: Brierley Hill, West Midlands, England, 20 January, 1947 — RB

League Club	Source	Date Signed	Seasons Played	Apps	Subs	Gls
Birmingham C	App	01/64	66	5	0	1

ISHERWOOD Roy Edward
Born: Blackburn, Greater Manchester, England, 24 January, 1934 — RW

League Club	Source	Date Signed	Seasons Played	Apps	Subs	Gls
Blackburn Rov	Nelson	10/57	57-61	49	-	9

ISLA Mauricio Anibal
Born: Santiago, Chile, 12 June, 1988 — RB
Chile: 66/Youth

League Club	Source	Date Signed	Seasons Played	Apps	Subs	Gls
Queens Park Rgrs (L)	Juventus (ITA)	08/14	14	24	2	0

ISMAEL Valerien
Born: Strasbourg, France, 28 September, 1975 — CD

League Club	Source	Date Signed	Seasons Played	Apps	Subs	Gls
Crystal Palace	Strasbourg (FRA)	01/98	97	13	0	0

ISMAIL Zeli
Born: Kukes, Albania, 12 December, 1993 — RW
England: Youth

League Club	Source	Date Signed	Seasons Played	Apps	Subs	Gls
Wolverhampton W	Sch	12/10	13	5	4	0
MK Dons	L	11/12	12	1	6	0
Burton A	L	01/14	13	10	5	3
Notts Co	L	07/14	14	10	4	4

ISSA Pierre Sanitarib
Born: Johannesburg, South Africa, 11 August, 1975 — CD
South Africa: 47

League Club	Source	Date Signed	Seasons Played	Apps	Subs	Gls
Watford	Olymp Marseille (FRA)	09/01	01	12	3	1

ISTEAD Steven Brian
Born: South Shields, Tyne and Wear, England, 23 April, 1986 — M

League Club	Source	Date Signed	Seasons Played	Apps	Subs	Gls
Hartlepool U	Sch	07/05	02-05	5	59	3

ITHELL William James (Jimmy)
Born: Hawarden, Flintshire, Wales, 7 February, 1916 — CH
Died: Trowbridge, Wiltshire, England, 3 January, 1986

League Club	Source	Date Signed	Seasons Played	Apps	Subs	Gls
Bolton W		11/36				
Swindon T	Tr	05/46	46-49	107	-	1

IVANOVIC Branislav
Born: Sremska Mitrovica, Yugoslavia, 22 February, 1984 — D
Serbia: 79/U21-38

League Club	Source	Date Signed	Seasons Played	Apps	Subs	Gls
Chelsea	Lokomotiv Moscow (RUS)	01/08	08-14	201	14	20

IVERSEN Steffen
Born: Oslo, Norway, 10 November, 1976 — F
Norway: 79/U21-23/Youth

League Club	Source	Date Signed	Seasons Played	Apps	Subs	Gls
Tottenham H	Rosenborg (NOR)	12/96	96-02	112	31	36
Wolverhampton W	Tr	08/03	03	11	5	4
Crystal Palace	Rosenborg (NOR)	01/11	10-11	11	9	2

IVERSON Robert Thomas James (Bob)
Born: Folkestone, Kent, England, 17 October, 1910 — WH/IF
Died: Birmingham, England, 19 June, 1953

League Club	Source	Date Signed	Seasons Played	Apps	Subs	Gls
Tottenham H	Folkestone	05/32				
Lincoln C	Ramsgate Press	09/33	33-34	41	-	13
Wolverhampton W	Tr	02/35	34-36	35	-	7
Aston Villa	Tr	12/36	36-47	135	-	9

IVEY George Harrison
Born: Stanley, County Durham, England, 29 October, 1923 — W
Died: Hartlepool, Cleveland, England, November, 1979

League Club	Source	Date Signed	Seasons Played	Apps	Subs	Gls
York C	West Stanley U	06/48	48-50	79	-	13

League Club	Source	Date Signed	Seasons Played	Apps	Subs	Gls
IVEY Paul Henry Winspear						
Born: Westminster, Central London, England, 1 April, 1961						F
Birmingham C	App	01/79	78-80	4	3	0
Chesterfield	Kettering T	12/82	82	0	6	0
IWELUMO Christopher Robert (Chris)						
Born: Coatbridge, Lanarkshire, Scotland, 1 August, 1978						F
Scotland: 4/B-1						
Stoke C	Aarhus Fremad (DEN)	03/00	99-03	40	44	16
York C	L	11/00	00	11	1	2
Cheltenham T	L	02/01	00	2	2	1
Brighton & HA	Tr	03/04	03	10	0	4
Colchester U	Alem'ia Aachen (GER)	07/05	05-06	87	5	35
Charlton Ath	Tr	07/07	07	32	14	10
Wolverhampton W	Tr	07/08	08-09	27	19	14
Bristol C	L	02/10	09	7	0	2
Burnley	Tr	07/10	10	29	16	11
Watford	Tr	07/11	11-12	25	21	4
Notts Co	L	11/12	12	5	0	0
Oldham Ath	L	01/13	12	4	3	1
Scunthorpe U	Tr	07/13	13	4	8	2
IZZET Kemal						
Born: Mile End, E London, England, 29 September, 1980						M
Charlton Ath	YT	01/99				
Colchester U	Tr	03/01	00-12	375	47	18
IZZET Mustafa Kemal (Muzzy)						
Born: Mile End, E London, England, 31 October, 1974						M
Turkey: 9						
Chelsea	YT	05/93				
Leicester C	Tr	03/96	95-03	265	4	38
Birmingham C	Tr	07/04	04-05	20	6	1

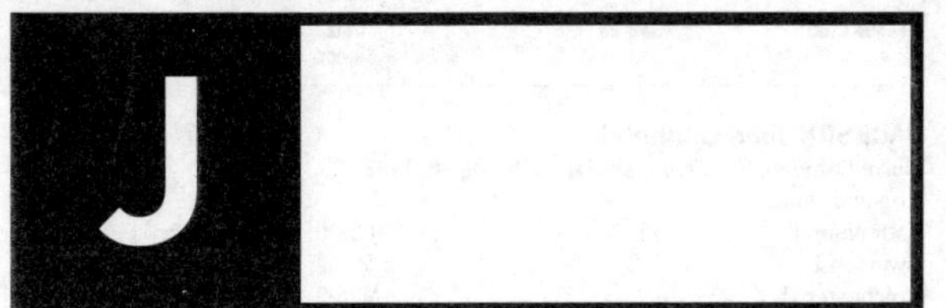

League Club	Source	Date Signed	Seasons Played	Apps	Subs	Gls
JAASKELAINEN Jussi						
Born: Vaasa, Finland, 19 April, 1975						G
Finland: 56/U21-14/Youth						
Bolton W	VPS Vaasa (FIN)	11/97	98-11	473	1	0
West Ham U	Tr	07/12	12-14	56	1	0
JACK Andrew Mackintosh						
Born: Glasgow, Scotland, 30 June, 1923						CF
Tranmere Rov	Wishaw Jnrs	06/48	48	3	-	3
JACK James Ross (Ross)						
Born: Avoch, Highlands, Scotland, 21 March, 1959						F
Everton	App	02/77	78	1	0	1
Norwich C	Tr	12/79	80-82	31	25	10
Lincoln C	Tr	08/83	83-84	52	8	16
JACK Kelvin Kyron						
Born: Arouca, Trinidad, 29 April, 1976						G
Trinidad & Tobago: 33						
Reading	San Juan Jab'h (TRD)	03/04				
Gillingham	Dundee	07/06	06	9	0	0
JACK Michael Lawrence						
Born: Carlisle, Cumbria, England, 2 October, 1982						M
Carlisle U	YT	06/01	01-03	19	23	0
JACK Rodney Alphonso						
Born: Kingstown, Saint Vincent And The Grenadines, 28 September, 1972						F
Saint Vincent And The Grenadines: 45						
Torquay U	Lambada (SVG)	10/95	95-97	82	5	24
Crewe Alex	Tr	08/98	98-02	140	23	33
Rushden & D	Tr	07/03	03	44	1	12
Oldham Ath	Tr	07/04	04	5	5	2
Crewe Alex	Waterford U (ROI)	08/06	06	19	11	1
JACK Vincent (Vince)						
Born: Rosemarkie, Highlands, Scotland, 6 August, 1933						CH
Died: New South Wales, Australia, 22 September, 2006						
Bury	Inverness Jnrs	04/54	55-56	10	-	0
Swindon T	Tr	10/56	56-58	26	-	0
Accrington Stan	Tr	07/59	59	22	-	0
JACKETT Frank						
Born: Ystalyfera, Neath Port Talbot, Wales, 5 July, 1927						WH
Died: Hertford, England, 14 April, 2010						
Watford	Pontardawe Ath	11/49	49-52	14	-	0
Leyton Orient	Tr	07/53	53	4	-	0
JACKETT Kenneth Francis (Kenny)						
Born: Watford, Hertfordshire, England, 5 January, 1962						M/LB
Wales: 31/U21-2/Youth						
Watford	App	01/80	79-89	328	7	25
JACKMAN Clive Edward James						
Born: Farnborough, Hampshire, England, 21 February, 1936						G
Aldershot	Jnr	05/53	52-56	38	-	0
West Bromwich A	Tr	06/57	57-58	21	-	0
JACKMAN Daniel James (Danny)						
Born: Worcester, England, 3 January, 1983						LB/M
Aston Villa	YT	04/01				
Cambridge U	L	02/02	01	5	2	1
Stockport Co	Tr	10/03	03-04	51	9	4
Gillingham	Tr	08/05	05-06	65	8	1
Northampton T	Tr	07/07	07-08	76	6	9
Gillingham	Tr	08/09	09-12	79	10	6
JACKMAN Derek Clive						
Born: Colchester, Essex, England, 20 August, 1927						WH
Crystal Palace	Chelmsford C	03/45				
West Ham U	Tr	08/48	48-50	8	-	0
JACKS George Charles						
Born: Stepney, E London, England, 14 March, 1946						M
Queens Park Rgrs	App	01/64	64	1	-	0
Millwall	Tr	07/65	65-70	144	7	5
Gillingham	Tr	07/72	72-75	159	0	20

League Club	Source	Date Signed	Seasons Played	Apps	Subs	Gls
JACKSON Alan						
Born: Swadlincote, Derbyshire, England, 22 August, 1938						RW
Wolverhampton W	Jnr	08/55	57-58	4	-	1
Bury	Tr	06/59	59-62	124	-	43
Brighton & HA	Tr	11/62	62-63	21	-	5
JACKSON Alan Edward						
Born: Scunthorpe, North Lincolnshire, England, 14 February, 1938						W
Died: Scunthorpe, North Lincolnshire, England, 9 April, 1996						
Lincoln C	Brigg T	11/58	58-60	4	-	0
JACKSON Albert						
Born: Manchester, England, 12 September, 1943						CF/CH
Died: Oldham, Greater Manchester, England, 2 December, 2014						
Oldham Ath	Manchester U (Jnr)	12/62	63-65	22	0	4
JACKSON Alec						
Born: Tipton, West Midlands, England, 29 May, 1937						RW/IF
England: FLge-1						
West Bromwich A	WG Allen's	09/54	54-63	192	-	50
Birmingham C	Tr	06/64	64-66	78	0	11
Walsall	Tr	02/67	66-67	36	2	7
JACKSON Alexander James (Alex)						
Born: Glasgow, Scotland, 28 November, 1935						CF
Birmingham C	Heart of Midlothian	04/58	58	6	-	6
Plymouth Arg	Tr	03/60	59-63	67	-	23
JACKSON Alexander Wilson (Alec)						
Born: Lesmahagow, Lanarkshire, Scotland, 2 October, 1921						WH/IF
York C	Huddersfield T (Am)	09/46	46-49	50	-	5
JACKSON Arnold						
Born: Manchester, England, 10 November, 1925						IF
Shrewsbury T		10/49	50-53	144	-	39
Stockport Co	Tr	06/54	54-58	153	-	48
JACKSON Benjamin Robert (Ben)						
Born: Peterlee, County Durham, England, 22 October, 1985						M
Doncaster Rov	Newcastle U (Sch)	01/04	04	0	1	0
JACKSON Brian						
Born: Maltby, South Yorkshire, England, 2 February, 1936						WH/RB
Died: Manchester, England, May, 1992						
Rotherham U	Maltby Main	09/54	55-64	131	-	6
Barnsley	Tr	07/65	65	29	0	0
JACKSON Brian Harvill						
Born: Walton-on-Thames, Surrey, England, 1 April, 1933						W
England: Schools						
Leyton Orient	Arsenal (Am)	10/50	50-51	38	-	2
Liverpool	Tr	11/51	51-57	124	-	12
Port Vale	Tr	07/58	58-61	159	-	29
Peterborough U	Tr	07/62	62-63	47	-	4
Lincoln C	Tr	05/64	64	10	-	1
JACKSON Charles Barry (Barry)						
Born: Askrigg, North Yorkshire, England, 2 February, 1938						CH
York C	Cliftonville, York	12/56	58-69	481	1	9
JACKSON Christopher Dean (Chris)						
Born: Barnsley, South Yorkshire, England, 16 January, 1976						F
England: Youth/Schools						
Barnsley	YT	01/93	92-95	16	7	2
JACKSON Clifford (Cliff)						
Born: Swindon, England, 3 September, 1941						LW/IF
England: Schools						
Swindon T	Jnr	09/58	58-62	91	-	30
Plymouth Arg	Tr	06/63	63-66	72	0	19
Crystal Palace	Tr	09/66	66-69	100	6	25
Torquay U	Tr	08/70	70-73	114	13	13
JACKSON Craig						
Born: Renishaw, Derbyshire, England, 17 January, 1969						CD
Notts Co	App	08/86	85-86	3	2	0
JACKSON Darren						
Born: Edinburgh, Scotland, 25 July, 1966						M/F
Scotland: 28/B-1						
Newcastle U	Meadowbank Thistle	10/86	86-88	53	16	7
Coventry C (L)	Glasgow Celtic	11/98	98	0	3	0
JACKSON Darren William						
Born: Keynsham, Avon, England, 24 September, 1971						D
Oxford U	YT	05/90	89-93	11	3	0
Reading	L	02/93	92	5	0	0
JACKSON David						
Born: Stoke-on-Trent, England, 23 January, 1937						IF/WH

League Club	Source	Date Signed	Seasons Played	Apps	Subs	Gls
Wrexham (Am)	Jnr	07/54	54	7	-	1
Bradford C	Marine	03/55	54-60	250	-	61
Tranmere Rov	Tr	07/61	61-62	38	-	5
Halifax T	Tr	07/63	63-64	66	-	2

JACKSON David Kenneth George
Born: Solihull, West Midlands, England, 22 August, 1978 — FB

League Club	Source	Date Signed	Seasons Played	Apps	Subs	Gls
Shrewsbury T	YT	-	95	0	1	0

JACKSON David Patrick
Born: Bradford, England, 16 September, 1958 — F
Died: Bradford, England, August, 2009

League Club	Source	Date Signed	Seasons Played	Apps	Subs	Gls
Manchester U	App	09/75				
Bradford C	Tr	09/78	78	9	3	3

JACKSON Dennis Leonard
Born: Birmingham, England, 8 March, 1932 — RB
Died: 20 March, 2014

League Club	Source	Date Signed	Seasons Played	Apps	Subs	Gls
Aston Villa	Hednesford T	10/54	56-58	8	-	0
Millwall	Tr	05/59	59-60	80	-	0

JACKSON Elliot
Born: Swindon, England, 27 August, 1977 — G

League Club	Source	Date Signed	Seasons Played	Apps	Subs	Gls
Oxford U	YT	07/96	96-98	7	0	0

JACKSON Ernest
Born: Sheffield, England, 11 June, 1914 — RH
Died: Sheffield, England, February, 1996

League Club	Source	Date Signed	Seasons Played	Apps	Subs	Gls
Sheffield U	Atlas & Norfolk	09/32	32-48	229	-	8

JACKSON Gary Andrew
Born: Swinton, Greater Manchester, England, 30 September, 1964 — M

League Club	Source	Date Signed	Seasons Played	Apps	Subs	Gls
Manchester C	Jnr	10/81	81	6	2	0
Exeter C	Tr	09/85	85-86	34	1	2

JACKSON George
Born: Liverpool, England, 14 January, 1911 — FB
Died: Wrexham, Wales, January, 2002

League Club	Source	Date Signed	Seasons Played	Apps	Subs	Gls
Everton	Walton Parish Church	05/32	34-47	75	-	0

JACKSON George
Born: Stretford, Greater Manchester, England, 10 February, 1952 — M

League Club	Source	Date Signed	Seasons Played	Apps	Subs	Gls
Stoke C	App	07/69	71	8	0	0

JACKSON Harold
Born: Halifax, West Yorkshire, England, 20 July, 1917 — LB
Died: Nailsea, Somerset, England, 13 June, 1996

League Club	Source	Date Signed	Seasons Played	Apps	Subs	Gls
Halifax T	Sowerby Bridge WE	08/36	36-46	83	-	3
Stockport Co	Tr	08/47	47	2	-	0

JACKSON Harry
Born: Blackburn, Greater Manchester, England, 30 December, 1918 — CF
Died: Bury, Greater Manchester, England, 19 August, 1984

League Club	Source	Date Signed	Seasons Played	Apps	Subs	Gls
Burnley	Darwen	01/42				
Manchester C	Tr	06/46	46-47	8	-	2
Preston NE	Tr	12/47	47-48	18	-	5
Blackburn Rov	Tr	12/48	48	1	-	0
Chester C	Tr	07/49	49	21	-	10

JACKSON Harry
Born: Renishaw, Derbyshire, England, 12 May, 1934 — CF

League Club	Source	Date Signed	Seasons Played	Apps	Subs	Gls
Oldham Ath	Jnr	06/51	51-55	10	-	1
Rochdale	Tr	10/55	55	1	-	1

JACKSON James (Jimmy)
Born: Glasgow, Scotland, 1 January, 1921 — IF
Died: Paisley, Renfrewshire, Scotland, 25 March, 2002

League Club	Source	Date Signed	Seasons Played	Apps	Subs	Gls
Bolton W	Glasgow St Mungo	06/39	47-49	11	-	1
Carlisle U	Tr	07/50	50-54	100	-	23

JACKSON James (Jimmy)
Born: Glasgow, Scotland, 26 March, 1931 — CF
Died: York, England, 2 March, 2013

League Club	Source	Date Signed	Seasons Played	Apps	Subs	Gls
Notts Co	Mapperley Celtic	03/49	48-57	113	-	47

JACKSON James Peter
Born: Glasgow, Scotland, 4 August, 1924 — WH

League Club	Source	Date Signed	Seasons Played	Apps	Subs	Gls
Bury	Third Lanark	05/50	50	1	-	0

JACKSON James William (Jimmy)
Born: Ashington, Northumberland, England, 30 December, 1933 — LB
Died: Northumberland, England, July, 2012
England: Schools

League Club	Source	Date Signed	Seasons Played	Apps	Subs	Gls
Newcastle U	Jnr	01/51				
Aldershot	Tr	07/55	55-60	197	-	19

JACKSON Jamie Noel Emmanuel Donnelly
Born: Sheffield, England, 1 November, 1986 — RW

League Club	Source	Date Signed	Seasons Played	Apps	Subs	Gls
Chesterfield	Sch	07/06	05-07	1	19	0

JACKSON John (Johnnie)
Born: Camden, N London, England, 15 August, 1982 — M
England: Youth

League Club	Source	Date Signed	Seasons Played	Apps	Subs	Gls
Tottenham H	YT	03/00	03-05	12	8	1
Swindon T	L	09/02	02	12	1	1
Colchester U	L	03/03	02	8	0	0
Coventry C	L	11/03	03	2	3	2
Watford	L	12/04	04	14	1	0
Derby Co	L	09/05	05	3	3	0
Colchester U	Tr	07/06	06-08	92	15	13
Notts Co	Tr	08/09	09	20	4	2
Charlton Ath	L	02/10	09	4	0	0
Charlton Ath	Tr	07/10	10-14	164	9	44

JACKSON John
Born: Newcastle-under-Lyme, Potteries, England, 7 January, 1923 — CF
Died: Leek, Staffordshire, England, June, 1992

League Club	Source	Date Signed	Seasons Played	Apps	Subs	Gls
Stoke C	Alsager	05/41	46-47	4	-	3

JACKSON John Keith
Born: Hammersmith, W London, England, 5 September, 1942 — G
England: FLge-2/Youth

League Club	Source	Date Signed	Seasons Played	Apps	Subs	Gls
Crystal Palace	Jnr	03/62	64-73	346	0	0
Leyton Orient	Tr	10/73	73-78	226	0	0
Millwall	Tr	08/79	79-80	79	0	0
Ipswich T	Tr	08/81	81	1	0	0
Hereford U	Tr	08/82	82	4	0	0

JACKSON Josef John (Joe)
Born: Barrow in Furness, Cumbria, England, 3 February, 1993 — F

League Club	Source	Date Signed	Seasons Played	Apps	Subs	Gls
Burnley	Sch	07/11	11	0	1	0

JACKSON Joseph George (Joe)
Born: Wolverhampton, England, 22 April, 1966 — M

League Club	Source	Date Signed	Seasons Played	Apps	Subs	Gls
Wolverhampton W	Jnr	08/83	83	1	0	0

JACKSON Justin Jonathan
Born: Nottingham, England, 10 December, 1974 — F
England: Semi Pro-2

League Club	Source	Date Signed	Seasons Played	Apps	Subs	Gls
Notts Co	Woking	09/97	97-98	7	18	1
Rotherham U	L	01/99	98	2	0	1
Halifax T	Tr	02/99	98-99	16	1	4
Rushden & D	Morecambe	06/00	01	5	0	0

JACKSON Kirk Stewart Samuel
Born: Barnsley, South Yorkshire, England, 16 October, 1976 — F
England: Semi Pro-6

League Club	Source	Date Signed	Seasons Played	Apps	Subs	Gls
Sheffield Wed	YT	05/95				
Scunthorpe U	Tr	07/96	96	0	4	1
Chesterfield	Tr	08/97	97	0	3	0
Darlington	Worksop T	03/01	00-01	6	15	1
Yeovil T	Stevenage Bor	11/02	03	19	11	5

JACKSON Leonard (Len)
Born: Stockport, Greater Manchester, England, 10 May, 1923 — RB
Died: Stockport, Greater Manchester, England, 20 May, 1968

League Club	Source	Date Signed	Seasons Played	Apps	Subs	Gls
Manchester C		01/45				
Rochdale	Tr	09/45	46-47	61	-	0

JACKSON Leonard Wilfred (Len)
Born: Birmingham, England, 6 September, 1922 — RB
Died: Birmingham, England, 14 May, 1990

League Club	Source	Date Signed	Seasons Played	Apps	Subs	Gls
Birmingham C		09/46				
Northampton T	Tr	07/48	48	2	-	0

JACKSON Mark Graham
Born: Barnsley, South Yorkshire, England, 30 September, 1977 — CD
England: Youth

League Club	Source	Date Signed	Seasons Played	Apps	Subs	Gls
Leeds U	YT	07/95	95-97	11	8	0
Huddersfield T	L	10/98	98	5	0	0
Barnsley	L	01/00	99	1	0	0
Scunthorpe U	Tr	03/00	99-04	127	9	4
Kidderminster Hrs	Tr	02/05	04	13	0	0
Rochdale	Kidderminster Hrs	01/06	05-06	20	4	0

JACKSON Mark Philip
Born: Preston, Lancashire, England, 3 February, 1986 — F

League Club	Source	Date Signed	Seasons Played	Apps	Subs	Gls
Preston NE	Sch	08/04	03-04	0	3	0
Shrewsbury T	L	10/05	05	2	3	0

JACKSON Marlon Michael
Born: Bristol, England, 6 December, 1990 — F

League Club	Source	Date Signed	Seasons Played	Apps	Subs	Gls
Bristol C	Sch	07/09	10	0	4	0
Hereford U	L	08/09	09	2	3	0
Aldershot T	L	11/09	09	18	4	1
Aldershot T	L	09/10	10	4	5	0
Northampton T	L	09/11	11	5	1	1
Cheltenham T	L	11/11	11	0	1	0
Bury	Hereford U	07/13	13	2	6	1

JACKSON Matthew Alan (Matt)
Born: Leeds, England, 19 October, 1971 — CD
England: U21-10/Schools

League Club	Source	Date Signed	Seasons Played	Apps	Subs	Gls
Luton T	Jnr	07/90	91	7	2	0
Preston NE	L	03/91	90	3	1	0
Everton	Tr	10/91	91-95	132	6	4
Charlton Ath	L	03/96	95	8	0	0
Queens Park Rgrs	L	08/96	96	7	0	0
Birmingham C	L	10/96	96	10	0	0
Norwich C	Tr	12/96	96-00	158	3	6
Wigan Ath	Tr	10/01	01-06	157	10	4
Watford	Tr	05/07	07	6	0	0
Blackpool	L	10/07	07	2	1	0

JACKSON Maurice
Born: Royston, South Yorkshire, England, 6 November, 1928 — FB/WH
Died: Barnsley, South Yorkshire, England, 1971

League Club	Source	Date Signed	Seasons Played	Apps	Subs	Gls
Barnsley	Carlton U	09/49	49-55	34	-	0
Barrow	Tr	08/56	56-58	74	-	0

JACKSON Michael Douglas
Born: Cheltenham, Gloucestershire, England, 26 June, 1980 — M

League Club	Source	Date Signed	Seasons Played	Apps	Subs	Gls
Cheltenham T	YT	08/97	99-01	2	7	0
Swansea C	Tr	07/02	02	0	1	0

JACKSON Michael James
Born: Runcorn, Cheshire, England, 4 December, 1973 — CD
England: Youth

League Club	Source	Date Signed	Seasons Played	Apps	Subs	Gls
Crewe Alex	YT	07/92	91-92	5	0	0
Bury	Tr	08/93	93-96	123	2	9
Preston NE	Tr	03/97	96-03	237	8	17
Tranmere Rov	L	12/02	02	6	0	0
Tranmere Rov	Tr	07/04	04-05	84	0	8
Blackpool	Tr	07/06	06-07	65	3	1
Shrewsbury T	Tr	07/08	08	21	0	2

JACKSON Nigel Anthony
Born: Pudsey, West Yorkshire, England, 27 June, 1950 — LB/M

League Club	Source	Date Signed	Seasons Played	Apps	Subs	Gls
Scunthorpe U	App	07/68	68-72	112	4	5

JACKSON Norman Edward
Born: Bradford, England, 6 July, 1925 — FB
Died: Chesterfield, Derbyshire, England, September, 2003

League Club	Source	Date Signed	Seasons Played	Apps	Subs	Gls
Sheffield Wed	Manningham Mills	10/48	49-52	31	-	0
Bristol C	Tr	06/54	54-55	8	-	0
Oldham Ath	Tr	07/56	56	2	-	0

JACKSON Peter
Born: Stoke-on-Trent, England, 23 January, 1937 — RH
Died: Leeds, England, 6 September, 1991

League Club	Source	Date Signed	Seasons Played	Apps	Subs	Gls
Wrexham (Am)	Jnr	07/54	54	7	-	1
Bradford C	Marine	03/55	54-60	199	-	15
Tranmere Rov	Tr	07/61	61-64	81	-	3

JACKSON Peter Allan
Born: Shelf, West Yorkshire, England, 6 April, 1961 — CD

League Club	Source	Date Signed	Seasons Played	Apps	Subs	Gls
Bradford C	App	04/79	78-86	267	11	24
Newcastle U	Tr	10/86	86-88	60	0	3
Bradford C	Tr	09/88	88-89	55	3	5
Huddersfield T	Tr	09/90	90-93	152	3	3
Chester C	Tr	09/94	94-96	100	0	3

JACKSON Philip John (Phil)
Born: Manchester, England, 8 September, 1958 — M

League Club	Source	Date Signed	Seasons Played	Apps	Subs	Gls
Stockport Co	Manchester C (App)	08/76	76-77	15	3	1

JACKSON Richard
Born: Whitby, North Yorkshire, England, 18 April, 1980 — RB

League Club	Source	Date Signed	Seasons Played	Apps	Subs	Gls
Scarborough	YT	03/98	97-98	21	1	0
Derby Co	Tr	03/99	99-06	98	20	0
Luton T	Tr	08/07	07	27	2	0
Hereford U	Tr	09/08	08	24	1	0
Burton A	Whitby T	12/09	09	4	1	0

JACKSON Richard George
Born: Rotherham, South Yorkshire, England, 13 December, 1932 — G

League Club	Source	Date Signed	Seasons Played	Apps	Subs	Gls
Rotherham U	Jnr	07/51				
York C	Tr	08/54				
Rotherham U		07/56	56	1	-	0

JACKSON Robert (Bob)
Born: Middleton, Greater Manchester, England, 5 June, 1934 — D

League Club	Source	Date Signed	Seasons Played	Apps	Subs	Gls
Oldham Ath	Jnr	08/51	51-54	29	-	1
Lincoln C	Tr	03/55	55-63	235	-	0

JACKSON Robert Gary (Robbie)
Born: Altrincham, Greater Manchester, England, 9 February, 1973 — F

League Club	Source	Date Signed	Seasons Played	Apps	Subs	Gls
Walsall	Manchester C (YT)	03/91	90-91	8	2	2

JACKSON Robert Gristwood (Bob)
Born: Cornsay, County Durham, England, 12 May, 1915 — CH
Died: Southend-on-Sea, England, October, 1991

League Club	Source	Date Signed	Seasons Played	Apps	Subs	Gls
Southend U	Stanley U	07/34	35-47	93	-	0

JACKSON Ronald (Ron)
Born: Crook, County Durham, England, 15 October, 1919 — LB
Died: Althorpe, Northamptonshire, England, 28 February, 1980

League Club	Source	Date Signed	Seasons Played	Apps	Subs	Gls
Wrexham		09/45	46-49	108	-	0
Leicester C	Tr	12/49	49-54	161	-	0

JACKSON Royston Leonard (Roy)
Born: Swindon, England, 22 October, 1931 — RH

League Club	Source	Date Signed	Seasons Played	Apps	Subs	Gls
Swindon T	Pinehurst YC	11/53	54	2	-	0

JACKSON Ryan Oliver
Born: Streatham, S London, England, 31 July, 1990 — RB/M
England: Semi Pro-2

League Club	Source	Date Signed	Seasons Played	Apps	Subs	Gls
AFC Wimbledon	Jnr	04/10	11	3	4	0
Newport Co	Macclesfield T	07/13	13-14	57	6	0

JACKSON Simeon Alexander
Born: Kingston, Jamaica, 28 March, 1987 — F
Canada: 44/Youth

League Club	Source	Date Signed	Seasons Played	Apps	Subs	Gls
Rushden & D	Sch	05/06	04-05	8	9	5
Gillingham	Tr	01/08	07-09	85	16	35
Norwich C	Tr	07/10	10-12	35	38	17
Millwall	Eint B'schweig (GER)	02/14	13	3	11	2
Coventry C	Tr	08/14	14	12	16	3

JACKSON Thomas (Tommy)
Born: Belfast, Northern Ireland, 3 November, 1946 — M
Northern Ireland: 35/U23-1

League Club	Source	Date Signed	Seasons Played	Apps	Subs	Gls
Everton	Glentoran	02/68	67-70	30	2	0
Nottingham F	Tr	10/70	70-74	73	8	6
Manchester U	Tr	07/75	75-76	18	1	0

JACKSON Thomas Anthony (Tony)
Born: Tarleton, Lancashire, England, 16 August, 1942 — RB

League Club	Source	Date Signed	Seasons Played	Apps	Subs	Gls
Southport	Lostock Hall	08/62	62-64	12	-	0

JACKSON William Patrick (Pat)
Born: Liverpool, England, 8 December, 1924 — IF/LH
Died: Crosby, Merseyside, England, 6 September, 1974

League Club	Source	Date Signed	Seasons Played	Apps	Subs	Gls
Swindon T	Tranmere Rov (Am)	10/47	48-49	4	-	1
Tranmere Rov	Tr	04/51	51-53	14	-	1

JACOB Liam
Born: Sydney, Australia, 18 August, 1994 — G

League Club	Source	Date Signed	Seasons Played	Apps	Subs	Gls
Oldham Ath	Manchester U (Sch)	07/12	12	0	1	0

JACOBS Devante Rogea
Born: Kingston, Jamaica, 17 April, 1996 — F

League Club	Source	Date Signed	Seasons Played	Apps	Subs	Gls
Oldham Ath	Blackburn Rov (Sch)	07/14	14	0	2	0

JACOBS Francis Arthur (Frank)
Born: Bristol, England, 22 April, 1940 — LH
Died: Kingswood, Avon, England, 8 November, 2009

League Club	Source	Date Signed	Seasons Played	Apps	Subs	Gls
Bristol C	Jnr	05/58	59-60	5	-	0

JACOBS Kyle Keith
Born: Manchester, England, 18 October, 1986 — RB

League Club	Source	Date Signed	Seasons Played	Apps	Subs	Gls
Mansfield T	Oldham Ath (Sch)	05/05	05	4	1	0

JACOBS Michael Edward
Born: Rothwell, Northamptonshire, England, 22 March, 1992 — LW

League Club	Source	Date Signed	Seasons Played	Apps	Subs	Gls
Northampton T	Sch	07/10	10-11	78	9	11
Derby Co	Tr	07/12	12-13	13	28	2
Wolverhampton W	Tr	11/13	13-14	31	11	8
Blackpool	L	03/15	14	5	0	1

JACOBS Stephen Douglas (Steve)
Born: West Ham, E London, England, 5 July, 1961 — FB/M

League Club	Source	Date Signed	Seasons Played	Apps	Subs	Gls
Coventry C	App	11/78	79-83	94	7	0
Brighton & HA	Tr	06/84	84-85	47	1	3
Charlton Ath	Tr	08/86				
Gillingham	Tr	12/86	86	6	1	0

JACOBS Trevor Frederick
Born: Bristol, England, 28 November, 1946 — RB
Died: Bristol, England, 18 January, 2014

League Club	Source	Date Signed	Seasons Played	Apps	Subs	Gls
Bristol C	Jnr	07/65	66-72	130	1	3
Plymouth Arg	L	09/72	72	4	0	0
Bristol Rov	Tr	05/73	73-75	82	0	3

JACOBS Wayne Graham
Born: Sheffield, England, 3 February, 1969 — LB

League Club	Source	Date Signed	Seasons Played	Apps	Subs	Gls
Sheffield Wed	App	01/87	87	5	1	0
Hull C	Tr	03/88	87-91	127	2	4
Rotherham U	Tr	08/93	93	40	2	2
Bradford C	Tr	08/94	94-04	302	16	12

JACOBSEN Anders
Born: Oslo, Norway, 18 April, 1968 CD

League Club	Source	Date Signed	Seasons Played	Apps	Subs	Gls
Sheffield U	IK Start (NOR)	12/98	98	8	4	0
Stoke C	Tr	08/99	99	29	4	2
Notts Co	Tr	09/00	00	27	2	2

JACOBSEN Lars Christian
Born: Odense, Germany, 20 September, 1979 RB
Denmark: 75/U21-26/Youth

League Club	Source	Date Signed	Seasons Played	Apps	Subs	Gls
Everton	FC Nuremburg (GER)	07/08	08	4	1	0
Blackburn Rov	Tr	06/09	09	11	2	0
West Ham U	Tr	08/10	10	22	2	0

JACOBSEN Viggo Lund
Born: Copenhagen, Denmark, 11 August, 1953 M

League Club	Source	Date Signed	Seasons Played	Apps	Subs	Gls
Charlton Ath	Kastrup (DEN)	11/79	79	9	0	0

JACOBSON Joseph Mark (Joe)
Born: Cardiff, Wales, 17 November, 1986 LB
Wales: U21-14

League Club	Source	Date Signed	Seasons Played	Apps	Subs	Gls
Cardiff C	Sch	07/06	05	0	1	0
Accrington Stan	L	11/06	06	6	0	1
Bristol Rov	Tr	02/07	06-08	49	24	1
Oldham Ath	Tr	07/09	09-10	14	2	0
Accrington Stan	Tr	11/10	10	26	0	2
Shrewsbury T	Tr	07/11	11-13	106	4	7
Wycombe W	Tr	07/14	14	42	0	3

JACQUES Anthony (Tony)
Born: Oddington, Oxfordshire, England, 10 October, 1942 LH

League Club	Source	Date Signed	Seasons Played	Apps	Subs	Gls
Oxford U	Jnr	08/60	62	7	-	0

JACQUES Joseph (Joe)
Born: Consett, County Durham, England, 12 September, 1944 CD
Died: Darlington, County Durham, England, 14 February, 1981

League Club	Source	Date Signed	Seasons Played	Apps	Subs	Gls
Preston NE	Jnr	09/61				
Lincoln C	Tr	05/64	64	22	-	0
Darlington	Tr	07/65	65-69	151	3	5
Southend U	Tr	10/69	69-72	85	2	0
Gillingham	Tr	11/72	72-74	73	0	1
Hartlepool U	Dartford	01/76	75	5	0	0

JAGGER George Newman
Born: Great Houghton, South Yorkshire, England, 30 September, 1941 LW

League Club	Source	Date Signed	Seasons Played	Apps	Subs	Gls
Barnsley	Houghton Main	06/60	60-62	45	-	2

JAGIELKA Philip Nikodem (Phil)
Born: Sale, Greater Manchester, England, 17 August, 1982 CD
England: 36/B-1/U21-6/Youth

League Club	Source	Date Signed	Seasons Played	Apps	Subs	Gls
Sheffield U	YT	05/00	99-06	231	23	18
Everton	Tr	07/07	07-14	230	12	10

JAGIELKA Stephen (Steve)
Born: Sale, Greater Manchester, England, 10 March, 1978 M

League Club	Source	Date Signed	Seasons Played	Apps	Subs	Gls
Stoke C	YT	07/96				
Shrewsbury T	Tr	07/97	97-02	89	76	17
Sheffield U	Tr	11/03				

JAGO Benjamin (Ben)
Born: Widnes, Cheshire, England, 4 September, 1996 M

League Club	Source	Date Signed	Seasons Played	Apps	Subs	Gls
Tranmere Rov	Sch	06/15	14	0	2	0

JAGO Gordon Harold
Born: Poplar, E London, England, 22 October, 1932 CH
England: Youth/Schools

League Club	Source	Date Signed	Seasons Played	Apps	Subs	Gls
Charlton Ath	Dulwich Hamlet	05/51	54-61	137	-	1

JAHRALDO-MARTIN Calaum
Born: Hemel Hempstead, Hertfordshire, England, 27 April, 1993 F
Antigua & Barbuda: 9

League Club	Source	Date Signed	Seasons Played	Apps	Subs	Gls
Hull C	Dulwich Hamlet	03/13				
Tranmere Rov	L	11/14	14	1	1	0

JAIDI Radhi Ben Abdelmajid
Born: Tunis, Tunisia, 30 August, 1975 CD
Tunisia: 101

League Club	Source	Date Signed	Seasons Played	Apps	Subs	Gls
Bolton W	Esperance Tunis (TUN)	07/04	04-05	35	8	8
Birmingham C	Tr	08/06	06-08	86	0	6
Southampton	Tr	09/09	09-10	57	1	4

JAIMEZ-RUIZ Mikhael Aimar
Born: Merida, Venezuela, 12 July, 1984 G
Venezuela: 1

League Club	Source	Date Signed	Seasons Played	Apps	Subs	Gls
Aldershot T	Northwood	06/07	08-09	43	1	0
AFC Wimbledon	Dover Ath	08/12	12	1	0	0

JAKEMAN Leslie (Mick)
Born: Nuneaton, Warwickshire, England, 14 March, 1930 WH

League Club	Source	Date Signed	Seasons Played	Apps	Subs	Gls
Derby Co	Atherstone T	06/47				
Leicester C	Hinckley Ath	05/51	54	1	-	0

JAKOBSSON Andreas
Born: Lund, Sweden, 6 October, 1972 CD
Sweden: 36

League Club	Source	Date Signed	Seasons Played	Apps	Subs	Gls
Southampton	Brondby (DEN)	08/04	04	24	3	2

JAKUB Yanek (Joe)
Born: Falkirk, Scotland, 7 December, 1956 M/FB

League Club	Source	Date Signed	Seasons Played	Apps	Subs	Gls
Burnley	App	12/73	75-79	42	0	0
Bury	Tr	10/80	80-86	262	3	27
Chester C	AZ67 Alkmaar (NED)	08/88	88	42	0	1
Burnley	Tr	07/89	89-92	161	2	8
Chester C	Tr	08/93	93	35	1	0
Wigan Ath	Colwyn Bay	09/94	94	16	0	0

JAKUBIAK Alex Louis
Born: Hounslow, SW London, England, 27 August, 1996 F
Scotland: Youth

League Club	Source	Date Signed	Seasons Played	Apps	Subs	Gls
Watford	Sch	02/14	13	1	0	0
Oxford U	L	08/14	14	2	7	1
Dagenham & Red	L	11/14	14	6	17	4

JAKUPOVIC Eldin
Born: Kozarac, Bosnia & Herzegovina, 2 October, 1984 G
Bosnia & Herzegovina: U21-2//Switzerland: 1/U21-1

League Club	Source	Date Signed	Seasons Played	Apps	Subs	Gls
Hull C	Aris Salonika (GRE)	07/12	12-14	8	1	0
Leyton Orient	L	01/14	13	13	0	0

JALAL Shwan Saman
Born: Baghdad, Iraq, 14 August, 1983 G
England: Semi Pro-5

League Club	Source	Date Signed	Seasons Played	Apps	Subs	Gls
Tottenham H	Hastings T	07/01				
Peterborough U	Woking	01/07	06-07	8	0	0
Morecambe	L	01/08	07	12	0	0
Bournemouth	Tr	08/08	08-12	147	1	0
Leyton Orient	L	02/14	13	2	0	0
Bury	Tr	06/14	14	5	0	0
Northampton T	Tr	02/15	14	4	0	0

JALES Richard Alexander (Dick)
Born: Chiswick, W London, England, 3 April, 1922 LB/LH
Died: Leicester, England, July, 2004

League Club	Source	Date Signed	Seasons Played	Apps	Subs	Gls
Bradford C	No 1 Bomber Group	06/45				
Aldershot	Tr	05/46	46-50	78	-	1

JALINK Nicolaas (Nico)
Born: Rotterdam, Netherlands, 22 June, 1964 M

League Club	Source	Date Signed	Seasons Played	Apps	Subs	Gls
Port Vale	RKC Waalwijk (NED)	07/91	91	20	8	1

JAMES Anthony (Tony)
Born: Cwmbran, Torfaen, Wales, 9 October, 1978 CD

League Club	Source	Date Signed	Seasons Played	Apps	Subs	Gls
West Bromwich A	YT	07/97				
Burton A	Weymouth	05/07	09-11	96	3	1
Hereford U	L	11/10	10	6	0	0
Newport Co	Tr	06/12	13	5	1	0

JAMES Anthony Craig (Tony)
Born: Sheffield, England, 27 June, 1967 CD

League Club	Source	Date Signed	Seasons Played	Apps	Subs	Gls
Lincoln C	Gainsborough Trinity	08/88	88-89	24	5	0
Leicester C	Tr	08/89	89-93	79	30	11
Hereford U	Tr	07/94	94-95	35	0	4
Plymouth Arg	Tr	08/96	96	34	0	1

JAMES Anthony Ralph (Tony)
Born: Swansea, Wales, 24 February, 1960 M

League Club	Source	Date Signed	Seasons Played	Apps	Subs	Gls
Swansea C	App	12/77	77-79	6	5	1

JAMES Christopher (Chris)
Born: Sheffield, England, 16 January, 1969 RB

League Club	Source	Date Signed	Seasons Played	Apps	Subs	Gls
Scarborough	Worksop T	08/91	91	12	1	0

JAMES Christopher Paul (Chris)
Born: Wellington, New Zealand, 4 July, 1987 M
England: Youth//New Zealand: 12

League Club	Source	Date Signed	Seasons Played	Apps	Subs	Gls
Fulham	Sch	07/05				
Barnet	Tampere U (FIN)	03/10	09	0	2	0

JAMES Clement Junior
Born: Bracknell, Berkshire, England, 10 March, 1981 W

League Club	Source	Date Signed	Seasons Played	Apps	Subs	Gls
Brentford	YT	06/99	99	0	1	0

JAMES Craig Peter
Born: Middlesbrough, England, 15 November, 1982 LB/M

League Club	Source	Date Signed	Seasons Played	Apps	Subs	Gls
Sunderland	YT	07/00	03	1	0	0
Darlington	L	11/03	03	10	0	1
Port Vale	Tr	03/04	03-05	61	12	1
Darlington	Tr	08/06	06	22	1	0

JAMES David (Dai)
Born: Swansea, Wales, 29 September, 1917 CF
Died: Swansea, Wales, 12 December, 1981

League Club	Source	Date Signed	Seasons Played	Apps	Subs	Gls
Leeds U	Midland Ath	10/34				
Bradford C	Tr	05/35	36	5	-	0
Chelsea	Mossley	04/38				
Swansea C	Tr	06/47	47	12	-	7

JAMES David
Born: Cambuslang, Glasgow, Scotland, 12 December, 1942 RW

League Club	Source	Date Signed	Seasons Played	Apps	Subs	Gls
Brighton & HA	Blantyre Victoria	05/62	62	5	-	0

JAMES David Benjamin
Born: Welwyn Garden City, Hertfordshire, England, 1 August, 1970 G
England: 53/B-1/U21-10/Youth

League Club	Source	Date Signed	Seasons Played	Apps	Subs	Gls
Watford	YT	07/88	90-91	89	0	0
Liverpool	Tr	07/92	92-98	213	1	0
Aston Villa	Tr	06/99	99-00	67	0	0
West Ham U	Tr	07/01	01-03	91	0	0
Manchester C	Tr	01/04	03-05	93	0	0
Portsmouth	Tr	08/06	06-09	134	0	0
Bristol C	Tr	08/10	10-11	81	0	0
Bournemouth	Tr	09/12	12	19	0	0

JAMES David John
Born: Southend-on-Sea, England, 11 March, 1948 LB/M

League Club	Source	Date Signed	Seasons Played	Apps	Subs	Gls
West Ham U	App	03/65				
Torquay U	Tr	05/67	67	8	0	0

JAMES Edward Glyn (Glyn)
Born: Llangollen, Denbighshire, Wales, 17 December, 1941 CH
Wales: 9/U23-2

League Club	Source	Date Signed	Seasons Played	Apps	Subs	Gls
Blackpool	Jnr	05/59	60-74	395	6	22

JAMES John Brian
Born: Stone, Staffordshire, England, 24 October, 1948 F/RH

League Club	Source	Date Signed	Seasons Played	Apps	Subs	Gls
Port Vale	Jnr	04/66	65-72	202	8	39
Chester C	Tr	02/73	72-75	97	1	40
Tranmere Rov	Tr	09/75	75-77	59	14	24

JAMES John Edward
Born: Birmingham, England, 19 February, 1934 LH/IF

League Club	Source	Date Signed	Seasons Played	Apps	Subs	Gls
Birmingham C	Paget Rgrs	03/51	52-53	5	-	2
Torquay U	Tr	06/55	55-60	125	-	11

JAMES John Stanley (Stan)
Born: South Shields, Tyne and Wear, England, 12 September, 1923 LB
Died: Merton, S London, England, April, 2003

League Club	Source	Date Signed	Seasons Played	Apps	Subs	Gls
Bradford Park Ave	South Shields	08/44	49-50	13	-	1

JAMES Joseph (Joe)
Born: Bootle, Merseyside, England, 9 September, 1954 CD

League Club	Source	Date Signed	Seasons Played	Apps	Subs	Gls
Liverpool	Jnr	01/74				
Southport	Tr	07/75	75	11	2	0

JAMES Julian Colin
Born: Tring, Hertfordshire, England, 22 March, 1970 RB
England: U21-2

League Club	Source	Date Signed	Seasons Played	Apps	Subs	Gls
Luton T	YT	07/88	87-97	262	20	13
Preston NE	L	09/91	91	6	0	0

JAMES Keith Andrew
Born: Hillingdon, W London, England, 18 August, 1961 RB
Died: December, 2014
England: Youth

League Club	Source	Date Signed	Seasons Played	Apps	Subs	Gls
Portsmouth	App	07/79	78-79	5	1	0

JAMES Kevin Ernest
Born: Southwark, S London, England, 3 January, 1980 M

League Club	Source	Date Signed	Seasons Played	Apps	Subs	Gls
Charlton Ath	YT	07/98				
Gillingham	Tr	08/00	00-03	18	31	4
Nottingham F	Tr	06/04	04	2	5	0
Boston U	L	12/04	04	6	0	0
Walsall	L	01/06	05	12	3	1
Yeovil T	L	08/06	06	2	4	0
Grimsby T	L	10/06	06	2	0	0
Swindon T	L	03/07	06	0	2	0

JAMES Kingsley Tyrone
Born: Rotherham, South Yorkshire, England, 17 February, 1992 M

League Club	Source	Date Signed	Seasons Played	Apps	Subs	Gls
Sheffield U	Sch	07/10				
Port Vale	Tr	07/11	11-12	3	8	0

JAMES Leighton
Born: Loughor, Swansea, Wales, 16 February, 1953 LW
Wales: 54/U23-7/Schools

League Club	Source	Date Signed	Seasons Played	Apps	Subs	Gls
Burnley	App	02/70	70-75	180	1	44
Derby Co	Tr	10/75	75-77	67	1	15
Queens Park Rgrs	Tr	10/77	77-78	27	1	4
Burnley	Tr	09/78	78-79	76	0	9
Swansea C	Tr	04/80	79-82	88	10	27
Sunderland	Tr	01/83	82-83	50	2	4
Bury	Tr	08/84	84	46	0	5
Newport Co	Tr	08/85	85	21	7	2
Burnley	Tr	08/86	86-88	75	4	13

JAMES Leslie
Born: United Kingdom W

League Club	Source	Date Signed	Seasons Played	Apps	Subs	Gls
Darlington (Am)		05/53	53	4	-	0

JAMES Lloyd Roger Stuart
Born: Bristol, England, 16 February, 1988 DM
Wales: U21-10/Youth

League Club	Source	Date Signed	Seasons Played	Apps	Subs	Gls
Southampton	Sch	07/05	08-09	68	3	2
Colchester U	Tr	07/10	10-11	34	17	1
Crawley T	L	03/12	11	6	0	0
Leyton Orient	Tr	07/12	12-14	74	9	4

JAMES Luke Myers
Born: Amble, Northumberland, England, 4 November, 1994 F

League Club	Source	Date Signed	Seasons Played	Apps	Subs	Gls
Hartlepool U	Sch	11/11	11-14	57	33	19
Peterborough U	Tr	09/14	14	21	11	1

JAMES Lutel Malik
Born: Manchester, England, 2 June, 1972 F
St Kitts & Nevis: 3

League Club	Source	Date Signed	Seasons Played	Apps	Subs	Gls
Scarborough	Yorkshire Amats	02/93	92	0	6	0
Bury	Hyde U	10/98	98-00	34	34	4

JAMES Martin Christopher
Born: Slough, Berkshire, England, 18 February, 1953 CD

League Club	Source	Date Signed	Seasons Played	Apps	Subs	Gls
Reading	Jnr	08/71	71	21	0	0

JAMES Martin Joseph
Born: Formby, Merseyside, England, 18 May, 1971 LB/M

League Club	Source	Date Signed	Seasons Played	Apps	Subs	Gls
Preston NE	YT	07/89	90-92	92	6	11
Stockport Co	Tr	03/93	92-93	13	19	0
Rotherham U	Tr	08/94	94-96	40	4	0

JAMES Matthew Lee
Born: Bacup, Lancashire, England, 22 July, 1991 M
England: Youth

League Club	Source	Date Signed	Seasons Played	Apps	Subs	Gls
Manchester U	Sch	07/09				
Preston NE	L	02/10	09	17	1	2
Preston NE	L	07/10	10	10	0	0
Leicester C	Tr	05/12	12-14	68	18	4

JAMES Oliver David (Olly)
Born: Birkenhead, Wirral, England, 30 January, 1987 RB

League Club	Source	Date Signed	Seasons Played	Apps	Subs	Gls
Tranmere Rov	Sch	07/04	05	0	1	0

JAMES Paul John
Born: Cardiff, Wales, 11 November, 1963 M
Canada: 47

League Club	Source	Date Signed	Seasons Played	Apps	Subs	Gls
Doncaster Rov	Hamilton Steel's (CAN)	11/87	87	7	1	0

JAMES Percy George Burge
Born: Ystrad Rhondda, Rhondda Cynon Taff, Wales, 9 March, 1917 LW
Died: Oxford, England, 1 June, 1993
Wales: Amateur

League Club	Source	Date Signed	Seasons Played	Apps	Subs	Gls
Luton T	Oxford C	08/49	49	2	-	1

JAMES Reece
Born: Bacup, Lancashire, England, 7 November, 1993 LB/M

League Club	Source	Date Signed	Seasons Played	Apps	Subs	Gls
Manchester U	Sch	07/12				
Carlisle U	L	07/13	13	1	0	0
Rotherham U	L	11/14	14	7	0	0
Huddersfield T	L	03/15	14	6	0	1

JAMES Robert Mark (Robbie)
Born: Gorseinon, Swansea, Wales, 23 March, 1957 M/F
Died: Llanelli, Carmarthenshire, Wales, 18 February, 1998
Wales: 47/U21-3

League Club	Source	Date Signed	Seasons Played	Apps	Subs	Gls
Swansea C	App	04/74	72-82	385	8	102
Stoke C	Tr	07/83	83-84	48	0	6
Queens Park Rgrs	Tr	10/84	84-86	78	9	5
Leicester C	Tr	06/87	87	21	2	0
Swansea C	Tr	01/88	87-89	82	8	16
Bradford C	Tr	08/90	90-91	89	0	6
Cardiff C	Tr	08/92	92-93	51	0	2

JAMES Ronald (Ron)
Born: Birmingham, England, 16 March, 1922 WH

League Club	Source	Date Signed	Seasons Played	Apps	Subs	Gls
Wolverhampton W		08/39				
Birmingham C	Tr	10/47				
Northampton T	Tr	07/48	48	4	-	1

JAMES Royston William (Roy)
Born: Bristol, England, 19 February, 1941 CF
Died: Bristol, England, 7 April, 1990

League Club	Source	Date Signed	Seasons Played	Apps	Subs	Gls
Bristol Rov	Old Georgians	07/60	60	1	-	0

League Club	Source	Date Signed	Seasons Played	Career Record Apps	Subs	Gls

JAMES Steven Robert (Steve)
Born: Coseley, West Midlands, England, 29 November, 1949 CD
England: Youth

League Club	Source	Date Signed	Seasons Played	Apps	Subs	Gls
Manchester U	App	12/66	68-74	129	0	4
York C	Tr	01/76	75-79	105	0	1

JAMES Thomas Albert George (Tony)
Born: Mountain Ash, Rhondda Cynon Taff, Wales, 16 September, 1919 IF
Died: Thornbury, Avon, England, 25 April, 1981

League Club	Source	Date Signed	Seasons Played	Apps	Subs	Gls
Brighton & HA	Folkestone	06/39	46-48	69	-	20
Bristol Rov	Tr	06/49	49-50	21	-	5

JAMES Thomas Lynn (Tom)
Born: Cardiff, Wales, 15 April, 1996 D
Wales: Youth

League Club	Source	Date Signed	Seasons Played	Apps	Subs	Gls
Cardiff C	Sch	-	13	0	1	0

JAMES Tyrone Selwyn
Born: Paddington, Central London, England, 19 September, 1956 D

League Club	Source	Date Signed	Seasons Played	Apps	Subs	Gls
Fulham	Jnr	09/74	75-77	18	2	0
Plymouth Arg	Tr	03/78	77-81	77	4	0
Torquay U	L	03/83	82	13	0	1

JAMES Walter George (George)
Born: Swansea, Wales, 15 June, 1924 FB/IF
Died: Swansea, Wales, November, 1998
Wales: Schools

League Club	Source	Date Signed	Seasons Played	Apps	Subs	Gls
Swansea C	Tawe U	08/42	49	4	-	0
Newport Co	Tr	07/50	50-51	13	-	5

JAMES William John (Billy)
Born: Cardiff, Wales, 18 October, 1921 CF
Died: Cardiff, Wales, 27 July, 1980
Wales: War-2

League Club	Source	Date Signed	Seasons Played	Apps	Subs	Gls
Cardiff C	Cardiff Corinthians	08/39	46	6	-	3

JAMES-LEWIS Merrick Anthony
Born: Lambeth, S London, England, 21 May, 1992 M

League Club	Source	Date Signed	Seasons Played	Apps	Subs	Gls
Southend U	Sch	08/10	11	0	1	0
Colchester U	Tr	07/12				

JAMESON Arron Thomas
Born: Sheffield, England, 7 November, 1989 G

League Club	Source	Date Signed	Seasons Played	Apps	Subs	Gls
Sheffield Wed	Sch	07/08	10	2	0	0

JAMESON John Charles
Born: Belfast, Northern Ireland, 11 March, 1958 W

League Club	Source	Date Signed	Seasons Played	Apps	Subs	Gls
Huddersfield T	Bangor	03/77	77	1	0	0

JAMESON Nathan
Born: Middlesbrough, England, 20 March, 1985 W

League Club	Source	Date Signed	Seasons Played	Apps	Subs	Gls
Walsall	Sch	07/04				
Darlington	Durham C	08/05	05	1	4	0

JAMIESON Ian
Born: Edinburgh, Scotland, 22 October, 1934 IF

League Club	Source	Date Signed	Seasons Played	Apps	Subs	Gls
Crewe Alex	Third Lanark	08/56	56	4	-	2
Birmingham C	Tr	07/57				

JAMIESON John Wallace (Iain)
Born: Dumbarton, Dunbartonshire, Scotland, 14 October, 1928 WH
Died: Kirkcudbright, Dumfries & Galloway, Scotland, 19 October, 2012

League Club	Source	Date Signed	Seasons Played	Apps	Subs	Gls
Coventry C	Aberdeen	01/49	48-57	181	-	6

JANKO Saidy
Born: Zurich, Switzerland, 22 October, 1995 RB/M
Switzerland: U21-1/Youth

League Club	Source	Date Signed	Seasons Played	Apps	Subs	Gls
Manchester U	FC Zurich (SUI)	09/13				
Bolton W	L	02/15	14	6	4	1

JANKOVIC Bozo
Born: Sarajevo, Yugoslavia, 22 May, 1951 F
Died: Kotor, Montenegro, October, 1993
Yugoslavia: 2

League Club	Source	Date Signed	Seasons Played	Apps	Subs	Gls
Middlesbrough	Zeljeznicar (YUG)	02/79	78-80	42	8	16

JANMAAT Daryl
Born: Leidschendam, Netherlands, 22 July, 1989 RB
Netherlands: 25/U21-11/Youth

League Club	Source	Date Signed	Seasons Played	Apps	Subs	Gls
Newcastle U	Feyenoord (NED)	07/14	14	37	0	1

JANNEY Mark
Born: Romford, E London, England, 2 December, 1977 M

League Club	Source	Date Signed	Seasons Played	Apps	Subs	Gls
Tottenham H	YT	07/96				
Brentford	L	03/97	96	1	1	1

JANSEN Matthew Brooke (Matt)
Born: Carlisle, Cumbria, England, 20 October, 1977 F
England: U21-6/Youth

League Club	Source	Date Signed	Seasons Played	Apps	Subs	Gls
Carlisle U	YT	01/96	96-97	26	16	10
Crystal Palace	Tr	02/98	97-98	23	3	10
Blackburn Rov	Tr	01/99	98-05	104	49	44
Coventry C	L	02/03	02	8	1	2
Bolton W	Tr	01/06	05	3	3	0

JANSSON Jan
Born: Oland, Sweden, 26 January, 1968 M
Sweden: 7

League Club	Source	Date Signed	Seasons Played	Apps	Subs	Gls
Port Vale	IFK Norrkoping (SWE)	11/96	96-98	37	14	6

JANSSON Oscar
Born: Orebro, Sweden, 23 December, 1990 G
Sweden: U21-2/Youth

League Club	Source	Date Signed	Seasons Played	Apps	Subs	Gls
Tottenham H	Sch	01/08				
Exeter C	L	09/09	09	7	0	0
Northampton T	L	08/10	10	4	0	0
Bradford C	L	08/11	11	1	0	0

JANTUNEN Pertti Kalevi
Born: Lahti, Finland, 25 June, 1952 M
Finland: 26

League Club	Source	Date Signed	Seasons Played	Apps	Subs	Gls
Bristol C	Eskilstuna (SWE)	03/79	78-79	7	1	1

JANUZAJ Adnan
Born: Brussels, Belgium, 5 February, 1995 W
Belgium: 5

League Club	Source	Date Signed	Seasons Played	Apps	Subs	Gls
Manchester U	Sch	02/12	13-14	22	23	4

JARA Gonzalo Alejandro
Born: Concepcion, Chile, 29 August, 1985 DM
Chile: 78

League Club	Source	Date Signed	Seasons Played	Apps	Subs	Gls
West Bromwich A	Colo Colo (CHL)	08/09	09-12	45	11	2
Brighton & HA	L	10/11	11	4	0	0
Brighton & HA	L	01/12	11	10	0	0
Nottingham F	Tr	01/13	12-13	43	6	0

[JARDEL] RIBEIRO DE ALMEIDA Mario Jardel
Born: Fortaleza, Brazil, 18 September, 1973 F
Brazil: 10

League Club	Source	Date Signed	Seasons Played	Apps	Subs	Gls
Bolton W	Sporting Lisbon (POR)	08/03	03	0	7	0

JARDINE Alexander (Alex)
Born: Cleland, Lanarkshire, Scotland, 12 April, 1926 RB
Died: SE London, England, 6 June, 1978

League Club	Source	Date Signed	Seasons Played	Apps	Subs	Gls
Millwall	Dundee U	08/50	50-57	299	-	25

JARDINE Frederick (Fred)
Born: Edinburgh, Scotland, 27 September, 1941 LB

League Club	Source	Date Signed	Seasons Played	Apps	Subs	Gls
Luton T	Dundee	05/61	61-69	218	2	9
Torquay U	Tr	02/71	70-71	11	0	0

JARMAN Harold James
Born: Bristol, England, 4 May, 1939 W

League Club	Source	Date Signed	Seasons Played	Apps	Subs	Gls
Bristol Rov	Victoria Ath	08/59	59-72	440	12	127
Newport Co	Tr	05/73	73	34	6	8

JARMAN John Emlyn
Born: Rhymney, Caerphilly, Wales, 4 February, 1931 WH
Died: Mansfield, Nottinghamshire, England, 21 October, 2009

League Club	Source	Date Signed	Seasons Played	Apps	Subs	Gls
Wolverhampton W	Lowhill YC	07/49				
Barnsley	Wellington T	10/50	51-55	45	-	1
Walsall	Tr	06/56	56-57	37	-	2

JARMAN Lee
Born: Cardiff, Wales, 16 December, 1977 D
Wales: U21-9/Youth

League Club	Source	Date Signed	Seasons Played	Apps	Subs	Gls
Cardiff C	YT	08/95	95-99	78	16	1
Exeter C	Merthyr Tydfil	03/00	99	7	0	0
Oxford U	Tr	07/00	00	15	6	1

JARMAN Nathan George
Born: Scunthorpe, North Lincolnshire, England, 19 September, 1986 F

League Club	Source	Date Signed	Seasons Played	Apps	Subs	Gls
Barnsley	Sch	05/05	04-05	1	14	0
Bury	L	01/06	05	1	1	0
Grimsby T	Tr	09/07	07-09	32	15	6

JARMAN William Brynmor (Bill)
Born: Pontypridd, Rhondda Cynon Taff, Wales, 18 July, 1920 IF
Died: Merthyr Tydfil, Wales, February, 1984

League Club	Source	Date Signed	Seasons Played	Apps	Subs	Gls
Bury	Llanbradach	10/46	46	10	-	1

JAROSIK Jiri
Born: Usti nad Labem, Czech Republic, 27 October, 1977 M
Czech Republic: 23

League Club	Source	Date Signed	Seasons Played	Apps	Subs	Gls
Chelsea	CSKA Moscow (RUS)	01/05	04	3	11	0
Birmingham C	L	08/05	05	19	5	5

JARRETT Albert Ojumiri
Born: Freetown, Sierra Leone, 23 October, 1984 LW
Sierra Leone: 2

League Club	Source	Date Signed	Seasons Played	Apps	Subs	Gls
Wimbledon	Dulwich Hamlet	04/03	03	3	6	0
Brighton & HA	Tr	08/04	04-05	12	11	1
Swindon T	L	01/06	05	2	4	0
Watford	Tr	08/06	06	0	1	0
Boston U	L	02/07	06	5	0	2
MK Dons	L	03/07	06	2	3	0
Gillingham	Tr	09/08	08	11	5	0
Barnet	Tr	08/09	09	33	12	2
Lincoln C	Tr	07/10	10	19	3	1
Aldershot T	L	02/11	10	2	2	0

JARRETT Jason Lee Mee
Born: Bury, Greater Manchester, England, 14 September, 1979 — M

League Club	Source	Date Signed	Seasons Played	Apps	Subs	Gls
Blackpool	YT	07/98	98	2	0	0
Wrexham	Tr	10/99	99	1	0	0
Bury	Tr	07/00	00-01	45	17	4
Wigan Ath	Tr	03/02	01-04	67	28	1
Stoke C	L	01/05	04	2	0	0
Norwich C	Tr	07/05	05	6	5	0
Plymouth Arg	L	11/05	05	7	0	0
Preston NE	Tr	03/06	05-08	12	6	1
Hull C	L	11/06	06	3	0	0
Leicester C	L	02/07	06	13	0	0
Queens Park Rgrs	L	09/07	07	1	1	0
Oldham Ath	L	01/08	07	12	3	3
Brighton & HA	Tr	01/09	08	11	2	0
Port Vale	Tr	09/09	09	7	2	0
Oldham Ath		07/10	10	7	1	0

JARRIE Frederick (Fred)
Born: Hartlepool, Cleveland, England, 2 August, 1922 — G
Died: Hartlepool, Cleveland, England, 1 February, 2004

League Club	Source	Date Signed	Seasons Played	Apps	Subs	Gls
Hartlepool U (Am)	Deaf Hill	08/47	47	1	-	0

JARVIE Paul
Born: Aberdeen, Scotland, 14 June, 1982 — G

League Club	Source	Date Signed	Seasons Played	Apps	Subs	Gls
Torquay U	Dundee U	02/05	04	1	0	0

JARVIS Alan Leslie
Born: Wrexham, Wales, 4 August, 1943 — M
Wales: 3

League Club	Source	Date Signed	Seasons Played	Apps	Subs	Gls
Everton	Jnr	07/61				
Hull C	Tr	06/64	65-70	148	11	12
Mansfield T	Tr	03/71	70-72	76	6	0

JARVIS Antony (Tony)
Born: Radcliffe, Greater Manchester, England, 19 March, 1964 — F

League Club	Source	Date Signed	Seasons Played	Apps	Subs	Gls
Oldham Ath	Irlam T	03/86				
Crewe Alex	Tr	10/86	86	6	3	1

JARVIS Harry
Born: Maltby, South Yorkshire, England, 8 October, 1928 — LH

League Club	Source	Date Signed	Seasons Played	Apps	Subs	Gls
Notts Co	Worksop T	05/51	52-54	29	-	0

JARVIS John Brian (Brian)
Born: Bangor-on-Dee, Wrexham, Wales, 26 August, 1933 — WH
Died: Shrewsbury, Shropshire, England, January, 2004

League Club	Source	Date Signed	Seasons Played	Apps	Subs	Gls
Wrexham		07/52	53-58	64	-	3
Oldham Ath	Tr	07/59	59-62	88	-	2

JARVIS Joseph
Born: Farnworth, Greater Manchester, England, 27 June, 1929 — RB
Died: Bolton, Greater Manchester, England, May, 2009

League Club	Source	Date Signed	Seasons Played	Apps	Subs	Gls
Stockport Co		09/53	54-56	43	-	0

JARVIS Matthew Thomas (Matt)
Born: Middlesbrough, England, 22 May, 1986 — LW
England: 1

League Club	Source	Date Signed	Seasons Played	Apps	Subs	Gls
Gillingham	Sch	05/04	03-06	78	32	12
Wolverhampton W	Tr	07/07	07-12	135	29	19
West Ham U	Tr	08/12	12-14	56	19	4

JARVIS Mervin John
Born: Bristol, England, 20 October, 1924 — LW
Died: Bristol, England, April, 1994

League Club	Source	Date Signed	Seasons Played	Apps	Subs	Gls
Bristol C	Douglas	05/48	48	4	-	0

JARVIS Nathaniel Stephen (Nat)
Born: Cardiff, Wales, 20 October, 1991 — F

League Club	Source	Date Signed	Seasons Played	Apps	Subs	Gls
Cardiff C	Sch	08/10				
Southend U	L	09/10	10	0	6	0

JARVIS Nicholas Charles (Nick)
Born: Mansfield, Nottinghamshire, England, 19 September, 1955 — LB

League Club	Source	Date Signed	Seasons Played	Apps	Subs	Gls
Scunthorpe U	Grantham	07/80	80	21	0	0

JARVIS Nigel Brian
Born: Totnes, Devon, England, 6 November, 1963 — RB

League Club	Source	Date Signed	Seasons Played	Apps	Subs	Gls
Plymouth Arg	App	11/81				
Torquay U	Yeovil T	02/85	84	8	3	0

JARVIS Ross Anthony (Rossi)
Born: Fakenham, Norfolk, England, 11 March, 1988 — M
England: Semi Pro-3/Youth

League Club	Source	Date Signed	Seasons Played	Apps	Subs	Gls
Norwich C	Sch	01/06	05-07	4	3	0
Torquay U	L	01/07	06	2	2	0
Rotherham U	L	03/07	06	10	0	0
Luton T	Tr	08/08	08	31	4	1
Barnet	Tr	07/10	10	12	10	0

JARVIS Ryan Robert
Born: Fakenham, Norfolk, England, 11 July, 1986 — F
England: Youth

League Club	Source	Date Signed	Seasons Played	Apps	Subs	Gls
Norwich C	Sch	08/03	02-07	5	24	3
Colchester U	L	03/05	04	2	4	0
Leyton Orient	L	02/07	06	14	0	6
Notts Co	L	01/08	07	17	0	2
Leyton Orient	Tr	07/08	08-10	52	32	10
Northampton T	L	11/10	10	3	0	0
Walsall	Tr	07/11	11	9	10	2
Torquay U	Tr	03/12	11-12	29	23	9
York C	Tr	07/13	13-14	26	17	8

JASPER Brian
Born: Plymouth, England, 25 November, 1933 — RB

League Club	Source	Date Signed	Seasons Played	Apps	Subs	Gls
Plymouth Arg	Astor Inst	07/54	56	2	-	0

JASPER Dale William
Born: Croydon, S London, England, 14 January, 1964 — M

League Club	Source	Date Signed	Seasons Played	Apps	Subs	Gls
Chelsea	App	01/82	83-84	10	0	0
Brighton & HA	Tr	05/86	86-87	44	5	6
Crewe Alex	Tr	07/88	88-91	103	8	2

JASZCZUN Antony John (Tommy)
Born: Kettering, Northamptonshire, England, 16 September, 1977 — LB

League Club	Source	Date Signed	Seasons Played	Apps	Subs	Gls
Aston Villa	YT	07/96				
Blackpool	Tr	01/00	99-03	107	15	0
Northampton T	Tr	07/04	04	24	8	0
Rochdale	Tr	08/05	05	12	5	0

JAVARY Jean-Phillipe
Born: Montpellier, France, 10 January, 1978 — M
France: Youth

League Club	Source	Date Signed	Seasons Played	Apps	Subs	Gls
Brentford	Raith Rov	08/00	00	4	2	0
Plymouth Arg	Tr	02/01	00	4	0	0
Sheffield U	Raith Rov	03/02	01-02	8	5	1

JAY Matthew William (Matt)
Born: Ashburton, Devon, England, 27 February, 1996 — F

League Club	Source	Date Signed	Seasons Played	Apps	Subs	Gls
Exeter C	Sch	12/13	13-14	2	3	0

JAYES Alfred Gordon (Gordon)
Born: Leicester, England, 26 November, 1923 — CF
Died: Leicester, England, 26 March, 1997
England: Schools

League Club	Source	Date Signed	Seasons Played	Apps	Subs	Gls
Notts Co	Leicester C (Am)	11/46	46-47	27	-	7

JAYES Brian
Born: Leicester, England, 13 December, 1932 — RH
Died: Leicester, England, 12 January, 1978

League Club	Source	Date Signed	Seasons Played	Apps	Subs	Gls
Leicester C	Jnr	07/54	55	3	-	0
Mansfield T	Tr	07/56	56-59	115	-	1

JAYES Carl Geoffrey
Born: Leicester, England, 15 March, 1954 — G
England: Schools

League Club	Source	Date Signed	Seasons Played	Apps	Subs	Gls
Leicester C	Jnr	06/71	74	5	0	0
Northampton T	Tr	11/77	77-79	68	0	0

JEAN Earl Jude
Born: Castries, Saint Lucia, 9 October, 1971 — F
Saint Lucia: 11

League Club	Source	Date Signed	Seasons Played	Apps	Subs	Gls
Ipswich T	Felguieras (POR)	12/96	96	0	1	0
Rotherham U	Tr	01/97	96	7	11	6
Plymouth Arg	Tr	08/97	97-98	37	28	7

JEANNE Leon Charles
Born: Cardiff, Wales, 17 November, 1980 — W
Wales: U21-8/Youth

League Club	Source	Date Signed	Seasons Played	Apps	Subs	Gls
Queens Park Rgrs	YT	11/97	98-99	8	4	0
Cardiff C	Tr	07/01	01	0	2	0

JEANNIN Alexandre Roger Magin (Alex)
Born: Troyes, France, 30 December, 1977 — LB

League Club	Source	Date Signed	Seasons Played	Apps	Subs	Gls
Darlington	Troyes AC (FRA)	03/01	00-01	22	0	0
Bristol Rov (L)	Exeter C	05/05	04	1	0	0
Hereford U	Tr	06/05	06	11	1	1

JEAVONS Patrick William Peter (Pat)
Born: Deptford, SE London, England, 5 July, 1946 — G

League Club	Source	Date Signed	Seasons Played	Apps	Subs	Gls
Lincoln C	Gravesend & Northfleet	02/66	65	1	0	0

JEBB Jack McCauley
Born: Kensington, Central London, England, 11 September, 1995 — M
England: Youth

League Club	Source	Date Signed	Seasons Played	Apps	Subs	Gls
Arsenal	Sch	09/12				
Stevenage	L	10/14	14	2	2	0
Stevenage	L	03/15	14	2	3	0

JEDINAK Michael John (Mile)
Born: Sydney, Australia, 3 August, 1984 — M
Australia: 59/Youth

League Club	Source	Date Signed	Seasons Played	Apps	Subs	Gls
Crystal Palace	Genclerbirligi (TKY)	08/11	11-14	132	2	10

JEFFELS Simon
Born: Darton, South Yorkshire, England, 18 January, 1966 — CD
England: Youth

League Club	Source	Date Signed	Seasons Played	Apps	Subs	Gls
Barnsley	App	01/84	83-87	39	3	0
Preston NE	L	10/87	87	1	0	0
Carlisle U	Tr	07/88	88-91	75	1	5

JEFFERIES Alfred James (Alf)
Born: Oxford, England, 9 February, 1922 — G
Died: Oxford, England, 9 February, 1998

League Club	Source	Date Signed	Seasons Played	Apps	Subs	Gls
Brentford	Oxford C	09/47	49-53	116	-	0
Torquay U	Tr	06/54	54	45	-	0

JEFFERS Francis
Born: Liverpool, England, 25 January, 1981 — F
England: 1/U21-16/Youth/Schools

League Club	Source	Date Signed	Seasons Played	Apps	Subs	Gls
Everton	YT	02/98	97-00	37	12	18
Arsenal	Tr	06/01	01-02	4	18	4
Everton	L	09/03	03	5	13	0
Charlton Ath	Tr	08/04	04	9	11	3
Blackburn Rov	Tr	07/06	06	3	7	0
Ipswich T	L	03/07	06	7	2	4
Sheffield Wed	Tr	08/07	07-09	28	26	5
Accrington Stan	Newcastle Jets (AUS)	03/13	12	4	3	2

JEFFERS John Joseph
Born: Liverpool, England, 5 October, 1968 — LW
England: Schools

League Club	Source	Date Signed	Seasons Played	Apps	Subs	Gls
Liverpool	App	10/86				
Port Vale	Tr	12/88	88-94	147	33	10
Shrewsbury T	L	01/95	94	3	0	1
Stockport Co	Tr	11/95	95-96	46	11	6

JEFFERS Shaun Elliot
Born: Bedford, England, 14 April, 1992 — F
England: Youth

League Club	Source	Date Signed	Seasons Played	Apps	Subs	Gls
Coventry C	Sch	06/10	09-11	0	7	0
Cheltenham T	L	08/10	10	3	19	1
Peterborough U	Tranmere Rov (NC)	10/13	13	3	5	1
Newport Co	Tr	01/14	13-14	15	20	2

JEFFERSON Arthur
Born: Goldthorpe, South Yorkshire, England, 14 December, 1916 — LB
Died: Hounslow, SW London, England, July, 1997

League Club	Source	Date Signed	Seasons Played	Apps	Subs	Gls
Queens Park Rgrs	Peterborough U	02/36	36-49	211	-	1
Aldershot	Tr	03/50	49-54	170	-	0

JEFFERSON Derek
Born: Morpeth, Northumberland, England, 5 September, 1948 — CD

League Club	Source	Date Signed	Seasons Played	Apps	Subs	Gls
Ipswich T	App	02/66	67-72	163	3	1
Wolverhampton W	Tr	10/72	72-75	41	1	0
Sheffield Wed	L	10/76	76	5	0	0
Hereford U	Tr	11/76	76-77	39	0	0

JEFFERSON Stanley (Stan)
Born: Goldthorpe, South Yorkshire, England, 26 June, 1931 — RB
Died: Aldershot, Hampshire, England, 10 February, 1973

League Club	Source	Date Signed	Seasons Played	Apps	Subs	Gls
Aldershot	Dearne Ath	08/52	52-57	80	-	0
Southend U	Tr	07/58				

JEFFERY Jack Charles
Born: Gravesend, Kent, England, 13 August, 1989 — F

League Club	Source	Date Signed	Seasons Played	Apps	Subs	Gls
West Ham U	Sch	07/07				
Leyton Orient	L	09/08	08	0	1	0

JEFFREY Alick James
Born: Rawmarsh, South Yorkshire, England, 29 January, 1939 — F
Died: Benidorm, Spain, November, 2000
England: U23-2/Amateur-3/Youth/Schools

League Club	Source	Date Signed	Seasons Played	Apps	Subs	Gls
Doncaster Rov	Jnr	02/56	54-56	71	-	34
Doncaster Rov	Skegness T	12/63	63-68	190	1	93
Lincoln C	Tr	01/69	68-69	19	3	3

JEFFREY Andrew Samuel (Andy)
Born: Bellshill, Lanarkshire, Scotland, 15 January, 1972 — RB

League Club	Source	Date Signed	Seasons Played	Apps	Subs	Gls
Leicester C	YT	02/90				
Cambridge U	Cambridge C	07/93	93-95	82	13	2

JEFFREY Anthony Lamar Malcolm
Born: Hendon, N London, England, 3 October, 1994 — RW

League Club	Source	Date Signed	Seasons Played	Apps	Subs	Gls
Arsenal	Sch	02/13				
Stevenage	L	03/13	12	0	1	0
Wycombe W	Tr	01/14	13	1	10	0

JEFFREY Michael Richard (Mike)
Born: Liverpool, England, 11 August, 1971 — F

League Club	Source	Date Signed	Seasons Played	Apps	Subs	Gls
Bolton W	YT	02/89	88-91	9	6	0
Doncaster Rov	Tr	03/92	91-93	48	1	19
Newcastle U	Tr	10/93	93	2	0	0
Rotherham U	Tr	06/95	95	22	0	5
Grimsby T	Kilmarnock	08/00	00-01	19	28	2
Scunthorpe U	L	03/02	01	4	2	1

JEFFREY Robert (Bob)
Born: Aberdeen, Scotland, 24 May, 1920 — WH
Died: Johnshaven, Aberdeenshire, Scotland, 8 August, 1992

League Club	Source	Date Signed	Seasons Played	Apps	Subs	Gls
Derby Co	Aberdeen	12/43				
Exeter C	Montrose	10/47	47	7	-	0

JEFFREY William Greenwood (Billy)
Born: Clydebank, Dunbartonshire, Scotland, 25 October, 1956 — M

League Club	Source	Date Signed	Seasons Played	Apps	Subs	Gls
Oxford U	App	10/73	73-81	311	3	24
Blackpool	Tr	06/82	82	12	2	1
Northampton T	Tr	03/83	82-83	53	1	6

JEFFRIES Derek
Born: Manchester, England, 22 March, 1951 — CD

League Club	Source	Date Signed	Seasons Played	Apps	Subs	Gls
Manchester C	App	08/68	69-72	64	9	0
Crystal Palace	Tr	09/73	73-75	107	0	1
Peterborough U	L	10/76	76	7	0	0
Millwall	L	03/77	76	10	1	0
Chester C	Tr	07/77	77-80	116	5	2

JEFFRIES Ronald James (Ron)
Born: Birmingham, England, 24 March, 1930 — CF

League Club	Source	Date Signed	Seasons Played	Apps	Subs	Gls
Aston Villa	Moor Green	12/50	50	2	-	0
Walsall	Tr	11/53	53	3	-	0

JEFFRIES William Arthur (Billy)
Born: Acton, W London, England, 11 March, 1921 — IF
Died: Hull, England, 1981

League Club	Source	Date Signed	Seasons Played	Apps	Subs	Gls
Mansfield T	Army	03/46	46	2	-	0
Hull C	Tr	01/47				

JELAVIC Nikica
Born: Capljina, Croatia, 27 August, 1985 — F
Croatia: 36/Youth

League Club	Source	Date Signed	Seasons Played	Apps	Subs	Gls
Everton	Glasgow Rangers	01/12	11-13	41	18	16
Hull C	Tr	01/14	13-14	37	5	12

JELLEYMAN Gareth Anthony
Born: Holywell, Flintshire, Wales, 14 November, 1980 — LB
Wales: U21-1/Youth

League Club	Source	Date Signed	Seasons Played	Apps	Subs	Gls
Peterborough U	YT	08/98	99-04	80	21	0
Boston U	L	08/04	04	3	0	0
Mansfield T	Tr	01/05	04-07	123	4	1

JELLY Horace Edward (Ted)
Born: Leicester, England, 28 August, 1921 — RB
Died: Leicester, England, 16 January, 2000

League Club	Source	Date Signed	Seasons Played	Apps	Subs	Gls
Leicester C	Belgrave U	05/46	46-50	56	-	1
Plymouth Arg	Tr	08/51	52-53	11	-	0

JEMSON Nigel Bradley
Born: Preston, Lancashire, England, 10 August, 1969 — F
England: U21-1

League Club	Source	Date Signed	Seasons Played	Apps	Subs	Gls
Preston NE	YT	07/87	85-87	28	4	8
Nottingham F	Tr	03/88	89-91	45	2	13
Bolton W	L	12/88	88	4	1	0
Preston NE	L	03/89	88	6	3	2
Sheffield Wed	Tr	09/91	91-93	26	25	9
Grimsby T	L	09/93	93	6	0	2
Notts Co	Tr	09/94	94-95	7	7	1
Watford	L	01/95	94	3	1	0
Rotherham U	L	02/96	95	16	0	5
Oxford U	Tr	07/96	96-97	68	0	27
Bury	Tr	02/98	97-98	17	12	1
Oxford U	Ayr U	01/00	99	13	5	0
Shrewsbury T	Tr	07/00	00-02	107	2	36

JENAS Jermaine Anthony
Born: Nottingham, England, 18 February, 1983 — M
England: 21/U21-9/Youth

League Club	Source	Date Signed	Seasons Played	Apps	Subs	Gls
Nottingham F	YT	02/00	00-01	29	0	4
Newcastle U	Tr	02/02	01-05	86	24	9
Tottenham H	Tr	08/05	05-12	133	22	21
Aston Villa	L	08/11	11	1	2	0

League Club	Source	Date Signed	Seasons Played	Apps	Subs	Gls
Nottingham F	L	09/12	12	1	5	1
Queens Park Rgrs	Tr	01/13	12-13	23	15	4

JENKIN Kenneth (Ken)
Born: Grimsby, North Lincolnshire, England, 27 November, 1931 — RW

League Club	Source	Date Signed	Seasons Played	Apps	Subs	Gls
Grimsby T	Jnr	07/50	50-53	23	-	6

JENKINS Brian
Born: Treherbert, Rhondda Cynon Taff, Wales, 1 August, 1935 — LW

League Club	Source	Date Signed	Seasons Played	Apps	Subs	Gls
Cardiff C	Cwmparc	04/56	56-60	29	-	7
Exeter C	Tr	06/61	61-62	73	-	11
Bristol Rov	Tr	07/63	63	7	-	0

JENKINS David John
Born: Bristol, England, 2 September, 1946 — F

League Club	Source	Date Signed	Seasons Played	Apps	Subs	Gls
Arsenal	App	10/63	67-68	16	1	3
Tottenham H	Tr	10/68	68-69	11	3	2
Brentford	Tr	07/72	72	13	5	1
Hereford U	Tr	03/73	72-73	18	4	3
Newport Co	L	03/74	73	6	0	1
Shrewsbury T	Tr	08/74	74	2	0	1
Workington	Durban C (RSA)	10/75	75	6	0	0

JENKINS Iain
Born: Prescot, Merseyside, England, 24 November, 1972 — D
Northern Ireland: 6/B-1

League Club	Source	Date Signed	Seasons Played	Apps	Subs	Gls
Everton	YT	06/91	90-92	3	2	0
Bradford C	L	12/92	92	6	0	0
Chester C	Tr	08/93	93-97	155	5	1
Shrewsbury T	Dundee U	07/00	00-01	19	2	0

JENKINS Iorweth Clifford (Iori)
Born: Neath, Wales, 11 December, 1959 — RB
Wales: Schools

League Club	Source	Date Signed	Seasons Played	Apps	Subs	Gls
Chelsea	App	12/77				
Brentford	Tr	11/79	79-80	12	3	1

JENKINS James Lindley (Lindley)
Born: West Bromwich, West Midlands, England, 6 April, 1954 — M

League Club	Source	Date Signed	Seasons Played	Apps	Subs	Gls
Birmingham C	App	07/71	73	2	0	0
Walsall	Tr	07/74	74	3	0	0

JENKINS Jamie
Born: Pontypool, Torfaen, Wales, 1 January, 1979 — M

League Club	Source	Date Signed	Seasons Played	Apps	Subs	Gls
Bournemouth	YT	07/97	98	0	1	0

JENKINS Lee David
Born: Pontypool, Torfaen, Wales, 28 June, 1979 — RB
Wales: U21-9/Youth/Schools

League Club	Source	Date Signed	Seasons Played	Apps	Subs	Gls
Swansea C	YT	12/96	96-03	125	44	3
Kidderminster Hrs	Tr	12/03	03-04	36	3	0

JENKINS Lee Robert
Born: West Bromwich, West Midlands, England, 17 March, 1961 — M
England: Youth

League Club	Source	Date Signed	Seasons Played	Apps	Subs	Gls
Aston Villa	App	01/79	78-79	0	3	0
Port Vale	Tr	11/80	80	1	0	0
Birmingham C	Rovaniemi (FIN)	10/85	85	1	0	0

JENKINS Neil
Born: Carshalton, S London, England, 6 January, 1982 — M/LB
England: Youth

League Club	Source	Date Signed	Seasons Played	Apps	Subs	Gls
Wimbledon	YT	07/00				
Southend U	Tr	08/02	02-03	36	14	8

JENKINS Peter Leslie
Born: Bow, E London, England, 7 February, 1947 — LB

League Club	Source	Date Signed	Seasons Played	Apps	Subs	Gls
Charlton Ath	Chelsea (App)	03/65	65	2	0	0

JENKINS Randolph Joseph
Born: Sligo, Republic of Ireland, 5 September, 1925 — IF

League Club	Source	Date Signed	Seasons Played	Apps	Subs	Gls
Walsall	Linfield	01/45				
Northampton T	Tr	06/46	46-47	18	-	6
Fulham	Tr	05/48				
Gillingham	Tr	06/50	50	2	-	0

JENKINS Reginald (Reg)
Born: Millbrook, Cornwall, England, 7 October, 1938 — F
Died: Tenerife, Spain, 29 January, 2013

League Club	Source	Date Signed	Seasons Played	Apps	Subs	Gls
Plymouth Arg	Truro C	10/57	58-59	16	-	3
Exeter C	Tr	12/60	60	20	-	6
Torquay U	Tr	07/61	61-63	88	-	23
Rochdale	Tr	06/64	64-72	294	11	118

JENKINS Ross Aden
Born: Watford, Hertfordshire, England, 9 November, 1990 — M
England: Youth

League Club	Source	Date Signed	Seasons Played	Apps	Subs	Gls
Watford	Sch	09/08	08-11	66	15	2
Plymouth Arg	L	09/12	12	2	0	1
Barnet	L	03/13	12	3	2	1

JENKINS Ross Anthony
Born: Kensington, Central London, England, 4 November, 1951 — F

League Club	Source	Date Signed	Seasons Played	Apps	Subs	Gls
Crystal Palace	App	11/69	71-72	15	0	2
Watford	Tr	11/72	72-82	312	27	118

JENKINS Stephen Matthew (Steve)
Born: Bristol, England, 2 January, 1980 — LB

League Club	Source	Date Signed	Seasons Played	Apps	Subs	Gls
Southampton	YT	01/98				
Brentford	L	03/99	98	0	1	0
Brentford	Tr	07/99	99	2	3	0

JENKINS Stephen Robert (Steve)
Born: Merthyr Tydfil, Wales, 16 July, 1972 — RB
Wales: 16/U21-2/Youth

League Club	Source	Date Signed	Seasons Played	Apps	Subs	Gls
Swansea C	YT	07/90	90-95	155	10	1
Huddersfield T	Tr	11/95	95-02	257	1	4
Birmingham C	L	12/00	00	3	0	0
Cardiff C	Tr	02/03	02	4	0	0
Notts Co	Tr	08/03	03	17	0	0
Peterborough U	Tr	01/04	03-04	11	3	1
Swindon T	Tr	10/04	04-05	41	7	1

JENKINS Thomas Ernest (Tom)
Born: Bethnal Green, E London, England, 2 December, 1947 — LW

League Club	Source	Date Signed	Seasons Played	Apps	Subs	Gls
Leyton Orient		01/66	65	1	0	0
West Ham U	Tr	12/67				
Reading	Margate	07/69	69	21	0	5
Southampton	Tr	12/69	69-72	84	0	4
Swindon T	Tr	11/72	72-75	89	11	4

JENKINS Thomas Frederick (Tom)
Born: Stockton-on-Tees, Cleveland, England, 5 December, 1925 — IF
Died: Sunderland, England, 7 May, 2009

League Club	Source	Date Signed	Seasons Played	Apps	Subs	Gls
Chelsea	Queen of the South	07/49	49	5	-	0
Leicester C	Kettering T	07/54				

JENKINSON Carl Daniel
Born: Harlow, Essex, England, 8 February, 1992 — RB
England: 1/U21-14/Youth//Finland: U21-1/Youth

League Club	Source	Date Signed	Seasons Played	Apps	Subs	Gls
Charlton Ath	Sch	07/10	10	7	1	0
Arsenal	Tr	05/11	11-13	26	11	1
West Ham U	L	07/14	14	29	3	0

JENKINSON Leigh
Born: Thorne, South Yorkshire, England, 9 July, 1969 — LW
Wales: B-1

League Club	Source	Date Signed	Seasons Played	Apps	Subs	Gls
Hull C	App	06/87	87-92	95	35	13
Rotherham U	L	09/90	90	5	2	0
Coventry C	Tr	03/93	92-94	22	10	1
Birmingham C	L	11/93	93	2	1	0
Wigan Ath	St Johnstone	07/98	98	3	4	0

JENNINGS Connor Joseph
Born: Manchester, England, 21 January, 1991 — F
England: Semi Pro-1

League Club	Source	Date Signed	Seasons Played	Apps	Subs	Gls
Scunthorpe U	Stalybridge Celtic	01/12	11-12	2	14	0

JENNINGS Dale
Born: Liverpool, England, 21 December, 1992 — LW

League Club	Source	Date Signed	Seasons Played	Apps	Subs	Gls
Tranmere Rov	Sch	10/10	10	25	4	6
Barnsley	Bayern Munich (GER)	06/13	13-14	33	14	4
MK Dons	L	11/13	13	6	0	0

JENNINGS Dennis Bernard
Born: Kidderminster, Worcestershire, England, 20 July, 1910 — RW/LB
Died: Wadebridge, Cornwall, England, 29 February, 1996

League Club	Source	Date Signed	Seasons Played	Apps	Subs	Gls
Huddersfield T	Kidderminster Hrs	10/30	30-32	33	-	5
Grimsby T	Tr	09/32	32-35	99	-	29
Birmingham C	Tr	01/36	35-49	192	-	12

JENNINGS Henry William (Bill)
Born: Norwich, England, 7 January, 1920 — CF
Died: Leamington, Warwickshire, England, 4 September, 1969

League Club	Source	Date Signed	Seasons Played	Apps	Subs	Gls
Northampton T	Kingsthorpe Grove	10/38	38-46	11	-	2
Ipswich T	Tr	05/47	47-50	102	-	41
Rochdale	Tr	06/51	51	3	-	1
Crystal Palace	Tr	09/51				

JENNINGS James Ryan
Born: Manchester, England, 2 September, 1987 — LB/M

League Club	Source	Date Signed	Seasons Played	Apps	Subs	Gls
Macclesfield T	Sch	07/06	06-08	23	15	0
Mansfield T	Cambridge U	07/13	13	32	1	4

JENNINGS Kentoine
Born: Bermuda, 15 October, 1971 — D
Bermuda: 15

League Club	Source	Date Signed	Seasons Played	Apps	Subs	Gls
Hereford U	Pembroke (BER)	08/91	91-92	11	5	0

JENNINGS Nicholas (Nicky)
Born: Wellington, Somerset, England, 18 January, 1946 — LW

League Club	Source	Date Signed	Seasons Played	Apps	Subs	Gls
Plymouth Arg	Wellington, Somerset	08/63	63-66	98	0	11
Portsmouth	Tr	01/67	66-73	199	8	44
Aldershot	L	11/73	73	4	0	1
Exeter C	Tr	05/74	74-77	119	5	15

JENNINGS Patrick Anthony (Pat)
Born: Newry, Armagh, Northern Ireland, 12 June, 1945 — G
Northern Ireland: 119/U23-1/Youth

League Club	Source	Date Signed	Seasons Played	Apps	Subs	Gls
Watford	Newry T	05/63	62-63	48	-	0
Tottenham H	Tr	06/64	64-76	472	0	0
Arsenal	Tr	08/77	77-84	237	0	0

JENNINGS Roy Thomas Edward
Born: Swindon, England, 31 December, 1931 — CH
England: Youth

League Club	Source	Date Signed	Seasons Played	Apps	Subs	Gls
Brighton & HA	Southampton (Am)	05/52	52-63	276	-	22

JENNINGS Steven John (Steve)
Born: Liverpool, England, 28 October, 1984 — DM

League Club	Source	Date Signed	Seasons Played	Apps	Subs	Gls
Tranmere Rov	Sch	10/02	03-08	112	28	6
Hereford U	L	01/07	06	11	0	0
Coventry C	Motherwell	08/12	12	36	3	0
Tranmere Rov	Tr	10/13	13	23	2	1
Port Vale	Tr	07/14	14	1	3	0
Tranmere Rov	Tr	10/14	14	30	0	1

JENNINGS William John (Billy)
Born: Hackney, E London, England, 20 February, 1952 — F
England: Youth

League Club	Source	Date Signed	Seasons Played	Apps	Subs	Gls
Watford	Jnr	04/70	70-74	80	13	33
West Ham U	Tr	09/74	74-78	89	10	34
Leyton Orient	Tr	08/79	79-81	64	3	21
Luton T	Tr	03/82	81	0	2	1

JENSEN Brian Paldon
Born: Copenhagen, Denmark, 8 June, 1975 — G

League Club	Source	Date Signed	Seasons Played	Apps	Subs	Gls
West Bromwich A	AZ Alkmaar (NED)	03/00	99-01	46	0	0
Burnley	Tr	07/03	03-12	267	4	0
Bury	Tr	09/13	13	36	0	0
Crawley T	Tr	05/14	14	19	1	0

JENSEN Claus William
Born: Nykobing Falster, Denmark, 29 April, 1977 — M
Denmark: 47/U21-17/Youth

League Club	Source	Date Signed	Seasons Played	Apps	Subs	Gls
Bolton W	Lyngby (DEN)	07/98	98-99	85	1	8
Charlton Ath	Tr	07/00	00-03	112	10	16
Fulham	Tr	07/04	04-06	31	4	4

JENSEN Hans Viggo (Viggo)
Born: Skagen, Denmark, 29 March, 1921 — LB/IF
Died: Denmark, 30 November, 2005
Denmark: 15

League Club	Source	Date Signed	Seasons Played	Apps	Subs	Gls
Hull C	Esbjerg (DEN)	10/48	48-56	308	-	51

JENSEN John Faxe
Born: Copenhagen, Denmark, 3 May, 1965 — M
Denmark: 69

League Club	Source	Date Signed	Seasons Played	Apps	Subs	Gls
Arsenal	Brondby (DEN)	08/92	92-95	93	5	1

JENSEN Niclas Christian Monberg
Born: Copenhagen, Denmark, 17 August, 1974 — LB
Denmark: 62/U21-18/Youth

League Club	Source	Date Signed	Seasons Played	Apps	Subs	Gls
Manchester C	FC Copenhagen (DEN)	01/02	01-02	48	3	2
Fulham	Bor Dortmund (GER)	07/05	05	14	2	0

JEPHCOTT Avun Cyd
Born: Coventry, England, 16 October, 1983 — F

League Club	Source	Date Signed	Seasons Played	Apps	Subs	Gls
Coventry C	Sch	02/03	02	0	1	0

JEPPSON Hans (Hasse)
Born: Kungsbacka, Sweden, 10 May, 1925 — CF
Died: Rome, Italy, 21 February, 2013
Sweden:

League Club	Source	Date Signed	Seasons Played	Apps	Subs	Gls
Charlton Ath (Am)	Djurgaardens (SWE)	01/51	50	11	-	9

JEPSON Arthur
Born: Selston, Nottinghamshire, England, 12 July, 1915 — G
Died: Mansfield, Nottinghamshire, England, 17 July, 1997

League Club	Source	Date Signed	Seasons Played	Apps	Subs	Gls
Mansfield T (Am)	Newark T	11/34	34	2	-	0
Port Vale	Grantham	06/38	38	39	-	0
Stoke C	Tr	09/46	46-47	28	-	0
Lincoln C	Tr	12/48	48-49	58	-	0

JEPSON Charles Barry (Barry)
Born: Alfreton, Derbyshire, England, 29 December, 1929 — CF
Died: Swanwick, Derbyshire, England, 8 December, 2001

League Club	Source	Date Signed	Seasons Played	Apps	Subs	Gls
Chesterfield	Alfreton T	11/48				
Mansfield T	Ilkeston T	03/54	53-56	55	-	36
Chester C	Tr	01/57	56-59	89	-	42
Southport	Tr	11/59	59	24	-	7

JEPSON Ronald Francis (Ronnie)
Born: Audley, Staffordshire, England, 12 May, 1963 — F

League Club	Source	Date Signed	Seasons Played	Apps	Subs	Gls
Port Vale	Nantwich T	03/89	88-90	12	10	0
Peterborough U	L	01/90	89	18	0	5
Preston NE	Tr	02/91	90-91	36	2	8
Exeter C	Tr	07/92	92-93	51	3	21
Huddersfield T	Tr	12/93	93-95	95	12	36
Bury	Tr	07/96	96-97	31	16	9
Oldham Ath	Tr	01/98	97	9	0	4
Burnley	Tr	07/98	98-00	4	55	3

JERKAN Nikola
Born: Split, Croatia, 8 December, 1964 — CD
Croatia: 31

League Club	Source	Date Signed	Seasons Played	Apps	Subs	Gls
Nottingham F	Real Oviedo (SPN)	06/96	96	14	0	0

JERMYN Mark Stephen
Born: Rinteln, Germany, 16 April, 1981 — FB

League Club	Source	Date Signed	Seasons Played	Apps	Subs	Gls
Torquay U	YT	07/99	98	0	1	0

JEROME Cameron Zishan
Born: Huddersfield, West Yorkshire, England, 14 August, 1986 — F
England: U21-10

League Club	Source	Date Signed	Seasons Played	Apps	Subs	Gls
Cardiff C	Middlesbrough (Jnr)	01/04	04-05	68	8	24
Birmingham C	Tr	06/06	06-11	128	53	37
Stoke C	Tr	08/11	11-13	15	35	7
Crystal Palace	L	09/13	13	20	8	2
Norwich C	Tr	08/14	14	32	9	18

[JERONIMO] MORALES Jeronimo
Born: Godoy Cruz, Argentina, 3 June, 1986 — F

League Club	Source	Date Signed	Seasons Played	Apps	Subs	Gls
Barnsley	Estudiantes (ARG)	07/10	10	0	5	0

JERVIS David John
Born: Stretford, Greater Manchester, England, 18 January, 1982 — LB

League Club	Source	Date Signed	Seasons Played	Apps	Subs	Gls
Mansfield T	YT	07/00	00-02	21	9	0

JERVIS Jake Mario
Born: Wolverhampton, England, 17 September, 1991 — F

League Club	Source	Date Signed	Seasons Played	Apps	Subs	Gls
Birmingham C	Sch	02/10	12	0	2	0
Hereford U	L	03/10	09	5	2	2
Notts Co	L	08/10	10	1	9	0
Hereford U	L	01/11	10	3	1	0
Swindon T	L	09/11	11	10	2	3
Preston NE	L	01/12	11	3	2	2
Carlisle U	L	08/12	12	5	0	3
Tranmere Rov	L	10/12	12	4	0	1
Portsmouth	L	11/12	12	1	2	1
Portsmouth	Elazigspor (TKY)	01/14	13	12	3	4

JERVIS William John
Born: Liverpool, England, 22 January, 1942 — RW

League Club	Source	Date Signed	Seasons Played	Apps	Subs	Gls
Blackburn Rov	Jnr	01/59				
Gillingham	Tr	07/61	61	1	-	0

JESS Eoin
Born: Portsoy, Aberdeenshire, Scotland, 13 December, 1970 — M
Scotland: 18/B-2/U21-14

League Club	Source	Date Signed	Seasons Played	Apps	Subs	Gls
Coventry C	Aberdeen	02/96	95-96	28	11	1
Bradford C	Aberdeen	12/00	00-01	60	2	17
Nottingham F	Tr	08/02	02-04	54	32	7
Northampton T	Tr	07/05	05-06	57	7	2

JESSOP Thomas Stanley (Stan)
Born: Liverpool, England, 5 August, 1932 — LW
Died: Brisbane, Australia, 29 February, 1996

League Club	Source	Date Signed	Seasons Played	Apps	Subs	Gls
Southport	Kidderminster Hrs	08/53	53	11	-	1

JESSOP William (Willie)
Born: Preston, Lancashire, England, 2 April, 1922 — LW
Died: Stafford, England, May, 1994

League Club	Source	Date Signed	Seasons Played	Apps	Subs	Gls
Preston NE	Jnr	09/40	46	4	-	0
Stockport Co	Tr	04/47	46-47	17	-	4
Oldham Ath	Tr	02/48	47-50	94	-	16
Wrexham	Tr	06/51	51	14	-	2

JEST Sydney Thomas (Syd)
Born: Ramsgate, Kent, England, 4 June, 1943 — RB

League Club	Source	Date Signed	Seasons Played	Apps	Subs	Gls
Brighton & HA	Ramsgate Ath	12/61	61-62	12	-	0

JEVONS Philip (Phil)
Born: Liverpool, England, 1 August, 1979 — F

League Club	Source	Date Signed	Seasons Played	Apps	Subs	Gls
Everton	YT	11/97	98-00	2	6	0
Grimsby T	Tr	07/01	01-03	46	17	18
Hull C	L	09/02	02	13	11	3
Yeovil T	Tr	07/04	04-05	80	4	42
Bristol C	Tr	07/06	06-07	31	12	11
Huddersfield T	Tr	11/07	07-08	29	15	9
Bury	L	03/09	08	3	4	2

League Club	Source	Date Signed	Seasons Played	Apps	Subs	Gls
Morecambe	L	08/09	09	40	0	18
Morecambe	Tr	07/10	10-11	41	24	12
JEWELL Paul						
Born: Liverpool, England, 28 September, 1964						F
Liverpool	App	09/82				
Wigan Ath	Tr	12/84	84-87	117	20	35
Bradford C	Tr	07/88	88-95	217	52	56
Grimsby T	L	08/95	95	2	3	1
JEWELL Ronald Percival (Ron)						
Born: Plymouth, England, 6 December, 1920						W
Died: Yealmpton, Devon, England, 14 February, 2000						
Torquay U	Plymouth Arg (Am)	09/46	46	1	-	0
JEZZARD Bedford Alfred George						
Born: Clerkenwell, Central London, England, 19 October, 1927						CF
Died: Alton, Hampshire, England, 21 May, 2005						
England: 2/B-3/FLge-3						
Fulham	Croxley BC	10/48	48-55	292	-	154
JI Dong-Won						
Born: Jeju, South Korea, 28 May, 1991						F
South Korea: 31						
Sunderland	Chunnam Dragons (KOR)	07/11	11-13	4	20	2
JIMENEZ Luis Antonio						
Born: Santiago, Chile, 17 June, 1984						RW
Chile: 26						
West Ham U (L)	Inter Milan (ITA)	07/09	09	6	5	1
JINKS James Thomas (Jimmy)						
Born: Camberwell, S London, England, 19 August, 1916						CF
Died: Eltham, SE London, England, 23 November, 1981						
Millwall	Downham Common	11/38	38-47	45	-	16
Fulham	Tr	08/48	48-49	11	-	3
Luton T	Tr	03/50	49-50	9	-	2
Aldershot	Tr	09/51	51	5	-	0
JIRANEK Martin						
Born: Liberec, Czech Republic, 25 May, 1979						CD
Czech Republic: 31/U21-20						
Birmingham C	Spartak Moscow (RUS)	08/10	10	10	0	0
[JO] ALVES DE ASSIS SILVA Joao						
Born: Sao Paulo, Brazil, 20 March, 1987						F
Brazil: 20/U23-7						
Manchester C	CSKA Moscow (RUS)	07/08	08-10	9	12	1
Everton	L	01/09	08	11	1	5
Everton	L	08/09	09	6	9	0
JOACHIM Julian Kevin						
Born: Boston, Lincolnshire, England, 20 September, 1974						F
England: U21-9/Youth						
Leicester C	YT	09/92	92-95	77	22	25
Aston Villa	Tr	02/96	95-00	90	51	39
Coventry C	Tr	07/01	01-03	41	15	11
Leeds U	Tr	07/04	04	10	17	2
Walsall	L	03/05	04	8	0	6
Boston U	Tr	07/05	05-06	44	2	17
Darlington	Tr	08/06	06-07	66	10	13
JOB Joseph-Desire						
Born: Lyon, France, 1 December, 1977						F/M
Cameroon: 52						
Middlesbrough	RC Lens (FRA)	08/00	00-05	62	29	16
JOBLING Keith Allen						
Born: Grimsby, North Lincolnshire, England, 26 March, 1934						CH
Grimsby T	New Waltham	07/53	53-68	450	0	5
JOBLING Kevin Andrew						
Born: Sunderland, England, 1 January, 1968						M/LB
Leicester C	App	01/86	86-87	4	5	0
Grimsby T	Tr	02/88	87-97	251	34	10
Shrewsbury T	Tr	07/98	98-99	66	3	3
JOBSON Richard Ian						
Born: Cottingham, East Riding of Yorkshire, England, 9 May, 1963						CD
England: B-2						
Watford	Burton A	11/82	82-84	26	2	4
Hull C	Tr	02/85	84-90	219	2	17
Oldham Ath	Tr	08/90	90-95	188	1	10
Leeds U	Tr	10/95	95-96	22	0	1
Southend U	L	01/98	97	8	0	1
Manchester C	Tr	03/98	97-99	49	1	4
Watford	L	11/00	00	2	0	0
Tranmere Rov	Tr	12/00	00-01	17	0	0
Rochdale	Tr	09/01	01-02	49	2	3
JOEL Stephen Philip (Steve)						
Born: Liverpool, England, 13 October, 1954						M
Southport	Portmadoc	11/77	77	0	1	0
JOHANNESON Albert Louis						
Born: Germiston, South Africa, 12 March, 1940						W
Died: Leeds, England, 29 September, 1995						
Leeds U	Germiston Cal'n (RSA)	04/61	60-69	170	2	48
York C	Tr	07/70	70-71	26	0	3
JOHANSEN Eirik Holmen						
Born: Tonsberg, Norway, 12 July, 1992						G
Norway: U21-7/Youth						
Manchester C	Sch	07/11				
Scunthorpe U	L	03/13	12	8	0	0
JOHANSEN Martin Bro						
Born: Copenhagen, Denmark, 22 July, 1972						M
Denmark: 1/U21-7/Youth						
Coventry C	FC Copenhagen (DEN)	06/97	97	0	2	0
JOHANSEN Michael Bro						
Born: Copenhagen, Denmark, 22 July, 1972						RW
Denmark: 2						
Bolton W	FC Copenhagen (DEN)	08/96	96-99	112	25	16
JOHANSEN Rune Buer						
Born: Oslo, Norway, 4 September, 1973						F
Bristol Rov (L)	Tromso (NOR)	11/00	00	0	2	0
JOHANSEN Stig						
Born: Svolvaer, Lofoten Island, Norway, 13 June, 1972						F
Norway: 3						
Southampton	FK Bodo/Glimpt (NOR)	08/97	97	3	3	0
Bristol C	L	02/98	97	2	1	0
JOHANSSON Jonatan Lillebror (JJ)						
Born: Stockholm, Sweden, 16 August, 1975						F
Finland: 105/U21-7						
Charlton Ath	Glasgow Rangers	08/00	00-05	90	58	27
Norwich C	L	01/06	05	6	6	3
JOHANSSON Nils-Eric Claes						
Born: Stockholm, Sweden, 13 January, 1980						D
Sweden: 4/U21-21/Youth						
Blackburn Rov	Nuremburg (GER)	10/01	01-04	59	27	0
Leicester C	Tr	07/05	05-06	75	0	1
JOHANSSON Roy Johan Andreas (Andreas)						
Born: Vanersborg, Sweden, 5 July, 1978						F
Sweden: 16/U21-2						
Wigan Ath	Djurgaardens (SWE)	01/05	04-06	10	19	4
JOHN Alistair Alexander						
Born: Croydon, S London, England, 28 November, 1987						W
Charlton Ath	Sch	05/06				
Brighton & HA	L	11/06	06	1	3	0
Torquay U	L	02/07	06	6	1	0
JOHN Collins						
Born: Zwedru, Liberia, 17 October, 1985						F
Netherlands: 2/U21-9/Youth						
Fulham	FC Twente (NED)	01/04	03-07	41	54	20
Leicester C	L	09/07	07	7	4	2
Watford	L	01/08	07	3	2	0
Barnet	Mes Sarcheshmeh (IRA)	09/12	12	1	0	0
JOHN Declan Christopher						
Born: Merthyr Tydfil, Wales, 30 June, 1995						LB
Wales: 2/U21-3/Youth						
Cardiff C	Sch	08/12	13-14	18	8	0
Barnsley	L	03/15	14	8	1	0
JOHN Dennis Carl						
Born: Swansea, Wales, 27 January, 1935						RB
Died: Cardiff, Wales, 9 April, 2013						
Plymouth Arg	Jnr	02/52	55-56	3	-	0
Swansea C	Tr	08/58	58	4	-	0
Scunthorpe U	Tr	08/59	59-61	88	-	0
Millwall	Tr	06/62	62-65	101	5	6
JOHN Dilwyn						
Born: Tonypandy, Rhondda Cynon Taff, Wales, 3 June, 1944						G
Wales: U23-1						
Cardiff C	Jnr	06/61	61-66	88	0	0
Swansea C	Tr	03/67	66-69	80	0	0
JOHN Malcolm						
Born: Bridgend, Wales, 9 December, 1950						F/M
Bristol Rov	Swansea C (Am)	09/71	71-73	4	1	2
Northampton T	Tr	03/74	73-74	34	7	9

JOHN Raymond Charles (Ray)
Born: Swansea, Wales, 22 November, 1932 RH/IF
Died: Westgate-on-Sea, Kent, England, 7 July, 2009

League Club	Source	Date Signed	Seasons Played	Apps	Subs	Gls
Barnsley	Tottenham H (Am)	05/53				
Exeter C	Tr	07/54	54-58	144	-	18
Oldham Ath	Tr	12/58	58-59	32	-	5

JOHN Stephen Paul (Steve)
Born: Brentwood, Essex, England, 22 December, 1966 D

League Club	Source	Date Signed	Seasons Played	Apps	Subs	Gls
Leyton Orient	App	12/84	85-86	23	0	0

JOHN Stern
Born: Tunapuna, Trinidad, 30 October, 1976 F
Trinidad & Tobago: 109

League Club	Source	Date Signed	Seasons Played	Apps	Subs	Gls
Nottingham F	Columbus Crew (USA)	11/99	99-01	49	23	18
Birmingham C	Tr	02/02	01-04	42	35	16
Coventry C	Tr	09/04	04-06	65	13	26
Derby Co	L	09/05	05	6	1	0
Sunderland	Tr	01/07	06-07	10	6	5
Southampton	Tr	08/07	07-08	39	8	19
Bristol C	L	10/08	08	13	11	2
Crystal Palace	Tr	07/09	09	7	9	2
Ipswich T	L	11/09	09	5	2	1

JOHN-LEWIS Lennell Nicholas (Lenny)
Born: Hammersmith, W London, England, 17 May, 1989 RW

League Club	Source	Date Signed	Seasons Played	Apps	Subs	Gls
Lincoln C	Sch	12/07	07-09	43	29	8
Bury	Tr	08/10	10-12	19	64	9

JOHNROSE Leonard (Lenny)
Born: Preston, Lancashire, England, 29 November, 1969 M

League Club	Source	Date Signed	Seasons Played	Apps	Subs	Gls
Blackburn Rov	YT	06/88	87-91	20	22	11
Preston NE	L	01/92	91	1	2	1
Hartlepool U	Tr	02/92	91-93	59	7	11
Bury	Tr	12/93	93-98	181	7	19
Burnley	Tr	02/99	98-02	51	27	4
Bury	Tr	10/02	02	5	1	0
Swansea C	Tr	01/03	02-03	36	4	3
Burnley	Tr	03/04	03	4	3	0

JOHNS Francis Stanley (Stan)
Born: Liverpool, England, 28 June, 1924 IF
Died: Warrington, Cheshire, England, 13 May, 1986

League Club	Source	Date Signed	Seasons Played	Apps	Subs	Gls
West Ham U	South Liverpool	08/50	50	6	-	2

JOHNS Jasper Nathaniel
Born: Stafford, England, 6 February, 1995 LB
England: Youth//Northern Ireland: Youth

League Club	Source	Date Signed	Seasons Played	Apps	Subs	Gls
Sheffield U	Everton (Sch)	07/13	13	0	1	0

JOHNS Mark
Born: Bristol, England, 17 May, 1959 F

League Club	Source	Date Signed	Seasons Played	Apps	Subs	Gls
Bristol Rov	Bristol Manor Farm	09/86	86	2	0	1

JOHNS Nicholas Paul (Nicky)
Born: Bristol, England, 8 June, 1957 G

League Club	Source	Date Signed	Seasons Played	Apps	Subs	Gls
Millwall	Minehead	02/76	76-77	50	0	0
Sheffield U	Tampa Bay R's (USA)	09/78	78	1	0	0
Charlton Ath	Tr	12/78	78-87	288	0	0
Queens Park Rgrs	Tr	12/87	87-88	10	0	0
Maidstone U	Tr	10/89	89-90	42	0	0

JOHNSEN Erland
Born: Fredrikstad, Norway, 5 April, 1967 CD
Norway: 24/U21-16/Youth

League Club	Source	Date Signed	Seasons Played	Apps	Subs	Gls
Chelsea	Bayern Munich (GER)	12/89	89-96	135	10	1

JOHNSEN Jean Ronny (Ronny)
Born: Sandefjord, Norway, 10 June, 1969 CD
Norway: 62

League Club	Source	Date Signed	Seasons Played	Apps	Subs	Gls
Manchester U	Besiktas (TKY)	07/96	96-01	85	14	7
Aston Villa	Tr	08/02	02-03	46	3	1
Newcastle U	Tr	09/04	04	3	0	0

JOHNSON Adam
Born: Sunderland, England, 14 July, 1987 W
England: 12/U21-19/Youth

League Club	Source	Date Signed	Seasons Played	Apps	Subs	Gls
Middlesbrough	Sch	05/05	05-09	49	47	13
Leeds U	L	10/06	06	4	1	0
Watford	L	09/07	07	11	1	5
Manchester C	Tr	02/10	09-11	39	34	11
Sunderland	Tr	08/12	12-14	86	17	17

JOHNSON Alan
Born: Stoke-on-Trent, England, 13 March, 1947 RW

League Club	Source	Date Signed	Seasons Played	Apps	Subs	Gls
Port Vale	Jnr	09/64	65	2	0	1

JOHNSON Alan Keith
Born: St Helens, Merseyside, England, 19 February, 1971 CD

League Club	Source	Date Signed	Seasons Played	Apps	Subs	Gls
Wigan Ath	YT	04/89	88-93	163	17	13
Lincoln C	Tr	02/94	93-95	57	6	0
Preston NE	L	09/95	95	2	0	0
Rochdale	Tr	08/96	96-98	59	3	4

JOHNSON Albert
Born: Morpeth, Northumberland, England, 7 September, 1923 FB
Died: Northampton, England, December, 1989

League Club	Source	Date Signed	Seasons Played	Apps	Subs	Gls
Bradford C	Ashington	05/47	46-49	35	-	0

JOHNSON Albert
Born: Weaverham, Cheshire, England, 15 July, 1920 W
Died: Weaverham, Cheshire, England, 22 June, 2011

League Club	Source	Date Signed	Seasons Played	Apps	Subs	Gls
Everton	PCI	05/39	46-47	9	-	0
Chesterfield	Tr	09/48	48	19	-	1

JOHNSON Andrew (Andy)
Born: Bedford, England, 10 February, 1981 F
England: 8/Youth

League Club	Source	Date Signed	Seasons Played	Apps	Subs	Gls
Birmingham C	Jnr	03/98	98-01	44	39	8
Crystal Palace	Tr	08/02	02-05	134	6	74
Everton	Tr	06/06	06-07	52	9	17
Fulham	Tr	08/08	08-11	65	21	13
Queens Park Rgrs	Tr	07/12	12-13	12	8	2
Crystal Palace	Tr	09/14				

JOHNSON Andrew James (Andy)
Born: Bath, England, 2 May, 1974 M
England: Youth//Wales: 15

League Club	Source	Date Signed	Seasons Played	Apps	Subs	Gls
Norwich C	YT	03/92	91-96	56	10	13
Nottingham F	Tr	07/97	97-01	102	17	9
West Bromwich A	Tr	09/01	01-05	121	11	7
Leicester C	Tr	07/06	06	21	1	1
Barnsley	Tr	06/07	07	4	0	0

JOHNSON Arthur
Born: Liverpool, England, 23 January, 1933 G
Died: Chorley, Lancashire, England, 20 June, 2011

League Club	Source	Date Signed	Seasons Played	Apps	Subs	Gls
Blackburn Rov	Jnr	01/50	51	1	-	0
Halifax T	Tr	03/55	54-59	215	-	0
Wrexham	Tr	06/60	60-61	52	-	0
Chester C	L	08/62	62	3	-	0

JOHNSON Bradley Paul (Brad)
Born: Hackney, E London, England, 28 April, 1987 M

League Club	Source	Date Signed	Seasons Played	Apps	Subs	Gls
Cambridge U	Jnr	11/04	04	0	1	0
Northampton T	Tr	05/05	05-07	44	9	8
Leeds U	Tr	01/08	07-10	91	26	15
Brighton & HA	L	10/08	08	10	0	4
Norwich C	Tr	07/11	11-14	130	8	21

JOHNSON Brett
Born: Hammersmith, W London, England, 15 August, 1985 LB

League Club	Source	Date Signed	Seasons Played	Apps	Subs	Gls
Northampton T	Aldershot T	07/05	05-07	14	12	0
Brentford	Tr	08/08	08	7	3	0
AFC Wimbledon	Tr	08/09	11	14	4	0

JOHNSON Brian
Born: Gateshead, Tyne and Wear, England, 20 March, 1936 CF

League Club	Source	Date Signed	Seasons Played	Apps	Subs	Gls
Millwall		10/57	57	7	-	2

JOHNSON Brian
Born: Newcastle-upon-Tyne, England, 12 November, 1948 RW

League Club	Source	Date Signed	Seasons Played	Apps	Subs	Gls
Sunderland	App	11/65				
Luton T	Tr	07/66	66-67	9	1	0

JOHNSON Brian Arthur Bentley
Born: Northwich, Cheshire, England, 28 May, 1930 W
Died: Cheshire, England, November, 2013

League Club	Source	Date Signed	Seasons Played	Apps	Subs	Gls
Wrexham		04/50	50-51	14	-	2

JOHNSON Brian Frederick
Born: Isleworth, W London, England, 21 October, 1955 W

League Club	Source	Date Signed	Seasons Played	Apps	Subs	Gls
Plymouth Arg	App	08/73	73-80	186	11	40
Torquay U	L	01/79	78	5	0	2
Torquay U	L	09/81	81	2	0	0

JOHNSON Brian Joseph
Born: Huyton, Merseyside, England, 29 October, 1948 M

League Club	Source	Date Signed	Seasons Played	Apps	Subs	Gls
Tranmere Rov	Jnr	05/67	68	0	1	0

JOHNSON Christopher (Chris)
Born: Brighton, England, 25 January, 1979 M

League Club	Source	Date Signed	Seasons Played	Apps	Subs	Gls
Watford	YT	02/97	96	1	0	0

JOHNSON Damien Michael
Born: Lisburn, Belfast, Northern Ireland, 18 November, 1978 DM
Northern Ireland: 56/U21-11/Youth

League Club	Source	Date Signed	Seasons Played	Apps	Subs	Gls
Blackburn Rov	YT	02/96	98-01	43	17	3
Nottingham F	L	01/98	97	5	1	0
Birmingham C	Tr	03/02	01-09	184	9	4

League Club	Source	Date Signed	Seasons Played	Apps	Subs	Gls
Plymouth Arg	Tr	02/10	09	20	0	2
Huddersfield T	L	08/10	10	14	2	0
Huddersfield T	L	07/11	11	16	2	0
Fleetwood T	Tr	07/12	12	17	5	0

JOHNSON Daniel (Danny)
Born: Middlesbrough, England, 2 April, 1993 — F

League Club	Source	Date Signed	Seasons Played	Apps	Subs	Gls
Cardiff C	Guisborough T	08/14				
Tranmere Rov	L	10/14	14	4	0	0
Stevenage	L	02/15	14	1	3	0

JOHNSON Daniel Anthony
Born: Kingston, Jamaica, 8 October, 1992 — M

League Club	Source	Date Signed	Seasons Played	Apps	Subs	Gls
Aston Villa	Sch	01/11				
Yeovil T	L	10/12	12	3	2	0
Chesterfield	L	08/14	14	7	4	0
Oldham Ath	L	11/14	14	5	1	3
Preston NE	Tr	01/15	14	20	0	8

JOHNSON David
Born: South Shields, Tyne and Wear, England, 19 November, 1955 — F
England: Youth

League Club	Source	Date Signed	Seasons Played	Apps	Subs	Gls
Bristol C	Doncaster Rov (Am)	05/74				
Hartlepool U	Tr	02/75	74	1	0	0

JOHNSON David
Born: Blackburn, Greater Manchester, England, 17 April, 1950 — G

League Club	Source	Date Signed	Seasons Played	Apps	Subs	Gls
Tranmere Rov	Atherstone T	07/74	74	3	0	0
Southport	L	01/76	75	6	0	0

JOHNSON David Alan
Born: Dinnington, South Yorkshire, England, 29 October, 1970 — F

League Club	Source	Date Signed	Seasons Played	Apps	Subs	Gls
Sheffield Wed	YT	07/89	91	5	1	0
Hartlepool U	L	10/91	91	7	0	2
Hartlepool U	L	11/92	92	3	0	0
Lincoln C	Tr	08/93	93-95	75	14	13

JOHNSON David Anthony
Born: Kingston, Jamaica, 15 August, 1976 — F
England: B-1/Schools//Jamaica: 4

League Club	Source	Date Signed	Seasons Played	Apps	Subs	Gls
Manchester U	YT	07/94				
Bury	Tr	07/95	95-97	72	25	18
Ipswich T	Tr	11/97	97-00	121	10	55
Nottingham F	Tr	01/01	00-05	122	26	46
Sheffield Wed	L	02/02	01	7	0	2
Burnley	L	03/02	01	8	0	5
Sheffield U	L	03/05	04	0	4	0

JOHNSON David Donald
Born: Northampton, England, 10 March, 1967 — LB

League Club	Source	Date Signed	Seasons Played	Apps	Subs	Gls
Northampton T	Irthlingborough D	07/89	89-91	23	24	0

JOHNSON David Edward
Born: Liverpool, England, 23 October, 1951 — F
England: 8

League Club	Source	Date Signed	Seasons Played	Apps	Subs	Gls
Everton	App	04/69	70-72	47	2	11
Ipswich T	Tr	11/72	72-75	134	2	35
Liverpool	Tr	08/76	76-81	128	20	55
Everton	Tr	08/82	82-83	32	8	4
Barnsley	L	02/84	83	4	0	1
Manchester C	Tr	03/84	83	4	2	1
Preston NE	Tulsa Roughnecks (USA)	10/84	84	20	4	3

JOHNSON David Nicholas Conrad
Born: Gloucester, England, 26 December, 1962 — RW

League Club	Source	Date Signed	Seasons Played	Apps	Subs	Gls
Watford	Redhill	03/82	81-83	4	3	0
Peterborough U	Tr	08/84	84-85	28	7	4

JOHNSON Dennis
Born: Sunderland, England, 20 May, 1934 — IF
Died: Sunderland, England, February, 2007

League Club	Source	Date Signed	Seasons Played	Apps	Subs	Gls
Hartlepool U	Seaham CW	02/54	57	2	-	0

JOHNSON Edward Abraham (Eddie)
Born: Daytona, Florida, USA, 31 March, 1984 — F
USA: 63/U23-7/Youth

League Club	Source	Date Signed	Seasons Played	Apps	Subs	Gls
Fulham	Sport'g Kansas C (USA)	01/08	07-10	5	14	0
Cardiff C	L	08/08	08-08	5	25	2
Preston NE	L	01/11	10	15	1	0

JOHNSON Edward William (Eddie)
Born: Chester, England, 20 September, 1984 — F
England: Youth

League Club	Source	Date Signed	Seasons Played	Apps	Subs	Gls
Manchester U	YT	10/01				
Coventry C	L	07/04	04	20	6	5
Crewe Alex	L	07/05	05	16	6	5
Bradford C	Tr	07/06	06-07	47	17	7
Chester C	Tr	10/08	08	7	3	1

JOHNSON Elliot George
Born: Hendon, N London, England, 17 August, 1994 — LB

League Club	Source	Date Signed	Seasons Played	Apps	Subs	Gls
Barnet	Sch	07/12	12	25	1	1

JOHNSON Eric
Born: Moulton, Cheshire, England, 25 May, 1927 — W/LH
Died: Isle of Wight, England, May, 1992

League Club	Source	Date Signed	Seasons Played	Apps	Subs	Gls
Coventry C	Winsford U	09/52	52-56	90	-	6
Torquay U	Tr	07/57	57-58	49	-	1

JOHNSON Eric
Born: Birkenhead, Wirral, England, 16 December, 1944 — LH

League Club	Source	Date Signed	Seasons Played	Apps	Subs	Gls
Wrexham	Everton (Am)	06/63	63-65	28	0	0

JOHNSON Gary Jack
Born: Peckham, SE London, England, 14 September, 1959 — F

League Club	Source	Date Signed	Seasons Played	Apps	Subs	Gls
Chelsea	App	09/77	78-80	16	3	9
Brentford	Tr	12/80	80-82	55	5	13
Aldershot	Plate Glass Rgrs (RSA)	08/85	85-87	73	2	20

JOHNSON Gavin
Born: Stowmarket, Suffolk, England, 10 October, 1970 — LB/M

League Club	Source	Date Signed	Seasons Played	Apps	Subs	Gls
Ipswich T	YT	03/89	88-94	114	18	11
Luton T	Tr	07/95	95	4	1	0
Wigan Ath	Tr	12/95	95-97	82	2	8
Colchester U	Dunfermline Ath	11/99	99-04	134	13	13
Boston U	Tr	07/05	05	3	1	0
Northampton T	Tr	08/05	05	22	2	1

JOHNSON George
Born: Davyhulme, Greater Manchester, England, 27 April, 1936 — IF
Died: Bolton, Greater Manchester, England, November, 2011

League Club	Source	Date Signed	Seasons Played	Apps	Subs	Gls
Rochdale	Gerrards	12/54	54	1	-	0
Southport	Ashton U	01/63	62	6	-	0

JOHNSON George
Born: Esh Winning, County Durham, England, 6 October, 1932 — LW
Died: Lincoln, England, 11 August, 2002

League Club	Source	Date Signed	Seasons Played	Apps	Subs	Gls
Lincoln C	Langley Park Jnrs	09/51	51	3	-	1

JOHNSON Glen McLeod
Born: Greenwich, SE London, England, 23 August, 1984 — RB
England: 54/U21-14/Youth

League Club	Source	Date Signed	Seasons Played	Apps	Subs	Gls
West Ham U	YT	08/01	02	14	1	0
Millwall	L	10/02	02	7	1	0
Chelsea	Tr	07/03	03-05	35	7	3
Portsmouth	L	07/06	06	25	1	0
Portsmouth	Tr	08/07	07-08	58	0	4
Liverpool	Tr	06/09	09-14	154	6	8

JOHNSON Glenn Paul
Born: Sydney, Australia, 16 July, 1972 — F

League Club	Source	Date Signed	Seasons Played	Apps	Subs	Gls
Cardiff C	Blacktown C (AUS)	03/96	95	1	4	0

JOHNSON Glenn William
Born: Barrow, Cumbria, England, 7 March, 1952 — G
England: Youth

League Club	Source	Date Signed	Seasons Played	Apps	Subs	Gls
Arsenal	App	07/69				
Doncaster Rov	Tr	06/70	70-72	95	0	0
Walsall	L	12/72	72	3	0	0
Aldershot	Tr	07/73	73-82	424	0	0

JOHNSON Howard
Born: Sheffield, England, 17 July, 1925 — CD
Died: Lincolnshire, England, 16 June, 2015

League Club	Source	Date Signed	Seasons Played	Apps	Subs	Gls
Sheffield U	Norton Woodseats	03/51	50-56	92	-	0
York C	Tr	08/57	57	28	-	0

JOHNSON Huw Alastair Beswick
Born: Hammersmith, W London, England, 22 June, 1993 — M

League Club	Source	Date Signed	Seasons Played	Apps	Subs	Gls
AFC Wimbledon	Jnr	12/11	11-12	1	8	0

JOHNSON Ian
Born: Oldham, Greater Manchester, England, 11 November, 1960 — FB

League Club	Source	Date Signed	Seasons Played	Apps	Subs	Gls
Rochdale	Chadderton	09/84	84-86	74	7	1

JOHNSON Ian
Born: Newcastle-upon-Tyne, England, 14 February, 1969 — CD

League Club	Source	Date Signed	Seasons Played	Apps	Subs	Gls
Northampton T	Gateshead	11/87	88	2	1	0
Torquay U	Whitley Bay	11/92	92	9	0	1

JOHNSON Ian
Born: Sunderland, England, 1 September, 1975 — W

League Club	Source	Date Signed	Seasons Played	Apps	Subs	Gls
Middlesbrough	YT	01/94	93	1	1	0
Bradford C	Tr	01/95	94	1	1	0

JOHNSON Ian Grant (Grant)
Born: Dundee, Scotland, 24 March, 1972 — M
Scotland: U21-6

League Club	Source	Date Signed	Seasons Played	Apps	Subs	Gls
Huddersfield T	Dundee U	11/97	97-98	64	1	5

JOHNSON James (Jim)
Born: Stockton-on-Tees, Cleveland, England, 26 March, 1923 — CF
Died: Stockton-on-Tees, Cleveland, England, May, 1987

League Club	Source	Date Signed	Seasons Played	Apps	Subs	Gls
Grimsby T	York C (Am)	03/45	46-49	6	-	1
Carlisle U	Tr	03/51	50	8	-	0

JOHNSON Jeffrey (Jeff)
Born: Manchester, England, 29 October, 1950 — M
England: Semi Pro-18

League Club	Source	Date Signed	Seasons Played	Apps	Subs	Gls
Stockport Co	Hyde U	09/76	76	6	2	0

JOHNSON Jeffrey David (Jeff)
Born: Cardiff, Wales, 26 November, 1953 — M
Wales: Schools

League Club	Source	Date Signed	Seasons Played	Apps	Subs	Gls
Manchester C	App	12/70	70-71	4	2	0
Swansea C	L	07/72	72	37	1	5
Crystal Palace	Tr	12/73	73-75	82	5	4
Sheffield Wed	Tr	07/76	76-80	175	5	6
Newport Co	Tr	08/81	81	34	0	2
Gillingham	Tr	09/82	82-84	85	3	4
Port Vale	Tr	07/85	85	10	0	1

JOHNSON Jemal Pierre
Born: Paterson, New Jersey, USA, 3 May, 1984 — F

League Club	Source	Date Signed	Seasons Played	Apps	Subs	Gls
Blackburn Rov	Sch	05/02	04-05	0	6	0
Preston NE	L	10/05	05	2	1	1
Darlington	L	03/06	05	9	0	3
Wolverhampton W	Tr	08/06	06	14	6	3
Leeds U	L	02/07	06	3	2	0
MK Dons	Tr	08/07	07-10	50	46	12
Stockport Co	L	01/10	09	14	2	2
Port Vale	L	09/10	10	1	5	0
Southend U	Lokomotiv Sofia (BUL)	07/11	11	1	4	0

JOHNSON Jermaine
Born: Kingston, Jamaica, 25 June, 1980 — RW
Jamaica: 74

League Club	Source	Date Signed	Seasons Played	Apps	Subs	Gls
Bolton W	Tivoli Gardens (JAM)	09/01	01-02	4	8	0
Oldham Ath	Tr	11/03	03-04	31	8	9
Bradford C	Tivoli Gardens (JAM)	07/06	06	26	1	4
Sheffield Wed	Tr	01/07	06-13	146	85	25

JOHNSON John (Johnny)
Born: Stockport, Greater Manchester, England, 11 December, 1921 — RW
Died: Kent, England, October, 2003

League Club	Source	Date Signed	Seasons Played	Apps	Subs	Gls
Stockport Co		01/41				
Millwall	Tr	12/45	46-54	294	-	42
Millwall	Tonbridge	11/55	55-56	15	-	4

JOHNSON John Edward (Edward)
Born: South Shields, Tyne and Wear, England, 4 February, 1929 — IF

League Club	Source	Date Signed	Seasons Played	Apps	Subs	Gls
Manchester C	South Shields	05/49				
Gateshead	North Shields	01/51	50-54	75	-	13

JOHNSON John James
Born: Middlesbrough, England, 16 September, 1988 — RB

League Club	Source	Date Signed	Seasons Played	Apps	Subs	Gls
Middlesbrough	Sch	05/08	08	0	1	0
Tranmere Rov	L	11/08	08	4	0	0
Northampton T	L	09/09	09	36	0	5
Northampton T	Tr	07/10	10-12	97	6	9

JOHNSON John William (Jack)
Born: Newcastle-upon-Tyne, England, 12 February, 1919 — RW
Died: Leicester, England, 1975

League Club	Source	Date Signed	Seasons Played	Apps	Subs	Gls
Huddersfield T	Leicester Nomads	06/36	36-38	18	-	2
Grimsby T	Tr	04/39	46-47	44	-	2

JOHNSON Joseph (Joe)
Born: South Kirkby, West Yorkshire, England, 16 May, 1916 — RH
Died: Huddersfield, West Yorkshire, England, 16 January, 2011

League Club	Source	Date Signed	Seasons Played	Apps	Subs	Gls
Doncaster Rov	Scarborough	12/38				
Southport	Folkestone	12/46	46	5	-	0

JOHNSON Joseph Robert (Joe)
Born: Greenock, Inverclyde, Scotland, 13 September, 1920 — IF

League Club	Source	Date Signed	Seasons Played	Apps	Subs	Gls
Lincoln C	Glasgow Rangers	11/52	52	11	-	2
Workington	Tr	07/53	53	38	-	5

JOHNSON Josh Thor
Born: Carenage, Trinidad, 16 April, 1981 — W
Trinidad & Tobago: U23-1

League Club	Source	Date Signed	Seasons Played	Apps	Subs	Gls
Wrexham	San Juan Jab'h (TRD)	08/06	06-07	10	19	1

JOHNSON Kenneth (Ken)
Born: Hartlepool, Cleveland, England, 15 February, 1931 — IF/WH
Died: Hartlepool, Cleveland, England, 29 December, 2011

League Club	Source	Date Signed	Seasons Played	Apps	Subs	Gls
Hartlepool U	Seaton Holy Trinity	05/49	49-63	384	-	98

JOHNSON Kevin Peter
Born: Doncaster, South Yorkshire, England, 29 August, 1952 — LM

League Club	Source	Date Signed	Seasons Played	Apps	Subs	Gls
Sheffield Wed	App	07/70	71	0	1	0
Southend U	Tr	09/72	72-73	12	4	1
Gillingham	L	02/74	73	1	0	0
Workington	Tr	07/74	74	15	0	1
Hartlepool U	Tr	02/75	74-76	60	1	8
Huddersfield T	Tr	09/76	76-77	80	1	23
Halifax T	Tr	08/78	78-80	51	6	10
Hartlepool U	Tr	01/81	80-83	74	13	3

JOHNSON Lee David
Born: Newmarket, Suffolk, England, 7 June, 1981 — M
England: Semi Pro-5

League Club	Source	Date Signed	Seasons Played	Apps	Subs	Gls
Watford	YT	10/98				
Brighton & HA	Tr	09/00				
Yeovil T	Brentford (NC)	07/01	03-05	115	0	14
Bristol C	Heart of Midlothian	08/06	06-10	155	19	11
Derby Co	L	01/10	09	4	0	0
Chesterfield	L	08/11	11	11	0	0

JOHNSON Leon Dean
Born: Shoreditch, Central London, England, 10 May, 1981 — CD
Grenada: 5

League Club	Source	Date Signed	Seasons Played	Apps	Subs	Gls
Southend U	YT	11/99	00-01	43	5	3
Gillingham	Tr	08/02	02-06	80	18	2
Wycombe W	Tr	07/07	07-13	172	7	4

JOHNSON Lloyd Glenn (Glenn)
Born: Vancouver, Canada, 22 April, 1951 — F
Canada: 9

League Club	Source	Date Signed	Seasons Played	Apps	Subs	Gls
West Bromwich A	Vancouver Sp'ans (CAN)	10/69	70-71	2	2	0

JOHNSON Marvin Anthony
Born: Wembley, NW London, England, 29 October, 1968 — CD

League Club	Source	Date Signed	Seasons Played	Apps	Subs	Gls
Luton T	App	11/86	87-01	352	21	7

JOHNSON Michael (Mick)
Born: York, England, 4 October, 1933 — LW
Died: Wollongong, NSW, Australia, 19 July, 2004

League Club	Source	Date Signed	Seasons Played	Apps	Subs	Gls
Newcastle U	Jnr	04/51				
Brighton & HA	Blyth Spartans	12/55	56	2	-	0
Fulham	Gloucester C	08/58	58-61	23	-	6
Doncaster Rov	Tr	07/62	62	15	-	2
Barrow	Tr	03/63	62	12	-	2

JOHNSON Michael
Born: Urmston, Greater Manchester, England, 3 March, 1988 — M
England: U21-2/Youth

League Club	Source	Date Signed	Seasons Played	Apps	Subs	Gls
Manchester C	Sch	01/06	06-09	36	1	2
Leicester C	L	07/11	11	3	4	0

JOHNSON Michael George (Mike)
Born: Swansea, Wales, 13 October, 1941 — CH
Died: Newport, Wales, October, 1991
Wales: 1/U23-2

League Club	Source	Date Signed	Seasons Played	Apps	Subs	Gls
Swansea C	Jnr	10/58	59-65	165	0	0

JOHNSON Michael James (Mike)
Born: Oxford, England, 24 February, 1928 — IF
Died: Blackpool, Lancashire, England, December, 2006

League Club	Source	Date Signed	Seasons Played	Apps	Subs	Gls
Preston NE	Lytham St Annes	09/50				
Accrington Stan	Tr	06/51	51	3	-	0

JOHNSON Michael Owen
Born: Nottingham, England, 4 July, 1973 — CD
Jamaica: 12

League Club	Source	Date Signed	Seasons Played	Apps	Subs	Gls
Notts Co	YT	07/91	91-94	102	5	0
Birmingham C	Tr	09/95	95-02	227	35	13
Derby Co	Tr	08/03	03-07	127	11	4
Sheffield Wed	L	09/07	07	13	0	0
Notts Co	Tr	02/08	07-08	40	1	3

JOHNSON Neil Joseph
Born: Grimsby, North Lincolnshire, England, 3 December, 1946 — RW

League Club	Source	Date Signed	Seasons Played	Apps	Subs	Gls
Tottenham H	App	06/64	65-70	27	7	5
Charlton Ath	L	02/71	70	1	0	0
Torquay U	Tr	07/71	71	5	1	1

JOHNSON Nigel Meridon
Born: Rotherham, South Yorkshire, England, 23 June, 1964 — CD

League Club	Source	Date Signed	Seasons Played	Apps	Subs	Gls
Rotherham U	App	08/82	82-84	89	0	1
Manchester C	Tr	06/85	85	4	0	0
Rotherham U	Tr	07/87	87-92	172	3	9

JOHNSON Oliver Tobias (Oli)
Born: Wakefield, England, 6 November, 1987 — F

League Club	Source	Date Signed	Seasons Played	Apps	Subs	Gls
Stockport Co	Nostell MW	10/08	08-09	13	27	7
Norwich C	Tr	01/10	09-10	4	17	4
Yeovil T	L	01/11	10	16	1	3
Yeovil T	L	09/11	11	5	1	0
Oxford U	Tr	01/12	11	8	9	3
York C	Tr	07/12	12	0	4	0

JOHNSON Owen Edmund
Born: Grimsby, North Lincolnshire, England, 13 November, 1919 — LW
Died: Salt Lake City, Utah, USA, 6 August, 2001

League Club	Source	Date Signed	Seasons Played	Apps	Subs	Gls
Derby Co	Stoke C (Am)	11/37				
Bradford C	Tr	10/46	46	10	-	1

JOHNSON Paul
Born: Scunthorpe, North Lincolnshire, England, 10 May, 1963 — G

League Club	Source	Date Signed	Seasons Played	Apps	Subs	Gls
Scunthorpe U	App	05/81	81	2	0	0
Scunthorpe U		01/85	85	12	0	0

JOHNSON Paul
Born: Stoke-on-Trent, England, 25 May, 1959 — LB

League Club	Source	Date Signed	Seasons Played	Apps	Subs	Gls
Stoke C	App	05/77	78-80	33	1	0
Shrewsbury T	Tr	05/81	81-86	178	2	3
York C	Tr	07/87	87-88	83	0	1

JOHNSON Paul Anthony
Born: Stoke-on-Trent, England, 19 September, 1955 — M

League Club	Source	Date Signed	Seasons Played	Apps	Subs	Gls
Stoke C	App	06/73	76-81	51	5	0
Chester C	Tr	08/82	82	18	1	0

JOHNSON Paul Anthony
Born: Sunderland, England, 5 April, 1992 — CD

League Club	Source	Date Signed	Seasons Played	Apps	Subs	Gls
Hartlepool U	Sch	07/10	10	1	0	0

JOHNSON Peter
Born: Rotherham, South Yorkshire, England, 31 July, 1931 — RB
Died: Rotherham, South Yorkshire, England, March, 2009

League Club	Source	Date Signed	Seasons Played	Apps	Subs	Gls
Rotherham U	Rawmarsh Welfare	03/53	53-57	153	-	23
Sheffield Wed	Tr	12/57	57-64	181	-	6
Peterborough U	Tr	07/65	65-66	42	0	1

JOHNSON Peter Edward
Born: Harrogate, North Yorkshire, England, 5 October, 1958 — LB

League Club	Source	Date Signed	Seasons Played	Apps	Subs	Gls
Middlesbrough	App	10/76	77-79	42	1	0
Newcastle U	Tr	10/80	80	16	0	0
Bristol C	L	09/82	82	20	0	0
Doncaster Rov	Tr	03/83	82	12	0	0
Darlington	Tr	08/83	83-84	89	0	2
Crewe Alex	Whitby T	10/85	85	8	0	0
Exeter C	Whitby T	03/86	85	5	0	0
Southend U	Tr	08/86	86-88	126	0	3
Gillingham	Tr	08/89	89-90	67	2	2
Peterborough U	Airdrieonians	10/91	91	11	0	0

JOHNSON Peter James
Born: Hackney, E London, England, 18 February, 1954 — W

League Club	Source	Date Signed	Seasons Played	Apps	Subs	Gls
Leyton Orient	Tottenham H (Am)	04/72	71-72	1	2	0
Crystal Palace	AEK Athens (GRE)	10/74	74-75	5	2	0
Bournemouth	Tr	06/76	76-78	99	8	11

JOHNSON Reda
Born: Marseille, France, 21 March, 1988 — LB
Benin: 10

League Club	Source	Date Signed	Seasons Played	Apps	Subs	Gls
Plymouth Arg	Amiens SC (FRA)	07/09	09-10	38	4	2
Sheffield Wed	Tr	01/11	10-13	70	5	18
Coventry C	Tr	07/14	14	20	0	5

JOHNSON Richard Mark
Born: Kurri Kurri, NSW, Australia, 27 April, 1974 — M
Australia: 1

League Club	Source	Date Signed	Seasons Played	Apps	Subs	Gls
Watford	YT	05/92	91-02	210	32	20
Northampton T	L	02/03	02	5	1	1
Stoke C	Tr	11/03	03	3	4	0
Queens Park Rgrs	Tr	02/04	03-04	16	1	0
MK Dons	L	10/04	04	2	0	0

JOHNSON Richard Raymond (Dickie)
Born: Liverpool, England, 20 February, 1953 — G

League Club	Source	Date Signed	Seasons Played	Apps	Subs	Gls
Tranmere Rov	Jnr	08/72	71-81	355	0	0

JOHNSON Robert Emmerson Oliver (Bob)
Born: Fencehouses, County Durham, England, 25 October, 1911 — CH
Died: Burnley, Lancashire, England, 5 March, 1982

League Club	Source	Date Signed	Seasons Played	Apps	Subs	Gls
Burnley	Bishop Auckland	09/34	34-48	78	-	0

JOHNSON Robert Nicholas (Robbie)
Born: Kensington, Central London, England, 30 March, 1962 — FB

League Club	Source	Date Signed	Seasons Played	Apps	Subs	Gls
Arsenal	App	02/80				
Brentford	Tr	03/81	80-81	2	0	0

JOHNSON Robert Simon (Rob)
Born: Bedford, England, 22 February, 1962 — FB

League Club	Source	Date Signed	Seasons Played	Apps	Subs	Gls
Luton T	App	08/79	83-88	91	6	0
Lincoln C	L	08/83	83	4	0	0
Leicester C	Tr	08/89	89-90	19	6	0
Barnet	Tr	08/91	91	2	0	0

JOHNSON Rodney (Rod)
Born: Leeds, England, 8 January, 1945 — M/F
England: Youth

League Club	Source	Date Signed	Seasons Played	Apps	Subs	Gls
Leeds U	Jnr	03/62	62-67	18	4	4
Doncaster Rov	Tr	03/68	67-70	106	1	23
Rotherham U	Tr	12/70	70-73	108	2	8
Bradford C	Tr	12/73	73-78	190	2	16

JOHNSON Roger
Born: Ashford, Surrey, England, 28 April, 1983 — CD

League Club	Source	Date Signed	Seasons Played	Apps	Subs	Gls
Wycombe W	YT	07/01	99-05	146	11	19
Cardiff C	Tr	07/06	06-08	112	7	12
Birmingham C	Tr	07/09	09-10	76	0	2
Wolverhampton W	Tr	07/11	11-12	68	1	2
Sheffield Wed	L	09/13	13	17	0	0
West Ham U	L	01/14	13	2	2	0
Charlton Ath	Tr	02/15	14	14	0	0

JOHNSON Ross Yorke
Born: Brighton, England, 2 February, 1976 — CD

League Club	Source	Date Signed	Seasons Played	Apps	Subs	Gls
Brighton & HA	YT	07/94	93-99	113	19	2
Colchester U	Tr	01/00	99-01	47	5	1

JOHNSON Roy
Born: Swindon, England, 18 May, 1933 — CF
Died: Bath, England, December, 2004

League Club	Source	Date Signed	Seasons Played	Apps	Subs	Gls
Swindon T	Chippenham U	04/52	52-55	31	-	4

JOHNSON Ryan
Born: Birmingham, England, 2 October, 1996 — LB

League Club	Source	Date Signed	Seasons Played	Apps	Subs	Gls
Stevenage	Sch	07/14	13-14	1	4	0

JOHNSON Samuel (Sam)
Born: Barnton, Cheshire, England, 10 February, 1919 — RB
Died: Goostrey, Cheshire, England, 15 November, 1994

League Club	Source	Date Signed	Seasons Played	Apps	Subs	Gls
Hull C	Northwich Victoria	04/47	46-47	10	-	0

JOHNSON Samuel William (Sam)
Born: Newcastle-under-Lyme, Potteries, England, 1 December, 1992 — G

League Club	Source	Date Signed	Seasons Played	Apps	Subs	Gls
Port Vale	Sch	06/11	13-14	21	2	0

JOHNSON Seth Art Maurice
Born: Birmingham, England, 12 March, 1979 — M
England: 1/U21-15/Youth

League Club	Source	Date Signed	Seasons Played	Apps	Subs	Gls
Crewe Alex	YT	07/96	96-98	89	4	6
Derby Co	Tr	05/99	99-01	73	0	2
Leeds U	Tr	10/01	01-04	43	11	4
Derby Co	Tr	08/05	05-06	47	10	4

JOHNSON Simon Ainsley
Born: West Bromwich, West Midlands, England, 9 March, 1983 — F
England: Youth

League Club	Source	Date Signed	Seasons Played	Apps	Subs	Gls
Leeds U	YT	07/00	02-04	3	8	0
Hull C	L	08/02	02	4	8	2
Blackpool	L	12/03	03	3	1	1
Sunderland	L	09/04	04	1	4	0
Doncaster Rov	L	12/04	04	8	3	3
Barnsley	L	02/05	04	10	1	2
Darlington	Tr	07/05	05-06	43	23	9
Hereford U	Tr	07/07	07-08	30	32	5
Bury	Tr	08/09	09	1	3	0

JOHNSON Stephen Anthony (Steve)
Born: Liverpool, England, 23 June, 1957 — F

League Club	Source	Date Signed	Seasons Played	Apps	Subs	Gls
Bury	Altrincham	11/77	77-82	139	15	52
Rochdale	Tr	08/83	83	17	2	7
Wigan Ath	Tr	02/84	83-84	50	1	18
Bristol C	Tr	03/85	84-85	14	7	3
Rochdale	L	12/85	85	3	3	1
Chester C	L	03/86	85	10	0	6
Scunthorpe U	Tr	07/86	86-87	59	13	20
Chester C	Tr	08/88	88	35	3	10
Rochdale	Husqvarna (SWE)	10/89	89	20	4	4

JOHNSON Steven (Steve)
Born: Nottingham, England, 23 March, 1961 — LB

League Club	Source	Date Signed	Seasons Played	Apps	Subs	Gls
Mansfield T	App	03/79	80	1	0	0

JOHNSON Terence (Terry)
Born: Newcastle-upon-Tyne, England, 30 August, 1949 — W/M

League Club	Source	Date Signed	Seasons Played	Apps	Subs	Gls
Newcastle U	Longbenton Jnrs	05/67				
Darlington	L	11/69	69	4	0	1
Southend U	Tr	01/71	70-74	156	2	35
Brentford	Tr	11/74	74-76	98	3	27

JOHNSON Thomas (Tom)
Born: Ecclesfield, South Yorkshire, England, 4 May, 1911 — CH
Died: Sheffield, England, 19 August, 1983

League Club	Source	Date Signed	Seasons Played	Apps	Subs	Gls
Sheffield U	Ecclesfield U	09/28	29-38	183	-	0
Lincoln C	Tr	03/46	46-48	75	-	0

JOHNSON Thomas (Tommy)
Born: Newcastle-upon-Tyne, England, 15 January, 1971 — F
England: U21-7

League Club	Source	Date Signed	Seasons Played	Apps	Subs	Gls
Notts Co	YT	01/89	88-91	100	18	47
Derby Co	Tr	03/92	91-94	91	7	30
Aston Villa	Tr	01/95	94-96	38	19	13
Everton (L)	Glasgow Celtic	09/99	99	0	3	0
Sheffield Wed	Glasgow Celtic	09/01	01	8	0	3
Gillingham	Kilmarnock	08/02	02-04	20	29	7
Sheffield U	Tr	02/05	04	1	0	0
Scunthorpe U	Tr	07/05	05	3	11	1

JOHNSON Thomas (Tom)
Born: Stockton-on-Tees, Cleveland, England, 5 March, 1926 — LH

League Club	Source	Date Signed	Seasons Played	Apps	Subs	Gls
Middlesbrough	Seaton Holy Trinity	01/45				
Darlington	Tr	08/47	47	6	-	1
Bradford Park Ave	Horden CW	08/52	52	1	-	0

JOHNSON Thomas (Tucker)
Born: Gateshead, Tyne and Wear, England, 21 September, 1921 — IF
Died: Poole, Dorset, England, 8 March, 1999

League Club	Source	Date Signed	Seasons Played	Apps	Subs	Gls
Gateshead		09/41	46-47	52	-	19
Nottingham F	Tr	08/48	48-51	68	-	27

JOHNSON Victor Ralph (Ralph)
Born: Hethersett, Norfolk, England, 15 April, 1922 — CF
Died: Norwich, England, 23 April, 2013

League Club	Source	Date Signed	Seasons Played	Apps	Subs	Gls
Norwich C	Chesterfield (Am)	05/46	46	18	-	8
Leyton Orient	Tr	04/47	47-48	7	-	2

JOHNSON William Herbert (Bert)
Born: Stockton-on-Tees, Cleveland, England, 4 June, 1916 — LH
Died: Kent, England, 30 June, 2009
England: War-2

League Club	Source	Date Signed	Seasons Played	Apps	Subs	Gls
Charlton Ath	Spennymoor U	03/39	46-52	142	-	1

JOHNSSON Julian Schantz
Born: Torshavn, Faroe Islands, 24 February, 1975 — M
Faroe Islands: 62

League Club	Source	Date Signed	Seasons Played	Apps	Subs	Gls
Hull C	Sogndal IF (NOR)	06/01	01	38	2	4

JOHNSTON Alan Keith
Born: Workington, Cumbria, England, 23 September, 1944 — RB

League Club	Source	Date Signed	Seasons Played	Apps	Subs	Gls
Blackpool	Jnr	10/61				
Workington	Tr	07/62	62-64	65	-	0

JOHNSTON Allan
Born: Glasgow, Scotland, 14 December, 1973 — LW
Scotland: 18/B-2/U21-3

League Club	Source	Date Signed	Seasons Played	Apps	Subs	Gls
Sunderland	Stade Rennais (FRA)	03/97	96-98	82	4	19
Birmingham C	L	10/99	99	7	2	0
Bolton W	Tr	01/00	99	17	2	3
Middlesbrough	Glasgow Rangers	09/01	01	13	4	1
Sheffield Wed	L	12/02	02	12	0	2

JOHNSTON Christopher Patrick (Pat)
Born: Dublin, Republic of Ireland, 16 July, 1924 — LH
Died: Grimsby, North Lincolnshire, England, 25 May, 1971
Republic of Ireland: LoI-3

League Club	Source	Date Signed	Seasons Played	Apps	Subs	Gls
Middlesbrough	Shelbourne (ROI)	12/47	47-48	3	-	0
Grimsby T	Tr	02/49	48-56	250	-	16

JOHNSTON Clement (Clem)
Born: Stoneyburn, West Lothian, Scotland, 3 September, 1933 — IF
Died: Melrose, Borders, Scotland, 13 February, 2012

League Club	Source	Date Signed	Seasons Played	Apps	Subs	Gls
Walsall	Haddington Ath	08/56	56	7	-	0

JOHNSTON Craig Peter
Born: Johannesburg, South Africa, 25 June, 1960 — M/F
England: B-1/U21-2

League Club	Source	Date Signed	Seasons Played	Apps	Subs	Gls
Middlesbrough	App	02/78	77-80	61	3	16
Liverpool	Tr	04/81	81-87	165	25	30

JOHNSTON David Douglas
Born: Scothern, Lincolnshire, England, 17 September, 1941 — FB

League Club	Source	Date Signed	Seasons Played	Apps	Subs	Gls
Leicester C	Bishop Auckland	02/60				
Exeter C	Tr	05/62	62	10	-	0
Stockport Co	Tr	07/63	63	26	-	0
Tranmere Rov	Tr	05/64				

JOHNSTON George
Born: Glasgow, Scotland, 21 March, 1947 — F

League Club	Source	Date Signed	Seasons Played	Apps	Subs	Gls
Cardiff C	Maryhill Harp	05/64	64-66	57	2	20
Arsenal	Tr	03/67	67-68	17	4	3
Birmingham C	Tr	05/69	69	6	3	1
Walsall	L	09/70	70	5	0	1
Fulham	Tr	10/70	70-71	33	6	12
Hereford U	Tr	08/72	72	15	3	5
Newport Co	Tr	09/73	73	2	1	0

JOHNSTON Henry (Harry)
Born: Manchester, England, 26 September, 1919 — RH/CH
Died: Blackpool, Lancashire, England, 12 October, 1973
England: 10/FLge-4

League Club	Source	Date Signed	Seasons Played	Apps	Subs	Gls
Blackpool	Droylsden Ath	10/36	37-54	387	-	11

JOHNSTON Ian
Born: Workington, Cumbria, England, 19 September, 1957 — CD

League Club	Source	Date Signed	Seasons Played	Apps	Subs	Gls
Workington	Jnr	08/75	74-76	46	2	0

JOHNSTON James Cruickshank (Jimmy)
Born: Aberdeen, Scotland, 12 April, 1923 — LH
Died: North Berwick, East Lothian, Scotland, 16 September, 2007

League Club	Source	Date Signed	Seasons Played	Apps	Subs	Gls
Leicester C	Peterhead	04/47	48-49	35	-	0
Reading	Tr	05/50	50-52	120	-	0
Swindon T	Tr	03/53	52-54	75	-	0

JOHNSTON John (Johnny)
Born: Belfast, Northern Ireland, 2 May, 1947 — M
Northern Ireland: U23-1

League Club	Source	Date Signed	Seasons Played	Apps	Subs	Gls
Blackpool	Glentoran	11/68	68-71	19	6	2
Halifax T	L	10/71	71	3	1	1
Bradford C	Tr	07/72	72-73	55	4	4
Southport	Tr	07/74	74-75	82	0	6
Halifax T	Tr	07/76	76-78	67	6	7

JOHNSTON Leslie Hamilton (Les)
Born: Glasgow, Scotland, 16 August, 1920 — IF
Died: Newcastle-under-Lyme, Potteries, England, 19 October, 2001
Scotland: 2

League Club	Source	Date Signed	Seasons Played	Apps	Subs	Gls
Stoke C	Glasgow Celtic	10/49	49-52	88	-	22
Shrewsbury T	Tr	07/53	53	16	-	6

JOHNSTON Maurice John Giblin (Mo)
Born: Glasgow, Scotland, 30 April, 1963 — F
Scotland: 38/U21-3

League Club	Source	Date Signed	Seasons Played	Apps	Subs	Gls
Watford	Partick Thistle	11/83	83-84	37	1	23
Everton	Glasgow Rangers	11/91	91-92	28	6	10

JOHNSTON Raymond (Ray)
Born: Thornbury, Avon, England, 5 May, 1981 — G
England: Schools

League Club	Source	Date Signed	Seasons Played	Apps	Subs	Gls
Bristol Rov	YT	06/99	98	1	0	0

JOHNSTON Robert
Born: Carlisle, Cumbria, England, 28 January, 1933 — WH

League Club	Source	Date Signed	Seasons Played	Apps	Subs	Gls
Carlisle U	Jnr	11/51	51-59	119	-	1

JOHNSTON Ronald (Ron)
Born: Glasgow, Scotland, 3 April, 1921 — CF
Died: Keighley, West Yorkshire, England, March, 1995

League Club	Source	Date Signed	Seasons Played	Apps	Subs	Gls
Rochdale	Glasgow Perthshire	11/47	47	17	-	7
Exeter C	Tr	06/48	48	10	-	2
Brighton & HA	Headington U	11/50	50	1	-	0

JOHNSTON Stanley (Stan)
Born: Wallsend, Tyne and Wear, England, 23 February, 1934 — IF

League Club	Source	Date Signed	Seasons Played	Apps	Subs	Gls
Fulham	Jnr	08/51				
Gateshead	Durham C	09/54	54	8	-	1

JOHNSTON Thomas Bourhill (Tommy)
Born: Loanhead, Midlothian, Scotland, 18 August, 1927 — CF
Died: New South Wales, Australia, 4 September, 2008

League Club	Source	Date Signed	Seasons Played	Apps	Subs	Gls
Darlington	Kilmarnock	04/51	51	27	-	9
Oldham Ath	Tr	03/52	51	5	-	3
Norwich C	Tr	06/52	52-54	60	-	28
Newport Co	Tr	10/54	54-55	63	-	46
Leyton Orient	Tr	02/56	55-57	87	-	70
Blackburn Rov	Tr	03/58	57-58	36	-	22
Leyton Orient	Tr	02/59	58-60	93	-	51
Gillingham	Tr	09/61	61	35	-	10

JOHNSTON Thomas Deans (Tom)
Born: Coldstream, Borders, Scotland, 30 December, 1918 — LW/LH
Died: Nottingham, England, 27 November, 1994

League Club	Source	Date Signed	Seasons Played	Apps	Subs	Gls
Nottingham F	Peterborough U	05/44	46-47	64	-	26
Notts Co	Tr	08/48	48-56	267	-	88

JOHNSTON William (Billy)
Born: United Kingdom — G

League Club	Source	Date Signed	Seasons Played	Apps	Subs	Gls
Barrow	Greenock Morton	04/47	46	1	-	0

JOHNSTON William Cecil (Billy)
Born: Coalisland, Tyrone, Northern Ireland, 21 May, 1942 — M
Northern Ireland: 2/NILge-7

League Club	Source	Date Signed	Seasons Played	Apps	Subs	Gls
Oldham Ath	Glenavon	06/66	66-68	28	1	6

JOHNSTON William James (Willie)
Born: Sunderland, England, 3 September, 1948 — F

League Club	Source	Date Signed	Seasons Played	Apps	Subs	Gls
Northampton T	Durham C	07/67	67	0	1	0

League Club	Source	Date Signed	Seasons Played	Apps	Subs	Gls
JOHNSTON William McClure (Willie)						
Born: Glasgow, Scotland, 19 December, 1946						W
Scotland: 22/SLge-2/U23-2						
West Bromwich A	Glasgow Rangers	12/72	72-78	203	4	18
Birmingham C	Vancouver W'caps (CAN)	10/79	79	15	0	0
JOHNSTONE Cyril						
Born: Hamilton, Lanarkshire, Scotland, 21 December, 1920						FB
Died: Hamilton, Lanarkshire, Scotland, 5 May, 1978						
Exeter C	Hamilton Academical	07/47	47-50	134	-	0
JOHNSTONE Denny						
Born: Dumfries, Scotland, 9 January, 1995						F
Scotland: Youth						
Birmingham C	Glasgow Celtic (Jnr)	08/14	14	0	2	0
Cheltenham T	L	02/15	14	4	1	1
Burton A	L	03/15	14	2	3	1
JOHNSTONE Derek Joseph						
Born: Dundee, Scotland, 4 November, 1953						F
Scotland: 14/SLge-2/U23-6						
Chelsea	Glasgow Rangers	09/83	83-84	1	3	0
JOHNSTONE Eric						
Born: Newcastle-upon-Tyne, England, 22 March, 1943						LW
Carlisle U	Tow Law T	06/63	63-64	15	-	3
Darlington	Tr	07/65	65-66	26	1	9
JOHNSTONE Glenn Paul						
Born: Kenya, 5 June, 1967						G
Preston NE	Lancaster C	01/93	92	10	0	0
JOHNSTONE Ian Donaldson						
Born: Galashiels, Borders, Scotland, 2 March, 1939						IF
Died: Suffolk, England, 7 November, 1993						
Colchester U	Ormiston Primrose	06/58	58-59	2	-	0
JOHNSTONE James Connelly (Jimmy)						
Born: Uddingston, Glasgow, Scotland, 30 September, 1944						W
Died: Uddingston, Lanarkshire, Scotland, 13 March, 2006						
Scotland: 23/SLge-4/U23-2						
Sheffield U	Glasgow Celtic	11/75	75-76	11	0	2
JOHNSTONE Robert (Bobby)						
Born: Selkirk, Borders, Scotland, 7 September, 1929						IF
Died: Selkirk, Borders, Scotland, 22 August, 2001						
Scotland: 17/SLge-6						
Manchester C	Hibernian	03/55	54-59	124	-	42
Oldham Ath	Hibernian	10/60	60-64	143	-	35
JOHNSTONE Robert Gordon (Bobby)						
Born: Edinburgh, Scotland, 19 November, 1934						LH
West Ham U	Ormiston Primrose	04/53	56	2	-	0
Ipswich T	Tr	07/57	57-58	35	-	4
JOHNSTONE Robert Rutherford						
Born: Cleland, Lanarkshire, Scotland, 13 September, 1918						FB
Died: Chester, England, 13 May, 2007						
Tranmere Rov	Raith Rov	09/46	46-47	40	-	0
JOHNSTONE Samuel Luke (Sam)						
Born: Preston, Lancashire, England, 25 March, 1993						G
England: Youth						
Manchester U	Sch	04/10				
Scunthorpe U	L	09/11	11	12	0	0
Walsall	L	03/13	12	7	0	0
Yeovil T	L	08/13	13	1	0	0
Doncaster Rov	L	01/14	13	18	0	0
Doncaster Rov	L	10/14	14	10	0	0
Preston NE	L	01/15	14	22	0	0
JOHNSTONE Stanley (Stan)						
Born: Shiremoor, Tyne and Wear, England, 28 October, 1940						LW
Died: Chester-le-Street, County Durham, England, 13 June, 2007						
Gateshead	Durham C	12/58	58	5	-	1
JOICEY Brian						
Born: Winlaton, Tyne and Wear, England, 19 December, 1945						F
Coventry C	North Shields	06/69	69-71	31	8	9
Sheffield Wed	Tr	08/71	71-75	144	1	48
Barnsley	Tr	07/76	76-78	77	16	43
JOKANOVIC Slavisa						
Born: Novi Sad, Yugoslavia, 16 August, 1968						DM
Yugoslavia: 64						
Chelsea	Depo la Coruna (SPN)	10/00	00-01	19	20	0
JOL Maarten Cornelius (Martin)						
Born: Den Haag, Netherlands, 16 January, 1956						DM
Netherlands: 3						

League Club	Source	Date Signed	Seasons Played	Apps	Subs	Gls
West Bromwich A	Twente Enschede (NED)	10/81	81-83	63	1	4
Coventry C	Tr	07/84	84	15	0	0
JOLLEY Charles (Charlie)						
Born: Bebington, Wirral, England, 3 March, 1936						CF
England: Youth						
Tranmere Rov	Liverpool (Am)	07/53	53-54	6	-	2
Chester C	Tr	05/55	55	7	-	3
JOLLEY Christian Anthony Hillard						
Born: Fleet, Hampshire, England, 12 May, 1988						F
AFC Wimbledon	Kingstonian	05/10	11-12	29	23	7
Newport Co	Tr	11/12	13-14	20	17	2
JOLLEY Terence Arthur (Terry)						
Born: Greenhithe, Kent, England, 13 April, 1959						F
Gillingham	Jnr	11/76	76-79	14	7	5
JOMBATI Sido Coelho						
Born: Lisbon, Portugal, 20 August, 1987						FB
Cheltenham T	Bath C	07/11	11-13	108	8	4
Wycombe W	Tr	05/14	14	35	0	0
JONES Alan						
Born: Grimethorpe, South Yorkshire, England, 21 January, 1951						RW/RB
Huddersfield T	App	12/68	70-72	30	2	0
Halifax T	Tr	08/73	73-76	109	0	6
Chesterfield	Tr	09/76	76-77	39	0	6
Lincoln C	Tr	11/77	77-78	24	2	4
Bradford C	Columbus Magic (USA)	09/79	79	16	3	1
Rochdale	Tr	08/80	80	40	4	5
JONES Alan						
Born: Caergwrle, Flintshire, Wales, 13 January, 1944						RW
Wrexham	Johnstown	07/64	64	2	-	0
JONES Alan Hugh						
Born: Wrexham, Wales, 22 September, 1949						CH
Wales: Schools						
Shrewsbury T	App	05/67	68	3	0	0
JONES Alan Michael						
Born: Swansea, Wales, 6 October, 1945						CD
Swansea C	App	10/63	64-67	61	0	6
Hereford U	Tr	07/68	72-73	52	1	2
Southport	Tr	08/74	74-75	49	0	2
JONES Alan William Edward						
Born: Edmonton, N London, England, 19 November, 1940						CF
Fulham	Jnr	04/58	59	7	-	3
JONES Alexander (Alex)						
Born: Blackburn, Greater Manchester, England, 27 November, 1964						CD
Oldham Ath	App	12/82	82-84	8	1	0
Stockport Co	L	10/84	84	3	0	0
Preston NE	Tr	06/86	86-89	100	1	3
Carlisle U	Tr	09/89	89-90	62	0	4
Rochdale	Tr	06/91	91	12	1	0
Rochdale	Motherwell	10/92	92-93	31	2	2
JONES Alfred (Alf)						
Born: Liverpool, England, 2 March, 1937						RB
Leeds U	Marine	04/60	60-61	25	-	0
Lincoln C	Tr	06/62	62-66	179	1	3
JONES Allan Powell						
Born: Flint, Wales, 6 January, 1940						FB
Died: Ealing, W London, England, September, 1993						
Wales: Schools						
Liverpool	Jnr	05/57	59-62	5	-	0
Brentford	Tr	08/63	63-69	244	4	3
JONES Allan Raymond						
Born: Burton-on-Trent, Staffordshire, England, 3 November, 1941						LW
Aston Villa	Jnr	11/58	61	1	-	0
JONES Andrai Ricardo						
Born: Liverpool, England, 1 January, 1992						RB
Bury	Sch	07/10	10-12	17	5	0
Barnsley	Tr	02/13	12	1	1	0
Tranmere Rov	L	08/13	13	1	1	0
JONES Andrew Mark (Andy)						
Born: Wrexham, Wales, 9 January, 1963						F
Wales: 6						
Port Vale	Rhyl	06/85	85-87	87	3	47
Charlton Ath	Tr	09/87	87-90	51	15	15
Port Vale	L	02/89	88	8	9	3
Bristol C	L	11/89	89	2	2	1
Bournemouth	Tr	10/90	90-91	36	4	8
Leyton Orient	Tr	10/91	91-92	44	15	13

JONES Andrew Stuart (Andy)
Born: Sutton-in-Ashfield, Nottinghamshire, England, 12 February, 1986 — M

League Club	Source	Date Signed	Seasons Played	Apps	Subs	Gls
Mansfield T	Sch	-	02	0	1	0

JONES Anthony Peter (Tony)
Born: Birmingham, England, 12 November, 1937 — IF/WH
Died: Lichfield, Staffordshire, England, April, 1990

League Club	Source	Date Signed	Seasons Played	Apps	Subs	Gls
Oxford U	Birmingham C (Am)	09/59	62-67	226	0	42
Newport Co	Tr	11/67	67-68	53	1	9

JONES Arthur
Born: Manchester, England, 23 April, 1920 — W
Died: Manchester, England, 8 September, 2001

League Club	Source	Date Signed	Seasons Played	Apps	Subs	Gls
Rochdale	Goslings	06/45	46	1	-	0

JONES Ashlee Ageron
Born: Walthamstow, NE London, England, 4 August, 1987 — G

League Club	Source	Date Signed	Seasons Played	Apps	Subs	Gls
Darlington	Kingstonian	10/09	09	1	0	0

JONES Barrie
Born: Barnsley, South Yorkshire, England, 31 October, 1938 — CF
Died: Sutton-in-Ashfield, Nottinghamshire, England, 23 November, 2013

League Club	Source	Date Signed	Seasons Played	Apps	Subs	Gls
Notts Co	Army	09/61	61-63	42	-	15

JONES Barrie Spencer
Born: Swansea, Wales, 10 October, 1941 — RW
Wales: 15/U23-8

League Club	Source	Date Signed	Seasons Played	Apps	Subs	Gls
Swansea C	Jnr	04/59	59-64	166	-	23
Plymouth Arg	Tr	09/64	64-66	98	0	9
Cardiff C	Tr	03/67	66-69	107	0	19

JONES Barry
Born: Prescot, Merseyside, England, 30 June, 1970 — D

League Club	Source	Date Signed	Seasons Played	Apps	Subs	Gls
Liverpool	Prescot Cables	01/89				
Wrexham	Tr	07/92	92-97	184	11	5
York C	Tr	12/97	97-00	130	4	5

JONES Benjamin (Ben)
Born: Connah's Quay, Flintshire, Wales, 11 September, 1992 — F

League Club	Source	Date Signed	Seasons Played	Apps	Subs	Gls
Chester C	Sch	-	08	2	13	0

JONES Benjamin James (Jimmy)
Born: Tonypandy, Rhondda Cynon Taff, Wales, 16 November, 1919 — LB
Died: Watford, Hertfordshire, England, 1976
Wales: Amateur

League Club	Source	Date Signed	Seasons Played	Apps	Subs	Gls
Watford	Slough T	09/47	47-53	158	-	0

JONES Bernard
Born: Coventry, England, 10 April, 1934 — IF

League Club	Source	Date Signed	Seasons Played	Apps	Subs	Gls
Northampton T	GEC Coventry Works	10/52	53-55	43	-	16
Cardiff C	Tr	03/56	55-56	9	-	0
Shrewsbury T	Tr	07/57	57-58	43	-	15

JONES Bernard
Born: Stoke-on-Trent, England, 29 September, 1924 — W
Died: Stafford, England, 23 May, 2000

League Club	Source	Date Signed	Seasons Played	Apps	Subs	Gls
Port Vale	Longport	10/48	48	6	-	0

JONES Bradley (Brad)
Born: Perth, Australia, 19 March, 1982 — G
Australia: 4/U23-6/Youth

League Club	Source	Date Signed	Seasons Played	Apps	Subs	Gls
Middlesbrough	YT	03/99	03-09	57	0	0
Stockport Co	L	12/02	02	1	0	0
Blackpool	L	11/03	03	5	0	0
Blackpool	L	11/04	04	12	0	0
Sheffield Wed	L	08/06	06	15	0	0
Liverpool	Tr	08/10	11-14	10	1	0
Derby Co	L	03/11	10	7	0	0

JONES Brian
Born: Doncaster, South Yorkshire, England, 5 September, 1933 — FB

League Club	Source	Date Signed	Seasons Played	Apps	Subs	Gls
Walsall		11/53	53	2	-	0

JONES Brian (Bryn)
Born: Barnsley, South Yorkshire, England, 15 September, 1938 — FB

League Club	Source	Date Signed	Seasons Played	Apps	Subs	Gls
Barnsley	Jnr	05/57	57-58	14	-	0
York C	Tr	05/59	59	1	-	0

JONES Bryn Edward
Born: Bagillt, Flintshire, Wales, 26 May, 1939 — LB

League Club	Source	Date Signed	Seasons Played	Apps	Subs	Gls
Watford	Holywell T	01/63	62	2	-	0
Chester C	Tr	08/64	64-66	30	0	0

JONES Brynley (Bryn)
Born: Llandrindod Wells, Powys, Wales, 8 February, 1948 — M
Wales: U23-1/Schools

League Club	Source	Date Signed	Seasons Played	Apps	Subs	Gls
Cardiff C	App	02/66	66-67	1	2	0
Newport Co	L	02/69	68	13	0	0
Bristol Rov	Tr	06/69	69-74	84	6	7

JONES Brynley (Bryn)
Born: Flint, Wales, 16 May, 1959 — M

League Club	Source	Date Signed	Seasons Played	Apps	Subs	Gls
Chester C	App	05/77	76-81	149	13	17

JONES Brynley Roy (Bryn)
Born: Swansea, Wales, 20 May, 1931 — LB/WH
Died: Winchmore Hill, N London, England, 5 October, 1990

League Club	Source	Date Signed	Seasons Played	Apps	Subs	Gls
Swansea C	Jnr	09/51	52-57	122	-	4
Newport Co	Tr	06/58	58-59	71	-	12
Bournemouth	Tr	02/60	59-63	118	-	5
Northampton T	Tr	10/63	63	7	-	0
Watford	Tr	11/63	63-66	90	1	1

JONES Brynmor (Bryn)
Born: Merthyr Tydfil, Wales, 14 February, 1912 — IF
Died: Wood Green, N London, England, 18 October, 1985
Wales: 17/War-8

League Club	Source	Date Signed	Seasons Played	Apps	Subs	Gls
Wolverhampton W	Aberaman Ath	10/33	33-37	163	-	52
Arsenal	Tr	08/38	38-48	71	-	7
Norwich C	Tr	06/49	49	23	-	1

JONES Carl Michael
Born: Chester-le-Street, County Durham, England, 3 September, 1986 — CD

League Club	Source	Date Signed	Seasons Played	Apps	Subs	Gls
Hartlepool U	Chester-le-Street T	05/05	05	1	0	0

JONES Charles Wilson (Charlie)
Born: Pentre Broughton, Wrexham, Wales, 29 April, 1914 — CF
Died: Birmingham, England, 9 January, 1986
Wales: 2

League Club	Source	Date Signed	Seasons Played	Apps	Subs	Gls
Wrexham	Brymbo Green	08/32	32-34	7	-	3
Birmingham C	Tr	09/34	34-46	135	-	63
Nottingham F	Tr	09/47	47	7	-	5

JONES Christopher Harry (Chris)
Born: Jersey, Channel Islands, 18 April, 1956 — F
England: U21-1

League Club	Source	Date Signed	Seasons Played	Apps	Subs	Gls
Tottenham H	App	05/73	74-81	149	15	37
Manchester C	Tr	09/82	82	3	0	0
Crystal Palace	Tr	11/82	82	18	0	3
Charlton Ath	Tr	09/83	83	17	6	2
Leyton Orient	Tr	09/84	84-86	106	1	19

JONES Christopher Martin Nigel (Chris)
Born: Altrincham, Greater Manchester, England, 19 November, 1945 — F

League Club	Source	Date Signed	Seasons Played	Apps	Subs	Gls
Manchester C	Jnr	05/64	66-67	6	1	2
Swindon T	Tr	07/68	68-71	49	19	18
Oldham Ath	L	01/72	71	3	0	1
Walsall	Tr	02/72	71-72	54	5	14
York C	Tr	06/73	73-75	94	1	33
Huddersfield T	Tr	08/76	76	9	5	2
Doncaster Rov	Tr	07/77	77-78	14	6	4
Darlington	L	01/78	77	14	2	3
Rochdale	Tr	12/78	78-79	51	5	19

JONES Christopher Trevor (Chris)
Born: Swansea, Wales, 12 September, 1989 — F
Wales: U21-1/Youth

League Club	Source	Date Signed	Seasons Played	Apps	Subs	Gls
Swansea C	Sch	10/06	06	0	7	0
Grimsby T	Tr	07/09	09	6	1	1

JONES Clifford William (Cliff)
Born: Swansea, Wales, 7 February, 1935 — W
England: FLge-3//Wales: 59/U23-1

League Club	Source	Date Signed	Seasons Played	Apps	Subs	Gls
Swansea C	Jnr	05/52	52-57	167	-	48
Tottenham H	Tr	02/58	57-68	314	4	135
Fulham	Tr	10/68	68-69	23	2	2

JONES Cobi N'Gai
Born: Detroit, Michigan, USA, 16 June, 1970 — M
USA: 164

League Club	Source	Date Signed	Seasons Played	Apps	Subs	Gls
Coventry C	UCLA Bruins (USA)	09/94	94	16	5	2

JONES Colin Malcolm
Born: Birmingham, England, 30 October, 1963 — LW

League Club	Source	Date Signed	Seasons Played	Apps	Subs	Gls
West Bromwich A	App	10/81				
Mansfield T		01/85	84	5	0	0

JONES Craig Nicholas
Born: Hereford, England, 12 December, 1989 — M

League Club	Source	Date Signed	Seasons Played	Apps	Subs	Gls
Hereford U	Jnr	01/08	08-09	2	2	0

JONES Craig Stephen
Born: Buckley, Flintshire, Wales, 20 March, 1987 — M/FB

League Club	Source	Date Signed	Seasons Played	Apps	Subs	Gls
Bury	The New Saints	08/12	12-14	65	37	5

JONES Cyril
Born: Johnstown, Wrexham, Wales, 17 July, 1920 — RB
Died: Johnstown, Wrexham, Wales, 27 November, 1995

League Club	Source	Date Signed	Seasons Played	Apps	Subs	Gls
Wrexham	Johnstown	02/42	46	29	-	0

JONES Daniel Jeffrey
Born: Rowley Regis, West Midlands, England, 14 July, 1986 — LB

League Club	Source	Date Signed	Seasons Played	Apps	Subs	Gls
Wolverhampton W	Sch	02/06	05-06	9	1	0
Northampton T	L	08/07	07	17	6	3
Northampton T	L	03/08	07	10	0	0
Oldham Ath	L	10/08	08	23	0	1
Notts Co	L	09/09	09	7	0	0
Bristol Rov	L	02/10	09	17	0	0
Sheffield Wed	Tr	07/10	10-12	23	14	0
Port Vale	Tr	01/13	12-13	33	3	1
Chesterfield	Tr	07/14	14	27	6	0

JONES Daniel John (Dan)
Born: Wallsend, Tyne and Wear, England, 14 December, 1994 — D

League Club	Source	Date Signed	Seasons Played	Apps	Subs	Gls
Hartlepool U	Sch	07/13	13-14	23	3	0

JONES Daniel John Gwilym (Gwilym)
Born: Cardigan, Wales, 3 April, 1925 — CF
Died: Swansea, Wales, July, 1992

League Club	Source	Date Signed	Seasons Played	Apps	Subs	Gls
Torquay U	Abergwynfi	09/47	47	6	-	1

JONES Darren Lee
Born: Newport, Wales, 28 August, 1983 — CD
Wales: Youth/Schools

League Club	Source	Date Signed	Seasons Played	Apps	Subs	Gls
Bristol C	YT	09/00	01	1	1	0
Cheltenham T	L	08/03	03	14	0	1
Hereford U	Forest Green Rov	06/09	09	40	1	3
Aldershot T	Tr	07/10	10-11	84	1	1
Shrewsbury T	Tr	07/12	12-13	52	1	1
AFC Wimbledon	Tr	01/14	13	17	1	1
Newport Co	Tr	05/14	14	43	0	4

JONES David
Born: Harrow, NW London, England, 3 July, 1964 — F

League Club	Source	Date Signed	Seasons Played	Apps	Subs	Gls
Chelsea		11/87				
Bury	Barnet	09/88	88	0	1	0
Leyton Orient	Barnet	12/88	88	0	2	0
Burnley	Barnet	02/89	88	4	0	0
Ipswich T		10/89				
Doncaster Rov	Tr	11/89	89-90	34	6	14
Bury	Tr	09/91	91	0	9	0
Hull C	Tr	02/93	92	11	1	1

JONES David
Born: Wrexham, Wales, 6 May, 1971 — W
Wales: Schools

League Club	Source	Date Signed	Seasons Played	Apps	Subs	Gls
Aston Villa	YT	06/89				
Wrexham	Tr	01/92	91	0	1	0

JONES David (Dai)
Born: Swansea, Wales, 3 March, 1935 — G
Died: Swansea, Wales, 29 June, 2014

League Club	Source	Date Signed	Seasons Played	Apps	Subs	Gls
Swansea C	REME	12/55	56-57	3	-	0

JONES David (Dave)
Born: Aberdare, Rhondda Cynon Taff, Wales, 7 January, 1932 — G

League Club	Source	Date Signed	Seasons Played	Apps	Subs	Gls
Brentford	Dover	12/51				
Reading	Tr	07/53	53-60	215	-	0
Aldershot	Tr	07/61	61-65	187	0	0

JONES David
Born: Whitwell, Derbyshire, England, 9 April, 1914 — WH
Died: Scarborough, North Yorkshire, England, 28 July, 1998

League Club	Source	Date Signed	Seasons Played	Apps	Subs	Gls
Bury	Worksop T	08/34	34-49	257	-	12

JONES David
Born: Blaenau Ffestiniog, Gwynedd, Wales, 8 September, 1914 — G

League Club	Source	Date Signed	Seasons Played	Apps	Subs	Gls
Stoke C	Colwyn Bay	03/37	38	1	-	0
Carlisle U	Tr	05/39	46-47	66	-	0
Rochdale	Tr	12/48				

JONES David Albert Brynmawr (Dai)
Born: Neath, Wales, 31 March, 1941 — F
Wales: Youth

League Club	Source	Date Signed	Seasons Played	Apps	Subs	Gls
Millwall	Ton Pentre	03/64	63-64	12	-	3
Newport Co	Tr	07/65	65-67	81	0	25
Mansfield T	Tr	11/67	67-71	116	14	32
Newport Co	Tr	11/71	71-73	43	4	11

JONES David Edward
Born: Saltney, Flintshire, Wales, 5 March, 1936 — LW

League Club	Source	Date Signed	Seasons Played	Apps	Subs	Gls
Wrexham	Saltney Jnrs	04/55	56-58	71	-	11
Crewe Alex	Tr	07/59	59	2	-	0

JONES David Edward
Born: Gosport, Hampshire, England, 11 February, 1952 — CD
Wales: 8/U23-4

League Club	Source	Date Signed	Seasons Played	Apps	Subs	Gls
Bournemouth	App	01/70	70-73	128	6	5
Nottingham F	Tr	08/74	74	36	0	1
Norwich C	Tr	09/75	75-79	120	3	4

JONES David Frank Lloyd
Born: Southport, Merseyside, England, 4 November, 1984 — DM
England: U21-1/Youth

League Club	Source	Date Signed	Seasons Played	Apps	Subs	Gls
Manchester U	Sch	07/03				
Preston NE	L	08/05	05	21	3	3
Derby Co	Tr	11/06	06-07	38	4	7
Wolverhampton W	Tr	07/08	08-10	58	8	6
Wigan Ath	Tr	08/11	11-12	21	8	0
Blackburn Rov	L	03/13	12	11	1	2
Burnley	Tr	08/13	13-14	82	0	1

JONES David Frederick (Davy)
Born: Brixham, Devon, England, 18 May, 1950 — M

League Club	Source	Date Signed	Seasons Played	Apps	Subs	Gls
Arsenal	App	02/68				
Middlesbrough	Tr	07/68				
Oxford U	Tr	10/68	68-70	17	4	0
Torquay U	Tr	07/72	72	0	1	0

JONES David Henry
Born: Tetbury, Gloucestershire, England, 4 August, 1937 — WH
Died: Leeds, England, January, 2013

League Club	Source	Date Signed	Seasons Played	Apps	Subs	Gls
Leeds U	Gloucester C	12/54				
Crewe Alex	Tr	05/60	60-61	16	-	0

JONES David Hilary
Born: Bradford, England, 29 December, 1950 — LW

League Club	Source	Date Signed	Seasons Played	Apps	Subs	Gls
Wolverhampton W		08/68				
York C	Tr	08/70	70	3	0	0

JONES David John
Born: Ruabon, Wrexham, Wales, 16 September, 1952 — F

League Club	Source	Date Signed	Seasons Played	Apps	Subs	Gls
Hereford U	Telford U	05/78	78-79	44	3	11

JONES David Owen (Dai)
Born: Cardiff, Wales, 28 October, 1910 — FB
Died: Oadby, Leicestershire, England, 25 May, 1971
Wales: 7

League Club	Source	Date Signed	Seasons Played	Apps	Subs	Gls
Leyton Orient	Ebbw Vale	08/31	31-32	55	-	0
Leicester C	Tr	05/33	33-46	226	-	4
Mansfield T	Tr	10/47	47-48	74	-	0

JONES David Richard
Born: Onllwyn, Neath Port Talbot, Wales, 18 January, 1946 — G

League Club	Source	Date Signed	Seasons Played	Apps	Subs	Gls
Derby Co		07/65				
Newport Co	Nuneaton Bor	05/68	67-68	3	0	0

JONES David Ronald (Dave)
Born: Liverpool, England, 17 August, 1956 — D
Died: Neath, Wales, 25 October, 2008
England: U21-1/Youth

League Club	Source	Date Signed	Seasons Played	Apps	Subs	Gls
Everton	App	05/74	75-78	79	7	1
Coventry C	Tr	06/79	79-80	8	3	0
Preston NE	Seiko Sports Ass (HKG)	08/83	83-84	50	0	1

JONES David Wilmott Llewellyn
Born: Kingsley, Cheshire, England, 9 April, 1940 — IF
Died: South Africa, 12 December, 2013
England: Youth

League Club	Source	Date Signed	Seasons Played	Apps	Subs	Gls
Crewe Alex	Jnr	05/56	56	10	-	1
Birmingham C	Tr	04/57	57-58	9	-	0
Millwall	Tr	12/59	59-63	165	-	71

JONES Denys John
Born: Aberdare, Rhondda Cynon Taff, Wales, 19 October, 1930 — W
Died: Norwich, England, May, 2003

League Club	Source	Date Signed	Seasons Played	Apps	Subs	Gls
Norwich C	Great Yarmouth T	04/51	51-52	5	-	2

JONES Desmond (Des)
Born: Ton Pentre, Rhondda Cynon Taff, Wales, 15 March, 1930 — W
Died: Bristol, England, April, 1987

League Club	Source	Date Signed	Seasons Played	Apps	Subs	Gls
Swansea C	Rhondda	01/48				
Bristol Rov	Tr	06/52	52	6	-	0
Workington	Tr	07/54	54-59	210	-	25

JONES Dilwyn Bowen
Born: Swansea, Wales, 2 January, 1937 — RH
Died: Pwllheli, Gwynedd, Wales, 13 July, 2011

League Club	Source	Date Signed	Seasons Played	Apps	Subs	Gls
Leeds U	Jnr	01/54				
Crewe Alex	Tr	02/58	57	15	-	1

JONES Edward William George (Eddie)
Born: Finchley, N London, England, 17 September, 1952 — LB
Wales: Schools

League Club	Source	Date Signed	Seasons Played	Apps	Subs	Gls
Tottenham H	Jnr	10/70				
Millwall	Tr	07/73	73-75	58	1	0

JONES Edwin Morris (Eddie)
Born: Abercynon, Rhondda Cynon Taff, Wales, 20 April, 1914 — RW
Died: Gloucester, England, April, 1984
Wales: Schools

League Club	Source	Date Signed	Seasons Played	Apps	Subs	Gls
Bolton W (Am)	Abercynon	04/33	33	1	-	1
Swindon T	Tr	05/36	36-46	124	-	17

JONES Eifion Pritchard
Born: Caernarfon, Gwynedd, Wales, 28 September, 1980 — CD
Wales: U21-1/Youth

League Club	Source	Date Signed	Seasons Played	Apps	Subs	Gls
Liverpool	YT	10/97				
Blackpool	Tr	03/00	99-00	5	3	0

JONES Eric
Born: Ulverston, Cumbria, England, 23 June, 1931 — W

League Club	Source	Date Signed	Seasons Played	Apps	Subs	Gls
Preston NE	Notts Co (Am)	01/52	53-54	13	-	0
Nottingham F	Tr	09/55	55-57	18	-	3
Doncaster Rov	Tr	03/58	57-58	15	-	2
Accrington Stan	Tr	07/59	59	18	-	0
Southport	Tr	07/60	60-61	76	-	18

JONES Eric John
Born: Dover, Kent, England, 5 March, 1938 — CH
Died: Cleveland, England, 13 March, 1987

League Club	Source	Date Signed	Seasons Played	Apps	Subs	Gls
Coventry C	Snowdown CW	05/55	56-60	14	-	0

JONES Eric Norman
Born: Birmingham, England, 5 February, 1915 — W
Died: Lincoln, England, 2 October, 1985

League Club	Source	Date Signed	Seasons Played	Apps	Subs	Gls
Wolverhampton W	Kidderminster Hrs	10/36	36	3	-	0
Portsmouth	Tr	11/37	37	1	-	0
Stoke C	Tr	09/38				
West Bromwich A	Tr	05/39				
Brentford	Tr	12/45				
Crewe Alex	Tr	07/46	46-47	37	-	9

JONES Eric Sidney (Sid)
Born: Wrexham, Wales, 10 October, 1921 — W
Died: Norwich, England, 25 April, 1981

League Club	Source	Date Signed	Seasons Played	Apps	Subs	Gls
Bolton W	Jnr	05/39				
Norwich C	Tr	12/45	46-47	40	-	9

JONES Ernest (Ernie)
Born: Ruabon, Wrexham, Wales, 9 December, 1919 — IF
Died: Ceredigion, Wales, May, 2011

League Club	Source	Date Signed	Seasons Played	Apps	Subs	Gls
Chester C	Bangor C	08/49	49-50	6	-	1

JONES Ernest George (Ernie)
Born: Bristol, England, 12 May, 1919 — LH
Died: North Somerset, Somerset, England, 10 December, 2010

League Club	Source	Date Signed	Seasons Played	Apps	Subs	Gls
Bristol C	Victoria Ath	08/39	46-47	27	-	1

JONES Ernest Peter (Peter)
Born: Manchester, England, 30 November, 1937 — RB/WH
England: Youth

League Club	Source	Date Signed	Seasons Played	Apps	Subs	Gls
Manchester U	Jnr	04/55	57	1	-	0
Wrexham	Tr	03/60	59-65	225	1	7
Stockport Co	Tr	07/66	66-67	51	3	1

JONES Frank
Born: Llandudno, Conwy, Wales, 3 October, 1960 — CD
Wales: U21-1

League Club	Source	Date Signed	Seasons Played	Apps	Subs	Gls
Wrexham	Jnr	07/79	78-80	8	0	0
Wrexham	Conwy U	09/84	84-86	30	1	0

JONES Frederick Arthur (Fred)
Born: Stoke-on-Trent, England, 21 October, 1922 — RB
Died: Rhyl, Denbighshire, Wales, December, 1989

League Club	Source	Date Signed	Seasons Played	Apps	Subs	Gls
Port Vale	South Liverpool	06/46	46	12	-	1

JONES Frederick George (Freddie)
Born: Gelligaer, Caerphilly, Wales, 11 January, 1938 — W
Died: Derby, England, 22 March, 2013
Wales: U23-2

League Club	Source	Date Signed	Seasons Played	Apps	Subs	Gls
Arsenal	Hereford U	01/58				
Brighton & HA	Tr	09/58	58-60	69	-	14
Swindon T	Tr	12/60	60	18	-	1
Grimsby T	Tr	07/61	61-62	58	-	9
Reading	Tr	07/63	63	30	-	5

JONES Frederick William Dennis (Derek)
Born: Ellesmere Port, Cheshire, England, 24 April, 1929 — FB/CF
Died: Ellesmere Port, Cheshire, England, 26 October, 2006

League Club	Source	Date Signed	Seasons Played	Apps	Subs	Gls
Tranmere Rov	Ellesmere Port T	07/53	53-60	155	-	19

JONES Gareth Anthony
Born: Cardiff, Wales, 18 June, 1952 — RW

League Club	Source	Date Signed	Seasons Played	Apps	Subs	Gls
Torquay U		10/72	72-73	11	5	0
Bournemouth	Tr	03/74	73-74	1	3	0

JONES Garry Edwin
Born: Wythenshawe, Greater Manchester, England, 11 December, 1950 — F

League Club	Source	Date Signed	Seasons Played	Apps	Subs	Gls
Bolton W	App	01/68	68-78	195	8	41
Sheffield U	L	02/75	74	3	0	1
Blackpool	Tr	11/78	78-79	18	9	5
Hereford U	Tr	08/80	80	21	4	4

JONES Gary
Born: Huddersfield, West Yorkshire, England, 6 April, 1969 — F

League Club	Source	Date Signed	Seasons Played	Apps	Subs	Gls
Doncaster Rov	Rossington Main	01/89	88-89	10	10	2
Southend U	Boston U	06/93	93-95	47	23	16
Lincoln C	L	09/93	93	0	4	2
Notts Co	Tr	03/96	95-98	103	14	38
Scunthorpe U	L	02/97	96	9	2	5
Hartlepool U	Tr	03/99	98-99	42	3	7
Halifax T	L	03/00	99	8	0	1
Halifax T	Tr	06/00	00-01	50	18	9

JONES Gary Kenneth
Born: Prescot, Merseyside, England, 5 January, 1951 — W

League Club	Source	Date Signed	Seasons Played	Apps	Subs	Gls
Everton	Jnr	10/68	70-75	76	6	12
Birmingham C	Tr	07/76	76-77	33	2	1

JONES Gary Roy
Born: Birkenhead, Wirral, England, 3 June, 1977 — M

League Club	Source	Date Signed	Seasons Played	Apps	Subs	Gls
Swansea C	Caernarfon T	07/97	97	3	5	0
Rochdale	Tr	01/98	97-01	123	17	22
Barnsley	Tr	11/01	01-02	56	0	2
Rochdale	Tr	11/03	03-11	326	4	52
Bradford C	Tr	07/12	12-13	81	3	8
Notts Co	Tr	08/14	14	39	4	3

JONES Gary Steven
Born: Chester, England, 10 May, 1975 — W/F

League Club	Source	Date Signed	Seasons Played	Apps	Subs	Gls
Tranmere Rov	YT	07/93	93-99	117	61	28
Nottingham F	Tr	07/00	00-01	24	12	2
Tranmere Rov	Tr	08/02	02-04	81	11	16
Grimsby T	Tr	08/05	05-07	78	37	25

JONES George
Born: Wrexham, Wales, 19 July, 1930 — RH

League Club	Source	Date Signed	Seasons Played	Apps	Subs	Gls
Wrexham		08/50	50-53	113	-	5

JONES George Alexander
Born: Radcliffe, Greater Manchester, England, 21 April, 1945 — F
England: Youth

League Club	Source	Date Signed	Seasons Played	Apps	Subs	Gls
Bury	App	06/62	61-63	63	-	15
Blackburn Rov	Tr	03/64	63-66	36	3	14
Bury	Tr	11/66	66-72	249	7	101
Oldham Ath	Tr	03/73	72-75	63	8	19
Halifax T	Tr	02/76	75-76	18	1	4
Southport	Tr	01/77	76-77	54	1	11

JONES George Colin (Colin)
Born: Chester, England, 8 September, 1940 — RH

League Club	Source	Date Signed	Seasons Played	Apps	Subs	Gls
Chester C	Jnr	03/60	59	3	-	0

JONES George Henry
Born: Sheffield, England, 27 November, 1918 — LW
Died: Sheffield, England, 10 March, 1995

League Club	Source	Date Signed	Seasons Played	Apps	Subs	Gls
Sheffield U	Woodburn Alliance	08/36	36-50	141	-	36
Barnsley	Tr	02/51	50-51	22	-	6

JONES Gerald (Gerry)
Born: Burslem, Potteries, England, 30 December, 1945 — LW

League Club	Source	Date Signed	Seasons Played	Apps	Subs	Gls
Stoke C	App	06/63	64-66	7	0	0

JONES Gerald Kenneth (Gerry)
Born: Newport, Wales, 21 April, 1950 — W

League Club	Source	Date Signed	Seasons Played	Apps	Subs	Gls
Luton T	Barry T	07/71				
Crewe Alex	L	02/73	72	6	1	1

JONES Gethin Wynne
Born: Perth, Australia, 13 October, 1995 — RB/M
Wales: U21-2/Youth

League Club	Source	Date Signed	Seasons Played	Apps	Subs	Gls
Everton	Sch	07/14				
Plymouth Arg	L	03/15	14	4	2	0

JONES Glanville (Glan)
Born: Merthyr Tydfil, Wales, 27 February, 1921 — LW

League Club	Source	Date Signed	Seasons Played	Apps	Subs	Gls
Hull C	Merthyr Tydfil	06/46	46	7	-	0
Bournemouth	Tr	05/47	48	9	-	3
Crewe Alex	Tr	03/49	48	10	-	1

JONES Glyn
Born: Rotherham, South Yorkshire, England, 8 April, 1936 — IF
England: Youth

League Club	Source	Date Signed	Seasons Played	Apps	Subs	Gls
Sheffield U	Rotherham U (Am)	06/54	55-57	29	-	4
Rotherham U	Tr	12/57	57-58	23	-	6
Mansfield T	Tr	07/59	59-60	45	-	18

JONES Glyn Alan
Born: Newport, Wales, 29 March, 1959 — G

League Club	Source	Date Signed	Seasons Played	Apps	Subs	Gls
Bristol Rov	App	03/77	77-79	9	0	0

League Club	Source	Date Signed	Seasons Played	Apps	Subs	Gls
Shrewsbury T	Tr	07/80				
Newport Co	Bath C	09/83	83	3	0	0

JONES Gordon Edward
Born: Sedgefield, County Durham, England, 6 March, 1943 — FB
England: U23-9/Youth

League Club	Source	Date Signed	Seasons Played	Apps	Subs	Gls
Middlesbrough	Jnr	03/60	60-72	457	5	4
Darlington	Tr	02/73	72-74	80	5	5

JONES Gordon Richard (Dick)
Born: Llanrwst, Conwy, Wales, 25 June, 1932 — LH/RB
Died: Rhuddlan, Denbighshire, Wales, 15 February, 2010

League Club	Source	Date Signed	Seasons Played	Apps	Subs	Gls
Crewe Alex	Holyhead	01/57	56-59	75	-	2

JONES Graeme Anthony
Born: Gateshead, Tyne and Wear, England, 13 March, 1970 — F

League Club	Source	Date Signed	Seasons Played	Apps	Subs	Gls
Doncaster Rov	Bridlington T	08/93	93-95	80	12	26
Wigan Ath	Tr	07/96	96-99	76	20	44
Southend U	St Johnstone	07/02	02	18	3	2
Boston U	Tr	03/03	02-03	33	3	7
Bury	Tr	07/04	04	1	2	1

JONES Graham
Born: Bradford, England, 5 October, 1957 — FB

League Club	Source	Date Signed	Seasons Played	Apps	Subs	Gls
Bradford C	Jnr	06/76	75-77	1	3	0

JONES Graham
Born: Worsley, Greater Manchester, England, 2 June, 1959 — D

League Club	Source	Date Signed	Seasons Played	Apps	Subs	Gls
Luton T	App	06/76	75-79	31	8	0
Torquay U	Tr	01/80	79-82	114	0	6
Stockport Co	Tr	07/83	83	32	3	2

JONES Graham Osborne
Born: Wrexham, Wales, 16 September, 1949 — CD

League Club	Source	Date Signed	Seasons Played	Apps	Subs	Gls
Wrexham	Jnr	10/67	67	3	0	0

JONES Grenville Arthur (Gren)
Born: Nuneaton, Warwickshire, England, 23 November, 1932 — RW
Died: Wrexham, Wales, 15 October, 1991
England: Youth/Schools

League Club	Source	Date Signed	Seasons Played	Apps	Subs	Gls
West Bromwich A	Jnr	12/49	53	2	-	0
Wrexham	Tr	06/55	55-60	240	-	36

JONES Griffith Thomas (Griff)
Born: Liverpool, England, 22 June, 1984 — F

League Club	Source	Date Signed	Seasons Played	Apps	Subs	Gls
Barnsley	Sch	09/03	02	0	2	0

JONES Gwyn
Born: Newport, Wales, 20 November, 1932 — IF
Died: Leeds, England, March, 2007

League Club	Source	Date Signed	Seasons Played	Apps	Subs	Gls
Leeds U	Llanelli	08/50				
York C	Tr	09/53				
Walsall	Tr	11/53	53	10	-	0

JONES Gwynfor (Gwyn)
Born: Llandwrog, Gwynedd, Wales, 20 March, 1935 — LB

League Club	Source	Date Signed	Seasons Played	Apps	Subs	Gls
Wolverhampton W	Caernarfon T	09/55	55-61	21	-	0
Bristol Rov	Tr	08/62	62-65	153	0	0

JONES Harold
Born: Liverpool, England, 22 May, 1933 — IF
Died: Warrington, Cheshire, England, 6 September, 2003

League Club	Source	Date Signed	Seasons Played	Apps	Subs	Gls
Liverpool	Jnr	02/52	53	1	-	0

JONES Harvey Cunningham
Born: Rhostyllen, Wrexham, Wales, 16 August, 1936 — RH

League Club	Source	Date Signed	Seasons Played	Apps	Subs	Gls
Wrexham	Liverpool (Am)	11/59	59	13	-	0
Chester C	Tr	08/60	60	19	-	0

JONES Haydn
Born: Caernarfon, Gwynedd, Wales, 8 May, 1946 — RB
Died: Bangor, Gwynedd, Wales, 31 August, 2010

League Club	Source	Date Signed	Seasons Played	Apps	Subs	Gls
Wrexham	Caernarfon T	06/64	64-65	13	1	1

JONES Henry (Jerry)
Born: Hartlepool, Cleveland, England, 28 September, 1918 — LH

League Club	Source	Date Signed	Seasons Played	Apps	Subs	Gls
Hartlepool U	Belle Vue Congs	09/46	46-48	75	-	1

JONES Herbert Neville
Born: Mold, Flintshire, Wales, 20 January, 1929 — IF

League Club	Source	Date Signed	Seasons Played	Apps	Subs	Gls
Wrexham	Colwyn Bay	07/51	51	1	-	0

JONES Ian Michael
Born: Germany, 26 August, 1976 — LB
Wales: Youth

League Club	Source	Date Signed	Seasons Played	Apps	Subs	Gls
Cardiff C	YT	07/95	93-95	3	0	0

JONES Idwal Gwyn
Born: Ton Pentre, Rhondda Cynon Taff, Wales, 3 August, 1924 — RW
Died: Bridgend, Wales, July, 1997

League Club	Source	Date Signed	Seasons Played	Apps	Subs	Gls
Swansea C	Ton Pentre	10/46	46	4	-	0

JONES Islwyn
Born: Merthyr Tydfil, Wales, 8 April, 1935 — LH

League Club	Source	Date Signed	Seasons Played	Apps	Subs	Gls
Cardiff C	Jnr	11/52	54-55	26	-	0

JONES Jake Ben
Born: Solihull, West Midlands, England, 6 April, 1993 — LM

League Club	Source	Date Signed	Seasons Played	Apps	Subs	Gls
Walsall	Sch	07/11	12	1	2	0

JONES James Alfred (Jimmy)
Born: Birkenhead, Wirral, England, 3 August, 1927 — G
Died: Horncastle, Lincolnshire, England, 5 May, 2015

League Club	Source	Date Signed	Seasons Played	Apps	Subs	Gls
Everton		12/45				
New Brighton	Tr	08/50	50	32	-	0
Lincoln C	Tr	08/51	51-53	76	-	0
Accrington Stan	Tr	02/54	53-54	46	-	0
Rochdale	Tr	09/55	55-60	177	-	0

JONES James Charles
Born: Winsford, Cheshire, England, 1 February, 1996 — M
Scotland: Youth

League Club	Source	Date Signed	Seasons Played	Apps	Subs	Gls
Crewe Alex	Sch	07/14	14	21	3	1

JONES James Lewis (Jamie)
Born: Kirkby, Merseyside, England, 18 February, 1989 — G

League Club	Source	Date Signed	Seasons Played	Apps	Subs	Gls
Everton	Sch	07/07				
Leyton Orient	Tr	07/08	08-13	151	0	0
Preston NE	Tr	06/14	14	17	0	0
Coventry C	L	01/15	14	4	0	0
Rochdale	L	02/15	14	13	0	0

JONES James Maurice
Born: Bolton, Greater Manchester, England, 23 October, 1925 — IF
Died: Bolton, Greater Manchester, England, 26 July, 1994

League Club	Source	Date Signed	Seasons Played	Apps	Subs	Gls
Hull C (Am)		05/47	46	1	-	0

JONES Jason Andrew
Born: Wrexham, Wales, 10 May, 1979 — G
Wales: U21-3/Youth

League Club	Source	Date Signed	Seasons Played	Apps	Subs	Gls
Swansea C	Liverpool (YT)	12/97	97-01	10	0	0

JONES Jermaine Junior
Born: Frankfurt, Germany, 3 November, 1981 — DM
Germany: 3/U21-4//USA: 50

League Club	Source	Date Signed	Seasons Played	Apps	Subs	Gls
Blackburn Rov (L)	Schalke 04 (GER)	01/11	10	15	0	0

JONES Jodi Jay Felice
Born: Bow, E London, England, 22 October, 1997 — F

League Club	Source	Date Signed	Seasons Played	Apps	Subs	Gls
Dagenham & Red	Sch	03/15	14	2	6	1

JONES John
Born: Gourock, Inverclyde, Scotland, 29 January, 1916 — IF
Died: Greenock, Inverclyde, Scotland, 11 March, 1999

League Club	Source	Date Signed	Seasons Played	Apps	Subs	Gls
Bradford C	Third Lanark	09/46	46	2	-	1

JONES John (Jack)
Born: Wrexham, Wales, 9 April, 1921 — IF
Died: Wrexham, Wales, May, 2001

League Club	Source	Date Signed	Seasons Played	Apps	Subs	Gls
Wrexham	Army	09/46	46-47	20	-	1
Doncaster Rov	Tr	07/48	48	6	-	0
New Brighton	Tr	08/49	49-50	77	-	11

JONES John Alan (Alan)
Born: Cefn Mawr, Wrexham, Wales, 12 September, 1939 — G

League Club	Source	Date Signed	Seasons Played	Apps	Subs	Gls
Cardiff C	Druids U	06/57	57	1	-	0
Exeter C	Tr	07/59	59-61	90	-	0
Norwich C	Tr	07/62	62	9	-	0
Wrexham	Tr	08/63	63	18	-	0

JONES John Edward (Jack)
Born: Bromborough, Wirral, England, 3 July, 1913 — FB
Died: Sunderland, England, 26 January, 1995

League Club	Source	Date Signed	Seasons Played	Apps	Subs	Gls
Everton	Ellesmere Port T	03/32	33-37	98	-	0
Sunderland	Tr	12/45	46	24	-	0

JONES John Ivor (Ivor)
Born: Ystrad Rhondda, Rhondda Cynon Taff, Wales, 1 April, 1925 — RW
Died: Sutton, S London, England, 24 October, 1999

League Club	Source	Date Signed	Seasons Played	Apps	Subs	Gls
Crystal Palace	Jnr	03/45	46	1	-	1
Arsenal	Croydon Rov	12/49				
Reading	Tr	02/50				

JONES John Mervyn (Mervyn)
Born: Bangor, Gwynedd, Wales, 30 April, 1931 — LW

League Club	Source	Date Signed	Seasons Played	Apps	Subs	Gls
Liverpool	Bangor C	12/51	51-52	4	-	0
Scunthorpe U	Tr	08/53	53-58	240	-	27
Crewe Alex	Tr	06/59	59-60	84	-	17
Chester C	Tr	08/61	61-62	63	-	10
Lincoln C	Tr	10/63	63	1	-	0

JONES John Morris (Johnny)
Born: Llanelli, Carmarthenshire, Wales, 31 October, 1924 — W

League Club	Source	Date Signed	Seasons Played	Apps	Subs	Gls
Fulham	Larne	01/47	47	1	-	0
Millwall	Tr	03/50	49-50	27	-	7

JONES John Thomas
Born: Holywell, Flintshire, Wales, 25 November, 1916 — G
Died: Holywell, Flintshire, Wales, 1978
Wales: Schools

League Club	Source	Date Signed	Seasons Played	Apps	Subs	Gls
Port Vale	Flint T	12/36	36	3	-	0
Northampton T	Tr	05/37	38-47	71	-	0
Oldham Ath	Tr	08/48	48	22	-	0

JONES Jonathan Berwyn (Jon)
Born: Wrexham, Wales, 27 October, 1978 — F

League Club	Source	Date Signed	Seasons Played	Apps	Subs	Gls
Chester C	YT	03/97	96-99	11	27	2

JONES Jordan Lewis
Born: Redcar, Cleveland, England, 24 October, 1994 — RW

League Club	Source	Date Signed	Seasons Played	Apps	Subs	Gls
Middlesbrough	Sch	10/12				
Hartlepool U	L	02/15	14	1	10	0

JONES Joseph Patrick (Joey)
Born: Llandudno, Conwy, Wales, 4 March, 1955 — LB
Wales: 72/U23-4

League Club	Source	Date Signed	Seasons Played	Apps	Subs	Gls
Wrexham	Jnr	01/73	72-74	98	0	2
Liverpool	Tr	07/75	75-77	72	0	3
Wrexham	Tr	10/78	78-82	145	1	6
Chelsea	Tr	10/82	82-84	76	2	2
Huddersfield T	Tr	08/85	85-86	67	1	3
Wrexham	Tr	08/87	87-91	131	1	11

JONES Keith
Born: Nantyglo, Blaenau Gwent, Wales, 23 October, 1928 — G
Died: Redditch, Worcestershire, England, 25 August, 2007
Wales: 1

League Club	Source	Date Signed	Seasons Played	Apps	Subs	Gls
Aston Villa	Kidderminster Hrs	05/46	47-56	185	-	0
Port Vale	Tr	07/57	57-58	64	-	0
Crewe Alex	Tr	04/59	58-59	46	-	0

JONES Keith Aubrey
Born: Dulwich, S London, England, 14 October, 1964 — M
England: Youth/Schools

League Club	Source	Date Signed	Seasons Played	Apps	Subs	Gls
Chelsea	App	08/83	82-86	43	9	7
Brentford	Tr	09/87	87-91	167	2	13
Southend U	Tr	10/91	91-94	88	2	11
Charlton Ath	Tr	09/94	94-99	142	17	6
Reading	Tr	07/00	00-01	28	11	0

JONES Kenneth (Ken)
Born: Aberdare, Rhondda Cynon Taff, Wales, 2 January, 1936 — LB
Died: Stoke-on-Trent, England, 18 January, 2013
Wales: U23-1

League Club	Source	Date Signed	Seasons Played	Apps	Subs	Gls
Cardiff C	Jnr	05/53	57-58	24	-	0
Scunthorpe U	Tr	12/58	58-63	168	-	0
Charlton Ath	Tr	09/64	64-65	25	0	0
Exeter C	Tr	06/66	66	17	0	0

JONES Kenneth (Ken)
Born: Easington, County Durham, England, 1 October, 1936 — FB
England: Schools

League Club	Source	Date Signed	Seasons Played	Apps	Subs	Gls
Sunderland	Jnr	10/53	59	10	-	0
Hartlepool U	Tr	01/61	60-61	33	-	0

JONES Kenneth (Ken)
Born: Havercroft, West Yorkshire, England, 26 June, 1944 — FB
Died: Chandler's Ford, Hampshire, England, 27 December, 2012

League Club	Source	Date Signed	Seasons Played	Apps	Subs	Gls
Bradford Park Ave	Monckton CW	10/61	62-64	100	-	3
Southampton	Tr	06/65	65-69	79	1	0
Cardiff C	Tr	07/71	71	6	0	0

JONES Kenneth Boothroyd (Ken)
Born: Rhosllanerchrugog, Wrexham, Wales, 11 May, 1937 — FB

League Club	Source	Date Signed	Seasons Played	Apps	Subs	Gls
Wrexham	Jnr	05/54	57-59	31	-	0
Crystal Palace	Tr	06/60	60	4	-	0
Swindon T	Tr	03/61	60-61	35	-	0

JONES Kenneth Brian (Ken)
Born: Keighley, West Yorkshire, England, 9 February, 1941 — M

League Club	Source	Date Signed	Seasons Played	Apps	Subs	Gls
Southend U	Army	10/60	60-63	87	-	34
Millwall	Tr	09/64	64-69	175	3	11
Colchester U	Tr	11/69	69-71	72	5	23

JONES Kenwyne Joel
Born: Point Fortin, Trinidad, 5 October, 1984 — F
Trinidad & Tobago: 68/U23/Youth

League Club	Source	Date Signed	Seasons Played	Apps	Subs	Gls
Southampton	West Connection (TRD)	05/04	04-07	44	27	19
Sheffield Wed	L	12/04	04	7	0	7
Stoke C	L	02/05	04	13	0	3
Sunderland	Tr	08/07	07-09	82	12	26
Stoke C	Tr	08/10	10-13	57	31	13
Cardiff C	Tr	01/14	13-14	31	14	12
Bournemouth	L	03/14	14	0	6	1

JONES Kevin Richard
Born: Wrexham, Wales, 16 February, 1974 — RB

League Club	Source	Date Signed	Seasons Played	Apps	Subs	Gls
Wrexham	YT	08/92	91-93	8	1	0

JONES Lee
Born: Pontypridd, Rhondda Cynon Taff, Wales, 9 August, 1970 — G

League Club	Source	Date Signed	Seasons Played	Apps	Subs	Gls
Swansea C	AFC Porth	03/94	94-97	6	0	0
Bristol Rov	Tr	03/98	97-99	76	0	0
Stockport Co	Tr	07/00	00-02	72	3	0
Blackpool	Tr	08/03	03-05	81	0	0
Bury	L	12/06	06	2	0	0
Darlington	Tr	01/07	06	9	0	0

JONES Leonard (Len)
Born: Barnsley, South Yorkshire, England, 9 June, 1913 — RW
Died: Chelmsford, England, 11 April, 1998

League Club	Source	Date Signed	Seasons Played	Apps	Subs	Gls
Barnsley	Wombwell	08/33	34-37	57	-	0
Plymouth Arg	Chelmsford C	05/39	46-48	39	-	2
Southend U	Tr	08/49	49	29	-	0
Colchester U	Tr	07/50	50-52	71	-	3
Ipswich T	Tr	07/53				

JONES Leslie (Les)
Born: Ynysybwl, Rhondda Cynon Taff, Wales, 8 December, 1922 — IF
Died: Pontypridd, Rhondda Cynon Taff, Wales, 1983
Wales: Amateur

League Club	Source	Date Signed	Seasons Played	Apps	Subs	Gls
Millwall	Barry T	12/47	48-51	7	-	1

JONES Leslie Albert (Les)
Born: Wrexham, Wales, 9 November, 1940 — IF
Wales: Schools

League Club	Source	Date Signed	Seasons Played	Apps	Subs	Gls
Bolton W	Jnr	11/57				
Tranmere Rov	Tr	07/62	62-64	68	-	29
Chester C	Tr	04/65	65-68	132	3	35

JONES Leslie Clifford (Les)
Born: Mountain Ash, Rhondda Cynon Taff, Wales, 1 January, 1930 — FB

League Club	Source	Date Signed	Seasons Played	Apps	Subs	Gls
Luton T	Craig Ath	10/50	50-57	98	-	1
Aston Villa	Tr	01/58	57	5	-	0

JONES Leslie Jenkin (Les)
Born: Aberdare, Rhondda Cynon Taff, Wales, 1 July, 1911 — IF
Died: Llanfymach, Pembrokeshire, Wales, 11 January, 1981
Wales: 11/War-5

League Club	Source	Date Signed	Seasons Played	Apps	Subs	Gls
Cardiff C	Aberdare & Aberaman	08/29	29-33	142	-	31
Coventry C	Tr	01/34	33-37	139	-	69
Arsenal	Tr	11/37	37-38	46	-	3
Swansea C	Tr	06/46	46	2	-	0
Brighton & HA	Barry T	08/48	48	3	-	0

JONES Linden
Born: New Tredegar, Caerphilly, Wales, 5 March, 1961 — RB/M
Wales: U21-3

League Club	Source	Date Signed	Seasons Played	Apps	Subs	Gls
Cardiff C	App	03/79	78-83	142	3	2
Newport Co	Tr	09/83	83-86	141	1	5
Reading	Tr	07/87	87-91	147	5	8

JONES Lloyd Richard
Born: Plymouth, England, 7 October, 1995 — CD
England: Youth//Wales: Youth

League Club	Source	Date Signed	Seasons Played	Apps	Subs	Gls
Liverpool	Sch	07/13				
Cheltenham T	L	01/15	14	5	1	0
Accrington Stan	L	03/15	14	11	0	1

JONES Luke Joseph
Born: Darwen, Lancashire, England, 10 April, 1987 — CD

League Club	Source	Date Signed	Seasons Played	Apps	Subs	Gls
Blackburn Rov	Sch	07/05				
Shrewsbury T	Ashton U	11/06	06-07	10	4	0
Stevenage	Mansfield T	05/13	13	21	5	0
Mansfield T	Tr	05/14				

JONES Marcus Lee
Born: Stone, Staffordshire, England, 24 June, 1974 — M

League Club	Source	Date Signed	Seasons Played	Apps	Subs	Gls
Cheltenham T	Scarborough	11/00	00	1	1	0

JONES Mark
Born: Romford, E London, England, 4 August, 1979 — LB

League Club	Source	Date Signed	Seasons Played	Apps	Subs	Gls
Southend U	YT	-	96	0	1	0

JONES Mark
Born: Bristol, England, 2 December, 1965 — M

League Club	Source	Date Signed	Seasons Played	Apps	Subs	Gls
Bristol C	App	-	82	0	1	0

JONES Mark
Born: Berinsfield, Oxfordshire, England, 26 September, 1961 — RM

League Club	Source	Date Signed	Seasons Played	Apps	Subs	Gls
Oxford U	App	09/79	79-85	101	28	7

League Club	Source	Date Signed	Seasons Played	Apps	Subs	Gls
Swindon T	Tr	09/86	86	39	1	9
Cardiff C	Tr	08/90	90-91	33	3	2

JONES Mark
Born: Brownhills, West Midlands, England, 4 January, 1968 RB/M

League Club	Source	Date Signed	Seasons Played	Apps	Subs	Gls
Walsall	App	01/86	87	6	2	0
Exeter C	L	11/88	88	5	0	0
Hereford U	Tr	08/89	89	40	2	8

JONES Mark
Born: Barnsley, South Yorkshire, England, 15 June, 1933 CH
Died: Munich, Germany, 6 February, 1958
England: Schools

League Club	Source	Date Signed	Seasons Played	Apps	Subs	Gls
Manchester U	Jnr	07/50	50-57	103	-	1

JONES Mark Alan
Born: Wrexham, Wales, 15 August, 1983 M
Wales: 2/U21-4

League Club	Source	Date Signed	Seasons Played	Apps	Subs	Gls
Wrexham	Sch	07/03	02-07	102	26	22
Rochdale	Tr	08/08	08	7	2	0

JONES Mark Andrew
Born: Walsall, West Midlands, England, 7 September, 1979 F
England: Youth/Schools

League Club	Source	Date Signed	Seasons Played	Apps	Subs	Gls
Wolverhampton W	YT	09/96	98-99	0	3	0
Cheltenham T	L	10/99	99	3	0	0
Chesterfield	Tr	08/00	00-01	1	8	0

JONES Mark Anthony Waldron
Born: Warley, West Midlands, England, 22 October, 1961 RB

League Club	Source	Date Signed	Seasons Played	Apps	Subs	Gls
Aston Villa	App	07/79	81-83	24	0	0
Brighton & HA	Tr	03/84	83-84	9	0	0
Birmingham C	Tr	10/84	84-86	33	1	0
Shrewsbury T	Tr	03/87				
Hereford U	Tr	06/87	87-90	155	1	2

JONES Mark David
Born: Doncaster, South Yorkshire, England, 2 October, 1958 M

League Club	Source	Date Signed	Seasons Played	Apps	Subs	Gls
Doncaster Rov	App	11/75	75-77	10	3	0

JONES Mark Richard
Born: Mansfield, Nottinghamshire, England, 21 December, 1965 CD

League Club	Source	Date Signed	Seasons Played	Apps	Subs	Gls
Notts Co	App	12/83	83-84	4	2	0

JONES Mark Thomas
Born: Liverpool, England, 16 September, 1960 FB

League Club	Source	Date Signed	Seasons Played	Apps	Subs	Gls
Preston NE	Runcorn	02/84	83-85	76	0	3

JONES Matthew Graham
Born: Llanelli, Carmarthenshire, Wales, 1 September, 1980 M
Wales: 13/B-1/U21-7/Youth

League Club	Source	Date Signed	Seasons Played	Apps	Subs	Gls
Leeds U	YT	09/97	98-00	11	12	0
Leicester C	Tr	12/00	00-02	19	8	1

JONES Matthew Leon (Matt)
Born: Chiswick, W London, England, 9 October, 1970 W

League Club	Source	Date Signed	Seasons Played	Apps	Subs	Gls
Southend U	YT	05/89	88-89	2	3	0

JONES Matthew Neil
Born: Shrewsbury, Shropshire, England, 11 October, 1980 M

League Club	Source	Date Signed	Seasons Played	Apps	Subs	Gls
Shrewsbury T	YT	07/99	98-00	5	2	0

JONES Matthew Ryan (Matt)
Born: Swindon, England, 30 November, 1995 LB

League Club	Source	Date Signed	Seasons Played	Apps	Subs	Gls
Swindon T	Sch	-	13	0	1	0

JONES Michael (Mick)
Born: Sunderland, England, 24 March, 1947 CD

League Club	Source	Date Signed	Seasons Played	Apps	Subs	Gls
Derby Co	Jnr	11/64				
Notts Co	Tr	07/69	69-72	82	18	1
Peterborough U	Tr	08/73	73-75	82	6	4

JONES Michael
Born: Liverpool, England, 3 December, 1987 G

League Club	Source	Date Signed	Seasons Played	Apps	Subs	Gls
Wrexham	Sch	08/06	04-07	9	2	0

JONES Michael Alan (Mick)
Born: Sutton-in-Ashfield, Nottinghamshire, England, 4 December, 1942 RB

League Club	Source	Date Signed	Seasons Played	Apps	Subs	Gls
Mansfield T	Mansfield CWS	10/60	62-65	91	0	0

JONES Michael David (Mike)
Born: Birkenhead, Wirral, England, 15 August, 1987 W

League Club	Source	Date Signed	Seasons Played	Apps	Subs	Gls
Tranmere Rov	Sch	04/06	05-07	5	5	1
Shrewsbury T	L	01/07	06	3	10	1
Bury	Tr	08/08	08-11	143	10	20
Sheffield Wed	Tr	01/12	11	6	4	0
Crawley T	Tr	08/12	12-13	75	7	4
Oldham Ath	Tr	06/14	14	45	0	6

JONES Michael David (Mick)
Born: Worksop, Nottinghamshire, England, 24 April, 1945 CF
England: 3/U23-9

League Club	Source	Date Signed	Seasons Played	Apps	Subs	Gls
Sheffield U	App	11/62	62-67	149	0	63
Leeds U	Tr	09/67	67-73	216	4	77

JONES Michael Howard (Mick)
Born: Llangurig, Powys, Wales, 25 August, 1938 RW

League Club	Source	Date Signed	Seasons Played	Apps	Subs	Gls
Shrewsbury T		07/59	58-61	22	-	1

JONES Michael Keith (Mick)
Born: Berkhamsted, Hertfordshire, England, 8 January, 1945 FB

League Club	Source	Date Signed	Seasons Played	Apps	Subs	Gls
Fulham	App	01/63				
Chelsea	Tr	12/64				
Leyton Orient	Tr	02/66	65-71	223	5	16
Charlton Ath	Tr	12/71	71-73	58	1	0

JONES Murray Lee
Born: Bexley, SE London, England, 7 October, 1964 F

League Club	Source	Date Signed	Seasons Played	Apps	Subs	Gls
Southend U	Jnr	09/82				
Crystal Palace	Carshalton Ath	10/89				
Bristol C	Tr	08/90				
Doncaster Rov	L	10/90	90	5	0	0
Exeter C	Tr	01/91	90	16	4	3
Grimsby T	Tr	07/91	91	14	14	3
Brentford	Tr	07/92	92	6	10	0

JONES Nathan Jason
Born: Ystrad Rhondda, Rhondda Cynon Taff, Wales, 28 May, 1973 LB/M

League Club	Source	Date Signed	Seasons Played	Apps	Subs	Gls
Luton T	Merthyr Tydfil	06/95				
Southend U	Numancia (SPN)	08/97	97-99	82	17	2
Scarborough	L	03/99	98	8	1	0
Brighton & HA	Tr	07/00	00-04	109	50	7
Yeovil T	Tr	07/05	05-11	168	17	2

JONES Norman Glyn
Born: Rhostyllen, Wrexham, Wales, 15 November, 1923 G
Died: Bristol, England, 25 June, 2003
Wales: Schools

League Club	Source	Date Signed	Seasons Played	Apps	Subs	Gls
Wrexham	Jnr	09/41	46	1	-	0

JONES Patrick James (Pat)
Born: Plymouth, England, 7 September, 1920 LB
Died: Plymouth, England, December, 1990

League Club	Source	Date Signed	Seasons Played	Apps	Subs	Gls
Plymouth Arg	Astor Inst	03/47	46-57	425	-	2

JONES Paul
Born: Snodland, Kent, England, 29 June, 1986 G
England: Semi Pro-1

League Club	Source	Date Signed	Seasons Played	Apps	Subs	Gls
Exeter C	Leyton Orient (Sch)	11/04	08-10	90	0	0
Peterborough U	L	01/11	10	1	0	0
Peterborough U	Tr	07/11	11	35	0	0
Crawley T	Tr	05/12	12-13	92	0	0
Portsmouth	Tr	06/14	14	46	0	0

JONES Paul Anthony
Born: Walsall, West Midlands, England, 6 September, 1965 M

League Club	Source	Date Signed	Seasons Played	Apps	Subs	Gls
Walsall	App	09/83	82-89	125	18	15
Wrexham	L	03/89	88	5	0	0
Wolverhampton W	Tr	11/89	89-90	7	7	0

JONES Paul Bernard
Born: Ellesmere Port, Cheshire, England, 13 May, 1953 CD

League Club	Source	Date Signed	Seasons Played	Apps	Subs	Gls
Bolton W	App	06/70	70-82	441	4	38
Huddersfield T	Tr	07/83	83-85	73	0	8
Oldham Ath	Tr	12/85	85-86	32	0	1
Blackpool	Tr	03/87	86-87	31	6	0
Rochdale	Galway C (ROI)	03/89	88	14	0	2
Stockport Co	Tr	06/89	89	25	0	0

JONES Paul Neil
Born: Liverpool, England, 3 June, 1978 CD

League Club	Source	Date Signed	Seasons Played	Apps	Subs	Gls
Tranmere Rov	YT	12/95				
Oldham Ath	Leigh RMI	11/99	99-00	26	2	3

JONES Paul Philip
Born: Birkenhead, Wirral, England, 2 October, 1976 LB

League Club	Source	Date Signed	Seasons Played	Apps	Subs	Gls
Wrexham	YT	07/95	96	6	0	0

JONES Paul Stanley
Born: Stockport, Greater Manchester, England, 10 September, 1953 M

League Club	Source	Date Signed	Seasons Played	Apps	Subs	Gls
Manchester U	App	12/70				
Mansfield T	Tr	06/73	73	15	5	1

JONES Paul Steven
Born: Chirk, Wrexham, Wales, 18 April, 1967 G
Wales: 50

League Club	Source	Date Signed	Seasons Played	Apps	Subs	Gls
Wolverhampton W	Kidderminster Hrs	07/91	92-95	33	0	0
Stockport Co	Tr	07/96	96	46	0	0
Southampton	Tr	07/97	97-03	192	1	0
Liverpool	L	01/04	03	2	0	0
Wolverhampton W	Tr	01/04	03-04	26	0	0

League Club	Source	Date Signed	Seasons Played	Apps	Subs	Gls
Watford	L	12/04	04	9	0	0
Millwall	L	08/05	05	3	0	0
Queens Park Rgrs	Tr	02/06	05-06	26	0	0

JONES Paul Timothy
Born: Solihull, West Midlands, England, 6 February, 1974 — W

League Club	Source	Date Signed	Seasons Played	Apps	Subs	Gls
Birmingham C	YT	02/92	91	0	1	0

JONES Peter
Born: Caerphilly, Wales, 22 September, 1957 — LB

League Club	Source	Date Signed	Seasons Played	Apps	Subs	Gls
Newport Co	Merthyr Tydfil	08/85	85-86	54	1	1

JONES Peter Alfred
Born: Ellesmere Port, Cheshire, England, 25 November, 1949 — D
England: Youth/Schools

League Club	Source	Date Signed	Seasons Played	Apps	Subs	Gls
Burnley	App	05/67	68-69	2	0	0
Swansea C	Tr	07/71	71-73	80	1	1

JONES Philip Andrew (Phil)
Born: Liverpool, England, 1 December, 1969 — RB

League Club	Source	Date Signed	Seasons Played	Apps	Subs	Gls
Everton	YT	06/88	87	0	1	0
Blackpool	L	03/90	89	6	0	0
Wigan Ath	Tr	01/91	90-92	84	4	2
Bury	Tr	08/93	93	4	0	0

JONES Philip Anthony (Phil)
Born: Preston, Lancashire, England, 21 February, 1992 — D/M
England: 17/U21-9/Youth

League Club	Source	Date Signed	Seasons Played	Apps	Subs	Gls
Blackburn Rov	Sch	10/09	09-10	31	4	0
Manchester U	Tr	06/11	11-14	86	8	2

JONES Philip Eric
Born: Ellesmere Port, Cheshire, England, 30 March, 1948 — W

League Club	Source	Date Signed	Seasons Played	Apps	Subs	Gls
Blackpool	Jnr	01/66				
Wrexham	Tr	05/67	66	1	0	0

JONES Philip Howard (Phil)
Born: Mansfield, Nottinghamshire, England, 12 September, 1961 — M

League Club	Source	Date Signed	Seasons Played	Apps	Subs	Gls
Sheffield U	App	06/79	78-80	25	3	1

JONES Philip Lee (Lee)
Born: Wrexham, Wales, 29 May, 1973 — F
Wales: 2/B-1/U21-14/Youth

League Club	Source	Date Signed	Seasons Played	Apps	Subs	Gls
Wrexham	YT	07/91	90-91	24	15	10
Liverpool	Tr	03/92	94-96	0	3	0
Crewe Alex	L	09/93	93	4	4	1
Wrexham	L	01/96	95	20	0	9
Wrexham	L	01/97	96	2	4	0
Tranmere Rov	Tr	03/97	96-99	58	28	16
Barnsley	Tr	07/00	00-01	17	23	5
Wrexham	Tr	03/02	01-03	25	24	14

JONES Philip Wayne (Wayne)
Born: Treorchy, Rhondda Cynon Taff, Wales, 20 October, 1948 — M
Wales: 1/U23-6

League Club	Source	Date Signed	Seasons Played	Apps	Subs	Gls
Bristol Rov	Jnr	10/66	66-72	218	5	28

JONES Ralph
Born: Maesteg, Bridgend, Wales, 19 May, 1921 — FB
Died: Bridgend, Wales, 18 January, 1997

League Club	Source	Date Signed	Seasons Played	Apps	Subs	Gls
Leicester C		10/44				
Newport Co	Tr	05/46	46-47	19	-	0
Bristol Rov	Tr	12/47	47-49	13	-	1

JONES Raymond Barry Bankote (Ray)
Born: East Ham, E London, England, 28 August, 1988 — F
Died: East Ham, E London, England, 25 August, 2007
England: Youth

League Club	Source	Date Signed	Seasons Played	Apps	Subs	Gls
Queens Park Rgrs	Sch	01/07	05-06	17	16	5

JONES Raymond Michael (Ray)
Born: Chester, England, 4 June, 1944 — RB
Died: Chester, England, 16 July, 2007

League Club	Source	Date Signed	Seasons Played	Apps	Subs	Gls
Chester C	Jnr	10/62	62-68	169	1	0

JONES Reece Nicholas
Born: Chessington, SW London, England, 22 July, 1992 — M
Wales: U21-1/Youth

League Club	Source	Date Signed	Seasons Played	Apps	Subs	Gls
AFC Wimbledon	Fulham (Sch)	08/10	11	1	0	0

JONES Richard Glynn (Richie)
Born: Manchester, England, 26 September, 1986 — RW
England: Youth

League Club	Source	Date Signed	Seasons Played	Apps	Subs	Gls
Manchester U	Sch	10/04				
Colchester U	L	10/06	06	0	6	0
Barnsley	L	02/07	06	1	3	0
Yeovil T	L	08/07	07	6	3	0
Hartlepool U	Tr	07/08	08-09	58	11	7
Oldham Ath	Tr	07/10	10	21	10	1
Bradford C	Tr	07/11	11-12	33	3	1
Rochdale	Tr	02/13	12	2	1	0

JONES Richard John
Born: Usk, Monmouthshire, Wales, 26 April, 1969 — M

League Club	Source	Date Signed	Seasons Played	Apps	Subs	Gls
Newport Co	YT	07/87	86-87	31	9	1
Hereford U	Tr	08/88	88-92	142	6	9
Swansea C	Tr	07/93	93	6	1	0

JONES Richard Kenneth (Ken)
Born: Llanelli, Carmarthenshire, Wales, 16 April, 1926 — RB
Died: Coventry, England, April, 2015

League Club	Source	Date Signed	Seasons Played	Apps	Subs	Gls
Coventry C	Llanelli	11/49	51-55	83	-	0

JONES Robert
Born: Coventry, England, 17 November, 1964 — F
England: Schools

League Club	Source	Date Signed	Seasons Played	Apps	Subs	Gls
Leicester C	Manchester C (App)	09/82	82-85	12	3	3
Walsall	Tr	08/86	86	1	4	0

JONES Robert Marc (Rob)
Born: Wrexham, Wales, 5 November, 1971 — RB
England: 8/U21-2/Youth//Wales: Schools

League Club	Source	Date Signed	Seasons Played	Apps	Subs	Gls
Crewe Alex	YT	12/88	87-91	59	16	2
Liverpool	Tr	10/91	91-97	182	1	0

JONES Robert Stanley (Bobby)
Born: Bristol, England, 28 October, 1938 — IF/W

League Club	Source	Date Signed	Seasons Played	Apps	Subs	Gls
Bristol Rov	Soundwell	05/56	57-66	250	0	64
Northampton T	Tr	09/66	66	17	0	1
Swindon T	Tr	02/67	66	11	0	0
Bristol Rov	Tr	08/67	67-72	159	9	36

JONES Robert Stuart
Born: Liverpool, England, 12 November, 1971 — M

League Club	Source	Date Signed	Seasons Played	Apps	Subs	Gls
Wrexham	YT	07/90	89-90	5	2	1

JONES Robert William (Bobby)
Born: Liverpool, England, 28 March, 1933 — G
Died: Blackburn, Greater Manchester, England, 27 August, 1998

League Club	Source	Date Signed	Seasons Played	Apps	Subs	Gls
Southport	Southport Boys Brigade	07/51	51-52	22	-	0
Chester C	Tr	08/53	53-57	166	-	0
Blackburn Rov	Tr	03/58	58-65	49	0	0

JONES Robert William (Rob)
Born: Stockton-on-Tees, Cleveland, England, 30 November, 1979 — CD

League Club	Source	Date Signed	Seasons Played	Apps	Subs	Gls
Stockport Co	Gateshead	04/03	03	14	2	2
Macclesfield T	L	10/03	03	1	0	0
Grimsby T	Tr	07/04	04-05	56	4	5
Scunthorpe U	Hibernian	07/09	09-10	41	1	2
Sheffield Wed	Tr	03/11	10-11	40	1	5
Doncaster Rov	Tr	07/12	12-14	66	0	10

JONES Roderick (Rod)
Born: Bassaleg, Monmouthshire, Wales, 14 June, 1946 — F/CD

League Club	Source	Date Signed	Seasons Played	Apps	Subs	Gls
Newport Co	Lovells Ath	10/69	69-78	271	16	67

JONES Rodney Ernest (Rod)
Born: Ashton-under-Lyne, Greater Manchester, England, 23 September, 1945 — G

League Club	Source	Date Signed	Seasons Played	Apps	Subs	Gls
Burnley	Ashton U	06/65				
Rotherham U	Tr	09/65	65-66	36	0	0
Burnley	Tr	03/67	67-68	9	0	0
Rochdale	Tr	06/71	71-73	19	0	0

JONES Roger
Born: Upton-on-Severn, Worcestershire, England, 8 November, 1946 — G
England: U23-1

League Club	Source	Date Signed	Seasons Played	Apps	Subs	Gls
Portsmouth	App	11/64				
Bournemouth	Tr	05/65	65-69	160	0	0
Blackburn Rov	Tr	01/70	69-75	242	0	0
Newcastle U	Tr	03/76	75	5	0	0
Stoke C	Tr	02/77	76-79	101	0	0
Derby Co	Tr	07/80	80-81	59	0	0
Birmingham C	L	02/82	81	4	0	0
York C	Tr	08/82	82-84	122	0	0

JONES Ronald (Ron)
Born: Crewe, Cheshire, England, 9 April, 1918 — LW
Died: Congleton, Cheshire, England, December, 1987

League Club	Source	Date Signed	Seasons Played	Apps	Subs	Gls
Crewe Alex	Heslington Victoria	05/37	36-46	22	-	7

JONES Ronald John (Ron)
Born: Ystrad Rhondda, Rhondda Cynon Taff, Wales, 27 February, 1926 — CF
Died: Pontypridd, Rhondda Cynon Taff, Wales, July, 1991

League Club	Source	Date Signed	Seasons Played	Apps	Subs	Gls
Swansea C		07/49				
Scunthorpe U	Tr	08/50	50	3	-	0

JONES Roy
Born: Stoke-on-Trent, England, 20 December, 1924 — CH
Died: Macclesfield, Cheshire, England, October, 2005

League Club	Source	Date Signed	Seasons Played	Apps	Subs	Gls
Stoke C	Jnr	10/43	47-49	7	-	0

JONES Roy John
Born: Clacton, Essex, England, 26 July, 1942 — G

League Club	Source	Date Signed	Seasons Played	Apps	Subs	Gls
Swindon T	RAF Brize Norton	10/67	67-71	34	0	0

JONES Ryan Anthony
Born: Sheffield, England, 23 July, 1973 — M
Wales: 1/B/U21-4

League Club	Source	Date Signed	Seasons Played	Apps	Subs	Gls
Sheffield Wed	YT	06/91	92-94	36	5	6
Scunthorpe U	L	01/96	95	11	0	3

JONES Samuel Stephen Thomas (Steve)
Born: Harrogate, North Yorkshire, England, 6 September, 1955 — G

League Club	Source	Date Signed	Seasons Played	Apps	Subs	Gls
Bradford C	App	09/73	72	2	0	0

JONES Scott
Born: Sheffield, England, 1 May, 1975 — M/D

League Club	Source	Date Signed	Seasons Played	Apps	Subs	Gls
Barnsley	YT	02/94	95-99	76	7	4
Mansfield T	L	08/97	97	6	0	0
Bristol Rov	Tr	08/00	00-01	51	7	3
York C	Tr	03/02	01-02	26	2	1

JONES Shane Graham
Born: Tredegar, Blaenau Gwent, Wales, 8 November, 1972 — M

League Club	Source	Date Signed	Seasons Played	Apps	Subs	Gls
Hereford U	YT	08/91	89-91	12	26	1

JONES Sidney (Sid)
Born: Rothwell, West Yorkshire, England, 15 February, 1921 — RB
Died: Colchester, Essex, England, 1977

League Club	Source	Date Signed	Seasons Played	Apps	Subs	Gls
Arsenal	Kippax Jnrs	05/39				
Walsall	Tr	07/48	48-51	146	-	1

JONES Simon Christopher
Born: Nettleham, Lincolnshire, England, 16 May, 1945 — G

League Club	Source	Date Signed	Seasons Played	Apps	Subs	Gls
Rochdale	Gainsborough Trinity	06/63	63-66	47	0	0
Chester C	Bangor C	10/67	67	3	0	0

JONES Stanley (Stan)
Born: United Kingdom — W

League Club	Source	Date Signed	Seasons Played	Apps	Subs	Gls
Crewe Alex		08/47	47	1	-	0

JONES Stanley George (Stan)
Born: Highley, Shropshire, England, 16 November, 1938 — CH

League Club	Source	Date Signed	Seasons Played	Apps	Subs	Gls
Walsall	Kidderminster Hrs	05/56	57-59	30	-	0
West Bromwich A	Tr	05/60	60-66	239	0	2
Walsall	Tr	03/68	67-72	204	2	7

JONES Stephen Alexander
Born: Plymouth, England, 11 March, 1974 — F

League Club	Source	Date Signed	Seasons Played	Apps	Subs	Gls
Plymouth Arg	YT	07/92	91	0	1	0

JONES Stephen Anthony (Steve)
Born: Wrexham, Wales, 28 November, 1962 — F

League Club	Source	Date Signed	Seasons Played	Apps	Subs	Gls
Wrexham	Jnr	08/81	80-81	3	2	0
Crewe Alex	Tr	08/82	82	6	4	1

JONES Stephen Gary (Steve)
Born: Cambridge, England, 17 March, 1970 — F

League Club	Source	Date Signed	Seasons Played	Apps	Subs	Gls
West Ham U	Billericay T	11/92	92-94	8	8	4
Bournemouth	Tr	10/94	94-95	71	3	26
West Ham U	Tr	05/96	96	5	3	0
Charlton Ath	Tr	02/97	96-99	28	24	8
Bournemouth	L	12/97	97	5	0	4
Bristol C	Tr	09/99	99-01	29	8	7
Brentford	L	01/00	99	6	2	0
Southend U	L	03/00	99	9	0	2
Wycombe W	L	07/00	00	5	0	0

JONES Stephen Graham (Steve)
Born: Derry, Northern Ireland, 25 October, 1976 — RW
England: Semi Pro-1//Northern Ireland: 29/B-1

League Club	Source	Date Signed	Seasons Played	Apps	Subs	Gls
Blackpool	Chadderton	10/95				
Bury	Tr	08/96				
Crewe Alex	Leigh RMI	07/01	01-05	122	37	39
Rochdale	L	02/02	01	6	3	1
Burnley	Tr	07/06	06-07	38	20	6
Crewe Alex	L	03/08	07	2	2	1
Huddersfield T	L	10/08	08	2	2	0
Bradford C	Tr	11/08	08	25	2	3
Walsall	Tr	07/09	09-10	34	9	9

JONES Stephen Robert (Steve)
Born: Bristol, England, 25 December, 1970 — RB

League Club	Source	Date Signed	Seasons Played	Apps	Subs	Gls
Swansea C	Cheltenham T	11/95	95-00	140	6	4
Cheltenham T	Tr	07/01	01-02	7	3	0

JONES Stephen Russell (Steve)
Born: Eastbourne, East Sussex, England, 25 July, 1957 — FB

League Club	Source	Date Signed	Seasons Played	Apps	Subs	Gls
Queens Park Rgrs	App	10/74				
Walsall	Tr	01/79	78	15	0	0
Wimbledon	Tr	07/79	79-82	77	2	1

JONES Steven (Steve)
Born: Stockton-on-Tees, Cleveland, England, 31 January, 1974 — G

League Club	Source	Date Signed	Seasons Played	Apps	Subs	Gls
Hartlepool U	YT	05/92	91-95	45	3	0

JONES Steven Francis (Steve)
Born: Liverpool, England, 18 October, 1960 — M

League Club	Source	Date Signed	Seasons Played	Apps	Subs	Gls
Manchester U	App	10/77				
Port Vale	Tr	05/79	79-80	24	1	3

JONES Steven Wynn (Steve)
Born: Wrexham, Wales, 23 October, 1964 — LB

League Club	Source	Date Signed	Seasons Played	Apps	Subs	Gls
Wrexham	Jnr	08/83	82-83	9	1	1

JONES Stuart Clive
Born: Bristol, England, 24 October, 1977 — G

League Club	Source	Date Signed	Seasons Played	Apps	Subs	Gls
Sheffield Wed	Weston-super-Mare	03/98				
Torquay U	Tr	02/00	99-00	32	0	0
Brighton & HA	Weston-super-Mare	02/04	03	2	1	0
Doncaster Rov	Tr	08/04	04	3	1	0

JONES Stuart John
Born: Aberystwyth, Ceredigion, Wales, 14 March, 1984 — FB/M
Wales: U21-1/Youth

League Club	Source	Date Signed	Seasons Played	Apps	Subs	Gls
Swansea C	Sch	07/03	02-04	23	11	0

JONES Tecwyn
Born: Holywell, Flintshire, Wales, 3 January, 1930 — FB
Died: Hammersmith, W London, England, 29 December, 2008

League Club	Source	Date Signed	Seasons Played	Apps	Subs	Gls
Brentford	Holywell T	03/50	51-52	5	-	0
Wrexham	Tr	07/53	53	4	-	0

JONES Tecwyn Lloyd
Born: Ruabon, Wrexham, Wales, 27 January, 1941 — WH
Wales: U23-1

League Club	Source	Date Signed	Seasons Played	Apps	Subs	Gls
Wrexham	Jnr	05/59	61-64	57	-	2
Colchester U	Tr	10/64	64-65	28	0	0
Crewe Alex	Tr	10/65	65	8	0	0

JONES Thomas (Tom)
Born: Aldershot, Hampshire, England, 7 October, 1964 — M
England: Semi Pro-1

League Club	Source	Date Signed	Seasons Played	Apps	Subs	Gls
Swindon T	Aberdeen	09/88	88-91	162	6	12
Reading	Tr	07/92	92-95	63	16	2

JONES Thomas Benjamin (Benny)
Born: Frodsham, Cheshire, England, 23 March, 1920 — LW
Died: Chelsea, W London, England, 21 December, 1972

League Club	Source	Date Signed	Seasons Played	Apps	Subs	Gls
Tranmere Rov	Ellesmere Port T	09/41	46-47	54	-	19
Chelsea	Tr	11/47	47-51	55	-	11
Accrington Stan	Tr	07/53	53	14	-	0

JONES Thomas Edwin (Tommy)
Born: Liverpool, England, 11 April, 1930 — CH
Died: Warrington, Cheshire, England, 5 June, 2010
England: Youth

League Club	Source	Date Signed	Seasons Played	Apps	Subs	Gls
Everton	Jnr	01/48	50-61	383	-	14

JONES Thomas George (Tommy)
Born: Connah's Quay, Flintshire, Wales, 12 October, 1917 — CH
Died: Bangor, Gwynedd, Wales, 3 January, 2004
Wales: 17/Schools/War-10

League Club	Source	Date Signed	Seasons Played	Apps	Subs	Gls
Wrexham	Llanerch Celts	11/34	35	6	-	0
Everton	Tr	03/36	36-49	165	-	4

JONES Thomas Gethin (Gethin)
Born: Llanbydder, Carmarthenshire, Wales, 8 August, 1981 — CD

League Club	Source	Date Signed	Seasons Played	Apps	Subs	Gls
Cardiff C	Carmarthen T	08/00	00-01	0	3	0

JONES Thomas Selwyn (Selwyn)
Born: Rhostyllen, Wrexham, Wales, 3 April, 1929 — RW
Died: Chesterfield, Derbyshire, England, September, 1995

League Club	Source	Date Signed	Seasons Played	Apps	Subs	Gls
Everton	Brentford (Am)	07/49				
Sheffield Wed	Dover	08/51				
Leyton Orient	Tr	07/52	52	6	-	0

JONES Thomas William (Tommy)
Born: Oakengates, Telford & Wrekin, England, 23 March, 1907 — IF
Died: Telford, England, 24 June, 1980

League Club	Source	Date Signed	Seasons Played	Apps	Subs	Gls
West Bromwich A	Oakengates T	07/29				
Burnley	Tr	11/30	30-33	94	-	24
Blackpool	Tr	09/33	33-37	153	-	38
Grimsby T	Tr	07/38	38-46	48	-	8
Accrington Stan		06/48				

JONES Trevor
Born: Aberdare, Rhondda Cynon Taff, Wales, 27 January, 1923 — W
Died: Merthyr Tydfil, Wales, March, 1983

League Club	Source	Date Signed	Seasons Played	Apps	Subs	Gls
Plymouth Arg	Aberaman	05/48				
Watford	Tr	08/49	49	15	-	2

League Club	Source	Date Signed	Seasons Played	Career Record Apps	Subs	Gls
JONES Vaughan						
Born: Tonyrefail, Rhondda Cynon Taff, Wales, 2 September, 1959						D
Wales: U21-2/Youth						
Bristol Rov	App	09/77	76-81	93	8	3
Newport Co	Tr	08/82	82-83	67	1	4
Cardiff C	Tr	07/84	84	11	0	1
Bristol Rov	Tr	12/84	84-92	277	3	9
JONES Vincent Peter (Vinnie)						
Born: Watford, Hertfordshire, England, 5 January, 1965						DM
Wales: 9						
Wimbledon	Wealdstone	11/86	86-88	77	0	9
Leeds U	Tr	06/89	89-90	44	2	5
Sheffield U	Tr	09/90	90-91	35	0	2
Chelsea	Tr	08/91	91-92	42	0	4
Wimbledon	Tr	09/92	92-97	171	6	12
Queens Park Rgrs	Tr	03/98	97-98	8	1	1
JONES Walter						
Born: Lurgan, Armagh, Northern Ireland, 4 April, 1925						RH
Blackpool	Linfield	12/47				
Doncaster Rov	Tr	06/50	50-52	69	-	2
Grimsby T	Tr	09/54				
York C	Tr	11/54	54	1	-	0
JONES Walter Schofield						
Born: Rochdale, Greater Manchester, England, 9 January, 1925						CF
Died: Rochdale, Greater Manchester, England, May, 2001						
Rochdale	St Chad's	11/46	46	2	-	2
JONES William (Billy)						
Born: Shrewsbury, Shropshire, England, 24 March, 1987						RB
England: Youth						
Crewe Alex	Sch	07/04	03-06	127	5	8
Preston NE	Tr	07/07	07-10	157	3	13
West Bromwich A	Tr	07/11	11-13	62	4	1
Sunderland	Tr	05/14	14	14	0	0
JONES William Ernest Arthur (Ernie)						
Born: Swansea, Wales, 12 November, 1920						RW
Died: Bolton, Greater Manchester, England, November, 2002						
Wales: 4/War-1						
Swansea C	Bolton W (Am)	10/43	46	37	-	3
Tottenham H	Tr	06/47	46-48	55	-	14
Southampton	Tr	05/49	49-51	44	-	4
Bristol C	Tr	11/51	51-53	50	-	7
JONES William Henry (Bill)						
Born: Macclesfield, Cheshire, England, 13 May, 1921						CD
Died: Bargoed, Caerphilly, Wales, 26 December, 2010						
England: 2/B-1/FLge-1						
Liverpool	Hayfield St Matthew's	09/38	46-53	257	-	17
JONES William John (Willie)						
Born: Aberbargoed, Caerphilly, Wales, 5 May, 1925						W
Died: Bargoed, Caerphilly, Wales, 17 October, 1999						
Ipswich T	Bargoed	04/49	49-54	33	-	1
JONES William John Beattie (Bill)						
Born: Liverpool, England, 6 June, 1924						CF
Died: Chester, England, April, 1995						
Manchester C		05/48	48-49	3	-	0
Chester C	Tr	06/51	51	29	-	4
JONES William Kenneth (Billy)						
Born: Gillingham, Kent, England, 26 March, 1983						LB
Leyton Orient	YT	07/01	00-03	68	4	0
Kidderminster Hrs	Tr	01/05	04	10	2	0
Crewe Alex	Exeter C	05/07	07-09	70	1	8
Exeter C	Tr	07/10	10-11	43	5	1
Cheltenham T	Tr	07/12	12	39	0	0
Newport Co	Tr	09/13	13	6	1	1
JONES William Morris (Morris)						
Born: Liverpool, England, 30 November, 1919						IF
Died: Crosby, Merseyside, England, July, 1993						
Port Vale	South Liverpool	06/46	46-47	53	-	26
Swindon T	Tr	11/47	47-49	94	-	48
Crystal Palace	Tr	05/50	50	17	-	3
Watford	Tr	03/51	50-51	27	-	7
JONK Wim						
Born: Volendam, Netherlands, 12 October, 1966						M
Netherlands: 49						
Sheffield Wed	PSV Eindhoven (NED)	08/98	98-00	69	1	5
JONSON Mattias						
Born: Orebro, Sweden, 16 January, 1974						RW
Sweden: 57						
Norwich C	Brondby (DEN)	08/04	04	19	9	0
JONSSON Egert Gunnthor						
Born: Reykjavik, Iceland, 18 August, 1988						RB
Iceland: 19/U21-15/Youth						
Wolverhampton W	Heart of Midlothian	01/12	11-12	2	2	0
Charlton Ath	L	11/12	12	1	1	0
JONSSON Sigurdur (Siggi)						
Born: Akranes, Iceland, 27 September, 1966						M
Iceland: 65/U21/Youth						
Sheffield Wed	IA Akranes (ICE)	02/85	84-88	59	8	4
Barnsley	L	01/86	85	5	0	0
Arsenal	Tr	07/89	89-90	2	6	1
JOPLING Joseph (Joe)						
Born: South Shields, Tyne and Wear, England, 21 April, 1951						D
Aldershot	Horton Westoe	08/69	69-70	35	0	2
Leicester C	Tr	09/70	70-73	2	1	0
Torquay U	L	01/74	73	6	0	0
Aldershot	Tr	03/74	73-83	321	11	11
JORDAN Andrew Joseph						
Born: Manchester, England, 14 December, 1979						CD
Scotland: U21-3						
Bristol C	YT	12/97	98-00	10	1	0
Cardiff C	Tr	10/00	00	3	2	0
Hartlepool U	Tr	08/03	03	4	1	0
JORDAN Brian Athol						
Born: Bentley, South Yorkshire, England, 31 January, 1932						LH
Derby Co		10/51				
Rotherham U	Denaby U	07/53	53-58	38	-	0
Middlesbrough	Tr	11/58	58	5	-	0
York C	Tr	07/60	60	8	-	0
JORDAN Clarence (Clarrie)						
Born: South Kirkby, West Yorkshire, England, 20 June, 1922						CF
Died: Doncaster, South Yorkshire, England, 16 February, 1992						
Doncaster Rov	Upton Colliery	04/40	46-47	60	-	48
Sheffield Wed	Tr	02/48	47-54	92	-	36
JORDAN Colin						
Born: Hemsworth, West Yorkshire, England, 2 June, 1934						RB
Bradford Park Ave	Fitzwilliam YC	04/52	53-56	27	-	0
JORDAN David Charles						
Born: Gillingham, Kent, England, 26 October, 1971						F
Gillingham	YT	06/90	90	0	2	0
JORDAN Gerald (Gerry)						
Born: Seaham, County Durham, England, 4 April, 1949						FB
Died: Warwickshire, England, April, 2012						
Northampton T	Jnr	06/66	66	1	0	0
JORDAN John (Jack)						
Born: Glasgow, Scotland, 25 February, 1924						RW
Died: Glasgow, Scotland, 23 June, 2007						
Reading	Alloa Ath	10/48	48	3	-	0
Brentford	Tr	09/49				
JORDAN John William (Johnny)						
Born: Romford, E London, England, 8 November, 1921						IF
Tottenham H	Grays Ath	08/47	47	24	-	10
Birmingham C	Juventus (ITA)	03/49	48-49	24	-	2
Sheffield Wed	Tr	09/50	50	10	-	2
JORDAN Joseph (Joe)						
Born: Carluke, Lanarkshire, Scotland, 15 December, 1951						F
Scotland: 52/U23-1						
Leeds U	Greenock Morton	10/70	71-77	139	30	35
Manchester U	Tr	01/78	77-80	109	0	37
Southampton	Verona (ITA)	08/84	84-86	48	0	12
Bristol C	Tr	02/87	86-89	38	19	8
JORDAN Michael John (Mike)						
Born: Exeter, England, 8 January, 1956						LW
Exeter C		07/75	75-76	15	3	3
JORDAN Michael William						
Born: Cheshunt, Hertfordshire, England, 7 April, 1986						G
Arsenal	Sch	04/04				
Chesterfield	Tr	08/06	06-07	7	0	0
JORDAN Roy Antony						
Born: Plymouth, England, 17 April, 1978						W
Hereford U	YT	-	96	1	0	0
JORDAN Scott Douglas						
Born: Newcastle-upon-Tyne, England, 19 July, 1975						M
York C	YT	10/92	92-00	123	44	12

JORDAN Stephen Robert (Steve)
Born: Warrington, Cheshire, England, 6 March, 1982 — LB

League Club	Source	Date Signed	Seasons Played	Apps	Subs	Gls
Manchester C	YT	03/99	02-06	49	4	0
Cambridge U	L	10/02	02	11	0	0
Burnley	Tr	07/07	07-09	69	4	0
Sheffield U	Tr	08/10	10	14	1	0
Huddersfield T	L	02/11	10	6	0	0
Rochdale	Rotherham U (NC)	10/11	11	17	2	0
Fleetwood T	Dunfermline Ath	07/13	13-14	50	2	1

JORDAN Thomas Michael (Tom)
Born: Manchester, England, 24 May, 1981 — FB

League Club	Source	Date Signed	Seasons Played	Apps	Subs	Gls
Bristol C	YT	03/01				
Southend U	Tr	08/02	02	0	1	0

JORDAN Timothy Edwin (Tim)
Born: Littleborough, Greater Manchester, England, 12 April, 1960 — F

League Club	Source	Date Signed	Seasons Played	Apps	Subs	Gls
Oldham Ath	Jnr	06/78	78-79	2	3	0

[JORDAO] BATISTA Adelino Jose Martins
Born: Malange, Angola, 30 August, 1971 — M
Portugal: U21-1

League Club	Source	Date Signed	Seasons Played	Apps	Subs	Gls
West Bromwich A	Sporting Braga (POR)	08/00	00-02	47	16	6

[JORDI] LOPEZ Jordi
Born: Barcelona, Spain, 28 February, 1981 — M

League Club	Source	Date Signed	Seasons Played	Apps	Subs	Gls
Queens Park Rgrs	RC Santander (SPN)	02/09	08	7	3	1
Swansea C	Tr	08/09	09-10	8	7	0

[JORDI GOMEZ] GOMEZ Jordi
Born: Barcelona, Spain, 24 May, 1985 — M

League Club	Source	Date Signed	Seasons Played	Apps	Subs	Gls
Swansea C	RCD Espanyol (SPN)	08/08	08	38	6	12
Wigan Ath	Tr	07/09	09-13	83	44	17
Sunderland	Tr	05/14	14	22	7	4

JORGENSEN Claus Beck
Born: Holstebro, Denmark, 27 April, 1979 — RW
Faroe Islands: 10

League Club	Source	Date Signed	Seasons Played	Apps	Subs	Gls
Bournemouth	AC Horsens (DEN)	07/99	99-00	77	10	14
Bradford C	Tr	07/01	01-02	41	9	12
Coventry C	Tr	08/03	03-05	30	22	6
Bournemouth	L	01/04	03	16	1	0
Blackpool	Tr	08/06	06-08	72	28	6
Port Vale	Tr	08/09	09	0	4	0

JORGENSEN Henrik
Born: Bogense, Denmark, 12 January, 1979 — FB

League Club	Source	Date Signed	Seasons Played	Apps	Subs	Gls
Notts Co	Boldklubben 1909 (DEN)	10/00	00-01	3	4	0

JORONEN Jesse Pekka
Born: Helsinki, Finland, 21 March, 1993 — G
Finland: 1/U21-10/Youth

League Club	Source	Date Signed	Seasons Played	Apps	Subs	Gls
Fulham	Sch	07/10	14	4	0	0
Accrington Stan	L	10/14	14	4	0	0

[JOSE ENRIQUE] DIAZ Jose Enrique
Born: Valencia, Spain, 23 January, 1986 — LB
Spain: U21-3/Youth

League Club	Source	Date Signed	Seasons Played	Apps	Subs	Gls
Newcastle U	Villarreal (SPN)	08/07	07-10	111	8	1
Liverpool	Tr	08/11	11-14	66	10	2

[JOSEMI] GONZALEZ Jose Miguel
Born: Torremolinos, Spain, 15 November, 1979 — RB

League Club	Source	Date Signed	Seasons Played	Apps	Subs	Gls
Liverpool	Malaga (SPN)	07/04	04-05	16	5	0

JOSEPH David
Born: Les Abymes, Guadeloupe, 22 November, 1976 — F

League Club	Source	Date Signed	Seasons Played	Apps	Subs	Gls
Notts Co (L)	Montpellier (FRA)	08/00	00	13	14	4

JOSEPH Francis
Born: Kilburn, NW London, England, 6 March, 1960 — F

League Club	Source	Date Signed	Seasons Played	Apps	Subs	Gls
Wimbledon	Hillingdon Bor	11/80	80-81	42	9	13
Brentford	Tr	07/82	82-86	103	7	43
Wimbledon	L	03/87	86	2	3	1
Reading	Tr	07/87	87	5	6	2
Bristol Rov	L	01/88	87	3	0	0
Aldershot	L	03/88	87	9	1	2
Sheffield U	Tr	07/88	88	5	8	3
Gillingham	Tr	03/89	88-89	12	6	1
Crewe Alex	Tr	12/89	89	9	7	2
Fulham	Tr	08/90	90	2	2	0
Barnet	Tampa Bay R's (USA)	10/91	91	1	0	0

JOSEPH Leon
Born: Stepney, E London, England, 26 February, 1920 — LW
Died: Barnet, N London, England, June, 1983
England: Amateur-12

League Club	Source	Date Signed	Seasons Played	Apps	Subs	Gls
Tottenham H (Am)	Leytonstone	02/47	46	1	-	0

JOSEPH Marc Ellis
Born: Leicester, England, 10 November, 1976 — CD

League Club	Source	Date Signed	Seasons Played	Apps	Subs	Gls
Cambridge U	YT	05/95	95-00	136	17	0
Peterborough U	Tr	07/01	01-02	60	1	2
Hull C	Tr	11/02	02-05	81	8	1
Bristol C	L	11/05	05	3	0	0
Blackpool	Tr	01/06	05-06	18	6	0
Rotherham U	Tr	07/07	07-09	58	18	4

JOSEPH Matthew Nathaniel Adolphus (Matt)
Born: Bethnal Green, E London, England, 30 September, 1972 — D
Barbados: 2//England: Youth

League Club	Source	Date Signed	Seasons Played	Apps	Subs	Gls
Arsenal	YT	11/90				
Gillingham	Tr	12/92				
Cambridge U	FC Ilves (FIN)	11/93	93-97	157	2	6
Leyton Orient	Tr	01/98	97-03	219	5	2

JOSEPH Ricardo Raymondo
Born: Kingston, Jamaica, 17 January, 1987 — LB

League Club	Source	Date Signed	Seasons Played	Apps	Subs	Gls
Rushden & D	Sch	-	05	1	0	0

JOSEPH Roger Anthony
Born: Paddington, Central London, England, 24 December, 1965 — RB
England: B-2

League Club	Source	Date Signed	Seasons Played	Apps	Subs	Gls
Brentford	Southall	10/84	84-87	103	1	2
Wimbledon	Tr	08/88	88-94	155	7	0
Millwall	L	03/95	94	5	0	0
Leyton Orient	Tr	11/96	96	15	0	0
West Bromwich A	Tr	02/97	96	0	2	0
Leyton Orient	Tr	08/97	97-99	26	24	0

JOSLIN Philip James (Phil)
Born: Kingsteignton, Devon, England, 1 September, 1916 — G
Died: Cardiff, Wales, 31 January, 1980

League Club	Source	Date Signed	Seasons Played	Apps	Subs	Gls
Torquay U	Kingsteignton Ath	01/36	35-47	135	-	0
Cardiff C	Tr	05/48	48-50	108	-	0

JOSLYN Roger Douglas William
Born: Colchester, Essex, England, 7 May, 1950 — M

League Club	Source	Date Signed	Seasons Played	Apps	Subs	Gls
Colchester U	Jnr	05/68	67-70	92	7	4
Aldershot	Tr	10/70	70-74	186	0	17
Watford	Tr	11/74	74-79	178	4	17
Reading	Tr	11/79	79-81	67	1	1

[JOTA] PELETEIRO Jose Ignacio
Born: A Pobra de Caraminal, Spain, 16 June, 1991 — W

League Club	Source	Date Signed	Seasons Played	Apps	Subs	Gls
Brentford	Celta Vigo (SPN)	08/14	14	37	5	11

JOVANOVIC Milan
Born: Bajina Basta, Yugoslavia, 18 April, 1981 — LW
Serbia: 44

League Club	Source	Date Signed	Seasons Played	Apps	Subs	Gls
Liverpool	Tr	05/10	10	5	5	0

JOVANOVIC Nikola
Born: Cetinje, Yugoslavia, 18 September, 1952 — CD
Yugoslavia: 7

League Club	Source	Date Signed	Seasons Played	Apps	Subs	Gls
Manchester U	R Star Belgrade (YUG)	01/80	79-80	20	1	4

JOVETIC Stevan
Born: Titograd, Yugoslavia, 2 November, 1989 — F
Montenegro: 36/U21-7

League Club	Source	Date Signed	Seasons Played	Apps	Subs	Gls
Manchester C	Fiorentina (ITA)	07/13	13-14	11	19	8

JOWETT Harold Uttley (Harry)
Born: Halifax, West Yorkshire, England, 15 November, 1923 — RW
Died: Halifax, West Yorkshire, England, April, 2005

League Club	Source	Date Signed	Seasons Played	Apps	Subs	Gls
Halifax T	Elland U	09/50	50	9	-	1

JOWETT Kenneth Stuart (Ken)
Born: Bradford, England, 9 March, 1927 — RW
Died: Bradford, England, March, 1993

League Club	Source	Date Signed	Seasons Played	Apps	Subs	Gls
Halifax T	Fryston CW	02/47	46-48	29	-	2

JOWETT Sylvester James (Jim)
Born: Sheffield, England, 27 January, 1926 — LW

League Club	Source	Date Signed	Seasons Played	Apps	Subs	Gls
York C	Sheffield U (Am)	09/46	46	1	-	0

JOWSEY James Robert
Born: Filey, North Yorkshire, England, 24 November, 1983 — G

League Club	Source	Date Signed	Seasons Played	Apps	Subs	Gls
Manchester U	YT	11/00				
Cambridge U	Scarborough	09/04	04	1	0	0

JOY Bernard
Born: Fulham, W London, England, 29 October, 1911 — CH
Died: Kenton, NW London, England, 18 July, 1984
England: 1/Amateur/War-1

League Club	Source	Date Signed	Seasons Played	Apps	Subs	Gls
Fulham (Am)	Casuals	02/31	33	1	-	0
Arsenal (Am)	Casuals	05/35	35-46	86	-	0

JOY Brian William
Born: Salford, England, 26 February, 1951 — FB/M

League Club	Source	Date Signed	Seasons Played	Apps	Subs	Gls
Blackburn Rov	Coventry C (Am)	08/68				
Torquay U	Tr	08/69	69	26	1	0
Tranmere Rov	Tr	06/70	70	21	0	1
Doncaster Rov	Tr	07/72	72	28	6	1
Exeter C	Tr	07/73	73-75	89	1	2
York C	San Diego Jaws (USA)	09/76	76	18	0	0

JOY David Frederick
Born: Barnard Castle, County Durham, England, 23 September, 1943 — FB
England: Youth

League Club	Source	Date Signed	Seasons Played	Apps	Subs	Gls
Huddersfield T	Evenwood T	07/62	65	1	0	0
York C	Tr	06/67	67	13	2	0

JOY Harold Cuthbert
Born: Ebbw Vale, Blaenau Gwent, Wales, 8 January, 1921 — CF
Died: Monmouthshire, Wales, 22 February, 2000

League Club	Source	Date Signed	Seasons Played	Apps	Subs	Gls
Norwich C	Lovells Ath	02/47	46	8	-	4
Ipswich T	Tr	12/47				
Newport Co	Tr	01/48	47	2	-	0

JOY Ian Paul
Born: San Diego, California, USA, 14 July, 1981 — LB

League Club	Source	Date Signed	Seasons Played	Apps	Subs	Gls
Tranmere Rov	YT	07/98				
Kidderminster Hrs	Montrose	08/01	01-02	15	7	0

JOYCE Anthony John (Tony)
Born: Wembley, NW London, England, 24 September, 1971 — FB

League Club	Source	Date Signed	Seasons Played	Apps	Subs	Gls
Queens Park Rgrs	YT	03/90				
Aldershot	Tr	05/91	90	3	0	0

JOYCE Ben Patrick
Born: Plymouth, England, 9 September, 1990 — F

League Club	Source	Date Signed	Seasons Played	Apps	Subs	Gls
Swindon T	Sch	02/08	07-08	1	3	1
Torquay U	Tr	07/09				

JOYCE Christopher (Chris)
Born: Dumbarton, Dunbartonshire, Scotland, 19 April, 1933 — IF
Died: Northampton, England, 20 December, 2002

League Club	Source	Date Signed	Seasons Played	Apps	Subs	Gls
Nottingham F	Vale of Leven	09/56	57	10	-	0
Notts Co	Tr	07/59	59-61	62	-	18

JOYCE Eric
Born: Durham, England, 3 July, 1924 — RH
Died: Chester-le-Street, County Durham, England, 1977

League Club	Source	Date Signed	Seasons Played	Apps	Subs	Gls
Bradford C	Eppleton CW	11/45	46	5	-	0

JOYCE Ian Francis
Born: Kinnelon, New Jersey, USA, 12 July, 1985 — G

League Club	Source	Date Signed	Seasons Played	Apps	Subs	Gls
Southend U	Watford (NC)	07/08	08-09	4	1	0

JOYCE John
Born: Easington, County Durham, England, 6 January, 1949 — RW

League Club	Source	Date Signed	Seasons Played	Apps	Subs	Gls
Hartlepool U (Am)	Peterlee Jnrs	03/67	66-68	4	0	0

JOYCE Joseph Patrick (Joe)
Born: Consett, County Durham, England, 18 March, 1961 — RB

League Club	Source	Date Signed	Seasons Played	Apps	Subs	Gls
Barnsley	Jnr	11/79	79-90	332	2	4
Scunthorpe U	Tr	02/91	90-92	91	0	2
Carlisle U	Tr	08/93	93-94	45	5	0
Darlington	L	09/93	93	4	0	0

JOYCE Luke James
Born: Bolton, Greater Manchester, England, 9 July, 1987 — M

League Club	Source	Date Signed	Seasons Played	Apps	Subs	Gls
Carlisle U	Wigan Ath (Sch)	08/06	06-08	12	14	2
Accrington Stan	Tr	07/09	09-14	237	9	8

JOYCE Nicholas John (Nick)
Born: Leeds, England, 27 July, 1947 — RW

League Club	Source	Date Signed	Seasons Played	Apps	Subs	Gls
Bradford C (Am)	Leeds Ashley Road	11/71	71	5	0	1

JOYCE Sean William
Born: Doncaster, South Yorkshire, England, 15 February, 1967 — M

League Club	Source	Date Signed	Seasons Played	Apps	Subs	Gls
Doncaster Rov	YT	07/85	85-87	39	2	2
Exeter C	L	11/86	86	1	0	0
Torquay U	Tr	08/88	88-92	143	15	15

JOYCE Walter
Born: Oldham, Greater Manchester, England, 10 September, 1937 — WH/LB
Died: Liverpool, England, October, 1999

League Club	Source	Date Signed	Seasons Played	Apps	Subs	Gls
Burnley	Jnr	10/54	60-63	70	-	3
Blackburn Rov	Tr	02/64	63-67	119	1	4
Oldham Ath	Tr	09/67	67-69	68	3	2

JOYCE Warren Garton
Born: Oldham, Greater Manchester, England, 20 January, 1965 — M

League Club	Source	Date Signed	Seasons Played	Apps	Subs	Gls
Bolton W	Jnr	06/82	82-87	180	4	17
Preston NE	Tr	10/87	87-91	170	7	35
Plymouth Arg	Tr	05/92	92	28	2	3
Burnley	Tr	07/93	93-95	65	5	9
Hull C	L	01/95	94	9	0	3
Hull C	Tr	07/96	96-99	137	1	12

JOYNES Nathan
Born: Hoyland, South Yorkshire, England, 7 August, 1985 — F

League Club	Source	Date Signed	Seasons Played	Apps	Subs	Gls
Barnsley	Sch	02/05	04	0	1	0
Boston U	L	01/07	06	9	1	1
Bradford C	L	07/07	07	1	1	0

[JUAN] MALDONDO DUARTE Juan
Born: Sao Paulo, Brazil, 6 February, 1982 — FB

League Club	Source	Date Signed	Seasons Played	Apps	Subs	Gls
Arsenal	Sao Paulo (BRA)	07/01				
Millwall	L	08/03	03	2	1	0

JUAN Jimmy Dominique Jacky
Born: Valence, France, 10 June, 1983 — M

League Club	Source	Date Signed	Seasons Played	Apps	Subs	Gls
Ipswich T (L)	AS Monaco (FRA)	01/05	05	24	10	5
Chesterfield	Grenoble (FRA)	12/11	11	6	1	1

[JUANJO] PEREZ Juanjo Carricondo
Born: Barcelona, Spain, 4 May, 1977 — F

League Club	Source	Date Signed	Seasons Played	Apps	Subs	Gls
Bradford C	Heart of Midlothian	10/01	01-02	7	19	1

JUDD Jeremy Laurence
Born: Bristol, England, 18 June, 1965 — G

League Club	Source	Date Signed	Seasons Played	Apps	Subs	Gls
Bournemouth	Jnr	07/82				
Torquay U	Dorchester T	08/84	84	2	0	0

JUDD Michael David (Mike)
Born: Southampton, England, 18 June, 1948 — LW

League Club	Source	Date Signed	Seasons Played	Apps	Subs	Gls
Southampton	App	08/65	67-69	14	1	3

JUDD Walter James
Born: Salisbury, Wiltshire, England, 25 October, 1926 — CF
Died: New Forest, Hampshire, England, 17 December, 1964

League Club	Source	Date Signed	Seasons Played	Apps	Subs	Gls
Southampton	Nomansland	08/49	50-52	34	-	13

JUDGE Alan Christopher
Born: Dublin, Republic of Ireland, 11 November, 1988 — W
Republic of Ireland: U23-4/U21-13/Youth

League Club	Source	Date Signed	Seasons Played	Apps	Subs	Gls
Blackburn Rov	Sch	11/06				
Plymouth Arg	L	01/09	08	15	2	2
Plymouth Arg	L	08/09	09	28	9	5
Notts Co	Tr	08/10	10-12	95	6	16
Blackburn Rov	Tr	07/13	13	7	4	0
Brentford	Tr	01/14	13-14	55	4	10

JUDGE Alan Graham
Born: Kingsbury, NW London, England, 14 May, 1960 — G

League Club	Source	Date Signed	Seasons Played	Apps	Subs	Gls
Luton T	Jnr	01/78	79-82	11	0	0
Reading	L	09/82	82	3	0	0
Reading	Tr	11/82	82-84	74	0	0
Oxford U	Tr	12/84	85-90	80	0	0
Lincoln C	L	11/85	85	2	0	0
Cardiff C	L	10/87	87	8	0	0
Hereford U	Tr	07/91	91-93	105	0	0
Swindon T	Banbury U	12/02				
Oxford U	Tr	03/03	02-04	2	0	0

JUDGE Matthew Peter (Matt)
Born: Barking, E London, England, 18 January, 1985 — F
Republic of Ireland: Youth

League Club	Source	Date Signed	Seasons Played	Apps	Subs	Gls
Luton T	Sch	-	02-03	0	2	0

JUDGES Barry John
Born: Rainham, Kent, England, 23 September, 1940 — CH

League Club	Source	Date Signed	Seasons Played	Apps	Subs	Gls
Gillingham	Jnr	12/57	57-58	3	-	0

JUKES Norman Geoffrey
Born: Leeds, England, 14 October, 1932 — RB

League Club	Source	Date Signed	Seasons Played	Apps	Subs	Gls
Huddersfield T	Apperley Bridge	07/51				
York C	Tr	10/53	53	1	-	0

JULES Mark Anthony
Born: Bradford, England, 5 September, 1971 — LB/M

League Club	Source	Date Signed	Seasons Played	Apps	Subs	Gls
Bradford C	YT	07/90				
Scarborough	Tr	08/91	91-92	57	20	16
Chesterfield	Tr	05/93	93-98	155	31	4
Halifax T	Tr	07/99	99-01	88	9	1

JULIAN Alan John
Born: Ashford, Kent, England, 11 March, 1983 — G
Northern Ireland: U21-1/Youth

League Club	Source	Date Signed	Seasons Played	Apps	Subs	Gls
Brentford	YT	07/01	02-03	16	0	0
Gillingham	Stevenage Bor	07/08	08-10	73	0	0
Stevenage	Tr	07/11	11	2	1	0

JULIANS Leonard Bruce (Len)
Born: Tottenham, N London, England, 19 June, 1933 — CF

Died: Southend-on-Sea, England, 17 December, 1993

League Club	Source	Date Signed	Seasons Played	Apps	Subs	Gls
Leyton Orient	Walthamstow Ave	06/55	55-58	66	-	35
Arsenal	Tr	12/58	58-59	18	-	7
Nottingham F	Tr	06/60	60-63	58	-	24
Millwall	Tr	01/64	63-66	125	0	58

[JULIO CESAR] SANTOS-CORREIA Julio Cesar
Born: Sao Luis, Brazil, 18 November, 1978 CD

League Club	Source	Date Signed	Seasons Played	Apps	Subs	Gls
Bolton W	Real Madrid (SPN)	08/04	04	4	1	0

[JULIO CESAR] SOARES DE ESPINDONA Julio Cesar
Born: Rio de Janeiro, Brazil, 3 September, 1979 G
Brazil: 87

League Club	Source	Date Signed	Seasons Played	Apps	Subs	Gls
Queens Park Rgrs	Inter Milan (ITA)	08/12	12	24	0	0

JULIUSSEN Albert Laurence
Born: Blyth, Northumberland, England, 20 February, 1920 CF

League Club	Source	Date Signed	Seasons Played	Apps	Subs	Gls
Huddersfield T	Dundee North End	10/38				
Portsmouth	Dundee	03/48	47	7	-	4
Everton	Tr	09/48	48	10	-	1

JUMP Stewart Paul
Born: Crumpsall, Greater Manchester, England, 27 January, 1952 D/M

League Club	Source	Date Signed	Seasons Played	Apps	Subs	Gls
Stoke C	App	07/69	70-73	36	8	1
Crystal Palace	Tr	12/73	73-75	67	1	2
Crystal Palace	New York Cosmos (USA)	09/76	76-77	12	1	0
Fulham	L	01/77	76	3	0	0

[JUNINHO] JUNIOR Osvaldo Giroldo
Born: Sao Paulo, Brazil, 22 February, 1973 F/M
Brazil: 50

League Club	Source	Date Signed	Seasons Played	Apps	Subs	Gls
Middlesbrough	Sao Paulo (BRA)	11/95	95-96	54	2	14
Middlesbrough (L)	Atletico Madrid (SPN)	09/99	99	24	4	4
Middlesbrough	Atletico Madrid (SPN)	08/02	02-03	35	6	11

[JUNIOR] GUIMARAES SANIBIO Jose Luis
Born: Fortaleza, Brazil, 20 July, 1976 F

League Club	Source	Date Signed	Seasons Played	Apps	Subs	Gls
Walsall	Treze (BRA)	08/02	02	28	8	15
Derby Co	Tr	08/03	03-04	11	19	4
Rotherham U	L	10/04	04	12	0	2

[JUNIOR] N'GALULA MBUYI Gabriel
Born: Kinshasa, DR Congo, 1 June, 1982 M

League Club	Source	Date Signed	Seasons Played	Apps	Subs	Gls
Stoke C (L)	Anderlecht (BEL)	07/05	05	16	6	0

[JUNIOR] SANTOS DA SILVA JUNIOR Francisco
Born: Bissau, Guinea-Bissau, 18 January, 1992 DM
Portugal: U21-2/Youth

League Club	Source	Date Signed	Seasons Played	Apps	Subs	Gls
Everton	Benfica Jnrs (POR)	02/12				
Port Vale	L	03/15	14	1	0	0

JUPP Duncan Alan
Born: Haslemere, Surrey, England, 25 January, 1975 RB
Scotland: U21-9

League Club	Source	Date Signed	Seasons Played	Apps	Subs	Gls
Fulham	YT	07/93	92-95	101	4	2
Wimbledon	Tr	06/96	96-01	23	7	0
Notts Co	Tr	11/02	02	6	2	0
Luton T	Tr	02/03	02	2	3	0
Southend U	Tr	07/03	03-05	96	4	0
Gillingham	Tr	07/06	06-07	28	1	0

JURYEFF Ian Martin
Born: Gosport, Hampshire, England, 24 November, 1962 F

League Club	Source	Date Signed	Seasons Played	Apps	Subs	Gls
Southampton	App	11/80	83	0	2	0
Mansfield T	L	03/84	83	12	0	5
Reading	L	11/84	84	7	0	2
Leyton Orient	Tr	02/85	84-88	106	5	44
Ipswich T	L	02/89	88	0	2	0
Halifax T	Tr	08/89	89	15	2	7
Hereford U	Tr	12/89	89-90	25	3	4
Halifax T	Tr	09/90	90-92	72	0	13
Darlington	Tr	08/92	92-93	26	8	6
Scunthorpe U	Tr	08/93	93-94	41	3	13

JUSTHAM Elliot
Born: Dagenham, E London, England, 18 August, 1990 G

League Club	Source	Date Signed	Seasons Played	Apps	Subs	Gls
Luton T	East Thurrock U	05/13	14	15	0	0

JUTKIEWICZ Lukas Isaac Paul
Born: Southampton, England, 20 March, 1989 F

League Club	Source	Date Signed	Seasons Played	Apps	Subs	Gls
Swindon T	Sch	07/06	05-06	16	22	5
Everton	Tr	05/07	08	0	1	0
Plymouth Arg	L	01/08	07	1	2	0
Huddersfield T	L	02/09	08	6	1	0
Coventry C	Tr	07/10	10-11	59	8	18
Middlesbrough	Tr	01/12	11-13	47	18	11
Bolton W	L	01/14	13	16	4	7
Burnley	Tr	07/14	14	10	15	0

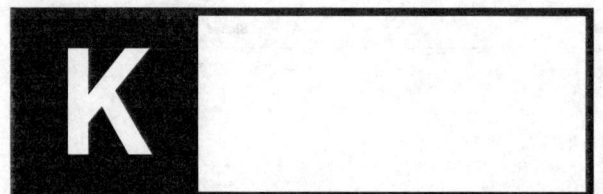

KAAK Anton Christian (Tom)
Born: Winterswijk, Netherlands, 31 March, 1978 M

League Club	Source	Date Signed	Seasons Played	Apps	Subs	Gls
Darlington	Heracles Almelo (NED)	07/00	00	7	1	2

KAAMARK Pontus Sven
Born: Vasteras, Sweden, 5 April, 1969 D
Sweden: 57

League Club	Source	Date Signed	Seasons Played	Apps	Subs	Gls
Leicester C	IFK Goteberg (SWE)	11/95	95-98	60	5	0

KABBA Sorfitu Stephen Tejan (Steve)
Born: Lambeth, S London, England, 7 March, 1981 F

League Club	Source	Date Signed	Seasons Played	Apps	Subs	Gls
Crystal Palace	YT	06/99	99-02	2	8	1
Luton T	L	03/02	01	0	3	0
Grimsby T	L	08/02	02	13	0	6
Sheffield U	Tr	11/02	02-06	46	32	18
Watford	Tr	01/07	06-07	13	12	1
Blackpool	L	07/08	08	12	5	2
Oldham Ath	L	02/09	08	7	1	0
Brentford	Tr	08/09	09	3	7	0
Burton A	L	11/09	09	18	5	6
Barnet	Tr	07/10	10-11	28	4	12

KABIA James Paul (Jim)
Born: Mansfield, Nottinghamshire, England, 11 November, 1954 F

League Club	Source	Date Signed	Seasons Played	Apps	Subs	Gls
Chesterfield	App	11/72	72-73	10	1	1

KABIA Jason Thomas
Born: Sutton-in-Ashfield, Nottinghamshire, England, 28 May, 1969 F

League Club	Source	Date Signed	Seasons Played	Apps	Subs	Gls
Lincoln C	Oakham U	01/92	91-92	17	11	4
Doncaster Rov	L	01/93	92	5	0	0

KABOUL Younes
Born: Annemasse, France, 4 January, 1986 CD
France: 5/U21-18

League Club	Source	Date Signed	Seasons Played	Apps	Subs	Gls
Tottenham H	AJ Auxerre (FRA)	07/07	07	19	2	3
Portsmouth	Tr	08/08	08-09	36	3	4
Tottenham H	Tr	01/10	09-14	83	6	3

KACANIKLIC Alexander (Alex)
Born: Helsingborg, Sweden, 13 August, 1991 LM
Sweden: 19/Youth

League Club	Source	Date Signed	Seasons Played	Apps	Subs	Gls
Liverpool	Sch	01/09				
Fulham	Tr	08/10	11-14	41	20	6
Watford	L	01/12	11	11	1	1
Burnley	L	03/13	12	6	0	0

KACHLOUL Hassan
Born: Agadir, Morocco, 19 February, 1973 M
Morocco: 12

League Club	Source	Date Signed	Seasons Played	Apps	Subs	Gls
Southampton	FC Metz (FRA)	10/98	98-00	73	13	14
Aston Villa	Tr	07/01	01	17	5	2
Wolverhampton W	L	09/03	03	0	4	0

KADAR Tamas
Born: Veszprom, Hungary, 14 March, 1990 LB
Hungary: 22/U21-16/Youth

League Club	Source	Date Signed	Seasons Played	Apps	Subs	Gls
Newcastle U	Zalaegerszegi (HUN)	01/08	09	6	7	0
Huddersfield T	L	01/11	10	2	0	0

KADOCH Ran
Born: Ma'ale Adumim, Palestinian Territory, 4 October, 1985 G

League Club	Source	Date Signed	Seasons Played	Apps	Subs	Gls
Barnet	Nes Tziana (ISR)	08/08	08	11	1	0

KAEBI Hossein
Born: Ahvas, Iran, 23 September, 1985 RW
Iran: 65

League Club	Source	Date Signed	Seasons Played	Apps	Subs	Gls
Leicester C	Persepolis (IRA)	08/07	07	2	1	0

KAGAWA Shinji
Born: Kobe, Japan, 17 March, 1989 M
Japan: 58/U23-3/Youth

League Club	Source	Date Signed	Seasons Played	Apps	Subs	Gls
Manchester U	Bor Dortmund (GER)	07/12	12-13	31	7	6

KAIKAI Sulaiman Borbor (Sulley)
Born: Southwark, S London, England, 26 August, 1995 F/W

League Club	Source	Date Signed	Seasons Played	Apps	Subs	Gls
Crystal Palace	Sch	01/13				
Crawley T	L	02/14	13	2	3	0
Cambridge U	L	11/14	14	11	14	5

KAILE Gordon Walter
Born: Dorset, England, 7 December, 1924 LW
Died: Blandford Forum, Dorset, England, 28 February, 1988

League Club	Source	Date Signed	Seasons Played	Apps	Subs	Gls
Nottingham F	RAOC Chilwell	05/45	47-49	65	-	8
Preston NE	Tr	07/51	51-53	7	-	1
Exeter C	Tr	08/54	54	6	-	1

KAISER Rudolph Hendrick (Rudi)
Born: Amsterdam, Netherlands, 26 December, 1960 RW

League Club	Source	Date Signed	Seasons Played	Apps	Subs	Gls
Coventry C	Royal Antwerp (BEL)	08/81	81	11	5	3

KAKU Blessing
Born: Ughelli, Nigeria, 5 March, 1978 M
Nigeria:

League Club	Source	Date Signed	Seasons Played	Apps	Subs	Gls
Bolton W	MS Ashdod (NIG)	08/04	04	0	1	0
Derby Co	L	11/04	04	3	1	0

KAKUTA Gael
Born: Lille, France, 21 June, 1991 LW
France: U21-18/Youth

League Club	Source	Date Signed	Seasons Played	Apps	Subs	Gls
Chelsea	Sch	07/08	09-10	1	5	0
Fulham	L	01/11	10	2	5	1
Bolton W	L	08/11	11	0	4	0

KALAC Zeljko
Born: Sydney, Australia, 16 December, 1972 G
Australia: 65

League Club	Source	Date Signed	Seasons Played	Apps	Subs	Gls
Leicester C	Sydney U (AUS)	10/95	95	1	0	0

KALAS Tomas
Born: Olomouc, Czech Republic, 15 May, 1993 CD
Czech Republic: 1/U21-17

League Club	Source	Date Signed	Seasons Played	Apps	Subs	Gls
Chelsea	Sigma Olomouc (CZE)	01/11	13	2	0	0
Middlesbrough	L	01/15	14	16	1	0

KALINIC Nikola
Born: Split, Croatia, 5 January, 1988 F
Croatia: 21/U21-9

League Club	Source	Date Signed	Seasons Played	Apps	Subs	Gls
Blackburn Rov	Hajduk Split (CRO)	08/09	09-10	29	15	7

KALLIO Toni
Born: Tampere, Finland, 9 August, 1978 LB
Finland: 49/U21-5

League Club	Source	Date Signed	Seasons Played	Apps	Subs	Gls
Fulham	Young Boys Bern (SUI)	01/08	08-09	2	2	0
Sheffield U	L	11/09	09	2	0	0
Sheffield U	L	02/10	09	6	0	0

KALLSTROM Kim Mikael
Born: Sandviken, Sweden, 24 August, 1982 M
Sweden: 120/U21-21/Youth

League Club	Source	Date Signed	Seasons Played	Apps	Subs	Gls
Arsenal (L)	Spartak Moscow (RUS)	01/14	13	1	2	0

KALOGERACOS Vasilios (Vas)
Born: Perth, Australia, 21 March, 1975 F
Australia: Youth

League Club	Source	Date Signed	Seasons Played	Apps	Subs	Gls
Birmingham C	Australian IOS (AUS)	12/93				
Stockport Co	Perth Glory (AUS)	08/97	97	0	2	0

KALOU Salomon Armand Magloire
Born: Oume, Ivory Coast, 3 August, 1985 F
Ivory Coast: 79

League Club	Source	Date Signed	Seasons Played	Apps	Subs	Gls
Chelsea	Feyenoord (NED)	07/06	06-11	94	62	37

KALVENES Christian
Born: Bergen, Norway, 8 March, 1977 LB

League Club	Source	Date Signed	Seasons Played	Apps	Subs	Gls
Burnley	Dundee U	07/08	08-09	24	3	1

KAMARA Abdul Salam
Born: Southampton, England, 10 February, 1974 M

League Club	Source	Date Signed	Seasons Played	Apps	Subs	Gls
Southampton	Norwich C (YT)	08/92				
Bristol C	Tr	03/93	93	0	1	0

KAMARA Alan
Born: Sheffield, England, 15 July, 1958 D

League Club	Source	Date Signed	Seasons Played	Apps	Subs	Gls
York C	Kiveton Park	07/79	79	10	0	0
Darlington	Tr	06/80	80-82	134	0	1
Scarborough	Burton A	11/87	87-90	158	1	2
Halifax T	Tr	08/91	91-92	34	2	0

KAMARA Christopher (Chris)
Born: Middlesbrough, England, 25 December, 1957 M

League Club	Source	Date Signed	Seasons Played	Apps	Subs	Gls
Portsmouth	App	12/75	75-76	56	7	7
Swindon T	Tr	08/77	77-80	133	14	21
Portsmouth	Tr	08/81	81	11	0	0
Brentford	Tr	10/81	81-84	150	2	28
Swindon T	Tr	08/85	85-87	86	1	6
Stoke C	Tr	07/88	88-89	60	0	5
Leeds U	Tr	01/90	89-91	15	5	1
Luton T	Tr	11/91	91-92	49	0	0
Sheffield U	L	11/92	92	6	2	0

League Club	Source	Date Signed	Seasons Played	Apps	Subs	Gls
Middlesbrough	L	02/93	92	3	2	0
Sheffield U	Tr	07/93	93	15	1	0
Bradford C	Tr	07/94	94	22	1	3

KAMARA Diomansy Mehdi
Born: Paris, France, 8 November, 1980 — F
Senegal: 51

League Club	Source	Date Signed	Seasons Played	Apps	Subs	Gls
Portsmouth (L)	Modena (ITA)	09/04	04	15	10	4
West Bromwich A	Modena (ITA)	08/05	05-06	54	6	21
Fulham	Tr	07/07	07-10	32	27	12
Leicester C	L	03/11	10	5	2	2

KAMARA Foday Ishmael (Ishmael)
Born: Issia, Sierra Leone, 29 October, 1987 — F
Sierra Leone: 5

League Club	Source	Date Signed	Seasons Played	Apps	Subs	Gls
Barnet	Dulwich Hamlet	09/12	12	0	1	0

KAMARA Kei Ansu
Born: Kenema, Sierra Leone, 1 September, 1984 — F
Sierra Leone: 21

League Club	Source	Date Signed	Seasons Played	Apps	Subs	Gls
Norwich C (L)	Sport'g Kansas C (USA)	01/13	12	7	4	1
Middlesbrough	Sport'g Kansas C (USA)	09/13	13	16	9	4

KAMARA Malvin Ginah
Born: Plumstead, SE London, England, 17 November, 1983 — W

League Club	Source	Date Signed	Seasons Played	Apps	Subs	Gls
Wimbledon	Sch	07/03	02-03	15	14	2
MK Dons	Wimbledon relocation	07/04	04-05	22	26	3
Cardiff C	Tr	07/06	06	3	12	1
Port Vale	Tr	01/07	06	14	4	1
Huddersfield T	Tr	07/07	07	33	12	3
Grimsby T	L	09/08	08	1	1	0

KAMDJO Clovis Tchoumbou
Born: Cameroon, 15 December, 1990 — DM

League Club	Source	Date Signed	Seasons Played	Apps	Subs	Gls
Barnet	Reading (Sch)	08/09	09-12	104	10	5

KAMINSKY Jason Mario George
Born: Leicester, England, 5 December, 1973 — F
Died: Leicester, England, 28 September, 2005

League Club	Source	Date Signed	Seasons Played	Apps	Subs	Gls
Nottingham F	YT	07/91	91	0	1	0

KAMUDIMBA KALALA Jean-Paul
Born: Lubumbashi, DR Congo, 16 March, 1982 — M
DR Congo: 8

League Club	Source	Date Signed	Seasons Played	Apps	Subs	Gls
Grimsby T	OGC Nice (FRA)	07/05	05	14	7	5
Yeovil T	Tr	07/06	06	35	3	1
Oldham Ath	Tr	07/07	07	14	6	0
Grimsby T	L	10/08	08	21	0	2
Yeovil T	Tr	09/09	09-10	45	4	1
Bristol Rov	Tr	01/11	10	10	1	0
Southend U	Tr	08/11	11	23	1	1

KANCHELSKIS Andrei
Born: Kirowograd, Ukraine, 23 January, 1969 — RW
Commonwealth of Independent States: 6//Russia: 36//Soviet Union: 17

League Club	Source	Date Signed	Seasons Played	Apps	Subs	Gls
Manchester U	Shakhtar Donetsk (UKR)	03/91	90-94	96	27	28
Everton	Tr	08/95	95-96	52	0	20
Manchester C (L)	Glasgow Rangers	01/01	00	7	3	0
Southampton	Glasgow Rangers	08/02	02	0	1	0

KANDOL Tresor Osmar
Born: Banga, DR Congo, 30 August, 1981 — F
DR Congo: 1

League Club	Source	Date Signed	Seasons Played	Apps	Subs	Gls
Luton T	YT	09/98	98-00	9	12	3
Cambridge U	Tr	08/01	01	2	2	0
Bournemouth	Heybridge Swifts	10/01	01	3	9	0
Darlington (L)	Dagenham & Red	11/05	05	6	1	2
Barnet	Tr	01/06	05-06	27	2	10
Leeds U	Tr	11/06	06-09	43	26	14
Millwall	L	08/08	08	16	2	8
Charlton Ath	L	01/09	08	10	3	2

KANE Alan
Born: Falkirk, Scotland, 20 January, 1957 — M

League Club	Source	Date Signed	Seasons Played	Apps	Subs	Gls
Portsmouth	Hibernian	03/75	74-75	6	1	0

KANE Anthony Michael (Tony)
Born: Belfast, Northern Ireland, 29 August, 1987 — RB
Republic of Ireland: U21-5//Northern Ireland: U21-5/Youth

League Club	Source	Date Signed	Seasons Played	Apps	Subs	Gls
Blackburn Rov	Sch	11/04				
Stockport Co	L	11/06	06	4	0	0
Stockport Co	L	10/08	08	3	0	0
Carlisle U	Tr	02/09	08-10	7	7	0
Darlington	L	09/09	09	4	0	0

KANE Harry Edward
Born: Chingford, NE London, England, 28 July, 1993 — F
England: 2/U21-14/Youth

League Club	Source	Date Signed	Seasons Played	Apps	Subs	Gls
Tottenham H	Sch	07/10	12-14	34	11	24
Leyton Orient	L	01/11	10	9	9	5
Millwall	L	01/12	11	19	3	7
Norwich C	L	08/12	12	1	2	0
Leicester C	L	02/13	12	5	8	2

KANE John Peter
Born: Hackney, E London, England, 15 December, 1960 — CD

League Club	Source	Date Signed	Seasons Played	Apps	Subs	Gls
Leyton Orient	App	12/78	78	0	1	0

KANE Leonard Russell (Len)
Born: Belfast, Northern Ireland, 27 January, 1926 — FB
Northern Ireland: NILge-3

League Club	Source	Date Signed	Seasons Played	Apps	Subs	Gls
Preston NE	Glentoran	05/47	48-49	5	-	0
Plymouth Arg	Tr	01/50				

KANE Paul James
Born: Edinburgh, Scotland, 20 August, 1965 — M
Scotland: Youth

League Club	Source	Date Signed	Seasons Played	Apps	Subs	Gls
Oldham Ath	Hibernian	01/91	90-91	13	8	0
Barnsley (L)	Aberdeen	08/95	95	4	0	0

KANE Peter
Born: Petershill, Glasgow, Scotland, 4 April, 1939 — IF

League Club	Source	Date Signed	Seasons Played	Apps	Subs	Gls
Northampton T	Queen's Park	10/59	59	28	-	16
Arsenal	Tr	07/60	60	4	-	1
Northampton T	Tr	09/63	63	18	-	8
Crewe Alex	Tr	03/64	63-66	82	1	29

KANE Robert (Bob)
Born: Cambuslang, Glasgow, Scotland, 11 May, 1911 — CH
Died: Cambuslang, Glasgow, Scotland, 27 January, 1985

League Club	Source	Date Signed	Seasons Played	Apps	Subs	Gls
Leeds U	St Roch's	08/35	35-46	57	-	0

KANE Todd Arthur Lucien
Born: Huntingdon, Cambridgeshire, England, 17 September, 1993 — RB
England: Youth

League Club	Source	Date Signed	Seasons Played	Apps	Subs	Gls
Chelsea	Sch	07/11				
Preston NE	L	11/12	12	3	0	0
Blackburn Rov	L	01/13	12	13	1	0
Blackburn Rov	L	06/13	13	23	4	2
Bristol C	L	11/14	14	1	4	0
Nottingham F	L	01/15	14	7	1	1

KANOUTE Frederic Oumar
Born: Lyon, France, 2 September, 1977 — F
France: B-1/U21-16//Mali: 39

League Club	Source	Date Signed	Seasons Played	Apps	Subs	Gls
West Ham U	Olymp Lyonnais (FRA)	03/00	99-02	79	5	29
Tottenham H	Tr	08/03	03-05	41	19	14

KANOUTE Samba
Born: Paris, France, 30 July, 1991 — D

League Club	Source	Date Signed	Seasons Played	Apps	Subs	Gls
Hereford U	AJ Auxerre Jnrs (FRA)	08/10	10	0	1	0

KANU Christopher Ogbonnaya (Chris)
Born: Owerri, Nigeria, 4 December, 1979 — RB
Nigeria: 3

League Club	Source	Date Signed	Seasons Played	Apps	Subs	Gls
Peterborough U	TOP Oss (NED)	08/03	03-04	25	9	0

KANU Nwankwo
Born: Owerri, Nigeria, 1 August, 1976 — F
Nigeria: 86/U23-6/Youth

League Club	Source	Date Signed	Seasons Played	Apps	Subs	Gls
Arsenal	Inter Milan (ITA)	02/99	98-03	63	56	30
West Bromwich A	Tr	07/04	04-05	38	15	7
Portsmouth	Tr	07/06	06-11	70	73	20

KANYUKA Patrick Elamenji
Born: Kinshasa, DR Congo, 19 July, 1987 — CD

League Club	Source	Date Signed	Seasons Played	Apps	Subs	Gls
Queens Park Rgrs	Jnr	07/04	04-06	8	4	0
Swindon T	Tr	01/08	07-08	19	1	1
Northampton T	Tr	10/09	09	3	0	0
Lincoln C	CFR Cluj (ROM)	01/11	10	2	4	0

KAPENGWE Emment
Born: Kabwe, Zambia, 27 March, 1943 — W
Died: Lusaka, Zambia, 17 September, 1988
Zambia: 42

League Club	Source	Date Signed	Seasons Played	Apps	Subs	Gls
Aston Villa	Atlanta Chiefs (USA)	09/69	69	3	0	0

KAPLER Konrad
Born: Tychy, Poland, 25 February, 1925 — LW
Died: Rochdale, Greater Manchester, England, 23 October, 1991

League Club	Source	Date Signed	Seasons Played	Apps	Subs	Gls
Rochdale	Glasgow Celtic	05/49	49	4	-	0

KAPO Narcisse-Olivier (Olivier)
Born: Abidjan, Ivory Coast, 27 September, 1980 — LW
France: 9/U21-14

League Club	Source	Date Signed	Seasons Played	Apps	Subs	Gls
Birmingham C	Juventus (ITA)	07/07	07	22	4	5
Wigan Ath	Tr	07/08	08-09	10	10	1

KAPRIELIAN Mickael
Born: Marseille, France, 6 October, 1980 — F

League Club	Source	Date Signed	Seasons Played	Career Record Apps	Subs	Gls
France: Youth						
Bolton W	Martigues (FRA)	01/00	99	0	1	0

KARAA Roch Di
Born: Sousse, Tunisia, 3 April, 1964 — G
Tunisia: U21/Youth

League Club	Source	Date Signed	Seasons Played	Apps	Subs	Gls
Darlington	ES Sahel (TUN)	03/85	84	1	0	0

KARACAN Jem Paul
Born: Catford, SE London, England, 21 February, 1989 — M
Turkey: U21-3/Youth

League Club	Source	Date Signed	Seasons Played	Apps	Subs	Gls
Reading	Sch	07/07	08-14	142	13	11
Bournemouth	L	10/07	07	11	2	1
Millwall	L	03/08	07	7	0	0

KARADAS Azar
Born: Nordfjord, Norway, 9 August, 1981 — F
Norway: 10/U21-33

League Club	Source	Date Signed	Seasons Played	Apps	Subs	Gls
Portsmouth (L)	Benfica (POR)	07/05	05	4	13	1

KARAGOUNIS Georgios
Born: Pyrgos, Greece, 6 March, 1977 — M
Greece: 139/U21-39

League Club	Source	Date Signed	Seasons Played	Apps	Subs	Gls
Fulham	Panathinaikos (GRE)	09/12	12-13	26	13	1

KARAM Amine
Born: Besancon, France, 3 January, 1984 — W

League Club	Source	Date Signed	Seasons Played	Apps	Subs	Gls
Oxford U	Sochaux (FRA)	02/04	04	0	2	0

KARBASSIYOON Daniel (Danny)
Born: Roanoke, Virginia, USA, 10 August, 1984 — LB
USA: Youth

League Club	Source	Date Signed	Seasons Played	Apps	Subs	Gls
Arsenal	Roanoke Star (USA)	08/03				
Ipswich T	L	12/04	04	3	2	0
Burnley	Tr	07/05	05	0	5	0

KARELSE John
Born: Kapelle, Netherlands, 17 May, 1970 — G

League Club	Source	Date Signed	Seasons Played	Apps	Subs	Gls
Newcastle U	NAC Breda (NED)	08/99	99	3	0	0

KAREMBEU Christian Lali
Born: Lifou, New Caledonia, 3 December, 1970 — DM
France: 53

League Club	Source	Date Signed	Seasons Played	Apps	Subs	Gls
Middlesbrough	Real Madrid (SPN)	08/00	00	31	2	4

KARIC Amir
Born: Doboj, Yugoslavia, 31 December, 1973 — CD
Slovenia: 64

League Club	Source	Date Signed	Seasons Played	Apps	Subs	Gls
Ipswich T	NK Maribor (SVN)	09/00				
Crystal Palace	L	03/01	00	3	0	0

KARL Steffen
Born: Hohenmoelsen, Saxony, Germany, 3 February, 1970 — M
Germany: U21-1

League Club	Source	Date Signed	Seasons Played	Apps	Subs	Gls
Manchester C (L)	Bor Dortmund (GER)	03/94	93	4	2	1

KARLSEN Kent
Born: Oslo, Norway, 17 February, 1973 — CD
Norway: U21

League Club	Source	Date Signed	Seasons Played	Apps	Subs	Gls
Luton T	FC Valerenga (NOR)	11/00	00	4	2	0

KARLSSON Par
Born: Gothenburg, Sweden, 29 May, 1978 — M
Sweden: U21

League Club	Source	Date Signed	Seasons Played	Apps	Subs	Gls
Wimbledon	IFK Goteberg (SWE)	09/00	00-02	10	16	0

KASAMI Pajtim
Born: Struga, Macedonia, 2 June, 1992 — M
Switzerland: 6/U23-4/U21-31/Youth

League Club	Source	Date Signed	Seasons Played	Apps	Subs	Gls
Fulham	Palermo (ITA)	07/11	11-13	23	15	3

KASHKET Scott Connor
Born: Chigwell, Essex, England, 6 July, 1995 — M

League Club	Source	Date Signed	Seasons Played	Apps	Subs	Gls
Leyton Orient	Jnr	02/14	14	0	1	0

KASIM Yaser Safa
Born: Baghdad, Iraq, 10 May, 1991 — M
Iraq: 15/U23-1

League Club	Source	Date Signed	Seasons Played	Apps	Subs	Gls
Brighton & HA	Tottenham H (Sch)	10/10	10	1	0	0
Swindon T	Tr	07/13	13-14	62	10	4

KASULE Victor Peter (Vic)
Born: Glasgow, Scotland, 28 May, 1965 — RW

League Club	Source	Date Signed	Seasons Played	Apps	Subs	Gls
Shrewsbury T	Meadowbank Thistle	01/88	87-89	28	12	4

KATALINIC Ivan
Born: Trogir, Croatia, 17 May, 1951 — G
Yugoslavia: 13

League Club	Source	Date Signed	Seasons Played	Apps	Subs	Gls
Southampton	Hadjuk Split (YUG)	02/80	79-81	48	0	0

KATAN Yaniv
Born: Haifa, Israel, 27 January, 1981 — W
Israel: 31/U21-17/Youth

League Club	Source	Date Signed	Seasons Played	Apps	Subs	Gls
West Ham U (L)	Maccabi Haifa (ISR)	01/06	05	2	4	0

KATCHOURO Petr
Born: Orsha, Belarus, 2 August, 1972 — F
Belarus: 29

League Club	Source	Date Signed	Seasons Played	Apps	Subs	Gls
Sheffield U	Dynamo Minsk (BLR)	07/96	96-99	50	45	19

KAVANAGH Eamonn Anthony
Born: Manchester, England, 5 January, 1954 — M

League Club	Source	Date Signed	Seasons Played	Apps	Subs	Gls
Manchester C	Jnr	06/71				
Rochdale	Tr	10/73	73	2	2	0
Workington	Bury (NC)	03/74	73-76	123	6	12
Scunthorpe U	Tr	08/77	77-79	68	8	3

KAVANAGH Edward Mark (Eddie)
Born: Glasgow, Scotland, 20 July, 1941 — RW

League Club	Source	Date Signed	Seasons Played	Apps	Subs	Gls
Notts Co	Cambuslang Rgrs	05/64	64	25	-	4

KAVANAGH Graham Anthony
Born: Dublin, Republic of Ireland, 2 December, 1973 — M
Republic of Ireland: 16/B-1/U21-9/Youth/Schools

League Club	Source	Date Signed	Seasons Played	Apps	Subs	Gls
Middlesbrough	Home Farm (ROI)	08/91	92-95	22	13	3
Darlington	L	02/94	93	5	0	0
Stoke C	Tr	09/96	96-00	198	8	35
Cardiff C	Tr	07/01	01-04	140	2	28
Wigan Ath	Tr	03/05	04-06	43	5	0
Sunderland	Tr	08/06	06	10	4	1
Sheffield Wed	L	09/07	07	7	0	1
Sheffield Wed	L	01/08	07	14	2	1
Carlisle U	Tr	10/08	08-10	62	2	7

KAVANAGH Jason Colin
Born: Birmingham, England, 23 November, 1971 — RB
England: Youth/Schools

League Club	Source	Date Signed	Seasons Played	Apps	Subs	Gls
Derby Co	YT	12/88	90-95	74	25	1
Wycombe W	Tr	11/96	96-98	84	6	1
Stoke C	Tr	03/99	98	8	0	0
Cambridge U	Tr	12/99	99	19	0	0

KAVANAGH Michael (Micky)
Born: Dublin, Republic of Ireland, 31 December, 1927 — LW
Died: Hove, East Sussex, England, 30 November, 2013

League Club	Source	Date Signed	Seasons Played	Apps	Subs	Gls
Brighton & HA	Bohemians (ROI)	02/48	48-49	26	-	7

KAVANAGH Peter John
Born: Ilford, E London, England, 3 November, 1938 — LW

League Club	Source	Date Signed	Seasons Played	Apps	Subs	Gls
Fulham	Dagenham	10/56				
Everton	Romford	02/61	60	6	-	0

KAVANAGH Sean
Born: Dublin, Republic of Ireland, 24 January, 1994 — LB/M
Republic of Ireland: U21-2/Youth

League Club	Source	Date Signed	Seasons Played	Apps	Subs	Gls
Fulham	Belvedere (ROI)	09/11	14	14	5	1

KAVELASHVILI Mikhail Guramovich
Born: Tbilisi, Georgia, 22 July, 1971 — F
Georgia: 46

League Club	Source	Date Signed	Seasons Played	Apps	Subs	Gls
Manchester C	Dinamo Tbilisi (GEO)	03/96	95-96	9	19	3

KAVIEDES Jaime Ivan (Ivan)
Born: Santo Domingo, Ecuador, 24 October, 1977 — F
Ecuador: 57

League Club	Source	Date Signed	Seasons Played	Apps	Subs	Gls
Crystal Palace (L)	Barcelona DG (ECU)	08/04	04	1	3	0

KAWAGUCHI Yoshikatsu
Born: Fuji, Japan, 15 August, 1975 — G
Japan: 116/U23-10

League Club	Source	Date Signed	Seasons Played	Apps	Subs	Gls
Portsmouth	Yokohama Marinos (JPN)	10/01	01-02	11	1	0

KAY Adam Bernard
Born: Burnley, Lancashire, England, 5 March, 1990 — M

League Club	Source	Date Signed	Seasons Played	Apps	Subs	Gls
Burnley	Sch	06/08				
Accrington Stan	L	03/09	08	1	2	0

KAY Anthony Herbert (Tony)
Born: Sheffield, England, 13 May, 1937 — LH
England: 1/FLge-4/U23-7

League Club	Source	Date Signed	Seasons Played	Apps	Subs	Gls
Sheffield Wed	Jnr	05/54	54-62	179	-	10
Everton	Tr	12/62	62-63	50	-	4

KAY Antony Roland
Born: Barnsley, South Yorkshire, England, 21 October, 1982 — M
England: Youth

League Club	Source	Date Signed	Seasons Played	Apps	Subs	Gls
Barnsley	YT	10/99	00-06	156	18	11
Tranmere Rov	Tr	07/07	07-08	74	8	17
Huddersfield T	Tr	06/09	09-11	84	11	10
MK Dons	Tr	08/12	12-14	104	4	4

KAY James (Jim)
Born: Preston, Lancashire, England, 3 May, 1932 — IF
Died: Preston, Lancashire, England, July, 1986

League Club	Source	Date Signed	Seasons Played	Apps	Subs	Gls
Stockport Co	Leyland Motors	05/53	54-55	9	-	3
Crewe Alex	Tr	12/56	56	6	-	0

KAY John
Born: Great Lumley, County Durham, England, 29 January, 1964 — RB

League Club	Source	Date Signed	Seasons Played	Apps	Subs	Gls
Arsenal	App	08/81	82-83	13	1	0
Wimbledon	Tr	07/84	84-86	63	0	2
Middlesbrough	L	01/85	84	8	0	0
Sunderland	Tr	07/87	87-93	196	3	0
Shrewsbury T	L	03/96	95	7	0	0
Preston NE	Tr	08/96	96	7	0	0
Scarborough	Tr	09/96	96-98	97	1	0

KAY Kenneth (Ken)
Born: Newark, Nottinghamshire, England, 9 March, 1920 — LW
Died: Newark, Nottinghamshire, England, July, 1986

League Club	Source	Date Signed	Seasons Played	Apps	Subs	Gls
Mansfield T	Ransome & Marles	06/47	47	1	-	0

KAY Matthew Paul (Matty)
Born: Blackpool, Lancashire, England, 12 October, 1989 — M

League Club	Source	Date Signed	Seasons Played	Apps	Subs	Gls
Blackpool	Sch	10/06	05	0	1	0

KAY Michael Joseph
Born: Consett, County Durham, England, 12 September, 1989 — RB

League Club	Source	Date Signed	Seasons Played	Apps	Subs	Gls
Sunderland	Sch	07/07				
Tranmere Rov	L	01/11	10	22	0	1
Tranmere Rov	Tr	07/11	11-12	7	5	0

KAY Robert (Roy)
Born: Edinburgh, Scotland, 24 October, 1949 — FB

League Club	Source	Date Signed	Seasons Played	Apps	Subs	Gls
York C	Glasgow Celtic	07/78	78-81	160	0	8

KAY Scott John David
Born: Denton, Greater Manchester, England, 18 September, 1989 — M

League Club	Source	Date Signed	Seasons Played	Apps	Subs	Gls
Manchester C	Sch	09/07				
Macclesfield T	Tr	07/11	11	10	5	0
Huddersfield T	Tr	08/12				

KAYAL Beram
Born: Acre, Israel, 2 May, 1988 — M
Israel: 26/U21-11/Youth

League Club	Source	Date Signed	Seasons Played	Apps	Subs	Gls
Brighton & HA	Glasgow Celtic	01/15	14	17	1	1

KAYE Arthur
Born: South Yorkshire, England, 9 May, 1933 — RW
Died: Barnsley, South Yorkshire, England, October, 2003
England: FLge-1/U23-1/Schools

League Club	Source	Date Signed	Seasons Played	Apps	Subs	Gls
Barnsley	Jnr	05/50	50-58	265	-	54
Blackpool	Tr	05/59	59-60	48	-	9
Middlesbrough	Tr	11/60	60-64	164	-	38
Colchester U	Tr	06/65	65-66	48	1	2

KAYE David Nicholas
Born: Huddersfield, West Yorkshire, England, 14 November, 1959 — G

League Club	Source	Date Signed	Seasons Played	Apps	Subs	Gls
Rotherham U		11/77				
Chester C	Mexborough T	03/85	84-85	10	0	0

KAYE George Henry (Harry)
Born: Liverpool, England, 19 April, 1919 — WH
Died: Liverpool, England, November, 1992

League Club	Source	Date Signed	Seasons Played	Apps	Subs	Gls
Liverpool		04/41	46	1	-	0
Swindon T	Tr	05/47	47-52	170	-	5

KAYE John
Born: Goole, East Riding of Yorkshire, England, 3 March, 1940 — CF/CD
England: FLge-2

League Club	Source	Date Signed	Seasons Played	Apps	Subs	Gls
Scunthorpe U	Goole T	09/60	60-62	77	-	25
West Bromwich A	Tr	06/63	63-71	281	3	45
Hull C	Tr	11/71	71-73	71	1	9

KAYE Peter John
Born: Huddersfield, West Yorkshire, England, 4 February, 1979 — F

League Club	Source	Date Signed	Seasons Played	Apps	Subs	Gls
Huddersfield T	YT	09/96	96	0	1	0

KAZIBONI Gregory (Greg)
Born: Kampala, Uganda, 16 May, 1992 — M

League Club	Source	Date Signed	Seasons Played	Apps	Subs	Gls
Northampton T	Sch	07/11	10-11	0	5	0

KAZIM-RICHARDS Colin
Born: Walthamstow, NE London, England, 26 August, 1986 — W
Turkey: 36/U21-5

League Club	Source	Date Signed	Seasons Played	Apps	Subs	Gls
Bury	Sch	-	04	10	20	3
Brighton & HA	Tr	07/05	05-06	25	18	6
Sheffield U	Tr	08/06	06	15	12	1
Blackburn Rov (L)	Galatasaray (TKY)	08/12	12	22	6	3

KAZIMIERCZAK Przemsylaw Tadeusz (Prez)
Born: Lodz, Poland, 22 February, 1988 — G

League Club	Source	Date Signed	Seasons Played	Apps	Subs	Gls
Bolton W	Sch	07/06				
Accrington Stan	L	01/07	06	7	1	0
Darlington	Tr	01/08	07-08	7	2	0

KAZMIERCZAK Przemyslaw (Prez)
Born: Lodz, Poland, 5 May, 1982 — M
Poland: 11

League Club	Source	Date Signed	Seasons Played	Apps	Subs	Gls
Derby Co	FC Porto (POR)	07/08	08	12	10	2

KEAN Jacob Kendall (Jake)
Born: Derby, England, 4 February, 1991 — G
England: Youth

League Club	Source	Date Signed	Seasons Played	Apps	Subs	Gls
Blackburn Rov	Derby Co (Sch)	05/10	11-13	37	0	0
Hartlepool U	L	09/10	10	19	0	0
Rochdale	L	08/11	11	14	0	0
Yeovil T	L	09/14	14	5	0	0
Oldham Ath	L	01/15	14	11	0	0

KEAN Robert Steven (Rob)
Born: Luton, England, 3 June, 1978 — M

League Club	Source	Date Signed	Seasons Played	Apps	Subs	Gls
Luton T	YT	05/96	97	0	1	0

KEAN Stephen (Steve)
Born: Glasgow, Scotland, 30 September, 1967 — W

League Club	Source	Date Signed	Seasons Played	Apps	Subs	Gls
Swansea C (L)	Glasgow Celtic	02/87	86	3	1	0

KEANE Cieran Macauley
Born: Nottingham, England, 14 August, 1996 — LB
Republic of Ireland: Youth

League Club	Source	Date Signed	Seasons Played	Apps	Subs	Gls
Notts Co	Wolverhampton W (Sch)	07/14	14	2	0	0

KEANE Keith Francis
Born: Luton, England, 20 November, 1986 — DM
Republic of Ireland: U21-4/Youth

League Club	Source	Date Signed	Seasons Played	Apps	Subs	Gls
Luton T	Sch	08/04	03-08	114	15	4
Preston NE	Tr	07/12	12-13	53	11	3
Crawley T	L	09/14	14	12	0	0
Stevenage	L	03/15	14	5	2	0

KEANE Michael Thomas Joseph
Born: Dublin, Republic of Ireland, 29 December, 1982 — M
England: U21-20/Youth//Republic of Ireland: Youth

League Club	Source	Date Signed	Seasons Played	Apps	Subs	Gls
Preston NE	YT	08/00	00-03	39	18	3
Grimsby T	L	03/03	02	7	0	2
Hull C	Tr	06/04	04	12	8	3
Rotherham U	Tr	03/05	04-06	51	9	0

KEANE Michael Vincent
Born: Stockport, Greater Manchester, England, 11 January, 1993 — CD
England: U21-19/Youth//Republic of Ireland: Youth

League Club	Source	Date Signed	Seasons Played	Apps	Subs	Gls
Manchester U	Sch	07/11	14	0	1	0
Leicester C	L	11/12	12	22	0	2
Derby Co	L	11/13	13	4	3	0
Blackburn Rov	L	03/14	13	13	0	3
Burnley	Tr	09/14	14	17	4	0

KEANE Robert David (Robbie)
Born: Dublin, Republic of Ireland, 8 July, 1980 — F
Republic of Ireland: 140/B-1/Youth

League Club	Source	Date Signed	Seasons Played	Apps	Subs	Gls
Wolverhampton W	YT	07/97	97-99	66	7	24
Coventry C	Tr	08/99	99	30	1	12
Leeds U	Inter Milan (ITA)	12/00	00-02	28	18	13
Tottenham H	Tr	08/02	02-07	158	39	80
Liverpool	Tr	07/08	08	16	3	5
Tottenham H	Tr	02/09	08-10	31	10	11
West Ham U	L	01/11	10	5	4	2
Aston Villa (L)	Los Angeles G'xy (USA)	01/12	11	5	1	3

KEANE Roy Maurice
Born: Cork, Republic of Ireland, 10 August, 1971 — M
Republic of Ireland: 67/U21-4/Youth/Schools

League Club	Source	Date Signed	Seasons Played	Apps	Subs	Gls
Nottingham F	Cobh Ramblers (ROI)	06/90	90-92	114	0	22
Manchester U	Tr	07/93	93-05	309	17	33

KEANE Thomas Joseph (Tommy)
Born: Galway, Republic of Ireland, 16 September, 1968 — M
Died: Galway, Republic of Ireland, 28 December, 2012
Republic of Ireland: Youth

League Club	Source	Date Signed	Seasons Played	Apps	Subs	Gls
Bournemouth	App	09/86	85-87	1	2	0
Colchester U	Tr	12/87	87	9	7	0

KEANE Thomas Roderick (Rory)
Born: Limerick, Republic of Ireland, 31 August, 1922 — RB
Died: Swansea, Wales, 13 February, 2004
Republic of Ireland: 4//Northern Ireland: 1

League Club	Source	Date Signed	Seasons Played	Apps	Subs	Gls
Swansea C	Limerick C (ROI)	06/47	47-54	163	-	0

League Club	Source	Date Signed	Seasons Played	Career Record Apps	Subs	Gls
KEANE William David (Will)						
Born: Stockport, Greater Manchester, England, 11 January, 1993						F
England: U21-6/Youth						
Manchester U	Sch	07/11	11	0	1	0
Wigan Ath	L	11/13	13	2	2	0
Queens Park Rgrs	L	01/14	13	6	4	0
Sheffield Wed	L	01/15	14	12	1	3
KEAR Michael Philip (Mike)						
Born: Coleford, Gloucestershire, England, 27 May, 1943						RW
Newport Co	Cinderford T	08/63	63	6	-	0
Nottingham F	Tr	12/63	63-66	26	1	5
Middlesbrough	Tr	09/67	67-69	56	2	7
Barnsley	L	08/70	70	6	0	1
KEARNEY Alan						
Born: Cork, Republic of Ireland, 22 September, 1987						M
Everton	Sch	09/05				
Chester C	L	02/07	06	4	2	0
KEARNEY Mark James						
Born: Ormskirk, Lancashire, England, 12 June, 1962						M
Everton	Marine	10/81				
Mansfield T	Tr	03/83	82-90	248	2	29
Bury	L	01/91	90	13	0	1
Bury	Tr	03/91	90-93	96	4	4
KEARNEY Michael Joseph (Mike)						
Born: Glasgow, Scotland, 18 February, 1953						F
Shrewsbury T	Petershill Jnrs	12/72	72-76	143	6	41
Chester C	Tr	03/77	76-77	37	1	5
Reading	Tr	01/78	77-79	78	9	24
Chester C	Tr	07/80	80	9	0	0
Reading	Tr	10/80	80-82	57	1	12
KEARNEY Noel Michael						
Born: Ipswich, England, 7 October, 1942						W
Ipswich T	Jnr	10/60				
Colchester U	Tr	09/64	64	3	-	0
KEARNEY Sydney Francis (Syd)						
Born: Liverpool, England, 28 March, 1917						LH
Died: Chelsea, W London, England, 1982						
Leicester C	Crowndale	08/36				
Tranmere Rov	Tr	05/37	37-38	9	-	2
Accrington Stan	Tr	11/38	38-46	30	-	7
Bristol C	Tr	01/47	46-49	65	-	5
KEARNEY Thomas James (Tom)						
Born: Liverpool, England, 7 October, 1981						M
Everton	YT	10/99				
Bradford C	Tr	03/02	01-05	46	8	2
KEARNS Daniel Anthony (Danny)						
Born: Belfast, Northern Ireland, 26 August, 1991						M
Republic of Ireland: LoI-1/U23-1/U21-3/Youth//Northern Ireland: Youth						
West Ham U	Sch	07/09				
Peterborough U	Dundalk (ROI)	08/11	11-13	10	22	0
York C	L	10/12	12	8	1	0
Rotherham U	L	01/13	12	5	5	0
Chesterfield	L	03/14	13	6	4	0
Carlisle U	Tr	07/14	14	3	7	0
KEARNS Frederick Thomas (Freddie)						
Born: Cork, Republic of Ireland, 8 November, 1927						CF
Died: Margate, Kent, England, 7 January, 1987						
Republic of Ireland: 1						
West Ham U	Shamrock Rov (ROI)	05/48	49-53	43	-	14
Norwich C	Tr	06/54	54-55	28	-	11
KEARNS Jamie Adam						
Born: Hammersmith, W London, England, 28 October, 1971						FB
Cambridge U	YT	07/90	90	1	0	0
KEARNS Michael (Mick)						
Born: Banbury, Oxfordshire, England, 26 November, 1950						G
Republic of Ireland: 18						
Oxford U	App	07/68	69-71	67	0	0
Plymouth Arg	L	10/72	72	1	0	0
Charlton Ath	L	02/73	72	4	0	0
Walsall	Tr	07/73	73-78	249	0	0
Wolverhampton W	Tr	07/79	79-80	9	0	0
Walsall	Tr	08/82	82-84	26	0	0
KEARNS Michael David (Mike)						
Born: Nuneaton, Warwickshire, England, 10 March, 1938						FB/WH
Coventry C	Stockingford Victoria	09/55	57-67	344	0	14
KEARNS Oliver Anthony (Ollie)						
Born: Banbury, Oxfordshire, England, 12 June, 1956						F

League Club	Source	Date Signed	Seasons Played	Career Record Apps	Subs	Gls
Reading	Banbury U	03/77	76-79	75	11	40
Oxford U	Tr	08/81	81	9	9	4
Walsall	Tr	08/82	82	31	7	11
Hereford U	Tr	06/83	83-87	166	4	58
Wrexham	Tr	12/87	87-89	36	10	14
KEARNS Peter Vincent						
Born: Wellingborough, Northamptonshire, England, 26 March, 1937						IF
Died: Weymouth, Dorset, England, 6 July, 2014						
Plymouth Arg	Wellingborough T	04/56	56-59	64	-	8
Aldershot	Corby T	12/62	62-67	184	1	64
Lincoln C	Tr	03/68	67-68	45	1	11
KEARTON Jason Brett						
Born: Ipswich, Queensland, Australia, 9 July, 1969						G
Everton	Brisbane Lions (AUS)	10/88	92-94	3	3	0
Stoke C	L	08/91	91	16	0	0
Blackpool	L	01/92	91	14	0	0
Notts Co	L	01/95	94	10	0	0
Crewe Alex	Tr	10/96	96-00	190	1	0
KEARY Patrick (Pat)						
Born: Patchway, Avon, England, 22 November, 1993						CD
Bristol Rov	YT	06/13	13	0	1	0
KEATES Dean Scott						
Born: Wasall, West Midlands, England, 30 June, 1978						M
Walsall	YT	08/96	96-01	125	34	9
Hull C	Tr	08/02	02-03	45	5	4
Kidderminster Hrs	Tr	02/04	03-04	48	1	7
Lincoln C	Tr	07/05	05	19	2	4
Walsall	Tr	01/06	05-06	50	3	15
Peterborough U	Tr	07/07	07-09	72	12	11
Wycombe W	Tr	01/10	09	13	0	1
KEATING Brian Alfred						
Born: Lewisham, SE London, England, 19 March, 1935						CF
Died: Australia, 2005						
Crewe Alex (Am)	Barry T	07/56	56-57	8	-	1
KEATING Dennis Joseph						
Born: Cork, Republic of Ireland, 18 October, 1940						LW
Chester C	Saltney Jnrs	06/62	62	1	-	0
KEATING Patrick Joseph (Pat)						
Born: Cork, Republic of Ireland, 17 September, 1930						LW
Died: Sheffield, England, 1981						
Sheffield U	Cork Ath (ROI)	02/50	50	3	-	0
Chesterfield	Tr	08/53	53-56	95	-	21
Swindon T	Wisbech T	08/53				
Bradford Park Ave	Tr	09/53	53	2	-	0
KEATING Robert						
Born: Oldham, Greater Manchester, England, 24 June, 1917						W
Died: Oldham, Greater Manchester, England, June, 1985						
Oldham Ath		08/41				
Accrington Stan	Hereford U	12/46	46	5	-	0
KEAVENY Jonathan Mark						
Born: Swansea, Wales, 24 May, 1981						F
Swansea C	Carmarthen T	07/02	02	4	5	0
KEAY John Paul (Jack)						
Born: Glasgow, Scotland, 14 June, 1960						CD
Shrewsbury T	Glasgow Celtic (Jnr)	07/77	77-81	152	3	20
Wrexham	Tr	09/82	82-85	156	0	9
KEBE Jimmy Boubou						
Born: Paris, France, 19 January, 1984						RW
Mali: 8						
Reading	RC Lens (FRA)	01/08	07-12	149	26	29
Crystal Palace	Tr	08/13	13	2	4	0
Leeds U	L	01/14	13	9	0	1
KEDWELL Daniel Trevor (Danny)						
Born: Gillingham, Kent, England, 3 August, 1983						F
Gillingham	AFC Wimbledon	07/11	11-14	97	22	40
KEE Billy Rodney						
Born: Loughborough, Leicestershire, England, 1 December, 1990						F
Northern Ireland: U21-10/Youth						
Leicester C	Sch	07/09				
Accrington Stan	L	08/09	09	15	22	9
Torquay U	Tr	07/10	10-11	18	26	9
Burton A	Tr	08/11	11-14	70	29	39
Scunthorpe U	Tr	08/14	14	0	12	0
Mansfield T	L	01/15	14	8	5	2
KEE Paul James						
Born: Derry, Northern Ireland, 21 February, 1967						F

League Club	Source	Date Signed	Seasons Played	Career Record Apps	Subs	Gls
Northern Ireland: Youth						
Mansfield T	App	01/84	83	0	1	0

KEE Paul Victor
Born: Belfast, Northern Ireland, 8 November, 1969 — G
Northern Ireland: 9/U21-1/Youth

Oxford U	Ards	05/88	89-93	56	0	0

KEEBLE Brian Beverley
Born: Holbeach, Lincolnshire, England, 11 July, 1938 — LB

Grimsby T	Holbeach U	05/59	59-64	172	-	1
Darlington	Tr	07/65	65-68	154	0	2

KEEBLE Christopher Mark (Chris)
Born: Colchester, Essex, England, 17 September, 1978 — M

Ipswich T	YT	06/97	97	0	1	0
Colchester U	Tr	03/00	99-02	12	12	2

KEEBLE Matthew
Born: Chipping Norton, Oxfordshire, England, 8 September, 1972 — F

Oxford U	YT	05/91	92-93	1	1	0

KEEBLE Victor Albert William (Vic)
Born: Colchester, Essex, England, 25 June, 1930 — CF

Colchester U	Arsenal (Am)	09/47	50-51	46	-	23
Newcastle U	Tr	02/52	51-57	104	-	56
West Ham U	Tr	10/57	57-59	76	-	45

KEEBLE Walter Frederick (Fred)
Born: Coventry, England, 30 August, 1919 — IF
Died: Nuneaton, Warwickshire, England, 8 May, 1987

Grimsby T	Albion Rov	09/46	46	7	-	0
Notts Co	Tr	07/47	47	4	-	1

KEEFE David Edward
Born: Dagenham, E London, England, 23 June, 1957 — W

Southend U	App	07/75	74-75	4	2	1
Torquay U	Tr	08/77	77	2	0	0

KEEGAN Gerard Anthony (Ged)
Born: Bradford, England, 3 October, 1955 — M
England: U21-1

Manchester C	App	03/73	74-78	32	5	2
Oldham Ath	Tr	02/79	78-82	139	5	5
Mansfield T	Tr	10/83	83	18	0	1
Rochdale	Tr	07/84	84	2	0	0

KEEGAN John Kevin Paul
Born: Liverpool, England, 5 August, 1981 — FB

York C	YT	-	99	2	1	0

KEEGAN Jordan Lee
Born: Dublin, Republic of Ireland, 5 February, 1992 — LW

Scunthorpe U	Monaghan U (ROI)	08/12	12	0	3	0

KEEGAN Joseph Kevin (Kevin)
Born: Armthorpe, South Yorkshire, England, 14 February, 1951 — F
England: 63/U23-5

Scunthorpe U	App	12/68	68-70	120	4	18
Liverpool	Tr	05/71	71-76	230	0	68
Southampton	Hamburger SV (GER)	07/80	80-81	68	0	37
Newcastle U	Tr	08/82	82-83	78	0	48

KEEGAN Michael Jerard (Mike)
Born: Wallasey, Wirral, England, 12 May, 1981 — M

Swansea C	YT	07/99	99-01	7	3	0

KEEGAN Paul Anthony
Born: Dublin, Republic of Ireland, 5 July, 1984 — DM
Republic of Ireland: U23-3/U21-5/Youth

Leeds U	YT	07/01				
Scunthorpe U	L	10/03	03	0	2	0
Doncaster Rov	Bohemians (ROI)	01/11	10-14	96	7	1

KEELAN Kevin Damien
Born: Calcutta, India, 5 January, 1941 — G

Aston Villa	Carpet Tr's, K'minster	07/58	59-60	5	-	0
Stockport Co	Tr	04/61	60	3	-	0
Wrexham	Kidderminster Hrs	11/61	61-62	68	-	0
Norwich C	Tr	07/63	63-79	571	0	0

KEELER Justin Jack
Born: Hillingdon, W London, England, 17 April, 1978 — W

Bournemouth	Christchurch	01/00	99-00	0	4	0

KEELEY Andrew James (Andy)
Born: Basildon, England, 16 September, 1956 — D
England: Youth

Tottenham H	App	01/74	76	5	1	0
Sheffield U	Tr	12/77	77-80	28	0	0
Scunthorpe U	Tr	07/81	81-82	75	2	1

KEELEY Damian
Born: Salford, England, 14 February, 1963 — F

Torquay U		09/81	81	1	2	0

KEELEY Glenn Matthew
Born: Basildon, England, 1 September, 1954 — CD
England: Youth

Ipswich T	App	08/72	72-73	4	0	0
Newcastle U	Tr	07/74	74-75	43	1	2
Blackburn Rov	Tr	08/76	76-86	365	5	23
Everton	L	10/82	82	1	0	0
Oldham Ath	Tr	08/87	87	10	1	0
Colchester U	L	02/88	87	4	0	0
Bolton W	Tr	09/88	88	20	0	0

KEELEY John Henry
Born: Plaistow, E London, England, 27 July, 1961 — G

Southend U	App	07/79	79-84	63	0	0
Brighton & HA	Chelmsford C	08/86	86-89	138	0	0
Oldham Ath	Tr	08/90	91-92	2	0	0
Oxford U	L	11/91	91	6	0	0
Reading	L	02/92	91	6	0	0
Chester C	L	08/92	92	4	0	0
Colchester U	Tr	07/93	93	15	0	0
Stockport Co	Chelmsford C	03/94	93-94	20	0	0
Peterborough U	Tr	01/95	94	3	0	0

KEELEY John James (Jackie)
Born: Liverpool, England, 18 October, 1936 — IF
Died: Liverpool, England, December, 2007
England: Youth/Schools

Everton	Jnr	05/54	57	4	-	1
Accrington Stan	Tr	07/59	59	10	-	1
Southport	Tr	12/59	59	4	-	0

KEELEY Nolan Bruce
Born: East Barsham, Norfolk, England, 24 May, 1951 — M

Scunthorpe U	Great Yarmouth T	04/73	72-79	255	4	37
Lincoln C	Tr	01/80	79-80	52	0	3

KEELEY Raymond (Ray)
Born: Battersea, SW London, England, 25 December, 1946 — RW/IF

Charlton Ath	App	12/64	64	1	-	0
Exeter C	Tr	03/66	65-66	45	1	10
Mansfield T	Crawley T	06/68	68-69	48	4	5

KEELEY Walter
Born: Manchester, England, 1 April, 1921 — IF
Died: Accrington, Lancashire, England, March, 1995

Accrington Stan	Chesterfield (Am)	12/44	46-47	48	-	21
Bury	Tr	10/47	47	7	-	0
Port Vale	Tr	01/48	47-48	18	-	3
Accrington Stan	Tr	09/48	48-51	101	-	35
Rochdale	Tr	10/51	51	4	-	0

KEEN Alan
Born: Barrow, Cumbria, England, 29 May, 1930 — IF

Barrow	Barrow Social	05/49	49-53	93	-	14
Chesterfield	Tr	07/54	54-55	54	-	12
Bradford Park Ave	Cheltenham T	02/57	56	11	-	1
Carlisle U	Cheltenham T	09/58	58-59	7	-	0

KEEN Herbert (Bert)
Born: Barrow, Cumbria, England, 9 September, 1926 — LW
Died: Barrow, Cumbria, England, November, 1993

Barrow	Netherfield	07/53	53	8	-	0

KEEN John (Jack)
Born: Barrow, Cumbria, England, 26 January, 1929 — WH
Died: Barrow, Cumbria, England, October, 2009

Barrow	West Bromwich A (Am)	01/48	47-58	275	-	20
Workington	Tr	07/59	59	19	-	0

KEEN Kevin Ian
Born: Amersham, Buckinghamshire, England, 25 February, 1967 — RM
England: Youth/Schools

West Ham U	App	03/84	86-92	187	32	21
Wolverhampton W	Tr	07/93	93-94	37	5	7
Stoke C	Tr	10/94	94-99	147	30	10
Macclesfield T	Tr	09/00	00-01	59	3	2

KEEN Michael Andrew Charles (Mike)
Born: Wrexham, Wales, 12 February, 1953 — G
Wales: Schools

Chester C	App	09/81				
Wrexham	Lex X1	06/85	85	5	0	0

KEEN Michael Thomas (Mike)
Born: High Wycombe, Buckinghamshire, England, 19 March, 1940 — M

Died: Flackwell Heath, Buckinghamshire, England, 17 April, 2009

League Club	Source	Date Signed	Seasons Played	Apps	Subs	Gls
Queens Park Rgrs	Jnr	06/58	59-68	393	0	39
Luton T	Tr	01/69	68-71	143	1	11
Watford	Tr	07/72	72-74	124	2	5

KEEN Nigel John
Born: Barrow, Cumbria, England, 23 October, 1961 RM

League Club	Source	Date Signed	Seasons Played	Apps	Subs	Gls
Manchester U	App	02/79				
Preston NE	Barrow	05/85	85	24	0	0

KEEN Peter Alan
Born: Middlesbrough, England, 16 November, 1976 G

League Club	Source	Date Signed	Seasons Played	Apps	Subs	Gls
Newcastle U	YT	03/96				
Carlisle U	Tr	08/99	99-03	60	1	1
Darlington	L	03/01	00	7	0	0

KEENAN Gerald Patrick (Gerry)
Born: Liverpool, England, 25 July, 1954 RB

League Club	Source	Date Signed	Seasons Played	Apps	Subs	Gls
Bury	Skelmersdale U	04/75	74-78	69	2	3
Port Vale	Tr	09/78	78-81	105	1	7
Rochdale	Ashton U	09/82	82-83	35	0	1

KEENAN Joseph John (Joe)
Born: Southampton, England, 14 October, 1982 M
England: Youth

League Club	Source	Date Signed	Seasons Played	Apps	Subs	Gls
Chelsea	YT	10/99	01-02	0	2	0
Brentford	L	08/05	05	0	3	0

KEENAN William George
Born: Llanelli, Carmarthenshire, Wales, 29 December, 1918 LW
Died: Llanelli, Carmarthenshire, Wales, May, 1993

League Club	Source	Date Signed	Seasons Played	Apps	Subs	Gls
Everton	Hereford U	01/39				
Newport Co	Tr	06/46	46	4	-	1

KEENE Douglas Charles (Doug)
Born: Hendon, N London, England, 30 August, 1928 W
Died: Kirkcaldy, Fife, Scotland, 21 January, 1986

League Club	Source	Date Signed	Seasons Played	Apps	Subs	Gls
Brentford	Jnr	09/47	48-49	13	-	1
Brighton & HA	Tr	06/50	50-52	61	-	10
Colchester U	Tr	07/53	53	22	-	1

KEENE James Duncan
Born: Wells, Somerset, England, 26 December, 1985 F

League Club	Source	Date Signed	Seasons Played	Apps	Subs	Gls
Portsmouth	Sch	09/04	04	1	1	0
Kidderminster Hrs	L	10/04	04	5	0	0
Bournemouth	L	09/05	05	6	5	2
Boston U	L	01/06	05	6	0	1
Portsmouth	Elfsborg (SWE)	02/13	12	6	3	1

KEEP Vernon
Born: Chester, England, 23 May, 1963 M

League Club	Source	Date Signed	Seasons Played	Apps	Subs	Gls
Wrexham	Connah's Quay Nomads	10/84	84	0	1	0

KEERS James (Jim)
Born: Stanley, County Durham, England, 10 December, 1931 RW

League Club	Source	Date Signed	Seasons Played	Apps	Subs	Gls
Darlington	Evenwood T	03/52	51-55	74	-	15

KEERY Stanley (Stan)
Born: Derby, England, 9 September, 1931 RH/IF
Died: Crewe, Cheshire, England, 7 March, 2013

League Club	Source	Date Signed	Seasons Played	Apps	Subs	Gls
Shrewsbury T	Wilmorton	08/52	52	15	-	2
Newcastle U	Tr	11/52	52-56	19	-	1
Mansfield T	Tr	05/57	57-58	53	-	17
Crewe Alex	Tr	10/58	58-64	252	-	21

KEETCH Robert David (Bobby)
Born: Tottenham, N London, England, 25 October, 1941 CH
Died: Mortlake, SW London, England, 29 June, 1996

League Club	Source	Date Signed	Seasons Played	Apps	Subs	Gls
Fulham	West Ham U (Am)	04/59	62-65	106	0	2
Queens Park Rgrs	Tr	11/66	66-68	49	3	0

KEETLEY Ernest Albert (Albert)
Born: Nottingham, England, 22 February, 1930 FB

League Club	Source	Date Signed	Seasons Played	Apps	Subs	Gls
Bury	Keyworth U (Am)	03/50	50	4	-	0
Bournemouth	Tr	07/52	53-57	86	-	0

KEETON Albert (Bob)
Born: Chesterfield, Derbyshire, England, 15 January, 1918 RB
Died: Torbay, Devon, England, January, 1996

League Club	Source	Date Signed	Seasons Played	Apps	Subs	Gls
Torquay U	Mosborough Trinity	06/37	37-47	77	-	0

KEIGHLEY John Paul (Paul)
Born: Ribchester, Lancashire, England, 15 February, 1961 M

League Club	Source	Date Signed	Seasons Played	Apps	Subs	Gls
Bolton W	App	02/79				
Crewe Alex	Tr	08/81	81	25	4	0

KEINAN Dekel
Born: Rosh Hanikra, Israel, 15 September, 1984 CD
Israel: 27

League Club	Source	Date Signed	Seasons Played	Apps	Subs	Gls
Blackpool	Maccabi Haifa (ISR)	08/10	10	3	3	0
Cardiff C	Tr	01/11	10-11	18	1	2
Crystal Palace	L	11/11	11	3	0	0
Bristol C	L	03/12	11	0	1	0

KEIR Colin William
Born: Bournemouth, England, 14 January, 1938 RW

League Club	Source	Date Signed	Seasons Played	Apps	Subs	Gls
Portsmouth	Jnr	05/55				
Workington	Tr	06/59	59	4	-	0

KEIRS John
Born: Drongan, Ayrshire, Scotland, 14 August, 1947 CD
Died: Hastings, East Sussex, England, 27 December, 1995

League Club	Source	Date Signed	Seasons Played	Apps	Subs	Gls
Charlton Ath	Annbank U	06/65	65-70	73	5	1

KEISTER John Edward Samuel
Born: Manchester, England, 11 November, 1970 DM
Sierra Leone: 7

League Club	Source	Date Signed	Seasons Played	Apps	Subs	Gls
Walsall	Faweh Tigres (SLE)	09/93	93-99	78	28	2
Chester C	Tr	01/00	99	8	2	0
Shrewsbury T	Tr	10/00	00	8	0	0

KEITH Adrian John
Born: Colchester, Essex, England, 16 December, 1962 CD

League Club	Source	Date Signed	Seasons Played	Apps	Subs	Gls
West Ham U	App	12/80				
Colchester U	Tr	12/82	82	4	0	0

KEITH Joseph Richard (Joe)
Born: Plaistow, E London, England, 1 October, 1978 LB/M

League Club	Source	Date Signed	Seasons Played	Apps	Subs	Gls
West Ham U	YT	07/97				
Colchester U	Tr	07/99	99-04	178	30	23
Bristol C	L	03/05	04	3	0	0
Leyton Orient	Tr	06/05	05-06	49	4	2
Shrewsbury T	L	10/06	06	1	0	0
Brentford	Tr	01/07	06	17	1	2

KEITH Marino
Born: Peterhead, Aberdeenshire, Scotland, 16 December, 1974 F

League Club	Source	Date Signed	Seasons Played	Apps	Subs	Gls
Plymouth Arg	Livingston	11/01	01-04	67	50	30
Colchester U	Tr	03/05	04	12	0	4

KEITH Richard Matthewson (Dick)
Born: Belfast, Northern Ireland, 15 May, 1933 RB
Died: Bournemouth, England, 28 February, 1967
Northern Ireland: 23/B/NILge-4

League Club	Source	Date Signed	Seasons Played	Apps	Subs	Gls
Newcastle U	Linfield	09/56	56-63	208	-	2
Bournemouth	Tr	02/64	63-65	47	0	0

KEIZERWEERD Orpheo Henk (Henk)
Born: Paramaribo, Suriname, 2 November, 1968 F

League Club	Source	Date Signed	Seasons Played	Apps	Subs	Gls
Oldham Ath	Rodez (FRA)	03/93	92	0	1	0

KELL George Allan (Allan)
Born: Spennymoor, County Durham, England, 9 April, 1949 WH

League Club	Source	Date Signed	Seasons Played	Apps	Subs	Gls
Darlington (Am)		08/66	67	0	2	0

KELL Leonard William (Len)
Born: Billingham, Cleveland, England, 27 May, 1932 IF

League Club	Source	Date Signed	Seasons Played	Apps	Subs	Gls
Chelsea	Jnr	02/52	53	3	-	0
Norwich C	Tr	06/54	54	2	-	0

KELL Richard
Born: Crook, County Durham, England, 15 September, 1979 M
England: Schools

League Club	Source	Date Signed	Seasons Played	Apps	Subs	Gls
Middlesbrough	YT	07/98				
Torquay U	Tr	02/01	00	15	0	3
Scunthorpe U	Tr	09/01	01-04	80	3	8
Barnsley	Tr	07/05	05	0	1	0

KELLARD Robert Sydney William (Bobby)
Born: Edmonton, N London, England, 1 March, 1943 M
England: Youth

League Club	Source	Date Signed	Seasons Played	Apps	Subs	Gls
Southend U	Jnr	05/60	59-62	106	-	15
Crystal Palace	Tr	09/63	63-65	77	0	6
Ipswich T	Tr	11/65	65	13	0	3
Portsmouth	Tr	03/66	65-67	91	0	8
Bristol C	Tr	07/68	68-69	77	0	6
Leicester C	Tr	08/70	70-71	49	0	8
Crystal Palace	Tr	09/71	71-72	44	2	4
Portsmouth	Tr	12/72	72-74	62	1	6
Hereford U	L	01/75	74	3	0	1
Torquay U	Durban C (RSA)	09/75	75	2	0	0

KELLER Francois
Born: Colmar, France, 27 October, 1973 M

League Club	Source	Date Signed	Seasons Played	Apps	Subs	Gls
Fulham	RC Strasbourg (FRA)	12/98	98	0	1	0

KELLER Kasey C
Born: Olympia, Washington, USA, 27 November, 1969 G
USA: 102

League Club	Source	Date Signed	Seasons Played	Apps	Subs	Gls
Millwall	Portland Univ (USA)	02/92	91-95	176	0	0

League Club	Source	Date Signed	Seasons Played	Apps	Subs	Gls
Leicester C	Tr	08/96	96-98	99	0	0
Tottenham H	Rayo Vallecano (SPN)	08/01	01-03	85	0	0
Southampton	L	11/04	04	4	0	0
Fulham	Borussia M'bach (GER)	08/07	07	13	0	0

KELLER Marc
Born: Colmar, France, 14 January, 1968 — M
France: 6

League Club	Source	Date Signed	Seasons Played	Apps	Subs	Gls
West Ham U	Karlsruhe (GER)	07/98	98-99	36	8	5
Portsmouth	L	09/00	00	3	0	0
Blackburn Rov	Tr	01/01	00	0	2	0

KELLETT Andrew Paul (Andy)
Born: Bolton, Greater Manchester, England, 10 November, 1993 — LB/M

League Club	Source	Date Signed	Seasons Played	Apps	Subs	Gls
Bolton W	Sch	07/12	13-14	1	3	0
Plymouth Arg	L	10/14	14	12	0	1

KELLEY Alan William
Born: Bootle, Merseyside, England, 24 December, 1952 — LB

League Club	Source	Date Signed	Seasons Played	Apps	Subs	Gls
Southport	App	12/70	70-71	17	6	2
Crewe Alex	Tr	08/72	72-75	105	2	0

KELLEY Stanley Robert (Stan)
Born: Foleshill, Warwickshire, England, 14 June, 1920 — FB
Died: Coventry, England, December, 1993

League Club	Source	Date Signed	Seasons Played	Apps	Subs	Gls
Coventry C	Herberts Ath	08/39	46	4	-	0

KELLOCK William (Billy)
Born: Glasgow, Scotland, 7 February, 1954 — M/F
Scotland: Schools

League Club	Source	Date Signed	Seasons Played	Apps	Subs	Gls
Cardiff C	Aston Villa (App)	02/72	71-72	33	2	2
Norwich C	Tr	06/73	73	1	2	0
Millwall	Tr	07/74				
Peterborough U	Kettering T	08/79	79-81	134	0	43
Luton T	Tr	07/82	82	2	5	0
Wolverhampton W	Tr	03/83	82-83	12	0	3
Southend U	Tr	09/83	83-84	53	0	8
Port Vale	Tr	12/84	84	10	1	4
Halifax T	Tr	07/85	85	41	2	17

KELLOW Tony
Born: Falmouth, Cornwall, England, 1 May, 1952 — F
Died: Truro, Cornwall, England, 20 February, 2011

League Club	Source	Date Signed	Seasons Played	Apps	Subs	Gls
Exeter C	Falmouth	07/76	76-78	107	0	40
Blackpool	Tr	11/78	78-79	57	0	23
Exeter C	Tr	03/80	79-83	140	3	61
Plymouth Arg	Tr	11/83	83	8	2	2
Swansea C	Tr	10/84	84	0	1	0
Newport Co	Tr	11/84	84	17	3	8
Exeter C	Tr	07/85	85-87	51	31	28

KELLY Alan James Alexander
Born: Dublin, Republic of Ireland, 5 July, 1936 — G
Died: Maryland, USA, 20 May, 2009
Republic of Ireland: 47/LoI-6

League Club	Source	Date Signed	Seasons Played	Apps	Subs	Gls
Preston NE	Drumcondra (ROI)	04/58	60-73	447	0	0

KELLY Alan Thomas
Born: Preston, Lancashire, England, 11 August, 1968 — G
Republic of Ireland: 34/U23-1/U21-3/Youth

League Club	Source	Date Signed	Seasons Played	Apps	Subs	Gls
Preston NE	App	09/85	85-91	142	0	0
Sheffield U	Tr	07/92	92-98	213	3	0
Blackburn Rov	Tr	07/99	99-02	39	1	0
Stockport Co	L	04/01	00	2	0	0
Birmingham C	L	08/01	01	6	0	0

KELLY Anthony Gerald (Tony)
Born: Prescot, Merseyside, England, 1 October, 1964 — M

League Club	Source	Date Signed	Seasons Played	Apps	Subs	Gls
Liverpool	App	09/82				
Wigan Ath	Prescot Cables	01/84	83-85	98	3	15
Stoke C	Tr	04/86	85-86	33	3	4
West Bromwich A	Tr	07/87	87	26	0	1
Chester C	L	09/88	88	5	0	0
Colchester U	L	10/88	88	13	0	2
Shrewsbury T	Tr	01/89	88-90	100	1	15
Bolton W	Tr	08/91	91-94	103	3	5
Port Vale	L	09/94	94	3	1	1
Millwall	Tr	10/94	94	1	1	0
Wigan Ath	Tr	11/94				
Peterborough U	Tr	12/94	94	12	1	2
Wigan Ath	Tr	07/95	95	2	0	0

KELLY Arthur
Born: Belfast, Northern Ireland, 12 March, 1914 — CF
Died: Belfast, Northern Ireland, 1973

League Club	Source	Date Signed	Seasons Played	Apps	Subs	Gls
Barrow	Belfast Celtic	09/46	46	8	-	2

KELLY Ashley Craig
Born: Ashton-under-Lyne, Greater Manchester, England, 22 December, 1988 — M

League Club	Source	Date Signed	Seasons Played	Apps	Subs	Gls
Oldham Ath	Sch	07/07	07	0	1	0

KELLY Bernard (Bernie)
Born: Carfin, Lanarkshire, Scotland, 21 October, 1932 — IF
Died: Detroit, Michigan, USA, 8 October, 2004
Scotland: B/SLge-1

League Club	Source	Date Signed	Seasons Played	Apps	Subs	Gls
Leicester C	Raith Rov	07/58	58	24	-	13
Nottingham F	Tr	04/59	58	2	-	0

KELLY Bernard Alexander
Born: Kensington, Central London, England, 21 August, 1928 — RW

League Club	Source	Date Signed	Seasons Played	Apps	Subs	Gls
Brentford	Bath C	06/50	50	1	-	1

KELLY Brian Leslie
Born: Ilkley, West Yorkshire, England, 22 May, 1943 — RB

League Club	Source	Date Signed	Seasons Played	Apps	Subs	Gls
Bradford C	Jnr	05/60	61-64	83	-	2
Doncaster Rov	Tr	01/65	64-67	130	1	3
York C	Tr	07/68	68-69	32	1	0

KELLY Christopher Miles (Chris)
Born: Epsom, Surrey, England, 14 October, 1948 — F
England: Amateur-1

League Club	Source	Date Signed	Seasons Played	Apps	Subs	Gls
Millwall	Leatherhead	01/75	74	9	2	0

KELLY Danny Michael
Born: Huntingdon, Cambridgeshire, England, 18 October, 1990 — CD/F
Republic of Ireland: Youth

League Club	Source	Date Signed	Seasons Played	Apps	Subs	Gls
Norwich C	Sch	07/09				
Barnet	Tr	07/10	10	0	3	0

KELLY Darren
Born: Derry, Northern Ireland, 30 June, 1979 — CD

League Club	Source	Date Signed	Seasons Played	Apps	Subs	Gls
Carlisle U	Derry C (ROI)	08/02	02-03	39	3	2

KELLY David Thomas
Born: Birmingham, England, 25 November, 1965 — F
Republic of Ireland: 26/B-3/U23-1/U21-3

League Club	Source	Date Signed	Seasons Played	Apps	Subs	Gls
Walsall	Alvechurch	12/83	83-87	115	32	63
West Ham U	Tr	08/88	88-89	29	12	7
Leicester C	Tr	03/90	89-91	63	3	22
Newcastle U	Tr	12/91	91-92	70	0	35
Wolverhampton W	Tr	06/93	93-95	76	7	26
Sunderland	Tr	09/95	95-96	32	2	2
Tranmere Rov	Tr	08/97	97-99	69	19	21
Sheffield U	Tr	07/00	00	21	14	6
Mansfield T	Motherwell	01/02	01	11	6	4

KELLY Dean
Born: Dublin, Republic of Ireland, 18 September, 1991 — F

League Club	Source	Date Signed	Seasons Played	Apps	Subs	Gls
Oldham Ath	Crumlin U	08/10	10	1	12	1

KELLY Desmond Charles James Jude (Des)
Born: Limerick, Republic of Ireland, 1 November, 1950 — G

League Club	Source	Date Signed	Seasons Played	Apps	Subs	Gls
Norwich C	Limerick (ROI)	07/70				
Colchester U	Tr	06/72	72	1	0	0

KELLY Donald Joseph (Don)
Born: Market Harborough, Leicestershire, England, 2 July, 1922 — CF
Died: Stafford, England, 24 May, 2009

League Club	Source	Date Signed	Seasons Played	Apps	Subs	Gls
Torquay U	Coventry C (Am)	07/47	46-47	5	-	3

KELLY Douglas Cain (Doug)
Born: Barnsley, South Yorkshire, England, 30 May, 1934 — CF

League Club	Source	Date Signed	Seasons Played	Apps	Subs	Gls
Barnsley	Jnr	08/51	52-54	18	-	7
Bradford C	Tr	06/55	55-56	43	-	14
Chesterfield	Tr	06/57	57	1	-	1

KELLY Edward Patrick (Eddie)
Born: Glasgow, Scotland, 7 February, 1951 — M
Scotland: U23-3

League Club	Source	Date Signed	Seasons Played	Apps	Subs	Gls
Arsenal	Possilpark YMCA	02/68	69-75	168	8	13
Queens Park Rgrs	Tr	09/76	76	28	0	1
Leicester C	Tr	07/77	77-79	85	0	4
Notts Co	Tr	07/80	80	26	1	1
Bournemouth	Tr	08/81	81	13	0	0
Leicester C	Tr	12/81	81-82	34	0	0
Torquay U	Melton T	10/84	84-85	35	0	1

KELLY Errington Edison
Born: Sandy Bay, Saint Vincent And The Grenadines, 8 April, 1958 — F/W

League Club	Source	Date Signed	Seasons Played	Apps	Subs	Gls
Bristol Rov	Ledbury T	09/81	81-82	12	6	3
Lincoln C	Tr	01/83	82	0	2	0
Bristol C	Tr	03/83	82	4	1	1
Coventry C	Tr	08/83				
Peterborough U	Tr	03/84	83-85	59	13	22
Peterborough U	Sweden	12/86	86-87	36	10	6

KELLY Frederick Charles (Fred)
Born: Wednesbury, West Midlands, England, 11 February, 1921 — CF
Died: Sandwell, West Midlands, England, 15 June, 2006

League Club	Source	Date Signed	Seasons Played	Apps	Subs	Gls
Walsall		12/45	46-47	16	-	6

KELLY Gary Alexander
Born: Preston, Lancashire, England, 3 August, 1966 — G
Republic of Ireland: B-1/U23-1/U21-8

League Club	Source	Date Signed	Seasons Played	Apps	Subs	Gls
Newcastle U	App	06/84	86-89	53	0	0
Blackpool	L	10/88	88	5	0	0
Bury	Tr	10/89	89-95	236	0	0
Oldham Ath	Tr	08/96	96-01	224	1	0
Sheffield U	Northwich Victoria	03/03	02	1	0	0

KELLY Gary Oliver
Born: Drogheda, Republic of Ireland, 9 July, 1974 — RB
Republic of Ireland: 52/U21-5/Youth/Schools

League Club	Source	Date Signed	Seasons Played	Apps	Subs	Gls
Leeds U	Home Farm (ROI)	09/91	91-06	419	11	2

KELLY Gavin John
Born: Beverley, East Riding of Yorkshire, England, 29 September, 1968 — G

League Club	Source	Date Signed	Seasons Played	Apps	Subs	Gls
Hull C	App	05/87	88-89	11	0	0
Bristol Rov	Tr	07/90	90-93	30	0	0
Scarborough	Tr	07/94	94-95	30	0	0

KELLY George Lawson
Born: Aberdeen, Scotland, 29 June, 1933 — IF
Died: Aberdeen, Scotland, 26 October, 1998

League Club	Source	Date Signed	Seasons Played	Apps	Subs	Gls
Stoke C	Aberdeen	02/56	55-57	67	-	35
Cardiff C	Tr	05/58	58	8	-	4
Stockport Co	Tr	07/59	59	34	-	4

KELLY Hugh Redmond
Born: Belfast, Northern Ireland, 17 August, 1919 — G
Died: Belfast, Northern Ireland, 30 September, 1977
Northern Ireland: 4/NILge-8

League Club	Source	Date Signed	Seasons Played	Apps	Subs	Gls
Fulham	Belfast Celtic	03/49	49	25	-	0
Southampton	Tr	08/50	50	28	-	0
Exeter C	Tr	06/52	52-55	99	-	0

KELLY Hugh Thomas
Born: Valleyfield, Fife, Scotland, 23 July, 1923 — LH
Died: Blackpool, Lancashire, England, 28 March, 2009
Scotland: 1/B

League Club	Source	Date Signed	Seasons Played	Apps	Subs	Gls
Blackpool	Jeanfield Swifts	08/44	46-59	429	-	8

KELLY James (Jimmy)
Born: Liverpool, England, 14 February, 1973 — M

League Club	Source	Date Signed	Seasons Played	Apps	Subs	Gls
Wrexham	YT	07/91	90-91	11	10	0
Wolverhampton W	Tr	02/92	91-93	4	3	0
Walsall	L	03/93	92	7	3	2
Wrexham	L	03/94	93	9	0	0

KELLY James (Jimmy)
Born: Crumlin, Antrim, Northern Ireland, 6 February, 1954 — LW

League Club	Source	Date Signed	Seasons Played	Apps	Subs	Gls
Wolverhampton W	Cliftonville	12/71	73-77	20	2	0
Wrexham	L	09/75	75	4	0	0
Walsall	Tr	08/78	78-79	19	7	3

KELLY James (Jimmy)
Born: Morpeth, Northumberland, England, 11 August, 1931 — RH
Died: Fleetwood, Lancashire, England, August, 2003

League Club	Source	Date Signed	Seasons Played	Apps	Subs	Gls
Watford	Blyth Spartans	03/49	50-54	119	-	4
Blackpool	Tr	10/54	54-60	198	-	9

KELLY James (Jimmy)
Born: Bellshill, Lanarkshire, Scotland, 4 June, 1933 — CF

League Club	Source	Date Signed	Seasons Played	Apps	Subs	Gls
Preston NE	Peterborough U	05/55				
Swindon T	Tr	02/58	57-58	30	-	14
Walsall	Tr	02/59	58	8	-	1

KELLY James
Born: Bradford, England, 1 July, 1938 — RH

League Club	Source	Date Signed	Seasons Played	Apps	Subs	Gls
Halifax T	Queensbury U	10/62	63	3	-	0

KELLY James (Jimmy)
Born: United Kingdom — WH

League Club	Source	Date Signed	Seasons Played	Apps	Subs	Gls
Barrow		02/46	46	1	-	0

KELLY James Edward (Jimmy)
Born: Seaham, County Durham, England, 29 December, 1907 — FB
Died: Oldham, Greater Manchester, England, 27 July, 1984

League Club	Source	Date Signed	Seasons Played	Apps	Subs	Gls
Southport	Murton CW	11/28	28-30	7	-	0
Barrow	Tr	08/31	31-32	55	-	0
Grimsby T	Tr	03/33	32-37	160	-	3
Bradford Park Ave	Tr	05/38	38	2	-	0
York C	Tr	12/38	38	24	-	0
Barrow	Trondheim (NOR)	06/46	46	1	-	0

KELLY James Lawrence (Jim)
Born: Holborn, Central London, England, 14 July, 1926 — W
Died: Wickford, Essex, England, 12 March, 1996

League Club	Source	Date Signed	Seasons Played	Apps	Subs	Gls
Gillingham	Dartford	05/51	51	3	-	0

KELLY James Patrick (Jimmy)
Born: Sacriston, County Durham, England, 22 November, 1951 — LB

League Club	Source	Date Signed	Seasons Played	Apps	Subs	Gls
Hartlepool U		08/70	71	5	0	0

KELLY James Patrick
Born: Drogheda, Republic of Ireland, 16 February, 1925 — LW
Republic of Ireland: LoI-2//Northern Ireland: NILge-4

League Club	Source	Date Signed	Seasons Played	Apps	Subs	Gls
Tottenham H	Glenavon	07/49				
Carlisle U	Tr	02/50	49-51	42	-	6

KELLY James Philip Vincent (Phil)
Born: Dublin, Republic of Ireland, 10 July, 1939 — RB
Died: Norwich, England, 16 August, 2012
Republic of Ireland: 5

League Club	Source	Date Signed	Seasons Played	Apps	Subs	Gls
Wolverhampton W	Sheldon T	09/57	58-61	16	-	0
Norwich C	Tr	08/62	62-66	114	1	2

KELLY James William (Jimmy)
Born: Carlisle, Cumbria, England, 2 May, 1957 — M

League Club	Source	Date Signed	Seasons Played	Apps	Subs	Gls
Manchester U	App	05/74	75	0	1	0

KELLY John
Born: Bebington, Wirral, England, 20 October, 1960 — W/M
Republic of Ireland: U21-2

League Club	Source	Date Signed	Seasons Played	Apps	Subs	Gls
Tranmere Rov	Cammell Laird	09/79	79-81	55	9	9
Preston NE	Tr	10/81	81-84	120	10	27
Chester C	Tr	08/85	85-86	85	0	17
Swindon T	Tr	06/87	87	3	4	1
Oldham Ath	Tr	11/87	87-88	51	1	6
Walsall	Tr	08/89	89-90	36	3	1
Huddersfield T	L	03/90	89	9	1	1
Huddersfield T	Tr	02/91	90-91	16	2	0
Chester C	Tr	07/92	92	24	7	1

KELLY John Carmichael (Johnny)
Born: Paisley, Renfrewshire, Scotland, 21 February, 1920 — LW
Died: Paisley, Renfrewshire, Scotland, 2 January, 2001
Scotland: 2/War-1

League Club	Source	Date Signed	Seasons Played	Apps	Subs	Gls
Barnsley	Greenock Morton	12/45	46-52	217	-	25
Halifax T	Greenock Morton	07/56	56-57	38	-	2

KELLY John Gerald
Born: Glasgow, Scotland, 14 December, 1935 — RH
Scotland: Schools

League Club	Source	Date Signed	Seasons Played	Apps	Subs	Gls
Crewe Alex	Third Lanark	08/59	59	20	-	1
Barnsley	Greenock Morton	09/63				

KELLY Julian James
Born: Enfield, N London, England, 6 September, 1989 — RB

League Club	Source	Date Signed	Seasons Played	Apps	Subs	Gls
Reading	Sch	07/08	08	4	3	0
Wycombe W	L	02/10	09	9	0	1
Lincoln C	L	01/11	10	21	0	0
Notts Co	Tr	07/11	11-12	49	5	4

KELLY Lawrence John (Laurie)
Born: Wolverhampton, England, 28 April, 1925 — LB
Died: Dudley, West Midlands, England, 1972

League Club	Source	Date Signed	Seasons Played	Apps	Subs	Gls
Wolverhampton W	Jnr	03/43	47-49	60	-	0
Huddersfield T	Tr	10/50	50-56	225	-	2

KELLY Leon Michael
Born: Coventry, England, 26 June, 1978 — M

League Club	Source	Date Signed	Seasons Played	Apps	Subs	Gls
Cambridge U	Atherstone U	08/01	01	1	1	0

KELLY Liam Mark
Born: Milton Keynes, England, 10 February, 1990 — M
Scotland: 1/U21-9/Youth

League Club	Source	Date Signed	Seasons Played	Apps	Subs	Gls
Bristol C	Kilmarnock	01/13	12-13	19	2	0
Oldham Ath	Tr	06/14	14	37	0	1

KELLY Marcus Philip
Born: Kettering, Northamptonshire, England, 16 March, 1986 — LW
England: Semi Pro-1

League Club	Source	Date Signed	Seasons Played	Apps	Subs	Gls
Rushden & D	Jnr	11/03	03-05	46	14	3

KELLY Mark David
Born: Blackpool, Lancashire, England, 7 October, 1966 — M

League Club	Source	Date Signed	Seasons Played	Apps	Subs	Gls
Shrewsbury T	Burnley (YT)	12/85				
Cardiff C	Tr	06/87	87-89	93	12	2
Fulham	Tr	06/90	90-92	55	9	2

KELLY Mark John
Born: Sutton, S London, England, 27 November, 1969 — LW
England: Youth//Republic of Ireland: 4/U23-2/U21-3

League Club	Source	Date Signed	Seasons Played	Apps	Subs	Gls
Portsmouth	App	11/86	87-90	24	25	2

KELLY Martin Ronald
Born: Bolton, Greater Manchester, England, 27 April, 1990 — FB
England: 1/U21-8/Youth

League Club	Source	Date Signed	Seasons Played	Apps	Subs	Gls
Liverpool	Sch	12/07	09-13	26	7	0

League Club	Source	Date Signed	Seasons Played	Apps	Subs	Gls
Huddersfield T	L	03/09	08	7	0	1
Crystal Palace	Tr	08/14	14	27	4	0

KELLY Michael (Mike)
Born: United Kingdom — LW

League Club	Source	Date Signed	Seasons Played	Apps	Subs	Gls
Wolverhampton W		06/39				
Crewe Alex	Tr	11/45	46	15	-	2

KELLY Michael John (Mike)
Born: Northampton, England, 18 October, 1942 — G
England: Amateur-1

League Club	Source	Date Signed	Seasons Played	Apps	Subs	Gls
Queens Park Rgrs	Wimbledon	03/66	67-69	54	0	0
Birmingham C	Tr	08/70	70-74	62	0	0

KELLY Michael Lawrence (Mike)
Born: Belvedere, SE London, England, 22 October, 1954 — M

League Club	Source	Date Signed	Seasons Played	Apps	Subs	Gls
Millwall	App	10/72	72-74	16	2	2
Charlton Ath	Tr	12/74	74	10	0	3

KELLY Noel
Born: Dublin, Republic of Ireland, 28 December, 1921 — IF
Died: Poulton-le-Fylde, Lancashire, England, 11 August, 1991
Republic of Ireland: 1//Northern Ireland: NILge-2

League Club	Source	Date Signed	Seasons Played	Apps	Subs	Gls
Arsenal	Glentoran	10/47	49	1	-	0
Crystal Palace	Tr	03/50	49-50	42	-	5
Nottingham F	Tr	08/51	51-54	48	-	11
Tranmere Rov	Tr	07/55	55-56	52	-	7

KELLY Norman
Born: Belfast, Northern Ireland, 10 October, 1970 — M
Northern Ireland: U21-1/Youth

League Club	Source	Date Signed	Seasons Played	Apps	Subs	Gls
Oldham Ath	YT	07/89	87-88	0	2	0
Wigan Ath	L	10/89	89	0	4	0

KELLY Nyrere Anthony Okpara (Tony)
Born: Coleshill, Warwickshire, England, 14 February, 1966 — W

League Club	Source	Date Signed	Seasons Played	Apps	Subs	Gls
Bristol C	Jnr	09/82	82	2	4	1
Stoke C	St Albans C	01/90	89-92	33	25	5
Hull C	L	01/92	91	6	0	1
Cardiff C	L	10/92	92	5	0	1
Bury	Tr	09/93	93-94	53	4	10
Leyton Orient	Tr	07/95	95-96	38	5	4
Colchester U	L	10/96	96	2	1	0

KELLY Patrick (Paddy)
Born: Kirkcaldy, Fife, Scotland, 26 April, 1978 — CD
Scotland: Youth

League Club	Source	Date Signed	Seasons Played	Apps	Subs	Gls
Newcastle U	Glasgow Celtic	08/97				
Reading	L	03/98	97	3	0	0

KELLY Patrick Michael (Pat)
Born: Johannesburg, South Africa, 9 April, 1918 — G
Died: Rochdale, Greater Manchester, England, 7 September, 1985
Northern Ireland: 1

League Club	Source	Date Signed	Seasons Played	Apps	Subs	Gls
Barnsley	Aberdeen	10/46	46-50	144	-	0
Crewe Alex	Tr	02/52	51-52	38	-	0

KELLY Paul Anthony
Born: Eccles, Greater Manchester, England, 6 March, 1971 — M

League Club	Source	Date Signed	Seasons Played	Apps	Subs	Gls
Manchester C	YT	02/90				
Crewe Alex	Tr	02/92	91	0	1	0

KELLY Paul Leon Marvin
Born: Hillingdon, W London, England, 24 February, 1974 — M

League Club	Source	Date Signed	Seasons Played	Apps	Subs	Gls
Fulham	YT	07/92	91-93	4	2	0

KELLY Paul Michael
Born: Bexley, SE London, England, 12 October, 1969 — M
England: Youth/Schools

League Club	Source	Date Signed	Seasons Played	Apps	Subs	Gls
West Ham U	YT	06/88	89	0	1	0

KELLY Peter Anthony
Born: East Kilbride, Lanarkshire, Scotland, 6 December, 1956 — RB

League Club	Source	Date Signed	Seasons Played	Apps	Subs	Gls
Newcastle U	App	07/74	74-80	31	2	0

KELLY Raymond (Ray)
Born: Athlone, Republic of Ireland, 29 December, 1976 — F
Republic of Ireland: U21-4

League Club	Source	Date Signed	Seasons Played	Apps	Subs	Gls
Manchester C	Athlone T (ROI)	08/94	97	1	0	0
Wrexham	L	10/97	97	5	1	1
Wrexham	L	03/98	97	0	4	0

KELLY Robert (Bob)
Born: Kirkcaldy, Fife, Scotland, 16 November, 1919 — WH
Died: Bedford, England, November, 2001

League Club	Source	Date Signed	Seasons Played	Apps	Subs	Gls
Millwall	Raith Rov	06/46	46-47	52	-	1
Bury	Tr	05/48	48	9	-	0

KELLY Robert Anthony
Born: Birmingham, England, 21 December, 1964 — M

League Club	Source	Date Signed	Seasons Played	Apps	Subs	Gls
Leicester C	App	12/82	83-86	17	7	1
Tranmere Rov	L	12/84	84	5	0	2
Wolverhampton W	Tr	03/87	86-88	13	3	2

KELLY Russell
Born: Ballymoney, Antrim, Northern Ireland, 10 August, 1976 — M
Republic of Ireland: Youth/Schools

League Club	Source	Date Signed	Seasons Played	Apps	Subs	Gls
Chelsea	YT	07/95				
Leyton Orient	L	03/96	95	5	1	0
Darlington	Tr	09/96	96	13	10	2

KELLY Seamus
Born: Tullamore, Offaly, Republic of Ireland, 6 May, 1974 — G

League Club	Source	Date Signed	Seasons Played	Apps	Subs	Gls
Cardiff C	UC Dublin (ROI)	08/98	98-99	12	1	0

KELLY Shaun David
Born: Liverpool, England, 11 December, 1988 — CD

League Club	Source	Date Signed	Seasons Played	Apps	Subs	Gls
Chester C	Sch	05/07	06-08	30	9	1
Burton A	Tr	03/10	09	2	2	0

KELLY Stephen Michael David
Born: Dublin, Republic of Ireland, 6 September, 1983 — RB
Republic of Ireland: 38/U21-15/Youth

League Club	Source	Date Signed	Seasons Played	Apps	Subs	Gls
Tottenham H	YT	09/00	03-05	29	8	2
Southend U	L	01/03	02	10	0	0
Queens Park Rgrs	L	03/03	02	7	0	0
Watford	L	09/03	03	13	0	0
Birmingham C	Tr	07/06	06-08	75	4	0
Stoke C	L	02/09	08	2	4	0
Fulham	Tr	07/09	09-12	36	8	0
Reading	Tr	01/13	12-14	40	6	1

KELLY Terence James (Terry)
Born: Gateshead, Tyne and Wear, England, 14 May, 1942 — CF

League Club	Source	Date Signed	Seasons Played	Apps	Subs	Gls
Newcastle U	Jnr	05/60				
Lincoln C	Tr	07/62	62	8	-	2

KELLY Terence William John (Terry)
Born: Luton, England, 16 January, 1932 — CH
Died: Luton, England, 2 August, 2007

League Club	Source	Date Signed	Seasons Played	Apps	Subs	Gls
Luton T	Vauxhall Motors	04/50	54-62	136	-	1

KELLY Thomas John (Tom)
Born: Bellshill, Lanarkshire, Scotland, 28 March, 1964 — LB/M

League Club	Source	Date Signed	Seasons Played	Apps	Subs	Gls
Hartlepool U	Queen of the South	08/85	85	14	1	0
Torquay U	Tr	07/86	86-88	116	4	0
York C	Tr	07/89	89	35	0	2
Exeter C	Tr	03/90	89-92	76	12	9
Torquay U	Tr	01/93	92-95	109	8	8

KELLY Thomas William (Tom)
Born: Darlington, County Durham, England, 22 November, 1919 — D
Died: Northallerton, North Yorkshire, England, 18 January, 1970

League Club	Source	Date Signed	Seasons Played	Apps	Subs	Gls
Darlington	Deneside Jnrs	11/37	37-50	157	-	2
York C	Tr	08/51				

KELLY Walter Muir
Born: Cowdenbeath, Fife, Scotland, 15 April, 1929 — CF
Died: Dunfermline, Fife, Scotland, 16 February, 1993

League Club	Source	Date Signed	Seasons Played	Apps	Subs	Gls
Bury	Raith Rov	08/52	52-56	159	-	77
Doncaster Rov	Tr	06/57	57	29	-	6
Stockport Co	Tr	03/58	57-59	47	-	12
Chester C	Tr	08/59	59-60	56	-	24

KELLY William Brian (Brian)
Born: Isleworth, W London, England, 25 September, 1937 — CF
Died: Redbridge, E London, England, March, 2013

League Club	Source	Date Signed	Seasons Played	Apps	Subs	Gls
Queens Park Rgrs	Dover	11/58	58	6	-	0

KELLY William Muir (Willie)
Born: Cowdenbeath, Fife, Scotland, 14 August, 1922 — CH
Died: Blackburn, Greater Manchester, England, 11 July, 1996

League Club	Source	Date Signed	Seasons Played	Apps	Subs	Gls
Blackburn Rov	Airdrieonians	09/51	51-56	186	-	1
Accrington Stan	Mossley	09/57	57	24	-	0

KELSALL Charles (Charlie)
Born: Hawarden, Flintshire, Wales, 15 April, 1921 — LB

League Club	Source	Date Signed	Seasons Played	Apps	Subs	Gls
Wrexham	Buckley	08/39	46-51	39	-	0

KELSEY Alfred John (Jack)
Born: Llansamlet, Swansea, Wales, 19 November, 1929 — G
Died: Barnet, N London, England, 18 March, 1992
England: FLge-1//Wales: 41

League Club	Source	Date Signed	Seasons Played	Apps	Subs	Gls
Arsenal	Winch Wen	08/49	50-61	327	-	0

KELTIE Clark Stuart
Born: Newcastle-upon-Tyne, England, 31 August, 1983 — M

League Club	Source	Date Signed	Seasons Played	Apps	Subs	Gls
Darlington	Walker Central	09/01	01-07	129	32	9
Rochdale	Tr	07/08	08	26	5	1
Lincoln C	Tr	01/10	09-10	25	4	0

KEMBER Stephen Dennis (Steve)
Born: Croydon, S London, England, 8 December, 1948 M
England: U23-3

League Club	Source	Date Signed	Seasons Played	Apps	Subs	Gls
Crystal Palace	App	12/65	65-71	216	2	35
Chelsea	Tr	09/71	71-74	125	5	13
Leicester C	Tr	07/75	75-78	115	2	6
Crystal Palace	Tr	10/78	78-79	39	3	1

KEMP David Michael
Born: Harrow, NW London, England, 20 February, 1953 F

League Club	Source	Date Signed	Seasons Played	Apps	Subs	Gls
Crystal Palace	Slough T	04/75	74-76	32	3	10
Portsmouth	Tr	11/76	76-77	63	1	30
Carlisle U	Tr	03/78	77-79	60	1	22
Plymouth Arg	Tr	09/79	79-81	82	2	39
Gillingham	L	12/81	81	9	0	2
Brentford	L	03/82	81	3	0	1

KEMP Frederick George (Fred)
Born: Salerno, Italy, 27 February, 1946 M

League Club	Source	Date Signed	Seasons Played	Apps	Subs	Gls
Wolverhampton W	App	06/63	64	3	-	0
Southampton	Tr	06/65	65-69	58	3	10
Blackpool	Tr	11/70	70-71	19	2	1
Halifax T	Tr	12/71	71-73	106	5	10
Hereford U	Tr	07/74	74	12	1	2

KEMP John
Born: Clydebank, Dunbartonshire, Scotland, 11 April, 1934 LW

League Club	Source	Date Signed	Seasons Played	Apps	Subs	Gls
Leeds U	Clyde	12/57	58	1	-	0
Barrow	Tr	03/59	58-63	170	-	45
Crewe Alex	Tr	12/63	63-65	47	0	7

KEMP Raymond William (Ray)
Born: Bristol, England, 18 January, 1922 G
Died: Thurrock, Essex, England, February, 1989

League Club	Source	Date Signed	Seasons Played	Apps	Subs	Gls
Reading (Am)	Grays Ath	09/49	49	3	-	0

KEMP Robert McAlpine (Roy)
Born: Falkirk, Scotland, 15 August, 1941 LW

League Club	Source	Date Signed	Seasons Played	Apps	Subs	Gls
Carlisle U	Falkirk	11/60	60	1	-	0

KEMP Samuel Patrick (Sam)
Born: Stockton-on-Tees, Cleveland, England, 29 August, 1932 RW
Died: Stockton-on-Tees, Cleveland, England, 2 August, 1987

League Club	Source	Date Signed	Seasons Played	Apps	Subs	Gls
Sunderland	Whitby T	03/52	52-56	17	-	2
Sheffield U	Tr	02/57	56-57	16	-	1
Mansfield T	Tr	05/58	58	3	-	1
Gateshead	Tr	10/58	58	7	-	1

KEMP Stephen Duncan (Steve)
Born: Shrewsbury, Shropshire, England, 2 May, 1955 CD
Died: Shrewsbury, Shropshire, England, 13 January, 2008

League Club	Source	Date Signed	Seasons Played	Apps	Subs	Gls
Shrewsbury T	App	07/73	72-73	7	1	0

KEMPSON Darran Kaya
Born: Blackpool, Lancashire, England, 6 December, 1984 CD
England: Semi Pro-2

League Club	Source	Date Signed	Seasons Played	Apps	Subs	Gls
Preston NE	Sch	07/04				
Crewe Alex	Morecambe	07/06	06	6	1	0
Bury	L	02/07	06	12	0	0
Shrewsbury T	Tr	07/07	07	18	5	0
Accrington Stan	L	02/08	07	8	0	1
Accrington Stan	Wrexham	08/09	09	40	0	1

KENDAL Stephen James (Steve)
Born: Birtley, Tyne and Wear, England, 4 August, 1961 LM

League Club	Source	Date Signed	Seasons Played	Apps	Subs	Gls
Nottingham F	App	08/79	81	1	0	0
Chesterfield	Tr	12/82	82-86	122	3	14
Torquay U	Tr	10/86	86	4	0	0

KENDALL Harold Arnold (Arnold)
Born: Halifax, West Yorkshire, England, 6 April, 1925 W
Died: Bradford, England, December, 2003

League Club	Source	Date Signed	Seasons Played	Apps	Subs	Gls
Bradford C	Salts	02/49	48-52	113	-	13
Rochdale	Tr	09/53	53-56	111	-	25
Bradford Park Ave	Tr	09/56	56-58	90	-	12

KENDALL Howard
Born: Ryton-on-Tyne, Tyne and Wear, England, 22 May, 1946 M
Died: Southport, Merseyside, England, 17 October, 2015
England: FLge-1/U23-6/Youth/Schools

League Club	Source	Date Signed	Seasons Played	Apps	Subs	Gls
Preston NE	App	05/63	62-66	104	0	13
Everton	Tr	03/67	66-73	227	2	21
Birmingham C	Tr	02/74	73-76	115	0	16
Stoke C	Tr	08/77	77-78	82	0	9
Blackburn Rov	Tr	07/79	79-80	79	0	6
Everton	Tr	08/81	81	4	0	0

KENDALL Ian
Born: Blackburn, Greater Manchester, England, 11 December, 1947 LW
Died: Blackburn, Greater Manchester, England, August, 2010

League Club	Source	Date Signed	Seasons Played	Apps	Subs	Gls
Blackburn Rov	App	12/65				
Southport	Tr	08/67	67	1	1	0

KENDALL James Briden (Jimmy)
Born: Birtley, Tyne and Wear, England, 4 October, 1922 IF

League Club	Source	Date Signed	Seasons Played	Apps	Subs	Gls
Barrow	Gateshead U	05/47	46-48	44	-	16
Gateshead	Tr	11/48	48-51	57	-	20
Barrow	Tr	10/51	51-52	22	-	6
Accrington Stan	Tr	09/52	52	26	-	8

KENDALL Mark
Born: Blackwood, Caerphilly, Wales, 20 September, 1958 G
Died: Blackwood, Caerphilly, Wales, 1 May, 2008
Wales: U21-1/Youth/Schools

League Club	Source	Date Signed	Seasons Played	Apps	Subs	Gls
Tottenham H	App	07/76	78-80	29	0	0
Chesterfield	L	11/79	79	9	0	0
Newport Co	Tr	09/80	80-86	272	0	0
Wolverhampton W	Tr	12/86	86-89	147	0	0
Swansea C	Tr	07/90	90-91	12	0	0
Burnley	L	12/91	91	2	0	0

KENDALL Mark Ivor
Born: Nuneaton, Warwickshire, England, 10 December, 1961 G
England: Youth

League Club	Source	Date Signed	Seasons Played	Apps	Subs	Gls
Aston Villa	App	11/79				
Northampton T	Tr	06/82	82	11	0	0
Birmingham C	Tr	02/84	83	1	0	0

KENDALL Paul Scott
Born: Halifax, West Yorkshire, England, 19 October, 1964 CD

League Club	Source	Date Signed	Seasons Played	Apps	Subs	Gls
Halifax T	App	10/82	81-85	91	15	4
Scarborough	Tr	07/86	87	22	5	1
Halifax T	Tr	03/88	87	9	1	0

KENDALL Ryan Paul
Born: Hull, England, 14 September, 1989 F

League Club	Source	Date Signed	Seasons Played	Apps	Subs	Gls
Hull C	Sch	08/08				
Bradford C	L	03/10	09	2	4	2

KENDRICK Joseph (Joe)
Born: Dublin, Republic of Ireland, 26 June, 1983 LB
Republic of Ireland: U21-1/Youth

League Club	Source	Date Signed	Seasons Played	Apps	Subs	Gls
Newcastle U	YT	07/00				
Darlington	1860 Munich (GER)	08/04	04-05	40	12	1

KENNA Jeffrey Jude (Jeff)
Born: Dublin, Republic of Ireland, 27 August, 1970 RB
Republic of Ireland: 27/B-1/U21-8/Youth/Schools

League Club	Source	Date Signed	Seasons Played	Apps	Subs	Gls
Southampton	YT	04/89	90-94	110	4	4
Blackburn Rov	Tr	03/95	94-00	153	2	1
Tranmere Rov	L	03/01	00	11	0	0
Wigan Ath	L	11/01	01	6	0	1
Birmingham C	Tr	12/01	01-03	71	4	3
Derby Co	Tr	03/04	03-05	64	1	0

KENNEDY Alan Philip
Born: Sunderland, England, 31 August, 1954 LB
England: 2/B-7/U23-6

League Club	Source	Date Signed	Seasons Played	Apps	Subs	Gls
Newcastle U	App	08/72	72-77	155	3	9
Liverpool	Tr	08/78	78-85	249	2	15
Sunderland	Tr	09/85	85-86	54	0	2
Hartlepool U	Germ'l Beerschot (BEL)	10/87	87	4	1	0
Wigan Ath	Grantham T	12/87	87	22	0	0
Wrexham	Colne Dynamoes	03/90	89-90	15	1	0

KENNEDY Andrew John (Andy)
Born: Stirling, Scotland, 8 October, 1964 F
Scotland: Youth

League Club	Source	Date Signed	Seasons Played	Apps	Subs	Gls
Birmingham C	Seiko Sports Ass (HKG)	03/85	84-87	51	25	18
Sheffield U	L	03/87	86	8	1	1
Blackburn Rov	Tr	06/88	88-89	49	10	23
Watford	Tr	08/90	90-91	17	8	4
Bolton W	L	10/91	91	1	0	0
Brighton & HA	Tr	09/92	92-93	34	8	10
Gillingham	Tr	09/94	94	0	2	0

KENNEDY Benjamin James (Ben)
Born: Lisburn, Belfast, Northern Ireland, 12 January, 1997 M/F
Northern Ireland: Youth

League Club	Source	Date Signed	Seasons Played	Apps	Subs	Gls
Stevenage	Sch	02/15	14	6	9	4

KENNEDY Callum Ewan
Born: Chertsey, Surrey, England, 9 November, 1989 LB

League Club	Source	Date Signed	Seasons Played	Apps	Subs	Gls
Swindon T	Sch	02/08	08-11	27	6	1
Gillingham	L	11/10	10	3	0	0
Rotherham U	L	02/11	10	4	1	0
Scunthorpe U	Tr	07/12	12	11	6	0
AFC Wimbledon	Tr	07/13	13-14	41	7	0

KENNEDY David
Born: Sunderland, England, 30 November, 1950 — CD

League Club	Source	Date Signed	Seasons Played	Apps	Subs	Gls
Leeds U	App	05/68	69	2	0	1
Lincoln C	Tr	07/71	71	6	2	1

KENNEDY David (Dave)
Born: Birkenhead, Wirral, England, 14 February, 1949 — W/M

League Club	Source	Date Signed	Seasons Played	Apps	Subs	Gls
Tranmere Rov	Jnr	05/67	67-69	16	1	0
Chester C	Tr	05/70	70-73	79	8	9
Torquay U	Tr	09/73	73-76	144	7	7

KENNEDY Gordon McKay
Born: Dundee, Scotland, 15 April, 1924 — LB
Died: Dundee, Scotland, 24 October, 1999

League Club	Source	Date Signed	Seasons Played	Apps	Subs	Gls
Blackpool	Dundee Elmwood	10/43	46-49	8	-	0
Bolton W	Tr	09/50	50	17	-	0
Stockport Co	Tr	08/53	53	20	-	1

KENNEDY Jason Brian
Born: Stockton-on-Tees, Cleveland, England, 11 September, 1986 — M

League Club	Source	Date Signed	Seasons Played	Apps	Subs	Gls
Middlesbrough	Sch	02/05	04-05	1	3	0
Boston U	L	11/06	06	13	0	1
Bury	L	03/07	06	12	0	0
Darlington	Tr	02/08	07-08	57	2	7
Rochdale	Tr	05/09	09-12	166	11	12
Bradford C	Tr	07/13	13-14	22	6	3
Rochdale	L	01/14	13	4	3	0
Carlisle U	Tr	03/15	14	11	0	3

KENNEDY John
Born: Newtownards, Down, Northern Ireland, 4 September, 1939 — G
Northern Ireland: NILge-3

League Club	Source	Date Signed	Seasons Played	Apps	Subs	Gls
Lincoln C	Glentoran	07/67	67-73	251	0	0

KENNEDY John (Jack)
Born: Kilwinning, Ayrshire, Scotland, 26 February, 1941 — IF

League Club	Source	Date Signed	Seasons Played	Apps	Subs	Gls
Charlton Ath	Saltcoats Victoria	03/62	61-64	46	-	8
Exeter C	Tr	11/65	65-66	40	1	6

KENNEDY John
Born: Airdrie, Lanarkshire, Scotland, 18 August, 1983 — CD
Scotland: 1/U21-15

League Club	Source	Date Signed	Seasons Played	Apps	Subs	Gls
Norwich C (L)	Glasgow Celtic	08/08	08	15	1	2

KENNEDY John Neil
Born: Newmarket, Suffolk, England, 19 August, 1978 — RB

League Club	Source	Date Signed	Seasons Played	Apps	Subs	Gls
Ipswich T	YT	06/97	97-98	6	2	0

KENNEDY Jonathan (Jon)
Born: Rotherham, South Yorkshire, England, 30 November, 1980 — G

League Club	Source	Date Signed	Seasons Played	Apps	Subs	Gls
Sunderland	Worksop T	05/00				
Blackpool	L	10/00	00	6	0	0

KENNEDY Joseph Peter (Joe)
Born: Cleator Moor, Cumbria, England, 15 November, 1925 — CH
Died: West Bromwich, West Midlands, England, 12 September, 1986
England: B-2

League Club	Source	Date Signed	Seasons Played	Apps	Subs	Gls
West Bromwich A	Altrincham	12/48	48-60	364	-	3
Chester C	Tr	06/61	61	35	-	0

KENNEDY Keith Vernon
Born: Sunderland, England, 5 March, 1952 — LB

League Club	Source	Date Signed	Seasons Played	Apps	Subs	Gls
Newcastle U	App	07/70	71	1	0	0
Bury	Tr	10/72	72-81	405	0	4
Mansfield T	Tr	08/82	82	32	2	0

KENNEDY Luke Daniel
Born: Peterborough, England, 22 May, 1986 — M

League Club	Source	Date Signed	Seasons Played	Apps	Subs	Gls
Rushden & D	Sch	07/05	04	1	2	0

KENNEDY Malcolm Stephen John
Born: Swansea, Wales, 13 October, 1939 — LH

League Club	Source	Date Signed	Seasons Played	Apps	Subs	Gls
Swansea C	Jnr	05/57	57-60	18	-	0
Carlisle U	Tr	06/61				

KENNEDY Mark John
Born: Dublin, Republic of Ireland, 15 May, 1976 — LB/LW
Republic of Ireland: 34/U21-7/Youth/Schools

League Club	Source	Date Signed	Seasons Played	Apps	Subs	Gls
Millwall	YT	05/92	92-94	37	6	9
Liverpool	Tr	03/95	94-97	5	11	0
Queens Park Rgrs	L	01/98	97	8	0	2
Wimbledon	Tr	03/98	97-98	11	10	0
Manchester C	Tr	07/99	99-00	56	10	8
Wolverhampton W	Tr	07/01	01-05	157	10	12
Crystal Palace	Tr	07/06	06-07	42	4	1
Cardiff C	Tr	07/08	08-09	60	6	0
Ipswich T	Tr	08/10	10-11	30	3	0

KENNEDY Matthew
Born: Kilmarnock, Ayrshire, Scotland, 1 November, 1994 — RW
Scotland: U21-1/Youth

League Club	Source	Date Signed	Seasons Played	Apps	Subs	Gls
Everton	Kilmarnock	08/12				
Tranmere Rov	L	01/14	13	8	0	0
MK Dons	L	03/14	13	7	0	1
Cardiff C	Tr	02/15	14	9	5	0

KENNEDY Michael Francis Martin (Mick)
Born: Salford, England, 9 April, 1961 — M
Republic of Ireland: 2/U21-4

League Club	Source	Date Signed	Seasons Played	Apps	Subs	Gls
Halifax T	App	01/79	78-79	74	2	4
Huddersfield T	Tr	08/80	80-81	80	1	9
Middlesbrough	Tr	08/82	82-83	68	0	5
Portsmouth	Tr	06/84	84-87	129	0	4
Bradford C	Tr	01/88	87-88	45	0	2
Leicester C	Tr	03/89	88	9	0	0
Luton T	Tr	08/89	89	30	2	0
Stoke C	Tr	08/90	90-91	51	1	3
Chesterfield	Tr	08/92	92	19	8	1
Wigan Ath	Tr	07/93	93	15	2	1

KENNEDY Patrick Antony (Pat)
Born: Dublin, Republic of Ireland, 9 October, 1934 — LB
Died: Urmston, Greater Manchester, England, 18 March, 2007

League Club	Source	Date Signed	Seasons Played	Apps	Subs	Gls
Manchester U	Johnville (ROI)	02/53	54	1	-	0
Blackburn Rov	Tr	08/56	57	3	-	0
Southampton	Tr	07/59	59	2	-	0
Oldham Ath	Tr	07/60				

KENNEDY Peter Henry James
Born: Lurgan, Armagh, Northern Ireland, 10 September, 1973 — LB/M
Northern Ireland: 20/B-1

League Club	Source	Date Signed	Seasons Played	Apps	Subs	Gls
Notts Co	Portadown	08/96	96	20	2	0
Watford	Tr	07/97	97-00	108	7	18
Wigan Ath	Tr	07/01	01-03	60	5	2
Derby Co	L	10/03	03	5	0	1
Peterborough U	Tr	08/04	04-05	25	6	2

KENNEDY Raymond (Ray)
Born: Seaton Delaval, Northumberland, England, 28 July, 1951 — M/F
England: 17/U23-6

League Club	Source	Date Signed	Seasons Played	Apps	Subs	Gls
Arsenal	App	11/68	69-73	156	2	53
Liverpool	Tr	07/74	74-81	272	3	51
Swansea C	Tr	01/82	81-83	42	0	2
Hartlepool U	Tr	11/83	83	18	5	3

KENNEDY Richard Joseph
Born: Waterford, Republic of Ireland, 28 August, 1978 — M

League Club	Source	Date Signed	Seasons Played	Apps	Subs	Gls
Crystal Palace	YT	03/97				
Wycombe W	Tr	10/98				
Brentford	Tr	07/99	99-00	5	5	0

KENNEDY Robert (Bobby)
Born: Motherwell, Lanarkshire, Scotland, 23 June, 1937 — WH/FB
Scotland: U23-1

League Club	Source	Date Signed	Seasons Played	Apps	Subs	Gls
Manchester C	Kilmarnock	07/61	61-68	216	3	9
Grimsby T	Tr	03/69	68-70	84	0	1

KENNEDY Stephen (Steve)
Born: Denton, Greater Manchester, England, 22 July, 1965 — D

League Club	Source	Date Signed	Seasons Played	Apps	Subs	Gls
Burnley	App	07/83	83-86	18	0	0

KENNEDY Terry
Born: Barnsley, South Yorkshire, England, 14 November, 1993 — CD

League Club	Source	Date Signed	Seasons Played	Apps	Subs	Gls
Sheffield U	Sch	11/10	10-14	14	4	0

KENNEDY Thomas Gordon (Tom)
Born: Bury, Greater Manchester, England, 24 June, 1985 — LB

League Club	Source	Date Signed	Seasons Played	Apps	Subs	Gls
Bury	Sch	11/02	03-06	131	12	5
Rochdale	Tr	07/07	07-09	132	0	9
Leicester C	Tr	07/10	10-11	5	1	0
Rochdale	L	11/10	10	6	0	0
Peterborough U	L	01/11	10	14	0	0
Peterborough U	L	09/11	11	8	2	0
Barnsley	Tr	09/12	12-13	67	1	1
Rochdale	Tr	08/14	14	22	1	0
Bury	L	10/14	14	1	1	0
Blackpool	L	11/14	14	5	0	0

KENNERLEY Kevin Robert
Born: Chester, England, 26 April, 1954 — M

League Club	Source	Date Signed	Seasons Played	Apps	Subs	Gls
Burnley	Arsenal (App)	05/72	75	6	0	1
Port Vale	Tr	05/76	76-77	16	8	1
Swansea C	L	02/78	77	2	0	0

KENNETH Garry
Born: Dundee, Scotland, 21 June, 1987 — CD
Scotland: 2/U21-8/Youth

League Club	Source	Date Signed	Seasons Played	Apps	Subs	Gls
Bristol Rov	Dundee U	07/12	12	18	0	1

KENNING Michael John (Mike)
Born: Erdington, West Midlands, England, 18 August, 1940 RW

League Club	Source	Date Signed	Seasons Played	Apps	Subs	Gls
Aston Villa	Brookhill	10/59	60	3	-	0
Shrewsbury T	Tr	05/61	61-62	62	-	17
Charlton Ath	Tr	11/62	62-66	152	1	43
Norwich C	Tr	12/66	66-67	44	0	9
Wolverhampton W	Tr	01/68	67-68	35	6	5
Charlton Ath	Tr	03/69	68-71	59	7	12
Watford	Tr	12/71	71-72	35	6	2

KENNON Neil Sandilands (Sandy)
Born: Johannesburg, South Africa, 28 November, 1933 G
Died: 17 August, 2015

League Club	Source	Date Signed	Seasons Played	Apps	Subs	Gls
Huddersfield T	Queens Park (RHO)	08/56	56-58	78	-	0
Norwich C	Tr	02/59	58-64	213	-	0
Colchester U	Tr	03/65	64-66	76	0	0

KENNY Frederick (Fred)
Born: Manchester, England, 14 January, 1923 FB
Died: Cyprus, 22 June, 1985

League Club	Source	Date Signed	Seasons Played	Apps	Subs	Gls
Stockport Co	Manchester C (Am)	12/47	48-56	204	-	0

KENNY Patrick Joseph (Paddy)
Born: Halifax, West Yorkshire, England, 17 May, 1978 G
Republic of Ireland: 7

League Club	Source	Date Signed	Seasons Played	Apps	Subs	Gls
Bury	Bradford Park Ave	08/98	99-01	133	0	0
Sheffield U	Tr	07/02	02-09	278	0	0
Queens Park Rgrs	Tr	06/10	10-11	77	0	0
Leeds U	Tr	07/12	12-13	76	0	0
Bolton W	Tr	09/14				
Oldham Ath	L	11/14	14	3	0	0
Ipswich T	Tr	01/15				

KENNY Vincent (Vince)
Born: Sheffield, England, 29 December, 1924 LB
Died: Sheffield, England, 24 February, 2006

League Club	Source	Date Signed	Seasons Played	Apps	Subs	Gls
Sheffield Wed	Atlas & Norfolk	11/45	46-54	144	-	0
Carlisle U	Tr	07/55	55-57	112	-	3

KENNY William Aidan (Billy)
Born: Liverpool, England, 23 October, 1951 M
England: Youth

League Club	Source	Date Signed	Seasons Played	Apps	Subs	Gls
Everton	App	07/69	70-74	10	2	0
Tranmere Rov	Tr	03/75	74-76	36	18	5

KENNY William Aidan (Billy)
Born: Liverpool, England, 19 September, 1973 M
England: U23-1

League Club	Source	Date Signed	Seasons Played	Apps	Subs	Gls
Everton	YT	06/92	92	16	1	1
Oldham Ath	Tr	08/94	94	4	0	0

KENT Frankie
Born: Shenfield, Essex, England, 21 November, 1995 CD

League Club	Source	Date Signed	Seasons Played	Apps	Subs	Gls
Colchester U	Sch	10/13	13-14	9	2	0

KENT Kevin John
Born: Stoke-on-Trent, England, 19 March, 1965 RW

League Club	Source	Date Signed	Seasons Played	Apps	Subs	Gls
West Bromwich A	App	12/82	83	1	1	0
Newport Co	Tr	07/84	84	23	10	1
Mansfield T	Tr	08/85	85-90	223	5	37
Port Vale	Tr	03/91	90-95	87	28	7

KENT Michael John (Mike)
Born: North Anston, South Yorkshire, England, 12 January, 1951 RW

League Club	Source	Date Signed	Seasons Played	Apps	Subs	Gls
Wolverhampton W	Wath W	08/68	69-71	0	2	0
Gillingham	L	03/71	70	11	0	0
Sheffield Wed	Tr	09/73	73	4	0	0

KENT Paul
Born: Rotherham, South Yorkshire, England, 23 February, 1954 LB

League Club	Source	Date Signed	Seasons Played	Apps	Subs	Gls
Norwich C	App	02/72	73	1	2	0
Halifax T	Tr	08/76	76	12	0	0

KENT Terence Ian (Terry)
Born: Battersea, SW London, England, 21 October, 1939 LW

League Club	Source	Date Signed	Seasons Played	Apps	Subs	Gls
Southend U		05/58	58	1	-	0
Millwall	Tr	08/60				

KENTON Darren Edward
Born: Wandsworth, SW London, England, 13 September, 1978 D

League Club	Source	Date Signed	Seasons Played	Apps	Subs	Gls
Norwich C	YT	07/97	97-02	142	16	9
Southampton	Tr	05/03	03-05	24	5	0
Leicester C	L	03/05	04	9	1	0
Leicester C	Tr	07/06	06-07	26	7	2
Leeds U	Tr	01/08	07	16	0	0
Cheltenham T	Tr	10/08	08	13	0	1

KENWORTHY Anthony David (Tony)
Born: Leeds, England, 30 October, 1958 CD
England: Youth

League Club	Source	Date Signed	Seasons Played	Apps	Subs	Gls
Sheffield U	App	07/76	75-85	281	5	34
Mansfield T	Tr	03/86	85-89	98	2	0

KENWORTHY Jonathan Raymond (Jon)
Born: St Asaph, Flintshire, Wales, 18 August, 1974 RW
Wales: U21-4/Youth

League Club	Source	Date Signed	Seasons Played	Apps	Subs	Gls
Tranmere Rov	YT	07/93	93-95	14	12	2
Chester C	L	12/95	95	5	2	1

KENWORTHY Stephen (Steve)
Born: Wrexham, Wales, 6 November, 1959 LB
Died: Wrexham, Wales, 26 June, 2001

League Club	Source	Date Signed	Seasons Played	Apps	Subs	Gls
Wrexham	Jnr	11/77	77-80	19	1	0
Bury	Tr	08/81	82	14	0	0

KENYON Alexander George (Alex)
Born: Euxton, Lancashire, England, 17 July, 1992 DM

League Club	Source	Date Signed	Seasons Played	Apps	Subs	Gls
Morecambe	Stockport Co	06/13	13-14	62	14	3

KENYON Frederick (Fred)
Born: Carlisle, Cumbria, England, 14 September, 1922 CH
Died: Carlisle, Cumbria, England, 20 December, 1998

League Club	Source	Date Signed	Seasons Played	Apps	Subs	Gls
Carlisle U		09/43	47-48	4	-	0

KENYON John Francis
Born: Blackburn, Greater Manchester, England, 2 December, 1953 F

League Club	Source	Date Signed	Seasons Played	Apps	Subs	Gls
Blackburn Rov	Great Harwood T	12/72	72-75	32	14	7

KENYON Roger Norton
Born: Blackpool, Lancashire, England, 4 January, 1949 CD

League Club	Source	Date Signed	Seasons Played	Apps	Subs	Gls
Everton	App	09/66	67-78	254	13	6
Bristol C	Vancouver W'caps (CAN)	10/79	79	4	0	0

KENYON Roy
Born: Manchester, England, 10 March, 1933 IF

League Club	Source	Date Signed	Seasons Played	Apps	Subs	Gls
Leeds U	Bolton W (Am)	12/50				
Southport	Worcester C	09/54	54	1	-	0

KEOGH Andrew Declan (Andy)
Born: Dublin, Republic of Ireland, 16 May, 1986 F
Republic of Ireland: 30/B-1/U21-9/Youth

League Club	Source	Date Signed	Seasons Played	Apps	Subs	Gls
Leeds U	Sch	05/03				
Scunthorpe U	L	08/04	04	9	3	2
Bury	L	01/05	04	4	0	2
Scunthorpe U	Tr	02/05	04-06	69	17	19
Wolverhampton W	Tr	01/07	06-10	79	37	19
Cardiff C	L	08/10	10	11	5	2
Bristol C	L	01/11	10	4	5	1
Leeds U	L	08/11	11	17	5	2
Millwall	Tr	01/12	11-13	47	23	17
Blackpool	L	01/14	13	9	5	3

KEOGH Richard John
Born: Harlow, Essex, England, 11 August, 1986 CD
Republic of Ireland: 8/U21-8

League Club	Source	Date Signed	Seasons Played	Apps	Subs	Gls
Stoke C	Sch	01/05				
Bristol C	Tr	07/05	05-06	24	16	3
Wycombe W	L	11/05	05	2	1	0
Huddersfield T	L	08/07	07	9	0	1
Carlisle U	L	10/07	07	7	0	0
Cheltenham T	L	03/08	07	10	0	0
Carlisle U	Tr	08/08	08-09	72	1	4
Coventry C	Tr	07/10	10-11	91	0	1
Derby Co	Tr	07/12	12-14	132	0	5

KEOHANE James Clifford John (Jimmy)
Born: Kilkenny, Republic of Ireland, 22 January, 1991 M

League Club	Source	Date Signed	Seasons Played	Apps	Subs	Gls
Bristol C	Wexford Youths (ROI)	09/10				
Exeter C	Tr	08/11	11-14	36	44	9

KEOUGH Daniel Peter (Danny)
Born: Rawtenstall, Lancashire, England, 31 January, 1963 DM

League Club	Source	Date Signed	Seasons Played	Apps	Subs	Gls
Manchester U	App	02/80				
Exeter C	Bury (NC)	10/85	85-86	71	1	0

KEOWN Martin Raymond
Born: Oxford, England, 24 July, 1966 CD
England: 43/B-1/U21-8/Youth

League Club	Source	Date Signed	Seasons Played	Apps	Subs	Gls
Arsenal	App	02/84	85	22	0	0
Brighton & HA	L	02/85	84	16	0	0
Brighton & HA	L	08/85	85	5	2	1
Aston Villa	Tr	06/86	86-88	109	3	3
Everton	Tr	08/89	89-92	92	4	0
Arsenal	Tr	02/93	92-03	282	28	4
Leicester C	Tr	07/04	04	16	1	0
Reading	Tr	01/05	04	3	2	0

KEOWN Niall Martin
Born: Oxford, England, 5 April, 1995 D

League Club	Source	Date Signed	Seasons Played	Apps	Subs	Gls
Reading	Sch	07/13	14	1	1	0

[KEPA] BLANCO Kepa
Born: Marbella, Spain, 13 January, 1984 — F
Spain: U21-8/Youth

League Club	Source	Date Signed	Seasons Played	Apps	Subs	Gls
West Ham U (L)	Sevilla (SPN)	01/07	06	1	7	1

KERFOOT Eric
Born: Ashton-under-Lyne, Greater Manchester, England, 31 July, 1924 — WH
Died: Dukinfield, Greater Manchester, England, 4 March, 1980

League Club	Source	Date Signed	Seasons Played	Apps	Subs	Gls
Leeds U	Stalybridge Celtic	12/49	49-58	336	-	9
Chesterfield	Tr	07/59	59	9	-	0

KERFOOT Jason John Thomas
Born: Preston, Lancashire, England, 17 April, 1973 — M

League Club	Source	Date Signed	Seasons Played	Apps	Subs	Gls
Preston NE	YT	07/91	90-91	0	4	0

KERKAR Salim
Born: Givors, France, 4 August, 1987 — M

League Club	Source	Date Signed	Seasons Played	Apps	Subs	Gls
Charlton Ath	Glasgow Rangers	08/12	12	15	7	1

KERLEY Adam Lewis
Born: Sutton-in-Ashfield, Nottinghamshire, England, 25 February, 1985 — F

League Club	Source	Date Signed	Seasons Played	Apps	Subs	Gls
Lincoln C	Sch	08/04	04	0	1	0

KERMORGANT Yann Alain
Born: Vannes, France, 8 November, 1981 — F

League Club	Source	Date Signed	Seasons Played	Apps	Subs	Gls
Leicester C	Stade de Reims (FRA)	08/09	09	9	11	1
Charlton Ath	Tr	09/11	11-13	78	11	29
Bournemouth	Tr	01/14	13-14	37	17	24

KERNAGHAN Alan Nigel
Born: Otley, West Yorkshire, England, 25 April, 1967 — CD/F
Republic of Ireland: 22//Northern Ireland: Schools

League Club	Source	Date Signed	Seasons Played	Apps	Subs	Gls
Middlesbrough	App	03/85	84-93	172	40	16
Charlton Ath	L	01/91	90	13	0	0
Manchester C	Tr	09/93	93-97	55	8	1
Bolton W	L	08/94	94	9	2	0
Bradford C	L	02/96	95	5	0	0

KERNAN Anthony Paul (Tony)
Born: Letterkenny, Donegal, Republic of Ireland, 31 August, 1963 — M
Republic of Ireland: Youth

League Club	Source	Date Signed	Seasons Played	Apps	Subs	Gls
Wolverhampton W	App	01/81	81	1	0	0

KERNICK Dudley Henry John
Born: Camelford, Cornwall, England, 29 August, 1921 — IF

League Club	Source	Date Signed	Seasons Played	Apps	Subs	Gls
Torquay U	Tintagel	01/39	46-47	38	-	7
Northampton T	Tr	08/48				
Birmingham C	Tr	12/48				

KERR Albert Wigham
Born: Lanchester, County Durham, England, 11 August, 1917 — W
Died: Consett, County Durham, England, 4 February, 1979

League Club	Source	Date Signed	Seasons Played	Apps	Subs	Gls
Aston Villa	Medomsley Jnrs	07/36	36-46	29	-	4

KERR Andrew (Andy)
Born: Cumnock, Ayrshire, Scotland, 29 June, 1931 — CF
Died: Aberdeen, Scotland, 24 December, 1997
Scotland: 2/B/SLge-2

League Club	Source	Date Signed	Seasons Played	Apps	Subs	Gls
Manchester C	Partick Thistle	06/59	59	10	-	0
Sunderland	Kilmarnock	04/63	62-63	18	-	5

KERR Andrew Alphonso (Andy)
Born: West Bromwich, West Midlands, England, 7 April, 1966 — D

League Club	Source	Date Signed	Seasons Played	Apps	Subs	Gls
Shrewsbury T	App	04/84	84-85	9	1	0
Cardiff C	Tr	08/86	86	31	0	1
Wycombe W	Telford U	09/88	93	12	2	3

KERR Archibald (Archie)
Born: Motherwell, Lanarkshire, Scotland, 30 August, 1935 — RW
Died: Denny, Falkirk, Scotland, 3 December, 2000

League Club	Source	Date Signed	Seasons Played	Apps	Subs	Gls
Shrewsbury T	Motherwell	01/57	56	13	-	0

KERR Brian
Born: Motherwell, Lanarkshire, Scotland, 12 October, 1981 — M
Scotland: 3/B-2/U21-14/Youth/Schools

League Club	Source	Date Signed	Seasons Played	Apps	Subs	Gls
Newcastle U	YT	12/98	00-02	4	5	0
Coventry C	L	10/02	02	2	1	0
Coventry C	L	03/04	03	5	4	0

KERR Charles Currie
Born: Glasgow, Scotland, 10 December, 1933 — RW
Died: Manchester, England, 19 July, 2011

League Club	Source	Date Signed	Seasons Played	Apps	Subs	Gls
Carlisle U	Greenock Morton	08/56	56-57	9	-	3
Barrow	Tonbridge	07/59	59	20	-	3

KERR David
Born: Govan, Glasgow, Scotland, 4 December, 1936 — IF

League Club	Source	Date Signed	Seasons Played	Apps	Subs	Gls
Liverpool	Bridgeton Waverley	04/56				
Southport	Tr	07/58	58	32	-	4

KERR David William
Born: Dumfries, Scotland, 6 September, 1974 — M/D

League Club	Source	Date Signed	Seasons Played	Apps	Subs	Gls
Manchester C	YT	09/91	92-95	4	2	0
Mansfield T	L	09/95	95	4	1	0
Mansfield T	Tr	07/96	96-99	56	24	4

KERR Dylan
Born: Valetta, Malta, 14 January, 1967 — FB

League Club	Source	Date Signed	Seasons Played	Apps	Subs	Gls
Sheffield Wed	Jnr	09/84				
Leeds U	Arcadia Shep's (RSA)	02/89	88-92	6	7	0
Doncaster Rov	L	08/91	91	7	0	1
Blackpool	L	12/91	91	12	0	1
Reading	Tr	07/93	93-95	84	5	5
Carlisle U	Tr	09/96	96	0	1	0
Kidderminster Hrs	Kilmarnock	09/00	00	0	1	0
Exeter C	Hamilton Academical	08/01	01	5	0	1

KERR George Adams McDonald
Born: Alexandria, Dunbartonshire, Scotland, 9 January, 1943 — IF

League Club	Source	Date Signed	Seasons Played	Apps	Subs	Gls
Barnsley	Renton Select	05/60	61-65	166	0	40
Bury	Tr	03/66	65-66	15	0	2
Oxford U	Tr	09/66	66-67	40	0	5
Scunthorpe U	Tr	02/68	67-72	151	6	31

KERR James (Jimmy)
Born: Lemington, Tyne and Wear, England, 3 March, 1932 — LW
Died: Newcastle-upon-Tyne, England, May, 1994

League Club	Source	Date Signed	Seasons Played	Apps	Subs	Gls
Lincoln C	Blyth Spartans	11/52	52-53	15	-	1
Oldham Ath	Tr	06/54	54-55	34	-	4

KERR James Peter (Jimmy)
Born: Glasgow, Scotland, 2 September, 1949 — M
Scotland: Schools

League Club	Source	Date Signed	Seasons Played	Apps	Subs	Gls
Bury	Jnr	09/66	65-69	150	2	38
Blackburn Rov	Tr	05/70	70	11	0	0

KERR James Stewart Robert (Stewart)
Born: Bellshill, Lanarkshire, Scotland, 13 November, 1974 — G
Scotland: U21-10

League Club	Source	Date Signed	Seasons Played	Apps	Subs	Gls
Brighton & HA (L)	Glasgow Celtic	11/94	94	2	0	0
Wigan Ath	Glasgow Celtic	08/01	01	8	0	0

KERR John
Born: Birkenhead, Wirral, England, 23 November, 1959 — F
Died: Spain, 4 June, 2006

League Club	Source	Date Signed	Seasons Played	Apps	Subs	Gls
Tranmere Rov	App	11/77	78-82	145	9	38
Bristol C	Tr	08/83	83	13	1	4
Stockport Co	Tr	01/84	83-84	47	0	16
Bury	Tr	03/85	84-85	21	10	4

KERR John Joseph
Born: Toronto, Canada, 6 March, 1965 — F
USA: 16

League Club	Source	Date Signed	Seasons Played	Apps	Subs	Gls
Portsmouth	Harrow Bor	08/87	87	2	2	0
Peterborough U	L	12/87	87	10	0	1
Millwall	Chertsey T	02/93	92-94	21	22	8
Walsall	Tr	11/95	95	0	1	0

KERR Nathaniel James (Nathan)
Born: Manchester, England, 31 October, 1987 — CD

League Club	Source	Date Signed	Seasons Played	Apps	Subs	Gls
Crewe Alex	Sch	07/06				
Rotherham U	Tr	01/07	06	1	2	0

KERR Paul Andrew
Born: Portsmouth, England, 9 June, 1964 — M

League Club	Source	Date Signed	Seasons Played	Apps	Subs	Gls
Aston Villa	App	05/82	83-86	16	8	3
Middlesbrough	Tr	01/87	86-90	114	11	13
Millwall	Tr	03/91	90-91	42	2	14
Port Vale	Tr	07/92	92-93	58	5	15
Leicester C	L	03/94	93	4	3	2
Wycombe W	Tr	10/94	94	0	1	1

KERR Peter
Born: Paisley, Renfrewshire, Scotland, 25 September, 1943 — IF

League Club	Source	Date Signed	Seasons Played	Apps	Subs	Gls
Reading	Third Lanark	05/63	63-64	41	-	7

KERR Peter
Born: Glasgow, Scotland, 3 January, 1928 — WH
Died: Glasgow, Scotland, 3 May, 1996

League Club	Source	Date Signed	Seasons Played	Apps	Subs	Gls
Hartlepool U	Maryhill Harp	09/49	49	2	-	0

KERR Robert (Bobby)
Born: Alexandria, Dunbartonshire, Scotland, 16 November, 1947 — M

League Club	Source	Date Signed	Seasons Played	Apps	Subs	Gls
Sunderland	Balloch Jnrs	11/64	66-78	355	13	57
Blackpool	Tr	03/79	78-79	18	4	2
Hartlepool U	Tr	07/80	80-81	48	1	2

KERR Robert James
Born: Coatbridge, Lanarkshire, Scotland, 29 November, 1929 — IF
Died: Edinburgh, Scotland, 13 May, 2012

League Club	Source	Date Signed	Seasons Played	Apps	Subs	Gls
Darlington	Third Lanark	10/52	52	10	-	2

KERR Robert Sneddon
Born: West Lothian, Scotland, 10 July, 1942 — CF
Died: Bo'ness, Falkirk, Scotland, 3 March, 1998

League Club	Source	Date Signed	Seasons Played	Apps	Subs	Gls
Millwall	Arbroath	08/62	62	1	-	0

KERR Scott Anthony
Born: Leeds, England, 11 December, 1981 — M
England: Semi Pro-9

League Club	Source	Date Signed	Seasons Played	Apps	Subs	Gls
Bradford C	YT	07/00	00	0	1	0
Hull C	Tr	06/01				
Lincoln C	Scarborough	07/05	05-10	209	12	8
York C	Tr	01/11	12	26	2	0

KERRAY James Ridley (Jimmy)
Born: Stirling, Scotland, 2 December, 1935 — IF

League Club	Source	Date Signed	Seasons Played	Apps	Subs	Gls
Huddersfield T	Dunfermline Ath	08/60	60-61	54	-	12
Newcastle U	Tr	02/62	61-62	38	-	10

KERRIGAN Daniel Anthony (Danny)
Born: Basildon, England, 4 July, 1982 — M

League Club	Source	Date Signed	Seasons Played	Apps	Subs	Gls
Southend U	YT	07/00	99-01	6	9	0

KERRIGAN Donald McDonald (Don)
Born: West Kilbride, Ayrshire, Scotland, 7 May, 1941 — IF
Died: Glasgow, Scotland, 29 December, 1990

League Club	Source	Date Signed	Seasons Played	Apps	Subs	Gls
Fulham	Dunfermline Ath	02/68	67-68	4	2	1
Lincoln C	L	03/69	68	12	0	0

KERRIGAN Steven John (Steve)
Born: Baillieston, Glasgow, Scotland, 9 October, 1972 — F

League Club	Source	Date Signed	Seasons Played	Apps	Subs	Gls
Shrewsbury T	Ayr U	01/98	97-99	63	13	15
Halifax T	Tr	03/00	99-01	70	8	22

KERRINS Patrick Michael (Pat)
Born: Fulham, W London, England, 13 September, 1936 — LW

League Club	Source	Date Signed	Seasons Played	Apps	Subs	Gls
Queens Park Rgrs	Jnr	12/53	53-59	146	-	30
Crystal Palace	Tr	06/60	60	5	-	0
Southend U	Tr	07/61	61	11	-	0

KERRINS Wayne Michael
Born: Brentwood, Essex, England, 5 August, 1965 — M/FB

League Club	Source	Date Signed	Seasons Played	Apps	Subs	Gls
Fulham	App	08/83	84-88	51	15	1
Port Vale	L	03/85	84	6	2	0
Leyton Orient	L	03/89	88	3	0	0

KERROUCHE Mehdi
Born: Douai, France, 11 October, 1985 — F

League Club	Source	Date Signed	Seasons Played	Apps	Subs	Gls
Swindon T	Al-Oruba (UAE)	08/11	11	9	4	6
Oxford U	L	02/12	11	1	3	0

KERRY Brian Philip
Born: Maltby, South Yorkshire, England, 18 December, 1948 — F

League Club	Source	Date Signed	Seasons Played	Apps	Subs	Gls
Grimsby T	App	01/66	65	0	1	0
Huddersfield T	Tr	04/67				

KERRY Christopher Brian (Chris)
Born: Chesterfield, Derbyshire, England, 15 April, 1976 — F

League Club	Source	Date Signed	Seasons Played	Apps	Subs	Gls
Mansfield T	YT	07/94	93	1	1	0

KERRY David Thomas (Dave)
Born: Derby, England, 6 February, 1937 — CF
England: Youth

League Club	Source	Date Signed	Seasons Played	Apps	Subs	Gls
Preston NE	Derby Co (Am)	05/55				
Chesterfield	Tr	07/61	61-62	55	-	23
Rochdale	Tr	07/63	63	12	-	4

KERRY Lloyd
Born: Chesterfield, Derbyshire, England, 22 January, 1988 — M

League Club	Source	Date Signed	Seasons Played	Apps	Subs	Gls
Sheffield U	Sch	07/06				
Torquay U	L	02/07	06	6	1	1
Chesterfield	Tr	02/08	07-08	36	10	5

KERSHAW Alan Derek
Born: Southport, Merseyside, England, 23 April, 1954 — RB

League Club	Source	Date Signed	Seasons Played	Apps	Subs	Gls
Preston NE	App	04/72				
Southport	Tr	07/74	74	19	5	0

KERSLAKE David
Born: Stepney, E London, England, 19 June, 1966 — RB
England: U21-1/Youth/Schools

League Club	Source	Date Signed	Seasons Played	Apps	Subs	Gls
Queens Park Rgrs	App	06/83	84-89	38	20	6
Swindon T	Tr	11/89	89-92	133	2	1
Leeds U	Tr	03/93	92	8	0	0
Tottenham H	Tr	09/93	93-95	34	3	0
Swindon T	L	11/96	96	8	0	0
Ipswich T	Tr	08/97	97	2	5	0
Wycombe W	L	12/97	97	9	1	0
Swindon T	Tr	03/98	97-98	22	2	0

KERSLAKE Michael Leslie (Mickey)
Born: Bethnal Green, E London, England, 27 February, 1958 — FB
England: Youth

League Club	Source	Date Signed	Seasons Played	Apps	Subs	Gls
Fulham	App	10/75	75-77	1	2	0
Brighton & HA	Tr	06/78				

KETSBAIA Temuri
Born: Abkhazia, Georgia, 18 March, 1968 — F/M
Georgia: 52

League Club	Source	Date Signed	Seasons Played	Apps	Subs	Gls
Newcastle U	AEK Athens (GRE)	07/97	97-99	41	37	8
Wolverhampton W	Tr	08/00	00-01	14	10	3

KETTERIDGE Stephen Jack (Steve)
Born: Stevenage, Hertfordshire, England, 7 November, 1959 — M

League Club	Source	Date Signed	Seasons Played	Apps	Subs	Gls
Wimbledon	Derby Co (App)	04/78	78-84	229	8	33
Crystal Palace	Tr	08/85	85-86	58	1	6
Leyton Orient	Tr	07/87	87-88	26	5	2
Cardiff C	L	10/88	88	6	0	2

KETTINGS Christopher David (Chris)
Born: Bolton, Greater Manchester, England, 25 October, 1992 — G
Scotland: U21-3/Youth

League Club	Source	Date Signed	Seasons Played	Apps	Subs	Gls
Blackpool	Sch	06/11				
Morecambe	L	01/12	11	2	0	0
Crystal Palace	Tr	06/14				

KETTLE Albert Henry
Born: Colchester, Essex, England, 3 June, 1922 — RB
Died: Fordham, Essex, England, 1 March, 1999

League Club	Source	Date Signed	Seasons Played	Apps	Subs	Gls
Colchester U	Arclight Sports	08/46	50-54	23	-	0

KETTLE Brian
Born: Prescot, Merseyside, England, 22 April, 1956 — LB
England: Youth

League Club	Source	Date Signed	Seasons Played	Apps	Subs	Gls
Liverpool	App	05/73	75-76	3	0	0
Wigan Ath	Houston Hurr'ne (USA)	09/80	80	14	0	1

KETTLEBOROUGH Keith Frank
Born: Rotherham, South Yorkshire, England, 29 June, 1935 — WH/IF
Died: Rotherham, South Yorkshire, England, 2 November, 2009

League Club	Source	Date Signed	Seasons Played	Apps	Subs	Gls
Rotherham U	Rotherham YMCA	12/55	55-60	118	-	20
Sheffield U	Tr	12/60	60-65	154	0	17
Newcastle U	Tr	12/65	65-66	30	0	0
Doncaster Rov	Tr	12/66	66-67	35	1	0
Chesterfield	Tr	11/67	67-68	66	0	3

KETTLEY Spencer Charles
Born: Ystrad Rhondda, Rhondda Cynon Taff, Wales, 22 May, 1921 — IF
Died: Desborough, Northamptonshire, England, 21 October, 2010

League Club	Source	Date Signed	Seasons Played	Apps	Subs	Gls
Luton T	Newbury T	08/44	46	1	-	0

KEVAN David John
Born: Wigtown, Dumfries & Galloway, Scotland, 31 August, 1968 — M

League Club	Source	Date Signed	Seasons Played	Apps	Subs	Gls
Notts Co	App	08/86	85-89	82	7	3
Cardiff C	L	09/89	89	6	1	0
Stoke C	Tr	01/90	89-93	78	3	2
Maidstone U	L	02/91	90	3	0	0
Bournemouth	L	03/94	93	0	1	0

KEVAN Derek Tennyson
Born: Ripon, North Yorkshire, England, 6 March, 1935 — IF
Died: Birmingham, England, 4 January, 2013
England: 14/FLge-1/U23-4

League Club	Source	Date Signed	Seasons Played	Apps	Subs	Gls
Bradford Park Ave	Ripon YMCA	10/52	52	15	-	8
West Bromwich A	Tr	07/53	55-62	262	-	157
Chelsea	Tr	03/63	62	7	-	1
Manchester C	Tr	08/63	63-64	67	-	48
Crystal Palace	Tr	07/65	65	21	0	5
Peterborough U	Tr	03/66	65-66	16	1	2
Luton T	Tr	12/66	66	11	0	4
Stockport Co	Tr	03/67	66-67	38	2	10

KEWELL Harold (Harry)
Born: Sydney, Australia, 22 September, 1978 — LW
Australia: 56/Youth

League Club	Source	Date Signed	Seasons Played	Apps	Subs	Gls
Leeds U	NSW Soccer Acad (AUS)	12/95	95-02	169	12	45
Liverpool	Tr	07/03	03-07	81	12	12

KEWLEY John Kevin (Kevin)
Born: Liverpool, England, 2 March, 1955 — M

League Club	Source	Date Signed	Seasons Played	Apps	Subs	Gls
Liverpool	App	03/72	77	0	1	0

KEWLEY-GRAHAM Jesse James
Born: Hounslow, SW London, England, 15 June, 1993 — M

League Club	Source	Date Signed	Seasons Played	Apps	Subs	Gls
Wycombe W	Sch	07/11	11-13	3	6	0

KEY Daniel Charles (Danny)
Born: Darlington, County Durham, England, 2 November, 1977 — M

League Club	Source	Date Signed	Seasons Played	Apps	Subs	Gls
Darlington	YT	07/96	96	0	3	0

League Club	Source	Date Signed	Seasons Played	Apps	Subs	Gls
KEY John Peter (Johnny)						
Born: Chelsea, W London, England, 5 November, 1937						RW
Fulham	Jnr	05/56	58-65	163	0	29
Coventry C	Tr	05/66	66-67	27	1	7
Leyton Orient	Tr	03/68	67-68	9	1	0
KEY Lance William						
Born: Kettering, Northamptonshire, England, 13 May, 1968						G
Sheffield Wed	Histon	04/90				
Oldham Ath	L	10/93	93	2	0	0
Oxford U	L	01/95	94	6	0	0
Lincoln C	L	08/95	95	5	0	0
Hartlepool U	L	12/95	95	1	0	0
Rochdale	L	03/96	95	14	0	0
Sheffield U	Dundee U	03/97				
Rochdale	Tr	08/97	97	19	0	0
KEY Richard Martin						
Born: Coventry, England, 13 April, 1956						G
Exeter C	Coventry C (Jnr)	07/75	75-77	109	0	0
Cambridge U	Tr	08/78	78-82	52	0	0
Northampton T	L	11/82	82	2	0	0
Leyton Orient	Tr	08/83	83	42	0	0
Brentford	Tr	08/84	84	1	0	0
Sunderland	Tr	10/84				
Cambridge U	L	03/85	84	13	0	0
Brentford	Swindon T (NC)	08/85	85	3	0	0
KEYES Anthony Joseph (Tony)						
Born: Salford, England, 29 October, 1953						M
Stockport Co	Witton A	10/71	71-73	7	1	0
KEYS Paul Andrew						
Born: Ipswich, England, 4 September, 1962						F
Luton T	Westerfield	07/81				
Halifax T	L	03/82	81	1	1	0
KEYWORTH Kenneth (Ken)						
Born: Rotherham, South Yorkshire, England, 24 February, 1934						CF/WH
Died: Rotherham, South Yorkshire, England, 7 January, 2000						
Rotherham U	Wolverhampton W (Am)	01/52	55-57	85	-	6
Leicester C	Tr	05/58	58-64	177	-	63
Coventry C	Tr	12/64	64	7	-	3
Swindon T	Tr	08/65	65	6	0	0
KEZMAN Mateja						
Born: Belgrade, Yugoslavia, 12 April, 1979						F
Serbia: 49						
Chelsea	PSV Eindhoven (NED)	07/04	04	6	19	4
KHAN Otis Jan Mohammed						
Born: Ashton-under-Lyne, Greater Manchester, England, 5 September, 1995						M
Sheffield U	Sch	07/14	13	0	2	0
KHARINE Dimitri Viktorovich						
Born: Moscow, Russia, 16 August, 1968						G
Commonwealth of Independent States: 9//Russia: 23//Soviet Union: 6						
Chelsea	CSKA Moscow (RUS)	12/92	92-98	118	0	0
KHELA Inderpaul Singh						
Born: Birmingham, England, 6 October, 1983						D
Kidderminster Hrs	Bedworth U	08/02	02	0	1	0
KHIZANISHVILI Zurab						
Born: Tbilisi, Georgia, 6 October, 1981						CD
Georgia: 91						
Blackburn Rov	Glasgow Rangers	08/05	05-09	54	8	1
Newcastle U	L	09/09	09	6	1	0
Reading	L	01/10	09	12	3	0
Reading	L	08/10	10	21	1	0
KHUMALO Bongani Sandile						
Born: Manzini, Swaziland, 6 January, 1987						CD
South Africa: 42						
Tottenham H	Supersport U (RSA)	01/11				
Preston NE	L	03/11	10	6	0	0
Reading	L	07/11	11	4	0	0
Doncaster Rov	L	07/13	13	30	0	0
Colchester U	L	03/15	14	10	0	0
KI Sung-Yeung						
Born: Gwangju, South Korea, 24 January, 1989						M
South Korea: 74/U23-21/Youth						
Swansea C	Glasgow Celtic	08/12	12-14	50	13	8
Sunderland	L	08/13	13	25	2	3
KICHENBRAND Donald Basil (Don)						
Born: Germiston, South Africa, 13 August, 1933						CF
Sunderland	Glasgow Rangers	03/58	57-59	53	-	28
KIDD Brian						
Born: Manchester, England, 29 May, 1949						F
England: 2/FLge-1/U23-10/Youth						
Manchester U	App	06/66	67-73	195	8	52
Arsenal	Tr	08/74	74-75	77	0	30
Manchester C	Tr	07/76	76-78	97	1	44
Everton	Tr	03/79	78-79	40	0	12
Bolton W	Tr	05/80	80-81	40	3	14
KIDD John Oliver						
Born: Birkenhead, Wirral, England, 15 January, 1936						IF
Tranmere Rov	Everton (Am)	08/55	55-58	34	-	4
KIDD Ryan Andrew						
Born: Heywood, Greater Manchester, England, 6 October, 1971						CD
Port Vale	YT	07/90	91	1	0	0
Preston NE	Tr	07/92	92-01	241	18	9
KIDD William Edward (Billy)						
Born: Pegswood, Northumberland, England, 31 January, 1907						LB
Died: Chesterfield, Derbyshire, England, 18 September, 1978						
Chesterfield	Pegswood U	03/32	31-47	316	-	2
KIELY Dean Laurence						
Born: Salford, England, 10 October, 1970						G
England: Youth/Schools//Republic of Ireland: 11/B-1						
Coventry C	App	10/87				
York C	Tr	03/90	90-95	210	0	0
Bury	Tr	08/96	96-98	137	0	0
Charlton Ath	Tr	05/99	99-05	222	0	0
Portsmouth	Tr	01/06	05	15	0	0
Luton T	L	11/06	06	11	0	0
West Bromwich A	Tr	01/07	06-09	67	2	0
KIERAN Leonard Vincent (Len)						
Born: Birkenhead, Wirral, England, 25 July, 1926						LH
Died: Birkenhead, Wirral, England, 24 July, 1981						
Tranmere Rov	Jnr	09/43	47-56	342	-	6
KIERNAN Brendan Jason						
Born: Lambeth, S London, England, 10 November, 1992						M
AFC Wimbledon	Jnr	12/10	11-12	3	12	0
KIERNAN Daniel James						
Born: Northampton, England, 16 December, 1973						M
Northampton T	YT	09/91	91	6	3	0
KIERNAN Frederick William (Fred)						
Born: Dublin, Republic of Ireland, 7 July, 1919						G
Died: Southampton, England, December, 1981						
Republic of Ireland: 5/LoI-2						
Southampton	Shamrock Rov (ROI)	10/51	51-55	132	-	0
KIERNAN Joseph (Joe)						
Born: Coatbridge, Lanarkshire, Scotland, 22 October, 1942						LH
Died: Northampton, England, 1 August, 2006						
Sunderland	Jnr	11/59	62	1	-	0
Northampton T	Tr	07/63	63-71	305	3	13
KIERNAN Robert Samuel (Rob)						
Born: Rickmansworth, Hertfordshire, England, 13 January, 1991						CD
Republic of Ireland: U21-14/Youth						
Watford	Sch	09/08				
Yeovil T	L	07/10	10	1	2	0
Bradford C	L	11/10	10	6	2	0
Wycombe W	L	02/11	10	2	0	0
Wigan Ath	Tr	07/11	13-14	23	6	1
Accrington Stan	L	03/12	11	3	0	0
Burton A	L	09/12	12	6	0	0
Brentford	L	11/12	12	5	3	0
Southend U	L	10/13	13	11	1	0
Birmingham C	L	02/15	14	11	1	1
KIERNAN Thomas (Tommy)						
Born: Coatbridge, Lanarkshire, Scotland, 20 October, 1918						IF
Died: Coatbridge, Lanarkshire, Scotland, 26 June, 1991						
Scotland: SLge-1						
Stoke C	Glasgow Celtic	09/47	47-48	28	-	6
Luton T	Tr	11/48	48-50	55	-	10
KIERNAN William Edward (Billy)						
Born: Penge, S London, England, 22 May, 1925						LW
Died: Tunbridge Wells, Kent, England, 2 April, 2006						
England: B-1						
Charlton Ath	Royal Ulster Rifles	07/49	49-60	378	-	89
KIGHTLY Michael John						
Born: Basildon, England, 24 January, 1986						RW
England: U21-7						
Southend U	Sch	12/03	02-04	2	11	0

League Club	Source	Date Signed	Seasons Played	Apps	Subs	Gls
Wolverhampton W	Grays Ath	11/06	06-11	99	15	23
Watford	L	10/11	11	11	1	3
Stoke C	Tr	08/12	12	14	8	3
Burnley	Tr	09/13	13-14	42	11	6

[KIKE] GARCIA Enrique
Born: Motilla del Palancar, Spain, 25 November, 1989 — F
Spain: Youth

League Club	Source	Date Signed	Seasons Played	Apps	Subs	Gls
Middlesbrough	Real Murcia (SPN)	07/14	14	25	17	9

[KIKO] CHARANA BAPTISTA GOMES Manuel Henrique
Born: Porto, Portugal, 24 October, 1976 — M

League Club	Source	Date Signed	Seasons Played	Apps	Subs	Gls
Stockport Co	Belenenses (POR)	12/96	96	0	3	0

KILBANE Farrell Noel
Born: Preston, Lancashire, England, 21 October, 1974 — CD

League Club	Source	Date Signed	Seasons Played	Apps	Subs	Gls
Preston NE	Cambridge U (YT)	07/93	93	0	1	0

KILBANE Kevin Daniel
Born: Preston, Lancashire, England, 1 February, 1977 — LW/FB
Republic of Ireland: 110/U21-11

League Club	Source	Date Signed	Seasons Played	Apps	Subs	Gls
Preston NE	YT	07/95	95-96	39	8	3
West Bromwich A	Tr	06/97	97-99	105	1	15
Sunderland	Tr	12/99	99-03	102	11	8
Everton	Tr	09/03	03-06	86	18	4
Wigan Ath	Tr	08/06	06-08	62	14	2
Hull C	Tr	01/09	08-10	41	10	2
Huddersfield T	L	01/11	10	23	1	2
Derby Co	L	08/11	11	7	2	1
Coventry C	Tr	07/12	12	8	1	0

KILBEY Thomas Charles (Tom)
Born: Walthamstow, NE London, England, 19 October, 1990 — M

League Club	Source	Date Signed	Seasons Played	Apps	Subs	Gls
Portsmouth	Sch	02/08	10	0	2	0
Lincoln C	L	03/11	10	6	1	0

KILCLINE Brian
Born: Nottingham, England, 7 May, 1962 — CD
England: U21-2

League Club	Source	Date Signed	Seasons Played	Apps	Subs	Gls
Notts Co	App	04/80	79-83	156	2	9
Coventry C	Tr	06/84	84-90	173	0	28
Oldham Ath	Tr	08/91	91	8	0	0
Newcastle U	Tr	02/92	91-93	20	12	0
Swindon T	Tr	01/94	93-94	16	1	0
Mansfield T	Tr	12/95	95-96	48	2	3

KILEY Thomas James (Tom)
Born: Swansea, Wales, 15 June, 1924 — CH
Died: Swansea, Wales, 9 September, 2000

League Club	Source	Date Signed	Seasons Played	Apps	Subs	Gls
Swansea C	RAF	06/47	49-56	129	-	2

KILFORD Ian Anthony
Born: Bristol, England, 6 October, 1973 — M

League Club	Source	Date Signed	Seasons Played	Apps	Subs	Gls
Nottingham F	YT	04/91	93	0	1	0
Wigan Ath	L	12/93	93	7	1	3
Wigan Ath	Tr	07/94	94-01	170	43	29
Bury	Tr	08/02				
Scunthorpe U	Tr	11/02	02-03	38	8	3

KILFORD John Douglas
Born: Derby, England, 8 November, 1938 — FB
Died: Lewisham, SE London, England, 8 October, 2012

League Club	Source	Date Signed	Seasons Played	Apps	Subs	Gls
Notts Co	Derby Corinthians	07/57	58	26	-	0
Leeds U	Tr	02/59	58-61	21	-	0

KILGALLON Mark Christopher
Born: Glasgow, Scotland, 20 December, 1962 — CD

League Club	Source	Date Signed	Seasons Played	Apps	Subs	Gls
Hull C	Ipswich T (App)	08/80	80	0	1	0

KILGALLON Matthew Shaun (Matt)
Born: York, England, 8 January, 1984 — CD
England: U21-5/Youth

League Club	Source	Date Signed	Seasons Played	Apps	Subs	Gls
Leeds U	YT	01/01	02-06	73	7	3
West Ham U	L	08/03	03	1	2	0
Sheffield U	Tr	01/07	06-09	105	2	4
Sunderland	Tr	01/10	09-12	21	2	0
Middlesbrough	L	08/10	10	2	0	0
Doncaster Rov	L	01/11	10	7	5	0
Blackburn Rov	Tr	07/13	13-14	45	2	2

KILGANNON John
Born: Stenhousemuir, Falkirk, Scotland, 26 June, 1936 — IF
Died: Falkirk, Scotland, 27 February, 1967

League Club	Source	Date Signed	Seasons Played	Apps	Subs	Gls
Luton T	Stenhousemuir	04/59	58-59	13	-	1

KILGANNON Sean
Born: Stirling, Scotland, 8 March, 1981 — M

League Club	Source	Date Signed	Seasons Played	Apps	Subs	Gls
Middlesbrough	YT	07/99	99	0	1	0

KILHEENEY Ciaran Joseph
Born: Stockport, Greater Manchester, England, 9 January, 1984 — F

League Club	Source	Date Signed	Seasons Played	Apps	Subs	Gls
Manchester C	YT	07/01				
Exeter C	Mossley	03/03	02	0	4	0

KILKELLY Thomas Francis (Tom)
Born: Galway, Republic of Ireland, 22 August, 1955 — CD
Republic of Ireland: Youth

League Club	Source	Date Signed	Seasons Played	Apps	Subs	Gls
Leicester C	App	07/73				
Northampton T	L	09/74	74	2	2	0

KILKENNY James (Jim)
Born: Stanley, County Durham, England, 21 November, 1934 — WH
Died: Doncaster, South Yorkshire, England, April, 2003

League Club	Source	Date Signed	Seasons Played	Apps	Subs	Gls
Doncaster Rov	Annfield Plain	05/52	55-60	132	-	1

KILKENNY Neil Martin
Born: Enfield, N London, England, 19 December, 1985 — M
Australia: 14/U23-10//England: Youth

League Club	Source	Date Signed	Seasons Played	Apps	Subs	Gls
Birmingham C	Arsenal (Sch)	01/04	05-06	6	20	0
Oldham Ath	L	11/04	04	24	3	4
Oldham Ath	L	08/07	07	19	1	1
Leeds U	Tr	01/08	07-10	96	22	8
Bristol C	Tr	07/11	11-13	50	18	1
Preston NE	Tr	11/13	13-14	48	14	2

KILLARNEY Arthur
Born: Huddersfield, West Yorkshire, England, 26 February, 1921 — LH
Died: Huddersfield, West Yorkshire, England, June, 2011

League Club	Source	Date Signed	Seasons Played	Apps	Subs	Gls
Halifax T		05/46	46	2	-	0

KILLEEN Lewis Keith
Born: Peterborough, England, 23 September, 1982 — F

League Club	Source	Date Signed	Seasons Played	Apps	Subs	Gls
Sheffield U	YT	07/01	01	0	1	0

KILLEN Christopher John (Chris)
Born: Wellington, New Zealand, 8 October, 1981 — F
New Zealand: 48/U23/Youth

League Club	Source	Date Signed	Seasons Played	Apps	Subs	Gls
Manchester C	Miramar Rgrs (NZL)	03/99	01	0	3	0
Wrexham	L	09/00	00	11	1	3
Port Vale	L	09/01	01	8	1	6
Oldham Ath	Tr	07/02	02-05	53	25	17
Norwich C (L)	Glasgow Celtic	02/09	08	0	4	0
Middlesbrough	Glasgow Celtic	01/10	09	15	2	3

KILLIN Harold Roy (Roy)
Born: Toronto, Canada, 18 July, 1929 — LB

League Club	Source	Date Signed	Seasons Played	Apps	Subs	Gls
Manchester U		04/49				
Lincoln C	Tr	08/52	53	7	-	0

KILLOCK Shane Adam
Born: Huddersfield, West Yorkshire, England, 12 March, 1989 — CD

League Club	Source	Date Signed	Seasons Played	Apps	Subs	Gls
Huddersfield T	Sch	01/08	07	1	0	0

KILLOUGHERY Graham Anthony
Born: Westminster, Central London, England, 22 July, 1984 — M

League Club	Source	Date Signed	Seasons Played	Apps	Subs	Gls
Torquay U	Sch	07/03	02-03	1	5	0

KILMORE Kevin
Born: Scunthorpe, North Lincolnshire, England, 11 November, 1959 — M
England: Youth

League Club	Source	Date Signed	Seasons Played	Apps	Subs	Gls
Scunthorpe U	Jnr	01/77	76-79	93	9	28
Grimsby T	Tr	09/79	79-82	70	32	27
Rotherham U	Tr	08/83	83-84	82	2	20
Lincoln C	KFC Geel (BEL)	01/86	85-86	40	6	6

KILNER Andrew William (Andy)
Born: Bolton, Greater Manchester, England, 11 October, 1966 — LW
England: Youth

League Club	Source	Date Signed	Seasons Played	Apps	Subs	Gls
Burnley	App	07/84	85	2	3	0
Stockport Co	Jonsered (SWE)	12/90	90-91	34	8	14
Rochdale	L	01/92	91	3	0	0
Bury	Tr	08/92	92	4	1	0

KILNER John Ian
Born: Bolton, Greater Manchester, England, 3 October, 1959 — G

League Club	Source	Date Signed	Seasons Played	Apps	Subs	Gls
Preston NE	App	10/77				
Halifax T	L	02/79	78	21	0	0
Halifax T	Tr	09/79	79-81	93	0	0
Wigan Ath	Bangor C	07/83	83	4	0	0

KILSHAW Edmund Ainsworth (Eddie)
Born: Prescot, Merseyside, England, 25 December, 1919 — RW
Died: Huyton, Merseyside, England, 24 July, 2006

League Club	Source	Date Signed	Seasons Played	Apps	Subs	Gls
Bury	Prescot Cables	10/37	37-48	147	-	17
Sheffield Wed	Tr	12/48	48	17	-	1

KILSHAW Frederick (Fred)
Born: Wrexham, Wales, 24 August, 1916 — IF

League Club	Source	Date Signed	Seasons Played	Apps	Subs	Gls
Leicester C	RAOC	01/45				
New Brighton	Tr	07/46	46	8	-	1

KILTY Mark Thomas
Born: Sunderland, England, 24 June, 1981 — CD

League Club	Source	Date Signed	Seasons Played	Apps	Subs	Gls
Darlington	YT	07/99	98-01	20	3	1

KIM Bo-Kyung
Born: Suncheon, South Korea, 6 October, 1989 — W
South Korea: 32/U23-20

League Club	Source	Date Signed	Seasons Played	Apps	Subs	Gls
Cardiff C	Cerezo Osaka (JPN)	07/12	12-14	43	15	3
Wigan Ath	Tr	02/15	14	17	1	2

KIM Do-Heon
Born: Dongducheon, South Korea, 14 July, 1982 — M
South Korea: 62/U23

League Club	Source	Date Signed	Seasons Played	Apps	Subs	Gls
West Bromwich A	Seongnam (KOR)	01/08	07-08	10	10	1

KIMBERLEY Samuel Kenneth (Ken)
Born: Walsall, West Midlands, England, 7 August, 1920 — G
Died: Walsall, West Midlands, England, 21 December, 1987

League Club	Source	Date Signed	Seasons Played	Apps	Subs	Gls
Walsall	Cannock Colliery	05/46	46	1	-	0

KIMBLE Alan Frank
Born: Dagenham, E London, England, 6 August, 1966 — LB

League Club	Source	Date Signed	Seasons Played	Apps	Subs	Gls
Charlton Ath	Jnr	08/84	84	6	0	0
Exeter C	L	08/85	85	1	0	0
Cambridge U	Tr	08/86	86-92	295	4	24
Wimbledon	Tr	07/93	93-01	196	19	0
Peterborough U	L	03/02	01	3	0	0
Luton T	Tr	08/02	02	8	4	0

KIMBLE Garry Leslie
Born: Dagenham, E London, England, 6 August, 1966 — LW

League Club	Source	Date Signed	Seasons Played	Apps	Subs	Gls
Charlton Ath	Jnr	08/84	84	7	2	1
Exeter C	L	08/85	85	1	0	0
Cambridge U	Tr	08/86	86-87	39	2	2
Doncaster Rov	Tr	10/87	87-88	60	5	1
Fulham	Tr	08/89	89	1	2	0
Maidstone U	Tr	10/89				
Gillingham	St Albans C	02/90	89-90	35	13	1
Peterborough U	Tr	07/91	91	30	0	4

KINDER Vladimir
Born: Bratislava, Slovakia, 9 March, 1969 — LB
Czechoslovakia: 1//Slovakia: 39

League Club	Source	Date Signed	Seasons Played	Apps	Subs	Gls
Middlesbrough	Slov Bratislava (SVK)	01/97	96-98	29	8	5

KINDON Stephen Michael (Steve)
Born: Warrington, Cheshire, England, 17 December, 1950 — F
England: Youth

League Club	Source	Date Signed	Seasons Played	Apps	Subs	Gls
Burnley	App	12/67	68-71	102	7	28
Wolverhampton W	Tr	07/72	72-77	111	17	28
Burnley	Tr	11/77	77-79	73	3	18
Huddersfield T	Tr	12/79	79-81	69	4	35

KINET Christophe
Born: Huy, Belgium, 31 December, 1972 — LW

League Club	Source	Date Signed	Seasons Played	Apps	Subs	Gls
Millwall	RC Strasbourg (FRA)	02/00	99-02	39	28	7

KING Adam
Born: Hillingdon, W London, England, 4 October, 1969 — M
England: Youth

League Club	Source	Date Signed	Seasons Played	Apps	Subs	Gls
West Ham U	YT	06/88				
Plymouth Arg	Tr	03/90	89-90	9	7	0

KING Alan
Born: Gateshead, Tyne and Wear, England, 25 November, 1947 — W

League Club	Source	Date Signed	Seasons Played	Apps	Subs	Gls
Hartlepool U (Am)	Horden CW	08/67	67	0	1	0

KING Alan John
Born: Birkenhead, Wirral, England, 18 January, 1945 — CD

League Club	Source	Date Signed	Seasons Played	Apps	Subs	Gls
Tranmere Rov	Jnr	07/63	62-71	341	0	35

KING Andrew Edward (Andy)
Born: Luton, England, 14 August, 1956 — M
Died: Luton, England, 27 May, 2015
England: U21-2

League Club	Source	Date Signed	Seasons Played	Apps	Subs	Gls
Luton T	App	07/74	74-75	30	3	9
Everton	Tr	04/76	75-79	150	1	38
Queens Park Rgrs	Tr	09/80	80-81	28	2	9
West Bromwich A	Tr	09/81	81	21	4	4
Everton	Tr	07/82	82-83	43	1	11
Wolverhampton W	SC Cambuur (NED)	01/85	84-85	28	0	10
Luton T	Tr	12/85	85	3	0	0
Aldershot	Tr	08/86	86	36	0	11

KING Andrew John (Andy)
Born: Thatcham, Berkshire, England, 30 March, 1970 — F

League Club	Source	Date Signed	Seasons Played	Apps	Subs	Gls
Reading	YT	06/88	88	0	1	0

KING Andrew Philip (Andy)
Born: Barnstaple, Devon, England, 29 October, 1988 — M
Wales: 29/U21-10/Youth

League Club	Source	Date Signed	Seasons Played	Apps	Subs	Gls
Leicester C	Sch	05/07	07-14	230	40	51

KING Barry
Born: Chesterfield, Derbyshire, England, 30 March, 1935 — RW

League Club	Source	Date Signed	Seasons Played	Apps	Subs	Gls
Chelsea	Norton Woodseats	02/58				
Reading	Tr	03/58	57	3	-	0

KING Christopher (Chris)
Born: Birkenhead, Wirral, England, 14 November, 1980 — LB

League Club	Source	Date Signed	Seasons Played	Apps	Subs	Gls
Accrington Stan	The New Saints	08/08	08-09	28	0	0

KING Craig Stuart
Born: Chesterfield, Derbyshire, England, 6 October, 1990 — W
Scotland: Youth

League Club	Source	Date Signed	Seasons Played	Apps	Subs	Gls
Leicester C	Sch	09/08				
Hereford U	L	09/09	09	22	4	3
Northampton T	L	11/10	10	3	4	0

KING David John (Dave)
Born: Hull, England, 24 October, 1940 — IF
Died: Hull, England, 16 July, 2010

League Club	Source	Date Signed	Seasons Played	Apps	Subs	Gls
Hull C	Jnr	10/58	59-62	65	-	24

KING David Martin (Dave)
Born: Colchester, Essex, England, 18 September, 1962 — M

League Club	Source	Date Signed	Seasons Played	Apps	Subs	Gls
Derby Co	App	09/80				
York C	Gresley Rov	03/83	82	0	1	0

KING Dennis
Born: Bearpark, County Durham, England, 16 September, 1932 — W
Died: Durham, England, June, 1988

League Club	Source	Date Signed	Seasons Played	Apps	Subs	Gls
Bradford Park Ave	Kimblesworth Jnrs	09/50				
Oldham Ath	Spennymoor U	05/54	54-55	22	-	7

KING Derek Albert
Born: Hackney, E London, England, 15 August, 1929 — CH
Died: Huntingdon, Cambridgeshire, England, 16 June, 2003

League Club	Source	Date Signed	Seasons Played	Apps	Subs	Gls
Tottenham H	Jnr	08/50	51-54	19	-	0
Swansea C	Tr	08/56	56	5	-	0

KING Frederick Alfred Robert (Bobby)
Born: Northampton, England, 19 September, 1919 — RW
Died: Northampton, England, 20 May, 2003

League Club	Source	Date Signed	Seasons Played	Apps	Subs	Gls
Northampton T	Northampton Nomads	10/37	37-38	42	-	6
Wolverhampton W	Tr	11/39	46	6	-	3
Northampton T	Tr	12/47	47-49	56	-	17

KING Gary Ian
Born: Grimsby, North Lincolnshire, England, 27 January, 1990 — F

League Club	Source	Date Signed	Seasons Played	Apps	Subs	Gls
Lincoln C	Sch	07/08	07-08	5	6	1
Accrington Stan	Tr	08/09	09	3	5	1

KING George
Born: Warkworth, Northumberland, England, 5 January, 1923 — CF
Died: Ely, Cambridgeshire, England, 10 February, 2002

League Club	Source	Date Signed	Seasons Played	Apps	Subs	Gls
Newcastle U	RAF	08/46	46	2	-	0
Hull C	Tr	03/48	47-48	3	-	0
Port Vale	Tr	04/49	48-49	10	-	5
Barrow	Tr	02/50	49-51	86	-	37
Bradford C	Tr	01/52	51-52	23	-	9
Gillingham	Tr	10/52	52	19	-	5

KING Gerald Henry (Gerry)
Born: Radnor, Powys, Wales, 7 April, 1947 — LW
Wales: Schools

League Club	Source	Date Signed	Seasons Played	Apps	Subs	Gls
Cardiff C	Jnr	06/64	64	6	-	0
Torquay U	Tr	06/65	65	18	0	2
Luton T	Tr	06/66	66	21	1	4
Newport Co	Tr	07/67	67-68	49	3	9

KING Jack Andrew
Born: Oxford, England, 20 August, 1985 — CD/M

League Club	Source	Date Signed	Seasons Played	Apps	Subs	Gls
Preston NE	Woking	07/12	12-14	64	14	7

KING Jeffrey (Jeff)
Born: Fauldhouse, West Lothian, Scotland, 9 November, 1953 — M

League Club	Source	Date Signed	Seasons Played	Apps	Subs	Gls
Derby Co	Albion Rov	04/74	75-77	12	2	0
Notts Co	L	01/76	75	3	0	0
Portsmouth	L	03/76	75	4	0	0
Walsall	Tr	11/77	77-78	50	1	4
Sheffield Wed	Tr	08/79	79-81	54	3	5
Sheffield U	Tr	01/82	81-82	35	2	5
Chesterfield	Tr	10/83	83	1	0	0

KING John
Born: Ferndale, Rhondda Cynon Taff, Wales, 29 November, 1933 — G
Died: Sydney, Australia, December, 1982
Wales: 1/WLge-3/Schools

League Club	Source	Date Signed	Seasons Played	Apps	Subs	Gls
Swansea C	Jnr	02/51	50-63	363	-	0

KING John (Jake)
Born: Glasgow, Scotland, 29 January, 1955 RB

League Club	Source	Date Signed	Seasons Played	Apps	Subs	Gls
Shrewsbury T	App	01/73	72-81	304	2	20
Wrexham	Tr	08/82	82-84	91	1	5
Cardiff C	Tr	11/84	84-85	30	0	0

KING John Aitken (Ian)
Born: Loanhead, Midlothian, Scotland, 27 May, 1937 CH
Scotland: Schools

League Club	Source	Date Signed	Seasons Played	Apps	Subs	Gls
Leicester C	Arniston Rgrs	06/57	57-65	244	0	6
Charlton Ath	Tr	03/66	65-67	63	0	0

KING John Allen (Johnny)
Born: Liverpool, England, 15 April, 1938 RH

League Club	Source	Date Signed	Seasons Played	Apps	Subs	Gls
Everton	Jnr	03/56	57-59	48	-	1
Bournemouth	Tr	07/60	60	21	-	1
Tranmere Rov	Tr	02/61	60-67	240	2	4
Port Vale	Tr	07/68	68-70	99	2	0

KING John Charles (Johnny)
Born: Great Gidding, Cambridgeshire, England, 5 November, 1926 LH
Died: Cambridge, England, 11 January, 2010

League Club	Source	Date Signed	Seasons Played	Apps	Subs	Gls
Leicester C	Peterborough U	09/44	46-54	197	-	5

KING John William (Johnny)
Born: Wrenbury, Cheshire, England, 9 August, 1932 CF

League Club	Source	Date Signed	Seasons Played	Apps	Subs	Gls
Crewe Alex	Jnr	10/49	50-53	48	-	17
Stoke C	Tr	09/53	53-60	284	-	106
Cardiff C	Tr	08/61	61	33	-	6
Crewe Alex	Tr	06/62	62-66	178	0	45

KING Joshua Christian Kojo (Josh)
Born: Oslo, Norway, 15 January, 1992 F
Norway: 17/U21-8/Youth

League Club	Source	Date Signed	Seasons Played	Apps	Subs	Gls
Manchester U	Sch	01/09				
Preston NE	L	08/10	10	6	2	0
Hull C	L	01/12	11	8	10	1
Blackburn Rov	Tr	11/12	12-14	36	28	5

KING Ledley Brenton
Born: Bow, E London, England, 12 October, 1980 CD
England: 21/U21-12/Youth

League Club	Source	Date Signed	Seasons Played	Apps	Subs	Gls
Tottenham H	YT	07/98	98-11	264	4	10

KING Liam
Born: Rainworth, Nottinghamshire, England, 31 December, 1987 M

League Club	Source	Date Signed	Seasons Played	Apps	Subs	Gls
Rotherham U	Sch	07/06	06-07	4	3	0

KING Mark
Born: Liverpool, England, 6 June, 1988 LB/M

League Club	Source	Date Signed	Seasons Played	Apps	Subs	Gls
Blackburn Rov	Sch	10/07				
Accrington Stan	Tr	01/08	07	4	2	0

KING Marlon Francis
Born: Dulwich, S London, England, 26 April, 1980 F
Jamaica: 24

League Club	Source	Date Signed	Seasons Played	Apps	Subs	Gls
Barnet	YT	09/98	98-99	36	17	14
Gillingham	Tr	06/00	00-03	82	19	40
Nottingham F	Tr	11/03	03-04	40	10	10
Leeds U	L	03/05	04	4	5	0
Watford	Tr	07/05	05-07	77	4	36
Wigan Ath	Tr	01/08	07-09	8	10	1
Hull C	L	08/08	08	19	1	5
Middlesbrough	L	01/09	08	9	4	2
Coventry C	Unattached	09/10	10	24	4	12
Birmingham C	Tr	07/11	11-12	60	7	29
Sheffield U	Tr	09/13	13	7	1	1

KING Martyn Noel Geoffrey
Born: Birmingham, England, 23 August, 1937 CF

League Club	Source	Date Signed	Seasons Played	Apps	Subs	Gls
Colchester U	Pegasus	05/56	56-64	212	-	130
Wrexham	Tr	10/64	64-65	45	0	15

KING Michael Bryan (Bryan)
Born: Bishops Stortford, Hertfordshire, England, 18 May, 1947 G

League Club	Source	Date Signed	Seasons Played	Apps	Subs	Gls
Millwall	Chelmsford C	06/67	67-74	302	0	0
Coventry C	Tr	08/75	75	23	0	0

KING Peter
Born: Liverpool, England, 5 July, 1964 M
Died: Liverpool, England, 28 February, 2012

League Club	Source	Date Signed	Seasons Played	Apps	Subs	Gls
Liverpool	App	07/82				
Crewe Alex	Tr	08/83	83-84	55	9	5

KING Peter Charles
Born: Worcester, England, 3 April, 1943 F

League Club	Source	Date Signed	Seasons Played	Apps	Subs	Gls
Cardiff C	Worcester C	09/60	61-73	351	5	67

KING Philip Geoffrey (Phil)
Born: Bristol, England, 28 December, 1967 LB
England: B-1

League Club	Source	Date Signed	Seasons Played	Apps	Subs	Gls
Exeter C	App	01/85	84-85	24	3	0
Torquay U	Tr	07/86	86	24	0	3
Swindon T	Tr	02/87	86-89	112	4	4
Sheffield Wed	Tr	11/89	89-93	124	5	2
Notts Co	L	10/93	93	6	0	0
Aston Villa	Tr	08/94	94	13	3	0
West Bromwich A	L	10/95	95	4	0	0
Swindon T	Tr	03/97	96	5	0	0
Blackpool	L	10/97	97	6	0	0
Brighton & HA	Tr	03/99	98	3	0	0

KING Raymond (Ray)
Born: Amble, Northumberland, England, 15 August, 1924 G
Died: Bangkok, Thailand, 19 July, 2014
England: B-1

League Club	Source	Date Signed	Seasons Played	Apps	Subs	Gls
Newcastle U	Amble Welfare	04/42				
Leyton Orient	Tr	10/46	46	1	-	0
Port Vale	Ashington	05/49	49-56	252	-	0

KING Robert David
Born: Merthyr Tydfil, Wales, 2 September, 1977 RB
Wales: Youth

League Club	Source	Date Signed	Seasons Played	Apps	Subs	Gls
Swansea C	Torquay U (YT)	07/96	96	2	0	0

KING Robert Edward (Bobby)
Born: Edinburgh, Scotland, 7 September, 1941 LB

League Club	Source	Date Signed	Seasons Played	Apps	Subs	Gls
Southend U	Glasgow Rangers	08/63	63-65	77	2	2

KING Robert James (Robbie)
Born: Chelmsford, England, 1 October, 1986 M

League Club	Source	Date Signed	Seasons Played	Apps	Subs	Gls
Colchester U	Sch	07/06	05	0	3	0

KING Simon
Born: Ebbw Vale, Blaenau Gwent, Wales, 19 July, 1964 FB

League Club	Source	Date Signed	Seasons Played	Apps	Subs	Gls
Newport Co	Cwmbran	10/84	84	1	0	0

KING Simon Daniel Roy
Born: Oxford, England, 11 April, 1983 CD
England: Semi Pro-3

League Club	Source	Date Signed	Seasons Played	Apps	Subs	Gls
Oxford U	YT	12/00	00-01	3	1	0
Barnet	Tr	07/03	05-06	74	1	2
Gillingham	Tr	07/07	07-11	93	5	3
Plymouth Arg	L	08/11	11	6	0	0

KING Thomas Frederick (Tommy)
Born: Barrow, Cumbria, England, 2 April, 1934 WH

League Club	Source	Date Signed	Seasons Played	Apps	Subs	Gls
Barrow	Holker Central OB	03/53	52-59	73	-	1

KING Thomas Henderson (Tommy)
Born: Edinburgh, Scotland, 18 July, 1933 G

League Club	Source	Date Signed	Seasons Played	Apps	Subs	Gls
Watford	Ormiston Primrose	03/54	55	20	-	0

KINGSHOTT Frederick John (Freddie)
Born: St Pancras, Central London, England, 20 June, 1929 G
Died: Queensland, Australia, 6 April, 2009

League Club	Source	Date Signed	Seasons Played	Apps	Subs	Gls
Doncaster Rov	Eastbourne U	02/53	52	2	-	0
Gillingham	Tr	11/55	55-56	45	-	0

KINGSLEY Stephen
Born: Stirling, Scotland, 23 July, 1994 LB/M
Scotland: U21-1/Youth

League Club	Source	Date Signed	Seasons Played	Apps	Subs	Gls
Swansea C	Falkirk	06/14				
Yeovil T	L	02/15	14	12	0	0

KINGSNORTH Thomas Henry (Tom)
Born: Sittingbourne, Kent, England, 16 April, 1917 CH
Died: Sittingbourne, Kent, England, February, 1992

League Club	Source	Date Signed	Seasons Played	Apps	Subs	Gls
Gillingham	Lloyds Paper Mills	09/46	50	28	-	0

KINGSON Richard Paul Franck
Born: Accra, Ghana, 13 June, 1978 G
Ghana: 90

League Club	Source	Date Signed	Seasons Played	Apps	Subs	Gls
Birmingham C	Ankaraspor (TKY)	07/07	07	1	0	0
Wigan Ath	Tr	09/08	08	3	1	0
Blackpool	Tr	09/10	10	19	1	0

KINGSTON Andrew Keith (Andy)
Born: Oxford, England, 21 February, 1959 RB
England: Youth/Schools

League Club	Source	Date Signed	Seasons Played	Apps	Subs	Gls
Oxford U	App	10/76	76-81	44	6	0

KINK Tarmo
Born: Tallinn, Estonia, 6 October, 1985 LW
Estonia: 82

League Club	Source	Date Signed	Seasons Played	Apps	Subs	Gls
Middlesbrough	Gyori ETO (HUN)	07/10	10-11	8	14	4

KINKLADZE Georgiou (Georgi)
Born: Tbilisi, Georgia, 6 November, 1973 M
Georgia: 49

League Club	Source	Date Signed	Seasons Played	Apps	Subs	Gls
Manchester C	Mretebi Tibilisi (GEO)	08/95	95-97	105	1	20
Derby Co	Ajax (NED)	11/99	99-02	60	33	7

KINLOCH Thomas Sutherland (Tommy)
Born: Anderston, Glasgow, Scotland, 22 February, 1927 — RH
Died: Milngavie, Dunbartonshire, Scotland, 13 February, 1994

League Club	Source	Date Signed	Seasons Played	Apps	Subs	Gls
Carlisle U	Falkirk	05/50	50-55	184	-	15
Workington	Tr	07/56	56-57	70	-	12
Southport	Tr	02/58	57-58	53	-	0

KINNAIRD Paul
Born: Glasgow, Scotland, 11 November, 1966 — W
Scotland: Youth

League Club	Source	Date Signed	Seasons Played	Apps	Subs	Gls
Norwich C	Possilpark YMCA	11/84				
Shrewsbury T (L)	Partick Thistle	02/93	92	4	0	1
Scarborough	Dunfermline Ath	10/95	95	3	0	0

KINNEAR Joseph Patrick (Joe)
Born: Dublin, Republic of Ireland, 27 December, 1946 — RB
Republic of Ireland: 26

League Club	Source	Date Signed	Seasons Played	Apps	Subs	Gls
Tottenham H	St Albans C	02/65	65-75	189	7	2
Brighton & HA	Tr	08/75	75	15	1	1

KINNELL George
Born: Cowdenbeath, Fife, Scotland, 22 December, 1937 — CH

League Club	Source	Date Signed	Seasons Played	Apps	Subs	Gls
Stoke C	Aberdeen	11/63	63-65	89	2	6
Oldham Ath	Tr	08/66	66	12	0	8
Sunderland	Tr	10/66	66-68	67	2	3
Middlesbrough	Tr	10/68	68	12	1	1

KINNIBURGH Steven Steel
Born: Glasgow, Scotland, 13 June, 1989 — LB

League Club	Source	Date Signed	Seasons Played	Apps	Subs	Gls
Oxford U	Glasgow Rangers	07/10	10-11	10	2	0

KINSELL Thomas Henry (Harry)
Born: Cannock, Staffordshire, England, 31 May, 1921 — LB
Died: Dudley, West Midlands, England, 14 August, 2000
England: War-2

League Club	Source	Date Signed	Seasons Played	Apps	Subs	Gls
West Bromwich A	Jnr	06/38	46-48	83	-	0
Bolton W	Tr	06/49	49	17	-	0
Reading	Tr	05/50	50	12	-	0
West Ham U	Tr	01/51	50-54	101	-	2

KINSELLA Antony Steven (Tony)
Born: Grays, Essex, England, 30 October, 1961 — LW
Republic of Ireland: U21-2

League Club	Source	Date Signed	Seasons Played	Apps	Subs	Gls
Millwall	App	11/78	78-80	55	6	1
Ipswich T	Tampa Bay R's (USA)	04/82	82-83	7	2	0
Millwall	Tr	06/84	84-85	20	2	1
Doncaster Rov	Enfield	02/87	86-87	29	1	4

KINSELLA Leonard (Len)
Born: Alexandria, Dunbartonshire, Scotland, 14 May, 1946 — M

League Club	Source	Date Signed	Seasons Played	Apps	Subs	Gls
Burnley	App	05/63	65-69	7	6	0
Carlisle U	Tr	09/70	70-71	9	4	0
Rochdale	Tr	09/71	71-73	82	3	4

KINSELLA Lewis
Born: Watford, Hertfordshire, England, 1 January, 1995 — LB

League Club	Source	Date Signed	Seasons Played	Apps	Subs	Gls
Aston Villa	Sch	07/13				
Luton T	L	03/15	14	2	1	0

KINSELLA Liam Mark
Born: Colchester, Essex, England, 23 February, 1996 — RB

League Club	Source	Date Signed	Seasons Played	Apps	Subs	Gls
Walsall	Sch	04/14	14	4	0	0

KINSELLA Mark Anthony
Born: Dublin, Republic of Ireland, 12 August, 1972 — M
Republic of Ireland: 48/B-1/U21-8/Youth

League Club	Source	Date Signed	Seasons Played	Apps	Subs	Gls
Colchester U	Home Farm (ROI)	08/89	89-96	174	6	27
Charlton Ath	Tr	09/96	96-01	200	8	19
Aston Villa	Tr	08/02	02-03	17	4	0
West Bromwich A	Tr	01/04	03	15	3	1
Walsall	Tr	07/04	04-06	35	7	1

KINSELLA Patrick Gerard (Pat)
Born: Liverpool, England, 8 November, 1943 — M

League Club	Source	Date Signed	Seasons Played	Apps	Subs	Gls
Liverpool	Jnr	11/60				
Tranmere Rov	Bangor C	08/66	66	1	0	0
Stockport Co	Rhyl	10/68	68	12	1	0

KINSEY Albert John
Born: Liverpool, England, 19 September, 1945 — F
England: Schools

League Club	Source	Date Signed	Seasons Played	Apps	Subs	Gls
Manchester U	App	10/62				
Wrexham	Tr	03/66	65-72	245	8	84
Crewe Alex	Tr	03/73	72-74	30	2	1

KINSEY Brian Robert
Born: Charlton, SE London, England, 4 March, 1938 — LB/LW

League Club	Source	Date Signed	Seasons Played	Apps	Subs	Gls
Charlton Ath	Bromley	09/56	56-70	371	6	19

KINSEY Noel
Born: Treorchy, Rhondda Cynon Taff, Wales, 24 December, 1925 — IF/WH
Wales: 7

League Club	Source	Date Signed	Seasons Played	Apps	Subs	Gls
Cardiff C	Jnr	06/44				
Norwich C	Tr	05/47	47-52	223	-	57
Birmingham C	Tr	05/53	53-57	149	-	48
Port Vale	Tr	02/58	57-60	72	-	6

KINSEY Stephen (Steve)
Born: Manchester, England, 2 January, 1963 — W/F
England: Youth

League Club	Source	Date Signed	Seasons Played	Apps	Subs	Gls
Manchester C	App	01/80	80-85	87	14	15
Chester C	L	09/82	82	3	0	1
Chesterfield	L	11/82	82	3	0	0
Rochdale	Tampa Bay R's (USA)	10/91	91	3	3	1

KIPPAX Dennis Hobson
Born: Sheffield, England, 7 August, 1926 — RW
Died: Sheffield, England, 18 March, 1970

League Club	Source	Date Signed	Seasons Played	Apps	Subs	Gls
Sheffield Wed	Stocksbridge Works	03/46	46	1	-	0

KIPPAX Frederick Peter (Peter)
Born: Burnley, Lancashire, England, 17 July, 1922 — LW
Died: Lytham St Annes, Lancashire, England, 21 September, 1987
England: FLge-2/Amateur-1

League Club	Source	Date Signed	Seasons Played	Apps	Subs	Gls
Burnley (Am)	Jnr	07/46	46-47	32	-	6
Liverpool (Am)	Tr	01/49	48	1	-	0

KIPPE Frode
Born: Oslo, Norway, 17 January, 1978 — CD
Norway: 8/B-1/U21-27

League Club	Source	Date Signed	Seasons Played	Apps	Subs	Gls
Liverpool	Lillestrom (NOR)	01/99				
Stoke C	L	12/99	99	15	0	1
Stoke C	L	10/00	00	15	4	0

KIRALY Gabor Ferenc
Born: Szombathely, Hungary, 1 April, 1976 — G
Hungary: 95/U21-10

League Club	Source	Date Signed	Seasons Played	Apps	Subs	Gls
Crystal Palace	Hertha Berlin (GER)	08/04	04-06	104	0	0
Aston Villa	L	12/06	06	5	0	0
Burnley	Tr	07/07	07	27	0	0
Fulham	1860 Munich (GER)	08/14	14	3	1	0

KIRBY Alan
Born: Barrow, Cumbria, England, 19 December, 1926 — G
Died: Barrow, Cumbria, England, 30 April, 2003

League Club	Source	Date Signed	Seasons Played	Apps	Subs	Gls
Notts Co	Holker Central OB	05/45				
Barrow		09/47	50-51	21	-	0

KIRBY Denis
Born: Leeds, England, 8 November, 1924 — WH
Died: Leeds, England, April, 2009

League Club	Source	Date Signed	Seasons Played	Apps	Subs	Gls
Leeds U	Jnr	09/42	47	8	-	0
Halifax T	Scarborough	08/50				

KIRBY Eric
Born: Sheffield, England, 12 October, 1926 — WH

League Club	Source	Date Signed	Seasons Played	Apps	Subs	Gls
Sheffield Wed		12/49	50	1	-	0
York C	Tr	08/52	52	1	-	0

KIRBY George
Born: Liverpool, England, 20 December, 1933 — CF
Died: Elland, West Yorkshire, England, 24 March, 2000

League Club	Source	Date Signed	Seasons Played	Apps	Subs	Gls
Everton	Jnr	06/52	55-57	26	-	9
Sheffield Wed	Tr	03/59	59	3	-	0
Plymouth Arg	Tr	01/60	59-62	93	-	38
Southampton	Tr	09/62	62-63	63	-	28
Coventry C	Tr	03/64	63-64	18	-	10
Swansea C	Tr	10/64	64	25	-	8
Walsall	Tr	05/65	65-66	74	1	25
Brentford	New York Gen'ls (USA)	10/68	68	5	0	1

KIRBY Jake Antony
Born: Liverpool, England, 1 May, 1994 — M

League Club	Source	Date Signed	Seasons Played	Apps	Subs	Gls
Tranmere Rov	Sch	05/12	11-14	26	27	3

KIRBY Ryan Mark
Born: Chingford, NE London, England, 6 September, 1974 — RB

League Club	Source	Date Signed	Seasons Played	Apps	Subs	Gls
Arsenal	YT	07/93				
Doncaster Rov	Tr	07/94	94-95	73	5	0
Wigan Ath	Crewe Alex (NC)	08/96	96	5	1	0
Northampton T	Tr	09/96	96	0	1	0

KIRK Andrew Robert (Andy)
Born: Belfast, Northern Ireland, 29 May, 1979 — F
Northern Ireland: 11/U21-9/Youth/Schools

League Club	Source	Date Signed	Seasons Played	Apps	Subs	Gls
Boston U	Heart of Midlothian	07/04	04	25	0	19
Northampton T	Tr	03/05	04-07	82	24	30
Yeovil T	Tr	01/08	07	15	4	4

League Club	Source	Date Signed	Seasons Played	Apps	Subs	Gls

KIRK Henry Joseph (Harry)
Born: Saltcoats, Ayrshire, Scotland, 25 August, 1944 — LW

League Club	Source	Date Signed	Seasons Played	Apps	Subs	Gls
Middlesbrough	Ardeer Rec	05/63	63	1	-	0
Darlington	Dumbarton	06/67	67-69	59	2	7
Hartlepool U	Tr	10/69	69-70	42	3	5
Scunthorpe U	Tr	11/70	70-72	112	0	16
Stockport Co	Tr	09/73	73-74	60	8	7

KIRK James (Jimmy)
Born: Tarbolton, Ayrshire, Scotland, 12 November, 1925 — G

League Club	Source	Date Signed	Seasons Played	Apps	Subs	Gls
Bury	St Mirren	08/51	51-53	80	-	0
Colchester U	Tr	06/54	54	32	-	0
Torquay U	Tr	08/55	55	39	-	0
Aldershot	Tr	07/56	56	5	-	0

KIRK John Francis
Born: Leicester, England, 7 February, 1922 — LW
Died: Leicester, England, October, 2006

League Club	Source	Date Signed	Seasons Played	Apps	Subs	Gls
Nottingham F	Army	08/48				
Darlington	Tr	08/51	51	30	-	4

KIRK John McCrae
Born: Winnipeg, Canada, 13 March, 1930 — IF

League Club	Source	Date Signed	Seasons Played	Apps	Subs	Gls
Portsmouth	Montrose	01/51				
Accrington Stan	Tr	03/53	52-53	14	-	1

KIRK Roy
Born: Shuttlewood, Derbyshire, England, 11 June, 1929 — D
Died: Peterborough, England, 5 November, 1984

League Club	Source	Date Signed	Seasons Played	Apps	Subs	Gls
Leeds U	Bolsover Colliery	10/48	50-51	34	-	1
Coventry C	Tr	03/52	51-59	330	-	6

KIRK Stephen David (Steve)
Born: Kirkcaldy, Fife, Scotland, 3 January, 1963 — FB

League Club	Source	Date Signed	Seasons Played	Apps	Subs	Gls
Stoke C	East Fife	05/80	81	12	0	0

KIRKALDIE John (Jack)
Born: Coventry, England, 2 August, 1917 — RW
Died: Coventry, England, July, 1985

League Club	Source	Date Signed	Seasons Played	Apps	Subs	Gls
Southend U	Leamington St John's	02/36	36	1	-	0
West Ham U	Tr	02/37	36-38	11	-	1
Doncaster Rov	Tr	04/39	38-47	53	-	17

KIRKBY John
Born: USA, 29 November, 1929 — RB
Died: Wrexham, Wales, 4 April, 1953

League Club	Source	Date Signed	Seasons Played	Apps	Subs	Gls
Stoke C	Banks o' Dee	12/46	48	1	-	0
Wrexham	Tr	08/51	51-52	5	-	0

KIRKHAM John (Jack)
Born: Ellesmere Port, Cheshire, England, 16 June, 1918 — CF
Died: Staffordshire, England, 1982

League Club	Source	Date Signed	Seasons Played	Apps	Subs	Gls
Wolverhampton W	Ellesmere Port T	03/36	37-38	13	-	5
Bournemouth	Tr	10/38	38-46	48	-	27

KIRKHAM John Kenneth
Born: Wednesbury, West Midlands, England, 13 May, 1941 — WH
England: U23-2/Youth

League Club	Source	Date Signed	Seasons Played	Apps	Subs	Gls
Wolverhampton W	Ellesmere Port T	05/58	59-64	100	-	12
Peterborough U	Tr	11/65	65-67	46	0	2
Exeter C	Tr	07/68	68	31	1	6

KIRKHAM Paul
Born: Manchester, England, 5 July, 1969 — F

League Club	Source	Date Signed	Seasons Played	Apps	Subs	Gls
Huddersfield T	Manchester U (YT)	09/87	87	0	1	0

KIRKHAM Peter Jonathan
Born: Newcastle-upon-Tyne, England, 28 October, 1974 — W

League Club	Source	Date Signed	Seasons Played	Apps	Subs	Gls
Darlington	Newcastle U (YT)	08/93	93-94	5	8	0

KIRKHAM Raymond Neville (Ray)
Born: Thorne, South Yorkshire, England, 16 December, 1934 — G

League Club	Source	Date Signed	Seasons Played	Apps	Subs	Gls
Mansfield T	Thorne T	12/57	57-59	42	-	0

KIRKHAM Reginald (Reg)
Born: Ormskirk, Lancashire, England, 8 May, 1919 — FB
Died: Burnley, Lancashire, England, May, 1999

League Club	Source	Date Signed	Seasons Played	Apps	Subs	Gls
Wolverhampton W	Ormskirk	05/39				
Burnley	Tr	03/47	48-50	13	-	1

KIRKHAM Royce
Born: Ollerton, Nottinghamshire, England, 17 October, 1937 — FB
Died: 24 January, 2015

League Club	Source	Date Signed	Seasons Played	Apps	Subs	Gls
Notts Co	Ollerton Colliery	05/55	56	1	-	0

KIRKLAND Christopher Edmund (Chris)
Born: Barwell, Leicestershire, England, 2 May, 1981 — G
England: 1/U21-8/Youth

League Club	Source	Date Signed	Seasons Played	Apps	Subs	Gls
Coventry C	YT	05/98	00-01	24	0	0
Liverpool	Tr	08/01	01-04	25	0	0
West Bromwich A	L	07/05	05	10	0	0
Wigan Ath	Tr	07/06	06-10	131	0	0
Leicester C	L	11/10	10	3	0	0
Doncaster Rov	L	10/11	11	1	0	0
Sheffield Wed	Tr	07/12	12-14	84	1	0

KIRKLAND James William (Jim)
Born: Bedford, England, 30 October, 1946 — LB

League Club	Source	Date Signed	Seasons Played	Apps	Subs	Gls
Grimsby T	Aberdeen	07/70	70	12	0	0

KIRKMAN Alan John
Born: Bolton, Greater Manchester, England, 21 June, 1936 — IF/CD
Died: Bolton, Greater Manchester, England, 14 January, 2011

League Club	Source	Date Signed	Seasons Played	Apps	Subs	Gls
Manchester C	Bacup Bor	02/56	56-58	7	-	6
Rotherham U	Tr	03/59	58-63	142	-	58
Newcastle U	Tr	09/63	63	5	-	1
Scunthorpe U	Tr	12/63	63-64	32	-	5
Torquay U	Tr	07/65	65-66	59	0	8
Workington	Tr	01/67	66-67	56	0	3

KIRKMAN Kenneth Roy (Ken)
Born: Farnworth, Greater Manchester, England, 20 March, 1931 — RW
Died: Ormskirk, Lancashire, England, 11 December, 2000

League Club	Source	Date Signed	Seasons Played	Apps	Subs	Gls
Bournemouth	Lomax's	07/51				
Southport	Tr	08/53	53	1	-	0

KIRKMAN Norman
Born: Bolton, Greater Manchester, England, 6 March, 1920 — LB
Died: Bolton, Greater Manchester, England, 17 November, 1995

League Club	Source	Date Signed	Seasons Played	Apps	Subs	Gls
Burnley	Padiham Central	09/39				
Rochdale	Tr	09/46	46-47	53	-	0
Chesterfield	Tr	12/47	47-48	41	-	0
Leicester C	Tr	08/49	49	12	-	0
Southampton	Tr	07/50	50-51	20	-	0
Exeter C	Tr	03/52	51-52	11	-	1

KIRKPATRICK John Garfield
Born: Slamannan, Falkirk, Scotland, 3 March, 1919 — IF/WH

League Club	Source	Date Signed	Seasons Played	Apps	Subs	Gls
Carlisle U		11/37	46	33	-	2

KIRKPATRICK Roger Whitworth
Born: Hull, England, 29 May, 1923 — WH/LW
Died: Stockport, Greater Manchester, England, May, 2013

League Club	Source	Date Signed	Seasons Played	Apps	Subs	Gls
Chester C		08/47	47-52	111	-	26

KIRKUP Brian Alexander
Born: Burnham, Buckinghamshire, England, 16 April, 1932 — CF/RH

League Club	Source	Date Signed	Seasons Played	Apps	Subs	Gls
Reading	Bedford T	08/55	55-57	55	-	19
Northampton T	Tr	07/58	58-59	26	-	7
Aldershot	Tr	11/59	59-61	59	-	15

KIRKUP Frank William
Born: Spennymoor, County Durham, England, 12 January, 1939 — LW
Died: Spennymoor, County Durham, England, April, 2009

League Club	Source	Date Signed	Seasons Played	Apps	Subs	Gls
Blackburn Rov	Spennymoor U	02/57				
Workington	Tr	06/59	59-62	140	-	31
Carlisle U	Tr	12/62	62-64	76	-	13
Notts Co	Tr	06/65	65	29	0	3
Workington	Tr	11/66	66	8	0	0

KIRKUP Graeme Stuart
Born: Cramlington, Northumberland, England, 31 May, 1965 — RB

League Club	Source	Date Signed	Seasons Played	Apps	Subs	Gls
Exeter C	App	05/83	81-85	103	4	1

KIRKUP Joseph Robert (Joe)
Born: Hexham, Northumberland, England, 17 December, 1939 — RB
England: U23-3/Youth

League Club	Source	Date Signed	Seasons Played	Apps	Subs	Gls
West Ham U	Jnr	05/57	58-65	165	0	6
Chelsea	Tr	03/66	65-67	48	5	2
Southampton	Tr	02/68	67-73	169	0	3

KIRKWOOD Ian
Born: Edinburgh, Scotland, 29 November, 1932 — IF

League Club	Source	Date Signed	Seasons Played	Apps	Subs	Gls
Reading	Wokingham T	02/53	52-54	5	-	1

KIRKWOOD John Fleming
Born: Falkirk, Scotland, 27 February, 1932 — G

League Club	Source	Date Signed	Seasons Played	Apps	Subs	Gls
Reading	Blairhall Colliery	12/49	52-53	31	-	0

KIRMAN Harold
Born: Hull, England, 3 December, 1930 — RB
Died: Hull, England, 17 July, 2011

League Club	Source	Date Signed	Seasons Played	Apps	Subs	Gls
Hull C	Francis Askew YC	12/50				
Gillingham	Tr	07/52	53	8	-	0
Hull C	Tr	01/55	55	2	-	0

KIROVSKI Jovan
Born: Escondido, California, USA, 18 March, 1976 — LW
USA: 62

League Club	Source	Date Signed	Seasons Played	Apps	Subs	Gls
Manchester U	La Jolla Nomads (USA)	07/95				

League Club	Source	Date Signed	Seasons Played	Apps	Subs	Gls
Crystal Palace	Sporting Lisbon (POR)	08/01	01	25	11	5
Birmingham C	Tr	08/02	02-03	5	18	2

KIRSTEN Kenneth (Ken)
Born: Pietermaritzburg, South Africa, 28 October, 1922 — LB

League Club	Source	Date Signed	Seasons Played	Apps	Subs	Gls
Charlton Ath	Park Villa (RSA)	03/48				
Aldershot	Tr	08/51	51	5	-	0

KIRTLEY John Henry (Harry)
Born: Washington, Tyne and Wear, England, 23 May, 1930 — IF
Died: Rhyl, Denbighshire, Wales, 8 December, 2007

League Club	Source	Date Signed	Seasons Played	Apps	Subs	Gls
Sunderland	Fatfield Jnrs	05/48	48-54	95	-	18
Cardiff C	Tr	05/55	55	38	-	4
Gateshead	Tr	03/57	56-59	95	-	16

KIRTON John (Jock)
Born: Aberdeen, Scotland, 4 March, 1916 — LH
Died: Stoke-on-Trent, England, 13 March, 1996
Scotland: War-1

League Club	Source	Date Signed	Seasons Played	Apps	Subs	Gls
Stoke C	Banks o' Dee	11/35	36-52	219	-	2
Bradford C	Tr	07/53	53	8	-	0

KISBY Christopher Nigel (Chris)
Born: Horsforth, West Yorkshire, England, 7 November, 1952 — FB

League Club	Source	Date Signed	Seasons Played	Apps	Subs	Gls
Scunthorpe U	App	10/70	70-72	30	9	2
Workington	Tr	08/73	73-76	162	2	2
Southport	Tr	08/77	77	42	0	1

KISHISHEV Radostin Prodanov
Born: Bourgas, Bulgaria, 30 July, 1974 — DM
Bulgaria: 88

League Club	Source	Date Signed	Seasons Played	Apps	Subs	Gls
Charlton Ath	Liteks Lovech (BUL)	08/00	00-06	149	30	2
Leeds U	L	03/07	06	10	0	0
Leicester C	Tr	07/07	07	2	5	0
Leeds U	L	10/07	07	5	2	0
Brighton & HA	Liteks Lovech (BUL)	07/10	10	21	11	0

KISNORBO Patrick Fabio Maxime
Born: Melbourne, Australia, 24 March, 1981 — CD
Australia: 18/U23-3/Youth

League Club	Source	Date Signed	Seasons Played	Apps	Subs	Gls
Leicester C	Heart of Midlothian	07/05	05-08	122	4	9
Leeds U	Tr	07/09	09-11	47	2	1
Ipswich T	L	01/13	12	1	2	0

KISS Filip
Born: Dunajska Streda, Slovakia, 13 October, 1990 — M
Slovakia: 8/U21-19/Youth

League Club	Source	Date Signed	Seasons Played	Apps	Subs	Gls
Cardiff C (L)	Slov Bratislava (SVK)	07/11	11	13	13	1
Cardiff C	Slov Bratislava (SVK)	07/12	12	0	2	0

KISSOCK John Paul
Born: Liverpool, England, 2 December, 1989 — LW
England: Semi Pro-1

League Club	Source	Date Signed	Seasons Played	Apps	Subs	Gls
Everton	Sch	12/06				
Accrington Stan	L	01/09	08	5	0	0
Oldham Ath (L)	Macclesfield T	01/14	13	2	2	0

KITAMIRIKE Joel Derick
Born: Kampala, Uganda, 5 April, 1984 — CD
England: Youth

League Club	Source	Date Signed	Seasons Played	Apps	Subs	Gls
Chelsea	YT	04/01				
Brentford	L	09/03	03	21	1	0
Mansfield T	Hornchurch	12/04	04	2	0	0

KITCHEN Ashley James
Born: Edwinstowe, Nottinghamshire, England, 10 October, 1988 — LB

League Club	Source	Date Signed	Seasons Played	Apps	Subs	Gls
Mansfield T	Sch	07/07	06-07	5	0	0

KITCHEN Benjamin (Ben)
Born: Bolton, Greater Manchester, England, 19 August, 1986 — M

League Club	Source	Date Signed	Seasons Played	Apps	Subs	Gls
Rochdale	Sch	07/05	04-05	3	6	0

KITCHEN David Edward (Sam)
Born: Rinteln, Germany, 11 June, 1967 — D

League Club	Source	Date Signed	Seasons Played	Apps	Subs	Gls
Leyton Orient	Frickley Ath	08/92	92-93	35	8	1
Doncaster Rov	Tr	02/94	93-94	21	1	1

KITCHEN John (Jack)
Born: Whitehaven, Cumbria, England, 28 February, 1925 — CH
Died: Scarborough, North Yorkshire, England, August, 1992

League Club	Source	Date Signed	Seasons Played	Apps	Subs	Gls
Barnsley	Kells Ath	10/44	46-51	53	-	0

KITCHEN Michael Peter (Peter)
Born: Mexborough, South Yorkshire, England, 16 February, 1952 — F

League Club	Source	Date Signed	Seasons Played	Apps	Subs	Gls
Doncaster Rov	Jnr	07/70	70-76	221	7	89
Leyton Orient	Tr	07/77	77-78	64	1	28
Fulham	Tr	02/79	78-79	21	3	6
Cardiff C	Tr	08/80	80-81	64	3	21
Leyton Orient	Happy Valley (HKG)	12/82	82-83	46	3	21
Chester C	Dagenham	03/85	84	3	2	1

KITCHENER Barry Raymond
Born: Dagenham, E London, England, 11 December, 1947 — CD
Died: Great Yarmouth, Norfolk, England, 30 March, 2012

League Club	Source	Date Signed	Seasons Played	Apps	Subs	Gls
Millwall	App	08/65	66-81	518	5	25

KITCHENER Raymond Alan (Ray)
Born: Baldock, Hertfordshire, England, 31 October, 1930 — LW
Died: Hitchin, Hertfordshire, England, June, 2013

League Club	Source	Date Signed	Seasons Played	Apps	Subs	Gls
Chelsea	Hitchin T	07/54	55	1	-	0
Norwich C	Tr	09/56	56	18	-	0

KITCHENER William Harry (Bill)
Born: Arlesey, Bedfordshire, England, 3 November, 1946 — D

League Club	Source	Date Signed	Seasons Played	Apps	Subs	Gls
West Ham U	App	11/63	66-67	11	0	0
Torquay U	L	09/66	66	25	0	3
Torquay U	Tr	12/67	67-70	142	0	5
Bournemouth	Tr	07/71	71	36	0	2

KITCHING Phillip John (Phil)
Born: Lewisham, SE London, England, 30 September, 1967 — M

League Club	Source	Date Signed	Seasons Played	Apps	Subs	Gls
York C	Bradford C (NC)	08/87	87	7	6	0

KITE Philip David (Phil)
Born: Bristol, England, 26 October, 1962 — G
England: Youth/Schools

League Club	Source	Date Signed	Seasons Played	Apps	Subs	Gls
Bristol Rov	App	10/80	80-83	96	0	0
Southampton	Tr	08/84	84-85	4	0	0
Middlesbrough	L	03/86	85	2	0	0
Gillingham	Tr	02/87	86-88	70	0	0
Bournemouth	Tr	08/89	89	7	0	0
Sheffield U	Tr	08/90	90-91	11	0	0
Mansfield T	L	11/91	91	11	0	0
Plymouth Arg	L	09/92	92	2	0	0
Rotherham U	L	10/92	92	1	0	0
Crewe Alex	L	11/92	92	5	0	0
Stockport Co	L	03/93	92	5	0	0
Cardiff C	Tr	07/93	93	17	1	0
Bristol C	Tr	08/94	94-95	5	1	0

KITSON David Barry (Dave)
Born: Hitchin, Hertfordshire, England, 21 January, 1980 — F

League Club	Source	Date Signed	Seasons Played	Apps	Subs	Gls
Cambridge U	Arlesey T	03/01	00-03	97	5	40
Reading	Tr	12/03	03-07	111	24	54
Stoke C	Tr	07/08	08-09	20	14	3
Reading	L	03/09	08	9	1	2
Middlesbrough	L	11/09	09	6	0	3
Portsmouth	Tr	08/10	10-11	57	11	12
Sheffield U	Tr	08/12	12	30	3	11
Oxford U	Tr	06/13	13	27	5	4

KITSON Neal
Born: New York, USA, 4 January, 1986 — G

League Club	Source	Date Signed	Seasons Played	Apps	Subs	Gls
Northampton T	Rochester Rhinos (USA)	01/12	11	8	0	0

KITSON Paul
Born: Murton, County Durham, England, 9 January, 1971 — F
England: U21-7

League Club	Source	Date Signed	Seasons Played	Apps	Subs	Gls
Leicester C	YT	12/88	89-91	39	11	6
Derby Co	Tr	03/92	91-94	105	0	36
Newcastle U	Tr	09/94	94-96	26	10	10
West Ham U	Tr	02/97	96-01	46	17	18
Charlton Ath	L	03/00	99	2	4	1
Crystal Palace	L	09/00	00	4	0	0
Brighton & HA	Tr	08/02	02	7	3	2
Rushden & D	Tr	09/03	03	18	10	5

KIWOMYA Andrew Alexander (Alex)
Born: Sheffield, England, 20 May, 1996 — F
England: Youth

League Club	Source	Date Signed	Seasons Played	Apps	Subs	Gls
Chelsea	Sch	11/13				
Barnsley	L	01/15	14	3	2	0

KIWOMYA Andrew Derek Bara (Andy)
Born: Huddersfield, West Yorkshire, England, 1 October, 1967 — LW
England: Youth

League Club	Source	Date Signed	Seasons Played	Apps	Subs	Gls
Barnsley	App	07/85	85	1	0	0
Sheffield Wed	Tr	10/86				
Rotherham U	Dundee	10/93	93	4	3	0
Scunthorpe U	Halifax T	03/95	94	9	0	3
Bradford C	Tr	07/95	95-96	27	16	3
Luton T	L	03/97	96	5	0	1
Burnley	L	09/97	97	1	2	0
Notts Co	Tr	12/97	97	0	2	0

KIWOMYA Christopher Maurends (Chris)
Born: Huddersfield, West Yorkshire, England, 2 December, 1969 — F

League Club	Source	Date Signed	Seasons Played	Apps	Subs	Gls
Ipswich T	App	03/87	88-94	197	28	51
Arsenal	Tr	01/95	94	5	9	3
Queens Park Rgrs	Selangor (MLY)	08/98	98-00	74	12	25

League Club	Source	Date Signed	Seasons Played	Career Record Apps	Subs	Gls

KJELDBJERG Jakob
Born: Fredrikstad, Norway, 21 October, 1969 — CD
Denmark: 14/U21-20

Chelsea	Silkeborg (NOR)	08/93	93-94	52	0	2

KLASNIC Ivan
Born: Hamburg, Germany, 29 January, 1980 — F
Croatia: 41/U21-3/Youth

Bolton W	FC Nantes (FRA)	09/09	09-11	28	50	20

[KLEBERSON] PEREIRA KLEBERSON Jose
Born: Urai, Brazil, 19 June, 1979 — M
Brazil: 32

Manchester U	Atlet Paraense (BRA)	08/03	03-04	16	4	2

KLEIN-DAVIES Joshua David (Josh)
Born: Bristol, England, 6 July, 1989 — F
Wales: Youth

Bristol Rov	Bristol C (Sch)	07/07	07	2	8	1
Luton T	L	08/08	08	0	1	0

KLETZENBAUER Carl Frank (Frank)
Born: Coventry, England, 21 July, 1936 — FB
Died: Nuneaton, Warwickshire, England, 8 August, 1996

Coventry C	Municipal Sports	03/56	56-63	122	-	3
Walsall	Tr	03/64	63-64	12	-	0

KLINSMANN Jurgen
Born: Goppingen, Germany, 30 July, 1964 — F
Germany: 108//West Germany: 28/U23-14/U21-8

Tottenham H	AS Monaco (FRA)	08/94	94	41	0	20
Tottenham H (L)	Sampdoria (ITA)	12/97	97	15	0	9

KLONER Hymie
Born: Johannesburg, South Africa, 23 May, 1929 — WH

Birmingham C	Marist Brothers (RSA)	11/50	50	1	-	0

KLUG Bryan Paul
Born: Coventry, England, 8 October, 1960 — M
England: Youth

Ipswich T	App	11/77				
Wimbledon	L	03/80	79	10	1	0
Chesterfield	Tr	08/83	83	27	7	2
Peterborough U	Tr	08/84	84	39	0	2

KLUIVERT Patrick Stephan
Born: Amsterdam, Netherlands, 1 July, 1976 — F
Netherlands: 79/Youth

Newcastle U	Barcelona (SPN)	07/04	04	15	10	6

KLUKOWSKI Yan
Born: Chippenham, Wiltshire, England, 1 January, 1987 — M

Newport Co	Forest Green Rov	05/14	14	24	14	4

KNAPP Anthony (Tony)
Born: Newstead, Nottinghamshire, England, 13 October, 1936 — CH
England: FLge-1

Leicester C	Jnr	12/53	55-60	86	-	0
Southampton	Tr	08/61	61-66	233	0	2
Coventry C	Tr	08/67	67	11	0	0
Tranmere Rov	Los Angeles Wolv (USA)	10/69	69-70	36	0	1

KNIGHT Alan Edward
Born: Balham, S London, England, 3 June, 1961 — G
England: U21-2/Youth

Portsmouth	App	03/79	77-99	683	0	0

KNIGHT Anthony (Tony)
Born: Romford, E London, England, 6 March, 1959 — G

Luton T	App	05/76	76-77	6	0	0

KNIGHT Arnold William
Born: Guisborough, Cleveland, England, 30 May, 1919 — IF
Died: Redcar, Cleveland, England, 8 October, 2003

Leeds U	Tottenham H (Am)	10/37				
Plymouth Arg	Tr	07/47	47	7	-	0
Bradford C	Tr	02/48	47-48	7	-	0

KNIGHT Brian James
Born: Dundee, Scotland, 28 March, 1949 — M/FB

Huddersfield T	Dundee	07/69				
Northampton T	Tr	10/69	69	9	3	0

KNIGHT Brian Thomas Arthur
Born: High Wycombe, Buckinghamshire, England, 14 November, 1946 — LW

Reading	App	11/64	64-65	4	0	1

KNIGHT Craig
Born: Wrexham, Wales, 24 October, 1973 — CD

Wrexham	YT	07/92	91	1	0	0

KNIGHT David Sean
Born: Houghton-le-Spring, Tyne and Wear, England, 15 January, 1987 — G

Middlesbrough	Sch	02/05				
Darlington	L	12/05	05	3	0	0
Oldham Ath	L	08/06	06	2	0	0
Swansea C	Tr	08/07				
Middlesbrough	Billingham Synthonia	11/08				
Darlington	Tr	08/09	09	7	0	0

KNIGHT Frank
Born: Hucknall, Nottinghamshire, England, 26 October, 1921 — LH
Died: Nottingham, England, 8 December, 1993

Nottingham F	Hucknall T	05/43	46-49	48	-	1

KNIGHT George Rollinson
Born: Bolton, Greater Manchester, England, 12 May, 1921 — IF
Died: Birmingham, England, August, 2011

Burnley	Holdens Temperance	05/38	38-46	9	-	2

KNIGHT Graham John
Born: Rochester, Kent, England, 5 January, 1952 — RB/M

Gillingham	App	01/70	70-78	229	16	10

KNIGHT Ian John
Born: Hartlepool, Cleveland, England, 26 October, 1966 — CD
England: U21-2

Barnsley	App	10/84				
Sheffield Wed	Tr	08/85	85-88	21	0	0
Scunthorpe U	L	08/89	89	2	0	0
Grimsby T	Tr	01/90	89-91	16	5	2
Carlisle U	Tr	08/92	92	1	0	0

KNIGHT Jason George
Born: Melbourne, Australia, 16 September, 1974 — M

Doncaster Rov	Hinckley Ath	08/95	95	1	3	0

KNIGHT Jeffrey William (Jeff)
Born: Sudbury, Derbyshire, England, 10 December, 1926 — IF
Died: Allestree, Derbyshire, England, 10 March, 2002

Derby Co	Derby Corinthians	05/46				
Walsall	Tr	08/52	52	4	-	0

KNIGHT John (Jackie)
Born: Bolton, Greater Manchester, England, 12 September, 1922 — IF
Died: Bath, England, 28 January, 1996

Burnley	Jnr	08/45	46-48	26	-	5
Preston NE	Tr	12/48	48-49	39	-	7
Chesterfield	Tr	07/51	51	35	-	6
Exeter C	Tr	08/52	52-53	56	-	6

KNIGHT Keith
Born: Cheltenham, Gloucestershire, England, 16 February, 1969 — RW
England: Schools

Reading	Cheltenham T	09/88	88-90	39	4	8

KNIGHT Leon Leroy
Born: Hackney, E London, England, 16 September, 1982 — F
England: Youth

Chelsea	YT	09/99				
Queens Park Rgrs	L	03/01	00	10	1	0
Huddersfield T	L	10/01	01	31	0	16
Sheffield Wed	L	07/02	02	14	10	3
Brighton & HA	Tr	07/03	03-05	98	10	34
Swansea C	Tr	01/06	05-06	20	8	15
Barnsley	L	11/06	06	6	3	0
MK Dons	Tr	01/07	06-07	22	11	5
Wycombe W	Tr	01/08	07	12	8	5

KNIGHT Lyndon Alan
Born: Lydbrook, Gloucestershire, England, 3 February, 1961 — G

Hereford U	App	02/79	78	2	0	0

KNIGHT Peter Richard
Born: Brighton, England, 12 November, 1939 — W

Brighton & HA	Lewes	01/64	63-65	9	1	1

KNIGHT Peter Robert
Born: Ilford, E London, England, 26 December, 1937 — RW

Southend U		06/58				
Nottingham F	Tr	08/59	59	4	-	0
Oxford U	Tr	07/60	62-64	94	-	12
Reading	Tr	11/64	64-65	26	0	3

KNIGHT Richard
Born: Burton-on-Trent, Staffordshire, England, 31 August, 1974 — RB

Walsall	YT	03/92	92-93	27	2	1

KNIGHT Richard
Born: Burton-on-Trent, Staffordshire, England, 3 August, 1979 — G
England: Youth

League Club	Source	Date Signed	Seasons Played	Career Record Apps	Subs	Gls
Derby Co	Burton A	06/97				
Carlisle U	L	03/99	98	6	0	0
Hull C	L	10/99	99	1	0	0
Macclesfield T	L	12/99	99	3	0	0
Oxford U	L	01/00	99	12	1	0
Oxford U	Tr	06/00	00-01	36	0	0
Colchester U	L	03/02	01	1	0	0
KNIGHT Terrie George						
Born: Camden, N London, England, 1 February, 1932						G
Aldershot (Am)	Alton T	10/58	58	4	-	0
KNIGHT Zatyiah (Zat)						
Born: Solihull, West Midlands, England, 2 May, 1980						CD
England: 2/U21-4						
Fulham	Rushall Olympic	02/99	01-07	140	10	3
Peterborough U	L	02/00	99	8	0	0
Aston Villa	Tr	08/07	07-08	38	2	2
Bolton W	Tr	08/09	09-13	157	11	4
Reading	Colorado Rapids (USA)	03/15	14	2	0	0
KNIGHT-PERCIVAL Nathaniel Lawrence (Nat)						
Born: Cambridge, England, 31 March, 1987						CD
England: Semi Pro-1						
Peterborough U	Wrexham	05/12	12-13	41	5	1
Shrewsbury T	Tr	05/14	14	28	0	1
KNIGHTON Kenneth (Ken)						
Born: Darton, South Yorkshire, England, 20 February, 1944						M
Wolverhampton W	App	02/61	64-66	13	3	0
Oldham Ath	Tr	11/66	66-67	45	0	4
Preston NE	Tr	11/67	67-68	62	0	4
Blackburn Rov	Tr	06/69	69-70	70	0	11
Hull C	Tr	03/71	70-72	79	1	9
Sheffield Wed	Tr	08/73	73-75	71	5	2
KNIGHTS Anthony Frank (Tony)						
Born: Grimsby, North Lincolnshire, England, 13 March, 1940						LH
Died: Cleethorpes, North Lincolnshire, England, 16 August, 2001						
Grimsby T	Jnr	06/58	59-63	75	-	1
Luton T	Tr	08/64	64	2	-	0
Aldershot	Tr	07/65	65	20	0	0
KNIGHTS Darryl James						
Born: Ipswich, England, 1 May, 1988						F
England: Youth						
Ipswich T	Sch	05/05	04	0	1	0
Yeovil T	L	02/07	06	0	4	0
Yeovil T	Tr	07/07	07	0	3	0
KNILL Alan Richard						
Born: Slough, Berkshire, England, 8 October, 1964						CD
Wales: 1/Youth						
Southampton	App	10/82				
Halifax T	Tr	07/84	84-86	118	0	6
Swansea C	Tr	08/87	87-88	89	0	3
Bury	Tr	08/89	89-93	141	3	9
Cardiff C	L	09/93	93	4	0	0
Scunthorpe U	Tr	11/93	93-96	131	0	8
Rotherham U	Tr	07/97	97-98	73	1	6
KNOCKAERT Anthony						
Born: Roubaix, France, 20 November, 1991						RW
France: U21-3/Youth						
Leicester C	EA Guingamp (FRA)	08/12	12-14	72	21	13
KNOTT Billy Steven						
Born: Canvey Island, Essex, England, 28 November, 1992						M
England: Youth						
Sunderland	Sch	01/11	12	0	1	0
AFC Wimbledon	L	01/12	11	14	6	3
Wycombe W	L	08/13	13	15	2	1
Port Vale	L	01/14	13	13	5	2
Bradford C	Tr	05/14	14	31	9	3
KNOTT Gareth Raymond						
Born: Blackwood, Caerphilly, Wales, 19 January, 1976						M
Wales: U21-1/Youth						
Tottenham H	YT	07/94				
Gillingham	L	02/95	94	5	0	0
KNOTT Herbert (Bert)						
Born: Goole, East Riding of Yorkshire, England, 5 December, 1914						IF
Died: Spilsby, Lincolnshire, England, June, 1986						
Brentford	Goole T	09/36				
Walsall	Brierley Hill Alliance	08/37	37	9	-	2
Hull C	Brierley Hill Alliance	10/40				
Bradford Park Ave	Tr	09/45				
Hull C	Tr	10/46	46	6	-	1

League Club	Source	Date Signed	Seasons Played	Career Record Apps	Subs	Gls
KNOTT William Francis (Billy)						
Born: Leeds, England, 16 March, 1934						IF
Died: Keighley, West Yorkshire, England, 17 November, 1996						
England: Youth						
Leeds U	Jnr	05/51				
Walsall	Tr	02/55	54	1	-	0
KNOWLES Cameron						
Born: Ripon, North Yorkshire, England, 19 September, 1969						M
Chesterfield	Sheffield Univ	08/93	93	1	0	0
KNOWLES Christopher James (Chris)						
Born: Stone, Staffordshire, England, 4 February, 1978						G
Chester C	Peterborough U (YT)	08/96	96	2	0	0
KNOWLES Cyril Barry						
Born: Fitzwilliam, West Yorkshire, England, 13 September, 1944						LB
Died: Middlesbrough, England, 31 August, 1991						
England: 4/FLge-1/U23-6						
Middlesbrough	Monckton CW	10/62	62-63	37	-	0
Tottenham H	Tr	05/64	64-75	402	1	15
KNOWLES Darren Thomas						
Born: Sheffield, England, 8 October, 1970						RB/M
Sheffield U	YT	07/89				
Stockport Co	Tr	09/89	89-92	51	12	0
Scarborough	Tr	08/93	93-96	139	5	2
Hartlepool U	Tr	03/97	96-00	164	4	2
KNOWLES Dominic Thomas						
Born: Accrington, Lancashire, England, 13 February, 1992						F
Burnley	Sch	06/10				
Burton A	Harrogate T	06/13	13-14	14	25	3
KNOWLES Harold Frederick (Harry)						
Born: Hednesford, Staffordshire, England, 6 September, 1932						LW
Walsall	Excelsior	09/50	50	9	-	1
Cardiff C	Worcester C	02/59	58-59	8	-	0
KNOWLES James (Jimmy)						
Born: Preston, Lancashire, England, 31 July, 1934						G
Preston NE	Jnr	10/57	57	2	-	0
Barrow	Tr	08/58	58-59	11	-	0
KNOWLES James Barry (Barry)						
Born: Wigan, Greater Manchester, England, 25 April, 1959						LB
Wigan Ath	Bangor C	10/84	84-87	124	3	3
KNOWLES John David (David)						
Born: Halifax, West Yorkshire, England, 11 April, 1941						G
Died: Brighouse, Yorkshire, England, 26 January, 2011						
Halifax T	Jnr	12/58	58-62	72	-	0
Bury	Tr	07/63	64	1	-	0
Bradford C	Tr	08/66	66	21	0	0
KNOWLES Peter						
Born: Fitzwilliam, West Yorkshire, England, 30 September, 1945						IF
England: U23-4/Youth						
Wolverhampton W	App	10/62	63-69	171	3	61
KNOWLES Raymond (Ray)						
Born: Willesden, NW London, England, 30 September, 1952						F
Wimbledon	Southall	07/78	78-79	31	8	6
KNOX James Hay (Jimmy)						
Born: Brechin, Angus, Scotland, 26 November, 1935						IF
Died: Coventry, England, 24 December, 2012						
Coventry C	Raith Rov	05/57	57	2	-	0
KNOX Robert Preston (Bobby)						
Born: Ulverston, Cumbria, England, 26 February, 1946						F/D
Died: Barrow, Cumbria, England, July, 2006						
Barrow	Jnr	07/65	64-71	94	14	19
KNOX Thomas (Tommy)						
Born: Glasgow, Scotland, 5 September, 1939						LW
Chelsea	East Stirlingshire	06/62	62-64	20	-	0
Newcastle U	Tr	02/65	64-66	24	1	1
Mansfield T	Tr	03/67	66-67	34	0	5
Northampton T	Tr	11/67	67-68	28	2	0
KNOX William Jess (Willie)						
Born: Kilmarnock, Ayrshire, Scotland, 9 September, 1937						WH
Scotland: Schools						
Barrow	Third Lanark	07/59	59	1	-	0
KOEJOE Samuel (Sammy)						
Born: Paramaribo, Suriname, 17 August, 1974						F
Queens Park Rgrs	RB Salzburg (AUT)	11/99	99-01	13	21	3

KOENEN Franciscus Leonardus Albertus (Frans)
Born: Waalwijk, Netherlands, 4 November, 1958 — M
Netherlands: U21

League Club	Source	Date Signed	Seasons Played	Apps	Subs	Gls
Newcastle U	NEC Nimegen (NED)	08/80	80	11	1	1

KOFFMAN Sidney John (Jack)
Born: Prestwich, Greater Manchester, England, 3 August, 1920 — LW
Died: Chelsea, W London, England, 1977

League Club	Source	Date Signed	Seasons Played	Apps	Subs	Gls
Manchester U	Northwich Victoria	08/45				
Hull C	Tr	06/46	46	4	-	0
Oldham Ath	Congleton T	06/47	47	3	-	0

KOLAR Martin
Born: Prague, Czech Republic, 18 September, 1983 — LW
Czech Republic: U21-8

League Club	Source	Date Signed	Seasons Played	Apps	Subs	Gls
Stoke C (L)	Anderlecht (BEL)	08/05	05	12	2	1

KOLAROV Aleksandar
Born: Belgrade, Yugoslavia, 10 November, 1985 — LB
Serbia: 55/U21-11

League Club	Source	Date Signed	Seasons Played	Apps	Subs	Gls
Manchester C	SS Lazio (ITA)	07/10	10-14	77	30	7

KOLINKO Alexanders (Alex)
Born: Riga, Latvia, 18 June, 1975 — G
Latvia: 88

League Club	Source	Date Signed	Seasons Played	Apps	Subs	Gls
Crystal Palace	Skonto Riga (LAT)	09/00	00-02	79	3	0

KOLKKA Joonas Einan
Born: Lahti, Finland, 28 September, 1974 — LW
Finland: 98

League Club	Source	Date Signed	Seasons Played	Apps	Subs	Gls
Crystal Palace	Borussia M'bach (GER)	07/04	04-05	21	5	3

KOMPANY Vincent Jean Mpoy
Born: Brussels, Belgium, 10 April, 1986 — CD
Belgium: 68/Youth

League Club	Source	Date Signed	Seasons Played	Apps	Subs	Gls
Manchester C	Hamburger SV (GER)	08/08	08-14	200	6	11

KONCHESKY Paul Martyn
Born: Barking, E London, England, 15 May, 1981 — LB
England: 2/U21-15/Youth

League Club	Source	Date Signed	Seasons Played	Apps	Subs	Gls
Charlton Ath	YT	05/98	97-04	91	58	5
Tottenham H	L	09/03	03	10	2	0
West Ham U	Tr	07/05	05-06	58	1	1
Fulham	Tr	07/07	07-10	97	0	2
Liverpool	Tr	08/10	10	15	0	0
Nottingham F	L	01/11	10	14	1	1
Leicester C	Tr	07/11	11-14	138	0	5

KONE Arouna
Born: Abidjan, Ivory Coast, 11 November, 1983 — F
Ivory Coast: 39

League Club	Source	Date Signed	Seasons Played	Apps	Subs	Gls
Wigan Ath	Sevilla (SPN)	08/12	12	32	2	11
Everton	Tr	07/13	13-14	7	10	1

KONJIC Muhamed
Born: Tuzla, Yugoslavia, 14 May, 1970 — CD
Bosnia & Herzegovina: 39

League Club	Source	Date Signed	Seasons Played	Apps	Subs	Gls
Coventry C	AS Monaco (FRA)	02/99	98-03	130	8	4
Derby Co	Tr	05/04	04	13	3	0

KONSTANTINIDIS Kostas
Born: Schorndorf, Germany, 31 August, 1972 — CD
Greece: 38

League Club	Source	Date Signed	Seasons Played	Apps	Subs	Gls
Bolton W (L)	Hertha Berlin (GER)	03/02	01	3	0	0

KONSTANTOPOULOS Dimitrios (Dimi)
Born: Thessalonika, Greece, 29 November, 1978 — G
Greece: 1/U21-9

League Club	Source	Date Signed	Seasons Played	Apps	Subs	Gls
Hartlepool U	SC Farense (POR)	01/04	04-06	117	0	0
Coventry C	Tr	07/07	07-09	23	1	0
Swansea C	L	10/08	08	4	0	0
Cardiff C	L	02/09	08	6	0	0
Middlesbrough	AEK Athens (GRE)	08/13	13-14	52	0	0

KONTE Amadou
Born: Bamako, Mali, 23 January, 1981 — F
Mali: Youth

League Club	Source	Date Signed	Seasons Played	Apps	Subs	Gls
Cambridge U	Paterno Calcio (ITA)	10/04	04	6	3	3

KOO-BOOTHE Nathan Djebril
Born: Westminster, Central London, England, 18 July, 1985 — CD

League Club	Source	Date Signed	Seasons Played	Apps	Subs	Gls
Watford	Hayes	02/03				
MK Dons	Tr	07/04	04	1	0	0

KOOGI Anders Bo
Born: Roskilde, Denmark, 8 September, 1979 — M
Denmark: Youth

League Club	Source	Date Signed	Seasons Played	Apps	Subs	Gls
Peterborough U	YT	07/97	98-99	0	2	0

KOORDES Rogier
Born: Haarlem, Netherlands, 13 June, 1972 — M

League Club	Source	Date Signed	Seasons Played	Apps	Subs	Gls
Port Vale	Telstar (NED)	02/97	96-98	29	9	0

KOPEL Frank
Born: Falkirk, Scotland, 28 March, 1949 — FB
Died: Kirriemuir, Angus, Scotland, 16 April, 2014
Scotland: Schools

League Club	Source	Date Signed	Seasons Played	Apps	Subs	Gls
Manchester U	Jnr	04/66	67-68	8	2	0
Blackburn Rov	Tr	03/69	68-71	23	2	0

KOPEL Scott Andrew
Born: Blackburn, Greater Manchester, England, 25 February, 1970 — M

League Club	Source	Date Signed	Seasons Played	Apps	Subs	Gls
Chesterfield	Dundee U	05/93	92	1	0	0

KOPTEFF Peter
Born: Helsinki, Finland, 10 April, 1979 — LW
Finland: 39

League Club	Source	Date Signed	Seasons Played	Apps	Subs	Gls
Stoke C	Viking Stavanger (NOR)	01/06	05	3	3	0

KORANTENG Nathan Papa Kwabena
Born: Hackney, E London, England, 26 May, 1992 — RW

League Club	Source	Date Signed	Seasons Played	Apps	Subs	Gls
Peterborough U	Sch	03/10	09	3	1	0

KOREN Robert
Born: Ljubljana, Slovenia, 20 September, 1980 — M
Slovenia: 61/U21-12

League Club	Source	Date Signed	Seasons Played	Apps	Subs	Gls
West Bromwich A	Lillestrom (NOR)	01/07	06-09	113	14	16
Hull C	Tr	08/10	10-13	127	16	28

KORNILENKO Sergei Aleksandrovich
Born: Vitebsk, Belarus, 14 June, 1983 — F
Belarus: 60/U21-17

League Club	Source	Date Signed	Seasons Played	Apps	Subs	Gls
Blackpool (L)	Zenit St P'burg (RUS)	01/11	10	3	3	0

KOROMA Omar Alieu
Born: Banjul, Gambia, 22 October, 1989 — F
Gambia: 2

League Club	Source	Date Signed	Seasons Played	Apps	Subs	Gls
Portsmouth	Banjul Hawks (GAM)	08/08				
Norwich C	L	08/08	08	2	3	0

KOROMAN Ognjien
Born: Belgrade, Yugoslavia, 19 September, 1978 — RW
Serbia: 36

League Club	Source	Date Signed	Seasons Played	Apps	Subs	Gls
Portsmouth	Terek Grozny (RUS)	01/06	05-06	1	3	1

KORSTEN Willem
Born: Boxtel, Netherlands, 21 January, 1975 — M
Netherlands: U21

League Club	Source	Date Signed	Seasons Played	Apps	Subs	Gls
Leeds U (L)	Vitesse Arnhem (NED)	01/99	98	4	3	2
Tottenham H	Vitesse Arnhem (NED)	07/99	99-00	12	11	3

KOSCIELNY Laurent
Born: Tulle, France, 10 September, 1985 — CD
France: 23

League Club	Source	Date Signed	Seasons Played	Apps	Subs	Gls
Arsenal	Lorient (FRA)	07/10	10-14	141	6	11

KOSKELA Toni
Born: Helsinki, Finland, 16 February, 1983 — M
Finland: U21-5/Youth

League Club	Source	Date Signed	Seasons Played	Apps	Subs	Gls
Cardiff C	Koo Tee Pee (FIN)	01/05	04	0	2	0

KOSMINA Alexander John (John)
Born: Adelaide, Australia, 17 August, 1956 — F
Australia: 60

League Club	Source	Date Signed	Seasons Played	Apps	Subs	Gls
Arsenal	Adelaide C (AUS)	03/78	78	0	1	0

KOSOWSKI Kamil
Born: Ostrawiecz, Poland, 30 August, 1977 — M
Poland: 54/U21-15

League Club	Source	Date Signed	Seasons Played	Apps	Subs	Gls
Southampton (L)	Wisla Krakow (POL)	08/05	05	12	6	1

KOTTILA Mika
Born: Helsinki, Finland, 22 September, 1974 — F
Finland: 31

League Club	Source	Date Signed	Seasons Played	Apps	Subs	Gls
Hereford U (L)	Rovaniemi (FIN)	11/96	96	11	2	1

KOTWICA Zachariah Jozef (Zach)
Born: Gloucester, England, 17 January, 1996 — W

League Club	Source	Date Signed	Seasons Played	Apps	Subs	Gls
Cheltenham T	Sch	08/13	13-14	9	26	2

KOUMANTARAKIS Georgios (George)
Born: Athens, Greece, 27 March, 1974 — F
South Africa: 13

League Club	Source	Date Signed	Seasons Played	Apps	Subs	Gls
Preston NE	FC Basel (SUI)	01/03	02-03	11	6	4

KOUMAS Jason
Born: Wrexham, Wales, 25 September, 1979 — M
Wales: 34

League Club	Source	Date Signed	Seasons Played	Apps	Subs	Gls
Tranmere Rov	YT	11/97	98-02	96	31	25
West Bromwich A	Tr	08/02	02-06	103	20	23

League Club	Source	Date Signed	Seasons Played	Apps	Subs	Gls
Cardiff C	L	08/05	05	42	2	12
Wigan Ath	Tr	07/07	07-09	32	22	2
Cardiff C	L	08/10	10	5	18	2
Tranmere Rov	Rtd	08/13	13-14	32	19	3

KOUYATE Cheikhou
Born: Dakar, Senegal, 21 December, 1989 — DM
Senegal: 17/Youth

League Club	Source	Date Signed	Seasons Played	Apps	Subs	Gls
West Ham U	Anderlecht (BEL)	06/14	14	30	1	4

KOVAC Radoslav
Born: Prague, Czech Republic, 27 November, 1979 — M
Czech Republic: 31/U21-15

League Club	Source	Date Signed	Seasons Played	Apps	Subs	Gls
West Ham U	Spartak Moscow (RUS)	02/09	08-10	42	11	3

KOVACEVIC Darko
Born: Kovin, Yugoslavia, 18 November, 1973 — F
Yugoslavia:

League Club	Source	Date Signed	Seasons Played	Apps	Subs	Gls
Sheffield Wed	R Star Belgrade (YUG)	12/95	95	8	8	4

KOVACS Janos
Born: Budapest, Hungary, 11 September, 1985 — CD

League Club	Source	Date Signed	Seasons Played	Apps	Subs	Gls
Chesterfield	MTK Budapest (HUN)	08/05	05-07	55	2	2
Lincoln C	Tr	07/08	08-09	59	0	4
Hereford U	Luton T	07/10	10	21	4	2

KOWALSKI Andrew Michael (Andy)
Born: Warsop, Nottinghamshire, England, 26 February, 1953 — M

League Club	Source	Date Signed	Seasons Played	Apps	Subs	Gls
Chesterfield	Worksop T	02/73	72-82	354	11	30
Doncaster Rov	Tr	07/83	83-84	45	7	1
Peterborough U	Tr	08/85	85	35	0	3
Chesterfield	Burton A	08/86	86	19	9	1

KOWENICKI Ryszard Stefan
Born: Lodz, Poland, 22 December, 1948 — M

League Club	Source	Date Signed	Seasons Played	Apps	Subs	Gls
Oldham Ath	Widzew Lodz (POL)	12/79	79-80	40	2	5

KOZAK Jan
Born: Kosice, Slovakia, 22 April, 1980 — W
Slovakia: 25

League Club	Source	Date Signed	Seasons Played	Apps	Subs	Gls
West Bromwich A (L)	Slov Bratislava (SVK)	01/06	05	4	2	0

KOZAK Libor
Born: Opava, Czech Republic, 30 May, 1989 — F
Czech Republic: 8/U21-14/Youth

League Club	Source	Date Signed	Seasons Played	Apps	Subs	Gls
Aston Villa	SS Lazio (ITA)	09/13	13	8	6	4

KOZLUK Robert (Robbie)
Born: Sutton-in-Ashfield, Nottinghamshire, England, 5 August, 1977 — RB
England: U21-2

League Club	Source	Date Signed	Seasons Played	Apps	Subs	Gls
Derby Co	YT	02/96	97-98	9	7	0
Sheffield U	Tr	03/99	98-06	193	20	2
Huddersfield T	L	09/00	00	14	0	0
Preston NE	L	01/05	04	0	1	0
Barnsley	Tr	07/07	07-09	72	3	0
Sheffield U	Tr	07/10	10	2	6	1
Port Vale	Tr	09/11	11	4	2	0
Bradford C	Tr	01/12	11	17	0	0

KOZMA Istvan
Born: Paszto, Hungary, 3 December, 1964 — M
Hungary: 40//Scotland: SLge-1

League Club	Source	Date Signed	Seasons Played	Apps	Subs	Gls
Liverpool	Dunfermline Ath	02/92	91-92	3	3	0

KPEKAWA Cole Desmond
Born: Blackpool, Lancashire, England, 20 May, 1996 — LB

League Club	Source	Date Signed	Seasons Played	Apps	Subs	Gls
Queens Park Rgrs	Sch	04/14	14	0	1	0
Colchester U	L	11/14	14	3	1	0
Portsmouth	L	03/15	14	2	0	0

KRAAY Hans
Born: Utrecht, Netherlands, 22 December, 1959 — DM

League Club	Source	Date Signed	Seasons Played	Apps	Subs	Gls
Brighton & HA	NAC Breda (NED)	02/84	83-84	19	4	3

KRAMARIC Andrej
Born: Zagreb, Croatia, 19 June, 1991 — F
Croatia: 6/U21-9/Youth

League Club	Source	Date Signed	Seasons Played	Apps	Subs	Gls
Leicester C	NK Rijeka (CRO)	01/15	14	6	7	2

KRANJCAR Niko
Born: Vienna, Austria, 13 August, 1984 — LM
Croatia: 81/U21-15/Youth

League Club	Source	Date Signed	Seasons Played	Apps	Subs	Gls
Portsmouth	Hajduk Split (CRO)	08/06	06-09	62	21	9
Tottenham H	Tr	08/09	09-11	30	19	9
Queens Park Rgrs (L)	Dynamo Kiev (UKR)	09/13	13	21	8	2
Queens Park Rgrs (L)	Dynamo Kiev (UKR)	09/14	14	11	11	2

KRAUSE James Richard (Jamie)
Born: Haverhill, Suffolk, England, 9 January, 1987 — LB

League Club	Source	Date Signed	Seasons Played	Apps	Subs	Gls
Ipswich T	Sch	07/06				
Carlisle U	L	11/06	06	3	0	0

KRETZSCHMAR Max Alexander
Born: Kingston-on-Thames, SW London, England, 12 October, 1993 — W

League Club	Source	Date Signed	Seasons Played	Apps	Subs	Gls
Wycombe W	Sch	05/12	13-14	29	22	6

KRISTENSEN Bjorn
Born: Aarhus, Denmark, 10 October, 1963 — M
Denmark: 20/U21-12

League Club	Source	Date Signed	Seasons Played	Apps	Subs	Gls
Newcastle U	Aarhus GF (DEN)	03/89	88-91	69	11	4
Bristol C	L	11/92	92	4	0	0
Portsmouth	Tr	03/93	92-94	56	15	1

KRISTINSSON Birkir
Born: Vestmannaeyjar, Iceland, 15 March, 1964 — G
Iceland: 74

League Club	Source	Date Signed	Seasons Played	Apps	Subs	Gls
Stoke C	IBV (ICE)	11/00	00	18	0	0

KRIZAN Ales
Born: Maribor, Slovenia, 25 July, 1971 — CD
Slovenia: 25

League Club	Source	Date Signed	Seasons Played	Apps	Subs	Gls
Barnsley	Branik Maribor (SVN)	07/97	97-98	13	0	0

KROLDRUP Per Billeskov
Born: Viborg, Denmark, 31 July, 1979 — CD
Denmark: 33

League Club	Source	Date Signed	Seasons Played	Apps	Subs	Gls
Everton	Udinese (ITA)	07/05	05	1	0	0

KROMHEER Elroy Patrick
Born: Amsterdam, Netherlands, 15 January, 1970 — CD

League Club	Source	Date Signed	Seasons Played	Apps	Subs	Gls
Reading	PEC Zwolle (NED)	08/98	98	11	0	0

KROMKAMP Jan
Born: Heerenveen, Netherlands, 17 August, 1980 — RB
Netherlands: 16

League Club	Source	Date Signed	Seasons Played	Apps	Subs	Gls
Liverpool	Villarreal (SPN)	01/06	05-06	7	7	0

KRUL Timothy Michael (Tim)
Born: Den Haag, Netherlands, 3 April, 1988 — G
Netherlands: 7/U21-12/Youth

League Club	Source	Date Signed	Seasons Played	Apps	Subs	Gls
Newcastle U	ADO Den Haag (NED)	08/05	09-14	149	3	0
Carlisle U	L	11/08	08	9	0	0

KRUSE Patrick Karl (Pat)
Born: Arlesey, Bedfordshire, England, 30 November, 1953 — CD

League Club	Source	Date Signed	Seasons Played	Apps	Subs	Gls
Leicester C	App	11/71	73	2	0	0
Mansfield T	L	09/74	74	6	0	1
Torquay U	Tr	03/75	74-76	79	0	4
Brentford	Tr	03/77	76-81	186	0	12
Northampton T	L	02/82	81	18	0	0

KRUSZYNSKI Zbigniew (Detsi)
Born: Tczew, Poland, 14 October, 1961 — M

League Club	Source	Date Signed	Seasons Played	Apps	Subs	Gls
Wimbledon	FC08 Homburg (GER)	12/88	88-91	65	6	4
Brentford	L	03/92	91	8	0	0
Brentford	Tr	08/92	92	5	1	0
Coventry C	Saarbrucken (GER)	09/93	93	1	1	0
Peterborough U	Tr	12/93	93	2	1	0

KRYSIAK Artur Lukasz
Born: Lodz, Poland, 11 August, 1989 — G
Poland: Youth

League Club	Source	Date Signed	Seasons Played	Apps	Subs	Gls
Birmingham C	Sch	09/06				
Swansea C	L	09/08	08	2	0	0
Burton A	L	08/09	09	38	0	0
Exeter C	Tr	07/10	10-13	127	0	0
Yeovil T	Tr	06/14	14	15	0	0

KRZYWICKI Ryszard Lech (Dick)
Born: Penley, Wrexham, Wales, 2 February, 1947 — RW
Wales: 8/U23-8

League Club	Source	Date Signed	Seasons Played	Apps	Subs	Gls
West Bromwich A	App	02/65	64-69	51	6	9
Huddersfield T	Tr	03/70	69-73	39	8	7
Scunthorpe U	L	02/73	72	2	0	0
Northampton T	L	11/73	73	8	0	3
Lincoln C	Tr	07/74	74-75	55	13	11

KUBICKI Dariusz Jan
Born: Kozuchow, Poland, 6 June, 1963 — FB
Poland: 46

League Club	Source	Date Signed	Seasons Played	Apps	Subs	Gls
Aston Villa	Legia Warsaw (POL)	08/91	91-93	24	1	0
Sunderland	Tr	03/94	93-96	135	1	0
Wolverhampton W	Tr	08/97	97	12	0	0
Tranmere Rov	L	03/98	97	12	0	0
Carlisle U	Tr	07/98	98	7	0	0
Darlington	Tr	10/98	98	2	1	0

KUBICKI Eryk
Born: Nysa, Poland, 18 August, 1925 — W

League Club	Source	Date Signed	Seasons Played	Apps	Subs	Gls
York C (Am)	Polish Army (POL)	10/46	46	5	-	0

KUDJODJI Ebenezer Joseph Tettley (Ben)
Born: Dunstable, Bedfordshire, England, 23 April, 1989 — F

League Club	Source	Date Signed	Seasons Played	Apps	Subs	Gls
Crystal Palace	Sch	07/07	07	0	1	0

KUDUZOVIC Fahrudin
Born: Vlasenica, Yugoslavia, 10 October, 1984 — M

League Club	Source	Date Signed	Seasons Played	Apps	Subs	Gls
Notts Co	Derby Co (Sch)	09/04	04	0	3	0

KUHL Aaron John
Born: Paulton, Somerset, England, 30 January, 1996 — M
England: Youth

League Club	Source	Date Signed	Seasons Played	Apps	Subs	Gls
Reading	Sch	12/13	14	3	3	0

KUHL Martin
Born: Frimley, Surrey, England, 10 January, 1965 — M

League Club	Source	Date Signed	Seasons Played	Apps	Subs	Gls
Birmingham C	App	01/83	82-86	103	8	5
Sheffield U	Tr	03/87	86-87	38	0	4
Watford	Tr	02/88	87	4	0	0
Portsmouth	Tr	09/88	88-92	146	11	27
Derby Co	Tr	09/92	92-94	68	0	1
Notts Co	L	09/94	94	2	0	0
Bristol C	Tr	12/94	94-96	85	9	7

KUIPERS Michel
Born: Amsterdam, Netherlands, 26 June, 1974 — G

League Club	Source	Date Signed	Seasons Played	Apps	Subs	Gls
Bristol Rov	SDW Amsterdam (NED)	01/99	98	1	0	0
Brighton & HA	Tr	07/00	00-09	246	1	0
Hull C	L	08/03	03	3	0	0
Boston U	L	11/05	05	4	0	0
Boston U	L	03/06	05	11	0	0
Crawley T	Tr	07/10	11	15	0	0

KULCSAR Giorgy (George)
Born: Budapest, Hungary, 12 August, 1967 — DM
Australia: 3

League Club	Source	Date Signed	Seasons Played	Apps	Subs	Gls
Bradford C	Royal Antwerp (BEL)	03/97	96-97	23	3	1
Queens Park Rgrs	Tr	12/97	97-00	42	14	1

KULKOV Vasili Sergeyevich
Born: Moscow, Russia, 11 June, 1966 — M
Russia: 21//Soviet Union: 21

League Club	Source	Date Signed	Seasons Played	Apps	Subs	Gls
Millwall (L)	FC Porto (POR)	01/96	95	6	0	0

KUQI Njazi
Born: Vushtrri, Kosovo, 25 March, 1983 — F
Finland: 12/U21-8

League Club	Source	Date Signed	Seasons Played	Apps	Subs	Gls
Birmingham C	FC Lahti (FIN)	01/05				
Blackpool	L	01/06	05	1	3	0
Peterborough U	L	03/06	05	1	0	0
Stevenage	TUS Koblenz (GER)	08/10	10	0	1	0

KUQI Shefki
Born: Vushtrri, Kosovo, 10 November, 1976 — F
Finland: 62

League Club	Source	Date Signed	Seasons Played	Apps	Subs	Gls
Stockport Co	FC Jokerit (FIN)	01/01	00-01	32	3	11
Sheffield Wed	Tr	01/02	01-03	58	6	19
Ipswich T	Tr	09/03	03-04	69	10	30
Blackburn Rov	Tr	06/05	05-06	15	19	7
Crystal Palace	Tr	08/06	06-08	46	32	17
Fulham	L	08/07	07	3	7	0
Ipswich T	L	03/08	07	2	2	0
Swansea C	TUS Koblenz (GER)	01/10	09-10	14	8	5
Derby Co	L	09/10	10	8	4	2
Newcastle U	Tr	02/11	10	0	6	0
Oldham Ath	Tr	08/11	11	39	1	11

KURILA John
Born: Glasgow, Scotland, 10 April, 1941 — WH

League Club	Source	Date Signed	Seasons Played	Apps	Subs	Gls
Northampton T	Glasgow Celtic	08/62	62	40	-	1
Bristol C	Tr	08/63	63	6	-	0
Northampton T	Tr	11/63	63-67	105	3	3
Southend U	Tr	07/68	68-69	87	1	1
Colchester U	Tr	05/70	70-71	53	0	4
Lincoln C	Tr	12/71	71	23	1	0

KURUCZ Peter
Born: Budapest, Hungary, 30 May, 1988 — G
Hungary: U21-11

League Club	Source	Date Signed	Seasons Played	Apps	Subs	Gls
West Ham U	Ujpest (HUN)	02/09	09	0	1	0
Rochdale	L	01/12	11	11	0	0

KURZ Frederick John (Fred)
Born: Grimsby, North Lincolnshire, England, 3 September, 1918 — CF
Died: Grimsby, North Lincolnshire, England, 28 November, 1978

League Club	Source	Date Signed	Seasons Played	Apps	Subs	Gls
Grimsby T	Grimsby YMCA	05/36	38	3	-	0
Crystal Palace	Tr	12/45	46-50	148	-	48

KUS Marcin Robert
Born: Warsaw, Poland, 2 September, 1981 — RB
Poland: 7

League Club	Source	Date Signed	Seasons Played	Apps	Subs	Gls
Queens Park Rgrs (L)	Lech Poznan (POL)	01/06	05	3	0	0

KUSUNGA Genseric
Born: Geneva, Switzerland, 12 March, 1988 — CD
Angola: 9

League Club	Source	Date Signed	Seasons Played	Apps	Subs	Gls
Oldham Ath	FC Basel (SUI)	09/13	13-14	30	6	2

KUSZCZAK Tomasz
Born: Krosno Odrzanskie, Poland, 20 March, 1982 — G
Poland: 11/U21-14/Youth

League Club	Source	Date Signed	Seasons Played	Apps	Subs	Gls
West Bromwich A	Hertha Berlin (GER)	08/04	04-05	30	1	0
Manchester U	Tr	08/06	06-11	30	2	0
Watford	L	02/12	11	13	0	0
Brighton & HA	Tr	07/12	12-13	84	0	0
Wolverhampton W		11/14	14	13	0	0

KUYT Dirk
Born: Katwijk, Netherlands, 22 July, 1980 — F
Netherlands: 104

League Club	Source	Date Signed	Seasons Played	Apps	Subs	Gls
Liverpool	Feyenoord (NED)	08/06	06-11	176	32	51

KVARME Bjorn Tore
Born: Trondheim, Norway, 17 June, 1972 — CD
Norway: 1/U21-11

League Club	Source	Date Signed	Seasons Played	Apps	Subs	Gls
Liverpool	Rosenborg (NOR)	01/97	96-98	39	6	0

KVIST William
Born: Aarhus, Denmark, 24 February, 1985 — DM
Denmark: 57/U21-5/Youth

League Club	Source	Date Signed	Seasons Played	Apps	Subs	Gls
Fulham (L)	VfB Stuttgart (GER)	01/14	13	7	1	0
Wigan Ath	VfB Stuttgart (GER)	09/14	14	18	8	0

KWIATKOWSKI Richard (Dick)
Born: Peterborough, England, 7 April, 1948 — M/FB

League Club	Source	Date Signed	Seasons Played	Apps	Subs	Gls
Peterborough U	Jnr	07/67	67-71	49	11	0

KYD Michael Robert
Born: Hackney, E London, England, 21 May, 1977 — F

League Club	Source	Date Signed	Seasons Played	Apps	Subs	Gls
Cambridge U	YT	05/95	94-99	88	36	23

KYDD David Richard
Born: Penge, S London, England, 22 December, 1945 — WH

League Club	Source	Date Signed	Seasons Played	Apps	Subs	Gls
Brighton & HA	App	09/63	65	2	0	0

KYLE Kevin Alistair
Born: Stranraer, Dumfries & Galloway, Scotland, 7 June, 1981 — F
Scotland: 10/B-3/U21-12

League Club	Source	Date Signed	Seasons Played	Apps	Subs	Gls
Sunderland	Ayr Boswell	09/98	00-06	59	32	11
Huddersfield T	L	09/00	00	0	4	0
Darlington	L	11/00	00	5	0	1
Rochdale	L	01/01	00	3	3	0
Coventry C	Tr	08/06	06-07	25	19	5
Wolverhampton W	L	01/08	07	3	9	1
Hartlepool U	L	10/08	08	15	0	5

KYLE Maurice
Born: Darlington, County Durham, England, 8 November, 1937 — CH
Died: Oxford, England, 16 January, 1981

League Club	Source	Date Signed	Seasons Played	Apps	Subs	Gls
Wolverhampton W	Jnr	09/55				
Oxford U	Tr	02/59	62-69	275	0	2
Southend U	L	03/70	69	8	0	0

KYNMAN David John
Born: Hull, England, 20 May, 1962 — M

League Club	Source	Date Signed	Seasons Played	Apps	Subs	Gls
Hull C	App	05/80	80-81	11	0	0

KYRATZOGLOU Alexandros Bassilios (Alex)
Born: Armidale, NSW, Australia, 27 August, 1974 — F

League Club	Source	Date Signed	Seasons Played	Apps	Subs	Gls
Oldham Ath	AEK Athens (GRE)	10/97	97	0	1	0

KYRGIAKOS Sotirios
Born: Trikala, Greece, 23 July, 1979 — CD
Greece: 61/U21-9

League Club	Source	Date Signed	Seasons Played	Apps	Subs	Gls
Liverpool	AEK Athens (GRE)	08/09	09-10	23	7	3
Sunderland (L)	VfL Wolfsburg (GER)	01/12	11	2	1	0

KYZERIDIS Nicos
Born: Thessalonika, Greece, 20 April, 1971 — M
Greece: 1

League Club	Source	Date Signed	Seasons Played	Apps	Subs	Gls
Portsmouth	Paniliakos (GRE)	07/98	98	2	2	0

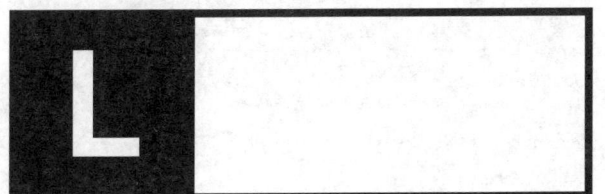

League Club	Source	Date Signed	Seasons Played	Career Record Apps	Subs	Gls

LABADIE Joss Christopher
Born: Croydon, S London, England, 31 August, 1990 M

League Club	Source	Date Signed	Seasons Played	Apps	Subs	Gls
West Bromwich A	Sch	07/08				
Shrewsbury T	L	01/09	08	1	0	0
Shrewsbury T	L	08/09	09	11	2	5
Cheltenham T	L	11/09	09	11	0	0
Tranmere Rov	Tr	03/10	09-11	43	27	10
Notts Co	Tr	07/12	12-13	23	16	3
Torquay U	L	03/13	12	7	0	4
Torquay U	Tr	01/14	13	10	0	1
Dagenham & Red	Tr	07/14	14	16	8	2

LABANT Vladimir
Born: Cadca, Czechoslovakia, 8 June, 1974 LB
Slovakia: 27

League Club	Source	Date Signed	Seasons Played	Apps	Subs	Gls
West Ham U	Sparta Prague (CZE)	01/02	01-02	7	6	0

LABARTHE Albert Gianfranco Tome (Gianfranco)
Born: Lima, Peru, 20 September, 1984 F
Peru: Youth

League Club	Source	Date Signed	Seasons Played	Apps	Subs	Gls
Huddersfield T	Sport Boys (PER)	01/03	02	0	3	0
Derby Co	Tr	08/03	03	0	3	0

LABONE Brian Leslie
Born: Liverpool, England, 23 January, 1940 CH
Died: Liverpool, England, 24 April, 2006
England: 26/FLge-5/U23-7

League Club	Source	Date Signed	Seasons Played	Apps	Subs	Gls
Everton	Jnr	07/57	57-71	451	0	2

LACEY Alexander Lawrence (Alex)
Born: Milton Keynes, England, 31 May, 1993 CD

League Club	Source	Date Signed	Seasons Played	Apps	Subs	Gls
Luton T	Sch	11/10	14	10	8	0

LACEY Anthony John (Tony)
Born: Leek, Staffordshire, England, 18 March, 1944 M/FB

League Club	Source	Date Signed	Seasons Played	Apps	Subs	Gls
Stoke C	Leek County School OB	10/65	67-68	2	2	0
Port Vale	Tr	02/70	69-74	194	7	9
Rochdale	Tr	07/75	75-76	83	0	0

LACEY Damien James
Born: Bridgend, Wales, 3 August, 1977 M/RB

League Club	Source	Date Signed	Seasons Played	Apps	Subs	Gls
Swansea C	YT	07/96	96-02	75	29	2

LACEY Desmond (Des)
Born: Dublin, Republic of Ireland, 3 August, 1925 RW
Died: Chester, England, 1974

League Club	Source	Date Signed	Seasons Played	Apps	Subs	Gls
Chester C (Am)	Jnr	07/46	46	1	-	0

LACEY William (Bill)
Born: Tynemouth, Tyne and Wear, England, 17 November, 1931 CF
Died: Reading, England, 9 May, 1988

League Club	Source	Date Signed	Seasons Played	Apps	Subs	Gls
Middlesbrough	North Shields YMCA	05/52				
Aldershot	Tr	02/53	52-58	210	-	59
Reading	Tr	07/59	59-62	90	-	40

LACK Harry
Born: Bolsover, Derbyshire, England, 29 November, 1930 LW

League Club	Source	Date Signed	Seasons Played	Apps	Subs	Gls
Leeds U	Mansfield T (Am)	07/51				
Blackburn Rov	Tr	08/52				
Chesterfield	Tr	08/53	53	1	-	0

LACKENBY George
Born: Newcastle-upon-Tyne, England, 22 May, 1931 D
Died: Newcastle-upon-Tyne, England, 3 April, 2004

League Club	Source	Date Signed	Seasons Played	Apps	Subs	Gls
Newcastle U	Jnr	10/50	51-56	19	-	0
Exeter C	Tr	12/56	56	24	-	4
Carlisle U	Tr	07/57	57-58	46	-	0
Gateshead	Tr	07/59	59	43	-	2
Hartlepool U	Tr	08/60	60-62	86	-	1

LACY John
Born: Liverpool, England, 14 August, 1951 CD

League Club	Source	Date Signed	Seasons Played	Apps	Subs	Gls
Fulham	Kingstonian	06/71	72-77	164	4	7
Tottenham H	Tr	07/78	78-82	99	5	2
Crystal Palace	Tr	08/83	83	24	3	0

LACZKO Zsolt
Born: Szeged, Hungary, 18 December, 1986 LB/M
Hungary: 22/U21-5

League Club	Source	Date Signed	Seasons Played	Apps	Subs	Gls
Leicester C	Olympiakos (GRE)	01/08	07	5	4	0

League Club	Source	Date Signed	Seasons Played	Career Record Apps	Subs	Gls

LADAPO Olayinka Fredrick Oladotun (Freddie)
Born: Romford, E London, England, 1 February, 1993 F

League Club	Source	Date Signed	Seasons Played	Apps	Subs	Gls
Colchester U	Sch	03/12	12-13	0	6	0

LADD Ian Martin
Born: Peterborough, England, 22 November, 1958 CD

League Club	Source	Date Signed	Seasons Played	Apps	Subs	Gls
Notts Co	Peterborough U (NC)	09/77	77	1	0	0

LAFAYETTE Ross
Born: Watford, Hertfordshire, England, 22 November, 1985 F

League Club	Source	Date Signed	Seasons Played	Apps	Subs	Gls
Luton T	Welling U	06/14	14	1	10	0

LAFFERTY Daniel
Born: Derry, Northern Ireland, 1 April, 1989 LB
Northern Ireland: 12/B-1/U21-6

League Club	Source	Date Signed	Seasons Played	Apps	Subs	Gls
Burnley	Derry C (ROI)	01/12	11-14	34	6	0
Rotherham U	L	03/15	14	11	0	0

LAFFERTY Kyle
Born: Enniskillen, Fermanagh, Northern Ireland, 21 July, 1987 F
Northern Ireland: 44/U21-2

League Club	Source	Date Signed	Seasons Played	Apps	Subs	Gls
Burnley	Sch	12/05	05-07	52	31	10
Darlington	L	01/06	05	9	0	3
Norwich C	Palermo (ITA)	07/14	14	11	7	1

LAHTINEN Aki Arimo
Born: Jyvaskyla, Finland, 31 October, 1958 CD
Finland: 56

League Club	Source	Date Signed	Seasons Played	Apps	Subs	Gls
Notts Co	Oulu Palloseura (FIN)	09/81	81-84	37	8	2

LAIDLAW John
Born: Aldershot, Hampshire, England, 5 July, 1936 RB

League Club	Source	Date Signed	Seasons Played	Apps	Subs	Gls
Colchester U	Easthouses Lily MW	06/57	59-60	41	-	1

LAIDLAW Joseph Daniel (Joe)
Born: Whickham, Tyne and Wear, England, 12 July, 1950 M/F

League Club	Source	Date Signed	Seasons Played	Apps	Subs	Gls
Middlesbrough	App	08/67	67-71	104	5	20
Carlisle U	Tr	07/72	72-75	146	5	44
Doncaster Rov	Tr	06/76	76-78	127	1	27
Portsmouth	Tr	06/79	79-80	60	0	19
Hereford U	Tr	12/80	80-81	61	1	8
Mansfield T	Tr	07/82	82	4	0	0

LAIDLER John Ralph (Jackie)
Born: Windermere, Cumbria, England, 5 January, 1919 LW
Died: Kendal, Cumbria, England, 8 October, 2009

League Club	Source	Date Signed	Seasons Played	Apps	Subs	Gls
Barrow	Windermere	09/36	36-38	40	-	6
Carlisle U	Netherfield	06/46	46	27	-	3

LAIDMAN Frederick (Fred)
Born: Durham, England, 20 June, 1913 IF
Died: Durham, England, June, 1987

League Club	Source	Date Signed	Seasons Played	Apps	Subs	Gls
Everton	Wigan Ath	12/36				
Bristol C	Tr	06/38	38	10	-	1
Darlington	Stockton	07/48	49	2	-	0

LAIGHT Ellis Stanley
Born: Birmingham, England, 30 June, 1976 F

League Club	Source	Date Signed	Seasons Played	Apps	Subs	Gls
Torquay U	YT	07/95	93-96	18	23	3

LAIGHT Ryan David
Born: Barnsley, South Yorkshire, England, 16 November, 1985 CD

League Club	Source	Date Signed	Seasons Played	Apps	Subs	Gls
Barnsley	Sch	07/05	05	0	1	0

LAING David (Davie)
Born: Strathmiglo, Fife, Scotland, 20 February, 1925 LH
Scotland: SLge-3

League Club	Source	Date Signed	Seasons Played	Apps	Subs	Gls
Gillingham	Hibernian	08/57	57-58	82	-	5

LAING James Frederick (Freddie)
Born: Glasgow, Scotland, 25 February, 1920 IF
Died: Glasgow, Scotland, 12 May, 1975

League Club	Source	Date Signed	Seasons Played	Apps	Subs	Gls
Luton T	Ashfield Jnrs	06/38				
Middlesbrough	Shelbourne (ROI)	07/47				
Bristol Rov	Tr	07/48	48	2	-	0

LAING Louis Mark
Born: Newcastle-upon-Tyne, England, 6 March, 1993 CD
England: Youth

League Club	Source	Date Signed	Seasons Played	Apps	Subs	Gls
Sunderland	Sch	03/10	10	0	1	0
Wycombe W	L	01/12	11	10	1	0
Nottingham F	Tr	06/14				
Notts Co	L	09/14	14	10	0	0

LAING Robert Smith (Bobby)
Born: Glasgow, Scotland, 1 February, 1925 LW
Died: Birmingham, England, September, 1985

League Club	Source	Date Signed	Seasons Played	Apps	Subs	Gls
Birmingham C	Falkirk	03/46	47-49	19	-	2
Watford	Tr	06/50	50-51	60	-	8

League Club	Source	Date Signed	Seasons Played	Career Record Apps	Subs	Gls

LAINTON Robert Paul (Rob)
Born: Ashton-under-Lyne, Greater Manchester, England, 12 October, 1989 G

Bolton W	Sch	07/09				
Bury	Tr	07/13	13-14	21	0	0
Burton A	L	02/14	13	14	0	0

LAIRD Alexander (Alex)
Born: Newmains, Lanarkshire, Scotland, 2 June, 1926 RW

Chelsea	Stirling A	11/51				
Notts Co	Tr	07/53	53	1	-	0

LAIRD Alexander Watson (Alec)
Born: Edinburgh, Scotland, 23 October, 1928 FB

Barrow	Dunfermline Ath	11/57	57	22	-	0
Scunthorpe U	Tr	08/58				

LAIRD David Sands
Born: Rutherglen, Glasgow, Scotland, 11 February, 1936 IF

Aldershot	St Mirren	07/57				
Northampton T	St Mirren	06/60	60	12	-	1

LAIRD David Wilson (Davie)
Born: Clackmannan, Stirlingshire, Scotland, 9 May, 1926 RH/IF
Died: Falkirk, Scotland, 7 November, 1999

Aldershot	Alloa Ath	05/48	48-53	127	-	22

LAIRD Kamu
Born: Port of Spain, Trinidad, 23 December, 1975 F
Trinidad & Tobago: 23

Chester C	Dulwich Hamlet	12/99	99	2	1	1

LAIRD Marc James Peter
Born: Edinburgh, Scotland, 23 January, 1986 M

Manchester C	Sch	01/04				
Northampton T	L	01/07	06	2	4	0
Port Vale	L	11/07	07	7	0	1
Millwall	Tr	01/08	07-10	63	13	6
Brentford	L	01/11	10	4	0	1
Walsall	L	03/11	10	8	0	0
Leyton Orient	Tr	08/11	11-12	11	12	2
Southend U	Tr	10/12	12-13	31	11	1
Tranmere Rov	Tr	07/14	14	27	7	1

LAIRD Scott Benjamin
Born: Bridgwater, Somerset, England, 15 May, 1988 LB
England: Semi Pro-1//Scotland: Youth

Plymouth Arg	Sch	07/06				
Stevenage	Tr	01/08	10-11	88	2	12
Preston NE	Tr	07/12	12-14	77	7	5

LAISBY Jonathan (John)
Born: Ulverston, Cumbria, England, 27 March, 1957 G

Liverpool	App	04/75				
Workington	Barrow	03/77	76	2	0	0

LAITT David John
Born: Colchester, Essex, England, 1 November, 1946 FB

Colchester U	Colchester Casuals	08/65	65	0	1	0

LAKE Huw Gilwyn Taylor
Born: Swansea, Wales, 20 August, 1963 M
Wales: Schools

Swansea C	App	08/81	82-83	14	5	2

LAKE Leslie Eric (Les)
Born: Luton, England, 29 January, 1923 FB
Died: Albuquerque, New Mexico, USA, 1976

Luton T	Holly Rgrs	09/41	46-50	59	-	0

LAKE Michael Charles (Mike)
Born: Manchester, England, 16 November, 1966 M
England: Semi Pro-1

Sheffield U	Macclesfield T	10/89	89-92	19	16	4
Wrexham	Tr	11/92	92-94	56	2	6

LAKE Paul Andrew
Born: Manchester, England, 28 October, 1968 M
England: B-1/U21-5

Manchester C	YT	05/87	86-92	106	4	7

LAKIN Barry
Born: Dartford, Kent, England, 19 September, 1973 M

Leyton Orient	YT	07/92	92-95	41	13	2

LAKING George Edward
Born: Harthill, South Yorkshire, England, 17 March, 1913 FB
Died: Codsall, Staffordshire, England, 5 June, 1997

Wolverhampton W	Dinnington	05/34	35-36	27	-	0
Middlesbrough	Tr	10/36	36-46	94	-	1

LAKIS Vasilios
Born: Thessalonika, Greece, 10 September, 1976 RW
Greece: 35

Crystal Palace	AEK Athens (GRE)	10/04	04	6	12	0

LALKOVIC Milan
Born: Kosice, Slovakia, 9 December, 1992 W
Slovakia: U21-16/Youth

Chelsea	Sch	07/10				
Doncaster Rov	L	08/11	11	1	5	0
Walsall	L	07/13	13	30	8	6
Barnsley	Tr	01/15	14	13	4	0

LALLANA Adam David
Born: St Albans, Hertfordshire, England, 10 May, 1988 F/W
England: 15/U21-1/Youth

Southampton	Sch	12/05	06-13	213	22	48
Bournemouth	L	10/07	07	2	1	0
Liverpool	Tr	07/14	14	23	4	5

LALLY Patrick Anthony (Pat)
Born: Paddington, Central London, England, 11 January, 1952 M/CD

Millwall	App	01/70	69	1	0	0
York C	Tr	07/71	71-72	64	7	5
Swansea C	Tr	08/73	73-78	153	8	10
Aldershot	L	10/75	75	3	0	0
Doncaster Rov	Tr	09/78	78-81	118	4	0

LAMA Bernard Pascal Maurice
Born: Tours, France, 7 April, 1963 G
France: 44

West Ham U	Paris St-Germain (FRA)	12/97	97	12	0	0

LAMAH Roland Conde
Born: Abidjan, Ivory Coast, 31 December, 1987 LW
Belgium: 5/U21-8/Youth

Swansea C (L)	CA Osasuna (SPN)	01/13	12-13	5	9	2

LAMB Alan
Born: Gateshead, Tyne and Wear, England, 30 January, 1970 F

Nottingham F	YT	02/88				
Hereford U	L	03/89	88	9	1	2
Hartlepool U	Tr	09/89	89-90	4	10	0

LAMB Alan David
Born: Falkirk, Scotland, 3 July, 1952 M
Scotland: U23-1

Preston NE	App	05/70	71-76	76	4	2
Port Vale	Tr	03/77	76-77	54	0	3

LAMB Harold Thomas (Harry)
Born: Kingswinford, West Midlands, England, 20 April, 1928 RB
Died: Monmouthshire, Wales, November, 2001

Aston Villa	Wordsley	10/49				
Scunthorpe U	Tr	06/54	54-55	36	-	0

LAMB Harry Edward
Born: Bebington, Wirral, England, 3 June, 1925 IF
Died: Bebington, Wirral, England, 9 August, 1982

Tranmere Rov	Everton (Am)	08/42	47-52	88	-	12

LAMB Paul David
Born: Plumstead, SE London, England, 12 September, 1974 M

Northampton T	YT	-	92	2	1	0

LAMB Stephen Percy (Steve)
Born: Leigh-on-Sea, Essex, England, 2 October, 1955 M

Southend U	App	10/73	74-75	6	1	0

LAMBDEN Victor David (Vic)
Born: Bristol, England, 24 October, 1925 CF
Died: Bristol, England, 3 July, 1996

Bristol Rov	Oldland	10/45	46-54	269	-	117

LAMBE Reginald Everard Vibert (Reggie)
Born: Hamilton, Bermuda, 4 February, 1991 RM
Bermuda: 15

Ipswich T	Sch	07/09	10	0	2	0
Bristol Rov	L	03/11	10	1	6	0
Mansfield T	Nykopings (SWE)	09/14	14	20	10	5

LAMBERT Anton James
Born: Nottingham, England, 29 November, 1959 M

Scunthorpe U	Long Eaton U	07/80	80-81	35	4	3

LAMBERT Brian
Born: Sutton-in-Ashfield, Nottinghamshire, England, 10 July, 1936 LB
Died: Kirkby in Ashfield, Nottinghamshire, England, 27 December, 2007

Mansfield T	Sutton T	10/54	54-59	24	-	0

LAMBERT Christopher James (James)
Born: Henley-on-Thames, Oxfordshire, England, 14 September, 1973 W/M

League Club	Source	Date Signed	Seasons Played	Apps	Subs	Gls
Reading	Jnr	07/92	92-98	77	48	16
Walsall	L	10/98	98	4	2	0
Oxford U	Tr	08/99	99	8	5	2

LAMBERT David
Born: Ruabon, Wrexham, Wales, 7 July, 1939 LB

League Club	Source	Date Signed	Seasons Played	Apps	Subs	Gls
Cardiff C	Druids U	03/59				
Wrexham	Tr	07/63	63	5	-	0

LAMBERT Eric Victor
Born: Derby, England, 4 August, 1920 CD
Died: Derby, England, 1979

League Club	Source	Date Signed	Seasons Played	Apps	Subs	Gls
Derby Co	Nottingham F (Am)	10/44				
Hartlepool U	Tr	06/46	46	16	-	0

LAMBERT John Gilbert (Gil)
Born: Preston, Lancashire, England, 16 March, 1937 LW
Died: Preston, Lancashire, England, 8 April, 1986

League Club	Source	Date Signed	Seasons Played	Apps	Subs	Gls
Preston NE	Jnr	03/55	58-60	22	-	4

LAMBERT Kenneth (Ken)
Born: Sheffield, England, 7 June, 1928 IF
Died: Sheffield, England, 29 June, 2002

League Club	Source	Date Signed	Seasons Played	Apps	Subs	Gls
Barnsley	Ecclesfield Red Rose	01/50	50-51	11	-	2
Gillingham	Tr	07/52	52	37	-	10
Swindon T	Tr	07/53	53-54	30	-	5
Bradford C	Tr	11/54	54	19	-	4

LAMBERT Kyle Mathew
Born: Wigan, Greater Manchester, England, 26 March, 1990 M

League Club	Source	Date Signed	Seasons Played	Apps	Subs	Gls
Rochdale	Sch	07/08	08	0	1	0

LAMBERT Martin Craig
Born: Southampton, England, 24 September, 1965 F
England: Youth/Schools

League Club	Source	Date Signed	Seasons Played	Apps	Subs	Gls
Brighton & HA	App	08/83	83	2	1	0
Torquay U	Tr	07/85	85	4	2	2
Brighton & HA	Sedan (FRA)	07/89	89	0	1	0

LAMBERT Matthew Roy
Born: Morecambe, Lancashire, England, 28 September, 1971 LB

League Club	Source	Date Signed	Seasons Played	Apps	Subs	Gls
Preston NE	YT	07/90	90-91	11	5	2
Bury	Tr	06/92				

LAMBERT Michael Arnold (Mick)
Born: Balsham, Cambridgeshire, England, 20 May, 1950 LW

League Club	Source	Date Signed	Seasons Played	Apps	Subs	Gls
Ipswich T	Newmarket	11/67	68-78	180	30	39
Peterborough U	Tr	07/79	79-80	15	6	2

LAMBERT Raymond (Ray)
Born: Bagillt, Flintshire, Wales, 18 July, 1922 RB
Died: Queensferry, Flintshire, Wales, 22 October, 2009
Wales: 5/Schools/War-4

League Club	Source	Date Signed	Seasons Played	Apps	Subs	Gls
Liverpool	Jnr	07/39	46-55	308	-	2

LAMBERT Rickie Lee
Born: Kirkby, Merseyside, England, 16 February, 1982 F
England: 11

League Club	Source	Date Signed	Seasons Played	Apps	Subs	Gls
Blackpool	YT	07/00	99	0	3	0
Macclesfield T	Tr	03/01	00-01	36	8	8
Stockport Co	Tr	04/03	02-04	88	10	18
Rochdale	Tr	02/05	04-06	61	3	28
Bristol Rov	Tr	08/06	06-09	114	14	52
Southampton	Tr	08/09	09-13	197	10	106
Liverpool	Tr	06/14	14	7	18	2

LAMBERT Roy
Born: Hoyland, South Yorkshire, England, 16 July, 1933 RH

League Club	Source	Date Signed	Seasons Played	Apps	Subs	Gls
Rotherham U	Thorncliffe Welfare	07/54	56-64	307	-	6
Barnsley	Tr	11/65	65	3	0	0

LAMBLE John
Born: Reading, England, 10 November, 1948 M

League Club	Source	Date Signed	Seasons Played	Apps	Subs	Gls
Reading	App	11/66	67	3	2	0

LAMBOURDE Bernard
Born: Pointe-a-Pitre, Guadeloupe, France, 11 May, 1971 D

League Club	Source	Date Signed	Seasons Played	Apps	Subs	Gls
Chelsea	Bordeaux (FRA)	07/97	97-00	29	11	2
Portsmouth	L	09/00	00	6	0	0

LAMBOURNE Dennis James
Born: Swansea, Wales, 7 October, 1945 CF

League Club	Source	Date Signed	Seasons Played	Apps	Subs	Gls
Wrexham	Llanelli	07/64	64-65	15	0	4

LAMBTON George Colin (Colin)
Born: Newcastle-upon-Tyne, England, 21 February, 1942 RH

League Club	Source	Date Signed	Seasons Played	Apps	Subs	Gls
Newcastle U	Chester Moor	02/60				
Doncaster Rov	Tr	07/63	63	6	-	0

LAMBTON William Ernest (Bill)
Born: Nottingham, England, 2 December, 1914 G
Died: Sherwood, Nottinghamshire, England, 16 September, 1976

League Club	Source	Date Signed	Seasons Played	Apps	Subs	Gls
Nottingham F	Basford North End	05/35				
Exeter C	Peterborough U	04/46				
Doncaster Rov	Tr	10/46	46	3	-	0

LAMBU Goma
Born: Kinshasa, DR Congo, 10 November, 1984 W
England: Youth

League Club	Source	Date Signed	Seasons Played	Apps	Subs	Gls
Millwall	YT	12/01				
Mansfield T	Redbridge	01/05	04	1	0	0

LAMELA Erik Manuel
Born: Buenos Aires, Argentina, 4 March, 1992 RW
Argentina: 12/Youth

League Club	Source	Date Signed	Seasons Played	Apps	Subs	Gls
Tottenham H	AS Roma (ITA)	08/13	13-14	28	14	2

LAMEY Michael
Born: Amsterdam, Netherlands, 29 November, 1979 RB
Netherlands: U21-4

League Club	Source	Date Signed	Seasons Played	Apps	Subs	Gls
Leicester C	Arm'ia Bielefeld (GER)	08/10	10	2	2	0

LAMEY Nathan James
Born: Leeds, England, 14 October, 1980 F

League Club	Source	Date Signed	Seasons Played	Apps	Subs	Gls
Wolverhampton W	YT	10/97				
Cambridge U	Tr	08/99	99-00	2	4	0

LAMIE Robert (Bob)
Born: Newarthill, Lanarkshire, Scotland, 28 December, 1928 W
Died: Northampton, England, 1981

League Club	Source	Date Signed	Seasons Played	Apps	Subs	Gls
Cardiff C	Stonehouse Violet	10/49	49-50	6	-	1
Swansea C	Tr	03/51	51	2	-	0

LAMONT David
Born: Glasgow, Scotland, 2 April, 1949 M

League Club	Source	Date Signed	Seasons Played	Apps	Subs	Gls
Colchester U	App	04/67	67	0	1	0

LAMONT William Turnbull (Bill)
Born: Glasgow, Scotland, 25 December, 1926 FB
Died: Glasgow, Scotland, 6 November, 1996

League Club	Source	Date Signed	Seasons Played	Apps	Subs	Gls
New Brighton	Kilmarnock	07/50	50	27	-	0
Tranmere Rov	Tr	09/51	51-55	143	-	3

LAMPARD Frank James
Born: Romford, E London, England, 20 June, 1978 M
England: 106/B-1/U21-19/Youth

League Club	Source	Date Signed	Seasons Played	Apps	Subs	Gls
West Ham U	YT	07/95	95-00	132	16	24
Swansea C	L	10/95	95	8	1	1
Chelsea	Tr	07/01	01-13	404	25	147
Manchester C (L)	New York C (USA)	08/14	14	10	22	6

LAMPARD Frank Richard George
Born: East Ham, E London, England, 20 September, 1948 LB
England: 2/U23-4/Youth

League Club	Source	Date Signed	Seasons Played	Apps	Subs	Gls
West Ham U	App	09/65	67-84	546	5	18
Southend U	Tr	08/85	85	33	0	1

LAMPE Derek Stanley
Born: Edmonton, N London, England, 20 May, 1937 CH
England: Youth

League Club	Source	Date Signed	Seasons Played	Apps	Subs	Gls
Fulham	Jnr	05/54	56-62	88	-	0

LAMPKIN Kevin
Born: Liverpool, England, 20 December, 1972 M

League Club	Source	Date Signed	Seasons Played	Apps	Subs	Gls
Liverpool	YT	05/91				
Huddersfield T	Tr	07/92	92	13	0	0
Mansfield T	Tr	02/94	93-95	35	7	3

LAMPKIN Stephen Charles Arthur (Steve)
Born: Silsden, West Yorkshire, England, 15 October, 1964 M

League Club	Source	Date Signed	Seasons Played	Apps	Subs	Gls
Bradford C	Silsden AFC	03/83	82-83	5	2	1

LAMPTEY Nii Odartey
Born: Accra, Ghana, 10 December, 1974 F
Ghana: 38

League Club	Source	Date Signed	Seasons Played	Apps	Subs	Gls
Aston Villa	PSV Eindhoven (NED)	08/94	94	1	5	0
Coventry C	Tr	08/95	95	3	3	0

LANCASHIRE Carl Peter
Born: Blackpool, Lancashire, England, 17 January, 1969 M

League Club	Source	Date Signed	Seasons Played	Apps	Subs	Gls
Blackpool	App	06/87	87	2	5	0

LANCASHIRE Graham
Born: Blackpool, Lancashire, England, 19 October, 1972 F

League Club	Source	Date Signed	Seasons Played	Apps	Subs	Gls
Burnley	YT	07/91	90-94	11	20	8
Halifax T	L	11/92	92	2	0	0
Chester C	L	01/94	93	10	1	7
Preston NE	Tr	12/94	94-95	11	12	2
Wigan Ath	L	01/96	95	4	0	3

League Club	Source	Date Signed	Seasons Played	Apps	Subs	Gls
Wigan Ath	Tr	03/96	95-97	16	10	9
Rochdale	Tr	10/97	97-00	54	29	23

LANCASHIRE Oliver James (Ollie)
Born: Basingstoke, Hampshire, England, 13 December, 1988 CD

League Club	Source	Date Signed	Seasons Played	Apps	Subs	Gls
Southampton	Sch	07/06	08-09	11	2	0
Grimsby T	L	10/09	09	24	1	1
Walsall	Tr	07/10	10-11	45	4	1
Aldershot T	Tr	07/12	12	10	2	0
Rochdale	Tr	07/13	13-14	54	5	0

LANCASTER Brian
Born: Bradford-on-Avon, Wiltshire, England, 8 May, 1939 CH

League Club	Source	Date Signed	Seasons Played	Apps	Subs	Gls
Torquay U		07/60	61	18	-	0

LANCASTER Cameron Paul
Born: Camden, N London, England, 5 November, 1992 F

League Club	Source	Date Signed	Seasons Played	Apps	Subs	Gls
Tottenham H	Sch	02/11	11	0	1	0
Dagenham & Red	L	03/11	10	0	4	0
Stevenage	Tr	08/14	14	4	1	1

LANCASTER David (Dave)
Born: Preston, Lancashire, England, 8 September, 1961 F

League Club	Source	Date Signed	Seasons Played	Apps	Subs	Gls
Blackpool	Colne Dynamoes	08/90	90	7	1	1
Chesterfield	L	02/91	90	12	0	4
Chesterfield	Tr	08/91	91-92	66	3	16
Rochdale	Tr	07/93	93	37	3	14
Bury	Halifax T	03/95	94-95	4	6	1
Rochdale	Tr	02/96	95-96	14	6	2

LANCASTER Desmond Charles (Des)
Born: Burnley, Lancashire, England, 16 July, 1937 LW
Died: Burnley, Lancashire, England, October, 2000

League Club	Source	Date Signed	Seasons Played	Apps	Subs	Gls
Burnley	Jnr	08/54	56	1	-	0
Darlington	Tr	03/58	57-58	31	-	18
Tranmere Rov	Tr	06/59	59	1	-	0

LANCASTER Joseph Gerard (Joe)
Born: Stockport, Greater Manchester, England, 28 April, 1926 G

League Club	Source	Date Signed	Seasons Played	Apps	Subs	Gls
Manchester U	Heaton Mersey OB	02/50	49	2	-	0
Accrington Stan	Tr	11/50	50	1	-	0

LANCASTER Martyn Neil
Born: Wigan, Greater Manchester, England, 10 November, 1980 CD

League Club	Source	Date Signed	Seasons Played	Apps	Subs	Gls
Chester C	YT	01/99	98-99	22	6	0

LANCASTER Raymond (Ray)
Born: Rotherham, South Yorkshire, England, 17 August, 1941 WH

League Club	Source	Date Signed	Seasons Played	Apps	Subs	Gls
Rotherham U	Jnr	11/58	60-64	64	-	2
Grimsby T	Tr	12/64	64-66	16	2	0
Lincoln C	Tr	01/67	66-67	24	0	0

LANCASTER Samuel John (Sam)
Born: Leicester, England, 17 February, 1986 M

League Club	Source	Date Signed	Seasons Played	Apps	Subs	Gls
Chesterfield	Sch	07/05	05	0	1	0

LANCELOTTE Eric Charles Harker
Born: India, 26 February, 1917 IF
Died: Canterbury, England, 1 September, 2007

League Club	Source	Date Signed	Seasons Played	Apps	Subs	Gls
Charlton Ath	Romford	05/35	37-47	40	-	6
Brighton & HA	Tr	02/48	47-49	60	-	14

LANDON Richard John
Born: Worthing, West Sussex, England, 22 March, 1970 F

League Club	Source	Date Signed	Seasons Played	Apps	Subs	Gls
Plymouth Arg	Bedworth U	01/94	93-94	21	9	12
Stockport Co	Tr	07/95	95-96	7	6	5
Rotherham U	L	03/97	96	7	1	0
Macclesfield T	Tr	07/97	97-98	16	16	9

LANDSBOROUGH Murray
Born: Thornhill, Dumfries & Galloway, Scotland, 30 December, 1915 FB
Died: Thornhill, Dumfries & Galloway, Scotland, 15 July, 1987

League Club	Source	Date Signed	Seasons Played	Apps	Subs	Gls
Carlisle U	Kilmarnock	08/47	47	1	-	0

LANDZAAT Denny Domingues
Born: Amsterdam, Netherlands, 6 May, 1976 M
Netherlands: 38

League Club	Source	Date Signed	Seasons Played	Apps	Subs	Gls
Wigan Ath	AZ Alkmaar (NED)	07/06	06-07	48	4	5

LANE Frank (Frankie)
Born: Wallasey, Wirral, England, 20 July, 1948 G
Died: Saughall Massie, Wirral, England, 19 May, 2011

League Club	Source	Date Signed	Seasons Played	Apps	Subs	Gls
Tranmere Rov	Stanley Arms	08/68	69-71	76	0	0
Liverpool	Tr	09/71	72	1	0	0
Notts Co	Tr	07/75	75	2	0	0

LANE Henry (Harry)
Born: Hednesford, Staffordshire, England, 21 March, 1909 IF
Died: Cannock, Staffordshire, England, March, 1977

League Club	Source	Date Signed	Seasons Played	Apps	Subs	Gls
Birmingham C	Bloxwich Strollers	12/29	30	2	-	0
Southend U	Tr	05/33	33-37	155	-	50
Plymouth Arg	Tr	03/38	37-38	47	-	8
Southend U	Tr	05/46	46-48	65	-	14

LANE John George (Jackie)
Born: Birmingham, England, 10 November, 1931 CF

League Club	Source	Date Signed	Seasons Played	Apps	Subs	Gls
Birmingham C	Boldmere St Michael's	09/49	52-55	46	-	14
Notts Co	Tr	07/56	56-58	57	-	19

LANE Kevin John
Born: Willenhall, West Midlands, England, 11 May, 1957 F

League Club	Source	Date Signed	Seasons Played	Apps	Subs	Gls
Torquay U	Walsall (App)	08/75	75-76	17	13	5

LANE Martin John
Born: Altrincham, Greater Manchester, England, 12 April, 1961 D

League Club	Source	Date Signed	Seasons Played	Apps	Subs	Gls
Manchester U	Jnr	05/79				
Chester C	Tr	08/82	82-86	175	0	3
Coventry C	Tr	01/87	86-87	0	3	0
Wrexham	L	10/88	88	6	0	0
Chester C	Tr	01/89	88-90	97	2	0
Walsall	Tr	08/91	91	6	4	0

LANE Michael Edward (Mick)
Born: Wellington, Somerset, England, 6 December, 1966 RB

League Club	Source	Date Signed	Seasons Played	Apps	Subs	Gls
Exeter C	App	12/84	83	1	0	0

LANE Sean Brendon
Born: Bristol, England, 16 January, 1964 M
England: Schools

League Club	Source	Date Signed	Seasons Played	Apps	Subs	Gls
Hereford U	App	03/81	80-82	39	11	3
Derby Co	Tr	05/83	83	1	0	0

LANG Gavin
Born: Larkhall, Lanarkshire, Scotland, 21 March, 1926 LW
Died: Wrexham, Wales, 19 February, 1989

League Club	Source	Date Signed	Seasons Played	Apps	Subs	Gls
Chester C	Spalding U	08/56	56	3	-	0

LANG Gavin Thomas
Born: Hereford, England, 10 November, 1951 LW

League Club	Source	Date Signed	Seasons Played	Apps	Subs	Gls
Chester C	Newcastle U (App)	11/69				
Crewe Alex	Tr	09/70	70	3	0	1

LANG Malcolm Christian
Born: Barnsley, South Yorkshire, England, 14 January, 1941 LW

League Club	Source	Date Signed	Seasons Played	Apps	Subs	Gls
York C	Bridlington T	08/63	63	12	-	2

LANG Thomas (Tommy)
Born: Larkhall, Lanarkshire, Scotland, 3 April, 1905 LW
Died: Cleland, Lanarkshire, Scotland, 12 May, 1988

League Club	Source	Date Signed	Seasons Played	Apps	Subs	Gls
Newcastle U	Larkhall Thistle	10/26	27-34	215	-	53
Huddersfield T	Tr	12/34	34-35	24	-	5
Manchester U	Tr	12/35	35-36	12	-	1
Swansea C	Tr	04/37	37	33	-	1
Ipswich T	Queen of the South	10/46	46	5	-	1

LANGAN David Francis
Born: Dublin, Republic of Ireland, 15 February, 1957 RB
Republic of Ireland: 25

League Club	Source	Date Signed	Seasons Played	Apps	Subs	Gls
Derby Co	App	02/75	76-79	143	0	1
Birmingham C	Tr	07/80	80-82	92	0	3
Oxford U	Tr	08/84	84-87	112	2	2
Leicester C	L	10/87	87	5	0	0
Bournemouth	Tr	12/87	87	19	1	0
Peterborough U	Tr	08/88	88	18	1	0

LANGAN Kevin
Born: Jersey, Channel Islands, 7 April, 1978 RB

League Club	Source	Date Signed	Seasons Played	Apps	Subs	Gls
Bristol C	YT	07/96	97-98	1	3	0

LANGE Anthony Stephen (Tony)
Born: West Ham, E London, England, 10 December, 1964 G

League Club	Source	Date Signed	Seasons Played	Apps	Subs	Gls
Charlton Ath	App	12/82	83-85	12	0	0
Aldershot	L	08/85	85	7	0	0
Aldershot	Tr	07/86	86-88	125	0	0
Wolverhampton W	Tr	07/89	89-90	8	0	0
Aldershot	L	11/90	90	2	0	0
Torquay U	L	09/91	91	1	0	0
West Bromwich A	Tr	08/92	92-94	45	3	0
Fulham	Tr	07/95	95-96	59	0	0

LANGE Rune
Born: Tromso, Norway, 24 June, 1977 F
Norway: 1

League Club	Source	Date Signed	Seasons Played	Apps	Subs	Gls
Hartlepool U	Tromso (NOR)	02/09	08	2	1	1

LANGFORD Craig Brian
Born: Solihull, West Midlands, England, 12 March, 1975 CD

League Club	Source	Date Signed	Seasons Played	Apps	Subs	Gls
Hereford U	YT	07/93	92-93	4	1	0

League Club	Source	Date Signed	Seasons Played	Apps	Subs	Gls

LANGFORD John William
Born: Kirkby-in-Ashfield, Nottinghamshire, England, 4 August, 1937 — LW

Nottingham F	Leicester C (Am)	08/55	55	4	-	0
Notts Co	Tr	08/58	58	16	-	0

LANGFORD Timothy (Tim)
Born: Kingswinford, West Midlands, England, 12 September, 1965 — F

Wycombe W	Telford U	03/93	93-94	19	16	8

LANGLAND John (Johnny)
Born: Easington, County Durham, England, 9 November, 1929 — F

Sunderland	Silksworth Jnrs	06/48				
Chesterfield	Consett	01/51	52-53	7	-	0
Hartlepool U	Blyth Spartans	07/58	58-59	38	-	11

LANGLEY Ernest James (Jimmy)
Born: Kilburn, NW London, England, 7 February, 1929 — LB
Died: Yiewsley, W London, England, 9 December, 2007
England: 3/B-3/FLge-1

Leeds U	Guildford C	06/52	52	9	-	3
Brighton & HA	Tr	07/53	53-56	166	-	14
Fulham	Tr	02/57	56-64	323	-	31
Queens Park Rgrs	Tr	07/65	65-66	86	1	9

LANGLEY Geoffrey Ralph (Geoff)
Born: Gateshead, Tyne and Wear, England, 31 March, 1962 — F

Bolton W	App	03/80	81	3	3	0

LANGLEY Kevin James
Born: St Helens, Merseyside, England, 24 May, 1964 — M

Wigan Ath	App	05/82	81-85	156	4	6
Everton	Tr	07/86	86	16	0	2
Manchester C	Tr	03/87	86	9	0	0
Chester C	L	01/88	87	9	0	0
Birmingham C	Tr	03/88	87-89	74	2	2
Wigan Ath	Tr	09/90	90-93	151	6	6

LANGLEY Richard Barrington Michael
Born: Harlesden, NW London, England, 27 December, 1979 — M
England: Youth//Jamaica: 17

Queens Park Rgrs	YT	12/96	98-03	123	10	18
Cardiff C	Tr	08/03	03-04	63	6	8
Queens Park Rgrs	Tr	08/05	05	22	11	3
Luton T	Tr	07/06	06-07	18	12	1

LANGLEY Richard John
Born: Lambeth, S London, England, 20 March, 1965 — RB

Fulham	Corinthian Casuals	11/86	86-90	43	7	0

LANGLEY Thomas William (Tommy)
Born: Lambeth, S London, England, 8 February, 1958 — F
England: B-3/U21-1/Youth/Schools

Chelsea	App	04/75	74-79	129	13	40
Queens Park Rgrs	Tr	08/80	80	24	1	8
Crystal Palace	Tr	03/81	80-82	54	5	9
Coventry C	AEK Athens (GRE)	03/84	83	2	0	0
Wolverhampton W	Tr	07/84	84	22	1	4
Aldershot	L	03/85	84	16	0	4
Aldershot	South China (HKG)	08/86	86-87	80	1	21
Exeter C	Tr	07/88	88	14	7	2

LANGMAN Hedley Neil (Neil)
Born: Bere Alston, Devon, England, 21 February, 1932 — CF

Plymouth Arg	Tavistock	09/53	53-57	96	-	49
Colchester U	Tr	11/57	57-60	128	-	50

LANGMAN Peter John Henry
Born: Bere Alston, Devon, England, 1 April, 1928 — CH

Plymouth Arg	Tavistock	06/51	54-57	90	-	0

LANGMEAD Kelvin Steven
Born: Coventry, England, 23 March, 1985 — CD

Preston NE	Sch	02/04	04	0	1	0
Carlisle U	L	02/04	03	3	8	1
Kidderminster Hrs	L	09/04	04	9	1	1
Shrewsbury T	Tr	11/04	04-09	210	21	19
Peterborough U	Tr	06/10	10	28	4	3
Northampton T	Tr	08/11	11-14	82	8	11

LANGRIDGE John
Born: Newcastle-upon-Tyne, England, 14 November, 1957 — F

Hartlepool U	Easington Colliery	10/82	82	5	1	0

LANGSTRETH Horace Lawrence (Lol)
Born: Blackburn, Greater Manchester, England, 19 July, 1931 — LB
Died: Plymouth, England, December, 1990

Accrington Stan	Blackburn Rov (Am)	07/53	53	3	-	0
Torquay U	Netherfield	08/56	56	1	-	0

LANGTON Robert (Bobby)
Born: Burscough, Lancashire, England, 8 September, 1918 — LW
Died: Burscough, Lancashire, England, 13 January, 1996
England: 11/B-3/FLge-9//Northern Ireland: NILge-1

Blackburn Rov	Burscough Victoria	09/38	38-47	107	-	24
Preston NE	Tr	08/48	48-49	55	-	14
Bolton W	Tr	11/49	49-52	118	-	16
Blackburn Rov	Tr	09/53	53-55	105	-	33

LANSBURY Henri George
Born: Enfield, N London, England, 12 October, 1990 — M
England: U21-16/Youth

Arsenal	Sch	07/08	09-11	0	3	0
Scunthorpe U	L	01/09	08	12	4	4
Watford	L	08/09	09	34	3	5
Norwich C	L	11/10	10	15	8	4
West Ham U	L	08/11	11	13	9	1
Nottingham F	Tr	08/12	12-14	88	12	22

LANSDOWNE William (Billy)
Born: Epping, Essex, England, 28 April, 1959 — F

West Ham U	Jnr	06/78	78-79	5	4	1
Charlton Ath	Tr	07/81	81-82	28	4	4
Gillingham	Tr	01/83	82	6	0	2

LANSDOWNE William Thomas Michael (Bill)
Born: Shoreditch, Central London, England, 9 November, 1935 — LH

West Ham U	Woodford T	02/56	55-62	57	-	5

LANZANO Mattia
Born: Grosseto, Italy, 4 July, 1990 — G

Swindon T	Gavorrano (ITA)	08/11	11	5	1	0

LANZONI Matteo
Born: Como, Italy, 18 July, 1988 — RB

Oldham Ath	Sampdoria (ITA)	08/13	13	10	0	1
Yeovil T	Tr	01/14	13	2	4	0
Cambridge U	Tr	08/14	14	3	0	0
Hartlepool U	L	11/14	14	1	0	0

LAPHAM Kyle Jonathan
Born: Swindon, England, 5 January, 1986 — RB

Swindon T	Sch	07/05	04	2	0	0

LAPOT Stanley (Stan)
Born: Edinburgh, Scotland, 20 January, 1944 — LH

Preston NE	Raith Rov	06/62	62-66	15	3	2

LAPPER Michael Steven (Mike)
Born: Los Angeles, California, USA, 28 August, 1970 — CD
USA: 44

Southend U	VfL Wolfsburg (GER)	08/95	95-96	46	6	1

LAPPIN Simon
Born: Glasgow, Scotland, 25 January, 1983 — M
Scotland: U21-10

Norwich C	St Mirren	01/07	06-11	99	10	2
Cardiff C	Tr	11/12	12	2	0	0
Sheffield U	L	10/13	13	7	2	0

LAPSLIE Thomas William Cavendish (Tom)
Born: Ongar, Essex, England, 5 May, 1995 — M

Colchester U	Sch	07/13	14	11	0	1

LARAMAN Peter Kenneth
Born: Rochester, Kent, England, 24 October, 1940 — IF
England: Youth

Charlton Ath	Jnr	02/58	58-59	2	-	1
Torquay U	Tr	07/61	61	9	-	5

LARGE Frank
Born: Leeds, England, 26 January, 1940 — CF/LH
Died: Louisburgh, County Mayo, Republic of Ireland, 8 August, 2003

Halifax T	Halifax British Rail	06/59	58-61	134	-	50
Queens Park Rgrs	Tr	06/62	62	18	-	5
Northampton T	Tr	03/63	62-63	47	-	30
Swindon T	Tr	03/64	63-64	17	-	4
Carlisle U	Tr	09/64	64-65	50	0	18
Oldham Ath	Tr	12/65	65-66	34	0	18
Northampton T	Tr	12/66	66-67	37	0	15
Leicester C	Tr	11/67	67	26	0	8
Fulham	Tr	06/68	68-69	20	4	3
Northampton T	Tr	08/69	69-72	133	2	42
Chesterfield	Tr	11/72	72-73	46	0	15

LARKIN Anthony Gerard (Tony)
Born: Liverpool, England, 12 January, 1956 — D

Wrexham	Jnr	07/75				
Shrewsbury T	Tr	07/78	78-80	54	1	0
Carlisle U	Tr	07/81	81-82	47	2	2
Hereford U	Tr	03/83	82-84	28	7	2

LARKIN Bernard Patrick (Bunny)
Born: Birmingham, England, 11 January, 1936 IF/WH

League Club	Source	Date Signed	Seasons Played	Apps	Subs	Gls
Birmingham C	Lea Hall YC	07/54	56-59	79	-	23
Norwich C	Tr	03/60	59-61	41	-	12
Doncaster Rov	Tr	09/61	61	25	-	12
Watford	Tr	06/62	62-64	49	-	3
Lincoln C	Tr	11/64	64-65	25	2	3

LARKIN Colin
Born: Dundalk, Republic of Ireland, 27 April, 1982 F
Republic of Ireland: Youth

League Club	Source	Date Signed	Seasons Played	Apps	Subs	Gls
Wolverhampton W	YT	05/99	99-00	1	2	0
Kidderminster Hrs	L	09/01	01	31	2	6
Mansfield T	Tr	08/02	02-04	61	31	25
Chesterfield	Tr	07/05	05-06	58	22	11
Northampton T	Tr	07/07	07-08	23	31	3
Hartlepool U	Tr	08/09	09-11	27	27	4

LARKIN Gordon Thomas
Born: Hartlepool, Cleveland, England, 12 October, 1958 LW

League Club	Source	Date Signed	Seasons Played	Apps	Subs	Gls
Hartlepool U	Billingham Synthonia	07/77	77-79	5	9	1

LARKIN James Thomas (Jim)
Born: Toronto, Canada, 23 October, 1975 G

League Club	Source	Date Signed	Seasons Played	Apps	Subs	Gls
Cambridge U	Virginia CU (USA)	01/98	97	1	0	0

LARKINS Jake
Born: Barking, E London, England, 11 January, 1994 G

League Club	Source	Date Signed	Seasons Played	Apps	Subs	Gls
West Ham U	Sch	07/12				
Leyton Orient	Tr	07/13	13	2	0	0

LARMOUR Albert Andrew James
Born: Belfast, Northern Ireland, 27 May, 1951 CD

League Club	Source	Date Signed	Seasons Played	Apps	Subs	Gls
Cardiff C	Linfield	07/72	72-78	152	2	0
Torquay U	Tr	06/79	79-81	46	4	4

LARMOUR David James
Born: Belfast, Northern Ireland, 23 August, 1977 F
Northern Ireland: Youth/Schools

League Club	Source	Date Signed	Seasons Played	Apps	Subs	Gls
Doncaster Rov	Liverpool (YT)	08/96	96	3	17	0

LARNACH Ian James
Born: Ferryhill, County Durham, England, 10 July, 1951 F

League Club	Source	Date Signed	Seasons Played	Apps	Subs	Gls
Darlington	App	07/69	69	1	1	1

LARNACH Michael David (Mike)
Born: Lybster, Highlands, Scotland, 9 November, 1952 F

League Club	Source	Date Signed	Seasons Played	Apps	Subs	Gls
Newcastle U	Clydebank	12/77	77	12	1	0

LA RONDE Everald
Born: East Ham, E London, England, 24 January, 1963 FB

League Club	Source	Date Signed	Seasons Played	Apps	Subs	Gls
West Ham U	App	01/81	81	6	1	0
Bournemouth	Tr	09/83	83-84	24	0	0
Peterborough U	L	01/85	84	8	0	0

LARRIEU Romain
Born: Mont-de-Marsan, France, 31 August, 1976 G

League Club	Source	Date Signed	Seasons Played	Apps	Subs	Gls
Plymouth Arg	ASOA Valence (FRA)	11/00	00-11	288	4	0
Gillingham	L	01/07	06	14	0	0
Yeovil T	L	09/07	07	6	0	0

LARROSA Ruben Dario (Dario)
Born: Buenos Aires, Argentina, 4 December, 1979 F

League Club	Source	Date Signed	Seasons Played	Apps	Subs	Gls
Walsall	Perlis (MLY)	07/05	05	2	5	0

LARSEN Stig Olav
Born: Bergen, Norway, 26 September, 1973 F

League Club	Source	Date Signed	Seasons Played	Apps	Subs	Gls
Hartlepool U	Fana IL (NOR)	12/97	97	0	4	0

LARSSON Henrik Edward
Born: Helsingborg, Sweden, 10 September, 1971 F
Sweden: 106

League Club	Source	Date Signed	Seasons Played	Apps	Subs	Gls
Manchester U (L)	Helsingborgs (SWE)	01/07	06	5	2	1

LARSSON Sebastian Bengt Ulf
Born: Eskilstuna, Sweden, 6 June, 1985 RM
Sweden: 74/U21-12

League Club	Source	Date Signed	Seasons Played	Apps	Subs	Gls
Arsenal	Sch	07/02	05	2	1	0
Birmingham C	Tr	08/06	06-10	151	33	19
Sunderland	Tr	07/11	11-14	128	9	12

LARUSSON Bjarnolfur (Bjarni)
Born: Vestmannaeyjar, Iceland, 11 March, 1976 M
Iceland: U21-10/Youth

League Club	Source	Date Signed	Seasons Played	Apps	Subs	Gls
Walsall	Hibernian	09/98	98-99	45	14	3
Scunthorpe U	Tr	09/00	00	33	0	4

LARYEA Benjamin Michael (Benny)
Born: Ghana, 20 March, 1962 F

League Club	Source	Date Signed	Seasons Played	Apps	Subs	Gls
Torquay U	Maidenhead U	03/84	83-84	10	2	3

LASCELLES Jamaal
Born: Derby, England, 11 November, 1993 CD
England: U21-1/Youth

League Club	Source	Date Signed	Seasons Played	Apps	Subs	Gls
Nottingham F	Sch	01/11	11-13	30	2	2
Stevenage	L	03/12	11	5	2	1
Newcastle U	Tr	07/14				
Nottingham F	L	08/14	14	20	6	1

LASIMANT Yohann
Born: Besancon, France, 4 September, 1989 W

League Club	Source	Date Signed	Seasons Played	Apps	Subs	Gls
Leyton Orient	Egri FC (HUN)	07/13	13	1	10	2

LASKEY Russell George
Born: Norwich, England, 17 March, 1937 IF

League Club	Source	Date Signed	Seasons Played	Apps	Subs	Gls
Norwich C	Gothic FC	01/56	56	4	-	2

LASLANDES Lilian
Born: Pauillac, Gironde, France, 4 September, 1971 F
France: 7

League Club	Source	Date Signed	Seasons Played	Apps	Subs	Gls
Sunderland	Bordeaux (FRA)	07/01	01	5	7	0

LASLEY Keith William Robert
Born: Paisley, Renfrewshire, Scotland, 21 September, 1979 M

League Club	Source	Date Signed	Seasons Played	Apps	Subs	Gls
Plymouth Arg	Motherwell	06/04	04-05	14	15	0
Blackpool	L	02/06	05	4	4	0

LASTUVKA Jan
Born: Ostrava, Czech Republic, 7 July, 1982 G
Czech Republic: 3/U21-17/Youth

League Club	Source	Date Signed	Seasons Played	Apps	Subs	Gls
Fulham (L)	Shakhtar Donetsk (UKR)	08/06	06	7	1	0

LATCHAM Leslie Arnold (Les)
Born: Crook, County Durham, England, 22 December, 1942 M/LB

League Club	Source	Date Signed	Seasons Played	Apps	Subs	Gls
Burnley	Jnr	01/60	64-70	149	4	10
Plymouth Arg	Tr	07/71	71-72	83	0	13
Bradford C	Tr	07/73	73	15	0	2

LATCHFORD David Barry (Dave)
Born: Birmingham, England, 9 April, 1949 G

League Club	Source	Date Signed	Seasons Played	Apps	Subs	Gls
Birmingham C	App	07/66	68-77	206	0	0
Bury	Motherwell	03/79	78	2	0	0

LATCHFORD Peter William
Born: Birmingham, England, 27 September, 1952 G
England: U23-2

League Club	Source	Date Signed	Seasons Played	Apps	Subs	Gls
West Bromwich A	App	10/69	72-74	81	0	0

LATCHFORD Robert Dennis (Bob)
Born: Birmingham, England, 18 January, 1951 F
England: 12/FLge-1/U23-6/Youth

League Club	Source	Date Signed	Seasons Played	Apps	Subs	Gls
Birmingham C	App	08/68	68-73	158	2	68
Everton	Tr	02/74	73-80	235	1	106
Swansea C	Tr	07/81	81-83	87	0	35
Coventry C	NAC Breda (NED)	07/84	84	11	1	2
Lincoln C	Tr	08/85	85	14	1	2
Newport Co	Tr	01/86	85	20	0	5

LATHAM David Colin
Born: Droylsden, Greater Manchester, England, 17 October, 1943 LW/IF

League Club	Source	Date Signed	Seasons Played	Apps	Subs	Gls
Manchester U	App	10/61				
Southport	Tr	07/63	63	22	-	0

LATHAM Harold (Harry)
Born: Sheffield, England, 9 January, 1921 CH
Died: Rotherham, South Yorkshire, England, 25 July, 1983

League Club	Source	Date Signed	Seasons Played	Apps	Subs	Gls
Sheffield U	Jnr	10/38	46-52	190	-	1

LATHAM Leslie (Les)
Born: Coventry, England, 31 December, 1917 CD
Died: Bedworth, Warwickshire, England, 4 September, 2001
England: Schools

League Club	Source	Date Signed	Seasons Played	Apps	Subs	Gls
Aston Villa	Newdigate Colliery	10/36				
Coventry C	Tr	10/46	46	1	-	0

LATHAN John George
Born: Sunderland, England, 12 April, 1952 M

League Club	Source	Date Signed	Seasons Played	Apps	Subs	Gls
Sunderland	App	04/69	69-73	41	12	14
Mansfield T	Tr	02/74	73-75	72	2	14
Carlisle U	Tr	02/76	75-77	55	6	8
Barnsley	L	02/77	76	6	1	0
Portsmouth	Tr	03/78	77-79	56	2	4
Mansfield T	Tr	08/79	79	29	0	1

LATHROPE Damon Len
Born: Stevenage, Hertfordshire, England, 28 October, 1989 DM

League Club	Source	Date Signed	Seasons Played	Apps	Subs	Gls
Norwich C	Sch	01/08				
Torquay U	Tr	07/10	10-13	85	24	0

LATIMER Frank Jackson
Born: Sunderland, England, 3 October, 1923 D
Died: Durham, England, November, 1994

League Club	Source	Date Signed	Seasons Played	Apps	Subs	Gls
Brentford	Snowdown CW	11/45	46-55	171	-	3

LATKA Martin
Born: Cesko Budojovice, Czech Republic, 28 September, 1984 — CD
Czech Republic: U21-25

League Club	Source	Date Signed	Seasons Played	Apps	Subs	Gls
Birmingham C (L)	Slavia Prague (CZE)	01/06	05	6	0	0

LATTE-YEDO Igor
Born: Dabou, Ivory Coast, 14 December, 1978 — CD

League Club	Source	Date Signed	Seasons Played	Apps	Subs	Gls
Cambridge U	Marseille End'me (FRA)	08/04	04	5	6	0

LAUDRUP Brian
Born: Vienna, Austria, 22 February, 1969 — W
Denmark: 82/U21-5/Youth

League Club	Source	Date Signed	Seasons Played	Apps	Subs	Gls
Chelsea	Glasgow Rangers	06/98	98	5	2	0

LAUGHTON Dennis
Born: Dingwall, Highlands, Scotland, 22 January, 1948 — D

League Club	Source	Date Signed	Seasons Played	Apps	Subs	Gls
Newcastle U	Greenock Morton	10/73	73-74	7	0	0

LAUNDERS Brian Terence
Born: Dublin, Republic of Ireland, 8 June, 1976 — M
Republic of Ireland: U21-9/Youth

League Club	Source	Date Signed	Seasons Played	Apps	Subs	Gls
Crystal Palace	Cherry Orchard (ROI)	09/93	94-95	1	3	0
Crewe Alex	Tr	08/96	96	6	3	0
Derby Co	BV Veendam (NED)	09/98	98	0	1	0
Colchester U	Tr	03/99	98-99	7	0	0
Crystal Palace	Tr	10/99	99	1	1	0
Sheffield U	Tr	11/99	99	0	1	0

LAUREL John Albert
Born: Dartford, Kent, England, 11 June, 1935 — CH
England: Youth

League Club	Source	Date Signed	Seasons Played	Apps	Subs	Gls
Tottenham H	Jnr	07/52				
Ipswich T	Tr	06/59	60-62	4	-	0

[LAUREN] BISAN-ETAME MAYER Laureano
Born: Kribi, Cameroon, 19 January, 1977 — RB
Cameroon: 25/U23-6

League Club	Source	Date Signed	Seasons Played	Apps	Subs	Gls
Arsenal	RCD Mallorca (SPN)	06/00	00-05	152	7	6
Portsmouth	Tr	01/07	06-07	20	5	0

LAURENT Francis
Born: Paris, France, 6 January, 1986 — W

League Club	Source	Date Signed	Seasons Played	Apps	Subs	Gls
Southend U	FSV Mainz 05 (GER)	08/08	08-09	38	18	9
Northampton T	Compiegne (FRA)	01/11	10	3	3	0

LAURENT Pierre
Born: Tulle, Correze, France, 13 December, 1970 — F

League Club	Source	Date Signed	Seasons Played	Apps	Subs	Gls
Leeds U	SC Bastia (FRA)	03/97	96	2	2	0

LAURSEN Jacob Thaysen
Born: Vejle, Denmark, 6 October, 1971 — CD
Denmark: 25/U21-24/Youth

League Club	Source	Date Signed	Seasons Played	Apps	Subs	Gls
Derby Co	Silkeborg (DEN)	07/96	96-99	135	2	3
Leicester C	FC Copenhagen (DEN)	01/02	01	10	0	0

LAURSEN Martin
Born: Silkeborg, Denmark, 26 July, 1977 — CD
Denmark: 53/U21-14/Youth

League Club	Source	Date Signed	Seasons Played	Apps	Subs	Gls
Aston Villa	AC Milan (ITA)	07/04	04-08	82	2	8

LAVERICK Michael George (Micky)
Born: Castle Eden, County Durham, England, 13 March, 1954 — M

League Club	Source	Date Signed	Seasons Played	Apps	Subs	Gls
Mansfield T	Jnr	01/72	72-75	73	16	13
Southend U	Tr	10/76	76-78	108	2	18
Huddersfield T	Tr	07/79	79-81	74	0	9
York C	Tr	01/82	81-82	38	3	6
Huddersfield T	L	01/83	82	2	0	0

LAVERICK Peter Henry
Born: Cleethorpes, North Lincolnshire, England, 29 January, 1939 — IF
Died: Scartho, North Lincolnshire, England, 29 March, 2013

League Club	Source	Date Signed	Seasons Played	Apps	Subs	Gls
Grimsby T	Jnr	03/56	57-60	4	-	0

LAVERICK Robert (Bobby)
Born: Castle Eden, County Durham, England, 11 June, 1938 — W
England: Youth

League Club	Source	Date Signed	Seasons Played	Apps	Subs	Gls
Chelsea	Jnr	06/55	56-57	7	-	0
Everton	Tr	02/59	58-59	22	-	6
Brighton & HA	Tr	06/60	60-61	63	-	20
Coventry C	Tr	07/62	62	4	-	0

LAVERTY Patrick James (Pat)
Born: Gorseinon, Swansea, Wales, 24 May, 1934 — IF

League Club	Source	Date Signed	Seasons Played	Apps	Subs	Gls
Sheffield U	Wellington T	05/56	56-59	7	-	0
Southend U	Tr	07/60	60	21	-	6

LAVERY Caolan Owen
Born: Red Deer, Alberta, Canada, 22 October, 1992 — F
Northern Ireland: U21-7/Youth

League Club	Source	Date Signed	Seasons Played	Apps	Subs	Gls
Sheffield Wed	Ipswich T (Sch)	05/12	13-14	16	18	6
Southend U	L	01/13	12	0	3	0
Plymouth Arg	L	11/13	13	4	4	3
Chesterfield	L	02/15	14	6	2	3

LAVERY James (Jim)
Born: Lennoxtown, Dunbartonshire, Scotland, 13 December, 1948 — G

League Club	Source	Date Signed	Seasons Played	Apps	Subs	Gls
Scunthorpe U		08/66	67	15	0	0
Scunthorpe U	Brigg T	08/74	74	11	0	0

LAVERY John
Born: Belfast, Northern Ireland, 24 November, 1919 — LW
Republic of Ireland: LoI-1//Northern Ireland: Schools

League Club	Source	Date Signed	Seasons Played	Apps	Subs	Gls
Bradford C	Dundalk (ROI)	08/48	48	5	-	0
Halifax T	Tr	09/48	48	3	-	1

LAVILLE Florent
Born: Valence, France, 7 August, 1973 — CD
France: U23-1

League Club	Source	Date Signed	Seasons Played	Apps	Subs	Gls
Bolton W	Olymp Lyonnais (FRA)	02/03	02-03	15	0	0
Coventry C	L	10/04	04	5	1	0

LAVIN Gerard
Born: Corby, Northamptonshire, England, 5 February, 1974 — RB
Scotland: U21-7

League Club	Source	Date Signed	Seasons Played	Apps	Subs	Gls
Watford	YT	05/92	91-95	121	5	3
Millwall	Tr	11/95	95-98	67	7	0
Bristol C	Tr	08/99	99-00	21	1	0
Wycombe W	L	01/01	00	2	0	0
Northampton T	Tr	05/01	01	2	0	0

LAW Brian John
Born: Merthyr Tydfil, Wales, 1 January, 1970 — CD
Wales: 1/U21-2/Youth/Schools

League Club	Source	Date Signed	Seasons Played	Apps	Subs	Gls
Queens Park Rgrs	YT	08/87	87-90	19	1	0
Wolverhampton W	Rtd	12/94	94-96	26	5	1
Millwall	Tr	07/97	97-98	45	0	4

LAW Cecil Richard
Born: Salisbury, Wiltshire, England, 10 March, 1930 — W

League Club	Source	Date Signed	Seasons Played	Apps	Subs	Gls
Derby Co	Alexandra (RHO)	08/51	52-53	33	-	2
Bury	Tr	05/54	54-55	44	-	5

LAW Denis
Born: Aberdeen, Scotland, 24 February, 1940 — IF
England: FLge-2//Italy: ILge-2//Scotland: 55/U23-3

League Club	Source	Date Signed	Seasons Played	Apps	Subs	Gls
Huddersfield T	Jnr	02/57	56-59	81	-	16
Manchester C	Tr	03/60	59-60	44	-	21
Manchester U	Torino (ITA)	08/62	62-72	305	4	171
Manchester C	Tr	07/73	73	22	2	9

LAW Gareth Martin
Born: Torquay, Devon, England, 20 August, 1982 — F

League Club	Source	Date Signed	Seasons Played	Apps	Subs	Gls
Torquay U	YT	11/00	00-01	2	13	1

LAW Graeme Christopher
Born: Kirkcaldy, Fife, Scotland, 6 October, 1984 — RB
Scotland: Youth

League Club	Source	Date Signed	Seasons Played	Apps	Subs	Gls
York C	Sch	07/04	03	2	2	0

LAW Marcus William
Born: Coventry, England, 28 September, 1975 — G

League Club	Source	Date Signed	Seasons Played	Apps	Subs	Gls
Bristol Rov	YT	07/94	94	2	0	0

LAW Nicholas (Nicky)
Born: Greenwich, SE London, England, 8 September, 1961 — CD
England: Schools

League Club	Source	Date Signed	Seasons Played	Apps	Subs	Gls
Arsenal	App	07/79				
Barnsley	Tr	08/81	81-85	113	1	1
Blackpool	Tr	08/85	85-86	64	2	1
Plymouth Arg	Tr	03/87	86-87	37	1	5
Notts Co	Tr	06/88	88-89	44	3	4
Scarborough	L	11/89	89	12	0	0
Rotherham U	Tr	08/90	90-93	126	2	4
Chesterfield	Tr	10/93	93-96	108	3	11
Hereford U	Tr	10/96	96	14	0	0

LAW Nicholas (Nicky)
Born: Nottingham, England, 29 March, 1988 — M
England: Youth

League Club	Source	Date Signed	Seasons Played	Apps	Subs	Gls
Sheffield U	Sch	11/05	06-07	2	3	0
Yeovil T	L	02/07	06	5	1	0
Bradford C	L	10/07	07	10	0	2
Bradford C	L	10/08	08	30	3	3
Rotherham U	Tr	07/09	09-10	85	1	6

LAWFORD Craig Brian
Born: Dewsbury, West Yorkshire, England, 25 November, 1972 — LB/M

League Club	Source	Date Signed	Seasons Played	Apps	Subs	Gls
Bradford C	YT	07/91	89-93	13	7	1
Hull C	Tr	08/94	94-95	45	17	3

LAWLER Christopher (Chris)
Born: Liverpool, England, 20 October, 1943 — RB
England: 4/FLge-2/U23-4/Youth/Schools

League Club	Source	Date Signed	Seasons Played	Apps	Subs	Gls
Liverpool	Jnr	10/60	62-74	406	0	41
Portsmouth	Tr	10/75	75-76	35	1	0
Stockport Co	Tr	08/77	77	33	3	3

LAWLER James Henry (Jimmy)
Born: Dublin, Republic of Ireland, 20 November, 1923 — LH

League Club	Source	Date Signed	Seasons Played	Apps	Subs	Gls
Portsmouth	Glentoran	10/47				
Southend U	Tr	01/49	48-56	269	-	17

LAWLER Joseph Frederick (Robin)
Born: Dublin, Republic of Ireland, 28 August, 1925 — LB/WH
Died: Fulham, W London, England, 17 April, 1998
Republic of Ireland: 8//Northern Ireland: NILge-2

League Club	Source	Date Signed	Seasons Played	Apps	Subs	Gls
Fulham	Belfast Celtic	03/49	49-61	281	-	0

LAWLESS Alexander Graham (Alex)
Born: Tonypandy, Rhondda Cynon Taff, Wales, 26 March, 1985 — RB/M
Wales: U21-1/Youth

League Club	Source	Date Signed	Seasons Played	Apps	Subs	Gls
Fulham	Jnr	08/03				
Torquay U	Tr	07/05	05	11	3	0
Luton T	York C	11/10	14	7	8	3

LAWLESS Arthur Trevor (Trevor)
Born: Cottam, Nottinghamshire, England, 23 March, 1932 — CH

League Club	Source	Date Signed	Seasons Played	Apps	Subs	Gls
Plymouth Arg	Worcester C	07/55	55	8	-	0
Oldham Ath	Tr	07/56	56	9	-	0
Aldershot	Tr	07/57	57	2	-	0
Southport	Tr	07/58	58	15	-	0

LAWLOR James Joseph (Jimmy)
Born: Dublin, Republic of Ireland, 10 May, 1933 — CH
Died: Bradford, England, 5 April, 2012
Northern Ireland: NILge-1

League Club	Source	Date Signed	Seasons Played	Apps	Subs	Gls
Doncaster Rov	Drumcondra (ROI)	08/52	54	10	-	0
Bradford C	Coleraine	03/57	56-61	153	-	5

LAWLOR John Boscoe (Johnny)
Born: Bellshill, Lanarkshire, Scotland, 30 January, 1937 — LW
Scotland: Schools

League Club	Source	Date Signed	Seasons Played	Apps	Subs	Gls
Aldershot	Kilmarnock	05/59	59-60	57	-	18

LAWLOR John Christopher (Kit)
Born: Dublin, Republic of Ireland, 3 December, 1922 — IF
Died: Dublin, Republic of Ireland, 8 June, 2004
Republic of Ireland: 3/LoI-6

League Club	Source	Date Signed	Seasons Played	Apps	Subs	Gls
Doncaster Rov	Drumcondra (ROI)	06/50	50-54	127	-	47

LAWRENCE Byron Alfredo
Born: Cambridge, England, 12 March, 1996 — M

League Club	Source	Date Signed	Seasons Played	Apps	Subs	Gls
Ipswich T	Sch	07/13	11	0	1	0
Colchester U	Tr	09/14	14	0	1	0

LAWRENCE Cyril
Born: Salford, England, 12 June, 1920 — RW

League Club	Source	Date Signed	Seasons Played	Apps	Subs	Gls
Blackpool		10/38				
Rochdale	Tr	04/47	46-49	44	-	5
Wrexham	Tr	09/50	50-51	50	-	9

LAWRENCE David
Born: Poole, Dorset, England, 12 May, 1933 — RB
Died: Bristol, England, 14 July, 2006

League Club	Source	Date Signed	Seasons Played	Apps	Subs	Gls
Bristol Rov	Poole T	06/55	56	5	-	0
Reading	Tr	06/57	57-58	23	-	0

LAWRENCE David William (Dai)
Born: Swansea, Wales, 18 January, 1947 — RB
Died: Swansea, Wales, 21 July, 2009
Wales: Amateur

League Club	Source	Date Signed	Seasons Played	Apps	Subs	Gls
Swansea C	Merthyr Tydfil	05/67	67-70	93	4	2

LAWRENCE Dennis William
Born: Port of Spain, Trinidad, 1 August, 1974 — CD
Trinidad & Tobago: 89

League Club	Source	Date Signed	Seasons Played	Apps	Subs	Gls
Wrexham	Defence Force (TRD)	03/01	00-06	190	8	14
Swansea C	Tr	08/06	06-07	77	2	7
Crewe Alex	L	09/08	08	26	0	2

LAWRENCE George Randolph
Born: Kensington, Central London, England, 14 September, 1962 — RW

League Club	Source	Date Signed	Seasons Played	Apps	Subs	Gls
Southampton	App	09/80	81-82	7	3	1
Oxford U	L	03/82	81	15	0	4
Oxford U	Tr	11/82	82-84	63	0	21
Southampton	Tr	01/85	84-86	58	12	11
Millwall	Tr	07/87	87-88	26	2	4
Bournemouth	Tr	08/89	89-91	47	28	5
Portsmouth	Weymouth	02/93	92	0	12	0

LAWRENCE Jamal Courtney
Born: Gloucester, England, 18 November, 1996 — RW

League Club	Source	Date Signed	Seasons Played	Apps	Subs	Gls
Cheltenham T	Sch	02/15	14	0	1	0

LAWRENCE James Hubert (Jamie)
Born: Balham, S London, England, 8 March, 1970 — W
Jamaica: 24

League Club	Source	Date Signed	Seasons Played	Apps	Subs	Gls
Sunderland	Cowes	10/93	93	2	2	0
Doncaster Rov	Tr	03/94	93-94	16	9	3
Leicester C	Tr	01/95	94-96	21	26	1
Bradford C	Tr	06/97	97-02	133	22	12
Walsall	Tr	03/03	02-03	12	10	1
Wigan Ath	L	11/03	03	0	4	0
Grimsby T	Tr	03/04	03	5	0	1
Brentford	Tr	09/04	04	8	6	0

LAWRENCE Keith Derek
Born: Orpington, SE London, England, 25 March, 1954 — CD

League Club	Source	Date Signed	Seasons Played	Apps	Subs	Gls
Chelsea	App	07/71				
Brentford	Tr	05/74	74-75	78	0	1

LAWRENCE Leslie Oliver (Les)
Born: Rowley Regis, West Midlands, England, 18 May, 1957 — F

League Club	Source	Date Signed	Seasons Played	Apps	Subs	Gls
Shrewsbury T	Stourbridge	02/75	75-76	10	4	2
Torquay U	Telford U	07/77	77-81	170	19	46
Port Vale	Tr	08/82	82	5	3	0
Aldershot	Tr	07/83	83	39	0	23
Rochdale	Tr	08/84	84	15	0	4
Burnley	Tr	11/84	84-85	22	9	8
Peterborough U	Tr	07/86	86-87	28	5	8
Cambridge U	Tr	02/88	87	11	2	0

LAWRENCE Liam
Born: Retford, Nottinghamshire, England, 14 December, 1981 — RW
Republic of Ireland: 15

League Club	Source	Date Signed	Seasons Played	Apps	Subs	Gls
Mansfield T	YT	07/00	99-03	120	16	34
Sunderland	Tr	08/04	04-06	49	24	10
Stoke C	Tr	11/06	06-09	99	14	23
Portsmouth	Tr	09/10	10-11	51	3	7
Cardiff C	L	03/12	11	12	1	1
Barnsley	PAOK Salonika (GRE)	01/14	13	10	4	1
Shrewsbury T	Tr	07/14	14	30	3	5

LAWRENCE Mark
Born: Stockton-on-Tees, Cleveland, England, 4 December, 1958 — M

League Club	Source	Date Signed	Seasons Played	Apps	Subs	Gls
Hartlepool U	Nunthorpe Ath	08/77	77-83	155	13	24
Port Vale	L	03/83	82	10	1	0

LAWRENCE Matthew James (Matt)
Born: Northampton, England, 19 June, 1974 — D
England: Schools

League Club	Source	Date Signed	Seasons Played	Apps	Subs	Gls
Wycombe W	Grays Ath	01/96	95-96	13	3	1
Fulham	Tr	02/97	96-98	57	2	0
Wycombe W	Tr	10/98	98-99	63	0	4
Millwall	Tr	03/00	99-05	213	11	0
Crystal Palace	Tr	08/06	06-09	109	12	1
Gillingham	Tr	08/10	10-11	65	4	0

LAWRENCE Thomas Johnstone (Tommy)
Born: Dailly, Ayrshire, Scotland, 14 May, 1940 — G
Scotland: 3/U23-1

League Club	Source	Date Signed	Seasons Played	Apps	Subs	Gls
Liverpool	Rylands YC	10/57	62-70	306	0	0
Tranmere Rov	Tr	09/71	71-73	80	0	0

LAWRENCE Thomas Morris (Tom)
Born: Wrexham, Wales, 13 January, 1994 — F
Wales: U21-8/Youth

League Club	Source	Date Signed	Seasons Played	Apps	Subs	Gls
Manchester U	Sch	07/12	13	1	0	0
Carlisle U	L	11/13	13	8	1	3
Yeovil T	L	01/14	13	17	2	2
Leicester C	Tr	09/14	14	0	3	0
Rotherham U	L	11/14	14	6	0	1

LAWRENSON Mark Thomas
Born: Preston, Lancashire, England, 2 June, 1957 — CD
Republic of Ireland: 39

League Club	Source	Date Signed	Seasons Played	Apps	Subs	Gls
Preston NE	Jnr	08/74	74-76	73	0	2
Brighton & HA	Tr	07/77	77-80	152	0	5
Liverpool	Tr	08/81	81-87	233	7	11

LAWRENSON Thomas (Tommy)
Born: Preston, Lancashire, England, 24 May, 1929 — W
Died: Fleetwood, Lancashire, England, 7 May, 1996

League Club	Source	Date Signed	Seasons Played	Apps	Subs	Gls
Preston NE	Leyland Motors	04/49	54	1	-	0
Southport	Tr	07/55	55-56	37	-	0

LAWRIE James
Born: Belfast, Northern Ireland, 18 December, 1990 — F
Northern Ireland: 3/B-1/U21-8/Youth

League Club	Source	Date Signed	Seasons Played	Apps	Subs	Gls
Port Vale	Sch	01/08	07-09	8	19	2

League Club	Source	Date Signed	Seasons Played	Career Record Apps	Subs	Gls

LAWRIE Samuel (Sam)
Born: Glasgow, Scotland, 15 December, 1934 RW
Died: Bradford, England, 26 August, 1979

League Club	Source	Date Signed	Seasons Played	Apps	Subs	Gls
Middlesbrough	Bedlay Jnrs	02/52	51-56	36	-	5
Charlton Ath	Tr	11/56	56-62	193	-	70
Bradford Park Ave	Tr	10/62	62-65	72	1	16

LAWS Brian
Born: Wallsend, Tyne and Wear, England, 14 October, 1961 RB
England: B-1/FLge

League Club	Source	Date Signed	Seasons Played	Apps	Subs	Gls
Burnley	App	10/79	79-82	125	0	12
Huddersfield T	Tr	08/83	83-84	56	0	1
Middlesbrough	Tr	03/85	84-87	103	5	12
Nottingham F	Tr	07/88	88-93	136	11	4
Grimsby T	Tr	12/94	94-96	30	16	2
Darlington	Tr	11/96	96	10	0	0
Scunthorpe U	Tr	01/97	96-97	11	7	0

LAWS Jonathan
Born: Peterborough, England, 1 September, 1964 M

League Club	Source	Date Signed	Seasons Played	Apps	Subs	Gls
Wolverhampton W	App	09/82				
Mansfield T	Tr	03/83	82	0	1	0

LAWSON Allan
Born: Lennoxtown, Dunbartonshire, Scotland, 13 September, 1941 CD

League Club	Source	Date Signed	Seasons Played	Apps	Subs	Gls
Oldham Ath	Glasgow Celtic	06/64	64-69	128	10	1

LAWSON David
Born: Wallsend, Tyne and Wear, England, 22 December, 1947 G

League Club	Source	Date Signed	Seasons Played	Apps	Subs	Gls
Newcastle U	Jnr	04/66				
Shrewsbury T	Tr	08/67				
Bradford Park Ave	Tr	10/67	67-68	13	0	0
Huddersfield T	Tr	05/69	70-71	51	0	0
Everton	Tr	06/72	72-76	124	0	0
Luton T	Tr	10/78	78	5	0	0
Stockport Co	Tr	03/79	78-80	106	0	0

LAWSON Frederick Ian Allison (Ian)
Born: Ouston, County Durham, England, 24 March, 1939 IF
England: Youth

League Club	Source	Date Signed	Seasons Played	Apps	Subs	Gls
Burnley	Jnr	03/56	56-60	23	-	7
Leeds U	Tr	03/62	61-64	44	-	17
Crystal Palace	Tr	06/65	65	15	2	6
Port Vale	Tr	08/66	66	7	1	0

LAWSON Ian James
Born: Huddersfield, West Yorkshire, England, 4 November, 1977 F

League Club	Source	Date Signed	Seasons Played	Apps	Subs	Gls
Huddersfield T	YT	01/95	96-98	13	29	5
Blackpool	L	11/98	98	5	0	3
Blackpool	L	01/99	98	4	0	0
Bury	Tr	07/99	99	20	5	11
Stockport Co	Tr	02/00	99-00	14	11	4
Bury	Tr	09/01	01-02	15	16	7

LAWSON James Joseph (Jimmy)
Born: Middlesbrough, England, 11 December, 1947 M

League Club	Source	Date Signed	Seasons Played	Apps	Subs	Gls
Middlesbrough	Jnr	12/64	65-67	25	6	3
Huddersfield T	Tr	08/68	68-75	234	11	42
Halifax T	Tr	06/76	76-78	93	0	9

LAWSON James Peter (Jimmy)
Born: Basildon, England, 21 January, 1987 W

League Club	Source	Date Signed	Seasons Played	Apps	Subs	Gls
Southend U	Sch	09/05	04-06	7	19	2
Grimsby T	L	09/06	06	0	1	0
Bournemouth	L	01/07	06	2	2	0

LAWSON John Richard
Born: York, England, 3 February, 1925 RW
Died: York, England, 31 August, 1990

League Club	Source	Date Signed	Seasons Played	Apps	Subs	Gls
York C	Dringhouses	08/44	46	1	-	0

LAWSON Norman
Born: Houghton-le-Spring, Tyne and Wear, England, 6 April, 1935 LW
Died: Swansea, Wales, 25 September, 2011

League Club	Source	Date Signed	Seasons Played	Apps	Subs	Gls
Bury	Hednesford T	09/55	55-57	56	-	8
Swansea C	Tr	07/58	58-59	24	-	3

LAWSON William (Willie)
Born: Dundee, Scotland, 28 November, 1947 LW

League Club	Source	Date Signed	Seasons Played	Apps	Subs	Gls
Sheffield Wed	Brechin C	10/69	69-70	9	1	0

LAWTHER William Ian (Ian)
Born: Belfast, Northern Ireland, 20 October, 1939 CF
Died: Oxford, England, 25 April, 2010
Northern Ireland: 4/B

League Club	Source	Date Signed	Seasons Played	Apps	Subs	Gls
Sunderland	Crusaders	03/58	59-60	75	-	41
Blackburn Rov	Tr	07/61	61-62	59	-	21
Scunthorpe U	Tr	07/63	63-64	60	-	22
Brentford	Tr	11/64	64-67	138	1	43
Halifax T	Tr	08/68	68-70	87	14	24
Stockport Co	Tr	07/71	71-75	158	6	29

LAWTON Craig Thomas
Born: Deeside, Flintshire, Wales, 5 January, 1972 M
Wales: B/U21-1/Youth/Schools

League Club	Source	Date Signed	Seasons Played	Apps	Subs	Gls
Manchester U	YT	07/90				
Port Vale	Tr	08/94	94-95	2	1	0

LAWTON Hubert Malcolm (Malcolm)
Born: Leeds, England, 7 November, 1935 LB

League Club	Source	Date Signed	Seasons Played	Apps	Subs	Gls
Leeds U	Jnr	11/52				
Bradford Park Ave	Tr	06/57	57-62	113	-	0

LAWTON James Michael (Jimmy)
Born: Middlesbrough, England, 6 July, 1942 CF

League Club	Source	Date Signed	Seasons Played	Apps	Subs	Gls
Darlington	Middlesbrough (Am)	10/61	61-65	121	0	58
Swindon T	Tr	09/65	65-66	11	0	3
Watford	Tr	03/67	66-67	10	3	1
Darlington	Tr	03/68	67-68	21	0	5

LAWTON John Kenneth
Born: Woore, Shropshire, England, 6 July, 1936 CF

League Club	Source	Date Signed	Seasons Played	Apps	Subs	Gls
Stoke C	Crewe Alex (Am)	06/54	55	9	-	3

LAWTON Norbert (Nobby)
Born: Manchester, England, 25 March, 1940 M
Died: Oldham, Greater Manchester, England, 23 April, 2006

League Club	Source	Date Signed	Seasons Played	Apps	Subs	Gls
Manchester U	Jnr	04/58	59-62	36	-	6
Preston NE	Tr	03/63	62-67	144	0	22
Brighton & HA	Tr	09/67	67-70	112	0	12
Lincoln C	Tr	02/71	70-71	20	0	0

LAWTON Peter
Born: Barnsley, South Yorkshire, England, 25 February, 1944 LB

League Club	Source	Date Signed	Seasons Played	Apps	Subs	Gls
Barnsley	Jnr	05/62	62-63	2	-	0

LAWTON Thomas (Tommy)
Born: Bolton, Greater Manchester, England, 6 October, 1919 CF
Died: Nottingham, England, 6 November, 1996
England: 23/FLge-3/War-23

League Club	Source	Date Signed	Seasons Played	Apps	Subs	Gls
Burnley	Rossendale U	03/36	35-36	25	-	16
Everton	Tr	01/37	36-38	87	-	65
Chelsea	Tr	11/45	46-47	42	-	30
Notts Co	Tr	11/47	47-51	151	-	90
Brentford	Tr	03/52	51-53	50	-	17
Arsenal	Tr	09/53	53-55	35	-	13

LAWTON William (Bill)
Born: Ashton-under-Lyne, Greater Manchester, England, 4 June, 1920 WH
Died: Brighton, England, 14 August, 2008

League Club	Source	Date Signed	Seasons Played	Apps	Subs	Gls
Oldham Ath	Ferranti	02/45	46-48	10	-	0
Chester C	Tr	10/49				

LAY Peter John
Born: Stratford, E London, England, 4 December, 1931 FB

League Club	Source	Date Signed	Seasons Played	Apps	Subs	Gls
Nottingham F	RAF Watnall	04/53	54	1	-	0
Queens Park Rgrs	Tr	07/56	56	1	-	0

LAYBOURNE Keith Ernest
Born: Sunderland, England, 27 January, 1959 FB

League Club	Source	Date Signed	Seasons Played	Apps	Subs	Gls
Lincoln C	Lambton Street BC	07/77	77-78	18	0	1

LAYNE David Richard (Bronco)
Born: Sheffield, England, 29 July, 1939 F

League Club	Source	Date Signed	Seasons Played	Apps	Subs	Gls
Rotherham U	Jnr	07/57	57-58	11	-	4
Swindon T	Tr	06/59	59-60	41	-	28
Bradford C	Tr	12/60	60-61	65	-	44
Sheffield Wed	Tr	06/62	62-63	74	-	52
Sheffield Wed	Rtd	06/72				
Hereford U	L	12/72	72	4	0	0

LAYTON Alan
Born: Bury, Greater Manchester, England, 27 November, 1928 RW

League Club	Source	Date Signed	Seasons Played	Apps	Subs	Gls
Bolton W		04/49				
Barrow	Tr	10/50	50-55	144	-	19

LAYTON John Henry
Born: Hereford, England, 29 June, 1951 CD

League Club	Source	Date Signed	Seasons Played	Apps	Subs	Gls
Hereford U	Kidderminster Hrs	09/74	74-79	198	2	13
Newport Co	Trowbridge T	01/84	83	1	0	0

LAYTON William Herbert (Bill)
Born: Shirley, West Midlands, England, 13 January, 1915 LH/IF
Died: Ipswich, England, February, 1984

League Club	Source	Date Signed	Seasons Played	Apps	Subs	Gls
Reading	Shirley T	03/37	37-46	51	-	17
Bradford Park Ave	Tr	01/47	46-48	47	-	5
Colchester U	Tr	08/49	50	7	-	0

LAYUN Miguel Arturo
Born: Cordoba, Mexico, 25 June, 1988 — M
Mexico: 25

League Club	Source	Date Signed	Seasons Played	Apps	Subs	Gls
Watford	Club America (MEX)	01/15	14	14	3	0

LAZARIDIS Stanley (Stan)
Born: Perth, Australia, 16 August, 1972 — LW
Australia: 59/U23/Youth

League Club	Source	Date Signed	Seasons Played	Apps	Subs	Gls
West Ham U	West Adelaide (AUS)	09/95	95-98	53	16	3
Birmingham C	Tr	07/99	99-05	142	49	8

LAZARUS Mark
Born: Stepney, E London, England, 5 December, 1938 — W

League Club	Source	Date Signed	Seasons Played	Apps	Subs	Gls
Leyton Orient	Barking	11/57	58-60	20	-	4
Queens Park Rgrs	Tr	09/60	60-61	37	-	19
Wolverhampton W	Tr	09/61	61	9	-	3
Queens Park Rgrs	Tr	02/62	61-63	81	-	28
Brentford	Tr	01/64	63-65	62	0	20
Queens Park Rgrs	Tr	11/65	65-67	86	2	29
Crystal Palace	Tr	11/67	67-69	63	0	17
Leyton Orient	Tr	10/69	69-71	81	1	14

LAZARUS Paul
Born: Stepney, E London, England, 4 September, 1962 — F

League Club	Source	Date Signed	Seasons Played	Apps	Subs	Gls
Charlton Ath	Jnr	08/80	80	2	0	1
Wimbledon	Kuopion Elo (FIN)	10/81	81	17	1	6

LEA Cyril
Born: Moss, Wrexham, Wales, 5 August, 1934 — LH
Wales: 2/Amateur

League Club	Source	Date Signed	Seasons Played	Apps	Subs	Gls
Leyton Orient	Bradley Rgrs	07/57	57-64	205	-	0
Ipswich T	Tr	11/64	64-68	103	4	2

LEA Harold
Born: Wigan, Greater Manchester, England, 14 September, 1931 — G

League Club	Source	Date Signed	Seasons Played	Apps	Subs	Gls
Stockport Co	Horwich RMI	05/58	58-63	117	-	0

LEA Leslie (Les)
Born: Manchester, England, 5 October, 1942 — W/M

League Club	Source	Date Signed	Seasons Played	Apps	Subs	Gls
Blackpool	Jnr	10/59	60-67	158	2	13
Cardiff C	Tr	11/67	67-69	75	1	6
Barnsley	Tr	08/70	70-75	198	7	32

LEA William Thomas (Billy)
Born: Wigan, Greater Manchester, England, 27 May, 1924 — IF

League Club	Source	Date Signed	Seasons Played	Apps	Subs	Gls
Stockport Co (Am)		11/59	59	1	-	0

LEABURN Carl Winston
Born: Lewisham, SE London, England, 30 March, 1969 — F
England: Youth

League Club	Source	Date Signed	Seasons Played	Apps	Subs	Gls
Charlton Ath	App	04/87	86-97	276	46	53
Northampton T	L	03/90	89	9	0	0
Wimbledon	Tr	01/98	97-00	36	23	4
Queens Park Rgrs	Tr	12/01	01	0	1	0

LEACH Albert
Born: Bolton, Greater Manchester, England, 10 July, 1931 — G
Died: Bolton, Greater Manchester, England, 12 October, 2004

League Club	Source	Date Signed	Seasons Played	Apps	Subs	Gls
Shrewsbury T		11/51	51	2	-	0

LEACH Brian Ernest
Born: Reading, England, 20 July, 1932 — LH
Died: Caversham, Berkshire, England, 7 March, 2013

League Club	Source	Date Signed	Seasons Played	Apps	Subs	Gls
Reading	Coley BC	11/50	52-56	108	-	1

LEACH Daniel James
Born: Perth, Australia, 5 January, 1986 — CD

League Club	Source	Date Signed	Seasons Played	Apps	Subs	Gls
Barnet	Portland Timbers (USA)	07/09	09-11	35	2	2

LEACH John Norman (Johnny)
Born: Whitehaven, Cumbria, England, 17 January, 1919 — LW

League Club	Source	Date Signed	Seasons Played	Apps	Subs	Gls
Barrow	Barrow Celtic	09/47	47-49	74	-	12

LEACH Marc Thomas
Born: Hemel Hempstead, Hertfordshire, England, 12 July, 1983 — CD

League Club	Source	Date Signed	Seasons Played	Apps	Subs	Gls
Wycombe W	YT	-	01	1	0	0

LEACH Michael John Christopher (Mick)
Born: Clapton, NE London, England, 16 January, 1947 — M/F
Died: West London, W London, England, 13 January, 1992
England: Youth

League Club	Source	Date Signed	Seasons Played	Apps	Subs	Gls
Queens Park Rgrs	App	02/64	64-77	291	22	61
Cambridge U	Detroit Express (USA)	09/78	78	18	1	1

LEACOCK Dean Graham
Born: Croydon, S London, England, 10 June, 1984 — CD
England: Youth

League Club	Source	Date Signed	Seasons Played	Apps	Subs	Gls
Fulham	Sch	07/02	03-05	8	1	0
Coventry C	L	09/04	04	12	1	0
Derby Co	Tr	08/06	06-10	103	14	1
Leyton Orient	Tr	01/12	11	15	0	0
Notts Co	Tr	07/12	12-13	67	1	2
Crawley T	Tr	07/14	14	23	0	1

LEADBEATER Richard Paul
Born: Dudley, West Midlands, England, 21 October, 1977 — F

League Club	Source	Date Signed	Seasons Played	Apps	Subs	Gls
Wolverhampton W	YT	07/96	96	0	1	0

LEADBETTER Albert
Born: Newton-le-Willows, Merseyside, England, 17 August, 1921 — LW
Died: Liverpool, England, May, 1994

League Club	Source	Date Signed	Seasons Played	Apps	Subs	Gls
Accrington Stan (Am)	Earlestown	12/46	46	4	-	0

LEADBETTER James Hunter (Jimmy)
Born: Edinburgh, Scotland, 15 July, 1928 — LW/WH
Died: Edinburgh, Scotland, 18 July, 2006

League Club	Source	Date Signed	Seasons Played	Apps	Subs	Gls
Chelsea	Edinburgh Thistle	07/49	51	3	-	0
Brighton & HA	Tr	08/52	52-54	107	-	29
Ipswich T	Tr	06/55	55-64	344	-	43

LEADBITTER Christopher Jonathan (Chris)
Born: Middlesbrough, England, 17 October, 1967 — LM

League Club	Source	Date Signed	Seasons Played	Apps	Subs	Gls
Grimsby T	App	09/85				
Hereford U	Tr	08/86	86-87	32	4	1
Cambridge U	Tr	08/88	88-92	144	32	18
Bournemouth	Tr	08/93	93-94	45	9	3
Plymouth Arg	Tr	07/95	95-96	46	6	1
Torquay U	Dorchester T	11/97	97-98	58	5	2
Plymouth Arg	Tr	07/99	99-00	37	3	2

LEADBITTER Daniel William
Born: Newcastle-upon-Tyne, England, 7 October, 1990 — RB

League Club	Source	Date Signed	Seasons Played	Apps	Subs	Gls
Newcastle U	Sch	07/10				
Torquay U	Tr	06/11	11-12	9	6	0

LEADBITTER Grant
Born: Chester-le-Street, County Durham, England, 7 January, 1986 — M
England: U21-3/Youth

League Club	Source	Date Signed	Seasons Played	Apps	Subs	Gls
Sunderland	Sch	01/03	05-09	61	50	11
Rotherham U	L	09/05	05	3	2	1
Ipswich T	Tr	09/09	09-11	112	4	13
Middlesbrough	Tr	07/12	12-14	119	5	21

LEADBITTER John
Born: Sunderland, England, 7 May, 1953 — CD

League Club	Source	Date Signed	Seasons Played	Apps	Subs	Gls
Sunderland	App	05/70				
Darlington	Tr	08/72	72	15	4	0

LEAF Andrew Keith (Andy)
Born: York, England, 18 January, 1962 — FB

League Club	Source	Date Signed	Seasons Played	Apps	Subs	Gls
York C	App	01/80	79	1	0	0

LEAH John David
Born: Shrewsbury, Shropshire, England, 3 August, 1978 — M

League Club	Source	Date Signed	Seasons Played	Apps	Subs	Gls
Darlington	Newtown	07/98	98	7	0	1

LEAHY Stephen David (Steve)
Born: Battersea, SW London, England, 23 September, 1959 — F
England: Schools

League Club	Source	Date Signed	Seasons Played	Apps	Subs	Gls
Crystal Palace	App	10/76	80-81	3	1	0

LEAKE Albert George
Born: Stoke-on-Trent, England, 7 April, 1930 — RH/IF
Died: Stoke-on-Trent, England, 24 July, 1999
England: Youth

League Club	Source	Date Signed	Seasons Played	Apps	Subs	Gls
Port Vale	Stoke C (Am)	02/50	50-59	269	-	34

LEAMON Frederick William (Fred)
Born: Jersey, Channel Islands, 11 May, 1919 — CF
Died: City of London, England, 27 August, 1981

League Club	Source	Date Signed	Seasons Played	Apps	Subs	Gls
Newport Co	Bath C	02/46	46	4	-	3
Bristol Rov	Tr	10/46	46-47	43	-	21
Brighton & HA	Tr	07/49	49	11	-	4

LEAN David Reginald
Born: Plymouth, England, 28 April, 1945 — CD

League Club	Source	Date Signed	Seasons Played	Apps	Subs	Gls
Plymouth Arg	Embankment	08/69	69-70	44	1	0

LEANING Andrew John (Andy)
Born: Howden, East Riding of Yorkshire, England, 18 May, 1963 — G

League Club	Source	Date Signed	Seasons Played	Apps	Subs	Gls
York C	Rowntree-Mack'sh	07/85	85-86	69	0	0
Sheffield U	Tr	05/87	87	21	0	0
Bristol C	Tr	09/88	88-92	75	0	0
Lincoln C	Tr	03/94	93-95	36	0	0
Chesterfield	Dundee	10/96	96-99	22	0	0

LEAR Graham John
Born: Exeter, England, 18 December, 1930 — G

League Club	Source	Date Signed	Seasons Played	Apps	Subs	Gls
Exeter C (Am)	Exeter T	06/50	50-51	20	-	0

LEARY Michael Antonio
Born: Ealing, W London, England, 17 April, 1983 — M

Republic of Ireland: Youth

League Club	Source	Date Signed	Seasons Played	Apps	Subs	Gls
Luton T	Jnr	08/01	03-04	9	13	2
Bristol Rov	L	08/05	05	12	1	0
Walsall	L	01/06	05	12	3	1
Torquay U	L	11/06	06	0	2	0
Brentford	L	01/07	06	17	0	0
Barnet	Tr	07/07	07-08	43	7	3
Grimsby T	Tr	07/09	09	19	9	0

LEARY Stuart Edward
Born: Cape Town, South Africa, 30 April, 1933 — CF
Died: Cape Town, South Africa, 21 August, 1988
England: U23-1

League Club	Source	Date Signed	Seasons Played	Apps	Subs	Gls
Charlton Ath	Clyde (RSA)	02/50	51-61	376	-	153
Queens Park Rgrs	Tr	12/62	62-65	94	0	29

LEATH Terence Charles (Terry)
Born: West Derby, Merseyside, England, 6 November, 1934 — RB

League Club	Source	Date Signed	Seasons Played	Apps	Subs	Gls
Southport	Birchfield Rov	03/59	58-59	17	-	0

LEATHER Maurice Peate
Born: Eastleigh, Hampshire, England, 9 November, 1929 — G
England: Youth

League Club	Source	Date Signed	Seasons Played	Apps	Subs	Gls
Portsmouth	Southampton (Am)	01/50	50-52	18	-	0

LEATHER Scott Ashley
Born: Sale, Greater Manchester, England, 30 September, 1992 — RB

League Club	Source	Date Signed	Seasons Played	Apps	Subs	Gls
Preston NE	Sch	07/11	10	2	0	0

LEAVER Derek
Born: Blackburn, Greater Manchester, England, 13 November, 1930 — IF
Died: Blackburn, Greater Manchester, England, 24 March, 2013

League Club	Source	Date Signed	Seasons Played	Apps	Subs	Gls
Blackburn Rov	Burnley (Am)	05/49	50-54	14	-	5
Bournemouth	Tr	07/55	55	29	-	5
Crewe Alex	Tr	03/56	55-56	28	-	5

LEAVY Stephen Francis (Steve)
Born: Longford, Republic of Ireland, 18 June, 1925 — RB
Died: Swansea, Wales, 26 January, 1996
Republic of Ireland: LoI-3

League Club	Source	Date Signed	Seasons Played	Apps	Subs	Gls
Swansea C	Sligo Rov (ROI)	07/50	50-57	37	-	1

LE BIHAN Neil Ernest
Born: Croydon, S London, England, 14 March, 1976 — M

League Club	Source	Date Signed	Seasons Played	Apps	Subs	Gls
Peterborough U	Tottenham H (YT)	07/94	94-96	21	10	0

LEBOEUF Frank Alain James
Born: Marseille, France, 22 January, 1968 — CD
France: 50

League Club	Source	Date Signed	Seasons Played	Apps	Subs	Gls
Chelsea	RC Strasbourg (FRA)	07/96	96-00	142	2	17

LECK Derek Alan
Born: Deal, Kent, England, 8 February, 1937 — RH/CF
Died: Brighton, England, 11 July, 2011

League Club	Source	Date Signed	Seasons Played	Apps	Subs	Gls
Millwall	Leyton YC	05/55	55-57	7	-	2
Northampton T	Tr	06/58	58-65	246	0	45
Brighton & HA	Tr	11/65	65-66	29	1	0

LECOINTE Matthew Robert (Matt)
Born: Plymouth, England, 29 October, 1994 — F
England: Youth

League Club	Source	Date Signed	Seasons Played	Apps	Subs	Gls
Plymouth Arg	Sch	05/12	11-12	11	14	2

LE CORNU Craig Douglas
Born: Birkenhead, Wirral, England, 17 September, 1960 — M

League Club	Source	Date Signed	Seasons Played	Apps	Subs	Gls
Liverpool	App	09/78				
Tranmere Rov	Tr	12/80	80	3	3	0

LECSINEL Jean-Francois
Born: Cayenne, French Guiana, 2 October, 1986 — LB
Haiti: 3

League Club	Source	Date Signed	Seasons Played	Apps	Subs	Gls
Swindon T	EA Guingamp (FRA)	01/09	08-10	45	11	1
Sheffield U	Tr	07/11	11	22	3	0

LEDESMA Emmanuel Jorge
Born: Quilmes, Argentina, 24 May, 1988 — W

League Club	Source	Date Signed	Seasons Played	Apps	Subs	Gls
Queens Park Rgrs (L)	Genoa (ITA)	08/08	08	11	6	1
Walsall	Genoa (ITA)	03/11	10	5	5	1
Walsall	Defensa Justicia (ARG)	03/12	11	9	1	4
Middlesbrough	Tr	07/12	12-14	31	25	8
Rotherham U	L	11/14	14	6	1	1
Brighton & HA	L	02/15	14	2	2	0

LEDGARD Ian
Born: Stockport, Greater Manchester, England, 9 February, 1948 — LB

League Club	Source	Date Signed	Seasons Played	Apps	Subs	Gls
Blackburn Rov	Leeds U (Am)	07/67				
Stockport Co	Tr	10/67	67-68	4	4	0

LEDGER Robert Hardy (Bob)
Born: Craghead, County Durham, England, 5 October, 1937 — CF/RW

League Club	Source	Date Signed	Seasons Played	Apps	Subs	Gls
Huddersfield T	Jnr	10/54	55-61	58	-	7
Oldham Ath	Tr	05/62	62-67	221	1	37
Mansfield T	Tr	11/67	67-69	51	6	15
Barrow	Tr	10/69	69	21	1	2

LEDGER Roy
Born: Barnsley, South Yorkshire, England, 9 December, 1930 — IF
Died: Barnsley, South Yorkshire, England, March, 1992

League Club	Source	Date Signed	Seasons Played	Apps	Subs	Gls
Barnsley	Smithies U	04/48	50	1	-	0

LEDGERTON Terence (Terry)
Born: Liverpool, England, 7 October, 1930 — LW
Died: Colchester, Essex, England, December, 2004

League Club	Source	Date Signed	Seasons Played	Apps	Subs	Gls
Brentford	Huyton	05/50	51-53	40	-	8
Millwall	Tr	05/54	54	6	-	2

LEDGISTER Aaron Turone
Born: Hong Kong, 9 October, 1987 — LW

League Club	Source	Date Signed	Seasons Played	Apps	Subs	Gls
Cheltenham T	Bristol C (Sch)	07/07	08	0	1	0

LEDLEY Joseph Christopher (Joe)
Born: Cardiff, Wales, 23 January, 1987 — LM
Wales: 57/U21-5/Youth

League Club	Source	Date Signed	Seasons Played	Apps	Subs	Gls
Cardiff C	Sch	10/04	04-09	213	13	25
Crystal Palace	Glasgow Celtic	01/14	13-14	44	2	4

LEE Alan Desmond
Born: Galway, Republic of Ireland, 21 August, 1978 — F
Republic of Ireland: 10/U21-5

League Club	Source	Date Signed	Seasons Played	Apps	Subs	Gls
Aston Villa	YT	08/95				
Torquay U	L	11/98	98	6	1	2
Port Vale	L	03/99	98	7	4	2
Burnley	Tr	07/99	99	2	13	0
Rotherham U	Tr	09/00	00-03	105	6	37
Cardiff C	Tr	08/03	03-05	47	39	10
Ipswich T	Tr	06/05	05-08	91	12	31
Crystal Palace	Tr	08/08	08-10	46	15	11
Norwich C	L	03/09	08	6	1	2
Huddersfield T	Tr	08/10	10-12	36	44	9
Ipswich T	Tr	08/13				

LEE Alan Robert
Born: Wegburg, Germany, 19 June, 1960 — LW

League Club	Source	Date Signed	Seasons Played	Apps	Subs	Gls
Leicester C	Philadelphia F'y (USA)	02/79	78-79	6	0	0

LEE Alfred (Alf)
Born: Farnworth, Greater Manchester, England, 11 June, 1927 — WH
Died: Boston, Lincolnshire, England, March, 1991

League Club	Source	Date Signed	Seasons Played	Apps	Subs	Gls
Bolton W		10/48				
Oldham Ath	Tr	07/50	50	3	-	1

LEE Andrew Gerard (Andy)
Born: Liverpool, England, 14 September, 1962 — RB/M
England: Semi Pro/Schools

League Club	Source	Date Signed	Seasons Played	Apps	Subs	Gls
Tranmere Rov	Stafford Rgrs	07/84	84	14	4	0
Cambridge U		09/85	85	8	1	0

LEE Andrew Jack (Andy)
Born: Bradford, England, 18 August, 1982 — M

League Club	Source	Date Signed	Seasons Played	Apps	Subs	Gls
Bradford C	YT	07/01	01-02	0	2	0

LEE Anthony (Tony)
Born: Manchester, England, 4 June, 1937 — LW

League Club	Source	Date Signed	Seasons Played	Apps	Subs	Gls
Southport (Am)	Cheadle Rov	02/58	57-58	10	-	1

LEE Charlie
Born: Whitechapel, Central London, England, 5 January, 1987 — M/RB

League Club	Source	Date Signed	Seasons Played	Apps	Subs	Gls
Tottenham H	Sch	07/05				
Millwall	L	11/06	06	4	1	0
Peterborough U	Tr	07/07	07-10	125	28	14
Gillingham	L	11/10	10	4	0	1
Gillingham	Tr	07/11	11-13	72	23	10
Stevenage	Tr	07/14	14	38	6	9

LEE Christian Earl
Born: Aylesbury, Buckinghamshire, England, 8 October, 1976 — F

League Club	Source	Date Signed	Seasons Played	Apps	Subs	Gls
Northampton T	Doncaster Rov (YT)	07/95	95-98	25	34	8
Gillingham	Tr	08/99	99	1	2	0
Rochdale	L	10/00	00	2	3	1
Leyton Orient	L	03/01	00	2	1	0
Bristol Rov	Tr	03/01	00	8	1	2
Rushden & D	Farnborough T	09/01	01	1	0	0

LEE Christopher (Chris)
Born: Batley, West Yorkshire, England, 18 June, 1971 — M

League Club	Source	Date Signed	Seasons Played	Apps	Subs	Gls
Bradford C	YT	07/89				
Rochdale	Tr	06/90	90	24	2	2
Scarborough	Tr	03/91	90-92	75	3	3
Hull C	Tr	07/93	93-95	104	12	5

LEE Chung-Yong
Born: Seoul, South Korea, 2 July, 1988 — RW
South Korea: 67

League Club	Source	Date Signed	Seasons Played	Apps	Subs	Gls
Bolton W	FC Seoul (KOR)	08/09	09-14	140	36	17
Crystal Palace	Tr	02/15	14	1	2	0

LEE Colin
Born: Torquay, Devon, England, 12 June, 1956 — F/RB

League Club	Source	Date Signed	Seasons Played	Apps	Subs	Gls
Bristol C	App	06/74				
Hereford U	L	11/74	74	7	2	0
Torquay U	Tr	01/77	76-77	35	0	14
Tottenham H	Tr	10/77	77-79	57	5	18
Chelsea	Tr	01/80	79-86	167	18	36
Brentford	Tr	07/87	87-88	20	4	1

LEE David John
Born: Kingswood, Avon, England, 26 November, 1969 — CD/M
England: U21-10/Youth

League Club	Source	Date Signed	Seasons Played	Apps	Subs	Gls
Chelsea	YT	07/88	88-97	119	32	11
Reading	L	01/92	91	5	0	5
Plymouth Arg	L	03/92	91	9	0	1
Portsmouth	L	08/94	94	4	1	0
Sheffield U	L	12/97	97	5	0	0
Bristol Rov	Tr	12/98	98	10	1	1
Crystal Palace	Tr	10/99				
Colchester U	Tr	01/00				
Exeter C	Tr	02/00	99	3	1	0

LEE David John Francis
Born: Basildon, England, 28 March, 1980 — RM

League Club	Source	Date Signed	Seasons Played	Apps	Subs	Gls
Tottenham H	YT	07/98				
Southend U	Tr	08/00	00	37	5	8
Hull C	Tr	06/01	01	2	9	1
Brighton & HA	Tr	01/02	01-03	1	5	0
Bristol Rov	L	10/02	02	5	0	0
Oldham Ath	Thurrock	10/04	04	5	2	0

LEE David Mark
Born: Manchester, England, 5 November, 1967 — RW

League Club	Source	Date Signed	Seasons Played	Apps	Subs	Gls
Bury	Jnr	08/86	85-91	203	5	35
Southampton	Tr	08/91	91-92	11	9	0
Bolton W	Tr	11/92	92-96	124	31	17
Wigan Ath	Tr	07/97	97-99	61	22	11
Blackpool	L	10/99	99	9	0	1
Carlisle U	Tr	08/00	00	1	12	0

LEE Dong-Gook
Born: Pohang, South Korea, 29 April, 1979 — F
South Korea: 71

League Club	Source	Date Signed	Seasons Played	Apps	Subs	Gls
Middlesbrough	Pohang Steelers (KOR)	01/07	06-07	8	15	0

LEE Dwayne Anthony
Born: Hillingdon, W London, England, 26 November, 1979 — M

League Club	Source	Date Signed	Seasons Played	Apps	Subs	Gls
Barnet	Exeter C	08/04	05	24	3	4

LEE Elliot Robert
Born: Durham, England, 16 December, 1994 — F

League Club	Source	Date Signed	Seasons Played	Apps	Subs	Gls
West Ham U	Sch	12/11	13-14	0	2	0
Colchester U	L	10/13	13	4	0	1
Luton T	L	02/15	14	9	2	3

LEE Eric George
Born: Chester, England, 18 October, 1922 — CH
England: Amateur-3

League Club	Source	Date Signed	Seasons Played	Apps	Subs	Gls
Chester C	Jnr	05/46	46-56	363	-	10

LEE Francis (Frank)
Born: Chorley, Lancashire, England, 17 February, 1944 — W

League Club	Source	Date Signed	Seasons Played	Apps	Subs	Gls
Preston NE	Horwich RMI	11/61	63-70	143	10	22
Southport	Tr	11/70	70-73	115	0	21
Stockport Co	Tr	07/74	74	13	0	1

LEE Francis Henry
Born: Westhoughton, Greater Manchester, England, 29 April, 1944 — F
England: 27/FLge-1/Youth

League Club	Source	Date Signed	Seasons Played	Apps	Subs	Gls
Bolton W	Jnr	05/61	60-67	189	0	92
Manchester C	Tr	10/67	67-73	248	1	112
Derby Co	Tr	08/74	74-75	62	0	24

LEE Frederick Stuart (Stuart)
Born: Manchester, England, 11 February, 1953 — F

League Club	Source	Date Signed	Seasons Played	Apps	Subs	Gls
Bolton W	App	02/71	71-74	77	8	20
Wrexham	Tr	11/75	75-77	46	8	12
Stockport Co	Tr	08/78	78-79	49	0	21
Manchester C	Tr	09/79	79	6	1	2

LEE Garth
Born: Sheffield, England, 30 September, 1943 — LW
England: Youth

League Club	Source	Date Signed	Seasons Played	Apps	Subs	Gls
Sheffield U	Jnr	05/61				
Chester C	Tr	09/63	63-64	28	-	7

LEE Gary
Born: Doncaster, South Yorkshire, England, 30 April, 1966 — CD

League Club	Source	Date Signed	Seasons Played	Apps	Subs	Gls
Doncaster Rov	YT	07/84	84	1	0	0

LEE George Thomas
Born: York, England, 4 June, 1919 — LW
Died: Norwich, England, 2 April, 1991

League Club	Source	Date Signed	Seasons Played	Apps	Subs	Gls
York C	Scarborough	06/36	36-46	37	-	11
Nottingham F	Tr	08/47	47-48	76	-	20
West Bromwich A	Tr	07/49	49-57	271	-	59

LEE Gordon Francis
Born: Hednesford, Staffordshire, England, 13 July, 1934 — FB

League Club	Source	Date Signed	Seasons Played	Apps	Subs	Gls
Aston Villa	Hednesford T	10/55	58-64	118	-	2
Shrewsbury T	Tr	07/66	66	2	0	0

LEE Graeme Barry
Born: Middlesbrough, England, 31 May, 1978 — CD

League Club	Source	Date Signed	Seasons Played	Apps	Subs	Gls
Hartlepool U	YT	07/96	95-02	208	11	19
Sheffield Wed	Tr	07/03	03-05	63	4	5
Doncaster Rov	Tr	01/06	05-07	56	4	5
Hartlepool U	L	02/08	07	3	0	0
Shrewsbury T	L	03/08	07	4	1	0
Bradford C	Tr	07/08	08	44	0	2
Notts Co	Tr	07/09	09-10	45	5	4

LEE Harold (Harry)
Born: Mexborough, South Yorkshire, England, 13 January, 1933 — IF

League Club	Source	Date Signed	Seasons Played	Apps	Subs	Gls
Derby Co	Thomas Hill YC	10/50				
Doncaster Rov	Margate	07/55				
Mansfield T	Tr	08/55	55	3	-	2

LEE Harry Bertie
Born: Hackney, E London, England, 20 March, 1995 — M

League Club	Source	Date Signed	Seasons Played	Apps	Subs	Gls
Leyton Orient	Sch	07/13	12-14	0	3	0

LEE Jake Alexander
Born: Cirencester, Gloucestershire, England, 18 September, 1991 — F

League Club	Source	Date Signed	Seasons Played	Apps	Subs	Gls
Cheltenham T	Sch	07/10	08-09	2	2	0

LEE James (Jimmy)
Born: Rotherham, South Yorkshire, England, 26 January, 1926 — FB
Died: Hereford, England, 15 May, 2001

League Club	Source	Date Signed	Seasons Played	Apps	Subs	Gls
Wolverhampton W	Wath W	02/45				
Hull C	Tr	10/48	49	3	-	1
Halifax T	Tr	02/51	50-51	26	-	0
Chelsea	Tr	10/51				
Leyton Orient	Tr	07/54	54-55	67	-	1
Swindon T	Tr	11/56	56-58	35	-	0

LEE Jason Benedict
Born: Forest Gate, E London, England, 9 May, 1971 — F

League Club	Source	Date Signed	Seasons Played	Apps	Subs	Gls
Charlton Ath	YT	06/89	89	0	1	0
Stockport Co	L	02/91	90	2	0	0
Lincoln C	Tr	03/91	90-92	86	7	21
Southend U	Tr	08/93	93	18	6	3
Nottingham F	Tr	03/94	93-96	41	35	14
Charlton Ath	L	02/97	96	7	1	3
Grimsby T	L	03/97	96	2	5	2
Watford	Tr	06/97	97-98	36	1	11
Chesterfield	Tr	08/98	98-99	17	11	1
Peterborough U	Tr	01/00	99-02	49	29	17
Boston U	Falkirk	08/04	04-05	43	13	11
Northampton T	Tr	01/06	05	8	3	1
Notts Co	Tr	06/06	06-07	59	10	16

LEE Jeffrey Wreathall (Jeff)
Born: Dewsbury, West Yorkshire, England, 3 October, 1945 — LB

League Club	Source	Date Signed	Seasons Played	Apps	Subs	Gls
Halifax T	Huddersfield T (Am)	01/65	64-72	233	9	3
Peterborough U	Tr	08/73	73-77	170	2	12

LEE John (Jack)
Born: Sileby, Leicestershire, England, 4 November, 1920 — CF
Died: Rugby, Warwickshire, England, 16 January, 1995
England: 1

League Club	Source	Date Signed	Seasons Played	Apps	Subs	Gls
Leicester C	Quorn Meth's	02/41	46-49	123	-	74
Derby Co	Tr	07/50	50-53	93	-	54
Coventry C	Tr	11/54	54	15	-	8

LEE John Anthony (Tony)
Born: Middlesbrough, England, 26 November, 1947 — RW

League Club	Source	Date Signed	Seasons Played	Apps	Subs	Gls
Leicester C		10/65				
Bradford C	Tr	07/67	67	6	2	3
Darlington	Stockton	05/68	68	11	3	1
Hartlepool U	South Shields	08/70				

LEE Kieran Christopher
Born: Stalybridge, Greater Manchester, England, 22 June, 1988 — DM

League Club	Source	Date Signed	Seasons Played	Apps	Subs	Gls
Manchester U	Sch	07/06	06	1	0	0

League Club	Source	Date Signed	Seasons Played	Apps	Subs	Gls
Queens Park Rgrs	L	01/08	07	2	5	0
Oldham Ath	Tr	07/08	08-11	108	9	5
Sheffield Wed	Tr	07/12	12-14	70	12	7

LEE Martyn James
Born: Guildford, Surrey, England, 10 September, 1980 — W

League Club	Source	Date Signed	Seasons Played	Apps	Subs	Gls
Wycombe W	YT	01/99	98-02	22	19	3
Cheltenham T	L	03/02	01	2	3	0

LEE Michael James (Mike)
Born: Mold, Flintshire, Wales, 27 June, 1938 — LW
Wales: Schools

League Club	Source	Date Signed	Seasons Played	Apps	Subs	Gls
West Bromwich A	Saltney Jnrs	08/56	56	1	-	0
Crewe Alex	Tr	06/58	58	1	-	0

LEE Norman Thomas
Born: Trealaw, Rhondda Cynon Taff, Wales, 29 May, 1939 — LH

League Club	Source	Date Signed	Seasons Played	Apps	Subs	Gls
Tottenham H	Jnr	11/57				
Bournemouth	Tr	09/61				
Southend U	Tr	02/62	61-62	22	-	1

LEE Oliver Robert (Olly)
Born: Hornchurch, E London, England, 11 July, 1991 — M

League Club	Source	Date Signed	Seasons Played	Apps	Subs	Gls
West Ham U	Sch	07/09				
Dagenham & Red	L	03/11	10	4	1	0
Dagenham & Red	L	08/11	11	15	1	3
Gillingham	L	02/12	11	5	3	0
Barnet	Tr	07/12	12	6	5	0
Birmingham C	Tr	03/13	13	14	2	1
Plymouth Arg	L	01/15	14	9	6	2

LEE Paul Andrew
Born: Oxford, England, 30 May, 1952 — F

League Club	Source	Date Signed	Seasons Played	Apps	Subs	Gls
Hereford U	Oxford C	09/72	73-74	21	7	5

LEE Raymond Maurice (Ray)
Born: Bristol, England, 19 September, 1970 — W

League Club	Source	Date Signed	Seasons Played	Apps	Subs	Gls
Arsenal	YT	10/88				
Scarborough	Swindon T (NC)	02/91	90	2	8	0

LEE Richard (Dick)
Born: Sheffield, England, 11 September, 1944 — LH

League Club	Source	Date Signed	Seasons Played	Apps	Subs	Gls
Rotherham U	Jnr	05/63				
Notts Co	Tr	06/64				
Mansfield T	Tr	08/65	65	3	1	1
Halifax T	Tr	07/66	66-67	14	0	0

LEE Richard Anthony
Born: Oxford, England, 5 October, 1982 — G
England: Youth

League Club	Source	Date Signed	Seasons Played	Apps	Subs	Gls
Watford	YT	03/00	02-08	89	3	0
Brentford	Tr	07/10	10-13	66	0	0

LEE Robert
Born: Newcastle-upon-Tyne, England, 23 December, 1957 — M

League Club	Source	Date Signed	Seasons Played	Apps	Subs	Gls
Doncaster Rov	App	05/74	74	1	0	0
Scunthorpe U	Tr	07/76	76-77	17	2	0

LEE Robert Gordon (Bob)
Born: Melton Mowbray, Leicestershire, England, 2 February, 1953 — F

League Club	Source	Date Signed	Seasons Played	Apps	Subs	Gls
Leicester C	Blaby BC	02/72	71-76	55	8	17
Doncaster Rov	L	08/74	74	14	0	4
Sunderland	Tr	09/76	76-79	101	6	32
Bristol Rov	Tr	08/80	80	19	4	2
Carlisle U	Tr	08/81	81-82	47	8	12
Southampton	Tr	03/83				
Darlington	Tr	08/83	83	5	0	0

LEE Robert Martin (Rob)
Born: West Ham, E London, England, 1 February, 1966 — M
England: 21/B-1/U21-2

League Club	Source	Date Signed	Seasons Played	Apps	Subs	Gls
Charlton Ath	Hornchurch	07/83	83-92	274	24	59
Newcastle U	Tr	09/92	92-01	292	11	44
Derby Co	Tr	02/02	01-02	47	1	2
West Ham U	Tr	08/03	03	12	4	0
Oldham Ath	Tr	11/04				
Wycombe W	Tr	03/05	04-05	34	4	0

LEE Samuel (Sammy)
Born: Liverpool, England, 7 February, 1959 — M
England: 14/U21-6/Youth

League Club	Source	Date Signed	Seasons Played	Apps	Subs	Gls
Liverpool	App	04/76	77-85	190	7	13
Queens Park Rgrs	Tr	08/86	86	29	1	0
Southampton	CA Osasuna (SPN)	01/90	89	0	2	0
Bolton W	Tr	10/90	90	4	0	0

LEE Tadanari
Born: Tokyo, Japan, 19 December, 1985 — F
Japan: 10

League Club	Source	Date Signed	Seasons Played	Apps	Subs	Gls
Southampton	Sanfrecce (JPN)	01/12	11	4	3	1

LEE Terence William George (Terry)
Born: Stepney, E London, England, 20 September, 1952 — G
Died: Torquay, Devon, England, 22 June, 1996

League Club	Source	Date Signed	Seasons Played	Apps	Subs	Gls
Tottenham H	Jnr	05/70	73	1	0	0
Torquay U	Tr	07/75	75-77	106	0	0
Newport Co	Tr	11/78	78	1	0	0

LEE Thomas Edward (Tommy)
Born: Keighley, West Yorkshire, England, 3 January, 1986 — G

League Club	Source	Date Signed	Seasons Played	Apps	Subs	Gls
Manchester U	Sch	07/05				
Macclesfield T	Tr	01/06	05-07	62	1	0
Rochdale	L	03/08	07	11	0	0
Chesterfield	Tr	08/08	08-14	275	0	0

LEE Thomas Joseph (Tommy)
Born: Horden, County Durham, England, 19 December, 1949 — M

League Club	Source	Date Signed	Seasons Played	Apps	Subs	Gls
Hartlepool U	Sunderland College	11/68	69	6	0	0

LEE Trevor Carl
Born: Lewisham, SE London, England, 3 July, 1954 — F

League Club	Source	Date Signed	Seasons Played	Apps	Subs	Gls
Millwall	Epsom & Ewell	10/75	75-78	99	9	22
Colchester U	Tr	11/78	78-80	95	1	35
Gillingham	Tr	01/81	80-82	43	4	14
Leyton Orient	L	10/82	82	5	0	0
Bournemouth	Tr	11/82	82-83	28	6	9
Cardiff C	Tr	12/83	83	21	0	5
Northampton T	Tr	07/84	84	24	0	0
Fulham	Tr	03/85	84	1	0	0

LEE William Richard (Billy)
Born: Darwen, Lancashire, England, 24 October, 1919 — RH
Died: Barrow, Cumbria, England, 14 November, 1996

League Club	Source	Date Signed	Seasons Played	Apps	Subs	Gls
Blackburn Rov	Pleasington	08/38	38	1	-	0
Barrow	Tr	05/47	46-52	158	-	1

LEE Young-Pyo
Born: Hong Chung, South Korea, 23 April, 1977 — LB
South Korea: 118

League Club	Source	Date Signed	Seasons Played	Apps	Subs	Gls
Tottenham H	PSV Eindhoven (NED)	07/05	05-07	68	2	0

LEE-BARRETT Arran
Born: Ipswich, England, 28 February, 1984 — G
England: Semi Pro-1

League Club	Source	Date Signed	Seasons Played	Apps	Subs	Gls
Cardiff C	Norwich C (Sch)	03/03				
Coventry C	Weymouth	01/07				
Hartlepool U	Tr	07/07	07-08	55	0	0
Ipswich T	Tr	08/09	09-11	36	2	0
Bolton W	Millwall (NC)	10/13				

LEEBROOK Peter David
Born: Saltburn, Cleveland, England, 18 September, 1968 — RB

League Club	Source	Date Signed	Seasons Played	Apps	Subs	Gls
Burnley	App	05/87	86-87	52	0	0

LEECH Fred
Born: Stalybridge, Greater Manchester, England, 5 December, 1923 — CF
Died: Tameside, Greater Manchester, England, December, 2001

League Club	Source	Date Signed	Seasons Played	Apps	Subs	Gls
Bradford C	Hurst	12/45	46	7	-	2

LEECH Vincent Graham (Vince)
Born: Littleborough, Greater Manchester, England, 6 December, 1940 — RH/FB

League Club	Source	Date Signed	Seasons Played	Apps	Subs	Gls
Blackburn Rov	Burnley (Am)	04/59				
Bury	Tr	07/61	61-67	108	3	0
Rochdale	Tr	07/68	68-70	59	0	1

LEEDER Frederick (Fred)
Born: New Hartley, Northumberland, England, 15 September, 1936 — RB

League Club	Source	Date Signed	Seasons Played	Apps	Subs	Gls
Everton	New Delaval Jnrs	03/55	57	1	-	0
Darlington	Tr	07/58	58-59	21	-	0
Southport	Tr	07/60	60-61	63	-	0

LEEDHAM John Richard
Born: Carshalton, S London, England, 8 November, 1942 — CH

League Club	Source	Date Signed	Seasons Played	Apps	Subs	Gls
Millwall	Epsom & Ewell	10/62	62-63	9	-	0
Walsall	Tr	05/64	64	13	-	0
Leyton Orient	Tr	08/65				

LEEK Kenneth (Ken)
Born: Ynysybwl, Rhondda Cynon Taff, Wales, 26 July, 1935 — IF
Died: Daventry, Northamptonshire, England, 19 November, 2007
Wales: 13/U23-1

League Club	Source	Date Signed	Seasons Played	Apps	Subs	Gls
Northampton T	Pontypridd YC	08/52	55-57	71	-	27
Leicester C	Tr	05/58	58-60	93	-	34
Newcastle U	Tr	06/61	61	13	-	6
Birmingham C	Tr	11/61	61-64	104	-	49
Northampton T	Tr	12/64	64-65	16	0	4
Bradford C	Tr	11/65	65-67	99	0	25

LEEMING Clifford (Cliff)
Born: Edgworth, Lancashire, England, 2 February, 1920 — LW
Died: Bolton, Greater Manchester, England, February, 2014

League Club	Source	Date Signed	Seasons Played	Apps	Subs	Gls
Bury	Bolton W (Am)	10/46	46	1	-	0
Tranmere Rov	Tr	07/47	47	13	-	2

LEES Alfred (Alf)
Born: Worsley, Greater Manchester, England, 28 July, 1923 — CH

League Club	Source	Date Signed	Seasons Played	Apps	Subs	Gls
Bolton W		05/47	47	2	-	0
New Brighton	Tr	08/49	49-50	72	-	0
Crewe Alex	Tr	09/51	51-55	186	-	5

LEES Geoffrey (Geoff)
Born: Rotherham, South Yorkshire, England, 1 October, 1933 — WH

League Club	Source	Date Signed	Seasons Played	Apps	Subs	Gls
Barnsley	Jnr	03/51				
Bradford C	Tr	07/55	55	3	-	0

LEES Norman
Born: Newcastle-upon-Tyne, England, 18 November, 1948 — M/D

League Club	Source	Date Signed	Seasons Played	Apps	Subs	Gls
Hull C	App	11/66	66-70	4	1	0
Hartlepool U	L	12/70	70	20	0	1
Darlington	Tr	07/71	71-76	108	12	5

LEES Terence (Terry)
Born: Stoke-on-Trent, England, 30 June, 1952 — M/D

League Club	Source	Date Signed	Seasons Played	Apps	Subs	Gls
Stoke C	App	07/69	70-73	17	7	0
Crewe Alex	L	03/75	74	6	0	0
Port Vale	San Jose E'quake (USA)	08/75	75	40	1	2
Birmingham C	Roda JC (NED)	07/79	79-80	11	1	0
Newport Co	Tr	08/81	81	25	0	0
Scunthorpe U	Stafford Rgrs	09/84	84	30	1	0

LEES Thomas James (Tom)
Born: Warwick, England, 28 November, 1990 — CD
England: U21-6

League Club	Source	Date Signed	Seasons Played	Apps	Subs	Gls
Leeds U	Sch	01/09	11-13	119	4	3
Accrington Stan	L	09/09	09	39	0	0
Bury	L	07/10	10	45	0	4
Sheffield Wed	Tr	08/14	14	44	0	0

LEES Walter Joseph
Born: Glasgow, Scotland, 2 February, 1947 — CD

League Club	Source	Date Signed	Seasons Played	Apps	Subs	Gls
Watford	Kilsyth Rgrs	06/68	68-75	220	6	10

LEESE Lars
Born: Cologne, Germany, 18 August, 1969 — G

League Club	Source	Date Signed	Seasons Played	Apps	Subs	Gls
Barnsley	Bayer Leverkusen (GER)	07/97	97-98	16	1	0

LEESE William (Billy)
Born: Stoke-on-Trent, England, 10 March, 1961 — CD

League Club	Source	Date Signed	Seasons Played	Apps	Subs	Gls
Port Vale	App	03/79	79	1	0	0

LEESON Donald (Don)
Born: Askern, South Yorkshire, England, 25 August, 1935 — G
Died: Grimsby, North Lincolnshire, England, 15 February, 2009

League Club	Source	Date Signed	Seasons Played	Apps	Subs	Gls
Barnsley	Askern Welfare	05/54	56-60	97	-	0

LEET Norman David
Born: Leicester, England, 13 March, 1962 — LB
England: Schools

League Club	Source	Date Signed	Seasons Played	Apps	Subs	Gls
Leicester C	Shepshed Charterhouse	06/80	80-82	19	0	0

LE FLEM Richard Peter (Dick)
Born: Bradford-on-Avon, Wiltshire, England, 12 July, 1942 — LW
England: U23-1

League Club	Source	Date Signed	Seasons Played	Apps	Subs	Gls
Nottingham F	Jnr	05/60	60-63	132	-	18
Wolverhampton W	Tr	01/64	63-64	19	-	5
Middlesbrough	Tr	02/65	64-65	9	0	1
Leyton Orient	Tr	03/66	65-66	11	0	2

LE FONDRE Adam
Born: Stockport, Greater Manchester, England, 2 December, 1986 — F

League Club	Source	Date Signed	Seasons Played	Apps	Subs	Gls
Stockport Co	Sch	02/05	04-06	29	34	17
Rochdale	L	01/07	06	7	0	4
Rochdale	Tr	07/07	07-09	58	33	33
Rotherham U	Tr	08/09	09-11	87	6	52
Reading	Tr	08/11	11-13	53	51	39
Cardiff C	Tr	05/14	14	19	4	3
Bolton W	L	01/15	14	16	1	8

LEGATE Roland Arthur (Roly)
Born: Arlesey, Bedfordshire, England, 4 May, 1939 — LW

League Club	Source	Date Signed	Seasons Played	Apps	Subs	Gls
Luton T	Arlesey T	05/56	56-61	15	-	8

LEGG Andrew (Andy)
Born: Neath, Wales, 28 July, 1966 — LW
Wales: 6

League Club	Source	Date Signed	Seasons Played	Apps	Subs	Gls
Swansea C	Briton Ferry	08/88	88-92	155	8	29
Notts Co	Tr	07/93	93-95	85	4	9
Birmingham C	Tr	02/96	95-96	31	14	5
Ipswich T	L	11/97	97	6	0	1
Reading	Tr	02/98	97-98	12	0	0
Peterborough U	L	10/98	98	5	0	0
Cardiff C	Tr	12/98	98-02	152	23	12
Peterborough U	Tr	07/03	03-04	76	5	5

LEGG Richard Desmond
Born: Chippenham, Wiltshire, England, 23 April, 1952 — F

League Club	Source	Date Signed	Seasons Played	Apps	Subs	Gls
Swindon T	Chippenham T	08/71	71-73	13	7	3

LEGG William Campbell (Billy)
Born: Bradford, England, 17 April, 1948 — LB

League Club	Source	Date Signed	Seasons Played	Apps	Subs	Gls
Huddersfield T	App	05/65	64-68	54	2	4

LEGGAT Graham
Born: Aberdeen, Scotland, 20 June, 1934 — RW
Died: Canada, 29 August, 2015
Scotland: 18/SLge-5/U23-1

League Club	Source	Date Signed	Seasons Played	Apps	Subs	Gls
Fulham	Aberdeen	08/58	58-66	251	3	127
Birmingham C	Tr	01/67	66-67	13	3	4
Rotherham U	Tr	07/68	68	13	2	7

LEGGE Leon Clinton
Born: Bexhill, East Sussex, England, 1 July, 1985 — CD

League Club	Source	Date Signed	Seasons Played	Apps	Subs	Gls
Brentford	Tonbridge Angels	07/09	09-12	81	13	9
Gillingham	Tr	01/13	12-14	79	2	8

LEGGETT Peter Robert
Born: Newton-le-Willows, Merseyside, England, 16 December, 1943 — RW

League Club	Source	Date Signed	Seasons Played	Apps	Subs	Gls
Swindon T	Weymouth	05/62	63-64	15	-	1
Brighton & HA	Tr	07/65	65	2	1	0
Cambridge U	Chelmsford C	01/70	70	21	0	3

LEGWINSKI Sylvain
Born: Clermont-Ferrand, France, 6 October, 1973 — M
France: B-3/U21-4

League Club	Source	Date Signed	Seasons Played	Apps	Subs	Gls
Fulham	Bordeaux (FRA)	08/01	01-05	116	12	8
Ipswich T	Tr	08/06	06-07	40	7	7

LEGZDINS Adam Richard
Born: Penkridge, Staffordshire, England, 28 November, 1986 — G

League Club	Source	Date Signed	Seasons Played	Apps	Subs	Gls
Birmingham C	Sch	07/06				
Crewe Alex	Tr	06/08	09	6	0	0
Burton A	Tr	08/10	10	46	0	0
Derby Co	Tr	07/11	11-12	32	3	0
Burton A	L	03/12	11	1	0	0
Leyton Orient	Tr	06/14	14	11	0	0

LEHMANN Dirk Johannes
Born: Aachen, Germany, 16 August, 1971 — F

League Club	Source	Date Signed	Seasons Played	Apps	Subs	Gls
Fulham	Energie Cottbuss (GER)	08/98	98	16	10	2
Brighton & HA	Hibernian	06/01	01	3	4	0

LEHMANN Jens Gerhard
Born: Essen, Germany, 10 November, 1969 — G
Germany: 61/U21-6/Youth

League Club	Source	Date Signed	Seasons Played	Apps	Subs	Gls
Arsenal	Bor Dortmund (GER)	08/03	03-07	146	1	0
Arsenal	VfB Stuttgart (GER)	03/11	10	1	0	0

LEIGERTWOOD Mikele Benjamin
Born: Enfield, N London, England, 12 November, 1982 — DM
Antigua & Barbuda: 11

League Club	Source	Date Signed	Seasons Played	Apps	Subs	Gls
Wimbledon	YT	06/01	01-03	55	1	2
Leyton Orient	L	11/01	01	8	0	0
Crystal Palace	Tr	02/04	03-05	41	18	1
Sheffield U	Tr	07/06	06-07	17	4	0
Queens Park Rgrs	Tr	08/07	07-10	108	23	12
Reading	Tr	11/10	10-13	93	4	7

LEIGH Dennis
Born: Barnsley, South Yorkshire, England, 26 February, 1949 — LB

League Club	Source	Date Signed	Seasons Played	Apps	Subs	Gls
Doncaster Rov	App	03/67	66-67	34	3	1
Rotherham U	Tr	02/68	67-72	153	7	10
Lincoln C	Tr	02/73	72-78	201	4	3

LEIGH Gregory Alex (Greg)
Born: Sale, Greater Manchester, England, 30 September, 1994 — LB/M
England: Youth

League Club	Source	Date Signed	Seasons Played	Apps	Subs	Gls
Manchester C	Sch	07/13				
Crewe Alex	L	08/14	14	36	2	1

LEIGH Ian Reginald
Born: Ilfracombe, Devon, England, 11 June, 1962 — G

League Club	Source	Date Signed	Seasons Played	Apps	Subs	Gls
Bournemouth	Swaythling	10/79	81-85	123	0	0
Bristol C	L	01/85	84	1	0	0
Torquay U	L	09/85	85	4	0	0

LEIGH Mark Brian
Born: Manchester, England, 4 October, 1961 — M

League Club	Source	Date Signed	Seasons Played	Apps	Subs	Gls
Stockport Co	Manchester C (App)	11/79	80-83	6	5	1

LEIGH Peter
Born: Wythenshawe, Greater Manchester, England, 4 March, 1939 — LB

League Club	Source	Date Signed	Seasons Played	Apps	Subs	Gls
Manchester C	Stamford Lads	08/57	59	2	-	0
Crewe Alex	Tr	06/61	61-71	432	0	3

League Club	Source	Date Signed	Seasons Played	Career Record Apps	Subs	Gls
LEIGHTON Anthony (Tony)						
Born: Leeds, England, 27 November, 1939						CF
Died: Dewsbury, West Yorkshire, England, 4 April, 1978						
Leeds U	Leeds Ashley Road Jnrs	12/56				
Doncaster Rov	Tr	06/59	59-61	84	-	44
Barnsley	Tr	05/62	62-64	107	-	59
Huddersfield T	Tr	01/65	64-67	89	1	40
Bradford C	Tr	03/68	67-69	84	4	23
LEIGHTON James (Jim)						
Born: Johnstone, Renfrewshire, Scotland, 24 July, 1958						G
Scotland: 91/U21-1						
Manchester U	Aberdeen	05/88	88-89	73	0	0
Reading	L	11/91	91	8	0	0
LEIJER Adrian						
Born: Dubbo, NSW, Australia, 25 March, 1986						CD
Fulham	Melbourne Vic (AUS)	08/07				
Norwich C	L	02/09	08	1	3	0
LEIPER John						
Born: Aberdeen, Scotland, 26 June, 1938						G
Plymouth Arg	Aberdeen East End	04/58	60-66	75	0	0
LEISHMAN Graham						
Born: Salford, England, 6 April, 1968						F
Mansfield T	Irlam T	12/88	88-90	8	19	3
LEISHMAN Thomas (Tommy)						
Born: Stenhousemuir, Falkirk, Scotland, 3 September, 1937						LH
Liverpool	St Mirren	11/59	59-62	107	-	6
LEITAO Jorge Manuel Vasconcelos						
Born: Cinfaes, Portugal, 14 January, 1974						F
Walsall	CD Feirense (POR)	08/00	00-05	190	40	57
LEITCH Andrew Buchanan (Andy)						
Born: Exeter, England, 27 March, 1950						F
Swansea C	Cadbury Heath	07/75	75	15	2	6
LEITCH Donald Scott (Scott)						
Born: Motherwell, Lanarkshire, Scotland, 6 October, 1969						DM
Swindon T	Heart of Midlothian	03/96	95-99	119	3	1
LEITCH Grant						
Born: South Africa, 31 October, 1972						W
Blackpool	Jnr	08/90	91-93	13	12	1
LEITCH-SMITH A-Jay (Jay)						
Born: Crewe, Cheshire, England, 6 March, 1990						F
Crewe Alex	Sch	05/08	09-13	74	29	19
Yeovil T	Tr	06/14	14	21	12	2
LEIVERS William Ernest (Bill)						
Born: Bolsover, Derbyshire, England, 29 January, 1932						D
Chesterfield	Jnr	02/50	51-52	27	-	0
Manchester C	Tr	11/53	54-63	250	-	4
Doncaster Rov	Tr	07/64	64-65	24	0	1
LEKAJ Rexhap (Rocky)						
Born: Pec, Kosovo, 12 October, 1989						LW
Norway: Youth						
Sheffield Wed	Sch	10/07	06-08	0	4	0
LELAN Joshua Kipkemboi (Josh)						
Born: Burton-on-Trent, Staffordshire, England, 21 December, 1994						CD
Derby Co	Sch	07/12				
Swindon T	L	07/14	14	2	3	0
LELLO Cyril Frank						
Born: Ludlow, Shropshire, England, 24 February, 1920						LH
Died: Liverpool, England, August, 1997						
Northern Ireland: NILge-1						
Lincoln C	Shrewsbury T	02/44				
Everton	Shrewsbury T	09/47	47-56	237	-	9
Rochdale	Tr	11/56	56	11	-	0
LEMAN Dennis						
Born: Newcastle-upon-Tyne, England, 1 December, 1954						M
England: Schools						
Manchester C	App	12/71	73-75	10	7	1
Sheffield Wed	Tr	12/76	76-81	89	15	9
Wrexham	L	02/82	81	17	0	1
Scunthorpe U	Tr	08/82	82-83	38	0	3
LEMARCHAND Stephane						
Born: Saint-Lo, Normandy, France, 6 August, 1971						M
Carlisle U	Louhans Cuiseaux (FRA)	09/00	00	4	1	1
LEMON Arthur						
Born: Neath, Wales, 25 January, 1932						CF
Nottingham F	Neath OB	02/51	52-54	24	-	1

League Club	Source	Date Signed	Seasons Played	Career Record Apps	Subs	Gls
LEMON Paul Andrew						
Born: Middlesbrough, England, 3 June, 1966						M
Sunderland	App	05/84	84-88	91	16	15
Carlisle U	L	12/84	84	2	0	0
Walsall	L	11/89	89	2	0	0
Reading	L	12/89	89	3	0	0
Chesterfield	Tr	09/90	90-92	80	5	10
LENAGH Steven Michael (Steve)						
Born: Durham, England, 21 March, 1979						M
Chesterfield	Sheffield Wed (YT)	11/97	97-98	6	7	1
LENARDUZZI Robert Italo (Bob)						
Born: Vancouver, Canada, 1 May, 1955						D
Canada: 47						
Reading	App	05/73	71-75	63	4	2
LENG Michael (Mike)						
Born: Rotherham, South Yorkshire, England, 14 June, 1952						D
Rotherham U	App	06/70	71-75	94	7	2
Workington	Tr	07/76	76	43	0	2
LENIHAN Brian						
Born: Cork, Republic of Ireland, 8 June, 1994						RB
Republic of Ireland: U21-2						
Hull C	Cork C (ROI)	08/14				
Blackpool	L	11/14	14	2	0	0
LENIHAN Darragh						
Born: Dublin, Republic of Ireland, 16 March, 1994						M
Republic of Ireland: U21-4/Youth						
Blackburn Rov	Belvedere (ROI)	10/11	14	2	1	0
Burton A	L	10/14	14	15	2	1
LENIHAN Michael Martin (Micky)						
Born: Swansea, Wales, 15 October, 1946						F
Swansea C	Swansea GPO	08/72	72-73	9	3	0
LENNARD David (Dave)						
Born: Manchester, England, 31 December, 1944						M
Bolton W	Jnr	12/61	62-68	114	5	3
Halifax T	Tr	07/69	69-71	97	0	16
Blackpool	Tr	10/71	71-72	42	3	9
Cambridge U	Tr	08/73	73-74	39	1	6
Chester C	Tr	09/74	74-75	73	2	11
Stockport Co	Tr	07/76	76	39	0	4
Bournemouth	Tr	09/77	77-78	56	3	4
LENNON Aaron Justin						
Born: Leeds, England, 16 April, 1987						RW
England: 21/B-2/U21-3/Youth						
Leeds U	Sch	07/03	03-04	19	19	1
Tottenham H	Tr	07/05	05-14	220	46	26
Everton	L	02/15	14	12	2	2
LENNON Alexander Vincent (Alex)						
Born: Glasgow, Scotland, 25 October, 1925						IF
Died: Stevenage, Hertfordshire, England, October, 1992						
Rotherham U	Caledonians	11/44				
Queens Park Rgrs	Selby T	01/47	48	1	-	0
Mansfield T	Tr	02/49	48	3	-	0
LENNON Harry George						
Born: Romford, E London, England, 16 December, 1994						CD
Charlton Ath	Sch	12/12	13	1	1	0
Cambridge U	L	07/14	14	0	2	0
Gillingham	L	11/14	14	2	0	0
LENNON Neil Francis						
Born: Lurgan, Armagh, Northern Ireland, 25 June, 1971						M
Northern Ireland: 40/B-3/U23-1/U21-2/Youth						
Manchester C	YT	08/89	87	1	0	0
Crewe Alex	Tr	08/90	90-95	142	5	15
Leicester C	Tr	02/96	95-00	169	1	6
Nottingham F	Glasgow Celtic	07/07	07	15	3	0
Wycombe W	Tr	01/08	07	8	1	0
LENNON Steven						
Born: Irvine, Ayrshire, Scotland, 20 January, 1988						M/RB
Scotland: U21-6						
Lincoln C (L)	Glasgow Rangers	01/10	09	15	4	3
LENNOX Joe Michael						
Born: Bristol, England, 22 November, 1991						RW
Bristol C	Sch	07/10				
Plymouth Arg	Tr	01/12	11-12	6	13	1
LENNOX Stephen John Martin (Steve)						
Born: Aberdeen, Scotland, 14 November, 1964						RW
Stoke C	App	12/81	82	1	1	0
Torquay U	L	12/83	83	11	0	0

LEON Diego
Born: Palencia, Spain, 16 January, 1983 — LW

League Club	Source	Date Signed	Seasons Played	Apps	Subs	Gls
Barnsley	G'hopper Zurich (SUI)	01/08	07-08	31	6	2

LEONARD Carleton Craig
Born: Oswestry, Shropshire, England, 3 February, 1958 — LB

League Club	Source	Date Signed	Seasons Played	Apps	Subs	Gls
Shrewsbury T	Jnr	09/75	75-82	224	3	1
Hereford U	Tr	06/83	83-84	29	1	0
Cardiff C	Tr	07/85	85	4	0	0

LEONARD Christopher (Chris)
Born: Jarrow, Tyne and Wear, England, 11 July, 1927 — CH

League Club	Source	Date Signed	Seasons Played	Apps	Subs	Gls
Darlington	South Shields	03/52	51-53	26	-	0

LEONARD Gary Alan
Born: Newcastle-upon-Tyne, England, 28 November, 1965 — M

League Club	Source	Date Signed	Seasons Played	Apps	Subs	Gls
West Bromwich A	App	11/83				
Shrewsbury T	Tr	07/85	85-87	48	19	1
Hereford U	L	03/88	87	11	0	1
Bury	Tr	07/88	88	4	5	1
Stockport Co	Tr	03/89	88-89	15	2	1

LEONARD Gary Edward
Born: Northampton, England, 23 March, 1962 — M

League Club	Source	Date Signed	Seasons Played	Apps	Subs	Gls
Northampton T	App	03/80	79-80	2	0	0

LEONARD Henry (Harry)
Born: Jarrow, Tyne and Wear, England, 19 May, 1924 — FB
Died: Jarrow, Tyne and Wear, England, 23 January, 2006

League Club	Source	Date Signed	Seasons Played	Apps	Subs	Gls
Bradford Park Ave	Darlington (Am)	05/45	47	1	-	0
Hartlepool U	Tr	11/48	48	2	-	0

LEONARD Keith Andrew
Born: Birmingham, England, 10 November, 1950 — F

League Club	Source	Date Signed	Seasons Played	Apps	Subs	Gls
Aston Villa	Highgate U	04/72	72-75	36	2	11
Port Vale	L	11/73	73	12	1	1

LEONARD Mark Anthony
Born: St Helens, Merseyside, England, 27 September, 1962 — F
England: Schools

League Club	Source	Date Signed	Seasons Played	Apps	Subs	Gls
Everton	Witton A	02/82				
Tranmere Rov	L	03/83	82	6	1	0
Crewe Alex	Tr	06/83	83-84	51	3	15
Stockport Co	Tr	02/85	84-86	73	0	23
Bradford C	Tr	09/86	86-91	120	37	29
Rochdale	Tr	03/92	91	9	0	1
Preston NE	Tr	08/92	92	19	3	1
Chester C	Tr	08/93	93	28	4	8
Wigan Ath	Tr	09/94	94-95	60	4	12
Rochdale	Tr	07/96	96-98	74	6	6

LEONARD Michael Christopher (Mick)
Born: Carshalton, S London, England, 9 May, 1959 — G

League Club	Source	Date Signed	Seasons Played	Apps	Subs	Gls
Halifax T	Epsom & Ewell	07/76	76-79	69	0	0
Notts Co	Tr	09/79	79-88	204	0	0
Chesterfield	Tr	03/89	88-93	175	1	0
Halifax T	L	11/90	90	3	0	0

LEONARD Patrick Desmond (Paddy)
Born: Dublin, Republic of Ireland, 25 July, 1929 — IF

League Club	Source	Date Signed	Seasons Played	Apps	Subs	Gls
Bristol Rov	Bath C	07/52	52-53	14	-	2
Colchester U	Tr	07/54	54	34	-	5

LEONARD Ryan Ian
Born: Plympton, Devon, England, 24 May, 1992 — M

League Club	Source	Date Signed	Seasons Played	Apps	Subs	Gls
Plymouth Arg	Sch	07/10	09	0	1	0
Southend U	Tr	08/11	11-14	110	13	11

LEONARD Stanley (Stan)
Born: Hawarden, Flintshire, Wales, 8 October, 1924 — RW
Died: Petersfield, Hampshire, England, 1 August, 1995

League Club	Source	Date Signed	Seasons Played	Apps	Subs	Gls
Chester C (Am)	Fleet Air Arm	01/47	46	1	-	0

LEONHARDSEN Oyvind
Born: Kristiansund, Norway, 17 August, 1970 — M
Norway: 86/U21-14/Youth

League Club	Source	Date Signed	Seasons Played	Apps	Subs	Gls
Wimbledon	Rosenborg (NOR)	11/94	94-96	73	3	13
Liverpool	Tr	06/97	97-98	34	3	7
Tottenham H	Tr	08/99	99-01	46	8	7
Aston Villa	Tr	08/02	02	13	6	3

LEONI Stephane
Born: Metz, France, 1 September, 1976 — RB
France: U21

League Club	Source	Date Signed	Seasons Played	Apps	Subs	Gls
Bristol Rov	FC Metz (FRA)	08/98	98-99	27	11	0

LE PEN Ulrich
Born: Auray, Brittany, France, 21 January, 1974 — M
France: U21

League Club	Source	Date Signed	Seasons Played	Apps	Subs	Gls
Ipswich T	Lorient (FRA)	11/01	01	0	1	0

LEPOINT Christophe
Born: Brussels, Belgium, 24 October, 1984 — M
Belgium: 2/U21-20/Youth

League Club	Source	Date Signed	Seasons Played	Apps	Subs	Gls
Charlton Ath	KAA Gent (BEL)	01/15	14	1	5	0

LE ROUX Daniel Leow
Born: Port Shepstone, South Africa, 25 November, 1933 — RW
South Africa: Amateur

League Club	Source	Date Signed	Seasons Played	Apps	Subs	Gls
Arsenal	Queen's Park (RSA)	02/57	57	5	-	0

LE SAUX Graeme Pierre
Born: St Helier, Jersey, Channel Islands, 17 October, 1968 — LB
England: 36/B-2/U21-4

League Club	Source	Date Signed	Seasons Played	Apps	Subs	Gls
Chelsea	St Paul's, Jersey	12/87	88-92	77	13	8
Blackburn Rov	Tr	03/93	92-96	127	2	7
Chelsea	Tr	08/97	97-02	133	7	4
Southampton	Tr	07/03	03-04	43	1	1

LESCOTT Aaron Anthony
Born: Birmingham, England, 2 December, 1978 — FB
England: Schools

League Club	Source	Date Signed	Seasons Played	Apps	Subs	Gls
Aston Villa	YT	07/96				
Lincoln C	L	03/00	99	3	2	0
Sheffield Wed	Tr	10/00	00-01	19	18	0
Stockport Co	Tr	11/01	01-03	65	7	1
Bristol Rov	Tr	03/04	03-09	197	10	5
Cheltenham T	L	03/10	09	7	1	0
Walsall	Tr	07/10	10	34	0	1

LESCOTT Joleon Patrick
Born: Birmingham, England, 16 August, 1982 — CD
England: 26/B-1/U21-2/Youth

League Club	Source	Date Signed	Seasons Played	Apps	Subs	Gls
Wolverhampton W	YT	08/99	00-05	206	6	13
Everton	Tr	06/06	06-09	109	4	14
Manchester C	Tr	08/09	09-13	92	15	7
West Bromwich A	Tr	06/14	14	34	0	1

LESLIE John Alexander
Born: Plumstead, SE London, England, 25 October, 1955 — F

League Club	Source	Date Signed	Seasons Played	Apps	Subs	Gls
Wimbledon	Dulwich Hamlet	12/75	77-82	242	11	86
Gillingham	Tr	08/83	83-84	60	5	12
Millwall	Tr	08/85	85-86	12	8	2

LESLIE Lawrence Grant (Lawrie)
Born: Edinburgh, Scotland, 17 March, 1935 — G
Scotland: 5/SLge-3

League Club	Source	Date Signed	Seasons Played	Apps	Subs	Gls
West Ham U	Airdrieonians	06/61	61-62	57	-	0
Stoke C	Tr	10/63	63-65	78	0	0
Millwall	Tr	07/66	66-67	67	0	0
Southend U	Tr	07/68	68	13	0	0

LESLIE Maurice Harrington
Born: India, 19 August, 1923 — FB

League Club	Source	Date Signed	Seasons Played	Apps	Subs	Gls
Swindon T	Army	06/47	46	1	-	0

LESLIE Steven
Born: Dumfries, Scotland, 6 February, 1976 — M

League Club	Source	Date Signed	Seasons Played	Apps	Subs	Gls
Stoke C	Jnr	03/93	94	0	1	0

LESLIE Steven Robert William (Steve)
Born: Hornsey, N London, England, 4 September, 1952 — M
England: Youth

League Club	Source	Date Signed	Seasons Played	Apps	Subs	Gls
Colchester U	Jnr	05/71	70-83	411	21	40

LESLIE Steven William
Born: Glasgow, Scotland, 5 November, 1987 — LM

League Club	Source	Date Signed	Seasons Played	Apps	Subs	Gls
Shrewsbury T	Jnr	07/06	05-10	53	49	7
Hereford U	L	03/11	10	10	1	2
Hereford U	L	10/11	11	10	0	2

LESSLIE Kenneth Gordon (Ken)
Born: West Ham, E London, England, 4 January, 1923 — W
Died: Southend-on-Sea, England, 15 December, 1991

League Club	Source	Date Signed	Seasons Played	Apps	Subs	Gls
Ipswich T		08/47				
Watford	Tr	07/48	48	7	-	1

LESTER Abraham Bennett (Benny)
Born: Sheffield, England, 10 February, 1920 — CF
Died: Sheffield, England, December, 1958

League Club	Source	Date Signed	Seasons Played	Apps	Subs	Gls
Hull C	Selby T	09/46	46-47	27	-	17
Lincoln C	Tr	01/48	47-48	37	-	10
Stockport Co	Ransome & Marles	08/49	49	8	-	2

LESTER Christopher James (Chris)
Born: Salford, England, 27 October, 1994 — W
Northern Ireland: U21-1

League Club	Source	Date Signed	Seasons Played	Apps	Subs	Gls
Bolton W	Sch	07/13	13	0	1	0

LESTER Jack William
Born: Sheffield, England, 8 October, 1975 — F

England: Schools

League Club	Source	Date Signed	Seasons Played	Apps	Subs	Gls
Grimsby T	Jnr	07/94	94-99	93	40	17
Doncaster Rov	L	09/96	96	5	6	1
Nottingham F	Tr	01/00	99-02	73	26	21
Sheffield U	Tr	08/03	03-04	26	18	12
Nottingham F	Tr	11/04	04-06	42	34	12
Chesterfield	Tr	07/07	07-12	155	42	83

LESTER Leslie James (Danny)
Born: Cardiff, Wales, 17 November, 1923 — LH
Died: Barry, Vale of Glamorgan, Wales, February, 1991

League Club	Source	Date Signed	Seasons Played	Apps	Subs	Gls
Cardiff C	Cardiff Corinthians	04/44				
Torquay U	Tr	08/48	48-49	31	-	1
Newport Co	Tr	09/50	50	2	-	0

LESTER Michael John Anthony (Mike)
Born: Manchester, England, 4 August, 1954 — M

League Club	Source	Date Signed	Seasons Played	Apps	Subs	Gls
Oldham Ath	App	08/72	72-73	26	1	2
Manchester C	Tr	11/73	73-76	1	1	0
Stockport Co	L	08/75	75	8	1	1
Grimsby T	Washington Dip's (USA)	11/77	77-79	45	3	10
Barnsley	Tr	10/79	79-80	64	0	11
Exeter C	Tr	08/81	81	18	1	6
Bradford C	Tr	02/82	81-82	46	3	2
Scunthorpe U	Tr	03/83	82-85	106	0	9
Hartlepool U	L	01/86	85	11	0	1
Stockport Co	Tr	09/86	86	11	0	0
Blackpool	Ludvika FK (SWE)	12/87	87	11	0	1

LE TALLEC Anthony
Born: Hennebont, Brittany, France, 3 October, 1984 — M
France: U21-34/Youth

League Club	Source	Date Signed	Seasons Played	Apps	Subs	Gls
Liverpool	Le Havre (FRA)	07/03	03-04	5	12	0
Sunderland	L	08/05	05	12	15	3

LETHERAN Glanville (Glan)
Born: Llanelli, Carmarthenshire, Wales, 1 May, 1956 — G
Wales: U23-1/U21-2

League Club	Source	Date Signed	Seasons Played	Apps	Subs	Gls
Leeds U	App	05/73	74	1	0	0
Scunthorpe U	L	08/76	76	27	0	0
Chesterfield	Tr	12/77	77-79	63	0	0
Swansea C	Tr	09/79	79	21	0	0

LE TISSIER Matthew Paul
Born: St Peter Port, Guernsey, Channel Islands, 14 October, 1968 — F/W
England: 8/B-6/Youth

League Club	Source	Date Signed	Seasons Played	Apps	Subs	Gls
Southampton	App	10/86	86-01	377	66	161

LEUTWILER Jayson
Born: Neuchatel, Switzerland, 25 April, 1989 — G
Switzerland: Youth

League Club	Source	Date Signed	Seasons Played	Apps	Subs	Gls
Middlesbrough	FC Basel (SUI)	08/12	13	1	2	0
Shrewsbury T	Tr	06/14	14	46	0	0

LEUTY Leon Harry
Born: Shrewsbury, Shropshire, England, 23 October, 1920 — CH
Died: Nottingham, England, 19 December, 1955
England: B-3/FLge-2

League Club	Source	Date Signed	Seasons Played	Apps	Subs	Gls
Derby Co	Rolls Royce	05/44	46-49	131	-	1
Bradford Park Ave	Tr	03/50	49-50	19	-	0
Notts Co	Tr	09/50	50-55	188	-	3

LEVEN Peter McDonald
Born: Glasgow, Scotland, 27 September, 1983 — M
Scotland: U21-2

League Club	Source	Date Signed	Seasons Played	Apps	Subs	Gls
Chesterfield	Kilmarnock	08/07	07	42	0	6
MK Dons	Tr	07/08	08-10	103	8	22
Oxford U	Tr	08/11	11-12	52	7	10

LEVER Arthur Richard
Born: Cardiff, Wales, 25 March, 1920 — RB
Died: Cardiff, Wales, 20 August, 2004
Wales: 1

League Club	Source	Date Signed	Seasons Played	Apps	Subs	Gls
Cardiff C	Cardiff Corinthians	08/43	46-50	155	-	9
Leicester C	Tr	09/50	50-53	119	-	0
Newport Co	Tr	07/54	54-56	72	-	0

LEVER Mark
Born: Beverley, East Riding of Yorkshire, England, 29 March, 1970 — CD

League Club	Source	Date Signed	Seasons Played	Apps	Subs	Gls
Grimsby T	YT	08/88	87-99	343	18	8
Bristol C	Tr	07/00	00-01	28	3	1
Mansfield T	Tr	08/02	02	15	0	0

LEVERTON Roland (Tot)
Born: Whitwell, Derbyshire, England, 8 May, 1926 — IF
Died: Nottingham, England, 19 August, 2003

League Club	Source	Date Signed	Seasons Played	Apps	Subs	Gls
Nottingham F	Jnr	10/43	46-53	103	-	36
Notts Co	Tr	10/53	53-55	45	-	5
Walsall	Tr	07/56	56	17	-	3

LEVY Anthony Samuel (Tony)
Born: Edmonton, N London, England, 20 October, 1959 — M

League Club	Source	Date Signed	Seasons Played	Apps	Subs	Gls
Plymouth Arg	App	10/77	78	0	1	0
Torquay U	Tr	07/79	79	8	5	1

LEVY Leonard (Len)
Born: Stepney, E London, England, 24 December, 1926 — G
Died: Kettering, Northamptonshire, England, 13 August, 2001

League Club	Source	Date Signed	Seasons Played	Apps	Subs	Gls
Aldershot	Guildford C	10/50	50	2	-	0

LEWIN Dennis Ronald (Ron)
Born: Edmonton, N London, England, 21 June, 1920 — FB
Died: Cockermouth, Cumbria, England, September, 1985

League Club	Source	Date Signed	Seasons Played	Apps	Subs	Gls
Bradford C	Enfield	09/43				
Fulham	Tr	06/46	46-48	41	-	0
Gillingham	Tr	06/50	50-54	191	-	1

LEWIN Derek James
Born: Manchester, England, 18 May, 1930 — IF
England: Amateur-5

League Club	Source	Date Signed	Seasons Played	Apps	Subs	Gls
Oldham Ath (Am)	St Annes Ath	08/53	53-54	10	-	1
Accrington Stan (Am)	Bishop Auckland	10/57	57	1	-	0

LEWINGTON Christopher John (Chris)
Born: Sidcup, SE London, England, 23 August, 1988 — G

League Club	Source	Date Signed	Seasons Played	Apps	Subs	Gls
Dagenham & Red	Leatherhead	08/09	10-13	127	0	0
Colchester U	Tr	07/14	14	1	0	0

LEWINGTON Dean Scott
Born: Kingston-on-Thames, SW London, England, 18 May, 1984 — LB

League Club	Source	Date Signed	Seasons Played	Apps	Subs	Gls
Wimbledon	Sch	07/03	02-03	28	1	1
MK Dons	Wimbledon relocation	07/04	04-14	469	0	18

LEWINGTON Raymond (Ray)
Born: Lambeth, S London, England, 7 September, 1956 — M

League Club	Source	Date Signed	Seasons Played	Apps	Subs	Gls
Chelsea	App	02/74	75-78	80	5	4
Wimbledon	Vancouver W'caps (CAN)	09/79	79	23	0	0
Fulham	Tr	03/80	79-84	172	2	20
Sheffield U	Tr	07/85	85	36	0	0
Fulham	Tr	07/86	86-89	58	2	1

LEWIS Alan Trevor
Born: Oxford, England, 19 August, 1954 — LB
England: Youth

League Club	Source	Date Signed	Seasons Played	Apps	Subs	Gls
Derby Co	App	05/72	72	2	0	0
Peterborough U	L	03/74	73	10	0	1
Brighton & HA	Tr	01/75	74	3	0	0
Reading	Tr	07/77	77-81	145	4	5

LEWIS Allan
Born: Pontypridd, Rhondda Cynon Taff, Wales, 31 May, 1971 — D/M

League Club	Source	Date Signed	Seasons Played	Apps	Subs	Gls
Cardiff C	YT	07/89	89-91	27	23	0

LEWIS Benjamin (Ben)
Born: Chelmsford, England, 22 June, 1977 — CD

League Club	Source	Date Signed	Seasons Played	Apps	Subs	Gls
Colchester U	YT	03/96	95	1	1	0
Southend U	Tr	08/97	97	14	0	1

LEWIS Bernard (Bernie)
Born: Aberfan, Merthyr Tydfil, Wales, 12 March, 1945 — LW
Wales: U23-5

League Club	Source	Date Signed	Seasons Played	Apps	Subs	Gls
Cardiff C	Jnr	04/64	63-67	87	1	7
Watford	Tr	12/67	67-69	41	10	9
Southend U	Tr	09/70	70-71	55	3	6

LEWIS Brian
Born: Woking, Surrey, England, 26 January, 1943 — M
Died: Bournemouth, England, 17 December, 1998

League Club	Source	Date Signed	Seasons Played	Apps	Subs	Gls
Crystal Palace	Jnr	04/60	60-62	32	-	4
Portsmouth	Tr	07/63	63-66	134	0	24
Coventry C	Tr	01/67	66-67	33	2	2
Luton T	Tr	07/68	68-69	45	5	22
Oxford U	Tr	01/70	69-70	12	2	4
Colchester U	Tr	12/70	70-71	46	0	17
Portsmouth	Tr	04/72	71-74	44	16	8

LEWIS Charles Reginald
Born: Liverpool, England, 11 May, 1921 — LW
Died: Liverpool, England, August, 1999

League Club	Source	Date Signed	Seasons Played	Apps	Subs	Gls
Halifax T	South Liverpool	10/47	47-48	24	-	4

LEWIS Daniel
Born: Redditch, Worcestershire, England, 18 June, 1982 — G

League Club	Source	Date Signed	Seasons Played	Apps	Subs	Gls
Kidderminster Hrs	Studley	07/04	04	1	0	0

LEWIS David Sandbrook
Born: Cardigan, Wales, 12 February, 1936 — IF
Died: Swansea, Wales, 30 October, 2007

League Club	Source	Date Signed	Seasons Played	Apps	Subs	Gls
Swansea C	St Jude's	12/57	57-58	19	-	1
Torquay U	Tr	07/60	60	16	-	2

LEWIS Dennis George
Born: Treherbert, Rhondda Cynon Taff, Wales, 21 April, 1925 RH/IF
Died: Torbay, Devon, England, November, 1996

League Club	Source	Date Signed	Seasons Played	Apps	Subs	Gls
Swansea C		08/46				
Torquay U	Tr	08/47	47-58	442	-	31

LEWIS Derek Ivor Edwin
Born: Edmonton, N London, England, 10 June, 1929 IF
Died: St Albans, Hertfordshire, England, 13 July, 1953

League Club	Source	Date Signed	Seasons Played	Apps	Subs	Gls
Gillingham	Bury T	05/50	50-51	48	-	31
Preston NE	Tr	02/52	51-52	37	-	14

LEWIS Dudley Keith
Born: Swansea, Wales, 17 November, 1962 CD
Wales: 1/U21-9/Schools

League Club	Source	Date Signed	Seasons Played	Apps	Subs	Gls
Swansea C	App	11/79	80-88	228	2	2
Huddersfield T	Tr	07/89	89-90	32	2	0
Halifax T	L	10/91	91	11	0	0
Wrexham	Tr	03/92	91	8	1	0
Halifax T	Tr	08/92	92	10	3	0
Torquay U	Tr	12/92	92	9	0	0

LEWIS Edward (Eddie)
Born: Manchester, England, 3 January, 1935 LB/CF
Died: Johannesburg, South Africa, 3 May, 2011

League Club	Source	Date Signed	Seasons Played	Apps	Subs	Gls
Manchester U	Jnr	01/52	52-55	20	-	9
Preston NE	Tr	12/55	55-56	12	-	2
West Ham U	Tr	11/56	56-57	31	-	12
Leyton Orient	Tr	06/58	58-63	143	-	5

LEWIS Edward (Eddie)
Born: West Bromwich, West Midlands, England, 21 June, 1926 G

League Club	Source	Date Signed	Seasons Played	Apps	Subs	Gls
West Bromwich A	Jnr	11/44				
Leyton Orient	Tr	03/46	46	5	-	0

LEWIS Edward James (Eddie)
Born: Los Angeles, California, USA, 17 May, 1974 LW
USA: 82

League Club	Source	Date Signed	Seasons Played	Apps	Subs	Gls
Fulham	San Jose Clash (USA)	03/00	99-01	8	8	0
Preston NE	Tr	09/02	02-04	97	14	15
Leeds U	Tr	07/05	05-07	83	2	8
Derby Co	Tr	08/07	07	22	2	0

LEWIS Frederick Arthur (Fred)
Born: Melksham, Wiltshire, England, 26 July, 1923 LB
Died: Aylesbury, Buckinghamshire, England, 1975

League Club	Source	Date Signed	Seasons Played	Apps	Subs	Gls
Chelsea	Aylesbury T	03/46	46-52	23	-	0
Colchester U	Tr	07/53	53-54	85	-	0

LEWIS Frederick John (Jack)
Born: Long Eaton, Derbyshire, England, 22 March, 1948 F
Wales: U23-1

League Club	Source	Date Signed	Seasons Played	Apps	Subs	Gls
Lincoln C	Long Eaton U	03/67	66-69	47	15	9
Grimsby T	Tr	01/70	69-76	231	27	74
Blackburn Rov	Tr	08/77	77	24	4	6
Doncaster Rov	Tr	08/78	78-79	48	16	10

LEWIS Glyndwr (Glyn)
Born: Abertillery, Blaenau Gwent, Wales, 3 July, 1921 W
Died: Blaina, Blaenau Gwent, Wales, 2 September, 1992

League Club	Source	Date Signed	Seasons Played	Apps	Subs	Gls
Crystal Palace	RAF	05/42	46-47	60	-	4
Bristol C	Tr	07/48	48	18	-	0

LEWIS Graham
Born: Reading, England, 15 February, 1982 F

League Club	Source	Date Signed	Seasons Played	Apps	Subs	Gls
Lincoln C	YT	07/00	99-00	3	4	0

LEWIS Gwynfor (Gwyn)
Born: Bangor, Gwynedd, Wales, 22 April, 1931 CF
Died: Bangor, Gwynedd, Wales, May, 1995
Wales: Youth

League Club	Source	Date Signed	Seasons Played	Apps	Subs	Gls
Everton	Jnr	05/48	51-55	10	-	6
Rochdale	Tr	06/56	56	27	-	11
Chesterfield	Tr	02/57	56-60	123	-	58

LEWIS Idris
Born: Tonypandy, Rhondda Cynon Taff, Wales, 26 August, 1915 RW
Died: Swansea, Wales, March, 1996

League Club	Source	Date Signed	Seasons Played	Apps	Subs	Gls
Swansea C	Gelli Colliery	05/35	35-37	66	-	4
Sheffield Wed	Tr	08/38	38	18	-	7
Swansea C	Tr	03/39				
Bristol Rov	Tr	07/46	46	13	-	2
Newport Co	Tr	10/46	46-47	27	-	4

LEWIS James Leonard (Jim)
Born: Hackney, E London, England, 26 June, 1927 W/CF
Died: Kelvedon Hatch, Essex, England, 21 November, 2011
England: Amateur-49

League Club	Source	Date Signed	Seasons Played	Apps	Subs	Gls
Leyton Orient (Am)	Walthamstow Ave	11/50	50	4	-	0
Chelsea (Am)	Walthamstow Ave	09/52	52-57	90	-	38

LEWIS John
Born: New Tredegar, Caerphilly, Wales, 15 October, 1955 M
Wales: U21-1

League Club	Source	Date Signed	Seasons Played	Apps	Subs	Gls
Cardiff C	Pontllanfraith	08/78	78-83	135	5	9
Newport Co	Tr	09/83	83-87	153	0	8
Swansea C	Tr	10/87	87	25	0	0

LEWIS John (Jack)
Born: Walsall, West Midlands, England, 6 October, 1923 LH
Died: Walsall, West Midlands, England, December, 2002

League Club	Source	Date Signed	Seasons Played	Apps	Subs	Gls
West Bromwich A	Jnr	10/45				
Mansfield T	Tr	08/48	48-52	163	-	11

LEWIS John (Jack)
Born: Tamworth, Staffordshire, England, 1 May, 1920 G
Died: Tamworth, Staffordshire, England, 10 October, 1988

League Club	Source	Date Signed	Seasons Played	Apps	Subs	Gls
Walsall	Boldmere St Michael's	12/45	46-52	271	-	0

LEWIS John (Jack)
Born: Walsall, West Midlands, England, 26 August, 1919 WH
Died: Walsall, West Midlands, England, 25 December, 2005

League Club	Source	Date Signed	Seasons Played	Apps	Subs	Gls
West Bromwich A	Jnr	04/37				
Crystal Palace	Tr	07/38	38-49	124	-	5
Bournemouth	Tr	11/49	49-50	45	-	1
Reading	Tr	07/51	51-52	74	-	17

LEWIS John George
Born: Hackney, E London, England, 9 May, 1954 M
England: Youth

League Club	Source	Date Signed	Seasons Played	Apps	Subs	Gls
Leyton Orient	Tottenham H (Am)	07/72	72	0	2	0

LEWIS Joseph Peter (Joe)
Born: Bungay, Suffolk, England, 6 October, 1987 G
England: U21-5/Youth

League Club	Source	Date Signed	Seasons Played	Apps	Subs	Gls
Norwich C	Sch	10/04				
Stockport Co	L	03/07	06	5	0	0
Morecambe	L	08/07	07	19	0	0
Peterborough U	Tr	01/08	07-11	167	0	0
Cardiff C	Tr	07/12	13	1	0	0
Blackpool	L	08/14	14	34	0	0

LEWIS Karl Junior (Junior)
Born: Wembley, NW London, England, 9 October, 1973 M

League Club	Source	Date Signed	Seasons Played	Apps	Subs	Gls
Fulham	YT	07/92	92	4	2	0
Gillingham	Hendon	08/99	99-00	47	12	8
Leicester C	Tr	01/01	00-02	24	6	1
Brighton & HA	L	02/02	01	14	1	3
Swindon T	L	03/03	02	9	0	0
Swindon T	L	10/03	03	4	0	0
Hull C	Tr	02/04	03-04	44	8	3
Brentford	Tr	08/05	05	11	3	0

LEWIS Kenneth (Ken)
Born: Cardiff, Wales, 7 November, 1924 LB
Died: Merthyr Tydfil, Wales, 1978

League Club	Source	Date Signed	Seasons Played	Apps	Subs	Gls
Torquay U	Sengenhydd	01/50	50-52	27	-	0

LEWIS Kenneth (Kenny)
Born: Bangor, Gwynedd, Wales, 12 October, 1929 IF
Died: Bangor, Gwynedd, Wales, 25 April, 1990

League Club	Source	Date Signed	Seasons Played	Apps	Subs	Gls
Walsall	Bangor C	03/54	53-54	19	-	1
Scunthorpe U	Worcester C	08/56	56	1	-	0

LEWIS Kevin
Born: Hull, England, 17 October, 1970 FB

League Club	Source	Date Signed	Seasons Played	Apps	Subs	Gls
Stoke C	YT	-	87	0	1	0

LEWIS Kevin
Born: Ellesmere Port, Cheshire, England, 19 September, 1940 RW
England: Youth

League Club	Source	Date Signed	Seasons Played	Apps	Subs	Gls
Sheffield U	Jnr	10/57	57-59	62	-	23
Liverpool	Tr	06/60	60-62	71	-	39
Huddersfield T	Tr	08/63	63-64	45	-	13

LEWIS Kevin William
Born: Hull, England, 25 September, 1952 FB
England: Schools

League Club	Source	Date Signed	Seasons Played	Apps	Subs	Gls
Manchester U	App	09/69				
Stoke C	Tr	07/72	72-75	15	0	0
Crewe Alex	Tr	06/79	79-81	117	5	2

LEWIS Matthew Thomas (Matt)
Born: Coventry, England, 20 March, 1984 F

League Club	Source	Date Signed	Seasons Played	Apps	Subs	Gls
Kidderminster Hrs	Marconi, Coventry	07/01	01-03	1	7	0

LEWIS Michael (Mickey)
Born: Birmingham, England, 15 February, 1965 M
England: Youth

League Club	Source	Date Signed	Seasons Played	Career Record Apps	Subs	Gls
West Bromwich A	App	02/82	81-84	22	2	0
Derby Co	Tr	11/84	84-87	37	6	1
Oxford U	Tr	08/88	88-99	279	26	7
LEWIS Morgan Rees						
Born: Bournemouth, England, 8 September, 1965						M
Bournemouth	Jnr	07/84	83-86	11	1	0
LEWIS Neil Anthony						
Born: Wolverhampton, England, 28 June, 1974						LB
Leicester C	YT	07/92	92-96	53	14	1
Peterborough U	Tr	06/97	97	31	3	0
LEWIS Norman						
Born: Oakengates, Telford & Wrekin, England, 28 May, 1927						LB
Shrewsbury T	Oakengates T	04/48	50-52	62	-	0
Newport Co	Gravesend & Northfleet	06/54	54	15	-	0
LEWIS Paul Samuel						
Born: Ystrad Rhondda, Rhondda Cynon Taff, Wales, 27 September, 1956						G
Wales: Youth						
Bristol Rov	App	10/74	75	1	0	0
LEWIS Reginald (Reg)						
Born: Bilston, West Midlands, England, 7 March, 1920						CF
Died: Chadwell Heath, E London, England, 2 April, 1997						
England: B-1						
Arsenal	Dulwich Hamlet	03/37	37-51	154	-	103
LEWIS Roland						
Born: Sandbach, Cheshire, England, 21 September, 1925						CF
Died: Crewe, Cheshire, England, September, 1999						
Port Vale	Congleton T	03/50	50-53	7	-	0
LEWIS Ronald (Ron)						
Born: Belfast, Northern Ireland, 10 February, 1932						IF
Burnley	Glentoran	06/49				
Barrow	Weymouth	05/54	54	5	-	1
LEWIS Russell						
Born: Blaengwynfi, Neath Port Talbot, Wales, 15 September, 1956						CD
Swindon T	Everwarm, Bridgend	10/76	76-82	175	6	7
Northampton T	Tr	08/83	83-85	131	1	6
LEWIS Stuart Allan						
Born: Welwyn Garden City, Hertfordshire, England, 15 October, 1987						M
England: Semi Pro-1/Youth/Schools						
Tottenham H	Sch	07/05				
Barnet	Tr	01/07	06	2	2	0
Gillingham	Stevenage Bor	01/08	07-09	35	16	1
Dagenham & Red	Tr	07/10	10	7	3	0
Wycombe W	Tr	11/10	10-14	143	9	8
LEWIS Terence John (Terry)						
Born: Newport, Wales, 22 October, 1950						CD
Wales: Schools						
Cardiff C	App	10/68	68-69	3	0	0
LEWIS Terrell Dayne						
Born: Brent, NW London, England, 1 September, 1988						W
Chesterfield	Chalfont St Peter	10/09	09	0	1	0
LEWIS Theo Anthony						
Born: Oxford, England, 10 August, 1991						M
Cheltenham T	Sch	07/10	08-11	18	22	0
LEWIS Thomas George (George)						
Born: New Tredegar, Caerphilly, Wales, 20 October, 1913						CF
Died: Hemel Hempstead, Hertfordshire, England, 6 August, 1981						
Watford	New Tredegar	05/34	36-38	25	-	11
Southampton	Tr	07/46	46-47	43	-	12
Brighton & HA	Tr	06/48	48	24	-	8
LEWIS Trevor						
Born: Blackwood, Caerphilly, Wales, 6 January, 1921						RW
Died: Coventry, England, 12 April, 2015						
Coventry C	Redditch T	02/48	47-52	11	-	0
Gillingham	Tr	02/53	52-54	26	-	2
LEWIS William (Billy)						
Born: Cardiff, Wales, 4 July, 1923						RW
Died: Cardiff, Wales, 27 July, 2013						
Cardiff C	Jnr	07/41	46-47	10	-	0
Newport Co	Tr	10/47	47-49	49	-	11
LEWIS William Albert (Bill)						
Born: Silvertown, E London, England, 23 November, 1921						LB
Died: Thorpe, Surrey, England, 27 August, 1998						
England: Schools						
Blackpool	West Ham U (Am)	07/45	46-49	31	-	0
Norwich C	Tr	11/49	49-55	232	-	1

League Club	Source	Date Signed	Seasons Played	Career Record Apps	Subs	Gls
LEWORTHY David John (Dave)						
Born: Portsmouth, England, 22 October, 1962						F
Portsmouth	App	09/80	81	0	1	0
Tottenham H	Fareham T	08/84	84-85	8	3	3
Oxford U	Tr	12/85	85-88	25	12	8
Shrewsbury T	L	10/87	87	6	0	3
Reading	Tr	07/89	89-91	23	21	7
LEY Oliver Albert George (George)						
Born: Exminster, Devon, England, 7 April, 1946						LB
Exeter C	Hitchin T	09/63	63-66	93	0	7
Portsmouth	Tr	05/67	66-72	183	1	10
Brighton & HA	Tr	09/72	72-73	47	0	0
Gillingham	Tr	08/74	74-75	87	0	3
LEYDEN Darren Spencer						
Born: Warley, West Midlands, England, 20 February, 1970						D
Torquay U	YT	07/88	88	7	2	0
LEYFIELD John George (Jack)						
Born: Chester, England, 5 August, 1923						WH
Died: Guildford, Surrey, England, 21 December, 2014						
Wrexham	Chester C (Am)	07/46	46-49	34	-	1
Southport	Tr	08/50	50	26	-	0
LEYLAND Harry Kenneth						
Born: Liverpool, England, 12 May, 1930						G
Died: Hoylake, Wirral, England, 7 December, 2006						
Everton	Jnr	08/50	51-55	36	-	0
Blackburn Rov	Tonbridge	08/56	56-60	166	-	0
Tranmere Rov	Tr	03/61	60-65	180	0	0
L'HELGOUALCH Cyrille						
Born: St Nazaire, France, 25 September, 1970						CD
Walsall	Angers SCO (FRA)	11/98				
Mansfield T	Tr	12/98	98	3	1	1
LIBBRA Marc						
Born: Toulon, France, 5 August, 1972						F
Norwich C	Toulouse (FRA)	08/01	01	17	17	7
LIBURD Patrece Ovel						
Born: Leeds, England, 1 March, 1988						CD
Macclesfield T	Dorchester T	03/09	08	1	0	0
LIBURD Richard John						
Born: Nottingham, England, 26 September, 1973						FB
Middlesbrough	Eastwood T	03/93	93	41	0	1
Bradford C	Tr	07/94	94-96	75	3	3
Carlisle U	Tr	02/98	97	9	0	0
Notts Co	Tr	08/98	98-02	127	27	9
Lincoln C	Tr	08/03	03	19	5	0
LICHAJ Eric Joseph						
Born: Chicago, Illinois, USA, 17 November, 1988						FB
USA: 10/Youth						
Aston Villa	Sch	07/07	10-12	21	11	1
Lincoln C	L	10/09	09	6	0	0
Leyton Orient	L	03/10	09	9	0	1
Leeds U	L	01/11	10	16	0	0
Nottingham F	Tr	07/13	13-14	58	8	0
LICKA Mario						
Born: Ostrava, Czech Republic, 30 April, 1982						M
Czech Republic: 3/U21-16						
Southampton	FC Slovacko (CZE)	08/06	06-07	17	10	1
LIDDELL Andrew Mark (Andy)						
Born: Leeds, England, 28 June, 1973						F
Scotland: U21-12						
Barnsley	YT	07/91	91-98	142	56	34
Wigan Ath	Tr	10/98	98-03	206	11	70
Sheffield U	Tr	07/04	04	26	7	3
Oldham Ath	Tr	06/06	05-08	107	18	29
Rotherham U	Tr	08/09	09	0	2	0
LIDDELL Garry						
Born: Bannockburn, Stirlingshire, Scotland, 27 August, 1954						F
Died: Falkirk, Scotland, April, 2015						
Leeds U	App	09/71	72-74	2	1	0
Grimsby T	Tr	03/77	76-80	90	15	22
Doncaster Rov	Heart of Midlothian	03/82	81-82	25	12	4
LIDDELL John Cairney						
Born: Stirling, Scotland, 13 December, 1933						CF
Died: Grangemouth, Falkirk, Scotland, 16 March, 1999						
Oldham Ath	St Johnstone	09/60	60-61	23	-	10
LIDDELL John Gilbert Hay						
Born: Edinburgh, Scotland, 17 April, 1915						IF

League Club	Source	Date Signed	Seasons Played	Apps	Subs	Gls

Died: Greenwich, SE London, England, March, 1986

League Club	Source	Date Signed	Seasons Played	Apps	Subs	Gls
Leyton Orient		03/44				
Bolton W	Tr	09/46				
Brighton & HA	Tr	03/47	46	4	-	1

LIDDELL William Beveridge (Billy)
Born: Dunfermline, Fife, Scotland, 10 January, 1922 — W/CF
Died: Liverpool, England, 3 July, 2001
Scotland: 28/War-8

League Club	Source	Date Signed	Seasons Played	Apps	Subs	Gls
Liverpool	Lochgelly Violet	04/39	46-60	494	-	216

LIDDLE Bryan
Born: Durham, England, 23 June, 1961 — LB

League Club	Source	Date Signed	Seasons Played	Apps	Subs	Gls
Hartlepool U	Brandon U	08/84	84	12	1	0

LIDDLE Craig George
Born: Chester-le-Street, County Durham, England, 21 October, 1971 — CD

League Club	Source	Date Signed	Seasons Played	Apps	Subs	Gls
Aston Villa	YT	07/90				
Middlesbrough	Blyth Spartans	07/94	94-97	20	5	0
Darlington	Tr	02/98	97-04	284	1	17

LIDDLE Daniel Hamilton Sneddon (Danny)
Born: Bo'ness, Falkirk, Scotland, 19 February, 1912 — LW
Died: Wigston, Leicestershire, England, 9 June, 1982
Scotland: 3

League Club	Source	Date Signed	Seasons Played	Apps	Subs	Gls
Leicester C	East Fife	05/32	32-38	255	-	64
Mansfield T	Tr	07/46	46	1	-	0

LIDDLE David
Born: Bedford, England, 21 May, 1957 — M/D

League Club	Source	Date Signed	Seasons Played	Apps	Subs	Gls
Northampton T	App	05/75	77-78	28	3	3

LIDDLE Gary Daniel
Born: Middlesbrough, England, 15 June, 1986 — CD/M
England: Youth

League Club	Source	Date Signed	Seasons Played	Apps	Subs	Gls
Middlesbrough	Sch	07/03				
Hartlepool U	Tr	08/06	06-11	239	8	18
Notts Co	Tr	07/12	12-13	78	0	4
Bradford C	Tr	06/14	14	39	2	1

LIDDLE Gavin
Born: Houghton-le-Spring, Tyne and Wear, England, 9 May, 1963 — FB

League Club	Source	Date Signed	Seasons Played	Apps	Subs	Gls
Darlington	Hartlepool U (App)	01/81	81-82	33	4	0

LIDDLE Kenneth (Ken)
Born: Gateshead, Tyne and Wear, England, 6 October, 1928 — IF
Died: Gateshead, Tyne and Wear, England, 21 January, 1998

League Club	Source	Date Signed	Seasons Played	Apps	Subs	Gls
Sunderland		12/49				
Darlington	Tr	06/50	50	1	-	0

LIDDLE Michael William
Born: Hounslow, SW London, England, 25 December, 1989 — LB
Republic of Ireland: U21-5

League Club	Source	Date Signed	Seasons Played	Apps	Subs	Gls
Sunderland	Sch	07/07				
Carlisle U	L	11/08	08	21	1	0
Leyton Orient	L	08/10	10	1	0	0
Accrington Stan	Tr	02/12	11-14	62	16	0

LIDDLE Thomas Blenkarn (Tom)
Born: Middleton, Greater Manchester, England, 22 April, 1921 — FB
Died: Bournemouth, England, 28 October, 1994

League Club	Source	Date Signed	Seasons Played	Apps	Subs	Gls
Bournemouth	Carlisle U (Am)	02/47	47	1	-	0

LIEVESLEY Dennis
Born: Chesterfield, Derbyshire, England, 19 September, 1919 — CH
Died: Aldershot, Hampshire, England, April, 1997

League Club	Source	Date Signed	Seasons Played	Apps	Subs	Gls
Aldershot	Rossington Main	08/46	46-48	8	-	0

LIGGITT Norman
Born: Thornaby, Cleveland, England, 21 July, 1941 — CH

League Club	Source	Date Signed	Seasons Played	Apps	Subs	Gls
Middlesbrough	Jnr	08/59				
Southend U	Tr	07/62	62	1	-	0

LIGHT Daniel (Danny)
Born: Chiswick, W London, England, 10 July, 1948 — F/W
Died: 20 October, 2014

League Club	Source	Date Signed	Seasons Played	Apps	Subs	Gls
Crystal Palace	App	12/65	66-67	18	1	5
Colchester U	Tr	08/68	68-69	65	2	14

LIGHT James Power (Jimmy)
Born: Oxford, England, 13 January, 1954 — RB

League Club	Source	Date Signed	Seasons Played	Apps	Subs	Gls
Oxford U	App	01/72	72-75	64	0	1

LIGHTBOURNE Kyle Lavince
Born: Hamilton, Bermuda, 29 September, 1968 — F
Bermuda: 22/Youth

League Club	Source	Date Signed	Seasons Played	Apps	Subs	Gls
Scarborough	Pembroke Zebras (BER)	12/92	92	11	8	3
Walsall	Tr	09/93	93-96	158	7	65
Coventry C	Tr	07/97	97	1	6	0
Fulham	L	01/98	97	4	0	2
Stoke C	Tr	02/98	97-00	83	28	21
Swindon T	L	01/01	00	2	0	0
Cardiff C	L	02/01	00	2	1	0
Macclesfield T	Tr	07/01	01-02	61	12	14
Hull C	L	03/02	01	3	1	0

LIGHTBOWN Trevor
Born: Blackburn, Greater Manchester, England, 21 November, 1939 — W

League Club	Source	Date Signed	Seasons Played	Apps	Subs	Gls
Accrington Stan (Am)	Burnley (Am)	08/59	59	8	-	0
Bradford Park Ave (Am)	Tr	08/60	60	2	-	0

LIGHTENING Arthur Douglas
Born: Durban, South Africa, 1 August, 1936 — G
Died: Durban, South Africa, October, 2001

League Club	Source	Date Signed	Seasons Played	Apps	Subs	Gls
Nottingham F	Queen's Park (RSA)	12/56	57-58	6	-	0
Coventry C	Tr	11/58	58-62	150	-	0
Middlesbrough	Tr	08/62	62	15	-	0

LIGHTFOOT Christopher Ian (Chris)
Born: Penketh, Cheshire, England, 1 April, 1970 — CD/M

League Club	Source	Date Signed	Seasons Played	Apps	Subs	Gls
Chester C	YT	07/88	87-94	263	14	32
Wigan Ath	Tr	07/95	95	11	3	1
Crewe Alex	Tr	03/96	95-99	63	24	4
Oldham Ath	L	09/00	00	3	0	0

LIGHTLY Brian Sydney
Born: Portsmouth, England, 12 May, 1936 — RH

League Club	Source	Date Signed	Seasons Played	Apps	Subs	Gls
Exeter C	Portsmouth (Am)	06/57	57	4	-	0

LIGHTOWLER Gerald Anthony (Gerry)
Born: Bradford, England, 5 September, 1940 — LB
Died: Dewsbury, West Yorkshire, England, 26 July, 2008

League Club	Source	Date Signed	Seasons Played	Apps	Subs	Gls
Bradford Park Ave	St Bede's	12/58	58-67	207	2	1
Bradford C	Los Angeles Wolv (USA)	10/68	68	11	0	0

LILEY Henry John Gerald (Harry)
Born: Trowbridge, Wiltshire, England, 19 August, 1918 — G
Died: Weston-super-Mare, Somerset, England, 17 September, 2001

League Club	Source	Date Signed	Seasons Played	Apps	Subs	Gls
Bristol Rov	Dockland Settlement	10/46	46-49	27	-	0

LILL David Arthur
Born: Aldbrough, East Riding of Yorkshire, England, 17 February, 1947 — M

League Club	Source	Date Signed	Seasons Played	Apps	Subs	Gls
Hull C	Jnr	03/65	66-69	16	2	2
Rotherham U	Tr	10/69	69-70	33	5	6
Cambridge U	Tr	07/71	71-75	166	6	22

LILL James Alfred
Born: Barnsley, South Yorkshire, England, 4 June, 1933 — LW

League Club	Source	Date Signed	Seasons Played	Apps	Subs	Gls
Mansfield T	Wentworth	03/54	53-55	3	-	0

LILL Michael James (Mickey)
Born: Barking, E London, England, 3 August, 1936 — LW
Died: Johannesburg, South Africa, September, 2004
England: Youth

League Club	Source	Date Signed	Seasons Played	Apps	Subs	Gls
Wolverhampton W	Storey Ath	06/54	57-59	30	-	15
Everton	Tr	02/60	59-61	31	-	11
Plymouth Arg	Tr	06/62	62	21	-	7
Portsmouth	Tr	03/63	62-64	39	-	5

LILLEY Derek Symon
Born: Paisley, Renfrewshire, Scotland, 9 February, 1974 — F
Scotland: Youth

League Club	Source	Date Signed	Seasons Played	Apps	Subs	Gls
Leeds U	Greenock Morton	03/97	96-98	4	17	1
Bury	L	03/99	98	5	0	1
Oxford U	Tr	08/99	99-00	51	12	9

LILLIS Jason Warren
Born: Chatham, Kent, England, 1 October, 1969 — F

League Club	Source	Date Signed	Seasons Played	Apps	Subs	Gls
Gillingham	YT	10/87	87-88	15	14	3
Maidstone U	FF Jaro (FIN)	07/89	89-91	57	18	18
Carlisle U	L	02/91	90	4	0	1
Walsall	Sittingbourne	10/93	93-94	14	11	6
Cambridge U	Tr	09/94	94	14	5	4

LILLIS Joshua Mark (Josh)
Born: Derby, England, 24 June, 1987 — G

League Club	Source	Date Signed	Seasons Played	Apps	Subs	Gls
Scunthorpe U	Sch	07/06	06-11	33	5	0
Notts Co	L	01/09	08	5	0	0
Grimsby T	L	09/09	09	4	0	0
Rochdale	L	10/09	09	1	0	0
Rochdale	L	07/10	10	23	0	0
Rochdale	Tr	07/12	12-14	105	2	0

LILLIS Mark Anthony
Born: Manchester, England, 17 January, 1960 — F/M

League Club	Source	Date Signed	Seasons Played	Apps	Subs	Gls
Huddersfield T	Manchester C (Jnr)	07/78	78-84	199	7	56
Manchester C	Tr	06/85	85	39	0	11
Derby Co	Tr	08/86	86-87	6	9	1
Aston Villa	Tr	09/87	87-88	30	1	4
Scunthorpe U	Tr	09/89	89-90	62	6	23
Stockport Co	Tr	09/91	91	9	2	2

LILWALL Stephen (Steve)
Born: Solihull, West Midlands, England, 5 February, 1970 — FB

League Club	Source	Date Signed	Seasons Played	Apps	Subs	Gls
West Bromwich A	Kidderminster Hrs	06/92	92-94	71	2	0

LILYGREEN Christopher Laurence (Chris)
Born: Newport, Wales, 9 June, 1965 — F

League Club	Source	Date Signed	Seasons Played	Apps	Subs	Gls
Newport Co	Newport YMCA	08/83	83-84	18	13	4

LIM Harvey Choun
Born: Halesworth, Suffolk, England, 30 August, 1967 — G

League Club	Source	Date Signed	Seasons Played	Apps	Subs	Gls
Norwich C	App	07/85				
Gillingham	Ornskoldsvik (SWE)	11/89	89-92	90	0	0

LIMBER Nicholas (Nick)
Born: Doncaster, South Yorkshire, England, 23 January, 1974 — LB

League Club	Source	Date Signed	Seasons Played	Apps	Subs	Gls
Doncaster Rov	YT	01/92	90-91	13	0	1
Manchester C	Tr	01/92				
Peterborough U	L	10/92	92	2	0	0
Doncaster Rov	Tr	03/94	93	3	1	0

LIMBERT Marc
Born: Deeside, Flintshire, Wales, 3 October, 1973 — RB

League Club	Source	Date Signed	Seasons Played	Apps	Subs	Gls
Chester C	YT	07/92	92	12	2	0

LIMPAR Anders Erik
Born: Solna, Sweden, 24 September, 1965 — LW
Sweden: 58

League Club	Source	Date Signed	Seasons Played	Apps	Subs	Gls
Arsenal	Cremonese (ITA)	08/90	90-93	76	20	17
Everton	Tr	03/94	93-96	51	15	5
Birmingham C	Tr	01/97	96	3	1	0

LINACRE John Edward
Born: Middlesbrough, England, 13 December, 1955 — M

League Club	Source	Date Signed	Seasons Played	Apps	Subs	Gls
Hartlepool U	Whitby T	07/77	77-81	192	4	12
Hartlepool U	Hamrun Spartans (MLT)	12/83	83	15	0	0

LINACRE Philip (Phil)
Born: Middlesbrough, England, 17 May, 1962 — F

League Club	Source	Date Signed	Seasons Played	Apps	Subs	Gls
Hartlepool U	Coventry C (App)	08/80	80-82	59	4	10
Hartlepool U	Whitby T	01/84	83	19	0	7
Darlington	Newcastle Blue Star	03/90	90	6	2	3

LINACRE William (Billy)
Born: Chesterfield, Derbyshire, England, 10 August, 1924 — RW
Died: Middlesbrough, England, 8 January, 2010

League Club	Source	Date Signed	Seasons Played	Apps	Subs	Gls
Chesterfield	Jnr	02/44	46-47	22	-	3
Manchester C	Tr	10/47	47-49	75	-	6
Middlesbrough	Tr	09/49	49-51	31	-	2
Hartlepool U	Goole T	08/53	53-55	89	-	10
Mansfield T	Tr	10/55	55	13	-	0

LINAKER John Edward (Johnny)
Born: Southport, Merseyside, England, 14 January, 1927 — RW
Died: Shipton, North Yorkshire, England, 14 June, 2013

League Club	Source	Date Signed	Seasons Played	Apps	Subs	Gls
Manchester C	Everton (Am)	08/45				
Southport	Tr	11/46	46	15	-	1
Nottingham F	Tr	09/47	48-49	15	-	2
York C	Tr	06/50	50-51	59	-	16
Hull C	Tr	10/51	51-52	26	-	3
York C	Tr	05/53	53-55	39	-	4
Crewe Alex	Scarborough	07/57	57	34	-	3

LINCOLN Greg Dean
Born: Cheshunt, Hertfordshire, England, 23 March, 1980 — M
England: Youth

League Club	Source	Date Signed	Seasons Played	Apps	Subs	Gls
Arsenal	YT	07/98				
Northampton T	Hammarby IF (SWE)	07/02	02-03	9	10	1

LINDEGAARD Anders Rosenkrantz
Born: Odense, Denmark, 13 April, 1984 — G
Denmark: 5/Youth

League Club	Source	Date Signed	Seasons Played	Apps	Subs	Gls
Manchester U	Aalesunds FK (NOR)	01/11	11-13	19	0	0

LINDEGAARD Andrew Rindom (Andy)
Born: Taunton, Somerset, England, 10 September, 1980 — M/RB

League Club	Source	Date Signed	Seasons Played	Apps	Subs	Gls
Yeovil T	Westlands Sports	06/00	03-06	57	32	3
Cheltenham T	Tr	07/07	07-08	42	14	2
Aldershot T	L	02/09	08	6	0	1
Yeovil T	Tr	08/09	09	2	3	0

LINDEROTH Tobias Jan Hakan
Born: Marseille, France, 21 April, 1979 — DM
Sweden: 76/U21-22

League Club	Source	Date Signed	Seasons Played	Apps	Subs	Gls
Everton	Stabaek (NOR)	02/02	01-03	29	11	0

LINDFIELD Craig Anthony
Born: Greasby, Wirral, England, 7 September, 1988 — W
England: Youth

League Club	Source	Date Signed	Seasons Played	Apps	Subs	Gls
Liverpool	Sch	08/06				
Notts Co	L	11/07	07	3	0	1
Chester C	L	01/08	07	5	2	0
Bournemouth	L	08/08	08	1	2	1
Accrington Stan	L	01/09	08	17	3	2
Macclesfield T	Tr	12/09	09	12	6	2
Accrington Stan	Tr	07/10	10-12	49	35	5

LINDLEY Edwin
Born: Epworth, North Lincolnshire, England, 22 April, 1931 — IF
Died: Scunthorpe, North Lincolnshire, England, 9 October, 1951

League Club	Source	Date Signed	Seasons Played	Apps	Subs	Gls
Nottingham F	Scunthorpe U	10/49	49	1	-	0
Scunthorpe U	Tr	08/51				

LINDLEY James Edward (Jim)
Born: Sutton-in-Ashfield, Nottinghamshire, England, 23 July, 1981 — G

League Club	Source	Date Signed	Seasons Played	Apps	Subs	Gls
Notts Co	YT	07/99	99-00	2	1	0

LINDLEY William Maurice (Maurice)
Born: Keighley, West Yorkshire, England, 5 December, 1915 — CH
Died: Leeds, England, 22 July, 1994

League Club	Source	Date Signed	Seasons Played	Apps	Subs	Gls
Everton	Keighley T	03/36	47-51	51	-	0

LINDORES William Robert Hope (Billy)
Born: Newcastleton, Borders, Scotland, 3 May, 1933 — FB
Died: Gullane, East Lothian, Scotland, January, 2011
Scotland: Schools

League Club	Source	Date Signed	Seasons Played	Apps	Subs	Gls
Barrow	Heart of Midlothian	07/59	59	4	-	0

LINDSAY Alec
Born: Bury, Greater Manchester, England, 27 February, 1948 — LB
England: 4/Youth

League Club	Source	Date Signed	Seasons Played	Apps	Subs	Gls
Bury	App	03/65	64-68	127	0	13
Liverpool	Tr	03/69	69-76	168	2	12
Stoke C	Tr	08/77	77	20	0	3

LINDSAY David (Dave)
Born: Dumbarton, Dunbartonshire, Scotland, 23 September, 1919 — RB
Died: March, Cambridgeshire, England, January, 1993

League Club	Source	Date Signed	Seasons Played	Apps	Subs	Gls
Luton T	St Mirren	05/48	48	7	-	0
Barnsley	Tr	11/48	48-51	78	-	3

LINDSAY David
Born: Cambuslang, Glasgow, Scotland, 29 June, 1922 — FB

League Club	Source	Date Signed	Seasons Played	Apps	Subs	Gls
Sunderland	Blantyre Victoria	08/46	46	1	-	0
Southend U	Tr	05/48	48-50	52	-	1

LINDSAY David James
Born: Romford, E London, England, 17 May, 1966 — LB

League Club	Source	Date Signed	Seasons Played	Apps	Subs	Gls
Crystal Palace	App	05/84	83-85	18	3	0

LINDSAY Hugh Murray
Born: Ickenham, W London, England, 23 August, 1938 — IF
England: Amateur-29

League Club	Source	Date Signed	Seasons Played	Apps	Subs	Gls
Southampton (Am)	Kingstonian	07/60	60	2	-	0

LINDSAY Ian
Born: Canonbie, Dumfries & Galloway, Scotland, 10 February, 1944 — G

League Club	Source	Date Signed	Seasons Played	Apps	Subs	Gls
Workington	Hearts of Liddlesdale	11/64	64	9	-	0
Carlisle U		11/66				

LINDSAY James Young (Jimmy)
Born: Hamilton, Lanarkshire, Scotland, 12 July, 1949 — M

League Club	Source	Date Signed	Seasons Played	Apps	Subs	Gls
West Ham U	Possilpark YMCA	08/66	68-70	36	3	2
Watford	Tr	08/71	71-73	64	1	12
Colchester U	Tr	07/74	74	45	0	6
Hereford U	Tr	08/75	75-76	79	0	6
Shrewsbury T	Tr	08/77	77-80	80	6	0

LINDSAY John McArthur (Jack)
Born: Cambuslang, Glasgow, Scotland, 11 December, 1921 — CF
Died: Carlisle, Cumbria, England, 9 February, 2006

League Club	Source	Date Signed	Seasons Played	Apps	Subs	Gls
Sheffield Wed	Greenock Morton	03/45	46	1	-	1
Bury	Tr	10/46	46	11	-	7
Carlisle U	Tr	08/47	47-50	103	-	46
Southport	Tr	03/51	50-51	50	-	20
Carlisle U	Wigan Ath	01/55	54	13	-	2

LINDSAY John Smith (Jack)
Born: Auchinleck, Ayrshire, Scotland, 8 August, 1924 — LB
Died: Liverpool, England, December, 1991

League Club	Source	Date Signed	Seasons Played	Apps	Subs	Gls
Everton	Glasgow Rangers	03/51	50-53	105	-	2
Bury	Worcester C	05/56	56	7	-	0

LINDSAY Lawrence (Laurie)
Born: Dumbarton, Dunbartonshire, Scotland, 7 October, 1921 — CH
Died: Alexandria, Dunbartonshire, Scotland, 5 February, 1985

League Club	Source	Date Signed	Seasons Played	Apps	Subs	Gls
Crewe Alex	Dundee	01/48	47-49	40	-	0

LINDSAY Malcolm (Mal)
Born: Ashington, Northumberland, England, 26 September, 1940 — F

League Club	Source	Date Signed	Seasons Played	Apps	Subs	Gls
Cambridge U	King's Lynn	02/70	70	6	0	1

LINDSAY Mark Edward
Born: Lambeth, S London, England, 6 March, 1955 — M

League Club	Source	Date Signed	Seasons Played	Apps	Subs	Gls
Crystal Palace	App	03/73	73-74	27	3	0

LINDSEY Barry
Born: Scunthorpe, North Lincolnshire, England, 17 April, 1944 — IF/RH

League Club	Source	Date Signed	Seasons Played	Apps	Subs	Gls
Scunthorpe U	App	05/61	61-70	210	6	13

LINDSEY Keith
Born: Scunthorpe, North Lincolnshire, England, 25 November, 1946 — RB
Died: Scunthorpe, North Lincolnshire, England, 12 February, 2003

League Club	Source	Date Signed	Seasons Played	Apps	Subs	Gls
Scunthorpe U	App	12/64	65	15	0	0
Doncaster Rov	Tr	07/66	66	16	2	1
Southend U	Cambridge U	01/69	68-71	89	2	4
Port Vale	Tr	12/71	71-72	24	0	0
Gillingham	Tr	12/72	72-74	73	0	5

LINDSEY Scott
Born: Walsall, West Midlands, England, 4 May, 1972 — M/RB

League Club	Source	Date Signed	Seasons Played	Apps	Subs	Gls
Gillingham	Bridlington T	07/94	94	11	1	0

LINEKER Gary Winston
Born: Leicester, England, 30 November, 1960 — F
England: 80/B-1

League Club	Source	Date Signed	Seasons Played	Apps	Subs	Gls
Leicester C	App	11/79	78-84	187	7	95
Everton	Tr	07/85	85	41	0	30
Tottenham H	Barcelona (SPN)	07/89	89-91	105	0	67

LINES Barry
Born: Bletchley, Buckinghamshire, England, 16 May, 1942 — LW

League Club	Source	Date Signed	Seasons Played	Apps	Subs	Gls
Northampton T	Bletchley T	09/60	60-69	260	6	48

LINES Christopher John (Chris)
Born: Bristol, England, 30 November, 1988 — M

League Club	Source	Date Signed	Seasons Played	Apps	Subs	Gls
Bristol Rov	Jnr	01/06	05-10	156	12	20
Sheffield Wed	Tr	08/11	11-12	41	6	3
MK Dons	L	01/13	12	11	5	0
Port Vale	Tr	07/13	13-14	52	9	3

LINEY Patrick (Pat)
Born: Paisley, Renfrewshire, Scotland, 14 July, 1936 — G

League Club	Source	Date Signed	Seasons Played	Apps	Subs	Gls
Bradford Park Ave	St Mirren	06/66	66	11	0	0
Bradford C	Tr	09/67	67-71	147	0	0

LINFORD John Russell
Born: Norwich, England, 6 December, 1957 — F

League Club	Source	Date Signed	Seasons Played	Apps	Subs	Gls
Ipswich T	Gorleston	08/81				
Colchester U	L	01/83	82	7	0	0
Southend U	L	03/83	82	6	0	3
Birmingham C (L)	Dordrecht DS79 (NED)	11/84	84	1	1	0

LING Martin
Born: West Ham, E London, England, 15 July, 1966 — M

League Club	Source	Date Signed	Seasons Played	Apps	Subs	Gls
Exeter C	App	01/84	82-85	109	8	14
Swindon T	Tr	07/86	86	2	0	0
Southend U	Tr	10/86	86-90	124	12	30
Mansfield T	L	01/91	90	3	0	0
Swindon T	Tr	03/91	90-95	132	18	10
Leyton Orient	Tr	07/96	96-99	143	5	8
Brighton & HA	Tr	03/00	99	2	6	1

LINGANZI Amine
Born: Algiers, Algeria, 16 November, 1989 — M
Congo: 4

League Club	Source	Date Signed	Seasons Played	Apps	Subs	Gls
Blackburn Rov	Saint-Etienne (FRA)	01/10	09-10	1	1	0
Preston NE	L	01/11	10	1	0	0
Accrington Stan	Tr	02/13	12	10	3	0
Gillingham	Tr	07/13	13-14	19	8	1

LINGARD Jesse Ellis
Born: Warrington, Cheshire, England, 15 December, 1992 — M
England: U21-11/Youth

League Club	Source	Date Signed	Seasons Played	Apps	Subs	Gls
Manchester U	Sch	07/11	14	1	0	0
Leicester C	L	11/12	12	0	5	0
Birmingham C	L	09/13	13	13	0	6
Brighton & HA	L	02/14	13	15	0	3
Derby Co	L	02/15	14	6	8	2

LINGER Paul Hayden
Born: Stepney, E London, England, 20 December, 1974 — M

League Club	Source	Date Signed	Seasons Played	Apps	Subs	Gls
Charlton Ath	YT	07/93	92-95	5	18	1
Leyton Orient	Tr	09/97	97	1	2	0
Brighton & HA	Tr	12/97	97	17	2	0

LINIGHAN Andrew (Andy)
Born: Hartlepool, Cleveland, England, 18 June, 1962 — CD
England: B-4

League Club	Source	Date Signed	Seasons Played	Apps	Subs	Gls
Hartlepool U	Henry Smith's BC	09/80	80-83	110	0	4
Leeds U	Tr	05/84	84-85	66	0	3
Oldham Ath	Tr	01/86	85-87	87	0	6
Norwich C	Tr	03/88	87-89	86	0	8
Arsenal	Tr	07/90	90-96	101	17	5
Crystal Palace	Tr	01/97	96-00	108	3	4
Queens Park Rgrs	L	03/99	98	4	3	0
Oxford U	Tr	10/00	00	12	1	0

LINIGHAN Brian
Born: Hartlepool, Cleveland, England, 2 November, 1973 — CD

League Club	Source	Date Signed	Seasons Played	Apps	Subs	Gls
Sheffield Wed	YT	07/92	93	1	0	0
Bury	Tr	07/97	99	2	1	0

LINIGHAN David
Born: Hartlepool, Cleveland, England, 9 January, 1965 — CD
England: FLge

League Club	Source	Date Signed	Seasons Played	Apps	Subs	Gls
Hartlepool U	Jnr	03/82	81-85	84	7	5
Derby Co	Tr	08/86				
Shrewsbury T	Tr	12/86	86-87	65	0	2
Ipswich T	Tr	06/88	88-95	275	2	12
Blackpool	Tr	11/95	95-97	97	3	5
Mansfield T	Dunfermline Ath	03/99	98-99	38	0	0

LINIGHAN William Brian (Brian)
Born: Hartlepool, Cleveland, England, 17 May, 1936 — CH
Died: Hartlepool, Cleveland, England, May, 2004

League Club	Source	Date Signed	Seasons Played	Apps	Subs	Gls
Lincoln C	St Joseph's, Hart'pool	12/53				
Darlington	L	10/58	58	1	-	1

LINK Thomas Henry (Tom)
Born: Halifax, West Yorkshire, England, 15 December, 1918 — RW
Died: Halifax, West Yorkshire, England, May, 1990

League Club	Source	Date Signed	Seasons Played	Apps	Subs	Gls
Bradford C		05/48	47-48	6	-	0

LINNECOR Albert Roy (Bert)
Born: Birmingham, England, 30 November, 1933 — LH/IF
Died: Lincoln, England, 25 November, 2012

League Club	Source	Date Signed	Seasons Played	Apps	Subs	Gls
Birmingham C	Brookhill Jnrs	05/52	55-56	17	-	0
Lincoln C	Tr	04/57	56-63	264	-	52

LINNELL John Lovell Leonard
Born: Holcot, Northamptonshire, England, 2 January, 1944 — RH

League Club	Source	Date Signed	Seasons Played	Apps	Subs	Gls
Northampton T	Jnr	09/63				
Peterborough U	Tr	07/67	67	24	2	1

LINNEY David William
Born: Birmingham, England, 5 September, 1961 — RB

League Club	Source	Date Signed	Seasons Played	Apps	Subs	Gls
Birmingham C	App	09/79	81	0	1	0
Oxford U	Tr	08/82	82	26	0	0

LINSTREM Kenneth Richard (Ken)
Born: Salford, England, 12 October, 1928 — WH
Died: Folkestone, Kent, England, 11 December, 1996

League Club	Source	Date Signed	Seasons Played	Apps	Subs	Gls
Crewe Alex	Stockport Co (Am)	06/50	50-51	13	-	1
Bournemouth	Tr	08/52				

LINTERN Melvin (Mel)
Born: Seaton Delaval, Northumberland, England, 17 May, 1950 — WH

League Club	Source	Date Signed	Seasons Played	Apps	Subs	Gls
Port Vale	Jnr	03/68	66	0	1	0

LINTON Desmond Martin (Des)
Born: Birmingham, England, 5 September, 1971 — RB/M

League Club	Source	Date Signed	Seasons Played	Apps	Subs	Gls
Leicester C	YT	01/90	89-91	6	5	0
Luton T	Tr	10/91	91-96	65	18	1
Peterborough U	Tr	03/97	96-98	41	5	0
Swindon T	L	03/99	98	7	1	0

LINTON Ivor
Born: West Bromwich, West Midlands, England, 20 November, 1959 — M

League Club	Source	Date Signed	Seasons Played	Apps	Subs	Gls
Aston Villa	App	09/77	76-81	16	11	0
Peterborough U	Tr	08/82	82-83	24	3	3
Birmingham C	Tr	12/83	83	3	1	0

LINTON James Alfred (Jimmy)
Born: Glasgow, Scotland, 2 December, 1930 — G

League Club	Source	Date Signed	Seasons Played	Apps	Subs	Gls
Notts Co	Kirkintilloch Rob Roy	11/52	52-58	114	-	0
Watford	Tr	07/59	59-62	71	-	0

LINTON Malcolm Wilton
Born: Southend-on-Sea, England, 13 February, 1952 — CD

League Club	Source	Date Signed	Seasons Played	Apps	Subs	Gls
Leyton Orient	Southend U (Am)	08/72	72-74	14	5	0

LINTON Thomas Neilson Goodwin (Tommy)
Born: Falkirk, Scotland, 15 October, 1920 — FB
Died: Lowestoft, Suffolk, England, 17 July, 2002

League Club	Source	Date Signed	Seasons Played	Apps	Subs	Gls
Southend U	Crittall Ath	05/45	46-48	67	-	0

LINWOOD Alexander Bryce (Alec)
Born: Drongan, Ayrshire, Scotland, 13 March, 1920 — CF
Died: Renfrew, Renfrewshire, Scotland, 26 October, 2003
Scotland: 1/SLge-1/War-1

League Club	Source	Date Signed	Seasons Played	Apps	Subs	Gls
Middlesbrough	St Mirren	06/46	46	14	-	3

LINWOOD Paul Anthony
Born: Birkenhead, Wirral, England, 24 October, 1983 — CD

League Club	Source	Date Signed	Seasons Played	Apps	Subs	Gls
Tranmere Rov	Sch	04/02	03-05	34	10	0
Wrexham	L	08/05	05	8	1	0
Chester C	Tr	07/06	06-08	118	4	4
Grimsby T	Tr	07/09	09	23	5	1

LIPA Andreas
Born: Vienna, Austria, 26 April, 1971 — LB
Austria: 1

League Club	Source	Date Signed	Seasons Played	Apps	Subs	Gls
Port Vale	Xanthi (GRE)	07/03	03-04	27	5	2

LIPTAK Zoltan
Born: Salgotarjan, Hungary, 10 December, 1984 — CD
Hungary: 17/U21-15

League Club	Source	Date Signed	Seasons Played	Apps	Subs	Gls
Southend U	Lombard-Papa (HUN)	08/07				
Southampton (L)	Ujpest (HUN)	02/09	08	0	7	0

LIPTROTT David (Dave)
Born: Stockport, Greater Manchester, England, 26 February, 1965 — F

League Club	Source	Date Signed	Seasons Played	Apps	Subs	Gls
Stockport Co	Jnr	09/82	82	0	1	0

LISBIE Kevin Anthony
Born: Hackney, E London, England, 17 October, 1978 — F
England: Youth//Jamaica: 10

League Club	Source	Date Signed	Seasons Played	Apps	Subs	Gls
Charlton Ath	YT	05/96	96-06	62	93	16
Gillingham	L	03/99	98	4	3	4
Reading	L	11/99	99	1	1	0
Queens Park Rgrs	L	12/00	00	1	1	0
Norwich C	L	09/05	05	4	2	1
Derby Co	L	12/06	06	7	0	1
Colchester U	Tr	08/07	07	39	3	17
Ipswich T	Tr	07/08	08	24	17	6
Colchester U	L	08/09	09	35	6	13
Millwall	L	07/10	10	10	10	4
Leyton Orient	Tr	09/11	11-14	97	14	46
Stevenage	L	03/15	14	3	0	0

LISHMAN Douglas John (Doug)
Born: Birmingham, England, 14 September, 1923 — IF
Died: Stoke-on-Trent, England, 21 December, 1994
England: B-1/FLge-1

League Club	Source	Date Signed	Seasons Played	Apps	Subs	Gls
Walsall	Paget Rgrs	08/46	46-47	59	-	26
Arsenal	Tr	07/48	48-55	226	-	125
Nottingham F	Tr	03/56	55-56	38	-	22

LISTER Alexander Duncan (Sandy)
Born: Glasgow, Scotland, 20 January, 1924 — IF

League Club	Source	Date Signed	Seasons Played	Apps	Subs	Gls
Rochdale	Alloa Ath	05/52	52	2	-	0

LISTER Eric
Born: Willenhall, West Midlands, England, 13 August, 1933 — LW
Died: Belper, Derbyshire, England, 22 March, 2004

League Club	Source	Date Signed	Seasons Played	Apps	Subs	Gls
Notts Co	Wolverhampton W (Am)	09/51	54-56	8	-	0

LISTER Herbert Francis (Bert)
Born: Manchester, England, 4 October, 1939 — CF
Died: Blackley, Greater Manchester, England, 15 July, 2007

League Club	Source	Date Signed	Seasons Played	Apps	Subs	Gls
Manchester C	Jnr	11/57	58	2	-	0
Oldham Ath	Tr	10/60	60-64	135	-	76
Rochdale	Tr	01/65	64-66	56	0	16
Stockport Co	Tr	01/67	66	16	0	11

LISTER Stephen Haley (Steve)
Born: Doncaster, South Yorkshire, England, 17 November, 1961 — CD/M

League Club	Source	Date Signed	Seasons Played	Apps	Subs	Gls
Doncaster Rov	App	05/79	78-84	228	9	30
Scunthorpe U	Tr	07/85	85-91	176	6	30
York C	L	03/91	90	4	0	1

LITA Leroy Halirou Bohari
Born: Kinshasa, DR Congo, 28 December, 1984 — F
England: U21-9

League Club	Source	Date Signed	Seasons Played	Apps	Subs	Gls
Bristol C	Sch	03/03	02-04	44	41	31
Reading	Tr	07/05	05-08	60	23	20
Charlton Ath	L	03/08	07	8	0	3
Norwich C	L	10/08	08	16	0	7
Middlesbrough	Tr	08/09	09-10	51	27	20
Swansea C	Tr	08/11	11-13	4	14	2
Birmingham C	L	09/12	12	9	1	3
Sheffield Wed	L	01/13	12	13	4	6
Brighton & HA	L	10/13	13	0	5	1
Barnsley	Tr	08/14	14	11	8	2
Notts Co	L	03/15	14	3	3	0

LITCHFIELD Peter
Born: Manchester, England, 27 July, 1956 — G

League Club	Source	Date Signed	Seasons Played	Apps	Subs	Gls
Preston NE	Droylsden	01/79	80-84	107	0	0
Bradford C	Tr	07/85	85-88	88	0	0
Oldham Ath	L	10/88	88	3	0	0
Scunthorpe U	Tr	07/89	89-90	25	0	0

LITHGO Gordon
Born: Hartlepool, Cleveland, England, 14 August, 1942 — LW

League Club	Source	Date Signed	Seasons Played	Apps	Subs	Gls
Hartlepool U	Seaton Holy Trinity	08/59	60-63	37	-	8

LI TIE (Li)
Born: Liaoning, China, 18 September, 1977 — DM
China: 92

League Club	Source	Date Signed	Seasons Played	Apps	Subs	Gls
Everton	Liaoning Bodao (CHN)	08/02	02-03	32	2	0

LITMANEN Jari Olaui
Born: Lahti, Finland, 20 February, 1971 — F/M
Finland: 137

League Club	Source	Date Signed	Seasons Played	Apps	Subs	Gls
Liverpool	Barcelona (SPN)	01/01	00-01	12	14	5

LITT Stephen Eric (Steve)
Born: Carlisle, Cumbria, England, 21 May, 1954 — CD

League Club	Source	Date Signed	Seasons Played	Apps	Subs	Gls
Luton T	Blackpool (App)	06/72	73-75	15	0	0
Northampton T	Minnesota Kicks (USA)	09/77	77	19	1	0

LITTLE Alan
Born: Horden, County Durham, England, 5 February, 1955 — M

League Club	Source	Date Signed	Seasons Played	Apps	Subs	Gls
Aston Villa	App	01/73	74	2	1	0
Southend U	Tr	12/74	74-76	102	1	12
Barnsley	Tr	08/77	77-79	91	0	14
Doncaster Rov	Tr	12/79	79-82	84	1	11
Torquay U	Tr	10/82	82-83	51	0	4
Halifax T	Tr	11/83	83-84	68	0	6
Hartlepool U	Tr	07/85	85	12	0	1

LITTLE Andrew (Andy)
Born: Enniskillen, Fermanagh, Northern Ireland, 12 May, 1989 — F
Northern Ireland: 9/B-1/U21-6/Youth

League Club	Source	Date Signed	Seasons Played	Apps	Subs	Gls
Port Vale (L)	Glasgow Rangers	08/11	11	2	5	0
Preston NE	Glasgow Rangers	06/14	14	5	7	1

LITTLE Barry Brian
Born: Greenwich, SE London, England, 25 August, 1964 — M
Died: Greenwich, SE London, England, 18 September, 1994
England: Youth

League Club	Source	Date Signed	Seasons Played	Apps	Subs	Gls
Charlton Ath	App	07/82	82	2	0	1

LITTLE Brian
Born: Horden, County Durham, England, 25 November, 1953 — F
England: 1

League Club	Source	Date Signed	Seasons Played	Apps	Subs	Gls
Aston Villa	App	03/71	71-79	242	5	60

LITTLE Colin Campbell
Born: Wythenshawe, Greater Manchester, England, 4 November, 1972 — F

League Club	Source	Date Signed	Seasons Played	Apps	Subs	Gls
Crewe Alex	Hyde U	02/96	95-02	135	58	33
Mansfield T	L	10/02	02	5	0	0
Macclesfield T	L	12/02	02	1	0	0
Macclesfield T	Tr	03/03	02-03	21	8	6

LITTLE George
Born: Newcastle-upon-Tyne, England, 1 December, 1915 — W
Died: Doncaster, South Yorkshire, England, March, 2002

League Club	Source	Date Signed	Seasons Played	Apps	Subs	Gls
Doncaster Rov	Throckley Welfare	08/36	36-47	49	-	11
York C	Tr	12/47	47	15	-	2

LITTLE Glen Matthew
Born: Wimbledon, SW London, England, 15 October, 1975 — RW

League Club	Source	Date Signed	Seasons Played	Apps	Subs	Gls
Crystal Palace	YT	07/94				
Burnley	Glentoran	11/96	96-03	211	35	32
Reading	L	03/03	02	6	0	1
Bolton W	L	09/03	03	0	4	0
Reading	Tr	05/04	04-07	81	15	5
Portsmouth	Tr	07/08	08	4	1	0
Reading	L	03/09	08	5	3	0
Sheffield U	Tr	08/09	09	7	9	0
Aldershot T	Tr	08/10	10	13	1	1

LITTLE John Adams (Jackie)
Born: Gateshead, Tyne and Wear, England, 17 May, 1912 — LW
Died: Ipswich, England, 15 October, 2007

League Club	Source	Date Signed	Seasons Played	Apps	Subs	Gls
Ipswich T	Needham Market	11/37	38-49	146	-	20

LITTLE Mark Daniel
Born: Worcester, England, 20 August, 1988 — RB
England: Youth

League Club	Source	Date Signed	Seasons Played	Apps	Subs	Gls
Wolverhampton W	Sch	08/05	06-07	19	8	0
Northampton T	L	01/08	07	17	0	0
Northampton T	L	08/08	08	9	0	0
Chesterfield	L	10/09	09	12	0	0
Peterborough U	Tr	03/10	09-13	139	18	3
Bristol C	Tr	07/14	14	35	2	1

LITTLE Ronald (Ronnie)
Born: Carlisle, Cumbria, England, 24 January, 1934 — RW
Died: Carlisle, Cumbria, England, 28 November, 2002

League Club	Source	Date Signed	Seasons Played	Apps	Subs	Gls
Carlisle U (Am)	Longsowerby Hearts	05/55	55	5	-	0

League Club	Source	Date Signed	Seasons Played	Career Record Apps	Subs	Gls
LITTLE Roy						
Born: Manchester, England, 1 June, 1931						LB
Died: Manchester, England, 2 February, 2015						
Manchester C	Greenwood Victoria	08/49	52-58	168	-	2
Brighton & HA	Tr	10/58	58-60	83	-	0
Crystal Palace	Tr	05/61	61-62	38	-	1
LITTLEJOHN Adrian Sylvester						
Born: Wolverhampton, England, 26 September, 1970						F
England: Youth						
Walsall	West Bromwich A (YT)	05/89	89-90	26	18	1
Sheffield U	Tr	08/91	91-94	44	25	12
Plymouth Arg	Tr	09/95	95-97	100	10	29
Oldham Ath	Tr	03/98	97-98	16	5	5
Bury	Tr	11/98	98-00	69	30	14
Sheffield U	Tr	10/01	01	1	2	0
Port Vale		02/03	02-03	36	13	10
Lincoln C	Tr	08/04	04	1	7	0
Rushden & D	Tr	01/05	04	8	7	0
Mansfield T	Tr	09/05	05	0	7	0
LITTLEJOHN Roy Derek						
Born: Bournemouth, England, 2 June, 1933						RW
England: Amateur-2						
Bournemouth (Am)	Jnr	05/52	52	9	-	0
Bournemouth (Am)	Oxford C	06/55	55	13	-	2
LITTLEJOHNS Colin						
Born: Liverpool, England, 8 September, 1968						M
Cambridge U	YT	10/85	85-86	10	2	0
LITTLER Joseph Eric (Eric)						
Born: St Helens, Merseyside, England, 14 April, 1929						CF
Died: Billinge, Merseyside, England, 18 December, 2009						
Leicester C	St Helens T	05/51	51-54	5	-	2
Lincoln C	Tr	12/54	54	6	-	2
Wrexham	Tr	06/55	55	12	-	1
Crewe Alex	Tr	12/55	55	10	-	2
LITTLER Thomas (Tom)						
Born: Stockport, Greater Manchester, England, 6 March, 1936						LW
Died: Poulton-le-Fylde, Lancashire, England, 26 April, 2006						
Stockport Co		04/55	55	1	-	0
LIVERMORE David						
Born: Edmonton, N London, England, 20 May, 1980						M
Arsenal	YT	07/98				
Millwall	Tr	07/99	99-05	269	4	12
Leeds U	Tr	07/06				
Hull C	Tr	08/06	06-07	33	12	5
Oldham Ath	L	01/08	07	10	0	1
Brighton & HA	Tr	07/08	08	12	4	0
Luton T	L	03/09	08	8	0	0
Barnet	Tr	02/10	09	11	3	1
LIVERMORE Douglas Ernest (Doug)						
Born: Prescot, Merseyside, England, 27 December, 1947						M
Liverpool	Jnr	11/65	67-70	13	3	0
Norwich C	Tr	11/70	70-74	113	1	4
Bournemouth	L	03/75	74	10	0	0
Cardiff C	Tr	08/75	75-77	84	4	5
Chester C	Tr	10/77	77-78	71	0	6
LIVERMORE Jake Cyril						
Born: Edmonton, N London, England, 14 November, 1989						M
England: 1						
Tottenham H	Sch	11/06	09-12	11	25	0
MK Dons	L	02/08	07	0	5	0
Derby Co	L	08/09	09	11	5	1
Peterborough U	L	01/10	09	9	0	1
Ipswich T	L	09/10	10	8	4	0
Leeds U	L	03/11	10	4	1	0
Hull C	Tr	08/13	13-14	69	2	4
LIVERSIDGE Nicholas James (Nick)						
Born: Hull, England, 18 July, 1988						G
Darlington	Rotherham U (Jnr)	11/07	09	13	0	0
Burnley	Whitby T	06/13				
LIVERSIDGE Ronnie						
Born: Huddersfield, West Yorkshire, England, 12 September, 1934						CF
Died: Huddersfield, West Yorkshire, England, May, 1997						
Bradford C	Ossett T	10/56	56-58	48	-	27
LIVESEY Charles Edward (Charlie)						
Born: West Ham, E London, England, 6 February, 1938						CF
Died: City of London, England, 26 February, 2005						
Southampton	Wolverhampton W (Am)	03/56	58	25	-	14
Chelsea	Tr	05/59	59-60	39	-	17
Gillingham	Tr	08/61	61-62	47	-	17
Watford	Tr	10/62	62-63	64	-	26
Northampton T	Tr	08/64	64-65	28	0	4
Brighton & HA	Tr	09/65	65-68	124	2	28
LIVESEY Daniel Richard (Danny)						
Born: Salford, England, 31 December, 1984						CD
Bolton W	Sch	08/02	02	0	2	0
Notts Co	L	09/03	03	9	2	0
Rochdale	L	02/04	03	11	2	0
Blackpool	L	08/04	04	1	0	0
Carlisle U	Tr	12/04	05-13	247	16	17
LIVESEY John (Jack)						
Born: Preston, Lancashire, England, 8 March, 1924						IF
Died: Bury, Greater Manchester, England, 20 March, 1988						
Preston NE	Jnr	04/44				
Bury	Tr	05/46	46	7	-	1
Doncaster Rov	Tr	01/47	47	3	-	0
Rochdale	Tr	04/48	47-50	113	-	36
Southport	Tr	07/51	51	31	-	9
LIVETT Simon Robert						
Born: East Ham, E London, England, 8 January, 1969						M
West Ham U	App	01/87	90	1	0	0
Leyton Orient	Tr	08/92	92-93	16	8	0
Cambridge U	Tr	10/93	93-94	12	0	0
Southend U	Grays Ath	07/98	98	19	4	1
LIVIE Gordon						
Born: Billingham, Cleveland, England, 10 June, 1932						D
Died: Leicester, England, April, 2004						
Leicester C	Jnr	12/49				
Mansfield T	Tr	07/52	52-53	21	-	0
LIVINGSTONE Archibald (Archie)						
Born: Pencaitland, East Lothian, Scotland, 15 November, 1915						IF
Died: Edinburgh, Scotland, 12 August, 1961						
Newcastle U	Dundee	05/35	35-37	33	-	5
Bury	Tr	06/38	38	24	-	8
Everton	Peterborough U	05/46	46	4	-	2
Southport	Tr	06/47	47	23	-	2
LIVINGSTONE Glen						
Born: Birmingham, England, 13 October, 1972						G
England: Youth/Schools						
Aston Villa	YT	01/91				
Walsall	York C (NC)	03/94	93	2	1	0
LIVINGSTONE Joseph (Joe)						
Born: Middlesbrough, England, 18 June, 1942						CF
Died: New Marske, Cleveland, England, 1 August, 2009						
Middlesbrough	Jnr	01/60	60-62	20	-	7
Carlisle U	Tr	11/62	62-65	81	1	42
Hartlepool U	Tr	05/66	65-66	15	0	5
LIVINGSTONE Stephen Carl (Steve)						
Born: Middlesbrough, England, 8 September, 1968						F
Coventry C	App	07/86	86-90	17	14	5
Blackburn Rov	Tr	01/91	90-92	25	5	10
Chelsea	Tr	03/93	92	0	1	0
Port Vale	L	09/93	93	4	1	0
Grimsby T	Tr	10/93	93-02	226	63	43
Carlisle U	Tr	08/03	03	6	0	0
LIVINGSTONE Wilfred Egerton (Wilf)						
Born: Barrow, Cumbria, England, 22 October, 1919						CF
Died: Lancaster, England, January, 2002Jul						
Barrow	Holker Central OB	09/47	47-48	4	-	0
LIVINGSTONE William (Billy)						
Born: Coventry, England, 13 August, 1964						F
Scotland: Youth						
Wolverhampton W	App	08/82	82-83	21	3	4
Derby Co	Tr	07/84				
LIVINGSTONE William Rennison (Billy)						
Born: Greenock, Inverclyde, Scotland, 8 February, 1929						CH
Died: Reading, England, March, 2011						
Reading	Ardeer Rec	04/49	49-54	49	-	2
Chelsea	Tr	06/55	56-57	20	-	0
Brentford	Tr	07/59	59	19	-	0
LIVSEY Gordon William						
Born: Keighley, West Yorkshire, England, 24 January, 1947						G
Wrexham	Kettering T	01/67	67-70	79	0	0
Chester C	Tr	08/71	71	44	0	0
Hartlepool U	Workington	12/77	77	6	0	0
LJUNGBERG Karl Fredrik (Freddie)						
Born: Markaryd, Sweden, 16 April, 1977						W

Sweden: 75/U21-12/Youth

League Club	Source	Date Signed	Seasons Played	Apps	Subs	Gls
Arsenal	Halmstads BK (SWE)	09/98	98-06	188	28	46
West Ham U	Tr	07/07	07	22	3	2

LLERA Miguel Angel
Born: Seville, Spain, 7 August, 1979 — CD

League Club	Source	Date Signed	Seasons Played	Apps	Subs	Gls
MK Dons	Hercul Alicante (SPN)	09/08	08	34	0	2
Charlton Ath	Tr	07/09	09-10	37	3	5
Blackpool	Tr	08/11				
Brentford	L	09/11	11	10	1	0
Sheffield Wed	Tr	11/11	11-13	74	9	10
Scunthorpe U	Tr	07/14	14	15	0	1

LLEWELLYN Andrew David (Andy)
Born: Bristol, England, 26 February, 1966 — RB
England: Youth

League Club	Source	Date Signed	Seasons Played	Apps	Subs	Gls
Bristol C	App	02/84	82-93	296	12	3
Exeter C	L	03/94	93	15	0	0
Hereford U	Tr	10/94	94	3	1	0

LLEWELLYN Christopher Mark (Chris)
Born: Merthyr Tydfil, Wales, 29 August, 1979 — LW
Wales: 6/B-1/U21-14/Youth

League Club	Source	Date Signed	Seasons Played	Apps	Subs	Gls
Norwich C	YT	01/97	97-02	103	39	17
Bristol Rov	L	02/03	02	14	0	3
Wrexham	Tr	08/03	03-04	91	0	15
Hartlepool U	Tr	07/05	05	24	5	0
Wrexham	Tr	08/06	06-07	77	2	12
Grimsby T	Tr	07/08	08	13	15	0

LLEWELLYN David John
Born: Cardiff, Wales, 9 August, 1949 — M
Wales: U23-1

League Club	Source	Date Signed	Seasons Played	Apps	Subs	Gls
West Ham U	Jnr	08/66	69-71	2	4	0
Peterborough U	Tr	08/73	73-74	11	2	3
Mansfield T	L	08/74	74	6	2	0

LLEWELLYN Herbert Arthur (Bert)
Born: Golborne, Greater Manchester, England, 5 February, 1939 — CF
England: Youth

League Club	Source	Date Signed	Seasons Played	Apps	Subs	Gls
Everton	Jnr	05/56	56-57	11	-	2
Crewe Alex	Tr	07/58	58-60	96	-	49
Port Vale	Tr	11/60	60-62	88	-	42
Northampton T	Tr	02/63	62	1	-	0
Walsall	Tr	02/64	63-64	17	-	6

LLORIS Hugo
Born: Nice, France, 26 December, 1986 — G
France: 67/U21-5/Youth

League Club	Source	Date Signed	Seasons Played	Apps	Subs	Gls
Tottenham H	Olymp Lyonnais (FRA)	08/12	12-14	99	0	0

LLOYD Anthony Francis (Tony)
Born: Taunton, Somerset, England, 14 March, 1984 — LB

League Club	Source	Date Signed	Seasons Played	Apps	Subs	Gls
Huddersfield T	Sch	08/03	03-04	40	2	3
Torquay U	Tr	11/05	05	19	1	0

LLOYD Barry David
Born: Hillingdon, W London, England, 19 February, 1949 — M
England: Youth

League Club	Source	Date Signed	Seasons Played	Apps	Subs	Gls
Chelsea	App	02/66	66-68	8	2	0
Fulham	Tr	12/68	68-75	249	8	29
Hereford U	Tr	10/76	76	12	2	0
Brentford	Tr	06/77	77	26	5	4

LLOYD Brian William
Born: Rhyl, Denbighshire, Wales, 18 March, 1948 — G
Wales: 3/U23-2

League Club	Source	Date Signed	Seasons Played	Apps	Subs	Gls
Stockport Co	Rhyl	03/67	67-68	32	0	0
Southend U	Tr	09/69	69-70	46	0	0
Wrexham	Tr	08/71	71-77	266	0	0
Chester C	Tr	09/77	77-79	94	0	0
Port Vale	L	02/81	80	16	0	0
Stockport Co	Tr	08/81	81-82	91	0	1

LLOYD Callum
Born: Nottingham, England, 1 January, 1986 — M

League Club	Source	Date Signed	Seasons Played	Apps	Subs	Gls
Mansfield T	Sch	05/05	04-06	16	25	4

LLOYD Clifford (Cliff)
Born: Frodsham, Cheshire, England, 14 November, 1916 — LB
Died: Frodsham, Cheshire, England, 8 January, 2000

League Club	Source	Date Signed	Seasons Played	Apps	Subs	Gls
Liverpool		11/37				
Wrexham		10/41				
Fulham	Tr	12/45	46	2	-	0
Bristol Rov	Tr	05/50				

LLOYD David
Born: Gateshead, Tyne and Wear, England, 1 June, 1928 — CF
Died: Gateshead, Tyne and Wear, England, January, 2000

League Club	Source	Date Signed	Seasons Played	Apps	Subs	Gls
Sheffield U	North Fenham	09/49				
York C	Tr	03/51	50	1	-	0

LLOYD Frank
Born: Darton, South Yorkshire, England, 16 January, 1928 — LH
Died: Barnsley, South Yorkshire, England, 8 March, 2009

League Club	Source	Date Signed	Seasons Played	Apps	Subs	Gls
Bradford C	Barnsley (Am)	07/51	51-53	24	-	0

LLOYD Grahame
Born: Liverpool, England, 10 January, 1951 — G

League Club	Source	Date Signed	Seasons Played	Apps	Subs	Gls
Liverpool	App	01/68				
Portsmouth	Motherwell	07/75	75-76	73	0	0

LLOYD Harold Demane
Born: Flint, Wales, 12 March, 1920 — G
Died: Rhyl, Denbighshire, Wales, June, 1984

League Club	Source	Date Signed	Seasons Played	Apps	Subs	Gls
Tranmere Rov	Flint T	10/45	46-56	188	-	0

LLOYD John David
Born: Hitchin, Hertfordshire, England, 10 December, 1944 — LB

League Club	Source	Date Signed	Seasons Played	Apps	Subs	Gls
Swindon T	App	01/62				
Oxford U	Tr	10/64	65-68	68	4	0
Aldershot	Tr	02/69	68-69	11	2	0

LLOYD John Walter
Born: Rossett, Wrexham, Wales, 15 February, 1948 — RW

League Club	Source	Date Signed	Seasons Played	Apps	Subs	Gls
Wrexham (Am)	Jnr	08/65	65-66	2	0	0

LLOYD Joseph Millington (Joe)
Born: Connah's Quay, Flintshire, Wales, 30 September, 1910 — LH
Died: Shotton, Flintshire, Wales, 1 April, 1996

League Club	Source	Date Signed	Seasons Played	Apps	Subs	Gls
Everton	Connah's Quay	02/31				
Swansea C	Tr	08/32	33-38	211	-	1
Wrexham	Tr	07/46	46	20	-	0

LLOYD Kevin Gareth
Born: Llanidloes, Powys, Wales, 26 September, 1970 — LB

League Club	Source	Date Signed	Seasons Played	Apps	Subs	Gls
Hereford U	Caersws	11/94	94-95	49	2	3
Cardiff C	Tr	08/96	96-97	27	6	1

LLOYD Kevin John James
Born: Wolverhampton, England, 12 June, 1958 — F

League Club	Source	Date Signed	Seasons Played	Apps	Subs	Gls
Cardiff C	Darlaston	05/79	79	0	1	0
Gillingham	Tr	07/80	80	0	1	0

LLOYD Laurence Valentine (Larry)
Born: Bristol, England, 6 October, 1948 — CD
England: 4/U23-8/Youth

League Club	Source	Date Signed	Seasons Played	Apps	Subs	Gls
Bristol Rov	Jnr	07/67	68	43	0	1
Liverpool	Tr	04/69	69-73	150	0	4
Coventry C	Tr	08/74	74-76	50	0	5
Nottingham F	Tr	10/76	76-80	148	0	6
Wigan Ath	Tr	03/81	80-82	52	0	2

LLOYD Norman Philip
Born: Neath, Wales, 8 March, 1930 — LH
Died: Exeter, England, 22 April, 2011

League Club	Source	Date Signed	Seasons Played	Apps	Subs	Gls
Cardiff C		03/48				
Torquay U	Tr	09/49	52-56	29	-	1

LLOYD Norman William McLean (Norrie)
Born: Torrance, Dunbartonshire, Scotland, 6 September, 1949 — M

League Club	Source	Date Signed	Seasons Played	Apps	Subs	Gls
Preston NE	Twechar YC	09/66	68-70	17	2	6
Stockport Co	L	01/71	70	10	0	0
Southport	Tr	07/71	71-73	93	10	13
Stockport Co	Tr	07/74	74	36	2	2

LLOYD Paul Laurence
Born: Preston, Lancashire, England, 26 March, 1987 — W

League Club	Source	Date Signed	Seasons Played	Apps	Subs	Gls
Morecambe	Jnr	07/05	07	1	6	0

LLOYD Peter John
Born: Pattingham, Staffordshire, England, 26 April, 1933 — LW

League Club	Source	Date Signed	Seasons Played	Apps	Subs	Gls
Walsall	Pattingham	03/51	53	5	-	0

LLOYD Philip Rowan (Phil)
Born: Hemsworth, West Yorkshire, England, 26 December, 1964 — CD

League Club	Source	Date Signed	Seasons Played	Apps	Subs	Gls
Middlesbrough	App	12/82				
Barnsley	Tr	09/83				
Darlington	Tr	03/84	83-86	127	0	3
Torquay U	Tr	08/87	87-91	169	1	7

LLOYD Robert Clive (Clive)
Born: Merthyr Tydfil, Wales, 4 September, 1945 — IF

League Club	Source	Date Signed	Seasons Played	Apps	Subs	Gls
Norwich C	App	09/62				
Cardiff C	Tr	08/64	64	2	-	0

LLOYD Robert Geoffrey (Geoff)
Born: Wrexham, Wales, 18 August, 1942 — CF

League Club	Source	Date Signed	Seasons Played	Apps	Subs	Gls
Wrexham	Llangollen	10/66	66	13	1	5
Bradford Park Ave	Tr	07/67	67	32	0	10

LLOYD Ryan Anthony
Born: Newcastle-under-Lyme, Potteries, England, 1 February, 1994 — M

League Club	Source	Date Signed	Seasons Played	Apps	Subs	Gls
Port Vale	Sch	07/12	10-13	2	10	0

LLOYD William Frederick (Bill)
Born: Poplar, E London, England, 10 July, 1934 — G

League Club	Source	Date Signed	Seasons Played	Apps	Subs	Gls
Millwall	Bromley	08/56	56-57	74	-	0

LLOYD William Lorraine (Billy)
Born: Ystrad Rhondda, Rhondda Cynon Taff, Wales, 22 May, 1915 — D
Died: Swindon, England, 1978

League Club	Source	Date Signed	Seasons Played	Apps	Subs	Gls
Swindon T	Milford Haven	08/39	46-50	107	-	2

LLOYD William Stanley (Stan)
Born: West Auckland, County Durham, England, 1 October, 1924 — RW
Died: Cleethorpes, North Lincolnshire, England, 6 July, 2011
England: Schools

League Club	Source	Date Signed	Seasons Played	Apps	Subs	Gls
Sunderland	Silksworth Jnrs	12/41	46-47	24	-	5
Grimsby T	Tr	08/48	48-52	148	-	23
Scunthorpe U	Worksop T	07/54	54	1	-	0

LOACH Scott James
Born: Nottingham, England, 27 May, 1988 — G
England: U21-14

League Club	Source	Date Signed	Seasons Played	Apps	Subs	Gls
Watford	Lincoln C (Sch)	05/06	08-11	153	1	0
Morecambe	L	01/08	07	2	0	0
Bradford C	L	02/08	07	20	0	0
Ipswich T	Tr	07/12	12-13	27	1	0
Rotherham U	Tr	06/14	14	2	0	0
Bury	L	11/14	14	2	0	0
Peterborough U	L	01/15	14	5	0	0
Yeovil T	L	03/15	14	6	0	0

LOADWICK Derek
Born: Middlesbrough, England, 4 October, 1956 — M/D

League Club	Source	Date Signed	Seasons Played	Apps	Subs	Gls
Leeds U	App	10/73				
Stockport Co	Tr	07/76	76-78	84	0	0
Hartlepool U	Tr	10/78	78-79	49	2	1

LOASBY Alan Arthur
Born: Wellingborough, Northamptonshire, England, 19 March, 1937 — W

League Club	Source	Date Signed	Seasons Played	Apps	Subs	Gls
Luton T	Jnr	04/54				
Northampton T	Tr	07/58	58	2	-	0

LOBBETT Patrick Sidney John (John)
Born: Exeter, England, 8 January, 1938 — G

League Club	Source	Date Signed	Seasons Played	Apps	Subs	Gls
Exeter C	Barnstaple T	03/56	58-60	44	-	0

LOBJOIT Billy Jay
Born: Edgware, NW London, England, 3 September, 1993 — F

League Club	Source	Date Signed	Seasons Played	Apps	Subs	Gls
Leyton Orient	Sch	07/12	11	0	1	0

LOCHERTY Joseph (Joe)
Born: Dundee, Scotland, 5 September, 1925 — WH
Died: Dundee, Scotland, 20 June, 2000

League Club	Source	Date Signed	Seasons Played	Apps	Subs	Gls
Sheffield Wed	Lochee Harp	09/47	48-49	10	-	0
Colchester U	Tr	07/50	50	10	-	1

LOCHHEAD Andrew Lorimar (Andy)
Born: Lenzie, Dunbartonshire, Scotland, 9 March, 1941 — CF
Scotland: U23-1

League Club	Source	Date Signed	Seasons Played	Apps	Subs	Gls
Burnley	Renfrew Jnrs	12/58	60-68	225	1	101
Leicester C	Tr	10/68	68-69	40	4	12
Aston Villa	Tr	02/70	69-72	127	4	34
Oldham Ath	Tr	08/73	73-74	44	1	10

LOCK Anthony Charles (Tony)
Born: Harlow, Essex, England, 3 September, 1976 — F

League Club	Source	Date Signed	Seasons Played	Apps	Subs	Gls
Colchester U	YT	04/95	94-00	44	58	13

LOCK Frank William
Born: Whitechapel, Central London, England, 12 March, 1922 — LB
Died: Colchester, Essex, England, 17 March, 1985

League Club	Source	Date Signed	Seasons Played	Apps	Subs	Gls
Charlton Ath	Finchley	12/45	46-53	222	-	8
Liverpool	Tr	12/53	53-54	41	-	0
Watford	Tr	06/55	55-56	42	-	1

LOCK Kevin Joseph
Born: Plaistow, E London, England, 27 December, 1953 — CD
England: U23-4/Youth

League Club	Source	Date Signed	Seasons Played	Apps	Subs	Gls
West Ham U	App	12/71	71-77	122	10	2
Fulham	Tr	05/78	78-84	210	1	27
Southend U	Tr	08/85	85	10	0	0

LOCK Matthew John
Born: Barnstaple, Devon, England, 10 March, 1984 — M

League Club	Source	Date Signed	Seasons Played	Apps	Subs	Gls
Exeter C	Sch	08/02	02	1	2	0

LOCKE Adam Spencer
Born: Croydon, S London, England, 20 August, 1970 — M/RB

League Club	Source	Date Signed	Seasons Played	Apps	Subs	Gls
Crystal Palace	YT	06/88				
Southend U	Tr	08/90	90-93	56	17	4
Colchester U	L	10/93	93	4	0	0
Colchester U	Tr	09/94	94-96	64	15	8
Bristol C	Tr	07/97	97-98	61	4	4
Luton T	Tr	08/99	99-01	45	17	5

LOCKE Gary
Born: Edinburgh, Scotland, 16 June, 1975 — M
Scotland: U21-10

League Club	Source	Date Signed	Seasons Played	Apps	Subs	Gls
Bradford C	Heart of Midlothian	01/01	00-01	32	6	2

LOCKE Gary Robert
Born: Kingsbury, NW London, England, 12 July, 1954 — RB
England: Youth

League Club	Source	Date Signed	Seasons Played	Apps	Subs	Gls
Chelsea	App	07/71	72-82	270	2	3
Crystal Palace	Tr	01/83	82-85	84	0	1

LOCKE Leslie Cameron (Les)
Born: Perth, Scotland, 24 January, 1934 — IF
Died: Johannesburg, South Africa, 1996
Scotland: Amateur

League Club	Source	Date Signed	Seasons Played	Apps	Subs	Gls
Queens Park Rgrs	Bromley	05/58	56-59	76	-	24

LOCKER Stephen (Steve)
Born: Ashington, Northumberland, England, 5 November, 1970 — CD

League Club	Source	Date Signed	Seasons Played	Apps	Subs	Gls
Hartlepool U	Nottingham F (YT)	09/88	88	0	1	0

LOCKETT Philip Barry (Phil)
Born: Stockport, Greater Manchester, England, 6 September, 1972 — M

League Club	Source	Date Signed	Seasons Played	Apps	Subs	Gls
Rochdale	YT	07/91	89-90	1	2	0

LOCKETT Ryan David Carl William
Born: Cambridge, England, 11 November, 1986 — F

League Club	Source	Date Signed	Seasons Played	Apps	Subs	Gls
Cambridge U	Sch	-	03	1	1	0

LOCKHART Crichton (Jock)
Born: Perth, Scotland, 6 March, 1930 — W

League Club	Source	Date Signed	Seasons Played	Apps	Subs	Gls
Southend U	Chertsey	08/50	50-56	45	-	11
Rochdale	Tr	06/57	57	40	-	11

LOCKHART Keith Samuel
Born: Wallsend, Tyne and Wear, England, 19 July, 1964 — M

League Club	Source	Date Signed	Seasons Played	Apps	Subs	Gls
Cambridge U	App	07/82	81-85	55	3	8
Wolverhampton W	Tr	03/86	85-86	24	1	4
Hartlepool U	Tr	12/86	86	2	0	0

LOCKHART Norman
Born: Belfast, Northern Ireland, 4 March, 1924 — LW
Died: Belfast, Northern Ireland, 19 January, 1993
Northern Ireland: 8

League Club	Source	Date Signed	Seasons Played	Apps	Subs	Gls
Swansea C	Linfield	10/46	46-47	47	-	13
Coventry C	Tr	10/47	47-52	182	-	41
Aston Villa	Tr	09/52	52-55	74	-	10
Bury	Tr	11/56	56-57	41	-	6

LOCKHART-ADAMS Kofi Wesley
Born: London, Ontario, Canada, 9 October, 1992 — F

League Club	Source	Date Signed	Seasons Played	Apps	Subs	Gls
Barnet	Sch	-	09	0	1	0

LOCKIE Alexander James (Alex)
Born: South Shields, Tyne and Wear, England, 11 April, 1915 — CH
Died: Sunderland, England, March, 1974

League Club	Source	Date Signed	Seasons Played	Apps	Subs	Gls
Sunderland	Reyrolles	09/35	36-38	40	-	1
Notts Co	Tr	09/46	46	23	-	0

LOCKIER Maurice Reginald
Born: Bristol, England, 27 November, 1924 — LW
Died: Bristol, England, 23 December, 2001

League Club	Source	Date Signed	Seasons Played	Apps	Subs	Gls
Bristol Rov		07/47	49	2	-	0

LOCKWOOD Adam Brian
Born: Wakefield, England, 26 October, 1981 — CD
England: Semi Pro-2

League Club	Source	Date Signed	Seasons Played	Apps	Subs	Gls
Reading	YT	03/99				
Yeovil T	Tr	10/01	03-05	67	6	4
Torquay U	L	11/05	05	9	0	3
Doncaster Rov	Tr	07/06	06-11	127	24	8
Bury	Tr	07/12	12-13	18	0	1
Oldham Ath	Guiseley	01/14	13-14	29	2	2

LOCKWOOD Edward
Born: Goldthorpe, South Yorkshire, England, 4 August, 1925 — LB
Died: Barnsley, South Yorkshire, England, December, 2005

League Club	Source	Date Signed	Seasons Played	Apps	Subs	Gls
Scunthorpe U	Denaby U	06/51	51-52	9	-	0

LOCKWOOD Matthew Dominic (Matt)
Born: Southend-on-Sea, England, 17 October, 1976 — LB

League Club	Source	Date Signed	Seasons Played	Apps	Subs	Gls
Queens Park Rgrs	Southend U (YT)	05/95				
Bristol Rov	Tr	07/96	96-97	58	5	1

League Club	Source	Date Signed	Seasons Played	Apps	Subs	Gls
Leyton Orient	Tr	08/98	98-06	319	9	50
Nottingham F	Tr	07/07	07	11	0	0
Colchester U	Tr	06/08	08-09	6	0	0
Barnet	L	02/09	08	12	0	0
Dagenham & Red	L	10/09	09	4	0	0
Barnet	L	01/10	09	19	0	2

LOCKWOOD Roy
Born: Barnsley, South Yorkshire, England, 20 June, 1933 — LB
England: Youth

League Club	Source	Date Signed	Seasons Played	Apps	Subs	Gls
Sheffield Wed	Jnr	04/51				
Norwich C	Tr	09/55	55-57	36	-	0

LOCKYER Thomas Alun (Tom)
Born: Barry, Vale of Glamorgan, Wales, 3 December, 1994 — D/M

League Club	Source	Date Signed	Seasons Played	Apps	Subs	Gls
Bristol Rov	Sch	07/13	12-13	38	7	1

LODGE Andrew Robert (Andy)
Born: Peterborough, England, 17 July, 1978 — FB

League Club	Source	Date Signed	Seasons Played	Apps	Subs	Gls
Boston U	Stamford AFC	01/00	02	1	1	0

LODGE Frank
Born: Oldham, Greater Manchester, England, 28 November, 1919 — CF
Died: Formby, Merseyside, England, 15 October, 1973

League Club	Source	Date Signed	Seasons Played	Apps	Subs	Gls
Stockport Co (Am)	Ward Street OB	03/47	46	1	-	0

LODGE George Raymond (Ray)
Born: Wallsend, Tyne and Wear, England, 27 January, 1943 — LW

League Club	Source	Date Signed	Seasons Played	Apps	Subs	Gls
Workington		12/61				
Newcastle U	Tr	07/62				
Barrow	Tr	07/63	63	6	-	0

LODGE Joe Thomas
Born: Skelmanthorpe, West Yorkshire, England, 16 April, 1921 — LH
Died: Skelmanthorpe, West Yorkshire, England, 9 July, 2012

League Club	Source	Date Signed	Seasons Played	Apps	Subs	Gls
Huddersfield T	Jnr	08/39	46-47	2	-	0

LODGE Paul
Born: Liverpool, England, 13 February, 1961 — M
England: Schools

League Club	Source	Date Signed	Seasons Played	Apps	Subs	Gls
Everton	App	02/79	80-81	20	4	0
Wigan Ath	L	08/82	82	5	0	1
Rotherham U	L	01/83	82	4	0	0
Preston NE	Tr	02/83	82-83	36	2	0
Bolton W	Tr	07/84	84	4	0	0
Port Vale	L	11/84	84	3	0	0
Stockport Co	Tr	03/85	84-85	10	3	2

LODGE Robert William (Bobby)
Born: Retford, Nottinghamshire, England, 1 July, 1941 — W

League Club	Source	Date Signed	Seasons Played	Apps	Subs	Gls
Sheffield Wed	Jnr	05/59	60	3	-	2
Doncaster Rov	Tr	05/61	61	23	-	4

LOFT Douglas James (Doug)
Born: Maidstone, Kent, England, 26 December, 1986 — DM

League Club	Source	Date Signed	Seasons Played	Apps	Subs	Gls
Brighton & HA	Hastings U	01/06	05-08	13	26	2
Dagenham & Red	L	02/09	08	10	1	0
Port Vale	Tr	07/09	09-13	156	18	18
Gillingham	Tr	06/14	14	36	0	1

LOFTHOUSE Nathaniel (Nat)
Born: Bolton, Greater Manchester, England, 27 August, 1925 — CF
Died: Bolton, Greater Manchester, England, 15 January, 2011
England: 33/B-1/FLge-15

League Club	Source	Date Signed	Seasons Played	Apps	Subs	Gls
Bolton W	Jnr	08/42	46-60	452	-	255

LOFTUS Robert (Bob)
Born: Liverpool, England, 15 December, 1931 — RW

League Club	Source	Date Signed	Seasons Played	Apps	Subs	Gls
Bradford Park Ave	Llanelli	12/55	55	3	-	0

LOFTUS-CHEEK Ruben Ira
Born: Lewisham, SE London, England, 23 January, 1996 — M
England: Youth

League Club	Source	Date Signed	Seasons Played	Apps	Subs	Gls
Chelsea	Sch	01/13	14	2	1	0

LOFTY James Kenneth (Jim)
Born: Farnham, Surrey, England, 5 December, 1945 — LW

League Club	Source	Date Signed	Seasons Played	Apps	Subs	Gls
Reading	Jnr	05/63	63	2	-	0
Birmingham C	Tr	07/64				

LOGAN Carlos Sean
Born: Wythenshawe, Greater Manchester, England, 7 November, 1985 — LW

League Club	Source	Date Signed	Seasons Played	Apps	Subs	Gls
Manchester C	Sch	07/04				
Chesterfield	L	03/05	04	6	3	1
Darlington	Tr	08/05	05-06	27	15	4
Bradford C	L	01/07	06	3	1	0

LOGAN Conrad Joseph
Born: Letterkenny, Republic of Ireland, 18 April, 1986 — G
Republic of Ireland: Youth

League Club	Source	Date Signed	Seasons Played	Apps	Subs	Gls
Leicester C	Sch	07/03	06-10	21	2	0
Boston U	L	12/05	05	10	0	0
Boston U	L	04/06	05	3	0	0
Stockport Co	L	08/07	07	34	0	0
Luton T	L	08/08	08	22	0	0
Stockport Co	L	03/09	08	7	0	0
Bristol Rov	L	02/11	10	16	0	0
Rotherham U	L	07/11	11	19	0	0
Rochdale	L	08/14	14	19	0	0

LOGAN David
Born: Middlesbrough, England, 5 December, 1963 — LB

League Club	Source	Date Signed	Seasons Played	Apps	Subs	Gls
Mansfield T	Whitby T	06/84	84-86	67	0	1
Northampton T	Tr	02/87	86-87	39	2	1
Halifax T	Tr	08/88	88	3	0	0
Stockport Co	Tr	10/88	88-89	60	0	4
Scarborough	Tr	08/90	90-91	54	1	1

LOGAN Douglas (Doug)
Born: Aberdeen, Scotland, 30 August, 1933 — LH
Died: London, England, June, 1984

League Club	Source	Date Signed	Seasons Played	Apps	Subs	Gls
Southampton	RAF Lamport	01/54	55-57	21	-	0

LOGAN Gordon Taylor
Born: Kirkliston, Edinburgh, Scotland, 3 October, 1949 — RB
Scotland: Youth

League Club	Source	Date Signed	Seasons Played	Apps	Subs	Gls
Port Vale	Tynecastle Ath	03/67	66-69	33	2	1

LOGAN Joel Alexander
Born: Manchester, England, 25 January, 1995 — W

League Club	Source	Date Signed	Seasons Played	Apps	Subs	Gls
Rochdale	Sch	07/13	12-14	4	9	0

LOGAN John William
Born: Horden, County Durham, England, 16 August, 1912 — WH
Died: Barnsley, South Yorkshire, England, 1980

League Club	Source	Date Signed	Seasons Played	Apps	Subs	Gls
Charlton Ath	Horden CW	07/34				
Darlington	Tr	05/35	35-36	65	-	5
Barnsley	Tr	03/37	36-46	99	-	5
Sheffield Wed	Tr	01/47	46	4	-	0

LOGAN Richard Adam
Born: Washington, Tyne and Wear, England, 18 February, 1988 — F

League Club	Source	Date Signed	Seasons Played	Apps	Subs	Gls
Darlington	Sch	-	04	0	1	0

LOGAN Richard Anthony
Born: Barnsley, South Yorkshire, England, 24 May, 1969 — M

League Club	Source	Date Signed	Seasons Played	Apps	Subs	Gls
Huddersfield T	Gainsborough Trinity	11/93	93-95	35	10	1
Plymouth Arg	Tr	10/95	95-97	67	19	12
Scunthorpe U	Tr	07/98	98-99	77	3	7
Lincoln C	Tr	07/00	00-02	14	3	1

LOGAN Richard James
Born: Bury St Edmunds, Suffolk, England, 4 January, 1982 — F
England: Youth/Schools

League Club	Source	Date Signed	Seasons Played	Apps	Subs	Gls
Ipswich T	YT	01/99	98-99	0	3	0
Cambridge U	L	01/01	00	5	0	1
Torquay U	L	12/01	01	16	0	4
Boston U	Tr	11/02	02-03	30	5	10
Peterborough U	Tr	09/03	03-05	40	43	15
Shrewsbury T	L	09/04	04	5	0	1
Lincoln C	L	11/05	05	8	0	2
Exeter C	Weymouth	01/07	08-11	55	77	24
Wycombe W	Tr	07/12	12	3	5	0

LOGAN Shaleum Narval (Shay)
Born: Wythenshawe, Greater Manchester, England, 29 January, 1988 — RB

League Club	Source	Date Signed	Seasons Played	Apps	Subs	Gls
Manchester C	Sch	07/06	08	1	0	0
Grimsby T	L	10/07	07	5	0	2
Scunthorpe U	L	11/07	07	4	0	0
Stockport Co	L	02/08	07	6	1	0
Tranmere Rov	L	07/09	09	32	1	0
Brentford	Tr	07/11	11-13	81	9	4

LOGGIE David McKie
Born: Newbiggin, Northumberland, England, 31 May, 1957 — F

League Club	Source	Date Signed	Seasons Played	Apps	Subs	Gls
Burnley	App	06/74	75-77	6	1	0
York C	Tr	06/78	78-79	47	3	11

LOGIE James Tullis (Jimmy)
Born: Edinburgh, Scotland, 23 November, 1919 — IF
Died: London, England, 30 April, 1984
Scotland: 1

League Club	Source	Date Signed	Seasons Played	Apps	Subs	Gls
Arsenal	Lochore Welfare	06/39	46-54	296	-	68

LOGUE Samuel Walker (Sam)
Born: Glasgow, Scotland, 9 April, 1934 — IF
Died: Paisley, Renfrewshire, Scotland, 25 October, 2004

League Club	Source	Date Signed	Seasons Played	Apps	Subs	Gls
Accrington Stan	Clyde	06/60	60	2	-	0

LOHMAN Johannes Hermanus Petrus (Jan)
Born: Dussen, Netherlands, 18 February, 1959 — M

Netherlands: U21

League Club	Source	Date Signed	Seasons Played	Apps	Subs	Gls
Watford	Lokeren (BEL)	10/81	81-85	51	12	6

LOLLEY Joseph (Joe)
Born: Redditch, Worcestershire, England, 25 August, 1992 — F
England: Semi Pro-1

League Club	Source	Date Signed	Seasons Played	Apps	Subs	Gls
Huddersfield T	Kidderminster Hrs	01/14	13-14	4	19	3

LOMAS Albert (Bert)
Born: Tyldesley, Greater Manchester, England, 14 October, 1924 — G
Died: Bolton, Greater Manchester, England, April, 2014

League Club	Source	Date Signed	Seasons Played	Apps	Subs	Gls
Leeds U	Bolton W (Am)	09/48	48	1	-	0
Rochdale	Mossley	05/50	50	9	-	0
Chesterfield	Tr	07/51	51	29	-	0

LOMAS Andrew James (Andy)
Born: Hartlepool, Cleveland, England, 26 April, 1965 — G

League Club	Source	Date Signed	Seasons Played	Apps	Subs	Gls
Cambridge U (L)	Stevenage Bor	03/95	94	2	0	0

LOMAS Clive Ian
Born: Ealing, W London, England, 18 January, 1947 — LH

League Club	Source	Date Signed	Seasons Played	Apps	Subs	Gls
Watford	App	01/65	65	6	1	0

LOMAS James Duncan (Jamie)
Born: Chesterfield, Derbyshire, England, 18 October, 1977 — M

League Club	Source	Date Signed	Seasons Played	Apps	Subs	Gls
Chesterfield	YT	09/96	96-99	17	13	0
Mansfield T	Tr	08/00	00	4	2	0

LOMAS Peter
Born: Royton, Greater Manchester, England, 9 May, 1933 — RB
Died: Southport, Merseyside, England, 15 November, 2006

League Club	Source	Date Signed	Seasons Played	Apps	Subs	Gls
Southport	Royton Amats	04/52	51-56	18	-	0

LOMAS Stephen Martin (Steve)
Born: Hannover, Germany, 18 January, 1974 — M
Northern Ireland: 45/B-1/Youth/Schools

League Club	Source	Date Signed	Seasons Played	Apps	Subs	Gls
Manchester C	YT	01/91	93-96	102	9	8
West Ham U	Tr	03/97	96-04	179	8	10
Queens Park Rgrs	Tr	08/05	05-06	44	11	2
Gillingham	L	08/07	07	8	0	0

LOMAX Geoffrey William (Geoff)
Born: Droylsden, Greater Manchester, England, 6 July, 1964 — D

League Club	Source	Date Signed	Seasons Played	Apps	Subs	Gls
Manchester C	Jnr	07/81	82-84	23	2	1
Wolverhampton W	L	10/85	85	5	0	0
Carlisle U	Tr	12/85	85-86	37	0	0
Rochdale	Tr	07/87	87-88	70	1	0

LOMAX Kelvin
Born: Bury, Greater Manchester, England, 12 November, 1986 — FB

League Club	Source	Date Signed	Seasons Played	Apps	Subs	Gls
Oldham Ath	Sch	07/05	03-09	65	17	0
Rochdale	L	09/07	07	10	0	0
Chesterfield	L	11/10	10	3	1	0
Shrewsbury T	Tr	01/11	10	0	1	0

LOMAX Michael John (Mike)
Born: Manchester, England, 7 December, 1979 — FB

League Club	Source	Date Signed	Seasons Played	Apps	Subs	Gls
Macclesfield T	Blackburn Rov (YT)	07/98	98	0	1	0

LOMBARDO Attilio
Born: Santa Marta, Caserta, Italy, 6 January, 1966 — W
Italy: 18

League Club	Source	Date Signed	Seasons Played	Apps	Subs	Gls
Crystal Palace	Juventus (ITA)	08/97	97-98	40	3	8

LONERGAN Andrew Michael (Andy)
Born: Preston, Lancashire, England, 19 October, 1983 — G
England: Youth//Republic of Ireland: Youth

League Club	Source	Date Signed	Seasons Played	Apps	Subs	Gls
Preston NE	YT	10/00	00-10	208	0	1
Darlington	L	12/02	02	2	0	0
Wycombe W	L	10/05	05	2	0	0
Swindon T	L	11/06	06	1	0	0
Leeds U	Tr	07/11	11	35	0	0
Bolton W	Tr	07/12	12-14	50	1	0

LONERGAN Darren
Born: Cork, Republic of Ireland, 28 January, 1974 — CD

League Club	Source	Date Signed	Seasons Played	Apps	Subs	Gls
Oldham Ath	Waterford (ROI)	09/94	95	1	1	0
Macclesfield T	Bury (NC)	08/98				

LONG Christopher (Chris)
Born: Hatfield, Hertfordshire, England, 7 February, 1948 — LW

League Club	Source	Date Signed	Seasons Played	Apps	Subs	Gls
Luton T	Hatfield T	02/66	65	1	0	0

LONG Christopher Michael (Chris)
Born: Huyton, Merseyside, England, 25 February, 1995 — F
England: Youth

League Club	Source	Date Signed	Seasons Played	Apps	Subs	Gls
Everton	Sch	07/13				
MK Dons	L	01/14	13	4	0	1
Brentford	L	01/15	14	2	8	4

LONG George Martin
Born: Sheffield, England, 5 November, 1993 — G
England: Youth

League Club	Source	Date Signed	Seasons Played	Apps	Subs	Gls
Sheffield U	Sch	02/12	10-13	65	1	0
Oxford U	L	07/14	14	10	0	0

LONG Herbert Raymond (Ray)
Born: Stickney, Lincolnshire, England, 4 October, 1936 — CH

League Club	Source	Date Signed	Seasons Played	Apps	Subs	Gls
Lincoln C	Louth U	12/58	59	1	-	0

LONG John William
Born: Southampton, England, 8 May, 1921 — FB

League Club	Source	Date Signed	Seasons Played	Apps	Subs	Gls
Exeter C	Chester C (Am)	04/46	46	1	-	0

LONG Kevin Finbarr
Born: Cork, Republic of Ireland, 18 August, 1990 — CD

League Club	Source	Date Signed	Seasons Played	Apps	Subs	Gls
Burnley	Cork C (ROI)	02/10	12-14	18	4	0
Accrington Stan	L	10/10	10	11	4	0
Accrington Stan	L	08/11	11	24	0	4
Rochdale	L	01/12	11	16	0	0
Portsmouth	L	08/12	12	5	0	0

LONG Nigel
Born: Doncaster, South Yorkshire, England, 31 March, 1955 — M

League Club	Source	Date Signed	Seasons Played	Apps	Subs	Gls
Doncaster Rov	Frickley Colliery	05/74	74	1	0	0

LONG Samuel Patrick Robert (Sam)
Born: Oxford, England, 16 January, 1995 — CD

League Club	Source	Date Signed	Seasons Played	Apps	Subs	Gls
Oxford U	Sch	06/13	12-14	11	3	1

LONG Shane Patrick
Born: Gortnahoe, Tipperary, Republic of Ireland, 22 January, 1987 — F
Republic of Ireland: 54/B-1/U21-1/Youth

League Club	Source	Date Signed	Seasons Played	Apps	Subs	Gls
Reading	Cork C (ROI)	06/05	05-11	95	79	44
West Bromwich A	Tr	08/11	11-13	60	21	19
Hull C	Tr	01/14	13	15	0	4
Southampton	Tr	08/14	14	16	16	5

LONG Stacy William
Born: Bromley, SE London, England, 11 January, 1985 — LW
England: Semi Pro-1/Youth

League Club	Source	Date Signed	Seasons Played	Apps	Subs	Gls
Charlton Ath	Sch	01/02				
Notts Co	Tr	08/05	05	7	12	1
Stevenage	Gravesend & Northfleet	06/09	10-11	37	15	3
AFC Wimbledon	Tr	07/12	12	23	5	3

LONG Terence Anthony (Terry)
Born: Tylers Green, Buckinghamshire, England, 17 November, 1934 — D

League Club	Source	Date Signed	Seasons Played	Apps	Subs	Gls
Crystal Palace	Wycombe W	05/55	55-68	432	10	16

LONG Trevor George
Born: Smethwick, West Midlands, England, 1 July, 1931 — LW
Died: Bideford, Devon, England, 15 November, 2006

League Club	Source	Date Signed	Seasons Played	Apps	Subs	Gls
Wolverhampton W	Mitchell & Butlers	12/50				
Gillingham	Tr	07/52	52-54	67	-	15
Reading	Tr	07/55	55	12	-	5

LONG Wilfred Roy (Wilf)
Born: Wallasey, Wirral, England, 28 December, 1922 — LW
Died: Wallasey, Wirral, England, February, 1993

League Club	Source	Date Signed	Seasons Played	Apps	Subs	Gls
New Brighton	Everton (Am)	07/46	46	2	-	0

LONGBOTTOM (LANGLEY) Arthur
Born: Leeds, England, 30 January, 1933 — IF

League Club	Source	Date Signed	Seasons Played	Apps	Subs	Gls
Queens Park Rgrs	Methley U	03/54	54-60	201	-	62
Port Vale	Tr	05/61	61-62	52	-	18
Millwall	Tr	01/63	62	10	-	1
Oxford U	Tr	08/63	63-64	34	-	14
Colchester U	Tr	10/64	64	33	-	12

LONGDEN Colin
Born: Rotherham, South Yorkshire, England, 21 July, 1933 — RW
England: Schools

League Club	Source	Date Signed	Seasons Played	Apps	Subs	Gls
Rotherham U	Jnr	08/50	52	3	-	0
York C	Tr	08/55	57	2	-	0

LONGDEN David Paul (Paul)
Born: East Ardsley, West Yorkshire, England, 28 September, 1962 — LB

League Club	Source	Date Signed	Seasons Played	Apps	Subs	Gls
Barnsley	App	09/80	81-82	5	0	0
Scunthorpe U	Tr	08/83	83-92	364	4	0

LONGDON Charles William (Charlie)
Born: Mansfield, Nottinghamshire, England, 6 May, 1917 — CF
Died: Truro, Cornwall, England, 19 November, 1986

League Club	Source	Date Signed	Seasons Played	Apps	Subs	Gls
Brighton & HA	Folkestone T	05/39				
Bournemouth	Tr	05/46	46	9	-	1
Rochdale	Tr	07/47	47	2	-	0

LONGHORN Dennis
Born: Hythe, Hampshire, England, 12 September, 1950 — M

League Club	Source	Date Signed	Seasons Played	Apps	Subs	Gls
Bournemouth	App	08/68	67-71	23	7	1
Mansfield T	Tr	12/71	71-73	93	3	5
Sunderland	Tr	02/74	73-76	35	5	3

League Club	Source	Date Signed	Seasons Played	Apps	Subs	Gls
Sheffield U	Tr	10/76	76-77	34	2	1
Aldershot	Tr	02/78	77-79	46	7	3
Colchester U	Tr	05/80	80-82	62	9	0

LONGHURST David John
Born: Northampton, England, 15 January, 1965 — F
Died: York, England, September, 1990

League Club	Source	Date Signed	Seasons Played	Apps	Subs	Gls
Nottingham F	App	01/83				
Halifax T	Tr	07/85	85-86	85	0	24
Northampton T	Tr	06/87	87-88	34	3	7
Peterborough U	Tr	10/88	88-89	51	7	7
York C	Tr	01/90	89-90	6	0	2

LONGLAND John (Johnny)
Born: Southampton, England, 24 September, 1932 — LH
Died: West Sussex, England, January, 2014

League Club	Source	Date Signed	Seasons Played	Apps	Subs	Gls
Brighton & HA		04/54	54	3	-	0

LONGLEY Nicholas (Nick)
Born: Mexborough, South Yorkshire, England, 21 May, 1961 — G

League Club	Source	Date Signed	Seasons Played	Apps	Subs	Gls
Crewe Alex	Whitchurch Alport	05/81	81-85	23	0	0

LONGLEY Scott Edward
Born: Wakefield, England, 16 July, 1973 — M

League Club	Source	Date Signed	Seasons Played	Apps	Subs	Gls
Halifax T	YT	07/92	91	1	0	0

LONGRIDGE George Paterson
Born: Glasgow, Scotland, 23 August, 1931 — G
Died: Pennsylvania, USA, 8 June, 1998

League Club	Source	Date Signed	Seasons Played	Apps	Subs	Gls
Leyton Orient	Denistoun Waverley	07/50				
Darlington	Tr	09/51	51	2	-	0

LONGWORTH Steven Paul (Steve)
Born: Leyland, Lancashire, England, 6 February, 1980 — F

League Club	Source	Date Signed	Seasons Played	Apps	Subs	Gls
Blackpool	YT	07/98	97	0	2	0

LONSDALE Joseph Stanley (Stan)
Born: Washington, Tyne and Wear, England, 13 April, 1931 — LB/W
Died: Huddersfield, West Yorkshire, England, 26 September, 2003

League Club	Source	Date Signed	Seasons Played	Apps	Subs	Gls
Huddersfield T	Seaham Jnrs	12/48				
Halifax T	Tr	03/55	54-59	202	-	21
Hartlepool U	Tr	11/60	60	9	-	0

LOOVENS Glen
Born: Doetinchem, Netherlands, 22 September, 1983 — CD
Netherlands: 2/U21-2

League Club	Source	Date Signed	Seasons Played	Apps	Subs	Gls
Cardiff C	Feyenoord (NED)	08/05	05-08	99	1	3
Sheffield Wed	Real Zaragoza (SPN)	12/13	13-14	47	1	0

LOPES Osvaldo
Born: Frejus, France, 6 April, 1980 — M

League Club	Source	Date Signed	Seasons Played	Apps	Subs	Gls
Plymouth Arg	Draguignan (FRA)	08/02	02	4	5	0
Torquay U	Cork C (ROI)	01/05	04	1	0	0

LOPES Richard (Richie)
Born: Waterford, Republic of Ireland, 10 August, 1981 — M

League Club	Source	Date Signed	Seasons Played	Apps	Subs	Gls
Sheffield U	YT	07/00				
Northampton T	Tr	03/01	00	3	3	0

LOPEZ Carlos
Born: Mexico City, Mexico, 18 April, 1970 — FB

League Club	Source	Date Signed	Seasons Played	Apps	Subs	Gls
Wycombe W	Chester C	01/02	01	1	0	0

LOPEZ Daniel (Dani)
Born: Madrid, Spain, 25 October, 1985 — F

League Club	Source	Date Signed	Seasons Played	Apps	Subs	Gls
Stevenage	CD Badajoz (SPN)	08/12	12-13	8	6	3
Aldershot T	L	11/12	12	11	1	6
Barnet	L	02/13	12	5	0	3

LOPEZ David
Born: Logrono, Spain, 10 September, 1982 — M

League Club	Source	Date Signed	Seasons Played	Apps	Subs	Gls
Brighton & HA	Atletico Bilbao (SPN)	08/12	12-13	53	12	12

LOPEZ Rik Alexander
Born: Harrow, NW London, England, 25 October, 1979 — RB

League Club	Source	Date Signed	Seasons Played	Apps	Subs	Gls
Queens Park Rgrs	YT	04/97				
Bristol Rov	Uniao Leiria (POR)	08/01	01	5	2	0

LOPEZ Walter Alberto
Born: Montevideo, Uruguay, 15 October, 1985 — FB/M
Uruguay: 3

League Club	Source	Date Signed	Seasons Played	Apps	Subs	Gls
West Ham U	River Plate (UGY)	09/08	08	0	5	0

LORAM Mark Julian
Born: Paignton, Devon, England, 13 August, 1967 — F/M

League Club	Source	Date Signed	Seasons Played	Apps	Subs	Gls
Torquay U	Brixham Villa	01/85	84-85	50	2	8
Queens Park Rgrs	Tr	05/86				
Torquay U	Tr	03/87	86-91	188	21	40
Stockport Co	L	03/92	91	1	3	0
Exeter C	L	09/92	92	2	1	0
Torquay U	Minehead	08/93	93	0	1	0

LORAN Tyrone Gabriel
Born: Amsterdam, Netherlands, 29 June, 1981 — RB
Netherlands Antilles: 5//Netherlands: U21

League Club	Source	Date Signed	Seasons Played	Apps	Subs	Gls
Manchester C	Volendam (NED)	07/02				
Tranmere Rov	Tr	12/02	02-04	42	5	0
Port Vale	L	12/04	04	6	0	0

LORD Albert Ernest
Born: Farnworth, Greater Manchester, England, 10 September, 1944 — G

League Club	Source	Date Signed	Seasons Played	Apps	Subs	Gls
Bolton W	Jnr	01/63				
Southport	Tr	03/66	65	16	0	0

LORD Barry
Born: Goole, East Riding of Yorkshire, England, 17 November, 1937 — G

League Club	Source	Date Signed	Seasons Played	Apps	Subs	Gls
Hull C	Goole Buchanan	04/56	58-60	5	-	0

LORD Frank
Born: Chadderton, Greater Manchester, England, 13 March, 1936 — CF
Died: Cape Town, South Africa, 11 June, 2005

League Club	Source	Date Signed	Seasons Played	Apps	Subs	Gls
Rochdale	Royton Amats	10/53	53-60	122	-	54
Crewe Alex	Tr	07/61	61-63	108	-	68
Plymouth Arg	Tr	11/63	63-65	69	0	23
Stockport Co	Tr	02/66	65-66	27	0	18
Blackburn Rov	Tr	12/66	66	10	0	1
Chesterfield	Tr	06/67	67	12	0	6
Plymouth Arg	Tr	10/67	68	6	0	2

LORD Malcolm
Born: Driffield, East Riding of Yorkshire, England, 25 October, 1946 — M
England: Schools

League Club	Source	Date Signed	Seasons Played	Apps	Subs	Gls
Hull C	Jnr	08/65	66-78	271	27	24

LORD Walter
Born: Grimsby, North Lincolnshire, England, 1 November, 1933 — IF

League Club	Source	Date Signed	Seasons Played	Apps	Subs	Gls
Grimsby T	Jnr	08/51	52-53	7	-	1
Lincoln C	Tr	05/56	56	1	-	0

LORD William Graham (Graham)
Born: Rawtenstall, Lancashire, England, 9 July, 1936 — LB

League Club	Source	Date Signed	Seasons Played	Apps	Subs	Gls
Accrington Stan	Rossendale U	07/57	58-60	67	-	0

LORENSON Roy Vincent
Born: Liverpool, England, 8 April, 1932 — WH/CH

League Club	Source	Date Signed	Seasons Played	Apps	Subs	Gls
Halifax T	St Elizabeth's	02/52	51-60	217	-	7
Tranmere Rov	Tr	10/60	60-61	14	-	0

LORENZO Nestor Gabriel
Born: Buenos Aires, Argentina, 28 February, 1966 — CD
Argentina: 13

League Club	Source	Date Signed	Seasons Played	Apps	Subs	Gls
Swindon T	Bari (ITA)	10/90	90-91	20	4	2

LORIMER Peter Patrick
Born: Dundee, Scotland, 14 December, 1946 — F/M
Scotland: 21/U23-2/Youth/Schools

League Club	Source	Date Signed	Seasons Played	Apps	Subs	Gls
Leeds U	Jnr	12/63	62-78	429	20	151
York C	Toronto Blizzard (CAN)	09/79	79	29	0	8
Leeds U	Vancouver W'caps (CAN)	03/84	83-85	74	2	17

LORMOR Anthony (Tony)
Born: Ashington, Northumberland, England, 29 October, 1970 — F

League Club	Source	Date Signed	Seasons Played	Apps	Subs	Gls
Newcastle U	YT	02/88	87-88	6	2	3
Lincoln C	Tr	01/90	89-93	90	10	30
Peterborough U	Tr	07/94	94	2	3	0
Chesterfield	Tr	12/94	94-97	97	16	35
Preston NE	Tr	11/97	97	9	3	3
Notts Co	L	02/98	97	2	5	0
Mansfield T	Tr	07/98	98-99	68	6	20
Hartlepool U	Tr	08/00	00-01	26	22	9
Shrewsbury T	L	02/02	01	7	0	2

LORNIE John (Jackie)
Born: Aberdeen, Scotland, 2 March, 1939 — IF/W
Died: Inverness, Scotland, 16 December, 2014
Scotland: Schools

League Club	Source	Date Signed	Seasons Played	Apps	Subs	Gls
Leicester C	Banks o' Dee	03/58	58-60	8	-	3
Luton T	Tr	06/61	61-62	19	-	6
Carlisle U	Tr	06/63	63	4	-	0
Tranmere Rov	Tr	06/64	64-65	33	2	6

LOSKA Anthony Stephen Patrick (Tony)
Born: Chesterton, Potteries, England, 11 February, 1950 — LB

League Club	Source	Date Signed	Seasons Played	Apps	Subs	Gls
Shrewsbury T	App	03/68	68-70	12	0	0
Port Vale	Tr	07/71	71-73	74	6	5
Chester C	Tr	12/73	73-76	103	7	5
Halifax T	Tr	10/76	76-78	101	1	0

LOSS Colin Paul
Born: Brentwood, Essex, England, 15 August, 1973 — M

League Club	Source	Date Signed	Seasons Played	Apps	Subs	Gls
Derby Co	Norwich C (YT)	11/91				
Bristol C	Gresley Rov	03/94	94	3	2	0

League Club	Source	Date Signed	Seasons Played	Career Record Apps	Subs	Gls

LOUGH John Douglas
Born: Gateshead, Tyne and Wear, England, 31 October, 1922 — LW
Died: Gateshead, Tyne and Wear, England, July, 1987

League Club	Source	Date Signed	Seasons Played	Apps	Subs	Gls
Gateshead (Am)		09/46	46	1	-	0

LOUGHLAN Antony John (Tony)
Born: Croydon, S London, England, 19 January, 1970 — W

League Club	Source	Date Signed	Seasons Played	Apps	Subs	Gls
Nottingham F	Leicester U	08/89	90	2	0	1
Lincoln C	Kettering T	10/93	93	4	8	2

LOUGHLAN John
Born: Coatbridge, Lanarkshire, Scotland, 12 June, 1943 — LB

League Club	Source	Date Signed	Seasons Played	Apps	Subs	Gls
Leicester C		08/61				
Crystal Palace	Greenock Morton	09/68	68-71	58	2	0
Wrexham	L	03/72	71	5	0	0

LOUGHNANE John Brian (Brian)
Born: Manchester, England, 16 August, 1930 — W
Died: Shropshire, England, July, 2014

League Club	Source	Date Signed	Seasons Played	Apps	Subs	Gls
Leeds U	Witton A	08/52				
Shrewsbury T	Tr	07/53	53-55	42	-	7
Bournemouth	Tr	07/56	56-58	43	-	5

LOUGHNANE Peter Brian
Born: Bournemouth, England, 18 March, 1958 — W

League Club	Source	Date Signed	Seasons Played	Apps	Subs	Gls
Manchester U	App	03/75				
Shrewsbury T	Tr	02/77	76-78	24	7	4

LOUGHRAN Joseph Lane (Joe)
Born: Consett, County Durham, England, 12 August, 1915 — RB
Died: Hove, East Sussex, England, 23 August, 1994

League Club	Source	Date Signed	Seasons Played	Apps	Subs	Gls
Birmingham C	Dudley College	08/33	35-36	31	-	2
Luton T	Tr	05/37	37-38	25	-	0
Burnley	Tr	07/39	46-49	65	-	0
Southend U	Tr	09/49	49-52	147	-	1

LOUGHTON Michael George (Mick)
Born: Colchester, Essex, England, 8 December, 1942 — CH

League Club	Source	Date Signed	Seasons Played	Apps	Subs	Gls
Colchester U	Jnr	08/61	64-67	121	1	7

LOUIS Jefferson Lee
Born: Harrow, NW London, England, 22 February, 1979 — F

League Club	Source	Date Signed	Seasons Played	Apps	Subs	Gls
Oxford U	Thame U	03/02	01-04	18	38	8
Bristol Rov	Woking	05/05	04-05	3	6	0
Mansfield T	Weymouth	01/08	07	14	4	4

LOUIS-JEAN Mathieu
Born: Rouen, France, 22 February, 1976 — RB
France: U21-4/Youth

League Club	Source	Date Signed	Seasons Played	Apps	Subs	Gls
Nottingham F	Le Havre (FRA)	09/98	98-04	188	10	3
Norwich C	Tr	07/05	05	2	0	0

LOUKES Gordon
Born: Sheffield, England, 15 June, 1928 — LW
Died: Sheffield, England, 18 March, 2006

League Club	Source	Date Signed	Seasons Played	Apps	Subs	Gls
Sheffield U		04/49	50	1	-	0
Southend U	Tr	07/51	51	2	-	0

[LOURENCO] DA SILVA Louis Carlos Lourenco
Born: Luanda, Angola, 5 June, 1983 — F
Portugal: Youth

League Club	Source	Date Signed	Seasons Played	Apps	Subs	Gls
Bristol C (L)	Sporting Lisbon (POR)	03/01	00	1	2	1
Oldham Ath (L)	Sporting Lisbon (POR)	07/02	02	1	6	1

LOVATT John
Born: Middlesbrough, England, 21 January, 1962 — RB

League Club	Source	Date Signed	Seasons Played	Apps	Subs	Gls
Derby Co	App	01/80	81	2	2	0

LOVATT John (Jack)
Born: Burton-on-Trent, Staffordshire, England, 23 August, 1941 — CF

League Club	Source	Date Signed	Seasons Played	Apps	Subs	Gls
West Bromwich A	Jnr	12/58	60-62	18	-	5

LOVE Alistair James
Born: Edinburgh, Scotland, 9 May, 1955 — M

League Club	Source	Date Signed	Seasons Played	Apps	Subs	Gls
West Bromwich A	Melbourne Thistle	03/73				
Southend U	Tr	05/74	74	6	5	0
Newport Co	Tr	07/75	75	41	1	2

LOVE Andrew Mark (Andy)
Born: Grimsby, North Lincolnshire, England, 28 March, 1979 — G

League Club	Source	Date Signed	Seasons Played	Apps	Subs	Gls
Grimsby T	YT	07/96	96-98	12	0	0

LOVE Ian James
Born: Cardiff, Wales, 1 March, 1958 — F

League Club	Source	Date Signed	Seasons Played	Apps	Subs	Gls
Swansea C	Barry T	08/86	86-88	33	8	9
Torquay U	Tr	03/89	88	8	1	0
Cardiff C	Tr	09/89	89	1	1	0

LOVE John (Johnny)
Born: Keynsham, Avon, England, 11 March, 1937 — LW
Died: Oxfordshire, England, 19 November, 2010

League Club	Source	Date Signed	Seasons Played	Apps	Subs	Gls
Oxford U	Wolverhampton W (Am)	03/55	62-63	25	-	5

LOVE John Ernest
Born: Hillingdon, W London, England, 22 April, 1951 — CD

League Club	Source	Date Signed	Seasons Played	Apps	Subs	Gls
Crystal Palace	Staines T	01/75	74	1	0	0

LOVE John Thomson (Jack)
Born: Edinburgh, Scotland, 18 March, 1924 — IF
Died: Glenfarg, Perthshire, Scotland, 14 June, 2007

League Club	Source	Date Signed	Seasons Played	Apps	Subs	Gls
Nottingham F	Albion Rov	02/49	48-51	59	-	21
Walsall	Llanelli	03/55	54-55	40	-	10

LOVE Michael John (Mickey)
Born: Stockport, Greater Manchester, England, 27 November, 1973 — M

League Club	Source	Date Signed	Seasons Played	Apps	Subs	Gls
Wigan Ath	Hinckley Ath	01/96	96	0	3	0

LOVELL Alan John
Born: Swansea, Wales, 17 May, 1940 — LW
Died: Swansea, Wales, 18 March, 2013

League Club	Source	Date Signed	Seasons Played	Apps	Subs	Gls
Swansea C	Jnr	06/57				
Stockport Co	Tr	07/60	60	1	-	0

LOVELL Frederick (Fred)
Born: Crewe, Cheshire, England, 18 June, 1929 — IF

League Club	Source	Date Signed	Seasons Played	Apps	Subs	Gls
Notts Co (Am)	Loughborough College	04/53	52-53	7	-	2

LOVELL Mark
Born: Bromley, SE London, England, 16 July, 1983 — FB

League Club	Source	Date Signed	Seasons Played	Apps	Subs	Gls
Gillingham	YT	04/01	00	0	1	0

LOVELL Mark Anthony
Born: Kensington, Central London, England, 20 January, 1961 — M

League Club	Source	Date Signed	Seasons Played	Apps	Subs	Gls
Fulham	App	08/78	77-78	4	2	0

LOVELL Michael Graham (Mike)
Born: Doncaster, South Yorkshire, England, 28 October, 1946 — LB

League Club	Source	Date Signed	Seasons Played	Apps	Subs	Gls
Doncaster Rov	App	10/64	65	2	0	0

LOVELL Stephen John (Steve)
Born: Swansea, Wales, 16 July, 1960 — F/M
Wales: 6/Schools

League Club	Source	Date Signed	Seasons Played	Apps	Subs	Gls
Crystal Palace	App	08/77	80-82	68	6	3
Stockport Co	L	10/79	79	12	0	0
Millwall	Tr	03/83	82-85	143	3	43
Swansea C	L	02/87	86	2	0	1
Gillingham	Tr	02/87	86-92	222	11	94
Bournemouth	Tr	11/92	92	3	0	0

LOVELL Stephen William Henry (Steve)
Born: Amersham, Buckinghamshire, England, 6 December, 1980 — F

League Club	Source	Date Signed	Seasons Played	Apps	Subs	Gls
Bournemouth	YT	07/99	98-99	1	7	0
Portsmouth	Tr	08/99	99-01	13	19	3
Exeter C	L	03/00	99	4	1	1
Sheffield U	L	03/02	01	3	2	1
Bournemouth	Partick Thistle	07/10	10-11	6	3	1

LOVELL Stuart Andrew
Born: Sydney, Australia, 9 January, 1972 — F
Australia: 2

League Club	Source	Date Signed	Seasons Played	Apps	Subs	Gls
Reading	YT	07/90	90-97	177	50	58

LOVELL Trevor
Born: Halifax, West Yorkshire, England, 19 January, 1940 — RW

League Club	Source	Date Signed	Seasons Played	Apps	Subs	Gls
Halifax T (Am)	Jnr	08/60	60-62	8	-	0

LOVEMAN Robert Leith (Bobby)
Born: Greenock, Inverclyde, Scotland, 30 September, 1921 — G
Died: Greenock, Inverclyde, Scotland, 23 August, 1986

League Club	Source	Date Signed	Seasons Played	Apps	Subs	Gls
Newport Co	Baillieston Jnrs	03/48	47-48	20	-	0
Aldershot	Ayr U	08/50				

LOVENKRANDS Peter Rosenkrands
Born: Copenhagen, Denmark, 29 January, 1980 — F
Denmark: 22/U21-13/Youth

League Club	Source	Date Signed	Seasons Played	Apps	Subs	Gls
Newcastle U	Schalke 04 (GER)	01/09	08-11	47	28	22
Birmingham C	Tr	07/12	12-13	16	21	4

LOVERIDGE James
Born: Llanelli, Carmarthenshire, Wales, 16 May, 1994 — F
Wales: Youth

League Club	Source	Date Signed	Seasons Played	Apps	Subs	Gls
Swansea C	Sch	07/12				
MK Dons	L	03/14	13	2	5	0
Newport Co	L	10/14	14	2	5	0

LOVERIDGE James Charles (Jimmy)
Born: Swansea, Wales, 19 October, 1962 — M
Wales: U21-3/Schools

League Club	Source	Date Signed	Seasons Played	Apps	Subs	Gls
Swansea C	App	11/79	79-84	39	8	4
Charlton Ath	Tr	06/85	85	5	1	0

League Club	Source	Date Signed	Seasons Played	Career Record Apps	Subs	Gls

LOVERIDGE John
Born: Wolverhampton, England, 28 February, 1959 — M

West Bromwich A	App	03/77				
Walsall	Tr	08/81	81	23	3	2

LOVERING John (Jack)
Born: Nuneaton, Warwickshire, England, 10 December, 1922 — LH

Coventry C	Holbrooks OB	06/46	46-47	6	-	0

LOVESEY William Samuel
Born: Marylebone, Central London, England, 8 December, 1922 — WH
Died: Southsea, Hampshire, England, 10 January, 1994

Swindon T	Wolverhampton W (Am)	05/45	46	4	-	0

LOVETT Eric
Born: Radcliffe, Greater Manchester, England, 20 August, 1925 — CH
Died: Shrewsbury, Shropshire, England, May, 1998

Accrington Stan		11/49	49-50	41	-	1

LOVETT Graham John
Born: Birmingham, England, 5 August, 1947 — M

West Bromwich A	App	11/64	64-70	106	8	8
Southampton	L	11/71	71	3	0	0

LOVETT Jay
Born: Brighton, England, 22 January, 1978 — FB

Brentford	Crawley T	02/00	00-02	24	4	0

LOVETT John Ernest
Born: Portsmouth, England, 31 October, 1940 — RW

Portsmouth		09/58				
Millwall	Tr	03/60	59	6	-	2

LOVETT Percival Reginald (Percy)
Born: Shrewsbury, Shropshire, England, 1 August, 1921 — G
Died: Shrewsbury, Shropshire, England, 1982

Everton	Kenwood Jnrs	08/38				
Wrexham	Tr	02/47	46	13	-	0

LOVIE James Theirs Harrison (Jim)
Born: Peterhead, Aberdeenshire, Scotland, 19 September, 1932 — W/WH

Bury	Peterhead	01/57	57-59	51	-	10
Bournemouth	Tr	07/60	60	9	-	0
Chesterfield	Tr	07/61	61-63	95	-	7

LOVRE Goran
Born: Zagreb, Croatia, 23 March, 1982 — M
Serbia: U21-7

Barnsley	Groningen (NED)	05/10	10	19	2	2

LOVREN Dejan
Born: Zenica, Bosnia & Herzegovina, 5 July, 1989 — CD
Croatia: 30/U21-20/Youth

Southampton	Olymp Lyonnais (FRA)	06/13	13	31	0	2
Liverpool	Tr	07/14	14	22	4	0

LOW Anthony Roy (Roy)
Born: Watford, Hertfordshire, England, 8 July, 1944 — M
England: Schools

Tottenham H	Jnr	07/61	64-66	6	2	1
Watford	Tr	02/67	66-68	25	1	4

LOW Gordon Alexander
Born: Aberdeen, Scotland, 11 July, 1940 — LH

Huddersfield T	Jnr	07/57	57-60	67	-	6
Bristol C	Tr	03/61	60-67	203	2	12
Stockport Co	Tr	07/68	68-69	63	1	7
Crewe Alex	Tr	08/70	70	5	0	0

LOW Joshua David (Josh)
Born: Bristol, England, 15 February, 1979 — RW
Wales: U21-4/Youth

Bristol Rov	YT	08/96	95-98	11	11	0
Leyton Orient	Tr	05/99	99	2	3	1
Cardiff C	Tr	11/99	99-01	54	21	6
Oldham Ath	Tr	08/02	02	19	2	3
Northampton T	Tr	08/03	03-05	90	12	15
Leicester C	Tr	07/06	06	12	4	0
Peterborough U	L	01/07	06-07	26	8	3
Cheltenham T	Tr	08/08	08-11	102	20	14

LOW Norman Harvey
Born: Aberdeen, Scotland, 23 March, 1914 — CH
Died: Toronto, Canada, 21 May, 1994

Liverpool	Rosehill Villa	10/33	34-36	13	-	0
Newport Co	Tr	11/36	36-46	112	-	0
Norwich C	Tr	10/46	46-49	150	-	0

LOWDEN George
Born: Isleworth, W London, England, 2 March, 1933 — FB

Brentford	Jnr	05/51	53-56	29	-	0

LOWDER Thomas William (Tommy)
Born: Worksop, Nottinghamshire, England, 17 October, 1924 — LW
Died: Boston, Lincolnshire, England, 13 May, 1999

Rotherham U	Worksop T	08/47	48	8	-	5
Southampton	Boston U	10/49	49-52	39	-	2
Southend U	Tr	05/53	53	21	-	3

LOWE Daniel James (Danny)
Born: Barnsley, South Yorkshire, England, 12 January, 1984 — M/LB

Northampton T	YT	-	00	0	4	0

LOWE David Anthony
Born: Liverpool, England, 30 August, 1965 — RW
England: U21-2/Youth

Wigan Ath	App	06/83	82-86	179	9	40
Ipswich T	Tr	06/87	87-91	121	13	37
Port Vale	L	03/92	91	8	1	2
Leicester C	Tr	07/92	92-95	68	26	22
Port Vale	L	02/94	93	18	1	5
Wigan Ath	Tr	03/96	95-98	85	23	26
Wrexham	Tr	07/99	99	4	6	1

LOWE Edward (Eddie)
Born: Halesowen, West Midlands, England, 11 July, 1925 — LH
Died: Nottingham, England, 9 March, 2009
England: 3

Aston Villa	Kynoch Works	05/45	46-49	104	-	3
Fulham	Tr	05/50	50-62	473	-	8
Notts Co	Tr	09/63	63-64	9	-	0

LOWE Garry
Born: Prescot, Merseyside, England, 21 February, 1967 — M

Bury		10/85	85	3	1	0

LOWE Gary Walter
Born: Manchester, England, 25 September, 1959 — M

Crystal Palace	App	10/76				
Manchester C	Tr	12/79				
Hereford U	Tr	06/80	80	9	0	0

LOWE Jamal Akua
Born: Brent, NW London, England, 21 July, 1994 — F

Barnet	Sch	10/12	12	3	5	0

LOWE Jason John
Born: Wigan, Greater Manchester, England, 2 September, 1991 — DM
England: U21-11/Youth

Blackburn Rov	Sch	10/09	10-14	110	10	1
Oldham Ath	L	03/11	10	7	0	2

LOWE Keith Stephen
Born: Wolverhampton, England, 13 September, 1985 — CD

Wolverhampton W	Sch	11/04	04-05	14	0	0
Burnley	L	08/05	05	10	6	0
Queens Park Rgrs	L	01/06	05	1	0	0
Swansea C	L	03/06	05	4	0	0
Cheltenham T	L	09/06	06	7	1	0
Cheltenham T	L	01/07	06	7	1	1
Port Vale	L	07/07	07	24	4	3
Hereford U	Kidderminster Hrs	07/09	09	17	2	1
Cheltenham T	Tr	07/10	10-13	96	14	7
York C	Tr	11/13	13-14	76	0	7

LOWE Kenneth (Kenny)
Born: Billingham, Cleveland, England, 6 November, 1961 — M
England: Semi Pro-2

Hartlepool U	App	11/78	81-83	50	4	3
Scarborough (L)	Barrow	01/88	87	4	0	0
Barnet	Barrow	03/91	91-92	55	17	5
Stoke C	Tr	08/93	93	3	6	0
Birmingham C	Tr	12/93	93-95	14	7	3
Carlisle U	L	09/94	94	1	1	0
Hartlepool U	L	08/95	95	13	0	3
Darlington	Gateshead	03/97	96-97	10	4	0

LOWE Matthew Ian
Born: Birmingham, England, 25 February, 1974 — G

Torquay U	YT	07/92	91-93	30	0	0

LOWE Matthew Thomas (Matt)
Born: Stoke-on-Trent, England, 20 October, 1990 — RB

Macclesfield T	Sch	07/09	09-10	7	4	0

LOWE Nicholas Paul (Nick)
Born: Oxford, England, 28 October, 1952 — CD

Oxford U	App	07/70	72-76	71	0	3
Halifax T	L	08/74	74	9	0	0

LOWE Onandi
Born: Kingston, Jamaica, 2 December, 1973 — F
Jamaica: 65/U23/Youth

League Club	Source	Date Signed	Seasons Played	Apps	Subs	Gls
Port Vale (L)	Rochester Rhinos (USA)	02/01	00	4	1	1
Rushden & D	Kansas C Wizards (USA)	11/01	01-03	87	3	49
Coventry C	Tr	03/04	03	1	1	1
LOWE Reginald (Reg)						
Born: Halesowen, West Midlands, England, 15 December, 1926						LB
Aston Villa	Finchley	08/44				
Fulham	Tr	05/50	50-52	66	-	0
LOWE Ryan Thomas						
Born: Liverpool, England, 18 September, 1978						F
Shrewsbury T	Burscough	07/00	00-04	81	56	23
Chester C	Tr	03/05	04-05	36	4	14
Crewe Alex	Tr	05/06	06-07	47	17	12
Stockport Co	L	03/08	07	4	0	0
Chester C	Tr	07/08	08	45	0	16
Bury	Tr	06/09	09-11	85	5	49
Sheffield Wed	Tr	08/11	11	11	15	8
MK Dons	Tr	08/12	12	28	14	11
Tranmere Rov	Tr	06/13	13	44	1	19
Bury	Tr	05/14	14	23	11	9
LOWE Simon John						
Born: Westminster, Central London, England, 26 December, 1962						F
Barnsley	Ossett T	12/83	83	2	0	0
Halifax T	Tr	07/84	84-85	74	3	19
Hartlepool U	Tr	08/86	86	12	2	1
Colchester U	Tr	12/86	86-87	32	4	8
Scarborough	Tr	11/87	87	14	2	3
LOWE Terence John (Terry)						
Born: Cheadle, Staffordshire, England, 27 May, 1943						RB
Port Vale	Stoke C (Am)	06/60	61-65	55	0	0
LOWELL Eric James						
Born: Cheadle, Staffordshire, England, 8 March, 1935						IF
Derby Co	Jnr	03/52	53	1	-	1
Stoke C	Tr	05/55	55	7	-	3
LOWERY Anthony William (Tony)						
Born: Wallsend, Tyne and Wear, England, 6 July, 1961						M
West Bromwich A	Ashington	03/81	81	1	0	0
Walsall	L	02/82	81	4	2	1
Mansfield T	Tr	04/83	82-90	249	3	19
Walsall	L	10/90	90	6	0	0
Carlisle U	Tr	10/91	91	6	1	0
LOWERY Harry						
Born: Moor Row, Cumbria, England, 26 February, 1918						WH/CH
Died: Dewsbury, West Yorkshire, England, 2 October, 2004						
West Bromwich A	Cleator Moor Celtic	05/35	37	17	-	0
Northampton T	Tr	11/45	46-48	76	-	2
LOWERY Jeremiah (Jerry)						
Born: Newcastle-upon-Tyne, England, 19 October, 1924						G
Died: Lowestoft, Suffolk, England, October, 2007						
Newcastle U	CA Parsons Ath	06/47	49-51	6	-	0
Lincoln C	Tr	03/52	52-53	51	-	0
Barrow	Peterborough U	06/56	56-57	86	-	0
Crewe Alex	Tr	07/58	58	4	-	0
LOWERY Stewart						
Born: Thornaby, Cleveland, England, 21 February, 1951						F
Watford	Bishop Auckland	10/70				
Walsall	L	11/70	70	0	2	0
LOWES Arnold Richardson						
Born: Sunderland, England, 27 February, 1919						WH
Died: Sheffield, England, 2 July, 1994						
Sheffield Wed	Washington Chemicals	10/37	38-47	42	-	8
Doncaster Rov	Tr	02/48	47-50	72	-	3
LOWES Barry Thomas						
Born: Barrow, Cumbria, England, 16 March, 1939						RW
Died: Barrow, Cumbria, England, 8 May, 2012						
Barrow	Holker Central OB	01/60	59-61	55	-	15
Blackpool	Tr	11/61				
Workington	Tr	08/62	62-65	121	0	34
Bury	Tr	02/66	65-66	33	0	6
Coventry C	Tr	03/67	66	3	0	0
Swindon T	Tr	08/67	67	2	0	0
LOWEY John Anthony						
Born: Manchester, England, 7 March, 1958						M
Manchester U	App	03/75				
Blackburn Rov	Chicago Sting (USA)	07/77				
Port Vale	Tr	12/77				
Sheffield Wed	California Sun (USA)	10/78	78-79	35	7	4
Blackburn Rov	Tr	11/80	80-85	136	5	14
Wigan Ath	Tr	07/86	86	1	2	0

League Club	Source	Date Signed	Seasons Played	Apps	Subs	Gls
Chesterfield	L	11/86	86	2	0	0
York C	L	03/87	86	3	3	0
Preston NE	Tr	08/87	87	4	0	1
Chester C	Tr	03/88	87	9	0	0
LOWIS Paul Noble						
Born: Shap, Cumbria, England, 17 October, 1937						LH
Blackpool	BABC	05/57				
Stockport Co	Tr	06/59	59	9	-	0
LOWNDES Nathan Peter						
Born: Salford, England, 2 June, 1977						F
Leeds U	YT	04/95				
Watford	Tr	10/95	96-97	1	6	0
Rotherham U (L)	Livingstone	03/02	01	2	0	0
Plymouth Arg	Livingstone	07/02	02-04	25	28	10
Port Vale	Tr	11/04	04-06	38	21	6
Chester C	Tr	07/07	07	8	4	0
LOWNDES Stephen Robert (Steve)						
Born: Cwmbran, Torfaen, Wales, 17 June, 1960						LM
Wales: 10/U21-4						
Newport Co	Jnr	10/77	77-82	200	8	39
Millwall	Tr	08/83	83-85	95	1	16
Barnsley	Tr	08/86	86-89	108	8	20
Hereford U	Tr	10/90	90-91	45	4	4
LOWNDS Mark Usher						
Born: Sunderland, England, 28 November, 1940						LH
Luton T	Ryehope CW	01/60	61-64	59	-	3
LOWREY Patrick (Pat)						
Born: Newcastle-upon-Tyne, England, 11 October, 1950						M
England: Schools						
Sunderland	Newcastle U (App)	12/67	68-71	13	2	3
Darlington	RU St-Gilloise (BEL)	08/75	75	14	6	2
Workington	Tr	07/76	76	15	0	3
LOWRIE George						
Born: Tonypandy, Rhondda Cynon Taff, Wales, 19 December, 1919						CF
Died: Kingswood, Avon, England, 3 May, 1989						
Wales: 4/War-9						
Swansea C	Tonypandy	01/37	36-37	19	-	3
Preston NE	Tr	12/37	37	5	-	0
Coventry C	Tr	06/39	46-47	56	-	44
Newcastle U	Tr	03/48	47-49	12	-	5
Bristol C	Tr	09/49	49-51	48	-	21
Coventry C	Tr	02/52	51-52	27	-	12
LOWRIE Thomas (Tommy)						
Born: Glasgow, Scotland, 14 January, 1928						RH
Died: Bellshill, Lanarkshire, Scotland, 24 April, 2009						
Manchester U	Troon Ath	08/47	47-49	13	-	0
Oldham Ath	Aberdeen	08/52	52-54	79	-	5
LOWRY Brian Thomas						
Born: Manchester, England, 12 December, 1936						RW
Grimsby T	Manchester U (Am)	08/54	54-55	12	-	1
LOWRY Jamie						
Born: Newquay, Cornwall, England, 18 March, 1987						RM
Chesterfield	Sch	07/06	06-11	99	15	11
Crewe Alex	L	11/11	11	9	1	0
Plymouth Arg	Tr	07/12	12	6	3	0
LOWRY Shane Thomas						
Born: Perth, Australia, 12 June, 1989						CD
Republic of Ireland: U21-2/Youth						
Aston Villa	Sch	07/07				
Plymouth Arg	L	09/09	09	13	0	0
Leeds U	L	01/10	09	11	0	0
Sheffield U	L	01/11	10	17	0	0
Millwall	Tr	11/11	11-13	80	3	2
Leyton Orient	Tr	07/14	14	31	3	0
LOWRY Thomas (Tommy)						
Born: Liverpool, England, 26 August, 1945						RB
Liverpool	App	04/63	64	1	-	0
Crewe Alex	Tr	07/66	66-77	435	1	2
LOWTHER Shaun						
Born: North Shields, Tyne and Wear, England, 24 January, 1962						FB
Peterborough U	Middlesbrough (NC)	01/85	84	1	0	0
LOWTHORPE Adam						
Born: Hull, England, 7 August, 1975						RB
Hull C	YT	07/93	93-97	70	11	3
LOWTON Matthew John						
Born: Chesterfield, Derbyshire, England, 9 June, 1989						RB

League Club	Source	Date Signed	Seasons Played	Apps	Subs	Gls
Sheffield U	Sch	07/07	09-11	66	12	10
Aston Villa	Tr	07/12	12-14	63	9	2

LOXLEY Anthony Dale (Tony)
Born: Nottingham, England, 14 December, 1959 — CD

League Club	Source	Date Signed	Seasons Played	Apps	Subs	Gls
Lincoln C	App	12/77	78	1	0	0

LOXLEY Herbert (Bert)
Born: Matlock, Derbyshire, England, 3 February, 1934 — CH/WH
Died: Lincoln, England, 9 October, 2008

League Club	Source	Date Signed	Seasons Played	Apps	Subs	Gls
Notts Co	Bonsall	03/52	54-63	245	-	9
Mansfield T	Tr	07/64				
Lincoln C	Lockheed Leamington	10/66	66	7	0	0

LOY Rory James
Born: Dumfries, Scotland, 19 March, 1988 — F
Scotland: U21-5

League Club	Source	Date Signed	Seasons Played	Apps	Subs	Gls
Carlisle U	Glasgow Rangers	01/11	10-12	35	15	7

LOYDEN Edward (Eddie)
Born: Liverpool, England, 22 December, 1945 — F

League Club	Source	Date Signed	Seasons Played	Apps	Subs	Gls
Blackpool	Jnr	12/63	64	2	-	0
Carlisle U	Tr	06/66				
Chester C	Tr	07/67	67	37	0	22
Shrewsbury T	Tr	05/68	68	11	1	2
Barnsley	Tr	12/68	68-70	64	1	23
Chester C	Tr	11/70	70-71	62	0	26
Tranmere Rov	Tr	06/72	72-73	61	0	22

LOZA Jamar Kasheef
Born: Kingston, Jamaica, 10 May, 1994 — F
Jamaica: 5

League Club	Source	Date Signed	Seasons Played	Apps	Subs	Gls
Norwich C	Sch	08/12	13-14	0	3	1
Coventry C	L	10/13	13	0	1	0
Leyton Orient	L	01/14	13	1	2	0
Southend U	L	03/14	13	4	3	1
Yeovil T	L	01/15	14	4	1	0

LUA LUA Kazenga
Born: Kinshasa, DR Congo, 10 December, 1990 — RW

League Club	Source	Date Signed	Seasons Played	Apps	Subs	Gls
Newcastle U	Sch	05/08	07-10	0	8	0
Doncaster Rov	L	03/09	08	2	2	0
Brighton & HA	L	02/10	09	9	2	0
Brighton & HA	L	08/10	10	7	4	4
Brighton & HA	Tr	07/11	11-14	45	70	10

LUA LUA Lumana Tresor
Born: Kinshasa, DR Congo, 28 December, 1980 — F
DR Congo: 28

League Club	Source	Date Signed	Seasons Played	Apps	Subs	Gls
Colchester U	Leyton College	09/98	98-00	37	24	15
Newcastle U	Tr	09/00	00-03	14	45	5
Portsmouth	Tr	02/04	03-06	62	25	19
Blackpool	AC Omonia (CYP)	09/11	11	18	11	4

[LUCAS] PEZZINI-LEIVA Lucas
Born: Dourados, Brazil, 9 January, 1987 — DM
Brazil: 24

League Club	Source	Date Signed	Seasons Played	Apps	Subs	Gls
Liverpool	Gremio (BRA)	07/07	07-14	161	35	1

LUCAS Alec Leroy
Born: Wrexham, Wales, 1 December, 1945 — FB
Wales: U23-1

League Club	Source	Date Signed	Seasons Played	Apps	Subs	Gls
Wrexham	Bradley Rgrs	08/65	65-66	51	4	0

LUCAS Brian Andrew
Born: Farnborough, Hampshire, England, 31 January, 1961 — M
Died: Basingstoke, Hampshire, England, 23 March, 2009

League Club	Source	Date Signed	Seasons Played	Apps	Subs	Gls
Aldershot	Jnr	07/78	79-83	112	13	19

LUCAS David Anthony
Born: Preston, Lancashire, England, 23 November, 1977 — G
England: Youth

League Club	Source	Date Signed	Seasons Played	Apps	Subs	Gls
Preston NE	YT	12/94	95-03	117	5	0
Darlington	L	12/95	95	6	0	0
Darlington	L	10/96	96	7	0	0
Scunthorpe U	L	12/96	96	6	0	0
Sheffield Wed	L	10/03	03	17	0	0
Sheffield Wed	Tr	06/04	04-05	52	0	0
Barnsley		01/07	06	2	1	0
Leeds U	Tr	09/07	07-08	16	0	0
Swindon T	Tr	07/09	09-10	61	1	0
Rochdale	Tr	08/11	11	16	0	0
Birmingham C	Tr	07/12				
Fleetwood T	Tr	01/13	12	1	1	0

LUCAS Frederick Charles (Fred)
Born: Slade Green, SE London, England, 29 September, 1933 — LH/IF

League Club	Source	Date Signed	Seasons Played	Apps	Subs	Gls
Charlton Ath	Jnr	01/52	55-63	185	-	29
Crystal Palace	Tr	10/63	63-64	16	-	0

LUCAS Jamie Alexander
Born: Pontypridd, Rhondda Cynon Taff, Wales, 6 December, 1995 — F

League Club	Source	Date Signed	Seasons Played	Apps	Subs	Gls
Bristol Rov	Sch	04/13	13	0	1	0

LUCAS Lee Paul
Born: Aberdare, Rhondda Cynon Taff, Wales, 10 June, 1992 — M
Wales: U21-19/Youth

League Club	Source	Date Signed	Seasons Played	Apps	Subs	Gls
Swansea C	Sch	07/10	10	0	1	0
Burton A	L	01/12	11	1	0	0
Cheltenham T	L	01/14	13	2	0	0

LUCAS Oliver Henry
Born: Paisley, Renfrewshire, Scotland, 14 January, 1923 — FB

League Club	Source	Date Signed	Seasons Played	Apps	Subs	Gls
Leyton Orient	St Mirren	07/48	48-49	2	-	0

LUCAS Paul
Born: Coseley, West Midlands, England, 27 April, 1936 — LW
Died: Sandwell, West Midlands, England, July, 1992

League Club	Source	Date Signed	Seasons Played	Apps	Subs	Gls
Aston Villa	Jnr	04/54				
Gillingham	Tr	08/56	56-57	44	-	7

LUCAS Peter Malcolm (Mal)
Born: Wrexham, Wales, 7 October, 1938 — RH
Wales: 4/U23-1

League Club	Source	Date Signed	Seasons Played	Apps	Subs	Gls
Leyton Orient	Bradley Rgrs	09/58	58-64	157	-	6
Norwich C	Tr	09/64	64-69	180	3	8
Torquay U	Tr	03/70	69-73	118	4	3

LUCAS Richard
Born: Chapeltown, South Yorkshire, England, 22 September, 1970 — LB

League Club	Source	Date Signed	Seasons Played	Apps	Subs	Gls
Sheffield U	YT	07/89	90-91	8	2	0
Preston NE	Tr	12/92	92-93	47	3	0
Lincoln C	L	10/94	94	4	0	0
Scarborough	Tr	07/95	95-96	63	9	0
Hartlepool U	Tr	03/97	96-97	49	0	2
Halifax T	Tr	08/98	98-99	39	9	0

LUCAS Richard John (Dick)
Born: Witney, Oxfordshire, England, 22 January, 1948 — RB

League Club	Source	Date Signed	Seasons Played	Apps	Subs	Gls
Oxford U	Jnr	07/65	67-74	190	1	2

LUCAS Robert Walter (Bob)
Born: Bethnal Green, E London, England, 6 January, 1925 — G
Died: Dorchester, Dorset, England, 12 March, 2010

League Club	Source	Date Signed	Seasons Played	Apps	Subs	Gls
Crystal Palace	Hendon	06/46	46	4	-	0

LUCAS William Henry (Billy)
Born: Newport, Wales, 15 January, 1918 — IF/WH
Died: Newport, Wales, 29 October, 1998
Wales: 7/WLge-3/War-8

League Club	Source	Date Signed	Seasons Played	Apps	Subs	Gls
Wolverhampton W	Treharris	05/36				
Swindon T	Tr	05/37	37-47	141	-	32
Swansea C	Tr	03/48	47-53	205	-	35
Newport Co	Tr	12/53	53-57	93	-	6

[LUCAS PIAZON] PIAZON Gustavo Lucas Domingues
Born: Curitiba, Brazil, 20 January, 1994 — M
Brazil: Youth

League Club	Source	Date Signed	Seasons Played	Apps	Subs	Gls
Chelsea	Sch	11/11	12	0	1	0

LUCIC Teddy Mark Sime
Born: Gothenburg, Sweden, 15 April, 1973 — CD
Sweden: 86

League Club	Source	Date Signed	Seasons Played	Apps	Subs	Gls
Leeds U (L)	AIK Solna (SWE)	08/02	02	16	1	1

LUCKETT Paul
Born: Coventry, England, 12 January, 1957 — FB

League Club	Source	Date Signed	Seasons Played	Apps	Subs	Gls
Halifax T	Coventry C (App)	08/74	74-75	26	1	0
Hartlepool U	Tr	03/76	75-76	19	0	0

LUCKETTI Christopher James (Chris)
Born: Littleborough, Greater Manchester, England, 28 September, 1971 — CD

League Club	Source	Date Signed	Seasons Played	Apps	Subs	Gls
Rochdale	YT	-	88	1	0	0
Stockport Co	Tr	08/90				
Halifax T	Tr	07/91	91-92	73	5	2
Bury	Tr	10/93	93-98	235	0	8
Huddersfield T	Tr	06/99	99-01	68	0	1
Preston NE	Tr	08/01	01-05	184	5	10
Sheffield U	Tr	03/06	05-07	14	3	0
Southampton	L	03/08	07	4	0	0
Huddersfield T	Tr	07/08	08	12	1	0

LUDDEN Dominic James
Born: Basildon, England, 30 March, 1974 — LB
England: Schools

League Club	Source	Date Signed	Seasons Played	Apps	Subs	Gls
Leyton Orient	Billericay T	07/92	92-93	50	8	1
Watford	Tr	08/94	94-96	28	5	0
Preston NE	Tr	07/98	98-00	29	8	0
Halifax T	Tr	07/01	01	2	0	0

League Club	Source	Date Signed	Seasons Played	Career Record Apps	Subs	Gls

LUDFORD George Albert
Born: Barnet, N London, England, 22 March, 1915 WH
Died: Enfield, N London, England, 2 January, 2001

Tottenham H	Jnr	05/36	36-49	75	-	7

LUDLAM Craig
Born: Sheffield, England, 8 November, 1976 RB

Sheffield Wed	YT	05/95				
Notts Co	L	10/96	96	1	0	0

LUDLAM Steven John (Steve)
Born: Chesterfield, Derbyshire, England, 18 October, 1955 M

Sheffield U	App	01/73	75-76	26	1	1
Carlisle U	Tr	05/77	77-79	90	6	11
Chester C	Tr	07/80	80-82	100	2	12

LUER Gregory Roland (Greg)
Born: Brighton, England, 6 December, 1994 F

Hull C	Burgess Hill T	11/14				
Port Vale	L	02/15	14	0	2	0

LUFF Neil John
Born: Bletchley, Buckinghamshire, England, 9 April, 1969 M

Gillingham	Jnr	06/87	87	0	1	0

LUGANO Diego Alfredo
Born: Canelones, Uruguay, 2 November, 1980 CD
Uruguay: 95

West Bromwich A	Paris St-Germain (FRA)	08/13	13	7	2	1

LUGG Raymond (Ray)
Born: Jarrow, Tyne and Wear, England, 18 July, 1948 M

Middlesbrough	Jnr	07/65	66-69	34	3	3
Watford	Tr	11/69	69-71	51	8	3
Plymouth Arg	Tr	07/72	72	22	2	1
Crewe Alex	Tr	07/73	73-77	183	2	10
Bury	Tr	07/78	78-79	68	3	2

[LUIS ALBERTO] ROMERO Luis Alberto
Born: Arcos de la Frontera, Spain, 28 September, 1992 LW
Spain: U21-1/Youth

Liverpool	Sevilla (SPN)	07/13	13	0	9	0

LUKAKU Romelu Menama
Born: Antwerp, Belgium, 13 May, 1993 F
Belgium: 39/U21-5

Chelsea	Anderlecht (BEL)	08/11	11-13	1	9	0
West Bromwich A	L	08/12	12	20	15	17
Everton	Tr	09/13	13-14	61	6	25

LUKE George
Born: Hetton-le-Hole, Tyne and Wear, England, 9 November, 1948 WH
England: Schools

Newcastle U	App	03/66				
Chelsea	Tr	03/67	66	1	0	0

LUKE George Baron
Born: Lanchester, County Durham, England, 20 October, 1932 CF
Died: County Durham, England, 10 December, 2001

Sheffield U	Esh Winning	01/52	53-54	7	-	0
Scunthorpe U	Tr	05/56	56	18	-	6

LUKE George Thomas
Born: Newcastle-upon-Tyne, England, 17 December, 1933 LW
Died: Newcastle-upon-Tyne, England, 23 March, 2010

Newcastle U	Jnr	12/50				
Hartlepool U	Tr	10/53	53-59	186	-	60
Newcastle U	Tr	10/59	59-60	27	-	4
Darlington	Tr	01/61	60-62	68	-	11

LUKE Noel Emmanuel
Born: Birmingham, England, 28 December, 1964 RB/M

West Bromwich A	App	04/82	82-83	8	1	1
Mansfield T	Tr	07/84	84-85	41	7	9
Peterborough U	Tr	08/86	86-92	270	7	27
Rochdale	Tr	03/93	92	2	1	0

LUKE William (Billy)
Born: Aberdeen, Scotland, 19 April, 1932 IF
Died: Aberdeen, Scotland, 28 February, 2014

Crewe Alex	East Fife	10/55	55	1	-	0

LUKIC Jovan (John)
Born: Chesterfield, Derbyshire, England, 11 December, 1960 G
England: B-1/U21-7/Youth

Leeds U	App	12/78	79-82	146	0	0
Arsenal	Tr	07/83	83-89	223	0	0
Leeds U	Tr	06/90	90-95	209	0	0
Arsenal	Tr	07/96	96-00	18	0	0

LUMBY James Anthony (Jim)
Born: Grimsby, North Lincolnshire, England, 2 October, 1954 F

Grimsby T	Jnr	10/72	73-74	28	3	12
Scunthorpe U	Brigg T	03/77	76-77	55	0	28
Carlisle U	Tr	04/78	77-78	24	3	7
Tranmere Rov	Tr	07/79	79-80	43	3	21
Mansfield T	Tr	01/81	80-81	49	2	18

LUMLEY Ilderton Thomas (Tommy)
Born: Consett, County Durham, England, 9 December, 1924 IF
Died: Consett, County Durham, England, 17 December, 2009

Charlton Ath	Consett	12/48	48-51	37	-	10
Barnsley	Tr	03/52	51-55	146	-	36
Darlington	Tr	08/56	56	15	-	3

LUMLEY Joseph Patrick (Joe)
Born: Harlow, Essex, England, 15 February, 1995 G

Queens Park Rgrs	Sch	04/13				
Accrington Stan	L	08/14	14	5	0	0

LUMLEY Robert (Bobby)
Born: Consett, County Durham, England, 6 January, 1933 IF

Charlton Ath	Jnr	01/50	53-54	6	-	0
Hartlepool U	Tr	02/55	54-57	107	-	19
Chesterfield	Tr	12/57	57-58	25	-	2
Gateshead	Tr	06/59	59	40	-	6
Hartlepool U	Tr	07/60	60	38	-	6

LUMLEY William Daniel (Billy)
Born: Loughton, Essex, England, 28 December, 1989 G

Northampton T	Wolverhampton W (Sch)	12/09	09	2	0	0

LUMSDEN Alexander (Alex)
Born: Falkirk, Scotland, 24 May, 1946 IF

Southend U	Camelon Jnrs	02/66	65-66	2	0	0

LUMSDEN James Murdoch (Jimmy)
Born: Glasgow, Scotland, 7 November, 1947 M

Leeds U	Jnr	11/64	66-69	3	1	0
Southend U	Tr	09/70	70	12	0	0

LUMSDEN John David
Born: Newcastle-under-Lyme, Potteries, England, 30 July, 1956 RB

Stoke C	App	08/73	75-77	26	2	0
Port Vale	L	03/78	77	5	0	0

LUMSDEN John Ivor
Born: Heanor, Derbyshire, England, 1 July, 1942 LB
Died: Derby, England, 19 February, 2014

Aston Villa	Jnr	07/59				
Workington	Tr	02/62	61-67	251	2	6
Chesterfield	Tr	03/68	67-70	94	0	0

LUMSDEN John Watson
Born: Edinburgh, Scotland, 15 December, 1960 M

Stoke C	East Fife	02/80	79-81	2	4	0

LUMSDON Christopher (Chris)
Born: Newcastle-upon-Tyne, England, 15 December, 1979 M

Sunderland	YT	07/97	97-99	2	0	0
Blackpool	L	02/00	99	6	0	1
Crewe Alex	L	09/00	00	14	2	0
Barnsley	Tr	10/01	01-03	70	15	13
Carlisle U	Tr	08/04	05-08	115	9	9
Darlington	Tr	08/09	09	2	0	0

LUNA Antonio Manuel
Born: Son Servera, Mallorca, Spain, 17 March, 1991 LB
Spain: Youth

Aston Villa	Sevilla (SPN)	07/13	13	16	1	1

LUNAN Daniel Dean (Danny)
Born: Bromley, SE London, England, 14 March, 1984 FB

Southend U	YT	-	01	0	1	0

LUND Andreas
Born: Kristiansand, Norway, 7 May, 1975 F
Norway: 8

Wimbledon	Molde FK (NOR)	02/00	99	10	2	2

LUND Gary James
Born: Grimsby, North Lincolnshire, England, 13 September, 1964 F
England: U21-3/Schools

Grimsby T	Jnr	07/83	83-85	47	13	24
Lincoln C	Tr	08/86	86	41	3	13
Notts Co	Tr	06/87	87-94	223	25	62
Hull C	L	08/92	92	5	0	2
Hull C	L	01/93	92	6	0	1
Hull C	L	03/95	94	11	0	3
Chesterfield	Tr	12/95	95-96	13	5	1

LUND Matthew Charles (Matty)
Born: Manchester, England, 21 November, 1990 — M
Northern Ireland: U21-6

League Club	Source	Date Signed	Seasons Played	Apps	Subs	Gls
Stoke C	Crewe Alex (Sch)	07/09				
Hereford U	L	11/10	10	1	1	0
Oldham Ath	L	07/11	11	2	1	0
Bristol Rov	L	01/12	11	9	4	2
Bristol Rov	L	07/12	12	14	4	2
Southend U	L	02/13	12	10	2	1
Rochdale	Tr	06/13	13-14	52	2	10

LUND Mitchell Perry
Born: Leeds, England, 27 August, 1996 — RB

League Club	Source	Date Signed	Seasons Played	Apps	Subs	Gls
Doncaster Rov	Sch	07/14	14	4	0	0

LUNDEKVAM Claus
Born: Austevoll, Norway, 22 February, 1973 — CD
Norway: 40/U21-16

League Club	Source	Date Signed	Seasons Played	Apps	Subs	Gls
Southampton	SK Brann Bergen (NOR)	09/96	96-06	350	7	2

LUNDIN Paul Michael
Born: Osby, Sweden, 21 November, 1964 — G

League Club	Source	Date Signed	Seasons Played	Apps	Subs	Gls
Oxford U	Osters IF (SWE)	03/99	98-99	28	1	0

LUNDON Sean
Born: Liverpool, England, 7 March, 1969 — M/LB

League Club	Source	Date Signed	Seasons Played	Apps	Subs	Gls
Chester C	YT	12/86	86-90	48	8	4

LUNDSTRAM John David
Born: Liverpool, England, 18 February, 1994 — M
England: Youth

League Club	Source	Date Signed	Seasons Played	Apps	Subs	Gls
Everton	Sch	02/12				
Doncaster Rov	L	02/13	12	14	0	0
Yeovil T	L	11/13	13	13	1	2
Leyton Orient	L	03/14	13	6	1	0
Blackpool	L	08/14	14	16	1	0
Leyton Orient	L	01/15	14	3	1	0
Scunthorpe U	L	03/15	14	5	2	0

LUNDSTRUM Colin Francis
Born: Colchester, Essex, England, 9 October, 1938 — RW

League Club	Source	Date Signed	Seasons Played	Apps	Subs	Gls
Ipswich T	West Ham U (Am)	11/56	57-59	13	-	1
Colchester U	Tr	08/61	61	1	-	0

LUNN Dennis
Born: Barnsley, South Yorkshire, England, 20 November, 1938 — CH

League Club	Source	Date Signed	Seasons Played	Apps	Subs	Gls
Doncaster Rov	Wombwell	10/58	59-61	85	-	0

LUNN George
Born: Bolton-on-Dearne, South Yorkshire, England, 28 June, 1915 — CH
Died: Birmingham, England, January, 2000

League Club	Source	Date Signed	Seasons Played	Apps	Subs	Gls
Aston Villa	Frickley Colliery	05/38				
Birmingham C	Tr	09/46				
Watford	Tr	10/47	47	5	-	0

LUNN Grant
Born: Guildford, Surrey, England, 26 August, 1967 — G

League Club	Source	Date Signed	Seasons Played	Apps	Subs	Gls
Aldershot	Farnborough T	08/85	85	9	0	0

LUNN Henry (Harry)
Born: Lurgan, Armagh, Northern Ireland, 20 March, 1925 — RW
Died: Swindon, England, 2 February, 1980

League Club	Source	Date Signed	Seasons Played	Apps	Subs	Gls
Notts Co	Glenavon	07/46	46	24	-	5
Portsmouth	Tr	07/47	47	1	-	0
Swindon T	Tr	05/48	48-53	196	-	30

LUNN Jack (Jackie)
Born: Barnsley, South Yorkshire, England, 14 October, 1937 — LW
Died: Huddersfield, West Yorkshire, England, November, 1988

League Club	Source	Date Signed	Seasons Played	Apps	Subs	Gls
Barnsley	Jnr	05/56	56-60	56	-	19
Chesterfield	Tr	07/61	61	40	-	13

LUNN William John (Billy)
Born: Lurgan, Armagh, Northern Ireland, 8 May, 1923 — IF
Died: Bournemouth, England, 19 January, 2000
Northern Ireland: Schools

League Club	Source	Date Signed	Seasons Played	Apps	Subs	Gls
West Bromwich A	Glenavon	02/46	46-47	10	-	5
Bournemouth	Tr	02/48	47-49	47	-	19
Newport Co	Tr	07/50	50-51	6	-	1

LUNNISS Roy Evan
Born: Islington, N London, England, 4 November, 1939 — FB
Died: Tower Hamlets, E London, England, January, 2010

League Club	Source	Date Signed	Seasons Played	Apps	Subs	Gls
Crystal Palace	Carshalton Ath	04/60	59-62	25	-	1
Portsmouth	Tr	06/63	63-65	69	0	1
Luton T	Addington (RSA)	12/66	66	1	0	0

LUNT Kenneth Vincent (Kenny)
Born: Runcorn, Cheshire, England, 20 November, 1979 — M
England: Youth/Schools

League Club	Source	Date Signed	Seasons Played	Apps	Subs	Gls
Crewe Alex	YT	06/97	97-05	343	30	35
Sheffield Wed	Tr	05/06	06-07	33	8	0
Crewe Alex	L	02/08	07	14	0	0
Crewe Alex	L	11/08	08	2	1	0
Hereford U	Tr	07/09	09-11	104	5	1

LUNT Robert John
Born: Widnes, Cheshire, England, 11 December, 1973 — W

League Club	Source	Date Signed	Seasons Played	Apps	Subs	Gls
Wrexham	YT	-	90-91	1	8	0

LUNTALA Tresor
Born: Dreux, France, 31 May, 1982 — M
DR Congo: 15

League Club	Source	Date Signed	Seasons Played	Apps	Subs	Gls
Birmingham C	Stade Rennais (FRA)	08/99	01	9	6	0

LUONGO Massimo Corey
Born: Sydney, Australia, 25 September, 1992 — M
Australia: 12/Youth

League Club	Source	Date Signed	Seasons Played	Apps	Subs	Gls
Tottenham H	Rushden & D	01/11				
Ipswich T	L	07/12	12	6	3	0
Swindon T	L	03/13	12	7	0	1
Swindon T	Tr	07/13	13-14	77	1	12

LUPOLI Arturo
Born: Brescia, Italy, 24 June, 1987 — F
Italy: U21-5/Youth

League Club	Source	Date Signed	Seasons Played	Apps	Subs	Gls
Arsenal	Sch	09/04	05	0	1	0
Derby Co	L	08/06	06	18	17	7
Norwich C (L)	Fiorentina (ITA)	08/08	08	7	10	4
Sheffield U (L)	Fiorentina (ITA)	02/09	08	2	7	2

LUQUE Albert
Born: Terrassa, Spain, 11 March, 1978 — W
Spain: 18/U21-13

League Club	Source	Date Signed	Seasons Played	Apps	Subs	Gls
Newcastle U	Depo la Coruna (SPN)	08/05	05-06	6	15	1

LUSCOMBE Lee James
Born: Guernsey, Channel Islands, 16 July, 1971 — W

League Club	Source	Date Signed	Seasons Played	Apps	Subs	Gls
Southampton	YT	04/89				
Brentford	Tr	10/91	91-92	29	13	6
Millwall	Tr	06/93	93	0	2	0
Doncaster Rov	Tr	02/94	93	5	3	0

LUSCOMBE Nathan John
Born: Gateshead, Tyne and Wear, England, 6 November, 1989 — LW

League Club	Source	Date Signed	Seasons Played	Apps	Subs	Gls
Sunderland	Sch	07/08				
Hartlepool U	Tr	07/11	11-12	5	21	1

LUSTED Leslie Reginald (Les)
Born: Reading, England, 20 September, 1931 — IF
Died: Weymouth, Dorset, England, 23 August, 2015

League Club	Source	Date Signed	Seasons Played	Apps	Subs	Gls
Leyton Orient	Harwich & Parkeston	12/52	52-53	23	-	6
Aldershot	Tr	07/54	54-55	10	-	1

LUTTON Robert John (Bertie)
Born: Banbridge, Down, Northern Ireland, 13 July, 1950 — W
Northern Ireland: 6

League Club	Source	Date Signed	Seasons Played	Apps	Subs	Gls
Wolverhampton W	Jnr	09/67	68-70	16	5	1
Brighton & HA	Tr	09/71	71-72	18	11	4
West Ham U	Tr	01/73	72-73	8	4	1

LUZHNY Oleg
Born: Lviv, Ukraine, 5 August, 1968 — D
Soviet Union: 8//Ukraine: 52

League Club	Source	Date Signed	Seasons Played	Apps	Subs	Gls
Arsenal	Dynamo Kiev (UKR)	07/99	99-02	58	17	0
Wolverhampton W	Tr	07/03	03	4	2	0

LUZI BERNARDI Patrice
Born: Ajaccio, France, 8 July, 1980 — G

League Club	Source	Date Signed	Seasons Played	Apps	Subs	Gls
Liverpool	AS Monaco (FRA)	08/02	03	0	1	0

LYALL George
Born: Berwick-on-Tweed, Northumberland, England, 4 May, 1947 — M

League Club	Source	Date Signed	Seasons Played	Apps	Subs	Gls
Preston NE	Raith Rov	03/66	65-71	91	14	16
Nottingham F	Tr	05/72	72-75	108	8	24
Hull C	Tr	12/75	75-76	42	0	5

LYALL John Angus
Born: Ilford, E London, England, 24 February, 1940 — LB
Died: Ipswich, England, 18 April, 2006
England: Youth

League Club	Source	Date Signed	Seasons Played	Apps	Subs	Gls
West Ham U	Jnr	05/57	59-62	31	-	0

LYDERSEN Pal
Born: Kristiansand, Norway, 10 September, 1965 — RB
Norway: 20

League Club	Source	Date Signed	Seasons Played	Apps	Subs	Gls
Arsenal	IK Start (NOR)	11/91	91-92	12	3	0

LYDIATE Jason Lee
Born: Manchester, England, 29 October, 1971 — CD

League Club	Source	Date Signed	Seasons Played	Apps	Subs	Gls
Manchester U	YT	07/90				
Bolton W	Tr	03/92	91-94	29	1	0
Blackpool	Tr	03/95	94-97	81	5	2
Scarborough	Tr	08/98	98	26	1	1
Rochdale	L	02/99	98	14	0	1

LYDON George Michael (Micky)
Born: Sunderland, England, 25 November, 1933 — IF/LH
England: Schools

League Club	Source	Date Signed	Seasons Played	Apps	Subs	Gls
Sunderland	Hylton Colliery Jnrs	12/50				
Leeds U	Tr	06/54	54	4	-	1
Gateshead	Tr	11/55	55-58	106	-	24

LYMAN Colin Charles
Born: Northampton, England, 9 March, 1914 — LW
Died: Cambridge, England, 9 May, 1986

League Club	Source	Date Signed	Seasons Played	Apps	Subs	Gls
Southend U	Rushden T	03/34	33	1	-	0
Northampton T	Tr	11/34	34-37	86	-	29
Tottenham H	Tr	10/37	37-38	46	-	10
Port Vale	Tr	05/46	46	11	-	1
Nottingham F	Tr	10/46	46	23	-	9
Notts Co	Tr	08/47	47	21	-	5

LYNAM Christopher Anthony (Chris)
Born: Manchester, England, 22 January, 1962 — W

League Club	Source	Date Signed	Seasons Played	Apps	Subs	Gls
Manchester U	App	01/80				
Carlisle U	Ryoden (HKG)	08/86	86	1	1	0

LYNCH Alexander Patrick (Alex)
Born: Holyhead, Anglesey, Wales, 4 April, 1995 — G
Wales: Youth

League Club	Source	Date Signed	Seasons Played	Apps	Subs	Gls
Peterborough U	Sch	07/13				
Wycombe W	Tr	07/14	14	0	1	0

LYNCH Anthony Junior (Tony)
Born: Paddington, Central London, England, 20 January, 1966 — W

League Club	Source	Date Signed	Seasons Played	Apps	Subs	Gls
Brentford	Maidstone U	01/84	83-85	35	10	6
Barnet	Wealdstone	10/90	91-93	18	18	4

LYNCH Barry John
Born: Birmingham, England, 8 June, 1951 — FB

League Club	Source	Date Signed	Seasons Played	Apps	Subs	Gls
Aston Villa	App	01/69	68-69	2	0	0
Grimsby T	Tr	06/72	72	10	4	0
Scunthorpe U	Tr	07/73	73-74	62	2	0
Torquay U	Portland Timbers (USA)	09/75	75-76	67	3	2

LYNCH Christopher John (Chris)
Born: Middlesbrough, England, 18 November, 1974 — M/LB

League Club	Source	Date Signed	Seasons Played	Apps	Subs	Gls
Hartlepool U	Halifax T (YT)	08/93	92-95	38	12	2

LYNCH Craig Thomas
Born: Chester-le-Street, County Durham, England, 25 March, 1992 — F

League Club	Source	Date Signed	Seasons Played	Apps	Subs	Gls
Sunderland	Sch	07/10	10	0	2	0
Hartlepool U	L	09/12	12	2	4	1
Rochdale	Tr	02/14	13	0	1	0

LYNCH Gavin
Born: Chester, England, 7 September, 1985 — F

League Club	Source	Date Signed	Seasons Played	Apps	Subs	Gls
Chester C	YT	-	04	0	1	0

LYNCH Jack William
Born: Blackburn, Greater Manchester, England, 22 June, 1995 — M

League Club	Source	Date Signed	Seasons Played	Apps	Subs	Gls
Carlisle U	Sch	05/13	13	0	1	0

LYNCH Jay Anthony
Born: Salford, England, 31 March, 1993 — G

League Club	Source	Date Signed	Seasons Played	Apps	Subs	Gls
Bolton W	Sch	07/12				
Accrington Stan	Tr	08/14	14	1	1	0

LYNCH Joel John
Born: Eastbourne, East Sussex, England, 3 October, 1987 — LB
England: Youth//Wales: 1

League Club	Source	Date Signed	Seasons Played	Apps	Subs	Gls
Brighton & HA	Sch	03/06	05-08	68	11	2
Nottingham F	Tr	09/08	08-11	65	15	3
Huddersfield T	Tr	07/12	12-14	81	4	6

LYNCH John
Born: Uddingston, Glasgow, Scotland, 22 September, 1917 — G
Died: Airdrie, Lanarkshire, Scotland, 5 January, 1985

League Club	Source	Date Signed	Seasons Played	Apps	Subs	Gls
Workington	Dunfermline Ath	10/52	52	2	-	0

LYNCH Mark John
Born: Manchester, England, 2 September, 1981 — RB

League Club	Source	Date Signed	Seasons Played	Apps	Subs	Gls
Manchester U	YT	07/01				
Sunderland	Tr	07/04	04	5	6	0
Hull C	Tr	06/05	05	15	1	0
Yeovil T	Tr	08/06	06-07	29	2	0
Rotherham U	Tr	07/08	08-09	28	3	2
Stockport Co	Tr	08/10	10	30	1	0

LYNCH Patrick (Pat)
Born: Belfast, Northern Ireland, 22 January, 1950 — CD

League Club	Source	Date Signed	Seasons Played	Apps	Subs	Gls
Middlesbrough	Cliftonville	06/70	71	0	1	0

LYNCH Ryan Patrick
Born: Birmingham, England, 13 March, 1987 — FB

League Club	Source	Date Signed	Seasons Played	Apps	Subs	Gls
Coventry C	Sch	07/06				
Crewe Alex	Tr	07/07	07	1	1	0

LYNCH Simon George
Born: Montreal, Canada, 19 May, 1982 — F
Scotland: B-2/U21-13

League Club	Source	Date Signed	Seasons Played	Apps	Subs	Gls
Preston NE	Glasgow Celtic	01/03	02-04	14	31	2
Stockport Co	L	12/03	03	9	0	3
Blackpool	L	12/04	04	5	2	0

LYNCH Terence John (Terry)
Born: Newport, Wales, 17 May, 1952 — G

League Club	Source	Date Signed	Seasons Played	Apps	Subs	Gls
Newport Co	Jnr	11/69	69-71	56	0	0

LYNCH Thomas Michael (Tommy)
Born: Limerick, Republic of Ireland, 10 October, 1964 — LB/M

League Club	Source	Date Signed	Seasons Played	Apps	Subs	Gls
Sunderland	Limerick (ROI)	08/88	88	4	0	0
Shrewsbury T	Tr	01/90	89-95	220	14	14

LYNE Neil George Francis
Born: Leicester, England, 4 April, 1970 — W

League Club	Source	Date Signed	Seasons Played	Apps	Subs	Gls
Nottingham F	Leicester U	08/89				
Walsall	L	03/90	89	6	1	0
Shrewsbury T	L	03/91	90	16	0	6
Shrewsbury T	Tr	07/91	91-92	61	3	11
Cambridge U	Tr	01/93	92-93	5	12	0
Chesterfield	L	09/93	93	5	1	1
Hereford U	Tr	07/94	94-95	49	14	2
Northampton T	Tr	08/96	96	1	0	0

LYNESS Dean James
Born: Halesowen, West Midlands, England, 20 July, 1991 — G
England: Youth

League Club	Source	Date Signed	Seasons Played	Apps	Subs	Gls
Burton A	Kidderminster Hrs	08/12	12-14	35	2	0

LYNEX Steven Charles (Steve)
Born: West Bromwich, West Midlands, England, 23 January, 1958 — W/M

League Club	Source	Date Signed	Seasons Played	Apps	Subs	Gls
West Bromwich A	App	01/76				
Birmingham C	Shamrock Rov (ROI)	04/79	78-80	28	18	10
Leicester C	Tr	02/81	80-86	200	13	57
Birmingham C	L	10/86	86	10	0	2
West Bromwich A	Tr	03/87	86-87	26	3	3
Cardiff C	Tr	07/88	88-89	56	6	2

LYNG Ciaran
Born: Wexford, Republic of Ireland, 24 July, 1985 — M
Republic of Ireland: Youth

League Club	Source	Date Signed	Seasons Played	Apps	Subs	Gls
Preston NE	Sch	09/03	03			
Shrewsbury T	Tr	12/04	04-05	0	5	0

LYNN Francis (Frank)
Born: Consett, County Durham, England, 29 May, 1929 — LW
Died: Grimsby, North Lincolnshire, England, August, 2011

League Club	Source	Date Signed	Seasons Played	Apps	Subs	Gls
Grimsby T	Blackhall CW	12/47	48	2	-	0

LYNN Joseph (Joe)
Born: Seaton Sluice, Northumberland, England, 31 January, 1925 — WH/IF
Died: South Tyneside, Tyne and Wear, England, June, 1992

League Club	Source	Date Signed	Seasons Played	Apps	Subs	Gls
Huddersfield T	Cramlington	05/47	49	5	-	0
Exeter C	Tr	06/50	50	29	-	2
Rochdale	Tr	07/51	51-55	193	-	23

LYNN Samuel (Sammy)
Born: St Helens, Merseyside, England, 25 December, 1920 — WH
Died: Salford, England, January, 1995

League Club	Source	Date Signed	Seasons Played	Apps	Subs	Gls
Manchester U	Jnr	01/38	47-49	13	-	0
Bradford Park Ave	Tr	02/51	50-52	73	-	0

LYNN Stanley (Stan)
Born: Bolton, Greater Manchester, England, 18 June, 1928 — FB
Died: Bromsgrove, Worcestershire, England, 28 April, 2002

League Club	Source	Date Signed	Seasons Played	Apps	Subs	Gls
Accrington Stan	Whitworths	07/47	46-49	35	-	2
Aston Villa	Tr	03/50	50-61	281	-	36
Birmingham C	Tr	10/61	61-65	131	0	26

LYNN William (Billy)
Born: Newcastle-upon-Tyne, England, 20 January, 1947 — LW

League Club	Source	Date Signed	Seasons Played	Apps	Subs	Gls
Huddersfield T		07/65	65-66	4	0	0
Rotherham U	Tr	04/67				

LYNNE Michael George Anthony (Mike)
Born: Kettering, Northamptonshire, England, 20 March, 1938 — G

League Club	Source	Date Signed	Seasons Played	Apps	Subs	Gls
Preston NE	Jnr	03/56	58	2	-	0

League Club	Source	Date Signed	Seasons Played	Apps	Subs	Gls
Bournemouth	Tr	06/59	59-60	17	-	0
Brighton & HA	Tr	07/61				

LYON David Edward
Born: Oldham, Greater Manchester, England, 21 November, 1948 — M

League Club	Source	Date Signed	Seasons Played	Apps	Subs	Gls
Bolton W	App	11/66				
Bury	Tr	08/67				
Southport	Mossley	09/76	76	11	2	1

LYON David George
Born: Altrincham, Greater Manchester, England, 18 January, 1951 — CD
Died: Cambridge, England, 29 April, 1999

League Club	Source	Date Signed	Seasons Played	Apps	Subs	Gls
Bury	App	01/69	68-71	65	6	0
Huddersfield T	Tr	09/71	71-73	24	1	0
Mansfield T	L	11/73	73	2	0	0
Cambridge U	Tr	07/74	74-76	84	1	11
Northampton T	Tr	10/77	77	6	0	0

LYON Thomas King (Tom)
Born: Clydebank, Dunbartonshire, Scotland, 17 March, 1915 — IF
Died: Old Kilpatrick, Dunbartonshire, Scotland, 26 November, 1998

League Club	Source	Date Signed	Seasons Played	Apps	Subs	Gls
Blackpool	Albion Rov	03/37	36-37	6	-	0
Chesterfield	Tr	09/38	38-47	41	-	22
New Brighton	Tr	07/48	48	36	-	7

LYONS Albert Edward (Eddie)
Born: Rochdale, Greater Manchester, England, 20 May, 1920 — LB
Died: Bracknell, Berkshire, England, November, 1996

League Club	Source	Date Signed	Seasons Played	Apps	Subs	Gls
Bury	Stockport Co (Am)	04/45	47-48	2	-	0
Millwall	Tr	03/50	49-51	6	-	0
Crewe Alex	Tr	07/52	52-53	23	-	0
Rochdale	Tr	12/53	53-54	19	-	1

LYONS Andrew (Andy)
Born: Blackpool, Lancashire, England, 19 October, 1966 — LW

League Club	Source	Date Signed	Seasons Played	Apps	Subs	Gls
Crewe Alex	Fleetwood T	10/92	92-93	7	4	2
Wigan Ath	Tr	10/93	93-95	79	8	27

LYONS Barry
Born: Shirebrook, Derbyshire, England, 14 March, 1945 — RW

League Club	Source	Date Signed	Seasons Played	Apps	Subs	Gls
Rotherham U	Jnr	09/62	63-66	125	0	23
Nottingham F	Tr	11/66	66-72	201	2	28
York C	Tr	09/73	73-75	80	5	11
Darlington	Tr	07/76	76-78	97	0	10

LYONS Brian
Born: Darfield, South Yorkshire, England, 3 December, 1948 — CH

League Club	Source	Date Signed	Seasons Played	Apps	Subs	Gls
Bradford Park Ave (Am)	Houghton Main	03/68	67	3	0	0

LYONS Darren Peter
Born: Manchester, England, 9 November, 1966 — RW

League Club	Source	Date Signed	Seasons Played	Apps	Subs	Gls
Bury	Ashton U	03/92	91-92	23	13	7

LYONS George William
Born: Rochdale, Greater Manchester, England, 1 May, 1935 — RW

League Club	Source	Date Signed	Seasons Played	Apps	Subs	Gls
Rochdale		12/53	53-56	29	-	4

LYONS John Patrick
Born: Buckley, Flintshire, Wales, 8 November, 1956 — F
Died: Colchester, Essex, England, 11 November, 1982

League Club	Source	Date Signed	Seasons Played	Apps	Subs	Gls
Wrexham	Jnr	06/75	74-78	63	23	23
Millwall	Tr	07/79	79-80	55	0	20
Cambridge U	Tr	10/80	80-81	20	1	6
Colchester U	Tr	02/82	81-82	31	2	9

LYONS Michael (Mick)
Born: Liverpool, England, 8 December, 1951 — CD
England: B-1/U23-5

League Club	Source	Date Signed	Seasons Played	Apps	Subs	Gls
Everton	App	07/69	70-81	364	25	48
Sheffield Wed	Tr	08/82	82-85	129	0	12
Grimsby T	Tr	11/85	85-86	50	0	4

LYONS Michael Charles (Mike)
Born: Iron Acton, Avon, England, 31 January, 1932 — RB

League Club	Source	Date Signed	Seasons Played	Apps	Subs	Gls
Bristol C	Jnr	06/50	50-51	2	-	0
Bristol Rov	Tr	07/53	53	2	-	0
Bournemouth	Tr	07/56	56-58	105	-	0
Swindon T	Tr	11/59	59	2	-	0

LYONS Paul
Born: Leigh, Greater Manchester, England, 24 June, 1977 — LB

League Club	Source	Date Signed	Seasons Played	Apps	Subs	Gls
Rochdale	Manchester U (YT)	09/95	95	1	2	0

LYONS Simon Ronald
Born: Watchet, Somerset, England, 2 December, 1982 — CD

League Club	Source	Date Signed	Seasons Played	Apps	Subs	Gls
Torquay U	YT	07/01	00	0	9	1

LYONS Terence (Terry)
Born: Bradford, England, 14 April, 1929 — LW
Died: Nelson, Lancashire, England, April, 1986

League Club	Source	Date Signed	Seasons Played	Apps	Subs	Gls
Burnley	Swain House U	10/49	50	12	-	3
Bradford Park Ave	Tr	09/51	51-52	38	-	6

LYSKE James Herbert Alexander (Jimmy)
Born: Lurgan, Armagh, Northern Ireland, 7 October, 1932 — LB

League Club	Source	Date Signed	Seasons Played	Apps	Subs	Gls
Sunderland	Glenavon	11/57				
Darlington	Tr	02/58	57-58	16	-	0

LYTHGOE Arnold
Born: Bolton, Greater Manchester, England, 7 March, 1922 — WH
Died: Norwich, England, June, 2005

League Club	Source	Date Signed	Seasons Played	Apps	Subs	Gls
Accrington Stan	Linfield	09/45	46	10	-	0

LYTHGOE Derrick
Born: Bolton, Greater Manchester, England, 5 May, 1933 — IF
Died: Norwich, England, 30 December, 2012

League Club	Source	Date Signed	Seasons Played	Apps	Subs	Gls
Blackpool	Jnr	05/50	55-57	4	-	1
Norwich C	Tr	03/58	57-61	62	-	22
Bristol C	Tr	08/62	62-63	13	-	2

LYTHGOE Philip (Phil)
Born: Norwich, England, 18 December, 1959 — M

League Club	Source	Date Signed	Seasons Played	Apps	Subs	Gls
Norwich C	App	12/77	77-79	9	3	1
Bristol Rov	L	09/78	78	6	0	0
Oxford U	Tr	08/80	80-81	23	5	3

LYTTLE Desmond (Des)
Born: Wolverhampton, England, 24 September, 1971 — W

League Club	Source	Date Signed	Seasons Played	Apps	Subs	Gls
Leicester C	YT	09/90				
Swansea C	Worcester C	07/92	92	46	0	1
Nottingham F	Tr	07/93	93-98	177	8	3
Port Vale	L	11/98	98	7	0	0
Watford	Tr	07/99	99	11	0	0
West Bromwich A	Tr	03/00	99-02	61	15	1
Northampton T	Stourport Swifts	11/03	03	23	4	0

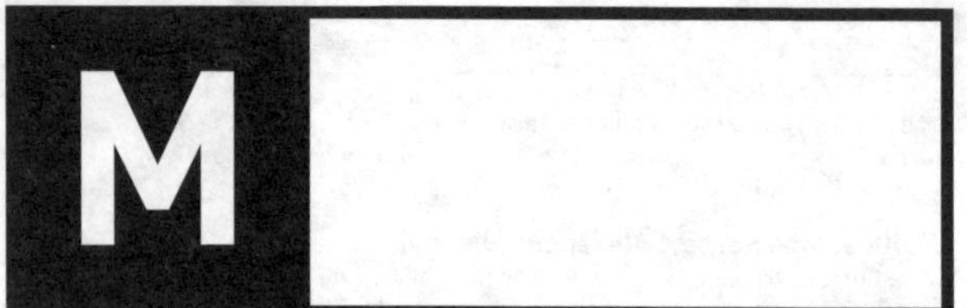

League Club	Source	Date Signed	Seasons Played	Career Record Apps	Subs	Gls
MABBUTT Gary Vincent						
Born: Bristol, England, 23 August, 1961						CD/M
England: 16/B-9/U21-7/Youth						
Bristol Rov	App	01/79	78-81	122	9	10
Tottenham H	Tr	08/82	82-97	458	19	27
MABBUTT Kevin Richard						
Born: Bristol, England, 5 December, 1958						F
England: Schools						
Bristol C	App	01/76	77-81	112	17	29
Crystal Palace	Tr	10/81	81-84	67	8	22
MABBUTT Raymond William (Ray)						
Born: Aylesbury, Buckinghamshire, England, 13 March, 1936						F/LH
Bristol Rov	Yorkshire Amats	08/56	57-68	392	2	27
Newport Co	Tr	09/69	69-70	39	6	14
MABEE Gary Lee						
Born: Oxford, England, 1 February, 1955						F
Tottenham H	App	02/72				
Northampton T	Tr	08/74	74-75	29	4	13
MABIZELA Oldjohn Mbulelo (Mbulelo)						
Born: Pietermaritzburg, South Africa, 16 September, 1980						CD
South Africa: 45						
Tottenham H	Orlando Pirates (RSA)	08/03	03-04	1	6	1
MACARI Luigi (Lou)						
Born: Edinburgh, Scotland, 7 June, 1949						M/F
Scotland: 24/U23-2						
Manchester U	Glasgow Celtic	01/73	72-83	311	18	78
Swindon T	Tr	07/84	84-85	33	3	3
MACARI Michael						
Born: Kilwinning, Ayrshire, Scotland, 4 February, 1973						F
Stoke C	West Ham U (YT)	07/91	96	15	15	3
MACARI Paul						
Born: Manchester, England, 23 August, 1976						F
Stoke C	Jnr	08/93	97	0	3	0
Sheffield U	Tr	12/98				
Huddersfield T	Tr	07/00	01-02	0	11	0
MACCARONE Massimo						
Born: Novara, Italy, 6 September, 1979						F
Italy: 2/U21-15/Youth						
Middlesbrough	Empoli (ITA)	07/02	02-06	46	35	18
MACCIOCHI David Andrew						
Born: Harlow, Essex, England, 14 January, 1972						LW
Queens Park Rgrs	YT	01/90				
Brighton & HA	Tr	09/92	92	0	2	0
MACEDO Elliot (Tony)						
Born: Gibraltar, 22 February, 1938						G
England: U23-10						
Fulham	Jnr	10/55	57-67	346	0	0
Colchester U	Tr	09/68	68	38	0	0
MACEY John Robert Thornbury						
Born: Bristol, England, 13 November, 1947						G
England: Schools						
Bristol C	App	05/65				
Grimsby T	Tr	07/68	68-69	36	1	0
Newport Co	Tr	07/70	70-75	194	0	0
MACEY Matthew Ryan (Matt)						
Born: Bath, England, 9 September, 1994						G
Tottenham H	Bristol Rov (Sch)	10/13				
Accrington Stan	L	01/15	14	4	0	0
MACHEDA Federico						
Born: Rome, Italy, 22 August, 1991						F
Italy: U21-10/Youth						
Manchester U	Sch	08/08	08-11	5	14	4
Queens Park Rgrs	L	01/12	11	0	3	0
Doncaster Rov	L	09/13	13	12	3	3
Birmingham C	L	01/14	13	10	8	10
Cardiff C	Tr	05/14	14	13	8	6

League Club	Source	Date Signed	Seasons Played	Career Record Apps	Subs	Gls
MACHENT Stanley Charles (Stan)						
Born: Chesterfield, Derbyshire, England, 23 March, 1921						WH/IF
Died: Chesterfield, Derbyshire, England, 17 December, 2012						
Sheffield U	Chesterfield Ramblers	10/38	46-47	22	-	2
Chesterfield	Tr	11/47	47-48	21	-	7
MACHIN Alex Harold						
Born: Hampstead, NW London, England, 6 July, 1920						WH/IF
Died: Truro, Cornwall, England, 18 February, 2005						
Chelsea	Royal Hampshire Reg't	10/44	46-47	53	-	8
Plymouth Arg	Tr	06/48	48-50	26	-	1
MACHIN Ernest (Ernie)						
Born: Walkden, Greater Manchester, England, 26 April, 1944						M
Died: Coventry, England, 22 July, 2012						
Coventry C	Nelson	03/62	62-72	255	2	33
Plymouth Arg	Tr	12/72	72-73	57	0	6
Brighton & HA	Tr	08/74	74-75	64	0	2
MACHIN Melvyn (Mel)						
Born: Newcastle-under-Lyme, Potteries, England, 16 April, 1945						M/RB
Port Vale	Jnr	07/62	62-65	29	1	6
Gillingham	Tr	07/66	66-70	155	1	11
Bournemouth	Tr	12/70	70-73	110	0	7
Norwich C	Tr	12/73	73-77	93	3	4
MACHO Jurgen						
Born: Vienna, Austria, 24 August, 1977						G
Austria: 26/U21-7						
Sunderland	First Vienna (AUT)	07/00	00-02	20	2	0
Chelsea	Tr	07/03				
MACOWAT Ian Stuart						
Born: Oxford, England, 19 November, 1965						D
England: Youth/Schools						
Everton	App	11/83				
Gillingham	Tr	01/85	84-85	4	1	0
Crewe Alex	Tr	07/86	86-88	64	8	1
MACROW Geoffrey Cyril (Geoff)						
Born: East Harling, Norfolk, England, 26 September, 1932						RW
Died: Ipswich, England, April, 1987						
Ipswich T	Thetford T	08/55	55-56	2	-	0
McADAM David Frederick						
Born: Hereford, England, 3 April, 1923						WH
Leeds U	Stapenhill WMC	05/48	48-49	24	-	0
Wrexham	Tr	05/50	50	10	-	0
McADAM Neil Bernard						
Born: East Kilbride, Lanarkshire, Scotland, 30 July, 1957						G
Port Vale	Northwich Victoria	08/82	82	2	0	0
McADAM Steven (Steve)						
Born: Portadown, Armagh, Northern Ireland, 2 April, 1960						LB
Burnley	Portadown	05/78	79	5	0	0
Wigan Ath	Barnsley (NC)	11/80	80-81	26	0	0
McADAM Thomas Ian (Tom)						
Born: Glasgow, Scotland, 9 April, 1954						CD
Scotland: SLge-1						
Stockport Co	Glasgow Celtic	08/86	86	5	0	1
McADAMS William John (Billy)						
Born: Belfast, Northern Ireland, 20 January, 1934						CF
Died: Barrow, Cumbria, England, 13 October, 2002						
Northern Ireland: 15						
Manchester C	Distillery	12/53	53-59	127	-	62
Bolton W	Tr	09/60	60-61	44	-	26
Leeds U	Tr	12/61	61	11	-	3
Brentford	Tr	07/62	62-64	75	-	36
Queens Park Rgrs	Tr	09/64	64-65	33	0	11
Barrow	Tr	07/66	66-67	53	0	9
McALEA Robert Joseph						
Born: Belfast, Northern Ireland, 13 September, 1920						IF
Bradford C	Ballymoney U	07/48	48	4	-	0
McALEER Francis (Frank)						
Born: Glasgow, Scotland, 16 October, 1945						M
Shrewsbury T	Greenock Morton	03/70				
Barrow	Tr	08/70	70	9	1	0
McALENY Conor Michael						
Born: Prescot, Merseyside, England, 12 August, 1992						F
Everton	Sch	02/10	11	0	2	0
Scunthorpe U	L	03/12	11	2	1	0
Brentford	L	07/13	13	3	1	0
Cardiff C	L	02/15	14	6	2	2

McALINDEN James (Jimmy)
Born: Belfast, Northern Ireland, 31 December, 1917 — IF
Died: Belfast, Northern Ireland, 18 November, 1993
Republic of Ireland: 2/LoI-1//Northern Ireland: 4/NILge-13

League Club	Source	Date Signed	Seasons Played	Apps	Subs	Gls
Portsmouth	Belfast Celtic	12/38	38-47	53	-	9
Stoke C	Tr	09/47	47-48	33	-	2
Southend U	Tr	10/48	48-53	217	-	12

McALINDEN Liam James
Born: Cannock, Staffordshire, England, 26 September, 1993 — M
Republic of Ireland: U21-1//Northern Ireland: U21-3/Youth

League Club	Source	Date Signed	Seasons Played	Apps	Subs	Gls
Wolverhampton W	Sch	09/10	12-14	3	11	1
Shrewsbury T	L	10/13	13	5	4	3
Fleetwood T	L	10/14	14	3	2	2
Fleetwood T	L	01/15	14	7	7	2

McALINDEN Robert (Bobby)
Born: Salford, England, 22 May, 1946 — W

League Club	Source	Date Signed	Seasons Played	Apps	Subs	Gls
Manchester C	Aston Villa (App)	05/64	63	1	-	0
Port Vale	Toronto C (CAN)	09/65				
Bournemouth	Los Angeles Azt (USA)	09/76	76	1	0	0

McALINDON Gareth Edward
Born: Hexham, Northumberland, England, 6 April, 1977 — W

League Club	Source	Date Signed	Seasons Played	Apps	Subs	Gls
Carlisle U	Newcastle U (YT)	07/95	95-98	22	37	5

McALINDON John (Johnny)
Born: Carlisle, Cumbria, England, 25 December, 1930 — CF
Died: Glasgow, Scotland, 10 February, 2002

League Club	Source	Date Signed	Seasons Played	Apps	Subs	Gls
Shrewsbury T	Glasgow Celtic	05/57	57	12	-	3

McALISKEY John James
Born: Huddersfield, West Yorkshire, England, 2 September, 1984 — F
Republic of Ireland: U21-1

League Club	Source	Date Signed	Seasons Played	Apps	Subs	Gls
Huddersfield T	Sch	05/04	03-06	15	28	7
Torquay U	L	09/05	05	3	0	0
Wrexham	L	09/06	06	3	0	0
Mansfield T	Tr	07/07	07	9	7	2

McALISTER Thomas Gerald (Tom)
Born: Clydebank, Dunbartonshire, Scotland, 10 December, 1952 — G

League Club	Source	Date Signed	Seasons Played	Apps	Subs	Gls
Sheffield U	App	05/70	71-75	63	0	0
Rotherham U	Tr	01/76	75-78	159	0	0
Blackpool	Tr	07/79	79	16	0	0
Swindon T	Tr	05/80	80	1	0	0
Bristol Rov	L	02/81	80	13	0	0
West Ham U	Tr	05/81	81-88	85	0	0
Colchester U	L	02/89	88	20	0	0

McALLE John Edward
Born: Liverpool, England, 31 January, 1950 — CD

League Club	Source	Date Signed	Seasons Played	Apps	Subs	Gls
Wolverhampton W	App	02/67	67-80	394	12	0
Sheffield U	Tr	08/81	81	18	0	0
Derby Co	Tr	04/82	81-83	51	7	1

McALLISTER Brian
Born: Glasgow, Scotland, 30 November, 1970 — D
Scotland: 3

League Club	Source	Date Signed	Seasons Played	Apps	Subs	Gls
Wimbledon	YT	03/89	89-97	74	11	0
Plymouth Arg	L	12/90	90	7	1	0
Crewe Alex	L	03/96	95	13	0	1

McALLISTER Craig
Born: Glasgow, Scotland, 28 June, 1980 — F
England: Semi Pro-2

League Club	Source	Date Signed	Seasons Played	Apps	Subs	Gls
Exeter C	Oxford U	07/08	08-09	8	26	7
Barnet	L	11/09	09	4	1	0
Rotherham U	L	03/10	09	7	1	0

McALLISTER David James
Born: Drogheda, Republic of Ireland, 29 December, 1988 — M

League Club	Source	Date Signed	Seasons Played	Apps	Subs	Gls
Sheffield U	St Patricks Ath (ROI)	01/11	10-12	14	6	2
Shrewsbury T	L	01/12	11	15	0	0
Shrewsbury T	Tr	01/13	12-13	30	11	2
Stevenage	Tr	10/14	14	13	3	0

McALLISTER Donald (Don)
Born: Radcliffe, Greater Manchester, England, 26 May, 1953 — CD

League Club	Source	Date Signed	Seasons Played	Apps	Subs	Gls
Bolton W	App	06/70	69-74	155	1	2
Tottenham H	Tr	02/75	74-80	168	4	9
Charlton Ath	Tr	08/81	81-82	55	0	6
Rochdale	Vitoria Setubal (POR)	11/84	84	3	0	0

McALLISTER Gary
Born: Motherwell, Lanarkshire, Scotland, 25 December, 1964 — M
Scotland: 57/B-2/U21-1

League Club	Source	Date Signed	Seasons Played	Apps	Subs	Gls
Leicester C	Motherwell	08/85	85-89	199	2	46
Leeds U	Tr	07/90	90-95	230	1	31
Coventry C	Tr	07/96	96-99	119	0	20
Liverpool	Tr	07/00	00-01	35	20	5
Coventry C	Tr	07/02	02-03	55	0	10

McALLISTER James (Jimmy)
Born: Barrhead, Renfrewshire, Scotland, 30 October, 1931 — IF
Died: Glasgow, Scotland, 5 February, 1997

League Club	Source	Date Signed	Seasons Played	Apps	Subs	Gls
Millwall	Neilston Jnrs	06/54	54-55	20	-	6
Bradford Park Ave	Greenock Morton	05/59	59-60	43	-	14

McALLISTER James Reynolds (Jamie)
Born: Glasgow, Scotland, 26 April, 1978 — LB
Scotland: 1

League Club	Source	Date Signed	Seasons Played	Apps	Subs	Gls
Bristol C	Heart of Midlothian	08/06	06-11	179	7	3
Preston NE	L	01/12	11	4	0	0
Yeovil T	Tr	07/12	12-13	68	4	0
Exeter C	Kerala Blasters (IND)	01/15	14	13	1	0

McALLISTER Kevin
Born: Falkirk, Scotland, 8 November, 1962 — RW

League Club	Source	Date Signed	Seasons Played	Apps	Subs	Gls
Chelsea	Falkirk	05/85	85-90	78	28	7

McALLISTER Sean Brian
Born: Bolton, Greater Manchester, England, 15 August, 1987 — M

League Club	Source	Date Signed	Seasons Played	Apps	Subs	Gls
Sheffield Wed	Sch	07/06	05-09	48	20	4
Mansfield T	L	09/07	07	5	2	0
Shrewsbury T	Tr	08/10	10-11	29	6	1
Port Vale	Tr	11/12	12	0	2	0
Scunthorpe U	Cowdenbeath	07/13	13-14	50	12	0

McALONE Robert (Bob)
Born: Whitehaven, Cumbria, England, 16 February, 1928 — CH
Died: Salisbury, Wiltshire, England, 25 February, 2010

League Club	Source	Date Signed	Seasons Played	Apps	Subs	Gls
Workington	Kells	07/50	51-53	68	-	3

McALOON Gerald Padua (Gerry)
Born: Glasgow, Scotland, 13 September, 1916 — IF
Died: Bridgeton, Glasgow, Scotland, 13 April, 1987

League Club	Source	Date Signed	Seasons Played	Apps	Subs	Gls
Brentford	St Francis Jnrs	06/34	37-38	21	-	8
Wolverhampton W	Tr	03/39	38	2	-	1
Brentford	Tr	12/45	46	7	-	4

McANDREW Anthony (Tony)
Born: Glasgow, Scotland, 11 April, 1956 — CD

League Club	Source	Date Signed	Seasons Played	Apps	Subs	Gls
Middlesbrough	App	08/73	73-81	245	2	13
Chelsea	Tr	09/82	82-83	20	0	4
Middlesbrough	Tr	09/84	84-85	66	0	2
Darlington	Willington	11/88	88	11	0	0
Hartlepool U	Tr	03/89	88	4	0	0

MacANDREW Robert (Bob)
Born: Derby, England, 6 April, 1943 — LB

League Club	Source	Date Signed	Seasons Played	Apps	Subs	Gls
Derby Co	Jnr	06/61	63	1	-	0

McANEARNEY James (Jim)
Born: Dundee, Scotland, 20 March, 1935 — IF

League Club	Source	Date Signed	Seasons Played	Apps	Subs	Gls
Sheffield Wed	St Stephen's, Dundee	03/52	53-58	38	-	10
Plymouth Arg	Tr	01/60	59-63	135	-	34
Watford	Tr	11/63	63-66	84	2	19
Bradford C	Tr	09/66	66-67	41	4	5

McANEARNEY Thomas (Tom)
Born: Dundee, Scotland, 6 January, 1933 — RH
Died: Sheffield, England, 14 February, 2012

League Club	Source	Date Signed	Seasons Played	Apps	Subs	Gls
Sheffield Wed	Dundee North End	10/51	52-64	352	-	19
Peterborough U	Tr	11/65	65	12	0	0
Aldershot	Tr	03/66	65-68	106	0	3

McANESPIE Kieran Liam
Born: Gosport, Hampshire, England, 11 September, 1979 — W
Scotland: U21-4/Youth

League Club	Source	Date Signed	Seasons Played	Apps	Subs	Gls
Fulham	St Johnstone	08/00				
Bournemouth	L	02/02	01	3	4	1
Plymouth Arg	Tr	03/03	02	2	2	0

McANESPIE Stephen (Steve)
Born: Kilmarnock, Ayrshire, Scotland, 1 February, 1972 — RB
Scotland: Youth

League Club	Source	Date Signed	Seasons Played	Apps	Subs	Gls
Bolton W	Raith Rov	09/95	95-97	19	5	0
Fulham	Tr	11/97	97-98	3	4	0
Bradford C	L	03/98	97	7	0	0
Cambridge U	Tr	08/00	00-01	20	4	0

McANUFF Joel Joshua Frederick (Jobi)
Born: Edmonton, N London, England, 9 November, 1981 — W
Jamaica: 12

League Club	Source	Date Signed	Seasons Played	Apps	Subs	Gls
Wimbledon	YT	07/00	01-03	76	20	13
West Ham U	Tr	02/04	03-04	4	9	1
Cardiff C	Tr	08/04	04	42	1	2
Crystal Palace	Tr	06/05	05-06	66	9	12
Watford	Tr	06/07	07-09	68	14	5

League Club	Source	Date Signed	Seasons Played	Apps	Subs	Gls
Reading	Tr	08/09	09-13	182	7	14
Leyton Orient	Tr	07/14	14	25	9	3

McARDLE Rory Alexander
Born: Doncaster, South Yorkshire, England, 1 May, 1987 — D
Northern Ireland: 7/U21-19/Youth

League Club	Source	Date Signed	Seasons Played	Apps	Subs	Gls
Sheffield Wed	Sch	06/05	06	0	1	0
Rochdale	L	07/05	05	16	3	1
Rochdale	Tr	11/06	06-09	125	4	4
Bradford C	Aberdeen	06/12	12-14	122	2	8

McAREAVEY Paul
Born: Belfast, Northern Ireland, 3 December, 1980 — M
Northern Ireland: U21-7/Youth

League Club	Source	Date Signed	Seasons Played	Apps	Subs	Gls
Swindon T	YT	07/99	97-01	10	14	1

McAREE Rodney Joseph (Rod)
Born: Dungannon, Tyrone, Northern Ireland, 19 August, 1974 — M
Northern Ireland: Youth/Schools

League Club	Source	Date Signed	Seasons Played	Apps	Subs	Gls
Liverpool	YT	08/91				
Bristol C	Tr	07/94	94	4	2	0
Fulham	Dungannon Swifts	12/95	95-97	22	6	3

McARTHUR Barry
Born: Nottingham, England, 4 May, 1947 — CF

League Club	Source	Date Signed	Seasons Played	Apps	Subs	Gls
Nottingham F	Jnr	05/65	65	7	1	4
Barrow	Tr	07/69	69	6	2	0
York C	Tr	12/69	69	1	0	0

McARTHUR Duncan Edward
Born: Brighton, England, 6 May, 1981 — W

League Club	Source	Date Signed	Seasons Played	Apps	Subs	Gls
Brighton & HA	YT	-	98	3	0	0

McARTHUR James McFarlane
Born: Glasgow, Scotland, 7 October, 1987 — M
Scotland: 19/U21-2

League Club	Source	Date Signed	Seasons Played	Apps	Subs	Gls
Wigan Ath	Hamilton Academical	07/10	10-14	87	42	11
Crystal Palace	Tr	09/14	14	29	3	2

McARTHUR Thomas (Tom)
Born: Neilston, Renfrewshire, Scotland, 23 April, 1925 — CH
Died: Leicester, England, April, 1994

League Club	Source	Date Signed	Seasons Played	Apps	Subs	Gls
Leicester C	Neilston Victoria	01/47	46-53	97	-	0
Plymouth Arg	Tr	01/54	53	2	-	0

McARTHUR Walter (Wally)
Born: Denaby, South Yorkshire, England, 21 March, 1912 — WH
Died: Bristol, England, 10 September, 1980

League Club	Source	Date Signed	Seasons Played	Apps	Subs	Gls
Bristol Rov	Goldthorpe U	01/33	32-49	261	-	14

McATEER Andrew William (Andy)
Born: Preston, Lancashire, England, 24 April, 1961 — LB

League Club	Source	Date Signed	Seasons Played	Apps	Subs	Gls
Preston NE	App	04/79	79-86	236	2	8
Blackpool	Tr	12/86	86-87	37	4	0
Preston NE	Tr	05/88	88	11	2	1

McATEER Jason Wynn
Born: Birkenhead, Wirral, England, 18 June, 1971 — RB/M
Republic of Ireland: 52/B-1

League Club	Source	Date Signed	Seasons Played	Apps	Subs	Gls
Bolton W	Marine	01/92	92-95	109	5	8
Liverpool	Tr	09/95	95-98	84	16	3
Blackburn Rov	Tr	01/99	98-01	58	14	4
Sunderland	Tr	10/01	01-03	53	0	5
Tranmere Rov	Tr	07/04	04-06	65	16	4

McAUGHTRIE Craig James
Born: Burton-on-Trent, Staffordshire, England, 3 March, 1981 — CD

League Club	Source	Date Signed	Seasons Played	Apps	Subs	Gls
Sheffield U	YT	07/99				
Carlisle U	Tr	08/00	00-01	2	8	1

McAUGHTRIE David
Born: Cumnock, Ayrshire, Scotland, 30 January, 1963 — CD

League Club	Source	Date Signed	Seasons Played	Apps	Subs	Gls
Stoke C	App	01/81	80-83	48	3	2
Carlisle U	Tr	07/84	84	28	0	1
York C	Tr	06/85	85-86	64	0	1
Darlington	Tr	07/87	87-88	36	3	0

MACAULAY Archibald Renwick (Archie)
Born: Falkirk, Scotland, 30 July, 1915 — WH/IF
Died: Knowle, West Midlands, England, 10 June, 1993
Scotland: 7/War-5

League Club	Source	Date Signed	Seasons Played	Apps	Subs	Gls
West Ham U	Glasgow Rangers	06/37	37-46	83	-	29
Brentford	Tr	10/46	46	26	-	2
Arsenal	Tr	07/47	47-49	103	-	1
Fulham	Tr	06/50	50-52	49	-	4

MACAULAY James Austin Russell (Jimmy)
Born: Edinburgh, Scotland, 19 October, 1922 — WH
Died: Romford, E London, England, November, 2000

League Club	Source	Date Signed	Seasons Played	Apps	Subs	Gls
Chelsea	Edinburgh Thistle	10/46	46-49	86	-	5
Aldershot	Tr	08/51	51	31	-	3

McAULEY Gareth Gerald
Born: Larne, Antrim, Northern Ireland, 5 December, 1979 — CD
Northern Ireland: 51/B-1/Schools

League Club	Source	Date Signed	Seasons Played	Apps	Subs	Gls
Lincoln C	Coleraine	08/04	04-05	65	7	8
Leicester C	Tr	06/06	06-07	70	4	5
Ipswich T	Tr	06/08	08-10	114	1	7
West Bromwich A	Tr	07/11	11-14	124	0	8

McAULEY Hugh Albert
Born: Bootle, Merseyside, England, 8 January, 1953 — LW

League Club	Source	Date Signed	Seasons Played	Apps	Subs	Gls
Liverpool	App	01/70				
Tranmere Rov	L	08/73	73	13	0	1
Plymouth Arg	Tr	10/74	74-76	76	1	7
Charlton Ath	Tr	12/76	76-77	55	0	9
Tranmere Rov	Tr	08/78	78	41	2	0
Carlisle U	Tr	07/79	79-80	14	3	1

McAULEY Hugh Francis
Born: Plymouth, England, 13 May, 1976 — M

League Club	Source	Date Signed	Seasons Played	Apps	Subs	Gls
Cheltenham T	Leek T	07/99	99-02	70	30	9
Kidderminster Hrs	Tr	03/03	02	0	4	0

MACAULEY Joshua Lee (Josh)
Born: Liverpool, England, 2 March, 1991 — F

League Club	Source	Date Signed	Seasons Played	Apps	Subs	Gls
Tranmere Rov	Sch	04/09	08	0	1	0

McAULEY Patrick Comerford (Pat)
Born: Barrhead, Renfrewshire, Scotland, 31 July, 1921 — LH
Died: Newharthill, Lanarkshire, England, 16 March, 1970
Scotland: SLge-1

League Club	Source	Date Signed	Seasons Played	Apps	Subs	Gls
Luton T	Glasgow Celtic	12/50	50	8	-	1

McAULEY Sean
Born: Sheffield, England, 23 June, 1972 — LB
Scotland: U21-1/Youth

League Club	Source	Date Signed	Seasons Played	Apps	Subs	Gls
Manchester U	YT	07/90				
Chesterfield (L)	St Johnstone	11/94	94	1	0	1
Hartlepool U	St Johnstone	07/95	95-96	84	0	1
Scunthorpe U	Tr	03/97	96-99	63	6	1
Scarborough	L	03/99	98	6	1	0
Rochdale	Tr	02/00	99-01	34	3	0

MACAULEY Stephen Roy (Steve)
Born: Lytham, Lancashire, England, 4 March, 1969 — CD

League Club	Source	Date Signed	Seasons Played	Apps	Subs	Gls
Manchester C	YT	11/87				
Crewe Alex	Fleetwood T	03/92	91-01	247	14	26
Macclesfield T	L	12/01	01	4	0	0
Macclesfield T	L	02/02	01	8	0	0
Rochdale	Tr	07/02	02	6	0	0
Macclesfield T	L	11/02	02	3	0	1
Macclesfield T	Tr	01/03	02-03	33	0	0

McAVENNIE Frank
Born: Glasgow, Scotland, 22 November, 1959 — F
Scotland: 5/B-1/U21-5/Youth

League Club	Source	Date Signed	Seasons Played	Apps	Subs	Gls
West Ham U	St Mirren	06/85	85-87	85	0	33
West Ham U	Glasgow Celtic	03/89	88-91	49	19	16
Aston Villa	Tr	08/92	92	0	3	0
Swindon T (L)	Glasgow Celtic	02/94	93	3	4	0

McAVOY Alan Joseph
Born: Wigton, Cumbria, England, 4 October, 1963 — M
Died: Maryport, Cumbria, England, 6 December, 2001

League Club	Source	Date Signed	Seasons Played	Apps	Subs	Gls
Blackpool		02/81	81	6	0	0

McAVOY Andrew David (Andy)
Born: Middlesbrough, England, 28 August, 1979 — M

League Club	Source	Date Signed	Seasons Played	Apps	Subs	Gls
Blackburn Rov	YT	07/97				
Hartlepool U	Tr	11/99	99-00	7	14	0
Macclesfield T	Tr	08/01	01	4	6	0

McAVOY Douglas Haig (Doug)
Born: Kilmarnock, Ayrshire, Scotland, 29 November, 1918 — IF
Died: Kilmarnock, Ayrshire, Scotland, 15 April, 1988

League Club	Source	Date Signed	Seasons Played	Apps	Subs	Gls
Liverpool	Kilmarnock	12/47	47-48	2	-	0

McAVOY Lawrence David (Larry)
Born: Lambeth, S London, England, 7 September, 1979 — FB

League Club	Source	Date Signed	Seasons Played	Apps	Subs	Gls
Cambridge U	YT	05/98	98	1	0	0

McBAIN Alan
Born: Aberdeen, Scotland, 10 February, 1940 — FB
Died: Hampshire, England, February, 2013

League Club	Source	Date Signed	Seasons Played	Apps	Subs	Gls
Swansea C	Aberdeen East End	01/59				
Carlisle U	Tr	06/60	60-62	70	-	0
Luton T	Tr	06/63	63-64	60	-	0

McBAIN Gordon Archibald
Born: Blantyre, Lanarkshire, Scotland, 4 December, 1934 — W
Died: East Kilbride, Lanarkshire, Scotland, 19 December, 1984

League Club	Source	Date Signed	Seasons Played	Apps	Subs	Gls
Rochdale	Kilmarnock	05/58	58	10	-	1

League Club	Source	Date Signed	Seasons Played	Career Record Apps	Subs	Gls

McBAIN Neil
Born: Campbeltown, Argyll & Bute, Scotland, 15 November, 1895 — CH
Died: Ayr, Scotland, 13 May, 1974
Scotland: 3

League Club	Source	Date Signed	Seasons Played	Apps	Subs	Gls
Manchester U	Ayr U	11/21	21-22	42	-	2
Everton	Tr	01/23	22-25	97	-	1
Liverpool	St Johnstone	03/28	27-28	12	-	0
Watford	Tr	11/28	28-30	85	-	5
New Brighton	Rtd	03/47	46	1	-	0

MacBENNETT James Congall (Seamus)
Born: Newcastle, Down, Northern Ireland, 16 November, 1925 — RW
Died: Lambeth, S London, England, 23 February, 1995

League Club	Source	Date Signed	Seasons Played	Apps	Subs	Gls
Cardiff C	Belfast Celtic	09/47	47	4	-	2
Tranmere Rov	Tr	11/48	48-49	12	-	1

McBETH George
Born: Belfast, Northern Ireland, 4 September, 1954 — RW

League Club	Source	Date Signed	Seasons Played	Apps	Subs	Gls
Manchester C	App	10/71				
Stockport Co	Tr	07/76	76-77	51	5	3

McBLAIN Andrew
Born: Bo'ness, Falkirk, Scotland, 11 August, 1926 — WH
Died: Bo'ness, Falkirk, Scotland, 7 November, 2013

League Club	Source	Date Signed	Seasons Played	Apps	Subs	Gls
Newport Co	Forth W	02/47	46-48	36	-	1

McBREEN Daniel James (Danny)
Born: Burnley, Lancashire, England, 23 April, 1977 — F

League Club	Source	Date Signed	Seasons Played	Apps	Subs	Gls
Scunthorpe U	Falkirk	08/06	06	1	6	0

McBRIDE Andrew David (Andy)
Born: Nakuru, Kenya, 15 March, 1954 — CD

League Club	Source	Date Signed	Seasons Played	Apps	Subs	Gls
Crystal Palace	App	10/71	73	1	0	0

McBRIDE Brian Robert
Born: Chicago, Illinois, USA, 19 June, 1972 — F
USA: 96

League Club	Source	Date Signed	Seasons Played	Apps	Subs	Gls
Preston NE (L)	Columbus Crew (USA)	09/00	00	8	1	1
Everton (L)	Columbus Crew (USA)	02/03	02	7	1	4
Fulham	Columbus Crew (USA)	01/04	03-07	102	38	32

McBRIDE John
Born: Kilsyth, Lanarkshire, Scotland, 31 December, 1923 — G

League Club	Source	Date Signed	Seasons Played	Apps	Subs	Gls
Reading	Third Lanark	03/48	47-52	100	-	0
Shrewsbury T	Tr	12/52	52-55	78	-	0

McBRIDE Joseph (Joe)
Born: Glasgow, Scotland, 17 August, 1960 — LW
Scotland: U21-1/Schools

League Club	Source	Date Signed	Seasons Played	Apps	Subs	Gls
Everton	App	08/78	79-81	51	6	9
Rotherham U	Tr	08/82	82-83	45	0	12
Oldham Ath	Tr	09/83	83-84	28	8	5

McBRIDE Joseph (Joe)
Born: Kilmarnock, Ayrshire, Scotland, 10 June, 1938 — CF
Died: Glasgow, Scotland, 11 July, 2012
Scotland: 2/SLge-4

League Club	Source	Date Signed	Seasons Played	Apps	Subs	Gls
Wolverhampton W	Kilmarnock	12/59				
Luton T	Tr	02/60	59-60	25	-	9

McBRIDE Kevin
Born: Airdrie, Lanarkshire, Scotland, 14 June, 1981 — DM

League Club	Source	Date Signed	Seasons Played	Apps	Subs	Gls
Darlington	Motherwell	05/07	07	3	3	1

McBRIDE Peter Patrick
Born: Motherwell, Lanarkshire, Scotland, 22 December, 1946 — M

League Club	Source	Date Signed	Seasons Played	Apps	Subs	Gls
Manchester U	North Motherwell BC	12/63				
Southport	Tr	07/66	66	1	2	0
Bradford Park Ave	Tr	07/67	67	5	2	0

McBRIDE Vincent (Vince)
Born: Manchester, England, 21 January, 1934 — G
Died: Sandbach, Cheshire, England, 20 May, 2005

League Club	Source	Date Signed	Seasons Played	Apps	Subs	Gls
Walsall	Ashton U	05/54	54	11	-	0
Aston Villa	Tr	03/56				
Mansfield T	Tr	07/58	58	10	-	0

McBRIDE William (Bill)
Born: Brampton, Cumbria, England, 8 November, 1913 — LB
Died: Carlisle, Cumbria, England, January, 1985

League Club	Source	Date Signed	Seasons Played	Apps	Subs	Gls
Carlisle U		02/46	46	14	-	1

McBURNEY Michael Leslie (Mike)
Born: Wrexham, Wales, 12 September, 1953 — F
Wales: Schools

League Club	Source	Date Signed	Seasons Played	Apps	Subs	Gls
Wrexham	Jnr	07/71	70-72	20	4	4
Bolton W	Tr	05/73	73	1	0	0
Hartlepool U	L	11/74	74	5	1	1
Tranmere Rov	L	03/75	74	4	1	0

McBURNIE Oliver Robert
Born: Leeds, England, 4 June, 1996 — F

League Club	Source	Date Signed	Seasons Played	Apps	Subs	Gls
Bradford C	Sch	08/13	13-14	2	13	0

MacCABE Andrew Bruce (Andy)
Born: Glasgow, Scotland, 22 February, 1935 — RW
Died: Chesterfield, Derbyshire, England, 17 December, 1963

League Club	Source	Date Signed	Seasons Played	Apps	Subs	Gls
Chesterfield	Corby T	11/54	55-58	53	-	7

McCABE James Joseph (Jim)
Born: Draperstown, Derry, Northern Ireland, 17 September, 1918 — WH
Died: South Bank, Cleveland, England, 8 July, 1989
Northern Ireland: 6

League Club	Source	Date Signed	Seasons Played	Apps	Subs	Gls
Middlesbrough	South Bank East End	05/37	46-47	34	-	0
Leeds U	Tr	03/48	47-53	152	-	0

McCABE Rhys
Born: West Calder, West Lothian, Scotland, 24 July, 1992 — M
Scotland: U21-3

League Club	Source	Date Signed	Seasons Played	Apps	Subs	Gls
Sheffield Wed	Glasgow Rangers	08/12	12-14	18	12	1
Portsmouth	L	03/14	13	2	2	0

McCAFFERTY James (Jim)
Born: Motherwell, Lanarkshire, Scotland, 10 July, 1957 — W

League Club	Source	Date Signed	Seasons Played	Apps	Subs	Gls
Hereford U	Bristol C (App)	04/75	75	0	3	0

McCAFFERTY Neil
Born: Derry, Northern Ireland, 19 July, 1984 — M

League Club	Source	Date Signed	Seasons Played	Apps	Subs	Gls
Charlton Ath	YT	08/01				
Cambridge U	L	12/03	03	5	1	0
Rushden & D	Tr	01/05	04-05	35	4	0

McCAFFERY Aidan
Born: Jarrow, Tyne and Wear, England, 30 August, 1957 — CD
England: Youth

League Club	Source	Date Signed	Seasons Played	Apps	Subs	Gls
Newcastle U	App	01/74	74-77	57	2	4
Derby Co	Tr	08/78	78-79	31	6	4
Bristol Rov	Tr	08/80	80-84	183	1	11
Bristol C	L	02/82	81	6	0	1
Torquay U	L	03/85	84	6	0	0
Exeter C	Tr	07/85	85-86	55	3	0
Hartlepool U	Tr	02/87	86	6	0	1
Carlisle U	Whitley Bay	01/88	87	14	0	0

McCAFFREY James (Jim)
Born: Luton, England, 12 October, 1951 — LW
England: Youth

League Club	Source	Date Signed	Seasons Played	Apps	Subs	Gls
Nottingham F	App	03/69	69	2	6	1
Mansfield T	Tr	07/72	72-76	170	8	21
Huddersfield T	Tr	01/77	76-77	23	4	0
Portsmouth	Tr	02/78	77-78	11	1	1
Northampton T	Tr	12/78	78-79	56	1	6

McCAIG Robert Alexander Marshall (Bobby)
Born: Lockerbie, Dumfries & Galloway, Scotland, 15 August, 1923 — RW
Died: Stockport, Greater Manchester, England, 14 January, 1986

League Club	Source	Date Signed	Seasons Played	Apps	Subs	Gls
Carlisle U	Queen of the South	08/48	48	5	-	0
Blackburn Rov	Tr	12/48	48-50	30	-	2
Stockport Co	Tr	08/51	51	15	-	2
Halifax T	Tr	01/52	51	17	-	2
Crewe Alex	Tr	08/52	52-53	19	-	1

McCALDON Ian
Born: Liverpool, England, 14 September, 1974 — G

League Club	Source	Date Signed	Seasons Played	Apps	Subs	Gls
Oxford U	Livingston	08/01	01	28	0	0

McCALL Alexander Noteman (Alex)
Born: Slamannan, Falkirk, Scotland, 26 March, 1939 — WH

League Club	Source	Date Signed	Seasons Played	Apps	Subs	Gls
Carlisle U		09/58	59	1	-	0

McCALL Andrew (Andy)
Born: Hamilton, Lanarkshire, Scotland, 15 March, 1925 — IF/W
Died: Leeds, England, December, 2014

League Club	Source	Date Signed	Seasons Played	Apps	Subs	Gls
Blackpool	Blantyre Celtic	07/47	47-50	87	-	15
West Bromwich A	Tr	01/51	50-51	31	-	3
Leeds U	Tr	08/52	52-54	62	-	8
Halifax T	Lovells Ath	07/56	56-59	139	-	15

McCALL Andrew Stuart Murray (Stuart)
Born: Leeds, England, 10 June, 1964 — M
England: Youth//Scotland: 40/U21-2

League Club	Source	Date Signed	Seasons Played	Apps	Subs	Gls
Bradford C	App	06/82	82-87	235	3	37
Everton	Tr	06/88	88-90	99	4	6
Bradford C	Glasgow Rangers	06/98	98-01	154	3	8
Sheffield U	Tr	07/02	02-03	69	2	2

McCALL Anthony Edward (Tony)
Born: Thatcham, Berkshire, England, 15 January, 1936 — W

League Club	Source	Date Signed	Seasons Played	Apps	Subs	Gls
Reading	Jnr	05/53	55-56	8	-	1

McCALL David
Born: Carlisle, Cumbria, England, 24 January, 1948 RW

League Club	Source	Date Signed	Seasons Played	Apps	Subs	Gls
Workington	Jnr	01/66	66	1	0	0

McCALL Ian Holland
Born: Dumfries, Scotland, 13 September, 1964 M

League Club	Source	Date Signed	Seasons Played	Apps	Subs	Gls
Bradford C	Glasgow Rangers	01/90	89	11	1	1

McCALL John (Johnny)
Born: Glasgow, Scotland, 29 September, 1918 IF
Died: Leeds, England, March, 1992

League Club	Source	Date Signed	Seasons Played	Apps	Subs	Gls
Bradford Park Ave	Workington	09/37	37-47	41	-	5

McCALL Peter
Born: West Ham, E London, England, 11 September, 1936 RH

League Club	Source	Date Signed	Seasons Played	Apps	Subs	Gls
Bristol C	King's Lynn	04/55	57-61	78	-	1
Oldham Ath	Tr	05/62	62-64	108	-	5

McCALL Robert Henry (Bob)
Born: Worksop, Nottinghamshire, England, 29 December, 1915 FB
Died: Worksop, Nottinghamshire, England, 6 February, 1992

League Club	Source	Date Signed	Seasons Played	Apps	Subs	Gls
Nottingham F	Worksop T	02/35	35-51	162	-	1

McCALL Stephen Harold (Steve)
Born: Carlisle, Cumbria, England, 15 October, 1960 M
England: B-1/U21-6/Youth

League Club	Source	Date Signed	Seasons Played	Apps	Subs	Gls
Ipswich T	App	10/78	79-86	249	8	7
Sheffield Wed	Tr	06/87	87-90	21	8	2
Carlisle U	L	02/90	89	6	0	0
Plymouth Arg	Tr	03/92	91-95	97	3	5
Torquay U	Tr	07/96	96-97	43	8	2
Plymouth Arg	Tr	08/98	98-99	28	5	1

McCALL William (Willie)
Born: Glasgow, Scotland, 14 November, 1920 LW
Died: Glasgow, Scotland, 1 June, 1985

League Club	Source	Date Signed	Seasons Played	Apps	Subs	Gls
Newcastle U	Aberdeen	01/48	47-48	16	-	4

McCALLIOG James (Jim)
Born: Glasgow, Scotland, 23 September, 1946 M
Scotland: 5/U23-2/Schools

League Club	Source	Date Signed	Seasons Played	Apps	Subs	Gls
Chelsea	Leeds (Jnr)	09/63	64-65	7	0	2
Sheffield Wed	Tr	10/65	65-68	150	0	19
Wolverhampton W	Tr	08/69	69-73	158	5	34
Manchester U	Tr	03/74	73-74	31	0	7
Southampton	Tr	02/75	74-76	70	2	8
Lincoln C	Lyn Oslo (NOR)	09/78	78	9	0	0

McCALLUM Gavin Kirk
Born: Toronto, Canada, 24 August, 1987 W
Canada: 1/Youth

League Club	Source	Date Signed	Seasons Played	Apps	Subs	Gls
Yeovil T	Jnr	01/06	06	0	1	0
Hereford U	Sutton U	08/09	09	20	7	8
Lincoln C	Tr	07/10	10	24	12	3
Barnet	L	11/11	11	0	2	0

McCALLUM Paul Leon Miller
Born: Streatham, S London, England, 28 July, 1993 F

League Club	Source	Date Signed	Seasons Played	Apps	Subs	Gls
West Ham U	Dulwich Hamlet	01/11				
AFC Wimbledon	L	11/12	12	6	3	4
Aldershot T	L	03/13	12	6	3	3
Torquay U	L	10/13	13	4	1	3
Portsmouth	L	01/15	14	0	7	0

McCALLUM Stewart
Born: Bearsden, Dunbartonshire, Scotland, 9 May, 1927 WH
Died: Bodelwyddan, Denbighshire, Wales, December, 2008

League Club	Source	Date Signed	Seasons Played	Apps	Subs	Gls
Wrexham	Rhyl	06/50	50-52	67	-	0
Workington	Kettering T	06/54	54-55	10	-	1
Coventry C	Tr	02/56				
Hartlepool U	Tr	07/56	56	2	-	0
Southport	Tr	08/57	57	9	-	0

McCALMAN Donald Stuart (Don)
Born: Greenock, Inverclyde, Scotland, 18 October, 1935 CH

League Club	Source	Date Signed	Seasons Played	Apps	Subs	Gls
Bradford Park Ave	Hibernian	06/59	59-65	297	0	5
Barrow	Tr	07/66	66	13	0	0

McCAMBRIDGE David Thomas (Dave)
Born: Larne, Antrim, Northern Ireland, 26 July, 1921 CH
Died: Barrow, Cumbria, England, 1982

League Club	Source	Date Signed	Seasons Played	Apps	Subs	Gls
Barrow	Larne T	09/46	46-49	16	-	1

McCAMMON Mark Jason
Born: Barnet, N London, England, 7 August, 1978 F
Barbados: 5

League Club	Source	Date Signed	Seasons Played	Apps	Subs	Gls
Cambridge U	Cambridge C	12/96	97-98	1	3	0
Charlton Ath	Cambridge C	03/99	99	1	3	0
Swindon T	L	01/00	99	4	0	0
Brentford	Tr	07/00	00-02	46	29	10
Millwall	Tr	03/03	02-04	15	7	2
Brighton & HA	Tr	12/04	04-05	19	6	3
Bristol C	L	02/06	05	8	3	4
Doncaster Rov	Tr	08/06	06-07	37	17	6
Gillingham	Tr	07/08	08-10	24	26	5
Bradford C	L	02/10	09	2	2	0

McCANCE Daren
Born: Consett, County Durham, England, 13 September, 1973 CD

League Club	Source	Date Signed	Seasons Played	Apps	Subs	Gls
Reading	YT	07/92	92	1	0	0

McCANN Albert
Born: Maidenhead, Berkshire, England, 1 November, 1941 W/IF
Died: Havant, Hampshire, England, 9 January, 2014

League Club	Source	Date Signed	Seasons Played	Apps	Subs	Gls
Luton T	Jnr	04/59	59-60	6	-	0
Coventry C	Tr	08/61	61	22	-	3
Portsmouth	Tr	08/62	62-73	331	7	83

McCANN Christopher John (Chris)
Born: Dublin, Republic of Ireland, 21 July, 1987 DM
Republic of Ireland: Youth

League Club	Source	Date Signed	Seasons Played	Apps	Subs	Gls
Burnley	Sch	01/06	05-12	213	25	27
Wigan Ath	Tr	07/13	13-14	33	11	4

McCANN Gavin Peter
Born: Blackpool, Lancashire, England, 10 January, 1978 M
England: 1

League Club	Source	Date Signed	Seasons Played	Apps	Subs	Gls
Everton	YT	07/95	97	5	6	0
Sunderland	Tr	11/98	98-02	106	10	8
Aston Villa	Tr	07/03	03-06	108	2	3
Bolton W	Tr	06/07	07-09	56	19	1

McCANN Grant Samuel
Born: Belfast, Northern Ireland, 14 April, 1980 M
Northern Ireland: 39/U21-11

League Club	Source	Date Signed	Seasons Played	Apps	Subs	Gls
West Ham U	YT	07/98	00-01	0	4	0
Notts Co	L	08/00	00	2	0	0
Cheltenham T	L	10/00	00	27	3	3
Cheltenham T	Tr	10/02	02-06	162	1	32
Barnsley	Tr	11/06	06-07	28	13	4
Scunthorpe U	Tr	01/08	07-09	91	8	18
Peterborough U	Tr	07/10	10-14	128	32	29

McCANN Henry Austin (Austin)
Born: Clydebank, Dunbartonshire, Scotland, 21 January, 1980 LB

League Club	Source	Date Signed	Seasons Played	Apps	Subs	Gls
Boston U	Clyde	08/04	04-05	76	4	1
Notts Co	Tr	07/06	06-07	56	9	0

McCANN James (Jim)
Born: Dundee, Scotland, 20 May, 1954 F

League Club	Source	Date Signed	Seasons Played	Apps	Subs	Gls
Nottingham F	App	05/72	74-75	2	4	1
Stockport Co	L	10/75	75	4	1	0
Halifax T	L	10/76	76	2	0	1

McCANN John (Johnny)
Born: Govan, Glasgow, Scotland, 27 July, 1934 LW
Scotland: B

League Club	Source	Date Signed	Seasons Played	Apps	Subs	Gls
Barnsley	Bridgeton Waverley	12/55	55-58	118	-	17
Bristol C	Tr	05/59	59-60	30	-	0
Huddersfield T	Tr	10/60	60-62	20	-	1
Derby Co	Tr	09/62	62-63	55	-	2
Darlington	Tr	08/64	64	4	-	0
Chesterfield	Tr	10/64	64-65	41	0	9

McCANN Neil Doherty
Born: Greenock, Inverclyde, Scotland, 11 August, 1974 LW
Scotland: 26/B-2/U21-9

League Club	Source	Date Signed	Seasons Played	Apps	Subs	Gls
Southampton	Glasgow Rangers	08/03	03-05	21	19	0

McCANN Ryan Patrick
Born: Blantyre, Lanarkshire, Scotland, 21 September, 1981 M/RB

League Club	Source	Date Signed	Seasons Played	Apps	Subs	Gls
Hartlepool U	Glasgow Celtic	08/03	03	0	4	0
Morecambe	Queen of the South	07/08	08	11	2	0

McCAREY Aaron
Born: Monaghan, Republic of Ireland, 14 January, 1992 G
Republic of Ireland: U21-10/Youth

League Club	Source	Date Signed	Seasons Played	Apps	Subs	Gls
Wolverhampton W	Monaghan U (ROI)	01/10	13	5	0	0
Walsall	L	11/12	12	14	0	0
York C	L	11/13	13	5	0	0

McCARRICK Mark Bernard
Born: Liverpool, England, 4 February, 1962 LB

League Club	Source	Date Signed	Seasons Played	Apps	Subs	Gls
Birmingham C	Witton A	05/83	83	12	3	0
Lincoln C	Tr	07/84	84-85	42	2	0
Crewe Alex	Tr	02/86	85	10	1	0
Tranmere Rov	Runcorn	08/87	87-90	125	0	14

McCARRISON Dugald McFarlane
Born: Lanark, Scotland, 22 December, 1969 F

League Club	Source	Date Signed	Seasons Played	Apps	Subs	Gls
Darlington (L)	Glasgow Celtic	10/91	91	5	0	2

League Club	Source	Date Signed	Seasons Played	Apps	Subs	Gls
McCARRON Francis Paul (Frank)						
Born: Glasgow, Scotland, 1 October, 1943						D
Carlisle U	Glasgow Celtic	07/67	67	7	2	1
McCARTAN Seamus Vincent (Shay)						
Born: Newry, Armagh, Northern Ireland, 18 May, 1994						F
Northern Ireland: U21-3/Youth						
Burnley	Sch	06/12	11	0	1	0
Accrington Stan	Tr	07/13	13-14	17	32	7
McCARTEN James Philip						
Born: Liverpool, England, 8 November, 1990						CD
Everton	Sch	10/08				
Accrington Stan	L	03/10	09	1	0	0
McCARTER James Joseph (Jim)						
Born: Glasgow, Scotland, 19 March, 1923						LW
Died: Weymouth, Dorset, England, 22 August, 2002						
Sheffield Wed	Vale of Clyde	01/46	46	6	-	0
Mansfield T	Tr	08/48	48-49	67	-	10
McCARTHY Alan James						
Born: Wandsworth, SW London, England, 11 January, 1972						CD
England: Youth//Wales: B/U21-3						
Queens Park Rgrs	YT	12/89	90-94	8	3	0
Watford	L	11/93	93	8	1	0
Plymouth Arg	L	02/94	93	1	1	0
Leyton Orient	Tr	08/95	95-96	43	4	0
McCARTHY Alex Simon						
Born: Guildford, Surrey, England, 3 December, 1989						G
England: U21-3						
Reading	Sch	07/08	10-13	69	1	0
Aldershot T	L	02/09	08	3	1	0
Yeovil T	L	02/09	09	44	0	0
Brentford	L	08/10	10	3	0	0
Leeds U	L	11/11	11	6	0	0
Ipswich T	L	01/12	11	10	0	0
Queens Park Rgrs	Tr	08/14	14	2	1	0
McCARTHY Anthony Paul (Tony)						
Born: Dublin, Republic of Ireland, 9 November, 1969						CD
Republic of Ireland: U21-5/Youth						
Millwall	Shelbourne (ROI)	06/92	92-94	20	1	1
Crewe Alex	L	12/94	94	2	0	0
Colchester U	Tr	03/95	94-96	88	1	1
McCARTHY Benedict Saul (Benni)						
Born: Cape Town, South Africa, 12 November, 1977						F
South Africa: 83						
Blackburn Rov	FC Porto (POR)	07/06	06-09	82	27	37
West Ham U	Tr	02/10	09-10	2	9	0
McCARTHY Daniel John Anthony (Danny)						
Born: Abergavenny, Monmouthshire, Wales, 26 September, 1942						W
Cardiff C	Abergavenny Thursday	07/60	61	7	-	0
McCARTHY Gerard (Gerry)						
Born: Limerick, Republic of Ireland, 30 March, 1934						CH
Republic of Ireland: LoI-1						
Charlton Ath	Limerick (ROI)	07/56	56	4	-	0
McCARTHY Ian						
Born: Porth, Rhondda Cynon Taff, Wales, 4 September, 1960						F
Swansea C	Coventry C (App)	03/78	77	0	1	0
McCARTHY James Patrick						
Born: Glasgow, Scotland, 12 November, 1990						DM
Republic of Ireland: 27/U21-5						
Wigan Ath	Hamilton Academical	07/09	09-13	119	1	7
Everton	Tr	09/13	13-14	58	4	3
McCARTHY Jason Sean						
Born: Southampton, England, 7 November, 1995						CD
Southampton	Sch	11/12	14	0	1	0
McCARTHY John						
Born: Dunmanway, Cork, Republic of Ireland, 22 January, 1922						CF
Republic of Ireland: LoI-4						
Bristol C	Cork U (ROI)	07/49	49	3	-	0
McCARTHY Jonathan David (Jon)						
Born: Middlesbrough, England, 18 August, 1970						RW
Northern Ireland: 18/B-2						
Hartlepool U	Jnr	11/87	87	0	1	0
York C	Shepshed Charterhouse	03/90	90-94	198	1	31
Port Vale	Tr	08/95	95-97	93	1	11
Birmingham C	Tr	09/97	97-01	107	17	8
Sheffield Wed	L	03/02	01	4	0	0
Port Vale	Tr	08/02	02	5	3	0
York C	Doncaster Rov	11/02	02	1	0	0
Carlisle U	Tr	11/02	02	19	2	1
McCARTHY Kevin John						
Born: Bethnal Green, E London, England, 24 December, 1957						M
Watford	App	01/76	75-77	35	1	1
McCARTHY Luke Joseph						
Born: Bolton, Greater Manchester, England, 7 July, 1993						RM
Bury	Sch	07/11	10	0	1	0
McCARTHY Michael Joseph (Mick)						
Born: Barnsley, South Yorkshire, England, 7 February, 1959						CD
Republic of Ireland: 57/U23-1						
Barnsley	App	07/77	77-83	272	0	7
Manchester C	Tr	12/83	83-86	140	0	2
Millwall	Olymp Lyonnais (FRA)	03/90	89-91	31	4	2
McCARTHY Patrick Richard (Paddy)						
Born: Dublin, Republic of Ireland, 31 May, 1983						CD
Republic of Ireland: B-1/U21-7/Youth						
Manchester C	YT	06/00				
Boston U	L	11/02	02	11	1	0
Notts Co	L	03/03	02	6	0	0
Leicester C	Tr	03/05	04-06	69	3	3
Charlton Ath	Tr	06/07	07	27	2	2
Crystal Palace	Tr	06/08	08-13	130	4	6
Sheffield U	L	10/14	14	10	1	1
Bolton W	L	03/15	14	5	0	0
McCARTHY Paul Jason						
Born: Cork, Republic of Ireland, 4 August, 1971						CD
Republic of Ireland: U21-10/Youth/Schools						
Brighton & HA	YT	04/89	89-95	180	1	6
Wycombe W	Tr	07/96	96-02	199	13	9
Oxford U	Tr	03/03	02-03	34	1	3
McCARTHY Philip (Phil)						
Born: Liverpool, England, 19 February, 1943						LW
Died: Liverpool, England, December, 1996						
Oldham Ath	Skelmersdale U	07/65	65	2	1	0
Halifax T	Tr	01/66	65-70	179	1	18
McCARTHY Robert Zepp (Bob)						
Born: Lyndhurst, Hampshire, England, 2 November, 1948						RB
Southampton	App	11/65	67-74	112	0	2
McCARTHY Roydon Stuart (Roy)						
Born: Barugh Green, South Yorkshire, England, 17 January, 1945						RW
Barnsley	Barugh Green Sports	05/62	61-62	3	-	0
Barrow	Tr	07/64	64-68	189	0	41
Southport	Tr	06/69	69	33	1	4
McCARTHY Sean Casey						
Born: Bridgend, Wales, 12 September, 1967						F
Wales: B-1						
Swansea C	Bridgend T	10/85	85-87	76	15	25
Plymouth Arg	Tr	08/88	88-89	67	3	19
Bradford C	Tr	07/90	90-93	127	4	60
Oldham Ath	Tr	12/93	93-97	117	23	42
Bristol C	L	03/98	97	7	0	1
Plymouth Arg	Tr	08/98	98-00	66	16	19
Exeter C	Tr	07/01	01	18	8	6
McCARTHY William Edward (Bill)						
Born: Bootle, Merseyside, England, 25 November, 1941						CD
England: Schools						
Liverpool	Jnr	12/58				
Southport	Tr	10/60	60-62	27	-	1
McCARTNEY George						
Born: Belfast, Northern Ireland, 29 April, 1981						LB
Northern Ireland: 34/U21-5/Youth/Schools						
Sunderland	YT	05/98	00-05	117	17	0
West Ham U	Tr	08/06	06-08	54	7	1
Sunderland	Tr	09/08	08-09	36	5	0
Leeds U	L	09/10	10	32	0	0
West Ham U	L	08/11	11	36	2	1
West Ham U	Tr	07/12	12-13	29	5	0
McCARTNEY Michael (Mike)						
Born: Musselburgh, East Lothian, Scotland, 28 September, 1954						LB
Scotland: Schools						
West Bromwich A	App	12/71				
Carlisle U	Tr	05/73	73-79	148	8	17
Southampton	Tr	07/80	80	22	0	1
Plymouth Arg	Tr	08/81	81-82	49	0	5
Carlisle U	Tr	03/83	82-86	130	1	7

McCARTNEY William Raymond (Willie)
Born: Newcraighall, Edinburgh, Scotland, 1 August, 1947 — CF

League Club	Source	Date Signed	Seasons Played	Apps	Subs	Gls
Port Vale	Glasgow Rangers	06/66	66	14	1	1

McCAVANA William Terence (Terry)
Born: Belfast, Northern Ireland, 24 January, 1921 — FB
Northern Ireland: 3/NILge-6/Amateur

League Club	Source	Date Signed	Seasons Played	Apps	Subs	Gls
Notts Co (Am)	Coleraine	08/48	48	3	-	0

McCHRYSTAL Mark Thomas
Born: Derry, Northern Ireland, 26 June, 1984 — CD
Northern Ireland: U21-9/Youth

League Club	Source	Date Signed	Seasons Played	Apps	Subs	Gls
Wolverhampton W	Sch	07/02				
Tranmere Rov	Derry C (ROI)	01/11	10-11	38	3	1
Scunthorpe U	L	11/12	12	3	0	0
Bristol Rov	Tr	01/13	12-13	56	0	0

McCLAIR Brian John
Born: Airdrie, Lanarkshire, Scotland, 8 December, 1963 — F
Scotland: 30/B/U21-8/Youth

League Club	Source	Date Signed	Seasons Played	Apps	Subs	Gls
Manchester U	Glasgow Celtic	07/87	87-97	296	59	88

McCLARE Sean Patrick
Born: Rotherham, South Yorkshire, England, 12 January, 1978 — M
Republic of Ireland: U21-3/Youth

League Club	Source	Date Signed	Seasons Played	Apps	Subs	Gls
Barnsley	YT	07/96	98-00	29	21	6
Rochdale	L	03/00	99	5	4	0
Port Vale	Tr	10/01	01-02	28	12	1
Rochdale	Tr	07/03	03	33	5	0

McCLAREN Christopher (Chris)
Born: Bristol, England, 14 March, 1963 — M

League Club	Source	Date Signed	Seasons Played	Apps	Subs	Gls
Darlington	Walton & Hersham	03/87	86	1	2	0

McCLAREN Stephen (Steve)
Born: York, England, 3 May, 1961 — M

League Club	Source	Date Signed	Seasons Played	Apps	Subs	Gls
Hull C	App	04/79	79-84	171	7	16
Derby Co	Tr	08/85	85-87	23	2	0
Lincoln C	L	02/87	86	8	0	0
Bristol C	Tr	02/88	87-88	60	1	2
Oxford U	Tr	08/89	89-91	27	6	0

McCLATCHEY Derek Heywood
Born: Huyton, Merseyside, England, 29 April, 1956 — F

League Club	Source	Date Signed	Seasons Played	Apps	Subs	Gls
Liverpool	App	05/73				
Southport	L	02/76	75	2	1	0

McCLEAN Christian Alphonso
Born: Colchester, Essex, England, 17 October, 1963 — F

League Club	Source	Date Signed	Seasons Played	Apps	Subs	Gls
Bristol Rov	Clacton T	03/88	87-90	28	23	6
Swansea C	Tr	07/91	91	4	0	0
Northampton T	Tr	11/91	91	19	0	3

McCLEAN James Joseph
Born: Derry, Northern Ireland, 22 April, 1989 — LW
Republic of Ireland: 29//Northern Ireland: U21-4

League Club	Source	Date Signed	Seasons Played	Apps	Subs	Gls
Sunderland	Derry C (ROI)	08/11	11-12	44	15	7
Wigan Ath	Tr	08/13	13-14	53	20	9

McCLEARY Garath James
Born: Oxford, England, 15 May, 1987 — W
Jamaica: 12

League Club	Source	Date Signed	Seasons Played	Apps	Subs	Gls
Nottingham F	Bromley	01/08	07-11	46	65	13
Reading	Tr	05/12	12-14	72	27	9

McCLELLAN Sidney Benjamin (Sid)
Born: Bow, E London, England, 11 June, 1925 — W/IF
Died: Barking, E London, England, 15 December, 2000

League Club	Source	Date Signed	Seasons Played	Apps	Subs	Gls
Tottenham H	Chelmsford C	08/49	50-55	68	-	29
Portsmouth	Tr	11/56	56-57	37	-	9
Leyton Orient	Tr	07/58	58	12	-	4

McCLELLAND Charles (Charlie)
Born: Lochgelly, Fife, Scotland, 8 January, 1924 — W

League Club	Source	Date Signed	Seasons Played	Apps	Subs	Gls
Blackburn Rov	Hyde U	12/46	46-48	13	-	2
Exeter C	Tr	07/49	49-54	183	-	60

McCLELLAND David
Born: Newcastle-upon-Tyne, England, 25 December, 1941 — RW

League Club	Source	Date Signed	Seasons Played	Apps	Subs	Gls
Port Vale	Bishop Auckland	08/67	67	2	2	0
Carlisle U	Tr	09/68				

McCLELLAND John (Jack)
Born: Lurgan, Armagh, Northern Ireland, 19 May, 1940 — G
Died: Lurgan, Armagh, Northern Ireland, 15 March, 1976
Northern Ireland: 6/NILge-2

League Club	Source	Date Signed	Seasons Played	Apps	Subs	Gls
Arsenal	Glenavon	10/60	60-63	46	-	0
Fulham	Tr	12/64	65-68	51	0	0
Lincoln C	L	12/68	68	12	0	0

McCLELLAND John
Born: Belfast, Northern Ireland, 7 December, 1955 — CD
England: FLge//Northern Ireland: 53

League Club	Source	Date Signed	Seasons Played	Apps	Subs	Gls
Cardiff C	Portadown	02/74	74	1	3	1
Mansfield T	Bangor C	05/78	78-80	122	3	8
Watford	Glasgow Rangers	11/84	84-88	184	0	3
Leeds U	Tr	06/89	89-91	22	2	0
Watford	L	01/90	89	1	0	0
Notts Co	L	03/92	91	6	0	0
Darlington	Rtd	10/96	96	1	0	0

McCLELLAND John Bonar
Born: Bradford, England, 5 March, 1935 — RW

League Club	Source	Date Signed	Seasons Played	Apps	Subs	Gls
Manchester C	Manchester YMCA	03/53	56-58	8	-	2
Lincoln C	Tr	09/58	58-61	121	-	32
Queens Park Rgrs	Tr	09/61	61-62	71	-	22
Portsmouth	Tr	05/63	62-67	136	1	35
Newport Co	Tr	07/68	68	36	0	10

McCLELLAND John William (Johnny)
Born: Colchester, Essex, England, 11 August, 1930 — IF
Died: Colchester, Essex, England, June, 2004

League Club	Source	Date Signed	Seasons Played	Apps	Subs	Gls
Colchester U	Lexden	09/51				
Stoke C	Tr	06/52	52	4	-	0
Swindon T	Tr	06/54	54	14	-	1
Rochdale	Tr	06/55	55	24	-	5

McCLELLAND Joseph (Joe)
Born: Edinburgh, Scotland, 12 October, 1935 — LB
Died: Edinburgh, Scotland, 24 April, 1999

League Club	Source	Date Signed	Seasons Played	Apps	Subs	Gls
Wrexham	Hibernian	06/64	64	32	-	0

McCLEN James David (Jamie)
Born: Newcastle-upon-Tyne, England, 13 May, 1979 — M

League Club	Source	Date Signed	Seasons Played	Apps	Subs	Gls
Newcastle U	YT	07/97	98-02	7	7	0
Carlisle U	Tr	08/05	05	0	2	0
Shrewsbury T	Blyth Spartans	02/06	05	4	0	0

McCLENAGHAN Albert (Bert)
Born: Derry, Northern Ireland, 7 July, 1954 — D

League Club	Source	Date Signed	Seasons Played	Apps	Subs	Gls
Watford	Larne T	12/77	77	2	0	0

McCLENAHAN Trent James
Born: Sydney, Australia, 4 February, 1985 — RB/M
Australia: U23-18/Youth

League Club	Source	Date Signed	Seasons Played	Apps	Subs	Gls
West Ham U	Sch	01/05	04	0	2	0
MK Dons	L	03/05	04	7	1	0
MK Dons	L	08/05	05	24	5	0
Hereford U	Tr	08/06	06-07	62	2	2
Scunthorpe U	Hamilton Academical	08/10	10	0	1	0

McCLURE Douglas Hugh (Doug)
Born: Islington, N London, England, 6 September, 1964 — LB
England: Youth/Schools

League Club	Source	Date Signed	Seasons Played	Apps	Subs	Gls
Queens Park Rgrs	App	08/82				
Exeter C	Tr	11/84	84	0	1	0
Torquay U	Tr	12/84	84	3	1	0
Wimbledon	Tr	01/85	84	2	0	0
Peterborough U	Canada	10/85	85	4	0	0
Crewe Alex	Tr	01/86	85	3	0	0

McCLURE Matthew Glen (Matt)
Born: Slough, Berkshire, England, 17 November, 1991 — F
Northern Ireland: U21-1/Youth

League Club	Source	Date Signed	Seasons Played	Apps	Subs	Gls
Wycombe W	Sch	07/10	10-14	62	48	24

McCLURE William (Willie)
Born: Shotts, Lanarkshire, Scotland, 16 May, 1921 — LW
Died: Shotts, Lanarkshire, Scotland, 15 November, 1992

League Club	Source	Date Signed	Seasons Played	Apps	Subs	Gls
Preston NE	Albion Rov	12/47	47	12	-	2
New Brighton	Tr	07/48	48-49	45	-	7
Carlisle U	Tr	10/49	49	8	-	0
Hartlepool U	Greenock Morton	08/50	50-52	118	-	24

McCLUSKEY Andrew (Andy)
Born: Manchester, England, 29 March, 1951 — M

League Club	Source	Date Signed	Seasons Played	Apps	Subs	Gls
Hartlepool U	St Joseph's	09/69	69	4	2	0

McCLUSKEY George McKinlay Cassidy
Born: Hamilton, Lanarkshire, Scotland, 19 September, 1957 — F
Scotland: U21-6

League Club	Source	Date Signed	Seasons Played	Apps	Subs	Gls
Leeds U	Glasgow Celtic	08/83	83-85	57	16	16

McCLUSKEY Ronald (Ronnie)
Born: Johnstone, Renfrewshire, Scotland, 3 November, 1936 — G
Died: Dunbar, East Lothian, Scotland, 23 June, 2011

League Club	Source	Date Signed	Seasons Played	Apps	Subs	Gls
Accrington Stan	East Fife	11/60	60	4	-	0

McCLUSKIE James Alexander Joseph (Jim)
Born: Rawtenstall, Lancashire, England, 29 September, 1966 — F

League Club	Source	Date Signed	Seasons Played	Apps	Subs	Gls
Rochdale	Jnr	07/84	83-85	14	5	0

McCOIST Alistair Murdoch (Ally)
Born: Motherwell, Lanarkshire, Scotland, 24 September, 1962 — F
Scotland: 61/U21-1/Youth

League Club	Source	Date Signed	Seasons Played	Apps	Subs	Gls
Sunderland	St Johnstone	08/81	81-82	38	18	8

McCOLE John
Born: Glasgow, Scotland, 18 September, 1936 — CF
Died: Gweedore, Donegal, Republic of Ireland, 1982

League Club	Source	Date Signed	Seasons Played	Apps	Subs	Gls
Bradford C	Falkirk	09/58	58-59	42	-	32
Leeds U	Tr	09/59	59-61	78	-	45
Bradford C	Tr	10/61	61-62	46	-	15
Rotherham U	Tr	12/62	62	14	-	5
Newport Co	Shelbourne (ROI)	10/64	64	6	-	2

McCOLL Duncan John
Born: Glasgow, Scotland, 28 December, 1945 — IF

League Club	Source	Date Signed	Seasons Played	Apps	Subs	Gls
Barnsley	Partick Thistle	01/66	65	5	0	0

McCOLL Thomas Gunn (Tommy)
Born: Glasgow, Scotland, 19 September, 1945 — IF

League Club	Source	Date Signed	Seasons Played	Apps	Subs	Gls
Colchester U	Denistoun Waverley	06/63	63-64	11	-	2
Chelsea	Tr	12/64				

McCOLLIN Andre Stefan
Born: Lambeth, S London, England, 1 April, 1985 — F

League Club	Source	Date Signed	Seasons Played	Apps	Subs	Gls
Yeovil T	Fisher Ath	08/08	08-09	0	13	1

McCOMBE Jamie Paul
Born: Pontefract, West Yorkshire, England, 1 January, 1983 — CD

League Club	Source	Date Signed	Seasons Played	Apps	Subs	Gls
Scunthorpe U	YT	11/01	01-03	42	21	1
Lincoln C	Tr	03/04	03-05	83	4	7
Bristol C	Tr	06/06	06-09	100	19	9
Huddersfield T	Tr	07/10	10-11	51	3	8
Preston NE	L	11/11	11	6	0	0
Doncaster Rov	Tr	08/12	12-14	49	4	2

McCOMBE John Paul
Born: Pontefract, West Yorkshire, England, 7 May, 1985 — CD

League Club	Source	Date Signed	Seasons Played	Apps	Subs	Gls
Huddersfield T	Sch	07/04	02-06	10	4	0
Hereford U	Tr	07/07	07	23	4	0
Port Vale	Tr	07/08	08-12	180	5	14
Mansfield T	Tr	06/13	13	5	0	2
York C	Tr	01/14	13-14	45	5	3

McCONNELL Barry
Born: Exeter, England, 1 January, 1977 — RB/M

League Club	Source	Date Signed	Seasons Played	Apps	Subs	Gls
Exeter C	YT	08/95	95-02	108	54	15

McCONNELL Peter
Born: Reddish, Greater Manchester, England, 3 March, 1937 — WH

League Club	Source	Date Signed	Seasons Played	Apps	Subs	Gls
Leeds U	Jnr	03/54	58-61	48	-	4
Carlisle U	Tr	08/62	62-68	271	1	26
Bradford C	Tr	07/69	69-70	76	3	0

McCONVILLE Ian John
Born: Doncaster, South Yorkshire, England, 1 May, 1959 — LW

League Club	Source	Date Signed	Seasons Played	Apps	Subs	Gls
Doncaster Rov	App	04/77	75-77	9	2	1

McCONVILLE Sean Joseph
Born: Burscough, Lancashire, England, 6 March, 1989 — W

League Club	Source	Date Signed	Seasons Played	Apps	Subs	Gls
Accrington Stan	Skelmersdale U	02/09	08-10	53	23	14
Rochdale (L)	Stockport Co	03/12	11	2	2	0

McCORD Brian John
Born: Derby, England, 24 August, 1968 — M/RB

League Club	Source	Date Signed	Seasons Played	Apps	Subs	Gls
Derby Co	App	06/87	87-89	3	2	0
Barnsley	L	11/89	89	5	0	0
Barnsley	Tr	03/90	89-91	35	3	2
Mansfield T	L	08/92	92	11	0	1
Stockport Co	Tr	12/92	92	4	4	0

McCORKINDALE John
Born: Campbeltown, Argyll & Bute, Scotland, 10 August, 1934 — LW
Died: Campbeltown, Argyll & Bute, Scotland, 22 June, 2004

League Club	Source	Date Signed	Seasons Played	Apps	Subs	Gls
Gillingham	Tonbridge	10/57	57	8	-	0

McCORMACK Alan
Born: Dublin, Republic of Ireland, 10 January, 1984 — M/RB
Republic of Ireland: Youth/Schools

League Club	Source	Date Signed	Seasons Played	Apps	Subs	Gls
Preston NE	Stella Maris BC (ROI)	08/02	03-06	2	9	0
Leyton Orient	L	08/03	03	8	2	0
Southend U	L	03/05	04	5	2	2
Southend U	Tr	11/06	06-09	128	11	16
Charlton Ath	Tr	07/10	10	18	6	1
Swindon T	Tr	07/11	11-12	76	4	2
Brentford	Tr	07/13	13-14	57	4	2

McCORMACK Francis Adamson (Frank)
Born: Glasgow, Scotland, 25 September, 1924 — CH
Died: Glasgow, Scotland, 6 April, 2011

League Club	Source	Date Signed	Seasons Played	Apps	Subs	Gls
Oldham Ath	Clyde	11/49	49	14	-	0

McCORMACK John Cecil (Cec)
Born: Chester-le-Street, County Durham, England, 15 February, 1922 — CF
Died: Australia, 1995

League Club	Source	Date Signed	Seasons Played	Apps	Subs	Gls
Gateshead	Newburn	09/41	46	29	-	19
Middlesbrough	Tr	04/47	46-48	37	-	15
Barnsley	Chelmsford C	07/50	50-51	50	-	42
Notts Co	Tr	11/51	51-55	82	-	35

McCORMACK Murdoch
Born: Glasgow, Scotland, 7 October, 1920 — LW
Died: Glasgow, Scotland, 22 April, 1951

League Club	Source	Date Signed	Seasons Played	Apps	Subs	Gls
Manchester C	Glasgow Rangers	04/47	46	1	-	0
Blackpool	Tr	07/47	47	12	-	3
Crewe Alex	Tr	07/48	48	31	-	3

McCORMACK Ross
Born: Glasgow, Scotland, 18 August, 1986 — F
Scotland: 11/B-1/U21-13/Youth

League Club	Source	Date Signed	Seasons Played	Apps	Subs	Gls
Doncaster Rov (L)	Glasgow Rangers	01/06	05	12	7	4
Cardiff C	Motherwell	07/08	08-10	53	21	25
Leeds U	Tr	08/10	10-13	119	25	53
Fulham	Tr	07/14	14	43	1	17

McCORMICK David
Born: Halifax, West Yorkshire, England, 3 November, 1920 — G
Died: Chester, England, 1983

League Club	Source	Date Signed	Seasons Played	Apps	Subs	Gls
Halifax T	St Malachy's	10/47	47-54	118	-	0

McCORMICK David
Born: Southwark, S London, England, 29 December, 1951 — F

League Club	Source	Date Signed	Seasons Played	Apps	Subs	Gls
Peterborough U	Biggleswade T	08/75	75	1	0	0

McCORMICK Henry (Harry)
Born: Coleraine, Derry, Northern Ireland, 10 January, 1924 — LW
Northern Ireland: NILge-1

League Club	Source	Date Signed	Seasons Played	Apps	Subs	Gls
Derby Co	Coleraine	10/46	46-47	7	-	0
Everton	Tr	07/48	48	4	-	0

McCORMICK James (Jimmy)
Born: Rotherham, South Yorkshire, England, 26 September, 1912 — RW
Died: Marbella, Spain, 4 January, 1968

League Club	Source	Date Signed	Seasons Played	Apps	Subs	Gls
Rotherham U	Rotherham YMCA	03/31	30-31	19	-	2
Chesterfield	Scarborough	08/32	32	15	-	2
Tottenham H	Tr	03/33	32-38	137	-	26
Fulham	Tr	04/46	46	9	-	2
Lincoln C	Tr	08/47	47-48	64	-	6
Crystal Palace	Tr	02/49	48	13	-	2

McCORMICK James
Born: Rotherham, South Yorkshire, England, 1 April, 1937 — RW

League Club	Source	Date Signed	Seasons Played	Apps	Subs	Gls
Sheffield U		10/56	56	1	-	0
Rotherham U	Tr	07/57				

McCORMICK John
Born: Glasgow, Scotland, 18 July, 1936 — CD

League Club	Source	Date Signed	Seasons Played	Apps	Subs	Gls
Crystal Palace	Aberdeen	05/66	66-72	194	0	6

McCORMICK Joseph Michael (Joe)
Born: Holywell, Flintshire, Wales, 15 July, 1916 — WH

League Club	Source	Date Signed	Seasons Played	Apps	Subs	Gls
Bolton W		10/37				
Rochdale	Tr	05/46	46-47	66	-	0
Scunthorpe U	Boston U	07/49	50	7	-	0

McCORMICK Luke Martin
Born: Coventry, England, 15 August, 1983 — G

League Club	Source	Date Signed	Seasons Played	Apps	Subs	Gls
Plymouth Arg	Sch	07/02	00-07	137	1	0
Boston U	L	10/04	04	2	0	0
Oxford U	Truro C	01/13	12	15	0	0
Plymouth Arg	Tr	05/13	13-14	73	0	0

McCORMICK Stephen (Steve)
Born: Dumbarton, Dunbartonshire, Scotland, 14 August, 1969 — F

League Club	Source	Date Signed	Seasons Played	Apps	Subs	Gls
Leyton Orient (L)	Dundee	09/98	98	1	3	0

McCOURT Francis Joseph (Frank)
Born: Portadown, Armagh, Northern Ireland, 9 December, 1925 — WH
Northern Ireland: 6

League Club	Source	Date Signed	Seasons Played	Apps	Subs	Gls
Bristol Rov	Shamrock Rov (ROI)	11/45				
Bristol Rov	Shamrock Rov (ROI)	03/49	49	32	-	1
Manchester C	Tr	12/50	50-53	61	-	4
Colchester U	Tr	06/54	54	12	-	0

McCOURT Jak
Born: Leicester, England, 6 July, 1995 — M

League Club	Source	Date Signed	Seasons Played	Apps	Subs	Gls
Leicester C	Sch	07/13				
Torquay U	L	10/13	13	10	1	0

McCOURT Patrick James (Paddy)
Born: Derry, Northern Ireland, 16 December, 1983 — W
Northern Ireland: 17/B-1/U21-8

League Club	Source	Date Signed	Seasons Played	Apps	Subs	Gls
Rochdale	Sch	02/02	01-04	31	48	8
Barnsley	Glasgow Celtic	08/13	13	15	8	2
Brighton & HA	Tr	08/14	14	0	10	0
Notts Co	L	02/15	14	11	1	1

McCOY Marvin Anthony Michael
Born: Walthamstow, NE London, England, 2 October, 1988 — RB
Antigua & Barbuda: 7

League Club	Source	Date Signed	Seasons Played	Apps	Subs	Gls
Hereford U	Watford (Sch)	08/07				
Wycombe W	Wealdstone	07/10	10-13	82	9	0
York C	Tr	06/14	14	30	1	0

McCOY Michael Paul (Mick)
Born: Sunderland, England, 29 January, 1934 — IF
Died: County Durham, England, June, 2002

League Club	Source	Date Signed	Seasons Played	Apps	Subs	Gls
Burnley	Silksworth CW	10/53				
Southport	Tr	07/57	57	5	-	1

McCOY Peter Joseph
Born: Wingate, County Durham, England, 31 July, 1923 — FB
Died: County Durham, England, 31 July, 1986

League Club	Source	Date Signed	Seasons Played	Apps	Subs	Gls
Newcastle U	Shotton Jnrs	09/46				
Norwich C	Tr	02/49	48	6	-	0

McCOY Wilfred (Wilf)
Born: Birmingham, England, 4 March, 1921 — CH
Died: Brighton, England, January, 2005

League Club	Source	Date Signed	Seasons Played	Apps	Subs	Gls
Portsmouth	Brighton & HA (Am)	08/46	46-47	18	-	0
Northampton T	Tr	12/48	48-49	60	-	0
Brighton & HA	Tr	01/51	50-53	112	-	0

McCRACKEN David
Born: Glasgow, Scotland, 16 October, 1981 — CD
Scotland: U21-5

League Club	Source	Date Signed	Seasons Played	Apps	Subs	Gls
Wycombe W	Dundee U	07/07	07-08	74	2	2
MK Dons	Tr	07/09	09	41	0	1
Brentford	Tr	07/10	10	1	1	0
Bristol Rov	L	01/11	10	5	5	0

McCRAE Alexander (Alex)
Born: Stoneyburn, West Lothian, Scotland, 2 January, 1920 — IF
Died: Livingston, West Lothian, Scotland, 8 October, 2009
Northern Ireland: NILge-1

League Club	Source	Date Signed	Seasons Played	Apps	Subs	Gls
Charlton Ath	Heart of Midlothian	05/47	47-48	43	-	8
Middlesbrough	Tr	11/48	48-52	122	-	47

McCRAE Ian
Born: West Ham, E London, England, 1 October, 1935 — LB

League Club	Source	Date Signed	Seasons Played	Apps	Subs	Gls
Accrington Stan		07/57	59-60	14	-	0

McCRAE Romone Curtis
Born: Southwark, S London, England, 25 August, 1991 — M

League Club	Source	Date Signed	Seasons Played	Apps	Subs	Gls
Peterborough U	Crawley T	07/09	09	0	2	0

McCREADIE Edward Graham (Eddie)
Born: Glasgow, Scotland, 15 April, 1940 — LB
Scotland: 23

League Club	Source	Date Signed	Seasons Played	Apps	Subs	Gls
Chelsea	East Stirlingshire	04/62	62-73	327	4	4

McCREADIE Edward James (Eddie)
Born: Alexandria, Dunbartonshire, Scotland, 23 February, 1924 — LW

League Club	Source	Date Signed	Seasons Played	Apps	Subs	Gls
Walsall	Elgin C	09/53	53	4	-	0

McCREADIE William Harvey (Harvey)
Born: Glenluce, Dumfries & Galloway, Scotland, 1 October, 1942 — CF
Died: Dumfries, Scotland, 30 September, 2008

League Club	Source	Date Signed	Seasons Played	Apps	Subs	Gls
Accrington Stan	Stranraer	10/59	58-59	28	-	10
Luton T	Tr	01/60	59	1	-	0
Wrexham	Tr	11/60	60	10	-	2

McCREADY Bernard Thomas
Born: Dumbarton, Dunbartonshire, Scotland, 23 April, 1937 — G

League Club	Source	Date Signed	Seasons Played	Apps	Subs	Gls
Rochdale	Glasgow Celtic	05/57	57-58	29	-	0
Oldham Ath	Tr	03/59	58	7	-	0

McCREADY Christopher James (Chris)
Born: Ellesmere Port, Cheshire, England, 5 September, 1981 — CD
England: Schools

League Club	Source	Date Signed	Seasons Played	Apps	Subs	Gls
Crewe Alex	YT	05/00	01-05	59	17	0
Tranmere Rov	Tr	07/06	06	42	0	1
Crewe Alex	Tr	07/07	07-08	36	3	2
Northampton T	Tr	07/09	09	13	1	0
Tranmere Rov	L	01/10	09	8	0	0
Morecambe	Tr	07/10	10-13	138	6	6

McCREADY Thomas (Tommy)
Born: Johnstone, Renfrewshire, Scotland, 19 October, 1943 — FB
Scotland: Schools

League Club	Source	Date Signed	Seasons Played	Apps	Subs	Gls
Watford	Hibernian	07/63	63	1	-	0

McCREADY Thomas (Tommy)
Born: Port Glasgow, Inverclyde, Scotland, 28 September, 1923 — IF
Died: Lincoln, England, 19 February, 2004

League Club	Source	Date Signed	Seasons Played	Apps	Subs	Gls
Hartlepool U	Cowdenbeath	08/49	49	34	-	3
Lincoln C	Tr	08/50	50	11	-	1

McCREADY Thomas Richard (Tom)
Born: Ellesmere Port, Merseyside, England, 7 June, 1991 — M

League Club	Source	Date Signed	Seasons Played	Apps	Subs	Gls
Morecambe	Limestone C'ge (USA)	07/14	14	1	6	0
Exeter C	Tr	02/15	14	1	2	0

McCREDIE Norman James (Norrie)
Born: Glasgow, Scotland, 17 May, 1928 — LB
Died: Oswaldtwistle, Lancashire, England, 8 June, 2006

League Club	Source	Date Signed	Seasons Played	Apps	Subs	Gls
Accrington Stan	Partick Thistle	05/55	55-56	51	-	3
Southport	Tr	08/57	57	33	-	2
Barrow	Tr	08/58	58	23	-	0

McCREERY David
Born: Belfast, Northern Ireland, 16 September, 1957 — M
Northern Ireland: 67/U21-1/Youth/Schools

League Club	Source	Date Signed	Seasons Played	Apps	Subs	Gls
Manchester U	App	10/74	74-78	48	39	7
Queens Park Rgrs	Tr	08/79	79-80	56	1	4
Newcastle U	Tulsa Roughnecks (USA)	10/82	82-88	237	6	2
Hartlepool U	Heart of Midlothian	08/91	91	27	3	0
Carlisle U	Coleraine	10/92	92-93	25	10	0
Hartlepool U	Tr	10/94	94	7	2	0

McCREESH Andrew (Andy)
Born: Billingham, Cleveland, England, 8 September, 1962 — FB
Died: Billingham, Cleveland, England, 5 February, 2009

League Club	Source	Date Signed	Seasons Played	Apps	Subs	Gls
Middlesbrough	App	09/80	81	2	0	0

McCRINDLE William (Willie)
Born: Kilmarnock, Ayrshire, Scotland, 28 June, 1923 — FB
Died: Great Yarmouth, Norfolk, England, 1982

League Club	Source	Date Signed	Seasons Played	Apps	Subs	Gls
Newport Co	Pollok Jnrs	12/48	48-49	5	-	0

McCROHAN Roy
Born: Reading, England, 22 September, 1930 — WH
Died: Exmouth, Devon, England, 3 March, 2015

League Club	Source	Date Signed	Seasons Played	Apps	Subs	Gls
Reading	Jnr	01/49	49-50	4	-	1
Norwich C	Tr	08/51	51-61	385	-	20
Colchester U	Tr	09/62	62-63	75	-	4
Bristol Rov	Tr	08/64	64	10	-	1

McCRORY Damien Paul
Born: Limerick, Republic of Ireland, 23 February, 1990 — LB
Republic of Ireland: Youth

League Club	Source	Date Signed	Seasons Played	Apps	Subs	Gls
Plymouth Arg	Sch	07/08				
Port Vale	L	10/08	08	10	2	0
Port Vale	L	08/09	09	2	3	0
Grimsby T	L	11/09	09	10	0	0
Dagenham & Red	Tr	02/10	09-11	74	2	1
Burton A	Tr	07/12	12-14	114	2	7

McCRORY Samuel McKee (Sammy)
Born: Belfast, Northern Ireland, 11 October, 1924 — IF
Died: Donaghadee, Down, Northern Ireland, 4 May, 2011
Northern Ireland: 1/B/NILge-1

League Club	Source	Date Signed	Seasons Played	Apps	Subs	Gls
Swansea C	Linfield	10/46	46-49	105	-	47
Ipswich T	Tr	03/50	49-51	97	-	39
Plymouth Arg	Tr	08/52	52-54	50	-	11
Southend U	Tr	06/55	55-59	205	-	91

McCRYSTAL Dennis
Born: Watford, Hertfordshire, England, 13 January, 1932 — G
Died: Watford, Hertfordshire, England, 4 January, 2006

League Club	Source	Date Signed	Seasons Played	Apps	Subs	Gls
Watford	Kingsway YC	03/50	50	1	-	0
Fulham	Tr	11/51				

McCUBBIN Robert (Bert)
Born: Kilmarnock, Ayrshire, Scotland, 13 February, 1943 — RW

League Club	Source	Date Signed	Seasons Played	Apps	Subs	Gls
Hartlepool U	Ayr U	06/63	63	2	-	0

McCUE Alexander Brian (Alec)
Born: Greenock, Inverclyde, Scotland, 25 November, 1927 — LW
Died: Ashford, Kent, England, October, 1989

League Club	Source	Date Signed	Seasons Played	Apps	Subs	Gls
Carlisle U	Falkirk	10/50	50	32	-	11
Grimsby T	Tr	07/51	51-52	37	-	15
Shrewsbury T	Tr	05/53	53-55	91	-	28

McCUE John William
Born: Stoke-on-Trent, England, 22 August, 1922 — FB
Died: Barlaston, Staffordshire, England, 19 November, 1999

League Club	Source	Date Signed	Seasons Played	Apps	Subs	Gls
Stoke C	Jnr	04/40	46-59	502	-	2
Oldham Ath	Tr	09/60	60-61	56	-	0

McCULLAGH Paul Andrew
Born: Brigg, North Lincolnshire, England, 6 February, 1974 — D

League Club	Source	Date Signed	Seasons Played	Apps	Subs	Gls
Scunthorpe U	YT	07/92	92	5	0	1

McCULLOCH Adam Andrew Ball Ross
Born: Crossford, Lanarkshire, Scotland, 4 June, 1920 — CF
Died: Farnham, Surrey, England, 8 June, 2004

League Club	Source	Date Signed	Seasons Played	Apps	Subs	Gls
Northampton T	Third Lanark	06/49	49-51	89	-	37
Shrewsbury T	Tr	01/52	51-52	46	-	18
Aldershot	Tr	02/53	52-54	79	-	32

McCULLOCH Andrew (Andy)
Born: Northampton, England, 3 January, 1950 — F

League Club	Source	Date Signed	Seasons Played	Apps	Subs	Gls
Queens Park Rgrs	Walton & Hersham	10/70	70-72	30	12	10
Cardiff C	Tr	10/72	72-73	58	0	24
Oxford U	Tr	07/74	74-75	41	0	9
Brentford	Tr	03/76	75-78	115	2	48
Sheffield Wed	Tr	06/79	79-82	122	3	44
Crystal Palace	Tr	08/83	83	25	0	3
Aldershot	Tr	11/84	84	16	0	2

McCULLOCH David (Dave)
Born: Hamilton, Lanarkshire, Scotland, 5 October, 1911 — CF
Died: East Kilbride, Lanarkshire, Scotland, 21 June, 1979
Scotland: 7/SLge-1/War-1

League Club	Source	Date Signed	Seasons Played	Apps	Subs	Gls
Brentford	Heart of Midlothian	11/35	35-38	117	-	85
Derby Co	Tr	10/38	38	31	-	16
Leicester C	Tr	08/46	46	4	-	2

McCULLOCH John Balfour (Iain)
Born: Kilmarnock, Ayrshire, Scotland, 28 December, 1954 — RW/F
Scotland: U21-2

League Club	Source	Date Signed	Seasons Played	Apps	Subs	Gls
Notts Co	Kilmarnock	04/78	78-83	212	3	51

McCULLOCH Lee Henry
Born: Coatbridge, Lanarkshire, Scotland, 14 May, 1978 — LW
Scotland: 18/B-1/U21-14/Youth

League Club	Source	Date Signed	Seasons Played	Apps	Subs	Gls
Wigan Ath	Motherwell	03/01	00-06	192	32	44

McCULLOCH Scott Anderson James
Born: Cumnock, Ayrshire, Scotland, 29 November, 1975 — LB
Scotland: Schools

League Club	Source	Date Signed	Seasons Played	Apps	Subs	Gls
Cardiff C	Dundee U	09/00	00	9	12	1

McCULLOCH Thomas (Tommy)
Born: Glasgow, Scotland, 25 December, 1921 — W
Died: Lennoxtown, Dunbartonshire, Scotland, 2 October, 2001

League Club	Source	Date Signed	Seasons Played	Apps	Subs	Gls
Northampton T	Queen of the South	12/49	49	2	-	0
Bradford C	Tr	01/51	50-53	109	-	9
Crewe Alex	Tr	07/54	54	28	-	5

McCULLOCH William Duncan (Billy)
Born: Edinburgh, Scotland, 25 June, 1922 — WH/FB
Died: Manchester, England, 1961

League Club	Source	Date Signed	Seasons Played	Apps	Subs	Gls
Stockport Co	RAF Woodford	03/44	46-53	309	-	4
Rochdale	Tr	07/54	54-57	140	-	2

McCULLOUGH Luke
Born: Portadown, Armagh, Northern Ireland, 15 February, 1994 — CD
Northern Ireland: 4/U21-6

League Club	Source	Date Signed	Seasons Played	Apps	Subs	Gls
Manchester U	Sch	07/12				
Cheltenham T	L	01/13	12	0	1	0
Doncaster Rov	Tr	07/13	13-14	46	1	0

McCULLOUGH Paul James
Born: Birmingham, England, 26 October, 1959 — G

League Club	Source	Date Signed	Seasons Played	Apps	Subs	Gls
Reading	Brixham	09/78				
Brentford	Dawlish T	07/80	80	7	0	0

McCULLOUGH William James (Billy)
Born: Carrickfergus, Antrim, Northern Ireland, 27 July, 1935 — LB
Northern Ireland: 10/NILge-1

League Club	Source	Date Signed	Seasons Played	Apps	Subs	Gls
Arsenal	Portadown	09/58	58-65	253	0	4
Millwall	Tr	08/66	66	17	2	0

McCUNNELL Barry
Born: Hull, England, 20 September, 1948 — W

League Club	Source	Date Signed	Seasons Played	Apps	Subs	Gls
Hull C	Endike Jnrs	10/66	69	0	1	0

McCUNNIE Jamie Patrick
Born: Glasgow, Scotland, 15 April, 1983 — RB
Scotland: B-1/U21-20

League Club	Source	Date Signed	Seasons Played	Apps	Subs	Gls
Hartlepool U	Dunfermline Ath	06/07	07-08	33	11	1

McCURDY Colin Charles
Born: Belfast, Northern Ireland, 18 July, 1954 — F
Northern Ireland: 1/NILge-1

League Club	Source	Date Signed	Seasons Played	Apps	Subs	Gls
Fulham	Larne T	11/77	77	1	0	0

McCURLEY Kevin
Born: Consett, County Durham, England, 2 April, 1926 — CF
Died: Broadstairs, Kent, England, 5 May, 2000

League Club	Source	Date Signed	Seasons Played	Apps	Subs	Gls
Brighton & HA	Worthing	09/48	48-50	21	-	9
Liverpool	Tr	06/51				
Colchester U	Tr	03/52	51-59	224	-	92
Oldham Ath	Tr	06/60	60	1	-	0

McCUSKER James (Jim)
Born: Maghera, Derry, Northern Ireland, 27 December, 1939 — G

League Club	Source	Date Signed	Seasons Played	Apps	Subs	Gls
Bradford C	Jnr	02/57	58	7	-	0
Stockport Co	Tr	08/59	59	2	-	0

McDAID David Gerard
Born: Derry, Northern Ireland, 3 December, 1990 — F
Republic of Ireland: Youth

League Club	Source	Date Signed	Seasons Played	Apps	Subs	Gls
York C	Derry C (ROI)	01/13	12	0	4	0

McDAID Sean Andrew
Born: Harrogate, North Yorkshire, England, 6 March, 1986 — LB

League Club	Source	Date Signed	Seasons Played	Apps	Subs	Gls
Leeds U	Sch	03/03				
Doncaster Rov	Tr	07/05	05-09	65	15	1
Carlisle U	Tr	07/10	10	12	0	0

McDERMENT William Stirling (Billy)
Born: Paisley, Renfrewshire, Scotland, 5 January, 1943 — D

League Club	Source	Date Signed	Seasons Played	Apps	Subs	Gls
Leicester C	Johnstone Burgh	05/61	62-66	20	3	1
Luton T	Tr	07/67	67-68	28	12	1
Notts Co	Tr	05/69	69	2	1	0

McDERMOTT Andrew (Andy)
Born: Sydney, Australia, 24 March, 1977 — RB
Australia: U23

League Club	Source	Date Signed	Seasons Played	Apps	Subs	Gls
Queens Park Rgrs	Australian IOS (AUS)	08/95	96	6	0	2
West Bromwich A	Tr	03/97	96-99	49	3	1
Notts Co	Tr	08/00	00	20	5	0

McDERMOTT Brian James
Born: Slough, Berkshire, England, 8 April, 1961 — W/M
England: Youth

League Club	Source	Date Signed	Seasons Played	Apps	Subs	Gls
Arsenal	App	02/79	78-83	38	23	12
Fulham	L	03/83	82	0	3	0
Oxford U	Tr	12/84	84-86	16	8	2
Huddersfield T	L	10/86	86	4	0	1
Cardiff C	Tr	08/87	87-88	49	2	8
Exeter C	Tr	02/89	88-90	65	3	4

McDERMOTT David Anthony
Born: Stourbridge, West Midlands, England, 6 February, 1988 — W

League Club	Source	Date Signed	Seasons Played	Apps	Subs	Gls
Walsall	Sch	07/06	05-07	1	13	0

McDERMOTT Donal Jeremiah
Born: Ashbourne, Meath, Republic of Ireland, 19 October, 1989 — W
Republic of Ireland: Youth

League Club	Source	Date Signed	Seasons Played	Apps	Subs	Gls
Manchester C	Sch	10/07				
MK Dons	L	09/08	08	0	1	0
Chesterfield	L	08/09	09	13	2	5
Scunthorpe U	L	01/10	09	4	5	0
Bournemouth	L	03/11	10	6	3	1
Huddersfield T	Tr	07/11	11	6	3	0
Bournemouth	Tr	01/12	11-12	12	8	1

McDERMOTT James Lawrence (Jimmy)
Born: Earlestown, Merseyside, England, 25 May, 1932 — W
Died: Knowsley, Merseyside, England, 29 August, 2006

League Club	Source	Date Signed	Seasons Played	Apps	Subs	Gls
Southport	Crompton's Rec	07/55	55-58	157	-	30

McDERMOTT John
Born: Middlesbrough, England, 3 February, 1969 — RB

League Club	Source	Date Signed	Seasons Played	Apps	Subs	Gls
Grimsby T	App	06/87	86-06	626	21	11

McDERMOTT John Charles
Born: Manchester, England, 14 October, 1959 — M

League Club	Source	Date Signed	Seasons Played	Apps	Subs	Gls
Manchester U	App	10/76				
Rochdale	Wigan Ath (NC)	09/79	79	5	3	1

McDERMOTT Maurice Patrick
Born: Chester-le-Street, County Durham, England, 21 February, 1923 — LB
Died: Stockton-on-Tees, Cleveland, England, 9 February, 1988

League Club	Source	Date Signed	Seasons Played	Apps	Subs	Gls
Sunderland	Consett	11/45				
York C	Consett	07/47	47	7	-	0

McDERMOTT Neale Terence
Born: Newcastle-upon-Tyne, England, 8 March, 1985 — M
England: Youth

League Club	Source	Date Signed	Seasons Played	Apps	Subs	Gls
Newcastle U	Sch	05/02				
Fulham	Tr	01/03				
Swindon T	L	08/05	05	9	4	2
Darlington	L	02/06	05	1	2	0
Carlisle U	Tr	08/06	06	6	9	3

McDERMOTT Steven (Steve)
Born: Gateshead, Tyne and Wear, England, 30 December, 1964 — F

League Club	Source	Date Signed	Seasons Played	Apps	Subs	Gls
Darlington	Sunderland (App)	11/82	82	0	2	0

McDERMOTT Terence (Terry)
Born: Kirkby, Merseyside, England, 8 December, 1951 — M
England: 25/B-1/U23-1

League Club	Source	Date Signed	Seasons Played	Apps	Subs	Gls
Bury	App	10/69	69-72	83	7	8
Newcastle U	Tr	02/73	72-74	55	1	6
Liverpool	Tr	11/74	74-82	221	11	54
Newcastle U	Tr	09/82	82-83	74	0	12

McDEVITT Kenneth Richard (Kenny)
Born: Liverpool, England, 4 March, 1929 — RW/IF

League Club	Source	Date Signed	Seasons Played	Apps	Subs	Gls
Tranmere Rov	Unity BC	01/50	51-59	237	-	40

McDONAGH Seamus Martin (Jim)
Born: Rotherham, South Yorkshire, England, 6 October, 1952 — G
England: Youth//Republic of Ireland: 24

League Club	Source	Date Signed	Seasons Played	Apps	Subs	Gls
Rotherham U	App	10/70	70-75	121	0	0
Bolton W	Tr	08/76	76-79	161	0	0
Everton	Tr	07/80	80	40	0	0
Bolton W	Tr	08/81	81-82	81	0	1
Notts Co	Tr	07/83	83-84	35	0	0
Birmingham C	L	09/84	84	1	0	0
Gillingham	L	03/85	84	10	0	0
Sunderland	L	08/85	85	7	0	0
Scarborough	Wichita Wings (USA)	11/87	87	9	0	0
Huddersfield T	L	01/88	87	6	0	0

McDONAGH William (Willie)
Born: Dublin, Republic of Ireland, 14 March, 1983 — M

League Club	Source	Date Signed	Seasons Played	Apps	Subs	Gls
Carlisle U	Bohemians (ROI)	10/01	01-03	40	23	4

McDONALD Alan
Born: Belfast, Northern Ireland, 12 October, 1963 — CD
Died: Lisburn, Belfast, Northern Ireland, 23 June, 2012
Northern Ireland: 52/Youth/Schools

League Club	Source	Date Signed	Seasons Played	Apps	Subs	Gls
Queens Park Rgrs	App	08/81	83-96	395	7	13
Charlton Ath	L	03/83	82	9	0	0
Swindon T	Tr	07/97	97	30	3	1

MacDONALD Alexander (Alex)
Born: Warrington, Cheshire, England, 14 April, 1990 — W
Scotland: U21-6/Youth

League Club	Source	Date Signed	Seasons Played	Apps	Subs	Gls
Burnley	Sch	06/08	07-12	0	11	0
Plymouth Arg	L	01/12	11	15	3	4
Plymouth Arg	L	08/12	12	14	2	1
Burton A	Tr	01/13	12-14	51	20	7
Oxford U	Tr	02/15	14	14	1	3

MacDONALD Angus Lees
Born: Winchester, Hampshire, England, 15 October, 1992 — CD

League Club	Source	Date Signed	Seasons Played	Apps	Subs	Gls
Reading	Sch	07/11				
Torquay U	L	02/12	11	1	1	0
AFC Wimbledon	L	07/12	12	2	2	0
Torquay U	L	11/12	12	10	4	0

MacDONALD Charles Lea (Charlie)
Born: Southwark, S London, England, 13 February, 1981 — F

League Club	Source	Date Signed	Seasons Played	Apps	Subs	Gls
Charlton Ath	YT	11/98	99-01	1	7	1
Cheltenham T	L	03/01	00	7	1	2
Torquay U	L	02/02	01	5	0	0
Colchester U	L	03/02	01	2	2	1
Southend U	Gravesend & Northfleet	07/07	07	11	14	1
Brentford	Tr	08/08	08-11	105	6	40
MK Dons	Tr	08/11	11-12	36	18	11
Leyton Orient	Tr	01/13	12	17	3	3
Oldham Ath	Tr	07/13	13	15	15	5

McDONALD Christopher William (Chris)
Born: Edinburgh, Scotland, 14 October, 1975 — M/D
Scotland: Schools

League Club	Source	Date Signed	Seasons Played	Apps	Subs	Gls
Arsenal	YT	12/93				
Stoke C	Tr	08/95				
Hartlepool U	Tr	08/96	96-98	18	2	0

McDONALD Clayton Rodney
Born: Liverpool, England, 26 December, 1988 — CD

League Club	Source	Date Signed	Seasons Played	Apps	Subs	Gls
Manchester C	Sch	07/07				
Macclesfield T	L	08/08	08	2	0	0
Chesterfield	L	02/09	08	1	1	0
Walsall	Tr	09/09	09-10	31	9	1
Port Vale	Tr	07/11	11-12	43	9	0
Bristol Rov	L	01/13	12	4	2	0
Tranmere Rov	Tr	08/14	14	0	1	0

McDONALD Cody Darren John
Born: Witham, Essex, England, 30 May, 1986 — F

League Club	Source	Date Signed	Seasons Played	Apps	Subs	Gls
Norwich C	Dartford	02/09	08-09	5	19	4
Gillingham	L	07/10	10	41	0	25
Coventry C	Tr	08/11	11-12	25	18	7
Gillingham	L	01/13	12	6	1	4
Gillingham	Tr	07/13	13-14	73	14	33

McDONALD Colin
Born: Edinburgh, Scotland, 10 April, 1974 — F
Scotland: U21-5/Schools

League Club	Source	Date Signed	Seasons Played	Apps	Subs	Gls
Swansea C	Falkirk	03/96	95-96	6	12	0

McDONALD Colin Agnew
Born: Ramsbottom, Greater Manchester, England, 15 October, 1930 — G
England: 8/FLge-3

League Club	Source	Date Signed	Seasons Played	Apps	Subs	Gls
Burnley	Hawkshaw St Mary's	10/48	53-58	186	-	0

McDONALD Colin Barry
Born: Norwich, England, 15 May, 1950 — M

League Club	Source	Date Signed	Seasons Played	Apps	Subs	Gls
Norwich C	App	07/67	67	4	0	0
Scunthorpe U	Tr	07/70	70-72	77	8	11

McDONALD Curtis Earl
Born: Cardiff, Wales, 24 March, 1988 — LB/M
Wales: U21-3/Youth

League Club	Source	Date Signed	Seasons Played	Apps	Subs	Gls
Cardiff C	Sch	11/06	05	0	1	0

McDONALD David Anderson
Born: Dundee, Scotland, 9 May, 1931 — G

League Club	Source	Date Signed	Seasons Played	Apps	Subs	Gls
Crystal Palace	Dundee Violet	03/51	52-54	30	-	0

McDONALD David Hugh
Born: Dublin, Republic of Ireland, 2 January, 1971 — RB
Republic of Ireland: B/U21-3/Youth/Schools

League Club	Source	Date Signed	Seasons Played	Apps	Subs	Gls
Tottenham H	YT	08/88	92	2	0	0
Gillingham	L	09/90	90	10	0	0
Bradford C	L	08/92	92	7	0	0
Reading	L	03/93	92	11	0	0
Peterborough U	Tr	08/93	93	28	1	0
Barnet	Tr	03/94	93-97	86	10	0

McDONALD Dean Louis
Born: Lambeth, S London, England, 19 February, 1986 — F

League Club	Source	Date Signed	Seasons Played	Apps	Subs	Gls
Ipswich T	Arsenal (Sch)	02/05	05	4	10	1
Hartlepool U	L	11/05	05	4	1	1
Gillingham	Tr	07/06	06	16	10	6

MacDONALD Garry
Born: Middlesbrough, England, 26 March, 1962 — F/D

League Club	Source	Date Signed	Seasons Played	Apps	Subs	Gls
Middlesbrough	App	03/80	80-83	40	13	5
Carlisle U	Tr	07/84	84	7	2	0
Darlington	Tr	10/84	84-88	153	9	35
Stockport Co	Tr	07/89	89	1	0	0
Hartlepool U	Tr	12/89	89-90	10	8	1

McDONALD Gary
Born: Sunderland, England, 20 November, 1969 — F

League Club	Source	Date Signed	Seasons Played	Apps	Subs	Gls
Mansfield T	Ipswich T (YT)	08/89	89	1	1	0

MacDONALD Gary
Born: Iserlohn, Germany, 25 October, 1979 — CD

League Club	Source	Date Signed	Seasons Played	Apps	Subs	Gls
Portsmouth	YT	07/98				
Peterborough U	Havant & Waterlooville	02/01	00-02	13	4	1

McDONALD Gary Matthew
Born: Irvine, Ayrshire, Scotland, 10 April, 1982 — M
Scotland: B-1

League Club	Source	Date Signed	Seasons Played	Apps	Subs	Gls
Oldham Ath	Kilmarnock	07/06	06-07	70	8	11
Morecambe	Hamilton Academical	06/11	11-12	79	6	6

McDONALD Gavin James
Born: Salford, England, 6 October, 1970 — F

League Club	Source	Date Signed	Seasons Played	Apps	Subs	Gls
Chesterfield	YT	-	88	5	7	1

McDONALD Gerard (Gerry)
Born: Milnthorpe, Cumbria, England, 3 December, 1952 — M
Died: Preston, Lancashire, England, April, 2005

League Club	Source	Date Signed	Seasons Played	Apps	Subs	Gls
Blackburn Rov	App	12/70	71	19	2	2
Halifax T	Tr	08/73	73	10	3	0

McDONALD Gordon
Born: Hampstead, NW London, England, 7 February, 1932 — LB
Died: Hastings, East Sussex, England, 1995

League Club	Source	Date Signed	Seasons Played	Apps	Subs	Gls
Crystal Palace	Eastbourne	12/54	54-56	13	-	0
Swindon T	Tr	07/57	57	10	-	0

McDONALD Harry
Born: Salford, England, 11 September, 1926 — LB
Died: Horton Kirby, Kent, England, 16 December, 2004

League Club	Source	Date Signed	Seasons Played	Apps	Subs	Gls
Crystal Palace	Ashton U	09/50	50-54	140	-	1

McDONALD Ian
Born: Inverness, Scotland, 5 February, 1951 — M

League Club	Source	Date Signed	Seasons Played	Apps	Subs	Gls
Wolverhampton W	Jnr	08/68				
Darlington	Tr	09/70	70	21	4	3

MacDONALD Ian Campbell Aitken
Born: Rinteln, Germany, 30 August, 1953 — CD

League Club	Source	Date Signed	Seasons Played	Apps	Subs	Gls
Carlisle U	St Johnstone	05/76	76-80	186	1	7

McDONALD Ian Clifford
Born: Barrow, Cumbria, England, 10 May, 1953 — M

League Club	Source	Date Signed	Seasons Played	Apps	Subs	Gls
Barrow	App	05/71	70-71	31	5	2
Workington	Tr	02/73	72-73	42	0	4
Liverpool	Tr	01/74				
Colchester U	L	02/75	74	5	0	2
Mansfield T	Tr	07/75	75-76	47	9	4
York C	Tr	11/77	77-81	175	0	29
Aldershot	Tr	11/81	81-88	340	0	50

MacDONALD Jack
Born: Liverpool, England, 1 September, 1921 — LB
Died: Liverpool, England, December, 1999

League Club	Source	Date Signed	Seasons Played	Apps	Subs	Gls
Liverpool		08/44				
Tranmere Rov	Tr	06/49	49-51	89	-	0

McDONALD James
Born: Greenock, Inverclyde, Scotland, 18 April, 1932 — W

League Club	Source	Date Signed	Seasons Played	Apps	Subs	Gls
Gillingham	Dumbarton	08/56	56	1	-	0

MacDONALD John
Born: Glasgow, Scotland, 15 April, 1961 — F
Scotland: U21-8/Youth/Schools

League Club	Source	Date Signed	Seasons Played	Apps	Subs	Gls
Charlton Ath (L)	Glasgow Rangers	09/86	86	2	0	0
Barnsley	Glasgow Rangers	11/86	86-89	87	7	20
Scarborough	Tr	11/89	89-90	39	1	6

McDONALD John Christopher (Jack)
Born: Maltby, South Yorkshire, England, 27 August, 1921 — LW
Died: Ryde, Isle of Wight, England, 28 June, 2007

League Club	Source	Date Signed	Seasons Played	Apps	Subs	Gls
Wolverhampton W	Jnr	09/38	38	2	-	0
Bournemouth	Tr	05/39	46-47	80	-	36
Fulham	Tr	06/48	48-51	75	-	19
Southampton	Tr	08/52	52	16	-	4
Southend U	Tr	05/53	53-54	28	-	6

MacDONALD John Sutherland
Born: Edinburgh, Scotland, 23 September, 1922 — LB

League Club	Source	Date Signed	Seasons Played	Apps	Subs	Gls
Notts Co	Carshalton Ath	08/48	48	1	-	0
Queens Park Rgrs	Tr	03/49				

McDONALD Joseph (Joe)
Born: Blantyre, Lanarkshire, Scotland, 10 February, 1929 — LB
Died: Australia, 7 September, 2003
Scotland: 2

League Club	Source	Date Signed	Seasons Played	Apps	Subs	Gls
Sunderland	Falkirk	03/54	53-57	137	-	1
Nottingham F	Tr	07/58	58-60	109	-	0

McDONALD Kevin David
Born: Carnoustie, Angus, Scotland, 4 November, 1988 — M
Scotland: U21-14/Youth

League Club	Source	Date Signed	Seasons Played	Apps	Subs	Gls
Burnley	Dundee	07/08	08-09	24	27	2
Scunthorpe U	L	10/10	10	3	2	1
Notts Co	L	02/11	10	10	1	0
Sheffield U	Tr	08/11	11-13	76	1	5
Wolverhampton W	Tr	08/13	13-14	84	3	5

MacDONALD Kevin Duncan
Born: Inverness, Scotland, 22 November, 1960 — M

League Club	Source	Date Signed	Seasons Played	Apps	Subs	Gls
Leicester C	Inverness CT	05/80	80-84	133	5	8
Liverpool	Tr	11/84	84-88	29	11	1
Leicester C	L	12/87	87	3	0	0
Coventry C	Tr	07/89	89-90	26	5	0
Cardiff C	L	03/91	90	8	0	0
Walsall	Tr	07/91	91-92	48	5	6

MacDONALD Leslie (Les)
Born: Newcastle-upon-Tyne, England, 2 April, 1934 — LB
Died: Portchester, Hampshire, England, 19 August, 2014

League Club	Source	Date Signed	Seasons Played	Apps	Subs	Gls
Portsmouth	Jnr	05/55				
Exeter C	Tr	06/57	57-65	294	0	0

McDONALD Malcolm
Born: Glasgow, Scotland, 26 October, 1913 — RB
Died: Bonnyrigg, Scotland, Scotland, 26 September, 1999
Scotland: SLge-1/War-3

League Club	Source	Date Signed	Seasons Played	Apps	Subs	Gls
Brentford	Kilmarnock	10/46	46-48	87	-	1

MACDONALD Malcolm Ian
Born: Fulham, W London, England, 7 January, 1950 — F
England: 14/FLge-1/U23-4

League Club	Source	Date Signed	Seasons Played	Apps	Subs	Gls
Fulham	Tonbridge	08/68	68	10	3	5
Luton T	Tr	07/69	69-70	88	0	49
Newcastle U	Tr	05/71	71-75	187	0	95
Arsenal	Tr	08/76	76-78	84	0	42

MacDONALD Martin
Born: Kilsyth, Lanarkshire, Scotland, 5 September, 1931 — RH

League Club	Source	Date Signed	Seasons Played	Apps	Subs	Gls
Portsmouth	Jnr	11/48				
Bournemouth	Tr	11/51	52-55	51	-	1

McDONALD Martin Joseph
Born: Irvine, Ayrshire, Scotland, 4 December, 1973 — M
England: Semi Pro-1

League Club	Source	Date Signed	Seasons Played	Apps	Subs	Gls
Stockport Co	Bramhall	08/92				
Doncaster Rov	Southport	08/96	96-97	48	0	4
Macclesfield T	Tr	12/97	97-98	45	0	3

McDONALD Michael Flynn (Mike)
Born: Glasgow, Scotland, 8 November, 1950 — G

League Club	Source	Date Signed	Seasons Played	Apps	Subs	Gls
Stoke C	Clydebank	10/72	72-73	5	0	0

McDONALD Neil
Born: Barrow, Cumbria, England, 27 May, 1954 — F

League Club	Source	Date Signed	Seasons Played	Apps	Subs	Gls
Workington	Barrow	03/77	76	5	1	0

McDONALD Neil Raymond
Born: Willington Quay, Tyne and Wear, England, 2 November, 1965 — RB/M
England: U21-5/Youth/Schools

League Club	Source	Date Signed	Seasons Played	Apps	Subs	Gls
Newcastle U	App	02/83	82-87	163	17	24
Everton	Tr	08/88	88-91	76	14	4
Oldham Ath	Tr	10/91	91-93	19	5	1
Bolton W	Tr	07/94	94	4	0	0
Preston NE	Tr	11/95	95-96	20	13	0

McDONALD Paul Thomas
Born: Motherwell, Lanarkshire, Scotland, 20 April, 1968 — LW

League Club	Source	Date Signed	Seasons Played	Apps	Subs	Gls
Southampton	Hamilton Academical	06/93	94-95	0	3	0
Burnley	L	09/95	95	8	1	1
Brighton & HA	Tr	02/96	95-97	52	9	5

McDONALD Richard Robertson (Rikki)
Born: Paisley, Renfrewshire, Scotland, 18 December, 1933 — CF
Died: Paisley, Renfrewshire, Scotland, 6 April, 2003

League Club	Source	Date Signed	Seasons Played	Apps	Subs	Gls
Barnsley	Saltcoats Victoria	12/57	58	1	-	0

MacDONALD Robert (Bob)
Born: Old Kilpatrick, Dunbartonshire, Scotland, 26 October, 1935 — RB

League Club	Source	Date Signed	Seasons Played	Apps	Subs	Gls
Manchester C	Vale of Leven	09/56	61	5	-	0
Bournemouth	Tr	09/63	63	1	-	0

McDONALD Robert Roderick (Rob)
Born: Hull, England, 22 January, 1959 — F

League Club	Source	Date Signed	Seasons Played	Apps	Subs	Gls
Hull C	App	01/77	76-79	17	8	2
Newcastle U	Racing Jet (BEL)	11/88	88	6	4	1

McDONALD Robert Wood (Bobby)
Born: Aberdeen, Scotland, 13 April, 1955 — LB

League Club	Source	Date Signed	Seasons Played	Apps	Subs	Gls
Aston Villa	App	09/72	72-75	33	6	3
Coventry C	Tr	08/76	76-80	161	0	14
Manchester C	Tr	10/80	80-82	96	0	11
Oxford U	Tr	09/83	83-86	93	1	14
Leeds U	Tr	02/87	86-87	18	0	1
Wolverhampton W	L	02/88	87	6	0	0

McDONALD Rodney (Rod)
Born: Westminster, Central London, England, 20 March, 1967 — F

League Club	Source	Date Signed	Seasons Played	Apps	Subs	Gls
Walsall	Colne Dynamoes	08/90	90-93	142	7	41
Chester C	Southport	11/96	96-97	43	10	11

McDONALD Roger Brown
Born: Glasgow, Scotland, 2 February, 1933 — FB
Died: Glasgow, Scotland, 22 October, 1996

League Club	Source	Date Signed	Seasons Played	Apps	Subs	Gls
Mansfield T	St Mirren	03/55	54-55	13	-	0
Crystal Palace	Cheltenham T	01/58				

McDONALD Scott Douglas
Born: Melbourne, Australia, 21 August, 1983 — F
Australia: 26/U23-2/Youth

League Club	Source	Date Signed	Seasons Played	Apps	Subs	Gls
Southampton	Eastern Pride (AUS)	08/00	01	0	2	0
Huddersfield T	L	07/02	02	7	6	1
Bournemouth	Tr	03/03	02	3	4	1
Wimbledon	Tr	08/03	03	0	2	0
Middlesbrough	Glasgow Celtic	02/10	09-12	102	14	37
Millwall	Tr	07/13	13-14	44	12	5

McDONALD Shaquille Alphonso (Shaq)
Born: Birmingham, England, 19 July, 1995 — F

League Club	Source	Date Signed	Seasons Played	Apps	Subs	Gls
Peterborough U	Chasetown	12/12				
York C	Tr	01/14				
Derby Co	Tr	07/14				
Cheltenham T	L	03/15	14	3	1	0

MacDONALD Shaun Benjamin
Born: Swansea, Wales, 17 June, 1988 — M
Wales: 1/U21-25/Youth

League Club	Source	Date Signed	Seasons Played	Apps	Subs	Gls
Swansea C	Sch	04/06	05-09	9	15	0
Yeovil T	L	01/09	08	4	0	2
Yeovil T	L	09/09	09	31	0	3
Yeovil T	L	08/10	10	15	0	0
Yeovil T	L	03/11	10	11	0	4
Bournemouth	Tr	08/11	11-14	55	26	1

MacDONALD Sherjill
Born: Amsterdam, Netherlands, 20 November, 1984 — F
Netherlands: U21-2

League Club	Source	Date Signed	Seasons Played	Apps	Subs	Gls
West Bromwich A	Apeldoorn (NED)	01/07	06-08	0	24	0
Hereford U	L	02/08	07	7	0	6

McDONALD Terence (Terry)
Born: Belfast, Northern Ireland, 5 February, 1947 — RB

League Club	Source	Date Signed	Seasons Played	Apps	Subs	Gls
Middlesbrough	Jnr	02/64				
Southport	Tr	07/65	65-66	33	0	1
Barrow	Tr	07/67	67-68	34	1	0

McDONALD Terence James (Terry)
Born: Limehouse, E London, England, 12 November, 1938 — LW
England: Youth

League Club	Source	Date Signed	Seasons Played	Apps	Subs	Gls
West Ham U	Jnr	04/56				
Leyton Orient	Tr	07/59	59-64	152	-	23
Reading	Tr	05/65	65	13	0	2

McDONALD Thomas (Tom)
Born: Walthamstow, NE London, England, 15 September, 1980 — RB

League Club	Source	Date Signed	Seasons Played	Apps	Subs	Gls
Southend U	YT	08/99	99-00	1	3	0

McDONALD Thomas (Tommy)
Born: Cowdenbeath, Fife, Scotland, 24 May, 1930 — RW
Died: Dunfermline, Fife, Scotland, 24 August, 2004
Scotland: B-1

League Club	Source	Date Signed	Seasons Played	Apps	Subs	Gls
Wolverhampton W	Hibernian	04/54	54-55	5	-	1
Leicester C	Tr	07/56	56-59	113	-	27

McDONALD William Love
Born: Longriggend, Lanarkshire, Scotland, 30 August, 1918 — WH
Died: Carlisle, Cumbria, England, February, 1997

League Club	Source	Date Signed	Seasons Played	Apps	Subs	Gls
Carlisle U	Airdrieonians	08/46	46	3	-	0

McDONNELL Charles (Charlie)
Born: Birkenhead, Wirral, England, 15 July, 1936 — IF
Died: Birkenhead, Wirral, England, 7 June, 2010

League Club	Source	Date Signed	Seasons Played	Apps	Subs	Gls
Tranmere Rov	Stork	09/57	57-60	68	-	26
Stockport Co	Tr	06/61	61-63	84	-	32
Tranmere Rov	Tr	10/63	63-64	45	-	25
Southport	Tr	07/65	65	10	0	1

McDONNELL Joseph Patrick (Joe)
Born: Basingstoke, Hampshire, England, 19 May, 1994 — G

League Club	Source	Date Signed	Seasons Played	Apps	Subs	Gls
AFC Wimbledon	Basingstoke T	07/14	14	3	1	0

McDONNELL Martin Henry
Born: Newton-le-Willows, Merseyside, England, 27 April, 1924 — CH
Died: Bedford, England, 7 April, 1988

League Club	Source	Date Signed	Seasons Played	Apps	Subs	Gls
Everton	Haydock C&B	08/42				
Southport	Earlestown	08/46	46	38	-	0
Birmingham C	Tr	05/47	47-49	32	-	0
Coventry C	Tr	10/49	49-54	232	-	0
Derby Co	Tr	07/55	55-57	93	-	0
Crewe Alex	Tr	07/58	58	17	-	0

McDONNELL Peter Anthony
Born: Kendal, Cumbria, England, 11 June, 1953 — G

League Club	Source	Date Signed	Seasons Played	Apps	Subs	Gls
Bury	Netherfield	10/73	73	1	0	0
Liverpool	Tr	08/74				
Oldham Ath	Tr	08/78	78-81	137	0	0

McDONOUGH Darron Karl
Born: Antwerp, Belgium, 7 November, 1962 — M/CD

League Club	Source	Date Signed	Seasons Played	Apps	Subs	Gls
Oldham Ath	App	01/80	80-86	178	5	14
Luton T	Tr	09/86	86-91	88	17	5
Newcastle U	Tr	03/92	91	2	1	0

McDONOUGH Roy
Born: Solihull, West Midlands, England, 16 October, 1958 — F

League Club	Source	Date Signed	Seasons Played	Apps	Subs	Gls
Birmingham C	App	10/76	76	2	0	1
Walsall	Tr	09/78	78-80	76	6	15
Chelsea	Tr	10/80				
Colchester U	Tr	02/81	80-82	89	4	24
Southend U	Tr	08/83	83	22	0	4
Exeter C	Tr	01/84	83-84	19	1	1
Cambridge U	Tr	10/84	84	30	2	5
Southend U	Tr	08/85	85-89	163	23	30
Colchester U	Tr	10/90	92-93	57	6	16

McDOUGALD David Eugene Junior (Junior)
Born: Big Spring, Texas, USA, 12 January, 1975 — F
England: Youth

League Club	Source	Date Signed	Seasons Played	Apps	Subs	Gls
Tottenham H	YT	07/93				
Brighton & HA	Tr	05/94	94-95	71	7	14
Chesterfield	L	03/96	95	9	0	3
Rotherham U	Tr	07/96	96	14	4	2
Millwall	Cambridge C	07/98	98	0	1	0
Leyton Orient	Tr	10/98	98	3	5	0

MacDOUGALL Edward John (Ted)
Born: Inverness, Scotland, 8 January, 1947 — F
Scotland: 7

League Club	Source	Date Signed	Seasons Played	Apps	Subs	Gls
Liverpool	ICI Rec	01/66				
York C	Tr	07/67	67-68	84	0	34
Bournemouth	Tr	07/69	69-72	146	0	103
Manchester U	Tr	09/72	72	18	0	5
West Ham U	Tr	03/73	72-73	24	0	5
Norwich C	Tr	12/73	73-76	112	0	51
Southampton	Tr	09/76	76-78	86	0	42
Bournemouth	Tr	11/78	78-79	51	1	16
Blackpool	Tr	03/80	79-80	11	2	0

McDOUGALL Laybourne
Born: Tynemouth, Tyne and Wear, England, 12 May, 1917 — FB
Died: Blyth, Northumberland, England, 28 January, 1994

League Club	Source	Date Signed	Seasons Played	Apps	Subs	Gls
Derby Co		02/35				
Carlisle U	Tr	06/37	37	3	-	0
Preston NE	Tr	03/38				
Blackpool	Tr	05/39				
Gateshead	Tr	10/46	46-48	60	-	0

McDOWALL Daniel (Danny)
Born: Kirkintilloch, Dunbartonshire, Scotland, 22 May, 1929 — IF
Died: Whitehaven, Cumbria, England, February, 2000

League Club	Source	Date Signed	Seasons Played	Apps	Subs	Gls
Middlesbrough	Kirkintilloch Rob Roy	02/47				
Workington	Glasgow Celtic	08/51	51-52	82	-	23
Lincoln C	Tr	07/53	53	17	-	4
Millwall	Tr	06/54	54-55	10	-	1

MacDOWALL Duncan John
Born: Paddington, Central London, England, 18 December, 1963 — F

League Club	Source	Date Signed	Seasons Played	Apps	Subs	Gls
Birmingham C	App	08/81	81	2	0	0

McDOWALL James Cowan (Jim)
Born: Glasgow, Scotland, 25 October, 1940 — G

League Club	Source	Date Signed	Seasons Played	Apps	Subs	Gls
Notts Co	Baillieston Jnrs	09/59				
Scunthorpe U	Boston U	12/61	61	1	-	0

McDOWALL Kenneth Francis (Ken)
Born: Manchester, England, 6 May, 1938 — LW

League Club	Source	Date Signed	Seasons Played	Apps	Subs	Gls
Manchester U	Rhyl	09/59				
Rochdale	Tr	10/60	60	6	-	0

McDOWALL Leslie John (Les)
Born: Gunga Pur, India, 25 October, 1912 — CD
Died: Tarporley, Cheshire, England, 18 August, 1991

League Club	Source	Date Signed	Seasons Played	Apps	Subs	Gls
Sunderland	Glentyne Thistle	12/32	34-37	13	-	0
Manchester C	Tr	03/38	37-48	117	-	8
Wrexham	Tr	11/49	49	3	-	0

McDOWELL John Alfred
Born: East Ham, E London, England, 7 September, 1951 — RB
England: U23-13/Youth

League Club	Source	Date Signed	Seasons Played	Apps	Subs	Gls
West Ham U	App	08/69	70-78	243	6	8
Norwich C	Tr	08/79	79-80	40	1	1

McEACHRAN Joshua Mark (Josh)
Born: Oxford, England, 1 March, 1993 — M
England: U21-15/Youth

League Club	Source	Date Signed	Seasons Played	Apps	Subs	Gls
Chelsea	Sch	07/10	10-11	1	10	0
Swansea C	L	01/12	11	1	3	0
Middlesbrough	L	08/12	12	35	3	0
Watford	L	09/13	13	5	2	0
Wigan Ath	L	01/14	13	5	3	0

McELHATTON Michael Terrence (Mike)
Born: Killarney, Republic of Ireland, 16 April, 1975 — M
Republic of Ireland: Schools

League Club	Source	Date Signed	Seasons Played	Apps	Subs	Gls
Bournemouth	YT	07/93	92-95	21	21	2
Scarborough	Tr	09/96	96-97	64	6	7
Rushden & D	Tr	07/98	01	4	3	1

McELHINNEY Gerard (Gerry)
Born: Derry, Northern Ireland, 19 September, 1956 — CD
Northern Ireland: 6

League Club	Source	Date Signed	Seasons Played	Apps	Subs	Gls
Bolton W	Distillery	09/80	80-84	107	2	2
Rochdale	L	11/82	82	20	0	1
Plymouth Arg	Tr	01/85	84-87	90	1	2
Peterborough U	Tr	08/88	88-90	87	0	1

McELHOLM Brendan Anthony
Born: Omagh, Tyrone, Northern Ireland, 7 July, 1982 — CD
Northern Ireland: Youth

League Club	Source	Date Signed	Seasons Played	Apps	Subs	Gls
Leyton Orient	YT	07/00	99-01	6	11	0

McELVANEY David Anthony
Born: Chesterfield, Derbyshire, England, 3 November, 1954 — M

League Club	Source	Date Signed	Seasons Played	Apps	Subs	Gls
Chesterfield	Derbyshire Times	10/75	75	4	0	1

McEVELEY James Michael (Jay)
Born: Liverpool, England, 11 February, 1985 — LB
England: U21-1//Scotland: 3/B-1

League Club	Source	Date Signed	Seasons Played	Apps	Subs	Gls
Blackburn Rov	Sch	07/02	02-06	17	1	0
Burnley	L	12/03	03	0	4	0
Gillingham	L	03/05	04	10	0	1
Ipswich T	L	08/05	05	17	2	1
Derby Co	Tr	01/07	06-09	77	15	4
Preston NE	L	09/08	08	7	0	0
Charlton Ath	L	11/08	08	6	0	0
Barnsley	Tr	07/10	10-11	40	6	1
Swindon T	Tr	03/12	11-13	66	2	0
Sheffield U	Tr	08/14	14	31	3	1

McEVILLY Lee Richard
Born: Liverpool, England, 15 April, 1982 — F
Northern Ireland: 1/U23-1/U21-9

League Club	Source	Date Signed	Seasons Played	Apps	Subs	Gls
Rochdale	Burscough	12/01	01-03	55	30	25
Wrexham	Accrington Stan	07/05	05-06	33	18	14
Accrington Stan	Tr	07/07	07	3	8	0
Rochdale	L	11/07	07	3	4	3
Rochdale	Cambridge U	11/08	08	4	12	5

McEVOY Donald William (Don)
Born: Golcar, West Yorkshire, England, 3 December, 1928 — CH
Died: Halifax, West Yorkshire, England, 9 October, 2004

League Club	Source	Date Signed	Seasons Played	Apps	Subs	Gls
Huddersfield T	Bradley U	09/47	49-54	148	-	3
Sheffield Wed	Tr	12/54	54-57	105	-	1
Lincoln C	Tr	01/59	58-59	23	-	0
Barrow	Tr	07/60	60-61	74	-	1

McEVOY Kenneth (Kenny)
Born: Waterford, Republic of Ireland, 4 September, 1994 — RM
Republic of Ireland: U21-3/Youth

League Club	Source	Date Signed	Seasons Played	Apps	Subs	Gls
Tottenham H	Sch	07/13				
Peterborough U	L	07/14	14	2	5	1
Colchester U	L	01/15	14	0	1	0

McEVOY Matthew Andrew (Andy)
Born: Dublin, Republic of Ireland, 15 July, 1938 — IF/WH
Died: Bray, Republic of Ireland, 7 May, 1994
Republic of Ireland: 17/LoI-4

League Club	Source	Date Signed	Seasons Played	Apps	Subs	Gls
Blackburn Rov	Bray W (ROI)	10/56	58-66	183	0	89

McEVOY Richard Patrick (Ricky)
Born: Gibraltar, 6 August, 1967 — M
Republic of Ireland: Youth

League Club	Source	Date Signed	Seasons Played	Apps	Subs	Gls
Luton T	App	08/85	86	0	1	0
Cambridge U	L	02/87	86	10	1	1

MacEWAN James (Jimmy)
Born: Dundee, Scotland, 22 March, 1929 — W

League Club	Source	Date Signed	Seasons Played	Apps	Subs	Gls
Aston Villa	Raith Rov	07/59	59-65	143	0	28
Walsall	Tr	08/66	66	10	0	1

MacEWAN Malcolm Peter (Peter)
Born: Johannesburg, South Africa, 23 May, 1933 — CF

League Club	Source	Date Signed	Seasons Played	Apps	Subs	Gls
Luton T	Germiston Cal'n (RSA)	02/54	53-55	26	-	11

McEWAN Stanley (Stan)
Born: Wishaw, Lanarkshire, Scotland, 8 June, 1957 — CD/M

League Club	Source	Date Signed	Seasons Played	Apps	Subs	Gls
Blackpool	App	07/74	74-81	204	10	24
Exeter C	Tr	07/82	82-83	65	0	15
Hull C	Tr	03/84	83-87	113	0	25
Wigan Ath	Tr	12/87	87-88	26	3	4
Hartlepool U	Tr	08/89	89	14	0	2

McEWAN Stephen (Steve)
Born: Selkirk, Borders, Scotland, 28 March, 1930 — IF

League Club	Source	Date Signed	Seasons Played	Apps	Subs	Gls
Liverpool	Bournemouth (Am)	07/50				
Accrington Stan	Tr	08/51	51	2	-	1

McEWAN William (Billy)
Born: Glasgow, Scotland, 29 August, 1914 — W
Died: Gravesend, Kent, England, December, 1991

League Club	Source	Date Signed	Seasons Played	Apps	Subs	Gls
Queens Park Rgrs	Petershill	06/38	38-49	96	-	17
Leyton Orient	Tr	02/50	49-50	21	-	3

McEWAN William Johnston McGowan (Billy)
Born: Cleland, Lanarkshire, Scotland, 20 June, 1951 — M

League Club	Source	Date Signed	Seasons Played	Apps	Subs	Gls
Blackpool	Hibernian	05/73	73	4	0	0
Brighton & HA	Tr	02/74	73-74	27	0	3
Chesterfield	Tr	11/74	74-76	79	1	7
Mansfield T	Tr	01/77	76-77	32	0	3
Peterborough U	Tr	11/77	77-78	62	1	3
Rotherham U	Tr	07/79	79-83	86	9	10

McEWEN David (Dave)
Born: Westminster, Central London, England, 2 November, 1977 — F

League Club	Source	Date Signed	Seasons Played	Apps	Subs	Gls
Tottenham H	Dulwich Hamlet	01/00	99-00	0	4	0
Queens Park Rgrs	Tr	07/01	01	2	3	0

McEWEN Francis Kevin (Frank)
Born: Dublin, Republic of Ireland, 15 February, 1948 — M
Republic of Ireland: LoI-1/U23-1

League Club	Source	Date Signed	Seasons Played	Apps	Subs	Gls
Manchester U	App	05/65				
Rochdale	Tr	11/66	66-67	17	0	2

McFADDEN Anthony (Tony)
Born: Hexham, Northumberland, England, 18 May, 1957 — F

League Club	Source	Date Signed	Seasons Played	Apps	Subs	Gls
Darlington	Reyrolles	08/81	81-82	44	3	10

McFADDEN James Henry
Born: Glasgow, Scotland, 14 April, 1983 — F
Scotland: 48/B-1/U21-7

League Club	Source	Date Signed	Seasons Played	Apps	Subs	Gls
Everton	Motherwell	09/03	03-07	53	56	11
Birmingham C	Tr	01/08	07-10	67	15	13
Everton	Tr	10/11	11	2	5	0
Sunderland	Tr	10/12	12	0	3	0

McFADZEAN Callum Jeffrey
Born: Sheffield, England, 16 January, 1994 — LB/M
England: Youth//Scotland: U21-1

League Club	Source	Date Signed	Seasons Played	Apps	Subs	Gls
Sheffield U	Sch	01/11	12-13	5	10	0
Chesterfield	L	11/13	13	2	2	0
Burton A	L	03/14	13	7	0	1
Burton A	L	07/14	14	7	2	1

McFADZEAN Clive Stuart
Born: Kilmarnock, Ayrshire, Scotland, 11 March, 1958 — F

League Club	Source	Date Signed	Seasons Played	Apps	Subs	Gls
Bradford C	App	03/76	75-76	3	1	2

McFADZEAN John Paul
Born: Sheffield, England, 2 April, 1966 — F

League Club	Source	Date Signed	Seasons Played	Apps	Subs	Gls
Rotherham U	App	-	83	0	1	0

McFADZEAN Kyle John
Born: Sheffield, England, 20 February, 1987 — LB
England: Semi Pro-3

League Club	Source	Date Signed	Seasons Played	Apps	Subs	Gls
Sheffield U	Sch	07/04				
Crawley T	Alfreton T	08/10	11-13	94	2	6
MK Dons	Tr	06/14	14	41	0	3

McFALL David Patrick (Dave)
Born: Ballymena, Antrim, Northern Ireland, 14 March, 1935 — IF

League Club	Source	Date Signed	Seasons Played	Apps	Subs	Gls
Aldershot	Sittingbourne	10/58	58	3	-	0

McFARLAND Roy Leslie
Born: Liverpool, England, 5 April, 1948 — CD
England: 28/FLge-6/U23-5

League Club	Source	Date Signed	Seasons Played	Apps	Subs	Gls
Tranmere Rov	Edge Hill BC	07/66	66-67	35	0	0
Derby Co	Tr	08/67	67-80	434	0	44
Bradford C	Tr	06/81	81-82	40	0	1
Derby Co	Tr	08/83	83	3	5	0

McFARLANE Andrew Antonie (Andy)
Born: Wolverhampton, England, 30 November, 1966 — F

League Club	Source	Date Signed	Seasons Played	Apps	Subs	Gls
Portsmouth	Cradley T	11/90	91	0	2	0
Swansea C	Tr	08/92	92-94	33	22	8
Scunthorpe U	Tr	08/95	95-96	48	12	19
Torquay U	Tr	01/97	96-98	42	14	11

McFARLANE Ian
Born: Lanark, Scotland, 26 January, 1933 — FB

League Club	Source	Date Signed	Seasons Played	Apps	Subs	Gls
Chelsea	Aberdeen	08/56	56-57	40	-	0
Leicester C	Tr	05/58	58	1	-	0

McFARLANE Robert Robertson (Bobby)
Born: Bo'ness, Falkirk, Scotland, 12 October, 1913 — WH
Died: Doncaster, South Yorkshire, England, 1971

League Club	Source	Date Signed	Seasons Played	Apps	Subs	Gls
Arsenal	Margate	03/36				
Doncaster Rov	Tr	05/37	37-47	131	-	4

McFARLANE William Noel (Noel)
Born: Bray, Republic of Ireland, 20 December, 1934 — W

League Club	Source	Date Signed	Seasons Played	Apps	Subs	Gls
Manchester U	Jnr	04/52	53	1	-	0

McFAUL Shane
Born: Dublin, Republic of Ireland, 23 May, 1986 — M
Republic of Ireland: U21-1/Youth

League Club	Source	Date Signed	Seasons Played	Apps	Subs	Gls
Notts Co	Sch	02/04	03-04	19	11	0
Brighton & HA	UC Dublin (ROI)	01/08	07	0	1	0

McFAUL William Stewart (Iam)
Born: Coleraine, Derry, Northern Ireland, 1 October, 1943 — G
Northern Ireland: 6/Amateur

League Club	Source	Date Signed	Seasons Played	Apps	Subs	Gls
Newcastle U	Linfield	11/66	66-74	290	0	0

McFEAT Archibald (Archie)
Born: Kincardine, Fife, Scotland, 23 January, 1924 — G
Died: Falkirk, Scotland, 1 April, 1996

League Club	Source	Date Signed	Seasons Played	Apps	Subs	Gls
Torquay U	Dumbarton	05/48	48	9	-	0

McFLYNN Terence Martin (Terry)
Born: Magherafelt, Derry, Northern Ireland, 27 March, 1981 — M
Northern Ireland: U21-7/Youth/Schools

League Club	Source	Date Signed	Seasons Played	Apps	Subs	Gls
Queens Park Rgrs	YT	05/98	00	1	1	0

McGAHEY Harrison
Born: Preston, Lancashire, England, 26 September, 1995 — CD

League Club	Source	Date Signed	Seasons Played	Apps	Subs	Gls
Blackpool	Sch	04/14	13	4	0	0
Sheffield U	Tr	07/14	14	11	4	0
Tranmere Rov	L	02/15	14	2	2	0

McGAIRY Thomas (Tom)
Born: Glasgow, Scotland, 25 November, 1927 — IF

League Club	Source	Date Signed	Seasons Played	Apps	Subs	Gls
Walsall	Dumbarton	08/54	54	7	-	1

McGANN William Thomas Arden
Born: Wilmslow, Cheshire, England, 12 July, 1923 — FB
Died: Macclesfield, Cheshire, England, 2 September, 1986

League Club	Source	Date Signed	Seasons Played	Apps	Subs	Gls
Stockport Co		05/48	49-50	14	-	0
Bournemouth	Tr	07/51				

McGARRIGLE Dennis
Born: Luton, England, 4 November, 1936 — G
Died: Crewe, Cheshire, England, April, 2004

League Club	Source	Date Signed	Seasons Played	Apps	Subs	Gls
Bristol C	Gourock Jnrs	02/60				
Crewe Alex	Tr	06/60	60-61	12	-	0

McGARRIGLE Kevin
Born: Newcastle-upon-Tyne, England, 9 April, 1977 — CD

League Club	Source	Date Signed	Seasons Played	Apps	Subs	Gls
Brighton & HA	YT	07/94	93-96	34	11	1

McGARRITY Thomas Welsh (Tom)
Born: Scotstoun, Glasgow, Scotland, 24 November, 1922 — IF
Died: Oxford, England, 17 March, 1999

League Club	Source	Date Signed	Seasons Played	Apps	Subs	Gls
Southampton	Greenock Morton	11/52	52	5	-	1

McGARRY Ronald James (Ron)
Born: Whitehaven, Cumbria, England, 5 December, 1937 — IF

League Club	Source	Date Signed	Seasons Played	Apps	Subs	Gls
Workington	Whitehaven	10/58	58-61	93	-	26
Bolton W	Tr	02/62	61-62	27	-	7
Newcastle U	Tr	12/62	62-66	118	3	41
Barrow	Tr	03/67	66-67	30	0	4
Barrow	Balgownie (AUS)	09/70	70	14	3	4

McGARRY William Harry (Bill)
Born: Stoke-on-Trent, England, 10 June, 1927 — RH
Died: South Africa, 15 March, 2005
England: 4/B-1/FLge-1

League Club	Source	Date Signed	Seasons Played	Apps	Subs	Gls
Port Vale	Northwood Mission	06/45	46-50	146	-	5
Huddersfield T	Tr	03/51	50-60	363	-	25
Bournemouth	Tr	03/61	60-62	78	-	2

McGARVEY Scott Thomas
Born: Glasgow, Scotland, 22 April, 1963 — F
Scotland: U21-4

League Club	Source	Date Signed	Seasons Played	Apps	Subs	Gls
Manchester U	App	04/80	80-82	13	12	3
Wolverhampton W	L	03/84	83	13	0	2
Portsmouth	Tr	07/84	84-85	17	6	6
Carlisle U	L	01/86	85	10	0	3
Carlisle U	Tr	07/86	86	25	0	8
Grimsby T	Tr	03/87	86-87	49	1	7
Bristol C	Tr	09/88	88	20	6	9
Oldham Ath	Tr	05/89	89	2	2	1
Wigan Ath	L	09/89	89	3	0	0

McGAVIN Steven James (Steve)
Born: North Walsham, Norfolk, England, 24 January, 1969 — F

League Club	Source	Date Signed	Seasons Played	Apps	Subs	Gls
Ipswich T	App	01/87				
Colchester U	Sudbury T	03/91	92-93	55	3	17
Birmingham C	Tr	01/94	93-94	16	7	2
Wycombe W	Tr	03/95	94-98	103	17	14
Southend U	Tr	02/99	98	4	7	0
Northampton T	Tr	07/99				
Colchester U	Tr	10/99	99-00	49	26	18

McGEACHIE George
Born: Falkirk, Scotland, 9 September, 1939 — LW

League Club	Source	Date Signed	Seasons Played	Apps	Subs	Gls
Darlington	Dundee	01/64	63-66	119	0	9

McGEACHIE George
Born: Calderbank, Lanarkshire, Scotland, 26 October, 1918 — WH
Died: Stirling, Scotland, 12 November, 1972

League Club	Source	Date Signed	Seasons Played	Apps	Subs	Gls
New Brighton	St Johnstone	07/46	46-47	63	-	4
Leyton Orient	Tr	07/48				
Rochdale	Tr	12/48	48-50	90	-	6
Crystal Palace	Tr	06/51	51	46	-	5

McGEACHY Joseph (Joe)
Born: Glasgow, Scotland, 21 April, 1920 — LW
Died: Glasgow, Scotland, 24 June, 1985

League Club	Source	Date Signed	Seasons Played	Apps	Subs	Gls
Leyton Orient	Third Lanark	05/48	48-50	74	-	4
Workington	Hereford U	09/52	52	2	-	1

McGEADY Aiden John
Born: Paisley, Renfrewshire, Scotland, 4 April, 1986 — LW
Republic of Ireland: 76

League Club	Source	Date Signed	Seasons Played	Apps	Subs	Gls
Everton	Spartak Moscow (RUS)	01/14	13-14	14	18	1

McGEADY John Thomas
Born: Glasgow, Scotland, 17 April, 1958 — RW

League Club	Source	Date Signed	Seasons Played	Apps	Subs	Gls
Sheffield U	Third Lanark	01/76	75-76	13	3	0
Newport Co	S California L's (USA)	10/78	78	2	0	0

McGEE Joseph Vincent (Joe)
Born: Liverpool, England, 6 March, 1993 — M

League Club	Source	Date Signed	Seasons Played	Apps	Subs	Gls
Morecambe	Jnr	07/11	11-13	4	11	0

McGEE Owen Edward
Born: Middlesbrough, England, 29 April, 1970 — FB

League Club	Source	Date Signed	Seasons Played	Apps	Subs	Gls
Middlesbrough	YT	07/88	89-90	18	3	1
Scarborough	Leicester C (NC)	03/92	91-92	21	3	0

McGEE Paul
Born: Dublin, Republic of Ireland, 17 May, 1968 — W
Republic of Ireland: U21-4

League Club	Source	Date Signed	Seasons Played	Apps	Subs	Gls
Colchester U	Bohemians (ROI)	02/89	88	3	0	0
Wimbledon	Tr	03/89	88-92	54	6	9
Peterborough U	L	03/94	93	5	1	0

McGEE Paul Gerard
Born: Sligo, Republic of Ireland, 19 June, 1954 — F
Republic of Ireland: 15/U21-2

League Club	Source	Date Signed	Seasons Played	Apps	Subs	Gls
Queens Park Rgrs	Sligo Rov (ROI)	11/77	77-78	31	8	7
Preston NE	Tr	10/79	79-81	62	4	13
Burnley	Tr	11/81	81-82	33	1	9
Preston NE	Shamrock Rov (ROI)	11/84	84	2	0	0

McGEEHAN Cameron Alexander
Born: Kingston-on-Thames, SW London, England, 6 April, 1995 — M
Northern Ireland: U21-3/Youth

League Club	Source	Date Signed	Seasons Played	Apps	Subs	Gls
Norwich C	Sch	07/13				
Cambridge U	L	01/15	14	4	0	3
Luton T	L	02/15	14	13	2	3

McGEENEY Patrick Michael (Paddy)
Born: Sheffield, England, 31 October, 1966 — M/D

League Club	Source	Date Signed	Seasons Played	Apps	Subs	Gls
Sheffield U	App	10/84	84-85	15	1	0
Rochdale	L	11/86	86	3	0	0
Chesterfield	Tr	08/87	87-88	45	4	1

McGEORGE James Lumley (Jimmy)
Born: Sunderland, England, 8 June, 1945 — RW

League Club	Source	Date Signed	Seasons Played	Apps	Subs	Gls
Leyton Orient	Spennymoor U	03/64	64-65	16	0	0
Mansfield T	Tr	07/66	66	5	4	0

McGEOUCH Dylan
Born: Glasgow, Scotland, 15 January, 1993 — M
Scotland: U21-10/Youth

League Club	Source	Date Signed	Seasons Played	Apps	Subs	Gls
Coventry C (L)	Glasgow Celtic	01/14	13	0	8	0

McGEOUGH James (Jimmy)
Born: Belfast, Northern Ireland, 14 July, 1946 — M
Republic of Ireland: LoI-5//Northern Ireland: NILge-2

League Club	Source	Date Signed	Seasons Played	Apps	Subs	Gls
Lincoln C	Waterford (ROI)	06/72	72-74	61	4	0
Hartlepool U	L	03/73	72	1	1	0

McGETTIGAN John Anthony
Born: Motherwell, Lanarkshire, Scotland, 28 November, 1945 — LW

League Club	Source	Date Signed	Seasons Played	Apps	Subs	Gls
Workington	Meadow Thistle	03/68	67-68	13	1	0

McGETTIGAN Lawrence (Larry)
Born: Hackney, E London, England, 25 December, 1952 — RW
Died: Watford, Hertfordshire, England, January, 1994

League Club	Source	Date Signed	Seasons Played	Apps	Subs	Gls
Watford	App	11/70	71-74	40	10	3

McGHEE David Christopher
Born: Worthing, West Sussex, England, 19 June, 1976 — CD

League Club	Source	Date Signed	Seasons Played	Apps	Subs	Gls
Brentford	YT	07/94	94-97	95	22	8
Leyton Orient	Stevenage Bor	11/99	99-03	108	7	7

McGHEE James William (Jim)
Born: Motherwell, Lanarkshire, Scotland, 21 August, 1930 — LW

League Club	Source	Date Signed	Seasons Played	Apps	Subs	Gls
Darlington	Kilmarnock	07/52	52	15	-	4
Newport Co	Barry T	05/54	54	11	-	1

McGHEE Jamie Graeme
Born: Grantham, Lincolnshire, England, 29 August, 1989 — W

League Club	Source	Date Signed	Seasons Played	Apps	Subs	Gls
Mansfield T	Sch	11/08	06	0	2	0

McGHEE Mark Edward
Born: Glasgow, Scotland, 20 May, 1957 — F
Scotland: 4/U21-1

League Club	Source	Date Signed	Seasons Played	Apps	Subs	Gls
Newcastle U	Greenock Morton	12/77	77-78	21	7	5
Newcastle U	Glasgow Celtic	08/89	89-90	63	4	24
Reading	IK Brage (SWE)	05/91	91-92	32	13	7

McGHEE Thomas Edward (Tommy)
Born: Manchester, England, 10 May, 1929 — RB
England: B-1/Amateur-3

League Club	Source	Date Signed	Seasons Played	Apps	Subs	Gls
Portsmouth	Wealdstone	05/54	54-58	136	-	0
Reading	Tr	07/59	59	8	-	0

McGHIE William Lambert (Billy)
Born: Lanark, Scotland, 19 January, 1958 — M
Scotland: Youth

League Club	Source	Date Signed	Seasons Played	Apps	Subs	Gls
Leeds U	App	01/76	76	2	0	1
York C	Tr	12/79	79-81	39	4	1

McGIBBON Douglas (Doug)
Born: Netley, Hampshire, England, 24 February, 1919 — CF
Died: Aylesbury, Buckinghamshire, England, 25 October, 2002

League Club	Source	Date Signed	Seasons Played	Apps	Subs	Gls
Southampton	Hamble AST	12/38	38-46	13	-	9
Fulham	Tr	01/47	46-47	42	-	18
Bournemouth	Tr	09/48	48-50	103	-	65

McGIBBON Patrick Colm (Pat)
Born: Lurgan, Armagh, Northern Ireland, 6 September, 1973 — CD
Northern Ireland: 7/B-5/U21-1/Schools

League Club	Source	Date Signed	Seasons Played	Apps	Subs	Gls
Manchester U	Portadown	08/92				
Swansea C	L	09/96	96	1	0	0
Wigan Ath	Tr	03/97	96-01	163	10	11
Scunthorpe U	L	02/02	01	6	0	0
Tranmere Rov	Tr	08/02	02	4	0	0

McGIFFORD Grahame Leslie
Born: Carshalton, S London, England, 1 May, 1955 — RB

League Club	Source	Date Signed	Seasons Played	Apps	Subs	Gls
Huddersfield T	App	07/72	72-75	41	1	0
Hull C	Tr	05/76	76	1	0	0
Port Vale	Tr	06/77	77	20	0	0

McGILL Andrew
Born: Glasgow, Scotland, 11 July, 1924 — RH
Died: Beverley, East Riding of Yorkshire, England, September, 1988

League Club	Source	Date Signed	Seasons Played	Apps	Subs	Gls
Bradford C	Clyde	11/47	47-51	164	-	24
Scunthorpe U	Tr	07/52	52-56	183	-	15

McGILL Austin Michael
Born: Dumfries, Scotland, 29 January, 1935 — CF

League Club	Source	Date Signed	Seasons Played	Apps	Subs	Gls
Carlisle U	Queen of the South	08/59	59	30	-	12

McGILL Brendan
Born: Dublin, Republic of Ireland, 22 March, 1981 — M
Republic of Ireland: Youth

League Club	Source	Date Signed	Seasons Played	Apps	Subs	Gls
Sunderland	R'r Valley Rgrs (ROI)	07/98				
Carlisle U	L	09/01	01	27	1	2
Carlisle U	Tr	08/02	02-05	82	22	13

McGILL Derek
Born: Lanark, Scotland, 14 October, 1975 — F

League Club	Source	Date Signed	Seasons Played	Apps	Subs	Gls
Port Vale	Queen's Park	10/98	98	0	3	0

McGILL James (Jimmy)
Born: Kilsyth, Lanarkshire, Scotland, 10 March, 1926 — IF
Died: Cumbernauld, Lanarkshire, Scotland, 21 April, 2013

League Club	Source	Date Signed	Seasons Played	Apps	Subs	Gls
Bury	Maryhill Harp	12/45	46	1	-	0
Derby Co	Tr	03/47	46-47	8	-	0

McGILL James Hopkins (Jimmy)
Born: Bellshill, Lanarkshire, Scotland, 2 October, 1939 — RB/RH
Died: Chester, England, October, 2006

League Club	Source	Date Signed	Seasons Played	Apps	Subs	Gls
Oldham Ath	Partick Thistle	05/59	59	38	-	2
Crewe Alex	Tr	08/60	60-62	81	-	2
Chester C	Tr	10/62	62-63	32	-	0
Wrexham	Tr	10/63	63	17	-	0

McGILL James Morrison (Jimmy)
Born: Glasgow, Scotland, 27 November, 1946 — M
Died: Leeds, England, 25 March, 2015

League Club	Source	Date Signed	Seasons Played	Apps	Subs	Gls
Arsenal	Possilpark YMCA	07/65	65-66	6	4	0
Huddersfield T	Tr	09/67	67-71	161	3	8
Hull C	Tr	10/71	71-75	141	6	2
Halifax T	Tr	02/76	75-76	31	1	0

McGILLIVRAY Craig
Born: Harrogate, North Yorkshire, England, 12 January, 1993 — G

League Club	Source	Date Signed	Seasons Played	Apps	Subs	Gls
Walsall	Harrogate T	06/14	14	2	0	0

McGILLIVRAY Findlay
Born: Newtongrange, Midlothian, Scotland, 19 March, 1940 — RB

League Club	Source	Date Signed	Seasons Played	Apps	Subs	Gls
Bradford Park Ave	Glasgow Rangers	05/66	66	38	1	0

McGINLAY John
Born: Inverness, Scotland, 8 April, 1964 — F
Scotland: 13/B-2

League Club	Source	Date Signed	Seasons Played	Apps	Subs	Gls
Shrewsbury T	Elgin C	02/89	88-89	58	2	27
Bury	Tr	07/90	90	16	9	9
Millwall	Tr	01/91	90-92	27	7	10
Bolton W	Tr	09/92	92-97	180	12	87
Bradford C	Tr	11/97	97	12	5	3
Oldham Ath	Tr	10/98	98	4	3	1

McGINLAY Patrick David (Pat)
Born: Glasgow, Scotland, 30 May, 1967 — M
Scotland: B-1/B-1

League Club	Source	Date Signed	Seasons Played	Apps	Subs	Gls
Blackpool	Bearsden BC	05/85	86	2	10	1

McGINLEY John
Born: Rowlands Gill, Tyne and Wear, England, 11 June, 1959 — W

League Club	Source	Date Signed	Seasons Played	Apps	Subs	Gls
Sunderland	Gateshead	02/82	81	3	0	0
Lincoln C	Nairn Co	09/84	84-86	69	2	11
Rotherham U	Tr	09/86	86	1	2	0
Hartlepool U	L	01/87	86	2	0	0
Lincoln C	Tr	01/87	86-88	36	5	7
Doncaster Rov	Tr	06/89	89	4	6	0

McGINLEY William David (Billy)
Born: Dumfries, Scotland, 12 November, 1954 — M
Scotland: Schools

League Club	Source	Date Signed	Seasons Played	Apps	Subs	Gls
Leeds U	App	01/72	72	0	1	0
Huddersfield T	Tr	09/74	74	11	4	1
Bradford C	Tr	06/75	75-76	52	8	11
Crewe Alex	Tr	08/77	77	36	2	2

McGINN Francis (Frank)
Born: Cambuslang, Glasgow, Scotland, 2 March, 1919 — LW
Died: Toronto, Canada, December, 1995

League Club	Source	Date Signed	Seasons Played	Apps	Subs	Gls
Wrexham	Bradford C (Am)	04/47	46	2	-	0
Ipswich T	Tr	08/48	48	8	-	2

McGINN Niall
Born: Dungannon, Tyrone, Northern Ireland, 20 July, 1987 — W
Northern Ireland: 36/B-1/U23-2

League Club	Source	Date Signed	Seasons Played	Apps	Subs	Gls
Brentford (L)	Glasgow Celtic	07/11	11	27	10	5

McGINN Stephen
Born: Glasgow, Scotland, 2 December, 1988 — M
Scotland: U21-8

League Club	Source	Date Signed	Seasons Played	Apps	Subs	Gls
Watford	St Mirren	01/10	09-10	26	12	2
Shrewsbury T	L	01/13	12	12	6	2
Sheffield U	Tr	06/13	13	23	7	0

McGINN William Bell (Billy)
Born: Ardrossan, Ayrshire, Scotland, 2 February, 1943 — LB

League Club	Source	Date Signed	Seasons Played	Apps	Subs	Gls
Oldham Ath	Ardrossan Winton Rov	11/63	63-65	37	1	0

McGINTY Brian
Born: East Kilbride, Lanarkshire, Scotland, 10 December, 1976 — M

League Club	Source	Date Signed	Seasons Played	Apps	Subs	Gls
Hull C	Glasgow Rangers	11/97	97-98	43	10	6

McGINTY Sean Andrew
Born: Maidstone, Kent, England, 11 August, 1993 — LB
Republic of Ireland: U21-10/Youth

League Club	Source	Date Signed	Seasons Played	Apps	Subs	Gls
Manchester U	Sch	08/10				
Morecambe	L	02/12	11	4	0	0
Carlisle U	L	11/12	12	0	1	0
Tranmere Rov	L	03/13	12	3	0	0
Sheffield U	Tr	06/13	13	2	0	0
Northampton T	L	01/14	13	2	0	0
Rochdale	Tr	03/14	13	0	1	0

McGIVEN Michael (Mick)
Born: Newcastle-upon-Tyne, England, 7 February, 1951 — CD/M

League Club	Source	Date Signed	Seasons Played	Apps	Subs	Gls
Sunderland	Jnr	07/68	69-73	107	6	9
West Ham U	Tr	11/73	73-77	46	2	0

McGIVERN Leighton Terence
Born: Liverpool, England, 2 June, 1984 — F

League Club	Source	Date Signed	Seasons Played	Apps	Subs	Gls
Rochdale	Vauxhall Motors	07/04	04	2	23	1
Accrington Stan	Vauxhall Motors	11/06	06-07	5	14	2

McGIVERN Ryan
Born: Newry, Armagh, Northern Ireland, 8 January, 1990 — LB
Northern Ireland: 23/B-1/U21-6/Youth

League Club	Source	Date Signed	Seasons Played	Apps	Subs	Gls
Manchester C	Sch	11/07	10	0	1	0
Morecambe	L	10/08	08	5	0	1
Leicester C	L	08/09	09	9	3	0
Walsall	L	08/10	10	15	0	0
Crystal Palace	L	08/11	11	5	0	0
Bristol C	L	09/11	11	26	5	0
Port Vale	Hibernian	06/14	14	18	2	0

McGLASHAN Jermaine Dave
Born: Croydon, S London, England, 14 April, 1988 — RW

League Club	Source	Date Signed	Seasons Played	Apps	Subs	Gls
Aldershot T	Ashford T, Surrey	08/10	10-11	41	20	5
Cheltenham T	Tr	01/12	11-13	85	19	12
Gillingham	Tr	06/14	14	23	17	5

McGLASHAN John
Born: Dundee, Scotland, 3 June, 1967 — M
Scotland: Youth

League Club	Source	Date Signed	Seasons Played	Apps	Subs	Gls
Millwall	Montrose	08/90	90-91	9	7	0
Fulham	L	12/92	92	5	0	1
Cambridge U	L	01/93	92	0	1	0
Peterborough U	Tr	01/93	92-93	44	2	3
Rotherham U	Tr	11/94	94-96	68	6	5

McGLEISH John Joseph
Born: Airdrie, Lanarkshire, Scotland, 9 November, 1951 — M

League Club	Source	Date Signed	Seasons Played	Apps	Subs	Gls
Northampton T	Jnr	11/68	70-72	7	1	0

McGLEISH Scott
Born: Barnet, N London, England, 10 February, 1974 — F

League Club	Source	Date Signed	Seasons Played	Apps	Subs	Gls
Charlton Ath	Edgware T	05/94	94	0	6	0
Leyton Orient	L	03/95	94	4	2	1
Peterborough U	Tr	07/95	95-96	3	10	0
Colchester U	L	02/96	95	1	5	2
Colchester U	L	03/96	95	9	0	4
Cambridge U	L	09/96	96	10	0	7
Leyton Orient	Tr	11/96	96-97	36	0	7
Barnet	Tr	10/97	97-00	106	28	36
Colchester U	Tr	01/01	00-03	118	26	38
Northampton T	Tr	05/04	04-06	106	5	42
Wycombe W	Tr	01/07	06-08	66	9	33
Northampton T	L	10/08	08	7	2	1
Leyton Orient	Tr	02/09	08-10	78	19	30
Bristol Rov	Tr	07/11	11	14	13	7
Barnet	L	03/12	11	5	4	0

McGLEN William (Bill)
Born: Bedlington, Northumberland, England, 27 April, 1921 — LH
Died: Burgh-le-Marsh, Lincolnshire, England, December, 1999

League Club	Source	Date Signed	Seasons Played	Apps	Subs	Gls
Manchester U	Blyth Spartans	05/46	46-51	110	-	2
Lincoln C	Tr	07/52	52	13	-	0
Oldham Ath	Tr	02/53	52-55	68	-	3

McGLENNON Thomas (Tom)
Born: Bearpark, County Durham, England, 20 October, 1933 — LH

League Club	Source	Date Signed	Seasons Played	Apps	Subs	Gls
Blackpool	Jnr	11/50				
Rochdale	Tr	05/57	57-58	61	-	2
Barrow	Burton A	11/59	59-60	61	-	6

McGLINCHEY Brian Kevin
Born: Derry, Northern Ireland, 26 October, 1977 — LB
Northern Ireland: B-1/U21-14/Youth

League Club	Source	Date Signed	Seasons Played	Apps	Subs	Gls
Manchester C	YT	12/95				
Port Vale	Tr	07/98	98	10	5	1
Gillingham	Tr	08/99	99-00	7	7	1
Plymouth Arg	Tr	12/00	00-02	54	14	2
Torquay U	Tr	09/03	03-05	70	2	0

McGOLDRICK David James
Born: Nottingham, England, 29 November, 1987 — F
Republic of Ireland: 2

League Club	Source	Date Signed	Seasons Played	Apps	Subs	Gls
Notts Co	Jnr	-	03	2	2	0
Southampton	Sch	07/05	05-08	49	15	12
Notts Co	L	09/05	05	4	2	0
Bournemouth	L	02/07	06	12	0	6
Port Vale	L	08/07	07	15	2	2
Nottingham F	Tr	06/09	09-11	31	32	8
Sheffield Wed	L	09/11	11	3	1	1
Coventry C	L	08/12	12	21	1	16
Ipswich T	Tr	01/13	12-14	67	3	25

McGOLDRICK Edward John Paul (Eddie)
Born: Islington, N London, England, 30 April, 1965 — W/M
Republic of Ireland: 15/B

League Club	Source	Date Signed	Seasons Played	Apps	Subs	Gls
Northampton T	Nuneaton Bor	08/86	86-88	97	10	9
Crystal Palace	Tr	01/89	88-92	139	8	11
Arsenal	Tr	06/93	93-95	32	6	0
Manchester C	Tr	09/96	96-97	39	1	0
Stockport Co	L	03/98	97	2	0	0

McGOLDRICK John
Born: Coatbridge, Lanarkshire, Scotland, 23 September, 1963 — RB

League Club	Source	Date Signed	Seasons Played	Apps	Subs	Gls
Leeds U	Glasgow Celtic	06/83	83	7	0	0

McGOLDRICK Thomas Joseph (Tom)
Born: Doncaster, South Yorkshire, England, 20 September, 1929 — CF

League Club	Source	Date Signed	Seasons Played	Apps	Subs	Gls
Rotherham U	Maltby Main	11/49	51	5	-	2
Chesterfield	Tr	05/53	53-54	36	-	16

McGONIGAL Robert Edwin (Bert)
Born: Cookstown, Derry, Northern Ireland, 2 May, 1942 — G
Died: 12 September, 2014
Northern Ireland: NILge-2/Schools

League Club	Source	Date Signed	Seasons Played	Apps	Subs	Gls
Brighton & HA	Glentoran	02/62	62-65	57	0	0

McGORRIGHAN Francis Owen (Frank)
Born: Easington, County Durham, England, 20 November, 1921 — IF
Died: Hull, England, 1 October, 1998

League Club	Source	Date Signed	Seasons Played	Apps	Subs	Gls
Middlesbrough	Easington CW	04/44				
Carlisle U	Tr	10/45				
Hull C	Tr	08/46	46	20	-	1
Blackburn Rov	Tr	02/47	46-47	5	-	0
Hull C	Tr	09/47	47	6	-	0
Southport	Tr	08/48	48	4	-	0

McGORRY Brian Paul
Born: Liverpool, England, 16 April, 1970 — M

League Club	Source	Date Signed	Seasons Played	Apps	Subs	Gls
Bournemouth	Weymouth	08/91	91-93	56	5	11
Peterborough U	Tr	02/94	93-94	44	8	6
Wycombe W	Tr	08/95	95	0	4	0
Cardiff C	L	03/96	95	7	0	0
Hereford U	Tr	03/97	96	7	0	1
Torquay U	Tr	07/98	98	31	3	1

McGOVERN Brendan
Born: Camborne, Cornwall, England, 9 February, 1980 — M

League Club	Source	Date Signed	Seasons Played	Apps	Subs	Gls
Plymouth Arg	YT	07/98	98	0	2	0

McGOVERN Brian
Born: Dublin, Republic of Ireland, 28 April, 1980 — CD
Republic of Ireland: U21-2/Youth

League Club	Source	Date Signed	Seasons Played	Apps	Subs	Gls
Arsenal	Cherry Orchard (ROI)	09/97	99	0	1	0
Queens Park Rgrs	L	12/99	99	3	2	0
Norwich C	Tr	07/00	00-01	8	13	1
Peterborough U	Tr	11/02	02	1	0	0

McGOVERN John Prescott
Born: Montrose, Angus, Scotland, 28 October, 1949 — M
Scotland: U23-2

League Club	Source	Date Signed	Seasons Played	Apps	Subs	Gls
Hartlepool U	App	11/66	65-68	69	3	5
Derby Co	Tr	09/68	68-73	186	4	16
Leeds U	Tr	08/74	74	4	0	0
Nottingham F	Tr	02/75	74-81	249	4	6
Bolton W	Tr	06/82	82-83	16	0	0

McGOVERN Jon-Paul
Born: Glasgow, Scotland, 3 October, 1980 — M

League Club	Source	Date Signed	Seasons Played	Apps	Subs	Gls
Sheffield U (L)	Glasgow Celtic	08/02	02	11	4	1
Sheffield Wed	Livingston	06/04	04-05	49	4	6
MK Dons	Tr	07/06	06-07	42	5	3
Swindon T	Tr	08/07	07-10	131	19	8
Carlisle U	Tr	07/11	11-12	77	6	4

McGOVERN Michael John (Mick)
Born: Hayes, W London, England, 15 February, 1951 — M

League Club	Source	Date Signed	Seasons Played	Apps	Subs	Gls
Queens Park Rgrs	App	11/68	67-71	10	2	0
Watford	L	08/72	72	4	0	0
Swindon T	Tr	02/73	72-74	28	4	2
Aldershot	L	03/75	74	6	0	1

McGOVERN Patrick Munro (Paddy)
Born: Edinburgh, Scotland, 14 May, 1948 — M

League Club	Source	Date Signed	Seasons Played	Apps	Subs	Gls
Notts Co	Royston BC	07/67	67	1	2	0

McGOVERN Simon
Born: Bradford, England, 25 February, 1965 — M

League Club	Source	Date Signed	Seasons Played	Apps	Subs	Gls
Bradford C	Jnr	08/82	82	1	0	0

McGOWAN Aaron Joseph
Born: Maghull, Merseyside, England, 1 August, 1996 — RM

League Club	Source	Date Signed	Seasons Played	Apps	Subs	Gls
Morecambe	Jnr	07/14	12-14	4	7	1

McGOWAN Aloysius (Ally)
Born: Airdrie, Lanarkshire, Scotland, 22 January, 1930 — FB
Died: Wrexham, Wales, 5 July, 2005

League Club	Source	Date Signed	Seasons Played	Apps	Subs	Gls
Wrexham	St Johnstone	05/53	53-64	408	-	2

League Club	Source	Date Signed	Seasons Played	Career Record Apps	Subs	Gls

McGOWAN Andrew (Andy)
Born: Corby, Northamptonshire, England, 17 July, 1956 — M
Died: Corby, Northamptonshire, England, 5 May, 1999
England: Youth

League Club	Source	Date Signed	Seasons Played	Apps	Subs	Gls
Northampton T	Corby T	06/75	75-77	93	12	15

McGOWAN Daniel (Danny)
Born: Dublin, Republic of Ireland, 8 November, 1924 — IF/WH
Died: Plaistow, E London, England, March, 1994
Republic of Ireland: 3

League Club	Source	Date Signed	Seasons Played	Apps	Subs	Gls
West Ham U	Shelbourne (ROI)	05/48	48-53	81	-	8

McGOWAN Gavin Gregory
Born: Blackheath, SE London, England, 16 January, 1976 — LB
England: Youth/Schools

League Club	Source	Date Signed	Seasons Played	Apps	Subs	Gls
Arsenal	YT	07/94	92-97	3	3	0
Luton T	L	03/97	96	2	0	0
Luton T	L	07/97	97	6	2	0
Luton T	Tr	07/98	98-00	42	8	0

McGOWAN George
Born: Carluke, Lanarkshire, Scotland, 30 November, 1943 — CF
Died: Wrexham, Wales, 20 November, 2009

League Club	Source	Date Signed	Seasons Played	Apps	Subs	Gls
Preston NE	Wishaw Jnrs	08/62				
Chester C	Tr	03/63	62-63	18	-	3
Stockport Co	Tr	09/64	64	5	-	0

McGOWAN Gerard James (Gerry)
Born: Kilwinning, Ayrshire, Scotland, 4 August, 1944 — W

League Club	Source	Date Signed	Seasons Played	Apps	Subs	Gls
Oldham Ath	Ardeer Rec	11/63	65	5	0	1

McGOWAN James (Jimmy)
Born: Cambuslang, Glasgow, Scotland, 12 January, 1924 — IF/WH
Died: Southampton, England, 28 March, 1984

League Club	Source	Date Signed	Seasons Played	Apps	Subs	Gls
Grimsby T	Dumbarton	07/46	46-48	34	-	4
Southampton	Tr	03/50	49-57	78	-	9

McGOWAN James (Jimmy)
Born: Glasgow, Scotland, 31 July, 1939 — RW

League Club	Source	Date Signed	Seasons Played	Apps	Subs	Gls
Mansfield T	St Johnstone	06/61	61	3	-	0

McGOWAN Kenneth (Ken)
Born: Wolverhampton, England, 13 May, 1920 — CF

League Club	Source	Date Signed	Seasons Played	Apps	Subs	Gls
Walsall		10/47	47-48	11	-	4

McGOWAN Neil William
Born: Glasgow, Scotland, 15 April, 1977 — LB

League Club	Source	Date Signed	Seasons Played	Apps	Subs	Gls
Oxford U	Albion Rov	08/99	99-00	26	5	0

McGRAIL Christopher Francis (Chris)
Born: Preston, Lancashire, England, 25 February, 1988 — F

League Club	Source	Date Signed	Seasons Played	Apps	Subs	Gls
Preston NE	Sch	11/06				
Accrington Stan	L	01/07	06	0	2	0
Accrington Stan	L	08/07	07	0	1	0

McGRANDLES Conor
Born: Falkirk, Scotland, 24 September, 1995 — RW

League Club	Source	Date Signed	Seasons Played	Apps	Subs	Gls
Norwich C	Falkirk	08/14	14	0	1	0

McGRATH Derek Brendan Joseph
Born: Dublin, Republic of Ireland, 21 January, 1972 — M
Republic of Ireland: U21-9

League Club	Source	Date Signed	Seasons Played	Apps	Subs	Gls
Brighton & HA	YT	12/89	89-90	2	4	0

McGRATH James
Born: Belfast, Northern Ireland, 15 November, 1921 — WH
Died: Barrow, Cumbria, England, September, 2000

League Club	Source	Date Signed	Seasons Played	Apps	Subs	Gls
Barrow	Bohemians (ROI)	08/45	46	3	-	0

McGRATH John
Born: Tidworth, Wiltshire, England, 21 March, 1932 — IF/WH

League Club	Source	Date Signed	Seasons Played	Apps	Subs	Gls
Notts Co	Aldershot (Am)	08/53	55-57	54	-	5
Darlington	Tr	05/58	58	25	-	6

McGRATH John Matthew
Born: Limerick, Republic of Ireland, 27 March, 1980 — M
Republic of Ireland: U21-5

League Club	Source	Date Signed	Seasons Played	Apps	Subs	Gls
Aston Villa	Belvedere (ROI)	09/99	00	0	3	0
Doncaster Rov	Tr	07/03	03	4	7	0
Shrewsbury T	L	08/04	04	7	1	0
Kidderminster Hrs	Tr	01/05	04	18	1	0
Burton A	Tamworth	07/07	09-12	111	12	4
York C	L	02/13	12	9	0	0

McGRATH John Thomas
Born: Manchester, England, 23 August, 1938 — CH
Died: Manchester, England, 25 December, 1998
England: FLge-1/U23-1

League Club	Source	Date Signed	Seasons Played	Apps	Subs	Gls
Bury	Miles Platting Swifts	10/55	56-60	148	-	2
Newcastle U	Tr	02/61	60-67	169	1	2
Southampton	Tr	02/68	67-73	167	1	1
Brighton & HA	L	12/72	72	3	0	0

McGRATH Lloyd Anthony
Born: Birmingham, England, 24 February, 1965 — M
England: U21-1/Youth

League Club	Source	Date Signed	Seasons Played	Apps	Subs	Gls
Coventry C	App	12/82	83-93	200	14	4
Portsmouth	Sing Tao (HKG)	10/94	94	15	3	0

McGRATH Martin Lawrence
Born: Hendon, N London, England, 15 October, 1960 — M
England: Schools

League Club	Source	Date Signed	Seasons Played	Apps	Subs	Gls
Southampton	App	10/78	79	0	1	0
Bournemouth	Tr	06/80	80	17	5	0

McGRATH Michael (Mick)
Born: Dublin, Republic of Ireland, 7 April, 1936 — LH
England: FLge-1//Republic of Ireland: 22/B

League Club	Source	Date Signed	Seasons Played	Apps	Subs	Gls
Blackburn Rov	Home Farm (ROI)	08/54	55-65	268	0	8
Bradford Park Ave	Tr	03/66	65-66	50	0	2

McGRATH Paul
Born: Greenford, W London, England, 4 December, 1959 — CD
England: FLge//Republic of Ireland: 83

League Club	Source	Date Signed	Seasons Played	Apps	Subs	Gls
Manchester U	St Patrick's Ath (ROI)	04/82	82-88	159	4	12
Aston Villa	Tr	08/89	89-95	248	5	9
Derby Co	Tr	10/96	96	23	1	0
Sheffield U	Tr	08/97	97	12	0	0

McGRATH Phillip John Hosford
Born: Banbridge, Down, Northern Ireland, 7 April, 1992 — M
Northern Ireland: Youth

League Club	Source	Date Signed	Seasons Played	Apps	Subs	Gls
Oldham Ath	Sch	04/10	10	0	1	0

McGRATH Roland Christopher (Chris)
Born: Belfast, Northern Ireland, 29 November, 1954 — W
Northern Ireland: 21

League Club	Source	Date Signed	Seasons Played	Apps	Subs	Gls
Tottenham H	App	01/72	73-75	30	8	5
Millwall	L	02/76	75	15	0	3
Manchester U	Tr	10/76	76-80	12	16	1

McGRAW John (Ian)
Born: Glasgow, Scotland, 30 August, 1926 — G
Died: Leicester, England, October, 2014

League Club	Source	Date Signed	Seasons Played	Apps	Subs	Gls
Leicester C	Arbroath	12/48	48-50	13	-	0

McGREAL John
Born: Birkenhead, Wirral, England, 2 June, 1972 — CD

League Club	Source	Date Signed	Seasons Played	Apps	Subs	Gls
Tranmere Rov	YT	07/90	91-98	193	2	1
Ipswich T	Tr	08/99	99-03	120	3	4
Burnley	Tr	08/04	04-06	92	4	1

McGREEVEY Brian Edmund
Born: Prestwich, Greater Manchester, England, 29 September, 1935 — RW

League Club	Source	Date Signed	Seasons Played	Apps	Subs	Gls
Arsenal	Preston NE (Am)	03/54				
Stockport Co	Tr	03/57	56	1	-	0

McGREGOR Alexander George Penman (Alex)
Born: Glasgow, Scotland, 12 November, 1950 — LW

League Club	Source	Date Signed	Seasons Played	Apps	Subs	Gls
Shrewsbury T	Hibernian	01/75	74-75	46	3	7
Aldershot	Tr	09/76	76-81	168	9	17

McGREGOR Allan James
Born: Edinburgh, Scotland, 31 January, 1982 — G
Scotland: 33/B-1/U21-6

League Club	Source	Date Signed	Seasons Played	Apps	Subs	Gls
Hull C	Besiktas (TKY)	07/13	13-14	52	0	0

McGREGOR Callum William
Born: Edinburgh, Scotland, 14 June, 1993 — W
Scotland: U21-5/Youth

League Club	Source	Date Signed	Seasons Played	Apps	Subs	Gls
Notts Co (L)	Glasgow Celtic	08/13	13	32	5	12

MacGREGOR Colin
Born: Bradford, England, 13 November, 1940 — RW

League Club	Source	Date Signed	Seasons Played	Apps	Subs	Gls
Bradford Park Ave	Bradford C (Am)	03/58	58-59	3	-	0

MacGREGOR James Peter (Peter)
Born: Hartlepool, Cleveland, England, 22 December, 1931 — IF
Died: Cleveland, England, March, 1994

League Club	Source	Date Signed	Seasons Played	Apps	Subs	Gls
Hartlepool U	Elwick Road	02/50	53-54	2	-	0

McGREGOR John Reid
Born: Airdrie, Lanarkshire, Scotland, 5 January, 1963 — CD

League Club	Source	Date Signed	Seasons Played	Apps	Subs	Gls
Liverpool	Queen's Park	06/82				
Leeds U	L	10/85	85	5	0	0

McGREGOR Mark Dale Thomas
Born: Chester, England, 16 February, 1977 — D

League Club	Source	Date Signed	Seasons Played	Apps	Subs	Gls
Wrexham	YT	07/95	94-00	237	7	11
Burnley	Tr	07/01	01-03	46	8	2
Blackpool	Tr	07/04	04-05	52	7	0
Port Vale	Tr	01/06	05-07	58	8	0

McGREGOR Paul Anthony
Born: Liverpool, England, 17 December, 1974 — F

League Club	Source	Date Signed	Seasons Played	Apps	Subs	Gls
Nottingham F	YT	12/91	94-96	7	23	3
Carlisle U	L	09/98	98	9	1	3
Preston NE	Tr	03/99	98	1	3	0
Plymouth Arg	Tr	07/99	99-00	75	2	19
Northampton T	Tr	07/01	01-02	54	8	5

MacGREGOR Terence James (Terry)
Born: Hartlepool, Cleveland, England, 24 May, 1938 — WH

League Club	Source	Date Signed	Seasons Played	Apps	Subs	Gls
Hartlepool U	Jnr	12/56	56-62	47	-	2

McGREGOR William (Willie)
Born: Paisley, Renfrewshire, Scotland, 1 December, 1923 — RB

League Club	Source	Date Signed	Seasons Played	Apps	Subs	Gls
Leicester C	Mossdale YMCA	04/47	47-51	9	-	0
Mansfield T	Tr	09/53	53-55	119	-	0

McGRELLIS Francis (Frank)
Born: Falkirk, Scotland, 5 October, 1958 — F

League Club	Source	Date Signed	Seasons Played	Apps	Subs	Gls
Coventry C	App	10/76				
Huddersfield T	L	08/78	78	4	1	0
Hereford U	Tr	03/79	78-81	80	5	24

McGROARTY James Martin (Jim)
Born: Derry, Northern Ireland, 30 August, 1957 — RW

League Club	Source	Date Signed	Seasons Played	Apps	Subs	Gls
Stoke C	Finn Harps (ROI)	09/77	77-78	6	1	2

McGROGAN Hugh
Born: Dumbarton, Dunbartonshire, Scotland, 1 March, 1957 — RW
Died: Bicester, Oxfordshire, England, 1 September, 1998

League Club	Source	Date Signed	Seasons Played	Apps	Subs	Gls
Oxford U	App	03/75	74-79	101	25	13
Carlisle U	Tr	05/80	80	1	1	0

McGRORY Shaun Patrick
Born: Coventry, England, 29 February, 1968 — LB

League Club	Source	Date Signed	Seasons Played	Apps	Subs	Gls
Coventry C	App	07/86				
Burnley	Tr	07/87	87-89	34	12	2

McGROTTY William (Willie)
Born: Glasgow, Scotland, 12 August, 1952 — W

League Club	Source	Date Signed	Seasons Played	Apps	Subs	Gls
Blackpool	Yoker Ath	06/70	70-72	2	2	1

McGUCKIN George Kay Whyte
Born: Dundee, Scotland, 11 August, 1938 — WH

League Club	Source	Date Signed	Seasons Played	Apps	Subs	Gls
Cardiff C	Dundee Shamrock	12/55	57	4	-	0

McGUCKIN Thomas Ian (Ian)
Born: Middlesbrough, England, 24 April, 1973 — CD

League Club	Source	Date Signed	Seasons Played	Apps	Subs	Gls
Hartlepool U	YT	06/91	91-96	147	5	8
Fulham	Tr	06/97				
Hartlepool U	L	12/98	98	8	0	0
Oxford U	Tr	07/00	00	6	1	0

McGUFFIE Alwyn Scott
Born: Drummore, Dumfries & Galloway, Scotland, 13 April, 1937 — WH/IF

League Club	Source	Date Signed	Seasons Played	Apps	Subs	Gls
Luton T	Queen of the South	09/54	55-63	79	-	10

McGUGAN John Hannah (Jackie)
Born: Airdrie, Lanarkshire, Scotland, 12 June, 1939 — CH

League Club	Source	Date Signed	Seasons Played	Apps	Subs	Gls
Leeds U	St Mirren	08/60	60	1	-	0
Tranmere Rov	Tr	02/61	60-61	35	-	0

McGUGAN Lewis Shay
Born: Long Eaton, Derbyshire, England, 25 October, 1988 — M
England: Youth

League Club	Source	Date Signed	Seasons Played	Apps	Subs	Gls
Nottingham F	Sch	11/06	06-12	140	62	40
Watford	Tr	07/13	13-14	36	4	10
Sheffield Wed	L	11/14	14	7	0	0
Sheffield Wed	L	02/15	14	14	1	3

McGUGAN Paul Joseph
Born: Glasgow, Scotland, 17 July, 1964 — CD

League Club	Source	Date Signed	Seasons Played	Apps	Subs	Gls
Barnsley	Glasgow Celtic	10/87	87-88	47	2	2
Chesterfield	Tr	01/91	90-93	74	3	6

McGUIGAN James (Jimmy)
Born: Addiewell, West Lothian, Scotland, 1 March, 1924 — W/WH
Died: Chesterfield, Derbyshire, England, 30 March, 1988

League Club	Source	Date Signed	Seasons Played	Apps	Subs	Gls
Sunderland	Hamilton Academical	06/47	47-48	3	-	1
Stockport Co	Tr	06/49	49-50	43	-	9
Crewe Alex	Tr	08/50	50-55	209	-	32
Rochdale	Tr	08/56	56-58	70	-	2

McGUIGAN John Joseph
Born: Motherwell, Lanarkshire, Scotland, 29 October, 1932 — LW/IF
Died: Bellshill, Lanarkshire, Scotland, 12 August, 2004

League Club	Source	Date Signed	Seasons Played	Apps	Subs	Gls
Southend U	St Mirren	05/55	55-57	125	-	34
Newcastle U	Tr	07/58	58-61	50	-	15
Scunthorpe U	Tr	01/62	61-62	57	-	17
Southampton	Tr	08/63	63-64	33	-	8
Swansea C	Tr	03/65	64-65	28	0	4

McGUIGAN Thomas (Tommy)
Born: Whitburn, West Lothian, Scotland, 22 November, 1922 — IF
Died: Hartlepool, Cleveland, England, 14 December, 1997

League Club	Source	Date Signed	Seasons Played	Apps	Subs	Gls
Hartlepool U	Ayr U	08/50	50-57	325	-	75

McGUINNESS Hendy Alistair Johnstone (Harry)
Born: Saltcoats, Ayrshire, Scotland, 17 February, 1928 — CD
Died: Torbay, Devon, England, 15 May, 1997

League Club	Source	Date Signed	Seasons Played	Apps	Subs	Gls
Torquay U	RM Devonport	03/48	49-54	81	-	0

McGUINNESS Paul
Born: Manchester, England, 2 March, 1966 — M

League Club	Source	Date Signed	Seasons Played	Apps	Subs	Gls
Manchester U	Jnr	07/84				
Crewe Alex	Tr	08/86	86	11	2	0
Manchester U	Loughborough Univ	07/89				
Chester C	Bury (NC)	07/91	91	3	4	0

McGUINNESS Robert Francis (Bobby)
Born: Motherwell, Lanarkshire, Scotland, 29 January, 1954 — F

League Club	Source	Date Signed	Seasons Played	Apps	Subs	Gls
Portsmouth	Motherwell	07/75	75-76	27	4	3

McGUINNESS Wilfred (Wilf)
Born: Manchester, England, 25 October, 1937 — WH
England: 2/FLge-1/U23-4/Youth/Schools

League Club	Source	Date Signed	Seasons Played	Apps	Subs	Gls
Manchester U	Jnr	11/54	55-59	81	-	2

McGUIRE Bernard Patrick
Born: Liverpool, England, 23 November, 1932 — RW

League Club	Source	Date Signed	Seasons Played	Apps	Subs	Gls
Shrewsbury T		07/53	53	2	-	0

McGUIRE Douglas John (Dougie)
Born: Bathgate, West Lothian, Scotland, 6 September, 1967 — W
Scotland: Youth

League Club	Source	Date Signed	Seasons Played	Apps	Subs	Gls
Sunderland (L)	Glasgow Celtic	03/88	87	1	0	0
Coventry C	Glasgow Celtic	08/88	89	1	3	0

McGUIRE James Gary (Gary)
Born: Campsall, South Yorkshire, England, 30 September, 1938 — G

League Club	Source	Date Signed	Seasons Played	Apps	Subs	Gls
Torquay U	Sydney Hakoah (AUS)	02/66	65-66	32	0	0

McGUIRE Jamie Anthony
Born: Birkenhead, Wirral, England, 13 November, 1983 — M

League Club	Source	Date Signed	Seasons Played	Apps	Subs	Gls
Fleetwood T	Droylsden	05/09	12	34	3	1
Mansfield T	Tr	07/13	13-14	50	6	3

McGUIRE Leslie George Robert (Les)
Born: Bethnal Green, E London, England, 31 January, 1929 — IF

League Club	Source	Date Signed	Seasons Played	Apps	Subs	Gls
Gillingham	Army	08/49	50-51	6	-	2

McGUIRE Michael James (Mick)
Born: Blackpool, Lancashire, England, 4 September, 1952 — M
England: Youth

League Club	Source	Date Signed	Seasons Played	Apps	Subs	Gls
Coventry C	Jnr	11/69	71-74	60	12	1
Norwich C	Tr	01/75	74-82	172	10	11
Barnsley	Tr	03/83	82-84	44	3	6
Oldham Ath	Tr	01/85	84-86	65	4	3

McGUIRE Philip
Born: Glasgow, Scotland, 4 March, 1980 — D
Scotland: U21-2

League Club	Source	Date Signed	Seasons Played	Apps	Subs	Gls
Doncaster Rov	Aberdeen	07/05	05	11	0	0

McGUIRE Reginald (Reg)
Born: Birkenhead, Wirral, England, 24 August, 1959 — F

League Club	Source	Date Signed	Seasons Played	Apps	Subs	Gls
Tranmere Rov	Cammell Laird	08/82	82	0	4	0

McGURK Adam Michael
Born: Larne, Antrim, Northern Ireland, 24 January, 1989 — F
Northern Ireland: U21-1

League Club	Source	Date Signed	Seasons Played	Apps	Subs	Gls
Aston Villa	Sch	01/06				
Tranmere Rov	Hednesford T	08/10	10-12	48	31	10
Burton A	Tr	08/13	13-14	58	13	15

McGURK David Michael
Born: Middlesbrough, England, 30 September, 1982 — CD

League Club	Source	Date Signed	Seasons Played	Apps	Subs	Gls
Darlington	Sch	08/02	01-05	46	10	6
York C	Tr	07/06	12-13	32	2	1

McHALE Christopher Mark (Chris)
Born: Birmingham, England, 4 November, 1984 — M

League Club	Source	Date Signed	Seasons Played	Apps	Subs	Gls
Kidderminster Hrs	Jnr	03/04	03-04	11	4	0

McHALE John (Sam)
Born: Oldham, Greater Manchester, England, 7 May, 1954 — CD

League Club	Source	Date Signed	Seasons Played	Apps	Subs	Gls
Reading (Am)	Alton T	01/75	74	1	0	0

McHALE John Kevin (Kevin)
Born: Darfield, South Yorkshire, England, 1 October, 1939 — RW
England: Youth/Schools

League Club	Source	Date Signed	Seasons Played	Apps	Subs	Gls
Huddersfield T	Jnr	10/56	56-67	345	0	60
Crewe Alex	Tr	01/68	67-70	116	0	22
Chester C	Tr	10/70	70-71	61	3	4

McHALE Raymond (Ray)
Born: Sheffield, England, 12 August, 1950 — M

League Club	Source	Date Signed	Seasons Played	Apps	Subs	Gls
Chesterfield	Hillsborough BC	08/69	71-74	123	1	27
Halifax T	Tr	10/74	74-76	86	0	21
Swindon T	Tr	09/76	76-79	171	2	33
Brighton & HA	Tr	05/80	80	9	2	0
Barnsley	Tr	03/81	80-81	52	1	1
Sheffield U	Tr	08/82	82-84	66	1	2
Bury	L	02/83	82	6	0	0
Swansea C	Tr	01/85	84-85	45	2	1
Rochdale	Scarborough	08/86	86	6	1	0
Scarborough	Tr	12/86	87	25	0	3

McHALE Thomas Anthony (Tom)
Born: Liverpool, England, 3 September, 1951 — RB

League Club	Source	Date Signed	Seasons Played	Apps	Subs	Gls
Bradford C	Prescot Cables	09/71	71-72	34	2	0

McHALE William
Born: Kelty, Fife, Scotland, 9 August, 1929 — IF
Died: Carlisle, Cumbria, England, April, 2002

League Club	Source	Date Signed	Seasons Played	Apps	Subs	Gls
Carlisle U	Dunfermline Ath	08/53	53	1	-	0
Halifax T		03/55	54	3	-	0

M'CHANGAMA Youssouf Yacoub
Born: Marseille, France, 29 August, 1990 — M
Comoros: 6

League Club	Source	Date Signed	Seasons Played	Apps	Subs	Gls
Oldham Ath	Troyes AC (FRA)	03/12	11-12	18	8	2

McHARD Archibald (Archie)
Born: Dumbarton, Dunbartonshire, Scotland, 10 June, 1934 — RW

League Club	Source	Date Signed	Seasons Played	Apps	Subs	Gls
Bradford Park Ave	Clyde	05/59	59-60	27	-	3

McHUGH Carl Gerard
Born: Lettermacaward, Donegal, Republic of Ireland, 5 February, 1993 — LB
Republic of Ireland: U21-2/Youth

League Club	Source	Date Signed	Seasons Played	Apps	Subs	Gls
Reading	Sch	07/11				
Bradford C	Tr	08/12	12-13	23	7	2
Plymouth Arg	Tr	06/14	14	43	1	2

McHUGH Frazer Joseph
Born: Nottingham, England, 14 July, 1981 — M

League Club	Source	Date Signed	Seasons Played	Apps	Subs	Gls
Swindon T	YT	08/99	98-00	13	6	0
Bradford C	Halesowen T	03/03	02-03	5	0	0
Notts Co	Tr	01/04	03	9	4	0

McHUGH Michael Bernard
Born: Letterkenny, Donegal, Republic of Ireland, 3 April, 1971 — F

League Club	Source	Date Signed	Seasons Played	Apps	Subs	Gls
Bradford C		09/89	90-93	18	13	4
Scarborough	Tr	03/94	93	1	2	0

McILHARGEY Stephen (Steve)
Born: Glasgow, Scotland, 23 August, 1963 — G

League Club	Source	Date Signed	Seasons Played	Apps	Subs	Gls
Walsall	Blantyre Celtic	07/87				
Blackpool	Tr	08/89	89-93	100	1	0
Chester C	L	09/93	93	1	0	0

McILHATTON John
Born: Stevenston, Ayrshire, Scotland, 3 January, 1921 — RW
Died: Ardrossan, Ayrshire, Scotland, 13 February, 1954

League Club	Source	Date Signed	Seasons Played	Apps	Subs	Gls
Everton	Albion Rov	04/46	46-48	55	-	1

McILMOYLE Hugh
Born: Cambuslang, Glasgow, Scotland, 29 January, 1940 — CF

League Club	Source	Date Signed	Seasons Played	Apps	Subs	Gls
Leicester C	Port Glasgow Ath	08/59	60-61	20	-	5
Rotherham U	Tr	07/62	62	12	-	4
Carlisle U	Tr	03/63	62-64	77	-	47
Wolverhampton W	Tr	10/64	64-66	90	0	35
Bristol C	Tr	03/67	66-67	20	0	4
Carlisle U	Tr	09/67	67-69	79	0	30
Middlesbrough	Tr	09/69	69-70	69	1	19
Preston NE	Tr	07/71	71-72	59	1	10
Carlisle U	Greenock Morton	07/74	74	15	3	2

McILROY James (Jimmy)
Born: Lisburn, Belfast, Northern Ireland, 25 October, 1931 — IF
England: FLge-2//Northern Ireland: 55

League Club	Source	Date Signed	Seasons Played	Apps	Subs	Gls
Burnley	Glentoran	03/50	50-62	439	-	116
Stoke C	Tr	03/63	62-65	96	2	16
Oldham Ath	Tr	03/66	65-67	35	4	1

McILROY Samuel Baxter (Sammy)
Born: Belfast, Northern Ireland, 2 August, 1954 — M
Northern Ireland: 88

League Club	Source	Date Signed	Seasons Played	Apps	Subs	Gls
Manchester U	App	08/71	71-81	320	22	57
Stoke C	Tr	02/82	81-84	132	1	14
Manchester C	Tr	08/85	85	12	0	1
Manchester C	Orgryte IS (SWE)	11/86	86	1	0	0
Bury	Tr	03/87	86-87	43	0	6
Bury	VFB Modling (AUT)	08/88	88-89	52	5	2
Preston NE	Tr	02/90	89	20	0	0

McILVENNY Edward Joseph (Ed)
Born: Greenock, Inverclyde, Scotland, 21 October, 1924 — RW
Died: Eastbourne, East Sussex, England, 18 May, 1989
Republic of Ireland: LoI-3//USA:

League Club	Source	Date Signed	Seasons Played	Apps	Subs	Gls
Wrexham	Greenock Morton	03/47	46-47	7	-	1
Manchester U	Philadelphia N's (USA)	08/50	50	2	-	0

McILVENNY Harold Jowett (Harry)
Born: Bradford, England, 5 October, 1922 — CF
Died: Bradford, England, 29 June, 2009
England: Amateur-7

League Club	Source	Date Signed	Seasons Played	Apps	Subs	Gls
Bradford Park Ave (Am)	Yorkshire Amats	08/46	46-49	43	-	17

McILVENNY John Anthony
Born: Barnstaple, Devon, England, 2 March, 1930 — RW
Died: Basingstoke, Hampshire, England, 25 September, 2006

League Club	Source	Date Signed	Seasons Played	Apps	Subs	Gls
West Bromwich A	Stafford Rgrs	10/49				
Bristol Rov	Cheltenham T	07/52	52-58	80	-	11
Reading	Tr	06/59	59-60	77	-	4

McILVENNY Patrick Dennis (Paddy)
Born: Belfast, Northern Ireland, 11 September, 1924 — RH
Died: West Sussex, England, March, 2013

League Club	Source	Date Signed	Seasons Played	Apps	Subs	Gls
Cardiff C	Merthyr Tydfil	05/50				
Brighton & HA	Tr	07/51	51-54	60	-	5
Aldershot	Tr	12/55	55-56	16	-	0

McILVENNY Robert (Bobby)
Born: Belfast, Northern Ireland, 7 July, 1926 — IF

League Club	Source	Date Signed	Seasons Played	Apps	Subs	Gls
Oldham Ath	Merthyr Tydfil	03/50	49-53	139	-	36
Bury	Tr	08/54	54	12	-	1
Southport	Tr	08/55	55-56	77	-	16
Barrow	Tr	07/57	57-58	43	-	11

McILWAINE Matthew (Matt)
Born: Glasgow, Scotland, 20 September, 1920 — WH
Died: Kettering, Northamptonshire, England, March, 1997

League Club	Source	Date Signed	Seasons Played	Apps	Subs	Gls
Bolton W	Dundee U	08/51	52	2	-	0

McILWRAITH James McLean (Jimmy)
Born: Troon, Ayrshire, Scotland, 17 April, 1954 — M

League Club	Source	Date Signed	Seasons Played	Apps	Subs	Gls
Bury	Motherwell	09/75	75-77	80	9	21
Portsmouth	Tr	07/78	78	16	3	0
Bury	Tr	07/79	79	28	1	3
Halifax T	Tr	10/80	80-81	33	3	6

McINALLY Alan Bruce
Born: Ayr, Scotland, 10 February, 1963 — F
Scotland: 8

League Club	Source	Date Signed	Seasons Played	Apps	Subs	Gls
Aston Villa	Glasgow Celtic	07/87	87-88	50	9	18

McINALLY Charles (Charlie)
Born: Glasgow, Scotland, 1 February, 1939 — WH

League Club	Source	Date Signed	Seasons Played	Apps	Subs	Gls
Brentford	St Roch's	09/58	59	1	-	0

McINALLY James Edward (Jim)
Born: Glasgow, Scotland, 19 February, 1964 — RB
Scotland: 10/U21-1/Youth

League Club	Source	Date Signed	Seasons Played	Apps	Subs	Gls
Nottingham F	Glasgow Celtic	06/84	84-85	36	0	0
Coventry C	Tr	01/86	85	5	0	0

McINALLY John Stewart
Born: Gatehouse of Fleet, Dumfries & Galloway, Scotland, 26 September, 1951 — G
Died: Gatehouse of Fleet, Dumfries & Galloway, Scotland, 5 June, 2012
Scotland: Schools

League Club	Source	Date Signed	Seasons Played	Apps	Subs	Gls
Manchester U	Jnr	03/69				
Lincoln C	Tr	08/70	70-71	22	0	0
Colchester U	Tr	11/72	72	27	0	0

McINCH James Reid (Jim)
Born: Glasgow, Scotland, 27 June, 1953 — F

League Club	Source	Date Signed	Seasons Played	Apps	Subs	Gls
Cardiff C	Jnr	08/70	72-74	11	2	0

McINDEWAR Archibald (Archie)
Born: Glasgow, Scotland, 26 July, 1921 — G
Died: Peterhead, Aberdeenshire, Scotland, 13 October, 2004

League Club	Source	Date Signed	Seasons Played	Apps	Subs	Gls
Workington	Stirling A	08/51	51	20	-	0

McINDOE Michael
Born: Edinburgh, Scotland, 2 December, 1979 — LW
Scotland: B-2

League Club	Source	Date Signed	Seasons Played	Apps	Subs	Gls
Luton T	YT	04/98	98-99	19	20	0
Doncaster Rov	Yeovil T	08/03	03-05	117	5	28
Derby Co	L	03/06	05	6	2	0
Barnsley	Tr	07/06	06	18	0	4
Wolverhampton W	Tr	11/06	06	25	2	3
Bristol C	Tr	07/07	07-08	88	2	12
Coventry C	Tr	08/09	09-10	38	8	1
MK Dons	L	11/10	10	8	0	0

McINERNEY Ian
Born: Limerick, Republic of Ireland, 1 September, 1972 — F

League Club	Source	Date Signed	Seasons Played	Apps	Subs	Gls
Peterborough U	YT	07/91	91	3	7	1

McINERNEY Ian Dominic
Born: Liverpool, England, 26 January, 1964 — W

League Club	Source	Date Signed	Seasons Played	Apps	Subs	Gls
Huddersfield T	Newcastle Blue Star	08/88	88	5	5	1
Stockport Co	Tr	07/89	89-90	37	5	8
Rochdale	L	02/91	90	4	0	1

McINNES Derek John
Born: Paisley, Renfrewshire, Scotland, 5 July, 1971 — M
Scotland: 2

League Club	Source	Date Signed	Seasons Played	Apps	Subs	Gls
Stockport Co (L)	Glasgow Rangers	11/98	98	13	0	0
West Bromwich A	Toulouse (FRA)	08/00	00-02	87	1	6
Millwall	Dundee U	07/06	07	7	6	1

McINNES Graham James
Born: Aberdeen, Scotland, 7 April, 1938 — IF

League Club	Source	Date Signed	Seasons Played	Apps	Subs	Gls
Bury	Aberdeen	06/59	60	1	-	0

McINNES Ian
Born: Hamilton, Lanarkshire, Scotland, 22 March, 1967 — RW

League Club	Source	Date Signed	Seasons Played	Apps	Subs	Gls
Rotherham U	App	09/84	83-84	6	3	0
Lincoln C	Tr	01/86	85-86	38	5	4

McINNES John
Born: Ayr, Scotland, 29 March, 1923 — IF

League Club	Source	Date Signed	Seasons Played	Apps	Subs	Gls
Bradford C	Raith Rov	05/49	49-50	21	-	6

McINNES John Smith
Born: Glasgow, Scotland, 11 August, 1927 — W
Died: Bedford, England, 1973

League Club	Source	Date Signed	Seasons Played	Apps	Subs	Gls
Chelsea	Greenock Morton	05/47	46-49	37	-	7

McINNES Joseph Clarke (Joe)
Born: Glasgow, Scotland, 9 December, 1932 — LW

League Club	Source	Date Signed	Seasons Played	Apps	Subs	Gls
Accrington Stan	Partick Thistle	03/56	55	14	-	2

McINNES William (Willie)
Born: Douglas, Lanarkshire, Scotland, 20 May, 1931 — G

League Club	Source	Date Signed	Seasons Played	Apps	Subs	Gls
Accrington Stan	Lesmahagow	10/55	55-60	153	-	0
Southport	Tr	07/61	61-62	26	-	0

McINTOSH Alan
Born: Llandudno, Conwy, Wales, 29 July, 1939 — W
Wales: Amateur

League Club	Source	Date Signed	Seasons Played	Apps	Subs	Gls
Cardiff C	Llandudno	02/62	61-63	64	-	11

McINTOSH Albert (Bert)
Born: Dundee, Scotland, 6 April, 1930 — CF
Died: Dundee, Scotland, 19 December, 2008

League Club	Source	Date Signed	Seasons Played	Apps	Subs	Gls
Swansea C	Dundee Downfield	03/54	53-57	15	-	3

McINTOSH Alexander (Alex)
Born: Dunfermline, Fife, Scotland, 14 April, 1916 — IF
Died: Cannock, Staffordshire, England, December, 1965

League Club	Source	Date Signed	Seasons Played	Apps	Subs	Gls
Wolverhampton W	Folkestone	10/37	37-46	44	-	7
Birmingham C	Tr	01/47	46-47	23	-	4
Coventry C	Tr	02/48	47-48	20	-	3

McINTOSH Alexander James (Alex)
Born: Inverurie, Aberdeenshire, Scotland, 19 October, 1923 — RB
Died: Carlisle, Cumbria, England, 19 October, 1998

League Club	Source	Date Signed	Seasons Played	Apps	Subs	Gls
Barrow	Dundee	04/47	46-49	89	-	1
Carlisle U	Tr	10/49	49-54	227	-	4

McINTOSH Austin James
Born: Newham, E London, England, 5 November, 1987 — RB

League Club	Source	Date Signed	Seasons Played	Apps	Subs	Gls
Mansfield T	Sch	07/06	04	1	0	0

McINTOSH David (Dave)
Born: Girvan, Ayrshire, Scotland, 4 May, 1925 — G
Died: Glenrothes, Fife, Scotland, 24 July, 1995

League Club	Source	Date Signed	Seasons Played	Apps	Subs	Gls
Sheffield Wed	Girvan Ath	10/47	47-57	293	-	0
Doncaster Rov	Tr	01/58	57-58	15	-	0

McINTOSH James McLauchlan (Jimmy)
Born: Dumfries, Scotland, 5 April, 1918 — CF
Died: Berwick-on-Tweed, Northumberland, England, 4 April, 2000
Northern Ireland: NILge-1

League Club	Source	Date Signed	Seasons Played	Apps	Subs	Gls
Blackpool	Droylsden	09/35	35-37	5	-	0
Preston NE	Tr	11/37	37-38	27	-	3
Blackpool	Tr	05/46	46-48	66	-	22
Everton	Tr	03/49	48-50	58	-	19

McINTOSH James William (Jim)
Born: Forfar, Angus, Scotland, 19 August, 1950 — W

League Club	Source	Date Signed	Seasons Played	Apps	Subs	Gls
Nottingham F	Montrose	10/70	70-75	45	7	2
Chesterfield	L	01/76	75	3	0	0
Hull C	Tr	03/76	75-76	20	0	1

McINTOSH John McGregor (Ian)
Born: Glasgow, Scotland, 14 September, 1933 — IF

League Club	Source	Date Signed	Seasons Played	Apps	Subs	Gls
Bury	Partick Thistle	12/57	57-58	29	-	14

McINTOSH Malcolm Patrick
Born: Oxford, England, 6 July, 1959 — D

League Club	Source	Date Signed	Seasons Played	Apps	Subs	Gls
Oxford U	App	07/77	78-80	53	3	0
Oxford U	Kettering T	08/82	82	2	0	0

McINTOSH Martin Wyllie
Born: East Kilbride, Lanarkshire, Scotland, 19 March, 1971 — CD
Scotland: B-2/Schools

League Club	Source	Date Signed	Seasons Played	Apps	Subs	Gls
Stockport Co	Hamilton Academical	08/97	97-99	96	3	5
Rotherham U	Hibernian	08/01	01-04	122	0	16
Huddersfield T	Tr	07/05	05-06	44	4	4
Grimsby T	L	08/06	06	4	0	0
Mansfield T	Tr	08/07	07	9	2	1

McINTOSH William Dowling (Willie)
Born: Glasgow, Scotland, 7 December, 1919 — CF
Died: Glasgow, Scotland, 24 February, 1990

League Club	Source	Date Signed	Seasons Played	Apps	Subs	Gls
Preston NE	St Johnstone	05/46	46-48	91	-	46
Blackpool	Tr	01/49	48-51	51	-	15
Stoke C	Tr	09/51	51-52	26	-	5
Walsall	Tr	11/52	52	22	-	9

McINTYRE James (Jimmy)
Born: Alexandria, Dunbartonshire, Scotland, 24 May, 1972 — W/F
Scotland: B

League Club	Source	Date Signed	Seasons Played	Apps	Subs	Gls
Bristol C	Duntocher BC	10/91	91	1	0	0
Exeter C	L	02/93	92	12	3	3
Reading	Kilmarnock	03/98	97-00	68	29	14

McINTYRE James Hobbs (Jim)
Born: Motherwell, Lanarkshire, Scotland, 22 March, 1933 — G

League Club	Source	Date Signed	Seasons Played	Apps	Subs	Gls
Accrington Stan	Albion Rov	03/57	56	4	-	0

McINTYRE Joseph Gerald (Joe)
Born: Manchester, England, 19 June, 1971 — LB

League Club	Source	Date Signed	Seasons Played	Apps	Subs	Gls
Rochdale	YT	10/88	88	2	2	0

McINTYRE Kevin
Born: Liverpool, England, 23 December, 1977 — LB
England: Semi Pro-4

League Club	Source	Date Signed	Seasons Played	Apps	Subs	Gls
Tranmere Rov	YT	11/96	97	0	2	0
Chester C	Doncaster Rov	05/02	04	9	1	0
Macclesfield T	Tr	12/04	04-07	130	4	16
Shrewsbury T	Tr	01/08	07-10	108	16	4
Accrington Stan	Tr	07/11	11	44	1	2
Rochdale	Tr	07/12	12	37	1	1

McINTYRE Patrick Finucane
Born: Aylesham, Kent, England, 14 March, 1943 — RB

League Club	Source	Date Signed	Seasons Played	Apps	Subs	Gls
Gillingham	Jnr	07/61	60-62	10	-	0

McINTYRE Stephen (Steve)
Born: Ayr, Scotland, 15 May, 1966 — RB

League Club	Source	Date Signed	Seasons Played	Apps	Subs	Gls
Hereford U	Ayr U	07/91	91	12	0	0

McIVER Frederick (Fred)
Born: Birtley, Tyne and Wear, England, 14 February, 1952 — M

League Club	Source	Date Signed	Seasons Played	Apps	Subs	Gls
Sunderland	App	04/69	71	1	0	0
Sheffield Wed	Racing Jet (BEL)	07/74	74-75	34	3	0

MacIVOR Ronald William (Ron)
Born: Edinburgh, Scotland, 23 March, 1951 — FB

League Club	Source	Date Signed	Seasons Played	Apps	Subs	Gls
Wigan Ath	East Fife	10/79	79	3	0	1

McJANNET William Leslie (Les)
Born: Cumnock, Ayrshire, Scotland, 2 August, 1961 — RB

League Club	Source	Date Signed	Seasons Played	Apps	Subs	Gls
Mansfield T	Jnr	08/79	79-81	73	1	0
Scarborough	Matlock T	08/87	87-88	29	5	0
Darlington	Tr	12/88	88-91	83	2	5

McJARROW Hugh
Born: Motherwell, Lanarkshire, Scotland, 29 January, 1928 — CF
Died: Brigstock, Northamptonshire, England, 25 July, 1987

League Club	Source	Date Signed	Seasons Played	Apps	Subs	Gls
Chesterfield	Newarthill Hearts	03/46	46-49	33	-	11
Sheffield Wed	Tr	03/50	49-51	46	-	21
Luton T	Tr	02/52	51-53	15	-	10
Plymouth Arg	Tr	12/53	53-55	30	-	3

MACKAIL-SMITH Craig Anthony Robert
Born: Watford, Hertfordshire, England, 25 February, 1984 — F
England: Semi Pro-7//Scotland: 7

League Club	Source	Date Signed	Seasons Played	Apps	Subs	Gls
Peterborough U	Dagenham & Red	01/07	06-10	173	12	80
Brighton & HA	Tr	07/11	11-14	79	30	21
Peterborough U	L	11/14	14	3	0	0

McKAIN Devante Nathaniel
Born: Hanwell, W London, England, 26 June, 1994 CD

League Club	Source	Date Signed	Seasons Played	Apps	Subs	Gls
Gillingham	Maidenhead U	11/12	12-13	0	2	0

MACKAY Angus MacDougall
Born: Glasgow, Scotland, 24 April, 1925 IF
Died: Exeter, England, 9 June, 2000

League Club	Source	Date Signed	Seasons Played	Apps	Subs	Gls
Ipswich T	Hamilton Academical	05/46	46	5	-	0
Exeter C	Tr	09/47	47-54	257	-	79
Millwall	Tr	06/55	55	17	-	4

MACKAY David
Born: Rutherglen, Glasgow, Scotland, 2 May, 1981 FB

League Club	Source	Date Signed	Seasons Played	Apps	Subs	Gls
Oxford U	Dundee	07/04	04	44	0	0

MACKAY David Craig (Dave)
Born: Musselburgh, East Lothian, Scotland, 14 November, 1934 LH
Died: Nottingham, England, 2 March, 2015
England: FLge-2//Scotland: 22/SLge-3/U23-4/Schools

League Club	Source	Date Signed	Seasons Played	Apps	Subs	Gls
Tottenham H	Heart of Midlothian	03/59	58-67	268	0	42
Derby Co	Tr	07/68	68-70	122	0	5
Swindon T	Tr	05/71	71	25	1	1

McKAY Derek
Born: Banff, Aberdeenshire, Scotland, 13 December, 1949 RW
Died: Pattaya, Thailand, 19 April, 2008

League Club	Source	Date Signed	Seasons Played	Apps	Subs	Gls
Barrow	Aberdeen	09/71	71	18	0	0

MACKAY Donald Scrimgeour (Don)
Born: Glasgow, Scotland, 19 March, 1940 G

League Club	Source	Date Signed	Seasons Played	Apps	Subs	Gls
Southend U	Dundee U	07/72	72-73	13	0	0

McKAY Jack
Born: Glasgow, Scotland, 19 November, 1996 F

League Club	Source	Date Signed	Seasons Played	Apps	Subs	Gls
Doncaster Rov	Sch	11/14	14	1	3	0

McKAY James (Jim)
Born: Stirling, Scotland, 11 June, 1918 CF
Died: Denny, Falkirk, Scotland, 14 November, 1986

League Club	Source	Date Signed	Seasons Played	Apps	Subs	Gls
Tranmere Rov	Cowdenbeath	08/49	49	12	-	1

McKAY Joffre
Born: Conon Bridge, Highlands, Scotland, 21 January, 1937 G

League Club	Source	Date Signed	Seasons Played	Apps	Subs	Gls
Bury	Ross Co	12/58				
Rochdale	Tr	07/60	60	9	-	0

McKAY John (Johnny)
Born: Port Glasgow, Inverclyde, Scotland, 27 June, 1927 LW
Died: Yeovil, Somerset, England, December, 1988

League Club	Source	Date Signed	Seasons Played	Apps	Subs	Gls
Queens Park Rgrs	Irvine Meadow	03/49	49-51	17	-	1

MACKAY Malcolm George (Malky)
Born: Coatbridge, Lanarkshire, Scotland, 19 February, 1972 CD
Scotland: 5

League Club	Source	Date Signed	Seasons Played	Apps	Subs	Gls
Norwich C	Glasgow Celtic	09/98	98-03	198	14	15
West Ham U	Tr	09/04	04	17	1	2
Watford	Tr	08/05	05-06	48	4	3

McKAY Mark Brian
Born: Edinburgh, Scotland, 12 November, 1967 W

League Club	Source	Date Signed	Seasons Played	Apps	Subs	Gls
Doncaster Rov	Dalkeith Jnrs	01/90	89	0	1	0

McKAY Matthew Paul (Matt)
Born: Warrington, Cheshire, England, 21 January, 1981 M

League Club	Source	Date Signed	Seasons Played	Apps	Subs	Gls
Chester C	YT	-	97	3	2	0
Everton	Tr	03/98				

MACKAY Michael
Born: Chester-le-Street, County Durham, England, 11 October, 1982 F

League Club	Source	Date Signed	Seasons Played	Apps	Subs	Gls
Hartlepool U	Consett	02/07	06-10	20	32	7

McKAY Paul Wilson
Born: Banbury, Oxfordshire, England, 28 January, 1971 RB/M

League Club	Source	Date Signed	Seasons Played	Apps	Subs	Gls
Burnley		11/89	89	8	4	0

McKAY Peter Walker
Born: Newburgh, Fife, Scotland, 23 February, 1925 CF
Died: Corby, Northamptonshire, England, 23 November, 2000

League Club	Source	Date Signed	Seasons Played	Apps	Subs	Gls
Burnley	Dundee U	05/54	54-56	60	-	36

MACKAY Robert (Bobby)
Born: Harthill, Lanarkshire, Scotland, 6 May, 1948 M

League Club	Source	Date Signed	Seasons Played	Apps	Subs	Gls
Leicester C	Harthill Jnrs	05/65	68	6	1	1

McKAY William (Billy)
Born: Rothesay, Isle of Bute, Scotland, 10 March, 1927 RW
Died: Largs, Ayrshire, Scotland, 2 July, 1996

League Club	Source	Date Signed	Seasons Played	Apps	Subs	Gls
Queens Park Rgrs	Deal T	07/55	55	6	-	0

McKAY William Robert (Billy)
Born: Corby, Northamptonshire, England, 22 October, 1988 F

Northern Ireland: 10/U21-7/Youth

League Club	Source	Date Signed	Seasons Played	Apps	Subs	Gls
Leicester C	Sch	07/07				
Northampton T	Tr	07/09	09-10	53	21	13
Wigan Ath	Inverness CT	01/15	14	1	8	0

McKEARNEY David Jonathan
Born: Crosby, Merseyside, England, 20 June, 1968 LB/M

League Club	Source	Date Signed	Seasons Played	Apps	Subs	Gls
Bolton W	Prescot Cables	11/87				
Crewe Alex	Northwich Victoria	10/89	89-92	95	13	12
Wigan Ath	Tr	07/93	93-94	45	4	9

McKECHNIE Ian Hector
Born: Lenzie, Dunbartonshire, Scotland, 4 October, 1941 G
Died: Brantingham, East Riding of Yorkshire, England, 9 June, 2015

League Club	Source	Date Signed	Seasons Played	Apps	Subs	Gls
Arsenal	Lenzie	05/59	61-63	23	-	0
Southend U	Tr	05/64	64-65	62	0	0
Hull C	Tr	08/66	66-73	255	0	0

McKECHNIE Thomas Sharp (Tommy)
Born: Milngavie, Dunbartonshire, Scotland, 9 February, 1940 IF
Died: Old Kilpatrick, Dunbartonshire, Scotland, 6 April, 2009

League Club	Source	Date Signed	Seasons Played	Apps	Subs	Gls
Luton T	Kirkintilloch Rob Roy	05/61	61-65	129	2	31
Bournemouth	Tr	07/66	66	14	0	2
Colchester U	Tr	09/67	67	22	1	5

McKEE Colin
Born: Glasgow, Scotland, 22 August, 1973 F

League Club	Source	Date Signed	Seasons Played	Apps	Subs	Gls
Manchester U	YT	06/91	93	1	0	0
Bury	L	01/93	92	2	0	0

McKEE Francis Joseph (Frank)
Born: Cowdenbeath, Fife, Scotland, 25 January, 1923 LH
Died: Slough, Berkshire, England, 24 July, 1988

League Club	Source	Date Signed	Seasons Played	Apps	Subs	Gls
Birmingham C	Dundee U	02/48	48-50	22	-	0
Gillingham	Tr	07/52	52-54	53	-	0

McKEE Raymond Trevor (Ray)
Born: Plaistow, E London, England, 16 June, 1926 G

League Club	Source	Date Signed	Seasons Played	Apps	Subs	Gls
Northampton T	Finchley	03/47	46	5	-	0

McKEE Stephen (Steve)
Born: Belfast, Northern Ireland, 15 April, 1956 LW

League Club	Source	Date Signed	Seasons Played	Apps	Subs	Gls
Sheffield U	Linfield	12/76	76	4	3	0

McKEE William Andrew (Bill)
Born: Burtonwood, Cheshire, England, 6 June, 1928 WH
Died: Blackburn, Greater Manchester, England, 21 April, 1999

League Club	Source	Date Signed	Seasons Played	Apps	Subs	Gls
Blackburn Rov	Earlestown	11/49	50	1	-	0

McKEENAN Alexander Peter (Peter)
Born: Port Glasgow, Inverclyde, Scotland, 26 February, 1924 IF

League Club	Source	Date Signed	Seasons Played	Apps	Subs	Gls
Leyton Orient	Port Glasgow	06/46	46	1	-	0

McKEEVER Mark Anthony
Born: Derry, Northern Ireland, 16 November, 1978 LW
Republic of Ireland: U21-4//Northern Ireland: Youth

League Club	Source	Date Signed	Seasons Played	Apps	Subs	Gls
Peterborough U	YT	-	96	2	1	0
Sheffield Wed	Tr	04/97	98-99	2	3	0
Bristol Rov	L	12/98	98	5	2	0
Reading	L	03/99	98	6	1	2
Bristol Rov	Tr	02/01	00-02	20	16	0

McKELLAR David Norwood
Born: Ardrossan, Ayrshire, Scotland, 22 May, 1956 G
Scotland: Youth

League Club	Source	Date Signed	Seasons Played	Apps	Subs	Gls
Ipswich T	App	03/74				
Derby Co	Ardrossan Winton Rov	04/78	78-79	41	0	0
Brentford	Tr	09/80	80-81	84	0	0
Carlisle U	Tr	08/83	83-84	82	0	0
Newcastle U (L)	Hibernian	02/86	85	10	0	0
Hartlepool U (L)	Dunfermline Ath	08/88	88	5	0	0
Carlisle U	Dunfermline Ath	10/88	88-89	69	0	0

MACKEN Anthony (Tony)
Born: Dublin, Republic of Ireland, 30 July, 1950 RB
Republic of Ireland: 1/LoI-1/U23-1

League Club	Source	Date Signed	Seasons Played	Apps	Subs	Gls
Derby Co	Waterford (ROI)	08/74	75-77	20	3	1
Portsmouth	L	11/75	75	5	0	0
Portsmouth	L	02/76	75	5	0	1
Walsall	Tr	10/77	77-81	190	0	1

MACKEN Jonathan Paul (Jon)
Born: Manchester, England, 7 September, 1977 F
England: Youth//Republic of Ireland: 1

League Club	Source	Date Signed	Seasons Played	Apps	Subs	Gls
Manchester U	YT	07/96				
Preston NE	Tr	07/97	97-01	155	29	63
Manchester C	Tr	03/02	01-04	27	24	7
Crystal Palace	Tr	06/05	05-06	14	11	2
Ipswich T	L	08/06	06	13	1	4
Derby Co	Tr	01/07	06-07	4	7	0

League Club	Source	Date Signed	Seasons Played	Apps	Subs	Gls
Barnsley	L	11/07	07	11	0	3
Barnsley	Tr	01/08	07-09	81	13	18
Walsall	Tr	08/10	10-11	68	8	16

McKENNA Alan Millar
Born: Edinburgh, Scotland, 4 August, 1961 — F

League Club	Source	Date Signed	Seasons Played	Apps	Subs	Gls
Millwall	App	10/78	78-81	23	7	4

McKENNA Benjamin James (Ben)
Born: Burnley, Lancashire, England, 16 January, 1993 — M
Northern Ireland: Youth

League Club	Source	Date Signed	Seasons Played	Apps	Subs	Gls
Carlisle U	Sch	06/11	10	0	1	0

McKENNA Brian Francis
Born: Dublin, Republic of Ireland, 30 January, 1972 — G
Republic of Ireland: U21-4

League Club	Source	Date Signed	Seasons Played	Apps	Subs	Gls
Brighton & HA	Home Farm (ROI)	07/89	90	1	0	0

McKENNA Francis (Frank)
Born: Blaydon, Tyne and Wear, England, 8 January, 1933 — W
England: Amateur-3

League Club	Source	Date Signed	Seasons Played	Apps	Subs	Gls
Leeds U	Bishop Auckland	07/56	56	6	-	4
Carlisle U	Tr	02/58	57-58	46	-	11
Hartlepool U	Tr	07/59	59	32	-	5

McKENNA John (Johnny)
Born: Belfast, Northern Ireland, 6 June, 1926 — W
Died: Blackpool, Lancashire, England, 28 October, 1980
Northern Ireland: 7/NILge-3/War-2

League Club	Source	Date Signed	Seasons Played	Apps	Subs	Gls
Huddersfield T	Linfield	09/48	48-52	134	-	8
Blackpool	Tr	07/54	54-56	24	-	2
Southport	Tr	07/57	57	15	-	1

McKENNA Kenneth Michael (Kenny)
Born: Birkenhead, Wirral, England, 2 July, 1960 — F

League Club	Source	Date Signed	Seasons Played	Apps	Subs	Gls
Tranmere Rov	Poulton Victoria	08/82	82	2	2	0
Tranmere Rov	Telford U	08/87	87-88	13	3	3

McKENNA Michael Joseph (Mike)
Born: Darkley, Armagh, Northern Ireland, 3 November, 1916 — WH
Died: Portadown, Armagh, Northern Ireland, 30 September, 1974

League Club	Source	Date Signed	Seasons Played	Apps	Subs	Gls
Northampton T	Bromsgrove Rov	07/46	46	4	-	0

McKENNA Patrick (Pat)
Born: Glasgow, Scotland, 26 April, 1920 — FB
Died: Aberdeen, Scotland, 16 November, 1995

League Club	Source	Date Signed	Seasons Played	Apps	Subs	Gls
Plymouth Arg	Aberdeen	08/52	52	1	-	0

McKENNA Paul Stephen
Born: Eccleston, Lancashire, England, 20 October, 1977 — M

League Club	Source	Date Signed	Seasons Played	Apps	Subs	Gls
Preston NE	YT	02/96	96-08	400	22	30
Nottingham F	Tr	07/09	09-10	65	2	3
Hull C	Tr	07/11	11-12	43	7	0
Fleetwood T	L	01/13	12	15	0	0

McKENNA Thomas (Tom)
Born: Paisley, Renfrewshire, Scotland, 11 November, 1919 — WH
Died: Chelmsford, England, December, 2008

League Club	Source	Date Signed	Seasons Played	Apps	Subs	Gls
Reading	St Mirren	06/46	46-47	28	-	1
Grimsby T	Tr	06/48	48-49	50	-	2

McKENNAN Peter Stewart
Born: Airdrie, Lanarkshire, Scotland, 16 July, 1918 — IF
Died: Dundonald, Ayrshire, Scotland, 28 September, 1991
Northern Ireland: NILge-2//Scotland: SLge-2

League Club	Source	Date Signed	Seasons Played	Apps	Subs	Gls
West Bromwich A	Partick Thistle	10/47	47	11	-	4
Leicester C	Tr	03/48	47-48	18	-	7
Brentford	Tr	09/48	48	24	-	6
Middlesbrough	Tr	05/49	49-50	40	-	18
Oldham Ath	Tr	07/51	51-53	78	-	28

MacKENZIE Aiden
Born: Athlone, Republic of Ireland, 15 July, 1959 — F

League Club	Source	Date Signed	Seasons Played	Apps	Subs	Gls
Lincoln C	Galway Rov (ROI)	12/78	79	4	2	0

MacKENZIE Christopher Neil (Chris)
Born: Northampton, England, 14 May, 1972 — G

League Club	Source	Date Signed	Seasons Played	Apps	Subs	Gls
Hereford U	Corby T	07/94	94-95	59	1	1
Leyton Orient	Tr	10/97	97-98	30	0	0
Chester C	Telford U	07/04	04-05	53	1	0
Shrewsbury T	Tr	07/06	06	20	0	0

MacKENZIE Donald Alexander (Don)
Born: Liverpool, England, 30 January, 1942 — W

League Club	Source	Date Signed	Seasons Played	Apps	Subs	Gls
Everton		01/63				
Rochdale	Tr	10/63	63-64	41	-	7

McKENZIE Donald Cameron (Don)
Born: Glasgow, Scotland, 9 June, 1927 — IF

League Club	Source	Date Signed	Seasons Played	Apps	Subs	Gls
Grimsby T	Glasgow Rangers	08/51	51	4	-	0

McKENZIE Duncan
Born: Grimsby, North Lincolnshire, England, 10 June, 1950 — F

League Club	Source	Date Signed	Seasons Played	Apps	Subs	Gls
Nottingham F	Old Clee	07/68	69-73	105	6	41
Mansfield T	L	03/70	69	7	3	3
Mansfield T	L	02/73	72	6	0	7
Leeds U	Tr	08/74	74-75	64	2	27
Everton	Anderlecht (BEL)	12/76	76-77	48	0	14
Chelsea	Tr	09/78	78	15	0	4
Blackburn Rov	Tr	03/79	78-80	74	0	16

MacKENZIE Gary
Born: Lanark, Scotland, 15 October, 1985 — CD

League Club	Source	Date Signed	Seasons Played	Apps	Subs	Gls
MK Dons	Dundee	07/10	10-12	60	3	3
Blackpool	Tr	03/13	12-13	47	0	3
Bradford C	L	02/15	14	9	3	1

MacKENZIE Hamish James Todd
Born: Denny, Falkirk, Scotland, 11 March, 1945 — LB

League Club	Source	Date Signed	Seasons Played	Apps	Subs	Gls
Liverpool	App	03/62				
Brentford	Dunfermline Ath	08/64	65-66	19	0	0

McKENZIE Ian Edward
Born: Wallsend, Tyne and Wear, England, 22 August, 1966 — LB

League Club	Source	Date Signed	Seasons Played	Apps	Subs	Gls
Barnsley	Newcastle U (App)	08/85	85	1	0	0
Stockport Co	Tr	09/86	86-88	51	8	0

MacKENZIE Ian Stanley
Born: Rotherham, South Yorkshire, England, 27 September, 1950 — CD

League Club	Source	Date Signed	Seasons Played	Apps	Subs	Gls
Sheffield U	Jnr	06/68	69-74	43	2	1
Southend U	L	03/75	74	5	1	0
Mansfield T	Tr	07/75	75-77	69	1	1

MacKENZIE John Archibald (Johnny)
Born: Glasgow, Scotland, 4 September, 1925 — RW
Scotland: 9/SLge-2

League Club	Source	Date Signed	Seasons Played	Apps	Subs	Gls
Bournemouth	Partick Thistle	08/47	47	38	-	9

MacKENZIE Kyrtis
Born: Newham, E London, England, 17 October, 1993 — CD

League Club	Source	Date Signed	Seasons Played	Apps	Subs	Gls
Torquay U	Sch	05/12	12	1	0	0

McKENZIE Leon Mark
Born: Croydon, S London, England, 17 May, 1978 — F

League Club	Source	Date Signed	Seasons Played	Apps	Subs	Gls
Crystal Palace	YT	10/95	95-00	44	41	7
Fulham	L	10/97	97	1	2	0
Peterborough U	L	08/98	98	4	0	3
Peterborough U	L	11/98	98	10	0	5
Peterborough U	Tr	10/00	00-03	83	7	45
Norwich C	Tr	12/03	03-06	47	32	20
Coventry C	Tr	08/06	06-09	42	20	12
Charlton Ath	Tr	09/09	09	0	12	0
Northampton T	Tr	09/10	10	17	10	10

McKENZIE Malcolm James
Born: Edinburgh, Scotland, 1 May, 1950 — LW

League Club	Source	Date Signed	Seasons Played	Apps	Subs	Gls
Port Vale	Jnr	05/67	65-67	7	1	1

MacKENZIE Matthew Laurence (Laurence)
Born: Old Kilpatrick, Dunbartonshire, Scotland, 7 July, 1924 — WH/IF
Died: Sheffield, England, March, 2010

League Club	Source	Date Signed	Seasons Played	Apps	Subs	Gls
Sheffield Wed	Clydebank Ath	12/45	46-47	6	-	0
Grimsby T	Tr	07/49	49-50	58	-	11

MacKENZIE Neil David
Born: Birmingham, England, 15 April, 1976 — M

League Club	Source	Date Signed	Seasons Played	Apps	Subs	Gls
Stoke C	West Bromwich A (YT)	11/95	96-99	15	27	1
Cambridge U	L	03/99	98	3	1	1
Cambridge U	Tr	10/99	99-00	20	8	0
Kidderminster Hrs	Tr	11/00	00	20	3	3
Blackpool	Tr	07/01	01	6	8	1
Mansfield T	Tr	08/02	02-04	50	21	4
Macclesfield T	Tr	11/04	04-05	20	4	1
Scunthorpe U	Tr	11/05	05-06	22	16	4
Hereford U	L	10/06	06	7	0	0
Notts Co	Tr	07/07	07-08	24	6	6
Port Vale	L	11/08	08	2	0	0

McKENZIE Paul
Born: Aberdeen, Scotland, 4 October, 1969 — M

League Club	Source	Date Signed	Seasons Played	Apps	Subs	Gls
Sunderland	YT	07/87				
Burnley	Peterhead	02/92	91	1	3	0

McKENZIE Robert Alexander
Born: Hexham, Northumberland, England, 22 March, 1979 — M/RB

League Club	Source	Date Signed	Seasons Played	Apps	Subs	Gls
Rotherham U	YT	06/97	96	6	5	0

McKENZIE Roger Mark
Born: Sheffield, England, 27 January, 1973 — F

League Club	Source	Date Signed	Seasons Played	Apps	Subs	Gls
Doncaster Rov	YT	07/91	91	7	10	1
Scarborough	Tr	08/92	92	0	1	0

MacKENZIE Stephen (Steve)
Born: Romford, E London, England, 23 November, 1961 — M
England: B-1/U21-3/Youth

League Club	Source	Date Signed	Seasons Played	Apps	Subs	Gls
Crystal Palace	App	07/79				
Manchester C	Tr	07/79	79-80	56	2	8
West Bromwich A	Tr	08/81	81-86	153	3	23
Charlton Ath	Tr	06/87	87-90	92	8	7
Sheffield Wed	Tr	02/91	90-91	5	10	2
Shrewsbury T	Tr	12/91	91-93	19	5	1

McKENZIE Stuart Ronald
Born: Hull, England, 19 September, 1967 — RB

League Club	Source	Date Signed	Seasons Played	Apps	Subs	Gls
York C	App	12/85	85-87	30	2	0

McKENZIE Taylor Joshua
Born: Enfield, N London, England, 30 May, 1994 — D

League Club	Source	Date Signed	Seasons Played	Apps	Subs	Gls
Sheffield Wed	Norwich C (Sch)	10/12				
Notts Co	Tr	05/14	14	2	2	0

McKEOWN Gary Joseph
Born: Oxford, England, 19 October, 1970 — M
England: Youth/Schools

League Club	Source	Date Signed	Seasons Played	Apps	Subs	Gls
Arsenal	YT	11/88				
Shrewsbury T	L	03/92	91	8	0	1
Exeter C (L)	Dundee	12/96	96	3	0	0

McKEOWN Isaac Lindsay (Lindsay)
Born: Belfast, Northern Ireland, 11 July, 1957 — M
Northern Ireland: NILge-2

League Club	Source	Date Signed	Seasons Played	Apps	Subs	Gls
Manchester U	App	07/74				
Sheffield Wed	Tr	07/76	76-77	6	5	0

McKEOWN James Karl
Born: Walsall, West Midlands, England, 24 July, 1989 — G

League Club	Source	Date Signed	Seasons Played	Apps	Subs	Gls
Peterborough U	Walsall (Sch)	07/07	07-09	2	4	0

McKEOWN Joseph Francis (Joe)
Born: Bannockburn, Stirlingshire, Scotland, 9 April, 1924 — IF
Died: Bannockburn, Stirlingshire, Scotland, 20 April, 1974

League Club	Source	Date Signed	Seasons Played	Apps	Subs	Gls
Hartlepool U	Stirling A	08/50	50	46	-	7

McKEOWN Thomas (Tom)
Born: Cleland, Lanarkshire, Scotland, 2 October, 1930 — RW
Died: Holytown, Lanarkshire, Scotland, 22 June, 1995

League Club	Source	Date Signed	Seasons Played	Apps	Subs	Gls
Accrington Stan	Queen of the South	05/54	54	12	-	2

McKERNON Craig Andrew
Born: Gloucester, England, 23 February, 1968 — FB

League Club	Source	Date Signed	Seasons Played	Apps	Subs	Gls
Mansfield T	App	02/86	84-89	79	14	0
Arsenal	Tr	12/89				

MACKEY Benjamin Michael (Ben)
Born: Leamington Spa, Warwickshire, England, 27 October, 1986 — F

League Club	Source	Date Signed	Seasons Played	Apps	Subs	Gls
Coventry C	Jnr	-	02	0	3	0

MACKIE James Charles (Jamie)
Born: Dorking, Surrey, England, 22 September, 1985 — F/W
Scotland: 9

League Club	Source	Date Signed	Seasons Played	Apps	Subs	Gls
Wimbledon	Leatherhead	01/04	03	8	5	0
MK Dons	Wimbledon relocation	07/04	04	0	3	0
Plymouth Arg	Exeter C	01/08	07-09	81	17	16
Queens Park Rgrs	Tr	05/10	10-12	66	19	18
Nottingham F	Tr	07/13	13	38	7	4
Reading	L	08/14	14	18	14	5

MACKIE John George
Born: Whitechapel, Central London, England, 5 July, 1976 — CD

League Club	Source	Date Signed	Seasons Played	Apps	Subs	Gls
Reading	Sutton U	11/99	00-03	61	10	3
Leyton Orient	Tr	01/04	03-06	119	3	11
Brentford	Tr	07/07	07	14	0	0

MACKIE Thomas Forbes (Tom)
Born: Burntisland, Fife, Scotland, 30 March, 1918 — LB
Died: Burntisland, Fife, Scotland, 2 February, 1989

League Club	Source	Date Signed	Seasons Played	Apps	Subs	Gls
New Brighton	St Johnstone	05/47	47	2	-	0
Chester C	Tr	08/48	48	5	-	0

McKIM John (Johnny)
Born: Greenock, Inverclyde, Scotland, 22 January, 1926 — IF
Died: Colchester, Essex, England, 20 June, 2000

League Club	Source	Date Signed	Seasons Played	Apps	Subs	Gls
Chelsea	Port Glasgow	06/47				
Colchester U	Tr	08/50	50-54	129	-	44

MACKIN John
Born: Glasgow, Scotland, 18 November, 1943 — RB

League Club	Source	Date Signed	Seasons Played	Apps	Subs	Gls
Northampton T		11/63	65-68	94	7	11
Lincoln C	Tr	07/69	69	3	0	0
York C	Tr	09/69	69-72	157	3	7
Darlington	L	03/73	72	2	0	0

MACKIN Levi Alan
Born: Chester, England, 4 April, 1986 — M
Wales: U21-1

League Club	Source	Date Signed	Seasons Played	Apps	Subs	Gls
Wrexham	Sch	07/05	05-07	18	27	1

McKINLAY Ian Joseph
Born: Huyton, Merseyside, England, 21 June, 1949 — RW

League Club	Source	Date Signed	Seasons Played	Apps	Subs	Gls
Southport	Wrexham (Am)	09/66	66-67	11	1	1

McKINLAY Robert (Bobby)
Born: Lochgelly, Fife, Scotland, 10 October, 1932 — CH
Died: West Bridgford, Nottinghamshire, England, August, 2002

League Club	Source	Date Signed	Seasons Played	Apps	Subs	Gls
Nottingham F	Bowhill Rov	10/49	51-69	611	3	9

McKINLAY Thomas Valley (Tosh)
Born: Glasgow, Scotland, 3 December, 1964 — LB
Scotland: 22/B/U21-6/Youth

League Club	Source	Date Signed	Seasons Played	Apps	Subs	Gls
Stoke C (L)	Glasgow Celtic	01/98	97	3	0	0

McKINLAY William James Alexander (Billy)
Born: Glasgow, Scotland, 22 April, 1969 — M
Scotland: 29/B-1/U21-6/Youth/Schools

League Club	Source	Date Signed	Seasons Played	Apps	Subs	Gls
Blackburn Rov	Dundee U	10/95	95-98	76	14	3
Bradford C	Tr	11/00	00	10	1	0
Preston NE	Tr	09/01				
Leicester C	Clydebank	08/02	02-03	44	9	1
Fulham	Tr	07/04	04	1	1	0

McKINNEY Richard
Born: Ballymoney, Antrim, Northern Ireland, 18 May, 1979 — G

League Club	Source	Date Signed	Seasons Played	Apps	Subs	Gls
Manchester C	Ballymena U	08/99				
Swindon T	Tr	07/01	01	1	0	0
Colchester U	Tr	08/02	02-03	25	1	0
Walsall	Tr	07/04	04	3	0	0

McKINNEY William (Bill)
Born: Newcastle-upon-Tyne, England, 20 July, 1936 — RB

League Club	Source	Date Signed	Seasons Played	Apps	Subs	Gls
Newcastle U	Wallsend St Luke's	05/56	57-64	85	-	6
Bournemouth	Tr	08/65	65	17	0	0
Mansfield T	Tr	07/66	66-67	51	1	2

McKINNON Paul John
Born: Frimley, Surrey, England, 1 August, 1958 — F

League Club	Source	Date Signed	Seasons Played	Apps	Subs	Gls
Blackburn Rov	Sutton U	12/86	86	5	0	0

McKINNON Raymond (Ray)
Born: Dundee, Scotland, 5 August, 1970 — M
Scotland: U21-6/Schools

League Club	Source	Date Signed	Seasons Played	Apps	Subs	Gls
Nottingham F	Dundee U	07/92	92	5	1	1
Luton T	Dundee U	08/98	98-99	29	4	2

McKINNON Robert (Rob)
Born: Glasgow, Scotland, 31 July, 1966 — LB
Scotland: 3/B-2

League Club	Source	Date Signed	Seasons Played	Apps	Subs	Gls
Newcastle U	Rutherglen Glencairn	11/84	85	1	0	0
Hartlepool U	Tr	08/86	86-91	246	1	7
Hartlepool U (L)	Heart of Midlothian	02/99	98	7	0	0
Carlisle U (L)	Heart of Midlothian	02/00	99	8	0	0

McKINVEN John James
Born: Campbeltown, Argyll & Bute, Scotland, 1 May, 1941 — LW

League Club	Source	Date Signed	Seasons Played	Apps	Subs	Gls
Southend U	Raith Rov	05/60	60-69	284	2	62
Cambridge U	Tr	12/69	70	18	0	2

MACKLEWORTH Colin
Born: Bow, E London, England, 24 March, 1947 — G

League Club	Source	Date Signed	Seasons Played	Apps	Subs	Gls
West Ham U	App	04/64	66	3	0	0
Leicester C	Tr	11/67	67-70	6	0	0

MACKLIN Lloyd Joshua
Born: Camberley, Surrey, England, 2 August, 1991 — W

League Club	Source	Date Signed	Seasons Played	Apps	Subs	Gls
Swindon T	Sch	08/08	08-09	1	10	0
Torquay U	L	02/10	09	3	1	0
Torquay U	Tr	07/10	10-12	7	23	0

McKNIGHT Allen Darrell
Born: Antrim, Northern Ireland, 27 January, 1964 — G
Northern Ireland: 10/U23-1

League Club	Source	Date Signed	Seasons Played	Apps	Subs	Gls
West Ham U	Glasgow Celtic	07/88	88	23	0	0
Rotherham U	Airdrieonians	10/91	91	3	0	0
Walsall	Tr	11/91	91	8	0	0
Exeter C	South China (HKG)	03/94	93	9	1	0

McKNIGHT George
Born: Newtownards, Down, Northern Ireland, 17 November, 1923 — IF
Died: Blackpool, Lancashire, England, 28 September, 1996

League Club	Source	Date Signed	Seasons Played	Apps	Subs	Gls
Blackpool	Coleraine	06/46	46-53	40	-	9
Chesterfield	Northwich Victoria	07/55	55	5	-	1
Southport	Tr	09/57	57	1	-	0

McKNIGHT Philip (Phil)
Born: Camlachie, Glasgow, Scotland, 15 June, 1924 LH

League Club	Source	Date Signed	Seasons Played	Apps	Subs	Gls
Chelsea	Alloa Ath	01/47	47-53	33	-	1
Leyton Orient	Tr	07/54	54-58	161	-	2

McKOP Henry George
Born: Bulawayo, Zimbabwe, 8 July, 1967 CD
Zimbabwe: 18

League Club	Source	Date Signed	Seasons Played	Apps	Subs	Gls
Bristol C	Bonner SC (ZIM)	02/94	93-94	2	3	0

McKOY Nicholas Paul (Nick)
Born: Newham, E London, England, 3 September, 1986 M

League Club	Source	Date Signed	Seasons Played	Apps	Subs	Gls
Wimbledon	Sch	-	03	1	2	0
MK Dons	Wimbledon relocation	07/05	05	5	11	0
Cardiff C	Tr	07/06				
Torquay U	L	01/07	06	1	3	0
Northampton T	Kettering T	07/11	11	5	4	0

MACKRETH Stephen Francis (Steve)
Born: Rossett, Wrexham, Wales, 1 July, 1950 FB

League Club	Source	Date Signed	Seasons Played	Apps	Subs	Gls
Wrexham	Jnr	10/67	68	1	1	0

McLACHLAN Dugald
Born: Falkirk, Scotland, 10 September, 1953 F

League Club	Source	Date Signed	Seasons Played	Apps	Subs	Gls
Preston NE	App	11/71				
Halifax T	L	10/72	72	1	1	0
Peterborough U	Tr	07/73	73	1	0	0

McLACHLAN Fraser Malcolm
Born: Manchester, England, 9 November, 1982 M

League Club	Source	Date Signed	Seasons Played	Apps	Subs	Gls
Stockport Co	YT	07/01	01-03	43	10	4
Mansfield T	Tr	11/04	04-05	23	6	0
Morecambe	Tr	03/06	07-10	23	6	0

McLACHLAN Stephen (Steve)
Born: Kirkcudbright, Dumfries & Galloway, Scotland, 19 September, 1918 RH
Died: Kirkcudbright, Dumfries & Galloway, Scotland, 26 July, 1990

League Club	Source	Date Signed	Seasons Played	Apps	Subs	Gls
Derby Co	Dalbeattie Star	03/38	38-52	58	-	1

McLAFFERTY Maurice
Born: Lanark, Scotland, 7 August, 1922 LB
Died: Worthing, West Sussex, England, January, 1999

League Club	Source	Date Signed	Seasons Played	Apps	Subs	Gls
Sheffield U	St Mirren	08/51	51	18	-	0
Brighton & HA	Tr	07/52	52	21	-	0

McLAGGON Kayne Simeon
Born: Barry, Vale of Glamorgan, Wales, 21 September, 1990 F
Wales: Youth

League Club	Source	Date Signed	Seasons Played	Apps	Subs	Gls
Southampton	Sch	09/07	08	1	6	1
Bristol Rov	Salisbury C	07/11	11	0	1	0

McLAIN Thomas (Tommy)
Born: Morpeth, Northumberland, England, 19 January, 1922 LH/CF
Died: Northumberland, England, December, 1995

League Club	Source	Date Signed	Seasons Played	Apps	Subs	Gls
Sunderland	Ashington	08/46	46-51	67	-	1
Northampton T	Tr	07/52	52-55	96	-	11

McLAREN Andrew (Andy)
Born: Larkhall, Lanarkshire, Scotland, 24 January, 1922 IF
Died: Northwich, Cheshire, England, 14 December, 1996
Scotland: 4

League Club	Source	Date Signed	Seasons Played	Apps	Subs	Gls
Preston NE	Larkhall Thistle	02/39	46-48	69	-	29
Burnley	Tr	12/48	48	3	-	1
Sheffield U	Tr	03/49	48-50	31	-	4
Barrow	Tr	02/51	50-54	155	-	52
Bradford Park Ave	Tr	10/54	54	18	-	7
Southport	Tr	06/55	55	4	-	1
Rochdale	Tr	11/55	55-56	44	-	12

McLAREN Andrew (Andy)
Born: Glasgow, Scotland, 5 June, 1973 M
Scotland: 1/U21-4/Schools

League Club	Source	Date Signed	Seasons Played	Apps	Subs	Gls
Reading	Dundee U	03/99	98-99	9	0	1

MacLAREN David (Dave)
Born: Auchterarder, Perthshire, Scotland, 12 June, 1934 G

League Club	Source	Date Signed	Seasons Played	Apps	Subs	Gls
Leicester C	Dundee	01/57	56-59	85	-	0
Plymouth Arg	Tr	06/60	60-64	131	-	0
Wolverhampton W	Tr	01/65	64-66	44	0	0
Southampton	Tr	09/66	66	22	0	0

McLAREN Edward (Eddie)
Born: Dundee, Scotland, 8 September, 1929 RB/WH

League Club	Source	Date Signed	Seasons Played	Apps	Subs	Gls
Blackpool	Dunkeld Jnrs	06/48				
Reading	Tr	10/52	53-58	184	-	2

McLAREN Hugh
Born: Hamilton, Lanarkshire, Scotland, 24 June, 1926 LW
Died: Derby, England, 8 December, 1965

League Club	Source	Date Signed	Seasons Played	Apps	Subs	Gls
Derby Co	Kilmarnock	10/49	49-53	119	-	53
Nottingham F	Tr	01/54	53-54	33	-	15
Walsall	Tr	07/55	55	31	-	8

McLAREN James Danks
Born: Birkenhead, Wirral, England, 29 July, 1936 RW

League Club	Source	Date Signed	Seasons Played	Apps	Subs	Gls
Chesterfield	Wigan Ath	06/58	59	11	-	2

MacLAREN James Scott (Jimmy)
Born: Crieff, Perthshire, Scotland, 26 November, 1921 G
Died: Blairgowrie, Perthshire, Scotland, 20 July, 2004

League Club	Source	Date Signed	Seasons Played	Apps	Subs	Gls
Chester C	Berwick Rgrs	01/47	46-48	30	-	0
Carlisle U	Tr	12/48	48-54	262	-	0

MacLAREN John James Roy (Roy)
Born: Auchterarder, Perthshire, Scotland, 12 February, 1930 G

League Club	Source	Date Signed	Seasons Played	Apps	Subs	Gls
Bury	St Johnstone	12/55	55-58	86	-	0
Sheffield Wed	Tr	10/58	58-63	31	-	0

McLAREN Paul Andrew
Born: High Wycombe, Buckinghamshire, England, 17 November, 1976 M

League Club	Source	Date Signed	Seasons Played	Apps	Subs	Gls
Luton T	YT	01/94	93-00	137	30	4
Sheffield Wed	Tr	06/01	01-03	83	13	8
Rotherham U	Tr	08/04	04-05	67	5	4
Tranmere Rov	Tr	07/06	06-07	85	0	5
Bradford C	Tr	07/08	08	32	2	3
Tranmere Rov	Tr	07/09	09-10	42	2	0
Oxford U	Tr	01/11	10-11	40	2	2

McLAREN Robert (Bobby)
Born: Chryston, Lanarkshire, Scotland, 5 August, 1929 IF
Died: Blackpool, Lancashire, England, 8 October, 2010

League Club	Source	Date Signed	Seasons Played	Apps	Subs	Gls
Cardiff C	Barry T	02/50	49	1	-	0
Scunthorpe U	Barry T	08/51	51	6	-	0

MacLAREN Ross
Born: Edinburgh, Scotland, 14 April, 1962 CD

League Club	Source	Date Signed	Seasons Played	Apps	Subs	Gls
Shrewsbury T	Glasgow Rangers	08/80	80-84	158	3	18
Derby Co	Tr	07/85	85-87	113	9	4
Swindon T	Tr	08/88	88-94	195	2	9

McLAREN Thomas (Tommy)
Born: Livingston, West Lothian, Scotland, 1 June, 1949 M
Died: Telford, England, 23 July, 1978

League Club	Source	Date Signed	Seasons Played	Apps	Subs	Gls
Port Vale	Berwick Rgrs	11/67	67-76	301	32	28

McLARTY Jesse Jones
Born: Ayr, Scotland, 3 March, 1920 IF
Died: Chester, England, July, 2001

League Club	Source	Date Signed	Seasons Played	Apps	Subs	Gls
Wrexham	Chester C (Am)	09/45	46-47	24	-	9

McLAUGHLAN Alexander Donaldson (Sandy)
Born: Kilwinning, Ayrshire, Scotland, 17 July, 1936 G
Died: Kilwinning, Ayrshire, Scotland, 13 April, 1990
Scotland: SLge-1

League Club	Source	Date Signed	Seasons Played	Apps	Subs	Gls
Sunderland	Kilmarnock	09/64	64-65	43	0	0

McLAUGHLAN John Montgomery Lamont
Born: Clarkston, Renfrewshire, Scotland, 12 April, 1936 G

League Club	Source	Date Signed	Seasons Played	Apps	Subs	Gls
Shrewsbury T (L)	Third Lanark	09/63	63	5	-	0

McLAUGHLIN Brian
Born: Airdrie, Lanarkshire, Scotland, 14 May, 1974 M
Died: Falkirk, Scotland, 13 August, 2009
Scotland: U21-8

League Club	Source	Date Signed	Seasons Played	Apps	Subs	Gls
Wigan Ath	Dundee U	07/99	00	13	5	0

McLAUGHLIN Conor Gerard
Born: Belfast, Northern Ireland, 26 July, 1991 RB
Northern Ireland: 6/U21-7

League Club	Source	Date Signed	Seasons Played	Apps	Subs	Gls
Preston NE	Linfield	01/10	10-11	15	9	0
Shrewsbury T	L	03/12	11	4	0	0
Fleetwood T	Tr	07/12	12-14	83	10	1

McLAUGHLIN Hugh
Born: Glasgow, Scotland, 2 September, 1943 WH

League Club	Source	Date Signed	Seasons Played	Apps	Subs	Gls
Brentford	St Roch's	09/61	63-65	4	1	0

McLAUGHLIN James
Born: Paisley, Renfrewshire, Scotland, 11 February, 1926 IF
Died: Glasgow, Scotland, 6 May, 2006

League Club	Source	Date Signed	Seasons Played	Apps	Subs	Gls
Walsall	Glenavon	06/48	48-49	14	-	0

McLAUGHLIN James Charles (Jimmy)
Born: Stirling, Scotland, 10 December, 1926 LW
Died: Newton Mearns, Renfrewshire, Scotland, 27 March, 1981

League Club	Source	Date Signed	Seasons Played	Apps	Subs	Gls
Hartlepool U	Alloa Ath	07/53	53	13	-	2

McLAUGHLIN James Christopher (Jim)
Born: Derry, Northern Ireland, 22 December, 1940 W/F
Northern Ireland: 12/U23-2

League Club	Source	Date Signed	Seasons Played	Apps	Subs	Gls
Birmingham C	Derry C (ROI)	06/58				

League Club	Source	Date Signed	Seasons Played	Apps	Subs	Gls
Shrewsbury T	Tr	07/60	60-62	124	-	56
Swansea C	Tr	05/63	63-66	133	3	45
Peterborough U	Tr	03/67	66	8	0	2
Shrewsbury T	Tr	09/67	67-72	159	14	21
Swansea C	Tr	11/72	72-73	20	7	2

McLAUGHLIN John
Born: Edmonton, N London, England, 29 October, 1954 FB
England: Youth

League Club	Source	Date Signed	Seasons Played	Apps	Subs	Gls
Colchester U	App	05/72	71-73	66	0	2
Swindon T	Tr	12/73	73-78	199	3	8
Portsmouth	Tr	07/79	79-83	172	0	1

McLAUGHLIN John
Born: Lennoxtown, Dunbartonshire, Scotland, 13 November, 1936 LB

League Club	Source	Date Signed	Seasons Played	Apps	Subs	Gls
Millwall	Greenock Morton	07/63	63	21	-	5

McLAUGHLIN John Ian
Born: Stirling, Scotland, 3 January, 1948 LB

League Club	Source	Date Signed	Seasons Played	Apps	Subs	Gls
Everton	Falkirk	10/71	71-75	59	2	1

McLAUGHLIN John Thomas
Born: Liverpool, England, 25 February, 1952 M

League Club	Source	Date Signed	Seasons Played	Apps	Subs	Gls
Liverpool	App	02/69	69-73	38	2	2
Portsmouth	L	10/75	75	5	0	0

McLAUGHLIN Jonathan Peter (Jon)
Born: Edinburgh, Scotland, 9 September, 1987 G

League Club	Source	Date Signed	Seasons Played	Apps	Subs	Gls
Bradford C	Harrogate T	07/08	08-13	125	0	0
Burton A	Tr	07/14	14	45	0	0

McLAUGHLIN Joseph (Joe)
Born: Greenock, Inverclyde, Scotland, 2 June, 1960 CD
Scotland: U21-10

League Club	Source	Date Signed	Seasons Played	Apps	Subs	Gls
Chelsea	Greenock Morton	06/83	83-88	220	0	5
Charlton Ath	Tr	08/89	89	31	0	0
Watford	Tr	08/90	90-91	46	0	2

McLAUGHLIN Michael Anthony (Mick)
Born: Newport, Wales, 5 January, 1943 CD

League Club	Source	Date Signed	Seasons Played	Apps	Subs	Gls
Newport Co	Nash U	11/61				
Newport Co	Lovells Ath	08/68	68-69	90	0	3
Hereford U	Tr	08/70	72-74	84	0	1
Newport Co	Cheltenham T	03/78	77	7	0	0

McLAUGHLIN Patrick Joseph (Pat)
Born: Larne, Antrim, Northern Ireland, 14 January, 1991 M
Northern Ireland: U21-10/Youth

League Club	Source	Date Signed	Seasons Played	Apps	Subs	Gls
Newcastle U	Sch	05/08				
York C	Tr	07/11	12	26	4	3

McLAUGHLIN Robert (Bobby)
Born: Belfast, Northern Ireland, 6 December, 1925 WH
Died: Southampton, England, April, 2003
Northern Ireland: NILge-1

League Club	Source	Date Signed	Seasons Played	Apps	Subs	Gls
Wrexham	Distillery	01/50	49	17	-	0
Cardiff C	Tr	04/50	50-53	48	-	3
Southampton	Tr	10/53	53-58	169	-	5

McLAUGHLIN Ryan
Born: Belfast, Northern Ireland, 30 September, 1994 RB
Northern Ireland: 2/U21-1/Youth

League Club	Source	Date Signed	Seasons Played	Apps	Subs	Gls
Liverpool	Sch	10/11				
Barnsley	L	01/14	13	9	0	0

McLAUGHLIN Stephen Antony
Born: Inishowen, Donegal, Republic of Ireland, 14 June, 1990 LW

League Club	Source	Date Signed	Seasons Played	Apps	Subs	Gls
Nottingham F	Derry C (ROI)	01/13	13-14	4	5	0
Bristol C	L	09/13	13	0	5	0
Notts Co	L	09/14	14	13	0	0
Southend U	L	03/15	14	6	0	1

McLAUGHLIN William James
Born: USA, 31 January, 1918 WH
Died: Crewe, Cheshire, England, 13 January, 1972

League Club	Source	Date Signed	Seasons Played	Apps	Subs	Gls
Crewe Alex		10/46	46	1	-	0

McLEAN Aaron
Born: Hammersmith, W London, England, 25 May, 1983 F
England: Semi Pro-5

League Club	Source	Date Signed	Seasons Played	Apps	Subs	Gls
Leyton Orient	YT	07/01	99-02	5	35	2
Peterborough U	Grays Ath	10/06	06-10	149	8	71
Hull C	Tr	12/10	10-13	49	28	8
Ipswich T	L	01/13	12	4	3	1
Birmingham C	L	11/13	13	2	5	0
Bradford C	Tr	01/14	13-14	25	8	6
Peterborough U	L	11/14	14	10	8	1

McLEAN Angus (Gus)
Born: Queensferry, Edinburgh, Scotland, 20 September, 1925 FB
Died: Shaw, Greater Manchester, England, 1 July, 1979

League Club	Source	Date Signed	Seasons Played	Apps	Subs	Gls
Wolverhampton W	Aberystwyth	11/42	46-50	144	-	2
Bury	Bromsgrove Rov	05/53	53	12	-	0
Crewe Alex	Tr	06/54	54	44	-	10

McLEAN Brian Stuart
Born: Rutherglen, Glasgow, Scotland, 28 February, 1985 CD
Northern Ireland: 1

League Club	Source	Date Signed	Seasons Played	Apps	Subs	Gls
Preston NE	Falkirk	08/11	11	15	1	1

McLEAN Colin
Born: Stirling, Scotland, 16 May, 1928 IF
Died: Stirling, Scotland, 26 June, 2000

League Club	Source	Date Signed	Seasons Played	Apps	Subs	Gls
Southport	Forfar Ath	06/52	52-53	59	-	18
Crewe Alex	Tr	07/54	54	11	-	1

McLEAN David John
Born: Newcastle-upon-Tyne, England, 24 November, 1957 M
England: Schools

League Club	Source	Date Signed	Seasons Played	Apps	Subs	Gls
Newcastle U	App	11/75	75-77	7	2	0
Carlisle U	Tr	03/78	77-78	9	6	0
Darlington	Tr	08/79	79-85	289	5	46
Scunthorpe U	Tr	07/86	86-87	23	1	3
Hartlepool U	L	03/87	86	6	0	0

McLEAN George Roy
Born: Paisley, Renfrewshire, Scotland, 16 September, 1937 CF

League Club	Source	Date Signed	Seasons Played	Apps	Subs	Gls
Norwich C	Glasgow Rangers	03/62				
Grimsby T	Tr	09/62	62-64	91	-	41
Exeter C	Tr	06/65	65-66	47	0	12
Workington	Tr	01/67	66-67	53	0	15
Barrow	Tr	06/68	68	26	1	9

MacLEAN Hugh
Born: Stornaway, Lewis, Western Isles, Scotland, 20 January, 1952 M

League Club	Source	Date Signed	Seasons Played	Apps	Subs	Gls
West Bromwich A	Tantallon U	02/69	71-72	4	2	0
Swindon T	Tr	07/74	74	17	2	0

MacLEAN Ian
Born: Paisley, Renfrewshire, Scotland, 13 August, 1966 CD
Canada: 3

League Club	Source	Date Signed	Seasons Played	Apps	Subs	Gls
Bristol Rov	Metro-Ford (CAN)	09/93	93-95	21	14	2
Cardiff C	L	09/94	94	4	0	0
Rotherham U	L	01/96	95	9	0	0

McLEAN Ian James
Born: Leeds, England, 13 September, 1978 LB

League Club	Source	Date Signed	Seasons Played	Apps	Subs	Gls
Bradford C	YT	01/97				
Oldham Ath	Tr	10/98	98-99	6	0	0

McLEAN James
Born: Alloa, Stirlingshire, Scotland, 3 April, 1934 IF
Died: Dunfermline, Fife, Scotland, 27 August, 1995

League Club	Source	Date Signed	Seasons Played	Apps	Subs	Gls
Port Vale	Alva Albion Rov	03/58	57	3	-	0

McLEAN John Derek (Derek)
Born: Brotton, Cleveland, England, 21 December, 1932 IF

League Club	Source	Date Signed	Seasons Played	Apps	Subs	Gls
Middlesbrough	North Skelton	10/52	55-61	119	-	30
Hartlepool U	Tr	10/61	61-63	89	-	16

McLEAN Peter Young
Born: Lochgelly, Fife, Scotland, 27 November, 1923 WH

League Club	Source	Date Signed	Seasons Played	Apps	Subs	Gls
Reading	Lochgelly Violet	01/49	49-52	70	-	6
Exeter C	Tr	08/53	53	15	-	0

MacLEAN Steven George (Steve)
Born: Edinburgh, Scotland, 23 August, 1982 F
Scotland: U21-4

League Club	Source	Date Signed	Seasons Played	Apps	Subs	Gls
Scunthorpe U (L)	Glasgow Rangers	08/03	03	37	5	23
Sheffield Wed	Glasgow Rangers	07/04	04-06	60	23	32
Cardiff C	Tr	07/07	07	6	9	1
Plymouth Arg	Tr	01/08	07-10	32	16	5
Oxford U	L	11/10	10	26	5	6
Yeovil T	Tr	07/11	11	14	6	3
Cheltenham T	L	03/12	11	3	0	1

McLEAN Stewart Duff
Born: Barrhead, Renfrewshire, Scotland, 30 August, 1923 IF
Died: Banff, Aberdeenshire, Scotland, 11 September, 2011

League Club	Source	Date Signed	Seasons Played	Apps	Subs	Gls
Rotherham U	Partick Thistle	05/46	46-47	35	-	20

McLEAN William (Billy)
Born: Liverpool, England, 14 August, 1931 RW

League Club	Source	Date Signed	Seasons Played	Apps	Subs	Gls
Blackburn Rov	Burscough	02/53	53	12	-	0

McLEAN William (Willie)
Born: Larkhall, Lanarkshire, Scotland, 18 December, 1922 RW
Died: Larkhall, Lanarkshire, Scotland, 24 May, 1986

League Club	Source	Date Signed	Seasons Played	Apps	Subs	Gls
New Brighton	Queen of the South	06/47	47	12	-	2

McLEAN William Graham
Born: Dumbarton, Dunbartonshire, Scotland, 14 October, 1933 — IF
Died: Alexandria, Dunbartonshire, Scotland, 9 June, 1996

League Club	Source	Date Signed	Seasons Played	Apps	Subs	Gls
Walsall	RAMC Kidderminster	02/54	53	2	-	0

McLEARY Alan Terry
Born: Lambeth, S London, England, 6 October, 1964 — CD
England: B-2/U21-1/Youth

League Club	Source	Date Signed	Seasons Played	Apps	Subs	Gls
Millwall	App	10/81	82-92	289	18	5
Sheffield U	L	07/92	92	3	0	0
Wimbledon	L	10/92	92	4	0	0
Charlton Ath	Tr	05/93	93-94	66	0	3
Bristol C	Tr	07/95	95-96	31	3	0
Millwall	Tr	02/97	96-98	36	0	0

McLEISH Hugh
Born: Shotts, Lanarkshire, Scotland, 10 June, 1948 — F
Died: Fleetwood, Lancashire, England, December, 2004

League Club	Source	Date Signed	Seasons Played	Apps	Subs	Gls
Sunderland	Dundee U	08/67				
Luton T	Tr	11/67	67	1	1	0

McLELLAN Alistair Alexander Angus
Born: Glasgow, Scotland, 16 April, 1922 — IF
Died: Birkenhead, Wirral, England, September, 2010

League Club	Source	Date Signed	Seasons Played	Apps	Subs	Gls
New Brighton	Albion Rov	08/46	46-47	34	-	7
Tranmere Rov	Tr	05/48	48	2	-	0

MacLEOD Alexander Hector McMillan (Alisdair)
Born: Glasgow, Scotland, 1 January, 1951 — F

League Club	Source	Date Signed	Seasons Played	Apps	Subs	Gls
Southampton	St Mirren	05/73	73	2	1	0
Huddersfield T	L	10/74	74	3	1	1

MacLEOD Alistair Reid (Ally)
Born: Glasgow, Scotland, 26 February, 1931 — LW
Died: Ayr, Scotland, 1 February, 2004

League Club	Source	Date Signed	Seasons Played	Apps	Subs	Gls
Blackburn Rov	St Mirren	06/56	56-60	193	-	47

McLEOD George James
Born: Inverness, Scotland, 30 November, 1932 — LW

League Club	Source	Date Signed	Seasons Played	Apps	Subs	Gls
Luton T	Clachnacuddin	01/55	55-58	51	-	6
Brentford	Tr	10/58	58-63	207	-	20
Queens Park Rgrs	Tr	01/64	63-64	41	-	4

McLEOD Izale Michael
Born: Birmingham, England, 15 October, 1984 — F
England: U21-1

League Club	Source	Date Signed	Seasons Played	Apps	Subs	Gls
Derby Co	Sch	02/03	02-03	24	15	4
Sheffield U	L	03/04	03	1	6	0
MK Dons	Tr	08/04	04-06	105	11	54
Charlton Ath	Tr	08/07	07-09	7	24	3
Colchester U	L	02/08	07	0	2	0
Millwall	L	01/09	08	5	2	2
Peterborough U	L	01/10	09	2	2	0
Barnet	Tr	09/10	10-11	68	5	32
Portsmouth	Tr	08/12	12	23	1	10
MK Dons	Tr	01/13	12-13	23	26	8
Northampton T	L	11/13	13	4	0	1
Crawley T	Tr	06/14	14	41	1	19

MacLEOD Jack Ross
Born: Epsom, Surrey, England, 3 July, 1988 — M

League Club	Source	Date Signed	Seasons Played	Apps	Subs	Gls
Hereford U	Carshalton Ath	01/08	08	2	4	0

MacLEOD John Murdoch (Johnny)
Born: Edinburgh, Scotland, 23 November, 1938 — RW
Scotland: 4/SLge-1/U23-1

League Club	Source	Date Signed	Seasons Played	Apps	Subs	Gls
Arsenal	Hibernian	07/61	61-64	101	-	23
Aston Villa	Tr	09/64	64-67	123	2	16

McLEOD Kevin Andrew
Born: Liverpool, England, 12 September, 1980 — LW

League Club	Source	Date Signed	Seasons Played	Apps	Subs	Gls
Everton	YT	09/98	00	0	5	0
Queens Park Rgrs	L	03/03	02	8	0	2
Queens Park Rgrs	Tr	08/03	03-04	30	29	4
Swansea C	Tr	02/05	04-06	32	12	7
Colchester U	Tr	08/06	06-07	34	18	7
Brighton & HA	Tr	07/08	08-09	13	13	0
Wycombe W	Tr	02/10	09	8	3	0

McLEOD Mark
Born: Sunderland, England, 15 December, 1986 — M

League Club	Source	Date Signed	Seasons Played	Apps	Subs	Gls
Darlington	Sch	07/06	05-06	4	2	0

McLEOD Norman Andrew
Born: Manchester, England, 29 July, 1930 — LB
Died: Rochester, Kent, England, April, 2012

League Club	Source	Date Signed	Seasons Played	Apps	Subs	Gls
Crewe Alex	Hyde U	08/57	57-58	25	-	1

McLEOD Robert Alexander (Bobby)
Born: Inverness, Scotland, 24 February, 1947 — CH

League Club	Source	Date Signed	Seasons Played	Apps	Subs	Gls
Hartlepool U	Sunderland College	11/65	65-68	23	5	0

McLEOD Robert Boyd (Bob)
Born: Fraserburgh, Aberdeenshire, Scotland, 22 January, 1919 — IF
Died: Macclesfield, Cheshire, England, August, 2000

League Club	Source	Date Signed	Seasons Played	Apps	Subs	Gls
Brighton & HA		11/47	47	1	-	0

McLEOD Samuel Mark (Sammy)
Born: Glasgow, Scotland, 4 January, 1934 — IF
Died: Adelaide, Australia, 29 July, 1973

League Club	Source	Date Signed	Seasons Played	Apps	Subs	Gls
Colchester U	Easthouses Lily	06/55	55-62	152	-	23

McLEOD Thomas (Tommy)
Born: Musselburgh, East Lothian, Scotland, 26 December, 1920 — IF/LH
Died: Inveresk, East Lothian, Scotland, 16 August, 1999

League Club	Source	Date Signed	Seasons Played	Apps	Subs	Gls
Liverpool	BAOR Germany	10/45	46-48	7	-	0
Chesterfield	Tr	07/51	51	25	-	3

McLINTOCK Francis (Frank)
Born: Glasgow, Scotland, 28 December, 1939 — WH/CD
Scotland: 9/U23-1

League Club	Source	Date Signed	Seasons Played	Apps	Subs	Gls
Leicester C	Shawfield Jnrs	01/57	59-64	168	-	25
Arsenal	Tr	10/64	64-72	312	2	26
Queens Park Rgrs	Tr	06/73	73-76	126	1	5

McLOUGHLIN Alan Francis
Born: Manchester, England, 20 April, 1967 — M
Republic of Ireland: 42/B-3

League Club	Source	Date Signed	Seasons Played	Apps	Subs	Gls
Manchester U	App	04/85				
Swindon T	Tr	08/86	86-90	101	5	19
Torquay U	L	03/87	86	16	0	1
Torquay U	L	08/87	87	5	3	3
Southampton	Tr	12/90	90-91	22	2	1
Portsmouth	Tr	02/92	91-99	297	12	54
Wigan Ath	Tr	12/99	99-01	12	10	1
Rochdale	Tr	12/01	01	15	3	1

McLOUGHLIN Anthony Joseph (Tony)
Born: Liverpool, England, 24 September, 1946 — LW
Died: Runcorn, Cheshire, England, August, 2012

League Club	Source	Date Signed	Seasons Played	Apps	Subs	Gls
Everton	Jnr	02/64				
Wrexham	Tr	07/66	66-67	27	2	9
Chester C	Tr	10/67	67	2	2	0

McLOUGHLIN Ian Michael
Born: Dublin, Republic of Ireland, 9 August, 1991 — G
Republic of Ireland: U21-10/Youth

League Club	Source	Date Signed	Seasons Played	Apps	Subs	Gls
Ipswich T	St Francis YC (ROI)	01/09				
Stockport Co	L	02/11	10	5	0	0
MK Dons	Tr	07/11	11-14	28	5	0
Walsall	L	01/13	12	6	0	0
Newport Co	L	03/14	13	12	0	0

McLOUGHLIN Paul Brendan
Born: Bristol, England, 23 December, 1963 — F/W

League Club	Source	Date Signed	Seasons Played	Apps	Subs	Gls
Cardiff C	Gisborne C (NZL)	12/84	84-85	40	9	4
Bristol C	Osters Vaxjo (SWE)	01/87				
Hereford U	Tr	06/87	87-88	72	2	14
Wolverhampton W	Tr	07/89	89-91	12	16	4
Walsall	L	09/91	91	9	0	4
York C	L	01/92	91	1	0	0
Mansfield T	Tr	01/92	91-93	49	12	9

McLUCKIE George Robertson
Born: Falkirk, Scotland, 19 September, 1931 — LW
Died: Ipswich, England, 1 January, 2011

League Club	Source	Date Signed	Seasons Played	Apps	Subs	Gls
Blackburn Rov	Lochore Welfare	08/52	52	20	-	2
Ipswich T	Tr	05/53	53-57	141	-	24
Reading	Tr	06/58	58-60	85	-	8

McLUCKIE Robert John (Sandy)
Born: Doncaster, South Yorkshire, England, 5 October, 1955 — M

League Club	Source	Date Signed	Seasons Played	Apps	Subs	Gls
Doncaster Rov	App	10/73	72-73	2	3	0

McMAHON Anthony (Tony)
Born: Bishop Auckland, County Durham, England, 24 March, 1986 — RB
England: Youth

League Club	Source	Date Signed	Seasons Played	Apps	Subs	Gls
Middlesbrough	Sch	02/05	04-11	104	15	3
Blackpool	L	11/07	07	2	0	0
Sheffield Wed	L	08/08	08	14	1	1
Sheffield U	Tr	07/12	12-13	61	0	2
Blackpool	Tr	01/14	13-14	46	4	1
Bradford C	L	03/15	14	4	4	1

McMAHON Daryl
Born: Dublin, Republic of Ireland, 10 October, 1983 — M
Republic of Ireland: Youth

League Club	Source	Date Signed	Seasons Played	Apps	Subs	Gls
West Ham U	YT	10/00				
Torquay U	L	03/04	03	0	1	0
Port Vale	Tr	09/04	04	1	4	0
Leyton Orient	Tr	11/04	04-06	42	23	5
Notts Co	L	11/06	06	3	4	0

McMAHON David
Born: Dublin, Republic of Ireland, 17 January, 1981 — F
Republic of Ireland: Youth

League Club	Source	Date Signed	Seasons Played	Apps	Subs	Gls
Newcastle U	YT	02/98				
Darlington	L	12/00	00	5	3	1

McMAHON Desmond (Des)
Born: Reading, England, 22 March, 1956 — F

League Club	Source	Date Signed	Seasons Played	Apps	Subs	Gls
Reading	Hungerford T	08/82	82	0	2	0

McMAHON Francis Gerard (Frank)
Born: Belfast, Northern Ireland, 4 January, 1950 — M

League Club	Source	Date Signed	Seasons Played	Apps	Subs	Gls
Coventry C	Distillery	10/69				
Lincoln C	Waterford (ROI)	07/71	71-72	54	2	2
Darlington	Tr	03/73	72-73	19	4	1
Hartlepool U	L	10/73	73	7	0	0

McMAHON Gerard Joseph (Gerry)
Born: Belfast, Northern Ireland, 29 December, 1973 — W
Northern Ireland: 17/B/U21-1/Youth/Schools

League Club	Source	Date Signed	Seasons Played	Apps	Subs	Gls
Tottenham H	Glenavon	07/92	94-95	9	7	0
Barnet	L	10/94	94	10	0	2
Stoke C	Tr	09/96	96-97	38	14	3

McMAHON Hugh (Hughie)
Born: Grangetown, Cleveland, England, 24 September, 1909 — LW
Died: Middlesbrough, England, October, 1986

League Club	Source	Date Signed	Seasons Played	Apps	Subs	Gls
Reading	Mexborough T	09/32	32	1	-	0
Southend U	Tr	05/33	33	10	-	3
Reading	Tr	06/34	34-35	10	-	2
Queens Park Rgrs	Tr	05/36	36-37	41	-	3
Sunderland	Tr	11/37	37-38	8	-	1
Hartlepool U	Tr	06/45	46-47	28	-	7
Rotherham U	Tr	09/47	47-48	59	-	8

McMAHON Ian David
Born: Wells, Somerset, England, 7 October, 1964 — M/D

League Club	Source	Date Signed	Seasons Played	Apps	Subs	Gls
Oldham Ath	App	10/82	82	2	0	0
Rochdale	Tr	01/84	83-85	89	2	8

McMAHON John
Born: Manchester, England, 7 December, 1949 — RB

League Club	Source	Date Signed	Seasons Played	Apps	Subs	Gls
Preston NE	App	12/67	70-78	256	1	7
Southend U	L	09/70	70	4	0	0
Chesterfield	L	09/79	79	1	0	0
Crewe Alex	Tr	10/79	79-80	67	0	2
Wigan Ath	Tr	08/81	81-82	71	0	5
Tranmere Rov	Tr	08/83	83	39	1	0

McMAHON John Albert
Born: Middlesbrough, England, 25 October, 1965 — F

League Club	Source	Date Signed	Seasons Played	Apps	Subs	Gls
Middlesbrough	App	10/83				
Darlington	Tr	03/85	84	0	4	0

McMAHON Kevin
Born: Tantobie, County Durham, England, 1 March, 1946 — F

League Club	Source	Date Signed	Seasons Played	Apps	Subs	Gls
Newcastle U	Consett	08/67				
York C	Tr	05/69	69-71	85	8	31
Bolton W	L	03/72	71	4	2	1
Barnsley	Tr	07/72	72	4	1	0
Hartlepool U	Tr	07/73	73-75	104	3	29

McMAHON Lewis James
Born: Doncaster, South Yorkshire, England, 2 May, 1985 — M

League Club	Source	Date Signed	Seasons Played	Apps	Subs	Gls
Sheffield Wed	Sch	07/04	03-04	22	3	2
Notts Co	L	07/05	05	23	6	0

McMAHON Patrick (Pat)
Born: Kilsyth, Lanarkshire, Scotland, 19 September, 1945 — M

League Club	Source	Date Signed	Seasons Played	Apps	Subs	Gls
Aston Villa	Glasgow Celtic	06/69	69-74	121	9	25

McMAHON Peter John
Born: Marylebone, Central London, England, 30 April, 1934 — WH

League Club	Source	Date Signed	Seasons Played	Apps	Subs	Gls
Leyton Orient	Chase of Chertsey	05/51	51-57	66	-	1
Aldershot	Tr	10/58	58-59	39	-	0

McMAHON Samuel Keiron (Sam)
Born: Newark, Nottinghamshire, England, 10 February, 1976 — M

League Club	Source	Date Signed	Seasons Played	Apps	Subs	Gls
Leicester C	YT	07/94	94-97	1	4	1
Cambridge U	Tr	03/99	98	1	2	0

McMAHON Stephen Joseph
Born: Southport, Merseyside, England, 31 July, 1984 — M

League Club	Source	Date Signed	Seasons Played	Apps	Subs	Gls
Blackpool	Sch	07/03	02-03	10	8	0
Kidderminster Hrs	L	09/04	04	3	2	0

McMAHON Stephen Joseph (Steve)
Born: Liverpool, England, 20 August, 1961 — M
England: 17/B-2/FLge/U21-6

League Club	Source	Date Signed	Seasons Played	Apps	Subs	Gls
Everton	App	08/79	80-82	99	1	11
Aston Villa	Tr	05/83	83-85	74	1	7
Liverpool	Tr	09/85	85-91	202	2	29
Manchester C	Tr	12/91	91-94	83	4	1
Swindon T	Tr	12/94	94-97	38	4	0

McMAHON Steven (Steve)
Born: Glasgow, Scotland, 22 April, 1970 — F

League Club	Source	Date Signed	Seasons Played	Apps	Subs	Gls
Swansea C	Ferguslie	08/91	92	2	0	0
Carlisle U	Tr	07/93	93	2	0	0
Darlington	Partick Thistle	01/96	95	6	4	1

McMANAMAN Callum Henry
Born: Huyton, Merseyside, England, 25 April, 1991 — W
England: Youth

League Club	Source	Date Signed	Seasons Played	Apps	Subs	Gls
Wigan Ath	Sch	07/09	08-14	44	35	10
Blackpool	L	10/11	11	9	5	2
West Bromwich A	Tr	01/15	14	5	3	0

McMANAMAN Steven (Steve)
Born: Bootle, Merseyside, England, 11 February, 1972 — W
England: 37/U21-7/Youth

League Club	Source	Date Signed	Seasons Played	Apps	Subs	Gls
Liverpool	YT	02/90	90-98	258	14	46
Manchester C	Real Madrid (SPN)	08/03	03-04	25	10	0

McMANUS Brendan
Born: Kilkeel, Down, Northern Ireland, 2 December, 1923 — G
Died: Oldham, Greater Manchester, England, September, 2010

League Club	Source	Date Signed	Seasons Played	Apps	Subs	Gls
Huddersfield T	Newry T	10/45	46	1	-	0
Oldham Ath	Tr	07/47	47	35	-	0
Bradford C	Tr	10/48	48-52	125	-	0

McMANUS Charles Eric (Eric)
Born: Limavady, Derry, Northern Ireland, 14 November, 1950 — G
Northern Ireland: Amateur

League Club	Source	Date Signed	Seasons Played	Apps	Subs	Gls
Coventry C	Coleraine	08/68	69-71	6	0	0
Notts Co	Tr	05/72	72-78	229	0	0
Stoke C	Tr	10/79	81	4	0	0
Lincoln C	L	12/79	79	21	0	0
Bradford C	Tr	08/82	82-84	113	0	0
Middlesbrough	L	01/86	85	2	0	0
Peterborough U	L	03/86	85	18	0	0
Tranmere Rov	Tr	08/86	86	3	0	0

McMANUS Edward James (Eddie)
Born: Ramsgate, Kent, England, 8 August, 1937 — RW

League Club	Source	Date Signed	Seasons Played	Apps	Subs	Gls
Bournemouth	Dover	08/54	58-59	4	-	0
Gillingham	Tr	08/60	60	3	-	0

McMANUS Paul James
Born: Liverpool, England, 22 April, 1990 — F

League Club	Source	Date Signed	Seasons Played	Apps	Subs	Gls
Chester C	Sch	10/07	07-08	15	13	3

McMANUS Scott Harrison
Born: Prestwich, Greater Manchester, England, 28 May, 1989 — LB/M

League Club	Source	Date Signed	Seasons Played	Apps	Subs	Gls
Crewe Alex	Curzon Ashton	08/08	08	3	3	1

McMANUS Stanley (Stan)
Born: Carlisle, Cumbria, England, 31 October, 1932 — LW

League Club	Source	Date Signed	Seasons Played	Apps	Subs	Gls
Bury	Canterbury C	01/56				
Southport	Tr	07/57	57	5	-	0

McMANUS Stephen David
Born: Lanark, Scotland, 10 September, 1982 — CD
Scotland: 26

League Club	Source	Date Signed	Seasons Played	Apps	Subs	Gls
Middlesbrough	Glasgow Celtic	01/10	09-12	66	5	2
Bristol C	L	02/12	11	6	0	0
Bristol C	L	10/12	12	11	0	1

McMANUS Steven
Born: Nottingham, England, 8 March, 1975 — M

League Club	Source	Date Signed	Seasons Played	Apps	Subs	Gls
Walsall	YT	05/93	92	0	1	0

McMANUS Stuart Joseph
Born: Falkirk, Scotland, 19 March, 1965 — F

League Club	Source	Date Signed	Seasons Played	Apps	Subs	Gls
Southampton	Jnr	07/84	85	2	0	1
Newport Co	L	08/85	85	4	1	0

McMANUS Thomas Kelly (Tom)
Born: Glasgow, Scotland, 28 February, 1981 — F
Scotland: U21-14

League Club	Source	Date Signed	Seasons Played	Apps	Subs	Gls
Boston U (L)	Hibernian	08/04	04	5	3	0

McMASTER Christopher (Chris)
Born: Darlington, County Durham, England, 16 June, 1959 — F

League Club	Source	Date Signed	Seasons Played	Apps	Subs	Gls
Hartlepool U	App	07/77	76-77	3	1	0

McMASTER Jamie
Born: Sydney, Australia, 29 November, 1982 — F

League Club	Source	Date Signed	Seasons Played	Apps	Subs	Gls
Leeds U	YT	11/99	02-04	0	11	0
Coventry C	L	11/02	02	2	0	0

League Club	Source	Date Signed	Seasons Played	Apps	Subs	Gls
Chesterfield	L	01/04	03	4	2	2
Swindon T	L	09/04	04	2	2	1
Peterborough U	L	01/05	04	3	0	0
Chesterfield	Tr	03/05	04	6	2	0
McMENAMIN Christopher (Chris)						
Born: Donegal, Republic of Ireland, 27 December, 1973						RB
Coventry C	Hitchin T	09/96				
Peterborough U	Tr	08/97	97-98	29	4	0
McMENAMIN Colin						
Born: Glasgow, Scotland, 12 February, 1981						F
Newcastle U	Annan Ath	01/01				
Shrewsbury T	Livingston	07/05	05	40	3	10
McMENEMY Paul Christopher						
Born: Farnborough, Hampshire, England, 5 November, 1966						F
West Ham U	App	11/84				
Aldershot	L	03/86	85	10	0	5
Northampton T	L	01/87	86	4	0	2
McMICHAEL Alfred (Alf)						
Born: Belfast, Northern Ireland, 1 October, 1927						LB
Died: Bangor, Down, Northern Ireland, 7 January, 2006						
Northern Ireland: 40/NILge-8						
Newcastle U	Linfield	09/49	49-62	402	-	1
McMILLAN Duncan						
Born: Glasgow, Scotland, 18 January, 1922						CH
Died: Grimsby, North Lincolnshire, England, 20 May, 1992						
Grimsby T	Glasgow Celtic	03/49	48-54	188	-	2
McMILLAN Eric						
Born: Beverley, East Riding of Yorkshire, England, 2 November, 1936						LH/IF
Died: Hull, England, March, 2006						
Chelsea	RAF High Wycombe	04/58	59	5	-	0
Hull C	Tr	07/60	60-63	150	-	3
Halifax T	Tr	07/65	65-66	49	1	8
McMILLAN George Sneddon						
Born: Motherwell, Lanarkshire, Scotland, 15 March, 1930						LW
Wrexham	Aberdeen	05/52	52	1	-	0
McMILLAN George Sorbie						
Born: Stonehouse, Lanarkshire, Scotland, 10 August, 1929						G
Died: East Kilbride, Lanarkshire, Scotland, 13 May, 2013						
Ipswich T	Newarthill Hearts	02/53	54-57	53	-	0
McMILLAN John Shaw						
Born: Renton, Dunbartonshire, Scotland, 14 April, 1937						RW
Cardiff C	Dumbarton	02/58	60	2	-	0
Exeter C	Tr	10/61	61-62	20	-	1
McMILLAN Lyndon Andre (Andy)						
Born: Bloemfontein, South Africa, 22 June, 1968						RB
York C	North'd & St Peters	10/87	87-98	409	12	5
McMILLAN Paul Anthony						
Born: Lennoxtown, Dunbartonshire, Scotland, 13 July, 1950						F
Chelsea	Jnr	08/67	67	1	0	0
McMILLAN Samuel Thomas (Sammy)						
Born: Belfast, Northern Ireland, 29 September, 1941						IF/WH
Northern Ireland: 2/U23-1						
Manchester U	Boyland BC	11/59	61-62	15	-	6
Wrexham	Tr	12/63	63-67	149	0	52
Southend U	Tr	09/67	67-69	76	4	5
Chester C	Tr	12/69	69	16	2	0
Stockport Co	Tr	07/70	70-71	74	0	29
McMILLAN Stephen Thomas (Steve)						
Born: Edinburgh, Scotland, 19 January, 1976						LB
Scotland: U21-4						
Wigan Ath	Motherwell	03/01	00-05	81	11	0
McMILLAN Thomas (Tommy)						
Born: Glasgow, Scotland, 12 February, 1931						LW
Died: Glasgow, Scotland, 4 October, 1999						
Norwich C	Glasgow Celtic	07/54	54	19	-	2
Workington	Tr	09/55	55	1	-	0
McMILLAN Thomas Pearson (Tommy)						
Born: Auchinleck, Ayrshire, Scotland, 16 January, 1936						IF/WH
Watford	Maybole Jnrs	09/56	56-57	33	-	13
Carlisle U	Tr	07/58	58-60	89	-	7
McMILLEN Walter						
Born: Belfast, Northern Ireland, 24 November, 1913						RH
Died: Larne, Antrim, Northern Ireland, 11 May, 1987						
Northern Ireland: 7/NILge-5/Amateur						
Manchester U	Cliftonville	08/33	33-34	27	-	2

League Club	Source	Date Signed	Seasons Played	Apps	Subs	Gls
Chesterfield	Tr	12/36	36-38	85	-	17
Millwall	Tr	05/39	46-49	91	-	0
McMINN Kevin Clifton (Ted)						
Born: Castle Douglas, Dumfries & Galloway, Scotland, 28 September, 1962						W
Derby Co	Sevilla (SPN)	02/88	87-92	108	15	9
Birmingham C	Tr	07/93	93	19	3	0
Burnley	Tr	04/94	93-95	38	8	3
McMINN Robert William (Bob)						
Born: Doncaster, South Yorkshire, England, 9 October, 1946						RB
Doncaster Rov	App	10/64	63-65	4	1	0
McMORDIE Alexander (Eric)						
Born: Belfast, Northern Ireland, 12 August, 1946						M
Northern Ireland: 21/U23-1						
Middlesbrough	Dundela	09/64	65-73	231	10	22
Sheffield Wed	L	10/74	74	9	0	6
York C	Tr	05/75	75-76	42	0	2
Hartlepool U	Tr	12/76	76-77	46	1	2
McMORRAN Edward James (Eddie)						
Born: Larne, Antrim, Northern Ireland, 2 September, 1923						IF
Died: Larne, Antrim, Northern Ireland, 16 September, 1984						
Northern Ireland: 15/NILge-3/Schools						
Manchester C	Belfast Celtic	08/47	47-48	33	-	12
Leeds U	Tr	01/49	48-49	38	-	6
Barnsley	Tr	07/50	50-52	104	-	32
Doncaster Rov	Tr	02/53	52-57	128	-	32
Crewe Alex	Tr	11/57	57	26	-	6
McMORRAN James Wilson (Jimmy)						
Born: Muirkirk, Ayrshire, Scotland, 29 October, 1942						IF
Scotland: Schools						
Aston Villa	Jnr	10/59	60-61	11	-	1
Walsall	Third Lanark	11/64	64-67	93	1	9
Swansea C	Tr	06/68	68	14	0	1
Walsall	Tr	11/68	68	9	1	1
Notts Co	Tr	07/69	69	6	0	0
McMORRAN John						
Born: Forth, Lanarkshire, Scotland, 11 May, 1934						IF
Died: Biggar, Lanarkshire, England, 10 January, 2001						
Bradford C	Forth W	12/54	54	1	-	0
McMORRAN Robert						
Born: Forth, Lanarkshire, Scotland, 12 March, 1926						RW
Died: Paisley, Renfrewshire, Scotland, 16 September, 1990						
Manchester U	Glasgow Rangers	02/47				
Walsall	Tr	02/50	49	8	-	1
McMULLEN David						
Born: Harrington, Cumbria, England, 6 January, 1936						WH
Died: Whitehaven, Cumbria, England, 4 June, 1999						
Workington		08/59	59	1	-	0
McMULLEN David						
Born: Denny, Falkirk, Scotland, 13 June, 1960						M
Wigan Ath	Cumbernauld U	02/80	79-80	20	7	1
McMULLEN Ian						
Born: Hoylake, Wirral, England, 17 November, 1965						M
Tranmere Rov		09/84	84	2	0	0
McMURRAY John Daniel						
Born: Billingham, Cleveland, England, 5 October, 1931						WH
Died: Billingham, Cleveland, England, 21 May, 1982						
Middlesbrough	Billingham Synthonia	05/49	53-54	3	-	0
McNAB Alexander (Sandy)						
Born: Glasgow, Scotland, 27 December, 1911						WH
Died: Halesowen, West Midlands, England, September, 1962						
Scotland: 2						
Sunderland	Pollok Jnrs	05/32	32-37	97	-	6
West Bromwich A	Tr	03/38	37-38	49	-	2
Newport Co	Tr	04/46	46	3	-	0
McNAB Alexander Duncan (Alex)						
Born: Birmingham, England, 6 April, 1932						WH
Died: Birmingham, England, 1974						
Scotland: Schools						
Shrewsbury T		12/54	54-56	4	-	0
McNAB James (Jimmy)						
Born: Denny, Falkirk, Scotland, 13 April, 1940						LB/LH
Died: Sunderland, England, 29 June, 2006						
Scotland: Schools						
Sunderland	Kilsyth Rgrs	06/57	58-66	284	1	13
Preston NE	Tr	03/67	66-73	222	2	6
Stockport Co	Tr	07/74	74-75	30	0	1

McNAB Neil
Born: Greenock, Inverclyde, Scotland, 4 June, 1957 — M
Scotland: U21-1/Schools

League Club	Source	Date Signed	Seasons Played	Apps	Subs	Gls
Tottenham H	Greenock Morton	02/74	73-78	63	9	3
Bolton W	Tr	11/78	78-79	33	2	4
Brighton & HA	Tr	02/80	79-82	100	3	4
Leeds U	L	12/82	82	5	0	0
Manchester C	Tr	07/83	83-89	216	5	16
Tranmere Rov	Tr	01/90	89-92	94	11	6
Huddersfield T	L	01/92	91	11	0	0
Darlington	Ayr U	09/93	93	4	0	0

McNAB Robert (Bob)
Born: Huddersfield, West Yorkshire, England, 20 July, 1943 — LB
England: 4/FLge-1

League Club	Source	Date Signed	Seasons Played	Apps	Subs	Gls
Huddersfield T	Moldgreen Civic YC	04/62	63-66	68	0	0
Arsenal	Tr	10/66	66-74	277	1	4
Wolverhampton W	Tr	07/75	75	13	0	0

McNAB Samuel (Sam)
Born: Glasgow, Scotland, 20 October, 1926 — IF
Died: Glasgow, Scotland, 2 November, 1995

League Club	Source	Date Signed	Seasons Played	Apps	Subs	Gls
Sheffield U	Dalry Thistle	01/52	52-53	11	-	4
York C	Tr	05/54	54	19	-	3

McNAB Thomas Copeland (Tom)
Born: Glasgow, Scotland, 15 July, 1933 — WH/IF
Died: Otahuhu, New Zealand, 5 April, 2006

League Club	Source	Date Signed	Seasons Played	Apps	Subs	Gls
Nottingham F	Partick Thistle	03/54				
Wrexham	Partick Thistle	03/57	56-58	43	-	5
Barrow	Tr	03/59	58-60	43	-	4

McNAIR Patrick James Coleman (Paddy)
Born: Ballyclare, Antrim, Northern Ireland, 27 April, 1995 — CD
Northern Ireland: 2/U21-2/Youth

League Club	Source	Date Signed	Seasons Played	Apps	Subs	Gls
Manchester U	Sch	07/13	14	12	4	0

McNALLY Bernard Anthony
Born: Shrewsbury, Shropshire, England, 17 February, 1963 — M
Northern Ireland: 5

League Club	Source	Date Signed	Seasons Played	Apps	Subs	Gls
Shrewsbury T	App	02/81	80-88	278	4	23
West Bromwich A	Tr	07/89	89-94	137	19	10

McNALLY Errol Alexander
Born: Lurgan, Armagh, Northern Ireland, 27 August, 1943 — G

League Club	Source	Date Signed	Seasons Played	Apps	Subs	Gls
Chelsea	Portadown	12/61	61-63	9	-	0

McNALLY John Brendan (Brendan)
Born: Dublin, Republic of Ireland, 22 January, 1935 — RB
Died: Luton, England, July, 2011
Republic of Ireland: 3/B

League Club	Source	Date Signed	Seasons Played	Apps	Subs	Gls
Luton T	Shelbourne (ROI)	05/56	56-62	134	-	3

McNALLY Mark
Born: Motherwell, Lanarkshire, Scotland, 10 March, 1971 — CD
Scotland: U21-2

League Club	Source	Date Signed	Seasons Played	Apps	Subs	Gls
Southend U	Glasgow Celtic	12/95	95-96	52	2	2
Stoke C	Tr	03/97	96-97	6	1	0

McNALLY Paul Anthony
Born: Consett, County Durham, England, 19 December, 1949 — M

League Club	Source	Date Signed	Seasons Played	Apps	Subs	Gls
Bradford C	Consett Jnrs	07/67	68	1	2	0

McNALLY Ross Jonathan
Born: Dublin, Republic of Ireland, 6 September, 1978 — CD

League Club	Source	Date Signed	Seasons Played	Apps	Subs	Gls
Brighton & HA	YT	07/97	97	1	1	0

McNAMARA Anthony (Tony)
Born: Liverpool, England, 3 October, 1929 — RW
Died: Liverpool, England, 30 May, 2015

League Club	Source	Date Signed	Seasons Played	Apps	Subs	Gls
Everton	St Matthew's	05/50	51-57	111	-	22
Liverpool	Tr	12/57	57	10	-	3
Crewe Alex	Tr	07/58	58	9	-	2
Bury	Tr	09/58	58	14	-	0

McNAMARA Anthony Dennis (Dennis)
Born: Liverpool, England, 8 March, 1935 — RW

League Club	Source	Date Signed	Seasons Played	Apps	Subs	Gls
Tranmere Rov		11/54	54	1	-	0

McNAMARA Brett Robert James
Born: Newark, Nottinghamshire, England, 8 July, 1972 — F

League Club	Source	Date Signed	Seasons Played	Apps	Subs	Gls
Northampton T	Stamford T	08/94	94	0	1	0

McNAMARA John (Jackie)
Born: Glasgow, Scotland, 24 October, 1973 — D
Scotland: 33/U21-12

League Club	Source	Date Signed	Seasons Played	Apps	Subs	Gls
Wolverhampton W	Glasgow Celtic	07/05	05-06	28	1	0

McNAMARA Niall Anthony
Born: Limerick, Republic of Ireland, 26 January, 1982 — F
Republic of Ireland: Youth

League Club	Source	Date Signed	Seasons Played	Apps	Subs	Gls
Nottingham F	YT	02/99				
Notts Co	Tr	07/01	01	0	4	0
Lincoln C	Belper T	08/03	03-04	2	9	0

McNAMEE Anthony
Born: Kensington, Central London, England, 13 July, 1984 — LW
England: Youth

League Club	Source	Date Signed	Seasons Played	Apps	Subs	Gls
Watford	Sch	04/02	01-06	34	57	2
Crewe Alex	L	03/07	06	5	0	0
Swindon T	Tr	01/08	07-09	62	17	3
Norwich C	Tr	11/09	09-10	12	22	1
MK Dons	Tr	08/11	11	0	7	0
Wycombe W	Tr	11/11	11	11	4	2
Aldershot T	Macclesfield T	02/13	12	0	1	0

McNAMEE David Kenneth
Born: Glasgow, Scotland, 10 October, 1980 — RB
Scotland: 4/B-1

League Club	Source	Date Signed	Seasons Played	Apps	Subs	Gls
Blackburn Rov	St Mirren	03/99				
Coventry C	Livingston	06/06	06-07	28	1	0
Plymouth Arg	Tr	07/08	08-09	11	8	0

McNAMEE Gerard (Ged)
Born: Consett, County Durham, England, 16 August, 1960 — W

League Club	Source	Date Signed	Seasons Played	Apps	Subs	Gls
Hartlepool U		11/79	79-82	2	2	1

McNAMEE John
Born: Coatbridge, Lanarkshire, Scotland, 11 June, 1941 — CD

League Club	Source	Date Signed	Seasons Played	Apps	Subs	Gls
Newcastle U	Hibernian	12/66	66-71	115	2	8
Blackburn Rov	Tr	11/71	71-72	56	0	9
Hartlepool U	Greenock Morton	12/73	73	2	0	0
Workington	Lancaster C	08/75	75	2	0	0

MacNAMEE John James
Born: Edinburgh, Scotland, 31 July, 1942 — LW

League Club	Source	Date Signed	Seasons Played	Apps	Subs	Gls
Reading	Montrose	12/64				
Tranmere Rov	Corby T	08/67	67-69	67	5	12

McNAMEE Peter
Born: Glasgow, Scotland, 20 March, 1935 — LW

League Club	Source	Date Signed	Seasons Played	Apps	Subs	Gls
Peterborough U	Lanark Ath	05/55	60-65	192	0	60
Notts Co	King's Lynn	01/66	65	3	0	0

McNAUGHT John
Born: Glasgow, Scotland, 19 June, 1964 — M
Died: Hamilton, Lanarkshire, Scotland, 7 June, 1997

League Club	Source	Date Signed	Seasons Played	Apps	Subs	Gls
Chelsea	Hamilton Academical	04/86	85-87	9	1	2

McNAUGHT Kenneth (Ken)
Born: Kirkcaldy, Fife, Scotland, 11 January, 1955 — CD

League Club	Source	Date Signed	Seasons Played	Apps	Subs	Gls
Everton	App	05/72	74-76	64	2	3
Aston Villa	Tr	08/77	77-82	207	0	8
West Bromwich A	Tr	08/83	83	42	0	1
Manchester C	L	12/84	84	7	0	0
Sheffield U	Tr	07/85	85	34	0	5

McNAUGHTON Callum James
Born: Harlow, Essex, England, 25 October, 1991 — CD

League Club	Source	Date Signed	Seasons Played	Apps	Subs	Gls
West Ham U	Sch	07/10				
AFC Wimbledon	Tr	09/11	11-12	19	0	0

McNAUGHTON Kevin Paul
Born: Dundee, Scotland, 28 August, 1982 — LB
Scotland: 4/B-2/U21-1

League Club	Source	Date Signed	Seasons Played	Apps	Subs	Gls
Cardiff C	Aberdeen	07/06	06-13	245	10	1
Bolton W	L	10/13	13	13	0	1
Bolton W	L	07/14	14	8	1	0

McNAUGHTON Michael Ian
Born: Blackpool, Lancashire, England, 29 January, 1980 — CD

League Club	Source	Date Signed	Seasons Played	Apps	Subs	Gls
Scarborough	YT	07/98	98	22	9	1

McNEE Terence Allan (Terry)
Born: Birkenhead, Wirral, England, 5 June, 1925 — G
Died: Birkenhead, Wirral, England, October, 1999

League Club	Source	Date Signed	Seasons Played	Apps	Subs	Gls
Wrexham	Park Villa	12/46	46	11	-	0

McNEICE Vincent (Vince)
Born: Cricklewood, NW London, England, 25 October, 1938 — CH

League Club	Source	Date Signed	Seasons Played	Apps	Subs	Gls
Watford	Jnr	03/57	57-63	231	-	0

McNEIL David (Dave)
Born: Chester, England, 14 May, 1921 — LB
Died: Chester, England, 21 April, 1993

League Club	Source	Date Signed	Seasons Played	Apps	Subs	Gls
Chester C	Hoole Alex	05/42	46-50	114	-	1

McNEIL Hamish Grant
Born: Alva, Stirlingshire, Scotland, 16 November, 1934 — IF

League Club	Source	Date Signed	Seasons Played	Apps	Subs	Gls
Colchester U	Bonnyrigg Rose	08/57	57	2	-	1

McNEIL Mark John
Born: Bethnal Green, E London, England, 3 December, 1962 — M

League Club	Source	Date Signed	Seasons Played	Apps	Subs	Gls
Leyton Orient	App	12/79	81-84	76	13	13
Aldershot	Tr	12/84	84-85	20	5	2

McNEIL Martin James
Born: Rutherglen, Glasgow, Scotland, 28 September, 1980 — CD

League Club	Source	Date Signed	Seasons Played	Apps	Subs	Gls
Cambridge U	YT	12/98	98-00	38	3	0
Torquay U	Tr	08/01	01	16	0	0

McNEIL Matthew (Matty)
Born: Manchester, England, 14 July, 1976 — F

League Club	Source	Date Signed	Seasons Played	Apps	Subs	Gls
Macclesfield T	Hyde U	03/06	05-06	41	6	6
Stockport Co	Tr	08/07	07-09	36	5	5

McNEIL Matthew Alexander (Matt)
Born: Glasgow, Scotland, 28 July, 1927 — CH
Died: Newcastle-upon-Tyne, England, 23 April, 1977

League Club	Source	Date Signed	Seasons Played	Apps	Subs	Gls
Newcastle U	Hibernian	12/49	50	9	-	0
Barnsley	Tr	08/51	51-52	68	-	1
Brighton & HA	Tr	07/53	53-55	53	-	0
Norwich C	Tr	03/56	55-56	44	-	2

McNEIL Michael (Mick)
Born: Middlesbrough, England, 7 February, 1940 — LB
England: 9/FLge-1/U23-9

League Club	Source	Date Signed	Seasons Played	Apps	Subs	Gls
Middlesbrough	Jnr	06/57	58-63	178	-	3
Ipswich T	Tr	07/64	64-71	141	5	4

McNEIL Richard (Dixie)
Born: Melton Mowbray, Leicestershire, England, 16 January, 1947 — F

League Club	Source	Date Signed	Seasons Played	Apps	Subs	Gls
Leicester C	Holwell Works	11/64				
Exeter C	Tr	06/66	66	31	0	11
Northampton T	Corby T	05/69	69-71	85	1	33
Lincoln C	Tr	01/72	71-73	96	1	53
Hereford U	Tr	08/74	74-77	128	1	85
Wrexham	Tr	09/77	77-82	166	1	54
Hereford U	Tr	10/82	82	12	0	3

McNEIL Robert Muirhead (Bobby)
Born: Hamilton, Lanarkshire, Scotland, 1 November, 1962 — RB

League Club	Source	Date Signed	Seasons Played	Apps	Subs	Gls
Hull C	App	11/80	80-84	135	3	3
Lincoln C	Blackpool (NC)	10/85	85	4	0	0
Preston NE	Tr	12/85	85-86	43	0	0
Carlisle U	Tr	08/87	87	18	1	0

McNEILL Alexander (Alan)
Born: Belfast, Northern Ireland, 16 August, 1945 — M
Northern Ireland: Amateur

League Club	Source	Date Signed	Seasons Played	Apps	Subs	Gls
Middlesbrough	Crusaders	08/67	67-68	3	0	0
Huddersfield T	Tr	11/68	68	1	1	0
Oldham Ath	Tr	10/69	69-74	154	16	19
Stockport Co	Tr	07/75	75-76	69	2	1

McNEILL Brian
Born: Newcastle-upon-Tyne, England, 1 April, 1956 — FB

League Club	Source	Date Signed	Seasons Played	Apps	Subs	Gls
Bristol C	App	04/74	75-76	0	3	0
Plymouth Arg	Tr	12/78	78-80	47	0	0

McNEILL Edward Vincent (Ted)
Born: Warrenpoint, Down, Northern Ireland, 26 March, 1929 — G

League Club	Source	Date Signed	Seasons Played	Apps	Subs	Gls
Sunderland	Portadown	12/51	53	7	-	0

McNEILL John McKeand (Ian)
Born: Baillieston, Glasgow, Scotland, 24 February, 1932 — IF

League Club	Source	Date Signed	Seasons Played	Apps	Subs	Gls
Leicester C	Aberdeen	03/56	55-58	72	-	26
Brighton & HA	Tr	03/59	58-61	116	-	12
Southend U	Tr	07/62	62-63	41	-	3

McNEISH Samuel (Sam)
Born: Bo'ness, Falkirk, Scotland, 4 August, 1930 — IF
Died: Falkirk, Scotland, 29 November, 1998

League Club	Source	Date Signed	Seasons Played	Apps	Subs	Gls
Leeds U	Linlithgow Rose	02/51	50	1	-	0

McNICHOL James Anthony (Jim)
Born: Glasgow, Scotland, 9 June, 1958 — CD
Scotland: U21-7

League Club	Source	Date Signed	Seasons Played	Apps	Subs	Gls
Luton T	Ipswich T (App)	07/76	76-78	13	2	0
Brentford	Tr	10/78	78-83	151	4	22
Exeter C	Tr	07/84	84-85	87	0	10
Torquay U	Tr	07/86	86-88	124	0	13
Exeter C	Tr	08/89	89-90	42	0	8
Torquay U	Tr	07/91	91	2	0	0

McNICHOL John (Johnny)
Born: Kilmarnock, Ayrshire, Scotland, 20 August, 1925 — IF/D
Died: Uckfield, East Sussex, England, 17 March, 2007

League Club	Source	Date Signed	Seasons Played	Apps	Subs	Gls
Newcastle U	Hurlford Jnrs	08/46				
Brighton & HA	Tr	08/48	48-51	158	-	37
Chelsea	Tr	08/52	52-57	181	-	59
Crystal Palace	Tr	03/58	57-62	189	-	15

McNICHOL Robert Hugh (Bob)
Born: Dumbarton, Dunbartonshire, Scotland, 13 February, 1933 — RB
Died: Tenerife, Spain, 25 April, 1980

League Club	Source	Date Signed	Seasons Played	Apps	Subs	Gls
Accrington Stan	Stirling A	05/56	56-58	134	-	5
Brighton & HA	Tr	06/59	59-61	93	-	0
Carlisle U	Gravesend & Northfleet	10/63	63	1	-	0

McNICHOLAS John
Born: Preston, Lancashire, England, 30 October, 1949 — M

League Club	Source	Date Signed	Seasons Played	Apps	Subs	Gls
Blackpool		10/68	70	0	1	0

McNICOL Alexander Hogarth (Alex)
Born: Baillieston, Glasgow, Scotland, 10 October, 1919 — IF
Died: Dover, Kent, England, December, 2001

League Club	Source	Date Signed	Seasons Played	Apps	Subs	Gls
Aldershot	Dunfermline Ath	08/47	47-50	110	-	20
Rochdale	Tr	01/51	50	17	-	3

McNISH Callum Leander William
Born: Oxford, England, 25 May, 1992 — LM

League Club	Source	Date Signed	Seasons Played	Apps	Subs	Gls
Southampton	Sch	05/09	09	0	1	0
Exeter C	Tr	07/11	11	2	3	0

McNIVEN David Jonathan
Born: Leeds, England, 27 May, 1978 — F

League Club	Source	Date Signed	Seasons Played	Apps	Subs	Gls
Oldham Ath	YT	10/95	96-99	8	18	2
York C	Tr	08/00	00	25	16	8

McNIVEN David Scott
Born: Stonehouse, Lanarkshire, Scotland, 9 September, 1955 — F
Scotland: U21-3

League Club	Source	Date Signed	Seasons Played	Apps	Subs	Gls
Leeds U	App	09/72	75-77	15	5	6
Bradford C	Tr	02/78	77-82	202	10	64
Blackpool	Tr	02/83	82-83	45	4	11
Halifax T	Pittsburg Spirit (USA)	03/85	84	12	0	4

McNIVEN Scott Andrew
Born: Leeds, England, 27 May, 1978 — RB
Scotland: U21-1/Youth

League Club	Source	Date Signed	Seasons Played	Apps	Subs	Gls
Oldham Ath	YT	10/95	94-01	204	18	3
Oxford U	Tr	07/02	02-03	85	0	1
Mansfield T	Tr	07/04	04	24	1	0
Chester C	Tr	07/05	05	41	0	1

McNULTY James (Jimmy)
Born: Runcorn, Cheshire, England, 13 February, 1985 — CD
Scotland: Youth

League Club	Source	Date Signed	Seasons Played	Apps	Subs	Gls
Macclesfield T	Caernarfon T	08/06	06-07	28	6	1
Stockport Co	Tr	01/08	07-08	37	0	1
Brighton & HA	Tr	02/09	08-09	10	3	1
Scunthorpe U	L	03/10	09	2	1	0
Scunthorpe U	L	07/10	10	5	1	0
Barnsley	Tr	06/11	11-12	53	3	2
Tranmere Rov	L	10/13	13	12	0	0
Bury	Tr	01/14	13-14	43	3	0

McNULTY Joseph (Joe)
Born: Dundalk, Republic of Ireland, 17 July, 1923 — G
Died: New York, USA, 14 March, 1986

League Club	Source	Date Signed	Seasons Played	Apps	Subs	Gls
Burnley	Ards	05/49	50-51	8	-	0
Sheffield U	Tr	06/52				

McNULTY Marc
Born: Edinburgh, Scotland, 14 September, 1992 — F

League Club	Source	Date Signed	Seasons Played	Apps	Subs	Gls
Sheffield U	Livingston	07/14	14	11	20	9

McNULTY Stephen Michael (Steve)
Born: Liverpool, England, 26 September, 1983 — CD

League Club	Source	Date Signed	Seasons Played	Apps	Subs	Gls
Liverpool	Sch	07/01				
Fleetwood T	Barrow	06/09	12	16	0	2
Luton T	Tr	01/13	14	41	0	0

McNULTY Thomas (Tom)
Born: Salford, England, 30 December, 1929 — RB
Died: Salford, England, April, 1979

League Club	Source	Date Signed	Seasons Played	Apps	Subs	Gls
Manchester U	Jnr	06/47	49-53	57	-	0
Liverpool	Tr	02/54	53-57	36	-	0

McNULTY William George
Born: Edinburgh, Scotland, 9 February, 1949 — G

League Club	Source	Date Signed	Seasons Played	Apps	Subs	Gls
Port Vale	Jnr	04/66	66	1	0	0
Chesterfield	Tr	07/68	68	6	0	0

McPAKE James
Born: Airdrie, Lanarkshire, Scotland, 24 June, 1984 — CD
Northern Ireland: 1

League Club	Source	Date Signed	Seasons Played	Apps	Subs	Gls
Coventry C	Livingston	02/09	08-11	34	4	1

McPARLAND Anthony Patrick
Born: Rutherglen, Glasgow, Scotland, 20 September, 1982 — W
Scotland: U21-1/Youth

League Club	Source	Date Signed	Seasons Played	Apps	Subs	Gls
Barnsley	Glasgow Celtic	02/06	05	0	8	0
Wycombe W	Tr	12/06	06	1	3	0

McPARLAND Ian John
Born: Tranent, East Lothian, Scotland, 4 October, 1961 — F

League Club	Source	Date Signed	Seasons Played	Apps	Subs	Gls
Notts Co	Ormiston Primrose	12/80	80-88	190	31	69
Hull C	Tr	03/89	88-90	31	16	7
Walsall	Tr	03/91	90	11	0	6
Lincoln C	Dunfermline Ath	08/92	92	3	1	0
Northampton T	Tr	10/92	92	11	0	3

McPARLAND Peter James
Born: Newry, Armagh, Northern Ireland, 25 April, 1934 — LW
England: FLge-1//Northern Ireland: 34

League Club	Source	Date Signed	Seasons Played	Apps	Subs	Gls
Aston Villa	Dundalk (ROI)	09/52	52-61	294	-	97
Wolverhampton W	Tr	01/62	61-62	24	-	10
Plymouth Arg	Tr	01/63	62-63	38	-	14

McPARTLAND Desmond (Des)
Born: Middlesbrough, England, 5 October, 1947 — G
Died: Middlesbrough, England, 22 April, 2006
England: Youth

League Club	Source	Date Signed	Seasons Played	Apps	Subs	Gls
Middlesbrough	App	10/64	65-67	35	0	0
Carlisle U	Tr	12/67	67	5	0	0
Northampton T	Tr	07/69	69	6	0	0
Hartlepool U	Tr	03/70	69-70	56	0	0

McPEAKE Matthew (Matt)
Born: Ballymena, Antrim, Northern Ireland, 19 June, 1919 — LH
Died: Plymouth, England, January, 2007

League Club	Source	Date Signed	Seasons Played	Apps	Subs	Gls
Everton	Ballymena U	07/46				
Grimsby T	Tr	06/47				
New Brighton	Tr	07/48	48-49	50	-	2

MacPHAIL John
Born: Dundee, Scotland, 7 December, 1955 — CD

League Club	Source	Date Signed	Seasons Played	Apps	Subs	Gls
Sheffield U	Dundee	01/79	78-82	135	0	7
York C	Tr	02/83	82-85	141	1	24
Bristol C	Tr	07/86	86	26	0	1
Sunderland	Tr	07/87	87-90	130	0	22
Hartlepool U	Tr	09/90	90-94	159	4	4

McPHAIL Stephen John Paul
Born: Westminster, Central London, England, 9 December, 1979 — M
Republic of Ireland: 10/B-1/U21-7/Youth

League Club	Source	Date Signed	Seasons Played	Apps	Subs	Gls
Leeds U	YT	12/96	97-03	52	26	3
Millwall	L	03/02	01	3	0	0
Nottingham F	L	08/03	03	13	1	0
Barnsley	Tr	07/04	04-05	66	4	4
Cardiff C	Tr	07/06	06-12	167	19	3
Sheffield Wed	Tr	09/13	13	13	0	0

McPHEAT William (Willie)
Born: Caldercruix, Lanarkshire, Scotland, 4 September, 1942 — IF

League Club	Source	Date Signed	Seasons Played	Apps	Subs	Gls
Sunderland	Calder Jnrs	09/59	60-62	58	-	19
Hartlepool U	Tr	09/65	65	13	2	2

McPHEE Christopher Simon (Chris)
Born: Eastbourne, East Sussex, England, 20 March, 1983 — F/M
England: Semi Pro-3

League Club	Source	Date Signed	Seasons Played	Apps	Subs	Gls
Brighton & HA	Sch	06/02	99-05	27	33	4
Swindon T	L	03/06	05	6	2	0
Torquay U	Tr	07/06	06	11	26	0
Torquay U	Kidderminster Hrs	07/11	11	6	20	2

McPHEE John
Born: Motherwell, Lanarkshire, Scotland, 21 November, 1937 — CD/WH/IF
Died: Hambleton, Lancashire, England, 4 January, 2015

League Club	Source	Date Signed	Seasons Played	Apps	Subs	Gls
Blackpool	Motherwell	07/62	62-69	249	10	15
Barnsley	Tr	06/70	70	26	0	3
Southport	Tr	07/71	71-72	85	0	1

McPHEE Magnus George (Tony)
Born: Edinburgh, Scotland, 30 April, 1914 — CF
Died: Basingstoke, Hampshire, England, 1960

League Club	Source	Date Signed	Seasons Played	Apps	Subs	Gls
Bradford Park Ave	Workington	10/36	36	30	-	18
Coventry C	Tr	06/37	37	12	-	6
Reading	Tr	05/38	38-48	132	-	90

McPHEE Stephen (Steve)
Born: Glasgow, Scotland, 5 June, 1981 — F
Scotland: U21-1

League Club	Source	Date Signed	Seasons Played	Apps	Subs	Gls
Coventry C	YT	11/98				
Port Vale	Tr	07/01	01-03	125	5	39
Hull C	Beira Mar (POR)	06/05	05-07	18	17	2
Blackpool	Tr	01/08	07-08	16	8	4

McPHEE Stewart Douglas
Born: Middlesbrough, England, 5 January, 1965 — M

League Club	Source	Date Signed	Seasons Played	Apps	Subs	Gls
Darlington	Whitby T	09/86	86	7	2	1

McPHERSON Albert
Born: Salford, England, 8 July, 1927 — CH
Died: 11 January, 2015

League Club	Source	Date Signed	Seasons Played	Apps	Subs	Gls
Bury	Salford LC	06/49				
Walsall	Stalybridge Celtic	05/54	54-63	351	-	8

MacPHERSON Angus Ian
Born: Glasgow, Scotland, 11 October, 1968 — LB

League Club	Source	Date Signed	Seasons Played	Apps	Subs	Gls
Exeter C (L)	Glasgow Rangers	03/90	89	11	0	1

McPHERSON Ian Buchanan
Born: Glasgow, Scotland, 26 July, 1920 — W
Died: St Albans, Hertfordshire, England, 20 March, 1983

League Club	Source	Date Signed	Seasons Played	Apps	Subs	Gls
Notts Co	Glasgow Rangers	08/45				
Arsenal	Tr	08/46	46-50	152	-	19
Notts Co	Tr	08/51	51-52	50	-	7
Brentford	Tr	07/53	53	4	-	0

McPHERSON Keith Anthony
Born: Greenwich, SE London, England, 11 September, 1963 — CD

League Club	Source	Date Signed	Seasons Played	Apps	Subs	Gls
West Ham U	App	09/81	84	1	0	0
Cambridge U	L	09/85	85	11	0	1
Northampton T	Tr	01/86	85-89	182	0	8
Reading	Tr	08/90	90-98	264	7	8
Brighton & HA	Tr	03/99	98-99	33	2	1

McPHERSON Kenneth (Ken)
Born: Hartlepool, Cleveland, England, 25 March, 1927 — CF/CH

League Club	Source	Date Signed	Seasons Played	Apps	Subs	Gls
Notts Co	Hartlepool U (Am)	08/50	50-52	26	-	10
Middlesbrough	Tr	08/53	53-55	33	-	15
Coventry C	Tr	11/55	55-57	88	-	38
Newport Co	Tr	06/58	58-60	128	-	51
Swindon T	Tr	08/61	61-64	107	-	3

McPHERSON Malcolm
Born: Glasgow, Scotland, 19 December, 1974 — M/RB

League Club	Source	Date Signed	Seasons Played	Apps	Subs	Gls
West Ham U	Yeovil T	01/94				
Brentford	Tr	06/96	96-97	9	3	0

McPHILLIPS Terence Peter (Terry)
Born: Manchester, England, 1 October, 1968 — F

League Club	Source	Date Signed	Seasons Played	Apps	Subs	Gls
Halifax T	Liverpool (App)	09/87	87-90	61	32	28
Northampton T	L	11/89	89	0	1	0
Crewe Alex	Tr	08/91	91	5	1	0

McQUADE Alexander Michael (Alex)
Born: Manchester, England, 7 November, 1992 — CD

League Club	Source	Date Signed	Seasons Played	Apps	Subs	Gls
Bolton W	Sch	07/12				
Shrewsbury T	Tr	07/13	13	0	1	0

McQUADE James (Jim)
Born: Barrhead, Renfrewshire, Scotland, 14 October, 1933 — IF
Northern Ireland: NILge-2

League Club	Source	Date Signed	Seasons Played	Apps	Subs	Gls
Halifax T	Dumbarton	08/57	57	9	-	2

McQUADE John
Born: Glasgow, Scotland, 8 July, 1970 — W

League Club	Source	Date Signed	Seasons Played	Apps	Subs	Gls
Port Vale	Hamilton Academical	07/98	98	0	3	0

McQUADE Terence James (Terry)
Born: Holborn, Central London, England, 24 February, 1941 — LW

League Club	Source	Date Signed	Seasons Played	Apps	Subs	Gls
Millwall	Enfield	10/61	61-62	34	-	7
Queens Park Rgrs	Tr	07/63	63	20	-	2
Millwall	Dover	11/65	65	3	0	1

McQUAID Thomas Joseph (Tom)
Born: Dublin, Republic of Ireland, 1 February, 1936 — LH
Died: Bradford, England, 1981

League Club	Source	Date Signed	Seasons Played	Apps	Subs	Gls
Bradford C	Thackley	11/57	58-59	23	-	2

McQUARRIE Andrew (Andy)
Born: Glasgow, Scotland, 2 October, 1939 — IF

League Club	Source	Date Signed	Seasons Played	Apps	Subs	Gls
Chesterfield	Albion Rov	11/62	62-63	38	-	12
Brighton & HA	Tr	07/64	64	2	-	1

McQUEEN Gordon
Born: Kilbirnie, Ayrshire, Scotland, 26 June, 1952 — CD
Scotland: 30

League Club	Source	Date Signed	Seasons Played	Apps	Subs	Gls
Leeds U	St Mirren	09/72	72-77	140	0	15
Manchester U	Tr	02/78	77-84	184	0	20

McQUEEN Ian David
Born: Manchester, England, 4 February, 1946 — CF
Died: Stockport, Greater Manchester, England, 28 May, 1985

League Club	Source	Date Signed	Seasons Played	Apps	Subs	Gls
Rochdale		01/66	65-66	14	2	4

McQUEEN Thomas (Tommy)
Born: West Calder, West Lothian, Scotland, 21 February, 1929 — G
Died: 10 February, 2015

League Club	Source	Date Signed	Seasons Played	Apps	Subs	Gls
Accrington Stan	Queen of the South	06/54	54-56	80	-	0

McQUEEN Thomas Feeney (Tommy)
Born: Bellshill, Lanarkshire, Scotland, 1 April, 1963 — LB

League Club	Source	Date Signed	Seasons Played	Apps	Subs	Gls
West Ham U	Aberdeen	03/87	86-89	24	6	0

McQUILKIN James Robbie Leonard
Born: Tipton, West Midlands, England, 9 January, 1989 — M
Northern Ireland: U21-1/Youth

League Club	Source	Date Signed	Seasons Played	Apps	Subs	Gls
Hereford U	Tescoma Zlin (CZE)	08/09	09-11	54	13	5
Walsall	Hereford U	07/13	13	2	7	0

McQUILLAN Dennis
Born: Derby, England, 16 March, 1934 — W
Died: Derby, England, August, 2014

League Club	Source	Date Signed	Seasons Played	Apps	Subs	Gls
Derby Co	Jnr	03/51	52-55	18	-	1
Aldershot	Tr	07/56				

McQUILLAN Patrick Gerard (Pat)
Born: Belfast, Northern Ireland, 27 June, 1961 — RB

League Club	Source	Date Signed	Seasons Played	Apps	Subs	Gls
Swansea C	Pembroke Bor	08/79				
Swansea C	Pembroke Bor	12/83	83-84	25	1	1

McQUOID Joshua Joseph Brian (Josh)
Born: Southampton, England, 15 December, 1989 — W/F
Northern Ireland: 5/B-1/U21-8/Youth

League Club	Source	Date Signed	Seasons Played	Apps	Subs	Gls
Bournemouth	Jnr	07/08	06-10	31	38	10
Millwall	Tr	11/10	10-11	8	8	1
Burnley	L	01/12	11	9	8	1
Bournemouth	Tr	05/12	12-13	22	13	3
Peterborough U	L	02/14	13	8	6	1
Coventry C	L	08/14	14	12	2	3

MacRAE Keith Alexander
Born: Glasgow, Scotland, 5 February, 1951 — G
Scotland: SLge-1/U23-2

League Club	Source	Date Signed	Seasons Played	Apps	Subs	Gls
Manchester C	Motherwell	10/73	73-80	56	0	0

MACREADY Brian Leslie
Born: Leicester, England, 25 March, 1942 — IF

League Club	Source	Date Signed	Seasons Played	Apps	Subs	Gls
West Bromwich A	Hull C (Am)	02/60	60-63	14	-	1
Mansfield T	Tr	07/64	64-65	49	1	11

McREADY John Lewis
Born: South Shields, Tyne and Wear, England, 24 July, 1992 — M

League Club	Source	Date Signed	Seasons Played	Apps	Subs	Gls
Darlington	Sch	05/10	09	3	1	0
York C	Tr	06/12	12	0	4	0

McROBERT Lee Peter
Born: Bromley, SE London, England, 4 October, 1972 — M

League Club	Source	Date Signed	Seasons Played	Apps	Subs	Gls
Millwall	Sittingbourne	02/95	94-97	12	11	1

McSEVENEY John Haddon
Born: Shotts, Lanarkshire, Scotland, 8 February, 1931 — LW

League Club	Source	Date Signed	Seasons Played	Apps	Subs	Gls
Sunderland	Hamilton Academical	10/51	51-54	35	-	3
Cardiff C	Tr	05/55	55-56	75	-	19
Newport Co	Tr	07/57	57-60	172	-	53
Hull C	Tr	07/61	61-64	161	-	60

McSHANE Anthony (Tony)
Born: Belfast, Northern Ireland, 28 February, 1927 — WH
Died: Plymouth, England, 12 December, 2012

League Club	Source	Date Signed	Seasons Played	Apps	Subs	Gls
Plymouth Arg	Brantwood	12/48	49-54	85	-	2
Swindon T	Tr	06/55	55-56	41	-	0

McSHANE Henry (Harry)
Born: Holytown, Lanarkshire, Scotland, 8 April, 1920 — LW
Died: Manchester, England, 7 November, 2012

League Club	Source	Date Signed	Seasons Played	Apps	Subs	Gls
Blackburn Rov	Bellshill Ath	04/37	37	2	-	0
Huddersfield T	Tr	09/46	46	15	-	1
Bolton W	Tr	07/47	47-50	93	-	6
Manchester U	Tr	09/50	50-53	56	-	8
Oldham Ath	Tr	02/54	53-54	41	-	5

McSHANE Paul David
Born: Greystones, Wicklow, Republic of Ireland, 6 January, 1986 — D
Republic of Ireland: 33/U21-9/Youth

League Club	Source	Date Signed	Seasons Played	Apps	Subs	Gls
Manchester U	Sch	01/03				
Walsall	L	12/04	04	3	1	1
Brighton & HA	L	08/05	05	38	0	3
West Bromwich A	Tr	08/06	06	31	1	2
Sunderland	Tr	07/07	07-08	20	4	0
Hull C	L	09/08	08	17	0	1
Hull C	Tr	09/09	09-14	88	14	3
Barnsley	L	02/11	10	10	0	1
Crystal Palace	L	01/12	11	9	2	0

McSHEFFREY Gary
Born: Coventry, England, 13 August, 1982 — LW/F
England: Youth

League Club	Source	Date Signed	Seasons Played	Apps	Subs	Gls
Coventry C	YT	08/99	98-06	108	35	44
Stockport Co	L	11/01	01	3	2	1
Luton T	L	08/03	03	18	0	9
Luton T	L	09/04	04	1	4	1
Birmingham C	Tr	08/06	06-09	68	15	16
Nottingham F	L	03/09	08	4	0	0
Leeds U	L	01/10	09	9	1	1
Coventry C	Tr	07/10	10-12	93	11	17
Chesterfield	Tr	09/13	13	2	7	1
Scunthorpe U	Tr	01/14	13-14	44	10	7

McSPORRAN Jermaine
Born: Manchester, England, 1 January, 1977 — F

League Club	Source	Date Signed	Seasons Played	Apps	Subs	Gls
Wycombe W	Oxford C	11/98	98-03	117	41	30
Walsall	Tr	03/04	03	2	4	0
Doncaster Rov	Tr	06/04	04-05	17	11	1
Boston U	L	02/06	05	0	2	0
Chester C	Tr	07/06	06	0	1	0

McSTAY Henry Matthew Patrick
Born: Lurgan, Armagh, Northern Ireland, 6 March, 1985 — D
Republic of Ireland: U21-4//Northern Ireland: Youth

League Club	Source	Date Signed	Seasons Played	Apps	Subs	Gls
Leeds U	Sch	03/02				
Morecambe	Royal Antwerp (BEL)	01/08	07-09	29	6	1

McSTAY James Gerald (Jimmy)
Born: Newry, Armagh, Northern Ireland, 4 August, 1922 — W
Died: North Yorkshire, England, 17 January, 2007
Republic of Ireland: LoI-1

League Club	Source	Date Signed	Seasons Played	Apps	Subs	Gls
Grimsby T	Dundalk (ROI)	08/48	48-50	61	-	2

McSTAY Raymond James (Ray)
Born: Hamilton, Lanarkshire, Scotland, 16 May, 1970 — M
Scotland: Schools

League Club	Source	Date Signed	Seasons Played	Apps	Subs	Gls
Cardiff C	Hamilton Academical	12/96	96	1	0	0

McSTAY William John (Willie)
Born: Hamilton, Lanarkshire, Scotland, 26 November, 1961 — RB/M

League Club	Source	Date Signed	Seasons Played	Apps	Subs	Gls
Huddersfield T	Glasgow Celtic	03/87	86-87	4	5	0
Notts Co	Tr	02/88	87-89	33	12	1
Hartlepool U	L	11/89	89	3	0	0

McSWEENEY David (Dave)
Born: Basildon, England, 28 December, 1981 — D

League Club	Source	Date Signed	Seasons Played	Apps	Subs	Gls
Southend U	YT	04/01	00-03	54	16	1

McSWEENEY Leon
Born: Cork, Republic of Ireland, 19 February, 1983 — FB/M

League Club	Source	Date Signed	Seasons Played	Apps	Subs	Gls
Leicester C	Jnr	08/01				
Stockport Co	Cork C (ROI)	01/08	07-08	33	14	5
Hartlepool U	Tr	06/09	09-10	48	29	3
Leyton Orient	Tr	07/11	11-12	57	4	0
Carlisle U	Tr	09/13	13	8	0	0
Northampton T	Tr	01/14	13	16	2	0

McSWEGAN Gary John
Born: Glasgow, Scotland, 24 September, 1970 — F
Scotland: 2/Youth/Schools

League Club	Source	Date Signed	Seasons Played	Apps	Subs	Gls
Notts Co	Glasgow Rangers	07/93	93-95	47	15	21
Barnsley (L)	Heart of Midlothian	12/01	01	1	4	0
Luton T (L)	Heart of Midlothian	02/02	01	2	1	0

McTAFF Stephen (Steve)
Born: Tanfield, County Durham, England, 11 March, 1922 — WH
Died: Bradford, England, 1983

League Club	Source	Date Signed	Seasons Played	Apps	Subs	Gls
Bradford Park Ave	Eden Colliery	05/45	46-47	29	-	0
New Brighton	Tr	07/48	48-50	100	-	3
York C	East Bierley	10/51				

McTAVISH John Robert
Born: Glasgow, Scotland, 2 February, 1932 — CH

League Club	Source	Date Signed	Seasons Played	Apps	Subs	Gls
Manchester C	Dalry Thistle	06/52	53-59	93	-	0

McTURK John
Born: Cumnock, Ayrshire, Scotland, 11 July, 1936 — LB

League Club	Source	Date Signed	Seasons Played	Apps	Subs	Gls
Wrexham	St Mirren	07/57	57	2	-	0

McVAY David Reid
Born: Workington, Cumbria, England, 5 March, 1955 — FB/M
England: Schools

League Club	Source	Date Signed	Seasons Played	Apps	Subs	Gls
Notts Co	Ilkeston T	07/73	73-78	101	12	2
Torquay U	L	09/77	77	8	0	0
Peterborough U	Tr	07/79	79-80	47	2	1
Lincoln C	Tr	08/81	81	13	0	0

McVEIGH James (Jim)
Born: Bamford, Derbyshire, England, 2 July, 1949 — FB

League Club	Source	Date Signed	Seasons Played	Apps	Subs	Gls
Wolverhampton W	Wath W	05/68	68	2	0	0
Gillingham	Tr	10/70	70-71	48	0	1

McVEIGH Paul Francis
Born: Belfast, Northern Ireland, 6 December, 1977 — LW

Northern Ireland: 20/U21-11/Youth/Schools

League Club	Source	Date Signed	Seasons Played	Apps	Subs	Gls
Tottenham H	YT	07/96	96	2	1	1
Norwich C	Tr	03/00	99-06	148	68	36
Burnley	L	03/07	06	6	2	3
Luton T	Tr	08/07	07-08	24	14	3
Norwich C	Tr	07/09	09	4	5	0

McVICAR Donald Frederick (Don)
Born: Perth, Scotland, 6 November, 1962 — D
Died: Dundee, Scotland, 31 January, 2006

League Club	Source	Date Signed	Seasons Played	Apps	Subs	Gls
Tranmere Rov	St Johnstone	08/85	85	7	0	0

MacVINISH Thomas (Tommy)
Born: Inverness, Scotland, 1 January, 1921 — LW
Died: Aberdeen, Scotland, 19 September, 1965

League Club	Source	Date Signed	Seasons Played	Apps	Subs	Gls
Preston NE	Hamilton Academical	08/48				
Darlington	Tr	08/50	50	1	-	0

McVITIE George James
Born: Carlisle, Cumbria, England, 7 September, 1948 — RW
England: Schools

League Club	Source	Date Signed	Seasons Played	Apps	Subs	Gls
Carlisle U	App	12/65	65-70	124	3	21
West Bromwich A	Tr	08/70	70-71	42	0	5
Oldham Ath	Tr	08/72	72-75	108	5	19
Carlisle U	Tr	12/75	75-80	191	7	20

McWHINNIE Archibald (Archie)
Born: Glasgow, Scotland, 17 July, 1926 — WH
Died: East Kilbride, Lanarkshire, Scotland, 21 March, 1971

League Club	Source	Date Signed	Seasons Played	Apps	Subs	Gls
Wrexham	Rutherglen Glencairn	05/51	51	2	-	0

MADAR Mickael Raymond
Born: Paris, France, 8 May, 1968 — F
France: 3

League Club	Source	Date Signed	Seasons Played	Apps	Subs	Gls
Everton	Depo la Coruna (SPN)	12/97	97-98	17	2	6

MADDEN Craig Anthony
Born: Manchester, England, 25 September, 1958 — F

League Club	Source	Date Signed	Seasons Played	Apps	Subs	Gls
Bury	Northern Nomads	03/78	77-85	278	19	128
West Bromwich A	Tr	03/86	85-86	10	2	3
Blackpool	Tr	02/87	86-89	73	18	24
Wrexham	L	01/90	89	6	2	0
York C	Tr	03/90	89	3	1	0

MADDEN David John
Born: Stepney, E London, England, 6 January, 1963 — M

League Club	Source	Date Signed	Seasons Played	Apps	Subs	Gls
Southampton	App	01/81				
Bournemouth	L	01/83	82	5	0	0
Arsenal	Tr	08/83	83	2	0	0
Charlton Ath	Tr	06/84	84	19	1	1
Reading	Los Angeles Laz (USA)	11/87	87	7	2	1
Crystal Palace	Tr	08/88	88-89	19	8	5
Birmingham C	L	01/90	89	5	0	1
Maidstone U	Tr	06/90	90	10	0	0

MADDEN Lawrence David (Lawrie)
Born: Hackney, E London, England, 28 September, 1955 — CD

League Club	Source	Date Signed	Seasons Played	Apps	Subs	Gls
Mansfield T	Manchester Univ	03/75	74-75	9	1	0
Charlton Ath	Boston U	03/78	77-81	109	4	7
Millwall	Tr	03/82	81-82	44	3	1
Sheffield Wed	Tr	08/83	83-90	200	12	2
Leicester C	L	01/91	90	3	0	0
Wolverhampton W	Tr	08/91	91-92	62	5	1
Darlington	Tr	09/93	93	5	0	0
Chesterfield	Tr	10/93	93-95	37	0	1

MADDEN Neil
Born: Luton, England, 6 February, 1962 — M

League Club	Source	Date Signed	Seasons Played	Apps	Subs	Gls
Luton T	App	12/79	79	1	0	0

MADDEN Patrick (Paddy)
Born: Dublin, Republic of Ireland, 4 March, 1990 — F
Republic of Ireland: 1/U21-1/Youth

League Club	Source	Date Signed	Seasons Played	Apps	Subs	Gls
Carlisle U	Bohemians (ROI)	01/11	10-12	7	25	2
Yeovil T	Tr	10/12	12-13	42	2	22
Scunthorpe U	Tr	01/14	13-14	63	4	19

MADDEN Peter
Born: Bradford, England, 31 October, 1934 — CH

League Club	Source	Date Signed	Seasons Played	Apps	Subs	Gls
Rotherham U	Thornton	10/55	55-65	309	2	7
Bradford Park Ave	Tr	07/66	66	25	3	1
Aldershot	Tr	07/67	67	26	1	1

MADDEN Simon Francis
Born: Dublin, Republic of Ireland, 1 May, 1988 — RB
Republic of Ireland: LoI-1/U21-3

League Club	Source	Date Signed	Seasons Played	Apps	Subs	Gls
Leeds U	Sch	05/06				
Darlington	Shamrock Rov (ROI)	01/10	09	13	2	0

MADDICK Kevin Andrew
Born: Newcastle-upon-Tyne, England, 18 September, 1974 — F

League Club	Source	Date Signed	Seasons Played	Apps	Subs	Gls
Darlington	Middlesbrough (YT)	09/92	92-93	1	2	0

MADDISON Donald (Don)
Born: Washington, Tyne and Wear, England, 15 February, 1927 — G

League Club	Source	Date Signed	Seasons Played	Apps	Subs	Gls
Bradford Park Ave	Sunderland (Am)	06/46				
Blackpool	Tr	02/48				
Darlington	Tr	08/50	50	1	-	0

MADDISON Frank
Born: Worksop, Nottinghamshire, England, 6 May, 1934 — LB
Died: Chesterfield, Derbyshire, England, 31 October, 1993

League Club	Source	Date Signed	Seasons Played	Apps	Subs	Gls
Notts Co		08/53	56-57	15	-	0

MADDISON George
Born: Hull, England, 6 October, 1930 — G
Died: Hull, England, December, 1987

League Club	Source	Date Signed	Seasons Played	Apps	Subs	Gls
Aldershot	Hull C (Am)	08/48	48	2	-	0
York C	Tr	09/52	53	11	-	0

MADDISON James (Jimmy)
Born: South Shields, Tyne and Wear, England, 9 November, 1924 — LW
Died: South Shields, Tyne and Wear, England, 7 June, 1992

League Club	Source	Date Signed	Seasons Played	Apps	Subs	Gls
Middlesbrough	Jnr	12/45	46	1	-	0
Darlington	Tr	08/49	49	41	-	7
Grimsby T	Tr	06/50	50-58	272	-	40
Chesterfield	Tr	03/59	58-60	98	-	16

MADDISON James Daniel
Born: Coventry, England, 23 November, 1996 — F

League Club	Source	Date Signed	Seasons Played	Apps	Subs	Gls
Coventry C	Sch	07/14	14	2	10	2

MADDISON John Anthony (Jack)
Born: Barrow, Cumbria, England, 1 October, 1940 — RW

League Club	Source	Date Signed	Seasons Played	Apps	Subs	Gls
Barrow	Holker Central OB	07/60	61-64	88	-	18

MADDISON Lee Robert
Born: Bristol, England, 5 October, 1972 — LB

League Club	Source	Date Signed	Seasons Played	Apps	Subs	Gls
Bristol Rov	YT	07/91	91-94	68	5	0
Northampton T	Tr	09/95	95-96	55	0	0
Carlisle U	Dundee	10/00	00-03	59	5	1
Oxford U	L	02/02	01	11	0	0

MADDISON Marcus Harley
Born: Trimdon, County Durham, England, 26 September, 1993 — F/W
England: Semi Pro-2

League Club	Source	Date Signed	Seasons Played	Apps	Subs	Gls
Newcastle U	Sch	07/12				
Peterborough U	Gateshead	08/14	14	23	6	7

MADDISON Neil Stanley
Born: Darlington, County Durham, England, 2 October, 1969 — M

League Club	Source	Date Signed	Seasons Played	Apps	Subs	Gls
Southampton	YT	04/88	88-97	149	20	19
Middlesbrough	Tr	10/97	97-99	32	24	4
Barnsley	L	11/00	00	3	0	0
Bristol C	L	03/01	00	4	3	1
Darlington	Tr	07/01	01-05	100	15	4

MADDISON Ralph
Born: Bentley, South Yorkshire, England, 28 August, 1918 — LW
Died: Bentley, South Yorkshire, England, 19 May, 1994

League Club	Source	Date Signed	Seasons Played	Apps	Subs	Gls
Doncaster Rov	Bentley Colliery	01/46	46-47	61	-	19
Stockport Co	Tr	05/48	48	5	-	0
Southport	Tr	02/49	48-49	34	-	4

MADDISON William Hartley (Hartley)
Born: Sunderland, England, 6 April, 1954 — RW

League Club	Source	Date Signed	Seasons Played	Apps	Subs	Gls
Hartlepool U (Am)		08/73	73-74	3	1	0

MADDIX Daniel Shawn (Danny)
Born: Ashford, Surrey, England, 11 October, 1967 — CD
Jamaica: 2

League Club	Source	Date Signed	Seasons Played	Apps	Subs	Gls
Tottenham H	App	07/85				
Southend U	L	11/86	86	2	0	0
Queens Park Rgrs	Tr	07/87	87-00	259	35	13
Sheffield Wed	Tr	07/01	01-02	55	4	2

MADDREN William Dixon (Willie)
Born: Billingham, Cleveland, England, 11 January, 1951 — CD
Died: Stockton-on-Tees, Cleveland, England, 29 August, 2000
England: U23-5

League Club	Source	Date Signed	Seasons Played	Apps	Subs	Gls
Middlesbrough	App	06/68	68-77	293	3	19

MADDY Paul Michael
Born: Cwmcarn, Caerphilly, Wales, 17 August, 1962 — M
Wales: U21-1

League Club	Source	Date Signed	Seasons Played	Apps	Subs	Gls
Cardiff C	App	08/80	80-82	35	8	3
Hereford U	L	03/83	82	9	0	1
Swansea C	Tr	08/83	83	18	2	3
Hereford U	Tr	03/84	83-85	75	2	16

League Club	Source	Date Signed	Seasons Played	Apps	Subs	Gls
Brentford	Tr	07/86	86	29	2	5
Chester C	Tr	07/87	87	17	1	1
Hereford U	Tr	03/88	87-88	27	8	1

MADELEY Paul Edward
Born: Leeds, England, 20 September, 1944 — M/D
England: 24/FLge-1/Youth

League Club	Source	Date Signed	Seasons Played	Apps	Subs	Gls
Leeds U	Farsley Celtic	05/62	63-80	528	8	25

MADINE Gary Lee
Born: Gateshead, Tyne and Wear, England, 24 August, 1990 — F

League Club	Source	Date Signed	Seasons Played	Apps	Subs	Gls
Carlisle U	Sch	12/07	07-10	28	38	13
Rochdale	L	03/09	08	1	2	0
Coventry C	L	10/09	09	0	9	0
Chesterfield	L	02/10	09	2	2	0
Sheffield Wed	Tr	01/11	10-14	67	34	26
Carlisle U	L	03/14	13	5	0	2
Coventry C	L	10/14	14	11	0	3
Blackpool	L	02/15	14	14	1	3

MADJO Guy Bertrand
Born: Douala, Cameroon, 1 June, 1984 — F
Cameroon: U23-1/Youth

League Club	Source	Date Signed	Seasons Played	Apps	Subs	Gls
Bristol C	Petersfield T	09/05	05	1	4	0
Cheltenham T (L)	Crawley T	11/07	07	2	3	0
Shrewsbury T	Crawley T	01/08	07	10	5	3
Stevenage	KS Bylis (ALB)	07/11	11	0	1	0
Port Vale	L	11/11	11	5	1	4
Aldershot T	Tr	01/12	11	15	8	8
Plymouth Arg	L	09/12	12	9	5	3
Tranmere Rov	Looktabfah (THA)	11/14	14	0	2	0

MADRICK Carl James
Born: Bolton, Greater Manchester, England, 20 September, 1968 — F

League Club	Source	Date Signed	Seasons Played	Apps	Subs	Gls
Huddersfield T	App	06/87	87	3	5	1
Peterborough U	Tr	09/88	88	3	5	0

MADSEN Peter Planch
Born: Roskilde, Denmark, 26 April, 1978 — F
Denmark: 13/U21-25/Youth

League Club	Source	Date Signed	Seasons Played	Apps	Subs	Gls
Southampton (L)	FC Koln (GER)	01/06	05	8	1	2

MAFFEY Denis
Born: Sunderland, England, 22 February, 1922 — CF
Died: Ipswich, England, 28 August, 1995

League Club	Source	Date Signed	Seasons Played	Apps	Subs	Gls
Ipswich T	Walton U	07/47	47	5	-	1

MAGEE Eric
Born: Lurgan, Armagh, Northern Ireland, 24 August, 1947 — RW/IF
Northern Ireland: NILge-2/Amateur

League Club	Source	Date Signed	Seasons Played	Apps	Subs	Gls
Oldham Ath	Glenavon	05/67	67-68	41	4	9
Port Vale	Tr	07/69	69	11	7	1

MAGEE Kevin
Born: Bathgate, West Lothian, Scotland, 10 April, 1971 — W

League Club	Source	Date Signed	Seasons Played	Apps	Subs	Gls
Preston NE	Partick Thistle	05/93	93-95	23	3	1
Plymouth Arg	Tr	09/95	95	0	4	0
Scarborough	Tr	12/95	95	26	2	1

MAGENNIS Joshua Brendan David (Josh)
Born: Bangor, Down, Northern Ireland, 15 August, 1990 — F
Northern Ireland: 11/U21-16/Youth

League Club	Source	Date Signed	Seasons Played	Apps	Subs	Gls
Cardiff C	Sch	07/09	09	1	8	0
Grimsby T	L	10/09	09	1	1	0

MAGENNIS Mark Arthur
Born: Newtownards, Down, Northern Ireland, 15 March, 1983 — M
Northern Ireland: Youth

League Club	Source	Date Signed	Seasons Played	Apps	Subs	Gls
Coventry C	YT	04/01				
Carlisle U	Linfield	10/02	02	6	0	1

MAGERA Lukas
Born: Opava, Czech Republic, 17 January, 1983 — F
Czech Republic: 4/U21-13

League Club	Source	Date Signed	Seasons Played	Apps	Subs	Gls
Swindon T	Poli Timisoara (ROM)	08/11	11	7	5	1

MAGGIORE Anthony (Tony)
Born: Sunderland, England, 28 October, 1957 — FB

League Club	Source	Date Signed	Seasons Played	Apps	Subs	Gls
Hartlepool U	Sunderland (App)	11/75	75-76	24	4	0

MAGHOMA Jacques Ilonda
Born: Lubumbashi, DR Congo, 23 October, 1987 — LW
DR Congo: 2

League Club	Source	Date Signed	Seasons Played	Apps	Subs	Gls
Tottenham H	Sch	07/05				
Burton A	Tr	07/09	09-12	138	17	26
Sheffield Wed	Tr	06/13	13-14	46	11	2

MAGILL Edward James (Jimmy)
Born: Lurgan, Armagh, Northern Ireland, 17 May, 1939 — FB
Northern Ireland: 26/U23-1

League Club	Source	Date Signed	Seasons Played	Apps	Subs	Gls
Arsenal	Portadown	05/59	59-64	116	-	0
Brighton & HA	Tr	10/65	65-67	50	0	1

MAGILTON James (Jim)
Born: Belfast, Northern Ireland, 6 May, 1969 — M
Northern Ireland: 52/U23-2/U21-1/Youth/Schools

League Club	Source	Date Signed	Seasons Played	Apps	Subs	Gls
Liverpool	App	05/86				
Oxford U	Tr	10/90	90-93	150	0	34
Southampton	Tr	02/94	93-97	124	6	13
Sheffield Wed	Tr	09/97	97-98	14	13	1
Ipswich T	Tr	01/99	98-05	243	30	16

MAGNAY Carl Ronald Joseph
Born: Gateshead, Tyne and Wear, England, 20 January, 1989 — RB
Northern Ireland: U21-1

League Club	Source	Date Signed	Seasons Played	Apps	Subs	Gls
Chelsea	Leeds U (Jnr)	01/07				
MK Dons	L	01/09	08	0	2	0
Northampton T	L	03/09	08	2	0	0

MAGUIRE Christopher Jack (Chris)
Born: Airdrie, Lanarkshire, Scotland, 16 January, 1989 — RW
Scotland: 2/U21-12

League Club	Source	Date Signed	Seasons Played	Apps	Subs	Gls
Derby Co	Aberdeen	07/11	11	2	5	1
Portsmouth	L	03/12	11	10	1	3
Sheffield Wed	Tr	06/12	12-14	59	20	18
Coventry C	L	11/13	13	1	1	2

MAGUIRE Danny
Born: Bermondsey, SE London, England, 9 September, 1989 — M

League Club	Source	Date Signed	Seasons Played	Apps	Subs	Gls
Queens Park Rgrs	Sch	07/08				
Yeovil T	L	03/09	08	1	0	0

MAGUIRE Gavin Terence
Born: Hammersmith, W London, England, 24 November, 1967 — CD
Wales: 7/B

League Club	Source	Date Signed	Seasons Played	Apps	Subs	Gls
Queens Park Rgrs	App	10/85	86-88	33	7	0
Portsmouth	Tr	01/89	88-92	87	4	0
Newcastle U	L	10/91	91	3	0	0
Millwall	Tr	03/93	92-93	12	0	0
Scarborough	L	03/94	93	2	0	0

MAGUIRE Jacob Harry (Harry)
Born: Mosborough, South Yorkshire, England, 5 March, 1993 — CD
England: U21-1

League Club	Source	Date Signed	Seasons Played	Apps	Subs	Gls
Sheffield U	Sch	03/11	10-13	133	1	9
Hull C	Tr	07/14	14	0	3	0
Wigan Ath	L	02/15	14	16	0	1

MAGUIRE James Edward (Teddy)
Born: Brandon, County Durham, England, 23 July, 1917 — RW
Died: Brandon, County Durham, England, 16 September, 2000

League Club	Source	Date Signed	Seasons Played	Apps	Subs	Gls
Wolverhampton W	Willington	11/35	36-38	79	-	7
Swindon T	Tr	05/47	47	28	-	4
Halifax T	Tr	10/48	48-49	55	-	7

MAGUIRE James Smith (Jim)
Born: Eaglesham, Renfrewshire, Scotland, 3 February, 1932 — W

League Club	Source	Date Signed	Seasons Played	Apps	Subs	Gls
Rochdale	Queen of the South	08/58	58	15	-	0

MAGUIRE Paul Bernard
Born: Glasgow, Scotland, 21 August, 1956 — LW

League Club	Source	Date Signed	Seasons Played	Apps	Subs	Gls
Shrewsbury T	Kilbirnie Ladeside	08/76	76-79	143	8	35
Stoke C	Tr	09/80	80-83	93	14	24
Port Vale	Tacoma Stars (USA)	07/85	85-87	101	14	22

MAGUIRE Peter Jason
Born: Holmfirth, West Yorkshire, England, 11 September, 1969 — F

League Club	Source	Date Signed	Seasons Played	Apps	Subs	Gls
Leeds U	YT	06/88	87	2	0	0
Huddersfield T	Tr	09/89	89-90	1	6	1
Stockport Co	L	09/90	90	0	2	0

MAGUIRE Sean Patrick
Born: Luton, England, 1 May, 1994 — F
Republic of Ireland: U21-1/Youth

League Club	Source	Date Signed	Seasons Played	Apps	Subs	Gls
West Ham U	Waterford U (ROI)	01/13				
Accrington Stan	L	09/14	14	29	4	7

MAGUIRE Thomas (Tommy)
Born: Dublin, Republic of Ireland, 22 July, 1955 — M

League Club	Source	Date Signed	Seasons Played	Apps	Subs	Gls
Liverpool	App	11/72				
Crewe Alex	Tr	08/73	73-75	23	4	1

MAHER Aiden
Born: Liverpool, England, 1 December, 1946 — LW
England: Schools

League Club	Source	Date Signed	Seasons Played	Apps	Subs	Gls
Everton	App	12/64	67	1	0	0
Plymouth Arg	Tr	10/68	68-70	64	0	3
Tranmere Rov	Tr	06/71	71	2	5	1

League Club	Source	Date Signed	Seasons Played	Career Record Apps	Subs	Gls
MAHER John (Johnny)						
Born: Manchester, England, 6 November, 1933						IF
Died: Lancashire, England, June, 2014						
Walsall	Manchester C (Am)	05/54	54	1	-	0
Gillingham	Tr	07/55	55	2	-	1
MAHER Kevin Andrew						
Born: Ilford, E London, England, 17 October, 1976						M
Republic of Ireland: U21-4						
Tottenham H	YT	07/95				
Southend U	Tr	01/98	97-07	375	8	22
Gillingham	L	03/08	07	7	0	0
Oldham Ath	Tr	07/08	08	21	7	1
Gillingham	Tr	07/09	09-10	57	5	0
Dagenham & Red	Tr	07/11	11-12	15	1	0
MAHER Niall Callum James Peter						
Born: Manchester, England, 31 July, 1995						FB
Bolton W	Sch	07/14				
Blackpool	L	01/15	14	6	4	0
MAHER Shaun Patrick						
Born: Dublin, Republic of Ireland, 20 June, 1978						CD
Fulham	Bohemians (ROI)	12/97				
Bournemouth	Bohemians (ROI)	08/01	01-06	96	21	5
MAHER Stephen John						
Born: Dublin, Republic of Ireland, 3 March, 1988						M
Republic of Ireland: U21-3/Youth						
Yeovil T	Dublin C (ROI)	07/06	06-07	4	3	0
MAHON Alan Joseph						
Born: Dublin, Republic of Ireland, 4 April, 1978						M
Republic of Ireland: 2/U21-18/Youth/Schools						
Tranmere Rov	YT	04/95	95-99	84	36	13
Blackburn Rov	Sporting Lisbon (POR)	12/00	00-03	25	11	1
Cardiff C	L	01/03	02	13	2	2
Ipswich T	L	09/03	03	7	4	1
Wigan Ath	Tr	02/04	03-05	39	8	9
Burnley	Tr	03/06	05-08	30	37	4
Blackpool	L	03/09	08	1	0	0
Tranmere Rov	Tr	07/09	09	8	8	1
MAHON Craig Derek						
Born: Dublin, Republic of Ireland, 21 June, 1989						W
Republic of Ireland: Youth						
Wigan Ath	Sch	07/08				
Accrington Stan	L	11/08	08	0	2	0
MAHON Gavin Andrew						
Born: Birmingham, England, 2 January, 1977						M
Wolverhampton W	YT	07/95				
Hereford U	Tr	07/96	96	10	1	1
Brentford	Tr	11/98	98-01	140	1	8
Watford	Tr	03/02	01-07	180	9	6
Queens Park Rgrs	Tr	01/08	07-09	45	13	4
Notts Co	Tr	08/11	11-12	26	17	0
Stevenage	L	02/13	12	8	1	0
Portsmouth	Tr	10/13	13	0	1	0
MAHON Michael John (Mick)						
Born: Manchester, England, 17 September, 1944						W
England: Amateur-3						
Port Vale	North Shields	05/66	66-68	91	0	21
York C	Tr	07/69	69	27	2	10
Colchester U	Tr	05/70	70-73	131	5	26
MAHONEY Anthony Joseph (Tony)						
Born: Barking, E London, England, 29 September, 1959						F
England: Youth						
Fulham	App	08/77	76-80	53	6	10
Northampton T	L	10/81	81	6	0	0
Brentford	Tr	07/82	82-83	33	8	12
Crystal Palace	Tr	06/84	84	17	1	4
MAHONEY Brian						
Born: Tantobie, County Durham, England, 12 May, 1952						F
Huddersfield T	App	11/69	70-71	18	2	2
Barnsley	Tr	03/72	71-74	82	8	16
MAHONEY Connor Anthony						
Born: Blackburn, Greater Manchester, England, 12 February, 1997						W
England: Youth						
Accrington Stan	Sch	-	13	1	3	0
Blackburn Rov	Sch	02/14				
MAHONEY John Francis						
Born: Cardiff, Wales, 20 September, 1946						M
Wales: 51/U23-3						
Crewe Alex	Ashton U	03/66	65-66	16	2	5
Stoke C	Tr	03/67	66-76	270	12	25
Middlesbrough	Tr	08/77	77-78	77	0	1
Swansea C	Tr	07/79	79-82	106	4	1
MAHONEY Michael James (Mike)						
Born: Bristol, England, 25 October, 1950						G
Bristol C	App	08/68	67-69	4	0	0
Torquay U	Tr	08/70	70-74	157	0	0
Newcastle U	Tr	03/75	74-78	108	0	0
MAHONEY-JOHNSON Michael Anthony						
Born: Paddington, Central London, England, 6 November, 1976						F
Queens Park Rgrs	YT	04/95	96-97	0	3	0
Wycombe W	L	08/96	96	2	2	2
Brighton & HA	L	02/98	97	3	1	0
MAHORN Paul Gladstone						
Born: Leytonstone, NE London, England, 13 August, 1973						F
Tottenham H	YT	01/92	93-97	3	0	0
Fulham	L	09/93	93	1	2	0
Burnley	L	03/96	95	3	5	1
Port Vale	Tr	03/98	97	0	1	0
MAHREZ Riyad						
Born: Paris, France, 21 February, 1991						W
Algeria: 17						
Leicester C	Le Havre (FRA)	01/14	13-14	37	12	7
MAHY Barry						
Born: Doncaster, South Yorkshire, England, 21 January, 1942						IF
Scunthorpe U	Islanders, Guernsey	05/63	63-66	21	1	2
[MAICON] SISENANDO Douglas Maicon						
Born: Novo Hamburgo, Brazil, 26 July, 1981						RB
Brazil: 76/Youth						
Manchester C	Inter Milan (ITA)	08/12	12	4	5	0
MAIDENS Michael Douglas						
Born: Middlesbrough, England, 7 May, 1987						RW
Died: Skelton, Cleveland, England, 19 October, 2007						
Hartlepool U	Sch	07/06	04-06	11	14	1
MAIDMENT Ian Michael						
Born: Newbury, Berkshire, England, 9 August, 1947						LW
Reading	App	08/65	65	7	0	0
MAIERHOFER Stefan						
Born: Vienna, Austria, 16 August, 1982						F
Austria: 19						
Wolverhampton W	Rapid Vienna (AUT)	09/09	09	1	8	1
Bristol C	L	03/10	09	1	2	0
Millwall	FC Koln (GER)	03/14	13	7	4	2
Millwall	Wiener Neustadt (AUT)	01/15	14	6	4	1
MAIGA Modibo						
Born: Bamako, Mali, 3 September, 1987						F
Mali: 40						
West Ham U	Sochaux (FRA)	07/12	12-13	13	18	3
Queens Park Rgrs	L	01/14	13	2	6	1
MAIL David						
Born: Bristol, England, 12 September, 1962						CD
Aston Villa	App	07/80				
Blackburn Rov	Tr	01/82	82-89	200	6	4
Hull C	Tr	07/90	90-94	140	10	2
MAILER Ronald George (Ron)						
Born: Auchterarder, Perthshire, Scotland, 18 May, 1932						IF
Darlington	Dunfermline Ath	03/54	54	11	-	2
MAILEY William (Willie)						
Born: Duntocher, Dunbartonshire, Scotland, 13 June, 1943						G
Died: Crewe, Cheshire, England, June, 1992						
Scotland: Schools						
Everton	Jnr	06/60				
Crewe Alex	Tr	03/63	63-69	216	0	0
MAIN Curtis Lee						
Born: South Shields, Tyne and Wear, England, 20 June, 1992						F
Darlington	Sch	08/09	07-09	17	28	5
Middlesbrough	Tr	05/11	11-13	13	35	6
Shrewsbury T	L	08/13	13	4	1	0
Doncaster Rov	Tr	07/14	14	23	15	8
MAIN Ian Roy						
Born: Weston-super-Mare, Somerset, England, 31 October, 1959						G
Died: Exeter, England, 16 September, 1998						
England: Schools						
Exeter C	Gloucester C	09/78	78-81	78	0	0

League Club	Source	Date Signed	Seasons Played	Apps	Subs	Gls
MAINWARING Carl Andrew						
Born: Swansea, Wales, 15 March, 1980						F
Swansea C	YT	07/98	97	2	1	0
MAINWARING Matthew Thomas (Matty)						
Born: Salford, England, 28 March, 1990						W
Stockport Co	Preston NE (Sch)	07/08	08-10	26	6	1
Hull C	Tr	12/11				
MAIORANA Giuliano						
Born: Cambridge, England, 18 April, 1969						LW
Manchester U	Histon	11/88	88-89	2	5	0
MAIR Gordon						
Born: Bothwell, Lanarkshire, Scotland, 18 December, 1958						LW
Scotland: Schools						
Notts Co	App	12/76	76-83	123	8	15
Lincoln C	Tr	08/84	84-85	57	0	3
MAIR Lee						
Born: Aberdeen, Scotland, 9 December, 1980						CD
Stockport Co	Dundee	06/04	04	9	5	0
MAITLAND Lloyd Curtis						
Born: Coleshill, Warwickshire, England, 21 March, 1957						RW
Huddersfield T	App	03/74	74-76	31	8	2
Darlington	Tr	03/77	76-78	58	13	6
MAITLAND-NILES Ainsley Cory						
Born: Ilford, E London, England, 29 August, 1997						W
England: Youth						
Arsenal	Sch	10/14	14	0	1	0
MAJEWSKI Radoslav						
Born: Pruszkow, Poland, 15 December, 1986						M
Poland: 9/U23-2/U21-9						
Nottingham F	Polonia Warsaw (POL)	07/09	09-13	119	25	16
Huddersfield T	L	07/14	14	3	5	0
MAJOR John Leonard (Jack)						
Born: Islington, N London, England, 12 March, 1929						W
Died: Hull, England, 22 August, 1986						
England: Amateur-3						
Hull C (Am)	Hull Amats	04/47	46	3	-	0
Hull C	Bishop Auckland	06/55	55-56	10	-	0
MAJOR Leslie Dennis (Les)						
Born: Yeovil, Somerset, England, 25 January, 1926						G
Died: Derby, England, 10 December, 2001						
Leicester C	Brush Sports	06/43	47-48	26	-	0
Plymouth Arg	Tr	05/49	49-55	75	-	0
MAKEL Lee Robert						
Born: Sunderland, England, 11 January, 1973						M
Newcastle U	YT	02/91	90-91	6	6	1
Blackburn Rov	Tr	07/92	92-95	1	5	0
Huddersfield T	Tr	10/95	95-97	62	3	5
Bradford C	Heart of Midlothian	08/01	01	2	11	0
Plymouth Arg	Livingston	06/04	04	13	6	0
MAKELELE Claude						
Born: Kinshasa, DR Congo, 18 February, 1973						DM
France: 71/B-4/U21-11						
Chelsea	Real Madrid (SPN)	09/03	03-07	132	12	2
MAKEPEACE Brian						
Born: Rossington, South Yorkshire, England, 6 October, 1931						RB
Doncaster Rov	Rossington Main	03/49	50-60	353	-	0
MAKIN Christopher Gregory (Chris)						
Born: Prestwich, Greater Manchester, England, 8 May, 1973						LB
England: U21-5/Youth/Schools						
Oldham Ath	YT	11/91	93-95	93	1	4
Wigan Ath	L	08/92	92	14	1	2
Sunderland	Olymp Marseille (FRA)	08/97	97-00	115	5	1
Ipswich T	Tr	03/01	00-03	78	0	0
Leicester C	Tr	08/04	04	21	0	0
Derby Co	Tr	02/05	04	13	0	0
Reading	Tr	08/05	05	11	1	0
Southampton	Tr	08/06	06-07	24	3	0
MAKIN Joseph (Joe)						
Born: Manchester, England, 21 September, 1950						RB
Oldham Ath	App	10/67	66-67	6	0	0
MAKIN Samuel Hansbrew (Sammy)						
Born: Radcliffe, Greater Manchester, England, 14 November, 1925						W
Died: Bury, Greater Manchester, England, 1981						
Rochdale	Moss Rov	05/44	46	5	-	1
MAKOFO Serge						
Born: Kinshasa, DR Congo, 22 October, 1986						W
MK Dons	Sch	07/05	04	0	1	0
Burton A	Grays Ath	09/09	09	0	2	0
MAKOUN Jean II						
Born: Yaounde, Cameroon, 29 May, 1983						M
Cameroon: 68						
Aston Villa	Olymp Lyonnais (FRA)	01/11	10	7	0	0
MAKSIMENKO Vitalijs						
Born: Riga, Latvia, 8 December, 1990						LB
Latvia: 14/U21-11						
Brighton & HA	Skonto Riga (LAT)	01/13	13	1	0	0
Yeovil T	L	03/13	12	2	1	0
MAKUKULA Ariza						
Born: Kinshasa, DR Congo, 4 March, 1981						F
Portugal: 4/U21-14						
Bolton W (L)	Benfica (POR)	01/09	08	4	2	0
MALAGA Kevin Marc-Francois						
Born: Toulon, France, 24 June, 1987						CD
Coventry C	OGC Nice (FRA)	07/12	12	2	0	0
MALAM Albert						
Born: Liverpool, England, 20 January, 1913						IF
Died: Kendal, Cumbria, England, 3 February, 1992						
Chesterfield	Colwyn Bay	11/32	32-34	58	-	25
Huddersfield T	Tr	09/34	34	21	-	11
Doncaster Rov	Tr	09/36	36-38	95	-	26
Wrexham	Tr	02/46	46	6	-	1
MALAN Norman Frederick						
Born: Johannesburg, South Africa, 23 November, 1923						G
Middlesbrough	Defos (RSA)	10/45	46	2	-	0
Darlington	Tr	08/48				
Scunthorpe U	Tr	08/49	50-55	136	-	0
Bradford Park Ave	Tr	07/56	56	24	-	0
MALBON Anthony Jordan						
Born: Stoke-on-Trent, England, 14 October, 1991						F
Port Vale	Sch	07/10	08-10	0	3	0
MALBRANQUE Steed						
Born: Mouscron, Belgium, 6 January, 1980						M
France: U21-7						
Fulham	Olymp Lyonnais (FRA)	08/01	01-06	160	12	32
Tottenham H	Tr	08/06	06-07	53	9	6
Sunderland	Tr	08/08	08-10	88	14	1
MALCOLM Alexander Anderson (Alex)						
Born: Hamilton, Lanarkshire, Scotland, 13 February, 1956						LB
Luton T	App	07/73				
Northampton T	Tr	08/76	76	2	0	0
MALCOLM Alexander Mitchell (Alex)						
Born: Alloa, Stirlingshire, Scotland, 15 December, 1921						LW
Died: Barnsley, South Yorkshire, England, 26 December, 1987						
Barnsley	Alloa Ath	06/46	46-47	5	-	0
MALCOLM Andrew (Andy)						
Born: West Ham, E London, England, 4 May, 1933						RH
Died: Port Elizabeth, South Africa, 26 December, 2013						
England: FLge-1/Youth/Schools						
West Ham U	Jnr	07/50	53-61	283	-	4
Chelsea	Tr	11/61	61	27	-	1
Queens Park Rgrs	Tr	10/62	62-64	84	-	5
MALCOLM John Moore						
Born: Clackmannan, Stirlingshire, Scotland, 20 May, 1917						LH
Accrington Stan		10/44	46	25	-	0
Tranmere Rov	Tr	07/47	47	22	-	0
MALCOLM Kenneth Campbell (Ken)						
Born: Aberdeen, Scotland, 25 July, 1926						LB
Died: Ipswich, England, May, 2006						
Ipswich T	Arbroath	05/54	54-62	274	-	2
MALCOLM Michael Dehaney						
Born: Harrow, NW London, England, 13 October, 1988						F
England: Youth						
Tottenham H	Sch	10/02				
Stockport Co	Tr	08/05	05-06	20	21	5
MALCOLM Paul Anthony						
Born: Felling, Tyne and Wear, England, 11 December, 1964						G
Newcastle U	App	12/82				
Rochdale	Durham C	09/84	84	24	0	0
Shrewsbury T	Tr	07/85				

League Club	Source	Date Signed	Seasons Played	Apps	Subs	Gls
Barnsley	Tr	08/86	86	3	0	0
Doncaster Rov	Tr	07/88	88	34	0	0

MALCOLM Robert (Bob)
Born: Glasgow, Scotland, 12 December, 1980 — DM
Scotland: B-3/U21-1

League Club	Source	Date Signed	Seasons Played	Apps	Subs	Gls
Derby Co	Glasgow Rangers	09/06	06-07	7	3	0
Queens Park Rgrs	L	10/07	07	10	1	0

MALCOLM Stuart Ross
Born: Edinburgh, Scotland, 2 August, 1979 — CD

League Club	Source	Date Signed	Seasons Played	Apps	Subs	Gls
Plymouth Arg	St Johnstone	08/02	02	3	0	0

MALCOLM Walter Grant Lees (Grant)
Born: Musselburgh, East Lothian, Scotland, 25 October, 1940 — W
Scotland: Schools

League Club	Source	Date Signed	Seasons Played	Apps	Subs	Gls
Newcastle U	Dalkeith Thistle	11/57	59	1	-	0

MALE Charles George (George)
Born: Plaistow, E London, England, 8 May, 1910 — RB
Died: Ontario, Canada, 19 February, 1998
England: 19/FLge-2

League Club	Source	Date Signed	Seasons Played	Apps	Subs	Gls
Arsenal	Clapton	05/30	30-47	285	-	0

MALE Norman Alfred
Born: West Bromwich, West Midlands, England, 27 May, 1917 — FB
Died: Sandwell, West Midlands, England, December, 1992

League Club	Source	Date Signed	Seasons Played	Apps	Subs	Gls
West Bromwich A	Bush Rov	10/34	37	3	-	1
Walsall	Tr	03/38	38-48	70	-	2

MALESSA Antony George (Tony)
Born: Ascot, Berkshire, England, 13 November, 1980 — G

League Club	Source	Date Signed	Seasons Played	Apps	Subs	Gls
Bristol C	Southampton (YT)	02/99	00	0	1	0

MALEY Mark
Born: Newcastle-upon-Tyne, England, 26 January, 1981 — D
England: Youth/Schools

League Club	Source	Date Signed	Seasons Played	Apps	Subs	Gls
Sunderland	YT	01/98				
Blackpool	L	10/00	00	2	0	0
Northampton T	L	11/00	00	2	0	0
York C	L	09/01	01	11	2	0

MALKIN Christopher Gregory (Chris)
Born: Hoylake, Wirral, England, 4 June, 1967 — F

League Club	Source	Date Signed	Seasons Played	Apps	Subs	Gls
Tranmere Rov	Stork	07/87	87-94	184	48	59
Millwall	Tr	07/95	95-96	46	6	14
Blackpool	Tr	10/96	96-98	45	19	6

MALKIN John (Jack)
Born: Longton, Potteries, England, 9 November, 1925 — RW
Died: Stoke-on-Trent, England, 19 May, 1994

League Club	Source	Date Signed	Seasons Played	Apps	Subs	Gls
Stoke C	Army	07/47	47-55	175	-	24

MALLENDER Gary
Born: Barnsley, South Yorkshire, England, 12 March, 1959 — M

League Club	Source	Date Signed	Seasons Played	Apps	Subs	Gls
Barnsley	App	03/77	76-78	0	2	0

MALLENDER Kenneth (Ken)
Born: Thrybergh, South Yorkshire, England, 10 December, 1943 — D

League Club	Source	Date Signed	Seasons Played	Apps	Subs	Gls
Sheffield U	App	02/61	61-68	141	2	2
Norwich C	Tr	10/68	68-70	46	0	1
Hereford U	Tr	07/71	72-73	71	1	1

MALLENDER Paul Richard
Born: Norwich, England, 30 November, 1969 — CD

League Club	Source	Date Signed	Seasons Played	Apps	Subs	Gls
Hereford U	App	09/86	87	0	1	0

MALLETT Joseph (Joe)
Born: Gateshead, Tyne and Wear, England, 8 January, 1916 — LH
Died: St Leonards, East Sussex, England, 8 February, 2004

League Club	Source	Date Signed	Seasons Played	Apps	Subs	Gls
Charlton Ath	Dunston Colliery	11/35				
Queens Park Rgrs	Tr	10/37	37	29	-	4
Charlton Ath	Tr	07/38	38	2	-	0
Queens Park Rgrs	Tr	02/39	38-46	41	-	7
Southampton	Tr	02/47	46-52	215	-	3
Leyton Orient	Tr	07/53	53-54	27	-	1

MALLEY Philip (Phil)
Born: Felling, Tyne and Wear, England, 1 November, 1965 — M/D

League Club	Source	Date Signed	Seasons Played	Apps	Subs	Gls
Hartlepool U	Sunderland (App)	11/83	83	0	1	0
Burnley	Berwick Rgrs	02/84	83-87	91	4	5
Stockport Co	L	11/84	84	3	0	0

MALLINSON David John
Born: Sheffield, England, 7 July, 1946 — WH

League Club	Source	Date Signed	Seasons Played	Apps	Subs	Gls
Mansfield T	Jnr	03/65	65	10	1	1

MALLINSON Trevor
Born: Huddersfield, West Yorkshire, England, 25 April, 1945 — LB

League Club	Source	Date Signed	Seasons Played	Apps	Subs	Gls
Halifax T (Am)	Huddersfield T (App)	12/64	64	3	-	0

MALLON James Gillan (Jim)
Born: Glasgow, Scotland, 28 August, 1938 — FB/CF
Died: Glasgow, Scotland, 9 May, 2012

League Club	Source	Date Signed	Seasons Played	Apps	Subs	Gls
Oldham Ath	Partick Thistle	03/59	58-59	31	-	8
Barrow	Greenock Morton	10/65	65-68	149	1	3

MALLON Ryan
Born: Sheffield, England, 22 March, 1983 — W

League Club	Source	Date Signed	Seasons Played	Apps	Subs	Gls
Sheffield U	Jnr	07/01	01	0	1	0

MALLORY Richard James Leroy (Dick)
Born: Bermuda, 10 August, 1942 — LW

League Club	Source	Date Signed	Seasons Played	Apps	Subs	Gls
Cardiff C	Pemb'ke Hamilton (BER)	05/63	63	3	-	0

MALLOY Daniel (Danny)
Born: Dennyloanhead, Falkirk, Scotland, 6 November, 1930 — CH
Died: Larbert, Falkirk, Scotland, 14 January, 2015
Scotland: B/SLge-1

League Club	Source	Date Signed	Seasons Played	Apps	Subs	Gls
Cardiff C	Dundee	10/55	55-60	226	-	1
Doncaster Rov	Tr	08/61	61	42	-	0

MALONE Richard Philip (Dick)
Born: Carfin, Lanarkshire, Scotland, 22 August, 1947 — RB
Scotland: U23-1

League Club	Source	Date Signed	Seasons Played	Apps	Subs	Gls
Sunderland	Ayr U	10/70	70-76	235	1	2
Hartlepool U	Tr	07/77	77-78	36	0	2
Blackpool	Tr	11/78	78-79	48	0	1

MALONE Scott Liam
Born: Rowley Regis, West Midlands, England, 25 March, 1991 — LB/M
England: Youth

League Club	Source	Date Signed	Seasons Played	Apps	Subs	Gls
Wolverhampton W	Sch	02/09				
Southend U	L	11/09	09	15	2	0
Burton A	L	10/10	10	18	4	1
Bournemouth	Tr	07/11	11	28	4	5
Millwall	Tr	05/12	12-14	62	6	5
Cardiff C	Tr	01/15	14	12	1	0

MALONEY Derek Thomas
Born: Newton-le-Willows, Merseyside, England, 27 March, 1936 — LH

League Club	Source	Date Signed	Seasons Played	Apps	Subs	Gls
Crewe Alex	St Helens T	02/58	57	15	-	0

MALONEY Jack Levi
Born: Ryde, Isle of Wight, England, 8 December, 1994 — W

League Club	Source	Date Signed	Seasons Played	Apps	Subs	Gls
Portsmouth	Sch	07/13	12-13	1	9	0

MALONEY Jonathan Duncan (Jon)
Born: Leeds, England, 3 March, 1985 — CD

League Club	Source	Date Signed	Seasons Played	Apps	Subs	Gls
Doncaster Rov	Sch	07/03	03-04	1	2	0

MALONEY Joseph John (Joe)
Born: Liverpool, England, 26 January, 1934 — CH
Died: Crewe, Cheshire, England, 17 October, 2006

League Club	Source	Date Signed	Seasons Played	Apps	Subs	Gls
Liverpool	Jnr	01/51	52-53	12	-	0
Shrewsbury T	Tr	07/54	54-59	237	-	1
Port Vale	Tr	07/61	61	1	-	0
Crewe Alex	Tr	08/61	61-62	26	-	0

MALONEY Paul John
Born: Rossington, South Yorkshire, England, 13 January, 1952 — M

League Club	Source	Date Signed	Seasons Played	Apps	Subs	Gls
York C	Huddersfield T (App)	02/70	69-71	3	5	0

MALONEY Sean
Born: Hyde, Greater Manchester, England, 4 October, 1962 — F

League Club	Source	Date Signed	Seasons Played	Apps	Subs	Gls
Stockport Co	Jnr	08/79	79	0	1	0

MALONEY Shaun Richard
Born: Miri, Sarawak, Malaysia, 24 January, 1983 — W/F
Scotland: 40/B-1/U21-21

League Club	Source	Date Signed	Seasons Played	Apps	Subs	Gls
Aston Villa	Glasgow Celtic	01/07	06-07	16	14	5
Wigan Ath	Glasgow Celtic	08/11	11-14	61	18	14

MALOUDA Florent Johan
Born: Cayenne, French Guiana, 13 June, 1980 — LW
France: 80

League Club	Source	Date Signed	Seasons Played	Apps	Subs	Gls
Chelsea	Olymp Lyonnais (FRA)	07/07	07-11	110	39	35

MALOY Kenneth Frederick (Ken)
Born: Edmonton, N London, England, 16 September, 1940 — LW

League Club	Source	Date Signed	Seasons Played	Apps	Subs	Gls
Plymouth Arg	Ilford	09/59	60-63	62	-	11
Peterborough U	Tr	07/64	64	6	-	1
Aldershot	Tr	07/65	65-66	51	1	11

MALOY Kevin William
Born: Aldershot, Hampshire, England, 12 November, 1966 — G

League Club	Source	Date Signed	Seasons Played	Apps	Subs	Gls
Exeter C	Taunton T	07/91	91	4	0	0

MALPASS Frank Love
Born: Consett, County Durham, England, 16 October, 1932 — G
Died: Consett, County Durham, England, 10 October, 2012

League Club	Source	Date Signed	Seasons Played	Apps	Subs	Gls
Gateshead	Jnr	10/49	49	3	-	0

League Club | Source | Date Signed | Seasons Played | Career Record Apps | Subs | Gls

MALPASS Samuel Thomas (Sam)
Born: Consett, County Durham, England, 12 September, 1918 — FB
Died: Wisbech, Cambridgeshire, England, 17 August, 1983

League Club	Source	Date Signed	Seasons Played	Apps	Subs	Gls
Huddersfield T	Eden Colliery	10/36				
Fulham	Tr	05/39	46	2	-	0
Watford	Tr	01/47	46-48	41	-	0

MALSOM Samuel Andrew (Sam)
Born: Teignmouth, Devon, England, 10 November, 1987 — F

League Club	Source	Date Signed	Seasons Played	Apps	Subs	Gls
Plymouth Arg	Sch	07/06				
Hereford U	Motala AIF (SWE)	08/10	10	1	3	0

MALT Robert
Born: Ryhope, Tyne and Wear, England, 4 November, 1951 — F

League Club	Source	Date Signed	Seasons Played	Apps	Subs	Gls
Leeds U	App	11/68				
Darlington	Tr	06/70	70	2	2	0

MALTBY John (Jack)
Born: Leadgate, County Durham, England, 31 July, 1939 — IF

League Club	Source	Date Signed	Seasons Played	Apps	Subs	Gls
Sunderland	Crookhall Jnrs	08/57	56-60	22	-	4
Darlington	Tr	06/61	61-64	114	-	32
Bury	Tr	07/65	65-66	56	1	8

MALZ Stefan
Born: Ludwigshafen, Germany, 15 June, 1972 — M

League Club	Source	Date Signed	Seasons Played	Apps	Subs	Gls
Arsenal	TSV Munich (GER)	07/99	99-00	2	4	1

MAMBO Yado Massaya
Born: Kilburn, NW London, England, 22 October, 1991 — CD

League Club	Source	Date Signed	Seasons Played	Apps	Subs	Gls
Charlton Ath	Sch	07/10				
AFC Wimbledon	L	10/12	12	13	0	0
Shrewsbury T	L	01/13	12	13	2	1

MAMOUN Blaise Noel Emmanuel
Born: Bamenda, Cameroon, 25 December, 1979 — F
Cameroon: Youth

League Club	Source	Date Signed	Seasons Played	Apps	Subs	Gls
Scunthorpe U	Saint-Etienne (FRA)	08/00	00	0	1	0

MANANGU Eric Mavambu
Born: Kinshasa, DR Congo, 9 September, 1985 — F

League Club	Source	Date Signed	Seasons Played	Apps	Subs	Gls
Rushden & D	Sch	-	03	0	1	0

MANCIENNE Michael Ian
Born: Feltham, SW London, England, 8 January, 1988 — CD
England: U21-30/Youth

League Club	Source	Date Signed	Seasons Played	Apps	Subs	Gls
Chelsea	Sch	01/06	08	2	2	0
Queens Park Rgrs	L	10/06	06	26	2	0
Queens Park Rgrs	L	08/07	07	26	4	0
Wolverhampton W	L	10/08	08	8	2	0
Wolverhampton W	L	08/09	09	22	8	0
Wolverhampton W	L	08/10	10	13	3	0
Nottingham F	Hamburger SV (GER)	07/14	14	34	2	0

MANCINI Andrea
Born: Genoa, Italy, 13 September, 1992 — M

League Club	Source	Date Signed	Seasons Played	Apps	Subs	Gls
Manchester C	Bologna Jnrs (ITA)	11/10				
Oldham Ath	L	11/11	11	0	1	0

MANCINI Michael (Mike)
Born: Hammersmith, W London, England, 8 June, 1956 — F

League Club	Source	Date Signed	Seasons Played	Apps	Subs	Gls
Leyton Orient	Hendon	03/84	83	2	0	0

MANCINI Roberto
Born: Jesi. Ancona, Italy, 27 November, 1964 — M
Italy: 36/U21-26

League Club	Source	Date Signed	Seasons Played	Apps	Subs	Gls
Leicester C (L)	SS Lazio (ITA)	01/01	00	3	1	0

MANCINI Terence John (Terry)
Born: Camden, N London, England, 4 October, 1942 — CD
Republic of Ireland: 5

League Club	Source	Date Signed	Seasons Played	Apps	Subs	Gls
Watford	Jnr	07/61	61-65	66	1	0
Leyton Orient	Port Elizabeth C (RSA)	11/67	67-71	167	0	16
Queens Park Rgrs	Tr	10/71	71-74	94	0	3
Arsenal	Tr	10/74	74-75	52	0	1
Aldershot	Tr	09/76	76	21	0	0

MANDERS Ronald Ernest (Ron)
Born: Shrewsbury, Shropshire, England, 13 November, 1931 — CH
Died: Stoke-on-Trent, England, 1980

League Club	Source	Date Signed	Seasons Played	Apps	Subs	Gls
Shrewsbury T	Jnr	12/54	54-56	6	-	0

MANDERSON David Anthony
Born: Glasgow, Scotland, 18 October, 1973 — M

League Club	Source	Date Signed	Seasons Played	Apps	Subs	Gls
Scarborough	YT	08/92	91	0	1	0

MANDEVILLE Liam
Born: Lincoln, England, 17 February, 1997 — F

League Club	Source	Date Signed	Seasons Played	Apps	Subs	Gls
Doncaster Rov	Sch	11/14	14	0	3	0

MANDRON Mikael Yann Mathieu
Born: Boulogne, France, 11 October, 1994 — F

League Club	Source	Date Signed	Seasons Played	Apps	Subs	Gls
Sunderland	Sch	10/11	12-14	0	3	0
Fleetwood T	L	01/14	13	4	7	1
Shrewsbury T	L	01/15	14	2	1	0

MANE Sadio
Born: Sedhiou, Senegal, 10 April, 1992 — LW
Senegal: 22

League Club	Source	Date Signed	Seasons Played	Apps	Subs	Gls
Southampton	RB Salzburg (AUT)	09/14	14	24	6	10

[MANEL] MARTINEZ FERNANDEZ Manuel
Born: Barcelona, Spain, 3 November, 1973 — F

League Club	Source	Date Signed	Seasons Played	Apps	Subs	Gls
Derby Co	RCD Espanyol (SPN)	01/04	03	12	4	3

MANGA Marc Andre
Born: Cameroon, 16 January, 1988 — M

League Club	Source	Date Signed	Seasons Played	Apps	Subs	Gls
Rochdale	Stade Lavallois (FRA)	10/09	09	0	2	0

MANGALA Eliaquim
Born: Paris, France, 13 February, 1991 — CD
France: 5/U21-23

League Club	Source	Date Signed	Seasons Played	Apps	Subs	Gls
Manchester C	FC Porto (POR)	08/14	14	24	1	0

MANGAN Andrew Francis
Born: Liverpool, England, 30 August, 1986 — F
England: Semi Pro-2

League Club	Source	Date Signed	Seasons Played	Apps	Subs	Gls
Blackpool	Sch	-	03	0	2	0
Accrington Stan	Tr	08/05	06	6	28	4
Bury	Tr	07/07	07	7	13	4
Accrington Stan	L	02/08	07	3	4	1
Fleetwood T	Wrexham	06/11	12	7	5	4
Shrewsbury T	Forest Green Rov	07/14	14	10	20	8

MANGANE Abdou Kader (Kader)
Born: Dakar, Senegal, 23 March, 1983 — CD
Senegal: 23

League Club	Source	Date Signed	Seasons Played	Apps	Subs	Gls
Sunderland (L)	Al-Hilal (SAU)	01/13	12	0	2	0

[MANICHE] OLIVEIRA RIBEIRO Nuno Ricardo
Born: Lisbon, Portugal, 11 November, 1977 — M
Portugal: 58/U21-11

League Club	Source	Date Signed	Seasons Played	Apps	Subs	Gls
Chelsea (L)	Dynamo Moscow (RUS)	01/06	05	3	5	0

MANKELOW Jamie Anthony
Born: Clapton, NE London, England, 4 September, 1964 — F

League Club	Source	Date Signed	Seasons Played	Apps	Subs	Gls
Leyton Orient	App	09/82	82	1	1	0

MANKTELOW Brian
Born: Farnham, Surrey, England, 29 March, 1951 — F

League Club	Source	Date Signed	Seasons Played	Apps	Subs	Gls
Aldershot	App	-	68	1	0	0

MANLEY Malcolm Richardson
Born: Johnstone, Renfrewshire, Scotland, 1 December, 1949 — CD
Scotland: Schools

League Club	Source	Date Signed	Seasons Played	Apps	Subs	Gls
Leicester C	Johnstone Burgh	01/67	67-72	107	10	5
Portsmouth	Tr	12/73	73-74	11	0	0

MANLEY Thomas Ronald (Tom)
Born: Northwich, Cheshire, England, 7 October, 1912 — WH/LW
Died: Brentwood, Essex, England, 4 July, 1988

League Club	Source	Date Signed	Seasons Played	Apps	Subs	Gls
Manchester U	Northwich Victoria	05/31	31-38	188	-	40
Brentford	Tr	07/39	46-50	116	-	7

MANN Adrian Gary
Born: Northampton, England, 12 July, 1967 — M

League Club	Source	Date Signed	Seasons Played	Apps	Subs	Gls
Northampton T	App	05/85	83-87	71	11	5
Torquay U	L	03/87	86	6	2	0
Newport Co	Tr	11/87	87	17	0	1

MANN Arthur Fraser
Born: Burntisland, Fife, Scotland, 23 January, 1948 — M/LB
Died: Birmingham, England, 3 February, 1999

League Club	Source	Date Signed	Seasons Played	Apps	Subs	Gls
Manchester C	Heart of Midlothian	11/68	68-70	32	3	0
Blackpool	L	11/71	71	3	0	0
Notts Co	Tr	07/72	72-78	243	10	21
Shrewsbury T	Tr	06/79	79	8	0	1
Mansfield T	Tr	10/79	79-81	114	2	3

MANN James Arthur (Jimmy)
Born: Goole, East Riding of Yorkshire, England, 15 December, 1952 — M

League Club	Source	Date Signed	Seasons Played	Apps	Subs	Gls
Leeds U	App	12/69	71-72	2	0	0
Bristol C	Tr	05/74	74-81	205	26	31
Barnsley	Tr	02/82	81-82	14	1	0
Scunthorpe U	Tr	01/83	82	2	0	0
Doncaster Rov	Tr	02/83	82	13	0	0

MANN Neil
Born: Nottingham, England, 9 November, 1972 — M

League Club	Source	Date Signed	Seasons Played	Apps	Subs	Gls
Grimsby T	Notts Co (Jnr)	09/90				
Hull C	Grantham T	07/93	93-00	138	37	10

MANN Ronald Harold (Ron)
Born: Nottingham, England, 8 October, 1932 — LB
Died: Nottingham, England, 30 November, 2008

League Club	Source	Date Signed	Seasons Played	Apps	Subs	Gls
Notts Co	Meadow BC	12/50	50	1	-	0
Aldershot	Tr	07/56	56-57	24	-	4

MANNERS Peter John
Born: Sunderland, England, 31 July, 1959 — M

League Club	Source	Date Signed	Seasons Played	Apps	Subs	Gls
Newcastle U	App	07/77	78	2	0	0

MANNERS Wingrove Austin
Born: Barbados, 7 March, 1955 — F
Died: Leeds, England, 22 April, 2014

League Club	Source	Date Signed	Seasons Played	Apps	Subs	Gls
Bradford C	App	-	71	1	0	0

MANNING John Joseph
Born: Liverpool, England, 11 December, 1940 — CF

League Club	Source	Date Signed	Seasons Played	Apps	Subs	Gls
Tranmere Rov	Liverpool (Am)	05/62	62-66	130	0	70
Shrewsbury T	Tr	10/66	66-67	39	0	18
Norwich C	Tr	09/67	67-68	60	0	21
Bolton W	Tr	03/69	68-70	27	2	7
Walsall	Tr	07/71	71	13	1	6
Tranmere Rov	Tr	03/72	71	5	0	1
Crewe Alex	Tr	08/72	72	37	1	6
Barnsley	Tr	09/73	73-74	41	4	7
Crewe Alex	Tr	11/75	75	7	0	5

MANNING Paul James
Born: Lewisham, SE London, England, 21 January, 1974 — FB

League Club	Source	Date Signed	Seasons Played	Apps	Subs	Gls
Millwall	YT	10/91	92	1	0	0

MANNINGER Alexander (Alex)
Born: Salzburg, Austria, 4 June, 1977 — G
Austria: 33/Youth

League Club	Source	Date Signed	Seasons Played	Apps	Subs	Gls
Arsenal	Grazer AK (AUT)	06/97	97-00	38	1	0

MANNINI Moreno
Born: Imola, Italy, 15 August, 1962 — D
Italy: 10

League Club	Source	Date Signed	Seasons Played	Apps	Subs	Gls
Nottingham F	Sampdoria (ITA)	08/99	99	7	1	0

MANNION Gerard Patrick (Gerry)
Born: Burtonwood, Cheshire, England, 21 December, 1939 — RW
Died: Warrington, Cheshire, England, 15 June, 1994
England: U23-2/Youth

League Club	Source	Date Signed	Seasons Played	Apps	Subs	Gls
Wolverhampton W	Jnr	11/57	59-60	17	-	7
Norwich C	Tr	09/61	61-67	100	0	17
Chester C	Tr	01/68	67	6	0	0

MANNION Sean
Born: Dublin, Republic of Ireland, 3 March, 1980 — M

League Club	Source	Date Signed	Seasons Played	Apps	Subs	Gls
Stockport Co	Stella Maris (ROI)	02/98	98	0	1	0

MANNION Wilfred James (Wilf)
Born: South Bank, Cleveland, England, 16 May, 1918 — IF
Died: Redcar, Cleveland, England, 14 April, 2000
England: 26/B-2/FLge-8/War-4

League Club	Source	Date Signed	Seasons Played	Apps	Subs	Gls
Middlesbrough	South Bank St Peter's	09/36	36-53	341	-	100
Hull C	Tr	12/54	54	16	-	1

MANNIX David Christopher
Born: Winsford, Cheshire, England, 24 August, 1985 — M
England: Youth

League Club	Source	Date Signed	Seasons Played	Apps	Subs	Gls
Liverpool	Sch	06/03				
Accrington Stan	L	11/06	06	1	0	0
Accrington Stan	Ham Kam (NOR)	01/08	07	9	3	0
Chester C	Tr	07/08	08	10	3	2

MANNONE Vito
Born: Milan, Italy, 2 March, 1988 — G
Italy: U21-7

League Club	Source	Date Signed	Seasons Played	Apps	Subs	Gls
Arsenal	Atalanta (ITA)	07/05	08-12	15	0	0
Barnsley	L	08/06	06	1	1	0
Hull C	L	10/10	10	10	0	0
Hull C	L	01/12	11	21	0	0
Sunderland	Tr	07/13	13-14	38	1	0

MANNS Paul Henry
Born: Great Haywood, Staffordshire, England, 15 April, 1961 — M

League Club	Source	Date Signed	Seasons Played	Apps	Subs	Gls
Notts Co	Cardiff C (NC)	08/79	79-80	5	2	1
Chester C	Tr	03/83	82-83	28	0	3

MANOLEV Stanislav
Born: Blagoevgrad, Bulgaria, 16 December, 1985 — RB/M
Bulgaria: 44/Youth

League Club	Source	Date Signed	Seasons Played	Apps	Subs	Gls
Fulham (L)	PSV Eindhoven (NED)	01/13	12	4	1	0

MANQUILLO Javier (Javi)
Born: Madrid, Spain, 5 May, 1994 — RB
Spain: U21-4/Youth

League Club	Source	Date Signed	Seasons Played	Apps	Subs	Gls
Liverpool (L)	Atletico Madrid (SPN)	08/14	14	10	0	0

MANSARAM Darren Timothy
Born: Doncaster, South Yorkshire, England, 25 June, 1984 — F

League Club	Source	Date Signed	Seasons Played	Apps	Subs	Gls
Grimsby T	Sch	09/02	02-04	35	38	6

MANSELL George William
Born: Doncaster, South Yorkshire, England, 19 January, 1943 — CF

League Club	Source	Date Signed	Seasons Played	Apps	Subs	Gls
Doncaster Rov		09/62	62	1	-	0

MANSELL John (Jack)
Born: Salford, England, 22 August, 1927 — LB
England: B-2/FLge-2//Wales: WLge-1

League Club	Source	Date Signed	Seasons Played	Apps	Subs	Gls
Brighton & HA	Manchester U (Am)	03/49	48-52	116	-	10
Cardiff C	Tr	10/52	52-53	25	-	0
Portsmouth	Tr	11/53	53-57	134	-	7

MANSELL Lee Richard Samuel
Born: Gloucester, England, 28 October, 1982 — M

League Club	Source	Date Signed	Seasons Played	Apps	Subs	Gls
Luton T	YT	05/01	00-04	35	12	8
Oxford U	Tr	07/05	05	44	0	1
Torquay U	Tr	07/06	06-13	251	8	22

MANSELL Ronald Barrington (Barry)
Born: Petersfield, Hampshire, England, 8 March, 1932 — FB

League Club	Source	Date Signed	Seasons Played	Apps	Subs	Gls
Portsmouth	Hillside YC	08/49	51-53	16	-	0
Reading	Tr	02/54	53-55	84	-	0
Bournemouth	Tr	06/57				

MANSET Mathieu
Born: Metz, France, 5 August, 1989 — F

League Club	Source	Date Signed	Seasons Played	Apps	Subs	Gls
Hereford U	Le Havre (FRA)	10/09	09-10	34	16	10
Reading	Tr	01/11	10-11	8	20	5
Carlisle U	FC Sion (SUI)	03/13	12	0	7	0
Coventry C	Tr	08/13	13	0	9	1
Walsall	Royal Antwerp (BEL)	08/14	14	4	15	0
Cheltenham T	Tr	02/15	14	8	4	0

MANSFIELD Frederick Charles Adam (Fred)
Born: Cambridge, England, 9 March, 1915 — RB
Died: Cambridge, England, 1 January, 1992

League Club	Source	Date Signed	Seasons Played	Apps	Subs	Gls
Brentford	Cambridge T	04/39				
Norwich C	Tr	02/47	46-47	34	-	0

MANSFIELD John Vincent
Born: Colchester, Essex, England, 13 September, 1946 — IF

League Club	Source	Date Signed	Seasons Played	Apps	Subs	Gls
Colchester U	Jnr	08/64	64-68	28	6	3

MANSFIELD Ronald William (Ron)
Born: Romford, E London, England, 31 December, 1923 — LW
Died: Romford, E London, England, April, 1997

League Club	Source	Date Signed	Seasons Played	Apps	Subs	Gls
Millwall	Ilford	04/41	46-52	97	-	25
Southend U	Tr	11/52	52	8	-	3

MANSLEY Allan
Born: Liverpool, England, 31 August, 1946 — LW
Died: Southport, Merseyside, England, 4 February, 2001

League Club	Source	Date Signed	Seasons Played	Apps	Subs	Gls
Blackpool	Skelmersdale U	06/67				
Brentford	Tr	01/68	67-70	94	1	24
Fulham	Tr	12/70	70	1	0	0
Notts Co	Tr	03/71	71	11	0	2
Lincoln C	L	12/71	71	3	0	0

MANSLEY Chad Andrew
Born: Newcastle, NSW, Australia, 13 November, 1980 — M
Australia: Schools

League Club	Source	Date Signed	Seasons Played	Apps	Subs	Gls
Leyton Orient	Newcastle Br'ers (AUS)	11/00	00	0	1	0

MANSLEY Vincent Clifford (Cliff)
Born: Skipton, North Yorkshire, England, 5 April, 1921 — RH
Died: Lancashire, England, August, 2006

League Club	Source	Date Signed	Seasons Played	Apps	Subs	Gls
Preston NE	School Lane Mills	09/40				
Barnsley	Tr	11/45	46-47	30	-	0
Chester C	Tr	06/48	48	22	-	0
Leyton Orient	Yeovil T	07/52	52	10	-	0

MANSOURI Yazid
Born: Revin, Ardennes, France, 25 February, 1978 — M
Algeria: 67

League Club	Source	Date Signed	Seasons Played	Apps	Subs	Gls
Coventry C (L)	Le Havre (FRA)	08/03	03	9	5	0

MANTOM Samuel Stephen (Sam)
Born: Stourbridge, West Midlands, England, 20 February, 1992 — M
England: Youth

League Club	Source	Date Signed	Seasons Played	Apps	Subs	Gls
West Bromwich A	Sch	07/10				
Tranmere Rov	L	11/10	10	2	0	0
Oldham Ath	L	02/11	10	3	1	0
Walsall	L	03/12	11	13	0	3
Walsall	Tr	11/12	12-14	78	6	7

[MANUCHO] ALBERTO Mateus Contreiras
Born: Luanda, Angola, 7 March, 1983 — LW

League Club	Source	Date Signed	Seasons Played	Career Record Apps	Subs	Gls

Angola: 52

League Club	Source	Date Signed	Seasons Played	Apps	Subs	Gls
Manchester U	Petro Atletico (ANG)	01/08	08	0	1	0
Hull C	L	01/09	08	6	7	2

MANUEL William Albert James (Billy)
Born: Hackney, E London, England, 28 June, 1969 — M/LB

League Club	Source	Date Signed	Seasons Played	Apps	Subs	Gls
Tottenham H	YT	07/87				
Gillingham	Tr	02/89	88-90	74	13	5
Brentford	Tr	06/91	91-93	83	11	1
Cambridge U	Stevenage Bor	10/94	94	10	0	0
Peterborough U	Tr	02/95	94-95	27	0	2
Gillingham	Tr	01/96	95-96	9	12	0
Barnet	Tr	07/97	97-98	13	16	1

MAPES Charles Edward (Charlie)
Born: Camden, N London, England, 4 July, 1982 — M

League Club	Source	Date Signed	Seasons Played	Apps	Subs	Gls
Cardiff C	Tottenham H (YT)	09/00				
Wycombe W	Berkhamsted T	07/03	03	10	5	3

MAPSON John (Johnny)
Born: Birkenhead, Wirral, England, 2 May, 1917 — G
Died: Sunderland, England, 19 August, 1999
England: War-1

League Club	Source	Date Signed	Seasons Played	Apps	Subs	Gls
Reading	Swindon T (Am)	04/35	35	2	-	0
Sunderland	Tr	03/36	35-52	346	-	0

MARANGONI Claudio Oscar
Born: Rosario, Argentina, 17 November, 1954 — M
Argentina: 9

League Club	Source	Date Signed	Seasons Played	Apps	Subs	Gls
Sunderland	San Lorenzo (ARG)	12/79	79-80	19	1	3

[MARCELINO] ELENA Marcelino
Born: Gijon, Spain, 26 September, 1971 — CD
Spain: 5

League Club	Source	Date Signed	Seasons Played	Apps	Subs	Gls
Newcastle U	RCD Mallorca (SPN)	07/99	99-00	15	2	0

MARCELLE Clinton Sherwin (Clint)
Born: Port of Spain, Trinidad, 9 November, 1968 — W
Trinidad & Tobago: 11

League Club	Source	Date Signed	Seasons Played	Apps	Subs	Gls
Barnsley	Felgueiras (POR)	08/96	96-98	37	32	8
Scunthorpe U	L	10/99	99	8	2	0
Hull C	Goole AFC	09/00	00	16	7	2
Darlington	Tr	02/01	00-01	8	7	0
Grimsby T	Scarborough	08/04	04	0	3	0

[MARCELO] DOS SANTOS CIPRIANO Marcelo
Born: Rio de Janeiro, Brazil, 11 October, 1969 — F

League Club	Source	Date Signed	Seasons Played	Apps	Subs	Gls
Sheffield U	Dep Alaves (SPN)	10/97	97-99	47	19	24
Birmingham C	Tr	10/99	99-01	47	30	24
Walsall	Tr	02/02	01	9	0	1

MARCH John Edmund
Born: Norwich, England, 12 May, 1940 — LB

League Club	Source	Date Signed	Seasons Played	Apps	Subs	Gls
Norwich C	Jnr	05/57				
Bradford Park Ave	Tr	06/61	61-62	62	-	1

MARCH Solomon Benjamin (Solly)
Born: Eastbourne, East Sussex, England, 20 July, 1994 — LW
England: U21-4

League Club	Source	Date Signed	Seasons Played	Apps	Subs	Gls
Brighton & HA	Sch	02/13	13-14	13	21	1

MARCH Stanley (Stan)
Born: Manchester, England, 26 December, 1938 — IF

League Club	Source	Date Signed	Seasons Played	Apps	Subs	Gls
Port Vale	Altrincham	08/59	59	1	-	0

MARCH William (Billy)
Born: Chester-le-Street, County Durham, England, 28 February, 1925 — LB
Died: Barnsley, South Yorkshire, England, 11 June, 1974

League Club	Source	Date Signed	Seasons Played	Apps	Subs	Gls
Barnsley	Ferryhill Ath	11/47	51	2	-	0
Gateshead	Tr	07/52	52-56	134	-	0

MARCHANT Marwood Godfrey
Born: Milford Haven, Pembrokeshire, Wales, 18 June, 1922 — IF
Died: Milford Haven, Pembrokeshire, Wales, 28 June, 1972

League Club	Source	Date Signed	Seasons Played	Apps	Subs	Gls
Cardiff C	Milford U	01/51	50	12	-	3
Torquay U	Tr	11/51	51-52	40	-	19

MARCHI Anthony Vittorio (Tony)
Born: Edmonton, N London, England, 21 January, 1933 — LH
England: B-1/Youth/Schools

League Club	Source	Date Signed	Seasons Played	Apps	Subs	Gls
Tottenham H	Jnr	06/50	49-56	131	-	2
Tottenham H	Torino (ITA)	07/59	59-64	101	-	5

MARCOLIN Dario
Born: Brescia, Italy, 28 October, 1971 — M
Italy: U23-10/U21-22/Youth

League Club	Source	Date Signed	Seasons Played	Apps	Subs	Gls
Blackburn Rov (L)	SS Lazio (ITA)	10/98	98	5	5	1

MARDEN Reuben John (Ben)
Born: Fulham, W London, England, 10 February, 1927 — LW
Died: Chelmsford, England, 1 February, 2000

League Club	Source	Date Signed	Seasons Played	Apps	Subs	Gls
Arsenal	Chelmsford C	02/50	50-54	42	-	11
Watford	Tr	06/55	55-56	41	-	11

MARDENBOROUGH Stephen Alexander (Steve)
Born: Birmingham, England, 11 September, 1964 — W

League Club	Source	Date Signed	Seasons Played	Apps	Subs	Gls
Coventry C	App	08/82				
Wolverhampton W	Tr	09/83	83	9	0	1
Cambridge U	L	02/84	83	6	0	0
Swansea C	Tr	07/84	84	32	4	7
Newport Co	Tr	07/85	85-86	50	14	11
Cardiff C	Tr	03/87	86-87	18	14	1
Hereford U	Tr	07/88	88	20	7	0
Darlington	Cheltenham T	07/90	90-92	79	27	18
Lincoln C	Tr	07/93	93	14	7	2
Scarborough	Tr	02/95	94	0	1	0
Colchester U	Stafford Rgrs	08/95	95	4	8	2
Swansea C	Tr	12/95	95	1	0	0

MARDON Paul Jonathan
Born: Bristol, England, 14 September, 1969 — CD
Wales: 1/B-1

League Club	Source	Date Signed	Seasons Played	Apps	Subs	Gls
Bristol C	YT	01/88	87-90	29	13	0
Doncaster Rov	L	09/90	90	3	0	0
Birmingham C	Tr	08/91	91-93	54	10	1
West Bromwich A	Tr	11/93	93-98	125	14	3
Oldham Ath	L	01/99	98	12	0	3
Plymouth Arg	L	09/00	00	3	0	1
Wrexham	L	10/00	00	6	1	0

MARESCA Vincenzo (Enzo)
Born: Salerno, Italy, 10 February, 1980 — M
Italy: U21-5/Youth

League Club	Source	Date Signed	Seasons Played	Apps	Subs	Gls
West Bromwich A	Cagliari (ITA)	08/98	98-99	28	19	5

MARGAS Javier Luciano
Born: Santiago, Chile, 10 May, 1969 — CD
Chile: 63

League Club	Source	Date Signed	Seasons Played	Apps	Subs	Gls
West Ham U	Catolica Univ (CHL)	08/98	98-00	21	3	1

MARGERISON Lee
Born: Bradford, England, 10 September, 1973 — M

League Club	Source	Date Signed	Seasons Played	Apps	Subs	Gls
Bradford C	YT	07/92	92	1	2	0

MARGERRISON John William
Born: Bushey, Hertfordshire, England, 20 October, 1955 — M

League Club	Source	Date Signed	Seasons Played	Apps	Subs	Gls
Tottenham H	App	12/72				
Fulham	Tr	07/75	75-78	63	8	9
Leyton Orient	Tr	07/79	79-81	77	3	6

MARGETSON Martyn Walter
Born: Neath, Wales, 8 September, 1971 — G
Wales: 1/B-1/U21-7/Youth/Schools

League Club	Source	Date Signed	Seasons Played	Apps	Subs	Gls
Manchester C	YT	07/90	90-97	51	0	0
Bristol Rov	L	12/93	93	2	1	0
Southend U	Tr	08/98	98	32	0	0
Huddersfield T	Tr	08/99	00-01	47	1	0
Cardiff C	Tr	08/02	02-04	31	1	0

MARGETTS Jonathan Gary
Born: Doncaster, South Yorkshire, England, 28 September, 1993 — F

League Club	Source	Date Signed	Seasons Played	Apps	Subs	Gls
Hull C	Sch	07/12				
Cambridge U	L	03/15	14	0	1	0

MARGINSON Karl Kevin
Born: Manchester, England, 11 November, 1970 — LW

League Club	Source	Date Signed	Seasons Played	Apps	Subs	Gls
Rotherham U	Ashton U	03/93	92-94	11	4	1

MARGREITTER Georg
Born: Bludenz, Austria, 7 November, 1988 — CD
Austria: U21-11/Youth

League Club	Source	Date Signed	Seasons Played	Apps	Subs	Gls
Wolverhampton W	Austria Vienna (AUT)	08/12	12	0	1	0
Chesterfield	L	09/14	14	11	2	1

MARIAPPA Adrian Joseph
Born: Harrow, NW London, England, 3 October, 1986 — CD
Jamaica: 25

League Club	Source	Date Signed	Seasons Played	Apps	Subs	Gls
Watford	Sch	07/05	05-11	196	20	4
Reading	Tr	07/12	12	29	0	1
Crystal Palace	Tr	09/13	13-14	31	5	1

MARIC Silvio
Born: Zagreb, Croatia, 20 March, 1975 — M
Croatia: 19

League Club	Source	Date Signed	Seasons Played	Apps	Subs	Gls
Newcastle U	Croatia Zagreb (CRO)	02/99	98-99	12	11	0

MARIN Marko
Born: Bosanska Gradiska, Bosnia & Herzegovina, 13 March, 1989 — LM
Germany: 16/U21-12/Youth

League Club	Source	Date Signed	Seasons Played	Apps	Subs	Gls
Chelsea	Werder Bremen (GER)	07/12	12	2	4	1

League Club	Source	Date Signed	Seasons Played	Apps	Subs	Gls
MARIN Nicolas						
Born: Marseille, France, 29 August, 1980						RM
Plymouth Arg (L)	Lorient (FRA)	09/08	08	1	5	0
MARINELLI Carlos Ariel						
Born: Buenos Aires, Argentina, 14 March, 1982						M
Argentina: Youth						
Middlesbrough	Boca Juniors (ARG)	10/99	99-03	18	25	3
MARINELLO Peter						
Born: Edinburgh, Scotland, 20 February, 1950						RW
Scotland: SLge-1/U23-2						
Arsenal	Hibernian	01/70	69-72	32	6	3
Portsmouth	Tr	07/73	73-75	92	3	7
Fulham	Motherwell	12/78	78-79	25	2	1
MARINER Paul						
Born: Bolton, Greater Manchester, England, 22 May, 1953						F
England: 35/B-7						
Plymouth Arg	Chorley	07/73	73-76	134	1	56
Ipswich T	Tr	09/76	76-83	260	0	96
Arsenal	Tr	02/84	83-85	52	8	14
Portsmouth	Tr	07/86	86-87	49	7	9
MARINKOV Alexandre (Alex)						
Born: Grenoble, France, 2 December, 1967						CD
Scarborough	Raon L'Etape (FRA)	08/98	98	22	0	4
MARIS George Thomas						
Born: Sheffield, England, 6 March, 1996						F
Barnsley	Sch	05/14	14	1	1	0
MARKER Nicholas Robert (Nicky)						
Born: Budleigh Salterton, Devon, England, 3 May, 1965						CD/M
Exeter C	App	05/83	81-87	196	6	3
Plymouth Arg	Tr	10/87	87-92	201	1	13
Blackburn Rov	Tr	09/92	92-96	41	13	1
Sheffield U	Tr	07/97	97-98	60	1	5
Plymouth Arg	L	02/99	98	4	0	0
MARKHAM Colin						
Born: Clowne, Derbyshire, England, 2 March, 1916						LH
Died: Bovey Tracey, Devon, England, 16 February, 1967						
Torquay U	Redhill	02/38	37-46	25	-	1
MARKHAM Leo Sargent						
Born: High Wycombe, Buckinghamshire, England, 22 March, 1953						CD/F
Watford	Marlow	08/72	72-74	22	11	3
MARKHAM Peter						
Born: Scunthorpe, North Lincolnshire, England, 18 March, 1954						RB
Scunthorpe U	App	03/72	71-76	121	1	1
MARKIE John						
Born: Bo'ness, Falkirk, Scotland, 16 December, 1944						RH
Scotland: Schools						
Newcastle U	App	04/62	63	2	-	0
MARKLEW Roger Kelsey						
Born: Sheffield, England, 30 January, 1940						LW
Died: Norwich, England, December, 2006						
Sheffield Wed	Sheffield U (Am)	05/58				
Accrington Stan	Tr	05/59				
Grimsby T	Tr	08/60	60	6	-	1
MARKMAN Damien Liam						
Born: Ascot, Berkshire, England, 7 January, 1978						F
Wycombe W	Slough T	11/95	95-96	0	4	0
MARKOVIC Lazar						
Born: Cacak, Serbia, 2 March, 1994						RW
Serbia: 20/U21-2/Youth						
Liverpool	Benfica (POR)	07/14	14	11	8	2
MARKS Charles William Alfred (Charlie)						
Born: Eccles, Kent, England, 21 December, 1919						RB
Died: Larkfield, Kent, England, 25 January, 2005						
Gillingham	Tooting & Mitcham U	08/43	50-56	265	-	8
MARKS Jamie						
Born: Belfast, Northern Ireland, 18 March, 1977						M
Northern Ireland: Youth/Schools						
Leeds U	YT	04/95				
Hull C	Tr	02/96	95-96	11	4	0
MARKS Michael David (Mike)						
Born: Lambeth, S London, England, 23 March, 1968						F
Millwall	App	07/86	86	36	0	10
Mansfield T	L	01/88	87	0	1	0
Leyton Orient	Tr	02/88	87	3	0	0
MARKS William George (George)						
Born: Amesbury, Wiltshire, England, 9 April, 1915						G
Died: Salisbury, Wiltshire, England, 22 January, 1998						
England: War-8						
Arsenal	Salisbury Corinthians	03/36	38	2	-	0
Blackburn Rov	Tr	08/46	46-47	67	-	0
Bristol C	Tr	08/48	48	9	-	0
Reading	Tr	10/48	48-52	118	-	0
MARKSTEDT Peter						
Born: Vasteras, Sweden, 11 January, 1972						CD
Barnsley	Vasteras SK (SWE)	11/97	97-98	8	1	0
MARLET Steve						
Born: Pithiviers, France, 10 January, 1974						F
France: 23/B-1						
Fulham	Olymp Lyonnais (FRA)	09/01	01-03	50	5	11
MARLEY Allan						
Born: Durham, England, 29 February, 1956						RB
Grimsby T	App	11/73	74-75	39	1	2
MARLEY George						
Born: Gateshead, Tyne and Wear, England, 22 April, 1921						IF
Died: Gateshead, Tyne and Wear, England, November, 1992						
Gateshead		09/47	47-49	22	-	2
MARLOW Frederick (Fred)						
Born: Sheffield, England, 9 November, 1928						LH/IF
Died: Suffolk, England, March, 2013						
Arsenal	Hillsborough BC	09/47				
Sheffield Wed	Tr	09/50				
Grimsby T	Buxton	08/51	51	12	-	6
York C	Boston U	10/53	53-54	24	-	0
MARLOW Geoffrey Arthur (Geoff)						
Born: Worksop, Nottinghamshire, England, 13 December, 1914						LW
Died: Lincoln, England, 8 November, 1978						
Lincoln C	Dinnington Ath	05/37	37-38	16	-	5
Lincoln C	Newark T	11/40	46-48	64	-	21
MARLOWE (MARKOWSKI) Richard Ronald (Ricky)						
Born: Edinburgh, Scotland, 10 August, 1950						F
Derby Co	Bonnyrigg Rose	06/69				
Shrewsbury T	Tr	12/73	73	31	0	4
Brighton & HA	Tr	07/74	74	24	1	5
Aldershot	L	01/76	75	2	0	0
MARMON Neale Gordon						
Born: Bournemouth, England, 21 April, 1961						CD
Torquay U	Plymouth Arg (NC)	03/80	79	4	0	0
Colchester U	Hannover 96 (GER)	01/90	89	22	0	4
MARNEY Daniel Gary (Danny)						
Born: Sidcup, SE London, England, 2 October, 1981						RW
Brighton & HA	YT	08/01	02-03	6	9	0
Southend U	L	12/02	02	13	4	0
MARNEY Dean Edward						
Born: Barking, E London, England, 31 January, 1984						M
England: U21-1						
Tottenham H	Sch	07/02	03-04	4	4	2
Swindon T	L	12/02	02	8	1	0
Queens Park Rgrs	L	01/04	03	1	1	0
Gillingham	L	11/04	04	3	0	0
Norwich C	L	08/05	05	12	1	0
Hull C	Tr	07/06	06-09	102	23	9
Burnley	Tr	05/10	10-14	159	10	8
MAROSI Marko						
Born: Slovakia, 23 October, 1993						G
Slovakia: U21-1						
Wigan Ath	Barnoldswick T	03/13				
Doncaster Rov	Tr	08/14	14	2	1	0
MARPLES Christopher (Chris)						
Born: Chesterfield, Derbyshire, England, 3 August, 1964						G
Chesterfield	Goole T	03/84	84-86	84	0	0
Stockport Co	Tr	03/87	86-87	57	0	0
York C	Tr	07/88	88-92	138	0	0
Scunthorpe U	L	02/92	91	1	0	0
Chesterfield	Tr	12/92	92-94	57	0	0
MARPLES Simon James						
Born: Sheffield, England, 30 July, 1975						RB
England: Semi Pro-2						
Doncaster Rov	Stocksbridge Pk Steels	09/99	03-05	40	3	0
Chester C	Tr	07/06	06-07	40	6	0

MARQUIS John Edward
Born: Lewisham, SE London, England, 16 May, 1992 — F

League Club	Source	Date Signed	Seasons Played	Apps	Subs	Gls
Millwall	Sch	05/10	09-14	20	22	5
Portsmouth	L	09/13	13	4	1	1
Torquay U	L	11/13	13	5	0	3
Northampton T	L	02/14	13	12	2	2
Cheltenham T	L	08/14	14	8	5	1
Gillingham	L	01/15	14	18	3	8

MARQUIS Paul Raymond
Born: Enfield, N London, England, 29 August, 1972 — CD

League Club	Source	Date Signed	Seasons Played	Apps	Subs	Gls
West Ham U	YT	07/91	93	0	1	0
Doncaster Rov	Tr	03/94	93-96	28	1	1

MARRIOTT Adam James
Born: Brandon, Suffolk, England, 14 April, 1991 — F

League Club	Source	Date Signed	Seasons Played	Apps	Subs	Gls
Stevenage	Cambridge C	07/14	14	8	5	3

MARRIOTT Alan
Born: Bedford, England, 3 September, 1978 — G

League Club	Source	Date Signed	Seasons Played	Apps	Subs	Gls
Tottenham H	YT	07/97				
Lincoln C	Tr	08/99	99-07	351	0	0
Mansfield T	Rushden & D	01/09	13	40	0	0

MARRIOTT Andrew (Andy)
Born: Sutton-in-Ashfield, Nottinghamshire, England, 11 October, 1970 — G
England: U21-1/Youth/Schools//Wales: 5

League Club	Source	Date Signed	Seasons Played	Apps	Subs	Gls
Arsenal	YT	10/88				
Nottingham F	Tr	06/89	91-92	11	0	0
West Bromwich A	L	09/89	89	3	0	0
Blackburn Rov	L	12/89	89	2	0	0
Colchester U	L	03/90	89	10	0	0
Burnley	L	08/91	91	15	0	0
Wrexham	Tr	10/93	93-97	213	0	0
Sunderland	Tr	08/98	98-99	2	0	0
Barnsley	Tr	03/01	01-02	53	1	0
Birmingham C	Tr	03/03	02	1	0	0
Coventry C	Beira Mar (POR)	08/04				
Colchester U	Tr	10/04				
Bury	Tr	11/04	04	19	0	0
Torquay U	Tr	03/05	04-05	57	0	0
Boston U	Tr	07/06	06	46	0	0
Exeter C	Tr	06/07	09	13	0	0

MARRIOTT Ernest (Ernie)
Born: Sutton-in-Ashfield, Nottinghamshire, England, 25 January, 1913 — FB
Died: Hove, East Sussex, England, 6 September, 1989

League Club	Source	Date Signed	Seasons Played	Apps	Subs	Gls
Brighton & HA	Sutton Junction	01/34	34-47	163	-	1

MARRIOTT Jack (Jackie)
Born: Sheffield, England, 16 July, 1915 — IF
Died: Sheffield, England, 22 April, 1989

League Club	Source	Date Signed	Seasons Played	Apps	Subs	Gls
Doncaster Rov	Normanton Sports	02/45	46-47	6	-	0
Southport	Tr	12/47	47-48	23	-	5

MARRIOTT Jack David
Born: Beverley, East Riding of Yorkshire, England, 9 September, 1994 — F

League Club	Source	Date Signed	Seasons Played	Apps	Subs	Gls
Ipswich T	Sch	07/13	12-13	0	2	0
Gillingham	L	01/14	13	0	1	0
Carlisle U	L	08/14	14	3	1	0
Colchester U	L	01/15	14	0	5	1

MARRIOTT John Leonard (Jack)
Born: Scunthorpe, North Lincolnshire, England, 1 April, 1928 — RW

League Club	Source	Date Signed	Seasons Played	Apps	Subs	Gls
Sheffield Wed	Scunthorpe U	02/47	46-54	153	-	19
Huddersfield T	Tr	07/55	55-56	38	-	4
Scunthorpe U	Tr	06/57	57-63	212	-	26

MARRIOTT Paul William
Born: Liverpool, England, 26 September, 1973 — F

League Club	Source	Date Signed	Seasons Played	Apps	Subs	Gls
Cardiff C	YT	-	91	0	1	0

MARRIOTT Stanley (Stan)
Born: Rochdale, Greater Manchester, England, 21 July, 1929 — CF
Died: Rochdale, Greater Manchester, England, January, 2002

League Club	Source	Date Signed	Seasons Played	Apps	Subs	Gls
Rochdale (Am)	Rochdale YMCA	12/52	52	6	-	2

MARRISON Colin Ian
Born: Sheffield, England, 23 September, 1985 — F

League Club	Source	Date Signed	Seasons Played	Apps	Subs	Gls
Sheffield U	Sch	07/05				
Bury	L	01/06	05	8	8	0

MARRON Christopher (Chris)
Born: Jarrow, Tyne and Wear, England, 7 February, 1925 — CF
Died: Mansfield, Nottinghamshire, England, June, 1986

League Club	Source	Date Signed	Seasons Played	Apps	Subs	Gls
Chesterfield	South Shields	10/47	47-51	108	-	44
Mansfield T	Tr	07/52	52-53	53	-	25
Bradford Park Ave	Tr	07/54	54	2	-	1

MARROW Alexander James (Alex)
Born: Tyldesley, Greater Manchester, England, 21 January, 1990 — DM

League Club	Source	Date Signed	Seasons Played	Apps	Subs	Gls
Blackburn Rov	Ashton Ath	02/08				
Oldham Ath	L	08/09	09	26	6	1
Crystal Palace	Tr	08/10	10-12	23	3	0
Preston NE	L	01/12	11	3	1	0
Fleetwood T	L	08/12	12	13	7	0
Blackburn Rov	Tr	07/13	13	2	1	0
Fleetwood T	L	01/14	13	6	1	1
Carlisle U	L	07/14	14	4	0	0

MARSDEN Anthony Joseph (Tony)
Born: Bolton, Greater Manchester, England, 11 September, 1948 — F
Died: Rochdale, Greater Manchester, England, September, 2010

League Club	Source	Date Signed	Seasons Played	Apps	Subs	Gls
Blackpool	App	07/66	67-68	4	1	0
Doncaster Rov	Tr	07/69	69-70	14	3	2
Grimsby T	L	11/69	69	2	0	0

MARSDEN Christopher (Chris)
Born: Sheffield, England, 3 January, 1969 — M

League Club	Source	Date Signed	Seasons Played	Apps	Subs	Gls
Sheffield U	App	01/87	87	13	3	1
Huddersfield T	Tr	07/88	88-93	113	8	9
Coventry C	L	11/93	93	5	2	0
Wolverhampton W	Tr	01/94	93	8	0	0
Notts Co	Tr	11/94	94-95	10	0	0
Stockport Co	Tr	01/96	95-97	63	2	3
Birmingham C	Tr	10/97	97-98	51	1	3
Southampton	Tr	02/99	98-03	118	11	6
Sheffield Wed	Busan Icons (KOR)	06/04	04	15	0	0

MARSDEN Eric
Born: Bolsover, Derbyshire, England, 3 January, 1930 — CF

League Club	Source	Date Signed	Seasons Played	Apps	Subs	Gls
Crystal Palace	Winchester C	04/50	50-52	34	-	11
Southend U	Tr	10/52	52	14	-	6
Shrewsbury T	Tr	03/53	52-53	11	-	0

MARSDEN Frederick (Fred)
Born: Blackburn, Greater Manchester, England, 6 September, 1911 — FB
Died: Bournemouth, England, November, 1989

League Club	Source	Date Signed	Seasons Played	Apps	Subs	Gls
Accrington Stan	Manchester Central	10/34	34	5	-	0
Wolverhampton W	Tr	01/35	35	1	-	0
Bournemouth	Tr	05/36	36-48	194	-	1

MARSDEN Jack
Born: Leeds, England, 17 December, 1931 — CH
Died: Leeds, England, February, 2014

League Club	Source	Date Signed	Seasons Played	Apps	Subs	Gls
Leeds U	Osmondthorpe YMCA	08/50	52-58	71	-	0
Barrow	Tr	03/59	58-59	47	-	0
Carlisle U	Tr	09/60	60-63	89	-	0
Doncaster Rov	Tr	07/64	64	2	-	0

MARSDEN James Richard
Born: Rotherham, South Yorkshire, England, 10 April, 1928 — IF

League Club	Source	Date Signed	Seasons Played	Apps	Subs	Gls
Rotherham U	Parkgate Welfare	08/52	52-54	11	-	2

MARSDEN John Edward
Born: Liverpool, England, 9 December, 1992 — F

League Club	Source	Date Signed	Seasons Played	Apps	Subs	Gls
Shrewsbury T	Woodley Sports	07/13	13	1	2	0

MARSDEN Keith
Born: Darley Dale, Derbyshire, England, 10 April, 1934 — CF
Died: South Africa, November, 1986

League Club	Source	Date Signed	Seasons Played	Apps	Subs	Gls
Chesterfield	Youlgreave BC	06/52	53-54	22	-	15
Manchester C	Tr	07/55	55-57	14	-	1
Accrington Stan	Tr	08/59				

MARSDEN Liam Robert
Born: Creswell, Derbyshire, England, 21 November, 1994 — RB

League Club	Source	Date Signed	Seasons Played	Apps	Subs	Gls
Mansfield T	Matlock T	07/13	13-14	11	1	0

MARSDEN Liddle
Born: Washington, Tyne and Wear, England, 13 May, 1936 — RH

League Club	Source	Date Signed	Seasons Played	Apps	Subs	Gls
Workington	South Shields	11/56	56	2	-	0

MARSH Adam
Born: Sheffield, England, 20 February, 1982 — F

League Club	Source	Date Signed	Seasons Played	Apps	Subs	Gls
Darlington	Worksop T	11/00	00-01	2	6	0

MARSH Arthur
Born: Rowley Regis, West Midlands, England, 4 May, 1947 — CD

League Club	Source	Date Signed	Seasons Played	Apps	Subs	Gls
Bolton W	App	05/65	66-70	71	2	0
Rochdale	Tr	12/71	71-73	89	1	0
Darlington	Tr	07/74	74	23	0	1

MARSH Christopher Jonathan (Chris)
Born: Sedgley, West Midlands, England, 14 January, 1970 — M/FB

League Club	Source	Date Signed	Seasons Played	Apps	Subs	Gls
Walsall	YT	07/88	87-00	355	37	23
Wycombe W	Tr	03/01	00-01	11	1	0
Northampton T	Tr	09/01	01-02	41	0	0

League Club	Source	Date Signed	Seasons Played	Career Record Apps	Subs	Gls

MARSH Clifford (Cliff)
Born: Atherton, Greater Manchester, England, 29 December, 1920 — IF
Died: Bournemouth, England, December, 1990

League Club	Source	Date Signed	Seasons Played	Apps	Subs	Gls
Leeds U	Winsford U	09/48	48	4	-	1
Bournemouth	Tr	05/49	49-51	39	-	2

MARSH Frank Kitchener
Born: Bolton, Greater Manchester, England, 7 June, 1916 — WH
Died: Caernarvon, Gwynedd, Wales, 17 January, 1978

League Club	Source	Date Signed	Seasons Played	Apps	Subs	Gls
Crewe Alex	Stafford Rgrs	07/36				
Bolton W	Tr	05/38	38	3	-	0
Chester C	Tr	05/39	46-47	69	-	2

MARSH Ian James
Born: Swansea, Wales, 27 October, 1969 — LB

League Club	Source	Date Signed	Seasons Played	Apps	Subs	Gls
Swansea C	YT	07/88	87	1	0	0
Bradford C	Tr	07/89				

MARSH John Henry (Jackie)
Born: Stoke-on-Trent, England, 31 May, 1948 — RB

League Club	Source	Date Signed	Seasons Played	Apps	Subs	Gls
Stoke C	App	06/65	67-78	346	9	2

MARSH John Kirk (Jack)
Born: Mansfield, Nottinghamshire, England, 8 October, 1922 — IF
Died: Mansfield, Nottinghamshire, England, 5 December, 1997

League Club	Source	Date Signed	Seasons Played	Apps	Subs	Gls
Notts Co	Mansfield BC	08/42	46-48	42	-	18
Coventry C	Tr	09/48	48-49	20	-	7
Leicester C	Tr	03/50	49-50	14	-	4
Chesterfield	Tr	09/50	50	26	-	4

MARSH John Stanley
Born: Farnworth, Greater Manchester, England, 31 August, 1940 — IF

League Club	Source	Date Signed	Seasons Played	Apps	Subs	Gls
Oldham Ath	Little Hulton	10/57	59	2	-	0

MARSH John William (Jack)
Born: Leeds, England, 17 December, 1947 — G

League Club	Source	Date Signed	Seasons Played	Apps	Subs	Gls
Bradford C	New Farnley Jnrs	05/66	66-67	12	0	0

MARSH Kevin William
Born: Liverpool, England, 27 July, 1949 — F

League Club	Source	Date Signed	Seasons Played	Apps	Subs	Gls
Liverpool	App	03/66				
Southport	Tr	05/70	70	35	2	8

MARSH Michael Andrew (Mike)
Born: Liverpool, England, 21 July, 1969 — RM

League Club	Source	Date Signed	Seasons Played	Apps	Subs	Gls
Liverpool	Kirkby T	08/87	88-93	42	27	2
West Ham U	Tr	09/93	93-94	46	3	1
Coventry C	Tr	12/94	94	15	0	2
Southend U	Galatasaray (TKY)	09/95	95-97	84	0	11

MARSH Rodney William
Born: Hatfield, Hertfordshire, England, 11 October, 1944 — F
England: 9/U23-2

League Club	Source	Date Signed	Seasons Played	Apps	Subs	Gls
Fulham	Jnr	10/62	62-65	63	0	22
Queens Park Rgrs	Tr	03/66	65-71	211	0	106
Manchester C	Tr	03/72	71-75	116	2	36
Fulham	Tampa Bay R's (USA)	08/76	76	16	0	5

MARSH Simon Thomas Peter
Born: Ealing, W London, England, 29 January, 1977 — LB
England: U21-1

League Club	Source	Date Signed	Seasons Played	Apps	Subs	Gls
Oxford U	YT	11/94	94-98	49	7	3
Birmingham C	Tr	12/98	98	6	1	0
Brentford	L	09/00	00	3	1	0

MARSH Tyrone Kallum
Born: Bedford, England, 24 December, 1993 — F

League Club	Source	Date Signed	Seasons Played	Apps	Subs	Gls
Oxford U	Sch	06/12	12-13	0	7	0

MARSH Wilson Edmund (Eddie)
Born: Dundee, Scotland, 14 December, 1927 — G
Died: Cheshire, England, 7 April, 2010

League Club	Source	Date Signed	Seasons Played	Apps	Subs	Gls
Charlton Ath	Erith & Belvedere	12/45	50-56	26	-	0
Luton T	Tr	06/57	57-58	2	-	0
Torquay U	Tr	07/59	59-61	61	-	0

MARSH-BROWN Keanu Marqheal
Born: Hammersmith, W London, England, 10 August, 1992 — RM
England: Semi Pro-3/Youth

League Club	Source	Date Signed	Seasons Played	Apps	Subs	Gls
Fulham	Sch	08/09				
MK Dons	L	01/11	10	12	5	2
Oldham Ath	Tr	01/12	11	5	6	1
Yeovil T	Tr	07/12	12	14	7	1
Barnet	Tr	03/13	12	3	2	1

MARSHALL Alexander Stewart (Alex)
Born: Alloa, Stirlingshire, Scotland, 27 November, 1935 — IF

League Club	Source	Date Signed	Seasons Played	Apps	Subs	Gls
Accrington Stan	Stirling A	10/60	60	8	-	2

MARSHALL Alfred George (Alf)
Born: Dagenham, E London, England, 21 May, 1933 — RB

League Club	Source	Date Signed	Seasons Played	Apps	Subs	Gls
Colchester U	Dagenham	10/57	58-60	30	-	0

MARSHALL Andrew John (Andy)
Born: Bury St Edmunds, Suffolk, England, 14 April, 1975 — G
England: U21-4/Youth

League Club	Source	Date Signed	Seasons Played	Apps	Subs	Gls
Norwich C	YT	07/93	94-00	194	1	0
Bournemouth	L	09/96	96	11	0	0
Gillingham	L	11/96	96	5	0	0
Ipswich T	Tr	07/01	01-02	53	0	0
Millwall	Tr	01/04	03-05	66	1	0
Coventry C	Tr	07/06	06-08	57	2	0

MARSHALL Ben
Born: Salford, England, 29 March, 1991 — W
England: U21-2

League Club	Source	Date Signed	Seasons Played	Apps	Subs	Gls
Stoke C	Crewe Alex (Sch)	07/09				
Northampton T	L	08/09	09	11	4	2
Cheltenham T	L	11/09	09	6	0	2
Carlisle U	L	02/10	09	11	9	3
Carlisle U	L	08/10	10	27	6	3
Sheffield Wed	L	08/11	11	22	0	5
Leicester C	Tr	01/12	11-12	36	20	7
Blackburn Rov	Tr	08/13	13-14	50	10	8

MARSHALL Brian
Born: Bolton-on-Dearne, South Yorkshire, England, 20 September, 1954 — CD

League Club	Source	Date Signed	Seasons Played	Apps	Subs	Gls
Huddersfield T	App	12/71	72-74	30	2	0
Scunthorpe U	L	10/74	74	3	0	0

MARSHALL Clifford (Cliff)
Born: Liverpool, England, 4 November, 1955 — W
England: Schools

League Club	Source	Date Signed	Seasons Played	Apps	Subs	Gls
Everton	App	11/73	74-75	6	1	0
Southport	Miami Toros (USA)	09/76	76	11	2	0

MARSHALL Colin
Born: Glasgow, Scotland, 1 November, 1969 — F

League Club	Source	Date Signed	Seasons Played	Apps	Subs	Gls
Barnsley	YT	04/88	88-90	0	4	0
Wrexham	L	09/91	91	3	0	0
Scarborough	L	03/92	91	4	0	1

MARSHALL Daniel John (Danny)
Born: Newark, Nottinghamshire, England, 18 December, 1975 — M

League Club	Source	Date Signed	Seasons Played	Apps	Subs	Gls
Chesterfield	Notts Co (YT)	08/94	94	0	1	0

MARSHALL David Howard
Born: Manchester, England, 12 November, 1955 — M

League Club	Source	Date Signed	Seasons Played	Apps	Subs	Gls
Workington	Headley Colliery	11/76	76	2	0	0

MARSHALL David James
Born: Glasgow, Scotland, 5 March, 1985 — G
Scotland: 19/B-1/U21-10

League Club	Source	Date Signed	Seasons Played	Apps	Subs	Gls
Norwich C (L)	Glasgow Celtic	01/07	06	2	0	0
Norwich C	Glasgow Celtic	07/07	07-08	92	0	0
Cardiff C	Tr	05/09	09-14	220	0	0

MARSHALL Dwight Wayne
Born: Castries, Saint Lucia, 3 October, 1965 — F

League Club	Source	Date Signed	Seasons Played	Apps	Subs	Gls
Plymouth Arg	Grays Ath	08/91	91-93	93	6	27
Middlesbrough	L	03/93	92	0	3	0
Luton T	Tr	07/94	94-98	90	38	28
Plymouth Arg	Tr	10/98	98	25	3	12

MARSHALL Ernest (Ernie)
Born: Dinnington, South Yorkshire, England, 23 May, 1918 — WH
Died: Pwlheli, Gwynedd, Wales, 1983

League Club	Source	Date Signed	Seasons Played	Apps	Subs	Gls
Sheffield U	Dinnington Ath	05/35	36-37	13	-	0
Cardiff C	Tr	05/39	46	1	-	0

MARSHALL Frank
Born: Sheffield, England, 26 January, 1929 — RH

League Club	Source	Date Signed	Seasons Played	Apps	Subs	Gls
Rotherham U	Scarborough	05/51	51-56	117	-	5
Scunthorpe U	Tr	07/57	57-58	80	-	0
Doncaster Rov	Tr	10/59	59-61	35	-	0

MARSHALL Gary
Born: Bristol, England, 20 April, 1964 — W

League Club	Source	Date Signed	Seasons Played	Apps	Subs	Gls
Bristol C	Shepton Mallet	07/83	83-87	48	20	7
Torquay U	L	12/84	84	7	0	1
Carlisle U	Tr	07/88	88	18	3	2
Scunthorpe U	Tr	07/89	89-90	38	3	3
Exeter C	Tr	10/90	90-91	48	12	6

MARSHALL Gordon
Born: Farnham, Surrey, England, 2 July, 1939 — G
England: U23-1

League Club	Source	Date Signed	Seasons Played	Apps	Subs	Gls
Newcastle U	Heart of Midlothian	06/63	63-67	177	0	0
Nottingham F	Tr	10/68	68	7	0	0

MARSHALL Gordon George Banks
Born: Edinburgh, Scotland, 19 April, 1964 — G
Scotland: 1

League Club	Source	Date Signed	Seasons Played	Apps	Subs	Gls
Stoke C (L)	Glasgow Celtic	12/93	93	10	0	0

MARSHALL Ian Paul
Born: Liverpool, England, 20 March, 1966 — CD/F

League Club	Source	Date Signed	Seasons Played	Apps	Subs	Gls
Everton	App	03/84	85-87	9	6	1
Oldham Ath	Tr	03/88	87-92	165	5	36
Ipswich T	Tr	08/93	93-96	79	5	32
Leicester C	Tr	08/96	96-99	49	34	18
Bolton W	Tr	08/00	00-01	13	25	6
Blackpool	Tr	11/01	01	21	0	1

MARSHALL John
Born: Rawtenstall, Lancashire, England, 1 November, 1938 — G

League Club	Source	Date Signed	Seasons Played	Apps	Subs	Gls
Accrington Stan		05/57	57-58	7	-	0

MARSHALL John Gilmore (Jack)
Born: Edgworth, Lancashire, England, 29 May, 1917 — FB
Died: Burnley, Lancashire, England, 6 January, 1998

League Club	Source	Date Signed	Seasons Played	Apps	Subs	Gls
Burnley	Bacup Bor	11/36	38-46	26	-	0

MARSHALL John James
Born: Glasgow, Scotland, 12 February, 1949 — LW

League Club	Source	Date Signed	Seasons Played	Apps	Subs	Gls
Preston NE		02/67				
Rotherham U	Ross Co	09/68	68	4	0	0

MARSHALL John Philip
Born: Balham, S London, England, 18 August, 1964 — M/RB

League Club	Source	Date Signed	Seasons Played	Apps	Subs	Gls
Fulham	App	08/82	83-95	393	18	28

MARSHALL Jordan
Born: Gateshead, Tyne and Wear, England, 10 May, 1993 — F

League Club	Source	Date Signed	Seasons Played	Apps	Subs	Gls
Darlington	Sch	-	09	0	3	0

MARSHALL Julian Paul
Born: Swansea, Wales, 6 July, 1957 — CD

League Club	Source	Date Signed	Seasons Played	Apps	Subs	Gls
Hereford U	Merthyr Tydfil	08/75	76-79	91	1	4
Bristol C	Tr	08/80	80-81	29	0	0
Blackburn Rov	Tr	05/82				
Walsall	Tr	08/82	82	10	0	0

MARSHALL Lee Alan
Born: Nottingham, England, 1 August, 1975 — M

League Club	Source	Date Signed	Seasons Played	Apps	Subs	Gls
Nottingham F	YT	08/92				
Stockport Co	Tr	03/95	94	1	0	0
Scunthorpe U	Eastwood T	06/97	97-99	18	27	2

MARSHALL Lee James
Born: Gloucester, England, 21 November, 1996 — M

League Club	Source	Date Signed	Seasons Played	Apps	Subs	Gls
Swindon T	Sch	10/14	14	1	1	0

MARSHALL Lee Keith
Born: Islington, N London, England, 21 January, 1979 — M/RB
England: U21-1

League Club	Source	Date Signed	Seasons Played	Apps	Subs	Gls
Norwich C	Enfield	03/97	97-00	95	22	11
Leicester C	Tr	03/01	00-02	37	8	0
West Bromwich A	Tr	08/02	02	4	5	1
Hull C	L	01/04	03	10	1	0

MARSHALL Marcus Joseph Lewis
Born: Hammersmith, W London, England, 7 October, 1989 — W

League Club	Source	Date Signed	Seasons Played	Apps	Subs	Gls
Blackburn Rov	Sch	04/08				
Rotherham U	Tr	01/10	09-11	47	26	4
Macclesfield T	L	01/12	11	13	1	1
Bury	Tr	07/12	12	4	5	0
Morecambe	Tr	06/13	13	6	9	0

MARSHALL Mark Anthony
Born: Mandeville, Jamaica, 9 May, 1986 — W

League Club	Source	Date Signed	Seasons Played	Apps	Subs	Gls
Swindon T	Eastleigh	08/08	08-09	1	18	0
Hereford U	L	09/09	09	8	0	0
Barnet	Tr	08/10	10-11	69	2	7
Coventry C	Unattached	02/14	13	6	8	0
Port Vale	Tr	07/14	14	45	1	7

MARSHALL Paul Anthony
Born: Manchester, England, 9 July, 1989 — LW
England: Youth

League Club	Source	Date Signed	Seasons Played	Apps	Subs	Gls
Manchester C	Sch	07/07				
Blackpool	L	01/09	08	1	1	0
Port Vale	L	03/09	08	13	0	1
Walsall	Tr	07/10	10	12	6	1
Rochdale	Tr	08/11	11	0	1	0
Port Vale	Droylsden	02/12	11	10	5	0

MARSHALL Peter
Born: Barrow, Cumbria, England, 2 October, 1947 — RW
Died: Barrow, Cumbria, England, June, 1996

League Club	Source	Date Signed	Seasons Played	Apps	Subs	Gls
Barrow	Holker Central OB	01/66	65-66	4	0	1

MARSHALL Peter William
Born: Worksop, Nottinghamshire, England, 5 December, 1934 — G

League Club	Source	Date Signed	Seasons Played	Apps	Subs	Gls
Scunthorpe U	Worksop T	09/54	54-56	64	-	0

MARSHALL Ralph
Born: Baillieston, Glasgow, Scotland, 30 January, 1944 — RB

League Club	Source	Date Signed	Seasons Played	Apps	Subs	Gls
Crewe Alex	Glasgow Rangers	09/64	64-66	72	1	0

MARSHALL Richard (Dickie)
Born: Hinckley, Leicestershire, England, 23 November, 1945 — RW
Died: Ontario, Canada, 15 March, 1992

League Club	Source	Date Signed	Seasons Played	Apps	Subs	Gls
Leicester C	App	08/63				
Southport	Tr	07/65	65-66	29	2	7

MARSHALL Roy Cyril
Born: Fulham, W London, England, 22 May, 1932 — G
Died: Brighton, England, November, 2002

League Club	Source	Date Signed	Seasons Played	Apps	Subs	Gls
Brighton & HA	Jnr	06/50				
Aldershot	Tr	08/57	57-60	34	-	0

MARSHALL Scott Roderick
Born: Edinburgh, Scotland, 1 May, 1973 — CD
Scotland: U21-5/Youth

League Club	Source	Date Signed	Seasons Played	Apps	Subs	Gls
Arsenal	YT	03/91	92-97	19	5	1
Rotherham U	L	12/93	93	10	0	1
Sheffield U	L	08/94	94	17	0	0
Southampton	Tr	08/98	98	2	0	0
Brentford	Tr	10/99	99-02	73	2	3
Wycombe W	Tr	11/03	03	8	0	0

MARSHALL Shaun Andrew
Born: Fakenham, Norfolk, England, 3 October, 1978 — G

League Club	Source	Date Signed	Seasons Played	Apps	Subs	Gls
Cambridge U	YT	02/97	96-04	150	5	0
Notts Co	Tr	08/05	05	1	0	0

MARSHALL Stanley Kenneth (Stan)
Born: Goole, East Riding of Yorkshire, England, 20 April, 1946 — F

League Club	Source	Date Signed	Seasons Played	Apps	Subs	Gls
Middlesbrough	Goole T	08/63	65	2	0	0
Notts Co	Tr	06/66	66-67	43	6	17

MARSHALL Terence William James (Terry)
Born: Whitechapel, Central London, England, 26 December, 1935 — RW

League Club	Source	Date Signed	Seasons Played	Apps	Subs	Gls
Newcastle U	Wisbech T	12/58	58-60	5	-	1

MARSHALL William Forsyth (Willie)
Born: Rutherglen, Glasgow, Scotland, 9 May, 1933 — CF

League Club	Source	Date Signed	Seasons Played	Apps	Subs	Gls
Bradford C	Rutherglen Glencairn	01/57	56-58	33	-	16
Swindon T	Tr	02/59	58-59	30	-	12

MARSHALL William Frederick (Billy)
Born: Belfast, Northern Ireland, 11 July, 1936 — FB
Died: Hartlepool, Cleveland, England, 20 April, 2007
Northern Ireland: B-2

League Club	Source	Date Signed	Seasons Played	Apps	Subs	Gls
Burnley	Distillery	10/53	59-60	6	-	0
Oldham Ath	Tr	08/62	62-63	57	-	0
Hartlepool U	Tr	08/64	64-65	57	0	0

MARSLAND Gordon
Born: Blackpool, Lancashire, England, 20 March, 1945 — LH/RB
Died: Blackpool, Lancashire, England, 4 January, 2009

League Club	Source	Date Signed	Seasons Played	Apps	Subs	Gls
Blackpool	App	05/62				
Carlisle U	Tr	06/65	65-68	63	2	4
Bristol Rov	Tr	06/69	69	16	0	1
Crewe Alex	L	09/70	70	5	0	0
Oldham Ath	L	03/71	70	1	3	0

MARSTON James Edward (Joe)
Born: Sydney, Australia, 7 January, 1926 — CH
England: FLge-1

League Club	Source	Date Signed	Seasons Played	Apps	Subs	Gls
Preston NE	Leichhardt (AUS)	02/50	50-54	185	-	0

MARSTON Maurice
Born: Trimdon, County Durham, England, 24 March, 1929 — FB
Died: Kettering, Northamptonshire, England, 28 January, 2002

League Club	Source	Date Signed	Seasons Played	Apps	Subs	Gls
Sunderland	Silksworth Jnrs	06/49	51-52	9	-	0
Northampton T	Tr	07/53	53-56	149	-	2

MARTEINSSON Petur Haflidi
Born: Reykjavik, Iceland, 14 July, 1973 — M/D
Iceland: 36/U21-19/Youth

League Club	Source	Date Signed	Seasons Played	Apps	Subs	Gls
Stoke C	Stabaek IF (NOR)	01/02	01-03	12	6	2

MARTIN Aaron
Born: Cowes, Isle of Wight, England, 29 September, 1989 — CD
England: Schools

League Club	Source	Date Signed	Seasons Played	Apps	Subs	Gls
Southampton	Eastleigh	11/09	09-11	13	7	1
Crystal Palace	L	07/12	12	3	1	0
Coventry C	L	02/13	12	12	0	0
Birmingham C	Tr	01/14	13	6	2	0
Yeovil T	Tr	06/14	14	12	0	3
Coventry C	Tr	10/14	14	26	1	0

MARTIN Alan Andrew
Born: Glasgow, Scotland, 1 January, 1989 — G
Scotland: U21-10

League Club	Source	Date Signed	Seasons Played	Apps	Subs	Gls
Leeds U	Motherwell	08/07				
Accrington Stan	L	07/09	09	7	0	0
Crewe Alex	Ayr U	07/11	12-13	32	1	0

MARTIN Alvin Edward
Born: Bootle, Merseyside, England, 29 July, 1958 — CD
England: 17/B-2/Youth

League Club	Source	Date Signed	Seasons Played	Apps	Subs	Gls
West Ham U	App	07/76	77-95	462	7	27
Leyton Orient	Tr	06/96	96	16	1	0

MARTIN Andrew Peter (Andy)
Born: Cardiff, Wales, 28 February, 1980 — F
Wales: U21-1/Youth

League Club	Source	Date Signed	Seasons Played	Apps	Subs	Gls
Crystal Palace	YT	02/97	98-99	12	10	2
Torquay U	Tr	03/02	01	5	0	0

MARTIN Barrie
Born: Birmingham, England, 29 September, 1935 — LB

League Club	Source	Date Signed	Seasons Played	Apps	Subs	Gls
Blackpool	Highfield YC	12/53	57-63	189	-	1
Oldham Ath	Tr	08/64	64	42	-	4
Tranmere Rov	Tr	06/65	65-67	99	4	0

MARTIN Carl Clarke
Born: Camden, N London, England, 24 October, 1986 — D

League Club	Source	Date Signed	Seasons Played	Apps	Subs	Gls
Crewe Alex	Wealdstone	10/09	09-11	27	8	1

MARTIN Christopher Hugh (Chris)
Born: Beccles, Suffolk, England, 4 November, 1988 — F
England: Youth//Scotland: 5

League Club	Source	Date Signed	Seasons Played	Apps	Subs	Gls
Norwich C	Sch	04/07	06-12	76	26	25
Luton T	L	08/08	08	39	1	11
Crystal Palace	L	11/11	11	20	6	7
Swindon T	L	11/12	12	6	6	1
Derby Co	Tr	02/13	12-14	87	5	40

MARTIN Christopher Joseph (Chris)
Born: Mansfield, Nottinghamshire, England, 21 July, 1990 — G

League Club	Source	Date Signed	Seasons Played	Apps	Subs	Gls
Port Vale	Sch	05/08	07-11	71	3	0

MARTIN Cornelius Joseph (Con)
Born: Dublin, Republic of Ireland, 20 March, 1923 — CH/G
Died: Rush, County Dublin, Republic of Ireland, 24 April, 2013
Republic of Ireland: 30//Northern Ireland: 6

League Club	Source	Date Signed	Seasons Played	Apps	Subs	Gls
Leeds U	Glentoran	01/47	46-48	47	-	1
Aston Villa	Tr	10/48	48-55	194	-	1

MARTIN Daniel Ashley (Dan)
Born: Derby, England, 24 September, 1986 — M

League Club	Source	Date Signed	Seasons Played	Apps	Subs	Gls
Derby Co	Sch	09/04				
Notts Co	Tr	07/05	05-06	28	23	8
Mansfield T	Tr	07/07	07	21	5	0

MARTIN David (Dave)
Born: East Ham, E London, England, 25 April, 1963 — M/D
England: Youth

League Club	Source	Date Signed	Seasons Played	Apps	Subs	Gls
Millwall	App	05/80	79-84	131	9	6
Wimbledon	Tr	09/84	84-85	30	6	3
Southend U	Tr	08/86	86-92	212	9	20
Bristol C	Tr	07/93	93-94	36	2	1
Northampton T	L	02/95	94	7	0	1
Gillingham	Tr	08/95	95	27	4	1
Leyton Orient	Tr	07/96	96	8	0	0
Northampton T	Tr	11/96	96	10	2	0
Brighton & HA	L	03/97	96	1	0	0

MARTIN David Edward
Born: Romford, E London, England, 22 January, 1986 — G
England: Youth

League Club	Source	Date Signed	Seasons Played	Apps	Subs	Gls
Wimbledon	Sch	01/04	03	2	0	0
MK Dons	Wimbledon relocation	07/04	04	15	0	0
Liverpool	Tr	01/06				
Accrington Stan	L	01/07	06	10	0	0
Leicester C	L	08/08	08	25	0	0
Tranmere Rov	L	10/09	09	3	0	0
Derby Co	L	03/10	09	2	0	0
MK Dons	Tr	07/10	10-14	199	0	0

MARTIN David John (Dave)
Born: Erith, SE London, England, 3 June, 1985 — LW

League Club	Source	Date Signed	Seasons Played	Apps	Subs	Gls
Crystal Palace	Dartford	01/07	06-07	2	12	0
Millwall	Tr	01/08	07-09	60	15	9
Derby Co	Tr	02/10	09-10	2	11	1
Notts Co	L	01/11	10	7	3	0
Walsall	L	09/11	11	4	0	0
Southend U	Tr	01/12	11-12	21	10	4
Luton T	Tr	01/13				
Stevenage	Tr	02/15	14	9	1	1

MARTIN Dean Edward
Born: Islington, N London, England, 31 August, 1972 — F/M

League Club	Source	Date Signed	Seasons Played	Apps	Subs	Gls
West Ham U	Fisher Ath	06/91	91	1	1	0
Colchester U	L	12/92	92	8	0	2
Brentford	KA Akureyri (ICE)	10/95	95	14	5	1

MARTIN Dean Stacey
Born: Halifax, West Yorkshire, England, 9 September, 1967 — M

League Club	Source	Date Signed	Seasons Played	Apps	Subs	Gls
Halifax T	App	09/85	86-90	149	4	7
Scunthorpe U	Tr	07/91	91-94	100	6	7
Rochdale	Tr	01/95	94-96	45	8	0

MARTIN Dennis Victor
Born: Eastleigh, Hampshire, England, 8 November, 1928 — LH
Died: Poole, Dorset, England, February, 2008

League Club	Source	Date Signed	Seasons Played	Apps	Subs	Gls
Bournemouth	Jnr	08/47	48-53	23	-	0

MARTIN Dennis William
Born: Edinburgh, Scotland, 27 October, 1947 — W/M

League Club	Source	Date Signed	Seasons Played	Apps	Subs	Gls
West Bromwich A	Kettering T	07/67	67-69	14	2	1
Carlisle U	Tr	07/70	70-77	271	4	48
Newcastle U	Tr	10/77	77	9	2	2
Mansfield T	Tr	03/78	77-78	46	0	3

MARTIN Donnan (Don)
Born: Corby, Northamptonshire, England, 15 February, 1944 — F
Died: Wellington, Somerset, England, 14 November, 2009
England: Youth

League Club	Source	Date Signed	Seasons Played	Apps	Subs	Gls
Northampton T	Jnr	07/62	62-67	136	0	52
Blackburn Rov	Tr	02/68	67-75	218	6	57
Northampton T	Tr	11/75	75-77	77	15	17

MARTIN Edward (Eddie)
Born: Baillieston, Glasgow, Scotland, 30 March, 1921 — IF

League Club	Source	Date Signed	Seasons Played	Apps	Subs	Gls
Accrington Stan	Alloa Ath	08/50	50	2	-	0

MARTIN Eliot James
Born: Plumstead, SE London, England, 27 September, 1972 — LB

League Club	Source	Date Signed	Seasons Played	Apps	Subs	Gls
Gillingham	YT	05/91	91-93	52	1	1
Gillingham	Chelmsford C	03/95	94	7	0	0

MARTIN Eric
Born: Perth, Scotland, 31 March, 1946 — G

League Club	Source	Date Signed	Seasons Played	Apps	Subs	Gls
Southampton	Dunfermline Ath	03/67	66-74	248	0	0

MARTIN Frederick (Fred)
Born: Nottingham, England, 13 December, 1925 — CF

League Club	Source	Date Signed	Seasons Played	Apps	Subs	Gls
Nottingham F	Cinderhill Colliery	10/44	47-48	5	-	0

MARTIN Frederick John (Fred)
Born: Nottingham, England, 14 April, 1925 — WH

League Club	Source	Date Signed	Seasons Played	Apps	Subs	Gls
Blackburn Rov	Sutton T	12/49				
Accrington Stan	Tr	07/50	50-51	64	-	0

MARTIN Geoffrey (Geoff)
Born: Tupton, Derbyshire, England, 9 March, 1940 — LW

League Club	Source	Date Signed	Seasons Played	Apps	Subs	Gls
Chesterfield	Parkhouse Colliery	10/58	58	2	-	0
Leeds U	Tr	05/60				
Darlington	Tr	07/61	61	20	-	6
Carlisle U	Tr	05/62	61-62	15	-	2
Workington	Tr	12/62	62-66	144	0	24
Grimsby T	Tr	11/66	66-67	71	0	5
Chesterfield	Tr	07/68	68-69	43	0	2

MARTIN Harold John
Born: Blackburn, Greater Manchester, England, 15 March, 1955 — D/M

League Club	Source	Date Signed	Seasons Played	Apps	Subs	Gls
Bolton W		11/73				
Rochdale	Tr	07/74	74	11	2	0

MARTIN Jae Andrew
Born: Hampstead, NW London, England, 5 February, 1976 — W

League Club	Source	Date Signed	Seasons Played	Apps	Subs	Gls
Southend U	YT	05/93	93-94	1	7	0
Leyton Orient	L	09/94	94	1	3	0
Birmingham C	Tr	07/95	95	1	6	0
Lincoln C	Tr	08/96	96-97	29	12	5
Peterborough U	Tr	07/98	98-99	7	12	1

MARTIN James
Born: Glasgow, Scotland, 3 March, 1937 — LW
Died: Glasgow, Scotland, 10 September, 1994

League Club	Source	Date Signed	Seasons Played	Apps	Subs	Gls
Nottingham F	Baillieston Jnrs	06/58	58	1	-	0

MARTIN James Caird (Jimmy)
Born: Dundee, Scotland, 27 May, 1938 — CF

League Club	Source	Date Signed	Seasons Played	Apps	Subs	Gls
Blackpool	Evenwood T	12/61				
Reading	Tr	06/62	62-63	22	-	6

MARTIN John (Johnny)
Born: Ashington, Northumberland, England, 4 December, 1946 — LW
Died: Tenerife, Spain, 16 November, 2013

League Club	Source	Date Signed	Seasons Played	Apps	Subs	Gls
Aston Villa	App	07/64	64	1	-	0
Colchester U	Tr	05/66	66-68	77	1	11
Workington	Chelmsford C	07/69	69-73	206	2	32
Southport	Tr	08/74	74-75	54	9	7

MARTIN John (Johnny)
Born: Bethnal Green, E London, England, 15 July, 1981 M

League Club	Source	Date Signed	Seasons Played	Apps	Subs	Gls
Leyton Orient	YT	08/98	97-02	74	18	5

MARTIN John Alan (Alan)
Born: Burslem, Potteries, England, 23 November, 1923 IF/WH
Died: Stoke-on-Trent, England, June, 2005

League Club	Source	Date Signed	Seasons Played	Apps	Subs	Gls
Port Vale	Nettlebank Villa	12/42	46-51	169	-	28
Stoke C	Tr	09/51	51-54	104	-	6
Port Vale	Bangor C	07/57	57-58	19	-	0

MARTIN John Grieve
Born: Dundee, Scotland, 20 August, 1935 RB

League Club	Source	Date Signed	Seasons Played	Apps	Subs	Gls
Sheffield Wed	Dundee North End	02/54	54-60	63	-	0
Rochdale	Tr	06/62	62-63	24	-	1

MARTIN John Rowland (Jackie)
Born: Hamstead, West Midlands, England, 5 August, 1914 IF
Died: Hednesford, Staffordshire, England, 3 March, 1996
England: War-2

League Club	Source	Date Signed	Seasons Played	Apps	Subs	Gls
Aston Villa	Hednesford T	01/36	36-48	81	-	22

MARTIN Joseph John (Joe)
Born: Dagenham, E London, England, 29 November, 1988 LB
England: Youth

League Club	Source	Date Signed	Seasons Played	Apps	Subs	Gls
Tottenham H	Sch	12/05				
Blackpool	Tr	03/08	07-09	15	7	0
Gillingham	Tr	12/10	10-14	150	11	8

MARTIN Kevin
Born: Bromsgrove, Worcestershire, England, 22 June, 1976 G

League Club	Source	Date Signed	Seasons Played	Apps	Subs	Gls
Scarborough	YT	07/95	94-97	23	0	0

MARTIN Lee Andrew
Born: Hyde, Greater Manchester, England, 5 February, 1968 LB
England: U21-2

League Club	Source	Date Signed	Seasons Played	Apps	Subs	Gls
Manchester U	App	05/86	87-93	56	17	1
Bristol Rov	Glasgow Celtic	08/96	96	25	0	0
Huddersfield T	L	09/97	97	2	1	0

MARTIN Lee Brendan
Born: Huddersfield, West Yorkshire, England, 9 September, 1968 G
England: Schools

League Club	Source	Date Signed	Seasons Played	Apps	Subs	Gls
Huddersfield T	YT	07/87	87-91	54	0	0
Blackpool	Tr	07/92	92-94	98	0	0
Rochdale	Tr	11/96				
Halifax T	Tr	08/97	98	37	0	0
Macclesfield T	Tr	07/99	99-02	52	1	0

MARTIN Lee Robert
Born: Taunton, Somerset, England, 9 February, 1987 LM
England: Youth

League Club	Source	Date Signed	Seasons Played	Apps	Subs	Gls
Manchester U	Sch	02/05	08	1	0	0
Stoke C	L	01/07	06	4	9	1
Plymouth Arg	L	10/07	07	10	2	2
Sheffield U	L	01/08	07	5	1	0
Nottingham F	L	08/08	08	9	4	1
Ipswich T	Tr	07/09	09-12	85	15	6
Charlton Ath	L	08/10	10	14	6	2
Millwall	Tr	07/13	13-14	38	15	2

MARTIN Lilian
Born: Valreas, Vaucluse, France, 28 May, 1971 RB

League Club	Source	Date Signed	Seasons Played	Apps	Subs	Gls
Derby Co	Olymp Marseille (FRA)	11/00	00	7	2	0

MARTIN Lionel John
Born: Ludlow, Shropshire, England, 15 May, 1947 M

League Club	Source	Date Signed	Seasons Played	Apps	Subs	Gls
Aston Villa	App	07/64	66-71	36	11	4
Doncaster Rov	L	03/71	70	2	0	0

MARTIN Malaury
Born: Nice, France, 25 August, 1988 M
France: U21-1/Youth

League Club	Source	Date Signed	Seasons Played	Apps	Subs	Gls
Blackpool	AS Monaco (FRA)	08/10				
Middlesbrough	Tr	07/11	11	0	15	3

MARTIN Michael Paul (Mick)
Born: Dublin, Republic of Ireland, 9 July, 1951 M
Republic of Ireland: 51/LoI-1/U23-1/Amateur

League Club	Source	Date Signed	Seasons Played	Apps	Subs	Gls
Manchester U	Bohemians (ROI)	01/73	72-74	33	7	2
West Bromwich A	Tr	10/75	75-78	85	4	11
Newcastle U	Tr	12/78	78-82	139	8	5
Cardiff C	Willington	11/84	84	7	0	0
Peterborough U	Tr	01/85	84	13	0	0
Rotherham U	Tr	08/85	85	5	0	0
Preston NE	Tr	09/85	85	35	0	0

MARTIN Neil
Born: Tranent, East Lothian, Scotland, 20 October, 1940 CF
Scotland: 3/SLge-2/U23-1

League Club	Source	Date Signed	Seasons Played	Apps	Subs	Gls
Sunderland	Hibernian	10/65	65-67	86	0	38
Coventry C	Tr	02/68	67-70	106	0	40
Nottingham F	Tr	02/71	70-74	116	3	28
Brighton & HA	Tr	07/75	75	13	4	8
Crystal Palace	Tr	03/76	75	8	1	1

MARTIN Peter
Born: South Shields, Tyne and Wear, England, 29 December, 1950 LW

League Club	Source	Date Signed	Seasons Played	Apps	Subs	Gls
Middlesbrough	Chilton BC	06/69				
Darlington	Tr	07/71	71	3	0	0
Barnsley	Tr	10/71	71-72	18	8	6

MARTIN Raymond Barry (Ray)
Born: Coseley, West Midlands, England, 23 January, 1945 RB

League Club	Source	Date Signed	Seasons Played	Apps	Subs	Gls
Birmingham C	App	05/62	63-75	325	8	1

MARTIN Richard William
Born: Chelmsford, England, 1 September, 1987 G

League Club	Source	Date Signed	Seasons Played	Apps	Subs	Gls
Brighton & HA	Sch	09/04				
Manchester C	Tr	09/07				
Yeovil T	Tr	08/09	09	2	1	0

MARTIN Roy
Born: Kilbirnie, Ayrshire, Scotland, 16 May, 1929 LB

League Club	Source	Date Signed	Seasons Played	Apps	Subs	Gls
Birmingham C	Kilwinning Rgrs	03/50	50-55	69	-	0
Derby Co	Tr	03/56	55-59	81	-	0
Chesterfield	Tr	07/60				

MARTIN Russell Kenneth Alexander
Born: Brighton, England, 4 January, 1986 D
Scotland: 19

League Club	Source	Date Signed	Seasons Played	Apps	Subs	Gls
Wycombe W	Lewes	08/04	04-07	88	28	5
Peterborough U	Tr	07/08	08-09	54	2	1
Norwich C	Tr	11/09	09-14	206	6	12

MARTIN Thomas (Tommy)
Born: Glasgow, Scotland, 21 December, 1924 IF/RH
Died: Blantyre, Lanarkshire, Scotland, 6 August, 1996

League Club	Source	Date Signed	Seasons Played	Apps	Subs	Gls
Doncaster Rov	Stirling A	07/50	50-52	71	-	9
Nottingham F	Tr	11/52	52-54	48	-	4
Hull C	Tr	06/55	55-56	32	-	2

MARTIN Wayne Lawrence
Born: Basildon, England, 16 December, 1965 FB

League Club	Source	Date Signed	Seasons Played	Apps	Subs	Gls
Crystal Palace	App	07/82	83	1	0	0

MARTINDALE David (Dave)
Born: Liverpool, England, 9 April, 1964 M

League Club	Source	Date Signed	Seasons Played	Apps	Subs	Gls
Tranmere Rov	Caernarfon T	07/87	87-93	128	38	9

MARTINDALE Gary
Born: Liverpool, England, 24 June, 1971 F

League Club	Source	Date Signed	Seasons Played	Apps	Subs	Gls
Bolton W	Burscough	03/94				
Peterborough U	Tr	07/95	95	26	5	15
Notts Co	Tr	03/96	95-97	34	32	13
Mansfield T	L	02/97	96	5	0	2
Rotherham U	Tr	03/98	97-99	17	10	6

MARTINDALE Leonard (Len)
Born: Bolton, Greater Manchester, England, 30 June, 1920 WH
Died: Chorley, Lancashire, England, 9 October, 1971

League Club	Source	Date Signed	Seasons Played	Apps	Subs	Gls
Burnley	Jnr	07/37	37-50	69	-	2
Accrington Stan	Tr	12/51	51	16	-	0

MARTINEZ Angel
Born: Girona, Spain, 31 January, 1986 M
Spain: U21-3/Youth

League Club	Source	Date Signed	Seasons Played	Apps	Subs	Gls
Blackpool	Girona (SPN)	08/11	11-13	45	17	1
Millwall	Tr	09/14	14	4	0	0

MARTINEZ Damian Emiliano
Born: Mar del Plata, Argentina, 2 September, 1992 G
Argentina: Youth

League Club	Source	Date Signed	Seasons Played	Apps	Subs	Gls
Arsenal	Independiente (ARG)	09/10	14	3	1	0
Oxford U	L	05/12	11	1	0	0
Sheffield Wed	L	10/13	13	11	0	0
Rotherham U	L	03/15	14	8	0	0

MARTINEZ Eugene
Born: Chelmsford, England, 6 July, 1957 LW

League Club	Source	Date Signed	Seasons Played	Apps	Subs	Gls
Bradford C	Harrogate Railway Ath	07/77	77-79	38	14	5
Rochdale	Tr	07/80	80-82	110	6	16
Newport Co	Tr	08/83	83	18	2	1
Northampton T	L	02/84	83	12	0	2

MARTINEZ Jairo Manfredo
Born: La Ceiba, Honduras, 14 May, 1978 F

League Club	Source	Date Signed	Seasons Played	Apps	Subs	Gls
Honduras: 38						
Coventry C	CD Motagua (HON)	10/00	01	5	6	3
MARTINEZ Roberto						
Born: Balaguer , Spain, 13 July, 1973						M
Wigan Ath	CF Balaguer (SPN)	07/95	95-00	148	39	17
Walsall	Motherwell	08/02	02	1	5	0
Swansea C	Tr	01/03	02-05	111	11	4
Chester C	Tr	07/06	06	31	0	3
MARTINEZ Williams Guillermo						
Born: Montevideo, Uruguay, 18 December, 1982						CD
Uruguay: 1						
West Bromwich A (L)	Defensor (UGY)	01/06	05	1	1	1
MARTINS Obafemi Akinwunmi (Oba)						
Born: Lagos, Nigeria, 28 October, 1984						F
Nigeria: 39						
Newcastle U	Inter Milan (ITA)	08/06	06-08	76	12	28
Birmingham C (L)	Rubin Kazan (RUS)	01/11	10	3	1	0
MARTIS Shelton						
Born: Willemstad, Curacao, Netherlands Antilles, 29 November, 1982						CD
Netherlands Antilles: 3						
Darlington	Eindhoven FC (NED)	08/05	05	41	1	2
West Bromwich A	Hibernian	07/07	07-09	18	4	2
Scunthorpe U	L	01/08	07	3	0	0
Doncaster Rov	L	10/08	08	5	0	1
Doncaster Rov	Tr	02/10	09-12	54	10	2
MARTOT David						
Born: Fecamp, France, 1 February, 1981						RW
Brighton & HA (L)	Le Havre (FRA)	08/07	07	17	9	1
MARTYN Antony Nigel (Nigel)						
Born: St Austell, Cornwall, England, 11 August, 1966						G
England: 23/B-6/U21-11						
Bristol Rov	St Blazey	08/87	87-89	101	0	0
Crystal Palace	Tr	11/89	89-95	272	0	0
Leeds U	Tr	07/96	96-01	207	0	0
Everton	Tr	09/03	03-05	85	1	0
MARUSTIK Christopher (Chris)						
Born: Swansea, Wales, 10 August, 1961						M/FB
Died: Morriston, Swansea, Wales, 12 August, 2015						
Wales: 6/U21-7/Schools						
Swansea C	App	08/78	78-85	143	9	11
Cardiff C	Tr	10/85	85-86	43	5	1
MARVEAUX Sylvain						
Born: Vannes, France, 15 April, 1986						M
France: U21-11						
Newcastle U	Stade Rennais (FRA)	07/11	11-13	13	25	1
MARVIN Walter						
Born: Derby, England, 6 July, 1920						CF
Died: Trafford, Greater Manchester, England, October, 1997						
Accrington Stan	Newport Co (Am)	12/46	46-47	9	-	3
MARWOOD Brian						
Born: Seaham, County Durham, England, 5 February, 1960						W
England: 1						
Hull C	App	02/78	79-83	154	4	51
Sheffield Wed	Tr	08/84	84-87	125	3	27
Arsenal	Tr	03/88	87-89	52	0	16
Sheffield U	Tr	09/90	90-91	14	8	3
Middlesbrough	L	10/91	91	3	0	0
Swindon T	Tr	03/93	92	6	5	1
Barnet	Tr	08/93	93	18	5	0
MASCARELL Omar						
Born: Tenerife, Spain, 2 February, 1993						DM
Spain: Youth						
Derby Co (L)	Real Madrid B (SPN)	08/14	14	18	5	0
MASCHERANO Javier Alejandro						
Born: Santa Fe, Argentina, 8 June, 1984						DM
Argentina: 117						
West Ham U	Corinthians (BRA)	08/06	06	3	2	0
Liverpool	Tr	01/07	06-09	90	3	1
MASEFIELD Keith Leonard						
Born: Birmingham, England, 26 February, 1957						FB
Aston Villa	App	10/74	74-76	1	3	0
MASEFIELD Paul Darren						
Born: Lichfield, Staffordshire, England, 21 October, 1970						RB
Birmingham C	YT	07/89				
Exeter C	Cheltenham T	02/92	91	1	0	0
Stockport Co	Bromsgrove Rov	08/92	92	7	0	0

League Club	Source	Date Signed	Seasons Played	Apps	Subs	Gls
Doncaster Rov	Tr	02/93	92	8	1	0
Preston NE	Tr	08/93	93	6	0	0
MASIELLO Luciano						
Born: Benevento, Italy, 2 January, 1951						W
Charlton Ath	App	01/69	69-70	6	0	0
MASINGA Philomen Raul (Phil)						
Born: Klerksdorp, South Africa, 28 June, 1969						F
South Africa: 58						
Leeds U	Mamelodi Sund'ns (RSA)	08/94	94-95	20	11	5
MASKELL Craig Dell						
Born: Aldershot, Hampshire, England, 10 April, 1968						F
Southampton	App	04/86	85-86	2	4	1
Huddersfield T	Tr	05/88	88-89	86	1	43
Reading	Tr	08/90	90-91	60	12	26
Swindon T	Tr	07/92	92-93	40	7	22
Southampton	Tr	02/94	93-95	8	9	1
Bristol C	L	12/95	95	5	0	1
Brighton & HA	Tr	03/96	95-97	68	1	20
Leyton Orient	Happy Valley (HKG)	03/98	97-98	15	8	2
MASKELL Dennis						
Born: Mountain Ash, Rhondda Cynon Taff, Wales, 16 April, 1931						LW
Watford		09/51	51	5	-	0
MASKELL Michael Richard (Mike)						
Born: Keynsham, Avon, England, 25 January, 1952						FB
Chelsea	App	02/69				
Brentford	Tr	07/70	70	1	0	0
MASKERY Christopher Paul (Chris)						
Born: Stoke-on-Trent, England, 25 September, 1964						M
Stoke C	App	09/82	82-86	82	10	3
MASON Andrew (Andy)						
Born: Stretford, Greater Manchester, England, 26 October, 1966						M
Crewe Alex	YT	08/84	84	1	1	0
MASON Andrew John (Andy)						
Born: Bolton, Greater Manchester, England, 22 November, 1974						F
Bolton W	YT	05/93				
Hull C	Tr	06/95	95-96	14	12	4
Chesterfield	Tr	03/97	96	1	1	0
Macclesfield T	Tr	08/97	97	7	5	0
MASON Christopher Joseph (Chris)						
Born: Newton Aycliffe, County Durham, England, 26 June, 1986						FB
Darlington	Sch	-	03	0	1	0
MASON Clifford Ernest (Cliff)						
Born: York, England, 27 November, 1929						LB
Died: Sheffield, England, 22 August, 2013						
Sunderland		01/50				
Darlington	Tr	07/52	52-54	107	-	0
Sheffield U	Tr	08/55	55-61	97	-	2
Leeds U	Tr	03/62	61-62	31	-	0
Scunthorpe U	Tr	02/64	63	12	-	1
Chesterfield	Tr	07/64	64	5	-	0
MASON Gary Ronald						
Born: Edinburgh, Scotland, 15 October, 1979						M
Scotland: U21-2/Schools						
Manchester C	YT	10/96	98	18	1	0
Hartlepool U	L	11/99	99	5	1	0
MASON George William						
Born: Birmingham, England, 5 September, 1913						CH
Died: Coventry, England, 12 August, 1993						
England: Schools/War-2						
Coventry C	Redhill Amats	11/31	31-51	330	-	6
MASON James (Jimmy)						
Born: Glasgow, Scotland, 17 April, 1933						LW/LH
Accrington Stan	Dundee	06/55	55-56	14	-	1
Chester C	Tr	06/57	57-58	64	-	7
Crystal Palace	Chelmsford C	05/60				
MASON John Francis						
Born: Birmingham, England, 23 January, 1943						F
England: Amateur-1						
Peterborough U	Alvechurch	05/66	66-67	37	0	18
MASON Joseph (Joe)						
Born: Plymouth, England, 13 May, 1991						F
Republic of Ireland: U21-3/Youth						
Plymouth Arg	Sch	07/09	09-10	31	22	10
Cardiff C	Tr	07/11	11-14	40	34	16
Bolton W	L	11/13	13	5	3	1

League Club	Source	Date Signed	Seasons Played	Apps	Subs	Gls
Bolton W	L	02/14	13	7	1	5
Bolton W	L	08/14	14	9	3	4
MASON Keith Michael						
Born: Leicester, England, 19 July, 1958						G
Huddersfield T	Enderby T	07/82	82-85	30	0	0
MASON Maurice						
Born: Sedgefield, County Durham, England, 25 June, 1927						WH
Died: County Durham, England, June, 2008						
Huddersfield T		01/48				
Darlington	Blackhall CW	07/52	52	3	-	0
MASON Michael Barry (Mike)						
Born: Bloxwich, West Midlands, England, 20 October, 1944						IF
Walsall	App	09/62	63	4	-	0
West Bromwich A	Tr	07/64				
MASON Paul David						
Born: Liverpool, England, 3 September, 1963						M
Ipswich T	Aberdeen	06/93	93-97	103	10	25
MASON Richard James (Dick)						
Born: Arley, Warwickshire, England, 2 April, 1918						LB
Died: Nuneaton, Warwickshire, England, November, 1992						
Coventry C	Nuneaton Bor	05/46	46-53	253	-	2
MASON Robert Henry (Bobby)						
Born: Tipton, West Midlands, England, 22 March, 1936						IF
Wolverhampton W	Jnr	05/53	55-61	143	-	44
Leyton Orient	Chelmsford C	03/63	62-63	23	-	0
MASON Ryan Glen						
Born: Enfield, N London, England, 13 June, 1991						M
England: 1/Youth						
Tottenham H	Sch	08/08	14	29	2	1
Yeovil T	L	07/09	09	26	2	6
Doncaster Rov	L	08/10	10	5	10	0
Doncaster Rov	L	07/11	11	2	2	0
Millwall	L	01/12	11	3	2	0
Swindon T	L	07/13	13	13	5	5
MASON Stuart James						
Born: Whitchurch, Shropshire, England, 2 June, 1948						D
Died: Wrexham, Wales, 5 February, 2006						
England: Youth						
Wrexham	Jnr	07/66	65-66	28	0	0
Liverpool	Tr	10/66				
Doncaster Rov	L	11/67	67	1	0	0
Wrexham	Tr	06/68	68-72	144	13	3
Chester C	Tr	06/73	73-77	132	5	7
Rochdale	L	12/76	76	2	0	0
Crewe Alex	L	10/77	77	4	0	1
MASON Thomas Herbert Andrew (Tommy)						
Born: Buxton, Derbyshire, England, 20 February, 1953						M
Derby Co	App	07/72				
Brighton & HA	Tr	09/74	74	23	2	2
MASON Thomas Joseph Robert (Tom)						
Born: Fulham, W London, England, 19 June, 1960						LB
Fulham	App	01/78	77-79	6	0	0
Brighton & HA	Tr	06/81				
MASON Thomas William (Tom)						
Born: Hartlepool, Cleveland, England, 21 April, 1925						RH
Hartlepool U	Railway Ath	05/46	46	5	-	0
MASSART David Louis (Dave)						
Born: Birmingham, England, 2 November, 1919						CF
Died: Weymouth, Dorset, England, December, 1993						
Birmingham C	Bells Ath	02/39	46	3	-	0
Walsall	Tr	06/47	47	27	-	23
Bury	Tr	03/48	47-50	85	-	44
Chesterfield	Tr	02/51	50	11	-	5
MASSEY Andrew Thomas (Andy)						
Born: New Cross, SE London, England, 20 October, 1961						M
Republic of Ireland: Youth						
Millwall	Jnr	03/79	80-83	73	15	8
Port Vale	L	03/84	83	4	0	1
Aldershot	Tr	05/84	84-85	65	6	3
MASSEY Bernard Kendrick Woolley						
Born: Ripley, Derbyshire, England, 5 November, 1920						IF/W
Died: Belper, Derbyshire, England, 27 May, 2006						
Halifax T	Peterborough U	09/38	38-50	82	-	7
MASSEY Eric						
Born: Derby, England, 11 September, 1923						LB
Died: Bury, Greater Manchester, England, 3 May, 2009						
Bury	Spartan Ath	09/46	46-56	201	-	6
MASSEY Gavin Alexander						
Born: Watford, Hertfordshire, England, 14 October, 1992						F
Watford	Sch	07/10	09-11	0	7	0
Yeovil T	L	09/11	11	8	8	3
Colchester U	L	01/12	11	2	1	0
Colchester U	L	02/12	11	2	3	0
Colchester U	Tr	08/12	12-14	95	21	16
MASSEY Kevin James						
Born: Gainsborough, Lincolnshire, England, 30 November, 1965						M
Cambridge U	App	12/83	83-85	9	7	1
MASSEY Richard						
Born: Seisdon, Staffordshire, England, 11 October, 1968						CD
Exeter C	App	07/86	85-87	22	6	1
MASSEY Robert William (Bob)						
Born: Marylebone, Central London, England, 6 April, 1940						RB
Bournemouth	Jnr	05/58	59-60	5	-	0
MASSEY Roy						
Born: Mexborough, South Yorkshire, England, 10 September, 1943						CF
England: Youth						
Rotherham U	Arsenal (Am)	07/64	64-66	15	1	6
Leyton Orient	Tr	09/67	67-68	58	5	13
Colchester U	Tr	07/69	69-70	30	4	11
MASSEY Stephen (Steve)						
Born: Manchester, England, 28 March, 1958						F
Stockport Co	App	07/75	74-77	87	14	20
Bournemouth	Tr	07/78	78-80	85	12	19
Peterborough U	Tr	08/81	81	13	5	3
Northampton T	Tr	02/82	81-82	60	0	26
Hull C	Tr	07/83	83-84	34	8	9
Cambridge U	Tr	08/85	85	28	3	11
Wrexham	Tr	07/86	86-87	38	5	10
MASSEY Stuart Anthony						
Born: Crawley, West Sussex, England, 17 November, 1964						M
Crystal Palace	Sutton U	07/92	92-93	1	1	0
Oxford U	Tr	07/94	94-97	82	21	8
MASSIE Leslie (Les)						
Born: Aberdeen, Scotland, 20 July, 1935						IF
Huddersfield T	Banks o' Dee	08/53	56-66	334	1	100
Darlington	Tr	10/66	66	20	0	2
Halifax T	Tr	06/67	67-68	89	0	40
Bradford Park Ave	Tr	08/69	69	14	0	2
Workington	Tr	12/69	69-70	62	0	15
MASSIMO Franco						
Born: Horsham, West Sussex, England, 23 September, 1968						F
Brighton & HA	App	09/86	85	0	1	0
MASSON Donald Sandison (Don)						
Born: Banchory, Aberdeenshire, Scotland, 26 August, 1946						M
Scotland: 17						
Middlesbrough	Jnr	09/63	64-67	50	3	6
Notts Co	Tr	09/68	68-74	273	0	81
Queens Park Rgrs	Tr	12/74	74-77	116	0	18
Derby Co	Tr	10/77	77	23	0	1
Notts Co	Tr	08/78	78-81	129	0	11
MASTERS Clark John						
Born: Hastings, East Sussex, England, 31 May, 1987						G
Brentford	Sch	06/06	06-07	11	1	0
Southend U	Tr	01/08				
Aldershot T	Tr	08/09	09	0	1	0
MASTERS Graham						
Born: Bristol, England, 13 August, 1931						W
Bristol C	Jnr	08/48	51	9	-	1
MASTERS Neil Bradley						
Born: Lisburn, Belfast, Northern Ireland, 25 May, 1972						LB
Northern Ireland: Youth						
Bournemouth	YT	08/90	92-93	37	1	2
Wolverhampton W	Tr	12/93	93-95	10	2	0
Gillingham	Tr	04/97	97	11	0	0
MATA Juan Manuel						
Born: Burgos, Spain, 28 April, 1988						F/W
Spain: 34/U21-20/Youth						
Chelsea	Valencia (SPN)	08/11	11-13	71	11	18
Manchester U	Tr	01/14	13-14	41	7	15

MATEJOVSKY Marek
Born: Brandys nad Labem, Czechoslovakia, 30 December, 1981 — M
Czech Republic: 15

League Club	Source	Date Signed	Seasons Played	Apps	Subs	Gls
Reading	Mlada Boleslav (CZE)	01/08	07-09	34	17	2

MATERAZZI Marco
Born: Lecce, Italy, 19 August, 1973 — CD
Italy: 41

League Club	Source	Date Signed	Seasons Played	Apps	Subs	Gls
Everton	Perugia (ITA)	07/98	98	26	1	1

MATEU Jose-Luis
Born: Castellon, Spain, 15 January, 1966 — LW

League Club	Source	Date Signed	Seasons Played	Apps	Subs	Gls
Torquay U	Castellon (SPN)	10/95	95	5	5	1

MATHER Harold (Harry)
Born: Bolton, Greater Manchester, England, 24 January, 1921 — LB
Died: Burnley, Lancashire, England, 1 March, 1999

League Club	Source	Date Signed	Seasons Played	Apps	Subs	Gls
Burnley	Jnr	05/38	46-54	301	-	0

MATHER Shaun
Born: Hereford, England, 9 September, 1965 — M

League Club	Source	Date Signed	Seasons Played	Apps	Subs	Gls
Newport Co	Presteigne	08/83	83	0	1	0

MATHEWS Francis John (Frank)
Born: London, England, 7 January, 1948 — FB

League Club	Source	Date Signed	Seasons Played	Apps	Subs	Gls
Southend U	App	01/66	65-67	20	6	0
Torquay U	Tr	06/68	68	6	1	0

MATHIAS Raymond (Ray)
Born: Liverpool, England, 13 December, 1946 — D

League Club	Source	Date Signed	Seasons Played	Apps	Subs	Gls
Tranmere Rov	App	12/64	67-84	557	10	6

MATHIE Alexander (Alex)
Born: Bathgate, West Lothian, Scotland, 20 December, 1968 — F
Scotland: Youth

League Club	Source	Date Signed	Seasons Played	Apps	Subs	Gls
Port Vale (L)	Greenock Morton	03/93	92	0	3	0
Newcastle U	Greenock Morton	07/93	93-94	3	22	4
Ipswich T	Tr	02/95	94-98	90	19	38
Preston NE (L)	Dundee U	09/99	99	5	7	2
York C	Dundee U	09/00	00-02	26	26	3

MATHIE David
Born: Motherwell, Lanarkshire, Scotland, 15 August, 1919 — CF
Died: Motherwell, Lanarkshire, Scotland, 3 January, 1954

League Club	Source	Date Signed	Seasons Played	Apps	Subs	Gls
Workington	Kilmarnock	10/53	53	2	-	0

MATIAS Pedro Manuel Miguel
Born: Madrid, Spain, 11 October, 1973 — M
Spain: U21-1

League Club	Source	Date Signed	Seasons Played	Apps	Subs	Gls
Macclesfield T	CD Logrones (SPN)	12/98	98	21	1	2
Tranmere Rov	Tr	08/99	99	1	3	0
Walsall	Tr	10/99	99-03	105	36	24
Blackpool	L	03/04	03	7	0	1
Kidderminster Hrs	Bristol Rov (NC)	11/04	04	4	1	1

MATIC Nemanja
Born: Sabac, Serbia, 1 August, 1988 — DM
Serbia: 21/U21-11

League Club	Source	Date Signed	Seasons Played	Apps	Subs	Gls
Chelsea	MFK Kosice (SVK)	08/09	09	0	2	0
Chelsea	Benfica (POR)	01/14	13-14	50	3	1

MATIER Gerald (Gerry)
Born: Lisburn, Belfast, Northern Ireland, 1 December, 1912 — G
Died: Lisburn, Belfast, Northern Ireland, 9 September, 1984
Republic of Ireland: LoI-7

League Club	Source	Date Signed	Seasons Played	Apps	Subs	Gls
Blackburn Rov	Coleraine	07/37	37-38	20	-	0
Bradford C	Glentoran	08/39				
Plymouth Arg	Tr	09/46				
Torquay U	Tr	11/46	46	17	-	0

MATRECANO Salvatore
Born: Naples, Italy, 5 October, 1970 — CD
Italy: U21

League Club	Source	Date Signed	Seasons Played	Apps	Subs	Gls
Nottingham F	Perugia (ITA)	08/99	99	11	0	0

MATT Jamille Antonio
Born: Jamaica, 2 December, 1990 — F

League Club	Source	Date Signed	Seasons Played	Apps	Subs	Gls
Fleetwood T	Kidderminster Hrs	01/13	12-13	25	14	11

MATTEO Dominic
Born: Dumfries, Scotland, 24 April, 1974 — CD
England: B-1/U21-4/Youth//Scotland: 6

League Club	Source	Date Signed	Seasons Played	Apps	Subs	Gls
Liverpool	YT	05/92	93-99	112	15	1
Sunderland	L	03/95	94	1	0	0
Leeds U	Tr	08/00	00-03	115	0	2
Blackburn Rov	Tr	06/04	04-05	31	3	0
Stoke C	Tr	01/07	06-07	23	0	1

MATTHEW Damian
Born: Islington, N London, England, 23 September, 1970 — M
England: U21-9

League Club	Source	Date Signed	Seasons Played	Apps	Subs	Gls
Chelsea	YT	06/89	89-92	13	8	0
Luton T	L	09/92	92	3	2	0
Crystal Palace	Tr	02/94	93-95	17	7	1
Bristol Rov	L	01/96	95	8	0	0
Burnley	Tr	07/96	96-97	50	9	7
Northampton T	Tr	07/98	98-99	1	1	0

MATTHEWS Adam James
Born: Gorseinon, Swansea, Wales, 13 January, 1992 — RB
Wales: 12/U21-5/Youth

League Club	Source	Date Signed	Seasons Played	Apps	Subs	Gls
Cardiff C	Sch	01/09	09-10	26	14	1

MATTHEWS David
Born: Hackney, E London, England, 20 November, 1965 — F

League Club	Source	Date Signed	Seasons Played	Apps	Subs	Gls
West Ham U	App	11/82				
Walsall	Basildon U	11/87				
Southend U	Tr	03/88	88	1	5	0

MATTHEWS David Ivor (Dai)
Born: Pontygwaith, Rhondda Cynon Taff, Wales, 24 September, 1921 — G
Died: Pontypridd, Rhondda Cynon Taff, Wales, 7 March, 1986

League Club	Source	Date Signed	Seasons Played	Apps	Subs	Gls
Cardiff C		09/47				
Newport Co	Tr	04/48	48	6	-	0

MATTHEWS George Terence Leonard (Terry)
Born: Leyton, NE London, England, 25 February, 1936 — IF

League Club	Source	Date Signed	Seasons Played	Apps	Subs	Gls
West Ham U	Jnr	02/53	55	9	-	1
Aldershot	Tr	07/57	57-61	62	-	20
Gillingham	Tr	08/62	62	10	-	1

MATTHEWS Graham
Born: Newcastle-under-Lyme, Potteries, England, 2 November, 1942 — IF

League Club	Source	Date Signed	Seasons Played	Apps	Subs	Gls
Stoke C	Jnr	11/59	60-62	16	-	3
Walsall	Tr	08/63	63-64	67	-	21
Crewe Alex	Tr	08/65	65-67	56	2	19

MATTHEWS Jason Lee
Born: Paulton, Somerset, England, 13 March, 1975 — G

League Club	Source	Date Signed	Seasons Played	Apps	Subs	Gls
Exeter C	Taunton T	08/99	99	11	1	0

MATTHEWS John Barry (Barry)
Born: Sheffield, England, 18 January, 1926 — LW
Died: Corby, Northamptonshire, England, 6 May, 1995

League Club	Source	Date Signed	Seasons Played	Apps	Subs	Gls
Lincoln C (Am)	Sheffield U (Am)	10/49	49	2	-	0

MATTHEWS John Keith (Keith)
Born: Wrexham, Wales, 7 March, 1934 — W
Died: Wrexham, Wales, January, 2008

League Club	Source	Date Signed	Seasons Played	Apps	Subs	Gls
Wrexham	Llay U	12/52	52-54	9	-	0

MATTHEWS John Melvin
Born: Camden, N London, England, 1 November, 1955 — M/D

League Club	Source	Date Signed	Seasons Played	Apps	Subs	Gls
Arsenal	App	08/73	74-77	38	7	2
Sheffield U	Tr	08/78	78-81	98	5	14
Mansfield T	Tr	08/82	82-83	70	2	6
Chesterfield	Tr	08/84	84	38	0	1
Plymouth Arg	Tr	08/85	85-88	131	4	4
Torquay U	Tr	07/89	89	22	3	0

MATTHEWS Lee Joseph
Born: Middlesbrough, England, 16 January, 1979 — F
England: Youth

League Club	Source	Date Signed	Seasons Played	Apps	Subs	Gls
Leeds U	YT	02/96	97	0	3	0
Notts Co	L	09/98	98	4	1	0
Gillingham	L	03/00	99	2	3	0
Bristol C	Tr	03/01	00-03	14	29	9
Darlington	L	12/03	03	6	0	1
Bristol Rov	L	01/04	03	9	0	0
Yeovil T	L	03/04	03	2	2	0
Port Vale	Tr	07/04	04-05	21	13	10
Crewe Alex	Tr	08/06	06	0	10	0

MATTHEWS Mark
Born: Reading, England, 17 September, 1961 — M

League Club	Source	Date Signed	Seasons Played	Apps	Subs	Gls
Reading		07/81	81-83	5	3	1

MATTHEWS Michael (Mike)
Born: Hull, England, 25 September, 1960 — M

League Club	Source	Date Signed	Seasons Played	Apps	Subs	Gls
Wolverhampton W	App	10/78	80-83	72	4	7
Scunthorpe U	Tr	02/84	83-85	56	2	5
Halifax T	North Ferriby U	09/86	86-88	98	1	8
Scarborough	Tr	12/88	88	7	0	1
Stockport Co	Tr	02/89	88-89	35	0	3
Scarborough	Tr	12/89	89-90	64	2	3
Hull C	Tr	08/91	91	10	6	2
Halifax T	Tr	08/92	92	23	0	2

MATTHEWS Neil
Born: Grimsby, North Lincolnshire, England, 19 September, 1966 — F

League Club	Source	Date Signed	Seasons Played	Apps	Subs	Gls
Grimsby T	App	09/84	84-86	9	2	1
Scunthorpe U	L	11/85	85	1	0	0
Halifax T	L	10/86	86	9	0	2
Bolton W	L	03/87	86	1	0	0
Halifax T	Tr	08/87	87-89	99	6	29
Stockport Co	Tr	06/90	90-92	27	16	15
Halifax T	L	09/91	91	3	0	0
Lincoln C	Tr	12/92	92-94	69	14	20
Bury	L	12/94	94	2	0	1
MATTHEWS Neil Peter						
Born: Manchester, England, 3 December, 1967						D/M
Northern Ireland: B/U21-1/Youth						
Blackpool	App	12/85	85-89	67	9	1
Cardiff C	Tr	08/90	90-92	60	6	2
Rochdale	Tr	07/93	93-94	15	4	0
MATTHEWS Paul William						
Born: Leicester, England, 30 September, 1946						M
Leicester C	App	08/64	64-70	56	5	5
Southend U	L	09/72	72	1	0	0
Mansfield T	Tr	12/72	72-77	121	3	6
Rotherham U	Tr	10/77	77	8	0	0
Northampton T	L	03/79	78	13	1	0
MATTHEWS Reginald Derrick (Reg)						
Born: Coventry, England, 20 December, 1932						G
Died: Coventry, England, 7 October, 2001						
England: 5/B-2/FLge-2/U23-4						
Coventry C	Jnr	05/50	52-56	111	-	0
Chelsea	Tr	11/56	56-60	135	-	0
Derby Co	Tr	10/61	61-67	225	0	0
MATTHEWS Robert David (Rob)						
Born: Slough, Berkshire, England, 14 October, 1970						W
England: Schools						
Notts Co	Loughborough Univ	03/92	91-94	23	20	11
Luton T	Tr	03/95	94	6	5	0
York C	Tr	09/95	95	14	3	1
Bury	Tr	01/96	95-98	54	20	11
Stockport Co	Tr	11/98	98-00	29	9	4
Blackpool	L	12/99	99	5	1	2
Halifax T	L	02/01	00	8	0	2
Hull C	Tr	03/01	00-01	17	6	3
MATTHEWS Roy Henderson						
Born: Slough, Berkshire, England, 29 March, 1940						IF
Charlton Ath	Arbroath Victoria	04/57	59-66	160	0	46
MATTHEWS Stanley						
Born: Hanley, Potteries, England, 1 February, 1915						RW
Died: Stoke-on-Trent, England, 23 February, 2000						
England: 54/FLge-14/Schools/War-29						
Stoke C	Jnr	02/32	31-46	259	-	51
Blackpool	Tr	05/47	47-61	380	-	17
Stoke C	Tr	10/61	61-64	59	-	3
MATTHEWS Wayne John						
Born: Cardiff, Wales, 11 September, 1964						M
Cardiff C	Jnr	01/83	83	4	10	0
MATTHEWSON Reginald (Reg)						
Born: Sheffield, England, 6 August, 1939						CD
Sheffield U	Jnr	06/58	61-67	146	3	3
Fulham	Tr	02/68	67-72	156	2	1
Chester C	Tr	01/73	72-75	86	1	1
MATTHEWSON Robert (Bob)						
Born: Newcastle-upon-Tyne, England, 13 April, 1930						CD
Died: Bolton, Greater Manchester, England, November, 2000						
Bolton W	Byker YC	03/48	50-52	3	-	0
Lincoln C	Tr	06/53				
MATTHEWSON Trevor						
Born: Sheffield, England, 12 February, 1963						CD
Sheffield Wed	App	02/81	80-82	3	0	0
Newport Co	Tr	10/83	83-84	73	2	0
Stockport Co	Tr	09/85	85-86	79	1	0
Lincoln C	Tr	08/87	88	43	0	2
Birmingham C	Tr	08/89	89-92	167	1	12
Preston NE	Tr	08/93	93	12	0	1
Bury	Tr	09/94	94-95	34	0	0
Hereford U	Witton A	10/96	96	35	0	2
MATTHIAS Terence (Terry)						
Born: Wrexham, Wales, 10 November, 1949						CD
Wales: Schools						
Shrewsbury T	App	05/67	65-73	96	2	0

League Club	Source	Date Signed	Seasons Played	Apps	Subs	Gls
MATTINSON Harry						
Born: Ireby, Cumbria, England, 20 July, 1925						CH
Died: South Shields, Tyne and Wear, England, 8 June, 2001						
Middlesbrough	Sunderland (Am)	11/45	46	3	-	0
Preston NE	Tr	03/49	48-58	124	-	0
MATTIS Dwayne Antony						
Born: Huddersfield, West Yorkshire, England, 31 July, 1981						M
Republic of Ireland: U21-2/Youth						
Huddersfield T	YT	07/99	98-03	50	19	2
Bury	Tr	07/04	04-06	93	4	11
Barnsley	Tr	01/07	06-07	3	1	0
Walsall	L	09/07	07	4	0	0
Walsall	Tr	07/08	08-09	67	4	6
Chesterfield	Tr	07/10	10-11	41	4	3
Macclesfield T	Tr	01/12	11	1	0	1
MATTISON Paul Andrew						
Born: Wakefield, England, 24 April, 1973						RM
Darlington	Ferrybridge	08/94	94-95	5	12	0
MATTOCK Joseph William (Joe)						
Born: Leicester, England, 15 May, 1990						LB
England: U21-5/Youth						
Leicester C	Sch	04/07	06-08	54	12	1
West Bromwich A	Tr	08/09	09	26	3	0
Sheffield U	L	01/11	10	12	1	0
Portsmouth	L	11/11	11	7	0	0
Brighton & HA	L	01/12	11	14	1	1
Sheffield Wed	Tr	07/12	12-14	50	7	2
MATTSSON Jesper Bo						
Born: Visby, Sweden, 18 April, 1968						CD
Sweden: 1						
Nottingham F	Halmstad (SWE)	12/98	98	5	1	0
MAUCHLEN Alistair Henry (Ally)						
Born: Kilwinning, Ayrshire, Scotland, 29 June, 1960						M/RB
Leicester C	Motherwell	08/85	85-91	228	11	11
MAUGE Ronald Carlton (Ronnie)						
Born: Islington, N London, England, 10 March, 1969						DM
Trinidad & Tobago: 8						
Charlton Ath	YT	07/87				
Fulham	Tr	09/88	88-89	47	3	2
Bury	Tr	07/90	90-94	92	16	10
Plymouth Arg	Tr	07/95	95-98	119	16	14
Bristol Rov	Tr	07/99	99-01	50	3	0
MAUGHAN Wesley James (Wes)						
Born: Southampton, England, 17 February, 1939						CF
Southampton	Cowes, Isle of Wight	05/57	58-61	6	-	1
Reading	Tr	03/62	61-62	16	-	3
MAUND John Henry (Jack)						
Born: Hednesford, Staffordshire, England, 5 January, 1916						RW
Died: Hednesford, Staffordshire, England, 19 August, 1994						
Aston Villa	Hednesford T	10/34	35-37	47	-	8
Nottingham F	Tr	05/39				
Walsall	Tr	10/46	46-47	32	-	7
MAUTONE Stefano (Steve)						
Born: Myrtleford, Victoria, Australia, 10 August, 1970						G
Australia: U23-2						
West Ham U	Canberra Cosmos (AUS)	03/96	96	1	0	0
Crewe Alex	L	09/96	96	3	0	0
Reading	Tr	02/97	96-97	29	0	0
Wolverhampton W	Tr	08/99				
Crystal Palace	Tr	11/99	99	2	0	0
Gillingham	Tr	03/00	99	1	0	0
MAVRAK Darko						
Born: Mostar, Bosnia & Herzegovina, 19 January, 1969						M
Walsall	Falkenberg (SWE)	01/99	98-99	13	4	2
MAVRIAS Charalampos (Charis)						
Born: Zakynthos, Greece, 21 February, 1994						W
Greece: 5/U21-16/Youth						
Sunderland	Panathinaikos (GRE)	08/13	13	1	3	0
MAW John Rex						
Born: Scunthorpe, North Lincolnshire, England, 22 December, 1934						LB
Scunthorpe U		06/57	57	1	-	0
MAWENE Samy-Oyame (Sammy)						
Born: Caen, France, 12 November, 1984						M
Millwall	SM Caen (FRA)	08/06	06	4	0	0
MAWENE Youl						
Born: Caen, France, 16 July, 1979						CD

League Club	Source	Date Signed	Seasons Played	Apps	Subs	Gls
Derby Co	RC Lens (FRA)	08/00	00-03	54	1	1
Preston NE	Tr	08/04	04-09	164	10	8
Fleetwood T	Aberdeen	07/12	12	19	0	0

MAWER Shaun Kerry
Born: Ulceby, North Lincolnshire, England, 6 August, 1959 — RB
Died: Hull, England, 17 July, 2010

League Club	Source	Date Signed	Seasons Played	Apps	Subs	Gls
Grimsby T	App	08/77	77-79	57	3	0

MAWSON Alfie Robert John
Born: Hillingdon, W London, England, 19 January, 1994 — CD

League Club	Source	Date Signed	Seasons Played	Apps	Subs	Gls
Brentford	Sch	06/12				
Wycombe W	L	08/14	14	45	0	6

MAWSON Craig John
Born: Skipton, North Yorkshire, England, 16 May, 1979 — G

League Club	Source	Date Signed	Seasons Played	Apps	Subs	Gls
Burnley	YT	07/97				
Halifax T	Tr	02/01	00	9	0	0
Oldham Ath	Morecambe	08/04	04	3	1	0

MAWSON Joseph (Joe)
Born: Workington, Cumbria, England, 7 January, 1934 — LW
Died: Cockermouth, Cumbria, England, August, 2011

League Club	Source	Date Signed	Seasons Played	Apps	Subs	Gls
Workington (Am)		06/55	55	1	-	0

MAWSON Ronald (Ron)
Born: Bishop Auckland, County Durham, England, 16 September, 1914 — G
Died: Coventry, England, 1981

League Club	Source	Date Signed	Seasons Played	Apps	Subs	Gls
Crewe Alex	RAF Tern Hill	06/45	46-47	23	-	0
Wrexham	Tr	09/48	48	6	-	0

MAXFIELD John (Jack)
Born: Carlisle, Cumbria, England, 17 June, 1919 — RW
Died: Carlisle, Cumbria, England, 14 January, 2004

League Club	Source	Date Signed	Seasons Played	Apps	Subs	Gls
Carlisle U		08/39	46-50	26	-	4
Workington	Tr	07/51	51	13	-	4

MAXFIELD Scott
Born: Doncaster, South Yorkshire, England, 13 July, 1976 — LB

League Club	Source	Date Signed	Seasons Played	Apps	Subs	Gls
Doncaster Rov	YT	07/94	94-95	22	7	1
Hull C	Tr	03/96	95-97	23	12	0

MAXWELL Alistair Elspie (Ally)
Born: Hamilton, Lanarkshire, Scotland, 16 February, 1965 — G

League Club	Source	Date Signed	Seasons Played	Apps	Subs	Gls
Bolton W (L)	Motherwell	03/92	91	3	0	0

MAXWELL Christopher Ethan (Chris)
Born: Llandudno, Conwy, Wales, 30 July, 1990 — G
Wales: U21-16/Youth

League Club	Source	Date Signed	Seasons Played	Apps	Subs	Gls
Fleetwood T	Wrexham	05/12	13-14	64	0	0

MAXWELL Hugh
Born: Riggend, Lanarkshire, Scotland, 14 May, 1938 — IF
Died: Kidlington, Oxfordshire, England, 25 January, 2010

League Club	Source	Date Signed	Seasons Played	Apps	Subs	Gls
Bradford Park Ave	Stirling A	04/62	61-62	12	-	5

MAXWELL Jason Dean
Born: Scunthorpe, North Lincolnshire, England, 1 September, 1972 — F

League Club	Source	Date Signed	Seasons Played	Apps	Subs	Gls
Scunthorpe U	Appleby Frodingham	01/93	92	0	2	0

MAXWELL Kenneth (Ken)
Born: Glasgow, Scotland, 11 February, 1928 — FB

League Club	Source	Date Signed	Seasons Played	Apps	Subs	Gls
Northampton T	Kilmarnock	06/49	50	2	-	0
Bradford Park Ave	East Stirlingshire	11/57	57	2	-	0

MAXWELL Leyton Jonathan
Born: Dyserth, Denbighshire, Wales, 3 October, 1979 — F/M
Wales: U21-14/Youth

League Club	Source	Date Signed	Seasons Played	Apps	Subs	Gls
Liverpool	YT	07/97				
Stockport Co	L	07/00	00	8	12	2
Cardiff C	Tr	08/01	01-03	10	24	1
Swansea C	Tr	03/04	03	1	2	0
Mansfield T	Newport Co	12/04	04	1	0	0

MAXWELL Patrick (Pat)
Born: Ayr, Scotland, 10 January, 1929 — LW/CF
Died: Kilmarnock, Ayrshire, Scotland, 9 March, 2000

League Club	Source	Date Signed	Seasons Played	Apps	Subs	Gls
Chesterfield	Saltcoats Victoria	08/51	51-52	18	-	3

MAY Adam John
Born: Southampton, England, 6 December, 1997 — M

League Club	Source	Date Signed	Seasons Played	Apps	Subs	Gls
Portsmouth	Sch	-	14	0	1	0

MAY Andrew Michael Peter (Andy)
Born: Bury, Greater Manchester, England, 26 February, 1964 — M
England: U21-1/Schools

League Club	Source	Date Signed	Seasons Played	Apps	Subs	Gls
Manchester C	App	01/82	80-86	141	9	8
Huddersfield T	Tr	07/87	87-89	112	2	5
Bolton W	L	03/88	87	9	1	2
Bristol C	Tr	08/90	90-91	88	2	4
Millwall	Tr	06/92	92-94	49	5	1

MAY Benjamin Steven (Ben)
Born: Gravesend, Kent, England, 10 March, 1984 — F

League Club	Source	Date Signed	Seasons Played	Apps	Subs	Gls
Millwall	YT	05/01	02-07	43	35	14
Colchester U	L	03/03	02	4	2	0
Brentford	L	08/03	03	38	3	7
Colchester U	L	08/04	04	5	9	1
Brentford	L	12/04	04	7	3	1
Scunthorpe U	Tr	09/07	07-09	11	34	3
Stevenage	Tr	10/10	10-11	9	18	1
Barnet	L	03/12	11	9	2	4

MAY Christopher John (Chris)
Born: Wakefield, England, 2 September, 1985 — G

League Club	Source	Date Signed	Seasons Played	Apps	Subs	Gls
Brighton & HA	Sch	-	04	0	1	0

MAY Daniel William (Danny)
Born: Watford, Hertfordshire, England, 19 January, 1988 — RB/M

League Club	Source	Date Signed	Seasons Played	Apps	Subs	Gls
Northampton T	Sch	07/07	06-07	2	3	0

MAY David
Born: Oldham, Greater Manchester, England, 24 June, 1970 — CD

League Club	Source	Date Signed	Seasons Played	Apps	Subs	Gls
Blackburn Rov	YT	06/88	88-93	123	0	3
Manchester U	Tr	07/94	94-02	68	17	6
Huddersfield T	L	12/99	99	1	0	0
Burnley	Tr	08/03	03	34	1	4

MAY Donald Ivor (Don)
Born: Broseley, Shropshire, England, 31 May, 1931 — RH/IF

League Club	Source	Date Signed	Seasons Played	Apps	Subs	Gls
Bury	Broseley	03/51	51-61	134	-	11

MAY Edward Skillion (Eddie)
Born: Edinburgh, Scotland, 30 August, 1967 — M
Scotland: U21-2/Youth

League Club	Source	Date Signed	Seasons Played	Apps	Subs	Gls
Brentford	Hibernian	07/89	89-90	46	1	10

MAY Edwin Charles (Eddie)
Born: Epping, Essex, England, 19 May, 1943 — CD
Died: Barry, Vale of Glamorgan, Wales, 14 April, 2012

League Club	Source	Date Signed	Seasons Played	Apps	Subs	Gls
Southend U	Dagenham	01/65	64-67	106	4	3
Wrexham	Tr	06/68	68-75	330	4	35
Swansea C	Tr	08/76	76-77	90	0	8

MAY Gary Colin
Born: Darlington, County Durham, England, 7 May, 1967 — M

League Club	Source	Date Signed	Seasons Played	Apps	Subs	Gls
Darlington		11/86	86	1	1	0

MAY Harry
Born: Glasgow, Scotland, 15 October, 1928 — LB
Died: Frampton-on-Severn, Gloucestershire, England, 9 July, 2007

League Club	Source	Date Signed	Seasons Played	Apps	Subs	Gls
Cardiff C	Thorniewood U	08/48	49	1	-	0
Swindon T	Tr	06/50	50-51	78	-	1
Barnsley	Tr	05/52	52-54	105	-	0
Southend U	Tr	09/55	55	19	-	1

MAY Jonathan (John)
Born: Crosby, Merseyside, England, 28 January, 1960 — CD
England: Schools

League Club	Source	Date Signed	Seasons Played	Apps	Subs	Gls
Blackpool	App	11/78	78	4	0	0
Exeter C	Tr	08/80				

MAY Lawrence Charles (Larry)
Born: Sutton Coldfield, West Midlands, England, 26 December, 1958 — CD

League Club	Source	Date Signed	Seasons Played	Apps	Subs	Gls
Leicester C	App	12/76	76-82	180	7	12
Barnsley	Tr	09/83	83-86	122	0	3
Sheffield Wed	Tr	02/87	86-87	30	1	1
Brighton & HA	Tr	09/88	88	24	0	3

MAY Leroy Armstrong
Born: Wolverhampton, England, 12 August, 1969 — F
England: Semi Pro-1

League Club	Source	Date Signed	Seasons Played	Apps	Subs	Gls
Walsall	Tividale	01/92	91	1	3	0
Hereford U	Tividale	01/93	92-93	16	5	3

MAY Rory Joseph
Born: Birmingham, England, 25 November, 1984 — F

League Club	Source	Date Signed	Seasons Played	Apps	Subs	Gls
Lincoln C	Coventry C (Sch)	08/03	03	1	4	0

MAY Steven (Stevie)
Born: Newburgh, Fife, Scotland, 3 November, 1992 — F
Scotland: 1/U21-8/Youth

League Club	Source	Date Signed	Seasons Played	Apps	Subs	Gls
Sheffield Wed	St Johnstone	08/14	14	26	13	7

MAY Warren Derek
Born: Southend-on-Sea, England, 31 December, 1964 — D

League Club	Source	Date Signed	Seasons Played	Apps	Subs	Gls
Southend U	App	01/83	82-85	77	12	4

MAYBANK Edward Glen (Teddy)
Born: Lambeth, S London, England, 11 October, 1956 — F

League Club	Source	Date Signed	Seasons Played	Apps	Subs	Gls
Chelsea	App	02/74	74-76	28	0	6
Fulham	Tr	11/76	76-77	27	0	14

League Club	Source	Date Signed	Seasons Played	Apps	Subs	Gls
Brighton & HA	Tr	11/77	77-79	62	2	16
Fulham	Tr	12/79	79	19	0	3

MAYBURY Alan Paul
Born: Dublin, Republic of Ireland, 8 August, 1978 — RB
Republic of Ireland: 10/B-1/U21-8/Youth

League Club	Source	Date Signed	Seasons Played	Apps	Subs	Gls
Leeds U	St Kevins BC (ROI)	08/95	95-01	10	4	0
Reading	L	03/99	98	8	0	0
Crewe Alex	L	10/00	00	6	0	0
Leicester C	Heart of Midlothian	01/05	04-07	83	2	3
Colchester U		12/08	08-09	26	1	0

MAYE Daniel Peter Christopher (Danny)
Born: Leicester, England, 14 July, 1982 — LW

League Club	Source	Date Signed	Seasons Played	Apps	Subs	Gls
Port Vale	YT	09/01	01	0	2	0
Southend U	Tr	07/02	02	0	2	0

MAYERS Alan
Born: Delamere, Cheshire, England, 20 April, 1937 — RW

League Club	Source	Date Signed	Seasons Played	Apps	Subs	Gls
Chester C	Jnr	05/55	55	1	-	0

MAYERS Derek
Born: Liverpool, England, 24 January, 1935 — RW

League Club	Source	Date Signed	Seasons Played	Apps	Subs	Gls
Everton	Jnr	08/52	52-56	18	-	7
Preston NE	Tr	05/57	57-60	118	-	26
Leeds U	Tr	06/61	61	20	-	5
Bury	Tr	07/62	62-63	32	-	6
Wrexham	Tr	10/63	63	21	-	2

MAYES Alan Kenneth
Born: Edmonton, N London, England, 11 December, 1953 — F

League Club	Source	Date Signed	Seasons Played	Apps	Subs	Gls
Queens Park Rgrs	App	07/71				
Watford	Tr	11/74	74-78	110	23	31
Northampton T	L	01/76	75	10	0	4
Swindon T	Tr	02/79	78-80	89	0	38
Chelsea	Tr	12/80	80-82	61	5	18
Swindon T	Tr	07/83	83-84	52	10	27
Carlisle U	Tr	07/85	85	8	2	2
Newport Co	L	02/86	85	3	0	1
Blackpool	Tr	09/86	86	12	1	6

MAYFIELD Leslie (Les)
Born: Mansfield, Nottinghamshire, England, 19 January, 1926 — RB
Died: Nottinghamshire, England, March, 2014

League Club	Source	Date Signed	Seasons Played	Apps	Subs	Gls
Mansfield T	Ilkeston	09/48	49-52	34	-	0

MAYLE John Robert (Bobby)
Born: Montgomery, Powys, Wales, 18 December, 1938 — CF

League Club	Source	Date Signed	Seasons Played	Apps	Subs	Gls
Shrewsbury T	Sentinel Jnrs	05/57	57	8	-	0

MAYLETT Bradley (Brad)
Born: Manchester, England, 24 December, 1980 — RW

League Club	Source	Date Signed	Seasons Played	Apps	Subs	Gls
Burnley	YT	02/99	98-02	3	42	0
Swansea C	L	03/03	02	6	0	0
Swansea C	Tr	06/03	03-04	30	19	5
Boston U	Tr	03/05	04-06	35	33	4
Chester C	L	03/07	06	3	2	1

MAYMAN Paul Francis
Born: Crewe, Cheshire, England, 29 May, 1958 — M
England: Semi Pro-2

League Club	Source	Date Signed	Seasons Played	Apps	Subs	Gls
Crewe Alex	Jnr	07/76	75-76	42	1	3

MAYNARD Kelvin
Born: Paramaribo, Suriname, 29 May, 1987 — RB

League Club	Source	Date Signed	Seasons Played	Apps	Subs	Gls
Burton A	Royal Antwerp (BEL)	11/14	14	5	5	1

MAYNARD Michael Clements (Mike)
Born: Georgetown, Guyana, 7 January, 1947 — FB

League Club	Source	Date Signed	Seasons Played	Apps	Subs	Gls
Crystal Palace	Hounslow T	03/66				
Peterborough U	Tr	07/67	67	2	1	0

MAYNARD Nicholas David (Nicky)
Born: Winsford, Cheshire, England, 11 December, 1986 — F

League Club	Source	Date Signed	Seasons Played	Apps	Subs	Gls
Crewe Alex	Sch	06/05	05-07	52	7	31
Bristol C	Tr	08/08	08-11	111	14	45
West Ham U	Tr	01/12	11	9	5	2
Cardiff C	Tr	08/12	12-14	6	16	2
Wigan Ath	L	01/14	13	11	5	4

MAYO Joseph (Joe)
Born: Tipton, West Midlands, England, 25 May, 1952 — F

League Club	Source	Date Signed	Seasons Played	Apps	Subs	Gls
Walsall	Dudley T	09/72	72	2	5	1
West Bromwich A	Tr	02/73	73-76	67	5	16
Leyton Orient	Tr	03/77	76-81	150	5	36
Cambridge U	Tr	09/81	81-82	35	1	14
Blackpool	L	10/82	82	5	0	1

MAYO Kerry
Born: Haywards Heath, West Sussex, England, 21 September, 1977 — LB

League Club	Source	Date Signed	Seasons Played	Apps	Subs	Gls
Brighton & HA	YT	07/96	96-08	329	39	12

MAYO Paul
Born: Lincoln, England, 13 October, 1981 — LB

League Club	Source	Date Signed	Seasons Played	Apps	Subs	Gls
Lincoln C	YT	04/00	99-03	92	14	6
Watford	Tr	03/04	03-04	25	0	0
Lincoln C	Tr	06/05	05-06	53	9	4
Notts Co	Tr	07/07	07-08	37	4	0
Darlington	L	01/08	07	7	0	1

MAYOR Daniel John (Danny)
Born: Leyland, Lancashire, England, 18 October, 1990 — W

League Club	Source	Date Signed	Seasons Played	Apps	Subs	Gls
Preston NE	Sch	12/08	09-11	31	33	2
Tranmere Rov	L	03/09	08	3	0	0
Sheffield Wed	Tr	08/12	12	1	7	0
Southend U	L	02/13	12	4	1	0
Bury	Tr	07/13	13-14	73	10	13

MAYRLEB Christian
Born: Wels, Austria, 8 June, 1972 — F
Austria: 29

League Club	Source	Date Signed	Seasons Played	Apps	Subs	Gls
Sheffield Wed	FC Tirol (AUT)	01/98	97	0	3	0

MAYS Albert Edward
Born: Ynyshir, Rhondda Cynon Taff, Wales, 18 April, 1929 — RH
Died: Derby, England, 5 July, 1973

League Club	Source	Date Signed	Seasons Played	Apps	Subs	Gls
Derby Co	Jnr	05/46	49-59	272	-	21
Chesterfield	Tr	07/60	60	37	-	5

MAYUKA Emmanuel
Born: Kabwe, Zambia, 21 November, 1990 — F
Zambia: 56

League Club	Source	Date Signed	Seasons Played	Apps	Subs	Gls
Southampton	Young Boys Bern (SUI)	08/12	12-14	1	15	0

MAZZARELLI Giuseppe
Born: Uster, Zurich, Switzerland, 14 August, 1972 — D
Switzerland:

League Club	Source	Date Signed	Seasons Played	Apps	Subs	Gls
Manchester C (L)	FC Zurich (SUI)	03/96	95	0	2	0

MAZZINA Jorge Nicolas (Nicolas)
Born: Buenos Aires, Argentina, 31 January, 1979 — M
Argentina: U21/Youth

League Club	Source	Date Signed	Seasons Played	Apps	Subs	Gls
Swansea C	AC Kimberley (ARG)	08/01	01	3	0	0
York C	Tr	09/02	02	0	3	0

MAZZON Giorgio
Born: Waltham Cross, Hertfordshire, England, 4 September, 1960 — D/M

League Club	Source	Date Signed	Seasons Played	Apps	Subs	Gls
Tottenham H	Hertford T	04/79	80-82	3	1	0
Aldershot	Tr	08/83	83-88	184	11	6

MBESUMA Collins
Born: Luanshya, Zambia, 3 February, 1984 — F
Zambia: 36

League Club	Source	Date Signed	Seasons Played	Apps	Subs	Gls
Portsmouth	Kaiser Chiefs (RSA)	08/05	05	0	4	0

MBIA Stephane Stephane
Born: Yaounde, Cameroon, 20 May, 1986 — DM
Cameroon: 61

League Club	Source	Date Signed	Seasons Played	Apps	Subs	Gls
Queens Park Rgrs	Olymp Marseille (FRA)	08/12	12	29	0	0

M'BOMA Henri Patrick (Patrick)
Born: Douala, Cameroon, 15 November, 1970 — F
Cameroon: 57

League Club	Source	Date Signed	Seasons Played	Apps	Subs	Gls
Sunderland (L)	Parma (ITA)	02/02	01	5	4	1

M'BOME Herve Kingsley (Kingsley)
Born: Yaounde, Cameroon, 21 November, 1981 — M
Cameroon: Youth

League Club	Source	Date Signed	Seasons Played	Apps	Subs	Gls
Sheffield U	Saint-Etienne (FRA)	04/00				
Cambridge U	Gap (FRA)	09/04	04	12	1	1

MEACHAM Jeffrey (Jeff)
Born: Bristol, England, 6 February, 1962 — F

League Club	Source	Date Signed	Seasons Played	Apps	Subs	Gls
Bristol Rov	Trowbridge T	03/87	86-87	19	7	9

MEACHIN Paul
Born: Bebington, Wirral, England, 17 July, 1956 — F

League Club	Source	Date Signed	Seasons Played	Apps	Subs	Gls
Southport (Am)	Ashville	10/74	74	3	0	0

MEACOCK Kevin Michael
Born: Bristol, England, 16 September, 1963 — F

League Club	Source	Date Signed	Seasons Played	Apps	Subs	Gls
Cardiff C	Devizes T	12/84	84-85	20	5	3

MEAD Peter Sidney
Born: Luton, England, 9 September, 1956 — LB

League Club	Source	Date Signed	Seasons Played	Apps	Subs	Gls
Luton T	App	07/74				
Northampton T	Tr	08/77	77-78	75	1	4

MEADE Raphael Joseph
Born: Islington, N London, England, 22 November, 1962 — F

League Club	Source	Date Signed	Seasons Played	Apps	Subs	Gls
Arsenal	App	06/80	81-84	25	16	14
Luton T	Dundee U	03/89	88	2	2	0

League Club	Source	Date Signed	Seasons Played	Apps	Subs	Gls
Ipswich T	Odense BK (DEN)	01/90	89	0	1	0
Plymouth Arg	Odense BK (DEN)	01/91	90	2	3	0
Brighton & HA	Tr	08/91	91	35	5	9
Brighton & HA	Ernest Borel (HKG)	08/94	94	0	3	0

MEADES Jonathan Charles
Born: Cardiff, Wales, 2 March, 1992 M/LB
Wales: U21-4/Youth

League Club	Source	Date Signed	Seasons Played	Apps	Subs	Gls
Cardiff C	Sch	08/10				
Bournemouth	Tr	08/12				
AFC Wimbledon	L	11/12	12	26	0	1
Oxford U	Tr	05/13	14	5	2	0

MEADOWS Frank
Born: Maltby, South Yorkshire, England, 27 June, 1933 WH
Died: South Molton, Devon, England, 5 February, 2001

League Club	Source	Date Signed	Seasons Played	Apps	Subs	Gls
Rotherham U		04/52	53-55	8	-	0
Coventry C	Tr	06/56	56	8	-	0

MEADOWS James (Jimmy)
Born: Bolton, Greater Manchester, England, 21 July, 1931 W
Died: Manchester, England, 1 January, 1994
England: 1/FLge-1

League Club	Source	Date Signed	Seasons Played	Apps	Subs	Gls
Southport	Bolton YMCA	03/49	48-50	60	-	6
Manchester C	Tr	03/51	50-54	130	-	30

MEADOWS John Alfred (Johnny)
Born: Hoxton, Central London, England, 13 November, 1930 WH/IF

League Club	Source	Date Signed	Seasons Played	Apps	Subs	Gls
Watford	St Albans C	06/51	51-59	222	-	42

MEADOWS John Ronald (Ron)
Born: Lancaster, England, 4 December, 1920 G

League Club	Source	Date Signed	Seasons Played	Apps	Subs	Gls
Burnley	Glasson Dock	09/46				
Bournemouth	Tr	04/50	50-51	16	-	0
Accrington Stan	Tr	07/52	52	18	-	0

MEADOWS Robert (Bobby)
Born: Melton Mowbray, Leicestershire, England, 25 April, 1938 FB

League Club	Source	Date Signed	Seasons Played	Apps	Subs	Gls
Stoke C	Jnr	05/55				
Doncaster Rov	Northwich Victoria	12/62	62-63	43	-	0

MEAGAN John George
Born: Shap, Cumbria, England, 11 November, 1935 CH

League Club	Source	Date Signed	Seasons Played	Apps	Subs	Gls
Workington	Jnr	12/52	54	1	-	0

MEAGAN Michael Kevin (Mick)
Born: Dublin, Republic of Ireland, 29 May, 1934 LH/LB
Republic of Ireland: 17/B/LoI-2/Schools

League Club	Source	Date Signed	Seasons Played	Apps	Subs	Gls
Everton	Johnville Jnrs	09/52	57-63	165	-	1
Huddersfield T	Tr	07/64	64-67	118	1	1
Halifax T	Tr	07/68	68	23	0	0

MEAGAN Thomas Patrick (Tom)
Born: Liverpool, England, 14 November, 1959 M

League Club	Source	Date Signed	Seasons Played	Apps	Subs	Gls
Doncaster Rov	App	11/77	77-78	32	5	1
Doncaster Rov	FC Haka (FIN)	09/82	82	2	0	0

MEAKER Michael John
Born: Greenford, W London, England, 18 August, 1971 W
Wales: B-1/U21-2

League Club	Source	Date Signed	Seasons Played	Apps	Subs	Gls
Queens Park Rgrs	YT	02/90	90-94	21	13	1
Plymouth Arg	L	11/91	91	4	0	0
Reading	Tr	07/95	95-97	46	21	2
Bristol Rov	Tr	08/98	98-00	19	8	2
Swindon T	L	03/00	99	6	0	0
Plymouth Arg	Tr	02/01	00	5	6	1

MEAKIN Harry
Born: Stoke-on-Trent, England, 8 September, 1919 FB
Died: Stoke-on-Trent, England, 18 January, 1986

League Club	Source	Date Signed	Seasons Played	Apps	Subs	Gls
Stoke C	Summerbank	11/45	46-49	35	-	0

MEALAND Kenneth Barry (Barry)
Born: Carshalton, S London, England, 24 January, 1943 RB
Died: Tunbridge Wells, Kent, England, 4 April, 2013

League Club	Source	Date Signed	Seasons Played	Apps	Subs	Gls
Fulham	Jnr	10/61	61-67	28	1	0
Rotherham U	Tr	08/68	68-69	44	1	0

MEAN Scott James
Born: Crawley, West Sussex, England, 13 December, 1973 M

League Club	Source	Date Signed	Seasons Played	Apps	Subs	Gls
Bournemouth	YT	08/92	92-95	52	22	8
West Ham U	Tr	11/96	97	0	3	0
Port Vale	L	08/98	98	1	0	0
Bournemouth	Tr	07/99	99	26	6	4

MEANEY John Francis
Born: Stoke-on-Trent, England, 19 November, 1919 WH/IF
Died: Newcastle-under-Lyme, Potteries, England, 13 January, 2000

League Club	Source	Date Signed	Seasons Played	Apps	Subs	Gls
Crewe Alex	Ravensdale	03/47	46-53	284	-	37

MEANEY Terence (Terry)
Born: Stoke-on-Trent, England, 25 May, 1922 CF
Died: Stoke-on-Trent, England, September, 1999

League Club	Source	Date Signed	Seasons Played	Apps	Subs	Gls
Bury	Ravensdale	05/44	46	4	-	2
Crewe Alex	Tr	07/47	47	4	-	3

MEARA James Stephen (Jim)
Born: Hammersmith, W London, England, 7 October, 1972 M

League Club	Source	Date Signed	Seasons Played	Apps	Subs	Gls
Watford	YT	04/91	92	1	1	0
Doncaster Rov	Tr	07/94	94-95	14	2	1

MEARS Tyrone
Born: Stockport, Greater Manchester, England, 18 February, 1983 RB
Jamaica: 1

League Club	Source	Date Signed	Seasons Played	Apps	Subs	Gls
Manchester C	Jnr	07/00	01	0	1	0
Preston NE	Tr	07/02	02-05	50	20	4
West Ham U	Tr	07/06	06	3	2	0
Derby Co	Tr	01/07	06-08	33	8	2
Burnley	Tr	07/09	09-10	82	0	1
Bolton W	Tr	07/11	11-13	27	1	0

MEASHAM Ian
Born: Barnsley, South Yorkshire, England, 14 December, 1964 RB

League Club	Source	Date Signed	Seasons Played	Apps	Subs	Gls
Huddersfield T	App	12/82	84	17	0	0
Lincoln C	L	10/85	85	6	0	0
Rochdale	L	03/86	85	12	0	0
Cambridge U	Tr	08/86	86	46	0	0
Burnley	Barnet	11/88	88-93	181	1	2
Doncaster Rov	Tr	09/93	93-95	29	3	0

MEASURES George Allan
Born: Walthamstow, NE London, England, 17 December, 1958 F

League Club	Source	Date Signed	Seasons Played	Apps	Subs	Gls
Cambridge U	Bowers U	11/83	83	4	0	0

MEATH Trevor John
Born: Wednesbury, West Midlands, England, 20 March, 1944 M/F

League Club	Source	Date Signed	Seasons Played	Apps	Subs	Gls
Walsall	Darlaston	05/64	64-69	59	7	16
Lincoln C	Tr	10/69	69-71	42	1	5

MEDD Gordon Ernest
Born: Birmingham, England, 17 August, 1925 W
Died: Blackpool, Lancashire, England, January, 1996

League Club	Source	Date Signed	Seasons Played	Apps	Subs	Gls
Birmingham C	Worcester C	10/46				
Walsall	Worcester C	06/49	49	22	-	2
Rochdale	Tr	07/50	50	5	-	1
York C	Tr	01/51	50	1	-	0

MEDEL Gary Alexis
Born: Santiago, Chile, 3 August, 1987 DM
Chile: 80/U23-8/Youth

League Club	Source	Date Signed	Seasons Played	Apps	Subs	Gls
Cardiff C	Sevilla (SPN)	08/13	13	34	0	0

MEDHURST Henry Edward Pafford (Harry)
Born: Byfleet, Surrey, England, 5 February, 1916 G
Died: Woking, Surrey, England, 9 April, 1984

League Club	Source	Date Signed	Seasons Played	Apps	Subs	Gls
West Ham U	Woking	11/36	38-46	24	-	0
Chelsea	Tr	01/47	46-51	143	-	0
Brighton & HA	Tr	11/52	52	12	-	0

MEDLEY Leslie Dennis (Les)
Born: Edmonton, N London, England, 3 September, 1920 LW
Died: Ontario, Canada, 22 February, 2001
England: 6/FLge-1/Schools

League Club	Source	Date Signed	Seasons Played	Apps	Subs	Gls
Tottenham H	Jnr	09/36	46-52	150	-	45

MEDLEY Luke Anthony Cleve
Born: Greenwich, SE London, England, 21 June, 1989 F

League Club	Source	Date Signed	Seasons Played	Apps	Subs	Gls
Bradford C	Tottenham H (Sch)	07/07	07	1	8	2
Barnet	Tr	07/08	08-09	5	14	1
Aldershot T (L)	Mansfield T	02/11	10	0	4	0

MEDLIN Nicholas Ryan Maxwell (Nicky)
Born: Camborne, Cornwall, England, 23 November, 1976 M

League Club	Source	Date Signed	Seasons Played	Apps	Subs	Gls
Exeter C	YT	08/95	95-97	20	17	1

MEDLOCK Owen Wilfred
Born: Whittlesey, Cambridgeshire, England, 8 March, 1938 G

League Club	Source	Date Signed	Seasons Played	Apps	Subs	Gls
Chelsea	Jnr	05/55				
Swindon T	Tr	02/59	59	3	-	0
Oxford U	Tr	12/59	62	19	-	0

[MEDO] KAMARA Mohamed
Born: Bo, Sierra Leone, 16 November, 1987 DM
Sierra Leone: 18

League Club	Source	Date Signed	Seasons Played	Apps	Subs	Gls
Bolton W	Part'n Belgrade (SRB)	01/13	12-14	41	11	3

MEDOU-OTYE Andre Parfait (Parfait)
Born: Ekoundendi, Cameroon, 29 November, 1976 FB

France: Youth

League Club	Source	Date Signed	Seasons Played	Apps	Subs	Gls
Kidderminster Hrs	Greenock Morton	11/00	00-01	18	1	0

MEDWIN Terence Cameron (Terry)
Born: Swansea, Wales, 25 September, 1932 — RW/CF
Wales: 30/WLge-1/Schools

League Club	Source	Date Signed	Seasons Played	Apps	Subs	Gls
Swansea C	Jnr	11/49	51-55	147	-	57
Tottenham H	Tr	04/56	56-62	197	-	65

MEE Benjamin Thomas (Ben)
Born: Sale, Greater Manchester, England, 21 September, 1989 — CD
England: U21-2/Youth

League Club	Source	Date Signed	Seasons Played	Apps	Subs	Gls
Manchester C	Sch	09/07				
Leicester C	L	01/11	10	15	0	0
Burnley	Tr	07/11	11-14	115	6	3

MEE George Edwin
Born: Blackpool, Lancashire, England, 20 May, 1923 — IF
Died: Nottingham, England, 1974

League Club	Source	Date Signed	Seasons Played	Apps	Subs	Gls
Nottingham F	Jnr	05/40	46	9	-	1

MEECHAN Alexander Thomas (Alex)
Born: Plymouth, England, 29 January, 1980 — F

League Club	Source	Date Signed	Seasons Played	Apps	Subs	Gls
Swindon T	YT	-	97	0	1	0
Bristol C	Tr	07/98	98-99	5	8	4
Chester C	Forest Green Rov	01/07	06	2	6	0

MEECHAN David Anderson
Born: Loganlea, West Lothian, Scotland, 10 November, 1943 — CF

League Club	Source	Date Signed	Seasons Played	Apps	Subs	Gls
Sheffield Wed	Burnley (Am)	12/60				
Scunthorpe U	Tr	06/61				
York C	Tr	06/63	63	6	-	0

MEEK George Jackson
Born: Glasgow, Scotland, 15 February, 1934 — W

League Club	Source	Date Signed	Seasons Played	Apps	Subs	Gls
Leeds U	Hamilton Academical	08/52	52-59	195	-	19
Walsall	L	01/54	53	18	-	2
Walsall	L	08/54	54	26	-	4
Leicester C	Tr	08/60	60	13	-	0
Walsall	Tr	07/61	61-64	128	-	22

MEENS Harold
Born: Doncaster, South Yorkshire, England, 15 October, 1919 — CH
Died: Beverley, East Riding of Yorkshire, England, September, 1987

League Club	Source	Date Signed	Seasons Played	Apps	Subs	Gls
Hull C	Shepherd's Road Club	10/38	38-51	146	-	0

MEESON David John (Dave)
Born: Oxford, England, 6 July, 1934 — G
Died: Oxford, England, June, 1991

League Club	Source	Date Signed	Seasons Played	Apps	Subs	Gls
Wolverhampton W	Oxford C	02/52				
Reading	Tr	08/54	54-62	156	-	0
Coventry C	Tr	09/62	62-64	24	-	0

MEGSON Donald Harry (Don)
Born: Sale, Greater Manchester, England, 12 June, 1936 — LB
England: FLge-1

League Club	Source	Date Signed	Seasons Played	Apps	Subs	Gls
Sheffield Wed	Mossley	06/53	59-69	386	0	6
Bristol Rov	Tr	03/70	69-70	31	0	1

MEGSON Gary John
Born: Manchester, England, 2 May, 1959 — M

League Club	Source	Date Signed	Seasons Played	Apps	Subs	Gls
Plymouth Arg	App	05/77	77-79	78	0	10
Everton	Tr	12/79	79-80	20	2	2
Sheffield Wed	Tr	08/81	81-83	123	0	13
Nottingham F	Tr	08/84				
Newcastle U	Tr	11/84	84-85	21	3	1
Sheffield Wed	Tr	12/85	85-88	107	3	12
Manchester C	Tr	01/89	88-91	78	4	2
Norwich C	Tr	07/92	92-94	42	4	1
Lincoln C	Tr	07/95	95	2	0	0
Shrewsbury T	Tr	09/95	95	2	0	0

MEGSON Kevin Craig
Born: Halifax, West Yorkshire, England, 1 July, 1971 — RB/M

League Club	Source	Date Signed	Seasons Played	Apps	Subs	Gls
Bradford C	YT	07/89	89-90	24	3	0
Halifax T	Tr	03/91	90-92	37	4	1

MEHEW David Stephen
Born: Camberley, Surrey, England, 29 October, 1967 — M

League Club	Source	Date Signed	Seasons Played	Apps	Subs	Gls
Bristol Rov	Leeds U (YT)	07/85	85-92	195	27	63
Exeter C	L	03/94	93	5	2	0
Walsall	Tr	07/94	94	6	7	0

MEHMET David Nedjate (Dave)
Born: Camberwell, S London, England, 2 December, 1960 — M

League Club	Source	Date Signed	Seasons Played	Apps	Subs	Gls
Millwall	App	12/77	76-80	97	17	15
Charlton Ath	Tampa Bay R's (USA)	01/82	81-82	29	0	2
Gillingham	Tr	03/83	82-85	128	4	39
Millwall	Tr	07/86	86-87	17	1	1

MEIJER Erik
Born: Maastricht, Netherlands, 2 August, 1969 — F
Netherlands: 1

League Club	Source	Date Signed	Seasons Played	Apps	Subs	Gls
Liverpool	Bayer Leverkusen (GER)	07/99	99-00	7	17	0
Preston NE	L	10/00	00	9	0	0

MEIJER Geert
Born: Sellingen, Netherlands, 15 March, 1951 — LW

League Club	Source	Date Signed	Seasons Played	Apps	Subs	Gls
Bristol C	Ajax (NED)	03/79	78-79	12	3	2

MEIKLE Lindon Levi
Born: Nottingham, England, 21 March, 1988 — W
England: Semi Pro-3

League Club	Source	Date Signed	Seasons Played	Apps	Subs	Gls
Mansfield T	Eastwood T	05/11	13	2	26	1
York C	Tr	07/14	14	13	15	0

MEIRELES Raul Jose Trinidade
Born: Porto, Portugal, 17 March, 1983 — M
Portugal: 76/U21-26

League Club	Source	Date Signed	Seasons Played	Apps	Subs	Gls
Liverpool	FC Porto (POR)	08/10	10	32	3	5
Chelsea	Tr	08/11	11-12	24	7	2

MEIRELLES Bruno
Born: Leiria, Portugal, 23 February, 1982 — M

League Club	Source	Date Signed	Seasons Played	Apps	Subs	Gls
Torquay U	ED Amadora (POR)	08/04	04	5	4	0

MEITE Abdoulaye (Abdou)
Born: Paris, France, 6 October, 1980 — CD
Ivory Coast: 48

League Club	Source	Date Signed	Seasons Played	Apps	Subs	Gls
Bolton W	Olymp Marseille (FRA)	08/06	06-07	56	0	0
West Bromwich A	Tr	08/08	08-10	44	4	0
Doncaster Rov	FC Honka (FIN)	01/14	13	21	0	1

MEJIAS Tomas
Born: Madrid, Spain, 30 January, 1989 — G
Spain: Youth

League Club	Source	Date Signed	Seasons Played	Apps	Subs	Gls
Middlesbrough	Real Madrid B (SPN)	02/14	13-14	7	1	0

MEKKI Adam Rhys
Born: Chester, England, 24 December, 1991 — RW

League Club	Source	Date Signed	Seasons Played	Apps	Subs	Gls
Aldershot T	Sch	04/11	10-12	32	30	3

MELAUGH Gavin Mark John
Born: Derry, Northern Ireland, 9 July, 1981 — M
Northern Ireland: U21-8

League Club	Source	Date Signed	Seasons Played	Apps	Subs	Gls
Aston Villa	YT	07/98				
Rochdale	Tr	11/02	02	17	2	1

MELCHIOT Mario
Born: Amsterdam, Netherlands, 4 November, 1976 — RB
Netherlands: 22/U21-13/Youth

League Club	Source	Date Signed	Seasons Played	Apps	Subs	Gls
Chelsea	Ajax (NED)	07/99	99-03	117	13	4
Birmingham C	Tr	07/04	04-05	55	2	2
Wigan Ath	Stade Rennais (FRA)	07/07	07-09	96	1	0

MELDRUM Colin
Born: Glasgow, Scotland, 26 November, 1941 — FB

League Club	Source	Date Signed	Seasons Played	Apps	Subs	Gls
Arsenal	Jnr	12/58				
Watford	Tr	12/60	60-62	32	-	0
Reading	Tr	04/63	62-69	265	1	8
Cambridge U	Tr	10/69	70	36	1	4
Workington	Rtd	12/74	74	0	2	0

MELIA James (Jimmy)
Born: Liverpool, England, 1 November, 1937 — M
England: 2/FLge-1/Youth/Schools

League Club	Source	Date Signed	Seasons Played	Apps	Subs	Gls
Liverpool	Jnr	11/54	55-63	269	-	76
Wolverhampton W	Tr	03/64	63-64	24	-	4
Southampton	Tr	11/64	64-68	139	0	11
Aldershot	Tr	11/68	68-71	135	0	14
Crewe Alex	Tr	02/72	71	2	2	0

MELL Stewart Albert
Born: Doncaster, South Yorkshire, England, 15 October, 1957 — F
England: Semi Pro-1

League Club	Source	Date Signed	Seasons Played	Apps	Subs	Gls
Doncaster Rov	Appleby Frodingham	02/80	79-82	62	14	14
Halifax T	Tr	07/83	83	22	8	8
Scarborough	Burton A	07/86	87-88	30	9	8

MELLANBY Daniel (Danny)
Born: Bishop Auckland, County Durham, England, 17 July, 1979 — F

League Club	Source	Date Signed	Seasons Played	Apps	Subs	Gls
Darlington	Bishop Auckland	07/01	01-03	33	11	8

MELLBERG Erik Olof (Olof)
Born: Gullspang, Sweden, 3 September, 1977 — CD
Sweden: 117/U21-27

League Club	Source	Date Signed	Seasons Played	Apps	Subs	Gls
Aston Villa	RC Santander (SPN)	07/01	01-07	231	1	8

MELLEDEW Stephen Thomas (Steve)
Born: Rochdale, Greater Manchester, England, 28 November, 1945 — F/M

League Club	Source	Date Signed	Seasons Played	Apps	Subs	Gls
Rochdale	Whipp & Bourne	12/66	66-69	88	9	23
Everton	Tr	09/69				
Aldershot	Tr	07/71	71-73	90	2	27
Bury	Tr	11/73	73-74	14	6	2
Crewe Alex	Tr	10/74	74-75	49	7	2
Rochdale	Tr	07/76	76-77	76	2	12

MELLIGAN John James
Born: Dublin, Republic of Ireland, 11 February, 1982 — M
Republic of Ireland: U21-1/Youth

League Club	Source	Date Signed	Seasons Played	Apps	Subs	Gls
Wolverhampton W	YT	07/00	02	0	2	0
Bournemouth	L	11/01	01	7	1	0
Kidderminster Hrs	L	09/02	02	10	0	5
Kidderminster Hrs	L	12/02	02	18	1	5
Kidderminster Hrs	L	10/03	03	5	0	1
Doncaster Rov	L	11/03	03	21	0	2
Cheltenham T	Tr	07/04	04-06	101	13	15
Leyton Orient	Tr	07/07	07-09	64	19	6
Cheltenham T	Dundalk (ROI)	08/10	10	14	13	0

MELLING Terence (Terry)
Born: Haverton Hill, Cleveland, England, 24 January, 1940 — F

League Club	Source	Date Signed	Seasons Played	Apps	Subs	Gls
Newcastle U	Tow Law T	12/65				
Watford	Tr	05/66	65-66	23	1	5
Newport Co	Tr	02/67	66-67	34	0	14
Mansfield T	Tr	11/67	67-68	33	0	7
Rochdale	Tr	09/68	68	20	0	8
Darlington	Tr	03/69	68-69	20	0	6

MELLIS Jacob Alexander
Born: Nottingham, England, 8 January, 1991 — M
England: Youth

League Club	Source	Date Signed	Seasons Played	Apps	Subs	Gls
Chelsea	Sch	07/08				
Southampton	L	08/09	09	7	5	0
Barnsley	L	01/11	10	14	1	2
Barnsley	Tr	07/12	12-13	56	10	6
Blackpool	Tr	07/14	14	4	9	0
Oldham Ath	L	01/15	14	2	5	0

MELLISH Stuart Michael
Born: Hyde, Greater Manchester, England, 19 November, 1969 — M

League Club	Source	Date Signed	Seasons Played	Apps	Subs	Gls
Rochdale	YT	07/88	87-88	24	3	1

MELLON Michael Joseph (Mickey)
Born: Paisley, Renfrewshire, Scotland, 18 March, 1972 — M

League Club	Source	Date Signed	Seasons Played	Apps	Subs	Gls
Bristol C	YT	12/89	89-92	26	9	1
West Bromwich A	Tr	02/93	92-94	38	7	6
Blackpool	Tr	11/94	94-97	123	1	14
Tranmere Rov	Tr	10/97	97-98	45	12	3
Burnley	Tr	01/99	98-00	72	12	5
Tranmere Rov	Tr	03/01	00-03	102	15	3
Kidderminster Hrs	Tr	08/04	04	5	2	0

MELLOR David Anthony
Born: Oldham, Greater Manchester, England, 10 July, 1993 — LB

League Club	Source	Date Signed	Seasons Played	Apps	Subs	Gls
Oldham Ath	Sch	08/11	11-14	40	8	1

MELLOR Ian
Born: Sale, Greater Manchester, England, 19 February, 1950 — LW

League Club	Source	Date Signed	Seasons Played	Apps	Subs	Gls
Manchester C	Wythenshawe Amats	12/69	70-72	36	4	7
Norwich C	Tr	03/73	72-73	28	1	2
Brighton & HA	Tr	04/74	74-77	116	6	31
Chester C	Tr	02/78	77-78	38	2	11
Sheffield Wed	Tr	06/79	79-81	54	16	11
Bradford C	Tr	06/82	82-83	27	9	4

MELLOR John Allan (Allan)
Born: Droylsden, Greater Manchester, England, 16 October, 1921 — LH
Died: Southampton, England, August, 1997

League Club	Source	Date Signed	Seasons Played	Apps	Subs	Gls
Hull C	Ashton U	05/47	47-51	104	-	4

MELLOR Kelvin
Born: Copenhagen, Denmark, 25 January, 1991 — RB/M

League Club	Source	Date Signed	Seasons Played	Apps	Subs	Gls
Crewe Alex	Nantwich T	02/08	10-13	62	14	2
Plymouth Arg	Tr	06/14	14	36	1	1

MELLOR Kenneth Edward (Ken)
Born: Leicester, England, 22 August, 1934 — CH

League Club	Source	Date Signed	Seasons Played	Apps	Subs	Gls
Leicester C		07/55				
Mansfield T	Tr	07/57	57-58	66	-	0
Swindon T	Tr	07/59	59-60	32	-	4

MELLOR Neil Andrew
Born: Sheffield, England, 4 November, 1982 — F

League Club	Source	Date Signed	Seasons Played	Apps	Subs	Gls
Liverpool	Sch	02/02	02-04	7	5	2
West Ham U	L	08/03	03	8	8	2
Wigan Ath	L	01/06	05	3	0	1
Preston NE	Tr	08/06	06-11	78	52	38
Sheffield Wed	L	07/10	10	24	9	13

MELLOR Peter Joseph
Born: Prestbury, Cheshire, England, 20 November, 1947 — G
England: Youth

League Club	Source	Date Signed	Seasons Played	Apps	Subs	Gls
Burnley	Witton A	04/69	69-71	69	0	0
Chesterfield	L	01/72	71	4	0	0
Fulham	Tr	02/72	71-76	190	0	0
Hereford U	Tr	09/77	77	32	0	0
Portsmouth	Tr	07/78	78-80	129	0	0

MELLOR Robert Brett (Brett)
Born: Huddersfield, West Yorkshire, England, 4 February, 1960 — CD

League Club	Source	Date Signed	Seasons Played	Apps	Subs	Gls
Huddersfield T	App	02/78	77	1	0	0
Barnsley	Tr	08/80				

MELLOR William (Bill)
Born: Manchester, England, 29 June, 1925 — RB

League Club	Source	Date Signed	Seasons Played	Apps	Subs	Gls
Accrington Stan	Droylsden	06/50	50-53	138	-	2

MELLOWS Michael Anthony (Mick)
Born: Epsom, Surrey, England, 14 November, 1947 — M
England: Amateur-15/Youth/Schools

League Club	Source	Date Signed	Seasons Played	Apps	Subs	Gls
Reading (Am)	Sutton U	09/70	70	14	2	2
Portsmouth	Winchester C	09/73	73-77	174	8	16

MELO Filipe Joaquim
Born: Espinho, Portugal, 3 November, 1989 — DM

League Club	Source	Date Signed	Seasons Played	Apps	Subs	Gls
Sheffield Wed	Moreirense (POR)	02/15	14	4	2	0

MELONO Alejandro Gabriel (Alex)
Born: Montevideo, Uruguay, 4 November, 1982 — CD

League Club	Source	Date Signed	Seasons Played	Apps	Subs	Gls
Yeovil T	Chacaritos (ARG)	09/05	05	1	0	0

MELROSE James Millsopp (Jim)
Born: Glasgow, Scotland, 7 October, 1958 — F
Scotland: SLge-1/U21-8/Schools

League Club	Source	Date Signed	Seasons Played	Apps	Subs	Gls
Leicester C	Partick Thistle	07/80	80-82	57	15	21
Coventry C	Tr	09/82	82	21	3	8
Wolverhampton W (L)	Glasgow Celtic	09/84	84	6	1	2
Manchester C	Glasgow Celtic	11/84	84-85	27	7	8
Charlton Ath	Tr	03/86	85-87	44	4	19
Leeds U	Tr	09/87	87	3	1	0
Shrewsbury T	Tr	02/88	87-89	27	22	3

MELTON Stephen (Steve)
Born: Lincoln, England, 3 October, 1978 — M

League Club	Source	Date Signed	Seasons Played	Apps	Subs	Gls
Nottingham F	YT	10/95	98-99	2	1	0
Stoke C	Tr	02/00	99	0	5	0
Brighton & HA	Tr	08/00	00-02	21	25	3
Hull C	Tr	12/02	02-03	19	11	0
Boston U	Tr	03/04	03-05	14	7	2

MELVANG Lars Mandrup
Born: Seattle, Washington, USA, 3 April, 1969 — RB

League Club	Source	Date Signed	Seasons Played	Apps	Subs	Gls
Watford	Silkeborg (DEN)	08/97	97	4	0	1

MELVILLE Alan Allistair
Born: Hartlepool, Cleveland, England, 13 March, 1941 — CH

League Club	Source	Date Signed	Seasons Played	Apps	Subs	Gls
Hartlepool U	St Joseph's	09/60	60-61	5	-	0

MELVILLE Andrew Roger (Andy)
Born: Swansea, Wales, 29 November, 1968 — CD
Wales: 65/B-1/U21-2

League Club	Source	Date Signed	Seasons Played	Apps	Subs	Gls
Swansea C	App	07/86	85-89	165	10	22
Oxford U	Tr	07/90	90-92	135	0	13
Sunderland	Tr	08/93	93-98	204	0	14
Bradford C	L	02/98	97	6	0	1
Fulham	Tr	07/99	99-03	150	3	4
West Ham U	Tr	01/04	03-04	14	3	0
Nottingham F	L	02/05	04	13	0	0

MELVILLE Leslie (Les)
Born: Ormskirk, Lancashire, England, 29 November, 1930 — LH
Died: Stockport, Greater Manchester, England, 1 February, 2009
England: Youth

League Club	Source	Date Signed	Seasons Played	Apps	Subs	Gls
Everton	Jnr	04/50				
Bournemouth	Tr	07/56	56-57	25	-	0
Oldham Ath	Tr	03/58	57	2	-	0

MENDES Albert Junior Hillyard Andrew (Junior)
Born: Balham, S London, England, 15 September, 1976 — F
Montserrat: 9

League Club	Source	Date Signed	Seasons Played	Apps	Subs	Gls
Chelsea	YT	07/95				
Carlisle U (L)	St Mirren	11/98	98	5	1	1
Mansfield T	St Mirren	01/03	02-03	54	3	12
Huddersfield T	Tr	07/04	04-05	13	17	5
Northampton T	L	10/05	05	9	3	2
Grimsby T	L	01/06	05	8	7	0
Notts Co	Tr	07/06	06	22	15	5
Lincoln C	L	03/07	06	4	5	0
Aldershot T	FC Mika (ARM)	02/08	08	1	5	0

MENDES Miguel Pedro (Pedro)
Born: Guimaraes, Portugal, 26 February, 1979 — M
Portugal: 12

League Club	Source	Date Signed	Seasons Played	Apps	Subs	Gls
Tottenham H	FC Porto (POR)	07/04	04-05	25	5	1
Portsmouth	Tr	01/06	05-07	53	5	5

MENDES Nuno Alexandre
Born: Guimaraes, Portugal, 7 April, 1978 — M
Portugal: U21-4

League Club	Source	Date Signed	Seasons Played	Apps	Subs	Gls
Plymouth Arg	Santa Clara (POR)	07/05	05	2	0	0

MENDEZ Gabriel
Born: Buenos Aires, Argentina, 12 March, 1973 — M
Australia: 9

League Club	Source	Date Signed	Seasons Played	Apps	Subs	Gls
Notts Co (L)	Parrametta (AUS)	03/97	96	2	1	0

MENDEZ-LAING Nathaniel Otis
Born: Birmingham, England, 15 April, 1992 — RW
England: Youth

League Club	Source	Date Signed	Seasons Played	Apps	Subs	Gls
Wolverhampton W	Sch	09/09				
Peterborough U	L	07/10	10	8	25	5
Sheffield U	L	08/11	11	4	4	1
Peterborough U	Tr	07/12	12-14	22	29	4
Portsmouth	L	11/12	12	5	3	0
Shrewsbury T	L	01/14	13	3	3	0
Cambridge U	L	02/15	14	10	1	1

MENDEZ RODRIGUEZ Alberto
Born: Nuremburg, Germany, 24 October, 1974 — F

League Club	Source	Date Signed	Seasons Played	Apps	Subs	Gls
Arsenal	FC Feucht (GER)	07/97	97-98	1	3	0

MENDHAM Peter Stanley
Born: King's Lynn, Norfolk, England, 9 April, 1960 — M

League Club	Source	Date Signed	Seasons Played	Apps	Subs	Gls
Norwich C	App	04/78	78-86	200	11	23

MENDIETA Gaizka
Born: Bilbao, Spain, 27 March, 1974 — M
Spain: 40/U23-2/U21-13/Youth

League Club	Source	Date Signed	Seasons Played	Apps	Subs	Gls
Middlesbrough (L)	SS Lazio (ITA)	08/03	03	30	1	2
Middlesbrough	SS Lazio (ITA)	07/04	04-06	26	5	2

MENDONCA Clive Paul
Born: Islington, N London, England, 9 September, 1968 — F

League Club	Source	Date Signed	Seasons Played	Apps	Subs	Gls
Sheffield U	App	09/86	86-87	8	5	4
Doncaster Rov	L	02/88	87	2	0	0
Rotherham U	Tr	03/88	87-90	71	13	27
Sheffield U	Tr	08/91	91	4	6	1
Grimsby T	L	01/92	91	10	0	3
Grimsby T	Tr	06/92	92-96	151	5	58
Charlton Ath	Tr	05/97	97-99	78	6	40

MENDY Arnaud
Born: Evreux, France, 10 February, 1990 — M
Guinea-Bissau: 2

League Club	Source	Date Signed	Seasons Played	Apps	Subs	Gls
Derby Co	Rouen (FRA)	09/08	09	0	1	0
Grimsby T	L	10/09	09	1	0	0
Tranmere Rov	L	08/10	10	11	1	1
Macclesfield T	Tr	07/11	11	23	5	2

MENDY Bernard
Born: Evreux, France, 20 August, 1981 — RB
France: 3/U21-2/Youth

League Club	Source	Date Signed	Seasons Played	Apps	Subs	Gls
Bolton W (L)	Paris St-Germain (FRA)	07/02	02	20	1	0
Hull C	Paris St-Germain (FRA)	07/08	08-09	30	19	2

MENDY Formose
Born: Guediawaye, Senegal, 23 March, 1989 — RM
Guinea-Bissau: 1

League Club	Source	Date Signed	Seasons Played	Apps	Subs	Gls
Blackpool	Sporting Gijon (SPN)	09/14	14	1	2	0

MENDY Jules
Born: Pikine, Senegal, 4 September, 1973 — F

League Club	Source	Date Signed	Seasons Played	Apps	Subs	Gls
Torquay U	Racing Club Paris (FRA	08/00	00	7	14	2

MENDY Noel Alexandre (Alex)
Born: Paris, France, 14 December, 1983 — W

League Club	Source	Date Signed	Seasons Played	Apps	Subs	Gls
Chesterfield	Mlada Boleslav (CZE)	08/11	11	31	3	2

MENETRIER Mickael
Born: Reims, France, 23 September, 1978 — G

League Club	Source	Date Signed	Seasons Played	Apps	Subs	Gls
Bournemouth	FC Metz (FRA)	08/00	00-01	12	1	0

MENMUIR William Fraser
Born: Glasgow, Scotland, 3 February, 1952 — M

League Club	Source	Date Signed	Seasons Played	Apps	Subs	Gls
Bristol C	Sandyhills	06/69	69-70	1	1	0

MENSAH Bernard Ayitey
Born: Hounslow, SW London, England, 29 December, 1994 — F

League Club	Source	Date Signed	Seasons Played	Apps	Subs	Gls
Watford	Sch	12/11	13-14	0	2	0

MENSAH John
Born: Obuasi, Ghana, 29 November, 1982 — CD
Ghana: 86

League Club	Source	Date Signed	Seasons Played	Apps	Subs	Gls
Sunderland (L)	Olymp Lyonnais (FRA)	08/09	09	14	2	1
Sunderland (L)	Olymp Lyonnais (FRA)	08/10	10	15	3	0

MENSEGUEZ Juan Carlos
Born: Cordoba, Argentina, 18 February, 1984 — W

League Club	Source	Date Signed	Seasons Played	Apps	Subs	Gls
West Bromwich A (L)	San Lorenzo (ARG)	02/09	08	3	4	1

MENZIES Adam Ross (Ross)
Born: Rutherglen, Glasgow, Scotland, 31 October, 1934 — WH
Scotland: Schools

League Club	Source	Date Signed	Seasons Played	Apps	Subs	Gls
Cardiff C	Glasgow Rangers	08/57	57	1	-	0

MENZIES Norman
Born: Washington, Tyne and Wear, England, 20 June, 1926 — IF
Died: Rake, West Sussex, England, 20 June, 2005

League Club	Source	Date Signed	Seasons Played	Apps	Subs	Gls
Barnsley	Hexham Hearts	10/49				
Aldershot	Tr	05/50	50-57	221	-	91

MEOLA Antonio Michael (Tony)
Born: Belleville, New Jersey, USA, 21 February, 1969 — G
USA: 100

League Club	Source	Date Signed	Seasons Played	Apps	Subs	Gls
Brighton & HA	Missouri Ath (USA)	08/90	90	1	0	0

MEPPEN-WALTER Courtney Alister
Born: Bury, Greater Manchester, England, 2 August, 1994 — CD
England: Youth

League Club	Source	Date Signed	Seasons Played	Apps	Subs	Gls
Manchester C	Sch	08/11				
Carlisle U	Unattached	11/13	13-14	33	6	2

MERCER Arthur David (David)
Born: Hull, England, 14 February, 1918 — LW
Died: Newton Abbot, Devon, England, April, 1986

League Club	Source	Date Signed	Seasons Played	Apps	Subs	Gls
Torquay U	RAF Volunteer Reserve	02/46	46-48	66	-	8

MERCER James Robertson (Jimmy)
Born: Dunfermline, Fife, Scotland, 17 March, 1935 — RW

League Club	Source	Date Signed	Seasons Played	Apps	Subs	Gls
Bury	Rosyth Rec	06/57	57-58	18	-	1
Crewe Alex	Tr	06/59	59	3	-	0

MERCER Joseph (Joe)
Born: Ellesmere Port, Cheshire, England, 9 August, 1914 — LH
Died: Hoylake, Wirral, England, 9 August, 1990
England: 5/FLge-2/War-27

League Club	Source	Date Signed	Seasons Played	Apps	Subs	Gls
Everton	Ellesmere Port T	09/32	32-46	170	-	1
Arsenal	Tr	12/46	46-53	247	-	2

MERCER Keith
Born: Lewisham, SE London, England, 14 October, 1956 — F

League Club	Source	Date Signed	Seasons Played	Apps	Subs	Gls
Watford	App	09/74	72-79	109	25	46
Southend U	Tr	02/80	79-82	131	0	35
Blackpool	Tr	08/83	83	31	0	9

MERCER Stanley (Stan)
Born: Birkenhead, Wirral, England, 11 September, 1919 — CF
Died: Fleetwood, Lancashire, England, 4 October, 2003

League Club	Source	Date Signed	Seasons Played	Apps	Subs	Gls
Leicester C	Blackpool (Am)	11/44	46	1	-	0
Accrington Stan	Tr	01/47	46-48	68	-	36
Mansfield T	Tr	10/48	48	12	-	6

MERCER Stephen Jack (Steve)
Born: Barking, E London, England, 1 May, 1965 — RB

League Club	Source	Date Signed	Seasons Played	Apps	Subs	Gls
Peterborough U	Cambridge U (NC)	09/82	82	3	0	0

MERCER William (Billy)
Born: Liverpool, England, 22 May, 1969 — G

League Club	Source	Date Signed	Seasons Played	Apps	Subs	Gls
Liverpool	YT	08/87				
Rotherham U	Tr	02/89	89-94	104	0	0
Sheffield U	Tr	10/94	94-95	4	0	0
Chesterfield	Tr	09/95	95-98	149	0	0
Bristol C	Tr	10/99	99	25	0	0

MEREDITH James Gregory
Born: Albury, NSW, Australia, 4 April, 1988 — LB

League Club	Source	Date Signed	Seasons Played	Apps	Subs	Gls
Derby Co	Sch	06/06				
Chesterfield	L	02/07	06	1	0	0
Shrewsbury T	Sligo Rov (ROI)	01/08	07	3	0	0
Bradford C	York C	06/12	12-14	94	4	1

MEREDITH John Frederick
Born: Hatfield, South Yorkshire, England, 23 September, 1940 — LW

League Club	Source	Date Signed	Seasons Played	Apps	Subs	Gls
Doncaster Rov	Jnr	01/58	58-60	59	-	8
Sheffield Wed	Tr	02/61	60	1	-	0
Chesterfield	Tr	07/62	62-63	81	-	6
Gillingham	Tr	03/64	63-68	227	1	7
Bournemouth	Tr	08/69	69-70	51	0	1

MEREDITH Robert Garfield
Born: Swansea, Wales, 3 September, 1917 — RW
Died: Merton, S London, England, May, 1994
Wales: Schools

League Club	Source	Date Signed	Seasons Played	Apps	Subs	Gls
Notts Co	Carlisle U (Am)	11/45				
Carlisle U	Tr	01/47	46	1	-	0

MEREDITH Thomas James Anthony (Tom)
Born: Enfield, N London, England, 27 October, 1977 — RB

League Club	Source	Date Signed	Seasons Played	Apps	Subs	Gls
Peterborough U	YT	07/96	95	1	1	0

MEREDITH Trevor George
Born: Bridgnorth, Shropshire, England, 25 December, 1936 — RW

League Club	Source	Date Signed	Seasons Played	Apps	Subs	Gls
Burnley	Kidderminster Hrs	11/57	59-63	37	-	8
Shrewsbury T	Tr	04/64	64-71	229	6	41

MERIDA Francisco (Fran)
Born: Barcelona, Spain, 4 March, 1990 — M
Spain: U21-6/Youth

League Club	Source	Date Signed	Seasons Played	Apps	Subs	Gls
Arsenal	Sch	03/07	08-09	0	6	1

MERINO Carlos Alberto
Born: Bilbao, Spain, 15 March, 1980 — M

League Club	Source	Date Signed	Seasons Played	Apps	Subs	Gls
Nottingham F	Jnr	09/97	99	3	6	0

MERKEL Alexander
Born: Almaty, Kazakhstan, 22 February, 1992 — M
Germany: Youth

League Club	Source	Date Signed	Seasons Played	Apps	Subs	Gls
Watford (L)	Udinese (ITA)	01/14	13	7	4	1

MERRICK Alan Ronald
Born: Birmingham, England, 20 June, 1950 — D
England: Youth

League Club	Source	Date Signed	Seasons Played	Apps	Subs	Gls
West Bromwich A	App	08/67	68-75	131	8	5
Peterborough U	L	09/75	75	5	0	0

MERRICK Geoffrey (Geoff)
Born: Bristol, England, 29 April, 1951 — CD
England: Schools

League Club	Source	Date Signed	Seasons Played	Apps	Subs	Gls
Bristol C	App	08/68	67-81	361	6	10

MERRICK Gilbert Harold (Gil)
Born: Birmingham, England, 26 January, 1922 — G
Died: Solihull, West Midlands, England, 3 February, 2010
England: 23/FLge-11

League Club	Source	Date Signed	Seasons Played	Apps	Subs	Gls
Birmingham C	Solihull T	08/39	46-59	485	-	0

MERRICK Neil Gilbert
Born: Birmingham, England, 6 April, 1952 — CD
England: Semi Pro-2

League Club	Source	Date Signed	Seasons Played	Apps	Subs	Gls
Bournemouth	Worcester C	09/74	74	13	2	0

MERRIFIELD Frankie Edward Peter
Born: Hackney, E London, England, 8 January, 1994 — M

League Club	Source	Date Signed	Seasons Played	Apps	Subs	Gls
AFC Wimbledon	Jnr	05/12	12	1	4	0

MERRIFIELD Royston Gordon (Roy)
Born: Mile End, E London, England, 11 October, 1931 — LW
Died: Blackpool, Lancashire, England, 29 January, 2011

League Club	Source	Date Signed	Seasons Played	Apps	Subs	Gls
Chelsea	Rainham T	02/54				
Millwall	Tr	06/56	56	2	-	0

MERRINGTON David Robert (Dave)
Born: Newcastle-upon-Tyne, England, 26 January, 1945 — CH

League Club	Source	Date Signed	Seasons Played	Apps	Subs	Gls
Burnley	App	02/62	64-70	96	2	1

MERRIS David Andrew (Dave)
Born: Rotherham, South Yorkshire, England, 13 October, 1980 — LB

League Club	Source	Date Signed	Seasons Played	Apps	Subs	Gls
York C	Harrogate T	08/03	03	42	2	0

MERRITT Harold George
Born: Ormskirk, Lancashire, England, 22 September, 1920 — IF
Died: Poole, Dorset, England, March, 2004

League Club	Source	Date Signed	Seasons Played	Apps	Subs	Gls
Everton	Jnr	12/37				
Leyton Orient	Tr	09/46	46	1	-	0

MERSON Paul Charles
Born: Harlesden, NW London, England, 20 March, 1968 — F/M
England: 21/B-4/U21-4/Youth

League Club	Source	Date Signed	Seasons Played	Apps	Subs	Gls
Arsenal	App	12/85	86-96	289	38	78
Brentford	L	01/87	86	6	1	0
Middlesbrough	Tr	07/97	97-98	48	0	11
Aston Villa	Tr	09/98	98-01	101	16	18
Portsmouth	Tr	08/02	02	44	1	12
Walsall	Tr	08/03	03-05	68	9	6

MERTESACKER Per
Born: Hanover, Germany, 29 September, 1984 — CD
Germany: 104/U21-3

League Club	Source	Date Signed	Seasons Played	Apps	Subs	Gls
Arsenal	Werder Bremen (GER)	08/11	11-14	124	1	5

[MESCA] TUE NA BANGA Buomesca Tue
Born: Guinea-Bissau, 6 May, 1993 — W
Portugal: Youth

League Club	Source	Date Signed	Seasons Played	Apps	Subs	Gls
Fulham	Chelsea (Sch)	09/11	13	0	1	0
Crewe Alex	L	11/13	13	6	0	1

MESLIEN Sylvain
Born: Paris, France, 7 August, 1981 — LB

League Club	Source	Date Signed	Seasons Played	Apps	Subs	Gls
Swansea C	Saint-Etienne (FRA)	11/06	06	0	1	0

MESSER Gary Michael
Born: Consett, County Durham, England, 22 September, 1979 — F

League Club	Source	Date Signed	Seasons Played	Apps	Subs	Gls
Doncaster Rov	YT	-	96-97	4	10	1
Bury	Tr	09/98				

METCALF Colin Christopher Anthony
Born: Norwich, England, 3 March, 1939 — CH

League Club	Source	Date Signed	Seasons Played	Apps	Subs	Gls
Norwich C	Norman YC	07/60	62-63	12	-	1
Southend U	Tr	09/64	64	3	-	0

METCALF Mark Peter
Born: Norwich, England, 25 September, 1965 — M
England: Schools

League Club	Source	Date Signed	Seasons Played	Apps	Subs	Gls
Norwich C	App	09/83	82	0	1	0

METCALF Matthew Adam
Born: Norwich, England, 28 July, 1969 — F

League Club	Source	Date Signed	Seasons Played	Apps	Subs	Gls
Brentford	Braintree T	09/93	93	3	4	0

METCALF Michael (Mickey)
Born: Liverpool, England, 24 May, 1939 — IF

League Club	Source	Date Signed	Seasons Played	Apps	Subs	Gls
Wrexham	Everton (Am)	05/57	57-63	121	-	58
Chester C	Tr	12/63	63-68	221	0	68

METCALFE John
Born: Birmingham, England, 2 June, 1935 — LW
Died: Birmingham, England, February, 1996

League Club	Source	Date Signed	Seasons Played	Apps	Subs	Gls
Birmingham C	Jnr	10/52	52	2	-	0
York C	Tr	06/57	57	3	-	2
Walsall	Tr	07/58	58	2	-	0

METCALFE Ronald
Born: South Shields, Tyne and Wear, England, 8 December, 1947 — W

League Club	Source	Date Signed	Seasons Played	Apps	Subs	Gls
Derby Co	Marsden Colliery Jnrs	01/65	66	1	0	0

METCALFE Stuart Michael
Born: Blackburn, Greater Manchester, England, 6 October, 1950 — M
England: Youth

League Club	Source	Date Signed	Seasons Played	Apps	Subs	Gls
Blackburn Rov	App	01/68	67-79	375	11	21
Carlisle U	Tr	07/80	80	23	2	3
Blackburn Rov	Carolina Light'g (USA)	10/82				
Crewe Alex	Tr	01/83	82	3	0	0
Blackburn Rov	Tr	02/83	82	1	0	0

METCALFE Victor (Vic)
Born: Barrow, Cumbria, England, 3 February, 1922 — LW
Died: Huddersfield, West Yorkshire, England, 6 April, 2003
England: 2/FLge-2

League Club	Source	Date Signed	Seasons Played	Apps	Subs	Gls
Huddersfield T	Ravensthorpe A	01/40	46-57	434	-	87
Hull C	Tr	06/58	58-59	6	-	3

METCHICK David John (Dave)
Born: Bakewell, Derbyshire, England, 14 August, 1943 — M
England: Youth

League Club	Source	Date Signed	Seasons Played	Apps	Subs	Gls
Fulham	Jnr	08/61	61-64	47	-	9
Leyton Orient	Tr	12/64	64-66	75	0	15
Peterborough U	Tr	03/67	66-67	38	0	6
Queens Park Rgrs	Tr	08/68	68-69	0	3	1
Arsenal	Tr	09/70				
Brentford	Atlanta Apollos (USA)	09/73	73-74	57	4	4

METGOD Johannes Anthonius Bernardus (Johnny)
Born: Amsterdam, Netherlands, 27 February, 1958 — M/CD
Netherlands: 21

League Club	Source	Date Signed	Seasons Played	Apps	Subs	Gls
Nottingham F	Real Madrid (SPN)	08/84	84-86	113	3	15
Tottenham H	Tr	07/87	87	5	7	0

METHLEY Irvin
Born: Worsbrough, South Yorkshire, England, 22 September, 1925 — FB
Died: Walsall, West Midlands, England, 9 July, 2004

League Club	Source	Date Signed	Seasons Played	Apps	Subs	Gls
Wolverhampton W	Jnr	10/42				
Walsall	Tr	03/46	46-50	113	-	1

METHVEN Colin John
Born: India, 10 December, 1955 — CD

League Club	Source	Date Signed	Seasons Played	Apps	Subs	Gls
Wigan Ath	East Fife	10/79	79-85	295	1	21
Blackpool	Tr	07/86	86-89	166	7	11
Carlisle U	L	09/90	90	12	0	0
Walsall	Tr	11/90	90-92	97	0	3

METTAM Leon
Born: Lincoln, England, 9 December, 1986 — F

League Club	Source	Date Signed	Seasons Played	Apps	Subs	Gls
Lincoln C	Sch	07/06	05-06	1	4	1

METTIOUI Ahmed
Born: Tangier, Morocco, 3 November, 1965 — W

League Club	Source	Date Signed	Seasons Played	Apps	Subs	Gls
Crewe Alex	Fath Union SC (MOR)	07/92	92	1	2	0

METTOMO Lucien
Born: Douala, Cameroon, 19 April, 1977 — CD
Cameroon: 30

League Club	Source	Date Signed	Seasons Played	Apps	Subs	Gls
Manchester C	Saint-Etienne (FRA)	10/01	01-02	20	7	1

MEYER Adrian Michael
Born: Yate, Avon, England, 22 September, 1970 — CD

League Club	Source	Date Signed	Seasons Played	Apps	Subs	Gls
Scarborough	YT	06/89	89-94	114	0	9

MEYER Barrie John
Born: Bournemouth, England, 21 August, 1932 — IF
Died: Durban, South Africa, September, 2015

League Club	Source	Date Signed	Seasons Played	Apps	Subs	Gls
Bristol Rov	Sneyd Park	11/49	50-57	139	-	60
Plymouth Arg	Tr	08/58	58	8	-	5
Newport Co	Tr	02/59	58-60	70	-	27
Bristol C	Tr	09/61	61-62	11	-	8

MEYLER David John
Born: Cork, Republic of Ireland, 29 May, 1989 — M
Republic of Ireland: 13/U21-9

League Club	Source	Date Signed	Seasons Played	Apps	Subs	Gls
Sunderland	Cork C (ROI)	07/08	09-12	14	11	0
Hull C	Tr	11/12	12-14	71	15	8

MEZAGUE Valery
Born: Marseille, France, 8 December, 1983 — M
Died: Toulon, France, 15 November, 2014
Cameroon: 7

League Club	Source	Date Signed	Seasons Played	Apps	Subs	Gls
Portsmouth (L)	Montpellier (FRA)	09/04	04	3	8	0
Bury	Panetolikos (GRE)	01/13	12	2	5	0

MICALLEF Constantinous (Tarki)
Born: Cardiff, Wales, 24 January, 1961 — M
Wales: U21-3/Schools

League Club	Source	Date Signed	Seasons Played	Apps	Subs	Gls
Cardiff C	App	01/79	78-82	67	14	11
Newport Co	Tr	09/83	83	22	2	2
Gillingham	Tr	08/84	84	2	0	1
Cardiff C	Tr	09/84	84-85	26	14	1
Bristol Rov	Tr	08/86	86	15	3	1

MICHAEL James David (Jamie)
Born: Pontypridd, Rhondda Cynon Taff, Wales, 28 October, 1978 — W
Wales: Youth

League Club	Source	Date Signed	Seasons Played	Apps	Subs	Gls
Cardiff C	YT	-	96	0	1	0

MICHALIK Lubomir (Lubo)
Born: Cadca, Czechoslovakia, 13 August, 1983 — CD
Slovakia: 7

League Club	Source	Date Signed	Seasons Played	Apps	Subs	Gls
Bolton W	FC Senec (SVK)	01/07	06-07	8	3	1
Leeds U	L	03/07	06	7	0	1
Leeds U	Tr	01/08	07-09	39	10	1
Carlisle U	Tr	08/10	10-11	65	3	2
Portsmouth	Tr	09/12	12	17	1	1

[MICHEL] MADERA Miguel Marcos
Born: Oviedo, Spain, 9 November, 1985 — DM

League Club	Source	Date Signed	Seasons Played	Apps	Subs	Gls
Birmingham C	Sporting Gijon (SPN)	01/10	09	3	6	0

MICHOPOULOS Nikolaos (Nik)
Born: Karditsa, Greece, 20 February, 1970 — G
Greece: 15

League Club	Source	Date Signed	Seasons Played	Apps	Subs	Gls
Burnley	PAOK Salonika (GRE)	08/00	00-02	85	0	0
Crystal Palace	L	09/02	02	5	0	0

[MICHU] PEREZ Miguel
Born: Oviedo, Spain, 21 March, 1986 — F
Spain: 1

League Club	Source	Date Signed	Seasons Played	Apps	Subs	Gls
Swansea C	Rayo Vallecano (SPN)	07/12	12-13	50	2	20

MICKLEWHITE Gary
Born: Southwark, S London, England, 21 March, 1961 — RM

League Club	Source	Date Signed	Seasons Played	Apps	Subs	Gls
Manchester U	App	03/78				
Queens Park Rgrs	Tr	07/79	80-84	97	9	11
Derby Co	Tr	02/85	84-92	223	17	31
Gillingham	Tr	07/93	93-95	78	17	3

MICKLEWRIGHT Andrew Alfred Joseph (Andy)
Born: Birmingham, England, 31 January, 1931 — IF
Died: Brixham, Devon, England, 5 August, 2006

League Club	Source	Date Signed	Seasons Played	Apps	Subs	Gls
Bristol Rov	Smethwick Highfield	01/52	51-52	8	-	1
Bristol C	Tr	05/53	53-54	39	-	17
Swindon T	Tr	09/55	55-58	114	-	31
Exeter C	Tr	07/59	59	38	-	11

MICKLEWRIGHT John Leslie (Les)
Born: Stoke-on-Trent, England, 13 October, 1915 — WH
Died: Haslingden, Lancashire, England, 19 May, 1991

League Club	Source	Date Signed	Seasons Played	Apps	Subs	Gls
Crewe Alex	Stafford Rgrs	09/46	46-49	71	-	0

MIDDLEBROUGH Alan
Born: Wardle, Greater Manchester, England, 4 December, 1925 — CF
Died: Keighley, West Yorkshire, England, February, 2004

League Club	Source	Date Signed	Seasons Played	Apps	Subs	Gls
Bolton W	Morecambe Services	07/46	46-47	5	-	1
Bradford C	Tr	08/48	48	4	-	0
Rochdale	Tr	10/48	48-51	47	-	25

MIDDLEMASS Clive
Born: Leeds, England, 25 August, 1944 — LH

League Club	Source	Date Signed	Seasons Played	Apps	Subs	Gls
Leeds U	Jnr	08/62				
Workington	Tr	11/63	63-69	168	1	6

MIDDLEMISS Ernest (Ernie)
Born: Newcastle-upon-Tyne, England, 30 August, 1920 — CF
Died: Kettering, Northamptonshire, England, February, 1999

League Club	Source	Date Signed	Seasons Played	Apps	Subs	Gls
Lincoln C	South Shields	06/48	48	2	-	0

MIDDLETON Craig Dean
Born: Nuneaton, Warwickshire, England, 10 September, 1970 — M

League Club	Source	Date Signed	Seasons Played	Apps	Subs	Gls
Coventry C	YT	05/89	89-92	2	1	0
Cambridge U	Tr	07/93	93-95	55	4	10
Cardiff C	Tr	08/96	96-99	95	24	8
Plymouth Arg	L	01/00	99	6	0	2
Halifax T	Tr	03/00	99-01	66	10	8

MIDDLETON Derek
Born: Ashby-de-la-Zouch, Leicestershire, England, 30 May, 1934 — WH

League Club	Source	Date Signed	Seasons Played	Apps	Subs	Gls
York C	Burton A	11/58	58	1	-	0

MIDDLETON Doyle Lewis Christie
Born: Southport, Merseyside, England, 11 April, 1994 — M
Scotland: Youth

League Club	Source	Date Signed	Seasons Played	Apps	Subs	Gls
Preston NE	Sch	-	10-11	1	2	0

MIDDLETON Frederick Thomas (Fred)
Born: West Hartlepool, County Durham, England, 2 August, 1930 — RH

League Club	Source	Date Signed	Seasons Played	Apps	Subs	Gls
Newcastle U	Jnr	04/48				
Lincoln C	Tr	05/54	54-62	300	-	16

MIDDLETON Harry Oliver
Born: Doncaster, South Yorkshire, England, 12 April, 1995 — M

League Club	Source	Date Signed	Seasons Played	Apps	Subs	Gls
Doncaster Rov	Sch	07/13	14	1	3	0

MIDDLETON Henry (Harry)
Born: Birmingham, England, 18 March, 1937 — CF
England: Youth

League Club	Source	Date Signed	Seasons Played	Apps	Subs	Gls
Wolverhampton W	Jnr	08/54	55	1	-	0
Scunthorpe U	Tr	09/59	59-60	29	-	11
Portsmouth	Tr	06/61	61	17	-	5
Shrewsbury T	Tr	02/62	61-64	85	-	36
Mansfield T	Tr	11/64	64-65	45	1	24
Walsall	Tr	03/66	65-67	56	2	27

MIDDLETON James
Born: Blackridge, West Lothian, Scotland, 25 April, 1922 — WH
Died: Bathgate, West Lothian, Scotland, 4 October, 1997

League Club	Source	Date Signed	Seasons Played	Apps	Subs	Gls
Bradford C	Third Lanark	05/49	49	8	-	0

MIDDLETON John
Born: Skegness, Lincolnshire, England, 24 December, 1956 — G
England: U21-3/Youth

League Club	Source	Date Signed	Seasons Played	Apps	Subs	Gls
Nottingham F	App	11/74	74-77	90	0	0
Derby Co	Tr	09/77	77-79	73	0	0

MIDDLETON John
Born: Rawmarsh, South Yorkshire, England, 11 July, 1955 — CD

League Club	Source	Date Signed	Seasons Played	Apps	Subs	Gls
Bradford C	App	07/73	72-78	188	4	5

MIDDLETON Lee John
Born: Nuneaton, Warwickshire, England, 10 September, 1970 — FB

League Club	Source	Date Signed	Seasons Played	Apps	Subs	Gls
Coventry C	YT	05/89	89	0	2	0
Swindon T	Tr	07/92				
Cambridge U	Tr	11/95	95	1	2	0

MIDDLETON Matthew Young (Matt)
Born: Boldon, Tyne and Wear, England, 24 October, 1907 — G
Died: Sunderland, England, 19 April, 1979

League Club	Source	Date Signed	Seasons Played	Apps	Subs	Gls
Southport	Boldon CW	02/31	31-32	63	-	0
Sunderland	Tr	08/33	33-38	56	-	0
Plymouth Arg	Tr	05/39				
Bradford C	Horden CW	08/46	46-48	94	-	0
York C	Tr	02/49	48-49	55	-	0

MIDDLETON Peter Watson
Born: Rawmarsh, South Yorkshire, England, 13 September, 1948 — M

Died: Doncaster, South Yorkshire, England, April, 1977

League Club	Source	Date Signed	Seasons Played	Apps	Subs	Gls
Sheffield Wed	App	09/65				
Bradford C	Tr	06/68	68-72	127	4	25
Plymouth Arg	Tr	09/72	72	1	0	1

MIDDLETON Raymond (Ray)
Born: Boldon, Tyne and Wear, England, 6 September, 1919 — G
Died: Boston, Lincolnshire, England, 12 April, 1977
England: B-4

League Club	Source	Date Signed	Seasons Played	Apps	Subs	Gls
Chesterfield	North Shields	10/37	38-50	250	-	0
Derby Co	Tr	06/51	51-53	116	-	0

MIDDLETON Robert Rex (Ray)
Born: Stretford, Greater Manchester, England, 8 December, 1933 — IF

League Club	Source	Date Signed	Seasons Played	Apps	Subs	Gls
Southend U	Bulford U	11/57	57	5	-	1
Workington	Tr	10/58	58	2	-	0
Swindon T	Tr	12/58	58	5	-	0
Aldershot	Tr	07/59	59	5	-	0

MIDDLETON Stephen Roy (Steve)
Born: Portsmouth, England, 28 March, 1953 — G

League Club	Source	Date Signed	Seasons Played	Apps	Subs	Gls
Southampton	App	07/70	73-76	24	0	0
Torquay U	L	03/75	74	10	0	0
Portsmouth	Tr	07/77	77	26	0	0

MIDGLEY Craig Steven
Born: Bradford, England, 24 May, 1976 — F

League Club	Source	Date Signed	Seasons Played	Apps	Subs	Gls
Bradford C	YT	07/95	94-97	0	11	1
Scarborough	L	12/95	95	14	2	1
Scarborough	L	03/97	96	6	0	2
Darlington	L	12/97	97	1	0	0
Hartlepool U	Tr	03/98	97-00	61	35	18
Halifax T	Tr	07/01	01	12	12	3

MIDGLEY Neil Alan
Born: Cambridge, England, 21 October, 1978 — F

League Club	Source	Date Signed	Seasons Played	Apps	Subs	Gls
Ipswich T	YT	06/97	99	1	3	1
Luton T	L	09/99	99	8	2	3
Barnet	Tr	03/01	00	3	1	0

[MIDO] HOSSAM Ahmed Abdel Hamid
Born: Cairo, Egypt, 23 February, 1983 — F
Egypt: 51

League Club	Source	Date Signed	Seasons Played	Apps	Subs	Gls
Tottenham H	AS Roma (ITA)	01/05	04-06	35	13	14
Middlesbrough	Tr	08/07	07-08	13	12	6
Wigan Ath	L	01/09	08	10	2	2
West Ham U	L	01/10	09	5	4	0
Barnsley	El Zamalek (EGY)	06/12	12	0	1	0

MIDSON Jack William
Born: Stevenage, Hertfordshire, England, 12 September, 1983 — F

League Club	Source	Date Signed	Seasons Played	Apps	Subs	Gls
Oxford U	Histon	06/09	10	11	10	6
Southend U	L	11/10	10	4	0	2
Barnet	L	03/11	10	3	2	0
AFC Wimbledon	Tr	07/11	11-13	100	26	38

MIDWOOD Michael Adrian
Born: Burnley, Lancashire, England, 19 April, 1976 — F

League Club	Source	Date Signed	Seasons Played	Apps	Subs	Gls
Huddersfield T	YT	07/94				
Huddersfield T	Halifax T	08/97	97	0	1	0

MIELCZAREK Raymond (Ray)
Born: Caernarfon, Gwynedd, Wales, 10 February, 1946 — CD
Died: Wrexham, Wales, 30 October, 2013
Wales: 1/U23-2

League Club	Source	Date Signed	Seasons Played	Apps	Subs	Gls
Wrexham	Jnr	05/64	64-67	76	0	0
Huddersfield T	Tr	09/67	67-70	25	1	1
Rotherham U	Tr	01/71	70-73	114	1	7

MIFSUD Michael
Born: Valletta, Malta, 17 April, 1981 — F
Malta: 88

League Club	Source	Date Signed	Seasons Played	Apps	Subs	Gls
Coventry C	Lillestrom (NOR)	01/07	06-08	65	21	16
Barnsley	L	02/09	08	11	4	2

MIGLIORANZI Stefani
Born: Pocos de Caldas, Brazil, 20 September, 1977 — M

League Club	Source	Date Signed	Seasons Played	Apps	Subs	Gls
Portsmouth	St John's Univ (USA)	03/99	98-01	25	10	2
Swindon T	Tr	08/02	02-05	111	13	8

MIGNOLET Simon
Born: Sint-Truiden, Belgium, 6 May, 1988 — G
Belgium: 14/U21-8

League Club	Source	Date Signed	Seasons Played	Apps	Subs	Gls
Sunderland	Sint Truidense (BEL)	07/10	10-12	90	0	0
Liverpool	Tr	06/13	13-14	73	1	0

[MIGUEL] VITOR Miguel Angelo Leonardo
Born: Torres Vedras, Portugal, 30 June, 1989 — CD
Portugal: U21-16/Youth

League Club	Source	Date Signed	Seasons Played	Apps	Subs	Gls
Leicester C (L)	Benfica (POR)	08/10	10	13	2	3

MIHAILOV Borislav Biserov
Born: Sofia, Bulgaria, 12 February, 1963 — G
Bulgaria: 102

League Club	Source	Date Signed	Seasons Played	Apps	Subs	Gls
Reading	Botev Plovdiv (BUL)	09/95	95-96	24	0	0

MIHALY Ronald Raymond (Ron)
Born: Chesterfield, Derbyshire, England, 14 October, 1952 — CD
England: Schools

League Club	Source	Date Signed	Seasons Played	Apps	Subs	Gls
Chesterfield	Jnr	08/71	71	4	0	0

MIKAELSSON Tobias Lars
Born: Gothenburg, Sweden, 17 November, 1988 — F

League Club	Source	Date Signed	Seasons Played	Apps	Subs	Gls
Aston Villa	Sch	11/05				
Port Vale	L	01/08	07	5	1	0

MIKE Adrian Roosevelt (Adie)
Born: Manchester, England, 16 November, 1973 — F
England: Youth/Schools

League Club	Source	Date Signed	Seasons Played	Apps	Subs	Gls
Manchester C	YT	07/92	91-94	5	11	2
Bury	L	03/93	92	5	2	1
Stockport Co	Tr	08/95	95-96	4	5	0
Hartlepool U	L	10/96	96	7	0	1
Doncaster Rov	L	02/97	96	5	0	1
Doncaster Rov	Tr	08/97	97	42	0	4
Lincoln C	Stalybridge Celtic	08/02	02	5	12	2

MIKE Leon Jonathan
Born: Manchester, England, 4 September, 1981 — F
England: Youth/Schools

League Club	Source	Date Signed	Seasons Played	Apps	Subs	Gls
Manchester C	YT	09/98	01	1	1	0
Oxford U	L	09/00	00	1	2	0
Halifax T	L	02/01	00	2	5	0

[MIKEL OBI] OBINNA John Michael
Born: Jos, Nigeria, 22 April, 1987 — DM
Nigeria: 64

League Club	Source	Date Signed	Seasons Played	Apps	Subs	Gls
Chelsea	Lyn Oslo (NOR)	07/06	06-14	164	60	1

MIKLOSKO Ludek (Ludo)
Born: Ostrava, Czech Republic, 9 December, 1961 — G
Czechoslovakia: 42/B-1/U23

League Club	Source	Date Signed	Seasons Played	Apps	Subs	Gls
West Ham U	Banik Ostrava (CZE)	02/90	89-97	315	0	0
Queens Park Rgrs	Tr	10/98	98-00	57	0	0

MIKOLANDA Petr
Born: Prague, Czech Republic, 12 September, 1984 — F

League Club	Source	Date Signed	Seasons Played	Apps	Subs	Gls
West Ham U	Viktoria Zizkov (CZE)	07/05				
Northampton T	L	09/05	05	2	0	0
Swindon T	L	11/05	05	1	4	0
Rushden & D	L	01/06	05	7	2	1

MILANESE Mauro
Born: Trieste, Italy, 17 September, 1971 — LB

League Club	Source	Date Signed	Seasons Played	Apps	Subs	Gls
Queens Park Rgrs	Perugia (ITA)	08/05	05-06	36	4	0

MILBOURNE Ian
Born: Hexham, Northumberland, England, 21 January, 1979 — F

League Club	Source	Date Signed	Seasons Played	Apps	Subs	Gls
Newcastle U	YT	07/97				
Scarborough	Tr	08/98	98	2	14	0

MILBURN George William
Born: Ashington, Northumberland, England, 24 June, 1910 — RB
Died: Chesterfield, Derbyshire, England, 24 June, 1980

League Club	Source	Date Signed	Seasons Played	Apps	Subs	Gls
Leeds U	Ashington	03/28	28-36	157	-	1
Chesterfield	Tr	05/37	37-47	105	-	16

MILBURN James (Jim)
Born: Ashington, Northumberland, England, 21 June, 1919 — LB
Died: Wakefield, England, January, 1985

League Club	Source	Date Signed	Seasons Played	Apps	Subs	Gls
Leeds U	Ashington	10/36	46-51	207	-	15
Bradford Park Ave	Tr	06/52	52-54	90	-	10

MILBURN John (Jack)
Born: Ashington, Northumberland, England, 18 March, 1908 — LB
Died: Leeds, England, 21 August, 1979

League Club	Source	Date Signed	Seasons Played	Apps	Subs	Gls
Leeds U	Spen Black & White	11/27	29-38	386	-	28
Norwich C	Tr	02/39	38	15	-	0
Bradford C	Tr	10/46	46	14	-	3

MILBURN John Edward Thompson (Jackie)
Born: Ashington, Northumberland, England, 11 May, 1924 — CF
Died: Ashington, Northumberland, England, 9 October, 1988
England: 13/FLge-3//Northern Ireland: NILge-4

League Club	Source	Date Signed	Seasons Played	Apps	Subs	Gls
Newcastle U	Ashington ATC	08/43	46-56	353	-	177

MILBURN Stanley (Stan)
Born: Ashington, Northumberland, England, 27 October, 1926 — RB
Died: Rochdale, Greater Manchester, England, 30 July, 2010
England: B-1/FLge-2

League Club	Source	Date Signed	Seasons Played	Apps	Subs	Gls
Chesterfield	Ashington	01/47	46-51	179	-	0

League Club	Source	Date Signed	Seasons Played	Apps	Subs	Gls
Leicester C	Tr	03/52	51-57	173	-	1
Rochdale	Tr	01/59	58-64	238	-	26

MILBURN William Renton Wakenshaw (Bill)
Born: Sunniside, Tyne and Wear, England, 25 January, 1932 — WH

League Club	Source	Date Signed	Seasons Played	Apps	Subs	Gls
Gateshead		04/55	56	2	-	0

MILD Stig Hakan (Hakan)
Born: Trollhattan, Sweden, 14 June, 1971 — M
Sweden: 74/U23-4

League Club	Source	Date Signed	Seasons Played	Apps	Subs	Gls
Wimbledon	IFK Goteberg (SWE)	11/01	01	8	1	0

MILDENHALL Stephen James (Steve)
Born: Swindon, England, 13 May, 1978 — G

League Club	Source	Date Signed	Seasons Played	Apps	Subs	Gls
Swindon T	YT	07/96	96-00	29	4	0
Notts Co	Tr	07/01	01-04	75	1	0
Oldham Ath	Tr	12/04	04	6	0	0
Grimsby T	Tr	07/05	05	46	0	0
Yeovil T	Tr	07/06	06-07	75	0	0
Southend U	Tr	07/08	08-09	78	0	0
Millwall	Tr	07/10	11	9	1	0
Scunthorpe U	L	11/12	12	9	0	0
Bristol Rov	Tr	01/13	12-13	68	0	0

MILES Andrew (Andy)
Born: New Tredegar, Caerphilly, Wales, 25 May, 1961 — W

League Club	Source	Date Signed	Seasons Played	Apps	Subs	Gls
Newport Co	Ebbw Vale	08/85	85	3	1	2

MILES (PLUCK) Colin Ian
Born: Edmonton, N London, England, 6 September, 1978 — CD

League Club	Source	Date Signed	Seasons Played	Apps	Subs	Gls
Watford	YT	02/97	97	1	0	0
Yeovil T	Dover Ath	07/01	03-05	74	13	4
Port Vale	Tr	07/06	06-07	24	8	0

MILES Denis
Born: Normanton, West Yorkshire, England, 6 August, 1936 — RW

League Club	Source	Date Signed	Seasons Played	Apps	Subs	Gls
Bradford Park Ave	Snydale Ath	09/53	53-54	24	-	1
Southport	Tr	06/55	55-56	51	-	12

MILES Jeffrey (Jeff)
Born: Caldicot, Monmouthshire, Wales, 17 January, 1949 — G

League Club	Source	Date Signed	Seasons Played	Apps	Subs	Gls
Newport Co (Am)	Cheltenham T	04/68	67-68	4	0	0

MILES John Francis
Born: Fazakerley, Merseyside, England, 28 September, 1981 — W

League Club	Source	Date Signed	Seasons Played	Apps	Subs	Gls
Liverpool	YT	04/99				
Stoke C	Tr	03/02	01	0	1	0
Crewe Alex	Tr	08/02	02	0	5	1
Macclesfield T	Tr	03/03	02-06	75	47	21
Accrington Stan	Tr	07/07	07-09	86	9	6
MK Dons	L	01/08	07	7	5	0

MILES Jonathan David
Born: Colchester, Essex, England, 29 March, 1993 — G

League Club	Source	Date Signed	Seasons Played	Apps	Subs	Gls
Tottenham H	Sch	07/12				
Dagenham & Red	L	03/13	12	2	0	0

MILES Sidney George (Sid)
Born: Bournemouth, England, 16 May, 1934 — CH
Died: Bournemouth, England, 31 January, 2014

League Club	Source	Date Signed	Seasons Played	Apps	Subs	Gls
Bournemouth	RASC Malaya	12/56	57	1	-	0

MILES Terence (Terry)
Born: Stoke-on-Trent, England, 7 May, 1937 — LH

League Club	Source	Date Signed	Seasons Played	Apps	Subs	Gls
Port Vale	Milton YC	06/55	56-67	358	7	17

MILIJAS Nenad
Born: Belgrade, Serbia, 30 April, 1983 — M
Serbia: 25/U21-13

League Club	Source	Date Signed	Seasons Played	Apps	Subs	Gls
Wolverhampton W	R Star Belgrade (SRB)	07/09	09-11	38	24	4

MILKINS Albert John (John)
Born: Dagenham, E London, England, 3 January, 1944 — G
England: Youth

League Club	Source	Date Signed	Seasons Played	Apps	Subs	Gls
Portsmouth	Jnr	05/61	60-73	344	0	0
Oxford U	Tr	08/74	74-78	53	0	0

MILLAR Albert James (James)
Born: Falkirk, Scotland, 21 December, 1927 — LB
Died: Staffordshire, England, 4 April, 1997

League Club	Source	Date Signed	Seasons Played	Apps	Subs	Gls
Crewe Alex	Deal T	08/58	58-59	56	-	2

MILLAR Alistair (Ally)
Born: Glasgow, Scotland, 15 January, 1952 — M

League Club	Source	Date Signed	Seasons Played	Apps	Subs	Gls
Barnsley	Benburb Jnrs	02/71	70-79	273	16	17
York C	Tr	07/80	80	11	1	0

MILLAR Christian Dale
Born: Stoke-on-Trent, England, 27 November, 1989 — M

League Club	Source	Date Signed	Seasons Played	Apps	Subs	Gls
Macclesfield T	Sch	07/08	07-08	0	4	0

MILLAR John
Born: Coatbridge, Lanarkshire, Scotland, 8 December, 1966 — LB/M

League Club	Source	Date Signed	Seasons Played	Apps	Subs	Gls
Chelsea	Jnr	08/84	85-86	11	0	0
Northampton T	L	01/87	86	1	0	0
Blackburn Rov	Tr	07/87	87-90	122	4	1

MILLAR John
Born: Cardenden, Fife, Scotland, 31 December, 1927 — IF
Died: Lincoln, England, November, 1991

League Club	Source	Date Signed	Seasons Played	Apps	Subs	Gls
Bradford C	Queen of the South	10/48	49-51	44	-	7
Grimsby T	Tr	05/52	52	5	-	2

MILLAR John Ross
Born: Armadale, West Lothian, Scotland, 25 October, 1923 — CF
Died: Bathgate, West Lothian, Scotland, 2 February, 1986

League Club	Source	Date Signed	Seasons Played	Apps	Subs	Gls
Bradford C	Albion Rov	06/49	49	3	-	1

MILLAR Kirk Steven
Born: Belfast, Northern Ireland, 7 July, 1992 — W
Northern Ireland: U21-10

League Club	Source	Date Signed	Seasons Played	Apps	Subs	Gls
Oldham Ath	Sch	04/10	09-13	8	30	1

MILLAR Thomas Thomson (Tommy)
Born: Edinburgh, Scotland, 3 December, 1938 — FB
Died: Edinburgh, Scotland, 29 July, 2001

League Club	Source	Date Signed	Seasons Played	Apps	Subs	Gls
Colchester U	Bo'ness U	06/59	59-61	44	-	4

MILLAR William (Billy)
Born: Mansfield, Nottinghamshire, England, 7 February, 1952 — G

League Club	Source	Date Signed	Seasons Played	Apps	Subs	Gls
Doncaster Rov (Am)	Folkhouse OB	02/75	74	1	0	0

MILLAR William (Willie)
Born: Irvine, Ayrshire, Scotland, 24 July, 1924 — LW/IF
Died: Accrington, Lancashire, England, March, 1995

League Club	Source	Date Signed	Seasons Played	Apps	Subs	Gls
Swindon T	Stirling A	08/50	50-52	75	-	18
Gillingham	Tr	07/53	53-55	91	-	35
Accrington Stan	Tr	07/56	56	26	-	11

MILLAR William Paul (Paul)
Born: Belfast, Northern Ireland, 16 November, 1966 — M/F
Northern Ireland: U23-1

League Club	Source	Date Signed	Seasons Played	Apps	Subs	Gls
Port Vale	Portadown	12/88	89-90	19	21	5
Hereford U	L	10/90	90	5	0	2
Cardiff C	Tr	08/91	91-94	91	29	17

MILLARD Lance Julian
Born: Bristol, England, 24 June, 1938 — G

League Club	Source	Date Signed	Seasons Played	Apps	Subs	Gls
Aldershot	Bristol C (Am)	09/60	60	12	-	0
Barrow	Tr	07/64	64-65	52	0	0

MILLARD Leonard (Len)
Born: Coseley, West Midlands, England, 7 March, 1919 — LB
Died: Dudley, West Midlands, England, 3 March, 1997

League Club	Source	Date Signed	Seasons Played	Apps	Subs	Gls
West Bromwich A	Sunbeam	05/37	46-57	436	-	7

MILLARD Robert (Ray)
Born: South Shields, Tyne and Wear, England, 2 June, 1927 — IF

League Club	Source	Date Signed	Seasons Played	Apps	Subs	Gls
Middlesbrough		12/45				
Reading	Blyth Spartans	06/49	49	2	-	0
Walsall	Tr	06/50	50	10	-	1
Crystal Palace		08/55				

MILLBANK Aaron Craig
Born: Ramsgate, Kent, England, 4 February, 1995 — F

League Club	Source	Date Signed	Seasons Played	Apps	Subs	Gls
Gillingham	Sch	04/14	13	0	1	0

MILLBANK Joseph Henry (Joe)
Born: Edmonton, N London, England, 30 September, 1919 — CH
Died: Truro, Cornwall, England, February, 2002

League Club	Source	Date Signed	Seasons Played	Apps	Subs	Gls
Wolverhampton W		07/38				
Crystal Palace	Tr	08/39	46-47	38	-	1
Queens Park Rgrs	Tr	07/48	48	1	-	0

MILLEN Keith Derek
Born: Croydon, S London, England, 26 September, 1966 — CD

League Club	Source	Date Signed	Seasons Played	Apps	Subs	Gls
Brentford	Jnr	08/84	84-92	301	4	17
Watford	Tr	03/94	93-98	163	2	5
Bristol C	Tr	11/99	99-02	59	1	4

MILLER Adam Edward
Born: Hemel Hempstead, Hertfordshire, England, 19 February, 1982 — M
England: Semi Pro-1

League Club	Source	Date Signed	Seasons Played	Apps	Subs	Gls
Queens Park Rgrs	Aldershot T	11/04	04-05	10	5	0
Peterborough U	L	09/05	05	2	0	0
Gillingham	Stevenage Bor	11/07	07-09	80	9	13
Dagenham & Red	L	11/09	09	8	0	0

MILLER Alan John
Born: Epping, Essex, England, 29 March, 1970 — G
England: U21-4/Youth/Schools

League Club	Source	Date Signed	Seasons Played	Apps	Subs	Gls
Arsenal	YT	05/88	92-93	6	2	0
Plymouth Arg	L	11/88	88	13	0	0
West Bromwich A	L	08/91	91	3	0	0
Birmingham C	L	12/91	91	15	0	0
Middlesbrough	Tr	08/94	94-96	57	0	0
Grimsby T	L	01/97	96	3	0	0
West Bromwich A	Tr	02/97	96-99	98	0	0
Blackburn Rov	Tr	02/00	99	1	0	0
Bristol C	L	08/00	00	4	0	0
Coventry C	L	11/00	00	0	1	0

MILLER Alan John
Born: Preston, Lancashire, England, 13 September, 1970 LW

League Club	Source	Date Signed	Seasons Played	Apps	Subs	Gls
Torquay U	Bury (YT)	08/89	89	3	1	0

MILLER Alfred George Abraham (Alf)
Born: Portsmouth, England, 5 March, 1917 WH
Died: Southsea, Hampshire, England, 2 August, 1999

League Club	Source	Date Signed	Seasons Played	Apps	Subs	Gls
Portsmouth	Jnr	11/35				
Bristol Rov	Margate	07/37				
Southport	Tr	10/37	37-38	32	-	2
Plymouth Arg	Tr	07/39	46-47	9	-	0

MILLER Anthony William (Tony)
Born: Chelmsford, England, 26 October, 1937 IF

League Club	Source	Date Signed	Seasons Played	Apps	Subs	Gls
Colchester U	Jnr	05/58	59-63	3	-	0

MILLER Archibald (Archie)
Born: Larkhall, Lanarkshire, Scotland, 5 September, 1913 WH
Died: Motherwell, Lanarkshire, Scotland, 14 July, 2006
Scotland: 1/SLge-1/War-1

League Club	Source	Date Signed	Seasons Played	Apps	Subs	Gls
Blackburn Rov	Heart of Midlothian	11/47	47	6	-	0
Carlisle U	Kilmarnock	09/50	50	1	-	0
Workington	Heart of Midlothian	02/52	51	1	-	0

MILLER Ashley Jordan
Born: Dover, Kent, England, 8 June, 1994 F

League Club	Source	Date Signed	Seasons Played	Apps	Subs	Gls
Gillingham	Sch	09/11	10-11	2	4	1

MILLER Barry Steven
Born: Northolt, W London, England, 29 March, 1976 CD

League Club	Source	Date Signed	Seasons Played	Apps	Subs	Gls
Gillingham	Farnborough T	08/99	99	1	3	0

MILLER Brian George
Born: Hapton, Lancashire, England, 19 January, 1937 LH/CH
Died: Burnley, Lancashire, England, 7 April, 2007
England: 1/FLge-2/U23-3

League Club	Source	Date Signed	Seasons Played	Apps	Subs	Gls
Burnley	Jnr	02/54	55-66	379	0	29

MILLER Charles (Charlie)
Born: Glasgow, Scotland, 18 March, 1976 M
Scotland: 1/U21-8/Schools

League Club	Source	Date Signed	Seasons Played	Apps	Subs	Gls
Leicester C (L)	Glasgow Rangers	03/99	98	1	3	0
Watford	Glasgow Rangers	10/99	99	9	5	0

MILLER Colin Fyfe
Born: Hamilton, Ontario, Canada, 4 October, 1964 M/LB
Canada: 61/Youth

League Club	Source	Date Signed	Seasons Played	Apps	Subs	Gls
Doncaster Rov	Glasgow Rangers	12/86	86-87	61	0	3

MILLER David (Dave)
Born: Middlesbrough, England, 21 January, 1921 LH
Died: Doncaster, South Yorkshire, England, 28 May, 1989

League Club	Source	Date Signed	Seasons Played	Apps	Subs	Gls
Middlesbrough	Jnr	09/38				
Wolverhampton W	Tr	08/45	46	2	-	0
Derby Co	Tr	04/47	47	1	-	0
Doncaster Rov	Tr	01/48	47-52	140	-	3
Aldershot	Tr	03/54	53	11	-	0

MILLER David Brian (Dave)
Born: Burnley, Lancashire, England, 8 January, 1964 CD/M

League Club	Source	Date Signed	Seasons Played	Apps	Subs	Gls
Burnley	App	01/82	82-84	27	5	3
Crewe Alex	L	03/83	82	3	0	0
Tranmere Rov	Tr	07/85	85	25	4	1
Preston NE	Colne Dynamoes	12/86	86-89	50	8	2
Burnley	L	02/89	88	4	0	0
Carlisle U	Tr	09/89	89-91	108	1	7
Stockport Co	Tr	03/92	91-94	72	9	1
Wigan Ath	Tr	10/94	94-95	35	3	3

MILLER Edward (Eddie)
Born: Ulverston, Cumbria, England, 21 June, 1920 IF
Died: Barrow, Cumbria, England, 21 September, 2002

League Club	Source	Date Signed	Seasons Played	Apps	Subs	Gls
Barrow	Ulverston	05/46	46-50	124	-	30

MILLER Ernest George (George)
Born: Pretoria, South Africa, 17 October, 1927 IF

League Club	Source	Date Signed	Seasons Played	Apps	Subs	Gls
Leeds U	Arcadia Shep's (RSA)	11/50	50-51	13	-	1
Workington	Tr	03/52	51	11	-	0

MILLER George
Born: Larkhall, Lanarkshire, Scotland, 20 May, 1939 LH
Died: Wishaw, Lanarkshire, Scotland, 26 December, 2008
Scotland: SLge-1

League Club	Source	Date Signed	Seasons Played	Apps	Subs	Gls
Wolverhampton W	Dunfermline Ath	10/64	64-65	37	0	3

MILLER George Thomas
Born: Eccleston, Lancashire, England, 25 November, 1991 M

League Club	Source	Date Signed	Seasons Played	Apps	Subs	Gls
Preston NE	Sch	02/10	10-11	2	5	0
Accrington Stan	Tr	07/12	12-13	26	3	3

MILLER Graham Joseph Patrick
Born: South Africa, 25 August, 1927 CF

League Club	Source	Date Signed	Seasons Played	Apps	Subs	Gls
Workington		12/52	52	10	-	1
Aldershot	Tr	07/53				

MILLER Ian
Born: Perth, Scotland, 13 May, 1955 RW

League Club	Source	Date Signed	Seasons Played	Apps	Subs	Gls
Bury	Jeanfield Swifts	08/73	73	9	6	0
Nottingham F	Tr	08/74				
Doncaster Rov	Tr	08/75	75-77	124	0	14
Swindon T	Tr	07/78	78-80	123	4	9
Blackburn Rov	Tr	08/81	81-88	252	16	16
Port Vale	Tr	07/89	89	14	7	1
Scunthorpe U	Tr	08/90	90	8	4	0

MILLER Ian Jonathan
Born: Colchester, Essex, England, 23 November, 1983 CD

League Club	Source	Date Signed	Seasons Played	Apps	Subs	Gls
Ipswich T	Bury T	09/06	06	0	1	0
Boston U	L	11/06	06	12	0	0
Darlington	L	02/07	06	7	0	1
Darlington	Tr	07/07	07-09	74	15	4
Cambridge U	Grimsby T	06/13	14	8	0	0

MILLER Ishmael Anthony
Born: Manchester, England, 5 March, 1987 F

League Club	Source	Date Signed	Seasons Played	Apps	Subs	Gls
Manchester C	Sch	03/05	05-06	3	14	0
West Bromwich A	Tr	08/07	07-10	39	31	14
Queens Park Rgrs	L	01/11	10	4	8	1
Nottingham F	Tr	08/11	11	13	12	3
Middlesbrough	L	08/12	12	14	11	5
Yeovil T	L	11/13	13	19	0	10
Blackpool	Tr	08/14	14	16	6	2
Huddersfield T	Tr	02/15	14	9	7	3

MILLER James Alistair Williamson (Alistair)
Born: Glasgow, Scotland, 24 January, 1936 LW

League Club	Source	Date Signed	Seasons Played	Apps	Subs	Gls
Brighton & HA	St Mirren	04/62	61	1	-	0
Norwich C	Tr	05/62	62-63	23	-	2

MILLER John Tony (Johnny)
Born: Ipswich, England, 21 September, 1950 RW

League Club	Source	Date Signed	Seasons Played	Apps	Subs	Gls
Ipswich T	Jnr	07/68	68-73	38	13	2
Norwich C	Tr	10/74	74-75	22	1	3
Mansfield T	Tr	07/76	76-79	109	4	14
Port Vale	Tr	09/80	80	22	4	4

MILLER Joseph McSpirits
Born: Glasgow, Scotland, 2 October, 1934 LW

League Club	Source	Date Signed	Seasons Played	Apps	Subs	Gls
Swindon T	Hamilton Academical	06/56	56	12	-	0

MILLER Joseph Paul (Paul)
Born: Wolverhampton, England, 9 December, 1940 G
Died: Nuneaton, Warwickshire, England, 18 June, 1963

League Club	Source	Date Signed	Seasons Played	Apps	Subs	Gls
Shrewsbury T	St Nicholas BC	07/59	59-62	77	-	0

MILLER Justin James
Born: Johannesburg, South Africa, 16 December, 1980 CD

League Club	Source	Date Signed	Seasons Played	Apps	Subs	Gls
Ipswich T	Jnr	11/99				
Leyton Orient	L	09/02	02	13	0	0
Leyton Orient	Tr	01/03	02-06	138	12	5
Port Vale	Tr	07/07	07	12	2	0

MILLER Keith Raymond
Born: Lewisham, SE London, England, 26 January, 1948 LB/M

League Club	Source	Date Signed	Seasons Played	Apps	Subs	Gls
West Ham U	Walthamstow Ave	09/65	68-69	1	2	0
Bournemouth	Tr	07/70	70-79	381	2	19

MILLER Kenneth (Kenny)
Born: Edinburgh, Scotland, 23 December, 1979 F
Scotland: 69/B-1/U21-7

League Club	Source	Date Signed	Seasons Played	Apps	Subs	Gls
Wolverhampton W (L)	Glasgow Rangers	09/01	01	3	2	2
Wolverhampton W	Glasgow Rangers	12/01	01-05	128	34	50
Derby Co	Glasgow Celtic	08/07	07	30	0	4
Cardiff C	Bursaspor (TKY)	07/11	11	41	2	10

MILLER Kern Aaron
Born: Skegness, Lincolnshire, England, 2 September, 1991 CD

League Club	Source	Date Signed	Seasons Played	Apps	Subs	Gls
Lincoln C	Sch	07/10	08	0	1	0
Barnsley	Tr	01/11				
Accrington Stan	L	07/11	11	2	0	0

League Club	Source	Date Signed	Seasons Played	Apps	Subs	Gls
MILLER Kevin						
Born: Falmouth, Cornwall, England, 15 March, 1969						G
Exeter C	Newquay	03/89	88-92	163	0	0
Birmingham C	Tr	05/93	93	24	0	0
Watford	Tr	08/94	94-96	128	0	0
Crystal Palace	Tr	07/97	97-98	66	0	0
Barnsley	Tr	08/99	99-01	115	0	0
Exeter C	Tr	08/02	02	46	0	0
Bristol Rov	Tr	07/03	03-04	72	0	0
Southampton	Rtd	02/06	05	7	0	0
Torquay U	Tr	01/07	06	7	0	0
MILLER Lee Adamson						
Born: Lanark, Scotland, 18 May, 1983						F
Scotland: 3/B-3						
Bristol C	Falkirk	07/03	03-04	34	15	8
Middlesbrough	Aberdeen	02/10	09-10	6	5	0
Notts Co	L	11/10	10	5	1	2
Scunthorpe U	L	01/11	10	12	6	1
Carlisle U	Tr	08/11	11-13	84	6	28
MILLER Liam William Peter						
Born: Cork, Republic of Ireland, 13 February, 1981						M
Republic of Ireland: 21/U21-15						
Manchester U	Glasgow Celtic	07/04	04-05	3	6	0
Leeds U	L	11/05	05	26	2	1
Sunderland	Tr	08/06	06-08	41	16	3
Queens Park Rgrs	L	01/09	08	11	2	0
MILLER Lumley Robert (Bob)						
Born: Blaydon, Tyne and Wear, England, 3 August, 1938						W/IF
Sheffield U		07/62				
Hartlepool U	Tr	11/62	62	9	-	2
MILLER Mark John						
Born: Tynemouth, Tyne and Wear, England, 22 September, 1962						RW
Gillingham	Whitley Bay	10/81	81-82	5	4	1
Doncaster Rov	Whitley Bay	08/83	83	21	9	4
Darlington	Tr	08/84	84	4	3	1
MILLER Paul Anthony						
Born: Bisley, Surrey, England, 31 January, 1968						M/F
Wimbledon	Yeovil T	08/87	87-92	65	15	10
Newport Co	L	10/87	87	6	0	2
Bristol C	L	01/90	89	0	3	0
Bristol Rov	Tr	08/94	94-96	100	5	22
Lincoln C	Tr	08/97	97-00	93	22	11
MILLER Paul Richard						
Born: Stepney, E London, England, 11 October, 1959						CD
Tottenham H	App	05/77	78-86	206	2	7
Charlton Ath	Tr	02/87	86-88	40	2	2
Watford	Tr	10/88	88	20	0	1
Bournemouth	Tr	08/89	89-90	43	4	1
Brentford	L	11/89	89	3	0	0
Swansea C	Tr	01/91	90	8	4	0
MILLER Peter Derek						
Born: Hoyland, South Yorkshire, England, 4 December, 1929						CF/D
Died: Huddersfield, West Yorkshire, England, 17 July, 2012						
Bradford C		08/52	52-55	18	-	2
MILLER Ralph Ernest						
Born: Slough, Berkshire, England, 22 June, 1941						D
Died: 2014						
Charlton Ath	Slough T	09/63	64	8	-	0
Gillingham	Tr	05/65	65-67	103	0	4
Bournemouth	Tr	07/68	68-70	71	1	1
MILLER Ricky Howard						
Born: Hatfield, Hertfordshire, England, 13 March, 1989						F
Luton T	Boston U	06/14	14	2	10	1
MILLER Robert (Robbie)						
Born: Bedford, England, 28 March, 1980						M
Coventry C	West Ham U (YT)	08/98				
Cambridge U	Tr	08/99	99	0	1	0
MILLER Robert James						
Born: Manchester, England, 3 November, 1972						LB
Oldham Ath	YT	07/91				
Hull C	Tr	10/92	92-93	22	6	0
MILLER Roger Lucas						
Born: Rushden, Northamptonshire, England, 18 August, 1938						IF
Northampton T	Jnr	11/56	56-58	4	-	1
MILLER Shaun Robert						
Born: Alsager, Cheshire, England, 25 September, 1987						F
Crewe Alex	Sch	07/06	06-11	111	52	38
Sheffield U	Tr	07/12	12-13	12	16	4

League Club	Source	Date Signed	Seasons Played	Apps	Subs	Gls
Shrewsbury T	L	03/14	13	5	3	3
Coventry C	Tr	07/14	14	1	11	1
Crawley T	L	11/14	14	4	1	0
York C	L	03/15	14	2	4	0
MILLER Thomas William (Tommy)						
Born: Shotton Colliery, County Durham, England, 8 January, 1979						M
Hartlepool U	YT	07/97	97-00	130	7	35
Ipswich T	Tr	07/01	01-04	101	16	30
Sunderland	Tr	07/05	05-06	30	3	3
Preston NE	L	11/06	06	4	3	0
Ipswich T	Tr	07/07	07-08	58	11	10
Sheffield Wed	Tr	07/09	09-10	39	15	10
Huddersfield T	Tr	07/11	11	24	2	1
Swindon T	Tr	07/12	12	28	6	1
Bury	Tr	08/13	13	25	3	0
Hartlepool U	Tr	08/14	14	14	1	0
MILLER Walter						
Born: Cornforth, County Durham, England, 11 August, 1930						WH
Died: Durham, England, December, 2014						
Hartlepool U		09/48	49	1	-	0
Luton T	Spennymoor U	02/52				
MILLER William Nesbit (Willie)						
Born: Edinburgh, Scotland, 1 November, 1969						RB
Scotland: U21-7						
Wrexham (L)	Dundee	09/01	01	5	0	0
MILLETT Glynne Alexander						
Born: Crickhowell, Powys, Wales, 13 October, 1968						M
Newport Co	YT	07/87	86-87	23	13	2
MILLETT Michael Paul						
Born: Wigan, Greater Manchester, England, 22 September, 1977						CD
Died: Wigan, Greater Manchester, England, March, 1995						
England: Youth/Schools						
Wigan Ath	YT	10/94	94	1	2	0
MILLIGAN Charles Campbell (Chic)						
Born: Ardrossan, Ayrshire, Scotland, 26 July, 1930						CH
Colchester U	Ardrossan Winton Rov	05/56	56-60	185	-	3
MILLIGAN Dudley						
Born: Johannesburg, South Africa, 7 November, 1916						CF
Died: South Africa, 1971						
Northern Ireland: 1						
Chesterfield	Clyde (RSA)	11/38	38-46	47	-	18
Bournemouth	Tr	08/47	47-48	45	-	25
Walsall	Tr	10/48	48	5	-	1
MILLIGAN Jamie						
Born: Blackpool, Lancashire, England, 3 January, 1980						LM
England: Youth						
Everton	YT	06/97	98-99	0	4	0
Blackpool	Tr	03/01	00-02	10	20	1
Fleetwood T	Hyde U	11/05	12	3	5	0
MILLIGAN Laurence Courtney (Laurie)						
Born: Liverpool, England, 20 April, 1958						LB
Blackpool	App	04/76	76-78	19	0	0
Portsmouth	L	03/79	78	7	0	0
Rochdale	Aldershot (NC)	10/79	79	8	1	0
MILLIGAN Michael Joseph (Mike)						
Born: Manchester, England, 20 February, 1967						M
Republic of Ireland: 1/B-2/U23-1/U21-1						
Oldham Ath	App	03/85	85-89	161	1	17
Everton	Tr	08/90	90	16	1	1
Oldham Ath	Tr	07/91	91-93	117	0	6
Norwich C	Tr	06/94	94-99	113	11	5
Blackpool	Tr	07/00	00-01	25	3	1
MILLIGAN Ross						
Born: Dumfries, Scotland, 2 June, 1978						FB
Carlisle U	Glasgow Rangers	07/97	97	2	5	0
MILLIGAN Stephen Jonathan Francis (Steve)						
Born: Hyde, Greater Manchester, England, 13 June, 1973						D/M
Rochdale	YT	-	89	5	0	1
MILLIGAN Terence John (Terry)						
Born: Manchester, England, 10 January, 1966						M
Manchester C	App	11/83				
Oldham Ath	Finland	02/86				
Crewe Alex	Tr	07/86	86-87	71	6	5
MILLIN Alfred (Alf)						
Born: Rotherham, South Yorkshire, England, 18 December, 1933						LW
Derby Co	Jnr	08/51	55	1	-	0

MILLINGTON Anthony Horace (Tony)
Born: Hawarden, Flintshire, Wales, 5 June, 1943 — G
Died: Wrexham, North Wales, Wales, 5 August, 2015
Wales: 21/U23-4

League Club	Source	Date Signed	Seasons Played	Apps	Subs	Gls
West Bromwich A	Sutton T	07/60	61-62	40	-	0
Crystal Palace	Tr	10/64	64-65	16	0	0
Peterborough U	Tr	03/66	66-68	118	0	0
Swansea C	Tr	07/69	69-73	178	0	0

MILLINGTON Grenville Rodney (Gren)
Born: Queensferry, Flintshire, Wales, 10 December, 1951 — G
Wales: Amateur

League Club	Source	Date Signed	Seasons Played	Apps	Subs	Gls
Chester C (Am)	Rhyl	07/68	68	1	0	0
Chester C	Witton A	09/73	73-82	289	0	0
Wrexham	Oswestry T	12/83	83	13	0	0

MILLINGTON John Henry
Born: Coseley, West Midlands, England, 21 February, 1930 — LH
Died: Dudley, West Midlands, England, 5 January, 2010

League Club	Source	Date Signed	Seasons Played	Apps	Subs	Gls
Aston Villa	Jnr	09/48				
Walsall	Tr	07/51	51-52	23	-	0

MILLINGTON Ralph Victor
Born: Neston, Wirral, England, 18 June, 1930 — CH
Died: Heswall, Wirral, England, 21 December, 1999

League Club	Source	Date Signed	Seasons Played	Apps	Subs	Gls
Tranmere Rov	Neston	01/50	50-60	357	-	3

MILLION Esmond
Born: Ashington, Northumberland, England, 15 March, 1938 — G

League Club	Source	Date Signed	Seasons Played	Apps	Subs	Gls
Middlesbrough	Amble Jnrs	05/56	56-61	52	-	0
Bristol Rov	Tr	06/62	62	38	-	0

MILLS Ben
Born: Stoke-on-Trent, England, 23 March, 1989 — F

League Club	Source	Date Signed	Seasons Played	Apps	Subs	Gls
Macclesfield T	Nantwich T	01/12	11	5	7	0

MILLS Brian
Born: Stone, Staffordshire, England, 26 December, 1971 — F
England: Youth

League Club	Source	Date Signed	Seasons Played	Apps	Subs	Gls
Port Vale	YT	04/90	90-91	14	9	4

MILLS Daniel John (Danny)
Born: Norwich, England, 18 May, 1977 — RB
England: 19/U21-14/Youth

League Club	Source	Date Signed	Seasons Played	Apps	Subs	Gls
Norwich C	YT	11/94	95-97	46	20	0
Charlton Ath	Tr	03/98	97-98	45	0	3
Leeds U	Tr	07/99	99-02	96	5	3
Middlesbrough	L	08/03	03	28	0	0
Manchester C	Tr	07/04	04-06	47	4	1
Hull C	L	09/06	06	9	0	0
Charlton Ath	L	08/07	07	19	0	0
Derby Co	L	01/08	07	2	0	0

MILLS Daniel Peter (Danny)
Born: Croydon, S London, England, 2 June, 1991 — F

League Club	Source	Date Signed	Seasons Played	Apps	Subs	Gls
Peterborough U	Crawley T (Jnr)	07/09	09	1	2	0
Torquay U	L	09/09	09	0	2	0

MILLS Daniel Raymond (Danny)
Born: Sidcup, SE London, England, 13 February, 1975 — W

League Club	Source	Date Signed	Seasons Played	Apps	Subs	Gls
Charlton Ath	YT	07/93				
Barnet	Tr	09/95	95-97	10	17	0
Brighton & HA	Tr	07/98	98	1	1	0

MILLS David John
Born: Robin Hood's Bay, North Yorkshire, England, 6 December, 1951 — F
England: B/U23-8

League Club	Source	Date Signed	Seasons Played	Apps	Subs	Gls
Middlesbrough	App	12/68	68-78	278	18	76
West Bromwich A	Tr	01/79	78-82	44	15	6
Newcastle U	L	01/82	81	23	0	4
Sheffield Wed	Tr	01/83	82	15	0	3
Newcastle U	Tr	08/83	83	10	6	5
Middlesbrough	Tr	06/84	84	31	1	14
Darlington	Whitby T	08/86	86	12	5	2

MILLS Donald (Don)
Born: Maltby, South Yorkshire, England, 17 August, 1926 — IF
Died: Paignton, Devon, England, 17 February, 1994

League Club	Source	Date Signed	Seasons Played	Apps	Subs	Gls
Queens Park Rgrs	Maltby Main	08/46	46-50	76	-	9
Torquay U	L	03/49	48	12	-	4
Torquay U	L	08/49	49	22	-	9
Cardiff C	Tr	02/51	50	1	-	0
Leeds U	Tr	09/51	51-52	34	-	9
Torquay U	Tr	12/52	52-61	308	-	68

MILLS Gary Leonard
Born: Sheerness, Kent, England, 20 May, 1981 — M

League Club	Source	Date Signed	Seasons Played	Apps	Subs	Gls
Rushden & D	Jnr	07/99	01-05	65	22	2

MILLS Gary Roland
Born: Northampton, England, 11 November, 1961 — M
England: U21-2/Youth/Schools

League Club	Source	Date Signed	Seasons Played	Apps	Subs	Gls
Nottingham F	App	11/78	78-81	50	8	8
Derby Co (L)	Seattle Sounders (USA)	10/82	82	18	0	2
Nottingham F	Seattle Sounders (USA)	03/83	83-86	63	15	4
Notts Co	Tr	08/87	87-88	75	0	8
Leicester C	Tr	03/89	88-94	195	5	15
Notts Co	Tr	09/94	94-95	44	3	0

MILLS Gregory Adam (Greg)
Born: Leicester, England, 18 September, 1990 — W

League Club	Source	Date Signed	Seasons Played	Apps	Subs	Gls
Derby Co	Sch	07/09	09	0	2	0
Macclesfield T	L	01/10	09	0	1	0

MILLS Harry
Born: Bishop Auckland, County Durham, England, 23 July, 1922 — IF
Died: Gateshead, Tyne and Wear, England, July, 2003

League Club	Source	Date Signed	Seasons Played	Apps	Subs	Gls
Sheffield U	Consett	06/46	46	3	-	2
Rotherham U	Tr	03/48	47	6	-	3
Rochdale	Tunbridge Wells	04/51	50	1	-	0
Halifax T	Tr	08/52				

MILLS Henry Owen (Harry)
Born: Blyth, Northumberland, England, 23 August, 1922 — G
Died: Blyth, Northumberland, England, August, 1990

League Club	Source	Date Signed	Seasons Played	Apps	Subs	Gls
Huddersfield T	Blyth Spartans	03/48	47-55	157	-	0
Halifax T	Tr	12/55	55-56	27	-	0

MILLS James
Born: Rotherham, South Yorkshire, England, 30 September, 1915 — LH
Died: Rotherham, South Yorkshire, England, 14 January, 1994

League Club	Source	Date Signed	Seasons Played	Apps	Subs	Gls
Rotherham U	Dinnington Ath	08/37	37-38	54	-	4
Hull C	Tr	10/46	46-47	42	-	1
Halifax T	Tr	12/47	47	19	-	0

MILLS Jamie Mark
Born: Swindon, England, 31 August, 1981 — M

League Club	Source	Date Signed	Seasons Played	Apps	Subs	Gls
Swindon T	YT	07/99	00	0	2	0

MILLS John (Jack)
Born: Bagillt, Flintshire, Wales, 19 December, 1920 — RB
Died: Louth, Lincolnshire, England, 1982

League Club	Source	Date Signed	Seasons Played	Apps	Subs	Gls
Chester C		05/46	46	3	-	0

MILLS Joseph Nathan
Born: Swindon, England, 30 October, 1989 — LB

League Club	Source	Date Signed	Seasons Played	Apps	Subs	Gls
Southampton	Sch	11/06	08-10	14	12	0
Scunthorpe U	L	02/09	08	13	1	0
Doncaster Rov	L	10/10	10	17	1	2
Reading	Tr	08/11	11	13	2	0
Burnley	Tr	07/12	12	9	1	0
Oldham Ath	L	08/13	13	11	0	0
Shrewsbury T	L	01/14	13	12	1	0
Oldham Ath	Tr	06/14	14	28	2	0

MILLS Keith
Born: Newcastle-upon-Tyne, England, 30 December, 1963 — M

League Club	Source	Date Signed	Seasons Played	Apps	Subs	Gls
Carlisle U	North Shields	02/88	87	0	1	0

MILLS Keith David
Born: Egham, Surrey, England, 29 December, 1942 — RH

League Club	Source	Date Signed	Seasons Played	Apps	Subs	Gls
Grimsby T	Jnr	01/60	60	2	-	0

MILLS Leigh
Born: Winchester, Hampshire, England, 8 February, 1988 — CD

League Club	Source	Date Signed	Seasons Played	Apps	Subs	Gls
Tottenham H	Sch	07/05				
Gillingham	L	08/08	08	6	1	1

MILLS Matthew Claude (Matt)
Born: Swindon, England, 14 July, 1986 — CD
England: Youth

League Club	Source	Date Signed	Seasons Played	Apps	Subs	Gls
Southampton	Sch	07/04	05	3	1	0
Coventry C	L	09/04	04	4	0	0
Bournemouth	L	02/05	04	12	0	3
Manchester C	Tr	01/06	05-06	1	1	0
Colchester U	L	01/07	06	8	1	0
Doncaster Rov	L	08/07	07	13	1	2
Doncaster Rov	Tr	01/08	07-08	57	4	1
Reading	Tr	08/09	09-10	60	1	4
Leicester C	Tr	07/11	11	25	0	1
Bolton W	Tr	07/12	12-14	84	3	6

MILLS Michael Dennis (Mick)
Born: Godalming, Surrey, England, 4 January, 1949 — FB
England: 42/FLge-2/U23-5/Youth

League Club	Source	Date Signed	Seasons Played	Apps	Subs	Gls
Ipswich T	Portsmouth (App)	02/66	65-82	588	3	22
Southampton	Tr	11/82	82-84	103	0	3
Stoke C	Tr	07/85	85-87	38	0	0

MILLS Neil
Born: Littleborough, Greater Manchester, England, 27 October, 1963 — F

League Club	Source	Date Signed	Seasons Played	Apps	Subs	Gls
Rochdale	Tim Bobbin	08/86	86	4	6	0
Stockport Co	Tr	08/87	87	5	2	0

MILLS Pablo Simeon Ishmael
Born: Birmingham, England, 27 May, 1984 — CD
England: Youth

League Club	Source	Date Signed	Seasons Played	Apps	Subs	Gls
Derby Co	Sch	07/02	02-05	40	18	0
MK Dons	L	08/05	05	16	0	1
Walsall	L	02/06	05	14	0	0
Rotherham U	Tr	07/06	06-09	127	9	3
Crawley T	Tr	07/10	11	19	2	2
Rotherham U	Macclesfield T	08/13	13	4	6	0
Bury	Tr	01/14	13-14	39	0	0
Cheltenham T	L	02/15	14	8	0	0

MILLS Robert Brian (Bobby)
Born: Edmonton, N London, England, 16 March, 1955 — M

League Club	Source	Date Signed	Seasons Played	Apps	Subs	Gls
Colchester U	App	12/72	71-73	20	6	0

MILLS Roland Walter George (Roly)
Born: Daventry, Northamptonshire, England, 22 June, 1933 — WH/F
Died: Northampton, England, 8 February, 2010
England: Youth

League Club	Source	Date Signed	Seasons Played	Apps	Subs	Gls
Northampton T	Jnr	05/51	54-63	305	-	30

MILLS Rowan Lee (Lee)
Born: Mexborough, South Yorkshire, England, 10 July, 1970 — F

League Club	Source	Date Signed	Seasons Played	Apps	Subs	Gls
Wolverhampton W	Stocksbridge Pk Steels	12/92	93-94	12	13	2
Derby Co	Tr	02/95	94	16	0	7
Port Vale	Tr	08/95	95-97	81	28	35
Bradford C	Tr	08/98	98-99	63	2	28
Manchester C	L	03/00	99	1	2	0
Portsmouth	Tr	08/00	00-01	24	2	4
Coventry C	Tr	11/01	01-02	30	8	7
Stoke C	Tr	01/03	02	7	4	2

MILLS Sean Douglas
Born: Ebbw Vale, Blaenau Gwent, Wales, 1 June, 1968 — M

League Club	Source	Date Signed	Seasons Played	Apps	Subs	Gls
Newport Co	Sunderland (App)	08/86	86	5	2	0

MILLS Simon Ashley
Born: Sheffield, England, 16 August, 1964 — RB/M
England: Youth

League Club	Source	Date Signed	Seasons Played	Apps	Subs	Gls
Sheffield Wed	App	08/82	82-84	1	4	0
York C	Tr	06/85	85-87	97	2	5
Port Vale	Tr	12/87	87-92	180	4	8

MILLS Stephen John (Steve)
Born: Portsmouth, England, 9 December, 1953 — FB
Died: Southampton, England, 7 August, 1988
England: U23-1

League Club	Source	Date Signed	Seasons Played	Apps	Subs	Gls
Southampton	App	07/71	72-76	57	4	0

MILLWARD Horace Douglas (Doug)
Born: Sheffield, England, 10 August, 1931 — IF
Died: Baltimore, Maryland, USA, 23 October, 2000

League Club	Source	Date Signed	Seasons Played	Apps	Subs	Gls
Southampton	Doncaster Rov (Am)	02/52				
Ipswich T	Tr	07/55	55-62	143	-	35

MILNE Alexander Soutar (Alec)
Born: Dundee, Scotland, 4 June, 1937 — FB
Scotland: U23-1

League Club	Source	Date Signed	Seasons Played	Apps	Subs	Gls
Cardiff C	Arbroath	03/57	57-64	172	-	1

MILNE Andrew Alexander
Born: York, England, 30 September, 1990 — CD
Scotland: Youth

League Club	Source	Date Signed	Seasons Played	Apps	Subs	Gls
Leeds U	Sch	07/09				
Darlington	L	11/09	09	12	1	0

MILNE Gordon
Born: Preston, Lancashire, England, 29 March, 1937 — RH
England: 14/FLge-2

League Club	Source	Date Signed	Seasons Played	Apps	Subs	Gls
Preston NE	Morecambe	01/56	56-60	81	-	3
Liverpool	Tr	09/60	60-66	234	2	18
Blackpool	Tr	05/67	67-69	60	4	4

MILNE John Buchanan (Johnny)
Born: Rosehearty, Aberdeenshire, Scotland, 27 April, 1911 — RB
Died: Cheadle, Greater Manchester, England, 6 September, 1994

League Club	Source	Date Signed	Seasons Played	Apps	Subs	Gls
Plymouth Arg	Fraserburgh	05/33	34-36	3	-	0
Southend U	Tr	06/37	37-38	66	-	1
Barrow	Tr	08/46	46	32	-	0
Oldham Ath	Tr	08/47	47	13	-	0

MILNE Kenneth (Kenny)
Born: Alloa, Stirlingshire, Scotland, 26 August, 1979 — CD
Scotland: U21-1

League Club	Source	Date Signed	Seasons Played	Apps	Subs	Gls
Scunthorpe U	Falkirk	07/08	08-09	5	0	0

MILNE Maurice
Born: Dundee, Scotland, 21 October, 1932 — LW
Died: Tayport, Fife, Scotland, 10 August, 1998

League Club	Source	Date Signed	Seasons Played	Apps	Subs	Gls
Norwich C	Dundee U	05/57	57	5	-	0

MILNE Michael (Mike)
Born: Aberdeen, Scotland, 17 August, 1959 — FB

League Club	Source	Date Signed	Seasons Played	Apps	Subs	Gls
Sunderland	App	05/77				
Rochdale		02/79	78	1	1	0

MILNE Ralph
Born: Dundee, Scotland, 13 May, 1961 — RW
Died: Dundee, Scotland, 6 September, 2015
Scotland: U21-3/Youth

League Club	Source	Date Signed	Seasons Played	Apps	Subs	Gls
Charlton Ath	Dundee U	01/87	86-87	19	3	0
Bristol C	Tr	01/88	87-88	29	1	6
Manchester U	Tr	11/88	88-89	19	4	3

MILNE Steven Craig
Born: Forfar, Angus, Scotland, 5 May, 1980 — F

League Club	Source	Date Signed	Seasons Played	Apps	Subs	Gls
Plymouth Arg	Dundee	07/04	04	0	12	0

MILNER Alfred John George (Alf)
Born: Harrogate, North Yorkshire, England, 6 February, 1919 — RW
Died: Bury St Edmunds, Suffolk, England, 20 December, 2002

League Club	Source	Date Signed	Seasons Played	Apps	Subs	Gls
Aldershot	Aldershot Garrison	08/46	46	7	-	1
Darlington	Tr	03/48	47-48	28	-	5
Hartlepool U	Stockton	11/51				

MILNER Andrew John (Andy)
Born: Kendal, Cumbria, England, 10 February, 1967 — F/W

League Club	Source	Date Signed	Seasons Played	Apps	Subs	Gls
Manchester C	Netherfield	01/89				
Rochdale	Tr	01/90	89-93	103	24	25
Chester C	Tr	08/94	94-97	106	19	24

MILNER James Edward (Jimmy)
Born: Newcastle-upon-Tyne, England, 3 February, 1933 — IF

League Club	Source	Date Signed	Seasons Played	Apps	Subs	Gls
Burnley	Blyth Spartans	12/52	53	1	-	0
Darlington	Tr	12/57	57-60	149	-	27
Accrington Stan	Tr	09/61				
Tranmere Rov	Tr	06/62	62	18	-	3

MILNER James Philip
Born: Leeds, England, 4 January, 1986 — RM
England: 53/U21-46/Youth/Schools

League Club	Source	Date Signed	Seasons Played	Apps	Subs	Gls
Leeds U	Sch	02/03	02-03	28	20	5
Swindon T	L	09/03	03	6	0	2
Newcastle U	Tr	07/04	04-08	72	22	6
Aston Villa	L	08/05	05	27	0	1
Aston Villa	Tr	08/08	08-10	68	5	11
Manchester C	Tr	08/10	10-14	89	58	13

MILNER John
Born: Huddersfield, West Yorkshire, England, 14 May, 1942 — RH

League Club	Source	Date Signed	Seasons Played	Apps	Subs	Gls
Huddersfield T	Jnr	05/59	60-62	17	-	0
Lincoln C	Tr	10/63	63-66	109	0	6
Bradford Park Ave	Tr	02/67	66	6	2	0

MILNER Jonathan Robert
Born: Mansfield, Nottinghamshire, England, 30 March, 1981 — F

League Club	Source	Date Signed	Seasons Played	Apps	Subs	Gls
Mansfield T	YT	-	97	1	6	0

MILNER Marcus Raglan Webb
Born: Kingston, Jamaica, 28 November, 1991 — M

League Club	Source	Date Signed	Seasons Played	Apps	Subs	Gls
Southend U	Sch	-	09	0	1	0

MILNER Michael (Mike)
Born: Hull, England, 21 September, 1939 — CH

League Club	Source	Date Signed	Seasons Played	Apps	Subs	Gls
Hull C	Jnr	07/57	58-67	160	0	0
Stockport Co	Tr	07/68	68	41	0	0
Barrow	Tr	09/69	69	11	0	0
Bradford C	Tr	12/69	69	0	1	0

MILOSAVLJEVIC Goran
Born: Kraljevo, Yugoslavia, 11 April, 1967 — M

League Club	Source	Date Signed	Seasons Played	Apps	Subs	Gls
Chester C	US Montelimar (FRA)	09/99	99	11	1	0

MILOSEVIC Dejan (Danny)
Born: Melbourne, Australia, 26 June, 1978 — G
Australia: U23/Youth

League Club	Source	Date Signed	Seasons Played	Apps	Subs	Gls
Leeds U	Perth Glory (AUS)	01/00				
Plymouth Arg	L	11/02	02	1	0	0
Crewe Alex	L	01/03	02	1	0	0

MILOSEVIC Savo
Born: Bijeljina, Bosnia & Herzegovina, 2 September, 1973 — F
Serbia: 102

League Club	Source	Date Signed	Seasons Played	Apps	Subs	Gls
Aston Villa	Part'n Belgrade (YUG)	07/95	95-97	84	6	28

MILSOM Paul Jason
Born: Bristol, England, 5 October, 1974 — F

League Club	Source	Date Signed	Seasons Played	Apps	Subs	Gls
Bristol C	YT	07/93	93	1	2	0
Cardiff C	Tr	03/95	94	1	2	0

MILSOM Robert Steven (Rob)
Born: Redhill, Surrey, England, 2 January, 1987 — M

League Club	Source	Date Signed	Seasons Played	Apps	Subs	Gls
Fulham	Sch	12/05	08	0	1	0
Brentford	L	02/08	07	5	1	0
Southend U	L	11/08	08	6	0	0
Rotherham U	Aberdeen	06/13	13-14	21	14	1
Bury	L	11/14	14	2	0	0

MILTON Clement Arthur (Arthur)
Born: Bristol, England, 10 March, 1928 — RW
Died: Bristol, England, 25 April, 2007
England: 1

League Club	Source	Date Signed	Seasons Played	Apps	Subs	Gls
Arsenal	Jnr	07/46	50-54	75	-	18
Bristol C	Tr	02/55	54	14	-	3

MILTON Roy
Born: Brixham, Devon, England, 27 November, 1934 — G

League Club	Source	Date Signed	Seasons Played	Apps	Subs	Gls
Bury	Jnr	10/52				
Torquay U	Tr	08/56	56	1	-	0

MILTON Russell Maurice
Born: Folkestone, Kent, England, 12 January, 1969 — M
England: Semi Pro-2

League Club	Source	Date Signed	Seasons Played	Apps	Subs	Gls
Arsenal	App	02/87				
Cheltenham T	Dover Ath	08/97	99-02	108	9	14

MILTON Simon Charles
Born: Fulham, W London, England, 23 August, 1963 — M

League Club	Source	Date Signed	Seasons Played	Apps	Subs	Gls
Ipswich T	Bury T	07/87	87-97	217	64	48
Exeter C	L	11/87	87	2	0	3
Torquay U	L	03/88	87	4	0	1

MILTON Stephen (Steve)
Born: Fulham, W London, England, 13 April, 1963 — F

League Club	Source	Date Signed	Seasons Played	Apps	Subs	Gls
West Ham U	App	04/81				
Fulham	Whyteleafe	10/89	89-91	39	19	9

MIMMS Robert Andrew (Bobby)
Born: York, England, 12 October, 1963 — G
England: U21-3

League Club	Source	Date Signed	Seasons Played	Apps	Subs	Gls
Halifax T	App	08/81				
Rotherham U	Tr	11/81	81-84	83	0	0
Everton	Tr	05/85	85-87	29	0	0
Notts Co	L	03/86	85	2	0	0
Sunderland	L	12/86	86	4	0	0
Blackburn Rov	L	01/87	86	6	0	0
Manchester C	L	09/87	87	3	0	0
Tottenham H	Tr	02/88	87-89	37	0	0
Blackburn Rov	Tr	12/90	90-95	126	2	0
Crystal Palace	Tr	08/96	96	1	0	0
Preston NE	Tr	09/96	96	27	0	0
Rotherham U	Tr	08/97	97	43	0	0
York C	Tr	08/98	98-99	63	0	0
Mansfield T	Tr	03/00	99-00	45	0	0

[MINEIRO] DA SILVA Carlos Luciano
Born: Porto Alegre, Brazil, 2 August, 1975 — M
Brazil: 24

League Club	Source	Date Signed	Seasons Played	Apps	Subs	Gls
Chelsea	Hertha Berlin (GER)	09/08	08	0	1	0

MINETT Jason Keith
Born: Peterborough, England, 12 August, 1971 — LB/M

League Club	Source	Date Signed	Seasons Played	Apps	Subs	Gls
Norwich C	YT	07/89	90-92	0	3	0
Exeter C	Tr	03/93	92-94	83	5	3
Lincoln C	Tr	07/95	95-96	41	5	5
Exeter C	Tr	01/97	96-97	19	0	0

MINGOIA Pietro (Piero)
Born: Enfield, N London, England, 20 October, 1991 — W

League Club	Source	Date Signed	Seasons Played	Apps	Subs	Gls
Watford	Sch	07/10	10	2	3	0
Accrington Stan	L	09/12	12	4	3	1
Accrington Stan	Tr	08/13	13-14	65	8	9

MINGS Tyrone Deon
Born: Bath, England, 13 March, 1993 — LB

League Club	Source	Date Signed	Seasons Played	Apps	Subs	Gls
Ipswich T	Chippenham T	12/12	12-14	43	14	1

MINIHAN Samuel Joseph (Sam)
Born: Rochdale, Greater Manchester, England, 16 February, 1994 — CD

League Club	Source	Date Signed	Seasons Played	Apps	Subs	Gls
Rochdale	Sch	07/12	11	1	0	0

MINNOCK John Joseph
Born: Tullamore, Republic of Ireland, 12 November, 1949 — W
Republic of Ireland: LoI-2/U23-2

League Club	Source	Date Signed	Seasons Played	Apps	Subs	Gls
Charlton Ath	St Patrick's Ath (ROI)	02/69	69	0	1	0

MINSHULL Lee Benjamin
Born: Chatham, Kent, England, 11 November, 1985 — M

League Club	Source	Date Signed	Seasons Played	Apps	Subs	Gls
AFC Wimbledon	Tonbridge Angels	06/10	11	13	5	0
Newport Co	Tr	01/12	13-14	68	11	7

MINSHULL Raymond (Ray)
Born: Bolton, Greater Manchester, England, 15 July, 1920 — G
Died: Southport, Merseyside, England, 15 February, 2005

League Club	Source	Date Signed	Seasons Played	Apps	Subs	Gls
Liverpool	Southport (Am)	09/46	46-49	28	-	0
Southport	Tr	07/51	51-57	217	-	0
Bradford Park Ave	Tr	12/57	57-58	28	-	0

MINTO Scott Christopher
Born: Bromborough, Wirral, England, 6 August, 1971 — LB
England: U21-6/Youth

League Club	Source	Date Signed	Seasons Played	Apps	Subs	Gls
Charlton Ath	YT	02/89	88-93	171	9	7
Chelsea	Tr	05/94	94-96	53	1	4
West Ham U	Benfica (POR)	01/99	98-02	44	7	0
Rotherham U	Tr	08/03	03-05	46	6	0

MINTON Albert Edward
Born: Walsall, West Midlands, England, 22 September, 1937 — CF
England: Youth

League Club	Source	Date Signed	Seasons Played	Apps	Subs	Gls
Blackpool	Derby Co (Am)	10/54				
Scunthorpe U	Tr	07/57	57-58	5	-	2
Doncaster Rov	Tr	12/58	58	11	-	2

MINTON Jeffrey Simon Thompson (Jeff)
Born: Hackney, E London, England, 28 December, 1973 — M

League Club	Source	Date Signed	Seasons Played	Apps	Subs	Gls
Tottenham H	YT	01/92	91	2	0	1
Brighton & HA	Tr	07/94	94-98	167	7	31
Port Vale	Tr	07/99	99-00	34	2	4
Rotherham U	Tr	03/01	00	5	4	2
Leyton Orient	Tr	07/01	01	32	1	5

MINTON Roger Christopher
Born: Birmingham, England, 4 June, 1951 — RB

League Club	Source	Date Signed	Seasons Played	Apps	Subs	Gls
West Bromwich A	App	06/69	70-74	24	2	1

MIOTTO Simon Jonathan
Born: Launceston, Tasmania, Australia, 5 September, 1969 — G

League Club	Source	Date Signed	Seasons Played	Apps	Subs	Gls
Hartlepool U	Riverside Olym'c (AUS)	07/98	98	5	0	0

MIQUEL-PONS Ignasi
Born: Barcelona, Spain, 28 September, 1992 — CD
Spain: Youth

League Club	Source	Date Signed	Seasons Played	Apps	Subs	Gls
Arsenal	Sch	10/09	11-12	1	4	0
Leicester C	L	08/13	13	6	1	0
Norwich C	Tr	09/14				

MIRALLAS Kevin Antonio Joel Gislain
Born: Liege, Belgium, 5 October, 1987 — LW
Belgium: 49/U21-5/Youth

League Club	Source	Date Signed	Seasons Played	Apps	Subs	Gls
Everton	Olympiakos (GRE)	08/12	12-14	69	19	21

MIRANDA Jose Silvio Lima Gomes
Born: Lisbon, Portugal, 2 April, 1974 — M

League Club	Source	Date Signed	Seasons Played	Apps	Subs	Gls
Rotherham U	FC Felgueiras (POR)	08/01	01	2	0	0

[MIRANDINHA] DA SILVA Francisco Ernandi Lima
Born: Fortaleza, Brazil, 2 July, 1959 — F
Brazil: 4

League Club	Source	Date Signed	Seasons Played	Apps	Subs	Gls
Newcastle U	Palmeiras (BRA)	08/87	87-88	47	7	20

MIRFIN David Matthew
Born: Sheffield, England, 18 April, 1985 — CD

League Club	Source	Date Signed	Seasons Played	Apps	Subs	Gls
Huddersfield T	Sch	12/03	02-07	141	20	9
Scunthorpe U	Tr	08/08	08-10	92	1	4
Watford	Tr	07/11	11	3	1	0
Scunthorpe U	Tr	01/12	11-13	87	7	3
Hartlepool U	L	02/15	14	15	0	0

MIROCEVIC Anton (Ante)
Born: Titograd, Yugoslavia, 6 August, 1952 — M
Yugoslavia: 6

League Club	Source	Date Signed	Seasons Played	Apps	Subs	Gls
Sheffield Wed	FC Budocnost (YUG)	10/80	80-82	58	3	6

MIRZA Nicolas
Born: Paris, France, 21 July, 1985 — M
Martinique: 3

League Club	Source	Date Signed	Seasons Played	Apps	Subs	Gls
Yeovil T	Paris St-Germain (FRA)	07/04	04	0	3	0

MISKELLY David Thomas
Born: Newtownards, Down, Northern Ireland, 3 September, 1979 — G
Northern Ireland: U21-11/Youth

League Club	Source	Date Signed	Seasons Played	Apps	Subs	Gls
Oldham Ath	YT	07/97	98-02	17	3	0

MISON Michael
Born: Southwark, S London, England, 8 November, 1975 — M

League Club	Source	Date Signed	Seasons Played	Apps	Subs	Gls
Fulham	YT	07/94	93-96	35	20	5

MISSE-MISSE Jean-Jacques
Born: Yaounde, Cameroon, 7 August, 1968 — F
Cameroon: 10

League Club	Source	Date Signed	Seasons Played	Apps	Subs	Gls
Chesterfield	Dundee U	03/98	97	1	0	0

MITCHEL-KING Matthew John (Matt)
Born: Reading, England, 12 September, 1983 — CD

League Club	Source	Date Signed	Seasons Played	Apps	Subs	Gls
Crewe Alex	Histon	06/09	09-10	40	6	0
AFC Wimbledon	Tr	07/11	11-12	46	1	2

MITCHELL Adam John
Born: Barnard Castle, County Durham, England, 3 April, 1993 — W

League Club	Source	Date Signed	Seasons Played	Apps	Subs	Gls
Sunderland	Sch	10/11	12	0	1	0

MITCHELL Albert James (Bert)
Born: Hanley, Potteries, England, 22 January, 1922 — LW
Died: Leek, Staffordshire, England, 4 April, 1997
England: B-1

League Club	Source	Date Signed	Seasons Played	Apps	Subs	Gls
Stoke C	Burslem A	05/41	46-47	10	-	2
Blackburn Rov	Tr	02/48	47	3	-	0
Northampton T	Kettering T	05/49	49-50	81	-	21
Luton T	Tr	07/51	51-54	106	-	41
Middlesbrough	Tr	09/54	54-55	50	-	6
Southport	Tr	08/56	56	16	-	3

MITCHELL Alexander Russell (Alec)
Born: Greenock, Inverclyde, Scotland, 24 May, 1918 — FB
Died: Ipswich, England, 13 October, 1990

League Club	Source	Date Signed	Seasons Played	Apps	Subs	Gls
Ipswich T	Bute Ath	08/46	47-49	42	-	2

MITCHELL Andrew Barry (Andy)
Born: Rotherham, South Yorkshire, England, 12 September, 1976 — FB

League Club	Source	Date Signed	Seasons Played	Apps	Subs	Gls
Aston Villa	YT	09/93				
Chesterfield	Tr	09/96	96	1	1	0

MITCHELL Andrew John (Andy)
Born: Liverpool, England, 18 April, 1990 — RW

League Club	Source	Date Signed	Seasons Played	Apps	Subs	Gls
Chester C	Sch	10/08	07	0	4	0

MITCHELL Anthony John (Tony)
Born: Redruth, Cornwall, England, 7 September, 1956 — RB

League Club	Source	Date Signed	Seasons Played	Apps	Subs	Gls
Exeter C	Leatherhead	07/77	78-81	60	0	0

MITCHELL Arnold
Born: Rotherham, South Yorkshire, England, 1 December, 1929 — WH/LB
Died: Exeter, England, 19 October, 2014

League Club	Source	Date Signed	Seasons Played	Apps	Subs	Gls
Derby Co	Sheffield Wed (Am)	02/48				
Nottingham F	Tr	03/50				
Notts Co	Tr	05/51	51	1	-	0
Exeter C	Tr	07/52	52-65	495	0	44

MITCHELL Barrie Horace
Born: Aberdeen, Scotland, 15 March, 1947 — F

League Club	Source	Date Signed	Seasons Played	Apps	Subs	Gls
Tranmere Rov	Aberdeen	02/74	73-75	77	6	10
Preston NE	Tr	07/76	76	7	4	2
York C	Tr	09/77	77	1	2	0

MITCHELL Charles Brian (Brian)
Born: Stonehaven, Aberdeenshire, Scotland, 16 July, 1963 — RB
Scotland: Schools

League Club	Source	Date Signed	Seasons Played	Apps	Subs	Gls
Bradford C	Aberdeen	02/87	86-91	170	8	9
Bristol C	Tr	07/92	92	15	1	0
Hull C	Tr	08/93	93	9	0	0

MITCHELL Christopher Philip (Chris)
Born: Stirling, Scotland, 21 July, 1988 — RB/M
Scotland: U21-7

League Club	Source	Date Signed	Seasons Played	Apps	Subs	Gls
Bradford C	Falkirk	07/11	11	10	1	1

MITCHELL Craig Richard
Born: Mansfield, Nottinghamshire, England, 6 May, 1985 — F

League Club	Source	Date Signed	Seasons Played	Apps	Subs	Gls
Mansfield T	Sch	07/03	02-03	3	13	1

MITCHELL David John (Dave)
Born: Stoke-on-Trent, England, 24 August, 1945 — CF

League Club	Source	Date Signed	Seasons Played	Apps	Subs	Gls
Port Vale	Jnr	03/64	64-65	21	0	4
Ipswich T	Tr	08/66	66	0	2	0

MITCHELL David Stuart
Born: Glasgow, Scotland, 13 June, 1962 — F
Australia: 44/Youth

League Club	Source	Date Signed	Seasons Played	Apps	Subs	Gls
Chelsea	Feyenoord (NED)	01/89	88-90	7	0	0
Newcastle U	L	01/91	90	2	0	1
Swindon T	Tr	07/91	91-92	61	7	16
Millwall	Altay Izmir (TKY)	10/93	93-94	49	6	15

MITCHELL Frank Rollason
Born: Goulburn, NSW, Australia, 3 June, 1922 — LH
Died: Warwick, England, 2 April, 1984

League Club	Source	Date Signed	Seasons Played	Apps	Subs	Gls
Birmingham C	Coventry C (Am)	09/43	46-48	93	-	6
Chelsea	Tr	01/49	48-51	75	-	1
Watford	Tr	08/52	52-56	193	-	0

MITCHELL Graham Lee
Born: Shipley, West Yorkshire, England, 16 February, 1968 — CD

League Club	Source	Date Signed	Seasons Played	Apps	Subs	Gls
Huddersfield T	App	06/86	86-94	235	9	2
Bournemouth	L	12/93	93	4	0	0
Bradford C	Tr	12/94	94-96	64	1	1
Cardiff C	Raith Rov	08/98	98	46	0	0
Halifax T	Tr	07/99	99-01	128	2	3

MITCHELL Ian David
Born: Tredegar, Blaenau Gwent, Wales, 1 October, 1971 — F

League Club	Source	Date Signed	Seasons Played	Apps	Subs	Gls
Hereford U	Merthyr Tydfil	10/90	90	0	3	0

MITCHELL James (Jamie)
Born: Glasgow, Scotland, 6 November, 1976 — F

League Club	Source	Date Signed	Seasons Played	Apps	Subs	Gls
Norwich C	YT	07/95				
Scarborough	Tr	08/96	96-97	31	47	10

MITCHELL James Donald
Born: Heanor, Derbyshire, England, 1 July, 1937 — G

League Club	Source	Date Signed	Seasons Played	Apps	Subs	Gls
Derby Co	Ilkeston T	10/58	58-59	6	-	0

MITCHELL James Robert (Jimmy)
Born: Liverpool, England, 13 June, 1967 — FB

League Club	Source	Date Signed	Seasons Played	Apps	Subs	Gls
Wigan Ath	App	06/85	84	2	0	0

MITCHELL John (Ian)
Born: Falkirk, Scotland, 9 May, 1946 — LW
Died: Dundee, Scotland, 2 April, 1996
Scotland: U23-2/Schools

League Club	Source	Date Signed	Seasons Played	Apps	Subs	Gls
Newcastle U	Dundee U	07/70	70	2	1	0

MITCHELL John
Born: St Albans, Hertfordshire, England, 12 March, 1952 — F

League Club	Source	Date Signed	Seasons Played	Apps	Subs	Gls
Fulham	St Albans C	02/72	72-77	158	12	57
Millwall	Tr	06/78	78-80	78	3	18

MITCHELL John Desmond
Born: Titchfield, Hampshire, England, 19 November, 1928 — LW
Died: Portsmouth, England, 20 April, 2000

League Club	Source	Date Signed	Seasons Played	Apps	Subs	Gls
Southampton	Gosport Bor	03/49	50	7	-	0

MITCHELL John George
Born: Gateshead, Tyne and Wear, England, 1 August, 1919 — CF
Died: Billingham, Cleveland, England, 14 July, 1977

League Club	Source	Date Signed	Seasons Played	Apps	Subs	Gls
Hartlepool U	Billingham Synthonia	11/46	46	3	-	2

MITCHELL Kenneth (Kenny)
Born: Sunderland, England, 26 May, 1957 — D/M

League Club	Source	Date Signed	Seasons Played	Apps	Subs	Gls
Newcastle U	App	04/75	76-80	61	5	2
Darlington	Tr	08/81	81	12	1	1

MITCHELL Kenneth Samuel (Ken)
Born: Wearhead, County Durham, England, 26 December, 1933 — CF
Died: Stockton-on-Tees, Cleveland, England, February, 2010

League Club	Source	Date Signed	Seasons Played	Apps	Subs	Gls
Plymouth Arg	Whitby Rov	03/56	55-56	8	-	4

MITCHELL Liam
Born: Nottingham, England, 18 September, 1992 — G

League Club	Source	Date Signed	Seasons Played	Apps	Subs	Gls
Notts Co	Sch	07/11				
Mansfield T	Tr	08/13	13	1	0	0

MITCHELL Neil Nicholas
Born: Lytham, Lancashire, England, 7 November, 1974 — F
England: Schools

League Club	Source	Date Signed	Seasons Played	Apps	Subs	Gls
Blackpool	YT	11/92	91-94	39	28	8
Rochdale	L	12/95	95	3	1	0
Macclesfield T	Tr	07/96	97	2	4	0

MITCHELL Norman
Born: Sunderland, England, 7 November, 1931 — RW
Died: Washington, Tyne and Wear, England, 1 October, 2010

League Club	Source	Date Signed	Seasons Played	Apps	Subs	Gls
Chesterfield	West Stanley	10/51	51-52	66	-	7
Workington	West Stanley	11/53	53-57	140	-	23
Hartlepool U	Tr	03/58	57-58	23	-	6

MITCHELL Paul Alexander
Born: Stalybridge, Greater Manchester, England, 26 August, 1981 — DM

League Club	Source	Date Signed	Seasons Played	Apps	Subs	Gls
Wigan Ath	YT	07/00	00-04	30	34	0
Halifax T	L	03/01	00	11	0	0
Swindon T	L	09/04	04	7	0	0
MK Dons	L	12/04	04	13	0	0
MK Dons	Tr	07/05	05-06	52	7	0
Wrexham	L	01/07	06	5	0	0
Barnet	L	08/08	08	3	0	0

MITCHELL Paul Robert
Born: Nottingham, England, 8 November, 1978 — CD

League Club	Source	Date Signed	Seasons Played	Apps	Subs	Gls
Notts Co	YT	07/97	96-97	1	1	0

MITCHELL Paul Robert
Born: Bournemouth, England, 20 October, 1971 M/RB
England: Youth/Schools

League Club	Source	Date Signed	Seasons Played	Apps	Subs	Gls
Bournemouth	YT	08/89	90-92	6	6	0
West Ham U	Tr	08/93	93	0	1	0
Bournemouth	Tr	03/96	95	2	2	0
Torquay U	Tr	08/96	96-97	33	5	1

MITCHELL Peter
Born: Oldham, Greater Manchester, England, 5 August, 1946 FB

League Club	Source	Date Signed	Seasons Played	Apps	Subs	Gls
Oldham Ath	St Patrick's, Oldham	07/66	65	0	1	0

MITCHELL Robert (Bobby)
Born: Petersfield, Hampshire, England, 17 December, 1948 F

League Club	Source	Date Signed	Seasons Played	Apps	Subs	Gls
Aldershot	Alton T	05/69	69-70	6	7	1

MITCHELL Robert (Bobby)
Born: South Shields, Tyne and Wear, England, 4 January, 1955 M

League Club	Source	Date Signed	Seasons Played	Apps	Subs	Gls
Sunderland	App	01/72	73-75	1	2	0
Blackburn Rov	Tr	07/76	76-77	17	12	6
Grimsby T	Tr	06/78	78-81	142	0	6
Carlisle U	Tr	08/82	82	2	0	0
Rotherham U	Tr	03/83	82-84	86	9	2
Lincoln C	Hamrun Spartans (MLT)	01/86	85-86	41	3	2

MITCHELL Robert Barr (Bobby)
Born: Campbeltown, Argyll & Bute, Scotland, 17 January, 1927 CF
Died: Taunton, Somerset, England, April, 2002

League Club	Source	Date Signed	Seasons Played	Apps	Subs	Gls
Exeter C	Third Lanark	07/51	51	3	-	0

MITCHELL Robert Carmichael (Bobby)
Born: Glasgow, Scotland, 16 August, 1924 LW
Died: Newcastle-upon-Tyne, England, 4 January, 1993
Scotland: 2/SLge-2

League Club	Source	Date Signed	Seasons Played	Apps	Subs	Gls
Newcastle U	Third Lanark	02/49	48-60	367	-	95

MITCHELL Ronald Gilbert (Ron)
Born: Morecambe, Lancashire, England, 13 February, 1935 RB

League Club	Source	Date Signed	Seasons Played	Apps	Subs	Gls
Leeds U	Morecambe	11/58	58	4	-	0

MITCHELL Ronald James (Ron)
Born: Barrhead, Renfrewshire, Scotland, 27 May, 1925 RW

League Club	Source	Date Signed	Seasons Played	Apps	Subs	Gls
Exeter C	Glasgow Celtic	08/49	49	2	-	0

MITCHELL Roy
Born: Liverpool, England, 10 March, 1964 M

League Club	Source	Date Signed	Seasons Played	Apps	Subs	Gls
Stockport Co		10/86	86	2	1	0

MITCHELL Scott Andrew
Born: Ely, Cambridgeshire, England, 2 September, 1985 CD

League Club	Source	Date Signed	Seasons Played	Apps	Subs	Gls
Ipswich T	Sch	03/04	03	0	2	0
Peterborough U (L)	Livingston	01/08	07	1	4	0

MITCHELL Stewart Anderson
Born: Glasgow, Scotland, 3 March, 1933 G

League Club	Source	Date Signed	Seasons Played	Apps	Subs	Gls
Newcastle U	Benburb Jnrs	09/53	54-62	45	-	0

MITCHELSON Kenneth Gordon (Ken)
Born: Edmonton, N London, England, 16 May, 1928 RB
Died: Hornsey, N London, England, February, 2005

League Club	Source	Date Signed	Seasons Played	Apps	Subs	Gls
Charlton Ath	Tottenham H (Am)	09/47				
Bristol C	Tr	05/49	49-52	28	-	0

MITCHESON Francis John (Frank)
Born: Stalybridge, Greater Manchester, England, 10 March, 1924 IF
Died: Tameside, Greater Manchester, England, 24 October, 1981

League Club	Source	Date Signed	Seasons Played	Apps	Subs	Gls
Doncaster Rov	Droylsden	05/44	46-48	22	-	5
Crewe Alex	Tr	11/48	48-53	180	-	34
Rochdale	Tr	06/54	54-55	50	-	8

MITCHINSON Thomas William (Tommy)
Born: Sunderland, England, 24 February, 1943 M
Died: Sunderland, England, 20 April, 2006

League Club	Source	Date Signed	Seasons Played	Apps	Subs	Gls
Sunderland	Jnr	12/60	62-65	16	3	2
Mansfield T	Tr	01/66	65-67	76	0	15
Aston Villa	Tr	08/67	67-68	49	0	9
Torquay U	Tr	05/69	68-71	108	0	9
Bournemouth	Tr	12/71	71-72	31	1	1

MITCHLEY Daniel James (Danny)
Born: Liverpool, England, 7 October, 1989 F

League Club	Source	Date Signed	Seasons Played	Apps	Subs	Gls
Blackpool	Sch	04/08	08	0	2	0

MITROGLOU Konstantinos (Kostas)
Born: Kavala, Greece, 12 March, 1988 F
Greece: 40/U21-16/Youth

League Club	Source	Date Signed	Seasons Played	Apps	Subs	Gls
Fulham	Olympiakos (GRE)	01/14	13	1	2	0

MITTEN Charles (Charlie)
Born: Rangoon, Burma, 17 January, 1921 W
Died: Stockport, Greater Manchester, England, 2 January, 2002

League Club	Source	Date Signed	Seasons Played	Apps	Subs	Gls
Manchester U	Strathallan Hawthorn	01/38	46-49	142	-	50
Fulham	Santa Fe (COL)	01/52	51-55	154	-	32
Mansfield T	Tr	02/56	55-57	100	-	25

MITTEN Charles (Charlie)
Born: Altrincham, Greater Manchester, England, 14 December, 1943 IF

League Club	Source	Date Signed	Seasons Played	Apps	Subs	Gls
Manchester U	Newcastle U (App)	11/61				
Halifax T	Altrincham	10/65	65	1	0	0

MITTEN John
Born: Davyhulme, Greater Manchester, England, 30 March, 1941 LW
England: Youth/Schools

League Club	Source	Date Signed	Seasons Played	Apps	Subs	Gls
Mansfield T	Jnr	01/58	57	3	-	0
Newcastle U	Tr	09/58	58-60	9	-	3
Leicester C	Tr	09/61	61	12	-	0
Coventry C	Tr	08/63	63-66	34	2	5
Plymouth Arg	Tr	01/67	66-67	43	0	8
Exeter C	Tr	07/68	68-70	96	4	17

MITTON Gilbert Keith (Keith)
Born: Leyland, Lancashire, England, 30 December, 1928 G
Died: Preston, Lancashire, England, 1 May, 1995

League Club	Source	Date Signed	Seasons Played	Apps	Subs	Gls
Preston NE	Leyland Motors	05/50	53	2	-	0
Carlisle U	Tr	06/54	54-56	47	-	0

MIYAICHI Ryo
Born: Okazaki, Japan, 14 December, 1992 LW
Japan: 2/Youth

League Club	Source	Date Signed	Seasons Played	Apps	Subs	Gls
Arsenal	Jnr	01/11	13	0	1	0
Bolton W	L	01/12	11	8	4	0
Wigan Ath	L	08/12	12	0	4	0

MKANDIWIRE Tamika Paul
Born: Mzuzu, Malawi, 28 May, 1983 W
England: Semi Pro-2

League Club	Source	Date Signed	Seasons Played	Apps	Subs	Gls
West Bromwich A	Sch	05/02				
Hereford U	Tr	07/04	06	39	0	2
Leyton Orient	Tr	07/07	07-09	114	0	15
Millwall	Tr	07/10	10-11	44	4	1
Southend U	L	11/12	12	11	0	0
Southend U	L	03/13	12	7	0	0
Shrewsbury T	Tr	07/13	13	38	1	1

MOBLEY David Leslie
Born: Oxford, England, 24 August, 1948 LB

League Club	Source	Date Signed	Seasons Played	Apps	Subs	Gls
Sheffield Wed	Jnr	09/65				
Grimsby T	Tr	07/69	69	26	1	0

MOBLEY Victor John (Vic)
Born: Oxford, England, 11 October, 1943 CD
England: FLge-1/U23-13

League Club	Source	Date Signed	Seasons Played	Apps	Subs	Gls
Sheffield Wed	Oxford C	09/61	63-69	187	0	8
Queens Park Rgrs	Tr	10/69	69-70	24	1	0

MOCHAN Dennis
Born: Falkirk, Scotland, 12 December, 1935 FB

League Club	Source	Date Signed	Seasons Played	Apps	Subs	Gls
Nottingham F	Raith Rov	06/62	62-65	108	0	1
Colchester U	Tr	09/66	66-69	113	3	2

MOCHAN Neil
Born: Larbert, Falkirk, Scotland, 6 April, 1927 CF
Died: Falkirk, Scotland, 28 August, 1994
Scotland: 3/B

League Club	Source	Date Signed	Seasons Played	Apps	Subs	Gls
Middlesbrough	Greenock Morton	05/51	51-52	38	-	14

MOCKLER Andrew James
Born: Stockton-on-Tees, Cleveland, England, 18 November, 1970 M

League Club	Source	Date Signed	Seasons Played	Apps	Subs	Gls
Arsenal	YT	11/88				
Scarborough	Tr	07/90	90-93	66	8	10

MOCQUET William (Will)
Born: Cherbourg, France, 23 January, 1983 W

League Club	Source	Date Signed	Seasons Played	Apps	Subs	Gls
Sunderland	Le Havre (FRA)	08/06				
Rochdale	L	11/06	06	6	1	1
Bury	L	03/07	06	9	0	0

MODEST Nathan Daniel
Born: Sheffield, England, 29 September, 1991 F

League Club	Source	Date Signed	Seasons Played	Apps	Subs	Gls
Sheffield Wed	Sch	07/10	08	1	3	0

MODESTE Anthony Mbu Agogo
Born: Cannes, France, 14 April, 1988 F
France: U21-16

League Club	Source	Date Signed	Seasons Played	Apps	Subs	Gls
Blackburn Rov (L)	Bordeaux (FRA)	01/12	11	3	6	0

MODRIC Luka
Born: Zadar, Croatia, 9 September, 1985 M
Croatia: 84/U21-15/Youth

League Club	Source	Date Signed	Seasons Played	Apps	Subs	Gls
Tottenham H	Dinamo Zagreb (CRO)	07/08	08-11	123	4	13

MOEN Petter Vaagan
Born: Hamar, Norway, 5 February, 1984 — LW
Norway: 9/U21-18

League Club	Source	Date Signed	Seasons Played	Apps	Subs	Gls
Queens Park Rgrs	SK Brann (NOR)	01/11	10	1	6	0

MOFFAT Adam
Born: Lochgelly, Fife, Scotland, 1 April, 1941 — IF

League Club	Source	Date Signed	Seasons Played	Apps	Subs	Gls
Newport Co	East Fife	10/61	61	17	-	5

MOFFATT Gregory Thomas (Greg)
Born: Liverpool, England, 8 January, 1964 — RB

League Club	Source	Date Signed	Seasons Played	Apps	Subs	Gls
Chester C	App	01/82	82	6	1	0

MOFFATT John Black (Johnny)
Born: Greenock, Inverclyde, Scotland, 22 December, 1929 — RW

League Club	Source	Date Signed	Seasons Played	Apps	Subs	Gls
Brighton & HA	Bellshill Ath	12/51	52	2	-	0

MOFFATT Robert Wallace (Bob)
Born: Portsmouth, England, 7 October, 1945 — LW/WH

League Club	Source	Date Signed	Seasons Played	Apps	Subs	Gls
Portsmouth	App	10/63				
Gillingham	Tr	05/65	65-67	24	1	1

MOFFITT Kenneth (Ken)
Born: Newcastle-upon-Tyne, England, 2 February, 1933 — LB/LH

League Club	Source	Date Signed	Seasons Played	Apps	Subs	Gls
Brentford	Berwick Rgrs	08/53				
Gateshead	Berwick Rgrs	09/57	57-59	76	-	2

MOGFORD Reginald William James (Reg)
Born: Newport, Wales, 12 June, 1919 — CF
Died: Worcester, England, 28 September, 1992

League Club	Source	Date Signed	Seasons Played	Apps	Subs	Gls
Newport Co	Jnr	06/38	38-47	20	-	9

MOHAMED Kaid Yusef
Born: Cardiff, Wales, 23 July, 1984 — F

League Club	Source	Date Signed	Seasons Played	Apps	Subs	Gls
Swindon T	Carmarthen T	08/07	07	3	8	0
Cheltenham T	Bath C	07/11	11-12	63	21	15
Port Vale	Tr	06/13	13	3	3	0
AFC Wimbledon	L	11/13	13	5	0	0
Bristol Rov	L	01/14	13	20	1	4
Northampton T	L	06/14	14	17	6	4

MOHAN Nicholas (Nicky)
Born: Middlesbrough, England, 6 October, 1970 — CD

League Club	Source	Date Signed	Seasons Played	Apps	Subs	Gls
Middlesbrough	Jnr	11/87	88-93	93	6	4
Hull C	L	09/92	92	5	0	1
Leicester C	Tr	07/94	94	23	0	0
Bradford C	Tr	07/95	95-96	83	0	4
Wycombe W	Tr	08/97	97-98	58	0	2
Stoke C	Tr	03/99	98-00	92	0	6
Hull C	Tr	07/01	01	26	1	1

MOHSNI Bilel
Born: Paris, France, 21 July, 1987 — CD/F
Tunisia: 4

League Club	Source	Date Signed	Seasons Played	Apps	Subs	Gls
Southend U	Sainte-Genevieve (FRA)	08/10	10-12	52	10	18
Ipswich T	L	10/12	12	0	5	0

MOILANEN Teuvo Johannes (Tepi)
Born: Oulu, Finland, 12 December, 1973 — G
Finland: 3/U21/Youth

League Club	Source	Date Signed	Seasons Played	Apps	Subs	Gls
Preston NE	FF Jaro (FIN)	12/95	95-02	155	3	0
Scarborough	L	12/96	96	4	0	0
Darlington	L	01/97	96	16	0	0

MOIR Ian
Born: Aberdeen, Scotland, 30 June, 1943 — W
Died: 26 March, 2015

League Club	Source	Date Signed	Seasons Played	Apps	Subs	Gls
Manchester U	Jnr	07/60	60-64	45	-	5
Blackpool	Tr	02/65	64-66	61	0	12
Chester C	Tr	05/67	67	25	0	3
Wrexham	Tr	01/68	67-71	144	6	20
Shrewsbury T	Tr	03/72	71-72	22	3	2
Wrexham	Tr	07/73	73-74	11	4	0

MOIR James (Jim)
Born: Newcastle-upon-Tyne, England, 23 March, 1918 — CF
Died: Durham, England, June, 2000

League Club	Source	Date Signed	Seasons Played	Apps	Subs	Gls
Accrington Stan	Newcastle West End	10/37	37-38	20	-	9
Carlisle U	Tr	08/46	46-47	42	-	20

MOIR Richard John (Ricky)
Born: Glasgow, Scotland, 22 October, 1945 — M

League Club	Source	Date Signed	Seasons Played	Apps	Subs	Gls
Shrewsbury T	Cumnock Jnrs	03/69	69-73	159	6	27
Halifax T	Tr	07/74	74	16	3	5

MOIR William (Willie)
Born: Bucksburn, Aberdeenshire, Scotland, 19 April, 1922 — IF
Died: Bolton, Greater Manchester, England, 9 May, 1988
Scotland: 1/B

League Club	Source	Date Signed	Seasons Played	Apps	Subs	Gls
Bolton W	RAF Kirkham	04/43	46-55	325	-	118
Stockport Co	Tr	09/55	55-57	70	-	26

MOKOENA Aaron Teboho
Born: Johannesburg, South Africa, 25 November, 1980 — CD
South Africa: 107

League Club	Source	Date Signed	Seasons Played	Apps	Subs	Gls
Blackburn Rov	KRC Genk (BEL)	01/05	04-08	55	46	0
Portsmouth	Tr	07/09	07-11	65	13	2

MOKONE Stephen Madi (Steve)
Born: Pretoria, South Africa, 23 March, 1932 — W
Died: Washington DC, USA, 20 March, 2015

League Club	Source	Date Signed	Seasons Played	Apps	Subs	Gls
Coventry C	Durban Bush B'ks (RSA)	10/56	56	4	-	1
Cardiff C	Heracles (NED)	06/59	59	3	-	1

MOLANGO Maheta Matteo
Born: St Imier, Switzerland, 24 July, 1982 — F

League Club	Source	Date Signed	Seasons Played	Apps	Subs	Gls
Brighton & HA	SV Burghausen (AUT)	07/04	04-06	4	2	1
Lincoln C	L	08/05	05	5	5	0
Oldham Ath	L	08/06	06	3	2	1
Wrexham	L	11/06	06	3	0	0

MOLBY Jan
Born: Kolding, Denmark, 4 July, 1963 — M
Denmark: 33/U21-7/Youth

League Club	Source	Date Signed	Seasons Played	Apps	Subs	Gls
Liverpool	Ajax (NED)	08/84	84-94	195	23	44
Barnsley	L	09/95	95	5	0	0
Norwich C	L	12/95	95	3	0	0
Swansea C	Tr	02/96	95-97	39	2	8

MOLDOVAN Viorel Dinu
Born: Bistrita, Romania, 8 July, 1972 — F
Romania: 70

League Club	Source	Date Signed	Seasons Played	Apps	Subs	Gls
Coventry C	G'hopper Zurich (SUI)	01/98	97	5	5	1

MOLENAAR Robert
Born: Zaandam, Netherlands, 27 February, 1969 — CD

League Club	Source	Date Signed	Seasons Played	Apps	Subs	Gls
Leeds U	FC Volendam (NED)	01/97	96-98	47	4	5
Bradford C	Tr	12/00	00-02	70	1	2

MOLESKI George Kyriakos
Born: Hillingdon, W London, England, 24 July, 1987 — RW

League Club	Source	Date Signed	Seasons Played	Apps	Subs	Gls
Brentford	Sch	-	04	0	1	0

MOLESLEY Mark Clifford
Born: Hillingdon, W London, England, 11 March, 1981 — M
England: Semi Pro-4

League Club	Source	Date Signed	Seasons Played	Apps	Subs	Gls
Bournemouth	Grays Ath	10/08	08-11	36	16	5
Aldershot T	L	03/12	11	2	6	1
Plymouth Arg	L	11/12	12	3	2	0
Exeter C	Tr	01/13	12	11	0	0

MOLLATT Ronald Vincent (Ron)
Born: Edwinstowe, Nottinghamshire, England, 24 February, 1932 — WH
Died: Bishopthorpe, North Yorkshire, England, 16 January, 2001

League Club	Source	Date Signed	Seasons Played	Apps	Subs	Gls
Leeds U	Thoresby CW	02/50	51-54	17	-	0
York C	Tr	07/55	55-59	124	-	1
Bradford C	Tr	07/60	60-62	88	-	0

MOLLER Jan Borje
Born: Malmo, Sweden, 17 September, 1953 — G
Sweden: 17

League Club	Source	Date Signed	Seasons Played	Apps	Subs	Gls
Bristol C	FF Malmo (SWE)	12/80	80-81	48	0	0

MOLLER-NIELSEN Peter
Born: Fredrikshavn, Denmark, 23 March, 1972 — F
Denmark: 17/U21-22/Youth

League Club	Source	Date Signed	Seasons Played	Apps	Subs	Gls
Fulham (L)	Real Oviedo (SPN)	01/01	00	2	3	1

MOLLOY David Anthony
Born: Newcastle-upon-Tyne, England, 29 August, 1986 — W

League Club	Source	Date Signed	Seasons Played	Apps	Subs	Gls
Carlisle U	Sch	-	03	3	4	0

MOLLOY George William (Billy)
Born: Coventry, England, 28 August, 1929 — W

League Club	Source	Date Signed	Seasons Played	Apps	Subs	Gls
Southampton	Ludgershall Army Camp	10/49	49	1	-	0
Newport Co	Lockheed Leamington	11/50	50	3	-	0

MOLLOY Gerard (Gerry)
Born: Rochdale, Greater Manchester, England, 13 March, 1936 — LH/LW

League Club	Source	Date Signed	Seasons Played	Apps	Subs	Gls
Rochdale	Jnr	11/55	55-56	6	-	0

MOLLOY Peter
Born: Athlone, Republic of Ireland, 1 January, 1921 — CH
Republic of Ireland: LoI-2//Northern Ireland: NILge-4

League Club	Source	Date Signed	Seasons Played	Apps	Subs	Gls
Notts Co	Distillery	04/48	47	1	-	0

MOLLOY Trevor
Born: Dublin, Republic of Ireland, 14 April, 1977 — F

League Club	Source	Date Signed	Seasons Played	Apps	Subs	Gls
Carlisle U	Shelbourne (ROI)	08/02	02	7	0	1

MOLONEY Brendan Anthony
Born: Killarney, Republic of Ireland, 18 January, 1989 — RB
Republic of Ireland: U21-6

League Club	Source	Date Signed	Seasons Played	Apps	Subs	Gls
Nottingham F	Sch	03/06	06-12	26	16	0
Chesterfield	L	01/08	07	8	1	1
Notts Co	L	07/09	09	18	0	1
Scunthorpe U	L	01/10	09	1	2	0
Bristol C	Tr	01/13	12-13	44	5	0
Yeovil T	Tr	07/14	14	4	1	0
Northampton T	Tr	01/15	14	22	0	1

MOLYNEAUX Lee Alexander
Born: Portsmouth, England, 16 January, 1983 — D/M

League Club	Source	Date Signed	Seasons Played	Apps	Subs	Gls
Portsmouth	YT	12/01				
Oxford U	Weymouth	07/04	04	6	10	0

MOLYNEUX Bernard
Born: Prescot, Merseyside, England, 17 September, 1933 — LW

League Club	Source	Date Signed	Seasons Played	Apps	Subs	Gls
Everton	Jnr	12/51				
Tranmere Rov	Tr	05/56	56	11	-	3

MOLYNEUX Frederick George (Fred)
Born: Wallasey, Wirral, England, 25 July, 1944 — CD

League Club	Source	Date Signed	Seasons Played	Apps	Subs	Gls
Liverpool	Jnr	06/62				
Southport	Tr	08/65	65-68	123	0	1
Plymouth Arg	Tr	08/68	68-70	79	0	5
Exeter C	L	02/71	70	2	0	0
Tranmere Rov	Tr	02/71	70-72	71	1	0
Southport	Tr	07/73	73	32	1	1

MOLYNEUX Geoffrey Barry (Geoff)
Born: Warrington, Cheshire, England, 23 January, 1943 — RW

League Club	Source	Date Signed	Seasons Played	Apps	Subs	Gls
Chester C (Am)	Rylands YC	05/62	62	1	-	0

MOLYNEUX John Allan
Born: Warrington, Cheshire, England, 3 February, 1931 — RB
England: Youth

League Club	Source	Date Signed	Seasons Played	Apps	Subs	Gls
Chester C	Orford YC	02/49	49-54	178	-	1
Liverpool	Tr	06/55	55-61	229	-	2
Chester C	Tr	08/62	62-64	67	-	0

MOLYNEUX Lee Robert
Born: Huyton, Merseyside, England, 24 February, 1989 — LM
England: Youth

League Club	Source	Date Signed	Seasons Played	Apps	Subs	Gls
Everton	Sch	03/06				
Southampton	Tr	01/09	08	4	0	0
Plymouth Arg	Tr	08/10	10	7	2	0
Accrington Stan	Tr	08/12	12	33	6	8
Crewe Alex	Tr	07/13	13-14	6	4	0
Rochdale	L	08/13	13	0	3	0
Accrington Stan	L	01/14	13	14	3	6
Accrington Stan	L	10/14	14	7	3	1
Tranmere Rov	Tr	01/15	14	7	4	0

MOLYNEUX Raymond (Ray)
Born: Kearsley, Greater Manchester, England, 13 June, 1930 — W
Died: Bolton, Greater Manchester, England, October, 2014
England: Youth

League Club	Source	Date Signed	Seasons Played	Apps	Subs	Gls
Bradford C	Ashton U	12/48	48	2	-	1

MOLYNEUX William Stanley (Billy)
Born: Liverpool, England, 10 January, 1944 — G

League Club	Source	Date Signed	Seasons Played	Apps	Subs	Gls
Liverpool	Earle	11/63	64	1	-	0
Oldham Ath	Tr	06/67	68	8	0	0

MONAGHAN Derek James
Born: Bromsgrove, Worcestershire, England, 20 January, 1959 — F
England: Youth

League Club	Source	Date Signed	Seasons Played	Apps	Subs	Gls
West Bromwich A	App	01/77	79-83	14	5	2
Port Vale	Tr	07/84	84	4	3	0

MONAGHAN William
Born: Glasgow, Scotland, 2 September, 1919 — RB
Died: Largs, Ayrshire, Scotland, 9 June, 1989

League Club	Source	Date Signed	Seasons Played	Apps	Subs	Gls
Bury	Alloa Ath	08/46				
Carlisle U	Ayr U	08/47	47-49	19	-	0

MONAKANA Jeffrey
Born: Edmonton, N London, England, 5 November, 1993 — RW

League Club	Source	Date Signed	Seasons Played	Apps	Subs	Gls
Preston NE	Arsenal (Sch)	07/12	12-13	23	17	4
Colchester U	L	09/13	13	6	3	1
Brighton & HA	Tr	01/14				
Crawley T	L	03/14	13	0	4	0
Mansfield T	L	02/15	14	2	4	0
Carlisle U	L	03/15	14	1	0	0

MONCRIEFF James Conradi
Born: Todmorden, West Yorkshire, England, 14 June, 1922 — CF
Died: Halifax, West Yorkshire, England, 5 February, 1975

League Club	Source	Date Signed	Seasons Played	Apps	Subs	Gls
Halifax T (Am)	Oxford Univ	06/46	46-54	42	-	13

MONCRIEFFE Prince
Born: Jamaica, 27 February, 1977 — F

League Club	Source	Date Signed	Seasons Played	Apps	Subs	Gls
Doncaster Rov	Hyde U	07/97	97	30	8	8

MONCUR George Anthony
Born: Swindon, England, 18 August, 1993 — M
England: Youth

League Club	Source	Date Signed	Seasons Played	Apps	Subs	Gls
West Ham U	Sch	09/10				
AFC Wimbledon	L	01/12	11	20	0	2
Colchester U	Tr	08/14	14	34	7	8

MONCUR John Frederick
Born: Stepney, E London, England, 22 September, 1966 — M

League Club	Source	Date Signed	Seasons Played	Apps	Subs	Gls
Tottenham H	App	08/84	86-90	10	11	1
Doncaster Rov	L	09/86	86	4	0	0
Cambridge U	L	03/87	86	3	1	0
Portsmouth	L	03/89	88	7	0	0
Brentford	L	10/89	89	5	0	1
Ipswich T	L	10/91	91	5	1	0
Swindon T	Tr	03/92	91-93	53	5	5
West Ham U	Tr	06/94	94-02	131	44	6

MONCUR Robert (Bobby)
Born: Perth, Scotland, 19 January, 1945 — CD
Scotland: 16/U23-1/Schools

League Club	Source	Date Signed	Seasons Played	Apps	Subs	Gls
Newcastle U	App	04/62	62-73	293	3	3
Sunderland	Tr	06/74	74-76	86	0	2
Carlisle U	Tr	11/76	76	11	0	0

MONCUR Thomas James (TJ)
Born: Hackney, E London, England, 23 September, 1987 — RB

League Club	Source	Date Signed	Seasons Played	Apps	Subs	Gls
Fulham	Sch	09/05				
Bradford C	L	01/08	07	6	1	0
Bradford C	L	08/08	08	11	3	0
Wycombe W	Tr	01/09	08-09	4	2	0

MONEY Richard
Born: Lowestoft, Suffolk, England, 13 October, 1955 — CD
England: B-1

League Club	Source	Date Signed	Seasons Played	Apps	Subs	Gls
Scunthorpe U	Lowestoft T	07/73	73-77	165	8	4
Fulham	Tr	12/77	77-79	106	0	3
Liverpool	Tr	04/80	80	12	2	0
Derby Co	L	12/81	81	5	0	0
Luton T	Tr	03/82	81-82	44	0	1
Portsmouth	Tr	08/83	83-85	17	0	0
Scunthorpe U	Tr	10/85	85-89	105	1	0

MONINGTON Mark David
Born: Bilsthorpe, Nottinghamshire, England, 21 October, 1970 — CD

League Club	Source	Date Signed	Seasons Played	Apps	Subs	Gls
Burnley	Jnr	03/89	88-93	65	19	5
Rotherham U	Tr	11/94	94-97	75	4	3
Rochdale	Tr	07/98	98-00	90	5	12
Boston U	Tr	07/01	02	1	0	0

MONK Brian
Born: Leeds, England, 15 May, 1937 — IF

League Club	Source	Date Signed	Seasons Played	Apps	Subs	Gls
Leeds U	Jnr	02/55				
Crewe Alex	Tr	05/58	58	5	-	0

MONK Frederick John (Fred)
Born: Brighton, England, 9 October, 1920 — RB/CF
Died: Aldershot, Hampshire, England, October, 1987
England: Schools

League Club	Source	Date Signed	Seasons Played	Apps	Subs	Gls
Brentford	Guildford C	03/48	47-53	206	-	47
Aldershot	Tr	07/54	54-55	49	-	0

MONK Garry Alan
Born: Bedford, England, 6 March, 1979 — CD

League Club	Source	Date Signed	Seasons Played	Apps	Subs	Gls
Torquay U	YT	-	95	4	1	0
Southampton	Tr	05/97	98-02	9	2	0
Torquay U	L	09/98	98	6	0	0
Stockport Co	L	09/99	99	2	0	0
Oxford U	L	01/01	00	5	0	0
Sheffield Wed	L	12/02	02	15	0	0
Barnsley	Tr	11/03	03	14	3	0
Swansea C	Tr	07/04	04-12	214	6	3

MONKHOUSE Alan Thompson William
Born: Stockton-on-Tees, Cleveland, England, 23 October, 1930 — CF
Died: Stockton-on-Tees, Cleveland, England, February, 1982

League Club	Source	Date Signed	Seasons Played	Apps	Subs	Gls
Millwall	Thornaby	08/50	49-53	65	-	20
Newcastle U	Tr	10/53	53-55	21	-	9
York C	Tr	06/56	56	12	-	1

MONKHOUSE Andrew William (Andy)
Born: Leeds, England, 23 October, 1980 — LW

League Club	Source	Date Signed	Seasons Played	Apps	Subs	Gls
Rotherham U	YT	11/98	98-05	68	60	9
Swindon T	Tr	07/06	06	9	1	2
Hartlepool U	Tr	11/06	06-13	267	31	47

MONKHOUSE Graham
Born: Carlisle, Cumbria, England, 26 April, 1954 — G

League Club	Source	Date Signed	Seasons Played	Apps	Subs	Gls
Workington	Penrith	08/76	76	4	0	0

MONKOU Kenneth John (Ken)
Born: Nickerie, Suriname, 29 November, 1964 — CD

League Club	Source	Date Signed	Seasons Played	Apps	Subs	Gls
Chelsea	Feyenoord (NED)	03/89	88-91	92	2	2
Southampton	Tr	08/92	92-98	190	8	10
Huddersfield T	Tr	08/99	99-00	21	0	1

MONKS John
Born: Stockport, Greater Manchester, England, 3 June, 1921 — LB
Died: Stockport, Greater Manchester, England, 17 December, 1983

League Club	Source	Date Signed	Seasons Played	Apps	Subs	Gls
Stockport Co		04/47	46-52	91	-	0

MONREAL Ignacio (Nacho)
Born: Pamplona, Spain, 26 February, 1986 — LB
Spain: 16/U21-9/Youth

League Club	Source	Date Signed	Seasons Played	Apps	Subs	Gls
Arsenal	Malaga (SPN)	01/13	12-14	48	13	1

MONTAGUE Ross Philip
Born: Twickenham, W London, England, 1 November, 1988 — F

League Club	Source	Date Signed	Seasons Played	Apps	Subs	Gls
Brentford	Sch	06/07	06-07	7	7	1

MONTANO Cristian Alexis
Born: Cali, Colombia, 11 December, 1991 — LW

League Club	Source	Date Signed	Seasons Played	Apps	Subs	Gls
West Ham U	Sch	07/10				
Notts Co	L	08/11	11	4	7	4
Swindon T	L	10/11	11	3	1	1
Dagenham & Red	L	11/11	11	10	0	3
Notts Co	L	02/12	11	1	3	0
Oxford U	L	03/12	11	6	3	2
Oldham Ath	Tr	08/12	12-13	31	9	3

MONTELLA Vincenzo
Born: Naples, Italy, 18 June, 1974 — F
Italy: 20

League Club	Source	Date Signed	Seasons Played	Apps	Subs	Gls
Fulham (L)	AS Roma (ITA)	01/07	06	3	7	2

MONTENEGRO Brian Guillermo
Born: Ascuncion, Paraguay, 18 June, 1993 — F
Paraguay: Youth

League Club	Source	Date Signed	Seasons Played	Apps	Subs	Gls
West Ham U	Depo Maldonado (PAR)	08/11				
Leeds U (L)	Nat Ascuncion (PAR)	09/14	14	0	5	0

MONTERO Jefferson Antonio
Born: Babahoyo, Ecuador, 1 September, 1989 — LW
Ecuador: 49

League Club	Source	Date Signed	Seasons Played	Apps	Subs	Gls
Swansea C	Monarcas Morelia (MEX)	07/14	14	15	15	1

MONTGOMERY Alec Webster
Born: Tamworth, Staffordshire, England, 16 September, 1926 — LB

League Club	Source	Date Signed	Seasons Played	Apps	Subs	Gls
Walsall	Baddesley	08/49	51-52	29	-	0

MONTGOMERY Derek
Born: Houghton-le-Spring, Tyne and Wear, England, 5 May, 1950 — M

League Club	Source	Date Signed	Seasons Played	Apps	Subs	Gls
Leeds U	App	12/67				
Bradford C	Tr	08/68	68	4	0	0

MONTGOMERY Gary Stephen
Born: Leamington Spa, Warwickshire, England, 8 October, 1982 — G

League Club	Source	Date Signed	Seasons Played	Apps	Subs	Gls
Coventry C	YT	01/01	02	8	0	0
Kidderminster Hrs	L	03/02	01	2	0	0
Rotherham U	Tr	07/03	03-06	33	2	0
Grimsby T	Tr	07/07	07	4	1	0

MONTGOMERY Graeme
Born: Enfield, N London, England, 3 March, 1988 — LW

League Club	Source	Date Signed	Seasons Played	Apps	Subs	Gls
Dagenham & Red	Wealdstone	01/09	08-09	4	18	2
Aldershot T	Tr	08/11				

MONTGOMERY James (Jim)
Born: Sunderland, England, 9 October, 1943 — G
England: U23-6/Youth

League Club	Source	Date Signed	Seasons Played	Apps	Subs	Gls
Sunderland	Jnr	10/60	61-76	537	0	0
Southampton	L	10/76	76	5	0	0
Birmingham C	Tr	02/77	76-78	66	0	0
Nottingham F	Tr	08/79				
Sunderland	Tr	08/80				

MONTGOMERY Nicholas Anthony (Nick)
Born: Leeds, England, 28 October, 1981 — DM
Scotland: B-1/U21-2

League Club	Source	Date Signed	Seasons Played	Apps	Subs	Gls
Sheffield U	YT	07/00	00-11	278	71	9
Millwall	L	03/12	11	0	2	0

MONTGOMERY Stanley William (Stan)
Born: West Ham, E London, England, 7 July, 1920 — CH
Died: Cardiff, Wales, 6 October, 2000
Wales: WLge-1

League Club	Source	Date Signed	Seasons Played	Apps	Subs	Gls
Hull C	Romford	09/44	46	5	-	0
Southend U	Tr	09/46	46-48	96	-	7
Cardiff C	Tr	12/48	48-54	230	-	4
Newport Co	Worcester C	11/55	55	9	-	0

MONTROSE Lewis Robert Egerton
Born: Manchester, England, 17 November, 1988 — M

League Club	Source	Date Signed	Seasons Played	Apps	Subs	Gls
Wigan Ath	Sch	07/07				
Cheltenham T	L	09/08	08	5	0	0
Chesterfield	L	02/09	08	11	1	0
Wycombe W	Tr	07/09	09-10	38	12	4
Gillingham	Tr	07/11	11-12	40	12	5
Oxford U	L	01/13	12	5	0	0
York C	Tr	06/13	13-14	36	11	1

MOODY Adrian James Harkin
Born: Birkenhead, Wirral, England, 29 September, 1982 — CD

League Club	Source	Date Signed	Seasons Played	Apps	Subs	Gls
Wrexham	YT	-	00-01	2	2	0

MOODY Alan
Born: Middlesbrough, England, 18 January, 1951 — D
England: Schools

League Club	Source	Date Signed	Seasons Played	Apps	Subs	Gls
Middlesbrough	App	01/68	68-72	44	2	0
Southend U	Tr	10/72	72-83	444	2	41

MOODY Kenneth George (Ken)
Born: Grimsby, North Lincolnshire, England, 12 November, 1924 — RB
Died: Sheffield, England, 14 September, 1990

League Club	Source	Date Signed	Seasons Played	Apps	Subs	Gls
Grimsby T	Humber U	10/42	47-50	114	-	0

MOODY Paul
Born: Portsmouth, England, 13 June, 1967 — F

League Club	Source	Date Signed	Seasons Played	Apps	Subs	Gls
Southampton	Waterlooville	07/91	91-93	7	5	0
Reading	L	12/92	92	5	0	1
Oxford U	Tr	02/94	93-96	98	38	49
Fulham	Tr	07/97	97-98	29	11	19
Millwall	Tr	07/99	99-01	45	15	24
Oxford U	Tr	09/01	01	29	6	13

MOODY Vincent Roy (Roy)
Born: Worksop, Nottinghamshire, England, 12 March, 1923 — RW

League Club	Source	Date Signed	Seasons Played	Apps	Subs	Gls
Lincoln C	Worksop T	11/46	46	1	-	0

MOONEY Brian John
Born: Dublin, Republic of Ireland, 2 February, 1966 — RW
Republic of Ireland: U23-2/U21-4/Youth

League Club	Source	Date Signed	Seasons Played	Apps	Subs	Gls
Liverpool	Home Farm (ROI)	08/83				
Wrexham	L	12/85	85	9	0	2
Preston NE	Tr	10/87	87-90	125	3	20
Sunderland	Tr	02/91	90-92	21	6	1
Burnley	L	09/92	92	6	0	0

MOONEY David (Dave)
Born: Dublin, Republic of Ireland, 30 October, 1984 — F
Republic of Ireland: U23-2

League Club	Source	Date Signed	Seasons Played	Apps	Subs	Gls
Reading	Cork C (ROI)	08/08				
Stockport Co	L	01/09	08	2	0	0
Norwich C	L	03/09	08	8	1	3
Charlton Ath	L	08/09	09	20	8	5
Colchester U	L	08/10	10	37	2	9
Leyton Orient	Tr	07/11	11-14	104	36	38

MOONEY Dean Francis
Born: Paddington, Central London, England, 24 July, 1956 — F

League Club	Source	Date Signed	Seasons Played	Apps	Subs	Gls
Leyton Orient	App	07/74	74-75	16	6	3
Bournemouth	GAIS Gothenburg (SWE)	12/80	80-81	27	0	10
Torquay U	Trowbridge T	08/84	84	15	0	2

MOONEY Francis (Frank)
Born: Fauldhouse, West Lothian, Scotland, 1 January, 1932 — RW

League Club	Source	Date Signed	Seasons Played	Apps	Subs	Gls
Manchester U	Bathgate St Mary's	05/49				
Blackburn Rov	Tr	02/54	53-55	58	-	19
Carlisle U	Tr	05/56	56-59	124	-	24

MOONEY Jason Bryan
Born: Newtownards, Down, Northern Ireland, 26 February, 1989 — G

League Club	Source	Date Signed	Seasons Played	Apps	Subs	Gls
Wycombe W	Comber Rec	08/11				
Tranmere Rov	Tr	07/12	12-13	4	0	0
York C	Tr	05/14	14	3	1	0

MOONEY John (Johnny)
Born: Fauldhouse, West Lothian, Scotland, 21 February, 1926 — RW
Died: Doncaster, South Yorkshire, England, July, 2000

League Club	Source	Date Signed	Seasons Played	Apps	Subs	Gls
Doncaster Rov	Hamilton Academical	05/53	53-58	168	-	32

MOONEY Kevin William
Born: Liverpool, England, 23 August, 1959 — D

League Club	Source	Date Signed	Seasons Played	Apps	Subs	Gls
Bury	Bangor C	03/80	80	1	0	0
Tranmere Rov	Telford U	08/82	82	21	1	0

MOONEY Thomas (Tom)
Born: Newry, Armagh, Northern Ireland, 14 December, 1973 — M

League Club	Source	Date Signed	Seasons Played	Apps	Subs	Gls
Huddersfield T	YT	06/92	92	1	0	0

MOONEY Thomas John (Tommy)
Born: Billingham, Cleveland, England, 11 August, 1971 F

League Club	Source	Date Signed	Seasons Played	Apps	Subs	Gls
Aston Villa	YT	11/89				
Scarborough	Tr	08/90	90-92	96	11	30
Southend U	Tr	07/93	93	9	5	5
Watford	Tr	03/94	93-00	221	29	60
Birmingham C	Tr	07/01	01-02	29	5	13
Stoke C	L	09/02	02	11	1	3
Sheffield U	L	01/03	02	2	1	0
Derby Co	L	03/03	02	7	1	0
Swindon T	Tr	07/03	03	41	4	19
Oxford U	Tr	07/04	04	42	0	15
Wycombe W	Tr	07/05	05-06	85	2	29
Walsall	Tr	07/07	07	36	0	11

MOOR Anthony John (Tony)
Born: Scarborough, North Yorkshire, England, 18 January, 1940 G

League Club	Source	Date Signed	Seasons Played	Apps	Subs	Gls
York C	Scarborough	05/62	62-64	57	-	0
Darlington	Tr	07/65	65-71	239	0	0

MOOR Reinier Sean
Born: Den Haag, Netherlands, 12 June, 1983 F
Republic of Ireland: Youth

League Club	Source	Date Signed	Seasons Played	Apps	Subs	Gls
Exeter C	Sch	08/02	01-02	2	17	3

MOORCROFT David Stanley (Dave)
Born: Liverpool, England, 16 March, 1947 CD

League Club	Source	Date Signed	Seasons Played	Apps	Subs	Gls
Tranmere Rov	Skelmersdale U	12/68	68-71	107	1	1

MOORCROFT Maurice
Born: Chesterfield, Derbyshire, England, 4 November, 1929 G
Died: Derbyshire, England, August, 2013
England: Youth

League Club	Source	Date Signed	Seasons Played	Apps	Subs	Gls
Sheffield U	Jnr	07/48				
Gillingham	Tr	07/52	52	8	-	0

MOORE Alan
Born: Dublin, Republic of Ireland, 25 November, 1974 LW
Republic of Ireland: 8/U21-4/Youth/Schools

League Club	Source	Date Signed	Seasons Played	Apps	Subs	Gls
Middlesbrough	YT	12/91	92-98	98	20	14
Barnsley	L	10/98	98	4	1	0
Burnley	Tr	07/01	01-03	42	27	4

MOORE Alan
Born: Hebburn, Tyne and Wear, England, 7 March, 1927 RW
Died: Cambridge, England, 7 April, 2008

League Club	Source	Date Signed	Seasons Played	Apps	Subs	Gls
Sunderland	South Shields	05/46				
Chesterfield	Spennymoor U	12/48	48-50	67	-	2
Hull C	Tr	07/51	51	13	-	4
Nottingham F	Tr	01/52	51-54	102	-	38
Coventry C	Tr	12/54	54-56	57	-	13
Swindon T	Tr	07/57	57-58	19	-	3
Rochdale	Tr	11/58	58	11	-	2

MOORE Andrew (Andy)
Born: Wantage, Oxfordshire, England, 2 October, 1964 M

League Club	Source	Date Signed	Seasons Played	Apps	Subs	Gls
Reading	App	-	81	0	1	0

MOORE Andrew Roy (Andy)
Born: Cleethorpes, North Lincolnshire, England, 14 November, 1965 CD

League Club	Source	Date Signed	Seasons Played	Apps	Subs	Gls
Grimsby T	App	11/83	83-86	62	2	1

MOORE Anthony Paul (Tony)
Born: York, England, 7 February, 1943 CF

League Club	Source	Date Signed	Seasons Played	Apps	Subs	Gls
York C (Am)	Heworth	05/62	62	2	-	0

MOORE Anthony Peter (Tony)
Born: Wolverhampton, England, 19 September, 1957 RB

League Club	Source	Date Signed	Seasons Played	Apps	Subs	Gls
Sheffield U	Burton A	07/79	79-81	29	0	0
Crewe Alex	Tr	08/82	82	17	0	2
Rochdale	Goole T	10/84	84	1	2	0

MOORE Anthony Peter (Tony)
Born: Scarborough, North Yorkshire, England, 4 September, 1947 W/M

League Club	Source	Date Signed	Seasons Played	Apps	Subs	Gls
Chesterfield	App	01/65	64-70	148	7	13
Grimsby T	L	03/71	70	2	1	0
Chester C	Tr	08/71	71	9	4	3

MOORE Bernard John
Born: Brighton, England, 18 December, 1923 CF
Died: Bedford, England, July, 2014

League Club	Source	Date Signed	Seasons Played	Apps	Subs	Gls
Brighton & HA	Jnr	09/45	47	8	-	2
Luton T	Hastings U	01/51	50-53	74	-	31
Brighton & HA	Tr	03/54	53-54	29	-	10

MOORE Brian
Born: Hemsworth, West Yorkshire, England, 24 December, 1938 W

League Club	Source	Date Signed	Seasons Played	Apps	Subs	Gls
Mansfield T (Am)	Loughborough College	09/60	60	4	-	0
Notts Co	Loughborough College	12/61	61-62	27	-	3
Doncaster Rov	Tr	07/63	63	1	-	0

MOORE Brian McGowan
Born: Belfast, Northern Ireland, 29 December, 1933 IF
Died: Cambridge, England, 8 September, 2006
Northern Ireland: NILge-1

League Club	Source	Date Signed	Seasons Played	Apps	Subs	Gls
West Ham U	Glentoran	02/55	54-55	9	-	1

MOORE Byron Curtis
Born: Stoke-on-Trent, England, 24 August, 1988 W

League Club	Source	Date Signed	Seasons Played	Apps	Subs	Gls
Crewe Alex	Sch	05/07	07-13	195	67	31
Port Vale	Tr	07/14	14	9	6	1

MOORE Christian (Chris)
Born: Derby, England, 4 November, 1972 F

League Club	Source	Date Signed	Seasons Played	Apps	Subs	Gls
Stockport Co	Leicester C (YT)	08/91	91	0	1	0

MOORE Christopher Charles (Chris)
Born: Hammersmith, W London, England, 13 January, 1980 F

League Club	Source	Date Signed	Seasons Played	Apps	Subs	Gls
Brentford	Dagenham & Red	07/06	06	8	8	2
Dagenham & Red	Tr	01/07	07	13	13	2

MOORE Craig Andrew
Born: Sydney, Australia, 12 December, 1975 CD
Australia: 52/U23-11/Youth

League Club	Source	Date Signed	Seasons Played	Apps	Subs	Gls
Crystal Palace	Glasgow Rangers	10/98	98	23	0	3
Newcastle U	Borussia M'bach (GER)	07/05	05-06	25	0	0

MOORE Darren Mark
Born: Birmingham, England, 22 April, 1974 CD
Jamaica: 3

League Club	Source	Date Signed	Seasons Played	Apps	Subs	Gls
Torquay U	YT	11/92	91-94	102	1	8
Doncaster Rov	Tr	07/95	95-96	76	0	7
Bradford C	Tr	06/97	97-98	62	0	3
Portsmouth	Tr	11/99	99-01	58	1	2
West Bromwich A	Tr	09/01	01-05	93	11	6
Derby Co	Tr	01/06	05-07	71	9	3
Barnsley	Tr	07/08	08-09	70	3	2
Burton A	Tr	08/10	10-11	33	5	0

MOORE David
Born: Grimsby, North Lincolnshire, England, 17 December, 1959 RB

League Club	Source	Date Signed	Seasons Played	Apps	Subs	Gls
Grimsby T	App	12/77	78-82	136	0	2
Carlisle U	Tr	08/83	83	13	0	1
Blackpool	Tr	12/83	83-86	114	1	1
Grimsby T	Tr	12/86	86-87	3	1	0
Darlington	Tr	08/88	88	25	5	1

MOORE David Leon
Born: Worsley, Greater Manchester, England, 4 April, 1985 F

League Club	Source	Date Signed	Seasons Played	Apps	Subs	Gls
Wigan Ath	Sch	07/04				
Bury	L	01/05	04	0	3	0

MOORE Eric
Born: St Helens, Merseyside, England, 16 July, 1926 RB
Died: St Helens, Merseyside, England, 5 August, 2004

League Club	Source	Date Signed	Seasons Played	Apps	Subs	Gls
Everton	Haydock	02/49	49-56	171	-	0
Chesterfield	Tr	01/57	56	6	-	0
Tranmere Rov	Tr	07/57	57	36	-	0

MOORE Gary
Born: Greenwich, SE London, England, 29 December, 1968 F

League Club	Source	Date Signed	Seasons Played	Apps	Subs	Gls
Maidstone U	Alma Swanley	03/91	90	0	5	1

MOORE Gary
Born: South Hetton, County Durham, England, 4 November, 1945 F

League Club	Source	Date Signed	Seasons Played	Apps	Subs	Gls
Sunderland	Jnr	11/62	64-66	13	0	2
Grimsby T	Tr	02/67	66-68	52	1	15
Southend U	Tr	11/68	68-73	156	8	46
Colchester U	L	03/74	73	11	0	7
Chester C	Tr	08/74	74-75	29	14	4
Swansea C	Tr	07/76	76-77	30	4	9

MOORE Gordon Alexander
Born: Greenock, Inverclyde, Scotland, 27 June, 1968 W

League Club	Source	Date Signed	Seasons Played	Apps	Subs	Gls
Bristol C	Jnr	06/86	85	0	1	0

MOORE Graham
Born: Hengoed, Caerphilly, Wales, 7 March, 1941 M
England: FLge-1//Wales: 21/U23-9

League Club	Source	Date Signed	Seasons Played	Apps	Subs	Gls
Cardiff C	Jnr	05/58	58-61	85	-	23
Chelsea	Tr	12/61	61-63	68	-	13
Manchester U	Tr	11/63	63	18	-	4
Northampton T	Tr	12/65	65-66	53	0	10
Charlton Ath	Tr	06/67	67-70	110	0	8
Doncaster Rov	Tr	09/71	71-73	67	2	3

MOORE Howard
Born: Canterbury, England, 5 March, 1947 RW
Died: Southend-on-Sea, England, 9 October, 2012

League Club	Source	Date Signed	Seasons Played	Apps	Subs	Gls
Coventry C	Ashford T, Kent	03/66				

League Club	Source	Date Signed	Seasons Played	Apps	Subs	Gls
Gillingham	Tr	07/67	67	17	0	0
Southend U	Tr	01/68	67-68	6	1	0

MOORE James Christopher (Chris)
Born: Newcastle-upon-Tyne, England, 17 January, 1984 — W

League Club	Source	Date Signed	Seasons Played	Apps	Subs	Gls
Darlington	Whitley Bay	03/10	09	8	3	0

MOORE Joe-Max
Born: Tulsa, Oklahoma, USA, 23 February, 1971 — F
USA: 100/U21

League Club	Source	Date Signed	Seasons Played	Apps	Subs	Gls
Everton	New England Rev (USA)	12/99	99-01	22	30	8

MOORE John
Born: Harthill, Lanarkshire, Scotland, 21 December, 1943 — CD

League Club	Source	Date Signed	Seasons Played	Apps	Subs	Gls
Luton T	Motherwell	05/65	65-72	264	9	13
Brighton & HA	L	10/72	72	5	0	0
Northampton T	Tr	08/74	74	14	0	0

MOORE John
Born: Consett, County Durham, England, 1 October, 1966 — F

League Club	Source	Date Signed	Seasons Played	Apps	Subs	Gls
Sunderland	App	10/84	84-87	4	12	1
Newport Co	L	12/85	85	2	0	0
Darlington	L	11/86	86	2	0	1
Mansfield T	L	03/87	86	5	0	1
Rochdale	L	01/88	87	10	0	2
Hull C	Tr	06/88	88	11	3	1
Sheffield U	L	03/89	88	4	1	0
Shrewsbury T	FC Utrecht (NED)	07/90	90	7	1	1
Crewe Alex	Tr	01/91	90	0	1	0
Scarborough	Tr	08/91	91	3	4	1

MOORE John
Born: Liverpool, England, 9 September, 1945 — CD

League Club	Source	Date Signed	Seasons Played	Apps	Subs	Gls
Stoke C	Everton (App)	07/63	67	12	1	0
Shrewsbury T	Tr	08/68	68-72	147	0	1
Swansea C	Tr	01/73	72-73	31	0	0

MOORE John Frederick Beriah (Beriah)
Born: Cardiff, Wales, 25 December, 1919 — LW
Died: Bangor, Gwynedd, Wales, May, 2005

League Club	Source	Date Signed	Seasons Played	Apps	Subs	Gls
Cardiff C	Cardiff Corinthians	09/41	47-48	6	-	4
Newport Co	Bangor C	07/50	50-52	121	-	45

MOORE John Leslie (Leslie)
Born: Sheffield, England, 7 July, 1933 — CH
Died: Sheffield, England, 15 October, 1992

League Club	Source	Date Signed	Seasons Played	Apps	Subs	Gls
Derby Co	Worksop T	11/57	57-63	144	-	3
Lincoln C	Boston U	10/65	65-66	59	0	0

MOORE John Michael
Born: Carlton, Nottinghamshire, England, 1 February, 1943 — RW
Died: Calverton, Nottinghamshire, England, 4 November, 2009

League Club	Source	Date Signed	Seasons Played	Apps	Subs	Gls
Lincoln C	Arnold St Mary's	11/61	61-64	30	-	5

MOORE John William Michael
Born: Chiswick, W London, England, 25 September, 1923 — WH
Died: Wandsworth, SW London, England, September, 2012

League Club	Source	Date Signed	Seasons Played	Apps	Subs	Gls
Brentford	Fleet Air Arm	09/46	46-47	4	-	0
Colchester U	Gloucester C	07/49	51	2	-	0

MOORE Jonathan (Jon)
Born: Cardiff, Wales, 17 November, 1955 — LB
Wales: Youth/Schools

League Club	Source	Date Signed	Seasons Played	Apps	Subs	Gls
Bristol Rov	App	11/73				
Millwall	Tr	12/74	74-78	119	0	5
Bournemouth	Tr	05/79	79-80	36	0	2

MOORE Karl
Born: Dublin, Republic of Ireland, 9 November, 1988 — LM
Republic of Ireland: U21-4/Youth

League Club	Source	Date Signed	Seasons Played	Apps	Subs	Gls
Manchester C	Sch	07/06				
Millwall	L	08/08	08	2	4	0

MOORE Kenneth (Ken)
Born: Bradford, England, 13 September, 1921 — RB
Died: Bradford, England, June, 2004

League Club	Source	Date Signed	Seasons Played	Apps	Subs	Gls
Halifax T	Bradford C (Am)	11/47	47-49	32	-	2

MOORE Kevin
Born: Loughborough, Leicestershire, England, 20 October, 1957 — M

League Club	Source	Date Signed	Seasons Played	Apps	Subs	Gls
Shrewsbury T	App	10/75	74-77	15	3	1

MOORE Kevin John
Born: Blackpool, Lancashire, England, 30 January, 1956 — LW

League Club	Source	Date Signed	Seasons Played	Apps	Subs	Gls
Blackpool	App	10/73	74-76	33	6	3
Bury	L	12/76	76	4	0	0
Swansea C	Tr	07/77	77-78	51	4	6
Newport Co	Tr	02/79	78-82	140	8	13
Swindon T	L	03/83	82	1	0	0

MOORE Kevin Thomas
Born: Grimsby, North Lincolnshire, England, 29 April, 1958 — CD
Died: Hedge End, Hampshire, England, 29 April, 2013
England: Schools

League Club	Source	Date Signed	Seasons Played	Apps	Subs	Gls
Grimsby T	Jnr	07/76	76-86	397	3	28
Oldham Ath	Tr	02/87	86	13	0	1
Southampton	Tr	08/87	87-93	144	4	10
Bristol Rov	L	01/92	91	7	0	0
Bristol Rov	L	10/92	92	4	0	1
Fulham	Tr	07/94	94-95	48	3	4

MOORE Kieffer Robert Francisco
Born: Torquay, Devon, England, 8 August, 1992 — F

League Club	Source	Date Signed	Seasons Played	Apps	Subs	Gls
Yeovil T	Dorchester T	07/13	13-14	30	20	7

MOORE Liam Simon
Born: Loughborough, Leicestershire, England, 31 January, 1993 — CD
England: U21-15/Youth

League Club	Source	Date Signed	Seasons Played	Apps	Subs	Gls
Leicester C	Sch	07/11	11-14	48	11	1
Bradford C	L	08/11	11	16	1	0
Brentford	L	02/13	12	6	1	0
Brentford	L	02/15	14	3	0	0

MOORE Luke Isaac
Born: Birmingham, England, 13 February, 1986 — F
England: U21-5/Youth

League Club	Source	Date Signed	Seasons Played	Apps	Subs	Gls
Aston Villa	Sch	02/03	03-07	36	51	14
Wycombe W	L	12/03	03	6	0	4
West Bromwich A	Tr	02/08	07-09	31	26	5
Derby Co	L	09/10	10	9	4	4
Swansea C	Tr	01/11	10-12	18	34	8

MOORE Luke Robert
Born: Gravesend, Kent, England, 27 April, 1988 — F
England: Semi Pro-1

League Club	Source	Date Signed	Seasons Played	Apps	Subs	Gls
AFC Wimbledon	Ebbsfleet U	06/09	11-13	81	24	16

MOORE Malcolm
Born: Sunderland, England, 18 December, 1948 — F

League Club	Source	Date Signed	Seasons Played	Apps	Subs	Gls
Sunderland	App	12/65	67-68	10	2	3
Crewe Alex	L	03/70	69	8	0	0
Tranmere Rov	Tr	07/70	70-72	83	10	21
Hartlepool U	Tr	08/73	73-75	127	2	34
Workington	Tr	08/76	76	22	0	2

MOORE Mark Steven
Born: Bradford, England, 9 July, 1972 — M

League Club	Source	Date Signed	Seasons Played	Apps	Subs	Gls
Cambridge U	N Hampshire C'ge (USA)	03/98	97	0	1	0

MOORE Martin Terence
Born: Middlesbrough, England, 10 January, 1966 — LW

League Club	Source	Date Signed	Seasons Played	Apps	Subs	Gls
Peterborough U	Stockton	01/90	89	6	1	0

MOORE Michael (Micky)
Born: Chorley, Lancashire, England, 20 July, 1952 — F

League Club	Source	Date Signed	Seasons Played	Apps	Subs	Gls
Preston NE	Blackburn Rov (Am)	06/70				
Southport	Tr	07/71	71-73	62	21	11
Port Vale	Wigan Ath	03/78	77	13	0	0
Wigan Ath	Tr	08/78	78-79	57	7	12

MOORE Michael Thomas
Born: Birmingham, England, 7 October, 1973 — F

League Club	Source	Date Signed	Seasons Played	Apps	Subs	Gls
Derby Co	YT	06/92				
Swansea C	Tr	06/93	93	0	1	0

MOORE Neil
Born: Liverpool, England, 21 September, 1972 — CD

League Club	Source	Date Signed	Seasons Played	Apps	Subs	Gls
Everton	YT	06/91	92-93	4	1	0
Blackpool	L	09/94	94	7	0	0
Oldham Ath	L	02/95	94	5	0	0
Carlisle U	L	08/95	95	13	0	0
Rotherham U	L	03/96	95	10	1	0
Norwich C	Tr	01/97	96	2	0	0
Burnley	Tr	08/97	97-98	48	4	3
Macclesfield T	Tr	12/99	99	12	3	2
Mansfield T	Telford U	07/02	02	18	0	0

MOORE Norman Woodliffe
Born: Grimsby, North Lincolnshire, England, 15 October, 1919 — CF
Died: Grimsby, North Lincolnshire, England, 14 March, 2007

League Club	Source	Date Signed	Seasons Played	Apps	Subs	Gls
Grimsby T	Jnr	03/39	46	7	-	1
Hull C	Tr	04/47	46-49	81	-	46
Blackburn Rov	Tr	03/50	49-50	7	-	1
Bury	Tr	08/51	51	2	-	0

MOORE Raymond (Ray)
Born: Workington, Cumbria, England, 2 November, 1956 — W

League Club	Source	Date Signed	Seasons Played	Apps	Subs	Gls
Workington	Sekers	11/75	75	3	0	0

MOORE Robert

Born: Campsall, South Yorkshire, England, 14 December, 1932 — IF

League Club	Source	Date Signed	Seasons Played	Apps	Subs	Gls
Rotherham U	Worksop T	05/55	55-56	19	-	2
Chesterfield	Tr	10/56	56-58	19	-	3

MOORE Robert Frederick Chelsea (Bobby)

Born: Barking, E London, England, 12 April, 1941 — CD
Died: Putney, SW London, England, 24 February, 1993
England: 108/FLge-12/U23-8/Youth

League Club	Source	Date Signed	Seasons Played	Apps	Subs	Gls
West Ham U	Jnr	06/58	58-73	543	1	24
Fulham	Tr	03/74	73-76	124	0	1

MOORE Ronald David (Ronnie)

Born: Liverpool, England, 29 January, 1953 — F

League Club	Source	Date Signed	Seasons Played	Apps	Subs	Gls
Tranmere Rov	Jnr	05/71	71-78	248	1	72
Cardiff C	Tr	02/79	78-79	54	2	6
Rotherham U	Tr	08/80	80-83	124	1	52
Charlton Ath	Tr	09/83	83-84	60	2	13
Rochdale	Tr	07/85	85	43	0	9
Tranmere Rov	Tr	07/86	86-88	75	0	6

MOORE Samuel Christopher (Sammy)

Born: Birmingham, England, 6 September, 1934 — W
Died: Dover, Kent, England, 1 March, 1994

League Club	Source	Date Signed	Seasons Played	Apps	Subs	Gls
Wolverhampton W	Aldershot (Am)	11/54				
Walsall	Tr	05/55	55-57	64	-	10
Gillingham	Tr	06/58	58-59	33	-	9

MOORE Samuel Leslie (Sammy)

Born: Deal, Kent, England, 7 September, 1987 — M

League Club	Source	Date Signed	Seasons Played	Apps	Subs	Gls
Ipswich T	Sch	07/06	06	0	1	0
Brentford	L	07/07	07	13	7	2
AFC Wimbledon	Dover Ath	07/10	11-14	130	9	12

MOORE Simon William

Born: Sandown, Isle of Wight, England, 19 May, 1990 — G

League Club	Source	Date Signed	Seasons Played	Apps	Subs	Gls
Brentford	Farnborough T	08/09	09-12	61	3	0
Cardiff C	Tr	07/13	14	8	2	0
Bristol C	L	01/14	13	11	0	0

MOORE Stefan Leroy

Born: Birmingham, England, 28 September, 1983 — F
England: Youth

League Club	Source	Date Signed	Seasons Played	Apps	Subs	Gls
Aston Villa	YT	10/00	02-04	9	13	2
Chesterfield	L	10/01	01	1	1	0
Millwall	L	08/04	04	3	3	0
Leicester C	L	03/05	04	2	5	0
Queens Park Rgrs	Tr	06/05	05-07	19	20	3
Port Vale	L	08/06	06	8	4	1
Walsall	Tr	01/08	07	3	2	1

MOORE Stephen John (Steve)

Born: Chester, England, 17 December, 1969 — F

League Club	Source	Date Signed	Seasons Played	Apps	Subs	Gls
Chester C	YT	-	87	0	1	0

MOORE Thomas Lynch (Tom)

Born: Trimdon, County Durham, England, 25 July, 1936 — G

League Club	Source	Date Signed	Seasons Played	Apps	Subs	Gls
Darlington (Am)	Trimdon	08/56	56	1	-	0

MOORE Thomas Roy (Roy)

Born: Grimsby, North Lincolnshire, England, 17 December, 1923 — CH
Died: Winchester, Hampshire, England, December, 1991

League Club	Source	Date Signed	Seasons Played	Apps	Subs	Gls
Grimsby T	Jnr	06/47	48-49	3	-	0

MOORE Watson Evans (Wattie)

Born: Hartlepool, Cleveland, England, 30 August, 1925 — CH
Died: Hartlepool, Cleveland, England, 1967

League Club	Source	Date Signed	Seasons Played	Apps	Subs	Gls
Hartlepool U	Oxford Street OB	05/48	48-59	447	-	3

MOORE-TAYLOR Jordan Alan

Born: Exeter, England, 21 January, 1994 — D

League Club	Source	Date Signed	Seasons Played	Apps	Subs	Gls
Exeter C	Sch	07/12	12-14	54	8	3

MOORES Ian Richard

Born: Newcastle-under-Lyme, Potteries, England, 5 October, 1954 — F
Died: Stoke-on-Trent, England, 13 January, 1998
England: U23-2

League Club	Source	Date Signed	Seasons Played	Apps	Subs	Gls
Stoke C	App	06/72	73-75	40	10	15
Tottenham H	Tr	08/76	76-78	25	4	6
Leyton Orient	Tr	10/78	78-81	110	7	26
Bolton W	Tr	07/82	82	23	3	3
Barnsley	L	02/83	82	3	0	0

MOORES James Craig (Craig)

Born: Macclesfield, Cheshire, England, 1 February, 1961 — F

League Club	Source	Date Signed	Seasons Played	Apps	Subs	Gls
Bolton W	App	02/79	80	0	1	0
Swindon T	Tr	07/81	81	1	1	0

MOORHOUSE Alan

Born: Wardle, Greater Manchester, England, 12 October, 1925 — W
Died: Blackpool, Lancashire, England, November, 2013

League Club	Source	Date Signed	Seasons Played	Apps	Subs	Gls
Rochdale	Blackburn Rov (Am)	03/47	46-47	17	-	3

MOORS Christopher Anthony (Chris)

Born: Yeovil, Somerset, England, 18 August, 1976 — F

League Club	Source	Date Signed	Seasons Played	Apps	Subs	Gls
Torquay U	West Ham U (YT)	11/95	95	0	1	0

MORAH Olisa Henry (Ollie)

Born: Islington, N London, England, 3 September, 1972 — F
England: Youth/Schools

League Club	Source	Date Signed	Seasons Played	Apps	Subs	Gls
Tottenham H	YT	07/91				
Hereford U	L	11/91	91	0	2	0
Swindon T	Tr	11/92				
Cambridge U	Sutton U	06/94	94	8	6	2
Torquay U	L	03/95	94	2	0	0

MORAIS Felipe Alexandre

Born: Lisbon, Portugal, 21 November, 1985 — RW
Portugal: U21-2

League Club	Source	Date Signed	Seasons Played	Apps	Subs	Gls
Chelsea	Jnr	07/03				
MK Dons	L	01/06	05	11	2	0
Millwall	Tr	06/06	06	8	4	1
Oldham Ath	St Johnstone	10/10	10-11	43	16	8
Stevenage	Tr	07/12	12-13	39	16	7
Bradford C	Tr	08/14	14	22	8	3

MORAIS Nuno Miguel Barbosa

Born: Penafiel, Portugal, 29 January, 1984 — CD
Portugal: U21-14/Youth

League Club	Source	Date Signed	Seasons Played	Apps	Subs	Gls
Chelsea	Penafiel (POR)	08/04	04-06	0	4	0

MORALEE Jamie David

Born: Wandsworth, SW London, England, 2 December, 1971 — F

League Club	Source	Date Signed	Seasons Played	Apps	Subs	Gls
Crystal Palace	YT	07/90	91	2	4	0
Millwall	Tr	09/92	92-93	56	11	19
Watford	Tr	07/94	94-95	40	9	7
Crewe Alex	Tr	08/96	96-97	10	6	0
Brighton & HA	Tr	08/98	98	22	9	3
Colchester U	Tr	07/99	99	20	7	1

MORAN Brian Joseph

Born: Hemsworth, West Yorkshire, England, 3 June, 1947 — RW

League Club	Source	Date Signed	Seasons Played	Apps	Subs	Gls
Barnsley	Jnr	01/67	66	1	0	0

MORAN Douglas Walter (Doug)

Born: Musselburgh, East Lothian, Scotland, 29 July, 1934 — IF

League Club	Source	Date Signed	Seasons Played	Apps	Subs	Gls
Ipswich T	Falkirk	07/61	61-63	104	-	31

MORAN Edward (Eddie)

Born: Cleland, Lanarkshire, Scotland, 20 July, 1930 — IF
Died: Stockport, Greater Manchester, England, 1 July, 2013

League Club	Source	Date Signed	Seasons Played	Apps	Subs	Gls
Leicester C	Cleland Jnrs	09/47	48-50	8	-	1
Stockport Co	Tr	10/51	51-56	110	-	44
Rochdale	Tr	02/57	56-58	43	-	13
Crewe Alex	Tr	09/58	58	23	-	7

MORAN James (Jimmy)

Born: Cleland, Lanarkshire, Scotland, 6 March, 1935 — IF

League Club	Source	Date Signed	Seasons Played	Apps	Subs	Gls
Leicester C	Wishaw Jnrs	12/55	56	3	-	1
Norwich C	Tr	11/57	57-59	36	-	17
Northampton T	Tr	01/61	60-61	24	-	6
Darlington	Tr	08/62	62	26	-	6
Workington	Tr	07/63	63-65	100	0	21

MORAN John

Born: Cleland, Lanarkshire, Scotland, 9 March, 1933 — IF
Died: Wishaw, Lanarkshire, Scotland, 8 April, 2015

League Club	Source	Date Signed	Seasons Played	Apps	Subs	Gls
Derby Co	Coltness U	11/54	54	2	-	0

MORAN Kevin Bernard

Born: Dublin, Republic of Ireland, 29 April, 1956 — CD
Republic of Ireland: 71

League Club	Source	Date Signed	Seasons Played	Apps	Subs	Gls
Manchester U	Pegasus, Dublin (ROI)	02/78	78-87	228	3	21
Blackburn Rov	Sporting Gijon (SPN)	01/90	89-93	143	4	10

MORAN Lister Ferguson

Born: Ryton-on-Tyne, Tyne and Wear, England, 3 June, 1930 — LH
Died: Penrith, Cumbria, England, May, 2005

League Club	Source	Date Signed	Seasons Played	Apps	Subs	Gls
Gateshead	Wearmouth CW	10/50	53-56	19	-	0

MORAN Michael Edward (Mike)

Born: Leek, Staffordshire, England, 26 December, 1935 — IF

League Club	Source	Date Signed	Seasons Played	Apps	Subs	Gls
Port Vale		07/54				
Crewe Alex	Tr	07/57	57	13	-	3

MORAN Paul

Born: Enfield, N London, England, 22 May, 1968 — W

League Club	Source	Date Signed	Seasons Played	Apps	Subs	Gls
Tottenham H	App	07/85	86-93	14	22	2
Portsmouth	L	01/89	88	3	0	0
Leicester C	L	11/89	89	10	0	1
Newcastle U	L	02/91	90	1	0	0
Southend U	L	03/91	90	1	0	0
Peterborough U	Tr	07/94	94	5	2	0

League Club	Source	Date Signed	Seasons Played	Career Record Apps	Subs	Gls

MORAN Richard (Richie)
Born: Hammersmith, W London, England, 9 September, 1963 — F

Birmingham C	Fujita Tokyo (JPN)	08/90	90	2	6	1

MORAN Ronald (Ronnie)
Born: Liverpool, England, 28 February, 1934 — LB
England: FLge-2

Liverpool	Jnr	01/52	52-64	343	-	14

MORAN Stephen James (Steve)
Born: Croydon, S London, England, 10 January, 1961 — F
England: U21-2/Schools

Southampton	Jnr	08/79	79-85	173	7	78
Leicester C	Tr	09/86	86-87	35	8	14
Reading	Tr	11/87	87-90	91	25	30
Exeter C	Tr	08/91	91-92	50	7	27
Hull C	Tr	08/93	93	11	6	5

MORAN Thomas (Tommy)
Born: Glasgow, Scotland, 31 May, 1924 — RH

Accrington Stan	Ayr U	08/53	53	7	-	0

MORAN Thomas (Tom)
Born: Edinburgh, Scotland, 5 February, 1930 — LW
Died: Edinburgh, Scotland, February, 2011

Carlisle U	Cowdenbeath	05/54	54-55	35	-	4
Darlington	Tr	05/56	56-57	70	-	13

MORAS Evangelos (Vangelis)
Born: Larissa, Greece, 26 August, 1981 — CD
Greece: 16/U21-9

Swansea C	Bologna (ITA)	09/11	11	0	1	0

MORDUE James (Jimmy)
Born: Seaton Delaval, Northumberland, England, 18 February, 1924 — WH

Bradford Park Ave	North Shields	09/46	48	2	-	0

MORDUE William (Billy)
Born: Sacriston, County Durham, England, 23 February, 1937 — D
Died: Doncaster, South Yorkshire, England, 23 September, 2010

Doncaster Rov	Bentley Colliery	03/58	57-60	78	-	0

MOREAU Fabrice
Born: Paris, France, 7 October, 1967 — M
Cameroon: 7

Notts Co	Airdrieonians	03/01	00	2	3	0

MOREFIELD William John Thomas (John)
Born: Gloucester, England, 26 October, 1922 — FB
Died: Wakefield, England, 17 December, 1997

Halifax T	Coney Hill	05/46	46-48	65	-	0

MOREIRA Fabio da Silva
Born: Rio de Janeiro, Brazil, 14 March, 1972 — M

Middlesbrough	GF Chaves (POR)	02/97	97	1	0	0

MOREIRA Joao Manuel Silva
Born: Angola, 30 June, 1970 — LB

Swansea C	Benfica (POR)	06/96	96-97	15	0	0

MORELAND Victor (Vic)
Born: Belfast, Northern Ireland, 15 June, 1957 — DM
Northern Ireland: 6/U21-1

Derby Co	Glentoran	09/78	78-79	38	4	1

MORELINE David John (Dave)
Born: Stepney, E London, England, 2 December, 1950 — D

Fulham	App	01/68	68-73	63	7	0
Reading	Tr	06/74	74-80	166	0	0

MOREMONT Ralph
Born: Sheffield, England, 24 September, 1924 — WH/IF
Died: Sheffield, England, 1982

Sheffield U	Hampton's Sports	09/46	49	2	-	0
Chester C	Tr	05/50	50-52	121	-	19
Rochdale		08/55	55	1	-	0

[MORENO] DA CUNHA TEIXEIRA Joao Miguel
Born: Guimaraes, Portugal, 19 August, 1981 — DM

Leicester C	Vit Guimaraes (POR)	08/10	10	3	0	0

MORENO Alberto
Born: Seville, Spain, 5 July, 1992 — LB
Spain: 3/U21-10

Liverpool	Sevilla (SPN)	08/14	14	26	2	2

MORENO Jaime Morales
Born: Santa Cruz, Bolivia, 19 January, 1974 — M
Bolivia: 75

Middlesbrough	Blooming (BOL)	09/94	94-95	8	13	1
Middlesbrough (L)	Washington DC U (USA)	12/97	97	1	4	1

MORENO Marcelo
Born: Santa Cruz de la Sierra, Bolivia, 18 June, 1987 — F
Bolivia: 37

Wigan Ath (L)	Shakhtar Donetsk (UKR)	02/10	09	9	3	0

MORENO Valera Javier (Javi)
Born: Valencia, Spain, 10 September, 1974 — F
Spain: 5/Youth

Bolton W (L)	Atletico Madrid (SPN)	01/04	03	1	7	0

MORGAN Adam James
Born: Liverpool, England, 21 April, 1994 — F
England: Youth

Liverpool	Sch	07/11				
Rotherham U	L	01/13	12	1	0	0
Yeovil T	Tr	11/13	13-14	6	12	1

MORGAN Alan
Born: Swansea, Wales, 2 January, 1936 — CH
Died: Swansea, Wales, November, 2009

Leeds U		01/54				
Crewe Alex	Tr	09/56	56	5	-	0

MORGAN Alan Meredith
Born: Aberystwyth, Ceredigion, Wales, 2 November, 1973 — M
Wales: U21-2/Youth/Schools

Tranmere Rov	YT	05/92	95-01	42	23	1

MORGAN Alan William
Born: Musselburgh, East Lothian, Scotland, 27 November, 1983 — M
Scotland: Youth

Blackburn Rov	YT	12/00				
Darlington	L	10/03	03	4	1	1
Cheltenham T	L	03/05	04	8	0	0

MORGAN Alfred Stanley (Stan)
Born: Abergwynfi, Neath Port Talbot, Wales, 10 October, 1920 — IF
Died: Walthamstow, NE London, England, 1971

Arsenal	Gwynfi Welfare	12/41	46	2	-	0
Walsall	Tr	06/48	48	10	-	1
Millwall	Tr	12/48	48-52	156	-	41
Leyton Orient	Tr	05/53	53-55	96	-	24

MORGAN Arthur Robert
Born: Ogmore Vale, Bridgend, Wales, 13 September, 1930 — IF/LB
Died: Barry, Vale of Glamorgan, Wales, 13 October, 2000

Swansea C	Army	12/48	50-52	12	-	0
Plymouth Arg	Tr	11/53	53-56	36	-	4

MORGAN Christopher Paul (Chris)
Born: Barnsley, South Yorkshire, England, 9 November, 1977 — CD

Barnsley	YT	07/96	97-02	182	3	7
Sheffield U	Tr	08/03	03-10	240	7	13

MORGAN Clifford Ivor (Cliff)
Born: Bristol, England, 26 September, 1913 — RH
Died: Bristol, England, 31 July, 1975

Bristol C	Bristol Boys Brigade	06/30	31-48	245	-	11

MORGAN Craig
Born: Flint, Wales, 18 June, 1985 — CD
Wales: 23/U21-12/Youth

Wrexham	Sch	07/03	01-04	33	19	1
MK Dons	Tr	07/05	05-06	41	2	0
Wrexham	L	10/06	06	1	0	0
Peterborough U	Tr	11/06	06-09	122	3	4
Preston NE	Tr	07/10	10-11	48	2	3
Rotherham U	Tr	09/12	12-14	89	2	1

MORGAN Daniel Frederick (Danny)
Born: Stepney, E London, England, 4 November, 1984 — F

Oxford U	Wimbledon (Sch)	07/04	04-05	1	5	1

MORGAN Darren Joseph
Born: Camberwell, S London, England, 5 November, 1967 — M
Wales: Youth

Millwall	App	11/85	86-90	35	8	2
Bradford C	L	03/90	89	2	0	0
Peterborough U	L	03/91	90	5	0	0
Bradford C	Tr	08/91	91	9	2	0

MORGAN David Bari Rees (Bari)
Born: Aberaeron, Ceredigion, Wales, 13 August, 1980 — M

Swansea C	YT	07/99	00	0	5	0

MORGAN Dean Lance
Born: Enfield, N London, England, 3 October, 1983 — W
Montserrat: 3

Colchester U	YT	08/01	00-02	23	48	6
Reading	Tr	11/03	03-04	13	18	3

League Club	Source	Date Signed	Seasons Played	Apps	Subs	Gls
Luton T	Tr	07/05	05-07	54	34	11
Southend U	L	11/07	07	6	2	0
Crewe Alex	L	03/08	07	7	2	1
Leyton Orient	L	08/08	08	18	14	5
MK Dons	Grays Ath	10/09	09	1	8	1
Aldershot T	L	03/10	09	8	1	4
Chesterfield	Tr	08/10	10-11	28	10	4
Oxford U	L	03/12	11	10	0	1
Wycombe W	Tr	09/12	12-13	48	14	15
Crawley T	Woking	01/15	14	3	10	0

MORGAN Denley James
Born: Llanelli, Carmarthenshire, Wales, 13 February, 1951 — LB

League Club	Source	Date Signed	Seasons Played	Apps	Subs	Gls
Swansea C	Jnr	05/69	68-71	14	0	0

MORGAN Donald (Don)
Born: Huddersfield, West Yorkshire, England, 8 June, 1925 — WH
Died: Huddersfield, West Yorkshire, England, 1976

League Club	Source	Date Signed	Seasons Played	Apps	Subs	Gls
Accrington Stan	Huddersfield T (Am)	06/47	46-47	8	-	1
Tranmere Rov	Tr	05/48				

MORGAN Ernest (Ernie)
Born: Barnsley, South Yorkshire, England, 13 January, 1927 — IF
Died: Rainham, Kent, England, 3 October, 2013

League Club	Source	Date Signed	Seasons Played	Apps	Subs	Gls
Lincoln C	Rawmarsh Welfare	09/49	52	3	-	0
Gillingham	Tr	08/53	53-56	155	-	73

MORGAN Gary
Born: Consett, County Durham, England, 1 April, 1961 — LB

League Club	Source	Date Signed	Seasons Played	Apps	Subs	Gls
Darlington	Berwick Rgrs	07/85	85-88	146	0	3

MORGAN George William
Born: Cardiff, Wales, 28 March, 1923 — W
Died: Norwich, England, 3 October, 1989

League Club	Source	Date Signed	Seasons Played	Apps	Subs	Gls
Norwich C	Cardiff C (Am)	01/47	46-49	65	-	15
Newport Co	Tr	06/50				

MORGAN Gerald (Gerry)
Born: Llanidloes, Powys, Wales, 23 February, 1950 — G

League Club	Source	Date Signed	Seasons Played	Apps	Subs	Gls
Walsall (Am)		03/74	73	1	0	0

MORGAN Huw
Born: Neath, Wales, 20 August, 1964 — M

League Club	Source	Date Signed	Seasons Played	Apps	Subs	Gls
Swansea C	App	08/82	83	5	2	0

MORGAN Ian Arthur
Born: Walthamstow, NE London, England, 14 November, 1946 — RW

League Club	Source	Date Signed	Seasons Played	Apps	Subs	Gls
Queens Park Rgrs	App	09/64	64-72	161	12	26
Watford	Tr	10/73	73	15	1	1

MORGAN James Alexander (Jamie)
Born: Plymouth, England, 1 October, 1975 — M

League Club	Source	Date Signed	Seasons Played	Apps	Subs	Gls
Plymouth Arg	YT	06/94	92-94	9	2	0
Exeter C	Tr	08/95	95	2	4	0

MORGAN Jonathan Peter (Jon)
Born: Cardiff, Wales, 10 July, 1970 — M
Wales: Youth

League Club	Source	Date Signed	Seasons Played	Apps	Subs	Gls
Cardiff C	YT	07/88	88-90	43	12	3

MORGAN Keith
Born: Trowbridge, Wiltshire, England, 19 February, 1940 — RH

League Club	Source	Date Signed	Seasons Played	Apps	Subs	Gls
Swindon T	Westbury U	08/58	58-66	325	0	6

MORGAN Kenneth Sidney (Ken)
Born: Swansea, Wales, 28 July, 1932 — RW
Died: Watford, Hertfordshire, England, 20 December, 2008

League Club	Source	Date Signed	Seasons Played	Apps	Subs	Gls
Fulham	Rickmansworth	09/50				
Watford	Tr	09/52				
Northampton T	Tr	09/54				
Brentford	Tr	08/55				
Crystal Palace	Tr	10/55	55	1	-	0

MORGAN Kerry David
Born: Merthyr Tydfil, Wales, 31 October, 1988 — W

League Club	Source	Date Signed	Seasons Played	Apps	Subs	Gls
Swansea C	Sch	07/08	09	1	2	0

MORGAN Laurence (Lol)
Born: Rotherham, South Yorkshire, England, 5 May, 1931 — LB

League Club	Source	Date Signed	Seasons Played	Apps	Subs	Gls
Huddersfield T	Sheffield U (Am)	03/49	49-50	7	-	0
Rotherham U	Tr	08/54	54-63	291	-	0
Darlington	Tr	07/64	64-65	30	1	0

MORGAN Lewis (Lew)
Born: Cowdenbeath, Fife, Scotland, 30 April, 1911 — RB
Died: Portsmouth, England, 22 September, 1988
Scotland: SLge-1

League Club	Source	Date Signed	Seasons Played	Apps	Subs	Gls
Portsmouth	Dundee	08/35	35-38	123	-	0
Watford	Tr	07/46	46-47	50	-	0

MORGAN Lionel Anthony
Born: Tottenham, N London, England, 17 February, 1983 — M
England: Youth

League Club	Source	Date Signed	Seasons Played	Apps	Subs	Gls
Wimbledon	YT	08/00	00-03	13	17	2

MORGAN Mark Paul Thomas (Paul)
Born: Belfast, Northern Ireland, 23 October, 1978 — CD
Northern Ireland: U21-1

League Club	Source	Date Signed	Seasons Played	Apps	Subs	Gls
Preston NE	YT	05/97				
Lincoln C	Tr	07/01	01-06	203	9	2
Bury	Tr	07/07	07	20	0	0
Macclesfield T	L	07/08	08	38	1	1
Macclesfield T	Tr	08/09	09-11	64	3	0

MORGAN Marvin Newlon
Born: Manchester, England, 13 April, 1983 — W

League Club	Source	Date Signed	Seasons Played	Apps	Subs	Gls
Aldershot T	Woking	06/08	08-10	77	14	26
Dagenham & Red	L	01/11	10	5	7	0
Shrewsbury T	Tr	06/11	11-12	63	19	15
Plymouth Arg	Tr	07/13	13-14	16	21	2
Hartlepool U	L	02/15	14	4	1	1

MORGAN Nicholas (Nicky)
Born: East Ham, E London, England, 30 October, 1959 — F

League Club	Source	Date Signed	Seasons Played	Apps	Subs	Gls
West Ham U	App	11/77	78-82	14	7	2
Portsmouth	Tr	03/83	82-86	79	16	32
Stoke C	Tr	11/86	86-89	73	15	20
Bristol C	Tr	03/90	89-92	75	5	23
Bournemouth	L	10/92	92	6	0	1
Exeter C	Tr	02/94	93	12	0	4

MORGAN Peter William
Born: Cardiff, Wales, 28 October, 1951 — CD

League Club	Source	Date Signed	Seasons Played	Apps	Subs	Gls
Cardiff C	Jnr	11/69	72	16	0	0
Hereford U	Tr	08/74	74	16	0	0
Newport Co	Tr	03/76	75-76	22	2	1

MORGAN Philip Jonathan (Phil)
Born: Stoke-on-Trent, England, 18 December, 1974 — G
England: Youth/Schools

League Club	Source	Date Signed	Seasons Played	Apps	Subs	Gls
Ipswich T	YT	07/93	94	1	0	0
Stoke C	Tr	07/95				
Chesterfield	L	10/96	96	2	0	0

MORGAN Richard Dennis (Dennis)
Born: Seven Sisters, Neath Port Talbot, Wales, 22 September, 1925 — RB
Died: Dover, Kent, England, 4 July, 1980

League Club	Source	Date Signed	Seasons Played	Apps	Subs	Gls
Cardiff C	Briton Ferry	04/44				
Norwich C	Tr	10/46	46-55	225	-	3

MORGAN Richard Leslie (Richie)
Born: Cardiff, Wales, 3 October, 1946 — CD
Wales: U23-1/Schools

League Club	Source	Date Signed	Seasons Played	Apps	Subs	Gls
Cardiff C	Cardiff Corinthians	02/66	67-76	68	0	0

MORGAN Roger Ernest
Born: Walthamstow, NE London, England, 14 November, 1946 — LW
England: U23-1/Youth

League Club	Source	Date Signed	Seasons Played	Apps	Subs	Gls
Queens Park Rgrs	App	09/64	64-68	180	0	39
Tottenham H	Tr	02/69	68-71	66	2	8

MORGAN Ronald (Ron)
Born: Merthyr Tydfil, Wales, 6 September, 1915 — CF
Died: Wolverhampton, England, June, 1990

League Club	Source	Date Signed	Seasons Played	Apps	Subs	Gls
Wolverhampton W	Merthyr T (Am)	01/34				
Bournemouth	Tr	06/35	35	2	-	1
Doncaster Rov	Northfleet	05/37	37-38	6	-	1
Accrington Stan	Tr	06/39	46	4	-	0

MORGAN Ryan Stephen
Born: Bristol, England, 12 July, 1978 — M

League Club	Source	Date Signed	Seasons Played	Apps	Subs	Gls
Bristol Rov	YT	03/97	96	1	0	0

MORGAN Samuel John (Sammy)
Born: Belfast, Northern Ireland, 3 December, 1946 — F
Northern Ireland: 18

League Club	Source	Date Signed	Seasons Played	Apps	Subs	Gls
Port Vale	Gorleston	07/70	69-72	109	5	25
Aston Villa	Tr	08/73	73-75	35	5	9
Brighton & HA	Tr	12/75	75-76	19	16	8
Cambridge U	Tr	08/77	77	34	3	4

MORGAN Scott
Born: Colchester, Essex, England, 22 March, 1975 — CD

League Club	Source	Date Signed	Seasons Played	Apps	Subs	Gls
Brentford	Bournemouth (YT)	08/93	93	1	0	0

MORGAN Sidney Samuel
Born: Bristol, England, 1 August, 1926 — G
Died: Bristol, England, 28 May, 2009

League Club	Source	Date Signed	Seasons Played	Apps	Subs	Gls
Bristol C	AG Farmers	12/47	48-53	71	-	0
Millwall	Tr	03/58	57-58	16	-	0

League Club	Source	Date Signed	Seasons Played	Apps	Subs	Gls
MORGAN Simon Charles						
Born: Birmingham, England, 5 September, 1966						D
England: U21-2						
Leicester C	App	11/84	85-89	147	13	3
Fulham	Tr	10/90	90-00	343	10	48
Brighton & HA	Tr	07/01	01	42	0	1
MORGAN Simon Dean						
Born: Merthyr Tydfil, Wales, 3 September, 1970						M
Newport Co	YT	-	87	0	2	0
MORGAN Stephen Alphonso (Steve)						
Born: Oldham, Greater Manchester, England, 19 September, 1968						LB
England: Youth						
Blackpool	App	08/86	85-89	135	9	10
Plymouth Arg	Tr	07/90	90-92	120	1	6
Coventry C	Tr	07/93	93-94	65	3	2
Bristol Rov	L	03/96	95	5	0	0
Wigan Ath	Tr	07/96	96-97	31	5	2
Bury	L	09/97	97	5	0	0
Burnley	Tr	08/98	98	17	0	0
Hull C	Tr	07/99	99	17	2	1
Halifax T	Tr	09/00	00	1	0	0
MORGAN Stephen James (Steve)						
Born: Wrexham, Wales, 28 December, 1970						W
Wales: Youth						
Oldham Ath	YT	07/89	87-88	1	1	0
Wrexham	L	03/90	89	7	0	1
Rochdale	Tr	03/91	90-91	12	11	3
MORGAN Stuart Edward						
Born: Swansea, Wales, 23 September, 1949						CD
West Ham U	Jnr	03/67				
Torquay U	L	02/69	68	14	0	0
Reading	Tr	11/69	69-71	42	4	1
Colchester U	Tr	08/72	72-74	79	2	10
Bournemouth	Tr	03/75	74-76	80	1	5
MORGAN Trevor James						
Born: Forest Gate, E London, England, 30 September, 1956						F
Bournemouth	Leytonstone & Ilford	09/80	80-81	53	0	13
Mansfield T	Tr	11/81	81	12	0	6
Bournemouth	Tr	03/82	81-83	88	0	33
Bristol C	Tr	03/84	83-84	32	0	8
Exeter C	Tr	11/84	84-85	30	0	9
Bristol Rov	Tr	09/85	85-86	54	1	24
Bristol C	Tr	01/87	86	19	0	7
Bolton W	Tr	06/87	87-88	65	12	17
Colchester U	Tr	10/89	89	31	1	12
Exeter C	Happy Valley (HKG)	11/90	90	14	3	3
Birmingham C	South China (HKG)	10/93	93	0	1	0
Exeter C	Rtd	09/94	94	4	5	1
MORGAN Wendell						
Born: Gorseinon, Swansea, Wales, 22 April, 1935						LW/WH
Cardiff C	Grovesend Welfare	05/52				
Brentford	Tr	06/54	55-57	47	-	6
Gillingham	Tr	09/57	57	34	-	3
Swansea C	Tr	07/58	58	7	-	0
Newport Co	Tr	06/59	59	26	-	3
Carlisle U	Tr	06/60	60	36	-	2
MORGAN Westley Nathan (Wes)						
Born: Nottingham, England, 21 January, 1984						CD
Jamaica: 15						
Nottingham F	Dunkirk, Nottingham	07/02	03-11	335	17	12
Kidderminster Hrs	L	02/03	02	5	0	1
Leicester C	Tr	01/12	11-14	142	2	5
MORGAN William (Willie)						
Born: Alloa, Stirlingshire, Scotland, 2 October, 1944						W
Scotland: 21/U23-1						
Burnley	Fishcross	10/61	62-67	183	0	19
Manchester U	Tr	08/68	68-74	236	2	25
Burnley	Tr	06/75	75	12	1	0
Bolton W	Tr	03/76	75-79	154	1	10
Blackpool	Tr	09/80	80-81	41	1	4
MORGAN William Alfred (Bill)						
Born: Rotherham, South Yorkshire, England, 26 September, 1926						WH
Died: Halifax, West Yorkshire, England, 12 July, 2007						
Wolverhampton W	Jnr	11/43				
Sheffield U	Tr	09/46				
Halifax T	Tr	08/48	48-52	110	-	3
Rochdale	Tr	07/53	53-54	28	-	0
MORGAN William James (Jimmy)						
Born: Bristol, England, 19 June, 1922						IF

League Club	Source	Date Signed	Seasons Played	Apps	Subs	Gls
Died: Bristol, England, 11 February, 1975						
Bristol Rov	Barton Hill Settlement	04/46	46-51	104	-	24
MORGAN Wynffrwd (Gwyn)						
Born: Abergwynfi, Neath Port Talbot, Wales, 7 August, 1925						RW
Died: Blaengwynfi, Neath Port Talbot, Wales, 9 April, 2006						
Bristol Rov (Am)	Coventry C (Am)	12/46	46	2	-	0
MORGAN-SMITH Amari Aaron						
Born: Wolverhampton, England, 3 April, 1989						F
England: Semi Pro-2						
Stockport Co	Crewe Alex (Sch)	08/07	07	0	1	0
Oldham Ath	Kidderminster Hrs	07/14	14	3	10	2
MORGANS Jeffrey (Jeff)						
Born: Farnborough, Hampshire, England, 12 August, 1942						IF
Died: Crewe, Cheshire, England, 14 January, 1995						
Crewe Alex	Jnr	09/59	60-61	9	-	2
MORGANS Kenneth Godfrey (Kenny)						
Born: Swansea, Wales, 16 March, 1939						W
Died: Swansea, Wales, 18 November, 2012						
Wales: U23-2						
Manchester U	Jnr	04/56	57-60	17	-	0
Swansea C	Tr	03/61	60-63	54	-	8
Newport Co	Tr	06/64	64-66	125	0	44
MORGANS Morgan Gwyn (Gwyn)						
Born: Blaenau Ffestiniog, Gwynedd, Wales, 20 April, 1932						WH
Northampton T	Blaenau Ffestiniog	08/55				
Wrexham	Tr	07/56	56-57	28	-	2
Southport	Tr	07/58	58	14	-	0
MORIAS Junior Augustus						
Born: Kingston, Jamaica, 3 July, 1995						F
Wycombe W	Sch	07/12	12-13	0	28	0
MORIENTES Fernando						
Born: Caceres, Spain, 5 April, 1976						F
Spain: 47						
Liverpool	Real Madrid (SPN)	01/05	04-05	32	9	8
MORINI Emanuele						
Born: Rome, Italy, 31 January, 1982						F
Bolton W	AS Roma (ITA)	09/00	00	1	1	0
MORISON Steven William (Steve)						
Born: Enfield, N London, England, 29 August, 1983						F
England: Semi Pro-8//Wales: 20						
Northampton T	Sch	07/03	01-04	7	16	3
Millwall	Stevenage Bor	05/09	09-10	82	1	35
Norwich C	Tr	06/11	11-12	26	27	10
Leeds U	Tr	01/13	12-14	30	11	5
Millwall	L	07/13	13	25	16	8
MORITZ Andre Francisco						
Born: Florianopolis, Brazil, 6 August, 1986						M
Crystal Palace	Mersin I'yurdu (TKY)	08/12	12	12	15	5
Bolton W	Tr	08/13	13	7	16	7
MORLEY Benjamin (Ben)						
Born: Hull, England, 20 December, 1980						RB
Hull C	YT	12/98	97-01	7	19	0
Boston U	Tr	08/02	02	1	1	0
MORLEY Brian James						
Born: Fleetwood, Lancashire, England, 4 October, 1960						LB
Blackburn Rov	App	10/78	78-79	20	0	0
Tranmere Rov	Tr	08/81	81	10	6	2
MORLEY David Thomas						
Born: St Helens, Merseyside, England, 25 September, 1977						CD
Manchester C	YT	01/96	97	1	2	1
Southend U	Tr	08/98	98-00	63	13	0
Carlisle U	Tr	01/01	00-01	37	4	1
Oxford U	Tr	12/01	01	16	2	3
Doncaster Rov	Tr	07/02	03-04	24	6	1
Macclesfield T	Tr	01/05	04-07	101	2	7
MORLEY Trevor William						
Born: Nottingham, England, 20 March, 1961						F
England: Semi Pro						
Northampton T	Nuneaton Bor	06/85	85-87	107	0	39
Manchester C	Tr	01/88	87-89	69	3	18
West Ham U	Tr	12/89	89-94	159	19	57
Reading	Tr	08/95	95-97	67	10	31
MORLEY William (Bill)						
Born: Nottingham, England, 30 July, 1925						RH
Died: Nottingham, England, 12 July, 1978						
Nottingham F	Mapperley Celtic	08/45	46-58	282	-	10

MORLEY William Anthony (Tony)
Born: Ormskirk, Lancashire, England, 26 August, 1954 — W
England: 6/B-2/U23-1/Youth

League Club	Source	Date Signed	Seasons Played	Apps	Subs	Gls
Preston NE	App	08/72	72-75	78	6	15
Burnley	Tr	02/76	75-78	78	13	5
Aston Villa	Tr	06/79	79-83	128	9	25
West Bromwich A	Tr	12/83	83-84	33	0	4
Birmingham C	L	11/84	84	4	0	3
West Bromwich A	ADO Den Haag (NED)	08/87	87	27	1	7
Burnley	L	10/88	88	5	0	0

MORNAR Ivica
Born: Split, Croatia, 12 January, 1974 — F
Croatia: 22/U21-5

League Club	Source	Date Signed	Seasons Played	Apps	Subs	Gls
Portsmouth	Anderlecht (BEL)	01/04	03-05	4	6	1

MORONEY Thomas (Tommy)
Born: Cork, Republic of Ireland, 10 November, 1923 — WH/CF
Died: Cork, Republic of Ireland, 2 May, 1981
Republic of Ireland: 12/LoI-7

League Club	Source	Date Signed	Seasons Played	Apps	Subs	Gls
West Ham U	Cork U (ROI)	08/47	47-52	148	-	8

MORRAD Frank
Born: Brentford, W London, England, 28 February, 1920 — FB/CF

League Club	Source	Date Signed	Seasons Played	Apps	Subs	Gls
Notts Co	Southall	08/44	46	1	-	0
Leyton Orient	Tr	11/46	46	25	-	11
Fulham	Tr	08/47				
Brighton & HA	Tr	02/48	47-50	43	-	3
Brentford	Tr	08/51	51-52	6	-	2

MORRALL Alfred Douglas (Alf)
Born: Birmingham, England, 1 July, 1916 — WH/F
Died: Sutton Coldfield, West Midlands, England, 30 January, 1998

League Club	Source	Date Signed	Seasons Played	Apps	Subs	Gls
Northampton T	Redditch T	10/44	46-47	34	-	11
Newport Co	Tr	07/48	48	28	-	0

MORRALL Stephen Asbury (Steve)
Born: Torquay, Devon, England, 25 September, 1952 — W

League Club	Source	Date Signed	Seasons Played	Apps	Subs	Gls
Torquay U	Jnr	08/72	72-76	133	32	12

MORRALL Terence Stephen (Terry)
Born: Smethwick, West Midlands, England, 24 November, 1938 — CH

League Club	Source	Date Signed	Seasons Played	Apps	Subs	Gls
Aston Villa	Jnr	11/55	59-60	8	-	0
Shrewsbury T	Tr	05/61	60-62	31	-	0
Wrexham	Tr	07/63	63-64	42	-	0
Southport	Tr	07/65	65	1	0	0

MORRELL Andrew Jonathan (Andy)
Born: Doncaster, South Yorkshire, England, 28 September, 1974 — F

League Club	Source	Date Signed	Seasons Played	Apps	Subs	Gls
Wrexham	Newcastle Blue Star	12/98	98-02	76	34	40
Coventry C	Tr	07/03	03-05	53	45	17
Blackpool	Tr	08/06	06-07	57	21	21
Bury	Tr	08/08	08-09	56	17	18

MORRELL Paul David
Born: Poole, Dorset, England, 23 March, 1961 — LB

League Club	Source	Date Signed	Seasons Played	Apps	Subs	Gls
Bournemouth	Weymouth	06/83	83-92	337	6	8

MORRELL Robert Ian (Bobby)
Born: Hesleden, County Durham, England, 4 June, 1944 — RH

League Club	Source	Date Signed	Seasons Played	Apps	Subs	Gls
Hartlepool U	Blackhall CW	03/64	63-64	34	-	0

MORREY Bernard Joseph
Born: Liverpool, England, 8 April, 1927 — W
Died: Huyton, Merseyside, England, 23 March, 2011

League Club	Source	Date Signed	Seasons Played	Apps	Subs	Gls
Tranmere Rov	Jnr	08/44				
Newport Co	Llandudno	10/52	52-53	22	-	2
Chester C	Tr	12/53	53-54	30	-	6

MORRIN Anthony John (Tony)
Born: Swinton, Greater Manchester, England, 31 July, 1946 — M

League Club	Source	Date Signed	Seasons Played	Apps	Subs	Gls
Bury	App	10/63	63-64	3	-	0
Burnley	Tr	07/65				
Doncaster Rov	Tr	08/66				
Stockport Co	Tr	10/66	66-68	26	5	2
Barrow	Tr	03/69	68-70	97	0	6
Exeter C	Tr	07/71	71-76	180	2	15
Stockport Co	Tr	03/77	76	13	0	1
Rochdale	Tr	08/77	77-78	29	1	0

MORRIS Aaron John
Born: Cardiff, Wales, 30 December, 1989 — CD/M
Wales: U21-8/Youth

League Club	Source	Date Signed	Seasons Played	Apps	Subs	Gls
Cardiff C	Sch	11/08	09	0	1	0
Aldershot T	Tr	08/10	10-12	78	20	2
AFC Wimbledon	Tr	01/14	13	15	2	0
Gillingham	Tr	05/14	14	20	3	0

MORRIS Alan
Born: Swansea, Wales, 6 April, 1941 — RW
Died: Swansea, Wales, 29 March, 2007

League Club	Source	Date Signed	Seasons Played	Apps	Subs	Gls
Swansea C	Jnr	06/58	57-62	12	-	1
Reading	Tr	08/63	63	12	-	0

MORRIS Alan Geoffrey
Born: Chester, England, 15 July, 1954 — FB
Died: Chester, England, 31 December, 1998

League Club	Source	Date Signed	Seasons Played	Apps	Subs	Gls
Chester C	Bangor C	06/84	84	0	1	0

MORRIS Alfred (Alf)
Born: Cadishead, Greater Manchester, England, 7 December, 1924 — WH
Died: Okehampton, Devon, England, 2 September, 2012

League Club	Source	Date Signed	Seasons Played	Apps	Subs	Gls
Accrington Stan	Rochdale (Am)	10/45	46-47	15	-	0

MORRIS Andrew Dean (Andy)
Born: Sheffield, England, 17 November, 1967 — F

League Club	Source	Date Signed	Seasons Played	Apps	Subs	Gls
Rotherham U	Jnr	07/85	84-86	0	7	0
Chesterfield	Tr	01/88	87-98	225	41	56
Exeter C	L	03/92	91	4	3	2
Rochdale	Tr	12/98	98-99	26	6	7

MORRIS Bryn Andrew
Born: Hartlepool, Cleveland, England, 25 April, 1996 — M
England: Youth

League Club	Source	Date Signed	Seasons Played	Apps	Subs	Gls
Middlesbrough	Sch	07/13	12-13	0	2	0
Burton A	L	11/14	14	3	2	0

MORRIS Carlton John
Born: Cambridge, England, 16 December, 1995 — F
England: Youth

League Club	Source	Date Signed	Seasons Played	Apps	Subs	Gls
Norwich C	Sch	12/13	14	0	1	0
Oxford U	L	08/14	14	5	2	0
York C	L	11/14	14	0	8	0

MORRIS Christopher Barry (Chris)
Born: Newquay, Cornwall, England, 24 December, 1963 — FB
England: Schools//Republic of Ireland: 35

League Club	Source	Date Signed	Seasons Played	Apps	Subs	Gls
Sheffield Wed	Jnr	10/82	83-86	61	13	1
Middlesbrough	Glasgow Celtic	08/92	92-96	75	7	3

MORRIS Christopher Joe (Chris)
Born: Spilsby, Lincolnshire, England, 12 October, 1939 — RW
Died: York, England, 12 February, 1997

League Club	Source	Date Signed	Seasons Played	Apps	Subs	Gls
Hull C	Jnr	10/57	58-60	17	-	4
York C	Tr	06/61				

MORRIS Colin
Born: Blyth, Northumberland, England, 22 August, 1953 — RW

League Club	Source	Date Signed	Seasons Played	Apps	Subs	Gls
Burnley	App	08/71	74-75	9	1	0
Southend U	Tr	01/77	76-79	133	0	25
Blackpool	Tr	12/79	79-81	87	0	26
Sheffield U	Tr	02/82	81-87	235	5	67
Scarborough	Tr	07/88	88-89	20	4	3

MORRIS David
Born: Swansea, Wales, 20 September, 1957 — F

League Club	Source	Date Signed	Seasons Played	Apps	Subs	Gls
Manchester U	App	10/74				
York C	L	03/77	76	1	6	0

MORRIS David Kenneth
Born: Plumstead, SE London, England, 19 November, 1971 — CD

League Club	Source	Date Signed	Seasons Played	Apps	Subs	Gls
Bournemouth	YT	07/90	90	0	1	0
Hereford U	Tr	02/93	92-93	33	7	1

MORRIS Douglas (Doug)
Born: Durham, England, 29 July, 1925 — RW

League Club	Source	Date Signed	Seasons Played	Apps	Subs	Gls
Hartlepool U	Ushaw Moor	01/46	46-50	19	-	3

MORRIS Edward Eric (Eric)
Born: Mold, Flintshire, Wales, 15 April, 1940 — FB
Died: Wrexham, Wales, October, 2011

League Club	Source	Date Signed	Seasons Played	Apps	Subs	Gls
Chester C		06/60	60	1	-	0

MORRIS Edwin Keith (Ted)
Born: Pontypool, Torfaen, Wales, 6 May, 1921 — G
Died: Cardiff, Wales, March, 2000

League Club	Source	Date Signed	Seasons Played	Apps	Subs	Gls
Cardiff C	Barry T	05/48	48-50	8	-	0

MORRIS Elfed
Born: Colwyn Bay, Conwy, Wales, 9 June, 1942 — LW
Died: Colwyn Bay, Conwy, Wales, 4 November, 2013

League Club	Source	Date Signed	Seasons Played	Apps	Subs	Gls
Wrexham	Colwyn Bay	05/60	60-61	9	-	6
Chester C	Tr	06/62	62-67	164	3	69
Halifax T	Tr	03/68	67-68	9	0	2

MORRIS Ernest
Born: Stocksbridge, South Yorkshire, England, 11 May, 1921 — CF
Died: Barnsley, South Yorkshire, England, March, 2008

League Club	Source	Date Signed	Seasons Played	Apps	Subs	Gls
Nottingham F		08/47	47	4	-	1
York C	Tr	06/48				
Halifax T	Grantham	11/50	50	1	-	0

MORRIS Frank
Born: Penge, S London, England, 28 March, 1932 LW
Died: Bromley, SE London, England, November, 2002

League Club	Source	Date Signed	Seasons Played	Apps	Subs	Gls
Crystal Palace	Beckenham	03/56	56	8	-	0

MORRIS Frederick Alfred (Freddie)
Born: Sheffield, England, 11 March, 1920 IF
Died: Sheffield, England, 1973

League Club	Source	Date Signed	Seasons Played	Apps	Subs	Gls
Barnsley		09/46	46-48	23	-	9
Southend U	Tr	01/49	48-49	34	-	16

MORRIS Frederick William (Fred)
Born: Shropshire, England, 15 June, 1929 RW
Died: Shrewsbury, Shropshire, England, 20 November, 1997

League Club	Source	Date Signed	Seasons Played	Apps	Subs	Gls
Walsall	Oswestry T	05/50	50-56	213	-	44
Mansfield T	Tr	03/57	56-57	56	-	17
Liverpool	Tr	05/58	58-59	47	-	14
Crewe Alex	Tr	06/60	60	8	-	1
Gillingham	Tr	01/61	60	11	-	1
Chester C	Tr	07/61	61	29	-	3

MORRIS Geoffrey (Geoff)
Born: Birmingham, England, 8 February, 1949 LW
Died: Shrewsbury, Shropshire, England, 16 February, 2015

League Club	Source	Date Signed	Seasons Played	Apps	Subs	Gls
Walsall	App	02/66	65-72	172	5	35
Shrewsbury T	Tr	01/73	72-74	71	4	9
Port Vale	Tr	08/75	75	10	5	1

MORRIS George Edward
Born: Crewe, Cheshire, England, 22 November, 1929 FB

League Club	Source	Date Signed	Seasons Played	Apps	Subs	Gls
Crewe Alex	Crewe Cadets	08/48	48-53	28	-	0

MORRIS Glenn James
Born: Woolwich, SE London, England, 20 December, 1983 G

League Club	Source	Date Signed	Seasons Played	Apps	Subs	Gls
Leyton Orient	Sch	03/03	01-09	121	3	0
Southend U	Tr	08/10	10-11	57	0	0
Aldershot T	Tr	08/12	12	1	1	0
Gillingham	Tr	05/14	14	9	1	0

MORRIS Gordon John
Born: Wolverhampton, England, 27 June, 1926 IF
Died: Codsall, Staffordshire, England, September, 2011

League Club	Source	Date Signed	Seasons Played	Apps	Subs	Gls
West Bromwich A	East Park	11/44				
Walsall	Tr	07/49	49	6	-	2

MORRIS Ian
Born: Dublin, Republic of Ireland, 27 February, 1987 LW
Republic of Ireland: U21-4/Youth

League Club	Source	Date Signed	Seasons Played	Apps	Subs	Gls
Leeds U	Sch	03/05				
Blackpool	L	09/05	05	21	9	3
Scunthorpe U	Tr	08/06	06-10	44	32	7
Carlisle U	L	03/09	08	4	2	0
Chesterfield	L	11/09	09	7	0	0
Chesterfield	L	07/10	10	13	6	1
Torquay U	Tr	07/11	11-12	42	6	3
Northampton T	Tr	06/13	13-14	23	12	3

MORRIS Ian Gwynfor
Born: Manchester, England, 10 June, 1948 W

League Club	Source	Date Signed	Seasons Played	Apps	Subs	Gls
Stockport Co	Bolton W (Am)	03/68	67	1	1	0

MORRIS James Henry
Born: St Helens, Merseyside, England, 15 November, 1915 CH
Died: St Helens, Merseyside, England, 1989

League Club	Source	Date Signed	Seasons Played	Apps	Subs	Gls
Stockport Co	St Helens T	08/39	46-48	61	-	3

MORRIS Jody Steven
Born: Hammersmith, W London, England, 22 December, 1978 M
England: U21-7/Youth/Schools

League Club	Source	Date Signed	Seasons Played	Apps	Subs	Gls
Chelsea	YT	01/96	95-02	82	42	5
Leeds U	Tr	07/03	03	11	1	0
Rotherham U	Tr	03/04	03	9	1	1
Millwall	Tr	07/04	04-06	60	5	5
Bristol C	St Johnstone	06/12	12	2	2	0

MORRIS John (Johnny)
Born: Radcliffe, Greater Manchester, England, 27 September, 1923 IF
Died: Bury, Greater Manchester, England, 6 April, 2011
England: 3/B-2/FLge-5

League Club	Source	Date Signed	Seasons Played	Apps	Subs	Gls
Manchester U	Jnr	03/41	46-48	83	-	32
Derby Co	Tr	03/49	48-52	130	-	44
Leicester C	Tr	10/52	52-57	206	-	33

MORRIS John Edward (Ed)
Born: Crewe, Cheshire, England, 27 November, 1937 RH

League Club	Source	Date Signed	Seasons Played	Apps	Subs	Gls
Crewe Alex	Jnr	12/54	54	2	-	0

MORRIS Joseph Richard (Joe)
Born: Canning Town, E London, England, 13 April, 1934 IF

League Club	Source	Date Signed	Seasons Played	Apps	Subs	Gls
Crewe Alex		08/54	54	3	-	0

MORRIS Joshua Francis (Josh)
Born: Preston, Lancashire, England, 30 September, 1991 LW
England: Youth

League Club	Source	Date Signed	Seasons Played	Apps	Subs	Gls
Blackburn Rov	Sch	09/10	10-13	7	13	0
Yeovil T	L	03/12	11	3	2	0
Rotherham U	L	10/12	12	5	0	0
Carlisle U	L	11/13	13	1	5	0
Fleetwood T	L	02/14	13	11	3	2
Fleetwood T	L	07/14	14	43	2	8

MORRIS Kevin George
Born: Much Wenlock, Shropshire, England, 22 September, 1953 RB

League Club	Source	Date Signed	Seasons Played	Apps	Subs	Gls
Shrewsbury T	App	07/71	70-71	9	0	0

MORRIS Kieron
Born: Leominster, Herefordshire, England, 3 June, 1994 LW

League Club	Source	Date Signed	Seasons Played	Apps	Subs	Gls
Walsall	Sch	07/12	13-14	10	6	2

MORRIS Lee
Born: Blackpool, Lancashire, England, 30 April, 1980 LW
England: U21-1/Youth

League Club	Source	Date Signed	Seasons Played	Apps	Subs	Gls
Sheffield U	YT	12/97	97-99	14	12	6
Derby Co	Tr	10/99	99-03	62	29	17
Huddersfield T	L	03/01	00	5	0	1
Leicester C	Tr	02/04	04	2	8	0
Yeovil T	Tr	08/06	06-07	23	11	5
Hereford U	Burton A	08/09	09	5	7	0

MORRIS Maldwyn Jones Gravell
Born: Swansea, Wales, 3 August, 1932 CF
Died: Pembroke Dock, Pembrokeshire, Wales, August, 2000

League Club	Source	Date Signed	Seasons Played	Apps	Subs	Gls
Swansea C	Pembroke Bor	10/56	56-57	14	-	5

MORRIS Mark
Born: Chester, England, 1 August, 1968 G

League Club	Source	Date Signed	Seasons Played	Apps	Subs	Gls
Wrexham	YT	08/87	85-93	101	0	0

MORRIS Mark John
Born: Morden, S London, England, 26 September, 1962 CD

League Club	Source	Date Signed	Seasons Played	Apps	Subs	Gls
Wimbledon	App	09/80	81-86	167	1	9
Aldershot	L	09/85	85	14	0	0
Watford	Tr	07/87	87-88	41	0	1
Sheffield U	Tr	07/89	89-90	53	3	3
Bournemouth	Tr	07/91	91-96	190	4	8
Gillingham	L	09/96	96	6	0	0
Brighton & HA	Tr	10/96	96-97	30	1	2

MORRIS Michael John (Mike)
Born: Plaistow, E London, England, 20 January, 1943 RW

League Club	Source	Date Signed	Seasons Played	Apps	Subs	Gls
Oxford U	Faversham T	07/64	64-66	89	1	15
Port Vale	Tr	08/67	67-71	176	8	24

MORRIS Neil Anthony
Born: Sheffield, England, 3 May, 1970 F

League Club	Source	Date Signed	Seasons Played	Apps	Subs	Gls
York C	Doncaster Rov (YT)	09/88	88	3	1	0
Doncaster Rov	Worksop T	02/92	91	0	1	0

MORRIS Paul Ian
Born: Bolton, Greater Manchester, England, 6 February, 1975 CD

League Club	Source	Date Signed	Seasons Played	Apps	Subs	Gls
Bury	YT	-	92	0	1	0

MORRIS Paul Whittington
Born: Llanelli, Carmarthenshire, Wales, 8 January, 1957 F

League Club	Source	Date Signed	Seasons Played	Apps	Subs	Gls
Hereford U	Llanelli	02/80	79-80	2	2	1

MORRIS Peter Andrew
Born: Farnworth, Greater Manchester, England, 23 November, 1958 W

League Club	Source	Date Signed	Seasons Played	Apps	Subs	Gls
Preston NE	App	10/76				
Blackburn Rov	Tr	07/78	78	2	2	0

MORRIS Peter John
Born: New Houghton, Derbyshire, England, 8 November, 1943 M

League Club	Source	Date Signed	Seasons Played	Apps	Subs	Gls
Mansfield T	Jnr	11/60	60-67	286	1	50
Ipswich T	Tr	03/68	67-73	213	7	13
Norwich C	Tr	06/74	74-75	66	0	1
Mansfield T	Tr	07/76	76-77	41	0	3
Peterborough U	Newcastle U (Coach)	08/79	79	1	0	0

MORRIS Ronald (Ronnie)
Born: Birmingham, England, 25 September, 1970 W
England: Schools

League Club	Source	Date Signed	Seasons Played	Apps	Subs	Gls
Birmingham C	YT	09/88	87-88	3	8	0

MORRIS Samuel (Sam)
Born: Warrington, Cheshire, England, 12 February, 1930 RH/CH
Died: 20 December, 2014

League Club	Source	Date Signed	Seasons Played	Apps	Subs	Gls
Chester C	Stockton Heath	12/51	51-56	90	-	0

MORRIS Stephen (Steve)
Born: Liverpool, England, 13 May, 1976 F

League Club	Source	Date Signed	Seasons Played	Apps	Subs	Gls
Wrexham	Liverpool (YT)	09/94	94-96	24	18	9

MORRIS Stephen Albert (Steve)
Born: Bristol, England, 6 July, 1949 — D/M

League Club	Source	Date Signed	Seasons Played	Apps	Subs	Gls
Bristol C	App	06/67				
Exeter C	Tr	06/69	69-71	61	11	2

MORRIS Steven Granville (Steve)
Born: Swansea, Wales, 8 October, 1958 — LB

League Club	Source	Date Signed	Seasons Played	Apps	Subs	Gls
Swansea C	App	06/76	75-78	33	6	1
Plymouth Arg	Tr	01/80				

MORRIS William (Billy)
Born: Radcliffe, Greater Manchester, England, 1 April, 1931 — RW

League Club	Source	Date Signed	Seasons Played	Apps	Subs	Gls
Bury	Jnr	05/48				
Derby Co	Tr	10/51				
Rochdale	Tr	11/52	52	4	-	1

MORRIS William (Billy)
Born: Llanddulas, Conwy, Wales, 30 July, 1918 — IF
Died: Bodelwyddan, Denbighshire, Wales, 31 December, 2002
Wales: 5/War-1

League Club	Source	Date Signed	Seasons Played	Apps	Subs	Gls
Burnley	Llandudno T	01/39	38-52	211	-	47

MORRIS William Henry (Billy)
Born: Swansea, Wales, 28 September, 1920 — LW
Died: Swansea, Wales, March, 1994

League Club	Source	Date Signed	Seasons Played	Apps	Subs	Gls
Swansea C		05/46	47-48	16	-	1
Brighton & HA	Tr	09/49	49-50	28	-	4

MORRIS William Walker (Billy)
Born: Birmingham, England, 26 March, 1913 — RB
Died: Dudley, West Midlands, England, January, 1995
England: 3

League Club	Source	Date Signed	Seasons Played	Apps	Subs	Gls
Wolverhampton W	Halesowen T	05/33	33-46	175	-	2

MORRISON Andrew Charles (Andy)
Born: Inverness, Scotland, 30 July, 1970 — CD/M

League Club	Source	Date Signed	Seasons Played	Apps	Subs	Gls
Plymouth Arg	YT	07/88	87-92	105	8	6
Blackburn Rov	Tr	08/93	93	1	4	0
Blackpool	Tr	12/94	94-95	47	0	3
Huddersfield T	Tr	07/96	96-98	43	2	2
Manchester C	Tr	10/98	98-00	36	1	4
Blackpool	L	09/00	00	6	0	1
Crystal Palace	L	10/00	00	5	0	0
Sheffield U	L	03/01	00	3	1	0

MORRISON Angus Cameron
Born: Dingwall, Highlands, Scotland, 26 April, 1924 — LW
Died: Derby, England, 18 December, 2002
Scotland: B-1

League Club	Source	Date Signed	Seasons Played	Apps	Subs	Gls
Derby Co	Ross Co	10/44	46-47	52	-	21
Preston NE	Tr	11/48	48-56	261	-	69
Millwall	Tr	10/57	57	15	-	4

MORRISON Charles
Born: Newton Aycliffe, County Durham, England, 12 January, 1953 — CD

League Club	Source	Date Signed	Seasons Played	Apps	Subs	Gls
Chelsea	App	08/70				
Doncaster Rov	Tr	07/72	72	5	1	0

MORRISON Clinton Hubert
Born: Tooting, SW London, England, 14 May, 1979 — F
Republic of Ireland: 36/U21-2

League Club	Source	Date Signed	Seasons Played	Apps	Subs	Gls
Crystal Palace	YT	03/97	97-01	141	16	62
Birmingham C	Tr	08/02	02-05	56	31	14
Crystal Palace	Tr	08/05	05-07	96	28	41
Coventry C	Tr	08/08	08-09	78	13	21
Sheffield Wed	Tr	07/10	10-11	29	25	7
MK Dons	L	09/11	11	5	1	3
Brentford	L	03/12	11	4	4	0
Colchester U	Tr	07/12	12-13	34	31	4
Exeter C	Long Eaton U	11/14	14	13	12	0

MORRISON David Ellis (Dave)
Born: Walthamstow, NE London, England, 30 November, 1974 — W

League Club	Source	Date Signed	Seasons Played	Apps	Subs	Gls
Peterborough U	Chelmsford C	05/94	94-96	59	18	12
Leyton Orient	Tr	03/97	96-99	21	25	3

MORRISON George Charles
Born: Ayr, Scotland, 27 November, 1924 — CH
Died: Darlington, County Durham, England, 9 October, 2005

League Club	Source	Date Signed	Seasons Played	Apps	Subs	Gls
Hartlepool U	St Johnstone	08/51	51	2	-	0

MORRISON James Clark
Born: Darlington, County Durham, England, 25 May, 1986 — M
England: Youth//Scotland: 39

League Club	Source	Date Signed	Seasons Played	Apps	Subs	Gls
Middlesbrough	Sch	07/03	03-06	40	27	3
West Bromwich A	Tr	08/07	07-14	193	44	25

MORRISON John
Born: Greenock, Inverclyde, Scotland, 4 August, 1929 — IF
Died: Greenock, Inverclyde, Scotland, 25 May, 2012

League Club	Source	Date Signed	Seasons Played	Apps	Subs	Gls
Torquay U	Greenock Morton	07/51	51	2	-	0

MORRISON John
Born: Kettering, Northamptonshire, England, 27 July, 1970 — M/RB

League Club	Source	Date Signed	Seasons Played	Apps	Subs	Gls
Torquay U	YT	07/88	88-89	24	8	0

MORRISON John Owen (Owen)
Born: Derry, Northern Ireland, 8 December, 1981 — W
Northern Ireland: U21-7/Youth/Schools

League Club	Source	Date Signed	Seasons Played	Apps	Subs	Gls
Sheffield Wed	YT	01/99	98-02	31	25	8
Hull C	L	08/02	02	1	1	0
Sheffield U	Tr	02/03	02	3	5	0
Stockport Co	Tr	08/03	03-04	11	12	1
Bradford C	Tr	12/04	04-05	24	8	2

MORRISON Michael Brian
Born: Bury St Edmunds, Suffolk, England, 3 March, 1988 — CD
England: Semi Pro-8

League Club	Source	Date Signed	Seasons Played	Apps	Subs	Gls
Leicester C	Cambridge U	07/08	08-10	72	5	5
Sheffield Wed	Tr	01/11	10	12	0	0
Charlton Ath	Tr	07/11	11-14	135	1	6
Birmingham C	Tr	10/14	14	21	0	0

MORRISON Murdoch (Murdo)
Born: Glasgow, Scotland, 9 October, 1924 — G
Died: Hillingdon, W London, England, 28 January, 1975

League Club	Source	Date Signed	Seasons Played	Apps	Subs	Gls
Luton T	Bellhaven Star	09/45	46	1	-	0
Leyton Orient	Tr	08/47	47	10	-	0

MORRISON Peter Anthony
Born: Manchester, England, 29 June, 1980 — LW

League Club	Source	Date Signed	Seasons Played	Apps	Subs	Gls
Bolton W	YT	07/98				
Scunthorpe U	Tr	05/00	00	8	10	0

MORRISON Ravel Ryan
Born: Wythenshawe, Greater Manchester, England, 2 February, 1993 — M/F
England: U21-4/Youth

League Club	Source	Date Signed	Seasons Played	Apps	Subs	Gls
Manchester U	Sch	02/10				
West Ham U	Tr	01/12	11-14	12	6	3
Birmingham C	L	08/12	12	23	4	3
Queens Park Rgrs	L	02/14	13	14	1	6
Cardiff C	L	09/14	14	1	6	0

MORRISON Robert Crosson
Born: Chapelhall, Lanarkshire, Scotland, 16 February, 1933 — IF
Died: Airdrie, Lanarkshire, Scotland, 6 October, 1999
Northern Ireland: NILge-1

League Club	Source	Date Signed	Seasons Played	Apps	Subs	Gls
Nottingham F	Glasgow Rangers	07/58	58	1	-	0
Workington	Tr	07/59	59-60	53	-	20

MORRISON Sean Joseph
Born: Plymouth, England, 8 January, 1991 — CD

League Club	Source	Date Signed	Seasons Played	Apps	Subs	Gls
Swindon T	Sch	02/08	07-10	46	4	6
Southend U	L	11/09	09	8	0	0
Reading	Tr	01/11	12-14	37	1	4
Huddersfield T	L	01/12	11	19	0	1
Cardiff C	Tr	08/14	14	41	0	6

MORRISON Thomas (Tommy)
Born: Croydon, S London, England, 6 March, 1943 — IF

League Club	Source	Date Signed	Seasons Played	Apps	Subs	Gls
Port Vale	Aberdeen	08/65	65	5	0	1

MORRISON William (Willie)
Born: Edinburgh, Scotland, 31 March, 1934 — RH
Died: Sharnbrook, Bedfordshire, England, 26 December, 2001

League Club	Source	Date Signed	Seasons Played	Apps	Subs	Gls
Sunderland	Merchiston Thistle	05/51	54-56	19	-	0
Southend U	Tr	01/58	57-59	60	-	4

MORRISON William (Willie)
Born: Croydon, S London, England, 10 October, 1939 — RB
Died: Glenboig, Lanarkshire, Scotland, 16 April, 2010

League Club	Source	Date Signed	Seasons Played	Apps	Subs	Gls
Portsmouth	Croy Guilds	05/58	58	3	-	0

MORRISON-HILL Jamie Steven (Steven)
Born: Plymouth, England, 8 June, 1981 — M

League Club	Source	Date Signed	Seasons Played	Apps	Subs	Gls
Plymouth Arg	YT	07/99	99	0	1	0

MORRISSEY Gearoid
Born: Cork, Republic of Ireland, 17 November, 1991 — M
Republic of Ireland: Youth

League Club	Source	Date Signed	Seasons Played	Apps	Subs	Gls
Blackburn Rov	Sch	11/08				
Cambridge U	Cork C (ROI)	12/14	14	3	5	0

MORRISSEY John Joseph (Johnny)
Born: Liverpool, England, 18 April, 1940 — LW
England: FLge-1/Schools

League Club	Source	Date Signed	Seasons Played	Apps	Subs	Gls
Liverpool	Jnr	05/57	57-60	36	-	6
Everton	Tr	09/62	62-71	257	2	43
Oldham Ath	Tr	05/72	72	6	0	1

MORRISSEY John Joseph
Born: Liverpool, England, 8 March, 1965 RW
England: Youth

League Club	Source	Date Signed	Seasons Played	Apps	Subs	Gls
Everton	App	03/83	84	1	0	0
Wolverhampton W	Tr	08/85	85	5	5	1
Tranmere Rov	Tr	10/85	85-98	396	74	50

MORRISSEY Patrick Joseph (Pat)
Born: Enniscorthy, Wexford, Republic of Ireland, 23 February, 1948 F
Died: Hammersmith, W London, England, 19 February, 2005
Republic of Ireland: U23-1

League Club	Source	Date Signed	Seasons Played	Apps	Subs	Gls
Coventry C	App	07/65	66-67	6	4	0
Torquay U	Tr	07/68	68	19	2	0
Crewe Alex	Tr	07/69	69-71	95	1	28
Chester C	Tr	10/71	71	9	0	1
Watford	Tr	12/71	71-74	101	6	27
Aldershot	Tr	11/74	74-76	109	0	27
Swansea C	L	10/77	77	3	1	0

MORRITT Gordon Raymond
Born: Rotherham, South Yorkshire, England, 8 February, 1942 G

League Club	Source	Date Signed	Seasons Played	Apps	Subs	Gls
Rotherham U	Steel Peach & Tozer	06/61	61-65	77	0	0
Doncaster Rov	Durban C (RSA)	09/67	67-68	40	0	0
Northampton T	Tr	08/68	68-69	42	0	0
York C	Tr	10/69	69-71	41	0	0
Rochdale	Tr	08/72	72	31	0	0
Darlington	Tr	08/73	73	34	0	0

MORROW Andrew Gareth (Andy)
Born: Bangor, Down, Northern Ireland, 5 October, 1980 LW
Northern Ireland: U21-1/Youth/Schools

League Club	Source	Date Signed	Seasons Played	Apps	Subs	Gls
Northampton T	YT	12/98	99-00	2	6	0

MORROW Grant Ralph
Born: Glasgow, Scotland, 4 October, 1970 F

League Club	Source	Date Signed	Seasons Played	Apps	Subs	Gls
Doncaster Rov	Rowntree-Mack'sh	07/89	89-92	46	18	7
Colchester U	Tr	08/93	93	0	1	0

MORROW Hugh (Hughie)
Born: Larne, Antrim, Northern Ireland, 9 July, 1930 RW

League Club	Source	Date Signed	Seasons Played	Apps	Subs	Gls
West Bromwich A	Nuneaton Bor	08/47	48	5	-	2
Northampton T	Lockheed Leamington	06/56	56	30	-	3

MORROW John James
Born: Belfast, Northern Ireland, 20 November, 1971 W
Northern Ireland: B/Youth

League Club	Source	Date Signed	Seasons Played	Apps	Subs	Gls
Oldham Ath	Glasgow Rangers	08/96	96	1	1	0

MORROW Samuel (Sam)
Born: Derry, Northern Ireland, 3 March, 1985 F
Northern Ireland: U21-4/Youth

League Club	Source	Date Signed	Seasons Played	Apps	Subs	Gls
Ipswich T	Sch	08/02				
Boston U	L	12/03	03	0	2	0
Tranmere Rov	Coleraine	08/10	10	2	3	0

MORROW Stephen Joseph (Steve)
Born: Bangor, Down, Northern Ireland, 2 July, 1970 D/M
Northern Ireland: 39/B-1/U23-2/Youth/Schools

League Club	Source	Date Signed	Seasons Played	Apps	Subs	Gls
Arsenal	YT	05/88	91-96	39	23	1
Reading	L	01/91	90	10	0	0
Watford	L	08/91	91	7	1	0
Reading	L	10/91	91	3	0	0
Barnet	L	03/92	91	1	0	0
Queens Park Rgrs	Tr	03/97	96-00	84	7	2
Peterborough U	L	03/01	00	11	0	0

MORSE Richard Anthony
Born: Newport, Wales, 17 December, 1966 CD

League Club	Source	Date Signed	Seasons Played	Apps	Subs	Gls
Newport Co	Jnr	08/83	83	0	1	0

MORSY Samy Syed (Sam)
Born: Wolverhampton, England, 10 September, 1991 DM

League Club	Source	Date Signed	Seasons Played	Apps	Subs	Gls
Port Vale	Sch	07/10	09-12	44	27	4
Chesterfield	Tr	07/13	13-14	73	0	3

MORTENSEN Henrik Ejehod
Born: Odder, Denmark, 12 February, 1968 F
Denmark: U21-1/Youth

League Club	Source	Date Signed	Seasons Played	Apps	Subs	Gls
Norwich C	Aarhus GF (DEN)	10/89	89-90	12	6	0

MORTENSEN Stanley Harding (Stan)
Born: South Shields, Tyne and Wear, England, 26 May, 1921 CF
Died: Blackpool, Lancashire, England, 22 May, 1991
England: 25/FLge-5/War-3//Wales: War-1

League Club	Source	Date Signed	Seasons Played	Apps	Subs	Gls
Blackpool	South Shields	05/38	46-55	319	-	197
Hull C	Tr	11/55	55-56	42	-	18
Southport	Tr	02/57	56-57	36	-	10

MORTIMER Alexander Barry (Alex)
Born: Manchester, England, 28 November, 1982 LB

League Club	Source	Date Signed	Seasons Played	Apps	Subs	Gls
Leicester C	YT	01/00				
Shrewsbury T	Tr	10/02	02	0	1	0

MORTIMER Dennis George
Born: Liverpool, England, 5 April, 1952 M
England: B-3/U23-6/Youth

League Club	Source	Date Signed	Seasons Played	Apps	Subs	Gls
Coventry C	App	09/69	69-75	179	14	10
Aston Villa	Tr	12/75	75-84	316	1	31
Sheffield U	L	12/84	84	7	0	0
Brighton & HA	Tr	08/85	85	40	0	2
Birmingham C	Tr	08/86	86	33	0	4

MORTIMER John McCormick (Johnny)
Born: Birkenhead, Wirral, England, 5 December, 1923 FB
Died: Wrexham, Wales, July, 2013

League Club	Source	Date Signed	Seasons Played	Apps	Subs	Gls
Wrexham	Chester C (Am)	01/47	46-48	23	-	0
New Brighton	Park Villa	10/49	49-50	5	-	0

MORTIMER Paul Henry
Born: Kensington, Central London, England, 8 May, 1968 M
England: U21-2

League Club	Source	Date Signed	Seasons Played	Apps	Subs	Gls
Charlton Ath	Farnborough T	09/87	87-90	108	5	17
Aston Villa	Tr	07/91	91	10	2	1
Crystal Palace	Tr	10/91	91-92	18	4	2
Brentford	L	01/93	92	6	0	0
Charlton Ath	Tr	07/94	94-98	67	19	15
Bristol C	Tr	08/99	99	22	1	0

MORTIMORE Charles Thomas Reginald (Charlie)
Born: Gosport, Hampshire, England, 12 April, 1928 CF
England: Amateur-17

League Club	Source	Date Signed	Seasons Played	Apps	Subs	Gls
Aldershot (Am)	RAF	08/49	49-52	66	-	28
Portsmouth (Am)	Woking	10/53	53	1	-	0
Aldershot (Am)	Woking	12/55	55	2	-	0

MORTIMORE John Henry
Born: Farnborough, Hampshire, England, 23 September, 1934 CH
England: Amateur-4/Youth

League Club	Source	Date Signed	Seasons Played	Apps	Subs	Gls
Chelsea	Woking	04/56	55-64	249	-	8
Queens Park Rgrs	Tr	09/65	65	10	0	0

MORTON Alan
Born: Peterborough, England, 6 March, 1942 IF

League Club	Source	Date Signed	Seasons Played	Apps	Subs	Gls
Arsenal	Peterborough U	04/59				
Peterborough U	Tr	10/61	61-62	7	-	2
Lincoln C	Wisbech T	07/63	63-64	58	-	20
Chesterfield	Tr	07/65	65	28	1	6

MORTON Alan
Born: Erith, SE London, England, 13 April, 1950 F

League Club	Source	Date Signed	Seasons Played	Apps	Subs	Gls
Crystal Palace	Woking	11/67				
Stockport Co	L	08/69	69	12	2	2
Fulham	Nuneaton Bor	08/70	70	1	0	1

MORTON Albert
Born: Newcastle-upon-Tyne, England, 27 July, 1919 G
Died: Sheffield, England, July, 1991

League Club	Source	Date Signed	Seasons Played	Apps	Subs	Gls
Sheffield Wed	St Peter's A	03/38	47-50	41	-	0
Rochdale	Tr	07/53	53-56	89	-	0

MORTON Geoffrey Dalgleish (Geoff)
Born: Acton, W London, England, 27 July, 1924 G
Died: Malvern, Worcestershire, England, 28 January, 2000

League Club	Source	Date Signed	Seasons Played	Apps	Subs	Gls
Watford	Chelmsford C	10/48	48-51	107	-	0
Southend U	Tr	02/52	51-52	25	-	0
Exeter C	Tr	09/54	54	6	-	0

MORTON George Edmund
Born: Liverpool, England, 30 September, 1943 IF
Died: Liverpool, England, 15 January, 2009

League Club	Source	Date Signed	Seasons Played	Apps	Subs	Gls
Everton	Jnr	10/60				
Rochdale	Tr	07/62	62-65	146	1	51

MORTON Gerald William (Gerry)
Born: Newcastle-upon-Tyne, England, 17 March, 1944 CH

League Club	Source	Date Signed	Seasons Played	Apps	Subs	Gls
Newcastle U	North Shields	08/62				
Workington	Tr	04/63	62-63	3	-	0

MORTON Keith
Born: Consett, County Durham, England, 11 August, 1934 W/CF

League Club	Source	Date Signed	Seasons Played	Apps	Subs	Gls
Crystal Palace (Am)	Army	08/53	53	5	-	3
Sunderland	Tr	07/54				
Darlington	Tr	05/55	55-60	171	-	49

MORTON Kenneth (Ken)
Born: Chorley, Lancashire, England, 19 May, 1947 LW
England: Schools

League Club	Source	Date Signed	Seasons Played	Apps	Subs	Gls
Manchester U	App	05/64				
York C	Tr	05/65	65	9	1	2
Blackpool	Tr	08/66				
Darlington	Fleetwood	07/68	68	4	1	0

League Club	Source	Date Signed	Seasons Played	Apps	Subs	Gls

MORTON Neil
Born: Congleton, Cheshire, England, 21 December, 1968 — F

League Club	Source	Date Signed	Seasons Played	Apps	Subs	Gls
Crewe Alex	YT	09/87	86-88	18	13	1
Chester C	Northwich Victoria	10/90	90-92	63	32	13
Wigan Ath	Tr	07/93	93-94	41	7	5

MORTON Norman
Born: Barnsley, South Yorkshire, England, 22 May, 1925 — CF
Died: Barnsley, South Yorkshire, England, 15 January, 1977

League Club	Source	Date Signed	Seasons Played	Apps	Subs	Gls
Leeds U	Woolley Colliery	12/47	47	1	-	0

MORTON Robert Hendy (Bob)
Born: Aston Clinton, Buckinghamshire, England, 25 September, 1927 — RH/CF
Died: Eaton Bray, Bedfordshire, England, 6 May, 2002
England: B-1

League Club	Source	Date Signed	Seasons Played	Apps	Subs	Gls
Luton T	Waterlows	02/46	48-63	495	-	48

MORTON Roy Steven
Born: Birmingham, England, 29 October, 1955 — M
England: Youth/Schools

League Club	Source	Date Signed	Seasons Played	Apps	Subs	Gls
Manchester U	App	11/72				
Birmingham C	Tr	09/73	74	3	0	0

MORTON William (Mick)
Born: Grangemouth, Falkirk, Scotland, 2 April, 1928 — CH
Died: North Surrey, England, March, 2007

League Club	Source	Date Signed	Seasons Played	Apps	Subs	Gls
Millwall		10/45	46-50	11	-	0

MOSBY Harold (Harry)
Born: Kippax, West Yorkshire, England, 25 June, 1926 — RW
Died: Rotherham, South Yorkshire, England, 15 June, 2007

League Club	Source	Date Signed	Seasons Played	Apps	Subs	Gls
Rotherham U	Huddersfield T (Am)	01/47	47-49	26	-	9
Scunthorpe U	Tr	07/50	50-54	149	-	21
Crewe Alex	Worksop T	08/56	56	38	-	4

MOSELEY Graham
Born: Manchester, England, 16 November, 1953 — G
England: Youth

League Club	Source	Date Signed	Seasons Played	Apps	Subs	Gls
Blackburn Rov	App	09/71				
Derby Co	Tr	09/71	72-76	32	0	0
Aston Villa	L	08/74	74	3	0	0
Walsall	L	10/77	77	3	0	0
Brighton & HA	Tr	11/77	77-85	189	0	0
Cardiff C	Tr	08/86	86-87	38	0	0

MOSES Adrian Paul (Adie)
Born: Doncaster, South Yorkshire, England, 4 May, 1975 — CD
England: U21-2

League Club	Source	Date Signed	Seasons Played	Apps	Subs	Gls
Barnsley	Jnr	07/93	94-00	137	14	3
Huddersfield T	Tr	12/00	00-02	63	6	1
Crewe Alex	Tr	07/03	03-05	46	11	0
Lincoln C	Tr	07/06	06-07	42	8	1

MOSES George
Born: High Spen, Tyne and Wear, England, 11 September, 1920 — IF
Died: Scarborough, North Yorkshire, England, 20 June, 1987

League Club	Source	Date Signed	Seasons Played	Apps	Subs	Gls
Newcastle U	Newburn	10/39				
Hartlepool U	Tr	08/46	46	19	-	4

MOSES Remi Mark
Born: Manchester, England, 14 November, 1960 — M
England: U21-8

League Club	Source	Date Signed	Seasons Played	Apps	Subs	Gls
West Bromwich A	App	11/78	79-81	63	0	5
Manchester U	Tr	09/81	81-87	143	7	7

MOSES Victor
Born: Kaduna, Nigeria, 12 December, 1990 — RW
England: U21-1/Youth//Nigeria: 24

League Club	Source	Date Signed	Seasons Played	Apps	Subs	Gls
Crystal Palace	Sch	12/07	07-09	42	16	11
Wigan Ath	Tr	02/10	09-12	47	27	8
Chelsea	Tr	08/12	12	12	11	1
Liverpool	L	09/13	13	6	13	1
Stoke C	L	08/14	14	19	0	3

MOSS Amos
Born: Birmingham, England, 28 August, 1921 — LH
Died: Aldridge, West Midlands, England, 8 April, 2004

League Club	Source	Date Signed	Seasons Played	Apps	Subs	Gls
Aston Villa	Jnr	05/39	46-55	102	-	5

MOSS Craig Anthony
Born: Birmingham, England, 11 March, 1961 — LW

League Club	Source	Date Signed	Seasons Played	Apps	Subs	Gls
Wolverhampton W	App	03/79	78-81	4	0	0

MOSS Darren Michael
Born: Wrexham, Wales, 24 May, 1981 — RB
Wales: U21-6/Youth

League Club	Source	Date Signed	Seasons Played	Apps	Subs	Gls
Chester C	YT	07/99	98-99	33	9	0
Shrewsbury T	Tr	07/01	01-04	84	13	10
Crewe Alex	Tr	03/05	04-06	54	5	2
Shrewsbury T	Tr	07/07	07-08	56	4	2
Morecambe	Tr	07/09	09-10	17	3	1

MOSS David Albert
Born: Doncaster, South Yorkshire, England, 15 November, 1968 — M

League Club	Source	Date Signed	Seasons Played	Apps	Subs	Gls
Doncaster Rov	Boston U	03/93	92-93	18	0	5
Chesterfield	Tr	10/93	93-95	59	12	16
Scunthorpe U	Tr	07/96	96	4	0	0
Swansea C	Falkirk	08/02	02	3	6	2

MOSS David John
Born: Witney, Oxfordshire, England, 18 March, 1952 — LW

League Club	Source	Date Signed	Seasons Played	Apps	Subs	Gls
Swindon T	Witney T	07/69	71-77	217	13	60
Luton T	Tr	05/78	78-84	218	3	88
Swindon T	Tr	07/85	85	4	0	0

MOSS Donald Richard (Don)
Born: Tamworth, Staffordshire, England, 27 June, 1925 — WH
Died: Cardiff, Wales, July, 1999

League Club	Source	Date Signed	Seasons Played	Apps	Subs	Gls
Cardiff C	Boldmere St Michael's	05/51				
Crystal Palace	Tr	05/53	53-56	56	-	2

MOSS Edward (Eddie)
Born: Skelmersdale, Lancashire, England, 27 October, 1939 — IF

League Club	Source	Date Signed	Seasons Played	Apps	Subs	Gls
Liverpool	Skelmersdale U	10/58				
Southport	Tr	07/59	59-60	51	-	15

MOSS Ernest (Ernie)
Born: Chesterfield, Derbyshire, England, 19 October, 1949 — F

League Club	Source	Date Signed	Seasons Played	Apps	Subs	Gls
Chesterfield	Chesterfield Tube W'ks	10/68	68-75	271	0	95
Peterborough U	Tr	01/76	75-76	34	1	9
Mansfield T	Tr	12/76	76-78	56	1	21
Chesterfield	Tr	01/79	78-80	105	2	33
Port Vale	Tr	06/81	81-82	74	0	23
Lincoln C	Tr	03/83	82	10	1	2
Doncaster Rov	Tr	06/83	83	41	3	15
Chesterfield	Tr	07/84	84-86	90	1	34
Stockport Co	Tr	12/86	86	26	0	7
Scarborough	Tr	08/87	87	22	1	4
Rochdale	L	03/88	87	10	0	2

MOSS Frank
Born: Aston, South Yorkshire, England, 16 September, 1917 — CH
Died: Looe, Cornwall, England, May, 1997

League Club	Source	Date Signed	Seasons Played	Apps	Subs	Gls
Sheffield Wed	Worcester C	11/35	36-37	22	-	0
Aston Villa	Tr	05/38	38-54	296	-	3

MOSS Jack (Jackie)
Born: Blackrod, Greater Manchester, England, 1 September, 1923 — IF
Died: Bolton, Greater Manchester, England, 1975

League Club	Source	Date Signed	Seasons Played	Apps	Subs	Gls
Bury	Horwich Central	12/43	46	7	-	2
Rochdale	Tr	01/47	46-48	58	-	17
Leeds U	Tr	01/49	48-50	23	-	2
Halifax T	Tr	01/51	50-53	124	-	11

MOSS Neil Graham
Born: New Milton, Hampshire, England, 10 May, 1975 — G

League Club	Source	Date Signed	Seasons Played	Apps	Subs	Gls
Bournemouth	YT	01/93	92-95	21	1	0
Southampton	Tr	12/95	96-01	22	2	0
Gillingham	L	08/97	97	10	0	0
Bournemouth	Tr	09/02	02-07	162	0	0

MOSS Paul Michael
Born: Birmingham, England, 2 August, 1957 — M

League Club	Source	Date Signed	Seasons Played	Apps	Subs	Gls
Wolverhampton W	Northfield Jnrs	07/76				
Hull C	Tr	09/79	79-80	53	1	7
Scunthorpe U	Tr	09/81	81	42	0	7

MOSS Robert (Bobby)
Born: Chigwell, Essex, England, 13 February, 1952 — F
Died: Romford, E London, England, 1 August, 2010

League Club	Source	Date Signed	Seasons Played	Apps	Subs	Gls
Leyton Orient	App	02/70	70	2	3	1
Colchester U	Tr	05/72	72	16	1	3

MOSS Robert Stephen (Bob)
Born: Kenton, NW London, England, 15 February, 1949 — RW

League Club	Source	Date Signed	Seasons Played	Apps	Subs	Gls
Fulham	App	02/66	67	8	1	3
Peterborough U	Tr	07/69	69-72	86	18	17

MOSS Roy Graham
Born: Maldon, Essex, England, 5 September, 1941 — IF
England: Schools

League Club	Source	Date Signed	Seasons Played	Apps	Subs	Gls
Tottenham H	Jnr	01/60				
Gillingham	Tr	09/62	62-63	14	-	3

MOSS Ryan James
Born: Dorchester, Dorset, England, 14 November, 1986 — F

League Club	Source	Date Signed	Seasons Played	Apps	Subs	Gls
Bournemouth	Jnr	08/04	04	0	1	0

MOSS Terence John (Terry)
Born: Bristol, England, 2 January, 1932 — LW

League Club	Source	Date Signed	Seasons Played	Apps	Subs	Gls
Swindon T (Am)		03/56	55	7	-	0

MOSSMAN David John

Born: Sheffield, England, 27 July, 1964 — LW
England: Schools

League Club	Source	Date Signed	Seasons Played	Apps	Subs	Gls
Sheffield Wed	Jnr	08/82				
Bradford C	L	03/85	84	0	3	1
Stockport Co	L	10/85	85	9	0	4
Rochdale	Tr	01/86	85	8	0	0
Stockport Co	Tr	03/86	85-86	28	2	1

MOSSOP Graham

Born: Cockermouth, Cumbria, England, 11 January, 1958 — F

League Club	Source	Date Signed	Seasons Played	Apps	Subs	Gls
Workington	Liverpool (App)	11/75	75	1	0	0
Carlisle U	Carlisle C	07/79	80	2	0	0

MOSTTO Miguel Angel

Born: Ica, Peru, 11 January, 1979 — F
Peru: 10

League Club	Source	Date Signed	Seasons Played	Apps	Subs	Gls
Barnsley	Cienciano (PER)	07/07	07-08	9	14	2

MOSTYN Roger

Born: Wrexham, Wales, 31 August, 1953 — F

League Club	Source	Date Signed	Seasons Played	Apps	Subs	Gls
Wrexham	Jnr	11/71	71-73	16	3	4

MOTTA Marco

Born: Merate, Italy, 14 May, 1986 — RB/M
Italy: 1/U21-36/Youth

League Club	Source	Date Signed	Seasons Played	Apps	Subs	Gls
Watford	Juventus (ITA)	02/15	14	7	2	0

MOTTERAM Carl

Born: Birmingham, England, 3 September, 1984 — M

League Club	Source	Date Signed	Seasons Played	Apps	Subs	Gls
Birmingham C	Sch	07/04				
Torquay U	Tr	07/06	06	1	6	0

MOTTERSHEAD Brian Leslie

Born: Rochdale, Greater Manchester, England, 13 July, 1935 — IF
Died: Rochdale, Greater Manchester, England, 8 October, 1985

League Club	Source	Date Signed	Seasons Played	Apps	Subs	Gls
Notts Co	Hamer YC	09/52				
Rochdale	Tr	08/53	53	1	-	0

MOTTERSHEAD Keith Anthony

Born: Stafford, England, 12 December, 1944 — RW

League Club	Source	Date Signed	Seasons Played	Apps	Subs	Gls
Doncaster Rov	Stafford Rgrs	10/66	66-67	34	6	0

MOTTLEY-HENRY Dylan

Born: Leeds, England, 2 August, 1997 — W

League Club	Source	Date Signed	Seasons Played	Apps	Subs	Gls
Bradford C	Sch	-	14	0	1	0

MOUGHTON Colin Edward

Born: Harrow, NW London, England, 30 December, 1947 — LH

League Club	Source	Date Signed	Seasons Played	Apps	Subs	Gls
Queens Park Rgrs	App	12/65	65-66	6	0	0
Colchester U	Tr	07/68	68	4	0	0

MOULD William (Billy)

Born: Tunstall, Potteries, England, 6 October, 1919 — RB
Died: Stoke-on-Trent, England, 1999

League Club	Source	Date Signed	Seasons Played	Apps	Subs	Gls
Stoke C	Summerbank	07/36	37-51	177	-	0
Crewe Alex	Tr	07/52	52-53	66	-	1

MOULDEN Anthony (Tony)

Born: Farnworth, Greater Manchester, England, 28 August, 1942 — IF

League Club	Source	Date Signed	Seasons Played	Apps	Subs	Gls
Bury	Blackburn Rov (Am)	05/60	60-61	4	-	0
Rochdale	Tr	06/62	62	5	-	1
Peterborough U	Tr	11/62	62-64	62	-	9
Notts Co	Tr	05/65	65	23	0	1
Rochdale	Tr	09/66	66	1	0	0

MOULDEN Paul Anthony Joseph

Born: Farnworth, Greater Manchester, England, 6 September, 1967 — F
England: Youth/Schools

League Club	Source	Date Signed	Seasons Played	Apps	Subs	Gls
Manchester C	App	09/84	85-88	48	16	18
Bournemouth	Tr	08/89	89	32	0	13
Oldham Ath	Tr	03/90	89-92	17	21	4
Brighton & HA	L	08/92	92	11	0	5
Birmingham C	Tr	03/93	92-93	18	2	5
Huddersfield T	Tr	03/95	94	0	2	0
Rochdale	Tr	08/95	95	6	10	1

MOULSON George Bernard

Born: Clogheen, Republic of Ireland, 6 August, 1914 — G
Died: Grimsby, North Lincolnshire, England, 11 November, 1994
Republic of Ireland: 3

League Club	Source	Date Signed	Seasons Played	Apps	Subs	Gls
Grimsby T	Weelsby Army Camp	07/36	46	1	-	0
Lincoln C	Tr	06/47	47-48	60	-	0

MOULT Louis Elliot

Born: Stoke-on-Trent, England, 14 May, 1992 — F

League Club	Source	Date Signed	Seasons Played	Apps	Subs	Gls
Stoke C	Sch	03/10	09	0	1	0
Bradford C	L	07/10	10	4	7	1
Accrington Stan	L	08/11	11	1	3	0
Northampton T	Tr	08/12	12	4	9	1

MOUNCER Frank Edmund

Born: Grimsby, North Lincolnshire, England, 22 November, 1920 — RB
Died: Grimsby, North Lincolnshire, England, 1977
England: Schools

League Club	Source	Date Signed	Seasons Played	Apps	Subs	Gls
Grimsby T	Humber U	09/38	46-48	22	-	0

MOUNTAIN Patrick Douglas (Pat)

Born: Pontypridd, Rhondda Cynon Taff, Wales, 1 August, 1976 — G
Wales: U21-2/Youth

League Club	Source	Date Signed	Seasons Played	Apps	Subs	Gls
Cardiff C	Barry T	07/95	96	5	0	0

MOUNTAIN Robert Brian (Bob)

Born: Wombwell, South Yorkshire, England, 11 September, 1956 — F

League Club	Source	Date Signed	Seasons Played	Apps	Subs	Gls
Huddersfield T	App	11/73	73	1	0	0

MOUNTFIELD Derek Neal

Born: Liverpool, England, 2 November, 1962 — CD
England: B-1/U21-1

League Club	Source	Date Signed	Seasons Played	Apps	Subs	Gls
Tranmere Rov	App	11/80	80-81	26	0	1
Everton	Tr	06/82	82-87	100	1	19
Aston Villa	Tr	06/88	88-91	88	2	9
Wolverhampton W	Tr	11/91	91-93	79	4	4
Carlisle U	Tr	08/94	94	30	1	3
Northampton T	Tr	10/95	95	4	0	0
Walsall	Tr	11/95	95-97	96	1	2
Scarborough	Bromsgrove Rov	01/99	98	5	1	0

MOUNTFORD David

Born: Hanley, Potteries, England, 9 January, 1931 — RW
Died: Stoke-on-Trent, England, September, 1985

League Club	Source	Date Signed	Seasons Played	Apps	Subs	Gls
Crewe Alex	Jnr	11/48	48-51	36	-	5
West Bromwich A	Tr	12/51	52	4	-	0
Crewe Alex	Tr	10/53	53-56	27	-	7

MOUNTFORD Derek

Born: Stoke-on-Trent, England, 24 March, 1934 — RH
Died: Stoke-on-Trent, England, January, 1994

League Club	Source	Date Signed	Seasons Played	Apps	Subs	Gls
Port Vale	Jnr	05/51	54-56	26	-	0
Crewe Alex	Tr	07/57	57	13	-	0

MOUNTFORD Frank

Born: Campsall, South Yorkshire, England, 30 March, 1923 — RH/RB
Died: Stoke-on-Trent, England, 27 June, 2006

League Club	Source	Date Signed	Seasons Played	Apps	Subs	Gls
Stoke C	Jnr	04/40	46-57	391	-	21

MOUNTFORD George Frederick

Born: Kidderminster, Worcestershire, England, 30 March, 1921 — RW
Died: Kidderminster, Worcestershire, England, 14 June, 1973

League Club	Source	Date Signed	Seasons Played	Apps	Subs	Gls
Stoke C	Kidderminster Hrs	09/38	46-49	123	-	25
Stoke C	Independiente (COL)	09/51	51-52	25	-	0
Queens Park Rgrs	Tr	10/52	52-53	35	-	2

MOUNTFORD Peter

Born: Stoke-on-Trent, England, 13 September, 1960 — M

League Club	Source	Date Signed	Seasons Played	Apps	Subs	Gls
Norwich C	App	09/78	81-82	1	3	0
Charlton Ath	Tr	09/83	83	10	1	1
Leyton Orient	Tr	01/85	84-86	27	6	2

MOUNTFORD Raymond (Ray)

Born: Mexborough, South Yorkshire, England, 28 April, 1958 — G

League Club	Source	Date Signed	Seasons Played	Apps	Subs	Gls
Manchester U	App	04/75				
Rotherham U	Tr	07/78	78-82	123	0	0
Bury	L	11/83	83	4	0	0

MOUNTFORD Robert William (Bob)

Born: Stoke-on-Trent, England, 23 February, 1952 — F
Died: New South Wales, Australia, 26 August, 2008

League Club	Source	Date Signed	Seasons Played	Apps	Subs	Gls
Port Vale	App	02/70	68-74	64	17	9
Scunthorpe U	L	10/74	74	1	2	0
Crewe Alex	L	12/74	74	5	0	0
Rochdale	Tr	01/75	74-77	97	1	37
Huddersfield T	Tr	10/77	77	12	2	4
Halifax T	Tr	03/78	77-79	56	6	11
Crewe Alex	Tr	08/80	80	3	0	0
Stockport Co	Tr	11/80	80	6	1	3

MOUSINHO John Michael Lewis

Born: Hounslow, SW London, England, 30 April, 1986 — M

League Club	Source	Date Signed	Seasons Played	Apps	Subs	Gls
Brentford	Notre Dame Univ (USA)	10/05	05-07	45	19	2
Wycombe W	Tr	06/08	08-09	58	15	3
Stevenage	Tr	07/10	10-11	50	7	10
Preston NE	Tr	05/12	12-13	16	10	1
Gillingham	L	11/13	13	4	0	1
Stevenage	L	01/14	13	15	1	1
Burton A	Tr	07/14	14	42	0	2

MOUSSA Franck Nyinzapa

Born: Brussels, Belgium, 24 July, 1989 — M

League Club	Source	Date Signed	Seasons Played	Apps	Subs	Gls
Southend U	Sch	02/07	05-09	74	16	7

League Club	Source	Date Signed	Seasons Played	Apps	Subs	Gls
Wycombe W	L	10/08	08	7	2	0
Leicester C	Tr	08/10	10	2	6	1
Doncaster Rov	L	02/11	10	14	0	2
Chesterfield	L	03/12	11	10	0	4
Coventry C	Tr	09/12	12-13	67	10	18
Charlton Ath	Tr	07/14	14	4	10	1
MOUSSADDIK Choukri (Chuck)						
Born: Meknes, Morocco, 23 February, 1970						G
Wycombe W	Wimbledon (Jnr)	08/90	95	1	0	0
MOUSSI Guy						
Born: Paris, France, 23 January, 1985						DM
Nottingham F	Angers SCO (FRA)	07/08	08-13	108	28	3
Millwall	L	11/13	13	3	0	0
Birmingham C		11/14	14	0	2	0
MOUTAOUAKIL Yassin (Yazz)						
Born: Nice, France, 18 July, 1986						RB
France: U21-5						
Charlton Ath	Chateauroux (FRA)	07/07	07-08	16	5	0
Portsmouth	Hayes & Yeading U	01/13	12-13	28	4	0
MOUYOKOLO Steven Stefan Fabrice						
Born: Melun, France, 24 January, 1987						CD
Hull C	US Boulogne (FRA)	01/09	09	19	2	1
Wolverhampton W	Tr	06/10	10	2	2	0
MOVERLEY Robert (Rob)						
Born: Batley, West Yorkshire, England, 18 January, 1969						G
Bradford C	App	06/87				
Hartlepool U	Tr	12/88	88-89	29	0	0
MOWATT Alex James						
Born: Doncaster, South Yorkshire, England, 13 February, 1995						M
England: Youth						
Leeds U	Sch	07/13	13-14	61	6	10
MOWBRAY Anthony Mark (Tony)						
Born: Saltburn, Cleveland, England, 22 November, 1963						CD
England: B-3						
Middlesbrough	App	11/81	82-91	345	3	26
Ipswich T	Glasgow Celtic	10/95	95-99	125	3	5
MOWBRAY Darren Karl						
Born: Middlesbrough, England, 24 January, 1978						CD
Scarborough	Middlesbrough (YT)	08/96	96	2	1	0
MOWBRAY Henry (Harry)						
Born: Hamilton, Lanarkshire, Scotland, 1 May, 1947						LB
Blackpool	Cowdenbeath	05/67	67-70	88	3	0
Bolton W	Tr	06/71	71-72	31	0	0
MOWER Kenneth Matthew (Ken)						
Born: Bloxwich, West Midlands, England, 1 December, 1960						LB
Walsall	App	11/78	78-90	410	5	8
MOWL Joseph William (William)						
Born: Bulwell, Nottinghamshire, England, 23 June, 1922						G
Notts Co	Sherwood	10/44	48	3	-	0
Mansfield T	Tr	07/49				
MOXEY Dean William						
Born: Exeter, England, 14 January, 1986						LB
England: Semi Pro-4						
Exeter C	Sch	07/04	08	41	2	4
Derby Co	Tr	07/09	09-10	47	5	2
Crystal Palace	Tr	01/11	10-13	75	16	1
Bolton W	Tr	07/14	14	14	6	1
MOXHAM Graham						
Born: Exeter, England, 3 January, 1949						LW
Bournemouth	Preston NE (App)	07/66				
Exeter C	Bideford T	07/75	75	4	2	0
MOXHAM Robert (Bob)						
Born: Barrow, Cumbria, England, 5 July, 1922						CF
Died: Barrow, Cumbria, England, February, 1990						
Barrow	Holker Central OB	09/48	48	5	-	1
MOYES David William						
Born: Bearsden, Dunbartonshire, Scotland, 25 April, 1963						CD
Scotland: Youth/Schools						
Cambridge U	Glasgow Celtic	10/83	83-85	79	0	1
Bristol C	Tr	10/85	85-87	83	0	6
Shrewsbury T	Tr	10/87	87-89	91	5	11
Preston NE	Hamilton Academical	09/93	93-97	142	1	15
MOYES John David						
Born: Heage, Derbyshire, England, 17 July, 1951						CD
Chesterfield	App	07/69	68-71	13	0	0

League Club	Source	Date Signed	Seasons Played	Apps	Subs	Gls
MOYLON Craig						
Born: Munster, Germany, 16 October, 1972						FB
Preston NE	Jnr	07/91	92	0	1	0
MOYO David Philani						
Born: Harare, Zimbabwe, 17 December, 1994						F
Northampton T	Jnr	06/12	12-14	2	12	1
MOYO-MODISE Clive Zwelibanzi						
Born: South Africa, 20 September, 1987						F
Rochdale	Jnr	09/05	05-06	2	26	1
MOYSE Alexander Rodney (Alec)						
Born: Mitcham, S London, England, 5 August, 1935						CF
Died: Australia, 1994						
Crystal Palace	Chatham	02/56	55-56	4	-	1
Swindon T	Tr	08/58	58	4	-	0
Millwall	Tr	09/58	58-59	22	-	3
MOYSE Ronald (Ron)						
Born: Portsmouth, England, 2 April, 1920						RB/RH
Died: Portsmouth, England, June, 1992						
Reading	Portsmouth (Am)	10/46	46-52	189	-	0
MOYSES Christopher Raymond (Chris)						
Born: Lincoln, England, 1 November, 1965						D/M
Lincoln C	App	11/83	83	2	2	0
Halifax T	Tr	07/84	84	21	4	0
MOZIKA Damien						
Born: Corbeil-Essonnes, France, 15 April, 1987						M
Chester C	AS Nancy (FRA)	07/08	08	21	1	2
Bury	Tarbiat Yazd (IRA)	08/10	10-11	35	2	3
Scunthorpe U	Tr	08/11	11-12	25	4	4
Torquay U	Tr	10/13	13	9	3	0
MOZLEY Bertram (Bert)						
Born: Derby, England, 23 September, 1923						RB
England: 3/FLge-1						
Derby Co	Nottingham F (Am)	06/46	46-54	297	-	2
MPENZA Emile Basunga Lokonda						
Born: Brussels, Belgium, 4 July, 1978						F
Belgium: 57						
Manchester C	Al Rayyan (QAT)	01/07	06-07	17	8	5
Plymouth Arg	Tr	09/08	08	3	6	2
MPOKU Paul-Jose						
Born: Kinshasa, DR Congo, 19 April, 1992						W
Belgium: U21-18/Youth						
Tottenham H	Sch	04/09				
Leyton Orient	L	09/10	10	9	18	2
MUAMBA Fabrice Ndala						
Born: Kinshasa, DR Congo, 6 April, 1988						DM
England: U21-33/Youth						
Arsenal	Sch	04/06				
Birmingham C	L	07/06	06	30	4	0
Birmingham C	Tr	05/07	07	37	0	2
Bolton W	Tr	06/08	08-11	118	12	3
MUCHA Jan						
Born: Snina, Slovakia, 5 December, 1982						G
Slovakia: 43						
Everton	Legia Warsaw (POL)	07/10	12	2	0	0
MUDD Paul Andrew						
Born: Hull, England, 13 November, 1970						LB
England: Schools						
Hull C	YT	07/89	88	1	0	0
Scarborough	Tr	07/90	90-92	95	3	2
Scunthorpe U	Tr	07/93	93-94	66	2	4
Lincoln C	Tr	07/95	95	2	2	0
MUDGE James Robert Mark (Jamie)						
Born: Exeter, England, 25 March, 1983						F
Exeter C	YT	-	00	0	3	0
MUDIE John Knight (Jackie)						
Born: Dundee, Scotland, 10 April, 1930						IF
Died: Stoke-on-Trent, England, 2 March, 1992						
Scotland: 17						
Blackpool	Lochee Harp	05/47	49-60	323	-	144
Stoke C	Tr	03/61	60-63	88	-	32
Port Vale	Tr	11/63	63-66	54	0	9
MUGGLETON Carl David						
Born: Leicester, England, 13 September, 1968						G
England: U21-1						
Leicester C	App	09/86	88-92	46	0	0
Chesterfield	L	09/87	87	17	0	0

League Club	Source	Date Signed	Seasons Played	Apps	Subs	Gls
Blackpool	L	02/88	87	2	0	0
Hartlepool U	L	10/88	88	8	0	0
Stockport Co	L	03/90	89	4	0	0
Stoke C	L	08/93	93	6	0	0
Stoke C	Glasgow Celtic	07/94	94-00	148	1	0
Rotherham U	L	11/95	95	6	0	0
Sheffield U	L	03/96	95	0	1	0
Mansfield T	L	09/99	99	9	0	0
Chesterfield	L	12/99	99	5	0	0
Cardiff C	L	03/01	00	6	0	0
Cheltenham T	Tr	07/01	01	7	0	0
Bradford C	L	12/01	01	4	0	0
Chesterfield	Tr	07/02	02-05	112	0	0
Mansfield T	Tr	07/06	06-07	52	0	0

MUGGLETON Samuel Alexander (Sam)
Born: Melton Mowbray, Leicestershire, England, 17 November, 1995 — LB

League Club	Source	Date Signed	Seasons Played	Apps	Subs	Gls
Gillingham	Sch	-	12-13	1	1	0

MUHREN Arnold Johannes Hyacinthus
Born: Volendam, Netherlands, 2 June, 1951 — M
Netherlands: 23

League Club	Source	Date Signed	Seasons Played	Apps	Subs	Gls
Ipswich T	Twente Enschede (NED)	08/78	78-81	161	0	21
Manchester U	Tr	08/82	82-84	65	5	13

MUIR Alexander Johnston (Alex)
Born: Inverkeithing, Fife, Scotland, 10 December, 1923 — RW
Died: Wallasey, Wirral, England, 4 September, 1995

League Club	Source	Date Signed	Seasons Played	Apps	Subs	Gls
Liverpool	Lochgelly Violet	07/47	47	4	-	0

MUIR Ian Baker
Born: Motherwell, Lanarkshire, Scotland, 16 June, 1929 — CH
Died: Bristol, England, 22 February, 2009

League Club	Source	Date Signed	Seasons Played	Apps	Subs	Gls
Bristol Rov	Motherwell	05/53	53-56	26	-	0
Oldham Ath	Tr	06/57	57	35	-	0

MUIR Ian James
Born: Coventry, England, 5 May, 1963 — F
England: Youth/Schools

League Club	Source	Date Signed	Seasons Played	Apps	Subs	Gls
Queens Park Rgrs	App	09/80	80	2	0	2
Burnley	L	10/82	82	1	1	1
Birmingham C	Tr	08/83	83	1	0	0
Brighton & HA	Tr	02/84	83-84	3	1	0
Swindon T	L	01/85	84	2	0	0
Tranmere Rov	Tr	07/85	85-94	283	31	140
Birmingham C	Tr	06/95	95	1	0	0
Darlington	L	09/95	95	4	0	1

MUIR John George
Born: Sedgley, West Midlands, England, 26 April, 1963 — F

League Club	Source	Date Signed	Seasons Played	Apps	Subs	Gls
Doncaster Rov	Dudley T	02/90	89-91	64	11	18
Stockport Co	Tr	02/92	91-92	10	3	3
Torquay U	L	02/93	92	7	5	0

MUIR Maurice Moyston
Born: Wimbledon, SW London, England, 19 March, 1963 — M
England: Schools

League Club	Source	Date Signed	Seasons Played	Apps	Subs	Gls
Northampton T	App	03/81	79-83	15	13	0

MUIR William Miller (Billy)
Born: Ayr, Scotland, 27 August, 1925 — W
Died: Yeovil, Somerset, England, January, 2005

League Club	Source	Date Signed	Seasons Played	Apps	Subs	Gls
Queens Park Rgrs	Irvine Meadow	02/49	48-52	17	-	4
Torquay U	Tr	10/52	52	9	-	0

MUIR William Nelson (Willie)
Born: Port Glasgow, Inverclyde, Scotland, 14 August, 1934 — RW
Died: Nuneaton, Warwickshire, England, May, 2000

League Club	Source	Date Signed	Seasons Played	Apps	Subs	Gls
Aldershot	St Mirren	05/56	56	8	-	4

MUIRHEAD Benjamin Robinson (Ben)
Born: Doncaster, South Yorkshire, England, 5 January, 1983 — RW
England: Youth

League Club	Source	Date Signed	Seasons Played	Apps	Subs	Gls
Manchester U	YT	01/00				
Bradford C	Tr	03/03	02-06	70	42	4
Rochdale	L	02/07	06	12	0	3
Rochdale	Tr	07/07	07	18	13	0

MUJANGI BIA Geoffrey (Geoff)
Born: Kinshasa, DR Congo, 12 August, 1989 — W
Belgium: 2/U21-6

League Club	Source	Date Signed	Seasons Played	Apps	Subs	Gls
Wolverhampton W (L)	RSC Charleroi (BEL)	01/10	09	1	2	0
Wolverhampton W (L)	RSC Charleroi (BEL)	06/10	10	0	1	0
Watford (L)	Standard Liege (BEL)	08/12	12	0	3	0

MUKENDI Henoc John
Born: Lubumbashi, DR Congo, 20 November, 1993 — F

League Club	Source	Date Signed	Seasons Played	Apps	Subs	Gls
Liverpool	Sch	07/12				
Northampton T	L	08/12	12	0	7	0

MUKENDI Vinny
Born: Manchester, England, 12 March, 1992 — F

League Club	Source	Date Signed	Seasons Played	Apps	Subs	Gls
Macclesfield T	Sch	04/10	08-11	20	27	3

MULDOON John Patrick Joseph
Born: Bebington, Wirral, England, 21 November, 1964 — M

League Club	Source	Date Signed	Seasons Played	Apps	Subs	Gls
Wrexham	Jnr	12/82	82-85	64	19	11

MULDOON Jonathan Jack (Jack)
Born: Scunthorpe, North Lincolnshire, England, 19 May, 1989 — F

League Club	Source	Date Signed	Seasons Played	Apps	Subs	Gls
Rochdale	Worksop T	05/14	14	2	1	0

MULDOON Oliver James
Born: Stepney, E London, England, 3 September, 1994 — RM

League Club	Source	Date Signed	Seasons Played	Apps	Subs	Gls
Charlton Ath	Sch	07/13				
Gillingham	L	03/15	14	3	0	0

MULDOON Terence (Terry)
Born: Ashington, Northumberland, England, 10 August, 1951 — W
Died: Scunthorpe, North Lincolnshire, England, 1971

League Club	Source	Date Signed	Seasons Played	Apps	Subs	Gls
Scunthorpe U (Am)		05/70	70	1	0	0

MULGREW Charles Patrick (Charlie)
Born: Glasgow, Scotland, 6 March, 1986 — D
Scotland: 17/U21-14/Youth

League Club	Source	Date Signed	Seasons Played	Apps	Subs	Gls
Wolverhampton W	Glasgow Celtic	08/06	06	5	1	0
Southend U	L	01/08	07	18	0	1

MULGREW Thomas (Tommy)
Born: Motherwell, Lanarkshire, Scotland, 13 April, 1929 — IF/LH

League Club	Source	Date Signed	Seasons Played	Apps	Subs	Gls
Northampton T	Greenock Morton	07/49	50-52	8	-	1
Newcastle U	Tr	10/52	52-53	14	-	1
Southampton	Tr	07/54	54-61	293	-	90
Aldershot	Tr	08/62	62-64	112	-	2

MULGROVE Keith Arnold
Born: Haltwhistle, Northumberland, England, 21 August, 1959 — CD

League Club	Source	Date Signed	Seasons Played	Apps	Subs	Gls
Newcastle U	App	07/77	78	0	1	0

MULHALL George
Born: Falkirk, Scotland, 8 May, 1936 — LW
Scotland: 3/SLge-3

League Club	Source	Date Signed	Seasons Played	Apps	Subs	Gls
Sunderland	Aberdeen	09/62	62-68	249	4	55

MULHEARN Kenneth John (Ken)
Born: Liverpool, England, 16 October, 1945 — G

League Club	Source	Date Signed	Seasons Played	Apps	Subs	Gls
Everton	App	07/63				
Stockport Co	Tr	08/64	64-67	100	0	0
Manchester C	Tr	09/67	67-69	50	0	0
Shrewsbury T	Tr	03/71	70-79	370	0	0
Crewe Alex	Tr	08/80	80-81	88	0	0

MULHERON Peter
Born: Glasgow, Scotland, 21 June, 1921 — IF
Died: Kent, England, March, 2009

League Club	Source	Date Signed	Seasons Played	Apps	Subs	Gls
Crystal Palace	Tonbridge	10/48	48-49	38	-	2

MULHOLLAND Francis Gerard (Frank)
Born: Belfast, Northern Ireland, 28 October, 1927 — LH
Died: Belfast, Northern Ireland, October, 2006
Northern Ireland: NILge-3

League Club	Source	Date Signed	Seasons Played	Apps	Subs	Gls
Middlesbrough	Glentoran	10/51	51-57	46	-	0

MULHOLLAND George Rush
Born: Paisley, Renfrewshire, Scotland, 4 August, 1928 — LB
Died: Stockton-on-Tees, Cleveland, England, December, 2001

League Club	Source	Date Signed	Seasons Played	Apps	Subs	Gls
Stoke C	Newcastle Catholics	07/50	50	3	-	0
Bradford C	Tr	07/53	53-59	277	-	0
Darlington	Tr	07/60	60-62	106	-	0

MULHOLLAND James (Jimmy)
Born: Knightswood, Glasgow, Scotland, 10 April, 1938 — IF
Died: Uddingston, Lanarkshire, Scotland, 21 June, 1994

League Club	Source	Date Signed	Seasons Played	Apps	Subs	Gls
Chelsea	East Stirlingshire	10/62	62-63	11	-	2
Barrow	Greenock Morton	08/65	65-68	132	2	46
Stockport Co	Tr	10/68	68-69	28	4	5
Crewe Alex	Tr	08/70	70	0	1	0

MULHOLLAND John Anthony
Born: Dumbarton, Dunbartonshire, Scotland, 20 January, 1932 — CF
Died: Winchester, Hampshire, England, July, 2000

League Club	Source	Date Signed	Seasons Played	Apps	Subs	Gls
Southampton	Condorrat Thistle	12/51				
Chester C	Tr	07/56	56	8	-	1
Halifax T	Tr	06/57	57	8	-	1

MULHOLLAND John Ross
Born: Dumbarton, Dunbartonshire, Scotland, 7 December, 1928 — W

League Club	Source	Date Signed	Seasons Played	Apps	Subs	Gls
Plymouth Arg	Renton BG	10/46				
Grimsby T	Tr	08/49	49-50	2	-	0
Scunthorpe U	Tr	10/50	50	6	-	1

MULHOLLAND Scott Rene
Born: Bexleyheath, SE London, England, 7 September, 1986 — M

League Club	Source	Date Signed	Seasons Played	Apps	Subs	Gls
Queens Park Rgrs	Sch	-	04	0	1	0

MULKERRIN James (Jimmy)
Born: Dumbarton, Dunbartonshire, Scotland, 25 December, 1931 — IF
Scotland: B-1

League Club	Source	Date Signed	Seasons Played	Apps	Subs	Gls
Accrington Stan	Hibernian	03/57	56-58	70	-	36
Tranmere Rov	Tr	08/59	59-60	38	-	8

MULLAN Brendan Gerald Joseph
Born: Coleraine, Derry, Northern Ireland, 2 January, 1950 — F
Northern Ireland: NILge-2/U23-1

League Club	Source	Date Signed	Seasons Played	Apps	Subs	Gls
Fulham	Coleraine	02/68	67-68	2	2	0
Millwall	Tr	07/69				

MULLARD Albert Thomas
Born: Walsall, West Midlands, England, 22 November, 1920 — IF
Died: Walsall, West Midlands, England, 27 May, 1984

League Club	Source	Date Signed	Seasons Played	Apps	Subs	Gls
Walsall	Hinckley Ath	11/45	46-48	61	-	12
Crewe Alex	Tr	06/49	49-50	44	-	15
Stoke C	Tr	08/50	50-51	21	-	3
Port Vale	Tr	09/51	51-55	163	-	22

MULLARKEY Samuel (Sam)
Born: Sleaford, Lincolnshire, England, 24 September, 1987 — F

League Club	Source	Date Signed	Seasons Played	Apps	Subs	Gls
Nottingham F	Sch	10/04				
Lincoln C	Grantham T	08/08	08	7	11	1

MULLEN Andrew (Andy)
Born: Newcastle-upon-Tyne, England, 28 July, 1928 — LW

League Club	Source	Date Signed	Seasons Played	Apps	Subs	Gls
Aston Villa	Royal Armoured Corps	07/48				
Brighton & HA	Tr	08/49				
Workington	Annfield Plain	08/51	51-52	66	-	5
Scunthorpe U	South Shields	08/55	55-56	10	-	1

MULLEN James (Jimmy)
Born: Jarrow, Tyne and Wear, England, 8 November, 1952 — CD

League Club	Source	Date Signed	Seasons Played	Apps	Subs	Gls
Sheffield Wed	App	10/70	70-79	222	7	10
Rotherham U	Tr	08/80	80-81	49	0	1
Preston NE	L	11/81	81	1	0	0
Cardiff C	Tr	03/82	81-85	128	5	12
Newport Co	Tr	06/86	86	19	0	0

MULLEN James (Jimmy)
Born: Newcastle-upon-Tyne, England, 6 January, 1923 — LW
Died: Wolverhampton, England, 13 October, 1987
England: 12/B-3/FLge-1/Schools/War-3

League Club	Source	Date Signed	Seasons Played	Apps	Subs	Gls
Wolverhampton W	Jnr	01/40	38-58	445	-	98

MULLEN James (Jimmy)
Born: Oxford, England, 16 March, 1947 — LW

League Club	Source	Date Signed	Seasons Played	Apps	Subs	Gls
Reading	Oxford C	11/66	66-67	8	0	1
Charlton Ath	Tr	11/67	67-68	7	0	0
Rotherham U	Tr	02/69	68-73	174	3	24
Blackburn Rov	Tr	08/74	74-75	6	4	0
Bury	Tr	06/76	76	2	2	0
Rochdale	L	03/77	76	6	2	1

MULLEN James Welsh
Born: Larne, Antrim, Northern Ireland, 10 January, 1921 — IF/LW
Died: Barrow, Cumbria, England, April, 2002

League Club	Source	Date Signed	Seasons Played	Apps	Subs	Gls
Barrow	Belfast Celtic	02/46	46-47	55	-	9
Crystal Palace	Tr	07/48	48	11	-	0
Bristol C	Tr	02/49	48-49	17	-	2
Barrow	Tr	09/50	50	9	-	0

MULLEN Roger Colin
Born: Cowbridge, Vale of Glamorgan, Wales, 2 March, 1966 — FB
Wales: Youth

League Club	Source	Date Signed	Seasons Played	Apps	Subs	Gls
Swansea C	App	03/84	83-84	2	1	0

MULLEN Stephen Anthony (Steve)
Born: Glasgow, Scotland, 8 September, 1959 — RW

League Club	Source	Date Signed	Seasons Played	Apps	Subs	Gls
Bury	Darwen	02/79	78-81	76	16	5

MULLER Adam Philip
Born: Leeds, England, 17 April, 1982 — F

League Club	Source	Date Signed	Seasons Played	Apps	Subs	Gls
Sheffield Wed	Ossett T	05/00	00	1	4	0

MULLER Heinz
Born: Frankfurt, Germany, 30 August, 1978 — G

League Club	Source	Date Signed	Seasons Played	Apps	Subs	Gls
Barnsley	Lillestrom (NOR)	08/07	07-08	64	0	0

MULLERY Alan Patrick
Born: Notting Hill, Central London, England, 23 November, 1941 — M
England: 35/FLge-2/U23-3

League Club	Source	Date Signed	Seasons Played	Apps	Subs	Gls
Fulham	Jnr	12/58	58-63	199	-	13
Tottenham H	Tr	03/64	63-71	312	0	25
Fulham	L	03/72	71	6	0	1
Fulham	Tr	07/72	72-75	158	1	23

MULLETT Joseph (Joe)
Born: Rowley Regis, West Midlands, England, 2 October, 1936 — LB/LH
Died: Sandwell, West Midlands, England, 3 March, 1995

League Club	Source	Date Signed	Seasons Played	Apps	Subs	Gls
Birmingham C	Malt Hill U	02/55	57	3	-	0
Norwich C	Tr	02/59	58-67	211	2	2

MULLEY James Anthony (Jim)
Born: Edgware, NW London, England, 30 September, 1988 — M

League Club	Source	Date Signed	Seasons Played	Apps	Subs	Gls
AFC Wimbledon	Chelmsford C	01/11	11	3	7	0

MULLIGAN David James (Dave)
Born: Fazakerley, Merseyside, England, 24 March, 1982 — RB
New Zealand: 28/U23/Youth

League Club	Source	Date Signed	Seasons Played	Apps	Subs	Gls
Barnsley	YT	10/00	01-03	59	6	1
Doncaster Rov	Tr	02/04	03-05	63	14	4
Scunthorpe U	Tr	07/06	06	20	4	1
Grimsby T	L	08/07	07	4	2	0
Port Vale	Tr	01/08	07	10	3	1

MULLIGAN Gary Thomas
Born: Dublin, Republic of Ireland, 23 April, 1985 — F
Republic of Ireland: U21-1

League Club	Source	Date Signed	Seasons Played	Apps	Subs	Gls
Wolverhampton W	Sch	07/02	04	0	1	0
Rushden & D	L	10/04	04	12	1	3
Sheffield U	Tr	07/05				
Port Vale	L	09/05	05	8	2	1
Gillingham	Tr	01/06	05-08	74	33	15
Northampton T	Tr	07/09	09	2	7	0

MULLIGAN James (Jimmy)
Born: Dublin, Republic of Ireland, 21 April, 1974 — F

League Club	Source	Date Signed	Seasons Played	Apps	Subs	Gls
Stoke C	YT	07/92				
Bury	L	11/93	93	2	1	1
Bury	Tr	07/94	94-95	9	8	2

MULLIGAN Lance Martin
Born: Sutton-in-Ashfield, Nottinghamshire, England, 21 October, 1985 — F

League Club	Source	Date Signed	Seasons Played	Apps	Subs	Gls
Mansfield T	Sch	-	03	0	1	0

MULLIGAN Nathan Michael
Born: Stockton-on-Tees, Cleveland, England, 15 September, 1986 — W

League Club	Source	Date Signed	Seasons Played	Apps	Subs	Gls
Darlington	Norton & Stockton Ancs	10/09	09	10	6	1

MULLIGAN Patrick Martin (Paddy)
Born: Dublin, Republic of Ireland, 17 March, 1945 — RB
Republic of Ireland: 50/LoI-5/U23-1

League Club	Source	Date Signed	Seasons Played	Apps	Subs	Gls
Chelsea	Shamrock Rov (ROI)	10/69	69-72	55	3	2
Crystal Palace	Tr	09/72	72-74	57	0	2
West Bromwich A	Tr	09/75	75-77	109	0	1

MULLIGAN Peter Granville
Born: Royston, South Yorkshire, England, 17 July, 1942 — RW

League Club	Source	Date Signed	Seasons Played	Apps	Subs	Gls
Barnsley	Jnr	10/59	59-63	9	-	0

MULLIN John Michael
Born: Bury, Greater Manchester, England, 11 August, 1975 — M

League Club	Source	Date Signed	Seasons Played	Apps	Subs	Gls
Burnley	Jnr	08/92	93-94	7	11	2
Sunderland	Tr	08/95	95-98	23	12	4
Preston NE	L	02/98	97	4	3	0
Burnley	L	03/98	97	6	0	0
Burnley	Tr	07/99	99-01	38	39	8
Rotherham U	Tr	10/01	01-05	159	21	12
Tranmere Rov	Tr	07/06	06-07	43	7	5
Accrington Stan	Tr	08/08	08-09	26	8	0

MULLIN Paul Bernard
Born: Bury, Greater Manchester, England, 16 March, 1974 — F

League Club	Source	Date Signed	Seasons Played	Apps	Subs	Gls
Accrington Stan	Radcliffe Bor	08/00	06-09	129	0	33
Bradford C	L	03/09	08-08	5	1	0
Morecambe	Tr	08/09	09-10	51	13	16

MULLIN Paul Philip
Born: Liverpool, England, 6 November, 1994 — F

League Club	Source	Date Signed	Seasons Played	Apps	Subs	Gls
Huddersfield T	Liverpool (Jnr)	09/12				
Morecambe	Tr	08/14	14	20	22	8

MULLINEUX Ian Joseph
Born: Salford, England, 10 November, 1968 — W

League Club	Source	Date Signed	Seasons Played	Apps	Subs	Gls
Bolton W	App	-	86	1	1	0

MULLINGS Darren
Born: Bristol, England, 3 March, 1987 — M
England: Schools

League Club	Source	Date Signed	Seasons Played	Apps	Subs	Gls
Bristol Rov	Jnr	01/06	05	0	4	0

MULLINGTON Philip Thomas (Phil)
Born: Oldham, Greater Manchester, England, 25 September, 1956 — M

League Club	Source	Date Signed	Seasons Played	Apps	Subs	Gls
Oldham Ath	App	09/74				

League Club	Source	Date Signed	Seasons Played	Apps	Subs	Gls
Rochdale	Tr	01/76	75-76	59	7	6
Crewe Alex	Northwich Victoria	01/78	77	1	0	0
Rochdale	Winsford U	08/78	78	8	1	0

MULLINS Hayden Ian
Born: Reading, England, 27 March, 1979 DM
England: U21-3

League Club	Source	Date Signed	Seasons Played	Apps	Subs	Gls
Crystal Palace	YT	02/97	98-03	219	3	18
West Ham U	Tr	10/03	03-08	152	28	4
Portsmouth	Tr	01/09	08-11	109	5	3
Reading	L	03/12	11	6	1	0
Birmingham C	Tr	07/12	12-13	29	7	2
Notts Co	L	01/14	13	15	1	1
Notts Co	Tr	06/14	14	32	0	0

MULLINS John Christopher (Johnny)
Born: Hampstead, NW London, England, 6 November, 1985 CD

League Club	Source	Date Signed	Seasons Played	Apps	Subs	Gls
Reading	Sch	11/04				
Kidderminster Hrs	L	12/04	04	21	0	2
Mansfield T	Tr	06/06	06-07	81	5	4
Stockport Co	Tr	07/08	08-09	67	2	4
Rotherham U	Tr	07/10	10-12	98	1	7
Oxford U	L	10/12	12	8	0	2
Oxford U	Tr	07/13	13-14	77	2	5

MULRAIN Steven (Steve)
Born: Lambeth, S London, England, 23 October, 1972 F
England: Schools

League Club	Source	Date Signed	Seasons Played	Apps	Subs	Gls
Leeds U	YT	07/91				
Rochdale	Charlton Ath (NC)	12/92	92-93	3	5	2

MULRANEY Ambrose Aloysius (Jock)
Born: Wishaw, Lanarkshire, Scotland, 18 May, 1916 RW
Died: Kinver, Staffordshire, England, 8 December, 2001

League Club	Source	Date Signed	Seasons Played	Apps	Subs	Gls
Ipswich T	Dartford	11/36	38	28	-	8
Birmingham C	Tr	10/45	46	27	-	8
Aston Villa	Kidderminster Hrs	09/48	48	12	-	2

MULRYNE Philip Patrick (Phil)
Born: Belfast, Northern Ireland, 1 January, 1978 M
Northern Ireland: 27/B-1/U21-3/Youth

League Club	Source	Date Signed	Seasons Played	Apps	Subs	Gls
Manchester U	YT	03/95	97	1	0	0
Norwich C	Tr	03/99	98-04	132	29	18
Cardiff C	Tr	08/05	05	1	3	0
Leyton Orient	Tr	02/07	06	1	1	0

MULUMBU Youssouf
Born: Kinshasa, DR Congo, 25 January, 1987 M
DR Congo: 26//France: U21-2

League Club	Source	Date Signed	Seasons Played	Apps	Subs	Gls
West Bromwich A	Paris St-Germain (FRA)	01/09	08-14	176	21	15

MULVANEY James (Jimmy)
Born: Airdrie, Lanarkshire, Scotland, 27 April, 1921 D
Died: Coventry, England, June, 1993

League Club	Source	Date Signed	Seasons Played	Apps	Subs	Gls
Luton T	Dumbarton	06/48	48-49	8	-	2
Brighton & HA	Tr	08/50	50	8	-	0
Bradford C	Tr	10/51	51	19	-	0
Halifax T	Bath C	11/52	52	1	-	0

MULVANEY James (Jimmy)
Born: Sunderland, England, 13 May, 1941 IF
Died: Sunderland, England, 15 August, 1982

League Club	Source	Date Signed	Seasons Played	Apps	Subs	Gls
Hartlepool U	Whitby T	08/65	65-67	67	2	31
Barrow	Tr	11/67	67-69	71	8	34
Stockport Co	Tr	07/70	70-71	38	2	8

MULVANEY Richard (Dick)
Born: Sunderland, England, 5 August, 1942 CD

League Club	Source	Date Signed	Seasons Played	Apps	Subs	Gls
Blackburn Rov	Billingham Synthonia	02/64	64-70	135	6	4
Oldham Ath	Tr	08/71	71-74	88	4	2
Rochdale	Tr	10/74	74-76	72	1	4

MULVEY Edward Patrick Noel (Paddy)
Born: Dublin, Republic of Ireland, 29 December, 1934 IF
Died: Dublin, Republic of Ireland, 11 February, 2009

League Club	Source	Date Signed	Seasons Played	Apps	Subs	Gls
Stockport Co	Glentoran	11/57	57-59	26	-	5

MULVOY Terence John (Terry)
Born: Manchester, England, 2 December, 1938 IF

League Club	Source	Date Signed	Seasons Played	Apps	Subs	Gls
Rochdale		02/56	56	2	-	0

MUMBY Peter
Born: Bradford, England, 22 February, 1969 F

League Club	Source	Date Signed	Seasons Played	Apps	Subs	Gls
Leeds U	YT	07/87	87-88	3	3	0
Burnley	Tr	07/89	89-91	36	10	9

MUMFORD Andrew Owen
Born: Neath, Wales, 18 June, 1981 M
Wales: U21-4/Youth/Schools

League Club	Source	Date Signed	Seasons Played	Apps	Subs	Gls
Swansea C	Llanelli	06/00	00-02	47	15	6

MUMFORD Wayne Ernest
Born: Rhymney, Caerphilly, Wales, 3 November, 1964 RB

League Club	Source	Date Signed	Seasons Played	Apps	Subs	Gls
Birmingham C	Manchester C (App)	09/82	82-83	5	2	0

MUNARI Gianni
Born: Sassuolo, Italy, 24 June, 1983 M

League Club	Source	Date Signed	Seasons Played	Apps	Subs	Gls
Watford (L)	Parma (ITA)	08/14	14	21	7	3

MUNCIE William Paul (Bill)
Born: Carluke, Lanarkshire, Scotland, 28 August, 1911 W
Died: Leicester, England, January, 1992

League Club	Source	Date Signed	Seasons Played	Apps	Subs	Gls
Leicester C	Shettleston Jnrs	08/34	34-37	42	-	11
Southend U	Tr	05/38	38	14	-	2
Crewe Alex	Hinckley U	10/46	46	1	-	0

MUNDAY Stuart Clifford
Born: Newham, E London, England, 28 September, 1972 RB

League Club	Source	Date Signed	Seasons Played	Apps	Subs	Gls
Brighton & HA	YT	07/90	91-95	78	17	4

MUNDEE Brian George
Born: Hammersmith, W London, England, 12 January, 1964 LB

League Club	Source	Date Signed	Seasons Played	Apps	Subs	Gls
Bournemouth	Hungerford T	01/82	82	3	1	0
Northampton T	Tr	10/83	83-85	96	4	3
Cambridge U	Tr	03/86	85-86	16	0	1

MUNDEE Dennis William John (Denny)
Born: Swindon, England, 10 October, 1968 M/D

League Club	Source	Date Signed	Seasons Played	Apps	Subs	Gls
Swindon T	Queens Park Rgrs (App)	08/86				
Bournemouth	Salisbury	03/88	88-92	76	24	6
Torquay U	L	09/89	89	9	0	0
Brentford	Tr	08/93	93-95	64	20	16
Brighton & HA	Tr	10/95	95-96	58	3	7

MUNDY Albert Edward
Born: Gosport, Hampshire, England, 12 May, 1926 IF/RH
Died: Portsmouth, England, 30 August, 2002

League Club	Source	Date Signed	Seasons Played	Apps	Subs	Gls
Portsmouth	Gosport Bor	01/51	50-53	51	-	12
Brighton & HA	Tr	11/53	53-57	165	-	87
Aldershot	Tr	02/58	57-60	130	-	12

MUNDY Harold James (Jimmy)
Born: Wythenshawe, Greater Manchester, England, 2 September, 1948 M

League Club	Source	Date Signed	Seasons Played	Apps	Subs	Gls
Manchester C	Ashland Rov	08/66	68-69	2	1	0
Oldham Ath	L	09/70	70	3	5	2

MUNGALL Steven Henry (Steve)
Born: Calderbank, Lanarkshire, Scotland, 22 May, 1958 D/M

League Club	Source	Date Signed	Seasons Played	Apps	Subs	Gls
Tranmere Rov	Motherwell	07/79	79-95	479	34	14

MUNIESA Marc
Born: Lloret de Mar, Spain, 27 March, 1992 LB
Spain: U21-9/Youth

League Club	Source	Date Signed	Seasons Played	Apps	Subs	Gls
Stoke C	Barcelona (SPN)	07/13	13-14	21	11	0

MUNKS David
Born: Sheffield, England, 29 April, 1947 CD
England: Youth

League Club	Source	Date Signed	Seasons Played	Apps	Subs	Gls
Sheffield U	App	08/64	65-68	108	4	1
Portsmouth	Tr	05/69	69-73	132	5	2
Swindon T	Tr	12/73	73-74	21	0	0
Exeter C	Tr	12/74	74-75	20	0	0

MUNRO Alexander (Alex)
Born: Glasgow, Scotland, 3 October, 1944 LH/LB
Died: St Austell, Cornwall, England, 24 May, 2009

League Club	Source	Date Signed	Seasons Played	Apps	Subs	Gls
Bristol Rov	Drumchapel Amats	10/62	62-70	159	9	11

MUNRO Alexander Dewar (Alex)
Born: Bo'ness, Falkirk, Scotland, 6 April, 1912 RW
Died: Blackpool, Lancashire, England, 29 August, 1986
Scotland: 3

League Club	Source	Date Signed	Seasons Played	Apps	Subs	Gls
Blackpool	Heart of Midlothian	03/37	36-48	144	-	17

MUNRO Alexander Iain Fordyce (Iain)
Born: Uddingston, Lanarkshire, Scotland, 24 August, 1951 LB
Scotland: 7/SLge-1

League Club	Source	Date Signed	Seasons Played	Apps	Subs	Gls
Stoke C	St Mirren	10/80	80	32	0	1
Sunderland	Tr	08/81	81-83	80	0	0

MUNRO Francis Michael (Frank)
Born: Broughty Ferry, Angus, Scotland, 25 October, 1947 CD
Died: Wolverhampton, England, 17 August, 2011
Scotland: 9/U23-4

League Club	Source	Date Signed	Seasons Played	Apps	Subs	Gls
Wolverhampton W	Aberdeen	01/68	67-76	290	6	14

MUNRO James Ferguson (Jimmy)
Born: Garmouth, Moray, Scotland, 25 March, 1926 RW
Died: Elgin, Moray, Scotland, 22 June, 1997

League Club	Source	Date Signed	Seasons Played	Apps	Subs	Gls
Manchester C	Waterford (ROI)	11/47	47-49	25	-	4
Oldham Ath	Tr	03/50	49-52	119	-	20

League Club	Source	Date Signed	Seasons Played	Apps	Subs	Gls
Lincoln C	Tr	02/53	52-57	161	-	24
Bury	Tr	01/58	57-58	41	-	7

MUNRO Malcolm George
Born: Melton Mowbray, Leicestershire, England, 21 May, 1953 CD
England: Youth/Schools

League Club	Source	Date Signed	Seasons Played	Apps	Subs	Gls
Leicester C	App	05/70	71-74	69	1	1

MUNRO Roderick Alexander (Roddie)
Born: Inverness, Scotland, 27 July, 1920 LB
Died: Cambridge, England, 1976

League Club	Source	Date Signed	Seasons Played	Apps	Subs	Gls
Brentford	Glasgow Rangers (Am)	05/46	46-52	199	-	0

MUNRO Stuart David
Born: Falkirk, Scotland, 15 September, 1962 LB
Scotland: B-2

League Club	Source	Date Signed	Seasons Played	Apps	Subs	Gls
Blackburn Rov	Glasgow Rangers	08/91	91	1	0	0
Bristol C	Tr	02/93	92-95	91	3	0

MUNRO William Davidson (Bill)
Born: Glasgow, Scotland, 21 June, 1934 IF

League Club	Source	Date Signed	Seasons Played	Apps	Subs	Gls
Barrow	Kilmarnock	06/59	59-60	15	-	2

MUNROE Karl Augustus
Born: Manchester, England, 23 September, 1979 CD

League Club	Source	Date Signed	Seasons Played	Apps	Subs	Gls
Swansea C	YT	07/98	97	0	1	0
Macclesfield T	Tr	10/99	99-03	94	25	1

MUNROE William James (Liam)
Born: Dublin, Republic of Ireland, 28 November, 1933 IF
Republic of Ireland: 1

League Club	Source	Date Signed	Seasons Played	Apps	Subs	Gls
Bristol C	Ards	12/57	57	1	-	0
Scunthorpe U	Tr	07/58				

MUNSON Nathan Wayne
Born: Colchester, Essex, England, 10 November, 1974 G

League Club	Source	Date Signed	Seasons Played	Apps	Subs	Gls
Colchester U	YT	06/93	92-93	3	1	0

MUNTARI Sulley Ali
Born: Konango, Ghana, 27 August, 1984 M
Ghana: 83/Youth

League Club	Source	Date Signed	Seasons Played	Apps	Subs	Gls
Portsmouth	Udinese (ITA)	07/07	07	27	2	4
Sunderland (L)	Inter Milan (ITA)	01/11	10	7	2	1

MURCHISON Ronald Angus (Ron)
Born: Kilmarnock, Ayrshire, Scotland, 12 February, 1927 WH
Died: Cambridgeshire, England, May, 2014

League Club	Source	Date Signed	Seasons Played	Apps	Subs	Gls
Ipswich T	Auchterarder Primrose	06/50	50-54	42	-	2

MURCOTT Stephen (Steve)
Born: Streetly, West Midlands, England, 17 January, 1961 G

League Club	Source	Date Signed	Seasons Played	Apps	Subs	Gls
Coventry C	App	11/78	79	1	0	0

MURDOCH Robert White (Bobby)
Born: Bothwell, Lanarkshire, Scotland, 17 August, 1944 M
Died: Glasgow, Scotland, 14 May, 2001
Scotland: 12/SLge-5/U23-1

League Club	Source	Date Signed	Seasons Played	Apps	Subs	Gls
Middlesbrough	Glasgow Celtic	09/73	73-75	93	2	6

MURDOCH Sean
Born: Edinburgh, Scotland, 31 July, 1986 G
Scotland: Youth

League Club	Source	Date Signed	Seasons Played	Apps	Subs	Gls
Accrington Stan	Hamilton Academical	08/11	11	12	1	0

MURDOCH Stewart
Born: Linlithgow, West Lothian, Scotland, 9 May, 1990 M

League Club	Source	Date Signed	Seasons Played	Apps	Subs	Gls
Fleetwood T	Falkirk	07/13	13-14	30	19	0
Northampton T	L	10/14	14	8	0	1

MURDOCH William Robert (Bobby)
Born: Garston, Merseyside, England, 25 January, 1936 IF

League Club	Source	Date Signed	Seasons Played	Apps	Subs	Gls
Liverpool	South Liverpool	05/57	57-58	17	-	5
Barrow	Tr	05/59	59	41	-	17
Stockport Co	Tr	08/60	60-61	58	-	17
Carlisle U	Tr	01/62	61	10	-	2
Southport	Tr	07/62	62	33	-	10

MURDOCK Colin James
Born: Ballymena, Antrim, Northern Ireland, 2 July, 1975 CD
Northern Ireland: 34/B-3/Youth/Schools

League Club	Source	Date Signed	Seasons Played	Apps	Subs	Gls
Manchester U	YT	07/92				
Preston NE	Tr	05/97	97-02	163	14	6
Crewe Alex	Hibernian	01/05	04	15	1	0
Rotherham U	Tr	07/05	05-06	43	0	2
Shrewsbury T	Tr	08/07	07	29	0	2
Accrington Stan	Tr	08/08	08	20	3	1

MURFIN Andrew John
Born: Doncaster, South Yorkshire, England, 26 November, 1976 LB

League Club	Source	Date Signed	Seasons Played	Apps	Subs	Gls
Scunthorpe U	Jnr	09/95	95	1	0	0

MURPHY Aidan
Born: Manchester, England, 17 September, 1967 M
England: Youth/Schools

League Club	Source	Date Signed	Seasons Played	Apps	Subs	Gls
Manchester U	App	09/84				
Lincoln C	L	10/86	86	2	0	0
Crewe Alex	Tr	05/87	87-91	94	19	13
Scarborough	Tr	08/92	92	7	1	0

MURPHY Andrew Colin (Andy)
Born: Preston, Lancashire, England, 18 October, 1966 M

League Club	Source	Date Signed	Seasons Played	Apps	Subs	Gls
Preston NE	App	07/84	83-84	9	1	0

MURPHY Bernard Anthony Paul (Ben)
Born: Dublin, Republic of Ireland, 19 November, 1947 IF

League Club	Source	Date Signed	Seasons Played	Apps	Subs	Gls
Torquay U	App	11/65	64-66	6	0	0

MURPHY Brian
Born: Waterford, Republic of Ireland, 7 May, 1983 G
Republic of Ireland: U21-3/Youth

League Club	Source	Date Signed	Seasons Played	Apps	Subs	Gls
Manchester C	YT	05/00				
Peterborough U	L	05/03	02	1	0	0
Swansea C	Waterford (ROI)	08/03	03-04	13	0	0
Ipswich T	Bohemians (ROI)	01/10	09-10	20	0	0
Queens Park Rgrs	Tr	08/11	13	1	1	0

MURPHY Christopher Patrick (Chris)
Born: Leamington Spa, Warwickshire, England, 8 March, 1983 M

League Club	Source	Date Signed	Seasons Played	Apps	Subs	Gls
Shrewsbury T	Sch	07/02	00-02	0	8	0
Cheltenham T	Telford U	07/04	04	0	4	0

MURPHY Daniel (Danny)
Born: Burtonwood, Cheshire, England, 10 May, 1922 LH
Died: Warrington, Cheshire, England, June, 2001

League Club	Source	Date Signed	Seasons Played	Apps	Subs	Gls
Bolton W	Burtonwood Ath	02/43	46-50	66	-	1
Crewe Alex	Tr	01/52	51-53	107	-	1
Rochdale	Tr	07/54	54-56	109	-	0

MURPHY Daniel Benjamin (Danny)
Born: Chester, England, 18 March, 1977 M
England: 9/U21-4/Youth/Schools

League Club	Source	Date Signed	Seasons Played	Apps	Subs	Gls
Crewe Alex	YT	03/94	93-96	110	24	27
Liverpool	Tr	07/97	97-03	114	56	25
Crewe Alex	L	02/99	98	16	0	1
Charlton Ath	Tr	08/04	04-05	54	2	7
Tottenham H	Tr	01/06	05-06	7	15	1
Fulham	Tr	08/07	07-11	161	8	17
Blackburn Rov	Tr	07/12	12	31	2	1

MURPHY Daniel Thomas (Danny)
Born: Southwark, S London, England, 4 December, 1982 LB
Republic of Ireland: Youth

League Club	Source	Date Signed	Seasons Played	Apps	Subs	Gls
Queens Park Rgrs	YT	12/99	01-02	14	9	0

MURPHY Darren
Born: Cork, Republic of Ireland, 28 July, 1985 M

League Club	Source	Date Signed	Seasons Played	Apps	Subs	Gls
Stevenage	Cork C (ROI)	01/09	10	1	4	0
Aldershot T	L	02/12	11	2	1	0
Port Vale	Tr	07/12	12	1	2	0

MURPHY Daryl
Born: Waterford, Republic of Ireland, 15 March, 1983 F
Republic of Ireland: 14/U21-4

League Club	Source	Date Signed	Seasons Played	Apps	Subs	Gls
Luton T	Jnr	11/00				
Sunderland	Waterford U (ROI)	06/05	05-09	60	50	14
Sheffield Wed	L	11/05	05	4	0	0
Ipswich T	L	02/10	09	18	0	6
Ipswich T (L)	Glasgow Celtic	08/11	11	31	2	4
Ipswich T	Glasgow Celtic	08/12	12-14	117	11	47

MURPHY David Paul
Born: Hartlepool, Cleveland, England, 1 March, 1984 LB
England: Youth

League Club	Source	Date Signed	Seasons Played	Apps	Subs	Gls
Middlesbrough	YT	07/01	01-02	4	9	0
Barnsley	L	03/04	03	10	0	2
Birmingham C	Hibernian	01/08	07-13	94	12	7

MURPHY Donal Patrick
Born: Dublin, Republic of Ireland, 23 February, 1955 LW

League Club	Source	Date Signed	Seasons Played	Apps	Subs	Gls
Coventry C	App	08/72	75-77	33	10	10
Millwall	L	10/77	77	3	0	0
Torquay U	Tr	05/78	78-79	81	4	20
Plymouth Arg	Tr	06/80	80-81	44	4	9
Torquay U	L	12/81	81	2	1	0
Blackburn Rov	Tr	02/82	81	1	2	0

MURPHY Edward (Eddie)
Born: Hamilton, Lanarkshire, Scotland, 13 May, 1924 IF
Died: Bridgwater, Somerset, England, 28 January, 2009

League Club	Source	Date Signed	Seasons Played	Apps	Subs	Gls
Northampton T	Greenock Morton	06/49	49-50	71	-	15

League Club	Source	Date Signed	Seasons Played	Career Record Apps	Subs	Gls
Barnsley	Tr	03/51	50-51	18	-	2
Exeter C	Tr	06/52	52-55	94	-	13
MURPHY Edward Cullinane (Eddie)						
Born: Glasgow, Scotland, 1 June, 1934						CH
Oldham Ath	Clyde	05/56	56-58	72	-	0
MURPHY Francis (Frank)						
Born: Glasgow, Scotland, 1 June, 1959						F
Barnet	Kettering T	08/88	91	3	12	5
MURPHY Francis John (John)						
Born: Edinburgh, Scotland, 16 August, 1949						M
Notts Co	Edina Hearts	08/67	67-68	17	2	2
MURPHY George						
Born: Cwmfelinfach, Caerphilly, Wales, 22 July, 1915						CF
Died: Ardsley, South Yorkshire, England, December, 1983						
Wales: War-2						
Bradford C	Cwmfelinfach Colts	11/34	34-47	180	-	43
Hull C	Tr	12/47	47	15	-	9
MURPHY Jacob						
Born: Wembley, NW London, England, 24 February, 1995						W
England: Youth						
Norwich C	Sch	01/13				
Swindon T	L	02/14	13	2	4	0
Southend U	L	03/14	13	4	3	1
Blackpool	L	11/14	14	8	1	2
Scunthorpe U	L	01/15	14	3	0	0
Colchester U	L	03/15	14	11	0	4
MURPHY James (Jamie)						
Born: Islington, N London, England, 17 November, 1971						M
Aldershot	Leyton Orient (YT)	07/90	90	1	2	0
MURPHY James (Jamie)						
Born: Glasgow, Scotland, 28 August, 1989						W
Scotland: U21-13/Youth						
Sheffield U	Motherwell	01/13	12-14	81	13	17
MURPHY James Anthony (Jamie)						
Born: Manchester, England, 25 February, 1973						CD
Blackpool	Jnr	08/90	92-94	48	7	1
Doncaster Rov	Tr	09/95	95-96	47	7	0
Halifax T	Tr	03/97	98	21	2	1
MURPHY James Baird (Jim)						
Born: Glasgow, Scotland, 29 November, 1942						IF
Notts Co	Raith Rov	02/68	67-68	33	0	7
MURPHY Jeremiah Michael (Jerry)						
Born: Stepney, E London, England, 23 September, 1959						M
England: Schools//Republic of Ireland: 3						
Crystal Palace	App	10/76	76-84	214	15	20
Chelsea	Tr	08/85	85-87	34	0	3
MURPHY John James						
Born: St Helens, Merseyside, England, 18 October, 1976						F
Chester C	YT	07/95	94-98	65	38	20
Blackpool	Tr	08/99	99-05	229	23	83
Macclesfield T	Tr	10/06	06	25	4	7
Chester C	Tr	07/07	07	39	0	9
MURPHY John William (Bill)						
Born: Birstall, West Yorkshire, England, 21 November, 1921						WH
Died: Bodmin, Cornwall, England, October, 2004						
Bradford C	Liverpool (Am)	09/46	46-51	144	-	9
MURPHY Jordan						
Born: Birmingham, England, 5 June, 1996						F
Walsall	Stourbridge	09/14	14	0	2	0
MURPHY Joseph (Joe)						
Born: Dublin, Republic of Ireland, 21 August, 1981						G
Republic of Ireland: 2/U21-14/Youth						
Tranmere Rov	YT	07/99	99-01	61	2	0
West Bromwich A	Tr	07/02	02-03	3	2	0
Walsall	L	10/04	04	25	0	0
Sunderland	Tr	08/05				
Walsall	L	10/05	05	14	0	0
Scunthorpe U	Tr	07/06	06-10	201	0	0
Coventry C	Tr	07/11	11-13	137	0	0
Huddersfield T	Tr	06/14	14	2	0	0
MURPHY Joseph Patrick						
Born: Waterford, Republic of Ireland, 30 March, 1924						FB
Brighton & HA	Shelbourne (ROI)	02/48				
Crystal Palace	Shelbourne (ROI)	02/49	48-50	37	-	0

League Club	Source	Date Signed	Seasons Played	Career Record Apps	Subs	Gls
MURPHY Joshua (Josh)						
Born: Wembley, NW London, England, 24 February, 1995						LW
England: Youth						
Norwich C	Sch	01/13	13-14	1	21	1
Wigan Ath	L	03/15	14	2	3	0
MURPHY Kieran Thomas						
Born: Kingston-on-Thames, SW London, England, 31 December, 1987						CD
Republic of Ireland: U21-2						
MK Dons	Sch	07/06	07	1	2	0
MURPHY Laurence Barry (Barry)						
Born: Consett, County Durham, England, 10 February, 1940						RB
Barnsley	South Shields	07/62	62-77	509	5	3
MURPHY Luke John						
Born: Alsager, Cheshire, England, 21 October, 1989						M
Crewe Alex	Sch	05/08	08-12	140	21	21
Leeds U	Tr	07/13	13-14	63	4	6
MURPHY Marcus Montagu						
Born: Tavistock, Devon, England, 16 November, 1914						IF
Died: Wisbech, Cambridgeshire, England, August, 2007						
Plymouth Arg	Plymouth U	08/46	46-47	15	-	1
MURPHY Matthew Simon (Matt)						
Born: Northampton, England, 20 August, 1971						M/F
Oxford U	Corby T	02/93	92-00	168	78	38
Scunthorpe U	L	12/97	97	1	2	0
Bury	Tr	08/01	01	5	4	0
Swansea C	Tr	07/02	02	9	3	2
MURPHY Michael (Mike)						
Born: Reading, England, 15 April, 1939						G
Reading (Am)	Thorneycroft Ath	04/58	57	1	-	0
MURPHY Michael John (Mick)						
Born: Slough, Berkshire, England, 5 May, 1977						F
Reading	Jnr	10/94	94	0	1	0
MURPHY Neil Anthony						
Born: Liverpool, England, 19 May, 1980						RB
England: Youth						
Liverpool	YT	10/97				
Blackpool	Tr	07/00	00-01	4	3	0
MURPHY Nicholas Michael (Nick)						
Born: West Bromwich, West Midlands, England, 25 December, 1946						M
Manchester U	Jnr	02/66				
Reading	Tr	07/70	70	3	1	0
MURPHY Patrick (Pat)						
Born: Merthyr Tydfil, Wales, 19 December, 1947						WH
Cardiff C	App	12/65	65	0	1	0
MURPHY Paul						
Born: Ashington, Northumberland, England, 16 March, 1954						F
Rotherham U	Ashington	02/72	73	1	0	0
Workington	L	08/73	73	10	2	1
MURPHY Peter						
Born: Hartlepool, Cleveland, England, 7 March, 1922						IF
Died: Coventry, England, 7 April, 1975						
Coventry C	Dunlop	05/46	46-49	115	-	37
Tottenham H	Tr	06/50	50-51	38	-	14
Birmingham C	Tr	01/52	51-59	245	-	107
MURPHY Peter James						
Born: Liverpool, England, 13 February, 1990						M/CD
Accrington Stan	Sch	08/08	07-13	134	21	18
Wycombe W	Tr	07/14	14	32	10	7
MURPHY Peter Michael						
Born: Dublin, Republic of Ireland, 27 October, 1980						CD
Republic of Ireland: 1/U21-2/Youth						
Blackburn Rov	YT	07/98				
Halifax T	L	10/00	00	18	3	1
Carlisle U	Tr	08/01	01-12	346	28	15
MURPHY Philip (Phil)						
Born: Liverpool, England, 21 November, 1960						F
Blackpool	CD Nacional (POR)	09/84	84	1	7	0
Burnley	Witton A	11/86	86	12	3	5
MURPHY Rhys Philip Elliot						
Born: Shoreham-by-Sea, West Sussex, England, 6 November, 1990						F
England: Youth						
Arsenal	Sch	07/08				
Brentford	L	11/09	09	1	4	0
Preston NE	L	01/12	11	1	4	0

League Club	Source	Date Signed	Seasons Played	Apps	Subs	Gls
Dagenham & Red	Telstar (NED)	07/13	13-14	38	3	14
Oldham Ath	Tr	02/15	14	3	8	0

MURPHY Shaun Peter
Born: Sydney, Australia, 5 November, 1970 CD
Australia: 18/U23/Youth

League Club	Source	Date Signed	Seasons Played	Apps	Subs	Gls
Notts Co	Perth Italia (AUS)	09/92	92-96	100	9	5
West Bromwich A	Tr	12/96	96-98	60	11	7
Sheffield U	Tr	07/99	99-02	157	1	10
Crystal Palace	L	02/02	01	11	0	0

MURPHY Stephen
Born: Dublin, Republic of Ireland, 5 April, 1978 M/D
Republic of Ireland: Youth

League Club	Source	Date Signed	Seasons Played	Apps	Subs	Gls
Huddersfield T	Belvedere (ROI)	05/95				
Halifax T	Tr	08/98	98-99	20	7	1

MURPHY Terence (Terry)
Born: Liverpool, England, 14 January, 1940 WH

League Club	Source	Date Signed	Seasons Played	Apps	Subs	Gls
Crewe Alex	Northwch Victoria	09/61	61	1	-	0

MURPHY Thomas Edwin (Eddie)
Born: South Bank, Cleveland, England, 25 March, 1921 IF
Died: Middlesbrough, England, 27 January, 2003

League Club	Source	Date Signed	Seasons Played	Apps	Subs	Gls
Middlesbrough	South Bank St Peter's	05/39	46-47	9	-	1
Blackburn Rov	Tr	12/47	47-48	31	-	6
Halifax T	Tr	03/49	48-53	217	-	29

MURPHY William Robinson (Billy)
Born: Barrhead, Renfrewshire, Scotland, 22 March, 1928 W

League Club	Source	Date Signed	Seasons Played	Apps	Subs	Gls
Exeter C	Stirling A	11/49	49	2	-	0
Bristol Rov	Tr	07/50	50	3	-	0

MURRAY Adam David
Born: Birmingham, England, 30 September, 1981 M
England: Youth

League Club	Source	Date Signed	Seasons Played	Apps	Subs	Gls
Derby Co	YT	10/98	98-02	25	31	0
Mansfield T	L	02/02	01	13	0	7
Kidderminster Hrs	L	08/03	03	3	0	0
Notts Co	Burton A	11/03	03	1	2	0
Kidderminster Hrs	Tr	01/04	03	16	3	3
Mansfield T	Tr	07/04	04	27	5	5
Carlisle U	Tr	03/05	05	29	8	1
Torquay U	Tr	08/06	06	21	0	0
Macclesfield T	Tr	01/07	06-07	30	4	0
Mansfield T	Luton T	10/10	13-14	27	5	2

MURRAY Alan
Born: Newcastle-upon-Tyne, England, 5 November, 1949 M

League Club	Source	Date Signed	Seasons Played	Apps	Subs	Gls
Middlesbrough	Wolverhampton W (App)	09/67	69-70	6	4	1
York C	L	01/72	71	4	0	0
Brentford	Tr	06/72	72	42	3	7
Doncaster Rov	Tr	07/73	73-76	133	13	21

MURRAY Alastair (Ally)
Born: Longtown, Cumbria, England, 22 December, 1943 IF

League Club	Source	Date Signed	Seasons Played	Apps	Subs	Gls
Sunderland	Jnr	01/61				
Barnsley	Tr	07/63	63	21	-	1
Carlisle U	Tr	07/64				
Hartlepool U	Tr	08/65				

MURRAY Albert George (Bert)
Born: Hoxton, Central London, England, 22 September, 1942 W
England: U23-6/Youth/Schools

League Club	Source	Date Signed	Seasons Played	Apps	Subs	Gls
Chelsea	Jnr	05/61	61-65	156	4	39
Birmingham C	Tr	08/66	66-70	126	6	22
Brighton & HA	Tr	02/71	70-73	99	3	25
Peterborough U	Tr	09/73	73-75	123	0	10

MURRAY Alexander James (Jimmy)
Born: Thornton, Lancashire, England, 4 February, 1945 W

League Club	Source	Date Signed	Seasons Played	Apps	Subs	Gls
Southport	Burscough	07/65	64	3	-	0

MURRAY Antonio James
Born: Cambridge, England, 15 September, 1984 M/F

League Club	Source	Date Signed	Seasons Played	Apps	Subs	Gls
Ipswich T	Sch	07/03	02	0	1	0

MURRAY Bruce Edward
Born: Germantown, Maryland, USA, 25 January, 1966 F
USA: 85

League Club	Source	Date Signed	Seasons Played	Apps	Subs	Gls
Millwall	US Soccer Fed (USA)	08/93	93	7	6	2
Stockport Co	L	03/94	93	2	1	0

MURRAY Daniel (Dan)
Born: Cambridge, England, 16 May, 1982 CD

League Club	Source	Date Signed	Seasons Played	Apps	Subs	Gls
Peterborough U	YT	03/00	99-00	3	2	0

MURRAY David Robert
Born: Chorley, Lancashire, England, 30 September, 1967 F

League Club	Source	Date Signed	Seasons Played	Apps	Subs	Gls
Chester C	Wigan Ath (Jnr)	09/85	85	3	3	1

MURRAY Dennis Patrick
Born: Stoke-on-Trent, England, 11 June, 1932 G
Died: Stoke-on-Trent, England, 2 October, 2006

League Club	Source	Date Signed	Seasons Played	Apps	Subs	Gls
Crewe Alex	Jnr	10/50	51	2	-	0

MURRAY Donald James (Don)
Born: Duffus, Moray, Scotland, 18 January, 1946 CD
Scotland: U23-1

League Club	Source	Date Signed	Seasons Played	Apps	Subs	Gls
Cardiff C	Burghead Thistle	01/63	62-74	406	0	6
Swansea C	L	10/74	74	5	0	0
Newport Co	Heart of Midlothian	10/76	76	16	2	0

MURRAY Edward James (Eddie)
Born: Crosby, Merseyside, England, 10 July, 1962 LW

League Club	Source	Date Signed	Seasons Played	Apps	Subs	Gls
Tranmere Rov	Stork	08/87	87-88	11	16	1

MURRAY Edwin John (Eddie)
Born: Ilford, E London, England, 31 August, 1973 D

League Club	Source	Date Signed	Seasons Played	Apps	Subs	Gls
Swindon T	YT	07/91	90-95	7	5	1

MURRAY Frederick Anthony (Fred)
Born: Clonmel, Republic of Ireland, 22 May, 1982 LB
Republic of Ireland: Youth

League Club	Source	Date Signed	Seasons Played	Apps	Subs	Gls
Blackburn Rov	YT	05/99				
Cambridge U	Tr	12/01	01-03	80	8	0
Northampton T	Tr	07/04	04	38	0	0
Exeter C	Stevenage Bor	09/08	08	3	3	0

MURRAY Glenn
Born: Maryport, Cumbria, England, 25 September, 1983 F

League Club	Source	Date Signed	Seasons Played	Apps	Subs	Gls
Carlisle U	Barrow	12/04	05-06	3	24	3
Stockport Co	L	08/06	06	11	0	3
Rochdale	Tr	10/06	06-07	50	4	25
Brighton & HA	Tr	01/08	07-10	101	17	54
Crystal Palace	Tr	07/11	11-14	79	32	44
Reading	L	09/14	14	18	0	8

MURRAY Hugh
Born: Dreghorn, Ayrshire, Scotland, 3 August, 1936 W

League Club	Source	Date Signed	Seasons Played	Apps	Subs	Gls
Manchester C	Dalry Thistle	04/55	55	1	-	0

MURRAY Ian David (David)
Born: Otterburn, Northumberland, England, 11 July, 1949 F

League Club	Source	Date Signed	Seasons Played	Apps	Subs	Gls
Workington	Corbridge U	03/74	73-75	79	3	22

MURRAY Ian William
Born: Edinburgh, Scotland, 20 March, 1981 DM
Scotland: 6/U21-15

League Club	Source	Date Signed	Seasons Played	Apps	Subs	Gls
Norwich C	Glasgow Rangers	08/07	07	8	1	0

MURRAY Ivan Hugh
Born: Ballymoney, Antrim, Northern Ireland, 29 May, 1944 LH
Northern Ireland: NILge-2

League Club	Source	Date Signed	Seasons Played	Apps	Subs	Gls
Fulham	Coleraine	02/68	67-68	4	1	0

MURRAY Jade Alan (Jay)
Born: Islington, N London, England, 23 September, 1981 F

League Club	Source	Date Signed	Seasons Played	Apps	Subs	Gls
Leyton Orient	YT	07/00	99	0	2	0

MURRAY James
Born: Motherwell, Lanarkshire, Scotland, 13 July, 1922 FB
Died: Yeovil, Somerset, England, February, 1998

League Club	Source	Date Signed	Seasons Played	Apps	Subs	Gls
Exeter C	Shawfield Jnrs	08/45	46	1	-	0

MURRAY James (Jimmy)
Born: Edinburgh, Scotland, 4 February, 1933 IF
Died: 10 July, 2015

League Club	Source	Date Signed	Seasons Played	Apps	Subs	Gls
Reading	Heart of Midlothian	02/54	53-54	7	-	3

MURRAY James Gerald (Jamie)
Born: Ayr, Scotland, 27 December, 1958 LB

League Club	Source	Date Signed	Seasons Played	Apps	Subs	Gls
Cambridge U	Rivet Spts, Aylesbury	09/76	76-83	213	16	3
Sunderland	L	03/84	83	1	0	0
Brentford	Tr	07/84	84-87	134	0	3
Cambridge U	Tr	09/87	87	13	0	0

MURRAY James Robert (Jimmy)
Born: Elvington, Kent, England, 11 October, 1935 CF
Died: Lichfield, Staffordshire, England, 27 September, 2008
England: FLge-1/U23-2

League Club	Source	Date Signed	Seasons Played	Apps	Subs	Gls
Wolverhampton W	Jnr	11/53	55-63	273	-	155
Manchester C	Tr	11/63	63-66	70	0	43
Walsall	Tr	05/67	66-68	53	4	13

MURRAY James William (Jimmy)
Born: Lambeth, S London, England, 16 March, 1935 IF
Died: Southwark, S London, England, 27 May, 2002

League Club	Source	Date Signed	Seasons Played	Apps	Subs	Gls
Crystal Palace	Jnr	07/55	55-57	37	-	13
Walsall	Tr	01/58	57-58	14	-	2

MURRAY John
Born: Newcastle-upon-Tyne, England, 2 March, 1948 RW/F

League Club	Source	Date Signed	Seasons Played	Apps	Subs	Gls
Burnley	Jnr	03/65	66-69	20	2	6
Blackpool	Tr	03/70	69-70	6	3	1
Bury	Tr	02/71	70-73	117	9	37
Reading	Tr	08/74	74-77	123	8	44
Brentford	Tr	02/78	77	2	3	1

MURRAY John Anthony
Born: Saltcoats, Ayrshire, Scotland, 5 February, 1949 FB

League Club	Source	Date Signed	Seasons Played	Apps	Subs	Gls
Cambridge U	Greenock Morton	07/71	71	3	0	0

MURRAY John George
Born: Lambeth, S London, England, 15 July, 1927 LB

League Club	Source	Date Signed	Seasons Played	Apps	Subs	Gls
Leyton Orient	Chelmsford C	08/49				
Gillingham	Sittingbourne	06/51	51	4	-	0

MURRAY John McCann
Born: Glasgow, Scotland, 9 March, 1945 LB
Died: Glasgow, Scotland, 3 October, 1997

League Club	Source	Date Signed	Seasons Played	Apps	Subs	Gls
Lincoln C	Stirling A	11/66	66	4	0	0

MURRAY Joseph Ernest (Joey)
Born: Liverpool, England, 5 November, 1971 M
England: Schools

League Club	Source	Date Signed	Seasons Played	Apps	Subs	Gls
Wrexham	Marine	03/91	90	11	0	0

MURRAY Karl Anthony
Born: Islington, N London, England, 24 June, 1982 M

League Club	Source	Date Signed	Seasons Played	Apps	Subs	Gls
Shrewsbury T	YT	02/00	99-02	77	32	5

MURRAY Kenneth (Ken)
Born: Darlington, County Durham, England, 2 April, 1928 IF
Died: Newcastle-upon-Tyne, England, 8 January, 1993

League Club	Source	Date Signed	Seasons Played	Apps	Subs	Gls
Darlington	Bishop Auckland	07/50	50-52	70	-	19
Mansfield T	Tr	07/53	53-56	140	-	60
Oldham Ath	Tr	03/57	56-57	35	-	14
Wrexham	Tr	02/58	57-58	32	-	10
Gateshead	Yeovil T	08/59	59	18	-	6

MURRAY Leslie (Les)
Born: Kinghorn, Fife, Scotland, 29 September, 1928 IF
Died: Blairgowrie, Perthshire, Scotland, 7 January, 1993

League Club	Source	Date Signed	Seasons Played	Apps	Subs	Gls
Rochdale	Arbroath	05/52	52	16	-	3

MURRAY Malcolm
Born: Buckie, Moray, Scotland, 26 July, 1964 RB

League Club	Source	Date Signed	Seasons Played	Apps	Subs	Gls
Hull C	Heart of Midlothian	03/89	88-89	9	2	0
Mansfield T	Tr	12/89	89-91	56	3	0

MURRAY Mark
Born: Manchester, England, 13 June, 1973 FB

League Club	Source	Date Signed	Seasons Played	Apps	Subs	Gls
Blackpool	Jnr	10/90	91-92	3	0	0

MURRAY Matthew (Matt)
Born: Paisley, Renfrewshire, Scotland, 25 December, 1929 LW

League Club	Source	Date Signed	Seasons Played	Apps	Subs	Gls
Barrow	St Mirren	08/58	58	33	-	2
Carlisle U	Tr	07/59	59	28	-	4

MURRAY Matthew William (Matt)
Born: Solihull, West Midlands, England, 2 May, 1981 G
England: U21-5/Youth

League Club	Source	Date Signed	Seasons Played	Apps	Subs	Gls
Wolverhampton W	YT	05/98	02-06	87	0	0
Tranmere Rov	L	03/06	05	2	0	0
Hereford U	L	11/08	08	3	0	0

MURRAY Maxwell (Max)
Born: Falkirk, Scotland, 7 November, 1935 CF
Scotland: U23-2/Amateur

League Club	Source	Date Signed	Seasons Played	Apps	Subs	Gls
West Bromwich A	Glasgow Rangers	11/62	62	3	-	0

MURRAY Neil Andrew
Born: Bellshill, Lanarkshire, Scotland, 21 February, 1973 M
Scotland: U21-16/Schools

League Club	Source	Date Signed	Seasons Played	Apps	Subs	Gls
Grimsby T (L)	FSV Mainz 05 (GER)	11/00	00	1	1	0

MURRAY Paul
Born: Carlisle, Cumbria, England, 31 August, 1976 M
England: B-1/U21-4/Youth

League Club	Source	Date Signed	Seasons Played	Apps	Subs	Gls
Carlisle U	YT	06/94	93-95	27	14	1
Queens Park Rgrs	Tr	03/96	95-00	115	25	7
Southampton	Tr	08/01	01	0	1	0
Oldham Ath	Tr	12/01	01-03	93	2	15
Carlisle U	Beira Mar (POR)	05/06	06	14	0	1
Shrewsbury T	Gretna	08/08	08-09	56	3	2
Hartlepool U	Tr	08/10	10-12	95	3	2
Oldham Ath	Tr	01/13				

MURRAY Robert James (Rob)
Born: Hammersmith, W London, England, 21 October, 1974 CD/F
Scotland: U21-1

League Club	Source	Date Signed	Seasons Played	Apps	Subs	Gls
Bournemouth	YT	01/93	92-97	88	59	12

MURRAY Robert Law (Bob)
Born: Kemnay, Aberdeenshire, Scotland, 24 April, 1932 D

League Club	Source	Date Signed	Seasons Played	Apps	Subs	Gls
Stockport Co	Inverurie Loco	11/51	52-62	465	-	32

MURRAY Ronan Michael
Born: Ennis, Republic of Ireland, 12 September, 1991 F
Republic of Ireland: U21-1/Youth

League Club	Source	Date Signed	Seasons Played	Apps	Subs	Gls
Ipswich T	Sch	07/10	10-12	1	8	0
Torquay U	L	03/11	10	4	3	1
Swindon T	L	11/11	11	9	11	3
Plymouth Arg	L	01/13	12	6	7	1
Notts Co	Tr	08/13	13-14	22	22	8

MURRAY Scott George
Born: Fraserburgh, Aberdeenshire, Scotland, 26 May, 1974 RW
Scotland: B-2

League Club	Source	Date Signed	Seasons Played	Apps	Subs	Gls
Aston Villa	Fraserburgh	03/94	95-96	4	0	0
Bristol C	Tr	12/97	97-02	193	31	46
Reading	Tr	07/03	03	25	9	5
Bristol C	Tr	03/04	03-08	91	39	28
Cheltenham T	L	09/08	08	12	1	2
Yeovil T	Tr	07/09	09	10	10	2

MURRAY Sean Michael
Born: Watford, Hertfordshire, England, 11 October, 1993 M
Republic of Ireland: U21-11/Youth

League Club	Source	Date Signed	Seasons Played	Apps	Subs	Gls
Watford	Sch	10/10	10-14	50	25	11

MURRAY Shaun
Born: Newcastle-upon-Tyne, England, 7 February, 1970 M
England: Youth/Schools

League Club	Source	Date Signed	Seasons Played	Apps	Subs	Gls
Tottenham H	YT	12/87				
Portsmouth	Tr	06/89	90-92	21	13	1
Scarborough	Tr	11/93	93	29	0	5
Bradford C	Tr	08/94	94-97	105	25	8
Notts Co	Tr	08/98	98-00	43	12	3

MURRAY Steven
Born: Kilmarnock, Ayrshire, Scotland, 1 December, 1967 M
Scotland: Youth

League Club	Source	Date Signed	Seasons Played	Apps	Subs	Gls
Nottingham F	App	04/85				
York C	L	09/86	86	2	1	0

MURRAY Terence (Terry)
Born: Dublin, Republic of Ireland, 22 May, 1928 IF
Republic of Ireland: 1/LoI-6

League Club	Source	Date Signed	Seasons Played	Apps	Subs	Gls
Hull C	Dundalk (ROI)	10/51	51-53	32	-	6
Bournemouth	Tr	03/54	53-54	13	-	1

MURRAY Thomas (Tommy)
Born: Airdrie, Lanarkshire, Scotland, 5 February, 1933 RW

League Club	Source	Date Signed	Seasons Played	Apps	Subs	Gls
Darlington	Headington U	06/56	56	3	-	0

MURRAY Thomas (Tommy)
Born: Bellshill, Lanarkshire, Scotland, 14 January, 1933 W

League Club	Source	Date Signed	Seasons Played	Apps	Subs	Gls
Leeds U	Queen of the South	08/60	60	7	-	2
Tranmere Rov	Tr	03/61	60-61	10	-	1

MURRAY Thomas (Tommy)
Born: Caldercruix, Lanarkshire, Scotland, 1 June, 1943 F

League Club	Source	Date Signed	Seasons Played	Apps	Subs	Gls
Carlisle U	Airdrieonians	03/67	66-70	123	11	38

MURRAY Thomas Alec (Tom)
Born: Barrow, Cumbria, England, 16 October, 1944 RB

League Club	Source	Date Signed	Seasons Played	Apps	Subs	Gls
Barrow	Jnr	07/64	63-64	8	-	0

MURRAY William Joseph (Billy)
Born: Burnley, Lancashire, England, 26 January, 1922 WH
Died: Stockport, Greater Manchester, England, October, 1992

League Club	Source	Date Signed	Seasons Played	Apps	Subs	Gls
Manchester C	Arbroath	01/47	46-49	20	-	1

MURTAGH Conall Francis
Born: Belfast, Northern Ireland, 29 June, 1985 W

League Club	Source	Date Signed	Seasons Played	Apps	Subs	Gls
Wrexham	Rhyl	07/07	07	3	1	0

MURTAGH Kieran Zac
Born: Wapping, E London, England, 29 October, 1988 M
Antigua & Barbuda: 14//Republic of Ireland: Youth

League Club	Source	Date Signed	Seasons Played	Apps	Subs	Gls
Yeovil T	Fisher Ath	07/08	08-09	29	24	3
Wycombe W	Tr	07/10	10	1	6	0
Mansfield T	Macclesfield T	06/13	13	2	1	0

MURTY Graeme Stuart
Born: Saltburn, Cleveland, England, 13 November, 1974 RB
Scotland: 4/B-1

League Club	Source	Date Signed	Seasons Played	Apps	Subs	Gls
York C	YT	03/93	93-97	106	11	7
Reading	Tr	07/98	98-07	295	11	2

League Club	Source	Date Signed	Seasons Played	Career Record Apps	Subs	Gls
Charlton Ath	L	01/09	08	8	0	0
Southampton	Tr	08/09	09	5	1	0
MURTY Joseph Dougan (Joe)						
Born: Glasgow, Scotland, 6 November, 1957						RW
Rochdale	App	11/75	74-75	15	5	2
Bury	Prestwich Heys	11/77	77	0	1	0
MUSAMPA Kizito (Kiki)						
Born: Kinshasa, DR Congo, 20 July, 1977						LW
Netherlands: U21-25/Youth						
Manchester C (L)	Atletico Madrid (SPN)	01/05	04-05	38	3	3
MUSCAT Kevin Vincent						
Born: Crawley, West Sussex, England, 7 August, 1973						RB
Australia: 46/U23-15/Youth						
Crystal Palace	South Melbourne (AUS)	08/96	96-97	51	2	2
Wolverhampton W	Tr	10/97	97-01	178	2	14
Millwall	Glasgow Rangers	08/03	03-04	52	1	0
MUSGRAVE David (Dave)						
Born: South Shields, Tyne and Wear, England, 20 April, 1928						LW
Died: Lancashire, England, September, 2009						
Manchester U	Hordens (RSA)	12/47				
New Brighton	Fleetwood	08/50	50	35	-	2
Preston NE	Tr	08/51				
Southport	Tr	10/51	51-52	52	-	7
Accrington Stan	Tr	09/53	53	30	-	7
MUSGROVE Malcolm Clarke						
Born: Lynemouth, Northumberland, England, 8 July, 1933						LW
Died: Torbay, Devon, England, 14 September, 2007						
West Ham U	Lynemouth Welfare	12/53	53-62	283	-	84
Leyton Orient	Tr	12/62	62-65	83	0	14
MUSGROVE Martin						
Born: Wanstead, NE London, England, 21 November, 1961						M
Torquay U	Heavitree U	03/82	81	1	1	0
MUSIAL Adam						
Born: Wielicza, Poland, 18 December, 1948						CD
Poland: 34						
Hereford U	Arka Gdynia (POL)	08/80	80-82	44	2	0
MUSKER Russell						
Born: Liverpool, England, 10 July, 1962						M/W
Bristol C	App	08/79	80-83	44	2	1
Exeter C	L	10/83	83	6	0	0
Gillingham	Tr	11/83	83-85	54	10	7
Torquay U	Tr	08/86	86-87	36	9	0
Torquay U	Dawlish T	07/90	90	20	1	1
Walsall	Tr	08/91	91	3	0	0
MUSSELWHITE Paul Stephen						
Born: Portsmouth, England, 22 December, 1968						G
Portsmouth	App	12/86				
Scunthorpe U	Tr	03/88	88-91	132	0	0
Port Vale	Tr	07/92	92-99	312	0	0
Hull C	Tr	09/00	00-03	94	1	0
Scunthorpe U	Tr	08/04	04-05	74	0	0
Lincoln C	Gateshead	08/09	10	0	1	0
MUSSON Ian Samuel						
Born: Lincoln, England, 13 December, 1953						W
Sheffield Wed	App	02/71				
Lincoln C	Tr	07/73	73	11	0	0
MUSSON Walter Urban (Chick)						
Born: Kilburn, Derbyshire, England, 8 October, 1920						LH
Died: Loughborough, Leicestershire, England, 22 April, 1955						
England: FLge-1						
Derby Co	Holbrook St Michael's	10/37	46-53	246	-	0
MUSTAFA Tarkan						
Born: Islington, N London, England, 28 August, 1973						RB
England: Semi Pro-2						
Barnet	Kettering T	08/97	97	2	9	0
Rushden & D	Kingstonian	06/00	01-02	31	3	1
MUSTAPHA Rahamat Riga (Riga)						
Born: Accra, Ghana, 10 October, 1981						W
Netherlands: U21-6/Youth						
Bolton W	Levante (SPN)	07/08	08-09	2	16	0
MUSTARD William (Bill)						
Born: South Shields, Tyne and Wear, England, 28 November, 1920						RW
Died: Exeter, England, 14 October, 1976						
Exeter C	Bath C	05/46	46	14	-	0
MUSTOE Jordan David						
Born: Birkenhead, Wirral, England, 28 January, 1991						LB
Wigan Ath	Sch	07/09				
Barnet	L	01/12	11	15	3	0
Morecambe	L	10/12	12	10	1	0
Carlisle U	L	02/13	12	14	0	1
Bury	L	10/13	13	6	0	0
Wycombe W	L	01/14	13	3	0	0
Morecambe	L	03/14	13	4	1	0
Accrington Stan	Tr	08/14	14	4	0	0
MUSTOE Neil John						
Born: Gloucester, England, 5 November, 1976						LM
Manchester U	YT	07/95				
Wigan Ath	Tr	01/98				
Cambridge U	Tr	07/98	98-01	71	28	4
MUSTOE Robin (Robbie)						
Born: Witney, Oxfordshire, England, 28 August, 1968						M
Oxford U	Jnr	07/86	86-89	78	13	10
Middlesbrough	Tr	07/90	90-01	327	38	25
Charlton Ath	Tr	08/02	02	6	0	0
Sheffield Wed	Tr	08/03	03	22	3	1
MUTCH Andrew Todd (Andy)						
Born: Liverpool, England, 28 December, 1963						F
England: B-3/U21-1						
Wolverhampton W	Southport	02/86	85-92	277	12	96
Swindon T	Tr	08/93	93-94	34	16	6
Wigan Ath	L	08/95	95	7	0	1
Stockport Co	Tr	03/96	95-97	28	36	10
MUTCH George						
Born: Aberdeen, Scotland, 21 September, 1912						IF
Died: Aberdeen, Scotland, 30 March, 2001						
Scotland: 1/Schools						
Manchester U	Arbroath	05/34	34-37	112	-	46
Preston NE	Tr	09/37	37-46	80	-	24
Bury	Tr	10/46	46	21	-	8
Southport	Tr	10/47	47	14	-	2
MUTCH Jordon James Edward Sydney						
Born: Derby, England, 2 December, 1991						M
England: U21-1/Youth						
Birmingham C	Sch	04/09	10-11	21	3	2
Hereford U	L	11/09	09	3	0	0
Doncaster Rov	L	01/10	09	5	12	2
Watford	L	08/10	10	21	2	5
Cardiff C	Tr	06/12	12-13	44	13	7
Queens Park Rgrs	Tr	08/14	14	6	3	0
Crystal Palace	Tr	01/15	14	4	3	0
MUTCHELL Robert David (Rob)						
Born: Solihull, West Midlands, England, 3 January, 1974						LB
Oxford U	YT	07/92				
Barnet	Tr	12/93	93-94	21	1	0
MUTRIE Leslie Alan (Les)						
Born: Newcastle-upon-Tyne, England, 1 April, 1952						F
England: Semi Pro-5						
Carlisle U	Gateshead	06/77	77	4	1	0
Hull C	Blyth Spartans	12/80	80-83	114	1	49
Doncaster Rov	L	12/83	83	6	0	1
Colchester U	Tr	01/84	83	10	4	2
Hartlepool U	Tr	08/84	84	18	0	4
MUTTOCK Jonathan Lee (Jon)						
Born: Oxford, England, 23 December, 1961						CD
Oxford U	YT	05/90	89	1	0	0
MUTTON Thomas James (Tommy)						
Born: Huddersfield, West Yorkshire, England, 17 January, 1978						F
Swansea C	Bangor C	09/99	99-00	4	3	0
MUTU Adrian						
Born: Arges, Romania, 8 January, 1979						F
Romania: 77/U21-12/Youth						
Chelsea	Parma (ITA)	08/03	03-04	21	6	6
MUXWORTHY Graham John						
Born: Bristol, England, 11 October, 1938						LW
Crystal Palace	Exeter U	09/57	57	2	-	0
Bristol Rov	Chippenham T	06/60	62	8	-	0
MUZINIC Drazen						
Born: Split, Yugoslavia, 25 January, 1953						D/M
Yugoslavia: 32						
Norwich C	Hajduk Split (YUG)	09/80	80-81	15	4	0

MVOTO Jean-Yves
Born: Paris, France, 6 September, 1988 CD
France: Youth

League Club	Source	Date Signed	Seasons Played	Apps	Subs	Gls
Sunderland	Paris St-Germain (FRA)	01/08				
Southend U	L	08/09	09	15	2	1
Oldham Ath	L	08/10	10	16	1	2
Oldham Ath	Tr	03/11	11-12	86	2	5
Barnsley	Tr	07/13	13-14	38	5	2

MVUEMBA Makengo Arnold (Arnold)
Born: Alencon, France, 28 January, 1985 M
France: U21-4

League Club	Source	Date Signed	Seasons Played	Apps	Subs	Gls
Portsmouth	Stade Rennais (FRA)	01/07	06-08	5	16	1

MWASILIE Joseph Kabina Gina (Joe)
Born: Basildon, England, 7 June, 1993 W

League Club	Source	Date Signed	Seasons Played	Apps	Subs	Gls
Morecambe	Jnr	07/11	11-13	3	27	0

MWILA Frederick (Freddie)
Born: Kasama, Zambia, 6 July, 1946 M

League Club	Source	Date Signed	Seasons Played	Apps	Subs	Gls
Aston Villa	Atlanta Chiefs (USA)	06/69	69	1	0	0

MYALL Stuart Thomas
Born: Eastbourne, East Sussex, England, 12 November, 1974 RB

League Club	Source	Date Signed	Seasons Played	Apps	Subs	Gls
Brighton & HA	YT	07/93	92-95	69	11	4
Brentford	Tr	06/96	97	2	0	0

MYCOCK Albert
Born: Manchester, England, 31 January, 1923 W
Died: Manchester, England, October, 2003

League Club	Source	Date Signed	Seasons Played	Apps	Subs	Gls
Manchester U	Goslings	05/44				
Crystal Palace	Tr	06/46	46-47	59	-	9
Barrow	Tr	07/48	48-49	42	-	4

MYCOCK David
Born: Sunderland, England, 30 August, 1921 CH/LH
Died: Halifax, West Yorkshire, England, October, 1990

League Club	Source	Date Signed	Seasons Played	Apps	Subs	Gls
Halifax T	Silksworth CW	05/46	46-51	169	-	17

MYCOCK David Christopher
Born: Todmorden, West Yorkshire, England, 18 September, 1969 LB

League Club	Source	Date Signed	Seasons Played	Apps	Subs	Gls
Rochdale	YT	07/88	87-88	19	3	0

MYCOCK John (Jack)
Born: Manchester, England, 11 February, 1936 W
Died: Bramhall, Greater Manchester, England, 17 May, 2006

League Club	Source	Date Signed	Seasons Played	Apps	Subs	Gls
Shrewsbury T (Am)	Congleton T	12/58	58	6	-	1

MYCOCK Thomas (Tommy)
Born: Ryhope, Tyne and Wear, England, 22 August, 1923 IF/WH
Died: Morecambe, Lancashire, England, 17 June, 1988
Northern Ireland: NILge-1

League Club	Source	Date Signed	Seasons Played	Apps	Subs	Gls
Southport	Silksworth CW	10/46	46	19	-	3
Aldershot	Tr	04/47	46-47	16	-	2
Brentford	Distillery	12/50				
Tranmere Rov	Tr	05/52	52-53	45	-	2
Bradford C	Tr	02/54	53-54	22	-	3

MYERS Alan William
Born: Newcastle-upon-Tyne, England, 12 February, 1928 G
Died: North Tyneside, Tyne and Wear, England, March, 2013

League Club	Source	Date Signed	Seasons Played	Apps	Subs	Gls
Gateshead		03/52	51	1	-	0

MYERS Andrew John (Andy)
Born: Hounslow, SW London, England, 3 November, 1973 LB
England: U21-4/Youth

League Club	Source	Date Signed	Seasons Played	Apps	Subs	Gls
Chelsea	YT	07/91	90-98	74	10	2
Bradford C	Tr	07/99	99-02	74	15	3
Portsmouth	L	03/00	99	4	4	0
Colchester U	Tr	07/03	03	21	0	0
Brentford	Tr	07/04	04	6	4	0

MYERS Christopher (Chris)
Born: Yeovil, Somerset, England, 1 April, 1969 M

League Club	Source	Date Signed	Seasons Played	Apps	Subs	Gls
Torquay U	App	06/87	86	8	1	0
Torquay U	Barnstaple T	08/90	90-92	88	8	7
Torquay U (L)	Dundee U	12/93	93	6	0	0
Scarborough	Dundee U	01/96	95	8	1	0
Exeter C	Tr	03/96	95-96	38	3	2

MYERS Clifford William (Cliff)
Born: Southwark, S London, England, 23 September, 1946 M

League Club	Source	Date Signed	Seasons Played	Apps	Subs	Gls
Charlton Ath	App	09/64	65-66	16	2	2
Brentford	Tr	06/67	67	7	3	0
Torquay U	Yeovil T	07/73	73-75	80	6	12

MYERS John Rodney (Rod)
Born: Sheffield, England, 16 February, 1939 LB

League Club	Source	Date Signed	Seasons Played	Apps	Subs	Gls
Doncaster Rov		01/63	63	20	-	0

MYERS Peter William
Born: Dronfield, Derbyshire, England, 15 September, 1982 M

League Club	Source	Date Signed	Seasons Played	Apps	Subs	Gls
Halifax T	YT	-	00	0	1	0

MYERSCOUGH William Henry (Billy)
Born: Bolton, Greater Manchester, England, 22 June, 1930 IF
Died: Glossop, Derbyshire, England, March, 1977

League Club	Source	Date Signed	Seasons Played	Apps	Subs	Gls
Walsall	Ashfield	06/54	54	26	-	6
Aston Villa	Tr	07/55	56-58	64	-	15
Rotherham U	Tr	07/59	59	38	-	11
Coventry C	Tr	07/60	60-61	58	-	16
Chester C	Tr	03/62	61-62	36	-	10
Wrexham	Tr	07/63	63	35	-	5

MYHILL Glyn Oliver (Boaz)
Born: Modesto. California, USA, 9 November, 1982 G
England: Youth//Wales: 20

League Club	Source	Date Signed	Seasons Played	Apps	Subs	Gls
Aston Villa	YT	11/00				
Bradford C	L	11/02	02	2	0	0
Macclesfield T	L	08/03	03	15	0	0
Stockport Co	L	11/03	03	2	0	0
Hull C	Tr	12/03	03-09	257	0	0
West Bromwich A	Tr	08/10	10-14	38	1	0
Birmingham C	L	07/11	11	42	0	0

MYHRE Thomas
Born: Sarpsborg, Norway, 16 October, 1973 G
Norway: 56/U21-27/Youth

League Club	Source	Date Signed	Seasons Played	Apps	Subs	Gls
Everton	Viking Stavanger (NOR)	11/97	97-00	70	0	0
Birmingham C	L	03/00	99	7	0	0
Tranmere Rov	L	11/00	00	3	0	0
Sunderland	Besiktas (TKY)	07/02	02-04	35	2	0
Crystal Palace	L	10/03	03	15	0	0
Charlton Ath	Fredrikstad (NOR)	08/05	05-06	21	0	0

MYLES Neil Thomson
Born: Falkirk, Scotland, 17 June, 1927 RH
Died: Ipswich, England, 15 November, 1993

League Club	Source	Date Signed	Seasons Played	Apps	Subs	Gls
Ipswich T	Third Lanark	08/49	49-59	223	-	15

MYNARD Leslie Daniel (Les)
Born: Bewdley, Worcestershire, England, 19 December, 1925 LW
Died: Worcester, England, 25 July, 2008

League Club	Source	Date Signed	Seasons Played	Apps	Subs	Gls
Wolverhampton W	Bewdley	05/45	47	3	-	0
Derby Co	Tr	07/49	49-50	14	-	2
Scunthorpe U	Tr	08/52	52	18	-	3

MYRIE-WILLIAMS Jennison Machisti
Born: Lambeth, S London, England, 17 May, 1988 LW
England: Youth

League Club	Source	Date Signed	Seasons Played	Apps	Subs	Gls
Bristol C	Sch	04/06	05-07	15	11	2
Cheltenham T	L	08/07	07	7	5	0
Tranmere Rov	L	11/07	07	21	4	3
Cheltenham T	L	08/08	08	5	0	1
Carlisle U	L	09/08	08	1	7	0
Hereford U	L	01/09	08	15	0	2
Stevenage	St Johnstone	07/11	11	3	14	0
Port Vale	L	11/11	11	6	0	1
Port Vale	Tr	07/12	12-13	69	13	16
Scunthorpe U	Tr	06/14	14	7	8	0
Tranmere Rov	L	01/15	14	16	2	3

MYTON Brian
Born: Strensall, North Yorkshire, England, 26 September, 1950 LB

League Club	Source	Date Signed	Seasons Played	Apps	Subs	Gls
Middlesbrough	App	09/67	68-70	10	0	0
Southend U	L	11/71	71	0	1	0

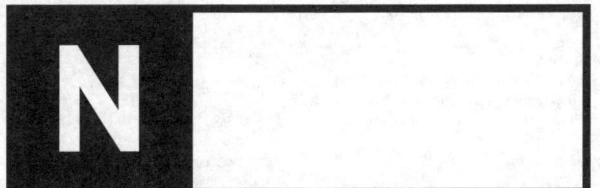

League Club	Source	Date Signed	Seasons Played	Career Record Apps	Subs	Gls
NACCA Francesco (Franco)						
Born: Venezuela, 9 November, 1982						M
Cambridge U	YT	04/01	02-03	11	15	0
NADE Christian Christian (Chris)						
Born: Paris, France, 18 September, 1984						W
France: U21-1						
Sheffield U	Troyes AC (FRA)	07/06	06	7	18	3
NADE Raphael						
Born: Abidjan, Ivory Coast, 18 October, 1980						F
Carlisle U	Woking	07/05	05	10	12	2
NAFTI Mehdi Ben Sedok						
Born: Toulouse, France, 28 November, 1978						DM
Tunisia: 44						
Birmingham C	RC Santander (SPN)	01/05	04-08	51	29	0
NAGY Miklos (Mick)						
Born: Budapest, Hungary, 1 May, 1929						IF
Scunthorpe U		01/51				
Swindon T	Tr	08/51	51	2	-	0
NAIL Desmond Roy (Roy)						
Born: St Columb, Cornwall, England, 28 December, 1924						CF
Died: Truro, Cornwall, England, 6 March, 1983						
Plymouth Arg	St Blazey	10/47	47	1	-	0
NAINBY Lewis John (Lew)						
Born: Seaton Delaval, Northumberland, England, 2 January, 1940						IF
Sheffield Wed		02/58				
Darlington	Tr	07/59	59	3	-	1
NAISBETT Philip (Phil)						
Born: Seaham, County Durham, England, 2 January, 1979						G
Sunderland	YT	04/97				
Scarborough	Gateshead	01/99	98	2	0	0
NAISBITT Daniel John (Danny)						
Born: Bishop Auckland, County Durham, England, 25 November, 1978						G
Walsall	YT	07/97				
Barnet	Tr	08/99	99-00	19	4	0
Carlisle U	L	08/02	02	1	0	0
NAISMITH Kal						
Born: Glasgow, Scotland, 18 February, 1992						W
Scotland: Youth						
Accrington Stan	Glasgow Rangers	08/13	13-14	54	19	14
NAISMITH Steven John						
Born: Stewarton, Ayrshire, Scotland, 14 September, 1986						M/F
Scotland: 38/B-3/U21-15						
Everton	Glasgow Rangers	07/12	12-14	48	45	15
NAKATA Hidetoshi						
Born: Yamanashi, Japan, 22 January, 1977						M
Japan: 77						
Bolton W (L)	Fiorentina (ITA)	08/05	05	14	7	1
NALIS Lilian Bernard Pierre						
Born: Paris, France, 29 September, 1971						M
Leicester C	Chievo Verona (ITA)	07/03	03-04	43	16	6
Sheffield U	Tr	07/05	05	3	1	0
Coventry C	L	10/05	05	5	1	2
Plymouth Arg	Tr	01/06	05-07	94	8	6
Swindon T	Tr	07/08	08	18	6	0
NANCEKIVELL Kevin William						
Born: Barnstaple, Devon, England, 22 October, 1971						F
Plymouth Arg	Tiverton T	08/00	00	0	6	1
NANGLE Romello Desmond						
Born: Nottingham, England, 8 January, 1995						F
Notts Co	Sch	07/13	12-13	0	8	1
[NANI] ALMEIDA DA CUNHA Luis Carlos						
Born: Praia, Cape Verde Islands, 17 November, 1986						W
Portugal: 86/U21-10						
Manchester U	Sporting Lisbon (POR)	07/07	07-14	111	36	26

League Club	Source	Date Signed	Seasons Played	Career Record Apps	Subs	Gls
NAPIER Alexander Stevenson (Alex)						
Born: Kirkcaldy, Fife, Scotland, 8 August, 1935						CF
Darlington	Raith Rov	05/55	55	1	-	0
NAPIER Christopher Robin Anthony (Kit)						
Born: Dunblane, Stirlingshire, Scotland, 26 September, 1943						CF
Blackpool	Jnr	11/60	62	2	-	0
Preston NE	Tr	06/63	63	1	-	0
Workington	Tr	07/64	64-65	58	0	26
Newcastle U	Tr	11/65	65	8	0	0
Brighton & HA	Tr	09/66	66-72	249	7	84
Blackburn Rov	Tr	08/72	72-73	53	1	10
NAPIER Robert John (John)						
Born: Lurgan, Armagh, Northern Ireland, 23 September, 1946						CD
Northern Ireland: 1/U23-2						
Bolton W	Jnr	09/63	64-66	69	0	2
Brighton & HA	Tr	08/67	67-72	218	1	5
Bradford C	Tr	10/72	72-74	106	0	3
Bradford C	San Diego Jaws (USA)	08/76	76	0	1	0
NARBETT Jonathan Vellenzer (Jon)						
Born: Birmingham, England, 21 November, 1968						M
Shrewsbury T	App	09/86	86-87	20	6	3
Hereford U	Tr	10/88	88-91	148	1	31
Oxford U	Tr	07/92	92-93	13	2	0
Chesterfield	Kalmar FF (SWE)	12/94	94-95	13	7	1
NARDIELLO Daniel Antony (Danny)						
Born: Coventry, England, 22 October, 1982						F
England: Youth/Schools//Wales: 1						
Manchester U	YT	11/99				
Swansea C	L	10/03	03	3	1	0
Barnsley	L	01/04	03	14	2	7
Barnsley	L	07/04	04	11	17	7
Barnsley	Tr	07/05	05-06	30	34	14
Queens Park Rgrs	Tr	07/07	07	4	4	0
Barnsley	L	01/08	07	8	3	1
Blackpool	Tr	07/08	08-09	1	6	0
Hartlepool U	L	01/09	08	8	4	3
Bury	L	11/09	09	6	0	4
Oldham Ath	L	03/10	09	2	0	0
Exeter C	Tr	07/10	10-11	43	23	19
Rotherham U	Tr	05/12	12-13	34	11	24
Bury	Tr	11/13	13-14	44	15	21
NARDIELLO Donato (Don)						
Born: Cardigan, Wales, 9 April, 1957						RW
Wales: 2/U21-1						
Coventry C	App	04/74	77-79	32	1	1
NARDIELLO Gerardo (Gerry)						
Born: Warley, West Midlands, England, 5 May, 1966						F
England: Youth						
Shrewsbury T	App	05/84	82-85	32	6	11
Cardiff C	L	03/86	85	7	0	4
Torquay U	Tr	07/86	86-87	28	9	11
NASH Carlo James						
Born: Bolton, Greater Manchester, England, 13 September, 1973						G
Crystal Palace	Clitheroe	07/96	96	21	0	0
Stockport Co	Tr	06/98	98-00	89	0	0
Manchester C	Tr	01/01	00-02	37	1	0
Middlesbrough	Tr	08/03	03-04	3	0	0
Preston NE	Tr	03/05	04-06	82	0	0
Wigan Ath	Tr	06/07				
Stoke C	L	01/08	07	10	0	0
Everton	Tr	08/08				
Stoke C	Tr	08/10				
Norwich C	Tr	07/13				
NASH Frank Cooper (Paddy)						
Born: South Bank, Cleveland, England, 30 June, 1918						G
Died: Middlesbrough, England, November, 1989						
Middlesbrough	South Bank East End	09/37	37-47	19	-	0
Southend U	Tr	12/47	47-50	57	-	0
NASH Gerard Thomas						
Born: Dublin, Republic of Ireland, 11 July, 1986						M
Republic of Ireland: Youth						
Ipswich T	Sch	07/03	03	0	1	0
Hartlepool U	L	01/06	05	3	0	0
NASH Marc						
Born: Newcastle-upon-Tyne, England, 13 May, 1978						F
Hartlepool U	Benfield Park	09/97	97	0	1	0
NASH Martin John						
Born: Regina, Saskatchewan, Canada, 27 December, 1975						M

Canada: 38/U23-11

League Club	Source	Date Signed	Seasons Played	Apps	Subs	Gls
Stockport Co	Vancouver 86ers (CAN)	11/96	96-97	0	11	0
Chester C	Vancouver 86ers (CAN)	09/99	99	12	4	0
Macclesfield T	Rochester Rhinos (USA)	01/03	02	1	4	0

NASH Robert Graham (Bobby)
Born: Hammersmith, W London, England, 8 February, 1946 — LB
Died: Crawley, West Sussex, England, 12 February, 1998

League Club	Source	Date Signed	Seasons Played	Apps	Subs	Gls
Queens Park Rgrs	Jnr	02/64	64	17	-	0
Exeter C	Tr	06/66	66	1	0	0

NASRI Samir
Born: Marseille, France, 26 June, 1987 — M
France: 41/U21-4/Youth

League Club	Source	Date Signed	Seasons Played	Apps	Subs	Gls
Arsenal	Olymp Marseille (FRA)	07/08	08-11	79	7	18
Manchester C	Tr	08/11	11-14	95	21	16

NASSARI Derek James
Born: Salford, England, 20 October, 1971 — M

League Club	Source	Date Signed	Seasons Played	Apps	Subs	Gls
Chester C	YT	07/88	89	0	1	0

NASTASIC Matija
Born: Valjevo, Serbia, 28 March, 1993 — CD
Serbia: 17/U21-8/Youth

League Club	Source	Date Signed	Seasons Played	Apps	Subs	Gls
Manchester C	Fiorentina (ITA)	08/12	12-13	32	2	0

NASTRI Carlo Luciano Raffaele
Born: Finchley, N London, England, 22 October, 1935 — RW

League Club	Source	Date Signed	Seasons Played	Apps	Subs	Gls
Crystal Palace	Kingstonian	07/58	58	2	-	0

NATTRASS Irving
Born: Fishburn, County Durham, England, 12 December, 1952 — RB
England: U23-1

League Club	Source	Date Signed	Seasons Played	Apps	Subs	Gls
Newcastle U	App	07/70	70-78	226	12	16
Middlesbrough	Tr	08/79	79-85	186	5	2

NATTRESS Clive
Born: Durham, England, 24 May, 1951 — D

League Club	Source	Date Signed	Seasons Played	Apps	Subs	Gls
Blackpool	Consett	08/70				
Darlington	Tr	08/72	72-79	297	5	15
Halifax T	Tr	06/80	80	37	0	5
Darlington	Bishop Auckland	08/85	85	1	0	0

NAUGHTON Kyle
Born: Sheffield, England, 11 November, 1988 — RB
England: U21-9

League Club	Source	Date Signed	Seasons Played	Apps	Subs	Gls
Sheffield U	Sch	03/07	08	39	1	1
Tottenham H	Tr	07/09	09-14	37	5	0
Middlesbrough	L	02/10	09	12	3	0
Leicester C	L	10/10	10	34	0	5
Norwich C	L	07/11	11	29	3	0
Swansea C	Tr	01/15	14	10	0	0

NAUGHTON William Balloch Stirling (Willie)
Born: Catrine, Ayrshire, Scotland, 20 March, 1962 — LW

League Club	Source	Date Signed	Seasons Played	Apps	Subs	Gls
Preston NE	App	03/80	79-84	148	14	10
Walsall	Tr	03/85	84-88	139	12	16
Shrewsbury T	Tr	08/89	89-90	43	6	4
Walsall	Tr	01/91	90	15	1	1

NAVARRO Alan Edward
Born: Liverpool, England, 31 May, 1981 — DM

League Club	Source	Date Signed	Seasons Played	Apps	Subs	Gls
Liverpool	YT	04/99				
Crewe Alex	L	03/01	00	5	3	1
Crewe Alex	L	08/01	01	7	0	0
Tranmere Rov	Tr	11/01	01-03	35	10	1
Chester C	L	08/04	04	3	0	0
Macclesfield T	L	12/04	04	11	0	1
Macclesfield T	Accrington Stan	10/05	05-06	55	4	2
MK Dons	Tr	07/07	07-08	70	7	4
Brighton & HA	Tr	08/09	09-11	57	16	1
Swindon T	Tr	07/12	12	12	5	0

NAVAS Jesus
Born: Seville, Spain, 21 November, 1985 — RW
Spain: 35/U21-5

League Club	Source	Date Signed	Seasons Played	Apps	Subs	Gls
Manchester C	Sevilla (SPN)	07/13	13-14	41	24	4

NAVAS Marco Antonio
Born: Seville, Spain, 21 September, 1982 — M

League Club	Source	Date Signed	Seasons Played	Apps	Subs	Gls
Bury	Rec'tivo Huelva (SPN)	08/13	13	1	1	0

NAYBET Noureddine
Born: Casablanca, Morocco, 10 February, 1970 — CD
Morocco: 115

League Club	Source	Date Signed	Seasons Played	Apps	Subs	Gls
Tottenham H	Depo la Coruna (SPN)	08/04	04-05	29	1	1

[NAYIM] AMAR Mohammed Ali
Born: Ceuta, Morocco, 5 November, 1968 — M
Spain: U21-1/Youth

League Club	Source	Date Signed	Seasons Played	Apps	Subs	Gls
Tottenham H	Barcelona (SPN)	11/88	88-92	95	17	11

NAYLOR Anthony Joseph (Tony)
Born: Manchester, England, 29 March, 1967 — F

League Club	Source	Date Signed	Seasons Played	Apps	Subs	Gls
Crewe Alex	Droylsden	03/90	89-93	104	18	45
Port Vale	Tr	07/94	94-00	207	46	71
Cheltenham T	Tr	08/01	01-02	62	12	18

NAYLOR Dominic John
Born: Watford, Hertfordshire, England, 12 August, 1970 — LB

League Club	Source	Date Signed	Seasons Played	Apps	Subs	Gls
Watford	YT	09/88				
Halifax T	Tr	12/89	89	5	1	1
Barnet	Hong Kong	08/91	91-92	50	1	0
Plymouth Arg	Tr	07/93	93-94	84	1	0
Gillingham	Tr	08/95	95	30	1	1
Leyton Orient	Tr	08/96	96-97	87	0	4

NAYLOR Edward Arnold
Born: Bradford, England, 24 December, 1921 — RH
Died: Huddersfield, West Yorkshire, England, December, 2000

League Club	Source	Date Signed	Seasons Played	Apps	Subs	Gls
Bradford Park Ave		05/45				
Halifax T	Tr	09/48	48	7	-	0

NAYLOR Geoffrey (Geoff)
Born: Goole, East Riding of Yorkshire, England, 28 December, 1949 — RH

League Club	Source	Date Signed	Seasons Played	Apps	Subs	Gls
Scunthorpe U	App	09/67	67	9	1	0

NAYLOR Glenn
Born: East Howden, East Riding of Yorkshire, England, 11 August, 1972 — F

League Club	Source	Date Signed	Seasons Played	Apps	Subs	Gls
York C	YT	03/90	89-96	78	33	30
Darlington	L	10/95	95	3	1	1
Darlington	Tr	09/96	96-02	157	52	46

NAYLOR Harold Francis
Born: Leeds, England, 6 June, 1928 — CF
Died: North Yorkshire, England, April, 2005

League Club	Source	Date Signed	Seasons Played	Apps	Subs	Gls
Oldham Ath (Am)	Mossley	04/51	50	1	-	0

NAYLOR Lee Martyn
Born: Bloxwich, West Midlands, England, 19 March, 1980 — LB
England: U21-3/Youth

League Club	Source	Date Signed	Seasons Played	Apps	Subs	Gls
Wolverhampton W	YT	10/97	97-06	270	23	7
Cardiff C	Glasgow Celtic	08/10	10-11	27	2	2
Accrington Stan	Rtd	09/13	13	13	0	0
Derby Co	Tr	02/14	13	0	4	0

NAYLOR Martyn Paul
Born: Walsall, West Midlands, England, 2 August, 1977 — RB

League Club	Source	Date Signed	Seasons Played	Apps	Subs	Gls
Shrewsbury T	Telford U	07/97	97	2	0	0

NAYLOR Richard Alan
Born: Leeds, England, 28 February, 1977 — F/CD

League Club	Source	Date Signed	Seasons Played	Apps	Subs	Gls
Ipswich T	YT	07/95	96-08	232	92	37
Millwall	L	01/02	01	2	1	0
Barnsley	L	03/02	01	7	1	0
Leeds U	Tr	01/09	08-10	64	2	4
Doncaster Rov	Tr	07/11	11	13	0	0
Rotherham U	Tr	01/12	11	5	0	0

NAYLOR Stuart William
Born: Wetherby, West Yorkshire, England, 6 December, 1962 — G
England: B-3/Youth

League Club	Source	Date Signed	Seasons Played	Apps	Subs	Gls
Lincoln C	Yorkshire Amats	06/80	81-85	49	0	0
Peterborough U	L	02/83	82	8	0	0
Crewe Alex	L	10/83	83	38	0	0
Crewe Alex	L	08/84	84	17	0	0
West Bromwich A	Tr	02/86	85-95	354	1	0
Bristol C	Tr	08/96	96-97	37	0	0
Mansfield T	L	12/98	98	6	0	0
Walsall	Tr	03/99				
Exeter C	Tr	08/99	99	30	0	0

NAYLOR Terence Michael Patrick (Terry)
Born: Islington, N London, England, 5 December, 1948 — D

League Club	Source	Date Signed	Seasons Played	Apps	Subs	Gls
Tottenham H	Smithfield Market	07/69	69-79	237	6	0
Charlton Ath	Tr	11/80	80-83	69	4	0

NAYLOR Thomas Keith (Tom)
Born: Sutton-in-Ashfield, Nottinghamshire, England, 28 June, 1991 — D

League Club	Source	Date Signed	Seasons Played	Apps	Subs	Gls
Derby Co	Mansfield T	11/11	11	8	0	0
Bradford C	L	11/12	12	4	1	0
Newport Co	L	08/13	13	24	9	1
Cambridge U	L	09/14	14	5	3	0
Burton A	L	01/15	14	13	4	0

NAYLOR Thomas Vincent (Tommy)
Born: Blackburn, Greater Manchester, England, 1 April, 1946 — CD
Died: Bournemouth, England, May, 2010

League Club	Source	Date Signed	Seasons Played	Apps	Subs	Gls
Bournemouth	App	10/63	64-70	139	4	3
Hereford U	Tr	08/72	72-74	73	2	4

NAYLOR Thomas William (Bill)
Born: Leeds, England, 7 December, 1924 — D
Died: Oldham, Greater Manchester, England, 18 June, 2011

League Club	Source	Date Signed	Seasons Played	Apps	Subs	Gls
Huddersfield T	Outwood Stormcocks	02/43				
Oldham Ath	Tr	03/48	47-58	224	-	0

NAYSMITH Gary Andrew
Born: Edinburgh, Scotland, 16 November, 1978 — LB
Scotland: 46/B-1/U21-27/Schools

League Club	Source	Date Signed	Seasons Played	Apps	Subs	Gls
Everton	Heart of Midlothian	10/00	00-06	113	21	6
Sheffield U	Tr	07/07	07-09	77	2	0
Huddersfield T	Tr	07/10	10-11	33	3	0

N'DA Julien
Born: Niort, France, 15 August, 1985 — RB

League Club	Source	Date Signed	Seasons Played	Apps	Subs	Gls
Accrington Stan	Rouen (FRA)	07/06	06	0	3	0

NDAH George Ehialimolisa
Born: Dulwich, S London, England, 23 December, 1974 — F
England: Youth

League Club	Source	Date Signed	Seasons Played	Apps	Subs	Gls
Crystal Palace	YT	08/92	92-97	33	45	8
Bournemouth	L	10/95	95	12	0	2
Gillingham	L	08/97	97	4	0	0
Swindon T	Tr	11/97	97-99	66	1	14
Wolverhampton W	Tr	10/99	99-05	50	37	15

NDAH Jamie Jidefor Ogoegbunan
Born: Camberwell, S London, England, 5 August, 1971 — F

League Club	Source	Date Signed	Seasons Played	Apps	Subs	Gls
Torquay U	Kingstonian	08/95	95-96	25	3	4
Barnet	Tr	02/97	96	12	2	4

N'DAW Guirane
Born: Rufisque, Senegal, 24 April, 1984 — DM
Senegal: 47

League Club	Source	Date Signed	Seasons Played	Apps	Subs	Gls
Birmingham C (L)	Saint-Etienne (FRA)	08/11	11	17	2	0
Ipswich T (L)	Saint-Etienne (FRA)	08/12	12	32	2	1

N'DIAYE Alassane
Born: Montbeliard, France, 25 February, 1990 — M

League Club	Source	Date Signed	Seasons Played	Apps	Subs	Gls
Crystal Palace	Toulouse Jnrs (FRA)	12/08	09-10	16	22	3
Swindon T	L	03/11	10	2	4	0
Southend U	L	07/11	11	0	1	0
Barnet	Tr	11/11	11	2	4	0

N'DIAYE Alfred John Momar
Born: Paris, France, 6 March, 1990 — DM
France: U21-7/Youth//Senegal: 8

League Club	Source	Date Signed	Seasons Played	Apps	Subs	Gls
Sunderland	Bursaspor (TKY)	01/13	12	15	1	0

N'DIAYE Sada (Pepe)
Born: Dakar, Senegal, 27 March, 1975 — F

League Club	Source	Date Signed	Seasons Played	Apps	Subs	Gls
Southend U	Troyes AC (FRA)	10/97	97	15	2	2

N'DIAYE Seyni
Born: Dakar, Senegal, 1 June, 1973 — F

League Club	Source	Date Signed	Seasons Played	Apps	Subs	Gls
Tranmere Rov	SM Caen (FRA)	03/01	00-01	11	8	4

NDIWA-LORD Kangana
Born: Maquela do Zambo, Angola, 28 February, 1984 — CD
DR Congo: 2//Sweden: Youth

League Club	Source	Date Signed	Seasons Played	Apps	Subs	Gls
Bolton W	Djurgaarden (SWE)	07/03				
Oldham Ath	L	08/03	03	3	1	0
Rochdale	L	02/04	03	0	1	0

NDLOVU Peter
Born: Bulawayo, Zimbabwe, 25 February, 1973 — W
Zimbabwe: 100

League Club	Source	Date Signed	Seasons Played	Apps	Subs	Gls
Coventry C	Highlanders (ZIM)	08/91	91-96	141	36	37
Birmingham C	Tr	07/97	97-00	78	29	22
Huddersfield T	L	12/00	00	6	0	4
Sheffield U	Tr	02/01	00-03	114	21	25

N'DOUR Alassane
Born: Dakar, Senegal, 12 December, 1981 — DM
Senegal: 8

League Club	Source	Date Signed	Seasons Played	Apps	Subs	Gls
West Bromwich A (L)	Saint-Etienne (FRA)	09/03	03	2	0	0
Walsall		02/08	07	3	6	1

N'DOYE Dame
Born: Thies, Senegal, 21 February, 1985 — F
Senegal: 26

League Club	Source	Date Signed	Seasons Played	Apps	Subs	Gls
Hull C	Lokomotiv Moscow (RUS)	02/15	14	13	2	5

N'DUMBU-NSUNGU Guylain
Born: Kinshasa, DR Congo, 26 December, 1982 — F
DR Congo: U21

League Club	Source	Date Signed	Seasons Played	Apps	Subs	Gls
Sheffield Wed	Amiens SC (FRA)	09/03	03-04	24	11	10
Preston NE	L	09/04	04	4	2	0
Colchester U	Tr	01/05	04	2	6	1
Darlington	Tr	08/05	05	11	10	10
Cardiff C	Tr	01/06	05	4	7	0
Gillingham	Tr	07/06	06	14	18	3
Bradford C	Tr	08/07	07	17	1	6
Darlington	Tr	01/08	07	4	4	3

NEAL Ashley James
Born: Northampton, England, 16 December, 1974 — D

League Club	Source	Date Signed	Seasons Played	Apps	Subs	Gls
Liverpool	YT	04/93				
Brighton & HA	L	09/96	96	8	0	0
Huddersfield T	Tr	12/96				
Peterborough U	Tr	03/97	96-97	6	2	0

NEAL Christopher (Chris)
Born: Kirkby-in-Ashfield, Nottinghamshire, England, 27 June, 1947 — RW

League Club	Source	Date Signed	Seasons Played	Apps	Subs	Gls
Darlington (Am)	Crook T	06/67	67	5	0	0

NEAL Christopher Michael (Chris)
Born: St Albans, Hertfordshire, England, 23 October, 1985 — G

League Club	Source	Date Signed	Seasons Played	Apps	Subs	Gls
Preston NE	Sch	12/04	04	0	1	0
Shrewsbury T	Tr	07/09	09-11	63	1	0
Port Vale	Tr	07/12	12-14	117	0	0

NEAL Dean John
Born: Edmonton, N London, England, 5 January, 1961 — F

League Club	Source	Date Signed	Seasons Played	Apps	Subs	Gls
Queens Park Rgrs	App	01/79	79-80	20	2	8
Millwall	Tulsa Roughnecks (USA)	10/81	81-84	101	19	42
Southend U	Tr	01/86	85-87	35	5	6
Cambridge U	L	12/87	87	4	0	0

NEAL George Charles
Born: Wellingborough, Northamptonshire, England, 29 December, 1919 — RH
Died: Wellingborough, Northamptonshire, England, August, 1997

League Club	Source	Date Signed	Seasons Played	Apps	Subs	Gls
Northampton T	Kettering T	01/45	46	3	-	0

NEAL John
Born: Seaham, County Durham, England, 3 April, 1932 — FB
Died: Rhosddu, Wrexham, Wales, 24 November, 2014

League Club	Source	Date Signed	Seasons Played	Apps	Subs	Gls
Hull C	Silksworth CW	08/49	49-55	60	-	1
Swindon T	King's Lynn	07/57	57-58	91	-	2
Aston Villa	Tr	07/59	59-62	96	-	0
Southend U	Tr	11/62	62-65	100	0	1

NEAL John James
Born: Hornsey, N London, England, 11 March, 1966 — F
England: Schools

League Club	Source	Date Signed	Seasons Played	Apps	Subs	Gls
Millwall	App	03/83	83	3	3	1

NEAL Lewis Ryan
Born: Leicester, England, 14 July, 1981 — LM

League Club	Source	Date Signed	Seasons Played	Apps	Subs	Gls
Stoke C	YT	07/98	00-04	29	41	2
Preston NE	Tr	08/05	05-07	24	41	5
Notts Co	L	10/08	08	4	0	0
Carlisle U	Tr	01/09	08	15	1	2
Shrewsbury T	Tr	07/09	09-10	21	10	2

NEAL Philip George (Phil)
Born: Irchester, Northamptonshire, England, 20 February, 1951 — RB
England: 50

League Club	Source	Date Signed	Seasons Played	Apps	Subs	Gls
Northampton T	App	12/68	68-74	182	2	29
Liverpool	Tr	10/74	74-85	453	2	41
Bolton W	Tr	12/85	85-88	56	8	3

NEAL Richard Marshall (Dick)
Born: Dinnington, South Yorkshire, England, 1 October, 1933 — LH
Died: Penkridge, Staffordshire, England, 21 February, 2013
England: U23-4

League Club	Source	Date Signed	Seasons Played	Apps	Subs	Gls
Wolverhampton W	Jnr	03/51				
Lincoln C	Tr	07/54	54-56	115	-	11
Birmingham C	Tr	04/57	56-61	165	-	15
Middlesbrough	Tr	10/61	61-62	33	-	4
Lincoln C	Tr	08/63	63-64	41	-	4

NEALE Duncan Frederick
Born: Portslade, East Sussex, England, 1 October, 1939 — WH

League Club	Source	Date Signed	Seasons Played	Apps	Subs	Gls
Newcastle U	Ilford	06/59	60-62	88	-	8
Plymouth Arg	Tr	08/63	63-69	141	5	8

NEALE John William
Born: Barnstaple, Devon, England, 15 January, 1949 — RW

League Club	Source	Date Signed	Seasons Played	Apps	Subs	Gls
Exeter C	Barnstaple T	03/72	71-74	51	14	5

NEALE Keith Ian
Born: Birmingham, England, 19 January, 1935 — IF

League Club	Source	Date Signed	Seasons Played	Apps	Subs	Gls
Birmingham C	Metropolitan Works	02/54	56-57	5	-	1
Lincoln C	Tr	11/57	57-58	8	-	1

NEALE Peter
Born: Bolsover, Derbyshire, England, 9 April, 1934 — CH/IF

League Club	Source	Date Signed	Seasons Played	Apps	Subs	Gls
Oldham Ath	Chesterfield (Jnr)	01/53	55-58	117	-	28
Scunthorpe U	Tr	10/58	58-66	221	5	7
Chesterfield	Tr	10/66	66-67	69	0	4

NEALE Philip Anthony (Phil)
Born: Scunthorpe, North Lincolnshire, England, 5 June, 1954 — LB/M

League Club	Source	Date Signed	Seasons Played	Apps	Subs	Gls
Lincoln C	Scunthorpe U (Am)	06/74	74-84	327	8	22

NEALE William Elwood (Billy)
Born: Wallsend, Tyne and Wear, England, 20 May, 1933 — LH
Died: North Tyneside, Tyne and Wear, England, October, 2001

League Club	Source	Date Signed	Seasons Played	Apps	Subs	Gls
Sunderland	Jnr	06/50				
Darlington	North Shields	05/57	57	15	-	0

NEARY Harold Frank (Frank)
Born: Aldershot, Hampshire, England, 6 March, 1921 — CF
Died: Sutton, S London, England, April, 2003

League Club	Source	Date Signed	Seasons Played	Apps	Subs	Gls
Queens Park Rgrs	Finchley	07/45	46	9	-	6
West Ham U	Tr	01/47	46-47	17	-	15
Leyton Orient	Tr	11/47	47-49	78	-	44
Queens Park Rgrs	Tr	10/49	49	18	-	5
Millwall	Tr	08/50	50-53	123	-	50

NEATE Derek George Stanbridge
Born: Uxbridge, W London, England, 1 October, 1927 — LW
Died: West Sussex, England, October, 2014

League Club	Source	Date Signed	Seasons Played	Apps	Subs	Gls
Brighton & HA	Hayes	04/56	55-56	24	-	6

NEATE Gordon
Born: Reading, England, 14 March, 1941 — FB

League Club	Source	Date Signed	Seasons Played	Apps	Subs	Gls
Reading	Jnr	03/58	58-65	99	0	2

NEAVE Ian James Gordon (Gordon)
Born: Glasgow, Scotland, 10 October, 1924 — WH
Died: Portsmouth, England, 2 August, 2003

League Club	Source	Date Signed	Seasons Played	Apps	Subs	Gls
Portsmouth	Pollok Jnrs	03/47				
Bournemouth	Tr	06/49	50-53	85	-	0
Aldershot	Tr	07/55	55-57	79	-	2
Portsmouth	Tr	09/58				

NEBBELING Gavin Mark
Born: Johannesburg, South Africa, 15 May, 1963 — CD

League Club	Source	Date Signed	Seasons Played	Apps	Subs	Gls
Crystal Palace	Arcadia Shep's (RSA)	08/81	81-88	145	6	8
Northampton T	L	10/85	85	11	0	0
Fulham	Tr	07/89	89-92	85	3	2
Hereford U	L	12/91	91	3	0	0
Preston NE	Tr	07/93	93	22	0	4

NEDERGAARD Steen
Born: Aalborg, Denmark, 25 February, 1970 — RB/M
Denmark: U21-14

League Club	Source	Date Signed	Seasons Played	Apps	Subs	Gls
Norwich C	OB Odense (DEN)	07/00	00-02	81	9	5

NEEDHAM Andrew Paul (Andy)
Born: Oldham, Greater Manchester, England, 13 September, 1955 — F

League Club	Source	Date Signed	Seasons Played	Apps	Subs	Gls
Birmingham C	App	08/73	75	2	1	1
Blackburn Rov	Tr	07/76	76	4	1	0
Aldershot	Tr	03/77	76-79	92	3	29

NEEDHAM Andrew Paul (Paul)
Born: Buxton, Derbyshire, England, 15 June, 1961 — RB

League Club	Source	Date Signed	Seasons Played	Apps	Subs	Gls
Chester C	App	06/79	80-82	55	2	1

NEEDHAM Anthony (Tony)
Born: Scunthorpe, North Lincolnshire, England, 4 January, 1941 — FB

League Club	Source	Date Signed	Seasons Played	Apps	Subs	Gls
Scunthorpe U	Jnr	07/59	59-64	33	-	0

NEEDHAM David William (Dave)
Born: Leicester, England, 21 May, 1949 — CD
England: B-6

League Club	Source	Date Signed	Seasons Played	Apps	Subs	Gls
Notts Co	App	07/66	65-76	429	1	32
Queens Park Rgrs	Tr	06/77	77	18	0	3
Nottingham F	Tr	12/77	77-81	81	5	9

NEEDHAM Liam Paul
Born: Sheffield, England, 19 October, 1985 — LW

League Club	Source	Date Signed	Seasons Played	Apps	Subs	Gls
Notts Co	Gainsborough Trinity	01/06	05-06	21	2	0

NEENAN Joseph Patrick (Joe)
Born: Manchester, England, 17 March, 1959 — G

League Club	Source	Date Signed	Seasons Played	Apps	Subs	Gls
York C	App	03/77	76-79	56	0	0
Scunthorpe U	Tr	01/80	79-84	191	0	0
Burnley	L	01/85	84	9	0	0
Burnley	Tr	07/85	85-86	81	0	0
Peterborough U	Tr	07/87	87-88	55	0	0
Scarborough	L	01/88	87	6	0	0

NEGO Loic
Born: Paris, France, 15 January, 1991 — RB
France: Youth

League Club	Source	Date Signed	Seasons Played	Apps	Subs	Gls
Charlton Ath	Ujpest (HUN)	01/14	13	1	0	0

NEGOUAI Christian
Born: Fort de France, Martinique, 20 January, 1975 — M

League Club	Source	Date Signed	Seasons Played	Apps	Subs	Gls
Manchester C	RSC Charleroi (BEL)	11/01	01-04	2	4	1
Coventry C	L	01/05	04	1	0	0

NEGREDO Alvaro
Born: Madrid, Spain, 20 August, 1985 — F
Spain: 21/U21-1

League Club	Source	Date Signed	Seasons Played	Apps	Subs	Gls
Manchester C	Sevilla (SPN)	07/13	13	21	11	9

NEIGHBOUR James Edward (Jimmy)
Born: Chingford, NE London, England, 15 November, 1950 — W
Died: Woodford Green, NE London, England, 11 April, 2009

League Club	Source	Date Signed	Seasons Played	Apps	Subs	Gls
Tottenham H	App	11/68	70-76	104	15	8
Norwich C	Tr	09/76	76-79	104	2	5
West Ham U	Tr	09/79	79-82	66	7	5
Bournemouth	L	01/83	82	6	0	0

NEIL Alexander Francis (Alex)
Born: Airdrie, Lanarkshire, Scotland, 9 June, 1981 — DM

League Club	Source	Date Signed	Seasons Played	Apps	Subs	Gls
Barnsley	Airdrieonians	07/00	00-03	83	38	4
Mansfield T	Tr	07/04	04	40	1	1

NEIL Gary Derek Campbell
Born: Glasgow, Scotland, 16 August, 1978 — M

League Club	Source	Date Signed	Seasons Played	Apps	Subs	Gls
Leicester C	YT	07/97				
Torquay U	Tr	03/99	98-00	19	8	1

NEIL Hugh Moorhead
Born: Cumnock, Ayrshire, Scotland, 2 October, 1936 — RB
Died: Carlisle, Cumbria, England, 1978
Scotland: Schools

League Club	Source	Date Signed	Seasons Played	Apps	Subs	Gls
Carlisle U	St Johnstone	06/61	61-68	247	2	2

NEIL James Darren (Jimmy)
Born: Bury St Edmunds, Suffolk, England, 28 February, 1976 — RB

League Club	Source	Date Signed	Seasons Played	Apps	Subs	Gls
Grimsby T	YT	07/94	95-96	1	1	0
Scunthorpe U	Tr	08/97	97	6	1	0

NEIL Patrick Thomas (Pat)
Born: Portsmouth, England, 24 October, 1937 — W
England: Amateur-10/Schools

League Club	Source	Date Signed	Seasons Played	Apps	Subs	Gls
Portsmouth (Am)	Jnr	06/55	55	9	-	3
Wolverhampton W (Am)	Tr	08/56	56	4	-	1
Portsmouth	Pegasus	05/62	62	1	-	0

NEIL William Marshbanks (Billy)
Born: Lanark, Scotland, 20 April, 1924 — IF

League Club	Source	Date Signed	Seasons Played	Apps	Subs	Gls
Bradford Park Ave	Greenock Morton	12/47	47	3	-	0

NEIL William Waugh (Billy)
Born: Roslin, Midlothian, Scotland, 10 November, 1944 — LW

League Club	Source	Date Signed	Seasons Played	Apps	Subs	Gls
Millwall	Bonnyrigg Rose	04/64	64-71	178	8	26

NEILL Lucas Edward
Born: Sydney, Australia, 9 March, 1978 — RB
Australia: 96/U23-12/Youth

League Club	Source	Date Signed	Seasons Played	Apps	Subs	Gls
Millwall	NSW Soccer Acad (AUS)	11/95	95-01	124	28	13
Blackburn Rov	Tr	09/01	01-06	184	4	5
West Ham U	Tr	01/07	06-08	79	0	1
Everton	Tr	09/09	09	10	2	0
Watford	Omiya Ardija (JPN)	02/14	13	0	1	0
Doncaster Rov	L	03/14	13	4	0	0

NEILL Thomas Kerr (Tommy)
Born: Methil, Fife, Scotland, 3 October, 1930 — WH/IF
Died: Bolton, Greater Manchester, England, 15 July, 1996

League Club	Source	Date Signed	Seasons Played	Apps	Subs	Gls
Bolton W	RAF Wharton	09/50	52-56	40	-	2
Bury	Tr	12/56	56-59	89	-	8
Tranmere Rov	Tr	10/60	60-62	79	-	2

NEILL Warren Anthony
Born: Acton, W London, England, 21 November, 1962 — RB
England: Schools

League Club	Source	Date Signed	Seasons Played	Apps	Subs	Gls
Queens Park Rgrs	App	09/80	80-87	177	4	3
Portsmouth	Tr	07/88	88-94	216	2	3
Watford	Tr	01/96	95	1	0	0

NEILL William John Terence (Terry)
Born: Belfast, Northern Ireland, 8 May, 1942 — CH
Northern Ireland: 59/U23-4/Schools

League Club	Source	Date Signed	Seasons Played	Apps	Subs	Gls
Arsenal	Bangor	12/59	60-69	240	1	8
Hull C	Tr	07/70	70-72	103	0	4

NEILSON Alan Bruce
Born: Wegburg, Germany, 26 September, 1972 — D
Wales: 5/B-2/U21-7

League Club	Source	Date Signed	Seasons Played	Apps	Subs	Gls
Newcastle U	YT	02/91	90-94	35	7	1
Southampton	Tr	06/95	95-97	42	13	0
Fulham	Tr	11/97	97-00	24	5	2
Grimsby T	Tr	10/01	01	8	2	0
Luton T	Tr	02/02	01-04	46	11	1

NEILSON Gordon
Born: Glasgow, Scotland, 28 May, 1947 — RW

League Club	Source	Date Signed	Seasons Played	Apps	Subs	Gls
Arsenal	Glasgow U	06/64	65-66	14	0	2
Brentford	Tr	10/68	68-71	80	12	15

NEILSON John Crane
Born: Hamilton, Lanarkshire, Scotland, 2 August, 1921 — CF
Died: Surrey, England, March, 1988

League Club	Source	Date Signed	Seasons Played	Apps	Subs	Gls
Bradford C	Clyde	10/47	47-48	29	-	11
Wrexham	Tr	10/48				

NEILSON Robert (Robbie)
Born: Paisley, Renfrewshire, Scotland, 19 June, 1980 — RB
Scotland: 1/B-1/U21-1

League Club	Source	Date Signed	Seasons Played	Apps	Subs	Gls
Leicester C	Heart of Midlothian	06/09	09-10	26	0	0
Brentford	L	02/11	10	15	0	0

NEILSON Scott Steven
Born: Enfield, N London, England, 15 May, 1987 — RW

League Club	Source	Date Signed	Seasons Played	Apps	Subs	Gls
Bradford C	Cambridge C	08/09	09	18	5	1
Crawley T	Tr	08/10	11	11	19	3

NEILSON Stephen Bruce (Steve)
Born: Newtongrange, Midlothian, Scotland, 25 April, 1931 — RH
Died: Rotherham, South Yorkshire, England, December, 2014

League Club	Source	Date Signed	Seasons Played	Apps	Subs	Gls
Rotherham U	Heart of Midlothian	07/55	56	9	-	0

NEILSON Thomas (Tom)
Born: Armadale, West Lothian, Scotland, 28 July, 1922 — WH
Died: Armadale, West Lothian, Scotland, 21 February, 1974

League Club	Source	Date Signed	Seasons Played	Apps	Subs	Gls
Ipswich T	Heart of Midlothian	05/48	48	1	-	0

NEKREWS Thomas John (Tommy)
Born: Chatham, Kent, England, 20 March, 1933 — CH

League Club	Source	Date Signed	Seasons Played	Apps	Subs	Gls
Gillingham	Chelsea (Am)	09/53	53-57	42	-	0
Watford	Tr	07/58				

NELMES Alan Victor
Born: Hackney, E London, England, 20 October, 1948 — D

League Club	Source	Date Signed	Seasons Played	Apps	Subs	Gls
Chelsea	Jnr	10/65				
Brentford	Tr	07/67	67-75	311	5	2

NELSEN Ryan
Born: Christchurch, New Zealand, 18 October, 1977 — CD
New Zealand: 45

League Club	Source	Date Signed	Seasons Played	Apps	Subs	Gls
Blackburn Rov	Washington DC U (USA)	01/05	04-11	169	3	8
Tottenham H	Tr	01/12	11	0	5	0
Queens Park Rgrs	Tr	07/12	12	21	0	1

NELSON Andrew Nesbitt (Andy)
Born: Canning Town, E London, England, 5 July, 1935 — CH

League Club	Source	Date Signed	Seasons Played	Apps	Subs	Gls
West Ham U	Jnr	12/53	57-58	15	-	1
Ipswich T	Tr	06/59	59-64	193	-	0
Leyton Orient	Tr	09/64	64-65	43	0	0
Plymouth Arg	Tr	10/65	65-67	94	0	1

NELSON Anthony James (Tony)
Born: Cardiff, Wales, 12 April, 1930 — CH
Wales: Amateur

League Club	Source	Date Signed	Seasons Played	Apps	Subs	Gls
Newport Co	RAF	01/52	51-53	19	-	6
Bristol C	Tr	05/54				
Bournemouth	Tr	06/56	56-64	194	-	1

NELSON Colin Armstrong
Born: Boldon, Tyne and Wear, England, 13 March, 1938 — RB

League Club	Source	Date Signed	Seasons Played	Apps	Subs	Gls
Sunderland	Usworth Colliery	03/58	58-64	146	-	2
Mansfield T	Tr	03/65	64-65	38	0	0

NELSON Curtis Alexander
Born: Newcastle-under-Lyme, Potteries, England, 21 May, 1993 — CD
England: Youth

League Club	Source	Date Signed	Seasons Played	Apps	Subs	Gls
Plymouth Arg	Sch	10/10	10-14	158	7	5

NELSON David (Dave)
Born: Douglas Water, Lanarkshire, Scotland, 3 February, 1918 — RH
Died: Connecticut, USA, April, 1988

League Club	Source	Date Signed	Seasons Played	Apps	Subs	Gls
Arsenal	St Bernard's	05/36	36-46	27	-	4
Fulham	Tr	12/46	46	23	-	3
Brentford	Tr	08/47	47-49	106	-	5
Queens Park Rgrs	Tr	02/50	49-50	31	-	0
Crystal Palace	Tr	03/52	51-52	12	-	0

NELSON Dennis Nicolson
Born: Edinburgh, Scotland, 25 February, 1950 — F/M

League Club	Source	Date Signed	Seasons Played	Apps	Subs	Gls
Crewe Alex	Dunfermline Ath	07/74	74-75	65	6	18
Reading	Tr	03/76	75-77	53	6	6
Crewe Alex	Tr	07/78	78-80	97	10	15

NELSON Fernando Jesus Vieira Alves
Born: Lisbon, Portugal, 5 November, 1971 — RB
Portugal: 10/U21-22/Youth

League Club	Source	Date Signed	Seasons Played	Apps	Subs	Gls
Aston Villa	Sporting Lisbon (POR)	06/96	96-97	54	5	0

NELSON Garry Paul
Born: Braintree, Essex, England, 16 January, 1961 — LW/F

League Club	Source	Date Signed	Seasons Played	Apps	Subs	Gls
Southend U	Jnr	07/79	79-82	106	23	17
Swindon T	Tr	08/83	83-84	78	1	7
Plymouth Arg	Tr	07/85	85-86	71	3	20
Brighton & HA	Tr	07/87	87-90	132	12	47
Notts Co	L	11/90	90	0	2	0
Charlton Ath	Tr	08/91	91-95	147	38	37
Torquay U	Tr	08/96	96	30	4	8

NELSON George
Born: Mexborough, South Yorkshire, England, 5 February, 1925 — WH
Died: Doncaster, South Yorkshire, England, 8 September, 2011

League Club	Source	Date Signed	Seasons Played	Apps	Subs	Gls
Sheffield U	Denaby Rov	08/43				
Lincoln C	Tr	09/46	46	1	-	0

NELSON James Frederick (Jimmy)
Born: Newcastle-upon-Tyne, England, 4 November, 1943 — FB

League Club	Source	Date Signed	Seasons Played	Apps	Subs	Gls
Sunderland		08/62				
Ipswich T	Tr	07/63				
Barrow	Tr	01/65	64-65	15	0	0

NELSON Michael John
Born: Gateshead, Tyne and Wear, England, 28 March, 1980 — CD

League Club	Source	Date Signed	Seasons Played	Apps	Subs	Gls
Bury	Bishop Auckland	03/01	00-02	68	4	8
Hartlepool U	Tr	07/03	03-08	255	4	14
Norwich C	Tr	07/09	09-10	35	4	5
Scunthorpe U	Tr	01/11	10-11	28	2	1
Bradford C	Kilmarnock	01/13	12	12	1	0
Cambridge U	Hibernian	08/14	14	33	0	3

NELSON Samuel (Sammy)
Born: Belfast, Northern Ireland, 1 April, 1949 — LB
Northern Ireland: 51/U23-1

League Club	Source	Date Signed	Seasons Played	Apps	Subs	Gls
Arsenal	Jnr	04/66	69-80	245	10	10
Brighton & HA	Tr	09/81	81-82	40	0	1

NELSON Samuel Edward (Sammy)
Born: Belfast, Northern Ireland, 26 May, 1924 — W
Northern Ireland: NILge-1/Schools

League Club	Source	Date Signed	Seasons Played	Apps	Subs	Gls
Blackpool	Linfield Swifts	10/46	46-47	13	-	0
Luton T	Tr	01/48	47-48	4	-	1

NELSON Sidney Raymond Kenneth (Sid)
Born: Lewisham, SE London, England, 1 January, 1996 — CD

League Club	Source	Date Signed	Seasons Played	Apps	Subs	Gls
Millwall	Sch	06/14	14	14	0	0

NELSON Stuart James
Born: Stroud, Gloucestershire, England, 17 September, 1981 — G

League Club	Source	Date Signed	Seasons Played	Apps	Subs	Gls
Millwall	Cirencester T	10/00				
Brentford	Hucknall T	02/04	03-06	115	1	0
Leyton Orient	Tr	07/07	07	30	0	0
Norwich C	Tr	08/08				
Notts Co	Aberdeen	07/10	10-11	78	1	0
Gillingham	Tr	07/12	12-14	115	0	0

NELSON William Edward (Bill)
Born: Silvertown, E London, England, 20 September, 1929 — FB

League Club	Source	Date Signed	Seasons Played	Apps	Subs	Gls
West Ham U		10/50	54	2	-	0
Queens Park Rgrs	Tr	07/55	55	9	-	0

NELSON-ADDY Ebby Godfried
Born: Milton Keynes, England, 13 September, 1992 — M

League Club	Source	Date Signed	Seasons Played	Apps	Subs	Gls
Aston Villa	Sch	07/11				
Hartlepool U	Brackley T	03/15	14	1	1	0

NELTHORPE Craig Robert
Born: Doncaster, South Yorkshire, England, 10 June, 1987 — LW

League Club	Source	Date Signed	Seasons Played	Apps	Subs	Gls
Doncaster Rov	Sch	06/06	04-07	3	7	1
Darlington	L	03/08	07	4	3	0

NEMETH Krisztian
Born: Gyor, Hungary, 5 January, 1989 — F
Hungary: 16/U21-5/Youth

League Club	Source	Date Signed	Seasons Played	Apps	Subs	Gls
Liverpool	MTK Budapest (HUN)	07/07				
Blackpool	L	01/09	08	0	1	0

NEMETH Szilard
Born: Komarno, Slovakia, 8 August, 1977 — F
Slovakia: 58

League Club	Source	Date Signed	Seasons Played	Apps	Subs	Gls
Middlesbrough	Inter Bratislava (SVK)	07/01	01-05	62	55	23

[NENE] CARVALHO Anderson Luiz
Born: Jundiai, Brazil, 19 July, 1981 — W
Brazil: U23-4

League Club	Source	Date Signed	Seasons Played	Apps	Subs	Gls
West Ham U	Al-Gharafa (QAT)	02/15	14	0	8	0

NESBIT Anthony (Tony)
Born: Sunderland, England, 26 January, 1968 — M
England: Schools

League Club	Source	Date Signed	Seasons Played	Apps	Subs	Gls
Newcastle U	App	01/86	86	1	2	0

NESBITT Edward (Eddie)
Born: Boldon, Tyne and Wear, England, 12 October, 1951 — G
Died: Northumberland, England, February, 2006

League Club	Source	Date Signed	Seasons Played	Apps	Subs	Gls
Hartlepool U (Am)	Longbenton Jnrs	08/71	71	1	0	0

NESBITT John
Born: Washington, Tyne and Wear, England, 24 September, 1933 — CH

League Club	Source	Date Signed	Seasons Played	Apps	Subs	Gls
Newcastle U	South Shields	12/55	57	3	-	0

NESBITT Mark Thomas
Born: Doncaster, South Yorkshire, England, 11 January, 1972 — RB

League Club	Source	Date Signed	Seasons Played	Apps	Subs	Gls
Middlesbrough	YT	01/90				
Hartlepool U	Tr	03/91	90-91	2	0	0

NESBITT Michael David (Mike)
Born: Doncaster, South Yorkshire, England, 8 January, 1969 — F
England: Youth

League Club	Source	Date Signed	Seasons Played	Apps	Subs	Gls
Doncaster Rov	App	01/86	85-87	6	5	1

NESBITT Teddy Moore
Born: East Ham, E London, England, 6 September, 1993 — LB

League Club	Source	Date Signed	Seasons Played	Apps	Subs	Gls
Southend U	Sch	07/11	10	0	2	0

NESS Hugh Preston
Born: Dunfermline, Fife, Scotland, 30 April, 1940 — LW

League Club	Source	Date Signed	Seasons Played	Apps	Subs	Gls
Accrington Stan	Raith Rov	07/59	59	14	-	1
Halifax T	Tr	06/60				

NESS Jamie
Born: Troon, Ayrshire, Scotland, 2 March, 1991 — M
Scotland: U21-2/Youth

League Club	Source	Date Signed	Seasons Played	Apps	Subs	Gls
Stoke C	Glasgow Rangers	07/12				
Leyton Orient	L	01/14	13	3	10	1
Crewe Alex	L	08/14	14	31	3	2

NETHERCOTT Kenneth Walter Samuel (Ken)
Born: Bristol, England, 22 July, 1925 — G
Died: Norwich, England, 14 December, 2007
England: B-1

League Club	Source	Date Signed	Seasons Played	Apps	Subs	Gls
Norwich C	Bristol C (Am)	04/47	47-58	378	-	0

NETHERCOTT Stuart David
Born: Ilford, E London, England, 21 March, 1973 — CD
England: U21-8

League Club	Source	Date Signed	Seasons Played	Apps	Subs	Gls
Tottenham H	YT	08/91	92-96	31	23	0
Maidstone U	L	09/91	91	13	0	1
Barnet	L	02/92	91	3	0	0
Millwall	Tr	01/98	97-03	206	9	10
Wycombe W	Tr	01/04	03-04	49	2	1

NETTLESHIP Reginald (Reg)
Born: Warsop, Nottinghamshire, England, 23 February, 1925 — IF
Died: Mansfield, Nottinghamshire, England, 16 September, 2001

League Club	Source	Date Signed	Seasons Played	Apps	Subs	Gls
Sheffield U	Welbeck Colliery	06/43				
Mansfield T	Tr	07/46	46	1	-	0

NETTLETON Ernest (Ernie)
Born: Sheffield, England, 7 January, 1918 — LW
Died: Pembroke, Wales, 5 March, 2005

League Club	Source	Date Signed	Seasons Played	Apps	Subs	Gls
Sheffield U	Hartlepool U (Am)	12/44				
York C	Tr	07/46	46	7	-	2

[NEUTON] PICCOLI Sergio Neuton
Born: Erechim, Brazil, 14 March, 1990 — LB

League Club	Source	Date Signed	Seasons Played	Apps	Subs	Gls
Watford (L)	Udinese (ITA)	08/12	12	7	1	0

NEVES Rui dos Santos Cordeiro (Rui)
Born: Vinhais, Portugal, 10 March, 1965 — F

League Club	Source	Date Signed	Seasons Played	Apps	Subs	Gls
Darlington	Famalicao (POR)	08/95	95	3	2	0

NEVILLE Christopher William (Chris)
Born: Downham Market, Norfolk, England, 22 October, 1970 — G

League Club	Source	Date Signed	Seasons Played	Apps	Subs	Gls
Ipswich T	YT	05/89	89	1	0	0

NEVILLE David Raymond (Dave)
Born: Birmingham, England, 8 January, 1929 — FB
Died: Manchester, England, 18 August, 1991

League Club	Source	Date Signed	Seasons Played	Apps	Subs	Gls
Bournemouth	Paget Rgrs	04/49				
Chelsea	Tr	07/50				
Rochdale	Burton A	08/55	55	1	-	0

NEVILLE Gary Alexander
Born: Bury, Greater Manchester, England, 18 February, 1975 — RB
England: 85/Youth

League Club	Source	Date Signed	Seasons Played	Apps	Subs	Gls
Manchester U	YT	01/93	93-10	380	20	5

NEVILLE Philip John (Phil)
Born: Bury, Greater Manchester, England, 21 January, 1977 — D/M
England: 59/U21-7/Youth/Schools

League Club	Source	Date Signed	Seasons Played	Apps	Subs	Gls
Manchester U	YT	06/94	94-04	210	53	5
Everton	Tr	08/05	05-12	237	5	4

NEVILLE Steven Francis (Steve)
Born: Walthamstow, NE London, England, 18 September, 1957 — W/F

League Club	Source	Date Signed	Seasons Played	Apps	Subs	Gls
Southampton	App	09/75	77	5	0	1
Exeter C	Tr	09/78	78-80	90	3	22
Sheffield U	Tr	10/80	80-81	40	9	6
Exeter C	Tr	10/82	82-84	89	3	27
Bristol C	Tr	11/84	84-87	128	6	40
Exeter C	Tr	07/88	88-90	115	5	39

NEVILLE William (Billy)
Born: Cork, Republic of Ireland, 15 May, 1935 — CF
Republic of Ireland: B

League Club	Source	Date Signed	Seasons Played	Apps	Subs	Gls
West Ham U	Wembley	11/56	57	3	-	0

NEVIN Patrick Kevin Francis Michael (Pat)
Born: Glasgow, Scotland, 6 September, 1963 — RW
Scotland: 28/B-4/U21-5/Youth

League Club	Source	Date Signed	Seasons Played	Apps	Subs	Gls
Chelsea	Clyde	07/83	83-87	190	3	36
Everton	Tr	07/88	88-91	81	28	16
Tranmere Rov	L	03/92	91	8	0	0
Tranmere Rov	Tr	08/92	92-96	181	12	30

NEVIN Paul Richard
Born: Lewisham, SE London, England, 23 June, 1969 — F

League Club	Source	Date Signed	Seasons Played	Apps	Subs	Gls
Carlisle U	Evansville Univ (USA)	09/91	91	2	6	0

NEVIN Ridley Walter
Born: Corbridge, Northumberland, England, 28 July, 1956 — M

League Club	Source	Date Signed	Seasons Played	Apps	Subs	Gls
Everton	App	05/74				
Workington	Tr	08/75	75	3	1	0

NEVINS Laurence (Laurie)
Born: Gateshead, Tyne and Wear, England, 2 July, 1920 — LW
Died: Gateshead, Tyne and Wear, England, June, 1972

League Club	Source	Date Signed	Seasons Played	Apps	Subs	Gls
Newcastle U		09/40				
Brighton & HA	Tr	05/47	47	5	-	0
Hartlepool U	Tr	03/48	47-48	18	-	8

NEVLAND Erik
Born: Stavanger, Norway, 10 November, 1977 — F
Norway: 8/U21-22/Youth

League Club	Source	Date Signed	Seasons Played	Apps	Subs	Gls
Manchester U (L)	Viking Stavanger (NOR)	07/97	97	0	1	0
Fulham	Groningen (NED)	01/08	07-09	18	34	9

NEW Martin Peter
Born: Swindon, England, 11 May, 1959 — G
England: Schools

League Club	Source	Date Signed	Seasons Played	Apps	Subs	Gls
Arsenal	App	03/77				
Mansfield T	Tr	06/78	78-79	21	0	0
Barnsley	Tr	06/80	80	24	0	0

NEWALL James Donald (Danny)
Born: Newport, Wales, 5 June, 1921 — WH
Died: Newport, Wales, 6 March, 1997

League Club	Source	Date Signed	Seasons Played	Apps	Subs	Gls
Newport Co	Melrose Stars	06/38	38-54	236	-	4

NEWBERY Peter John
Born: Derby, England, 4 March, 1938 — CF

League Club	Source	Date Signed	Seasons Played	Apps	Subs	Gls
Derby Co	Jnr	03/55	58-60	5	-	2

NEWBOLD Adam Charles
Born: Nottingham, England, 16 November, 1989 — F

League Club	Source	Date Signed	Seasons Played	Apps	Subs	Gls
Nottingham F	Sch	12/06	08	0	4	0

NEWBOLD Alfred (Alf)
Born: Hartlepool, Cleveland, England, 7 August, 1921 — RB
Died: Birmingham, England, 28 December, 2001

League Club	Source	Date Signed	Seasons Played	Apps	Subs	Gls
Huddersfield T	Ouston W	12/45	46	2	-	0
Newport Co	Tr	10/46	46	22	-	0

NEWBY Jonathan Philip Robert (Jon)
Born: Warrington, Cheshire, England, 28 November, 1978 — F

League Club	Source	Date Signed	Seasons Played	Apps	Subs	Gls
Liverpool	Jnr	05/97	99	0	1	0
Crewe Alex	L	03/00	99	5	1	0
Sheffield U	L	08/00	00	3	10	0
Bury	Tr	02/01	00-02	109	0	21
Huddersfield T	Tr	08/03	03	10	4	0
York C	L	03/04	03	6	1	0
Bury	Tr	08/04	04-05	21	25	5
Wrexham	Tr	08/06	06	2	9	0
Morecambe	Tr	08/07	07	11	21	6

NEWBY Thomas Geoffrey (Geoff)
Born: Barrow, Cumbria, England, 9 October, 1949 — LH

League Club	Source	Date Signed	Seasons Played	Apps	Subs	Gls
Barrow (Am)	Jnr	11/68	68	1	0	0

NEWCOMBE Bernard John (Len)
Born: Swansea, Wales, 28 February, 1931 — LW
Died: Swansea, Wales, March, 1996

League Club	Source	Date Signed	Seasons Played	Apps	Subs	Gls
Fulham	Jnr	05/48	51-54	23	-	3
Brentford	Tr	04/56	55-58	85	-	8

NEWCOMBE Giles Alan
Born: Doncaster, South Yorkshire, England, 7 September, 1968 — G

League Club	Source	Date Signed	Seasons Played	Apps	Subs	Gls
Rotherham U	App	06/87	86	6	0	0

NEWELL Edgar
Born: Swansea, Wales, 17 April, 1920 — FB

League Club	Source	Date Signed	Seasons Played	Apps	Subs	Gls
Swansea C	Hafod Ath	08/46	47-50	22	-	0

NEWELL George
Born: Rochdale, Greater Manchester, England, 17 March, 1936 — CH

League Club	Source	Date Signed	Seasons Played	Apps	Subs	Gls
Rochdale		04/57	57	1	-	0

NEWELL Joseph Peter (Joe)
Born: Tamworth, Staffordshire, England, 15 March, 1993 — W

League Club	Source	Date Signed	Seasons Played	Apps	Subs	Gls
Peterborough U	Sch	03/11	10-14	71	25	3

NEWELL Justin James
Born: Germany, 8 February, 1980 — F

League Club	Source	Date Signed	Seasons Played	Apps	Subs	Gls
Torquay U	YT	06/98	97	0	1	0

NEWELL Michael Colin (Mike)
Born: Liverpool, England, 27 January, 1965 — F
England: B-2/U21-4

League Club	Source	Date Signed	Seasons Played	Apps	Subs	Gls
Crewe Alex	Liverpool (Jnr)	09/83	83	3	0	0
Wigan Ath	Tr	10/83	83-85	64	8	25
Luton T	Tr	01/86	85-87	62	1	18
Leicester C	Tr	09/87	87-88	81	0	21
Everton	Tr	07/89	89-91	48	20	15
Blackburn Rov	Tr	11/91	91-95	113	17	28
Birmingham C	Tr	07/96	96	11	4	1
West Ham U	L	12/96	96	6	1	0
Bradford C	L	03/97	96	7	0	0
Crewe Alex	Aberdeen	03/99	98	1	3	0
Blackpool	Doncaster Rov	02/00	99-00	16	2	2

NEWELL Paul Clayton
Born: Woolwich, SE London, England, 23 February, 1969 — G

League Club	Source	Date Signed	Seasons Played	Apps	Subs	Gls
Southend U	App	06/87	87-88	15	0	0
Leyton Orient	Tr	08/90	90-93	61	0	0
Colchester U	L	08/92	92	14	0	0
Barnet	Tr	07/94	94-95	16	0	0
Darlington	Tr	01/96	95-96	41	0	0

NEWEY Thomas William (Tom)
Born: Huddersfield, West Yorkshire, England, 31 October, 1982 — LB

League Club	Source	Date Signed	Seasons Played	Apps	Subs	Gls
Leeds U	YT	08/00				
Cambridge U	L	02/03	02	6	0	0
Darlington	L	03/03	02	7	0	1
Leyton Orient	Tr	08/03	03-04	34	20	3
Cambridge U	Tr	01/05	04	15	1	0
Grimsby T	Tr	07/05	05-08	142	5	3
Rochdale	L	03/09	08	1	1	0
Bury	Tr	08/09	09	29	3	0
Rotherham U	Tr	07/10	10-11	53	5	0
Scunthorpe U	Tr	08/12	12	45	0	0
Oxford U	Tr	07/13	13-14	52	0	1
Northampton T	Tr	10/14	14	5	4	0

NEWHOUSE Aidan Robert
Born: Wallasey, Wirral, England, 23 May, 1972 — F
England: Youth

League Club	Source	Date Signed	Seasons Played	Apps	Subs	Gls
Chester C	YT	07/89	87-89	29	15	6
Wimbledon	Tr	02/90	89-92	7	16	3
Port Vale	L	01/94	93	0	2	0
Portsmouth	L	12/94	94	6	0	1
Torquay U	L	12/95	95	4	0	2
Fulham	Tr	06/97	97	7	1	1
Swansea C	Tr	10/97	97-98	8	6	0
Brighton & HA	Tr	08/99	99	1	11	2

NEWLAND Raymond James (Ray)
Born: Liverpool, England, 19 July, 1971 — G

League Club	Source	Date Signed	Seasons Played	Apps	Subs	Gls
Plymouth Arg	St Helens T	07/92	92-93	25	1	0
Chester C	Tr	07/94	94	9	1	0
Torquay U	Tr	01/96	95-96	28	0	0

NEWLANDS Douglas Haigh (Doug)
Born: Edinburgh, Scotland, 29 October, 1931 — W
Died: Perth, Scotland, 11 April, 2011

League Club	Source	Date Signed	Seasons Played	Apps	Subs	Gls
Burnley	Aberdeen	03/55	54-58	98	-	21
Stoke C	Tr	07/59	59	32	-	8

NEWLANDS Malcolm (Monty)
Born: Wishaw, Lanarkshire, Scotland, 28 March, 1925 — G
Died: Motherwell, Lancashire, Scotland, 10 February, 1996

League Club	Source	Date Signed	Seasons Played	Apps	Subs	Gls
Preston NE	St Mirren	07/48	48-52	80	-	0
Workington	Tr	11/52	52-59	250	-	0

NEWLOVE Peter
Born: Bradford, England, 27 December, 1947 — WH

League Club	Source	Date Signed	Seasons Played	Apps	Subs	Gls
Bradford C	App	01/66	64-66	2	1	0

NEWMAN Albert Dorcin
Born: Lichfield, Staffordshire, England, 1 March, 1915 — LH
Died: Walsall, West Midlands, England, 18 December, 1981

League Club	Source	Date Signed	Seasons Played	Apps	Subs	Gls
Walsall	Brierley Hill Alliance	11/39	46-49	135	-	2

NEWMAN Darren Lewis
Born: Brighton, England, 14 August, 1968 — CD

League Club	Source	Date Signed	Seasons Played	Apps	Subs	Gls
Brighton & HA	App	08/86	85	1	0	0

NEWMAN Eric Ivan Alfred
Born: Romford, E London, England, 24 November, 1924 — G
Died: Tenterden, Kent, England, January, 1971

League Club	Source	Date Signed	Seasons Played	Apps	Subs	Gls
Arsenal	Romford	10/46				
Ipswich T	Tr	09/50	52	18	-	0

NEWMAN Harry Maurice (Mick)
Born: London, Ontario, Canada, 2 April, 1932 — IF

League Club	Source	Date Signed	Seasons Played	Apps	Subs	Gls
West Ham U	Dagenham	02/57	56-57	7	-	2

NEWMAN John Henry George
Born: Hereford, England, 13 December, 1933 — CH/LH

League Club	Source	Date Signed	Seasons Played	Apps	Subs	Gls
Birmingham C	Jnr	03/51	51-57	60	-	0
Leicester C	Tr	11/57	57-59	61	-	2
Plymouth Arg	Tr	01/60	59-67	298	0	9
Exeter C	Tr	11/67	67-71	91	1	1

NEWMAN Keith
Born: Farnham, Surrey, England, 20 November, 1949 — WH
England: Schools

League Club	Source	Date Signed	Seasons Played	Apps	Subs	Gls
Aldershot	App	11/66	66-69	19	4	0
York C	Tr	07/70	70	3	1	0

NEWMAN Richard Adrian (Ricky)
Born: Guildford, Surrey, England, 5 August, 1970 — D/M

League Club	Source	Date Signed	Seasons Played	Apps	Subs	Gls
Crystal Palace	Jnr	01/88	92-94	43	5	3
Maidstone U	L	02/92	91	9	1	1
Millwall	Tr	07/95	95-99	144	6	5
Reading	Tr	03/00	99-04	98	23	1
Brentford	Tr	07/05	05	29	1	3
Aldershot T	Tr	07/06	08	10	7	0

NEWMAN Robert Nigel (Rob)
Born: Bradford-on-Avon, Wiltshire, England, 13 December, 1963 — D/M

League Club	Source	Date Signed	Seasons Played	Apps	Subs	Gls
Bristol C	App	10/81	81-90	382	12	52
Norwich C	Tr	07/91	91-97	181	19	14
Wigan Ath	L	03/98	97	8	0	0
Southend U	Tr	07/98	98-01	63	9	11

NEWMAN Ronald (Ron)
Born: Pontypridd, Rhondda Cynon Taff, Wales, 1 May, 1933 — IF

League Club	Source	Date Signed	Seasons Played	Apps	Subs	Gls
Northampton T	Ynysybwl	10/53	54-55	18	-	5
Coventry C	Tr	03/56	55-56	13	-	2
Torquay U	Tr	07/57	57	4	-	0

NEWMAN Ronald Vernon (Ron)
Born: Fareham, Hampshire, England, 19 January, 1934 — W/IF

League Club	Source	Date Signed	Seasons Played	Apps	Subs	Gls
Portsmouth	Woking	01/55	54-60	109	-	21
Leyton Orient	Tr	01/61	60-61	14	-	1
Crystal Palace	Tr	10/62	62	6	-	0
Gillingham	Tr	09/63	63-65	90	3	20

NEWSHAM Marc Anthony
Born: Hatfield, South Yorkshire, England, 24 March, 1987 — F

League Club	Source	Date Signed	Seasons Played	Apps	Subs	Gls
Rotherham U	Sch	07/06	04-07	14	34	7

NEWSHAM Stanley (Stan)
Born: Farnworth, Greater Manchester, England, 24 March, 1931 — IF
Died: Portsmouth, England, 4 May, 2001

League Club	Source	Date Signed	Seasons Played	Apps	Subs	Gls
Bournemouth	Bolton W (Am)	06/52	52-56	142	-	74
Notts Co	Tr	08/57	57-61	99	-	44

NEWSOME Jonathan (Jon)
Born: Sheffield, England, 6 September, 1970 — CD

League Club	Source	Date Signed	Seasons Played	Apps	Subs	Gls
Sheffield Wed	YT	07/89	89-90	6	1	0
Leeds U	Tr	06/91	91-93	62	14	3
Norwich C	Tr	06/94	94-95	61	1	7
Sheffield Wed	Tr	03/96	95-99	50	4	4
Bolton W	L	11/98	98	6	0	0

NEWSOME Robinson (Robin)
Born: Hebden Bridge, West Yorkshire, England, 25 September, 1919 — IF
Died: Dudley, West Midlands, England, 9 November, 1999

League Club	Source	Date Signed	Seasons Played	Apps	Subs	Gls
West Bromwich A	Congleton T	03/39				
Coventry C	Tr	06/47	47	7	-	2

NEWSON Mark Joseph
Born: Stepney, E London, England, 7 December, 1960 — D
England: Semi Pro-5

League Club	Source	Date Signed	Seasons Played	Apps	Subs	Gls
Charlton Ath	App	12/78				
Bournemouth	Maidstone U	05/85	85-89	172	5	23
Fulham	Tr	02/90	89-92	98	4	4
Barnet	Tr	08/93	93-94	58	1	4

NEWTON Adam Lee
Born: Grays, Essex, England, 4 December, 1980 — M/RB
England: U21-1//St Kitts & Nevis: 5

League Club	Source	Date Signed	Seasons Played	Apps	Subs	Gls
West Ham U	YT	07/99	99	0	2	0
Portsmouth	L	07/99	99	1	2	0
Notts Co	L	11/00	00	13	7	1
Leyton Orient	L	03/02	01	10	0	1
Peterborough U	Tr	07/02	02-07	191	27	8
Brentford	Tr	07/08	08	30	5	1

NEWTON Benjamin (Ben)
Born: Grimsby, North Lincolnshire, England, 10 October, 1934 — IF

League Club	Source	Date Signed	Seasons Played	Apps	Subs	Gls
Grimsby T	Jnr	07/53	53	3	-	0

NEWTON Christopher John (Chris)
Born: Leeds, England, 15 November, 1979 — F

League Club	Source	Date Signed	Seasons Played	Apps	Subs	Gls
Halifax T	YT	07/98	98-99	12	10	1

NEWTON Conor James
Born: Whickham, Tyne and Wear, England, 17 October, 1991 — M

League Club	Source	Date Signed	Seasons Played	Apps	Subs	Gls
Newcastle U	Sch	07/10				
Rotherham U	St Mirren	05/14	14	6	7	0

NEWTON Edward John Ikem (Eddie)
Born: Hammersmith, W London, England, 13 December, 1971 — M
England: U21-2

League Club	Source	Date Signed	Seasons Played	Apps	Subs	Gls
Chelsea	YT	05/90	91-98	139	26	8
Cardiff C	L	01/92	91	18	0	4
Birmingham C	Tr	07/99	99	2	2	0
Oxford U	Tr	03/00	99	7	0	0
Barnet	Tr	08/00	00	2	2	0

NEWTON Eric David
Born: Sheffield, England, 21 June, 1932 — IF

League Club	Source	Date Signed	Seasons Played	Apps	Subs	Gls
Halifax T	Norton Woodseats	12/54	54	10	-	3

NEWTON Graham Wilfred
Born: Bilston, West Midlands, England, 22 December, 1942 — M

League Club	Source	Date Signed	Seasons Played	Apps	Subs	Gls
Blackpool	Wolverhampton W (Am)	08/61				
Walsall	Tr	02/62	62-63	30	-	10
Coventry C	Tr	01/64	63	8	-	3
Bournemouth	Tr	12/64	64-66	27	1	3
Port Vale	Atlanta Chiefs (USA)	11/68	68	4	0	1

NEWTON Henry Albert
Born: Nottingham, England, 18 February, 1944 — M/LB
England: FLge-1/U23-4

League Club	Source	Date Signed	Seasons Played	Apps	Subs	Gls
Nottingham F	Jnr	06/61	63-70	282	0	17
Everton	Tr	10/70	70-73	76	0	5
Derby Co	Tr	09/73	73-76	111	6	5
Walsall	Tr	07/77	77	16	0	0

NEWTON John
Born: Edinburgh, Scotland, 19 January, 1940 — RH

League Club	Source	Date Signed	Seasons Played	Apps	Subs	Gls
Notts Co	Craiglea Thistle	10/57	58-60	5	-	0

NEWTON John Lawes (Jackie)
Born: Bishop Auckland, County Durham, England, 25 May, 1925 — WH
Died: County Durham, England, 30 January, 2010

League Club	Source	Date Signed	Seasons Played	Apps	Subs	Gls
Newcastle U	Cockton Hill Jnrs	05/44				
Hartlepool U	Tr	05/46	46-57	332	-	15

NEWTON Keith Robert
Born: Manchester, England, 23 June, 1941 — LB
Died: Blackburn, Greater Manchester, England, 15 June, 1998
England: 27/FLge-5/U23-4

League Club	Source	Date Signed	Seasons Played	Apps	Subs	Gls
Blackburn Rov	Jnr	10/58	60-69	306	0	9
Everton	Tr	12/69	69-71	48	1	1
Burnley	Tr	06/72	72-77	209	0	5

NEWTON Reginald William (Reg)
Born: Limehouse, E London, England, 30 June, 1926 — G

League Club	Source	Date Signed	Seasons Played	Apps	Subs	Gls
Leyton Orient	Dagenham Works	04/48	48	23	-	0
Brentford	Tr	07/49	49-56	87	-	0

NEWTON Robert (Bob)
Born: Chesterfield, Derbyshire, England, 23 November, 1956 — F

League Club	Source	Date Signed	Seasons Played	Apps	Subs	Gls
Huddersfield T	App	11/73	73-76	37	5	7
Hartlepool U	Tr	08/77	77-82	150	0	48
Port Vale	Tr	09/82	82-83	48	0	22
Chesterfield	Tr	10/83	83-84	78	0	29
Hartlepool U	Tr	07/85	85	8	3	2
Stockport Co	L	03/86	85	6	0	1
Bristol Rov	Chesterfield (NC)	02/87	86	7	1	0

NEWTON Robert Arthur (Bob)
Born: Earl Shilton, Leicestershire, England, 19 January, 1946 — W
Died: Hinckley, Leicestershire, England, 25 October, 2009

League Club	Source	Date Signed	Seasons Played	Apps	Subs	Gls
Leicester C	App	08/63	64	2	-	0
Bradford C	Tr	05/65	65	19	1	4

NEWTON Sean Michael
Born: Liverpool, England, 23 September, 1998 — LB
England: Semi Pro-5

League Club	Source	Date Signed	Seasons Played	Apps	Subs	Gls
Chester C	Jnr	05/07	07	2	0	0
Notts Co (L)	Lincoln C	02/15	14	6	2	0

NEWTON Shaun O'Neill
Born: Camberwell, S London, England, 20 August, 1975 — RW
England: U21-3

League Club	Source	Date Signed	Seasons Played	Apps	Subs	Gls
Charlton Ath	YT	07/93	92-00	189	51	20
Wolverhampton W	Tr	08/01	01-04	115	15	12
West Ham U	Tr	03/05	04-06	19	21	1
Leicester C	Tr	03/07	06-07	16	3	1

NEWTON Stanley Douglas (Doug)
Born: Newcastle-upon-Tyne, England, 16 January, 1959 — M
England: Semi Pro-3

League Club	Source	Date Signed	Seasons Played	Apps	Subs	Gls
Scarborough	Boston U	03/88	87	4	1	0

N'GALA Bondzanga (Bondz)
Born: Forest Gate, E London, England, 13 September, 1989 — D

League Club	Source	Date Signed	Seasons Played	Apps	Subs	Gls
West Ham U	Sch	02/08				
MK Dons	L	11/08	08	1	2	0
Scunthorpe U	L	09/09	09	0	2	0
Plymouth Arg	Tr	03/10	09-10	32	3	1
Yeovil T	Tr	07/11	11	24	7	2
Stevenage	Tr	07/12	12	21	4	0
Barnet	L	02/13	12	5	1	0
Portsmouth	Tr	08/13	13	24	3	3

NGATA Heremaia (Herry)
Born: Wanganui, New Zealand, 24 August, 1971 — F
New Zealand: 28

League Club	Source	Date Signed	Seasons Played	Apps	Subs	Gls
Hull C	Jnr	07/89	89-91	8	17	0

NGO BAHENG Wesley
Born: Dieppe, France, 23 September, 1989 — F

League Club	Source	Date Signed	Seasons Played	Apps	Subs	Gls
Newcastle U	Le Havre (FRA)	01/08				
Aldershot T	Tr	11/10	10	0	3	0
Hereford U	Tr	01/11	10	0	2	0

N'GOG David
Born: Paris, France, 1 April, 1989 — F
France: U21-17/Youth

League Club	Source	Date Signed	Seasons Played	Apps	Subs	Gls
Liverpool	Paris St-Germain (FRA)	07/08	08-10	21	42	9
Bolton W	Tr	08/11	11-13	57	24	14
Swansea C	Tr	01/14	13	0	3	0

N'GOMA Kalusivikako (Kalu)
Born: Kinshasa, DR Congo, 3 August, 1979 — M

League Club	Source	Date Signed	Seasons Played	Apps	Subs	Gls
Darlington	Libourne (FRA)	08/06	06	15	3	1

NGONGE Felix Michel (Michel)
Born: Huy, Belgium, 10 January, 1967 — F
DR Congo: 6

League Club	Source	Date Signed	Seasons Played	Apps	Subs	Gls
Watford	Samsunspor (TKY)	07/98	98-00	29	18	9
Huddersfield T	L	03/00	99	0	4	0
Queens Park Rgrs	Tr	12/00	00	7	6	3

N'GOO Michael Ayadeji
Born: Walthamstow, NE London, England, 23 October, 1992 — F
England: Youth

League Club	Source	Date Signed	Seasons Played	Apps	Subs	Gls
Liverpool	Sch	10/09				
Yeovil T	L	07/13	13	1	5	0
Walsall	L	01/14	13	4	10	1

N'GOTTY Bruno
Born: Lyon, France, 10 June, 1971 — CD
France: 6

League Club	Source	Date Signed	Seasons Played	Apps	Subs	Gls
Bolton W	Olymp Marseille (FRA)	09/01	01-05	143	5	4
Birmingham C	Tr	07/06	06	25	0	1
Leicester C	Tr	07/07	07	30	8	0
Hereford U	L	09/08	08	8	0	0

League Club	Source	Date Signed	Seasons Played	Career Record Apps	Subs	Gls
N'GOYI Granddi						
Born: Melun, France, 17 May, 1988						M
France: U21-6/Youth						
Leeds U (L)	Palermo (ITA)	01/15	14	1	0	0
N'GUESSAN Djombo Dany-Gael (Dany)						
Born: Paris, France, 11 August, 1987						W
Boston U (L)	Glasgow Rangers	08/06	06	13	10	5
Lincoln C	Glasgow Rangers	01/07	06-08	70	21	15
Leicester C	Tr	07/09	09-10	19	13	3
Scunthorpe U	L	11/10	10	3	0	1
Southampton	L	01/11	10	2	4	0
Millwall	Tr	08/11	11-13	12	17	2
Charlton Ath	L	03/12	11	6	1	4
Swindon T	Tr	09/13	13	14	10	8
Port Vale		10/14	14	10	1	2
N'GUESSAN Joseph David Ruhemann (Joe)						
Born: Lewisham, SE London, England, 15 July, 1995						RW
Stevenage	Sch	07/13	12-14	2	7	1
NIBLETT Victor (Vic)						
Born: Frimley, Surrey, England, 9 December, 1924						CH
Died: Gillingham, Kent, England, 1 October, 2004						
Reading	Jnr	08/44	46-49	6	-	0
West Ham U	Tr	06/50				
Gillingham	Tr	08/51	51-55	154	-	0
NIBLOE John Allister (Jack)						
Born: Sheffield, England, 1 June, 1939						CF
Died: Stocksbridge, South Yorkshire, England, 29 November, 1964						
Sheffield U		08/58	58-60	25	-	4
Stoke C	Tr	10/61	61-62	20	-	4
Doncaster Rov	Tr	10/62	62-63	36	-	7
Stockport Co	Tr	07/64	64	22	-	4
NIBLOE Joseph (Joe)						
Born: Glasgow, Scotland, 10 December, 1926						LB
Died: East Kilbride, Lanarkshire, Scotland, 23 September, 2007						
Cardiff C	Clydebank Jnrs	03/48	48	1	-	0
NICHOL Robert Wishart						
Born: Carlisle, Cumbria, England, 19 January, 1941						LW
Carlisle U (Am)	Jnr	06/58	58-59	3	-	1
NICHOLAS Andrew Peter						
Born: Liverpool, England, 10 October, 1983						LB
Swindon T	Liverpool (Sch)	07/03	03-07	105	21	4
Chester C	L	03/05	04	5	0	0
Rotherham U	Tr	08/08	08-09	26	0	0
NICHOLAS Anthony Wallace Long (Tony)						
Born: West Ham, E London, England, 16 April, 1938						IF
Died: Chelmsford, England, 25 September, 2005						
England: Youth						
Chelsea	Jnr	05/55	56-59	59	-	18
Brighton & HA	Tr	11/60	60-61	65	-	22
Leyton Orient	Chelmsford C	06/65	65	8	1	2
NICHOLAS Charles (Charlie)						
Born: Glasgow, Scotland, 30 December, 1961						F
Scotland: 20/U21-6/Youth						
Arsenal	Glasgow Celtic	07/83	83-87	145	6	34
NICHOLAS Charles Brian (Brian)						
Born: Aberdare, Rhondda Cynon Taff, Wales, 20 April, 1933						RH
England: Schools						
Queens Park Rgrs	Jnr	05/50	48-54	113	-	2
Chelsea	Tr	07/55	55-57	26	-	1
Coventry C	Tr	02/58	57-61	113	-	0
NICHOLAS George Anton						
Born: Watford, Hertfordshire, England, 19 December, 1992						M
Notts Co	Sch	07/11	10	0	1	0
NICHOLAS Glyn						
Born: Dartmouth, Devon, England, 2 December, 1946						CF
Plymouth Arg	App	09/64	64-65	2	0	0
Crewe Alex	L	03/66	65	2	0	1
NICHOLAS John Thomas (Jack)						
Born: Derby, England, 26 November, 1910						WH
Died: Nottingham, England, 14 February, 1977						
Wales: Schools						
Derby Co	Swansea C (Am)	12/27	28-46	347	-	14
NICHOLAS Kenneth William (Ken)						
Born: Northampton, England, 3 February, 1938						LB
Died: Blackheath, SE London, England, 24 March, 2007						
England: Youth/Schools						

League Club	Source	Date Signed	Seasons Played	Career Record Apps	Subs	Gls
Arsenal	Jnr	05/55				
Watford	Tr	05/59	59-64	198	-	4
NICHOLAS Peter						
Born: Newport, Wales, 10 November, 1959						DM
Wales: 73/U21-3/Schools						
Crystal Palace	App	12/76	77-80	127	0	7
Arsenal	Tr	03/81	80-82	57	3	1
Crystal Palace	Tr	10/83	83-84	47	0	7
Luton T	Tr	01/85	84-86	102	0	1
Chelsea	Aberdeen	08/88	88-90	79	1	2
Watford	Tr	03/91	90-91	40	0	1
NICHOLL Christopher John (Chris)						
Born: Wilmslow, Cheshire, England, 12 October, 1946						CD
Northern Ireland: 51						
Burnley	Jnr	04/65				
Halifax T	Witton A	06/68	68-69	42	0	3
Luton T	Tr	08/69	69-71	97	0	6
Aston Villa	Tr	03/72	71-76	210	0	11
Southampton	Tr	06/77	77-82	228	0	8
Grimsby T	Tr	08/83	83-84	70	0	0
NICHOLL James Michael (Jimmy)						
Born: Hamilton, Ontario, Canada, 28 December, 1956						RB
Northern Ireland: 73/U21-1/Schools						
Manchester U	App	02/74	74-81	188	9	3
Sunderland	L	12/81	81	3	0	0
Sunderland	Toronto Blizzard (CAN)	09/82	82	29	0	0
West Bromwich A	Glasgow Rangers	11/84	84-85	56	0	0
NICHOLL Terence John (Terry)						
Born: Wilmslow, Cheshire, England, 16 September, 1952						M
Crewe Alex		02/72	71-72	46	0	7
Sheffield U	Tr	03/73	73-74	12	10	1
Southend U	Tr	05/75	75-76	50	0	3
Gillingham	Tr	10/76	76-80	184	0	11
NICHOLLS Alan						
Born: Plymouth, England, 10 February, 1963						CD
Bristol C	App	02/80	80-82	70	0	5
NICHOLLS Alan						
Born: Sutton Coldfield, West Midlands, England, 28 August, 1973						G
Died: Peterborough, England, June, 1995						
England: U21-1						
Plymouth Arg	Cheltenham T	08/93	93-94	64	1	0
NICHOLLS Alexander Douglas (Alex)						
Born: Stourbridge, West Midlands, England, 9 December, 1987						W/F
Walsall	Sch	07/06	05-11	127	64	24
Northampton T	Tr	06/12	12-14	19	2	8
Exeter C	Tr	09/14	14	27	5	5
NICHOLLS Ashley Joseph						
Born: Ipswich, England, 30 October, 1981						DM
England: Schools						
Ipswich T	Ipswich W	07/00				
Darlington	Tr	08/02	02-03	65	2	6
Cambridge U	Tr	02/04	03-04	40	4	1
Rushden & D (L)	Cambridge U	08/05	05	11	0	0
Rushden & D	Tr	01/06	05	15	4	0
NICHOLLS David						
Born: Bradford, England, 3 November, 1956						M
England: Schools						
Huddersfield T	App	11/73				
Bradford C	Tr	08/75	75	0	4	0
NICHOLLS James Henry (Jim)						
Born: Coseley, West Midlands, England, 27 November, 1919						G
Died: Leeds, England, July, 2002						
Bradford Park Ave	Dudley T	05/46	46-49	36	-	0
Rochdale	Tr	08/51	51-52	50	-	0
NICHOLLS John (Johnny)						
Born: Wolverhampton, England, 3 April, 1931						IF
Died: Wolverhampton, England, 1 April, 1995						
England: 2/B-1/U23-1						
West Bromwich A	Heath Town U	08/51	51-56	131	-	58
Cardiff C	Tr	05/57	57	8	-	2
Exeter C	Tr	11/57	57-58	55	-	23
NICHOLLS Kevin John Richard						
Born: Newham, E London, England, 2 January, 1979						M
England: Youth						
Charlton Ath	YT	01/96	96-97	4	8	1
Brighton & HA	L	02/99	98	4	0	1
Wigan Ath	Tr	06/99	99-00	19	9	0
Luton T	Tr	08/01	01-05	173	2	31

League Club	Source	Date Signed	Seasons Played	Apps	Subs	Gls
Leeds U	Tr	07/06	06	12	1	0
Preston NE	Tr	07/07	07	17	1	0
Luton T	Tr	08/08	08	16	3	0

NICHOLLS Lee Anthony
Born: Huyton, Merseyside, England, 5 October, 1992 G
England: Youth

League Club	Source	Date Signed	Seasons Played	Apps	Subs	Gls
Wigan Ath	Sch	01/10	13-14	7	0	0
Accrington Stan	L	02/12	11	9	0	0
Northampton T	L	08/12	12	46	0	0

NICHOLLS Mark
Born: Hillingdon, W London, England, 30 May, 1977 F

League Club	Source	Date Signed	Seasons Played	Apps	Subs	Gls
Chelsea	YT	07/95	96-98	11	25	3
Reading	L	12/99	99	4	1	1
Grimsby T	L	02/00	99	6	0	0
Colchester U	L	10/00	00	3	1	0
Torquay U	Partick Thistle	09/01	01	4	5	1

NICHOLLS Philip Roy (Phil)
Born: Bilston, West Midlands, England, 22 June, 1952 CD

League Club	Source	Date Signed	Seasons Played	Apps	Subs	Gls
Wolverhampton W	App	07/70				
Crewe Alex	Tr	09/72	72-76	155	8	8
Bradford C	Tr	03/77	76-77	19	2	2
Crewe Alex	Tr	08/78	78	10	3	0

NICHOLLS Raymond Ian (Ray)
Born: Peterborough, England, 7 April, 1965 M

League Club	Source	Date Signed	Seasons Played	Apps	Subs	Gls
Cambridge U	App	08/82	81-83	18	5	1

NICHOLLS Ronald Bernard (Ron)
Born: Sharpness, Gloucestershire, England, 4 December, 1933 G
Died: Cheltenham, Gloucestershire, England, 29 August, 1994

League Club	Source	Date Signed	Seasons Played	Apps	Subs	Gls
Bristol Rov	Cheltenham T	11/54	55-57	71	-	0
Cardiff C	Tr	08/58	58-60	51	-	0
Bristol C	Tr	07/61	61-63	39	-	0

NICHOLLS Ronald Henry (Ron)
Born: Cannock, Staffordshire, England, 18 October, 1935 WH

League Club	Source	Date Signed	Seasons Played	Apps	Subs	Gls
West Bromwich A	Jnr	11/52				
Walsall	Tr	08/53	53	2	-	0

NICHOLLS Ryan Rhys
Born: Cardiff, Wales, 10 May, 1973 M
Wales: Schools

League Club	Source	Date Signed	Seasons Played	Apps	Subs	Gls
Leeds U	YT	07/91				
Cardiff C	Tr	01/95	94	6	6	1

NICHOLLS Wayne Keith
Born: Wolverhampton, England, 21 October, 1952 F
Died: Whitehaven, Cumbria, England, August, 2010

League Club	Source	Date Signed	Seasons Played	Apps	Subs	Gls
Leicester C	Wolverhampton W (App)	11/70				
Workington	Tr	08/71	71-72	21	12	1

NICHOLS Adam Anthony
Born: Ilford, E London, England, 14 September, 1962 CD

League Club	Source	Date Signed	Seasons Played	Apps	Subs	Gls
Ipswich T	App	10/79				
Colchester U	Wits Univ (RSA)	09/83	83	4	2	1

NICHOLS Brian Albert
Born: Dagenham, E London, England, 30 May, 1945 LB

League Club	Source	Date Signed	Seasons Played	Apps	Subs	Gls
Fulham	App	07/63	65-67	50	1	1
Millwall	Tr	07/68	68-69	9	1	0

NICHOLS Jonathan Anthony (Jon)
Born: Plymouth, England, 10 September, 1980 FB

League Club	Source	Date Signed	Seasons Played	Apps	Subs	Gls
Torquay U	YT	07/99	98-99	6	1	0

NICHOLS Tom Andrew
Born: Wellington, Somerset, England, 1 September, 1993 F

League Club	Source	Date Signed	Seasons Played	Apps	Subs	Gls
Exeter C	Sch	07/11	11-14	45	30	22

NICHOLSON Barry
Born: Dumfries, Scotland, 24 August, 1978 M
Scotland: 3/U21-7

League Club	Source	Date Signed	Seasons Played	Apps	Subs	Gls
Preston NE	Aberdeen	07/08	08-11	70	23	9
Fleetwood T	Tr	07/12	12	18	12	2

NICHOLSON Derek
Born: Harrow, NW London, England, 8 April, 1936 RW

League Club	Source	Date Signed	Seasons Played	Apps	Subs	Gls
Leyton Orient	Chase of Chertsey	11/53	57	6	-	0

NICHOLSON Gary Anthony
Born: Hexham, Northumberland, England, 4 November, 1960 LW

League Club	Source	Date Signed	Seasons Played	Apps	Subs	Gls
Newcastle U	App	11/78	78-80	7	5	0
Mansfield T	Tr	08/81	81-83	112	6	21
York C	Tr	07/84	84	23	1	4
Halifax T	Tr	07/85	85-86	54	5	4

NICHOLSON George Henry (Harry)
Born: Wetheral, Cumbria, England, 25 January, 1932 G

League Club	Source	Date Signed	Seasons Played	Apps	Subs	Gls
Grimsby T	Carlisle U (Am)	08/52	53	17	-	0
Nottingham F	Tr	07/55	55-56	72	-	0
Accrington Stan	Tr	03/58	58	1	-	0
Leyton Orient	Tr	03/59	59	4	-	0
Bristol C	Tr	07/60	60	1	-	0

NICHOLSON Jake Charlie
Born: Harrow, NW London, England, 19 July, 1992 M
England: Youth

League Club	Source	Date Signed	Seasons Played	Apps	Subs	Gls
Tottenham H	Sch	07/10				
Crystal Palace	Tr	07/13				
AFC Wimbledon	Tr	02/14	13-14	5	1	1

NICHOLSON James Joseph (Jimmy)
Born: Belfast, Northern Ireland, 27 February, 1943 M
Northern Ireland: 41/B-4/U23-4/Schools

League Club	Source	Date Signed	Seasons Played	Apps	Subs	Gls
Manchester U	Jnr	02/60	60-62	58	-	5
Huddersfield T	Tr	12/64	64-73	280	1	25
Bury	Tr	12/73	73-75	79	4	0

NICHOLSON John Purcel
Born: Liverpool, England, 2 September, 1936 CH
Died: Doncaster, South Yorkshire, England, 3 September, 1966

League Club	Source	Date Signed	Seasons Played	Apps	Subs	Gls
Liverpool		01/57	59	1	-	0
Port Vale	Tr	08/61	61-65	184	0	1
Doncaster Rov	Tr	09/65	65-66	41	0	0

NICHOLSON John Reay (Jack)
Born: Harrington, Cumbria, England, 23 November, 1928 LW
Died: Harrington, Cumbria, England, 3 June, 1993

League Club	Source	Date Signed	Seasons Played	Apps	Subs	Gls
Barrow	Frizington White Star	05/49	49	4	-	1

NICHOLSON Kevin John
Born: Derby, England, 2 October, 1980 LB
England: Semi Pro-8/Youth/Schools

League Club	Source	Date Signed	Seasons Played	Apps	Subs	Gls
Sheffield Wed	YT	10/97	00	0	1	0
Northampton T	Tr	01/01	00	6	1	0
Notts Co	Tr	03/01	00-03	74	21	3
Torquay U	Forest Green Rov	07/07	09-13	180	8	8

NICHOLSON Maximillian (Max)
Born: Leeds, England, 3 October, 1971 LW

League Club	Source	Date Signed	Seasons Played	Apps	Subs	Gls
Doncaster Rov	YT	06/90	89-91	23	4	2
Hereford U	Tr	05/92	92-93	52	11	7
Torquay U	Tr	09/94	94	1	0	0
Scunthorpe U	Tr	11/94	94-95	27	24	5

NICHOLSON Peter
Born: Cleator Moor, Cumbria, England, 12 January, 1951 FB/M

League Club	Source	Date Signed	Seasons Played	Apps	Subs	Gls
Blackpool	Carlisle U (App)	08/69	70	3	3	0
Bolton W	Tr	06/71	71-81	303	15	12
Rochdale	Lytham St Annes	11/82	82	7	0	0
Carlisle U	Lytham St Annes	03/83	82-83	1	2	0

NICHOLSON Peter William
Born: Hull, England, 11 December, 1936 CF

League Club	Source	Date Signed	Seasons Played	Apps	Subs	Gls
Hull C (Am)	Kingburn Ath	06/60	60	1	-	0

NICHOLSON Reece
Born: Bircotes, Nottinghamshire, England, 4 April, 1936 IF

League Club	Source	Date Signed	Seasons Played	Apps	Subs	Gls
Doncaster Rov	Jnr	09/53	54-57	28	-	8

NICHOLSON Shane Michael
Born: Newark, Nottinghamshire, England, 3 June, 1970 LB

League Club	Source	Date Signed	Seasons Played	Apps	Subs	Gls
Lincoln C	YT	07/88	86-91	122	11	7
Derby Co	Tr	04/92	92-95	73	1	1
West Bromwich A	Tr	02/96	95-97	50	2	0
Chesterfield	Tr	08/98	98	23	1	0
Stockport Co	Tr	06/99	99-00	73	4	3
Sheffield U	Tr	07/01	01	21	4	3
Tranmere Rov	Tr	07/02	02-03	45	9	6
Chesterfield	Tr	07/04	04-06	66	4	12
Lincoln C	L	11/06	06	7	1	0
Boston U	L	01/07	06	5	1	0

NICHOLSON Stanley (Stan)
Born: Middlesbrough, England, 20 August, 1931 IF

League Club	Source	Date Signed	Seasons Played	Apps	Subs	Gls
Middlesbrough	South Bank	05/49				
Leeds U	Tr	08/51				
Hartlepool U	Horden CW	07/58	58	7	-	1

NICHOLSON Stuart Ian
Born: Newcastle-upon-Tyne, England, 3 February, 1987 F

League Club	Source	Date Signed	Seasons Played	Apps	Subs	Gls
West Bromwich A	Sch	01/06	05-06	0	6	0
Bristol Rov	L	11/06	06	8	2	2
Bristol Rov	Tr	01/07	06	4	8	4
Shrewsbury T	L	08/07	07	6	8	1
Wrexham	L	01/08	07	9	4	0

NICHOLSON William Edward (Bill)
Born: Scarborough, North Yorkshire, England, 26 January, 1919 — RH
Died: Potters Bar, Hertfordshire, England, 23 October, 2004
England: 1/B-3/FLge-1

League Club	Source	Date Signed	Seasons Played	Apps	Subs	Gls
Tottenham H	Scarborough Y'g Libs	08/38	38-54	314	-	6

NICKALLS James Horatio (Jim)
Born: Amble, Northumberland, England, 29 May, 1934 — CH

League Club	Source	Date Signed	Seasons Played	Apps	Subs	Gls
Sunderland	Amble BC	04/53				
Darlington	Tr	05/54	54	18	-	0

NICKEAS Mark
Born: Southport, Merseyside, England, 20 October, 1956 — RB

League Club	Source	Date Signed	Seasons Played	Apps	Subs	Gls
Plymouth Arg	App	07/74				
Chester C	Tr	08/75	75-78	58	2	1

NICKLAS Charles (Charlie)
Born: Sunderland, England, 26 April, 1930 — CF

League Club	Source	Date Signed	Seasons Played	Apps	Subs	Gls
Hull C	Silksworth CW	12/50	51	6	-	1
Darlington	Tr	05/53	53	17	-	6

NICOL Bennett (Benny)
Born: Glasgow, Scotland, 10 March, 1921 — IF
Died: Bolton, Greater Manchester, England, January, 2000

League Club	Source	Date Signed	Seasons Played	Apps	Subs	Gls
Bolton W		11/46				
Rochdale	Winsford U	07/49	49	5	-	1

NICOL George Wallace
Born: Bannockburn, Stirlingshire, Scotland, 20 July, 1923 — G

League Club	Source	Date Signed	Seasons Played	Apps	Subs	Gls
Aldershot	Falkirk	08/51	51	19	-	0

NICOL Paul John
Born: Scunthorpe, North Lincolnshire, England, 31 October, 1967 — CD

League Club	Source	Date Signed	Seasons Played	Apps	Subs	Gls
Scunthorpe U	App	07/86	86-89	68	7	2

NICOL Robert Benjamin Mathieson (Bobby)
Born: Edinburgh, Scotland, 11 May, 1936 — RH
Died: Ontario, Canada, 11 July, 2012
Scotland: U23-2/Schools

League Club	Source	Date Signed	Seasons Played	Apps	Subs	Gls
Barnsley	Hibernian	08/62	62-63	37	-	1

NICOL Stephen (Steve)
Born: Troon, Ayrshire, Scotland, 11 December, 1961 — M/RB
Scotland: 27/U21-14

League Club	Source	Date Signed	Seasons Played	Apps	Subs	Gls
Liverpool	Ayr U	10/81	82-94	328	14	37
Notts Co	Tr	01/95	94-95	32	0	2
Sheffield Wed	Tr	11/95	95-97	41	8	0
West Bromwich A	L	03/98	97	9	0	0

NICOLAS Alexis Peter
Born: Westminster, Central London, England, 13 February, 1983 — M
Cyprus: U21-2

League Club	Source	Date Signed	Seasons Played	Apps	Subs	Gls
Aston Villa	YT	04/01				
Chelsea	Tr	12/01	03	1	1	0
Brighton & HA	Tr	08/04	04-05	33	11	0

NICOLAU Nicky George
Born: Camden, N London, England, 12 October, 1983 — LB/M

League Club	Source	Date Signed	Seasons Played	Apps	Subs	Gls
Arsenal	Sch	07/02				
Southend U	Tr	03/04	03-04	24	7	1
Swindon T	Tr	07/05	05	3	2	0
Barnet	Tr	08/06	06-08	60	21	4

NICOLL Paul
Born: Ellesmere Port, Cheshire, England, 10 November, 1966 — M

League Club	Source	Date Signed	Seasons Played	Apps	Subs	Gls
Wrexham	Jnr	07/84	84	0	1	0

NIEDZWIECKI Andrej Edward (Eddie)
Born: Bangor, Gwynedd, Wales, 3 May, 1959 — G
Wales: 2/Schools

League Club	Source	Date Signed	Seasons Played	Apps	Subs	Gls
Wrexham	Jnr	07/76	77-82	111	0	0
Chelsea	Tr	06/83	83-87	136	0	0

NIELSEN Allan
Born: Esbjerg, Denmark, 13 March, 1971 — M
Denmark: 44

League Club	Source	Date Signed	Seasons Played	Apps	Subs	Gls
Tottenham H	Brondby (DEN)	09/96	96-99	78	19	12
Wolverhampton W	L	03/00	99	7	0	2
Watford	Tr	08/00	00-02	95	6	19

NIELSEN David Jean
Born: Skagen, Denmark, 1 December, 1976 — F
Denmark: U21-8/Youth

League Club	Source	Date Signed	Seasons Played	Apps	Subs	Gls
Grimsby T (L)	FC Copenhagen (DEN)	10/00	00	16	1	5
Wimbledon	FC Copenhagen (DEN)	03/01	00-01	15	8	4
Norwich C	Tr	12/01	01-03	35	23	14

NIELSEN Gunnar
Born: Torshavn, Faroe Islands, 7 October, 1986 — G
Faroe Islands: 27

League Club	Source	Date Signed	Seasons Played	Apps	Subs	Gls
Blackburn Rov	BK Frem (FAR)	07/07				
Manchester C	Tr	02/09	09	0	1	0
Tranmere Rov	L	07/10	10	2	0	0

NIELSEN John Schmidt
Born: Aarhus, Denmark, 7 April, 1972 — M

League Club	Source	Date Signed	Seasons Played	Apps	Subs	Gls
Southend U	Ikast (DEN)	09/96	96-97	18	11	3

NIELSEN Kent
Born: Copenhagen, Denmark, 28 December, 1961 — CD
Denmark: 54/U21-11/Youth

League Club	Source	Date Signed	Seasons Played	Apps	Subs	Gls
Aston Villa	Brondby (DEN)	06/89	89-91	74	5	4

NIELSEN Martin Ulrich
Born: Aarhus, Denmark, 24 March, 1973 — M
Denmark: U21-9

League Club	Source	Date Signed	Seasons Played	Apps	Subs	Gls
Huddersfield T	FC Copenhagen (DEN)	03/98	97	0	3	0

NIELSEN Thomas
Born: Aarhus, Denmark, 25 March, 1972 — LB

League Club	Source	Date Signed	Seasons Played	Apps	Subs	Gls
Shrewsbury T	Aarhus Fremad (DEN)	08/96	96	19	3	1

NIELSON Norman Frederick
Born: Johannesburg, South Africa, 6 November, 1928 — CH
Died: Derby, England, 1 January, 2002

League Club	Source	Date Signed	Seasons Played	Apps	Subs	Gls
Charlton Ath	Arcadia Pretoria (RSA)	07/49	49	1	-	0
Derby Co	Tr	09/51	51-53	57	-	8
Bury	Tr	05/54	54-56	100	-	5
Hull C	Tr	04/57	56-57	25	-	0

NIEMI Antti Mikko
Born: Oulu, Finland, 31 May, 1972 — G
Finland: 67/U21-17/Youth

League Club	Source	Date Signed	Seasons Played	Apps	Subs	Gls
Southampton	Heart of Midlothian	08/02	02-05	106	0	0
Fulham	Tr	01/06	05-07	62	0	0
Portsmouth	Rtd	08/09				

NIESTROJ Robert Waldemar
Born: Opole, Poland, 2 December, 1974 — M

League Club	Source	Date Signed	Seasons Played	Apps	Subs	Gls
Wolverhampton W	Fort Dusseldorf (GER)	11/98	98-99	2	4	0

NIEUWENHUYS Berry
Born: Boksburg, South Africa, 5 November, 1911 — RW
Died: Johannesburg, South Africa, 12 June, 1984

League Club	Source	Date Signed	Seasons Played	Apps	Subs	Gls
Liverpool	Germiston Cal'n (RSA)	09/33	33-46	236	-	74

NIGHTINGALE Albert
Born: Thrybergh, South Yorkshire, England, 10 November, 1923 — IF
Died: Liverpool, England, 26 February, 2006

League Club	Source	Date Signed	Seasons Played	Apps	Subs	Gls
Sheffield U	Thurcroft	06/41	46-47	62	-	15
Huddersfield T	Tr	03/48	47-51	119	-	20
Blackburn Rov	Tr	10/51	51-52	35	-	5
Leeds U	Tr	10/52	52-56	130	-	48

NIGHTINGALE David Reginald
Born: Liverpool, England, 15 August, 1927 — RB

League Club	Source	Date Signed	Seasons Played	Apps	Subs	Gls
Tranmere Rov		09/46	46	3	-	0

NIGHTINGALE Luke Raymond
Born: Portsmouth, England, 22 December, 1980 — F

League Club	Source	Date Signed	Seasons Played	Apps	Subs	Gls
Portsmouth	YT	11/98	98-00	14	31	4
Swindon T	L	12/02	02	2	1	0
Southend U	Tr	08/03	03	0	4	0

NIGHTINGALE Mark Barry Douglas
Born: Salisbury, Wiltshire, England, 1 February, 1957 — D/M
England: Youth

League Club	Source	Date Signed	Seasons Played	Apps	Subs	Gls
Bournemouth	App	07/74	74-75	44	5	4
Crystal Palace	Tr	06/76				
Norwich C	Tr	07/77	77-81	28	7	0
Bournemouth	Bulova (HKG)	11/82	82-85	144	6	4
Peterborough U	Tr	07/86	86-87	71	7	3

NIGHTINGALE Ronald (Ron)
Born: Darwen, Lancashire, England, 27 January, 1937 — WH

League Club	Source	Date Signed	Seasons Played	Apps	Subs	Gls
Accrington Stan		07/57	58-60	14	-	0

NIGHTINGALE William John (Will)
Born: Wandsworth, SW London, England, 2 August, 1995 — CD

League Club	Source	Date Signed	Seasons Played	Apps	Subs	Gls
AFC Wimbledon	Sch	05/14	14	3	1	0

NIJHOLT Luc
Born: Zaandam, Netherlands, 29 July, 1961 — D

League Club	Source	Date Signed	Seasons Played	Apps	Subs	Gls
Swindon T	Motherwell	07/93	93-94	66	1	1

NIKOLIC Dusan
Born: Belgrade, Yugoslavia, 23 January, 1953 — RW
Yugoslavia: 4

League Club	Source	Date Signed	Seasons Played	Apps	Subs	Gls
Bolton W	R Star Belgrade (YUG)	10/80	80-81	22	0	2

NILIS Luc Gilbert Cyrille
Born: Hasselt, Belgium, 25 May, 1967 — F
Belgium: 56/U21-3/Youth

League Club	Source	Date Signed	Seasons Played	Apps	Subs	Gls
Aston Villa	PSV Eindhoven (NED)	07/00	00	3	0	1

NILSEN Roger
Born: Tromso, Norway, 8 August, 1969 — LB
Norway: 32/U21-19

League Club	Source	Date Signed	Seasons Played	Apps	Subs	Gls
Sheffield U	Viking Stavanger (NOR)	11/93	93-98	157	9	0
Tottenham H	Tr	03/99	98	3	0	0

NILSSON Mikael
Born: Kristianstad, Sweden, 24 June, 1978 — M
Sweden: 64

League Club	Source	Date Signed	Seasons Played	Apps	Subs	Gls
Southampton	Halmstads (SWE)	07/04	04	12	4	0

NILSSON Nils Lennart Roland (Roland)
Born: Helsingborg, Sweden, 27 November, 1963 — FB
Sweden: 116

League Club	Source	Date Signed	Seasons Played	Apps	Subs	Gls
Sheffield Wed	IFK Goteberg (SWE)	11/89	89-93	151	0	2
Coventry C	Helsingborg (SWE)	07/97	97-98	60	0	0
Coventry C	Helsingborg (SWE)	07/01	01	9	0	0

NIMANI Frederic
Born: Marseille, France, 8 October, 1988 — F
France: U21-8/Youth

League Club	Source	Date Signed	Seasons Played	Apps	Subs	Gls
Burnley (L)	AS Monaco (FRA)	01/10	09	0	2	0

NIMELY-TCHUIMENI Alex
Born: Monrovia, Liberia, 11 May, 1991 — F
England: Youth

League Club	Source	Date Signed	Seasons Played	Apps	Subs	Gls
Manchester C	Coton Sports (CMR)	07/08	09	0	1	0
Middlesbrough	L	09/11	11	0	9	0
Coventry C	L	01/12	11	16	1	1
Crystal Palace	L	01/13	12	1	1	0
Port Vale		11/14	14	0	1	0

NIMMO Ian Wallace
Born: Boston, Lincolnshire, England, 23 January, 1958 — F

League Club	Source	Date Signed	Seasons Played	Apps	Subs	Gls
Sheffield Wed	App	01/76	75-78	26	19	10
Peterborough U	L	01/77	76	4	0	1
Doncaster Rov	Tr	06/79	79-81	77	9	29

NIMMO Liam Wallace
Born: Boston, Lincolnshire, England, 28 December, 1984 — F

League Club	Source	Date Signed	Seasons Played	Apps	Subs	Gls
Grimsby T	Sch	10/03	03	0	2	0

NIMMO William Brown (Willie)
Born: Forth, Lanarkshire, Scotland, 11 January, 1934 — G
Died: Inveresk, East Lothian, Scotland, 17 August, 1991

League Club	Source	Date Signed	Seasons Played	Apps	Subs	Gls
Leeds U	Alloa Ath	02/56	57	1	-	0
Doncaster Rov	Tr	03/58	57-61	182	-	0
Mansfield T	Tr	07/62				

NIMNI Aviyahu (Avi)
Born: Tel Aviv, Israel, 26 April, 1972 — M
Israel: 80

League Club	Source	Date Signed	Seasons Played	Apps	Subs	Gls
Derby Co (L)	Maccabi Tel Aviv (ISR)	11/99	99	2	2	1

NISBET Gordon James Mackay
Born: Wallsend, Tyne and Wear, England, 18 September, 1951 — RB
England: U23-1

League Club	Source	Date Signed	Seasons Played	Apps	Subs	Gls
West Bromwich A	Willington Quay BC	09/68	69-75	136	0	0
Hull C	Tr	09/76	76-80	190	3	1
Plymouth Arg	Tr	12/80	80-86	281	0	14
Exeter C	Tr	06/87	87	12	0	0

NISH Colin John
Born: Musselburgh, East Lothian, Scotland, 7 March, 1981 — F

League Club	Source	Date Signed	Seasons Played	Apps	Subs	Gls
Hartlepool U	Hibernian	07/11	11	12	7	4

NISH David John
Born: Burton-on-Trent, Staffordshire, England, 26 September, 1947 — LB/M
England: 5/FLge-5/U23-10/Youth/Schools

League Club	Source	Date Signed	Seasons Played	Apps	Subs	Gls
Leicester C	Measham Social Welfare	07/66	66-72	228	0	25
Derby Co	Tr	08/72	72-78	184	4	10

NIVEN Derek Dunbar
Born: Falkirk, Scotland, 12 December, 1983 — M

League Club	Source	Date Signed	Seasons Played	Apps	Subs	Gls
Bolton W	Raith Rov	11/01				
Chesterfield	Tr	12/03	03-11	262	35	18
Northampton T	L	10/11	11	4	0	0

NIVEN Stuart Thomas
Born: Glasgow, Scotland, 24 December, 1978 — M
Scotland: Youth

League Club	Source	Date Signed	Seasons Played	Apps	Subs	Gls
Ipswich T	YT	09/96	96	2	0	0
Barnet	Tr	09/00	00	20	4	2

NIX Kyle Ashley
Born: Sydney, Australia, 21 January, 1986 — M
England: Semi Pro-2/Youth

League Club	Source	Date Signed	Seasons Played	Apps	Subs	Gls
Aston Villa	Sch	01/03				
Sheffield U	Tr	04/05				
Bradford C	Parkgate	08/07	07-08	37	19	6

NIX Peter
Born: Rotherham, South Yorkshire, England, 25 January, 1958 — LW

League Club	Source	Date Signed	Seasons Played	Apps	Subs	Gls
Rotherham U	Jnr	08/76	77-79	22	0	2

NIXON Eric Walter
Born: Manchester, England, 4 October, 1962 — G

League Club	Source	Date Signed	Seasons Played	Apps	Subs	Gls
Manchester C	Curzon Ashton	12/83	85-87	58	0	0
Wolverhampton W	L	08/86	86	16	0	0
Bradford C	L	11/86	86	3	0	0
Southampton	L	12/86	86	4	0	0
Carlisle U	L	01/87	86	16	0	0
Tranmere Rov	L	03/88	87	8	0	0
Tranmere Rov	Tr	07/88	88-96	333	0	0
Blackpool	L	02/96	95	20	0	0
Bradford C	L	09/96	96	12	0	0
Stockport Co	Tr	08/97	97	43	0	0
Wigan Ath	L	08/98	98	1	0	0
Wigan Ath	Tr	03/99	98	2	0	0
Tranmere Rov	Tr	07/99	99-02	1	4	0
Kidderminster Hrs	L	10/01	01	2	0	0
Sheffield Wed	Tr	09/03	03	0	1	0

NIXON Jonathan Charles (Jon)
Born: Ilkeston, Derbyshire, England, 20 January, 1948 — RW

League Club	Source	Date Signed	Seasons Played	Apps	Subs	Gls
Derby Co	Jnr	09/65				
Notts Co	Ilkeston T	10/69	69-74	167	12	32
Peterborough U	Tr	09/74	74-76	104	6	16
Shrewsbury T	Tr	08/77	77	21	2	3
Barnsley	Tr	03/78	77	6	4	0
Halifax T	Tr	06/78	78	12	7	1

NIXON Marc Steven
Born: Hexham, Northumberland, England, 29 January, 1984 — F

League Club	Source	Date Signed	Seasons Played	Apps	Subs	Gls
Carlisle U	Sch	07/02	02	3	4	0

NIXON Paul
Born: Seaham, County Durham, England, 23 September, 1963 — M
New Zealand: 4

League Club	Source	Date Signed	Seasons Played	Apps	Subs	Gls
Bristol Rov	Seaham Red Star	01/89	88-90	31	13	6

NIXON Thomas James (Tom)
Born: Backworth, Tyne and Wear, England, 25 March, 1931 — WH
Died: North Tyneside, Tyne and Wear, England, November, 2003

League Club	Source	Date Signed	Seasons Played	Apps	Subs	Gls
Darlington	Newcastle U (Am)	05/51	51	1	-	0

NIXON William John (Billy)
Born: Ballynahinch, Down, Northern Ireland, 28 September, 1941 — IF
Northern Ireland: Schools

League Club	Source	Date Signed	Seasons Played	Apps	Subs	Gls
Norwich C	Distillery	03/61	61	1	-	0
Shrewsbury T	Tr	03/62	61-64	17	-	1

NJIE Seedy Ishmail
Born: Lewisham, SE London, England, 1 December, 1994 — F

League Club	Source	Date Signed	Seasons Played	Apps	Subs	Gls
Southend U	Sch	07/13	12	0	1	0

NKUMU Archange
Born: Tottenham, N London, England, 5 November, 1993 — DM

League Club	Source	Date Signed	Seasons Played	Apps	Subs	Gls
Chelsea	Sch	07/11				
Yeovil T	L	08/12	12	0	1	0

NOAKE David John
Born: Yeovil, Somerset, England, 9 June, 1940 — W

League Club	Source	Date Signed	Seasons Played	Apps	Subs	Gls
Luton T	Dorchester T	11/59	59-60	17	-	0
Bristol C	Tr	06/61	61	11	-	3

NOAKES Alfred George Edward (Alfie)
Born: Stratford, E London, England, 14 August, 1933 — LB
Died: Portsmouth, England, 24 October, 2005

League Club	Source	Date Signed	Seasons Played	Apps	Subs	Gls
West Ham U	Jnr	08/50				
Crystal Palace	Sittingbourne	06/55	55-61	195	-	14
Portsmouth	Tr	07/62	62-63	13	-	0

NOBBS Alan Keith (Keith)
Born: Bishop Auckland, County Durham, England, 18 September, 1961 — RB

League Club	Source	Date Signed	Seasons Played	Apps	Subs	Gls
Middlesbrough	App	09/79	80	1	0	0
Halifax T	Tr	08/82	82-83	87	0	1
Hartlepool U	Bishop Auckland	08/85	85-92	274	6	1

NOBLE Alfred William Thomas (Alf)
Born: Hackney, E London, England, 18 September, 1924 — IF
Died: Norwich, England, 24 November, 1999
England: Amateur-18

League Club	Source	Date Signed	Seasons Played	Apps	Subs	Gls
Colchester U (Am)	Briggs Sports	09/55	55	1	-	0

NOBLE Barry
Born: Stockton-on-Tees, Cleveland, England, 5 June, 1951 — G

League Club	Source	Date Signed	Seasons Played	Apps	Subs	Gls
Hartlepool U	Jnr	08/70	71	1	0	0

NOBLE Daniel William (Danny)
Born: Hull, England, 2 September, 1970 — G

League Club	Source	Date Signed	Seasons Played	Apps	Subs	Gls
Stoke C	YT	07/89	89-90	3	0	0
Crewe Alex	Tr	06/91	91	7	0	0

NOBLE David James
Born: Hitchin, Hertfordshire, England, 2 February, 1982 — M
England: Youth//Scotland: B-1/U21-2

League Club	Source	Date Signed	Seasons Played	Apps	Subs	Gls
Arsenal	YT	03/01				
Watford	L	07/01	01	5	10	1
West Ham U	Tr	01/03	03	0	3	0
Boston U	Tr	02/04	03-05	54	3	5
Bristol C	Tr	11/05	05-08	62	23	7
Yeovil T	L	03/09	08	2	0	0
Exeter C		01/10	10-11	71	7	2
Rotherham U	Tr	07/12	12	20	2	3
Cheltenham T	L	09/13	13	25	4	0
Oldham Ath	Tr	08/14	14	0	2	0
Exeter C	Tr	09/14	14	8	7	0

NOBLE Frank
Born: Sheffield, England, 26 October, 1945 — RB

League Club	Source	Date Signed	Seasons Played	Apps	Subs	Gls
Sheffield Wed	Jnr	05/63	63-65	2	0	0
Peterborough U	Tr	07/67	67-71	205	2	1

NOBLE John
Born: Manchester, England, 20 May, 1919 — W
Died: Stockport, Greater Manchester, England, March, 1996

League Club	Source	Date Signed	Seasons Played	Apps	Subs	Gls
Stockport Co	Warte Villa	03/39	46	1	-	0

NOBLE Liam Thomas
Born: Newcastle-upon-Tyne, England, 8 May, 1991 — M

League Club	Source	Date Signed	Seasons Played	Apps	Subs	Gls
Sunderland	Sch	07/09				
Carlisle U	L	01/11	10	18	3	3
Carlisle U	Tr	07/11	11-13	92	17	17
Notts Co	Tr	06/14	14	30	3	5

NOBLE Mark James
Born: Canning Town, E London, England, 8 May, 1987 — M
England: U21-20/Youth

League Club	Source	Date Signed	Seasons Played	Apps	Subs	Gls
West Ham U	Sch	07/04	04-14	260	20	31
Hull C	L	02/06	05	4	1	0
Ipswich T	L	08/06	06	12	1	1

NOBLE Norman
Born: Barnsley, South Yorkshire, England, 8 August, 1923 — D
Died: Rotherham, South Yorkshire, England, 1973

League Club	Source	Date Signed	Seasons Played	Apps	Subs	Gls
Huddersfield T		06/43				
Bradford C	Tr	10/45				
Rotherham U	Ransome & Marles	05/48	48-57	326	-	21

NOBLE Peter
Born: Newcastle-upon-Tyne, England, 19 August, 1944 — F/M

League Club	Source	Date Signed	Seasons Played	Apps	Subs	Gls
Newcastle U	Consett	11/64	65-67	22	3	7
Swindon T	Tr	01/68	67-72	212	4	62
Burnley	Tr	06/73	73-79	241	2	63
Blackpool	Tr	01/80	79-82	92	5	14

NOBLE Robert (Bobby)
Born: South Gosforth, Tyne and Wear, England, 25 May, 1949 — CD
Died: Sydney, Australia, May, 2005

League Club	Source	Date Signed	Seasons Played	Apps	Subs	Gls
Newcastle U	App	04/67				
Barrow	L	08/69	69	19	0	3
Bury	Tr	08/70	70	6	0	0
Barrow	Tr	10/70	70-71	72	1	5
Colchester U	Tr	08/72	72	25	2	0
Southport	Tr	03/73	72-74	61	2	6
Darlington	Tr	08/75	75-76	54	0	3

NOBLE Robert (Bobby)
Born: Manchester, England, 18 December, 1945 — LB
England: Youth

League Club	Source	Date Signed	Seasons Played	Apps	Subs	Gls
Manchester U	App	12/62	65-66	31	0	0

NOBLE Ryan Andrew
Born: Sunderland, England, 16 August, 1993 — F
England: Youth

League Club	Source	Date Signed	Seasons Played	Apps	Subs	Gls
Sunderland	Sch	07/09	10-11	0	5	0
Derby Co	L	09/10	10	0	1	0
Derby Co	L	01/12	11	1	1	0
Hartlepool U	L	03/12	11	9	0	2
Hartlepool U	L	10/12	12	7	3	1
Burnley	Tr	07/13	13	0	1	0

NOBLE Stuart William
Born: Edinburgh, Scotland, 14 October, 1983 — F

League Club	Source	Date Signed	Seasons Played	Apps	Subs	Gls
Fulham	Sch	08/03				
Torquay U	L	08/04	04	2	1	0
Northampton T	L	02/05	04	0	4	0

NOBLE Wayne Ian
Born: Bristol, England, 11 June, 1967 — LM

League Club	Source	Date Signed	Seasons Played	Apps	Subs	Gls
Bristol Rov	App	03/85	85-86	16	6	1

NOBLE-LAZARUS Reuben Courtney
Born: Huddersfield, West Yorkshire, England, 16 August, 1993 — F

League Club	Source	Date Signed	Seasons Played	Apps	Subs	Gls
Barnsley	Sch	08/10	08-14	10	36	3
Scunthorpe U	L	11/13	13	2	2	0
Rochdale	Tr	10/14	14	7	12	1

NOCERINO Antonio
Born: Naples, Italy, 9 April, 1985 — M
Italy: 15/U21-10/Youth

League Club	Source	Date Signed	Seasons Played	Apps	Subs	Gls
West Ham U (L)	AC Milan (ITA)	01/14	13	2	8	0

NOEL-WILLIAMS Gifton Ruben Elisha
Born: Islington, N London, England, 21 January, 1980 — F
England: Youth

League Club	Source	Date Signed	Seasons Played	Apps	Subs	Gls
Watford	YT	02/97	96-02	107	62	33
Stoke C	Tr	05/03	03-04	81	7	23
Burnley	Tr	07/05	05-06	36	16	7
Brighton & HA	L	03/06	06	7	0	2
Millwall	Lorca Deportivo (SPN)	10/08	08	1	0	0
Yeovil T	L	11/08	08	6	0	0

NOGAN Kurt
Born: Cardiff, Wales, 9 September, 1970 — F
Wales: B-1/U21-2

League Club	Source	Date Signed	Seasons Played	Apps	Subs	Gls
Luton T	YT	07/89	89-91	17	16	3
Peterborough U	Tr	09/92				
Brighton & HA	Tr	10/92	92-94	97	0	49
Burnley	Tr	04/95	94-96	87	5	33
Preston NE	Tr	03/97	96-99	74	19	27
Cardiff C	Tr	03/00	99-00	4	14	1

NOGAN Lee Martin
Born: Cardiff, Wales, 21 May, 1969 — F
Wales: 2/B-1/U21-1

League Club	Source	Date Signed	Seasons Played	Apps	Subs	Gls
Oxford U	App	03/87	87-91	57	7	10
Brentford	L	03/87	86	10	1	2
Southend U	L	09/87	87	6	0	1
Watford	Tr	12/91	91-94	97	8	26
Southend U	L	03/94	93	4	1	0
Reading	Tr	01/95	94-96	71	20	26
Notts Co	L	02/97	96	6	0	0
Grimsby T	Tr	07/97	97-98	63	11	10
Darlington	Tr	07/99	99-00	37	12	6
Luton T	L	11/00	00	7	0	1
York C	Tr	02/01	00-03	133	10	32

NOGUERA Alberto
Born: Madrid, Spain, 24 September, 1989 — M

League Club	Source	Date Signed	Seasons Played	Apps	Subs	Gls
Blackpool	Atletico Madrid (SPN)	08/12	12	0	1	0

NOLAN David Joseph
Born: Liverpool, England, 24 February, 1968 — M

League Club	Source	Date Signed	Seasons Played	Apps	Subs	Gls
Chester C	Bromborough Pool	01/92	91	1	0	0

NOLAN Edward William (Eddie)
Born: Waterford, Republic of Ireland, 5 August, 1988 — LB
Republic of Ireland: 3/B-1/U21-13

League Club	Source	Date Signed	Seasons Played	Apps	Subs	Gls
Blackburn Rov	Sch	09/05				
Stockport Co	L	03/07	06	2	2	0
Hartlepool U	L	11/07	07	11	0	0
Preston NE	Tr	10/08	08-09	33	7	0
Sheffield Wed	L	02/10	09	14	0	1
Scunthorpe U	Tr	07/10	10-14	113	9	1

NOLAN George
Born: Liverpool, England, 9 December, 1925 — LH
Died: Liverpool, England, January, 2013

League Club	Source	Date Signed	Seasons Played	Apps	Subs	Gls
Southport	A1 Control	06/46	46	3	-	0

NOLAN Ian Robert
Born: Liverpool, England, 9 July, 1970 — LB
Northern Ireland: 18

League Club	Source	Date Signed	Seasons Played	Apps	Subs	Gls
Tranmere Rov	Marine	08/91	91-93	87	1	1
Sheffield Wed	Tr	08/94	94-99	164	1	4
Bradford C	Tr	07/00	00	17	4	0
Wigan Ath	Tr	08/01	01	5	3	0

NOLAN Kevin Anthony Jance
Born: Liverpool, England, 24 June, 1982 — M

England: U21-1/Youth

League Club	Source	Date Signed	Seasons Played	Apps	Subs	Gls
Bolton W	YT	01/00	99-08	257	39	40
Newcastle U	Tr	01/09	08-10	84	1	29
West Ham U	Tr	06/11	11-14	129	10	30

NOLAN Liam Joseph
Born: Liverpool, England, 20 September, 1994 — M
Northern Ireland: U21-1/Youth

League Club	Source	Date Signed	Seasons Played	Apps	Subs	Gls
Crewe Alex	Sch	04/13	13-14	14	12	0

NOLAN Matthew Lee (Matt)
Born: Hitchin, Hertfordshire, England, 25 February, 1982 — F

League Club	Source	Date Signed	Seasons Played	Apps	Subs	Gls
Peterborough U	Hitchin T	09/03	03	0	1	0

NOLAN Michael William (Mike)
Born: Dublin, Republic of Ireland, 8 July, 1950 — FB

League Club	Source	Date Signed	Seasons Played	Apps	Subs	Gls
Oldham Ath	App	08/67	66-67	2	0	0

NOLAN Philip (Phil)
Born: Edmonton, N London, England, 29 December, 1923 — CH
Died: Watford, Hertfordshire, England, 20 January, 2011

League Club	Source	Date Signed	Seasons Played	Apps	Subs	Gls
Watford	Hayes	10/47	47-54	91	-	8

NOLAN Terence Stephen (Terry)
Born: Prescot, Merseyside, England, 16 March, 1956 — F

League Club	Source	Date Signed	Seasons Played	Apps	Subs	Gls
Southport	Prescot Cables	02/78	77	0	1	0

NONDA Shabani Christophe
Born: Bujumbura, Burundi, 6 March, 1977 — F
DR Congo: 49

League Club	Source	Date Signed	Seasons Played	Apps	Subs	Gls
Blackburn Rov (L)	AS Roma (ITA)	08/06	06	17	9	7

NOON Harry
Born: Sutton-in-Ashfield, Nottinghamshire, England, 6 October, 1937 — LB/WH
Died: Sydney, Australia, 2 September, 1996

League Club	Source	Date Signed	Seasons Played	Apps	Subs	Gls
Notts Co	Bentinck Meth's	05/55	57-61	122	-	0
Bradford C	Tr	07/62	62	1	-	0

NOON Mark Richard
Born: Leamington Spa, Warwickshire, England, 23 September, 1983 — RB

League Club	Source	Date Signed	Seasons Played	Apps	Subs	Gls
Coventry C	YT	08/01	02	0	2	0

NOONE Craig Stephen
Born: Kirkby, Merseyside, England, 17 November, 1987 — LW

League Club	Source	Date Signed	Seasons Played	Apps	Subs	Gls
Plymouth Arg	Southport	08/08	08-10	22	33	5
Exeter C	L	09/09	09	7	0	2
Brighton & HA	Tr	10/11	10-12	31	28	4
Cardiff C	Tr	08/12	12-14	71	15	9

NORBURN Oliver Lewis
Born: Bolton, Greater Manchester, England, 26 October, 1992 — M

League Club	Source	Date Signed	Seasons Played	Apps	Subs	Gls
Leicester C	Sch	07/11				
Bristol Rov	L	09/11	11	1	4	0
Bristol Rov	Tr	07/12	12-13	41	10	3
Plymouth Arg	Tr	07/14	14	7	7	0

NORBURY Michael Shaun (Mick)
Born: Hemsworth, West Yorkshire, England, 22 January, 1969 — F

League Club	Source	Date Signed	Seasons Played	Apps	Subs	Gls
Scarborough	Ossett T	12/89				
Cambridge U	Bridlington T	02/92	91-92	11	15	3
Preston NE	Tr	12/92	92-93	32	10	13
Doncaster Rov	Tr	11/94	94-95	19	8	5

NORCROSS William (Bill)
Born: Preston, Lancashire, England, 29 December, 1937 — W

League Club	Source	Date Signed	Seasons Played	Apps	Subs	Gls
Southport (Am)	Chorley	07/59	59	1	-	0

NORFOLK Lee Richard
Born: Dunedin, New Zealand, 17 October, 1975 — M

League Club	Source	Date Signed	Seasons Played	Apps	Subs	Gls
Ipswich T	YT	07/94	94	1	2	0

NORMAN Albert Griffith (Griff)
Born: Cardiff, Wales, 20 February, 1926 — LH/CH
Died: Cardiff, Wales, 6 August, 2010

League Club	Source	Date Signed	Seasons Played	Apps	Subs	Gls
Cardiff C		04/50	51	1	-	0
Torquay U	Tr	10/52	52-57	216	-	6

NORMAN Anthony Joseph (Tony)
Born: Deeside, Flintshire, Wales, 24 February, 1958 — G
Wales: 5/B

League Club	Source	Date Signed	Seasons Played	Apps	Subs	Gls
Burnley	Jnr	08/76				
Hull C	Tr	02/80	79-88	372	0	0
Sunderland	Tr	12/88	88-94	198	0	0
Huddersfield T	Tr	07/95	95-96	6	0	0

NORMAN Derek Antony
Born: Birmingham, England, 11 February, 1946 — RH/IF
Died: Southampton, England, October, 2010
England: Youth

League Club	Source	Date Signed	Seasons Played	Apps	Subs	Gls
Southampton	Alvechurch	01/64				
Aldershot	Tr	05/65	65	22	1	0

NORMAN John
Born: Birkenhead, Wirral, England, 26 June, 1971 — F

League Club	Source	Date Signed	Seasons Played	Apps	Subs	Gls
Tranmere Rov	YT	02/90				
Bury	Heswall	10/92	92	1	1	0

NORMAN Malcolm Allen
Born: Cardiff, Wales, 24 October, 1934 — G

League Club	Source	Date Signed	Seasons Played	Apps	Subs	Gls
Bristol Rov	Cardiff Corinthians	05/58	58-61	69	-	0

NORMAN Maurice
Born: Mulbarton, Norfolk, England, 8 May, 1934 — CH
England: 23/FLge-1/U23-3

League Club	Source	Date Signed	Seasons Played	Apps	Subs	Gls
Norwich C	Wymondham OB	09/52	54-55	35	-	0
Tottenham H	Tr	11/55	55-65	357	0	16

NORMAN Richard (Richie)
Born: Throckley, Tyne and Wear, England, 5 September, 1935 — LB

League Club	Source	Date Signed	Seasons Played	Apps	Subs	Gls
Leicester C	Horden CW	11/58	59-67	303	0	2
Peterborough U	Tr	07/68	68	9	1	0

NORMAN Sean
Born: Lowestoft, Suffolk, England, 27 November, 1966 — M/LB

League Club	Source	Date Signed	Seasons Played	Apps	Subs	Gls
Colchester U	Lowestoft T	10/84	86-87	18	3	1

NORMANN Runar
Born: Harstad, Norway, 1 March, 1978 — W
Norway: U21-3/Youth

League Club	Source	Date Signed	Seasons Played	Apps	Subs	Gls
Coventry C	Lillestrom (NOR)	08/99	99-02	3	10	1

NORMANTON Graham Stephen
Born: Hartlepool, Cleveland, England, 13 November, 1959 — LB

League Club	Source	Date Signed	Seasons Played	Apps	Subs	Gls
Hartlepool U	Middlesbrough (App)	07/78	79-80	17	1	0

NORMANTON Sidney Albert (Skinner)
Born: Barnsley, South Yorkshire, England, 20 August, 1926 — WH
Died: Barnsley, South Yorkshire, England, 24 April, 1995

League Club	Source	Date Signed	Seasons Played	Apps	Subs	Gls
Barnsley	Barnsley Main	09/45	47-53	123	-	2
Halifax T	Tr	07/54	54	13	-	0

NORMINGTON Grant
Born: Hull, England, 9 May, 1990 — M

League Club	Source	Date Signed	Seasons Played	Apps	Subs	Gls
Grimsby T	Sch	07/08	08	0	1	0

NORRIE Craig Thomas
Born: Hull, England, 22 July, 1960 — F

League Club	Source	Date Signed	Seasons Played	Apps	Subs	Gls
Hull C	App	08/78	78-81	22	9	4

NORRIS David Martin
Born: Stamford, Lincolnshire, England, 22 February, 1981 — M

League Club	Source	Date Signed	Seasons Played	Apps	Subs	Gls
Bolton W	Boston U	02/00				
Hull C	L	03/02	01	3	3	1
Plymouth Arg	Tr	10/02	02-07	216	10	27
Ipswich T	Tr	01/08	07-10	103	3	13
Portsmouth	Tr	06/11	11	39	1	8
Leeds U	Tr	07/12	12	27	3	3
Peterborough U	Tr	02/15	14	3	5	0

NORRIS Derek
Born: Beighton, South Yorkshire, England, 19 June, 1935 — LH
Died: Sheffield, England, December, 1997

League Club	Source	Date Signed	Seasons Played	Apps	Subs	Gls
Peterborough U	Gainsborough Trinity	06/60	60	5	-	0

NORRIS George Albert
Born: Aldershot, Hampshire, England, 19 September, 1935 — CF

League Club	Source	Date Signed	Seasons Played	Apps	Subs	Gls
Aldershot	Farnborough T	12/58	58-63	106	-	59

NORRIS Graham John
Born: Hampton, W London, England, 8 February, 1954 — W

League Club	Source	Date Signed	Seasons Played	Apps	Subs	Gls
Crystal Palace	App	02/72				
Southend U	L	03/73	72	1	0	0

NORRIS (HACKER) Luke Michael
Born: Stevenage, Hertfordshire, England, 3 June, 1993 — F

League Club	Source	Date Signed	Seasons Played	Apps	Subs	Gls
Brentford	Sch	06/12	10-13	0	3	0
Northampton T	L	10/13	13	8	2	4
Dagenham & Red	L	01/14	13	16	3	4
Gillingham	Tr	07/14	14	13	24	6

NORRIS Michael (Mike)
Born: Mansfield, Nottinghamshire, England, 27 February, 1957 — G

League Club	Source	Date Signed	Seasons Played	Apps	Subs	Gls
Scunthorpe U	App	02/75	73-75	25	0	0

NORRIS Oliver Patrick (Ollie)
Born: Derry, Northern Ireland, 1 April, 1929 — CF
Died: Melbourne, Australia, 14 June, 2011

League Club	Source	Date Signed	Seasons Played	Apps	Subs	Gls
Middlesbrough	Jnr	07/48	51-53	12	-	2
Bournemouth	Worcester C	07/55	55-58	96	-	34
Northampton T	Tr	09/58	58	14	-	1
Rochdale	Ashford T, Kent	01/61	60	2	-	1

NORRIS Raymond George (Ray)
Born: Bristol, England, 15 July, 1922 — CH
Died: Bristol, England, 1972

League Club	Source	Date Signed	Seasons Played	Apps	Subs	Gls
Bristol C	Bedminster	05/47	47	3	-	0

NORRIS Robert Paul (Rob)
Born: Radcliffe-on-Trent, Nottinghamshire, England, 12 October, 1987 — W

League Club	Source	Date Signed	Seasons Played	Apps	Subs	Gls
Boston U	Sch	-	04-05	1	2	0

NORRIS Russell
Born: Kent, England, 1 February, 1971 — RB

League Club	Source	Date Signed	Seasons Played	Apps	Subs	Gls
Gillingham	YT	07/89	89	2	3	0

NORRIS Stephen Mark (Steve)
Born: Coventry, England, 22 September, 1961 — F
England: Semi Pro-1

League Club	Source	Date Signed	Seasons Played	Apps	Subs	Gls
Scarborough	Telford U	07/88	88-89	35	10	13
Notts Co	L	11/89	89	0	1	0
Carlisle U	Tr	12/89	89-90	21	8	5
Halifax T	Tr	10/90	90-91	56	0	35
Chesterfield	Tr	01/92	91-94	84	13	43
Scarborough	L	01/95	94	8	0	4

NORRIS William James (Will)
Born: Watford, Hertfordshire, England, 12 August, 1993 — G

League Club	Source	Date Signed	Seasons Played	Apps	Subs	Gls
Cambridge U	Royston T	07/12	14	3	0	0

NORTH Daniel Jamie (Danny)
Born: Grimsby, North Lincolnshire, England, 7 September, 1987 — F

League Club	Source	Date Signed	Seasons Played	Apps	Subs	Gls
Grimsby T	Sch	07/06	04-09	44	37	17

NORTH Eric
Born: Halifax, West Yorkshire, England, 6 October, 1923 — LW
Died: Burnley, Lancashire, England, August, 1992

League Club	Source	Date Signed	Seasons Played	Apps	Subs	Gls
Halifax T (Am)	Lee Mount	08/48	48	1	-	0

NORTH Marc Victor
Born: Ware, Hertfordshire, England, 29 May, 1966 — F
Died: Southend-on-Sea, England, 25 September, 2001

League Club	Source	Date Signed	Seasons Played	Apps	Subs	Gls
Luton T	App	03/84	85-86	11	7	3
Lincoln C	L	03/85	84	4	0	0
Scunthorpe U	L	01/87	86	4	1	2
Birmingham C	L	03/87	86	4	1	1
Grimsby T	Tr	08/87	87-88	64	3	17
Leicester C	Tr	03/89	88-90	51	20	9
Grimsby T	Luton T (NC)	08/91	91	0	1	0

NORTH Stacey Stewart
Born: Luton, England, 25 November, 1964 — CD
England: Youth

League Club	Source	Date Signed	Seasons Played	Apps	Subs	Gls
Luton T	App	08/82	83-87	24	1	0
Wolverhampton W	L	11/85	85	3	0	0
West Bromwich A	Tr	12/87	87-89	96	2	0
Fulham	Tr	10/90	90	38	0	0

NORTH Thomas Williamson (Tom)
Born: Barrow-on-Soar, Leicestershire, England, 31 October, 1919 — IF
Died: Barrow-on-Soar, Leicestershire, England, August, 1996

League Club	Source	Date Signed	Seasons Played	Apps	Subs	Gls
Nottingham F	Banbury Spencer	01/45	46	1	-	0

NORTHCOTT George Edward
Born: Torquay, Devon, England, 7 May, 1935 — CH
Died: Torquay, Devon, England, 15 November, 2010

League Club	Source	Date Signed	Seasons Played	Apps	Subs	Gls
Torquay U	Jnr	10/52	54-61	163	-	2
Exeter C	Cheltenham T	08/63	63	1	-	0

NORTHCOTT Thomas Theodore (Tommy)
Born: Torquay, Devon, England, 5 December, 1931 — CF
Died: Torbay, Devon, England, 26 September, 2008
England: Youth

League Club	Source	Date Signed	Seasons Played	Apps	Subs	Gls
Torquay U	Hele Spurs	12/48	48-52	60	-	10
Cardiff C	Tr	10/52	52-54	76	-	13
Lincoln C	Tr	07/55	55-57	94	-	34
Torquay U	Tr	11/57	57-65	348	2	126

NORTHMORE Ryan
Born: Plymouth, England, 5 September, 1980 — G

League Club	Source	Date Signed	Seasons Played	Apps	Subs	Gls
Torquay U	YT	07/99	99-00	26	2	0

NORTHOVER Stanley Oswald (Stan)
Born: Weymouth, Dorset, England, 3 July, 1926 — IF
Died: Weymouth, Dorset, England, 29 November, 1990

League Club	Source	Date Signed	Seasons Played	Apps	Subs	Gls
Luton T (Am)	Weymouth	02/50	49	1	-	0

NORTON David John (Dave)
Born: Gateshead, Tyne and Wear, England, 24 January, 1957 — D

League Club	Source	Date Signed	Seasons Played	Apps	Subs	Gls
Hartlepool U	Whickham	12/78	78-79	14	3	2

NORTON David Wayne
Born: Cannock, Staffordshire, England, 3 March, 1965 — RB/M
England: Youth

League Club	Source	Date Signed	Seasons Played	Apps	Subs	Gls
Aston Villa	App	03/83	84-87	42	2	2
Notts Co	Tr	08/88	88-90	22	5	1
Rochdale	L	10/90	90	9	0	0
Hull C	L	01/91	90	15	0	0
Hull C	Tr	08/91	91-93	134	0	5
Northampton T	Tr	08/94	94-95	78	4	0
Hereford U	Tr	08/96	96	45	0	0

NORTON Paul
Born: Mexborough, South Yorkshire, England, 17 September, 1969 — G

League Club	Source	Date Signed	Seasons Played	Apps	Subs	Gls
Hartlepool U	Sheffield U (YT)	08/88	88	5	0	0

NORTON Peter
Born: Manchester, England, 11 November, 1947 — RB

League Club	Source	Date Signed	Seasons Played	Apps	Subs	Gls
Bournemouth	Jnr	11/66	66-67	18	1	1
Crewe Alex	Tr	07/68				

NORTON Ralph
Born: Aylesham, Kent, England, 11 October, 1942 — WH/IF

League Club	Source	Date Signed	Seasons Played	Apps	Subs	Gls
Reading	Jnr	10/59	60-65	99	1	9
Bournemouth	Tr	07/66	66-67	44	3	4

NORVILLE Jason
Born: Sangre Grande, Trinidad, 9 September, 1983 — F
Trinidad & Tobago: 1

League Club	Source	Date Signed	Seasons Played	Apps	Subs	Gls
Watford	Sch	04/02	01-02	6	8	1
Barnet	Tr	08/05	05-07	13	20	3

NORWOOD James Thomas
Born: Eastbourne, East Sussex, England, 5 September, 1990 — RM
England: Semi Pro-7/Schools

League Club	Source	Date Signed	Seasons Played	Apps	Subs	Gls
Exeter C	Eastbourne T	07/09	09-10	3	1	0

NORWOOD Oliver James
Born: Burnley, Lancashire, England, 12 April, 1991 — M
England: Youth//Northern Ireland: 24/U21-11/Youth

League Club	Source	Date Signed	Seasons Played	Apps	Subs	Gls
Manchester U	Sch	07/09				
Carlisle U	L	09/10	10	4	2	0
Scunthorpe U	L	08/11	11	14	1	1
Coventry C	L	01/12	11	17	1	2
Huddersfield T	Tr	06/12	12-14	75	5	8
Reading	Tr	08/14	14	32	6	1

NOSWORTHY Nyron Paul Henry
Born: Brixton, S London, England, 11 October, 1980 — CD/M
Jamaica: 14

League Club	Source	Date Signed	Seasons Played	Apps	Subs	Gls
Gillingham	YT	12/98	98-04	151	23	5
Sunderland	Tr	07/05	05-09	103	11	0
Sheffield U	L	02/10	09	19	0	0
Sheffield U	L	07/10	10	31	1	0
Watford	Tr	10/11	11-13	55	1	2
Bristol C	L	03/13	13	10	0	1
Blackpool		11/14	14	5	0	0
Portsmouth	L	03/15	14	6	1	0

NOTEMAN Kevin Simon
Born: Preston, Lancashire, England, 15 October, 1969 — LW

League Club	Source	Date Signed	Seasons Played	Apps	Subs	Gls
Leeds U	YT	06/88	87	0	1	0
Doncaster Rov	Tr	11/89	89-91	105	1	20
Mansfield T	Tr	03/92	91-94	77	18	15
Doncaster Rov	Tr	08/95	95	4	0	1
Chester C	Tr	09/95	95-96	57	11	18

NOTMAN Alexander McKeachie (Alex)
Born: Dalkeith, Midlothian, Scotland, 10 December, 1979 — F
Scotland: U21-11/Youth/Schools

League Club	Source	Date Signed	Seasons Played	Apps	Subs	Gls
Manchester U	YT	12/96				
Sheffield U	L	01/00	99	7	3	3
Norwich C	Tr	11/00	00-03	18	36	1

NOTTINGHAM Steven Edward (Steve)
Born: Peterborough, England, 21 June, 1980 — CD

League Club	Source	Date Signed	Seasons Played	Apps	Subs	Gls
Scunthorpe U	YT	07/98	97	1	0	0

NOUBISSIE Patrick Benjamin
Born: Paris, France, 25 June, 1983 — DM
Cameroon: U23

League Club	Source	Date Signed	Seasons Played	Apps	Subs	Gls
Swindon T	RF Picardie (FRA)	01/07	06	1	2	0

NOUBLE Frank Herman
Born: Lewisham, SE London, England, 24 September, 1991 — F
England: Youth

League Club	Source	Date Signed	Seasons Played	Apps	Subs	Gls
West Ham U	Chelsea (Sch)	07/09	09-11	4	9	1
West Bromwich A	L	02/10	09	3	0	0
Swindon T	L	03/10	09	3	5	0
Swansea C	L	09/10	10	2	4	1
Barnsley	L	01/11	10	4	0	0
Charlton Ath	L	03/11	10	4	5	1
Gillingham	L	09/11	11	12	1	5

League Club	Source	Date Signed	Seasons Played	Apps	Subs	Gls
Barnsley	L	03/12	11	5	1	0
Wolverhampton W	Tr	06/12	12	0	2	0
Ipswich T	Tr	01/13	12-14	22	34	4
Coventry C	Tr	09/14	14	28	3	6

NOUBLE Joel Jonathan (Jon)
Born: Deptford, SE London, England, 19 January, 1996 — F

League Club	Source	Date Signed	Seasons Played	Apps	Subs	Gls
Dagenham & Red	Jnr	04/14	13	0	1	0

NOVACKI Jan
Born: Manchester, England, 4 December, 1958 — RW
England: Youth

League Club	Source	Date Signed	Seasons Played	Apps	Subs	Gls
Bolton W	App	12/76				
York C	L	12/77	77	24	1	3

NOVAK Lee Paul
Born: Newcastle-upon-Tyne, England, 28 September, 1988 — F

League Club	Source	Date Signed	Seasons Played	Apps	Subs	Gls
Huddersfield T	Gateshead	02/09	09-12	89	55	34
Birmingham C	Tr	07/13	13-14	42	17	9

NOVAKOVICH Andrija
Born: Milwaukee, Wisconsin, USA, 21 September, 1996 — F
USA: Youth

League Club	Source	Date Signed	Seasons Played	Apps	Subs	Gls
Reading	Sch	04/14	14	0	2	0

NOVO Ignacio Javier Gomez (Nacho)
Born: Ferrol, Spain, 26 March, 1979 — F

League Club	Source	Date Signed	Seasons Played	Apps	Subs	Gls
Carlisle U	Greenock Morton	02/14	13	2	4	0

NOWAK Tadeusz
Born: Trzcinsko, Poland, 28 November, 1948 — RW
Poland: 1

League Club	Source	Date Signed	Seasons Played	Apps	Subs	Gls
Bolton W	Legia Warsaw (POL)	03/79	78-80	22	2	1

NOWLAND Adam Christopher
Born: Preston, Lancashire, England, 6 July, 1981 — M/F

League Club	Source	Date Signed	Seasons Played	Apps	Subs	Gls
Blackpool	YT	01/99	97-00	18	51	5
Wimbledon	Tr	06/01	01-03	35	21	5
West Ham U	Tr	01/04	03-04	5	10	1
Gillingham	L	09/04	04	3	0	1
Nottingham F	Tr	11/04	04	5	0	0
Preston NE	Tr	08/05	05-06	9	5	3
Gillingham	L	09/07	07	4	1	0
Stockport Co	L	11/07	07	4	0	0
Notts Co	Lancaster C	07/08	08	16	4	0

NSIALA Aristote (Toto)
Born: Kinshasa, DR Congo, 25 March, 1992 — CD
DR Congo: 1

League Club	Source	Date Signed	Seasons Played	Apps	Subs	Gls
Everton	Sch	01/10				
Macclesfield T	L	10/10	10	10	0	0
Accrington Stan	Tr	01/12	11-12	34	2	0

NSUE Emilia
Born: Palma de Mallorca, Spain, 30 September, 1989 — RB/M
Spain: U21-8/Youth//Equatorial Guinea: 9

League Club	Source	Date Signed	Seasons Played	Apps	Subs	Gls
Middlesbrough	RCD Mallorca (SPN)	07/14	14	12	14	0

NTAMARK Charles Batmbog (Charlie)
Born: Paddington, Central London, England, 22 July, 1964 — M
Cameroon: 31

League Club	Source	Date Signed	Seasons Played	Apps	Subs	Gls
Walsall	Boreham Wood	08/90	90-96	256	20	12

NTIMBAN-ZEH Harry Dave
Born: Paris, France, 26 September, 1973 — CD

League Club	Source	Date Signed	Seasons Played	Apps	Subs	Gls
Wimbledon	Sporting Espinho (POR)	03/04	03	9	1	0
MK Dons	Wimbledon relocation	08/04	04	11	0	0

NTLHE Kgosietsile (Kgosi)
Born: Pretoria, South Africa, 21 February, 1994 — LB
South Africa: 1/Youth

League Club	Source	Date Signed	Seasons Played	Apps	Subs	Gls
Peterborough U	Sch	03/11	11-14	56	13	4

N'TOKO Chira Vusa
Born: Kinshasa, DR Congo, 30 January, 1988 — D

League Club	Source	Date Signed	Seasons Played	Apps	Subs	Gls
Barnet	ADO Den Haag (NED)	02/13	12	2	0	0

N'TOYA-ZOA Tcham
Born: Kinshasa, DR Congo, 3 November, 1983 — F

League Club	Source	Date Signed	Seasons Played	Apps	Subs	Gls
Chesterfield	Troyes AC (FRA)	03/04	03-05	22	26	8
Oxford U	L	03/06	05	7	1	4
Notts Co	Tr	06/06	06	4	17	1

NUGENT Arthur
Born: Glasgow, Scotland, 30 May, 1926 — RB
Died: Glasgow, Scotland, 6 October, 1995

League Club	Source	Date Signed	Seasons Played	Apps	Subs	Gls
Darlington	Canterbury C	06/56	56	5	-	0

NUGENT Ben William
Born: Welwyn Garden City, Hertfordshire, England, 29 November, 1992 — CD

League Club	Source	Date Signed	Seasons Played	Apps	Subs	Gls
Cardiff C	Sch	07/12	12	7	5	1
Peterborough U	L	02/14	13	11	0	0
Yeovil T	L	07/14	14	23	0	1

NUGENT David James
Born: Huyton, Merseyside, England, 2 May, 1985 — F
England: 1/U21-14/Youth

League Club	Source	Date Signed	Seasons Played	Apps	Subs	Gls
Bury	Sch	03/03	01-04	58	30	18
Preston NE	Tr	01/05	04-06	83	11	33
Portsmouth	Tr	07/07	07-10	62	16	16
Burnley	L	09/09	09	20	10	6
Leicester C	Tr	07/11	11-14	137	22	54

NUGENT Kevin Patrick
Born: Edmonton, N London, England, 10 April, 1969 — F
Republic of Ireland: Youth

League Club	Source	Date Signed	Seasons Played	Apps	Subs	Gls
Leyton Orient	YT	07/87	87-91	86	8	20
Plymouth Arg	Tr	03/92	91-95	124	7	32
Bristol C	Tr	09/95	95-96	48	22	14
Cardiff C	Tr	08/97	97-01	94	5	29
Leyton Orient	Tr	01/02	01-02	17	11	4
Swansea C	Tr	01/03	02-05	53	21	16

NUGENT Richard Joseph
Born: Birmingham, England, 20 March, 1964 — CD

League Club	Source	Date Signed	Seasons Played	Apps	Subs	Gls
Barnet	St Albans C	10/88	91	2	0	0

NUGENT Stephen (Steve)
Born: Orrell, Greater Manchester, England, 7 May, 1973 — F

League Club	Source	Date Signed	Seasons Played	Apps	Subs	Gls
Wigan Ath	YT	08/91	89-92	7	6	0

NUGENT William Clifford (Cliff)
Born: Islington, N London, England, 3 March, 1929 — LW

League Club	Source	Date Signed	Seasons Played	Apps	Subs	Gls
Cardiff C	Headington U	01/51	51-58	113	-	19
Mansfield T	Tr	11/58	58-59	52	-	7

NUHIU Atdhe
Born: Pristina, Kosovo, 29 July, 1989 — F
Austria: U21-13/Youth

League Club	Source	Date Signed	Seasons Played	Apps	Subs	Gls
Sheffield Wed	Rapid Vienna (AUT)	07/13	13-14	56	25	16

NULTY Geoffrey Owen (Geoff)
Born: Prescot, Merseyside, England, 13 February, 1949 — M

League Club	Source	Date Signed	Seasons Played	Apps	Subs	Gls
Stoke C	St Helens T	07/67				
Burnley	Tr	07/68	69-74	123	7	20
Newcastle U	Tr	12/74	74-77	101	0	11
Everton	Tr	07/78	78-79	22	5	2

NUNDY Jeffrey William (Jeff)
Born: Hull, England, 29 November, 1935 — CH

League Club	Source	Date Signed	Seasons Played	Apps	Subs	Gls
Huddersfield T	Bradford C (Jnr)	12/53				
Bradford C	Tr	07/57	57-59	32	-	0

NUNES Fabio Alexandre Silva
Born: Portimao, Portugal, 24 July, 1992 — LW
Portugal: Youth

League Club	Source	Date Signed	Seasons Played	Apps	Subs	Gls
Blackburn Rov	Portimanense (POR)	07/12	12-13	2	5	0

NUNEZ Antonio
Born: Madrid, Spain, 15 January, 1979 — M

League Club	Source	Date Signed	Seasons Played	Apps	Subs	Gls
Liverpool	Real Madrid (SPN)	08/04	04	8	10	0

NUNEZ Garcia Milton Omar (Milton)
Born: La Ceiba, Honduras, 30 October, 1972 — F
Honduras: 86

League Club	Source	Date Signed	Seasons Played	Apps	Subs	Gls
Sunderland	PAOK Salonika (GRE)	03/00	99	0	1	0

NUNEZ Ramon Fernando
Born: Tegucigalpa, Honduras, 14 November, 1985 — LW
Honduras: 44

League Club	Source	Date Signed	Seasons Played	Apps	Subs	Gls
Leeds U	Olimpia (HON)	09/10	10-11	6	15	1
Scunthorpe U	L	03/11	10	8	0	3

NUNN Benjamin Thomas (Ben)
Born: Cambridge, England, 25 October, 1989 — RB

League Club	Source	Date Signed	Seasons Played	Apps	Subs	Gls
Boston U	Sch	-	06	0	1	0

NUNN Walter
Born: Deptford, SE London, England, 16 January, 1920 — WH
Died: Camberwell, S London, England, 1965

League Club	Source	Date Signed	Seasons Played	Apps	Subs	Gls
Charlton Ath	Bexleyheath & Welling	05/39				
Swindon T	Tr	06/47	47	4	-	0

[NUNO GOMES] PEREIRA Nuno Miguel Soares
Born: Amarante, Portugal, 5 July, 1976 — F
Portugal: 78/U23-5/U21-13/Youth

League Club	Source	Date Signed	Seasons Played	Apps	Subs	Gls
Blackburn Rov	SC Braga (POR)	07/12	12	8	10	4

NURSE Jonathan David (Jon)
Born: Bridgetown, Barbados, 1 March, 1981 — F/W
Barbados: 6

League Club	Source	Date Signed	Seasons Played	Apps	Subs	Gls
Dagenham & Red	Stevenage Bor	05/07	07-11	129	50	27
Barnet	Tr	07/12	12	18	8	3

NURSE Melvyn Tudor George (Mel)
Born: Swansea, Wales, 11 October, 1937 — CH
Wales: 12/U23-2/Schools

League Club	Source	Date Signed	Seasons Played	Apps	Subs	Gls
Swansea C	Jnr	06/55	55-62	159	-	9
Middlesbrough	Tr	10/62	62-65	113	0	8
Swindon T	Tr	09/65	65-67	122	1	10
Swansea C	Tr	06/68	68-70	97	1	3

NUTE Stephen Leslie Rodney (Steve)
Born: Plymouth, England, 18 April, 1962 — G

League Club	Source	Date Signed	Seasons Played	Apps	Subs	Gls
Exeter C	App	04/80	80	5	0	0

NUTLEY Robert (Bobby)
Born: Paisley, Renfrewshire, Scotland, 10 September, 1916 — RW
Died: Paisley, Renfrewshire, Scotland, 14 July, 1996
Scotland: SLge-1

League Club	Source	Date Signed	Seasons Played	Apps	Subs	Gls
Portsmouth	Hibernian	08/46	46	9	-	1

NUTT Gordon Edward
Born: Birmingham, England, 8 November, 1932 — W
Died: Hobart, Tasmania, Australia, 25 February, 2014

League Club	Source	Date Signed	Seasons Played	Apps	Subs	Gls
Coventry C	Sheldon T	11/49	51-54	76	-	11
Cardiff C	Tr	12/54	54-55	17	-	4
Arsenal	Tr	09/55	55-59	49	-	10
Southend U	Tr	10/60	60	16	-	2

NUTT Philip James (Phil)
Born: Westminster, Central London, England, 18 May, 1958 — F

League Club	Source	Date Signed	Seasons Played	Apps	Subs	Gls
Queens Park Rgrs	App	07/75	75-76	0	4	1

NUTTALL James (Jimmy)
Born: Liverpool, England, 14 October, 1929 — CF

League Club	Source	Date Signed	Seasons Played	Apps	Subs	Gls
Southport	Skelmersdale U	05/50	50-52	67	-	29

NUTTALL Martin
Born: Oldham, Greater Manchester, England, 12 September, 1961 — F

League Club	Source	Date Signed	Seasons Played	Apps	Subs	Gls
Oldham Ath	App	09/79	80-81	8	5	1
Halifax T	Tr	08/82	82-83	39	11	10

NUTTALL William (Billy)
Born: Preston, Lancashire, England, 7 December, 1920 — FB

League Club	Source	Date Signed	Seasons Played	Apps	Subs	Gls
Preston NE	Jnr	07/46	46	2	-	0
Barrow	Tr	08/48	48-50	65	-	0

NUTTELL Michael John (Mike)
Born: Boston, Lincolnshire, England, 22 November, 1968 — F

League Club	Source	Date Signed	Seasons Played	Apps	Subs	Gls
Peterborough U	YT	08/87	85-87	12	9	0
Crewe Alex	L	12/87	87	2	1	1
Carlisle U	L	11/88	88	1	2	0

NUTTER John Robert William
Born: Burnham, Buckinghamshire, England, 13 June, 1982 — LB
England: Semi Pro-3

League Club	Source	Date Signed	Seasons Played	Apps	Subs	Gls
Wycombe W	YT	01/01	00	1	0	0
Gillingham	Stevenage Bor	11/07	07-10	130	8	3

NUTTON Michael William (Mickey)
Born: St Johns Wood, N London, England, 3 October, 1959 — CD

League Club	Source	Date Signed	Seasons Played	Apps	Subs	Gls
Chelsea	App	10/77	78-82	77	2	0
Reading	L	02/83	82	6	0	0
Millwall	Tr	03/83	82-85	81	1	4

NWADIKE Chukwuemeka Ibezimife (Emeka)
Born: Camberwell, S London, England, 9 August, 1978 — CD

League Club	Source	Date Signed	Seasons Played	Apps	Subs	Gls
Wolverhampton W	YT	07/96				
Shrewsbury T	Tr	12/96	96-97	2	1	0

NWAJIOBI Chukwuemeka (Emeka)
Born: Nibo Awka, Nigeria, 25 May, 1959 — F
England: Schools//Nigeria: 4

League Club	Source	Date Signed	Seasons Played	Apps	Subs	Gls
Luton T	Dulwich Hamlet	12/83	83-87	59	13	17

NWOKEJI Mark Obidozie Chukwuemeka
Born: Manchester, England, 30 January, 1982 — F

League Club	Source	Date Signed	Seasons Played	Apps	Subs	Gls
Dagenham & Red	Staines T	07/08	08	3	13	3

NYAFLI Nathan Setor Kofi
Born: Lambeth, S London, England, 24 December, 1993 — F

League Club	Source	Date Signed	Seasons Played	Apps	Subs	Gls
Gillingham	Sch	07/13	12	0	1	1

NYAMAH Kofi
Born: Islington, N London, England, 20 June, 1975 — LB/M

League Club	Source	Date Signed	Seasons Played	Apps	Subs	Gls
Cambridge U	YT	05/93	93-94	9	14	2
Stoke C	Kettering T	12/96	96-97	9	8	0
Luton T	Tr	08/98				
Exeter C	Kingstonian	08/99	99	23	12	1

NYARKO Alex
Born: Accra, Ghana, 15 October, 1973 — DM
Ghana: 11

League Club	Source	Date Signed	Seasons Played	Apps	Subs	Gls
Everton	RC Lens (FRA)	08/00	00-03	26	7	1

NYATANGA Lewin John
Born: Burton-on-Trent, Staffordshire, England, 18 August, 1988 — CD
Wales: 34/U21-10/Youth

League Club	Source	Date Signed	Seasons Played	Apps	Subs	Gls
Derby Co	Sch	08/05	05-08	57	6	4
Sunderland	L	10/06	06	9	2	0
Barnsley	L	02/07	06	10	0	1
Barnsley	L	07/07	07	24	1	0
Barnsley	L	01/08	07	16	0	1
Bristol C	Tr	07/09	09-12	97	8	4
Peterborough U	L	11/10	10	3	0	0
Barnsley	Tr	07/13	13-14	55	2	5

NYGAARD Marc Stephen Griffith
Born: Copenhagen, Denmark, 1 September, 1976 — M/F
Denmark: 7/U21-6/Youth

League Club	Source	Date Signed	Seasons Played	Apps	Subs	Gls
Queens Park Rgrs	Brescia (ITA)	07/05	05-07	43	26	13

NZAMBA Guy Roger
Born: Port Gentil, Gabon, 13 July, 1970 — F

League Club	Source	Date Signed	Seasons Played	Apps	Subs	Gls
Southend U	Trieste (ITA)	09/97	97	0	1	0

N'ZOGBIA Charles
Born: Le Havre, France, 28 May, 1986 — LW
France: 2/U21-13

League Club	Source	Date Signed	Seasons Played	Apps	Subs	Gls
Newcastle U	Le Havre (FRA)	09/04	04-08	86	32	9
Wigan Ath	Tr	02/09	08-10	80	3	15
Aston Villa	Tr	07/11	11-14	54	24	4

N'ZONZI Steven N'Kemboanza
Born: Paris, France, 15 December, 1988 — DM
France: U21-6

League Club	Source	Date Signed	Seasons Played	Apps	Subs	Gls
Blackburn Rov	Amiens SC (FRA)	07/09	09-11	77	9	5
Stoke C	Tr	08/12	12-14	107	2	6

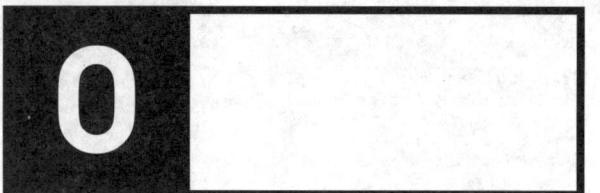

OAKES Alan Arthur
Born: Winsford, Cheshire, England, 7 September, 1942 — M
England: FLge-1

League Club	Source	Date Signed	Seasons Played	Apps	Subs	Gls
Manchester C	Jnr	09/59	59-75	561	3	26
Chester C	Tr	07/76	76-81	211	0	15
Port Vale	Rtd	10/83	83	1	0	0

OAKES Andrew Mark (Andy)
Born: Northwich, Cheshire, England, 11 January, 1977 — G

League Club	Source	Date Signed	Seasons Played	Apps	Subs	Gls
Hull C	Winsford U	12/98	98	19	0	0
Derby Co	Tr	06/99	00-03	43	0	0
Bolton W	L	08/04	04	1	0	0
Walsall	Tr	03/05	04-05	34	0	0
Swansea C	Tr	08/06	06	4	0	0
Darlington	Tr	07/07	07-08	16	0	0

OAKES Dennis Raymond
Born: Bedworth, Warwickshire, England, 10 April, 1946 — M

League Club	Source	Date Signed	Seasons Played	Apps	Subs	Gls
Coventry C	App	08/64				
Notts Co	Tr	06/67	67-70	107	12	0
Peterborough U	Tr	05/71	71-72	84	1	5

OAKES Donald Joseph (Don)
Born: Rhyl, Denbighshire, Wales, 8 October, 1928 — LH
Died: Islington, N London, England, 13 June, 1977

League Club	Source	Date Signed	Seasons Played	Apps	Subs	Gls
Arsenal	Downend ATC	07/46	52-54	11	-	1

OAKES George
Born: Orrell, Greater Manchester, England, 18 October, 1918 — RW
Died: Wigan, Greater Manchester, England, 1 May, 1990

League Club	Source	Date Signed	Seasons Played	Apps	Subs	Gls
Southport	Astley & Tyldesley	08/45	46	7	-	0

OAKES John (Jackie)
Born: Hamilton, Lanarkshire, Scotland, 6 December, 1919 — W
Died: Dumfries, Scotland, 3 December, 1995

League Club	Source	Date Signed	Seasons Played	Apps	Subs	Gls
Huddersfield T	Queen of the South	11/43				
Blackburn Rov	Queen of the South	02/47	46-47	35	-	9
Manchester C	Tr	06/48	48-50	77	-	9

OAKES John (Jack)
Born: Winsford, Cheshire, England, 13 September, 1905 — CH
Died: Perth, Australia, 20 March, 1992
England: War-1

League Club	Source	Date Signed	Seasons Played	Apps	Subs	Gls
Nottingham F	Cargo Fleet	08/28	29	2	-	0
Southend U	Crook T	05/31	31	2	-	0
Aldershot	Spennymoor U	08/34	34-35	61	-	19
Charlton Ath	Tr	03/36	35-46	130	-	3
Plymouth Arg	Tr	07/47	47	36	-	0

OAKES John Francis
Born: Hamilton, Lanarkshire, Scotland, 16 January, 1921 — W
Died: Whitehaven, Cumbria, England, June, 1987

League Club	Source	Date Signed	Seasons Played	Apps	Subs	Gls
Rochdale	Queen of the South	02/47	46	1	-	0

OAKES Keith Brian
Born: Bedworth, Warwickshire, England, 3 July, 1956 — CD

League Club	Source	Date Signed	Seasons Played	Apps	Subs	Gls
Peterborough U	App	07/73	72-77	48	13	2
Newport Co	Tr	09/78	78-83	232	0	27
Gillingham	Tr	08/84	84-86	84	2	7
Fulham	Tr	09/86	86-87	76	0	3
Peterborough U	Tr	08/88	88-90	95	2	9

OAKES Michael Christian (Mike)
Born: Northwich, Cheshire, England, 30 October, 1973 — G
England: U21-6

League Club	Source	Date Signed	Seasons Played	Apps	Subs	Gls
Aston Villa	Jnr	07/91	96-98	49	2	0
Scarborough	L	11/93	93	1	0	0
Wolverhampton W	Tr	10/99	99-05	198	1	0
Cardiff C	Tr	07/07	07	11	0	0

OAKES Scott John
Born: Leicester, England, 5 August, 1972 — W/M
England: U21-1

League Club	Source	Date Signed	Seasons Played	Apps	Subs	Gls
Leicester C	YT	05/90	89-91	1	1	0
Luton T	Tr	10/91	91-95	136	37	27
Sheffield Wed	Tr	08/96	96-98	7	17	1
Cambridge U	Tr	08/00	00	7	11	0
Leyton Orient	Tr	07/01	01	11	0	0

OAKES Stefan Trevor
Born: Leicester, England, 6 September, 1978 — LM

League Club	Source	Date Signed	Seasons Played	Apps	Subs	Gls
Leicester C	YT	07/97	98-02	39	25	2
Crewe Alex	L	03/03	02	3	4	0
Walsall	Tr	07/03	03	1	4	0
Notts Co	Tr	02/04	03-04	42	3	5
Wycombe W	Tr	07/05	05-07	83	25	5
Lincoln C	Tr	07/08	08-09	32	12	1

OAKES Thomas
Born: Manchester, England, 6 February, 1922 — RW
Died: Manchester, England, November, 1993

League Club	Source	Date Signed	Seasons Played	Apps	Subs	Gls
Manchester C	Manchester U (Am)	04/47	46	1	-	0

OAKEY Graham
Born: Droitwich, Worcestershire, England, 5 October, 1954 — RB

League Club	Source	Date Signed	Seasons Played	Apps	Subs	Gls
Coventry C	App	10/72	74-77	87	1	0

OAKLEY George
Born: Wandsworth, SW London, England, 18 November, 1995 — F

League Club	Source	Date Signed	Seasons Played	Apps	Subs	Gls
AFC Wimbledon	Sch	04/14	14	0	6	0

OAKLEY Kenneth (Ken)
Born: Rhymney, Caerphilly, Wales, 9 May, 1929 — CF

League Club	Source	Date Signed	Seasons Played	Apps	Subs	Gls
Cardiff C	Ebbw Vale	03/50	50-53	7	-	1
Northampton T	Tr	07/54	54	13	-	6

OAKLEY Matthew (Matt)
Born: Peterborough, England, 17 August, 1977 — M
England: U21-4

League Club	Source	Date Signed	Seasons Played	Apps	Subs	Gls
Southampton	YT	07/95	94-05	238	23	14
Derby Co	Tr	08/06	06-07	55	1	9
Leicester C	Tr	01/08	07-10	124	13	10
Exeter C	L	09/11	11	7	0	0
Exeter C	Tr	07/12	12-14	99	6	0

OAKLEY Norman
Born: Stockton-on-Tees, Cleveland, England, 4 June, 1939 — G

League Club	Source	Date Signed	Seasons Played	Apps	Subs	Gls
Doncaster Rov	Jnr	04/57				
Scunthorpe U	Tr	07/58				
Hartlepool U	Tr	09/58	58-63	182	-	0
Swindon T	Tr	03/64	63-64	21	-	0
Grimsby T	Tr	09/66	66	15	0	0

OAKLEY Royston James (Roy)
Born: Tipton, West Midlands, England, 5 January, 1928 — RB

League Club	Source	Date Signed	Seasons Played	Apps	Subs	Gls
Southampton	Guernsey Rgrs	11/50	53-55	6	-	0

OASTLER Joseph James (Joe)
Born: Portsmouth, England, 3 July, 1990 — RB

League Club	Source	Date Signed	Seasons Played	Apps	Subs	Gls
Queens Park Rgrs	Portsmouth (Sch)	07/08	09	0	1	0
Torquay U	Tr	10/10	10-12	99	9	1

OATES Graham
Born: Scunthorpe, North Lincolnshire, England, 4 December, 1943 — LW

League Club	Source	Date Signed	Seasons Played	Apps	Subs	Gls
Blackpool	App	05/61	61-68	119	3	26
Grimsby T	Tr	10/68	68-70	80	1	9

OATES Graham
Born: Bradford, England, 14 March, 1949 — M

League Club	Source	Date Signed	Seasons Played	Apps	Subs	Gls
Bradford C	Manningham Mills	02/70	69-73	158	3	19
Blackburn Rov	Tr	06/74	74-75	76	0	10
Newcastle U	Tr	03/76	75-77	26	9	3

OATES Rhys Derek
Born: Pontefract, West Yorkshire, England, 4 December, 1994 — F

League Club	Source	Date Signed	Seasons Played	Apps	Subs	Gls
Barnsley	Sch	07/13	14	0	9	0

OATES Robert Anthony (Bob)
Born: Leeds, England, 26 July, 1956 — CD
England: Youth

League Club	Source	Date Signed	Seasons Played	Apps	Subs	Gls
Scunthorpe U	Leeds Ashley Road	08/74	74-82	306	9	17
Rochdale	Tr	08/83	83	42	0	1

OATWAY Anthony Philip David (Charlie)
Born: Hammersmith, W London, England, 28 November, 1973 — M

League Club	Source	Date Signed	Seasons Played	Apps	Subs	Gls
Cardiff C	Yeading	08/94	94-95	29	3	0
Torquay U	Tr	12/95	95-97	65	2	1
Brentford	Tr	08/97	97-98	37	20	0
Lincoln C	L	10/98	98	3	0	0
Brighton & HA	Tr	07/99	99-05	200	24	9

OBADEYI Temitope Ayoluwa (Temi)
Born: Birmingham, England, 29 October, 1989 — F
England: Youth

League Club	Source	Date Signed	Seasons Played	Apps	Subs	Gls
Bolton W	Sch	11/06	08	0	3	0
Swindon T	L	08/09	09	9	3	2
Rochdale	L	01/10	09	5	6	1
Shrewsbury T	L	10/10	10	7	2	0
Chesterfield	L	11/11	11	3	2	0

League Club	Source	Date Signed	Seasons Played	Apps	Subs	Gls
Rochdale	L	03/12	11	3	3	1
Bury	Rio Ave (POR)	08/13	13	0	7	0
Plymouth Arg	L	11/13	13	5	9	1

OBAFEMI Alofabi (Affy)
Born: Walthamstow, NE London, England, 25 November, 1994 — F

League Club	Source	Date Signed	Seasons Played	Apps	Subs	Gls
Leyton Orient	Sch	07/11	11-12	0	9	0
Dagenham & Red	Tr	07/13	13	9	13	2

OBEBO Godfrey
Born: Lagos, Nigeria, 16 April, 1966 — F

League Club	Source	Date Signed	Seasons Played	Apps	Subs	Gls
Halifax T	Collier Row	03/93	92	0	3	0

OBENEY Henry Richard (Harry)
Born: Bethnal Green, E London, England, 9 March, 1938 — RH/CF

League Club	Source	Date Signed	Seasons Played	Apps	Subs	Gls
West Ham U	Briggs Sports	05/56	56-60	25	-	12
Millwall	Tr	06/61	61-63	76	-	10

OBENG Curtis
Born: Stretford, Greater Manchester, England, 14 February, 1989 — RB
England: Semi Pro-1/Youth

League Club	Source	Date Signed	Seasons Played	Apps	Subs	Gls
Manchester C	Sch	07/07				
Swansea C	Wrexham	01/12				
Fleetwood T	L	10/12	12	4	1	0
York C	L	01/13	12	4	0	0
Stevenage	L	02/14	13	15	0	0
Newport Co	L	10/14	14	4	1	0

O'BERG Paul John
Born: Hull, England, 8 May, 1958 — M

League Club	Source	Date Signed	Seasons Played	Apps	Subs	Gls
Scunthorpe U	Bridlington T	07/79	79-83	117	13	23
Wimbledon	Tr	08/84	84	2	1	0
Stockport Co	L	11/84	84	2	0	0
Chester C	L	12/84	84	5	0	1
Scunthorpe U	L	03/85	84	0	2	0

OBERSTELLER Jack Lewis
Born: Plaistow, E London, England, 10 October, 1988 — LB/M

League Club	Source	Date Signed	Seasons Played	Apps	Subs	Gls
Wycombe W	Millwall (Sch)	07/07				
Exeter C	Tr	07/08	08	3	4	0

OBERTAN Gabriel Antoine
Born: Paris, France, 26 February, 1989 — LW
France: U21-11/Youth

League Club	Source	Date Signed	Seasons Played	Apps	Subs	Gls
Manchester U	Bordeaux (FRA)	07/09	09-10	4	10	0
Newcastle U	Tr	08/11	11-14	30	23	2

OBI Anthony Lloyd (Tony)
Born: Birmingham, England, 15 September, 1965 — W
England: Youth

League Club	Source	Date Signed	Seasons Played	Apps	Subs	Gls
Aston Villa	App	09/83				
Walsall	L	12/84	84	1	1	0
Plymouth Arg	L	02/85	84	5	0	0
Bristol Rov	Tr	08/85	85	1	0	0
Oxford U	Tr	10/85	86	0	1	0
Brentford	L	08/86	86	10	0	0

OBIKA Jonathan Chiedozie
Born: Enfield, N London, England, 12 September, 1990 — F
England: Youth

League Club	Source	Date Signed	Seasons Played	Apps	Subs	Gls
Tottenham H	Sch	01/09				
Yeovil T	L	03/09	08	10	0	4
Yeovil T	L	08/09	09	13	9	6
Millwall	L	02/10	09	0	12	2
Crystal Palace	L	08/10	10	0	7	0
Peterborough U	L	01/11	10	0	1	1
Swindon T	L	02/11	10	3	2	0
Yeovil T	L	03/11	10	11	0	3
Yeovil T	L	08/11	11	24	3	4
Charlton Ath	L	02/13	12	2	8	3
Brighton & HA	L	01/14	13	0	5	0
Charlton Ath	L	04/14	13	3	9	0
Swindon T	Tr	09/14	14	21	11	8

OBILEYE Stephen Ayomide (Ayo)
Born: Hackney, E London, England, 2 September, 1994 — CD

League Club	Source	Date Signed	Seasons Played	Apps	Subs	Gls
Sheffield Wed	Sch	05/13				
Charlton Ath	Tr	10/14				
Dagenham & Red	L	11/14	14	25	1	2

OBINNA Eric Chukwynyely
Born: Owerri, Nigeria, 10 June, 1981 — F

League Club	Source	Date Signed	Seasons Played	Apps	Subs	Gls
Reading	Kaiserslautern (GER)	09/05	05	0	6	0

OBINNA Victor Nsofor
Born: Jos, Nigeria, 25 March, 1987 — W
Nigeria: 47/U23-6

League Club	Source	Date Signed	Seasons Played	Apps	Subs	Gls
West Ham U (L)	Inter Milan (ITA)	08/10	10	17	8	3

OBITA Jordan John
Born: Oxford, England, 8 December, 1993 — M/LB
England: U21-2/Youth

League Club	Source	Date Signed	Seasons Played	Apps	Subs	Gls
Reading	Sch	12/10	13-14	75	2	1
Barnet	L	01/12	11	3	2	0
Gillingham	L	03/12	11	5	1	3
Portsmouth	L	08/12	12	2	6	1
Oldham Ath	L	01/13	12	4	4	0

O'BRIEN Aiden Anthony
Born: Hornsey, N London, England, 4 October, 1993 — F
Republic of Ireland: U21-10/Youth

League Club	Source	Date Signed	Seasons Played	Apps	Subs	Gls
Millwall	Sch	10/10	14	13	6	2
Crawley T	L	02/13	12	0	9	0
Torquay U	L	01/14	13	0	3	0

O'BRIEN Alan
Born: Dublin, Republic of Ireland, 20 February, 1985 — LW
Republic of Ireland: 5/Youth

League Club	Source	Date Signed	Seasons Played	Apps	Subs	Gls
Newcastle U	Sch	04/02	05-06	1	4	0
Carlisle U	L	09/05	05	2	3	1
Swindon T	Hibernian	07/09	09-10	11	19	0
Yeovil T	Tr	08/11	11	8	5	0

O'BRIEN Andrew James (Andy)
Born: Harrogate, North Yorkshire, England, 29 June, 1979 — CD
England: U21-1/Youth//Republic of Ireland: 26/U21-8

League Club	Source	Date Signed	Seasons Played	Apps	Subs	Gls
Bradford C	YT	10/96	96-00	113	20	3
Newcastle U	Tr	03/01	00-04	114	6	6
Portsmouth	Tr	07/05	05-06	30	2	0
Bolton W	Tr	08/07	07-10	68	6	1
Leeds U	Tr	10/10	10-11	32	2	2

O'BRIEN Anthony (Tony)
Born: Liverpool, England, 4 September, 1956 — FB

League Club	Source	Date Signed	Seasons Played	Apps	Subs	Gls
Southport	St Theresa's	08/74	74-76	17	3	1

O'BRIEN Burton
Born: Johannesburg, South Africa, 10 June, 1981 — M
Scotland: U21-6/Youth

League Club	Source	Date Signed	Seasons Played	Apps	Subs	Gls
Blackburn Rov	St Mirren	07/99				
Sheffield Wed	Livingston	07/05	05-07	73	26	6

O'BRIEN Colin
Born: Dunfermline, Fife, Scotland, 19 April, 1956 — W

League Club	Source	Date Signed	Seasons Played	Apps	Subs	Gls
Bristol C	Swaythling	11/77				
Hereford U	L	12/78	78	1	1	0

O'BRIEN George
Born: Dunfermline, Fife, Scotland, 22 November, 1935 — IF

League Club	Source	Date Signed	Seasons Played	Apps	Subs	Gls
Leeds U	Dunfermline Ath	03/57	56-58	44	-	6
Southampton	Tr	07/59	59-65	244	0	154
Leyton Orient	Tr	03/66	65-66	17	0	3
Aldershot	Tr	12/66	66-67	38	3	8

O'BRIEN George
Born: Liverpool, England, 21 October, 1939 — IF
Died: Lambeth, S London, England, 14 February, 1995

League Club	Source	Date Signed	Seasons Played	Apps	Subs	Gls
Everton	Jnr	02/59				
Southport	Tr	07/60	60	3	-	1

O'BRIEN Gerald (Gerry)
Born: Glasgow, Scotland, 10 November, 1949 — W

League Club	Source	Date Signed	Seasons Played	Apps	Subs	Gls
Southampton	Clydebank	03/70	69-75	66	12	2
Bristol Rov	L	03/74	73	3	0	0
Swindon T	Tr	03/76	75-76	24	3	0

O'BRIEN James (Jamie)
Born: Dublin, Republic of Ireland, 8 June, 1990 — M
Republic of Ireland: Youth

League Club	Source	Date Signed	Seasons Played	Apps	Subs	Gls
Birmingham C	Sch	06/07				
Bradford C	Tr	08/09	09	15	8	2

O'BRIEN James John (Jim)
Born: Alexandria, Dunbartonshire, Scotland, 28 September, 1987 — W
Republic of Ireland: U21-6/Youth

League Club	Source	Date Signed	Seasons Played	Apps	Subs	Gls
Barnsley	Motherwell	06/10	10-13	83	40	7
Coventry C	Tr	07/14	14	43	1	6

O'BRIEN Jonathan Mark (Jon)
Born: Southend-on-Sea, England, 2 November, 1961 — G

League Club	Source	Date Signed	Seasons Played	Apps	Subs	Gls
Southend U	Tilbury	03/84	84	11	0	0

O'BRIEN Joseph (Joe)
Born: Dublin, Republic of Ireland, 9 May, 1924 — LW

League Club	Source	Date Signed	Seasons Played	Apps	Subs	Gls
Luton T	Dundalk (ROI)	11/47	47-48	11	-	3
Ipswich T	Tr	06/49	49-50	50	-	12

O'BRIEN Joseph Martin (Joey)
Born: Dublin, Republic of Ireland, 17 February, 1986 — RB/M

League Club	Source	Date Signed	Seasons Played	Apps	Subs	Gls

Republic of Ireland: 5/U21-6/Youth

League Club	Source	Date Signed	Seasons Played	Apps	Subs	Gls
Bolton W	Sch	11/04	04-08	42	8	0
Sheffield Wed	L	12/04	04	14	1	2
Sheffield Wed	L	03/11	10	3	1	0
West Ham U	Tr	07/11	11-14	78	13	3

O'BRIEN Liam Daniel
Born: Ruislip, W London, England, 30 November, 1991 G
England: Youth

League Club	Source	Date Signed	Seasons Played	Apps	Subs	Gls
Portsmouth	Sch	12/08				
Barnet	Tr	01/11	10-12	20	1	0
Brentford	Tr	08/13				
Dagenham & Red	Tr	05/14	14	9	1	0

O'BRIEN Luke
Born: Halifax, West Yorkshire, England, 11 September, 1988 LB

League Club	Source	Date Signed	Seasons Played	Apps	Subs	Gls
Bradford C	Sch	07/07	07-11	115	16	2
Exeter C	Tr	01/12	11	2	1	0
Oxford U	Tr	09/12	12	11	4	0

O'BRIEN Mark Leo
Born: Dublin, Republic of Ireland, 20 November, 1992 CD
Republic of Ireland: Youth

League Club	Source	Date Signed	Seasons Played	Apps	Subs	Gls
Derby Co	Sch	11/09	08-12	21	11	0

O'BRIEN Michael George (Mick)
Born: Liverpool, England, 25 September, 1979 M
England: Schools

League Club	Source	Date Signed	Seasons Played	Apps	Subs	Gls
Everton	YT	10/97				
Torquay U	Tr	07/99	99-01	32	20	5

O'BRIEN Noel William
Born: Islington, N London, England, 18 December, 1956 M

League Club	Source	Date Signed	Seasons Played	Apps	Subs	Gls
Arsenal	App	01/74				
Mansfield T	Tr	06/75	75	7	0	0

O'BRIEN Raymond Christopher (Ray)
Born: Dublin, Republic of Ireland, 21 May, 1951 LB
Republic of Ireland: 4/LoI-1/U23-2

League Club	Source	Date Signed	Seasons Played	Apps	Subs	Gls
Manchester U	Shelbourne (ROI)	05/73				
Notts Co	Tr	03/74	73-82	323	0	33
Derby Co	L	09/83	83	4	0	0

O'BRIEN Robert Louis (Rob)
Born: Leeds, England, 28 November, 1983 M

League Club	Source	Date Signed	Seasons Played	Apps	Subs	Gls
Doncaster Rov	Leeds U (Jnr)	01/03	03	1	0	0

O'BRIEN Roy Joseph
Born: Cork, Republic of Ireland, 27 November, 1974 CD
Republic of Ireland: Youth/Schools

League Club	Source	Date Signed	Seasons Played	Apps	Subs	Gls
Arsenal	YT	07/93				
Bournemouth	Tr	08/96	96	1	0	0
Yeovil T	Dorchester T	08/00	03-04	23	4	0

O'BRIEN William (Willie)
Born: Middlesbrough, England, 26 January, 1929 CH

League Club	Source	Date Signed	Seasons Played	Apps	Subs	Gls
Darlington		02/50	50	2	-	0

O'BRIEN William Francis (Liam)
Born: Dublin, Republic of Ireland, 5 September, 1964 M
Republic of Ireland: 16/U23-1/Youth/Schools

League Club	Source	Date Signed	Seasons Played	Apps	Subs	Gls
Manchester U	Shamrock Rov (ROI)	10/86	86-88	16	15	2
Newcastle U	Tr	11/88	88-93	131	20	19
Tranmere Rov	Tr	01/94	93-98	169	12	12

O'CALLAGHAN Brendan Richard
Born: Bradford, England, 23 July, 1955 F/CD
Republic of Ireland: 6/U21-1/Youth/Schools

League Club	Source	Date Signed	Seasons Played	Apps	Subs	Gls
Doncaster Rov	Jnr	07/73	73-77	184	3	65
Stoke C	Tr	03/78	77-84	255	10	44
Oldham Ath	Tr	02/85	84-85	10	0	0

O'CALLAGHAN Brian Patrick
Born: Limerick, Republic of Ireland, 24 February, 1981 D
Republic of Ireland: U21-4/Youth

League Club	Source	Date Signed	Seasons Played	Apps	Subs	Gls
Barnsley	Pike Rov (ROI)	07/98	00-03	58	17	1
Notts Co	Worksop T	07/05	05	30	3	1

O'CALLAGHAN George Paul
Born: Cork, Republic of Ireland, 5 September, 1979 M
Republic of Ireland: Youth

League Club	Source	Date Signed	Seasons Played	Apps	Subs	Gls
Port Vale	YT	07/98	98-01	22	12	4
Ipswich T	Cork C (ROI)	01/07	06-07	4	8	1
Brighton & HA	L	08/07	07	13	1	0
Tranmere Rov	Cork C (ROI)	07/08	08	4	2	0
Yeovil T	Dundalk (ROI)	07/09	09	7	5	0

O'CALLAGHAN Kevin
Born: Dagenham, E London, England, 19 October, 1961 LW
Republic of Ireland: 21/U21-1/Youth

League Club	Source	Date Signed	Seasons Played	Apps	Subs	Gls
Millwall	App	11/78	78-79	15	5	3
Ipswich T	Tr	01/80	79-84	72	43	4
Portsmouth	Tr	01/85	84-86	84	3	16
Millwall	Tr	06/87	87-90	65	11	14
Southend U	Tr	07/91	91-92	10	11	1

O'CARROLL Diarmuid
Born: Killarney, Republic of Ireland, 16 March, 1987 F
Republic of Ireland: Youth

League Club	Source	Date Signed	Seasons Played	Apps	Subs	Gls
Morecambe	Glasgow Celtic	07/08	08	15	14	5

O'CEARUILL Joseph Delpesh (Joe)
Born: Edmonton, N London, England, 9 February, 1987 CD
Republic of Ireland: 2/B-1/U21-9/Youth

League Club	Source	Date Signed	Seasons Played	Apps	Subs	Gls
Arsenal	Watford (Sch)	07/06				
Brighton & HA	L	01/07	06	6	2	0
Barnet	Tr	08/07	07	9	5	0

O'CONNELL Brendan John
Born: Lambeth, S London, England, 12 November, 1966 M/F

League Club	Source	Date Signed	Seasons Played	Apps	Subs	Gls
Portsmouth	App	07/85				
Exeter C	Tr	08/86	86-87	73	8	19
Burnley	Tr	07/88	88-89	62	2	17
Huddersfield T	L	11/89	89	11	0	1
Barnsley	Tr	03/90	89-95	212	28	35
Charlton Ath	Tr	07/96	96	33	5	2
Wigan Ath	Tr	08/97	97	17	0	5

O'CONNELL Brian Edward (Pat)
Born: Kensington, Central London, England, 13 September, 1937 LW

League Club	Source	Date Signed	Seasons Played	Apps	Subs	Gls
Fulham	Jnr	03/56	58-65	152	0	26
Crystal Palace	Tr	07/66	66	20	1	2

O'CONNELL Iain Andrew
Born: Southend-on-Sea, England, 9 October, 1970 CD

League Club	Source	Date Signed	Seasons Played	Apps	Subs	Gls
Southend U	YT	07/89	89	0	4	0

O'CONNELL Jack William
Born: Liverpool, England, 29 March, 1994 CD

League Club	Source	Date Signed	Seasons Played	Apps	Subs	Gls
Blackburn Rov	Sch	05/12				
Rotherham U	L	11/12	12	1	2	0
York C	L	01/13	12	18	0	0
Rochdale	L	07/13	13	38	0	0
Rochdale	L	09/14	14	17	0	3
Brentford	Tr	01/15				
Rochdale	L	02/15	14	11	1	2

O'CONNELL Seamus
Born: Carlisle, Cumbria, England, 1 January, 1930 IF
Died: Spain, 24 February, 2013
England: Amateur-4

League Club	Source	Date Signed	Seasons Played	Apps	Subs	Gls
Middlesbrough (Am)	Queen's Park	05/53	53	3	-	2
Chelsea (Am)	Bishop Auckland	08/54	54-55	16	-	11
Carlisle U (Am)	Crook T	02/58	57	4	-	2

O'CONNOR Aaron Derek
Born: Nottingham, England, 9 August, 1983 F

League Club	Source	Date Signed	Seasons Played	Apps	Subs	Gls
Scunthorpe U	Ilkeston T	12/02	02	0	3	0
Newport Co	Luton T	07/12	13-14	33	10	12

O'CONNOR Anthony Dean
Born: Cork, Republic of Ireland, 25 October, 1992 CD
Republic of Ireland: U21-8/Youth

League Club	Source	Date Signed	Seasons Played	Apps	Subs	Gls
Blackburn Rov	Sch	07/10				
Burton A	L	08/12	12	46	0	0
Torquay U	L	07/13	13	30	1	0
Plymouth Arg	Tr	08/14	14	40	0	3

O'CONNOR D'Arcy Christopher
Born: Oldham, Greater Manchester, England, 21 December, 1994 CD

League Club	Source	Date Signed	Seasons Played	Apps	Subs	Gls
Rochdale	Sch	07/13	12	1	0	0

O'CONNOR Derek Peter Luke
Born: Dublin, Republic of Ireland, 9 March, 1978 G
Republic of Ireland: U21-3/Youth/Schools

League Club	Source	Date Signed	Seasons Played	Apps	Subs	Gls
Huddersfield T	YT	05/95	97	1	0	0

O'CONNOR Douglas (Doug)
Born: Barnsley, South Yorkshire, England, 29 April, 1954 F

League Club	Source	Date Signed	Seasons Played	Apps	Subs	Gls
Barnsley	App	04/72	70-73	27	9	7
Mansfield T	Tr	07/74	74	11	6	2
Scunthorpe U	Tr	07/75	75-76	28	3	9

O'CONNOR Emmett
Born: Toronto, Canada, 13 September, 1992 M

League Club	Source	Date Signed	Seasons Played	Apps	Subs	Gls
Crawley T	Scarborough C (CAN)	07/14	14	1	3	0

O'CONNOR Garreth
Born: Dublin, Republic of Ireland, 10 November, 1978 M

League Club	Source	Date Signed	Seasons Played	Apps	Subs	Gls
Bournemouth	Bohemians (ROI)	06/00	00-04	109	59	24

League Club	Source	Date Signed	Seasons Played	Apps	Subs	Gls
Burnley	Tr	07/05	05-07	26	12	7
Bournemouth	L	08/07	07	5	1	0
Luton T	Tr	10/08	08	3	0	0

O'CONNOR Garry Lawrence

Born: Edinburgh, Scotland, 7 May, 1983 F

Scotland: 16/U21-8

League Club	Source	Date Signed	Seasons Played	Apps	Subs	Gls
Birmingham C	Lokomotiv Moscow (RUS)	07/07	07-10	22	30	9
Barnsley	Tr	09/10	10	19	3	4

O'CONNOR Gary

Born: Newtongrange, Midlothian, Scotland, 7 April, 1974 G

Scotland: Youth/Schools

League Club	Source	Date Signed	Seasons Played	Apps	Subs	Gls
Doncaster Rov	Heart of Midlothian	01/96	95-96	26	0	0

O'CONNOR James Francis Edward

Born: Birmingham, England, 20 November, 1984 RB

League Club	Source	Date Signed	Seasons Played	Apps	Subs	Gls
Aston Villa	Sch	05/03				
Port Vale	L	09/04	04	13	0	0
Bournemouth	Tr	02/05	04-05	43	2	1
Doncaster Rov	Tr	05/06	06-11	201	11	4
Derby Co	Tr	08/12	12	15	7	1
Bristol C	L	09/13	13	3	0	0
Walsall	Tr	06/14	14	30	2	1

O'CONNOR James Kelly (Jimmy)

Born: Coatbridge, Lanarkshire, Scotland, 27 June, 1951 W

League Club	Source	Date Signed	Seasons Played	Apps	Subs	Gls
Bury	Kirkstyle Thistle	07/70	70	7	0	2

O'CONNOR James Kevin

Born: Dublin, Republic of Ireland, 1 September, 1979 M

Republic of Ireland: U21-9/Youth

League Club	Source	Date Signed	Seasons Played	Apps	Subs	Gls
Stoke C	YT	09/96	98-02	176	0	16
West Bromwich A	Tr	08/03	03	27	3	0
Burnley	L	10/04	04	12	1	0
Burnley	Tr	03/05	04-07	117	9	11
Sheffield Wed	Tr	07/08	08-11	115	24	6

O'CONNOR Jonathan (Jon)

Born: Darlington, County Durham, England, 29 October, 1976 RB

England: U21-3/Youth

League Club	Source	Date Signed	Seasons Played	Apps	Subs	Gls
Everton	YT	10/93	95-97	3	2	0
Sheffield U	Tr	02/98	97-98	2	2	0
Blackpool	Lincoln C (NC)	10/00	00	10	1	0

O'CONNOR Kevin John Anthony

Born: Dublin, Republic of Ireland, 19 October, 1985 M

Republic of Ireland: U21-2/Youth

League Club	Source	Date Signed	Seasons Played	Apps	Subs	Gls
Wolverhampton W	Sch	07/03	06	3	0	0
Stockport Co	L	03/06	05	6	1	1

O'CONNOR Kevin Patrick

Born: Blackburn, Greater Manchester, England, 24 February, 1982 RB/M

Republic of Ireland: U21-6

League Club	Source	Date Signed	Seasons Played	Apps	Subs	Gls
Brentford	YT	03/00	99-13	368	52	32

O'CONNOR Malcolm Joseph

Born: Ashton-under-Lyne, Greater Manchester, England, 25 April, 1965 F

League Club	Source	Date Signed	Seasons Played	Apps	Subs	Gls
Rochdale	Curzon Ashton	03/83	82-83	12	4	3

O'CONNOR Mark Andrew

Born: Benfleet, Essex, England, 10 March, 1963 M

Republic of Ireland: U21-1

League Club	Source	Date Signed	Seasons Played	Apps	Subs	Gls
Queens Park Rgrs	App	06/80	81-82	2	1	0
Exeter C	L	10/83	83	38	0	1
Bristol Rov	Tr	08/84	84-85	79	1	10
Bournemouth	Tr	03/86	85-89	115	13	12
Gillingham	Tr	12/89	89-92	107	9	8
Bournemouth	Tr	07/93	93-94	56	2	3
Gillingham	Tr	08/95	95-96	36	4	1

O'CONNOR Martin John

Born: Walsall, West Midlands, England, 10 December, 1967 M

Cayman Islands: 2

League Club	Source	Date Signed	Seasons Played	Apps	Subs	Gls
Crystal Palace	Bromsgrove Rov	06/92	93	2	0	0
Walsall	L	03/93	92	10	0	1
Walsall	Tr	02/94	93-95	94	0	21
Peterborough U	Tr	07/96	96	18	0	3
Birmingham C	Tr	11/96	96-01	181	6	16
Walsall	Tr	02/02	01-02	45	3	2
Shrewsbury T	Tr	08/03	04	13	8	0

O'CONNOR Michael (Mike)

Born: Romford, E London, England, 11 January, 1952 W

League Club	Source	Date Signed	Seasons Played	Apps	Subs	Gls
Southend U	App	-	69	1	0	0

O'CONNOR Michael Joseph

Born: Belfast, Northern Ireland, 6 October, 1987 M

Northern Ireland: 11/B-1/U21-3/Youth

League Club	Source	Date Signed	Seasons Played	Apps	Subs	Gls
Crewe Alex	Sch	07/05	05-08	65	12	3
Lincoln C	L	03/09	08	9	1	1
Scunthorpe U	Tr	07/09	09-11	77	20	11
Rotherham U	Tr	05/12	12-13	47	17	8
Port Vale	Tr	07/14	14	44	0	6

O'CONNOR Patrick (Pat)

Born: Wishaw, Lanarkshire, Scotland, 1 May, 1934 CH

League Club	Source	Date Signed	Seasons Played	Apps	Subs	Gls
Barrow	Bellshill Ath	06/58	58-59	20	-	4

O'CONNOR Paul Daniel

Born: Easington, County Durham, England, 17 August, 1971 G

League Club	Source	Date Signed	Seasons Played	Apps	Subs	Gls
Leicester C	YT	03/89				
Hartlepool U	Blyth Spartans	04/96	95-96	31	0	0

O'CONNOR Philip Kelvin (Phil)

Born: Romford, E London, England, 10 October, 1953 W

Died: New South Wales, Australia, 23 September, 1985

Australia: 20/U21

League Club	Source	Date Signed	Seasons Played	Apps	Subs	Gls
Luton T	Bexley U	12/72	72	1	1	0
Lincoln C	L	01/75	74	4	0	1

O'CONNOR Robert Thomas

Born: Gateshead, Tyne and Wear, England, 9 August, 1940 LW

League Club	Source	Date Signed	Seasons Played	Apps	Subs	Gls
Gateshead (Am)	Jnr	05/58	58	2	-	0

O'CONNOR Shane Edward

Born: Cork, Republic of Ireland, 14 April, 1990 M

Republic of Ireland: U21-1/Youth

League Club	Source	Date Signed	Seasons Played	Apps	Subs	Gls
Ipswich T	Liverpool (Sch)	07/09	09-10	13	4	0

O'CONNOR Timothy Daniel (Tim)

Born: Neath, Wales, 3 October, 1967 M

Wales: Youth

League Club	Source	Date Signed	Seasons Played	Apps	Subs	Gls
Cardiff C	Afan Lido	01/85	85	1	1	0

O'CONNOR Turlough Luac

Born: Athlone, Republic of Ireland, 22 July, 1946 F

Republic of Ireland: 7/LoI-3/Amateur

League Club	Source	Date Signed	Seasons Played	Apps	Subs	Gls
Fulham	Bohemians (ROI)	05/66	67	1	0	0

O'CONNOR Vincent John (Jackie)

Born: Bearpark, County Durham, England, 12 March, 1929 W

League Club	Source	Date Signed	Seasons Played	Apps	Subs	Gls
Hartlepool U	Middlesbrough (Am)	12/47	48	2	-	0

O'DEA Darren

Born: Dublin, Republic of Ireland, 4 February, 1987 CD

Republic of Ireland: 20/U21-9

League Club	Source	Date Signed	Seasons Played	Apps	Subs	Gls
Reading (L)	Glasgow Celtic	09/09	09	7	1	0
Ipswich T (L)	Glasgow Celtic	08/10	10	17	3	0
Leeds U (L)	Glasgow Celtic	08/11	11	35	0	2
Blackpool	Metalurg Donetsk (UKR)	01/15	14	16	3	0

ODEJAYI Olukayode (Kayode)

Born: Ibadan, Nigeria, 21 February, 1982 F

Nigeria: 1

League Club	Source	Date Signed	Seasons Played	Apps	Subs	Gls
Bristol C	YT	07/00	99-00	0	6	0
Cheltenham T	Forest Green Rov	06/03	03-06	100	48	30
Barnsley	Tr	06/07	07-09	32	40	4
Scunthorpe U	L	02/09	08	1	5	1
Colchester U	Tr	09/09	09-11	70	45	17
Rotherham U	Tr	05/12	12	17	25	5
Accrington Stan	L	09/13	13	26	6	8
Tranmere Rov	Tr	06/14	14	27	13	5

O'DELL Andrew (Andy)

Born: Hull, England, 2 January, 1963 M

League Club	Source	Date Signed	Seasons Played	Apps	Subs	Gls
Grimsby T	App	01/81	81-82	18	2	0
Rotherham U	Tr	08/83	83-84	16	2	0
Torquay U	Tr	03/85	84	12	2	2
Darlington	North Ferriby U	09/87	87	1	2	0

O'DELL Robert Edward (Bobby)

Born: Newport, Isle of Wight, England, 10 December, 1934 CH

League Club	Source	Date Signed	Seasons Played	Apps	Subs	Gls
Reading	Jnr	07/52	53	2	-	0

ODELUSI Oluwasanmi Babafemi Oluwaseu (Sanmi)

Born: Newham, E London, England, 11 June, 1993 W

League Club	Source	Date Signed	Seasons Played	Apps	Subs	Gls
Bolton W	Sch	07/12	12-13	0	6	0
MK Dons	L	02/14	13	6	4	0
Coventry C	L	01/15	14	4	10	3

ODEMWINGIE Peter Osazemwinde

Born: Tashkent, Uzbekistan, 15 July, 1981 F

Nigeria: 65

League Club	Source	Date Signed	Seasons Played	Apps	Subs	Gls
West Bromwich A	Lokomotiv Moscow (RUS)	08/10	10-12	67	20	30
Cardiff C	Tr	09/13	13	11	4	1
Stoke C	Tr	01/14	13-14	16	6	5

ODHIAMBO Eric Geno Sije

Born: Oxford, England, 12 May, 1989 F

League Club	Source	Date Signed	Seasons Played	Apps	Subs	Gls
Leicester C	Sch	01/07				
Southend U	L	08/07	07	2	3	0
ODJIDJA-OFOE Vadis						
Born: Ghent, Belgium, 21 February, 1989						M
Belgium: 3/U21-10/Youth						
Norwich C	Club Brugge (BEL)	08/14	14	1	4	0
O'DOHERTY Kenneth Brendan (Ken)						
Born: Dublin, Republic of Ireland, 30 March, 1963						CD
Republic of Ireland: U21-1						
Crystal Palace	UC Dublin (ROI)	02/85	85-87	41	1	0
Huddersfield T	Tr	06/88	88-91	63	2	1
Exeter C	L	08/91	91	2	0	0
O'DONNELL Brian Francis						
Born: Port Glasgow, Inverclyde, Scotland, 8 August, 1957						M
Bristol Rov	Bournemouth (App)	05/76				
Bournemouth	Blacktown C (AUS)	01/82	81-82	9	5	0
Torquay U	Tr	10/82	82	19	0	0
O'DONNELL Christopher (Chris)						
Born: Newcastle-upon-Tyne, England, 26 May, 1968						D
Ipswich T	App	06/85	86-88	10	4	0
Northampton T	L	01/88	87	1	0	0
Leeds U	Tr	07/89	89	0	1	0
Exeter C	Tr	08/91	91	2	0	0
O'DONNELL Daniel (Danny)						
Born: Dumbarton, Dunbartonshire, Scotland, 27 February, 1939						IF
Brentford	Kirkintilloch Rob Roy	02/60	60-61	11	-	0
O'DONNELL Daniel (Danny)						
Born: Rainford, Merseyside, England, 10 March, 1986						CD
Liverpool	Sch	11/04				
Crewe Alex	L	08/06	06	21	4	1
Crewe Alex	Tr	06/07	07-09	68	10	2
Shrewsbury T	Tr	08/10	10	4	1	0
Stockport Co	Tr	01/11	10	7	0	0
O'DONNELL Edward (Eddie)						
Born: Barrow, Cumbria, England, 5 February, 1921						D
Died: Ulverston, Cumbria, England, 5 May, 1994						
Barrow	RAF	09/46	46-52	34	-	0
O'DONNELL Francis Joseph (Frank)						
Born: Buckhaven, Fife, Scotland, 31 August, 1911						CF
Died: Macclesfield, Cheshire, England, 4 September, 1952						
Scotland: 6						
Preston NE	Glasgow Celtic	05/35	35-37	92	-	36
Blackpool	Tr	11/37	37-38	30	-	17
Aston Villa	Tr	11/38	38	29	-	14
Nottingham F	Tr	01/46	46	11	-	5
O'DONNELL Hugh						
Born: Buckhaven, Fife, Scotland, 15 February, 1913						LW
Died: Preston, Lancashire, England, 9 May, 1965						
Preston NE	Glasgow Celtic	05/35	35-38	132	-	29
Blackpool	Tr	03/39	38-46	11	-	2
Rochdale	Tr	03/47	46-47	40	-	14
Halifax T	Tr	03/48	47-48	13	-	1
O'DONNELL James (Jimmy)						
Born: Methil, Fife, Scotland, 18 April, 1934						IF
Blackburn Rov	Wellesley Jnrs	05/52				
Oldham Ath	Tr	10/53	54-55	15	-	3
Leeds U	Stalybridge Celtic	01/57				
O'DONNELL Jonathan David (Jon)						
Born: Leeds, England, 21 March, 1954						RB/M
Died: Yeovil, Somerset, England, 4 April, 1997						
Leeds U	App	03/71				
Cambridge U	Tr	07/73	73-75	79	0	8
Colchester U	L	08/75	75	1	0	0
Hartlepool U	Tr	07/76	76	30	1	1
Scunthorpe U	Tr	07/77	77-79	60	0	0
O'DONNELL Neil						
Born: Glasgow, Scotland, 21 December, 1949						M
Norwich C	Jnr	12/66	67-73	31	19	2
Gillingham	Tr	08/74	74-75	18	6	0
Sheffield Wed	Tr	10/75	75-76	40	0	1
O'DONNELL Philip (Phil)						
Born: Motherwell, Lanarkshire, Scotland, 25 March, 1972						M
Died: Wishaw, Lanarkshire, Scotland, 29 December, 2007						
Scotland: 1/U21-8						
Sheffield Wed	Glasgow Celtic	07/99	99-01	13	7	0

League Club	Source	Date Signed	Seasons Played	Apps	Subs	Gls
O'DONNELL Ralph						
Born: Cudworth, South Yorkshire, England, 17 October, 1931						CH
Died: Weymouth, Dorset, England, 28 May, 2011						
Sheffield Wed	Upton Colliery	05/49	51-61	170	-	3
O'DONNELL Richard Mark						
Born: Sheffield, England, 12 September, 1988						G
Sheffield Wed	Sch	07/07	10-11	14	1	0
Oldham Ath	L	03/08	07	3	1	0
Macclesfield T	L	02/12	11	11	0	0
Chesterfield	Tr	05/12	12	14	0	0
Walsall	Tr	07/13	13-14	90	0	0
O'DONNELL Stephen James						
Born: Airdrie, Lanarkshire, Scotland, 10 July, 1983						M
Scotland: Youth						
Boston U	Dundee U	01/05	04	2	2	0
O'DONNELL William (Willie)						
Born: Clydebank, Dunbartonshire, Scotland, 9 August, 1924						IF
Died: Glasgow, Scotland, 20 August, 1989						
Northampton T	Partick Thistle	06/51	51-53	105	-	44
Shrewsbury T	Tr	07/54	54-57	130	-	45
O'DONOGHUE Michael Derry						
Born: Islington, N London, England, 18 January, 1996						LB
Colchester U	Sch	07/13	14	1	0	0
O'DONOGHUE Michael Gerard (Mike)						
Born: Islington, N London, England, 13 September, 1956						F
Southampton	Wembley	01/79				
Northampton T	L	11/79	79	4	0	1
O'DONOVAN Roy Simon						
Born: Cork, Republic of Ireland, 10 August, 1985						F
Republic of Ireland: B-2/U21-9						
Coventry C	Sch	08/02				
Sunderland	Cork C (ROI)	08/07	07	4	13	0
Blackpool	L	01/09	08	11	1	0
Southend U	L	09/09	09	3	1	1
Hartlepool U	L	02/10	09	15	0	9
Coventry C	Tr	07/10	10-12	6	11	0
Northampton T	Tr	01/13	12-13	25	6	6
O'DOWD Adrian Gregory						
Born: Solihull, West Midlands, England, 16 September, 1959						F
Aston Villa	App	08/77				
Oxford U	Tr	02/80	79-80	8	2	1
O'DOWD Gregory Henry (Greg)						
Born: Dublin, Republic of Ireland, 16 March, 1973						CD
Brighton & HA	YT	11/90	91	0	1	0
O'DOWDA Callum Joshua Ryan						
Born: Oxford, England, 23 April, 1995						LW
Republic of Ireland: U21-1						
Oxford U	Sch	06/13	13-14	24	25	4
O'DRISCOLL John Francis (Jack)						
Born: Cork, Republic of Ireland, 20 September, 1921						RW
Died: Swansea, Wales, 11 March, 1988						
Republic of Ireland: 3/LoI-1//Northern Ireland: 3						
Swansea C	Cork U (ROI)	05/47	47-51	118	-	24
O'DRISCOLL Sean Michael						
Born: Wolverhampton, England, 1 July, 1957						M
Republic of Ireland: 3/U21-3						
Fulham	Alvechurch	11/79	79-83	141	7	14
Bournemouth	Tr	02/84	83-94	409	12	19
ODUBADE Yemi						
Born: Lagos, Nigeria, 4 July, 1984						F
Yeovil T	Eastbourne T	07/04	04	0	4	0
Oxford U	Eastbourne Bor	01/06	05	4	4	1
Stevenage	Tr	05/09	10	5	10	1
ODUBAJO Moses Adeshina Ayoola Junior						
Born: Greenwich, SE London, England, 28 July, 1993						RB/M
England: Youth						
Leyton Orient	Sch	07/11	11-13	81	12	12
Brentford	Tr	06/14	14	44	1	3
ODUNSI Saheed Adeleke (Leke)						
Born: Walworth, S London, England, 5 December, 1980						M
Millwall	YT	02/99	98-01	5	12	0
Colchester U	L	08/02	02	3	3	0
Southend U	Carshalton Ath	07/03	03	12	0	1
ODUWA Kelede Nathan (Nathan)						
Born: Bloomsbury, London, England, 5 March, 1996						M

England: Youth

League Club	Source	Date Signed	Seasons Played	Apps	Subs	Gls
Tottenham H	Sch	07/13				
Luton T	L	02/15	14	3	8	0

OELOFSE Roelof Johannes Gysbertus (Ralph)
Born: Johannesburg, South Africa, 12 November, 1926 — CH
Died: Cape Town, South Africa, November, 2001

League Club	Source	Date Signed	Seasons Played	Apps	Subs	Gls
Chelsea	Berea Park (RSA)	10/51	51-52	8	-	0
Watford	Tr	07/53	53	15	-	0

O'FARRELL Francis (Frank)
Born: Cork, Republic of Ireland, 9 October, 1927 — LH
Republic of Ireland: 9

League Club	Source	Date Signed	Seasons Played	Apps	Subs	Gls
West Ham U	Cork U (ROI)	01/48	50-56	197	-	6
Preston NE	Tr	11/56	56-60	118	-	2

OFFIONG Richard
Born: South Shields, Tyne and Wear, England, 17 December, 1983 — F
England: Youth

League Club	Source	Date Signed	Seasons Played	Apps	Subs	Gls
Newcastle U	YT	09/01				
Darlington	L	11/02	02	7	0	2
York C	L	03/04	03	2	2	0
Doncaster Rov	Istanbulspor (TKY)	08/05	05	2	3	0
Carlisle U	Hamilton Academical	07/09	09	2	13	1

O'FLANAGAN Kevin Patrick
Born: Dublin, Republic of Ireland, 10 June, 1919 — W
Died: Dublin, Republic of Ireland, 26 May, 2006
Republic of Ireland: 10/LoI-8//Northern Ireland: Amateur/War-2

League Club	Source	Date Signed	Seasons Played	Apps	Subs	Gls
Arsenal (Am)	Bohemians (ROI)	10/45	46	14	-	3
Brentford (Am)	Barnet	11/49	49	6	-	0

O'FLYNN John
Born: Cobh, Republic of Ireland, 11 July, 1982 — F
Republic of Ireland: U21-6

League Club	Source	Date Signed	Seasons Played	Apps	Subs	Gls
Peterborough U	YT	07/01				
Barnet	Cork C (ROI)	09/08	08-09	63	7	29
Exeter C	Tr	07/10	10-13	69	54	23

O'FLYNN Stephen Joseph (Steve)
Born: Mallow, Cork, Republic of Ireland, 27 April, 1982 — F

League Club	Source	Date Signed	Seasons Played	Apps	Subs	Gls
Northampton T	Limerick C (ROI)	01/10	09	0	5	0

OFODILE Adolphus
Born: Enugu, Nigeria, 15 December, 1979 — F
Nigeria: U21

League Club	Source	Date Signed	Seasons Played	Apps	Subs	Gls
Walsall	FC Magdeburg (GER)	07/01	01	0	1	0

OFORI-TWUMASI Seth Nana (Nana)
Born: Accra, Ghana, 15 May, 1990 — RB
England: Youth

League Club	Source	Date Signed	Seasons Played	Apps	Subs	Gls
Chelsea	Sch	07/07				
Dagenham & Red	L	11/09	09	8	0	2
Peterborough U	Tr	07/10	10	6	5	0
Northampton T	Tr	03/11	10-11	15	1	0
Yeovil T	Tr	07/13	13-14	18	10	0

OGBOCHE Bartholomew
Born: Ogoja, Nigeria, 1 October, 1984 — F
Nigeria: 11

League Club	Source	Date Signed	Seasons Played	Apps	Subs	Gls
Middlesbrough	Kavala (GRE)	10/11	11	5	12	3

OGBURN Michael George (Mike)
Born: Portsmouth, England, 19 February, 1948 — RB

League Club	Source	Date Signed	Seasons Played	Apps	Subs	Gls
Brentford	Portsmouth (Jnr)	05/65	66	12	0	0

OGDEN Alan
Born: Thrybergh, South Yorkshire, England, 15 April, 1954 — LB

League Club	Source	Date Signed	Seasons Played	Apps	Subs	Gls
Sheffield U	App	05/71	71-73	6	6	0
York C	Tr	09/74	74	7	0	0
Huddersfield T		07/75				

OGDEN Christopher John (Chris)
Born: Oldham, Greater Manchester, England, 3 February, 1953 — G

League Club	Source	Date Signed	Seasons Played	Apps	Subs	Gls
Oldham Ath	Jnr	07/71	71-77	128	0	0
Swindon T	Tr	08/78	78-79	24	0	0
Rotherham U	Tr	11/79	79	3	0	0

OGDEN Frederick (Fred)
Born: Oldham, Greater Manchester, England, 3 April, 1925 — G
Died: Oldham, Greater Manchester, England, February, 2008

League Club	Source	Date Signed	Seasons Played	Apps	Subs	Gls
Oldham Ath	Edge Lane BC	12/47	47-54	151	-	0
Chesterfield	Tr	06/55				
Oldham Ath	Tr	03/56	55	5	-	0

OGDEN Neil
Born: Orrell, Greater Manchester, England, 29 November, 1975 — LB

League Club	Source	Date Signed	Seasons Played	Apps	Subs	Gls
Wigan Ath	YT	03/94	92-95	11	4	0

OGDEN Paul
Born: Leek, Staffordshire, England, 18 December, 1946 — W

League Club	Source	Date Signed	Seasons Played	Apps	Subs	Gls
Port Vale (Am)	Leek Castle	11/65	65	2	0	0

OGDEN Paul
Born: Salford, England, 16 October, 1969 — M

League Club	Source	Date Signed	Seasons Played	Apps	Subs	Gls
Hartlepool U	Oldham Ath (YT)	08/88	88-89	9	3	0

OGDEN Trevor
Born: Culcheth, Cheshire, England, 12 June, 1945 — CF

League Club	Source	Date Signed	Seasons Played	Apps	Subs	Gls
Manchester C		09/64	64	9	-	3
Doncaster Rov	Tr	06/65	65-66	39	0	14

OGHANI George William
Born: Manchester, England, 2 September, 1960 — F

League Club	Source	Date Signed	Seasons Played	Apps	Subs	Gls
Bury	Sheffield U (Jnr)	02/78				
Bolton W	Hyde U	10/83	83-86	86	13	27
Wrexham	L	03/87	86	6	1	0
Burnley	Tr	06/87	87-88	73	1	21
Stockport Co	Tr	06/89	89	5	3	2
Hereford U	Tr	10/89	89	7	1	2
Scarborough	Hyde U	02/90	89-90	43	7	18
Carlisle U	Evagoras (CYP)	08/92	92-93	45	8	15

OGILVIE Gary Francis
Born: Dundee, Scotland, 16 November, 1967 — LB

League Club	Source	Date Signed	Seasons Played	Apps	Subs	Gls
Sunderland	Dundee	03/88	88	0	1	0

OGILVIE John Forest
Born: Motherwell, Lanarkshire, Scotland, 28 October, 1928 — LB

League Club	Source	Date Signed	Seasons Played	Apps	Subs	Gls
Leicester C	Hibernian	09/55	55-58	82	-	2
Mansfield T	Tr	01/60	59-60	24	-	1

OGILVIE John Leofric
Born: Workington, Cumbria, England, 20 December, 1943 — D

League Club	Source	Date Signed	Seasons Played	Apps	Subs	Gls
Workington	Blackpool (Am)	04/63	62-74	386	4	15

OGLEY Alan
Born: Darton, South Yorkshire, England, 4 February, 1946 — G
England: Schools

League Club	Source	Date Signed	Seasons Played	Apps	Subs	Gls
Barnsley	App	03/63	62	9	-	0
Manchester C	Tr	07/63	63-67	51	0	0
Stockport Co	Tr	09/67	67-74	240	0	0
Darlington	Tr	08/75	75-76	80	0	0

OGLEY Mark Alan
Born: Barnsley, South Yorkshire, England, 10 March, 1967 — CD

League Club	Source	Date Signed	Seasons Played	Apps	Subs	Gls
Barnsley	App	03/85	85-86	19	0	0
Aldershot	L	12/87	87	6	2	0
Carlisle U	Tr	03/88	87-89	33	0	1
Aldershot	Tr	11/89	89-90	58	4	0

OGOGO Abumere Tafadzwa (Abu)
Born: Epsom, Surrey, England, 3 November, 1989 — DM

League Club	Source	Date Signed	Seasons Played	Apps	Subs	Gls
Arsenal	Sch	09/07				
Barnet	L	11/08	08	7	2	1
Dagenham & Red	Tr	07/09	09-14	218	7	17

O'GORMAN David John
Born: Chester, England, 20 June, 1972 — W

League Club	Source	Date Signed	Seasons Played	Apps	Subs	Gls
Wrexham	YT	07/90	90	8	9	0
Swansea C	Barry T	08/97	97-98	13	26	5

O'GRADY Christopher James (Chris)
Born: Nottingham, England, 25 January, 1986 — F
England: Youth

League Club	Source	Date Signed	Seasons Played	Apps	Subs	Gls
Leicester C	Sch	08/04	02-06	6	18	1
Notts Co	L	09/04	04	3	6	0
Rushden & D	L	08/05	05	20	2	4
Rotherham U	Tr	01/07	06-07	46	5	15
Oldham Ath	Tr	05/08	08	3	10	0
Bury	L	10/08	08	3	3	0
Bradford C	L	01/09	08	0	2	0
Stockport Co	L	02/09	08	17	1	2
Rochdale	Tr	08/09	09-11	88	2	31
Sheffield Wed	Tr	08/11	11-12	39	14	9
Barnsley	Tr	01/13	12-13	52	4	21
Brighton & HA	Tr	07/14	14	15	13	1
Sheffield U	L	11/14	14	4	0	1

O'GRADY Michael (Mike)
Born: Leeds, England, 11 October, 1942 — LW
England: 2/FLge-3/U23-3

League Club	Source	Date Signed	Seasons Played	Apps	Subs	Gls
Huddersfield T	Jnr	10/59	59-65	160	0	26
Leeds U	Tr	10/65	65-69	90	1	12
Wolverhampton W	Tr	09/69	69-72	28	5	5
Birmingham C	L	02/72	71	2	1	0
Rotherham U	Tr	11/72	72-73	24	0	2

OGRIZOVIC Steven (Steve)
Born: Mansfield, Nottinghamshire, England, 12 September, 1957 — G
England: FLge

League Club	Source	Date Signed	Seasons Played	Apps	Subs	Gls
Chesterfield	Old Newark Road BC	07/77	77	16	0	0

League Club	Source	Date Signed	Seasons Played	Apps	Subs	Gls
Liverpool	Tr	11/77	77-80	4	0	0
Shrewsbury T	Tr	08/82	82-83	84	0	0
Coventry C	Tr	06/84	84-99	507	0	1

OGSTON John Kessack
Born: Aberdeen, Scotland, 15 January, 1939 G
Scotland: U23-3

League Club	Source	Date Signed	Seasons Played	Apps	Subs	Gls
Liverpool	Aberdeen	08/65	66	1	0	0
Doncaster Rov	Tr	08/68	68-70	70	0	0

O'HAGAN Daniel Alexander Nicholas (Danny)
Born: Padstow, Cornwall, England, 24 April, 1976 F

League Club	Source	Date Signed	Seasons Played	Apps	Subs	Gls
Plymouth Arg	YT	06/94	94-95	1	8	1
Plymouth Arg	Weston-super-Mare	11/97	97	5	4	0

O'HAGAN Patrick John (Pat)
Born: Caerphilly, Wales, 15 March, 1971 G

League Club	Source	Date Signed	Seasons Played	Apps	Subs	Gls
Newport Co	YT	-	87	3	0	0
Cardiff C	Tr	07/89				

O'HALLORAN Keith James
Born: Dublin, Republic of Ireland, 10 November, 1975 M
Republic of Ireland: U21-3/Youth/Schools

League Club	Source	Date Signed	Seasons Played	Apps	Subs	Gls
Middlesbrough	Cherry Orchard (ROI)	09/94	94-95	3	1	0
Scunthorpe U	L	03/96	95	6	1	0
Cardiff C	L	11/96	96	8	0	0
Swindon T	St Johnstone	07/00	00-01	46	0	7

O'HALLORAN Matthew Vincent (Matt)
Born: Nottingham, England, 18 November, 1982 M

League Club	Source	Date Signed	Seasons Played	Apps	Subs	Gls
Derby Co	Sch	07/02				
Oldham Ath	Tr	08/03	03	2	11	1
Chesterfield	Tr	12/03	03	1	2	0
Boston U	Tr	08/04	04	5	3	1

O'HALLORAN Michael Francis
Born: Glasgow, Scotland, 6 January, 1991 F
Scotland: U21-2/Youth

League Club	Source	Date Signed	Seasons Played	Apps	Subs	Gls
Bolton W	Sch	06/10				
Sheffield U	L	03/12	11	1	6	0
Carlisle U	L	08/12	12	0	1	0
Tranmere Rov	L	11/12	12	17	6	3

O'HALLORAN Neil
Born: Cardiff, Wales, 21 June, 1933 IF
Died: Barry, Vale of Glamorgan, Wales, October, 1995

League Club	Source	Date Signed	Seasons Played	Apps	Subs	Gls
Cardiff C	Cardiff Corinthians	08/54	55-56	10	-	4
Newport Co	Tr	07/57	57	14	-	2

O'HALLORAN Stephen Edward
Born: Cobh, Republic of Ireland, 29 November, 1987 LB
Republic of Ireland: 2/U21-9

League Club	Source	Date Signed	Seasons Played	Apps	Subs	Gls
Aston Villa	Sch	11/05				
Wycombe W	L	11/06	06	9	2	0
Southampton	L	01/08	07	0	1	0
Swansea C	L	11/08	08	2	0	0
Coventry C	Tr	07/10	10	10	1	0
Carlisle U	Tr	07/11	11	3	0	0

OHANDJANIAN Demis Armen
Born: Manchester, England, 1 May, 1978 F

League Club	Source	Date Signed	Seasons Played	Apps	Subs	Gls
Doncaster Rov	Curzon Ashton	02/97	96	0	1	0

O'HANLON Joshua (Josh)
Born: Dublin, Republic of Ireland, 25 September, 1995 F

League Club	Source	Date Signed	Seasons Played	Apps	Subs	Gls
Bournemouth	Longford T (ROI)	01/14				
York C	L	03/15	14	0	3	0

O'HANLON Kelham Gerard
Born: Saltburn, Cleveland, England, 16 May, 1962 G
Republic of Ireland: 1/U21-2

League Club	Source	Date Signed	Seasons Played	Apps	Subs	Gls
Middlesbrough	App	05/80	82-84	87	0	0
Rotherham U	Tr	08/85	85-90	248	0	0
Carlisle U	Tr	08/91	91-92	83	0	0
Preston NE	Tr	07/93	93	23	0	0
Preston NE	Dundee U	09/96	96-00	13	1	0

O'HANLON Sean Philip
Born: Southport, Merseyside, England, 2 January, 1983 CD
England: Youth

League Club	Source	Date Signed	Seasons Played	Apps	Subs	Gls
Everton	YT	02/00				
Swindon T	Tr	01/04	03-05	97	2	9
MK Dons	Tr	07/06	06-10	145	12	15
Carlisle U	Hibernian	01/13	12-14	80	1	5

O'HARA Albert Edward (Eddie)
Born: Glasgow, Scotland, 28 October, 1935 LW
Scotland: U23-3/Schools

League Club	Source	Date Signed	Seasons Played	Apps	Subs	Gls
Everton	Falkirk	06/58	58-59	29	-	2
Rotherham U	Tr	02/60	59-60	20	-	3
Barnsley	Greenock Morton	07/62	62-64	127	-	36

O'HARA Daniel (Dan)
Born: Airdrie, Lanarkshire, Scotland, 28 September, 1937 IF

League Club	Source	Date Signed	Seasons Played	Apps	Subs	Gls
Mansfield T	Glasgow Celtic	06/61	61	3	-	1

O'HARA Edward Patrick
Born: Dublin, Republic of Ireland, 22 February, 1927 LW
Died: Birmingham, England, 8 March, 1987

League Club	Source	Date Signed	Seasons Played	Apps	Subs	Gls
Birmingham C	Dundalk (ROI)	11/49	49-50	6	-	0

O'HARA Gerald John (Gerry)
Born: Wolverhampton, England, 3 December, 1956 M

League Club	Source	Date Signed	Seasons Played	Apps	Subs	Gls
Wolverhampton W	App	12/74	75-76	7	2	0
Hereford U		08/78	78	1	0	0

O'HARA Jamie Darryl
Born: Dartford, Kent, England, 25 September, 1986 M
England: U21-7/Youth

League Club	Source	Date Signed	Seasons Played	Apps	Subs	Gls
Tottenham H	Sch	09/04	07-09	15	19	2
Chesterfield	L	01/06	05	19	0	5
Millwall	L	08/07	07	10	4	2
Portsmouth	L	08/09	09	25	1	2
Wolverhampton W	Tr	01/11	10-13	47	8	5
Blackpool		11/14	14	26	1	2

O'HARA Michael John (Mike)
Born: Coventry, England, 30 August, 1944 G

League Club	Source	Date Signed	Seasons Played	Apps	Subs	Gls
Luton T	App	11/61	60	2	-	0
Swindon T	Tr	11/61	61-62	30	-	0
Bournemouth	Tr	09/63				

O'HARA Stephen (Steve)
Born: Lanark, Scotland, 21 February, 1971 D/M

League Club	Source	Date Signed	Seasons Played	Apps	Subs	Gls
Walsall	YT	07/89	89-93	104	18	4

O'HARE Alan Patrick James
Born: Drogheda, Republic of Ireland, 31 July, 1982 D

League Club	Source	Date Signed	Seasons Played	Apps	Subs	Gls
Bolton W	YT	11/01				
Chesterfield	L	01/02	01	19	0	0
Chesterfield	Tr	10/02	02-07	107	28	3

O'HARE John
Born: Renton, Dunbartonshire, Scotland, 24 September, 1946 F
Scotland: 13/U23-3

League Club	Source	Date Signed	Seasons Played	Apps	Subs	Gls
Sunderland	Drumchapel Amats	10/63	64-66	51	0	14
Derby Co	Tr	08/67	67-73	247	1	65
Leeds U	Tr	08/74	74	6	0	1
Nottingham F	Tr	02/75	74-79	94	7	14

OJI Samuel Udoka (Sam)
Born: Westminster, Central London, England, 9 October, 1985 CD

League Club	Source	Date Signed	Seasons Played	Apps	Subs	Gls
Birmingham C	Arsenal (Sch)	04/04				
Doncaster Rov	L	11/05	05	1	3	0
Bristol Rov	L	02/07	06	5	0	0
Leyton Orient	Tr	08/07	07	9	4	0
Hereford U	Tr	08/08	08	4	0	0

OJO Oluwaseyi Babajide (Seyi)
Born: Hemel Hempstead, Hertfordshire, England, 19 June, 1997 W
England: Youth

League Club	Source	Date Signed	Seasons Played	Apps	Subs	Gls
Liverpool	Sch	07/14				
Wigan Ath	L	02/15	14	7	4	0

OKAFOR Samuel Amaechi
Born: Xtiam, Nigeria, 17 March, 1982 M

League Club	Source	Date Signed	Seasons Played	Apps	Subs	Gls
Colchester U	YT	-	98	0	1	0

OKAI Stephen Patrick
Born: Accra, Ghana, 3 December, 1973 M

League Club	Source	Date Signed	Seasons Played	Apps	Subs	Gls
Leyton Orient	Jnr	07/92	91-93	11	14	4

OKAKA CHUKA Stefano
Born: Perugia, Italy, 9 August, 1989 F
Italy: U21-7/Youth

League Club	Source	Date Signed	Seasons Played	Apps	Subs	Gls
Fulham (L)	AS Roma (ITA)	02/10	09	3	8	2

O'KAMBACK Joseph (Joe)
Born: Tottenham, N London, England, 13 March, 1915 WH
Died: Harlow, Essex, England, 1981

League Club	Source	Date Signed	Seasons Played	Apps	Subs	Gls
Millwall	Distillery	04/46	46	1	-	0

O'KANE Aiden
Born: Belfast, Northern Ireland, 24 November, 1979 M

League Club	Source	Date Signed	Seasons Played	Apps	Subs	Gls
York C	Cliftonville	08/01	01	11	1	0

O'KANE Eunan Charles
Born: Derry, Northern Ireland, 10 July, 1990 M
Republic of Ireland: U21-3//Northern Ireland: U21-4/Youth

League Club	Source	Date Signed	Seasons Played	Apps	Subs	Gls
Everton	Sch	08/07				
Torquay U	Coleraine	01/10	09-11	81	25	12
Bournemouth	Tr	07/12	12-14	73	12	2

O'KANE John Andrew
Born: Nottingham, England, 15 November, 1974 — RB

League Club	Source	Date Signed	Seasons Played	Apps	Subs	Gls
Manchester U	YT	01/93	95-96	1	1	0
Bury	L	10/96	96	2	2	2
Bury	L	01/97	96	9	0	1
Bradford C	L	10/97	97	7	0	0
Everton	Tr	01/98	97-98	14	0	0
Burnley	L	10/98	98	8	0	0
Bolton W	Tr	11/99	99-00	32	6	2
Blackpool	Tr	07/01	01-02	42	10	4

O'KANE Vincent (Vince)
Born: Stepney, E London, England, 20 November, 1952 — M

League Club	Source	Date Signed	Seasons Played	Apps	Subs	Gls
Charlton Ath	App	12/70	70-72	29	3	1

O'KANE William James (Liam)
Born: Derry, Northern Ireland, 17 June, 1948 — D
Northern Ireland: 20

League Club	Source	Date Signed	Seasons Played	Apps	Subs	Gls
Nottingham F	Derry C (ROI)	12/68	68-75	186	3	0

O'KEEFE Eamon Gerard
Born: Manchester, England, 13 October, 1953 — F
England: Semi Pro-2//Republic of Ireland: 5/U21-4

League Club	Source	Date Signed	Seasons Played	Apps	Subs	Gls
Plymouth Arg	Stalybridge Celtic	02/74				
Everton	Mossley	07/79	79-81	26	14	6
Wigan Ath	Tr	01/82	81-82	56	2	25
Port Vale	Tr	07/83	83-84	50	9	17
Blackpool	Tr	03/85	84-86	33	3	23
Chester C	St Patrick's Ath (ROI)	03/89	88-89	12	5	4

O'KEEFE James Vincent (Vince)
Born: Birmingham, England, 2 April, 1957 — G

League Club	Source	Date Signed	Seasons Played	Apps	Subs	Gls
Birmingham C	Paget Rgrs	07/75				
Walsall	Tr	07/76				
Exeter C	AP Leamington	06/78	78-79	53	0	0
Torquay U	Tr	02/80	79-81	108	0	0
Blackburn Rov	Tr	08/82	82-88	68	0	0
Bury	L	10/83	83	2	0	0
Blackpool	L	12/86	86	1	0	0
Blackpool	L	02/89	88	6	0	0
Wrexham	Tr	07/89	89-91	83	0	0
Exeter C	Tr	08/92	92	2	0	0

O'KEEFE Joshua Adam (Josh)
Born: Whalley, Lancashire, England, 22 December, 1988 — M
Republic of Ireland: U21-1

League Club	Source	Date Signed	Seasons Played	Apps	Subs	Gls
Blackburn Rov	Sch	01/06				
Walsall	Tr	07/09	09	8	5	0
Lincoln C	Tr	07/10	10	33	4	4

O'KEEFE Patrick John
Born: Peterborough, England, 17 July, 1967 — M

League Club	Source	Date Signed	Seasons Played	Apps	Subs	Gls
Peterborough U	App	07/85	84	0	1	0

O'KEEFE Stuart Antony Alan
Born: Eye, Suffolk, England, 4 March, 1991 — M

League Club	Source	Date Signed	Seasons Played	Apps	Subs	Gls
Southend U	Sch	10/08	08-09	4	6	0
Crystal Palace	Tr	08/10	10-14	19	17	1
Blackpool	L	11/14	14	3	1	0
Cardiff C	Tr	01/15	14	4	2	0

O'KELLY Richard Florence
Born: West Bromwich, West Midlands, England, 8 January, 1957 — F

League Club	Source	Date Signed	Seasons Played	Apps	Subs	Gls
Walsall	Alvechurch	10/79	80-85	189	15	56
Port Vale	Tr	07/86	86-87	26	2	4
Walsall	Tr	01/88	87	7	5	1
Grimsby T	Tr	07/88	88	38	1	10

OKENABIRHIE Fejiri Shaun China
Born: Hendon, N London, England, 25 February, 1996 — F

League Club	Source	Date Signed	Seasons Played	Apps	Subs	Gls
Stevenage	Jnr	09/13	13	1	2	0

OKENLA Folorunso (Foley)
Born: Ibadan, Nigeria, 9 October, 1967 — W

League Club	Source	Date Signed	Seasons Played	Apps	Subs	Gls
Birmingham C	Burnley (NC)	08/91	91	2	5	1

OKIMO Jerome Odike
Born: Ealing, W London, England, 8 June, 1988 — LB

League Club	Source	Date Signed	Seasons Played	Apps	Subs	Gls
Stevenage	Wealdstone	08/14	14	26	3	0

OKOCHA Augustine Jay Azuka (Jay)
Born: Enugu, Nigeria, 14 August, 1973 — M
Nigeria: 74

League Club	Source	Date Signed	Seasons Played	Apps	Subs	Gls
Bolton W	Paris St-Germain (FRA)	08/02	02-05	106	18	14
Hull C	Qatar SC (QAT)	09/07	07	10	8	0

OKOLI James Chuks
Born: Lagos, Nigeria, 11 January, 1976 — FB

League Club	Source	Date Signed	Seasons Played	Apps	Subs	Gls
York C		08/02	02	1	2	0

OKON Paul Michael
Born: Sydney, Australia, 5 April, 1972 — DM
Australia: 28/U23-3/Youth

League Club	Source	Date Signed	Seasons Played	Apps	Subs	Gls
Middlesbrough	Fiorentina (ITA)	08/00	00-01	24	4	0
Watford	Tr	01/02	01	14	1	0
Leeds U	Tr	08/02	02	15	0	0

OKORE Tetchi Jores Charlemagne Ulrich (Jores)
Born: Abidjan, Ivory Coast, 11 August, 1992 — CD
Denmark: 8/U21-7

League Club	Source	Date Signed	Seasons Played	Apps	Subs	Gls
Aston Villa	Nordsjaelland (DEN)	06/13	13-14	24	2	1

OKORIE Chima Ephraim
Born: Owerri, Nigeria, 8 October, 1968 — F
Nigeria:

League Club	Source	Date Signed	Seasons Played	Apps	Subs	Gls
Grimsby T	Peterborough U (NC)	09/93	93	0	5	0
Torquay U	Tr	03/94	93-94	32	4	6

OKORONKWO Isaac
Born: Lagos, Nigeria, 1 May, 1978 — CD
Nigeria: 26

League Club	Source	Date Signed	Seasons Played	Apps	Subs	Gls
Wolverhampton W	Shakhtar Donetsk (UKR)	07/03	03	7	0	0

OKUONGHAE Magnus Erharuyi
Born: Lagos, Nigeria, 16 February, 1986 — CD

League Club	Source	Date Signed	Seasons Played	Apps	Subs	Gls
Rushden & D	Sch	07/05	03-05	15	7	1
Dagenham & Red	Crawley T	07/07	07-08	54	1	2
Colchester U	Tr	07/09	09-14	194	2	8

OLAH Bela Josef
Born: Ozd, Hungary, 8 June, 1938 — RW

League Club	Source	Date Signed	Seasons Played	Apps	Subs	Gls
Northampton T	Bedford T	12/58	58-60	42	-	8

OLAOYE Dolapo (Dele)
Born: Lagos, Nigeria, 17 October, 1982 — M

League Club	Source	Date Signed	Seasons Played	Apps	Subs	Gls
Port Vale	YT	-	00	0	1	0

OLDBURY Marcus John
Born: Bournemouth, England, 29 March, 1976 — M

League Club	Source	Date Signed	Seasons Played	Apps	Subs	Gls
Norwich C	YT	07/94				
Bournemouth	Tr	07/95	95	2	11	0

OLDFIELD Craig
Born: Brentwood, Essex, England, 24 November, 1963 — F

League Club	Source	Date Signed	Seasons Played	Apps	Subs	Gls
Colchester U	Stowmarket T	03/83	83	0	3	0

OLDFIELD David Charles
Born: Perth, Australia, 30 May, 1968 — M
England: U21-1

League Club	Source	Date Signed	Seasons Played	Apps	Subs	Gls
Luton T	App	05/86	87-88	21	8	4
Manchester C	Tr	03/89	88-89	18	8	6
Leicester C	Tr	01/90	89-94	163	25	26
Millwall	L	02/95	94	16	1	6
Luton T	Tr	07/95	95-97	99	18	18
Stoke C	Tr	07/98	98-99	50	15	7
Peterborough U	Tr	03/00	99-01	68	10	4
Oxford U	Tr	08/02	02-03	20	11	2

OLDFIELD John Edward
Born: Helsby, Cheshire, England, 13 July, 1918 — RH
Died: Crewe, Cheshire, England, January, 2006

League Club	Source	Date Signed	Seasons Played	Apps	Subs	Gls
Port Vale	Helsby	03/46	46	1	-	0

OLDFIELD John Stephen
Born: Carlton in Lindrick, Nottinghamshire, England, 19 August, 1943 — G
Died: Leeds, England, October, 2002

League Club	Source	Date Signed	Seasons Played	Apps	Subs	Gls
Huddersfield T	Jnr	08/61	63-68	152	0	0
Wolverhampton W	Tr	12/69	69-70	19	0	0
Crewe Alex	L	11/71	71	5	0	0
Bradford C	Tr	12/71	71-72	31	0	0

OLDFIELD Terence James (Terry)
Born: Bristol, England, 1 April, 1939 — RH

League Club	Source	Date Signed	Seasons Played	Apps	Subs	Gls
Bristol Rov	Clifton St Vincent's	02/58	60-65	131	1	11
Wrexham	Tr	07/66	66	39	1	6

OLDHAM Eric
Born: Newcastle-upon-Tyne, England, 27 June, 1933 — LB
Died: Newcastle-upon-Tyne, England, 23 November, 1994

League Club	Source	Date Signed	Seasons Played	Apps	Subs	Gls
Bolton W	Seaton Delaval	10/53				
Gateshead	Tr	07/56	56-57	53	-	0
Hartlepool U	Kidderminster Hrs	06/59	59	12	-	0

OLDHAM George
Born: Tintwistle, Derbyshire, England, 20 April, 1920 — LB
Died: Luton, England, October, 1993

League Club	Source	Date Signed	Seasons Played	Apps	Subs	Gls
Stoke C	Mottram Central	10/37	38	2	-	0
Newport Co	Tr	09/46	46-47	63	-	0

OLDHAM John
Born: Nottingham, England, 24 October, 1949 — CF

League Club	Source	Date Signed	Seasons Played	Apps	Subs	Gls
Mansfield T	Nuthall BC	02/67	66	0	1	0

OLDHAM John (Jack)
Born: Oswaldtwistle, Lancashire, England, 30 January, 1926 — CH
Died: Blackburn, Greater Manchester, England, August, 2005

League Club	Source	Date Signed	Seasons Played	Apps	Subs	Gls
Accrington Stan	Oswaldtwistle Immanuel	08/50	50-52	10	-	0

OLDRIDGE Andrew Robert (Bob)
Born: Barton-on-Humber, North Lincolnshire, England, 17 November, 1957 — M

League Club	Source	Date Signed	Seasons Played	Apps	Subs	Gls
Grimsby T	Immingham T	01/76	75-76	9	6	1

OLDROYD Darren Robert
Born: Ormskirk, Lancashire, England, 1 November, 1966 — RB

League Club	Source	Date Signed	Seasons Played	Apps	Subs	Gls
Everton	App	11/84	84	0	1	0
Wolverhampton W	Tr	08/86	86	10	0	0

O'LEARY Daniel
Born: Cork, Republic of Ireland, 11 January, 1951 — IF

League Club	Source	Date Signed	Seasons Played	Apps	Subs	Gls
Millwall	App	05/68				
Fulham	Tr	07/69	69	0	1	0

O'LEARY David Anthony
Born: Stoke Newington, N London, England, 2 May, 1958 — CD
Republic of Ireland: 68

League Club	Source	Date Signed	Seasons Played	Apps	Subs	Gls
Arsenal	App	07/75	75-92	523	35	11
Leeds U	Tr	06/93	93	10	0	0

O'LEARY Donal Patrick
Born: Limehouse, E London, England, 24 June, 1936 — LW

League Club	Source	Date Signed	Seasons Played	Apps	Subs	Gls
Blackburn Rov	Blackrock (ROI)	10/54	55	6	-	1

O'LEARY Kristian Denis (Kris)
Born: Port Talbot, Wales, 30 August, 1977 — D/M
Wales: Youth

League Club	Source	Date Signed	Seasons Played	Apps	Subs	Gls
Swansea C	YT	07/96	95-07	238	46	10
Cheltenham T	L	11/06	06	5	0	1
Leyton Orient	L	08/09	09	1	2	0

O'LEARY Stephen Michael
Born: Barnet, N London, England, 12 February, 1985 — M
Republic of Ireland: Youth

League Club	Source	Date Signed	Seasons Played	Apps	Subs	Gls
Luton T	Sch	08/04	03-07	30	15	3
Tranmere Rov	L	10/05	05	19	2	3
Hereford U	Tr	08/08	08	11	4	1
Bradford C	Tr	08/09	09	4	3	0

OLEJNIK Robert (Bobby)
Born: Vienna, Austria, 26 November, 1986 — G
Austria: U21-13

League Club	Source	Date Signed	Seasons Played	Apps	Subs	Gls
Aston Villa	Sch	12/04				
Torquay U	Falkirk	07/11	11	46	0	0
Peterborough U	Tr	06/12	12-13	88	0	0
Scunthorpe U	L	07/14	14	13	0	0
York C	L	01/15	14	16	0	0

OLEKSEWYCZ Stephen Michael (Steve)
Born: Sowerby Bridge, West Yorkshire, England, 24 February, 1983 — F

League Club	Source	Date Signed	Seasons Played	Apps	Subs	Gls
Halifax T	Jnr	08/00	00-01	0	5	0

OLEMBE Rene Salomon (Salomon)
Born: Yaounde, Cameroon, 8 December, 1980 — LB/M
Cameroon: 64

League Club	Source	Date Signed	Seasons Played	Apps	Subs	Gls
Leeds U (L)	Olymp Marseille (FRA)	08/03	03	8	4	0
Wigan Ath	Olymp Marseille (FRA)	08/07	07	2	6	0

OLI Dennis Chiedozie
Born: Newham, E London, England, 28 January, 1984 — F/W
England: Semi Pro-5

League Club	Source	Date Signed	Seasons Played	Apps	Subs	Gls
Queens Park Rgrs	YT	10/01	01-03	8	15	0
Swansea C	Tr	08/04	04	0	1	0
Cambridge U	Tr	09/04	04	4	0	1
Gillingham	Grays Ath	11/07	07-11	67	66	14
Wycombe W	Tr	07/12	12	6	4	0

O'LINN (OLINSKY) Sydney (Syd)
Born: Oudtshoorn, South Africa, 5 May, 1927 — IF

League Club	Source	Date Signed	Seasons Played	Apps	Subs	Gls
Charlton Ath	Green Point (RSA)	12/47	47-56	187	-	32

OLINYK Peter
Born: Bolton, Greater Manchester, England, 4 October, 1953 — M

League Club	Source	Date Signed	Seasons Played	Apps	Subs	Gls
Bolton W	App	06/71	73-74	7	3	0
Stockport Co	L	11/74	74	4	0	0

OLIPHANT David
Born: Carlisle, Cumbria, England, 29 January, 1942 — RH
Died: Carlisle, Cumbria, England, 4 November, 2004

League Club	Source	Date Signed	Seasons Played	Apps	Subs	Gls
Wolverhampton W	Jnr	06/59				
Carlisle U	Tr	12/60	60-64	109	-	11

OLISADEBE Emmanuel
Born: Owerri, Nigeria, 22 December, 1978 — F
Poland: 25

League Club	Source	Date Signed	Seasons Played	Apps	Subs	Gls
Portsmouth (L)	Panathinaikos (GRE)	01/06	05	0	2	0

OLISEH Egutu Chukwuma
Born: Lagos, Nigeria, 18 November, 1980 — DM

League Club	Source	Date Signed	Seasons Played	Apps	Subs	Gls
Queens Park Rgrs	La Louviere (BEL)	08/06	06	2	0	0

OLIVE Robert Leslie (Les)
Born: Salford, England, 28 April, 1928 — G
Died: Oldham, Greater Manchester, England, 20 May, 2006

League Club	Source	Date Signed	Seasons Played	Apps	Subs	Gls
Manchester U (Am)	Jnr	01/53	52	2	-	0

OLIVEIRA Filipe Vilaca
Born: Braga, Portugal, 27 May, 1984 — RW
Portugal: U21-21/Youth

League Club	Source	Date Signed	Seasons Played	Apps	Subs	Gls
Chelsea	FC Porto (POR)	09/01	02-04	0	5	0
Preston NE	L	12/04	04	1	4	0

OLIVEIRA Nelson Miguel Castro
Born: Barcelos, Portugal, 8 August, 1991 — F
Portugal: 14/U21-4/Youth

League Club	Source	Date Signed	Seasons Played	Apps	Subs	Gls
Swansea C (L)	Benfica (POR)	01/15	14	4	6	1

OLIVEIRA Raul Miguel Silva
Born: Lisbon, Portugal, 26 August, 1972 — CD

League Club	Source	Date Signed	Seasons Played	Apps	Subs	Gls
Bradford C (L)	Depo Farense (POR)	03/97	96	2	0	0

OLIVER Adam
Born: West Bromwich, West Midlands, England, 25 October, 1980 — M
England: Youth

League Club	Source	Date Signed	Seasons Played	Apps	Subs	Gls
West Bromwich A	YT	08/98	98-00	2	21	1

OLIVER Antony John (Tony)
Born: Portsmouth, England, 22 September, 1967 — G

League Club	Source	Date Signed	Seasons Played	Apps	Subs	Gls
Brentford	Portsmouth (NC)	08/87	87	11	0	0

OLIVER Brian Charles
Born: Liverpool, England, 6 March, 1957 — G

League Club	Source	Date Signed	Seasons Played	Apps	Subs	Gls
Rochdale	Bury (App)	03/75	75	3	0	0
Southport	L	12/75	75	2	0	0

OLIVER Connor
Born: Newcastle-upon-Tyne, England, 17 January, 1994 — RB

League Club	Source	Date Signed	Seasons Played	Apps	Subs	Gls
Sunderland	Sch	07/12				
Hartlepool U	L	03/14	13	2	1	0
Blackpool	Tr	01/15	14	4	2	0

OLIVER Darren
Born: Liverpool, England, 1 November, 1971 — LB

League Club	Source	Date Signed	Seasons Played	Apps	Subs	Gls
Bolton W	YT	05/90	92	3	0	0
Rochdale	Tr	10/93	93-94	22	6	0

OLIVER Dean Colin
Born: Derby, England, 4 December, 1987 — F

League Club	Source	Date Signed	Seasons Played	Apps	Subs	Gls
Sheffield U	Sch	07/06				
Torquay U	L	03/07	06	0	1	0

OLIVER Edmund Alan (Ted)
Born: Manchester, England, 17 March, 1961 — M/FB

League Club	Source	Date Signed	Seasons Played	Apps	Subs	Gls
Rochdale	App	03/79	77-79	19	3	1

OLIVER Eric
Born: Spennymoor, County Durham, England, 8 July, 1940 — G

League Club	Source	Date Signed	Seasons Played	Apps	Subs	Gls
Darlington (Am)	West Auckland T	12/63	63	2	-	0

OLIVER Gavin Ronald
Born: Felling, Tyne and Wear, England, 6 September, 1962 — CD

League Club	Source	Date Signed	Seasons Played	Apps	Subs	Gls
Sheffield Wed	App	08/80	80-84	14	6	0
Tranmere Rov	L	01/83	82	17	0	1
Brighton & HA	L	08/85	85	15	1	0
Bradford C	Tr	11/85	85-94	308	5	9

OLIVER George
Born: Houghton-le-Spring, Tyne and Wear, England, 22 January, 1919 — LW
Died: Sunderland, England, 1981

League Club	Source	Date Signed	Seasons Played	Apps	Subs	Gls
Halifax T		10/45				
Gateshead	Tr	10/46	46	13	-	1

OLIVER Henry Spoors (Harry)
Born: Sunderland, England, 16 February, 1921 — CH
Died: Sunderland, England, 14 January, 1994
England: Schools

League Club	Source	Date Signed	Seasons Played	Apps	Subs	Gls
Hartlepool U	Houghton CW	03/38	37	9	-	0
Brentford	Tr	05/38	46-47	18	-	0
Watford	Tr	05/48	48-51	122	-	2

OLIVER Howard Derek
Born: Sunderland, England, 16 April, 1950 — W

League Club	Source	Date Signed	Seasons Played	Apps	Subs	Gls
Sheffield Wed	Jnr	04/67				
Hartlepool U	Tr	08/68	68	0	1	0

OLIVER James (Jim)
Born: Tain, Highlands, Scotland, 13 January, 1958 — M

League Club	Source	Date Signed	Seasons Played	Apps	Subs	Gls
Wigan Ath	Montrose	08/80	80	1	1	0

OLIVER James (Jim)
Born: Uxbridge, W London, England, 28 August, 1949 — LB

League Club	Source	Date Signed	Seasons Played	Apps	Subs	Gls
Crystal Palace	App	03/67	67-69	3	0	0

OLIVER James Henry Kenneth (Ken)
Born: Loughborough, Leicestershire, England, 10 August, 1924 — CH
Died: Derby, England, 13 May, 1994

League Club	Source	Date Signed	Seasons Played	Apps	Subs	Gls
Sunderland	Brush Sports	08/46	47-48	8	-	1
Derby Co	Tr	09/49	49-57	184	-	1
Exeter C	Tr	01/58	57-59	92	-	0

OLIVER James Robert (Jim)
Born: Falkirk, Scotland, 3 December, 1941 — IF/RW
Scotland: Schools

League Club	Source	Date Signed	Seasons Played	Apps	Subs	Gls
Norwich C	Falkirk	08/62	62-64	40	-	14
Brighton & HA	Tr	03/65	64-67	37	6	6
Colchester U	Tr	02/68	67-69	65	10	10

OLIVER John
Born: Red Row, Northumberland, England, 6 October, 1920 — IF/RW
Died: Morpeth, Northumberland, England, January, 2011

League Club	Source	Date Signed	Seasons Played	Apps	Subs	Gls
Chesterfield	Amble	10/46	46-47	24	-	5

OLIVER John (Jack)
Born: Bradford, England, 21 September, 1946 — LB

League Club	Source	Date Signed	Seasons Played	Apps	Subs	Gls
Bradford Park Ave (Am)	Jnr	03/66	65	1		00

OLIVER Joseph Allen (Allen)
Born: Blyth, Northumberland, England, 8 September, 1924 — LW

League Club	Source	Date Signed	Seasons Played	Apps	Subs	Gls
Derby Co	Crofton CW	10/46	47-49	16	-	2
Stockport Co	Tr	08/50	50-53	139	-	29
Gateshead	Tr	07/54	54-57	146	-	37

OLIVER Keith
Born: South Shields, Tyne and Wear, England, 15 January, 1976 — M

League Club	Source	Date Signed	Seasons Played	Apps	Subs	Gls
Hartlepool U	YT	07/94	93-95	25	7	0

OLIVER Kenneth (Ken)
Born: Pelton, County Durham, England, 26 November, 1938 — IF

League Club	Source	Date Signed	Seasons Played	Apps	Subs	Gls
Sunderland	Birtley ROF	05/58				
Barnsley	South Shields	02/60	59-62	94	-	38
Watford	Tr	07/63	63-64	58	-	26
Workington	Tr	02/65	64-66	84	0	18
Bournemouth	Tr	01/67	66	14	0	4

OLIVER Luke John
Born: Acton, W London, England, 1 May, 1984 — CD
England: Semi Pro-1

League Club	Source	Date Signed	Seasons Played	Apps	Subs	Gls
Wycombe W	Brook House	07/02	02-03	0	4	0
Yeovil T	Woking	07/05	05	0	3	0
Wycombe W	Stevenage Bor	01/09	08-09	20	11	0
Bradford C	Tr	03/10	09-13	105	2	4

OLIVER Michael
Born: Middlesbrough, England, 2 August, 1975 — M

League Club	Source	Date Signed	Seasons Played	Apps	Subs	Gls
Middlesbrough	YT	08/92				
Stockport Co	Tr	07/94	94-95	17	5	1
Darlington	Tr	07/96	96-99	135	16	14
Rochdale	Tr	07/00	00-02	87	16	9

OLIVER Neil
Born: Berwick-on-Tweed, Northumberland, England, 11 April, 1967 — FB

League Club	Source	Date Signed	Seasons Played	Apps	Subs	Gls
Blackburn Rov	Berwick Rgrs	08/89	89-90	5	1	0

OLIVER Peter Francis Raeside
Born: Dunfermline, Fife, Scotland, 14 August, 1948 — LB

League Club	Source	Date Signed	Seasons Played	Apps	Subs	Gls
York C	Heart of Midlothian	07/74	74-75	41	0	0
Huddersfield T	Tr	05/76	76	41	0	1

OLIVER Ralph John
Born: Tredegar, Blaenau Gwent, Wales, 30 March, 1934 — WH

League Club	Source	Date Signed	Seasons Played	Apps	Subs	Gls
Shrewsbury T	Hereford U	08/55	55-57	7	-	0

OLIVER Vadaine Aston James
Born: Sheffield, England, 21 October, 1991 — F

League Club	Source	Date Signed	Seasons Played	Apps	Subs	Gls
Sheffield Wed	Sch	07/10				
Crewe Alex	Lincoln C	06/13	13-14	16	18	3
Mansfield T	L	11/14	14	28	2	7

OLLERENSHAW John
Born: Stockport, Greater Manchester, England, 3 April, 1925 — RB

League Club	Source	Date Signed	Seasons Played	Apps	Subs	Gls
Arsenal	Manchester C (Am)	09/46				
Hartlepool U	Tr	06/50	50	2	-	0
Oldham Ath	Tr	03/51				

OLLERENSHAW Scott
Born: Sydney, Australia, 9 February, 1968 — F
Australia: 14

League Club	Source	Date Signed	Seasons Played	Apps	Subs	Gls
Walsall	APIA Leichhardt (AUS)	08/92	92	8	12	4

OLNEY Ian Douglas
Born: Luton, England, 17 December, 1969 — F
England: U21-10

League Club	Source	Date Signed	Seasons Played	Apps	Subs	Gls
Aston Villa	YT	07/88	88-91	62	26	16
Oldham Ath	Tr	07/92	92-95	43	2	13

OLNEY Kevin John
Born: Doncaster, South Yorkshire, England, 12 February, 1959 — D

League Club	Source	Date Signed	Seasons Played	Apps	Subs	Gls
Doncaster Rov	Jnr	08/76	76-78	65	1	1

OLOFINJANA Seyi
Born: Lagos, Nigeria, 30 June, 1980 — M
Nigeria: 44

League Club	Source	Date Signed	Seasons Played	Apps	Subs	Gls
Wolverhampton W	SK Brann Bergen (NOR)	08/04	04-07	123	12	16
Stoke C	Tr	07/08	08	14	4	2
Hull C	Tr	08/09	09-12	21	13	0
Cardiff C	L	08/10	10	38	1	6
Sheffield Wed	L	03/13	12	6	0	0
Sheffield Wed	Tr	10/13	13	6	1	0

O'LOUGHLIN Charles Michael Patrick (Charlie)
Born: Birmingham, England, 17 March, 1989 — CD

League Club	Source	Date Signed	Seasons Played	Apps	Subs	Gls
Port Vale	Sch	07/07	07	0	3	0

O'LOUGHLIN Nigel
Born: Rochdale, Greater Manchester, England, 19 January, 1954 — M

League Club	Source	Date Signed	Seasons Played	Apps	Subs	Gls
Shrewsbury T	Rhyl	08/72	72-75	23	10	7
Rochdale	Tr	08/76	76-81	242	3	17

O'LOUGHLIN William James (Billy)
Born: Bolton, Greater Manchester, England, 18 January, 1937 — W

League Club	Source	Date Signed	Seasons Played	Apps	Subs	Gls
Oldham Ath	Rossendale U	02/60	59-60	27	-	0

OLSEN Benjamin Robert (Ben)
Born: Harrisburg, Pennsylvania, USA, 15 March, 1977 — M
USA: 37

League Club	Source	Date Signed	Seasons Played	Apps	Subs	Gls
Nottingham F (L)	Washington DC U (USA)	10/00	00	14	4	2

OLSEN James Paul
Born: Bootle, Merseyside, England, 23 October, 1981 — W

League Club	Source	Date Signed	Seasons Played	Apps	Subs	Gls
Tranmere Rov	Liverpool (YT)	03/01	00-02	1	3	0
Macclesfield T	Tr	03/04	03	0	2	0

OLSEN Jesper
Born: Fakse, Denmark, 20 March, 1961 — LW
Denmark: 43

League Club	Source	Date Signed	Seasons Played	Apps	Subs	Gls
Manchester U	Ajax (NED)	07/84	84-88	119	20	21

OLSEN Kim Plougman
Born: Herning, Denmark, 11 February, 1979 — F

League Club	Source	Date Signed	Seasons Played	Apps	Subs	Gls
Sheffield Wed	Midtjylland (DEN)	02/04	03	6	4	0

OLSSON Jonas
Born: Landskrona, Sweden, 10 March, 1983 — CD
Sweden: 25/U21-19

League Club	Source	Date Signed	Seasons Played	Apps	Subs	Gls
West Bromwich A	NEC Nijmegen (NED)	09/08	08-14	205	4	11

OLSSON Marcus Jonas Munuhe
Born: Gavle, Sweden, 17 May, 1988 — LB/M
Sweden: 2/U21-1

League Club	Source	Date Signed	Seasons Played	Apps	Subs	Gls
Blackburn Rov	Halmstads (SWE)	01/12	11-14	74	10	1

OLSSON Martin Tony Waikwa
Born: Gavle, Sweden, 17 May, 1988 — LB
Sweden: 27/U21-23/Youth

League Club	Source	Date Signed	Seasons Played	Apps	Subs	Gls
Blackburn Rov	Hogaborgs BK (SWE)	01/06	07-12	100	17	3
Norwich C	Tr	07/13	13-14	75	1	1

OLSSON Paul
Born: Hull, England, 24 December, 1965 — M

League Club	Source	Date Signed	Seasons Played	Apps	Subs	Gls
Hull C	App	01/84				
Exeter C	Tr	03/87	86-87	38	5	2
Scarborough	Tr	08/88	88-89	34	14	5
Hartlepool U	Tr	12/89	89-93	162	9	13
Darlington	Tr	07/94	94-95	76	0	8

OLSZAR Sebastian
Born: Cieszyn, Poland, 10 December, 1981 — F

League Club	Source	Date Signed	Seasons Played	Apps	Subs	Gls
Portsmouth	Admira Modling (AUT)	01/04				
Coventry C	L	03/04	03	1	4	0

OLUFEMI David Oluwatosin (Tosin)
Born: Hackney, E London, England, 13 May, 1994 — W

League Club	Source	Date Signed	Seasons Played	Apps	Subs	Gls
Colchester U	Sch	07/12	12-13	5	9	0

League Club	Source	Date Signed	Seasons Played	Career Record Apps	Subs	Gls
OLUGBODI Jide Michael						
Born: Lagos, Nigeria, 20 November, 1977						M
Brentford	Austria Lustenau (AUT)	10/03	03	0	2	0
O'MAHONEY Francis Kevin (Frank)						
Born: Aldershot, Hampshire, England, 5 April, 1935						CF
Swindon T	Farnborough T	04/57	56-57	8	-	5
O'MAHONY Matthew Augustine (Matt)						
Born: Waterford, Republic of Ireland, 19 January, 1913						CH
Died: Norwich, England, 25 January, 1992						
Republic of Ireland: 6//Northern Ireland: 1						
Southport	Hoylake	04/35	34	12	-	0
Wolverhampton W	Tr	05/35				
Newport Co	Tr	03/36	35	8	-	0
Bristol Rov	Tr	05/36	36-38	101	-	6
Ipswich T	Tr	07/39	46-48	58	-	4
OMAN Alan John						
Born: Newcastle-upon-Tyne, England, 6 October, 1952						LB
Northampton T	App	10/70	70-74	83	5	3
O'MARA John						
Born: Farnworth, Greater Manchester, England, 19 March, 1947						F
Gillingham	Margate	10/65				
Brentford	Wimbledon	03/71	70-72	53	0	28
Blackburn Rov	Tr	09/72	72-73	30	5	10
Bradford C	Chelmsford C	12/74	74	3	0	1
O'MEARA Alan Michael						
Born: Grantham, Lincolnshire, England, 15 December, 1958						G
Died: Leicester, England, 18 January, 2013						
Scunthorpe U	App	07/76	75-76	41	0	0
OMERUO Josiak Kenneth Josiah (Kenneth)						
Born: Kaduna, Nigeria, 17 October, 1993						CD
Nigeria: 28/Youth						
Chelsea	Standard Liege (BEL)	01/12				
Middlesbrough	L	01/14	13-14	31	2	0
OMIGIE Joseph Eghodalo (Joe)						
Born: Shepherd's Bush, W London, England, 13 June, 1972						F
Brentford	Donna FC	08/94	95-97	10	14	1
OMMEL Sergio Melvin						
Born: Den Haag, Netherlands, 2 September, 1977						F
Bristol Rov	KR Reykjavik (ICE)	11/01	01	18	5	8
OMOTOLA Tolani						
Born: Germany, 16 April, 1998						F
Tranmere Rov	Sch	-	14	0	1	0
OMOYINMI Emmanuel (Manny)						
Born: Nigeria, 28 December, 1977						F
England: Schools						
West Ham U	YT	05/95	96-98	1	8	2
Bournemouth	L	09/96	96	5	2	0
Leyton Orient	L	03/99	98	3	1	1
Gillingham	L	09/99	99	7	2	3
Scunthorpe U	L	12/99	99	6	0	1
Barnet	L	02/00	99	1	5	0
Oxford U	Tr	07/00	00-03	32	35	9
OMOZUSI Elliott Junior Uyi						
Born: Hackney, E London, England, 15 December, 1988						RB
England: Youth						
Fulham	Jnr	12/05	07	8	0	0
Norwich C	L	07/08	08	20	1	0
Charlton Ath	L	10/09	09	7	2	0
Leyton Orient	Tr	07/10	10-11	47	3	0
Leyton Orient	Unattached	01/13	12-14	63	7	0
ONE Armand						
Born: Paris, France, 15 March, 1983						F
Cambridge U	FC Nantes (FRA)	09/01	01	18	14	4
Northampton T	L	09/02	02	6	0	1
Wrexham	Tr	09/03	03	2	1	0
O'NEIL Brian						
Born: Bedlington, Northumberland, England, 4 January, 1944						M
England: FLge-2/U23-1						
Burnley	Jnr	01/61	62-69	231	4	22
Southampton	Tr	05/71	70-74	148	1	16
Huddersfield T	Tr	10/74	74-75	60	1	3
O'NEIL Brian						
Born: Paisley, Renfrewshire, Scotland, 6 September, 1972						DM
Scotland: 7/U21-7/Youth/Schools						
Nottingham F (L)	Glasgow Celtic	03/97	96	4	1	0
Derby Co	VfL Wolfsburg (GER)	11/00	00-02	14	3	0
Preston NE	Tr	01/03	02-05	101	11	5

League Club	Source	Date Signed	Seasons Played	Career Record Apps	Subs	Gls
O'NEIL Gary Paul						
Born: Beckenham, SE London, England, 18 May, 1983						M
England: U21-9/Youth						
Portsmouth	YT	06/00	99-07	142	33	16
Walsall	L	09/03	03	7	0	0
Cardiff C	L	09/04	04	8	1	1
Middlesbrough	Tr	08/07	07-10	105	4	8
West Ham U	Tr	01/11	10-12	33	15	3
Queens Park Rgrs	Tr	08/13	13	23	6	1
Norwich C	Tr	08/14	14	10	11	0
O'NEIL Joseph (Joe)						
Born: Glasgow, Scotland, 15 August, 1931						WH/IF
Died: Trowbridge, Wiltshire, England, 16 February, 2005						
Southend U (L)	Aberdeen	11/52	52-53	24	-	11
Leicester C	Aberdeen	03/56	57	5	-	2
Northampton T	Tr	10/57	57-58	28	-	4
O'NEIL Liam Christian James						
Born: Cambridge, England, 31 July, 1993						DM
West Bromwich A	Histon	03/12	13	0	3	0
Scunthorpe U	L	11/14	14	21	1	2
O'NEIL Thomas Henry (Tommy)						
Born: Spennymoor, County Durham, England, 5 January, 1925						RB
Died: Newport, Wales, 1978						
Newcastle U	Spennymoor U	09/42				
Newport Co	Tr	04/48	48	9	-	0
O'NEIL Thomas Patrick (Tommy)						
Born: St Helens, Merseyside, England, 25 October, 1952						M
Died: St Helens, Merseyside, England, May, 2006						
England: Schools						
Manchester U	App	11/69	70-72	54	0	0
Blackpool	L	01/73	72	7	0	0
Southport	Tr	08/73	73-77	192	6	20
Tranmere Rov	Tr	06/78	78-79	74	0	10
Halifax T	Tr	08/80	80-81	39	1	2
O'NEILL Alan						
Born: Cork, Republic of Ireland, 27 August, 1973						F
Birmingham C	Cobh Ramblers (ROI)	02/92	91	2	2	0
O'NEILL (HOPE) Alan						
Born: Leadgate, County Durham, England, 13 November, 1937						IF
Sunderland	Jnr	02/55	56-60	74	-	27
Aston Villa	Tr	10/60	60-62	23	-	6
Plymouth Arg	Tr	11/62	62-63	40	-	14
Bournemouth	Tr	02/64	63-65	37	0	8
O'NEILL Frank Simon						
Born: Dublin, Republic of Ireland, 13 April, 1940						W
Republic of Ireland: 20/LoI-15						
Arsenal	Home Farm (ROI)	04/59	60	2	-	0
O'NEILL George						
Born: Port Glasgow, Inverclyde, Scotland, 26 July, 1942						LH
USA: 2						
Barrow	Glasgow Celtic	10/64	64	7	-	0
O'NEILL George Patrick						
Born: Liverpool, England, 21 July, 1923						IF
Died: Liverpool, England, 8 October, 2006						
Port Vale (Am)	Ellemere Port	11/48	48	5	-	0
O'NEILL James (Jimmy)						
Born: Larne, Antrim, Northern Ireland, 24 November, 1941						CF
Northern Ireland: 1/U23-1/Schools						
Sunderland	Jnr	11/58	61	7	-	6
Walsall	Tr	12/62	62-64	38	-	13
Darlington	Melbourne Hakoah (AUS)	10/67	67	21	3	4
O'NEILL James Anthony (Jimmy)						
Born: Dublin, Republic of Ireland, 13 October, 1931						G
Died: Ormskirk, Lancashire, England, 15 December, 2007						
Republic of Ireland: Youth-17						
Everton	Bulfin U (ROI)	05/49	50-59	201	-	0
Stoke C	Tr	07/60	60-63	130	-	0
Darlington	Tr	03/64	63-64	32	-	0
Port Vale	Tr	02/65	64-65	42	0	0
O'NEILL James Joseph (Sean)						
Born: Belfast, Northern Ireland, 24 February, 1952						D
Leeds U	App	05/69				
Chesterfield	Tr	07/74	74-85	437	5	6
O'NEILL John Joseph						
Born: Glasgow, Scotland, 3 January, 1974						F
Bournemouth	Glasgow Celtic	03/96	95-00	79	45	10

O'NEILL John Nicholas
Born: Dublin, Republic of Ireland, 9 September, 1935 — LB
Died: Blackpool, Lancashire, England, 23 September, 2012
Republic of Ireland: 1

League Club	Source	Date Signed	Seasons Played	Apps	Subs	Gls
Preston NE	Drumcondra (ROI)	04/58	58-62	50	-	0
Barrow	Tr	07/63	63	35	-	3

O'NEILL John Patrick
Born: Derry, Northern Ireland, 11 March, 1958 — CD
Northern Ireland: 39

League Club	Source	Date Signed	Seasons Played	Apps	Subs	Gls
Leicester C	Loughborough Univ	03/76	78-86	313	0	10
Queens Park Rgrs	Tr	07/87	87	2	0	0
Norwich C	Tr	12/87	87	1	0	0

O'NEILL Joseph (Joe)
Born: Clayton-Le-Moors, Lancashire, England, 28 October, 1982 — F

League Club	Source	Date Signed	Seasons Played	Apps	Subs	Gls
Preston NE	Sch	07/02	04	0	2	0
Bury	L	07/03	03	10	13	3
Mansfield T	L	08/04	04	3	12	0
Chester C	L	01/05	04	5	6	1

O'NEILL Keith Padre Gerard
Born: Dublin, Republic of Ireland, 16 February, 1976 — LM
Republic of Ireland: 13/U21-1/Youth/Schools

League Club	Source	Date Signed	Seasons Played	Apps	Subs	Gls
Norwich C	YT	07/94	94-98	54	19	9
Middlesbrough	Tr	03/99	98-00	32	5	0
Coventry C	Tr	08/01	01-03	7	5	0

O'NEILL Leslie Arthur (Les)
Born: Blyth, Northumberland, England, 4 December, 1943 — M

League Club	Source	Date Signed	Seasons Played	Apps	Subs	Gls
Newcastle U	Blyth Spartans	11/61	63	1	-	0
Darlington	Tr	01/65	64-69	178	2	35
Bradford C	Tr	03/70	69-71	95	2	17
Carlisle U	Tr	05/72	72-76	148	7	20

O'NEILL Luke Marcus
Born: Slough, Berkshire, England, 20 August, 1991 — RB
England: Youth

League Club	Source	Date Signed	Seasons Played	Apps	Subs	Gls
Leicester C	Sch	09/08	09	0	1	0
Tranmere Rov	L	02/10	09	4	0	0
Burnley	Mansfield T	06/12	12	0	1	0
York C	L	10/13	13	15	0	1
Southend U	L	01/14	13	1	0	0
Scunthorpe U	L	08/14	14	13	0	0
Leyton Orient	L	02/15	14	8	0	0

O'NEILL Martin Hugh Michael
Born: Kilrea, Derry, Northern Ireland, 1 March, 1952 — M
Northern Ireland: 64

League Club	Source	Date Signed	Seasons Played	Apps	Subs	Gls
Nottingham F	Distillery	10/71	71-80	264	21	48
Norwich C	Tr	02/81	80	11	0	1
Manchester C	Tr	06/81	81	12	1	0
Norwich C	Tr	01/82	81-82	54	1	11
Notts Co	Tr	08/83	83-84	63	1	5

O'NEILL Matthew Paul (Matt)
Born: Accrington, Lancashire, England, 25 June, 1984 — LW

League Club	Source	Date Signed	Seasons Played	Apps	Subs	Gls
Burnley	Sch	07/03	02-04	2	11	0

O'NEILL Michael Andrew Martin
Born: Portadown, Armagh, Northern Ireland, 5 July, 1969 — M/F
Northern Ireland: 31/B-2/U23-1/U21-1/Youth/Schools

League Club	Source	Date Signed	Seasons Played	Apps	Subs	Gls
Newcastle U	Coleraine	10/87	87-88	36	12	15
Coventry C	Hibernian	07/96	96-97	3	2	0
Reading	L	03/98	97	9	0	1
Wigan Ath	Tr	09/98	98-99	65	1	2

O'NEILL Paul Dennis
Born: Farnworth, Greater Manchester, England, 17 June, 1982 — CD

League Club	Source	Date Signed	Seasons Played	Apps	Subs	Gls
Macclesfield T	YT	07/00	99-02	23	13	0

O'NEILL Ryan
Born: Dungannon, Tyrone, Northern Ireland, 19 January, 1990 — RB
Northern Ireland: Youth

League Club	Source	Date Signed	Seasons Played	Apps	Subs	Gls
West Ham U	Sch	07/07				
Barnet	Tr	08/09	09	11	4	0

O'NEILL Thomas (Tommy)
Born: Kirkintilloch, Dunbartonshire, Scotland, 2 February, 1958 — M

League Club	Source	Date Signed	Seasons Played	Apps	Subs	Gls
Cambridge U	Ipswich T (App)	07/76	76-82	96	20	8
Northampton T	Tr	06/83	83	43	0	6

O'NEILL William (Willie)
Born: Glasgow, Scotland, 30 December, 1940 — CD
Died: Airdrie, Lanarkshire, Scotland, 28 April, 2011
Scotland: SLge-1

League Club	Source	Date Signed	Seasons Played	Apps	Subs	Gls
Carlisle U	Glasgow Celtic	05/69	69	15	0	0

O'NEILL William Anthony (Billy)
Born: Cork, Republic of Ireland, 29 December, 1919 — IF
Republic of Ireland: LoI-2//Northern Ireland: NILge-3

League Club	Source	Date Signed	Seasons Played	Apps	Subs	Gls
Burnley	Chelmsford C	06/49	50	1	-	1
Walsall	Tr	01/51	50-51	51	-	16

ONIBUJE Folawiyo (Fola)
Born: Lagos, Nigeria, 25 September, 1984 — F

League Club	Source	Date Signed	Seasons Played	Apps	Subs	Gls
Preston NE	Charlton Ath (Jnr)	11/02				
Huddersfield T	L	11/03	03	0	2	0
Barnsley	Tr	07/04	04	0	3	0
Peterborough U	Tr	03/05	04	0	2	0
Swindon T	Cambridge U	07/06	06	6	8	2
Brentford	L	11/06	06	0	2	0
Wycombe W	Tr	01/07	06	1	4	0
Shrewsbury T	Tr	08/07				
Macclesfield T	Tr	02/08	07	0	1	0
Accrington Stan	Tr	08/08	08	0	5	0

O'NIEN Luke Terry
Born: Hemel Hempstead, Hertfordshire, England, 21 November, 1994 — M

League Club	Source	Date Signed	Seasons Played	Apps	Subs	Gls
Watford	Sch	07/13	13	0	1	0

ONOVWIGUN Michael Richie
Born: Clapham, SW London, England, 9 April, 1996 — M

League Club	Source	Date Signed	Seasons Played	Apps	Subs	Gls
Chesterfield	Brentford (Sch)	07/14	14	0	2	0

ONSLOW Leslie Gordon (Les)
Born: Swindon, England, 29 August, 1926 — WH

League Club	Source	Date Signed	Seasons Played	Apps	Subs	Gls
Swindon T	South Marston	10/45	46-48	4	-	0

ONSLOW Roy Eric
Born: Swindon, England, 12 September, 1928 — IF
Died: Swindon, England, 31 July, 2007

League Club	Source	Date Signed	Seasons Played	Apps	Subs	Gls
Swindon T	South Marston	11/47	47-55	140	-	23

ONUOHA Chinedum (Nedum)
Born: Warri, Nigeria, 12 November, 1986 — RB
England: U21-21/Youth

League Club	Source	Date Signed	Seasons Played	Apps	Subs	Gls
Manchester C	Sch	11/04	04-11	72	23	3
Sunderland	L	08/10	10	31	0	1
Queens Park Rgrs	Tr	01/12	11-14	77	11	2

ONUORA Ifem (Iffy)
Born: Glasgow, Scotland, 28 July, 1967 — F

League Club	Source	Date Signed	Seasons Played	Apps	Subs	Gls
Huddersfield T	Bradford Univ	07/89	89-93	115	50	30
Mansfield T	Tr	07/94	94-95	17	11	8
Gillingham	Tr	08/96	96-97	53	9	23
Swindon T	Tr	03/98	97-99	64	9	25
Gillingham	Tr	01/00	99-01	69	17	26
Sheffield U	Tr	07/02	02	7	0	1
Wycombe W	L	08/03	03	6	0	0
Grimsby T	Tr	09/03	03	18	1	3
Tranmere Rov	Tr	02/04	03	1	2	0
Huddersfield T	Tr	03/04	03	0	3	0

ONWERE Udo Alozie
Born: Hammersmith, W London, England, 9 November, 1971 — M

League Club	Source	Date Signed	Seasons Played	Apps	Subs	Gls
Fulham	YT	07/90	90-93	66	19	7
Lincoln C	Tr	08/94	94-95	40	3	4
Blackpool	Dover Ath	09/96	96	5	4	0
Barnet	Tr	08/97	97-98	25	11	2

ONYEALI Elkanah Bollington
Born: Port Harcourt, Nigeria, 7 June, 1939 — CF
Died: Robeiro, Nigeria, 11 August, 2008
Nigeria: 11

League Club	Source	Date Signed	Seasons Played	Apps	Subs	Gls
Tranmere Rov	Birkenhead Tech.	08/60	60	13	-	8

ONYEDINMA Wilfred Oluwafemi (Fred)
Born: Lagos, Nigeria, 24 November, 1996 — W

League Club	Source	Date Signed	Seasons Played	Apps	Subs	Gls
Millwall	Sch	11/13	13-14	4	2	0
Wycombe W	L	11/14	14	20	5	8

ONYEWU Oguchialu Chijioke (Oguchi)
Born: Washington DC, USA, 13 May, 1982 — CD
USA: 69/Youth

League Club	Source	Date Signed	Seasons Played	Apps	Subs	Gls
Newcastle U (L)	Standard Liege (BEL)	01/07	06	7	4	0
Queens Park Rgrs	Sporting Lisbon (POR)	10/13				
Sheffield Wed	Tr	01/14	13	18	0	0
Charlton Ath		10/14	14	1	2	0

OOIJER Andre Antonius Maria
Born: Amsterdam, Netherlands, 11 July, 1974 — CD
Netherlands: 55

League Club	Source	Date Signed	Seasons Played	Apps	Subs	Gls
Blackburn Rov	PSV Eindhoven (NED)	08/06	06-08	73	6	2

OOSTHUIZEN Ronald (Ron)
Born: Johannesburg, South Africa, 16 March, 1936 — W

League Club	Source	Date Signed	Seasons Played	Apps	Subs	Gls
Charlton Ath	Marist Brothers (RSA)	09/53	55	1	-	0
Carlisle U	Yeovil T	09/59	59	1	-	0

League Club	Source	Date Signed	Seasons Played	Apps	Subs	Gls
OPARA Junior Lloyd (Lloyd)						
Born: Edmonton, N London, England, 6 January, 1984						F
Colchester U	YT	-	01-02	0	6	0
Cambridge U	Tr	04/03	02-03	1	9	1
Swindon T	Grays Ath	07/04				
Peterborough U	Cheshunt	03/06	05-06	8	11	2
OPARA Kelechi Chrysantus						
Born: Owerri, Nigeria, 21 December, 1981						F
Colchester U	YT	-	98-00	2	17	0
Leyton Orient	Tr	12/00	00	3	3	0
OPINEL Sacha Fernand Henry						
Born: Bourg-Saint-Maurice, France, 9 April, 1977						LB/M
Plymouth Arg	Raith Rov	12/00				
Leyton Orient	Tr	02/01	00	9	2	1
ORAM Dennis Graham						
Born: Bristol, England, 14 January, 1920						FB
Died: Bath, England, 9 April, 2007						
Bristol C (Am)	Knowle	08/46	46	3	-	0
ORD Brian Rigby						
Born: Dunston-on-Tyne, Tyne and Wear, England, 21 June, 1939						LB/LH
Charlton Ath	Bleach Green	11/57	61-62	13	-	1
ORD Kenneth (Ken)						
Born: South Shields, Tyne and Wear, England, 21 September, 1939						RH
Died: Camden, N London, England, 4 March, 1992						
Sunderland	Cleadon Colliery	11/57				
Chesterfield	Tr	06/61	61	3	-	0
ORD Richard John						
Born: Murton, County Durham, England, 3 March, 1970						CD
England: U21-3						
Sunderland	YT	07/87	87-97	223	20	7
York C	L	02/90	89	3	0	0
Queens Park Rgrs	Tr	07/98				
ORD Thomas (Tommy)						
Born: Woolwich, SE London, England, 15 October, 1952						F
Chelsea	Erith & Belvedere	12/72	72	3	0	1
O'REGAN Kieran Michael						
Born: Cork, Republic of Ireland, 9 November, 1963						M/D
Republic of Ireland: 4/U21-5/Youth						
Brighton & HA	Tramore Ath (ROI)	04/83	82-86	69	17	2
Swindon T	Tr	08/87	87	23	3	1
Huddersfield T	Tr	08/88	88-92	187	12	25
West Bromwich A	Tr	07/93	93-94	36	9	2
Halifax T	Tr	08/95	98	15	4	2
O'REILLY Alexander (Alex)						
Born: Loughton, Essex, England, 15 September, 1979						G
West Ham U	YT	08/98				
Northampton T	L	08/99	99	7	0	0
O'REILLY Gary Miles						
Born: Isleworth, W London, England, 21 March, 1961						CD
England: Schools//Republic of Ireland: Youth						
Tottenham H	Grays Ath	09/79	80-83	39	6	0
Brighton & HA	Tr	08/84	84-86	78	1	3
Crystal Palace	Tr	01/87	86-89	65	5	2
Birmingham C	L	03/91	90	1	0	0
Brighton & HA	Tr	07/91	91	28	0	3
ORENUGA Kenny Oluwafei Gbolahan Ademola (Femi)						
Born: Lewisham, SE London, England, 18 March, 1993						W
Everton	Sch	03/10				
Notts Co	L	10/11	11	0	2	0
ORGILL Harold (Harry)						
Born: Hucknall, Nottinghamshire, England, 1 October, 1920						G
Died: Nottingham, England, 1979						
Bolton W	Basford U	11/38				
Southport	Tr	06/39				
Nottingham F		04/47	46	7	-	0
Notts Co	Tr	06/47	47	2	-	0
ORHAN Remzi Yilmaz (Yilmaz)						
Born: Nicosia, Cyprus, 13 March, 1955						F
West Ham U	Aveley	10/72	75-76	6	2	0
O'RILEY Paul John						
Born: Prescot, Merseyside, England, 17 October, 1950						F
Hull C	App	10/68	68-73	19	11	2
Scunthorpe U	L	03/71	70	11	0	4
Barnsley	Tr	07/74	74	11	3	2
Southport	Goole T	03/75	74-76	19	11	4

League Club	Source	Date Signed	Seasons Played	Apps	Subs	Gls
ORIOL Eduard (Edu)						
Born: Tarragona, Spain, 5 November, 1986						W
Blackpool	AEL Limassol (CYP)	08/14	14	8	2	0
ORIOL Joan						
Born: Tarragona, Spain, 5 November, 1986						LB
Blackpool	CA Osasuna (SPN)	08/14	14	11	0	0
O'RIORDAN Donald Joseph (Donal)						
Born: Dublin, Republic of Ireland, 14 May, 1957						CD/M
Republic of Ireland: U21-1/Youth						
Derby Co	App	05/75	76-77	2	4	1
Doncaster Rov	L	01/78	77	2	0	0
Preston NE	Tulsa Roughnecks (USA)	10/78	78-82	153	5	8
Carlisle U	Tr	08/83	83-84	84	0	18
Middlesbrough	Tr	08/85	85	41	0	2
Grimsby T	Tr	08/86	86-87	86	0	14
Notts Co	Tr	07/88	88-92	102	7	5
Mansfield T	L	09/89	89	6	0	0
Torquay U	Tr	02/93	92-95	76	3	3
Scarborough	Tr	12/95	95	1	0	0
ORLANDI Andrea						
Born: Barcelona, Spain, 3 August, 1984						LB/M
Swansea C	Dep Alaves (SPN)	08/07	07-11	44	28	3
Brighton & HA	Tr	08/12	12-13	39	10	6
Blackpool	Tr	08/14	14	23	5	4
ORLYGSSON Thorvaldur (Toddi)						
Born: Odense, Denmark, 2 August, 1966						M
Iceland: 41						
Nottingham F	KA Akureyri (ICE)	12/89	89-92	31	6	2
Stoke C	Tr	08/93	93-95	86	4	16
Oldham Ath	Tr	12/95	95-98	65	11	1
ORMANDY John (Jack)						
Born: Liverpool, England, 25 January, 1912						LW
Died: Dewsbury, West Yorkshire, England, January, 1997						
Bradford C	Prescot Cables	06/32	32-35	63	-	9
Bury	Tr	06/36	36-38	87	-	18
Southend U	Tr	06/39				
Oldham Ath	Tr	07/46	46	30	-	5
Halifax T	Tr	07/47	47	7	-	0
ORMEROD Anthony						
Born: Middlesbrough, England, 31 March, 1979						W
England: Youth						
Middlesbrough	YT	05/96	97-99	8	11	3
Carlisle U	L	01/99	98	5	0	0
York C	L	09/99	99	9	3	0
Hartlepool U	L	09/01	01	2	0	0
ORMEROD Brett Ryan						
Born: Blackburn, Greater Manchester, England, 18 October, 1976						F
Blackpool	Accrington Stan	03/97	96-01	105	23	45
Southampton	Tr	12/01	01-05	62	37	12
Leeds U	L	09/04	04	6	0	0
Wigan Ath	L	03/05	04	3	3	2
Preston NE	Tr	01/06	05-07	37	25	13
Nottingham F	L	03/08	07	13	0	2
Oldham Ath	L	10/08	08	2	3	0
Blackpool	Tr	01/09	08-11	50	37	15
Rochdale	L	01/12	11	4	1	1
ORMEROD Mark Ian						
Born: Bournemouth, England, 5 February, 1976						G
Brighton & HA	YT	07/94	96-99	85	0	0
ORMOND John Lambie (Iain)						
Born: Harthill, Lanarkshire, Scotland, 10 August, 1947						W
New Zealand: 10						
Barnsley	Blockhouse Bay (NZL)	12/67	68	1	0	1
ORMOND William (Bill)						
Born: Greenock, Inverclyde, Scotland, 26 August, 1926						LW
Died: Greenock, Inverclyde, Scotland, 17 September, 1992						
Blackpool	Partick Thistle	10/47				
Oldham Ath	Tr	12/49	49-53	122	-	25
Barrow	Tr	02/54	53-57	140	-	20
Scunthorpe U	Tr	08/58	58	3	-	0
ORMONDROYD Ian						
Born: Bradford, England, 22 September, 1964						F
Bradford C	Thackley	09/85	85-88	72	15	20
Oldham Ath	L	03/87	86	8	2	1
Aston Villa	Tr	02/89	88-91	41	15	6
Derby Co	Tr	09/91	91	25	0	8
Leicester C	Tr	03/92	91-94	67	10	7
Hull C	L	01/95	94	10	0	6

League Club	Source	Date Signed	Seasons Played	Apps	Subs	Gls
Bradford C	Tr	07/95	95-96	28	10	6
Oldham Ath	Tr	09/96	96-97	26	5	8
Scunthorpe U	Tr	09/97	97	7	13	0

ORMROD Leslie (Les)
Born: Stockport, Greater Manchester, England, 8 October, 1952 FB
England: Schools

League Club	Source	Date Signed	Seasons Played	Apps	Subs	Gls
Stockport Co	Everton (App)	03/70	69-73	103	5	0

ORMSBY Brendan Thomas Christopher
Born: Birmingham, England, 1 October, 1960 CD
England: Youth/Schools

League Club	Source	Date Signed	Seasons Played	Apps	Subs	Gls
Aston Villa	App	10/78	78-85	115	2	4
Leeds U	Tr	02/86	85-88	46	0	5
Shrewsbury T	L	01/90	89	1	0	0
Doncaster Rov	Tr	07/90	90-91	78	0	8
Scarborough	Tr	08/92	92	15	1	1
Wigan Ath	Waterford (ROI)	08/94	94	2	0	0

ORMSTON Alexander (Alec)
Born: Stoke-on-Trent, England, 10 February, 1919 LW
Died: Stoke-on-Trent, England, 12 July, 1975
England: FLge-3

League Club	Source	Date Signed	Seasons Played	Apps	Subs	Gls
Stoke C	Summerbank	07/36	37-51	172	-	29

O'ROURKE James
Born: Glasgow, Scotland, 17 October, 1948 FB

League Club	Source	Date Signed	Seasons Played	Apps	Subs	Gls
Arsenal	Possilpark Jnrs	10/65				
Carlisle U	Tr	10/67	67	0	1	0

O'ROURKE John
Born: Northampton, England, 11 February, 1945 CF
England: U23-1/Youth/Schools

League Club	Source	Date Signed	Seasons Played	Apps	Subs	Gls
Chelsea	Arsenal (Jnr)	04/62				
Luton T	Tr	12/63	63-65	84	0	64
Middlesbrough	Tr	07/66	66-67	63	1	38
Ipswich T	Tr	02/68	67-69	69	0	30
Coventry C	Tr	11/69	69-71	52	2	17
Queens Park Rgrs	Tr	10/71	71-72	33	1	12
Bournemouth	Tr	01/74	73-74	21	1	4

O'ROURKE Kenneth (Ken)
Born: Lambeth, S London, England, 8 December, 1949 IF

League Club	Source	Date Signed	Seasons Played	Apps	Subs	Gls
Arsenal	Leyton Orient (App)	02/67				
Colchester U	Tr	08/68	68	1	0	0
Ipswich T	Tr	08/68				

O'ROURKE William James (Billy)
Born: Nottingham, England, 2 April, 1960 G
Died: Preston, Lancashire, England, 24 January, 2002

League Club	Source	Date Signed	Seasons Played	Apps	Subs	Gls
Burnley	App	02/78	79-82	14	0	0
Blackpool	L	08/83	83	6	0	0
Chester C	Tr	03/84	83	5	0	0
Blackpool	Tr	06/84	84-85	92	0	0
Tranmere Rov	L	09/86	86	15	0	0
Tranmere Rov	Tr	02/87	86-87	38	0	0

ORPHAN Leslie James (Les)
Born: Newport, Wales, 17 April, 1923 IF
Died: Newport, Wales, 11 September, 1995
Wales: Amateur

League Club	Source	Date Signed	Seasons Played	Apps	Subs	Gls
Newport Co	Girlings, Cwmbran	02/49	48	1	-	0

ORR Anderson (Alan)
Born: Glasgow, Scotland, 19 December, 1923 RH
Died: Lancaster, Pennsylvania, USA, 25 August, 1998

League Club	Source	Date Signed	Seasons Played	Apps	Subs	Gls
Nottingham F	Third Lanark	08/51	51-54	46	-	0

ORR Bradley James
Born: Liverpool, England, 1 November, 1982 RB

League Club	Source	Date Signed	Seasons Played	Apps	Subs	Gls
Newcastle U	YT	07/01				
Burnley	L	01/04	03	1	3	0
Bristol C	Tr	07/04	04-09	204	25	12
Queens Park Rgrs	Tr	07/10	10-11	31	8	1
Blackburn Rov	Tr	01/12	11-12	28	3	0
Ipswich T	L	11/12	12	13	0	0
Blackpool	L	09/13	13	3	1	0

ORR Douglas McDonald (Doug)
Born: Glasgow, Scotland, 8 November, 1937 LW
Scotland: Amateur

League Club	Source	Date Signed	Seasons Played	Apps	Subs	Gls
Queens Park Rgrs (Am)	Hendon	06/57	57	5	-	0

ORR Henry (Harry)
Born: Lisburn, Belfast, Northern Ireland, 31 October, 1936 LH

League Club	Source	Date Signed	Seasons Played	Apps	Subs	Gls
Sheffield U	Distillery	11/58	58-63	10	-	1
Peterborough U	Tr	07/64	64-66	47	1	0

ORR Neil Ian
Born: Greenock, Inverclyde, Scotland, 13 May, 1959 DM
Scotland: SLge-1/U21-7

League Club	Source	Date Signed	Seasons Played	Apps	Subs	Gls
West Ham U	Greenock Morton	01/82	81-87	133	13	4

ORRITT Bryan
Born: Caernarfon, Gwynedd, Wales, 22 February, 1937 IF/WH
Died: Johannesburg, South Africa, 24 March, 2014
Wales: U23-3

League Club	Source	Date Signed	Seasons Played	Apps	Subs	Gls
Birmingham C	Bangor C	01/56	56-61	99	-	23
Middlesbrough	Tr	03/62	61-65	115	3	22

OSANO Curtis
Born: Nakuru, Kenya, 8 March, 1987 RB

League Club	Source	Date Signed	Seasons Played	Apps	Subs	Gls
Reading	Sch	07/06				
AFC Wimbledon	Luton T	05/12	12	15	2	0

OSAWE Osayamen
Born: Lagos, Nigeria, 13 September, 1993 F

League Club	Source	Date Signed	Seasons Played	Apps	Subs	Gls
Blackburn Rov	Sch	07/12				
Accrington Stan	L	10/12	12	0	2	0

OSAYI-SAMUEL Bright
Born: Nigeria, 1 February, 1997 F

League Club	Source	Date Signed	Seasons Played	Apps	Subs	Gls
Blackpool	Jnr	-	14	1	5	0

OSBORN Benjamin Jarrod (Ben)
Born: Derby, England, 5 August, 1984 M
England: Youth

League Club	Source	Date Signed	Seasons Played	Apps	Subs	Gls
Nottingham F	Sch	07/12	13-14	33	12	3

OSBORN Kenneth George (Ken)
Born: Hampstead, NW London, England, 23 November, 1948 RW

League Club	Source	Date Signed	Seasons Played	Apps	Subs	Gls
Gillingham	Queens Park Rgrs (App)	06/66	68-69	2	0	0

OSBORN Mark
Born: Bletchley, Buckinghamshire, England, 18 June, 1981 G

League Club	Source	Date Signed	Seasons Played	Apps	Subs	Gls
Wycombe W	YT	03/99	99	1	0	0

OSBORN Simon Edward
Born: New Addington, S London, England, 19 January, 1972 M

League Club	Source	Date Signed	Seasons Played	Apps	Subs	Gls
Crystal Palace	YT	01/90	90-93	47	8	5
Reading	Tr	08/94	94	31	1	5
Queens Park Rgrs	Tr	07/95	95	6	3	1
Wolverhampton W	Tr	12/95	95-00	151	11	11
Tranmere Rov	Tr	03/01	00	9	0	1
Port Vale	Tr	09/01	01	7	0	0
Gillingham	Tr	10/01	01-02	38	8	5
Walsall	Tr	07/03	03-05	98	15	5
Hereford U	Tr	08/06	06	0	1	0

OSBORNE Glyn
Born: Crewe, Cheshire, England, 23 August, 1954 F

League Club	Source	Date Signed	Seasons Played	Apps	Subs	Gls
Crewe Alex	App	-	70-71	2	5	0

OSBORNE Ian Leonard
Born: Leicester, England, 28 October, 1952 RB

League Club	Source	Date Signed	Seasons Played	Apps	Subs	Gls
Birmingham C	App	10/70	75	10	0	0
Port Vale	Tr	06/76	76	14	1	0

OSBORNE John
Born: Barlborough, Derbyshire, England, 1 December, 1940 G
Died: Evesham, Worcestershire, England, 7 November, 1998
England: Schools

League Club	Source	Date Signed	Seasons Played	Apps	Subs	Gls
Chesterfield	Bolton W (Am)	09/60	60-66	110	0	0
West Bromwich A	Tr	01/67	66-76	250	0	0
Walsall	L	02/73	72	3	0	0

OSBORNE John (Johnny)
Born: Renfrew, Renfrewshire, Scotland, 14 October, 1919 IF
Died: Leicester, England, 19 September, 1981

League Club	Source	Date Signed	Seasons Played	Apps	Subs	Gls
Leicester C	Linwood Thistle	09/38				
Watford	Tr	02/48	47-48	34	-	12

OSBORNE Junior
Born: Watford, Hertfordshire, England, 12 February, 1988 RB

League Club	Source	Date Signed	Seasons Played	Apps	Subs	Gls
Watford	Sch	07/05	04-05	1	1	0
Aldershot T	Tr	08/08	08	8	0	0

OSBORNE Karleigh Anthony Jonathan
Born: Southall, W London, England, 19 March, 1988 CD

League Club	Source	Date Signed	Seasons Played	Apps	Subs	Gls
Brentford	Sch	06/06	04-11	139	22	6
Millwall	Tr	07/12	12-13	14	0	1
Bristol C	Tr	11/13	13-14	25	3	1
Colchester U	L	02/15	14	4	0	0

OSBORNE Lawrence William (Lawrie)
Born: Stratford, E London, England, 20 October, 1967 M

League Club	Source	Date Signed	Seasons Played	Apps	Subs	Gls
Arsenal	App	07/85				
Newport Co	Tr	11/87	87	15	0	0
Maidstone U	Redbridge Forest	07/90	90-91	49	4	8
Gillingham	Tr	12/91	91-92	5	1	1

League Club	Source	Date Signed	Seasons Played	Apps	Subs	Gls

OSBORNE Leon Aiden
Born: Doncaster, South Yorkshire, England, 28 October, 1991 — W

Bradford C	Sch	07/08	06-10	16	21	1

OSBORNE Roger Charles
Born: Otley, Suffolk, England, 9 March, 1950 — M

Ipswich T	Grundisburgh	03/71	73-80	109	15	9
Colchester U	Tr	02/81	80-85	196	10	11

OSBORNE Steven Colin (Steve)
Born: Middlesbrough, England, 3 March, 1969 — F

Peterborough U	South Bank	03/89	88-90	18	43	7
York C	Tr	08/91	91	6	3	0

OSBORNE Wayne
Born: Stockton-on-Tees, Cleveland, England, 14 January, 1977 — FB

York C	YT	06/95	95	5	1	0

OSBOURNE Calbert Gary James (Gary)
Born: Wolverhampton, England, 22 October, 1969 — RW

Shrewsbury T	YT	07/88	88	3	4	0

OSBOURNE Isaac Samuel
Born: Birmingham, England, 22 June, 1986 — DM

Coventry C	Sch	07/03	02-09	101	21	0
Crewe Alex	L	10/06	06	2	0	0

OSBOURNE Isaiah George
Born: Birmingham, England, 5 November, 1987 — M
England: Youth

Aston Villa	Sch	11/05	06-07	7	12	0
Nottingham F	L	03/09	08	7	1	0
Middlesbrough	L	11/09	09	9	0	0
Sheffield Wed	L	01/11	10	9	1	0
Blackpool	Hibernian	07/12	12-13	46	6	2
Scunthorpe U	L	10/14	14	24	4	0

[OSCAR] JUNIOR Oscar Dos Santos Emboaba
Born: Sao Paulo, Brazil, 9 September, 1991 — M
Brazil: 45/U23-6/Youth

Chelsea	Internacional (BRA)	07/12	12-14	74	21	18

OSCROFT Harry
Born: Mansfield, Nottinghamshire, England, 10 March, 1926 — LW
Died: Ipswich, England, 31 December, 2008

Mansfield T	Mansfield Colliery	04/47	46-49	113	-	41
Stoke C	Tr	01/50	49-58	326	-	103
Port Vale	Tr	09/59	59-60	47	-	12

OSEI-KUFFOUR Jonathan (Jo)
Born: Edmonton, N London, England, 17 November, 1981 — F

Arsenal	YT	07/00				
Swindon T	L	08/01	01	4	7	2
Torquay U	Beveren (BEL)	10/02	02-05	111	37	29
Brentford	Tr	07/06	06	38	1	12
Bournemouth	Tr	07/07	07	39	5	12
Bristol Rov	Tr	08/08	08-11	104	26	32
Gillingham	Tr	09/11	11	26	4	9
Wycombe W	Tr	09/12	12-13	33	23	5

OSGOOD Keith
Born: Isleworth, W London, England, 8 May, 1955 — CD
England: Youth/Schools

Tottenham H	App	05/72	73-77	112	1	13
Coventry C	Tr	01/78	77-78	24	0	1
Derby Co	Tr	10/79	79-81	61	8	10
Leyton Orient	Tr	12/81	81-83	36	0	0
Cambridge U	HJK Helsinki (FIN)	11/84	84-85	34	1	1

OSGOOD Peter Leslie
Born: Windsor, Berkshire, England, 20 February, 1947 — F
Died: Slough, Berkshire, England, 1 March, 2006
England: 4/FLge-3/U23-6/Youth

Chelsea	Jnr	09/64	65-73	276	3	103
Southampton	Tr	03/74	73-77	122	4	28
Norwich C	L	11/76	76	3	0	0
Chelsea	Philadelphia F'y (USA)	12/78	78-79	10	0	2

OSGOOD Stephen (Steve)
Born: Bracknell, Berkshire, England, 20 January, 1962 — G

Aldershot	Newbury T	02/89	88	1	0	0

O'SHAUGHNESSY Brian
Born: Wednesbury, West Midlands, England, 8 September, 1932 — IF
Died: Walsall, West Midlands, England, January, 1986

Walsall	Bloxwich Strollers	03/54	53	1	-	0

O'SHAUGHNESSY Michael John (Mike)
Born: Poplar, E London, England, 15 April, 1955 — G

Leyton Orient	App	08/73	73	1	0	0

O'SHAUGHNESSY Paul Joseph
Born: Bury, Greater Manchester, England, 3 October, 1981 — M

Bury	YT	07/01	01-03	27	18	1

O'SHAUGHNESSY Stephen (Steve)
Born: Wrexham, Wales, 13 October, 1967 — M/CD
Wales: Youth

Leeds U	App	10/85				
Bradford C	Tr	11/85	87	0	1	0
Rochdale	Tr	08/88	88-90	101	8	16
Exeter C	Tr	07/91	91	1	2	0
Darlington	Tr	01/92	91-93	88	0	2

O'SHEA Daniel Edward (Danny)
Born: Kennington, S London, England, 26 March, 1963 — D/M

Arsenal	App	12/80	82	6	0	0
Charlton Ath	L	02/84	83	9	0	0
Exeter C	Tr	08/84	84	45	0	2
Southend U	Tr	08/85	85-88	117	2	12
Cambridge U	Tr	08/89	89-94	186	17	1
Northampton T	Tr	03/95	94-96	73	7	1

O'SHEA James (Jay)
Born: Dublin, Republic of Ireland, 10 August, 1988 — W
Republic of Ireland: U21-7/Youth

Birmingham C	Galway U (ROI)	08/09	09	0	1	0
Middlesbrough	L	03/10	09	1	1	0
Stevenage	L	10/10	10	5	0	0
Port Vale	L	01/11	10	5	0	1
MK Dons	Tr	07/11	11-12	17	22	6
Chesterfield	Tr	11/12	12-14	79	28	23

O'SHEA John Francis
Born: Waterford, Republic of Ireland, 30 April, 1981 — D
Republic of Ireland: 102/U21-13/Youth

Manchester U	Waterford (ROI)	09/98	01-10	188	68	10
Bournemouth	L	01/00	99	10	0	1
Sunderland	Tr	07/11	11-14	133	0	3

O'SHEA Timothy James (Tim)
Born: Pimlico, Central London, England, 12 November, 1966 — D/M
Republic of Ireland: U21-2/Youth

Tottenham H	App	08/84	86-87	1	2	0
Newport Co	L	10/86	86	10	0	0
Leyton Orient	Tr	07/88	88	7	2	1
Gillingham	Tr	02/89	88-91	102	10	2

OSHILAJA Abdul-Yussuf Adedeji (Adedeji)
Born: Bermondsey, SE London, England, 26 February, 1993 — CD

Cardiff C	Sch	07/12				
Newport Co	L	10/13	13	8	0	0
Sheffield Wed	L	02/14	13	2	0	0
AFC Wimbledon	L	01/15	14	23	0	1

OSHODI Edward Abdullai Mobalaji Olatunji Afo (Eddie)
Born: Wembley, NW London, England, 14 January, 1992 — CD
England: Semi Pro-3/Youth

Watford	Sch	01/09	09	0	1	0

OSMAN Abdul-Haq Bin Seidu (Abdul)
Born: Accra, Ghana, 27 February, 1987 — M

Northampton T	Gretna	07/08	08-10	97	7	7
Crewe Alex	Kerkyra (GRE)	07/12	12-13	63	6	0

OSMAN Harold James (Harry)
Born: Alton, Hampshire, England, 29 January, 1911 — LW
Died: Florida, USA, 17 December, 1998

Plymouth Arg	Poole T	12/35	35-36	5	-	0
Southampton	Tr	06/37	37-38	70	-	31
Millwall	Tr	03/39	38-47	34	-	3
Bristol C	Tr	10/47	47	18	-	1

OSMAN Leon
Born: Orrell, Greater Manchester, England, 17 May, 1981 — M
England: 2/Youth/Schools

Everton	YT	08/98	02-14	293	50	44
Carlisle U	L	10/02	02	10	2	1
Derby Co	L	01/04	03	17	0	3

OSMAN Rex Charles Herbert
Born: Derby, England, 4 April, 1932 — WH
Died: Ipswich, England, 9 June, 2005
England: Youth

Derby Co	Jnr	07/49	53-54	2	-	0

OSMAN Russell Charles
Born: Repton, Derbyshire, England, 14 February, 1959 — CD
England: 11/B-2/U21-7/Youth

Ipswich T	App	03/76	77-84	294	0	17

League Club	Source	Date Signed	Seasons Played	Apps	Subs	Gls
Leicester C	Tr	07/85	85-87	108	0	8
Southampton	Tr	06/88	88-91	92	4	6
Bristol C	Tr	10/91	91-93	67	3	3
Plymouth Arg	Sudbury T	03/95				
Brighton & HA	Tr	09/95	95	11	1	0
Cardiff C	Tr	02/96	95	14	1	0

OSMOND Avery Noel
Born: Huddersfield, West Yorkshire, England, 25 December, 1924 — IF

League Club	Source	Date Signed	Seasons Played	Apps	Subs	Gls
Southend U	Peterborough U	05/48	48	2	-	0

OSMOND Colin Albert Eric
Born: Whitchurch, Hampshire, England, 15 May, 1937 — CH
England: Youth

League Club	Source	Date Signed	Seasons Played	Apps	Subs	Gls
Portsmouth	Jnr	05/54	57	1	-	0

OSPINA David
Born: Medellin, Colombia, 31 August, 1988 — G
Colombia: 57/Youth

League Club	Source	Date Signed	Seasons Played	Apps	Subs	Gls
Arsenal	OGC Nice (FRA)	07/14	14	18	0	0

OSTENSTAD Egil Johan
Born: Haugesund, Norway, 2 January, 1972 — F
Norway: 18/U21-27/Youth

League Club	Source	Date Signed	Seasons Played	Apps	Subs	Gls
Southampton	Viking Stavanger (NOR)	10/96	96-99	80	16	28
Blackburn Rov	Tr	08/99	99-02	38	24	12
Manchester C	L	02/01	00	1	3	0

OSTER John Morgan
Born: Boston, Lincolnshire, England, 8 December, 1978 — W
Wales: 13/B-1/U21-9/Youth

League Club	Source	Date Signed	Seasons Played	Apps	Subs	Gls
Grimsby T	YT	07/96	96	21	3	3
Everton	Tr	07/97	97-98	22	18	1
Sunderland	Tr	08/99	99-04	48	20	5
Barnsley	L	10/01	01	2	0	0
Grimsby T	L	11/02	02	10	0	5
Grimsby T	L	02/03	02	7	0	1
Leeds U	L	11/04	04	8	0	1
Burnley	Tr	01/05	04	12	3	1
Reading	Tr	08/05	05-07	29	47	2
Crystal Palace	Tr	08/08	08	27	4	3
Doncaster Rov	Tr	08/09	09-11	100	11	2
Barnet	Tr	09/12	12	23	5	2

OSTERGAARD John Brian (Johnny)
Born: Herning, Denmark, 6 February, 1955 — F

League Club	Source	Date Signed	Seasons Played	Apps	Subs	Gls
Charlton Ath	Ikast (DEN)	11/79	79-80	8	4	1

OSTLUND Alexander
Born: Akersberga, Sweden, 2 November, 1978 — RB
Sweden: 22

League Club	Source	Date Signed	Seasons Played	Apps	Subs	Gls
Southampton	Feyenoord (NED)	01/06	05-07	35	9	0

O'SULLIVAN Cyril John
Born: Lewisham, SE London, England, 22 February, 1920 — G
Died: Oxford, England, 14 March, 2003

League Club	Source	Date Signed	Seasons Played	Apps	Subs	Gls
Reading	Crown Villa	09/46	46-47	36	-	0

O'SULLIVAN John
Born: Cork, Republic of Ireland, 30 May, 1922 — RW

League Club	Source	Date Signed	Seasons Played	Apps	Subs	Gls
Swansea C	Waterford (ROI)	01/48	47	2	-	0
Aldershot	Lovells Ath	11/51				

O'SULLIVAN John Anthony James
Born: Birmingham, England, 18 September, 1993 — M
Republic of Ireland: U21-4/Youth

League Club	Source	Date Signed	Seasons Played	Apps	Subs	Gls
Blackburn Rov	Sch	07/11	12-14	1	2	0
Accrington Stan	L	09/14	14	13	0	4
Barnsley	L	02/15	14	7	1	0

O'SULLIVAN Peter Anthony
Born: Conway, Conwy, Wales, 4 March, 1951 — LW
Wales: 3/U23-6/Schools

League Club	Source	Date Signed	Seasons Played	Apps	Subs	Gls
Manchester U	App	03/68				
Brighton & HA	Tr	04/70	70-80	432	3	39
Fulham	Tr	06/81	81-82	45	1	1
Charlton Ath	L	10/82	82	5	0	0
Reading	L	11/82	82	9	0	0
Aldershot	Seiko Sports Ass (HKG)	07/83	83	13	1	0

O'SULLIVAN Thomas Paul (Tommy)
Born: Mountain Ash, Rhondda Cynon Taff, Wales, 18 December, 1994 — M
Wales: U21-6/Youth

League Club	Source	Date Signed	Seasons Played	Apps	Subs	Gls
Cardiff C	Sch	04/12				
Port Vale	L	02/15	14	1	4	0

O'SULLIVAN Wayne St John
Born: Akrotiri, Cyprus, 25 February, 1974 — RM
Republic of Ireland: U21-2

League Club	Source	Date Signed	Seasons Played	Apps	Subs	Gls
Swindon T	YT	05/93	94-96	65	24	3
Cardiff C	Tr	08/97	97-98	78	7	4
Plymouth Arg	Tr	07/99	99-00	83	2	3

O'SULLIVAN William Finbar (Willie)
Born: Lambeth, S London, England, 5 October, 1959 — W
Republic of Ireland: Youth

League Club	Source	Date Signed	Seasons Played	Apps	Subs	Gls
Charlton Ath	App	10/77	76-77	1	1	0

OSVALDO Pablo Daniel (Dani)
Born: Buenos Aires, Argentina, 12 January, 1986 — F
Italy: 14/U21-12

League Club	Source	Date Signed	Seasons Played	Apps	Subs	Gls
Southampton	AS Roma (ITA)	08/13	13	9	4	3

OSVOLD Kjetil
Born: Aalesund, Norway, 5 June, 1961 — LM
Norway: 37

League Club	Source	Date Signed	Seasons Played	Apps	Subs	Gls
Nottingham F	Lillestrom (NOR)	03/87	86-87	5	2	0
Leicester C	L	12/87	87	3	1	0

O'TOOLE Christopher Patrick (Pat)
Born: Dublin, Republic of Ireland, 2 January, 1965 — M

League Club	Source	Date Signed	Seasons Played	Apps	Subs	Gls
Leicester C	Shelbourne (ROI)	02/90				
Exeter C	L	12/90	90	6	0	0
Shrewsbury T	Tr	03/91	90-92	26	20	1
Torquay U	Cobh Ramblers (ROI)	08/93	93	3	0	0

O'TOOLE Gavin Francis
Born: Dublin, Republic of Ireland, 19 September, 1975 — M
Republic of Ireland: U21-2/Youth/Schools

League Club	Source	Date Signed	Seasons Played	Apps	Subs	Gls
Coventry C	YT	07/93				
Hereford U	L	11/96	96	1	0	0

O'TOOLE John Joseph (John-Joe)
Born: Harrow, NW London, England, 30 September, 1988 — M
Republic of Ireland: U21-5

League Club	Source	Date Signed	Seasons Played	Apps	Subs	Gls
Watford	Sch	09/07	07-08	37	20	10
Sheffield U	L	02/09	08	5	4	1
Colchester U	Tr	09/09	09-12	47	25	2
Bristol Rov	L	01/13	12	18	0	3
Bristol Rov	Tr	07/13	13	41	0	13
Northampton T	Tr	06/14	14	24	11	2
Southend U	L	11/14	14	2	0	0

OTSEMOBOR John
Born: Liverpool, England, 23 March, 1983 — RB
England: Youth

League Club	Source	Date Signed	Seasons Played	Apps	Subs	Gls
Liverpool	YT	03/00	03	4	0	0
Hull C	L	03/03	02	8	1	3
Bolton W	L	02/04	03	1	0	0
Crewe Alex	L	09/04	04	14	0	1
Rotherham U	Tr	07/05	05	4	6	0
Crewe Alex	Tr	01/06	05-06	43	0	0
Norwich C	Tr	07/07	07-09	88	5	2
Southampton	Tr	01/10	09	19	0	0
Sheffield Wed	Tr	07/10	10-11	21	5	0
MK Dons	Tr	07/12	12-13	42	2	1
Tranmere Rov	L	11/13	13	2	0	0

OTTA Walter Nicolas
Born: Cordoba, Argentina, 20 December, 1973 — M

League Club	Source	Date Signed	Seasons Played	Apps	Subs	Gls
Walsall	Deportes Temuco (CHL)	11/98	98	6	2	3

OTTEWELL Sidney (Sid)
Born: Horsley, Derbyshire, England, 23 October, 1919 — IF
Died: Eastwood, Nottinghamshire, England, 31 January, 2012

League Club	Source	Date Signed	Seasons Played	Apps	Subs	Gls
Chesterfield	Holbrook MW	11/36	36-46	42	-	12
Birmingham C	Tr	06/47	47	5	-	2
Luton T	Tr	12/47	47	15	-	4
Nottingham F	Tr	07/48	48-49	32	-	3
Mansfield T	Tr	01/50	49-51	67	-	21
Scunthorpe U	Tr	03/52	51-52	30	-	12

OTTO Hendrikus Matheus (Heini)
Born: Amsterdam, Netherlands, 24 August, 1954 — M
Netherlands: 1/U23

League Club	Source	Date Signed	Seasons Played	Apps	Subs	Gls
Middlesbrough	Twente Enschede (NED)	08/81	81-84	163	3	24

OTTO Ricky Junior
Born: Hackney, E London, England, 9 November, 1967 — LW

League Club	Source	Date Signed	Seasons Played	Apps	Subs	Gls
Leyton Orient	Haringey Bor	11/90	90-92	41	15	13
Southend U	Tr	07/93	93-94	63	1	17
Birmingham C	Tr	12/94	94-96	25	21	6
Charlton Ath	L	09/96	96	5	2	0
Peterborough U	L	02/97	96	15	0	4
Notts Co	L	09/97	97	4	0	0

OTTOSSON Ulf Peter
Born: Degerfors, Sweden, 2 July, 1968 — F

League Club	Source	Date Signed	Seasons Played	Apps	Subs	Gls
Norwich C (L)	Norrkoping (SWE)	01/97	96	4	3	1

OTULAKOWSKI Anton
Born: Dewsbury, West Yorkshire, England, 29 January, 1956 — M

League Club	Source	Date Signed	Seasons Played	Apps	Subs	Gls
Barnsley	Ossett T	03/75	74-76	42	0	2
West Ham U	Tr	10/76	76-77	10	7	0
Southend U	Tr	03/79	78-82	161	2	8
Millwall	Tr	03/83	82-85	114	0	14
Crystal Palace	Tr	08/86	86	12	0	1

OUADDOU Abdeslam
Born: Alnif, Morocco, 1 November, 1978 — D
Morocco: 57

League Club	Source	Date Signed	Seasons Played	Apps	Subs	Gls
Fulham	AS Nancy (FRA)	08/01	01-02	13	8	0

[OUBINA] MELENDEZ Borja Oubina
Born: Vigo, Spain, 17 May, 1982 — DM
Spain: 2

League Club	Source	Date Signed	Seasons Played	Apps	Subs	Gls
Birmingham C (L)	Celta Vigo (SPN)	08/07	07	1	1	0

OULARE Souleymane
Born: Conakry, Guinea, 16 October, 1972 — F
Guinea: 16

League Club	Source	Date Signed	Seasons Played	Apps	Subs	Gls
Stoke C	Fenerbahce (TKY)	12/01	01	0	1	0

OUTHART Anthony (Tony)
Born: Scarborough, North Yorkshire, England, 17 September, 1963 — F

League Club	Source	Date Signed	Seasons Played	Apps	Subs	Gls
Scarborough	Bridlington T	11/87	87-88	3	3	1

OUTHWAITE George
Born: Ferryhill, County Durham, England, 19 May, 1928 — G
Died: Spennymoor, County Durham, England, 27 July, 2006

League Club	Source	Date Signed	Seasons Played	Apps	Subs	Gls
Oldham Ath (Am)	Chilton Ath	03/56	55	4	-	0

OUTTERSIDE Mark Jeremy
Born: Hexham, Northumberland, England, 13 January, 1967 — RB

League Club	Source	Date Signed	Seasons Played	Apps	Subs	Gls
Sunderland	App	01/85	86	1	0	0
Darlington	Tr	07/87	87	37	1	0

OVARD Frank Colin
Born: Evesham, Worcestershire, England, 16 December, 1955 — F
England: Semi Pro-3

League Club	Source	Date Signed	Seasons Played	Apps	Subs	Gls
Gillingham	Maidstone U	12/81	81	4	2	0

OVENDALE Mark John
Born: Leicester, England, 22 November, 1973 — G
Died: Pontypridd, Rhondda Cynon Taff, Wales, 29 August, 2011

League Club	Source	Date Signed	Seasons Played	Apps	Subs	Gls
Northampton T	Wisbech T	08/94	94	6	0	0
Bournemouth	Barry T	05/98	98-99	89	0	0
Luton T	Tr	08/00	00-02	44	1	0
York C	Tr	08/03	03	41	0	0

OVER Eric
Born: Sheffield, England, 5 July, 1933 — LW
Died: Peterborough, England, 7 January, 2012

League Club	Source	Date Signed	Seasons Played	Apps	Subs	Gls
Sheffield U	Sheffield FC	11/54	54	2	-	0
Barrow	Tr	01/56	55-57	19	-	1
Oldham Ath	Tr	12/57	57	21	-	2

OVERFIELD Jack
Born: Leeds, England, 14 May, 1932 — LW

League Club	Source	Date Signed	Seasons Played	Apps	Subs	Gls
Leeds U	Yorkshire Amats	05/53	55-59	159	-	20
Sunderland	Tr	08/60	60-62	65	-	5
Peterborough U	Tr	02/63	62	1	-	0
Bradford C	Tr	07/64	64	11	-	0

OVERMARS Marc
Born: Emst, Netherlands, 29 March, 1973 — LW
Netherlands: 86

League Club	Source	Date Signed	Seasons Played	Apps	Subs	Gls
Arsenal	Ajax (NED)	07/97	97-99	91	9	25

OVERSON Richard John
Born: Kettering, Northamptonshire, England, 3 June, 1959 — CD

League Club	Source	Date Signed	Seasons Played	Apps	Subs	Gls
Burnley	App	06/77	77-79	5	1	0
Hereford U	Tr	05/80	80-81	6	5	1

OVERSON Vincent David (Vince)
Born: Kettering, Northamptonshire, England, 15 May, 1962 — CD
England: Youth

League Club	Source	Date Signed	Seasons Played	Apps	Subs	Gls
Burnley	App	11/79	79-85	207	4	6
Birmingham C	Tr	06/86	86-90	179	3	3
Stoke C	Tr	08/91	91-95	167	3	6
Burnley	Tr	08/96	96	6	2	0
Shrewsbury T	L	09/97	97	2	0	0

OVERTON John
Born: Rotherham, South Yorkshire, England, 2 May, 1956 — CD

League Club	Source	Date Signed	Seasons Played	Apps	Subs	Gls
Aston Villa	App	01/74	75	2	1	0
Halifax T	L	03/76	75	14	0	2
Gillingham	Tr	06/76	76-80	177	1	10

OVERTON Paul Henry
Born: Soham, Cambridgeshire, England, 18 April, 1961 — G

League Club	Source	Date Signed	Seasons Played	Apps	Subs	Gls
Ipswich T	App	07/78	77	1	0	0
Peterborough U	Tr	05/79				
Northampton T	Tr	06/80				

OVIEDO Bryan Josue
Born: Quesada, Costa Rica, 18 February, 1990 — LB/M
Costa Rica: 26/Youth

League Club	Source	Date Signed	Seasons Played	Apps	Subs	Gls
Everton	FC Copenhagen (DEN)	08/12	12-14	11	19	2

OWEN Aled Watkin
Born: Brynteg, Anglesey, Wales, 7 January, 1934 — RW

League Club	Source	Date Signed	Seasons Played	Apps	Subs	Gls
Tottenham H	Bangor C	09/53	53	1	-	0
Ipswich T	Tr	07/58	58-61	30	-	3
Wrexham	Tr	07/63	63	3	-	0

OWEN Brian Ernest
Born: Harefield, NW London, England, 2 November, 1944 — W

League Club	Source	Date Signed	Seasons Played	Apps	Subs	Gls
Watford	App	07/62	62-69	148	5	17
Colchester U	Tr	05/70	70-71	11	1	2
Wolverhampton W	Tr	01/72	72	4	0	0

OWEN Brian Gordon
Born: Bath, England, 7 July, 1942 — F

League Club	Source	Date Signed	Seasons Played	Apps	Subs	Gls
Hereford U	Bath C	07/70	72-73	46	11	13

OWEN Bryn
Born: Rochdale, Greater Manchester, England, 25 April, 1939 — RB

League Club	Source	Date Signed	Seasons Played	Apps	Subs	Gls
Rochdale	Turf Hill	08/60	60-61	6	-	0

OWEN Derek William
Born: Shrewsbury, Shropshire, England, 11 March, 1938 — RW

League Club	Source	Date Signed	Seasons Played	Apps	Subs	Gls
Shrewsbury T	Coton Rov	01/57	56-57	13	-	3

OWEN Gareth
Born: Chester, England, 21 October, 1971 — M
Wales: B-1/U21-8

League Club	Source	Date Signed	Seasons Played	Apps	Subs	Gls
Wrexham	YT	07/90	89-00	298	52	36

OWEN Gareth David
Born: Cheadle, Staffordshire, England, 21 September, 1982 — CD
Wales: Youth

League Club	Source	Date Signed	Seasons Played	Apps	Subs	Gls
Stoke C	YT	07/01	03-04	1	4	0
Oldham Ath	L	01/04	03	15	0	1
Torquay U	L	07/04	04	2	3	0
Oldham Ath	Tr	03/05	04-05	26	0	0
Stockport Co	L	07/06	06	39	0	0
Stockport Co	Tr	06/07	07-08	43	1	0
Yeovil T	L	10/08	08	7	0	0
Port Vale	Tr	11/08	08-12	109	5	1

OWEN Gary Alfred
Born: St Helens, Merseyside, England, 7 July, 1958 — M
England: B-7/U21-22/Youth

League Club	Source	Date Signed	Seasons Played	Apps	Subs	Gls
Manchester C	App	08/75	75-78	101	2	19
West Bromwich A	Tr	06/79	79-85	185	2	21
Sheffield Wed	Panionios (GRE)	08/87	87	12	5	0

OWEN Gordon
Born: Barnsley, South Yorkshire, England, 14 June, 1959 — RW

League Club	Source	Date Signed	Seasons Played	Apps	Subs	Gls
Sheffield Wed	Jnr	11/76	77-82	32	15	5
Rotherham U	L	03/80	79	9	0	0
Doncaster Rov	L	11/82	82	9	0	0
Chesterfield	L	03/83	82	6	0	2
Cardiff C	Tr	08/83	83	38	1	14
Barnsley	Tr	08/84	84-85	68	0	25
Bristol C	Tr	08/86	86-87	51	2	11
Hull C	L	12/87	87	3	0	0
Mansfield T	Tr	01/88	87-88	54	4	8
Blackpool	Tr	07/89	89-90	21	8	4
Carlisle U	L	10/90	90	4	1	0
Exeter C	L	12/90	90	4	0	0

OWEN James Vaughan
Born: Caernarfon, Gwynedd, Wales, 14 January, 1991 — M
Wales: Youth

League Club	Source	Date Signed	Seasons Played	Apps	Subs	Gls
Chester C	Sch	08/09	08	4	3	0

OWEN John Leslie (Les)
Born: Hawarden, Flintshire, Wales, 11 April, 1933 — FB

League Club	Source	Date Signed	Seasons Played	Apps	Subs	Gls
Chester C	Saltney Jnrs	07/54	56	1	-	0

OWEN Leslie Terence (Terry)
Born: Liverpool, England, 11 September, 1949 — F/W

League Club	Source	Date Signed	Seasons Played	Apps	Subs	Gls
Everton	App	12/66	67	2	0	0
Bradford C	Tr	06/70	70-71	41	11	6
Chester C	Tr	06/72	72-76	161	15	41
Cambridge U	Tr	08/77	77	1	0	0
Rochdale	Tr	09/77	77-78	80	2	21
Port Vale	Tr	07/79	79	14	4	3

OWEN Maurice
Born: Abingdon, Oxfordshire, England, 4 July, 1924 — CF/CH
Died: Abingdon, Oxfordshire, England, 8 July, 2000

League Club	Source	Date Signed	Seasons Played	Apps	Subs	Gls
Swindon T	Abingdon T	12/46	46-62	555	-	150

OWEN Michael James
Born: Chester, England, 14 December, 1979 — F
England: 89/U21-1/Youth/Schools

League Club	Source	Date Signed	Seasons Played	Apps	Subs	Gls
Liverpool	Jnr	12/96	96-03	193	23	118
Newcastle U	Real Madrid (SPN)	08/05	05-08	58	13	26
Manchester U	Tr	07/09	09-11	6	25	5
Stoke C	Tr	09/12	12	0	8	1

OWEN Neil
Born: Bury, Greater Manchester, England, 14 October, 1959 — M

League Club	Source	Date Signed	Seasons Played	Apps	Subs	Gls
Sheffield Wed	App	-	76	1	0	0

OWEN Robert (Bobby)
Born: Farnworth, Greater Manchester, England, 17 October, 1947 — F

League Club	Source	Date Signed	Seasons Played	Apps	Subs	Gls
Bury	App	08/65	64-67	81	3	36
Manchester C	Tr	07/68	68-69	18	4	3
Swansea C	L	03/70	69	5	1	1
Carlisle U	Tr	06/70	70-76	185	19	51
Northampton T	L	10/76	76	5	0	0
Workington	L	12/76	76	8	0	2
Bury	L	02/77	76	4	0	1
Doncaster Rov	Tr	07/77	77-78	74	3	22

OWEN Robert Gibson (Bobby)
Born: Sunderland, England, 5 May, 1924 — LH
Died: South Shields, Tyne and Wear, England, October, 1999

League Club	Source	Date Signed	Seasons Played	Apps	Subs	Gls
Huddersfield T	Murton CW	04/45				
Lincoln C	Murton CW	01/47	46-54	246	-	5

OWEN Ronald Derek (Derek)
Born: Ellesmere Port, Cheshire, England, 25 September, 1938 — G

League Club	Source	Date Signed	Seasons Played	Apps	Subs	Gls
Chester C (Am)	Ellesmere Port	05/58	58-60	7	-	0

OWEN Sydney William (Syd)
Born: Birmingham, England, 28 February, 1922 — CD
Died: Leeds, England, August, 1998
England: 3/FLge-2

League Club	Source	Date Signed	Seasons Played	Apps	Subs	Gls
Birmingham C	Birmingham YMCA	10/45	46	5	-	0
Luton T	Tr	06/47	47-58	388	-	3

OWEN Trefor
Born: Flint, Wales, 20 February, 1933 — CH
Died: Bath, England, July, 2001
Wales: Amateur

League Club	Source	Date Signed	Seasons Played	Apps	Subs	Gls
Leyton Orient	Tooting & Mitcham U	01/58	58-60	15	-	0

OWEN William (Billy)
Born: Llanfairfechan, Conwy, Wales, 30 June, 1914 — WH/F
Died: Isles of Scilly, England, 14 June, 1976

League Club	Source	Date Signed	Seasons Played	Apps	Subs	Gls
Manchester C	Northwich Victoria	06/34	35	9	-	3
Tranmere Rov	Tr	03/36	35	6	-	4
Newport Co	Tr	06/36	36-46	69	-	5
Exeter C	Tr	10/46	46	20	-	9

OWEN-EVANS Thomas George (Tom)
Born: Bristol, England, 18 March, 1997 — F

League Club	Source	Date Signed	Seasons Played	Apps	Subs	Gls
Newport Co	Sch	05/15	14	0	1	0

OWENS Andrew James
Born: Liverpool, England, 15 October, 1989 — CD

League Club	Source	Date Signed	Seasons Played	Apps	Subs	Gls
Accrington Stan	Rhyl	08/10	10	0	3	0

OWENS Graeme Adam
Born: Cramlington, Northumberland, England, 1 June, 1988 — W

League Club	Source	Date Signed	Seasons Played	Apps	Subs	Gls
Middlesbrough	Sch	07/07				
Chesterfield	L	03/08	07	2	2	0
Blackpool	L	01/09	08	1	7	0

OWENS John Gilbert
Born: Ynysybwl, Rhondda Cynon Taff, Wales, 25 March, 1932 — RH

League Club	Source	Date Signed	Seasons Played	Apps	Subs	Gls
Exeter C	Pontypridd	10/53	53-54	14	-	0
Bournemouth		09/56				

OWENS Thomas Leslie (Les)
Born: Sunderland, England, 17 October, 1919 — CF
Died: Norwich, England, 28 March, 1974

League Club	Source	Date Signed	Seasons Played	Apps	Subs	Gls
Charlton Ath	Washington Chemicals	09/37	37-38	12	-	5
Doncaster Rov	Tr	02/39	38-47	21	-	11
Southport	Tr	12/47	47-48	53	-	11
Hartlepool U	Tr	07/49	49	28	-	12
Norwich C	Tr	03/50	49-50	20	-	8
Reading	Tr	07/51	51	8	-	4
Brighton & HA	Tr	06/52	52	15	-	4

OWER John Campion Taylor (Ian)
Born: Glasgow, Scotland, 2 January, 1939 — G

League Club	Source	Date Signed	Seasons Played	Apps	Subs	Gls
Workington	St Johnstone	02/63	62-67	200	0	0

OWERS Adrian Richard
Born: Danbury, Essex, England, 26 February, 1965 — M

League Club	Source	Date Signed	Seasons Played	Apps	Subs	Gls
Southend U	App	02/83	82-84	19	9	0
Brighton & HA	Chelmsford C	12/87	87-90	32	8	4
Gillingham	L	03/91	90	9	1	0
Maidstone U	Tr	10/91	91	1	0	0

OWERS Gary
Born: Newcastle-upon-Tyne, England, 3 October, 1968 — M/RB
England: FLge

League Club	Source	Date Signed	Seasons Played	Apps	Subs	Gls
Sunderland	App	10/86	87-94	259	9	25
Bristol C	Tr	12/94	94-97	121	5	9
Notts Co	Tr	07/98	98-01	147	7	12

OWERS Philip (Phil)
Born: Bishop Auckland, County Durham, England, 28 April, 1955 — G

League Club	Source	Date Signed	Seasons Played	Apps	Subs	Gls
Darlington	Jnr	06/73	72-74	45	0	0
Gillingham	Tr	07/75	75	2	0	0
Darlington	Tr	07/76	76-79	69	0	0
Hartlepool U	Brandon U	08/87	87	2	0	0

OWUSU Ansah Ossei
Born: Hackney, E London, England, 22 November, 1979 — M

League Club	Source	Date Signed	Seasons Played	Apps	Subs	Gls
Wimbledon	YT	06/98	00	1	3	0
Bristol Rov	L	02/01	00	11	6	0

OWUSU Lloyd Magnus
Born: Slough, Berkshire, England, 12 December, 1976 — F
Ghana: 2

League Club	Source	Date Signed	Seasons Played	Apps	Subs	Gls
Brentford	Slough T	07/98	98-01	148	16	64
Sheffield Wed	Tr	07/02	02-03	24	28	9
Reading	Tr	12/03	03-04	25	16	10
Brentford	Tr	07/05	05-06	43	6	12
Yeovil T	Tr	07/07	07-08	31	16	10
Cheltenham T	Tr	09/08	08	16	6	7
Brighton & HA	L	03/09	08	13	1	7
Barnet	Luton T	09/11	11	0	5	0

OWUSU-ABEYIE Quincy Jamie
Born: Amsterdam, Netherlands, 15 April, 1986 — W
Ghana: 18//Netherlands: U21-7/Youth

League Club	Source	Date Signed	Seasons Played	Apps	Subs	Gls
Arsenal	Sch	07/04	04-05	1	4	0
Birmingham C (L)	Spartak Moscow (RUS)	08/08	08	12	7	2
Cardiff C (L)	Spartak Moscow (RUS)	02/09	08	0	5	0
Portsmouth (L)	Spartak Moscow (RUS)	01/10	09	3	7	0

OXBROW Darren William
Born: Ipswich, England, 1 September, 1969 — CD

League Club	Source	Date Signed	Seasons Played	Apps	Subs	Gls
Ipswich T	YT	06/88				
Maidstone U	Tr	08/89	89-91	84	1	2
Colchester U	Tr	08/92	92	12	4	4
Barnet	Tr	12/92	92	1	0	0

OXFORD Kenneth (Ken)
Born: Oldham, Greater Manchester, England, 14 November, 1929 — G
Died: Nottingham, England, 6 August, 1993
England: Youth

League Club	Source	Date Signed	Seasons Played	Apps	Subs	Gls
Manchester C	Ardwick LC	10/47	47	1	-	0
Derby Co	Tr	01/49				
Chesterfield	RAF	06/50				
Norwich C	Tr	07/51	53-57	128	-	0
Derby Co	Tr	12/57	57-62	151	-	0
Doncaster Rov	Tr	07/64	64	16	-	0
Port Vale	Tr	03/65				

OXLADE-CHAMBERLAIN Alexander Mark David (Alex)
Born: Portsmouth, England, 15 August, 1993 — M
England: 20/U21-8/Youth

League Club	Source	Date Signed	Seasons Played	Apps	Subs	Gls
Southampton	Sch	08/10	09-10	27	9	9
Arsenal	Tr	08/11	11-14	40	38	6

OXLEY Albert
Born: Gateshead, Tyne and Wear, England, 21 October, 1914 — IF
Died: Gateshead, Tyne and Wear, England, December, 1994

League Club	Source	Date Signed	Seasons Played	Apps	Subs	Gls
Gateshead	Windy Nook	01/35	34-46	120	-	25

OXLEY Mark Thomas
Born: Aston, South Yorkshire, England, 2 June, 1990 — G
England: Youth

League Club	Source	Date Signed	Seasons Played	Apps	Subs	Gls
Hull C	Rotherham U (Sch)	08/08	12	0	1	0
Grimsby T	L	02/10	09	3	0	0
Burton A	L	10/12	12	3	0	0
Oldham Ath	L	07/13	13	36	0	0

League Club	Source	Date Signed	Seasons Played	Career Record Apps	Subs	Gls
OXLEY Scott						
Born: Sheffield, England, 22 November, 1976						M
York C	YT	07/95	95	1	1	0
OXTOBY Richard (Dick)						
Born: Chesterfield, Derbyshire, England, 5 September, 1939						CH
Bolton W	Jnr	01/57	59	3	-	0
Tranmere Rov	Tr	07/63	63	5	-	0
OYEBANJO Olanrewaju Olusegun Mark (Lanre)						
Born: Hackney, E London, England, 27 April, 1990						RB
Republic of Ireland: U21-6/Youth						
York C	Histon	06/11	12-13	63	8	0
Crawley T	Tr	06/14	14	26	5	0
OYEDELE Ade Shola (Shola)						
Born: Kano, Nigeria, 14 September, 1984						D
Wimbledon	Sch	-	03	9	0	0
MK Dons	Wimbledon relocation	08/04	04-05	20	8	0
OYELEKE Emmanuel Oyedele Oluwaseun Opeoluwa						
Born: Wandsworth, SW London, England, 24 December, 1992						M
Brentford	Sch	06/12	11	1	0	0
Northampton T	L	01/13	12	1	1	0
OYEN Davy						
Born: Zutendaal, Belgium, 17 July, 1975						LB
Belgium: 3						
Nottingham F	Anderlecht (BEL)	01/03	02-03	4	4	0
OYENUGA Olalekan Kudus (Kudus)						
Born: Walthamstow, NE London, England, 18 March, 1993						F
Tottenham H	Sch	04/11				
Bury	L	08/11	11	0	1	0
OZIL Mesut						
Born: Gelsenkirchen, Germany, 15 October, 1988						M
Germany: 66/U21-16/Youth						
Arsenal	Real Madrid (SPN)	09/13	13-14	46	2	9
OZTUMER Erhan						
Born: Greenwich, SE London, England, 29 May, 1991						M
Peterborough U	Dulwich Hamlet	06/14	14	11	9	1

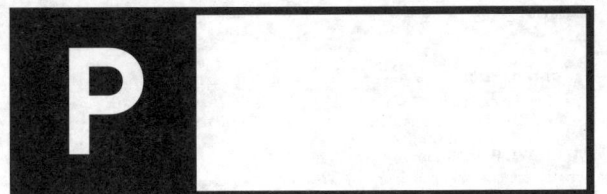

PAATELAINEN Mika Matti Petteri (Mixu)
Born: Helsinki, Finland, 3 February, 1967 — F
Finland: 69

League Club	Source	Date Signed	Seasons Played	Apps	Subs	Gls
Bolton W	Aberdeen	07/94	94-96	58	11	15
Wolverhampton W	Tr	08/97	97	10	13	0

PACE Derek John
Born: Bloxwich, West Midlands, England, 11 March, 1932 — CF
Died: Essington, Staffordshire, England, 17 October, 1989

League Club	Source	Date Signed	Seasons Played	Apps	Subs	Gls
Aston Villa	Bloxwich Strollers	09/49	50-57	98	-	40
Sheffield U	Tr	12/57	57-64	253	-	140
Notts Co	Tr	12/64	64-65	29	0	15
Walsall	Tr	07/66	66	4	1	1

PACEY David (Dave)
Born: Luton, England, 2 October, 1936 — WH
England: U23-1

League Club	Source	Date Signed	Seasons Played	Apps	Subs	Gls
Luton T	Hitchin T	08/56	57-64	246	-	16

PACEY Denis Frank
Born: Feltham, SW London, England, 27 September, 1928 — CF
Died: Chertsey, Surrey, England, 23 March, 2009

League Club	Source	Date Signed	Seasons Played	Apps	Subs	Gls
Leyton Orient	Walton & Hersham	12/51	51-54	120	-	46
Millwall	Tr	10/54	54-58	133	-	37
Aldershot	Tr	09/58	58-59	32	-	13

PACHECO Daniel (Dani)
Born: Malaga, Spain, 5 January, 1991 — F
Spain: U21-2/Youth

League Club	Source	Date Signed	Seasons Played	Apps	Subs	Gls
Liverpool	Sch	02/08	09-10	0	5	0
Norwich C	L	03/11	10	3	3	2

PACK Leonard John (Lenny)
Born: Salisbury, Wiltshire, England, 27 September, 1976 — M

League Club	Source	Date Signed	Seasons Played	Apps	Subs	Gls
Cambridge U	YT	07/95	94-96	5	10	0

PACK Marlon
Born: Portsmouth, England, 25 March, 1991 — M

League Club	Source	Date Signed	Seasons Played	Apps	Subs	Gls
Portsmouth	Sch	07/09	10	0	1	0
Wycombe W	L	08/09	09	7	1	0
Dagenham & Red	L	01/10	09	17	0	1
Cheltenham T	L	08/10	10	32	6	2
Cheltenham T	Tr	07/11	11-12	83	3	12
Bristol C	Tr	07/13	13-14	56	21	3

PACK Roy James
Born: Stoke Newington, N London, England, 20 September, 1946 — RB

League Club	Source	Date Signed	Seasons Played	Apps	Subs	Gls
Arsenal	App	11/63	65	1	0	0
Portsmouth	Tr	07/66	66-68	91	0	0
Oxford U	Tr	05/69				

PACKARD Edgar
Born: Mansfield, Nottinghamshire, England, 7 March, 1919 — CH
Died: Mansfield, Nottinghamshire, England, January, 1996

League Club	Source	Date Signed	Seasons Played	Apps	Subs	Gls
Sheffield Wed	Clipstone Welfare	12/36	46-51	124	-	1
Halifax T	Tr	08/52	52-53	85	-	0

PACKER Leslie John (Les)
Born: Sunderland, England, 8 April, 1959 — F

League Club	Source	Date Signed	Seasons Played	Apps	Subs	Gls
Doncaster Rov		09/78	78-79	5	2	2

PACKER Michael David (Mike)
Born: Willesden, NW London, England, 20 April, 1950 — D

League Club	Source	Date Signed	Seasons Played	Apps	Subs	Gls
Watford	App	04/68	68-72	57	11	2
Crewe Alex	L	03/72	71	12	0	0
Colchester U	Tr	07/73	73-82	337	7	20

PACKER Norman James
Born: Ynysybwl, Rhondda Cynon Taff, Wales, 14 June, 1931 — WH
Died: Exmouth, Devon, England, 25 September, 2009

League Club	Source	Date Signed	Seasons Played	Apps	Subs	Gls
Exeter C	Pontypridd	07/55	55-60	18	-	0

PACKHAM William Joseph (Will)
Born: Brighton, England, 13 January, 1981 — G

League Club	Source	Date Signed	Seasons Played	Apps	Subs	Gls
Brighton & HA	YT	06/99	00-01	1	1	0

PACKWOOD William James (Will)
Born: Concord, Massachusetts, USA, 21 May, 1993 — CD
USA: U23-3/Youth

League Club	Source	Date Signed	Seasons Played	Apps	Subs	Gls
Birmingham C	Sch	07/11	12-14	17	1	0
Bristol Rov	L	10/13	13	8	0	0
Colchester U	L	11/14	14	1	0	0
Cheltenham T	L	03/15	14	5	0	1

PACQUETTE Richard Francis
Born: Kilburn, NW London, England, 28 January, 1983 — F

League Club	Source	Date Signed	Seasons Played	Apps	Subs	Gls
Queens Park Rgrs	YT	02/00	00-03	13	18	6
Mansfield T	L	02/04	03	3	2	1
MK Dons	Tr	09/04	04	1	4	0
Brentford	Fisher Ath	11/04	04	1	0	0

PADDON Graham Charles
Born: Manchester, England, 24 August, 1950 — M
Died: Great Yarmouth, Norfolk, England, 19 November, 2007
England: U23-1

League Club	Source	Date Signed	Seasons Played	Apps	Subs	Gls
Coventry C	App	05/68	68-69	3	2	1
Norwich C	Tr	10/69	69-73	162	0	19
West Ham U	Tr	12/73	73-76	115	0	11
Norwich C	Tr	11/76	76-81	126	2	6
Millwall	L	12/81	81	5	0	1

PADELLI Daniele
Born: Lecco, Italy, 25 October, 1985 — G
Italy: U21-1/Youth

League Club	Source	Date Signed	Seasons Played	Apps	Subs	Gls
Liverpool (L)	Sampdoria (ITA)	01/07	06	1	0	0

PADOVANI Romain
Born: Nice, France, 15 October, 1989 — DM

League Club	Source	Date Signed	Seasons Played	Apps	Subs	Gls
Portsmouth	AS Monaco (FRA)	07/13	13	11	7	1

PADOVANO Michele
Born: Turin, Italy, 28 August, 1966 — F
Italy: 1

League Club	Source	Date Signed	Seasons Played	Apps	Subs	Gls
Crystal Palace	Juventus (ITA)	11/97	97-98	8	4	1

PADULA Diego Gino Mauro (Gino)
Born: Buenos Aires, Argentina, 11 July, 1976 — LB

League Club	Source	Date Signed	Seasons Played	Apps	Subs	Gls
Walsall	Xerez CD (SPN)	11/99	99	23	2	0
Wigan Ath	Tr	07/00	00	2	2	0
Queens Park Rgrs	Tr	07/02	02-04	81	9	4
Nottingham F	Tr	07/05	05	3	0	0

PAGAL Jean-Claude
Born: Yaounde, Cameroon, 15 September, 1964 — D
Cameroon: 17

League Club	Source	Date Signed	Seasons Played	Apps	Subs	Gls
Carlisle U		02/98	97	1	0	0

PAGE Donald Richard (Don)
Born: Manchester, England, 18 January, 1964 — F

League Club	Source	Date Signed	Seasons Played	Apps	Subs	Gls
Wigan Ath	Runcorn	03/89	88-90	62	12	15
Rotherham U	Tr	08/91	91-92	40	15	13
Rochdale	L	02/93	92	3	1	1
Doncaster Rov	Tr	11/93	93	18	4	4
Chester C	Tr	07/94	94	22	8	5
Scarborough	Tr	08/95	95	26	11	5

PAGE Jack Keith
Born: Purley, S London, England, 16 December, 1989 — M

League Club	Source	Date Signed	Seasons Played	Apps	Subs	Gls
Leyton Orient	Sch	-	06	0	1	0

PAGE John
Born: Frimley Green, Surrey, England, 21 October, 1934 — D
Died: Fair Oak, Hampshire, England, July, 2006

League Club	Source	Date Signed	Seasons Played	Apps	Subs	Gls
Southampton	Jnr	10/51	52-60	190	-	24

PAGE Malcolm Edward
Born: Knucklas, Powys, Wales, 5 February, 1947 — D/M
Wales: 28/U23-6/Schools

League Club	Source	Date Signed	Seasons Played	Apps	Subs	Gls
Birmingham C	App	09/64	64-80	328	8	8
Oxford U	Tr	02/81	80-81	14	0	1

PAGE Raymond Michael (Mick)
Born: Swindon, England, 26 September, 1930 — LB

League Club	Source	Date Signed	Seasons Played	Apps	Subs	Gls
Swindon T	Vickers Armstrong	04/51	50-54	32	-	0

PAGE Robert John (Rob)
Born: Llwynypia, Rhondda Cynon Taff, Wales, 3 September, 1974 — CD
Wales: 41/B-1/U21-6/Youth/Schools

League Club	Source	Date Signed	Seasons Played	Apps	Subs	Gls
Watford	YT	04/93	93-00	209	7	2
Sheffield U	Tr	08/01	01-03	106	1	1
Cardiff C	Tr	07/04	04	8	1	0
Coventry C	Tr	02/05	04-06	69	1	1
Huddersfield T	Tr	01/08	07	18	0	1
Chesterfield	Tr	07/08	08-10	54	2	1

PAGE Sam Terry
Born: Purley, S London, England, 30 October, 1987 — LB

League Club	Source	Date Signed	Seasons Played	Apps	Subs	Gls
MK Dons	Sch	07/06	06	0	1	0

PAHARS Marian
Born: Zolotonosha, Ukraine, 5 August, 1976 — F
Latvia: 75

League Club	Source	Date Signed	Seasons Played	Apps	Subs	Gls
Southampton	Skonto Riga (LAT)	03/99	98-05	110	27	43

PAINE Terence Lionel (Terry)
Born: Winchester, Hampshire, England, 23 March, 1939 — RW
England: 19/FLge-5/U23-4

League Club	Source	Date Signed	Seasons Played	Apps	Subs	Gls
Southampton	Winchester C	02/57	56-73	709	4	160
Hereford U	Tr	08/74	74-76	106	5	8

PAINTER Edward George (Eddie)
Born: Swindon, England, 23 June, 1921 — WH
Died: Swindon, England, 16 March, 2001

League Club	Source	Date Signed	Seasons Played	Apps	Subs	Gls
Swindon T	Marlborough Army Camp	10/38	46-50	77	-	0

PAINTER Ian John
Born: Wombourne, Staffordshire, England, 28 December, 1964 — F
England: U21-1/Youth

League Club	Source	Date Signed	Seasons Played	Apps	Subs	Gls
Stoke C	App	12/82	82-85	105	8	20
Coventry C	Tr	07/86	86	0	3	0

PAINTER Marcos David
Born: Solihull, West Midlands, England, 17 August, 1986 — LB
Republic of Ireland: U21-7/Youth

League Club	Source	Date Signed	Seasons Played	Apps	Subs	Gls
Birmingham C	Sch	07/05	05-06	3	2	0
Swansea C	Tr	11/06	06-09	66	2	0
Brighton & HA	Tr	01/10	09-12	89	1	1
Bournemouth	L	02/13	12	2	0	0
Portsmouth	Tr	08/13	13	17	0	0

PAINTER Peter Robert (Robbie)
Born: Wigan, Greater Manchester, England, 26 January, 1971 — F

League Club	Source	Date Signed	Seasons Played	Apps	Subs	Gls
Chester C	YT	07/88	87-90	58	26	8
Maidstone U	Tr	08/91	91	27	3	5
Burnley	Tr	03/92	91-92	16	10	2
Darlington	Tr	09/93	93-96	104	11	28
Rochdale	Tr	10/96	96-98	101	11	30
Halifax T	Tr	07/99	99-00	46	12	8

PAINTER Trevor Alfred
Born: Norwich, England, 2 July, 1949 — CH
Died: Drayton, Norfolk, England, 9 April, 2012

League Club	Source	Date Signed	Seasons Played	Apps	Subs	Gls
Norwich C	App	07/67	67	2	0	0
Colchester U	Tr	05/70	70	1	0	0

PAINTSIL John
Born: Berekum, Ghana, 15 June, 1981 — RB
Ghana: 88

League Club	Source	Date Signed	Seasons Played	Apps	Subs	Gls
West Ham U	Hapoel Tel Aviv (ISR)	08/06	06-07	7	12	0
Fulham	Tr	07/08	08-10	74	1	0
Leicester C	Tr	07/11	11	4	2	0

PAISLEY Robert (Bob)
Born: Hetton-le-Hole, Tyne and Wear, England, 23 January, 1919 — WH
Died: Knowsley, Merseyside, England, 14 February, 1996

League Club	Source	Date Signed	Seasons Played	Apps	Subs	Gls
Liverpool	Bishop Auckland	05/39	46-53	253	-	10

PALACIOS Wilson Roberto
Born: La Ceiba, Honduras, 29 July, 1984 — DM
Honduras: 95

League Club	Source	Date Signed	Seasons Played	Apps	Subs	Gls
Birmingham C (L)	Olimpia (HON)	08/07	07	4	3	0
Wigan Ath	Olimpia (HON)	01/08	07-08	37	0	0
Tottenham H	Tr	01/09	08-10	56	9	1
Stoke C	Tr	08/11	11-13	14	24	0

PALADINO Giuseppe (Joe)
Born: St Helens, Merseyside, England, 21 August, 1965 — G

League Club	Source	Date Signed	Seasons Played	Apps	Subs	Gls
Wigan Ath	St Helens T	12/90	90	7	0	0

PALAZUELOS Ruben
Born: Santander, Spain, 11 April, 1983 — DM

League Club	Source	Date Signed	Seasons Played	Apps	Subs	Gls
Yeovil T	FC Honka (FIN)	02/14	13	6	3	0

PALETHORPE Christopher Glynne (Chris)
Born: Maidenhead, Berkshire, England, 6 November, 1942 — RW
Died: Windsor, Berkshire, England, 21 May, 2010

League Club	Source	Date Signed	Seasons Played	Apps	Subs	Gls
Reading	Jnr	11/59	60-62	55	-	10
Aldershot	Tr	06/63	63-64	56	-	4

PALETHORPE Philip John (Phil)
Born: Liverpool, England, 17 September, 1986 — G

League Club	Source	Date Signed	Seasons Played	Apps	Subs	Gls
Tranmere Rov	Sch	09/03				
Chester C	Tr	08/06	07	0	1	0

PALETTA Gabriel Alejandro
Born: Buenos Aires, Argentina, 15 February, 1986 — CD
Argentina: Youth//Italy: 3

League Club	Source	Date Signed	Seasons Played	Apps	Subs	Gls
Liverpool	Atletic Banfield (ARG)	07/06	06	2	1	0

PALFREYMAN George Barry
Born: Sheffield, England, 13 March, 1933 — G

League Club	Source	Date Signed	Seasons Played	Apps	Subs	Gls
Halifax T (Am)	Sheffield FC	01/54	53	1	-	0

PALGRAVE Brian Uriel
Born: Birmingham, England, 12 July, 1966 — F

League Club	Source	Date Signed	Seasons Played	Apps	Subs	Gls
Walsall	Alvechurch	07/84	84-87	5	3	1

PALIN Grenville
Born: Armthorpe, South Yorkshire, England, 13 February, 1940 — RB

League Club	Source	Date Signed	Seasons Played	Apps	Subs	Gls
Wolverhampton W	Jnr	03/57				
Walsall	Tr	07/60	60-63	130	-	10

PALIN Leigh Grenville
Born: Worcester, England, 12 September, 1965 — M
England: Youth

League Club	Source	Date Signed	Seasons Played	Apps	Subs	Gls
Aston Villa	App	09/83				
Shrewsbury T	L	12/84	84	2	0	0
Nottingham F	Tr	11/85				
Bradford C	Tr	10/86	86-88	65	6	10
Stoke C	Tr	09/89	89	17	2	3
Hull C	Tr	03/90	89-91	57	0	7
Rochdale	L	10/91	91	3	0	0
Burnley	Tr	10/92	92	1	0	0

PALIOS Markos (Mark)
Born: Birkenhead, Wirral, England, 9 November, 1952 — M

League Club	Source	Date Signed	Seasons Played	Apps	Subs	Gls
Tranmere Rov	Jnr	07/73	73-79	177	13	25
Crewe Alex	Tr	01/80	79-82	114	4	23
Tranmere Rov	Tr	03/83	82-84	55	4	7

PALLISTER Gary Andrew
Born: Ramsgate, Kent, England, 30 June, 1965 — CD
England: 22/B-9/FLge

League Club	Source	Date Signed	Seasons Played	Apps	Subs	Gls
Middlesbrough	Billingham T	11/84	85-89	156	0	5
Darlington	L	10/85	85	7	0	0
Manchester U	Tr	08/89	89-97	314	3	12
Middlesbrough	Tr	07/98	98-00	55	0	1

PALLISTER Gordon
Born: Howden-le-Wear, County Durham, England, 2 April, 1917 — LB
Died: Barnsley, South Yorkshire, England, 24 November, 1999
England: FLge-1

League Club	Source	Date Signed	Seasons Played	Apps	Subs	Gls
Bradford C	Willington Jnrs	05/34	37-38	28	-	0
Barnsley	Tr	10/38	38-51	220	-	3

PALMER Aiden Witting
Born: Enfield, N London, England, 2 January, 1987 — LB

League Club	Source	Date Signed	Seasons Played	Apps	Subs	Gls
Leyton Orient	Sch	07/06	04-08	42	5	0
Dagenham & Red	L	01/09	08	3	0	0

PALMER Ashley John
Born: Pontefract, West Yorkshire, England, 9 November, 1992 — CD

League Club	Source	Date Signed	Seasons Played	Apps	Subs	Gls
Scunthorpe U	Sch	07/11	11	0	1	0

PALMER Calvin Ian
Born: Skegness, Lincolnshire, England, 21 October, 1940 — WH
Died: Brighton, England, 12 March, 2014

League Club	Source	Date Signed	Seasons Played	Apps	Subs	Gls
Nottingham F	Skegness T	03/58	58-63	91	-	14
Stoke C	Tr	09/63	63-67	165	0	24
Sunderland	Tr	02/68	67-69	35	5	5
Crewe Alex	Hellenic (RSA)	10/71	71	2	0	0

PALMER Carlton Lloyd
Born: Rowley Regis, West Midlands, England, 5 December, 1965 — M
England: 18/B-5/U21-4

League Club	Source	Date Signed	Seasons Played	Apps	Subs	Gls
West Bromwich A	App	12/84	85-88	114	7	4
Sheffield Wed	Tr	02/89	88-93	204	1	14
Leeds U	Tr	06/94	94-96	100	2	5
Southampton	Tr	09/97	97-98	44	1	3
Nottingham F	Tr	01/99	98-99	14	2	1
Coventry C	Tr	09/99	99-00	27	3	1
Watford	L	12/00	00	5	0	0
Sheffield Wed	L	02/01	00	12	0	0
Sheffield Wed	L	09/01	01	10	0	0
Stockport Co	Tr	11/01	01-02	42	1	4
Mansfield T	Dublin C (ROI)	08/05	05	1	0	0

PALMER Charles Anthony (Charlie)
Born: Aylesbury, Buckinghamshire, England, 10 July, 1963 — RB

League Club	Source	Date Signed	Seasons Played	Apps	Subs	Gls
Watford	App	07/81	83	10	0	1
Derby Co	Tr	07/84	84-85	51	0	2
Hull C	Tr	02/87	86-88	69	1	1
Notts Co	Tr	02/89	88-93	178	4	7
Walsall	Tr	07/94	94-95	54	0	2

PALMER Christopher Louis (Chris)
Born: Derby, England, 16 October, 1983 — LB/M

League Club	Source	Date Signed	Seasons Played	Apps	Subs	Gls
Derby Co	Sch	07/03				

League Club	Source	Date Signed	Seasons Played	Career Record Apps	Subs	Gls
Notts Co	Tr	07/04	04-05	48	6	5
Wycombe W	Tr	07/06	06-07	23	10	0
Darlington	L	08/07	07	4	0	0
Walsall	Tr	08/08	08	41	3	1
Gillingham	Tr	07/09	09-10	34	4	5
Burton A	Tr	07/11	11-12	23	20	3
PALMER David John						
Born: Bristol, England, 10 April, 1961						FB
Died: Bristol, England, 2 March, 2011						
Bristol Rov	App	01/79	78	1	0	0
PALMER Desmond Frederick (Des)						
Born: Swansea, Wales, 23 September, 1931						CF
Wales: 3						
Swansea C	Jnr	04/50	52-58	84	-	38
Liverpool	Tr	03/59				
Derby Co	Jo'burg Ramblers (RSA)	06/61	61	18	-	6
PALMER Frank						
Born: Sunderland, England, 29 October, 1923						LW
Gateshead (Am)	Bishop Auckland	02/51	50	2	-	1
PALMER Geoffrey (Geoff)						
Born: Barnsley, South Yorkshire, England, 12 November, 1940						FB
Bristol C	Doncaster Rov (Am)	08/58	61	1	-	0
PALMER Geoffrey (Geoff)						
Born: Cannock, Staffordshire, England, 11 July, 1954						RB
England: U23-12						
Wolverhampton W	App	07/72	73-84	389	5	13
Burnley	Tr	11/84	84-85	34	0	0
Wolverhampton W	Tr	12/85	85-86	21	1	0
PALMER Jermaine Ashley Clifton						
Born: Derby, England, 28 August, 1986						F
Stoke C	Sch	01/05	03-04	0	4	0
Grimsby T	Tr	07/05				
PALMER John Neville						
Born: Bristol, England, 1 July, 1958						M
Bristol C	Weston-super-Mare	03/83	82	2	6	0
PALMER Lee James						
Born: Gillingham, Kent, England, 19 September, 1970						LB
Gillingham	YT	07/89	87-94	109	11	5
Cambridge U	Tr	08/95	95-96	30	1	1
PALMER Leslie						
Born: Barrow, Cumbria, England, 16 December, 1923						WH
Died: Barrow, Cumbria, England, December, 2002						
Barrow	Holker Central OB	10/49	49	1	-	0
PALMER Leslie James (Les)						
Born: Birmingham, England, 5 September, 1971						F
West Bromwich A	YT	07/90	90-91	5	3	1
PALMER Liam Jordan						
Born: Worksop, Nottinghamshire, England, 19 September, 1991						RB/M
Scotland: U21-8/Youth						
Sheffield Wed	Sch	07/10	10-14	78	19	1
Tranmere Rov	L	07/12	12	42	1	0
PALMER Marcus James						
Born: Gloucester, England, 6 November, 1988						F
Hereford U	Cheltenham T (Sch)	08/06	06-07	1	3	0
PALMER Matthew Thomas (Matt)						
Born: Derby, England, 27 February, 1995						M
Burton A	Sch	07/13	12-14	52	23	4
PALMER Oliver James (Ollie)						
Born: Epsom, Surrey, England, 21 January, 1992						F
Mansfield T	Havant & Waterlooville	07/13	13-14	22	32	5
PALMER Roger Neil						
Born: Manchester, England, 30 January, 1959						F
Manchester C	App	01/77	77-80	22	9	9
Oldham Ath	Tr	11/80	80-93	419	47	141
PALMER Ryan Warren John						
Born: Dulwich, S London, England, 2 February, 1980						FB
Fulham	YT	07/98				
Brighton & HA	Tr	07/99	99	1	0	0
PALMER Stephen Leonard (Steve)						
Born: Brighton, England, 31 March, 1968						CD/M
England: Schools						
Ipswich T	Cambridge Univ	08/89	89-95	87	24	2
Watford	Tr	09/95	95-00	222	13	8
Queens Park Rgrs	Tr	07/01	01-03	116	11	9
MK Dons	Tr	07/04	04-05	28	6	1

League Club	Source	Date Signed	Seasons Played	Career Record Apps	Subs	Gls
PALSSON Guolaugur Victor (Victor)						
Born: Reykjavik, Iceland, 30 April, 1991						DM
Iceland: 4/U21-11						
Liverpool	Aarhus GF (DEN)	01/09				
Dagenham & Red	L	11/10	10	2	0	0
PAMAROT Louis Noe (Noe)						
Born: Paris, France, 14 April, 1979						D
Portsmouth (L)	OGC Nice (FRA)	09/99	99	1	1	0
Tottenham H	OGC Nice (FRA)	08/04	04-05	23	2	1
Portsmouth	Tr	01/06	05-08	50	15	3
PAMMENT Michael Ian (Mike)						
Born: Huddersfield, West Yorkshire, England, 12 May, 1945						CF
Died: Dewsbury, West Yorkshire, England, 16 July, 2006						
England: Youth						
Bradford C (Am)	Kirkburton YC	07/64	64	1	-	0
PAMPHLETT Tony John						
Born: Westminster, Central London, England, 13 April, 1960						CD
Maidstone U	Dartford	07/86	89	7	0	0
PANAYI Sofroni James (Jimmy)						
Born: Hammersmith, W London, England, 24 January, 1980						D
Watford	YT	07/98	99-01	10	3	0
PANAYIOTOU Harrison Andreas (Harry)						
Born: Leicester, England, 28 October, 1994						F
St Kitts & Nevis: 2						
Leicester C	Sch	04/12	11	0	1	1
PANCRATE Fabrice						
Born: Paris, France, 2 May, 1980						RW
Newcastle U	Paris St-Germain (FRA)	11/09	09	5	11	1
PANDIANI Walter Gerardo						
Born: Montevideo, Uruguay, 27 April, 1976						F
Uruguay: 4						
Birmingham C	Depo la Coruna (SPN)	02/05	04-05	20	11	6
PANES Simon Michael						
Born: Almondsbury, Avon, England, 22 February, 1960						F
Bristol C	Melksham T	08/82	82	2	2	0
PANOPOULOS Mikael (Mike)						
Born: Melbourne, Australia, 9 October, 1976						W
Greece: U21						
Portsmouth	Aris Salonika (GRE)	09/99	99-01	45	9	7
PANTER Derek						
Born: Blackpool, Lancashire, England, 22 November, 1943						IF
Died: Worsley, Greater Manchester, England, 13 August, 2013						
Manchester C	West Bromwich A (Am)	08/62	63	1	-	0
Torquay U	Tr	05/64	64	5	-	1
Southport	Tr	07/65				
PANTHER Emmanuel Ugochukwa Ezenwa (Manny)						
Born: Glasgow, Scotland, 11 May, 1984						M
Exeter C	York C	06/08	08	15	7	2
Morecambe	L	08/09	09	14	5	0
Aldershot T	Tr	07/10	10-11	20	4	0
PANTILIMON Costel Fane						
Born: Bacau, Romania, 1 February, 1987						G
Romania: 20/U21-2/Youth						
Manchester C	Poli Timisoara (ROM)	08/11	13	7	0	0
Sunderland	Tr	06/14	14	28	0	0
PANUCCI Christian						
Born: Savona, Italy, 12 April, 1973						RB
Italy: 57/U21-19						
Chelsea (L)	Inter Milan (ITA)	08/00	00	7	1	0
PAPACONSTANTINOU Loukas						
Born: Toronto, Canada, 10 May, 1974						G
Darlington	Alabama Saints (USA)	07/97	97	1	0	0
PAPADOPOULOS Dimitrios						
Born: Tashkent, Uzbekistan, 20 October, 1981						F
Greece: 22/U21-27/Youth						
Burnley	Akratitos (GRE)	07/01	01-02	7	33	3
PAPAVASILIOU Nicodemos (Nicky)						
Born: Limassol, Cyprus, 31 August, 1970						LW
Cyprus: 38						
Newcastle U	OF Iraklion (GRE)	07/93	93	7	0	0
[PAPA WAIGO] N'DIAYE Papa Waigo						
Born: Saint-Louis, Senegal, 20 January, 1984						W/F
Senegal: 15						
Southampton (L)	Fiorentina (ITA)	09/09	09	11	24	5

PAPE Andrew Maurice (Andy)
Born: Hammersmith, W London, England, 22 March, 1962 G
England: Semi Pro-15

League Club	Source	Date Signed	Seasons Played	Apps	Subs	Gls
Queens Park Rgrs	Feltham	03/80	79	1	0	0
Barnet	Enfield	08/91	91-93	40	0	0

PAPPOE Daniel Mills
Born: Accra, Ghana, 30 December, 1993 CD
Ghana: Youth

League Club	Source	Date Signed	Seasons Played	Apps	Subs	Gls
Chelsea	Sch	07/11				
Colchester U	L	07/13	13	0	2	0
Brighton & HA	Tr	08/14				

PARDEW Alan Scott
Born: Wimbledon, SW London, England, 18 July, 1961 M

League Club	Source	Date Signed	Seasons Played	Apps	Subs	Gls
Crystal Palace	Yeovil T	03/87	87-91	111	17	8
Charlton Ath	Tr	11/91	91-94	98	6	24
Barnet	Tr	07/95	95-96	64	3	0

PARDOE Glyn
Born: Winsford, Cheshire, England, 1 June, 1946 LB
England: U23-4/Schools

League Club	Source	Date Signed	Seasons Played	Apps	Subs	Gls
Manchester C	App	06/63	61-74	303	2	17

PAREDES Juan Carlos
Born: Esmeraldas, Ecuador, 8 July, 1987 RB
Ecuador: 52

League Club	Source	Date Signed	Seasons Played	Apps	Subs	Gls
Watford	Barcelona DG (ECU)	07/14	14	32	7	0

PAREJO Daniel
Born: Madrid, Spain, 16 April, 1989 M
Spain: U21-19/Youth

League Club	Source	Date Signed	Seasons Played	Apps	Subs	Gls
Queens Park Rgrs (L)	Real Madrid (SPN)	08/08	08	10	4	0

PARFITT Henry Edward (Harry)
Born: Cardiff, Wales, 26 September, 1929 RB
Died: Newport, Wales, 17 October, 2012

League Club	Source	Date Signed	Seasons Played	Apps	Subs	Gls
Cardiff C		05/49	53	1	-	0
Torquay U	L	10/52	52	28	-	0
Torquay U	L	08/53	53	30	-	0

PARIS Alan David
Born: Slough, Berkshire, England, 15 August, 1964 LB

League Club	Source	Date Signed	Seasons Played	Apps	Subs	Gls
Watford	Slough T	11/82				
Peterborough U	Tr	08/85	85-87	135	2	2
Leicester C	Tr	07/88	88-90	80	8	3
Notts Co	Tr	01/91	90-91	39	3	1

PARISH Elliot Charles
Born: Towcester, Northamptonshire, England, 20 May, 1990 G
England: Youth

League Club	Source	Date Signed	Seasons Played	Apps	Subs	Gls
Aston Villa	Sch	07/08				
Lincoln C	L	03/11	10	9	0	0
Cardiff C	Tr	09/11				
Wycombe W	L	09/12	12	2	0	0
Bristol C	Tr	07/13	13	19	0	0
Newport Co	L	02/14	13	7	0	0
Blackpool	Tr	08/14	14	12	1	0

PARK Cameron
Born: Marske, Cleveland, England, 6 July, 1992 LW
Scotland: U21-1/Youth

League Club	Source	Date Signed	Seasons Played	Apps	Subs	Gls
Middlesbrough	Sch	12/10	10	0	4	0
Barnsley	L	08/11	11	1	2	0
Crewe Alex	L	02/14	13	3	1	0

PARK Chu-Young
Born: Daegu, South Korea, 10 July, 1985 F
South Korea: 68/U23/Youth

League Club	Source	Date Signed	Seasons Played	Apps	Subs	Gls
Arsenal	AS Monaco (FRA)	08/11	11	0	1	0
Watford	L	01/14	13	1	1	0

PARK Colin Sidney John
Born: Swansea, Wales, 8 February, 1945 G

League Club	Source	Date Signed	Seasons Played	Apps	Subs	Gls
Swansea C	Jnr	09/63	63	1	-	0

PARK Ji-Sung
Born: Seoul, South Korea, 25 February, 1981 M
South Korea: 101

League Club	Source	Date Signed	Seasons Played	Apps	Subs	Gls
Manchester U	PSV Eindhoven (NED)	07/05	05-11	93	40	19
Queens Park Rgrs	Tr	07/12	12	15	5	0

PARK Robert (Bobby)
Born: Douglas, Lanarkshire, Scotland, 7 April, 1930 G
Died: Glasgow, Scotland, 12 September, 1998

League Club	Source	Date Signed	Seasons Played	Apps	Subs	Gls
Crewe Alex	Airdrieonians	08/55	55-56	61	-	0

PARK Robert (Bobby)
Born: Coatbridge, Lanarkshire, Scotland, 5 January, 1952 M

League Club	Source	Date Signed	Seasons Played	Apps	Subs	Gls
Sunderland	Jnr	01/69	69-71	50	14	4

PARK Robert Clydesdale (Bobby)
Born: Edinburgh, Scotland, 3 July, 1946 M

League Club	Source	Date Signed	Seasons Played	Apps	Subs	Gls
Aston Villa	App	07/63	64-68	60	14	7
Wrexham	Tr	05/69	69-71	98	4	8
Peterborough U	Tr	06/72	72	15	3	1
Northampton T	Tr	02/73	72-73	21	3	0
Hartlepool U	Tr	07/74	74	14	3	0

PARK Terence Charles (Terry)
Born: Liverpool, England, 7 February, 1957 M

League Club	Source	Date Signed	Seasons Played	Apps	Subs	Gls
Wolverhampton W	Jnr	03/74				
Stockport Co	Blackpool (NC)	07/76	76-79	87	3	8
Stockport Co	Minnesota Kicks (USA)	03/81	80-82	72	0	7
Manchester C	L	01/83	82	0	2	0
Bury	Tr	07/83	83	18	3	1

PARK William
Born: Gateshead, Tyne and Wear, England, 23 February, 1919 CH
Died: North Tyneside, Tyne and Wear, England, August, 1999

League Club	Source	Date Signed	Seasons Played	Apps	Subs	Gls
Blackpool	Felling Red Star	05/38	38	2	-	0
York C	Tr	09/46	46	22	-	1

PARKE John
Born: Bangor, Down, Northern Ireland, 6 August, 1937 FB
Died: Belfast, Northern Ireland, 27 August, 2011
Northern Ireland: 14/NILge-5

League Club	Source	Date Signed	Seasons Played	Apps	Subs	Gls
Sunderland	Hibernian	11/64	64-67	83	2	0

PARKER Albert Edward
Born: Liverpool, England, 13 September, 1927 FB
Died: Wrexham, Wales, 29 October, 2005

League Club	Source	Date Signed	Seasons Played	Apps	Subs	Gls
Crewe Alex	South Liverpool	12/48	48-51	113	-	0
Wrexham	Tr	11/51	51-58	216	-	1

PARKER Alexander Hershaw (Alex)
Born: Kirkconnel, Dumfries & Galloway, Scotland, 2 August, 1935 RB
Died: Gretna, Dumfries & Galloway, Scotland, 7 January, 2010
Scotland: 15/SLge-9/U23-6

League Club	Source	Date Signed	Seasons Played	Apps	Subs	Gls
Everton	Falkirk	06/58	58-64	198	-	5
Southport	Tr	09/65	65-67	76	0	0

PARKER Benjamin Brian Colin (Ben)
Born: Pontefract, West Yorkshire, England, 8 November, 1987 LB
England: Youth

League Club	Source	Date Signed	Seasons Played	Apps	Subs	Gls
Leeds U	Sch	11/04	07-10	32	7	0
Bradford C	L	07/06	06	35	4	0
Darlington	L	02/08	07	13	0	0
Carlisle U	L	01/12	11	5	0	1

PARKER Brian Thomas
Born: Chorley, Lancashire, England, 4 August, 1955 G
England: Semi Pro-1

League Club	Source	Date Signed	Seasons Played	Apps	Subs	Gls
Crewe Alex	Jnr	08/72	73	26	0	0
Arsenal	Tr	08/75				

PARKER Carl
Born: Burnley, Lancashire, England, 25 March, 1971 M

League Club	Source	Date Signed	Seasons Played	Apps	Subs	Gls
Rochdale	Rossendale U	02/92	91-92	9	7	1

PARKER Derek Sevastapool
Born: Wivenhoe, Essex, England, 23 June, 1926 RH
Died: Colchester, Essex, England, 8 April, 2011

League Club	Source	Date Signed	Seasons Played	Apps	Subs	Gls
West Ham U	Grays Ath	10/44	46-56	199	-	9
Colchester U	Tr	03/57	56-60	130	-	1

PARKER Garry Stuart
Born: Oxford, England, 7 September, 1965 M
England: B-1/U21-6/Youth

League Club	Source	Date Signed	Seasons Played	Apps	Subs	Gls
Luton T	App	05/83	82-85	31	11	3
Hull C	Tr	02/86	85-87	82	2	8
Nottingham F	Tr	03/88	87-91	99	4	17
Aston Villa	Tr	11/91	91-94	91	4	13
Leicester C	Tr	02/95	94-98	89	25	10

PARKER Graham Sydney
Born: Coventry, England, 23 May, 1946 M
England: Schools

League Club	Source	Date Signed	Seasons Played	Apps	Subs	Gls
Aston Villa	App	05/63	63-67	16	1	1
Rotherham U	Tr	12/67	67	3	0	0
Lincoln C	Tr	07/68	68	4	1	0
Exeter C	Tr	03/69	68-73	180	1	12
Torquay U	Tr	05/74	74-75	41	2	3

PARKER Harold (Harry)
Born: Blackburn, Greater Manchester, England, 8 February, 1933 RW

League Club	Source	Date Signed	Seasons Played	Apps	Subs	Gls
Blackburn Rov	Lower Darwen YC	08/51	51	3	-	0

PARKER Henry Clifford (Cliff)
Born: Denaby, South Yorkshire, England, 6 September, 1913 LW
Died: Isle of Wight, England, 1983

League Club	Source	Date Signed	Seasons Played	Apps	Subs	Gls
Doncaster Rov	Denaby U	08/31	31-33	52	-	11
Portsmouth	Tr	12/33	33-50	242	-	57

PARKER Herbert Derrick (Derrick)
Born: Wallsend, Tyne and Wear, England, 7 February, 1957 — F

League Club	Source	Date Signed	Seasons Played	Apps	Subs	Gls
Burnley	App	02/74	74-75	5	1	2
Southend U	Tr	02/77	76-79	129	3	43
Barnsley	Tr	02/80	79-82	104	3	32
Oldham Ath	Tr	08/83	83-84	54	3	11
Doncaster Rov	L	12/84	84	5	0	1
Burnley	Tr	10/85	85-86	43	0	10
Rochdale	Haka Valkeakoski (FIN)	10/87	87	6	1	1

PARKER Jeffrey Samuel (Jeff)
Born: Liverpool, England, 23 January, 1969 — M

League Club	Source	Date Signed	Seasons Played	Apps	Subs	Gls
Crewe Alex	YT	07/87	87	7	3	0

PARKER John William
Born: Birkenhead, Wirral, England, 5 July, 1925 — IF
Died: Blackpool, Lancashire, England, August, 1988

League Club	Source	Date Signed	Seasons Played	Apps	Subs	Gls
Everton	St Lawrence CYMS	12/48	50-55	167	-	82
Bury	Tr	05/56	56-58	82	-	43

PARKER Joseph Connor (Joe)
Born: Gloucester, England, 11 March, 1995 — F

League Club	Source	Date Signed	Seasons Played	Apps	Subs	Gls
Newport Co	Gloucester C	11/13	14	0	4	0

PARKER Joshua Kevin Stanley (Josh)
Born: Slough, Berkshire, England, 1 December, 1990 — W
Antigua & Barbuda: 16

League Club	Source	Date Signed	Seasons Played	Apps	Subs	Gls
Queens Park Rgrs	Sch	07/09	09-10	1	4	0
Northampton T	L	10/10	10	3	0	0
Wycombe W	L	11/10	10	0	1	0
Oldham Ath	Tr	08/11	11	7	6	0
Dagenham & Red	L	03/12	11	6	2	0
Oxford U	Windsor	12/12	12	5	10	0

PARKER Keigan
Born: Livingston, West Lothian, Scotland, 8 June, 1982 — F
Scotland: U21-1/Youth

League Club	Source	Date Signed	Seasons Played	Apps	Subs	Gls
Blackpool	St Johnstone	07/04	04-07	96	45	34
Huddersfield T	Tr	07/08	08	14	6	2
Hartlepool U	L	03/09	08	9	0	0
Oldham Ath	Tr	07/09	09	17	10	2
Bury	L	03/10	09	2	0	0

PARKER Kevin James
Born: Plymouth, England, 20 September, 1979 — F

League Club	Source	Date Signed	Seasons Played	Apps	Subs	Gls
Norwich C	YT	06/99				
Torquay U	Tr	08/00	00-01	8	9	2

PARKER Martin Thomas
Born: Exeter, England, 18 October, 1970 — M

League Club	Source	Date Signed	Seasons Played	Apps	Subs	Gls
Exeter C	YT	-	88	0	1	0

PARKER Neil
Born: Blackburn, Greater Manchester, England, 19 October, 1957 — FB

League Club	Source	Date Signed	Seasons Played	Apps	Subs	Gls
Leeds U	App	10/75	77	0	1	0

PARKER Patrick John (Pat)
Born: Bow, E London, England, 15 July, 1929 — CH
Died: Southampton, England, 28 January, 2014

League Club	Source	Date Signed	Seasons Played	Apps	Subs	Gls
Southampton	Newton Abbot	08/51	51-58	132	-	0

PARKER Paul Andrew
Born: West Ham, E London, England, 4 April, 1964 — D
England: 19/B-3/U21-8/Youth

League Club	Source	Date Signed	Seasons Played	Apps	Subs	Gls
Fulham	App	04/82	80-86	140	13	2
Queens Park Rgrs	Tr	06/87	87-90	121	4	1
Manchester U	Tr	08/91	91-95	100	5	1
Derby Co	Tr	08/96	96	4	0	0
Sheffield U	Tr	11/96	96	7	3	0
Fulham	Tr	01/97	96	3	0	0
Chelsea	Tr	03/97	96	1	3	0

PARKER Raymond Dennis (Ray)
Born: Doncaster, South Yorkshire, England, 27 January, 1925 — LB
Died: Rotherham, South Yorkshire, England, January, 2006

League Club	Source	Date Signed	Seasons Played	Apps	Subs	Gls
Chesterfield	Thurcroft	02/45	47	14	-	0
Sheffield Wed	Tr	04/48	48	1	-	0
Bradford C	Buxton	06/51	51-52	41	-	1

PARKER Reginald Ernest Arundel (Reg)
Born: Pontyclun, Rhondda Cynon Taff, Wales, 10 June, 1921 — CF
Died: Bridgend, Wales, 27 June, 1997
Wales: WLge-2

League Club	Source	Date Signed	Seasons Played	Apps	Subs	Gls
Cardiff C		11/46	47	2	-	0
Newport Co	Tr	08/48	48-53	201	-	99

PARKER Richard John
Born: Wolverhampton, England, 6 July, 1973 — F

League Club	Source	Date Signed	Seasons Played	Apps	Subs	Gls
Walsall	Cradley T	09/92	92	0	1	0

PARKER Robert (Bobby)
Born: Coventry, England, 11 November, 1952 — CD
England: Youth

League Club	Source	Date Signed	Seasons Played	Apps	Subs	Gls
Coventry C	App	05/70	69-73	77	3	0
Carlisle U	Tr	06/74	74-83	373	2	6

PARKER Robert William (Bob)
Born: Seaham, County Durham, England, 26 November, 1935 — RB

League Club	Source	Date Signed	Seasons Played	Apps	Subs	Gls
Huddersfield T	Murton CW	06/54	59-64	65	-	0
Barnsley	Tr	07/65	65-68	108	0	0

PARKER Samuel (Sam)
Born: Liverpool, England, 5 April, 1924 — RB/CF

League Club	Source	Date Signed	Seasons Played	Apps	Subs	Gls
Accrington Stan	Marine	07/48	48	13	-	6
Barnsley	Tr	12/48				
Accrington Stan	Tr	09/49	49-50	36	-	6
Crewe Alex	Tr	11/50	50-51	41	-	5

PARKER Scott Matthew
Born: Lambeth, S London, England, 13 October, 1980 — DM
England: 18/U21-12/Youth/Schools

League Club	Source	Date Signed	Seasons Played	Apps	Subs	Gls
Charlton Ath	YT	10/97	97-03	104	24	9
Norwich C	L	10/00	00	6	0	1
Chelsea	Tr	01/04	03-04	8	7	1
Newcastle U	Tr	06/05	05-06	54	1	4
West Ham U	Tr	06/07	07-11	109	4	10
Tottenham H	Tr	08/11	11-12	43	7	0
Fulham	Tr	08/13	13-14	62	4	5

PARKER Sean
Born: Newcastle-upon-Tyne, England, 23 August, 1973 — M

League Club	Source	Date Signed	Seasons Played	Apps	Subs	Gls
Northampton T	YT	07/91	91-92	9	1	0

PARKER Sonny
Born: Middlesbrough, England, 28 February, 1983 — RB
England: Youth

League Club	Source	Date Signed	Seasons Played	Apps	Subs	Gls
Birmingham C	YT	04/99				
Bristol Rov	Tr	12/02	02-03	26	4	1

PARKER Stanley Frederick (Stan)
Born: Worksop, Nottinghamshire, England, 31 July, 1920 — IF
Died: Bury St Edmunds, Suffolk, England, 14 November, 1994

League Club	Source	Date Signed	Seasons Played	Apps	Subs	Gls
Ipswich T	Worksop L Brigade OB	05/46	46-50	126	-	43
Norwich C	Tr	08/51				

PARKER Stuart John
Born: Preston, Lancashire, England, 16 February, 1954 — F

League Club	Source	Date Signed	Seasons Played	Apps	Subs	Gls
Blackpool	App	04/72	72-74	10	6	2
Southend U	Tr	07/75	75-76	62	2	23
Chesterfield	Tr	02/77	76-77	30	4	8
Blackburn Rov	Sparta Rotterdam (NED)	07/79	79	5	4	1
Bury	KV Mechelen (BEL)	09/82	82	26	8	9
Chester C	Tr	09/83	83	9	0	5
Stockport Co	Drogheda (ROI)	02/84	83	0	1	0

PARKER Stuart Kevin
Born: Nantwich, Cheshire, England, 13 April, 1963 — G

League Club	Source	Date Signed	Seasons Played	Apps	Subs	Gls
Wrexham	Jnr	08/81	82-84	31	0	0

PARKER Terence James (Terry)
Born: Southampton, England, 20 December, 1983 — M

League Club	Source	Date Signed	Seasons Played	Apps	Subs	Gls
Portsmouth	Sch	03/03				
Oxford U	Tr	07/04	04	6	2	0

PARKER Thomas Robertson (Tommy)
Born: Hartlepool, Cleveland, England, 13 February, 1924 — LH/IF
Died: Ipswich, England, 18 March, 1996

League Club	Source	Date Signed	Seasons Played	Apps	Subs	Gls
Ipswich T	HMS Ganges	08/46	46-56	428	-	86

PARKER Walter
Born: Doncaster, South Yorkshire, England, 28 June, 1929 — FB
Died: Doncaster, South Yorkshire, England, May, 2004

League Club	Source	Date Signed	Seasons Played	Apps	Subs	Gls
Hull C	Jnr	08/47				
Crewe Alex	Tr	08/51	51-55	59	-	0

PARKER Wesley Jaye (Wes)
Born: Skegness, Lincolnshire, England, 7 December, 1983 — FB

League Club	Source	Date Signed	Seasons Played	Apps	Subs	Gls
Grimsby T	Sch	07/02	02-03	1	8	0

PARKER William (Bill)
Born: Liverpool, England, 15 August, 1925 — IF/LW

League Club	Source	Date Signed	Seasons Played	Apps	Subs	Gls
Reading	Runcorn	06/50	50-52	32	-	6
Swindon T	Tr	02/53	52	10	-	0
Exeter C	Tr	07/53	53	18	-	2

League Club	Source	Date Signed	Seasons Played	Career Record Apps	Subs	Gls

PARKER William Frederick (Bill)
Born: Liverpool, England, 29 March, 1932 CH
Died: Prenton, Merseyside, England, 20 December, 2012

League Club	Source	Date Signed	Seasons Played	Apps	Subs	Gls
Liverpool	Burscough	04/53				
Southport	Shelbourne (ROI)	07/59	59	9	-	0

PARKER William Thomas (Billy)
Born: Bolsover, Derbyshire, England, 6 October, 1920 G
Died: Chesterfield, Derbyshire, England, 1953

League Club	Source	Date Signed	Seasons Played	Apps	Subs	Gls
Crewe Alex		07/47	47-48	18	-	0

PARKES Alan
Born: Hartlepool, Cleveland, England, 12 January, 1929 CF
Died: Stockton-on-Tees, Cleveland, England, 14 April, 2013

League Club	Source	Date Signed	Seasons Played	Apps	Subs	Gls
Charlton Ath	Murton CW	10/49				
Darlington	Tonbridge	03/55	54	1	-	0

PARKES Barry Joseph
Born: Hartlepool, Cleveland, England, 21 January, 1940 IF

League Club	Source	Date Signed	Seasons Played	Apps	Subs	Gls
Hartlepool U	Easington CW	11/60	60-62	29	-	7
Reading		10/63				

PARKES Henry Arthur (Harry)
Born: Birmingham, England, 4 January, 1920 FB
Died: Solihull, West Midlands, England, 4 March, 2009

League Club	Source	Date Signed	Seasons Played	Apps	Subs	Gls
Aston Villa	Boldmere St Michael's	04/39	46-54	320	-	3

PARKES Jordan David
Born: Watford, Hertfordshire, England, 26 July, 1989 LB
England: Youth

League Club	Source	Date Signed	Seasons Played	Apps	Subs	Gls
Watford	Sch	02/07	08	1	0	0
Brentford	L	01/08	07	0	1	0
Barnet	L	03/08	07	7	3	0
Barnet	Tr	07/10	10-11	48	3	1

PARKES Philip (Phil)
Born: West Bromwich, West Midlands, England, 14 July, 1947 G

League Club	Source	Date Signed	Seasons Played	Apps	Subs	Gls
Wolverhampton W	Jnr	09/64	66-77	303	0	0

PARKES Philip Benjamin Neil Frederick (Phil)
Born: Sedgley, West Midlands, England, 8 August, 1950 G
England: 1/B-1/U23-6/U21-1

League Club	Source	Date Signed	Seasons Played	Apps	Subs	Gls
Walsall	Brierley Hill Alliance	01/68	68-69	52	0	0
Queens Park Rgrs	Tr	06/70	70-78	344	0	0
West Ham U	Tr	02/79	78-89	344	0	0
Ipswich T	Tr	08/90	90	3	0	0

PARKES Sidney (Sid)
Born: Hartlepool, Cleveland, England, 20 September, 1919 G
Died: Hartlepool, Cleveland, England, October, 1989

League Club	Source	Date Signed	Seasons Played	Apps	Subs	Gls
Hartlepool U	Hetton U	08/46	46-47	6	-	0

PARKES Thomas Peter Wilson (Tom)
Born: Sutton-in-Ashfield, Nottinghamshire, England, 15 January, 1992 CD

League Club	Source	Date Signed	Seasons Played	Apps	Subs	Gls
Leicester C	Sch	10/09				
Burton A	L	01/10	09	21	1	1
Yeovil T	L	11/10	10	0	1	0
Burton A	L	03/11	10	4	1	0
Burton A	L	07/11	11	4	0	0
Bristol Rov	Tr	02/12	11-13	98	0	2

PARKES Tony
Born: Sheffield, England, 5 May, 1949 M

League Club	Source	Date Signed	Seasons Played	Apps	Subs	Gls
Blackburn Rov	Buxton	05/70	70-80	345	5	38

PARKHILL James Archibald
Born: Belfast, Northern Ireland, 27 July, 1934 G

League Club	Source	Date Signed	Seasons Played	Apps	Subs	Gls
Exeter C	Cliftonville	09/63	63	1	-	0

PARKHOUSE Richard McDonald
Born: Calne, Wiltshire, England, 30 August, 1914 FB
Died: Chippenham, Wiltshire, England, 29 June, 1992

League Club	Source	Date Signed	Seasons Played	Apps	Subs	Gls
Swindon T	Calne & Harris	10/35	35-46	27	-	0

PARKIN Albert Geoffrey (Geoffrey)
Born: Mansfield, Nottinghamshire, England, 11 April, 1928 F
Died: Chesterfield, Derbyshire, England, November, 2008

League Club	Source	Date Signed	Seasons Played	Apps	Subs	Gls
Derby Co	Jnr	05/46	49	9	-	0

PARKIN Brian
Born: Birkenhead, Wirral, England, 12 October, 1965 G

League Club	Source	Date Signed	Seasons Played	Apps	Subs	Gls
Oldham Ath	Jnr	03/83	83-84	6	0	0
Crewe Alex	Tr	11/84	84-87	98	0	0
Crystal Palace	Tr	07/88	88-89	20	0	0
Bristol Rov	Tr	11/89	89-95	241	0	0
Wycombe W	Tr	07/96	96-97	25	0	0
Notts Co	Tr	10/98	98	1	0	0
Bristol Rov	Yeovil T	10/99	99-00	2	3	0

PARKIN Derek
Born: Newcastle-upon-Tyne, England, 2 January, 1948 RB
England: FLge-1/U23-5

League Club	Source	Date Signed	Seasons Played	Apps	Subs	Gls
Huddersfield T	Jnr	05/65	64-67	60	1	1
Wolverhampton W	Tr	02/68	67-81	500	1	6
Stoke C	Tr	03/82	81-82	40	0	0

PARKIN Herbert Buttery
Born: Sheffield, England, 10 April, 1920 LB
Died: Sheffield, England, July, 1992

League Club	Source	Date Signed	Seasons Played	Apps	Subs	Gls
Sheffield U	Atlas & Norfolk	04/42	47-50	35	-	0
Chesterfield	Tr	08/51	51-52	55	-	0

PARKIN Jonathan (Jon)
Born: Barnsley, South Yorkshire, England, 30 December, 1981 F

League Club	Source	Date Signed	Seasons Played	Apps	Subs	Gls
Barnsley	YT	01/99	98-01	8	2	0
Hartlepool U	L	12/01	01	0	1	0
York C	Tr	02/02	01-03	64	10	14
Macclesfield T	Tr	02/04	03-05	63	2	30
Hull C	Tr	01/06	05-06	40	7	11
Stoke C	L	03/07	06	5	1	3
Stoke C	Tr	07/07	07	4	25	2
Preston NE	Tr	08/08	08-10	72	29	28
Cardiff C	Tr	01/11	10	2	9	1
Doncaster Rov	L	09/11	11	4	1	0
Huddersfield T	L	11/11	11	2	1	0
Scunthorpe U	L	02/12	11	13	1	6
Fleetwood T	Tr	06/12	12-13	28	25	17

PARKIN Maurice
Born: Sheffield, England, 8 September, 1949 RB

League Club	Source	Date Signed	Seasons Played	Apps	Subs	Gls
Leeds U	App	10/67				
Shrewsbury T	Tr	07/68	68	4	1	0

PARKIN Samuel (Sam)
Born: Roehampton, SW London, England, 14 March, 1981 F
England: Schools//Scotland: B-1

League Club	Source	Date Signed	Seasons Played	Apps	Subs	Gls
Chelsea	Jnr	08/98				
Millwall	L	09/00	00	5	2	4
Wycombe W	L	11/00	00	5	3	1
Oldham Ath	L	03/01	00	3	4	3
Northampton T	L	07/01	01	31	9	4
Swindon T	Tr	08/02	02-04	120	4	67
Ipswich T	Tr	07/05	05-06	17	5	5
Luton T	Tr	08/06	06-08	34	16	10
Leyton Orient	L	10/08	08	12	1	0
Walsall	Tr	07/09	09	7	17	3
Exeter C	St Mirren	07/13	13	17	9	3

PARKIN Stephen John (Steve)
Born: Mansfield, Nottinghamshire, England, 7 November, 1965 M/FB
England: U21-5/Youth/Schools

League Club	Source	Date Signed	Seasons Played	Apps	Subs	Gls
Stoke C	App	11/83	82-88	104	9	5
West Bromwich A	Tr	06/89	89-91	44	4	2
Mansfield T	Tr	07/92	92-95	84	3	3

PARKIN Thomas Aitchison (Tommy)
Born: Gateshead, Tyne and Wear, England, 1 February, 1956 M

League Club	Source	Date Signed	Seasons Played	Apps	Subs	Gls
Ipswich T	App	12/73	77-86	52	18	0
Grimsby T	L	03/76	75	6	0	0
Peterborough U	L	07/76	76	3	0	0

PARKIN Timothy John (Tim)
Born: Penrith, Cumbria, England, 31 December, 1957 CD

League Club	Source	Date Signed	Seasons Played	Apps	Subs	Gls
Blackburn Rov	App	03/76	76-78	13	0	0
Bristol Rov	Malmo FF (SWE)	08/81	81-85	205	1	12
Swindon T	Tr	07/86	86-89	109	1	6
Port Vale	Tr	12/89	89-91	41	7	1
Shrewsbury T	L	09/91	91	5	0	0
Darlington	Tr	08/92	92	40	0	2

PARKINSON Alan
Born: Dagenham, E London, England, 12 April, 1945 G

League Club	Source	Date Signed	Seasons Played	Apps	Subs	Gls
Leyton Orient (Am)	Aveley	03/67	66	1	0	0

PARKINSON Alan
Born: Normanton, West Yorkshire, England, 5 May, 1932 CF
Died: Pontefract, West Yorkshire, England, 7 September, 2002

League Club	Source	Date Signed	Seasons Played	Apps	Subs	Gls
Bradford Park Ave	Jnr	10/50	51-54	13	-	4

PARKINSON Alfred (Alf)
Born: Camden, N London, England, 30 April, 1922 RH
Died: Barnet, N London, England, August, 2003

League Club	Source	Date Signed	Seasons Played	Apps	Subs	Gls
Queens Park Rgrs		09/43	46-50	76	-	5

PARKINSON Allan Arnold
Born: Longton, Lancashire, England, 19 July, 1933 RB

League Club	Source	Date Signed	Seasons Played	Apps	Subs	Gls
Southport	Leyland Motors	08/53	53-58	106	-	0

League Club	Source	Date Signed	Seasons Played	Apps	Subs	Gls

PARKINSON Andrew James (Andy)
Born: Johannesburg, South Africa, 5 May, 1959 — RM
USA: 2

League Club	Source	Date Signed	Seasons Played	Apps	Subs	Gls
Newcastle U	Highlands Park (RSA)	03/78	77-78	0	3	0
Peterborough U	Tr	08/79	79	12	1	5

PARKINSON Andrew John (Andy)
Born: Liverpool, England, 27 May, 1979 — RW

League Club	Source	Date Signed	Seasons Played	Apps	Subs	Gls
Tranmere Rov	Liverpool (YT)	04/97	97-02	102	62	18
Sheffield U	Tr	07/03	03	3	4	0
Notts Co	L	01/04	03	5	0	3
Notts Co	L	03/04	03	5	4	0
Grimsby T	Tr	07/04	04-05	75	10	12
Notts Co	Tr	06/06	06-07	51	17	5
Accrington Stan	Gateshead	07/10	10	10	8	2

PARKINSON Daniel James (Dan)
Born: Preston, Lancashire, England, 2 November, 1992 — W

League Club	Source	Date Signed	Seasons Played	Apps	Subs	Gls
Morecambe	Jnr	07/11	11-12	0	6	0

PARKINSON Eric
Born: Longridge, Lancashire, England, 14 December, 1930 — WH

League Club	Source	Date Signed	Seasons Played	Apps	Subs	Gls
Preston NE	Longridge U	02/51				
Southport	Tr	06/56	57	4	-	0

PARKINSON Gary Anthony
Born: Thornaby, Cleveland, England, 10 January, 1968 — RB

League Club	Source	Date Signed	Seasons Played	Apps	Subs	Gls
Middlesbrough	Everton (Jnr)	01/86	86-92	194	8	5
Southend U	L	10/92	92	6	0	0
Bolton W	Tr	03/93	92-93	1	2	0
Burnley	Tr	01/94	93-96	134	1	4
Preston NE	Tr	05/97	97-00	82	2	6
Blackpool	Tr	03/01	00-01	22	2	0

PARKINSON John
Born: Trimdon, County Durham, England, 2 June, 1953 — M

League Club	Source	Date Signed	Seasons Played	Apps	Subs	Gls
Hartlepool U (Am)	Trimdon Village	09/71	71	1	0	0

PARKINSON Joseph Simon (Joe)
Born: Eccles, Greater Manchester, England, 11 June, 1971 — M

League Club	Source	Date Signed	Seasons Played	Apps	Subs	Gls
Wigan Ath	YT	04/89	88-92	115	4	6
Bournemouth	Tr	07/93	93	30	0	1
Everton	Tr	03/94	94-96	88	2	3

PARKINSON Keith James
Born: Preston, Lancashire, England, 28 January, 1956 — CD

League Club	Source	Date Signed	Seasons Played	Apps	Subs	Gls
Leeds U	App	02/73	75-80	25	6	0
Hull C	L	11/81	81	0	1	0
Doncaster Rov	Tr	01/82	81	5	0	0

PARKINSON Noel David
Born: Hull, England, 16 November, 1959 — M
England: Youth

League Club	Source	Date Signed	Seasons Played	Apps	Subs	Gls
Ipswich T	App	12/76				
Bristol Rov	L	11/79	79	5	0	1
Brentford	L	02/80	79	9	1	0
Mansfield T	Tr	07/80	80-81	66	4	13
Scunthorpe U	Tr	08/82	82-83	39	2	7
Colchester U	Tr	08/84	84-85	79	0	13

PARKINSON Philip John (Phil)
Born: Chorley, Lancashire, England, 1 December, 1967 — M

League Club	Source	Date Signed	Seasons Played	Apps	Subs	Gls
Southampton	App	12/85				
Bury	Tr	03/88	87-91	133	12	5
Reading	Tr	07/92	92-02	332	30	20

PARKINSON Stephen (Steve)
Born: Lincoln, England, 27 August, 1974 — M

League Club	Source	Date Signed	Seasons Played	Apps	Subs	Gls
Lincoln C	YT	05/93	92-93	1	4	0

PARKINSON Stuart George
Born: Fleetwood, Lancashire, England, 18 February, 1976 — M

League Club	Source	Date Signed	Seasons Played	Apps	Subs	Gls
Blackpool	Preston NE (YT)	03/94	94	0	1	0

PARKS Albert
Born: Lurgan, Armagh, Northern Ireland, 9 February, 1926 — IF

League Club	Source	Date Signed	Seasons Played	Apps	Subs	Gls
Notts Co	Glenavon	11/45	46-47	30	-	4

PARKS Anthony (Tony)
Born: Hackney, E London, England, 28 January, 1963 — G

League Club	Source	Date Signed	Seasons Played	Apps	Subs	Gls
Tottenham H	App	09/80	81-87	37	0	0
Oxford U	L	10/86	86	5	0	0
Gillingham	L	09/87	87	2	0	0
Brentford	Tr	08/88	88-90	71	0	0
Fulham	Tr	02/91	90	2	0	0
West Ham U	Tr	08/91	91	6	0	0
Stoke C	Tr	08/92	92	2	0	0
Blackpool	Falkirk	09/96				
Burnley	Tr	08/97				
Doncaster Rov	L	02/98	97	6	0	0
Scarborough	Barrow	02/99	98	15	0	0
Halifax T	Tr	07/99	99-00	5	1	0

PARKS John Alfred
Born: Wath-on-Dearne, South Yorkshire, England, 14 September, 1943 — CF

League Club	Source	Date Signed	Seasons Played	Apps	Subs	Gls
Sheffield U	App	11/60	63	1	-	0
Halifax T	Tr	09/66	66-67	41	0	14

PARLANE Derek James
Born: Helensburgh, Argyll & Bute, Scotland, 5 May, 1953 — F
Scotland: 12/SLge-2/U23-5/U21-1

League Club	Source	Date Signed	Seasons Played	Apps	Subs	Gls
Leeds U	Glasgow Rangers	03/80	79-82	45	5	10
Manchester C	Tr	08/83	83-84	47	1	20
Swansea C	Tr	01/85	84	21	0	3
Rochdale	Racing Jet (BEL)	12/86	86-87	42	0	10

PARLOUR Raymond (Ray)
Born: Romford, E London, England, 7 March, 1973 — M
England: 10/B-1/U21-12

League Club	Source	Date Signed	Seasons Played	Apps	Subs	Gls
Arsenal	YT	03/91	91-03	282	57	22
Middlesbrough	Tr	07/04	04-05	43	3	0
Hull C	Tr	02/07	06	14	1	0

PARMENTER Steven James (Steve)
Born: Chelmsford, England, 22 January, 1977 — F

League Club	Source	Date Signed	Seasons Played	Apps	Subs	Gls
Queens Park Rgrs	Southend U (YT)	05/95				
Bristol Rov	Tr	07/96	96-97	11	7	2

PARMENTER Terence Leslie (Terry)
Born: Romford, E London, England, 21 October, 1947 — LW/RB

League Club	Source	Date Signed	Seasons Played	Apps	Subs	Gls
Fulham	App	11/64	64-68	18	0	1
Leyton Orient	Tr	02/69	68-70	34	3	3
Gillingham	Tr	08/71	71-72	48	1	0

PARNABY Stuart
Born: Bishop Auckland, County Durham, England, 19 July, 1982 — RB
England: U21-4/Youth/Schools

League Club	Source	Date Signed	Seasons Played	Apps	Subs	Gls
Middlesbrough	YT	07/99	02-06	73	18	2
Halifax T	L	10/00	00	6	0	0
Birmingham C	Tr	07/07	07-10	34	13	0
Middlesbrough	Tr	07/12	12-13	11	6	0
Hartlepool U	Tr	06/14	14	5	0	0

PARNABY Thomas William (Tom)
Born: South Shields, Tyne and Wear, England, 6 January, 1922 — IF
Died: Totnes, Devon, England, 4 December, 2004

League Club	Source	Date Signed	Seasons Played	Apps	Subs	Gls
Plymouth Arg	Jnr	07/39				
Oldham Ath	Tr	02/47	47	7	-	1

PARNELL Denis Russell
Born: Farnborough, Hampshire, England, 17 January, 1940 — LW
England: Youth

League Club	Source	Date Signed	Seasons Played	Apps	Subs	Gls
Aldershot	West Bromwich A (Am)	08/58	58-60	66	-	11
Norwich C	Tr	07/61	61	2	-	0

PARNELL Francis William (Frank)
Born: Birkenhead, Wirral, England, 4 November, 1935 — CF

League Club	Source	Date Signed	Seasons Played	Apps	Subs	Gls
Tranmere Rov		01/56	55-56	4	-	3

PARNELL Roy
Born: Birkenhead, Wirral, England, 8 October, 1943 — RB

League Club	Source	Date Signed	Seasons Played	Apps	Subs	Gls
Everton	Jnr	10/60	60-63	3	-	0
Tranmere Rov	Tr	08/64	64-66	105	0	2
Bury	Tr	02/67	66-69	97	0	2

PARODI Leslie Vincent (Les)
Born: Lambeth, S London, England, 1 April, 1954 — LB

League Club	Source	Date Signed	Seasons Played	Apps	Subs	Gls
Bournemouth	Slough T	09/72	73-74	45	4	2

PARR Gordon John
Born: Bristol, England, 6 December, 1938 — WH

League Club	Source	Date Signed	Seasons Played	Apps	Subs	Gls
Bristol C	Jnr	02/57	57-71	281	6	4

PARR Henry Edward (Harry)
Born: Newark, Nottinghamshire, England, 23 October, 1915 — IF
Died: West Bridgford, Nottinghamshire, England, June, 2004
England: Amateur-1

League Club	Source	Date Signed	Seasons Played	Apps	Subs	Gls
Lincoln C (Am)	Ransome & Marles	08/46	46-50	112	-	13

PARR Jack (Jackie)
Born: Derby, England, 21 November, 1920 — LB
Died: Derby, England, 28 March, 1985

League Club	Source	Date Signed	Seasons Played	Apps	Subs	Gls
Derby Co	Holbrook St Michael's	03/38	46-52	112	-	0
Shrewsbury T	Tr	07/53	53-55	112	-	0

PARR John Barry
Born: Weston-super-Mare, Somerset, England, 23 November, 1942 — G

League Club	Source	Date Signed	Seasons Played	Apps	Subs	Gls
Nottingham F	Ransome & Marles	11/62	63	1	-	0

PARR Jonathan
Born: Oslo, Norway, 21 October, 1988 — LB

League Club	Source	Date Signed	Seasons Played	Career Record Apps	Subs	Gls

Norway: 9/U21-18

League Club	Source	Date Signed	Seasons Played	Apps	Subs	Gls
Crystal Palace	Aalesunds FK (NOR)	08/11	11-13	75	17	2
Ipswich T	Tr	07/14	14	24	7	2

PARR Stephen Valentine (Steve)
Born: Bamber Bridge, Lancashire, England, 22 December, 1926 — FB

League Club	Source	Date Signed	Seasons Played	Apps	Subs	Gls
Liverpool	Farington Villa	05/48	51-52	20	-	0
Exeter C	Tr	05/55	55-56	8	-	0
Rochdale	Tr	12/56	56-57	16	-	1

PARR Trevor William
Born: Bradford, England, 21 December, 1961 — D

League Club	Source	Date Signed	Seasons Played	Apps	Subs	Gls
Birmingham C	App	12/79				
Bradford C	Tr	07/80				
Huddersfield T	Tr	11/80				
Peterborough U	Boston U	11/84	84	0	1	0

PARRETT Dean Gary
Born: Hampstead, NW London, England, 16 November, 1991 — M
England: Youth

League Club	Source	Date Signed	Seasons Played	Apps	Subs	Gls
Tottenham H	Sch	12/08				
Aldershot T	L	09/09	09	4	0	0
Plymouth Arg	L	08/10	10	5	3	1
Charlton Ath	L	03/11	10	9	0	1
Yeovil T	L	01/12	11	9	1	0
Swindon T	L	03/13	12	3	0	0
Stevenage	Tr	10/13	13-14	36	6	5

PARRINO Elian Franco
Born: Perez, Argentina, 3 September, 1988 — RB

League Club	Source	Date Signed	Seasons Played	Apps	Subs	Gls
Sheffield U	Estudiantes (ARG)	09/10	10	7	1	0

PARRIS George Michael
Born: Ilford, E London, England, 11 September, 1964 — M/FB
England: Schools

League Club	Source	Date Signed	Seasons Played	Apps	Subs	Gls
West Ham U	App	09/82	84-92	211	28	12
Birmingham C	Tr	03/93	92-94	36	3	1
Brentford	L	08/94	94	5	0	0
Bristol C	L	12/94	94	6	0	0
Brighton & HA	L	02/95	94	18	0	2
Brighton & HA	Norrkoping (SWE)	09/95	95-96	55	1	3
Southend U	Tr	08/97	97	1	0	0

PARRISH Andrew Michael (Andy)
Born: Bolton, Greater Manchester, England, 22 June, 1988 — RB

League Club	Source	Date Signed	Seasons Played	Apps	Subs	Gls
Bury	Sch	09/05	05-07	29	14	1
Morecambe	Tr	07/08	08-14	220	16	1

PARRISH Donald Arthur (Don)
Born: Bilston, West Midlands, England, 22 November, 1944 — IF

League Club	Source	Date Signed	Seasons Played	Apps	Subs	Gls
Wrexham	Jnr	06/63	62-65	4	0	0

PARRISH Sean
Born: Wrexham, Wales, 14 March, 1972 — M

League Club	Source	Date Signed	Seasons Played	Apps	Subs	Gls
Shrewsbury T	YT	07/90	89-90	1	2	0
Doncaster Rov	Telford U	05/94	94-95	64	2	8
Northampton T	Tr	08/96	96-99	103	6	13
Chesterfield	Tr	07/00	00-01	44	11	11
Kidderminster Hrs	Tr	07/02	02-03	37	19	8

PARROTT John Frank
Born: Scunthorpe, North Lincolnshire, England, 5 June, 1934 — IF

League Club	Source	Date Signed	Seasons Played	Apps	Subs	Gls
Scunthorpe U		12/55	55	1	-	0

PARRY Anthony John (Tony)
Born: Burton-on-Trent, Staffordshire, England, 8 September, 1945 — CD
Died: Stafford, England, 23 November, 2009

League Club	Source	Date Signed	Seasons Played	Apps	Subs	Gls
Hartlepool U	Burton A	11/65	65-71	181	8	5
Derby Co	Tr	01/72	72	4	2	0
Mansfield T	L	01/74	73	0	1	0

PARRY Brinley John (Jack)
Born: Pontardawe, Swansea, Wales, 11 January, 1924 — G
Died: Chelmsford, England, 20 January, 2010
Wales: 1

League Club	Source	Date Signed	Seasons Played	Apps	Subs	Gls
Swansea C	Clydach	09/46	46-50	96	-	0
Ipswich T	Tr	08/51	51-54	138	-	0

PARRY Colin
Born: Stockport, Greater Manchester, England, 16 February, 1941 — CH

League Club	Source	Date Signed	Seasons Played	Apps	Subs	Gls
Stockport Co	Vernon Park	07/62	62-67	132	1	0
Bradford C	L	09/65	65	5	0	0
Rochdale	Tr	07/68	68-71	155	2	1

PARRY Cyril
Born: Derby, England, 13 December, 1937 — RW
England: Schools

League Club	Source	Date Signed	Seasons Played	Apps	Subs	Gls
Notts Co	Derby Co (Am)	05/55	57-58	12	-	2

PARRY David Edward (Dave)
Born: Southport, Merseyside, England, 11 February, 1948 — W

League Club	Source	Date Signed	Seasons Played	Apps	Subs	Gls
Blackpool	App	12/65				
Tranmere Rov	Tr	07/67	67	3	0	0
Halifax T	Tr	09/68	68	2	0	0

PARRY John (Jack)
Born: Derby, England, 29 July, 1931 — IF/WH

League Club	Source	Date Signed	Seasons Played	Apps	Subs	Gls
Derby Co	Jnr	07/48	48-65	482	1	105

PARRY John Ernan
Born: Holywell, Flintshire, Wales, 4 September, 1939 — FB

League Club	Source	Date Signed	Seasons Played	Apps	Subs	Gls
Liverpool	Jnr	09/56				
Doncaster Rov	Tr	09/61	61	14	-	0

PARRY Leslie Irvine (Les)
Born: Wallasey, Wirral, England, 13 November, 1953 — D

League Club	Source	Date Signed	Seasons Played	Apps	Subs	Gls
Tranmere Rov	Jnr	09/72	72-83	254	4	4

PARRY Mark
Born: Wrexham, Wales, 21 May, 1970 — W

League Club	Source	Date Signed	Seasons Played	Apps	Subs	Gls
Chester C	YT	-	87	4	1	1

PARRY Oswald (Ossie)
Born: Merthyr Tydfil, Wales, 16 August, 1908 — LB
Died: Ipswich, England, 3 April, 1991

League Club	Source	Date Signed	Seasons Played	Apps	Subs	Gls
Crystal Palace	Wimbledon	05/31	31-35	141	-	0
Ipswich T	Tr	06/36	38-48	104	-	0

PARRY Paul Ian
Born: Chepstow, Monmouthshire, Wales, 19 August, 1980 — LW
Wales: 12

League Club	Source	Date Signed	Seasons Played	Apps	Subs	Gls
Cardiff C	Hereford U	01/04	03-08	148	43	24
Preston NE	Tr	08/09	09-11	57	23	6
Shrewsbury T	Tr	07/12	12-13	54	16	11

PARRY Raymond Alan (Ray)
Born: Derby, England, 19 January, 1936 — IF
Died: Bolton, Greater Manchester, England, 23 May, 2003
England: 2/FLge-2/U23-4/Youth/Schools

League Club	Source	Date Signed	Seasons Played	Apps	Subs	Gls
Bolton W	Jnr	01/53	51-60	270	-	68
Blackpool	Tr	10/60	60-64	128	-	27
Bury	Tr	10/64	64-71	137	10	17

PARRY Stephen (Steve)
Born: Upton, West Yorkshire, England, 11 December, 1956 — G

League Club	Source	Date Signed	Seasons Played	Apps	Subs	Gls
Barnsley	App	12/74	73-74	5	0	0

PARRY William (Bill)
Born: Blaenau Ffestiniog, Gwynedd, Wales, 18 February, 1933 — RB
Died: Rochester, Kent, England, 20 May, 2009

League Club	Source	Date Signed	Seasons Played	Apps	Subs	Gls
Tottenham H	Portmadoc	09/53				
Gillingham	Tr	07/55	55-60	200	-	4

PARSELLE Norman John
Born: Newport, Wales, 8 January, 1970 — M

League Club	Source	Date Signed	Seasons Played	Apps	Subs	Gls
Newport Co	YT	-	87	4	6	0

PARSLEY Neil Robert
Born: Liverpool, England, 25 April, 1966 — RB

League Club	Source	Date Signed	Seasons Played	Apps	Subs	Gls
Leeds U	Witton A	11/88				
Chester C	L	12/89	89	6	0	0
Huddersfield T	Tr	07/90	90-92	55	2	0
Doncaster Rov	L	02/91	90	2	1	0
West Bromwich A	Tr	09/93	93-94	38	5	0
Exeter C	Tr	08/95	95	29	3	0

PARSLEY Wilfred Norman (Norman)
Born: Shildon, County Durham, England, 28 November, 1923 — WH
Died: Bishop Auckland, County Durham, England, 24 December, 1993

League Club	Source	Date Signed	Seasons Played	Apps	Subs	Gls
Darlington	Shildon	10/45	46-52	161	-	14

PARSLOW Daniel James (Danny)
Born: Caerphilly, Wales, 11 September, 1985 — CD
Wales: U21-4/Youth

League Club	Source	Date Signed	Seasons Played	Apps	Subs	Gls
Cardiff C	Sch	11/04				
York C	Tr	08/06	12-13	57	1	1

PARSONS Alexander Antony (Alex)
Born: Worthing, West Sussex, England, 7 September, 1992 — F

League Club	Source	Date Signed	Seasons Played	Apps	Subs	Gls
Bournemouth	Jnr	07/11	11	0	1	0

PARSONS David (Dave)
Born: Greenwich, SE London, England, 25 February, 1982 — M

League Club	Source	Date Signed	Seasons Played	Apps	Subs	Gls
Leyton Orient	YT	07/00	99	1	0	0

PARSONS Dennis Ronald
Born: Birmingham, England, 29 May, 1925 — G
Died: Solihull, West Midlands, England, 27 May, 1980

League Club	Source	Date Signed	Seasons Played	Apps	Subs	Gls
Wolverhampton W	BSA Cycles	11/44	48-51	23	-	0
Aston Villa	Hereford U	09/52	52-54	36	-	0

League Club	Source	Date Signed	Seasons Played	Apps	Subs	Gls

PARSONS Derek John
Born: Hammersmith, W London, England, 24 October, 1929 — WH
Died: Slough, Berkshire, England, 4 October, 2010

League Club	Source	Date Signed	Seasons Played	Apps	Subs	Gls
Queens Park Rgrs		02/50	52	2	-	1

PARSONS Edward John (Ted)
Born: Bristol, England, 22 March, 1928 — CF
Died: Brislington, Avon, England, 5 January, 1996

League Club	Source	Date Signed	Seasons Played	Apps	Subs	Gls
Bristol Rov	Frome T	08/49	49	5	-	2

PARSONS Eric George
Born: Worthing, West Sussex, England, 9 November, 1923 — RW
Died: Worthing, West Sussex, England, 7 February, 2011
England: B-2

League Club	Source	Date Signed	Seasons Played	Apps	Subs	Gls
West Ham U	Jnr	10/43	46-50	145	-	34
Chelsea	Tr	12/50	50-56	158	-	37
Brentford	Tr	11/56	56-60	118	-	18

PARSONS Frank Ronald
Born: Amersham, Buckinghamshire, England, 29 October, 1947 — G

League Club	Source	Date Signed	Seasons Played	Apps	Subs	Gls
Crystal Palace	Jnr	07/65	66	4	0	0
Cardiff C	Tr	08/70	70-72	17	0	0
Fulham	Tr	01/74				
Reading	Tr	09/74	74	1	0	0

PARSONS Geoffrey Roy (Geoff)
Born: Belper, Derbyshire, England, 2 August, 1931 — LW
Died: Mansfield, Nottinghamshire, England, 8 February, 1996

League Club	Source	Date Signed	Seasons Played	Apps	Subs	Gls
Mansfield T	Jnr	05/51				
Chesterfield	Tr	07/52	52	1	-	0

PARSONS John Stuart
Born: Cardiff, Wales, 10 December, 1950 — F
Wales: Schools

League Club	Source	Date Signed	Seasons Played	Apps	Subs	Gls
Cardiff C	App	12/68	70-72	7	8	6
Bournemouth	Tr	02/73	72-74	6	1	1
Newport Co	Tr	03/75	74-76	57	3	22

PARSONS Lindsay William
Born: Bristol, England, 20 March, 1946 — FB

League Club	Source	Date Signed	Seasons Played	Apps	Subs	Gls
Bristol Rov	App	04/64	63-76	354	5	0
Torquay U	Tr	08/77	77-78	56	0	0

PARSONS Mark Christopher
Born: Luton, England, 24 February, 1975 — RB

League Club	Source	Date Signed	Seasons Played	Apps	Subs	Gls
Northampton T	YT	07/93	91-93	51	0	0

PARSONS Matthew John (Matty)
Born: Catford, SE London, England, 23 December, 1991 — LB

League Club	Source	Date Signed	Seasons Played	Apps	Subs	Gls
Crystal Palace	Sch	07/10	10-11	5	1	0
Barnet	L	03/11	10	7	1	0
Wycombe W	L	08/12	12	4	0	0
Plymouth Arg	Tr	01/14	13	10	0	0

PARSONS Stephen Paul James (Steve)
Born: Hammersmith, W London, England, 7 October, 1957 — M

League Club	Source	Date Signed	Seasons Played	Apps	Subs	Gls
Wimbledon	Walton & Hersham	12/77	77-79	91	3	19
Leyton Orient	Tr	03/80	79-80	36	0	6

PARSONS Stuart
Born: Staveley, Derbyshire, England, 24 May, 1948 — IF

League Club	Source	Date Signed	Seasons Played	Apps	Subs	Gls
Chesterfield	Jnr	08/67	66	1	0	0

PARTINGTON Joseph Michael (Joe)
Born: Portsmouth, England, 1 April, 1990 — M
Wales: U21-8/Youth

League Club	Source	Date Signed	Seasons Played	Apps	Subs	Gls
Bournemouth	Jnr	07/08	07-12	21	31	2

PARTNER Andrew Neil (Andy)
Born: Colchester, Essex, England, 21 October, 1974 — CD

League Club	Source	Date Signed	Seasons Played	Apps	Subs	Gls
Colchester U	YT	06/93	92-94	0	2	0

PARTON Andrew (Andy)
Born: Doncaster, South Yorkshire, England, 29 September, 1983 — F

League Club	Source	Date Signed	Seasons Played	Apps	Subs	Gls
Scunthorpe U	Sch	07/03	01-05	4	15	0

PARTON Jeffrey John (Jeff)
Born: Swansea, Wales, 24 February, 1953 — G
Wales: U23-3/Schools

League Club	Source	Date Signed	Seasons Played	Apps	Subs	Gls
Burnley	App	03/70	71-73	3	0	0
Northampton T	Tr	07/75	75-77	25	0	0

PARTRIDGE Brendan David (Don)
Born: Manchester, England, 17 September, 1941 — LW

League Club	Source	Date Signed	Seasons Played	Apps	Subs	Gls
Stockport Co		11/60	60-61	31	-	6
Darlington	Tr	07/62	62	3	-	0

PARTRIDGE Cyril
Born: York, England, 12 October, 1931 — W
Died: Leeds, England, 4 April, 2014

League Club	Source	Date Signed	Seasons Played	Apps	Subs	Gls
Queens Park Rgrs	Yorkshire Amats	08/54				
Rotherham U	Bedford T	08/57	57	7	-	2

PARTRIDGE David William
Born: Westminster, Central London, England, 26 November, 1978 — LB
Wales: 7/U21-1

League Club	Source	Date Signed	Seasons Played	Apps	Subs	Gls
West Ham U	YT	07/97				
Leyton Orient (L)	Dundee U	01/02	01	6	1	0
Bristol C	Motherwell	07/05	05	11	0	0
MK Dons	L	01/06	05	18	0	0
Leyton Orient	L	07/06	06	1	0	0
Brentford	L	01/07	06	3	0	0

PARTRIDGE Donald (Don)
Born: Bolton, Greater Manchester, England, 22 October, 1925 — WH
Died: Blackpool, Lancashire, England, 11 August, 2003

League Club	Source	Date Signed	Seasons Played	Apps	Subs	Gls
Rochdale	Farnworth	10/45	46-55	103	-	2

PARTRIDGE John Thomas
Born: Chesterfield, Derbyshire, England, 14 September, 1962 — LB

League Club	Source	Date Signed	Seasons Played	Apps	Subs	Gls
Chesterfield	App	09/80	81-82	34	4	0
Mansfield T	L	09/83	83	1	0	0

PARTRIDGE Malcolm
Born: Calow, Derbyshire, England, 28 August, 1950 — F
England: Schools

League Club	Source	Date Signed	Seasons Played	Apps	Subs	Gls
Mansfield T	App	09/68	67-70	65	2	20
Leicester C	Tr	09/70	70-73	24	12	4
Charlton Ath	L	01/72	71	1	1	0
Grimsby T	Tr	03/75	74-78	134	4	25
Scunthorpe U	Tr	07/79	79-81	91	6	21

PARTRIDGE Matthew Nicholas (Matt)
Born: Thatcham, Berkshire, England, 24 October, 1993 — RB

League Club	Source	Date Signed	Seasons Played	Apps	Subs	Gls
Reading	Sch	06/12				
Dagenham & Red	Tr	07/14	14	20	4	1

PARTRIDGE Maurice Edward
Born: Birmingham, England, 20 February, 1941 — LB

League Club	Source	Date Signed	Seasons Played	Apps	Subs	Gls
Birmingham C	Jnr	03/58				
Walsall	Tr	07/61	61-62	3	-	0

PARTRIDGE Richard Joseph (Richie)
Born: Dublin, Republic of Ireland, 12 September, 1980 — W
Republic of Ireland: U21-8/Youth

League Club	Source	Date Signed	Seasons Played	Apps	Subs	Gls
Liverpool	YT	09/97				
Bristol Rov	L	03/01	00	4	2	1
Coventry C	L	09/02	02	23	4	4
Sheffield Wed	Tr	08/05	05	6	12	0
Rotherham U	Tr	07/06	06	30	3	3
Chester C	Tr	07/07	07-08	49	15	5
MK Dons	Tr	07/09	09	1	3	0
Stockport Co	Tr	01/10	09	20	2	1

PARTRIDGE Scott Malcolm
Born: Leicester, England, 13 October, 1974 — F

League Club	Source	Date Signed	Seasons Played	Apps	Subs	Gls
Bradford C	YT	07/92	92-93	0	5	0
Bristol C	Tr	02/94	93-96	24	33	7
Torquay U	L	10/95	95	5	0	2
Plymouth Arg	L	01/96	95	6	1	2
Scarborough	L	03/96	95	5	2	0
Cardiff C	Tr	02/97	96-97	29	8	2
Torquay U	Tr	03/98	97-98	33	1	12
Brentford	Tr	02/99	98-01	79	13	21
Rushden & D	Tr	09/01	01-02	28	16	5
Exeter C	L	12/02	02	2	2	2
Shrewsbury T	Tr	03/03	02	2	2	0

PARZYSZEK Piotr
Born: Torun, Poland, 8 September, 1993 — F
Poland: U21-3/Youth

League Club	Source	Date Signed	Seasons Played	Apps	Subs	Gls
Charlton Ath	De Graafschap (NED)	01/14	13	0	1	0

PASANEN Petri Mikael
Born: Lahti, Finland, 24 September, 1980 — CD
Finland: 76/U21-6/Youth

League Club	Source	Date Signed	Seasons Played	Apps	Subs	Gls
Portsmouth (L)	Ajax (NED)	01/04	03	11	1	0

PASCOE Colin James
Born: Port Talbot, Wales, 9 April, 1965 — LW
Wales: 10/U21-4/Youth/Schools

League Club	Source	Date Signed	Seasons Played	Apps	Subs	Gls
Swansea C	App	04/83	82-87	167	7	39
Sunderland	Tr	03/88	87-91	116	10	22
Swansea C	L	07/92	92	15	0	4
Swansea C	Tr	08/93	93-95	72	9	11
Blackpool	Tr	03/96	95	0	1	0

PASCOE Jason
Born: Jarrow, Tyne and Wear, England, 15 February, 1970 — RB

League Club	Source	Date Signed	Seasons Played	Apps	Subs	Gls
Northampton T	Clipstone Welfare	06/94	94	11	4	0

PASCOLO Marco
Born: Sion, Switzerland, 9 May, 1966 — G
Switzerland: 55

League Club	Source	Date Signed	Seasons Played	Apps	Subs	Gls
Nottingham F	Cagliari (ITA)	06/97	97	5	0	0

PASHLEY Robert Wilminson
Born: Sheffield, England, 9 September, 1937 — RW

League Club	Source	Date Signed	Seasons Played	Apps	Subs	Gls
Sheffield U	Sheffield Wed (Am)	01/56				
Rotherham U	Tr	07/58				
Scunthorpe U	Gainsborough Trinity	05/59	59	3	-	1
Barrow	Tr	06/60	60	26	-	2

PASHLEY Terence (Terry)
Born: Chesterfield, Derbyshire, England, 11 October, 1956 — LB
England: Schools

League Club	Source	Date Signed	Seasons Played	Apps	Subs	Gls
Burnley	App	10/73	75-77	16	2	0
Blackpool	Tr	08/78	78-82	201	0	7
Bury	Tr	08/83	83-88	205	12	5

PASKIN William John (John)
Born: Cape Town, South Africa, 1 February, 1962 — F

League Club	Source	Date Signed	Seasons Played	Apps	Subs	Gls
West Bromwich A	KV Kortrijk (BEL)	08/88	88	14	11	5
Wolverhampton W	Tr	06/89	89-91	21	13	3
Stockport Co	L	09/91	91	3	2	1
Birmingham C	L	11/91	91	8	2	3
Shrewsbury T	L	02/92	91	1	0	0
Wrexham	Tr	02/92	91-93	28	23	11
Bury	Tr	07/94	94-95	15	23	8

PASSEY Peter Thord John
Born: Birmingham, England, 13 July, 1952 — D
England: Youth

League Club	Source	Date Signed	Seasons Played	Apps	Subs	Gls
Birmingham C	App	07/69				
Newport Co	L	01/72	71	20	0	0
Newport Co	Tr	12/72	72-75	116	0	2

PASSI Franck
Born: Bergerac, France, 28 March, 1966 — M
France: U21

League Club	Source	Date Signed	Seasons Played	Apps	Subs	Gls
Bolton W	Compostella (SPN)	11/99	99-00	21	17	0

PASSLEY Joshua (Josh)
Born: Chelsea, W London, England, 21 November, 1994 — RB/M

League Club	Source	Date Signed	Seasons Played	Apps	Subs	Gls
Fulham	Sch	02/13				
Shrewsbury T	L	11/14	14	6	0	0
Portsmouth	L	01/15	14	12	0	0

PASSMOOR Thomas (Tom)
Born: Chester-le-Street, County Durham, England, 12 February, 1937 — CH
Died: Doncaster, South Yorkshire, England, 4 February, 1991

League Club	Source	Date Signed	Seasons Played	Apps	Subs	Gls
Sunderland	Jnr	05/54				
Scunthorpe U	South Shields	05/59	59-63	27	-	0
Carlisle U	Tr	12/63	63-69	241	2	0

PASSMORE Edward (Ernie)
Born: Hetton-le-Hole, Tyne and Wear, England, 28 April, 1922 — CF
Died: Durham, England, 5 December, 1988

League Club	Source	Date Signed	Seasons Played	Apps	Subs	Gls
Swansea C	Portsmouth (Am)	02/44	46	6	-	2
Gateshead	Tr	04/47	46-49	41	-	26

PASTON Mark Nelson
Born: Hastings, New Zealand, 13 December, 1976 — G
New Zealand: 36

League Club	Source	Date Signed	Seasons Played	Apps	Subs	Gls
Bradford C	Napier City Rgrs (NZL)	08/03	03	13	0	0
Walsall	Tr	06/04	04	8	1	0

PATCHING Martin
Born: Rotherham, South Yorkshire, England, 1 November, 1958 — M
England: Youth/Schools

League Club	Source	Date Signed	Seasons Played	Apps	Subs	Gls
Wolverhampton W	App	03/76	75-79	78	12	10
Watford	Tr	12/79	79-83	24	1	3
Northampton T	L	01/83	82	6	0	1

PATE Alexander Montgomerie (Sandy)
Born: Lennoxtown, Dunbartonshire, Scotland, 15 August, 1944 — RB

League Club	Source	Date Signed	Seasons Played	Apps	Subs	Gls
Watford	Renfrew Jnrs	03/65	64-66	14	1	0
Mansfield T	Tr	10/67	67-77	412	1	2

PATERSON Alexander (Alex)
Born: Duntocher, Dunbartonshire, Scotland, 18 March, 1922 — LH
Died: Stockport, Greater Manchester, England, 22 January, 1992

League Club	Source	Date Signed	Seasons Played	Apps	Subs	Gls
New Brighton	Alloa Ath	07/46	46-47	67	-	10
Stockport Co	Tr	03/48	47-52	160	-	7
Barrow	Tr	08/53				

PATERSON George Denholm
Born: Denny, Falkirk, Scotland, 26 September, 1914 — WH
Died: New Zealand, December, 1985
Scotland: 1/SLge-2/War-3

League Club	Source	Date Signed	Seasons Played	Apps	Subs	Gls
Brentford	Glasgow Celtic	10/46	46-49	62	-	0

PATERSON George Longmore
Born: Aberdeen, Scotland, 19 December, 1916 — IF
Died: Liverpool, England, June, 1996

League Club	Source	Date Signed	Seasons Played	Apps	Subs	Gls
Liverpool	Hall & Russell	05/37	38	2	-	0
Swindon T	Tr	10/46	46-49	53	-	6

PATERSON James Lee (Jim)
Born: Airdrie, Lanarkshire, Scotland, 25 September, 1979 — LB
Scotland: U21-9

League Club	Source	Date Signed	Seasons Played	Apps	Subs	Gls
Plymouth Arg	Motherwell	01/08	07-10	46	19	1
Bristol Rov	Shamrock Rov (ROI)	01/12	11-12	40	3	1

PATERSON Jamie Charles Stuart
Born: Coventry, England, 20 December, 1991 — W/F

League Club	Source	Date Signed	Seasons Played	Apps	Subs	Gls
Walsall	Sch	07/10	10-12	72	22	15
Nottingham F	Tr	07/13	13-14	26	27	9

PATERSON Jamie Ryan
Born: Dumfries, Scotland, 26 April, 1973 — W

League Club	Source	Date Signed	Seasons Played	Apps	Subs	Gls
Halifax T	YT	07/91	90-92	34	10	5
Scunthorpe U	Falkirk	10/95	95-96	34	21	2
Halifax T	Tr	07/97	98-99	56	8	17
Doncaster Rov	Tr	07/00	03	7	1	1

PATERSON Martin Andrew
Born: Tunstall, Potteries, England, 13 May, 1987 — F/W
Northern Ireland: 22/U21-2/Youth

League Club	Source	Date Signed	Seasons Played	Apps	Subs	Gls
Stoke C	Sch	06/06	04-06	2	13	1
Grimsby T	L	11/06	06	15	0	6
Scunthorpe U	Tr	07/07	07	34	6	13
Burnley	Tr	06/08	08-12	100	30	29
Huddersfield T	Tr	07/13	13-14	13	12	5
Bristol C	L	03/14	13	6	2	1
Fleetwood T	L	11/14	14	3	0	0

PATERSON Matthew (Matt)
Born: Dunfermline, Fife, Scotland, 18 October, 1989 — F
Scotland: Youth

League Club	Source	Date Signed	Seasons Played	Apps	Subs	Gls
Southampton	Sch	07/08	08-09	5	13	2
Southend U	Tr	01/10	09-10	13	14	2
Stockport Co	L	02/11	10	9	1	3
Burton A	Tr	08/12	12	15	16	7

PATERSON Scott Thomas
Born: Aberdeen, Scotland, 13 May, 1972 — CD

League Club	Source	Date Signed	Seasons Played	Apps	Subs	Gls
Liverpool	Cove Rgrs	03/92				
Bristol C	Tr	07/94	94-97	40	10	1
Cardiff C	L	11/97	97	5	0	0
Carlisle U	Tr	07/98	98	18	1	1
Cambridge U	Tr	09/99	99	6	0	0
Plymouth Arg	Tr	03/00	99	5	0	0

PATERSON Sean Patrick
Born: Greenock, Inverclyde, Scotland, 26 March, 1987 — F

League Club	Source	Date Signed	Seasons Played	Apps	Subs	Gls
Blackpool	Sch	07/06	04	0	2	0

PATERSON Steven William (Steve)
Born: Elgin, Moray, Scotland, 8 April, 1958 — CD

League Club	Source	Date Signed	Seasons Played	Apps	Subs	Gls
Manchester U	Nairn Co	07/75	76-79	3	3	0

PATERSON Thomas (Tommy)
Born: Lochore, Fife, Scotland, 3 April, 1927 — IF

League Club	Source	Date Signed	Seasons Played	Apps	Subs	Gls
Leicester C	Lochgelly Albert	03/48	48-49	17	-	4
Newcastle U	Tr	06/50	50-51	2	-	0
Watford	Tr	07/52	52-54	45	-	7

PATERSON Thomas (Tommy)
Born: Ashington, Northumberland, England, 30 March, 1954 — F

League Club	Source	Date Signed	Seasons Played	Apps	Subs	Gls
Middlesbrough	Leicester C (Am)	09/74	74	1	0	0
Bournemouth	Tr	04/76	76-77	45	12	10
Darlington	Tr	06/78	78	6	1	2

PATERSON Toby Lee
Born: Dumfries, Scotland, 15 May, 1971 — CD

League Club	Source	Date Signed	Seasons Played	Apps	Subs	Gls
Halifax T	YT	07/89	88	0	1	0

PATERSON William Alexander Kennedy (Bill)
Born: Kinlochleven, Highlands, Scotland, 25 February, 1930 — CH
Died: Inverness, Scotland, 9 November, 2002
Scotland: B

League Club	Source	Date Signed	Seasons Played	Apps	Subs	Gls
Doncaster Rov	Ransome & Marles	03/50	50-54	113	-	0
Newcastle U	Tr	10/54	54-57	22	-	1

PATERSON William Clarkson (Billy)
Born: Bellshill, Lanarkshire, Scotland, 6 October, 1927 — CF
Died: Carluke, Lanarkshire, Scotland, 8 February, 1987

League Club	Source	Date Signed	Seasons Played	Apps	Subs	Gls
Accrington Stan	Greenock Morton	08/49	49	1	-	0

PATES Colin George
Born: Carshalton, S London, England, 10 August, 1961 — CD

League Club	Source	Date Signed	Seasons Played	Apps	Subs	Gls
England: Youth						
Chelsea	App	07/79	79-88	280	1	10
Charlton Ath	Tr	10/88	88-89	37	1	0
Arsenal	Tr	01/90	89-92	12	9	0
Brighton & HA	L	03/91	90	17	0	0
Brighton & HA	Tr	08/93	93-94	49	1	0

PATMORE Warren James
Born: Kingsbury, NW London, England, 14 August, 1971 — F
England: Semi Pro-7

League Club	Source	Date Signed	Seasons Played	Apps	Subs	Gls
Cambridge U	Northwood	03/92	92	1	0	0
Millwall	Bashley	08/93	93	0	1	0
Northampton T	Tr	12/93	93-94	12	9	2
Rushden & D	Yeovil T	06/01	01	4	0	1

PATON David Samuel Craig (Dave)
Born: Saltcoats, Ayrshire, Scotland, 13 December, 1943 — CH

League Club	Source	Date Signed	Seasons Played	Apps	Subs	Gls
Southampton	St Mirren	07/63	63-67	13	0	0
Aldershot	Tr	11/69	69-70	30	0	0

PATON John Aloysius (Johnny)
Born: Glasgow, Scotland, 2 April, 1923 — LW

League Club	Source	Date Signed	Seasons Played	Apps	Subs	Gls
Chelsea	Glasgow Celtic	11/46	46	18	-	3
Brentford	Glasgow Celtic	09/49	49-51	90	-	14
Watford	Tr	07/52	52-54	84	-	17

PATON Robert Simpson Reid (Danny)
Born: West Calder, West Lothian, Scotland, 27 January, 1936 — IF
Died: Livingston, West Lothian, Scotland, 10 March, 2011

League Club	Source	Date Signed	Seasons Played	Apps	Subs	Gls
Oxford U	Heart of Midlothian	07/64	64	2	-	1

PATON Thomas Gracie (Tommy)
Born: Saltcoats, Ayrshire, Scotland, 22 December, 1918 — RH/IF
Died: Folkestone, Kent, England, 14 December, 1991

League Club	Source	Date Signed	Seasons Played	Apps	Subs	Gls
Wolverhampton W	Ardeer Thistle	06/37				
Swansea C	Tr	10/38	38	6	-	0
Bournemouth	Tr	02/39	38-47	46	-	8
Watford	Tr	01/48	47-51	141	-	1

PATRICK Alfred (Alf)
Born: York, England, 25 September, 1921 — CF

League Club	Source	Date Signed	Seasons Played	Apps	Subs	Gls
York C	New Earswick	09/46	46-52	228	-	109

PATRICK Bert (Bertie)
Born: Kilsyth, Lanarkshire, Scotland, 26 April, 1946 — RB
Died: Kilsyth, Lanarkshire, Scotland, March, 2015

League Club	Source	Date Signed	Seasons Played	Apps	Subs	Gls
Preston NE	Stirling A	08/63	64-69	50	0	1
Barrow	Tr	07/71	71	34	0	1

PATRICK Jordan Daniel
Born: Luton, England, 10 October, 1992 — W

League Club	Source	Date Signed	Seasons Played	Apps	Subs	Gls
Luton T	Sch	-	08	0	2	0

PATRICK Matthew (Matt)
Born: Slamannan, Falkirk, Scotland, 13 June, 1919 — W/FB
Died: York, England, 14 July, 2005

League Club	Source	Date Signed	Seasons Played	Apps	Subs	Gls
York C	Cowdenbeath	09/40	46-53	248	-	47

PATRICK Roy
Born: Overseal, Derbyshire, England, 4 December, 1935 — FB
Died: Glasgow, Scotland, 26 March, 1998

League Club	Source	Date Signed	Seasons Played	Apps	Subs	Gls
Derby Co	Jnr	02/52	52-55	49	-	0
Nottingham F	Tr	05/59	59-60	57	-	0
Southampton	Tr	06/61	61-62	31	-	0
Exeter C	Tr	03/63	62-64	50	-	0

PATRICK William Cecil Gibson (Bill)
Born: Lochgelly, Fife, Scotland, 12 March, 1932 — FB
Died: Kent, England, 18 April, 2003

League Club	Source	Date Signed	Seasons Played	Apps	Subs	Gls
Coventry C	Snowdown CW	11/54	55-57	44	-	6
Gillingham	Tr	06/58	58-59	47	-	14

PATTEN Kyle Anthony
Born: Barry, Vale of Glamorgan, Wales, 21 July, 1994 — M

League Club	Source	Date Signed	Seasons Played	Apps	Subs	Gls
Newport Co	Sch	07/13	14	0	1	0

PATTERSON Darren James
Born: Belfast, Northern Ireland, 15 October, 1969 — CD
Northern Ireland: 17/B-3/U21-1/Youth

League Club	Source	Date Signed	Seasons Played	Apps	Subs	Gls
West Bromwich A	YT	07/88				
Wigan Ath	Tr	04/89	89-91	69	28	6
Crystal Palace	Tr	07/92	94	22	0	1
Luton T	Tr	08/95	95-97	52	4	0
Preston NE	L	10/96	96	2	0	0
York C	Dundee U	12/00	00	4	2	0
Oxford U	Tr	02/01	00-01	20	0	1

PATTERSON Gary
Born: Newcastle-upon-Tyne, England, 27 November, 1972 — M

League Club	Source	Date Signed	Seasons Played	Apps	Subs	Gls
Notts Co	YT	07/91				
Shrewsbury T	Tr	07/93	93-94	52	5	2
Wycombe W	Tr	12/94	94-96	46	13	2
Barnet	L	01/97	96	3	0	0
Chesterfield	L	02/97	96	7	2	0

PATTERSON George Thomas
Born: Sunderland, England, 15 September, 1934 — RH

League Club	Source	Date Signed	Seasons Played	Apps	Subs	Gls
Hull C	Silksworth Jnrs	10/52	54-55	7	-	1
York C	South Shields	05/57	57-59	57	-	4
Hartlepool U	Tr	06/60	60	18	-	1

PATTERSON Ian Daniel
Born: Chatham, Kent, England, 4 April, 1973 — CD

League Club	Source	Date Signed	Seasons Played	Apps	Subs	Gls
Sunderland	YT	03/92				
Burnley	Tr	08/93	93	0	1	0
Wigan Ath	Tr	03/94	93	2	2	0

PATTERSON John George (Jack)
Born: Cramlington, Northumberland, England, 6 July, 1922 — G
Died: Blackburn, Greater Manchester, England, October, 2002

League Club	Source	Date Signed	Seasons Played	Apps	Subs	Gls
Blackburn Rov	North Shields	04/45	48-56	107	-	0

PATTERSON Mark
Born: Leeds, England, 13 September, 1968 — RB/M

League Club	Source	Date Signed	Seasons Played	Apps	Subs	Gls
Carlisle U	App	08/87	86-87	19	3	0
Derby Co	Tr	11/87	88-92	41	10	3
Plymouth Arg	Tr	07/93	93-96	131	3	3
Gillingham	Tr	10/97	97-02	118	6	2

PATTERSON Mark Andrew
Born: Darwen, Lancashire, England, 24 May, 1965 — M

League Club	Source	Date Signed	Seasons Played	Apps	Subs	Gls
Blackburn Rov	App	05/83	83-87	89	12	20
Preston NE	Tr	06/88	88-89	54	1	19
Bury	Tr	02/90	89-90	42	0	10
Bolton W	Tr	01/91	90-95	158	11	11
Sheffield U	Tr	12/95	95-97	72	2	4
Southend U	L	03/97	96	4	0	0
Bury	Tr	12/97	97-98	27	4	2
Blackpool	L	12/98	98	7	0	0
Southend U	Tr	03/99	98	5	0	0

PATTERSON Marlon Anthony
Born: Southwark, S London, England, 24 June, 1983 — LB

League Club	Source	Date Signed	Seasons Played	Apps	Subs	Gls
Dagenham & Red	Yeading	08/07	07	5	1	0

PATTERSON Robert Alexander
Born: Newcastle-upon-Tyne, England, 12 March, 1935 — G

League Club	Source	Date Signed	Seasons Played	Apps	Subs	Gls
Gateshead	Stanley U	03/59	58-59	26	-	0

PATTERSON Ronald Lindsay (Ron)
Born: Seaham, County Durham, England, 30 October, 1929 — LB

League Club	Source	Date Signed	Seasons Played	Apps	Subs	Gls
Middlesbrough	Whitehall Jnrs	06/49	51	1	-	0
Northampton T	Tr	06/52	52-61	300	-	5

PATTERSON Rory Christopher
Born: Strabane, Tyrone, Northern Ireland, 16 July, 1984 — F
Northern Ireland: 5

League Club	Source	Date Signed	Seasons Played	Apps	Subs	Gls
Rochdale	Sch	07/03	02-03	5	10	0
Plymouth Arg	Coleraine	07/10	10	21	14	4

PATTERSON Simon George
Born: Harrow, NW London, England, 4 September, 1982 — F
Died: Hammersmith, W London, England, 10 September, 2006

League Club	Source	Date Signed	Seasons Played	Apps	Subs	Gls
Watford	Wembley	09/00				
Wycombe W	L	07/03	03	3	1	2

PATTIMORE Michael Richard
Born: Newport, Wales, 15 March, 1979 — M
Wales: Youth

League Club	Source	Date Signed	Seasons Played	Apps	Subs	Gls
Swindon T	YT	07/97	96-97	0	3	0

PATTISON Frank McKay
Born: Barrhead, Renfrewshire, Scotland, 23 December, 1930 — LW

League Club	Source	Date Signed	Seasons Played	Apps	Subs	Gls
Barnsley	Alloa Ath	12/51	51-54	29	-	5

PATTISON John Morris (Johnny)
Born: Glasgow, Scotland, 19 December, 1918 — LW

League Club	Source	Date Signed	Seasons Played	Apps	Subs	Gls
Queens Park Rgrs	Motherwell	05/37	37-49	92	-	26
Leyton Orient	Tr	02/50	49-50	43	-	10

PATTISON John William Philip
Born: Portsmouth, England, 23 February, 1925 — RH
Died: Hampshire, England, 20 August, 1993

League Club	Source	Date Signed	Seasons Played	Apps	Subs	Gls
Reading	Portsmouth CS	07/45	46	2	-	0

PATTISON Matthew Joseph (Matty)
Born: Johannesburg, South Africa, 27 October, 1986 — M
South Africa: 5

League Club	Source	Date Signed	Seasons Played	Apps	Subs	Gls
Newcastle U	Sch	12/05	05-06	4	6	0
Norwich C	Tr	11/07	07-08	40	11	3

League Club	Source	Date Signed	Seasons Played	Career Record Apps	Subs	Gls
PATTON Aaron Anthony						
Born: Westminster, Central London, England, 27 February, 1979						FB
Wycombe W	YT	07/97	97	0	1	0
PATULEA Adrian Marian						
Born: Targoviste, Romania, 10 November, 1984						F
Lincoln C	Petrolul Ploesti (ROM)	09/08	08	17	14	11
Leyton Orient	Tr	07/09	09-10	4	18	1
Hereford U	Tr	03/11	10	0	6	0
PAUL Anthony George (Tony)						
Born: Islington, N London, England, 6 April, 1961						M
Crystal Palace	App	04/78	80	0	1	0
PAUL David Dryburgh						
Born: Kirkcaldy, Fife, Scotland, 19 February, 1936						G
Scotland: Schools						
Derby Co	Jnr	02/53	53-55	2	-	0
PAUL Ian Kevin						
Born: Wolverhampton, England, 23 January, 1961						M
Walsall	App	08/78	77-80	68	2	9
PAUL Martyn Leighton						
Born: Whalley, Lancashire, England, 2 February, 1975						F
Bristol Rov	YT	07/93	93-95	11	11	1
Doncaster Rov	Tr	07/96				
PAUL Roy						
Born: Ton Pentre, Rhondda Cynon Taff, Wales, 18 April, 1920						LH
Died: Treorchy, Rhondda Cynon Taff, Wales, 21 May, 2002						
Wales: 33						
Swansea C	Ton Pentre	10/38	46-49	159	-	13
Manchester C	Tr	07/50	50-56	270	-	9
PAUL Thomas (Tom)						
Born: Grimsby, North Lincolnshire, England, 14 May, 1933						RW
Grimsby T		05/55	58	1	-	0
[PAULINHO] MACIEL Jose Paulo Bezerra						
Born: Sao Paulo, Brazil, 25 July, 1988						M
Brazil: 32						
Tottenham H	Corinthians (BRA)	07/13	13-14	31	14	6
PAULO Pedro Saraiva Antonio						
Born: Luanda, Angola, 21 November, 1973						W
Died: Portugal, 23 February, 2000						
Darlington	Sporting Lisbon (POR)	08/95	95	4	2	0
[PAULO JORGE] GOMES PEREIRA Paulo Jorge						
Born: Braga, Portugal, 18 January, 1993						M
Portugal: Youth						
Blackburn Rov	FC Porto Jnrs (POR)	08/12	12	0	1	0
PAVEY Alfie Martin Kevin						
Born: Southwark, S London, England, 2 October, 1995						F
Millwall	Maidstone U	05/13	14	0	1	0
PAVITT William Ernest (Bill)						
Born: West Ham, E London, England, 30 June, 1920						CH
Died: Brentwood, Essex, England, 2 August, 1989						
Fulham	RAF Debden	08/46	49-52	50	-	1
Southend U	Tr	05/53	53-54	79	-	0
PAVLYUCHENKO Roman Anatolevich						
Born: Krasnodar, Russia, 15 December, 1981						F
Russia: 51						
Tottenham H	Spartak Moscow (RUS)	09/08	08-11	45	33	20
PAWSON Henry Anthony (Tony)						
Born: Chertsey, Surrey, England, 22 August, 1921						W
Died: Kent, England, 11 October, 2012						
England: Amateur-8						
Charlton Ath (Am)	Pegasus	12/51	51-52	2	-	1
PAXTON John William						
Born: Wolverhampton, England, 24 March, 1928						LB
Died: Wolverhampton, England, October, 2010						
Wolverhampton W	Jnr	04/45				
Notts Co	Tr	05/50	50	2	-	0
PAYE Michael Charles (Mike)						
Born: Orpington, SE London, England, 30 July, 1966						RB
Charlton Ath	App	08/84	83	2	0	0
PAYNE Albert Charles						
Born: Liverpool, England, 11 November, 1923						RH
Died: Mitcham, S London, England, 3 August, 2008						
Tranmere Rov		08/46	46-48	10	-	0
PAYNE Brian						
Born: Altrincham, Greater Manchester, England, 4 November, 1937						RW
Died: Sturminster Newton, Dorset, England, 19 August, 2013						
Huddersfield T	Jnr	10/55				
Gillingham	Tr	07/57	57-59	36	-	3
PAYNE Clive Edward						
Born: Aylsham, Norfolk, England, 2 March, 1950						RB
Norwich C	App	03/68	68-73	122	3	0
Bournemouth	Tr	12/73	73-75	101	0	3
PAYNE David Ronald						
Born: Thornton Heath, S London, England, 25 April, 1947						D
England: U23-1						
Crystal Palace	App	11/64	64-72	281	3	9
Leyton Orient	Tr	08/73	73-77	88	5	0
PAYNE Derek Richard						
Born: Edgware, NW London, England, 26 April, 1967						M
Barnet	Hayes	07/91	91-92	50	1	6
Southend U	Tr	07/93	93	32	3	0
Watford	Tr	07/94	94-95	33	3	1
Peterborough U	Tr	08/96	96-98	79	3	4
PAYNE Donald (Don)						
Born: Swansea, Wales, 18 November, 1950						G
Swansea C	Jnr	12/70	71	11	0	0
Torquay U	Tr	06/72				
Newport Co	Tr	08/73	73-74	32	0	0
PAYNE Frank Ernest						
Born: Ipswich, England, 18 March, 1926						G
Died: Ipswich, England, January, 2001						
Derby Co	Ollerton Colliery	10/47				
Hull C	Tr	08/48				
Lincoln C	Tr	08/49	49	5	-	0
PAYNE George Henry						
Born: Liverpool, England, 22 August, 1921						G
Died: Birkenhead, Wirral, England, 6 April, 1987						
Tranmere Rov		04/47	46-60	439	-	0
PAYNE Ian Neil						
Born: Crawley, West Sussex, England, 19 January, 1977						LB
Wales: Youth						
Plymouth Arg	YT	07/95	94	1	0	0
PAYNE Irving Ernest Henry (Joe)						
Born: Briton Ferry, Neath Port Talbot, Wales, 29 June, 1921						IF
Died: Daventry, Northamptonshire, England, 12 September, 2001						
Swansea C	Jnr	07/38	46-48	52	-	12
Newport Co	Tr	10/49	49	12	-	1
Scunthorpe U	Tr	07/50	50	40	-	2
Northampton T	Tr	08/51	51	32	-	6
PAYNE Jack						
Born: Stepney, E London, England, 25 October, 1994						M
Southend U	Sch	07/13	13-14	20	25	6
PAYNE Jack Stephen						
Born: Gravesend, Kent, England, 5 December, 1991						DM
Gillingham	Sch	02/09	08-12	83	18	5
Peterborough U	Tr	01/13	12-14	78	9	5
PAYNE James (Jim)						
Born: West Bromwich, West Midlands, England, 25 May, 1936						RB
Died: Walsall, West Midlands, England, October, 2008						
Walsall	West Bromwich A (Jnr)	08/55	55	1	-	0
PAYNE James Bolcherson (Jimmy)						
Born: Liverpool, England, 10 March, 1926						W
Died: Kendal, Cumbria, England, 22 January, 2013						
England: B-3						
Liverpool	Bootle ATC	11/44	48-55	224	-	37
Everton	Tr	04/56	55-56	5	-	2
PAYNE Jeremy (Jess)						
Born: Dartford, Kent, England, 7 March, 1958						CD
Leicester C	Jnr	07/76				
Torquay U	Tr	12/77	77-78	25	0	1
PAYNE Joseph (Joe)						
Born: Chesterfield, Derbyshire, England, 17 January, 1914						CF
Died: Luton, England, 22 April, 1975						
England: 1						
Luton T	Biggleswade T	06/34	34-37	72	-	82
Chelsea	Tr	03/38	37-38	36	-	21
West Ham U	Tr	12/46	46	10	-	6

PAYNE Joshua James (Josh)
Born: Basingstoke, Hampshire, England, 25 November, 1990 — M

League Club	Source	Date Signed	Seasons Played	Apps	Subs	Gls
West Ham U	Sch	07/08	08	0	2	0
Cheltenham T	L	09/08	08	9	2	1
Colchester U	L	10/09	09	2	1	0
Wycombe W	L	01/10	09	3	0	1
Doncaster Rov	Tr	07/10				
Oxford U	Tr	08/10	10-11	25	9	1
Aldershot T	Tr	01/12	11-12	23	9	3

PAYNE Lee John
Born: Luton, England, 12 December, 1966 — LW

League Club	Source	Date Signed	Seasons Played	Apps	Subs	Gls
Newcastle U	Barnet	09/88	88	6	1	0
Reading	Tr	03/89	88-89	25	2	3

PAYNE Mark Ian
Born: Swindon, England, 2 September, 1966 — W

League Club	Source	Date Signed	Seasons Played	Apps	Subs	Gls
Swindon T	App	09/84	84	0	3	0

PAYNE Mark Richard Crawford
Born: Cheltenham, Gloucestershire, England, 3 August, 1960 — M

League Club	Source	Date Signed	Seasons Played	Apps	Subs	Gls
Stockport Co	SC Cambuur (NED)	08/88	88-90	77	10	16
Rochdale	Tr	05/91	91-92	58	4	8

PAYNE Russell
Born: Wigan, Greater Manchester, England, 8 July, 1970 — RW

League Club	Source	Date Signed	Seasons Played	Apps	Subs	Gls
Liverpool	Skelmersdale U	03/90				
Crewe Alex	L	10/91	91	3	3	0

PAYNE Stefan Steve
Born: Lambeth, S London, England, 10 August, 1991 — F

League Club	Source	Date Signed	Seasons Played	Apps	Subs	Gls
Fulham	Sutton U	10/09				
Gillingham	Tr	07/10	10-11	1	27	1
Aldershot T	Tr	01/12	11	0	1	0

PAYNE Stephen John (Steve)
Born: Pontefract, West Yorkshire, England, 1 August, 1975 — CD
England: Semi Pro-1

League Club	Source	Date Signed	Seasons Played	Apps	Subs	Gls
Huddersfield T	YT	07/93				
Macclesfield T	Tr	12/94	97-98	71	6	2
Chesterfield	Tr	07/99	99-03	146	5	8
Macclesfield T	Tr	03/04	03	13	0	0

PAYNTER William Paul (Billy)
Born: Liverpool, England, 13 July, 1984 — F

League Club	Source	Date Signed	Seasons Played	Apps	Subs	Gls
Port Vale	Sch	07/02	00-05	119	25	30
Hull C	Tr	11/05	05	11	11	3
Southend U	Tr	08/06	06	5	4	0
Bradford C	L	01/07	06	15	0	4
Swindon T	Tr	08/07	07-09	102	18	45
Leeds U	Tr	07/10	10-11	10	17	3
Brighton & HA	L	10/11	11	6	4	0
Doncaster Rov	Tr	08/12	12-13	26	20	13
Sheffield U	L	01/14	13	6	7	0
Carlisle U	Tr	06/14	14	9	9	1

PAYTON Andrew Paul (Andy)
Born: Padiham, Lancashire, England, 23 October, 1967 — F

League Club	Source	Date Signed	Seasons Played	Apps	Subs	Gls
Hull C	App	07/85	86-91	116	27	55
Middlesbrough	Tr	11/91	91	8	11	3
Barnsley	Glasgow Celtic	11/93	93-95	100	8	41
Huddersfield T	Tr	07/96	96-97	42	1	17
Burnley	Tr	01/98	97-02	115	41	68
Blackpool	L	12/01	01	4	0	1

PAYTON Clifford Charles (Cliff)
Born: Brighton, England, 16 October, 1935 — IF

League Club	Source	Date Signed	Seasons Played	Apps	Subs	Gls
Accrington Stan	Wisbech T	07/56				
Gillingham	Tonbridge	03/59	58-59	24	-	5

PAZ Charquero Adrian (Adrian)
Born: Montevideo, Uruguay, 9 September, 1968 — F
Uruguay: 10

League Club	Source	Date Signed	Seasons Played	Apps	Subs	Gls
Ipswich T	Penarol (UGY)	09/94	94	13	4	1

PEACH David Sidney
Born: Bedford, England, 21 January, 1951 — LB
England: B-1/U21-6

League Club	Source	Date Signed	Seasons Played	Apps	Subs	Gls
Gillingham	App	01/69	69-73	186	1	30
Southampton	Tr	01/74	73-79	221	3	34
Swindon T	Tr	03/80	79-81	52	1	2
Leyton Orient	Tr	03/82	81-82	47	0	6

PEACH Geoffrey Leonard (Geoff)
Born: Torpoint, Cornwall, England, 11 October, 1932 — IF
Died: Torpoint, Cornwall, England, 11 December, 2003

League Club	Source	Date Signed	Seasons Played	Apps	Subs	Gls
Plymouth Arg	Millwall (Am)	07/56	56	1	-	0

PEACH John (Jack)
Born: Barnsley, South Yorkshire, England, 4 April, 1923 — IF
Died: Barnsley, South Yorkshire, England, February, 2013

League Club	Source	Date Signed	Seasons Played	Apps	Subs	Gls
Barnsley	York C (Am)	11/45				
Hull C	Selby T	10/46	46-47	19	-	2

PEACHEY John Michael
Born: Cambridge, England, 21 July, 1952 — F

League Club	Source	Date Signed	Seasons Played	Apps	Subs	Gls
York C	Hillingdon Bor	08/73	73-74	6	2	3
Barnsley	Tr	11/74	74-78	116	11	31
Darlington	L	12/75	75	5	1	3
Darlington	Tr	03/79	78-79	16	4	6
Plymouth Arg	Tr	07/80	80	1	2	0

PEACOCK Alan
Born: Middlesbrough, England, 29 October, 1937 — CF
England: 6/Youth

League Club	Source	Date Signed	Seasons Played	Apps	Subs	Gls
Middlesbrough	Jnr	11/54	55-63	218	-	125
Leeds U	Tr	02/64	63-66	54	0	27
Plymouth Arg	Tr	10/67	67	11	0	1

PEACOCK Anthony Lee
Born: Middlesbrough, England, 6 September, 1985 — M

League Club	Source	Date Signed	Seasons Played	Apps	Subs	Gls
Middlesbrough	Sch	07/03				
Darlington	Tr	08/05	05	17	10	0

PEACOCK Darren
Born: Bristol, England, 3 February, 1968 — CD

League Club	Source	Date Signed	Seasons Played	Apps	Subs	Gls
Newport Co	App	02/86	85-87	24	4	0
Hereford U	Tr	03/89	88-90	56	3	4
Queens Park Rgrs	Tr	12/90	90-93	123	3	6
Newcastle U	Tr	03/94	93-97	131	2	2
Blackburn Rov	Tr	07/98	98-99	42	5	1
Wolverhampton W	L	10/00	00	2	2	0

PEACOCK Dennis
Born: Lincoln, England, 19 April, 1953 — G

League Club	Source	Date Signed	Seasons Played	Apps	Subs	Gls
Nottingham F	App	04/71	72-74	22	0	0
Walsall	L	03/73	72	10	0	0
Doncaster Rov	Tr	07/75	75-79	199	0	0
Bolton W	Tr	03/80	80-81	16	0	0
Doncaster Rov	Tr	08/82	82-85	130	0	0
Burnley	L	09/85	85	8	0	0

PEACOCK Ernest Anderson (Ernie)
Born: Renfrew, Renfrewshire, Scotland, 10 August, 1942 — WH

League Club	Source	Date Signed	Seasons Played	Apps	Subs	Gls
Workington	St Mirren	01/64	63	1	-	0

PEACOCK Ernest Gilbert (Ernie)
Born: Bristol, England, 11 December, 1924 — RH/CH
Died: Bristol, England, 12 February, 1973

League Club	Source	Date Signed	Seasons Played	Apps	Subs	Gls
Notts Co	Syston	03/45				
Bristol C	Tr	10/46	46-58	343	-	7

PEACOCK Frank Edwin
Born: Bolton, Greater Manchester, England, 17 May, 1945 — WH

League Club	Source	Date Signed	Seasons Played	Apps	Subs	Gls
Stockport Co	Blackburn Rov (Am)	11/64	64	5	-	0

PEACOCK Gavin Keith
Born: Welling, SE London, England, 18 November, 1967 — M
England: Youth/Schools

League Club	Source	Date Signed	Seasons Played	Apps	Subs	Gls
Queens Park Rgrs	App	11/84	86-87	7	10	1
Gillingham	Tr	10/87	87-88	69	1	11
Bournemouth	Tr	08/89	89-90	56	0	8
Newcastle U	Tr	11/90	90-92	102	3	35
Chelsea	Tr	08/93	93-95	92	11	17
Queens Park Rgrs	Tr	11/96	96-01	182	8	35
Charlton Ath	L	08/01	01	1	4	0

PEACOCK George
Born: Pontypool, Torfaen, Wales, 10 February, 1924 — FB
Died: Pontypridd, Rhondda Cynon Taff, Wales, February, 1984

League Club	Source	Date Signed	Seasons Played	Apps	Subs	Gls
Bristol Rov	Pentwyn	05/46	46	7	-	0

PEACOCK John Charles
Born: Leeds, England, 27 March, 1956 — LB

League Club	Source	Date Signed	Seasons Played	Apps	Subs	Gls
Scunthorpe U	Jnr	08/74	74-79	185	5	1

PEACOCK Keith
Born: Barnehurst, SE London, England, 2 May, 1945 — M

League Club	Source	Date Signed	Seasons Played	Apps	Subs	Gls
Charlton Ath	Jnr	07/62	62-78	513	21	92

PEACOCK Lee Anthony
Born: Paisley, Renfrewshire, Scotland, 9 October, 1976 — M/F
Scotland: U21-1/Youth

League Club	Source	Date Signed	Seasons Played	Apps	Subs	Gls
Carlisle U	YT	03/95	93-97	52	24	11
Mansfield T	Tr	10/97	97-99	79	10	29
Manchester C	Tr	11/99	99	4	4	0
Bristol C	Tr	08/00	00-03	131	13	54
Sheffield Wed	Tr	07/04	04-05	37	14	6
Swindon T	Tr	01/06	05-09	104	21	20
Grimsby T	Tr	01/10	09	14	3	2

PEACOCK Michael Richards (Mike)
Born: Fishburn, County Durham, England, 28 September, 1940 — G

League Club	Source	Date Signed	Seasons Played	Apps	Subs	Gls
Darlington	Shildon	08/60	60-62	46	-	0

PEACOCK Richard John
Born: Sheffield, England, 29 October, 1972 — W

League Club	Source	Date Signed	Seasons Played	Apps	Subs	Gls
Hull C	Sheffield FC	10/93	93-98	144	30	21
Lincoln C	Tr	01/99	98-00	41	27	6

PEACOCK Robert John
Born: Rushden, Northamptonshire, England, 8 December, 1937 — WH

League Club	Source	Date Signed	Seasons Played	Apps	Subs	Gls
Northampton T	Rushden T	02/57	57	2	-	0

PEACOCK Terence McGhee (Terry)
Born: Hull, England, 18 April, 1935 — CF

League Club	Source	Date Signed	Seasons Played	Apps	Subs	Gls
Hull C	Jnr	12/52	55	2	-	0
Queens Park Rgrs	Tr	08/56	56-57	16	-	4

PEAD Craig George
Born: Bromsgrove, Worcestershire, England, 15 September, 1981 — RB/M
England: Youth

League Club	Source	Date Signed	Seasons Played	Apps	Subs	Gls
Coventry C	YT	09/98	01-03	24	18	3
Notts Co	L	09/04	04	4	1	0
Walsall	L	03/05	04-06	72	16	0
Brentford	Tr	07/07	07-08	32	6	0

PEAKE Andrew Michael (Andy)
Born: Market Harborough, Leicestershire, England, 1 November, 1961 — M
England: U21-1/Youth

League Club	Source	Date Signed	Seasons Played	Apps	Subs	Gls
Leicester C	App	01/79	78-84	141	6	13
Grimsby T	Tr	08/85	85-86	39	0	4
Charlton Ath	Tr	09/86	86-91	174	3	5
Middlesbrough	Tr	11/91	91-93	83	3	1

PEAKE Dudley John
Born: Swansea, Wales, 26 October, 1934 — CH
Died: Liverpool, England, May, 2012

League Club	Source	Date Signed	Seasons Played	Apps	Subs	Gls
Swansea C	Tawe U	04/56	55-57	57	-	2
Newport Co	Tr	06/58	58-62	129	-	0

PEAKE Jason William
Born: Coalville, Leicestershire, England, 29 September, 1971 — M/LW
England: Youth/Schools

League Club	Source	Date Signed	Seasons Played	Apps	Subs	Gls
Leicester C	YT	01/90	90	4	4	1
Hartlepool U	L	02/92	91	5	1	1
Halifax T	Tr	08/92	92	32	1	1
Rochdale	Tr	03/94	93-95	91	4	6
Brighton & HA	Tr	07/96	96	27	3	1
Bury	Tr	10/97	97	3	3	0
Rochdale	Tr	07/98	98-99	74	7	11
Plymouth Arg	Tr	07/00	00	7	3	2

PEAKE Trevor
Born: Nuneaton, Warwickshire, England, 10 February, 1957 — CD
England: Semi Pro-2

League Club	Source	Date Signed	Seasons Played	Apps	Subs	Gls
Lincoln C	Nuneaton Bor	06/79	79-82	171	0	7
Coventry C	Tr	07/83	83-91	276	1	6
Luton T	Tr	08/91	91-97	175	4	0

PEAPELL Frederick Dennis (Dennis)
Born: Swindon, England, 16 November, 1945 — RH/FB

League Club	Source	Date Signed	Seasons Played	Apps	Subs	Gls
Swindon T	App	11/63	64	2	-	0
Exeter C	Tr	07/65	65	23	1	1

PEARCE Alan James
Born: Middlesbrough, England, 25 October, 1965 — LW

League Club	Source	Date Signed	Seasons Played	Apps	Subs	Gls
York C	Jnr	10/83	83-86	76	2	9
Torquay U	Tr	08/87	87	20	7	2

PEARCE Alexander Gregory (Greg)
Born: Bolton, Greater Manchester, England, 26 May, 1980 — D

League Club	Source	Date Signed	Seasons Played	Apps	Subs	Gls
Chesterfield	YT	03/98	98-01	14	5	0

PEARCE Alexander James (Alex)
Born: Wallingford, Oxfordshire, England, 9 November, 1988 — CD
Republic of Ireland: 7//Scotland: U21-2/Youth

League Club	Source	Date Signed	Seasons Played	Apps	Subs	Gls
Reading	Sch	10/06	08-14	205	7	14
Northampton T	L	02/07	06	15	0	1
Bournemouth	L	11/07	07	11	0	0
Norwich C	L	01/08	07	8	3	0
Southampton	L	10/08	08	6	3	2

PEARCE Allan David
Born: Wellington, New Zealand, 7 April, 1983 — F
New Zealand: 1/U23-1/Youth

League Club	Source	Date Signed	Seasons Played	Apps	Subs	Gls
Lincoln C	Barnsley (YT)	10/02	02-03	9	10	1

PEARCE Andrew John (Andy)
Born: Bradford-on-Avon, Wiltshire, England, 20 April, 1966 — CD

League Club	Source	Date Signed	Seasons Played	Apps	Subs	Gls
Coventry C	Halesowen T	05/90	90-92	68	3	4
Sheffield Wed	Tr	06/93	93-95	66	3	3
Wimbledon	Tr	11/95	95	6	1	0

PEARCE Christopher Leslie (Chris)
Born: Newport, Wales, 7 August, 1961 — G
Wales: Youth/Schools

League Club	Source	Date Signed	Seasons Played	Apps	Subs	Gls
Blackburn Rov	Wolverhampton W (App)	10/79				
Rochdale	L	08/80	80	5	0	0
Rochdale	Tr	08/82	82	36	0	0
Port Vale	Tr	06/83	83-85	48	0	0
Wrexham	Tr	07/86	86	25	0	0
Burnley	Tr	07/87	87-91	181	0	0
Bradford C	Tr	07/92	92	9	0	0

PEARCE David
Born: Northolt, W London, England, 7 December, 1959 — F
England: Semi Pro-1

League Club	Source	Date Signed	Seasons Played	Apps	Subs	Gls
Millwall	Wealdstone	02/78	77	1	0	0

PEARCE David Gordon
Born: Scunthorpe, North Lincolnshire, England, 19 December, 1934 — WH
Died: Gainsborough, Lincolnshire, England, 22 September, 1999

League Club	Source	Date Signed	Seasons Played	Apps	Subs	Gls
Scunthorpe U		07/56	58	2	-	0

PEARCE Dennis Anthony
Born: Wolverhampton, England, 10 September, 1974 — LB

League Club	Source	Date Signed	Seasons Played	Apps	Subs	Gls
Aston Villa	YT	06/93				
Wolverhampton W	Tr	07/95	95-96	7	2	0
Notts Co	Tr	07/97	97-00	108	10	3
Peterborough U	Tr	05/01	01-03	11	3	0

PEARCE Graham Charles
Born: Hammersmith, W London, England, 8 July, 1959 — LB

League Club	Source	Date Signed	Seasons Played	Apps	Subs	Gls
Brighton & HA	Barnet	01/82	82-85	87	1	2
Gillingham	Tr	07/86	86-87	65	0	0
Brentford	Tr	09/88	88	11	7	0
Maidstone U	Tr	07/89	89	24	3	0

PEARCE Ian Anthony
Born: Bury St Edmunds, Suffolk, England, 7 May, 1974 — CD
England: U21-3/Youth

League Club	Source	Date Signed	Seasons Played	Apps	Subs	Gls
Chelsea	Jnr	08/91	90-92	0	4	0
Blackburn Rov	Tr	10/93	93-97	43	19	2
West Ham U	Tr	09/97	97-03	135	7	9
Fulham	Tr	01/04	03-07	55	2	1
Southampton	L	02/08	07	1	0	0
Lincoln C	Kingstonian	09/09	09-10	8	6	0

PEARCE James William (Jimmy)
Born: Tottenham, N London, England, 27 November, 1947 — W
England: Schools

League Club	Source	Date Signed	Seasons Played	Apps	Subs	Gls
Tottenham H	App	05/65	68-72	108	33	21

PEARCE Jason Daniel
Born: Hillingdon, W London, England, 6 December, 1987 — CD

League Club	Source	Date Signed	Seasons Played	Apps	Subs	Gls
Portsmouth	Sch	07/06				
Bournemouth	Tr	08/07	07-10	159	3	7
Portsmouth	Tr	07/11	11	43	0	2
Leeds U	Tr	05/12	12-14	91	8	2
Wigan Ath	Tr	01/15	14	16	0	2

PEARCE John
Born: Watford, Hertfordshire, England, 12 December, 1950 — FB

League Club	Source	Date Signed	Seasons Played	Apps	Subs	Gls
Watford	Jnr	07/69	70	0	1	0

PEARCE John Arthur
Born: Grimsby, North Lincolnshire, England, 29 February, 1940 — WH

League Club	Source	Date Signed	Seasons Played	Apps	Subs	Gls
Grimsby T	Jnr	12/58	58-61	48	-	0

PEARCE Krystian Mitchell Victor
Born: Birmingham, England, 5 January, 1990 — CD
England: Youth

League Club	Source	Date Signed	Seasons Played	Apps	Subs	Gls
Birmingham C	Sch	03/07				
Notts Co	L	11/07	07	8	0	1
Port Vale	L	01/08	07	11	1	0
Scunthorpe U	L	08/08	08	36	3	0
Peterborough U	L	07/09	09	0	2	0
Huddersfield T	Tr	01/10	09	0	1	0
Notts Co	Tr	07/10	10-12	53	3	5
Barnet	L	09/12	12	17	0	1
Torquay U	Tr	07/13	13	35	0	4

PEARCE Reginald Stanley (Reg)
Born: Liverpool, England, 12 January, 1930 — LH/IF
England: FLge-2

League Club	Source	Date Signed	Seasons Played	Apps	Subs	Gls
Luton T	Winsford U	11/54	54-57	75	-	5
Sunderland	Tr	02/58	57-60	61	-	4
Peterborough U	Cambridge C	08/63	63	28	-	2

PEARCE Stuart
Born: Shepherds Bush, W London, England, 24 April, 1962 — LB
England: 78/U21-1

League Club	Source	Date Signed	Seasons Played	Apps	Subs	Gls
Coventry C	Wealdstone	10/83	83-84	52	0	4
Nottingham F	Tr	06/85	85-96	401	0	63
Newcastle U	Tr	07/97	97-98	37	0	0
West Ham U	Tr	08/99	99-00	42	0	2
Manchester C	Tr	07/01	01	38	0	3

PEARCE Trevor George
Born: Canterbury, England, 30 May, 1949 — W

League Club	Source	Date Signed	Seasons Played	Apps	Subs	Gls
Arsenal	Folkestone T	02/70				
Aldershot	Tr	05/71	71-72	19	6	2

PEARCEY Jason Kevin
Born: Leamington Spa, Warwickshire, England, 23 July, 1971 — G

League Club	Source	Date Signed	Seasons Played	Apps	Subs	Gls
Mansfield T	YT	07/89	88-94	77	0	0
Grimsby T	Tr	11/94	94-97	49	0	0
Brentford	Tr	07/98	98-99	23	0	0

PEARS Jeffrey (Jeff)
Born: York, England, 14 June, 1920 — G
Died: York, England, 6 April, 2003

League Club	Source	Date Signed	Seasons Played	Apps	Subs	Gls
York C	Terry's	09/47	47-48	3	-	0

PEARS Richard James
Born: Exeter, England, 16 July, 1976 — F

League Club	Source	Date Signed	Seasons Played	Apps	Subs	Gls
Exeter C	YT	07/94	93-96	43	17	8

PEARS Stephen (Steve)
Born: Brandon, County Durham, England, 22 January, 1962 — G

League Club	Source	Date Signed	Seasons Played	Apps	Subs	Gls
Manchester U	App	01/79	84	4	0	0
Middlesbrough	L	11/83	83	12	0	0
Middlesbrough	Tr	07/85	85-94	327	0	0
Liverpool	Tr	08/95				
Hartlepool U	Tr	08/96	96	16	0	0

PEARSON Andrew John (Andy)
Born: Newmarket, Suffolk, England, 19 November, 1960 — F

League Club	Source	Date Signed	Seasons Played	Apps	Subs	Gls
Luton T	App	11/78	79	1	1	0

PEARSON Benjamin David (Ben)
Born: Oldham, Greater Manchester, England, 4 January, 1995 — M
England: Youth

League Club	Source	Date Signed	Seasons Played	Apps	Subs	Gls
Manchester U	Sch	07/13				
Barnsley	L	01/15	14	21	1	1

PEARSON David Aubrey John (Dave)
Born: Deeside, Flintshire, Wales, 13 October, 1947 — RB
Wales: U23-1/Schools

League Club	Source	Date Signed	Seasons Played	Apps	Subs	Gls
Everton	App	10/65				
Southport	Tr	08/67	67-69	91	2	0
Rochdale	Tr	09/70	70	3	0	0

PEARSON David Thomson (Dave)
Born: Dunfermline, Fife, Scotland, 9 November, 1932 — IF

League Club	Source	Date Signed	Seasons Played	Apps	Subs	Gls
Blackburn Rov	Jnr	11/49				
Ipswich T	Tr	05/54				
Oldham Ath	Darwen	08/56	56	25	-	12
Rochdale	Tr	03/57	56-57	32	-	17
Crewe Alex	Tr	05/58	58	9	-	2

PEARSON Donald James (Don)
Born: Swansea, Wales, 14 March, 1930 — LH
Died: Swansea, Wales, December, 2009

League Club	Source	Date Signed	Seasons Played	Apps	Subs	Gls
Swansea C	St Jude's	06/50	52-57	52	-	1
Aldershot	Tr	07/58	58	31	-	2

PEARSON Gary
Born: Houghton-le-Spring, Tyne and Wear, England, 7 December, 1976 — CD

League Club	Source	Date Signed	Seasons Played	Apps	Subs	Gls
Sheffield U	YT	07/95				
Darlington	Durham C	08/01	01-03	39	9	3

PEARSON Gregory Edward (Greg)
Born: Birmingham, England, 3 April, 1985 — F

League Club	Source	Date Signed	Seasons Played	Apps	Subs	Gls
West Ham U	Sch	07/03				
Lincoln C	L	08/04	04	1	2	0
Rushden & D	Tr	07/05	05	16	6	1
Burton A	Bishops Stortford	07/08	09-11	46	43	19
Aldershot T	L	11/11	11	1	4	0
Crewe Alex	L	01/12	11	8	1	3

PEARSON Ian Trevor
Born: Leeds, England, 18 September, 1950 — F

League Club	Source	Date Signed	Seasons Played	Apps	Subs	Gls
Plymouth Arg	Goole T	07/74	74-75	6	6	0
Millwall	Wycombe W	08/77	77-78	41	3	9
Exeter C	Tr	11/78	78-80	67	2	10
Plymouth Arg	Bideford	08/83	83	5	3	1

PEARSON James David
Born: Sheffield, England, 19 January, 1993 — RB

League Club	Source	Date Signed	Seasons Played	Apps	Subs	Gls
Leicester C	Rotherham U (Jnr)	09/12				
Carlisle U	L	03/14	13	3	0	0

PEARSON James Findlay (Jim)
Born: Falkirk, Scotland, 24 March, 1953 — F
Scotland: U23-6

League Club	Source	Date Signed	Seasons Played	Apps	Subs	Gls
Everton	St Johnstone	07/74	74-77	76	17	15
Newcastle U	Tr	08/78	78-79	11	0	3

PEARSON James Stuart (Stuart)
Born: Hull, England, 21 June, 1949 — F
England: 15/U23-1

League Club	Source	Date Signed	Seasons Played	Apps	Subs	Gls
Hull C	Jnr	07/68	69-73	126	3	44
Manchester U	Tr	05/74	74-77	138	1	55
West Ham U	Tr	08/79	79-81	28	6	6

PEARSON John
Born: Ferryhill, County Durham, England, 8 March, 1945 — F

League Club	Source	Date Signed	Seasons Played	Apps	Subs	Gls
Hartlepool U (Am)	Ferryhill Ath	01/69	68	1	0	0

PEARSON John
Born: Wigan, Greater Manchester, England, 18 October, 1946 — RW
England: Schools

League Club	Source	Date Signed	Seasons Played	Apps	Subs	Gls
Manchester U	App	11/63				
York C	Tr	07/65	65	14	1	4

PEARSON John Arthur
Born: Isleworth, W London, England, 23 April, 1935 — IF

League Club	Source	Date Signed	Seasons Played	Apps	Subs	Gls
Brentford	Jnr	11/52	55-56	5	-	0
Queens Park Rgrs	Tr	06/58	58-59	21	-	9

PEARSON John George
Born: Gateshead, Tyne and Wear, England, 10 April, 1931 — RB
Died: Gateshead, Tyne and Wear, England, July, 1996

League Club	Source	Date Signed	Seasons Played	Apps	Subs	Gls
Hartlepool U	Reyrolles	04/53	52	1	-	0

PEARSON John Stuart
Born: Sheffield, England, 1 September, 1963 — F
England: Youth

League Club	Source	Date Signed	Seasons Played	Apps	Subs	Gls
Sheffield Wed	App	05/81	80-84	64	41	24
Charlton Ath	Tr	05/85	85-86	52	9	15
Leeds U	Tr	01/87	86-90	51	48	12
Rotherham U	L	03/91	90	11	0	5
Barnsley	Tr	07/91	91-92	29	3	4
Hull C	L	01/92	91	15	0	0
Carlisle U	Tr	08/93	93-94	5	3	0
Mansfield T	Tr	11/94	94	0	2	0
Cardiff C	Tr	01/95	94	12	0	0

PEARSON Lawrence (Lawrie)
Born: Wallsend, Tyne and Wear, England, 2 July, 1965 — LB/M

League Club	Source	Date Signed	Seasons Played	Apps	Subs	Gls
Hull C	Gateshead	06/84	84-86	58	1	0
Bristol C	Tr	06/87				
Port Vale	Tr	08/87	87	3	0	0
Darlington	Barrow	08/93	93	26	2	4
Chesterfield	Tr	03/94	93	0	1	0

PEARSON Mark
Born: Sheffield, England, 28 October, 1939 — IF
England: Youth/Schools

League Club	Source	Date Signed	Seasons Played	Apps	Subs	Gls
Manchester U	Jnr	05/57	57-62	68	-	12
Sheffield Wed	Tr	10/63	63-64	39	-	9
Fulham	Tr	05/65	65-67	53	5	7
Halifax T	Tr	03/68	68	2	3	1

PEARSON Matthew Joe (Matty)
Born: Keighley, West Yorkshire, England, 3 August, 1993 — D/M

League Club	Source	Date Signed	Seasons Played	Apps	Subs	Gls
Blackburn Rov	Sch	07/11				
Rochdale	Tr	07/12	12	8	1	0

PEARSON Michael (Mike)
Born: Bilston, West Midlands, England, 5 December, 1942 — IF

League Club	Source	Date Signed	Seasons Played	Apps	Subs	Gls
Manchester C	Jnr	12/59				
Walsall	Tr	05/62	62	3	-	1

PEARSON Michael Thomas (Mike)
Born: Bangor, Gwynedd, Wales, 19 January, 1988 — CD

League Club	Source	Date Signed	Seasons Played	Apps	Subs	Gls
Oldham Ath	Sch	07/06	06-07	0	2	0

PEARSON Nigel Graham
Born: Nottingham, England, 21 August, 1963 — CD

League Club	Source	Date Signed	Seasons Played	Apps	Subs	Gls
Shrewsbury T	Heanor T	11/81	82-87	153	0	5
Sheffield Wed	Tr	10/87	87-93	176	9	14
Middlesbrough	Tr	07/94	94-97	115	1	5

PEARSON Richard (Ricky)
Born: Ulcombe, Kent, England, 18 October, 1970 — CD

League Club	Source	Date Signed	Seasons Played	Apps	Subs	Gls
Gillingham	YT	07/89	88-89	7	2	0

PEARSON Richard John (Dick)
Born: Portsmouth, England, 14 June, 1931 — WH

League Club	Source	Date Signed	Seasons Played	Apps	Subs	Gls
Portsmouth	Gosport Bor	05/49	53	4	-	1

PEARSON Stanley Clare (Stan)
Born: Salford, England, 11 January, 1919 — IF
Died: Alderley Edge, Cheshire, England, 20 February, 1997
England: 8/FLge-1

League Club	Source	Date Signed	Seasons Played	Apps	Subs	Gls
Manchester U	Adelphi LC	05/36	37-53	312	-	127
Bury	Tr	02/54	53-57	121	-	56
Chester C	Tr	10/57	57-58	57	-	16

PEARSON Stephen Paul
Born: Lanark, Scotland, 2 October, 1982 — W
Scotland: 10/B-1/U21-8

League Club	Source	Date Signed	Seasons Played	Apps	Subs	Gls
Derby Co	Glasgow Celtic	01/07	06-10	92	20	3
Stoke C	L	03/08	07	3	1	0
Bristol C	Tr	11/11	11-13	63	7	7

PEARSON Thomas Usher (Tommy)
Born: Edinburgh, Scotland, 6 March, 1914 — LW
Died: Edinburgh, Scotland, 1 March, 1999
England: FLge-1/War-1//Scotland: 2/SLge-1

League Club	Source	Date Signed	Seasons Played	Apps	Subs	Gls
Newcastle U	Murrayfield Amats	03/33	33-47	212	-	46

PEARSON Trevor
Born: Sheffield, England, 4 April, 1952 — G

League Club	Source	Date Signed	Seasons Played	Apps	Subs	Gls
Sheffield Wed (Am)	Woodseats WMC	03/72	71	4	0	0

PEARSON Walter (Wally)
Born: Ottershaw, Surrey, England, 13 November, 1928 — G
Died: Sutton, S London, England, December, 2008

League Club	Source	Date Signed	Seasons Played	Apps	Subs	Gls
Aldershot (Am)	Tooting & Mitcham U	03/61	60	1	-	0

PEARSON William George Arthur (Billy)
Born: Clonmel, Republic of Ireland, 23 October, 1921 — LW
Died: West Yorkshire, England, 23 May, 2009

League Club	Source	Date Signed	Seasons Played	Apps	Subs	Gls
Grimsby T	RAF	09/43	46-48	35	-	9
Chester C	Tr	06/49	49	12	-	3

PEART Robert Charles (Bob)
Born: Swindon, England, 17 December, 1926 — CF
Died: Swindon, England, 22 December, 1966

League Club	Source	Date Signed	Seasons Played	Apps	Subs	Gls
Swindon T	Pinehurst YC	04/48	49-51	13	-	5

PEART Ronald (Ron)
Born: Brandon, County Durham, England, 8 March, 1920 — CH
Died: Durham, England, April, 1999

League Club	Source	Date Signed	Seasons Played	Apps	Subs	Gls
Hartlepool U	Langley Moor	09/38	38	8	-	0
Derby Co	Tr	05/39	46	1	-	0
York C	Tr	06/48	48	5	-	0

PEAT James Leslie
Born: Birmingham, England, 29 May, 1951 — W

League Club	Source	Date Signed	Seasons Played	Apps	Subs	Gls
Workington	Cadbury's	08/73	73	0	1	0

PEAT John (Jack)
Born: United Kingdom — LW

League Club	Source	Date Signed	Seasons Played	Apps	Subs	Gls
Workington	Kilmarnock	10/53	53	1	-	0

PEAT Nathan Neil Martin
Born: Hull, England, 19 September, 1982 — LB

League Club	Source	Date Signed	Seasons Played	Apps	Subs	Gls
Hull C	Sch	07/02	02-03	0	2	0
Cambridge U	L	12/03	03	3	3	0
Lincoln C	L	07/04	04	6	4	0

PEAT William Arthur (Arthur)
Born: Liverpool, England, 1 September, 1940 — RH
Died: Southport, Merseyside, England, 16 July, 2012

League Club	Source	Date Signed	Seasons Played	Apps	Subs	Gls
Everton	Jnr	04/59				
Southport	Tr	07/61	61-71	401	0	27
Crewe Alex	Tr	07/72	72-73	82	0	5

PEATTIE Donald Simpson (Don)
Born: York, England, 5 April, 1963 — F

League Club	Source	Date Signed	Seasons Played	Apps	Subs	Gls
Sheffield U	Gretna	08/84	84	3	2	0
Doncaster Rov	L	01/86	85	3	1	0

PECK Dennis Trevor (Trevor)
Born: Llanelli, Carmarthenshire, Wales, 25 May, 1938 — FB
Died: Kettering, Northamptonshire, England, 19 May, 2014

League Club	Source	Date Signed	Seasons Played	Apps	Subs	Gls
Cardiff C	Llanelli	02/58	59-64	42	-	0

PECKETT Andrew Richard (Andy)
Born: Sheffield, England, 19 September, 1969 — M

League Club	Source	Date Signed	Seasons Played	Apps	Subs	Gls
Doncaster Rov	YT	06/88	87-88	2	7	0

PECNIK Nejc
Born: Dravograd, Slovenia, 3 January, 1986 — M
Slovenia: 23/U21-3

League Club	Source	Date Signed	Seasons Played	Apps	Subs	Gls
Sheffield Wed	CD Nacional (POR)	07/12	12	5	5	0

PEDDELTY John
Born: Bishop Auckland, County Durham, England, 2 April, 1955 — CD
England: Youth

League Club	Source	Date Signed	Seasons Played	Apps	Subs	Gls
Ipswich T	App	01/73	72-76	44	0	5
Plymouth Arg	Tr	10/76	76-77	30	3	1

PEDDELTY John Maurice (Maurice)
Born: Carlisle, Cumbria, England, 23 May, 1950 — M

League Club	Source	Date Signed	Seasons Played	Apps	Subs	Gls
Carlisle U	App	12/67	68-69	9	4	1
Darlington	Tr	07/70	70-71	51	5	1

PEDEN George Wright Watson
Born: Rosewell, Midlothian, Scotland, 12 April, 1943 — LB

League Club	Source	Date Signed	Seasons Played	Apps	Subs	Gls
Lincoln C	Heart of Midlothian	04/67	66-73	223	2	15

PEDERSEN Henrik
Born: Kjellerup, Denmark, 10 June, 1975 — F
Denmark: 3

League Club	Source	Date Signed	Seasons Played	Apps	Subs	Gls
Bolton W	Silkeborg (NOR)	07/01	01-06	93	50	22
Hull C	Tr	08/07	07	18	3	4

PEDERSEN Jan Ove
Born: Oslo, Norway, 12 November, 1968 — M
Norway: 16/U21-3/Youth

League Club	Source	Date Signed	Seasons Played	Apps	Subs	Gls
Hartlepool U (L)	SK Brann Bergen (NOR)	10/97	97	17	0	1

PEDERSEN Marcus
Born: Hamar, Norway, 8 June, 1990 — F
Norway: 7/U21-19/Youth

League Club	Source	Date Signed	Seasons Played	Apps	Subs	Gls
Barnsley (L)	Vitesse Arnhem (NED)	08/13	13	12	6	2

PEDERSEN Morten Gamst
Born: Vadso, Norway, 8 September, 1981 — LW
Norway: 80/U21-18/Youth

League Club	Source	Date Signed	Seasons Played	Apps	Subs	Gls
Blackburn Rov	Tromso (NOR)	08/04	04-12	257	31	35

PEDERSEN Per Werner
Born: Aalborg, Denmark, 30 March, 1969 — F
Denmark: 6/U21-2

League Club	Source	Date Signed	Seasons Played	Apps	Subs	Gls
Blackburn Rov	Odense (DEN)	02/97	96	6	5	1

PEDERSEN Rune
Born: Copenhagen, Denmark, 9 October, 1979 — G
Denmark: U21-8/Youth

League Club	Source	Date Signed	Seasons Played	Apps	Subs	Gls
Nottingham F	Aarhus GF (DEN)	07/05	05-06	18	1	0

PEDERSEN Tore Andre
Born: Fredrikstad, Norway, 29 September, 1969 — CD
Norway: 45

League Club	Source	Date Signed	Seasons Played	Apps	Subs	Gls
Oldham Ath	SK Brann Bergen (NOR)	10/93	93	7	3	0
Blackburn Rov	St Pauli (GER)	09/97	97	3	2	0
Wimbledon	Eintracht F'furt (GER)	06/99	99	6	0	0

PEDROZA Antonio Michael
Born: Chester, England, 20 February, 1991 — F

League Club	Source	Date Signed	Seasons Played	Apps	Subs	Gls
Crystal Palace	Jaguares (MEX)	08/11	11	1	3	0

PEEBLES Richard Winter (Dick)
Born: Glasgow, Scotland, 30 August, 1923 — IF
Died: Glasgow, Scotland, 1 June, 2004

League Club	Source	Date Signed	Seasons Played	Apps	Subs	Gls
Swindon T	St Johnstone	05/50	50	12	-	1

PEEK James (Jim)
Born: Hartlepool, Cleveland, England, 7 July, 1933 — RB
Died: Stockton-on-Tees, Cleveland, England, October, 2013

League Club	Source	Date Signed	Seasons Played	Apps	Subs	Gls
Hartlepool U (Am)	West View A	12/59	59	7	-	0

PEEL Kenneth (Ken)
Born: Manchester, England, 8 November, 1922 — IF
Died: Stockport, Greater Manchester, England, December, 2002

League Club	Source	Date Signed	Seasons Played	Apps	Subs	Gls
Crewe Alex	Rusholme	09/46	46	1	-	0

PEEL Nathan James
Born: Blackburn, Greater Manchester, England, 17 May, 1972 — F

League Club	Source	Date Signed	Seasons Played	Apps	Subs	Gls
Preston NE	YT	07/90	90	1	9	1
Sheffield U	Tr	08/91	91	0	1	0
Halifax T	L	02/93	92	3	0	0
Burnley	Tr	09/93	93-94	4	12	2
Rotherham U	L	03/95	94	9	0	4
Mansfield T	L	10/95	95	2	0	0
Doncaster Rov	L	02/96	95	2	0	0
Rotherham U	Tr	07/96				
Macclesfield T	Tr	01/97	97	10	4	3

PEEL Trevor
Born: Huddersfield, West Yorkshire, England, 25 October, 1945 — RB

League Club	Source	Date Signed	Seasons Played	Apps	Subs	Gls
Bradford Park Ave	Huddersfield T (Am)	04/67	66-67	11	0	0

PEER Dean
Born: Stourbridge, West Midlands, England, 8 August, 1969 — M

League Club	Source	Date Signed	Seasons Played	Apps	Subs	Gls
Birmingham C	YT	07/87	86-92	106	14	8
Mansfield T	L	12/92	92	10	0	0
Walsall	Tr	11/93	93-94	41	4	8
Northampton T	Tr	08/95	95-99	97	31	6
Shrewsbury T	Tr	01/00	99-00	53	3	0

PEERS Gavin Joseph
Born: Dublin, Republic of Ireland, 10 November, 1985 — RB
Republic of Ireland: U23-1

League Club	Source	Date Signed	Seasons Played	Apps	Subs	Gls
Blackburn Rov	Sch	11/02				
Mansfield T	Tr	08/05	05	12	1	2

PEETERS Bob
Born: Lier, Belgium, 10 January, 1974 — F
Belgium: 12

League Club	Source	Date Signed	Seasons Played	Apps	Subs	Gls
Millwall	Vitesse Arnhem (NED)	08/03	03-05	16	9	3

PEGG David
Born: Doncaster, South Yorkshire, England, 20 September, 1935 — LW
Died: Munich, Germany, 6 February, 1958
England: 1/B-1/U23-3/Schools

League Club	Source	Date Signed	Seasons Played	Apps	Subs	Gls
Manchester U	Jnr	09/52	52-57	127	-	24

PEGG James Kenneth (Jimmy)
Born: Salford, England, 4 January, 1926 — G
Died: Manchester, England, 25 August, 1999

League Club	Source	Date Signed	Seasons Played	Apps	Subs	Gls
Manchester U	Jnr	11/47	47	2	-	0
Torquay U	Tr	08/49	49	2	-	0
York C	Tr	08/50	50	1	-	0

PEHRSSON Magnus Karl
Born: Stockholm, Sweden, 25 May, 1976 — M

League Club	Source	Date Signed	Seasons Played	Apps	Subs	Gls
Bradford C (L)	Djurgaarden (SWE)	10/96	96	1	0	0

PEJIC Melvyn (Mel)
Born: Newcastle-under-Lyme, Potteries, England, 27 April, 1959 — CD

League Club	Source	Date Signed	Seasons Played	Apps	Subs	Gls
Stoke C	Jnr	01/77	79	1	0	0
Hereford U	Tr	06/80	80-91	404	8	14
Wrexham	Tr	01/92	91-94	103	3	3

PEJIC Michael (Mike)
Born: Newcastle-under-Lyme, Potteries, England, 25 January, 1950 — LB
England: 4/U23-8

League Club	Source	Date Signed	Seasons Played	Apps	Subs	Gls
Stoke C	App	01/68	68-76	274	0	6
Everton	Tr	02/77	76-78	76	0	2
Aston Villa	Tr	09/79	79	10	0	0

PEJIC Shaun Melvyn
Born: Hereford, England, 16 November, 1982 — CD
Wales: U21-6/Youth

League Club	Source	Date Signed	Seasons Played	Apps	Subs	Gls
Wrexham	Sch	08/02	00-07	161	13	0

PEKHART Tomas
Born: Suzice, Czech Republic, 26 May, 1989 — F
Czech Republic: 19/U21-26

League Club	Source	Date Signed	Seasons Played	Apps	Subs	Gls
Tottenham H	Slavia Prague (CZE)	08/06				
Southampton	L	08/08	08	2	7	1

[PELE] CARDOSO MONTEIRO Pedro Miguel
Born: Albufeira, Portugal, 7 May, 1978 — CD
Cape Verde Islands: 11

League Club	Source	Date Signed	Seasons Played	Apps	Subs	Gls
Southampton	Belenenses (POR)	07/06	06	34	3	1
West Bromwich A	Tr	08/07	07-08	14	10	0

PELL Dennis
Born: Normanton, West Yorkshire, England, 19 April, 1929 — LW
Died: Wakefield, England, January, 2003

League Club	Source	Date Signed	Seasons Played	Apps	Subs	Gls
Rotherham U	Methley	05/52	52-55	11	-	3
Grimsby T	Tr	10/55	55-56	3	-	1

PELL Harry David Belraj
Born: Tilbury, Essex, England, 21 October, 1991 — M

League Club	Source	Date Signed	Seasons Played	Apps	Subs	Gls
Bristol Rov	Charlton Ath (Sch)	07/10	10	7	3	0
Hereford U	L	01/11	10	5	2	0
Hereford U	Tr	07/11	11	22	8	3
AFC Wimbledon	Tr	01/13	12-14	45	14	5

PELL Robert Anthony
Born: Leeds, England, 5 February, 1979 — F

League Club	Source	Date Signed	Seasons Played	Apps	Subs	Gls
Rotherham U	YT	06/97	96	2	0	0
Doncaster Rov	L	11/97	97	6	4	1

PELLE Graziano
Born: Lecce, Italy, 15 July, 1985 — F
Italy: 4/U21-11/Youth

League Club	Source	Date Signed	Seasons Played	Apps	Subs	Gls
Southampton	Feyenoord (NED)	07/14	14	37	1	12

PELLEGRINO Mauricio Andres
Born: Cordoba, Argentina, 5 October, 1971 — CD
Argentina: 3/Youth

League Club	Source	Date Signed	Seasons Played	Apps	Subs	Gls
Liverpool (L)	Valencia (SPN)	01/05	04	11	1	0

PELLICORI Alessandro
Born: Cosenza, Italy, 22 July, 1981 — F

League Club	Source	Date Signed	Seasons Played	Apps	Subs	Gls
Queens Park Rgrs	Avellino (ITA)	08/09	09	1	7	0

PELTIER Lee Anthony
Born: Liverpool, England, 11 December, 1986 — D
England: Youth

League Club	Source	Date Signed	Seasons Played	Apps	Subs	Gls
Liverpool	Sch	11/04				
Hull C	L	03/07	06	5	2	0
Yeovil T	Tr	08/07	07-08	68	1	1
Huddersfield T	Tr	06/09	09-10	80	0	1
Leicester C	Tr	06/11	11	39	1	2
Leeds U	Tr	08/12	12-13	63	3	1
Nottingham F	L	03/14	13	7	0	0
Huddersfield T	Tr	06/14	14	8	3	0
Cardiff C	Tr	01/15	14	15	0	0

PEMBERTON James Henry Arthur (Jim)
Born: Wolverhampton, England, 30 April, 1916 — RB
Died: Wolverhampton, England, 10 February, 1996

League Club	Source	Date Signed	Seasons Played	Apps	Subs	Gls
West Bromwich A	Brownhills A	08/38	46-50	162	-	0

PEMBERTON James Thomas (Jim)
Born: Kingswinford, West Midlands, England, 14 November, 1925 — RH/LB

League Club	Source	Date Signed	Seasons Played	Apps	Subs	Gls
West Bromwich A	Round Oak	05/45				
Luton T	Stourbridge	11/47	50-56	92	-	8

PEMBERTON John Matthew
Born: Oldham, Greater Manchester, England, 18 November, 1964 — D

League Club	Source	Date Signed	Seasons Played	Apps	Subs	Gls
Rochdale	Chadderton	09/84	84	1	0	0
Crewe Alex	Chadderton	03/85	84-87	116	5	1
Crystal Palace	Tr	03/88	87-89	76	2	2
Sheffield U	Tr	07/90	90-93	67	1	0
Leeds U	Tr	11/93	93-95	44	9	0
Crewe Alex	Tr	08/97	97	1	0	0

PEMBERTON Martin Calvin
Born: Bradford, England, 1 February, 1976 — LB/M

League Club	Source	Date Signed	Seasons Played	Apps	Subs	Gls
Oldham Ath	YT	07/94	95-96	0	5	0
Doncaster Rov	Tr	03/97	96-97	33	2	2
Scunthorpe U	Tr	03/98	97	3	3	0
Hartlepool U	Tr	07/98	98	0	4	0
Mansfield T	Bradford Park Ave	08/00	00-01	49	7	5
Stockport Co	Tr	04/02	02-03	20	6	0
Rochdale	L	01/04	03	1	0	0

PEMBERTON Selwyn Robert
Born: Cardiff, Wales, 13 October, 1928 — RB
Died: Cardiff, Wales, May, 2005

League Club	Source	Date Signed	Seasons Played	Apps	Subs	Gls
Newport Co		03/52	52	1	-	0

PEMBERY Gordon Dennis
Born: Cardiff, Wales, 10 October, 1926 — LH/LW
Died: Swindon, England, 12 March, 2013

League Club	Source	Date Signed	Seasons Played	Apps	Subs	Gls
Norwich C	Cardiff Nomads	01/47	46	1	-	0
Cardiff C	Tr	08/48	49	1	-	0
Torquay U	Tr	06/50	50-51	51	-	7
Charlton Ath	Tr	01/52	51-55	18	-	1
Swindon T	Tr	06/56	56	37	-	2

PEMBLETON Martin John
Born: Scunthorpe, North Lincolnshire, England, 1 June, 1990 — M

League Club	Source	Date Signed	Seasons Played	Apps	Subs	Gls
Lincoln C	Sch	07/08	07	4	2	0

PEMBRIDGE Mark Anthony
Born: Merthyr Tydfil, Wales, 29 November, 1970 — M
Wales: 54/B-2/U21-1/Schools

League Club	Source	Date Signed	Seasons Played	Apps	Subs	Gls
Luton T	YT	07/89	90-91	60	0	6
Derby Co	Tr	06/92	92-94	108	2	28
Sheffield Wed	Tr	07/95	95-97	88	5	11
Everton	Benfica (POR)	08/99	99-03	82	9	4
Fulham	Tr	09/03	03-05	40	5	1

PENDER John Patrick
Born: Luton, England, 19 November, 1963 — CD
Republic of Ireland: U21-5/Youth

League Club	Source	Date Signed	Seasons Played	Apps	Subs	Gls
Wolverhampton W	App	11/81	81-84	115	2	3
Charlton Ath	Tr	07/85	85-87	41	0	0
Bristol C	Tr	10/87	87-89	83	0	3
Burnley	Tr	10/90	90-95	171	0	8
Wigan Ath	Tr	08/95	95-96	67	3	1
Rochdale	Tr	07/97	97	14	0	0

PENDERGAST William James (Bill)
Born: Pen-y-groes, Gwynedd, Wales, 13 April, 1915 — CF
Died: Rhyl, Denbighshire, Wales, May, 2001

League Club	Source	Date Signed	Seasons Played	Apps	Subs	Gls
Manchester U	Wrexham (Am)	12/35				
Wolverhampton W	Tr	01/36				
Bristol Rov	Tr	05/36	36-37	7	-	3

League Club	Source	Date Signed	Seasons Played	Apps	Subs	Gls
Chester C	Colchester U	07/38	38	34	-	26
New Brighton	Tr	08/46	46-47	69	-	26
PENDLEBURY Derek Keith (Keith)						
Born: Stockport, Greater Manchester, England, 22 January, 1934						LH
Stockport Co	Jnr	03/51	53	2	-	0
PENDLEBURY Ian David						
Born: Bolton, Greater Manchester, England, 3 September, 1983						LB
Wigan Ath	YT	08/01	01	4	0	0
PENDREY Gary James Sidney						
Born: Birmingham, England, 9 February, 1949						D
Birmingham C	App	10/66	68-78	287	19	4
West Bromwich A	Tr	08/79	79	18	0	0
Torquay U	Tr	08/81	81	12	0	0
Bristol Rov	Tr	12/81	81	1	0	0
Walsall	Tr	08/82	82	8	0	1
PENFOLD Mark						
Born: Woolwich, SE London, England, 10 December, 1956						RB
Charlton Ath	App	04/74	73-78	65	5	0
Leyton Orient	Tr	07/79	79	3	0	1
PENFORD Dennis Henry						
Born: Reading, England, 31 August, 1931						LB
Died: Torquay, Devon, England, 28 December, 2011						
Reading		05/52	53-58	101	-	6
Torquay U	Tr	06/59	59-61	77	-	0
PENFORD Thomas James (Tom)						
Born: Leeds, England, 5 January, 1985						M
Bradford C	Sch	07/04	02-07	26	12	1
PENGELLY Richard Norman Woodrow (Norman)						
Born: Looe, Cornwall, England, 6 October, 1919						CH
Died: Plymouth, England, 10 October, 2005						
Plymouth Arg	Looe	05/47	47-49	9	-	0
PENHALIGON Gary						
Born: St Austell, Cornwall, England, 13 May, 1970						G
Plymouth Arg	YT	07/88	88	1	0	0
PENIKET Richard James						
Born: Bromsgrove, Worcestershire, England, 4 March, 1993						F
Wales: U21-1/Youth						
Fulham	Sch	07/10				
Hereford U	L	10/11	11	4	3	0
PENK Henry (Harry)						
Born: Wigan, Greater Manchester, England, 19 July, 1934						W
Portsmouth	Wigan Ath	09/55	55-56	9	-	2
Plymouth Arg	Tr	06/57	57-59	104	-	14
Southampton	Tr	07/60	60-63	52	-	6
PENMAN Christopher (Chris)						
Born: Houghton-le-Spring, Tyne and Wear, England, 12 September, 1945						G
Darlington	Preston NE (App)	12/62	62-63	30	-	0
PENMAN William Salmond Thomson (Willie)						
Born: East Wemyss, Fife, Scotland, 7 August, 1939						IF
Newcastle U	Glasgow Rangers	04/63	62-65	62	1	18
Swindon T	Tr	09/66	66-69	87	11	18
Walsall	Tr	08/70	70-72	118	5	6
PENN Donald John (Don)						
Born: Smethwick, West Midlands, England, 15 March, 1960						F
Walsall	Warley Bor	01/78	77-82	132	9	54
PENN Frank Reginald						
Born: Edmonton, N London, England, 15 April, 1927						LW
Died: Chester, England, August, 2001						
Crystal Palace	Guildford C	09/49	49	1	-	0
PENN Russell Anthony (Russ)						
Born: Dudley, West Midlands, England, 8 November, 1985						DM
England: Semi Pro-8						
Burton A	Kidderminster Hrs	07/09	09-10	73	8	7
Cheltenham T	Tr	07/11	11-13	89	16	2
York C	Tr	01/14	13-14	66	0	2
PENNANT Jermaine Lloyd						
Born: Nottingham, England, 15 January, 1983						RW
England: U21-24/Youth/Schools						
Arsenal	Notts Co (Jnr)	03/00	02-04	2	10	3
Watford	L	01/02	01	9	0	2
Watford	L	11/02	02	12	0	0
Leeds U	L	08/03	03	34	2	2
Birmingham C	Tr	01/05	04-05	47	3	2
Liverpool	Tr	07/06	06-08	36	19	3
Portsmouth	L	01/09	08	9	4	0

League Club	Source	Date Signed	Seasons Played	Apps	Subs	Gls
Stoke C	Real Zaragoza (SPN)	08/10	10-13	45	20	4
Wolverhampton W	L	10/12	12	10	5	0
Wigan Ath	FC Pune C (IND)	02/15	14	12	1	3
PENNEY David Mark						
Born: Wakefield, England, 17 August, 1964						M
Derby Co	Pontefract Collieries	09/85	86-88	6	13	0
Oxford U	Tr	06/89	89-93	76	34	15
Swansea C	L	03/91	90	12	0	3
Swansea C	Tr	03/94	93-96	112	7	20
Cardiff C	Tr	07/97	97-98	33	2	5
PENNEY Steven Alexander (Steve)						
Born: Ballymena, Antrim, Northern Ireland, 6 January, 1964						RW
Northern Ireland: 17						
Brighton & HA	Ballymena U	11/83	83-88	125	13	15
Burnley	Heart of Midlothian	07/92	92	10	1	3
PENNICK Raymond (Ray)						
Born: Ferryhill, County Durham, England, 30 November, 1946						F
York C (Am)	Willington	03/69	68	0	1	0
PENNINGTON Jack						
Born: Tadcaster, North Yorkshire, England, 12 September, 1928						RW
Died: Huddersfield, West Yorkshire, England, July, 1987						
Halifax T	Marsden	11/53	53-54	7	-	2
PENNINGTON James (Jim)						
Born: Golborne, Greater Manchester, England, 26 April, 1939						RW
Manchester C	Jnr	08/56	58	1	-	0
Crewe Alex	Tr	03/61	60-62	34	-	3
Grimsby T	Tr	04/63	62-64	89	-	8
Oldham Ath	Tr	07/65	65	23	0	0
Rochdale	Tr	07/66	66	14	0	0
PENNINGTON James (Jimmy)						
Born: Burtonwood, Cheshire, England, 13 November, 1928						IF
Died: Weston, Shropshire, England, 12 September, 1976						
Huddersfield T	Burtonwood OB	08/49				
Southport	Tr	07/51	51-53	55	-	11
PENNINGTON Matthew						
Born: Warrington, Cheshire, England, 6 October, 1994						D
England: Youth						
Everton	Sch	07/13				
Tranmere Rov	L	01/14	13	17	0	2
Coventry C	L	11/14	14	24	0	0
PENNOCK Adrian Barry						
Born: Ipswich, England, 27 March, 1971						D/M
Norwich C	YT	07/89	89	1	0	0
Bournemouth	Tr	08/92	92-95	130	1	9
Gillingham	Tr	10/96	96-02	164	4	2
PENNOCK Anthony (Tony)						
Born: Swansea, Wales, 10 April, 1971						G
Stockport Co	Clydach U	08/90				
Wigan Ath	L	12/90	90	2	0	0
Wigan Ath	Tr	06/91	92	8	0	0
Hereford U	Tr	07/94	94	13	2	0
Rushden & D	Yeovil T	06/01	01	3	2	0
PENNY Christian Vincent (Chris)						
Born: Southend-on-Sea, England, 16 February, 1973						FB
Doncaster Rov	Brigg T	02/92	91	1	0	0
PENNY Diego Alonso Roberto						
Born: Lima, Peru, 22 April, 1984						G
Peru: 6						
Burnley	CC Bolognesi (PER)	07/08	08-09	1	1	0
PENNY John						
Born: Plymouth, England, 19 August, 1938						RW
Plymouth Arg	Jnr	11/55	57-59	7	-	0
PENNY Shaun						
Born: Bristol, England, 24 September, 1957						F
England: Schools						
Bristol C	App	09/74				
Bristol Rov	Tr	08/79	79-81	57	3	13
PENNYFATHER Glenn Julian						
Born: Billericay, Essex, England, 11 February, 1963						M
Southend U	App	02/81	80-87	232	6	36
Crystal Palace	Tr	11/87	87-88	31	3	1
Ipswich T	Tr	10/89	89-92	11	4	1
Bristol C	Tr	02/93	92-93	21	5	1
PENRHYN Norman Andrew						
Born: Lambeth, S London, England, 28 February, 1950						F
Plymouth Arg	App	-	67	0	1	0

PENRICE Gary Kenneth
Born: Bristol, England, 23 March, 1964 — F

League Club	Source	Date Signed	Seasons Played	Apps	Subs	Gls
Bristol Rov	Mangotsfield U	11/84	84-89	186	2	54
Watford	Tr	11/89	89-90	41	2	17
Aston Villa	Tr	03/91	90-91	14	6	1
Queens Park Rgrs	Tr	10/91	91-95	55	27	20
Watford	Tr	11/95	95-96	26	13	2
Bristol Rov	Tr	07/97	97-99	48	21	6

PENROSE Colin Richard
Born: Bradford, England, 1 November, 1949 — IF

League Club	Source	Date Signed	Seasons Played	Apps	Subs	Gls
Bradford Park Ave (Am)	Sedbergh YC	09/68	68	6	0	1

PENROSE Norman
Born: Consett, County Durham, England, 10 March, 1922 — RH
Died: Blyth, Northumberland, England, September, 2000
England: Schools

League Club	Source	Date Signed	Seasons Played	Apps	Subs	Gls
Grimsby T	Medomsley	05/39	46-47	9	-	0

PENSEE-BILLONG Michel
Born: Yaounde, Cameroon, 16 June, 1973 — CD
Cameroon: 7

League Club	Source	Date Signed	Seasons Played	Apps	Subs	Gls
MK Dons	San. Hiroshima (JPN)	01/05	04	18	0	1

PENTECOST Michael Eric (Mike)
Born: Hounslow, SW London, England, 13 April, 1948 — RB
Died: Durban, South Africa, 7 May, 2011

League Club	Source	Date Signed	Seasons Played	Apps	Subs	Gls
Fulham	Sutton U	08/66	66-72	81	6	0

PENTNEY Carl Benjamin
Born: Colchester, Essex, England, 3 February, 1989 — G

League Club	Source	Date Signed	Seasons Played	Apps	Subs	Gls
Leicester C	Sch	07/07	08	0	1	0
Colchester U	Tr	08/10				

PEPLOW Ronald Rupert (Ron)
Born: Willesden, NW London, England, 4 May, 1935 — WH

League Club	Source	Date Signed	Seasons Played	Apps	Subs	Gls
Brentford	Southall	08/55	55-60	61	-	5

PEPLOW Stephen Thomas (Steve)
Born: Liverpool, England, 8 January, 1949 — RW

League Club	Source	Date Signed	Seasons Played	Apps	Subs	Gls
Liverpool	App	01/66	69	2	0	0
Swindon T	Tr	05/70	70-72	37	3	11
Nottingham F	Tr	07/73	73	3	0	0
Mansfield T	L	12/73	73	4	0	3
Tranmere Rov	Tr	01/74	73-80	232	16	44

PEPPER Carl
Born: Darlington, County Durham, England, 26 July, 1980 — RB

League Club	Source	Date Signed	Seasons Played	Apps	Subs	Gls
Darlington	YT	07/98	98	5	1	0

PEPPER Colin Nigel (Nigel)
Born: Rotherham, South Yorkshire, England, 25 April, 1968 — M

League Club	Source	Date Signed	Seasons Played	Apps	Subs	Gls
Rotherham U	App	04/86	85-89	35	10	1
York C	Tr	07/90	90-96	223	12	39
Bradford C	Tr	02/97	96-98	47	5	11
Southend U (L)	Aberdeen	12/99	99	9	3	2
Scunthorpe U	Aberdeen	07/00	00-01	2	1	0

PEPPITT Sydney (Syd)
Born: Stoke-on-Trent, England, 8 September, 1919 — IF
Died: Stoke-on-Trent, England, 25 December, 1992
England: Schools

League Club	Source	Date Signed	Seasons Played	Apps	Subs	Gls
Stoke C	Jnr	09/36	36-49	94	-	29
Port Vale	Tr	05/50	50	11	-	3

PERALTA Sixto Raimundo
Born: Comodoro Rivadavia, Argentina, 16 April, 1979 — M
Argentina: Youth

League Club	Source	Date Signed	Seasons Played	Apps	Subs	Gls
Ipswich T (L)	Inter Milan (ITA)	08/01	01	16	6	3

PERCH James Robert
Born: Mansfield, Nottinghamshire, England, 29 September, 1985 — D/M

League Club	Source	Date Signed	Seasons Played	Apps	Subs	Gls
Nottingham F	Sch	11/02	04-09	163	27	12
Newcastle U	Tr	07/10	10-12	41	24	1
Wigan Ath	Tr	07/13	13-14	77	4	3

PERCIVAL Jason Charles
Born: Nuneaton, Warwickshire, England, 20 September, 1973 — F

League Club	Source	Date Signed	Seasons Played	Apps	Subs	Gls
Stoke C	YT	09/90				
Exeter C	Tr	07/93	93	0	4	0

PERCIVAL John Robert (Jack)
Born: Pittington, County Durham, England, 16 May, 1913 — LH
Died: Rochdale, Greater Manchester, England, January, 1976

League Club	Source	Date Signed	Seasons Played	Apps	Subs	Gls
Manchester C	Durham C	10/32	33-46	161	-	8
Bournemouth	Tr	05/47	47-48	52	-	1

PERCIVAL Ronald Frederick John (Jack)
Born: Norwood, S London, England, 19 April, 1924 — CH

League Club	Source	Date Signed	Seasons Played	Apps	Subs	Gls
Huddersfield T	Tunbridge Wells	02/48	47-49	8	-	0
Chesterfield	Tr	05/50	50	6	-	0

PERDOMO Jose Batile
Born: Salto, Uruguay, 6 January, 1965 — M
Uruguay: 27

League Club	Source	Date Signed	Seasons Played	Apps	Subs	Gls
Coventry C	Genoa (ITA)	08/90	90	4	0	0

PEREIRA Andreas Hugo
Born: Duffel, Belgium, 1 January, 1996 — M
Belgium: Youth//Brazil: Youth

League Club	Source	Date Signed	Seasons Played	Apps	Subs	Gls
Manchester U	Sch	01/13	14	0	1	0

PEREPLOTKINS Andrejs
Born: Kharkov, Ukraine, 27 December, 1984 — RW
Latvia: 28

League Club	Source	Date Signed	Seasons Played	Apps	Subs	Gls
Derby Co (L)	Skonto Riga (LAT)	08/08	08	2	0	0

PEREZ Ayoze
Born: Tenerife, Spain, 23 July, 1993 — F
Spain: U21-2

League Club	Source	Date Signed	Seasons Played	Apps	Subs	Gls
Newcastle U	CD Tenerife (SPN)	06/14	14	25	11	7

PEREZ Lionel
Born: Bagnols-sur-Ceze, France, 24 April, 1967 — G

League Club	Source	Date Signed	Seasons Played	Apps	Subs	Gls
Sunderland	Bordeaux (FRA)	08/96	96-97	74	1	0
Newcastle U	Tr	07/98				
Scunthorpe U	L	10/99	99	13	0	0
Cambridge U	Tr	03/00	99-01	87	1	0

PEREZ Sebastien
Born: Saint-Chamond, France, 24 November, 1973 — M

League Club	Source	Date Signed	Seasons Played	Apps	Subs	Gls
Blackburn Rov	SC Bastia (FRA)	07/98	98	4	1	1

PERGL Pavel
Born: Prague, Czech Republic, 14 November, 1977 — M

League Club	Source	Date Signed	Seasons Played	Apps	Subs	Gls
Preston NE	Sparta Prague (CZE)	02/07	06	6	0	1

PERICARD Vincent de Paul
Born: Efko, Cameroon, 3 October, 1982 — F
France: Youth

League Club	Source	Date Signed	Seasons Played	Apps	Subs	Gls
Portsmouth	Juventus (ITA)	07/02	02-05	21	23	9
Sheffield U	L	09/05	05	3	8	2
Plymouth Arg	L	02/06	05	14	1	4
Stoke C	Tr	07/06	06-08	20	18	2
Southampton	L	03/08	07	1	4	0
Millwall	L	02/09	08	2	0	0
Carlisle U	Tr	10/09	09	10	0	4
Swindon T	Tr	01/10	09-10	13	19	2

PERIFIMOU Christopher James (Chris)
Born: Enfield, N London, England, 27 November, 1975 — W

League Club	Source	Date Signed	Seasons Played	Apps	Subs	Gls
Leyton Orient	YT	-	94	3	1	0
Barnet	Tr	09/95				

PERKINS Christopher Paul (Chris)
Born: Stepney, E London, England, 1 March, 1980 — CD

League Club	Source	Date Signed	Seasons Played	Apps	Subs	Gls
Southend U	YT	07/98	97	3	2	0

PERKINS Christopher Peter (Chris)
Born: Nottingham, England, 9 January, 1974 — D/M

League Club	Source	Date Signed	Seasons Played	Apps	Subs	Gls
Mansfield T	YT	11/92	92-93	3	5	0
Chesterfield	Tr	07/94	94-98	136	11	3
Hartlepool U	Tr	07/99	99	7	1	0
Chesterfield	Tr	10/99	99-00	37	2	0
Lincoln C	Tr	01/01	00	11	1	0

PERKINS David Philip
Born: Heysham, Lancashire, England, 21 June, 1982 — DM
England: Semi Pro-9

League Club	Source	Date Signed	Seasons Played	Apps	Subs	Gls
Rochdale	Morecambe	01/07	06-07	54	4	4
Colchester U	Tr	07/08	08-10	71	8	7
Chesterfield	L	10/09	09	11	2	1
Stockport Co	L	01/10	09	22	0	0
Barnsley	Tr	07/11	11-13	84	7	2
Blackpool	Tr	01/14	13-14	65	0	0

PERKINS Declan Oliver
Born: Ilford, E London, England, 17 October, 1975 — W
Republic of Ireland: U21-4

League Club	Source	Date Signed	Seasons Played	Apps	Subs	Gls
Southend U	YT	05/94	94	1	5	0
Cambridge U	L	09/95	95	1	1	1

PERKINS Eric
Born: West Bromwich, West Midlands, England, 19 August, 1934 — LB
Died: Walsall, West Midlands, England, 30 December, 2008

League Club	Source	Date Signed	Seasons Played	Apps	Subs	Gls
West Bromwich A	Hill Top	06/52	55	2	-	0
Walsall	Tr	06/56	56-58	67	-	1

PERKINS Glen Stewart
Born: Northampton, England, 12 October, 1960 — M

League Club	Source	Date Signed	Seasons Played	Apps	Subs	Gls
Northampton T	App	10/78	78	0	1	0

PERKINS Stephen Arthur (Steve)
Born: Stepney, E London, England, 3 October, 1954 — FB

League Club	Source	Date Signed	Seasons Played	Apps	Subs	Gls
Chelsea	App	11/71				
Queens Park Rgrs	Tr	06/77	77	2	0	0
Wimbledon	Tr	10/78	78-80	52	0	0

PERKINS Steven William (Steve)
Born: St Helens, Merseyside, England, 5 November, 1975 — M

League Club	Source	Date Signed	Seasons Played	Apps	Subs	Gls
Plymouth Arg	Crediton U	02/97	96	1	3	0

PERKS Stephen John (Steve)
Born: Bridgnorth, Shropshire, England, 19 April, 1963 — G

League Club	Source	Date Signed	Seasons Played	Apps	Subs	Gls
Shrewsbury T	App	04/81	84-91	243	0	0

PERON Jean-Francois (Jeff)
Born: Saint-Omer, France, 11 October, 1965 — M

League Club	Source	Date Signed	Seasons Played	Apps	Subs	Gls
Walsall	Caen (FRA)	08/97	97	38	0	1
Portsmouth	Tr	09/98	98-99	46	2	3
Wigan Ath	Tr	11/99	99	19	4	0

PERONE Bruno Caldini
Born: Sao Paulo, Brazil, 6 July, 1987 — CD

League Club	Source	Date Signed	Seasons Played	Apps	Subs	Gls
Queens Park Rgrs	Tombense (BRA)	08/11	11	1	0	0

PERPETUINI David Peter
Born: Hitchin, Hertfordshire, England, 26 September, 1979 — LM

League Club	Source	Date Signed	Seasons Played	Apps	Subs	Gls
Watford	YT	07/97	98-00	17	2	1
Gillingham	Tr	08/01	01-04	55	31	5
Wycombe W	Tr	01/05	04	1	1	0
Walsall	Tr	03/05	04	7	0	0

PERRETT Darren John
Born: Cardiff, Wales, 29 December, 1969 — W

League Club	Source	Date Signed	Seasons Played	Apps	Subs	Gls
Swansea C	Cheltenham T	07/93	93-95	13	17	1

PERRETT George Richard
Born: Kennington, S London, England, 2 May, 1915 — RH
Died: Ipswich, England, 9 August, 1952

League Club	Source	Date Signed	Seasons Played	Apps	Subs	Gls
Fulham	Woking	04/34				
Ipswich T	Tr	06/36	38-49	131	-	4

PERRETT Russell (Russ)
Born: Barton-on-Sea, Hampshire, England, 18 June, 1973 — CD

League Club	Source	Date Signed	Seasons Played	Apps	Subs	Gls
Portsmouth	AFC Lymington	09/95	95-98	66	6	2
Cardiff C	Tr	07/99	99-00	28	1	1
Luton T	Tr	08/01	01-06	89	10	9
Bournemouth	Tr	07/07	07	10	0	0

PERRIN Steven Charles (Steve)
Born: Paddington, Central London, England, 13 February, 1952 — F
England: Schools

League Club	Source	Date Signed	Seasons Played	Apps	Subs	Gls
Crystal Palace	Wycombe W	03/76	76-77	45	3	13
Plymouth Arg	Tr	03/78	77-79	33	1	6
Portsmouth	Tr	11/79	79-80	18	10	3
Northampton T	Hillingdon Bor	12/81	81-82	22	0	5

PERRY Andrew (Andy)
Born: Dulwich, S London, England, 28 December, 1962 — RW

League Club	Source	Date Signed	Seasons Played	Apps	Subs	Gls
Portsmouth	Dulwich Hamlet	11/86	87	1	3	0
Gillingham	Tr	08/88	88	8	5	0

PERRY Arthur
Born: Doncaster, South Yorkshire, England, 15 October, 1932 — LB

League Club	Source	Date Signed	Seasons Played	Apps	Subs	Gls
Hull C	Jnr	12/50				
Bradford Park Ave	Tr	07/56	56-57	60	-	0
Rotherham U	Tr	07/58	58	2	-	0

PERRY Christopher John (Chris)
Born: Carshalton, S London, England, 26 April, 1973 — CD

League Club	Source	Date Signed	Seasons Played	Apps	Subs	Gls
Wimbledon	YT	07/91	93-98	158	9	2
Tottenham H	Tr	07/99	99-02	111	9	3
Charlton Ath	Tr	09/03	03-05	69	7	3
West Bromwich A	Tr	07/06	06	23	0	0
Luton T	Tr	07/07	07	35	0	1
Southampton	Tr	03/08	07-09	55	3	2

PERRY David
Born: Sheffield, England, 17 May, 1967 — D

League Club	Source	Date Signed	Seasons Played	Apps	Subs	Gls
Chesterfield	Jnr	08/85	85-87	12	5	0

PERRY Frederick Noel (Fred)
Born: Cheltenham, Gloucestershire, England, 30 October, 1933 — RB

League Club	Source	Date Signed	Seasons Played	Apps	Subs	Gls
Liverpool	Worthing	07/54	55	1	-	0

PERRY Jason
Born: Caerphilly, Wales, 2 April, 1970 — CD
Wales: 1/B-2/U21-3/Youth/Schools

League Club	Source	Date Signed	Seasons Played	Apps	Subs	Gls
Cardiff C	Jnr	08/87	86-96	278	3	5
Bristol Rov	Tr	07/97	97	24	1	0
Lincoln C	Tr	07/98	98	10	2	0
Hull C	Tr	12/98	98-00	14	1	0

PERRY Kyle Blain
Born: Wolverhampton, England, 5 March, 1986 — F

League Club	Source	Date Signed	Seasons Played	Apps	Subs	Gls
Port Vale	Chasetown	01/08	07-08	18	13	0

PERRY Leonard (Len)
Born: Walsall, West Midlands, England, 14 May, 1930 — FB
Died: Walsall, West Midlands, England, 14 January, 2004

League Club	Source	Date Signed	Seasons Played	Apps	Subs	Gls
Walsall	Jnr	10/50	53	3	-	0

PERRY Mark James
Born: Perivale, W London, England, 19 October, 1978 — D
England: Youth/Schools

League Club	Source	Date Signed	Seasons Played	Apps	Subs	Gls
Queens Park Rgrs	YT	10/95	96-01	54	12	1

PERRY Michael Alexander (Micky)
Born: Wimbledon, SW London, England, 4 April, 1964 — F

League Club	Source	Date Signed	Seasons Played	Apps	Subs	Gls
West Bromwich A	App	02/82	82-83	14	6	5
Torquay U	L	10/84	84	5	0	1
Northampton T	L	12/84	84	4	0	0
Torquay U	Tr	03/85	84-85	18	0	1

PERRY Peter
Born: Rotherham, South Yorkshire, England, 11 April, 1936 — RB
Died: Sheffield, England, 18 April, 2011

League Club	Source	Date Signed	Seasons Played	Apps	Subs	Gls
Rotherham U	Treeton Red Rose	07/56	57-61	99	-	12
York C	Tr	07/62	62	23	-	0

PERRY William (Bill)
Born: Johannesburg, South Africa, 10 September, 1930 — W
Died: Blackpool, Lancashire, England, 27 September, 2007
England: 3/B-2/FLge-1

League Club	Source	Date Signed	Seasons Played	Apps	Subs	Gls
Blackpool	Jo'burg Rgrs (RSA)	11/49	49-61	394	-	119
Southport	Tr	06/62	62	26	-	0

PERRYMAN Gerald (Gerry)
Born: West Haddon, Northamptonshire, England, 3 October, 1947 — FB

League Club	Source	Date Signed	Seasons Played	Apps	Subs	Gls
Northampton T	Jnr	09/66	66	1	0	0
Colchester U	Tr	07/68	68	1	1	0

PERRYMAN Stephen John (Steve)
Born: Ealing, W London, England, 21 December, 1951 — DM
England: 1/U23-17/Youth/Schools

League Club	Source	Date Signed	Seasons Played	Apps	Subs	Gls
Tottenham H	App	01/69	69-85	653	2	31
Oxford U	Tr	03/86	85-86	17	0	0
Brentford	Tr	11/86	86-89	44	9	0

PESCHISOLIDO Paolo Pasquale (Paul)
Born: Toronto, Canada, 25 May, 1971 — F
Canada: 53/U23-11/Youth

League Club	Source	Date Signed	Seasons Played	Apps	Subs	Gls
Birmingham C	Toronto FC (CAN)	11/92	92-93	37	6	16
Stoke C	Tr	08/94	94-95	59	7	19
Birmingham C	Tr	03/96	95	7	2	1
West Bromwich A	Tr	07/96	96-97	36	9	18
Fulham	Tr	10/97	97-99	69	26	24
Queens Park Rgrs	L	11/00	00	5	0	1
Sheffield U	L	01/01	00	4	1	2
Norwich C	L	03/01	00	3	2	0
Sheffield U	Tr	07/01	01-03	35	44	17
Derby Co	Tr	03/04	03-06	38	53	20
Luton T	Tr	07/07	07	2	2	0

PESZKO Slavomir
Born: Jaslo, Poland, 19 February, 1985 — W
Poland: 30/U21-3

League Club	Source	Date Signed	Seasons Played	Apps	Subs	Gls
Wolverhampton W (L)	FC Koln (GER)	08/12	12	7	6	0

PETCHEY George
Born: Whitechapel, Central London, England, 24 June, 1931 — WH

League Club	Source	Date Signed	Seasons Played	Apps	Subs	Gls
West Ham U	Jnr	08/48	52	2	-	0
Queens Park Rgrs	Tr	07/53	53-59	255	-	22
Crystal Palace	Tr	06/60	60-63	143	-	12

PETER Sergio Mario
Born: Ludwigshafen, Germany, 12 October, 1986 — W
Germany: U21-1

League Club	Source	Date Signed	Seasons Played	Apps	Subs	Gls
Blackburn Rov	Sch	11/04	05-06	2	15	0

PETERLIN Anton Alexander
Born: San Francisco, California, USA, 4 April, 1987 — DM

League Club	Source	Date Signed	Seasons Played	Apps	Subs	Gls
Everton	Ventura County (USA)	07/09				
Plymouth Arg	Tr	08/10	10	9	3	0
Walsall	Tr	07/11	11	20	6	0

PETERS Alan Gerard
Born: Newport, Wales, 14 October, 1958 — M

League Club	Source	Date Signed	Seasons Played	Apps	Subs	Gls
Hereford U	Aston Villa (App)	06/76	76	1	0	0

PETERS Gary David
Born: Carshalton, S London, England, 3 August, 1954 — D

League Club	Source	Date Signed	Seasons Played	Apps	Subs	Gls
Reading	Guildford C	05/75	75-78	150	6	7

League Club	Source	Date Signed	Seasons Played	Apps	Subs	Gls
Fulham	Tr	08/79	79-81	57	7	2
Wimbledon	Tr	07/82	82-83	83	0	7
Aldershot	Tr	07/84	84	17	0	1
Reading	Tr	02/85	84-87	93	7	4
Fulham	Tr	08/88	88-89	7	4	2

PETERS Jaime Bryant
Born: Pickering, Ontario, Canada, 4 May, 1987 — M
Canada: 26/U23-1/Youth

League Club	Source	Date Signed	Seasons Played	Apps	Subs	Gls
Ipswich T	Kaiserslautern (GER)	08/05	05-10	60	39	4
Yeovil T	L	01/08	07	12	2	1
Gillingham	L	01/09	08	1	2	0
Bournemouth	L	09/11	11	8	0	0

PETERS Jeffrey (Jeff)
Born: Wideopen, Tyne and Wear, England, 7 March, 1961 — LB

League Club	Source	Date Signed	Seasons Played	Apps	Subs	Gls
Middlesbrough	App	03/79	79	6	0	0

PETERS Mark
Born: Flint, Wales, 6 July, 1972 — CD
Wales: B/U21-3/Youth

League Club	Source	Date Signed	Seasons Played	Apps	Subs	Gls
Manchester C	YT	07/90				
Norwich C	Tr	09/92				
Peterborough U	Tr	08/93	93	17	2	0
Mansfield T	Tr	09/94	94-98	107	1	9
Rushden & D	Tr	07/99	01-02	65	2	1
Leyton Orient	Tr	09/03	03-04	39	2	2

PETERS Mark William
Born: Frimley, Surrey, England, 4 October, 1983 — F

League Club	Source	Date Signed	Seasons Played	Apps	Subs	Gls
Southampton	YT	10/00				
Brentford	Tr	02/02	02-03	5	15	1

PETERS Martin Stanford
Born: Plaistow, E London, England, 8 November, 1943 — M
England: 67/FLge-6/U23-5/Youth/Schools

League Club	Source	Date Signed	Seasons Played	Apps	Subs	Gls
West Ham U	App	11/60	61-69	302	0	81
Tottenham H	Tr	03/70	69-74	189	0	46
Norwich C	Tr	03/75	74-79	206	1	44
Sheffield U	Tr	08/80	80	23	1	4

PETERS Robert Anthony Angus (Rob)
Born: Kensington, Central London, England, 18 May, 1971 — M

League Club	Source	Date Signed	Seasons Played	Apps	Subs	Gls
Brentford	YT	07/89	89-93	16	14	1
Carlisle U	Tr	11/94	94	5	3	0

PETERS Roger Douglas (Lou)
Born: Cheltenham, Gloucestershire, England, 5 March, 1944 — W
England: Youth

League Club	Source	Date Signed	Seasons Played	Apps	Subs	Gls
Bristol C	App	03/61	60-67	158	0	25
Bournemouth	Tr	06/68	68-69	35	2	3

PETERS Ryan Vincent
Born: Wandsworth, SW London, England, 21 August, 1987 — RB

League Club	Source	Date Signed	Seasons Played	Apps	Subs	Gls
Brentford	Sch	07/05	04-07	2	34	2

PETERS Thomas James (Tom)
Born: Droylsden, Greater Manchester, England, 22 December, 1920 — IF
Died: Derby, England, April, 2010

League Club	Source	Date Signed	Seasons Played	Apps	Subs	Gls
Doncaster Rov	Stalybridge Celtic	05/44				
Southend U	Tr	05/45				
Bury	Tr	12/46	47	10	-	1
Leeds U	Tr	08/48				
Mansfield T	Tr	03/49	48	6	-	2
Accrington Stan	Droylsden	10/49	49	4	-	2

PETERSON Alexander (Alex)
Born: Doncaster, South Yorkshire, England, 17 October, 1994 — F

League Club	Source	Date Signed	Seasons Played	Apps	Subs	Gls
Doncaster Rov	Sch	07/13	13-14	1	5	0

PETERSON Eric Brian (Brian)
Born: Johannesburg, South Africa, 28 October, 1936 — IF

League Club	Source	Date Signed	Seasons Played	Apps	Subs	Gls
Blackpool	Berea Park (RSA)	10/56	56-61	103	-	16

PETERSON Frank Arthur
Born: Croydon, S London, England, 3 April, 1951 — F

League Club	Source	Date Signed	Seasons Played	Apps	Subs	Gls
Millwall	App	02/69	68	3	0	0

PETERSON Kristoffer Paul (Kris)
Born: Gothenburg, Sweden, 28 November, 1994 — RW
Sweden: U21-7/Youth

League Club	Source	Date Signed	Seasons Played	Apps	Subs	Gls
Liverpool	Sch	11/11				
Tranmere Rov	L	11/13	13	6	0	0

PETERSON Paul Wayne
Born: Hitchin, Hertfordshire, England, 22 December, 1949 — LB

League Club	Source	Date Signed	Seasons Played	Apps	Subs	Gls
Leeds U	App	12/66	69	3	1	0
Swindon T	Tr	06/71	71	1	0	0

PETHARD Frederick James (Freddie)
Born: Glasgow, Scotland, 7 October, 1950 — FB
Scotland: Schools

League Club	Source	Date Signed	Seasons Played	Apps	Subs	Gls
Cardiff C	Glasgow Celtic	08/69	71-78	161	10	0
Torquay U	Tr	08/79	79-81	104	1	0

PETHERBRIDGE George Ernest
Born: Devonport, Devon, England, 19 May, 1927 — RW
Died: Shepton Mallet, Somerset, England, 4 March, 2013

League Club	Source	Date Signed	Seasons Played	Apps	Subs	Gls
Bristol Rov	Colston Sports	10/45	46-61	452	-	85

PETHICK Robert John (Robbie)
Born: Tavistock, Devon, England, 8 September, 1970 — RB

League Club	Source	Date Signed	Seasons Played	Apps	Subs	Gls
Portsmouth	Weymouth	10/93	93-98	157	32	3
Bristol Rov	Tr	02/99	98-00	60	3	2
Brighton & HA	Tr	07/01	01-03	44	20	0

PETIT Emmanuel
Born: Dieppe, France, 22 September, 1970 — DM
France: 63

League Club	Source	Date Signed	Seasons Played	Apps	Subs	Gls
Arsenal	AS Monaco (FRA)	06/97	97-99	82	3	9
Chelsea	Barcelona (SPN)	07/01	01-03	52	3	2

PETRACHI Gianluca
Born: Lecce, Italy, 14 January, 1969 — M

League Club	Source	Date Signed	Seasons Played	Apps	Subs	Gls
Nottingham F	Perugia (ITA)	08/99	99	10	3	0

PETRASSO Michael Alexander (Mike)
Born: Toronto, Canada, 7 September, 1995 — W
Canada: Youth

League Club	Source	Date Signed	Seasons Played	Apps	Subs	Gls
Queens Park Rgrs	Toronto FC (CAN)	08/12	13	0	1	0
Oldham Ath	L	11/13	13	9	2	1
Coventry C	L	02/14	13	7	0	1
Leyton Orient	L	09/14	14	2	1	0
Notts Co	L	10/14	14	5	3	3

PETRESCU Daniel Vasile (Dan)
Born: Bucharest, Romania, 22 December, 1967 — RB
Romania: 95/U21

League Club	Source	Date Signed	Seasons Played	Apps	Subs	Gls
Sheffield Wed	Genoa (ITA)	08/94	94-95	28	9	3
Chelsea	Tr	11/95	95-99	134	16	18
Bradford C	Tr	08/00	00	16	1	1
Southampton	Tr	01/01	00-01	8	3	2

PETRESCU Tomi Christian
Born: Jyvaskyla, Finland, 24 July, 1986 — M
Finland: U21-7/Youth

League Club	Source	Date Signed	Seasons Played	Apps	Subs	Gls
Leicester C	Sch	08/03	02	0	1	0

PETRIC Gordan
Born: Belgrade, Yugoslavia, 30 July, 1969 — LB
Yugoslavia: 4

League Club	Source	Date Signed	Seasons Played	Apps	Subs	Gls
Crystal Palace	Glasgow Rangers	11/98	98	18	0	1

PETRIC Mladen
Born: Breko, Bosnia & Herzegovina, 1 January, 1981 — F
Switzerland: U21-1/Youth//Croatia: 45/U21-7

League Club	Source	Date Signed	Seasons Played	Apps	Subs	Gls
Fulham	Hamburger SV (GER)	07/12	12	9	14	5
West Ham U	Tr	09/13	13	0	3	0

PETROV Martin Petiov
Born: Vratza, Bulgaria, 15 January, 1979 — LW
Bulgaria: 89

League Club	Source	Date Signed	Seasons Played	Apps	Subs	Gls
Manchester C	Atletico Madrid (SPN)	07/07	07-09	46	13	9
Bolton W	Tr	07/10	10-12	54	19	10

PETROV Stiliyan Alypshev
Born: Sofia, Bulgaria, 5 July, 1979 — M
Bulgaria: 106

League Club	Source	Date Signed	Seasons Played	Apps	Subs	Gls
Aston Villa	Glasgow Celtic	08/06	06-11	174	11	9

PETROVIC Radosav
Born: Ub, Serbia, 8 March, 1989 — M
Serbia: 42/U21-3

League Club	Source	Date Signed	Seasons Played	Apps	Subs	Gls
Blackburn Rov	Part'n Belgrade (SRB)	08/11	11	10	9	0

PETROVIC Vladimir
Born: Belgrade, Yugoslavia, 1 July, 1955 — M
Yugoslavia: 34

League Club	Source	Date Signed	Seasons Played	Apps	Subs	Gls
Arsenal	R Star Belgrade (YUG)	12/82	82	10	3	2

PETRUCCI Davide
Born: Rome, Italy, 5 October, 1991 — M
Italy: Youth

League Club	Source	Date Signed	Seasons Played	Apps	Subs	Gls
Manchester U	Sch	10/08				
Peterborough U	L	01/13	12	4	0	1
Charlton Ath	L	03/14	13	0	5	0

PETT Thomas George (Tom)
Born: Potters Bar, Hertfordshire, England, 3 December, 1991 — W

League Club	Source	Date Signed	Seasons Played	Apps	Subs	Gls
Stevenage	Wealdstone	06/14	14	28	6	7

League Club	Source	Date Signed	Seasons Played	Career Record Apps	Subs	Gls

PETTA Alfred Manuel (Bobby)
Born: Rotterdam, Netherlands, 6 August, 1974 — LW

Ipswich T	Feyenoord (NED)	06/96	96-98	55	15	9
Fulham (L)	Glasgow Celtic	01/04	03	3	6	0
Darlington	Glasgow Celtic	01/05	04	12	0	1
Bradford C	Tr	06/05	05	23	4	4

PETTEFER Carl James
Born: Burnham, Buckinghamshire, England, 22 March, 1981 — DM

Portsmouth	YT	11/98	00-01	1	2	0
Exeter C	L	10/02	02	30	1	1
Southend U	Tr	02/04	03-05	62	6	0
Bournemouth	Oxford U	08/08	08	0	1	0

PETTERSON Andrew Keith (Andy)
Born: Fremantle, Australia, 29 September, 1969 — G
Australia: Youth

Luton T	East Freemantle (AUS)	12/88	92-93	16	3	0
Ipswich T	L	03/93	92	1	0	0
Charlton Ath	Tr	07/94	94-98	68	4	0
Bradford C	L	12/94	94	3	0	0
Ipswich T	L	09/95	95	1	0	0
Plymouth Arg	L	01/96	95	6	0	0
Colchester U	L	03/96	95	5	0	0
Portsmouth	L	11/98	98	13	0	0
Portsmouth	Tr	07/99	99-00	19	0	0
Torquay U	L	03/01	00	6	0	0
West Bromwich A	Tr	03/02				
Brighton & HA	Tr	08/02	02	6	1	0
Bournemouth	Tr	12/02				
Southend U	Derry C (ROI)	09/03	03	1	0	0
Walsall	Derry C (ROI)	01/04	03	3	0	0

PETTIGREW Adrian Robert James
Born: Clapton, NE London, England, 12 November, 1986 — CD

Chelsea	Sch	03/05				
Wycombe W	L	03/07	06	1	0	0
Brentford	L	08/07	07	9	2	0
Rotherham U	L	01/08	07	3	1	0

PETTINGER Andrew Richard (Andy)
Born: Scunthorpe, North Lincolnshire, England, 21 April, 1984 — G

Everton	YT	05/01				
Grimsby T	Tr	12/02	03	3	0	0

PETTINGER Paul Allen
Born: Barnsley, South Yorkshire, England, 1 October, 1975 — G
England: Youth/Schools

Leeds U	YT	10/92				
Torquay U	L	12/94	94	3	0	0
Rotherham U	L	08/95	95	0	1	0
Gillingham	Tr	03/96				
Carlisle U	Tr	08/96				
Rotherham U	Tr	08/97	97-00	16	0	0
Lincoln C	Tr	07/01	01	3	0	0

PETTIT Raymond John (Ray)
Born: Hull, England, 11 December, 1946 — CD

Hull C	App	12/64	66-71	78	1	0
Barnsley	Tr	09/72	72-73	49	2	1

PETTS John William Frederick James
Born: Edmonton, N London, England, 2 October, 1938 — WH
England: Youth

Arsenal	Jnr	05/56	57-61	32	-	0
Reading	Tr	10/62	62-64	34	-	0
Bristol Rov	Tr	07/65	65-69	88	4	3

PETTS Paul Andrew
Born: Hackney, E London, England, 27 September, 1961 — M
England: Youth

Bristol Rov	App	06/79	78-79	12	1	0
Shrewsbury T	Tr	08/80	80-84	138	11	16

PETTY Benjamin James (Ben)
Born: Solihull, West Midlands, England, 22 March, 1977 — M

Aston Villa	YT	05/95				
Stoke C	Tr	11/98	98-00	26	20	0
Hull C	Tr	07/01	01-02	24	5	0

PEVERELL John Richard
Born: Richmond, North Yorkshire, England, 17 September, 1941 — RB

Darlington	Ferryhill Ath	09/59	61-71	418	1	13

PEVERELL Nicholas John (Nicky)
Born: Middlesbrough, England, 28 April, 1973 — F

Middlesbrough	YT	07/91				
Hartlepool U	Tr	11/92	92-93	14	21	3
Hartlepool U	Kuitan Sports (HKG)	12/94	94	0	1	0
York C	Tr	02/95	94-95	13	16	2

PEYTON Gerald Joseph (Gerry)
Born: Birmingham, England, 20 May, 1956 — G
Republic of Ireland: 33/U21-2

Burnley	Atherstone T	05/75	75-76	30	0	0
Fulham	Tr	12/76	76-85	345	0	0
Southend U	L	09/83	83	10	0	0
Bournemouth	Tr	07/86	86-90	202	0	0
Everton	Tr	07/91				
Bolton W	L	02/92	91	1	0	0
Brentford	L	09/92	92	14	0	0
Chelsea	L	01/93	92	0	1	0
Brentford	Tr	03/93	92	5	0	0

PEYTON Noel
Born: Dublin, Republic of Ireland, 4 December, 1935 — IF
Republic of Ireland: 6/B/LoI-5

Leeds U	Shamrock Rov (ROI)	01/58	57-62	105	-	17
York C	Tr	07/63	63-64	37	-	4

PEYTON Robert Andrew
Born: Birmingham, England, 1 May, 1954 — M

Port Vale	Chelmsley T	01/72	71	1	1	0

PEYTON Warren
Born: Manchester, England, 13 December, 1979 — M
England: Semi Pro-2

Rochdale	Bolton W (NC)	10/99	99	1	0	0
Bury	Tr	09/00	00	0	1	0

PHELAN Albert
Born: Sheffield, England, 27 April, 1945 — CD

Chesterfield	Charlton U	07/64	64-74	386	5	14
Halifax T	Tr	10/74	74-76	118	0	4

PHELAN Leeyon
Born: Hammersmith, W London, England, 6 October, 1982 — F

Wycombe W	YT	07/01	00-01	0	3	0

PHELAN Michael Christopher (Mike)
Born: Nelson, Lancashire, England, 24 September, 1962 — DM
England: 1/Youth

Burnley	App	07/80	80-84	166	2	9
Norwich C	Tr	07/85	85-88	155	1	9
Manchester U	Tr	07/89	89-93	88	14	2
West Bromwich A	Tr	07/94	94-95	18	3	0

PHELAN Scott Richard
Born: Liverpool, England, 13 March, 1988 — M
England: Youth

Everton	Sch	07/05				
Bradford C	Tr	08/07	07	8	5	0

PHELAN Terence Michael (Terry)
Born: Manchester, England, 16 March, 1967 — LB
Republic of Ireland: 42/B-1/U23-1/U21-1/Youth

Leeds U	App	08/84	85	12	2	0
Swansea C	Tr	07/86	86	45	0	0
Wimbledon	Tr	07/87	87-91	155	4	1
Manchester C	Tr	08/92	92-95	102	1	1
Chelsea	Tr	11/95	95-96	13	2	0
Everton	Tr	01/97	96-99	23	2	0
Crystal Palace	L	10/99	99	14	0	0
Fulham	Tr	02/00	99-00	18	1	2
Sheffield U	Tr	08/01	01	8	0	0

PHENIX Michael James (Mike)
Born: Manchester, England, 15 March, 1989 — RW

Barnsley	AFC Telford U	10/14	14	0	2	0

PHENIX William Brian (Bill)
Born: Tyldesley, Greater Manchester, England, 10 December, 1937 — LW
Died: Manchester, England, 17 June, 1997

Southport	Boothstown Holy Family	12/57	57-58	15	-	3

PHILLIBEN John
Born: Stirling, Scotland, 14 March, 1964 — D
Scotland: Youth

Doncaster Rov	Stirling A	03/84	83-86	66	5	1
Cambridge U	L	12/85	85	6	0	0

PHILLIP Iain Frederick
Born: Dundee, Scotland, 14 February, 1951 — CD
Scotland: SLge-1/U23-1/Schools

Crystal Palace	Dundee	09/72	72-73	35	0	1

PHILLIPS Aaron Owen
Born: Warwick, England, 20 November, 1993 — RB

Coventry C	Sch	06/12	13-14	17	13	1

PHILLIPS Benjamin (Ben)
Born: Stockport, Greater Manchester, England, 9 June, 1960 — RB

Bury	Macclesfield T	09/80	80	14	0	0

PHILLIPS Brendon Ulysses
Born: St Catherine, Jamaica, 16 July, 1954 — M
England: Semi Pro-4

League Club	Source	Date Signed	Seasons Played	Apps	Subs	Gls
Leicester C	App	07/72				
Peterborough U	Tr	08/73	73	1	0	0
Mansfield T	Boston U	08/80	80	17	0	0

PHILLIPS Cornelius Patrick (Con)
Born: Liverpool, England, 10 May, 1938 — CF

League Club	Source	Date Signed	Seasons Played	Apps	Subs	Gls
Liverpool	Jnr	06/55				
Southport	Tr	07/57	57	19	-	6

PHILLIPS David Owen
Born: Wegburg, Germany, 29 July, 1963 — M/RB
Wales: 62/U21-4/Youth

League Club	Source	Date Signed	Seasons Played	Apps	Subs	Gls
Plymouth Arg	App	08/81	81-83	65	8	15
Manchester C	Tr	08/84	84-85	81	0	13
Coventry C	Tr	06/86	86-88	93	7	8
Norwich C	Tr	07/89	89-92	152	0	18
Nottingham F	Tr	08/93	93-96	116	10	5
Huddersfield T	Tr	11/97	97-98	44	8	3
Lincoln C	Tr	03/99	98-99	15	2	0

PHILLIPS Demar Constantine
Born: Kingston, Jamaica, 23 September, 1983 — LW
Jamaica: 62

League Club	Source	Date Signed	Seasons Played	Apps	Subs	Gls
Stoke C	Waterhouse (JAM)	08/07	07	0	2	0

PHILLIPS Donald (Don)
Born: Llanelli, Carmarthenshire, Wales, 3 March, 1933 — IF
Died: Bury St Edmunds, Suffolk, England, 26 November, 2009

League Club	Source	Date Signed	Seasons Played	Apps	Subs	Gls
Swansea C	Llanelli	12/56	56-57	3	-	0

PHILLIPS Edward John (Ted)
Born: Leiston, Suffolk, England, 21 August, 1933 — IF

League Club	Source	Date Signed	Seasons Played	Apps	Subs	Gls
Ipswich T	Leiston	12/53	53-63	269	-	161
Leyton Orient	Tr	03/64	63-64	36	-	17
Luton T	Tr	02/65	64	12	-	8
Colchester U	Tr	09/65	65	32	0	13

PHILLIPS Ernest (Ernie)
Born: North Shields, Tyne and Wear, England, 29 November, 1923 — RB
Died: York, England, 10 January, 2004

League Club	Source	Date Signed	Seasons Played	Apps	Subs	Gls
Manchester C	South Shields	01/47	48-51	80	-	0
Hull C	Tr	11/51	51-53	42	-	0
York C	Tr	06/54	54-57	164	-	2

PHILLIPS Gareth Russell
Born: Porth, Rhondda Cynon Taff, Wales, 19 August, 1979 — M
Wales: U21-3/Youth/Schools

League Club	Source	Date Signed	Seasons Played	Apps	Subs	Gls
Swansea C	YT	07/98	96-02	59	29	2

PHILLIPS Gary Christopher
Born: St Albans, Hertfordshire, England, 20 September, 1961 — G
England: Semi Pro-1

League Club	Source	Date Signed	Seasons Played	Apps	Subs	Gls
West Bromwich A	Brighton & HA (App)	06/79				
Brentford	Barnet	12/84	84-87	143	0	0
Reading	Tr	08/88	88	24	0	0
Hereford U	L	09/89	89	6	0	0
Barnet	Tr	12/89	91-94	117	0	0

PHILLIPS Gordon David
Born: Uxbridge, W London, England, 17 November, 1946 — G

League Club	Source	Date Signed	Seasons Played	Apps	Subs	Gls
Brentford	Hayes	11/63	64-72	206	0	0

PHILLIPS Horace Leonard (Len)
Born: Shoreditch, Central London, England, 11 September, 1922 — IF/RH
Died: Portsmouth, England, 9 December, 2011
England: 3/FLge-2

League Club	Source	Date Signed	Seasons Played	Apps	Subs	Gls
Portsmouth	Hillside YC	01/46	46-54	245	-	48

PHILLIPS Ian Alexander
Born: Cumnock, Ayrshire, Scotland, 23 April, 1959 — LB

League Club	Source	Date Signed	Seasons Played	Apps	Subs	Gls
Mansfield T	Ipswich T (App)	08/77	77-78	18	5	0
Peterborough U	Tr	08/79	79-81	97	0	3
Northampton T	Tr	08/82	82	42	0	1
Colchester U	Tr	09/83	83-86	150	0	10
Aldershot	Tr	08/87	87-89	106	0	2
Colchester U	Kettering T	07/91	92	0	1	0

PHILLIPS James Neil (Jimmy)
Born: Bolton, Greater Manchester, England, 8 February, 1966 — LB

League Club	Source	Date Signed	Seasons Played	Apps	Subs	Gls
Bolton W	App	08/83	83-86	103	5	2
Oxford U	Glasgow Rangers	08/88	88-89	79	0	7
Middlesbrough	Tr	03/90	89-92	139	0	6
Bolton W	Tr	07/93	93-99	210	11	3

PHILLIPS James Peter (Jimmy)
Born: Stoke-on-Trent, England, 20 September, 1989 — LW

League Club	Source	Date Signed	Seasons Played	Apps	Subs	Gls
Stoke C	Sch	07/08				
Burton A	Tr	08/09	09-14	78	43	3

PHILLIPS John Brian (Brian)
Born: Cadishead, Greater Manchester, England, 9 November, 1931 — CH
Died: Sutton in Ashfield, Nottinghamshire, England, 28 March, 2012

League Club	Source	Date Signed	Seasons Played	Apps	Subs	Gls
Middlesbrough	Altrincham	06/54	54-59	121	-	2
Mansfield T	Tr	06/60	60-62	103	-	3

PHILLIPS John Edgar
Born: Portsmouth, England, 4 March, 1937 — RH
Died: Portsmouth, England, 4 January, 2014

League Club	Source	Date Signed	Seasons Played	Apps	Subs	Gls
Portsmouth	Jnr	05/55	55-59	77	-	0

PHILLIPS Joseph Roy (Joe)
Born: Cardiff, Wales, 8 July, 1923 — FB
Died: Bridgend, Wales, 13 October, 1992

League Club	Source	Date Signed	Seasons Played	Apps	Subs	Gls
Cardiff C	Cardiff Corinthians	04/42	46	2	-	0

PHILLIPS Justin Lee
Born: Derby, England, 17 December, 1971 — CD
England: Youth

League Club	Source	Date Signed	Seasons Played	Apps	Subs	Gls
Derby Co	YT	07/90	90	3	0	1

PHILLIPS Kalvin Mark
Born: Leeds, England, 2 December, 1995 — M

League Club	Source	Date Signed	Seasons Played	Apps	Subs	Gls
Leeds U	Sch	07/14	14	2	0	1

PHILLIPS Kevin Mark
Born: Hitchin, Hertfordshire, England, 25 July, 1973 — F
England: 8/B-1

League Club	Source	Date Signed	Seasons Played	Apps	Subs	Gls
Watford	Baldock T	12/94	94-96	54	5	24
Sunderland	Tr	07/97	97-02	207	1	113
Southampton	Tr	08/03	03-04	49	15	22
Aston Villa	Tr	07/05	05	20	3	4
West Bromwich A	Tr	08/06	06-07	60	11	38
Birmingham C	Tr	07/08	08-10	31	38	19
Blackpool	Tr	07/11	11-12	29	27	18
Crystal Palace	Tr	01/13	12-13	2	16	6
Leicester C	Tr	01/14	13	2	10	2

PHILLIPS Lee
Born: Aberdare, Rhondda Cynon Taff, Wales, 18 March, 1979 — RB
Wales: Youth

League Club	Source	Date Signed	Seasons Played	Apps	Subs	Gls
Cardiff C	YT	07/97	96-99	11	5	0

PHILLIPS Lee Paul
Born: Penzance, Cornwall, England, 16 September, 1980 — F

League Club	Source	Date Signed	Seasons Played	Apps	Subs	Gls
Plymouth Arg	YT	07/98	96-00	18	32	1

PHILLIPS Leighton
Born: Briton Ferry, Neath Port Talbot, Wales, 25 September, 1949 — CD/M
Wales: 58/U23-4/U21-1/Schools

League Club	Source	Date Signed	Seasons Played	Apps	Subs	Gls
Cardiff C	App	04/67	66-74	169	13	11
Aston Villa	Tr	09/74	74-78	134	6	4
Swansea C	Tr	11/78	78-80	97	0	0
Charlton Ath	Tr	08/81	81-82	45	0	1
Exeter C	Tr	03/83	82	10	0	0

PHILLIPS Leslie Michael (Les)
Born: Lambeth, S London, England, 7 January, 1963 — M

League Club	Source	Date Signed	Seasons Played	Apps	Subs	Gls
Birmingham C	App	08/80	81-83	36	8	3
Oxford U	Tr	03/84	83-92	165	14	10
Northampton T	Tr	07/93	93	26	0	0

PHILLIPS Lionel Arthur Raymond
Born: Much Dewchurch, Herefordshire, England, 13 December, 1929 — IF

League Club	Source	Date Signed	Seasons Played	Apps	Subs	Gls
Portsmouth	Yeovil T	02/53	53	4	-	1

PHILLIPS Marcus Stuart
Born: Trowbridge, Wiltshire, England, 17 October, 1973 — W

League Club	Source	Date Signed	Seasons Played	Apps	Subs	Gls
Swindon T	YT	05/93				
Oxford U	Witney T	02/97	96	0	1	0

PHILLIPS Mark Ian
Born: Lambeth, S London, England, 27 January, 1982 — CD

League Club	Source	Date Signed	Seasons Played	Apps	Subs	Gls
Millwall	YT	05/00	01-06	60	7	1
Darlington	L	03/07	06	7	1	0
Brentford	Tr	08/08	08-09	47	8	1
Southend U	Tr	08/10	10-13	83	9	12
AFC Wimbledon	Tr	06/14	14	2	3	0

PHILLIPS Martin John
Born: Exeter, England, 13 March, 1976 — RW

League Club	Source	Date Signed	Seasons Played	Apps	Subs	Gls
Exeter C	YT	07/94	92-95	36	16	5
Manchester C	Tr	11/95	95-96	3	12	0
Scunthorpe U	L	01/98	97	2	1	0
Exeter C	L	03/98	97	7	1	0
Portsmouth	Tr	08/98	98-99	4	20	1
Bristol Rov	L	02/99	98	2	0	0
Plymouth Arg	Tr	08/00	00-03	90	24	10
Torquay U	Tr	07/04	04-06	52	18	6

League Club	Source	Date Signed	Seasons Played	Apps	Subs	Gls

PHILLIPS Matthew (Matt)
Born: Aylesbury, Buckinghamshire, England, 13 March, 1991 — RW
England: Youth//Scotland: 2

League Club	Source	Date Signed	Seasons Played	Apps	Subs	Gls
Wycombe W	Sch	07/08	08-10	38	40	8
Blackpool	Tr	08/10	10-12	59	35	12
Sheffield U	L	10/11	11	5	1	5
Queens Park Rgrs	Tr	08/13	13-14	33	13	6

PHILLIPS Michael Edward
Born: Dulwich, S London, England, 22 January, 1983 — M

League Club	Source	Date Signed	Seasons Played	Apps	Subs	Gls
Gillingham	YT	04/01	00	0	1	0

PHILLIPS Michael Shirkie (Mike)
Born: Cumnock, Ayrshire, Scotland, 18 January, 1933 — CF

League Club	Source	Date Signed	Seasons Played	Apps	Subs	Gls
Grimsby T	Cumnock Jnrs	01/55	54	6	-	1

PHILLIPS Nicholas (Nicky)
Born: West Ham, E London, England, 29 November, 1960 — M

League Club	Source	Date Signed	Seasons Played	Apps	Subs	Gls
Coventry C	App	08/78	79	4	1	0

PHILLIPS Peter Stuart
Born: Wellingborough, Northamptonshire, England, 29 June, 1946 — F
England: Amateur-2

League Club	Source	Date Signed	Seasons Played	Apps	Subs	Gls
Luton T	Bishops Stortford	06/69	69	2	3	0
Torquay U	L	01/71	70	2	0	1
Cambridge U	Tr	03/71	70-72	40	13	13

PHILLIPS Ralph
Born: Hetton-le-Hole, Tyne and Wear, England, 9 August, 1933 — FB/RH
Died: County Durham, England, September, 2011

League Club	Source	Date Signed	Seasons Played	Apps	Subs	Gls
Middlesbrough		05/54				
Northampton T	Tr	08/58	58-60	83	-	1
Darlington	Tr	06/61	61-62	29	-	2

PHILLIPS Reginald Roydon (Reg)
Born: Llanelli, Carmarthenshire, Wales, 9 March, 1921 — CF
Died: Shrewsbury, Shropshire, England, 1972

League Club	Source	Date Signed	Seasons Played	Apps	Subs	Gls
Crewe Alex	Shrewsbury T	05/49	49-51	63	-	35

PHILLIPS Ronald Daniel (Ron)
Born: Worsley, Greater Manchester, England, 30 March, 1947 — LW/M
Died: Walkden, Greater Manchester, England, 17 April, 2002

League Club	Source	Date Signed	Seasons Played	Apps	Subs	Gls
Bolton W	Jnr	10/65	66-74	135	10	17
Chesterfield	L	01/75	74	5	0	0
Bury	Tr	06/75	75-76	68	4	5
Chester C	Tr	09/77	77-80	128	2	21

PHILLIPS Russell George Thomas
Born: Exeter, England, 22 June, 1916 — W/IF
Died: Dorset, England, October, 2000

League Club	Source	Date Signed	Seasons Played	Apps	Subs	Gls
Millwall	Exeter C (Am)	01/45				
Torquay U	Tr	01/46	46	30	-	3

PHILLIPS Stephen Edward (Steve)
Born: Edmonton, N London, England, 4 August, 1954 — F/W
England: Youth

League Club	Source	Date Signed	Seasons Played	Apps	Subs	Gls
Birmingham C	App	08/71	71-75	15	5	1
Torquay U	L	12/74	74	6	0	0
Northampton T	Tr	10/75	75-76	50	1	8
Brentford	Tr	02/77	76-79	156	1	65
Northampton T	Tr	08/80	80-81	75	0	29
Southend U	Tr	03/82	81-85	157	1	66
Torquay U	Tr	01/86	85-86	32	0	11
Peterborough U	Tr	11/86	86-87	46	2	16
Exeter C	L	09/87	87	5	1	1
Chesterfield	L	01/88	87	9	0	2

PHILLIPS Steven John (Steve)
Born: Bath, England, 6 May, 1978 — G

League Club	Source	Date Signed	Seasons Played	Apps	Subs	Gls
Bristol C	Paulton Rov	11/96	98-05	254	3	0
Bristol Rov	Tr	07/06	06-08	136	0	0
Shrewsbury T	L	08/09	09	11	0	0
Crewe Alex	Tr	11/09	09-13	105	1	0

PHILLIPS Stewart Gavin
Born: Halifax, West Yorkshire, England, 30 December, 1961 — F

League Club	Source	Date Signed	Seasons Played	Apps	Subs	Gls
Hereford U	App	11/79	77-87	285	8	84
West Bromwich A	Tr	03/88	87-88	15	0	4
Swansea C	Tr	01/89	88-89	10	10	1
Hereford U	Tr	08/90	90	31	6	10
Wrexham	Tr	08/91	91	1	1	1

PHILLIPS Thomas John Seymour (John)
Born: Shrewsbury, Shropshire, England, 7 July, 1951 — G
Wales: 4/U23-4

League Club	Source	Date Signed	Seasons Played	Apps	Subs	Gls
Shrewsbury T	App	11/68	68-69	51	0	0
Aston Villa	Tr	10/69	69	15	0	0
Chelsea	Tr	08/70	70-78	125	0	0
Crewe Alex	L	08/79	79	6	0	0
Brighton & HA	Tr	03/80	80	1	0	0
Charlton Ath	Tr	07/81	81	2	0	0

PHILLIPS Trevor
Born: Rotherham, South Yorkshire, England, 18 September, 1952 — F
England: Youth

League Club	Source	Date Signed	Seasons Played	Apps	Subs	Gls
Rotherham U	App	03/70	69-78	289	32	80
Hull C	Tr	06/79	79	22	0	3
Chester C	Tr	03/80	79-81	57	7	11
Stockport Co	Tr	03/82	81-82	49	2	13
Chester C	Tr	08/83	83	9	1	2

PHILLIPS Wayne
Born: Caernarfon, Gwynedd, Wales, 15 December, 1970 — M
Wales: B-2

League Club	Source	Date Signed	Seasons Played	Apps	Subs	Gls
Wrexham	YT	08/89	89-97	184	23	16
Stockport Co	Tr	02/98	97-98	14	8	0
Wrexham	Tr	07/99	99-02	35	3	2

PHILLIPSON William Ernest (Bill)
Born: Barrow, Cumbria, England, 4 April, 1917 — G
Died: Ulverston, Cumbria, England, 1974

League Club	Source	Date Signed	Seasons Played	Apps	Subs	Gls
Barrow	Holker Central OB	10/38	46-47	14	-	0

PHILLIPSON-MASTERS Forbes Ernest
Born: Bournemouth, England, 14 November, 1955 — CD

League Club	Source	Date Signed	Seasons Played	Apps	Subs	Gls
Southampton	App	11/73	76-77	9	0	0
Exeter C	L	09/76	76	6	0	0
Bournemouth	L	09/77	77	7	0	2
Luton T	L	03/79	78	10	0	0
Plymouth Arg	Tr	08/79	79-82	119	0	0
Bristol C	Tr	11/82	82-84	94	0	4
Exeter C	L	03/85	84	5	2	1

PHILLISKIRK Anthony (Tony)
Born: Sunderland, England, 10 February, 1965 — F
England: Schools

League Club	Source	Date Signed	Seasons Played	Apps	Subs	Gls
Sheffield U	Jnr	08/83	83-87	62	18	20
Rotherham U	L	10/86	86	6	0	1
Oldham Ath	Tr	07/88	88	3	7	1
Preston NE	Tr	02/89	88	13	1	6
Bolton W	Tr	06/89	89-92	139	2	51
Peterborough U	Tr	10/92	92-93	37	6	15
Burnley	Tr	01/94	93-95	33	7	9
Carlisle U	L	10/95	95	3	0	1
Cardiff C	Tr	12/95	95-96	55	6	5
Macclesfield T	L	02/98	97	1	9	1

PHILLISKIRK Daniel (Danny)
Born: Oldham, Greater Manchester, England, 10 April, 1991 — F/M
England: Youth

League Club	Source	Date Signed	Seasons Played	Apps	Subs	Gls
Chelsea	Sch	09/08				
Oxford U	L	08/10	10	0	1	0
Sheffield U	L	01/11	10	0	3	0
Sheffield U	Tr	06/11	12	0	1	0
Oxford U	L	10/11	11	2	2	0
Coventry C	Tr	02/13	12	1	0	0
Oldham Ath	Tr	08/13	13-14	70	11	8

PHILO Mark William
Born: Bracknell, Berkshire, England, 5 October, 1984 — M
Died: Reading, England, 14 January, 2006

League Club	Source	Date Signed	Seasons Played	Apps	Subs	Gls
Wycombe W	Sch	07/03	03-04	6	11	0

PHILP David
Born: Fowey, Cornwall, England, 8 July, 1960 — G

League Club	Source	Date Signed	Seasons Played	Apps	Subs	Gls
Plymouth Arg	Newquay	07/84	84	7	0	0

PHILPOTT Alan
Born: Stoke-on-Trent, England, 8 November, 1942 — WH/FB
Died: Fenton, Potteries, England, 26 May, 2009

League Club	Source	Date Signed	Seasons Played	Apps	Subs	Gls
Stoke C	Jnr	11/59	60-67	41	4	1
Oldham Ath	Tr	11/67	67-68	28	3	1

PHILPOTT James Frederick (Jamie)
Born: Tunbridge Wells, Kent, England, 2 October, 1996 — F

League Club	Source	Date Signed	Seasons Played	Apps	Subs	Gls
Millwall	Sch	05/15	14	0	1	1

PHILPOTT Lee
Born: Barnet, N London, England, 21 February, 1970 — LM

League Club	Source	Date Signed	Seasons Played	Apps	Subs	Gls
Peterborough U	App	07/86	87-88	1	3	0
Cambridge U	Tr	05/89	89-92	118	16	17
Leicester C	Tr	11/92	92-95	57	18	3
Blackpool	Tr	03/96	95-97	51	20	5
Lincoln C	Tr	07/98	98-99	33	14	3
Hull C	Tr	08/00	00-02	45	9	2

PHILPOTTS David Ronald (Dave)
Born: Bromborough, Wirral, England, 31 March, 1954 — CD

League Club	Source	Date Signed	Seasons Played	Apps	Subs	Gls
Coventry C	App	10/71	73	3	0	0

League Club	Source	Date Signed	Seasons Played	Apps	Subs	Gls
Southport	L	01/74	73	8	0	0
Tranmere Rov	Tr	09/74	74-77	174	1	5
Tranmere Rov	Carolina Light'g (USA)	10/83	83-84	36	0	6

PHIPPS Harold James
Born: Dartford, Kent, England, 15 January, 1916 — CH
Died: Croydon, S London, England, 8 December, 2000

League Club	Source	Date Signed	Seasons Played	Apps	Subs	Gls
Charlton Ath	Middlesex Regiment	10/43	46-50	185	-	2
Watford	Tr	06/52	52-53	47	-	0

PHOENIX Peter Patrick
Born: Urmston, Greater Manchester, England, 31 December, 1936 — LW

League Club	Source	Date Signed	Seasons Played	Apps	Subs	Gls
Oldham Ath	Tamworth	02/58	57-62	161	-	26
Rochdale	Tr	10/62	62-63	36	-	4
Exeter C	Tr	10/63	63	15	-	1
Southport	Tr	01/64	63	10	-	0
Stockport Co	Tr	07/64	64	19	-	1

PHOENIX Ronald James (Ron)
Born: Stretford, Greater Manchester, England, 30 June, 1929 — WH

League Club	Source	Date Signed	Seasons Played	Apps	Subs	Gls
Manchester C	Humphrey Park	03/50	51-59	53	-	2
Rochdale	Tr	02/60	60-61	64	-	0

PHOENIX William Eric (Eric)
Born: Manchester, England, 20 January, 1932 — IF
Died: Stockport, Greater Manchester, England, November, 2011

League Club	Source	Date Signed	Seasons Played	Apps	Subs	Gls
Gillingham	Hastings U	07/54	54-55	17	-	2
Exeter C	Tr	07/56	56	5	-	0

PHYTHIAN Ernest Rixon (Ernie)
Born: Farnworth, Greater Manchester, England, 16 July, 1942 — CF
England: Youth

League Club	Source	Date Signed	Seasons Played	Apps	Subs	Gls
Bolton W	Jnr	07/59	59-61	10	-	3
Wrexham	Tr	03/62	61-64	134	-	44
Hartlepool U	Tr	06/65	65-67	124	0	51

PICK Gary Mark
Born: Leicester, England, 9 July, 1971 — M

League Club	Source	Date Signed	Seasons Played	Apps	Subs	Gls
Stoke C	Leicester U	08/92				
Hereford U	Tr	06/94	94-95	33	10	2
Cambridge U	Tr	03/96	95	2	2	0

PICKARD Leonard James (Len)
Born: Barnstaple, Devon, England, 29 November, 1924 — CF
Died: Barnstaple, Devon, England, 16 March, 2011

League Club	Source	Date Signed	Seasons Played	Apps	Subs	Gls
Bristol Rov	Barnstaple T	01/51	51	4	-	1
Bristol C	Tr	05/53				
Bradford Park Ave	Tr	10/53	53-55	76	-	31

PICKARD Owen Anthony
Born: Barnstaple, Devon, England, 18 November, 1969 — F
England: Semi Pro-1

League Club	Source	Date Signed	Seasons Played	Apps	Subs	Gls
Plymouth Arg	YT	07/88	88-91	6	10	1
Hereford U	Tr	07/92	92-93	66	7	14

PICKEN Allan
Born: Sydney, Australia, 17 September, 1981 — CD

League Club	Source	Date Signed	Seasons Played	Apps	Subs	Gls
Walsall	Newcastle Jets (AUS)	07/06	06	1	1	0

PICKEN Philip James (Phil)
Born: Droylsden, Greater Manchester, England, 12 November, 1985 — RB

League Club	Source	Date Signed	Seasons Played	Apps	Subs	Gls
Manchester U	Sch	07/04				
Chesterfield	L	08/05	05	32	0	1
Chesterfield	Tr	07/06	06-09	101	7	1
Notts Co	L	01/09	08	22	0	0
Bury	Tr	08/10	10-12	76	1	0

PICKERING Albert Gary (Ally)
Born: Manchester, England, 22 June, 1967 — RB

League Club	Source	Date Signed	Seasons Played	Apps	Subs	Gls
Rotherham U	Buxton	02/90	89-93	87	1	2
Coventry C	Tr	10/93	93-95	54	11	0
Stoke C	Tr	08/96	96-98	81	2	1
Burnley	Tr	12/98	98	21	0	1
Cambridge U	Altrincham	12/99				
Chester C	Tr	01/00	99	7	0	1

PICKERING Frederick (Fred)
Born: Blackburn, Greater Manchester, England, 19 January, 1941 — CF
England: 3/FLge-1/U23-3

League Club	Source	Date Signed	Seasons Played	Apps	Subs	Gls
Blackburn Rov	Jnr	01/58	59-63	123	-	59
Everton	Tr	03/64	63-66	97	0	56
Birmingham C	Tr	08/67	67-68	74	0	27
Blackpool	Tr	06/69	69-70	49	1	24
Blackburn Rov	Tr	03/71	70	11	0	2

PICKERING John
Born: Stockton-on-Tees, Cleveland, England, 7 November, 1944 — CD
Died: Hutton Rudby, North Yorkshire, England, 31 May, 2001

League Club	Source	Date Signed	Seasons Played	Apps	Subs	Gls
Newcastle U	Stockton	07/63				
Halifax T	Tr	09/65	65-73	364	3	5
Barnsley	Tr	07/74	74	42	1	2

PICKERING John (Jack)
Born: Chapeltown, South Yorkshire, England, 18 December, 1908 — IF
Died: Bournemouth, England, 1977
England: 1/FLge-1

League Club	Source	Date Signed	Seasons Played	Apps	Subs	Gls
Sheffield U	Mortomley St Saviours	12/25	26-47	344	-	103

PICKERING Michael John (Mike)
Born: Mirfield, West Yorkshire, England, 29 September, 1956 — CD

League Club	Source	Date Signed	Seasons Played	Apps	Subs	Gls
Barnsley	Jnr	10/74	74-76	100	0	1
Southampton	Tr	06/77	77-78	44	0	0
Sheffield Wed	Tr	10/78	78-82	106	4	1
Norwich C	L	09/83	83	0	1	0
Bradford C	L	11/83	83	4	0	0
Barnsley	L	12/83	83	3	0	0
Rotherham U	Tr	01/84	83-85	102	0	1
York C	Tr	07/86	86	31	1	1
Stockport Co	Tr	07/87	87-88	15	1	0

PICKERING Nicholas (Nick)
Born: Newcastle-upon-Tyne, England, 4 August, 1963 — M/LB
England: 1/U21-15/Youth

League Club	Source	Date Signed	Seasons Played	Apps	Subs	Gls
Sunderland	App	08/81	81-85	177	2	18
Coventry C	Tr	01/86	85-87	76	2	9
Derby Co	Tr	08/88	88-91	35	10	3
Darlington	Tr	10/91	91-92	57	0	7
Burnley	Tr	03/93	92	4	0	0

PICKERING Peter Barlow
Born: York, England, 24 March, 1926 — LB
Died: Cape Town, South Africa, 21 November, 2006

League Club	Source	Date Signed	Seasons Played	Apps	Subs	Gls
York C	New Earswick	04/44	46-47	49	-	0
Chelsea	Tr	05/48	48-50	27	-	0
Northampton T	Kettering T	07/55	55-57	86	-	0

PICKERING William Henry (Bill)
Born: Sheffield, England, 10 December, 1919 — FB
Died: Selby, North Yorkshire, England, 16 November, 1983

League Club	Source	Date Signed	Seasons Played	Apps	Subs	Gls
Sheffield Wed	Jnr	10/37	38	3	-	0
Oldham Ath	Tr	07/48	48-49	78	-	0

PICKETT Reginald Arthur (Reg)
Born: Boreilly, India, 6 January, 1927 — WH
Died: Rowlands Castle, Hampshire, England, 4 November, 2012

League Club	Source	Date Signed	Seasons Played	Apps	Subs	Gls
Portsmouth	Weymouth	03/49	49-56	123	-	3
Ipswich T	Tr	07/57	57-62	140	-	3

PICKFORD Jordan Lee
Born: Washington, Tyne and Wear, England, 7 March, 1994 — G
England: Youth

League Club	Source	Date Signed	Seasons Played	Apps	Subs	Gls
Sunderland	Sch	03/11				
Burton A	L	08/13	13	12	0	0
Carlisle U	L	02/14	13	18	0	0
Bradford C	L	07/14	14	33	0	0

PICKRELL Anthony David (Tony)
Born: Neath, Wales, 3 November, 1942 — LW

League Club	Source	Date Signed	Seasons Played	Apps	Subs	Gls
Cardiff C	Jnr	09/60	60-61	18	-	4

PICKUP John Antony (Tony)
Born: Wakefield, England, 3 December, 1931 — IF

League Club	Source	Date Signed	Seasons Played	Apps	Subs	Gls
Bradford Park Ave	Frickley Colliery	09/55	55	2	-	0

PICKUP Reginald John (Reg)
Born: Stoke-on-Trent, England, 6 September, 1929 — IF

League Club	Source	Date Signed	Seasons Played	Apps	Subs	Gls
Stoke C	Jnr	08/49	49	1	-	0

PICKWICK Donald Henry John (Don)
Born: Penygraig, Rhondda Cynon Taff, Wales, 7 February, 1925 — WH
Died: Queensland, Australia, 2 April, 2004

League Club	Source	Date Signed	Seasons Played	Apps	Subs	Gls
Norwich C	Bristol C (Am)	08/47	47-55	224	-	9

PIDCOCK Frederick Charles (Fred)
Born: Canada, 29 June, 1933 — G
Died: Leicester, England, January, 1999

League Club	Source	Date Signed	Seasons Played	Apps	Subs	Gls
Walsall (Am)	Moor Green	09/53	53	1	-	0

PIDGELEY Leonard James (Lenny)
Born: Twickenham, W London, England, 7 February, 1984 — G
England: Youth

League Club	Source	Date Signed	Seasons Played	Apps	Subs	Gls
Chelsea	Sch	07/03	04-05	1	1	0
Watford	L	09/03	03	26	1	0
Millwall	Tr	06/06	06-07	55	0	0
Carlisle U	Tr	07/09	09	17	0	0
Bradford C	Woking	10/10	10	21	0	0
Exeter C	Tr	07/11	11	8	2	0
Newport Co	Tr	08/12	13-14	29	0	0
Mansfield T	L	02/15	14	15	0	0

League Club	Source	Date Signed	Seasons Played	Apps	Subs	Gls

PIEARCE Stephen (Steve)
Born: Sutton Coldfield, West Midlands, England, 27 September, 1974 — F

League Club	Source	Date Signed	Seasons Played	Apps	Subs	Gls
Wolverhampton W	YT	07/93				
Doncaster Rov	Tr	07/96	96	8	11	1

PIECHNIK Torben
Born: Copenhagen, Denmark, 21 May, 1963 — CD
Denmark: 15

League Club	Source	Date Signed	Seasons Played	Apps	Subs	Gls
Liverpool	FC Copenhagen (DEN)	09/92	92-93	16	1	0

PIEKALNIETIS John Andrew
Born: Penrith, Cumbria, England, 23 September, 1951 — CD
England: Youth

League Club	Source	Date Signed	Seasons Played	Apps	Subs	Gls
Nottingham F	Jnr	03/69				
Southend U	Tr	04/71	70	1	0	0

PIENAAR Steven Jerome
Born: Johannesburg, South Africa, 17 March, 1982 — M
South Africa: 61

League Club	Source	Date Signed	Seasons Played	Apps	Subs	Gls
Everton	Bor Dortmund (GER)	07/07	07-10	100	4	9
Tottenham H	Tr	01/11	10-11	5	5	0
Everton	Tr	01/12	11-14	71	10	11

PIERCE David Edward
Born: Manchester, England, 4 October, 1975 — G

League Club	Source	Date Signed	Seasons Played	Apps	Subs	Gls
Rotherham U	Manchester U (YT)	08/94				
Chesterfield	Tr	08/95	95	1	0	0

PIERCE Gary
Born: Bury, Greater Manchester, England, 2 March, 1951 — G

League Club	Source	Date Signed	Seasons Played	Apps	Subs	Gls
Huddersfield T	Mossley	02/71	71-72	23	0	0
Wolverhampton W	Tr	08/73	73-78	98	0	0
Barnsley	Tr	07/79	79-82	81	0	0
Blackpool	Tr	08/83	83	27	0	0

PIERCE John Barry (Barry)
Born: Liverpool, England, 13 August, 1934 — IF

League Club	Source	Date Signed	Seasons Played	Apps	Subs	Gls
Crystal Palace	Truro C	08/55	55-58	85	-	23
Millwall	Tr	05/59	59-60	46	-	17
York C	Tr	07/61	61	12	-	5
Exeter C	Tr	07/62	62	28	-	4

PIERCY John William
Born: Forest Gate, E London, England, 18 September, 1979 — M
England: Youth

League Club	Source	Date Signed	Seasons Played	Apps	Subs	Gls
Tottenham H	YT	07/98	99-00	1	7	0
Brighton & HA	Tr	09/02	02-04	10	20	4

PIERGIANNI Carl Liam
Born: Peterborough, England, 3 May, 1992 — CD

League Club	Source	Date Signed	Seasons Played	Apps	Subs	Gls
Peterborough U	Sch	05/10	10	0	1	0

PIERRE Aaron Jordan
Born: Southall, W London, England, 17 February, 1993 — CD

League Club	Source	Date Signed	Seasons Played	Apps	Subs	Gls
Brentford	Fulham (Sch)	07/11				
Wycombe W	Tr	02/14	13-14	50	0	5

PIERRE Nigel Nigus
Born: Port of Spain, Trinidad, 2 June, 1979 — F
Trinidad & Tobago: 4/U23

League Club	Source	Date Signed	Seasons Played	Apps	Subs	Gls
Bristol Rov	Joe Public (TRD)	02/00	99	1	2	0

PIETERS Erik
Born: Tiel, Netherlands, 7 August, 1988 — LB
Netherlands: 17/U21-19/Youth

League Club	Source	Date Signed	Seasons Played	Apps	Subs	Gls
Stoke C	PSV Eindhoven (NED)	07/13	13-14	63	4	1

PIGGOTT Gary David
Born: Warley, West Midlands, England, 1 April, 1969 — F

League Club	Source	Date Signed	Seasons Played	Apps	Subs	Gls
West Bromwich A	Dudley T	03/91	91	3	2	0
Shrewsbury T	Tr	03/93	92	3	1	0

PIGOTT Joseph David Wozencroft (Joe)
Born: Maidstone, Kent, England, 24 November, 1993 — F

League Club	Source	Date Signed	Seasons Played	Apps	Subs	Gls
Charlton Ath	Sch	07/12	13-14	2	10	0
Gillingham	L	01/14	13	4	3	1
Newport Co	L	09/14	14	6	4	3
Southend U	L	01/15	14	17	3	6

PIKE Christopher (Chris)
Born: Cardiff, Wales, 19 October, 1961 — F

League Club	Source	Date Signed	Seasons Played	Apps	Subs	Gls
Fulham	Barry T	03/85	85-87	32	10	4
Cardiff C	L	12/86	86	6	0	2
Cardiff C	Tr	07/89	89-92	134	14	65
Hereford U	Tr	07/93	93-94	36	2	18
Gillingham	Tr	09/94	94	26	1	13

PIKE Geoffrey Alan (Geoff)
Born: Clapton, NE London, England, 28 September, 1956 — M

League Club	Source	Date Signed	Seasons Played	Apps	Subs	Gls
West Ham U	App	09/74	75-86	275	16	32
Notts Co	Tr	07/87	87-88	80	2	17
Leyton Orient	Tr	09/89	89-90	36	8	1

PIKE Martin Russell
Born: South Shields, Tyne and Wear, England, 21 October, 1964 — LB

League Club	Source	Date Signed	Seasons Played	Apps	Subs	Gls
West Bromwich A	App	10/82				
Peterborough U	Tr	08/83	83-85	119	7	8
Sheffield U	Tr	08/86	86-89	127	2	5
Tranmere Rov	L	11/89	89	2	0	0
Bolton W	L	12/89	89	5	0	1
Fulham	Tr	02/90	89-93	187	3	14
Rotherham U	Tr	08/94	94-95	7	2	0

PILGRIM John Alan (Alan)
Born: Billingborough, Lincolnshire, England, 20 July, 1947 — CD

League Club	Source	Date Signed	Seasons Played	Apps	Subs	Gls
Lincoln C	Billingborough	05/65	65-71	20	3	1

PILKINGTON Anthony Neil James
Born: Blackburn, Greater Manchester, England, 3 November, 1987 — W
Republic of Ireland: 8/U21-1

League Club	Source	Date Signed	Seasons Played	Apps	Subs	Gls
Stockport Co	Atherton Collieries	12/06	06-08	63	14	16
Huddersfield T	Tr	01/09	08-10	88	2	19
Norwich C	Tr	07/11	11-13	58	17	14
Cardiff C	Tr	08/14	14	15	5	1

PILKINGTON Brian
Born: Leyland, Lancashire, England, 12 February, 1933 — LW
England: 1/B-2/FLge-2

League Club	Source	Date Signed	Seasons Played	Apps	Subs	Gls
Burnley	Leyland Motors	04/51	52-60	300	-	67
Bolton W	Tr	03/61	60-63	82	-	11
Bury	Tr	02/64	63-64	20	-	0
Barrow	Tr	02/65	64-66	86	1	9

PILKINGTON Daniel Luke (Danny)
Born: Blackburn, Greater Manchester, England, 25 May, 1990 — W

League Club	Source	Date Signed	Seasons Played	Apps	Subs	Gls
Stockport Co	Myerscough College	07/08	08-10	11	27	1

PILKINGTON George
Born: Hemsworth, West Yorkshire, England, 3 June, 1926 — WH

League Club	Source	Date Signed	Seasons Played	Apps	Subs	Gls
Rotherham U	Great Houghton	11/48	49	1	-	0
Chester C	Tr	07/52	52	16	-	0
Stockport Co	Tr	05/53	53-55	77	-	4

PILKINGTON George Edward
Born: Rugeley, Staffordshire, England, 7 November, 1981 — CD
England: Youth

League Club	Source	Date Signed	Seasons Played	Apps	Subs	Gls
Everton	YT	11/98				
Exeter C	L	11/02	02	7	0	0
Port Vale	Tr	07/03	03-07	223	1	11
Luton T	Tr	08/08	08	18	0	0
Mansfield T	Tr	06/12	13	2	0	0

PILKINGTON Joel Thomas
Born: Accrington, Lancashire, England, 1 August, 1984 — M

League Club	Source	Date Signed	Seasons Played	Apps	Subs	Gls
Burnley	Sch	07/03	03-04	0	2	0

PILKINGTON Kevin William
Born: Hitchin, Hertfordshire, England, 8 March, 1974 — G
England: Schools

League Club	Source	Date Signed	Seasons Played	Apps	Subs	Gls
Manchester U	YT	07/92	94-97	4	2	0
Rochdale	L	02/96	95	6	0	0
Rotherham U	L	01/97	96	17	0	0
Port Vale	Tr	07/98	98-99	23	0	0
Mansfield T	Tr	09/00	00-04	167	0	0
Notts Co	Tr	07/05	05-08	141	0	0
Notts Co	Luton T	02/12	12-14	2	1	0

PILKINGTON Leslie (Les)
Born: Darwen, Lancashire, England, 23 June, 1925 — RW
Died: Darwen, Lancashire, England, 16 September, 1995

League Club	Source	Date Signed	Seasons Played	Apps	Subs	Gls
Arsenal	Darwen Corinthians	03/48				
Watford	Tr	03/50	49-50	5	-	0

PILLING Andrew James (Andy)
Born: Wigan, Greater Manchester, England, 30 June, 1969 — M

League Club	Source	Date Signed	Seasons Played	Apps	Subs	Gls
Preston NE	App	-	85	1	0	0
Wigan Ath	Tr	07/87	87-92	131	25	20

PILLING Anthony Stuart (Stuart)
Born: Sheffield, England, 26 March, 1951 — M/LB

League Club	Source	Date Signed	Seasons Played	Apps	Subs	Gls
Preston NE	Jnr	07/69				
Hull C	Tr	07/70				
Scunthorpe U	Tr	05/73	73-81	246	16	26

PILLING John James (Jack)
Born: St Helens, Merseyside, England, 4 June, 1913 — WH
Died: Knowsley, Merseyside, England, November, 1997

League Club	Source	Date Signed	Seasons Played	Apps	Subs	Gls
Manchester U	Peasley Cross	08/33				
Liverpool	Burscough	09/42				
Southport	Tr	02/46	46	9	-	0

PILLING Vincent John (Vince)
Born: Bolton, Greater Manchester, England, 8 January, 1932 — W
Died: Bolton, Greater Manchester, England, 9 February, 2007

League Club	Source	Date Signed	Seasons Played	Apps	Subs	Gls
Bolton W	Lomax's	10/52	52-54	7	-	0
Bradford Park Ave	Tr	08/55	55	9	-	1

PILVI Tero
Born: Vihti, Finland, 21 February, 1976 — M

League Club	Source	Date Signed	Seasons Played	Apps	Subs	Gls
Cambridge U	Airdrieonians	03/01	00	3	2	0

PIMBLETT Francis Roy (Frank)
Born: Liverpool, England, 12 March, 1957 — M
England: Schools

League Club	Source	Date Signed	Seasons Played	Apps	Subs	Gls
Aston Villa	App	10/74	74-75	9	0	0
Newport Co	L	03/76	75	7	0	0
Stockport Co	Tr	07/76	76	0	1	0
Hartlepool U	Brisbane C (AUS)	03/80	79	3	0	0

PIMBLEY Douglas William (Doug)
Born: King's Norton, West Midlands, England, 19 June, 1917 — IF/LH
Died: Nottingham, England, 18 January, 1988

League Club	Source	Date Signed	Seasons Played	Apps	Subs	Gls
Birmingham C	Stourbridge	07/46	46	2	-	0
Notts Co	Tr	03/48	47-49	23	-	1

PIMLOTT John Gordon
Born: Radcliffe, Greater Manchester, England, 21 January, 1939 — IF
Died: Bangor, Gwynedd, Wales, January, 1992

League Club	Source	Date Signed	Seasons Played	Apps	Subs	Gls
Bury		12/57				
Chester C	Tr	08/59	59-60	41	-	11

PINAMONTE Lorenzo
Born: Verona, Italy, 9 May, 1978 — F

League Club	Source	Date Signed	Seasons Played	Apps	Subs	Gls
Bristol C	Foggia (ITA)	09/98	98-99	3	4	1
Brighton & HA	L	12/99	99	8	1	2
Brentford	Tr	02/00	99-00	8	15	2
Leyton Orient	L	02/01	00	5	6	2

PINAULT Thomas
Born: Grasse, France, 4 December, 1981 — M

League Club	Source	Date Signed	Seasons Played	Apps	Subs	Gls
Colchester U	AS Cannes (FRA)	07/99	99-03	104	29	5
Grimsby T	Tr	07/04	04	32	11	7
Brentford	Tr	07/06	06	24	3	1

PINCHBECK Clifford Brian (Cliff)
Born: Cleethorpes, North Lincolnshire, England, 20 January, 1925 — CF
Died: Cleethorpes, North Lincolnshire, England, 2 November, 1996

League Club	Source	Date Signed	Seasons Played	Apps	Subs	Gls
Everton	Scunthorpe U	12/47	47	3	-	0
Brighton & HA	Tr	08/49	49	14	-	5
Port Vale	Tr	11/49	49-51	69	-	34
Northampton T	Tr	12/51	51	3	-	3

PINCOTT Frederick (Fred)
Born: Bristol, England, 19 March, 1913 — CH
Died: Winchester, Hampshire, England, February, 2000

League Club	Source	Date Signed	Seasons Played	Apps	Subs	Gls
Wolverhampton W	Bristol Royal Victoria	11/31	32	2	-	0
Bournemouth	Tr	05/34	34-38	196	-	0
Newport Co	Gravesend U	07/47	47	14	-	0

PINDER John James (Jack)
Born: York, England, 1 December, 1912 — RB
Died: York, England, 19 August, 2004
England: Schools

League Club	Source	Date Signed	Seasons Played	Apps	Subs	Gls
York C	Jnr	02/30	32-47	199	-	4

PINGEL Frank Mortensen
Born: Aarhus, Denmark, 9 May, 1964 — F
Denmark: 11

League Club	Source	Date Signed	Seasons Played	Apps	Subs	Gls
Newcastle U	AGF Aarhus (DEN)	01/89	88	13	1	1

PINKNEY Alan John
Born: Battersea, SW London, England, 1 January, 1947 — M
England: Schools

League Club	Source	Date Signed	Seasons Played	Apps	Subs	Gls
Exeter C	St Lukes College	02/68	67-68	7	0	1
Crystal Palace	Tr	07/69	69-73	19	5	0
Fulham	L	01/73	72	11	1	0

PINNER Michael John (Mike)
Born: Boston, Lincolnshire, England, 16 February, 1934 — G
England: Amateur-52

League Club	Source	Date Signed	Seasons Played	Apps	Subs	Gls
Aston Villa (Am)	Pegasus	05/54	54-56	4	-	0
Sheffield Wed (Am)	Arsenal (Am)	12/57	57-58	7	-	0
Queens Park Rgrs (Am)	Corinthian Casuals	07/59	59	19	-	0
Manchester U (Am)	Tr	02/61	60	4	-	0
Chelsea (Am)	Hendon	10/61	61	1	-	0
Swansea C (Am)	Hendon	05/62	61	1	-	0
Leyton Orient	Tr	10/62	62-64	77	-	0

PINNEY Nathaniel Barrington
Born: Norwood, S London, England, 16 November, 1990 — F

League Club	Source	Date Signed	Seasons Played	Apps	Subs	Gls
Crystal Palace	Sch	07/09	08	0	1	0
Dagenham & Red	L	10/10	10	0	1	0

PINNOCK James Edward
Born: Dartford, Kent, England, 1 August, 1978 — F

League Club	Source	Date Signed	Seasons Played	Apps	Subs	Gls
Gillingham	YT	07/97	96-99	0	9	0

PINNOCK Mitchell Bernard
Born: Gravesend, Kent, England, 12 December, 1994 — F

League Club	Source	Date Signed	Seasons Played	Apps	Subs	Gls
Southend U	Sch	01/13	12	0	2	0

PINTADO Gorka
Born: San Sebastian, Spain, 24 March, 1978 — F

League Club	Source	Date Signed	Seasons Played	Apps	Subs	Gls
Swansea C	Granada (SPN)	06/08	08-10	25	48	7

PINTO Sergio Paulo Viera
Born: Porto, Portugal, 8 January, 1973 — M

League Club	Source	Date Signed	Seasons Played	Apps	Subs	Gls
Bradford C	Boavista (POR)	10/96	96	7	11	0

PIPE David Ronald
Born: Caerphilly, Wales, 5 November, 1983 — RB/M
Wales: 1/U21-12/Youth

League Club	Source	Date Signed	Seasons Played	Apps	Subs	Gls
Coventry C	YT	11/00	02	11	10	1
Notts Co	Tr	01/04	03-06	138	3	4
Bristol Rov	Tr	07/07	07-09	78	8	3
Cheltenham T	L	11/09	09	7	1	0
Newport Co	Unattached	09/11	13	22	3	0

PIPER Gilbert Harold
Born: Northfleet, Kent, England, 21 June, 1921 — CH
Died: Gravesend, Kent, England, 1987

League Club	Source	Date Signed	Seasons Played	Apps	Subs	Gls
Tottenham H	Northfleet	01/40				
Gillingham	Tr	08/46	50	4	-	0

PIPER Leonard Henry (Lenny)
Born: Camberwell, S London, England, 8 August, 1977 — M
England: Youth

League Club	Source	Date Signed	Seasons Played	Apps	Subs	Gls
Wimbledon	YT	06/95				
Gillingham	Tr	07/96	96-97	4	16	1

PIPER Matthew James (Matt)
Born: Leicester, England, 29 September, 1981 — W

League Club	Source	Date Signed	Seasons Played	Apps	Subs	Gls
Leicester C	YT	08/99	01	14	2	1
Mansfield T	L	11/01	01	8	0	1
Sunderland	Tr	08/02	02-04	13	11	0

PIPER Norman John
Born: North Tawton, Devon, England, 8 January, 1948 — M
England: U23-4/Youth

League Club	Source	Date Signed	Seasons Played	Apps	Subs	Gls
Plymouth Arg	App	02/65	64-69	215	0	35
Portsmouth	Tr	05/70	70-77	309	4	51

PIPER Ronald David (Ron)
Born: Cresswell, Northumberland, England, 16 March, 1943 — IF

League Club	Source	Date Signed	Seasons Played	Apps	Subs	Gls
Tottenham H	Arsenal (Am)	10/60	62	1	-	0

PIPER Stephen Paul (Steve)
Born: Brighton, England, 2 November, 1953 — CD

League Club	Source	Date Signed	Seasons Played	Apps	Subs	Gls
Brighton & HA	Jnr	09/72	72-77	160	2	9
Portsmouth	Tr	02/78	77-78	27	2	2

PIQUE Gerard
Born: Barcelona, Spain, 2 February, 1987 — CD
Spain: 69/U21-12/Youth

League Club	Source	Date Signed	Seasons Played	Apps	Subs	Gls
Manchester U	Barcelona Jnrs (SPN)	02/05	05-07	6	6	0

PIQUIONNE Frederic
Born: Noumea, New Caledonia, 8 December, 1978 — F
France: 1

League Club	Source	Date Signed	Seasons Played	Apps	Subs	Gls
Portsmouth (L)	Olymp Lyonnais (FRA)	08/09	09	26	8	5
West Ham U	Olymp Lyonnais (FRA)	07/10	10-11	34	20	8
Doncaster Rov	L	03/12	11	8	0	2

PIRES Loick Barros Paiva
Born: Lisbon, Portugal, 20 November, 1989 — LW

League Club	Source	Date Signed	Seasons Played	Apps	Subs	Gls
Leyton Orient	Sch	07/08	08-09	0	15	0

PIRES Robert Emmanuel
Born: Reims, France, 29 October, 1973 — LW
France: 79/U21-12

League Club	Source	Date Signed	Seasons Played	Apps	Subs	Gls
Arsenal	Olymp Marseille (FRA)	07/00	00-05	159	30	62
Aston Villa	Villarreal (SPN)	11/10	10	2	7	0

[PIRI] MORI COSTA Francisco Javier
Born: Cangas de Onis, Spain, 10 November, 1970 — M

League Club	Source	Date Signed	Seasons Played	Apps	Subs	Gls
Barnsley (L)	Merida (SPN)	03/99	98	2	0	0

PIRIE Frederick William (Fred)
Born: Coupar Angus, Perthshire, Scotland, 19 January, 1934 — RB

League Club	Source	Date Signed	Seasons Played	Apps	Subs	Gls
Accrington Stan	Coupar Angus	01/54	54-59	17	-	0

[PISCU] LOPEZ Adrian
Born: As Pontes, Spain, 25 February, 1987 — CD

League Club	Source	Date Signed	Seasons Played	Apps	Subs	Gls
Wigan Ath	Depo la Coruna (SPN)	12/10	10-12	9	2	0

PISTONE Alessandro
Born: Milan, Italy, 27 July, 1975 — FB
Italy: U21-11

League Club	Source	Date Signed	Seasons Played	Apps	Subs	Gls
Newcastle U	Inter Milan (ITA)	07/97	97-99	45	1	1
Everton	Tr	07/00	00-05	94	9	1

PITCHER Darren Edward James
Born: Stepney, E London, England, 12 October, 1969 — RB/M
England: Youth

League Club	Source	Date Signed	Seasons Played	Apps	Subs	Gls
Charlton Ath	YT	01/88	90-93	170	3	8
Crystal Palace	Tr	07/94	94-96	60	4	0
Leyton Orient	L	01/98	97	1	0	0

PITCHER Geoffrey (Geoff)
Born: Sutton, S London, England, 15 August, 1975 — M
England: Semi Pro-6

League Club	Source	Date Signed	Seasons Played	Apps	Subs	Gls
Millwall	YT	03/93				
Watford	Tr	07/94	94-95	4	9	2
Colchester U	Kingstonian	02/97	96	0	1	0
Brighton & HA	Kingstonian	06/01	01	2	8	0

PITMAN Brett Douglas
Born: Jersey, Channel Islands, 31 January, 1988 — F

League Club	Source	Date Signed	Seasons Played	Apps	Subs	Gls
Bournemouth	St Paul's, Jersey	12/04	05-10	103	71	58
Bristol C	Tr	08/10	10-12	33	44	20
Bournemouth	Tr	11/12	12-14	53	41	37

PITMAN Jamie Roy
Born: Warminster, Wiltshire, England, 6 January, 1976 — M

League Club	Source	Date Signed	Seasons Played	Apps	Subs	Gls
Swindon T	YT	07/94	94	2	1	0
Hereford U	Tr	02/96	95-96	16	5	0

PITT Courtney Leon
Born: Westminster, Central London, England, 17 December, 1981 — LW

League Club	Source	Date Signed	Seasons Played	Apps	Subs	Gls
Chelsea	YT	07/00				
Portsmouth	Tr	07/01	01	29	10	3
Luton T	L	08/03	03	11	1	0
Coventry C	L	12/03	03	1	0	0
Oxford U	Tr	03/04	03	5	3	0
Boston U	Tr	08/04	04	20	12	4

PITT John Harry (Jackie)
Born: Willenhall, West Midlands, England, 20 May, 1920 — RH
Died: Bristol, England, 17 August, 2004

League Club	Source	Date Signed	Seasons Played	Apps	Subs	Gls
Bristol Rov	Aberavon	05/46	46-57	467	-	16

PITT Richard Ernest (Richie)
Born: Ryhope, Tyne and Wear, England, 22 October, 1951 — CD
England: Schools

League Club	Source	Date Signed	Seasons Played	Apps	Subs	Gls
Sunderland	Jnr	11/68	68-73	126	0	7

PITT Stephen William (Steve)
Born: Willesden, NW London, England, 1 August, 1948 — W

League Club	Source	Date Signed	Seasons Played	Apps	Subs	Gls
Tottenham H	App	08/65	65	1	0	0
Colchester U	Tr	06/69	69	4	2	0

PITTMAN Jon-Paul
Born: Oklahoma City, Oklahoma, USA, 24 October, 1986 — F
England: Semi Pro-1

League Club	Source	Date Signed	Seasons Played	Apps	Subs	Gls
Nottingham F	Sch	12/05				
Hartlepool U	L	01/06	05	2	1	0
Bury	L	08/06	06	5	4	1
Doncaster Rov	Tr	01/07				
Wycombe W	Crawley T	02/09	08-10	38	39	14
Oxford U	Tr	07/11	11-12	8	22	5
Crawley T	L	09/11	11	0	4	1
Wycombe W	Tr	06/13	13	2	8	0

PITTMAN Stephen Lee (Steve)
Born: Wilson, North Carolina, USA, 18 July, 1967 — LB

League Club	Source	Date Signed	Seasons Played	Apps	Subs	Gls
Shrewsbury T	East Fife	03/89	88-89	31	1	2

PITTS Matthew
Born: Middlesbrough, England, 25 December, 1979 — RB

League Club	Source	Date Signed	Seasons Played	Apps	Subs	Gls
Sunderland	YT	06/98				
Carlisle U	Tr	07/99	99-00	21	13	1

PIZANTI David
Born: Haifa, Israel, 27 May, 1962 — M/LB
Israel: 30

League Club	Source	Date Signed	Seasons Played	Apps	Subs	Gls
Queens Park Rgrs	FC Cologne (GER)	09/87	87-88	16	5	0

PIZARRO Claudio Miguel
Born: Lima, Peru, 31 October, 1978 — F
Peru: 81

League Club	Source	Date Signed	Seasons Played	Apps	Subs	Gls
Chelsea	Bayern Munich (GER)	06/07	07	4	17	2

PIZARRO David Marcelo
Born: Valparaiso, Chile, 11 September, 1979 — M
Chile: 40

League Club	Source	Date Signed	Seasons Played	Apps	Subs	Gls
Manchester C (L)	AS Roma (ITA)	01/12	11	1	4	0

PLACE Brendan Anthony
Born: Dublin, Republic of Ireland, 13 December, 1965 — CD

League Club	Source	Date Signed	Seasons Played	Apps	Subs	Gls
Gillingham	Athlone T (ROI)	10/89	89	3	1	0

PLACE Charles Arthur (Charlie)
Born: Ilkeston, Derbyshire, England, 26 November, 1937 — LW

League Club	Source	Date Signed	Seasons Played	Apps	Subs	Gls
Derby Co	Jnr	11/54	55	2	-	0

PLACE Mark Gerald
Born: Mansfield, Nottinghamshire, England, 16 November, 1969 — D

League Club	Source	Date Signed	Seasons Played	Apps	Subs	Gls
Mansfield T	YT	07/88	88-89	12	3	0
Doncaster Rov	Tr	08/90	90	1	0	0

PLANT Kenneth George (Ken)
Born: Nuneaton, Warwickshire, England, 15 August, 1925 — CF
Died: Nuneaton, Warwickshire, England, 22 March, 2014

League Club	Source	Date Signed	Seasons Played	Apps	Subs	Gls
Bury	Nuneaton Bor	02/50	49-53	119	-	54
Colchester U	Tr	01/54	53-58	189	-	82

PLASKETT Stephen Colin (Steve)
Born: Newcastle-upon-Tyne, England, 24 April, 1971 — RB

League Club	Source	Date Signed	Seasons Played	Apps	Subs	Gls
Hartlepool U	YT	07/89	88-89	19	1	0

PLASMATI Gianvito
Born: Matera, Italy, 28 January, 1983 — F

League Club	Source	Date Signed	Seasons Played	Apps	Subs	Gls
Leyton Orient	Siena (ITA)	10/14	14	7	7	2

PLATNAUER Nicholas Robert (Nicky)
Born: Leicester, England, 10 June, 1961 — LB/M

League Club	Source	Date Signed	Seasons Played	Apps	Subs	Gls
Bristol Rov	Bedford T	08/82	82	21	3	7
Coventry C	Tr	08/83	83-84	38	6	6
Birmingham C	Tr	12/84	84-85	23	5	2
Reading	L	01/86	85	7	0	0
Cardiff C	Tr	09/86	86-88	110	5	6
Notts Co	Tr	08/89	89-90	57	0	1
Port Vale	L	01/91	90	14	0	0
Leicester C	Tr	07/91	91-92	32	3	0
Scunthorpe U	Tr	03/93	92	14	0	2
Mansfield T	Kettering T	08/93	93	25	0	0
Lincoln C	Tr	02/94	93-95	26	1	0

PLATT Clive Linton
Born: Wolverhampton, England, 27 October, 1977 — F

League Club	Source	Date Signed	Seasons Played	Apps	Subs	Gls
Walsall	YT	07/96	95-98	18	14	4
Rochdale	Tr	08/99	99-02	151	18	30
Notts Co	Tr	08/03	03	19	0	3
Peterborough U	Tr	01/04	03-04	35	2	6
MK Dons	Tr	01/05	04-06	91	11	27
Colchester U	Tr	07/07	07-09	109	16	25
Coventry C	Tr	07/10	10-11	45	22	7
Northampton T	Tr	05/12	12-13	32	15	6
Bury	Tr	01/14	13-14	8	11	2

PLATT David Andrew
Born: Chadderton, Greater Manchester, England, 10 June, 1966 — M/F
England: 62/B-3/U21-3

League Club	Source	Date Signed	Seasons Played	Apps	Subs	Gls
Manchester U	Chadderton	07/84				
Crewe Alex	Tr	01/85	84-87	134	0	55
Aston Villa	Tr	02/88	87-90	121	0	50
Arsenal	Sampdoria (ITA)	07/95	95-97	65	23	13
Nottingham F	Rtd	08/99	99-00	3	2	1

PLATT Edward Hewitt (Ted)
Born: Newcastle-under-Lyme, Potteries, England, 26 March, 1921 — G
Died: Ilford, E London, England, 20 September, 1996

League Club	Source	Date Signed	Seasons Played	Apps	Subs	Gls
Arsenal	Colchester U	01/39	46-52	53	-	0
Portsmouth	Tr	09/53	53-54	31	-	0
Aldershot	Tr	08/55	55	16	-	0

PLATT James Archibald (Jim)
Born: Ballymoney, Antrim, Northern Ireland, 26 January, 1952 — G
Northern Ireland: 23/Amateur

League Club	Source	Date Signed	Seasons Played	Apps	Subs	Gls
Middlesbrough	Ballymena U	05/70	71-82	401	0	0
Hartlepool U	L	08/78	78	13	0	0
Cardiff C	L	11/78	78	4	0	0

PLATT John Roger
Born: Ashton-under-Lyne, Greater Manchester, England, 22 August, 1954 — G

League Club	Source	Date Signed	Seasons Played	Apps	Subs	Gls
Oldham Ath	Ashton U	06/72	75-80	109	0	0
Bury	Tr	08/81	81-82	20	0	0
Bolton W	Tr	07/83	83	10	0	0
Tranmere Rov	L	11/84	84	8	0	0
Preston NE	Tr	02/85	84-85	38	0	0

PLATT John Stephen
Born: Bermondsey, SE London, England, 29 January, 1942 — RW

League Club	Source	Date Signed	Seasons Played	Apps	Subs	Gls
Charlton Ath	Brookhill BC	06/61	61	2	-	0

PLATT Kristian Daniel
Born: Birkenhead, Wirral, England, 15 December, 1991 — CD

League Club	Source	Date Signed	Seasons Played	Apps	Subs	Gls
Chester C	Sch	-	08	0	1	0

PLATT Matthew
Born: Crewe, Cheshire, England, 15 October, 1983 — M

League Club	Source	Date Signed	Seasons Played	Apps	Subs	Gls
Crewe Alex	Sch	07/02	04	0	1	0

PLATT Thomas Christopher (Tom)
Born: Pontefract, West Yorkshire, England, 1 October, 1993 — M

League Club	Source	Date Signed	Seasons Played	Apps	Subs	Gls
York C	Sch	07/12	12-14	24	23	0

PLATTS Laurence (Laurie)
Born: Worksop, Nottinghamshire, England, 31 October, 1921 — G
Died: Bourne, Lincolnshire, England, 4 September, 2006

League Club	Source	Date Signed	Seasons Played	Apps	Subs	Gls
Nottingham F	Jnr	10/43	46-49	6	-	0
Chesterfield	Tr	07/51	51	11	-	0
Stockport Co	Buxton	02/53	52-53	28	-	0

PLATTS Mark Anthony
Born: Sheffield, England, 23 May, 1979 — LW
England: Youth/Schools

League Club	Source	Date Signed	Seasons Played	Apps	Subs	Gls
Sheffield Wed	YT	10/96	95	0	2	0
Torquay U	Tr	03/99	98-00	16	18	1

PLATTS Peter
Born: Dinnington, South Yorkshire, England, 14 January, 1928 — CF
Died: Scunthorpe, North Lincolnshire, England, November, 1987

League Club	Source	Date Signed	Seasons Played	Apps	Subs	Gls
Scunthorpe U (Am)	Lincolnshire Police	07/51	51	2	-	2

PLAYER Percival Roy Ivan (Roy)
Born: Portsmouth, England, 10 May, 1928 — CH
Died: Rutland, England, 15 April, 1992

League Club	Source	Date Signed	Seasons Played	Apps	Subs	Gls
Grimsby T	Portsmouth (Am)	08/52	52-58	57	-	0
Oldham Ath	Tr	05/59	59	2	-	0

PLEAT David John
Born: Nottingham, England, 15 January, 1945 — W
England: Youth/Schools

League Club	Source	Date Signed	Seasons Played	Apps	Subs	Gls
Nottingham F	Jnr	03/62	61-63	6	-	1
Luton T	Tr	08/64	64-66	67	3	9
Shrewsbury T	Tr	07/67	67	10	2	1
Exeter C	Tr	07/68	68-69	66	2	13
Peterborough U	Tr	07/70	70	28	1	2

PLENDERLEITH John Boyd (Jackie)
Born: Bellshill, Lanarkshire, Scotland, 6 October, 1937 — CH
Scotland: 1/U23-5/Schools

League Club	Source	Date Signed	Seasons Played	Apps	Subs	Gls
Manchester C	Hibernian	07/60	60-62	41	-	0

PLESSIS Damien Jerome Jean Richard
Born: Orleans, France, 5 March, 1988 — M
France: U21-1/Youth

League Club	Source	Date Signed	Seasons Played	Apps	Subs	Gls
Liverpool	Olymp Lyonnais (FRA)	08/07	07-08	3	0	0

PLLU Charles Lamont (Charlie)
Born: Saltcoats, Ayrshire, Scotland, 28 February, 1934 — G

League Club	Source	Date Signed	Seasons Played	Apps	Subs	Gls
Sheffield Wed	Scarborough	12/56	56-57	19	-	0

PLUCK Lee Kenneth
Born: Enfield, N London, England, 27 February, 1982 — FB

League Club	Source	Date Signed	Seasons Played	Apps	Subs	Gls
Barnet	YT	07/00	00	0	1	0

PLUCKROSE Alan
Born: Southwater, West Sussex, England, 3 July, 1963 — LB

League Club	Source	Date Signed	Seasons Played	Apps	Subs	Gls
Torquay U	Falmouth	03/83	82	3	0	0

PLUMB Richard Kevin (Dick)
Born: Swindon, England, 24 September, 1946 — CF

League Club	Source	Date Signed	Seasons Played	Apps	Subs	Gls
Swindon T	App	12/63				
Bristol Rov	Tr	04/65	65-68	39	0	8
Charlton Ath	Yeovil T	09/70	70-71	32	11	10
Exeter C	Tr	08/72	72-73	59	0	17

PLUME Richard William (Dickie)
Born: Tottenham, N London, England, 10 June, 1949 — M

League Club	Source	Date Signed	Seasons Played	Apps	Subs	Gls
Millwall	App	03/67	66-68	12	4	0
Leyton Orient	Tr	05/69	69-70	12	6	1

PLUMLEY Gary Edward
Born: Birmingham, England, 24 March, 1956 — G

League Club	Source	Date Signed	Seasons Played	Apps	Subs	Gls
Leicester C	App	03/74				
Newport Co	Tr	06/76	76-80	182	0	0
Hereford U	Happy Valley (HKG)	09/82	82	13	0	0
Newport Co	Tr	12/82	82	2	0	0
Cardiff C	Happy Valley (HKG)	08/83	83-84	25	0	0
Newport Co	L	08/84	84	2	0	0
Newport Co	Ebbw Vale	03/87	86	1	0	0

PLUMMER Calvin Anthony
Born: Nottingham, England, 14 February, 1963 — W

League Club	Source	Date Signed	Seasons Played	Apps	Subs	Gls
Nottingham F	App	02/81	81-82	10	2	2
Chesterfield	Tr	12/82	82	28	0	7
Derby Co	Tr	08/83	83	23	4	3
Barnsley	Tr	03/84	83-86	41	13	7
Nottingham F	Tr	12/86				
Nottingham F	Lahden Reipas (FIN)	10/87	87	8	0	2
Plymouth Arg	Tr	09/88	88	17	6	1
Chesterfield	Tr	07/89	89-90	67	4	12

PLUMMER Christopher Scott (Chris)
Born: Isleworth, W London, England, 12 October, 1976 — CD
England: U21-5/Youth

League Club	Source	Date Signed	Seasons Played	Apps	Subs	Gls
Queens Park Rgrs	YT	07/94	95-02	54	8	2
Bristol Rov	L	11/02	02	2	0	0
Peterborough U	Barnet	09/04	04-06	44	6	1

PLUMMER Dwayne Jermaine
Born: Bristol, England, 12 May, 1978 — W

League Club	Source	Date Signed	Seasons Played	Apps	Subs	Gls
Bristol C	YT	09/95	95-97	1	13	0
Bristol Rov	Chesham U	09/00	00-01	29	6	1

PLUMMER Ellis Kane
Born: Denton, Greater Manchester, England, 2 September, 1994 — LB

League Club	Source	Date Signed	Seasons Played	Apps	Subs	Gls
Manchester C	Sch	10/11				
Oldham Ath	L	11/13	13	3	0	0

PLUMMER Matthew Robert (Matt)
Born: Hull, England, 18 January, 1989 — CD

League Club	Source	Date Signed	Seasons Played	Apps	Subs	Gls
Hull C	Sch	12/06				
Darlington	Tr	08/09	09	5	3	0

PLUMMER Norman Leonard
Born: Leicester, England, 12 January, 1924 — CH
Died: Leicester, England, 25 October, 1999

League Club	Source	Date Signed	Seasons Played	Apps	Subs	Gls
Leicester C	Leicester ATC	11/42	47-51	66	-	1
Mansfield T	Tr	07/52	52-55	166	-	5

PLUMMER Tristan Daine
Born: Bristol, England, 30 January, 1990 — F
England: Youth

League Club	Source	Date Signed	Seasons Played	Apps	Subs	Gls
Bristol C	Sch	05/07				
Luton T	L	08/08	08	0	5	0
Hereford U	L	08/09	09	4	1	3
Gillingham	L	01/10	09	2	0	0

PLUNKETT Sidney Ernest (Sid)
Born: Norwich, England, 2 October, 1920 — W
Died: Norwich, England, 26 June, 1986

League Club	Source	Date Signed	Seasons Played	Apps	Subs	Gls
Norwich C	Norwich YMCA	04/38	38	3	-	0
Wolverhampton W	Tr	04/39				
Norwich C	Tr	02/46	46	28	-	7

POBORSKY Karel
Born: Jindrichuv-Hradec, Czech Republic, 30 March, 1972 — W
Czech Republic: 118

League Club	Source	Date Signed	Seasons Played	Apps	Subs	Gls
Manchester U	Slavia Prague (CZE)	06/96	96-97	18	14	5

POCOGNOLI Sebastien Jean
Born: Seraing, Belgium, 1 August, 1987 — LB
Belgium: 13/U21-12/Youth

League Club	Source	Date Signed	Seasons Played	Apps	Subs	Gls
West Bromwich A	Hannover 96 (GER)	07/14	14	15	0	0

PODD Cyril Casey Marcel (Ces)
Born: Basseterre, St Kitts, 7 August, 1952 — FB
St Kitts & Nevis:

League Club	Source	Date Signed	Seasons Played	Apps	Subs	Gls
Bradford C	Bradford Art College	08/70	70-83	494	8	3
Halifax T	Tr	08/84	84-85	52	5	0
Scarborough	Tr	07/86	87	3	0	0

PODMORE Edgar Vincent
Born: Fenton, Potteries, England, 20 April, 1918 — G
Died: Stoke-on-Trent, England, July, 1987

League Club	Source	Date Signed	Seasons Played	Apps	Subs	Gls
Stoke C		08/43				
Crewe Alex	Tr	08/47	47	1	-	0

PODOLSKI Lukas Josef
Born: Gliwice, Poland, 4 June, 1985 — F/W
Germany: 125/U21-5/Youth

League Club	Source	Date Signed	Seasons Played	Apps	Subs	Gls
Arsenal	FC Koln (GER)	07/12	12-14	39	21	19

POGATETZ Emanuel
Born: Steinbock, Austria, 16 January, 1983 — CD
Austria: 61

League Club	Source	Date Signed	Seasons Played	Apps	Subs	Gls
Middlesbrough	Bayer Leverkusen (GER)	08/05	05-09	119	4	4
West Ham U (L)	VfL Wolfsburg (GER)	01/13	12	1	5	0

League Club	Source	Date Signed	Seasons Played	Career Record Apps	Subs	Gls

POGBA Mathias Fassou
Born: Conakry, Guinea, 19 August, 1990 — F
Guinea: 2

League Club	Source	Date Signed	Seasons Played	Apps	Subs	Gls
Crewe Alex	Wrexham	07/12	12-13	48	8	17
Crawley T	Pescara (ITA)	02/15	14	14	3	2

POGBA Paul Labile
Born: Marne-la-Vallee, France, 15 March, 1993 — M
France: 23/Youth

League Club	Source	Date Signed	Seasons Played	Apps	Subs	Gls
Manchester U	Sch	03/10	11	0	3	0

POGLIACOMI Leslie Amado (Les)
Born: Sydney, Australia, 3 May, 1976 — G
Australia: Youth

League Club	Source	Date Signed	Seasons Played	Apps	Subs	Gls
Oldham Ath	Parramatta Power (AUS)	07/02	02-04	120	0	0
Blackpool	Tr	08/05	05	15	0	0
Oldham Ath	Tr	07/06	06	40	0	0

POGREBNYAK Pavel Viktorovich
Born: Moscow, Russia, 8 November, 1983 — F
Russia: 33

League Club	Source	Date Signed	Seasons Played	Apps	Subs	Gls
Fulham	VfB Stuttgart (GER)	01/12	11	12	0	6
Reading	Tr	07/12	12-14	77	17	24

POINTER Keith Cecil
Born: Norwich, England, 16 February, 1951 — M

League Club	Source	Date Signed	Seasons Played	Apps	Subs	Gls
West Ham U	Norwich C (Am)	06/68				
Cambridge U	Tr	03/72	71-72	6	2	2

POINTER Raymond (Ray)
Born: Cramlington, Northumberland, England, 10 October, 1936 — F
England: 3/FLge-2/U23-5

League Club	Source	Date Signed	Seasons Played	Apps	Subs	Gls
Burnley	Dudley Welfare	08/57	57-64	223	-	118
Bury	Tr	08/65	65	19	0	17
Coventry C	Tr	12/65	65-66	26	0	13
Portsmouth	Tr	01/67	66-72	148	4	31

POINTER Reginald Ernest (Reg)
Born: Norwich, England, 28 January, 1935 — CD

League Club	Source	Date Signed	Seasons Played	Apps	Subs	Gls
Norwich C	City of Norwich SOBU	06/56	56	11	-	0

POINTON Neil Geoffrey
Born: Church Warsop, Nottinghamshire, England, 28 November, 1964 — LB

League Club	Source	Date Signed	Seasons Played	Apps	Subs	Gls
Scunthorpe U	App	08/82	81-85	159	0	2
Everton	Tr	11/85	85-89	95	6	5
Manchester C	Tr	07/90	90-91	74	0	2
Oldham Ath	Tr	07/92	92-95	92	3	3
Walsall	Heart of Midlothian	07/98	98-99	61	0	0
Chesterfield	Tr	01/00	99	9	1	0

POINTON Raymond Evison (Ray)
Born: Birkenhead, Wirral, England, 6 November, 1947 — D
Died: Bebington, Wirral, England, 1 July, 2013

League Club	Source	Date Signed	Seasons Played	Apps	Subs	Gls
Tranmere Rov	App	11/65	67-70	41	6	0

POINTON William James (Bill)
Born: Hanley, Potteries, England, 25 November, 1920 — CF
Died: Portsmouth, England, 6 January, 2008

League Club	Source	Date Signed	Seasons Played	Apps	Subs	Gls
Port Vale		07/40	46-48	74	-	26
Queens Park Rgrs	Tr	01/49	48-49	26	-	6
Brentford	Tr	02/50	49-50	16	-	2

POKE Michael Harold
Born: Staines, Surrey, England, 21 November, 1985 — G

League Club	Source	Date Signed	Seasons Played	Apps	Subs	Gls
Southampton	Sch	01/04	07	3	1	0
Torquay U	L	09/09	09	28	1	0
Brighton & HA	Tr	07/10				
Bristol Rov	L	01/12	11	8	0	0
Torquay U	Tr	06/12	12-13	57	0	0
Portsmouth	Tr	06/14				

POKU Godfrey Akwasi
Born: Newham, E London, England, 22 July, 1990 — M

League Club	Source	Date Signed	Seasons Played	Apps	Subs	Gls
Mansfield T	Luton T	07/12	13	1	3	0

POLAND George
Born: Penarth, Vale of Glamorgan, Wales, 21 September, 1913 — G
Died: Penarth, Vale of Glamorgan, Wales, 6 October, 1988
Wales: 2/War-4

League Club	Source	Date Signed	Seasons Played	Apps	Subs	Gls
Cardiff C	Swindon T (Am)	11/35	35-36	24	-	0
Wrexham	Tr	07/38	38	39	-	0
Liverpool	Tr	07/39				
Cardiff C	Tr	08/46	46	2	-	0

POLE Harold Edward William (Ted)
Born: Kessingland, Suffolk, England, 25 March, 1922 — CF
Died: Felixstowe, Suffolk, England, 13 December, 2010

League Club	Source	Date Signed	Seasons Played	Apps	Subs	Gls
Ipswich T	Gorleston	10/46	46-50	39	-	13
Leyton Orient	Tr	07/51	51-52	12	-	0

POLEON Dominic Alfred
Born: Newham, E London, England, 7 September, 1993 — F

League Club	Source	Date Signed	Seasons Played	Apps	Subs	Gls
Leeds U	Sch	07/12	12-14	3	26	3
Bury	L	10/12	12	7	0	2
Sheffield U	L	02/13	12	3	4	0
Oldham Ath	Tr	09/14	14	21	14	4

POLK Stanley (Stan)
Born: Liverpool, England, 28 October, 1921 — IF/WH
Died: Liverpool, England, 12 October, 2009

League Club	Source	Date Signed	Seasons Played	Apps	Subs	Gls
Liverpool	South Liverpool	03/40	46-47	13	-	0
Port Vale	Tr	07/48	48-51	159	-	14

POLLARD Brian Edward
Born: York, England, 22 May, 1954 — W
England: Youth

League Club	Source	Date Signed	Seasons Played	Apps	Subs	Gls
York C	Jnr	03/72	71-77	151	11	34
Watford	Tr	11/77	77-79	68	3	8
Mansfield T	Tr	01/80	79-80	45	9	5
Blackpool	Tr	08/81	81	0	1	0
York C	Tr	09/81	81-83	98	4	26
Chesterfield	Scarborough (NC)	09/84	84	0	1	0
Hartlepool U	Scarborough (NC)	01/85	84	2	0	0

POLLARD Gary
Born: Staveley, Derbyshire, England, 30 December, 1959 — CD

League Club	Source	Date Signed	Seasons Played	Apps	Subs	Gls
Chesterfield	Jnr	07/77	77-82	83	4	1
Port Vale	Tr	06/83	83	17	1	0
Mansfield T	Tr	07/84	84-86	66	1	1
Peterborough U	Tr	08/87	87-88	20	0	0

POLLARD James
Born: Liverpool, England, 4 June, 1926 — LW

League Club	Source	Date Signed	Seasons Played	Apps	Subs	Gls
Newport Co	Tredomen	05/46				
Tranmere Rov		11/47	47-48	24	-	1

POLLARD Kelly John (John)
Born: Chelmsford, England, 17 November, 1971 — CD

League Club	Source	Date Signed	Seasons Played	Apps	Subs	Gls
Colchester U	YT	06/90	88-89	1	8	1

POLLET Ludovic (Ludo)
Born: Vieux-Conde, France, 18 June, 1970 — CD

League Club	Source	Date Signed	Seasons Played	Apps	Subs	Gls
Wolverhampton W	Le Havre (FRA)	09/99	99-02	74	4	7
Walsall	L	11/02	02	5	0	0

POLLITT John (Jack)
Born: Farnworth, Greater Manchester, England, 29 March, 1937 — CF
Died: Bolton, Greater Manchester, England, December, 2009

League Club	Source	Date Signed	Seasons Played	Apps	Subs	Gls
Bolton W	Jnr	12/54				
Bury	Tr	08/58	58	4	-	0
Accrington Stan	Tr	03/60	59	3	-	1
Rochdale	Tr	08/60	60	6	-	1

POLLITT Michael Francis (Mike)
Born: Farnworth, Greater Manchester, England, 29 February, 1972 — G

League Club	Source	Date Signed	Seasons Played	Apps	Subs	Gls
Manchester U	YT	07/90				
Bury	Tr	07/91				
Lincoln C	L	09/92	92	5	0	0
Lincoln C	Tr	12/92	92-93	52	0	0
Darlington	Tr	08/94	94-95	55	0	0
Notts Co	Tr	11/95	96-97	10	0	0
Oldham Ath	L	08/97	97	16	0	0
Gillingham	L	12/97	97	6	0	0
Brentford	L	01/98	97	5	0	0
Sunderland	Tr	02/98				
Rotherham U	Tr	07/98	98-99	92	0	0
Chesterfield	Tr	06/00	00	46	0	0
Rotherham U	Tr	05/01	01-04	175	0	0
Wigan Ath	Tr	06/05	05-10	31	5	0
Ipswich T	L	11/06	06	1	0	0
Burnley	L	01/07	06	4	0	0
Barnsley	L	08/13	13	2	0	0

POLLOCK Jamie
Born: Stockton-on-Tees, Cleveland, England, 16 February, 1974 — M
England: U21-3/Youth

League Club	Source	Date Signed	Seasons Played	Apps	Subs	Gls
Middlesbrough	YT	12/91	90-95	144	11	17
Bolton W	CA Osasuna (SPN)	11/96	96-97	43	3	5
Manchester C	Tr	03/98	97-99	49	9	5
Crystal Palace	Tr	08/00	00	29	2	4
Birmingham C	L	03/01	00	4	1	0

POLLOCK Maitland Alexander Inglis (Matt)
Born: Lochmaben, Dumfries & Galloway, Scotland, 31 October, 1952 — W
Scotland: Schools

League Club	Source	Date Signed	Seasons Played	Apps	Subs	Gls
Nottingham F	App	10/70				
Walsall	Tr	07/73	73	1	1	0
Luton T	Burton A	03/74	75	3	3	0
Portsmouth	Tr	07/76	76-77	50	4	10

POLLOCK Stewart
Born: Bellshill, Lanarkshire, Scotland, 25 September, 1933 — IF
Died: Wishaw, Lanarkshire, Scotland, 7 September, 2003

League Club	Source	Date Signed	Seasons Played	Apps	Subs	Gls
Gillingham	Motherwell	07/56	56	10	-	0

POLLOCK William (Bill)
Born: Barrhead, Renfrewshire, Scotland, 7 June, 1920 — RH
Died: Barrhead, Renfrewshire, Scotland, 29 February, 1968

League Club	Source	Date Signed	Seasons Played	Apps	Subs	Gls
Oldham Ath	Manchester U (Am)	07/47	47	4	-	0

POLSTON Andrew Alfred (Andy)
Born: Walthamstow, NE London, England, 26 July, 1970 — FB

League Club	Source	Date Signed	Seasons Played	Apps	Subs	Gls
Tottenham H	YT	07/88	89	0	1	0
Cambridge U	L	10/89	89	3	0	0
Gillingham	L	11/91	91	1	1	0

POLSTON John David
Born: Walthamstow, NE London, England, 10 June, 1968 — CD
England: Youth

League Club	Source	Date Signed	Seasons Played	Apps	Subs	Gls
Tottenham H	App	07/85	86-89	17	7	1
Norwich C	Tr	07/90	90-97	200	15	8
Reading	Tr	07/98	98-99	16	2	1

POLYCARPOU Andrew (Andy)
Born: Islington, N London, England, 15 August, 1958 — M

League Club	Source	Date Signed	Seasons Played	Apps	Subs	Gls
Southend U		09/76	76-80	41	20	10
Cambridge U	Tr	08/81	81	1	4	0
Cardiff C	Tr	03/82	81	7	0	0

POMPHREY Edric Alfred (Syd)
Born: Stretford, Greater Manchester, England, 31 May, 1916 — RB
Died: Stockport, Greater Manchester, England, 16 February, 1987

League Club	Source	Date Signed	Seasons Played	Apps	Subs	Gls
Notts Co	Hyde U	09/44				
Rochdale	Tr	10/45	46	9	-	0

POND Nathan Louis
Born: Preston, Lancashire, England, 5 January, 1985 — CD

League Club	Source	Date Signed	Seasons Played	Apps	Subs	Gls
Fleetwood T	Springfields	07/03	12-14	75	5	2

PONTE Raimondo
Born: Brugg, Switzerland, 4 April, 1955 — M
Switzerland: 34

League Club	Source	Date Signed	Seasons Played	Apps	Subs	Gls
Nottingham F	G'hopper Zurich (SUI)	08/80	80	17	4	3

PONTIN Keith
Born: Pontyclun, Rhondda Cynon Taff, Wales, 14 June, 1956 — CD
Wales: 2/U21-1

League Club	Source	Date Signed	Seasons Played	Apps	Subs	Gls
Cardiff C	App	05/74	76-82	193	0	5

POOK David Charles
Born: Plymouth, England, 16 January, 1955 — W

League Club	Source	Date Signed	Seasons Played	Apps	Subs	Gls
Torquay U	App	01/73	71-72	13	3	1

POOK Michael David
Born: Swindon, England, 22 October, 1985 — M

League Club	Source	Date Signed	Seasons Played	Apps	Subs	Gls
Swindon T	Sch	07/05	04-08	85	24	3
Cheltenham T	Tr	08/09	09-10	56	8	6

POOLE Andrew John (Andy)
Born: Chesterfield, Derbyshire, England, 6 July, 1960 — G

League Club	Source	Date Signed	Seasons Played	Apps	Subs	Gls
Northampton T	Mansfield T (App)	07/78	78-81	141	0	0
Wolverhampton W	Tr	08/82				
Port Vale	Tr	03/83	82	2	0	0

POOLE Cyril John
Born: Mansfield, Nottinghamshire, England, 13 March, 1921 — LB/LW
Died: Balderton, Nottinghamshire, England, 11 February, 1996

League Club	Source	Date Signed	Seasons Played	Apps	Subs	Gls
Mansfield T (Am)	Annesley Colliery	02/37	36	1	-	0
Mansfield T	Gillingham	02/44	49-50	16	-	1

POOLE David Andrew
Born: Manchester, England, 25 November, 1984 — RW

League Club	Source	Date Signed	Seasons Played	Apps	Subs	Gls
Manchester U	Sch	07/02				
Yeovil T	Tr	07/05	05-06	21	8	2
Stockport Co	Tr	09/06	06-07	43	10	6
Darlington	Tr	07/08	08	18	8	1
Stockport Co	Tr	08/09	09-10	51	14	2

POOLE Gary John
Born: Stratford, E London, England, 11 September, 1967 — RB

League Club	Source	Date Signed	Seasons Played	Apps	Subs	Gls
Tottenham H	YT	07/85				
Cambridge U	Tr	08/87	87-88	42	1	0
Barnet	Tr	03/89	91	39	1	2
Plymouth Arg	Tr	06/92	92	39	0	5
Southend U	Tr	07/93	93-94	43	1	2
Birmingham C	Tr	09/94	94-96	70	2	0
Charlton Ath	Tr	11/96	96	14	2	1

POOLE Glenn Stephen
Born: Barking, E London, England, 3 February, 1981 — LW

League Club	Source	Date Signed	Seasons Played	Apps	Subs	Gls
Rochdale (L)	Grays Ath	03/07	06	1	5	0
Brentford	Grays Ath	05/07	07-08	60	11	19
Barnet	AFC Wimbledon	06/10	10	6	4	1

POOLE Henry (Harry)
Born: Stoke-on-Trent, England, 31 January, 1935 — WH/IF

League Club	Source	Date Signed	Seasons Played	Apps	Subs	Gls
Port Vale	Oxford C	04/56	55-67	450	1	73

POOLE James Alexander
Born: Stockport, Greater Manchester, England, 20 March, 1990 — F

League Club	Source	Date Signed	Seasons Played	Apps	Subs	Gls
Manchester C	Sch	07/08				
Bury	L	03/10	09	4	5	0
Hartlepool U	L	10/10	10	0	3	1
Hartlepool U	Tr	07/11	11-13	58	38	14
Bury	Tr	08/14	14	0	4	0

POOLE John Arthur Frederick
Born: Stoke-on-Trent, England, 12 December, 1932 — G

League Club	Source	Date Signed	Seasons Played	Apps	Subs	Gls
Port Vale	Stoke C (Am)	09/53	55-60	33	-	0

POOLE Joseph
Born: Huddersfield, West Yorkshire, England, 25 May, 1923 — W
Died: Huddersfield, West Yorkshire, England, November, 1990

League Club	Source	Date Signed	Seasons Played	Apps	Subs	Gls
Huddersfield T	David Brown's Works	06/41	46	2	-	0
Bradford C	Tr	02/47	46-48	56	-	5

POOLE Kenneth James (Ken)
Born: Tredegar, Blaenau Gwent, Wales, 27 April, 1934 — LH

League Club	Source	Date Signed	Seasons Played	Apps	Subs	Gls
Swansea C	Jnr	11/53				
Northampton T	Tr	06/56	56	4	-	0

POOLE Kevin
Born: Bromsgrove, Worcestershire, England, 21 July, 1963 — G

League Club	Source	Date Signed	Seasons Played	Apps	Subs	Gls
Aston Villa	App	06/81	84-86	28	0	0
Northampton T	L	11/84	84	3	0	0
Middlesbrough	Tr	08/87	87-89	34	0	0
Hartlepool U	L	03/91	90	12	0	0
Leicester C	Tr	07/91	91-96	163	0	0
Birmingham C	Tr	08/97	97-00	56	0	0
Bolton W	Tr	10/01	01-04	4	1	0
Derby Co	Tr	07/05	05	6	0	0
Burton A	Tr	08/06	09	5	1	0

POOLE Michael David (Mike)
Born: Morley, West Yorkshire, England, 23 April, 1955 — G

League Club	Source	Date Signed	Seasons Played	Apps	Subs	Gls
Rochdale	Coventry C (App)	09/73	73-77	192	0	0
Rochdale	Portland Timbers (USA)	08/81	81	27	0	0

POOLE Regan Leslie
Born: Cardiff, Wales, 18 June, 1998 — CD
Wales: Youth

League Club	Source	Date Signed	Seasons Played	Apps	Subs	Gls
Newport Co	Sch	-	14	11	0	0

POOLE Richard John
Born: Heston, W London, England, 3 July, 1957 — F

League Club	Source	Date Signed	Seasons Played	Apps	Subs	Gls
Brentford	App	07/75	73-75	12	9	1
Watford	Tr	07/76	76	3	4	1

POOLE Roy
Born: Sheffield, England, 2 December, 1939 — CF/LB

League Club	Source	Date Signed	Seasons Played	Apps	Subs	Gls
Wolverhampton W	Jnr	01/57				
Rotherham U	Tr	07/58				
Chesterfield	Tr	07/61	61-63	50	-	14

POOLE Terence (Terry)
Born: Chesterfield, Derbyshire, England, 16 December, 1949 — G

League Club	Source	Date Signed	Seasons Played	Apps	Subs	Gls
Manchester U	Jnr	02/67				
Huddersfield T	Tr	08/68	68-76	207	0	0
Bolton W	Tr	01/77	80	29	0	0
Sheffield U	L	03/80	79	7	0	0

POOLE Terence (Terry)
Born: Sheffield, England, 8 December, 1937 — WH

League Club	Source	Date Signed	Seasons Played	Apps	Subs	Gls
Sheffield Wed	Jnr	04/55				
Darlington	Tr	07/59	59-60	41	-	3

POOLEY Dean
Born: Sidcup, SE London, England, 10 September, 1986 — CD

League Club	Source	Date Signed	Seasons Played	Apps	Subs	Gls
Millwall	Sch	04/06	05	0	1	0

POOM Mart
Born: Tallinn, Estonia, 3 February, 1972 — G
Estonia: 120

League Club	Source	Date Signed	Seasons Played	Apps	Subs	Gls
Portsmouth	FC Wil (SUI)	08/94	95	4	0	0
Derby Co	Flora Tallinn (EST)	03/97	96-02	143	3	0
Sunderland	Tr	11/02	02-04	58	0	1
Arsenal	Tr	08/05	06	1	0	0
Watford	Tr	05/07	07-08	19	0	0

League Club	Source	Date Signed	Seasons Played	Career Record Apps	Subs	Gls
POPE David William						
Born: Camden, N London, England, 8 January, 1936						RB
Crystal Palace		09/53				
Swansea C		09/56	57	2	-	0
POPE Neil Lester						
Born: Cambridge, England, 9 October, 1972						M
Peterborough U	Cambridge U (YT)	03/91	90	1	1	0
POPE Nicholas David (Nick)						
Born: Cambridge, England, 19 April, 1992						G
Charlton Ath	Bury T	07/11	12-14	7	2	0
York C	L	11/13	13	22	0	0
Bury	L	01/15	14	22	0	0
POPE Steven Anthony (Steve)						
Born: Mow Cop, Staffordshire, England, 8 September, 1976						CD
Crewe Alex	YT	06/95	97	2	4	0
POPE Terence John (Terry)						
Born: Newport, Wales, 27 January, 1926						G
Died: Liverpool, England, 7 September, 2003						
Newport Co	Bargoed U	07/50	50-54	83	-	0
POPE Thomas John (Tom)						
Born: Stoke-on-Trent, England, 27 August, 1985						F
Crewe Alex	Biddulph Victoria	09/05	06-08	32	24	17
Rotherham U	Tr	06/09	09-10	35	18	4
Port Vale	L	01/11	10	10	3	3
Port Vale	Tr	08/11	11-14	149	14	56
POPELY Peter Charles Francis						
Born: York, England, 7 April, 1943						LB
York C	Cliftonville, York	08/62	62-66	24	1	0
POPESCU Gheorghe (Gica)						
Born: Calafat, Romania, 9 October, 1967						DM
Romania: 115						
Tottenham H	PSV Eindhoven (NED)	09/94	94	23	0	3
POPOV Goran						
Born: Strumica, Macedonia, 2 October, 1984						LB
Macedonia: 46/U21-10/Youth						
West Bromwich A (L)	Dynamo Kiev (UKR)	09/12	12	10	2	0
West Bromwich A (L)	Dynamo Kiev (UKR)	07/13	13	1	1	0
POPOVIC Anthony (Tony)						
Born: Sydney, Australia, 4 July, 1973						CD
Australia: 58/U23-4/Youth						
Crystal Palace	Sanfrecce (JPN)	08/01	01-05	121	2	6
POPPITT John (Johnny)						
Born: West Sleekburn, Northumberland, England, 20 January, 1923						RB
Died: Derby, England, 12 February, 2014						
Derby Co	West Sleekburn	05/45	46-49	16	-	0
Queens Park Rgrs	Tr	09/50	50-53	106	-	0
POPPLETON David John						
Born: Doncaster, South Yorkshire, England, 19 December, 1979						M
Everton	YT	07/97				
Lincoln C	Tr	08/99	99	4	1	0
POPPY Arthur						
Born: Yeovil, Somerset, England, 6 January, 1961						CD
Northampton T	App	-	77	1	0	0
PORFIRIO Hugo Cardoso						
Born: Lisbon, Portugal, 29 September, 1973						W
Portugal: 3/U21-10/Youth						
West Ham U (L)	Sporting Lisbon (POR)	09/96	96	15	8	2
Nottingham F (L)	Benfica (POR)	01/99	98	3	6	1
PORIC Adem						
Born: Kensington, Central London, England, 22 April, 1973						M
Australia: Youth						
Sheffield Wed	St George-B'pest (AUS)	10/93	93-97	3	11	0
Southend U	L	02/97	96	7	0	0
Rotherham U	Tr	02/98	97	4	0	0
Notts Co	Tr	03/98	97	3	1	0
PORRITT Nathan John						
Born: Middlesbrough, England, 9 January, 1990						LW
Middlesbrough	Sch	07/08				
Darlington	L	08/09	09	4	1	0
PORRITT Walter						
Born: Heckmondwike, West Yorkshire, England, 19 July, 1914						RW
Died: Heckmondwike, West Yorkshire, England, July, 1993						
Huddersfield T		05/35				
York C	Tr	08/36	36-46	40	-	5

League Club	Source	Date Signed	Seasons Played	Career Record Apps	Subs	Gls
PORT Bernard Harry						
Born: Burton-on-Trent, Staffordshire, England, 14 December, 1925						G
Hull C	Newhall FC	09/50				
Chester C	Tr	08/51	51-52	9	-	0
PORTEOUS John Robert (Jack)						
Born: India, 12 January, 1933						IF/LH
Aldershot	Alton T	02/56	55	1	-	0
PORTEOUS John Robertson (Johnny)						
Born: Motherwell, Lanarkshire, Scotland, 5 December, 1921						WH
Died: Plymouth, England, August, 2007						
Plymouth Arg	Alloa Ath	07/49	49-55	215	-	13
Exeter C	Tr	03/56	55-56	40	-	0
PORTEOUS Trevor						
Born: Hull, England, 9 October, 1933						WH
Died: Stockport, Greater Manchester, England, 15 May, 1997						
Hull C	Jnr	10/50	51-55	61	-	1
Stockport Co	Tr	06/56	56-64	337	-	9
PORTER Andrew (Andy)						
Born: Stewarton, Ayrshire, Scotland, 21 January, 1937						RH
Watford	Darvel Jnrs	06/59	59-62	72	-	4
PORTER Andrew Michael (Andy)						
Born: Holmes Chapel, Cheshire, England, 17 September, 1968						M
Port Vale	App	06/87	86-97	313	44	22
Wigan Ath	Tr	07/98	98-99	8	13	1
Mansfield T	L	10/99	99	5	0	0
Chester C	L	02/00	99	16	0	0
Port Vale	Rtd	11/04	04-05	2	2	0
PORTER Christopher Ian (Chris)						
Born: Sunderland, England, 10 November, 1979						G
Sunderland	YT	08/98				
Darlington	Leiftur (ICE)	03/02	01-02	9	1	0
York C	Tr	07/03	03	5	0	0
PORTER Christopher John (Chris)						
Born: Wigan, Greater Manchester, England, 12 December, 1983						F
Bury	QEGS OB	03/03	02-04	48	23	18
Oldham Ath	Tr	07/05	05-06	52	14	28
Derby Co	Motherwell	02/09	08-10	20	24	9
Sheffield U	Tr	07/11	11-14	47	41	16
Shrewsbury T	L	02/13	12	4	1	1
Chesterfield	L	10/13	13	2	1	0
Colchester U	Tr	01/15	14	20	1	7
PORTER Christopher John (Chris)						
Born: North Petherton, Somerset, England, 30 April, 1949						RW
Swindon T	Bridgwater T	11/69	70-73	33	2	4
PORTER Derek						
Born: Ulverston, Cumbria, England, 22 June, 1936						W
Barrow	Dalton T	05/57	57-58	15	-	1
PORTER Gary Michael						
Born: Sunderland, England, 6 March, 1966						M
England: U21-12/Youth						
Watford	App	03/84	83-96	362	38	47
Walsall	Tr	06/97	97-98	39	5	1
Scarborough	Tr	02/99	98	11	2	0
PORTER George						
Born: Chirk, Wrexham, Wales, 5 February, 1935						W
Wrexham (Am)	Chirk AAA	05/59	59	1	-	0
PORTER George Edwards						
Born: Sidcup, SE London, England, 27 June, 1992						W
Leyton Orient	Cray W	07/10	10-11	9	26	1
Burnley	Tr	07/12				
Colchester U	L	01/13	12	13	6	1
AFC Wimbledon	L	07/13	13	17	4	0
Rochdale	Tr	01/14	13	1	1	0
Dagenham & Red	Tr	08/14	14	7	12	1
PORTER Joel William						
Born: Adelaide, Australia, 25 December, 1978						F
Australia: 4						
Hartlepool U	Olympic Sharks (AUS)	11/03	03-08	135	38	52
PORTER Leslie (Les)						
Born: Gateshead, Tyne and Wear, England, 5 May, 1923						WH
Died: Middlesbrough, England, November, 2002						
Newcastle U	Redheugh Steelworks	09/44				
York C	Tr	03/49	48-53	38	-	1
PORTER Levi Roger						
Born: Leicester, England, 6 April, 1987						LM

England: Youth

League Club	Source	Date Signed	Seasons Played	Apps	Subs	Gls
Leicester C	Sch	07/05	06-08	28	11	3

PORTER Max
Born: Grays, Essex, England, 29 June, 1987 — M
England: Semi Pro-6

League Club	Source	Date Signed	Seasons Played	Apps	Subs	Gls
Barnet	Bishops Stortford	06/07	07-08	44	12	1
AFC Wimbledon	Rushden & D	07/11	11	11	4	1
Newport Co	Tr	02/12	13-14	36	13	2

PORTER Michael Robert (Mike)
Born: Stoke-on-Trent, England, 19 May, 1945 — IF

League Club	Source	Date Signed	Seasons Played	Apps	Subs	Gls
Port Vale	Jnr	07/62	63-64	13	-	2

PORTER Trevor James
Born: Guildford, Surrey, England, 16 October, 1956 — G

League Club	Source	Date Signed	Seasons Played	Apps	Subs	Gls
Fulham	App	05/74				
Brentford	Slough T	08/78	78-79	15	0	0

PORTER William (Bill)
Born: Shotton Colliery, County Durham, England, 23 November, 1923 — LB
Died: Durham, England, 28 January, 1975

League Club	Source	Date Signed	Seasons Played	Apps	Subs	Gls
Hartlepool U	Horden CW	09/43	46	2	-	0

PORTERFIELD John (Ian)
Born: Dunfermline, Fife, Scotland, 11 February, 1946 — M
Died: Farnham, Surrey, England, 11 September, 2007

League Club	Source	Date Signed	Seasons Played	Apps	Subs	Gls
Sunderland	Raith Rov	12/67	67-75	217	12	17
Reading	L	11/76	76	5	0	0
Sheffield Wed	Tr	07/77	77-79	103	3	3

PORTEUS Joseph (Joe)
Born: Shildon, County Durham, England, 20 April, 1925 — LH
Died: Chesterfield, Derbyshire, England, 9 January, 1995

League Club	Source	Date Signed	Seasons Played	Apps	Subs	Gls
York C	Chesterfield (Am)	08/46	46	23	-	0

PORTWOOD Clifford (Cliff)
Born: Salford, England, 17 October, 1937 — IF
Died: Basingstoke, Hampshire, England, 10 January, 2012

League Club	Source	Date Signed	Seasons Played	Apps	Subs	Gls
Preston NE	Manchester Ath	02/55				
Port Vale	Tr	08/59	59-60	61	-	33
Grimsby T	Tr	07/61	61-63	92	-	35
Portsmouth	Tr	05/64	64-68	95	4	28

POSCHA Marcus Anthony
Born: Rochdale, Greater Manchester, England, 16 August, 1996 — FB

League Club	Source	Date Signed	Seasons Played	Apps	Subs	Gls
Bury	Sch	-	13	0	1	0

POSKETT Malcolm
Born: Middlesbrough, England, 19 July, 1953 — F

League Club	Source	Date Signed	Seasons Played	Apps	Subs	Gls
Middlesbrough	South Bank	04/73	73	0	1	0
Hartlepool U	Tr	07/74				
Hartlepool U	Whitby T	11/76	76-77	50	1	20
Brighton & HA	Tr	02/78	77-79	33	12	17
Watford	Tr	01/80	79-81	57	6	17
Carlisle U	Tr	08/82	82-84	108	2	40
Darlington	Tr	07/85	85	18	3	4
Stockport Co	Tr	01/86	85	8	0	1
Hartlepool U	L	03/86	85	4	1	0
Carlisle U	Tr	08/86	86-87	67	9	20

POSKETT Thomas William (Tom)
Born: Esh Winning, County Durham, England, 26 December, 1909 — G
Died: Crewe, Cheshire, England, 19 December, 1972

League Club	Source	Date Signed	Seasons Played	Apps	Subs	Gls
Grimsby T	Crook T	12/28	28-30	2	-	0
Lincoln C	Tr	05/32	33	10	-	0
Notts Co	Tr	05/34	34	10	-	0
Tranmere Rov	Tr	08/35	35-36	22	-	0
Crewe Alex	Tr	07/37	37-46	99	-	0

POSSEBON Rodrigo Pereira
Born: Porto Alegre, Brazil, 13 February, 1989 — M

League Club	Source	Date Signed	Seasons Played	Apps	Subs	Gls
Manchester U	Internacional (BRA)	01/08	08	0	3	0

POSSEE Derek James
Born: Southwark, S London, England, 14 February, 1946 — RW/F

League Club	Source	Date Signed	Seasons Played	Apps	Subs	Gls
Tottenham H	App	03/63	63-65	19	0	4
Millwall	Tr	08/67	67-72	222	1	79
Crystal Palace	Tr	01/73	72-73	51	2	13
Leyton Orient	Tr	07/74	74-76	77	3	11

POSTIGA Helder Manuel Marques
Born: Povoa de Varzim, Portugal, 2 August, 1982 — F
Portugal: 71/U21-16

League Club	Source	Date Signed	Seasons Played	Apps	Subs	Gls
Tottenham H	FC Porto (POR)	07/03	03	9	10	1

POSTLEWHITE Dennis John
Born: Birkenhead, Wirral, England, 13 October, 1957 — CD

League Club	Source	Date Signed	Seasons Played	Apps	Subs	Gls
Tranmere Rov	App	10/75	76-78	31	2	1

POSTMA Stefan
Born: Utrecht, Netherlands, 10 June, 1976 — G

League Club	Source	Date Signed	Seasons Played	Apps	Subs	Gls
Aston Villa	De Graafschap (NED)	05/02	02-04	7	4	0
Wolverhampton W	Tr	08/05	05	29	0	0

POTRAC Anthony Joseph (Tony)
Born: Victoria, Australia, 21 January, 1953 — W

League Club	Source	Date Signed	Seasons Played	Apps	Subs	Gls
Chelsea	App	08/70	71	1	0	0

POTTER Alfie James
Born: Hackney, E London, England, 9 January, 1989 — W

League Club	Source	Date Signed	Seasons Played	Apps	Subs	Gls
Peterborough U	Jnr	07/07	07	0	2	0
Oxford U	Tr	07/10	10-14	101	44	20
AFC Wimbledon	Tr	01/15	14	10	5	1

POTTER Daniel Raymond John (Danny)
Born: Ipswich, England, 18 March, 1979 — G

League Club	Source	Date Signed	Seasons Played	Apps	Subs	Gls
Colchester U	Chelsea (YT)	10/97				
Exeter C	Tr	08/98	98-99	10	0	0
Torquay U	Cambridge U	07/10	10	9	0	0

POTTER Darren Michael
Born: Liverpool, England, 21 December, 1984 — M
Republic of Ireland: 5/U21-11/Youth

League Club	Source	Date Signed	Seasons Played	Apps	Subs	Gls
Liverpool	Sch	04/02	04	0	2	0
Southampton	L	01/06	05	8	2	0
Wolverhampton W	Tr	08/06	06-07	46	10	0
Sheffield Wed	Tr	01/09	08-10	85	11	8
MK Dons	Tr	06/11	11-14	155	0	8

POTTER Frederick (Fred)
Born: Cradley Heath, West Midlands, England, 29 November, 1940 — G

League Club	Source	Date Signed	Seasons Played	Apps	Subs	Gls
Aston Villa	Cradley Heath	07/59	60	3	-	0
Doncaster Rov	Tr	07/62	62-65	123	0	0
Hereford U	Burton A	07/70	72-73	10	0	0

POTTER Gary Charles
Born: Chester, England, 6 August, 1952 — CD

League Club	Source	Date Signed	Seasons Played	Apps	Subs	Gls
Chester C	Jnr	07/73	73-74	11	0	0

POTTER George Ross
Born: Arbroath, Angus, Scotland, 7 October, 1946 — D

League Club	Source	Date Signed	Seasons Played	Apps	Subs	Gls
Luton T	Forfar Ath	03/68	67-68	3	5	0
Torquay U	Tr	07/69	69-70	32	4	0
Hartlepool U	Tr	07/71	71-76	211	2	4

POTTER Graham Stephen
Born: Solihull, West Midlands, England, 20 May, 1975 — LB
England: U21-1/Youth

League Club	Source	Date Signed	Seasons Played	Apps	Subs	Gls
Birmingham C	YT	07/92	92-93	23	2	2
Wycombe W	L	09/93	93	2	1	0
Stoke C	Tr	12/93	93-95	41	4	1
Southampton	Tr	07/96	96	2	6	0
West Bromwich A	Tr	02/97	96-99	31	12	0
Northampton T	L	10/97	97	4	0	0
Reading	L	12/99	99	4	0	0
York C	Tr	07/00	00-02	108	6	5
Boston U	Tr	07/03	03	11	1	0
Macclesfield T	Tr	02/04	03-04	55	2	8

POTTER Harold (Harry)
Born: Tyldesley, Greater Manchester, England, 20 May, 1923 — FB
Died: Rochdale, Greater Manchester, England, June, 1992

League Club	Source	Date Signed	Seasons Played	Apps	Subs	Gls
Shrewsbury T	Winsford U	07/49	50-51	67	-	0
Rochdale	Tr	06/52	52-53	52	-	0

POTTER James
Born: Belfast, Northern Ireland, 20 November, 1941 — RH

League Club	Source	Date Signed	Seasons Played	Apps	Subs	Gls
Sunderland	Jnr	11/58				
Darlington	Tr	09/63	63	19	-	1

POTTER Lee
Born: Salford, England, 3 September, 1978 — F

League Club	Source	Date Signed	Seasons Played	Apps	Subs	Gls
Bolton W	YT	07/97				
Halifax T	Tr	12/99	99-00	13	9	2

POTTER Luke Alexander
Born: Barnsley, South Yorkshire, England, 17 July, 1989 — LB

League Club	Source	Date Signed	Seasons Played	Apps	Subs	Gls
Barnsley	Sch	07/07	06-10	15	4	0

POTTER Raymond John (Ray)
Born: Beckenham, SE London, England, 7 May, 1936 — G
Died: Exeter, England, 7 August, 2005

League Club	Source	Date Signed	Seasons Played	Apps	Subs	Gls
Crystal Palace	Jnr	05/53	53-57	44	-	0
West Bromwich A	Tr	06/58	58-66	217	0	0
Portsmouth	Tr	05/67	67-69	3	0	0

POTTER Ronald Charles (Ron)
Born: Wolverhampton, England, 5 December, 1948 — CD

League Club	Source	Date Signed	Seasons Played	Apps	Subs	Gls
West Bromwich A	App	12/66	68-69	8	1	0
Swindon T	Tr	11/70	70-74	84	2	0

POTTER Stephen Derek (Steve)
Born: Belper, Derbyshire, England, 1 October, 1955 — G

League Club	Source	Date Signed	Seasons Played	Apps	Subs	Gls
Manchester C	App	10/73				
Swansea C	Tr	08/74	74-77	118	0	0

POTTS Bradley Michael (Brad)
Born: Haltwhistle, Northumberland, England, 3 July, 1994 — RB/M
England: Youth

League Club	Source	Date Signed	Seasons Played	Apps	Subs	Gls
Carlisle U	Sch	09/12	12-14	91	12	9

POTTS Brian
Born: Sunderland, England, 3 September, 1948 — RB

League Club	Source	Date Signed	Seasons Played	Apps	Subs	Gls
Leicester C	App	09/65	67-68	9	1	0
Peterborough U	Tr	07/69	69-70	49	1	0

POTTS Craig
Born: Carlisle, Cumbria, England, 25 February, 1974 — LW

League Club	Source	Date Signed	Seasons Played	Apps	Subs	Gls
Carlisle U	YT	09/92	91-92	9	5	0

POTTS Daniel (Danny)
Born: Barking, E London, England, 13 April, 1994 — LB
England: Youth

League Club	Source	Date Signed	Seasons Played	Apps	Subs	Gls
West Ham U	Sch	12/11	11-12	4	1	0
Colchester U	L	11/12	12	5	0	0
Portsmouth	L	11/13	13	5	0	0

POTTS Eric Thomas
Born: Liverpool, England, 16 March, 1950 — W

League Club	Source	Date Signed	Seasons Played	Apps	Subs	Gls
Sheffield Wed	Oswestry T	12/69	70-76	142	17	21
Brighton & HA	Tr	06/77	77	19	14	5
Preston NE	Tr	08/78	78-80	50	7	5
Burnley	Tr	09/80	80-81	48	8	5
Bury	Tr	10/82	82-83	46	5	7

POTTS Harry
Born: Hetton-le-Hole, Tyne and Wear, England, 22 October, 1920 — IF
Died: Burnley, Lancashire, England, 16 January, 1996

League Club	Source	Date Signed	Seasons Played	Apps	Subs	Gls
Burnley	Jnr	11/37	46-50	165	-	47
Everton	Tr	10/50	50-55	59	-	15

POTTS Henry James
Born: Carlisle, Cumbria, England, 23 January, 1925 — W
England: Amateur-8

League Club	Source	Date Signed	Seasons Played	Apps	Subs	Gls
Northampton T (Am)	Pegasus	08/50	50	10	-	0

POTTS Michael Craig Thomas
Born: Preston, Lancashire, England, 26 November, 1991 — M

League Club	Source	Date Signed	Seasons Played	Apps	Subs	Gls
Blackburn Rov	Sch	11/08				
York C	Tr	06/11	12	12	2	3

POTTS Reginald (Reg)
Born: Stoke-on-Trent, England, 31 July, 1927 — LB
Died: Stoke-on-Trent, England, 28 January, 1996

League Club	Source	Date Signed	Seasons Played	Apps	Subs	Gls
Port Vale	Northwood Mission	08/45	48-56	277	-	3

POTTS Steven John (Steve)
Born: Hartford, Connecticut, USA, 7 May, 1967 — D
England: Youth

League Club	Source	Date Signed	Seasons Played	Apps	Subs	Gls
West Ham U	App	05/84	84-00	362	37	1

POTTS Victor Ernest (Vic)
Born: Birmingham, England, 20 August, 1915 — RB
Died: Sutton Coldfield, West Midlands, England, 22 October, 1996

League Club	Source	Date Signed	Seasons Played	Apps	Subs	Gls
Tottenham H	Metro Welfare	08/34				
Doncaster Rov	Tr	08/38	37-38	27	-	0
Aston Villa	Tr	08/45	46-47	62	-	0

POULSEN Christian Bjornshoj
Born: Asnaes, Denmark, 28 February, 1980 — DM
Denmark: 92/U21-8/Youth

League Club	Source	Date Signed	Seasons Played	Apps	Subs	Gls
Liverpool	Juventus (ITA)	08/10	10	9	3	0

POULTON George Henry
Born: Holborn, Central London, England, 23 April, 1929 — LW
Died: Thurrock, Essex, England, 3 December, 2010

League Club	Source	Date Signed	Seasons Played	Apps	Subs	Gls
Gillingham	Army	08/49	51	5	-	1
Leyton Orient	Tr	07/52	52-54	61	-	24

POUND John Henry Kenneth (Ken)
Born: Portsmouth, England, 24 August, 1944 — W/IF

League Club	Source	Date Signed	Seasons Played	Apps	Subs	Gls
Swansea C	Yeovil T	07/64	64-65	25	1	4
Bournemouth	Tr	08/66	66-68	102	0	24
Gillingham	Tr	07/69	69-70	62	11	11

POUNDER Albert William
Born: Charlton, SE London, England, 27 July, 1931 — RW
Died: Bromley, SE London, England, May, 2009

League Club	Source	Date Signed	Seasons Played	Apps	Subs	Gls
Charlton Ath	Harvey Sports	02/50	52	1	-	0
Queens Park Rgrs	Tr	02/54	53-55	53	-	6

POUNDER Anthony Mark (Tony)
Born: Yeovil, Somerset, England, 11 March, 1966 — LW

League Club	Source	Date Signed	Seasons Played	Apps	Subs	Gls
Bristol Rov	Weymouth	07/90	90-93	102	11	10
Hereford U	Weymouth	09/94	94-95	54	8	4

POUNDER John Anthony (Tony)
Born: Sheffield, England, 16 March, 1935 — RW

League Club	Source	Date Signed	Seasons Played	Apps	Subs	Gls
Luton T	Atlas Sports	12/55	55-56	3	-	0
Coventry C	Tr	06/57	57	6	-	1
Crewe Alex	Yeovil T	12/57	57-58	29	-	5

POUNEWATCHY Stephane Zeusnagapa
Born: Paris, France, 10 February, 1968 — CD

League Club	Source	Date Signed	Seasons Played	Apps	Subs	Gls
Carlisle U	Gueugnon (FRA)	08/96	96-97	81	0	3
Port Vale	Dundee	08/98	98	2	0	0
Colchester U	Tr	02/99	98	15	0	1

POUNTNEY Craig Frank
Born: Bromsgrove, Worcestershire, England, 23 November, 1979 — F

League Club	Source	Date Signed	Seasons Played	Apps	Subs	Gls
Shrewsbury T	YT	04/98	97	0	1	0

POUNTNEY David Harold (Dave)
Born: Baschurch, Shropshire, England, 12 October, 1939 — WH/CH

League Club	Source	Date Signed	Seasons Played	Apps	Subs	Gls
Shrewsbury T	Myddle	09/57	57-63	175	-	11
Aston Villa	Tr	10/63	63-67	109	4	7
Shrewsbury T	Tr	02/68	67-69	54	4	1
Chester C	Tr	06/70	70-72	135	0	1

POUNTNEY Ronald Alan (Ron)
Born: Bilston, West Midlands, England, 19 March, 1955 — M

League Club	Source	Date Signed	Seasons Played	Apps	Subs	Gls
Walsall (Am)	Jnr	07/72	72	1	0	0
Port Vale	Tr	10/73				
Southend U	Bilston T	01/75	74-84	327	22	26

POUSO Omar Heber
Born: Montevideo, Uruguay, 28 February, 1980 — M
Uruguay: 8

League Club	Source	Date Signed	Seasons Played	Apps	Subs	Gls
Charlton Ath (L)	Penarol (UGY)	09/06	06	1	0	0

POUTCH Neil Anthony
Born: Dublin, Republic of Ireland, 27 November, 1969 — FB
Republic of Ireland: U21-8

League Club	Source	Date Signed	Seasons Played	Apps	Subs	Gls
Luton T	YT	11/87	89	0	1	0

POUTON Alan
Born: Newcastle-upon-Tyne, England, 1 February, 1977 — M

League Club	Source	Date Signed	Seasons Played	Apps	Subs	Gls
Oxford U	Newcastle U (YT)	11/95				
York C	Tr	12/95	96-98	79	11	7
Grimsby T	Tr	08/99	99-03	100	21	12
Gillingham	Tr	01/04	03-06	44	18	3
Hartlepool U	L	09/04	04	5	0	0

POVEY Neil Andrew
Born: Birmingham, England, 26 June, 1977 — M

League Club	Source	Date Signed	Seasons Played	Apps	Subs	Gls
Torquay U	YT	07/95	94-95	8	3	0

POVEY Victor Richard (Vic)
Born: Wolverhampton, England, 16 March, 1944 — RW

League Club	Source	Date Signed	Seasons Played	Apps	Subs	Gls
Wolverhampton W	Jnr	07/61				
Notts Co	Tr	08/63	63-64	35	-	3

POVEY William
Born: Billingham, Cleveland, England, 11 January, 1943 — W

League Club	Source	Date Signed	Seasons Played	Apps	Subs	Gls
Middlesbrough	Jnr	05/60	62	6	-	0
York C	Tr	03/64	64	3	-	0

POWEL Berry Leroy
Born: Utrecht, Netherlands, 2 May, 1980 — F

League Club	Source	Date Signed	Seasons Played	Apps	Subs	Gls
Millwall	FC Den Bosch (NED)	01/06	05	8	4	1

POWELL Andrew (Andy)
Born: Plymouth, England, 27 June, 1955 — G

League Club	Source	Date Signed	Seasons Played	Apps	Subs	Gls
Hereford U	Presteigne	10/82	82	4	0	0

POWELL Anthony (Tony)
Born: Severn Beach, Avon, England, 11 February, 1947 — CD

League Club	Source	Date Signed	Seasons Played	Apps	Subs	Gls
Bournemouth	Bath C	04/68	68-73	214	5	10
Norwich C	Tr	08/74	74-80	235	2	3

POWELL Aubrey
Born: Gurnos, Merthyr Tydfil, Wales, 19 April, 1918 — IF
Died: Leeds, England, 27 January, 2009
Wales: 8/War-4

League Club	Source	Date Signed	Seasons Played	Apps	Subs	Gls
Leeds U	Swansea C (Am)	11/35	36-47	112	-	25
Everton	Tr	07/48	48-49	35	-	5
Birmingham C	Tr	08/50	50	15	-	1

POWELL Baden
Born: Hebburn, Tyne and Wear, England, 17 June, 1931 — RW
Died: Sunderland, England, January, 2014

League Club	Source	Date Signed	Seasons Played	Apps	Subs	Gls
Darlington	South Shields ESB	10/50	50-53	9	-	0

League Club	Source	Date Signed	Seasons Played	Career Record Apps	Subs	Gls

POWELL Barry Ivor
Born: Kenilworth, Warwickshire, England, 29 January, 1954 — M
England: U23-4

League Club	Source	Date Signed	Seasons Played	Apps	Subs	Gls
Wolverhampton W	App	01/72	72-74	58	6	7
Coventry C	Tr	09/75	75-79	162	2	27
Derby Co	Tr	10/79	79-81	86	0	7
Burnley	Bulova (HKG)	07/84	84	9	2	0
Swansea C	Tr	02/85	84	8	0	0
Wolverhampton W	South China (HKG)	11/86	86-87	10	4	0

POWELL Brian John Edward (John)
Born: York, England, 10 March, 1936 — LW

League Club	Source	Date Signed	Seasons Played	Apps	Subs	Gls
York C	Cliftonville, York	09/56	56-59	27	-	5

POWELL Christopher George Robin (Chris)
Born: Lambeth, S London, England, 8 September, 1969 — LB
England: 5

League Club	Source	Date Signed	Seasons Played	Apps	Subs	Gls
Crystal Palace	YT	12/87	88	2	1	0
Aldershot	L	01/90	89	11	0	0
Southend U	Tr	08/90	90-95	246	2	3
Derby Co	Tr	01/96	95-97	89	2	1
Charlton Ath	Tr	07/98	98-03	190	10	1
West Ham U	Tr	09/04	04	35	1	0
Charlton Ath	Tr	07/05	05	25	2	0
Watford	Tr	07/06	06	9	6	0
Charlton Ath	Tr	07/07	07	16	1	1
Leicester C	Tr	08/08	08-09	14	5	0

POWELL Clifford George (Cliff)
Born: Watford, Hertfordshire, England, 21 February, 1968 — D

League Club	Source	Date Signed	Seasons Played	Apps	Subs	Gls
Watford	App	02/86				
Hereford U	L	12/87	87	7	0	0
Sheffield U	Tr	03/88	87-88	7	3	0
Doncaster Rov	L	03/89	88	4	0	0
Cardiff C	L	11/89	89	0	1	0

POWELL Colin David
Born: Hendon, N London, England, 7 July, 1948 — RW

League Club	Source	Date Signed	Seasons Played	Apps	Subs	Gls
Charlton Ath	Barnet	01/73	72-80	301	20	30
Gillingham	Tr	08/81	81-82	54	1	1

POWELL Conor
Born: Dublin, Republic of Ireland, 26 August, 1987 — LB
Republic of Ireland: U21-9

League Club	Source	Date Signed	Seasons Played	Apps	Subs	Gls
Colchester U	Bohemians (ROI)	01/11	10	2	0	0

POWELL Daniel Vendrys
Born: Luton, England, 12 March, 1991 — W

League Club	Source	Date Signed	Seasons Played	Apps	Subs	Gls
MK Dons	Sch	02/09	08-14	124	65	33

POWELL Darren David
Born: Hammersmith, W London, England, 10 March, 1976 — CD

League Club	Source	Date Signed	Seasons Played	Apps	Subs	Gls
Brentford	Hampton	07/98	98-01	128	0	6
Crystal Palace	Tr	08/02	02-04	53	2	2
West Ham U	L	11/04	04	5	0	1
Southampton	Tr	07/05	05-07	42	1	2
Derby Co	Tr	11/08	08	5	1	0
Brentford	Tr	03/09	08	3	1	0
MK Dons	Tr	08/09	09	19	5	0

POWELL Darryl Anthony
Born: Lambeth, S London, England, 15 January, 1971 — M
Jamaica: 21

League Club	Source	Date Signed	Seasons Played	Apps	Subs	Gls
Portsmouth	YT	12/88	88-94	83	49	16
Derby Co	Tr	07/95	95-01	187	20	10
Birmingham C	Tr	09/02	02	3	8	0
Sheffield Wed	Tr	01/03	02	8	0	0
Nottingham F	Colorado Rapids (USA)	02/05	04	11	0	0

POWELL David
Born: Dolgarrog, Conwy, Wales, 15 October, 1944 — WH
Wales: 11/U23-4

League Club	Source	Date Signed	Seasons Played	Apps	Subs	Gls
Wrexham	Gwydyr Rov	05/63	62-68	132	2	4
Sheffield U	Tr	09/68	68-70	89	0	2
Cardiff C	Tr	09/72	72-74	36	0	1

POWELL David Morgan (Dai)
Born: Swansea, Wales, 19 January, 1935 — LB

League Club	Source	Date Signed	Seasons Played	Apps	Subs	Gls
Blackpool		12/52				
Rochdale	Tr	07/58	58-60	76	-	1

POWELL David Robert
Born: Cannock, Staffordshire, England, 24 September, 1967 — G

League Club	Source	Date Signed	Seasons Played	Apps	Subs	Gls
West Bromwich A	Cherry Valley	04/86	87	2	0	0
Wrexham	L	02/87	86	2	0	0

POWELL Francis Michael (Franny)
Born: Burnley, Lancashire, England, 17 June, 1977 — W

League Club	Source	Date Signed	Seasons Played	Apps	Subs	Gls
Rochdale	Burnley (YT)	09/95	95	0	2	0

POWELL Gary
Born: Hoylake, Wirral, England, 2 April, 1969 — F

League Club	Source	Date Signed	Seasons Played	Apps	Subs	Gls
Everton	YT	07/87				
Lincoln C	L	09/90	90	11	0	0
Scunthorpe U	L	11/90	90	3	1	1
Wigan Ath	L	03/91	90	13	1	4
Wigan Ath	Tr	08/91	91-92	44	26	13
Bury	Tr	08/93	93	4	1	0

POWELL George Reginald
Born: Fulham, W London, England, 11 October, 1924 — RB
Died: Camden, N London, England, 19 February, 1989

League Club	Source	Date Signed	Seasons Played	Apps	Subs	Gls
Queens Park Rgrs	Fulham (Am)	12/46	47-52	145	-	0

POWELL Ivor Verdun
Born: Bargoed, Caerphilly, Wales, 5 July, 1916 — WH
Died: Bath, England, 6 November, 2012
Wales: 8/War-4

League Club	Source	Date Signed	Seasons Played	Apps	Subs	Gls
Queens Park Rgrs	Barnet	09/37	38-48	110	-	2
Aston Villa	Tr	12/48	48-50	79	-	5
Port Vale	Tr	08/51	51	6	-	0
Bradford C	Barry T	06/52	52-54	83	-	9

POWELL Jack Patrick
Born: Canning Town, E London, England, 29 January, 1994 — M

League Club	Source	Date Signed	Seasons Played	Apps	Subs	Gls
West Ham U	Sch	07/12				
Millwall	Tr	08/13	14	5	0	0

POWELL Kenneth (Kenny)
Born: Mansfield, Nottinghamshire, England, 2 March, 1920 — LW
Died: Southport, Merseyside, England, 14 April, 1976

League Club	Source	Date Signed	Seasons Played	Apps	Subs	Gls
Derby Co	Mansfield CWS	05/39	46	13	-	0
Southport	Tr	06/47	47-50	90	-	18

POWELL Kenneth Leigh (Ken)
Born: Chester, England, 25 September, 1924 — LH
Died: Chester, England, 17 January, 2005

League Club	Source	Date Signed	Seasons Played	Apps	Subs	Gls
Cardiff C	Chester C (Am)	09/47				
Exeter C	Tr	06/48	48-49	22	-	1
Bristol Rov	Tr	07/51	51	4	-	0

POWELL Lamar Levi
Born: Bristol, England, 3 September, 1993 — F

League Club	Source	Date Signed	Seasons Played	Apps	Subs	Gls
Bristol Rov	Sch	11/10	10	0	1	0

POWELL Lee
Born: Caerleon, Monmouthshire, Wales, 2 June, 1973 — W
Wales: U21-4

League Club	Source	Date Signed	Seasons Played	Apps	Subs	Gls
Southampton	YT	05/91	91-93	2	5	0

POWELL Michael (Mike)
Born: Newport, Wales, 26 April, 1951 — RB

League Club	Source	Date Signed	Seasons Played	Apps	Subs	Gls
Newport Co	Newport YMCA	01/76	75-77	7	2	0

POWELL Michael Philip (Mike)
Born: Slough, Berkshire, England, 18 April, 1933 — CH

League Club	Source	Date Signed	Seasons Played	Apps	Subs	Gls
Queens Park Rgrs	Jnr	01/51	52-58	105	-	0

POWELL Neville David
Born: Flint, Wales, 2 September, 1963 — RW

League Club	Source	Date Signed	Seasons Played	Apps	Subs	Gls
Tranmere Rov	App	08/81	80-84	76	10	4

POWELL Nicholas Edward (Nick)
Born: Crewe, Cheshire, England, 23 March, 1994 — M
England: U21-2/Youth

League Club	Source	Date Signed	Seasons Played	Apps	Subs	Gls
Crewe Alex	Sch	03/11	10-11	34	21	14
Manchester U	Tr	07/12	12	0	2	1
Wigan Ath	L	09/13	13	23	8	7
Leicester C	L	09/14	14	0	3	0

POWELL Paul
Born: Wallingford, Oxfordshire, England, 30 June, 1978 — LB

League Club	Source	Date Signed	Seasons Played	Apps	Subs	Gls
Oxford U	YT	07/96	95-02	143	35	17

POWELL Raymond (Ray)
Born: Swansea, Wales, 5 August, 1924 — CF
Died: Essex, England, May, 2014

League Club	Source	Date Signed	Seasons Played	Apps	Subs	Gls
Swansea C	Haverfordwest	05/47	47-50	18	-	5
Scunthorpe U	Tr	08/51	51	31	-	14

POWELL Richard
Born: Chesterfield, Derbyshire, England, 3 September, 1969 — G

League Club	Source	Date Signed	Seasons Played	Apps	Subs	Gls
Blackpool	YT	06/88	86-87	14	0	0

POWELL Ronald William Herbert (Ronnie)
Born: Knighton, Powys, Wales, 2 December, 1929 — G
Died: Rossall, Lancashire, England, 25 May, 1992

League Club	Source	Date Signed	Seasons Played	Apps	Subs	Gls
Manchester C	Knighton T	11/48	49	12	-	0
Chesterfield	Tr	06/52	52-64	471	-	0

POWELL Stephen (Steve)
Born: Derby, England, 20 September, 1955 — DM
England: U23-1/Youth/Schools

League Club	Source	Date Signed	Seasons Played	Apps	Subs	Gls
Derby Co	App	11/72	71-84	342	10	20

POWELL Thomas Ernest (Tommy)
Born: Derby, England, 12 April, 1925 — RW
Died: Birkenhead, Wirral, England, 9 September, 1998

League Club	Source	Date Signed	Seasons Played	Apps	Subs	Gls
Derby Co	Derby Corinthians	04/42	48-61	380	-	57

POWELL Wayne
Born: Caerphilly, Wales, 25 October, 1956 — F
Wales: Youth

League Club	Source	Date Signed	Seasons Played	Apps	Subs	Gls
Bristol Rov	App	10/74	75-77	25	7	10
Halifax T	L	10/77	77	4	0	1
Hereford U	Tr	06/78	78	6	0	2

POWER Alan Thomas Daniel
Born: Dublin, Republic of Ireland, 23 January, 1988 — M
Republic of Ireland: U21-1

League Club	Source	Date Signed	Seasons Played	Apps	Subs	Gls
Nottingham F	Sch	04/06				
Hartlepool U	Tr	07/08	08-09	0	6	0

POWER Graeme Richard
Born: Harrow, NW London, England, 7 March, 1977 — LB
England: Youth/Schools

League Club	Source	Date Signed	Seasons Played	Apps	Subs	Gls
Queens Park Rgrs	YT	04/95				
Bristol Rov	Tr	07/96	96-97	25	1	0
Exeter C	Tr	08/98	98-02	165	6	2

POWER John
Born: Chelsea, W London, England, 10 December, 1959 — G

League Club	Source	Date Signed	Seasons Played	Apps	Subs	Gls
Brentford	Kingstonian	03/87	86	2	0	0

POWER Lee Michael
Born: Lewisham, SE London, England, 30 June, 1972 — F
Republic of Ireland: B-1/U21-13/Youth

League Club	Source	Date Signed	Seasons Played	Apps	Subs	Gls
Norwich C	YT	07/90	89-93	28	16	10
Charlton Ath	L	12/92	92	5	0	0
Sunderland	L	08/93	93	1	2	0
Portsmouth	L	10/93	93	1	1	0
Bradford C	Tr	03/94	93-94	14	16	5
Peterborough U	Tr	07/95	95	25	13	6
Plymouth Arg	Hibernian	08/98	98	7	9	0
Halifax T	Tr	12/98	98-99	17	8	5

POWER Max McAuley
Born: Bebington, Wirral, England, 27 July, 1993 — M

League Club	Source	Date Signed	Seasons Played	Apps	Subs	Gls
Tranmere Rov	Sch	04/11	11-14	99	10	12

POWER Michael David (Mike)
Born: Stockport, Greater Manchester, England, 3 October, 1961 — F

League Club	Source	Date Signed	Seasons Played	Apps	Subs	Gls
Stockport Co	Jnr	08/80	80-85	67	4	16

POWER Paul Christopher
Born: Manchester, England, 30 October, 1953 — M/LB
England: B-1

League Club	Source	Date Signed	Seasons Played	Apps	Subs	Gls
Manchester C	Leeds Polytechnic	09/73	75-85	358	7	26
Everton	Tr	06/86	86-87	52	0	6

POWER Philip Damian (Phil)
Born: Salford, England, 25 July, 1966 — F

League Club	Source	Date Signed	Seasons Played	Apps	Subs	Gls
Crewe Alex	Northwich Victoria	08/85	85-86	18	9	3
Macclesfield T	Stalybridge Celtic	10/93	97	21	17	7

POWLING Richard Frederick (Richie)
Born: Barking, E London, England, 21 May, 1956 — D
England: Youth

League Club	Source	Date Signed	Seasons Played	Apps	Subs	Gls
Arsenal	App	07/73	73-77	50	5	3

POWNER Robert James (Bob)
Born: Newcastle-under-Lyme, Potteries, England, 2 July, 1967 — G

League Club	Source	Date Signed	Seasons Played	Apps	Subs	Gls
Crewe Alex	Jnr	08/88	85-86	6	0	0

POWNEY Brian William
Born: Seaford, East Sussex, England, 7 October, 1944 — G

League Club	Source	Date Signed	Seasons Played	Apps	Subs	Gls
Brighton & HA	App	11/61	61-73	351	0	0

POWTON Brian
Born: Newcastle-upon-Tyne, England, 29 August, 1929 — G
Died: Northumberland, England, June, 1985

League Club	Source	Date Signed	Seasons Played	Apps	Subs	Gls
Newcastle U	Heaton Stannington	10/50				
Preston NE	Tr	08/51				
Hartlepool U	Tr	07/52	52	4	-	0

POYET Diego
Born: Zaragoza, Spain, 8 April, 1995 — M
England: Youth

League Club	Source	Date Signed	Seasons Played	Apps	Subs	Gls
Charlton Ath	Sch	04/12	13	20	0	0
West Ham U	Tr	07/14	14	1	2	0
Huddersfield T	L	11/14	14	2	0	0

POYET Gustavo Augusto
Born: Montevideo, Uruguay, 15 November, 1967 — M
Uruguay: 26/Youth

League Club	Source	Date Signed	Seasons Played	Apps	Subs	Gls
Chelsea	Real Zaragoza (SPN)	07/97	97-00	79	26	36
Tottenham H	Tr	07/01	01-03	66	16	18

POYNER Robert Christopher (Bobby)
Born: Newport, Wales, 25 December, 1932 — CH
Died: Newport, Wales, 31 August, 1977
Wales: Youth/Schools

League Club	Source	Date Signed	Seasons Played	Apps	Subs	Gls
Newport Co	Jnr	01/51	50-51	2	-	0

POYNTON William (Bill)
Born: Shiremoor, Tyne and Wear, England, 30 June, 1944 — FB/IF

League Club	Source	Date Signed	Seasons Played	Apps	Subs	Gls
Burnley	Jnr	07/61				
Mansfield T	Tr	07/64	64-65	20	0	0
Lincoln C	Lockheed Leamington	10/66	66	0	1	0

POYSER George Henry
Born: Sutton-in-Ashfield, Nottinghamshire, England, 6 February, 1910 — LB
Died: Nottingham, England, 30 January, 1995

League Club	Source	Date Signed	Seasons Played	Apps	Subs	Gls
Wolverhampton W	Stanton Hill	05/28				
Port Vale	Mansfield T	05/31	31-33	72	-	0
Brentford	Tr	06/34	34-38	149	-	0
Plymouth Arg	Tr	04/46	46	3	-	0

POZO Jose Angel
Born: Malaga, Spain, 15 March, 1996 — F
Spain: Youth

League Club	Source	Date Signed	Seasons Played	Apps	Subs	Gls
Manchester C	Sch	03/13	14	1	2	0

POZUELO Alejandro
Born: Seville, Spain, 20 September, 1991 — RW

League Club	Source	Date Signed	Seasons Played	Apps	Subs	Gls
Swansea C	Real Betis (SPN)	07/13	13	7	15	0

PRAGG Michael Kenneth (Mickey)
Born: Shrewsbury, Shropshire, England, 8 October, 1941 — IF
England: Amateur-3

League Club	Source	Date Signed	Seasons Played	Apps	Subs	Gls
Shrewsbury T (Am)	Jnr	05/59	60-62	5	-	1

PRANGLEY Samuel (Sam)
Born: Newport, Wales, 30 September, 1924 — WH
Died: Newport, Wales, 25 July, 2009

League Club	Source	Date Signed	Seasons Played	Apps	Subs	Gls
Newport Co	Lovells Ath	11/46	46	7	-	0

PRASKI Josef
Born: France, 22 January, 1926 — RW
Died: Mansfield, Nottinghamshire, England, January, 1998

League Club	Source	Date Signed	Seasons Played	Apps	Subs	Gls
Notts Co	Jeanfield Swifts	03/49	48	3	-	0

PRATLEY Darren Antony
Born: Barking, E London, England, 22 April, 1985 — M

League Club	Source	Date Signed	Seasons Played	Apps	Subs	Gls
Fulham	Sch	04/02	03	0	1	0
Brentford	L	02/05	04	11	3	1
Brentford	L	08/05	05	25	7	4
Swansea C	Tr	06/06	06-10	158	19	26
Bolton W	Tr	07/11	11-14	75	23	9

PRATLEY Richard George (Dick)
Born: Banbury, Oxfordshire, England, 12 January, 1963 — CD

League Club	Source	Date Signed	Seasons Played	Apps	Subs	Gls
Derby Co	Banbury U	07/83	83-86	29	2	1
Scunthorpe U	L	03/84	83	10	0	0
Shrewsbury T	Tr	02/88	87-89	44	2	1

PRATT John Arthur
Born: Hackney, E London, England, 26 June, 1948 — M

League Club	Source	Date Signed	Seasons Played	Apps	Subs	Gls
Tottenham H	Jnr	11/65	68-79	307	24	39

PRATT John Leslie
Born: Atherstone, Warwickshire, England, 1 March, 1943 — G

League Club	Source	Date Signed	Seasons Played	Apps	Subs	Gls
Reading	Wycombe W	07/69	69-71	29	0	0

PRATT Lee Stuart
Born: Cleethorpes, North Lincolnshire, England, 31 March, 1970 — G

League Club	Source	Date Signed	Seasons Played	Apps	Subs	Gls
Grimsby T	YT	06/88	86	1	0	0

PRATT Michael Wayne (Mick)
Born: Newport, Wales, 15 January, 1966 — F
Wales: Youth

League Club	Source	Date Signed	Seasons Played	Apps	Subs	Gls
Newport Co	Jnr	08/83	83-84	4	5	2

PRATT Raymond Ernest (Ray)
Born: Burry Port, Carmarthenshire, Wales, 11 November, 1955 — F
Wales: Youth

League Club	Source	Date Signed	Seasons Played	Apps	Subs	Gls
Exeter C	Merthyr Tydfil	03/80	79-85	127	46	61

PRATT Thomas (Tom)
Born: Manchester, England, 3 June, 1995 — F

League Club	Source	Date Signed	Seasons Played	Apps	Subs	Gls
Bury	Sch	07/13	12	0	2	0

League Club	Source	Date Signed	Seasons Played	Career Record Apps	Subs	Gls
PRATT Wayne						
Born: Southampton, England, 1 March, 1960						M
Southampton	App	03/78	80	1	0	0
PRECIOUS Derek						
Born: Crewe, Cheshire, England, 2 June, 1931						IF
Died: Crewe, Cheshire, England, 16 November, 2006						
Crewe Alex	Whitchurch Alport	09/55	55-56	18	-	3
PREDIC Uros						
Born: Novi Sad, Serbia, 11 August, 1973						M
Doncaster Rov (L)	Hajduk Kula (SRB)	08/05	05	3	3	0
PREECE Andrew Paul (Andy)						
Born: Evesham, Worcestershire, England, 27 March, 1967						F
Northampton T	Evesham U	08/88	88	0	1	0
Wrexham	Worcester C	03/90	89-91	44	7	7
Stockport Co	Tr	12/91	91-93	89	8	42
Crystal Palace	Tr	06/94	94	17	3	4
Blackpool	Tr	07/95	95-97	114	12	35
Bury	Tr	07/98	98-03	87	81	27
Carlisle U	Tr	12/03	03	23	2	3
PREECE Brian James						
Born: Hereford, England, 16 February, 1958						W
Died: Malvern, Worcestershire, England, 27 April, 1992						
Hereford U	App	02/76	74-76	5	1	0
Newport Co	Tr	03/77	76-77	38	6	12
PREECE David Douglas						
Born: Sunderland, England, 26 August, 1976						G
Sunderland	YT	06/94				
Darlington	Tr	07/97	97-98	91	0	0
Barnsley	Odense BK (DEN)	07/09	09-11	6	1	0
PREECE David William						
Born: Much Wenlock, Shropshire, England, 28 May, 1963						M
Died: Luton, England, 20 July, 2007						
England: B-3						
Walsall	App	07/80	80-84	107	4	5
Luton T	Tr	12/84	84-94	328	8	21
Derby Co	Tr	08/95	95	10	3	1
Birmingham C	L	11/95	95	6	0	0
Swindon T	L	03/96	95	7	0	1
Cambridge U	Tr	09/96	96-00	40	35	2
Torquay U	Tr	10/01	01	4	2	0
PREECE John Causer (Jack)						
Born: Wolverhampton, England, 30 April, 1914						RB
Died: Chippenham, Wiltshire, England, 5 July, 2003						
Wolverhampton W	Sunbeam Motors	05/31	33	2	-	0
Bristol Rov	Tr	05/35	35-37	79	-	0
Bradford C	Tr	07/38	38	3	-	0
Southport	Tr	05/39	46	36	-	0
Swindon T	Tr	06/47	47	7	-	0
PREECE Paul William						
Born: Penarth, Vale of Glamorgan, Wales, 16 May, 1957						M
Newport Co	App	06/75	74-75	17	6	0
PREECE Roger						
Born: Much Wenlock, Shropshire, England, 9 June, 1968						M
Wrexham	Coventry C (Jnr)	08/86	86-89	89	21	12
Chester C	Tr	08/90	90-95	165	5	4
Shrewsbury T	Telford U	07/97	97-99	46	6	3
PREECE Ryan						
Born: Briton Ferry, Neath Port Talbot, Wales, 10 January, 1969						M
Newport Co	YT	10/87	87	7	3	2
PREEDY Philip Andrew (Phil)						
Born: Hereford, England, 20 November, 1975						M/LB
Hereford U	YT	07/94	93-96	31	20	4
PREEN Garyn Vernon						
Born: Tredegar, Blaenau Gwent, Wales, 25 October, 1991						W
Wales: Youth						
Burton A	Southampton (Sch)	07/10	10	0	1	0
[PREKI] RADOSAVLJEVIC Predrag						
Born: Belgrade, Yugoslavia, 24 June, 1963						W
USA: 28						
Everton	St Louis Storm (USA)	08/92	92-93	22	24	4
Portsmouth	Tr	07/94	94	30	10	5
PRENDERGAST Michael John (Mick)						
Born: Denaby, South Yorkshire, England, 24 November, 1950						F
Died: Mexborough, South Yorkshire, England, 29 April, 2010						
Sheffield Wed	App	11/67	68-77	170	13	53
Barnsley	Tr	05/78	77-78	12	8	2
Halifax T	L	10/78	78	4	0	1
PRENDERGAST Rory						
Born: Pontefract, West Yorkshire, England, 6 April, 1978						LW
Barnsley	YT	04/97				
York C	Tr	08/98	98	1	2	0
Blackpool	Accrington Stan	07/05	05-06	22	7	0
Rochdale	Tr	01/07	06-07	6	13	2
Darlington	L	03/07	06	5	3	0
PRENDERVILLE Barry James Robert						
Born: Dublin, Republic of Ireland, 16 October, 1976						CD
Republic of Ireland: Youth						
Coventry C	Cherry Orchard (ROI)	08/94				
Oldham Ath	St Patrick's Ath (ROI)	09/00	00-01	16	5	0
PRENTIS John						
Born: Liverpool, England, 22 March, 1939						RB
Blackpool		10/62	64-65	6	0	0
Stockport Co	Tr	10/66	66-67	16	3	0
PRESCOTT Francis Stephen (Frank)						
Born: Birkenhead, Wirral, England, 12 August, 1922						CF
Died: Birkenhead, Wirral, England, 1969						
Tranmere Rov	St Annes	10/46	46	2	-	0
PRESCOTT James Lawrence (Jimmy)						
Born: Golborne, Greater Manchester, England, 2 November, 1930						IF
Died: Warrington, Cheshire, England, 14 February, 2011						
Southport	Leeds U (Am)	03/54	53-54	53	-	9
York C	Tr	06/55	55	18	-	5
Southport	Tr	10/56	56	17	-	1
PRESLAND Edward Robert (Eddie)						
Born: Loughton, Essex, England, 27 March, 1943						LB
West Ham U	Jnr	10/60	64-65	6	0	1
Crystal Palace	Tr	01/67	66-68	61	0	0
Colchester U	L	10/69	69	5	0	0
PRESLEY Charles Derek (Derek)						
Born: Warminster, Wiltshire, England, 8 March, 1930						RH
Bristol C	Warminster T	03/50	50-51	9	-	0
Bristol Rov	Tr	05/52				
PRESSDEE James Stuart (Jim)						
Born: Swansea, Wales, 19 June, 1933						FB
Wales: Schools						
Swansea C	Jnr	08/51	53-55	8	-	0
PRESSLEY Steven John						
Born: Elgin, Moray, Scotland, 11 October, 1973						CD
Scotland: 32/U21-26						
Coventry C	Glasgow Rangers	10/94	94	18	1	1
PRESSMAN Kevin Paul						
Born: Fareham, Hampshire, England, 6 November, 1967						G
England: B-3/U21-1/Youth/Schools						
Sheffield Wed	App	11/85	87-03	400	4	0
Stoke C	L	03/92	91	4	0	0
Leicester C	Tr	07/04	04	13	0	0
Coventry C	Leeds U (NC)	03/05				
Mansfield T	Tr	08/05	05	41	0	0
PRESTON Carl William						
Born: Poole, Dorset, England, 25 April, 1991						W
Bournemouth	Jnr	08/08	08	2	0	0
PRESTON Daniel Sean (Dan)						
Born: Birmingham, England, 26 September, 1991						CD
Birmingham C	Sch	01/10				
Hereford U	Tr	02/10	09	4	0	0
PRESTON Matthew Eric (Matt)						
Born: Birmingham, England, 16 March, 1995						CD
Walsall	Sch	01/13	14	0	1	0
PRESTON Michael John						
Born: Plymouth, England, 22 November, 1977						RW
Torquay U	YT	07/96	95-96	4	6	0
PRESTON Richard Frank						
Born: Nottingham, England, 10 June, 1967						F
Scarborough	Stanton FC	03/88	87	1	3	0
PRESTON Richard John						
Born: Basildon, England, 7 May, 1976						FB
Northampton T	YT	08/94	93	1	0	0
PRICA Rade Stanislav						
Born: Ljungby, Sweden, 30 June, 1980						F
Sweden: 14/U21-13						
Sunderland	Aalborg BK (DEN)	01/08	07	0	6	1

PRICE Albert Edward
Born: Langwith, Derbyshire, England, 4 April, 1926 — G
Died: Mansfield, Nottinghamshire, England, 1983

League Club	Source	Date Signed	Seasons Played	Apps	Subs	Gls
Crewe Alex	Creswell Colliery	12/46	46	5	-	0

PRICE Albert James William (Billy)
Born: Hadley, Telford & Wrekin, England, 10 April, 1917 — CF
Died: Bradford, England, September, 1995

League Club	Source	Date Signed	Seasons Played	Apps	Subs	Gls
Huddersfield T	Wrockwardine Wood	10/37	37-47	51	-	23
Reading	Tr	10/47	47-48	15	-	2
Hull C	Tr	01/49	48	8	-	5
Bradford C	Tr	11/49	49-51	54	-	28

PRICE Allen Douglas
Born: Gelligaer, Caerphilly, Wales, 24 March, 1968 — FB
Wales: Youth

League Club	Source	Date Signed	Seasons Played	Apps	Subs	Gls
Cardiff C	Newport Co (Jnr)	08/85	85	2	0	0

PRICE Arthur
Born: Rowlands Gill, Tyne and Wear, England, 12 January, 1921 — WH
Died: Gateshead, Tyne and Wear, England, June, 1995

League Club	Source	Date Signed	Seasons Played	Apps	Subs	Gls
Newcastle U	Spen Black & White	08/40				
Leeds U	Consett	05/46	46	6	-	0

PRICE Brynley (Bryn)
Born: Treorchy, Rhondda Cynon Taff, Wales, 15 January, 1936 — RH

League Club	Source	Date Signed	Seasons Played	Apps	Subs	Gls
Barnsley	Treorchy BC	05/55	56-57	2	-	0

PRICE Cecil Albert
Born: Cardiff, Wales, 2 December, 1919 — LW
Died: Bridgend, Wales, February, 2008

League Club	Source	Date Signed	Seasons Played	Apps	Subs	Gls
Cardiff C	Tynte Rov	09/48	48	1	-	0
Bradford C	Tr	06/49	49	7	-	0

PRICE Christopher John (Chris)
Born: Hereford, England, 30 March, 1960 — RB
England: Youth

League Club	Source	Date Signed	Seasons Played	Apps	Subs	Gls
Hereford U	App	01/78	76-85	327	3	27
Blackburn Rov	Tr	07/86	86-87	83	0	11
Aston Villa	Tr	05/88	88-91	109	2	2
Blackburn Rov	Tr	02/92	91-92	13	6	3
Portsmouth	Tr	01/93	92-93	14	4	0

PRICE David James
Born: Caterham, Surrey, England, 23 June, 1955 — DM
England: Youth/Schools

League Club	Source	Date Signed	Seasons Played	Apps	Subs	Gls
Arsenal	App	08/72	72-80	116	10	16
Peterborough U	L	01/75	74	6	0	1
Crystal Palace	Tr	03/81	80-81	25	2	2
Leyton Orient	Tr	03/83	82	10	0	0

PRICE Derrick Valentine
Born: Wellington, Telford & Wrekin, England, 14 February, 1932 — RW

League Club	Source	Date Signed	Seasons Played	Apps	Subs	Gls
Shrewsbury T	Donnington Wood	02/53	53-57	125	-	28
Aldershot	Tr	07/58	58-59	4	-	1

PRICE Ernest (Ernie)
Born: Easington, County Durham, England, 12 May, 1926 — WH
Died: Taunton, Somerset, England, 25 February, 2013

League Club	Source	Date Signed	Seasons Played	Apps	Subs	Gls
Sunderland		01/45				
Darlington		12/48	48-50	69	-	0
Crystal Palace	Tr	07/51	51-52	34	-	5

PRICE Gareth Michael
Born: Swindon, England, 21 February, 1970 — M
Died: Nottingham, England, 31 August, 1998

League Club	Source	Date Signed	Seasons Played	Apps	Subs	Gls
Mansfield T	YT	07/88				
Bury	Tr	07/89	89-90	1	3	0

PRICE George
Born: Crewe, Cheshire, England, 2 December, 1929 — LW

League Club	Source	Date Signed	Seasons Played	Apps	Subs	Gls
Crewe Alex		02/54	53	4	-	0

PRICE Jack Alexander
Born: Shrewsbury, Shropshire, England, 19 December, 1992 — M

League Club	Source	Date Signed	Seasons Played	Apps	Subs	Gls
Wolverhampton W	Sch	06/11	13-14	39	10	1
Yeovil T	L	09/14	14	5	1	0
Leyton Orient	L	10/14	14	4	1	0

PRICE James Benjamin (Jamie)
Born: Normanton, West Yorkshire, England, 27 October, 1981 — RB

League Club	Source	Date Signed	Seasons Played	Apps	Subs	Gls
Doncaster Rov	YT	08/99	03-04	22	3	0

PRICE James Richard (Jamie)
Born: Preston, Lancashire, England, 1 February, 1978 — FB

League Club	Source	Date Signed	Seasons Played	Apps	Subs	Gls
Rochdale	YT	07/96	95	3	0	0

PRICE Jason Jeffrey
Born: Pontypridd, Rhondda Cynon Taff, Wales, 12 April, 1977 — RM
Wales: U21-7

League Club	Source	Date Signed	Seasons Played	Apps	Subs	Gls
Swansea C	Aberaman Ath	07/95	96-00	133	11	17
Brentford	Tr	08/01	01	15	0	1
Tranmere Rov	Tr	11/01	01-02	34	15	11
Hull C	Tr	07/03	03-05	45	30	13
Doncaster Rov	Tr	01/06	05-08	59	34	17
Millwall	Tr	03/09	08-09	11	12	4
Oldham Ath	L	02/10	09	7	0	1
Carlisle U	Tr	03/10	09-10	8	4	4
Bradford C	L	10/10	10	6	4	1
Walsall	L	01/11	10	4	1	0
Hereford U	L	03/11	10	1	3	0
Barnet	Tr	08/11	11	5	0	1
Morecambe	Tr	09/11	11	12	6	2

PRICE John (Johnny)
Born: Leadgate, County Durham, England, 14 April, 1947 — RW

League Club	Source	Date Signed	Seasons Played	Apps	Subs	Gls
Leeds U	App	05/65				
Southport	Tr	07/66	66	16	2	2

PRICE John
Born: Middlewich, Cheshire, England, 28 April, 1960 — M

League Club	Source	Date Signed	Seasons Played	Apps	Subs	Gls
Rochdale	Nantwich T	01/78	77-78	10	2	0

PRICE John (Johnny)
Born: Horden, County Durham, England, 25 October, 1943 — LW
Died: Stockport, Greater Manchester, England, 6 May, 1995

League Club	Source	Date Signed	Seasons Played	Apps	Subs	Gls
Burnley	Horden CW	11/60	63-64	21	-	2
Stockport Co	Tr	05/65	65-71	241	5	23
Blackburn Rov	Tr	09/71	71-73	63	13	12
Stockport Co	Tr	03/74	73-75	51	15	1

PRICE John (Jack)
Born: Shotton Colliery, County Durham, England, 29 August, 1918 — IF
Died: Horden, County Durham, England, 18 April, 2013

League Club	Source	Date Signed	Seasons Played	Apps	Subs	Gls
Portsmouth	Horden CW	09/36				
Hartlepool U	Tr	06/38	38-48	89	-	12
York C	Tr	12/48	48	2	-	2

PRICE John David (Jack)
Born: Camden, N London, England, 31 December, 1932 — CH

League Club	Source	Date Signed	Seasons Played	Apps	Subs	Gls
Tottenham H	Eastbourne U	09/54				
Aldershot	Tr	01/57	56-58	86	-	1
Watford	Tr	06/59	59	22	-	0

PRICE John Geraint
Born: Aberystwyth, Ceredigion, Wales, 22 November, 1936 — LB

League Club	Source	Date Signed	Seasons Played	Apps	Subs	Gls
Liverpool	Fordhouses YC	10/54	55	1	-	0
Aston Villa	Tr	03/57				
Walsall	Tr	07/57				
Shrewsbury T	Tr	07/58	58-59	9	-	0

PRICE Kenneth Edward (Ken)
Born: Ellesmere Port, Cheshire, England, 25 March, 1939 — CF

League Club	Source	Date Signed	Seasons Played	Apps	Subs	Gls
Aston Villa	Bromborough Pool	08/59				
Tranmere Rov	Tr	12/60	60	3	-	2
Hartlepool U	Tr	07/61	61	8	-	3

PRICE Kenneth Gordon (Ken)
Born: Dudley, West Midlands, England, 26 February, 1954 — F

League Club	Source	Date Signed	Seasons Played	Apps	Subs	Gls
Southend U	Dudley T	05/76	76	1	0	0
Gillingham	Tr	12/76	76-82	247	8	78
Reading	Tr	01/83	82-84	40	3	6

PRICE Leslie Eugene
Born: Consett, County Durham, England, 26 August, 1930 — W

League Club	Source	Date Signed	Seasons Played	Apps	Subs	Gls
Sunderland		08/50				
Gateshead	Tr	07/52	52-53	39	-	13

PRICE Lewis Peter
Born: Bournemouth, England, 19 July, 1984 — G
Wales: 11/U21-10/Youth

League Club	Source	Date Signed	Seasons Played	Apps	Subs	Gls
Ipswich T	Southampton (Jnr)	08/02	03-06	67	1	0
Cambridge U	L	11/04	04	6	0	0
Derby Co	Tr	07/07	07	6	0	0
MK Dons	L	10/08	08	2	0	0
Luton T	L	02/09	08	1	0	0
Brentford	L	07/09	09	13	0	0
Crystal Palace	Tr	07/10	10-12	5	1	0
Mansfield T	L	04/14	13	5	0	0
Crawley T	L	11/14	14	18	0	0

PRICE Mark Anthony
Born: Keighley, West Yorkshire, England, 15 October, 1973 — M

League Club	Source	Date Signed	Seasons Played	Apps	Subs	Gls
Scarborough	YT	-	91	2	1	1

PRICE Michael (Mike)
Born: Ashington, Northumberland, England, 3 April, 1983 — G

League Club	Source	Date Signed	Seasons Played	Apps	Subs	Gls
Leicester C	YT	02/01				
Darlington	Tr	08/03	03	36	0	0

PRICE Michael David (Mike)
Born: Wrexham, Wales, 29 April, 1982 — FB
Wales: U21-11

League Club	Source	Date Signed	Seasons Played	Apps	Subs	Gls
Everton	YT	01/00				
Hull C	Tr	07/01	01-02	1	3	0

PRICE Neil
Born: Hemel Hempstead, Hertfordshire, England, 15 February, 1964 — LB

League Club	Source	Date Signed	Seasons Played	Apps	Subs	Gls
Watford	App	02/82	83	7	1	0
Plymouth Arg	L	02/84	83	1	0	0
Blackpool	L	03/85	84	13	0	0
Swansea C	Tr	07/85	85	0	2	0

PRICE Paul Terence
Born: St Albans, Hertfordshire, England, 23 May, 1954 — CD
Wales: 25/U21-1

League Club	Source	Date Signed	Seasons Played	Apps	Subs	Gls
Luton T	Welwyn Garden C	07/71	72-80	206	1	8
Tottenham H	Tr	06/81	81-83	35	4	0
Swansea C	Minnesota S'kers (USA)	01/85	84-85	62	0	1
Peterborough U	Tr	08/86	86-87	86	0	0

PRICE Peter
Born: Tarbolton, Ayrshire, Scotland, 26 February, 1932 — IF

League Club	Source	Date Signed	Seasons Played	Apps	Subs	Gls
Darlington	Gloucester C	01/54	53-54	3	-	0

PRICE Peter William
Born: Wrexham, Wales, 17 August, 1949 — F
Wales: U23-4

League Club	Source	Date Signed	Seasons Played	Apps	Subs	Gls
Liverpool	App	08/66				
Peterborough U	Tr	07/68	68-71	114	5	62
Portsmouth	Tr	06/72	72-73	13	1	2
Peterborough U	L	07/74	74	2	0	0
Barnsley	Tr	11/74	74-77	72	7	28

PRICE Raymond (Ray)
Born: Hetton-le-Hole, Tyne and Wear, England, 18 May, 1944 — RB
Died: Sheffield, England, 18 November, 1990

League Club	Source	Date Signed	Seasons Played	Apps	Subs	Gls
Norwich C	Jnr	07/63	63	1	-	0
Colchester U	Tr	07/64	64-66	15	2	0

PRICE Raymond John (Ray)
Born: Northampton, England, 30 November, 1948 — F

League Club	Source	Date Signed	Seasons Played	Apps	Subs	Gls
Northampton T	App	12/66	66-67	7	0	0

PRICE Ryan
Born: Staffordshire, England, 13 March, 1970 — G
England: Semi Pro-6

League Club	Source	Date Signed	Seasons Played	Apps	Subs	Gls
Birmingham C	Stafford Rgrs	08/94				
Macclesfield T	Tr	11/95	97-99	99	1	0

PRICE Terence Edmund (Terry)
Born: Colchester, Essex, England, 11 October, 1945 — RB

League Club	Source	Date Signed	Seasons Played	Apps	Subs	Gls
Leyton Orient	App	08/63	64-67	86	1	18
Colchester U	Tr	09/67	67-68	55	2	5

PRICE Thomas Dudley (Duggie)
Born: Swansea, Wales, 17 November, 1931 — IF

League Club	Source	Date Signed	Seasons Played	Apps	Subs	Gls
Swansea C	Jnr	04/50	53-57	34	-	9
Southend U	Tr	01/58	57-60	91	-	41
Hull C	Tr	09/60	60-62	76	-	26
Bradford C	Tr	07/63	63-64	62	-	21

PRICE Trevor Henry Richard
Born: Ellesmere Port, Cheshire, England, 27 December, 1944 — LW

League Club	Source	Date Signed	Seasons Played	Apps	Subs	Gls
Workington		06/64	64	2	-	1

PRICE Walter Booth
Born: Neston, Wirral, England, 14 February, 1921 — CH
Died: Kings Lynn, Norfolk, England, February, 1984

League Club	Source	Date Signed	Seasons Played	Apps	Subs	Gls
Tranmere Rov		03/41	46	2	-	0
Rochdale	Tr	08/48	48	1	-	0

PRIDAY Marcus Albert
Born: Knighton, Powys, Wales, 16 October, 1971 — G
Wales: Youth

League Club	Source	Date Signed	Seasons Played	Apps	Subs	Gls
Hereford U	YT	08/90	89	3	0	0

PRIDAY Robert Herbert (Bob)
Born: Cape Town, South Africa, 29 March, 1925 — LW
Died: Johannesburg, South Africa, 30 September, 1998

League Club	Source	Date Signed	Seasons Played	Apps	Subs	Gls
Liverpool	Cape Town C (RSA)	12/45	46-48	34	-	6
Blackburn Rov	Tr	03/49	48-50	44	-	11
Accrington Stan	Northwich Victoria	12/52	52	5	-	0
Rochdale	Tr	08/53	53	5	-	1

PRIDDLE Sean Patrick
Born: Hammersmith, W London, England, 14 December, 1965 — M

League Club	Source	Date Signed	Seasons Played	Apps	Subs	Gls
Wimbledon	App	12/83				
Crewe Alex	Tr	02/85	84	6	5	0
Exeter C	Tooting & Mitcham U	07/86	86	18	0	1
Brentford	Tr	07/87	87	5	1	0

PRIDDY Paul Joseph
Born: Isleworth, W London, England, 11 July, 1953 — G

League Club	Source	Date Signed	Seasons Played	Apps	Subs	Gls
Brentford	Walton & Hersham	10/72	72-76	121	0	0
Wimbledon	Tooting & Mitcham U	10/78	78	1	0	0
Brentford	Hayes	08/81	81	1	0	0

PRIEST Christopher (Chris)
Born: Leigh, Greater Manchester, England, 18 October, 1973 — M

League Club	Source	Date Signed	Seasons Played	Apps	Subs	Gls
Everton	YT	06/92				
Chester C	L	09/94	94	11	0	1
Chester C	Tr	01/95	94-98	151	5	25
Macclesfield T	Tr	07/99	99-03	140	10	13

PRIEST Harry
Born: Clay Cross, Derbyshire, England, 26 October, 1935 — IF

League Club	Source	Date Signed	Seasons Played	Apps	Subs	Gls
Sheffield U	Clay Cross Works	02/54	56	2	-	1
Halifax T	Tr	01/58	57-58	30	-	12

PRIEST Philip (Phil)
Born: Warley, West Midlands, England, 9 September, 1966 — M
England: Youth/Schools

League Club	Source	Date Signed	Seasons Played	Apps	Subs	Gls
Chelsea	App	09/83				
Blackpool	L	12/86	86	1	0	0
Brentford	L	03/87	86	3	2	1
Shrewsbury T	Tr	07/87	87-89	54	6	3

PRIESTLEY Derek
Born: Queensbury, West Yorkshire, England, 22 December, 1926 — LW
Died: Bradford, England, June, 1999

League Club	Source	Date Signed	Seasons Played	Apps	Subs	Gls
Halifax T		10/50	51-55	145	-	19
Bradford Park Ave	Tr	07/56				

PRIESTLEY Gerald (Gerry)
Born: Halifax, West Yorkshire, England, 2 March, 1931 — RW/IF

League Club	Source	Date Signed	Seasons Played	Apps	Subs	Gls
Nottingham F	RAOC Chilwell	12/50				
Exeter C	Tr	06/53	53-54	42	-	6
Grimsby T	Tr	06/55	55-58	110	-	11
Crystal Palace	Tr	11/58	58-59	28	-	2
Halifax T	Tr	07/60	60-62	105	-	23

PRIESTLEY Jason Aaron
Born: Leeds, England, 25 October, 1970 — G

League Club	Source	Date Signed	Seasons Played	Apps	Subs	Gls
Carlisle U	YT	07/89	90	22	0	0
Hartlepool U	L	12/89	89	16	0	0
Scarborough	L	08/91	91	9	0	0

PRIESTLEY Maurice
Born: Bradford, England, 27 October, 1922 — CF
Died: Bradford, England, 3 April, 1986

League Club	Source	Date Signed	Seasons Played	Apps	Subs	Gls
Bradford Park Ave	Guiseley	09/46				
Halifax T	Tr	01/48	47-48	24	-	8

PRIESTLEY Philip Alan (Phil)
Born: Wigan, Greater Manchester, England, 30 March, 1976 — G

League Club	Source	Date Signed	Seasons Played	Apps	Subs	Gls
Rochdale	Atherton Laburnum Rov	09/98	98-99	2	1	0

PRIESTLEY Royston Maurice (Roy)
Born: Barnsley, South Yorkshire, England, 26 November, 1948 — F

League Club	Source	Date Signed	Seasons Played	Apps	Subs	Gls
Barnsley (Am)	Jnr	08/67	67	1	0	0

PRIET Nicolas
Born: Lyon, France, 31 January, 1983 — FB

League Club	Source	Date Signed	Seasons Played	Apps	Subs	Gls
Leicester C	Olymp Lyonnais (FRA)	07/03				
Doncaster Rov	Tr	07/04	04	7	0	0

PRIJOVIC Aleksandr
Born: St Gallen, Switzerland, 21 April, 1990 — F
Switzerland: U21-2/Youth//Serbia: Youth

League Club	Source	Date Signed	Seasons Played	Apps	Subs	Gls
Derby Co	Parma (ITA)	09/08				
Yeovil T	L	01/09	08	4	0	0
Northampton T	L	03/09	08	3	7	2

PRIMUS Linvoy Stephen
Born: Forest Gate, E London, England, 14 September, 1973 — CD

League Club	Source	Date Signed	Seasons Played	Apps	Subs	Gls
Charlton Ath	YT	08/92	92	4	0	0
Barnet	Tr	07/94	94-96	127	0	7
Reading	Tr	07/97	97-99	94	1	1
Portsmouth	Tr	08/00	00-08	189	9	5
Charlton Ath	L	09/08	08	10	0	1

PRINCE Eric
Born: Ipstones, Staffordshire, England, 11 December, 1924 — IF
Died: Stoke-on-Trent, England, 18 January, 2003

League Club	Source	Date Signed	Seasons Played	Apps	Subs	Gls
Port Vale	Ipstones	09/44	46	14	-	2

PRINCE Francis Anthony (Frankie)
Born: Penarth, Vale of Glamorgan, Wales, 1 December, 1949 — M
Wales: U23-4

League Club	Source	Date Signed	Seasons Played	Apps	Subs	Gls
Bristol Rov	App	12/67	67-79	360	2	23
Exeter C	Tr	07/80	80-81	27	4	2

League Club	Source	Date Signed	Seasons Played	Career Record Apps	Subs	Gls
PRINCE Harold						
Born: Stoke-on-Trent, England, 4 December, 1921						G
Died: Hanley, Potteries, England, 17 February, 2009						
Port Vale	Bucknall	08/44	47-48	5	-	0
PRINCE Neil Michael						
Born: Liverpool, England, 17 March, 1983						M
England: Youth						
Torquay U	Liverpool (YT)	08/02	02	3	4	0
PRINDIVILLE Steven Alan (Steve)						
Born: Harlow, Essex, England, 26 December, 1968						LB
Leicester C	App	12/86	87	0	1	0
Chesterfield	Tr	06/88	88	43	0	1
Mansfield T	Tr	06/89	89-90	26	2	0
Doncaster Rov	Hinckley Ath	02/92	91-93	58	1	2
PRING Dennis Frederick						
Born: Newport, Wales, 8 November, 1940						IF
Southampton	Newport YMCA	02/59	58	4	-	0
PRING Keith David						
Born: Newport, Wales, 11 March, 1943						LW
Wales: 3						
Newport Co	Nash U	11/61	61-64	62	-	3
Rotherham U	Tr	10/64	64-67	81	0	6
Notts Co	Tr	12/67	67-68	41	3	2
Southport	Tr	07/69	69-70	48	0	4
PRINGLE Benjamin Philip (Ben)						
Born: Whitley Bay, Tyne and Wear, England, 25 July, 1988						W
Derby Co	Ilkeston T	07/09	09-10	4	16	0
Torquay U	L	03/11	10	5	0	0
Rotherham U	Tr	06/11	11-14	136	11	19
PRINGLE Brian						
Born: Chathill, Northumberland, England, 12 March, 1949						M
Hartlepool U (Am)	Alnwick T	04/73	72	1	0	0
PRINGLE Ulf Martin (Martin)						
Born: Gothenburg, Sweden, 18 November, 1970						F
Sweden: 2/B-1						
Charlton Ath	Benfica (POR)	01/99	98-00	28	30	8
Grimsby T	L	02/02	01	2	0	0
PRINGLE William Alexander						
Born: Liverpool, England, 24 February, 1932						IF
Died: Chester, England, October, 2006						
Leeds U	Jnr	08/49				
Grimsby T	Tr	05/54	54	2	-	0
PRINS Jason						
Born: Wisbech, Cambridgeshire, England, 1 November, 1974						F
Carlisle U	YT	08/93	91-93	7	11	0
PRIOR Jason Christopher						
Born: Portsmouth, England, 20 December, 1988						F
AFC Wimbledon	Bognor Regis T	01/12	11-12	3	6	0
PRIOR Kenneth George (Ken)						
Born: Ashington, Northumberland, England, 13 October, 1932						LW
Newcastle U	Sunderland (Am)	03/52	51-52	8	-	3
Millwall	Tr	05/54	54-55	61	-	16
Newcastle U	Tr	07/56	56	2	-	0
PRIOR Spencer Justin						
Born: Southend-on-Sea, England, 22 April, 1971						CD
Southend U	YT	05/89	88-92	135	0	3
Norwich C	Tr	06/93	93-95	67	7	1
Leicester C	Tr	08/96	96-97	61	3	0
Derby Co	Tr	08/98	98-99	48	6	1
Manchester C	Tr	03/00	99-00	27	3	4
Cardiff C	Tr	07/01	01-03	72	9	2
Southend U	Tr	08/04	04-06	71	4	2
PRISCOTT Anthony John (Tony)						
Born: Eastleigh, Hampshire, England, 19 March, 1941						W/IF
Portsmouth	Jnr	07/59	59-61	35	-	6
Aldershot	Tr	08/62	62-65	141	0	44
Bournemouth	Tr	01/66	65-66	60	1	7
Aldershot	Tr	08/67	67-70	126	10	27
PRISKE Brian						
Born: Horsens, Denmark, 14 May, 1977						RB
Denmark: 24/U21-15						
Portsmouth	KRC Genk (BEL)	08/05	05	26	4	0
PRISKIN Tamas						
Born: Komarno, Slovakia, 27 September, 1986						F
Hungary: 49/U21-6						

League Club	Source	Date Signed	Seasons Played	Career Record Apps	Subs	Gls
Watford	Gyori ETO (HUN)	08/06	06-08	46	20	15
Preston NE	L	03/08	07	4	1	2
Ipswich T	Tr	08/09	09-11	28	23	5
Queens Park Rgrs	L	02/10	09	13	0	1
Swansea C	L	03/11	10	0	4	1
Derby Co	L	11/11	11	4	1	1
PRISO Carl Yaya						
Born: Cameroon, 10 July, 1979						F
Torquay U	Chemnitzer FC (GER)	08/05	05	1	2	0
PRITCHARD Alan Stewart						
Born: Chester, England, 24 August, 1943						IF
Chester C	Jnr	10/60	60-63	19	-	6
PRITCHARD Alex David						
Born: Grays, Essex, England, 3 May, 1993						F/M
England: U21-6/Youth						
Tottenham H	Sch	07/11	13	0	1	0
Peterborough U	L	01/13	12	2	4	0
Swindon T	L	07/13	13	33	3	6
Brentford	L	07/14	14	43	2	12
PRITCHARD Alfred Vincent (Alf)						
Born: Chester, England, 31 August, 1920						IF
Died: Chester, England, 9 May, 1995						
Millwall	Chester C (Am)	09/37				
Wrexham	Dumbarton	08/46	46-49	36	-	8
PRITCHARD Bradley						
Born: Harare, Zimbabwe, 19 December, 1985						RM
Charlton Ath	Hayes & Yeading U	05/11	11-13	58	21	3
Leyton Orient	Tr	07/14	14	22	9	0
PRITCHARD David Michael						
Born: Wolverhampton, England, 27 May, 1972						RB
Wales: B-1						
West Bromwich A	YT	07/90	91	1	4	0
Bristol Rov	Telford U	02/94	93-01	157	6	1
PRITCHARD Harvey John (Jack)						
Born: Meriden, Warwickshire, England, 30 January, 1918						W
Died: Beccles, Suffolk, England, May, 2000						
Coventry C	Exhall Colliery	10/35	36	5	-	2
Crystal Palace	Tr	06/37	37	30	-	6
Manchester C	Tr	03/38	37-38	22	-	5
Southend U	Tr	02/47	46-51	71	-	8
PRITCHARD Howard Keith						
Born: Cardiff, Wales, 18 October, 1958						W
Wales: 1/Youth						
Bristol C	App	08/76	78-80	31	7	2
Swindon T	Tr	08/81	81-82	59	6	11
Bristol C	Tr	08/83	83-85	117	2	22
Gillingham	Tr	08/86	86-87	84	4	20
Walsall	Tr	07/88	88-89	40	5	7
Maidstone U	Tr	10/89	89-90	29	4	6
PRITCHARD John Vincent						
Born: Manchester, England, 29 September, 1995						F
Oldham Ath	Sch	-	13	0	1	0
PRITCHARD Joseph Henry (Joe)						
Born: Birkenhead, Wirral, England, 4 September, 1943						M
Tranmere Rov	Liverpool (Am)	09/62	62-69	176	2	29
PRITCHARD Joshua Philip (Josh)						
Born: Stockport, Greater Manchester, England, 23 September, 1992						M
Wales: U21-3						
Fulham	Sch	07/11				
Gillingham	Tr	06/14	14	14	11	0
PRITCHARD Keith						
Born: Wallasey, Wirral, England, 20 October, 1919						IF
Died: Birkenhead, Wirral, England, October, 1998						
New Brighton (Am)	New Brighton Baptists	07/46	46-47	25	-	8
PRITCHARD Mark Owen						
Born: Tredegar, Blaenau Gwent, Wales, 23 November, 1985						F
Swansea C	Sch	07/05	03	1	3	0
PRITCHARD Philip John (Phil)						
Born: Wordsley, West Midlands, England, 9 January, 1965						G
Stoke C	App	01/82				
Southend U	L	03/84	83	9	0	0
PRITCHARD Raymond (Ray)						
Born: Liverpool, England, 23 June, 1954						RB
England: Schools						
Tranmere Rov	Everton (App)	08/72	72-73	13	1	0
Southport	L	01/74	73	3	0	0

PRITCHARD Roy Thomas
Born: Dawley, Telford & Wrekin, England, 9 May, 1925 — LB
Died: Walsall, West Midlands, England, March, 1993

League Club	Source	Date Signed	Seasons Played	Apps	Subs	Gls
Wolverhampton W	Jnr	05/42	46-54	202	-	0
Aston Villa	Tr	02/55	55-57	3	-	0
Notts Co	Tr	11/57	57	18	-	0
Port Vale	Tr	08/58	58-59	24	-	0

PRITCHETT Darrol
Born: Bentley, South Yorkshire, England, 22 March, 1933 — FB

League Club	Source	Date Signed	Seasons Played	Apps	Subs	Gls
Hull C	Jnr	01/51				
Walsall	Tr	05/54	54	1	-	0

PRITCHETT Keith Bernard
Born: Glasgow, Scotland, 8 November, 1953 — LB

League Club	Source	Date Signed	Seasons Played	Apps	Subs	Gls
Wolverhampton W	Drumchapel Amats	04/72				
Doncaster Rov	Tr	07/73	73	6	0	0
Queens Park Rgrs	Tr	03/74	74	4	0	0
Brentford	Tr	07/76	76	11	0	1
Watford	Tr	11/76	76-81	133	7	9
Blackpool	Tr	11/82	82-83	36	1	1

PRITTY George Joseph
Born: Birmingham, England, 4 March, 1915 — WH
Died: Birmingham, England, July, 1996

League Club	Source	Date Signed	Seasons Played	Apps	Subs	Gls
Aston Villa	HB Metro	05/33	36-37	3	-	0
Nottingham F	Tr	12/38	38-47	49	-	1

PROBERT Eric William
Born: South Kirkby, West Yorkshire, England, 17 February, 1952 — M
Died: Pontefract, West Yorkshire, England, September, 2004
England: Youth

League Club	Source	Date Signed	Seasons Played	Apps	Subs	Gls
Burnley	App	02/69	68-72	62	5	11
Notts Co	Tr	07/73	73-76	122	0	14
Darlington	Tr	07/78	78-79	20	1	0

PROBETS Ashley
Born: Bexleyheath, SE London, England, 13 December, 1984 — W

League Club	Source	Date Signed	Seasons Played	Apps	Subs	Gls
Arsenal	Sch	07/03				
Rochdale	Tr	07/04	04	4	5	0

PROCTER Andrew John (Andy)
Born: Blackburn, Greater Manchester, England, 13 March, 1983 — M
England: Semi Pro-1

League Club	Source	Date Signed	Seasons Played	Apps	Subs	Gls
Accrington Stan	Great Harwood T	02/02	06-11	221	14	29
Preston NE	Tr	01/12	11-12	25	9	0
Bury	Tr	07/13	13	23	9	2
Accrington Stan	Tr	09/14	14	29	0	0

PROCTOR David
Born: Belfast, Northern Ireland, 10 October, 1929 — RH

League Club	Source	Date Signed	Seasons Played	Apps	Subs	Gls
Blackpool	Portadown	08/49				
Norwich C	Tr	01/53	52-53	17	-	0
Barrow	Northwich Victoria	10/54	54-58	160	-	2
Wrexham	Tr	08/59	59	2	-	0

PROCTOR James Anthony
Born: Doncaster, South Yorkshire, England, 25 October, 1976 — W

League Club	Source	Date Signed	Seasons Played	Apps	Subs	Gls
Rochdale	Bradford C (YT)	10/95	95	1	2	0

PROCTOR Jamie Thomas
Born: Preston, Lancashire, England, 25 March, 1992 — F

League Club	Source	Date Signed	Seasons Played	Apps	Subs	Gls
Preston NE	Sch	02/10	09-11	24	13	4
Stockport Co	L	08/10	10	4	3	0
Swansea C	Tr	08/12				
Shrewsbury T	L	10/12	12	2	0	0
Crawley T	Tr	01/13	12-13	36	26	13
Fleetwood T	Tr	06/14	14	32	9	8

PROCTOR Mark Gerard
Born: Middlesbrough, England, 30 January, 1961 — M
England: U21-4/Youth

League Club	Source	Date Signed	Seasons Played	Apps	Subs	Gls
Middlesbrough	App	09/78	78-80	107	2	12
Nottingham F	Tr	08/81	81-82	60	4	5
Sunderland	L	03/83	82	5	0	0
Sunderland	Tr	08/83	83-87	110	2	19
Sheffield Wed	Tr	09/87	87-88	59	0	4
Middlesbrough	Tr	03/89	88-92	101	19	6
Tranmere Rov	Tr	03/93	92-93	31	0	1
Hartlepool U	South Shields	03/97	96	6	0	0

PROCTOR Michael Anthony
Born: Sunderland, England, 3 October, 1980 — F

League Club	Source	Date Signed	Seasons Played	Apps	Subs	Gls
Sunderland	YT	10/97	02-03	15	23	3
Halifax T	L	03/01	00	11	1	4
York C	L	08/01	01	40	1	14
Bradford C	L	08/02	02	10	2	4
Rotherham U	Tr	02/04	03-04	32	13	7
Swindon T	L	02/05	04	4	0	2
Hartlepool U	Tr	07/05	05-06	23	5	5
Wrexham	Tr	03/07	06-07	32	17	13

PROCTOR Michael Henry (Harry)
Born: Ushaw Moor, County Durham, England, 10 July, 1912 — WH
Died: Norwich, England, 6 February, 1984

League Club	Source	Date Signed	Seasons Played	Apps	Subs	Gls
Hartlepool U	Washington Colliery	07/32	32-33	61	-	14
Norwich C	Tr	05/34	34-46	108	-	3

PROKAS Richard
Born: Penrith, Cumbria, England, 22 January, 1976 — DM

League Club	Source	Date Signed	Seasons Played	Apps	Subs	Gls
Carlisle U	YT	07/94	94-00	184	20	3
Cambridge U	Tr	03/01	00-01	9	3	1

PROLZE Brian Joseph
Born: Altrincham, Greater Manchester, England, 11 April, 1932 — CF
Died: Altrincham, Greater Manchester, England, 31 October, 1996

League Club	Source	Date Signed	Seasons Played	Apps	Subs	Gls
Crewe Alex (Am)	Altrincham	02/54	53	1	-	0

PROPHETT Colin George
Born: Crewe, Cheshire, England, 8 March, 1947 — CD

League Club	Source	Date Signed	Seasons Played	Apps	Subs	Gls
Sheffield Wed	Crewe YC	06/68	69-72	111	8	7
Norwich C	Tr	06/73	73	34	1	0
Swindon T	Tr	09/74	74-77	158	2	10
Chesterfield	Tr	09/78	78-79	35	2	1
Crewe Alex	Tr	10/79	79-80	79	0	1

PROSCHWITZ Nick
Born: Weissenfels, Germany, 28 November, 1986 — F

League Club	Source	Date Signed	Seasons Played	Apps	Subs	Gls
Hull C	SC Paderborn 07 (GER)	07/12	12-13	5	24	3
Barnsley	L	01/14	13	8	6	4
Brentford	Tr	08/14	14	1	17	1
Coventry C	L	02/15	14	6	3	1

PROSINECKI Robert
Born: Schwenningen, Germany, 12 January, 1969 — M
Croatia: 49//Yugoslavia: 15

League Club	Source	Date Signed	Seasons Played	Apps	Subs	Gls
Portsmouth	Standard Liege (BEL)	08/01	01	30	3	9

PROSSER Luke Barrie
Born: Waltham Cross, Hertfordshire, England, 28 May, 1988 — CD

League Club	Source	Date Signed	Seasons Played	Apps	Subs	Gls
Port Vale	Sch	07/06	07-09	29	4	2
Southend U	Tr	08/10	10-14	107	11	5

PROSSER Neil Albert
Born: Edmonton, N London, England, 8 March, 1957 — F

League Club	Source	Date Signed	Seasons Played	Apps	Subs	Gls
Bournemouth	Harlow T	07/80	80	1	1	0
Tranmere Rov		09/82	82	1	1	0

PROUDLER Arthur
Born: Kingswinford, West Midlands, England, 3 October, 1929 — LH
Died: Ormskirk, Lancashire, England, October, 2000

League Club	Source	Date Signed	Seasons Played	Apps	Subs	Gls
Aston Villa	Halesowen T	12/47	54	1	-	0
Crystal Palace	Tr	06/56	56-58	26	-	2

PROUDLOCK Adam David
Born: Newport, Telford & Wrekin, England, 9 May, 1981 — F
England: Youth

League Club	Source	Date Signed	Seasons Played	Apps	Subs	Gls
Wolverhampton W	YT	07/99	00-02	42	29	13
Nottingham F	L	03/02	01	3	0	0
Tranmere Rov	L	10/02	02	5	0	0
Sheffield Wed	L	12/02	02	3	2	2
Sheffield Wed	Tr	09/03	03-05	37	13	9
Ipswich T	Tr	10/05	05	3	6	0
Stockport Co	Tr	08/06	06-07	32	24	11
Darlington	Tr	07/08	08	3	5	0
Grimsby T	Tr	11/08	08-09	36	19	9

PROUDLOCK George Thomas
Born: Morpeth, Northumberland, England, 19 September, 1919 — IF
Died: Northumberland, England, December, 2005

League Club	Source	Date Signed	Seasons Played	Apps	Subs	Gls
West Ham U	Amble Jnrs	11/37	38-47	18	-	5

PROUDLOCK Paul
Born: Hartlepool, Cleveland, England, 25 October, 1965 — W/M

League Club	Source	Date Signed	Seasons Played	Apps	Subs	Gls
Hartlepool U		09/84	84-85	8	7	0
Middlesbrough	South Bank	11/86	86-88	2	3	1
Carlisle U	Tr	03/89	88-92	137	18	20
Hartlepool U	L	09/92	92	3	3	0

PROUDLOVE Andrew George (Andy)
Born: Buxton, Derbyshire, England, 15 January, 1955 — W

League Club	Source	Date Signed	Seasons Played	Apps	Subs	Gls
Reading	App	-	71	4	1	0
Sheffield Wed	Buxton	09/75	75	10	5	0
Norwich C	Tr	02/76	76	0	1	0
Hereford U	Tr	05/77	77	6	5	0
Port Vale	Tr	11/78	78	5	0	0

PROUTON Ralph Oliver
Born: Southampton, England, 1 March, 1926 — LH

League Club	Source	Date Signed	Seasons Played	Apps	Subs	Gls
Arsenal	Romsey T	08/49				
Swindon T	Tr	08/52	52	13	-	0

PROVAN Andrew McKelvie Hughes (Andy)
Born: Greenock, Inverclyde, Scotland, 1 January, 1944 — LW

League Club	Source	Date Signed	Seasons Played	Apps	Subs	Gls
Barnsley	St Mirren	05/63	63	3	-	0
York C	Tr	08/64	64-68	159	1	49
Chester C	Tr	08/68	68-69	78	4	18
Wrexham	Tr	04/70	70-71	48	2	10
Southport	Tr	07/72	72-73	82	1	28
Torquay U	Tr	08/74	74-76	83	8	14

PROVAN David
Born: Falkirk, Scotland, 11 March, 1941 — D
Scotland: 5/SLge-1/U23-1

League Club	Source	Date Signed	Seasons Played	Apps	Subs	Gls
Crystal Palace	Glasgow Rangers	06/70	70	1	0	0
Plymouth Arg	Tr	03/71	70-74	128	1	10

PROVERBS Roy John
Born: Wednesbury, West Midlands, England, 8 July, 1932 — RB/WH

League Club	Source	Date Signed	Seasons Played	Apps	Subs	Gls
Coventry C	Stratford T	05/56	56	10	-	0
Bournemouth	Tr	07/57				
Gillingham	Tr	02/58	57-61	143	-	2

PROVETT Robert James (Jim)
Born: Trimdon, County Durham, England, 22 December, 1982 — G

League Club	Source	Date Signed	Seasons Played	Apps	Subs	Gls
Hartlepool U	Sch	04/02	03-04	66	0	0
Bury	Tr	08/07	07	32	0	0

PRUDHAM Charles Edward (Eddie)
Born: Felling, Tyne and Wear, England, 12 April, 1952 — F

League Club	Source	Date Signed	Seasons Played	Apps	Subs	Gls
Sheffield Wed	Jnr	07/69	70-74	14	5	2
Carlisle U	Tr	11/74	74-76	15	2	2
Hartlepool U	L	09/76	76	3	0	0
Workington	L	02/77	76	15	0	6
Stockport Co	Tr	07/77	77-79	80	7	22
Bournemouth	Tr	05/80	80	2	2	0

PRUDHOE Mark
Born: Washington, Tyne and Wear, England, 8 November, 1963 — G

League Club	Source	Date Signed	Seasons Played	Apps	Subs	Gls
Sunderland	App	09/81	82	7	0	0
Hartlepool U	L	11/83	83	3	0	0
Birmingham C	Tr	09/84	84	1	0	0
Walsall	Tr	02/86	85-86	26	0	0
Doncaster Rov	L	12/86	86	5	0	0
Grimsby T	L	03/87	86	8	0	0
Hartlepool U	L	08/87	87	13	0	0
Bristol C	L	11/87	87	3	0	0
Carlisle U	Tr	12/87	87-88	34	0	0
Darlington	Tr	03/89	88-92	146	0	0
Stoke C	Tr	06/93	93-96	82	0	0
Peterborough U	L	09/94	94	6	0	0
York C	L	02/97	96	2	0	0
Bradford C	Tr	07/97	97	8	0	0
Southend U	Tr	11/99	99	6	0	0

PRUNIER William
Born: Paris, France, 14 August, 1967 — CD
France: 1

League Club	Source	Date Signed	Seasons Played	Apps	Subs	Gls
Manchester U (L)	Bordeaux (FRA)	12/94	95	2	0	0

PRUTTON David Thomas Michael
Born: Hull, England, 12 September, 1981 — M
England: U21-25/Youth

League Club	Source	Date Signed	Seasons Played	Apps	Subs	Gls
Nottingham F	YT	10/98	99-02	141	2	7
Southampton	Tr	01/03	02-06	65	17	3
Nottingham F	L	01/07	06	11	1	2
Leeds U	Tr	08/07	07-09	47	18	4
Colchester U	Tr	01/10	09	18	1	3
Swindon T	Tr	07/10	10	31	10	3
Sheffield Wed	Tr	06/11	11-13	48	8	3
Scunthorpe U	L	08/12	12	13	0	0
Coventry C	L	03/14	13	8	0	0

PRYCE Idris
Born: Wrexham, Wales, 24 February, 1941 — LW

League Club	Source	Date Signed	Seasons Played	Apps	Subs	Gls
Wrexham	Jnr	09/59	59	3	-	0

PRYCE Ryan James
Born: Salisbury, Wiltshire, England, 20 September, 1989 — G

League Club	Source	Date Signed	Seasons Played	Apps	Subs	Gls
Bournemouth	Jnr	07/08	07-08	3	2	0

PRYDE David (Dave)
Born: Newtongrange, Midlothian, Scotland, 10 November, 1913 — LH
Died: Torbay, Devon, England, June, 1987

League Club	Source	Date Signed	Seasons Played	Apps	Subs	Gls
Arsenal	Peebles Rov	05/35	38	4	-	0
Torquay U	Tr	10/46	46-49	64	-	0

PRYDE Robert Ireland (Bob)
Born: Methil, Fife, Scotland, 25 April, 1913 — CH
Died: Blackpool, Lancashire, England, 30 June, 1998
England: FLge-2

League Club	Source	Date Signed	Seasons Played	Apps	Subs	Gls
Blackburn Rov	St Johnstone	05/33	33-48	320	-	11

PRYDE William (Bill)
Born: Falkirk, Scotland, 20 May, 1919 — WH
Died: Shieldhall, Falkirk, Scotland, 24 April, 1970

League Club	Source	Date Signed	Seasons Played	Apps	Subs	Gls
Southend U	Bo'ness	07/47	47-48	17	-	0

PRYER Terence (Terry)
Born: London, England, 4 December, 1967 — CD

League Club	Source	Date Signed	Seasons Played	Apps	Subs	Gls
Southend U		10/85	85	2	0	0

PUCKETT David Charles
Born: Southampton, England, 29 October, 1960 — F

League Club	Source	Date Signed	Seasons Played	Apps	Subs	Gls
Southampton	App	10/78	80-85	51	43	14
Bournemouth	Tr	07/86	86-88	29	6	14
Stoke C	L	03/88	87	7	0	0
Swansea C	L	11/88	88	7	1	3
Aldershot	Tr	01/89	88-90	113	0	50
Bournemouth	Tr	03/92	91	1	3	0

PUDDY Willem John Stanley (Will)
Born: Warminster, Wiltshire, England, 4 October, 1987 — G

League Club	Source	Date Signed	Seasons Played	Apps	Subs	Gls
Cheltenham T	Sch	07/07	08	1	0	0

PUDIL Daniel
Born: Prague, Czech Republic, 27 September, 1985 — LB/M
Czech Republic: 26/U21-16/Youth

League Club	Source	Date Signed	Seasons Played	Apps	Subs	Gls
Watford	Granada (SPN)	08/12	12-14	83	14	3

PUGH Andrew John (Andy)
Born: Gravesend, Kent, England, 26 January, 1989 — F

League Club	Source	Date Signed	Seasons Played	Apps	Subs	Gls
Gillingham	Sch	07/07	06-08	0	6	0

PUGH Daniel Adam (Danny)
Born: Cheadle Hulme, Greater Manchester, England, 19 October, 1982 — LM

League Club	Source	Date Signed	Seasons Played	Apps	Subs	Gls
Manchester U	YT	07/00	02	0	1	0
Leeds U	Tr	07/04	04-05	34	16	5
Preston NE	Tr	07/06	06-07	50	2	4
Stoke C	Tr	11/07	07-11	42	25	1
Preston NE	L	11/10	10	5	0	0
Leeds U	Tr	09/11	11-13	51	7	4
Sheffield Wed	L	01/13	12	16	0	1
Coventry C	Tr	07/14	14	5	0	0

PUGH Daral James
Born: Crynant, Neath Port Talbot, Wales, 5 June, 1961 — W/M
Wales: U21-2

League Club	Source	Date Signed	Seasons Played	Apps	Subs	Gls
Doncaster Rov	App	12/78	78-82	136	18	15
Huddersfield T	Tr	09/82	82-84	52	33	7
Rotherham U	Tr	07/85	85-87	106	6	6
Cambridge U	L	12/87	87	6	0	1
Torquay U	Tr	08/88	88-89	29	3	0

PUGH David
Born: Markham, Caerphilly, Wales, 22 January, 1947 — M
Wales: U23-2/Schools

League Club	Source	Date Signed	Seasons Played	Apps	Subs	Gls
Newport Co	Jnr	04/64	64-67	73	5	9
Chesterfield	Tr	12/67	67-72	212	1	12
Halifax T	Tr	08/73	73-75	91	5	3
Rotherham U	Tr	07/76	76-78	57	1	0
York C	Tr	11/78	78-80	73	4	2

PUGH David
Born: Liverpool, England, 19 September, 1964 — LW

League Club	Source	Date Signed	Seasons Played	Apps	Subs	Gls
Chester C	Runcorn	07/89	89-93	168	11	23
Bury	Tr	08/94	94-97	101	2	28

PUGH Gary
Born: Wrexham, Wales, 10 January, 1967 — W

League Club	Source	Date Signed	Seasons Played	Apps	Subs	Gls
Wrexham	Jnr	07/84	84	1	0	0

PUGH Gary Kevin
Born: Ramsgate, Kent, England, 11 February, 1961 — M

League Club	Source	Date Signed	Seasons Played	Apps	Subs	Gls
West Ham U	Jnr	02/78				
Bournemouth	Dover	01/81	80	0	3	1
Torquay U	Thanet U	11/84	84	4	0	0

PUGH John Graham (Graham)
Born: Chester, England, 12 February, 1948 — M
England: U23-1

League Club	Source	Date Signed	Seasons Played	Apps	Subs	Gls
Sheffield Wed	App	02/65	65-71	136	6	7
Huddersfield T	Tr	05/72	72-74	80	0	1
Chester C	Tr	02/75	74-76	67	2	3
Barnsley	Tr	10/76	76-79	128	2	8
Scunthorpe U	Tr	01/80	79-80	54	1	0

PUGH Kevin John
Born: Corbridge, Northumberland, England, 11 October, 1960 — M

League Club	Source	Date Signed	Seasons Played	Apps	Subs	Gls
Newcastle U	App	10/78	81	0	1	0
Darlington	Gateshead	09/83	83	0	2	0

PUGH Marc Anthony
Born: Bacup, Lancashire, England, 2 April, 1987 LW

League Club	Source	Date Signed	Seasons Played	Apps	Subs	Gls
Bury	Burnley (Sch)	03/06	05-06	30	11	4
Shrewsbury T	Tr	07/07	07-08	27	17	4
Luton T	L	09/08	08	3	1	0
Hereford U	Tr	03/09	08-09	47	2	14
Bournemouth	Tr	07/10	10-14	187	20	40

PUGH Stephen
Born: Bangor, Gwynedd, Wales, 27 November, 1973 F
Wales: U21-2/Youth

League Club	Source	Date Signed	Seasons Played	Apps	Subs	Gls
Wrexham	YT	07/92	92-94	3	8	0

PUGH Stephen John (Steve)
Born: Wolverhampton, England, 1 February, 1965 FB/M

League Club	Source	Date Signed	Seasons Played	Apps	Subs	Gls
Wolverhampton W	App	12/82				
Torquay U	Tr	09/83	83-85	115	5	4
Exeter C	Tr	08/86	86	23	1	1

PUGSLEY David George
Born: Merthyr Tydfil, Wales, 15 August, 1931 G

League Club	Source	Date Signed	Seasons Played	Apps	Subs	Gls
Newport Co (Am)	Gloucester C	03/53	52	1	-	0

PULIS Anthony James
Born: Bristol, England, 21 July, 1984 M
Wales: U21-5

League Club	Source	Date Signed	Seasons Played	Apps	Subs	Gls
Portsmouth	Sch	03/03				
Stoke C	Tr	12/04	06-07	0	2	0
Torquay U	L	12/04	04	1	2	0
Plymouth Arg	L	03/06	05	0	5	0
Grimsby T	L	11/06	06	9	0	0
Bristol Rov	L	02/08	07	0	1	0
Southampton	Tr	08/08				
Lincoln C	L	10/09	09	7	0	0
Stockport Co	L	10/10	10	9	1	1
Barnet	L	02/11	10	4	0	0
Aldershot T	Tr	08/11	11	1	4	0

PULIS Anthony Richard (Tony)
Born: Newport, Wales, 16 January, 1958 D/M

League Club	Source	Date Signed	Seasons Played	Apps	Subs	Gls
Bristol Rov	App	09/75	75-80	78	7	3
Bristol Rov	Happy Valley (HKG)	06/82	82-83	44	1	2
Newport Co	Tr	07/84	84-85	75	2	0
Bournemouth	Tr	08/86	86-88	68	6	3
Gillingham	Tr	08/89	89	16	0	0
Bournemouth	Tr	08/90	90-91	12	4	1

PULIS Raymond (Ray)
Born: Newport, Wales, 21 November, 1964 F

League Club	Source	Date Signed	Seasons Played	Apps	Subs	Gls
Newport Co	App	11/82	82	0	1	0

PULLAN Christopher John (Chris)
Born: Durham, England, 11 December, 1967 M

League Club	Source	Date Signed	Seasons Played	Apps	Subs	Gls
Watford	Jnr	07/86	86-90	5	7	0
Halifax T	L	02/89	88	5	0	1
Maidstone U	Tr	03/91	90	0	1	0

PULLAR David Harry (Dave)
Born: Durham, England, 13 February, 1959 W

League Club	Source	Date Signed	Seasons Played	Apps	Subs	Gls
Portsmouth	App	02/77	75-78	84	9	4
Exeter C	Tr	07/79	79-82	124	6	22
Crewe Alex	Tr	07/83	83-86	120	12	7

PULLEN James Daniel
Born: Chelmsford, England, 18 March, 1982 G

League Club	Source	Date Signed	Seasons Played	Apps	Subs	Gls
Ipswich T	Heybridge Swifts	10/99	02	1	0	0
Blackpool	L	08/01	01	16	0	0
Peterborough U	Tr	11/03	03	3	0	0

PULLEN Walter Ernest (Wally)
Born: Ripley, Derbyshire, England, 2 August, 1919 IF
Died: Luton, England, 1977

League Club	Source	Date Signed	Seasons Played	Apps	Subs	Gls
Leyton Orient	Fulham (Am)	01/46	46-50	117	-	37

PULLEY Gordon Albert
Born: Stourbridge, West Midlands, England, 18 September, 1936 LW

League Club	Source	Date Signed	Seasons Played	Apps	Subs	Gls
Millwall	Oswestry T	09/56	56-57	60	-	9
Gillingham	Tr	05/58	58-65	204	0	46
Peterborough U	Tr	11/65	65-66	16	1	4

PUNCHEON Jason David Ian
Born: Croydon, S London, England, 26 June, 1986 W

League Club	Source	Date Signed	Seasons Played	Apps	Subs	Gls
Wimbledon	Sch	-	03	6	2	0
MK Dons	Wimbledon relocation	10/04	04-05	9	17	1
Barnet	Lewes	08/06	06-07	71	7	15
Plymouth Arg	Tr	07/08	08	5	1	0
MK Dons	L	10/08	08	8	1	1
MK Dons	L	01/09	08	18	0	3
MK Dons	L	08/09	09	23	1	7
Southampton	Tr	01/10	09-12	63	11	9
Millwall	L	11/10	10	7	0	5
Blackpool	L	01/11	10	6	5	3
Queens Park Rgrs	L	08/11	11	0	2	0
Crystal Palace	Tr	08/13	13-14	60	11	13

PUNTER Brian
Born: Bromsgrove, Worcestershire, England, 16 August, 1935 CF/LW
England: Youth

League Club	Source	Date Signed	Seasons Played	Apps	Subs	Gls
Wolverhampton W	Jnr	09/53				
Leicester C	Bromsgrove Rov	05/58				
Lincoln C	Tr	11/59	59-63	75	-	21

PUNTON William (Bill)
Born: Morpeth, Northumberland, England, 18 December, 1957 G

League Club	Source	Date Signed	Seasons Played	Apps	Subs	Gls
Bradford C	Gainsborough Trinity	08/75	75-76	7	0	0

PUNTON William Hamilton (Bill)
Born: Ormiston, East Lothian, Scotland, 4 May, 1934 LW

League Club	Source	Date Signed	Seasons Played	Apps	Subs	Gls
Newcastle U	Portadown	02/54	53-57	23	-	1
Southend U	Tr	07/58	58	38	-	6
Norwich C	Tr	07/59	59-66	219	0	24
Sheffield U	Tr	11/66	66-67	16	0	1
Scunthorpe U	Tr	01/68	67-68	45	1	2

PURCELL Brian Patrick John
Born: Swansea, Wales, 23 November, 1938 D
Died: Hereford, England, 20 January, 1969

League Club	Source	Date Signed	Seasons Played	Apps	Subs	Gls
Swansea C	Tower U	01/58	59-67	164	1	1

PURCELL Daniel
Born: Chesterfield, Derbyshire, England, 15 September, 1948 F

League Club	Source	Date Signed	Seasons Played	Apps	Subs	Gls
Chesterfield (Am)	Jnr	05/65	65	0	1	0

PURCELL Tadhg
Born: Dublin, Republic of Ireland, 9 February, 1985 F

League Club	Source	Date Signed	Seasons Played	Apps	Subs	Gls
Darlington	Shamrock Rov (ROI)	01/10	09	22	0	9
Northampton T	Tr	07/10	10	1	3	0

PURCHES Stephen Richard (Steve)
Born: Ilford, E London, England, 14 January, 1980 RB

League Club	Source	Date Signed	Seasons Played	Apps	Subs	Gls
West Ham U	YT	07/98				
Bournemouth	Tr	07/00	00-06	221	23	10
Leyton Orient	Tr	07/07	07-09	107	3	5
Bournemouth	Tr	07/10	10-11	26	7	0

PURDIE Bernard Charles
Born: Wrexham, Wales, 20 April, 1949 F/FB

League Club	Source	Date Signed	Seasons Played	Apps	Subs	Gls
Wrexham	Jnr	10/67	68-69	7	3	3
Chester C	Tr	07/71	71-72	54	9	14
Crewe Alex	Tr	07/73	73-79	203	10	44
Huddersfield T	Tr	10/79	79-81	37	9	1
Crewe Alex	Tr	08/82	82	14	2	0

PURDIE Ian
Born: Larkhall, Lanarkshire, Scotland, 7 March, 1953 LW
Scotland: U23-1

League Club	Source	Date Signed	Seasons Played	Apps	Subs	Gls
Wigan Ath	Motherwell	07/78	78-79	54	1	12
Portsmouth	Tr	11/79	79	4	1	1

PURDIE James John (Jock)
Born: Berwick-on-Tweed, Northumberland, England, 24 May, 1918 G
Died: Margate, Kent, England, 29 February, 1988

League Club	Source	Date Signed	Seasons Played	Apps	Subs	Gls
Millwall	Airdrieonians	02/46	46-47	50	-	0
Southport	Kilmarnock	02/49	48	6	-	0
Aldershot	Tonbridge	10/50	50	16	-	0

PURDIE Jonathan (Jon)
Born: Corby, Northamptonshire, England, 22 February, 1967 W
England: Schools

League Club	Source	Date Signed	Seasons Played	Apps	Subs	Gls
Arsenal	App	01/85				
Wolverhampton W	Tr	07/85	85-87	82	7	12
Cambridge U	L	10/87	87	7	0	2
Oxford U	Tr	07/88	88	5	6	0
Brentford	Tr	03/89	88	5	1	0
Shrewsbury T	Tr	06/89	89	9	3	1

PURDIE Robert James (Rob)
Born: Wigston, Leicestershire, England, 28 September, 1982 M
England: Semi Pro-2

League Club	Source	Date Signed	Seasons Played	Apps	Subs	Gls
Hereford U	Leicester C (Sch)	07/02	06	43	1	6
Darlington	Tr	07/07	07-08	69	10	6
Oldham Ath	Tr	05/09				
Hereford U	Tr	10/10	10-11	52	7	7
Shrewsbury T	Tr	07/12	12	12	11	0

PURDON Edward John (Ted)
Born: Johannesburg, South Africa, 1 March, 1930 CF
Died: Toronto, Canada, 29 April, 2007

League Club	Source	Date Signed	Seasons Played	Apps	Subs	Gls
Birmingham C	Marist Brothers (RSA)	08/50	51-53	64	-	27
Sunderland	Tr	01/54	53-56	90	-	40
Workington	Tr	03/57	56-57	33	-	9
Barrow	Tr	03/58	57-58	37	-	12
Bristol Rov	Bath C	08/60	60	4	-	1

PURI Sander
Born: Tartu, Estonia, 7 May, 1988 — W
Estonia: 58/U21-3

League Club	Source	Date Signed	Seasons Played	Apps	Subs	Gls
York C	St Mirren	06/13	13	3	5	0

PURKISS Benjamin John (Ben)
Born: Sheffield, England, 1 April, 1984 — RB

League Club	Source	Date Signed	Seasons Played	Apps	Subs	Gls
Sheffield U	Sch	08/01				
Oxford U	York C	05/10	10	19	4	0
Hereford U	Tr	01/12	11	15	0	0
Walsall	Tr	08/12	12-14	66	7	0

PURNELL Philip (Phil)
Born: Bristol, England, 16 September, 1964 — LW

League Club	Source	Date Signed	Seasons Played	Apps	Subs	Gls
Bristol Rov	Mangotsfield U	09/85	85-91	130	23	22
Swansea C	L	12/91	91	5	0	1

PURRINGTON Ben
Born: Exeter, England, 5 May, 1996 — LB

League Club	Source	Date Signed	Seasons Played	Apps	Subs	Gls
Plymouth Arg	Sch	05/13	13-14	15	5	0

PURSE Darren John
Born: Stepney, E London, England, 14 February, 1977 — CD
England: U21-2

League Club	Source	Date Signed	Seasons Played	Apps	Subs	Gls
Leyton Orient	YT	02/94	93-95	48	7	3
Oxford U	Tr	07/96	96-97	52	7	5
Birmingham C	Tr	02/98	97-03	143	25	9
West Bromwich A	Tr	06/04	04	22	0	0
Cardiff C	Tr	08/05	05-08	103	8	10
Sheffield Wed	Tr	07/09	09-10	61	0	2
Millwall	Tr	01/11	10	9	4	1
Yeovil T	L	10/11	11	5	0	0
Plymouth Arg	Tr	11/11	11-12	45	0	2
Port Vale	Tr	01/13	12	17	0	2

PURSELL Robert Wilson
Born: Glasgow, Scotland, 28 September, 1919 — RB
Died: Minehead, Somerset, England, 8 August, 2006

League Club	Source	Date Signed	Seasons Played	Apps	Subs	Gls
Port Vale	Chesterton	12/39	46-47	39	-	0

PURSER Wayne Montague
Born: Basildon, England, 13 April, 1980 — F

League Club	Source	Date Signed	Seasons Played	Apps	Subs	Gls
Queens Park Rgrs	YT	04/97				
Barnet	Tr	08/00	00	4	14	3
Leyton Orient	Tr	03/03	02-04	36	14	9
Peterborough U	Hornchurch	11/04	04	15	11	6

PURVES Charles Reuben (Charlie)
Born: High Spen, Tyne and Wear, England, 17 February, 1921 — IF
Died: Southampton, England, 20 June, 2013

League Club	Source	Date Signed	Seasons Played	Apps	Subs	Gls
Charlton Ath	Spennymoor U	10/46	46-49	46	-	4
Southampton	Tr	06/51	51-53	30	-	2

PURVIS Bartholomew (Bart)
Born: Gateshead, Tyne and Wear, England, 15 October, 1919 — LB
Died: Gateshead, Tyne and Wear, England, June, 2001

League Club	Source	Date Signed	Seasons Played	Apps	Subs	Gls
Everton	North Shields	01/46				
Gateshead	Tr	10/46	46	1	-	0
Reading	Tr	03/47				
Plymouth Arg	Tr	06/47				
Notts Co	Tr	05/48	48-50	25	-	0
Carlisle U	Tr	08/51	51	4	-	0
Hartlepool U	Tr	08/52				

PURVIS William Youngson Rule (Willie)
Born: Berwick-on-Tweed, Northumberland, England, 14 December, 1938 — CF
Died: Cleethorpes, North Lincolnshire, England, 30 July, 2012

League Club	Source	Date Signed	Seasons Played	Apps	Subs	Gls
Grimsby T	Berwick Rgrs	08/61	61-62	7	-	2
Doncaster Rov	Tr	12/62	62	2	-	0

PUSIC Martin
Born: Vienna, Austria, 24 October, 1987 — W
Austria: Youth

League Club	Source	Date Signed	Seasons Played	Apps	Subs	Gls
Hull C	Rheindorf Altach (AUT)	08/11	11	2	0	0

PUTNEY Trevor Anthony
Born: Harold Hill, E London, England, 9 April, 1960 — M

League Club	Source	Date Signed	Seasons Played	Apps	Subs	Gls
Ipswich T	Brentwood & Warley	09/80	82-85	94	9	8
Norwich C	Tr	06/86	86-88	76	6	9
Middlesbrough	Tr	07/89	89-90	45	3	1
Watford	Tr	08/91	91-92	42	10	2
Leyton Orient	Tr	07/93	93	20	2	2
Colchester U	L	08/94	94	7	0	0
Colchester U	Tr	10/94	94	21	0	2

PUTTERILL Raymond Francis (Ray)
Born: Wallasey, Wirral, England, 2 March, 1989 — LW

League Club	Source	Date Signed	Seasons Played	Apps	Subs	Gls
Liverpool	Sch	07/07				
Accrington Stan	Halewood T	08/10	10	11	13	0
Rochdale	Southport	08/12	12	1	17	1

PUTTNAM David Paul
Born: Leicester, England, 3 February, 1967 — LW

League Club	Source	Date Signed	Seasons Played	Apps	Subs	Gls
Leicester C	Leicester U	02/89	88-89	4	3	0
Lincoln C	Tr	01/90	89-95	160	17	21
Gillingham	Tr	10/95	95-96	15	25	2
Swansea C	Tr	08/97	97	4	0	0

PUYGRENIER Sebastien Nicolas
Born: Limoges, France, 28 January, 1982 — CD

League Club	Source	Date Signed	Seasons Played	Apps	Subs	Gls
Bolton W (L)	Zenit St P'burg (RUS)	01/09	08	5	2	1

PYATT John Henry
Born: Barnet, N London, England, 26 September, 1948 — IF/FB

League Club	Source	Date Signed	Seasons Played	Apps	Subs	Gls
Liverpool	Chesham U	07/67				
Peterborough U	Tr	07/68	68	15	1	1

PYE Frederick (Fred)
Born: Stockport, Greater Manchester, England, 11 March, 1928 — IF
Died: Cheshire, England, 31 March, 2008

League Club	Source	Date Signed	Seasons Played	Apps	Subs	Gls
Accrington Stan	Stalybridge Celtic	04/48	47-48	4	-	0

PYE Jesse
Born: Treeton, South Yorkshire, England, 22 December, 1919 — CF
Died: Blackpool, Lancashire, England, 20 February, 1984
England: 1/B-3/FLge-1/War-1

League Club	Source	Date Signed	Seasons Played	Apps	Subs	Gls
Sheffield U	Treeton Rov	12/38				
Notts Co	Royal Engineers	08/45				
Wolverhampton W	Tr	05/46	46-51	188	-	90
Luton T	Tr	07/52	52-54	61	-	32
Derby Co	Tr	10/54	54-56	61	-	24

PYE William (Billy)
Born: Rainford, Merseyside, England, 8 November, 1930 — IF

League Club	Source	Date Signed	Seasons Played	Apps	Subs	Gls
Stockport Co		08/49				
Chester C	Tr	07/52	53-55	28	-	11

PYGALL David Allen
Born: Watford, Hertfordshire, England, 23 January, 1939 — IF

League Club	Source	Date Signed	Seasons Played	Apps	Subs	Gls
Watford	Jnr	01/56	55-60	20	-	2

PYKE Malcolm
Born: Eltham, SE London, England, 6 March, 1938 — WH

League Club	Source	Date Signed	Seasons Played	Apps	Subs	Gls
West Ham U	Jnr	03/55	56-57	17	-	0
Crystal Palace	Tr	06/59	59	2	-	0

PYLE Elijah St Quentin
Born: Chester-le-Street, County Durham, England, 22 September, 1918 — IF
Died: Durham, England, September, 2009

League Club	Source	Date Signed	Seasons Played	Apps	Subs	Gls
York C	West Stanley	11/47	47-48	10	-	3

PYLE Stephen (Steve)
Born: North Shields, Tyne and Wear, England, 28 September, 1963 — M/F

League Club	Source	Date Signed	Seasons Played	Apps	Subs	Gls
Cambridge U	App	07/81	80-85	56	13	8
Torquay U	Tr	12/85	85-86	27	6	5

PYLE Walter David (David)
Born: Trowbridge, Wiltshire, England, 12 December, 1936 — CH
Died: Trowbridge, Wiltshire, England, 3 February, 2002

League Club	Source	Date Signed	Seasons Played	Apps	Subs	Gls
Bristol Rov	Trowbridge T	07/55	56-61	139	-	0
Bristol C	Tr	07/62	62	8	-	0

PYM Christy James
Born: Exeter, England, 24 April, 1995 — G
England: Youth

League Club	Source	Date Signed	Seasons Played	Apps	Subs	Gls
Exeter C	Sch	07/13	13-14	34	0	0

PYM Ernest Frederick (Ernie)
Born: Torquay, Devon, England, 23 March, 1935 — LW
Died: Torbay, Devon, England, 22 October, 2004

League Club	Source	Date Signed	Seasons Played	Apps	Subs	Gls
Torquay U	St Marychurch	09/57	57-64	284	-	83

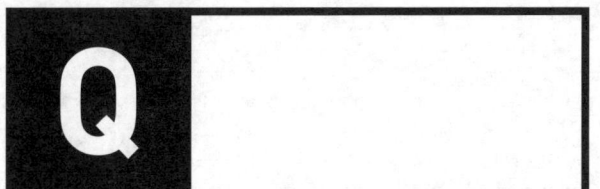

QUAILEY Brian Sullivan
Born: Leicester, England, 21 March, 1978 — F

League Club	Source	Date Signed	Seasons Played	Apps	Subs	Gls
West Bromwich A	Nuneaton Bor	09/97	97-98	1	6	0
Exeter C	L	12/98	98	8	4	2
Blackpool	L	12/99	99	1	0	0
Scunthorpe U	Tr	02/00	99-01	39	32	16

QUAIRNEY John (Jock)
Born: Girvan, Ayrshire, Scotland, 7 January, 1927 — G
Died: Girvan, Ayrshire, Scotland, 17 March, 2000

League Club	Source	Date Signed	Seasons Played	Apps	Subs	Gls
Rotherham U	Girvan Jnrs	07/48	48-59	260	-	0

QUAMINA Mark Ezzard
Born: Sutton, S London, England, 25 November, 1969 — M

League Club	Source	Date Signed	Seasons Played	Apps	Subs	Gls
Wimbledon	YT	07/88	88	1	0	0
Plymouth Arg	Tr	07/91	91	4	1	0

QUARESMA Ricardo
Born: Lisbon, Portugal, 26 September, 1983 — LW
Portugal: 40/U21-21

League Club	Source	Date Signed	Seasons Played	Apps	Subs	Gls
Chelsea (L)	Inter Milan (ITA)	02/09	08	1	3	0

QUARTERMAIN Patrick George (Pat)
Born: Oxford, England, 16 April, 1937 — LB

League Club	Source	Date Signed	Seasons Played	Apps	Subs	Gls
Oxford U	Jnr	09/55	62-66	184	1	0

QUASHIE Nigel Francis
Born: Peckham, SE London, England, 20 July, 1978 — M
England: B-1/U21-4/Youth//Scotland: 14

League Club	Source	Date Signed	Seasons Played	Apps	Subs	Gls
Queens Park Rgrs	YT	08/95	95-97	50	7	3
Nottingham F	Tr	08/98	98-99	37	7	2
Portsmouth	Tr	08/00	00-04	140	8	13
Southampton	Tr	01/05	04-05	37	0	5
West Bromwich A	Tr	01/06	05-06	26	3	1
West Ham U	Tr	01/07	06	7	0	0
Birmingham C	L	10/08	08	8	2	0
Wolverhampton W	L	01/09	08	3	0	0
MK Dons	L	11/09	09	6	1	2
Queens Park Rgrs	Tr	01/10	09	4	0	0

QUAYLE Mark Leslie
Born: Liverpool, England, 2 October, 1978 — F

League Club	Source	Date Signed	Seasons Played	Apps	Subs	Gls
Everton	YT	10/95				
Notts Co	Tr	06/98	98	2	3	0

QUEEN Gerald (Gerry)
Born: Glasgow, Scotland, 15 January, 1945 — F

League Club	Source	Date Signed	Seasons Played	Apps	Subs	Gls
Crystal Palace	Kilmarnock	07/69	69-72	101	7	25
Leyton Orient	Tr	09/72	72-76	149	7	34

QUESTED Wilfred Leonard (Len)
Born: Folkestone, Kent, England, 9 January, 1925 — WH
Died: Queensland, Australia, 20 August, 2012
England: B-1

League Club	Source	Date Signed	Seasons Played	Apps	Subs	Gls
Fulham	Folkestone	08/46	46-51	175	-	6
Huddersfield T	Tr	11/51	51-56	220	-	8

QUEUDRUE Franck
Born: Paris, France, 27 August, 1978 — LB
France: B-1

League Club	Source	Date Signed	Seasons Played	Apps	Subs	Gls
Middlesbrough	RC Lens (FRA)	10/01	01-05	145	5	11
Fulham	Tr	07/06	06	28	1	1
Birmingham C	Tr	08/07	07-09	43	4	3
Colchester U	L	03/10	09	3	0	0

QUIGLEY Damian
Born: Rochdale, Greater Manchester, England, 20 September, 1987 — M

League Club	Source	Date Signed	Seasons Played	Apps	Subs	Gls
Bury	Sch	06/06	05	0	1	0

QUIGLEY Edward (Eddie)
Born: Bury, Greater Manchester, England, 13 July, 1921 — IF
Died: Fleetwood, Lancashire, England, 16 April, 1997
England: B-1

League Club	Source	Date Signed	Seasons Played	Apps	Subs	Gls
Bury	Jnr	09/41	46-47	42	-	18
Sheffield Wed	Tr	10/47	47-49	74	-	49
Preston NE	Tr	12/49	49-51	52	-	17
Blackburn Rov	Tr	11/51	51-55	159	-	92
Bury	Tr	08/56	56	10	-	3

QUIGLEY Gilbert
Born: Ulverston, Cumbria, England, 17 February, 1921 — WH/LB
Died: Barrow, Cumbria, England, March, 2006

League Club	Source	Date Signed	Seasons Played	Apps	Subs	Gls
Barrow	Vickers Sports	12/45	46-48	27	-	0

QUIGLEY John (Johnny)
Born: Glasgow, Scotland, 28 June, 1935 — IF/RH
Died: Nottingham, England, 30 November, 2004

League Club	Source	Date Signed	Seasons Played	Apps	Subs	Gls
Nottingham F	Glasgow Celtic	07/57	57-64	236	-	51
Huddersfield T	Tr	02/65	64-66	66	1	4
Bristol C	Tr	10/66	66-67	66	0	7
Mansfield T	Tr	07/68	68-70	105	0	2

QUIGLEY Mark
Born: Dublin, Republic of Ireland, 27 October, 1985 — M
Republic of Ireland: U21-1/Youth

League Club	Source	Date Signed	Seasons Played	Apps	Subs	Gls
Millwall	Sch	11/02	03-04	4	5	0

QUIGLEY Michael Anthony Joseph (Mike)
Born: Manchester, England, 2 October, 1970 — M

League Club	Source	Date Signed	Seasons Played	Apps	Subs	Gls
Manchester C	YT	07/89	91-93	3	9	0
Wrexham	L	02/95	94	4	0	0
Hull C	Tr	07/95	95-97	36	15	3
Hull C	Altrincham	01/00	99	0	3	0

QUIGLEY Thomas Cook (Tommy)
Born: East Calder, West Lothian, Scotland, 26 March, 1932 — CF

League Club	Source	Date Signed	Seasons Played	Apps	Subs	Gls
Portsmouth	Barry T	12/55				
Queens Park Rgrs	Tr	06/56	56	16	-	7

QUINLAN Maurice Edward (Eddie)
Born: Clapton, NE London, England, 15 August, 1931 — LW
Died: Reading, England, 10 March, 2008

League Club	Source	Date Signed	Seasons Played	Apps	Subs	Gls
Tottenham H	Great Yarmouth T	03/52				
Reading	Tr	06/53	53-55	51	-	11

QUINLAN Michael (Mike)
Born: Barnsley, South Yorkshire, England, 4 December, 1941 — CH

League Club	Source	Date Signed	Seasons Played	Apps	Subs	Gls
Bristol C	Doncaster Rov (Am)	03/59	60	2	-	0

QUINLAN Philip Edward (Phil)
Born: Southport, Merseyside, England, 17 April, 1971 — F
England: Youth

League Club	Source	Date Signed	Seasons Played	Apps	Subs	Gls
Everton	YT	07/89				
Huddersfield T	L	03/91	90	7	1	2
Doncaster Rov	Tr	08/92	92	2	7	0

QUINN Alan
Born: Dublin, Republic of Ireland, 13 June, 1979 — W
Republic of Ireland: 8/U21-8/Youth

League Club	Source	Date Signed	Seasons Played	Apps	Subs	Gls
Sheffield Wed	Cherry Orchard (ROI)	12/97	97-03	147	10	16
Sunderland	L	10/03	03	5	1	0
Sheffield U	Tr	07/04	04-07	76	21	11
Ipswich T	Tr	01/08	07-09	50	19	3

QUINN Albert
Born: Lanchester, County Durham, England, 18 April, 1920 — IF
Died: Esh, County Durham, England, 26 June, 2008

League Club	Source	Date Signed	Seasons Played	Apps	Subs	Gls
Sunderland	Esh Winning Jnrs	11/46	47	6	-	2
Darlington	Tr	05/48	48-50	86	-	42

QUINN Anthony Michael (Tony)
Born: Liverpool, England, 24 July, 1959 — F

League Club	Source	Date Signed	Seasons Played	Apps	Subs	Gls
Wigan Ath	Everton (NC)	01/79	79-80	36	7	14

QUINN Barry Scott
Born: Dublin, Republic of Ireland, 9 May, 1979 — M
Republic of Ireland: 4/U21-17/Youth

League Club	Source	Date Signed	Seasons Played	Apps	Subs	Gls
Coventry C	YT	11/96	98-02	67	16	0
Rushden & D	L	01/04	03	4	0	0
Oxford U	Tr	03/04	03-05	83	3	2

QUINN Desmond (Des)
Born: Killyleagh, Down, Northern Ireland, 21 March, 1926 — RB
Died: Beckenham, SE London, England, 14 June, 1980

League Club	Source	Date Signed	Seasons Played	Apps	Subs	Gls
Blackburn Rov	Lytham	08/47	47	1	-	0
Millwall	Tr	06/49	49-54	43	-	0

QUINN Gordon Patrick
Born: Hammersmith, W London, England, 11 May, 1932 — IF

League Club	Source	Date Signed	Seasons Played	Apps	Subs	Gls
Queens Park Rgrs	Eastcote BC	08/52	52-56	22	-	1
Plymouth Arg	Tr	09/56	56-57	14	-	2

QUINN James (Jimmy)
Born: Kilsyth, Lanarkshire, Scotland, 23 November, 1946 — LB
Died: Glasgow, Scotland, 29 April, 2002

League Club	Source	Date Signed	Seasons Played	Apps	Subs	Gls
Sheffield Wed	Glasgow Celtic	01/75	74-75	46	0	1

QUINN James Martin (Jimmy)
Born: Belfast, Northern Ireland, 18 November, 1959 — F

Northern Ireland: 46/B-1

League Club	Source	Date Signed	Seasons Played	Apps	Subs	Gls
Swindon T	Oswestry T	12/81	81-83	34	15	10
Blackburn Rov	Tr	08/84	84-86	58	13	17
Swindon T	Tr	12/86	86-87	61	3	30
Leicester C	Tr	06/88	88	13	18	6
Bradford C	Tr	03/89	88-89	35	0	14
West Ham U	Tr	12/89	89-90	34	13	18
Bournemouth	Tr	08/91	91	43	0	19
Reading	Tr	07/92	92-96	149	33	71
Peterborough U	Tr	07/97	97-98	47	2	25
Swindon T	Tr	11/98	99	1	6	0

QUINN John David

Born: Widnes, Cheshire, England, 30 May, 1938 M

League Club	Source	Date Signed	Seasons Played	Apps	Subs	Gls
Sheffield Wed	Prescot Cables	05/59	59-67	166	7	20
Rotherham U	Tr	11/67	67-71	114	0	7
Halifax T	Tr	07/72	72-74	88	4	1

QUINN Michael (Mick)

Born: Liverpool, England, 2 May, 1962 F

League Club	Source	Date Signed	Seasons Played	Apps	Subs	Gls
Wigan Ath	Derby Co (App)	09/79	79-81	56	13	19
Stockport Co	Tr	07/82	82-83	62	1	39
Oldham Ath	Tr	01/84	83-85	78	2	34
Portsmouth	Tr	03/86	85-88	115	6	54
Newcastle U	Tr	07/89	89-92	110	5	59
Coventry C	Tr	11/92	92-94	57	7	25
Plymouth Arg	L	11/94	94	3	0	0
Watford	L	03/95	94	4	1	0

QUINN Niall John

Born: Dublin, Republic of Ireland, 6 October, 1966 F

Republic of Ireland: 91/B-1/U23-1/U21-6/Youth/Schools

League Club	Source	Date Signed	Seasons Played	Apps	Subs	Gls
Arsenal	Jnr	11/83	85-89	59	8	14
Manchester C	Tr	03/90	89-95	183	20	66
Sunderland	Tr	08/96	96-02	168	35	61

QUINN Noel Peter Anthony

Born: Dublin, Republic of Ireland, 2 November, 1949 RW

League Club	Source	Date Signed	Seasons Played	Apps	Subs	Gls
Oldham Ath	Blackburn Rov (Am)	01/67	67	4	0	0

QUINN Patrick (Pat)

Born: Glasgow, Scotland, 26 April, 1936 IF

Scotland: 4/SLge-6

League Club	Source	Date Signed	Seasons Played	Apps	Subs	Gls
Blackpool	Motherwell	11/62	62-63	34	-	9

QUINN Patrick Anthony (Pat)

Born: Kilsyth, Lanarkshire, Scotland, 18 June, 1918 IF

Died: Halifax, West Yorkshire, England, 15 May, 1979

League Club	Source	Date Signed	Seasons Played	Apps	Subs	Gls
Halifax T	Ashfield	07/46	46	25	-	6

QUINN Paul Charles

Born: Wishaw, Lanarkshire, Scotland, 21 July, 1985 RB

Scotland: U21-3

League Club	Source	Date Signed	Seasons Played	Apps	Subs	Gls
Cardiff C	Motherwell	07/09	09-11	38	8	1
Doncaster Rov	Tr	08/12	12-13	68	5	2

QUINN Robert John (Rob)

Born: Sidcup, SE London, England, 8 November, 1976 M

Republic of Ireland: B-1/U21-5

League Club	Source	Date Signed	Seasons Played	Apps	Subs	Gls
Crystal Palace	YT	03/95	95-97	18	5	1
Brentford	Tr	07/98	98-00	98	11	2
Oxford U	Tr	01/01	00-01	23	6	2
Bristol Rov	Tr	07/02	02-03	67	12	3

QUINN Stephen

Born: Dublin, Republic of Ireland, 4 April, 1986 M

Republic of Ireland: 13/U21-9

League Club	Source	Date Signed	Seasons Played	Apps	Subs	Gls
Sheffield U	Sch	07/05	06-12	190	16	20
MK Dons	L	09/05	05	6	0	0
MK Dons	L	11/05	05	7	2	0
Rotherham U	L	01/06	05	16	0	0
Hull C	Tr	08/12	12-14	62	23	4

QUINN Stephen James (James)

Born: Coventry, England, 15 December, 1974 F

Northern Ireland: 50/B-2/U21-1/Youth

League Club	Source	Date Signed	Seasons Played	Apps	Subs	Gls
Birmingham C	YT	-	92	1	3	0
Blackpool	Tr	07/93	93-97	128	23	37
Stockport Co	L	03/94	93	0	1	0
West Bromwich A	Tr	02/98	97-01	85	29	9
Notts Co	L	11/01	01	6	0	3
Bristol Rov	L	03/02	01	6	0	1
Sheffield Wed	Willem II (NED)	01/05	04	10	5	2
Peterborough U	Tr	08/05	05	21	3	7
Bristol C	L	10/05	05	2	1	1
Northampton T	Tr	08/06	06	5	13	1

QUINN Wayne Richard

Born: Hayle, Cornwall, England, 19 November, 1976 LB

England: B-1/U21-2/Youth

League Club	Source	Date Signed	Seasons Played	Apps	Subs	Gls
Sheffield U	YT	12/94	97-00	131	8	6
Newcastle U	Tr	01/01	00	14	1	0
Sheffield U	L	01/03	02	6	0	0
West Ham U	Tr	09/03	03	22	0	0

QUINNEY Henry Jesse (Jesse)

Born: Rugby, Warwickshire, England, 15 October, 1922 FB

Died: Rugby, Warwickshire, England, 17 January, 2002

League Club	Source	Date Signed	Seasons Played	Apps	Subs	Gls
Northampton T	Wolverhampton W (Am)	01/43	46	3	-	0

QUINNEY John

Born: Rugby, Warwickshire, England, 2 October, 1932 FB

Died: Cheltenham, Gloucestershire, England, 15 March, 1986

League Club	Source	Date Signed	Seasons Played	Apps	Subs	Gls
Coventry C	Jnr	11/49	52	3	-	0

QUINTON Darren John

Born: Romford, E London, England, 28 April, 1986 M

League Club	Source	Date Signed	Seasons Played	Apps	Subs	Gls
Cambridge U	Sch	02/05	03-04	14	18	0

QUINTON Walter (Wally)

Born: North Anston, South Yorkshire, England, 13 December, 1917 LB

Died: Sheffield, England, 8 March, 1996

League Club	Source	Date Signed	Seasons Played	Apps	Subs	Gls
Rotherham U	Dinnington	07/38	38	32	-	0
Birmingham C	Tr	07/39	47	8	-	0
Brentford	Tr	04/49	48-50	42	-	0
Southend U	Tr	08/52				
Shrewsbury T	Tr	10/52	52	3	-	0

QUIRKE David

Born: Ballina, Mayo, Republic of Ireland, 11 January, 1947 CD

League Club	Source	Date Signed	Seasons Played	Apps	Subs	Gls
Gillingham	Bedford T	07/66	67-73	221	9	0

QUIRKE Michael James

Born: Coventry, England, 10 September, 1991 G

Republic of Ireland: U21-1

League Club	Source	Date Signed	Seasons Played	Apps	Subs	Gls
Coventry C	Sch	06/10	10	3	1	0

QUITONGO Jose Manuel

Born: Luanda, Angola, 18 November, 1974 W

League Club	Source	Date Signed	Seasons Played	Apps	Subs	Gls
Darlington	Norrkoping (SWE)	09/95	95	1	0	0

QUIXALL Albert

Born: Sheffield, England, 9 August, 1933 IF

England: 5/B-3/FLge-4/U23-1/Schools

League Club	Source	Date Signed	Seasons Played	Apps	Subs	Gls
Sheffield Wed	Jnr	08/50	50-58	241	-	64
Manchester U	Tr	09/58	58-63	165	-	50
Oldham Ath	Tr	09/64	64-65	36	0	11
Stockport Co	Tr	07/66	66	13	0	0

QUOW Trevor

Born: Peterborough, England, 28 September, 1960 M

League Club	Source	Date Signed	Seasons Played	Apps	Subs	Gls
Peterborough U	App	09/78	78-85	191	12	17
Gillingham	Tr	08/86	86-88	64	15	3
Northampton T	Tr	01/89	88-89	42	6	2
Northampton T	Kettering T	02/91	90-91	36	4	0

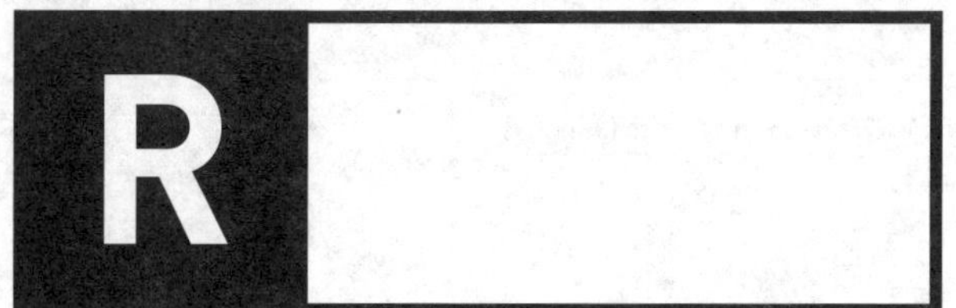

League Club	Source	Date Signed	Seasons Played	Career Record Apps	Subs	Gls

RABIHOU Amadou Dangadji
Born: Douala, Cameroon, 2 December, 1984 — F

Hereford U	SC Lustenau (AUT)	09/10	10	1	2	0

RABJOHN Christopher (Chris)
Born: Sheffield, England, 10 March, 1945 — M

Rotherham U	Jnr	07/63	65-67	76	2	5
Doncaster Rov	Tr	02/68	67-72	137	12	8

RACCHI Daniel Craig (Danny)
Born: Elland, West Yorkshire, England, 22 November, 1987 — W

Huddersfield T	Sch	06/06	06-07	0	6	0
Bury	Tr	07/08	08-09	10	33	0

RACHEL Adam
Born: Birmingham, England, 10 December, 1976 — G

Aston Villa	YT	05/95	98	0	1	0
Blackpool	Tr	09/99	99	1	0	0

RACHUBKA Paul Stephen
Born: San Luis Obispo, California, USA, 21 May, 1981 — G
England: Youth

Manchester U	YT	07/99	00	1	0	0
Oldham Ath	L	11/01	01	16	0	0
Charlton Ath	Tr	05/02				
Huddersfield T	L	03/04	03	13	0	0
MK Dons	L	08/04	04	4	0	0
Northampton T	L	09/04	04	10	0	0
Huddersfield T	Tr	11/04	04-05	63	0	0
Peterborough U	L	12/06	06	4	0	0
Blackpool	L	01/07	06	8	0	0
Blackpool	Tr	06/07	07-10	109	1	0
Leeds U	Tr	07/11	11	5	1	0
Tranmere Rov	L	11/11	11	10	0	0
Leyton Orient	L	03/12	11	8	0	0
Accrington Stan	L	11/12	12	21	0	0
Oldham Ath	Tr	09/13	13-14	32	0	0
Crewe Alex	Tr	02/15	14	14	1	0

RACKHAM Derrick Richard
Born: Norwich, England, 14 June, 1928 — LW
Died: Drayton, Norfolk, England, 24 March, 1996

Norwich C	Norman YC	11/49	51	8	-	2

RACKLEY Robert William (Bob)
Born: Teignmouth, Devon, England, 15 March, 1940 — LW

Exeter C	Newton Abbot Spurs	03/58				
Bristol Rov	Tr	07/60				
Oldham Ath	Tr	10/60	60	19	-	5

RACKSTRAW Charles (Charlie)
Born: Sheffield, England, 23 April, 1938 — F

Chesterfield	Boynton Sports	03/58	58-63	172	-	48
Gillingham	Tr	05/64	64-66	93	1	25
Bradford C	Tr	01/67	66-69	94	10	27

RACON Therry Norbert
Born: Paris, France, 1 May, 1984 — DM
Guadeloupe: 3

Charlton Ath	EA Guingamp (FRA)	08/07	07-10	90	8	7
Brighton & HA	L	03/08	07	8	0	0
Millwall	Tr	07/11	12	0	1	0
Portsmouth	L	02/13	12	16	0	0
Portsmouth	Tr	10/13	13	12	4	0

RADCLIFFE Mark
Born: Hyde, Greater Manchester, England, 26 October, 1919 — G
Died: Cheshire, England, March, 2013

Oldham Ath		12/42				
Fulham	Chelmsford C	08/46	46-47	11	-	0
Rochdale	Witton A	11/52	52	1	-	0

RADCLIFFE Vincent (Vince)
Born: Manchester, England, 9 June, 1945 — D
Died: Perth, Australia, 11 March, 2014

Portsmouth	App	06/63	64-66	10	0	0
Peterborough U	Tr	07/67	67	2	0	0
Rochdale	Tr	07/68	68	26	0	1

League Club	Source	Date Signed	Seasons Played	Career Record Apps	Subs	Gls

RADEBE Lucas Valeriu
Born: Soweto, South Africa, 12 April, 1969 — CD
South Africa: 70

Leeds U	Kaiser Chiefs (RSA)	09/94	94-04	180	20	0

RADFORD Arthur
Born: Rotherham, South Yorkshire, England, 7 October, 1925 — LB
Died: Rotherham, South Yorkshire, England, 1981

Huddersfield T		10/44				
Rotherham U		05/47	47-49	44	-	0
Rochdale	Tr	06/51	51	27	-	0
Swindon T	Frickley Colliery	08/52	52	16	-	0

RADFORD John
Born: Hemsworth, West Yorkshire, England, 22 February, 1947 — F
England: 2/FLge-2/U23-4

Arsenal	App	03/64	63-76	375	4	111
West Ham U	Tr	12/76	76-77	28	0	0
Blackburn Rov	Tr	02/78	77-78	36	0	10

RADFORD Mark
Born: Leicester, England, 20 December, 1968 — M/LB

Colchester U	Jnr	05/87	87-89	47	17	5

RADFORD Ronald (Ronnie)
Born: South Elmsall, West Yorkshire, England, 12 July, 1943 — M

Leeds U	Sheffield Wed (Am)	10/61				
Newport Co	Cheltenham T	07/69	69-70	63	3	7
Hereford U	Tr	07/71	72-73	61	0	6

RADFORD William Howard (Howard)
Born: Abercynon, Rhondda Cynon Taff, Wales, 8 September, 1930 — G

Bristol Rov	Penrhiwceiber	08/51	51-61	244	-	0

RADIGAN Neil Thomas
Born: Middlesbrough, England, 4 July, 1980 — M

Scarborough	YT	07/98	98	4	5	0
Darlington	Tr	07/99				

RADUCIOIU Florin Valeriu
Born: Bucharest, Romania, 17 March, 1970 — F
Romania: 40

West Ham U	RCD Espanyol (SPN)	06/96	96	6	5	2

RADZINSKI Tomasz
Born: Poznan, Poland, 14 December, 1973 — F
Canada: 46/U23-3

Everton	Anderlecht (BEL)	08/01	01-03	78	13	25
Fulham	Tr	08/04	04-06	73	30	10

RAE Alexander McFarlane (Alex)
Born: Glasgow, Scotland, 23 August, 1946 — M

Bury	East Fife	05/69	69	10	1	0

RAE Alexander Scott (Alex)
Born: Glasgow, Scotland, 30 September, 1969 — M
Scotland: B-4/U21-8

Millwall	Falkirk	08/90	90-95	205	13	63
Sunderland	Tr	06/96	96-01	90	24	12
Wolverhampton W	Tr	09/01	01-03	88	19	15
MK Dons	Dundee	07/09	09	2	1	0

RAE Gavin Paul
Born: Aberdeen, Scotland, 28 November, 1977 — M
Scotland: 14/U21-6

Cardiff C	Glasgow Rangers	07/07	07-10	109	21	7

RAE Ian Johnstone
Born: Grangemouth, Falkirk, Scotland, 19 January, 1933 — RB
Died: Wadhurst, East Sussex, England, 4 July, 2005
Scotland: B/U23-1

Bristol C	Falkirk	10/57	57	12	-	0

RAE Joseph (Joe)
Born: Glasgow, Scotland, 6 March, 1925 — CF
Died: Glasgow, Scotland, 1 May, 1987

Torquay U	Glasgow Celtic	07/48	48	20	-	4

[RAFAEL] DA SILVA Rafael Pereira
Born: Rio de Janeiro, Brazil, 9 July, 1990 — RB
Brazil: 2/Youth

Manchester U	Fluminense (BRA)	08/08	08-14	96	13	5

RAFFELL Stephen Christopher (Steve)
Born: Blyth, Northumberland, England, 27 April, 1970 — CD

Doncaster Rov	YT	06/88	87-89	45	9	0

RAFFERTY Andrew James (Andy)
Born: Sidcup, SE London, England, 27 May, 1988 — G

Hartlepool U	Guisborough T	07/10	10-13	5	0	0

RAFFERTY Bernard
Born: Manchester, England, 9 July, 1948 — IF

League Club	Source	Date Signed	Seasons Played	Apps	Subs	Gls
Bradford Park Ave		10/69	69	8	5	1

RAFFERTY James (Jim)
Born: Manchester, England, 7 November, 1930 — LH
Died: Manchester, England, May, 1999

League Club	Source	Date Signed	Seasons Played	Apps	Subs	Gls
Manchester C		12/48				
Bradford Park Ave	Tr	06/52	52	2	-	0

RAFFERTY Joseph Gerard (Joe)
Born: Liverpool, England, 6 October, 1993 — RB
Republic of Ireland: Youth

League Club	Source	Date Signed	Seasons Played	Apps	Subs	Gls
Rochdale	Liverpool (Sch)	07/12	12-14	79	4	1

RAFFERTY Kevin Brian
Born: Nairobi, Kenya, 9 November, 1960 — G

League Club	Source	Date Signed	Seasons Played	Apps	Subs	Gls
Crewe Alex	App	09/78	78-79	22	0	0

RAFFERTY Ronald (Ron)
Born: South Shields, Tyne and Wear, England, 6 May, 1934 — F/CH

League Club	Source	Date Signed	Seasons Played	Apps	Subs	Gls
Portsmouth	Wycombe W	07/54	54-56	23	-	5
Grimsby T	Tr	12/56	56-62	264	-	145
Hull C	Tr	07/63	63-64	16	-	6
Aldershot	Tr	07/66	66-68	79	2	10

RAFFERTY William Henry (Billy)
Born: Port Glasgow, Inverclyde, Scotland, 30 December, 1950 — F

League Club	Source	Date Signed	Seasons Played	Apps	Subs	Gls
Coventry C	Port Glasgow Rgrs	07/68	69-72	27	0	3
Blackpool	Tr	10/72	72-73	35	1	9
Plymouth Arg	Tr	03/74	73-75	89	1	35
Carlisle U	Tr	05/76	76-77	72	0	27
Wolverhampton W	Tr	03/78	77-79	41	3	6
Newcastle U	Tr	10/79	79-80	34	5	6
Portsmouth	Tr	12/80	80-82	98	4	40
Bournemouth	Tr	02/84	83-84	58	0	18

RAFTER Sean
Born: Southend-on-Sea, England, 20 May, 1957 — G

League Club	Source	Date Signed	Seasons Played	Apps	Subs	Gls
Southend U	App	06/75	75-77	23	0	0
Leicester C	Tr	01/78				
Leyton Orient	Tr	07/79	80	2	0	0

RAFTERY Patrick Thomas
Born: Stoke-on-Trent, England, 28 November, 1925 — IF

League Club	Source	Date Signed	Seasons Played	Apps	Subs	Gls
Port Vale	Ravensdale	01/49	48-49	5	-	0

RAGGETT Brian Charles
Born: Staincross, South Yorkshire, England, 11 January, 1949 — D

League Club	Source	Date Signed	Seasons Played	Apps	Subs	Gls
Barnsley	App	01/67	66-71	56	8	0

RAGLAN Charles Jordan Clark (Charlie)
Born: Wythenshawe, Greater Manchester, England, 28 April, 1993 — CD

League Club	Source	Date Signed	Seasons Played	Apps	Subs	Gls
Port Vale	Sch	06/11				
Chesterfield	FC United, Manchester	04/14	14	15	3	1

RAHIM Brent Dominic
Born: Diego Martin, Trinidad, 8 August, 1978 — M
Trinidad & Tobago: 49

League Club	Source	Date Signed	Seasons Played	Apps	Subs	Gls
West Ham U	Levski Sofia (BUL)	08/02				
Northampton T (L)	L	01/03	02	6	0	1

RAHMBERG Marino
Born: Orebro, Sweden, 7 August, 1974 — F
Sweden: 4

League Club	Source	Date Signed	Seasons Played	Apps	Subs	Gls
Derby Co	Degerfors (SWE)	01/97	96	0	1	0

RAINE David
Born: Darlington, County Durham, England, 28 March, 1937 — FB

League Club	Source	Date Signed	Seasons Played	Apps	Subs	Gls
Port Vale		05/57	56-61	144	-	0
Doncaster Rov	Tr	07/62	62-64	107	-	2
Colchester U	Tr	06/65	65-66	44	4	0

RAINE Robert Reginald (Bob)
Born: Chesterfield, Derbyshire, England, 17 November, 1927 — D

League Club	Source	Date Signed	Seasons Played	Apps	Subs	Gls
Chesterfield	Newbold Colliery	02/49	49	1	-	0
Aldershot	Kidderminster Hrs	02/51	50-53	47	-	21

RAINEY Hugh
Born: Dumbarton, Dunbartonshire, Scotland, 7 January, 1935 — RH
Died: Nantucket, Massachusetts, USA, 1 January, 2005

League Club	Source	Date Signed	Seasons Played	Apps	Subs	Gls
Portsmouth	Renton BG	06/53				
Queens Park Rgrs	Tr	06/55				
Aldershot	Tr	07/57	57	8	-	0

RAINFORD David John
Born: Stepney, E London, England, 21 April, 1979 — M

League Club	Source	Date Signed	Seasons Played	Apps	Subs	Gls
Colchester U	YT	07/97	98	0	1	0
Scarborough	L	12/98	98	0	2	0
Dagenham & Red	Bishops Stortford	07/06	07	28	1	8

RAINFORD John William (Johnny)
Born: Camden, N London, England, 11 December, 1930 — IF/WH
Died: Hounslow, SW London, England, May, 2001

League Club	Source	Date Signed	Seasons Played	Apps	Subs	Gls
Crystal Palace	Jnr	03/49	48-52	64	-	8
Cardiff C	Tr	05/53	53	3	-	1
Brentford	Tr	10/53	53-61	299	-	42

RAINFORD Kenneth Sydney (Ken)
Born: Saughall Massie, Wirral, England, 4 November, 1926 — CF
Died: Birkenhead, Wirral, England, 9 February, 1997

League Club	Source	Date Signed	Seasons Played	Apps	Subs	Gls
New Brighton	New Brighton Baptists	02/48	47	3	-	1

RAJCZI Peter
Born: Kaposvar, Hungary, 3 April, 1981 — F
Hungary: 12

League Club	Source	Date Signed	Seasons Played	Apps	Subs	Gls
Barnsley (L)	Ujpest (HUN)	01/07	06	8	7	2

RAJKOVIC Ante
Born: Vitez, Bosnia & Herzegovina, 17 August, 1952 — CD
Yugoslavia: 6

League Club	Source	Date Signed	Seasons Played	Apps	Subs	Gls
Swansea C	Sarajevo (YUG)	03/81	80-84	79	1	2

RALLS Joseph William (Joe)
Born: Aldershot, Hampshire, England, 13 October, 1993 — M
England: Youth

League Club	Source	Date Signed	Seasons Played	Apps	Subs	Gls
Cardiff C	Sch	09/11	11-14	21	21	3
Yeovil T	L	08/13	13	33	4	3

RALPH Nathanael Anthony (Nathan)
Born: Dunmow, Essex, England, 14 February, 1993 — LB

League Club	Source	Date Signed	Seasons Played	Apps	Subs	Gls
Peterborough U	Sch	07/11				
Yeovil T	Tr	07/12	12-14	14	21	1

RALSTON Peter
Born: Fauldhouse, West Lothian, Scotland, 31 January, 1929 — CH

League Club	Source	Date Signed	Seasons Played	Apps	Subs	Gls
Accrington Stan	Falkirk	08/57	57-58	6	-	0

RALSTON Walter (Wally)
Born: Glasgow, Scotland, 3 October, 1935 — LB
Died: Glasgow, Scotland, 4 October, 2009

League Club	Source	Date Signed	Seasons Played	Apps	Subs	Gls
Aldershot (L)	Partick Thistle	06/58	58	3	-	0

RAMAGE Alan
Born: Guisborough, Cleveland, England, 29 November, 1957 — CD

League Club	Source	Date Signed	Seasons Played	Apps	Subs	Gls
Middlesbrough	App	12/75	75-79	65	4	2
Derby Co	Tr	07/80	80-81	32	1	2

RAMAGE Andrew William (Andy)
Born: Barking, E London, England, 3 October, 1974 — M

League Club	Source	Date Signed	Seasons Played	Apps	Subs	Gls
Gillingham	Dagenham & Red	11/93	94	8	5	1

RAMAGE Craig Darren
Born: Derby, England, 30 March, 1970 — M/F
England: U21-3

League Club	Source	Date Signed	Seasons Played	Apps	Subs	Gls
Derby Co	YT	07/88	89-93	33	9	4
Wigan Ath	L	02/89	88	10	0	2
Watford	Tr	02/94	93-96	99	5	27
Peterborough U	L	02/97	96	7	0	0
Bradford C	Tr	06/97	97-98	24	11	1
Notts Co	Tr	08/99	99-00	50	5	7

RAMAGE George McIntosh
Born: Dalkeith, Midlothian, Scotland, 29 January, 1937 — G

League Club	Source	Date Signed	Seasons Played	Apps	Subs	Gls
Colchester U	Third Lanark	08/61	62-63	38	-	0
Leyton Orient	Tr	07/64	64	4	-	0
Luton T	Tr	11/65	65	7	0	0

RAMAGE Peter Iain
Born: Whitley Bay, Tyne and Wear, England, 22 November, 1983 — D

League Club	Source	Date Signed	Seasons Played	Apps	Subs	Gls
Newcastle U	Sch	07/03	04-07	45	6	0
Queens Park Rgrs	Tr	05/08	08-10	59	9	2
Crystal Palace	L	08/11	11	14	3	0
Birmingham C	L	02/12	11	14	0	0
Crystal Palace	Tr	08/12	12	39	1	4
Barnsley	L	09/13	13	24	0	0
Barnsley	L	10/14	14	19	0	3

RAMASUT Mahan William Thomas (Tom)
Born: Cardiff, Wales, 30 August, 1977 — M
Wales: B/U21-4/Youth

League Club	Source	Date Signed	Seasons Played	Apps	Subs	Gls
Norwich C		07/95				
Bristol Rov	Tr	09/96	96-97	30	12	6

[RAMIRES] SANTOS DO NASCIMENTO Ramires
Born: Rio de Janeiro, Brazil, 24 March, 1987 — M
Brazil: 51/U23-9

League Club	Source	Date Signed	Seasons Played	Apps	Subs	Gls
Chelsea	Benfica (POR)	08/10	10-14	118	29	15

RAMIREZ Gaston Ezequiel
Born: Fray Bentos, Uruguay, 2 December, 1990 — M

League Club	Source	Date Signed	Seasons Played	Apps	Subs	Gls

Uruguay: 34/Youth

League Club	Source	Date Signed	Seasons Played	Apps	Subs	Gls
Southampton	Bologna (ITA)	08/12	12-14	23	22	6
Hull C	L	09/14	14	11	11	1

RAMIS Ivan Andres
Born: Sa Pobla, Mallorca, Spain, 25 October, 1984 — CD
Spain: U23-4/U21-3/Youth

League Club	Source	Date Signed	Seasons Played	Apps	Subs	Gls
Wigan Ath	RCD Mallorca (SPN)	08/12	12-14	48	1	4

RAMMELL Andrew Victor (Andy)
Born: Nuneaton, Warwickshire, England, 10 February, 1967 — F

League Club	Source	Date Signed	Seasons Played	Apps	Subs	Gls
Manchester U	Atherstone U	09/89				
Barnsley	Tr	09/90	90-95	149	36	44
Southend U	Tr	02/96	95-97	50	19	13
Walsall	Tr	07/98	98-99	60	9	23
Wycombe W	Tr	09/00	00-02	69	5	25
Bristol Rov	Tr	03/03	02-03	8	4	6

RAMPLING Dennis
Born: Gainsborough, Lincolnshire, England, 25 November, 1923 — RW

League Club	Source	Date Signed	Seasons Played	Apps	Subs	Gls
Fulham	Napier & Sons	11/42	47	2	-	0
Bournemouth	Tr	07/48	48	24	-	4
Brentford	Tr	05/49	49	1	-	0

RAMPLING Edward (Eddie)
Born: Wigan, Greater Manchester, England, 17 February, 1948 — LW

League Club	Source	Date Signed	Seasons Played	Apps	Subs	Gls
Chester C	Newton-le-Willows YC	03/67	67	2	1	0

RAMSAY Craig James
Born: Dunfermline, Fife, Scotland, 19 September, 1962 — F

League Club	Source	Date Signed	Seasons Played	Apps	Subs	Gls
Lincoln C	App	09/80	79-80	3	2	2

RAMSAY George Albert
Born: Sunderland, England, 24 April, 1923 — RW
Died: Aberdeen, Scotland, 28 November, 1996

League Club	Source	Date Signed	Seasons Played	Apps	Subs	Gls
Gateshead	Raith Rov	11/46	46	9	-	1

RAMSAY John William
Born: Sunderland, England, 25 January, 1979 — M

League Club	Source	Date Signed	Seasons Played	Apps	Subs	Gls
Doncaster Rov	YT	10/97	97	2	8	0

RAMSAY Scott Alan
Born: Hastings, East Sussex, England, 16 October, 1980 — W

League Club	Source	Date Signed	Seasons Played	Apps	Subs	Gls
Brighton & HA	YT	06/99	99-00	10	25	2

RAMSBOTTOM Neil
Born: Blackburn, Greater Manchester, England, 25 February, 1946 — G

League Club	Source	Date Signed	Seasons Played	Apps	Subs	Gls
Bury	Jnr	07/64	65-70	174	0	0
Blackpool	Tr	02/71	70-71	12	0	0
Crewe Alex	L	01/72	71	3	0	0
Coventry C	Tr	03/72	72-74	51	0	0
Sheffield Wed	Tr	08/75	75	18	0	0
Plymouth Arg	Tr	07/76	76	39	0	0
Blackburn Rov	Tr	01/78	78	10	0	0
Sheffield U	New Jersey Am'ns (USA)	10/79	79	2	0	0
Bradford C	Tr	08/80	80-82	73	0	0
Bournemouth	Tr	08/83	83	4	0	0

RAMSCAR Frederick Thomas (Fred)
Born: Salford, England, 24 January, 1919 — IF
Died: Northampton, England, May, 2003
Northern Ireland: NILge-1

League Club	Source	Date Signed	Seasons Played	Apps	Subs	Gls
Wolverhampton W	Glentoran	09/45	46	16	-	1
Queens Park Rgrs	Tr	10/47	47-49	51	-	4
Preston NE	Tr	11/49	49-50	19	-	4
Northampton T	Tr	07/51	51-54	139	-	55
Millwall	Tr	09/54	54	30	-	5

RAMSDEN Bernard (Barney)
Born: Sheffield, England, 8 November, 1917 — FB
Died: Los Angeles, California, USA, March, 1976

League Club	Source	Date Signed	Seasons Played	Apps	Subs	Gls
Liverpool	Sheffield Victoria	03/35	37-47	57	-	0
Sunderland	Tr	03/48	47-48	12	-	0
Hartlepool U	Tr	01/50	49	13	-	0

RAMSDEN Simon Paul
Born: Newton Aycliffe, County Durham, England, 17 December, 1981 — RB

League Club	Source	Date Signed	Seasons Played	Apps	Subs	Gls
Sunderland	YT	08/00				
Notts Co	L	08/02	02	21	11	0
Grimsby T	Tr	08/04	04-05	31	6	0
Rochdale	Tr	01/06	05-08	107	5	6
Bradford C	Tr	07/09	09-11	48	2	1

RAMSEY Aaron James
Born: Bargoed, Caerphilly, Wales, 26 December, 1990 — M
Wales: 34/U21-12/Youth

League Club	Source	Date Signed	Seasons Played	Apps	Subs	Gls
Cardiff C	Sch	01/08	06-07	11	5	1
Arsenal	Tr	06/08	08-14	104	52	23
Nottingham F	L	11/10	10	2	3	0
Cardiff C	L	01/11	10	6	0	1

RAMSEY Alfred Ernest (Alf)
Born: Dagenham, E London, England, 22 January, 1920 — RB
Died: Ipswich, England, 28 April, 1999
England: 32/FLge-6

League Club	Source	Date Signed	Seasons Played	Apps	Subs	Gls
Southampton	Portsmouth (Am)	04/44	46-48	90	-	8
Tottenham H	Tr	05/49	49-54	226	-	24

RAMSEY Christopher Leroy (Chris)
Born: Birmingham, England, 28 April, 1962 — RB

League Club	Source	Date Signed	Seasons Played	Apps	Subs	Gls
Brighton & HA	Bristol C (App)	08/80	80-83	30	0	0
Swindon T	Tr	08/84	84-86	99	1	5
Southend U	Tr	08/87	87	8	5	0

RAMSEY Donald (Don)
Born: Manchester, England, 27 September, 1928 — RW

League Club	Source	Date Signed	Seasons Played	Apps	Subs	Gls
Oldham Ath		11/46	49	2	-	0

RAMSEY Paul Christopher
Born: Derry, Northern Ireland, 3 September, 1962 — M/RB
Northern Ireland: 14/Schools

League Club	Source	Date Signed	Seasons Played	Apps	Subs	Gls
Leicester C	App	04/80	80-90	278	12	13
Cardiff C	Tr	08/91	91-92	69	0	7
Cardiff C (L)	St Johnstone	11/94	94	11	0	0
Torquay U	Telford U	11/95	95	18	0	0

RAMSEY Robert (Bob)
Born: Sunderland, England, 24 February, 1935 — RB

League Club	Source	Date Signed	Seasons Played	Apps	Subs	Gls
Huddersfield T	Jnr	01/53				
York C	Tr	05/58	58-60	75	-	0

RANDALL Adrian John
Born: Amesbury, Wiltshire, England, 10 November, 1968 — M
England: Youth

League Club	Source	Date Signed	Seasons Played	Apps	Subs	Gls
Bournemouth	App	09/86	85-87	3	0	0
Aldershot	Tr	09/88	88-90	102	5	12
Burnley	Tr	12/91	91-95	105	20	8
York C	Tr	12/95	95-96	26	6	2
Bury	Tr	12/96	96-97	16	17	3

RANDALL Connor Steven
Born: Liverpool, England, 21 October, 1995 — RB
England: Youth

League Club	Source	Date Signed	Seasons Played	Apps	Subs	Gls
Liverpool	Sch	10/12				
Shrewsbury T	L	01/15	14	0	1	0

RANDALL Ernest Albert Walter (Ernie)
Born: Bognor Regis, West Sussex, England, 13 January, 1926 — CF

League Club	Source	Date Signed	Seasons Played	Apps	Subs	Gls
Chelsea	Bognor Regis T	12/50	51	3	-	1
Crystal Palace	Tr	06/53	53-54	22	-	11

RANDALL Jack Daniel
Born: Bromley, SE London, England, 7 July, 1992 — M

League Club	Source	Date Signed	Seasons Played	Apps	Subs	Gls
Aldershot T	Crystal Palace (Sch)	07/10	10	0	1	0

RANDALL Kevin
Born: Ashton-under-Lyne, Greater Manchester, England, 20 August, 1945 — F

League Club	Source	Date Signed	Seasons Played	Apps	Subs	Gls
Bury	Droylsden	10/65	65	4	0	0
Chesterfield	Tr	07/66	66-71	258	0	96
Notts Co	Tr	08/72	72-75	119	2	38
Mansfield T	Tr	11/75	75-77	62	4	20
York C	Tr	10/77	77-80	96	11	27

RANDALL Mark Leonard
Born: Milton Keynes, England, 28 September, 1989 — M
England: Youth

League Club	Source	Date Signed	Seasons Played	Apps	Subs	Gls
Arsenal	Sch	02/07	07-08	0	2	0
Burnley	L	01/08	07	2	8	0
MK Dons	L	01/10	09	12	4	0
Rotherham U	L	10/10	10	3	7	1
Chesterfield	Tr	07/11	11-12	28	17	2
MK Dons	Ascoli (ITA)	03/14	13-14	3	10	0

RANDALL Maurice
Born: Manchester, England, 4 August, 1919 — LB
Died: Pwllheli, Gwynedd, Wales, 2 June, 1976

League Club	Source	Date Signed	Seasons Played	Apps	Subs	Gls
Crewe Alex	Droylsden	02/47	46-48	41	-	0

RANDALL Paul
Born: Liverpool, England, 16 February, 1958 — F

League Club	Source	Date Signed	Seasons Played	Apps	Subs	Gls
Bristol Rov	Frome T	08/77	77-78	49	3	33
Stoke C	Tr	12/78	78-80	38	8	7
Bristol Rov	Tr	01/81	80-85	169	15	61

RANDALL-HURREN William George James (Will)
Born: Swindon, England, 2 May, 1997 — M

League Club	Source	Date Signed	Seasons Played	Apps	Subs	Gls
Swindon T	Sch	05/15	13-14	2	3	0

RANDELL Colin William
Born: Skewen, Neath Port Talbot, Wales, 12 December, 1952 — M/RB
Wales: U23-1/Schools

League Club	Source	Date Signed	Seasons Played	Apps	Subs	Gls
Coventry C	App	05/70				
Plymouth Arg	Tr	09/73	73-76	137	2	9
Exeter C	Tr	09/77	77-78	78	0	4
Plymouth Arg	Tr	07/79	79-81	110	0	8
Blackburn Rov	Tr	08/82	82-84	72	1	7
Newport Co	L	03/84	83	15	0	0
Swansea C	Tr	07/85	85-86	20	2	1

RANDLES Thomas (Tommy)
Born: Blackpool, Lancashire, England, 13 October, 1940 — IF

League Club	Source	Date Signed	Seasons Played	Apps	Subs	Gls
Stoke C	Ellesmere Port	02/60	61	2	-	0

RANDOLPH Darren Edward
Born: Bray, Republic of Ireland, 12 May, 1987 — G
Republic of Ireland: 2/B-1/U21-10

League Club	Source	Date Signed	Seasons Played	Apps	Subs	Gls
Charlton Ath	Sch	12/04	06-09	12	2	0
Gillingham	L	08/06	06	3	0	0
Bury	L	03/08	07	14	0	0
Hereford U	L	07/08	08	13	0	0
Birmingham C	Motherwell	07/13	13-14	91	0	0

RANEGIE Mathias
Born: Gothenburg, Sweden, 14 June, 1984 — F
Sweden: 5

League Club	Source	Date Signed	Seasons Played	Apps	Subs	Gls
Watford	Udinese (ITA)	01/14	13	8	2	4
Millwall	L	08/14	14	3	4	0

RANGEL Angel
Born: Tortosa, Spain, 28 October, 1982 — RB

League Club	Source	Date Signed	Seasons Played	Apps	Subs	Gls
Swansea C	Terrassa (SPN)	08/07	07-14	269	14	8

RANGER Nile
Born: Southgate, N London, England, 11 April, 1991 — F
England: Youth

League Club	Source	Date Signed	Seasons Played	Apps	Subs	Gls
Newcastle U	Southampton (Sch)	08/08	09-12	5	46	2
Barnsley	L	11/11	11	3	2	0
Sheffield Wed	L	03/12	11	7	1	2
Swindon T	Tr	08/13	13	19	4	8
Blackpool	Tr	08/14	14	5	9	2

RANKIN Andrew George (Andy)
Born: Bootle, Merseyside, England, 11 May, 1944 — G
England: U23-1

League Club	Source	Date Signed	Seasons Played	Apps	Subs	Gls
Everton	Jnr	10/61	63-70	85	0	0
Watford	Tr	11/71	71-79	299	0	0
Huddersfield T	Tr	12/79	79-81	71	0	0

RANKIN George
Born: Liverpool, England, 29 January, 1930 — LB
Died: Fazackerley, Merseyside, England, 22 September, 1989
England: Youth

League Club	Source	Date Signed	Seasons Played	Apps	Subs	Gls
Everton	Jnr	08/48	50-55	36	-	0
Southport	Tr	07/56	56-59	144	-	0

RANKIN Isaiah Marcus
Born: Edmonton, N London, England, 22 May, 1978 — F

League Club	Source	Date Signed	Seasons Played	Apps	Subs	Gls
Arsenal	YT	09/95	97	0	1	0
Colchester U	L	09/97	97	10	1	5
Bradford C	Tr	08/98	98-00	15	22	4
Birmingham C	L	01/00	99	11	2	4
Bolton W	L	08/00	00	9	7	2
Barnsley	Tr	01/01	00-03	18	29	8
Grimsby T	Tr	02/04	03	12	0	4
Brentford	Tr	07/04	04-05	64	14	15
Grimsby T	Tr	07/06	06-07	27	10	2
Macclesfield T	L	03/07	06	1	3	0

RANKIN James
Born: Gateshead, Tyne and Wear, England, 8 September, 1927 — RW
Died: Newcastle-upon-Tyne, England, 12 March, 1985

League Club	Source	Date Signed	Seasons Played	Apps	Subs	Gls
Newcastle U	Jnr	09/44				
Brighton & HA		08/49				
Grimsby T	Tr	01/50	49-50	5	-	1

RANKINE Michael Lee
Born: Doncaster, South Yorkshire, England, 15 January, 1985 — F

League Club	Source	Date Signed	Seasons Played	Apps	Subs	Gls
Scunthorpe U	Barrow	09/04	04	1	20	1
Bournemouth (L)	Rushden & D	10/08	08	3	0	0
Aldershot T	York C	07/11	11-12	31	15	3
York C	L	02/13	12	5	3	0

RANKINE Simon Mark (Mark)
Born: Doncaster, South Yorkshire, England, 30 September, 1969 — M

League Club	Source	Date Signed	Seasons Played	Apps	Subs	Gls
Doncaster Rov	YT	07/88	87-91	160	4	20
Wolverhampton W	Tr	01/92	91-95	112	20	1
Preston NE	Tr	09/96	96-02	217	16	12
Sheffield U	Tr	03/03	02-03	11	8	0
Tranmere Rov	Tr	07/04	04-05	61	4	0

RANKMORE Frank Edward John
Born: Cardiff, Wales, 21 July, 1939 — CH
Wales: 1/U23-2

League Club	Source	Date Signed	Seasons Played	Apps	Subs	Gls
Cardiff C	Cardiff Corinthians	12/57	61-62	67	-	0
Peterborough U	Tr	08/63	63-67	201	0	7
Northampton T	Tr	08/68	68-70	103	0	15

RANSHAW Jack William
Born: Nettleham, Lincolnshire, England, 19 December, 1916 — LW
Died: Nettleham, Lincolnshire, England, 1 May, 2003

League Club	Source	Date Signed	Seasons Played	Apps	Subs	Gls
Lincoln C	Grantham	03/46	46	3	-	0

RANSHAW Richard William Graham (Rick)
Born: Sleaford, Lincolnshire, England, 17 April, 1970 — F

League Club	Source	Date Signed	Seasons Played	Apps	Subs	Gls
Lincoln C	YT	08/88	88	0	1	0

RANSON Raymond (Ray)
Born: St Helens, Merseyside, England, 12 June, 1960 — RB
England: U21-10/Youth/Schools

League Club	Source	Date Signed	Seasons Played	Apps	Subs	Gls
Manchester C	App	06/77	78-83	181	3	1
Birmingham C	Tr	11/84	84-88	136	1	0
Newcastle U	Tr	12/88	88-92	78	5	1
Manchester C	Tr	01/93	92	17	0	0
Reading	Tr	07/93	93	22	2	0

RANTANEN Jari Juhani
Born: Helsinki, Finland, 31 December, 1961 — F
Finland: 29

League Club	Source	Date Signed	Seasons Played	Apps	Subs	Gls
Leicester C	IFK Goteberg (SWE)	09/87	87	10	3	3

RANTIE Tokelo Anthony
Born: Parys, South Africa, 8 September, 1990 — F
South Africa: 26

League Club	Source	Date Signed	Seasons Played	Apps	Subs	Gls
Bournemouth	Malmo FF (SWE)	08/13	13-14	14	27	5

RAPER Kenneth (Kenny)
Born: Stanley, County Durham, England, 15 May, 1956 — LM

League Club	Source	Date Signed	Seasons Played	Apps	Subs	Gls
Stoke C	App	06/73				
Torquay U	Tr	07/77	77-78	51	1	8

[RAPHAEL] ROSSI BRANCO Raphael
Born: Campinas, Brazil, 25 July, 1990 — CD

League Club	Source	Date Signed	Seasons Played	Apps	Subs	Gls
Swindon T	Whitehawk	07/13	13-14	39	5	3

RAPLEY Kevin John
Born: Reading, England, 21 September, 1977 — F

League Club	Source	Date Signed	Seasons Played	Apps	Subs	Gls
Brentford	YT	07/96	96-98	27	24	12
Southend U	L	11/98	98	9	0	4
Notts Co	Tr	02/99	98-00	21	31	4
Exeter C	L	11/00	00	6	1	0
Scunthorpe U	L	03/01	00	1	4	0
Colchester U	Tr	08/01	01-02	40	16	11
Chester C	Tr	07/03	04	12	9	2

RAPLEY Peter David
Born: Portsmouth, England, 24 October, 1936 — RW

League Club	Source	Date Signed	Seasons Played	Apps	Subs	Gls
Exeter C	Portsmouth (Am)	06/57	57-59	10	-	4

RAPONI Juan Pablo
Born: Santa Fe, Argentina, 7 May, 1980 — M

League Club	Source	Date Signed	Seasons Played	Apps	Subs	Gls
Oxford U	CO Bahia Blanco (ARG)	02/05	04	5	5	0

RASIAK Grzegorz
Born: Szczecin, Poland, 12 January, 1979 — F
Poland: 37

League Club	Source	Date Signed	Seasons Played	Apps	Subs	Gls
Derby Co	Dysk. Grodzik (POL)	09/04	04-05	41	0	18
Tottenham H	Tr	08/05	05	4	4	0
Southampton	Tr	02/06	05-09	58	20	28
Bolton W	L	01/08	07	2	5	0
Watford	L	08/08	08	12	9	8
Reading	Tr	08/09	09-10	14	16	9

RASMUSSEN Mark Alan
Born: Newcastle-upon-Tyne, England, 28 November, 1983 — M

League Club	Source	Date Signed	Seasons Played	Apps	Subs	Gls
Burnley	New Hartley	07/01	02	0	2	0

RASULO Giorgio Antonio
Born: Banbury, Oxfordshire, England, 23 January, 1997 — F
England: Youth

League Club	Source	Date Signed	Seasons Played	Apps	Subs	Gls
MK Dons	Sch	05/14	12-13	1	7	0
Oxford U	L	02/15	14	0	1	0

RAT Razvan Dinca
Born: Slatina, Romania, 26 May, 1981 — LB
Romania: 103/U21-16

League Club	Source	Date Signed	Seasons Played	Apps	Subs	Gls
West Ham U	Shakhtar Donetsk (UKR)	07/13	13	11	4	0

RATCLIFFE Beaumont (Bill)
Born: Barnburgh, South Yorkshire, England, 24 April, 1909 — CH
Died: Ellesmere Port, Cheshire, England, 30 March, 2003

League Club	Source	Date Signed	Seasons Played	Apps	Subs	Gls
New Brighton	Bradford Park Ave (Am)	10/31	31-34	131	-	4
Oldham Ath	Le Havre (FRA)	06/35	35-38	156	-	1
Reading	Tr	05/46	46-47	32	-	0
Watford	Tr	05/48	48	24	-	0

RATCLIFFE David
Born: Dewsbury, West Yorkshire, England, 9 March, 1957 — CD

League Club	Source	Date Signed	Seasons Played	Apps	Subs	Gls
Bradford C	App	03/75	74-77	17	11	1

RATCLIFFE Donald (Don)
Born: Newcastle-under-Lyme, Potteries, England, 13 November, 1934 — W/WH
Died: Crewe, Cheshire, England, 19 October, 2014

League Club	Source	Date Signed	Seasons Played	Apps	Subs	Gls
Stoke C	Jnr	05/53	54-63	238	-	16
Middlesbrough	Tr	09/63	63-65	65	0	3
Darlington	Tr	02/66	65-67	85	1	12
Crewe Alex	Tr	01/68	67-68	45	2	2

RATCLIFFE James Barrie (Barrie)
Born: Blackburn, Greater Manchester, England, 21 September, 1941 — LW

League Club	Source	Date Signed	Seasons Played	Apps	Subs	Gls
Blackburn Rov	Jnr	09/58	59-63	36	-	4
Scunthorpe U	Tr	05/64	64	26	-	7
Rochdale	Tr	07/65	65	12	0	1

RATCLIFFE Kevin
Born: Connah's Quay, Flintshire, Wales, 12 November, 1960 — CD
Wales: 59/U21-2/Youth/Schools

League Club	Source	Date Signed	Seasons Played	Apps	Subs	Gls
Everton	App	11/78	79-91	356	3	2
Everton	Dundee	10/92				
Cardiff C	Tr	01/93	92-93	25	0	1
Derby Co	Nottingham F (NC)	01/94	93	6	0	0
Chester C	Tr	07/94	94	23	0	0

RATCLIFFE Patrick Christopher (Paddy)
Born: Dublin, Republic of Ireland, 31 December, 1919 — RB
Died: Los Angeles, California, USA, 10 March, 1986

League Club	Source	Date Signed	Seasons Played	Apps	Subs	Gls
Notts Co	Bohemians (ROI)	11/45				
Wolverhampton W	Tr	06/46	46	2	-	0
Plymouth Arg	Tr	06/47	47-55	236	-	10

RATCLIFFE Raymond (Ray)
Born: St Helens, Merseyside, England, 3 November, 1929 — WH

League Club	Source	Date Signed	Seasons Played	Apps	Subs	Gls
Stockport Co		03/49	48	1	-	0

RATCLIFFE Simon
Born: Davyhulme, Greater Manchester, England, 8 February, 1967 — D/M
England: Youth/Schools

League Club	Source	Date Signed	Seasons Played	Apps	Subs	Gls
Manchester U	App	02/85				
Norwich C	Tr	06/87	87	6	3	0
Brentford	Tr	01/89	88-94	197	17	14
Gillingham	Tr	08/95	95-97	100	5	10

RATHBONE Graham Charles
Born: Newport, Wales, 22 August, 1942 — CD
Died: Newport, Wales, 8 January, 2012

League Club	Source	Date Signed	Seasons Played	Apps	Subs	Gls
Newport Co	Merthyr Tydfil	03/61	60-66	191	0	6
Grimsby T	Tr	11/66	66-72	232	1	11
Cambridge U	Tr	02/73	72-73	35	1	0

RATHBONE Michael John (Mike)
Born: Birmingham, England, 6 November, 1958 — LB
England: Youth

League Club	Source	Date Signed	Seasons Played	Apps	Subs	Gls
Birmingham C	App	11/76	76-78	17	3	0
Blackburn Rov	Tr	03/79	78-86	270	3	2
Preston NE	Tr	07/87	87-90	82	9	4

RATTLE Jonathan Paul (Jon)
Born: Woodbridge, Suffolk, England, 22 July, 1976 — M/LB

League Club	Source	Date Signed	Seasons Played	Apps	Subs	Gls
Cambridge U	YT	05/94	94	6	0	0
Cambridge U	Stevenage Bor	09/95	95	7	2	0

RATTRAY Kevin Winston
Born: Tottenham, N London, England, 6 October, 1968 — M

League Club	Source	Date Signed	Seasons Played	Apps	Subs	Gls
Gillingham	Woking	06/95	95	18	8	3
Barnet	Tr	09/96	96	9	0	0

RATTRAY Peter Kerr
Born: Bannockburn, Stirlingshire, Scotland, 7 November, 1925 — IF
Died: Stirling, Scotland, 5 December, 2004

League Club	Source	Date Signed	Seasons Played	Apps	Subs	Gls
Plymouth Arg	Dundee	09/50	50-51	54	-	22
Norwich C	Tr	06/52	52-53	24	-	5

RAVANELLI Fabrizio
Born: Perugia, Italy, 11 December, 1968 — F
Italy: 22

League Club	Source	Date Signed	Seasons Played	Apps	Subs	Gls
Middlesbrough	Juventus (ITA)	08/96	96-97	35	0	17
Derby Co	SS Lazio (ITA)	08/01	01-02	46	4	14

RAVEN David Haydn
Born: Birkenhead, Wirral, England, 10 March, 1985 — RB
England: Youth

League Club	Source	Date Signed	Seasons Played	Apps	Subs	Gls
Liverpool	Sch	05/02	04	0	1	0
Tranmere Rov	L	01/06	05	11	0	0
Carlisle U	Tr	07/06	06-09	134	2	1
Shrewsbury T	Tr	08/10	10	22	2	0
Tranmere Rov	Tr	08/11	11	17	0	0

RAVEN Paul Duncan
Born: Salisbury, Wiltshire, England, 28 July, 1970 — CD
England: Youth/Schools

League Club	Source	Date Signed	Seasons Played	Apps	Subs	Gls
Doncaster Rov	Jnr	06/88	87-88	52	0	4
West Bromwich A	Tr	03/89	88-99	249	10	15
Doncaster Rov	L	11/91	91	7	0	0
Rotherham U	L	10/98	98	11	0	2
Grimsby T	Tr	07/00	00-02	21	10	0
Carlisle U	Tr	02/03	02-03	24	0	1

RAVENHILL Richard John (Ricky)
Born: Doncaster, South Yorkshire, England, 16 January, 1981 — M

League Club	Source	Date Signed	Seasons Played	Apps	Subs	Gls
Barnsley	YT	06/99				
Doncaster Rov	Tr	01/02	03-05	58	40	9
Chester C	L	07/06	06	1	2	0
Grimsby T	Tr	08/06	06	15	2	2
Darlington	Tr	01/07	06-08	75	13	6
Notts Co	Tr	05/09	09-11	76	3	3
Bradford C	Tr	11/11	11-13	50	6	2
Northampton T	L	11/13	13	6	0	0
Northampton T	Tr	01/14	13-14	27	4	0
Mansfield T	Tr	01/15	14	12	1	0

RAVENSCROFT Craig Anthony
Born: Hammersmith, W London, England, 20 December, 1974 — F

League Club	Source	Date Signed	Seasons Played	Apps	Subs	Gls
Brentford	YT	07/93	93-95	6	3	1

RAWCLIFFE Frank
Born: Blackburn, Greater Manchester, England, 16 December, 1921 — CF
Died: Blackburn, Greater Manchester, England, 21 December, 1986

League Club	Source	Date Signed	Seasons Played	Apps	Subs	Gls
Tranmere Rov	Jnr	12/38				
Wolverhampton W	Tr	01/39				
Notts Co	Colchester U	02/43				
Newport Co	Tr	06/46	46	37	-	14
Swansea C	Tr	05/47	47	25	-	16
Aldershot	Tr	07/48	48	35	-	14

RAWCLIFFE Peter
Born: Cleethorpes, North Lincolnshire, England, 8 December, 1963 — F

League Club	Source	Date Signed	Seasons Played	Apps	Subs	Gls
Grimsby T	Louth U	09/86	86-87	9	13	2
Lincoln C	Holbeach U	08/90	90	0	1	0

RAWES Herbert
Born: Frizington, Cumbria, England, 23 November, 1932 — RW
Died: Farnborough, Hampshire, England, 21 January, 2010

League Club	Source	Date Signed	Seasons Played	Apps	Subs	Gls
Carlisle U		09/53	53-54	10	-	1

RAWLE Mark Anthony
Born: Leicester, England, 27 April, 1979 — F

League Club	Source	Date Signed	Seasons Played	Apps	Subs	Gls
Southend U	Boston U	02/01	00-02	69	9	15
Oxford U	Tr	07/03	03-04	10	27	8
Kidderminster Hrs	Tr	02/05	04	5	6	3

RAWLINGS Charles John (Charlie)
Born: Coleshill, Warwickshire, England, 4 November, 1932 — LH
Died: 28 September, 2014

League Club	Source	Date Signed	Seasons Played	Apps	Subs	Gls
West Bromwich A	Erdington A	03/50				
Walsall	Tr	06/56	56-62	200	-	5
Port Vale	Tr	07/63	63-64	31	-	2

RAWLINGS James Sydney Dean (Syd)
Born: Wombwell, South Yorkshire, England, 5 May, 1913 — RW
Died: Penarth, Vale of Glamorgan, Wales, 10 July, 1956

League Club	Source	Date Signed	Seasons Played	Apps	Subs	Gls
Preston NE	Dick Kerr's XI	03/32	33	12	-	0
Huddersfield T	Tr	03/34	33-34	11	-	2
West Bromwich A	Tr	03/35	34-35	10	-	1
Northampton T	Tr	06/36	36-37	48	-	18
Millwall	Tr	12/37	37-38	53	-	27
Everton	Tr	11/45				
Plymouth Arg	Tr	05/46	46-47	56	-	20

RAWLINGSON John Anderson
Born: Wallsend, Tyne and Wear, England, 7 April, 1944 — CH
Died: Newcastle-upon-Tyne, England, 14 March, 2006

League Club	Source	Date Signed	Seasons Played	Apps	Subs	Gls
Bury	Corinthian Jnrs	07/62	64	2	-	0
Barrow	Tr	07/65	65	19	0	2

RAWLINS David
Born: Llay, Wrexham, Wales, 12 December, 1943 — LW

League Club	Source	Date Signed	Seasons Played	Apps	Subs	Gls
Wrexham (Am)		11/65	65	1	0	0

RAWLINSON Mark David
Born: Bolton, Greater Manchester, England, 9 June, 1975 — M

League Club	Source	Date Signed	Seasons Played	Apps	Subs	Gls
Manchester U	YT	07/93				

League Club	Source	Date Signed	Seasons Played	Apps	Subs	Gls
Bournemouth	Tr	07/95	95-99	48	31	2
Exeter C	Tr	07/00	00	18	7	2

RAWSON Colin
Born: Shirebrook, Derbyshire, England, 12 November, 1926 LH
Died: Sutton in Ashfield, Nottinghamshire, England, April, 2009

League Club	Source	Date Signed	Seasons Played	Apps	Subs	Gls
Nottingham F	Welbeck Colliery	09/44	46	1	-	0
Rotherham U	Peterborough U	07/48	49-52	113	-	12
Sheffield U	Tr	03/53	53-55	70	-	1
Millwall	Tr	10/55	55-58	159	-	5
Torquay U	Tr	07/59	59-61	86	-	2

RAWSON Farrend James
Born: Nottingham, England, 11 July, 1996 CD

League Club	Source	Date Signed	Seasons Played	Apps	Subs	Gls
Derby Co	Sch	07/14				
Rotherham U	L	03/15	14	4	0	0

RAWSON John Kenneth (Ken)
Born: Nottingham, England, 31 March, 1921 CH
Died: Nottingham, England, 30 March, 2005

League Club	Source	Date Signed	Seasons Played	Apps	Subs	Gls
Nottingham F	Daybrook U	12/46	47-49	6	-	0

RAWSON Kenneth (Ken)
Born: Ripley, Derbyshire, England, 18 September, 1931 CH
Died: Belper, Derbyshire, England, June, 1986

League Club	Source	Date Signed	Seasons Played	Apps	Subs	Gls
Notts Co	Ripley	05/53	54-60	34	-	0

RAY Cecil Holmes
Born: West Grinstead, West Sussex, England, 25 October, 1911 CF
Died: Haywards Heath, West Sussex, England, October, 1995

League Club	Source	Date Signed	Seasons Played	Apps	Subs	Gls
Aldershot	Lewes U	01/36	35-46	89	-	39

RAY George Edward
Born: Warrington, Cheshire, England, 13 October, 1993 CD
Wales: U21-5

League Club	Source	Date Signed	Seasons Played	Apps	Subs	Gls
Crewe Alex	Sch	07/11	12-14	42	6	2

RAY John Dennis (Johnny)
Born: Wolverhampton, England, 7 November, 1946 WH

League Club	Source	Date Signed	Seasons Played	Apps	Subs	Gls
Shrewsbury T	Brereton Social	01/65	65	7	0	0

RAY John Walter
Born: Newmarket, Suffolk, England, 21 November, 1968 CD

League Club	Source	Date Signed	Seasons Played	Apps	Subs	Gls
Colchester U	YT	10/87	87	0	1	0

RAY Philip (Phil)
Born: Wallsend, Tyne and Wear, England, 21 November, 1964 RB

League Club	Source	Date Signed	Seasons Played	Apps	Subs	Gls
Burnley	App	11/82	82	1	0	0
Hartlepool U	L	10/83	83	5	0	1

RAYA David
Born: Barcelona, Spain, 15 September, 1995 G

League Club	Source	Date Signed	Seasons Played	Apps	Subs	Gls
Blackburn Rov	Sch	02/14	14	2	0	0

RAYBOULD Eric
Born: Manchester, England, 8 December, 1940 WH

League Club	Source	Date Signed	Seasons Played	Apps	Subs	Gls
Chester C		07/60	60-61	10	-	0

RAYBOULD Philip Edward (Phil)
Born: Caerphilly, Wales, 26 May, 1948 M
Wales: Amateur/Schools

League Club	Source	Date Signed	Seasons Played	Apps	Subs	Gls
Swansea C	Bridgend T	07/67	67-68	9	1	4
Newport Co	Tr	09/69	69	5	1	1

RAYMENT Joseph Watson (Joe)
Born: Hartlepool, Cleveland, England, 25 September, 1934 RW

League Club	Source	Date Signed	Seasons Played	Apps	Subs	Gls
Middlesbrough	Jnr	10/51	52-54	24	-	4
Hartlepool U	Tr	07/55	55-57	63	-	17
Darlington	Tr	07/58	58-64	173	-	31

RAYMENT Patrick John (Pat)
Born: Peterborough, England, 11 April, 1965 FB/M

League Club	Source	Date Signed	Seasons Played	Apps	Subs	Gls
Peterborough U	App	04/83	81-84	24	6	3
Cambridge U	Tr	10/84	84-86	42	6	2

RAYMOND Francis John (Frankie)
Born: Chislehurst, SE London, England, 18 November, 1992 M

League Club	Source	Date Signed	Seasons Played	Apps	Subs	Gls
Reading	Sch	07/10				
Dagenham & Red	Eastbourne Bor	07/14	14	2	0	1

RAYNER Albert Edward (Edward)
Born: Salford, England, 13 August, 1932 RH

League Club	Source	Date Signed	Seasons Played	Apps	Subs	Gls
Stoke C	Northwich Victoria	05/55	56-59	4	-	0

RAYNER Edward (Ted)
Born: Hemsworth, West Yorkshire, England, 28 September, 1916 G
Died: Halifax, West Yorkshire, England, April, 1988

League Club	Source	Date Signed	Seasons Played	Apps	Subs	Gls
Halifax T	Scarborough	10/40	46-50	137	-	0

RAYNER James Patrick (Jim)
Born: Cornsay, County Durham, England, 31 March, 1935 RH
Died: County Durham, England, 5 January, 2009

League Club	Source	Date Signed	Seasons Played	Apps	Subs	Gls
Grimsby T	Langley Park Jnrs	05/52	52-53	12	-	3
Bury	Tr	05/54				
Hartlepool U	Tr	11/54				
Bury	Tr	06/55				
Barrow	Tr	09/55	55	11	-	1
Peterborough U	Grantham	07/58	60-62	119	-	12
Notts Co	Grantham	09/64	64	32	-	13

RAYNER Simon Christopher
Born: Vancouver, Canada, 8 July, 1983 G
Canada: U23-2

League Club	Source	Date Signed	Seasons Played	Apps	Subs	Gls
Bournemouth	Jnr	08/01				
Lincoln C	Port Talbot T	08/04	04-05	4	0	0
Torquay U	L	03/07	06	10	0	0

RAYNER Warren Anthony
Born: Bradford, England, 24 April, 1957 RW

League Club	Source	Date Signed	Seasons Played	Apps	Subs	Gls
Bradford C	App	04/75	74-76	13	4	0

RAYNES John
Born: Sheffield, England, 4 November, 1928 LW
Died: Sheffield, England, December, 1995

League Club	Source	Date Signed	Seasons Played	Apps	Subs	Gls
Sheffield U	Jnr	11/45				
Rotherham U		03/49	49	5	-	1
Northampton T	Worksop T	07/51				

RAYNES Michael Bernard
Born: Wythenshawe, Greater Manchester, England, 15 October, 1987 CD

League Club	Source	Date Signed	Seasons Played	Apps	Subs	Gls
Stockport Co	Sch	03/05	04-09	123	17	5
Scunthorpe U	Tr	02/10	09-10	27	7	0
Rotherham U	Tr	08/11	11	31	2	0
Oxford U	Tr	07/12	12-14	64	5	1
Mansfield T	Tr	01/15	14	10	0	0

RAYNES William Arnold (Willie)
Born: Sheffield, England, 30 October, 1964 LW

League Club	Source	Date Signed	Seasons Played	Apps	Subs	Gls
Rotherham U	Heanor T	09/83	83-84	17	3	2
Stockport Co	L	01/85	84	2	0	0
Wolverhampton W	Tr	12/85	85	6	1	0

RAYNOR Paul Edward
Born: Chester, England, 3 September, 1957 FB

League Club	Source	Date Signed	Seasons Played	Apps	Subs	Gls
Chester C	App	09/75	76-81	196	1	9
Chester C	Oswestry T	08/83	83	3	0	0

RAYNOR Paul James
Born: Nottingham, England, 29 April, 1966 M

League Club	Source	Date Signed	Seasons Played	Apps	Subs	Gls
Nottingham F	App	04/84	84	3	0	0
Bristol Rov	L	03/85	84	7	1	0
Huddersfield T	Tr	08/85	85-86	38	12	9
Swansea C	Tr	03/87	86-91	170	21	27
Wrexham	L	10/88	88	6	0	0
Cambridge U	Tr	03/92	91-92	46	3	2
Preston NE	Tr	07/93	93-95	72	8	9
Cambridge U	Tr	09/95	95-96	78	1	7
Leyton Orient	Guang Deong (CHN)	02/98	97-98	6	9	0

RAYNOR Robert
Born: Nottingham, England, 30 August, 1940 G
Died: Nottingham, England, 7 March, 2007

League Club	Source	Date Signed	Seasons Played	Apps	Subs	Gls
Nottingham F		05/64				
Halifax T	Tr	08/65	65-66	17	0	0

RAZAK Abdul
Born: Bouake, Ivory Coast, 11 November, 1992 M
Ivory Coast: 5

League Club	Source	Date Signed	Seasons Played	Apps	Subs	Gls
Manchester C	Sch	01/11	10-12	0	5	0
Portsmouth	L	10/11	11	1	2	0
Brighton & HA	L	02/12	11	4	2	0
Charlton Ath	L	09/12	12	2	0	0
West Ham U	Anzhi Makhachk'a (RUS)	01/14				
Doncaster Rov	OFI Crete (GRE)	01/15	14	5	4	0

RAZAK Hamdi
Born: Paris, France, 8 October, 1985 F

League Club	Source	Date Signed	Seasons Played	Apps	Subs	Gls
Swindon T	FC Igny (FRA)	01/09	08	0	3	0

REA Kenneth Wilfred (Ken)
Born: Liverpool, England, 17 February, 1935 WH
Died: Liverpool, England, 10 April, 2014

League Club	Source	Date Signed	Seasons Played	Apps	Subs	Gls
Everton	Jnr	06/52	56-58	46	-	0

REA Simon
Born: Kenilworth, Warwickshire, England, 20 September, 1976 CD

League Club	Source	Date Signed	Seasons Played	Apps	Subs	Gls
Birmingham C	YT	01/95	95	0	1	0
Peterborough U	Tr	08/99	99-04	146	13	8
Cambridge U	L	01/05	04	4	0	0

REA Wallace
Born: Uddingston, Glasgow, Scotland, 21 June, 1935 W

Died: Bradford, England, May, 1998

League Club	Source	Date Signed	Seasons Played	Apps	Subs	Gls
Bradford C	Motherwell	07/59	59	11	-	2

REACH Adam Michael
Born: Chester-le-Street, County Durham, England, 3 February, 1993 — LM
England: Youth

League Club	Source	Date Signed	Seasons Played	Apps	Subs	Gls
Middlesbrough	Sch	07/11	10-14	37	22	5
Shrewsbury T	L	08/13	13	17	5	3
Bradford C	L	01/14	13	18	0	3

READ David Peter (Dave)
Born: Stafford, England, 15 January, 1941 — RW

League Club	Source	Date Signed	Seasons Played	Apps	Subs	Gls
Wolverhampton W	Jnr	10/58				
Chester C	Tr	10/62	62-66	68	4	6

READ John Anthony (Tony)
Born: Haydock, Merseyside, England, 5 July, 1942 — G/F

League Club	Source	Date Signed	Seasons Played	Apps	Subs	Gls
Sheffield Wed	Wolverhampton W (Am)	01/60				
Peterborough U	Tr	05/64	64	2	-	0
Luton T	Tr	03/65	65-71	195	4	12

READ Paul Colin
Born: Harlow, Essex, England, 25 September, 1973 — F
England: Schools

League Club	Source	Date Signed	Seasons Played	Apps	Subs	Gls
Arsenal	YT	10/91				
Leyton Orient	L	03/95	94	11	0	0
Southend U	L	10/95	95	3	1	1
Wycombe W	Tr	01/97	96-98	32	25	9
Luton T	OFK Ostersund (SWE)	12/99				
Exeter C	OFK Ostersund (SWE)	11/00	00-01	13	13	1

READER Peter Edward
Born: East Ham, E London, England, 8 March, 1941 — G
England: Youth

League Club	Source	Date Signed	Seasons Played	Apps	Subs	Gls
West Ham U	Jnr	06/59				
Millwall	Tr	06/61	61	1	-	0

READFERN Thomas Edward (Edward)
Born: Crook, County Durham, England, 9 July, 1944 — CF

League Club	Source	Date Signed	Seasons Played	Apps	Subs	Gls
West Bromwich A	Langley Park Jnrs	08/61	63	4	-	0

READY Karl
Born: Neath, Wales, 14 August, 1972 — D
Wales: 5/B-2/U21-5/Schools

League Club	Source	Date Signed	Seasons Played	Apps	Subs	Gls
Queens Park Rgrs	YT	08/90	91-00	206	20	10

REAGAN Charles Martin (Martin)
Born: Newcastle-on-Tyne, England, 12 May, 1924 — W

League Club	Source	Date Signed	Seasons Played	Apps	Subs	Gls
York C	Jnr	09/46	46	1	-	0
Hull C	Tr	04/47	46-47	18	-	1
Middlesbrough	Tr	02/48	47-50	24	-	4
Shrewsbury T	Tr	08/51	51-52	58	-	9
Portsmouth	Tr	01/53	52	5	-	0
Norwich C	Tr	06/54	54-55	34	-	4

REAM Timothy Michael (Tim)
Born: St Louis, Missouri, USA, 5 October, 1987 — CD
USA: 15

League Club	Source	Date Signed	Seasons Played	Apps	Subs	Gls
Bolton W	New York R Bulls (USA)	01/12	11-14	110	4	0

REANEY Paul
Born: Fulham, W London, England, 22 October, 1944 — RB
England: 3/FLge-3/U23-5

League Club	Source	Date Signed	Seasons Played	Apps	Subs	Gls
Leeds U	Jnr	10/61	62-77	549	7	6
Bradford C	Tr	06/78	78-79	37	1	0

REAY Edwin Peel (Ted)
Born: Tynemouth, Tyne and Wear, England, 5 August, 1914 — LB
Died: Australia, 1992

League Club	Source	Date Signed	Seasons Played	Apps	Subs	Gls
Sheffield U	North Shields	03/37				
Queens Park Rgrs	Tr	06/37	37-49	34	-	0

REAY Shaun
Born: Boldon, Tyne and Wear, England, 20 May, 1989 — F

League Club	Source	Date Signed	Seasons Played	Apps	Subs	Gls
Darlington	Sch	10/06	06-07	1	3	0

REBROV Sergei Stanislavovych
Born: Horlivka, Ukraine, 3 June, 1974 — F
Ukraine: 75/U21-17

League Club	Source	Date Signed	Seasons Played	Apps	Subs	Gls
Tottenham H	Dynamo Kiev (UKR)	06/00	00-01	37	22	10
West Ham U	Tr	08/04	04	12	14	1

RECK Sean Mark
Born: Oxford, England, 5 May, 1967 — M

League Club	Source	Date Signed	Seasons Played	Apps	Subs	Gls
Oxford U	App	04/85	86-88	11	3	0
Newport Co	L	08/85	85	15	0	0
Reading	L	03/86	85	1	0	0
Wrexham	Tr	07/89	89-90	41	4	2

RECKORD Jamie Vincent Junior
Born: Wolverhampton, England, 9 March, 1992 — LB
England: Youth

League Club	Source	Date Signed	Seasons Played	Apps	Subs	Gls
Wolverhampton W	Sch	07/10				
Northampton T	L	03/11	10	4	3	0
Scunthorpe U	L	01/12	11	17	0	0
Coventry C	L	09/12	12	7	2	0
Plymouth Arg	L	09/13	13	11	1	0
Swindon T	L	01/14	13	3	2	0

REDAN Iwan Benito Marvin
Born: Rotterdam, Netherlands, 21 August, 1980 — F

League Club	Source	Date Signed	Seasons Played	Apps	Subs	Gls
Cardiff C (L)	Willem II (NED)	01/07	06	0	2	0

REDDIE Thomas McGregor (Tom)
Born: Grangemouth, Falkirk, Scotland, 5 October, 1926 — D

League Club	Source	Date Signed	Seasons Played	Apps	Subs	Gls
Aldershot	Falkirk	07/51	51-56	96	-	1

REDDING Thomas Richard (Tom)
Born: Grimsby, North Lincolnshire, England, 17 March, 1932 — D
Died: Grimsby, North Lincolnshire, England, 1980

League Club	Source	Date Signed	Seasons Played	Apps	Subs	Gls
Grimsby T	Brigg T	07/54	54-56	4	-	0

REDDINGTON Stuart
Born: Lincoln, England, 21 February, 1978 — CD

League Club	Source	Date Signed	Seasons Played	Apps	Subs	Gls
Chelsea	Lincoln U	08/99				
Mansfield T	Tr	03/01	00-02	48	6	1

REDDISH Shane
Born: Bolsover, Derbyshire, England, 5 May, 1971 — M/FB

League Club	Source	Date Signed	Seasons Played	Apps	Subs	Gls
Mansfield T	YT	07/89				
Doncaster Rov	Tr	02/90	89-92	51	9	3
Carlisle U	Tr	07/93	93-94	35	2	1
Chesterfield	L	09/94	94	2	1	0
Hartlepool U	Tr	11/94	94-95	41	2	0

REDDY Michael
Born: Kilkenny, Republic of Ireland, 24 March, 1980 — F
Republic of Ireland: U21-8/Youth

League Club	Source	Date Signed	Seasons Played	Apps	Subs	Gls
Sunderland	Kilkenny C (ROI)	08/99	99-00	0	10	1
Swindon T	L	01/01	00	17	1	4
Hull C	L	09/01	01	1	4	4
York C	L	11/02	02	10	1	2
Sheffield Wed	L	01/03	02	13	2	3
Sheffield Wed	L	10/03	03	9	3	1
Grimsby T	Tr	08/04	04-06	70	24	22

REDFEARN Brian
Born: Bradford, England, 20 February, 1935 — LW

League Club	Source	Date Signed	Seasons Played	Apps	Subs	Gls
Bradford Park Ave	Jnr	08/52	52-57	130	-	32
Blackburn Rov	Tr	12/57				
Darlington	Tr	06/59	59-60	48	-	16
Halifax T	Tr	06/61	61-62	67	-	9
Bradford C	Tr	07/63	63	7	-	2

REDFEARN Neil David
Born: Dewsbury, West Yorkshire, England, 20 June, 1965 — M

League Club	Source	Date Signed	Seasons Played	Apps	Subs	Gls
Bolton W	Nottingham F (YT)	06/82	82-83	35	0	1
Lincoln C	Tr	03/84	83-85	96	4	13
Doncaster Rov	Tr	08/86	86	46	0	14
Crystal Palace	Tr	07/87	87-88	57	0	10
Watford	Tr	11/88	88-89	22	2	3
Oldham Ath	Tr	01/90	89-90	56	6	16
Barnsley	Tr	09/91	91-97	289	3	71
Charlton Ath	Tr	07/98	98	29	1	3
Bradford C	Tr	08/99	99	14	3	1
Wigan Ath	Tr	03/00	99-00	18	4	7
Halifax T	Tr	03/01	00-01	39	3	6
Boston U	Tr	08/02	02-03	46	8	12
Rochdale	Tr	03/04	03	9	0	0

REDFERN David
Born: Sheffield, England, 8 November, 1962 — G

League Club	Source	Date Signed	Seasons Played	Apps	Subs	Gls
Sheffield Wed	Jnr	06/81				
Rochdale	Tr	03/85	84-86	87	0	0
Wigan Ath	L	10/87	87	3	0	0
Stockport Co	Gainsborough Trinity	07/89	89-92	48	0	0

REDFERN Edward (Ted)
Born: Liverpool, England, 20 June, 1924 — RW/WH
Died: Birkenhead, Wirral, England, 14 April, 1994

League Club	Source	Date Signed	Seasons Played	Apps	Subs	Gls
New Brighton	Unity BC	01/48	47-49	22	-	0

REDFERN Frederick (Fred)
Born: Hyde, Greater Manchester, England, 28 September, 1914 — RB
Died: Tameside, Greater Manchester, England, July, 1989

League Club	Source	Date Signed	Seasons Played	Apps	Subs	Gls
Stockport Co	Hyde U	08/45	46-47	36	-	0

REDFERN James (Jimmy)
Born: Kirkby, Merseyside, England, 1 August, 1952 RW

League Club	Source	Date Signed	Seasons Played	Apps	Subs	Gls
Bolton W	App	08/69	69-72	19	5	2
Chester C	Tr	08/73	73-76	98	8	15

REDFERN Robert (Bob)
Born: Crook, County Durham, England, 3 March, 1918 RW
Died: Bournemouth, England, 3 July, 2002

League Club	Source	Date Signed	Seasons Played	Apps	Subs	Gls
Wolverhampton W	Tow Law T	05/36				
Bournemouth	Cradley Heath	02/37	36-46	89	-	4
Brighton & HA	Tr	08/47	47	5	-	1

REDFORD Ian Petrie
Born: Perth, Scotland, 5 April, 1960 M
Died: Irvine, Ayrshire, Scotland, 10 January, 2014
Scotland: U21-6/Youth

League Club	Source	Date Signed	Seasons Played	Apps	Subs	Gls
Ipswich T	Dundee U	11/88	88-90	59	9	8

REDHEAD William Sylvester (Bill)
Born: Newcastle-upon-Tyne, England, 10 October, 1935 WH
Died: Gosforth, Tyne and Wear, England, 15 September, 2000

League Club	Source	Date Signed	Seasons Played	Apps	Subs	Gls
Newcastle U	George Angus	08/54	56	1	-	0
Gateshead	Tr	08/59	59	20	-	0

REDKNAPP Henry James (Harry)
Born: Poplar, E London, England, 2 March, 1947 RW
England: Youth

League Club	Source	Date Signed	Seasons Played	Apps	Subs	Gls
West Ham U	App	03/64	65-71	146	3	7
Bournemouth	Tr	08/72	72-75	96	5	5
Brentford	Tr	09/76	76	1	0	0
Bournemouth	Rtd	09/82	82	1	0	0

REDKNAPP Jamie Frank
Born: Barton-on-Sea, Hampshire, England, 25 June, 1973 M
England: 17/B-1/U21-19/Youth/Schools

League Club	Source	Date Signed	Seasons Played	Apps	Subs	Gls
Bournemouth	YT	06/90	89-90	6	7	0
Liverpool	Tr	01/91	91-01	207	30	30
Tottenham H	Tr	04/02	02-04	37	11	4
Southampton	Tr	01/05	04	16	0	0

REDMAN William (Bill)
Born: Manchester, England, 29 January, 1928 LB
Died: Manchester, England, December, 1994

League Club	Source	Date Signed	Seasons Played	Apps	Subs	Gls
Manchester U	Jnr	11/46	50-53	36	-	0
Bury	Tr	06/54	54-55	37	-	1

REDMILE Matthew Ian (Matt)
Born: Nottingham, England, 12 November, 1976 CD
England: Semi Pro-3

League Club	Source	Date Signed	Seasons Played	Apps	Subs	Gls
Notts Co	YT	07/95	96-00	140	7	7
Shrewsbury T	Tr	11/00	00-02	107	0	6

REDMOND Daniel Nathan Jerome (Nathan)
Born: Birmingham, England, 6 March, 1994 W
England: U21-22/Youth

League Club	Source	Date Signed	Seasons Played	Apps	Subs	Gls
Birmingham C	Sch	07/11	11-12	27	35	7
Norwich C	Tr	07/13	13-14	56	21	5

REDMOND Daniel Stephen
Born: Liverpool, England, 2 March, 1991 M

League Club	Source	Date Signed	Seasons Played	Apps	Subs	Gls
Wigan Ath	Everton (Sch)	07/09				
Carlisle U	L	02/14	13	12	3	0

REDMOND Harold (Harry)
Born: Manchester, England, 24 March, 1933 RB
Died: Swansea, Wales, 21 September, 1985

League Club	Source	Date Signed	Seasons Played	Apps	Subs	Gls
Crystal Palace	Tavistock	04/57	57	2	-	0
Millwall	Tr	05/58	58-60	54	-	0

REDMOND Shane Patrick
Born: Dublin, Republic of Ireland, 23 March, 1989 G
Republic of Ireland: U21-13/Youth

League Club	Source	Date Signed	Seasons Played	Apps	Subs	Gls
Nottingham F	Sch	05/06				
Burton A	L	07/09	09	3	0	0
Darlington	L	01/10	09	19	0	0
Chesterfield	Tr	08/10				

REDMOND Stephen (Steve)
Born: Liverpool, England, 2 November, 1967 CD
England: U21-14/Youth

League Club	Source	Date Signed	Seasons Played	Apps	Subs	Gls
Manchester C	App	12/84	85-91	231	4	7
Oldham Ath	Tr	07/92	92-97	195	10	4
Bury	Tr	07/98	98-02	145	6	6

REDROBE William Eric (Eric)
Born: Wigan, Greater Manchester, England, 23 August, 1944 F
England: Youth

League Club	Source	Date Signed	Seasons Played	Apps	Subs	Gls
Bolton W	Jnr	02/62	63-65	4	0	1
Southport	Tr	08/66	66-72	186	6	55
Hereford U	Tr	10/72	72-75	75	11	17
Hereford U	Bath C	01/78	77	0	1	0

REDSHAW Jack
Born: Salford, England, 20 November, 1990 F

League Club	Source	Date Signed	Seasons Played	Apps	Subs	Gls
Manchester C	Sch	07/09				
Rochdale	Tr	07/10	10	0	2	0
Morecambe	Altrincham	01/12	11-14	74	46	36

REDSHAW Raymond (Ray)
Born: Salford, England, 23 December, 1958 F

League Club	Source	Date Signed	Seasons Played	Apps	Subs	Gls
Wigan Ath	Horwich RMI	07/84	84	2	2	0

REDWOOD Barry Keith
Born: Torquay, Devon, England, 11 September, 1946 CF

League Club	Source	Date Signed	Seasons Played	Apps	Subs	Gls
Exeter C	App	09/64	64	1	-	0

REDWOOD Toby Richard Barry
Born: Newton Abbot, Devon, England, 7 October, 1973 LB

League Club	Source	Date Signed	Seasons Played	Apps	Subs	Gls
Exeter C	YT	06/92	91-93	15	5	0

REECE Andrew John (Andy)
Born: Shrewsbury, Shropshire, England, 5 September, 1962 M

League Club	Source	Date Signed	Seasons Played	Apps	Subs	Gls
Bristol Rov	Dudley T	08/87	87-92	230	9	17
Walsall	L	11/92	92	9	0	1
Walsall	L	08/93	93	6	0	0
Hereford U	Tr	11/93	93-95	69	2	5

REECE Charles Thomas (Charlie)
Born: Birmingham, England, 8 September, 1988 M

League Club	Source	Date Signed	Seasons Played	Apps	Subs	Gls
Bristol Rov	Jnr	06/07	07-10	12	18	0

REECE Gilbert Ivor (Gil)
Born: Cardiff, Wales, 2 July, 1942 LW
Died: Cardiff, Wales, 20 December, 2003
Wales: 29/Schools

League Club	Source	Date Signed	Seasons Played	Apps	Subs	Gls
Cardiff C	Jnr	05/61				
Newport Co	Pembroke Bor	06/63	63-64	32	-	9
Sheffield U	Tr	04/65	65-72	197	14	59
Cardiff C	Tr	09/72	72-75	94	6	23
Swansea C	Tr	07/76	76	0	2	0

REECE Paul John
Born: Nottingham, England, 16 July, 1968 G

League Club	Source	Date Signed	Seasons Played	Apps	Subs	Gls
Stoke C	App	07/86	86	2	0	0
Grimsby T	Kettering T	07/88	88-91	54	0	0
Doncaster Rov	Kettering T	09/92	92	1	0	0
Oxford U	Tr	10/92	92-93	39	0	0
Notts Co	Tr	08/94	94	11	0	0
West Bromwich A	Tr	08/95	95	1	0	0

REECE Thomas Samuel (Tom)
Born: Wolverhampton, England, 17 May, 1919 LH
Died: Wolverhampton, England, May, 1990

League Club	Source	Date Signed	Seasons Played	Apps	Subs	Gls
Wolverhampton W		07/37				
Crystal Palace	Tr	09/38	38-47	76	-	5

REED Adam Maurice
Born: Bishop Auckland, County Durham, England, 18 February, 1975 M/D

League Club	Source	Date Signed	Seasons Played	Apps	Subs	Gls
Darlington	YT	07/93	91-94	45	7	1
Blackburn Rov	Tr	08/95				
Darlington	L	02/97	96	14	0	0
Rochdale	L	12/97	97	10	0	0
Darlington	Tr	07/98	98-02	80	14	2

REED Adam Michael
Born: Hartlepool, Cleveland, England, 8 May, 1991 M

League Club	Source	Date Signed	Seasons Played	Apps	Subs	Gls
Sunderland	Sch	07/09				
Brentford	L	02/11	10	8	3	0
Bradford C	L	09/11	11	4	0	0
Leyton Orient	L	03/12	11	10	1	0
Portsmouth	L	01/13	12	5	5	0
York C	L	03/13	12	6	0	2
Burton A	Tr	06/13	13	4	2	1
York C	Tr	01/14	13	17	2	0

REED Barry Reginald Frank
Born: Peterborough, England, 24 November, 1937 FB

League Club	Source	Date Signed	Seasons Played	Apps	Subs	Gls
Leicester C	St Neots	03/55				
Luton T	Tr	05/61	61	1	-	0

REED Frank Nicholas
Born: Seaham, County Durham, England, 12 October, 1933 G
Died: Tonbridge, Kent, England, 6 August, 1975

League Club	Source	Date Signed	Seasons Played	Apps	Subs	Gls
Charlton Ath	Murton CW	08/54	55-62	29	-	0

REED George
Born: Normanton, West Yorkshire, England, 16 July, 1938 CH

League Club	Source	Date Signed	Seasons Played	Apps	Subs	Gls
Halifax T	Swillington	08/61	62	2	-	0

REED Graham
Born: Doncaster, South Yorkshire, England, 24 June, 1961 RB

League Club	Source	Date Signed	Seasons Played	Apps	Subs	Gls
Barnsley	App	06/79	78-79	3	0	0
Northampton T	Frickley Ath	06/85	85-88	105	7	2

REED Graham Albert William
Born: King's Lynn, Norfolk, England, 6 February, 1938 — WH

League Club	Source	Date Signed	Seasons Played	Apps	Subs	Gls
Sunderland	King's Lynn	02/55	57	5	-	0

REED Harrison James (Harry)
Born: Worthing, West Sussex, England, 27 January, 1995 — M
England: Youth

League Club	Source	Date Signed	Seasons Played	Apps	Subs	Gls
Southampton	Sch	08/13	13-14	5	8	0

REED Hugh Dennett
Born: Dumbarton, Dunbartonshire, Scotland, 23 August, 1950 — RW
Died: Crewe, Cheshire, England, November, 1992

League Club	Source	Date Signed	Seasons Played	Apps	Subs	Gls
West Bromwich A	Jnr	08/67	68-70	5	3	2
Plymouth Arg	Tr	11/71	71-73	44	12	9
Brentford	L	10/73	73	3	1	0
Crewe Alex	Tr	07/74	74-75	38	9	9
Hartlepool U	Huddersfield T (NC)	10/76	76	6	0	1

REED Ian Paul
Born: Lichfield, Staffordshire, England, 4 September, 1975 — M

League Club	Source	Date Signed	Seasons Played	Apps	Subs	Gls
Shrewsbury T	YT	07/94	94-96	10	8	2

REED Jake
Born: Great Yarmouth, Norfolk, England, 13 May, 1991 — F

League Club	Source	Date Signed	Seasons Played	Apps	Subs	Gls
Dagenham & Red	Great Yarmouth T	07/11	11-13	13	18	1

REED Jamie Lee
Born: Deeside, Flintshire, Wales, 13 August, 1987 — F

League Club	Source	Date Signed	Seasons Played	Apps	Subs	Gls
Wrexham	Sch	07/05	05-06	0	7	0
York C	Bangor C	01/11	12	4	13	1

REED John Paul
Born: Rotherham, South Yorkshire, England, 27 August, 1972 — W

League Club	Source	Date Signed	Seasons Played	Apps	Subs	Gls
Sheffield U	YT	07/90	91-95	11	4	2
Scarborough	L	01/91	90	14	0	5
Scarborough	L	09/91	91	5	1	0
Darlington	L	03/93	92	8	2	2
Mansfield T	L	09/93	93	12	1	2
Blackpool	Tr	07/97	97	0	3	0

REED Kevin David
Born: Leicester, England, 22 September, 1960 — W

League Club	Source	Date Signed	Seasons Played	Apps	Subs	Gls
Leicester C	App	05/78	78	0	1	0

REED Louis Samuel
Born: Barnsley, South Yorkshire, England, 25 July, 1997 — M
England: Youth

League Club	Source	Date Signed	Seasons Played	Apps	Subs	Gls
Sheffield U	Sch	08/14	13-14	10	10	0

REED Martin John
Born: Scarborough, North Yorkshire, England, 10 January, 1978 — CD

League Club	Source	Date Signed	Seasons Played	Apps	Subs	Gls
York C	YT	07/96	96-00	39	7	0

REED Matthew James (Matt)
Born: Dartford, Kent, England, 24 December, 1986 — G

League Club	Source	Date Signed	Seasons Played	Apps	Subs	Gls
West Ham U	Sch	07/05				
Barnet	L	01/06	05	4	0	0

REED Stephen Eric (Steve)
Born: Doncaster, South Yorkshire, England, 6 January, 1956 — D

League Club	Source	Date Signed	Seasons Played	Apps	Subs	Gls
Doncaster Rov	App	01/74	72-78	137	3	2

REED Steven Leslie (Steve)
Born: Barnstaple, Devon, England, 18 June, 1985 — LB/M

League Club	Source	Date Signed	Seasons Played	Apps	Subs	Gls
Yeovil T	Jnr	09/02	03-04	4	4	0
Torquay U	Tr	03/06	05-06	21	5	0
Macclesfield T	Weymouth	07/09				

REED Thomas Roland (Ron)
Born: Haltwhistle, Northumberland, England, 4 October, 1934 — WH
Died: Manchester, England, October, 1998

League Club	Source	Date Signed	Seasons Played	Apps	Subs	Gls
Newport Co	Newport Barracks	01/54	53-54	2	-	0

REED William George (Billy)
Born: Ynyshir, Rhondda Cynon Taff, Wales, 25 January, 1928 — RW
Died: Swansea, Wales, January, 2003
Wales: 2/Amateur/Schools

League Club	Source	Date Signed	Seasons Played	Apps	Subs	Gls
Cardiff C	Rhondda Transport	07/47				
Brighton & HA	Tr	08/48	48-52	129	-	36
Ipswich T	Tr	07/53	53-57	155	-	43
Swansea C	Tr	02/58	57	8	-	0

REES Anthony Andrew (Tony)
Born: Merthyr Tydfil, Wales, 1 August, 1964 — F
Wales: 1/B/U21-1/Youth/Schools

League Club	Source	Date Signed	Seasons Played	Apps	Subs	Gls
Aston Villa	App	08/82				
Birmingham C	Tr	07/83	83-87	75	20	12
Peterborough U	L	10/85	85	5	0	2
Shrewsbury T	L	03/86	85	1	1	0
Barnsley	Tr	03/88	87-88	27	4	3
Grimsby T	Tr	08/89	89-93	124	17	33
West Bromwich A	Tr	11/94	94-95	11	12	2

REES Barrie Gwyn
Born: Rhyl, Denbighshire, Wales, 4 February, 1944 — RH
Died: Rhyl, Denbighshire, Wales, 27 March, 1965

League Club	Source	Date Signed	Seasons Played	Apps	Subs	Gls
Everton	Jnr	09/61	63-64	4	-	2
Brighton & HA	Tr	01/65	64	12	-	1

REES David Ian (Ian)
Born: Cross Hands, Carmarthenshire, Wales, 21 September, 1943 — F

League Club	Source	Date Signed	Seasons Played	Apps	Subs	Gls
Swansea C	Ammanford T	12/61	64	1	-	0
Swansea C	Ammanford T	08/68	68	1	1	0

REES Douglas Charles (Doug)
Born: Neath, Wales, 12 February, 1923 — CH
Died: Ipswich, England, 27 February, 2000
Wales: Amateur

League Club	Source	Date Signed	Seasons Played	Apps	Subs	Gls
Ipswich T	Troedyrhiw	02/49	48-58	356	-	1

REES Jason Mark
Born: Aberdare, Rhondda Cynon Taff, Wales, 22 December, 1969 — M/W
Wales: 1/B-1/U21-3/Youth/Schools

League Club	Source	Date Signed	Seasons Played	Apps	Subs	Gls
Luton T	YT	07/88	89-93	59	23	0
Mansfield T	L	12/93	93	15	0	1
Portsmouth	Tr	07/94	94-96	30	13	3
Exeter C	L	01/97	96	7	0	0
Cambridge U	Tr	08/97	97	17	3	0
Exeter C	Tr	07/98	98-99	86	1	5
Torquay U	Tiverton T	12/00	00-01	51	7	2

REES John Frederick
Born: Bedlinog, Merthyr Tydfil, Wales, 3 February, 1933 — CF
Died: Caerphilly, Wales, April, 2012
Wales: Amateur/Youth

League Club	Source	Date Signed	Seasons Played	Apps	Subs	Gls
Newport Co (Am)	Troedyrhiw	08/52	52	2	-	0

REES John Graham (Graham)
Born: Pontypridd, Rhondda Cynon Taff, Wales, 28 August, 1937 — W

League Club	Source	Date Signed	Seasons Played	Apps	Subs	Gls
Exeter C	Pontypridd YC	09/54	54-65	345	0	85

REES Joshua David (Josh)
Born: Hemel Hempstead, Hertfordshire, England, 4 October, 1993 — RM

League Club	Source	Date Signed	Seasons Played	Apps	Subs	Gls
Arsenal	Sch	09/11				
Nottingham F	Tr	09/13	13	0	1	0

REES Maldwyn James Francis (Mal)
Born: Neath, Wales, 21 April, 1924 — IF

League Club	Source	Date Signed	Seasons Played	Apps	Subs	Gls
Norwich C	Swansea C (Am)	05/47				
Brighton & HA	Tr	09/49	49	2	-	0
Scunthorpe U	Barry T	07/50	50	18	-	1

REES Mark
Born: Smethwick, West Midlands, England, 13 October, 1961 — RW
England: Schools

League Club	Source	Date Signed	Seasons Played	Apps	Subs	Gls
Walsall	App	08/79	78-89	188	49	37
Rochdale	L	10/86	86	2	1	0

REES Matthew Richard (Matt)
Born: Swansea, Wales, 2 September, 1982 — CD
Wales: U21-4

League Club	Source	Date Signed	Seasons Played	Apps	Subs	Gls
Millwall	YT	04/00				
Swansea C	L	03/04	03	3	0	1

REES Melvyn John (Mel)
Born: Cardiff, Wales, 25 January, 1967 — G
Died: Derby, England, 30 May, 1993
Wales: Youth

League Club	Source	Date Signed	Seasons Played	Apps	Subs	Gls
Cardiff C	App	09/84	84-86	31	0	0
Watford	Tr	07/87	87	3	0	0
Crewe Alex	L	08/89	89	6	0	0
Leyton Orient	L	01/90	89	9	0	0
West Bromwich A	Tr	09/90	90	18	0	0
Sheffield U	Tr	03/92	91	8	0	0

REES Nigel Richard
Born: Bridgend, Wales, 11 July, 1953 — LW

League Club	Source	Date Signed	Seasons Played	Apps	Subs	Gls
Cardiff C	Jnr	08/70	70-72	21	6	1

REES Peter Noel
Born: Machynlleth, Powys, Wales, 5 May, 1932 — W

League Club	Source	Date Signed	Seasons Played	Apps	Subs	Gls
Tranmere Rov (Am)	Llanidloes	10/56	56	9	-	4

REES Robert Clive (Clive)
Born: Nantymoel, Bridgend, Wales, 7 September, 1937 — G
Died: Swansea, Wales, 4 May, 1997

League Club	Source	Date Signed	Seasons Played	Apps	Subs	Gls
Newport Co (Am)	Caerau	03/63	62	4	-	0

REES Ronald Raymond (Ronnie)
Born: Ystradgynlais, Powys, Wales, 4 April, 1944 — W

Wales: 39/U23-7

League Club	Source	Date Signed	Seasons Played	Apps	Subs	Gls
Coventry C	App	05/62	62-67	230	0	42
West Bromwich A	Tr	03/68	67-68	34	1	9
Nottingham F	Tr	02/69	68-71	76	9	12
Swansea C	Tr	01/72	71-74	88	1	5

REES William (Billy)
Born: Blaengarw, Bridgend, Wales, 10 March, 1924 — IF
Died: Bridgend, Wales, 27 July, 1996
Wales: 4/War-1

League Club	Source	Date Signed	Seasons Played	Apps	Subs	Gls
Cardiff C	Caernarvon Rov	02/44	46-48	101	-	34
Tottenham H	Tr	06/49	49	11	-	3
Leyton Orient	Tr	07/50	50-55	184	-	58

REES William (Billy)
Born: Swansea, Wales, 30 September, 1937 — LW

League Club	Source	Date Signed	Seasons Played	Apps	Subs	Gls
Swansea C	Jnr	10/54	54-57	6	-	0
Crystal Palace	Peterborough U	05/59	59	17	-	1

REES William Derrick (Derrick)
Born: Swansea, Wales, 18 February, 1934 — IF/W
Died: Swansea, Wales, April, 1998

League Club	Source	Date Signed	Seasons Played	Apps	Subs	Gls
Portsmouth	Army	05/54	54-56	46	-	15
Ipswich T	Tr	05/57	57-60	90	-	29

REESON Maurice Anthony (Tony)
Born: Rotherham, South Yorkshire, England, 24 September, 1933 — IF
Died: Rotherham, South Yorkshire, England, 31 January, 1990

League Club	Source	Date Signed	Seasons Played	Apps	Subs	Gls
Rotherham U	Jnr	11/53	54	4	-	1
Grimsby T	Tr	06/55	55-57	76	-	20
Doncaster Rov	Tr	02/58	57-58	21	-	6
Southport	Tr	06/59	59	42	-	9

REET Daniel Steven (Danny)
Born: Sheffield, England, 31 January, 1987 — F

League Club	Source	Date Signed	Seasons Played	Apps	Subs	Gls
Sheffield Wed	Sch	07/05				
Bury	L	11/05	05	6	0	4
Mansfield T	Tr	01/06	05-07	24	17	11
Rochdale	L	03/07	06	0	6	0

REEVE Edward Gordon (Eddie)
Born: Islington, N London, England, 3 December, 1947 — IF/LH

League Club	Source	Date Signed	Seasons Played	Apps	Subs	Gls
Brentford	App	12/65	65-67	20	4	0

REEVE Frederick William (Fred)
Born: Clapton, NE London, England, 1 May, 1918 — LH
Died: Thanet, Kent, England, August, 1994

League Club	Source	Date Signed	Seasons Played	Apps	Subs	Gls
Crystal Palace	Ashford T, Kent	05/35	36	1	-	0
Tottenham H	Tr	05/37				
Rochdale	Tr	07/38	38	27	-	3
Grimsby T	Tr	07/39	46-47	46	-	0
Reading	Tr	06/48	48-49	34	-	1

REEVE James Michael (Jamie)
Born: Weymouth, Dorset, England, 26 November, 1975 — F

League Club	Source	Date Signed	Seasons Played	Apps	Subs	Gls
Bournemouth	YT	07/94	94	2	5	0
Hereford U	Tr	03/95	94	0	5	0

REEVE Kenneth Eric (Ken)
Born: Grimsby, North Lincolnshire, England, 13 January, 1921 — IF
Died: Saltfleet, Lincolnshire, England, 20 May, 2005

League Club	Source	Date Signed	Seasons Played	Apps	Subs	Gls
Grimsby T	Humber U	02/38	46-47	24	-	5
Doncaster Rov	Tr	07/48	48	30	-	12
Mansfield T	Tr	07/49	49-53	139	-	62

REEVES Alan
Born: Birkenhead, Wirral, England, 19 November, 1967 — CD

League Club	Source	Date Signed	Seasons Played	Apps	Subs	Gls
Norwich C	Heswall	09/88				
Gillingham	L	02/89	88	18	0	0
Chester C	Tr	08/89	89-90	31	9	2
Rochdale	Tr	07/91	91-94	119	2	9
Wimbledon	Tr	09/94	94-96	52	5	4
Swindon T	Tr	06/98	98-05	190	18	12

REEVES Benjamin Neil (Ben)
Born: Verwood, Dorset, England, 19 November, 1991 — M

League Club	Source	Date Signed	Seasons Played	Apps	Subs	Gls
Southampton	Sch	02/09	11-12	0	5	0
Dagenham & Red	L	02/12	11	5	0	0
Southend U	L	01/13	12	7	3	1
MK Dons	Tr	07/13	13-14	51	7	14

REEVES David
Born: Birkenhead, Wirral, England, 19 November, 1967 — F

League Club	Source	Date Signed	Seasons Played	Apps	Subs	Gls
Sheffield Wed	Heswall	08/86	88	8	9	2
Scunthorpe U	L	12/86	86	3	1	2
Scunthorpe U	L	10/87	87	6	0	4
Burnley	L	11/87	87	16	0	8
Bolton W	Tr	08/89	89-92	111	23	29
Notts Co	Tr	03/93	92-93	9	4	2
Carlisle U	Tr	10/93	93-96	127	0	48
Preston NE	Tr	10/96	96-97	45	2	12
Chesterfield	Tr	11/97	97-01	160	8	46
Oldham Ath	Tr	12/01	01	11	2	3
Chesterfield	Tr	08/02	02-03	54	17	12

REEVES Dennis John Richardson
Born: Lochmaben, Dumfries & Galloway, Scotland, 1 December, 1944 — G

League Club	Source	Date Signed	Seasons Played	Apps	Subs	Gls
Chester C		09/63	63-66	139	0	0
Wrexham	Tr	10/67	67-68	15	0	0

REEVES Derek Brian
Born: Poole, Dorset, England, 27 August, 1934 — CF
Died: Poole, Dorset, England, 22 May, 1995

League Club	Source	Date Signed	Seasons Played	Apps	Subs	Gls
Southampton	Bournemouth Gasworks	12/54	54-62	273	-	145
Bournemouth	Tr	11/62	62-64	35	-	8

REEVES Frank
Born: Peckham, SE London, England, 11 July, 1921 — WH
Died: Greenwich, SE London, England, November, 1993

League Club	Source	Date Signed	Seasons Played	Apps	Subs	Gls
Millwall	Sidcup	02/47	47-54	179	-	1

REEVES Jake Kenny
Born: Lewisham, SE London, England, 30 June, 1993 — M

League Club	Source	Date Signed	Seasons Played	Apps	Subs	Gls
Brentford	Sch	07/11	10-13	17	18	0
AFC Wimbledon	L	11/12	12	5	0	0
Swindon T	Tr	08/14	14	1	9	1
AFC Wimbledon	Tr	01/15	14	23	0	2

REEVES John Charles
Born: Hackney, E London, England, 8 July, 1963 — LM

League Club	Source	Date Signed	Seasons Played	Apps	Subs	Gls
Fulham	App	06/81	81-84	9	5	0
Colchester U	Tr	08/85	85-87	58	3	7

REEVES Kevin Philip
Born: Burley, Hampshire, England, 20 October, 1957 — F
England: 2/B-3/U21-10/Youth

League Club	Source	Date Signed	Seasons Played	Apps	Subs	Gls
Bournemouth	App	07/75	74-76	60	3	20
Norwich C	Tr	01/77	76-79	118	1	37
Manchester C	Tr	03/80	79-82	129	1	34
Burnley	Tr	07/83	83	20	1	12

REEVES Martin Lee
Born: Birmingham, England, 7 September, 1981 — M

League Club	Source	Date Signed	Seasons Played	Apps	Subs	Gls
Leicester C	YT	11/00	01-02	1	7	0
Hull C	L	03/03	02	5	3	1
Northampton T	Tr	06/03	03-04	9	6	0

REEVES Michael Randall (Mike)
Born: Saltash, Cornwall, England, 13 January, 1943 — FB

League Club	Source	Date Signed	Seasons Played	Apps	Subs	Gls
Plymouth Arg	Saltash U	06/61	62-69	107	3	0

REEVES Peter John
Born: Eltham, SE London, England, 7 February, 1949 — CD
England: Youth

League Club	Source	Date Signed	Seasons Played	Apps	Subs	Gls
Charlton Ath	App	02/66	65-73	263	5	2

REEVES Peter Philip
Born: Swansea, Wales, 20 January, 1959 — M
Wales: Schools

League Club	Source	Date Signed	Seasons Played	Apps	Subs	Gls
Coventry C	App	12/76				
Swansea C	Tr	07/78	78	2	2	0

REEVES Raymond Henry Ernest (Ray)
Born: Reading, England, 12 August, 1931 — LB
Died: Reading, England, 30 November, 2007
England: Youth

League Club	Source	Date Signed	Seasons Played	Apps	Subs	Gls
Reading	Jnr	05/49	52-60	284	-	29
Brentford	Tr	07/61	61	5	-	0

REEVES Thomas Brian (Brian)
Born: Skelmersdale, Lancashire, England, 18 February, 1939 — G
Died: Spain, April, 2014

League Club	Source	Date Signed	Seasons Played	Apps	Subs	Gls
Blackburn Rov	Burscough	08/60	60-61	12	-	0
Scunthorpe U	Tr	04/62	62-64	38	-	0
Southport	Tr	07/65	65-68	143	0	0

REEVES-JONES Adrian Kenneth
Born: Stoke-on-Trent, England, 18 October, 1966 — W

League Club	Source	Date Signed	Seasons Played	Apps	Subs	Gls
Port Vale	App	10/84	84	2	1	0

REGAN Carl Anthony
Born: Liverpool, England, 14 January, 1980 — RB
England: Youth

League Club	Source	Date Signed	Seasons Played	Apps	Subs	Gls
Everton	YT	01/98				
Barnsley	Tr	06/00	00-01	31	6	0
Hull C	Tr	08/02	02	33	5	0
Chester C	Droylsden	03/05	04-05	43	4	0
Macclesfield T	Tr	07/06	06-07	54	4	2
MK Dons	Tr	01/08	07-08	32	4	1
Bristol Rov	Tr	07/09	09-10	51	5	0

League Club	Source	Date Signed	Seasons Played	Apps	Subs	Gls
Notts Co	L	02/11	10	4	0	0
Shrewsbury T	Tr	08/11	11	12	1	0
Notts Co	Tr	08/12	12	9	2	0
Bury	Tr	01/13	12	9	1	0

REGAN Douglas John Thomas (Duggie)
Born: Stoke-under-Ham, Somerset, England, 3 June, 1922 LW
Died: Yeovil, Somerset, England, 13 December, 2006

League Club	Source	Date Signed	Seasons Played	Apps	Subs	Gls
Exeter C	Fleet Air Arm	03/45	46-52	206	-	63
Bristol C	Tr	12/52	52-55	39	-	11

REGAN James (Jim)
Born: Hemsworth, West Yorkshire, England, 7 December, 1927 RH
Died: Wakefield, England, April, 1977

League Club	Source	Date Signed	Seasons Played	Apps	Subs	Gls
Rotherham U	Moorthorpe Colliery	08/49	51-52	12	-	0
Bristol C	Tr	06/53	53-55	51	-	1
Coventry C	Tr	03/56	55-56	26	-	0

REGAN John Henry
Born: Dalton-in-Furness, Cumbria, England, 8 June, 1925 LW
Died: Askam-in-Furness, Cumbria, England, 10 February, 2006

League Club	Source	Date Signed	Seasons Played	Apps	Subs	Gls
Barrow	Swarth Moor	01/48	48-50	9	-	1

REGAN Matthew John
Born: Worcester, England, 18 June, 1944 CF

League Club	Source	Date Signed	Seasons Played	Apps	Subs	Gls
Birmingham C	Claines	09/61	62-63	5	-	2
Shrewsbury T	Tr	10/64	64-65	21	0	6
Brentford	Tr	03/66	65-66	14	0	5
Crewe Alex	Tr	11/66	66-68	47	3	18
Doncaster Rov	Tr	09/68	68-70	91	3	25

REGAN Terence (Terry)
Born: Bradford, England, 26 June, 1926 RW

League Club	Source	Date Signed	Seasons Played	Apps	Subs	Gls
Bradford C (Am)	Salts	10/48	48	1	-	0

REGIS Cyrille
Born: Maripasoula, French Guiana, 9 February, 1958 F
England: 5/B-3/U21-6

League Club	Source	Date Signed	Seasons Played	Apps	Subs	Gls
West Bromwich A	Hayes	05/77	77-84	233	4	82
Coventry C	Tr	10/84	84-90	231	6	47
Aston Villa	Tr	07/91	91-92	46	6	12
Wolverhampton W	Tr	08/93	93	8	11	2
Wycombe W	Tr	08/94	94	30	5	9
Chester C	Tr	08/95	95	29	0	7

REGIS David (Dave)
Born: Paddington, Central London, England, 3 March, 1964 F

League Club	Source	Date Signed	Seasons Played	Apps	Subs	Gls
Notts Co	Barnet	09/80	90-91	31	15	15
Plymouth Arg	Tr	11/91	91-92	28	3	4
Bournemouth	L	08/92	92	6	0	2
Stoke C	Tr	10/92	92-93	49	14	15
Birmingham C	Tr	08/94	94	4	2	2
Southend U	Tr	09/94	94-95	34	4	9
Barnsley	Tr	02/96	95-96	4	12	1
Peterborough U	L	09/96	96	4	3	1
Notts Co	L	02/97	96	7	3	2
Scunthorpe U	L	08/97	97	5	0	0
Leyton Orient	Tr	10/97	97	4	0	0
Lincoln C	Tr	12/97	97	0	1	0
Scunthorpe U	Wivenhoe T	02/98	97	4	0	2

REGIS Robert
Born: Huddersfield, West Yorkshire, England, 24 January, 1967 F

League Club	Source	Date Signed	Seasons Played	Apps	Subs	Gls
Burnley	Huddersfield T (Jnr)	08/86	86	3	1	1

REGTOP Hendrik Jan (Erik)
Born: Emmen, Netherlands, 16 February, 1968 F

League Club	Source	Date Signed	Seasons Played	Apps	Subs	Gls
Bradford C	Heerenveen (NED)	07/96	96	5	3	1

REHMAN Zeshan (Zesh)
Born: Birmingham, England, 14 October, 1983 CD
England: Youth//Pakistan: 18

League Club	Source	Date Signed	Seasons Played	Apps	Subs	Gls
Fulham	YT	06/01	03-05	18	3	0
Brighton & HA	L	09/03	03	9	2	2
Norwich C	L	01/06	05	5	0	0
Queens Park Rgrs	Tr	08/06	06-07	40	6	0
Brighton & HA	L	03/07	06	8	0	0
Blackpool	L	07/08	08	0	3	0
Bradford C	Tr	01/09	08-10	57	6	2

REHN Jan Stefan (Stefan)
Born: Stockholm, Sweden, 22 September, 1966 M
Sweden: 45/U21-17/Youth

League Club	Source	Date Signed	Seasons Played	Apps	Subs	Gls
Everton	Djurgaardens (SWE)	06/89	89	1	3	0

REICH Marco Franziscus Thomas
Born: Meisenheim, Germany, 30 December, 1977 W
Germany: 1/U21-11

League Club	Source	Date Signed	Seasons Played	Apps	Subs	Gls
Derby Co	Werder Bremen (GER)	01/04	03-04	36	14	7
Crystal Palace	Tr	09/05	05-06	18	9	2
Walsall	Kick's Offenbach (GER)	08/08	08	9	10	3

REID Andrew Matthew (Andy)
Born: Dublin, Republic of Ireland, 29 July, 1982 LM
Republic of Ireland: 29/U21-15/Youth

League Club	Source	Date Signed	Seasons Played	Apps	Subs	Gls
Nottingham F	YT	08/99	00-04	121	23	21
Tottenham H	Tr	01/05	04-05	20	6	1
Charlton Ath	Tr	08/06	06-07	36	2	7
Sunderland	Tr	01/08	07-10	49	19	4
Sheffield U	L	10/10	10	8	1	2
Blackpool	Tr	01/11	10	2	3	0
Nottingham F	Tr	07/11	11-14	97	22	16

REID Andrew Merrick (Andy)
Born: Urmston, Greater Manchester, England, 4 July, 1962 CD
England: Semi Pro-1

League Club	Source	Date Signed	Seasons Played	Apps	Subs	Gls
Bury	Altrincham	08/92	92-93	27	6	1

REID Anthony James (Tony)
Born: Nottingham, England, 9 May, 1963 M

League Club	Source	Date Signed	Seasons Played	Apps	Subs	Gls
Derby Co	App	05/80	80-82	27	3	1
Scunthorpe U	L	02/83	82	6	0	0
Newport Co	Tr	03/83	82-84	74	2	12
Chesterfield	Tr	07/85	85-87	63	4	7

REID Bobby Armani
Born: Bristol, England, 1 March, 1993 M

League Club	Source	Date Signed	Seasons Played	Apps	Subs	Gls
Bristol C	Sch	07/11	10-14	20	11	2
Cheltenham T	L	11/11	10	0	1	0
Oldham Ath	L	03/13	12	3	4	0
Plymouth Arg	L	09/14	14	7	0	0
Plymouth Arg	L	11/14	14	6	0	2
Plymouth Arg	L	01/15	14	20	0	1

REID Brian Robertson
Born: Paisley, Renfrewshire, Scotland, 15 June, 1970 CD
Scotland: U21-4

League Club	Source	Date Signed	Seasons Played	Apps	Subs	Gls
Burnley	Greenock Morton	09/98	98	30	1	3
Blackpool	Dunfermline Ath	10/00	00-01	55	0	2

REID Craig Kevin
Born: Coventry, England, 17 December, 1985 F

League Club	Source	Date Signed	Seasons Played	Apps	Subs	Gls
Coventry C	Ipswich T (Sch)	07/04				
Cheltenham T	Dunfermline Ath	01/07	06-07	2	12	0
Stevenage	Newport Co	01/11	10-11	38	11	8
Aldershot T	Tr	07/12	12	29	10	11
Southend U	Tr	08/13	13	0	6	0
Stevenage	Tr	02/14	13	1	3	0

REID David Alexander
Born: Glasgow, Scotland, 3 January, 1923 LH

League Club	Source	Date Signed	Seasons Played	Apps	Subs	Gls
Rochdale	Glasgow Perthshire	01/48	47-50	36	-	2
Bradford Park Ave	Tr	09/50	50-51	13	-	0
Workington	Tr	07/53	53	8	-	1
Crewe Alex	Tr	08/54	54	3	-	0

REID Dennis Alexander (Alex)
Born: Glasgow, Scotland, 2 March, 1947 M

League Club	Source	Date Signed	Seasons Played	Apps	Subs	Gls
Newcastle U	Dundee U	10/71	71-72	15	8	0

REID Ernest James (Ernie)
Born: Pentrebach, Merthyr Tydfil, Wales, 24 March, 1914 RB
Died: Kent, England, February, 2007

League Club	Source	Date Signed	Seasons Played	Apps	Subs	Gls
Swansea C	Plymouth U	07/32	32	1	-	0
Chelsea	Tr	09/37	38	1	-	0
Norwich C	Tr	07/39	46	5	-	0

REID Francis (Frank)
Born: Mauchline, Ayrshire, Scotland, 16 June, 1920 W
Died: Huddersfield, West Yorkshire, England, 2 February, 1970

League Club	Source	Date Signed	Seasons Played	Apps	Subs	Gls
Huddersfield T	Cumnock Jnrs	08/46	46-48	7	-	0
Stockport Co	Tr	06/49	49-50	23	-	0

REID Izak George
Born: Stafford, England, 8 July, 1987 RB/M

League Club	Source	Date Signed	Seasons Played	Apps	Subs	Gls
Macclesfield T	Sch	07/06	06-10	117	28	5
Morecambe	Tr	06/11	11-12	35	19	3

REID James Alexander
Born: Ashbourne, Derbyshire, England, 28 February, 1990 LW
England: Youth

League Club	Source	Date Signed	Seasons Played	Apps	Subs	Gls
Nottingham F	Sch	04/08	08	0	1	0

REID James Provan
Born: Dundee, Scotland, 14 December, 1935 IF

League Club	Source	Date Signed	Seasons Played	Apps	Subs	Gls
Bury	Dundee U	01/57	56-58	21	-	9
Stockport Co	Tr	03/59	58	11	-	2

REID James Tyrrell (Jamie)
Born: Ashburton, Devon, England, 15 July, 1994 F
Northern Ireland: U21-2

League Club	Source	Date Signed	Seasons Played	Apps	Subs	Gls
Exeter C	Sch	07/12	12-13	4	6	2

REID John
Born: Edinburgh, Scotland, 23 July, 1935 — W

League Club	Source	Date Signed	Seasons Played	Apps	Subs	Gls
Watford	Airdrieonians	12/56	56	1	-	1
Norwich C	Airdrieonians	06/58				
Barrow	Tr	07/59	59	20	-	4

REID John
Born: Newmains, Lanarkshire, Scotland, 20 August, 1932 — IF/WH

League Club	Source	Date Signed	Seasons Played	Apps	Subs	Gls
Bradford C	Hamilton Academical	12/57	57-61	147	-	32
Northampton T	Tr	11/61	61-63	85	-	14
Luton T	Tr	11/63	63-65	111	0	7
Torquay U	Tr	06/66	66	21	2	1
Rochdale	Tr	07/67	67	37	2	3

REID John Douglas Jamieson (Duggie)
Born: West Kilbride, Ayrshire, Scotland, 3 October, 1917 — IF
Died: Fareham, Hampshire, England, 8 February, 2002

League Club	Source	Date Signed	Seasons Played	Apps	Subs	Gls
Stockport Co	Heaton Chapel	08/35	36-38	84	-	23
Portsmouth	Tr	03/46	46-55	308	-	129

REID John Herkess
Born: Edinburgh, Scotland, 4 May, 1925 — F

League Club	Source	Date Signed	Seasons Played	Apps	Subs	Gls
Torquay U	Hibernian	05/49	49-51	51	-	10

REID Kyel Romane
Born: Deptford, SE London, England, 26 November, 1987 — LW
England: Youth

League Club	Source	Date Signed	Seasons Played	Apps	Subs	Gls
West Ham U	Sch	11/04	05-07	1	2	0
Barnsley	L	11/06	06	12	14	2
Crystal Palace	L	03/08	07	0	2	0
Blackpool	L	11/08	08	7	0	0
Wolverhampton W	L	01/09	08	3	5	1
Sheffield U	Tr	07/09	09	0	7	0
Charlton Ath	Tr	01/10	09-10	24	25	5
Bradford C	Tr	08/11	11-13	78	18	10
Preston NE	Tr	06/14	14	5	9	0

REID Levi Stanley Junior
Born: Stafford, England, 19 January, 1983 — M

League Club	Source	Date Signed	Seasons Played	Apps	Subs	Gls
Port Vale	Sch	07/03	02-04	28	14	0
Macclesfield T	Stafford Rgrs	08/07	07	29	2	2

REID Mark
Born: Kilwinning, Ayrshire, Scotland, 15 September, 1961 — LB
Scotland: U21-2/Youth

League Club	Source	Date Signed	Seasons Played	Apps	Subs	Gls
Charlton Ath	Glasgow Celtic	05/85	85-90	209	2	15

REID Michael James (Micky)
Born: Wolverhampton, England, 7 August, 1927 — CF
Died: Portsmouth, England, 10 April, 1975

League Club	Source	Date Signed	Seasons Played	Apps	Subs	Gls
Wolverhampton W		02/48				
Bournemouth	Tr	02/49	48	5	-	2
Portsmouth	Tr	07/50	50	5	-	1
Watford	Tr	12/52	52	19	-	8

REID Nicholas Scott (Nicky)
Born: Urmston, Greater Manchester, England, 30 October, 1960 — D/M
England: U21-6

League Club	Source	Date Signed	Seasons Played	Apps	Subs	Gls
Manchester C	App	11/78	78-86	211	5	2
Blackburn Rov	Tr	07/87	87-91	160	14	9
Bristol C	L	09/92	92	3	1	0
West Bromwich A	Tr	11/92	92-93	13	7	0
Wycombe W	Tr	03/94	93-94	6	2	0
Bury	Witton A	12/95	95-96	19	6	0

REID Paul James
Born: Sydney, Australia, 6 July, 1979 — RB/M
Australia: 2/Youth

League Club	Source	Date Signed	Seasons Played	Apps	Subs	Gls
Bradford C	Wollongong Wolv (AUS)	09/02	02	7	1	2
Brighton & HA	Tr	03/04	03-07	86	8	5

REID Paul Mark
Born: Carlisle, Cumbria, England, 18 February, 1982 — CD
England: Youth

League Club	Source	Date Signed	Seasons Played	Apps	Subs	Gls
Carlisle U	YT	02/99	99	17	2	0
Preston NE (L)	Glasgow Rangers	01/02	01	0	1	1
Northampton T (L)	Glasgow Rangers	12/02	02	19	0	0
Northampton T	Glasgow Rangers	06/03	03	33	0	2
Barnsley	Tr	07/04	04-07	107	7	3
Carlisle U	L	03/08	07	1	0	0
Colchester U	Tr	07/08	08-10	52	4	1
Scunthorpe U	Tr	01/11	10-12	74	0	2
Northampton T	Tr	09/13	13	16	0	0

REID Paul Robert
Born: Oldbury, West Midlands, England, 19 January, 1968 — W

League Club	Source	Date Signed	Seasons Played	Apps	Subs	Gls
Leicester C	App	01/86	86-91	140	22	21
Bradford C	L	03/92	91	7	0	0
Bradford C	Tr	07/92	92-93	80	2	15
Huddersfield T	Tr	05/94	94-96	70	7	6
Oldham Ath	Tr	03/97	96-98	93	0	6
Bury	Tr	07/99	99-01	102	8	9
Swansea C	Tr	07/02	02	18	2	1

REID Peter
Born: Huyton, Merseyside, England, 20 June, 1956 — DM
England: 13/U21-6

League Club	Source	Date Signed	Seasons Played	Apps	Subs	Gls
Bolton W	App	05/74	74-82	222	3	23
Everton	Tr	12/82	82-88	155	4	8
Queens Park Rgrs	Tr	02/89	88-89	29	0	1
Manchester C	Tr	12/89	89-93	90	13	1
Southampton	Tr	09/93	93	7	0	0
Notts Co	Tr	02/94	93	5	0	0
Bury	Tr	07/94	94	1	0	0

REID Reuben James
Born: Bristol, England, 26 July, 1988 — F

League Club	Source	Date Signed	Seasons Played	Apps	Subs	Gls
Plymouth Arg	Jnr	01/06	05-06	1	6	0
Rochdale	L	01/07	06	0	2	0
Torquay U	L	03/07	06	4	3	2
Wycombe W	L	08/07	07	1	10	1
Brentford	L	01/08	07	1	9	1
Rotherham U	Tr	08/08	08	38	3	18
West Bromwich A	Tr	08/09	09	0	4	0
Peterborough U	L	01/10	09	5	8	0
Walsall	L	08/10	10	13	5	3
Oldham Ath	Tr	01/11	10-12	28	11	7
Yeovil T	Tr	07/12	12	7	12	4
Plymouth Arg	L	01/13	12	18	0	2
Plymouth Arg	Tr	07/13	13-14	86	2	35

REID Robert (Bobby)
Born: Hamilton, Lanarkshire, Scotland, 19 February, 1911 — LW
Died: Hamilton, Lanarkshire, Scotland, 16 November, 1987
Scotland: 2/SLge-2

League Club	Source	Date Signed	Seasons Played	Apps	Subs	Gls
Brentford	Hamilton Academical	01/36	35-38	103	-	33
Sheffield U	Tr	02/39	38-46	14	-	4
Bury	Tr	11/46	46	17	-	1

REID Robert Bell Alexander
Born: Dundee, Scotland, 18 November, 1936 — G
Died: Kirkcaldy, Fife, Scotland, 29 July, 2000

League Club	Source	Date Signed	Seasons Played	Apps	Subs	Gls
Swansea C	Downfield Jnrs	09/57	57-59	17	-	0

REID Ronald Eric (Ron)
Born: Liversedge, West Yorkshire, England, 9 November, 1944 — RW

League Club	Source	Date Signed	Seasons Played	Apps	Subs	Gls
Chesterfield	Retford T	07/67	67	6	1	1

REID Shaun
Born: Huyton, Merseyside, England, 13 October, 1965 — M

League Club	Source	Date Signed	Seasons Played	Apps	Subs	Gls
Rochdale	YT	09/83	83-88	126	7	4
Preston NE	L	12/85	85	3	0	0
York C	Tr	12/88	88-91	104	2	7
Rochdale	Tr	08/92	92-94	106	1	10
Bury	Tr	07/95	95	20	1	0
Chester C	Tr	11/96	96-99	53	9	2

REID Steven John
Born: Kingston-on-Thames, SW London, England, 10 March, 1981 — W/RB
England: Youth//Republic of Ireland: 23/U21-3

League Club	Source	Date Signed	Seasons Played	Apps	Subs	Gls
Millwall	YT	05/98	97-02	115	24	18
Blackburn Rov	Tr	07/03	03-09	91	22	6
Queens Park Rgrs	L	11/09	09	1	1	0
West Bromwich A	Tr	03/10	09-13	71	11	3
Burnley	Tr	07/14	14	1	6	0

REID Wesley Andrew
Born: Lewisham, SE London, England, 10 September, 1968 — M

League Club	Source	Date Signed	Seasons Played	Apps	Subs	Gls
Arsenal	App	07/86				
Millwall	Tr	06/87	88-89	5	1	0
Bradford C	Tr	01/91	90-91	31	4	3

REID William Dunlop
Born: Ayr, Scotland, 13 January, 1920 — RH

League Club	Source	Date Signed	Seasons Played	Apps	Subs	Gls
Newport Co	Cumnock Jnrs	05/48	49	9	-	0

REID Winston Wiremu
Born: Auckland, New Zealand, 3 July, 1988 — CD
Denmark: U21-10//New Zealand: 18

League Club	Source	Date Signed	Seasons Played	Apps	Subs	Gls
West Ham U	Midtjylland (DEN)	08/10	10-14	113	10	6

REILLY Alan
Born: Dublin, Republic of Ireland, 22 August, 1980 — LW

League Club	Source	Date Signed	Seasons Played	Apps	Subs	Gls
Manchester C	YT	09/98				
Halifax T	Tr	12/99	99-01	30	15	2

REILLY Andrew Daniel (Andy)
Born: Luton, England, 26 October, 1985 — LB
Scotland: U21-1/Youth

League Club	Source	Date Signed	Seasons Played	Apps	Subs	Gls
Wycombe W	Sch	04/04	03	5	0	0

REILLY Callum Anthony
Born: Warrington, Cheshire, England, 3 October, 1993 — M
Republic of Ireland: U21-8

League Club	Source	Date Signed	Seasons Played	Apps	Subs	Gls
Birmingham C	Sch	07/12	12-14	39	21	2
Burton A	L	03/15	14	1	1	0

REILLY Daniel (Danny)
Born: Peterborough, England, 17 November, 1966 — M

League Club	Source	Date Signed	Seasons Played	Apps	Subs	Gls
Peterborough U	App	08/84	84	0	1	0

REILLY David John
Born: Chester, England, 24 November, 1966 — M

League Club	Source	Date Signed	Seasons Played	Apps	Subs	Gls
Wrexham	Jnr	07/84	84	0	1	0

REILLY Felix McCairney
Born: Wallyford, East Lothian, Scotland, 12 September, 1933 — IF

League Club	Source	Date Signed	Seasons Played	Apps	Subs	Gls
Bradford Park Ave	East Fife	03/60	59-61	31	-	12
Crewe Alex	Tr	12/61	61	6	-	1

REILLY George Gerard
Born: Motherwell, Lanarkshire, Scotland, 14 September, 1957 — F

League Club	Source	Date Signed	Seasons Played	Apps	Subs	Gls
Northampton T	Corby T	06/76	76-79	124	3	46
Cambridge U	Tr	11/79	79-82	136	2	36
Watford	Tr	08/83	83-84	46	2	14
Newcastle U	Tr	02/85	84-85	31	0	10
West Bromwich A	Tr	12/85	85-87	42	1	9
Cambridge U	Tr	07/88	88	20	0	7

REILLY Leonard Harold (Len)
Born: Rotherhithe, SE London, England, 31 January, 1917 — CH
Died: Queensland, Australia, 26 June, 1998

League Club	Source	Date Signed	Seasons Played	Apps	Subs	Gls
Norwich C	Diss T	02/36	37-46	30	-	0

REILLY Mark Francis
Born: Wishaw, Lanarkshire, Scotland, 30 March, 1969 — M
Scotland: B-1

League Club	Source	Date Signed	Seasons Played	Apps	Subs	Gls
Reading	Kilmarnock	07/98	98	4	2	0

REILLY Terence (Terry)
Born: High Valleyfield, Fife, Scotland, 1 July, 1924 — LB
Died: Glasgow, Scotland, 31 October, 2007

League Club	Source	Date Signed	Seasons Played	Apps	Subs	Gls
Chesterfield	Bo'ness U	03/49				
Southport	Tr	08/50	50-54	191	-	2
Bradford Park Ave	Tr	06/55	55	14	-	0

REINA Enrique Iglesia (Ricky)
Born: Folkestone, Kent, England, 2 October, 1971 — F

League Club	Source	Date Signed	Seasons Played	Apps	Subs	Gls
Brentford	Dover Ath	09/97	97	2	4	1

REINA Jose Manuel (Pepe)
Born: Madrid, Spain, 31 August, 1982 — G
Spain: 33/U21-20/Youth

League Club	Source	Date Signed	Seasons Played	Apps	Subs	Gls
Liverpool	Villarreal (SPN)	07/05	05-12	285	0	0

REINDORF Jesse Yapo
Born: Paris, France, 10 July, 1991 — F
Rwanda: 2

League Club	Source	Date Signed	Seasons Played	Apps	Subs	Gls
Bury	UR Namur (BEL)	07/13	13	1	3	1

REINELT Robert Squire (Robbie)
Born: Loughton, Essex, England, 11 March, 1974 — F

League Club	Source	Date Signed	Seasons Played	Apps	Subs	Gls
Aldershot	YT	-	90	3	2	0
Gillingham	Wivenhoe T	03/93	93-94	34	18	5
Colchester U	Tr	03/95	94-96	22	26	10
Brighton & HA	Tr	02/97	96-97	32	12	7
Leyton Orient	Tr	08/98	98	2	5	0

REIS Tijane Freitas
Born: Canchungo, Guinea-Bissau, 28 June, 1991 — LW
Portugal: U21-1

League Club	Source	Date Signed	Seasons Played	Apps	Subs	Gls
Swindon T	GF Chaves (POR)	07/13	13	2	4	0

REIZIGER Michael John
Born: Amsterdam, Netherlands, 3 May, 1973 — RB
Netherlands: 72

League Club	Source	Date Signed	Seasons Played	Apps	Subs	Gls
Middlesbrough	Barcelona (SPN)	07/04	04-05	19	3	1

REKIK Karim
Born: Den Haag, Netherlands, 2 December, 1994 — LB
Netherlands: 1/U21-7/Youth

League Club	Source	Date Signed	Seasons Played	Apps	Subs	Gls
Manchester C	Sch	12/11				
Portsmouth	L	03/12	11	8	0	0
Blackburn Rov	L	02/13	12	4	1	0

RELISH John Derek
Born: Huyton, Merseyside, England, 5 October, 1953 — LB

League Club	Source	Date Signed	Seasons Played	Apps	Subs	Gls
Chester C	App	10/71	72-73	10	1	1
Newport Co	Tr	06/74	74-86	319	19	9

REMY Christophe Philippe
Born: Besancon, France, 6 August, 1971 — RB/M

League Club	Source	Date Signed	Seasons Played	Apps	Subs	Gls
Oxford U	AJ Auxerre (FRA)	07/97	97-98	23	5	1

REMY Ellis Nathan
Born: Hastings, East Sussex, England, 13 February, 1984 — F

League Club	Source	Date Signed	Seasons Played	Apps	Subs	Gls
Wimbledon	Jnr	06/01				
Lincoln C	Hastings T	08/03	03	0	1	0

REMY Loic
Born: Lyon, France, 2 January, 1987 — F
France: 30/U21-11/Youth

League Club	Source	Date Signed	Seasons Played	Apps	Subs	Gls
Queens Park Rgrs	Olymp Marseille (FRA)	01/13	12-14	15	1	6
Newcastle U	L	08/13	13	24	2	14
Chelsea	Tr	09/14	14	6	13	7

RENDELL Scott David
Born: Ashford, Surrey, England, 21 October, 1986 — F

League Club	Source	Date Signed	Seasons Played	Apps	Subs	Gls
Reading	Sch	07/05				
Peterborough U	Cambridge U	02/08	07-08	5	8	4
Yeovil T	L	10/08	08	5	0	0
Torquay U	L	07/09	09	28	7	12
Wycombe W	Tr	07/10	10-11	26	17	15
Bristol Rov	L	10/11	11	4	1	0
Oxford U	L	01/12	11	15	3	3

RENNIE David
Born: Edinburgh, Scotland, 29 August, 1964 — CD/M
Scotland: Youth

League Club	Source	Date Signed	Seasons Played	Apps	Subs	Gls
Leicester C	App	05/82	83-85	21	0	1
Leeds U	Tr	01/86	85-88	95	6	5
Bristol C	Tr	07/89	89-91	101	3	8
Birmingham C	Tr	02/92	91-92	32	3	4
Coventry C	Tr	03/93	92-95	80	2	3
Northampton T	Tr	08/96	96-97	45	3	3
Peterborough U	Tr	12/97	97-98	27	0	0

RENNIE Paul Andrew
Born: Nantwich, Cheshire, England, 26 October, 1971 — RB

League Club	Source	Date Signed	Seasons Played	Apps	Subs	Gls
Crewe Alex	YT	-	89	1	1	0
Stoke C	Tr	05/90	90-91	4	0	0
Wigan Ath	Tr	08/93	93-94	36	4	3

RENNISON Graham Lee
Born: Northallerton, North Yorkshire, England, 2 October, 1978 — CD

League Club	Source	Date Signed	Seasons Played	Apps	Subs	Gls
York C	YT	07/98	97	1	0	0

RENNISON Shaun
Born: Northallerton, North Yorkshire, England, 23 November, 1980 — CD

League Club	Source	Date Signed	Seasons Played	Apps	Subs	Gls
Scarborough	YT	02/99	98	15	0	1

RENSHAW Derrick
Born: Gateshead, Tyne and Wear, England, 18 September, 1924 — RB
Died: Kettering, Northamptonshire, England, March, 1998

League Club	Source	Date Signed	Seasons Played	Apps	Subs	Gls
Sunderland		12/47				
Barrow	Tr	06/50	50-54	150	-	0

RENSHAW Ian Francis
Born: Chelmsford, England, 14 April, 1978 — FB

League Club	Source	Date Signed	Seasons Played	Apps	Subs	Gls
Scarborough	Basildon U	11/98	98	0	1	0

RENTMEISTER Jeffrey Christian
Born: Oupeye, Belgium, 11 July, 1984 — CD

League Club	Source	Date Signed	Seasons Played	Apps	Subs	Gls
Blackpool	KVC Westerlo (BEL)	08/14	14	7	1	0

RENTON Kris Joseph
Born: Musselburgh, East Lothian, Scotland, 12 July, 1990 — F
Scotland: Youth

League Club	Source	Date Signed	Seasons Played	Apps	Subs	Gls
Norwich C	Sch	07/08	06	1	2	0

RENTON William (Billy)
Born: Cardenden, Fife, Scotland, 4 February, 1942 — M

League Club	Source	Date Signed	Seasons Played	Apps	Subs	Gls
Southport	Dunfermline Ath	11/70				
Barrow	Tr	01/71	70-71	23	1	2

RENTS Samuel David (Sam)
Born: Brighton, England, 22 June, 1987 — LB
England: Semi Pro-1

League Club	Source	Date Signed	Seasons Played	Apps	Subs	Gls
Brighton & HA	Sch	06/06	06-07	23	7	0

RENWICK Craig
Born: Lanark, Scotland, 22 September, 1958 — CD

League Club	Source	Date Signed	Seasons Played	Apps	Subs	Gls
Sheffield U	East Stirlingshire	04/78	78-79	8	1	0

RENWICK Richard (Dick)
Born: Gilsland, Cumbria, England, 27 November, 1942 — LB

League Club	Source	Date Signed	Seasons Played	Apps	Subs	Gls
Grimsby T	Jnr	12/59				
Aldershot	Tr	07/63	63-68	203	2	4
Brentford	Tr	02/69	68-70	96	0	5
Stockport Co	Tr	10/71	71	30	0	1

League Club	Source	Date Signed	Seasons Played	Apps	Subs	Gls
Rochdale	Tr	07/72	72-73	48	1	0
Darlington	L	01/74	73	19	0	0

REO-COKER Nigel Shola Andre
Born: Thornton Heath, S London, England, 14 May, 1984 — M
England: U21-23/Youth

League Club	Source	Date Signed	Seasons Played	Apps	Subs	Gls
Wimbledon	Sch	07/02	01-03	57	1	6
West Ham U	Tr	01/04	03-06	113	7	11
Aston Villa	Tr	07/07	07-10	85	17	1
Bolton W	Tr	07/11	11	37	0	3
Ipswich T	Tr	10/12	12	8	2	0

REPKA Tomas
Born: Zlin, Czech Republic, 2 January, 1974 — CD
Czechoslovakia: 1//Czech Republic: 46/U21-2

League Club	Source	Date Signed	Seasons Played	Apps	Subs	Gls
West Ham U	Fiorentina (ITA)	09/01	01-05	164	0	0

RESCH Franz
Born: Vienna, Austria, 4 May, 1969 — LB/M
Austria: 2

League Club	Source	Date Signed	Seasons Played	Apps	Subs	Gls
Darlington	Motherwell	10/97	97	15	2	1

RESTARICK Stephen Leonard James (Steve)
Born: Barking, E London, England, 28 November, 1971 — F

League Club	Source	Date Signed	Seasons Played	Apps	Subs	Gls
Colchester U	YT	-	89	0	1	0

RETALLICK Graham
Born: Cambridge, England, 8 February, 1970 — M

League Club	Source	Date Signed	Seasons Played	Apps	Subs	Gls
Peterborough U	Histon	08/92	92	2	3	0

REUSER Martijn Franciscus
Born: Amsterdam, Netherlands, 1 February, 1975 — M
Netherlands: 1/U21-12

League Club	Source	Date Signed	Seasons Played	Apps	Subs	Gls
Ipswich T	Vitesse Arnhem (NED)	03/00	99-03	42	49	14

REVEILLERE Anthony Guy Marie
Born: Doue-la-Fontaine, France, 10 November, 1979 — FB
France: 20/U21-24/Youth

League Club	Source	Date Signed	Seasons Played	Apps	Subs	Gls
Sunderland	Napoli (ITA)	10/14	14	15	1	0

REVEL Gordon Harold
Born: Mansfield, Nottinghamshire, England, 19 September, 1927 — CH

League Club	Source	Date Signed	Seasons Played	Apps	Subs	Gls
Mansfield T	Westfield Folk House	08/50	52	1	-	0

REVELL Alexander David (Alex)
Born: Cambridge, England, 7 July, 1983 — F

League Club	Source	Date Signed	Seasons Played	Apps	Subs	Gls
Cambridge U	YT	04/01	00-03	19	38	5
Brighton & HA	Braintree T	07/06	06-07	48	11	13
Southend U	Tr	01/08	07-09	25	9	4
Swindon T	L	09/09	09	7	3	2
Wycombe W	L	01/10	09	11	4	6
Leyton Orient	Tr	07/10	10-11	39	5	13
Rotherham U	Tr	08/11	11-14	136	14	28
Cardiff C	Tr	01/15	14	8	8	2

REVELL Charles (Charlie)
Born: Belvedere, SE London, England, 5 June, 1919 — LH/LB
Died: Bromley, SE London, England, 11 December, 1999

League Club	Source	Date Signed	Seasons Played	Apps	Subs	Gls
Charlton Ath	Northfleet	05/39	46-50	104	-	15
Derby Co	Tr	03/51	50-51	22	-	2

REVIE Donald George (Don)
Born: Middlesbrough, England, 10 July, 1927 — IF
Died: Edinburgh, Scotland, 26 May, 1989
England: 6/B-1/FLge-2

League Club	Source	Date Signed	Seasons Played	Apps	Subs	Gls
Leicester C	Middlesbrough Swifts	08/44	46-49	96	-	25
Hull C	Tr	11/49	49-51	76	-	12
Manchester C	Tr	10/51	51-56	162	-	37
Sunderland	Tr	11/56	56-58	64	-	15
Leeds U	Tr	12/58	58-61	76	-	11

REW Roy Edward
Born: Belfast, Northern Ireland, 26 May, 1924 — CF
Died: Essex, England, October, 2014

League Club	Source	Date Signed	Seasons Played	Apps	Subs	Gls
Exeter C	Seamills	02/49	48-49	4	-	1

REWBURY Jamie Richard
Born: Wattstown, Rhondda Cynon Taff, Wales, 15 February, 1986 — FB
Wales: Youth

League Club	Source	Date Signed	Seasons Played	Apps	Subs	Gls
Swansea C	Sch	-	03	1	1	0

REYES Jose Antonio
Born: Utrera, Spain, 1 September, 1983 — LW
Spain: 21/U21-7/Youth

League Club	Source	Date Signed	Seasons Played	Apps	Subs	Gls
Arsenal	Sevilla (SPN)	01/04	03-05	54	15	16

REYNA Claudio
Born: Livingston, New Jersey, USA, 20 July, 1973 — DM
USA: 112

League Club	Source	Date Signed	Seasons Played	Apps	Subs	Gls
Sunderland	Glasgow Rangers	12/01	01-02	28	0	3
Manchester C	Tr	08/03	03-06	69	8	4

REYNOLDS Arthur Brayley (Brayley)
Born: Blackwood, Caerphilly, Wales, 30 May, 1935 — CF

League Club	Source	Date Signed	Seasons Played	Apps	Subs	Gls
Cardiff C	Lovells Ath	05/56	56-58	55	-	14
Swansea C	Tr	05/59	59-64	150	-	58

REYNOLDS Graham Edward Arthur
Born: Newport, Wales, 23 January, 1937 — CF
Died: Cardiff, Wales, 27 February, 2008
Wales: Amateur

League Club	Source	Date Signed	Seasons Played	Apps	Subs	Gls
Newport Co (Am)	Caerleon	10/56	56	4	-	1
Newport Co	Brecon Corries	07/63	63-66	42	1	11

REYNOLDS Hugh
Born: Wishaw, Lanarkshire, Scotland, 19 September, 1926 — RH
Died: Wishaw, Lanarkshire, Scotland, 10 August, 1998

League Club	Source	Date Signed	Seasons Played	Apps	Subs	Gls
Torquay U	Greenock Morton	05/48	48	3	-	0

REYNOLDS James Andrew (Jim)
Born: Swindon, England, 27 October, 1967 — M
England: Youth

League Club	Source	Date Signed	Seasons Played	Apps	Subs	Gls
Swindon T	App	09/85	84-86	0	2	0

REYNOLDS Joseph John (Joe)
Born: Cleland, Lanarkshire, Scotland, 13 February, 1939 — CH
Died: Bangor, Gwynedd, Wales, March, 1998

League Club	Source	Date Signed	Seasons Played	Apps	Subs	Gls
Crewe Alex		08/60	60	5	-	0

REYNOLDS Mark
Born: Motherwell, Lanarkshire, Scotland, 7 May, 1987 — CD
Scotland: B-1/U21-9/Youth

League Club	Source	Date Signed	Seasons Played	Apps	Subs	Gls
Sheffield Wed	Motherwell	01/11	10-11	10	0	0

REYNOLDS Mark David
Born: Glapwell, Derbyshire, England, 1 January, 1966 — FB

League Club	Source	Date Signed	Seasons Played	Apps	Subs	Gls
Mansfield T	App	-	82	4	0	0

REYNOLDS Richard John (Dick)
Born: Looe, Cornwall, England, 15 February, 1948 — M/F
England: Youth

League Club	Source	Date Signed	Seasons Played	Apps	Subs	Gls
Plymouth Arg	App	02/65	64-70	123	8	24
Portsmouth	Tr	07/71	71-75	134	7	24

REYNOLDS Ronald Sidney Maurice (Ron)
Born: Haslemere, Surrey, England, 2 June, 1928 — G
Died: Haslemere, Surrey, England, 2 June, 1999

League Club	Source	Date Signed	Seasons Played	Apps	Subs	Gls
Aldershot	Jnr	12/45	46-49	114	-	0
Tottenham H	Tr	07/50	53-57	86	-	0
Southampton	Tr	03/60	59-63	90	-	0

REYNOLDS Thomas (Tommy)
Born: Felling, Tyne and Wear, England, 2 October, 1922 — LW
Died: Gateshead, Tyne and Wear, England, March, 1998

League Club	Source	Date Signed	Seasons Played	Apps	Subs	Gls
Sunderland	Felling Jnrs	07/46	46-52	167	-	18
Darlington	King's Lynn	12/54	54-55	43	-	6

[REZA] GHOOCHANNEJHAD Reza
Born: Mashdad, Iran, 20 September, 1987 — F
Iran: 9//Netherlands: Youth

League Club	Source	Date Signed	Seasons Played	Apps	Subs	Gls
Charlton Ath	Standard Liege (BEL)	01/14	13	10	5	1

REZAI Carl Sarbaz
Born: Manchester, England, 16 October, 1982 — M

League Club	Source	Date Signed	Seasons Played	Apps	Subs	Gls
Halifax T	YT	10/00	00	8	3	1

RHEAD Matthew James (Matt)
Born: Stoke-on-Trent, England, 31 August, 1984 — F

League Club	Source	Date Signed	Seasons Played	Apps	Subs	Gls
Mansfield T	Corby T	01/12	13-14	44	28	9

RHOADES-BROWN Peter
Born: Hampton, W London, England, 2 January, 1962 — LW

League Club	Source	Date Signed	Seasons Played	Apps	Subs	Gls
Chelsea	App	07/79	79-83	86	10	4
Oxford U	Tr	01/84	83-88	87	25	13

RHODES Alan
Born: Bradford, England, 5 January, 1946 — WH

League Club	Source	Date Signed	Seasons Played	Apps	Subs	Gls
Bradford C (Am)	Salts	07/64	64-65	7	0	0

RHODES Albert
Born: North Anston, South Yorkshire, England, 29 April, 1936 — RB

League Club	Source	Date Signed	Seasons Played	Apps	Subs	Gls
Queens Park Rgrs	Worksop T	12/54	55-56	5	-	0

RHODES Alexander Graham (Alex)
Born: Cambridge, England, 23 January, 1982 — LW

League Club	Source	Date Signed	Seasons Played	Apps	Subs	Gls
Brentford	Newmarket T	11/03	03-06	17	40	5
Swindon T	L	10/06	06	0	4	0
Bradford C	Tr	08/07	07	11	17	3
Rotherham U	Tr	08/08	08	14	4	2

RHODES Andrew Charles (Andy)
Born: Askern, South Yorkshire, England, 23 August, 1964 — G

League Club	Source	Date Signed	Seasons Played	Apps	Subs	Gls
Barnsley	App	08/82	83-84	36	0	0

League Club	Source	Date Signed	Seasons Played	Apps	Subs	Gls
Doncaster Rov	Tr	10/85	85-87	106	0	0
Oldham Ath	Tr	03/88	87-89	69	0	0
Scarborough (L)	Airdrieonians	11/97	97	11	0	0

RHODES Benjamin Peter (Ben)
Born: York, England, 2 May, 1983 — M

League Club	Source	Date Signed	Seasons Played	Apps	Subs	Gls
York C	YT	-	01	0	1	0

RHODES Brian William
Born: Marylebone, Central London, England, 23 October, 1937 — G
Died: New Zealand, 17 November, 1993

League Club	Source	Date Signed	Seasons Played	Apps	Subs	Gls
West Ham U	Jnr	01/55	57-62	61	-	0
Southend U	Tr	09/63	63	11	-	0

RHODES Christopher Kyle (Chris)
Born: Mansfield, Nottinghamshire, England, 9 January, 1987 — M

League Club	Source	Date Signed	Seasons Played	Apps	Subs	Gls
Notts Co	Sch	-	03	0	1	0

RHODES John Anthony (Tony)
Born: Dover, Kent, England, 17 September, 1946 — CD

League Club	Source	Date Signed	Seasons Played	Apps	Subs	Gls
Derby Co	Jnr	10/63	64-70	5	0	0
Halifax T	Tr	11/70	70-75	233	0	9
Southport	Tr	08/76	76	7	2	0

RHODES Jordan Luke
Born: Oldham, Greater Manchester, England, 5 February, 1990 — F
Scotland: 13/U21-8

League Club	Source	Date Signed	Seasons Played	Apps	Subs	Gls
Ipswich T	Sch	08/07	07-08	0	10	1
Rochdale	L	09/08	08	5	0	2
Brentford	L	01/09	08	14	0	7
Huddersfield T	Tr	08/09	09-12	108	16	73
Blackburn Rov	Tr	08/12	12-14	127	7	73

RHODES Mark Nigel
Born: Sheffield, England, 26 August, 1957 — M

League Club	Source	Date Signed	Seasons Played	Apps	Subs	Gls
Rotherham U	App	08/75	75-84	235	11	13
Darlington	L	10/82	82	14	0	0
Mansfield T	L	03/83	82	4	0	0
Burnley	Tr	03/85	84-85	12	1	0

RHODES Stanley (Stan)
Born: Sheffield, England, 19 April, 1929 — IF
Died: Sheffield, England, October, 2013

League Club	Source	Date Signed	Seasons Played	Apps	Subs	Gls
Leeds U		05/48				
Sheffield U	Worksop T	11/51	51	1	-	0

RHODES Trevor Charles
Born: Southend-on-Sea, England, 9 August, 1948 — M

League Club	Source	Date Signed	Seasons Played	Apps	Subs	Gls
Arsenal	App	09/65				
Millwall	Tr	09/66	66	4	0	0
Bristol Rov	Tr	07/68	68	2	0	0

RIBEIRO Bruno Miguel Fernandes
Born: Setubal, Portugal, 22 October, 1975 — M
Portugal: U21-5

League Club	Source	Date Signed	Seasons Played	Apps	Subs	Gls
Leeds U	Vitoria Setubal (POR)	07/97	97-98	35	7	4
Sheffield U	Tr	10/99	99-00	12	13	1

RIBEIRO Bruno da Paula (Bruno)
Born: Tupa, Brazil, 1 April, 1983 — RB

League Club	Source	Date Signed	Seasons Played	Apps	Subs	Gls
Blackburn Rov	Gremio (BRA)	08/11	12	4	1	0

RIBEIRO Christian Michael
Born: Neath, Wales, 14 December, 1989 — RB
Wales: 2/U21-8/Youth

League Club	Source	Date Signed	Seasons Played	Apps	Subs	Gls
Bristol C	Sch	12/06	09-10	13	1	0
Stockport Co	L	11/09	09	7	0	0
Colchester U	L	01/10	09	2	0	0
Carlisle U	L	11/11	11	5	0	0
Scunthorpe U	Tr	01/12	11-13	56	3	2
Exeter C	Tr	08/14	14	33	4	2

RICARD Cuesta Hamilton (Hamilton)
Born: Quibdo, Colombia, 12 January, 1974 — F
Colombia: 27/U21

League Club	Source	Date Signed	Seasons Played	Apps	Subs	Gls
Middlesbrough	Depo Cali (COL)	03/98	97-01	92	23	33

[RICARDO] LOPEZ Ricardo Felipe
Born: Madrid, Spain, 30 December, 1971 — G
Spain: 2/Youth

League Club	Source	Date Signed	Seasons Played	Apps	Subs	Gls
Manchester U	Real Valladolid (SPN)	08/02	02	0	1	0

[RICARDO] SOARES PEREIRA Ricardo Alexandre Martins
Born: Montijo, Portugal, 11 March, 1976 — G
Portugal: 79/U21-1

League Club	Source	Date Signed	Seasons Played	Apps	Subs	Gls
Leicester C	Real Betis (SPN)	01/11	10	8	0	0

RICE Brian
Born: Bellshill, Lanarkshire, Scotland, 11 October, 1963 — LM
Scotland: U21-1/Youth

League Club	Source	Date Signed	Seasons Played	Apps	Subs	Gls
Nottingham F	Hibernian	08/85	85-90	86	5	9
Grimsby T	L	10/86	86	4	0	0
West Bromwich A	L	01/89	88	2	1	0
Stoke C	L	02/91	90	18	0	0

RICE Gary James
Born: Zambia, 25 September, 1975 — LB

League Club	Source	Date Signed	Seasons Played	Apps	Subs	Gls
Exeter C	YT	07/94	94-96	31	13	0

RICE Martin John
Born: Exeter, England, 7 March, 1986 — G
England: Semi Pro-1

League Club	Source	Date Signed	Seasons Played	Apps	Subs	Gls
Torquay U	Truro C	07/07	12-13	35	2	0

RICE Patrick James (Pat)
Born: Belfast, Northern Ireland, 17 March, 1949 — RB
Northern Ireland: 49/U23-2

League Club	Source	Date Signed	Seasons Played	Apps	Subs	Gls
Arsenal	Jnr	03/66	67-80	391	6	12
Watford	Tr	11/80	80-83	112	0	1

RICE Robert Anthony (Robbie)
Born: Stanmore, NW London, England, 23 February, 1989 — D

League Club	Source	Date Signed	Seasons Played	Apps	Subs	Gls
Wycombe W	Sch	07/07	07-08	0	2	0

RICE Ronald Henry (Ron)
Born: Birkenhead, Wirral, England, 13 April, 1923 — IF
Died: Wirral, England, 11 February, 2011

League Club	Source	Date Signed	Seasons Played	Apps	Subs	Gls
Bradford C	Huddersfield T (Am)	09/46	46	1	-	0
Tranmere Rov	Tr	10/46	46	5	-	1

RICHARD Fabrice
Born: Saintes, France, 16 August, 1973 — RB

League Club	Source	Date Signed	Seasons Played	Apps	Subs	Gls
Colchester U	AS Cannes (FRA)	03/99	98-99	23	1	0

RICHARDS Anthony Willis (Tony)
Born: Smethwick, West Midlands, England, 6 March, 1934 — CF
Died: Stafford, England, 4 March, 2010

League Club	Source	Date Signed	Seasons Played	Apps	Subs	Gls
Birmingham C	Hopes' Works	12/51				
Walsall	Tr	09/54	54-62	334	-	183
Port Vale	Tr	03/63	62-65	59	4	30

RICHARDS Ashley Darel Jazz (Jazz)
Born: Swansea, Wales, 12 April, 1991 — FB
Wales: 5/U21-16/Youth

League Club	Source	Date Signed	Seasons Played	Apps	Subs	Gls
Swansea C	Sch	07/09	09-14	29	10	0
Crystal Palace	L	01/13	12	10	1	0
Huddersfield T	L	09/13	13	7	2	0
Fulham	L	01/15	14	14	0	0

RICHARDS Carroll Lloyd (Carl)
Born: Port Maria, Jamaica, 12 January, 1960 — F
England: Semi Pro-1

League Club	Source	Date Signed	Seasons Played	Apps	Subs	Gls
Bournemouth	Enfield	07/86	86-88	57	14	16
Birmingham C	Tr	10/88	88	18	1	2
Peterborough U	Tr	07/89	89	16	4	5
Blackpool	Tr	01/90	89-91	32	9	8
Maidstone U	L	10/91	91	4	0	2

RICHARDS Craig Alan
Born: Neath, Wales, 10 October, 1959 — M

League Club	Source	Date Signed	Seasons Played	Apps	Subs	Gls
Queens Park Rgrs	App	07/77				
Wimbledon	Tr	06/79	79	2	0	0

RICHARDS Dane O'Brian
Born: Montego Bay, Jamaica, 14 December, 1983 — W
Jamaica: 45

League Club	Source	Date Signed	Seasons Played	Apps	Subs	Gls
Burnley	Vancouver W'caps (CAN)	01/13	12	0	1	0

RICHARDS Dean Ivor
Born: Bradford, England, 9 June, 1974 — CD
Died: Leeds, England, 26 February, 2011
England: U21-4

League Club	Source	Date Signed	Seasons Played	Apps	Subs	Gls
Bradford C	YT	07/92	91-94	82	4	4
Wolverhampton W	Tr	03/95	94-98	118	4	7
Southampton	Tr	07/99	99-01	67	0	3
Tottenham H	Tr	09/01	01-03	73	0	4

RICHARDS Eliot Allen
Born: New Tredegar, Caerphilly, Wales, 1 September, 1991 — F
Wales: U21-1/Youth

League Club	Source	Date Signed	Seasons Played	Apps	Subs	Gls
Bristol Rov	Jnr	07/09	09-13	59	53	16
Exeter C	L	02/14	13	11	6	5
Tranmere Rov	Tr	05/14	14	9	4	1
Cheltenham T	Tr	02/15	14	6	3	1

RICHARDS Garry
Born: Romford, E London, England, 11 June, 1986 — CD

League Club	Source	Date Signed	Seasons Played	Apps	Subs	Gls
Colchester U	Sch	07/05	05-06	15	5	1
Brentford	L	02/07	06	10	0	1
Southend U	Tr	08/07	07	8	2	0
Gillingham	Tr	01/08	07-11	93	14	4

RICHARDS Gary Vivian
Born: Swansea, Wales, 2 August, 1963 FB

League Club	Source	Date Signed	Seasons Played	Apps	Subs	Gls
Swansea C	App	08/81	81-84	63	3	1
Lincoln C	Jonkopings Sodra (SWE)	11/85	85	2	5	0
Cambridge U	Tr	03/86	85	8	0	0
Torquay U	Tr	07/86	86	24	1	1

RICHARDS Geoffrey Mottram (Geoff)
Born: Bilston, West Midlands, England, 24 April, 1929 IF
Died: Wolverhampton, England, 15 May, 2014

League Club	Source	Date Signed	Seasons Played	Apps	Subs	Gls
West Bromwich A	Albion Works	08/46	46-47	3	-	1

RICHARDS Gordon
Born: Rhostyllen, Wrexham, Wales, 23 October, 1933 LW
Died: Wrexham, Wales, 17 November, 1993

League Club	Source	Date Signed	Seasons Played	Apps	Subs	Gls
Wrexham	Ruabon	05/52	52-57	96	-	24
Chester C	Tr	01/58	57-60	74	-	16

RICHARDS Ian
Born: Barnsley, South Yorkshire, England, 5 October, 1979 M

League Club	Source	Date Signed	Seasons Played	Apps	Subs	Gls
Blackburn Rov	YT	07/97				
Halifax T	Tr	07/99	99-00	13	11	0

RICHARDS Jamie Alexander
Born: Southend-on-Sea, England, 24 June, 1994 D

League Club	Source	Date Signed	Seasons Played	Apps	Subs	Gls
Plymouth Arg	Sch	07/11	12-13	0	2	0

RICHARDS John Barrington
Born: West Bromwich, West Midlands, England, 14 June, 1931 IF
Died: Broxbourne, Hertfordshire, England, 30 November, 2001

League Club	Source	Date Signed	Seasons Played	Apps	Subs	Gls
Swindon T	RAPC Devizes	11/55	55-59	105	-	36
Norwich C	Tr	12/59	59	5	-	2
Aldershot	Tr	10/60	60	19	-	8

RICHARDS John Peter
Born: Warrington, Cheshire, England, 9 November, 1950 F
England: 1/B-3/FLge-1/U23-6/U21-1/Schools

League Club	Source	Date Signed	Seasons Played	Apps	Subs	Gls
Wolverhampton W	Jnr	07/69	69-82	365	20	144
Derby Co	L	11/82	82	10	0	2

RICHARDS Jordan
Born: Sunderland, England, 25 April, 1993 RB

League Club	Source	Date Signed	Seasons Played	Apps	Subs	Gls
Hartlepool U	Sch	07/11	11-14	26	15	0

RICHARDS Justin Donovan
Born: West Bromwich, West Midlands, England, 16 October, 1980 F
England: Semi Pro-3

League Club	Source	Date Signed	Seasons Played	Apps	Subs	Gls
West Bromwich A	YT	01/99	98	0	1	0
Bristol Rov	Tr	01/01	00-02	3	13	0
Colchester U	L	10/02	02	0	2	0
Peterborough U	Woking	05/06	06	4	9	1
Boston U	L	01/07	06	3	0	0
Cheltenham T	Kidderminster Hrs	07/09	09	39	5	15
Port Vale	Tr	07/10	10	37	5	9
Burton A	Tr	07/11	11-12	32	16	12
Oxford U	Tr	01/13	12	4	0	0

RICHARDS Lloyd George
Born: Kingston, Jamaica, 11 February, 1958 M

League Club	Source	Date Signed	Seasons Played	Apps	Subs	Gls
Notts Co	App	02/76	75-77	7	2	0
York C	Tr	06/80	80	17	1	1

RICHARDS Marc John
Born: Wolverhampton, England, 8 July, 1982 F
England: Youth

League Club	Source	Date Signed	Seasons Played	Apps	Subs	Gls
Blackburn Rov	YT	07/99				
Crewe Alex	L	08/01	01	1	3	0
Oldham Ath	L	10/01	01	3	2	0
Halifax T	L	02/02	01	5	0	0
Swansea C	L	11/02	02	14	3	7
Northampton T	Tr	07/03	03-04	35	18	10
Rochdale	L	03/05	04	4	1	2
Barnsley	Tr	08/05	05-06	51	18	18
Port Vale	Tr	07/07	07-11	162	19	68
Chesterfield	Tr	05/12	12-13	51	21	21
Northampton T	Tr	05/14	14	26	5	18

RICHARDS Matthew Lee (Matt)
Born: Harlow, Essex, England, 26 December, 1984 M
England: U21-1

League Club	Source	Date Signed	Seasons Played	Apps	Subs	Gls
Ipswich T	Sch	01/02	02-08	118	30	8
Brighton & HA	L	09/07	07	28	0	0
Brighton & HA	L	07/08	08	23	0	1
Walsall	Tr	08/09	09-10	85	1	12
Shrewsbury T	Tr	07/11	11-12	78	7	12
Cheltenham T	Tr	07/13	13-14	90	1	8

RICHARDS Matthew Washington (Matt)
Born: Derby, England, 1 December, 1989 M
England: Youth

League Club	Source	Date Signed	Seasons Played	Apps	Subs	Gls
Derby Co	Sch	12/06				
Wycombe W	Tr	01/09				
Notts Co	L	03/09	08	0	1	0

RICHARDS Micah Lincoln
Born: Birmingham, England, 24 June, 1988 RB
England: 13/U21-15/Youth

League Club	Source	Date Signed	Seasons Played	Apps	Subs	Gls
Manchester C	Sch	07/05	05-13	164	15	7

RICHARDS Michael James (Mike)
Born: Codsall, Staffordshire, England, 26 May, 1939 G

League Club	Source	Date Signed	Seasons Played	Apps	Subs	Gls
Oxford U	Wellington T	07/62	62-63	30	-	0
Shrewsbury T	Tr	11/63				

RICHARDS Peter (Pedro)
Born: Edmonton, N London, England, 11 November, 1956 RB
Died: Nottingham, England, 23 December, 2001

League Club	Source	Date Signed	Seasons Played	Apps	Subs	Gls
Notts Co	App	11/74	74-85	397	2	5

RICHARDS Stanley Verdun (Stan)
Born: Cardiff, Wales, 21 January, 1917 CF
Died: Cardiff, Wales, 19 April, 1987
Wales: 1

League Club	Source	Date Signed	Seasons Played	Apps	Subs	Gls
Cardiff C	Cardiff Corinthians	01/46	46-47	57	-	39
Swansea C	Tr	06/48	48-50	62	-	35

RICHARDS Stephen (Steve)
Born: Dundee, Scotland, 24 October, 1961 CD

League Club	Source	Date Signed	Seasons Played	Apps	Subs	Gls
Hull C	App	10/79	79-82	55	3	2
York C	Gainsborough Trinity	12/84	84	6	1	0
Lincoln C	Tr	08/85	85	21	0	0
Cambridge U	Tr	03/86	85	4	0	2
Scarborough	Tr	08/86	87-90	164	0	13
Halifax T	Tr	08/91	91	24	1	0
Doncaster Rov	Tr	05/92	92	36	2	3

RICHARDS Thomas Oliver (Tom)
Born: Guildford, Surrey, England, 16 October, 1994 LB

League Club	Source	Date Signed	Seasons Played	Apps	Subs	Gls
Fulham	Sch	07/13				
AFC Wimbledon	L	02/14	13	9	1	0

RICHARDS Tony
Born: New Houghton, Derbyshire, England, 9 June, 1944 WH

League Club	Source	Date Signed	Seasons Played	Apps	Subs	Gls
Mansfield T	App	06/62	61-63	3	-	0

RICHARDS Tony Spencer
Born: Newham, E London, England, 17 September, 1973 F

League Club	Source	Date Signed	Seasons Played	Apps	Subs	Gls
West Ham U	YT	08/92				
Cambridge U	Sudbury T	08/95	95-96	29	13	5
Leyton Orient	Tr	10/97	97-99	47	16	11
Barnet	Tr	08/00	00	27	6	8
Southend U	Tr	07/01	01	9	8	2

RICHARDS Wayne
Born: Scunthorpe, North Lincolnshire, England, 10 May, 1961 LB

League Club	Source	Date Signed	Seasons Played	Apps	Subs	Gls
Derby Co	App	05/79	79-81	16	3	0

RICHARDSON Anthony Frederick (Tony)
Born: Alford, Lincolnshire, England, 5 November, 1943 CF
Died: Spain, 29 August, 2007

League Club	Source	Date Signed	Seasons Played	Apps	Subs	Gls
Nottingham F	Jnr	11/60				
Bradford C (Am)	Cheltenham T	05/62	62	2	-	1

RICHARDSON Anthony Joseph (Tony)
Born: Southwark, S London, England, 7 January, 1932 FB

League Club	Source	Date Signed	Seasons Played	Apps	Subs	Gls
Queens Park Rgrs	Slough Sports Club	04/51	51	2	-	0

RICHARDSON Barry
Born: Wallsend, Tyne and Wear, England, 5 August, 1969 G

League Club	Source	Date Signed	Seasons Played	Apps	Subs	Gls
Sunderland	YT	05/88				
Scunthorpe U	Tr	03/89				
Scarborough	Tr	08/89	89-90	30	0	0
Northampton T	Stockport Co (NC)	09/91	91-93	96	0	0
Preston NE	Tr	07/94	94-95	20	0	0
Lincoln C	Tr	10/95	95-99	131	0	0
Mansfield T	L	08/99	99	6	0	0
Halifax T	Doncaster Rov	12/01	01	24	0	0

RICHARDSON Brian
Born: Sheffield, England, 5 October, 1934 RH

League Club	Source	Date Signed	Seasons Played	Apps	Subs	Gls
Sheffield U		12/54	55-64	291	-	9
Swindon T	Tr	01/66	65	11	0	0
Rochdale	Tr	07/66	66	19	0	1

RICHARDSON Craig Thomas
Born: Newham, E London, England, 8 October, 1979 FB

League Club	Source	Date Signed	Seasons Played	Apps	Subs	Gls
Leyton Orient	YT	-	97	1	0	0

RICHARDSON Damien John
Born: Dublin, Republic of Ireland, 2 August, 1947 — F
Republic of Ireland: 3/LoI-1

League Club	Source	Date Signed	Seasons Played	Apps	Subs	Gls
Gillingham	Shamrock Rov (ROI)	10/72	72-80	314	9	94

RICHARDSON David (Dave)
Born: Billingham, Cleveland, England, 11 March, 1932 — LB

League Club	Source	Date Signed	Seasons Played	Apps	Subs	Gls
Leicester C	Jnr	11/49	54	2	-	0
Grimsby T	Tr	06/55	55-59	175	-	1
Swindon T	Tr	06/60				
Barrow	Tr	07/61	61-62	31	-	0

RICHARDSON Derek
Born: Hackney, E London, England, 13 July, 1956 — G
England: Semi Pro-4/Youth

League Club	Source	Date Signed	Seasons Played	Apps	Subs	Gls
Chelsea	App	02/74				
Queens Park Rgrs	Tr	04/76	76-78	31	0	0
Sheffield U	Tr	12/79	79-80	42	0	0
Coventry C	Tr	03/82				

RICHARDSON Frazer
Born: Rotherham, South Yorkshire, England, 29 October, 1982 — RB
England: Youth

League Club	Source	Date Signed	Seasons Played	Apps	Subs	Gls
Leeds U	YT	11/99	03-08	122	27	3
Stoke C	L	01/03	02	6	1	0
Stoke C	L	11/03	03	6	0	1
Charlton Ath	Tr	07/09	09	37	1	1
Southampton	Tr	07/10	10-12	49	11	0
Middlesbrough	Tr	08/13	13	11	0	0
Ipswich T	L	01/14	13	3	4	0
Rotherham U	Tr	06/14	14	19	4	0

RICHARDSON Frederick (Fred)
Born: Spennymoor, County Durham, England, 18 August, 1925 — CF

League Club	Source	Date Signed	Seasons Played	Apps	Subs	Gls
Chelsea	Bishop Auckland	09/46	46	2	-	0
Hartlepool U	Tr	10/47	47-48	43	-	16
Barnsley	Tr	10/48	48-49	41	-	12
West Bromwich A	Tr	06/50	50-51	29	-	8
Chester C	Tr	02/52	51-52	23	-	6
Hartlepool U	Tr	11/52	52-55	106	-	19

RICHARDSON Garbutt
Born: Newcastle-upon-Tyne, England, 24 October, 1938 — CH/CF
Died: Rhuddlan, Denbighshire, Wales, 1980

League Club	Source	Date Signed	Seasons Played	Apps	Subs	Gls
Huddersfield T	Jnr	10/55				
Preston NE	Tr	07/57	59-60	15	-	1
Accrington Stan	Tr	07/61				
Carlisle U	Tr	07/62				
Halifax T	Tr	11/62	62-63	20	-	1
Barrow	Tr	07/64	64	30	-	5

RICHARDSON George
Born: Worksop, Nottinghamshire, England, 12 December, 1912 — IF
Died: Worksop, Nottinghamshire, England, 24 March, 1968

League Club	Source	Date Signed	Seasons Played	Apps	Subs	Gls
Huddersfield T	Manton Colliery	04/33	33	1	-	0
Sheffield U	Tr	05/34	35-38	32	-	9
Hull C	Tr	11/38	38-47	36	-	15

RICHARDSON Graham Charles
Born: Sedgefield, County Durham, England, 20 March, 1958 — G

League Club	Source	Date Signed	Seasons Played	Apps	Subs	Gls
Hartlepool U	Darlington (Am)	08/75	75-80	89	0	0

RICHARDSON Ian George
Born: Barking, E London, England, 22 October, 1970 — CD/M
England: Semi Pro-1

League Club	Source	Date Signed	Seasons Played	Apps	Subs	Gls
Birmingham C	Dagenham & Red	08/95	95	3	4	0
Notts Co	L	01/96	95	4	0	0
Notts Co	Tr	03/96	95-04	233	16	21

RICHARDSON Ian Paul
Born: Ely, Cambridgeshire, England, 9 May, 1964 — F

League Club	Source	Date Signed	Seasons Played	Apps	Subs	Gls
Watford	App	05/82	83-84	5	3	2
Blackpool	L	12/82	82	4	1	2
Rotherham U	L	02/85	84	5	0	2
Chester C	Tr	11/85	85-86	31	4	10
Scunthorpe U	Tr	10/86	86-88	11	7	4

RICHARDSON James Robert (Jimmy)
Born: Ashington, Northumberland, England, 8 February, 1911 — IF
Died: Bexley, SE London, England, 28 August, 1964
England: 2/FLge-1/Schools

League Club	Source	Date Signed	Seasons Played	Apps	Subs	Gls
Newcastle U	Blyth Spartans	04/28	29-34	136	-	42
Huddersfield T	Tr	10/34	34-37	120	-	32
Newcastle U	Tr	10/37	37	14	-	4
Millwall	Tr	03/38	37-38	52	-	16
Leyton Orient	Tr	01/48	47	15	-	0

RICHARDSON Jay Grant
Born: Bromley, SE London, England, 14 November, 1979 — M

League Club	Source	Date Signed	Seasons Played	Apps	Subs	Gls
Chelsea	YT	02/98				
Exeter C	Tr	07/01	01	5	13	0

RICHARDSON John (Jack)
Born: Birkenhead, Wirral, England, 24 May, 1933 — G

League Club	Source	Date Signed	Seasons Played	Apps	Subs	Gls
Southport	Canterbury C	07/56	56-59	103	-	0

RICHARDSON John
Born: Worksop, Nottinghamshire, England, 20 April, 1945 — FB

League Club	Source	Date Signed	Seasons Played	Apps	Subs	Gls
Derby Co	App	04/62	62-70	118	0	4
Notts Co	Tr	07/71	71	0	2	0

RICHARDSON John
Born: Durham, England, 28 July, 1966 — F

League Club	Source	Date Signed	Seasons Played	Apps	Subs	Gls
Colchester U	Chesham U	09/93	93	1	7	0

RICHARDSON John Pattinson
Born: Stannington, Northumberland, England, 5 February, 1949 — CD

League Club	Source	Date Signed	Seasons Played	Apps	Subs	Gls
Millwall	Jnr	-	65	1	0	0
Brentford	Tr	08/66	66-69	83	2	7
Fulham	Tr	08/69	69-72	61	10	6
Aldershot	Tr	07/73	73-76	120	1	6

RICHARDSON Jonathan Derek (Jon)
Born: Nottingham, England, 29 August, 1975 — CD

League Club	Source	Date Signed	Seasons Played	Apps	Subs	Gls
Exeter C	YT	07/94	93-99	242	5	8
Oxford U	Tr	08/00	00-01	57	2	2

RICHARDSON Joseph Arthur Searles (Joe)
Born: Sheffield, England, 17 March, 1942 — IF
Died: Liverpool, England, 1966

League Club	Source	Date Signed	Seasons Played	Apps	Subs	Gls
Birmingham C	Winsford U	09/59				
Sheffield U	Tr	01/60				
Rochdale	Tr	10/60	60-64	115	-	31
Tranmere Rov	Tr	07/65				

RICHARDSON Kevin
Born: Newcastle-upon-Tyne, England, 4 December, 1962 — DM
England: 1

League Club	Source	Date Signed	Seasons Played	Apps	Subs	Gls
Everton	App	12/80	81-86	95	15	16
Watford	Tr	09/86	86	39	0	2
Arsenal	Tr	08/87	87-89	88	8	5
Aston Villa	Real Sociedad (SPN)	08/91	91-94	142	1	13
Coventry C	Tr	02/95	94-97	75	3	0
Southampton	Tr	09/97	97	25	3	0
Barnsley	Tr	07/98	98-99	28	2	0
Blackpool	L	01/00	99	20	0	1

RICHARDSON Kieran Edward
Born: Greenwich, SE London, England, 21 October, 1984 — LB/M
England: 8/U21-12

League Club	Source	Date Signed	Seasons Played	Apps	Subs	Gls
Manchester U	Sch	08/03	02-06	20	21	2
West Bromwich A	L	01/05	04	11	1	3
Sunderland	Tr	07/07	07-12	124	10	14
Fulham	Tr	08/12	12-13	40	5	5
Aston Villa	Tr	07/14	14	16	6	0

RICHARDSON Leam Nathan
Born: Leeds, England, 19 November, 1979 — RB

League Club	Source	Date Signed	Seasons Played	Apps	Subs	Gls
Blackburn Rov	YT	12/97				
Bolton W	Tr	07/00	00-01	5	8	0
Notts Co	L	11/01	01	20	1	0
Blackpool	L	12/02	02	20	0	0
Blackpool	Tr	07/03	03-04	44	7	0
Accrington Stan	Tr	08/05	06-11	81	19	2

RICHARDSON Lee James
Born: Halifax, West Yorkshire, England, 12 March, 1969 — M

League Club	Source	Date Signed	Seasons Played	Apps	Subs	Gls
Halifax T	YT	07/87	86-88	43	13	2
Watford	Tr	02/89	88-89	40	1	1
Blackburn Rov	Tr	08/90	90-91	50	12	3
Oldham Ath	Aberdeen	08/94	94-96	82	6	21
Stockport Co	L	08/97	97	4	2	0
Huddersfield T	Tr	10/97	97-98	29	7	3
Bury	L	08/99	99	5	0	1
Chesterfield	Livingston	08/00	00-01	43	1	1

RICHARDSON Lloyd Matthew
Born: Dewsbury, West Yorkshire, England, 7 October, 1977 — M
England: Youth

League Club	Source	Date Signed	Seasons Played	Apps	Subs	Gls
Oldham Ath	YT	10/94	96	0	1	0

RICHARDSON Marcus Glenroy
Born: Reading, England, 31 August, 1977 — F

League Club	Source	Date Signed	Seasons Played	Apps	Subs	Gls
Cambridge U	Harrow Bor	03/01	00-01	7	9	2
Torquay U	Tr	09/01	01-02	21	18	8
Hartlepool U	Tr	10/02	02-03	23	4	5
Lincoln C	L	08/03	03	9	3	4
Lincoln C	Tr	12/03	03-04	32	8	10
Rochdale	L	02/05	04	1	1	0

League Club	Source	Date Signed	Seasons Played	Apps	Subs	Gls
Yeovil T	Tr	03/05	04	2	2	0
Chester C	Tr	07/05	05	22	12	4
Macclesfield T	L	03/06	05	8	0	3
Bury	Crawley T	08/07	07	1	0	0

RICHARDSON Michael Scott
Born: Newcastle-upon-Tyne, England, 17 March, 1992 — M

League Club	Source	Date Signed	Seasons Played	Apps	Subs	Gls
Newcastle U	Walker Central	08/10				
Leyton Orient	L	08/11	11	1	2	0
Gillingham	L	02/13	12	1	1	0
Accrington Stan	L	08/13	13	10	5	0

RICHARDSON Neil Thomas
Born: Sunderland, England, 3 March, 1968 — CD/M

League Club	Source	Date Signed	Seasons Played	Apps	Subs	Gls
Rotherham U	Brandon U	08/89	89-98	168	16	9
Exeter C	L	11/96	96	14	0	0
Mansfield T	Tr	08/99	99	31	0	0

RICHARDSON Nicholas John (Nick)
Born: Halifax, West Yorkshire, England, 11 April, 1967 — M

League Club	Source	Date Signed	Seasons Played	Apps	Subs	Gls
Halifax T	Emley	11/88	88-91	89	12	17
Cardiff C	Tr	08/92	92-94	106	5	13
Wrexham	L	10/94	94	4	0	2
Chester C	L	12/94	94	6	0	1
Bury	Tr	08/95	95	3	2	0
Chester C	Tr	09/95	95-99	158	11	11
York C	Tr	02/01	00-01	33	6	1

RICHARDSON Norman
Born: Hamsterley, County Durham, England, 15 April, 1915 — FB
Died: Bolton, Greater Manchester, England, 11 April, 1981

League Club	Source	Date Signed	Seasons Played	Apps	Subs	Gls
Bolton W	Medomsley Jnrs	05/33				
New Brighton	Tr	02/36	35-50	213	-	0

RICHARDSON Paul
Born: Selston, Nottinghamshire, England, 25 October, 1949 — M
England: Youth

League Club	Source	Date Signed	Seasons Played	Apps	Subs	Gls
Nottingham F	App	08/67	67-76	199	23	18
Chester C	Tr	10/76	76	28	0	2
Stoke C	Tr	06/77	77-80	124	3	10
Sheffield U	Tr	08/81	81-82	35	1	2
Blackpool	L	01/83	82	4	0	0
Swindon T	Tr	07/83	83	7	0	0
Swansea C	Tr	09/84	84	12	0	0

RICHARDSON Paul Andrew
Born: Hucknall, Nottinghamshire, England, 7 November, 1962 — M
England: Semi Pro-3

League Club	Source	Date Signed	Seasons Played	Apps	Subs	Gls
Derby Co	Nuneaton Bor	08/84	84	7	7	0

RICHARDSON Roderick Keith (Rod)
Born: Hunstanton, Norfolk, England, 1 October, 1942 — IF

League Club	Source	Date Signed	Seasons Played	Apps	Subs	Gls
Torquay U	Norwich C (Am)	07/62	62-63	7	-	1

RICHARDSON Russell Lee
Born: Sheffield, England, 21 October, 1964 — RB
England: Schools

League Club	Source	Date Signed	Seasons Played	Apps	Subs	Gls
Scunthorpe U	YT	08/83	83	2	0	0

RICHARDSON Stanley (Stan)
Born: Harrington, Cumbria, England, 28 April, 1924 — LW
Died: Whitehaven, Cumbria, England, April, 2005

League Club	Source	Date Signed	Seasons Played	Apps	Subs	Gls
Workington	Frizington White Star	08/51	51	9	-	1

RICHARDSON Steven Earl (Steve)
Born: Slough, Berkshire, England, 11 February, 1962 — LB

League Club	Source	Date Signed	Seasons Played	Apps	Subs	Gls
Southampton	App	02/80				
Reading	Tr	07/82	82-92	373	7	3

RICHARDSON Stuart
Born: Leeds, England, 12 June, 1938 — WH

League Club	Source	Date Signed	Seasons Played	Apps	Subs	Gls
Queens Park Rgrs	Methley U	11/56	58	1	-	0
Oldham Ath	Tr	07/59	59	22	-	0

RICHARDSON Thomas (Tommy)
Born: Reading, England, 1 February, 1931 — IF/D
Died: Aldershot, Hampshire, England, 18 February, 1976

League Club	Source	Date Signed	Seasons Played	Apps	Subs	Gls
Middlesbrough		09/52				
Southport	Tr	05/54				
Aldershot	Tr	07/55	55-57	41	-	9

RICHARDSON William (Bill)
Born: Bedlington, Northumberland, England, 25 October, 1943 — LB

League Club	Source	Date Signed	Seasons Played	Apps	Subs	Gls
Sunderland	Jnr	10/60				
Mansfield T	Tr	10/65	65-67	61	2	0
York C	Tr	06/68	68	24	0	0

RICHENS Michael Keith
Born: Bedford, England, 28 February, 1995 — RB

League Club	Source	Date Signed	Seasons Played	Apps	Subs	Gls
Peterborough U	Sch	07/12				
Stevenage	L	09/14	14	2	0	0

RICHES Steven Alexander (Steve)
Born: Sydney, Australia, 6 August, 1976 — W

League Club	Source	Date Signed	Seasons Played	Apps	Subs	Gls
Leyton Orient	Warringah D's (AUS)	09/96	96	2	3	0

RICHLEY Lionel (Len)
Born: Gateshead, Tyne and Wear, England, 2 July, 1924 — LH
Died: Newcastle-upon-Tyne, England, 1980

League Club	Source	Date Signed	Seasons Played	Apps	Subs	Gls
Hartlepool U	Tonbridge	06/51	51-53	72	-	0

RICHMAN Simon Andrew
Born: Ormskirk, Lancashire, England, 2 June, 1990 — RW

League Club	Source	Date Signed	Seasons Played	Apps	Subs	Gls
Port Vale	Sch	04/08	07-09	26	22	5

RICHMOND Andrew John (Andy)
Born: Nottingham, England, 9 January, 1983 — G

League Club	Source	Date Signed	Seasons Played	Apps	Subs	Gls
Chesterfield	Sch	07/02	02-04	7	1	0

RICHMOND John Frederick
Born: Derby, England, 17 September, 1938 — LH

League Club	Source	Date Signed	Seasons Played	Apps	Subs	Gls
Derby Co	Derby Corinthians	01/56	57-62	6	-	0

RICKABY Stanley (Stan)
Born: Stockton-on-Tees, Cleveland, England, 12 March, 1924 — RB
Died: Perth, Australia, 11 February, 2014
England: 1/FLge-1

League Club	Source	Date Signed	Seasons Played	Apps	Subs	Gls
Middlesbrough	South Bank	07/46	47-49	10	-	0
West Bromwich A	Tr	02/50	49-54	189	-	2

RICKARD Derek Bryan Philip
Born: Plymouth, England, 1 October, 1947 — F

League Club	Source	Date Signed	Seasons Played	Apps	Subs	Gls
Plymouth Arg	St Austell	12/69	69-73	101	9	41
Bournemouth	Tr	07/74	74-75	22	10	6

RICKARD Matthew Richard (Matt)
Born: Exeter, England, 29 January, 1993 — F

League Club	Source	Date Signed	Seasons Played	Apps	Subs	Gls
Plymouth Arg	Sch	-	10	0	1	0

RICKARDS Kenneth (Ken)
Born: Middlesbrough, England, 22 March, 1929 — CF

League Club	Source	Date Signed	Seasons Played	Apps	Subs	Gls
Hull C	Middlesbrough Park	05/47				
Darlington	Tr	01/50	49	8	-	0

RICKARDS Scott
Born: Sutton Coldfield, West Midlands, England, 3 November, 1981 — F

League Club	Source	Date Signed	Seasons Played	Apps	Subs	Gls
Kidderminster Hrs	Tamworth	12/03	03-04	5	12	1

RICKERS Paul Steven
Born: Pontefract, West Yorkshire, England, 9 May, 1975 — M/D

League Club	Source	Date Signed	Seasons Played	Apps	Subs	Gls
Oldham Ath	YT	07/93	94-01	242	19	20
Northampton T	Tr	07/02	02	8	3	0

RICKETT Horace Francis John
Born: Thurrock, Essex, England, 3 January, 1912 — G
Died: Colchester, Essex, England, January, 1989

League Club	Source	Date Signed	Seasons Played	Apps	Subs	Gls
Southend U	Chelmsford C	09/40				
Leyton Orient	Tr	02/43				
Fulham	Tr	11/45				
Reading	Chelmsford C	06/46	46-47	22	-	0

RICKETT Walter
Born: Sheffield, England, 20 March, 1917 — W
Died: Kettering, Northamptonshire, England, July, 1991
England: B-1

League Club	Source	Date Signed	Seasons Played	Apps	Subs	Gls
Sheffield U	Aqueduct	05/39	46-47	57	-	16
Blackpool	Tr	01/48	47-49	42	-	7
Sheffield Wed	Tr	10/49	49-52	95	-	13
Rotherham U	Tr	09/52	52	28	-	4
Halifax T	Tr	08/53	53	31	-	2

RICKETTS Alan
Born: Crawley, West Sussex, England, 30 October, 1962 — F

League Club	Source	Date Signed	Seasons Played	Apps	Subs	Gls
Crewe Alex	Wrexham (NC)	08/81	81	14	3	2

RICKETTS Donovan Damon
Born: Montego Bay, Jamaica, 7 June, 1977 — G
Jamaica: 100

League Club	Source	Date Signed	Seasons Played	Apps	Subs	Gls
Bolton W	Village U (JAM)	01/04				
Bradford C	Tr	08/04	04-07	108	0	0

RICKETTS Graham Anthony
Born: Oxford, England, 30 July, 1939 — WH
England: Youth

League Club	Source	Date Signed	Seasons Played	Apps	Subs	Gls
Bristol Rov	Jnr	08/56	56-60	32	-	0
Stockport Co	Tr	07/61	61-63	119	-	6
Doncaster Rov	Tr	07/64	64-67	143	7	16
Peterborough U	Tr	03/68	67-68	46	3	1

RICKETTS Mark James
Born: Sidcup, SE London, England, 7 January, 1984 — D/M

League Club	Source	Date Signed	Seasons Played	Apps	Subs	Gls
Charlton Ath	Sch	08/03				
MK Dons	L	11/05	05	4	1	0

RICKETTS Michael Barrington
Born: Birmingham, England, 4 December, 1978 — F
England: 1

League Club	Source	Date Signed	Seasons Played	Apps	Subs	Gls
Walsall	YT	09/96	95-99	31	45	14
Bolton W	Tr	07/00	00-02	63	35	37
Middlesbrough	Tr	01/03	02-03	12	20	3
Leeds U	Tr	07/04	04-05	10	15	0
Stoke C	L	02/05	04	1	10	0
Cardiff C	L	08/05	05	17	0	5
Burnley	L	01/06	05	12	1	2
Southend U	Tr	07/06	06	0	2	0
Preston NE	Tr	01/07	06	7	7	1
Oldham Ath	Tr	07/07	07	8	1	2
Walsall	L	11/07	07	12	0	3
Walsall		07/08	08	25	3	9
Tranmere Rov	Tr	08/09	09	7	5	2

RICKETTS Rohan Anthony
Born: Clapham, SW London, England, 22 December, 1982 — RB
England: Youth

League Club	Source	Date Signed	Seasons Played	Apps	Subs	Gls
Arsenal	YT	09/01				
Tottenham H	Tr	07/02	03-04	17	13	1
Coventry C	L	10/04	04	5	1	0
Wolverhampton W	L	03/05	04-06	35	16	1
Queens Park Rgrs	L	03/07	06	0	2	0
Barnsley	Tr	07/07	07	2	8	0
Exeter C	Shamrock Rov (ROI)	03/12	11	0	1	0

RICKETTS Samuel Derek (Sam)
Born: Aylesbury, Buckinghamshire, England, 11 October, 1981 — RB
England: Semi Pro-4//Wales: 52

League Club	Source	Date Signed	Seasons Played	Apps	Subs	Gls
Oxford U	YT	04/00	00-02	32	13	1
Swansea C	Telford U	06/04	04-05	85	1	1
Hull C	Tr	07/06	06-08	111	2	1
Bolton W	Tr	08/09	09-12	89	7	1
Wolverhampton W	Tr	07/13	13-14	46	2	2
Swindon T	L	03/15	14	8	1	0

RICKIS Victor Allen Fyfe Mann (Vic)
Born: Edinburgh, Scotland, 26 November, 1940 — LW

League Club	Source	Date Signed	Seasons Played	Apps	Subs	Gls
Millwall	Dalkeith Thistle	12/59	60	3	-	1

RIDDICK Gordon George
Born: Watford, Hertfordshire, England, 6 November, 1943 — M

League Club	Source	Date Signed	Seasons Played	Apps	Subs	Gls
Luton T	Jnr	04/61	62-66	101	1	16
Gillingham	Tr	03/67	66-69	114	0	24
Charlton Ath	Tr	11/69	69-70	26	3	5
Leyton Orient	Tr	10/70	70-72	13	8	3
Northampton T	Tr	12/72	72-73	28	0	3
Brentford	Tr	10/73	73-76	106	4	5

RIDEHALGH Liam Mark
Born: Halifax, West Yorkshire, England, 20 April, 1991 — LB

League Club	Source	Date Signed	Seasons Played	Apps	Subs	Gls
Huddersfield T	Sch	07/09	10	15	5	0
Swindon T	L	09/11	11	9	2	0
Chesterfield	L	01/12	11	20	0	1
Chesterfield	L	08/12	12	12	2	0
Rotherham U	L	11/12	12	19	1	0
Tranmere Rov	Tr	09/13	13-14	49	5	1

RIDEOUT Brian James
Born: Bristol, England, 15 September, 1940 — FB

League Club	Source	Date Signed	Seasons Played	Apps	Subs	Gls
Bristol Rov	Jnr	02/59	60	1	-	0

RIDEOUT Paul David
Born: Bournemouth, England, 14 August, 1964 — F
England: U21-5/Youth/Schools

League Club	Source	Date Signed	Seasons Played	Apps	Subs	Gls
Swindon T	App	08/81	80-82	90	5	38
Aston Villa	Tr	06/83	83-84	50	4	19
Southampton	Bari (ITA)	07/88	88-91	68	7	19
Swindon T	L	03/91	90	9	0	1
Notts Co	Tr	09/91	91	9	2	3
Everton	Glasgow Rangers	08/92	92-96	86	26	29
Tranmere Rov	Shengzhen (CHN)	07/00	00-01	42	4	6

RIDGE Roy
Born: Sheffield, England, 21 October, 1934 — RB

League Club	Source	Date Signed	Seasons Played	Apps	Subs	Gls
Sheffield U	Ecclesfield	11/51	53-60	11	-	0
Rochdale	Tr	08/64	64-65	85	0	0

RIDGEWELL Liam Matthew
Born: Bexleyheath, SE London, England, 21 July, 1984 — CD
England: U21-8/Youth

League Club	Source	Date Signed	Seasons Played	Apps	Subs	Gls
Aston Villa	YT	07/01	03-06	66	13	6
Bournemouth	L	10/02	02	2	3	0
Birmingham C	Tr	08/07	07-11	150	2	9
West Bromwich A	Tr	01/12	11-13	74	2	2
Wigan Ath (L)	Portland Timbers (USA)	01/15	14	6	0	0

RIDGWAY Ian David
Born: Reading, England, 28 December, 1975 — M

League Club	Source	Date Signed	Seasons Played	Apps	Subs	Gls
Notts Co	YT	07/94	94-96	3	4	0

RIDING Alan
Born: Preston, Lancashire, England, 14 March, 1945 — CF

League Club	Source	Date Signed	Seasons Played	Apps	Subs	Gls
Exeter C	Colchester U (Am)	07/64	65	1	0	0

RIDINGS David (Dave)
Born: Farnworth, Greater Manchester, England, 27 February, 1970 — M

League Club	Source	Date Signed	Seasons Played	Apps	Subs	Gls
Halifax T	Curzon Ashton	01/93	92	21	0	4
Lincoln C	Tr	02/94	93	10	0	0
Crewe Alex	Ashton U	07/95	95	1	0	0

RIDLER David George (Dave)
Born: Liverpool, England, 12 March, 1976 — CD

League Club	Source	Date Signed	Seasons Played	Apps	Subs	Gls
Wrexham	Rocky's, Liverpool	07/96	96-00	104	12	1
Macclesfield T	Tr	07/01	01-02	53	3	0
Shrewsbury T	Tr	07/03	04	6	3	0

RIDLEY David George Henry (Dave)
Born: Pontypridd, Rhondda Cynon Taff, Wales, 16 December, 1916 — CF
Died: Pontypridd, Rhondda Cynon Taff, Wales, 13 September, 1998

League Club	Source	Date Signed	Seasons Played	Apps	Subs	Gls
Millwall	Bedford T	01/45				
Brighton & HA	Tr	07/46	46	5	-	0

RIDLEY John
Born: Consett, County Durham, England, 27 April, 1952 — CD/M

League Club	Source	Date Signed	Seasons Played	Apps	Subs	Gls
Port Vale	Sheffield Univ	08/73	73-78	149	7	3
Leicester C	Tr	10/78	78	17	7	0
Chesterfield	Tr	08/79	79-81	121	3	8
Port Vale	Tr	08/82	82-84	105	9	5

RIDLEY Lee
Born: Scunthorpe, North Lincolnshire, England, 5 December, 1981 — LB

League Club	Source	Date Signed	Seasons Played	Apps	Subs	Gls
Scunthorpe U	YT	07/01	00-06	87	13	2
Cheltenham T	Tr	07/07	07-09	58	4	1
Darlington	L	11/07	07	6	0	0
Lincoln C	L	01/08	07	15	0	0

RIDLEY Robert Michael (Bob)
Born: Reading, England, 30 May, 1942 — W

League Club	Source	Date Signed	Seasons Played	Apps	Subs	Gls
Portsmouth	Jnr	06/60				
Gillingham	Tr	07/61	61-66	71	2	8

RIDYARD Alfred (Alf)
Born: Cudworth, South Yorkshire, England, 5 March, 1908 — CH
Died: Sandwell, West Midlands, England, 1981

League Club	Source	Date Signed	Seasons Played	Apps	Subs	Gls
Barnsley	Shafton	08/28	30-31	21	-	3
West Bromwich A	Tr	06/32	32-36	31	-	0
Queens Park Rgrs	Tr	03/38	37-47	28	-	0

RIEDLE Karl-Heinz
Born: Weiler-Simmerberg, Germany, 16 September, 1965 — F
Germany: 42/U21-4/Youth

League Club	Source	Date Signed	Seasons Played	Apps	Subs	Gls
Liverpool	Bor Dortmund (GER)	08/97	97-99	34	26	11
Fulham	Tr	09/99	99-00	16	19	6

RIEPER Marc Jensen
Born: Copenhagen, Denmark, 5 June, 1968 — CD
Denmark: 61/U21-4

League Club	Source	Date Signed	Seasons Played	Apps	Subs	Gls
West Ham U	Brondby (DEN)	12/94	94-97	83	7	5

RIERA Alberto (Albert)
Born: Manacor, Mallorca, Spain, 15 April, 1982 — LW
Spain: 16/U21-15

League Club	Source	Date Signed	Seasons Played	Apps	Subs	Gls
Manchester C (L)	RCD Espanyol (SPN)	01/06	05	12	3	1
Liverpool	RCD Espanyol (SPN)	09/08	08-09	33	7	3
Watford (L)	Udinese (ITA)	03/14	13	6	2	1

RIERA Arnau Caldenteny
Born: Manacor, Mallorca, Spain, 1 October, 1981 — M

League Club	Source	Date Signed	Seasons Played	Apps	Subs	Gls
Sunderland	Barcelona B (SPN)	11/06	06	0	1	0
Southend U	L	11/06	06	1	1	0

RIERA Oriol
Born: Vic, Spain, 3 July, 1986 — F

League Club	Source	Date Signed	Seasons Played	Apps	Subs	Gls
Wigan Ath	CA Osasuna (SPN)	06/14	14	6	7	1

RIETHER Sascha
Born: Lahr, Germany, 23 March, 1983 — RB
Germany: 2/U21-20

League Club	Source	Date Signed	Seasons Played	Apps	Subs	Gls
Fulham (L)	FC Koln (GER)	07/12	12	35	0	1
Fulham	FC Koln (GER)	07/13	13	30	1	0

RIGBY Anthony Angelo (Tony)
Born: Ormskirk, Lancashire, England, 10 August, 1972 — M

League Club	Source	Date Signed	Seasons Played	Apps	Subs	Gls
Crewe Alex	YT	05/90				
Bury	Barrow	01/93	92-98	120	46	19
Scarborough	L	02/97	96	5	0	1
Shrewsbury T	Tr	09/99	99	4	4	1

RIGBY Edward (Eddie)
Born: Atherton, Greater Manchester, England, 20 April, 1925 — RH/FB
Died: Shrewsbury, Shropshire, England, 13 February, 2012

League Club	Source	Date Signed	Seasons Played	Apps	Subs	Gls
Manchester C		02/48				
Barrow	Tr	07/49	49	19	-	0

RIGBY Ernest (Ernie)
Born: Kirkham, Lancashire, England, 8 April, 1928 — RB
Died: Fleetwood, Lancashire, England, 12 December, 1999

League Club	Source	Date Signed	Seasons Played	Apps	Subs	Gls
Accrington Stan	Blackpool (Am)	02/51	50-51	10	-	0

RIGBY Jack
Born: Golborne, Greater Manchester, England, 29 July, 1924 — CH
Died: Blackburn, Greater Manchester, England, November, 1997

League Club	Source	Date Signed	Seasons Played	Apps	Subs	Gls
Manchester C	Bryn Boys Brigade	12/46	46-52	100	-	0

RIGBY Jonathan Kendall (Jon)
Born: Bury St Edmunds, Suffolk, England, 31 January, 1965 — F

League Club	Source	Date Signed	Seasons Played	Apps	Subs	Gls
Norwich C	App	08/82	83-84	7	3	0
Aldershot	Tr	03/86	85	1	0	0
Cambridge U	Tr	10/86	86-87	28	3	5

RIGBY Lloyd Joseph
Born: Wigan, Greater Manchester, England, 27 February, 1989 — G

League Club	Source	Date Signed	Seasons Played	Apps	Subs	Gls
Rochdale	Sch	07/07				
Stockport Co	Vauxhall Motors	08/08	09	2	0	0

RIGBY Norman
Born: Warsop, Nottinghamshire, England, 23 May, 1923 — CH/LB
Died: Newark, Nottinghamshire, England, 21 August, 2001

League Club	Source	Date Signed	Seasons Played	Apps	Subs	Gls
Notts Co	Ransome & Marles	09/44	47-50	46	-	0
Peterborough U	Tr	07/51	60-61	55	-	0

RIGBY William (Bill)
Born: Chester, England, 9 June, 1921 — G
Died: Greasby, Wirral, England, 1 June, 2010

League Club	Source	Date Signed	Seasons Played	Apps	Subs	Gls
Chester C	Jnr	08/46	46	1	-	0

RIGG Sean Michael
Born: Bristol, England, 1 October, 1988 — LW

League Club	Source	Date Signed	Seasons Played	Apps	Subs	Gls
Bristol Rov	Jnr	06/06	06-08	15	42	2
Port Vale	Tr	11/09	09-11	58	35	16
Oxford U	Tr	05/12	12-13	61	11	7
AFC Wimbledon	Tr	05/14	14	39	5	5

RIGG Steven James
Born: Keswick, Cumbria, England, 30 June, 1992 — F

League Club	Source	Date Signed	Seasons Played	Apps	Subs	Gls
Carlisle U	Penrith	07/14	14	19	9	6

RIGG Thomas (Tommy)
Born: Bedlington, Northumberland, England, 20 February, 1920 — G
Died: Northumberland, England, May, 1995

League Club	Source	Date Signed	Seasons Played	Apps	Subs	Gls
Middlesbrough	Ashington	02/39				
Watford	Ashington	06/46	46-48	80	-	0
Gillingham	Consett	08/51	51-55	192	-	0

RIGGOTT Christopher Mark (Chris)
Born: Derby, England, 1 September, 1980 — CD
England: U21-8/Youth

League Club	Source	Date Signed	Seasons Played	Apps	Subs	Gls
Derby Co	YT	10/98	99-02	87	4	5
Middlesbrough	Tr	01/03	02-09	95	9	5
Stoke C	L	02/08	07	9	0	0
Cardiff C	Tr	09/10	10	2	0	0
Derby Co		08/11				

RIGGS Leslie John (Les)
Born: Portsmouth, England, 30 May, 1935 — WH

League Club	Source	Date Signed	Seasons Played	Apps	Subs	Gls
Gillingham	Jnr	06/52	53-57	152	-	3
Newport Co	Tr	06/58	58-60	110	-	3
Bury	Tr	06/61	61	6	-	0
Crewe Alex	Tr	02/63	62-63	67	-	6
Gillingham	Tr	09/64	64-65	17	1	1

RIGOGLIOSO Adriano
Born: Liverpool, England, 28 May, 1979 — W
England: Semi Pro-1

League Club	Source	Date Signed	Seasons Played	Apps	Subs	Gls
Doncaster Rov	Morecambe	11/03	03-04	7	22	0

RIGTERS Maceo
Born: Amsterdam, Netherlands, 22 January, 1984 — W
Netherlands: U21-9

League Club	Source	Date Signed	Seasons Played	Apps	Subs	Gls
Blackburn Rov	NAC Breda (NED)	07/07	07	0	2	0
Norwich C	L	03/08	07	0	2	0
Barnsley	L	08/08	08	4	15	0

RIIHILAHTI Aki Pasinpoika
Born: Helsinki, Finland, 9 September, 1976 — DM
Finland: 69/U21-2/Youth

League Club	Source	Date Signed	Seasons Played	Apps	Subs	Gls
Crystal Palace	Valerenga (NOR)	03/01	00-05	130	27	13

RIISE Bjorn Helge
Born: Aalesund, Norway, 21 June, 1983 — M
Norway: 35/U21-16

League Club	Source	Date Signed	Seasons Played	Apps	Subs	Gls
Fulham	Lillestrom (NOR)	07/09	09-10	5	10	0
Sheffield U	L	02/11	10	9	4	1
Portsmouth	L	09/11	11	2	0	0

RIISE John Arne
Born: Molde, Norway, 24 September, 1980 — LB/M
Norway: 110/U21-17/Youth

League Club	Source	Date Signed	Seasons Played	Apps	Subs	Gls
Liverpool	AS Monaco (FRA)	07/01	01-07	196	38	21
Fulham	AS Roma (ITA)	07/11	11-13	81	6	0

RILEY Brian Francis
Born: Bolton, Greater Manchester, England, 14 September, 1937 — LW

League Club	Source	Date Signed	Seasons Played	Apps	Subs	Gls
Bolton W	Jnr	12/54	56-58	8	-	1

RILEY Christopher John (Chris)
Born: Rhyl, Denbighshire, Wales, 19 January, 1939 — IF
Died: Rutland, England, 5 June, 1983

League Club	Source	Date Signed	Seasons Played	Apps	Subs	Gls
Crewe Alex	Rhyl	03/58	57-63	139	-	46
Tranmere Rov	Tr	07/64				

RILEY David Sydney
Born: Northampton, England, 8 December, 1960 — F

League Club	Source	Date Signed	Seasons Played	Apps	Subs	Gls
Nottingham F	Keyworth U	01/84	83-86	7	5	2
Darlington	L	02/87	86	6	0	2
Peterborough U	L	07/87	87	12	0	2
Port Vale	Tr	10/87	87-89	75	1	11
Peterborough U	Tr	03/90	89-91	73	11	21

RILEY Glyn
Born: Barnsley, South Yorkshire, England, 24 July, 1958 — F

League Club	Source	Date Signed	Seasons Played	Apps	Subs	Gls
Barnsley	App	07/76	74-81	103	28	16
Doncaster Rov	L	12/79	79	7	1	2
Bristol C	Tr	08/82	82-86	184	15	61
Torquay U	L	09/87	87	6	0	1
Aldershot	Tr	10/87	87-88	48	10	5

RILEY Howard
Born: Wigston, Leicestershire, England, 18 August, 1938 — W
England: U23-2/Youth

League Club	Source	Date Signed	Seasons Played	Apps	Subs	Gls
Leicester C	Jnr	08/55	55-64	193	-	38
Walsall	Tr	01/66	65	24	0	3
Barrow	Atlanta Chiefs (USA)	07/68	68	21	3	6

RILEY Hughen William
Born: Accrington, Lancashire, England, 12 June, 1947 — M

League Club	Source	Date Signed	Seasons Played	Apps	Subs	Gls
Rochdale		12/66	67-71	81	8	12
Crewe Alex	Tr	12/71	71-74	116	5	9
Bury	Tr	12/74	74-75	47	4	3
Bournemouth	Tr	04/76	76-77	69	3	7

RILEY Ian Michael
Born: Tollesbury, Essex, England, 8 February, 1947 — LB

League Club	Source	Date Signed	Seasons Played	Apps	Subs	Gls
Southend U	Maldon T	11/67	67-68	3	1	0

RILEY Joseph (Joe)
Born: Stockton-on-Tees, Cleveland, England — IF

League Club	Source	Date Signed	Seasons Played	Apps	Subs	Gls
Darlington (Am)	Stockton	08/49	49	8	-	2

RILEY Joseph Michael (Joe)
Born: Salford, England, 13 October, 1991 — RB

League Club	Source	Date Signed	Seasons Played	Apps	Subs	Gls
Bolton W	Sch	07/11	11	2	1	0
Oxford U	L	07/14	14	22	0	0
Bury	Tr	01/15	14	16	1	1

RILEY Martin James
Born: Wolverhampton, England, 5 December, 1986 — CD
England: Semi Pro-1/Youth

League Club	Source	Date Signed	Seasons Played	Apps	Subs	Gls
Wolverhampton W	Sch	03/05				
Cheltenham T	Kidderminster Hrs	07/10	10	26	0	0
Mansfield T	Wrexham	06/13	13-14	62	2	1

RILEY Paul Anthony
Born: Eastwood, Nottinghamshire, England, 29 September, 1982 — LB

League Club	Source	Date Signed	Seasons Played	Apps	Subs	Gls
Notts Co	YT	12/01	01-03	18	10	3

RILEY-LOWE Connor
Born: Paignton, Devon, England, 10 January, 1996 — LB

League Club	Source	Date Signed	Seasons Played	Apps	Subs	Gls
Exeter C	Sch	07/14	14	3	0	0

RIMMER Gilbert Henry (Gil)
Born: Southport, Merseyside, England, 14 July, 1932 — W
Died: Southport, Merseyside, England, December, 2008

League Club	Source	Date Signed	Seasons Played	Apps	Subs	Gls
Southport (Am)	Leyland Road	07/55	55	2	-	0

RIMMER John James (Jimmy)
Born: Southport, Merseyside, England, 10 February, 1948 — G
England: 1

League Club	Source	Date Signed	Seasons Played	Apps	Subs	Gls
Manchester U	App	05/65	67-72	34	0	0

League Club	Source	Date Signed	Seasons Played	Apps	Subs	Gls
Swansea C	L	10/73	73	17	0	0
Arsenal	Tr	02/74	73-76	124	0	0
Aston Villa	Tr	08/77	77-82	229	0	0
Swansea C	Tr	08/83	83-85	66	0	0

RIMMER Neill
Born: Liverpool, England, 13 November, 1967 — M
England: Youth/Schools

League Club	Source	Date Signed	Seasons Played	Apps	Subs	Gls
Everton	App	-	84	0	1	0
Ipswich T	Tr	08/85	85-87	19	3	3
Wigan Ath	Tr	07/88	88-95	184	6	10

RIMMER Raymond (Ray)
Born: Southport, Merseyside, England, 6 August, 1938 — LW

League Club	Source	Date Signed	Seasons Played	Apps	Subs	Gls
Southport (Am)	Formby Dons	08/55	55-57	8	-	0

RIMMER Stephen Anthony (Steve)
Born: Liverpool, England, 23 May, 1979 — CD

League Club	Source	Date Signed	Seasons Played	Apps	Subs	Gls
Manchester C	YT	05/96				
Port Vale	Tr	07/99	99	0	2	0

RIMMER Stuart Alan
Born: Southport, Merseyside, England, 12 October, 1964 — F
England: Youth

League Club	Source	Date Signed	Seasons Played	Apps	Subs	Gls
Everton	App	10/82	81-83	3	0	0
Chester C	Tr	01/85	84-87	110	4	67
Watford	Tr	03/88	87-88	10	0	1
Notts Co	Tr	11/88	88	3	1	2
Walsall	Tr	02/89	88-90	85	3	31
Barnsley	Tr	03/91	90	10	5	1
Chester C	Tr	08/91	91-97	213	33	67
Rochdale	L	09/94	94	3	0	0
Preston NE	L	12/94	94	0	2	0

RIMMER Warwick Robert
Born: Birkenhead, Wirral, England, 1 March, 1941 — D
England: Schools

League Club	Source	Date Signed	Seasons Played	Apps	Subs	Gls
Bolton W	Jnr	03/58	60-74	462	7	17
Crewe Alex	Tr	03/75	74-78	114	14	0

RIMMINGTON Norman
Born: Staincross, South Yorkshire, England, 29 November, 1923 — G

League Club	Source	Date Signed	Seasons Played	Apps	Subs	Gls
Barnsley	Mapplewell	02/45	46	27	-	0
Hartlepool U	Tr	12/47	47-51	124	-	0

RINALDI Douglas Medeiros
Born: Erval Seco, Brazil, 10 February, 1984 — M

League Club	Source	Date Signed	Seasons Played	Apps	Subs	Gls
Watford	Veranopolis (BRA)	01/07	06	6	1	1

RING Michael Paul (Mike)
Born: Brighton, England, 13 February, 1961 — W

League Club	Source	Date Signed	Seasons Played	Apps	Subs	Gls
Brighton & HA	App	02/79	81-83	1	4	0
Hull C	Ballymena U	07/84	84-85	17	7	2
Bolton W	L	03/86	85	1	2	0
Aldershot	Tr	07/86	86-88	53	26	16

RING Thomas (Tommy)
Born: Glasgow, Scotland, 8 August, 1930 — LW
Died: Glasgow, Scotland, 2 October, 1997
Scotland: 12/SLge-8

League Club	Source	Date Signed	Seasons Played	Apps	Subs	Gls
Everton	Clyde	01/60	59-60	27	-	6
Barnsley	Tr	11/61	61-62	21	-	1

RINGER Walter Albert
Born: Stanley, West Yorkshire, England, 7 October, 1941 — LW
Died: Leeds, England, September, 2007

League Club	Source	Date Signed	Seasons Played	Apps	Subs	Gls
Halifax T	Leeds U (Am)	12/59	59-60	6	-	0

RINGSTEAD Alfred (Alf)
Born: Dublin, Republic of Ireland, 14 October, 1927 — RW
Died: Sheffield, England, 15 January, 2000
Republic of Ireland: 20

League Club	Source	Date Signed	Seasons Played	Apps	Subs	Gls
Sheffield U	Northwich Victoria	11/50	50-58	247	-	101
Mansfield T	Tr	07/59	59	27	-	3

RINTANEN Mauno Olavi
Born: Helsinki, Finland, 28 April, 1925 — G
Died: Denmark, 13 July, 2000
Finland: 7

League Club	Source	Date Signed	Seasons Played	Apps	Subs	Gls
Hull C (Am)	HJK Helsinki (FIN)	09/56	56	4	-	0

RIOCH Bruce David
Born: Aldershot, Hampshire, England, 6 September, 1947 — M
Scotland: 24

League Club	Source	Date Signed	Seasons Played	Apps	Subs	Gls
Luton T	App	09/64	64-68	148	1	47
Aston Villa	Tr	07/69	69-73	149	5	34
Derby Co	Tr	02/74	73-76	106	0	34
Everton	Tr	12/76	76-77	30	0	3
Derby Co	Tr	11/77	77-79	40	1	4
Birmingham C	L	12/78	78	3	0	0
Sheffield U	L	03/79	78	8	0	1
Torquay U	Seattle Sounders (USA)	10/80	80-83	64	7	6

RIOCH Daniel Gordon (Neil)
Born: Paddington, Central London, England, 13 April, 1951 — CD
England: Youth

League Club	Source	Date Signed	Seasons Played	Apps	Subs	Gls
Luton T	App	07/68				
Aston Villa	Tr	09/69	69-74	17	5	3
York C	L	02/72	71	0	1	0
Northampton T	L	03/72	71	14	0	4
Plymouth Arg	Tr	05/75	75	3	2	0

RIOCH Gregor James (Greg)
Born: Sutton Coldfield, West Midlands, England, 24 June, 1975 — LB

League Club	Source	Date Signed	Seasons Played	Apps	Subs	Gls
Luton T	YT	07/93				
Barnet	L	09/93	93	3	0	0
Peterborough U	Tr	08/95	95	13	5	0
Hull C	Tr	07/96	96-98	86	5	6
Macclesfield T	Tr	07/99	99-00	58	1	6
Shrewsbury T	Tr	03/01	00-01	46	0	2

RIORDAN Derek George
Born: Edinburgh, Scotland, 16 January, 1983 — F
Scotland: 3/U21-5

League Club	Source	Date Signed	Seasons Played	Apps	Subs	Gls
Bristol Rov	St Johnstone	09/12	12	7	4	0

RIPLEY Andrew Ian (Andy)
Born: Middlesbrough, England, 10 December, 1975 — W

League Club	Source	Date Signed	Seasons Played	Apps	Subs	Gls
Darlington	YT	11/93	93	0	2	0

RIPLEY Connor James
Born: Stockton-on-Tees, Cleveland, England, 13 February, 1993 — G
England: Youth

League Club	Source	Date Signed	Seasons Played	Apps	Subs	Gls
Middlesbrough	Sch	01/11	10-11	1	1	0
Oxford U	L	04/12	11	1	0	0

RIPLEY Keith Anthony
Born: Normanton, West Yorkshire, England, 10 October, 1954 — LB

League Club	Source	Date Signed	Seasons Played	Apps	Subs	Gls
Huddersfield T	Gainsborough Trinity	08/78	78	2	3	0
Doncaster Rov	Tr	08/79	79	5	0	0

RIPLEY Stanley Keith (Keith)
Born: Normanton, West Yorkshire, England, 29 March, 1935 — WH
Died: Normanton, West Yorkshire, England, 5 November, 2012

League Club	Source	Date Signed	Seasons Played	Apps	Subs	Gls
Leeds U	Altofts YMCA	04/52	54-57	67	-	15
Norwich C	Tr	08/58	58	12	-	6
Mansfield T	Tr	11/58	58-59	31	-	5
Peterborough U	Tr	07/60	60-61	82	-	12
Doncaster Rov	Tr	08/62	62-65	123	5	7

RIPLEY Stuart Edward
Born: Middlesbrough, England, 20 November, 1967 — RW
England: 2/U21-8/Youth

League Club	Source	Date Signed	Seasons Played	Apps	Subs	Gls
Middlesbrough	App	12/85	84-91	210	39	26
Bolton W	L	02/86	85	5	0	1
Blackburn Rov	Tr	07/92	92-97	172	15	13
Southampton	Tr	07/98	98-01	36	17	1
Barnsley	L	11/00	00	8	2	1
Sheffield Wed	L	03/01	00	5	1	1

RISBRIDGER Gareth John
Born: High Wycombe, Buckinghamshire, England, 31 October, 1981 — M

League Club	Source	Date Signed	Seasons Played	Apps	Subs	Gls
Southend U	Yeovil T	07/01	01	0	1	0

RISDON Stanley William (Stan)
Born: Exeter, England, 13 August, 1913 — WH
Died: Hove, East Sussex, England, 2 August, 1979

League Club	Source	Date Signed	Seasons Played	Apps	Subs	Gls
Exeter C	St Mary's Majors	10/33	33-35	35	-	1
Brighton & HA	Tr	08/36	36-46	23	-	0

RISEBOROUGH Cyril
Born: Doncaster, South Yorkshire, England, 22 February, 1933 — RW

League Club	Source	Date Signed	Seasons Played	Apps	Subs	Gls
Swindon T	Silksworth CW	02/55	54-56	26	-	1

RISETH Vidar
Born: Levanger, Norway, 21 April, 1972 — F
Norway: 52

League Club	Source	Date Signed	Seasons Played	Apps	Subs	Gls
Luton T	Kongsvinger (NOR)	10/95	95	6	5	0

RISHWORTH Stephen Peter (Steve)
Born: Chester, England, 8 June, 1980 — M

League Club	Source	Date Signed	Seasons Played	Apps	Subs	Gls
Wrexham	Manchester C (YT)	08/98	98	0	4	0

RISOM Henrik
Born: Vildbjerg, Denmark, 24 July, 1968 — M
Denmark: 9

League Club	Source	Date Signed	Seasons Played	Apps	Subs	Gls
Stoke C	Vejle BK (DEN)	08/00	00	9	16	0

RISSER Oliver Hanjorge
Born: Windhoek, Namibia, 17 September, 1980 — M
Namibia: 27

League Club	Source	Date Signed	Seasons Played	Apps	Subs	Gls
Swindon T	Kuopio PS (FIN)	07/11	11	23	9	3
Stevenage	L	08/12	12	5	7	1
Aldershot T	Tr	01/13	12	11	3	0

RISSER Wilko Rudi
Born: Windhoek, Namibia, 11 August, 1982 — F
Namibia: 14

League Club	Source	Date Signed	Seasons Played	Apps	Subs	Gls
Aldershot T	SV Elversburg (GER)	02/12	11	8	8	3

RIST Frank Henry
Born: Leyton, NE London, England, 30 March, 1914 — CH
Died: Waltham Forest, NE London, England, 9 September, 2001

League Club	Source	Date Signed	Seasons Played	Apps	Subs	Gls
Leyton Orient	Grays Ath	08/32				
Charlton Ath	Tr	06/33	34-46	47	-	1

RITCHIE Andrew Timothy (Andy)
Born: Manchester, England, 28 November, 1960 — F
England: U21-1/Youth/Schools

League Club	Source	Date Signed	Seasons Played	Apps	Subs	Gls
Manchester U	App	12/77	77-80	26	7	13
Brighton & HA	Tr	10/80	80-82	82	7	23
Leeds U	Tr	03/83	82-86	127	9	40
Oldham Ath	Tr	08/87	87-94	187	30	82
Scarborough	Tr	08/95	95-96	59	9	17
Oldham Ath	Tr	02/97	96-98	14	12	2

RITCHIE David Mark
Born: Stoke-on-Trent, England, 20 January, 1971 — F

League Club	Source	Date Signed	Seasons Played	Apps	Subs	Gls
Stoke C	YT	07/89				
Stockport Co	Tr	03/90	89	0	1	0

RITCHIE John
Born: Paddington, Central London, England, 28 February, 1951 — F
England: Amateur-2

League Club	Source	Date Signed	Seasons Played	Apps	Subs	Gls
Arsenal	Slough T	04/72				
Hereford U	Tr	03/74	73-74	19	3	4

RITCHIE John
Born: Ashington, Northumberland, England, 10 April, 1944 — LB
Died: Staffordshire, England, 16 February, 2012
England: Amateur-1

League Club	Source	Date Signed	Seasons Played	Apps	Subs	Gls
Port Vale	Whitley Bay	12/65	65-66	50	0	3
Preston NE	Tr	04/67	66-71	94	0	5
Bradford C	Tr	03/72	71-72	20	0	0

RITCHIE John (Jack)
Born: Blairhall, Fife, Scotland, 31 March, 1927 — RH

League Club	Source	Date Signed	Seasons Played	Apps	Subs	Gls
Accrington Stan	Crossgates Primrose	06/49	49	13	-	0

RITCHIE John Brough
Born: Auchterderran, Fife, Scotland, 12 June, 1947 — G

League Club	Source	Date Signed	Seasons Played	Apps	Subs	Gls
Bradford C	Brechin C	07/71	71-73	64	0	0

RITCHIE John Henry
Born: Kettering, Northamptonshire, England, 12 July, 1941 — CF
Died: Newcastle-under-Lyme, Potteries, England, 23 February, 2007
England: FLge-1

League Club	Source	Date Signed	Seasons Played	Apps	Subs	Gls
Stoke C	Kettering T	06/62	62-66	110	0	64
Sheffield Wed	Tr	11/66	66-68	88	1	34
Stoke C	Tr	07/69	69-74	151	8	71

RITCHIE Matthew Thomas (Matt)
Born: Gosport, Hampshire, England, 10 September, 1989 — RW
Scotland: 4

League Club	Source	Date Signed	Seasons Played	Apps	Subs	Gls
Portsmouth	Sch	07/08	09-10	3	4	0
Dagenham & Red	L	09/08	08	36	1	11
Notts Co	L	09/09	09	12	4	3
Swindon T	L	02/10	09	0	4	0
Swindon T	Tr	10/10	10-12	101	2	26
Bournemouth	Tr	01/13	12-14	87	6	27

RITCHIE Paul Michael
Born: St Andrews, Fife, Scotland, 25 January, 1969 — F

League Club	Source	Date Signed	Seasons Played	Apps	Subs	Gls
Gillingham (L)	Dundee	02/93	92	6	0	3
Gillingham (L)	Dundee	09/94	94	5	0	1

RITCHIE Paul Simon
Born: Kirkcaldy, Fife, Scotland, 21 August, 1975 — CD
Scotland: 7/B/U21-7/Schools

League Club	Source	Date Signed	Seasons Played	Apps	Subs	Gls
Bolton W	Heart of Midlothian	12/99	99	13	1	0
Manchester C	Glasgow Rangers	08/00	00-01	11	9	0
Portsmouth	L	09/02	02	8	4	0
Derby Co	L	03/03	02	7	0	0
Walsall	Tr	08/03	03	33	0	1

RITCHIE Robert (Bob)
Born: Glasgow, Scotland, 1 February, 1920 — IF

League Club	Source	Date Signed	Seasons Played	Apps	Subs	Gls
Watford	Rickmansworth	02/48	48	1	-	0

RITCHIE Stephen Kilcar (Steve)
Born: Glasgow, Scotland, 17 February, 1954 — FB
Scotland: Schools

League Club	Source	Date Signed	Seasons Played	Apps	Subs	Gls
Bristol C	App	09/71	72	1	0	0
Hereford U	Greenock Morton	06/75	75-77	102	0	3
Torquay U	Aberdeen	03/79	78-79	58	0	2

RITCHIE Stuart Arthur
Born: Southampton, England, 20 May, 1968 — M

League Club	Source	Date Signed	Seasons Played	Apps	Subs	Gls
Aston Villa	App	05/86	86	0	1	0
Crewe Alex	Tr	06/87	87	13	5	0

RITCHIE Thomas (Tommy)
Born: Bangor, Down, Northern Ireland, 10 July, 1930 — IF

League Club	Source	Date Signed	Seasons Played	Apps	Subs	Gls
Manchester U	Bangor	12/50				
Reading	Tr	02/53	52-54	18	-	5
Grimsby T	Dartford	08/58	58	1	-	0
Barrow	Tr	12/58	58	16	-	6

RITCHIE Thomas Gibb (Tom)
Born: Edinburgh, Scotland, 2 January, 1952 — F

League Club	Source	Date Signed	Seasons Played	Apps	Subs	Gls
Bristol C	Bridgend Thistle	07/69	72-80	308	13	77
Sunderland	Tr	01/81	80-81	32	3	8
Carlisle U	L	03/82	81	14	1	0
Bristol C	Tr	06/82	82-84	92	1	25

RITCHIE William Saunders (Bill)
Born: Dundee, Scotland, 13 November, 1932 — CF

League Club	Source	Date Signed	Seasons Played	Apps	Subs	Gls
Bury	Stirling A	06/57	57-58	13	-	7
Stockport Co	Tr	03/59	58-60	52	-	12

RITSON John Albert
Born: Liverpool, England, 6 September, 1949 — RB

League Club	Source	Date Signed	Seasons Played	Apps	Subs	Gls
Bolton W	App	09/66	67-77	321	3	9
Bury	Tr	09/78	78-79	41	0	2

RITSON Ledger
Born: Gateshead, Tyne and Wear, England, 28 April, 1921 — LB
Died: Haringey, N London, England, 1977

League Club	Source	Date Signed	Seasons Played	Apps	Subs	Gls
Leyton Orient	Army	03/46	46-48	84	-	0

RIVEROS Cristian Miguel
Born: Posta Leiva, Paraguay, 16 October, 1982 — M
Paraguay: 90

League Club	Source	Date Signed	Seasons Played	Apps	Subs	Gls
Sunderland	Cruz Azul (MEX)	06/10	10	5	7	1

RIVERS Alan Desmond
Born: Portsmouth, England, 27 January, 1946 — CH

League Club	Source	Date Signed	Seasons Played	Apps	Subs	Gls
Luton T	App	01/64	65-66	25	5	1
Watford	Tr	09/67	67	0	2	0

RIVERS Mark Alan
Born: Crewe, Cheshire, England, 26 November, 1975 — W

League Club	Source	Date Signed	Seasons Played	Apps	Subs	Gls
Crewe Alex	YT	05/94	95-00	177	26	43
Norwich C	Tr	06/01	01-03	54	20	10
Crewe Alex	Tr	07/04	04-05	35	16	10
Carlisle U	Tr	01/06	05	2	2	0

RIVIERE Emmanuel Jose
Born: Le Lamentin, Martinique, 3 March, 1990 — F
France: U21-15/Youth

League Club	Source	Date Signed	Seasons Played	Apps	Subs	Gls
Newcastle U	AS Monaco (FRA)	07/14	14	15	8	1

RIX Benjamin (Ben)
Born: Wolverhampton, England, 11 December, 1982 — LM

League Club	Source	Date Signed	Seasons Played	Apps	Subs	Gls
Crewe Alex	YT	02/01	01-08	88	44	4
Bournemouth	L	01/06	05	7	4	0

RIX Graham Cyril
Born: Askern, South Yorkshire, England, 23 October, 1957 — LW
England: 17/B-3/U21-7

League Club	Source	Date Signed	Seasons Played	Apps	Subs	Gls
Arsenal	App	01/75	76-87	338	13	41
Brentford	L	12/87	87	6	0	0
Chelsea	Dundee	05/94	94	0	1	0

RIZA Omer Karime Ali
Born: Enfield, N London, England, 8 November, 1979 — LW
Turkey: B-1

League Club	Source	Date Signed	Seasons Played	Apps	Subs	Gls
Arsenal	YT	07/98				
West Ham U	Tr	12/99				
Barnet	L	10/00	00	7	3	4
Cambridge U	L	03/01	00	10	2	3
Cambridge U	Tr	08/02	02	43	3	11
Shrewsbury T	Trabzonspor (TKY)	04/09	08-09	1	9	0
Aldershot T	Tr	02/10	09	0	1	0

RIZZO Nicholas Anthony (Nicky)
Born: Sydney, Australia, 9 June, 1979 — W
Australia: 1/U23-9

League Club	Source	Date Signed	Seasons Played	Apps	Subs	Gls
Liverpool	Sydney Olympic (AUS)	09/96				
Crystal Palace	Tr	07/98	98-99	15	21	1
MK Dons	AC Prato (ITA)	11/04	04-06	28	22	4

League Club	Source	Date Signed	Seasons Played	Apps	Subs	Gls
Grimsby T	L	01/07	06	1	0	0
Chesterfield	L	03/07	06	2	2	0

ROACH Neville
Born: Reading, England, 29 September, 1978 — F

League Club	Source	Date Signed	Seasons Played	Apps	Subs	Gls
Reading	YT	05/97	96-98	5	11	1
Southend U	Tr	02/99	98-99	13	3	2
Oldham Ath	Eastern Pride (AUS)	03/01	00	0	1	0
Torquay U	Tr	08/01	01	5	7	1
Oxford U	Eastleigh	01/06	05	1	6	0

ROACHE Lee Paul
Born: Leytonstone, NE London, England, 30 April, 1984 — F

League Club	Source	Date Signed	Seasons Played	Apps	Subs	Gls
Barnet	Sch	08/03	05	2	6	1

ROAST Jesse
Born: Barking, E London, England, 16 March, 1964 — RB

League Club	Source	Date Signed	Seasons Played	Apps	Subs	Gls
Maidstone U	Barking	01/87	89-90	31	1	0

ROBB David Thomson
Born: Broughty Ferry, Angus, Scotland, 15 December, 1947 — F
Scotland: 5/SLge-3/U23-3

League Club	Source	Date Signed	Seasons Played	Apps	Subs	Gls
Norwich C	Tampa Bay R's (USA)	09/78	78	4	1	1

ROBB George
Born: Finsbury Park, N London, England, 1 June, 1926 — LW
Died: Haywards Heath, West Sussex, England, 25 December, 2011
England: 1/B-3/FLge-1/Amateur-17

League Club	Source	Date Signed	Seasons Played	Apps	Subs	Gls
Tottenham H	Finchley	12/51	51-58	182	-	53

ROBB Ian Alexander
Born: Doncaster, South Yorkshire, England, 1 June, 1955 — CD

League Club	Source	Date Signed	Seasons Played	Apps	Subs	Gls
York C	Jnr	02/73	73-74	4	0	0

ROBB William Lawson (Willie)
Born: Cambuslang, Glasgow, Scotland, 23 December, 1927 — LH
Died: Glasgow, Scotland, 18 May, 2002

League Club	Source	Date Signed	Seasons Played	Apps	Subs	Gls
Leyton Orient	Aberdeen	05/50	50	5	-	0
Bradford C	Albion Rov	10/54	54-57	127	-	4

ROBBEN Arjen
Born: Groningen, Netherlands, 23 January, 1984 — W
Netherlands: 86/U21-8/Youth

League Club	Source	Date Signed	Seasons Played	Apps	Subs	Gls
Chelsea	PSV Eindhoven (NED)	07/04	04-06	51	16	15

ROBBINS Gordon
Born: Barnsley, South Yorkshire, England, 7 February, 1936 — WH

League Club	Source	Date Signed	Seasons Played	Apps	Subs	Gls
Rotherham U	Wombwell	05/53				
Crewe Alex	Goole T	12/58	58	4	-	0

ROBBINS Robert (Robbie)
Born: Newton Abbot, Devon, England, 20 September, 1953 — G

League Club	Source	Date Signed	Seasons Played	Apps	Subs	Gls
Torquay U	Newton Abbot	08/76	76	19	0	0

ROBBINS Terence John (Terry)
Born: Southwark, S London, England, 14 January, 1965 — F
England: Semi Pro-6

League Club	Source	Date Signed	Seasons Played	Apps	Subs	Gls
Barnet	Welling U	07/95	95	9	6	1

ROBER Hans Jurgen (Jurgen)
Born: Gernrode, Germany, 25 December, 1953 — RM

League Club	Source	Date Signed	Seasons Played	Apps	Subs	Gls
Nottingham F	Calgary Boomers (CAN)	12/81	81	21	1	3

ROBERGE Valentin Sebastien Roger
Born: Paris, France, 9 June, 1987 — CD

League Club	Source	Date Signed	Seasons Played	Apps	Subs	Gls
Sunderland	CS Maritimo (POR)	07/13	13-14	8	2	0

ROBERT Fabien
Born: Lorient, France, 6 January, 1989 — W
France: Youth

League Club	Source	Date Signed	Seasons Played	Apps	Subs	Gls
Doncaster Rov (L)	Lorient (FRA)	01/12	11	7	6	2

ROBERT Laurent
Born: Saint-Benoit, Reunion, 21 May, 1975 — LW
France: 9/B-4/Youth

League Club	Source	Date Signed	Seasons Played	Apps	Subs	Gls
Newcastle U	Paris St-Germain (FRA)	08/01	01-04	110	19	22
Portsmouth	L	07/05	05	13	4	1
Derby Co	Levante (SPN)	01/08	07	3	1	0

ROBERTS Adam John
Born: Wythenshawe, Greater Manchester, England, 30 December, 1991 — M

League Club	Source	Date Signed	Seasons Played	Apps	Subs	Gls
Macclesfield T	Sch	05/10	10-11	1	3	0

ROBERTS Alan
Born: Bury, Greater Manchester, England, 23 April, 1946 — LB

League Club	Source	Date Signed	Seasons Played	Apps	Subs	Gls
Bradford Park Ave	Mossley	11/69	69	15	0	0

ROBERTS Alan
Born: Newcastle-upon-Tyne, England, 8 December, 1964 — RW

League Club	Source	Date Signed	Seasons Played	Apps	Subs	Gls
Middlesbrough	App	12/82	82-85	28	10	2
Darlington	Tr	09/85	85-87	116	3	19
Sheffield U	Tr	07/88	88-89	31	5	2
Lincoln C	Tr	10/89	89	10	0	0

ROBERTS Albert (Arthur)
Born: Goldthorpe, South Yorkshire, England, 27 January, 1907 — LB
Died: Elsecar, South Yorkshire, England, 27 January, 1957

League Club	Source	Date Signed	Seasons Played	Apps	Subs	Gls
Southampton	Ardsley Ath	08/29	30-37	156	-	0
Swansea C	Tr	08/38	38	16	-	0
York C	Tr	07/46	46	1	-	0

ROBERTS Andrew James (Andy)
Born: Dartford, Kent, England, 20 March, 1974 — M
England: U21-5

League Club	Source	Date Signed	Seasons Played	Apps	Subs	Gls
Millwall	YT	10/91	91-94	132	6	5
Crystal Palace	Tr	07/95	95-97	106	2	2
Wimbledon	Tr	03/98	97-01	92	9	6
Norwich C	L	01/02	01	4	1	0
Millwall	Tr	08/02	02-03	60	6	3

ROBERTS Anthony Mark (Tony)
Born: Holyhead, Anglesey, Wales, 4 August, 1969 — G
Wales: 2/B-2/U21-2/Youth

League Club	Source	Date Signed	Seasons Played	Apps	Subs	Gls
Queens Park Rgrs	YT	07/87	87-97	122	0	0
Millwall	Tr	08/98	98	8	0	0
Dagenham & Red	St Albans C	07/00	07-10	175	0	0

ROBERTS Benjamin James (Ben)
Born: Bishop Auckland, County Durham, England, 22 June, 1975 — G
England: U21-1

League Club	Source	Date Signed	Seasons Played	Apps	Subs	Gls
Middlesbrough	YT	03/93	96-97	15	1	0
Hartlepool U	L	10/95	95	4	0	0
Wycombe W	L	12/95	95	15	0	0
Bradford C	L	08/96	96	2	0	0
Millwall	L	02/99	98	11	0	0
Luton T	L	02/00	99	14	0	0
Charlton Ath	Tr	07/00	02	0	1	0
Reading	L	01/02	01	6	0	0
Luton T	L	08/02	02	5	0	0
Brighton & HA	L	01/03	02	3	0	0
Brighton & HA	Tr	07/03	03	32	0	0

ROBERTS Brian James
Born: Windsor, Berkshire, England, 3 February, 1967 — F

League Club	Source	Date Signed	Seasons Played	Apps	Subs	Gls
Reading	App	07/85	84-85	0	5	0

ROBERTS Brian Leslie Ford
Born: Manchester, England, 6 November, 1955 — FB

League Club	Source	Date Signed	Seasons Played	Apps	Subs	Gls
Coventry C	App	11/73	75-83	209	6	1
Hereford U	L	02/75	74	5	0	0
Birmingham C	Tr	03/84	83-89	182	5	0
Wolverhampton W	Tr	06/90	90	17	4	0

ROBERTS Christian John (Chris)
Born: Cardiff, Wales, 22 October, 1979 — F
Wales: U21-1/Youth

League Club	Source	Date Signed	Seasons Played	Apps	Subs	Gls
Cardiff C	YT	10/97	97-99	6	17	3
Exeter C	Tr	07/00	00-01	67	12	18
Bristol C	Tr	03/02	01-04	65	29	20
Swindon T	Tr	10/04	04-07	77	34	21

ROBERTS Cledwyn
Born: Colwyn Bay, Conwy, Wales, 12 August, 1947 — WH

League Club	Source	Date Signed	Seasons Played	Apps	Subs	Gls
Wrexham	Glan Conwy	08/65	65	1	0	0

ROBERTS Colin
Born: Castleford, West Yorkshire, England, 16 September, 1933 — WH

League Club	Source	Date Signed	Seasons Played	Apps	Subs	Gls
Bradford Park Ave	Altofts Welfare	05/51	53-55	75	-	0
Bradford C	Frickley Colliery	06/59	59-60	57	-	0

ROBERTS Connor Stuart
Born: Chirk, Wrexham, Wales, 8 December, 1992 — G
Wales: U21-6/Youth

League Club	Source	Date Signed	Seasons Played	Apps	Subs	Gls
Everton	Sch	12/09				
Cheltenham T	Tr	08/12	13	1	0	0

ROBERTS Darren Anthony
Born: Birmingham, England, 12 October, 1969 — F

League Club	Source	Date Signed	Seasons Played	Apps	Subs	Gls
Wolverhampton W	Burton A	04/92	92	12	9	5
Hereford U	L	03/94	93	5	1	5
Chesterfield	Tr	07/94	94-95	10	15	1
Darlington	Tr	07/96	96-98	76	20	33
Peterborough U	L	02/98	97	2	1	0
Scarborough	Tr	02/99	98	18	0	3
Exeter C	Tr	07/00	00	3	5	1

ROBERTS David (Dave)
Born: Birmingham, England, 21 December, 1946 — RW

League Club	Source	Date Signed	Seasons Played	Apps	Subs	Gls
Aston Villa	Jnr	12/63	65-67	15	1	1
Shrewsbury T	Tr	03/68	67-73	224	6	20
Swansea C	Tr	05/74	74	31	5	1

ROBERTS David Frazer
Born: Southampton, England, 26 November, 1949 — CD
Wales: 17/U23-4

League Club	Source	Date Signed	Seasons Played	Apps	Subs	Gls
Fulham	App	09/67	68-70	21	1	0
Oxford U	Tr	02/71	70-74	160	1	7
Hull C	Tr	02/75	74-77	86	0	4
Cardiff C	Tr	08/78	78-80	40	1	2

ROBERTS David Gordon
Born: Plymouth, England, 8 May, 1944 — RB

League Club	Source	Date Signed	Seasons Played	Apps	Subs	Gls
Plymouth Arg	App	12/61	61-63	11	-	0

ROBERTS Dean
Born: Mexborough, South Yorkshire, England, 12 January, 1967 — F

League Club	Source	Date Signed	Seasons Played	Apps	Subs	Gls
Bolton W	App	01/85				
Exeter C	Tr	07/86	86	23	2	7

ROBERTS Dennis
Born: West Bretton, West Yorkshire, England, 5 February, 1918 — CH
Died: Huddersfield, West Yorkshire, England, 8 April, 2001

League Club	Source	Date Signed	Seasons Played	Apps	Subs	Gls
Notts Co	Huddersfield T (Am)	08/37				
Bristol C	Tr	05/38	38-53	303	-	2

ROBERTS Donald Campbell (Don)
Born: Arlecdon, Cumbria, England, 3 February, 1933 — WH/IF

League Club	Source	Date Signed	Seasons Played	Apps	Subs	Gls
Workington	Whitehaven	07/52	52-53	21	-	0
Barrow		10/57	57-58	22	-	3

ROBERTS Douglas Gordon (Gordon)
Born: Coventry, England, 30 May, 1925 — W
Died: Northampton, England, October, 1991

League Club	Source	Date Signed	Seasons Played	Apps	Subs	Gls
Wolverhampton W	Jnr	09/42				
Northampton T	Tr	09/45	46-48	57	-	7
Brighton & HA	Tr	03/49	48-49	17	-	3
Accrington Stan	Tr	07/51	51	39	-	11

ROBERTS Dudley Edward
Born: Derby, England, 16 October, 1945 — F

League Club	Source	Date Signed	Seasons Played	Apps	Subs	Gls
Coventry C	Jnr	11/63	65-67	11	1	6
Mansfield T	Tr	03/68	67-73	194	6	66
Doncaster Rov	L	02/73	72	7	0	0
Scunthorpe U	Tr	02/74	73-75	56	3	17

ROBERTS Edward (Ted)
Born: Chesterfield, Derbyshire, England, 2 November, 1916 — CF
Died: Coventry, England, 12 August, 1970

League Club	Source	Date Signed	Seasons Played	Apps	Subs	Gls
Derby Co	Glapwell Colliery	04/34	35	4	-	0
Coventry C	Tr	03/37	36-51	211	-	85

ROBERTS Edward John (Eddie)
Born: Liverpool, England, 16 November, 1947 — G

League Club	Source	Date Signed	Seasons Played	Apps	Subs	Gls
Tranmere Rov	Harrowby Jnrs	05/67	68-69	8	0	0

ROBERTS Eric
Born: Batley, West Yorkshire, England, 16 January, 1921 — LW
Died: Dewsbury, West Yorkshire, England, 13 December, 1985

League Club	Source	Date Signed	Seasons Played	Apps	Subs	Gls
Halifax T	Altofts Colliery	08/47	47	5	-	1

ROBERTS Frederick (Fred)
Born: Rhyl, Denbighshire, Wales, 7 May, 1916 — RW
Died: Colwyn Bay, Conwy, Wales, June, 1985

League Club	Source	Date Signed	Seasons Played	Apps	Subs	Gls
Bury	Rhyl	04/38	38-46	12	-	5
Leyton Orient	Tr	11/46	46	18	-	2

ROBERTS Gareth Michael (Gary)
Born: Chester, England, 18 March, 1984 — LW
England: Semi Pro-4

League Club	Source	Date Signed	Seasons Played	Apps	Subs	Gls
Accrington Stan	Welshpool T	02/05	06	14	0	8
Ipswich T	Tr	10/06	06-07	40	14	3
Crewe Alex	L	02/08	07	4	0	0
Huddersfield T	Tr	07/08	08-11	145	17	31
Swindon T	Tr	07/12	12	29	10	4
Chesterfield	Tr	06/13	13-14	69	5	17

ROBERTS Gareth William
Born: Hull, England, 15 November, 1960 — W/M
Wales: U21-1

League Club	Source	Date Signed	Seasons Played	Apps	Subs	Gls
Hull C	App	11/78	78-90	409	5	47

ROBERTS Gareth Wyn
Born: Wrexham, Wales, 6 February, 1978 — LB
Wales: 9/B-1/U21-10

League Club	Source	Date Signed	Seasons Played	Apps	Subs	Gls
Liverpool	YT	05/96				
Tranmere Rov	Panionios (GRE)	08/99	99-05	276	5	13
Doncaster Rov	Tr	07/06	06-09	130	11	8
Derby Co	Tr	07/10	10-12	92	4	1
Bury	Tr	06/13	13	11	0	0
Notts Co	Tr	01/14	13	6	0	0

ROBERTS Gary Paul Michael
Born: Rhyl, Denbighshire, Wales, 5 April, 1960 — F

League Club	Source	Date Signed	Seasons Played	Apps	Subs	Gls
Brentford	Wembley	10/80	80-85	180	7	45

ROBERTS Gary Steven
Born: Chester, England, 4 February, 1987 — M
England: Youth

League Club	Source	Date Signed	Seasons Played	Apps	Subs	Gls
Crewe Alex	Sch	07/04	03-07	110	12	11
Yeovil T	Tr	08/08	08	27	3	2
Rotherham U		11/09	09	11	2	3
Port Vale	Tr	07/10	10-11	39	7	6

ROBERTS Geoffrey Michael (Geoff)
Born: Liverpool, England, 29 December, 1949 — LB

League Club	Source	Date Signed	Seasons Played	Apps	Subs	Gls
Bolton W	App	01/67	67-69	5	0	0

ROBERTS Glyn Shane
Born: Ipswich, England, 19 October, 1974 — M

League Club	Source	Date Signed	Seasons Played	Apps	Subs	Gls
Rotherham U	Norwich C (YT)	07/93	93-94	11	5	1

ROBERTS Gordon Richard
Born: Cardiff, Wales, 30 December, 1946 — W
Wales: Schools

League Club	Source	Date Signed	Seasons Played	Apps	Subs	Gls
Wolverhampton W	App	01/64				
Bury	Tr	09/65	65	2	0	0

ROBERTS Graham Paul
Born: Southampton, England, 3 July, 1959 — CD
England: 6/B-1

League Club	Source	Date Signed	Seasons Played	Apps	Subs	Gls
Portsmouth	Sholing Sports	03/77				
Tottenham H	Weymouth	05/80	80-86	200	9	23
Chelsea	Glasgow Rangers	08/88	88-89	70	0	18
West Bromwich A	Tr	11/90	90-91	39	0	6

ROBERTS Gryffydd Orthin (Griffith)
Born: Blaenau Ffestiniog, Gwynedd, Wales, 2 October, 1920 — G
Died: Barmouth, Gwynedd, Wales, November, 1991

League Club	Source	Date Signed	Seasons Played	Apps	Subs	Gls
Nottingham F	Blaenau Ffestiniog	05/46	46	9	-	0

ROBERTS Harold
Born: Liverpool, England, 12 January, 1920 — W
Died: Chesterfield, Derbyshire, England, 11 February, 2007

League Club	Source	Date Signed	Seasons Played	Apps	Subs	Gls
Chesterfield	Harrowby Jnrs	08/39	46-48	92	-	9
Birmingham C	Tr	11/48	48-50	34	-	2
Shrewsbury T	Tr	06/51	51-52	70	-	16
Scunthorpe U	Tr	07/53	53-54	17	-	1

ROBERTS Ian Mark
Born: Colwyn Bay, Conwy, Wales, 28 February, 1961 — M

League Club	Source	Date Signed	Seasons Played	Apps	Subs	Gls
Wrexham	Jnr	07/79	78-79	2	4	0

ROBERTS Ian Patterson
Born: Glasgow, Scotland, 28 September, 1955 — LB

League Club	Source	Date Signed	Seasons Played	Apps	Subs	Gls
Shrewsbury T	App	09/72	71-75	93	3	0
Crewe Alex	Tr	07/76	76-78	89	4	0

ROBERTS Iwan Wyn
Born: Caernarfon, Gwynedd, Wales, 26 June, 1968 — F
Wales: 15/B-1/Youth/Schools

League Club	Source	Date Signed	Seasons Played	Apps	Subs	Gls
Watford	YT	07/86	85-89	40	23	9
Huddersfield T	Tr	08/90	90-93	141	1	50
Leicester C	Tr	11/93	93-95	92	8	41
Wolverhampton W	Tr	07/96	96	24	9	12
Norwich C	Tr	07/97	97-03	232	46	84
Gillingham	Tr	07/04	04	11	9	3
Cambridge U	L	03/05	04	11	0	3

ROBERTS James Anthony
Born: Aylesbury, Buckinghamshire, England, 21 June, 1996 — F

League Club	Source	Date Signed	Seasons Played	Apps	Subs	Gls
Oxford U	Sch	06/14	14	5	20	3

ROBERTS James Dale (Dale)
Born: Newcastle-upon-Tyne, England, 8 October, 1956 — CD
Died: Deben, Suffolk, England, 5 February, 2003
England: Youth

League Club	Source	Date Signed	Seasons Played	Apps	Subs	Gls
Ipswich T	App	09/74	74-77	17	1	0
Hull C	Tr	02/80	79-84	149	4	6

ROBERTS James Nicoll (Jimmy)
Born: Falkirk, Scotland, 12 June, 1923 — LW

League Club	Source	Date Signed	Seasons Played	Apps	Subs	Gls
Ipswich T	Dundee	09/49	49-51	73	-	15
Barrow	Tr	07/52	52	11	-	2

ROBERTS Jamie Steven
Born: Doncaster, South Yorkshire, England, 11 April, 1974 — M

League Club	Source	Date Signed	Seasons Played	Apps	Subs	Gls
Doncaster Rov	YT	07/92	92	1	1	0

ROBERTS Jason Andre Davis
Born: Harlesden, NW London, England, 25 January, 1978 — F
Grenada: 22

League Club	Source	Date Signed	Seasons Played	Apps	Subs	Gls
Wolverhampton W	Hayes	09/97				
Torquay U	L	12/97	97	13	1	6
Bristol C	L	03/98	97	1	2	1
Bristol Rov	Tr	08/98	98-99	73	5	38

League Club	Source	Date Signed	Seasons Played	Career Record Apps	Subs	Gls
West Bromwich A	Tr	07/00	00-02	75	14	24
Portsmouth	L	09/03	03	4	6	1
Wigan Ath	Tr	01/04	03-05	93	0	37
Blackburn Rov	Tr	07/06	06-11	73	61	24
Reading	Tr	01/12	11-12	25	3	6

ROBERTS Jeremy
Born: Middlesbrough, England, 24 November, 1966 — G
England: Youth

League Club	Source	Date Signed	Seasons Played	Apps	Subs	Gls
Hartlepool U	Jnr	12/83	83	1	0	0
Leicester C	Tr	07/84	85	3	0	0
Darlington	Tr	03/87	86-87	29	0	0
Brentford	Tr	09/88	88	5	0	0

ROBERTS John Dilwyn (Dilwyn)
Born: Brynteg, Anglesey, Wales, 22 July, 1928 — RW
Died: Wrexham, Wales, 13 March, 2000

League Club	Source	Date Signed	Seasons Played	Apps	Subs	Gls
Wrexham (Am)	Brymbo Steel Works	04/51	50	1	-	0

ROBERTS John Griffith
Born: Abercynon, Rhondda Cynon Taff, Wales, 11 September, 1946 — CD/CF
Wales: 22/U23-5/U21-1

League Club	Source	Date Signed	Seasons Played	Apps	Subs	Gls
Swansea C	Abercynon Ath	07/64	65-67	36	1	16
Northampton T	Tr	11/67	67-68	62	0	11
Arsenal	Tr	05/69	69-72	56	3	4
Birmingham C	Tr	10/72	72-75	61	5	1
Wrexham	Tr	08/76	76-79	145	0	5
Hull C	Tr	08/80	80	26	0	1

ROBERTS John Hopkin (Jackie)
Born: Swansea, Wales, 30 June, 1918 — FB
Died: Swansea, Wales, June, 2001
Wales: 1/Schools

League Club	Source	Date Signed	Seasons Played	Apps	Subs	Gls
Bolton W	Cwmbwrla Jnrs	04/36	37-50	162	-	19
Swansea C	Tr	09/50	50	16	-	1

ROBERTS John Thomas
Born: Cessnock, NSW, Australia, 24 March, 1944 — G
Australia:

League Club	Source	Date Signed	Seasons Played	Apps	Subs	Gls
Blackburn Rov	APIA Leichhardt (AUS)	04/66	65	3	0	0
Chesterfield	L	08/67	67	46	0	0
Bradford C	Tr	08/68	68-70	44	0	0
Southend U	Tr	01/71	70-71	47	0	0
Northampton T	Tr	07/72	72	13	0	0

ROBERTS Jonathan Wesley (Jon)
Born: Llwynypia, Rhondda Cynon Taff, Wales, 30 December, 1968 — G
Wales: Youth

League Club	Source	Date Signed	Seasons Played	Apps	Subs	Gls
Cardiff C	YT	11/87	87-88	9	0	0

ROBERTS Jordan Stephen
Born: Watford, Hertfordshire, England, 5 January, 1994 — M

League Club	Source	Date Signed	Seasons Played	Apps	Subs	Gls
Aldershot T	Sch	03/12	11-12	2	7	0

ROBERTS Kenneth (Ken)
Born: Crewe, Cheshire, England, 10 March, 1931 — W/IF

League Club	Source	Date Signed	Seasons Played	Apps	Subs	Gls
Aston Villa	Crewe Villa	08/51	51-53	42	-	7

ROBERTS Kenneth Owen (Ken)
Born: Cefn Mawr, Wrexham, Wales, 27 March, 1936 — RW

League Club	Source	Date Signed	Seasons Played	Apps	Subs	Gls
Wrexham (Am)	Jnr	05/51	51	1	-	0
Aston Villa	Tr	05/53	53-57	38	-	3

ROBERTS Kevin
Born: Liverpool, England, 17 August, 1989 — RB

League Club	Source	Date Signed	Seasons Played	Apps	Subs	Gls
Chester C	Sch	05/07	07-08	74	7	7

ROBERTS Kevin John
Born: Bristol, England, 25 July, 1955 — G

League Club	Source	Date Signed	Seasons Played	Apps	Subs	Gls
Swindon T	Welton Rov	03/77	77	1	0	0

ROBERTS Lee John
Born: Market Drayton, Shropshire, England, 23 March, 1957 — CD

League Club	Source	Date Signed	Seasons Played	Apps	Subs	Gls
Shrewsbury T	App	01/75	73-77	9	6	1
Exeter C	L	03/77	76	5	2	0
Exeter C	Tr	09/77	77-82	135	9	12

ROBERTS Mark Alan
Born: Northwich, Cheshire, England, 16 October, 1983 — CD

League Club	Source	Date Signed	Seasons Played	Apps	Subs	Gls
Crewe Alex	Sch	07/03	04	3	3	0
Chester C	L	01/06	05	1	0	0
Accrington Stan	Northwich Victoria	07/07	07	33	1	0
Stevenage	Northwich Victoria	11/08	10-12	132	0	14
Fleetwood T	Tr	07/13	13-14	60	0	6

ROBERTS Maurice Ernest Stanley
Born: Bristol, England, 5 July, 1922 — LW
Died: Bristol, England, April, 1993

League Club	Source	Date Signed	Seasons Played	Apps	Subs	Gls
Brentford	Army	08/46	46	10	-	0
Bristol C	Tr	05/47				

ROBERTS Michael John (Mike)
Born: Birmingham, England, 21 May, 1960 — M

League Club	Source	Date Signed	Seasons Played	Apps	Subs	Gls
Shrewsbury T		07/78	78	0	1	0

ROBERTS Neil Wyn
Born: Wrexham, Wales, 7 April, 1978 — F
Wales: 3/B-1/U21-2/Youth

League Club	Source	Date Signed	Seasons Played	Apps	Subs	Gls
Wrexham	YT	07/96	97-99	58	17	17
Wigan Ath	Tr	02/00	99-03	64	61	19
Hull C	L	01/02	01	3	3	0
Bradford C	L	09/04	04	3	0	1
Doncaster Rov	Tr	10/04	04-05	47	14	8
Wrexham	Tr	08/06	06-07	52	3	11

ROBERTS Owen John
Born: Maerdy, Rhondda Cynon Taff, Wales, 16 February, 1919 — G
Died: Pontypridd, Rhondda Cynon Taff, Wales, June, 2000

League Club	Source	Date Signed	Seasons Played	Apps	Subs	Gls
Plymouth Arg	Maerdy	02/38				
Swansea C	Aberaman Ath	10/45	46-47	24	-	0
Newport Co	Tr	08/48	48	7	-	0

ROBERTS Patrick John Joseph
Born: Kingston-on-Thames, SW London, England, 5 February, 1997 — F
England: Youth

League Club	Source	Date Signed	Seasons Played	Apps	Subs	Gls
Fulham	Sch	02/14	13-14	2	17	0

ROBERTS Paul
Born: West Ham, E London, England, 27 April, 1962 — D

League Club	Source	Date Signed	Seasons Played	Apps	Subs	Gls
Millwall	App	04/79	78-82	142	4	0
Brentford	Tr	09/83	83-84	61	1	0
Swindon T	Finland	09/85	85	25	2	0
Southend U	Tr	07/86	86	38	0	0
Aldershot	Tr	08/87	87	36	3	0
Exeter C	Leytonstone & Ilford	12/88	88	3	0	0
Southend U	Tr	01/89	88-89	53	1	0
Colchester U	Fisher Ath	09/91	92-93	63	0	1

ROBERTS Paul Dorgham
Born: Criccieth, Gwynedd, Wales, 29 July, 1977 — F
Wales: U21-1

League Club	Source	Date Signed	Seasons Played	Apps	Subs	Gls
Wrexham		12/96	96	0	1	0

ROBERTS Peter
Born: Chesterfield, Derbyshire, England, 21 July, 1955 — W

League Club	Source	Date Signed	Seasons Played	Apps	Subs	Gls
Chesterfield	Chesterfield Tube W'ks	09/73	74-75	2	0	0

ROBERTS Peter Lorenzo
Born: Sherburn-in-Elmet, North Yorkshire, England, 16 July, 1925 — CF
Died: Buckinghamshire, England, November, 2008

League Club	Source	Date Signed	Seasons Played	Apps	Subs	Gls
Leeds U	Newcastle U (Am)	09/46				
New Brighton	Tr	07/48	48	3	-	0

ROBERTS Philip Stanley (Phil)
Born: Cardiff, Wales, 24 February, 1950 — RB
Wales: 4/U23-6

League Club	Source	Date Signed	Seasons Played	Apps	Subs	Gls
Bristol Rov	App	11/68	69-72	174	1	6
Portsmouth	Tr	05/73	73-77	152	1	1
Hereford U	Tr	07/78	78	3	0	0
Exeter C	Tr	02/79	78-81	103	2	0

ROBERTS Robert (Bobby)
Born: Edinburgh, Scotland, 2 September, 1940 — M
Scotland: SLge-1/U23-1

League Club	Source	Date Signed	Seasons Played	Apps	Subs	Gls
Leicester C	Motherwell	09/63	63-69	225	5	25
Mansfield T	Tr	09/70	70-71	76	4	4
Colchester U	Coventry C (Coach)	07/73	72	0	2	0

ROBERTS Ronald (Ronnie)
Born: Llay, Wrexham, Wales, 14 September, 1942 — LW
Wales: U23-2

League Club	Source	Date Signed	Seasons Played	Apps	Subs	Gls
Wrexham	Jnr	04/60	59-62	67	-	4
Tranmere Rov	Tr	03/63	62-63	56	-	2

ROBERTS Sean Joseph
Born: Durban, South Africa, 2 January, 1983 — G

League Club	Source	Date Signed	Seasons Played	Apps	Subs	Gls
Sheffield Wed	Wits Univ (RSA)	10/01	01	0	1	0

ROBERTS Stanley (Stan)
Born: Wrexham, Wales, 19 April, 1921 — F
Died: Wrexham, Wales, April, 1995

League Club	Source	Date Signed	Seasons Played	Apps	Subs	Gls
Wrexham	Cross Street	09/46	46-47	27	-	10
New Brighton	Tr	07/48	48-50	103	-	25

ROBERTS Stephen Wyn (Steve)
Born: Wrexham, Wales, 24 February, 1980 — CD
Wales: 1/U21-4/Youth

League Club	Source	Date Signed	Seasons Played	Apps	Subs	Gls
Wrexham	YT	01/98	99-04	143	7	6
Doncaster Rov	Tr	07/05	05-07	58	15	1
Walsall	Tr	07/08	08-09	16	0	1

ROBERTS Stuart Ian
Born: Llanelli, Carmarthenshire, Wales, 22 July, 1980 W
Wales: U21-13

League Club	Source	Date Signed	Seasons Played	Apps	Subs	Gls
Swansea C	YT	07/98	98-01	58	34	14
Wycombe W	Tr	10/01	01-03	37	33	4
Swansea C	Tr	02/04	03	8	4	1
Kidderminster Hrs	Tr	08/04	04	4	1	1

ROBERTS Stuart William
Born: Chirk, Wrexham, Wales, 25 March, 1967 G
Wales: Youth

League Club	Source	Date Signed	Seasons Played	Apps	Subs	Gls
Stoke C	App	03/85	84	3	0	0

ROBERTS Thomas (Tommy)
Born: Liverpool, England, 28 July, 1927 FB
Died: Birkenhead, Wirral, England, January, 2001

League Club	Source	Date Signed	Seasons Played	Apps	Subs	Gls
Blackburn Rov	Skelmersdale U	12/51	51-53	6	-	0
Watford	Tr	12/54	54	1	-	0
Chester C	Tr	02/56	55	5	-	0

ROBERTS Thomas (Tommy)
Born: Liverpool, England, 27 December, 1945 LW

League Club	Source	Date Signed	Seasons Played	Apps	Subs	Gls
Everton	App	11/63				
Stockport Co	Tr	03/65	64-65	20	0	0
Southport	Tr	07/66	66	4	0	1

ROBERTS Thomas Walter George (Tom)
Born: Reading, England, 11 June, 1932 IF

League Club	Source	Date Signed	Seasons Played	Apps	Subs	Gls
Birmingham C		05/53				
Barrow	Tr	10/55	55-56	40	-	14

ROBERTS Trevor Edwin
Born: Caernarfon, Gwynedd, Wales, 25 February, 1942 G
Died: Cambridge, England, 2 June, 1972
Wales: Amateur

League Club	Source	Date Signed	Seasons Played	Apps	Subs	Gls
Liverpool	Liverpool Univ	06/63				
Southend U	Tr	01/66	65-69	171	0	0
Cambridge U	Tr	08/70	70-71	36	0	0

ROBERTS Trevor Lee
Born: Southampton, England, 9 May, 1961 CD

League Club	Source	Date Signed	Seasons Played	Apps	Subs	Gls
Portsmouth	Southampton (App)	02/79	78-79	1	2	0

ROBERTS Walter (Wally)
Born: Wrexham, Wales, 23 November, 1917 WH
Died: Wrexham, Wales, March, 2006

League Club	Source	Date Signed	Seasons Played	Apps	Subs	Gls
Wrexham		08/38	38-47	60	-	1
Bournemouth	Tr	07/48	48-49	15	-	0

ROBERTS William Berwyn (Will)
Born: Rhyl, Denbighshire, Wales, 24 April, 1994 M

League Club	Source	Date Signed	Seasons Played	Apps	Subs	Gls
Coventry C	Sch	06/12	11	0	1	0

ROBERTS William Ernest (Bill)
Born: Flint, Wales, 22 October, 1918 G
Died: Connahs Quay, Flintshire, Wales, June, 1994

League Club	Source	Date Signed	Seasons Played	Apps	Subs	Gls
Rochdale		04/46	46-48	43	-	0

ROBERTS William John (Billy)
Born: Bradford, England, 9 April, 1963 F

League Club	Source	Date Signed	Seasons Played	Apps	Subs	Gls
Rochdale	Farsley Celtic	11/88	88	1	0	0

ROBERTS Winston
Born: Hartlepool, Cleveland, England, 5 July, 1939 IF

League Club	Source	Date Signed	Seasons Played	Apps	Subs	Gls
Hartlepool U	Caledonians	09/58	58	3	-	0

ROBERTSON Alexander (Sandy)
Born: Edinburgh, Scotland, 26 April, 1971 M
Scotland: U21-1

League Club	Source	Date Signed	Seasons Played	Apps	Subs	Gls
Coventry C	Glasgow Rangers	01/94	93-94	0	4	0

ROBERTSON Alistair Peter (Ally)
Born: Philpstoun, West Lothian, Scotland, 9 September, 1952 CD
Scotland: Schools

League Club	Source	Date Signed	Seasons Played	Apps	Subs	Gls
West Bromwich A	App	09/69	69-85	504	2	8
Wolverhampton W	Tr	09/86	86-89	107	0	0

ROBERTSON Andrew (Andy)
Born: Glasgow, Scotland, 11 March, 1994 LB
Scotland: 6/U21-3

League Club	Source	Date Signed	Seasons Played	Apps	Subs	Gls
Hull C	Dundee U	07/14	14	17	7	0

ROBERTSON Archibald Lamond (Lammie)
Born: Paisley, Renfrewshire, Scotland, 27 September, 1947 M

League Club	Source	Date Signed	Seasons Played	Apps	Subs	Gls
Burnley	Benburb Jnrs	09/66				
Bury	Tr	06/68	68	3	2	0
Halifax T	Tr	02/69	68-72	142	8	20
Brighton & HA	Tr	12/72	72-73	42	4	9
Exeter C	Tr	06/74	74-77	132	1	25
Leicester C	Tr	09/77	77	6	1	0
Peterborough U	Tr	08/78	78	12	3	1
Bradford C	Tr	01/79	78-80	41	2	3

ROBERTSON Christopher (Chris)
Born: Dundee, Scotland, 11 October, 1985 CD

League Club	Source	Date Signed	Seasons Played	Apps	Subs	Gls
Sheffield U	Sch	10/05				
Chester C	L	01/06	05	0	1	0
Torquay U	Tr	03/07	06-11	118	4	6
Preston NE	Tr	01/12	11-12	33	6	1
Port Vale	Tr	06/13	13-14	57	4	3

ROBERTSON David (Dave)
Born: Baillieston, Glasgow, Scotland, 12 January, 1945 RW

League Club	Source	Date Signed	Seasons Played	Apps	Subs	Gls
Crewe Alex	Motherwell	07/63	63	11	-	2

ROBERTSON David Alexander
Born: Aberdeen, Scotland, 17 October, 1968 FB
Scotland: 3/B/U21-7

League Club	Source	Date Signed	Seasons Played	Apps	Subs	Gls
Leeds U	Glasgow Rangers	06/97	97	24	2	0

ROBERTSON Edward Harold Yeoman (Eddie)
Born: Edinburgh, Scotland, 19 December, 1935 FB
Died: West Kirby, Wirral, England, 17 December, 1981

League Club	Source	Date Signed	Seasons Played	Apps	Subs	Gls
Bury	Linlithgow Rose	07/54	56-62	196	-	7
Wrexham	Tr	10/63	63	24	-	0
Tranmere Rov	Tr	07/64	64-68	143	4	1

ROBERTSON George Jenkins
Born: Falkirk, Scotland, 20 April, 1930 D
Died: Plymouth, England, 23 March, 2003

League Club	Source	Date Signed	Seasons Played	Apps	Subs	Gls
Plymouth Arg	Gairdoch Jnrs	01/50	50-63	358	-	2

ROBERTSON Graham Stuart
Born: Edinburgh, Scotland, 2 November, 1976 F

League Club	Source	Date Signed	Seasons Played	Apps	Subs	Gls
Millwall	Raith Rov	08/96	96-97	0	2	0

ROBERTSON Gregor Aedan
Born: Edinburgh, Scotland, 19 January, 1984 LB
Scotland: U21-15

League Club	Source	Date Signed	Seasons Played	Apps	Subs	Gls
Nottingham F	Heart of Midlothian	02/01	03-04	25	11	0
Rotherham U	Tr	07/05	05-06	46	7	1
Chesterfield	Tr	07/07	07-11	106	10	3
Crewe Alex	Tr	07/12	12-13	27	5	0
Northampton T	Tr	02/14	13-14	34	2	0

ROBERTSON Hugh Scott
Born: Aberdeen, Scotland, 19 March, 1975 LB/M
Scotland: U21-2

League Club	Source	Date Signed	Seasons Played	Apps	Subs	Gls
Hartlepool U	Ross Co	01/04	03-04	37	3	6

ROBERTSON James (Jimmy)
Born: Leith, Edinburgh, Scotland, 7 July, 1940 IF

League Club	Source	Date Signed	Seasons Played	Apps	Subs	Gls
Newport Co	Aberdeen	07/61	61	29	-	5

ROBERTSON James (Jim)
Born: Gateshead, Tyne and Wear, England, 24 November, 1969 RB

League Club	Source	Date Signed	Seasons Played	Apps	Subs	Gls
Carlisle U	YT	07/88	87-89	10	2	0

ROBERTSON James Gillen (Jimmy)
Born: Cardonald, Glasgow, Scotland, 17 December, 1944 RW
Scotland: 1/U23-4

League Club	Source	Date Signed	Seasons Played	Apps	Subs	Gls
Tottenham H	St Mirren	03/64	63-68	153	4	25
Arsenal	Tr	10/68	68-69	45	1	7
Ipswich T	Tr	03/70	69-71	87	0	10
Stoke C	Tr	06/72	72-76	99	15	12
Walsall	Tr	09/77	77	16	0	0
Crewe Alex	Tr	09/78	78	32	1	0

ROBERTSON James Wright (Jimmy)
Born: Falkirk, Scotland, 20 February, 1929 LW

League Club	Source	Date Signed	Seasons Played	Apps	Subs	Gls
Arsenal	Dunipace Thistle	06/48	51	1	-	0
Brentford	Tr	09/53	53-55	84	-	14

ROBERTSON John Alexander
Born: Ayr, Scotland, 28 March, 1976 RB

League Club	Source	Date Signed	Seasons Played	Apps	Subs	Gls
Oxford U	Ayr U	07/00	00	37	3	0

ROBERTSON John Craig (Jackie)
Born: Aberdeen, Scotland, 15 July, 1928 CF
Died: Ayr, Scotland, 2014

League Club	Source	Date Signed	Seasons Played	Apps	Subs	Gls
Portsmouth	Ayr U	08/55	55	12	-	4
York C	Tr	06/57	57	17	-	5
Barrow	Tr	08/58	58-61	156	-	47

ROBERTSON John Grant
Born: Edinburgh, Scotland, 2 October, 1964 F
Scotland: 16/B/U21-2

League Club	Source	Date Signed	Seasons Played	Apps	Subs	Gls
Newcastle U	Heart of Midlothian	04/88	88	7	5	0

ROBERTSON John Neilson
Born: Uddingston, Glasgow, Scotland, 20 January, 1953 W
Scotland: 28/Youth/Schools

League Club	Source	Date Signed	Seasons Played	Career Record Apps	Subs	Gls
Nottingham F	App	05/70	70-82	374	13	61
Derby Co	Tr	06/83	83-84	72	0	3
Nottingham F	Tr	08/85	85	10	1	0
ROBERTSON John Nicholas						
Born: Liverpool, England, 8 January, 1974						CD
Wigan Ath	YT	07/92	92-95	108	4	4
Lincoln C	Tr	12/95	95-97	38	2	1
ROBERTSON Jordan Steven						
Born: Sheffield, England, 12 February, 1988						F
Sheffield U	Sch	07/06				
Torquay U	L	11/06	06	5	4	2
Northampton T	L	01/07	06	9	8	3
Oldham Ath	L	02/08	07	2	1	1
Southampton	L	09/08	08	8	2	1
Bury	L	08/09	09	4	0	1
Scunthorpe U	St Johnstone	06/11	11	12	7	3
ROBERTSON Leonard Verdun (Len)						
Born: Middlesbrough, England, 1 March, 1916						IF
Died: Cleveland, England, 1979						
Watford	Stockton	06/46	46	6	-	2
Bradford C	Tr	03/47				
Hull C	Tr	04/47	46-47	9	-	2
Accrington Stan	Tr	07/48	48	3	-	0
ROBERTSON Mark William						
Born: Sydney, Australia, 6 April, 1977						M
Australia: 1/U23-5/Youth						
Burnley	Marconi Stall'ns (AUS)	10/97	97-99	27	9	1
Swindon T	L	08/00	00	4	6	1
Stockport Co	St Johnstone	01/04	03-04	27	5	1
ROBERTSON Paul						
Born: Stockport, Greater Manchester, England, 5 February, 1972						LB
Stockport Co	York C (YT)	08/89	89-90	7	3	0
Bury	Tr	07/91	91-92	8	0	0
Doncaster Rov	Runcorn	10/95	95-96	15	5	0
ROBERTSON Scott						
Born: Dundee, Scotland, 7 April, 1985						M
Scotland: 2						
Blackpool	Dundee U	07/12	12	1	0	0
ROBERTSON Stuart						
Born: Glasgow, Scotland, 29 September, 1959						M
Burnley	App	07/77	78-81	30	2	0
Exeter C	Tr	03/82	81	5	1	0
Doncaster Rov	Newcastle KBU (AUS)	10/82	82	25	0	0
ROBERTSON Stuart John						
Born: Nottingham, England, 16 December, 1946						CD
Nottingham F	Jnr	08/64				
Doncaster Rov	Tr	07/66	66-71	224	2	8
Northampton T	Tr	05/72	72-78	254	0	24
ROBERTSON Thomas Smith (Tom)						
Born: Coventry, England, 28 September, 1944						W
Crystal Palace	St Mirren	10/66	66	5	0	0
ROBERTSON William George						
Born: Glasgow, Scotland, 4 November, 1936						W
Middlesbrough	L Pieter's BC	11/53	54	5	-	2
ROBERTSON William Gibb (Bill)						
Born: Glasgow, Scotland, 13 November, 1928						G
Died: Sutton, S London, England, 26 June, 1973						
Chelsea	Arthurlie	07/46	50-59	199	-	0
Leyton Orient	Tr	09/60	60-62	47	-	0
ROBERTSON William Harold (Bill)						
Born: Crowthorne, Berkshire, England, 25 March, 1923						G
Died: Banstead, Surrey, England, 15 March, 2003						
Chelsea	RAF Lossiemouth	10/45	46-47	37	-	0
Birmingham C	Tr	12/48	48-51	2	-	0
Stoke C	Tr	06/52	52-59	238	-	0
ROBERTSON William James Tavendale (Willie)						
Born: Montrose, Angus, Scotland, 9 November, 1923						LH/LB
Died: Preston, Lancashire, England, 19 August, 2006						
Preston NE	Montrose Roselea	03/42	46-52	52	-	0
Southport	Tr	07/55	55	28	-	0
[ROBINHO] DE SOUZA Robson						
Born: Sao Vicente, Brazil, 29 January, 1984						F
Brazil: 95/U23-8						
Manchester C	Real Madrid (SPN)	09/08	08-09	36	5	14
ROBINS Ian						
Born: Bury, Greater Manchester, England, 22 February, 1952						F/W

League Club	Source	Date Signed	Seasons Played	Career Record Apps	Subs	Gls
Oldham Ath	App	02/70	69-76	202	18	40
Bury	Tr	07/77	77-78	49	0	5
Huddersfield T	Tr	08/78	78-81	145	11	59
ROBINS Mark Gordon						
Born: Ashton-under-Lyne, Greater Manchester, England, 22 December, 1969						F
England: U21-6						
Manchester U	App	12/86	88-91	19	29	11
Norwich C	Tr	08/92	92-94	57	10	20
Leicester C	Tr	01/95	94-96	40	16	12
Reading	L	08/97	97	5	0	0
Manchester C	Panionios (GRE)	03/99	98	0	2	0
Walsall	Tr	08/99	99	30	10	6
Rotherham U	Tr	07/00	00-03	84	24	44
Bristol C	L	02/03	02	6	0	4
Sheffield Wed	Tr	12/03	03	14	1	3
ROBINSON Alan						
Born: Grantham, Lincolnshire, England, 2 December, 1955						F
Sheffield Wed	App	12/73				
Scunthorpe U	Tr	08/75	75	1	0	0
ROBINSON Albert						
Born: Chester, England, 1 June, 1948						M
Died: Chester, England, June, 1995						
Chester C	Jnr	07/68	67-68	4	1	0
ROBINSON Andrew Craig (Andy)						
Born: Oldham, Greater Manchester, England, 10 March, 1966						M
England: Schools						
Manchester U	App	03/84				
Burnley	L	10/85	85	5	0	1
Bury	Tr	01/86	85-86	12	7	0
Carlisle U	Tr	03/87	86-87	43	3	3
ROBINSON Andrew Mark (Andy)						
Born: Birkenhead, Wirral, England, 3 November, 1979						LW
Tranmere Rov	Cammell Laird	11/02				
Swansea C	Tr	08/03	03-07	159	33	43
Leeds U	Tr	07/08	08-09	20	18	2
Tranmere Rov	L	03/10	09	3	2	1
Tranmere Rov	Tr	01/11	10-13	72	20	17
Shrewsbury T	Tr	07/14	14	0	2	0
ROBINSON Anthony (Tony)						
Born: Hebburn, Tyne and Wear, England, 5 November, 1958						W
Hartlepool U	Newcastle Blue Star	09/86	86	1	1	0
ROBINSON Anton Dale						
Born: Harrow, NW London, England, 17 February, 1986						M
England: Semi Pro-2						
Millwall	Sch	04/04				
Bournemouth	Weymouth	02/09	08-10	104	2	10
Huddersfield T	Tr	08/11	11-12	13	14	1
Gillingham	L	01/13	12	12	2	0
Coventry C	L	03/14	13	5	1	0
ROBINSON Ashley Paul Emmanuel						
Born: Croydon, S London, England, 5 December, 1989						F
Crystal Palace	Sch	-	07	0	6	0
ROBINSON Bernard Cecil						
Born: Cambridge, England, 5 December, 1911						RH/RB
Died: Sprowston, Norfolk, England, 29 November, 2004						
Norwich C	King's Lynn	12/31	31-48	360	-	13
ROBINSON Brian Thomas Arthur						
Born: Paddington, Central London, England, 2 April, 1946						G
Peterborough U	App	04/64	64-65	8	0	0
ROBINSON Callum Jack						
Born: Northampton, England, 2 February, 1995						LW
England: Youth						
Aston Villa	Sch	07/13	13	0	4	0
Preston NE	L	09/14	14	6	4	2
Preston NE	L	02/15	14	12	3	2
ROBINSON Carl Philip						
Born: Llandrindod Wells, Powys, Wales, 13 October, 1976						M
Wales: 52/B-2/U21-6/Youth						
Wolverhampton W	YT	07/95	96-01	129	35	19
Shrewsbury T	L	03/96	95	2	2	0
Portsmouth	Tr	07/02	02-03	11	5	0
Sheffield Wed	L	01/03	02	4	0	1
Walsall	L	02/03	02	10	1	1
Rotherham U	L	09/03	03	14	0	0
Sheffield U	L	01/04	03	4	1	0
Sunderland	Tr	03/04	03-05	49	3	5
Norwich C	Tr	11/05	05-06	44	5	2

ROBINSON Colin Roy
Born: Birmingham, England, 15 May, 1960 F

League Club	Source	Date Signed	Seasons Played	Apps	Subs	Gls
Shrewsbury T	Mile Oak Rov	11/82	82-87	176	18	41
Birmingham C	Tr	01/88	87-88	34	3	6
Hereford U	Tr	08/89	89-90	41	23	6

ROBINSON Cyril
Born: Nottingham, England, 4 March, 1929 LH

League Club	Source	Date Signed	Seasons Played	Apps	Subs	Gls
Blackpool	Mansfield T (Am)	09/49	51-54	22	-	2
Bradford Park Ave	Northwich Victoria	06/56	56-58	89	-	3
Southport	Tr	07/59	59	37	-	0

ROBINSON David (Dave)
Born: Birmingham, England, 14 July, 1948 CD

League Club	Source	Date Signed	Seasons Played	Apps	Subs	Gls
Birmingham C	App	07/66	68-71	110	2	2
Walsall	Tr	02/73	72-76	164	1	3

ROBINSON David Alan
Born: Haverton Hill, Cleveland, England, 14 January, 1965 CD

League Club	Source	Date Signed	Seasons Played	Apps	Subs	Gls
Hartlepool U	Billingham T	08/83	83-85	64	2	1
Halifax T	Tr	08/86	86-88	72	0	1
Peterborough U	Tr	07/89	89-92	95	0	9
Notts Co	Tr	09/92	92-93	3	0	1

ROBINSON David John
Born: Newcastle-upon-Tyne, England, 27 November, 1969 F

League Club	Source	Date Signed	Seasons Played	Apps	Subs	Gls
Newcastle U	YT	06/88	88-91	0	8	0
Peterborough U	L	02/91	90	7	0	3
Reading	Tr	03/92	91	8	0	0
Blackpool	Tr	07/92	92-93	21	5	4
Cambridge U	Bishop Auckland	12/95	95	4	13	1

ROBINSON David Stanley
Born: Exeter, England, 6 January, 1937 W
Died: Exeter, England, July, 2006

League Club	Source	Date Signed	Seasons Played	Apps	Subs	Gls
Exeter C	Whipton	12/54	57-58	16	-	4
Oldham Ath	Tr	07/59				

ROBINSON David William (Dave)
Born: Manchester, England, 25 November, 1921 LH
Died: Macclesfield, Cheshire, England, January, 2006

League Club	Source	Date Signed	Seasons Played	Apps	Subs	Gls
Shrewsbury T	Manchester U (Am)	08/49	50	10	-	0

ROBINSON Edward
Born: Prudhoe, Northumberland, England, 15 January, 1922 LB/LW
Died: Newcastle-upon-Tyne, England, June, 1987

League Club	Source	Date Signed	Seasons Played	Apps	Subs	Gls
Gateshead		11/45	46-52	91	-	7

ROBINSON Eric Michael
Born: Manchester, England, 1 July, 1935 IF
Died: Marple, Greater Manchester, England, 25 April, 2008

League Club	Source	Date Signed	Seasons Played	Apps	Subs	Gls
West Bromwich A	Altrincham	03/57	57	1	-	0
Rotherham U	Tr	01/59	58-59	13	-	1

ROBINSON Frederick James (Fred)
Born: Rotherham, South Yorkshire, England, 29 December, 1954 FB

League Club	Source	Date Signed	Seasons Played	Apps	Subs	Gls
Rotherham U	App	01/73	73	4	0	0
Doncaster Rov	Tr	07/75	75-78	111	8	3
Huddersfield T	Tr	08/79	79-80	72	0	2

ROBINSON George Dennis
Born: Liverpool, England, 28 May, 1937 RW

League Club	Source	Date Signed	Seasons Played	Apps	Subs	Gls
Southport	Unit Construction	02/59	58	2	-	0

ROBINSON George Frederick
Born: Melton Mowbray, Leicestershire, England, 17 June, 1925 LB
Died: Leicester, England, February, 2000

League Club	Source	Date Signed	Seasons Played	Apps	Subs	Gls
Notts Co	Holwell Works	08/44	46	29	-	0

ROBINSON George Henry
Born: Heanor, Derbyshire, England, 11 January, 1908 IF
Died: Blackheath, SE London, England, 15 January, 1963

League Club	Source	Date Signed	Seasons Played	Apps	Subs	Gls
Sunderland	Ilkeston U	04/27	27-30	31	-	8
Charlton Ath	Tr	06/31	31-32	40	-	5
Charlton Ath	Burton T	08/34	34-46	198	-	37

ROBINSON Henry (Harry)
Born: Southport, Merseyside, England, 14 September, 1947 RW

League Club	Source	Date Signed	Seasons Played	Apps	Subs	Gls
Blackpool	App	01/65				
Southport	Tr	02/66				
Burnley	Tr	09/66				
Newport Co	Tr	11/67	67-68	38	1	3

ROBINSON Herbert
Born: Padiham, Lancashire, England, 30 April, 1922 CF

League Club	Source	Date Signed	Seasons Played	Apps	Subs	Gls
Accrington Stan	Barnoldswick T	12/46	46	5	-	4

ROBINSON Ian Brendan
Born: Nottingham, England, 25 August, 1978 M

League Club	Source	Date Signed	Seasons Played	Apps	Subs	Gls
Mansfield T	YT	07/96	95-96	7	10	1

ROBINSON Jack
Born: Warrington, Cheshire, England, 1 September, 1993 LB
England: U21-10/Youth

League Club	Source	Date Signed	Seasons Played	Apps	Subs	Gls
Liverpool	Sch	09/10	09-10	1	2	0
Wolverhampton W	L	02/13	12	11	0	0
Blackpool	L	08/13	13	33	1	0
Queens Park Rgrs	Tr	07/14				
Huddersfield T	L	08/14	14	30	0	0

ROBINSON Jake David
Born: Brighton, England, 23 October, 1986 F

League Club	Source	Date Signed	Seasons Played	Apps	Subs	Gls
Brighton & HA	Sch	12/03	03-08	61	62	13
Aldershot T	L	02/09	08	19	0	4
Shrewsbury T	Tr	07/09	09-10	35	21	11
Torquay U	L	01/11	10	22	0	7
Northampton T	Tr	07/11	11-12	28	29	4

ROBINSON James Gilbert
Born: Prescot, Merseyside, England, 18 September, 1982 M

League Club	Source	Date Signed	Seasons Played	Apps	Subs	Gls
Crewe Alex	YT	11/01	02-03	1	9	1

ROBINSON Jamie
Born: Liverpool, England, 26 February, 1972 CD

League Club	Source	Date Signed	Seasons Played	Apps	Subs	Gls
Liverpool	YT	06/90				
Barnsley	Tr	07/92	92-93	8	1	0
Carlisle U	Tr	01/94	93-96	46	11	4
Torquay U	Tr	07/97	97-98	75	0	1
Exeter C	Tr	09/99	99	11	1	0
Chester C	Tr	01/00	99	9	0	0

ROBINSON John
Born: Lurgan, Armagh, Northern Ireland, 2 April, 1920 WH
Died: Wheaton Aston, Staffordshire, England, 24 October, 1981

League Club	Source	Date Signed	Seasons Played	Apps	Subs	Gls
Wolverhampton W	Glenavon	01/42				
Walsall	Tr	03/47	46-47	5	-	0

ROBINSON John (Johnny)
Born: Chorley, Lancashire, England, 18 April, 1936 RW

League Club	Source	Date Signed	Seasons Played	Apps	Subs	Gls
Bury	Leyland Motors	09/54	54-59	120	-	21
Oldham Ath	Tr	07/61	61	3	-	0

ROBINSON John
Born: Middlesbrough, England, 10 February, 1934 LH/IF

League Club	Source	Date Signed	Seasons Played	Apps	Subs	Gls
Middlesbrough	Jnr	10/51	53-54	3	-	0
Hartlepool U	Horden CW	06/59	59	9	-	0

ROBINSON John Allan (Jackie)
Born: Shiremoor, Tyne and Wear, England, 10 August, 1917 IF
Died: Shiremoor, Tyne and Wear, England, 30 July, 1972
England: 4/FLge-1

League Club	Source	Date Signed	Seasons Played	Apps	Subs	Gls
Sheffield Wed	Shiremoor	10/34	34-46	108	-	34
Sunderland	Tr	10/46	46-48	82	-	32
Lincoln C	Tr	10/49	49	8	-	5

ROBINSON John James (Jack)
Born: Oswaldtwistle, Lancashire, England, 23 April, 1918 G
Died: Accrington, Lancashire, England, April, 1993

League Club	Source	Date Signed	Seasons Played	Apps	Subs	Gls
Accrington Stan	Sacred Heart	05/35	35-36	16	-	0
Manchester C	Tr	04/37	38-46	2	-	0
Bury	Tr	11/46	46	12	-	0
Southend U	Tr	08/47	47	6	-	0

ROBINSON John Robert Campbell
Born: Bulawayo, Zimbabwe, 29 August, 1971 W
Wales: 30/U21-5

League Club	Source	Date Signed	Seasons Played	Apps	Subs	Gls
Brighton & HA	YT	04/89	89-92	57	5	6
Charlton Ath	Tr	09/92	92-02	296	36	35
Cardiff C	Tr	07/03	03-04	39	3	3
Gillingham	Tr	10/04	04	2	2	0

ROBINSON Joseph (Joe)
Born: Morpeth, Northumberland, England, 4 March, 1919 G
Died: Stockport, Greater Manchester, England, 3 July, 1991

League Club	Source	Date Signed	Seasons Played	Apps	Subs	Gls
Hartlepool U	Ashington	05/38	38	11	-	0
Blackpool	Tr	07/46	47-48	25	-	0
Hull C	Tr	02/49	48-52	70	-	0

ROBINSON Joseph (Joe)
Born: Lanchester, County Durham, England, 14 November, 1918 WH
Died: Hitchin, Hertfordshire, England, October, 1988

League Club	Source	Date Signed	Seasons Played	Apps	Subs	Gls
Norwich C	Ouston U	11/37	46	2	-	0

ROBINSON Joseph Norman (Norman)
Born: Middlesbrough, England, 5 January, 1921 CH
Died: Middlesbrough, England, April, 1990

League Club	Source	Date Signed	Seasons Played	Apps	Subs	Gls
Middlesbrough	South Bank St Peter's	01/46	46-47	16	-	0
Grimsby T	Tr	06/48	48	5	-	0

ROBINSON Joseph William (Billy)
Born: Chester-le-Street, County Durham, England, 13 April, 1932 RW

League Club	Source	Date Signed	Seasons Played	Apps	Subs	Gls
Newcastle U	Jnr	09/51				
Hartlepool U	West Stanley	07/54	55-57	43	-	11
Gateshead	Tr	08/58	58	22	-	5

ROBINSON Keith
Born: Bolton, Greater Manchester, England, 30 December, 1937 — IF

League Club	Source	Date Signed	Seasons Played	Apps	Subs	Gls
Oldham Ath		09/58	58-60	40	-	4

ROBINSON Leonard James (Len)
Born: Nottingham, England, 1 October, 1946 — FB

League Club	Source	Date Signed	Seasons Played	Apps	Subs	Gls
Notts Co	Nottingham F (Am)	03/64	63-64	4	-	0

ROBINSON Leslie (Les)
Born: Shirebrook, Derbyshire, England, 1 March, 1967 — RB

League Club	Source	Date Signed	Seasons Played	Apps	Subs	Gls
Mansfield T	Nottingham F (Jnr)	10/84	84-86	11	4	0
Stockport Co	Tr	11/86	86-87	67	0	3
Doncaster Rov	Tr	03/88	87-89	82	0	12
Oxford U	Tr	03/90	89-99	379	5	3
Mansfield T	Tr	07/00	00-01	80	0	0

ROBINSON Mark Andrew
Born: Guisborough, Cleveland, England, 24 July, 1981 — LB
England: Semi Pro-3

League Club	Source	Date Signed	Seasons Played	Apps	Subs	Gls
Hartlepool U	YT	07/99	00-03	80	5	0
Stockport Co	Hereford U	07/05	05-06	57	2	4
Torquay U	Tr	01/07	06	18	0	0

ROBINSON Mark James
Born: Rochdale, Greater Manchester, England, 21 November, 1968 — RB/M

League Club	Source	Date Signed	Seasons Played	Apps	Subs	Gls
West Bromwich A	App	01/87	85-86	2	0	0
Barnsley	Tr	06/87	87-92	117	20	6
Newcastle U	Tr	03/93	92-93	14	11	0
Swindon T	Tr	07/94	94-01	255	14	4

ROBINSON Mark Jeffrey
Born: Nottingham, England, 26 November, 1960 — F

League Club	Source	Date Signed	Seasons Played	Apps	Subs	Gls
Notts Co	Ilkeston T	01/85	84-85	12	14	1

ROBINSON Mark William
Born: Middlesbrough, England, 22 October, 1961 — M

League Club	Source	Date Signed	Seasons Played	Apps	Subs	Gls
Middlesbrough	App	10/79				
Hartlepool U	Guisborough T	01/83	82-83	34	1	4

ROBINSON Martin John
Born: Ilford, E London, England, 17 July, 1957 — F/W

League Club	Source	Date Signed	Seasons Played	Apps	Subs	Gls
Tottenham H	App	05/75	75-77	5	1	2
Charlton Ath	Tr	02/78	77-84	218	10	58
Reading	L	09/82	82	6	0	2
Gillingham	Tr	10/84	84-86	91	5	23
Southend U	Tr	07/87	87-88	43	13	14
Cambridge U	Tr	08/89	89	7	9	1

ROBINSON Marvin Leon St Clair
Born: Crewe, Cheshire, England, 11 April, 1980 — F
England: Schools

League Club	Source	Date Signed	Seasons Played	Apps	Subs	Gls
Derby Co	YT	07/98	98-02	3	9	1
Stoke C	L	09/00	00	3	0	1
Tranmere Rov	L	11/02	02	1	5	1
Chesterfield	Tr	09/03	03	17	15	6
Notts Co	Tr	09/04	04	1	1	0
Rushden & D	Tr	11/04	04	0	2	0
Walsall	Tr	12/04	04	4	6	4
Stockport Co	Tr	03/05	04	3	0	0
Lincoln C	Tr	08/05	05	20	12	7
Macclesfield T	Tr	07/06	06	5	0	0

ROBINSON Matthew Adam (Matt)
Born: Newmarket, Suffolk, England, 22 March, 1984 — F

League Club	Source	Date Signed	Seasons Played	Apps	Subs	Gls
Bournemouth	Ipswich T (Sch)	10/03				
Cambridge U	Tr	02/04	03-04	1	6	0

ROBINSON Matthew James (Matt)
Born: Leicester, England, 1 June, 1994 — M

League Club	Source	Date Signed	Seasons Played	Apps	Subs	Gls
Luton T	Leicester C (Sch)	07/12	14	7	2	0

ROBINSON Matthew Richard (Matt)
Born: Exeter, England, 23 December, 1974 — LB

League Club	Source	Date Signed	Seasons Played	Apps	Subs	Gls
Southampton	YT	07/93	94-97	3	11	0
Portsmouth	Tr	02/98	97-99	65	4	1
Reading	Tr	01/00	99-01	62	3	0
Oxford U	Tr	07/02	02-05	171	0	4

ROBINSON Maurice
Born: Newark, Nottinghamshire, England, 9 November, 1929 — LW

League Club	Source	Date Signed	Seasons Played	Apps	Subs	Gls
Leeds U	Ransome & Marles	04/49				
Doncaster Rov	Gainsborough Trinity	12/52	52-53	19	-	7
Northampton T	Kettering T	06/57	57	11	-	2

ROBINSON Michael Anthony (Mike)
Born: Sunderland, England, 30 October, 1968 — FB

League Club	Source	Date Signed	Seasons Played	Apps	Subs	Gls
Newcastle U	YT	08/87				
Darlington	Tr	07/88	88	0	1	0

ROBINSON Michael John
Born: Leicester, England, 12 July, 1958 — F
Republic of Ireland: 24

League Club	Source	Date Signed	Seasons Played	Apps	Subs	Gls
Preston NE	App	07/76	75-78	45	3	15
Manchester C	Tr	07/79	79	29	1	8
Brighton & HA	Tr	07/80	80-82	111	2	37
Liverpool	Tr	08/83	83-84	26	4	6
Queens Park Rgrs	Tr	12/84	84-86	41	7	5

ROBINSON Neil
Born: Liverpool, England, 20 April, 1957 — RB/M

League Club	Source	Date Signed	Seasons Played	Apps	Subs	Gls
Everton	App	05/74	75-78	13	3	1
Swansea C	Tr	10/79	79-84	114	9	7
Grimsby T	Tr	09/84	84-87	109	0	6
Darlington	Tr	07/88	88	35	2	1

ROBINSON Neil David
Born: Liverpool, England, 18 November, 1979 — F

League Club	Source	Date Signed	Seasons Played	Apps	Subs	Gls
Macclesfield T	Prescot Cables	07/02	02-03	2	9	0

ROBINSON Paul
Born: Seaton Delaval, Northumberland, England, 25 May, 1983 — F

League Club	Source	Date Signed	Seasons Played	Apps	Subs	Gls
Tranmere Rov	Sch	05/02				
Grimsby T	L	09/04	04	1	1	0

ROBINSON Paul
Born: Scarborough, North Yorkshire, England, 2 January, 1974 — G

League Club	Source	Date Signed	Seasons Played	Apps	Subs	Gls
Sheffield Wed	YT	07/92				
Scarborough	Tr	08/93	93	3	1	0

ROBINSON Paul
Born: Hampstead, NW London, England, 5 January, 1963 — LB
England: Youth/Schools

League Club	Source	Date Signed	Seasons Played	Apps	Subs	Gls
Millwall	App	01/80	79-83	56	3	2

ROBINSON Paul Derrick
Born: Sunderland, England, 20 November, 1978 — F

League Club	Source	Date Signed	Seasons Played	Apps	Subs	Gls
Darlington	YT	07/97	95-97	7	19	3
Newcastle U	Tr	03/98	99	2	9	0
Wimbledon	Tr	08/00	00-01	0	4	0
Burnley	L	10/00	00	0	4	0
Grimsby T	L	03/02	01	1	4	0
Grimsby T	L	08/02	02	5	7	1
Carlisle U	L	11/02	02	1	4	1
Blackpool	Tr	03/03	02	5	2	1
Hartlepool U	Tr	07/03	03	19	12	7
Torquay U	Whitley Bay	11/05	05	12	9	3

ROBINSON Paul James
Born: Nottingham, England, 21 February, 1971 — F

League Club	Source	Date Signed	Seasons Played	Apps	Subs	Gls
Scarborough	Bury (YT)	05/89	89	13	7	3
Plymouth Arg	Tr	05/90	90	7	4	3
Hereford U	Tr	06/91	91	7	4	0

ROBINSON Paul Mark James
Born: Barnet, N London, England, 7 January, 1982 — CD

League Club	Source	Date Signed	Seasons Played	Apps	Subs	Gls
Millwall	YT	10/00	02-13	295	16	17
Torquay U	L	12/04	04	12	0	0
Portsmouth	Tr	08/14	14	33	0	2

ROBINSON Paul Peter
Born: Watford, Hertfordshire, England, 14 December, 1978 — LB
England: U21-3

League Club	Source	Date Signed	Seasons Played	Apps	Subs	Gls
Watford	YT	02/97	96-03	201	18	8
West Bromwich A	Tr	10/03	03-08	211	3	4
Bolton W	Tr	07/09	09-11	74	3	0
Leeds U	L	03/12	11	9	1	0
Birmingham C	Tr	09/12	12-14	104	5	0

ROBINSON Paul William
Born: Beverley, East Riding of Yorkshire, England, 15 October, 1979 — G
England: 41/U21-11

League Club	Source	Date Signed	Seasons Played	Apps	Subs	Gls
Leeds U	YT	05/97	98-03	93	2	0
Tottenham H	Tr	05/04	04-07	137	0	1
Blackburn Rov	Tr	07/08	08-14	189	0	0

ROBINSON Peter
Born: Newbiggin, Northumberland, England, 4 September, 1957 — CD
England: Semi Pro-6

League Club	Source	Date Signed	Seasons Played	Apps	Subs	Gls
Burnley	Jnr	06/76	76-79	48	7	3
Rochdale	Blyth Spartans	03/85	84	9	3	0
Darlington	Tr	08/85	85-87	110	2	5
Halifax T	L	12/85	85	3	2	0

ROBINSON Peter
Born: Manchester, England, 29 January, 1922 — WH
Died: Manchester, England, 9 September, 2000

League Club	Source	Date Signed	Seasons Played	Apps	Subs	Gls
Manchester C	Jnr	05/40	46	1	-	0
Chesterfield	Tr	10/47	47-48	60	-	0
Notts Co	Buxton	02/50	49-52	82	-	1

ROBINSON Peter John
Born: St Ives, Cambridgeshire, England, 11 April, 1949 — CD

League Club	Source	Date Signed	Seasons Played	Apps	Subs	Gls
Southend U	Cambridge U	03/69	68-69	1	3	0

ROBINSON Philip Brian (Phil)
Born: Doncaster, South Yorkshire, England, 21 November, 1942 — RW
Died: Sheffield, England, 27 December, 1989

League Club	Source	Date Signed	Seasons Played	Apps	Subs	Gls
Huddersfield T	Montrose Victoria	04/60				
Doncaster Rov	Tr	08/61	61-65	157	0	19
Bradford Park Ave	Tr	07/66	66-68	108	8	8
Darlington	Tr	07/69	69	26	1	4

ROBINSON Philip Daniel (Phil)
Born: Manchester, England, 28 September, 1980 — CD

League Club	Source	Date Signed	Seasons Played	Apps	Subs	Gls
Blackpool	YT	01/99	98-99	6	5	0

ROBINSON Philip John (Phil)
Born: Stafford, England, 6 January, 1967 — M

League Club	Source	Date Signed	Seasons Played	Apps	Subs	Gls
Aston Villa	App	01/85	86	2	1	1
Wolverhampton W	Tr	07/87	87-88	63	8	8
Notts Co	Tr	08/89	89-91	65	1	5
Birmingham C	L	03/91	90	9	0	0
Huddersfield T	Tr	09/92	92-93	74	1	5
Northampton T	L	09/94	94	14	0	0
Chesterfield	Tr	12/94	94-95	60	1	17
Notts Co	Tr	08/96	96-97	63	14	5
Stoke C	Tr	06/98	98-99	53	9	2

ROBINSON Raymond (Ray)
Born: Durham, England, 2 December, 1950 — IF

League Club	Source	Date Signed	Seasons Played	Apps	Subs	Gls
Preston NE	App	12/68	68	2	0	0

ROBINSON Richard (Dicky)
Born: Whitburn, Tyne and Wear, England, 19 January, 1927 — D
Died: Barrow, Cumbria, England, 19 April, 2009
England: FLge-5

League Club	Source	Date Signed	Seasons Played	Apps	Subs	Gls
Middlesbrough	Marsden Colliery Jnrs	04/45	46-58	390	-	1
Barrow	Tr	06/59	59-62	139	-	0

ROBINSON Robert (Bobby)
Born: Ashington, Northumberland, England, 23 June, 1921 — G
Died: Newcastle-upon-Tyne, England, 28 March, 1975

League Club	Source	Date Signed	Seasons Played	Apps	Subs	Gls
Sunderland	Newbiggin	02/47	47-51	31	-	0
Newcastle U	Tr	08/52	52	5	-	0

ROBINSON Ronald (Ronnie)
Born: Sunderland, England, 22 October, 1966 — LB

League Club	Source	Date Signed	Seasons Played	Apps	Subs	Gls
Ipswich T	SC Vaux	11/84				
Leeds U	Tr	11/85	85-86	27	0	0
Doncaster Rov	Tr	02/87	86-88	76	2	5
West Bromwich A	Tr	03/89	88	1	0	0
Rotherham U	Tr	08/89	89-91	86	0	2
Peterborough U	Tr	12/91	91-92	44	3	0
Exeter C	Tr	07/93	93-94	37	2	1
Huddersfield T	L	01/94	93	2	0	0
Scarborough	Tr	08/95	95	1	0	0

ROBINSON Ryan
Born: Kendal, Cumbria, England, 13 October, 1982 — G

League Club	Source	Date Signed	Seasons Played	Apps	Subs	Gls
Blackburn Rov	Sch	01/02				
Southend U	Tr	07/03	03	2	0	0

ROBINSON Simon William
Born: West Bromwich, West Midlands, England, 6 April, 1965 — M

League Club	Source	Date Signed	Seasons Played	Apps	Subs	Gls
Blackpool	Alvechurch	12/90				
Walsall	Alvechurch	12/91	91	0	1	0

ROBINSON Spencer Liam (Liam)
Born: Bradford, England, 29 December, 1965 — F

League Club	Source	Date Signed	Seasons Played	Apps	Subs	Gls
Huddersfield T	App	01/84	83-85	17	4	2
Tranmere Rov	L	12/85	85	4	0	3
Bury	Tr	07/86	86-92	248	14	89
Bristol C	Tr	07/93	93	31	10	4
Burnley	Tr	07/94	94-96	43	20	9
Scarborough	Tr	08/97	97-98	45	20	7

ROBINSON Stephen (Steve)
Born: Lisburn, Belfast, Northern Ireland, 10 December, 1974 — M
Northern Ireland: 7/B-4/U21-1/Youth/Schools

League Club	Source	Date Signed	Seasons Played	Apps	Subs	Gls
Tottenham H	YT	01/93	93	1	1	0
Bournemouth	Tr	10/94	94-99	227	13	51
Preston NE	Tr	05/00	00-01	6	18	1
Bristol C	L	03/02	01	6	0	1
Luton T	Tr	06/02	02-07	170	15	9

ROBINSON Steven Eli (Steve)
Born: Nottingham, England, 17 January, 1975 — RM

League Club	Source	Date Signed	Seasons Played	Apps	Subs	Gls
Birmingham C	YT	06/93	94-00	53	28	0
Peterborough U	L	03/96	95	5	0	0
Swindon T	Tr	02/01	00-04	128	14	5
Lincoln C	Tr	07/05	05	11	1	0

ROBINSON Steven Martin
Born: Sheffield, England, 14 June, 1964 — M

League Club	Source	Date Signed	Seasons Played	Apps	Subs	Gls
Chesterfield	App	06/82	81-82	8	1	0

ROBINSON Stuart Alan
Born: Middlesbrough, England, 16 January, 1959 — LW

League Club	Source	Date Signed	Seasons Played	Apps	Subs	Gls
Newcastle U	App	07/77	77-78	11	1	2
Aldershot	Tr	07/80	80-82	71	6	10

ROBINSON Terence (Terry)
Born: Woodhams, Essex, England, 8 November, 1929 — CH
England: Amateur-10

League Club	Source	Date Signed	Seasons Played	Apps	Subs	Gls
Brentford (Am)	Loughborough College	09/54	54-56	35	-	1
Northampton T (Am)	Tr	07/57	57	13	-	0

ROBINSON Terence Allan Charles (Terry)
Born: Stewkley, Buckinghamshire, England, 24 March, 1954 — F

League Club	Source	Date Signed	Seasons Played	Apps	Subs	Gls
Luton T	App	03/72				
Cambridge U	L	09/72	72	6	0	1
Crewe Alex	Tr	12/72	72-73	7	4	1

ROBINSON Theo Larayan Ronaldo
Born: Birmingham, England, 22 January, 1989 — F
Jamaica: 5

League Club	Source	Date Signed	Seasons Played	Apps	Subs	Gls
Watford	Sch	02/07	05-08	0	5	0
Hereford U	L	08/07	07	32	11	13
Southend U	L	01/09	08	20	1	7
Huddersfield T	Tr	07/09	09-10	17	21	13
Millwall	Tr	09/10	10	8	3	3
Derby Co	Tr	02/11	10-12	48	32	20
Huddersfield T	L	02/13	12	4	2	0
Doncaster Rov	Tr	08/13	13-14	32	31	9
Scunthorpe U	L	03/15	14	8	0	3

ROBINSON Trevor Kymar
Born: Saint Catherine, Jamaica, 20 September, 1984 — W

League Club	Source	Date Signed	Seasons Played	Apps	Subs	Gls
Millwall	Sch	01/04	03-05	1	3	0

ROBINSON William (Bill)
Born: Whitburn, Tyne and Wear, England, 4 April, 1919 — CF
Died: Hartlepool, Cleveland, England, 7 October, 1992

League Club	Source	Date Signed	Seasons Played	Apps	Subs	Gls
Sunderland	Hylton Colliery Jnrs	04/36	37-38	24	-	14
Charlton Ath	Tr	05/46	46-48	52	-	16
West Ham U	Tr	01/49	48-51	101	-	60

ROBINSON William (Billy)
Born: Manchester, England, 17 November, 1925 — WH/LB
Died: Salford, England, 16 May, 1953

League Club	Source	Date Signed	Seasons Played	Apps	Subs	Gls
Stockport Co		08/49	49	9	-	2
Accrington Stan	Tr	12/50	50-52	96	-	2

ROBLEDO Edward Oliver (Ted)
Born: Iquique, Chile, 26 July, 1928 — LH
Died: 6 December, 1970

League Club	Source	Date Signed	Seasons Played	Apps	Subs	Gls
Notts Co	Brampton Ellis YC	09/45				
Barnsley	Tr	04/46	47-48	5	-	0
Newcastle U	Tr	02/49	49-52	37	-	0
Notts Co	Colo Colo (CHL)	09/57	57	2	-	0

ROBLEDO Jorge Oliver (George)
Born: Iquique, Chile, 14 April, 1926 — CF
Died: Dubai, United Arab Emirates, 1 April, 1989
Chile: 31

League Club	Source	Date Signed	Seasons Played	Apps	Subs	Gls
Barnsley	Huddersfield T (Am)	04/43	46-48	105	-	45
Newcastle U	Tr	01/49	48-52	146	-	82

ROBLES Joel
Born: Getafe, Spain, 17 June, 1990 — G
Spain: U23-1/U21-2/Youth

League Club	Source	Date Signed	Seasons Played	Apps	Subs	Gls
Wigan Ath (L)	Atletico Madrid (SPN)	01/13	12	9	0	0
Everton	Atletico Madrid (SPN)	07/13	13-14	7	2	0

ROBLES Louis Gabriel
Born: Liverpool, England, 11 September, 1996 — F

League Club	Source	Date Signed	Seasons Played	Apps	Subs	Gls
Wigan Ath	Sch	-	14	0	1	0

ROBLEY Keith
Born: Cockermouth, Cumbria, England, 3 June, 1944 — W

League Club	Source	Date Signed	Seasons Played	Apps	Subs	Gls
Workington (Am)	Flimby	08/65	65	2	0	0

ROBSHAW Henry William (Harry)
Born: Edmonton, N London, England, 10 May, 1927 — RH
Died: Yeovil, Somerset, England, 26 January, 1990

League Club	Source	Date Signed	Seasons Played	Apps	Subs	Gls
Tottenham H	Hendon	11/48	51	1	-	0
Reading	Tr	02/53	52-53	20	-	1

ROBSON Albert Proud (Bert)
Born: Crook, County Durham, England, 14 November, 1916 — CF
Died: Croydon, S London, England, January, 1990

League Club	Source	Date Signed	Seasons Played	Apps	Subs	Gls
Crystal Palace	Godalming	12/34	36-47	85	-	22

ROBSON Barry Gordon George
Born: Inverurie, Aberdeenshire, Scotland, 7 November, 1978 — LW
Scotland: 17/B-2

League Club	Source	Date Signed	Seasons Played	Apps	Subs	Gls
Middlesbrough	Glasgow Celtic	01/10	09-11	84	3	17
Sheffield U	Vancouver W'caps (CAN)	01/13	12	10	7	2

ROBSON Benjamin Thomas (Benny)
Born: Gateshead, Tyne and Wear, England, 3 January, 1922 — LB
Died: Gateshead, Tyne and Wear, England, 29 October, 1999

League Club	Source	Date Signed	Seasons Played	Apps	Subs	Gls
Southport	Aberdeen	08/49	49	2	-	0

ROBSON Bryan
Born: Witton Gilbert, County Durham, England, 11 January, 1957 — M
England: 90/B-3/FLge/U21-7/Youth

League Club	Source	Date Signed	Seasons Played	Apps	Subs	Gls
West Bromwich A	App	08/74	74-81	194	4	40
Manchester U	Tr	10/81	81-93	326	19	74
Middlesbrough	Tr	05/94	94-96	23	2	1

ROBSON Bryan Stanley (Pop)
Born: Sunderland, England, 11 November, 1945 — F
England: FLge-1/U23-2

League Club	Source	Date Signed	Seasons Played	Apps	Subs	Gls
Newcastle U	Jnr	11/62	64-70	205	1	82
West Ham U	Tr	02/71	70-73	120	0	47
Sunderland	Tr	07/74	74-76	90	0	34
West Ham U	Tr	10/76	76-78	107	0	47
Sunderland	Tr	06/79	79-80	49	3	23
Carlisle U	Tr	03/81	80-81	48	0	21
Chelsea	Tr	08/82	82	11	4	3
Carlisle U	L	03/83	82	11	0	4
Sunderland	Tr	08/83	83	7	5	3
Carlisle U	Tr	07/84	84-85	10	3	1

ROBSON Charles Leslie (Les)
Born: South Shields, Tyne and Wear, England, 1 November, 1931 — LW

League Club	Source	Date Signed	Seasons Played	Apps	Subs	Gls
Hull C	North Hull Jnrs	05/50	51	3	-	1
Darlington	Tr	05/53	53-54	66	-	19
Liverpool	Tr	07/55				
Crewe Alex	Tr	01/56	55	14	-	2

ROBSON David Mark
Born: Castle Eden, County Durham, England, 5 October, 1966 — M

League Club	Source	Date Signed	Seasons Played	Apps	Subs	Gls
Hartlepool U		11/86	86	1	0	0

ROBSON Gary
Born: Chester-le-Street, County Durham, England, 6 July, 1965 — M

League Club	Source	Date Signed	Seasons Played	Apps	Subs	Gls
West Bromwich A	App	05/83	82-92	184	34	28
Bradford C	Tr	07/93	93-95	72	3	3

ROBSON Glenn Alan
Born: Sunderland, England, 25 September, 1977 — F

League Club	Source	Date Signed	Seasons Played	Apps	Subs	Gls
Rochdale	Murton CW	11/96	96-97	0	10	0
Darlington	Blyth Spartans	08/03	03	3	3	0

ROBSON James (Jimmy)
Born: Pelton, County Durham, England, 23 January, 1939 — IF/CD
England: U23-1

League Club	Source	Date Signed	Seasons Played	Apps	Subs	Gls
Burnley	Jnr	01/56	56-64	202	-	79
Blackpool	Tr	03/65	64-67	60	4	14
Barnsley	Tr	01/68	67-69	87	0	15
Bury	Tr	08/70	70-72	100	3	3
Burnley	Tr	05/73				

ROBSON James Donald (Don)
Born: Winlaton, Tyne and Wear, England, 5 February, 1934 — CF

League Club	Source	Date Signed	Seasons Played	Apps	Subs	Gls
Doncaster Rov		07/51				
Gateshead	Tr	09/53	53-56	34	-	11

ROBSON John Dixon
Born: Consett, County Durham, England, 15 July, 1950 — LB
Died: Sutton Coldfield, West Midlands, England, 12 May, 2004
England: FLge-1/U23-7

League Club	Source	Date Signed	Seasons Played	Apps	Subs	Gls
Derby Co	Birtley YC	10/67	67-72	170	1	3
Aston Villa	Tr	10/72	72-77	141	3	1

ROBSON John Douglas
Born: Washington, Tyne and Wear, England, 20 July, 1942 — CH

League Club	Source	Date Signed	Seasons Played	Apps	Subs	Gls
Darlington		10/62	62-64	34	-	0

ROBSON Keith
Born: Hetton-le-Hole, Tyne and Wear, England, 15 November, 1953 — F/W

League Club	Source	Date Signed	Seasons Played	Apps	Subs	Gls
Newcastle U	Jnr	05/71	72-73	14	0	3
West Ham U	Tr	09/74	74-76	65	3	13
Cardiff C	Tr	08/77	77	21	0	5
Norwich C	Tr	02/78	77-80	61	4	13
Leicester C	Tr	09/81	81-82	8	1	0
Carlisle U	L	03/83	82	10	1	4

ROBSON Lancelot (Lance)
Born: Newcastle-upon-Tyne, England, 27 December, 1939 — WH/CF
Died: Cleveland, England, 30 November, 1987

League Club	Source	Date Signed	Seasons Played	Apps	Subs	Gls
Newcastle U	Stannington	10/58				
Darlington	Tr	07/60	60-63	144	-	47
Darlington	Blyth Spartans	07/68	68-69	69	0	18
Hartlepool U	Tr	02/70	69	8	0	2

ROBSON Mark Andrew
Born: Newham, E London, England, 22 May, 1969 — LW

League Club	Source	Date Signed	Seasons Played	Apps	Subs	Gls
Exeter C	App	12/86	86	26	0	7
Tottenham H	Tr	07/87	88-89	3	5	0
Reading	L	03/88	87	5	2	0
Watford	L	10/89	89	1	0	0
Plymouth Arg	L	12/89	89	7	0	0
Exeter C	L	01/92	91	7	1	1
West Ham U	Tr	08/92	92-93	42	5	8
Charlton Ath	Tr	11/93	93-96	79	26	9
Notts Co	Tr	06/97	97-99	26	6	4
Wycombe W	L	10/98	98	1	3	0

ROBSON Matthew (Matt)
Born: Easington, County Durham, England, 29 December, 1954 — CD

League Club	Source	Date Signed	Seasons Played	Apps	Subs	Gls
Sunderland	App	01/72				
Darlington	L	03/75	74	1	0	0

ROBSON Matthew James (Matty)
Born: Spennymoor, County Durham, England, 23 January, 1985 — M/LB

League Club	Source	Date Signed	Seasons Played	Apps	Subs	Gls
Hartlepool U	Sch	03/04	03-08	90	45	9
Carlisle U	Tr	07/09	09-14	160	27	20

ROBSON Robert William (Bobby)
Born: Sacriston, County Durham, England, 18 February, 1933 — IF
Died: County Durham, England, 31 July, 2009
England: 20/FLge-5/U23-1

League Club	Source	Date Signed	Seasons Played	Apps	Subs	Gls
Fulham	Middlesbrough (Am)	05/50	50-55	152	-	68
West Bromwich A	Tr	03/56	55-61	239	-	56
Fulham	Tr	08/62	62-66	192	0	9

ROBSON Ronald (Ron)
Born: Sunderland, England, 12 September, 1932 — RB
Died: Sunderland, England, October, 1993

League Club	Source	Date Signed	Seasons Played	Apps	Subs	Gls
Gateshead	Albion Sports Club	06/57	57-58	7	-	0

ROBSON Stewart Ian
Born: Billericay, Essex, England, 6 November, 1964 — M
England: U21-8/Youth

League Club	Source	Date Signed	Seasons Played	Apps	Subs	Gls
Arsenal	App	11/81	81-86	150	1	16
West Ham U	Tr	01/87	86-90	68	1	4
Coventry C	Tr	03/91	90-93	55	2	3

ROBSON Thomas (Tom)
Born: Sunderland, England, 1 February, 1936 — CH
Died: Sunderland, England, 1981

League Club	Source	Date Signed	Seasons Played	Apps	Subs	Gls
Sunderland	Jnr	09/57	58-59	5	-	0
Darlington	Tr	08/60	60	1	-	0

ROBSON Thomas Henry (Tommy)
Born: Gateshead, Tyne and Wear, England, 31 July, 1944 — LW
England: Youth

League Club	Source	Date Signed	Seasons Played	Apps	Subs	Gls
Northampton T	App	08/61	61-65	73	1	20
Chelsea	Tr	12/65	65	6	1	0
Newcastle U	Tr	12/66	66-68	46	2	11
Peterborough U	Tr	11/68	68-80	440	42	111

ROBSON Thomas Raymond (Ray)
Born: Newcastle-upon-Tyne, England, 11 August, 1928 — LB
Died: Hertfordshire, England, January, 2014

League Club	Source	Date Signed	Seasons Played	Apps	Subs	Gls
Cardiff C		02/49				
Bradford C	Tr	07/50	50-51	10	-	0
Grimsby T	Tr	06/52	52-54	58	-	2

ROBSON Trevor
Born: Stoke-on-Trent, England, 4 January, 1959 — F

League Club	Source	Date Signed	Seasons Played	Apps	Subs	Gls
Port Vale	App	01/77	75	0	1	0

ROBSON William Henderson
Born: Whitehaven, Cumbria, England, 13 October, 1931 — IF

League Club	Source	Date Signed	Seasons Played	Apps	Subs	Gls
Workington	Kells	08/51	51-59	128	-	55
Carlisle U	Tr	11/59	59	12	-	1

ROBSON-KANU Thomas Henry Alex (Hal)
Born: Acton, W London, England, 21 May, 1989 — W
England: Youth//Wales: 26/U21-4

League Club	Source	Date Signed	Seasons Played	Apps	Subs	Gls
Reading	Sch	07/07	09-14	93	77	21

League Club	Source	Date Signed	Seasons Played	Apps	Subs	Gls
Southend U	L	01/08	07	6	2	3
Southend U	L	08/08	08	12	2	2
Swindon T	L	01/09	08	20	0	4

ROBY Donald (Don)
Born: Wigan, Greater Manchester, England, 15 November, 1933 — RW
Died: Nottingham, England, 10 June, 2013

League Club	Source	Date Signed	Seasons Played	Apps	Subs	Gls
Notts Co	Orrell Bispham Meth's	02/51	50-60	226	-	37
Derby Co	Tr	08/61	61-62	70	-	6

ROCA Carlos Jose
Born: Manchester, England, 4 September, 1984 — RW

League Club	Source	Date Signed	Seasons Played	Apps	Subs	Gls
Oldham Ath	Sch	-	03	0	7	0

ROCASTLE Craig Aaron
Born: Lewisham, SE London, England, 17 August, 1981 — M
Grenada: 12

League Club	Source	Date Signed	Seasons Played	Apps	Subs	Gls
Chelsea	Slough T	09/03				
Barnsley	L	02/04	03	4	1	0
Lincoln C	L	03/04	03	0	2	0
Sheffield Wed	Tr	02/05	04-05	23	5	1
Yeovil T	L	03/06	05	5	3	0
Oldham Ath	Tr	07/06	06	17	18	2
Port Vale	Tr	07/07	07	17	6	1
Gillingham	L	01/08	07	2	0	0

ROCASTLE David Carlyle
Born: Lewisham, SE London, England, 2 May, 1967 — M
Died: Slough, Berkshire, England, 31 March, 2001
England: 14/B-2/U21-14

League Club	Source	Date Signed	Seasons Played	Apps	Subs	Gls
Arsenal	App	12/84	85-91	204	14	24
Leeds U	Tr	08/92	92-93	17	8	2
Manchester C	Tr	12/93	93	21	0	2
Chelsea	Tr	08/94	94-95	27	2	0
Norwich C	L	01/97	96	11	0	0
Hull C	L	10/97	97	10	0	1

ROCCA Jonathan Christian (Jon)
Born: Sheffield, England, 4 November, 1972 — RB

League Club	Source	Date Signed	Seasons Played	Apps	Subs	Gls
Scarborough	YT	06/91	91	3	0	0

ROCHA Carlos
Born: Lisbon, Portugal, 4 December, 1974 — F

League Club	Source	Date Signed	Seasons Played	Apps	Subs	Gls
Bury	Boston Bulldogs (USA)	08/99	99	0	3	0

ROCHA Ricardo Sergio
Born: Braga, Portugal, 3 October, 1978 — CD
Portugal: 6

League Club	Source	Date Signed	Seasons Played	Apps	Subs	Gls
Tottenham H	Benfica (POR)	01/07	06-07	13	1	0
Portsmouth	Standard Liege (BEL)	02/10	09-12	86	7	0

ROCHE Barry Christopher
Born: Dublin, Republic of Ireland, 6 April, 1982 — G
Republic of Ireland: Youth

League Club	Source	Date Signed	Seasons Played	Apps	Subs	Gls
Nottingham F	YT	06/99	00-04	10	3	0
Chesterfield	Tr	07/05	05-07	126	0	0
Morecambe	Tr	07/08	08-14	275	0	0

ROCHE David
Born: Wallsend, Tyne and Wear, England, 13 December, 1970 — M

League Club	Source	Date Signed	Seasons Played	Apps	Subs	Gls
Newcastle U	YT	08/88	88-91	23	13	0
Peterborough U	L	01/93	92	4	0	0
Doncaster Rov	Tr	10/93	93-94	49	1	8
Southend U	Tr	03/95	94	0	4	0

ROCHE John Anthony (Johnny)
Born: Poplar, E London, England, 18 May, 1932 — CF/RW
Died: Romford, E London, England, August, 1988

League Club	Source	Date Signed	Seasons Played	Apps	Subs	Gls
Millwall	Margate	06/57	57-58	25	-	14
Crystal Palace	Tr	05/59	59	36	-	11

ROCHE Lee Paul
Born: Bolton, Greater Manchester, England, 28 October, 1980 — RB
England: U21-1/Youth

League Club	Source	Date Signed	Seasons Played	Apps	Subs	Gls
Manchester U	YT	02/99	02	0	1	0
Wrexham	L	07/00	00	41	0	0
Burnley	Tr	07/03	03-04	38	16	2
Wrexham	Tr	07/05	05-06	43	2	1

ROCHE Patrick Joseph Christopher (Paddy)
Born: Dublin, Republic of Ireland, 4 January, 1951 — G
Republic of Ireland: 8/U23-1

League Club	Source	Date Signed	Seasons Played	Apps	Subs	Gls
Manchester U	Shelbourne (ROI)	10/73	74-81	46	0	0
Brentford	Tr	08/82	82-83	71	0	0
Halifax T	Tr	07/84	84-88	184	0	0

ROCHE Stephen Michael
Born: Dublin, Republic of Ireland, 2 October, 1978 — LB/M
Republic of Ireland: Youth/Schools

League Club	Source	Date Signed	Seasons Played	Apps	Subs	Gls
Millwall	Belvedere (ROI)	10/94	96-98	7	4	0

ROCHEMBACK Fabio
Born: Soledade, Brazil, 10 December, 1981 — M
Brazil: 7

League Club	Source	Date Signed	Seasons Played	Apps	Subs	Gls
Middlesbrough	Sporting Lisbon (POR)	08/05	05-07	60	8	5

ROCHFORD William (Bill)
Born: Esh Winning, County Durham, England, 23 May, 1913 — FB
Died: East Hedleyhope, County Durham, England, 9 March, 1984
England: FLge-1

League Club	Source	Date Signed	Seasons Played	Apps	Subs	Gls
Portsmouth	Esh Winning Jnrs	08/31	32-38	137	-	1
Southampton	Tr	07/46	46-49	128	-	0
Colchester U	Tr	07/50	50	2	-	0

ROCHINA Ruben
Born: Valencia, Spain, 23 March, 1991 — F
Spain: Youth

League Club	Source	Date Signed	Seasons Played	Apps	Subs	Gls
Blackburn Rov	Barcelona Jnrs (SPN)	01/11	10-13	23	23	7

[ROCHINHA] COSTA ROCHA Diogo Filipe
Born: Espinho, Portugal, 3 May, 1995 — M
Portugal: Youth

League Club	Source	Date Signed	Seasons Played	Apps	Subs	Gls
Bolton W (L)	Benfica B (POR)	01/15	14	4	0	0

ROCKETT Jason
Born: London, England, 26 September, 1969 — CD

League Club	Source	Date Signed	Seasons Played	Apps	Subs	Gls
Rotherham U	Hallam Univ	03/92				
Scarborough	Tr	08/93	93-97	171	1	11

ROCKETT Trevor Dennis
Born: Finchampstead, Berkshire, England, 8 October, 1951 — G

League Club	Source	Date Signed	Seasons Played	Apps	Subs	Gls
Aldershot	Fleet	07/76	76-77	5	0	0

RODALLEGA Hugo
Born: Valle del Cauta, Colombia, 25 July, 1985 — F
Colombia: 43

League Club	Source	Date Signed	Seasons Played	Apps	Subs	Gls
Wigan Ath	Necaxa (MEX)	01/09	08-11	92	20	24
Fulham	Tr	07/12	12-14	50	25	15

RODAWAY William Vincent (Billy)
Born: Liverpool, England, 26 September, 1954 — CD
England: Schools

League Club	Source	Date Signed	Seasons Played	Apps	Subs	Gls
Burnley	App	09/71	71-80	201	2	1
Peterborough U	Tr	07/81	81-82	80	1	0
Blackpool	Tr	08/83	83	41	0	0
Tranmere Rov	Tr	07/84	84-85	55	3	5
Burnley	Tr	08/86	86	44	0	2

RODDAN Craig John
Born: Kirkby, Merseyside, England, 22 April, 1993 — M

League Club	Source	Date Signed	Seasons Played	Apps	Subs	Gls
Liverpool	Sch	06/11				
Carlisle U	L	11/13	13	0	1	0
Accrington Stan		11/14				

RODDIE Andrew Robert (Andy)
Born: Glasgow, Scotland, 4 November, 1971 — M
Scotland: U21-5/Youth/Schools

League Club	Source	Date Signed	Seasons Played	Apps	Subs	Gls
Notts Co	Motherwell	01/97				
Carlisle U	Happy Valley (HKG)	08/99	99	1	1	0

RODDOM Joseph Norman (Joe)
Born: Spennymoor, County Durham, England, 16 May, 1924 — LH
Died: Macclesfield, Cheshire, England, August, 1998

League Club	Source	Date Signed	Seasons Played	Apps	Subs	Gls
Chesterfield	Blyth Spartans	01/48				
Darlington	Tr	06/50	50	6	-	0

RODGER Graham
Born: Glasgow, Scotland, 1 April, 1967 — CD
England: U21-4

League Club	Source	Date Signed	Seasons Played	Apps	Subs	Gls
Wolverhampton W	App	-	83	1	0	0
Coventry C	Tr	02/85	85-88	31	5	2
Luton T	Tr	08/89	89-91	27	1	2
Grimsby T	Tr	01/92	91-97	134	12	11

RODGER James McPhail (Jim)
Born: Cleland, Lanarkshire, Scotland, 15 September, 1933 — IF

League Club	Source	Date Signed	Seasons Played	Apps	Subs	Gls
Newport Co (L)	St Mirren	02/57	56-57	5	-	1

RODGER Richard John
Born: Hemsworth, West Yorkshire, England, 1 July, 1936 — LW/IF
Died: Calderdale, West Yorkshire, England, July, 2013

League Club	Source	Date Signed	Seasons Played	Apps	Subs	Gls
Halifax T	Jnr	09/54	54-56	15	-	3

RODGER Simon Lee
Born: Shoreham-by-Sea, West Sussex, England, 3 October, 1971 — LM

League Club	Source	Date Signed	Seasons Played	Apps	Subs	Gls
Crystal Palace	Bognor Regis T	07/90	91-01	242	34	11
Manchester C	L	10/96	96	8	0	1
Stoke C	L	02/97	96	5	0	0
Brighton & HA	Woking	10/02	02-03	34	2	2

RODGER William (Willie)
Born: Dalkeith, Midlothian, Scotland, 24 June, 1947 — W

League Club	Source	Date Signed	Seasons Played	Apps	Subs	Gls
Bradford Park Ave	Newtongrange Star	04/65	65-66	6	2	0

RODGERS Alwyn
Born: Chesterfield, Derbyshire, England, 29 May, 1938 — FB

League Club	Source	Date Signed	Seasons Played	Apps	Subs	Gls
Doncaster Rov		11/56	58	1	-	0

RODGERS Anton Michael
Born: Reading, England, 26 January, 1993 — M

League Club	Source	Date Signed	Seasons Played	Apps	Subs	Gls
Brighton & HA	Chelsea (Sch)	06/11				
Exeter C	L	03/13	12	1	1	0
Oldham Ath	Tr	07/13	13	2	5	0
Swindon T	Tr	07/14	14	7	3	2

RODGERS Arnold William
Born: Rotherham, South Yorkshire, England, 5 December, 1923 — CF
Died: Bristol, England, 6 October, 1993

League Club	Source	Date Signed	Seasons Played	Apps	Subs	Gls
Huddersfield T	Wickersley	03/42	46-49	28	-	17
Bristol C	Tr	10/49	49-55	195	-	106
Shrewsbury T	Tr	06/56	56	13	-	3

RODGERS Clifford Frederick (Cliff)
Born: Rotherham, South Yorkshire, England, 3 October, 1921 — LB
Died: Goole, East Riding of Yorkshire, England, 14 October, 1990

League Club	Source	Date Signed	Seasons Played	Apps	Subs	Gls
York C	RAF Pocklington	11/45	46	26	-	0

RODGERS David Michael
Born: Bristol, England, 28 February, 1952 — CD
England: Schools

League Club	Source	Date Signed	Seasons Played	Apps	Subs	Gls
Bristol C	Jnr	07/69	70-81	190	2	15
Torquay U	Tr	02/82	81	5	0	1
Lincoln C	Tr	03/82	81	3	0	0

RODGERS Luke John
Born: Birmingham, England, 1 January, 1982 — F
England: Semi Pro-2

League Club	Source	Date Signed	Seasons Played	Apps	Subs	Gls
Shrewsbury T	YT	07/00	99-04	122	20	52
Crewe Alex	Tr	07/05	05-06	18	20	9
Port Vale	Tr	01/07	06-08	45	14	15
Yeovil T	Tr	11/08	08	10	12	3
Notts Co	Tr	07/09	09-10	27	19	13
Portsmouth	Lillestrom (NOR)	08/12	12	6	4	2
Shrewsbury T	Tr	11/12	12	13	2	2

RODGERS Mark
Born: Broxburn, West Lothian, Scotland, 20 September, 1967 — M

League Club	Source	Date Signed	Seasons Played	Apps	Subs	Gls
Preston NE	YT	09/85	85	1	0	0

RODGERS Paul Leo Henry
Born: Edmonton, N London, England, 6 October, 1989 — RB

League Club	Source	Date Signed	Seasons Played	Apps	Subs	Gls
Arsenal	Sch	07/07				
Northampton T	L	01/09	08	9	2	0
Northampton T	Tr	08/09	09-10	39	17	0

RODGERSON Alan Ralph
Born: Easington, County Durham, England, 19 March, 1939 — IF
England: Schools

League Club	Source	Date Signed	Seasons Played	Apps	Subs	Gls
Middlesbrough	Jnr	05/56	58-60	13	-	3

RODGERSON Ian
Born: Hereford, England, 9 April, 1966 — RB/M

League Club	Source	Date Signed	Seasons Played	Apps	Subs	Gls
Hereford U	Pegasus Jnrs	07/85	85-87	95	5	6
Cardiff C	Tr	08/88	88-90	98	1	4
Birmingham C	Tr	12/90	90-92	87	8	13
Sunderland	Tr	07/93	93-94	5	5	0
Cardiff C	Tr	07/95	95-96	43	12	1

RODI Joseph (Joe)
Born: Glasgow, Scotland, 23 July, 1913 — RW
Died: Canada, 1965

League Club	Source	Date Signed	Seasons Played	Apps	Subs	Gls
Grimsby T	East Fife	04/45				
Rochdale	Boston U	04/46	46	9	-	3

RODIC Alexsander
Born: Hrvatska Dubica, Bosnia & Herzegovina, 26 December, 1979 — F
Slovenia: 9

League Club	Source	Date Signed	Seasons Played	Apps	Subs	Gls
Portsmouth	NK Gorica (SVN)	01/05	04	1	3	0

RODMAN Alexander James (Alex)
Born: Sutton Coldfield, West Midlands, England, 15 February, 1987 — W
England: Semi Pro-3

League Club	Source	Date Signed	Seasons Played	Apps	Subs	Gls
Aldershot T	Tamworth	01/11	10-12	33	10	7
York C	L	11/12	12	12	6	1

RODNEY Nialle Seyi
Born: Nottingham, England, 28 February, 1991 — F

League Club	Source	Date Signed	Seasons Played	Apps	Subs	Gls
Nottingham F	Sch	03/09	10	0	3	0
Burton A	L	03/11	10	0	3	0
Bradford C	Tr	07/11	11	0	5	0
Hartlepool U	AFC Telford U	07/13	13	1	12	0

RODON Christopher Peter (Chris)
Born: Swansea, Wales, 9 June, 1963 — F

League Club	Source	Date Signed	Seasons Played	Apps	Subs	Gls
Brighton & HA	Pontardawe	01/83	82	0	1	0
Cardiff C	L	08/83	83	4	0	0

RODON Peter Clive
Born: Swansea, Wales, 5 February, 1945 — CF
Died: Swansea, Wales, July, 2000

League Club	Source	Date Signed	Seasons Played	Apps	Subs	Gls
Swansea C	Jnr	11/62				
Bradford C	Tr	07/64	64-66	60	4	15

RODOSTHENOUS Michael
Born: Islington, N London, England, 25 August, 1976 — F

League Club	Source	Date Signed	Seasons Played	Apps	Subs	Gls
West Bromwich A	YT	07/95	96	0	1	0
Cambridge U	Tr	10/97	97	0	2	0

[RODRI] RIOS LOZANO Rodrigo
Born: Soria, Spain, 6 June, 1990 — F
Spain: U21-2

League Club	Source	Date Signed	Seasons Played	Apps	Subs	Gls
Sheffield Wed (L)	Barcelona B (SPN)	08/12	12	5	6	1

[RODRIGO] DE ALMEIDA Juliano Rodrigo
Born: Santos, Brazil, 7 August, 1976 — F

League Club	Source	Date Signed	Seasons Played	Apps	Subs	Gls
Everton (L)	Botafogo (BRA)	07/02	02	0	4	0

[RODRIGO] MORENO MACHADO Rodrigo
Born: Rio de Janeiro, Brazil, 6 March, 1991 — F
Spain: 1/U21-16/Youth

League Club	Source	Date Signed	Seasons Played	Apps	Subs	Gls
Bolton W (L)	Benfica (POR)	08/10	10	4	13	1

RODRIGUES Hugo Miguel
Born: Santa Maria da Feira, Portugal, 22 November, 1979 — CD

League Club	Source	Date Signed	Seasons Played	Apps	Subs	Gls
Yeovil T	Pedras Rubras (POR)	08/03	03	23	11	1

RODRIGUES Peter Joseph
Born: Cardiff, Wales, 21 January, 1944 — RB
Wales: 40/U23-5/Schools

League Club	Source	Date Signed	Seasons Played	Apps	Subs	Gls
Cardiff C	Jnr	05/61	63-65	85	0	2
Leicester C	Tr	01/66	65-70	138	0	6
Sheffield Wed	Tr	10/70	70-74	162	0	2
Southampton	Tr	07/75	75-76	59	0	3

RODRIGUEZ Bruno
Born: Bastia, Corsica, France, 25 November, 1972 — F

League Club	Source	Date Signed	Seasons Played	Apps	Subs	Gls
Bradford C (L)	Paris St-Germain (FRA)	09/99	99	0	2	0

RODRIGUEZ David
Born: Talavera de la Reina, Spain, 14 February, 1986 — F
Spain: Youth

League Club	Source	Date Signed	Seasons Played	Apps	Subs	Gls
Brighton & HA	Celta Vigo (SPN)	01/14	13	6	4	1

RODRIGUEZ Jay Enrique
Born: Burnley, Lancashire, England, 29 July, 1989 — F
England: 1/U21-1

League Club	Source	Date Signed	Seasons Played	Apps	Subs	Gls
Burnley	Sch	06/07	07-11	75	30	31
Barnsley	L	02/10	09	1	5	1
Southampton	Tr	06/12	12-13	54	14	21

RODRIGUEZ Maximiliano Ruben (Maxi)
Born: Rosario, Argentina, 2 January, 1981 — W
Argentina: 57/Youth

League Club	Source	Date Signed	Seasons Played	Apps	Subs	Gls
Liverpool	Atletico Madrid (SPN)	01/10	09-11	48	9	15

RODRIGUEZ Vicente
Born: Valencia, Spain, 16 July, 1981 — W
Spain: 38/U21-11/Youth

League Club	Source	Date Signed	Seasons Played	Apps	Subs	Gls
Brighton & HA	Valencia (SPN)	09/11	11-12	17	12	5

RODWELL Anthony (Tony)
Born: Southport, Merseyside, England, 26 August, 1962 — RW

League Club	Source	Date Signed	Seasons Played	Apps	Subs	Gls
Blackpool	Colne Dynamoes	08/90	90-94	137	5	17
Scarborough	Tr	12/94	94	6	2	1
Wigan Ath	L	01/95	94	5	0	1

RODWELL Jack Christian
Born: Southport, Merseyside, England, 11 March, 1991 — DM
England: 3/U21-21/Youth

League Club	Source	Date Signed	Seasons Played	Apps	Subs	Gls
Everton	Sch	03/08	07-11	51	34	4
Manchester C	Tr	08/12	12-13	7	9	2
Sunderland	Tr	08/14	14	17	6	3

RODWELL James Richard (Jimmy)
Born: Lincoln, England, 20 November, 1970 — CD

League Club	Source	Date Signed	Seasons Played	Apps	Subs	Gls
Darlington	YT	01/89	88	1	0	0
Rushden & D	Halesowen T	08/96	01	8	1	0
Boston U	Tr	02/02	02	2	1	0

RODWELL Joseph (Joe)
Born: Southport, Merseyside, England, 13 October, 1928 — W

League Club	Source	Date Signed	Seasons Played	Apps	Subs	Gls
Accrington Stan (Am)	Birkdale Ath	09/48	48	2	-	0

League Club	Source	Date Signed	Seasons Played	Apps	Subs	Gls

ROE John
Born: Broxburn, West Lothian, Scotland, 7 January, 1938 — RB
Died: Wandsworth, SW London, England, 20 February, 1996

League Club	Source	Date Signed	Seasons Played	Apps	Subs	Gls
Colchester U	West Calder	07/58	59	2	-	0

ROE Maurice Leonard (Len)
Born: Hayes, W London, England, 11 January, 1932 — WH

League Club	Source	Date Signed	Seasons Played	Apps	Subs	Gls
Brentford	Ruislip Manor	05/51	54-56	7	-	0

ROE Philip Michael (Phil)
Born: Chelmsford, England, 7 October, 1991 — LB

League Club	Source	Date Signed	Seasons Played	Apps	Subs	Gls
Sheffield U	Sch	07/10				
Port Vale	Tr	07/11	11	0	2	0

ROEDER Glenn Victor
Born: Woodford, NE London, England, 13 December, 1955 — CD
England: B-6

League Club	Source	Date Signed	Seasons Played	Apps	Subs	Gls
Leyton Orient	App	12/73	74-77	107	8	4
Queens Park Rgrs	Tr	08/78	78-83	157	0	17
Notts Co	L	11/83	83	4	0	0
Newcastle U	Tr	12/83	83-88	193	0	8
Watford	Tr	07/89	89-90	74	4	2
Leyton Orient	Tr	01/92	91	6	2	0
Gillingham	Purfleet	11/92	92	6	0	0

ROFE Dennis
Born: Epping, Essex, England, 1 June, 1950 — LB
England: U23-1

League Club	Source	Date Signed	Seasons Played	Apps	Subs	Gls
Leyton Orient	App	02/68	67-72	170	1	6
Leicester C	Tr	08/72	72-79	290	0	5
Chelsea	Tr	02/80	79-81	58	1	0
Southampton	Tr	07/82	82-83	18	1	0

ROFFEY William Robert (Bill)
Born: Stepney, E London, England, 6 February, 1954 — LB

League Club	Source	Date Signed	Seasons Played	Apps	Subs	Gls
Crystal Palace	App	05/71	72-73	24	0	0
Leyton Orient	Tr	10/73	73-83	324	4	8
Brentford	L	03/84	83	13	0	1
Millwall	Tr	08/84	84-85	36	1	2

ROFFI Guido Tomaso Angelo (George)
Born: Tyntetown, Rhondda Cynon Taff, Wales, 6 March, 1924 — RH/IF
Died: Pontypridd, Rhondda Cynon Taff, Wales, 27 February, 1973

League Club	Source	Date Signed	Seasons Played	Apps	Subs	Gls
Newport Co	Tynte Rov	02/47	46-50	112	-	27

ROGAN Anthony Gerard Patrick (Anton)
Born: Belfast, Northern Ireland, 25 March, 1966 — D
Northern Ireland: 18

League Club	Source	Date Signed	Seasons Played	Apps	Subs	Gls
Sunderland	Glasgow Celtic	10/91	91-92	45	1	1
Oxford U	Tr	08/93	93-94	56	2	3
Millwall	Tr	08/95	95-96	30	6	8
Blackpool	Tr	07/97	97-98	10	5	0

ROGAN Leslie Michael (Mike)
Born: Fleetwood, Lancashire, England, 29 May, 1948 — G

League Club	Source	Date Signed	Seasons Played	Apps	Subs	Gls
Workington	App	08/66	66-76	390	0	0
Stockport Co	Tr	06/77	77-80	73	0	0
Crewe Alex	L	03/79	78	3	0	0

ROGERS Alan
Born: Liverpool, England, 3 January, 1977 — LB
England: U21-3

League Club	Source	Date Signed	Seasons Played	Apps	Subs	Gls
Tranmere Rov	YT	07/95	95-96	53	4	2
Nottingham F	Tr	07/97	97-01	135	2	17
Leicester C	Tr	11/01	01-03	57	5	0
Wigan Ath	L	12/03	03	5	0	0
Nottingham F	Tr	02/04	03-04	44	1	0
Hull C	L	01/06	05	9	0	0
Bradford C	Tr	08/06	06	4	4	0
Accrington Stan	Tr	01/07	06	6	0	0

ROGERS Alan James
Born: Plymouth, England, 6 July, 1954 — LW

League Club	Source	Date Signed	Seasons Played	Apps	Subs	Gls
Plymouth Arg	App	07/72	73-78	107	10	5
Portsmouth	Tr	07/79	79-83	154	7	14
Southend U	Tr	03/84	83-85	84	3	4
Cardiff C	Tr	08/86	86	25	2	1

ROGERS Alfred (Alf)
Born: Ecclesfield, South Yorkshire, England, 10 April, 1921 — IF
Died: Sheffield, England, October, 1992

League Club	Source	Date Signed	Seasons Played	Apps	Subs	Gls
Sheffield Wed	Birley Carr	06/42	46-49	30	-	8

ROGERS Alfred Harper (Alf)
Born: Willenhall, West Midlands, England, 17 January, 1920 — RB
Died: Wolverhampton, England, 1981

League Club	Source	Date Signed	Seasons Played	Apps	Subs	Gls
Aldershot	West Bromwich A (Am)	05/46	46-53	317	-	5

ROGERS Andrew (Andy)
Born: Chatteris, Cambridgeshire, England, 1 December, 1956 — LW
England: Schools

League Club	Source	Date Signed	Seasons Played	Apps	Subs	Gls
Peterborough U	Chatteris T	07/76	75-77	25	4	1
Southampton	Hampton	02/80	79-81	0	5	0
Plymouth Arg	Tr	09/81	81-84	159	4	15
Reading	Tr	07/85	85-86	44	0	5
Southend U	Tr	10/86	86-87	40	5	2

ROGERS Darren John
Born: Birmingham, England, 9 April, 1970 — LB

League Club	Source	Date Signed	Seasons Played	Apps	Subs	Gls
West Bromwich A	YT	07/88	90-91	7	7	1
Birmingham C	Tr	07/92	92-93	15	3	0
Wycombe W	L	11/93	93	0	1	0
Walsall	Tr	07/94	94-97	48	10	0

ROGERS David Raymond (Dave)
Born: Liverpool, England, 25 August, 1975 — LB

League Club	Source	Date Signed	Seasons Played	Apps	Subs	Gls
Tranmere Rov	YT	07/94				
Chester C	Tr	08/95	95-96	18	7	1
Peterborough U (L)	Ayr U	10/00	00	1	2	0
Scunthorpe U	Ayr U	03/01	00	1	0	0
Carlisle U	Portadown	09/01	01	26	1	1

ROGERS Dennis
Born: Chorley, Lancashire, England, 28 March, 1936 — G

League Club	Source	Date Signed	Seasons Played	Apps	Subs	Gls
Accrington Stan	Netherfield	03/59	58	3	-	0

ROGERS Donald Edward (Don)
Born: Paulton, Somerset, England, 25 October, 1945 — LW
England: FLge-1/U23-2/Youth

League Club	Source	Date Signed	Seasons Played	Apps	Subs	Gls
Swindon T	App	10/62	62-72	400	0	146
Crystal Palace	Tr	11/72	72-74	69	1	28
Queens Park Rgrs	Tr	09/74	74	13	5	5
Swindon T	Tr	03/76	75-76	11	1	2

ROGERS Edward Eamonn (Eamonn)
Born: Dublin, Republic of Ireland, 16 April, 1947 — M
Republic of Ireland: 19/U23-1

League Club	Source	Date Signed	Seasons Played	Apps	Subs	Gls
Blackburn Rov	App	05/65	65-71	158	6	30
Charlton Ath	Tr	10/71	71-72	37	2	3
Northampton T	L	11/72	72	4	0	1

ROGERS Ehud (Tim)
Born: Chirk, Wrexham, Wales, 15 October, 1909 — RW
Died: Chirk, Wrexham, Wales, 25 January, 1996
Wales: Amateur/War-2

League Club	Source	Date Signed	Seasons Played	Apps	Subs	Gls
Wrexham	Oswestry T	05/34	34	11	-	2
Arsenal	Tr	01/35	34-35	16	-	5
Newcastle U	Tr	06/36	36-38	56	-	10
Swansea C	Tr	05/39				
Wrexham	Tr	12/45	46	1	-	0

ROGERS Graham Reginald
Born: Newport, Wales, 5 September, 1955 — CD

League Club	Source	Date Signed	Seasons Played	Apps	Subs	Gls
Newport Co	App	09/73	74	0	4	0
Newport Co	Barry T	08/85	85	6	1	0

ROGERS James Richard (Jimmy)
Born: Wednesbury, West Midlands, England, 31 December, 1929 — F
Died: Clevedon, Somerset, England, December, 1996

League Club	Source	Date Signed	Seasons Played	Apps	Subs	Gls
Wolverhampton W	Rubery Owen	05/48				
Bristol C	Tr	05/50	50-56	155	-	74
Coventry C	Tr	12/56	56-58	77	-	27
Bristol C	Tr	12/58	58-61	115	-	28

ROGERS John Charles
Born: Liverpool, England, 16 September, 1950 — F
England: Semi Pro-5

League Club	Source	Date Signed	Seasons Played	Apps	Subs	Gls
Port Vale	Wigan Ath	10/76	76	25	1	6
Wigan Ath	Altrincham	08/82	82	4	2	2

ROGERS Kenneth John (Kenny)
Born: Chatham, Kent, England, 21 November, 1954 — LW

League Club	Source	Date Signed	Seasons Played	Apps	Subs	Gls
Gillingham	App	11/72	72-73	11	2	1

ROGERS Kevin Perry
Born: Merthyr Tydfil, Wales, 23 September, 1963 — LM
Wales: Youth/Schools

League Club	Source	Date Signed	Seasons Played	Apps	Subs	Gls
Aston Villa	App	09/81				
Birmingham C	Tr	04/83	83	8	1	1
Wrexham	Tr	07/84	84	30	4	3

ROGERS Kristian Raleigh John
Born: Chester, England, 2 October, 1980 — G
England: Schools

League Club	Source	Date Signed	Seasons Played	Apps	Subs	Gls
Wrexham	Chester C (Jnr)	08/98	99-02	39	1	0
Sheffield U	Tr	07/03				

ROGERS Lee Julian
Born: Doncaster, South Yorkshire, England, 21 October, 1966 — D

League Club	Source	Date Signed	Seasons Played	Apps	Subs	Gls
Doncaster Rov	YT	07/84				
Chesterfield	Tr	08/86	86-97	310	24	1

League Club	Source	Date Signed	Seasons Played	Career Record Apps	Subs	Gls
ROGERS Lee Martyn						
Born: Bristol, England, 8 April, 1967						CD
Bristol C	App	12/84	84-86	30	0	0
Hereford U	L	03/87	86	13	0	0
York C	L	12/87	87	5	2	0
Exeter C	Tr	06/88	88-90	74	4	0
ROGERS Mark Alvin						
Born: Guelph, Ontario, Canada, 3 November, 1975						CD
Canada: 7						
Wycombe W	Burnaby Canad'ns (CAN)	12/98	99-03	123	16	4
ROGERS Martyn						
Born: Bristol, England, 7 March, 1955						RB
England: Youth						
Bristol C	App	03/73				
Exeter C	Bath C	07/79	79-84	129	3	5
ROGERS Martyn						
Born: Nottingham, England, 26 January, 1960						RB
Died: Ringwood, Hampshire, England, February, 1992						
England: Schools						
Manchester U	App	01/77	77	1	0	0
Queens Park Rgrs	Tr	07/79	79	2	0	0
ROGERS Paul Anthony						
Born: Portsmouth, England, 21 March, 1965						M
England: Semi Pro-6						
Sheffield U	Sutton U	01/92	91-95	120	5	10
Notts Co	Tr	12/95	95-96	21	1	2
Wigan Ath	L	12/96	96	7	2	3
Wigan Ath	Tr	03/97	96-98	85	6	2
Brighton & HA	Tr	07/99	99-02	105	14	15
ROGERS Peter Philip						
Born: Bristol, England, 22 April, 1953						F
Exeter C	Bath C	02/79	78-83	194	11	39
ROGERS Robert Hampton (Robbie)						
Born: Los Angeles, California, USA, 12 May, 1987						W
USA: 18/Youth						
Leeds U	Columbus Crew (USA)	01/12	11	1	3	0
Stevenage	L	08/12	12	1	5	0
ROGERS William (Billy)						
Born: Ulverston, Cumbria, England, 3 July, 1919						WH/IF
Died: Barrow, Cumbria, England, 8 February, 1974						
Preston NE	Swarth Moor	08/37				
Blackburn Rov	Tr	06/38	38-47	73	-	24
Barrow	Tr	10/47	47-52	196	-	14
ROGERSON Lee Antony						
Born: Darwen, Lancashire, England, 21 March, 1967						M
Wigan Ath	Clitheroe	01/90	89-90	1	3	0
ROGET Leo Thomas Earl						
Born: Ilford, E London, England, 1 August, 1977						CD
Southend U	YT	07/95	95-00	105	15	7
Stockport Co	Tr	03/01	00-01	28	3	1
Reading	L	02/02	01	1	0	0
Brentford	Tr	08/02	02-03	29	0	0
Rushden & D	Tr	01/04	03	16	1	0
Oxford U	Tr	07/04	04-05	67	1	4
ROGNE Thomas						
Born: Sandvika, Norway, 29 June, 1990						CD
Norway: 2/U21-17/Youth						
Wigan Ath	Glasgow Celtic	07/13	13	10	2	0
ROJO Faustino Marcos Alberto (Marcos)						
Born: La Plata, Argentina, 20 March, 1990						CD
Argentina: 37						
Manchester U	Sporting Lisbon (POR)	08/14	14	20	2	0
ROLES Albert James (Albie)						
Born: Southampton, England, 29 September, 1921						FB
Died: Southampton, England, 3 October, 2012						
Southampton	Albion BC	08/42	48	1	-	0
ROLFE James (Jimmy)						
Born: Liverpool, England, 8 February, 1932						RW
Liverpool	Jnr	07/52				
Chester C	Tr	07/53	53-54	50	-	4
Crewe Alex	Tr	08/55	55-57	101	-	11
Barrow	Tr	07/58	58	12	-	3
ROLLING Franck Jacques						
Born: Colmar, France, 23 August, 1968						CD
Leicester C	Ayr U	09/95	95-96	18	0	0
Bournemouth	Tr	08/97	97	26	4	4
Gillingham	Tr	09/98	98	1	0	0
ROLLINGS Andrew Nicholas (Andy)						
Born: Portishead, Avon, England, 14 December, 1954						CD
Norwich C	App	12/72	73	4	0	0
Brighton & HA	Tr	04/74	74-79	168	0	11
Swindon T	Tr	05/80	80	11	1	1
Portsmouth	Tr	05/81	81-82	29	0	1
Torquay U	Tr	08/83	83	2	0	0
Brentford	Tr	11/83	83	1	0	0
ROLLINS Kevin						
Born: Halifax, West Yorkshire, England, 2 January, 1947						FB
Halifax T	App	-	64	1	-	0
ROLLO Alexander (Alex)						
Born: Dumbarton, Dunbartonshire, Scotland, 18 September, 1926						LB
Died: Whitehaven, Cumbria, England, 5 October, 2004						
Scotland: SLge-1						
Workington	Dumbarton	06/57	57-59	126	-	3
ROLLO James Shepherd (Jimmy)						
Born: Helmsdale, Highlands, Scotland, 16 November, 1937						G
Died: Perth, Scotland, 15 October, 2012						
Oldham Ath	Poole T	05/60	60-62	59	-	0
Southport	Tr	07/63	63	38	-	0
Bradford C	Tr	07/64	64-65	37	0	0
ROLLO James Stuart (Jimmy)						
Born: Wisbech, Cambridgeshire, England, 22 May, 1976						FB
Walsall	YT	05/95				
Cardiff C	Yate T	01/97	96-97	6	9	0
ROLPH Andrew John Peter (Andy)						
Born: Coleshill, Warwickshire, England, 28 October, 1969						RW
Chesterfield	Mile Oak Rov	02/89	88-90	14	22	1
ROLPH Darren Gregory						
Born: Romford, E London, England, 19 November, 1968						FB
England: Schools						
Barnsley	King's Lynn	08/87	87	1	1	0
ROLPH Gary Leslie						
Born: Stepney, E London, England, 24 February, 1960						F
Brentford	App	02/78	76-78	8	4	1
ROMA Dominic Mark						
Born: Sheffield, England, 29 November, 1985						RB
England: Youth						
Sheffield U	Sch	07/04				
Boston U	L	02/05	04	2	0	0
ROMANO Serge						
Born: Metz, France, 25 May, 1964						FB
Wolverhampton W	Martigues (FRA)	08/96	96	1	3	0
ROMEO Mahlon Beresford Baker						
Born: Westminster, Central London, England, 19 September, 1995						RB
Gillingham	Sch	07/14	12	1	0	0
ROMEU Oriol						
Born: Ulldecona, Spain, 24 September, 1991						DM
Spain: U23-5/U21-10/Youth						
Chelsea	Barcelona (SPN)	08/11	11-12	15	7	0
ROMMEDAHL Dennis						
Born: Copenhagen, Denmark, 22 July, 1978						W
Denmark: 126/U21-15/Youth						
Charlton Ath	PSV Eindhoven (NED)	07/04	04-06	57	18	4
ROMO David						
Born: Nimes, France, 7 August, 1978						M
France: Youth						
Swansea C	EA Guingamp (FRA)	10/00	00-01	31	12	1
[RONALDO] AVEIRO DOS SANTOS Cristiano Ronaldo						
Born: Sao Joao da Madeira, Portugal, 5 February, 1985						W/F
Portugal: 120/U21-10/Youth						
Manchester U	Sporting Lisbon (POR)	08/03	03-08	157	39	84
RONALDSON Kenneth (Ken)						
Born: Leith, Edinburgh, Scotland, 27 September, 1945						IF
Bristol Rov	Aberdeen	07/65	65-68	72	4	15
Gillingham	Tr	11/69	69-70	6	0	0
RONSON Brian						
Born: Bearpark, County Durham, England, 7 August, 1935						G
Died: Durham, England, June, 2003						
Fulham	Willington	03/53	53	2	-	0
Southend U	Tr	08/56	56-58	30	-	0
Norwich C	Tr	08/59	59	1	-	0
Peterborough U	Tr	07/61	61-62	50	-	0

RONSON William (Billy)
Born: Fleetwood, Lancashire, England, 22 January, 1957 — M
Died: Maryland, USA, 8 April, 2015

League Club	Source	Date Signed	Seasons Played	Apps	Subs	Gls
Blackpool	App	02/74	74-78	124	4	12
Cardiff C	Tr	07/79	79-81	90	0	4
Wrexham	Tr	10/81	81	31	1	1
Barnsley	Tr	08/82	82-85	111	2	3
Birmingham C	L	11/85	85	2	0	0
Blackpool	Tr	01/86	85	3	0	0

ROOFE Kemar
Born: Walsall, West Midlands, England, 6 January, 1993 — W

League Club	Source	Date Signed	Seasons Played	Apps	Subs	Gls
West Bromwich A	Sch	01/12				
Northampton T	L	09/12	12	4	2	0
Cheltenham T	L	11/13	13	7	2	1
Colchester U	L	11/14	14	0	2	0
Oxford U	Tr	02/15	14	12	4	6

ROOKE Rodney
Born: Grays, Essex, England, 7 April, 1970 — LB

League Club	Source	Date Signed	Seasons Played	Apps	Subs	Gls
Colchester U	YT	06/88	89	4	0	0

ROOKE Ronald (Ron)
Born: Carlisle, Cumbria, England, 12 December, 1926 — RW
Died: Kendal, Cumbria, England, 29 November, 2011

League Club	Source	Date Signed	Seasons Played	Apps	Subs	Gls
Carlisle U (Am)	Carlisle Young Libs	09/49	49	1	-	0

ROOKE Ronald Leslie (Ronnie)
Born: Guildford, Surrey, England, 7 December, 1911 — CF
Died: Bedford, England, 9 June, 1985
England: War-1

League Club	Source	Date Signed	Seasons Played	Apps	Subs	Gls
Crystal Palace	Woking	03/33	33-36	18	-	6
Fulham	Tr	10/36	36-46	105	-	70
Arsenal	Tr	12/46	46-48	88	-	68
Crystal Palace	Tr	06/49	49-50	45	-	26

ROOKE Steven Alan (Steve)
Born: Carlisle, Cumbria, England, 21 September, 1982 — FB

League Club	Source	Date Signed	Seasons Played	Apps	Subs	Gls
Carlisle U	YT	06/01	01	0	1	0

ROOKES Philip William (Phil)
Born: Dulverton, Somerset, England, 23 April, 1919 — FB
Died: Portsmouth, England, 4 February, 2003

League Club	Source	Date Signed	Seasons Played	Apps	Subs	Gls
Bradford C	Worksop T	10/36	37	11	-	0
Portsmouth	Tr	01/38	38-50	114	-	0
Colchester U	Tr	07/51	51-52	68	-	0

ROOKS Richard (Dickie)
Born: Sunderland, England, 29 May, 1940 — CH

League Club	Source	Date Signed	Seasons Played	Apps	Subs	Gls
Sunderland	Jnr	06/57	60-64	34	-	2
Middlesbrough	Tr	08/65	65-68	136	0	14
Bristol C	Tr	06/69	69-71	96	0	4

ROONEY Adam Christopher
Born: Dublin, Republic of Ireland, 21 April, 1988 — F
Republic of Ireland: U21-9/Youth

League Club	Source	Date Signed	Seasons Played	Apps	Subs	Gls
Stoke C	Sch	08/06	05-06	2	13	4
Yeovil T	L	03/07	06	1	2	0
Chesterfield	L	08/07	07	11	11	7
Bury	L	02/08	07	10	6	3
Birmingham C	Inverness CT	07/11	11	6	12	4
Swindon T	L	08/12	12	11	18	9
Oldham Ath	Tr	08/13	13	16	8	4

ROONEY James (Jimmy)
Born: Dundee, Scotland, 10 December, 1945 — LW

League Club	Source	Date Signed	Seasons Played	Apps	Subs	Gls
Peterborough U	Lochee Harp	07/65	65-66	7	0	2

ROONEY John Richard
Born: Liverpool, England, 17 December, 1990 — F

League Club	Source	Date Signed	Seasons Played	Apps	Subs	Gls
Macclesfield T	Sch	08/08	07-09	25	16	3
Barnsley	Orlando C (USA)	10/12				
Bury	Tr	07/13	13	1	2	0

ROONEY Luke William
Born: Bermondsey, SE London, England, 28 December, 1990 — W

League Club	Source	Date Signed	Seasons Played	Apps	Subs	Gls
Gillingham	Sch	07/09	09-11	15	38	6
Swindon T	Tr	01/12	11-12	14	17	2
Burton A	L	09/12	12	3	0	0
Rotherham U	L	11/12	12	2	1	0
Crawley T	L	08/13	13	0	4	0
Luton T	Maidstone U	03/14	14	8	3	3

ROONEY Robert (Bob)
Born: Glasgow, Scotland, 26 October, 1920 — CH
Died: Cambuslang, Lanarkshire, Scotland, 10 November, 1992
Scotland: Schools

League Club	Source	Date Signed	Seasons Played	Apps	Subs	Gls
Leyton Orient	Falkirk	05/48	48-50	66	-	2
Workington	Tr	06/51	51	27	-	0

ROONEY Robert (Bobby)
Born: Cowie, Stirlingshire, Scotland, 8 July, 1938 — IF

League Club	Source	Date Signed	Seasons Played	Apps	Subs	Gls
Sheffield U	Clydebank	06/58	58-59	15	-	3
Doncaster Rov	Tr	10/62	62	5	-	1
Lincoln C	Tr	01/63	62-63	28	-	3

ROONEY Simon Anthony
Born: Manchester, England, 10 July, 1970 — M

League Club	Source	Date Signed	Seasons Played	Apps	Subs	Gls
Blackpool	YT	07/88	87-88	4	5	0

ROONEY Thomas Anthony (Tommy)
Born: Liverpool, England, 30 December, 1984 — F

League Club	Source	Date Signed	Seasons Played	Apps	Subs	Gls
Macclesfield T	Tranmere Rov (Sch)	06/04	04	0	1	0

ROONEY Wayne Mark
Born: Liverpool, England, 24 October, 1985 — F
England: 105/Youth

League Club	Source	Date Signed	Seasons Played	Apps	Subs	Gls
Everton	Sch	02/03	02-03	40	27	15
Manchester U	Tr	08/04	04-14	312	28	170

ROOST William Charles (Bill)
Born: Bristol, England, 22 March, 1924 — IF
Died: Bristol, England, 10 February, 2013

League Club	Source	Date Signed	Seasons Played	Apps	Subs	Gls
Bristol Rov	Stonehouse	09/48	48-56	177	-	49
Swindon T	Tr	05/57	57-58	18	-	3

ROPER Alan John
Born: Tipton, West Midlands, England, 21 May, 1939 — RB/WH

League Club	Source	Date Signed	Seasons Played	Apps	Subs	Gls
Walsall	Toll End Wesley	05/59	62-64	53	-	2

ROPER David
Born: Ilkley, West Yorkshire, England, 26 September, 1944 — G
Died: Leeds, England, November, 2005
England: Youth

League Club	Source	Date Signed	Seasons Played	Apps	Subs	Gls
Bradford C (Am)	Salts	09/62	62	13	-	0

ROPER Donald George Beaumont (Don)
Born: Botley, Hampshire, England, 14 December, 1922 — W
Died: Southampton, England, 8 June, 2001
England: B-1/FLge-1

League Club	Source	Date Signed	Seasons Played	Apps	Subs	Gls
Southampton	Bitterne Nomads	06/40	46	40	-	8
Arsenal	Tr	08/47	47-56	297	-	88
Southampton	Tr	01/57	56-58	80	-	32

ROPER Ian Robert
Born: Nuneaton, Warwickshire, England, 20 June, 1977 — CD

League Club	Source	Date Signed	Seasons Played	Apps	Subs	Gls
Walsall	YT	05/95	95-07	298	27	7
Luton T	Tr	08/08	08	18	1	3

ROQUE Mikel (Miki)
Born: Tremp, Spain, 8 July, 1988 — CD
Died: Barcelona, Spain, 24 June, 2012
Spain: Youth

League Club	Source	Date Signed	Seasons Played	Apps	Subs	Gls
Liverpool	UE Lleida (SPN)	08/05				
Oldham Ath	L	03/07	06	1	3	0

ROQUE JUNIOR Jose Victor
Born: Santa Rita do Sapucai, Brazil, 31 August, 1976 — CD
Brazil: 48

League Club	Source	Date Signed	Seasons Played	Apps	Subs	Gls
Leeds U (L)	AC Milan (ITA)	09/03	03	5	0	0

ROSA Denes
Born: Budapest, Hungary, 7 April, 1977 — W
Hungary: 10

League Club	Source	Date Signed	Seasons Played	Apps	Subs	Gls
Wolverhampton W	Ferencvaros (HUN)	01/06	05	6	3	2
Cheltenham T	L	03/07	06	3	1	0

ROSADO Diogo Jorge
Born: Peniche, Portugal, 21 February, 1990 — M
England: Youth//Portugal: U21-6

League Club	Source	Date Signed	Seasons Played	Apps	Subs	Gls
Blackburn Rov	Sporting Lisbon (POR)	08/12	12	1	1	0

ROSARIO Robert Michael
Born: Hammersmith, W London, England, 4 March, 1966 — F
England: U21-4/Youth

League Club	Source	Date Signed	Seasons Played	Apps	Subs	Gls
Norwich C	Hillingdon Bor	12/83	83-90	115	11	18
Wolverhampton W	L	12/85	85	2	0	1
Coventry C	Tr	03/91	90-92	54	5	8
Nottingham F	Tr	03/93	92-94	25	2	3

ROSCOE Andrew Ronald (Andy)
Born: Liverpool, England, 4 June, 1973 — W/LB

League Club	Source	Date Signed	Seasons Played	Apps	Subs	Gls
Bolton W	Liverpool (YT)	07/91	93	2	1	0
Rotherham U	Tr	10/94	94-98	184	18	18
Mansfield T	Tr	08/99	99	29	10	2
Exeter C	Tr	07/00	00-02	91	23	11

ROSCOE Philip (Phil)
Born: Barnsley, South Yorkshire, England, 3 March, 1934 — FB

League Club	Source	Date Signed	Seasons Played	Apps	Subs	Gls
Barnsley	Jnr	08/51				
Halifax T	Tr	07/56	56-63	258	-	5

ROSE Andrew Mark
Born: Ascot, Berkshire, England, 9 August, 1978 — D

League Club	Source	Date Signed	Seasons Played	Apps	Subs	Gls
Oxford U	YT	07/97	97-98	1	4	0

ROSE Colin James
Born: Winsford, Cheshire, England, 22 January, 1972 — M
England: Semi Pro-2

League Club	Source	Date Signed	Seasons Played	Apps	Subs	Gls
Crewe Alex	YT	04/90	90-91	17	5	1
Macclesfield T	Witton A	08/97	97	15	4	0

ROSE Daniel Antony (Danny)
Born: Barnsley, South Yorkshire, England, 10 December, 1993 — F

League Club	Source	Date Signed	Seasons Played	Apps	Subs	Gls
Barnsley	Sch	02/11	10-14	4	13	1
Bury	L	03/14	13	0	6	3
Bury	Tr	08/14	14	19	6	10

ROSE Daniel Lee (Danny)
Born: Doncaster, South Yorkshire, England, 2 June, 1990 — LB
England: U21-29/Youth

League Club	Source	Date Signed	Seasons Played	Apps	Subs	Gls
Tottenham H	Leeds U (Sch)	07/07	09-14	57	9	5
Watford	L	03/09	08	3	4	0
Peterborough U	L	09/09	09	4	2	0
Bristol C	L	09/10	10	13	4	0
Sunderland	L	08/12	12	25	2	1

ROSE Daniel Stephen (Danny)
Born: Bristol, England, 21 February, 1988 — RW
England: Semi Pro-2

League Club	Source	Date Signed	Seasons Played	Apps	Subs	Gls
Manchester U	Sch	07/06				
Fleetwood T	Newport Co	01/12				
Aldershot T	L	10/12	12	34	0	2
Oxford U	Tr	06/13	13-14	63	6	6

ROSE Frederick (Freddy)
Born: Stannington, Northumberland, England, 27 March, 1955 — W

League Club	Source	Date Signed	Seasons Played	Apps	Subs	Gls
Huddersfield T	App	04/72				
Workington	Tr	07/74	74	0	2	0

ROSE Gordon
Born: Sheffield, England, 22 March, 1935 — W

League Club	Source	Date Signed	Seasons Played	Apps	Subs	Gls
Sheffield U		10/56				
Halifax T	Scarborough	07/58	58	8	-	1

ROSE Jack
Born: Sheffield, England, 26 October, 1921 — RB
Died: Huntingdon, Cambridgeshire, England, January, 2005

League Club	Source	Date Signed	Seasons Played	Apps	Subs	Gls
Queens Park Rgrs	Peterborough U	03/45	46-47	17	-	0

ROSE Jack Joseph
Born: Solihull, West Midlands, England, 30 November, 1994 — G

League Club	Source	Date Signed	Seasons Played	Apps	Subs	Gls
West Bromwich A	Sch	07/13				
Accrington Stan	L	11/14	14	4	0	0

ROSE James (Jim)
Born: Clayton-Le-Moors, Lancashire, England, 4 March, 1918 — G
Died: Blackburn, Greater Manchester, England, March, 1989

League Club	Source	Date Signed	Seasons Played	Apps	Subs	Gls
Accrington Stan	Clayton Villa	02/39	38-46	20	-	0

ROSE John
Born: Woolwich, SE London, England, 12 August, 1920 — W

League Club	Source	Date Signed	Seasons Played	Apps	Subs	Gls
Bournemouth	Salisbury	02/46	46	1	-	0

ROSE Jordan
Born: Southampton, England, 22 November, 1989 — CD

League Club	Source	Date Signed	Seasons Played	Apps	Subs	Gls
Stockport Co	Paulton Rov	07/10	10	13	2	0

ROSE Karl Barrie
Born: Barnsley, South Yorkshire, England, 12 October, 1978 — F

League Club	Source	Date Signed	Seasons Played	Apps	Subs	Gls
Barnsley	Jnr	11/95	98	2	2	0
Mansfield T	L	03/99	98	0	1	0

ROSE Kenneth (Ken)
Born: Eckington, Derbyshire, England, 18 March, 1930 — CF
Died: Lichfield, Staffordshire, England, 7 November, 1996

League Club	Source	Date Signed	Seasons Played	Apps	Subs	Gls
Chesterfield		11/50				
Exeter C	Tr	06/52	52	11	-	3
Rochdale	Tr	07/53	53	11	-	0
Workington	Tr	06/54	54	6	-	2

ROSE Kevin Philip
Born: Evesham, Worcestershire, England, 23 November, 1960 — G

League Club	Source	Date Signed	Seasons Played	Apps	Subs	Gls
Lincoln C	Ledbury T	08/79				
Hereford U	Ledbury T	03/83	82-88	268	0	0
Bolton W	Tr	07/89	89-91	10	0	0
Carlisle U	L	03/90	89	11	0	0
Rochdale	L	02/91	90	3	0	0
Rochdale	Tr	11/91	91-92	68	0	0

ROSE Matthew David
Born: Dartford, Kent, England, 24 September, 1975 — CD
England: U21-2

League Club	Source	Date Signed	Seasons Played	Apps	Subs	Gls
Arsenal	YT	07/94	95-96	2	3	0
Queens Park Rgrs	Tr	05/97	97-06	220	22	8
Yeovil T	Tr	02/07	06-07	34	5	1

ROSE Michael Charles
Born: Salford, England, 28 July, 1982 — LB
England: Semi Pro-4

League Club	Source	Date Signed	Seasons Played	Apps	Subs	Gls
Manchester U	YT	09/99				
Yeovil T	Hereford U	05/04	04-05	37	4	1
Cheltenham T	L	08/05	05	3	0	0
Scunthorpe U	L	01/06	05	15	0	0
Stockport Co	Tr	07/06	06-09	94	10	8
Norwich C	L	01/10	09	11	1	1
Swindon T	Tr	07/10	10	27	8	3
Colchester U	Tr	05/11	11-12	34	2	2
Rochdale	Tr	02/13	12-14	78	10	7

ROSE Michael John (Mick)
Born: New Barnet, N London, England, 22 July, 1943 — G

League Club	Source	Date Signed	Seasons Played	Apps	Subs	Gls
Charlton Ath	St Albans C	07/63	63-66	75	0	0
Notts Co	Tr	03/67	66-69	109	0	0
Mansfield T	L	08/70	70	3	0	0

ROSE Mitchell Nigel (Mitch)
Born: Doncaster, South Yorkshire, England, 4 July, 1994 — M

League Club	Source	Date Signed	Seasons Played	Apps	Subs	Gls
Rotherham U	Sch	07/12	12	1	4	0
Crawley T	L	07/14	14	0	1	0

ROSE Richard Alan
Born: Tonbridge, Kent, England, 8 September, 1982 — D

League Club	Source	Date Signed	Seasons Played	Apps	Subs	Gls
Gillingham	YT	04/01	00-05	44	14	0
Bristol Rov	L	12/02	02	9	0	0
Hereford U	Tr	07/06	06-10	154	11	4
Dagenham & Red	Tr	07/11	11	9	1	1

ROSE Romone Alexander Adolphus
Born: Reading, England, 19 January, 1990 — W

League Club	Source	Date Signed	Seasons Played	Apps	Subs	Gls
Queens Park Rgrs	Sch	07/08	07-09	0	4	0
Northampton T	L	08/09	09	0	1	0
Cheltenham T	L	10/09	09	1	0	0
Torquay U	L	10/10	10	2	3	1

ROSENBERG Nils Markus (Markus)
Born: Malmo, Sweden, 27 September, 1982 — F
Sweden: 33/U21-9

League Club	Source	Date Signed	Seasons Played	Apps	Subs	Gls
West Bromwich A	Werder Bremen (GER)	08/12	12-13	6	22	0

ROSENIOR Leroy De Graft
Born: Balham, S London, England, 24 August, 1964 — F
England: Youth/Schools//Sierra Leone: 1

League Club	Source	Date Signed	Seasons Played	Apps	Subs	Gls
Fulham	Jnr	08/82	82-84	53	1	15
Queens Park Rgrs	Tr	08/85	85-86	27	11	8
Fulham	Tr	06/87	87	34	0	20
West Ham U	Tr	03/88	87-91	44	9	15
Fulham	L	09/90	90	11	0	3
Charlton Ath	L	11/91	91	3	0	0
Bristol C	Tr	03/92	91-93	35	16	12

ROSENIOR Liam James
Born: Wandsworth, SW London, England, 9 July, 1984 — RB
England: U21-7/Youth

League Club	Source	Date Signed	Seasons Played	Apps	Subs	Gls
Bristol C	YT	08/01	01-02	2	20	2
Fulham	Tr	11/03	04-06	76	3	0
Torquay U	L	03/04	03	9	1	0
Reading	Tr	08/07	07-09	62	2	0
Ipswich T	L	09/09	09	26	3	1
Hull C	Tr	10/10	10-14	112	32	1

ROSENTHAL Abram Wallace (Abe)
Born: Liverpool, England, 12 October, 1921 — IF
Died: Liverpool, England, February, 1986

League Club	Source	Date Signed	Seasons Played	Apps	Subs	Gls
Tranmere Rov	Liverpool (Am)	01/39	38-46	27	-	8
Bradford C	Tr	04/47	46-48	44	-	11
Oldham Ath	Tr	03/49				
Tranmere Rov	Tr	08/49	49-51	69	-	24
Bradford C	Tr	01/52	52-53	63	-	32
Tranmere Rov	Tr	07/54	54	21	-	3
Bradford C	Tr	07/55	55	1	-	0

ROSENTHAL Ronny
Born: Haifa, Israel, 11 October, 1963 — F
Israel: 60

League Club	Source	Date Signed	Seasons Played	Apps	Subs	Gls
Liverpool	Standard Liege (BEL)	03/90	89-93	32	42	21
Tottenham H	Tr	01/94	93-96	55	33	4
Watford	Tr	08/97	97-98	25	5	8

ROSICKY Tomas
Born: Prague, Czech Republic, 4 October, 1980 — M

League Club	Source	Date Signed	Seasons Played	Apps	Subs	Gls

Czech Republic: 100/U21-2/Youth

League Club	Source	Date Signed	Seasons Played	Apps	Subs	Gls
Arsenal	Bor Dortmund (GER)	05/06	06-14	107	63	19

ROSLER Uwe
Born: Altenberg, Germany, 15 November, 1968 — F
East Germany: 5/U21-6

League Club	Source	Date Signed	Seasons Played	Apps	Subs	Gls
Manchester C	FC Nurnberg (GER)	03/94	93-97	141	11	50
Southampton	Tennis Borussia (GER)	07/00	00-01	9	15	0
West Bromwich A	L	10/01	01	5	0	1

ROSS Alan
Born: Ellesmere Port, Cheshire, England, 7 February, 1933 — G

League Club	Source	Date Signed	Seasons Played	Apps	Subs	Gls
Oldham Ath (Am)	Bishop Auckland	09/56	56	3	-	0
Accrington Stan	Oldham Ath (Am)	03/59	58	1	-	0

ROSS Alexander Malcolm Cameron (Alex)
Born: Glasgow, Scotland, 17 December, 1923 — WH

League Club	Source	Date Signed	Seasons Played	Apps	Subs	Gls
West Bromwich A	Shawfield Jnrs	10/47				
Crystal Palace	Tr	08/48	48-50	34	-	0

ROSS Bryce Thomas
Born: Edinburgh, Scotland, 4 December, 1927 — IF
Died: Consett, County Durham, England, 1969

League Club	Source	Date Signed	Seasons Played	Apps	Subs	Gls
Newcastle U	Jnr	12/43				
Carlisle U		11/46	46-47	3	-	0

ROSS Colin
Born: Dailly, Ayrshire, Scotland, 29 August, 1962 — M

League Club	Source	Date Signed	Seasons Played	Apps	Subs	Gls
Middlesbrough	App	09/80	80-82	37	1	0
Chesterfield	L	03/83	82	6	0	0
Darlington	Tr	08/83	83-84	14	0	0

ROSS George
Born: Inverness, Scotland, 15 April, 1943 — RB

League Club	Source	Date Signed	Seasons Played	Apps	Subs	Gls
Preston NE	Hilton Ath	04/60	60-72	384	2	3
Southport	L	11/72	72	4	0	0
Southport	Tr	07/73	73	27	0	0

ROSS George Alfred
Born: Deptford, SE London, England, 1 November, 1920 — RH
Died: Kent, England, 22 February, 2014

League Club	Source	Date Signed	Seasons Played	Apps	Subs	Gls
Millwall	Metro Gas	01/46				
Carlisle U	Tr	05/47	47	9	-	0

ROSS Ian
Born: Glasgow, Scotland, 26 January, 1947 — M/CD

League Club	Source	Date Signed	Seasons Played	Apps	Subs	Gls
Liverpool	Possilpark YMCA	08/65	66-71	42	6	2
Aston Villa	Tr	02/72	71-75	175	0	3
Notts Co	L	10/76	76	4	0	1
Northampton T	L	11/76	76	2	0	0
Peterborough U	Tr	12/76	76-78	112	0	1
Wolverhampton W	Tr	08/79				
Hereford U	Rtd	10/82	82	15	0	0

ROSS Ian
Born: Sheffield, England, 13 January, 1986 — M
England: Youth

League Club	Source	Date Signed	Seasons Played	Apps	Subs	Gls
Sheffield U	Sch	07/04				
Boston U	L	08/05	05	13	1	4
Bury	L	03/06	05	6	1	0
Notts Co	L	07/06	06	26	10	1
Rotherham U	Tr	11/07	07	9	8	0

ROSS James Allan (Allan)
Born: Glasgow, Scotland, 26 May, 1942 — G
Died: Carlisle, Cumbria, England, 2 November, 1999

League Club	Source	Date Signed	Seasons Played	Apps	Subs	Gls
Luton T	Petershill Jnrs	04/62				
Carlisle U	Tr	06/63	63-78	465	1	0

ROSS John James (Jack)
Born: Falkirk, Scotland, 5 June, 1976 — RB

League Club	Source	Date Signed	Seasons Played	Apps	Subs	Gls
Hartlepool U	Clyde	07/04	04	21	3	0

ROSS Louis Alexander Purdie
Born: Dublin, Republic of Ireland, 19 September, 1920 — FB
Died: Walsall, West Midlands, England, 19 April, 1990

League Club	Source	Date Signed	Seasons Played	Apps	Subs	Gls
Walsall	Queen of the South	08/48	48	8	-	0

ROSS Maurice Alexander
Born: Dundee, Scotland, 3 February, 1981 — RB
Scotland: 13

League Club	Source	Date Signed	Seasons Played	Apps	Subs	Gls
Sheffield Wed	Glasgow Rangers	08/05	05	1	0	0
Wolverhampton W	Tr	10/05	05	13	5	0
Millwall	Tr	08/06	06	14	1	0

ROSS Michael Patrick (Micky)
Born: Southampton, England, 2 September, 1971 — F
England: Schools

League Club	Source	Date Signed	Seasons Played	Apps	Subs	Gls
Portsmouth	YT	12/88	88-91	0	4	0
Exeter C	Tr	08/93	93-94	27	1	9
Plymouth Arg	Tr	11/94	94	11	6	0
Exeter C	L	11/95	95	7	0	2

ROSS Neil James
Born: West Bromwich, West Midlands, England, 10 August, 1982 — F

League Club	Source	Date Signed	Seasons Played	Apps	Subs	Gls
Leeds U	YT	08/99				
Stockport Co	Tr	01/00	99-02	3	6	2
Bristol Rov	L	10/01	01	2	3	0
Macclesfield T	Tr	01/03	02-03	7	7	0

ROSS Robert (Bobby)
Born: Glasgow, Scotland, 2 February, 1917 — WH
Died: Sutton, S London, England, 21 August, 1994

League Club	Source	Date Signed	Seasons Played	Apps	Subs	Gls
Watford	Dumbarton	07/46	46	33	-	6

ROSS Robert Alexander (Bobby)
Born: Wishaw, Lanarkshire, Scotland, 25 May, 1927 — RB
Died: Leeds, England, March, 1992

League Club	Source	Date Signed	Seasons Played	Apps	Subs	Gls
Leeds U	Workington	08/50	51	5	-	0
Stockport Co	Tr	06/54	54	9	-	0

ROSS Robert Cochrane (Bobby)
Born: Edinburgh, Scotland, 9 September, 1941 — M

League Club	Source	Date Signed	Seasons Played	Apps	Subs	Gls
Grimsby T	St Mirren	06/65	65-70	208	4	18

ROSS Robert Herdman (Bobby)
Born: Edinburgh, Scotland, 18 May, 1942 — M/F

League Club	Source	Date Signed	Seasons Played	Apps	Subs	Gls
Shrewsbury T	Heart of Midlothian	06/63	63-65	99	0	29
Brentford	Tr	03/66	65-72	288	4	58
Cambridge U	Tr	10/72	72-73	57	8	14

ROSS Robert Russell
Born: Cowdenbeath, Fife, Scotland, 13 December, 1925 — CH
Died: Blackpool, Lancashire, England, April, 1984

League Club	Source	Date Signed	Seasons Played	Apps	Subs	Gls
Millwall	Dundee U	08/52	52	1	-	0

ROSS Stewart
Born: Woking, Surrey, England, 11 September, 1945 — D

League Club	Source	Date Signed	Seasons Played	Apps	Subs	Gls
Wolverhampton W		11/65	67-68	1	2	0

ROSS Thomas (Tommy)
Born: Tain, Highlands, Scotland, 27 February, 1947 — IF

League Club	Source	Date Signed	Seasons Played	Apps	Subs	Gls
Peterborough U	Lochee Harp	07/65	65-66	5	2	2
York C	Tr	06/67	67-68	56	5	20

ROSS Trevor William
Born: Ashton-under-Lyne, Greater Manchester, England, 16 January, 1957 — M
England: Schools//Scotland: U21-1

League Club	Source	Date Signed	Seasons Played	Apps	Subs	Gls
Arsenal	App	06/74	74-77	57	1	5
Everton	Tr	11/77	77-82	120	4	16
Portsmouth	L	10/82	82	5	0	0
Sheffield U	L	12/82	82	4	0	0
Sheffield U	AEK Athens (GRE)	01/84	83	4	0	0
Bury	Tr	08/84	84-86	96	2	11

ROSS William
Born: Glasgow, Scotland, 2 May, 1919 — CF
Died: Stockport, Greater Manchester, England, 6 August, 1990

League Club	Source	Date Signed	Seasons Played	Apps	Subs	Gls
Bradford C	Arbroath	07/50	50	4	-	2

ROSS William Bernard (Bernard)
Born: Swansea, Wales, 8 November, 1924 — IF
Died: Bangor, Gwynedd, Wales, February, 1999

League Club	Source	Date Signed	Seasons Played	Apps	Subs	Gls
Cardiff C	Towey U	03/43	46-47	8	-	2
Sheffield U	Tr	05/48	48	3	-	1
Southport	Tr	08/49	49-50	47	-	13

ROSS William Eric (Eric)
Born: Belfast, Northern Ireland, 19 September, 1944 — M
Northern Ireland: 1/NILge-1/U23-1

League Club	Source	Date Signed	Seasons Played	Apps	Subs	Gls
Newcastle U	Glentoran	08/67	67-68	2	0	0
Northampton T	Tr	08/69	69-71	51	4	5
Hartlepool U	L	11/71	71	2	0	0

ROSSER Douglas Richard (Doug)
Born: Swansea, Wales, 8 September, 1948 — CD

League Club	Source	Date Signed	Seasons Played	Apps	Subs	Gls
Swansea C	Jnr	05/67	68-70	28	1	1
Crewe Alex	Barry T	08/71	71	28	1	0

ROSSI Generoso
Born: Naples, Italy, 3 January, 1979 — G

League Club	Source	Date Signed	Seasons Played	Apps	Subs	Gls
Queens Park Rgrs	Palermo (ITA)	01/05	04	3	0	0

ROSSI Giuseppe
Born: Teaneck, New Jersey, USA, 1 February, 1987 — F
Italy: 30/U21-16

League Club	Source	Date Signed	Seasons Played	Apps	Subs	Gls
Manchester U	Sch	11/04	05	1	4	1
Newcastle U	L	08/06	06	3	8	0

ROSSITER Donald Paul (Don)
Born: Strood, Kent, England, 8 June, 1935 — IF

League Club	Source	Date Signed	Seasons Played	Career Record Apps	Subs	Gls
England: Youth						
Arsenal	Jnr	06/52				
Leyton Orient	Tr	03/56	56	1	-	0
Gillingham	Dartford	07/57	57	1	-	0
ROSSITER Dudley John (John)						
Born: Kingsbridge, Devon, England, 28 October, 1942						FB
Torquay U	Millfield School	07/61	62-63	24	-	0
ROSTRON John Wilfred (Wilf)						
Born: Sunderland, England, 29 September, 1956						LB
England: Schools						
Arsenal	App	10/73	74-76	12	5	2
Sunderland	Tr	07/77	77-79	75	1	17
Watford	Tr	10/79	79-88	306	11	22
Sheffield Wed	Tr	01/89	88	7	0	0
Sheffield U	Tr	09/89	89-90	33	3	3
Brentford	Tr	01/91	90-92	34	8	2
ROTHERY Gavin Marc						
Born: Morley, West Yorkshire, England, 22 September, 1987						M
England: Youth						
Leeds U	Sch	09/05				
Carlisle U	York C	02/09	08-09	0	2	0
ROTHWELL Edward (Teddy)						
Born: Atherton, Greater Manchester, England, 3 September, 1917						W/IF
Died: Horwich, Greater Manchester, England, 10 April, 2000						
Bolton W	Jnr	02/36	37-48	48	-	2
Southport	Tr	08/49	49-50	40	-	5
ROTHWELL George						
Born: Bolton, Greater Manchester, England, 22 November, 1923						WH
Died: Bolton, Greater Manchester, England, June, 2004						
Accrington Stan	Chorley	08/44	46-51	202	-	10
ROTHWELL John (Jack)						
Born: Kearsley, Greater Manchester, England, 29 March, 1920						CF
Died: Southport, Merseyside, England, 15 February, 1991						
Southport	St Thomas' S Sefton	11/38	38-46	18	-	9
Birmingham C	Tr	03/47				
Southport	Tr	08/49				
Crewe Alex	Tr	10/49	49	3	-	1
ROTHWELL Joseph Matthew (Joe)						
Born: Oldham, Greater Manchester, England, 11 January, 1995						M
England: Youth						
Manchester U	Sch	07/13				
Blackpool	L	01/15	14	1	2	0
ROTHWELL Ronald (Ron)						
Born: Bury, Greater Manchester, England, 10 July, 1920						FB
Rochdale	Dunfermline Ath	10/46	46-51	48	-	0
ROUGIER Anthony Leo (Tony)						
Born: La Brea, Trinidad, 17 July, 1971						W
Trinidad & Tobago: 67						
Port Vale	Hibernian	01/99	98-99	41	10	8
Reading	Tr	08/00	00-02	47	37	6
Brighton & HA	L	02/03	02	5	1	2
Brentford	Tr	08/03	03	29	2	4
Bristol C	Tr	03/04	03	5	1	1
ROUGVIE Douglas (Doug)						
Born: Ballingry, Fife, Scotland, 24 May, 1956						D
Scotland: 1						
Chelsea	Aberdeen	08/84	84-86	74	0	3
Brighton & HA	Tr	06/87	87	35	0	2
Shrewsbury T	Tr	08/88	88	20	1	3
Fulham	Tr	02/89	88	18	0	1
ROUND Frederick Leonard (Len)						
Born: Wallheath, West Midlands, England, 21 May, 1928						G
Died: Dudley, West Midlands, England, December, 2005						
Hull C	Ayr U	06/57	57	17	-	0
ROUND Paul Gordon						
Born: Blackburn, Greater Manchester, England, 22 June, 1959						CD/F
Blackburn Rov	App	08/77	76-80	41	10	5
ROUND Stephen Clive (Steve)						
Born: Dudley, West Midlands, England, 28 February, 1963						F
Walsall	App	03/80	81-82	5	19	3
ROUND Stephen John (Steve)						
Born: Burton-on-Trent, Staffordshire, England, 9 November, 1970						FB
Derby Co	YT	07/89	91-92	8	1	0
ROUNSEVELL Anthony Eldred (Tony)						
Born: Liskeard, Cornwall, England, 1 April, 1945						D
Plymouth Arg	App	12/62	63-67	34	2	0

League Club	Source	Date Signed	Seasons Played	Career Record Apps	Subs	Gls
ROUSE David Edward						
Born: South Woodham Ferrers, Essex, England, 6 March, 1976						G
Macclesfield T	Manchester U (Coach)	01/07	06	1	0	0
ROUSE Domaine Leroy						
Born: Stretford, Greater Manchester, England, 4 July, 1989						F
Bury	Sch	11/07	06-09	1	11	0
ROUSE Herbert (Bert)						
Born: Doncaster, South Yorkshire, England, 29 November, 1920						RB
Doncaster Rov		06/48	48-54	35	-	0
ROUSE Raymond Victor (Vic)						
Born: Swansea, Wales, 16 March, 1936						G
Wales: 1/U23-1						
Millwall	Jnr	03/53				
Crystal Palace	Tr	08/56	56-62	238	-	0
Northampton T	Tr	04/63				
Oxford U	Tr	08/63	63-64	22	-	0
Leyton Orient	Tr	07/65	65-66	40	0	0
ROUSE Shaun						
Born: Great Yarmouth, Norfolk, England, 28 February, 1972						M
England: Youth						
Bristol C	Glasgow Rangers	06/92				
Carlisle U	Weston-super-Mare	02/94	93	1	4	0
ROUSSEL Cedric						
Born: Mons, Belgium, 6 January, 1978						F
Belgium: 2/U21-12/Youth						
Coventry C	KAA Ghent (BEL)	10/99	99-00	28	11	8
Wolverhampton W	Tr	02/01	00-01	9	17	2
ROUTIS Christopher Pascal						
Born: Geneva, Switzerland, 3 March, 1990						CD
Bradford C	Servette (SUI)	08/14	14	16	2	2
ROUTLEDGE Jonathan Joseph (Jon)						
Born: Liverpool, England, 23 November, 1989						W
Wigan Ath	Liverpool (Sch)	07/08	08	0	1	0
ROUTLEDGE Ronald Wright (Ron)						
Born: Ashington, Northumberland, England, 14 October, 1937						G
Sunderland	Jnr	10/54	56-57	2	-	0
Bradford Park Ave	Tr	05/58	58-61	39	-	0
ROUTLEDGE Thomas Alan (Alan)						
Born: Wallsend, Tyne and Wear, England, 6 May, 1960						FB
Bristol Rov	Bath Univ	10/80	80	0	1	0
ROUTLEDGE Wayne Neville Anthony						
Born: Sidcup, SE London, England, 7 January, 1985						W
England: U21-12/Youth						
Crystal Palace	Sch	07/02	01-04	83	27	10
Tottenham H	Tr	07/05	05-07	3	2	0
Portsmouth	L	01/06	05	3	10	0
Fulham	L	08/06	06	13	11	0
Aston Villa	Tr	01/08	07-08	0	2	0
Cardiff C	L	11/08	08	9	0	2
Queens Park Rgrs	Tr	01/09	08-09	43	1	3
Newcastle U	Tr	01/10	09-10	25	9	3
Queens Park Rgrs	L	01/11	10	20	0	5
Swansea C	Tr	08/11	11-14	106	22	11
ROVDE Knut Marius (Marius)						
Born: Trondheim, Norway, 26 June, 1972						G
Wrexham	Ayr U	01/02	01	12	0	0
ROWAN Barry						
Born: Willesden, NW London, England, 24 April, 1942						RW
Brentford	Watford (Am)	10/60				
Millwall	Dover	07/64	64-66	72	0	13
Colchester U	Detroit Cougars (USA)	11/68	68	2	0	0
Reading	Durban U (RSA)	08/69	69	1	0	0
Plymouth Arg	Tr	09/69	69	10	0	1
Exeter C	Tr	07/70	70-72	76	5	14
ROWAN Brian						
Born: Glasgow, Scotland, 28 June, 1948						RB
Aston Villa	Baillieston Jnrs	04/69	69	1	0	0
Watford	Toronto Metros (CAN)	10/71	71	8	4	0
ROWAN Jonathan Robert						
Born: Grimsby, North Lincolnshire, England, 29 November, 1981						F
Grimsby T	YT	07/00	00-03	32	20	6
ROWBOTHAM Darren						
Born: Cardiff, Wales, 22 October, 1966						F
Wales: Youth						
Plymouth Arg	Jnr	11/84	84-87	22	24	2

League Club	Source	Date Signed	Seasons Played	Apps	Subs	Gls
Exeter C	Tr	10/87	87-91	110	8	47
Torquay U	Tr	09/91	91	14	0	3
Birmingham C	Tr	01/92	91-92	31	5	6
Mansfield T	L	12/92	92	4	0	0
Hereford U	L	03/93	92	8	0	2
Crewe Alex	Tr	07/93	93-94	59	2	21
Shrewsbury T	Tr	07/95	95-96	31	9	9
Exeter C	Tr	10/96	96-99	108	10	37
Leyton Orient	L	11/99	99	4	2	0

ROWBOTHAM Jason
Born: Cardiff, Wales, 3 January, 1969 — LB
Wales: Youth

League Club	Source	Date Signed	Seasons Played	Apps	Subs	Gls
Plymouth Arg	YT	07/87	87-88	8	1	0
Shrewsbury T	Tr	03/92				
Hereford U	Tr	10/92	92	3	2	1
Wycombe W	Raith Rov	09/95	95	27	0	0
Plymouth Arg	Tr	10/96	96-99	42	9	1
Torquay U	Dorchester T	10/00	00	4	1	0

ROWBOTHAM Joshua James (Josh)
Born: Stockton-on-Tees, Cleveland, England, 7 January, 1994 — RB

League Club	Source	Date Signed	Seasons Played	Apps	Subs	Gls
Hartlepool U	Sch	07/12	10-11	2	0	0

ROWBOTHAM Michael Grant (Mike)
Born: Sheffield, England, 2 September, 1965 — M

League Club	Source	Date Signed	Seasons Played	Apps	Subs	Gls
Manchester U	App	09/83				
Grimsby T	Tr	08/84	84	3	1	0

ROWDEN Leonard Albert (Len)
Born: Swansea, Wales, 31 May, 1927 — CF
Died: Swansea, Wales, April, 2013

League Club	Source	Date Signed	Seasons Played	Apps	Subs	Gls
Swansea C	Clydach	10/53	53	1	-	0

ROWE Benjamin Paul (Ben)
Born: Hull, England, 1 October, 1970 — F

League Club	Source	Date Signed	Seasons Played	Apps	Subs	Gls
Exeter C	Bristol C (Jnr)	09/89	89-90	5	7	2

ROWE Brian
Born: Sunderland, England, 24 October, 1971 — M/RB

League Club	Source	Date Signed	Seasons Played	Apps	Subs	Gls
Doncaster Rov	YT	10/90	90-92	42	12	1

ROWE Colwyn Roger
Born: Ipswich, England, 22 March, 1956 — W

League Club	Source	Date Signed	Seasons Played	Apps	Subs	Gls
Colchester U	Jnr	01/74	73-74	4	8	2

ROWE Daniel (Dan)
Born: Billingham, Cleveland, England, 24 October, 1995 — CD/M

League Club	Source	Date Signed	Seasons Played	Apps	Subs	Gls
Rotherham U	Sch	07/13				
Wycombe W	L	03/14	13	7	0	0
Wycombe W	L	07/14	14	5	3	0
Wycombe W	L	10/14	14	5	3	0

ROWE Daniel Martin
Born: Wythenshawe, Greater Manchester, England, 29 January, 1990 — M

League Club	Source	Date Signed	Seasons Played	Apps	Subs	Gls
Stockport Co	Sch	07/09	08-10	7	17	1

ROWE Dominic Ryan
Born: Leeds, England, 23 April, 1993 — W

League Club	Source	Date Signed	Seasons Played	Apps	Subs	Gls
Bradford C	Sch	07/11	10	1	1	0

ROWE Edwin Stanley (Stan)
Born: Exeter, England, 20 August, 1921 — LB
Died: Exeter, England, July, 1985

League Club	Source	Date Signed	Seasons Played	Apps	Subs	Gls
Exeter C	St Dennis	10/47	47-53	139	-	0

ROWE Ezekiel Bartholomew (Zeke)
Born: Stoke Newington, N London, England, 30 October, 1973 — F

League Club	Source	Date Signed	Seasons Played	Apps	Subs	Gls
Chelsea	YT	06/92				
Barnet	L	11/93	93	9	1	2
Brighton & HA	L	03/96	95	9	0	3
Peterborough U	Tr	07/96	96-98	13	22	3
Doncaster Rov	L	02/98	97	6	0	2

ROWE Graham Edward
Born: Southport, Merseyside, England, 28 August, 1945 — M/D

League Club	Source	Date Signed	Seasons Played	Apps	Subs	Gls
Blackpool	App	07/63	63-70	101	4	12
Tranmere Rov	L	11/70	70	6	1	0
Bolton W	Tr	05/71	71	4	2	0

ROWE James Anthony
Born: Christchurch, Dorset, England, 10 March, 1987 — M

League Club	Source	Date Signed	Seasons Played	Apps	Subs	Gls
Bournemouth	Jnr	07/04	04-05	0	4	0

ROWE James Michael
Born: Wantage, Oxfordshire, England, 21 October, 1991 — M

League Club	Source	Date Signed	Seasons Played	Apps	Subs	Gls
Reading	Sch	07/10				
Tranmere Rov	Forest Green Rov	07/13	13-14	10	16	3

ROWE Mark Terence
Born: Bodmin, Cornwall, England, 9 June, 1964 — M/D
England: Schools

League Club	Source	Date Signed	Seasons Played	Apps	Subs	Gls
Plymouth Arg	App	09/81	81-84	46	9	1
Torquay U	Saltash U	09/86	86	7	0	0

ROWE Norman
Born: Halesowen, West Midlands, England, 20 March, 1940 — W

League Club	Source	Date Signed	Seasons Played	Apps	Subs	Gls
Walsall	Aston Villa (Am)	03/59	59-60	6	-	0

ROWE Norman Terence Sinclair (Terry)
Born: Fulham, W London, England, 8 June, 1964 — RB

League Club	Source	Date Signed	Seasons Played	Apps	Subs	Gls
Brentford	App	06/82	81-84	63	3	1

ROWE Rodney Carl
Born: Huddersfield, West Yorkshire, England, 30 July, 1975 — F

League Club	Source	Date Signed	Seasons Played	Apps	Subs	Gls
Huddersfield T	YT	07/93	93-96	14	20	2
Scarborough	L	08/94	94	10	4	1
Bury	L	03/95	94	1	2	0
York C	Tr	02/97	96-99	74	23	20
Halifax T	L	09/99	99	7	2	2
Gillingham	Tr	11/99	99	8	14	4
Hull C	Tr	01/01	00-01	19	16	8

ROWE Thomas Malcolm (Tommy)
Born: Wythenshawe, Greater Manchester, England, 1 May, 1989 — M/LB

League Club	Source	Date Signed	Seasons Played	Apps	Subs	Gls
Stockport Co	Sch	03/07	06-08	60	12	13
Peterborough U	Tr	05/09	09-13	161	14	23
Wolverhampton W	Tr	06/14	14	7	7	0

ROWE Valentine Norman (Norman)
Born: Shouldham, Norfolk, England, 14 February, 1926 — RB
Died: Kings Lynn, Norfolk, England, September, 1988

League Club	Source	Date Signed	Seasons Played	Apps	Subs	Gls
Derby Co	King's Lynn	12/49	51	2	-	0
Walsall	Tr	08/52	52	25	-	0

ROWE-TURNER Lathaniel Alanzo
Born: Leicester, England, 12 November, 1989 — CD

League Club	Source	Date Signed	Seasons Played	Apps	Subs	Gls
Leicester C	Sch	10/07				
Cheltenham T	L	10/08	08	1	0	0
Torquay U	Tr	02/10	09-11	9	26	1

ROWELL Gary
Born: Seaham, County Durham, England, 6 June, 1957 — LW/F
England: U21-1

League Club	Source	Date Signed	Seasons Played	Apps	Subs	Gls
Sunderland	App	07/74	75-83	229	28	88
Norwich C	Tr	08/84	84	2	4	1
Middlesbrough	Tr	08/85	85	27	0	10
Brighton & HA	Tr	08/86	86-87	9	3	0
Carlisle U	Tr	03/88	87	7	0	0
Burnley	Tr	08/88	88-89	8	11	1

ROWELL John Frederick (Fred)
Born: Seaham, County Durham, England, 31 December, 1918 — IF
Died: Bournemouth, England, 9 March, 1988

League Club	Source	Date Signed	Seasons Played	Apps	Subs	Gls
Sunderland	Seaham CW	10/37				
Brentford	Tr	07/38				
Bournemouth	Army	09/41	46-47	31	-	11
Wrexham	Tr	07/48	48-49	41	-	5
Aldershot	Tr	08/50	50	5	-	0

ROWELL Jonathan Michael (Jonny)
Born: Newcastle-upon-Tyne, England, 10 September, 1989 — M

League Club	Source	Date Signed	Seasons Played	Apps	Subs	Gls
Hartlepool U	Sch	01/08	08-09	3	9	0

ROWETT Gary
Born: Bromsgrove, Worcestershire, England, 6 March, 1974 — D

League Club	Source	Date Signed	Seasons Played	Apps	Subs	Gls
Cambridge U	YT	09/91	91-93	51	12	9
Everton	Tr	05/94	93-94	2	2	0
Blackpool	L	01/95	94	17	0	0
Derby Co	Tr	07/95	95-97	101	4	2
Birmingham C	Tr	08/98	98-99	87	0	6
Leicester C	Tr	07/00	00-01	47	2	2
Charlton Ath	Tr	05/02	02-03	13	0	1

ROWLAND Alfred (Alf)
Born: Stokesley, North Yorkshire, England, 2 September, 1920 — CH
Died: Stokesley, North Yorkshire, England, November, 1997

League Club	Source	Date Signed	Seasons Played	Apps	Subs	Gls
Aldershot	Stockton	08/46	46-48	93	-	0
Cardiff C	Tr	02/49	48-49	3	-	0

ROWLAND Andrew Arthur (Andy)
Born: Derby, England, 8 September, 1954 — F
England: Youth

League Club	Source	Date Signed	Seasons Played	Apps	Subs	Gls
Derby Co	Jnr	09/72				
Bury	Tr	08/74	74-78	169	5	59
Swindon T	Tr	09/78	78-85	280	7	80

ROWLAND Andrew James (Andy)
Born: Taunton, Somerset, England, 1 October, 1965 — F
England: Schools

League Club	Source	Date Signed	Seasons Played	Apps	Subs	Gls
Southampton	Exmouth T	11/89				
Torquay U	Tr	03/91	90-91	9	7	1

ROWLAND David Charles
Born: Stotfold, Bedfordshire, England, 12 September, 1940 — IF
England: Schools

League Club	Source	Date Signed	Seasons Played	Apps	Subs	Gls
Luton T	Arlesey T	01/58	57	1	-	0

ROWLAND John Douglas
Born: Riddings, Derbyshire, England, 7 April, 1941 — W/CF
England: Youth

League Club	Source	Date Signed	Seasons Played	Apps	Subs	Gls
Nottingham F (Am)	Ironville Amats	04/61	60-61	26	-	3
Port Vale	Tr	08/62	62-66	147	2	40
Mansfield T	Tr	09/66	66-67	49	0	16
Tranmere Rov	Tr	07/68	68	25	1	3

ROWLAND John Oswald
Born: Newport, Wales, 16 March, 1936 — LB/LH
Died: Newport, Wales, 31 October, 2002
Wales: U23-1

League Club	Source	Date Signed	Seasons Played	Apps	Subs	Gls
Newport Co	Lovells Ath	06/58	58-68	461	1	11

ROWLAND Keith
Born: Portadown, Armagh, Northern Ireland, 1 September, 1971 — M/LB
Northern Ireland: 19/B-3/Youth

League Club	Source	Date Signed	Seasons Played	Apps	Subs	Gls
Bournemouth	YT	10/89	91-92	65	7	2
Coventry C	L	01/93	92	0	2	0
West Ham U	Tr	08/93	93-97	63	17	1
Queens Park Rgrs	Tr	01/98	97-00	32	24	3
Luton T	L	01/01	00	12	0	2
Chesterfield	Tr	08/01	01-02	6	6	0

ROWLAND Leonard Charles (Len)
Born: Manchester, England, 23 June, 1925 — LB
Died: Stockport, Greater Manchester, England, May, 2014
England: Amateur-6

League Club	Source	Date Signed	Seasons Played	Apps	Subs	Gls
Wrexham (Am)	Mansfield T (Am)	05/49	49-50	18	-	0
Stockport Co	Ashton U	12/52	52-56	61	-	0

ROWLAND Stephen John (Steve)
Born: Wrexham, Wales, 2 November, 1981 — RB

League Club	Source	Date Signed	Seasons Played	Apps	Subs	Gls
Port Vale	YT	07/01	01-05	103	18	1

ROWLANDS John Henry
Born: Liverpool, England, 7 February, 1945 — F/CD

League Club	Source	Date Signed	Seasons Played	Apps	Subs	Gls
Mansfield T		10/67	67	12	1	3
Torquay U	Tr	06/68	68	18	0	4
Exeter C	L	01/69	68	1	0	0
Stockport Co	Cape Town C (RSA)	08/69	69-70	45	1	11
Barrow	Tr	01/71	70-71	52	2	6
Workington	Tr	07/72	72-73	50	1	11
Crewe Alex	Tr	11/73	73-74	31	4	1
Hartlepool U	Seattle Sounders (USA)	09/75	75-76	47	2	10

ROWLANDS Martin Charles
Born: Hammersmith, W London, England, 8 February, 1979 — M
Republic of Ireland: 5/U21-8

League Club	Source	Date Signed	Seasons Played	Apps	Subs	Gls
Brentford	Farnborough T	08/98	98-02	128	21	20
Queens Park Rgrs	Tr	08/03	03-10	179	19	33
Millwall	L	02/11	10	0	1	0
Wycombe W	L	09/11	11	8	2	0
Colchester U	Tr	02/12	11	7	2	2
Leyton Orient	Tr	08/12	12	31	2	4

ROWLANDS Trevor Ivor
Born: Wattstown, Rhondda Cynon Taff, Wales, 2 February, 1922 — LB
Died: Norwich, England, 22 July, 1973
Wales: Schools

League Club	Source	Date Signed	Seasons Played	Apps	Subs	Gls
Norwich C	Cardiff Nomads	08/46	47-49	10	-	2
Colchester U	Tr	07/50	50-52	46	-	5

ROWLES Albert Edward James (Eddie)
Born: Gosport, Hampshire, England, 10 March, 1951 — M/F

League Club	Source	Date Signed	Seasons Played	Apps	Subs	Gls
Bournemouth	App	03/68	67-70	58	8	12
York C	Tr	07/71	71-72	61	6	14
Torquay U	Tr	06/73	73-74	54	5	13
Darlington	Tr	08/75	75-77	96	7	21
Colchester U	Tr	12/77	77-81	79	12	17

ROWLEY Antonio Camilio (Tony)
Born: Porthcawl, Bridgend, Wales, 19 September, 1929 — IF
Died: Bromborough, Wirral, England, 28 April, 2006
Wales: 1

League Club	Source	Date Signed	Seasons Played	Apps	Subs	Gls
Birmingham C	Wellington T	01/49				
Liverpool	Stourbridge	10/53	53-57	60	-	38
Tranmere Rov	Tr	03/58	57-60	100	-	45

ROWLEY Arthur
Born: Liverpool, England, 9 May, 1933 — IF
Died: Aintree, Merseyside, England, 18 February, 2014

League Club	Source	Date Signed	Seasons Played	Apps	Subs	Gls
Liverpool	Florence Melley BC	05/51	52	11	-	0
Wrexham	Tr	11/54	54-56	54	-	8
Crewe Alex	Tr	02/57	56-57	32	-	8
Tranmere Rov	Tr	09/58				

ROWLEY George Arthur (Arthur)
Born: Wolverhampton, England, 21 April, 1926 — IF
Died: Shrewsbury, Shropshire, England, 18 December, 2002
England: B-1/FLge-1

League Club	Source	Date Signed	Seasons Played	Apps	Subs	Gls
West Bromwich A	Blakenhall St Luke's	05/44	46-48	24	-	4
Fulham	Tr	12/48	48-49	56	-	26
Leicester C	Tr	07/50	50-57	303	-	251
Shrewsbury T	Tr	06/58	58-64	236	-	152

ROWLEY John
Born: Wolverhampton, England, 23 June, 1944 — LB

League Club	Source	Date Signed	Seasons Played	Apps	Subs	Gls
Bradford Park Ave	Wellington T	10/67	67	35	0	0

ROWLEY John Frederick (Jack)
Born: Wolverhampton, England, 7 October, 1918 — CF
Died: Shaw, Greater Manchester, England, 28 June, 1998
England: 6/B-1/FLge-3/War-1

League Club	Source	Date Signed	Seasons Played	Apps	Subs	Gls
Wolverhampton W	Dudley OB	11/35				
Bournemouth	Tr	02/37	36-37	23	-	12
Manchester U	Tr	10/37	37-54	380	-	182
Plymouth Arg	Tr	02/55	54-56	56	-	14

ROWLEY Kenneth Francis (Ken)
Born: Pelsall, West Midlands, England, 29 August, 1926 — IF
Died: Walsall, West Midlands, England, 28 May, 1995

League Club	Source	Date Signed	Seasons Played	Apps	Subs	Gls
Wolverhampton W	Elkingtons	10/47	49	1	-	0
Birmingham C	Tr	01/51	50-54	40	-	19
Coventry C	Tr	11/54	54	3	-	0

ROWNEY Christopher (Chris)
Born: Ashton-under-Lyne, Greater Manchester, England, 14 February, 1991 — M

League Club	Source	Date Signed	Seasons Played	Apps	Subs	Gls
Oldham Ath	Sch	07/09	09	0	1	0

ROWNTREE Adam Peter
Born: Lincoln, England, 23 November, 1988 — F

League Club	Source	Date Signed	Seasons Played	Apps	Subs	Gls
Boston U	Sch	-	06	0	3	0

ROWSON David Andrew
Born: Aberdeen, Scotland, 14 September, 1976 — DM
Scotland: U21-5

League Club	Source	Date Signed	Seasons Played	Apps	Subs	Gls
Stoke C	Aberdeen	07/01	01	8	5	0
Northampton T	Partick Thistle	07/04	04-05	48	18	2
Darlington	Tr	08/06	06	20	4	2
Boston U	L	11/06	06	6	0	0

ROXBURGH Alexander White (Alex)
Born: Manchester, England, 19 September, 1910 — G
Died: Prestwich, Greater Manchester, England, 5 December, 1985
England: War-1

League Club	Source	Date Signed	Seasons Played	Apps	Subs	Gls
Blackpool	St Annes & S Shore Wed	03/31	32-38	57	-	0
Barrow	Tr	08/46	46-47	69	-	0

ROY Andrew (Andy)
Born: Tillicoultry, Stirlingshire, Scotland, 14 July, 1928 — IF
Died: Stirling, Scotland, 13 March, 1999

League Club	Source	Date Signed	Seasons Played	Apps	Subs	Gls
Exeter C	Dunfermline Ath	08/49	49	2	-	0

ROY Bryan Edward Steven
Born: Amsterdam, Netherlands, 12 February, 1970 — W
Netherlands: 32

League Club	Source	Date Signed	Seasons Played	Apps	Subs	Gls
Nottingham F	Foggia (ITA)	08/94	94-96	70	15	24

ROY Eric Serge
Born: Nice, France, 26 September, 1967 — DM

League Club	Source	Date Signed	Seasons Played	Apps	Subs	Gls
Sunderland	Olymp Marseille (FRA)	08/99	99-00	20	7	0

ROY John Robin (Jack)
Born: Southampton, England, 23 March, 1914 — RW
Died: Bournemouth, England, 24 November, 1980

League Club	Source	Date Signed	Seasons Played	Apps	Subs	Gls
Norwich C	Sholing Ath	08/33	34-35	6	-	0
Mansfield T	Tr	04/36	36	25	-	2
Sheffield Wed	Tr	02/37	36-37	15	-	1
Notts Co	Tr	03/38	37-38	15	-	0
Tranmere Rov	Tr	12/38	38	20	-	2
Ipswich T	Yeovil & Petters U	02/46	46	15	-	2

ROYCE Simon Ernest
Born: Forest Gate, E London, England, 9 September, 1971 — G

League Club	Source	Date Signed	Seasons Played	Apps	Subs	Gls
Southend U	Heybridge Swifts	10/91	91-97	147	2	0
Charlton Ath	Tr	07/98	98	8	0	0
Leicester C	Tr	07/00	00	16	3	0
Brighton & HA	L	12/01	01	6	0	0
Queens Park Rgrs	L	08/02	02	16	0	0
Charlton Ath	Tr	07/03	03	1	0	0
Luton T	L	10/04	04	2	0	0
Queens Park Rgrs	Tr	01/05	04-06	63	0	0
Gillingham	Tr	04/07	06-09	94	1	0
Brentford	Tr	08/10	10	1	1	0

ROYLE Joseph (Joe)
Born: Liverpool, England, 8 April, 1949 — F
England: 6/FLge-1/U23-10

League Club	Source	Date Signed	Seasons Played	Apps	Subs	Gls
Everton	App	08/66	65-74	229	3	102
Manchester C	Tr	12/74	74-77	98	1	23
Bristol C	Tr	11/77	77-79	100	1	18
Norwich C	Tr	08/80	80-81	40	2	9

ROYSTON Robert (Bob)
Born: Newcastle-upon-Tyne, England, 1 December, 1915 — RB
Died: Southwold, Suffolk, England, 12 February, 1996

League Club	Source	Date Signed	Seasons Played	Apps	Subs	Gls
Sunderland	Seaham CW	01/35				
Southport	Tr	10/36	37-38	70	-	2
Plymouth Arg	Tr	03/39	38-46	39	-	0

ROZEHNAL David Sebastian
Born: Olomouc, Czech Republic, 5 July, 1980 — CD
Czech Republic: 60

League Club	Source	Date Signed	Seasons Played	Apps	Subs	Gls
Newcastle U	Paris St-Germain (FRA)	07/07	07	16	5	0

RUARK Anthony (Tony)
Born: West Ham, E London, England, 23 March, 1933 — CH

League Club	Source	Date Signed	Seasons Played	Apps	Subs	Gls
Southend U		05/56	56	9	-	0

RUBINS Andrejs
Born: Riga, Latvia, 26 November, 1978 — LM
Latvia: 117

League Club	Source	Date Signed	Seasons Played	Apps	Subs	Gls
Crystal Palace	Skonto Riga (LAT)	10/00	00-02	17	14	0

RUDD Declan Thomas
Born: Diss, Norfolk, England, 16 January, 1991 — G
England: U21-1/Youth

League Club	Source	Date Signed	Seasons Played	Apps	Subs	Gls
Norwich C	Sch	07/08	09-11	6	4	0
Preston NE	L	01/13	12	14	0	0
Preston NE	L	07/13	13	46	0	0

RUDD Edward (Ted)
Born: Wigan, Greater Manchester, England, 7 January, 1929 — LH

League Club	Source	Date Signed	Seasons Played	Apps	Subs	Gls
Bolton W		08/50				
Accrington Stan	Tr	08/51	51	2	-	0

RUDD John James (Jimmy)
Born: Dublin, Republic of Ireland, 25 October, 1919 — LW
Died: Manchester, England, 13 December, 1985

League Club	Source	Date Signed	Seasons Played	Apps	Subs	Gls
Manchester C	Terenure Ath (ROI)	01/38	46	2	-	0
York C	Tr	03/47	46-48	83	-	23
Leeds U	Tr	02/49	48-49	18	-	1
Rotherham U	Tr	10/49	49-51	75	-	11
Scunthorpe U	Tr	10/51	51	32	-	4
Workington	Tr	09/52	52	17	-	1

RUDD William Thomas (Billy)
Born: Manchester, England, 13 December, 1941 — M

League Club	Source	Date Signed	Seasons Played	Apps	Subs	Gls
Birmingham C	Stalybridge Celtic	10/59	59-61	24	-	3
York C	Tr	11/61	61-65	193	0	30
Grimsby T	Tr	07/66	66-67	59	1	9
Rochdale	Tr	02/68	67-69	108	0	8
Bury	Tr	06/70	70-76	174	15	19

RUDDOCK Neil
Born: Wandsworth, SW London, England, 9 May, 1968 — CD
England: 1/B-1/U21-4/Youth

League Club	Source	Date Signed	Seasons Played	Apps	Subs	Gls
Millwall	App	03/86				
Tottenham H	Tr	04/86	86-87	7	2	0
Millwall	Tr	06/88	88	0	2	1
Southampton	Tr	02/89	88-91	100	7	9
Tottenham H	Tr	07/92	92	38	0	3
Liverpool	Tr	07/93	93-97	111	4	11
Queens Park Rgrs	L	03/98	97	7	0	0
West Ham U	Tr	07/98	98-99	39	3	2
Crystal Palace	Tr	07/00	00	19	1	2
Swindon T	Tr	08/01	01	14	1	1

RUDDOCK Pelly
Born: Hendon, N London, England, 4 January, 1993 — M

League Club	Source	Date Signed	Seasons Played	Apps	Subs	Gls
West Ham U	Boreham Wood	12/11				
Luton T	Tr	11/13	14	10	6	1

RUDDY John Thomas Gordon
Born: St Ives, Cambridgeshire, England, 24 October, 1986 — G
England: 1

League Club	Source	Date Signed	Seasons Played	Apps	Subs	Gls
Cambridge U	Sch	09/04	03-04	39	0	0
Everton	Tr	05/05	05	0	1	0
Walsall	L	09/05	05	5	0	0
Rushden & D	L	11/05	05	3	0	0
Chester C	L	12/05	05	4	0	0
Stockport Co	L	09/06	06	11	0	0
Wrexham	L	02/07	06	5	0	0
Bristol C	L	04/07	06	1	0	0
Stockport Co	L	02/08	07	12	0	0
Crewe Alex	L	01/09	08	19	0	0
Norwich C	Tr	07/10	10-14	181	0	0

RUDGE Dale Anthony
Born: Wolverhampton, England, 9 June, 1963 — M

League Club	Source	Date Signed	Seasons Played	Apps	Subs	Gls
Wolverhampton W	App	08/81	82-83	23	4	0
Preston NE	Tr	07/84	84-85	46	1	2

RUDGE David Harry (Dave)
Born: Wolverhampton, England, 21 January, 1948 — W

League Club	Source	Date Signed	Seasons Played	Apps	Subs	Gls
Aston Villa	App	05/65	66-69	49	6	10
Hereford U	Tr	08/72	72-75	75	7	8
Torquay U	Tr	12/75	75-77	60	4	4

RUDGE John Robert
Born: Wolverhampton, England, 21 October, 1944 — F

League Club	Source	Date Signed	Seasons Played	Apps	Subs	Gls
Huddersfield T	Jnr	11/61	62-66	5	0	0
Carlisle U	Tr	12/66	66-68	45	5	16
Torquay U	Tr	01/69	68-71	94	2	34
Bristol Rov	Tr	02/72	71-74	50	20	17
Bournemouth	Tr	03/75	74-76	18	3	2

RUDGE Simon James
Born: Warrington, Cheshire, England, 30 December, 1964 — M

League Club	Source	Date Signed	Seasons Played	Apps	Subs	Gls
Bolton W	App	12/82	82-85	77	14	14

RUDHAM Keith Robert (Doug)
Born: Johannesburg, South Africa, 3 May, 1926 — G
Died: Johannesburg, South Africa, 13 August, 1991
South Africa: Amateur

League Club	Source	Date Signed	Seasons Played	Apps	Subs	Gls
Liverpool	Jo'burg Rgrs (RSA)	11/54	54-59	63	-	0

RUDI Petter Normann
Born: Kristiansund, Norway, 17 September, 1973 — LW
Norway: 46/U21/Youth

League Club	Source	Date Signed	Seasons Played	Apps	Subs	Gls
Sheffield Wed	Molde FK (NOR)	10/97	97-00	70	7	8

RUDKIN Thomas William (Tommy)
Born: Peterborough, England, 16 June, 1919 — LW
Died: Wisbech, Cambridgeshire, England, 15 May, 1969

League Club	Source	Date Signed	Seasons Played	Apps	Subs	Gls
Wolverhampton W	Creswell	02/38				
Lincoln C	Tr	05/38	38	2	-	1
Arsenal	Peterborough U	01/47	46	5	-	2
Southampton	Tr	08/47	47-48	9	-	0
Bristol C	Tr	05/49	49-50	34	-	4

RUDMAN Harold
Born: Whitworth, Lancashire, England, 4 November, 1924 — FB
Died: Rochdale, Greater Manchester, England, 4 October, 2013

League Club	Source	Date Signed	Seasons Played	Apps	Subs	Gls
Burnley	Bacup Bor	12/42	46-56	71	-	0
Rochdale	Tr	07/57	57	21	-	2

RUDONJA Mladen
Born: Koper, Slovenia, 26 July, 1971 — M
Slovenia: 65

League Club	Source	Date Signed	Seasons Played	Apps	Subs	Gls
Portsmouth	St Truiden (BEL)	08/00	00-01	4	10	0

RUECROFT Jacob (Jake)
Born: Lanchester, County Durham, England, 1 May, 1915 — D
Died: Pontefract, West Yorkshire, England, February, 2005

League Club	Source	Date Signed	Seasons Played	Apps	Subs	Gls
Halifax T	Goole T	05/38	38-46	60	-	2
Bradford C	Scarborough	01/48	47-48	43	-	0

RUFFELS Joshua Andrew Bernard (Josh)
Born: Oxford, England, 23 October, 1993 — M

League Club	Source	Date Signed	Seasons Played	Apps	Subs	Gls
Coventry C	Sch	06/12	11	0	1	0
Oxford U	Tr	07/13	13-14	50	12	1

RUFFETT Raymond Douglas (Ray)
Born: Luton, England, 20 July, 1924 — WH

League Club	Source	Date Signed	Seasons Played	Apps	Subs	Gls
Luton T	Jnr	10/41	48	1	-	0

RUFUS Marvin Marcel
Born: Lewisham, SE London, England, 11 September, 1976 — M

League Club	Source	Date Signed	Seasons Played	Apps	Subs	Gls
Leyton Orient	Charlton Ath (YT)	11/94	94	5	2	0

RUFUS Richard Raymond
Born: Lewisham, SE London, England, 12 January, 1975 — CD
England: U21-6

League Club	Source	Date Signed	Seasons Played	Apps	Subs	Gls
Charlton Ath	YT	07/93	94-02	284	4	12

RUGGIERO John Salvatore
Born: Longton, Potteries, England, 26 November, 1954 — M

League Club	Source	Date Signed	Seasons Played	Apps	Subs	Gls
Stoke C	App	05/72	76	9	0	2
Workington	L	01/76	75	3	0	0
Brighton & HA	Tr	06/77	77	4	4	2
Portsmouth	L	12/77	77	6	0	1
Chester C	Tr	04/79	79	9	2	1

[RUI MARQUES] MARQUES Rui Manuel
Born: Luanda, Angola, 3 September, 1977 — CD
Angola: 19

League Club	Source	Date Signed	Seasons Played	Apps	Subs	Gls
Leeds U	CS Maritimo (POR)	08/05	06-09	85	5	4
Hull C	L	03/06	05	1	0	0

RUIZ Bryan Jafet
Born: San Jose, Costa Rica, 18 August, 1985 — W/F
Costa Rica: 76

League Club	Source	Date Signed	Seasons Played	Apps	Subs	Gls
Fulham	FC Twente (NED)	08/11	11-14	74	23	12

RULE Alan Henry
Born: Southampton, England, 10 January, 1930 — WH
Died: Carmarthen, Wales, November, 2008

League Club	Source	Date Signed	Seasons Played	Apps	Subs	Gls
Chelsea	Winchester C	11/52				
Norwich C	Tr	09/56	56	8	-	0
Bournemouth	Tr	06/57	57	25	-	0

RULE Glenn Paul
Born: Birkenhead, Wirral, England, 30 November, 1989 — FB

League Club	Source	Date Signed	Seasons Played	Apps	Subs	Gls
Chester C	Sch	10/08	07-08	20	6	0

RUMBLE Paul
Born: Hemel Hempstead, Hertfordshire, England, 14 March, 1969 — LB

League Club	Source	Date Signed	Seasons Played	Apps	Subs	Gls
Watford	App	03/87				
Scunthorpe U	L	08/88	88	8	0	1
Maidstone U	Tr	08/89	89-91	48	7	3

RUMBOLD George Arthur
Born: Alton, Hampshire, England, 10 July, 1911 — FB
Died: Ipswich, England, 12 December, 1995

League Club	Source	Date Signed	Seasons Played	Apps	Subs	Gls
Crystal Palace	Faringdon	10/34	35	5	-	0
Leyton Orient	Tr	06/37	37-38	52	-	0
Ipswich T	Tr	05/46	46-49	121	-	11

RUMNEY Joseph Edgar (Edgar)
Born: Abberton, Essex, England, 15 September, 1936 — RB/LH

League Club	Source	Date Signed	Seasons Played	Apps	Subs	Gls
Colchester U	Jnr	05/57	57-64	49	-	0

RUNDLE Adam
Born: South Shields, Tyne and Wear, England, 8 July, 1984 — LW

League Club	Source	Date Signed	Seasons Played	Apps	Subs	Gls
Darlington	YT	-	01-02	8	9	0
Carlisle U	Tr	12/02	02-03	25	19	1
Mansfield T	Dublin C (ROI)	01/05	04-05	45	8	9
Rochdale	Tr	07/06	06-09	95	32	17
Rotherham U	L	11/09	09	4	0	0
Chesterfield	Tr	02/10	09	12	4	0
Morecambe	Tr	07/10	10	8	9	0

RUNDLE Charles Rodney (Charlie)
Born: Fowey, Cornwall, England, 17 January, 1923 — IF
Died: Bodmin, Cornwall, England, 28 June, 1997

League Club	Source	Date Signed	Seasons Played	Apps	Subs	Gls
Tottenham H	St Blazey	02/46	46-48	28	-	12
Crystal Palace	Tr	06/50	50-51	38	-	2

RUNDLE Sidney Stewart Knight (Sid)
Born: Fowey, Cornwall, England, 19 October, 1921 — WH
Died: Truro, Cornwall, England, 10 July, 1987

League Club	Source	Date Signed	Seasons Played	Apps	Subs	Gls
Plymouth Arg	St Blazey	06/45	46-52	53	-	1

RUNSTROM Bjorn Sandro
Born: Stockholm, Sweden, 1 March, 1984 — F
Sweden: U21-20/Youth

League Club	Source	Date Signed	Seasons Played	Apps	Subs	Gls
Fulham	Hammarby IF (SWE)	08/06	06	0	1	0
Luton T	L	01/07	06	7	1	2

RUSH David
Born: Sunderland, England, 15 May, 1971 — F

League Club	Source	Date Signed	Seasons Played	Apps	Subs	Gls
Sunderland	YT	07/89	90-93	40	19	12
Hartlepool U	L	08/91	91	8	0	2
Peterborough U	L	10/93	93	2	2	1
Cambridge U	L	09/94	94	2	0	0
Oxford U	Tr	09/94	94-96	67	25	21
York C	Tr	01/97	96-97	2	3	0
Hartlepool U	Morpeth T	09/98	98	5	5	0

RUSH Ian James
Born: Flint, Wales, 20 October, 1961 — F
Wales: 73/U21-2/Schools

League Club	Source	Date Signed	Seasons Played	Apps	Subs	Gls
Chester C	App	09/79	78-79	33	1	14
Liverpool	Tr	05/80	80-86	224	0	139
Liverpool	Juventus (ITA)	07/86	88-95	223	22	89
Leeds U	Tr	05/96	96	34	2	3
Newcastle U	Tr	08/97	97	6	4	0
Sheffield U	L	02/98	97	4	0	0
Wrexham	Tr	08/98	98	12	5	0

RUSH Jonathan (Jon)
Born: Wellington, New Zealand, 13 October, 1961 — G

League Club	Source	Date Signed	Seasons Played	Apps	Subs	Gls
Blackpool	De La Salle C'ge (NZL)	11/79	80-81	11	0	0
Carlisle U	Tr	08/82				

RUSH Matthew James
Born: Dalston, N London, England, 6 August, 1971 — M
Republic of Ireland: U21-4

League Club	Source	Date Signed	Seasons Played	Apps	Subs	Gls
West Ham U	YT	03/90	90-94	29	19	5
Cambridge U	L	03/93	92	4	6	0
Swansea C	L	01/94	93	13	0	0
Norwich C	Tr	08/95	95-96	0	3	0
Northampton T	L	10/96	96	14	0	3
Oldham Ath	Tr	03/97	96-97	17	7	3

RUSHBURY Andrew James (Andy)
Born: Carlisle, Cumbria, England, 7 March, 1983 — M/LB

League Club	Source	Date Signed	Seasons Played	Apps	Subs	Gls
Chesterfield	Sch	07/02	00-03	23	17	1

RUSHBURY David Graham
Born: Wolverhampton, England, 20 February, 1956 — D

League Club	Source	Date Signed	Seasons Played	Apps	Subs	Gls
West Bromwich A	App	02/74	74-75	28	0	0
Sheffield Wed	Tr	11/76	76-78	111	1	7
Swansea C	Tr	07/79	79-80	51	1	0
Carlisle U	Tr	08/81	81-84	120	9	1
Gillingham	Tr	03/85	84	12	0	0
Doncaster Rov	Tr	07/85	85-86	66	0	2
Cambridge U	L	02/87	86	1	0	0
Bristol Rov	Tr	02/87	86	14	2	0

RUSHBY Alan
Born: Doncaster, South Yorkshire, England, 27 December, 1933 — CH

League Club	Source	Date Signed	Seasons Played	Apps	Subs	Gls
Doncaster Rov		01/52	53	1	-	0
Mansfield T	Tr	03/57	56-57	20	-	0
Bradford Park Ave	Tr	11/57	57-58	12	-	0

RUSHFELDT Sigurd (Siggi)
Born: Vadso, Norway, 11 December, 1972 — F
Norway: 38/U21-2

League Club	Source	Date Signed	Seasons Played	Apps	Subs	Gls
Birmingham C (L)	Tromso (NOR)	10/95	95	3	4	0

RUSHFORTH Peter
Born: Carlisle, Cumbria, England, 6 December, 1945 — D

League Club	Source	Date Signed	Seasons Played	Apps	Subs	Gls
Workington (Am)	Coronation BC	09/66	66	5	0	0

RUSHTON Brian William Eric
Born: Sedgley, West Midlands, England, 21 October, 1943 — RB

League Club	Source	Date Signed	Seasons Played	Apps	Subs	Gls
Birmingham C	App	10/60	62-63	12	-	0
Notts Co	Tr	06/67	67	2	1	0

RUSHWORTH Peter John
Born: Bristol, England, 12 April, 1927 — RH
Died: Christchurch, Dorset, England, 14 November, 2014

League Club	Source	Date Signed	Seasons Played	Apps	Subs	Gls
Leicester C	Cheltenham T	11/51				
Bournemouth	Tr	06/53	53-56	88	-	1

RUSK Simon Edward
Born: Peterborough, England, 17 December, 1981 — RB/M
Scotland: Youth

League Club	Source	Date Signed	Seasons Played	Apps	Subs	Gls
Boston U	Peterborough U (YT)	04/01	02-06	76	29	8

RUSLING Graham
Born: Keadby, North Lincolnshire, England, 4 April, 1948 — F

League Club	Source	Date Signed	Seasons Played	Apps	Subs	Gls
Scunthorpe U		01/67	66-70	71	9	17

RUSNAK Albert
Born: Kosice, Slovakia, 7 July, 1994 — RW
Slovakia: U21-1/Youth

League Club	Source	Date Signed	Seasons Played	Apps	Subs	Gls
Manchester C	Sch	03/12				
Oldham Ath	L	08/13	13	0	2	0
Birmingham C	L	01/14	13	3	0	0

RUSSELL Alec
Born: Bristol, England, 17 April, 1925 — IF

League Club	Source	Date Signed	Seasons Played	Apps	Subs	Gls
Bristol C		11/47	47-48	3	-	0

RUSSELL Alexander (Alex)
Born: Seaham, County Durham, England, 21 February, 1944 — M

League Club	Source	Date Signed	Seasons Played	Apps	Subs	Gls
Everton	Marsden Colliery Jnrs	12/61				
Southport	Tr	11/63	63-69	262	1	63
Blackburn Rov	Tr	08/70	70	22	2	4
Tranmere Rov	Tr	07/71	71-72	54	1	7
Crewe Alex	L	10/72	72	4	0	0
Southport	Tr	11/72	72-74	84	1	12

RUSSELL Alexander John (Alex)
Born: Crosby, Merseyside, England, 17 March, 1973 — M

League Club	Source	Date Signed	Seasons Played	Apps	Subs	Gls
Rochdale	Burscough	07/94	94-97	83	19	14
Cambridge U	Tr	08/98	98-00	72	9	8
Torquay U	Tr	08/01	01-04	152	1	21
Bristol C	Tr	07/05	05-07	42	14	6
Northampton T	L	08/07	07	11	2	1
Cheltenham T	L	01/08	07	12	1	2
Cheltenham T	Tr	07/08	08	19	4	0
Exeter C	L	02/09	08	7	0	0
Exeter C	Tr	07/09	09	27	2	1
Yeovil T	Bath C	01/11	10	2	12	0

RUSSELL Allan
Born: Aberdeen, Scotland, 16 November, 1953 — M

League Club	Source	Date Signed	Seasons Played	Apps	Subs	Gls
Peterborough U	Leicester C (App)	09/71	71-72	7	8	1

RUSSELL Allan John
Born: Glasgow, Scotland, 13 December, 1980 — F

League Club	Source	Date Signed	Seasons Played	Apps	Subs	Gls
Macclesfield T	St Mirren	08/05	05	12	1	2
Mansfield T	Tr	11/05	05	7	11	2

RUSSELL Colin
Born: Liverpool, England, 21 January, 1961 — F

League Club	Source	Date Signed	Seasons Played	Apps	Subs	Gls
Liverpool	App	04/78	80	0	1	0
Huddersfield T	Tr	09/82	82-83	64	2	23
Stoke C	L	03/84	83	11	0	2
Bournemouth	Tr	08/84	84-85	65	3	14
Doncaster Rov	Tr	07/86	86-87	43	0	5
Scarborough	Tr	10/87	87	12	1	2
Wigan Ath	Tr	07/88	88	8	0	3

RUSSELL Craig Stewart
Born: Jarrow, Tyne and Wear, England, 4 February, 1974 — F

League Club	Source	Date Signed	Seasons Played	Apps	Subs	Gls
Sunderland	YT	07/92	91-97	103	47	31
Manchester C	Tr	11/97	97-98	22	9	2
Tranmere Rov	L	08/98	98	3	1	0
Port Vale	L	01/99	98	8	0	1
Darlington	L	09/99	99	11	1	2
Oxford U	L	02/00	99	5	1	0
Carlisle U	St Johnstone	01/03	02-03	10	9	1
Darlington	Tr	01/04	03-04	21	19	2

RUSSELL Darel Francis Roy
Born: Mile End, E London, England, 22 October, 1980 — M
England: Youth

League Club	Source	Date Signed	Seasons Played	Apps	Subs	Gls
Norwich C	YT	11/97	97-02	99	33	7
Stoke C	Tr	08/03	03-06	166	5	16
Norwich C	Tr	07/07	07-09	102	10	11
Preston NE	Tr	08/10	10-11	23	4	0
Charlton Ath	L	11/11	11	8	3	2
Portsmouth	Tr	08/12	12	17	0	0

RUSSELL Edward Thomas (Eddie)
Born: Cranwell, Lincolnshire, England, 15 July, 1928 — WH

League Club	Source	Date Signed	Seasons Played	Apps	Subs	Gls
Wolverhampton W	St Chad's College	04/46	48-50	30	-	0
Middlesbrough	Tr	12/51	51-52	29	-	1
Leicester C	Tr	10/53	53-57	90	-	5
Notts Co	Tr	08/58	58	9	-	0

RUSSELL Guy Robert
Born: Solihull, West Midlands, England, 28 September, 1967 — F

League Club	Source	Date Signed	Seasons Played	Apps	Subs	Gls
Birmingham C	App	05/86	84-87	7	4	0
Carlisle U	L	03/87	86	9	3	2

RUSSELL Hugh William (Hughie)
Born: Redcar, Cleveland, England, 10 March, 1921 — IF/W
Died: Taunton, Somerset, England, December, 1991

League Club	Source	Date Signed	Seasons Played	Apps	Subs	Gls
Gillingham	Bishop Auckland	08/46	50-51	61	-	8

RUSSELL James Walker (Jim)
Born: Edinburgh, Scotland, 14 September, 1916 — IF
Died: Florida, USA, 17 August, 1994
Scotland: Schools

League Club	Source	Date Signed	Seasons Played	Apps	Subs	Gls
Sunderland	Murrayfield Amats	06/34	35-37	5	-	0
Norwich C	Tr	05/38	38-46	12	-	2
Crystal Palace	Tr	12/46	46-47	43	-	6
New Brighton	Tr	07/48	48	24	-	1

RUSSELL John Matthieson
Born: Plymouth, England, 22 April, 1938 — W
Died: Plymouth, England, March, 2009

League Club	Source	Date Signed	Seasons Played	Apps	Subs	Gls
Plymouth Arg	Jnr	01/59				
Southport	Tr	07/60	60	1	-	0

RUSSELL Johnathan Simpson Snedden (Johnny)
Born: Glasgow, Scotland, 8 April, 1990 — F
Scotland: 3/U21-11/Youth

League Club	Source	Date Signed	Seasons Played	Apps	Subs	Gls
Derby Co	Dundee U	06/13	13-14	50	28	15

RUSSELL Keith David
Born: Aldridge, West Midlands, England, 31 January, 1974 — F

League Club	Source	Date Signed	Seasons Played	Apps	Subs	Gls
Blackpool	Hednesford T	04/97	96	0	1	0

RUSSELL Kevin John
Born: Portsmouth, England, 6 December, 1966 — M/F
England: Youth

League Club	Source	Date Signed	Seasons Played	Apps	Subs	Gls
Portsmouth	Brighton & HA (App)	10/84	85-86	3	1	0
Wrexham	Tr	07/87	87-88	84	0	43
Leicester C	Tr	06/89	89-91	24	19	10
Peterborough U	L	09/90	90	7	0	3
Cardiff C	L	01/91	90	3	0	0
Hereford U	L	11/91	91	3	0	1
Stoke C	L	01/92	91	5	0	1
Stoke C	Tr	07/92	92	30	10	5
Burnley	Tr	06/93	93	26	2	6
Bournemouth	Tr	03/94	93-94	30	0	1
Notts Co	Tr	02/95	94	9	2	0
Wrexham	Tr	07/95	95-02	172	26	17

RUSSELL Lee Edward
Born: Southampton, England, 3 September, 1969 — D

League Club	Source	Date Signed	Seasons Played	Apps	Subs	Gls
Portsmouth	YT	07/88	88-97	103	20	3
Bournemouth	L	09/94	94	3	0	0
Torquay U	Tr	03/99	98-01	78	4	0

RUSSELL Malcolm
Born: Halifax, West Yorkshire, England, 9 November, 1945 — D

League Club	Source	Date Signed	Seasons Played	Apps	Subs	Gls
Halifax T	App	03/63	62-68	183	1	0
Southport	Tr	09/68	68-70	92	0	2
Barrow	Tr	12/70	70-71	64	0	2
Stockport Co	Tr	07/72	72	11	0	0

RUSSELL Martin Christopher
Born: Dublin, Republic of Ireland, 27 April, 1967 — M
Republic of Ireland: U23-1/U21-4/Youth

League Club	Source	Date Signed	Seasons Played	Apps	Subs	Gls
Manchester U	App	04/84				
Birmingham C	L	10/86	86	3	2	0
Leicester C	Tr	03/87	86-88	13	7	0
Scarborough	Tr	02/89	88-89	51	0	9
Middlesbrough	Tr	03/90	90	10	1	2

RUSSELL Matthew Lee (Matt)
Born: Dewsbury, West Yorkshire, England, 17 January, 1978 — RB/M

League Club	Source	Date Signed	Seasons Played	Apps	Subs	Gls
Scarborough	YT	07/96	96-98	21	23	3
Doncaster Rov	L	03/98	97	4	1	0
Halifax T	Tr	07/99	99	3	4	0

RUSSELL Raymond (Ray)
Born: Walsall, West Midlands, England, 9 March, 1930 — IF

League Club	Source	Date Signed	Seasons Played	Apps	Subs	Gls
West Bromwich A	Jnr	05/48				
Shrewsbury T	Burton A	05/54	54-59	168	-	55
Crewe Alex	Tr	03/60	59	13	-	4

RUSSELL Robert Inglis (Bobby)
Born: Aberdour, Fife, Scotland, 27 December, 1919 — WH
Died: Dunfermline, Fife, Scotland, 26 March, 2004

League Club	Source	Date Signed	Seasons Played	Apps	Subs	Gls
Chelsea	Airdrieonians	12/44	46	2	-	0
Notts Co	Tr	08/48	48	2	-	0
Leyton Orient	Tr	10/48				

RUSSELL Roger Francis
Born: Corby, Northamptonshire, England, 20 November, 1957 — F

League Club	Source	Date Signed	Seasons Played	Apps	Subs	Gls
Northampton T	Corby T	09/81	81	0	1	0

RUSSELL Samuel Ian (Sam)
Born: Middlesbrough, England, 4 October, 1982 — G

League Club	Source	Date Signed	Seasons Played	Apps	Subs	Gls
Middlesbrough	YT	07/00				
Darlington	L	12/02	02	1	0	0
Scunthorpe U	L	08/03	03	10	0	0
Darlington	Tr	08/04	04-06	107	0	0
Rochdale	Tr	08/07	07-08	38	0	0

RUSSELL Sidney Edward James (Sid)
Born: Feltham, SW London, England, 4 October, 1937 — FB
Died: Quebec, Canada, 18 June, 1994

League Club	Source	Date Signed	Seasons Played	Apps	Subs	Gls
Brentford	Jnr	08/56	56-59	54	-	0

RUSSELL Simon Craig
Born: Hull, England, 19 March, 1985 — M

League Club	Source	Date Signed	Seasons Played	Apps	Subs	Gls
Hull C	Sch	-	02	0	1	0
Kidderminster Hrs	Tr	07/04	04	18	10	2

RUSSELL Wayne Leonard
Born: Cardiff, Wales, 29 November, 1967 — G

League Club	Source	Date Signed	Seasons Played	Apps	Subs	Gls
Burnley	Ebbw Vale	10/93	94-96	22	2	0

RUSSELL William (Billy)
Born: Hounslow, SW London, England, 7 July, 1935 — IF
England: Amateur-4

League Club	Source	Date Signed	Seasons Played	Apps	Subs	Gls
Sheffield U	Rhyl	11/57	57-62	144	-	55
Bolton W	Tr	03/63	62-64	22	-	2
Rochdale	Tr	07/66	66-67	60	1	8

RUSSELL William Howie (Bill)
Born: Coatbridge, Lanarkshire, Scotland, 19 October, 1919 — IF
Died: Newcastle-upon-Tyne, England, 9 July, 1989

League Club	Source	Date Signed	Seasons Played	Apps	Subs	Gls
Hartlepool U		05/46	46-47	13	-	1

RUSSELL William McKnight (Billy)
Born: Glasgow, Scotland, 14 September, 1959 — RB
Scotland: Youth

League Club	Source	Date Signed	Seasons Played	Apps	Subs	Gls
Everton	App	07/77				

League Club	Source	Date Signed	Seasons Played	Apps	Subs	Gls
Doncaster Rov	Glasgow Celtic	07/79	79-84	241	3	15
Scunthorpe U	Tr	08/85	85-87	113	4	7
Rotherham U	Tr	08/88	88-91	103	2	2

RUSSELL William Peter (Peter)
Born: Gornal, West Midlands, England, 16 January, 1935 — CH

Wolverhampton W	Jnr	10/52	54-55	3	-	0
Notts Co	Tr	03/56	55-58	106	-	6

RUSSO Gary
Born: Hemsby, Norfolk, England, 2 August, 1956 — FB

Ipswich T	App	08/74				
Bournemouth	Tr	07/75	75	1	0	0

RUSSON Ronald (Ron)
Born: Wednesbury, West Midlands, England, 10 December, 1928 — CH
Died: Stourbridge, West Midlands, England, 1981

Wolverhampton W	Jnr	04/46				
Walsall	Hednesford T	05/48	48-54	145	-	1

RUST Nicholas Charles Irwin (Nicky)
Born: Ely, Cambridgeshire, England, 25 September, 1974 — G
England: Youth

Brighton & HA	Arsenal (YT)	07/93	93-97	177	0	0
Barnet	Tr	08/98	98	2	0	0

RUSTER Sebastien
Born: Marseille, France, 6 September, 1982 — F

Swindon T	AS Cannes (FRA)	10/03	03	0	2	0

RUTHERFORD Colin
Born: Rowlands Gill, Tyne and Wear, England, 11 July, 1944 — WH

Sunderland	Jnr	07/61				
Barnsley	Tr	06/63	63	1	-	0

RUTHERFORD Greg David
Born: North Shields, Tyne and Wear, England, 17 May, 1994 — RM

Hartlepool U	Sch	07/12	11-13	0	9	1

RUTHERFORD Ian Stewart
Born: Hitchin, Hertfordshire, England, 24 December, 1972 — F

Crewe Alex	Luton T (YT)	06/91	91	0	1	0

RUTHERFORD Jonathan Paul (Paul)
Born: Sunderland, England, 23 February, 1967 — F

Newcastle U	App	07/85				
Scarborough	Meadowbank Thistle	09/94	94	6	2	1

RUTHERFORD Joseph Henry Hamilton (Joe)
Born: Fatfield, Tyne and Wear, England, 20 September, 1914 — G
Died: Sutton Coldfield, West Midlands, England, 27 December, 1994

Southport	Birtley Colliery	10/36	36-38	88	-	0
Aston Villa	Tr	02/39	38-51	148	-	0

RUTHERFORD Mark Robin
Born: Birmingham, England, 25 March, 1972 — M

Birmingham C	YT	07/90	89-90	1	4	0
Shrewsbury T (L)	Shelbourne (ROI)	02/94	93	7	7	0
Shrewsbury T (L)	Shelbourne (ROI)	09/98	98	0	3	0

RUTHERFORD Michael Alan
Born: Sidcup, SE London, England, 6 June, 1972 — M

Queens Park Rgrs	YT	12/89	89	1	1	0

RUTHERFORD Paul Leslie
Born: Hoylake, Wirral, England, 10 July, 1987 — RW

Chester C	Jnr	10/05	05-08	22	35	1

RUTHERFORD Robert (Bobby)
Born: South Shields, Tyne and Wear, England, 20 April, 1922 — LW
Died: North Shields, Tyne and Wear, England, 23 October, 2004

Newcastle U	Wallsend St Luke's	03/44				
Gateshead	Tr	11/45	46-52	9	-	2

RUTHERFORD Robert Alan (Bobby)
Born: Carlisle, Cumbria, England, 28 July, 1953 — M
England: Schools

Leeds U	App	08/70				
Workington	Tr	11/72	72	1	1	0

RUTHERFORD William John (Bill)
Born: Bellshill, Lanarkshire, Scotland, 23 January, 1930 — LH
Died: Southport, Merseyside, England, 29 April, 1980

Darlington	Stirling A	07/52	52-58	251	-	3
Southport	Tr	07/59	59-63	176	-	7

RUTLEY Peter
Born: Exeter, England, 19 May, 1946 — RH/IF

Exeter C	App	07/63	62-64	16	-	0

RUTTER Charles Frederick (Charlie)
Born: Poplar, E London, England, 22 December, 1927 — RB
Died: Cardiff, Wales, 19 October, 2012
England: B-1

Cardiff C	Taunton T	09/49	50-57	118	-	0
Exeter C	Tr	08/58				

RUTTER Cyril Hutton
Born: Leeds, England, 21 February, 1933 — D

Portsmouth	Jnr	07/51	53-62	171	-	0

RUTTER David Brian (Brian)
Born: Poplar, E London, England, 11 May, 1933 — IF
Died: Essex, England, July, 2014

Crystal Palace	Cardiff C (Am)	11/54	54	3	-	1

RUTTER John Thomas
Born: Warrington, Cheshire, England, 13 September, 1952 — FB

Wolverhampton W	App	09/70				
Bournemouth	Tr	08/73	73	2	2	0
Exeter C	Tr	07/74	74-75	31	1	1
Stockport Co	Tr	08/76	76-85	400	4	10

RUTTER Keith Gregg
Born: Leeds, England, 10 September, 1931 — CH

Queens Park Rgrs	Methley U	07/54	54-62	339	-	1
Colchester U	Tr	02/63	62-63	63	-	0

RUTTER Stephen John (Steve)
Born: Erith, SE London, England, 24 July, 1968 — F

Maidstone U	Kettering T	02/92	91	0	1	0

RYALLS Brian
Born: Hemsworth, West Yorkshire, England, 7 July, 1932 — G
Died: Barnsley, South Yorkshire, England, 4 June, 2009

Sheffield Wed	Grimethorpe Colliery	01/53	53-57	41	-	0

RYAN Darragh Joseph
Born: Haywards Heath, West Sussex, England, 21 May, 1980 — F

Brighton & HA	YT	03/98	97-98	4	5	2

RYAN Darren Thomas
Born: Oswestry, Shropshire, England, 3 July, 1972 — LW

Shrewsbury T	YT	10/90	90-91	3	1	0
Chester C	Tr	08/92	92	5	12	2
Stockport Co	Tr	01/93	92-93	29	7	6
Rochdale	Tr	07/94	94-95	19	13	2
Chester C	Tr	03/96	95	2	2	1

RYAN David Peter
Born: Failsworth, Greater Manchester, England, 5 January, 1957 — G

Manchester U	App	07/74				
Port Vale	L	01/76	75	1	0	0
Southport	Tr	03/76	75-76	23	0	0

RYAN Derek Anthony
Born: Dublin, Republic of Ireland, 2 January, 1967 — M

Wolverhampton W	App	10/84	84-86	23	10	5

RYAN Eric William
Born: Oswestry, Shropshire, England, 6 January, 1933 — FB

Mansfield T	Oswestry T	05/51	54-56	20	-	0

RYAN George
Born: Glasgow, Scotland, 29 December, 1931 — CF

Sheffield U	Hull C (Am)	05/51				
Chesterfield	Third Lanark	07/54	54	3	-	0

RYAN Gerard Joseph (Gerry)
Born: Dublin, Republic of Ireland, 4 October, 1955 — W/F
Republic of Ireland: 16

Derby Co	Bohemians (ROI)	09/77	77-78	30	0	4
Brighton & HA	Tr	09/78	78-84	131	41	32

RYAN Jack Liam
Born: Barrow, Cumbria, England, 5 April, 1996 — F

Preston NE	Sch	07/14	14	0	1	0

RYAN James (Jimmy)
Born: Maghull, Merseyside, England, 6 September, 1988 — RW
Republic of Ireland: U21-4/Youth

Liverpool	Sch	07/06				
Shrewsbury T	L	08/07	07	0	1	0
Shrewsbury T	Tr	01/08	07	1	2	0
Accrington Stan	Tr	08/08	08-10	122	7	22
Scunthorpe U	Tr	07/11	11-12	61	8	4
Chesterfield	Tr	06/13	13-14	81	2	6

RYAN James (Jimmy)
Born: Stirling, Scotland, 12 May, 1945 — RW

Manchester U	Corrie Hearts	01/63	65-69	21	3	4
Luton T	Tr	04/70	70-76	172	12	21

RYAN James Patrick (Jimmy)
Born: Prestatyn, Denbighshire, Wales, 6 September, 1942 — CF
Wales: U23-1

League Club	Source	Date Signed	Seasons Played	Apps	Subs	Gls
Charlton Ath	Dulwich Hamlet	02/63	62-64	16	-	8
Millwall	Tr	02/65	64-65	12	0	2
Exeter C	Hastings U	01/67	66	20	0	5

RYAN John Bernard
Born: Failsworth, Greater Manchester, England, 18 February, 1962 LB/M
England: U21-1

League Club	Source	Date Signed	Seasons Played	Apps	Subs	Gls
Oldham Ath	App	02/80	81-82	77	0	8
Newcastle U	Tr	08/83	83-84	28	0	1
Sheffield Wed	Tr	09/84	84	5	3	1
Oldham Ath	Tr	08/85	85-86	20	3	0
Mansfield T	Tr	10/87	87-88	53	9	1
Chesterfield	Tr	06/89	89-90	81	1	6
Rochdale	Tr	06/91	91-93	64	6	2
Bury	Tr	12/93	93	8	1	0

RYAN John Gilbert
Born: Lewisham, SE London, England, 20 July, 1947 RB/M

League Club	Source	Date Signed	Seasons Played	Apps	Subs	Gls
Arsenal	Maidstone U	10/64				
Fulham	Tr	07/65	65-68	42	5	1
Luton T	Tr	07/69	69-75	264	2	10
Norwich C	Tr	08/76	76-79	113	3	26
Sheffield U	Seattle Sounders (USA)	09/80	80-81	56	0	2
Manchester C	Tr	01/82	81	19	0	0
Stockport Co	Tr	08/83	83	1	1	0
Chester C	Tr	09/83	83	4	0	0
Cambridge U	Tr	10/84	84	5	0	0

RYAN John Joseph (Buck)
Born: Alloa, Stirlingshire, Scotland, 16 October, 1930 IF
Died: Swindon, England, 19 August, 2008

League Club	Source	Date Signed	Seasons Played	Apps	Subs	Gls
Charlton Ath	Chippenham T	02/54	54-58	61	-	32
Newcastle U	Tr	03/59				
Bristol C	Tr	07/60	60	3	-	0

RYAN John Oliver
Born: Liverpool, England, 28 October, 1944 RW

League Club	Source	Date Signed	Seasons Played	Apps	Subs	Gls
Tranmere Rov		08/64				
Luton T	Wigan Ath	10/67	67-68	17	1	1
Notts Co	Tr	05/69	69	22	2	1

RYAN Keith James
Born: Northampton, England, 25 June, 1970 M

League Club	Source	Date Signed	Seasons Played	Apps	Subs	Gls
Wycombe W	Berkhamsted T	07/90	93-04	299	52	29

RYAN Kenneth (Ken)
Born: Accrington, Lancashire, England, 20 September, 1936 G

League Club	Source	Date Signed	Seasons Played	Apps	Subs	Gls
Accrington Stan (Am)	Accrington Collieries	04/59	58	1	-	0

RYAN Laurence John (Laurie)
Born: Watford, Hertfordshire, England, 15 October, 1963 F

League Club	Source	Date Signed	Seasons Played	Apps	Subs	Gls
Cambridge U	Dunstable	04/88	87-89	39	12	13

RYAN Leon Michael
Born: Sunderland, England, 8 November, 1982 CD

League Club	Source	Date Signed	Seasons Played	Apps	Subs	Gls
Scunthorpe U	Kotkan TP (FIN)	09/02	02	0	2	0

RYAN Michael Joseph (Mike)
Born: Welwyn Garden City, Hertfordshire, England, 14 October, 1930 RW
Died: Ealing, W London, England, September, 2006

League Club	Source	Date Signed	Seasons Played	Apps	Subs	Gls
Arsenal	Chase of Chertsey	07/48				
Lincoln C	Tr	06/52	52	7	-	0
York C	Tr	01/53	52	4	-	0

RYAN Michael Stuart (Mike)
Born: Stockport, Greater Manchester, England, 3 October, 1979 LB

League Club	Source	Date Signed	Seasons Played	Apps	Subs	Gls
Manchester U	YT	07/98				
Wrexham	Tr	03/99	99	4	3	0

RYAN Oliver Paul
Born: Boston, Lincolnshire, England, 26 September, 1985 F

League Club	Source	Date Signed	Seasons Played	Apps	Subs	Gls
Lincoln C	Sch	07/05	04-07	8	30	0

RYAN Reginald Alphonsus (Reg)
Born: Dublin, Republic of Ireland, 30 October, 1925 IF
Died: Birmingham, England, 13 February, 1997
Republic of Ireland: 16//Northern Ireland: 1

League Club	Source	Date Signed	Seasons Played	Apps	Subs	Gls
West Bromwich A	Nuneaton Bor	04/45	46-54	234	-	28
Derby Co	Tr	07/55	55-58	133	-	30
Coventry C	Tr	09/58	58-60	65	-	9

RYAN Richard (Richie)
Born: Kilkenny, Republic of Ireland, 6 January, 1985 DM
Republic of Ireland: Youth

League Club	Source	Date Signed	Seasons Played	Apps	Subs	Gls
Sunderland	Sch	01/02	02	0	2	0
Scunthorpe U	Tr	03/05	05	7	6	0
Boston U	Tr	07/06	06	9	4	0

RYAN Robert Paul (Robbie)
Born: Dublin, Republic of Ireland, 16 May, 1977 LB
Republic of Ireland: U21-12/Youth/Schools

League Club	Source	Date Signed	Seasons Played	Apps	Subs	Gls
Huddersfield T	Belvedere (ROI)	07/94	96-97	12	3	0
Millwall	Tr	01/98	97-03	209	17	2
Bristol Rov	Tr	07/04	04-05	53	1	0

RYAN Thomas Stanley (Tom)
Born: Windlesham, Surrey, England, 9 July, 1952 CD

League Club	Source	Date Signed	Seasons Played	Apps	Subs	Gls
Reading	App	05/70	70	1	0	0

RYAN Timothy James (Tim)
Born: Stockport, Greater Manchester, England, 10 December, 1974 CD
England: Semi Pro-14

League Club	Source	Date Signed	Seasons Played	Apps	Subs	Gls
Scunthorpe U	YT	04/93	92-93	1	1	0
Doncaster Rov	Buxton	08/96	96	22	6	0
Doncaster Rov	Southport	05/00	03-05	86	2	6
Peterborough U	Tr	03/06	05	6	1	0
Boston U	Tr	05/06	06	23	0	4
Darlington	Tr	01/07	06-08	38	4	1

RYAN Vaughan William
Born: Westminster, Central London, England, 2 September, 1968 M
England: Schools

League Club	Source	Date Signed	Seasons Played	Apps	Subs	Gls
Wimbledon	App	08/86	86-91	67	15	3
Sheffield U	L	01/89	88	2	1	0
Leyton Orient	Tr	08/92	92-94	40	4	0

RYDEN Hugh Johnston
Born: Dumbarton, Dunbartonshire, Scotland, 7 April, 1943 F/M

League Club	Source	Date Signed	Seasons Played	Apps	Subs	Gls
Leeds U	Yoker Ath	10/60				
Bristol Rov	Tr	06/62	62	8	-	4
Stockport Co	Greenock Morton	07/63	63	38	-	9
Chester C	Tr	06/64	64-67	140	1	44
Halifax T	Tr	11/67	67-69	54	1	6
Stockport Co	Tr	12/69	69-72	112	11	15

RYDEN John Johnston
Born: Dumbarton, Dunbartonshire, Scotland, 18 February, 1931 CH
Died: Keston, SE London, England, 16 August, 2013

League Club	Source	Date Signed	Seasons Played	Apps	Subs	Gls
Accrington Stan	Alloa Ath	02/54	53-55	80	-	1
Tottenham H	Tr	11/55	55-58	63	-	2
Watford	Tr	06/61	61	24	-	1

RYDER Derek Francis
Born: Leeds, England, 18 February, 1947 LB

League Club	Source	Date Signed	Seasons Played	Apps	Subs	Gls
Leeds U	Jnr	02/64				
Cardiff C	Tr	06/66	66	4	0	0
Rochdale	Tr	07/68	68-71	167	0	1
Southport	Tr	07/72	72-73	80	2	2

RYDER Robert (Bob)
Born: Bolton, Greater Manchester, England, 11 July, 1943 LB
Died: Oldham, Greater Manchester, England, December, 2000

League Club	Source	Date Signed	Seasons Played	Apps	Subs	Gls
Gillingham	Nantwich T	01/65	64-67	8	0	0

RYDER Stuart Henry
Born: Sutton Coldfield, West Midlands, England, 6 November, 1973 CD
England: U21-3

League Club	Source	Date Signed	Seasons Played	Apps	Subs	Gls
Walsall	YT	07/92	92-97	86	15	5
Mansfield T	Tr	07/98	98	18	4	2

RYDER Terence Roy (Terry)
Born: Norwich, England, 3 June, 1928 RW/IF
Died: Norwich, England, 24 January, 2012

League Club	Source	Date Signed	Seasons Played	Apps	Subs	Gls
Norwich C	City W	09/46	46-49	46	-	12
Portsmouth	Tr	10/50	50-51	14	-	4
Swindon T	Tr	07/52	52	33	-	13

RYECRAFT Frederick (Fred)
Born: Southall, W London, England, 29 August, 1939 G

League Club	Source	Date Signed	Seasons Played	Apps	Subs	Gls
Brentford	Southall	09/59	62-63	33	-	0

RYLANDS David Robert (Dave)
Born: Liverpool, England, 7 March, 1953 CD

League Club	Source	Date Signed	Seasons Played	Apps	Subs	Gls
Liverpool	App	03/70				
Hereford U	Tr	09/74	74-75	22	0	0
Newport Co	L	03/75	74	3	0	1
Hartlepool U	L	03/76	75	11	0	0
Halifax T	Tr	06/76	76	5	0	0

RYMER George Herbert
Born: Barnsley, South Yorkshire, England, 6 October, 1923 G

League Club	Source	Date Signed	Seasons Played	Apps	Subs	Gls
Barnsley	Ardsley Victoria	12/43	46	3	-	0
Accrington Stan	Tr	02/47	46	8	-	0

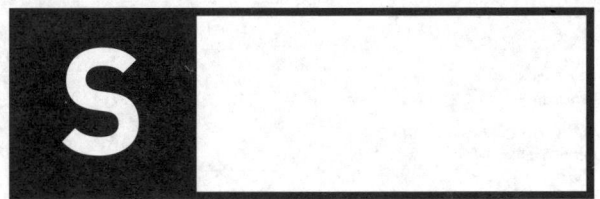

League Club	Source	Date Signed	Seasons Played	Career Record Apps	Subs	Gls

SA Orlando
Born: Barcelos, Portugal, 26 May, 1988 F
Portugal: 1/U21-7

League Club	Source	Date Signed	Seasons Played	Apps	Subs	Gls
Fulham	FC Porto (POR)	08/11	11	3	4	1

SAAH Brian Ebo
Born: Hornchurch, E London, England, 16 December, 1986 CD
England: Semi Pro-1

League Club	Source	Date Signed	Seasons Played	Apps	Subs	Gls
Leyton Orient	Sch	08/06	03-08	82	11	1
Torquay U	Cambridge U	08/11	11-12	78	0	2
Dagenham & Red	Tr	07/13	13-14	63	3	0

SABELLA Alejandro (Alex)
Born: Buenos Aires, Argentina, 5 November, 1954 LM
Argentina: 8

League Club	Source	Date Signed	Seasons Played	Apps	Subs	Gls
Sheffield U	River Plate (ARG)	08/78	78-79	76	0	8
Leeds U	Tr	06/80	80	22	1	2

SABIN Arthur Henry
Born: Kingstanding, West Midlands, England, 25 January, 1939 G
Died: Birmingham, England, March, 1958

League Club	Source	Date Signed	Seasons Played	Apps	Subs	Gls
Aston Villa	Jnr	01/57	56-57	2	-	0

SABIN Eric
Born: Paris, France, 22 January, 1975 F
Martinique: 3

League Club	Source	Date Signed	Seasons Played	Apps	Subs	Gls
Swindon T	Wasquehal (FRA)	07/01	01-02	60	13	9
Queens Park Rgrs	Tr	07/03	03	3	7	1
Boston U	L	03/04	03	2	0	0
Northampton T	Tr	03/04	03-05	41	16	13
Oxford U	Tr	08/05	05	28	1	7

SABORIO Alvaro Alberto
Born: Quesada, Costa Rica, 25 March, 1982 F
Costa Rica: 103/U23-15

League Club	Source	Date Signed	Seasons Played	Apps	Subs	Gls
Bristol C (L)	FC Sion (SUI)	09/09	09	11	8	2

SADDINGTON Nigel
Born: Sunderland, England, 9 December, 1965 CD

League Club	Source	Date Signed	Seasons Played	Apps	Subs	Gls
Doncaster Rov	SC Vaux	09/84	84	6	0	0
Sunderland	Roker FC	01/86	86	3	0	0
Carlisle U	Tr	02/88	87-89	97	0	15

SADLER David
Born: Yalding, Kent, England, 5 February, 1946 CD/CF
England: 4/FLge-2/U23-3/Amateur-2/Youth

League Club	Source	Date Signed	Seasons Played	Apps	Subs	Gls
Manchester U	Maidstone U	02/63	63-73	266	6	22
Preston NE	Tr	11/73	73-76	104	1	3

SADLER George Handel
Born: Whitwell, Derbyshire, England, 7 May, 1915 FB
Died: Burnley, Lancashire, England, 30 December, 2004

League Club	Source	Date Signed	Seasons Played	Apps	Subs	Gls
West Ham U	Gainsborough Trinity	12/38	46	1	-	0

SADLER Matthew (Matt)
Born: Birmingham, England, 26 February, 1985 LB
England: Youth

League Club	Source	Date Signed	Seasons Played	Apps	Subs	Gls
Birmingham C	Sch	04/02	02-07	49	2	0
Northampton T	L	11/03	03	7	0	0
Watford	Tr	01/08	07-08	29	1	0
Stockport Co	L	01/10	09	20	0	0
Shrewsbury T	L	07/10	10	46	0	0
Walsall	Tr	07/11	11	46	0	1
Crawley T	Tr	06/12	12-13	92	0	2
Rotherham U	Tr	06/14				
Crawley T	L	09/14	14	10	0	0
Oldham Ath	L	03/15	14	7	1	0

SADLIER Richard Thomas
Born: Dublin, Republic of Ireland, 14 January, 1979 F
Republic of Ireland: 1/U21-2/Youth

League Club	Source	Date Signed	Seasons Played	Apps	Subs	Gls
Millwall	Belvedere (ROI)	08/96	96-03	103	42	34

SAEIJS Jan-Paul Frederik Daniel
Born: Den Haag, Netherlands, 20 June, 1978 CD

League Club	Source	Date Signed	Seasons Played	Apps	Subs	Gls
Southampton (L)	Roda JC (NED)	01/09	08	20	0	2

SAFRI Youssef
Born: Casablanca, Morocco, 1 March, 1977 DM

League Club	Source	Date Signed	Seasons Played	Career Record Apps	Subs	Gls

Morocco: 77

League Club	Source	Date Signed	Seasons Played	Apps	Subs	Gls
Coventry C	Raja Casablanca (MOR)	08/01	01-03	87	4	1
Norwich C	Tr	07/04	04-06	68	15	3
Southampton	Tr	08/07	07	37	0	0

SAGANOWSKI Marek
Born: Lodz, Poland, 31 October, 1978 F
Poland: 35

League Club	Source	Date Signed	Seasons Played	Apps	Subs	Gls
Southampton	Troyes AC (FRA)	01/07	06-09	42	26	19

SAGAR Edward (Ted)
Born: Campsall, South Yorkshire, England, 7 February, 1910 G
Died: Liverpool, England, 16 October, 1986
England: 4/FLge-5//Northern Ireland: NILge-1

League Club	Source	Date Signed	Seasons Played	Apps	Subs	Gls
Everton	Thorne Colliery	03/29	29-52	463	-	0

SAGARE Jacob Kent (Jake)
Born: Yakima, Washington, USA, 5 April, 1980 F

League Club	Source	Date Signed	Seasons Played	Apps	Subs	Gls
Grimsby T	Portland Timbers (USA)	11/02	02	1	0	0

SAGBO Yannick Anister
Born: Marseille, France, 12 April, 1988 F
Ivory Coast: 2/U23-5

League Club	Source	Date Signed	Seasons Played	Apps	Subs	Gls
Hull C	ET Gaillard (FRA)	07/13	13-14	16	16	2
Wolverhampton W	L	09/14	14	1	3	0

SAGE Melvyn (Mel)
Born: Gillingham, Kent, England, 24 March, 1964 RB

League Club	Source	Date Signed	Seasons Played	Apps	Subs	Gls
Gillingham	App	03/82	81-85	126	6	5
Derby Co	Tr	08/86	86-91	137	3	4

SAGE Roland Frank (Frank)
Born: Chipping Sodbury, Avon, England, 31 May, 1924 WH
Died: Gloucester, England, December, 2000

League Club	Source	Date Signed	Seasons Played	Apps	Subs	Gls
Cardiff C		02/45				
Newport Co	Tr	04/48	47-48	3	-	0

SAGNA Bacary
Born: Sens, France, 14 February, 1983 RB
France: 49/U21-12

League Club	Source	Date Signed	Seasons Played	Apps	Subs	Gls
Arsenal	AJ Auxerre (FRA)	07/07	07-13	206	7	4
Manchester C	Tr	07/14	14	8	1	0

SAHA Louis Laurent
Born: Paris, France, 8 August, 1978 F
France: 20/U21-8/Youth

League Club	Source	Date Signed	Seasons Played	Apps	Subs	Gls
Newcastle U (L)	FC Metz (FRA)	01/99	98	5	6	1
Fulham	FC Metz (FRA)	06/00	00-03	100	17	53
Manchester U	Tr	01/04	03-07	52	34	28
Everton	Tr	09/08	08-11	65	32	27
Tottenham H	Tr	01/12	11	5	5	3
Sunderland	Tr	08/12	12	0	11	0

SAHAR Ben
Born: Halon, Israel, 10 August, 1989 F
Israel: 33/U21-16/Youth

League Club	Source	Date Signed	Seasons Played	Apps	Subs	Gls
Chelsea	Sch	07/07	06	0	3	0
Queens Park Rgrs	L	08/07	07	6	3	0
Sheffield Wed	L	02/08	07	8	4	3

SAHIN Nuri Kazim
Born: Ludenscheid, Germany, 5 September, 1988 M
Turkey: 47/U21-11/Youth

League Club	Source	Date Signed	Seasons Played	Apps	Subs	Gls
Liverpool (L)	Real Madrid (SPN)	08/12	12	7	0	1

SAHLIN Dan
Born: Falun, Sweden, 18 April, 1967 F
Sweden: 3

League Club	Source	Date Signed	Seasons Played	Apps	Subs	Gls
Birmingham C (L)	Hammarby IF (SWE)	11/95	95	0	1	0

SAHNOUN Nicolas Omar Mickael
Born: Bordeaux, France, 3 September, 1980 M

League Club	Source	Date Signed	Seasons Played	Apps	Subs	Gls
Fulham (L)	Bordeaux (FRA)	10/00	00	2	5	0

SAIB Moussa
Born: Tissemsilt, Algeria, 6 March, 1969 M
Algeria: 74

League Club	Source	Date Signed	Seasons Played	Apps	Subs	Gls
Tottenham H	Valencia (SPN)	02/98	97-98	3	10	1

SAILE Michael Anthony (Mike)
Born: Heywood, Greater Manchester, England, 31 December, 1950 LB
England: Youth

League Club	Source	Date Signed	Seasons Played	Apps	Subs	Gls
Bury	App	01/69	68-72	92	1	0

SAINSBURY Kim
Born: Reading, England, 21 September, 1957 F

League Club	Source	Date Signed	Seasons Played	Apps	Subs	Gls
Reading	App	-	74	0	1	0

ST AIMIE Kieron Lloyd Junior
Born: Wembley, NW London, England, 4 May, 1989 F

League Club	Source	Date Signed	Seasons Played	Apps	Subs	Gls
Queens Park Rgrs	Sch	05/07				
Barnet	Tr	01/08	05-08	6	7	0

SAINTE-LUCE Kevin Privat
Born: Point-a-Pitre, Guadeloupe, 28 April, 1993 — W

League Club	Source	Date Signed	Seasons Played	Apps	Subs	Gls
Cardiff C	Sch	07/12				
AFC Wimbledon	Tr	02/13	12-14	9	37	3

ST JOHN Ian
Born: Motherwell, Lanarkshire, Scotland, 7 June, 1938 — CF
Scotland: 21/SLge-4/U23-2

League Club	Source	Date Signed	Seasons Played	Apps	Subs	Gls
Liverpool	Motherwell	04/61	61-70	334	2	95
Coventry C	Hellenic (RSA)	09/71	71	18	0	3
Tranmere Rov	Cape Town C (RSA)	10/72	72	9	0	1

ST JUSTE Jason Valentine
Born: Leeds, England, 21 September, 1985 — LW

League Club	Source	Date Signed	Seasons Played	Apps	Subs	Gls
Darlington	Garforth T	09/04	04	9	6	2
Southampton	Garforth T	09/05				

ST LEDGER-HALL Sean Patrick
Born: Birmingham, England, 28 December, 1984 — CD
Republic of Ireland: 37

League Club	Source	Date Signed	Seasons Played	Apps	Subs	Gls
Peterborough U	Sch	07/03	02-05	77	2	1
Preston NE	Tr	07/06	06-10	181	4	10
Middlesbrough	L	09/09	09	14	1	2
Leicester C	Tr	07/11	11-13	32	4	0
Millwall	L	03/12	12	5	1	0

SAINTY John Albert
Born: Poplar, E London, England, 24 March, 1946 — F/M
England: Schools

League Club	Source	Date Signed	Seasons Played	Apps	Subs	Gls
Tottenham H	App	07/63				
Reading	Tr	08/67	67-69	63	8	19
Bournemouth	Tr	02/70	69-73	111	7	20
Mansfield T	L	11/72	72	3	0	0
Aldershot	Tr	08/74	74-75	26	3	0

SAKHO Diafra
Born: Guediawaye, Senegal, 24 December, 1989 — F
Senegal: 3

League Club	Source	Date Signed	Seasons Played	Apps	Subs	Gls
West Ham U	FC Metz (FRA)	08/14	14	20	3	10

SAKHO Lamine
Born: Dakar, Senegal, 28 September, 1977 — LW
France: U21//Senegal: 57

League Club	Source	Date Signed	Seasons Played	Apps	Subs	Gls
Leeds U (L)	Olymp Marseille (FRA)	08/03	03	9	8	1

SAKHO Mamadou
Born: Paris, France, 13 February, 1990 — CD
France: 26/U21-15/Youth

League Club	Source	Date Signed	Seasons Played	Apps	Subs	Gls
Liverpool	Paris St-Germain (FRA)	09/13	13-14	32	2	1

SAKIRI Artim
Born: Struga, Macedonia, 23 September, 1973 — M
Macedonia: 72

League Club	Source	Date Signed	Seasons Played	Apps	Subs	Gls
West Bromwich A	CSKA Sofia (BUL)	08/03	03-04	8	20	1

SAKO Bakary
Born: Paris, France, 26 April, 1988 — LW
France: U21-10//Mali: 14

League Club	Source	Date Signed	Seasons Played	Apps	Subs	Gls
Wolverhampton W	Saint-Etienne (FRA)	08/12	12-14	111	7	36

SAKO Marike
Born: Paris, France, 17 November, 1981 — W

League Club	Source	Date Signed	Seasons Played	Apps	Subs	Gls
Torquay U	Delemont (SUI)	07/05	05	10	15	3
Rochdale	Tr	08/06	06	14	3	3

SALAH Mohamed
Born: Basyoun, Egypt, 15 June, 1992 — W
Egypt: 37/U23-11/Youth

League Club	Source	Date Signed	Seasons Played	Apps	Subs	Gls
Chelsea	FC Basel (SUI)	01/13	13-14	6	7	2

SALAKO Andrew Olumide (Andy)
Born: Lagos, Nigeria, 8 November, 1972 — FB

League Club	Source	Date Signed	Seasons Played	Apps	Subs	Gls
Charlton Ath	YT	04/91	90	1	0	0

SALAKO John Akin
Born: Lagos, Nigeria, 11 February, 1969 — LW
England: 5

League Club	Source	Date Signed	Seasons Played	Apps	Subs	Gls
Crystal Palace	App	11/86	86-94	172	43	22
Swansea C	L	08/89	89	13	0	3
Coventry C	Tr	08/95	95-97	68	4	4
Bolton W	Tr	03/98	97	0	7	0
Fulham	Tr	07/98	98	7	3	1
Charlton Ath	Tr	08/99	99-01	10	37	2
Reading	Tr	11/01	01-03	96	15	13
Brentford	Tr	08/04	04	30	5	4

SALATHIEL David Neil (Neil)
Born: Wrexham, Wales, 19 November, 1962 — RB
Wales: Schools

League Club	Source	Date Signed	Seasons Played	Apps	Subs	Gls
Wrexham	Sheffield Wed (Jnr)	05/80	80	4	0	0
Crewe Alex	Tr	06/81	81-82	64	1	0
Wrexham	Arcadia Shep's (RSA)	12/83	83-89	239	1	3

SALCIDO Carlos Arnoldo
Born: Ocotlan, Mexico, 2 April, 1980 — LB
Mexico: 124/U23-9

League Club	Source	Date Signed	Seasons Played	Apps	Subs	Gls
Fulham	PSV Eindhoven (NED)	08/10	10	22	1	0

SALE Mark David
Born: Burton-on-Trent, Staffordshire, England, 27 February, 1972 — F

League Club	Source	Date Signed	Seasons Played	Apps	Subs	Gls
Stoke C	YT	07/90	89	0	2	0
Cambridge U	Tr	05/91				
Birmingham C	Rocester	03/92	91-92	11	10	0
Torquay U	Tr	03/93	92-93	30	14	8
Preston NE	Tr	07/94	94	10	3	7
Mansfield T	Tr	07/95	95-96	36	9	12
Colchester U	Tr	03/97	96-98	69	11	12
Plymouth Arg	L	03/99	98	8	0	1

SALEM Yannick
Born: Amiens, France, 29 March, 1983 — F
DR Congo: 3

League Club	Source	Date Signed	Seasons Played	Apps	Subs	Gls
Stockport Co	Eintracht Trier (GER)	10/10	10	2	3	0

SALES Ronald Duncan (Ronnie)
Born: South Shields, Tyne and Wear, England, 19 September, 1920 — CH
Died: South Shields, Tyne and Wear, England, August, 1995

League Club	Source	Date Signed	Seasons Played	Apps	Subs	Gls
Newcastle U	Reyrolles	07/42				
Leyton Orient	Tr	05/47	47-48	46	-	3
Hartlepool U	Colchester U	08/50	50	3	-	0

SALGADO Miguel Angel (Michel)
Born: Pontevedra, Spain, 22 October, 1975 — RB
Spain: 53/U21-10

League Club	Source	Date Signed	Seasons Played	Apps	Subs	Gls
Blackburn Rov	Real Madrid (SPN)	08/09	09-11	61	5	0

SALIFOU Moustapha
Born: Lome, Togo, 1 June, 1983 — M
Togo: 59

League Club	Source	Date Signed	Seasons Played	Apps	Subs	Gls
Aston Villa	FC Wil (SUI)	08/07	07	0	4	0

SALIHU Lumbardh
Born: Vitina, Yugoslavia, 18 November, 1992 — F

League Club	Source	Date Signed	Seasons Played	Apps	Subs	Gls
Northampton T	SV Wienerberg (AUT)	07/11	11	0	1	0

SALISBURY Gareth
Born: Caernarfon, Gwynedd, Wales, 11 March, 1941 — IF

League Club	Source	Date Signed	Seasons Played	Apps	Subs	Gls
Wrexham	Jnr	05/59	59-61	11	-	0
Norwich C	Tr	07/62				
Luton T	Tr	07/63	63	12	-	2
Colchester U	Tr	07/64	64	15	-	2
Chesterfield	Tr	07/65	65	34	0	9

SALL Abdou Ahmed
Born: Dakar, Senegal, 1 November, 1980 — CD

League Club	Source	Date Signed	Seasons Played	Apps	Subs	Gls
Kidderminster Hrs	Toulouse (FRA)	08/01	01-02	31	0	2
Oxford U	L	11/02	02	0	1	0
Kidderminster Hrs	Revel (FRA)	02/04	03-04	19	2	0

SALLI Janne
Born: Seinajoki, Finland, 14 December, 1977 — FB
Finland: 8/U21/Youth

League Club	Source	Date Signed	Seasons Played	Apps	Subs	Gls
Barnsley	Haka Valkeakoski (FIN)	11/00	00	6	1	0

SALMAN Danis Mahmut Mehmet
Born: Famagusta, Cyprus, 12 March, 1960 — D
England: Youth

League Club	Source	Date Signed	Seasons Played	Apps	Subs	Gls
Brentford	App	08/77	75-85	316	9	8
Millwall	Tr	08/86	86-89	85	8	4
Plymouth Arg	Tr	03/90	89-91	71	3	4
Peterborough U	L	03/92	91	1	0	0
Torquay U	Tr	09/92	92	20	0	0

SALMON Alexander Mark (Alex)
Born: Liverpool, England, 9 July, 1994 — F

League Club	Source	Date Signed	Seasons Played	Apps	Subs	Gls
Carlisle U	Sch	06/13	12	0	2	0

SALMON Leonard Alexander (Len)
Born: West Kirby, Wirral, England, 24 June, 1912 — WH
Died: Birkenhead, Wirral, England, February, 1995

League Club	Source	Date Signed	Seasons Played	Apps	Subs	Gls
New Brighton	Hoylake	10/34	34-35	30	-	2
Burnley	South Liverpool	09/41				
Tranmere Rov	Tr	09/46	46-47	30	-	1

SALMON Mark Maurice
Born: Dublin, Republic of Ireland, 31 October, 1988 — M
Republic of Ireland: Youth

League Club	Source	Date Signed	Seasons Played	Apps	Subs	Gls
Wolverhampton W	Sch	11/06				
Port Vale	L	11/07	07	8	1	0

SALMON Michael Bernard (Mike)
Born: Leyland, Lancashire, England, 14 July, 1964 — G

League Club	Source	Date Signed	Seasons Played	Apps	Subs	Gls
Blackburn Rov	Jnr	10/81	81	1	0	0
Chester C	L	10/82	82	16	0	0
Stockport Co	Tr	08/83	83-85	118	0	0
Bolton W	Tr	07/86	86	26	0	0
Wrexham	Tr	03/87	86-88	100	0	0
Charlton Ath	Tr	07/89	90-97	148	0	0
Oxford U	L	12/98	98	1	0	0

SALMONS Geoffrey (Geoff)
Born: Mexborough, South Yorkshire, England, 14 January, 1948 — M

League Club	Source	Date Signed	Seasons Played	Apps	Subs	Gls
Sheffield U	Jnr	02/66	67-73	170	10	8
Stoke C	Tr	07/74	74-77	115	3	14
Sheffield U	L	09/77	77	5	0	0
Leicester C	Tr	10/77	77	25	1	4
Chesterfield	Tr	08/78	78-81	119	1	15

SALT Philip Thomas (Phil)
Born: Huddersfield, West Yorkshire, England, 2 March, 1979 — M

League Club	Source	Date Signed	Seasons Played	Apps	Subs	Gls
Oldham Ath	YT	07/97	97-00	12	10	0

SALT Samuel John (Sammy)
Born: Southport, Merseyside, England, 30 December, 1938 — LH
Died: Poulton-le-Fylde, Lancashire, England, 18 May, 1999

League Club	Source	Date Signed	Seasons Played	Apps	Subs	Gls
Blackpool	Jnr	01/56	60	18	-	0

SALTER Kenneth (Ken)
Born: Cullompton, Devon, England, 16 November, 1933 — G
Died: Taunton, Somerset, England, October, 2006

League Club	Source	Date Signed	Seasons Played	Apps	Subs	Gls
Exeter C	Cullompton	11/50	50	1	-	0

SALTER Mark Charles
Born: Oxford, England, 16 March, 1980 — F

League Club	Source	Date Signed	Seasons Played	Apps	Subs	Gls
Southend U	Frome T	10/02	02	5	8	1

SALTON Darren Brian
Born: Edinburgh, Scotland, 16 March, 1972 — CD
Scotland: U21-6/Youth/Schools

League Club	Source	Date Signed	Seasons Played	Apps	Subs	Gls
Luton T	YT	03/89	91-92	17	1	0

SALTOR Bruno
Born: Barcelona, Spain, 1 October, 1980 — RB

League Club	Source	Date Signed	Seasons Played	Apps	Subs	Gls
Brighton & HA	Valencia (SPN)	07/12	12-14	93	5	5

[SALVA] BALLESTA Vialcho Salvador
Born: Zaragoza, Spain, 22 May, 1975 — F
Spain: 4/U23-4/U21-9

League Club	Source	Date Signed	Seasons Played	Apps	Subs	Gls
Bolton W (L)	Valencia (SPN)	01/03	02	1	5	0

SALVAGE Barry John
Born: Bristol, England, 21 December, 1946 — LW
Died: Eastbourne, East Sussex, England, October, 1986

League Club	Source	Date Signed	Seasons Played	Apps	Subs	Gls
Fulham	Eastbourne U	09/67	67-68	7	0	0
Millwall	Tr	03/69	68	1	1	0
Queens Park Rgrs	Tr	03/71	70-72	16	5	1
Brentford	Tr	02/73	72-74	87	0	8
Millwall	Tr	08/75	75-76	43	12	9

SALVATI Marc Robert
Born: Middlesbrough, England, 5 March, 1983 — M

League Club	Source	Date Signed	Seasons Played	Apps	Subs	Gls
York C	YT	-	01	1	7	1

SAM Hector McLeod
Born: San Juan, Trinidad, 25 February, 1978 — F
Trinidad & Tobago: 20

League Club	Source	Date Signed	Seasons Played	Apps	Subs	Gls
Wrexham	San Juan Jab'h (TRD)	08/00	00-04	77	73	35
Port Vale	Tr	07/05	05	0	4	0
Walsall	Tr	07/06	06	28	14	7
Notts Co	Tr	07/07	07	7	13	1

SAM Lloyd Ekow
Born: Leeds, England, 27 September, 1984 — W
England: Youth

League Club	Source	Date Signed	Seasons Played	Apps	Subs	Gls
Charlton Ath	Sch	07/02	04-09	95	24	6
Leyton Orient	L	01/04	03	5	5	0
Sheffield Wed	L	08/06	06	4	0	0
Southend U	L	03/07	06	0	2	0
Leeds U	Tr	07/10	10-11	10	25	2
Notts Co	L	03/12	11	8	2	5

SAM-YORKE Delano Ezra
Born: Hammersmith, W London, England, 20 January, 1989 — F

League Club	Source	Date Signed	Seasons Played	Apps	Subs	Gls
Cambridge U	Basingstoke T	05/13	14	0	2	0

SAMARAS Giorgios
Born: Iraklion, Crete, Greece, 21 February, 1985 — F
Greece: 81/U21-5

League Club	Source	Date Signed	Seasons Played	Apps	Subs	Gls
Manchester C	Heerenveen (NED)	01/06	05-07	28	27	8
West Bromwich A	Glasgow Celtic	08/14	14	0	5	0

SAMBA Cherno
Born: Banjul, Gambia, 10 January, 1985 — F
England: Youth//Gambia: 4

League Club	Source	Date Signed	Seasons Played	Apps	Subs	Gls
Millwall	Sch	02/02				
Plymouth Arg	Cadiz (SPN)	08/06	06	1	12	1
Wrexham	L	01/07	06	1	2	0

SAMBA Veijeany Christopher (Chris)
Born: Paris, France, 28 March, 1984 — CD
Congo: 26

League Club	Source	Date Signed	Seasons Played	Apps	Subs	Gls
Blackburn Rov	Hertha Berlin (GER)	01/07	06-11	160	1	16
Queens Park Rgrs	Anzhi Makhachk'a (RUS)	01/13	12	10	0	0

SAMBROOK Andrew John (Andy)
Born: Chatham, Kent, England, 13 July, 1979 — FB
England: Schools

League Club	Source	Date Signed	Seasons Played	Apps	Subs	Gls
Gillingham	Jnr	-	96	0	1	0
Rushden & D	Hartwick College (USA)	08/01	01-04	48	21	0

SAMBROOK Raymond (Ray)
Born: Wolverhampton, England, 21 May, 1933 — LW
Died: Newport, Wales, March, 1999

League Club	Source	Date Signed	Seasons Played	Apps	Subs	Gls
Coventry C	Wednesfield	09/53	54-57	96	-	26
Manchester C	Tr	01/58	57-61	62	-	13
Doncaster Rov	Tr	06/62	62	8	-	0

SAMMELS Jonathan Charles (Jon)
Born: Ipswich, England, 23 July, 1945 — M
England: FLge-1/U23-9/Youth

League Club	Source	Date Signed	Seasons Played	Apps	Subs	Gls
Arsenal	App	08/62	62-70	212	3	39
Leicester C	Tr	07/71	71-77	236	5	21

SAMMON Conor
Born: Dublin, Republic of Ireland, 6 November, 1986 — F
Republic of Ireland: 9/U21-3

League Club	Source	Date Signed	Seasons Played	Apps	Subs	Gls
Wigan Ath	Kilmarnock	01/11	10-11	9	23	1
Derby Co	Tr	08/12	12-14	45	38	10
Ipswich T	L	08/14	14	8	11	1
Rotherham U	L	01/15	14	11	4	3

SAMPLE James (Jim)
Born: Morpeth, Northumberland, England, 5 November, 1921 — IF
Died: Bradford, England, 7 January, 1992

League Club	Source	Date Signed	Seasons Played	Apps	Subs	Gls
Bradford C	Ashington	08/47	47-48	8	-	2

SAMPSON Ian
Born: Wakefield, England, 14 November, 1968 — CD

League Club	Source	Date Signed	Seasons Played	Apps	Subs	Gls
Sunderland	Goole T	11/90	91-93	13	4	1
Northampton T	L	12/93	93	8	0	0
Northampton T	Tr	08/94	94-03	372	10	26

SAMPSON Jack
Born: Wigan, Greater Manchester, England, 14 April, 1993 — F
England: Youth

League Club	Source	Date Signed	Seasons Played	Apps	Subs	Gls
Bolton W	Sch	04/11				
Southend U	L	01/12	11	5	4	0
Accrington Stan	L	10/12	12	2	3	0
Morecambe	Tr	07/13	13-14	34	24	5

SAMPSON Peter Stanley
Born: Great Wakering, Essex, England, 9 July, 1927 — LH
Died: Congresbury, Somerset, England, 16 May, 2009

League Club	Source	Date Signed	Seasons Played	Apps	Subs	Gls
Bristol Rov	Devizes T	06/48	48-60	339	-	4

SAMPSON Raymond Victor (Ray)
Born: Swindon, England, 6 February, 1935 — IF

League Club	Source	Date Signed	Seasons Played	Apps	Subs	Gls
Swindon T	Jnr	05/52	53-58	64	-	10

SAMPSON Thomas William (Tommy)
Born: Southwark, S London, England, 18 August, 1954 — CD

League Club	Source	Date Signed	Seasons Played	Apps	Subs	Gls
Millwall	App	06/72	72	0	1	0

SAMSON Craig Ian
Born: Darvel, Ayrshire, Scotland, 1 April, 1984 — G
Scotland: U21-6

League Club	Source	Date Signed	Seasons Played	Apps	Subs	Gls
Hereford U	Dundee	07/08	08	10	1	0

SAMUEL Dominic James
Born: Southwark, S London, England, 1 May, 1994 — F
England: Youth

League Club	Source	Date Signed	Seasons Played	Apps	Subs	Gls
Reading	Sch	12/11	12	0	1	0
Colchester U	L	01/13	12	2	0	0
Dagenham & Red	L	01/14	13	1	0	0
Coventry C	L	01/15	14	12	1	6

SAMUEL JLloyd
Born: San Fernando, Trinidad, 29 March, 1981 — LB
England: U21-7/Youth//Trinidad & Tobago: 2

League Club	Source	Date Signed	Seasons Played	Apps	Subs	Gls
Aston Villa	YT	02/99	99-06	144	25	2
Gillingham	L	10/01	01	7	1	0

League Club	Source	Date Signed	Seasons Played	Apps	Subs	Gls
Bolton W	Tr	06/07	07-09	64	7	0
Cardiff C	L	03/11	10	6	0	0

SAMUEL Randolf Fitzgerald (Randy)
Born: Point Fortin, Trinidad, 23 December, 1963 — CD
Canada: 82

League Club	Source	Date Signed	Seasons Played	Apps	Subs	Gls
Port Vale	Fortuna Sittard (NED)	11/95	95	9	0	1

SAMUEL Robert William Lewis (Bobby)
Born: Aberdeen, Scotland, 18 May, 1946 — W

League Club	Source	Date Signed	Seasons Played	Apps	Subs	Gls
Lincoln C	Aberdeen	07/67	67	3	1	0

SAMUELS Dean Walter
Born: Hackney, E London, England, 29 March, 1973 — F

League Club	Source	Date Signed	Seasons Played	Apps	Subs	Gls
Barnet	Boreham Wood	12/96	96-97	13	26	4

SAMUELS Leslie (Les)
Born: Oldham, Greater Manchester, England, 8 December, 1928 — IF
Died: Burnley, Lancashire, England, 3 May, 1998

League Club	Source	Date Signed	Seasons Played	Apps	Subs	Gls
Burnley	Tottenham H (Am)	12/49	50	2	-	0
Exeter C	Tr	07/53	53	12	-	1
Wrexham	Tr	03/54	53-54	26	-	11
Crewe Alex	Tr	11/54	54-55	40	-	14
Bradford C	Tr	12/55	55-57	84	-	38
Stockport Co	Tr	03/58	57-58	25	-	5

SAMWAYS Mark
Born: Doncaster, South Yorkshire, England, 11 November, 1968 — G

League Club	Source	Date Signed	Seasons Played	Apps	Subs	Gls
Doncaster Rov	YT	08/87	87-91	121	0	0
Scunthorpe U	Tr	03/92	91-96	180	0	0
York C	Tr	07/97	97	29	0	0
Darlington	Tr	07/98	99	33	1	0

SAMWAYS Vincent (Vinny)
Born: Bethnal Green, E London, England, 27 October, 1968 — M
England: U21-5/Youth

League Club	Source	Date Signed	Seasons Played	Apps	Subs	Gls
Tottenham H	App	11/85	86-93	165	28	11
Everton	Tr	08/94	94-95	17	6	2
Wolverhampton W	L	12/95	95	3	0	0
Birmingham C	L	02/96	95	12	0	0
Walsall	Sevilla (SPN)	02/03	02-03	42	0	2

SANAGHAN Joseph (Joe)
Born: Motherwell, Lanarkshire, Scotland, 12 December, 1914 — LB
Died: Northern Ireland, November, 1951

League Club	Source	Date Signed	Seasons Played	Apps	Subs	Gls
Bradford Park Ave	Blantyre Celtic	08/35	35	4	-	0
Bournemouth	Tr	06/37	37-48	169	-	0
Stockport Co	Tr	08/49	49-50	52	-	0

SANASY Kevin Roy
Born: Leeds, England, 2 November, 1984 — F

League Club	Source	Date Signed	Seasons Played	Apps	Subs	Gls
Bradford C	Sch	07/04	02-04	2	7	1

SANCHEZ Alexis Alejandro
Born: Tocopilla, Chile, 19 December, 1988 — F
Chile: 86/Youth

League Club	Source	Date Signed	Seasons Played	Apps	Subs	Gls
Arsenal	Barcelona (SPN)	07/14	14	34	1	16

SANCHEZ Carlos Alberto
Born: Quibdo, Colombia, 6 February, 1986 — DM
Colombia: 58

League Club	Source	Date Signed	Seasons Played	Apps	Subs	Gls
Aston Villa	Elche (SPN)	08/14	14	20	8	1

SANCHEZ John
Born: Paddington, Central London, England, 21 October, 1940 — LH
England: Youth/Schools

League Club	Source	Date Signed	Seasons Played	Apps	Subs	Gls
Arsenal	Jnr	10/57				
Watford	Tr	06/59	59-60	19	-	0

SANCHEZ Lawrence Phillip (Lawrie)
Born: Lambeth, S London, England, 22 October, 1959 — M
England: Schools//Northern Ireland: 3

League Club	Source	Date Signed	Seasons Played	Apps	Subs	Gls
Reading	Thatcham T	09/78	77-84	249	13	28
Wimbledon	Tr	12/84	84-93	254	16	33
Swindon T	Tr	03/94	93	6	2	0

SANCHEZ-LOPEZ Carlos
Born: Madrid, Spain, 22 July, 1979 — RB

League Club	Source	Date Signed	Seasons Played	Apps	Subs	Gls
Bristol Rov	Getafe (SPN)	02/02	01	6	0	0

SANCHO Brent
Born: Port of Spain, Trinidad, 13 March, 1977 — CD
Trinidad & Tobago: 43

League Club	Source	Date Signed	Seasons Played	Apps	Subs	Gls
Gillingham	Dundee	08/05	05-06	35	10	2

SAND Peter
Born: Hadsund, Denmark, 19 July, 1972 — M
Denmark: DLge

League Club	Source	Date Signed	Seasons Played	Apps	Subs	Gls
Barnsley	Midtjylland (DEN)	10/01	01	4	2	1

SANDAZA Francisco Jose
Born: Toledo, Spain, 30 November, 1984 — F

League Club	Source	Date Signed	Seasons Played	Apps	Subs	Gls
Brighton & HA	Dundee U	09/10	10	3	12	2

SANDELL Andrew Charles (Andy)
Born: Calne, Wiltshire, England, 8 September, 1983 — LB/W

League Club	Source	Date Signed	Seasons Played	Apps	Subs	Gls
Bristol Rov	Bath C	06/06	06	20	16	3
Aldershot T	Salisbury C	11/08	08-09	53	5	7
Wycombe W	Tr	07/10	10-11	41	2	7
Newport Co	Chippenham T	01/12	13-14	53	8	4

SANDEMAN Bradley Robert
Born: Northampton, England, 24 February, 1970 — RB

League Club	Source	Date Signed	Seasons Played	Apps	Subs	Gls
Northampton T	YT	07/88	87-90	28	30	3
Maidstone U	Tr	02/91	90-91	55	2	8
Port Vale	Tr	08/92	92-95	62	7	1
Rotherham U	Tr	07/96	96	20	1	2
Hereford U	Tr	03/97	96	7	0	0

SANDER Christopher Andrew (Chris)
Born: Swansea, Wales, 11 November, 1962 — G

League Club	Source	Date Signed	Seasons Played	Apps	Subs	Gls
Swansea C	App	11/79	81-83	20	0	0
Wrexham	L	09/84	84	5	0	0
Cardiff C	Tr	08/85	85	8	0	0
Cardiff C	Haverfordwest	03/86	85	5	0	0

SANDERCOCK Kenneth Leslie (Ken)
Born: Plymouth, England, 31 January, 1951 — M/RB

League Club	Source	Date Signed	Seasons Played	Apps	Subs	Gls
Torquay U	App	01/69	68-69	42	4	1
Leicester C	Tr	11/69	69	5	4	1
Torquay U	Tr	11/71	71-74	113	6	5

SANDERCOCK Philip John (Phil)
Born: Plymouth, England, 21 June, 1953 — LB

League Club	Source	Date Signed	Seasons Played	Apps	Subs	Gls
Torquay U	App	09/71	69-76	199	5	13
Huddersfield T	Tr	06/77	77-78	81	0	1
Northampton T	Tr	09/79	79-80	69	0	3

SANDERS Alan John
Born: Newport, Wales, 29 October, 1963 — M
Wales: Schools

League Club	Source	Date Signed	Seasons Played	Apps	Subs	Gls
Cardiff C	App	11/81	81	1	1	0

SANDERS Allan
Born: Salford, England, 31 January, 1934 — RB

League Club	Source	Date Signed	Seasons Played	Apps	Subs	Gls
Manchester C		08/55				
Everton	Tr	07/56	57-59	56	-	0
Swansea C	Tr	11/59	59-62	92	-	0
Brighton & HA	Tr	01/63	62-65	80	0	0

SANDERS James Albert (Jim)
Born: Holborn, Central London, England, 5 July, 1920 — G
Died: Tamworth, Staffordshire, England, 13 August, 2003

League Club	Source	Date Signed	Seasons Played	Apps	Subs	Gls
Charlton Ath	Longlands	02/44				
West Bromwich A	Tr	11/45	46-57	327	-	0
Coventry C	Tr	07/58	58	10	-	0

SANDERS James Charles Frederick (Jim)
Born: Marlborough, Wiltshire, England, 15 October, 1932 — LH
Died: Chichester, West Sussex, England, May, 2007

League Club	Source	Date Signed	Seasons Played	Apps	Subs	Gls
Bristol C		11/51				
Crystal Palace	Tr	03/55	55-58	46	-	0
Rochdale	Tr	10/60				
Exeter C	Cheltenham T	08/62	62	20	-	1

SANDERS Peter Charles William
Born: Newport, Wales, 7 September, 1942 — CF

League Club	Source	Date Signed	Seasons Played	Apps	Subs	Gls
Newport Co	Jnr	10/59	60	3	-	0
Gillingham	Tr	07/61	61	2	-	0

SANDERS Roy Joseph
Born: Stepney, E London, England, 22 September, 1940 — RW

League Club	Source	Date Signed	Seasons Played	Apps	Subs	Gls
Northampton T	Romford	05/62	62	15	-	2

SANDERS Steven (Steve)
Born: Halifax, West Yorkshire, England, 2 June, 1978 — FB

League Club	Source	Date Signed	Seasons Played	Apps	Subs	Gls
Huddersfield T	YT	07/96				
Doncaster Rov	Tr	08/97	97	19	6	0

SANDERSON Eric
Born: Chapeltown, South Yorkshire, England, 10 November, 1921 — FB
Died: Sheffield, England, October, 1988

League Club	Source	Date Signed	Seasons Played	Apps	Subs	Gls
Rotherham U	Parramore Sports	09/47	47	2	-	1

SANDERSON Ian
Born: Torquay, Devon, England, 26 August, 1956 — F

League Club	Source	Date Signed	Seasons Played	Apps	Subs	Gls
Torquay U	Upton Ath	08/77	77	0	1	0

SANDERSON John Robert McDevitt
Born: Carlisle, Cumbria, England, 5 February, 1918 — LB

League Club	Source	Date Signed	Seasons Played	Career Record Apps	Subs	Gls
Died: Luton, England, 14 May, 1993						
Carlisle U		05/38	38	15	-	0
Wolverhampton W	Tr	02/39				
Luton T	Tr	05/46	46	6	-	0
SANDERSON Jordan Ben Joseph						
Born: Chingford, NE London, England, 7 August, 1993						M
Colchester U	Sch	07/11	10-13	0	2	0
SANDERSON Keith						
Born: Hull, England, 9 October, 1940						M
Plymouth Arg	Bath C	08/64	64	29	-	2
Queens Park Rgrs	Tr	06/65	65-68	98	6	10
SANDERSON Michael (Mike)						
Born: Germany, 26 October, 1966						M
Darlington	Hartlepool U (App)	03/86	85	1	0	0
SANDERSON Paul David						
Born: Blackpool, Lancashire, England, 16 December, 1966						RW
Manchester C	Fleetwood T	11/83				
Chester C	Tr	12/83	83	24	0	3
Halifax T	Tr	08/84	84-86	88	16	5
Cardiff C	Tr	07/87	87	8	13	1
Walsall	Tr	03/88	87	0	3	0
SANDERSON Philip (Phil)						
Born: Barnsley, South Yorkshire, England, 1 November, 1953						LW
Barnsley	Worsbrough Bridge	10/74	74	2	0	1
SANDFORD Lee Robert						
Born: Lambeth, S London, England, 22 April, 1968						D
England: Youth						
Portsmouth	App	12/85	85-89	66	6	1
Stoke C	Tr	12/89	89-95	255	3	8
Sheffield U	Tr	07/96	96-01	142	9	4
Reading	L	09/97	97	5	0	0
Stockport Co	L	10/01	01	7	0	0
SANDIFORD Ian Robert						
Born: Chorley, Lancashire, England, 26 February, 1946						CF
Blackburn Rov	App	02/64				
Stockport Co	Tr	06/64	64-65	47	0	9
Crewe Alex	Tr	01/66	65-66	48	5	17
SANDLANDS Herbert						
Born: Nantwich, Cheshire, England, 9 August, 1931						CH
Died: Nantwich, Cheshire, England, 24 July, 2005						
Crewe Alex (Am)	Nantwich T	08/54	54	1	-	0
SANDOMIERSKI Grzegorz						
Born: Bialystok, Poland, 5 September, 1989						G
Poland: 3/U21-2/Youth						
Blackburn Rov (L)	Racing Genk (BEL)	08/12	12	7	1	0
[SANDRO] RANIERE Sandro						
Born: Minas Gerais, Brazil, 15 March, 1989						DM
Brazil: 17/U23-7/Youth						
Tottenham H	SC Internacional (BRA)	08/10	10-13	60	21	3
Queens Park Rgrs	Tr	09/14	14	17	0	1
SANDWITH Kevin						
Born: Workington, Cumbria, England, 30 April, 1978						LB
Carlisle U	YT	07/96	97	2	1	0
Lincoln C	Halifax T	03/04	03-04	35	5	2
Macclesfield T	Tr	07/05	05	34	1	3
Chester C	Tr	06/06	06-07	39	15	3
SANDY Adam						
Born: Peterborough, England, 22 September, 1958						M
Northampton T	Wolverton T	02/80	79-82	88	16	7
SANDYS Harold Albert (Harry)						
Born: Fulham, W London, England, 8 October, 1932						CF
Torquay U	Yeovil T	08/54	54	2	-	0
SANETTI Francesco						
Born: Rome, Italy, 11 January, 1979						F
Sheffield Wed	Genoa (ITA)	04/98	97-98	1	4	1
SANFORD Mark Alexander						
Born: Westminster, Central London, England, 10 September, 1960						F
Aldershot	Jnr	06/79	79-82	72	12	23
SANG Neil						
Born: Liverpool, England, 23 May, 1972						M
Everton	YT	05/90				
Torquay U	Tr	06/91	91	8	6	0
SANGARE Djoumin						
Born: Dunkerque, France, 16 December, 1983						CD
Oxford U	York C	03/11	10	2	2	0

League Club	Source	Date Signed	Seasons Played	Career Record Apps	Subs	Gls
SAN JUAN Jesus Garcia						
Born: Zaragoza, Spain, 22 August, 1971						M
Wolverhampton W (L)	Real Zaragoza (SPN)	09/97	97	4	0	0
SANKEY John (Jack)						
Born: Winsford, Cheshire, England, 19 March, 1912						D
Died: Birmingham, England, 16 April, 1985						
West Bromwich A	Winsford U	11/30	33-38	144	-	5
Northampton T	Tr	10/45	46-47	42	-	0
SANKEY Martin Andrew						
Born: Wellington, Telford & Wrekin, England, 4 May, 1964						F
Shrewsbury T	App	02/82	82	0	5	0
SANKOFA Osei Omari Kwende						
Born: Streatham, S London, England, 19 March, 1985						D
England: Youth						
Charlton Ath	Sch	11/02	02-07	12	3	0
Bristol C	L	09/05	05	8	0	0
Brentford	L	01/08	07	10	1	0
Southend U	Tr	07/08	08-09	33	6	0
SAN MIGUEL Xavier						
Born: Bilbao, Spain, 7 May, 1971						M
Cambridge U	Baracaldo FC (SPN)	08/96	96	0	1	0
SANOGO Yaya						
Born: Paris, France, 27 January, 1993						F
France: U21-8/Youth						
Arsenal	AJ Auxerre (FRA)	07/13	13-14	2	9	0
Crystal Palace	L	01/15	14	3	7	0
SANOKHO Amadou						
Born: Paris, France, 1 September, 1975						M
Burnley	Sanguistese (ITA)	09/04	04	0	3	0
Oldham Ath	Tr	03/05	04	0	1	0
SANSAM Christian (Chris)						
Born: Hull, England, 26 December, 1975						M
Scunthorpe U	YT	12/93	93-95	10	11	1
Scarborough	Halifax T	03/96	95	5	1	0
Bradford C	Tr	08/96	96	0	1	0
Hull C	Tr	11/96	96	2	1	0
SANSARA Netan Nico						
Born: Darlaston, West Midlands, England, 3 August, 1989						LB
Walsall	Sch	07/08	08-09	24	3	0
SANSBY Clifford Palmer (Cliff)						
Born: Peterborough, England, 24 November, 1934						LB
Peterborough U	March T	07/59	60	1	-	1
SANSOM Kenneth Graham (Kenny)						
Born: Camberwell, S London, England, 26 September, 1958						LB
England: 86/B-2/FLge/U21-8/Youth/Schools						
Crystal Palace	App	12/75	74-79	172	0	3
Arsenal	Tr	08/80	80-87	314	0	6
Newcastle U	Tr	12/88	88	20	0	0
Queens Park Rgrs	Tr	06/89	89-90	64	0	0
Coventry C	Tr	03/91	90-92	51	0	0
Everton	Tr	02/93	92	6	1	1
Brentford	Tr	03/93	92	8	0	0
Watford	Chertsey T	08/94	94	1	0	0
SANSOME Paul Eric						
Born: New Addington, S London, England, 6 October, 1961						G
Millwall	Crystal Palace (App)	04/80	81-87	156	0	0
Southend U	Tr	03/88	87-96	308	0	0
Birmingham C	L	01/96	95	1	0	0
SANTA CRUZ Roque Luis						
Born: Asuncion, Paraguay, 16 August, 1981						F
Paraguay: 104/Youth						
Blackburn Rov	Bayern Munich (GER)	07/07	07-08	53	4	23
Manchester C	Tr	06/09	09-10	6	14	3
Blackburn Rov	L	01/11	10	7	2	0
SANTON Davide						
Born: Ferrara, Italy, 2 January, 1991						LB
Italy: 8/U21-17/Youth						
Newcastle U	Inter Milan (ITA)	08/11	11-13	76	6	1
SANTOS Alefe						
Born: Sao Paulo, Brazil, 1 March, 1995						W
Bristol Rov	Sch	06/13	12-13	7	17	1
Derby Co	Tr	07/14	14			
Notts Co	L	01/15	14	1	2	0
SANTOS Andre Clarindo						
Born: Sao Paulo, Brazil, 8 March, 1983						LB/M

League Club	Source	Date Signed	Seasons Played	Apps	Subs	Gls

Brazil: 24

League Club	Source	Date Signed	Seasons Played	Apps	Subs	Gls
Arsenal	Fenerbahce (TKY)	08/11	11-12	13	10	2

SANTOS Georges
Born: Marseille, France, 15 August, 1970 — M/D
Cape Verde Islands: 4

League Club	Source	Date Signed	Seasons Played	Apps	Subs	Gls
Tranmere Rov	Toulon (FRA)	07/98	98-99	46	1	2
West Bromwich A	Tr	03/00	99	8	0	0
Sheffield U	Tr	07/00	00-01	37	24	6
Grimsby T	Tr	09/02	02	24	2	1
Ipswich T	Tr	08/03	03	28	6	1
Queens Park Rgrs	Tr	08/04	04-05	64	10	6
Brighton & HA	Tr	08/06	06	7	4	0

SANTOS Ricardo Alex Almeida
Born: Almada, Portugal, 18 June, 1995 — CD

League Club	Source	Date Signed	Seasons Played	Apps	Subs	Gls
Peterborough U	Thurrock	02/14	13-14	23	2	0

SANTOS Yazalde Damas (Ali)
Born: Jersey, Channel Islands, 30 July, 1975 — F

League Club	Source	Date Signed	Seasons Played	Apps	Subs	Gls
Bournemouth	Jersey Scots	11/95	95	0	3	0

SANTUS Paul Graham
Born: Billinge, Merseyside, England, 8 September, 1983 — M

League Club	Source	Date Signed	Seasons Played	Apps	Subs	Gls
Wigan Ath	Sch	07/02	01	0	1	0

SAPHIN Reginald Francis Edward (Reg)
Born: Kilburn, NW London, England, 8 August, 1916 — G
Died: Luton, England, 23 December, 2005

League Club	Source	Date Signed	Seasons Played	Apps	Subs	Gls
Queens Park Rgrs	Walthamstow Ave	06/46	46-50	30	-	0
Watford	Tr	07/51	51-53	57	-	0

SAPPLETON Reneil St Aubin (Ricky)
Born: Kingston, Jamaica, 8 December, 1989 — F

League Club	Source	Date Signed	Seasons Played	Apps	Subs	Gls
Leicester C	Queens Park Rgrs (Sch)	07/07	07	0	1	0
Bournemouth	L	08/08	08	1	2	1
Macclesfield T	Tr	08/09	09-10	19	15	8

SARA Juan Manuel
Born: Buenos Aires, Argentina, 13 October, 1978 — F

League Club	Source	Date Signed	Seasons Played	Apps	Subs	Gls
Coventry C (L)	Dundee	01/03	02	1	2	1

SARCEVIC Antoni Charles
Born: Manchester, England, 13 March, 1992 — M
England: Semi Pro-1

League Club	Source	Date Signed	Seasons Played	Apps	Subs	Gls
Crewe Alex	Woodley Sports	05/10	10-11	1	11	1
Fleetwood T	Chester FC	06/13	13-14	68	11	15

SARGENT Gary Stewart
Born: Bedford, England, 11 September, 1952 — F

League Club	Source	Date Signed	Seasons Played	Apps	Subs	Gls
Norwich C	App	09/70	71	0	1	0
Scunthorpe U	Tr	07/72	72	14	1	1
Peterborough U	Bedford T	07/77	77-78	27	7	5
Northampton T	Tr	06/79	79-80	41	2	4

SAROYA Nevin
Born: Hillingdon, W London, England, 15 September, 1980 — D

League Club	Source	Date Signed	Seasons Played	Apps	Subs	Gls
Brentford	YT	06/99	99	0	1	0

SARR Mass
Born: Monrovia, Liberia, 6 February, 1973 — F
Liberia: 79

League Club	Source	Date Signed	Seasons Played	Apps	Subs	Gls
Reading	Hajduk Split (CRO)	07/98	98-99	18	13	3

SARSON Albert
Born: Rossington, South Yorkshire, England, 31 December, 1930 — CF
Died: Doncaster, South Yorkshire, England, 1969

League Club	Source	Date Signed	Seasons Played	Apps	Subs	Gls
Doncaster Rov	Mansfield T (Am)	08/49	49-50	2	-	0

SARTORI Carlo Domenico
Born: Pinzolo, Italy, 10 February, 1948 — M

League Club	Source	Date Signed	Seasons Played	Apps	Subs	Gls
Manchester U	Jnr	02/65	68-71	26	13	4

SAS Marco
Born: Vlaardingden, Netherlands, 16 February, 1971 — CD
Netherlands: U21

League Club	Source	Date Signed	Seasons Played	Apps	Subs	Gls
Bradford C	NAC Breda (NED)	07/96	96	31	0	3

SATCHWELL Kenneth Raymond (Ken)
Born: Birmingham, England, 17 January, 1940 — W/CF

League Club	Source	Date Signed	Seasons Played	Apps	Subs	Gls
Coventry C	SU Carburettors	09/58	58-61	68	-	21
Walsall	Nuneaton Bor	01/65	64-66	54	3	7

SAUL Eric Michael
Born: Dublin, Republic of Ireland, 28 October, 1978 — M

League Club	Source	Date Signed	Seasons Played	Apps	Subs	Gls
Brighton & HA	YT	07/97	97	0	4	0

SAUL Frank Lander
Born: Canvey Island, Essex, England, 23 August, 1943 — F/M
England: Youth

League Club	Source	Date Signed	Seasons Played	Apps	Subs	Gls
Tottenham H	Jnr	08/60	60-67	112	4	37
Southampton	Tr	01/68	67-69	47	3	2
Queens Park Rgrs	Tr	05/70	70-71	40	3	4
Millwall	Tr	03/72	71-75	85	11	4

SAUNDERS Benjamin (Ben)
Born: Southwell, Nottinghamshire, England, 12 October, 1984 — F

League Club	Source	Date Signed	Seasons Played	Apps	Subs	Gls
Doncaster Rov	Southwell C	08/05				
Bury	L	01/06	05	1	0	0

SAUNDERS Callum Luke
Born: Istanbul, Turkey, 26 September, 1995 — F
Wales: Youth

League Club	Source	Date Signed	Seasons Played	Apps	Subs	Gls
Crewe Alex	Sch	07/14	14	1	3	0

SAUNDERS Carl Stephen
Born: Birmingham, England, 26 November, 1964 — F

League Club	Source	Date Signed	Seasons Played	Apps	Subs	Gls
Stoke C	Washwood	03/83	82-89	130	34	23
Bristol Rov	Tr	02/90	89-93	123	19	42
Oxford U	Tr	12/93	93	2	3	0
Walsall	Tr	02/94	93	1	1	0

SAUNDERS Dean Nicholas
Born: Swansea, Wales, 21 June, 1964 — F
England: FLge//Wales: 75

League Club	Source	Date Signed	Seasons Played	Apps	Subs	Gls
Swansea C	App	06/82	83-84	42	7	12
Cardiff C	L	03/85	84	3	1	0
Brighton & HA	Tr	08/85	85-86	66	6	20
Oxford U	Tr	03/87	86-88	57	2	22
Derby Co	Tr	10/88	88-90	106	0	42
Liverpool	Tr	07/91	91-92	42	0	11
Aston Villa	Tr	09/92	92-94	111	1	38
Nottingham F	Galatasaray (TKY)	07/96	96-97	39	4	5
Sheffield U	Tr	12/97	97-98	42	1	17
Bradford C	Benfica (POR)	08/99	99-00	32	12	3

SAUNDERS Dennis Fowler
Born: Scarborough, North Yorkshire, England, 19 December, 1924 — WH
Died: Malvern, Worcestershire, England, 16 February, 2003
England: Amateur-1

League Club	Source	Date Signed	Seasons Played	Apps	Subs	Gls
Newport Co (Am)	Huddersfield T (Am)	11/46	46	7	-	0

SAUNDERS Derek William
Born: Ware, Hertfordshire, England, 6 January, 1928 — LH
England: Amateur-6

League Club	Source	Date Signed	Seasons Played	Apps	Subs	Gls
Chelsea	Walthamstow Ave	07/53	53-58	203	-	9

SAUNDERS Francis John (Jack)
Born: Middlesbrough, England, 24 August, 1924 — CH

League Club	Source	Date Signed	Seasons Played	Apps	Subs	Gls
Darlington	Army	09/46	46-47	67	-	0
Chelsea	Tr	05/48	49-53	52	-	0
Crystal Palace	Tr	08/54	54-55	59	-	0
Chester C	Tr	05/57	57-58	67	-	3

SAUNDERS George Ernest
Born: Birkenhead, Wirral, England, 1 March, 1918 — RB
Died: Birkenhead, Wirral, England, 1982

League Club	Source	Date Signed	Seasons Played	Apps	Subs	Gls
Everton		02/39	46-51	133	-	0

SAUNDERS Glyn
Born: Nottingham, England, 16 June, 1956 — RB

League Club	Source	Date Signed	Seasons Played	Apps	Subs	Gls
Nottingham F	App	06/74	76	4	0	0

SAUNDERS John George
Born: Worksop, Nottinghamshire, England, 1 December, 1950 — CD
Died: Worksop, Nottinghamshire, England, 14 January, 1998

League Club	Source	Date Signed	Seasons Played	Apps	Subs	Gls
Mansfield T	App	12/68	69-72	89	0	2
Huddersfield T	Tr	10/72	72-75	121	0	1
Barnsley	L	12/75	75	9	0	0
Barnsley	Tr	03/76	75-78	140	0	7
Lincoln C	Tr	06/79	79	25	1	1
Doncaster Rov	Tr	08/80	80	27	1	2

SAUNDERS John Henry
Born: Maidenhead, Berkshire, England, 18 December, 1943 — RW

League Club	Source	Date Signed	Seasons Played	Apps	Subs	Gls
Charlton Ath	Jnr	08/62	62	1	-	0

SAUNDERS John Thomas
Born: Newport, Wales, 2 October, 1950 — CD
Wales: Schools

League Club	Source	Date Signed	Seasons Played	Apps	Subs	Gls
Newport Co	Birmingham C (App)	08/69	69-70	26	1	0
Leeds U	Tr	07/71				
Walsall	Tr	10/72	72-75	94	5	2

SAUNDERS Leonard James (Jimmy)
Born: Liverpool, England, 7 January, 1928 — CF
Died: Liverpool, England, July, 2009

League Club	Source	Date Signed	Seasons Played	Apps	Subs	Gls
New Brighton (Am)	Stoneycroft	01/51	50	4	-	2

SAUNDERS Mark Philip
Born: Reading, England, 23 July, 1971 — M

League Club	Source	Date Signed	Seasons Played	Apps	Subs	Gls
Plymouth Arg	Tiverton T	08/95	95-97	60	12	11
Gillingham	Tr	06/98	98-05	120	56	15

SAUNDERS Matthew (Matt)
Born: Chertsey, Surrey, England, 12 September, 1989 — M

League Club	Source	Date Signed	Seasons Played	Apps	Subs	Gls
Fulham	Sch	03/09				
Lincoln C	L	01/10	09	17	1	3
Dagenham & Red		02/12	11-13	39	2	4

SAUNDERS Neil Christopher
Born: Barking, E London, England, 7 May, 1983 — M

League Club	Source	Date Signed	Seasons Played	Apps	Subs	Gls
Watford	Sch	01/02				
Exeter C	Team Bath	06/07	08-09	17	6	3

SAUNDERS Paul Brian
Born: Watford, Hertfordshire, England, 17 December, 1959 — D

League Club	Source	Date Signed	Seasons Played	Apps	Subs	Gls
Watford	App	12/77				
Northampton T	Tr	07/78	78-82	114	12	5

SAUNDERS Robert Charles (Robbie)
Born: Poole, Dorset, England, 26 August, 1945 — W

League Club	Source	Date Signed	Seasons Played	Apps	Subs	Gls
Bournemouth	App	06/63	65	2	1	0

SAUNDERS Ronald (Ron)
Born: Birkenhead, Wirral, England, 6 November, 1932 — CF
England: Youth

League Club	Source	Date Signed	Seasons Played	Apps	Subs	Gls
Everton	Jnr	02/51	54	3	-	0
Gillingham	Tonbridge	05/57	57-58	49	-	20
Portsmouth	Tr	09/58	58-64	236	-	145
Watford	Tr	09/64	64-65	39	0	18
Charlton Ath	Tr	08/65	65-66	64	1	24

SAUNDERS Ronald Albert (Ron)
Born: Malmesbury, Wiltshire, England, 14 January, 1923 — CH
Died: Bristol, England, March, 1999

League Club	Source	Date Signed	Seasons Played	Apps	Subs	Gls
Swindon T (Am)	North Leaze Ath	04/48	47	1	-	0

SAUNDERS Roy
Born: Salford, England, 4 September, 1930 — WH
Died: Swansea, Wales, 29 January, 2009
England: Youth

League Club	Source	Date Signed	Seasons Played	Apps	Subs	Gls
Liverpool	Hull C (Am)	05/48	52-58	132	-	1
Swansea C	Tr	03/59	58-62	94	-	3

SAUNDERS Sam Daniel
Born: Erith, SE London, England, 29 August, 1983 — RW

League Club	Source	Date Signed	Seasons Played	Apps	Subs	Gls
Dagenham & Red	Carshalton Ath	05/05	07-08	61	1	14
Brentford	Tr	07/09	09-14	81	56	23
Wycombe W	L	02/15	14	11	0	2

SAUNDERS Steven John Peter (Steve)
Born: Warrington, Cheshire, England, 21 September, 1964 — F/M

League Club	Source	Date Signed	Seasons Played	Apps	Subs	Gls
Bolton W	App	09/82	83	3	0	0
Crewe Alex	Tr	07/85	85	15	7	1
Preston NE	Tr	08/86				
Grimsby T	Tr	08/87	87-88	70	6	13
Scarborough	Tr	08/89	89	23	9	1

SAUNDERS Wesley (Wes)
Born: Sunderland, England, 23 February, 1963 — CD
England: Schools

League Club	Source	Date Signed	Seasons Played	Apps	Subs	Gls
Newcastle U	Jnr	06/81	81-84	79	0	0
Bradford C	L	03/85	84	1	3	0
Carlisle U	Tr	08/85	85-87	97	0	11
Torquay U	Dundee	07/90	90-92	60	1	6

SAVA Facundo
Born: Buenos Aires, Argentina, 3 July, 1974 — F

League Club	Source	Date Signed	Seasons Played	Apps	Subs	Gls
Fulham	Gimnasia LP (ARG)	06/02	02-03	13	13	6

SAVAGE Basir Mohammed (Bas)
Born: Wandsworth, SW London, England, 7 January, 1982 — W

League Club	Source	Date Signed	Seasons Played	Apps	Subs	Gls
Reading	Walton & Hersham	02/02	01-03	6	10	0
Wycombe W	L	09/04	04	2	2	0
Bury	L	02/05	04	5	0	0
Bristol C	Walton & Hersham	11/05	05	15	8	1
Gillingham	Tr	09/06	06	8	6	1
Brighton & HA	Tr	02/07	06-07	31	5	9
Millwall	Tr	02/08	07	9	2	2
Tranmere Rov	Tr	07/08	08-09	48	7	9
Dagenham & Red	Tr	09/10	10	21	15	3
Northampton T	Tr	08/11	11	3	5	0

SAVAGE David Thomas Patrick (Dave)
Born: Dublin, Republic of Ireland, 30 July, 1973 — M
Republic of Ireland: 5/U21-5

League Club	Source	Date Signed	Seasons Played	Apps	Subs	Gls
Brighton & HA	Kilkenny C (ROI)	03/91				
Millwall	Longford T (ROI)	05/94	94-98	104	28	6
Northampton T	Tr	10/98	98-00	98	15	18
Oxford U	Tr	08/01	01-02	85	0	5
Bristol Rov	Tr	07/03	03-04	58	7	3
Rushden & D	Tr	07/05	05	30	2	2

SAVAGE John Alfred (Jack)
Born: Bromley, SE London, England, 14 December, 1929 — G
Died: Blackpool, Lancashire, England, January, 2009

League Club	Source	Date Signed	Seasons Played	Apps	Subs	Gls
Hull C	RAF	09/50	50	4	-	0
Halifax T	Tr	03/52	51-53	61	-	1
Manchester C	Tr	11/53	54-57	30	-	0
Walsall	Tr	01/58	57-58	51	-	0

SAVAGE Reginald (Reg)
Born: Eccles, Greater Manchester, England, 5 July, 1912 — G
Died: Salford, England, October, 1997

League Club	Source	Date Signed	Seasons Played	Apps	Subs	Gls
Leeds U	Stalybridge Celtic	02/31	34-38	79	-	0
Nottingham F	Queen of the South	05/46	46	20	-	0
Accrington Stan	Tr	08/47				
Accrington Stan	Tr	08/47				

SAVAGE Robert James (Robbie)
Born: Liverpool, England, 8 January, 1960 — M

League Club	Source	Date Signed	Seasons Played	Apps	Subs	Gls
Liverpool	App	01/78				
Wrexham	L	10/82	82	27	0	10
Stoke C	Tr	07/83	83	5	2	0
Bournemouth	Tr	12/83	83-86	80	2	18
Bradford C	Tr	12/86	86-87	11	0	0
Bolton W	Tr	09/87	87-89	83	4	11

SAVAGE Robert William (Robbie)
Born: Wrexham, Wales, 18 October, 1974 — M
Wales: 39/U21-5/Youth/Schools

League Club	Source	Date Signed	Seasons Played	Apps	Subs	Gls
Manchester U	YT	07/93				
Crewe Alex	Tr	07/94	94-96	74	3	10
Leicester C	Tr	07/97	97-01	160	12	8
Birmingham C	Tr	05/02	02-04	82	0	11
Blackburn Rov	Tr	01/05	04-07	74	2	1
Derby Co	Tr	01/08	07-10	118	6	7
Brighton & HA	L	10/08	08	6	0	0

SAVARESE Giovanni
Born: Caracas, Venezuela, 14 July, 1971 — F
Venezuela: 30

League Club	Source	Date Signed	Seasons Played	Apps	Subs	Gls
Swansea C	San Jose E'quake (USA)	10/00	00	28	3	12
Millwall	Tr	08/01	01	0	1	0

SAVIC Andelko
Born: Lausanne, Switzerland, 3 March, 1993 — F
Switzerland: U21-1/Youth

League Club	Source	Date Signed	Seasons Played	Apps	Subs	Gls
Sheffield Wed (L)	Sampdoria (ITA)	08/13	13	0	1	0

SAVIC Stefan
Born: Mojkovac, Montenegro, 8 January, 1991 — CD
Montenegro: 32/U21-5

League Club	Source	Date Signed	Seasons Played	Apps	Subs	Gls
Manchester C	FK Partizan (SRB)	07/11	11	5	6	1

SAVILLE Andrew Victor (Andy)
Born: Hull, England, 12 December, 1964 — F

League Club	Source	Date Signed	Seasons Played	Apps	Subs	Gls
Hull C	Jnr	09/83	83-88	74	27	18
Walsall	Tr	03/89	88-89	28	10	5
Barnsley	Tr	03/90	89-91	71	11	21
Hartlepool U	Tr	03/92	91-92	37	0	13
Birmingham C	Tr	03/93	92-94	51	8	17
Burnley	L	12/94	94	3	1	1
Preston NE	Tr	07/95	95-96	56	0	30
Wigan Ath	Tr	10/96	96-97	17	8	4
Cardiff C	Tr	10/97	97-98	34	1	12
Hull C	L	09/98	98	3	0	0
Scarborough	Tr	03/99	98	0	9	0

SAVILLE George Alan
Born: Camberley, Surrey, England, 1 June, 1993 — DM

League Club	Source	Date Signed	Seasons Played	Apps	Subs	Gls
Chelsea	Sch	07/10				
Millwall	L	02/13	12	2	1	0
Brentford	L	06/13	13	33	7	4
Wolverhampton W	Tr	08/14	14	5	2	0
Bristol C	L	01/15	14	1	6	1

SAVILLE Jack William
Born: Camberley, Surrey, England, 2 April, 1991 — CD

League Club	Source	Date Signed	Seasons Played	Apps	Subs	Gls
Southampton	Chelsea (Sch)	07/09				
Barnet	Tr	11/11	11-12	18	5	1

SAVILLE Peter William
Born: Dalbeattie, Dumfries & Galloway, Scotland, 29 August, 1948 — W

League Club	Source	Date Signed	Seasons Played	Apps	Subs	Gls
Carlisle U		07/66	67	1	0	0
Bradford Park Ave	Hawick Royal Albert	03/69	68-69	31	0	1

SAVIN Keith Anthony
Born: Oxford, England, 5 June, 1929 — LB
Died: Leicester, England, 18 December, 1992

League Club	Source	Date Signed	Seasons Played	Apps	Subs	Gls
Derby Co	Oxford C	05/50	50-55	65	-	0
Mansfield T	Tr	05/57	57-58	68	-	0

SAVINO Raymond John (Ray)
Born: Norwich, England, 16 November, 1938 — RW

League Club	Source	Date Signed	Seasons Played	Apps	Subs	Gls
Norwich C	Thorpe Village	02/57	56-61	22	-	3
Bristol C	Tr	07/62	62-67	75	0	2

[SAVIO] NSEREKO Savio Magala
Born: Kampala, Uganda, 27 July, 1989 — F
Germany: Youth

League Club	Source	Date Signed	Seasons Played	Apps	Subs	Gls
West Ham U	Brescia (ITA)	01/09	08	1	9	0

SAWARD Leonard Roderick (Len)
Born: Aldershot, Hampshire, England, 6 July, 1927 — CF

League Club	Source	Date Signed	Seasons Played	Apps	Subs	Gls
Crystal Palace	Beddington	03/49	48-50	9	-	1
Newport Co	Cambridge U	01/54	53-54	25	-	5

SAWARD Patrick (Pat)
Born: Cobh, Republic of Ireland, 17 August, 1928 — WH/IF
Died: Newark, Nottinghamshire, England, 21 September, 2002
Republic of Ireland: 18

League Club	Source	Date Signed	Seasons Played	Apps	Subs	Gls
Millwall	Beckenham	07/51	51-54	118	-	14
Aston Villa	Tr	08/55	55-60	152	-	2
Huddersfield T	Tr	03/61	60-62	59	-	1
Crawley T	Tr	10/63				

SAWBRIDGE John (Jack)
Born: Wigan, Greater Manchester, England, 20 September, 1920 — G
Died: Southport, Merseyside, England, 26 February, 1984

League Club	Source	Date Signed	Seasons Played	Apps	Subs	Gls
Oldham Ath	Crossens	12/45	46-47	8	-	0

SAWYER Brian
Born: Rotherham, South Yorkshire, England, 28 January, 1938 — CF/W

League Club	Source	Date Signed	Seasons Played	Apps	Subs	Gls
Rotherham U	Rawmarsh Welfare	01/58	57-62	90	-	31
Bradford C	Tr	12/62	62-63	15	-	2

SAWYER Gary Dean
Born: Bideford, Devon, England, 5 July, 1985 — LB

League Club	Source	Date Signed	Seasons Played	Apps	Subs	Gls
Plymouth Arg	Sch	07/04	06-09	88	7	5
Bristol C	L	03/10	09	2	0	0
Bristol Rov	Tr	07/10	10-11	60	1	0
Leyton Orient	Tr	05/12	12-14	62	7	1

SAWYER Lee Thomas
Born: Leytonstone, NE London, England, 10 September, 1989 — M
England: Youth

League Club	Source	Date Signed	Seasons Played	Apps	Subs	Gls
Chelsea	Sch	07/07				
Southend U	L	08/08	08	11	1	1
Coventry C	L	01/09	08	1	1	0
Wycombe W	L	03/09	08	8	1	1
Southend U	L	07/09	09	0	6	0
Barnet	Tr	01/10	09	4	3	1
Southend U	Woking	01/11	10-11	12	15	0

SAWYER Roy
Born: Barnsley, South Yorkshire, England, 29 March, 1940 — CD

League Club	Source	Date Signed	Seasons Played	Apps	Subs	Gls
Barnsley	Worsbrough Bridge	05/58	60-61	2	-	0

SAWYERS Keith Wilson
Born: Banbury, Oxfordshire, England, 14 June, 1960 — M

League Club	Source	Date Signed	Seasons Played	Apps	Subs	Gls
Carlisle U	Carlisle Spartans	01/78	77-79	5	4	0

SAWYERS Robert (Rob)
Born: Dudley, West Midlands, England, 20 November, 1978 — LB

League Club	Source	Date Signed	Seasons Played	Apps	Subs	Gls
Barnet	Wolverhampton W (YT)	10/97	97-00	78	6	3

SAWYERS Romaine Theodore
Born: Birmingham, England, 2 November, 1991 — M
St Kitts & Nevis: 10

League Club	Source	Date Signed	Seasons Played	Apps	Subs	Gls
West Bromwich A	Sch	07/09				
Port Vale	L	01/11	10	0	1	0
Shrewsbury T	L	01/12	11	2	5	0
Walsall	L	03/13	12	0	4	0
Walsall	Tr	07/13	13-14	66	20	10

SAXBY Gary Philip
Born: Clipstone, Nottinghamshire, England, 11 December, 1959 — M

League Club	Source	Date Signed	Seasons Played	Apps	Subs	Gls
Mansfield T	App	12/77	78	14	2	1
Northampton T	Tr	08/80	80-82	86	10	11

SAXBY Michael William (Mick)
Born: Clipstone, Nottinghamshire, England, 12 August, 1957 — CD

League Club	Source	Date Signed	Seasons Played	Apps	Subs	Gls
Mansfield T	App	01/75	75-78	76	3	5
Luton T	Tr	07/79	79-81	82	0	6
Grimsby T	L	03/83	82	10	0	0
Lincoln C	L	11/83	83	10	0	1
Newport Co	Tr	07/84	84	6	0	0
Middlesbrough	Tr	09/84	84	15	0	0

SAXTON Robert (Bobby)
Born: Doncaster, South Yorkshire, England, 6 September, 1943 — CD

League Club	Source	Date Signed	Seasons Played	Apps	Subs	Gls
Derby Co	Denaby U	02/62	64-67	94	2	1
Plymouth Arg	Tr	02/68	67-75	224	6	7
Exeter C	Tr	09/75	75-77	92	0	3

SAYER Andrew Clive (Andy)
Born: Brentwood, Essex, England, 6 June, 1966 — F

League Club	Source	Date Signed	Seasons Played	Apps	Subs	Gls
Wimbledon	App	06/84	83-87	46	12	15
Cambridge U	L	02/88	87	2	3	0
Fulham	Tr	08/88	88-89	44	9	15
Leyton Orient	Tr	02/90	89-91	23	7	6
Sheffield U	L	03/91	90	0	3	0

SAYER Peter Anthony
Born: Cardiff, Wales, 2 May, 1955 — W/M
Wales: 7/U21-2

League Club	Source	Date Signed	Seasons Played	Apps	Subs	Gls
Cardiff C	Jnr	07/73	73-77	70	12	14
Brighton & HA	Tr	02/78	77-79	46	9	6
Preston NE	Tr	08/80	80-83	42	3	6
Cardiff C	L	09/81	81	4	0	1
Chester C	Tr	07/84	84	35	1	6

SBRAGIA Richard (Ricky)
Born: Lennoxtown, Dunbartonshire, Scotland, 26 May, 1956 — CD

League Club	Source	Date Signed	Seasons Played	Apps	Subs	Gls
Birmingham C	App	05/74	74-77	14	1	1
Walsall	Tr	10/78	78-79	77	0	4
Blackpool	Tr	07/80	80-81	24	2	1
York C	Tr	08/82	82-86	149	0	7
Darlington	L	08/85	85	6	0	0

SCAIFE Nicholas Antony (Nicky)
Born: Middlesbrough, England, 14 May, 1975 — M

League Club	Source	Date Signed	Seasons Played	Apps	Subs	Gls
York C	Whitby T	03/95	94-95	0	2	0

SCAIFE Robert Henry (Bobby)
Born: Northallerton, North Yorkshire, England, 12 October, 1955 — M

League Club	Source	Date Signed	Seasons Played	Apps	Subs	Gls
Middlesbrough	App	10/72				
Halifax T	L	01/75	74	5	1	1
Hartlepool U	Tr	09/75	75-77	77	3	10
Rochdale	Tr	10/77	77-79	95	3	9

SCALES George
Born: Northwich, Cheshire, England, 14 March, 1923 — G
Died: Rhyl, Denbighshire, Wales, June, 1993

League Club	Source	Date Signed	Seasons Played	Apps	Subs	Gls
Chester C	Manchester C (Am)	08/44	46-48	81	-	0

SCALES John Robert
Born: Harrogate, North Yorkshire, England, 4 July, 1966 — CD
England: 3/B-2

League Club	Source	Date Signed	Seasons Played	Apps	Subs	Gls
Bristol Rov	Leeds U (YT)	07/85	85-86	68	4	2
Wimbledon	Tr	07/87	87-94	235	5	11
Liverpool	Tr	09/94	94-96	65	0	2
Tottenham H	Tr	12/96	96-99	29	4	0
Ipswich T	Tr	07/00	00	2	0	0

SCALES Terence Albert (Terry)
Born: Stratford, E London, England, 18 November, 1951 — D

League Club	Source	Date Signed	Seasons Played	Apps	Subs	Gls
West Ham U	App	08/69				
Brentford	Tr	07/71	71-76	212	0	5

SCALONI Lionel Sebastian
Born: Santa Fe, Argentina, 16 May, 1978 — RB
Argentina: 7/Youth

League Club	Source	Date Signed	Seasons Played	Apps	Subs	Gls
West Ham U (L)	Depo la Coruna (SPN)	01/06	05	13	0	0

SCANLON Albert Joseph
Born: Manchester, England, 10 October, 1935 — LW
Died: Salford, England, 21 December, 2009
England: FLge-1/U23-5

League Club	Source	Date Signed	Seasons Played	Apps	Subs	Gls
Manchester U	Jnr	12/52	54-60	115	-	34
Newcastle U	Tr	11/60	60-61	22	-	5
Lincoln C	Tr	02/62	61-62	47	-	11
Mansfield T	Tr	04/63	62-65	108	0	21

SCANLON John (Ian)
Born: Birkenshaw, Lanarkshire, Scotland, 13 July, 1952 — LW

League Club	Source	Date Signed	Seasons Played	Apps	Subs	Gls
Notts Co	East Stirlingshire	07/72	72-77	99	12	31

SCANNELL Damian
Born: Croydon, S London, England, 28 April, 1985 — W

League Club	Source	Date Signed	Seasons Played	Apps	Subs	Gls
Southend U	Eastleigh	01/08	07-09	21	32	2
Brentford	L	11/08	08	1	1	0
Dagenham & Red	Tr	07/10	10-11	21	13	2

SCANNELL Sean
Born: Croydon, S London, England, 19 September, 1990 — W
Republic of Ireland: B-1/U21-10/Youth

League Club	Source	Date Signed	Seasons Played	Apps	Subs	Gls
Crystal Palace	Sch	01/08	07-11	69	61	12
Huddersfield T	Tr	06/12	12-14	67	47	7

SCANNELL Thomas (Tommy)
Born: Youghal, Co. Cork, Republic of Ireland, 3 June, 1925 — G
Died: Stepney, E London, England, September, 1992
Republic of Ireland: 1

League Club	Source	Date Signed	Seasons Played	Apps	Subs	Gls
Southend U	Tilbury	12/49	50-54	98	-	0

SCAPUZZI Luca
Born: Milan, Italy, 15 April, 1991 — M

League Club	Source	Date Signed	Seasons Played	Apps	Subs	Gls
Manchester C	Portogruaro (ITA)	08/11				
Oldham Ath	L	11/11	11	8	2	1
Portsmouth	L	03/12	11	0	2	0

SCARBOROUGH Brian
Born: Ironville, Derbyshire, England, 11 December, 1941 — LW

League Club	Source	Date Signed	Seasons Played	Apps	Subs	Gls
Derby Co	Jnr	01/59	58-60	4	-	0

SCARBOROUGH James Albert (Jim)
Born: Nottingham, England, 10 June, 1931 — CF

League Club	Source	Date Signed	Seasons Played	Apps	Subs	Gls
Darlington	West Bromwich A (Am)	09/51	51-53	49	-	15

SCARGILL Wayne
Born: Barnsley, South Yorkshire, England, 30 April, 1968 — FB

League Club	Source	Date Signed	Seasons Played	Apps	Subs	Gls
Bradford C	Frickley Ath	11/93	94	1	0	0

SCARLETT Andre Pierre
Born: Wembley, NW London, England, 11 January, 1980 — M

League Club	Source	Date Signed	Seasons Played	Apps	Subs	Gls
Luton T	YT	07/98	98-00	9	9	1

SCARLETT John Edgar
Born: Wolverhampton, England, 1 August, 1934 — IF
Died: Wolverhampton, England, 20 February, 1960

League Club	Source	Date Signed	Seasons Played	Apps	Subs	Gls
Walsall		03/52	52-53	10	-	2

SCARROTT Alan Richard
Born: Malmesbury, Wiltshire, England, 22 November, 1944 — RW

League Club	Source	Date Signed	Seasons Played	Apps	Subs	Gls
West Bromwich A	Chippenham T	12/61				
Bristol Rov	Tr	06/64				
Reading	Tr	04/65	65-67	90	0	7

SCARTH James William (Jimmy)
Born: North Shields, Tyne and Wear, England, 26 August, 1926 — RW/CF
Died: Hertford, England, 12 December, 2000

League Club	Source	Date Signed	Seasons Played	Apps	Subs	Gls
Tottenham H	Percy Main	08/48	49-51	7	-	3
Gillingham	Tr	02/52	51-54	138	-	24

SCATTERGOOD Eric
Born: Worsbrough, South Yorkshire, England, 9 September, 1929 — LH
Died: Barnsley, South Yorkshire, England, June, 1998

League Club	Source	Date Signed	Seasons Played	Apps	Subs	Gls
Barnsley	Worsbrough DST	02/47	49-51	12	-	0

SCHARNER Paul Josef Herbert
Born: Scheibbs, Austria, 11 March, 1980 — CD/M
Austria: 40

League Club	Source	Date Signed	Seasons Played	Apps	Subs	Gls
Wigan Ath	SK Brann Bergen (NOR)	01/06	05-09	130	15	14
West Bromwich A	Tr	08/10	10-11	51	11	7
Wigan Ath (L)	Hamburger SV (GER)	01/13	12	14	0	0

SCHEMMEL Sebastian
Born: Nancy, France, 2 June, 1975 — RB

League Club	Source	Date Signed	Seasons Played	Apps	Subs	Gls
West Ham U	FC Metz (FRA)	01/01	00-02	60	3	1
Portsmouth	Tr	08/03	03	12	2	0

SCHIAVI Mark Antony
Born: Westminster, Central London, England, 1 May, 1964 — M
England: Youth

League Club	Source	Date Signed	Seasons Played	Apps	Subs	Gls
West Ham U	App	11/81				
Bournemouth	L	09/83	83	10	0	0
Bournemouth	Tr	07/84	84	14	5	0
Northampton T	Tr	07/85	85-86	31	4	5
Cambridge U	Tr	09/86	86	24	6	2

SCHLUPP Jeffrey
Born: Hamburg, Germany, 23 December, 1992 — M/LB
Germany: Youth//Ghana: 7

League Club	Source	Date Signed	Seasons Played	Apps	Subs	Gls
Leicester C	Sch	07/10	11-14	61	37	9
Brentford	L	03/11	10	6	3	6

SCHMEICHEL Kasper Peter
Born: Copenhagen, Denmark, 5 November, 1986 — G
Denmark: 12/U21-17

League Club	Source	Date Signed	Seasons Played	Apps	Subs	Gls
Manchester C	Sch	11/04	07-08	7	1	0
Darlington	L	01/06	05	4	0	0
Bury	L	02/06	05	15	0	0
Bury	L	08/06	06	14	0	0
Cardiff C	L	10/07	07	14	0	0
Coventry C	L	03/08	07	9	0	0
Notts Co	Tr	08/09	09	43	0	0
Leeds U	Tr	06/10	10	37	0	0
Leicester C	Tr	07/11	11-14	162	0	0

SCHMEICHEL Peter Boleslaw
Born: Gladsaxe, Denmark, 18 November, 1963 — G
Denmark: 129

League Club	Source	Date Signed	Seasons Played	Apps	Subs	Gls
Manchester U	Brondby (DEN)	08/91	91-98	292	0	0
Aston Villa	Sporting Lisbon (POR)	07/01	01	29	0	1
Manchester C	Tr	04/02	02	29	0	0

SCHMELTZ Sidney
Born: Nieuwegein, Netherlands, 8 June, 1989 — W

League Club	Source	Date Signed	Seasons Played	Apps	Subs	Gls
Oldham Ath	BV Veendam (NED)	07/13	13	5	12	0
Shrewsbury T	L	01/14	13	2	2	0
Hartlepool U		10/14	14	2	3	0

SCHMITZ Rafael
Born: Blumenau, Brazil, 17 December, 1980 — CD

League Club	Source	Date Signed	Seasons Played	Apps	Subs	Gls
Birmingham C (L)	OSC Lille (FRA)	07/07	07	12	3	0

SCHNEIDERLIN Morgan
Born: Obernai, France, 8 November, 1989 — DM
France: 9/U21-3/Youth

League Club	Source	Date Signed	Seasons Played	Apps	Subs	Gls
Southampton	Strasbourg (FRA)	07/08	08-14	201	30	14

SCHNOOR Stefan
Born: Neumunster, Germany, 24 April, 1971 — CD

League Club	Source	Date Signed	Seasons Played	Apps	Subs	Gls
Derby Co	Hamburger SV (GER)	07/98	98-00	48	12	2

SCHOFIELD Alan Stewart (Stewart)
Born: Blackburn, Greater Manchester, England, 24 July, 1933 — IF

League Club	Source	Date Signed	Seasons Played	Apps	Subs	Gls
Southport	Blackburn Rov (Am)	07/57	57-58	36	-	9

SCHOFIELD Daniel James (Danny)
Born: Doncaster, South Yorkshire, England, 10 April, 1980 — LW

League Club	Source	Date Signed	Seasons Played	Apps	Subs	Gls
Huddersfield T	Brodsworth Welfare	02/99	98-07	205	43	39
Yeovil T	Tr	07/08	08-09	38	5	5
Millwall	Tr	09/09	09-10	48	19	9
Rotherham U	Tr	07/11	11	35	2	1
Accrington Stan	L	09/12	12	6	2	0

SCHOFIELD Ernest (Ernie)
Born: Sheffield, England, 29 March, 1921 — IF

League Club	Source	Date Signed	Seasons Played	Apps	Subs	Gls
Bradford C	Sheffield Wed (Am)	06/45	46	1	-	1

SCHOFIELD Gary
Born: Eccles, Greater Manchester, England, 27 March, 1957 — FB

League Club	Source	Date Signed	Seasons Played	Apps	Subs	Gls
Stockport Co		03/78	77	0	1	0

SCHOFIELD Graham
Born: Manchester, England, 18 December, 1950 — CD

League Club	Source	Date Signed	Seasons Played	Apps	Subs	Gls
Oldham Ath	Brookdale Park YC	08/69	69	1	0	0

SCHOFIELD John David
Born: Barnsley, South Yorkshire, England, 16 May, 1965 — M

League Club	Source	Date Signed	Seasons Played	Apps	Subs	Gls
Lincoln C	Gainsborough Trinity	11/88	88-94	221	10	11
Doncaster Rov	Tr	11/94	94-96	107	3	12
Mansfield T	Tr	08/97	97-98	81	5	0
Hull C	Tr	07/99	99	13	12	0
Lincoln C	Tr	08/00	00	13	6	0

SCHOFIELD John Reginald
Born: Atherstone, Warwickshire, England, 8 February, 1931 — G
Died: Coventry, England, 2 November, 2006

League Club	Source	Date Signed	Seasons Played	Apps	Subs	Gls
Birmingham C	Nuneaton Bor	02/50	52-65	212	0	0
Wrexham	Tr	07/66	66-67	52	0	0

SCHOFIELD Malcolm
Born: Failsworth, Greater Manchester, England, 8 October, 1918 — G
Died: Truro, Cornwall, England, March, 1985

League Club	Source	Date Signed	Seasons Played	Apps	Subs	Gls
Oldham Ath	Newton Heath Ath	11/37	46	7	-	0

SCHOFIELD Mark Anthony
Born: Wigan, Greater Manchester, England, 10 October, 1966 — FB

League Club	Source	Date Signed	Seasons Played	Apps	Subs	Gls
Wigan Ath	App	10/84	83-84	1	1	0

SCHOFIELD Thomas (Tom)
Born: Halifax, West Yorkshire, England, 22 June, 1926 — G

League Club	Source	Date Signed	Seasons Played	Apps	Subs	Gls
Halifax T (Am)	Boothtown	10/52	52	1	-	0

SCHOLES Martin
Born: Barrow, Cumbria, England, 28 January, 1954 — CD

League Club	Source	Date Signed	Seasons Played	Apps	Subs	Gls
Workington		11/76	76	3	1	0

SCHOLES Paul
Born: Salford, England, 16 November, 1974 — M/F
England: 66/Youth

League Club	Source	Date Signed	Seasons Played	Apps	Subs	Gls
Manchester U	YT	01/93	94-12	404	95	107

SCHROEDER Nico Petrus
Born: Alkmaar, Netherlands, 19 November, 1947 — G
Died: Swansea, Wales, October, 2004

League Club	Source	Date Signed	Seasons Played	Apps	Subs	Gls
Swansea C	Bridgend T	07/76	76	1	0	0

SCHUMACHER Steven Thomas (Steve)
Born: Liverpool, England, 30 April, 1984 — M
England: Youth

League Club	Source	Date Signed	Seasons Played	Apps	Subs	Gls
Everton	YT	05/01				
Carlisle U	L	10/03	03	4	0	0
Bradford C	Tr	08/04	04-06	110	7	13
Crewe Alex	Tr	05/07	07-09	59	14	7
Bury	Tr	07/10	10-12	109	5	23
Fleetwood T	Tr	05/13	13-14	58	6	5

SCHURRLE Andre Horst
Born: Ludwigshafen, Germany, 6 November, 1990 — W/F
Germany: 46/U21-5/Youth

League Club	Source	Date Signed	Seasons Played	Apps	Subs	Gls
Chelsea	Bayer Leverkusen (GER)	07/13	13-14	20	24	11

SCHWARZ Hans-Jurgen Stefan (Stefan)
Born: Malmo, Sweden, 18 April, 1969 — M
Sweden: 69/U21

League Club	Source	Date Signed	Seasons Played	Apps	Subs	Gls
Arsenal	Benfica (POR)	05/94	94	34	0	2
Sunderland	Valencia (SPN)	08/99	99-01	62	5	3

SCHWARZER Mark
Born: Sydney, Australia, 6 October, 1972 — G
Australia: 109/Youth

League Club	Source	Date Signed	Seasons Played	Apps	Subs	Gls
Bradford C	Kaiserslautern (GER)	11/96	96	13	0	0
Middlesbrough	Tr	02/97	96-07	367	0	0
Fulham	Tr	07/08	08-12	172	0	0
Chelsea	Tr	07/13	13	4	0	0
Leicester C	Tr	01/15	14	6	0	0

SCHWINKENDORF Jorn
Born: Hamburg, Germany, 27 January, 1971 — CD

League Club	Source	Date Signed	Seasons Played	Apps	Subs	Gls
Cardiff C	Waldhof Mannheim (GER)	11/99	99	5	0	0

SCIMECA Riccardo (Riccy)
Born: Leamington Spa, Warwickshire, England, 13 June, 1975 — CD/M
England: B-1/U21-9

League Club	Source	Date Signed	Seasons Played	Apps	Subs	Gls
Aston Villa	YT	07/93	95-98	50	23	2
Nottingham F	Tr	07/99	99-02	147	4	7
Leicester C	Tr	07/03	03	28	1	1
West Bromwich A	Tr	05/04	04-05	29	6	0
Cardiff C	Tr	01/06	05-09	60	10	6

SCOCCO Ignacio Martin (Nacho)
Born: Santa Fe, Argentina, 29 May, 1985 — W
Argentina: 1/Youth

League Club	Source	Date Signed	Seasons Played	Apps	Subs	Gls
Sunderland	Internacional (BRA)	01/14	13	0	6	0

SCOFFHAM Stephen (Steve)
Born: Munster, Germany, 12 July, 1983 — F

League Club	Source	Date Signed	Seasons Played	Apps	Subs	Gls
Notts Co	Gedling T	02/04	03-05	29	23	7

SCONCE Mark Allan
Born: Wrexham, Wales, 18 February, 1968 — FB

League Club	Source	Date Signed	Seasons Played	Apps	Subs	Gls
Chester C	App	07/86	85	1	1	0

SCOPE David Frederick
Born: Newcastle-upon-Tyne, England, 10 May, 1967 — W

League Club	Source	Date Signed	Seasons Played	Apps	Subs	Gls
Northampton T	Blyth Spartans	09/89	89-91	6	13	1

SCOTHERN Ashley John
Born: Featherstone, West Yorkshire, England, 11 September, 1984 — F
England: Youth

League Club	Source	Date Signed	Seasons Played	Apps	Subs	Gls
Barnsley	YT	-	01	0	1	0

SCOTHORN Garry
Born: Hoyland, South Yorkshire, England, 6 June, 1950 — G

League Club	Source	Date Signed	Seasons Played	Apps	Subs	Gls
Sheffield Wed	App	06/67	67	1	0	0
Mansfield T	Sligo Rov (ROI)	08/74				

SCOTLAND Jason Kelvin
Born: Port of Spain, Trinidad, 18 February, 1979 — F
Trinidad & Tobago: 41

League Club	Source	Date Signed	Seasons Played	Apps	Subs	Gls
Swansea C	St Johnstone	07/07	07-08	82	8	45
Wigan Ath	Tr	07/09	09	14	18	1
Ipswich T	Tr	08/10	10-12	54	33	19
Barnsley	Tr	01/13	12-13	10	28	8

SCOTSON Reginald (Reg)
Born: Stockton-on-Tees, Cleveland, England, 22 September, 1919 — RH
Died: Grimsby, North Lincolnshire, England, February, 1999

League Club	Source	Date Signed	Seasons Played	Apps	Subs	Gls
Sunderland	Ouston Jnrs	04/39	46-50	61	-	1
Grimsby T	Tr	12/50	50-54	164	-	4

SCOTT Alexander MacNaughton (Sandy)
Born: Kingsbarns, Fife, Scotland, 17 November, 1922 — LB
Died: Glenrothes, Fife, Scotland, 27 August, 1995

League Club	Source	Date Signed	Seasons Played	Apps	Subs	Gls
Leicester C	Lochgelly Albert	03/47	47-49	31	-	1
Carlisle U	Tr	01/50	49-55	200	-	4

SCOTT Alexander Silcock (Alex)
Born: Falkirk, Scotland, 22 November, 1936 — RW
Died: Falkirk, Scotland, 12 September, 2001
Scotland: 16/B/SLge-7/U23-1

League Club	Source	Date Signed	Seasons Played	Apps	Subs	Gls
Everton	Glasgow Rangers	02/63	62-66	149	0	23

SCOTT Andrew (Andy)
Born: Epsom, Surrey, England, 2 August, 1972 — F/LB

League Club	Source	Date Signed	Seasons Played	Apps	Subs	Gls
Sheffield U	Sutton U	12/92	92-97	39	36	6
Chesterfield	L	10/96	96	4	1	3
Bury	L	03/97	96	2	6	0
Brentford	Tr	11/97	97-00	109	9	28
Oxford U	Tr	01/01	00-03	77	18	24
Leyton Orient	Tr	03/04	03-04	45	2	10

SCOTT Andrew Michael (Andy)
Born: Manchester, England, 27 June, 1975 — LB

League Club	Source	Date Signed	Seasons Played	Apps	Subs	Gls
Blackburn Rov	YT	01/93				
Cardiff C	Tr	08/94	94-96	14	2	1
Rochdale	Tr	08/97	97	1	2	0

SCOTT Anthony James Ernest (Tony)
Born: St Neots, Cambridgeshire, England, 1 April, 1941 — W
England: Youth

League Club	Source	Date Signed	Seasons Played	Apps	Subs	Gls
West Ham U	Jnr	05/58	59-65	83	0	16
Aston Villa	Tr	10/65	65-67	47	3	3
Torquay U	Tr	09/67	67-69	82	5	4
Bournemouth	Tr	07/70	70-71	60	2	6
Exeter C	Tr	06/72	72-73	51	0	2

SCOTT Augustus Fisher (Augie)
Born: Sunderland, England, 19 February, 1921 — IF
Died: Sunderland, England, 28 November, 1998

League Club	Source	Date Signed	Seasons Played	Apps	Subs	Gls
Luton T	Hylton CW	03/39				
Southampton	Tr	07/47	47-49	46	-	9
Colchester U	Tr	08/51	51-53	120	-	10

SCOTT Christopher (Chris)
Born: Wallsend, Tyne and Wear, England, 11 September, 1963 — CD

League Club	Source	Date Signed	Seasons Played	Apps	Subs	Gls
Northampton T	Blyth Spartans	07/87				
Lincoln C	Tr	03/88	88	4	0	0

SCOTT Christopher James (Chris)
Born: Burnley, Lancashire, England, 12 February, 1980 — RB

League Club	Source	Date Signed	Seasons Played	Apps	Subs	Gls
Burnley	YT	07/98	98	9	5	0

SCOTT Colin George
Born: Glasgow, Scotland, 19 May, 1970 — G

League Club	Source	Date Signed	Seasons Played	Apps	Subs	Gls
Brentford (L)	Glasgow Rangers	03/90	89	6	0	0

SCOTT David Perry
Born: Belfast, Northern Ireland, 6 June, 1918 — G
Died: Northampton, England, 21 December, 1977

League Club	Source	Date Signed	Seasons Played	Apps	Subs	Gls
Northampton T	Linfield	05/45	46-47	11	-	0

SCOTT Derek Edward
Born: Gateshead, Tyne and Wear, England, 8 February, 1958 — RB
England: Schools

League Club	Source	Date Signed	Seasons Played	Apps	Subs	Gls
Burnley	App	02/75	74-84	277	8	24
Bolton W	Tr	07/85	85-87	119	0	0

SCOTT Dion Elijah
Born: Warley, West Midlands, England, 24 December, 1980 — CD

League Club	Source	Date Signed	Seasons Played	Apps	Subs	Gls
Walsall	YT	05/99	00-01	0	2	0
Mansfield T	Tr	07/02				
Kidderminster Hrs	Tr	01/03	02	19	0	1

SCOTT Donald (Don)
Born: Elland, West Yorkshire, England, 20 October, 1922 — RW
Died: Halifax, West Yorkshire, England, 19 January, 2000

League Club	Source	Date Signed	Seasons Played	Apps	Subs	Gls
Halifax T		09/48	48-49	20	-	5

SCOTT Frederick Hind (Freddie)
Born: Fatfield, Tyne and Wear, England, 6 October, 1916 — RW
Died: Nottingham, England, September, 1995
England: Schools

League Club	Source	Date Signed	Seasons Played	Apps	Subs	Gls
Bolton W	Fatfield Jnrs	01/35				
Bradford Park Ave	Tr	05/36				
York C	Tr	02/37	36-46	74	-	16
Nottingham F	Tr	09/46	46-56	301	-	40

SCOTT Gary Craig
Born: Liverpool, England, 2 March, 1978 — FB

League Club	Source	Date Signed	Seasons Played	Apps	Subs	Gls
Tranmere Rov	YT	10/95				
Rotherham U	Tr	08/97	97-98	19	1	0

SCOTT Geoffrey Samuel (Geoff)
Born: Birmingham, England, 31 October, 1956 — D

League Club	Source	Date Signed	Seasons Played	Apps	Subs	Gls
Stoke C	Highgate U	04/77	77-79	76	2	3
Leicester C	Tr	02/80	79-81	39	0	0

League Club	Source	Date Signed	Seasons Played	Apps	Subs	Gls
Birmingham C	Tr	02/82	81-82	18	1	0
Charlton Ath	Tr	10/82	82	2	0	0
Middlesbrough	Tr	06/84	84	2	0	0
Northampton T	Tr	09/84	84	16	1	0
Cambridge U	Tr	07/85	85	19	0	0

SCOTT George William
Born: Aberdeen, Scotland, 25 October, 1944 — M

League Club	Source	Date Signed	Seasons Played	Apps	Subs	Gls
Liverpool	App	10/61				
Tranmere Rov	Port Elizabeth C (RSA)	11/68	68-69	35	1	0

SCOTT Ian
Born: Radcliffe, Greater Manchester, England, 20 September, 1967 — M
England: Schools

League Club	Source	Date Signed	Seasons Played	Apps	Subs	Gls
Manchester C	App	09/85	87-88	20	4	3
Stoke C	Tr	07/89	89-91	21	9	2
Crewe Alex	L	03/91	90	12	0	1
Bury	Tr	08/92	92	7	2	2

SCOTT Ian Richard
Born: Otley, West Yorkshire, England, 4 March, 1969 — D

League Club	Source	Date Signed	Seasons Played	Apps	Subs	Gls
Manchester U	App	03/87				
Stockport Co	Tr	09/87	87-88	23	2	0

SCOTT James (Jimmy)
Born: Hetton-le-Hole, Tyne and Wear, England, 7 September, 1934 — WH/LB
England: Schools

League Club	Source	Date Signed	Seasons Played	Apps	Subs	Gls
Burnley	Jnr	09/51	54-60	3	-	0
Oldham Ath	Tr	06/61	61-63	76	-	0

SCOTT James (Jim)
Born: Falkirk, Scotland, 21 August, 1940 — RW
Scotland: 1

League Club	Source	Date Signed	Seasons Played	Apps	Subs	Gls
Newcastle U	Hibernian	08/67	67-69	70	4	6
Crystal Palace	Tr	02/70	69-71	36	7	5

SCOTT James Adamson (Jamie)
Born: Newcastle-upon-Tyne, England, 28 February, 1960 — M

League Club	Source	Date Signed	Seasons Played	Apps	Subs	Gls
Newcastle U	App	03/78	77-78	9	1	0

SCOTT James Dennis
Born: Olney, Buckinghamshire, England, 5 September, 1945 — IF

League Club	Source	Date Signed	Seasons Played	Apps	Subs	Gls
Leyton Orient	Chelsea (Am)	11/62	63-65	22	1	6

SCOTT James John Wedderburn
Born: Glasgow, Scotland, 26 December, 1927 — IF

League Club	Source	Date Signed	Seasons Played	Apps	Subs	Gls
Workington	Alloa Ath	06/54	54	6	-	1

SCOTT John (Jackie)
Born: Belfast, Northern Ireland, 22 December, 1933 — RW
Died: Manchester, England, June, 1978
Northern Ireland: 2/B

League Club	Source	Date Signed	Seasons Played	Apps	Subs	Gls
Manchester U	Ormond Star	10/51	52-55	3	-	0
Grimsby T	Tr	06/56	56-62	240	-	51
York C	Tr	06/63	63	21	-	3

SCOTT John
Born: Normanton, West Yorkshire, England, 2 January, 1942 — IF

League Club	Source	Date Signed	Seasons Played	Apps	Subs	Gls
Bradford C	Jnr	08/60	61-62	11	-	2
Chesterfield	Tr	07/63	63	5	-	0

SCOTT John Alfred
Born: Maryport, Cumbria, England, 18 July, 1928 — G

League Club	Source	Date Signed	Seasons Played	Apps	Subs	Gls
Leeds U	Workington	05/50	50-54	111	-	0

SCOTT John Mather
Born: Edinburgh, Scotland, 21 August, 1953 — CD

League Club	Source	Date Signed	Seasons Played	Apps	Subs	Gls
Workington	Brechin C	08/75	75	1	1	0

SCOTT Joseph (Joe)
Born: Plymouth, England, 11 January, 1953 — F

League Club	Source	Date Signed	Seasons Played	Apps	Subs	Gls
Bournemouth	Falmouth	06/78	78	18	3	4

SCOTT Joseph Cumpson (Joe)
Born: Fatfield, Tyne and Wear, England, 9 January, 1930 — IF

League Club	Source	Date Signed	Seasons Played	Apps	Subs	Gls
Newcastle U		04/49				
Luton T	Spennymoor U	02/52	52-53	13	-	2
Middlesbrough	Tr	09/54	54-58	93	-	26
Hartlepool U	Tr	01/59	58-59	62	-	8
York C	Tr	06/60	60	17	-	2

SCOTT Joshua Daniel (Josh)
Born: Camden, N London, England, 10 May, 1985 — F

League Club	Source	Date Signed	Seasons Played	Apps	Subs	Gls
Dagenham & Red	Hayes & Yeading U	07/09	09-13	73	32	15

SCOTT Keith James
Born: Westminster, Central London, England, 19 June, 1967 — F

League Club	Source	Date Signed	Seasons Played	Apps	Subs	Gls
Lincoln C	Leicester U	03/90	89-90	7	9	2
Wycombe W	Tr	03/91	93	15	0	10
Swindon T	Tr	11/93	93-94	43	8	12
Stoke C	Tr	12/94	94-95	22	3	3
Norwich C	Tr	11/95	95-96	10	15	5
Bournemouth	L	02/96	95	8	0	1
Watford	L	02/97	96	6	0	2
Wycombe W	Tr	03/97	96-98	60	3	20
Reading	Tr	03/99	98-00	20	15	5
Colchester U	Tr	10/00	00	8	1	1

SCOTT Kenneth (Ken)
Born: Maltby, South Yorkshire, England, 13 August, 1931 — RW

League Club	Source	Date Signed	Seasons Played	Apps	Subs	Gls
Derby Co	Denaby U	08/50	50	2	-	0
Mansfield T	Denaby U	08/52	52	5	-	2

SCOTT Kevin
Born: Lincoln, England, 12 November, 1954 — CD

League Club	Source	Date Signed	Seasons Played	Apps	Subs	Gls
Lincoln C	Sheffield Polytechnic	02/74	73	1	0	0

SCOTT Kevin Watson
Born: Easington, County Durham, England, 17 December, 1966 — CD

League Club	Source	Date Signed	Seasons Played	Apps	Subs	Gls
Newcastle U	Durham C	12/84	86-93	227	0	8
Tottenham H	Tr	02/94	93-95	16	2	1
Port Vale	L	01/95	94	17	0	1
Charlton Ath	L	12/96	96	4	0	0
Norwich C	Tr	01/97	96-97	31	2	0
Darlington	L	01/99	98	4	0	0

SCOTT Lawrence (Laurie)
Born: Sheffield, England, 23 April, 1917 — RB
Died: Barnsley, South Yorkshire, England, 23 July, 1999
England: 17/B-4/FLge-5/War-16

League Club	Source	Date Signed	Seasons Played	Apps	Subs	Gls
Bradford C	Bolton Woods	05/35	35-36	39	-	0
Arsenal	Tr	02/37	46-51	115	-	0
Crystal Palace	Tr	10/51	51-52	28	-	0

SCOTT Lloyd Edward
Born: Stepney, E London, England, 13 October, 1961 — G

League Club	Source	Date Signed	Seasons Played	Apps	Subs	Gls
Leyton Orient	App	10/79				
Watford	Tr	02/82				
Blackpool	Tr	07/82	82	2	0	0

SCOTT Malcolm Ernest
Born: South Shields, Tyne and Wear, England, 8 May, 1936 — LH

League Club	Source	Date Signed	Seasons Played	Apps	Subs	Gls
Newcastle U	Cleadon Jnrs	09/55	56-60	25	-	2
Darlington	Tr	10/61	61-62	47	-	2
York C	Tr	10/63	63	19	-	0

SCOTT Martin
Born: Sheffield, England, 7 January, 1968 — LB

League Club	Source	Date Signed	Seasons Played	Apps	Subs	Gls
Rotherham U	App	01/86	84-90	93	1	3
Bristol C	Tr	12/90	90-94	171	0	14
Sunderland	Tr	12/94	94-98	104	2	9

SCOTT Melvyn Douglas (Mel)
Born: Claygate, Surrey, England, 26 September, 1939 — CD
Died: Colchester, Essex, England, August, 1997
England: U23-3/Youth

League Club	Source	Date Signed	Seasons Played	Apps	Subs	Gls
Chelsea	Jnr	11/56	57-61	97	-	0
Brentford	Tr	03/63	62-66	157	0	2

SCOTT Michael Ramsey (Mike)
Born: Newcastle-upon-Tyne, England, 4 December, 1945 — LW

League Club	Source	Date Signed	Seasons Played	Apps	Subs	Gls
Burnley	App	12/62				
Hartlepool U	Tr	07/64	64	2	-	0

SCOTT Morrys James
Born: Swansea, Wales, 17 December, 1970 — F

League Club	Source	Date Signed	Seasons Played	Apps	Subs	Gls
Cardiff C	YT	07/89	89	1	8	0
Southend U	Colchester U	10/90				
Plymouth Arg	Tr	06/91	91	3	3	0
Northampton T	Tr	08/92	92	10	7	2

SCOTT Paul
Born: Wakefield, England, 5 November, 1979 — RB

League Club	Source	Date Signed	Seasons Played	Apps	Subs	Gls
Huddersfield T	YT	07/98	02-03	18	14	2
Bury	Tr	08/04	04-09	204	9	13
Morecambe	Tr	07/10	10	6	2	0

SCOTT Paul David
Born: Burnley, Lancashire, England, 29 January, 1985 — FB

League Club	Source	Date Signed	Seasons Played	Apps	Subs	Gls
Burnley	Sch	07/04	03	0	2	0

SCOTT Peter Reginald
Born: Notting Hill, Central London, England, 1 October, 1963 — M

League Club	Source	Date Signed	Seasons Played	Apps	Subs	Gls
Fulham	App	10/81	81-91	268	9	27
Bournemouth	Tr	08/92	92	9	1	0
Barnet	Burnham	11/93	93-95	72	6	2

SCOTT Peter William
Born: Liverpool, England, 19 September, 1952 — FB
England: Youth//Northern Ireland: 10

League Club	Source	Date Signed	Seasons Played	Apps	Subs	Gls
Everton	App	07/70	71-74	42	2	1

League Club	Source	Date Signed	Seasons Played	Apps	Subs	Gls
Southport	L	01/74	73	4	0	0
York C	Tr	12/75	75-78	99	1	3
Aldershot	Tr	03/79	78-82	114	7	2

SCOTT Philip Campbell
Born: Perth, Scotland, 14 November, 1974 — M
Scotland: U21-4

League Club	Source	Date Signed	Seasons Played	Apps	Subs	Gls
Sheffield Wed	St Johnstone	03/99	98-99	2	7	1

SCOTT Richard Paul
Born: Dudley, West Midlands, England, 29 September, 1974 — M/D

League Club	Source	Date Signed	Seasons Played	Apps	Subs	Gls
Birmingham C	YT	05/93	92-94	11	1	0
Shrewsbury T	Tr	03/95	94-97	91	14	18
Peterborough U	Tr	07/98	98-00	65	16	7
Peterborough U	Stevenage Bor	12/02	02	13	3	1

SCOTT Richard Sydney Arthur (Dick)
Born: Thetford, Norfolk, England, 26 October, 1941 — WH

League Club	Source	Date Signed	Seasons Played	Apps	Subs	Gls
Norwich C	Jnr	11/58	60-62	28	-	1
Cardiff C	Tr	07/63	63-64	37	-	5
Scunthorpe U	Tr	09/64	64-65	47	0	8
Lincoln C	Tr	07/66	66	9	1	1

SCOTT Robert (Rob)
Born: Epsom, Surrey, England, 15 August, 1973 — RB/F

League Club	Source	Date Signed	Seasons Played	Apps	Subs	Gls
Sheffield U	Sutton U	08/93	94-95	2	4	1
Scarborough	L	03/95	94	8	0	3
Northampton T	L	11/95	95	5	0	0
Fulham	Tr	01/96	95-98	65	19	17
Carlisle U	L	08/98	98	7	0	3
Rotherham U	Tr	11/98	98-04	160	14	9
Oldham Ath	Tr	07/05	05	19	2	1
Macclesfield T	Tr	08/06	06	22	4	2

SCOTT Robert (Bert)
Born: Stonehouse, Lanarkshire, Scotland, 20 May, 1930 — W/IF

League Club	Source	Date Signed	Seasons Played	Apps	Subs	Gls
Accrington Stan	Alloa Ath	09/54	54-58	149	-	32
Wrexham	Tr	07/59	59	2	-	0
Oldham Ath	Tr	10/59	59	9	-	1

SCOTT Robert (Bob)
Born: Broxburn, West Lothian, Scotland, 13 January, 1964 — F

League Club	Source	Date Signed	Seasons Played	Apps	Subs	Gls
Colchester U	Whitburn Jnrs	03/89	88-89	26	11	8

SCOTT Robert Alexander
Born: Liverpool, England, 26 October, 1913 — G
Died: West Ham, E London, England, 1962
England: Schools

League Club	Source	Date Signed	Seasons Played	Apps	Subs	Gls
Liverpool	Jnr	05/31				
Burnley	Tr	05/33	33-35	57	-	0
Wolverhampton W	Tr	02/36	35-38	119	-	0
Crewe Alex	Tr	08/47	47-48	44	-	0

SCOTT Robert John (Bob)
Born: Dundee, Scotland, 16 March, 1937 — RH

League Club	Source	Date Signed	Seasons Played	Apps	Subs	Gls
Cardiff C	Dundee Violet	02/57	57	3	-	0
Swindon T	Tr	06/61				
Newport Co	Tr	11/61	61-62	18	-	0
Southport	Sankey's	07/63	63	3	-	0

SCOTT Robert William (Bobby)
Born: Liverpool, England, 22 February, 1953 — CD

League Club	Source	Date Signed	Seasons Played	Apps	Subs	Gls
Wrexham	Jnr	07/71	70-75	15	4	0
Reading	L	01/75	74	5	0	0
Hartlepool U	Tr	07/76	76	37	0	0
Rochdale	Tr	07/77	77-78	71	0	3
Crewe Alex	Tr	08/79	79-85	238	1	15
Wrexham	Northwich Victoria	01/86	85	2	1	0

SCOTT Ryan
Born: Cleveland, England, 20 March, 1976 — G

League Club	Source	Date Signed	Seasons Played	Apps	Subs	Gls
Darlington	YT	07/94	93	0	1	0

SCOTT Samuel Cooke Bricknell (Sammy)
Born: Ashington, Northumberland, England, 14 June, 1922 — IF
Died: Ashington, Northumberland, England, 14 October, 1988

League Club	Source	Date Signed	Seasons Played	Apps	Subs	Gls
Hartlepool U	Ashington	02/46	46-47	49	-	17

SCOTT Stephen Richard (Steve)
Born: Johnstown, Wrexham, Wales, 5 November, 1966 — CD

League Club	Source	Date Signed	Seasons Played	Apps	Subs	Gls
Wrexham	Oswestry T	03/86	87	0	2	0

SCOTT Stuart Robin (Robin)
Born: Shrewsbury, Shropshire, England, 31 March, 1946 — W/IF

League Club	Source	Date Signed	Seasons Played	Apps	Subs	Gls
Shrewsbury T	Jnr	04/64	63-65	18	0	2

SCOTT Walter
Born: Douglas, Lanarkshire, Scotland, 23 June, 1932 — G
Died: Stranraer, Dumfries & Galloway, Scotland, 6 June, 1988

League Club	Source	Date Signed	Seasons Played	Apps	Subs	Gls
Halifax T	Dumbarton	08/54	54	13	-	0

SCOTT William John (Bill)
Born: Preston, Lancashire, England, 14 June, 1921 — LB
Died: Chorley, Lancashire, England, 1 January, 2002

League Club	Source	Date Signed	Seasons Played	Apps	Subs	Gls
Preston NE	Jnr	05/39	46-53	208	-	0

SCOTT William Reed (Billy)
Born: Wallsend, Tyne and Wear, England, 6 December, 1907 — IF
Died: Southport, Merseyside, England, 12 January, 1969
England: 1

League Club	Source	Date Signed	Seasons Played	Apps	Subs	Gls
Middlesbrough	Howdon British Legion	05/27	30-31	26	-	5
Brentford	Tr	05/32	32-46	273	-	84
Aldershot	Tr	07/47	47	21	-	0

SCOTTING Allen
Born: Dartford, Kent, England, 22 April, 1966 — LB

League Club	Source	Date Signed	Seasons Played	Apps	Subs	Gls
Gillingham	Charlton Ath (Jnr)	02/84	83	2	0	0

SCOUGALL Stefan
Born: Edinburgh, Scotland, 7 December, 1992 — LM
Scotland: U21-2

League Club	Source	Date Signed	Seasons Played	Apps	Subs	Gls
Sheffield U	Livingston	01/14	13-14	33	7	3

SCOULAR James (Jimmy)
Born: Livingston, West Lothian, Scotland, 11 January, 1925 — RH
Died: Cardiff, Wales, 21 March, 1998
Scotland: 9

League Club	Source	Date Signed	Seasons Played	Apps	Subs	Gls
Portsmouth	Gosport Bor	12/45	46-52	247	-	8
Newcastle U	Tr	06/53	53-60	247	-	6
Bradford Park Ave	Tr	01/61	60-63	108	-	5

SCOWCROFT James Benjamin (Jamie)
Born: Bury St Edmunds, Suffolk, England, 15 November, 1975 — F
England: U21-5

League Club	Source	Date Signed	Seasons Played	Apps	Subs	Gls
Ipswich T	YT	07/94	95-00	163	39	47
Leicester C	Tr	07/01	01-04	127	6	24
Ipswich T	L	02/05	04	3	6	0
Coventry C	Tr	07/05	05	37	4	3
Crystal Palace	Tr	07/06	06-08	66	17	14
Leyton Orient	Tr	07/09	09	13	13	0

SCOWEN Joshua Charles (Josh)
Born: Cheshunt, Hertfordshire, England, 28 March, 1993 — M

League Club	Source	Date Signed	Seasons Played	Apps	Subs	Gls
Wycombe W	Sch	07/11	10-14	88	3	3
Barnsley	Tr	01/15	14	19	2	4

SCREEN Anthony Lewis (Tony)
Born: Swansea, Wales, 9 May, 1952 — FB/F
Wales: U23-1

League Club	Source	Date Signed	Seasons Played	Apps	Subs	Gls
Swansea C	App	05/70	68-74	125	3	10

SCREEN William Robert (Willie)
Born: Swansea, Wales, 8 November, 1948 — M
Wales: U23-2

League Club	Source	Date Signed	Seasons Played	Apps	Subs	Gls
Swansea C	Jnr	03/67	67-71	133	9	13
Newport Co	Tr	06/72	72-75	137	5	7

SCRIMGEOUR Brian
Born: Dundee, Scotland, 11 August, 1959 — D/M

League Club	Source	Date Signed	Seasons Played	Apps	Subs	Gls
Chesterfield	Dundee	07/83	83-86	117	4	16

SCRIMSHAW Stanley (Stan)
Born: Hartlepool, Cleveland, England, 7 August, 1915 — CH
Died: Halifax, West Yorkshire, England, March, 1988

League Club	Source	Date Signed	Seasons Played	Apps	Subs	Gls
Hartlepool U	Easington CW	01/36	35-36	17	-	1
Bradford C	Tr	06/37	37-46	20	-	0
Halifax T	Frickley Colliery	10/47	47-49	52	-	0

SCRINE Francis Henry (Frank)
Born: Swansea, Wales, 9 January, 1925 — IF
Died: Swansea, Wales, 5 October, 2001
Wales: 2

League Club	Source	Date Signed	Seasons Played	Apps	Subs	Gls
Swansea C		03/44	47-53	143	-	46
Oldham Ath	Tr	10/53	53-55	78	-	21

SCRIVENS Stephen (Steve)
Born: Ewell, Surrey, England, 11 March, 1957 — LW

League Club	Source	Date Signed	Seasons Played	Apps	Subs	Gls
Fulham	App	03/75	74-75	3	1	1
Brentford	L	12/76	76	5	0	0

SCRIVENS William
Born: Rotherham, South Yorkshire, England, 26 May, 1936 — G

League Club	Source	Date Signed	Seasons Played	Apps	Subs	Gls
Rotherham U		08/56	56	2	-	0

SCRUGHAM Robert
Born: Cleator Moor, Cumbria, England, 15 May, 1932 — G

League Club	Source	Date Signed	Seasons Played	Apps	Subs	Gls
Workington	Cleator Moor	08/53	53	3	-	0

SCULLION Stewart McNab Adam
Born: Bo'ness, Falkirk, Scotland, 18 April, 1946 — W

League Club	Source	Date Signed	Seasons Played	Apps	Subs	Gls
Charlton Ath	Chesham U	03/65				

League Club	Source	Date Signed	Seasons Played	Apps	Subs	Gls
Watford	Tr	02/66	65-70	217	8	30
Sheffield U	Tr	05/71	71-73	53	4	7
Watford	Tr	12/73	73-75	87	0	19
SCULLY Anthony Derek Thomas (Tony)						
Born: Dublin, Republic of Ireland, 12 June, 1976						W
Republic of Ireland: B-1/U21-10/Youth/Schools						
Crystal Palace	YT	12/93	95-96	0	3	0
Bournemouth	L	10/94	94	6	4	0
Cardiff C	L	01/96	95	13	1	0
Manchester C	Tr	08/97	97	1	8	0
Stoke C	L	01/98	97	7	0	0
Queens Park Rgrs	Tr	03/98	97-00	20	20	2
Cambridge U	Tr	07/01	01-02	20	11	2
Southend U	L	11/02	02	8	0	0
Peterborough U	Tr	03/03	02	0	3	0
Notts Co	Barnet	02/04	03-04	26	15	5
SCULLY Patrick Joseph (Pat)						
Born: Dublin, Republic of Ireland, 23 June, 1970						CD
Republic of Ireland: 1/B/U23-1/U21-9/Youth/Schools						
Arsenal	YT	09/87				
Preston NE	L	09/89	89	13	0	1
Northampton T	L	08/90	90	15	0	0
Southend U	Tr	01/91	90-93	114	1	6
Huddersfield T	Tr	03/94	93-95	74	0	2
SCURR David William						
Born: Netley, Hampshire, England, 25 September, 1939						LB
Died: Southampton, England, 26 July, 1991						
Southampton	Jnr	04/58	59-60	2	-	0
SCURR John Thomas (Jackie)						
Born: North Shields, Tyne and Wear, England, 30 September, 1940						IF
Died: Hertfordshire, England, February, 2013						
Arsenal	North Shields BC	09/59				
Carlisle U	Tr	01/61	60-61	14	-	1
SEABORNE Daniel Anthony (Danny)						
Born: Holsworthy, Devon, England, 5 March, 1987						CD
Exeter C	Sch	07/05	08-09	48	4	1
Southampton	Tr	01/10	09-11	29	15	0
Charlton Ath	L	11/12	12	7	0	0
Bournemouth	L	01/13	12	13	0	0
Yeovil T	Tr	07/13	13	10	0	0
Coventry C	Tr	11/13	13	18	3	1
SEABRIGHT Jordan						
Born: Poole, Dorset, England, 1 May, 1994						G
Bournemouth	Jnr	08/11				
Dagenham & Red	Tr	08/12	12-13	7	1	0
SEABURY Kevin						
Born: Shrewsbury, Shropshire, England, 24 November, 1973						RB
Shrewsbury T	YT	07/92	92-00	206	23	7
SEACOLE Jason Paul						
Born: Oxford, England, 11 April, 1960						F
England: Youth/Schools						
Oxford U	App	04/77	76-81	104	16	22
SEADEN John Charles						
Born: Southend-on-Sea, England, 4 June, 1967						M
Southend U	App	03/85	84-85	18	1	0
SEAGER Ryan Paul						
Born: Yeovil, Somerset, England, 5 February, 1996						F
England: Youth						
Southampton	Sch	02/13	14	0	1	0
SEAGRAVES Christopher Anthony (Chris)						
Born: Liverpool, England, 7 October, 1964						RB
Liverpool	App	09/82				
Grimsby T	Tr	08/84	84	22	1	0
SEAGRAVES Mark						
Born: Bootle, Merseyside, England, 22 October, 1966						CD
England: Youth/Schools						
Liverpool	App	11/83				
Norwich C	L	11/86	86	3	0	0
Manchester C	Tr	09/87	87-89	36	6	0
Bolton W	Tr	09/90	90-94	152	5	7
Swindon T	Tr	06/95	95-97	57	4	0
SEAL David						
Born: Penrith, NSW, Australia, 26 January, 1972						F
Australia: U23/Youth						
Bristol C	Aalst (BEL)	10/94	94-96	24	27	10
Northampton T	Tr	08/97	97-98	35	8	12

League Club	Source	Date Signed	Seasons Played	Apps	Subs	Gls
SEAL James (Jimmy)						
Born: Wakefield, England, 9 December, 1950						F
Wolverhampton W	Upton Robins	03/68	68	1	0	0
Walsall	L	01/70	69	17	0	8
Walsall	L	12/70	70	24	0	6
Barnsley	Tr	05/71	71	43	0	12
York C	Tr	07/72	72-76	152	9	43
Darlington	Tr	11/76	76-79	115	7	19
Rochdale	Tr	11/79	79-80	44	9	4
SEALEY Alan William						
Born: Canning Town, E London, England, 24 February, 1942						RW
Died: Romford, E London, England, February, 1996						
Leyton Orient	Memorial Sports	08/59	60	4	-	1
West Ham U	Tr	03/61	60-66	107	0	22
Plymouth Arg	Tr	09/67	67	4	0	0
SEALEY Arthur John (John)						
Born: Wallasey, Wirral, England, 27 December, 1945						RW
Liverpool	Warrington T	12/63	64	1	-	1
Chester C	Tr	06/66	66-67	3	1	0
SEALEY Leslie Jesse (Les)						
Born: Bethnal Green, E London, England, 29 September, 1957						G
Died: Southend-on-Sea, England, 19 August, 2001						
Coventry C	App	03/76	76-82	158	0	0
Luton T	Tr	08/83	83-88	207	0	0
Plymouth Arg	L	10/84	84	6	0	0
Manchester U	L	03/90	89	2	0	0
Manchester U	Tr	06/90	90	31	0	0
Aston Villa	Tr	07/91	91	18	0	0
Coventry C	L	03/92	91	2	0	0
Birmingham C	L	10/92	92	12	0	0
Manchester U	Tr	01/93				
Blackpool	Tr	07/94	94	7	0	0
West Ham U	Tr	11/94	95	1	1	0
Leyton Orient	Tr	07/96	96	12	0	0
West Ham U	Tr	11/96	96	1	1	0
SEALY Anthony John (Tony)						
Born: Hackney, E London, England, 7 May, 1959						F
Southampton	App	05/77	77-78	2	5	0
Crystal Palace	Tr	03/79	78-80	16	8	5
Port Vale	L	02/80	79	17	0	6
Queens Park Rgrs	Tr	03/81	80-83	57	6	18
Port Vale	L	02/82	81	6	0	4
Fulham	L	12/83	83	5	0	1
Fulham	Tr	08/84	84-85	17	3	10
Leicester C	Tr	09/85	85-86	28	11	7
Bournemouth	L	03/87	86	8	5	2
Brentford	SC Braga (POR)	03/89	88	11	1	4
Bristol Rov	Tr	09/89	89-90	21	16	7
Brentford	MyPa (FIN)	10/91	91	9	9	0
SEAMAN David Andrew						
Born: Rotherham, South Yorkshire, England, 19 September, 1963						G
England: 75/B-6/U21-10						
Leeds U	App	09/81				
Peterborough U	Tr	08/82	82-84	91	0	0
Birmingham C	Tr	10/84	84-85	75	0	0
Queens Park Rgrs	Tr	08/86	86-89	141	0	0
Arsenal	Tr	05/90	90-02	405	0	0
Manchester C	Tr	07/03	03	19	0	0
SEANLA Stephane Claude (Claude)						
Born: Abidjan, Ivory Coast, 2 June, 1988						F
Watford	Tottenham H (Sch)	06/06				
Barnet	Kettering T	08/07	07	1	2	0
SEAR Reginald Clifford (Cliff)						
Born: Rhostyllen, Wrexham, Wales, 22 September, 1936						LB
Died: Chester, England, 8 July, 2000						
Wales: 1/U23-2						
Manchester C	Oswestry T	01/57	56-65	248	0	1
Chester C	Tr	04/68	68-69	48	1	1
SEARGEANT Steven Charles (Steve)						
Born: Liverpool, England, 2 January, 1951						D
England: Schools						
Everton	App	07/68	71-77	77	3	1
SEARLE Damon Peter						
Born: Cardiff, Wales, 26 October, 1971						LB
Wales: B-1/U21-6/Youth/Schools						
Cardiff C	YT	08/90	90-95	232	2	3
Stockport Co	Tr	05/96	96-97	34	7	0
Carlisle U	Tr	07/98	98-99	57	9	3
Rochdale	L	09/99	99	13	1	0
Southend U	Tr	07/00	00-02	126	7	3
Chesterfield	Tr	08/03	03	4	1	0

League Club	Source	Date Signed	Seasons Played	Career Record Apps	Subs	Gls
SEARLE Eric Frederick						
Born: Guildford, Surrey, England, 20 July, 1925						G
Aldershot		10/47	47-49	14	-	0
SEARLE Stephen (Steve)						
Born: Lambeth, S London, England, 7 March, 1977						M
Barnet	Sittingbourne	08/97	97-99	67	17	5
SEARLE Stuart Andrew						
Born: Wimbledon, SW London, England, 27 February, 1979						G
Chelsea	Basingstoke T	07/07				
Watford	Tr	01/09				
MK Dons	Tr	07/09	09-10	6	0	0
SEARS Douglas Reginald (Doug)						
Born: Eton, Berkshire, England, 5 January, 1919						IF
Died: Slough, Berkshire, United Kingdom, March, 1995						
Grimsby T	Slough T	10/43				
Reading	Tr	05/46	46	5	-	0
Aldershot	Tr	06/47	47-49	46	-	13
SEARS Frederick David (Freddie)						
Born: Hornchurch, E London, England, 27 November, 1989						F
England: U21-3/Youth						
West Ham U	Sch	07/07	07-11	16	30	2
Crystal Palace	L	06/09	09	11	7	0
Coventry C	L	02/10	09	3	7	0
Scunthorpe U	L	10/10	10	9	0	0
Colchester U	Tr	02/12	11-14	76	26	31
Ipswich T	Tr	01/15	14	14	7	9
SEARS Gerald (Gerry)						
Born: Arkwright Town, Derbyshire, England, 13 January, 1935						LB
Died: Chesterfield, Derbyshire, England, 11 September, 2014						
Chesterfield	Jnr	01/52	52-67	413	0	4
SEARSON Harold Vincent (Harry)						
Born: Mansfield, Nottinghamshire, England, 3 June, 1924						G
Died: Corby, Northamptonshire, England, 9 January, 2013						
Sheffield Wed	Bilsthorpe Colliery	08/46				
Mansfield T	Tr	06/47	47-48	42	-	0
Leeds U	Tr	01/49	48-51	104	-	0
York C	Tr	11/52	52-53	62	-	0
SEARY Raymond Michael (Ray)						
Born: Slough, Berkshire, England, 18 September, 1952						LB
Died: Histon, Cambridgeshire, England, 5 December, 2001						
Queens Park Rgrs	App	09/70	71	0	1	0
Cambridge U	Tr	03/74	73-75	55	2	0
SEASMAN John						
Born: Liverpool, England, 21 February, 1955						M/F
Tranmere Rov	App	02/73	72-74	15	2	0
Luton T	Tr	01/75	74-75	7	1	2
Millwall	Tr	02/76	75-79	157	1	35
Rotherham U	Tr	08/80	80-83	93	7	25
Cardiff C	Tr	08/84	84	10	2	2
Rochdale	L	11/84	84	8	0	0
Chesterfield	Tr	01/85	84	8	2	1
Rochdale	Tr	07/85	85-87	86	1	4
SEATHERTON Raymond (Ray)						
Born: Tiverton, Devon, England, 20 May, 1932						CF
Died: Tiverton, Devon, England, 3 October, 2011						
Bristol Rov	Minehead	02/55	55	2	-	2
SEATON Gordon						
Born: Wick, Highlands, Scotland, 1 September, 1945						WH
Chester C	Rhyl	12/66	66-67	46	3	2
SEBA Jesus Hernandez						
Born: Zaragoza, Spain, 11 April, 1974						W
Spain: U21-3						
Wigan Ath	Real Zaragoza (SPN)	08/95	95-96	8	13	3
SEBOK Vilmos						
Born: Budapest, Hungary, 13 June, 1973						D
Hungary: 53/U23-12						
Bristol C	Ujpest (HUN)	01/99	98-99	18	5	0
SECK Mamadou						
Born: Rufisque, Senegal, 23 August, 1979						CD
Senegal: 6						
Sheffield U	Le Havre (FRA)	01/07				
Scunthorpe U	L	01/08	07	0	1	0
SEDDON Andrew (Andy)						
Born: Worsley, Greater Manchester, England, 23 November, 1959						FB
Stockport Co		08/77	78	1	3	0
Stockport Co		03/82	81-82	3	0	0

League Club	Source	Date Signed	Seasons Played	Career Record Apps	Subs	Gls
SEDDON Benjamin Paul (Ben)						
Born: Liverpool, England, 5 February, 1952						CD
Tranmere Rov	Formby	04/73	73	1	0	0
SEDDON David Andrew						
Born: Rochdale, Greater Manchester, England, 13 April, 1951						LB
Rochdale	Stafford Rgrs	01/74	73-74	18	2	0
SEDDON Frank Owen						
Born: Stockton-on-Tees, Cleveland, England, 1 May, 1928						CH
Notts Co	Primrose Hill, Stock'n	05/46				
Hull C		05/47	49	3	-	0
Halifax T	Tr	01/51	50-51	4	-	0
SEDDON Gareth Jonathan						
Born: Burnley, Lancashire, England, 23 May, 1980						F
England: Semi Pro-2						
Bury	RAF Codsall	08/01	01-03	53	26	17
Rushden & D	Tr	07/04				
SEDDON Ian Wright						
Born: Prestbury, Cheshire, England, 14 October, 1950						M
Bolton W	App	06/69	69-72	51	13	4
Chester C	Tr	09/73	73-75	62	11	7
Stockport Co	L	11/75	75	4	0	0
Chesterfield	L	01/76	75	2	0	0
Cambridge U	Tr	02/76	75-76	34	3	3
Rochdale	Tr	07/77	77	30	1	3
Wigan Ath	Tr	07/78	78	1	0	0
SEDDON Thomas (Tom)						
Born: Rotherham, South Yorkshire, England, 25 October, 1935						LB
Rotherham U		03/54	58	1	-	0
SEDGEMORE Benjamin Redwood (Ben)						
Born: Wolverhampton, England, 5 August, 1975						M
England: Schools						
Birmingham C	YT	05/93				
Northampton T	L	12/94	94	1	0	0
Mansfield T	L	08/95	95	4	5	0
Peterborough U	Tr	01/96	95	13	4	0
Mansfield T	Tr	09/96	96-97	58	9	6
Macclesfield T	Tr	03/98	97-00	84	18	6
Lincoln C	Tr	02/01	00-03	83	25	5
SEDGEMORE Jacob Oliver (Jake)						
Born: Wolverhampton, England, 10 October, 1978						W
England: Semi Pro-5						
Shrewsbury T	Northwich Victoria	07/03	04	25	6	5
Bury	Tr	07/05	05	3	6	0
SEDGLEY Stephen Philip (Steve)						
Born: Enfield, N London, England, 26 May, 1968						CD/M
England: U21-11						
Coventry C	App	06/86	86-88	81	3	3
Tottenham H	Tr	07/89	89-93	147	17	8
Ipswich T	Tr	06/94	94-96	105	0	15
Wolverhampton W	Tr	07/97	97-00	96	10	9
SEDGWICK Christopher Edward (Chris)						
Born: Sheffield, England, 28 April, 1980						RW
Rotherham U	YT	08/97	97-04	195	48	17
Preston NE	Tr	11/04	04-09	207	22	12
Sheffield Wed	Tr	07/10	10-11	29	14	5
Scunthorpe U	Tr	09/12	12	0	4	0
Bury	Hyde FC	07/13	13-14	33	24	2
SEDLAN Jason Mark						
Born: Peterborough, England, 5 August, 1979						M
Mansfield T	YT	07/98	97-98	1	5	0
SEDLOSKI Goce						
Born: Prilep, Macedonia, 10 April, 1974						CD
Macedonia: 100						
Sheffield Wed	Hadjuk Split (CRO)	03/98	97	3	1	0
SEED Trevance Frederick (Terry)						
Born: Preston, Lancashire, England, 3 September, 1923						CH
Died: Preston, Lancashire, England, December, 1994						
Preston NE	Jnr	07/46				
Carlisle U	Tr	12/46	46-49	81	-	0
Accrington Stan	Tr	09/50	50	1	-	0
SEEMLEY Ivor John						
Born: Sheffield, England, 30 June, 1929						FB
Died: Sheffield, England, 3 November, 2014						
Sheffield Wed	Jnr	07/46	53-54	15	-	0
Stockport Co	Tr	06/55	55-56	81	-	0
Chesterfield	Tr	06/57	57-58	77	-	0

League Club	Source	Date Signed	Seasons Played	Career Record Apps	Subs	Gls

SEGERS Johannes (Hans)
Born: Eindhoven, Netherlands, 30 October, 1961 G

Nottingham F	PSV Eindhoven (NED)	08/84	84-87	58	0	0
Stoke C	L	02/87	86	1	0	0
Sheffield U	L	11/87	87	10	0	0
Wimbledon	Tr	09/88	88-95	265	2	0
Wolverhampton W	Tr	08/96	97	11	0	0
Tottenham H	Tr	08/98	98	1	0	0

SEGURA Victor Abascal
Born: Zaragoza, Spain, 13 March, 1973 D

Norwich C	UE Lleida (SPN)	08/97	97-98	24	5	0

SEIDI Alberto Adulai
Born: Guinea-Bissau, 20 November, 1992 W

Southampton	Sch	04/11				
Aldershot T	L	11/12	12	0	1	0

SEIGEL Arnold William
Born: Islington, N London, England, 21 March, 1919 WH
Died: Edgware, NW London, England, December, 2008

Leyton Orient	Hendon	06/46	46	9	-	0

SEIP Marcel
Born: Winschoten, Netherlands, 5 April, 1982 CD
Netherlands: U21-1

Plymouth Arg	Heerenveen (NED)	08/06	06-10	130	4	6
Blackpool	L	09/09	09	7	0	2
Sheffield U	L	01/10	09	5	1	0
Bradford C	Tr	10/11	11	23	0	1

SEITH Robert (Bobby)
Born: Coatbridge, Lanarkshire, Scotland, 9 March, 1932 RH

Burnley	Monifieth Tayside	03/49	53-59	211	-	6

SEKAJJA Ibra
Born: Kampala, Uganda, 31 October, 1992 F
England: Youth

Crystal Palace	Sch	05/11	10-11	1	1	1
MK Dons	L	11/12	12	0	1	0
Barnet	L	01/13	12	3	1	0

SELBY Dennis
Born: Broughton, Flintshire, Wales, 15 October, 1920 W
Died: Chester, England, 5 August, 1969

Chester C (Am)		07/46	46	5	-	1

SELF Glenn Walter
Born: Norwich, England, 4 December, 1953 F

Norwich C	App	09/70	70-72	4	1	2
Torquay U	L	03/73	72	3	0	0

SELKIRK John (Jack)
Born: Doncaster, South Yorkshire, England, 20 January, 1923 RB
Died: Sleaford, Lincolnshire, England, 11 August, 1993

Rotherham U	Edlington CW	10/44	46-56	427	-	13

SELLARS Geoffrey (Geoff)
Born: Stockport, Greater Manchester, England, 20 May, 1930 RW

Leeds U	Altrincham	04/50				
Aston Villa	Tr	08/50	50	2	-	0

SELLARS John (Johnny)
Born: Stoke-on-Trent, England, 28 April, 1924 WH
Died: Stoke-on-Trent, England, 24 June, 1985

Stoke C	Jnr	10/41	46-57	384	-	14

SELLARS Peter
Born: Market Rasen, Lincolnshire, England, 15 March, 1958 M

Lincoln C	App	-	75	0	1	0

SELLARS Scott
Born: Sheffield, England, 27 November, 1965 LW
England: U21-3

Leeds U	App	07/83	82-85	72	4	12
Blackburn Rov	Tr	07/86	86-91	194	8	35
Leeds U	Tr	07/92	92	6	1	0
Newcastle U	Tr	03/93	92-95	56	5	5
Bolton W	Tr	12/95	95-98	106	5	15
Huddersfield T	Tr	07/99	99-00	29	19	1
Port Vale	Aarhus GF (DEN)	01/02				
Mansfield T	Tr	03/02	01-02	17	3	3

SELLEY Ian
Born: Chertsey, Surrey, England, 14 June, 1974 M
England: U21-3/Youth

Arsenal	YT	05/92	92-96	35	6	0
Southend U	L	12/96	96	3	1	0
Fulham	Tr	10/97	97	3	0	0
Wimbledon	Tr	08/00	00	1	3	0
Southend U	L	02/02	01	14	0	0
Southend U	L	08/02	02	11	0	0

SELLS Charles Edward
Born: Paddington, Central London, England, 24 June, 1939 IF

Exeter C	Wealdstone	08/62	62	14	-	3

SEMARK Robin Harry
Born: Portsmouth, England, 5 September, 1972 M

Cardiff C	YT	07/91	91	4	2	0

SEMBIE-FERRIS Dion Leonard
Born: Peterborough, England, 23 May, 1996 W

Colchester U	St Neots T	11/13	14	2	8	0

SEMEDO Jose Victor Moreira
Born: Setubal, Portugal, 11 January, 1985 DM
Portugal: U21-13/Youth

Charlton Ath	Sporting Lisbon (POR)	07/07	07-10	117	18	2
Sheffield Wed	Tr	07/11	11-14	107	17	1

SEMLEY Alan
Born: Barnsley, South Yorkshire, England, 21 February, 1966 F

Barnsley	App	02/84	83	1	3	0

SEMPLE Ryan
Born: Derry, Northern Ireland, 2 July, 1977 M

Peterborough U	YT	-	94	1	1	0

SEMPLE Ryan David
Born: Belfast, Northern Ireland, 4 July, 1985 RW

Peterborough U	Sch	08/02	02-05	15	26	3
Lincoln C	Tr	07/06	06	0	4	0
Chester C	L	11/06	06	0	3	0

SENDA Daniel Luke (Danny)
Born: Harrow, NW London, England, 17 April, 1981 RB
England: Youth

Wycombe W	Southampton (Jnr)	01/99	98-05	217	59	9
Millwall	Tr	08/06	06-07	73	3	1
Torquay U		09/10	10	2	0	0
Bristol Rov	Tr	02/11	10	15	0	0
Barnet	Tr	07/11	11	19	0	0

SENDALL Richard Adam
Born: Stamford, Lincolnshire, England, 10 July, 1967 F

Blackpool	Watford (App)	07/85	85-86	6	5	0
Carlisle U	Tr	07/88	88-92	48	36	14
Cardiff C	L	09/89	89	3	1	0

SENDEROS Philippe Sylvain
Born: Geneva, Switzerland, 14 February, 1985 CD
Switzerland: 54/U23-5/Youth

Arsenal	Servette (SUI)	07/03	04-07	54	10	4
Everton	L	01/10	09	1	1	0
Fulham	Tr	07/10	10-13	54	3	2
Aston Villa	Valencia (SPN)	06/14	14	7	1	0

SENDLES-WHITE Jamie Alex
Born: Kingston-on-Thames, SW London, England, 10 April, 1994 CD
Northern Ireland: U21-8/Youth

Queens Park Rgrs	Sch	01/12				
Mansfield T	L	10/14	14	7	0	0

SENE Saer
Born: Paris, France, 4 November, 1986 F

Blackpool	New York R Bulls (USA)	01/15	14	0	1	0

SENIOR Allan Gordon
Born: Dewsbury, West Yorkshire, England, 29 September, 1930 RH

Halifax T		08/52	52	1	-	0

SENIOR Colin
Born: Thornhill, West Yorkshire, England, 3 June, 1927 CH
Died: Leicester, England, 9 January, 2011

Huddersfield T	Stocksbridge Works	06/45	50	5	-	1
Accrington Stan	Tr	06/51	51	27	-	1

SENIOR Courtney Fitzroy
Born: Croydon, S London, England, 30 June, 1997 W

Brentford	Sch	12/14				
Wycombe W	L	01/15	14	0	1	0

SENIOR Karl Robert
Born: Northwich, Cheshire, England, 3 September, 1972 M

Chester C	YT	-	89	0	1	0

SENIOR Michael Graham (Mike)
Born: Huddersfield, West Yorkshire, England, 3 March, 1981 M

Huddersfield T	YT	07/99	00	0	4	0

SENIOR Philip Anthony (Phil)
Born: Huddersfield, West Yorkshire, England, 30 October, 1982 — G

League Club	Source	Date Signed	Seasons Played	Apps	Subs	Gls
Huddersfield T	YT	11/99	02-05	49	4	0

SENIOR Philip Malcolm (Malcolm)
Born: Mapplewell, South Yorkshire, England, 29 May, 1943 — D

League Club	Source	Date Signed	Seasons Played	Apps	Subs	Gls
Barnsley	Jnr	06/61				
Southport	Tr	07/63	63	2	-	0

SENIOR Stephen (Steve)
Born: Sheffield, England, 15 May, 1963 — RB

League Club	Source	Date Signed	Seasons Played	Apps	Subs	Gls
York C	App	05/81	80-86	158	10	6
Darlington	L	10/84	84	5	0	0
Northampton T	Tr	06/87	87	1	3	0
Wigan Ath	Tr	10/87	87-89	107	2	3
Preston NE	Tr	07/90	90-91	73	0	3

SENIOR Stuart
Born: Barnsley, South Yorkshire, England, 26 October, 1953 — W

League Club	Source	Date Signed	Seasons Played	Apps	Subs	Gls
Barnsley	App	11/71	72	1	1	0

SENIOR Trevor John
Born: Dorchester, Dorset, England, 28 November, 1961 — F

League Club	Source	Date Signed	Seasons Played	Apps	Subs	Gls
Portsmouth	Dorchester T	12/81	81-82	11	0	2
Aldershot	L	03/83	82	10	0	6
Reading	Tr	08/83	83-86	164	0	102
Watford	Tr	07/87	87	22	2	1
Middlesbrough	Tr	03/88	87-88	9	1	2
Reading	Tr	10/88	88-91	127	10	52

SENIOR Vincent Roy (Roy)
Born: Barnsley, South Yorkshire, England, 21 June, 1940 — W
Died: Barnsley, South Yorkshire, England, January, 2012

League Club	Source	Date Signed	Seasons Played	Apps	Subs	Gls
Doncaster Rov		08/60	60	12	-	5
Peterborough U	Tr	07/61	61-63	38	-	11
Millwall	Tr	03/64	63-64	15	-	3
Barnsley	Tr	11/64	64	21	-	4

SEOL Ki-Hyeon
Born: Jeongseon, South Korea, 8 January, 1979 — W
South Korea: 83/U23-21

League Club	Source	Date Signed	Seasons Played	Apps	Subs	Gls
Wolverhampton W	Anderlecht (BEL)	09/04	04-05	50	19	8
Reading	Tr	07/06	06-07	24	6	4
Fulham	Tr	08/07	07-09	6	12	1

SEPP Dennis
Born: Apeldoorn, Netherlands, 5 June, 1973 — W

League Club	Source	Date Signed	Seasons Played	Apps	Subs	Gls
Bradford C	HSC91 (NED)	06/97	97	0	3	0

SERCOMBE Liam Michael
Born: Exeter, England, 25 April, 1990 — M

League Club	Source	Date Signed	Seasons Played	Apps	Subs	Gls
Exeter C	Sch	03/08	08-14	205	31	23

SERELLA David Edward (Dave)
Born: King's Lynn, Norfolk, England, 24 September, 1952 — CD

League Club	Source	Date Signed	Seasons Played	Apps	Subs	Gls
Nottingham F	App	08/70	71-74	65	3	0
Walsall	Tr	11/74	75-81	262	2	12
Walsall	L	11/74	74	3	0	0
Blackpool	Tr	08/82	82-83	34	1	3

SEREMET Dino
Born: Ljubljana, Slovenia, 16 August, 1980 — G

League Club	Source	Date Signed	Seasons Played	Apps	Subs	Gls
Luton T	NK Maribor (SVN)	07/04	04	6	1	0
Doncaster Rov	L	11/05	05	1	0	0
Tranmere Rov	L	01/06	05	13	0	0

SERENI Matteo
Born: Parma, Italy, 11 February, 1975 — G
Italy: U21-4

League Club	Source	Date Signed	Seasons Played	Apps	Subs	Gls
Ipswich T	Sampdoria (ITA)	08/01	01	25	0	0

SERIOUX Adrian Roger
Born: Scarborough, Ontario, Canada, 12 May, 1979 — RB/M
Canada: 19

League Club	Source	Date Signed	Seasons Played	Apps	Subs	Gls
Millwall	Toronto Lynx (CAN)	08/04	04-05	12	12	0

SERMANNI Thomas Dorby (Tommy)
Born: Glasgow, Scotland, 1 July, 1954 — M
Scotland: Schools

League Club	Source	Date Signed	Seasons Played	Apps	Subs	Gls
Blackpool	Albion Rov	03/78	78	6	4	1
Torquay U	Dundee U	08/79	79-82	83	6	12

SERRAN Albert
Born: Barcelona, Spain, 17 July, 1989 — CD

League Club	Source	Date Signed	Seasons Played	Apps	Subs	Gls
Swansea C	RCD Espanyol (SPN)	08/08	08-10	18	12	0

SERRANT Carl
Born: Bradford, England, 12 September, 1975 — LB
England: B-1/U21-2/Youth

League Club	Source	Date Signed	Seasons Played	Apps	Subs	Gls
Oldham Ath	YT	07/94	95-97	84	6	1
Newcastle U	Tr	07/98	98-99	5	1	0
Bury	L	02/99	98	15	0	0

SERTORI Mark Anthony
Born: Manchester, England, 1 September, 1967 — CD

League Club	Source	Date Signed	Seasons Played	Apps	Subs	Gls
Stockport Co	East Manchester	02/87	86-87	3	1	0
Lincoln C	Tr	07/88	88-89	43	7	9
Wrexham	Tr	02/90	89-93	106	4	3
Bury	Tr	07/94	94-95	4	9	1
Scunthorpe U	Tr	07/96	96-97	82	1	2
Halifax T	Tr	07/98	98-99	44	1	0
York C	Tr	09/99	99-00	63	3	2
Shrewsbury T	Tr	03/01	00	0	1	0
Cheltenham T	Tr	03/01	00	10	0	0

SESAY Alie
Born: Enfield, N London, England, 25 July, 1993 — CD
Sierra Leone: 2

League Club	Source	Date Signed	Seasons Played	Apps	Subs	Gls
Leicester C	Sch	07/12				
Colchester U	L	01/14	13	2	1	0

SESSEGNON Stephane
Born: Bohicon, Benin, 1 June, 1984 — M/F
Benin: 51

League Club	Source	Date Signed	Seasons Played	Apps	Subs	Gls
Sunderland	Paris St-Germain (FRA)	01/11	10-13	85	2	17
West Bromwich A	Tr	09/13	13-14	43	11	6

SESTANOVICH Ashley Shane
Born: Lambeth, S London, England, 18 September, 1981 — LW

League Club	Source	Date Signed	Seasons Played	Apps	Subs	Gls
Sheffield U	Hampton & Richmond Bor	02/03	03	0	2	0
Grimsby T	L	06/04	04	17	5	2
Chester C	Tr	02/05	04	3	4	0

SETCHELL Gary John
Born: King's Lynn, Norfolk, England, 8 May, 1975 — LB

League Club	Source	Date Signed	Seasons Played	Apps	Subs	Gls
Rushden & D	Kettering T	06/00	01-02	20	13	1

SETTERS Maurice Edgar
Born: Honiton, Devon, England, 16 December, 1936 — WH
England: U23-16/Youth/Schools

League Club	Source	Date Signed	Seasons Played	Apps	Subs	Gls
Exeter C	Jnr	01/54	53-54	10	-	0
West Bromwich A	Tr	01/55	55-59	120	-	10
Manchester U	Tr	01/60	59-64	159	-	12
Stoke C	Tr	11/64	64-67	86	0	5
Coventry C	Tr	11/67	67-69	50	1	3
Charlton Ath	Tr	01/70	69	8	0	1

SEVERIN Scott Derek
Born: Stirling, Scotland, 15 February, 1979 — DM
Scotland: 15/U21-10

League Club	Source	Date Signed	Seasons Played	Apps	Subs	Gls
Watford	Aberdeen	07/09	09	4	5	0

SEVERN James Alexander Robert
Born: Nottingham, England, 10 October, 1991 — G
England: Youth

League Club	Source	Date Signed	Seasons Played	Apps	Subs	Gls
Derby Co	Sch	07/10	10	0	1	0
Scunthorpe U	Tr	06/12	12-14	1	2	0

SEWARD Bruce Walter
Born: Uxbridge, W London, England, 10 February, 1939 — IF

League Club	Source	Date Signed	Seasons Played	Apps	Subs	Gls
Brighton & HA	Yiewsley	05/57				
Aldershot	Tr	07/59	59	1	-	0

SEWARD Gary
Born: Paddington, Central London, England, 1 October, 1961 — F

League Club	Source	Date Signed	Seasons Played	Apps	Subs	Gls
Blackpool	App	11/79	79	0	1	0

SEWELL Arthur
Born: Cornforth, County Durham, England, 15 July, 1934 — IF

League Club	Source	Date Signed	Seasons Played	Apps	Subs	Gls
Bradford C (Am)	Bishop Auckland	06/54	54	1	-	0

SEWELL John (Jackie)
Born: Whitehaven, Cumbria, England, 24 January, 1927 — IF
England: 6/FLge-5//Zambia: 10

League Club	Source	Date Signed	Seasons Played	Apps	Subs	Gls
Notts Co	Whitehaven T	10/44	46-50	178	-	97
Sheffield Wed	Tr	03/51	50-55	164	-	87
Aston Villa	Tr	12/55	55-59	123	-	36
Hull C	Tr	10/59	59-60	44	-	8

SEWELL John David
Born: Brockley, SE London, England, 7 July, 1936 — RB

League Club	Source	Date Signed	Seasons Played	Apps	Subs	Gls
Charlton Ath	Bexleyheath & Welling	01/55	56-63	185	-	5
Crystal Palace	Tr	10/63	63-70	228	3	6
Leyton Orient	Tr	08/71	71	5	2	0

SEXTON David James (Dave)
Born: Islington, N London, England, 6 April, 1930 — IF
Died: Kenilworth, Warwickshire, England, 25 November, 2012

League Club	Source	Date Signed	Seasons Played	Apps	Subs	Gls
Luton T	Chelmsford C	06/51	51-52	9	-	1
West Ham U	Tr	04/53	52-55	74	-	27

League Club	Source	Date Signed	Seasons Played	Apps	Subs	Gls
Leyton Orient	Tr	06/56	56-57	24	-	4
Brighton & HA	Tr	10/57	57-58	49	-	26
Crystal Palace	Tr	05/59	59	27	-	11

SEYMOUR Christopher David (Chris)
Born: Reading, England, 14 September, 1971 — M/D

League Club	Source	Date Signed	Seasons Played	Apps	Subs	Gls
Reading	YT	07/90	90-91	10	3	0

SEYMOUR Ian Patrick
Born: Tunbridge Wells, Kent, England, 17 March, 1948 — G

League Club	Source	Date Signed	Seasons Played	Apps	Subs	Gls
Fulham	Tonbridge	08/66	66-70	64	0	0
Brighton & HA	L	02/71	70	3	0	0

SHAABAN Rami
Born: Stockholm, Sweden, 30 June, 1975 — G
Sweden: 16

League Club	Source	Date Signed	Seasons Played	Apps	Subs	Gls
Arsenal	Djurgaarden (SWE)	08/02	02	3	0	0
Brighton & HA	Tr	02/05	04	6	0	0

SHACKELL Jason Philip
Born: Stevenage, Hertfordshire, England, 27 August, 1983 — CD

League Club	Source	Date Signed	Seasons Played	Apps	Subs	Gls
Norwich C	Sch	01/03	02-08	112	7	3
Wolverhampton W	Tr	09/08	08	3	9	0
Norwich C	L	02/09	08	14	0	0
Doncaster Rov	L	08/09	09	20	1	1
Barnsley	Tr	05/10	10	44	0	3
Derby Co	Tr	07/11	11	46	0	1
Burnley	Tr	07/12	12-14	128	0	4

SHACKLETON Alan
Born: Padiham, Lancashire, England, 3 February, 1934 — CF
Died: Bromley, SE London, England, 6 May, 2009

League Club	Source	Date Signed	Seasons Played	Apps	Subs	Gls
Burnley	Bolton W (Am)	05/54	56-58	31	-	18
Leeds U	Tr	10/58	58-59	30	-	16
Everton	Tr	09/59	59	26	-	10
Oldham Ath	Nelson	08/61	61	10	-	7

SHACKLETON Leonard Francis (Len)
Born: Bradford, England, 3 May, 1922 — IF
Died: Kendal, Cumbria, England, 28 November, 2000
England: 5/B-1/FLge-2/Schools/War-1

League Club	Source	Date Signed	Seasons Played	Apps	Subs	Gls
Bradford Park Ave	Dartford	12/40	46	7	-	4
Newcastle U	Tr	10/46	46-47	57	-	26
Sunderland	Tr	02/48	47-57	320	-	97

SHADBOLT William Henry
Born: Shrewsbury, Shropshire, England, 4 August, 1932 — LW
Died: Shrewsbury, Shropshire, England, 1980

League Club	Source	Date Signed	Seasons Played	Apps	Subs	Gls
Sheffield Wed	Oswestry T	01/53	52	7	-	0
Halifax T	Tr	03/54	53	3	-	1

SHAHIN Jammal
Born: Grimsby, North Lincolnshire, England, 19 December, 1988 — W

League Club	Source	Date Signed	Seasons Played	Apps	Subs	Gls
Grimsby T	Armthorpe Welfare	10/09	09	4	1	0

SHAIL Mark Edward David
Born: Sandviken, Sweden, 15 October, 1966 — CD
England: Semi Pro-1

League Club	Source	Date Signed	Seasons Played	Apps	Subs	Gls
Bristol C	Yeovil T	03/93	92-99	117	11	4
Kidderminster Hrs	Tr	07/00	00-01	40	0	1

SHAKES Ricky Ulric
Born: Brixton, S London, England, 26 January, 1985 — W
Guyana: 10//Trinidad & Tobago: 1

League Club	Source	Date Signed	Seasons Played	Apps	Subs	Gls
Bolton W	Sch	07/04				
Bristol Rov	L	02/05	04	0	1	0
Bury	L	03/05	04	4	3	2
Swindon T	Tr	07/05	05-06	52	17	5
Brentford	Tr	08/07	07	25	14	3

SHAKESPEARE Craig Robert
Born: Birmingham, England, 26 October, 1963 — M

League Club	Source	Date Signed	Seasons Played	Apps	Subs	Gls
Walsall	App	11/81	82-88	276	8	45
Sheffield Wed	Tr	06/89	89	15	2	0
West Bromwich A	Tr	02/90	89-92	104	8	12
Grimsby T	Tr	07/93	93-96	84	22	10
Scunthorpe U	Tr	07/97	97	3	1	0

SHANAHAN Terence Christopher (Terry)
Born: Paddington, Central London, England, 5 December, 1951 — F

League Club	Source	Date Signed	Seasons Played	Apps	Subs	Gls
Ipswich T	Tottenham H (App)	07/69	70	3	1	0
Blackburn Rov	L	09/71	71	6	0	2
Halifax T	Tr	11/71	71-74	88	8	23
Chesterfield	Tr	10/74	74-75	56	4	28
Millwall	Tr	04/76	76	13	7	5
Bournemouth	Tr	07/77	77	14	4	1
Aldershot	Tr	07/78	78-79	16	0	4

SHANDRAN Anthony Mark
Born: North Shields, Tyne and Wear, England, 17 September, 1981 — F

League Club	Source	Date Signed	Seasons Played	Apps	Subs	Gls
Burnley	YT	11/00	00	0	1	0
York C	Tr	01/03	02	12	6	3

SHANKLAND Andrew John (Andy)
Born: Stoke-on-Trent, England, 8 April, 1964 — M

League Club	Source	Date Signed	Seasons Played	Apps	Subs	Gls
Port Vale	App	03/82	81-85	15	10	2

SHANKLY William (Bill)
Born: Glenbuck, Ayrshire, Scotland, 2 September, 1913 — RH
Died: Liverpool, England, 29 September, 1981
Scotland: 5/War-7

League Club	Source	Date Signed	Seasons Played	Apps	Subs	Gls
Carlisle U	Cronberry	07/32	32	16	-	0
Preston NE	Tr	07/33	33-48	297	-	13

SHANKS Donald (Don)
Born: Hammersmith, W London, England, 2 October, 1952 — FB
England: Youth

League Club	Source	Date Signed	Seasons Played	Apps	Subs	Gls
Luton T	Fulham (App)	07/70	71-74	89	1	2
Queens Park Rgrs	Tr	11/74	74-80	176	4	10
Brighton & HA	Tr	08/81	81-82	45	1	0
Wimbledon	Eastern AA (HKG)	01/84	83	1	0	0

SHANKS James (Jimmy)
Born: Barrow, Cumbria, England, 31 October, 1918 — LW
Died: Barrow, Cumbria, England, 10 April, 2011

League Club	Source	Date Signed	Seasons Played	Apps	Subs	Gls
Barrow	Vickers Sports	10/45	46	23	-	5

SHANKS Robert (Bob)
Born: Sunniside, Tyne and Wear, England, 14 December, 1911 — CH
Died: Swindon, England, December, 1989

League Club	Source	Date Signed	Seasons Played	Apps	Subs	Gls
Leeds U		05/33				
Swindon T	Tr	05/35	35-36	25	-	1
Crystal Palace	Tr	05/37	37-38	18	-	0
Swindon T	Spennymoor U	10/46	46	1	-	0

SHANKS Walter George (Wally)
Born: Valetta, Malta, 1 May, 1923 — LH/IF
Died: Luton, England, November, 2010

League Club	Source	Date Signed	Seasons Played	Apps	Subs	Gls
Chelsea	Elgin C	10/46				
Luton T	Tr	12/46	46-56	264	-	6

SHANNON David Leslie
Born: Liverpool, England, 4 May, 1953 — RB

League Club	Source	Date Signed	Seasons Played	Apps	Subs	Gls
Sunderland	App	05/70				
Stockport Co	Tr	07/73	73	3	1	1

SHANNON Leslie (Les)
Born: Liverpool, England, 12 March, 1926 — LH/IF
Died: Leighton Buzzard, Bedfordshire, England, 2 December, 2007
England: B-3

League Club	Source	Date Signed	Seasons Played	Apps	Subs	Gls
Liverpool	Jnr	11/44	47-48	11	-	1
Burnley	Tr	11/49	49-58	262	-	39

SHANNON Robert (Rab)
Born: Bellshill, Lanarkshire, Scotland, 20 April, 1966 — RB
Scotland: U21-7

League Club	Source	Date Signed	Seasons Played	Apps	Subs	Gls
Middlesbrough (L)	Dundee	09/91	91	0	1	0

SHARDLOW Paul Michael
Born: Stone, Staffordshire, England, 29 April, 1943 — G
Died: Stoke-on-Trent, England, 14 October, 1968

League Club	Source	Date Signed	Seasons Played	Apps	Subs	Gls
Stoke C	Northwich Victoria	05/66	66-67	3	0	0

SHARIFF Abdallah Mohamed (Mo)
Born: Newham, E London, England, 5 March, 1993 — LB

League Club	Source	Date Signed	Seasons Played	Apps	Subs	Gls
Queens Park Rgrs	Slough T	09/10				
Dagenham & Red	L	03/13	12	1	3	0
Bradford C	Tr	08/14	14	0	1	0

SHARKEY Dominic (Nick)
Born: Helensburgh, Argyll & Bute, Scotland, 4 May, 1943 — CF
Died: Sunderland, England, 9 February, 2015
Scotland: U23-2/Schools

League Club	Source	Date Signed	Seasons Played	Apps	Subs	Gls
Sunderland	Drumchapel Amats	05/60	59-66	99	0	51
Leicester C	Tr	10/66	66-67	6	0	5
Mansfield T	Tr	03/68	67-69	67	2	17
Hartlepool U	Tr	07/70	70-71	55	5	12

SHARKEY Patrick George Sharp (Pat)
Born: Omagh, Tyrone, Northern Ireland, 26 August, 1953 — M
Northern Ireland: 1

League Club	Source	Date Signed	Seasons Played	Apps	Subs	Gls
Ipswich T	Portadown	09/73	75-76	17	1	1
Millwall	L	11/76	76	7	0	0
Mansfield T	Tr	08/77	77	31	1	5
Colchester U	Tr	06/78	78	5	1	0
Peterborough U	Tr	03/79	78-79	15	0	0

SHARMAN Donald William (Joe)
Born: Rothwell, Northamptonshire, England, 2 February, 1932 — G

League Club	Source	Date Signed	Seasons Played	Apps	Subs	Gls
Derby Co	Symington's, Mkt Harb.	02/49	50	2	-	0
Bradford C	Gresley Rov	06/56				

SHARMAN Samuel Joseph (Sam)
Born: Hull, England, 7 November, 1977 — FB

League Club	Source	Date Signed	Seasons Played	Apps	Subs	Gls
Sheffield Wed	YT	05/96				
Hull C	Tr	03/97	96	2	2	0

SHARP Duncan
Born: Barnsley, South Yorkshire, England, 16 March, 1933 — CH

League Club	Source	Date Signed	Seasons Played	Apps	Subs	Gls
Barnsley	Woolley Colliery	05/50	53-61	213	-	0

SHARP Frank
Born: Edinburgh, Scotland, 28 May, 1947 — LW

League Club	Source	Date Signed	Seasons Played	Apps	Subs	Gls
Carlisle U	Heart of Midlothian	03/67	66-68	32	2	0
Cardiff C	Tr	02/69	68-69	14	1	1
Barnsley	Tr	08/70	70-72	125	0	7
Grimsby T	Tr	07/73	73	26	3	2
Port Vale	Tr	05/74	74	17	7	2

SHARP George Henry
Born: Bedlington, Northumberland, England, 20 July, 1935 — LW

League Club	Source	Date Signed	Seasons Played	Apps	Subs	Gls
Darlington (Am)		05/57	57	3	-	0
Oldham Ath (Am)	Tr	11/57	57	1	-	0

SHARP Graeme Marshall
Born: Glasgow, Scotland, 16 October, 1960 — F
Scotland: 12/U21-1

League Club	Source	Date Signed	Seasons Played	Apps	Subs	Gls
Everton	Dumbarton	04/80	79-90	306	16	111
Oldham Ath	Tr	07/91	91-94	103	6	30

SHARP James
Born: Reading, England, 2 January, 1976 — CD

League Club	Source	Date Signed	Seasons Played	Apps	Subs	Gls
Hartlepool U	Andover	08/00	00-01	44	5	2
Torquay U	Falkirk	07/05	05	30	2	0
Shrewsbury T	Tr	07/06				
Rochdale	Tr	08/06	06	12	0	1

SHARP John
Born: Knottingley, West Yorkshire, England, 25 April, 1937 — LW

League Club	Source	Date Signed	Seasons Played	Apps	Subs	Gls
Halifax T	Fryston CW	01/55	54-58	92	-	16

SHARP Kevin Philip
Born: Sarnia, Ontario, Canada, 19 September, 1974 — LB
England: Youth/Schools

League Club	Source	Date Signed	Seasons Played	Apps	Subs	Gls
Leeds U	AJ Auxerre (FRA)	10/92	92-95	11	6	0
Wigan Ath	Tr	11/95	95-01	156	22	10
Wrexham	Tr	11/01	01	12	3	0
Huddersfield T	Tr	08/02	02	38	1	0
Scunthorpe U	Tr	07/03	03-04	41	5	2
Shrewsbury T	Tr	07/05	05	27	3	1

SHARP Neil Anthony
Born: Hemel Hempstead, Hertfordshire, England, 19 January, 1978 — CD

League Club	Source	Date Signed	Seasons Played	Apps	Subs	Gls
Swansea C	Merthyr Tydfil	10/01	01-02	26	6	1

SHARP Norman Winslow
Born: Liverpool, England, 26 November, 1919 — IF
Died: Leeds, England, 9 May, 1977

League Club	Source	Date Signed	Seasons Played	Apps	Subs	Gls
Everton		11/38				
Wrexham	Tr	09/46	46-49	122	-	16

SHARP Raymond (Ray)
Born: Stirling, Scotland, 16 November, 1969 — LB
Scotland: U21-4

League Club	Source	Date Signed	Seasons Played	Apps	Subs	Gls
Preston NE	Dunfermline Ath	10/94	94-95	22	0	0

SHARP Ronald (Ronnie)
Born: Montreal, Canada, 22 November, 1932 — W

League Club	Source	Date Signed	Seasons Played	Apps	Subs	Gls
Doncaster Rov	Arbroath	10/58	58-59	58	-	11

SHARP Thomas Alexander (Tom)
Born: Newmains, Lanarkshire, Scotland, 30 July, 1957 — CD

League Club	Source	Date Signed	Seasons Played	Apps	Subs	Gls
Everton	App	08/75				
Brentford	Tr	01/76	75-76	4	12	1

SHARP William Louis (Billy)
Born: Sheffield, England, 5 February, 1986 — F

League Club	Source	Date Signed	Seasons Played	Apps	Subs	Gls
Sheffield U	Sch	07/04	04	0	2	0
Rushden & D	L	01/05	04	16	0	9
Scunthorpe U	Tr	08/05	05-06	80	2	53
Sheffield U	Tr	07/07	07-08	38	13	8
Doncaster Rov	L	09/09	09	32	1	15
Doncaster Rov	Tr	07/10	10-11	45	4	25
Southampton	Tr	01/12	11-12	11	6	9
Nottingham F	L	08/12	12	30	9	10
Reading	L	09/13	13	6	4	2
Doncaster Rov	L	02/14	13	15	1	4
Leeds U	Tr	08/14	14	17	16	5

SHARPE Frederick Arthur (Fred)
Born: Norwich, England, 26 January, 1924 — IF

League Club	Source	Date Signed	Seasons Played	Apps	Subs	Gls
Wrexham (Am)		05/48	48	1	-	0

SHARPE Frederick Charles (Freddie)
Born: Brockley, SE London, England, 11 November, 1937 — CH

League Club	Source	Date Signed	Seasons Played	Apps	Subs	Gls
Tottenham H	Jnr	05/56	58	2	-	1
Norwich C	Tr	07/63	63-68	107	4	0
Reading	Tr	07/69	69-70	64	0	1

SHARPE Gerald Ralph (Gerry)
Born: Gloucester, England, 17 March, 1946 — W/IF

League Club	Source	Date Signed	Seasons Played	Apps	Subs	Gls
Bristol C	App	03/64	64-70	149	4	48

SHARPE John James
Born: Birmingham, England, 9 August, 1975 — LW

League Club	Source	Date Signed	Seasons Played	Apps	Subs	Gls
Manchester C	YT	07/93				
Exeter C	Tr	02/96	95-96	28	7	2

SHARPE John William Henry
Born: Portsmouth, England, 9 October, 1957 — RB

League Club	Source	Date Signed	Seasons Played	Apps	Subs	Gls
Southampton	App	10/75	76-77	21	0	0
Gillingham	Tr	09/78	78-84	192	2	2
Swansea C	Southampton (NC)	09/85	85	5	0	0

SHARPE Lee Stuart
Born: Halesowen, West Midlands, England, 27 May, 1971 — LW
England: 8/B-1/U21-8

League Club	Source	Date Signed	Seasons Played	Apps	Subs	Gls
Torquay U	YT	05/88	87	9	5	3
Manchester U	Tr	06/88	88-95	160	33	21
Leeds U	Tr	08/96	96-98	28	2	5
Bradford C	Tr	03/99	98-01	36	20	4
Portsmouth	L	02/01	00	17	0	0
Exeter C	Tr	08/02	02	4	0	1

SHARPE Leonard Thomas (Len)
Born: Scunthorpe, North Lincolnshire, England, 29 November, 1932 — WH

League Club	Source	Date Signed	Seasons Played	Apps	Subs	Gls
Scunthorpe U	Ashby Inst	05/50	51-61	185	-	6
Hull C	Tr	06/62	62-65	58	0	4
Scunthorpe U	Goole T	03/67				

SHARPE Philip (Phil)
Born: Leeds, England, 26 January, 1968 — F

League Club	Source	Date Signed	Seasons Played	Apps	Subs	Gls
Halifax T	Doncaster Rov (App)	08/86	86	0	1	0

SHARPE Rhys Kehinde
Born: Nottingham, England, 17 October, 1994 — LB/M
Northern Ireland: U21-4/Youth

League Club	Source	Date Signed	Seasons Played	Apps	Subs	Gls
Derby Co	Sch	07/13				
Shrewsbury T	L	03/15	14	2	1	0

SHARPE Richard
Born: Wokingham, Berkshire, England, 14 January, 1967 — F

League Club	Source	Date Signed	Seasons Played	Apps	Subs	Gls
Rochdale	Cocoa Expos (USA)	10/94	94	9	7	2

SHARPE Robert
Born: Kirkcaldy, Fife, Scotland, 20 December, 1925 — RB
Died: Darlington, County Durham, England, 21 February, 2014

League Club	Source	Date Signed	Seasons Played	Apps	Subs	Gls
Darlington	Raith Rov	08/52	52	14	-	0

SHARPLES Brian
Born: Bradford, England, 6 September, 1944 — CD

League Club	Source	Date Signed	Seasons Played	Apps	Subs	Gls
Birmingham C	App	12/61	62-68	60	1	2
Exeter C	Tr	12/68	68-70	68	0	4

SHARPLES George Frank Vincent
Born: Ellesmere Port, Cheshire, England, 20 September, 1943 — WH
England: Youth/Schools

League Club	Source	Date Signed	Seasons Played	Apps	Subs	Gls
Everton	Jnr	09/60	60-63	10	-	0
Blackburn Rov	Tr	03/65	64-68	99	4	5
Southport	Tr	07/71	71	23	2	0

SHARPLES John
Born: Wolverhampton, England, 8 August, 1934 — LB
Died: Wolverhampton, England, 1 September, 2001

League Club	Source	Date Signed	Seasons Played	Apps	Subs	Gls
Aston Villa	Heath T	10/55	58	13	-	0
Walsall	Tr	08/59	59-63	124	-	1

SHARPLES John Benjamin
Born: Bury, Greater Manchester, England, 26 January, 1973 — CD

League Club	Source	Date Signed	Seasons Played	Apps	Subs	Gls
York C	Ayr U	03/96	95-96	38	0	1

SHARPLING Christopher Barry (Chris)
Born: Bromley, SE London, England, 21 April, 1981 — F

League Club	Source	Date Signed	Seasons Played	Apps	Subs	Gls
Crystal Palace	Jnr	08/98	99	1	5	0

SHARPS Ian William
Born: Warrington, Cheshire, England, 23 October, 1980 — CD

League Club	Source	Date Signed	Seasons Played	Apps	Subs	Gls
Tranmere Rov	YT	07/99	98-05	163	7	6
Rotherham U	Tr	07/06	06-09	160	0	8
Shrewsbury T	Tr	08/10	10-11	86	0	2
Rotherham U	Tr	05/12	12	23	0	1
Burton A	Tr	01/13	12-14	71	3	1

SHARRATT Christopher Michael (Chris)
Born: West Kirby, Wirral, England, 13 August, 1970 — F

League Club	Source	Date Signed	Seasons Played	Apps	Subs	Gls
Wigan Ath	Stalybridge Celtic	12/91	91-92	11	13	3

SHARRATT Harold (Harry)
Born: Wigan, Greater Manchester, England, 16 December, 1929 — G
Died: Lancaster, England, 19 August, 2002
England: Amateur-4

League Club	Source	Date Signed	Seasons Played	Apps	Subs	Gls
Blackpool (Am)	Yorkshire Amats	05/52	52	1	-	0
Oldham Ath (Am)	Bishop Auckland	03/56	55	1	-	0
Nottingham F (Am)	Bishop Auckland	01/58	57	1	-	0

SHARRATT Stuart Edgar
Born: Leek, Staffordshire, England, 26 February, 1942 — G

League Club	Source	Date Signed	Seasons Played	Apps	Subs	Gls
Port Vale	Oswestry T	03/66	65-71	143	0	0

SHARROCK Anthony (Tony)
Born: Warrington, Cheshire, England, 8 September, 1955 — G

League Club	Source	Date Signed	Seasons Played	Apps	Subs	Gls
Southport	Liverpool (Am)	11/73	73	1	0	0

SHARRY Luke Irvin
Born: Leeds, England, 9 March, 1990 — M

League Club	Source	Date Signed	Seasons Played	Apps	Subs	Gls
Bradford C	Sch	07/08	08-09	0	2	0

SHAW Adrian
Born: Murton, County Durham, England, 13 April, 1966 — M/LB

League Club	Source	Date Signed	Seasons Played	Apps	Subs	Gls
Nottingham F	App	12/83				
Halifax T	Tr	12/84	84-87	95	5	1
York C	Bridlington T	10/88	88	5	0	0
Chesterfield	Tr	12/88	88-90	40	10	3

SHAW Alan
Born: Preston, Lancashire, England, 9 October, 1943 — LW

League Club	Source	Date Signed	Seasons Played	Apps	Subs	Gls
Preston NE	Jnr	10/60				
Hull C	Tr	08/61	61-63	15	-	1

SHAW Alexander (Alex)
Born: United Kingdom — IF

League Club	Source	Date Signed	Seasons Played	Apps	Subs	Gls
Crewe Alex		12/44	46	14	-	4

SHAW Arthur
Born: Limehouse, E London, England, 9 April, 1924 — RH

League Club	Source	Date Signed	Seasons Played	Apps	Subs	Gls
Brentford	Hayes	05/46	46	4	-	0
Arsenal	Tr	04/48	49-54	57	-	0
Watford	Tr	06/55	55	3	-	0

SHAW Barry
Born: Chilton, County Durham, England, 31 October, 1948 — W

League Club	Source	Date Signed	Seasons Played	Apps	Subs	Gls
Darlington (Am)	Crowborough Ath	03/68	67	2	0	0

SHAW Bernard
Born: Selby, North Yorkshire, England, 4 September, 1929 — WH

League Club	Source	Date Signed	Seasons Played	Apps	Subs	Gls
Hull C	Buckley Jnrs	05/48				
Lincoln C	Goole T	10/53	53-54	9	-	1

SHAW Bernard
Born: Sheffield, England, 14 March, 1945 — LB
England: U23-2/Youth

League Club	Source	Date Signed	Seasons Played	Apps	Subs	Gls
Sheffield U	App	10/62	62-68	135	1	2
Wolverhampton W	Tr	07/69	69-72	113	3	2
Sheffield Wed	Tr	06/73	73-75	100	4	3

SHAW Cecil Ernest
Born: Mansfield, Nottinghamshire, England, 22 June, 1911 — LB
Died: Birmingham, England, 20 January, 1977
England: FLge-1

League Club	Source	Date Signed	Seasons Played	Apps	Subs	Gls
Wolverhampton W	Rufford Colliery	02/30	29-36	177	-	8
West Bromwich A	Tr	12/36	36-46	110	-	10

SHAW Christopher John (Chris)
Born: Bournemouth, England, 23 August, 1965 — M

League Club	Source	Date Signed	Seasons Played	Apps	Subs	Gls
Bournemouth	Jnr	06/83	82-85	13	12	2

SHAW Colin Michael
Born: St Albans, Hertfordshire, England, 19 June, 1943 — IF
England: Youth

League Club	Source	Date Signed	Seasons Played	Apps	Subs	Gls
Chelsea	Jnr	05/60	61	1	-	0
Norwich C	Tr	08/63	63-64	3	-	0
Leyton Orient	Tr	03/65	65	7	0	0

SHAW Eric Lewis
Born: Barnsley, South Yorkshire, England, 12 February, 1947 — RH

League Club	Source	Date Signed	Seasons Played	Apps	Subs	Gls
Barnsley	App	02/65	64	2	-	0

SHAW Gary Robert
Born: Birmingham, England, 21 January, 1961 — F
England: U21-7/Youth

League Club	Source	Date Signed	Seasons Played	Apps	Subs	Gls
Aston Villa	App	01/79	78-87	158	7	59
Blackpool	L	02/88	87	4	2	0
Walsall	SK Klagenfurt (AUT)	02/90	89	4	5	3
Shrewsbury T	Kilmarnock	09/90	90	20	2	5

SHAW George David (David)
Born: Huddersfield, West Yorkshire, England, 11 October, 1948 — F

League Club	Source	Date Signed	Seasons Played	Apps	Subs	Gls
Huddersfield T	Jnr	01/67	66-68	23	3	2
Oldham Ath	Tr	09/69	69-72	155	0	70
West Bromwich A	Tr	03/73	72-74	65	17	17
Oldham Ath	Tr	10/75	75-77	55	4	21

SHAW Gordon
Born: Ashton-in-Makerfield, Greater Manchester, England, 7 May, 1926 — RB

League Club	Source	Date Signed	Seasons Played	Apps	Subs	Gls
Southport (Am)	Haydock C&B	07/46	46	2	-	0

SHAW Graham Laurence
Born: Sheffield, England, 9 July, 1934 — LB
Died: Sheffield, England, 12 May, 1998
England: 5/FLge-4/U23-5

League Club	Source	Date Signed	Seasons Played	Apps	Subs	Gls
Sheffield U	Jnr	07/51	51-66	439	0	14
Doncaster Rov	Tr	09/67	67	22	0	0

SHAW Graham Paul
Born: Stoke-on-Trent, England, 7 June, 1967 — F

League Club	Source	Date Signed	Seasons Played	Apps	Subs	Gls
Stoke C	App	06/85	85-88	83	16	18
Preston NE	Tr	07/89	89-91	113	8	29
Stoke C	Tr	08/92	92-94	23	13	5
Plymouth Arg	L	08/94	94	6	0	0
Rochdale	Tr	03/95	94-95	13	9	0

SHAW Hugh
Born: Clydebank, Dunbartonshire, Scotland, 29 April, 1929 — WH
Died: Clydebank, Dunbartonshire, Scotland, 8 May, 1985

League Club	Source	Date Signed	Seasons Played	Apps	Subs	Gls
Tranmere Rov	Rhyl	06/55	55	3	-	0

SHAW John
Born: Stirling, Scotland, 4 February, 1954 — G

League Club	Source	Date Signed	Seasons Played	Apps	Subs	Gls
Leeds U	App	02/71				
Bristol C	Tr	05/74	76-84	295	0	0
Exeter C	Tr	07/85	85-87	109	0	0

SHAW John Stephen (Jack)
Born: Doncaster, South Yorkshire, England, 10 April, 1924 — CF
Died: Denaby, South Yorkshire, England, April, 2011

League Club	Source	Date Signed	Seasons Played	Apps	Subs	Gls
Rotherham U	Yorkshire Main	04/45	46-52	262	-	122
Sheffield Wed	Tr	06/53	53-57	56	-	21

SHAW Jonathan Steven (Jon)
Born: Sheffield, England, 10 November, 1983 — F
England: Semi Pro-6

League Club	Source	Date Signed	Seasons Played	Apps	Subs	Gls
Sheffield Wed	Sch	07/03	02-04	8	10	2
York C	L	11/03	03	5	3	0
Rochdale	Halifax T	07/08	08-09	5	2	1

SHAW Joseph (Joe)
Born: Murton, County Durham, England, 23 June, 1928 — CH
Died: Sheffield, England, 18 November, 2007
England: FLge-2

League Club	Source	Date Signed	Seasons Played	Apps	Subs	Gls
Sheffield U	Upton Colliery	07/45	48-65	632	0	7

SHAW Kenneth (Ken)
Born: Dukinfield, Greater Manchester, England, 15 December, 1920 — CF
Died: Stockport, Greater Manchester, England, 15 February, 2004

League Club	Source	Date Signed	Seasons Played	Apps	Subs	Gls
Stockport Co	Hyde U	10/42	46-47	41	-	18

SHAW Luke Paul Hoare
Born: Kingston-on-Thames, SW London, England, 12 July, 1995 — LB
England: 4/U21-5/Youth

League Club	Source	Date Signed	Seasons Played	Apps	Subs	Gls
Southampton	Sch	07/12	12-13	57	3	0
Manchester U	Tr	06/14	14	15	1	0

SHAW Mark
Born: St Helens, Merseyside, England, 15 October, 1964 — M

League Club	Source	Date Signed	Seasons Played	Apps	Subs	Gls
Wigan Ath	Jnr	11/82	82	3	0	0

SHAW Martin John
Born: Bristol, England, 14 September, 1960 — M

League Club	Source	Date Signed	Seasons Played	Apps	Subs	Gls
Bristol Rov	App	09/78	78	1	1	0

SHAW Matthew Alan (Matt)
Born: Blackpool, Lancashire, England, 17 May, 1984 — F

League Club	Source	Date Signed	Seasons Played	Apps	Subs	Gls
Sheffield Wed	Stockport Co (YT)	03/02				
Wrexham	Tr	10/04	04	0	1	0
Blackpool	Tr	12/04	04	2	8	0

SHAW Paul
Born: Burnham, Buckinghamshire, England, 4 September, 1973 — F
England: Youth

League Club	Source	Date Signed	Seasons Played	Apps	Subs	Gls
Arsenal	YT	09/91	94-96	1	11	2
Burnley	L	03/95	94	8	1	4
Cardiff C	L	08/95	95	6	0	0
Peterborough U	L	10/95	95	12	0	5
Millwall	Tr	09/97	97-99	88	21	26

League Club	Source	Date Signed	Seasons Played	Apps	Subs	Gls
Gillingham	Tr	07/00	00-03	118	17	26
Sheffield U	Tr	01/04	03-05	20	15	8
Rotherham U	L	08/04	04	9	0	2
Rotherham U	Tr	01/06	05	15	2	4
Chesterfield	Tr	07/06	06	23	7	4

SHAW Peter Kevin
Born: Northolt, W London, England, 9 January, 1956 — CD

League Club	Source	Date Signed	Seasons Played	Apps	Subs	Gls
Charlton Ath	Staines T	12/77	77-80	100	5	5
Exeter C	L	11/81	81	3	0	0
Gillingham	Tr	02/82	81-85	140	3	2

SHAW Raymond (Ray)
Born: Walsall, West Midlands, England, 18 May, 1913 — WH
Died: Kirby Muxloe, Leicestershire, England, 29 April, 1980

League Club	Source	Date Signed	Seasons Played	Apps	Subs	Gls
Birmingham C	Darlaston	04/37	37-46	12	-	0

SHAW Richard Edward
Born: Brentford, W London, England, 11 September, 1968 — CD

League Club	Source	Date Signed	Seasons Played	Apps	Subs	Gls
Crystal Palace	App	09/86	87-95	193	14	3
Hull C	L	12/89	89	4	0	0
Coventry C	Tr	11/95	95-05	296	21	1
Millwall	Tr	06/06	06-07	57	2	0

SHAW Ronald (Ron)
Born: Bolton-on-Dearne, South Yorkshire, England, 1 January, 1924 — RW
Died: Middlesbrough, England, November, 1991

League Club	Source	Date Signed	Seasons Played	Apps	Subs	Gls
Torquay U	Harrow T	02/47	46-57	384	-	99

SHAW Samuel (Sam)
Born: Caverswall, Staffordshire, England, 14 September, 1934 — IF

League Club	Source	Date Signed	Seasons Played	Apps	Subs	Gls
Crewe Alex	Foley	08/56	56	19	-	4

SHAW Simon Robert
Born: Middlesbrough, England, 21 September, 1973 — RB/M
England: Semi Pro-2

League Club	Source	Date Signed	Seasons Played	Apps	Subs	Gls
Darlington	YT	08/92	91-97	144	32	12

SHAW Steven (Steve)
Born: Manchester, England, 10 August, 1960 — LW

League Club	Source	Date Signed	Seasons Played	Apps	Subs	Gls
Rochdale	App	-	77	6	0	0

SHAW Stuart
Born: Chester, England, 9 October, 1944 — W

League Club	Source	Date Signed	Seasons Played	Apps	Subs	Gls
Everton	Aintree Villa Colts	12/61	64-65	3	0	0
Crystal Palace	Tr	12/66				
Southport	Tr	03/67	66-68	66	1	6
Port Vale	Tr	07/69	69	1	2	0

SHAW Thomas William (Tom)
Born: Nottingham, England, 1 December, 1986 — M
England: Semi Pro-2

League Club	Source	Date Signed	Seasons Played	Apps	Subs	Gls
Rushden & D	Sch	-	05	0	1	0

SHAWCROSS Francis David (David)
Born: Stretford, Greater Manchester, England, 3 July, 1941 — M
England: U23-1/Youth

League Club	Source	Date Signed	Seasons Played	Apps	Subs	Gls
Manchester C	Jnr	06/58	58-64	47	-	2
Stockport Co	Tr	06/65	65-66	59	1	14
Halifax T	Tr	03/67	66-69	126	6	21

SHAWCROSS Ryan James
Born: Buckley, Flintshire, Wales, 4 October, 1987 — CD
England: 1/U21-2

League Club	Source	Date Signed	Seasons Played	Apps	Subs	Gls
Manchester U	Sch	07/06				
Stoke C	Tr	08/08	07-14	272	4	19

SHAWKY Mohamed Ali Abu El Yazid
Born: Port Said, Egypt, 5 October, 1981 — M
Egypt: 66

League Club	Source	Date Signed	Seasons Played	Apps	Subs	Gls
Middlesbrough	Al Ahly (EGY)	08/07	07-08	14	4	0

SHEA Dane Brekken (Brek)
Born: Bryan, Texas, USA, 28 February, 1990 — LW
USA: 33/U23-3/Youth

League Club	Source	Date Signed	Seasons Played	Apps	Subs	Gls
Stoke C	FC Dallas (USA)	01/13	12-13	0	3	0
Barnsley	L	01/14	13	5	3	0
Birmingham C	L	09/14	14	2	4	0

SHEA James William
Born: Islington, N London, England, 16 June, 1991 — G

League Club	Source	Date Signed	Seasons Played	Apps	Subs	Gls
Arsenal	Sch	07/09				
Dagenham & Red	L	08/11	11	0	1	0
AFC Wimbledon	Harrow Bor	07/14	14	38	0	0

SHEARD Frank
Born: Spilsby, Lincolnshire, England, 29 January, 1922 — CH
Died: Leicester, England, 11 July, 1990

League Club	Source	Date Signed	Seasons Played	Apps	Subs	Gls
Leicester C	Skegness T	08/41				
Southend U	Tr	05/46	46-52	180	-	1

SHEARER Alan
Born: Newcastle-upon-Tyne, England, 13 August, 1970 — F
England: 63/B-1/U21-11/Youth

League Club	Source	Date Signed	Seasons Played	Apps	Subs	Gls
Southampton	YT	04/88	87-91	105	13	23
Blackburn Rov	Tr	07/92	92-95	132	6	112
Newcastle U	Tr	07/96	96-05	295	8	148

SHEARER David John
Born: Inverness, Scotland, 16 October, 1958 — F

League Club	Source	Date Signed	Seasons Played	Apps	Subs	Gls
Middlesbrough	Clachnacuddin	01/78	77-82	88	9	23
Wigan Ath	L	03/80	79	11	0	9
Grimsby T	Tr	08/83	83	1	3	0
Gillingham	Tr	08/84	84-87	82	11	42
Bournemouth	Tr	10/87	87	8	3	3
Scunthorpe U	Tr	02/88	87-88	16	0	7
Darlington	Tr	12/88	88	6	1	0

SHEARER Duncan Nichol
Born: Fort William, Highlands, Scotland, 28 August, 1962 — F
Scotland: 7

League Club	Source	Date Signed	Seasons Played	Apps	Subs	Gls
Chelsea	Clachnacuddin	11/83	85	2	0	1
Huddersfield T	Tr	03/86	85-87	80	3	38
Swindon T	Tr	06/88	88-91	156	3	78
Blackburn Rov	Tr	03/92	91	5	1	1

SHEARER John McMillan (Jock)
Born: Dunfermline, Fife, Scotland, 8 July, 1916 — IF
Died: Surrey, England, 3 April, 1979

League Club	Source	Date Signed	Seasons Played	Apps	Subs	Gls
Derby Co	Portadown	03/46				
Bradford C	Tr	10/46	46-48	75	-	17
Grimsby T	Tr	02/49	48-50	34	-	9

SHEARER Lee Sean
Born: Southend-on-Sea, England, 23 October, 1977 — CD

League Club	Source	Date Signed	Seasons Played	Apps	Subs	Gls
Leyton Orient	YT	07/95	94-96	14	4	1

SHEARER Peter Andrew
Born: Birmingham, England, 4 February, 1967 — M
England: Semi Pro-1

League Club	Source	Date Signed	Seasons Played	Apps	Subs	Gls
Birmingham C	App	02/85	84	2	2	0
Rochdale	Tr	07/86	86	1	0	0
Bournemouth	Cheltenham T	03/89	88-92	76	9	10
Birmingham C	Tr	01/94	93-94	22	3	7

SHEARER Scott
Born: Glasgow, Scotland, 15 February, 1981 — G
Scotland: B-1

League Club	Source	Date Signed	Seasons Played	Apps	Subs	Gls
Coventry C	Albion Rov	07/03	03-04	37	1	0
Rushden & D	L	02/05	04	3	0	0
Rushden & D	L	03/05	04	10	0	0
Bristol Rov	Tr	07/05	05-06	47	0	0
Shrewsbury T	L	10/06	06	20	0	0
Wycombe W	Tr	07/07	07-09	62	1	0
Crawley T	Wrexham	01/11	11	25	0	0
Rotherham U	Tr	05/12	12-13	31	0	0
Crewe Alex	Tr	07/14	14	2	0	0
Burton A	L	01/15	14	0	1	0

SHEARING Peter Fraser
Born: Uxbridge, W London, England, 26 August, 1938 — G

League Club	Source	Date Signed	Seasons Played	Apps	Subs	Gls
West Ham U	Hendon	06/60	60	6	-	0
Portsmouth	Tr	07/61	61-63	17	-	0
Exeter C	Tr	06/64	64-65	80	0	0
Plymouth Arg	Tr	06/66	66-67	24	0	0
Exeter C	Tr	07/68	68-70	79	0	0
Bristol Rov	Tr	02/71				
Gillingham	Tr	08/71	71-72	39	0	0

SHEAVILLS James Edward (Jimmy)
Born: Aylsham, Norfolk, England, 28 July, 1940 — RW
Died: Barnsley, South Yorkshire, England, 4 September, 2003

League Club	Source	Date Signed	Seasons Played	Apps	Subs	Gls
Leeds U	Jnr	09/57				
Peterborough U	Holbeach U	03/60	60-62	30	-	8
Barnsley	Tr	06/63	63-64	65	-	6

SHECHTER Itay Menachem
Born: Nazareth, Israel, 22 February, 1987 — F
Israel: 24/U21-16/Youth

League Club	Source	Date Signed	Seasons Played	Apps	Subs	Gls
Swansea C (L)	Kaiserslautern (GER)	08/12	12	7	11	1

SHEEDY Kevin Mark
Born: Builth Wells, Powys, Wales, 21 October, 1959 — M
Republic of Ireland: 46/U21-5/Youth

League Club	Source	Date Signed	Seasons Played	Apps	Subs	Gls
Hereford U	App	10/76	75-77	47	4	4
Liverpool	Tr	07/78	80-81	1	2	0
Everton	Tr	08/82	82-91	263	11	67
Newcastle U	Tr	03/92	91-92	36	1	4
Blackpool	Tr	07/93	93	25	1	1

SHEEHAN Alan Michael Anthony
Born: Athlone, Republic of Ireland, 14 September, 1986 — LB
Republic of Ireland: U21-5/Youth

League Club	Source	Date Signed	Seasons Played	Apps	Subs	Gls
Leicester C	Sch	09/04	04-07	20	3	1
Mansfield T	L	09/06	06	9	1	0
Leeds U	Tr	01/08	07-08	21	0	2
Crewe Alex	L	03/09	08	3	0	0
Oldham Ath	L	09/09	09	8	0	1
Swindon T	Tr	11/09	09-10	39	4	2
Notts Co	Tr	07/11	11-13	113	1	9
Bradford C	Tr	06/14	14	13	10	1
Peterborough U	L	03/15	14	1	1	0

SHEEHAN Joshua Luke (Josh)
Born: Burry Port, Carmarthenshire, Wales, 30 March, 1995 — M
Wales: U21-3/Youth

League Club	Source	Date Signed	Seasons Played	Apps	Subs	Gls
Swansea C	Sch	07/13				
Yeovil T	L	02/15	14	12	1	0

SHEEN John (Jock)
Born: Baillieston, Glasgow, Scotland, 30 August, 1920 — IF
Died: Sheffield, England, 5 July, 1997

League Club	Source	Date Signed	Seasons Played	Apps	Subs	Gls
Sheffield U	Baillieston Jnrs	09/37				
Hull C	Tr	07/46	46	5	-	1

SHEERAN Mark John
Born: Newcastle-upon-Tyne, England, 9 September, 1982 — F

League Club	Source	Date Signed	Seasons Played	Apps	Subs	Gls
Darlington	Sch	07/02	01-03	1	31	6

SHEERIN Joseph Earnan Raftery (Joe)
Born: Hammersmith, W London, England, 1 February, 1979 — F

League Club	Source	Date Signed	Seasons Played	Apps	Subs	Gls
Chelsea	YT	07/97	96	0	1	0
Bournemouth	Tr	02/00	99	3	3	1

SHEFFIELD Jonathan (Jon)
Born: Bedworth, Warwickshire, England, 1 February, 1969 — G

League Club	Source	Date Signed	Seasons Played	Apps	Subs	Gls
Norwich C	App	02/87	88	1	0	0
Aldershot	L	09/89	89	11	0	0
Aldershot	L	08/90	90	15	0	0
Cambridge U	Tr	03/91	90-94	56	0	0
Colchester U	L	12/93	93	6	0	0
Swindon T	L	01/94	93	2	0	0
Hereford U	L	09/94	94	8	0	0
Peterborough U	Tr	07/95	95-96	62	0	0
Plymouth Arg	Tr	07/97	97-00	155	0	0

SHEFFIELD Laurence Joseph (Laurie)
Born: Swansea, Wales, 27 April, 1939 — CF
Wales: Schools

League Club	Source	Date Signed	Seasons Played	Apps	Subs	Gls
Bristol Rov	Jnr	07/56				
Newport Co	Barry T	04/62	61-64	92	-	46
Doncaster Rov	Tr	08/65	65-66	58	0	36
Norwich C	Tr	11/66	66-67	27	0	16
Rotherham U	Tr	08/67	67	19	0	6
Oldham Ath	Tr	12/67	67	18	0	6
Luton T	Tr	07/68	68-69	31	4	12
Doncaster Rov	Tr	10/69	69	13	2	6
Peterborough U	Tr	08/70	70	17	1	6

SHELDON Gareth Richard
Born: Birmingham, England, 8 May, 1980 — W
England: Semi Pro-6

League Club	Source	Date Signed	Seasons Played	Apps	Subs	Gls
Scunthorpe U	YT	02/99	97-01	52	35	6
Exeter C	Tr	08/02	02	7	12	1
Hereford U	Kidderminster Hrs	06/06	06	3	5	1

SHELDON Kevin John
Born: Cheddleton, Staffordshire, England, 14 June, 1956 — RW

League Club	Source	Date Signed	Seasons Played	Apps	Subs	Gls
Stoke C	App	06/73	75-80	12	3	0
Wigan Ath	Tr	08/81	81-82	29	0	1
Port Vale	L	08/82	82	5	0	0
Crewe Alex	Tr	08/83	83	2	0	0

SHELIA Murtaz
Born: Tbilisi, Georgia, 25 March, 1969 — D
Georgia: 29

League Club	Source	Date Signed	Seasons Played	Apps	Subs	Gls
Manchester C	FCA Vladikavkaz (RUS)	11/97	97-98	15	0	2

SHELL Francis Harry (Frank)
Born: Hackney, E London, England, 2 January, 1912 — CF
Died: Axminster, Devon, England, July, 1988

League Club	Source	Date Signed	Seasons Played	Apps	Subs	Gls
Aston Villa	Ford Sports	05/37	37-38	23	-	8
Birmingham C	Tr	09/46				
Mansfield T	Hereford U	06/47	47	22	-	1

SHELLEY Brian
Born: Dublin, Republic of Ireland, 15 November, 1981 — RB
Republic of Ireland: U21-4

League Club	Source	Date Signed	Seasons Played	Apps	Subs	Gls
Carlisle U	Bohemians (ROI)	08/02	02-03	60	6	1

SHELLEY Daniel Steven (Danny)
Born: Stoke-on-Trent, England, 29 December, 1990 — M

League Club	Source	Date Signed	Seasons Played	Apps	Subs	Gls
Crewe Alex	Sch	01/09	08-11	39	34	8

SHELLITO Kenneth John (Ken)
Born: East Ham, E London, England, 18 April, 1940 — RB
England: 1/U23-1

League Club	Source	Date Signed	Seasons Played	Apps	Subs	Gls
Chelsea	Jnr	04/57	58-65	114	0	2

SHELTON Andrew Marc (Andy)
Born: Sutton Coldfield, West Midlands, England, 19 June, 1980 — M

League Club	Source	Date Signed	Seasons Played	Apps	Subs	Gls
Chester C	YT	07/98	97-99	14	21	1

SHELTON Gary
Born: Nottingham, England, 21 March, 1958 — M
England: U21-1

League Club	Source	Date Signed	Seasons Played	Apps	Subs	Gls
Walsall	App	03/76	75-77	12	12	0
Aston Villa	Tr	01/78	78-81	24	0	7
Notts Co	L	03/80	79	8	0	0
Sheffield Wed	Tr	03/82	81-86	195	3	18
Oxford U	Tr	07/87	87-88	60	5	1
Bristol C	Tr	08/89	89-93	149	1	24
Rochdale	L	02/94	93	3	0	0
Chester C	Tr	07/94	94-97	62	7	6

SHELTON John Benjamin Thomas (Jack)
Born: Stourbridge, West Midlands, England, 9 November, 1912 — FB
Died: Oxford, England, January, 1992

League Club	Source	Date Signed	Seasons Played	Apps	Subs	Gls
Wolverhampton W	Chase Terrace U	12/32				
Walsall	Hednesford T	08/34	34-46	103	-	5

SHELTON Luton George Kieshawn
Born: Kingston, Jamaica, 11 November, 1985 — W/F
Jamaica: 75

League Club	Source	Date Signed	Seasons Played	Apps	Subs	Gls
Sheffield U	Helsingborgs (SWE)	01/07	06-07	7	12	1

SHELVEY Jonjo
Born: Romford, E London, England, 27 February, 1992 — M
England: 1/U21-13/Youth

League Club	Source	Date Signed	Seasons Played	Apps	Subs	Gls
Charlton Ath	Sch	02/09	07-09	35	7	7
Liverpool	Tr	06/10	10-12	17	30	2
Blackpool	L	09/11	11	10	0	6
Swansea C	Tr	07/13	13-14	57	6	9

SHENTON Oliver Gregory (Ollie)
Born: Blythe Bridge, Potteries, England, 6 November, 1997 — M

League Club	Source	Date Signed	Seasons Played	Apps	Subs	Gls
Stoke C	Sch	11/14	14	0	1	0

SHEPHARD Christopher John (Chris)
Born: Exeter, England, 25 December, 1988 — W

League Club	Source	Date Signed	Seasons Played	Apps	Subs	Gls
Exeter C	Sch	07/07	08-11	7	6	0

SHEPHARD Liam Christopher
Born: Ton Pentre, Rhondda Cynon Taff, Wales, 22 November, 1994 — RB/M

League Club	Source	Date Signed	Seasons Played	Apps	Subs	Gls
Swansea C	Sch	07/13				
Yeovil T	L	01/15	14	20	0	0

SHEPHEARD Jonathan Thomas (Jon)
Born: Oxford, England, 31 March, 1981 — CD

League Club	Source	Date Signed	Seasons Played	Apps	Subs	Gls
Oxford U	YT	06/99	99-00	6	1	0

SHEPHERD Anthony (Tony)
Born: Glasgow, Scotland, 16 November, 1966 — M
Scotland: Youth/Schools

League Club	Source	Date Signed	Seasons Played	Apps	Subs	Gls
Bristol C (L)	Glasgow Celtic	12/88	88	2	1	0
Carlisle U	Glasgow Celtic	07/89	89-90	73	2	8

SHEPHERD Arthur Leslie
Born: Liverpool, England, 11 May, 1922 — W
Died: Liverpool, England, 7 October, 2002

League Club	Source	Date Signed	Seasons Played	Apps	Subs	Gls
Liverpool		01/43				
New Brighton	Tr	08/49	49-50	30	-	10

SHEPHERD Brian Albert
Born: Leicester, England, 29 January, 1935 — FB

League Club	Source	Date Signed	Seasons Played	Apps	Subs	Gls
Coventry C	Hinckley Ath	10/56	57-59	29	-	0

SHEPHERD Ernest (Ernie)
Born: Wombwell, South Yorkshire, England, 14 August, 1919 — LW
Died: Southend-on-Sea, England, 1 March, 2001

League Club	Source	Date Signed	Seasons Played	Apps	Subs	Gls
Fulham	Bradford Rov	04/38	46-48	72	-	13
West Bromwich A	Tr	12/48	48	4	-	0
Hull C	Tr	03/49	48-49	15	-	3
Queens Park Rgrs	Tr	08/50	50-55	219	-	51

SHEPHERD James (Jimmy)
Born: Aspull, Greater Manchester, England, 25 June, 1938 — LH/IF

League Club	Source	Date Signed	Seasons Played	Apps	Subs	Gls
Blackburn Rov	St John Baptist BC	11/55				

League Club	Source	Date Signed	Seasons Played	Apps	Subs	Gls
Everton	Tr	07/59				
Crewe Alex	Tr	06/60	60-63	49	-	4
Southport	Tr	02/64	63	13	-	6

SHEPHERD Jamie Greig (Greig)
Born: Edinburgh, Scotland, 29 September, 1960 — F

League Club	Source	Date Signed	Seasons Played	Apps	Subs	Gls
Norwich C	Musselburgh Windsor	03/79	79-81	13	3	2
Southend U	Eastern AA (HKG)	08/83	83-84	47	6	11
Peterborough U	Tr	12/84	84-86	53	2	14

SHEPHERD John Arthur
Born: Maltby, South Yorkshire, England, 20 September, 1945 — M

League Club	Source	Date Signed	Seasons Played	Apps	Subs	Gls
Rotherham U		05/66	65-67	22	0	2
York C	Tr	09/68	68	5	0	0
Oxford U		10/69	69	9	2	1

SHEPHERD John Herbert Edwin
Born: Kensington, Central London, England, 29 May, 1932 — IF

League Club	Source	Date Signed	Seasons Played	Apps	Subs	Gls
Millwall	RAF Sennen	10/52	52-57	149	-	63
Brighton & HA	Tr	06/58	58-59	45	-	19
Gillingham	Tr	02/60	59-60	53	-	23

SHEPHERD John William (Bill)
Born: Liverpool, England, 25 September, 1920 — RB
Died: Liverpool, England, March, 1983

League Club	Source	Date Signed	Seasons Played	Apps	Subs	Gls
Liverpool	Elm Park	12/45	48-51	53	-	0

SHEPHERD Paul David Edward
Born: Leeds, England, 17 November, 1977 — RB
England: Youth

League Club	Source	Date Signed	Seasons Played	Apps	Subs	Gls
Leeds U	YT	09/95	96	1	0	0
Tranmere Rov	L	02/99	98	0	1	0
Scunthorpe U	Keflavik (ICE)	09/00	00	0	1	0
Luton T	Tr	03/01	00	7	0	0

SHEPHERD Peter
Born: Ivybridge, Devon, England, 27 August, 1965 — G

League Club	Source	Date Signed	Seasons Played	Apps	Subs	Gls
Exeter C	Jnr	08/82	82	1	0	0

SHEPHERD Trevor
Born: Sutton-in-Ashfield, Nottinghamshire, England, 25 December, 1946 — F

League Club	Source	Date Signed	Seasons Played	Apps	Subs	Gls
Nottingham F	Jnr	12/63				
Coventry C	Tr	10/66	67-68	12	2	1
Torquay U	L	03/68	67	14	0	6
Plymouth Arg	Tr	06/69	69-70	36	3	4

SHEPHERDSON Harold
Born: Middlesbrough, England, 28 October, 1918 — CH
Died: Middlesbrough, England, 14 September, 1995

League Club	Source	Date Signed	Seasons Played	Apps	Subs	Gls
Middlesbrough	South Bank East End	05/36	36-46	17	-	0
Southend U	Tr	05/47				

SHEPPARD Horace Hedley (Hedley)
Born: West Ham, E London, England, 26 November, 1909 — FB
Died: Poole, Dorset, England, 12 December, 2006

League Club	Source	Date Signed	Seasons Played	Apps	Subs	Gls
West Ham U	Barking	11/32				
Aldershot	Tr	07/34	34-48	249	-	1

SHEPPARD Karl
Born: Dublin, Republic of Ireland, 14 February, 1991 — F
Republic of Ireland: U21-1

League Club	Source	Date Signed	Seasons Played	Apps	Subs	Gls
Everton	Sch	03/08				
Reading	Shamrock Rov (ROI)	01/12				
Accrington Stan	L	08/12	12	5	5	1

SHEPPARD Richard James (Dick)
Born: Bristol, England, 14 February, 1945 — G
Died: Bristol, England, 18 October, 1998

League Club	Source	Date Signed	Seasons Played	Apps	Subs	Gls
West Bromwich A	App	02/63	65-68	39	0	0
Bristol Rov	Tr	06/69	69-74	151	0	0
Torquay U	L	12/73	73	2	0	0

SHEPPARD Simon Andrew
Born: Clevedon, Somerset, England, 7 August, 1973 — G
England: Youth/Schools

League Club	Source	Date Signed	Seasons Played	Apps	Subs	Gls
Watford	YT	04/91	92-93	23	0	0
Scarborough	L	03/94	93	9	0	0
Reading	Tr	09/94	95	18	0	0

SHEPPEARD Howard Thomas
Born: Ynysybwl, Rhondda Cynon Taff, Wales, 31 January, 1933 — IF

League Club	Source	Date Signed	Seasons Played	Apps	Subs	Gls
Sunderland	Gnasyhard YC	12/51	53	1	-	0
Cardiff C	Tr	05/55				
Newport Co	Tr	06/56	56-57	31	-	5

SHEPSTONE Paul Thomas Adam
Born: Coventry, England, 8 November, 1970 — M
England: Youth

League Club	Source	Date Signed	Seasons Played	Apps	Subs	Gls
Coventry C	YT	11/87				
Birmingham C	Tr	07/89				
Blackburn Rov	Atherstone U	05/90	90-91	16	10	1
York C	L	03/92	91	2	0	0

SHERGOLD Wilfred Frederick (Wilf)
Born: Swindon, England, 18 September, 1943 — LH/IF

League Club	Source	Date Signed	Seasons Played	Apps	Subs	Gls
Swindon T	Jnr	10/60	63-65	37	0	0
Bradford C	Tr	06/66	66-67	22	6	2

SHERGOLD William Richard (Billy)
Born: Newport, Wales, 22 January, 1923 — IF/W
Died: Newport, Wales, 25 July, 1968
Wales: WLge-1/Amateur

League Club	Source	Date Signed	Seasons Played	Apps	Subs	Gls
Newport Co	Walthamstow Ave	07/47	47-55	273	-	48

SHERIDAN Alexander (Alex)
Born: Motherwell, Lanarkshire, Scotland, 19 July, 1948 — LB

League Club	Source	Date Signed	Seasons Played	Apps	Subs	Gls
Brighton & HA	Queen's Park	08/70	70	12	3	2

SHERIDAN Anthony Joseph (Tony)
Born: Dublin, Republic of Ireland, 21 October, 1974 — LW
Republic of Ireland: U21-5/Youth

League Club	Source	Date Signed	Seasons Played	Apps	Subs	Gls
Coventry C	Jnr	10/91	92-93	5	4	0

SHERIDAN Cillian
Born: Bailieborough, Cavan, Republic of Ireland, 23 February, 1989 — F
Republic of Ireland: 3/U21-10

League Club	Source	Date Signed	Seasons Played	Apps	Subs	Gls
Plymouth Arg (L)	Glasgow Celtic	08/09	09	5	8	0

SHERIDAN Darren Stephen
Born: Manchester, England, 8 December, 1967 — M

League Club	Source	Date Signed	Seasons Played	Apps	Subs	Gls
Barnsley	Winsford U	08/93	93-98	149	22	5
Wigan Ath	Tr	07/99	99-00	50	8	3
Oldham Ath	Tr	07/01	01-03	72	16	3

SHERIDAN Frank Michael
Born: Stepney, E London, England, 9 December, 1961 — M

League Club	Source	Date Signed	Seasons Played	Apps	Subs	Gls
Derby Co	App	07/78	80-81	41	2	5
Torquay U	Tr	08/82	82-83	24	3	3

SHERIDAN George Francis
Born: Wigan, Greater Manchester, England, 30 October, 1929 — RW
Died: Salford, England, December, 1986

League Club	Source	Date Signed	Seasons Played	Apps	Subs	Gls
Bolton W		09/50				
Bradford C	Colwyn Bay	01/52	51-52	12	-	1

SHERIDAN Jake
Born: Nottingham, England, 8 July, 1986 — M

League Club	Source	Date Signed	Seasons Played	Apps	Subs	Gls
Notts Co	Dunkirk, Nottingham	08/05	05-06	13	17	1

SHERIDAN John
Born: Ramsgate, Kent, England, 25 May, 1938 — RH

League Club	Source	Date Signed	Seasons Played	Apps	Subs	Gls
Notts Co	Linby Colliery	07/55	57-65	287	0	9
Hartlepool U	Tr	07/66	66-69	117	3	1

SHERIDAN John Joseph
Born: Stretford, Greater Manchester, England, 1 October, 1964 — M
Republic of Ireland: 34/B-1/U23-2/U21-2/Youth

League Club	Source	Date Signed	Seasons Played	Apps	Subs	Gls
Leeds U	Manchester C (Jnr)	03/82	82-88	225	5	47
Nottingham F	Tr	08/89				
Sheffield Wed	Tr	11/89	89-96	187	10	25
Birmingham C	L	02/96	95	1	1	0
Bolton W	Tr	11/96	96-97	24	8	2
Oldham Ath	Doncaster Rov	10/98	98-03	132	13	14

SHERINGHAM Charles Edward William (Charlie)
Born: Chingford, NE London, England, 17 April, 1988 — F

League Club	Source	Date Signed	Seasons Played	Apps	Subs	Gls
Crystal Palace	Ipswich T (Sch)	08/06				
Bournemouth	Dartford	10/11	11	2	4	1
AFC Wimbledon	Tr	06/13	13	8	7	1

SHERINGHAM Edward Paul (Teddy)
Born: Highams Park, NE London, England, 2 April, 1966 — F
England: 51/U21-1/Youth

League Club	Source	Date Signed	Seasons Played	Apps	Subs	Gls
Millwall	App	01/84	83-90	205	15	93
Aldershot	L	02/85	84	4	1	0
Nottingham F	Tr	07/91	91-92	42	0	14
Tottenham H	Tr	08/92	92-96	163	3	76
Manchester U	Tr	07/97	97-00	73	31	31
Tottenham H	Tr	07/01	01-02	67	3	22
Portsmouth	Tr	07/03	03	25	7	9
West Ham U	Tr	07/04	04-06	45	31	28
Colchester U	Tr	07/07	07	11	8	3

SHERLOCK Paul Grahame
Born: Wigan, Greater Manchester, England, 17 November, 1973 — LB

League Club	Source	Date Signed	Seasons Played	Apps	Subs	Gls
Notts Co	YT	07/92	93-94	8	4	1
Mansfield T	Tr	03/95	94-96	29	10	2

SHERLOCK Steven Edward (Steve)
Born: Birmingham, England, 10 May, 1959 — LB

League Club	Source	Date Signed	Seasons Played	Apps	Subs	Gls
Manchester C	App	05/77				
Luton T	Tr	06/78	78	2	0	0
Stockport Co	Tr	08/79	79-85	236	9	7
Cardiff C	Tr	07/86	86	14	1	0
Newport Co	L	12/86	86	5	0	0
Newport Co	Tr	03/87	86-87	42	2	2

SHERON Michael Nigel (Mike)
Born: St Helens, Merseyside, England, 11 January, 1972 — F
England: U21-16

League Club	Source	Date Signed	Seasons Played	Apps	Subs	Gls
Manchester C	YT	07/90	91-93	82	18	24
Bury	L	03/91	90	1	4	1
Norwich C	Tr	08/94	94-95	19	9	2
Stoke C	Tr	11/95	95-96	64	5	34
Queens Park Rgrs	Tr	07/97	97-98	57	6	19
Barnsley	Tr	01/99	98-02	114	38	33
Blackpool	Tr	07/03	03	28	10	8
Macclesfield T	Tr	08/04	04	14	12	3
Shrewsbury T	Tr	03/05	04	6	1	2

SHERRATT Brian
Born: Stoke-on-Trent, England, 29 March, 1944 — G

League Club	Source	Date Signed	Seasons Played	Apps	Subs	Gls
Stoke C	App	04/61	61	1	-	0
Oxford U	Tr	08/65	65-67	44	0	0
Nottingham F	L	10/68	68	1	0	0
Barnsley	Tr	06/69	69	15	0	0
Colchester U	Gainsborough Trinity	08/70	70	9	0	0

SHERRATT James Aaron (Jimmy)
Born: Warrington, Cheshire, England, 24 December, 1921 — CF/RB

League Club	Source	Date Signed	Seasons Played	Apps	Subs	Gls
Southampton		02/46				
Arsenal	Tr	12/46				
Hartlepool U	Tr	12/48	48	20	-	4
Leyton Orient	Tr	08/49	49-51	39	-	8
Workington	Tr	08/52	52-53	48	-	3

SHERRATT John Herbert
Born: Stoke-on-Trent, England, 9 March, 1923 — CF
Died: Birkenhead, Wirral, England, 27 July, 1975

League Club	Source	Date Signed	Seasons Played	Apps	Subs	Gls
Port Vale (Am)		03/49	48	2	-	0

SHERWOOD Alfred Thomas (Alf)
Born: Aberaman, Rhondda Cynon Taff, Wales, 13 November, 1924 — LB
Died: Pontypridd, Rhondda Cynon Taff, Wales, 12 March, 1990
Wales: 41/WLge-4/Schools/War-1

League Club	Source	Date Signed	Seasons Played	Apps	Subs	Gls
Cardiff C	Aberaman Ath	07/42	46-55	354	-	14
Newport Co	Tr	07/56	56-60	205	-	21

SHERWOOD Henry William (Jack)
Born: Reading, England, 3 September, 1913 — RH
Died: Reading, England, 29 October, 1985

League Club	Source	Date Signed	Seasons Played	Apps	Subs	Gls
Reading	Islington Corinthians	06/38	38	9	-	1
Aldershot	Tr	09/47	47-48	47	-	5
Crystal Palace	Tr	07/49	49	2	-	0

SHERWOOD Jeffrey (Jeff)
Born: Bristol, England, 5 October, 1959 — RB

League Club	Source	Date Signed	Seasons Played	Apps	Subs	Gls
Bristol Rov	Bath C	06/82	82	16	2	0

SHERWOOD Stephen (Steve)
Born: Selby, North Yorkshire, England, 10 December, 1953 — G

League Club	Source	Date Signed	Seasons Played	Apps	Subs	Gls
Chelsea	App	07/71	71-75	16	0	0
Millwall	L	10/73	73	1	0	0
Brentford	L	01/74	73	16	0	0
Brentford	L	08/74	74	46	0	0
Watford	Tr	11/76	76-86	211	0	1
Grimsby T	Tr	07/87	87-92	183	0	0
Northampton T	Tr	08/93	93	15	1	0
Lincoln C	Grimsby T (NC)	03/95	94	6	1	0

SHERWOOD Timothy Alan (Tim)
Born: St Albans, Hertfordshire, England, 6 February, 1969 — M
England: 3/B-1/U21-4

League Club	Source	Date Signed	Seasons Played	Apps	Subs	Gls
Watford	App	02/87	87-88	23	9	2
Norwich C	Tr	07/89	89-91	66	5	10
Blackburn Rov	Tr	02/92	91-98	239	7	25
Tottenham H	Tr	02/99	98-01	81	12	12
Portsmouth	Tr	01/03	02-03	24	6	1
Coventry C	Tr	08/04	04	10	1	0

SHEVCHENKO Andrei Mykolayovich
Born: Dvirkivschyna, Ukraine, 29 August, 1976 — F
Ukraine: 111/U21-7/Youth

League Club	Source	Date Signed	Seasons Played	Apps	Subs	Gls
Chelsea	AC Milan (ITA)	07/06	06-09	30	18	9

SHIELDS Anthony Gerald (Tony)
Born: Strabane, Tyrone, Northern Ireland, 4 June, 1980 — M

League Club	Source	Date Signed	Seasons Played	Apps	Subs	Gls
Peterborough U	YT	07/98	97-03	93	31	3

SHIELDS Duncan
Born: Dumbarton, Dunbartonshire, Scotland, 6 November, 1949 — CD

League Club	Source	Date Signed	Seasons Played	Apps	Subs	Gls
Workington	Possilpark YMCA	08/69	69	8	1	0

SHIELDS Greg
Born: Falkirk, Scotland, 21 August, 1976 — RB
Scotland: U21-2/Youth/Schools

League Club	Source	Date Signed	Seasons Played	Apps	Subs	Gls
Charlton Ath	Dunfermline Ath	08/99	99-00	23	2	2
Walsall	L	02/02	01	7	0	0

SHIELDS James (Jimmy)
Born: Glasgow, Scotland, 28 November, 1931 — IF
Died: Glasgow, Scotland, 29 March, 2001

League Club	Source	Date Signed	Seasons Played	Apps	Subs	Gls
Shrewsbury T	Hibernian	05/56	56	24	-	6

SHIELDS Paul Martin
Born: Dunfermline, Fife, Scotland, 15 August, 1981 — F

League Club	Source	Date Signed	Seasons Played	Apps	Subs	Gls
Gillingham	Forfar Ath	08/05	05	6	11	1

SHIELDS Robert James (Jimmy)
Born: Derry, Northern Ireland, 26 September, 1931 — CF
Northern Ireland: 1/NILge-1/Amateur

League Club	Source	Date Signed	Seasons Played	Apps	Subs	Gls
Sunderland	Crusaders	03/54				
Southampton	Tr	07/56	56-58	38	-	20

SHIELDS Samuel Miller (Sam)
Born: Denny, Falkirk, Scotland, 21 March, 1929 — IF
Died: Falkirk, Scotland, 13 September, 1986

League Club	Source	Date Signed	Seasons Played	Apps	Subs	Gls
Liverpool	Cowdenbeath	05/49	49	1	-	0
Darlington	Stirling A	06/52	52	21	-	2

SHIELDS Sean Patrick
Born: Enfield, N London, England, 21 January, 1992 — RW
Northern Ireland: U21-2

League Club	Source	Date Signed	Seasons Played	Apps	Subs	Gls
Dagenham & Red	St Albans C	01/13	12-13	2	11	0

SHIELDS Solomon Joel Anthony
Born: Leyton, NE London, England, 14 October, 1989 — RB/M

League Club	Source	Date Signed	Seasons Played	Apps	Subs	Gls
Leyton Orient	Sch	07/08	06	0	1	0

SHIELS Dean Andrew
Born: Magherafelt, Derry, Northern Ireland, 1 February, 1985 — M/F
Northern Ireland: 14/U21-6

League Club	Source	Date Signed	Seasons Played	Apps	Subs	Gls
Arsenal	Sch	07/02				
Doncaster Rov	Hibernian	02/09	08-10	46	37	10

SHIELS Dennis Patrick
Born: Belfast, Northern Ireland, 24 August, 1938 — CF/W
Northern Ireland: B

League Club	Source	Date Signed	Seasons Played	Apps	Subs	Gls
Sheffield U	Distillery	12/58	58-63	32	-	8
Peterborough U	Tr	07/64	64	12	-	4
Notts Co	Tr	07/65	65	28	1	6

SHIELS James Matthew (Jimmy)
Born: Derry, Northern Ireland, 24 February, 1938 — RB
Northern Ireland: B/NILge-1

League Club	Source	Date Signed	Seasons Played	Apps	Subs	Gls
Manchester U	Waterside BC	09/56				
Southend U	Tr	06/61	61	25	-	0

SHILTON Peter Leslie
Born: Leicester, England, 18 September, 1949 — G
England: 125/FLge-3/U23-13/Youth/Schools

League Club	Source	Date Signed	Seasons Played	Apps	Subs	Gls
Leicester C	App	09/66	65-74	286	0	1
Stoke C	Tr	11/74	74-77	110	0	0
Nottingham F	Tr	09/77	77-81	202	0	0
Southampton	Tr	08/82	82-86	188	0	0
Derby Co	Tr	07/87	87-91	175	0	0
Plymouth Arg	Tr	03/92	91-93	34	0	0
Bolton W	Wimbledon (NC)	03/95	94	0	1	0
Coventry C	Tr	07/95				
West Ham U	Tr	01/96				
Leyton Orient	Tr	11/96	96	9	0	0

SHILTON Samuel Roger (Sam)
Born: Nottingham, England, 21 July, 1978 — LW

League Club	Source	Date Signed	Seasons Played	Apps	Subs	Gls
Plymouth Arg	YT	-	94-95	1	2	0
Coventry C	Tr	10/95	97-98	3	4	0
Hartlepool U	Tr	07/99	99-00	45	9	7
Kidderminster Hrs	Tr	07/01	01-03	60	19	5

SHIMMIN Dominic Edward
Born: Bermondsey, SE London, England, 13 October, 1987 — D

League Club	Source	Date Signed	Seasons Played	Apps	Subs	Gls
Queens Park Rgrs	Arsenal (Sch)	03/05	05-06	2	1	0
Bournemouth	L	11/07	07	1	1	0

SHIMWELL Edmund (Eddie)
Born: Birchover, Derbyshire, England, 27 February, 1920 — RB
Died: Thornton Cleveleys, Lancashire, England, 3 October, 1988
England: 1

League Club	Source	Date Signed	Seasons Played	Apps	Subs	Gls
Sheffield U	Birchover	01/39	46	14	-	0

League Club	Source	Date Signed	Seasons Played	Apps	Subs	Gls
Blackpool	Tr	12/46	46-56	286	-	5
Oldham Ath	Tr	05/57	57	7	-	0

SHINER Roy Albert James
Born: Ryde, Isle of Wight, England, 15 November, 1924 — CF
Died: Ryde, Isle of Wight, England, 28 October, 1988

League Club	Source	Date Signed	Seasons Played	Apps	Subs	Gls
Huddersfield T	Cheltenham T	12/51	51-54	21	-	6
Sheffield Wed	Tr	07/55	55-59	153	-	93
Hull C	Tr	11/59	59	22	-	8

SHINNERS Paul
Born: Westminster, Central London, England, 8 January, 1959 — F

League Club	Source	Date Signed	Seasons Played	Apps	Subs	Gls
Gillingham	Fisher Ath	10/84	84	1	3	0
Colchester U	L	03/85	84	6	0	1
Leyton Orient	Tr	07/85	85-88	73	4	32

SHINNIE Andrew Murray
Born: Aberdeen, Scotland, 17 July, 1989 — M
Scotland: 1/U21-3/Youth

League Club	Source	Date Signed	Seasons Played	Apps	Subs	Gls
Birmingham C	Inverness CT	07/13	13-14	42	11	4

SHINTON Robert Thomas (Bobby)
Born: West Bromwich, West Midlands, England, 6 January, 1952 — F

League Club	Source	Date Signed	Seasons Played	Apps	Subs	Gls
Walsall	Lye T	03/72	71-73	78	1	20
Cambridge U	Tr	03/74	73-75	99	0	25
Wrexham	Tr	07/76	76-78	128	0	37
Manchester C	Tr	07/79	79	5	0	0
Millwall	L	02/80	79	5	0	3
Newcastle U	Tr	03/80	79-81	41	1	10
Millwall	Tr	03/82	81-82	29	5	4

SHIPLEY George Michael
Born: Newcastle-upon-Tyne, England, 7 March, 1959 — M

League Club	Source	Date Signed	Seasons Played	Apps	Subs	Gls
Southampton	App	03/77	79	2	1	0
Reading	L	03/79	78	11	1	1
Lincoln C	Tr	01/80	79-84	229	1	42
Charlton Ath	Tr	07/85	85-86	61	0	6
Gillingham	Tr	08/87	87-88	27	2	3

SHIPLEY Mark Edward
Born: South Elmsall, West Yorkshire, England, 11 February, 1959 — G

League Club	Source	Date Signed	Seasons Played	Apps	Subs	Gls
Blackburn Rov	App	08/77				
Doncaster Rov	Tr	08/79	79-80	6	0	0

SHIPPERLEY David John (Dave)
Born: Uxbridge, W London, England, 12 April, 1952 — CD

League Club	Source	Date Signed	Seasons Played	Apps	Subs	Gls
Charlton Ath	App	04/70	70-73	92	8	8
Plymouth Arg	L	02/74	73	1	0	0
Gillingham	Tr	05/74	74-77	144	0	10
Charlton Ath	Tr	02/78	77-79	53	0	6
Reading	Tr	09/79	79-80	18	1	0

SHIPPERLEY Neil Jason
Born: Chatham, Kent, England, 30 October, 1974 — F
England: U21-7

League Club	Source	Date Signed	Seasons Played	Apps	Subs	Gls
Chelsea	YT	09/92	92-94	26	11	7
Watford	L	12/94	94	5	1	1
Southampton	Tr	01/95	94-96	65	1	12
Crystal Palace	Tr	10/96	96-98	49	12	20
Nottingham F	Tr	09/98	98	12	8	1
Barnsley	Tr	07/99	99-00	70	8	27
Wimbledon	Tr	07/01	01-02	82	5	32
Crystal Palace	Tr	07/03	03-04	40	1	9
Sheffield U	Tr	07/05	05	34	5	11
Brentford	Tr	01/07	06	11	0	0

SHIPWRIGHT William Kenneth (Bill)
Born: Camden, N London, England, 22 December, 1932 — D

League Club	Source	Date Signed	Seasons Played	Apps	Subs	Gls
Watford	Chesham U	04/53	53-58	146	-	0
Aldershot	Tr	06/59	59-62	123	-	0

SHIRES Alan Jeffrey
Born: Leigh-on-Sea, Essex, England, 29 June, 1948 — RW

League Club	Source	Date Signed	Seasons Played	Apps	Subs	Gls
Southend U	App	-	65	0	1	0
Colchester U	Tr	07/66	66-67	23	0	3

SHIRES Corbin Carlos
Born: Sheffield, England, 31 December, 1997 — D

League Club	Source	Date Signed	Seasons Played	Apps	Subs	Gls
Mansfield T	Hallam	03/15	14	0	1	0

SHIRLEY Alexander Gordon (Alex)
Born: Milngavie, Dunbartonshire, Scotland, 31 October, 1921 — RW
Died: Northumberland, England, April, 1990

League Club	Source	Date Signed	Seasons Played	Apps	Subs	Gls
New Brighton	Dundee U	10/46	46	18	-	3
Bradford C	Tr	08/47	47	1	-	0

SHIRTLIFF Paul Robert
Born: Hoyland, South Yorkshire, England, 3 November, 1962 — RB
Died: Barnsley, South Yorkshire, England, 13 September, 2009
England: Semi Pro-15

League Club	Source	Date Signed	Seasons Played	Apps	Subs	Gls
Sheffield Wed	App	11/80	80-82	7	2	0
Northampton T	Tr	07/84	84	27	2	0

SHIRTLIFF Peter Andrew
Born: Hoyland, South Yorkshire, England, 6 April, 1961 — CD

League Club	Source	Date Signed	Seasons Played	Apps	Subs	Gls
Sheffield Wed	App	10/78	78-85	188	0	4
Charlton Ath	Tr	08/86	86-88	102	1	7
Sheffield Wed	Tr	07/89	89-92	104	0	4
Wolverhampton W	Tr	08/93	93-95	67	2	0
Barnsley	Tr	08/95	95-97	48	1	0
Carlisle U	L	10/96	96	5	0	0

SHITTU Daniel Olusola (Danny)
Born: Lagos, Nigeria, 2 September, 1980 — CD
Nigeria: 32

League Club	Source	Date Signed	Seasons Played	Apps	Subs	Gls
Charlton Ath	Carshalton Ath	09/99				
Blackpool	L	02/01	00	15	2	2
Queens Park Rgrs	Tr	10/01	01-05	166	3	17
Watford	Tr	08/06	06-07	64	5	8
Bolton W	Tr	08/08	08	9	1	0
Millwall	Tr	10/10	10	9	0	0
Queens Park Rgrs	Tr	01/11	10	5	2	0
Millwall	Tr	08/12	12-14	67	2	2

SHOEMAKE Kevin Paul
Born: Woodford, NE London, England, 28 January, 1965 — G

League Club	Source	Date Signed	Seasons Played	Apps	Subs	Gls
Leyton Orient	App	01/83	83	4	0	0
Peterborough U	Welling U	09/86	86-87	40	0	0

SHONE George Frederick
Born: Runcorn, Cheshire, England, 15 February, 1922 — CF
Died: Runcorn, Cheshire, England, September, 2009

League Club	Source	Date Signed	Seasons Played	Apps	Subs	Gls
Tranmere Rov		12/46	46	4	-	0

SHORE Andrew Jonathan (Drew)
Born: Poole, Dorset, England, 8 April, 1982 — M

League Club	Source	Date Signed	Seasons Played	Apps	Subs	Gls
Bristol Rov	YT	07/01	01	9	0	0

SHORE Brian
Born: Huddersfield, West Yorkshire, England, 1 February, 1935 — CF

League Club	Source	Date Signed	Seasons Played	Apps	Subs	Gls
Halifax T		10/56	56-57	9	-	3

SHORE Edward (Ted)
Born: Nuneaton, Warwickshire, England, 18 October, 1927 — LW
Died: Nuneaton, Warwickshire, England, 13 February, 1976

League Club	Source	Date Signed	Seasons Played	Apps	Subs	Gls
Port Vale		10/45	47	3	-	0
Coventry C	Tr	07/48	48-49	2	-	0

SHORE James Andrew (Jamie)
Born: Bristol, England, 1 September, 1977 — M
England: Youth

League Club	Source	Date Signed	Seasons Played	Apps	Subs	Gls
Norwich C	YT	09/94				
Bristol Rov	Tr	07/98	98	18	6	2

SHORE William Andrew (Andy)
Born: Kirkby-in-Ashfield, Nottinghamshire, England, 29 December, 1955 — CD

League Club	Source	Date Signed	Seasons Played	Apps	Subs	Gls
Mansfield T	Jnr	07/74	74	1	0	0

SHOREY Nicky Robert
Born: Romford, E London, England, 19 February, 1981 — LB
England: 2/B-1

League Club	Source	Date Signed	Seasons Played	Apps	Subs	Gls
Leyton Orient	YT	07/99	99-00	12	3	0
Reading	Tr	02/01	01-07	267	0	12
Aston Villa	Tr	08/08	08-09	22	2	0
Nottingham F	L	11/09	09	9	0	0
Fulham	L	02/10	09	9	0	0
West Bromwich A	Tr	08/10	10-11	47	6	0
Reading	Tr	07/12	12	16	1	0
Bristol C	Tr	08/13	13	11	3	0
Portsmouth	Tr	01/14	13-14	40	1	0

SHORT Alan John Moxley
Born: Plymouth, England, 5 July, 1928 — RW

League Club	Source	Date Signed	Seasons Played	Apps	Subs	Gls
Exeter C	Tamerton	08/50	50	5	-	1

SHORT Christian Mark (Chris)
Born: Munster, Germany, 9 May, 1970 — D

League Club	Source	Date Signed	Seasons Played	Apps	Subs	Gls
Scarborough	Pickering T	07/88	88-89	42	1	1
Notts Co	Tr	09/90	90-95	77	17	2
Huddersfield T	L	12/94	94	6	0	0
Sheffield U	Tr	12/95	95-97	40	4	0
Stoke C	Tr	07/98	98-99	33	2	0

SHORT Craig Jonathan
Born: Bridlington, East Riding of Yorkshire, England, 25 June, 1968 — CD
England: Schools

League Club	Source	Date Signed	Seasons Played	Apps	Subs	Gls
Scarborough	Pickering T	10/87	87-88	61	2	7
Notts Co	Tr	07/89	89-92	128	0	6
Derby Co	Tr	09/92	92-94	118	0	9
Everton	Tr	07/95	95-98	90	9	4

League Club	Source	Date Signed	Seasons Played	Apps	Subs	Gls
Blackburn Rov	Tr	08/99	99-04	131	3	4
Sheffield U	Tr	07/05	05	20	3	1

SHORT David
Born: St Neots, Cambridgeshire, England, 14 April, 1941 — LW

League Club	Source	Date Signed	Seasons Played	Apps	Subs	Gls
Lincoln C	St Neots T	11/58	58-59	4	-	0

SHORT John (Jack)
Born: Great Houghton, South Yorkshire, England, 18 February, 1928 — RB
Died: Barnsley, South Yorkshire, England, 1976

League Club	Source	Date Signed	Seasons Played	Apps	Subs	Gls
Wolverhampton W	Wath W	05/48	50-53	98	-	0
Stoke C	Tr	08/54	54-55	55	-	2
Barnsley	Tr	10/56	56-59	109	-	0

SHORT John David
Born: Gateshead, Tyne and Wear, England, 25 January, 1921 — RH/IF
Died: Nottingham, England, May, 1986

League Club	Source	Date Signed	Seasons Played	Apps	Subs	Gls
Leeds U	St Hilda's	01/38	46-48	60	-	18
Millwall	Tr	11/48	48-55	245	-	19

SHORT Maurice
Born: Middlesbrough, England, 29 December, 1949 — G

League Club	Source	Date Signed	Seasons Played	Apps	Subs	Gls
Middlesbrough	App	02/67	67-69	16	0	0
Oldham Ath	Tr	06/70	70	5	0	0
Grimsby T	L	01/71	70	10	0	0

SHORT Russell David Victor
Born: Ilford, E London, England, 4 September, 1968 — FB

League Club	Source	Date Signed	Seasons Played	Apps	Subs	Gls
Southend U	App	06/87	86	0	1	0

SHORTHOUSE William Henry (Bill)
Born: Bilston, West Midlands, England, 27 May, 1922 — CH
Died: Wolverhampton, England, 6 September, 2008

League Club	Source	Date Signed	Seasons Played	Apps	Subs	Gls
Wolverhampton W	St Martin's OB	04/46	47-56	344	-	1

SHORTT William Warren (Bill)
Born: Wrexham, Wales, 13 October, 1920 — G
Died: Plymouth, England, 20 September, 2004
Wales: 12/War-1

League Club	Source	Date Signed	Seasons Played	Apps	Subs	Gls
Chester C	Hoole Alex	05/39				
Plymouth Arg	Tr	02/46	46-55	342	-	0

SHOTTON John
Born: Hartlepool, Cleveland, England, 17 August, 1971 — M

League Club	Source	Date Signed	Seasons Played	Apps	Subs	Gls
Manchester U	YT	05/89				
Hartlepool U	Tr	09/90	90	0	1	0

SHOTTON Malcolm
Born: Newcastle-upon-Tyne, England, 16 February, 1957 — CD

League Club	Source	Date Signed	Seasons Played	Apps	Subs	Gls
Leicester C	App	02/75				
Oxford U	Nuneaton Bor	05/80	80-87	262	1	12
Portsmouth	Tr	08/87	87	10	0	0
Huddersfield T	Tr	02/88	87-88	16	0	1
Barnsley	Tr	09/88	88-89	64	2	6
Hull C	Tr	02/90	89-91	58	1	2
Barnsley	Ayr U	07/94	94-95	10	0	1

SHOTTON Ryan Colin
Born: Fenton, Potteries, England, 30 September, 1988 — D

League Club	Source	Date Signed	Seasons Played	Apps	Subs	Gls
Stoke C	Sch	03/07	10-12	34	14	1
Tranmere Rov	L	08/08	08	33	0	5
Barnsley	L	09/09	09	30	0	0
Wigan Ath	L	09/13	13	7	2	1
Derby Co	Tr	08/14	14	23	2	2

SHOULDER Alan
Born: Bishop Auckland, County Durham, England, 4 February, 1953 — F

League Club	Source	Date Signed	Seasons Played	Apps	Subs	Gls
Newcastle U	Blyth Spartans	12/78	78-81	99	8	35
Carlisle U	Tr	08/82	82-84	110	2	32
Hartlepool U	Tr	06/85	85-87	66	0	24

SHOULDER James (Jimmy)
Born: Esh Winning, County Durham, England, 11 September, 1946 — LB

League Club	Source	Date Signed	Seasons Played	Apps	Subs	Gls
Sunderland	Esh Winning Jnrs	02/64	66	3	0	0
Hartlepool U	Scarborough	08/73	73-74	62	1	3

SHOWELL George William
Born: Bilston, West Midlands, England, 9 February, 1934 — D
Died: Wrexham, Wales, 18 December, 2012

League Club	Source	Date Signed	Seasons Played	Apps	Subs	Gls
Wolverhampton W	Jnr	08/51	54-64	200	-	3
Bristol C	Tr	05/65	65	9	2	0
Wrexham	Tr	11/66	66-67	48	0	1

SHOWERS Derek
Born: Merthyr Tydfil, Wales, 28 January, 1953 — F
Wales: 2/U23-6/Schools

League Club	Source	Date Signed	Seasons Played	Apps	Subs	Gls
Cardiff C	Jnr	08/70	70-76	76	7	10
Bournemouth	Tr	07/77	77-78	58	2	19
Portsmouth	Tr	02/79	78-80	36	3	8
Hereford U	Tr	12/80	80-82	87	2	13

SHOWLER Kenneth (Ken)
Born: Doncaster, South Yorkshire, England, 3 February, 1933 — RW

League Club	Source	Date Signed	Seasons Played	Apps	Subs	Gls
Chesterfield	Bentley Colliery	11/52	53	7	-	0

SHOWLER Paul
Born: Doncaster, South Yorkshire, England, 10 October, 1966 — LW
England: Semi Pro-2

League Club	Source	Date Signed	Seasons Played	Apps	Subs	Gls
Barnet	Altrincham	08/91	91-92	69	2	12
Bradford C	Tr	08/93	93-95	72	16	15
Luton T	Tr	08/96	96-98	23	4	6

SHOWUNMI Enoch Olusesan
Born: Kilburn, NW London, England, 21 April, 1982 — F
Nigeria: 2

League Club	Source	Date Signed	Seasons Played	Apps	Subs	Gls
Luton T	Willesden Constantine	09/03	03-05	40	62	14
Bristol C	Tr	07/06	06-07	38	12	13
Sheffield Wed	L	01/08	07	6	4	0
Leeds U	Tr	07/08	08-09	3	12	2
Tranmere Rov	Falkirk	07/10	10-11	64	6	14
Notts Co	Tr	06/12	12-13	18	18	4
Torquay U	L	02/14	13	7	0	0
Plymouth Arg	L	03/14	13	2	5	0

SHREEVE John Thomas Thornton (Jack)
Born: Boldon, Tyne and Wear, England, 18 August, 1917 — FB
Died: Charlton, SE London, England, 30 July, 1966

League Club	Source	Date Signed	Seasons Played	Apps	Subs	Gls
Charlton Ath	Boldon Villa	01/35	36-50	145	-	0

SHREEVES Peter
Born: Neath, Wales, 30 November, 1940 — IF

League Club	Source	Date Signed	Seasons Played	Apps	Subs	Gls
Reading	Finchley	01/59	58-65	112	1	17

SHREWSBURY Philip (Phil)
Born: Heanor, Derbyshire, England, 25 March, 1947 — W
England: Youth

League Club	Source	Date Signed	Seasons Played	Apps	Subs	Gls
Notts Co	Jnr	09/65	66	1	1	0

SHROOT Robin Alexander Edward
Born: Hammersmith, W London, England, 26 March, 1988 — W
Northern Ireland: U21-4

League Club	Source	Date Signed	Seasons Played	Apps	Subs	Gls
Birmingham C	Harrow Bor	01/09				
Walsall	L	03/09	08	0	5	0
Burton A	L	07/09	09	4	3	0
Cheltenham T	L	08/10	10	4	3	1
Stevenage	Tr	07/11	11-13	28	33	9

SHRUBB Paul
Born: Guildford, Surrey, England, 1 August, 1955 — M/D

League Club	Source	Date Signed	Seasons Played	Apps	Subs	Gls
Fulham	App	08/72	72	1	0	0
Brentford	Hellenic (RSA)	03/77	76-81	170	12	8
Aldershot	Tr	08/82	82-86	165	9	5

SHTANIUK Sergei
Born: Minsk, Belarus, 11 January, 1972 — CD
Belarus: 42

League Club	Source	Date Signed	Seasons Played	Apps	Subs	Gls
Stoke C	Dynamo Moscow (RUS)	08/01	01-02	84	0	5

SHUFFLEBOTTOM Frank
Born: Chesterfield, Derbyshire, England, 9 October, 1917 — FB

League Club	Source	Date Signed	Seasons Played	Apps	Subs	Gls
Sheffield U	Norton Woodseats	12/34				
Ipswich T	Margate	06/38	38	2	-	0
Nottingham F	Tr	09/42	46	2	-	0
Bradford C	Tr	10/46	46-47	56	-	0

SHUKER Christopher Alan (Chris)
Born: Liverpool, England, 9 May, 1982 — W

League Club	Source	Date Signed	Seasons Played	Apps	Subs	Gls
Manchester C	YT	09/99	01-02	1	4	0
Macclesfield T	L	03/01	00	6	3	1
Walsall	L	02/03	02	3	2	0
Rochdale	L	08/03	03	14	0	1
Hartlepool U	L	12/03	03	14	0	1
Barnsley	Tr	03/04	03-05	93	7	17
Tranmere Rov	Tr	07/06	06-09	106	17	14
Morecambe	Tr	08/10	10	12	15	2
Port Vale		02/12	11-13	27	28	1
Tranmere Rov		12/14	14	1	2	0

SHUKER John
Born: Eccles, Greater Manchester, England, 8 May, 1942 — FB

League Club	Source	Date Signed	Seasons Played	Apps	Subs	Gls
Oxford U	Manchester C (Am)	12/61	62-76	473	5	46

SHUTE Philip (Phil)
Born: Darlington, County Durham, England, 15 December, 1953 — F

League Club	Source	Date Signed	Seasons Played	Apps	Subs	Gls
Darlington	Shildon	03/84	85	2	0	0

SHUTT Carl Steven
Born: Sheffield, England, 10 October, 1961 — F

League Club	Source	Date Signed	Seasons Played	Apps	Subs	Gls
Sheffield Wed	Spalding U	05/85	85-87	36	4	16
Bristol C	Tr	10/87	87-88	39	7	10
Leeds U	Tr	03/89	88-92	46	33	17

League Club	Source	Date Signed	Seasons Played	Apps	Subs	Gls
Birmingham C	Tr	08/93	93	18	8	4
Manchester C	L	12/93	93	5	1	0
Bradford C	Tr	08/94	94-96	60	28	15
Darlington	Tr	03/97	96-98	28	25	9

SHUTT Stephen James (Steve)
Born: Barnsley, South Yorkshire, England, 29 November, 1964 — M

League Club	Source	Date Signed	Seasons Played	Apps	Subs	Gls
Barnsley	App	11/82	82	1	0	0
Scunthorpe U	Goole T	02/85	84	2	0	1

SHUTTLEWORTH Barry
Born: Accrington, Lancashire, England, 9 July, 1977 — LB

League Club	Source	Date Signed	Seasons Played	Apps	Subs	Gls
Bury	YT	07/95				
Rotherham U	Tr	08/97				
Blackpool	Tr	08/98	98-99	16	3	1
Macclesfield T	Scarborough	10/01	01	0	3	0

SHYNE Christopher (Chris)
Born: Rochdale, Greater Manchester, England, 10 December, 1950 — G
Died: Rochdale, Greater Manchester, England, February, 2004

League Club	Source	Date Signed	Seasons Played	Apps	Subs	Gls
Rochdale	Dyers Arms	01/77	76-78	20	0	0
Wigan Ath	Tr	08/79	79	10	0	0

SIBBALD Robert Louis (Bobby)
Born: Hebburn, Tyne and Wear, England, 25 January, 1948 — FB/M

League Club	Source	Date Signed	Seasons Played	Apps	Subs	Gls
Leeds U	Jnr	01/65	66-67	1	1	0
York C	Tr	02/69	68-70	74	5	7
Southport	Tr	07/71	71-76	240	0	13

SIBIERSKI Antoine
Born: Lille, France, 5 August, 1974 — M/F
France: 1/B/U23-3

League Club	Source	Date Signed	Seasons Played	Apps	Subs	Gls
Manchester C	RC Lens (FRA)	08/03	03-05	64	28	11
Newcastle U	Tr	08/06	06	14	12	3
Wigan Ath	Tr	06/07	07-08	10	23	4
Norwich C	L	09/08	08	13	2	2

SIBLEY Albert (Joe)
Born: West Thurrock, Essex, England, 6 October, 1919 — RW
Died: Southend-on-Sea, England, 20 February, 2008

League Club	Source	Date Signed	Seasons Played	Apps	Subs	Gls
Southend U	Jnr	08/37	46	21	-	3
Newcastle U	Tr	02/47	46-49	31	-	6
Southend U	Tr	07/50	50-55	192	-	36

SIBLEY Eric Seymour
Born: Christchurch, Dorset, England, 17 November, 1915 — FB
Died: Bournemouth, England, May, 1996

League Club	Source	Date Signed	Seasons Played	Apps	Subs	Gls
Tottenham H	Jnr	05/34				
Bournemouth	Tr	08/37	37	7	-	0
Blackpool	Tr	10/37	37-46	82	-	0
Grimsby T	Tr	12/47	47-48	23	-	0
Chester C	Tr	07/49	49	7	-	0

SIBLEY Frank Philip
Born: Uxbridge, W London, England, 4 December, 1947 — LH
England: Youth

League Club	Source	Date Signed	Seasons Played	Apps	Subs	Gls
Queens Park Rgrs	App	02/65	63-70	140	3	3

SIBLEY Thomas Ivor (Tom)
Born: Porth, Rhondda Cynon Taff, Wales, 27 October, 1920 — LW
Died: Pontypridd, Rhondda Cynon Taff, Wales, November, 1994

League Club	Source	Date Signed	Seasons Played	Apps	Subs	Gls
Birmingham C	Ton Pentre	09/43				
Rochdale	Tr	03/47	46-47	23	-	3

SIBON Gerald
Born: Emmen, Netherlands, 19 April, 1974 — F
Netherlands: U23-4

League Club	Source	Date Signed	Seasons Played	Apps	Subs	Gls
Sheffield Wed	Ajax (NED)	07/99	99-02	98	31	36

SIDDALL Alfred Brian (Brian)
Born: Northwich, Cheshire, England, 2 May, 1930 — IF
Died: 2007

League Club	Source	Date Signed	Seasons Played	Apps	Subs	Gls
Stoke C	Northwich Victoria	02/51	50-53	59	-	10
Bournemouth	Tr	01/54	53-56	85	-	16
Ipswich T	Tr	05/57	57-60	58	-	6

SIDDALL Barry Alfred
Born: Ellesmere Port, Cheshire, England, 12 September, 1954 — G
England: Youth

League Club	Source	Date Signed	Seasons Played	Apps	Subs	Gls
Bolton W	App	01/72	72-76	137	0	0
Sunderland	Tr	09/76	76-81	167	0	0
Darlington	L	10/80	80	8	0	0
Port Vale	Tr	08/82	82-84	81	0	0
Blackpool	L	10/83	83	7	0	0
Stoke C	Tr	01/85	84-85	20	0	0
Tranmere Rov	L	10/85	85	12	0	0
Manchester C	L	03/86	85	6	0	0
Blackpool	Tr	08/86	86-88	110	0	0
Stockport Co	Tr	06/89	89	21	0	0
Hartlepool U	Tr	03/90	89	11	0	0
West Bromwich A	Tr	08/90				
Carlisle U	Mossley	11/90	90	24	0	0
Chester C	Tr	07/91	91	9	0	0
Preston NE	Northwich Victoria	11/92	92	1	0	0

SIDEBOTTOM Arnold
Born: Barnsley, South Yorkshire, England, 1 April, 1954 — CD

League Club	Source	Date Signed	Seasons Played	Apps	Subs	Gls
Manchester U	Jnr	02/72	72-74	16	0	0
Huddersfield T	Tr	01/76	75-77	56	5	5
Halifax T	Tr	10/78	78	21	0	2

SIDEBOTTOM Geoffrey (Geoff)
Born: Mapplewell, South Yorkshire, England, 29 December, 1936 — G
Died: Scunthorpe, North Lincolnshire, England, 3 November, 2008

League Club	Source	Date Signed	Seasons Played	Apps	Subs	Gls
Wolverhampton W	Jnr	09/54	58-60	28	-	0
Aston Villa	Tr	02/61	60-64	70	-	0
Scunthorpe U	Tr	01/65	64-66	59	0	0
Brighton & HA	New York Gen'ls (USA)	01/69	68-70	40	0	0

SIDIBE Mamady
Born: Kremis, Mali, 18 December, 1979 — F
Mali: 14

League Club	Source	Date Signed	Seasons Played	Apps	Subs	Gls
Swansea C	CAP Charenton (FRA)	07/01	01	26	5	7
Gillingham	Tr	08/02	02-04	80	26	10
Stoke C	Tr	07/05	05-10	148	20	24
Sheffield Wed	L	11/12	12	5	4	1
Tranmere Rov	L	02/13	12	10	0	0

SIDLOW Cyril
Born: Colwyn Bay, Conwy, Wales, 26 November, 1915 — G
Died: Wolverhampton, England, 12 April, 2005
Wales: 7/Amateur/War-11

League Club	Source	Date Signed	Seasons Played	Apps	Subs	Gls
Wolverhampton W	Llandudno	05/37	37-38	4	-	0
Liverpool	Tr	02/46	46-50	149	-	0

SIDWELL Steven James
Born: Wandsworth, SW London, England, 14 December, 1982 — M
England: U21-5/Youth

League Club	Source	Date Signed	Seasons Played	Apps	Subs	Gls
Arsenal	YT	07/01				
Brentford	L	10/01	01	29	1	4
Brighton & HA	L	11/02	02	11	1	5
Reading	Tr	01/03	02-06	164	4	29
Chelsea	Tr	07/07	07	7	8	0
Aston Villa	Tr	07/08	08-10	24	21	3
Fulham	Tr	01/11	10-13	82	10	14
Stoke C	Tr	06/14	14	5	7	0

SIEVWRIGHT George Edgar Smollett
Born: Broughty Ferry, Angus, Scotland, 10 September, 1937 — WH

League Club	Source	Date Signed	Seasons Played	Apps	Subs	Gls
Oldham Ath	Dundee U	06/63	63	37	-	4
Tranmere Rov	Tr	06/64				
Rochdale	Tr	07/65	65	31	1	1

SIGERE Jean-Michel Paul
Born: Fort-de-France, Martinique, 26 January, 1977 — F
France: Youth

League Club	Source	Date Signed	Seasons Played	Apps	Subs	Gls
Rushden & D	Bordeaux (FRA)	03/00	01	4	3	1

SIGURDARSON Bjorn Bergmann
Born: Akranes, Iceland, 26 February, 1991 — F
Iceland: 1/U21-7/Youth

League Club	Source	Date Signed	Seasons Played	Apps	Subs	Gls
Wolverhampton W	Lillestrom (NOR)	07/12	12-13	29	26	7

SIGURDSSON Gylfi Thor
Born: Reykjavik, Iceland, 8 September, 1989 — M
Iceland: 30/U21-3/Youth

League Club	Source	Date Signed	Seasons Played	Apps	Subs	Gls
Reading	Sch	07/07	09-10	36	6	18
Shrewsbury T	L	10/08	08	4	1	1
Crewe Alex	L	02/09	08	14	1	3
Swansea C (L)	TSG Hoffenheim (GER)	01/12	11	17	1	7
Tottenham H	TSG Hoffenheim (GER)	07/12	12-13	26	32	8
Swansea C	Tr	07/14	14	32	0	7

SIGURDSSON Hannes
Born: Reykjavik, Iceland, 10 April, 1983 — F
Iceland: 13

League Club	Source	Date Signed	Seasons Played	Apps	Subs	Gls
Stoke C	Viking Stavanger (NOR)	08/05	05-06	10	15	1

SIGURDSSON Larus Orri
Born: Akureyri, Iceland, 4 June, 1973 — CD
Iceland: 42/U21-16/Youth

League Club	Source	Date Signed	Seasons Played	Apps	Subs	Gls
Stoke C	Thor (ICE)	10/94	94-99	199	1	7
West Bromwich A	Tr	09/99	99-03	104	12	1

[SILAS] REBELO FERNANDES Jorge Manuel
Born: Lisbon, Portugal, 1 September, 1976 — M
Portugal: 3

League Club	Source	Date Signed	Seasons Played	Apps	Subs	Gls
Wolverhampton W	Uniao Leiria (POR)	07/03	03	2	7	0

SILENZI Andrea
Born: Rome, Italy, 10 February, 1966 — F
Italy: 1

League Club	Source	Date Signed	Seasons Played	Apps	Subs	Gls
Nottingham F	Torino (ITA)	08/95	95-96	4	8	0

SILK Gary Lee
Born: Newport, Isle of Wight, England, 13 September, 1984 — RB/M

League Club	Source	Date Signed	Seasons Played	Apps	Subs	Gls
Portsmouth	Sch	01/04				
Wycombe W	L	07/04	04	19	3	0
Boston U	L	01/06	05	11	3	0
Notts Co	Tr	07/06	06-07	46	17	2

SILK George Henry
Born: Liverpool, England, 18 October, 1916 — RB
Died: Plymouth, England, 6 February, 1969

League Club	Source	Date Signed	Seasons Played	Apps	Subs	Gls
Southport	Miranda FC	09/35	35-36	14	-	0
Plymouth Arg	Tr	08/37	37-50	86	-	1

SILKMAN Barry
Born: Stepney, E London, England, 29 June, 1952 — M

League Club	Source	Date Signed	Seasons Played	Apps	Subs	Gls
Hereford U	Barnet	08/74	74-75	18	19	2
Crystal Palace	Tr	08/76	76-78	40	8	6
Plymouth Arg	Tr	10/78	78	14	0	2
Luton T	L	02/79	78	3	0	0
Manchester C	Tr	03/79	78-79	19	0	3
Brentford	Tr	08/80	80	14	0	1
Queens Park Rgrs	Tr	10/80	80	22	1	2
Leyton Orient	Tr	09/81	81-84	133	7	14
Southend U	Tr	07/85	85	38	2	1
Crewe Alex	Tr	09/86	86	1	1	0

SILLE Leslie Taylor (Les)
Born: Liverpool, England, 12 April, 1928 — LW
Died: Liverpool, England, 7 April, 2007

League Club	Source	Date Signed	Seasons Played	Apps	Subs	Gls
Bournemouth (Am)	Tranmere Rov (Am)	03/47	46	1	-	0
Crystal Palace (Am)	Ipswich T (Am)	09/48	48	3	-	0
Tranmere Rov (Am)	Tr	02/49	48	1	-	0

SILLETT John Charles
Born: Southampton, England, 20 July, 1936 — RB
England: FLge-1

League Club	Source	Date Signed	Seasons Played	Apps	Subs	Gls
Chelsea	Southampton (Am)	04/54	56-61	93	-	0
Coventry C	Tr	04/62	61-65	108	1	1
Plymouth Arg	Tr	07/66	66-67	37	1	1

SILLETT Richard Peter Tudor (Peter)
Born: Southampton, England, 1 February, 1933 — FB
Died: Ashford, Kent, England, 13 March, 1998
England: 3/B-1/FLge-1/U23-3/Youth

League Club	Source	Date Signed	Seasons Played	Apps	Subs	Gls
Southampton	Jnr	06/50	51-52	59	-	4
Chelsea	Tr	06/53	53-61	260	-	29

SILLS Timothy (Tim)
Born: Romsey, Hampshire, England, 10 September, 1979 — F
England: Semi Pro-1

League Club	Source	Date Signed	Seasons Played	Apps	Subs	Gls
Oxford U	Aldershot T	01/06	05	9	4	1
Hereford U	Tr	07/06	06	22	14	2
Torquay U	Tr	07/07	09	12	6	2
Stevenage	Tr	01/10	10	1	0	0
Aldershot T	Tr	01/11	10	8	11	2

SILMAN David Alan
Born: Hampstead, NW London, England, 28 October, 1959 — CD

League Club	Source	Date Signed	Seasons Played	Apps	Subs	Gls
Brentford	Wolverhampton W (App)	02/78	78	1	0	0

SILMAN Roy
Born: Doncaster, South Yorkshire, England, 12 May, 1934 — FB

League Club	Source	Date Signed	Seasons Played	Apps	Subs	Gls
Rotherham U	Edlington CW	04/52	52-59	105	-	2
Barnsley	Tr	07/60				

SILVA David Josue Jimenez
Born: Gran Canaria, Spain, 8 January, 1986 — M
Spain: 91/U21-9

League Club	Source	Date Signed	Seasons Played	Apps	Subs	Gls
Manchester C	Valencia (SPN)	07/10	10-14	150	12	33

SILVA Debray Dario (Dario)
Born: Treinta y Tres, Uruguay, 2 November, 1972 — F
Uruguay: 49

League Club	Source	Date Signed	Seasons Played	Apps	Subs	Gls
Portsmouth	Sevilla (SPN)	08/05	05	13	0	2

SILVA Toni Brito
Born: Guinea-Bissau, 15 September, 1993 — RW
Portugal: Youth

League Club	Source	Date Signed	Seasons Played	Apps	Subs	Gls
Liverpool	Sch	09/10				
Northampton T	L	02/12	11	12	3	1
Barnsley	Tr	07/12	12	0	1	0
Dagenham & Red	L	03/13	12	4	0	0

SILVESTER Peter Dennis
Born: Wokingham, Berkshire, England, 19 February, 1948 — F

League Club	Source	Date Signed	Seasons Played	Apps	Subs	Gls
Reading	App	02/66	65-69	76	3	27
Norwich C	Tr	09/69	69-73	99	1	37
Colchester U	L	10/73	73	4	0	0
Southend U	Tr	02/74	73-76	79	2	32
Reading	L	03/75	74	2	0	0
Blackburn Rov	L	10/76	76	5	0	1
Cambridge U	Washington Dip's (USA)	08/77	77	2	2	1

SILVESTRE Mikael Samy
Born: Tours, France, 9 August, 1977 — CD
France: 40/U21-5/Youth

League Club	Source	Date Signed	Seasons Played	Apps	Subs	Gls
Manchester U	Inter Milan (ITA)	09/99	99-07	225	24	6
Arsenal	Tr	08/08	08-09	21	5	3

SILVESTRI Marco
Born: Reggio-Emilia, Italy, 2 March, 1991 — G
Italy: U21-1/Youth

League Club	Source	Date Signed	Seasons Played	Apps	Subs	Gls
Leeds U	Chievo Verona (ITA)	07/14	14	43	0	0

[SILVINHO] SILVIO DE CAMPOS Junior
Born: Sao Paulo, Brazil, 30 June, 1974 — LB
Brazil: 6

League Club	Source	Date Signed	Seasons Played	Apps	Subs	Gls
Arsenal	Corinthians (BRA)	07/99	99-00	46	9	3
Manchester C	Barcelona (SPN)	09/09	09	6	4	0

SIM John (Jock)
Born: Glasgow, Scotland, 4 December, 1922 — CF
Died: Chippenham, Wiltshire, England, 14 January, 2000

League Club	Source	Date Signed	Seasons Played	Apps	Subs	Gls
Plymouth Arg	Chippenham T	-				
Brighton & HA	Kirkintilloch Rob Roy	10/46	46-49	32	-	5

SIMB Jean-Pierre
Born: Paris, France, 4 September, 1974 — F

League Club	Source	Date Signed	Seasons Played	Apps	Subs	Gls
Torquay U	Paris Red Star (FRA)	03/99	98-99	4	16	1

SIMBA Amara Sylla
Born: Dakar, Senegal, 23 December, 1961 — F
France: 3

League Club	Source	Date Signed	Seasons Played	Apps	Subs	Gls
Leyton Orient	Leon (MEX)	10/98	98-99	27	10	13

SIMCOE Kenneth Edward (Ken)
Born: Nottingham, England, 14 February, 1937 — RW/CF
Died: Nottingham, England, 16 September, 2012

League Club	Source	Date Signed	Seasons Played	Apps	Subs	Gls
Nottingham F	Jnr	12/56	57	2	-	1
Coventry C	Tr	05/59	59	8	-	1
Notts Co	Tr	07/60	60	2	-	0

SIMEK Franklin Michael (Frankie)
Born: St Louis, Missouri, USA, 13 October, 1984 — RB
USA: 5/Youth

League Club	Source	Date Signed	Seasons Played	Apps	Subs	Gls
Arsenal	Sch	07/02				
Queens Park Rgrs	L	10/04	04	5	0	0
Bournemouth	L	03/05	04	8	0	0
Sheffield Wed	Tr	07/05	05-09	113	6	2
Carlisle U	Tr	07/10	10-12	107	2	0

SIMKIN Darren Spencer
Born: Walsall, West Midlands, England, 24 March, 1970 — FB

League Club	Source	Date Signed	Seasons Played	Apps	Subs	Gls
Wolverhampton W	Blakenall	12/91	92-93	14	1	0
Shrewsbury T	Tr	12/94	94	10	2	0

SIMM John (Johnny)
Born: Ashton-in-Makerfield, Greater Manchester, England, 24 November, 1929 — W

League Club	Source	Date Signed	Seasons Played	Apps	Subs	Gls
Bolton W		10/47	47	1	-	0
Bury	Tr	05/51	51-54	47	-	8
Bradford C	Tr	03/55	54-58	95	-	22

SIMMONDS Christopher Kenneth (Chris)
Born: Plymouth, England, 5 August, 1920 — IF
Died: Corby, Northamptonshire, England, June, 1982

League Club	Source	Date Signed	Seasons Played	Apps	Subs	Gls
Millwall	Barry T	05/47	46-49	67	-	14
Leyton Orient	Tr	06/50	50	15	-	1
Workington	Tr	06/51	51-53	119	-	33

SIMMONDS Daniel Brian (Danny)
Born: Eastbourne, East Sussex, England, 17 December, 1974 — M

League Club	Source	Date Signed	Seasons Played	Apps	Subs	Gls
Brighton & HA	YT	07/93	93-94	8	10	0

SIMMONDS Donovan Ashton
Born: Walthamstow, NE London, England, 12 October, 1988 — F

League Club	Source	Date Signed	Seasons Played	Apps	Subs	Gls
Coventry C	Charlton Ath (Sch)	07/07				
Gillingham	L	03/08	07	0	3	0

SIMMONDS Melvyn Robert (Mel)
Born: Reading, England, 20 December, 1951 — M
England: Schools

League Club	Source	Date Signed	Seasons Played	Apps	Subs	Gls
Reading	Manchester U (App)	01/69				
Bournemouth	Tr	07/69	69	4	2	0

SIMMONDS Robert Lyndon (Lyndon)
Born: Pontypool, Torfaen, Wales, 11 November, 1966 — F
Wales: Youth

League Club	Source	Date Signed	Seasons Played	Apps	Subs	Gls
Leeds U	App	11/84	84-85	6	3	3
Swansea C	L	10/86	86	7	1	1
Rochdale	Tr	02/87	86-87	65	0	22

SIMMONITE Gordon
Born: Sheffield, England, 25 April, 1957 — RB
England: Semi Pro

League Club	Source	Date Signed	Seasons Played	Apps	Subs	Gls
Sheffield Wed	Rotherham (App)	08/75	76	1	0	0
Blackpool	Boston U	09/80	80-82	63	0	1
Lincoln C	Tr	11/82	82-84	71	1	0

SIMMONS Anthony John (Tony)
Born: Stocksbridge, South Yorkshire, England, 9 February, 1965 — F
England: Youth

League Club	Source	Date Signed	Seasons Played	Apps	Subs	Gls
Sheffield Wed	App	02/83	81-82	1	3	0
Queens Park Rgrs	Tr	11/83				
Rotherham U	Tr	03/84	83-86	85	11	27
Lincoln C	Tr	09/86	86	14	5	5
Cardiff C	L	02/87	86	4	1	1

SIMMONS David John (Dave)
Born: Ryde, Isle of Wight, England, 24 October, 1948 — F
Died: Ely, Cambridgeshire, England, 3 July, 2007

League Club	Source	Date Signed	Seasons Played	Apps	Subs	Gls
Arsenal	App	11/65				
Bournemouth	L	11/68	68	7	0	3
Aston Villa	Tr	02/69	68-70	13	4	7
Walsall	L	10/70	70	5	0	2
Colchester U	Tr	12/70	70-72	57	5	11
Cambridge U	Tr	03/73	72-73	19	5	3
Brentford	Tr	03/74	73-75	47	5	17
Cambridge U	Tr	11/75	75	16	1	5

SIMMONS Paris Michael
Born: Lewisham, SE London, England, 2 January, 1990 — F

League Club	Source	Date Signed	Seasons Played	Apps	Subs	Gls
Derby Co	Sch	07/08	07	0	1	0

SIMMS Gordon
Born: Leamington Spa, Warwickshire, England, 20 December, 1936 — W

League Club	Source	Date Signed	Seasons Played	Apps	Subs	Gls
Coventry C (Am)	Flavell's	10/57	57	1	-	0

SIMMS Gordon Henry
Born: Larne, Antrim, Northern Ireland, 23 March, 1981 — CD
Northern Ireland: U21-14/Youth/Schools

League Club	Source	Date Signed	Seasons Played	Apps	Subs	Gls
Wolverhampton W	YT	04/98				
Hartlepool U	Tr	03/01	01-02	6	5	0

SIMNER Joseph (Joe)
Born: Sedgley, West Midlands, England, 13 March, 1923 — IF
Died: Stourbridge, West Midlands, England, June, 2000

League Club	Source	Date Signed	Seasons Played	Apps	Subs	Gls
Chelsea	Folkestone	10/47	47	1	-	0
Swindon T	Tr	07/49	49-50	30	-	12

SIMONS Alan Geoffrey
Born: Wrexham, Wales, 2 September, 1968 — G

League Club	Source	Date Signed	Seasons Played	Apps	Subs	Gls
Port Vale	YT	09/87	87	1	0	0

SIMONSEN Allan Rodenkam
Born: Vejle, Denmark, 15 December, 1952 — F
Denmark: 55/U21-6

League Club	Source	Date Signed	Seasons Played	Apps	Subs	Gls
Charlton Ath	Barcelona (SPN)	11/82	82	16	0	9

SIMONSEN Steven Preben Arthur (Steve)
Born: South Shields, Tyne and Wear, England, 3 April, 1979 — G
England: U21-4/Youth

League Club	Source	Date Signed	Seasons Played	Apps	Subs	Gls
Tranmere Rov	YT	10/96	97-98	35	0	0
Everton	Tr	09/98	99-03	28	2	0
Stoke C	Tr	08/04	04-09	160	6	0
Sheffield U	Tr	03/10	09-11	94	2	0
Preston NE	Tr	08/12	12	10	0	0

SIMPEMBA Ian Frederick
Born: Dublin, Republic of Ireland, 28 March, 1983 — D/M
Republic of Ireland: Youth

League Club	Source	Date Signed	Seasons Played	Apps	Subs	Gls
Wycombe W	YT	07/01	02-03	17	3	2

SIMPKIN Christopher John (Chris)
Born: Hull, England, 24 April, 1944 — M/CD

League Club	Source	Date Signed	Seasons Played	Apps	Subs	Gls
Hull C	App	04/62	62-71	284	1	19
Blackpool	Tr	10/71	71-72	31	3	1
Scunthorpe U	Tr	10/73	73-74	61	0	2
Huddersfield T	Tr	08/75	75	25	0	0
Hartlepool U	Tr	12/76	76-77	47	0	0

SIMPKIN Joseph (Joe)
Born: Skelmersdale, Lancashire, England, 26 September, 1921 — WH
Died: Skelmersdale, Lancashire, England, 17 January, 1969

League Club	Source	Date Signed	Seasons Played	Apps	Subs	Gls
Southport	Burscough	04/44	46-47	10	-	2

SIMPKINS Kenneth (Ken)
Born: Wrexham, Wales, 21 December, 1943 — G
Wales: U23-1

League Club	Source	Date Signed	Seasons Played	Apps	Subs	Gls
Wrexham	Jnr	05/62	62-63	4	-	0
Hartlepool U	Tr	03/64	63-67	121	0	1

SIMPKINS Michael James (Mike)
Born: Sheffield, England, 28 November, 1978 — CD

League Club	Source	Date Signed	Seasons Played	Apps	Subs	Gls
Sheffield Wed	YT	07/97				
Chesterfield	Tr	03/98	98-00	22	4	0
Cardiff C	Tr	05/01	01	13	4	0
Exeter C	L	09/02	02	4	1	0
Cheltenham T	L	12/02	02	2	0	0
Rochdale	Tr	08/03	03	25	2	0

SIMPSON Alexander (Alec)
Born: Glasgow, Scotland, 24 November, 1924 — LH
Died: Wombourne, Staffordshire, England, 16 June, 2008

League Club	Source	Date Signed	Seasons Played	Apps	Subs	Gls
Wolverhampton W	Benburb Jnrs	01/47	47-48	2	-	0
Notts Co	Tr	10/49	49-52	74	-	6
Southampton	Tr	11/52	52-54	68	-	1
Shrewsbury T	Tr	07/55	55-57	100	-	4

SIMPSON Archibald (Archie)
Born: Dundee, Scotland, 8 June, 1933 — RB
Scotland: Schools

League Club	Source	Date Signed	Seasons Played	Apps	Subs	Gls
Newcastle U	Dundee	07/55				
Barrow	Tr	07/56	56-58	76	-	1

SIMPSON Charles William (Charlie)
Born: Rochdale, Greater Manchester, England, 11 July, 1954 — M

League Club	Source	Date Signed	Seasons Played	Apps	Subs	Gls
Rochdale	App	07/72	72	1	0	1

SIMPSON Colin Robertson
Born: Oxford, England, 30 April, 1976 — F

League Club	Source	Date Signed	Seasons Played	Apps	Subs	Gls
Watford	YT	07/94	95	0	1	0
Leyton Orient	Hendon	12/97	97	9	5	3

SIMPSON Cyril
Born: Aylesham, Kent, England, 18 August, 1942 — IF

League Club	Source	Date Signed	Seasons Played	Apps	Subs	Gls
Gillingham	Jnr	06/60	59-61	18	-	0

SIMPSON Daniel Peter (Danny)
Born: Eccles, Greater Manchester, England, 4 January, 1987 — RB

League Club	Source	Date Signed	Seasons Played	Apps	Subs	Gls
Manchester U	Sch	01/06	07	1	2	0
Sunderland	L	01/07	06	13	1	0
Ipswich T	L	03/08	07	7	1	0
Blackburn Rov	L	08/08	08	10	2	0
Newcastle U	Tr	08/09	09-12	122	1	1
Queens Park Rgrs	Tr	06/13	13-14	33	1	0
Leicester C	Tr	08/14	14	13	1	0

SIMPSON Dennis Ewart
Born: Coventry, England, 1 November, 1919 — RW
Died: Coventry, England, 10 January, 2002

League Club	Source	Date Signed	Seasons Played	Apps	Subs	Gls
Coventry C	Salem Baptist	05/39	46-49	67	-	5
Reading	Tr	05/50	50-54	172	-	32
Exeter C	Tr	05/55	55-56	30	-	4

SIMPSON Elliott David
Born: York, England, 1 July, 1976 — LB

League Club	Source	Date Signed	Seasons Played	Apps	Subs	Gls
York C	YT	06/94	94	1	0	0

SIMPSON Fitzroy
Born: Bradford-on-Avon, Wiltshire, England, 26 February, 1970 — M
Jamaica: 36

League Club	Source	Date Signed	Seasons Played	Apps	Subs	Gls
Swindon T	YT	07/88	88-91	78	27	9
Manchester C	Tr	03/92	91-94	58	13	4
Bristol C	L	09/94	94	4	0	0
Portsmouth	Tr	08/95	95-99	139	9	10
Walsall	Heart of Midlothian	03/01	00-02	45	18	4

SIMPSON Gary
Born: Chesterfield, Derbyshire, England, 10 June, 1959 — F

League Club	Source	Date Signed	Seasons Played	Apps	Subs	Gls
Chesterfield	App	07/77	76-80	36	7	8
Chester C	Tr	08/81	81-82	57	6	18

SIMPSON Gary John
Born: Ashford, Surrey, England, 14 February, 1976 — CD

League Club	Source	Date Signed	Seasons Played	Apps	Subs	Gls
Luton T	YT	07/94				
Fulham	L	03/96	95	5	2	0

SIMPSON George Leonard
Born: Shirebrook, Derbyshire, England, 3 December, 1933 — IF
Died: Cleveleys, Lancashire, England, 23 February, 2012

League Club	Source	Date Signed	Seasons Played	Apps	Subs	Gls
Mansfield T	Jnr	08/51	52-53	8	-	0
Gillingham	Hereford U	08/56	56	8	-	1

SIMPSON Harold (Harry)
Born: Ashton-under-Lyne, Greater Manchester, England, 2 August, 1927 — LW

League Club	Source	Date Signed	Seasons Played	Apps	Subs	Gls
Accrington Stan (Am)	Lytham	04/49	48	1	-	0

SIMPSON Jacob David (Jake)
Born: Oxford, England, 27 October, 1990 RM

League Club	Source	Date Signed	Seasons Played	Apps	Subs	Gls
Shrewsbury T	Blackburn Rov (Sch)	07/09	09	14	4	0
Stockport Co	Tr	09/10	10	11	8	0

SIMPSON James (Jimmy)
Born: Clay Cross, Derbyshire, England, 8 December, 1923 IF
Died: Matlock, Derbyshire, England, 1 May, 2010

League Club	Source	Date Signed	Seasons Played	Apps	Subs	Gls
Chesterfield	Parkhouse Colliery	08/45	46	3	-	0

SIMPSON Jay-Alistaire Frederick (Jay)
Born: Enfield, N London, England, 1 December, 1988 F
England: Youth

League Club	Source	Date Signed	Seasons Played	Apps	Subs	Gls
Arsenal	Sch	07/07				
Millwall	L	08/07	07	34	7	6
West Bromwich A	L	01/09	08	9	4	1
Queens Park Rgrs	L	08/09	09	34	5	12
Hull C	Tr	08/10	10-12	46	32	12
Millwall	L	08/11	11	13	3	4
Leyton Orient	Buriram U (THA)	07/14	14	12	16	5

SIMPSON John
Born: Hedon, East Riding of Yorkshire, England, 27 October, 1918 LB
Died: Market Weighton, East Riding of Yorkshire, England, 21 June, 2000

League Club	Source	Date Signed	Seasons Played	Apps	Subs	Gls
Huddersfield T	Bridlington T	03/39	46	5	-	0
York C	Tr	03/48	47-53	207	-	0

SIMPSON John Lionel
Born: Appleby, Cumbria, England, 5 October, 1933 G
Died: Gillingham, Kent, England, 7 December, 1993

League Club	Source	Date Signed	Seasons Played	Apps	Subs	Gls
Lincoln C	Netherfield	03/57	56	5	-	0
Gillingham	Tr	06/57	57-71	571	0	0

SIMPSON Joshua Christopher (Josh)
Born: Vancouver, Canada, 15 May, 1983 LW
Canada: 43/U23-5/Youth

League Club	Source	Date Signed	Seasons Played	Apps	Subs	Gls
Millwall	Portland Univ (USA)	08/04	04-05	30	13	2

SIMPSON Joshua Richard (Josh)
Born: Harlow, Essex, England, 6 March, 1987 M
England: Semi Pro-4

League Club	Source	Date Signed	Seasons Played	Apps	Subs	Gls
Peterborough U	Histon	11/09	09	8	13	2
Southend U	L	08/10	10	17	0	1
Crawley T	Tr	01/11	11-14	106	16	9

SIMPSON Karl Edward
Born: Newmarket, Suffolk, England, 14 October, 1976 M

League Club	Source	Date Signed	Seasons Played	Apps	Subs	Gls
Norwich C	Jnr	07/95	95-97	4	6	0

SIMPSON Kenneth (Ken)
Born: Sheffield, England, 12 June, 1931 W

League Club	Source	Date Signed	Seasons Played	Apps	Subs	Gls
Rotherham U	Ransome & Marles	09/55	55-57	7	-	0

SIMPSON Luke Thomas
Born: Heywood, Greater Manchester, England, 23 September, 1994 G

League Club	Source	Date Signed	Seasons Played	Apps	Subs	Gls
Oldham Ath	Sch	07/13				
Accrington Stan	Tr	08/14	14	6	2	0

SIMPSON Michael
Born: Nottingham, England, 28 February, 1974 M

League Club	Source	Date Signed	Seasons Played	Apps	Subs	Gls
Notts Co	YT	07/92	93-96	39	10	3
Plymouth Arg	L	10/96	96	10	2	0
Wycombe W	Tr	12/96	96-03	267	18	16
Leyton Orient	Tr	07/04	04-06	105	0	4
Burton A		11/07	09	20	4	2

SIMPSON Neil Alexander
Born: Hackney, E London, England, 15 November, 1961 M
England: Youth//Scotland: 5/U21-11

League Club	Source	Date Signed	Seasons Played	Apps	Subs	Gls
Newcastle U	Aberdeen	07/90	90	1	3	0

SIMPSON Noel Harold
Born: Mansfield, Nottinghamshire, England, 23 December, 1922 LH
Died: Kirkby-in-Ashfield, Nottinghamshire, England, 21 November, 1987

League Club	Source	Date Signed	Seasons Played	Apps	Subs	Gls
Nottingham F	Raleigh Ath	05/45	46-47	47	-	3
Coventry C	Tr	08/48	48-56	258	-	8
Exeter C	Tr	02/57	56-57	33	-	0

SIMPSON Owen
Born: Prudhoe, Northumberland, England, 18 December, 1943 LB/M

League Club	Source	Date Signed	Seasons Played	Apps	Subs	Gls
Rotherham U	Clara Vale Jnrs	10/62	64-66	6	0	0
Leyton Orient	Tr	09/67	67	36	0	4
Colchester U	Tr	08/68	68	41	2	4
Southend U	Tr	08/69	69-70	64	0	1
Darlington	Tr	03/71	70	11	0	0
Grimsby T	Tr	08/71	71	6	1	0

SIMPSON Paul David
Born: Carlisle, Cumbria, England, 26 July, 1966 LW
England: U21-5/Youth

League Club	Source	Date Signed	Seasons Played	Apps	Subs	Gls
Manchester C	App	08/83	82-88	99	22	18
Oxford U	Tr	10/88	88-91	138	6	43
Derby Co	Tr	02/92	91-97	134	52	48
Sheffield U	L	12/96	96	2	4	0
Wolverhampton W	Tr	10/97	97-99	32	20	6
Walsall	L	09/98	98	4	0	1
Walsall	L	12/98	98	6	0	0
Blackpool	Tr	08/00	00-01	69	7	13
Rochdale	Tr	03/02	01-02	37	5	15
Carlisle U	Tr	08/03	03-05	29	5	6

SIMPSON Peter Frederick
Born: Gorleston, Norfolk, England, 13 January, 1945 CD

League Club	Source	Date Signed	Seasons Played	Apps	Subs	Gls
Arsenal	App	04/62	63-77	353	17	10

SIMPSON Peter Wilson
Born: Sunderland, England, 21 September, 1940 IF
England: Schools

League Club	Source	Date Signed	Seasons Played	Apps	Subs	Gls
Burnley	Jnr	11/57	61-62	3	-	0
Bury	Tr	08/63	63	4	-	0

SIMPSON Philip Mark (Phil)
Born: Lambeth, S London, England, 18 October, 1969 M

League Club	Source	Date Signed	Seasons Played	Apps	Subs	Gls
Barnet	Stevenage Bor	10/95	95-98	91	9	7

SIMPSON Reginald (Reg)
Born: Blackburn, Greater Manchester, England, 14 June, 1923 D
Died: Lytham St Annes, Lancashire, England, 25 March, 2007

League Club	Source	Date Signed	Seasons Played	Apps	Subs	Gls
Preston NE		11/43	46	4	-	0
Carlisle U	Tr	08/48	48	38	-	0

SIMPSON Robbie
Born: Poole, Dorset, England, 15 March, 1985 F

League Club	Source	Date Signed	Seasons Played	Apps	Subs	Gls
Coventry C	Cambridge U	07/07	07-08	24	37	4
Huddersfield T	Tr	06/09	09	4	9	0
Brentford	L	08/10	10	11	16	4
Oldham Ath	Tr	09/11	11-12	49	17	8
Leyton Orient	Tr	11/13	13	5	9	0
Cambridge U	Tr	06/14	14	23	12	8

SIMPSON Robert (Bobby)
Born: Bishop Auckland, County Durham, England, 15 September, 1915 LW
Died: Bishop Auckland, County Durham, England, 13 January, 1994

League Club	Source	Date Signed	Seasons Played	Apps	Subs	Gls
Darlington	West Auckland T	08/36	36-46	96	-	14
Hartlepool U	Tr	07/47	47	13	-	1

SIMPSON Robert Anthony (Robbie)
Born: Luton, England, 3 March, 1976 F
England: Youth

League Club	Source	Date Signed	Seasons Played	Apps	Subs	Gls
Tottenham H	YT	11/93				
Portsmouth	Tr	07/96	97	0	2	0

SIMPSON Ronald (Ron)
Born: Carlisle, Cumbria, England, 25 February, 1934 LW
Died: Carlisle, Cumbria, England, 11 November, 2010

League Club	Source	Date Signed	Seasons Played	Apps	Subs	Gls
Huddersfield T	Holme Head Works	02/51	51-57	110	-	24
Sheffield U	Tr	05/58	58-64	203	-	44
Carlisle U	Tr	12/64	64-65	46	0	6

SIMPSON Ronald Campbell (Ronnie)
Born: Glasgow, Scotland, 11 October, 1930 G
Died: Edinburgh, Scotland, 19 April, 2004
Scotland: 5/B/SLge-1/Amateur

League Club	Source	Date Signed	Seasons Played	Apps	Subs	Gls
Newcastle U	Third Lanark	02/51	51-59	262	-	0

SIMPSON Terence John Norman (Terry)
Born: Southampton, England, 8 October, 1938 WH

League Club	Source	Date Signed	Seasons Played	Apps	Subs	Gls
Southampton	Jnr	06/57	58-61	22	-	1
Peterborough U	Tr	06/62	62	45	-	4
West Bromwich A	Tr	06/63	63-66	71	1	3
Walsall	Tr	03/67	66-67	50	1	4
Gillingham	Tr	07/68	68	35	1	4

SIMPSON Thomas (Tommy)
Born: Airdrie, Lanarkshire, Scotland, 31 July, 1931 FB

League Club	Source	Date Signed	Seasons Played	Apps	Subs	Gls
Darlington	Dundee U	08/56	56-57	4	-	0

SIMPSON William
Born: Carlisle, Cumbria, England, 2 October, 1919 IF

League Club	Source	Date Signed	Seasons Played	Apps	Subs	Gls
Carlisle U	Tottenham H (Am)	08/46	46	12	-	2

SIMPSON William George
Born: Glasgow, Scotland, 22 May, 1928 CF/LH
Died: Epsom, Surrey, England, 8 August, 2002

League Club	Source	Date Signed	Seasons Played	Apps	Subs	Gls
Aston Villa	Trentside Jnrs, Nott'm	05/50				
Crystal Palace	Tr	08/52	52-54	38	-	13

SIMS David Nigel (Nigel)
Born: Coton-in-Elms, Derbyshire, England, 9 August, 1931 G
England: FLge-2

League Club	Source	Date Signed	Seasons Played	Apps	Subs	Gls
Wolverhampton W	Stapenhill	09/48	48-55	38	-	0
Aston Villa	Tr	03/56	55-63	264	-	0
Peterborough U	Tr	09/64	64	16	-	0

SIMS Frank
Born: Lincoln, England, 12 September, 1931 CH
Died: Nottingham, England, 28 November, 2001

League Club	Source	Date Signed	Seasons Played	Apps	Subs	Gls
Lincoln C	Ruston-Bucyrus	08/51	51-55	3	-	0

SIMS Harry Christopher (Chris)
Born: Liverpool, England, 6 December, 1939 FB

League Club	Source	Date Signed	Seasons Played	Apps	Subs	Gls
Blackburn Rov	Clitheroe	04/59	63-64	13	-	0

SIMS Jared Phillip John
Born: Truro, Cornwall, England, 16 October, 1993 F

League Club	Source	Date Signed	Seasons Played	Apps	Subs	Gls
Plymouth Arg	Sch	07/12	11	3	0	0

SIMS John
Born: Belper, Derbyshire, England, 14 August, 1952 F

League Club	Source	Date Signed	Seasons Played	Apps	Subs	Gls
Derby Co	App	08/70	72	2	1	0
Luton T	L	11/73	73	3	0	1
Oxford U	L	09/74	74	6	1	1
Colchester U	L	01/75	74	2	0	0
Notts Co	Tr	12/75	75-77	48	13	13
Exeter C	Tr	12/78	78-79	33	1	11
Plymouth Arg	Tr	10/79	79-82	161	2	43
Torquay U	Tr	08/83	83	30	0	8
Exeter C	Tr	02/84	83-84	23	2	6
Torquay U	Tr	11/84	84	15	2	3

SIMS Steven Frank (Steve)
Born: Lincoln, England, 2 July, 1957 CD
England: B-1/U21-10

League Club	Source	Date Signed	Seasons Played	Apps	Subs	Gls
Leicester C	App	08/74	75-78	78	1	3
Watford	Tr	12/78	78-83	150	2	4
Notts Co	Tr	09/84	84-86	85	0	5
Watford	Tr	10/86	86	19	0	1
Aston Villa	Tr	06/87	87-88	41	0	0
Lincoln C	Burton A	10/90	90	5	0	0

SINAMA-PONGOLLE Florent
Born: Saint-Pierre, Reunion, 20 October, 1984 F
France: 1/U21-37/Youth

League Club	Source	Date Signed	Seasons Played	Apps	Subs	Gls
Liverpool	Le Havre (FRA)	07/03	03-05	12	26	4
Blackburn Rov	L	01/06	05	8	2	1

SINCLAIR Brian William
Born: Liverpool, England, 2 August, 1958 M

League Club	Source	Date Signed	Seasons Played	Apps	Subs	Gls
Blackpool	Bury (NC)	08/77	77	0	2	0
Port Vale	Tr	08/78	78	14	4	2

SINCLAIR Colin MacLean
Born: Edinburgh, Scotland, 1 December, 1947 F
Scotland: Youth/Schools

League Club	Source	Date Signed	Seasons Played	Apps	Subs	Gls
Darlington	Raith Rov	06/71	71-76	201	2	59
Hereford U	Tr	10/76	76-77	20	2	2
Newport Co	Tr	01/78	77-78	29	1	5

SINCLAIR David
Born: Dunfermline, Fife, Scotland, 6 October, 1969 CD

League Club	Source	Date Signed	Seasons Played	Apps	Subs	Gls
Millwall	Raith Rov	07/96	96	6	2	0

SINCLAIR Dean Michael
Born: Luton, England, 17 December, 1984 M
England: Semi Pro-5

League Club	Source	Date Signed	Seasons Played	Apps	Subs	Gls
Norwich C	Sch	05/03	02	1	1	0
Barnet	Tr	07/04	05-06	81	5	8
Charlton Ath	Tr	07/07				
Cheltenham T	L	10/07	07	12	0	1
Cheltenham T	L	08/08	08	2	1	0
Grimsby T	L	01/09	08	9	0	1
Barnet	L	11/09	09	2	1	1
Grimsby T	L	01/10	09	16	0	3

SINCLAIR Dennis
Born: Middlesbrough, England, 20 November, 1931 RW
Died: Loughborough, Leicestershire, England, 25 June, 2011

League Club	Source	Date Signed	Seasons Played	Apps	Subs	Gls
Derby Co	Ilkeston T	05/52				
Mansfield T	Tr	07/53	53	1	-	0

SINCLAIR Emile Anthony
Born: Leeds, England, 29 December, 1987 F

League Club	Source	Date Signed	Seasons Played	Apps	Subs	Gls
Nottingham F	Bradford C (Jnr)	07/07	07-08	0	15	1
Brentford	L	11/07	07	1	3	0
Macclesfield T	L	01/09	08	6	0	1
Macclesfield T	Tr	03/09	08-11	71	18	13
Peterborough U	Tr	08/11	11-12	26	21	13
Barnsley	L	11/12	12	1	3	0
Doncaster Rov	L	01/13	12	1	3	0
Crawley T	Tr	08/13	13	9	6	2
Northampton T	Tr	01/14	13-14	16	14	3
York C	Tr	01/15	14	9	3	2

SINCLAIR Frank Mohammed
Born: Lambeth, S London, England, 3 December, 1971 D
Jamaica: 28

League Club	Source	Date Signed	Seasons Played	Apps	Subs	Gls
Chelsea	YT	05/90	90-97	163	6	7
West Bromwich A	L	12/91	91	6	0	1
Leicester C	Tr	08/98	98-03	153	11	3
Burnley	Tr	07/04	04-06	88	4	1
Huddersfield T	Tr	02/07	06-07	41	1	0
Lincoln C	Tr	07/08	08	21	2	0
Wycombe W	L	03/09	08	9	0	0

SINCLAIR Harvey Patrick (Harry)
Born: Bournemouth, England, 30 November, 1933 G

League Club	Source	Date Signed	Seasons Played	Apps	Subs	Gls
Fulham	Bournemouth (Am)	12/50				
Leicester C	Cambridge U	08/56	56	1	-	0
Bristol Rov	Yeovil T	09/58	58	1	-	0
Fulham	Yeovil T	07/59				

SINCLAIR Jade
Born: Cleveland, England, 6 November, 1971 M

League Club	Source	Date Signed	Seasons Played	Apps	Subs	Gls
Hartlepool U	YT	-	89	4	0	0

SINCLAIR James Alexander
Born: Newcastle-upon-Tyne, England, 22 October, 1987 RB

League Club	Source	Date Signed	Seasons Played	Apps	Subs	Gls
Bolton W	Sch	06/07	06	0	2	0

SINCLAIR James Graeme (Graeme)
Born: Paisley, Renfrewshire, Scotland, 1 July, 1957 FB
Scotland: SLge-1/U21-1

League Club	Source	Date Signed	Seasons Played	Apps	Subs	Gls
Manchester C (L)	Glasgow Celtic	11/84	84	1	0	0

SINCLAIR Jerome Terence
Born: Birmingham, England, 20 September, 1996 F
England: Youth

League Club	Source	Date Signed	Seasons Played	Apps	Subs	Gls
Liverpool	Sch	12/13	14	0	2	0
Wigan Ath	L	03/15	14	0	1	0

SINCLAIR John Evens Wright (Jackie)
Born: Culross, Fife, Scotland, 21 July, 1943 RW
Died: Dollar, Stirlingshire, Scotland, 2 September, 2010
Scotland: 1

League Club	Source	Date Signed	Seasons Played	Apps	Subs	Gls
Leicester C	Dunfermline Ath	05/65	65-67	103	0	50
Newcastle U	Tr	01/68	67-69	42	1	6
Sheffield Wed	Tr	12/69	69-72	97	4	14
Chesterfield	L	03/73	72	10	0	3

SINCLAIR Michael John (Mike)
Born: Grimsby, North Lincolnshire, England, 13 October, 1938 CF

League Club	Source	Date Signed	Seasons Played	Apps	Subs	Gls
Grimsby T	Jnr	09/57	57-60	6	-	1

SINCLAIR Nicholas John Thomas (Nick)
Born: Manchester, England, 3 January, 1960 RB
England: Schools

League Club	Source	Date Signed	Seasons Played	Apps	Subs	Gls
Oldham Ath	Jnr	06/78	78-84	73	2	1
Wolverhampton W	L	09/84	84	1	0	0
Tranmere Rov	Tr	10/84	84-85	22	0	1

SINCLAIR Robert Alan
Born: Greenwich, SE London, England, 9 April, 1974 F

League Club	Source	Date Signed	Seasons Played	Apps	Subs	Gls
Maidstone U	YT	-	91	1	0	0

SINCLAIR Robert Dunlop
Born: Winchburgh, West Lothian, Scotland, 29 June, 1915 RW
Died: Darlington, County Durham, England, 2 July, 1993

League Club	Source	Date Signed	Seasons Played	Apps	Subs	Gls
Chesterfield	Falkirk	05/39				
Darlington	Tr	06/46	46-47	68	-	11

SINCLAIR Robert James (Rob)
Born: Bedford, England, 29 August, 1989 W

League Club	Source	Date Signed	Seasons Played	Apps	Subs	Gls
Luton T	Sch	07/07				
Stevenage	Salisbury C	08/10	10	14	13	2
Aldershot T	L	03/12	11	1	3	0
Aldershot T	L	11/12	12	1	5	0

SINCLAIR Ronald McDonald (Ronnie)
Born: Stirling, Scotland, 19 November, 1964 G
Scotland: Youth/Schools

League Club	Source	Date Signed	Seasons Played	Apps	Subs	Gls
Nottingham F	App	10/82				
Wrexham	L	03/84	83	11	0	0
Leeds U	Tr	06/86	86	8	0	0
Halifax T	L	03/87	86	4	0	0
Halifax T	L	12/88	88	10	0	0
Bristol C	Tr	09/89	89-90	44	0	0
Walsall	L	09/91	91	10	0	0
Stoke C	Tr	11/91	91-95	78	2	0
Chester C	Tr	08/96	96-97	70	0	0

SINCLAIR Roy
Born: Liverpool, England, 10 December, 1944 M
Died: Liverpool, England, 12 January, 2013

League Club	Source	Date Signed	Seasons Played	Apps	Subs	Gls
Tranmere Rov	Liverpool (Am)	10/63	63-68	130	8	17
Watford	Tr	03/69	68-71	32	11	3
Chester C	L	12/71	71	5	0	2
Tranmere Rov	Tr	07/72	72	12	0	0

SINCLAIR Scott Andrew
Born: Bath, England, 26 March, 1989 LW
England: U21-7/Youth

League Club	Source	Date Signed	Seasons Played	Apps	Subs	Gls
Bristol Rov	Jnr	-	04	0	2	0
Chelsea	Sch	03/06	06-08	1	4	0
Plymouth Arg	L	01/07	06	8	7	2
Queens Park Rgrs	L	11/07	07	8	1	1
Charlton Ath	L	02/08	07	0	3	0
Crystal Palace	L	03/08	07	6	0	2
Birmingham C	L	01/09	08	8	6	0
Wigan Ath	L	08/09	09	1	17	1
Swansea C	Tr	08/10	10-12	74	8	28
Manchester C	Tr	08/12	12-14	2	11	0
West Bromwich A	L	08/13	13	4	4	0
Aston Villa	L	01/15	14	5	4	1

SINCLAIR Thomas (Tommy)
Born: Wigan, Greater Manchester, England, 13 October, 1921 W

League Club	Source	Date Signed	Seasons Played	Apps	Subs	Gls
Aldershot	Gainsborough Trinity	08/44	46-50	70	-	8
Brentford	Tr	08/50	50	16	-	5
Bradford C	Tr	08/51	51	9	-	0

SINCLAIR Tony Roy
Born: Lewisham, SE London, England, 5 March, 1985 CD

League Club	Source	Date Signed	Seasons Played	Apps	Subs	Gls
Gillingham	Woking	07/10	10	17	3	0

SINCLAIR Trevor Lloyd
Born: Dulwich, S London, England, 2 March, 1973 W
England: 12/B-1/U21-14/Youth

League Club	Source	Date Signed	Seasons Played	Apps	Subs	Gls
Blackpool	YT	08/90	89-92	84	28	15
Queens Park Rgrs	Tr	08/93	93-97	162	5	16
West Ham U	Tr	01/98	97-02	175	2	37
Manchester C	Tr	07/03	03-06	65	17	5
Cardiff C	Tr	07/07	07	14	7	1

SINCLAIR William (Billy)
Born: Southport, Merseyside, England, 11 September, 1920 W
Died: Ormskirk, Lancashire, England, 15 September, 1978

League Club	Source	Date Signed	Seasons Played	Apps	Subs	Gls
Southport	Blackburn Rov (Am)	09/45	46	15	-	1

SINCLAIR William Inglis (Billy)
Born: Glasgow, Scotland, 21 March, 1947 WH

League Club	Source	Date Signed	Seasons Played	Apps	Subs	Gls
Chelsea	Greenock Morton	09/64	64	1	-	0

SINCLAIR William Mearns (Willie)
Born: Blairhall, Fife, Scotland, 14 October, 1934 IF

League Club	Source	Date Signed	Seasons Played	Apps	Subs	Gls
Huddersfield T	Falkirk	12/58	58-59	15	-	5
Tranmere Rov	Tr	06/60	60	4	-	0
Halifax T	Tr	10/60	60	21	-	3

SINDALL Mark
Born: Shirebrook, Derbyshire, England, 3 September, 1964 M

League Club	Source	Date Signed	Seasons Played	Apps	Subs	Gls
Mansfield T	Notts Co (App)	10/82	82-83	18	3	0

SINGER Dennis James (Jimmy)
Born: Cefn Hengoed, Caerphilly, Wales, 30 August, 1937 IF
Died: Cefn Hengoed, Caerphilly, Wales, July, 2010

League Club	Source	Date Signed	Seasons Played	Apps	Subs	Gls
Newport Co	Fleur-de-Lis Welfare	05/56	57-60	52	-	27
Birmingham C	Tr	09/60	60-61	20	-	8
Bournemouth	Tr	09/62	62-63	59	-	22
Newport Co	Tr	07/64	64	8	-	5

SINGH Harpal
Born: Bradford, England, 15 September, 1981 LW

League Club	Source	Date Signed	Seasons Played	Apps	Subs	Gls
Leeds U	YT	09/98				
Bury	L	09/01	01	11	1	2
Bristol C	L	03/02	01	3	0	0
Bradford C	L	11/02	02	3	0	0
Bury	L	08/03	03	20	8	2
Stockport Co	Tr	02/05	04-05	24	6	1

SINGLETON Anthony Joseph (Tony)
Born: Preston, Lancashire, England, 30 March, 1936 CH
Died: Los Angeles, California, USA, 29 August, 2008

League Club	Source	Date Signed	Seasons Played	Apps	Subs	Gls
Preston NE	Jnr	05/55	60-67	286	1	0

SINGLETON Bernard (Barney)
Born: Conisbrough, South Yorkshire, England, 14 April, 1924 G
Died: Exeter, England, October, 1981

League Club	Source	Date Signed	Seasons Played	Apps	Subs	Gls
Wolverhampton W	Lincoln C (Am)	05/41				
Exeter C	Tr	01/46	46-53	177	-	1

SINGLETON Martin David
Born: Banbury, Oxfordshire, England, 2 August, 1963 M
England: Youth

League Club	Source	Date Signed	Seasons Played	Apps	Subs	Gls
Coventry C	App	01/81	81-84	20	3	1
Bradford C	Tr	12/84	84-86	69	2	3
West Bromwich A	Tr	12/86	86-87	15	4	1
Northampton T	Tr	11/87	87-89	45	5	4
Walsall	Tr	09/90	90	20	8	1

SINGLETON Thomas William (Tommy)
Born: Blackpool, Lancashire, England, 8 September, 1940 D
Died: Blackpool, Lancashire, England, 29 December, 2005

League Club	Source	Date Signed	Seasons Played	Apps	Subs	Gls
Blackpool	Jnr	11/58				
Peterborough U	Tr	06/62	62-64	85	-	1
Chester C	Tr	06/65	65-67	87	1	1
Bradford Park Ave	Tr	07/68	68	32	0	1

SINNOTT Jordan James
Born: Bradford, England, 14 February, 1995 DM

League Club	Source	Date Signed	Seasons Played	Apps	Subs	Gls
Huddersfield T	Sch	07/12	12-14	0	2	0
Bury	L	08/13	13	5	4	1

SINNOTT Lee
Born: Pelsall, West Midlands, England, 12 July, 1965 CD
England: U21-1/Youth

League Club	Source	Date Signed	Seasons Played	Apps	Subs	Gls
Walsall	App	11/82	81-83	40	0	2
Watford	Tr	09/83	83-86	71	7	2
Bradford C	Tr	07/87	87-90	173	0	6
Crystal Palace	Tr	08/91	91-92	53	2	0
Bradford C	Tr	12/93	93-94	34	0	1
Huddersfield T	Tr	12/94	94-96	86	1	1
Oldham Ath	Tr	07/97	97-98	25	6	0
Bradford C	L	03/98	97	7	0	0

SINTON Andrew (Andy)
Born: Cramlington, Northumberland, England, 19 March, 1966 LM
England: 12/B-3/FLge/Schools

League Club	Source	Date Signed	Seasons Played	Apps	Subs	Gls
Cambridge U	App	04/83	82-85	90	3	13
Brentford	Tr	12/85	85-88	149	0	28
Queens Park Rgrs	Tr	03/89	88-92	160	0	22
Sheffield Wed	Tr	08/93	93-95	54	6	3
Tottenham H	Tr	01/96	95-98	66	17	6
Wolverhampton W	Tr	07/99	99-01	62	10	3

SIRREL James (Jimmy)
Born: Glasgow, Scotland, 2 February, 1922 IF
Died: Nottingham, England, 25 September, 2008

League Club	Source	Date Signed	Seasons Played	Apps	Subs	Gls
Bradford Park Ave	Glasgow Celtic	05/49	49-50	12	-	2
Brighton & HA	Tr	08/51	51-53	55	-	16
Aldershot	Tr	08/54	54-56	31	-	2

SISSOKO Habib
Born: Essonne, France, 24 May, 1971 F

League Club	Source	Date Signed	Seasons Played	Apps	Subs	Gls
Preston NE	Louhans Cuiseaux (FRA)	02/98	97	4	3	0
Torquay U	Royal Capellen (BEL)	08/00	00	7	7	2

SISSOKO Mohamed Lamine (Momo)
Born: Rouen, France, 22 January, 1985 DM
Mali: 34

League Club	Source	Date Signed	Seasons Played	Apps	Subs	Gls
Liverpool	Valencia (SPN)	07/05	05-07	42	9	1

SISSOKO Moussa
Born: Paris, France, 16 August, 1989 M
France: 28/U21-20/Youth

League Club	Source	Date Signed	Seasons Played	Apps	Subs	Gls
Newcastle U	Toulouse (FRA)	01/13	12-14	81	0	10

SISSOKO Noe
Born: Bamako, Mali, 2 June, 1983 M

League Club	Source	Date Signed	Seasons Played	Apps	Subs	Gls
Notts Co	US Creteil (FRA)	01/06	05	1	2	0

SISSON Michael Anthony
Born: Mansfield, Nottinghamshire, England, 24 November, 1978 M

League Club	Source	Date Signed	Seasons Played	Apps	Subs	Gls
Mansfield T	YT	01/98	97-00	26	5	2

SISSONS John Graham (Graham)
Born: Chester-le-Street, County Durham, England, 20 May, 1934 D

League Club	Source	Date Signed	Seasons Played	Apps	Subs	Gls
Birmingham C	Country Girl	07/54	56-62	90	-	0
Peterborough U	Tr	12/61	62-64	68	-	0
Walsall	Tr	11/64	64-67	93	5	1

SISSONS John Leslie
Born: Hayes, W London, England, 30 September, 1945 LW
England: U23-10/Youth/Schools

League Club	Source	Date Signed	Seasons Played	Apps	Subs	Gls
West Ham U	App	10/62	62-69	210	3	37
Sheffield Wed	Tr	08/70	70-73	114	1	14
Norwich C	Tr	12/73	73	17	0	2
Chelsea	Tr	08/74	74	10	1	0

SITFORD Jack Anthony (Tony)
Born: Crowborough, East Sussex, England, 28 January, 1940 LB/CF

League Club	Source	Date Signed	Seasons Played	Apps	Subs	Gls
Brighton & HA	Tr	03/59	60-61	22	-	2

[SITO] CASTRO Luisito
Born: La Coruna, Spain, 21 May, 1980 — RB

League Club	Source	Date Signed	Seasons Played	Apps	Subs	Gls
Ipswich T	Racing Ferrol (SPN)	08/05	05-07	48	11	1

SITTON John Edmund
Born: Hackney, E London, England, 21 October, 1959 — CD

League Club	Source	Date Signed	Seasons Played	Apps	Subs	Gls
Chelsea	App	10/77	78-79	11	2	0
Millwall	Tr	02/80	79-80	43	2	1
Gillingham	Tr	09/81	81-84	102	5	5
Leyton Orient	Tr	07/85	85-90	166	4	7

SIVEBAEK John
Born: Vejle, Denmark, 25 October, 1961 — RB
Denmark: 87/U21-13/Youth

League Club	Source	Date Signed	Seasons Played	Apps	Subs	Gls
Manchester U	Vejle BK (DEN)	02/86	85-86	29	2	1

SIVELL Laurence (Laurie)
Born: Lowestoft, Suffolk, England, 8 February, 1951 — G

League Club	Source	Date Signed	Seasons Played	Apps	Subs	Gls
Ipswich T	App	02/69	69-83	141	0	0
Lincoln C	L	01/79	78	2	0	0

SIX Didier
Born: Lille, France, 21 August, 1954 — W
France: 52

League Club	Source	Date Signed	Seasons Played	Apps	Subs	Gls
Aston Villa	Mulhouse (FRA)	10/84	84	13	3	2

SJOBERG John
Born: Aberdeen, Scotland, 12 June, 1941 — D
Died: Leicester, England, 2 October, 2008
Scotland: Schools

League Club	Source	Date Signed	Seasons Played	Apps	Subs	Gls
Leicester C	Banks o' Dee	08/58	60-72	335	1	15
Rotherham U	Tr	06/73	73	6	0	0

SKACEL Rudolf (Rudi)
Born: Trutnov, Czech Republic, 17 July, 1979 — LW
Czech Republic: 7/U21-9

League Club	Source	Date Signed	Seasons Played	Apps	Subs	Gls
Southampton	Olymp Marseille (FRA)	07/06	06-08	73	8	5

SKARZ Joseph Peter (Joe)
Born: Huddersfield, West Yorkshire, England, 13 July, 1989 — LB

League Club	Source	Date Signed	Seasons Played	Apps	Subs	Gls
Huddersfield T	Sch	02/07	06-09	60	8	1
Hartlepool U	L	03/09	08	5	2	0
Shrewsbury T	L	01/10	09	20	0	0
Bury	Tr	07/10	10-12	130	0	4
Rotherham U	Tr	03/12	12-14	64	2	2
Oxford U	Tr	01/15	14	18	0	0

SKEDD Anthony Stuart (Tony)
Born: Hartlepool, Cleveland, England, 19 May, 1975 — M/LB

League Club	Source	Date Signed	Seasons Played	Apps	Subs	Gls
Hartlepool U	YT	10/93	92-94	39	7	1

SKEECH Henry Gordon (Gordon)
Born: Warrington, Cheshire, England, 15 March, 1934 — LB
Died: Newton le Willows, Merseyside, England, 13 May, 2008

League Club	Source	Date Signed	Seasons Played	Apps	Subs	Gls
Shrewsbury T	Runcorn	11/54	54-62	223	-	2

SKEELS Eric Thomas
Born: Eccles, Greater Manchester, England, 27 October, 1939 — D

League Club	Source	Date Signed	Seasons Played	Apps	Subs	Gls
Stoke C	Stockport Co (Am)	12/58	59-75	495	12	7
Port Vale	Seattle Sounders (USA)	09/76	76	5	0	1

SKEEN George Gray
Born: Gateshead, Tyne and Wear, England, 4 August, 1920 — LH
Died: Burton-on-Trent, Staffordshire, England, 10 May, 1984

League Club	Source	Date Signed	Seasons Played	Apps	Subs	Gls
Gateshead		10/46	46-49	86	-	3

SKEEN Kenneth Albert (Ken)
Born: Cheltenham, Gloucestershire, England, 20 March, 1942 — M/F

League Club	Source	Date Signed	Seasons Played	Apps	Subs	Gls
Swindon T	Trowbridge T	09/64	64-66	14	0	4
Oxford U	Tr	07/67	67-73	214	20	27

SKEET Stuart Christopher
Born: Edmonton, N London, England, 6 July, 1948 — G
Died: Enfield, N London, England, 1 February, 2011

League Club	Source	Date Signed	Seasons Played	Apps	Subs	Gls
Tottenham H	App	12/65				
Northampton T	L	03/69	68	1	0	0

SKEETE Leopold Anthony (Leo)
Born: Liverpool, England, 3 August, 1949 — F

League Club	Source	Date Signed	Seasons Played	Apps	Subs	Gls
Rochdale	Ellesmere Port	04/73	72-74	39	1	14

SKELLY Richard Brian
Born: Norwich, England, 24 March, 1972 — LB

League Club	Source	Date Signed	Seasons Played	Apps	Subs	Gls
Cambridge U	Newmarket T	01/94	93	2	0	0
Northampton T	Tr	06/94	94	3	0	0

SKELTON Aaron Matthew
Born: Welwyn Garden City, Hertfordshire, England, 22 November, 1974 — M

League Club	Source	Date Signed	Seasons Played	Apps	Subs	Gls
Luton T	YT	12/92	94-96	5	3	0
Colchester U	Tr	07/97	97-00	114	11	17
Luton T	Tr	07/01	01-02	14	3	2

SKELTON Craig Eric
Born: Redcar, Cleveland, England, 14 September, 1980 — F

League Club	Source	Date Signed	Seasons Played	Apps	Subs	Gls
Darlington	YT	07/99	00	0	1	0

SKELTON Gavin Richard
Born: Carlisle, Cumbria, England, 27 March, 1981 — M

League Club	Source	Date Signed	Seasons Played	Apps	Subs	Gls
Carlisle U	YT	05/99	99	1	6	0

SKELTON George Alfred
Born: Thurcroft, South Yorkshire, England, 27 November, 1919 — IF
Died: Thurcroft, South Yorkshire, England, September, 1994

League Club	Source	Date Signed	Seasons Played	Apps	Subs	Gls
Huddersfield T	Thurcroft Main	12/45	46	1	-	0
Leyton Orient	Tr	07/47	47	3	-	0

SKIDMORE William (Billy)
Born: Barnsley, South Yorkshire, England, 15 March, 1925 — LB
Died: Barnsley, South Yorkshire, England, 14 March, 2004

League Club	Source	Date Signed	Seasons Played	Apps	Subs	Gls
Wolverhampton W	Jnr	05/42				
Walsall	Tr	05/46	46-50	99	-	10

SKILLEN Keith
Born: Cockermouth, Cumbria, England, 26 May, 1948 — F
Died: Cockermouth, Cumbria, England, 7 August, 2013

League Club	Source	Date Signed	Seasons Played	Apps	Subs	Gls
Workington	Netherfield	12/73	73-74	56	8	9
Hartlepool U	Tr	07/75	75	4	2	1

SKINGLEY Brian George
Born: Romford, E London, England, 28 August, 1937 — RB
Died: Southend-on-Sea, England, August, 1999

League Club	Source	Date Signed	Seasons Played	Apps	Subs	Gls
Bristol Rov	Ilfracombe	01/55				
Crystal Palace	Tr	09/58	58	11	-	0
Queens Park Rgrs	Tr	07/59				

SKINNER Craig Richard
Born: Bury, Greater Manchester, England, 21 October, 1970 — RW

League Club	Source	Date Signed	Seasons Played	Apps	Subs	Gls
Blackburn Rov	YT	06/89	90-91	11	5	0
Plymouth Arg	Tr	08/92	92-94	42	11	4
Wrexham	Tr	07/95	95-98	70	17	10
York C	Tr	03/99	98-99	4	6	0

SKINNER George Edward Henry
Born: Belvedere, SE London, England, 26 June, 1917 — IF
Died: Eastbourne, East Sussex, England, 30 September, 2002

League Club	Source	Date Signed	Seasons Played	Apps	Subs	Gls
Tottenham H	Callenders	09/38	46	1	-	0
Brighton & HA	Tr	02/48				

SKINNER Justin
Born: Hounslow, SW London, England, 30 January, 1969 — M

League Club	Source	Date Signed	Seasons Played	Apps	Subs	Gls
Fulham	App	11/86	86-90	111	24	23
Bristol Rov	Tr	08/91	91-97	174	13	12
Walsall	L	09/97	97	10	0	0

SKINNER Justin James
Born: Dorking, Surrey, England, 17 September, 1972 — LB

League Club	Source	Date Signed	Seasons Played	Apps	Subs	Gls
Wimbledon	YT	07/91	92-95	2	0	0
Bournemouth	L	03/94	93	16	0	0
Wycombe W	L	08/94	94	4	1	0

SKINNER Stephen Karl (Steve)
Born: Whitehaven, Cumbria, England, 25 November, 1981 — W

League Club	Source	Date Signed	Seasons Played	Apps	Subs	Gls
Carlisle U	YT	06/00	99	0	2	0
Carlisle U (L)	Gretna	10/01	01	1	5	0

SKIPPER Peter Dennis
Born: Hull, England, 11 April, 1958 — CD

League Club	Source	Date Signed	Seasons Played	Apps	Subs	Gls
Hull C	Schultz YC	02/79	78-79	22	1	2
Scunthorpe U	L	02/80	79	0	1	0
Darlington	Tr	05/80	80-81	91	0	4
Hull C	Tr	08/82	82-88	264	1	17
Oldham Ath	Tr	10/88	88	27	0	1
Walsall	Tr	07/89	89-90	81	0	2
Wrexham	Tr	09/91	91	2	0	0
Wigan Ath	Tr	10/91	91	15	3	0
Wigan Ath	Stafford Rgrs	11/92	92-93	73	0	4

SKIRTON Alan Frederick Graham
Born: Bath, England, 23 January, 1939 — W

League Club	Source	Date Signed	Seasons Played	Apps	Subs	Gls
Arsenal	Bath C	01/59	60-66	144	1	53
Blackpool	Tr	09/66	66-68	76	1	25
Bristol C	Tr	11/68	68-70	75	3	14
Torquay U	Tr	07/71	71	36	2	7

SKIVERTON Terence John (Terry)
Born: Mile End, E London, England, 26 June, 1975 — CD
England: Semi Pro-4

League Club	Source	Date Signed	Seasons Played	Apps	Subs	Gls
Chelsea	YT	05/93				
Wycombe W	L	02/95	94	8	2	0
Wycombe W	Tr	03/96	95-96	5	5	1
Yeovil T	Welling U	06/99	03-08	188	7	21

League Club	Source	Date Signed	Seasons Played	Apps	Subs	Gls

SKIVINGTON Glenn
Born: Barrow, Cumbria, England, 19 January, 1962 — M
England: Semi Pro-5

League Club	Source	Date Signed	Seasons Played	Apps	Subs	Gls
Derby Co	Barrow	07/80	80-82	39	7	2
Halifax T	L	03/83	82	4	0	0
Southend U	Tr	08/83	83	2	1	0

SKIVINGTON Michael Noel (Mike)
Born: Glasgow, Scotland, 24 December, 1921 — CH
Died: Enfield, N London, England, 2 March, 2012
Republic of Ireland: LoI-1

League Club	Source	Date Signed	Seasons Played	Apps	Subs	Gls
Bury	Alloa Ath	06/47				
Rochdale	Tr	01/48	47	1	-	0
Leyton Orient	Dundalk (ROI)	10/49	49	5	-	0
Gillingham	Tr	07/50	50	8	-	0
Brentford	Tr	09/51				

SKOKO Josip
Born: Mount Gambier, South Australia, Australia, 10 December, 1975 — DM
Australia: 51/U23-3/Youth

League Club	Source	Date Signed	Seasons Played	Apps	Subs	Gls
Wigan Ath	Genclerbirligi (TKY)	08/05	05-07	34	11	0
Stoke C	L	02/06	05	9	0	2

SKOPELITIS Giannis Ioannis
Born: Thessalonika, Greece, 2 March, 1978 — M

League Club	Source	Date Signed	Seasons Played	Apps	Subs	Gls
Portsmouth	Aigaleo (GRE)	01/05	04-05	9	9	0

SKORA Eric
Born: Metz, France, 20 August, 1981 — M

League Club	Source	Date Signed	Seasons Played	Apps	Subs	Gls
Preston NE	AS Nancy (FRA)	10/01	01-04	37	14	0
Walsall	L	11/05	05	4	0	2

SKOUBO Morten
Born: Holstebro, Denmark, 30 June, 1980 — F
Denmark: 6/U21-8

League Club	Source	Date Signed	Seasons Played	Apps	Subs	Gls
West Bromwich A (L)	Borussia M'bach (GER)	02/04	03	0	2	0

SKOVBJERG Thomas
Born: Esbjerg, Denmark, 25 October, 1974 — RM

League Club	Source	Date Signed	Seasons Played	Apps	Subs	Gls
Kidderminster Hrs	Esbjerg (DEN)	08/99	00	7	5	1

SKRTEL Martin
Born: Handlova, Slovakia, 15 December, 1984 — CD
Slovakia: 73/U21-2/Youth

League Club	Source	Date Signed	Seasons Played	Apps	Subs	Gls
Liverpool	Zenit St P'burg (RUS)	01/08	07-14	212	8	15

SKULASON Olafur-Ingi (Oli)
Born: Reykjavik, Iceland, 1 April, 1983 — DM
Iceland: 25/U21-12/Youth

League Club	Source	Date Signed	Seasons Played	Apps	Subs	Gls
Arsenal	Fylkir (ICE)	10/01				
Brentford	Tr	07/05	05-06	12	0	1

SKULL John (Johnny)
Born: Swindon, England, 25 August, 1932 — RW
England: Youth

League Club	Source	Date Signed	Seasons Played	Apps	Subs	Gls
Wolverhampton W	Swindon T (Am)	06/50				
Swindon T	Banbury Spencer	09/57	57-58	33	-	11

SKUSE Cole
Born: Yate, Avon, England, 29 March, 1986 — DM

League Club	Source	Date Signed	Seasons Played	Apps	Subs	Gls
Bristol C	Sch	04/05	04-12	222	57	9
Ipswich T	Tr	05/13	13-14	83	0	1

SLABBER Jamie Andrew
Born: Enfield, N London, England, 31 December, 1984 — F
England: Semi Pro-1/Youth

League Club	Source	Date Signed	Seasons Played	Apps	Subs	Gls
Tottenham H	Sch	01/02	02	0	1	0
Swindon T	L	12/04	04	4	5	0

SLACK Andrew (Andy)
Born: Heywood, Greater Manchester, England, 9 June, 1959 — G

League Club	Source	Date Signed	Seasons Played	Apps	Subs	Gls
Rochdale	Bolton W (App)	01/78	77-78	15	0	0

SLACK Melvyn (Mel)
Born: Bishop Auckland, County Durham, England, 7 March, 1944 — WH

League Club	Source	Date Signed	Seasons Played	Apps	Subs	Gls
Sunderland	Bishop Auckland YC	03/61	64	2	-	1
Southend U	Tr	08/65	65-68	107	4	5
Cambridge U	Tr	01/69	70	33	2	0

SLACK Robert Geoffrey
Born: Morecambe, Lancashire, England, 13 July, 1934 — W
Died: Carnforth, Lancashire, England, 8 January, 2009

League Club	Source	Date Signed	Seasons Played	Apps	Subs	Gls
Stockport Co	Morecambe	11/58	58	8	-	1

SLACK Rodney
Born: Yaxley, Cambridgeshire, England, 11 April, 1940 — G

League Club	Source	Date Signed	Seasons Played	Apps	Subs	Gls
Leicester C	Fletton YC	09/58				
Queens Park Rgrs	Tr	03/61	61	1	-	0

SLACK Trevor Colin
Born: Peterborough, England, 26 September, 1962 — CD
England: Youth

League Club	Source	Date Signed	Seasons Played	Apps	Subs	Gls
Peterborough U	App	08/80	80-85	201	1	18
Rotherham U	Tr	08/86	86	14	1	1
Grimsby T	Tr	08/87	87	21	0	0
Northampton T	Tr	02/88	87	13	0	1
Chesterfield	Tr	09/88	88-89	23	0	0

SLADE Liam John
Born: Stourbridge, West Midlands, England, 14 May, 1995 — CD

League Club	Source	Date Signed	Seasons Played	Apps	Subs	Gls
Burton A	Sch	07/13	14	0	6	0

SLADE Robert Frederick
Born: Hounslow, SW London, England, 15 July, 1927 — G

League Club	Source	Date Signed	Seasons Played	Apps	Subs	Gls
Millwall (Am)	Acton T	10/48	48	1	-	0

SLADE Steven Anthony (Steve)
Born: Hackney, E London, England, 6 October, 1975 — F
England: U21-4

League Club	Source	Date Signed	Seasons Played	Apps	Subs	Gls
Tottenham H	YT	07/94	95	1	4	0
Queens Park Rgrs	Tr	07/96	96-99	27	41	6
Brentford	L	02/97	96	4	0	0
Cambridge U	Tr	08/00	00	4	5	1

SLAGER Denzel Jahfar
Born: Utrecht, Netherlands, 2 May, 1993 — RW

League Club	Source	Date Signed	Seasons Played	Apps	Subs	Gls
Coventry C	RKC Waalwijk (NED)	01/14	13	0	3	0

SLANE Paul
Born: Glasgow, Scotland, 25 November, 1991 — W
Scotland: Youth

League Club	Source	Date Signed	Seasons Played	Apps	Subs	Gls
MK Dons (L)	Glasgow Celtic	01/12	11	0	5	0

SLATER Christopher James (Chris)
Born: Lichfield, Staffordshire, England, 14 January, 1984 — CD

League Club	Source	Date Signed	Seasons Played	Apps	Subs	Gls
Port Vale	Chasetown	01/08	07-08	7	4	0

SLATER Darren
Born: Bishop Auckland, County Durham, England, 4 January, 1979 — M

League Club	Source	Date Signed	Seasons Played	Apps	Subs	Gls
Hartlepool U	YT	-	95	0	1	0

SLATER Frederick Benjamin (Fred)
Born: Burton-on-Trent, Staffordshire, England, 25 September, 1925 — CF
Died: Isle of Wight, England, September, 2002

League Club	Source	Date Signed	Seasons Played	Apps	Subs	Gls
Birmingham C	Burton A	11/47	48-49	5	-	1
York C	Tr	06/51	51	13	-	3

SLATER Jack
Born: Heywood, Greater Manchester, England, 8 May, 1917 — RH
Died: Rochdale, Greater Manchester, England, December, 1998

League Club	Source	Date Signed	Seasons Played	Apps	Subs	Gls
Rochdale		04/40				
Crewe Alex	Tr	08/46	46	3	-	0

SLATER James Jonathan (Jamie)
Born: Wrexham, Wales, 27 October, 1968 — F

League Club	Source	Date Signed	Seasons Played	Apps	Subs	Gls
Wrexham	YT	07/87	87	0	3	0

SLATER John Brian (Brian)
Born: Sheffield, England, 20 October, 1932 — IF
Died: Sheffield, England, 10 September, 1999

League Club	Source	Date Signed	Seasons Played	Apps	Subs	Gls
Sheffield Wed		05/51	52	3	-	0
Grimsby T	Tr	07/54	54	4	-	0
Rotherham U	Tr	09/55	56	17	-	5
Chesterfield	Tr	06/57	57	15	-	3

SLATER Malcolm Bruce
Born: Buckie, Moray, Scotland, 22 October, 1939 — RW

League Club	Source	Date Signed	Seasons Played	Apps	Subs	Gls
Southend U	Montrose	11/63	63-66	82	0	6
Leyton Orient	Tr	01/67	66-69	111	0	4
Colchester U	L	10/69	69	4	0	0

SLATER Raymond (Ray)
Born: Seaton Delaval, Northumberland, England, 22 August, 1931 — CF
Died: Newcastle-upon-Tyne, England, October, 2005

League Club	Source	Date Signed	Seasons Played	Apps	Subs	Gls
Chesterfield	South Shields	06/56	56	2	-	1
Gateshead	Tr	10/56	56	6	-	2

SLATER Robert (Bert)
Born: Musselburgh, East Lothian, Scotland, 5 May, 1936 — G
Died: Brechin, Angus, Scotland, 21 July, 2006
Scotland: U23-1

League Club	Source	Date Signed	Seasons Played	Apps	Subs	Gls
Liverpool	Falkirk	05/59	59-61	99	-	0
Watford	Dundee	05/65	65-68	134	0	0

SLATER Robert David (Robbie)
Born: Ormskirk, Lancashire, England, 22 November, 1964 — W
Australia: 44

League Club	Source	Date Signed	Seasons Played	Apps	Subs	Gls
Blackburn Rov	RC Lens (FRA)	08/94	94	12	6	0
West Ham U	Tr	08/95	95-96	18	7	2

League Club	Source	Date Signed	Seasons Played	Apps	Subs	Gls
Southampton	Tr	09/96	96-97	25	16	2
Wolverhampton W	Tr	03/98	97	4	2	0

SLATER Stuart Ian
Born: Sudbury, Suffolk, England, 27 March, 1969 LW
England: B-2/U21-3

League Club	Source	Date Signed	Seasons Played	Apps	Subs	Gls
West Ham U	App	04/87	87-91	134	7	11
Ipswich T	Glasgow Celtic	09/93	93-95	61	11	4
Watford	Leicester C (NC)	11/96	96-97	22	8	1

SLATER William John (Bill)
Born: Clitheroe, Lancashire, England, 29 April, 1927 WH
England: 12/Amateur-20

League Club	Source	Date Signed	Seasons Played	Apps	Subs	Gls
Blackpool (Am)	Jnr	05/49	49-51	30	-	9
Brentford (Am)	Tr	12/51	51	7	-	1
Wolverhampton W	Tr	08/52	52-62	310	-	20
Brentford	Tr	07/63	63	5	-	2

SLATTER Leslie Arthur Heber (Les)
Born: Reading, England, 22 November, 1931 RW

League Club	Source	Date Signed	Seasons Played	Apps	Subs	Gls
Luton T	Mount Pleasant YC	03/49	49	1	-	0
Aston Villa	Crusaders	08/53				
York C	Tr	07/54	54	13	-	0

SLATTER Neil John
Born: Cardiff, Wales, 30 May, 1964 D
Wales: 22/U21-6/Youth

League Club	Source	Date Signed	Seasons Played	Apps	Subs	Gls
Bristol Rov	App	05/82	80-84	147	1	4
Oxford U	Tr	07/85	85-89	88	3	6
Bournemouth	L	03/90	89	5	1	0

SLATTERY James Clive (Clive)
Born: Swansea, Wales, 21 July, 1946 W/M

League Club	Source	Date Signed	Seasons Played	Apps	Subs	Gls
Swansea C	North End	10/68	68-71	65	5	10
Hereford U	Tr	07/72	72	3	5	0

SLATTERY Joseph William (Joe)
Born: Newcastle-upon-Tyne, England, 3 June, 1926 CF

League Club	Source	Date Signed	Seasons Played	Apps	Subs	Gls
Accrington Stan	Hexham Hearts	06/50	50	13	-	2

SLAVCHEV Simeon Nenchev
Born: Sofia, Bulgaria, 25 September, 1993 M
Bulgaria: 4/U21-5/Youth

League Club	Source	Date Signed	Seasons Played	Apps	Subs	Gls
Bolton W (L)	Sporting Lisbon (POR)	02/15	14	0	1	0

SLAVEN Bernard Joseph (Bernie)
Born: Paisley, Renfrewshire, Scotland, 13 November, 1960 F
Republic of Ireland: 7

League Club	Source	Date Signed	Seasons Played	Apps	Subs	Gls
Middlesbrough	Albion Rov	09/85	85-92	286	21	118
Port Vale	Tr	03/93	92-93	29	4	9
Darlington	Tr	02/94	93-94	35	2	7

SLAVEN John Cameron Charles
Born: Edinburgh, Scotland, 8 October, 1985 F

League Club	Source	Date Signed	Seasons Played	Apps	Subs	Gls
Carlisle U	Jnr	11/02	01-02	0	3	0

SLAWSON Stephen Michael (Steve)
Born: Nottingham, England, 13 November, 1972 F

League Club	Source	Date Signed	Seasons Played	Apps	Subs	Gls
Notts Co	YT	07/91	91-94	16	22	4
Burnley	L	02/93	92	5	0	2
Shrewsbury T	L	10/94	94	6	0	0
Mansfield T	Tr	07/95	95	21	8	5
Rotherham U	Tr	07/96	96	2	3	0

SLEATH Daniel James (Danny)
Born: Matlock, Derbyshire, England, 14 December, 1986 LW

League Club	Source	Date Signed	Seasons Played	Apps	Subs	Gls
Mansfield T	Jnr	08/05	06-07	5	9	0

SLEE David Carl (Carl)
Born: Swansea, Wales, 30 November, 1947 D
Wales: Schools

League Club	Source	Date Signed	Seasons Played	Apps	Subs	Gls
Swansea C	Jnr	01/66	67-70	115	4	0

SLEEUWENHOEK John Cornelius
Born: Wednesfield, West Midlands, England, 26 February, 1944 CH
Died: Wolverhampton, England, 20 June, 1989
England: FLge-1/Youth-232/Schools

League Club	Source	Date Signed	Seasons Played	Apps	Subs	Gls
Aston Villa	App	03/61	60-67	226	0	1
Birmingham C	Tr	11/67	67-70	29	1	0
Torquay U	L	03/71	70	11	0	0
Oldham Ath	Tr	07/71	71	2	0	0

SLEIGHT Geoffrey (Geoff)
Born: Royston, South Yorkshire, England, 20 June, 1943 W

League Club	Source	Date Signed	Seasons Played	Apps	Subs	Gls
Bolton W	Barnsley (Jnr)	09/61	61	2	-	0

SLEW Jordan Michael
Born: Sheffield, England, 7 September, 1992 F
England: Youth

League Club	Source	Date Signed	Seasons Played	Apps	Subs	Gls
Sheffield U	Sch	11/10	10-11	8	3	3
Blackburn Rov	Tr	08/11	11	0	1	0
Stevenage	L	03/12	11	6	3	0
Oldham Ath	L	08/12	12	3	0	0
Rotherham U	L	01/13	12	2	5	0
Port Vale	L	08/14	14	5	4	2
Cambridge U	Tr	02/15	14	9	4	1

SLINGSBY Lee
Born: Rossington, South Yorkshire, England, 27 November, 1970 M

League Club	Source	Date Signed	Seasons Played	Apps	Subs	Gls
Scarborough	Doncaster Rov (YT)	07/89	89	0	1	0

SLINN Kevin Paul
Born: Northampton, England, 2 September, 1974 F

League Club	Source	Date Signed	Seasons Played	Apps	Subs	Gls
Watford	YT	04/93				
Stockport Co	Tr	07/94	94	2	2	1

SLOAN David
Born: Lisburn, Belfast, Northern Ireland, 28 October, 1941 RW
Northern Ireland: 2/U23-1/Amateur

League Club	Source	Date Signed	Seasons Played	Apps	Subs	Gls
Scunthorpe U	Bangor	11/63	63-67	133	3	42
Oxford U	Tr	02/68	67-72	166	8	28
Walsall	Tr	07/73	73-74	44	5	3

SLOAN James (Jimmy)
Born: Newcastle-upon-Tyne, England, 22 February, 1924 IF
Died: South Shields, Tyne and Wear, England, 28 November, 1990

League Club	Source	Date Signed	Seasons Played	Apps	Subs	Gls
Newcastle U	CA Parsons Ath	01/45				
Hartlepool U	Tr	10/46	46-51	83	-	28

SLOAN Josiah Walter (Paddy)
Born: Lurgan, Armagh, Northern Ireland, 30 April, 1920 WH/IF
Died: Melbourne, Australia, 7 January, 1993
Republic of Ireland: 2//Northern Ireland: 1/War-1

League Club	Source	Date Signed	Seasons Played	Apps	Subs	Gls
Manchester U	Glenavon	09/37				
Tranmere Rov	Tr	05/39				
Arsenal	Tr	05/46	46-47	33	-	1
Sheffield U	Tr	02/48	47	12	-	2
Norwich C	Brescia (ITA)	12/51	51	6	-	0

SLOAN Mark Scott (Scott)
Born: Wallsend, Tyne and Wear, England, 14 December, 1967 F

League Club	Source	Date Signed	Seasons Played	Apps	Subs	Gls
Newcastle U	Berwick Rgrs	07/90	90	11	5	1
Cambridge U (L)	Falkirk	02/94	93	4	0	1
Hartlepool U	Falkirk	08/94	94-95	27	8	2

SLOAN Thomas (Tom)
Born: Ballymena, Antrim, Northern Ireland, 10 July, 1959 M
Northern Ireland: 3/NILge-3/U21-1

League Club	Source	Date Signed	Seasons Played	Apps	Subs	Gls
Manchester U	Ballymena U	08/78	78-80	4	7	0
Chester C	Ballymena U	08/82	82	44	0	3

SLOCOMBE Michael (Mike)
Born: Bristol, England, 3 May, 1941 WH

League Club	Source	Date Signed	Seasons Played	Apps	Subs	Gls
Bristol Rov	Jnr	06/61	61-62	32	-	0

SLOCOMBE Sam Oliver
Born: Scunthorpe, North Lincolnshire, England, 5 June, 1988 G

League Club	Source	Date Signed	Seasons Played	Apps	Subs	Gls
Scunthorpe U	Bottesford T	08/08	09-14	112	3	0

SLOMA Samuel Mark (Sam)
Born: Finchley, N London, England, 29 October, 1982 LB/M

League Club	Source	Date Signed	Seasons Played	Apps	Subs	Gls
Dagenham & Red	Wingate & Finchley	07/06	07	22	7	2

SLORY Andwele Cedric (Andy)
Born: Paramaribo, Suriname, 27 September, 1982 RW
Netherlands: 2

League Club	Source	Date Signed	Seasons Played	Apps	Subs	Gls
West Bromwich A	Feyenoord (NED)	02/10	09	1	5	0

SLOTH Casper Bisgaard
Born: Aarhus, Denmark, 26 March, 1992 DM
Denmark: 8/U21-10/Youth

League Club	Source	Date Signed	Seasons Played	Apps	Subs	Gls
Leeds U	Aarhus GF (DEN)	08/14	14	7	6	0

SLOUGH Alan Peter
Born: Luton, England, 24 September, 1947 M/D

League Club	Source	Date Signed	Seasons Played	Apps	Subs	Gls
Luton T	App	05/65	65-72	265	10	28
Fulham	Tr	08/73	73-76	154	0	13
Peterborough U	Tr	07/77	77-80	104	1	10
Millwall	Tr	06/81	81	14	0	0

SLUSARSKI Bartosz
Born: Szamocin, Poland, 11 December, 1981 F
Poland: 2/U21-12

League Club	Source	Date Signed	Seasons Played	Apps	Subs	Gls
West Bromwich A	Dysk. Gradziak (POL)	08/07	07	0	1	0
Blackpool	L	11/07	07	4	2	1
Sheffield Wed	L	03/08	07	3	4	1
Sheffield Wed	L	11/08	08	4	3	1

SLYNN Frank (Frankie)
Born: Birmingham, England, 10 February, 1924 LH/W

Died: York, England, November, 2014

League Club	Source	Date Signed	Seasons Played	Apps	Subs	Gls
Sheffield Wed	Batchelors Sports	09/46	46-50	44	-	5
Bury	Tr	12/50	50-52	41	-	0
Walsall	Tr	09/53	53	10	-	0

SMALE Thomas Henry (Harry)
Born: Swansea, Wales, 16 July, 1928 — RB

League Club	Source	Date Signed	Seasons Played	Apps	Subs	Gls
Shrewsbury T	Derby Co (Am)	07/50	50-51	14	-	1
Aldershot	Tr	08/52	52	1	-	0

SMALES Kenneth (Ken)
Born: Hull, England, 3 May, 1932 — FB

League Club	Source	Date Signed	Seasons Played	Apps	Subs	Gls
Hull C	Brunswick Inst	05/53	56	1	-	0

SMALL Bryan
Born: Birmingham, England, 15 November, 1971 — FB
England: U21-12/Youth

League Club	Source	Date Signed	Seasons Played	Apps	Subs	Gls
Aston Villa	YT	07/90	91-94	31	5	0
Birmingham C	L	09/94	94	3	0	0
Bolton W	Tr	03/96	95-96	11	1	0
Luton T	L	09/97	97	15	0	0
Bradford C	L	12/97	97	5	0	0
Bury	Tr	01/98	97	18	0	1
Stoke C	Tr	07/98	98-99	40	5	0
Walsall	Brentford (NC)	01/01				

SMALL Colin
Born: Stockport, Greater Manchester, England, 9 November, 1970 — M
England: Schools

League Club	Source	Date Signed	Seasons Played	Apps	Subs	Gls
Rochdale	Manchester C (YT)	07/89	89	5	2	1

SMALL David
Born: Dundee, Scotland, 17 July, 1930 — RW
Died: Melrose, Borders, Scotland, 23 January, 2012

League Club	Source	Date Signed	Seasons Played	Apps	Subs	Gls
Watford	Dundee North End	06/50	50-51	5	-	0

SMALL John Hedley
Born: Billingham, Cleveland, England, 14 January, 1945 — G

League Club	Source	Date Signed	Seasons Played	Apps	Subs	Gls
Hartlepool U (Am)	H Wrightson, Thornaby	06/65	65	2	0	0

SMALL Martin Leonard (Len)
Born: Gateshead, Tyne and Wear, England, 2 February, 1920 — IF
Died: County Durham, England, October, 2009

League Club	Source	Date Signed	Seasons Played	Apps	Subs	Gls
Gateshead		08/46	46-51	94	-	29

SMALL Michael Anthony (Mike)
Born: Birmingham, England, 2 March, 1962 — F
England: Youth

League Club	Source	Date Signed	Seasons Played	Apps	Subs	Gls
Luton T	Bromsgrove Rov	10/79	81-82	0	4	0
Peterborough U	L	10/82	82	2	2	1
Brighton & HA	PAOK Salonika (GRE)	08/90	90	39	0	15
West Ham U	Tr	08/91	91-92	42	7	13
Wolverhampton W	L	09/93	93	2	1	1
Charlton Ath	L	02/94	93	1	1	0

SMALL Peter Victor
Born: Horsham, West Sussex, England, 23 October, 1924 — W
Died: Cambridge, England, 3 November, 2006

League Club	Source	Date Signed	Seasons Played	Apps	Subs	Gls
Luton T	Horsham	08/47	47-49	28	-	5
Leicester C	Tr	02/50	49-54	65	-	16
Nottingham F	Tr	09/54	54-56	87	-	20
Brighton & HA	Tr	07/57	57	8	-	3

SMALL Samuel John (Sam)
Born: Birmingham, England, 15 May, 1912 — CF/FB
Died: Birmingham, England, 19 December, 1993

League Club	Source	Date Signed	Seasons Played	Apps	Subs	Gls
Birmingham C	Bromsgrove Rov	05/34	34-36	6	-	0
West Ham U	Tr	01/37	36-47	108	-	39
Brighton & HA	Tr	03/48	47-49	38	-	0

SMALL Wade Kristopher
Born: Croydon, S London, England, 23 February, 1984 — RW

League Club	Source	Date Signed	Seasons Played	Apps	Subs	Gls
Wimbledon	Sch	07/03	03	23	4	1
MK Dons	Wimbledon relocation	07/04	04-05	65	7	11
Sheffield Wed	Tr	06/06	06-08	37	31	7
Blackpool	L	03/09	08	4	1	1
Chesterfield	Tr	08/09	09	24	3	4
Aldershot T	Tr	08/10	10	18	11	5

SMALLER Paul Andrew
Born: Scunthorpe, North Lincolnshire, England, 18 September, 1970 — M

League Club	Source	Date Signed	Seasons Played	Apps	Subs	Gls
Grimsby T	YT	07/89	88-89	1	1	0

SMALLEY Deane Alfie Michael
Born: Oldham, Greater Manchester, England, 5 September, 1988 — F/W

League Club	Source	Date Signed	Seasons Played	Apps	Subs	Gls
Oldham Ath	Sch	07/07	06-10	64	41	10
Rochdale	L	09/10	10	0	3	0
Chesterfield	L	11/10	10	22	6	12
Oxford U	Tr	07/11	11-13	46	35	13
Bradford C	L	01/12	11	7	6	0
Plymouth Arg	Tr	05/14	14	3	13	1

SMALLEY Mark Anthony
Born: Newark, Nottinghamshire, England, 2 January, 1965 — CD
England: Youth

League Club	Source	Date Signed	Seasons Played	Apps	Subs	Gls
Nottingham F	App	01/83	82-84	1	2	0
Birmingham C	L	03/86	85	7	0	0
Bristol Rov	L	08/86	86	10	0	0
Leyton Orient	Tr	02/87	86-89	59	5	4
Mansfield T	Tr	11/89	89-90	49	0	2
Maidstone U	Tr	05/91	91	33	1	2

SMALLEY Paul Thomas
Born: Nottingham, England, 17 November, 1966 — RB
England: Youth

League Club	Source	Date Signed	Seasons Played	Apps	Subs	Gls
Notts Co	App	11/84	85-87	112	6	0
Scunthorpe U	Tr	09/88	88-90	84	2	1
Blackpool	L	10/90	90	6	0	0
Leeds U	Tr	12/90				
Doncaster Rov	Tr	03/91	90	14	0	0

SMALLEY Thomas (Tom)
Born: Kinsley, West Yorkshire, England, 13 January, 1912 — RB
Died: Wolverhampton, England, 1 April, 1984
England: 1

League Club	Source	Date Signed	Seasons Played	Apps	Subs	Gls
Wolverhampton W	South Kirkby Colliery	05/31	31-37	179	-	11
Norwich C	Tr	08/38	38	42	-	1
Northampton T	Tr	10/45	46-50	200	-	2

SMALLING Christopher Lloyd (Chris)
Born: Greenwich, SE London, England, 22 November, 1989 — CD
England: 18/U21-14/Youth

League Club	Source	Date Signed	Seasons Played	Apps	Subs	Gls
Fulham	Maidstone U	07/08	08-09	9	4	0
Manchester U	Tr	07/10	10-14	77	23	6

SMALLMAN David Paul
Born: Connah's Quay, Flintshire, Wales, 22 March, 1953 — F
Wales: 7/U23-5

League Club	Source	Date Signed	Seasons Played	Apps	Subs	Gls
Wrexham	Jnr	11/71	72-74	100	1	38
Everton	Tr	03/75	74-76	19	2	6

SMALLWOOD James Wilson (Jim)
Born: Bearpark, County Durham, England, 1 September, 1925 — WH
Died: Chesterfield, Derbyshire, England, 29 January, 2010

League Club	Source	Date Signed	Seasons Played	Apps	Subs	Gls
Chesterfield	Spennymoor U	12/49	49-60	345	-	14

SMALLWOOD Neil
Born: York, England, 3 December, 1966 — G

League Club	Source	Date Signed	Seasons Played	Apps	Subs	Gls
York C	Jnr	06/85	86-87	13	0	0
Darlington	Tr	08/88	88	4	0	0

SMALLWOOD Richard
Born: Redcar, Cleveland, England, 29 December, 1990 — M
England: Youth

League Club	Source	Date Signed	Seasons Played	Apps	Subs	Gls
Middlesbrough	Sch	07/08	10-13	36	25	3
Rotherham U	L	01/14	13	17	1	0
Rotherham U	Tr	08/14	14	37	4	1

SMART Allan Andrew Colin
Born: Perth, Scotland, 8 July, 1974 — F

League Club	Source	Date Signed	Seasons Played	Apps	Subs	Gls
Preston NE	Inverness CT	11/94	94-95	17	4	6
Carlisle U	L	11/95	95	3	1	0
Northampton T	L	09/96	96	1	0	0
Carlisle U	Tr	10/96	96-97	41	3	16
Watford	Tr	07/98	98-00	48	9	12
Stoke C	L	11/01	01	0	2	0
Oldham Ath	Tr	11/01	01	14	7	6
Crewe Alex	Dundee U	08/03	03	0	6	0
MK Dons	Tr	07/04	04	15	3	4
Bury	Tr	07/05	05	11	2	1

SMART Andrew James
Born: Altrincham, Greater Manchester, England, 17 March, 1986 — LB

League Club	Source	Date Signed	Seasons Played	Apps	Subs	Gls
Macclesfield T	Jnr	07/04	05	7	2	0

SMART Gary James
Born: Totnes, Devon, England, 29 April, 1964 — FB

League Club	Source	Date Signed	Seasons Played	Apps	Subs	Gls
Oxford U	Wokingham T	07/88	88-93	170	5	0

SMART Gary Michael
Born: Bristol, England, 8 December, 1963 — M

League Club	Source	Date Signed	Seasons Played	Apps	Subs	Gls
Bristol Rov	Mangotsfield U	09/85	85-86	11	8	4

SMART James (Jim)
Born: Dundee, Scotland, 9 January, 1947 — W

League Club	Source	Date Signed	Seasons Played	Apps	Subs	Gls
Chelsea	Greenock Morton	02/65	64	1	-	0

SMART Jason
Born: Rochdale, Greater Manchester, England, 15 February, 1969 — CD

League Club	Source	Date Signed	Seasons Played	Apps	Subs	Gls
Rochdale	App	08/86	85-88	116	1	4
Crewe Alex	Tr	07/89	89-91	87	2	2

SMART Kevin Graham
Born: Newcastle-upon-Tyne, England, 17 October, 1958 RB

League Club	Source	Date Signed	Seasons Played	Apps	Subs	Gls
Plymouth Arg	App	10/76	76-77	32	0	0
Wigan Ath	Tr	07/78	78-79	48	1	1

SMART Mapidima Lesetja (Bally)
Born: Polokwane, South Africa, 27 April, 1989 W

League Club	Source	Date Signed	Seasons Played	Apps	Subs	Gls
Norwich C	Sch	07/07	06	0	1	0
MK Dons	L	09/07	07	0	8	0

SMART Richard (Dick)
Born: Bishop Auckland, County Durham, England, 19 June, 1921 IF
Died: Wisbech, Cambridgeshire, England, April, 2003

League Club	Source	Date Signed	Seasons Played	Apps	Subs	Gls
Exeter C	Stanley U	08/46	46-51	103	-	33

SMART Roger William
Born: Swindon, England, 25 March, 1943 M

League Club	Source	Date Signed	Seasons Played	Apps	Subs	Gls
Swindon T	Jnr	05/60	61-72	340	5	43
Charlton Ath	Tr	05/73	73	30	1	1

SMEDLEY Lawrence (Laurie)
Born: Sheffield, England, 7 May, 1922 IF
Died: Sheffield, England, 17 March, 2010

League Club	Source	Date Signed	Seasons Played	Apps	Subs	Gls
Lincoln C		05/45	46-48	11	-	7

SMEE Roger Guy
Born: Reading, England, 14 August, 1948 F

League Club	Source	Date Signed	Seasons Played	Apps	Subs	Gls
Chelsea	Jnr	03/66				
Reading	Tr	01/67	66-69	49	1	16
Reading	VG Ostend (BEL)	07/73	73	6	3	1

SMEETS Axel
Born: Brussels, Belgium, 12 April, 1974 M
Belgium: U21-25

League Club	Source	Date Signed	Seasons Played	Apps	Subs	Gls
Sheffield U	KV Kortrijk (BEL)	07/99	99	2	3	0

SMEETS Jorg
Born: Bussum, Netherlands, 5 November, 1970 M

League Club	Source	Date Signed	Seasons Played	Apps	Subs	Gls
Wigan Ath	Heracles Almelo (NED)	10/97	97-98	10	14	3
Chester C	L	03/99	98	1	2	0

SMELT Lee Adrian
Born: Edmonton, N London, England, 13 March, 1958 G
England: Schools

League Club	Source	Date Signed	Seasons Played	Apps	Subs	Gls
Colchester U	Jnr	07/75				
Nottingham F	Gravesend & Northfleet	06/80	80	1	0	0
Peterborough U	L	08/81	81	5	0	0
Halifax T	Tr	10/81	81-83	119	0	0
Cardiff C	Tr	08/84	84-85	37	0	0
Exeter C	L	03/85	84	13	0	0

SMELTZ Shane Edward
Born: Goppingen, Germany, 29 September, 1981 F
New Zealand: 51/U23-5/Youth

League Club	Source	Date Signed	Seasons Played	Apps	Subs	Gls
Mansfield T	Adelaide U (AUS)	01/05	04	1	4	0

SMERTIN Alexei
Born: Barnaul, Russia, 1 May, 1975 DM
Russia: 55

League Club	Source	Date Signed	Seasons Played	Apps	Subs	Gls
Chelsea	Bordeaux (FRA)	08/03	04	11	5	0
Portsmouth	L	08/03	03	23	3	0
Charlton Ath	L	07/05	05	18	0	0
Fulham	Dynamo Moscow (RUS)	01/07	06-07	17	5	0

SMETHURST Derek
Born: Durban, South Africa, 24 October, 1947 F

League Club	Source	Date Signed	Seasons Played	Apps	Subs	Gls
Chelsea	Durban C (RSA)	12/68	70-71	14	0	4
Millwall	Tr	09/71	71-74	66	4	9

SMETHURST Edward (Ted)
Born: Doncaster, South Yorkshire, England, 5 March, 1938 G

League Club	Source	Date Signed	Seasons Played	Apps	Subs	Gls
Chesterfield	Denaby U	08/59	59	19	-	0

SMETHURST Peter Joseph
Born: Durban, South Africa, 8 August, 1940 IF

League Club	Source	Date Signed	Seasons Played	Apps	Subs	Gls
Blackpool	Durban U (RSA)	02/60	59	1	-	0

SMEULDERS John
Born: Hackney, E London, England, 28 March, 1957 G
England: Youth

League Club	Source	Date Signed	Seasons Played	Apps	Subs	Gls
Leyton Orient	App	07/74				
Bournemouth	Tr	07/79	79-80	14	0	0
Bournemouth	Weymouth	01/84	83-85	75	0	0
Torquay U	Tr	07/86	86	18	0	0
Peterborough U	L	12/86	86	1	0	0
Bournemouth	Poole T	08/87	87	2	0	0
Brentford	Tr	10/88	88	8	0	0
Bournemouth	Tr	03/89	88	7	0	0

SMICER Vladimir (Vlad)
Born: Decin, Czech Republic, 24 May, 1973 M
Czechoslovakia: 1/U21-7//Czech Republic: 80

League Club	Source	Date Signed	Seasons Played	Apps	Subs	Gls
Liverpool	RC Lens (FRA)	07/99	99-04	69	52	10

SMIKLE Brian Junior
Born: Tipton, West Midlands, England, 3 November, 1985 RW

League Club	Source	Date Signed	Seasons Played	Apps	Subs	Gls
West Bromwich A	Sch	07/05				
Cheltenham T	Kidderminster Hrs	05/10	10-11	40	41	5

SMILLIE Andrew Thomas (Andy)
Born: Minster, Sheppey, Kent, England, 15 March, 1941 IF
England: Youth

League Club	Source	Date Signed	Seasons Played	Apps	Subs	Gls
West Ham U	Jnr	06/58	58-60	20	-	3
Crystal Palace	Tr	06/61	61-62	53	-	23
Scunthorpe U	Tr	07/63	63-64	13	-	2
Southend U	Tr	09/64	64-68	164	0	29
Gillingham	Tr	10/68	68-70	88	6	7

SMILLIE Neil
Born: Barnsley, South Yorkshire, England, 19 July, 1958 LW

League Club	Source	Date Signed	Seasons Played	Apps	Subs	Gls
Crystal Palace	App	10/75	76-81	71	12	7
Brentford	L	01/77	76	3	0	0
Brighton & HA	Tr	08/82	82-84	62	13	2
Watford	Tr	06/85	85	10	6	3
Reading	Tr	12/86	86-87	38	1	0
Brentford	Tr	08/88	88-92	163	9	18
Gillingham	Tr	07/93	93-94	53	0	3

SMILLIE Ronald Drummond (Ron)
Born: Grimethorpe, South Yorkshire, England, 27 September, 1933 RW
Died: Chelmsford, England, 17 August, 2005

League Club	Source	Date Signed	Seasons Played	Apps	Subs	Gls
Barnsley	Jnr	12/50	51-55	29	-	1
Lincoln C	Tr	06/56	56-59	91	-	15
Barnsley	Tr	07/60	60-61	85	-	16

SMIRK Alfred Henry (Alf)
Born: Pershore, Worcestershire, England, 14 March, 1917 IF
Died: Southend-on-Sea, England, November, 1996
England: Schools

League Club	Source	Date Signed	Seasons Played	Apps	Subs	Gls
Southend U	Sunderland DOC	05/38	38-47	100	-	26
Gateshead	Tr	03/48	47	11	-	4

SMITH Adam
Born: Lingwood, Norfolk, England, 11 September, 1985 LB

League Club	Source	Date Signed	Seasons Played	Apps	Subs	Gls
Peterborough U	Kings Lynn	11/06	06	5	4	1

SMITH Adam Clifford
Born: Sunderland, England, 23 November, 1992 G

League Club	Source	Date Signed	Seasons Played	Apps	Subs	Gls
Leicester C	Sch	03/11				
Mansfield T	L	01/15	14	4	0	0

SMITH Adam James
Born: Walthamstow, NE London, England, 29 April, 1991 RB
England: U21-11/Youth

League Club	Source	Date Signed	Seasons Played	Apps	Subs	Gls
Tottenham H	Sch	05/08	11	0	1	0
Wycombe W	L	08/09	09	3	0	0
Torquay U	L	11/09	09	16	0	0
Bournemouth	L	09/10	10	38	0	1
MK Dons	L	08/11	11	17	0	2
Leeds U	L	01/12	11	3	0	0
Millwall	L	11/12	12	24	1	1
Derby Co	L	07/13	13	7	1	0
Bournemouth	Tr	01/14	13-14	7	27	0

SMITH Adrian Jonathan (Adie)
Born: Birmingham, England, 11 August, 1973 CD
England: Semi Pro-3

League Club	Source	Date Signed	Seasons Played	Apps	Subs	Gls
Kidderminster Hrs	Bromsgrove Rov	06/97	00-03	112	10	8

SMITH Alan
Born: Newcastle-upon-Tyne, England, 15 October, 1921 LW

League Club	Source	Date Signed	Seasons Played	Apps	Subs	Gls
Arsenal		05/46	46	3	-	0
Brentford	Tr	12/46	46-48	13	-	4
Leyton Orient	Tr	07/49	49	6	-	1

SMITH Alan
Born: Rothwell, West Yorkshire, England, 28 October, 1980 F/M
England: 19/U21-10/Youth

League Club	Source	Date Signed	Seasons Played	Apps	Subs	Gls
Leeds U	YT	03/98	98-03	148	24	38
Manchester U	Tr	05/04	04-06	43	18	7
Newcastle U	Tr	08/07	07-11	68	16	0
MK Dons	Tr	01/12	11-13	37	30	2
Notts Co	Tr	05/14	14	20	3	0

SMITH Alan David
Born: Sheffield, England, 7 December, 1966 D

League Club	Source	Date Signed	Seasons Played	Apps	Subs	Gls
Sheffield Wed	App	12/84				
Darlington	Tr	09/86	86-88	26	5	1

SMITH Alan Frederick
Born: Newport, Wales, 3 September, 1949 — M
Wales: Youth

League Club	Source	Date Signed	Seasons Played	Apps	Subs	Gls
Newport Co	Cromwell Jnrs	09/66	66-71	89	12	7

SMITH Alan Martin
Born: Birmingham, England, 21 November, 1962 — F
England: 13/B-4/FLge/Semi Pro-3

League Club	Source	Date Signed	Seasons Played	Apps	Subs	Gls
Leicester C	Alvechurch	06/82	82-86	181	10	73
Arsenal	Tr	03/87	87-94	242	22	87
Leicester C	L	03/87	86	9	0	3

SMITH Alan Michael
Born: Harrogate, North Yorkshire, England, 1 September, 1950 — LW

League Club	Source	Date Signed	Seasons Played	Apps	Subs	Gls
York C (Am)	Harrogate Railway Ath	12/70	70	1	1	0

SMITH Albert Owen Stephen
Born: Blackwood, Caerphilly, Wales, 15 October, 1923 — G
Died: Haringey, N London, England, 8 April, 1976

League Club	Source	Date Signed	Seasons Played	Apps	Subs	Gls
Cardiff C	Oakdale	04/44				
Newport Co	Tr	05/47	46-47	27	-	0

SMITH Albert William
Born: Stoke-on-Trent, England, 27 August, 1918 — LH
Died: Gravesend, Kent, England, 9 June, 1992

League Club	Source	Date Signed	Seasons Played	Apps	Subs	Gls
Queens Park Rgrs	Shirley Jnrs	05/39	46-48	62	-	2

SMITH Alex Ralph
Born: Clapham, SW London, England, 31 October, 1991 — M

League Club	Source	Date Signed	Seasons Played	Apps	Subs	Gls
Fulham	Sch	07/09	12	0	1	0
Leyton Orient	L	11/12	12	0	2	0
Swindon T	Tr	07/13	13	5	3	1
Yeovil T		11/14	14	3	3	0

SMITH Alexander (Alex)
Born: Thornhill Lees, West Yorkshire, England, 11 May, 1947 — FB

League Club	Source	Date Signed	Seasons Played	Apps	Subs	Gls
Bradford C	Ossett A	12/64	65-67	91	2	2
Huddersfield T	Tr	03/68	67-68	29	0	0
Southend U	Tr	04/70	70-73	129	1	1
Colchester U	Tr	01/73	73-74	51	0	1
Halifax T	Tr	02/75	74-75	46	1	1

SMITH Alexander (Alec)
Born: Dundee, Scotland, 4 September, 1927 — RB
Died: Leigh, Greater Manchester, England, November, 1991

League Club	Source	Date Signed	Seasons Played	Apps	Subs	Gls
Blackpool	Dundee Elmwood	08/46				
Bradford Park Ave	Tr	06/49	49-50	5	-	0

SMITH Alexander (Alex)
Born: Lancaster, England, 29 October, 1938 — G

League Club	Source	Date Signed	Seasons Played	Apps	Subs	Gls
Accrington Stan	Weymouth	08/61				
Bolton W	Tr	03/62	62-67	19	0	0
Halifax T	Tr	01/68	67-75	341	0	0
Preston NE	Tr	05/76	76	8	0	0

SMITH Alexander Philip (Alex)
Born: Liverpool, England, 15 February, 1976 — LB/M

League Club	Source	Date Signed	Seasons Played	Apps	Subs	Gls
Everton	YT	07/94				
Swindon T	Tr	01/96	95-97	17	14	1
Huddersfield T	Tr	02/98	97	4	2	0
Chester C	Tr	07/98	98	32	0	2
Port Vale	Tr	03/99	98-00	52	6	2
Reading	Tr	07/01	01-02	12	2	2
Shrewsbury T	L	12/02	02	13	0	0
Wrexham	Chester C	07/04	04-05	32	12	0

SMITH Alfred (Alf)
Born: Wolverhampton, England — W

League Club	Source	Date Signed	Seasons Played	Apps	Subs	Gls
Walsall	Bilston	10/53	53	1	-	0

SMITH Allan
Born: United Kingdom — W

League Club	Source	Date Signed	Seasons Played	Apps	Subs	Gls
Hull C (Am)		09/46	46	1	-	0

SMITH Andrew Greg
Born: Burnley, Lancashire, England, 22 December, 1989 — F

League Club	Source	Date Signed	Seasons Played	Apps	Subs	Gls
Accrington Stan	Sch	08/08	07-08	0	2	0

SMITH Andrew William (Andy)
Born: Lisburn, Belfast, Northern Ireland, 25 September, 1980 — F
Northern Ireland: 18/B-1

League Club	Source	Date Signed	Seasons Played	Apps	Subs	Gls
Sheffield U	Ballyclare Comrades	09/99	00	0	6	0
Bury	L	11/00	00	2	0	0
Preston NE	Glentoran	07/04	04	3	11	0
Stockport Co	L	11/04	04	1	0	0
Cheltenham T	L	11/06	06	2	0	0
Bristol C	Tr	02/07	06	3	7	0

SMITH Anthony (Tony)
Born: Sunderland, England, 21 September, 1971 — LB
England: Youth

League Club	Source	Date Signed	Seasons Played	Apps	Subs	Gls
Sunderland	YT	07/90	90-94	19	1	0
Hartlepool U	L	01/92	91	4	1	0
Northampton T	Tr	08/95	95	2	0	0

SMITH Anthony (Tony)
Born: Sunderland, England, 20 February, 1957 — CD
England: Schools

League Club	Source	Date Signed	Seasons Played	Apps	Subs	Gls
Newcastle U	Jnr	07/75	77	1	1	0
Peterborough U	Tr	03/79	78-81	68	0	5
Halifax T	Tr	08/82	82-83	81	2	3
Hartlepool U	Tr	08/84	84-88	200	0	8

SMITH Anthony (Tony)
Born: Sunderland, England, 31 December, 1943 — F

League Club	Source	Date Signed	Seasons Played	Apps	Subs	Gls
West Ham U	Consett	11/63				
Watford	Tr	06/66	66	3	0	0
Hartlepool U		10/67	67	2	0	1

SMITH Archibald Nimmo (Archie)
Born: Larkhall, Lanarkshire, Scotland, 23 October, 1924 — CF
Died: Larkhall, Lanarkshire, Scotland, 16 May, 1995

League Club	Source	Date Signed	Seasons Played	Apps	Subs	Gls
Exeter C	Hamilton Academical	05/48	48-51	115	-	43
Carlisle U	Barnstaple T	08/52	52-53	31	-	8

SMITH Arthur Edward
Born: Bourne, Lincolnshire, England, 13 February, 1922 — FB
Died: Luton, England, 1982

League Club	Source	Date Signed	Seasons Played	Apps	Subs	Gls
Luton T		05/45				
Aldershot	Tr	08/47	47-48	2	-	0

SMITH Arthur Eric
Born: Whetstone, Leicestershire, England, 5 September, 1921 — IF
Died: Wolverhampton, England, September, 2005

League Club	Source	Date Signed	Seasons Played	Apps	Subs	Gls
Leicester C	Wolverhampton W (Am)	02/41	46-47	17	-	3
West Bromwich A	Tr	06/48	48-51	49	-	12
Plymouth Arg	Tr	08/52	52-53	28	-	9
Crewe Alex	Tr	06/54	54	5	-	0

SMITH Barry Anthony
Born: Colchester, Essex, England, 3 March, 1953 — G

League Club	Source	Date Signed	Seasons Played	Apps	Subs	Gls
Colchester U	Jnr	07/71	71-72	49	0	0

SMITH Barry Joseph
Born: Wigan, Greater Manchester, England, 21 September, 1969 — M

League Club	Source	Date Signed	Seasons Played	Apps	Subs	Gls
Wigan Ath	YT	-	87	0	1	0

SMITH Benjamin James (Ben)
Born: Whitley Bay, Tyne and Wear, England, 5 September, 1986 — G

League Club	Source	Date Signed	Seasons Played	Apps	Subs	Gls
Doncaster Rov	Newcastle U (Sch)	08/06	06-09	14	1	0
Lincoln C	L	11/07	07	9	0	0
Morecambe	L	10/09	09	3	0	0
Shrewsbury T	Tr	08/11	11	36	0	0
Rochdale	Tr	08/12				
Stevenage	Tr	08/13				

SMITH Benjamin Peter (Ben)
Born: Chelmsford, England, 23 November, 1978 — M

League Club	Source	Date Signed	Seasons Played	Apps	Subs	Gls
Reading	Arsenal (YT)	04/97	96	0	1	0
Southend U	Yeovil T	06/01	01	0	1	0
Shrewsbury T	Hereford U	06/04	04-05	19	5	4
Hereford U	Weymouth	01/07	06-08	89	10	7
Crawley T	Tr	08/09	11	3	2	1
Aldershot T	L	01/12	11	3	5	0

SMITH Bradley Shaun (Brad)
Born: Penrith, NSW, Australia, 9 April, 1994 — LB/M
Australia: 4/U23-3//England: Youth

League Club	Source	Date Signed	Seasons Played	Apps	Subs	Gls
Liverpool	Sch	08/11	13	0	1	0
Swindon T	L	08/14	14	7	0	0

SMITH Brian
Born: Bolton, Greater Manchester, England, 12 September, 1955 — M
Died: Blackpool, Lancashire, England, 3 September, 2013
England: Youth

League Club	Source	Date Signed	Seasons Played	Apps	Subs	Gls
Bolton W	App	09/73	74-78	43	6	3
Bradford C	L	10/77	77	8	0	0
Blackpool	Tr	08/79	79	18	1	1
Bournemouth	Tr	12/80	80-81	40	0	2
Bury	Tr	03/82	81	6	0	0

SMITH Brian
Born: Sheffield, England, 27 October, 1966 — D

League Club	Source	Date Signed	Seasons Played	Apps	Subs	Gls
Sheffield U	App	10/84	84-88	81	3	0
Scunthorpe U	L	03/87	86	6	0	1

SMITH Bryan James
Born: Swindon, England, 26 August, 1983 — FB

League Club	Source	Date Signed	Seasons Played	Apps	Subs	Gls
Swindon T	YT	-	99	0	1	0

League Club	Source	Date Signed	Seasons Played	Apps	Subs	Gls
SMITH Carl Paul						
Born: Sheffield, England, 15 January, 1979						M
Burnley	YT	09/97	97-98	5	6	0
SMITH Charles (Charlie)						
Born: Oswaldtwistle, Lancashire, England, 27 June, 1930						IF
Accrington Stan (Am)	Oswaldtwistle Immanuel	06/50	50	1	-	0
SMITH Charles Alan (Alan)						
Born: Salford, England, 7 June, 1940						G
Stockport Co	Manchester C (Am)	06/60	60	6	-	0
SMITH Charles James (Charlie)						
Born: Cardiff, Wales, 26 August, 1915						RW
Died: Torbay, Devon, England, 31 March, 1984						
Exeter C	Exeter Toc H	08/36	36	5	-	0
Torquay U	Aberdeen	04/46	46	23	-	0
SMITH Christian Daniel						
Born: Crewe, Cheshire, England, 10 December, 1987						M
Port Vale	Sch	07/06	06	0	1	0
SMITH Christopher Alan (Chris)						
Born: Derby, England, 30 June, 1981						CD
Reading	YT	06/99				
York C	Tr	07/01	01-03	71	8	0
York C	Mansfield T	10/10	12-13	53	1	4
SMITH Christopher David (Chris)						
Born: Stoke-on-Trent, England, 12 October, 1990						RB
Swindon T	Stone Dominoes	02/12	11	0	1	0
SMITH Christopher Gerald (Chris)						
Born: Birmingham, England, 3 January, 1977						M
Walsall	YT	05/95	95	0	1	0
SMITH Christopher James (Chris)						
Born: Christchurch, Dorset, England, 28 March, 1966						RB
Bristol Rov	Cheltenham T	05/85	84	1	0	0
SMITH Clifford Stephen (Steve)						
Born: Birmingham, England, 13 January, 1961						F
Walsall	Bromsgrove Rov	08/80	80-81	17	2	3
SMITH Colin						
Born: Bishop Auckland, County Durham, England, 30 November, 1951						CD
Leeds U	App	11/69				
Darlington	Shildon	09/84	84	2	0	0
SMITH Colin Richard						
Born: Ruddington, Nottinghamshire, England, 3 November, 1958						CD
England: Schools						
Nottingham F	Jnr	06/77				
Norwich C	Tr	08/82	82	2	2	0
Cardiff C	Sea Bee (HKG)	10/83	83-84	50	0	3
Aldershot	Tr	12/84	84-89	185	5	4
SMITH Connor Charles						
Born: Stockton-on-Tees, Cleveland, England, 14 October, 1996						W
Hartlepool U	Sch	04/15	13-14	3	6	0
SMITH Connor Michael						
Born: Mullingar, Republic of Ireland, 18 February, 1993						M
Republic of Ireland: U21-4/Youth						
Watford	Sch	09/12	12-13	3	5	0
Gillingham	L	01/14	13	6	4	0
SMITH Craig						
Born: Mansfield, Nottinghamshire, England, 2 August, 1976						F
Derby Co	YT	08/95				
Rochdale	L	08/97	97	1	2	0
SMITH Craig Mark						
Born: Bradford, England, 8 June, 1984						M
Halifax T	YT	-	01	0	2	0
SMITH Daniel (Danny)						
Born: Armadale, West Lothian, Scotland, 7 September, 1921						W
Died: Kettering, Northamptonshire, England, 8 October, 1998						
West Bromwich A	Coltness U	05/45	47	7	-	1
Chesterfield	Tr	06/48	48	15	-	4
Crewe Alex	Tr	08/49	49-51	110	-	15
SMITH Daniel (Dan)						
Born: Sunderland, England, 5 October, 1986						LB
Sunderland	Sch	10/03	05	1	2	0
Huddersfield T	L	01/06	05	7	1	0
SMITH Daniel Lee (Danny)						
Born: Southampton, England, 17 August, 1982						M
Bournemouth	YT	04/00	99-01	8	10	0

League Club	Source	Date Signed	Seasons Played	Apps	Subs	Gls
SMITH Daniel Philip (Dan)						
Born: Saltash, Cornwall, England, 5 October, 1989						RW
Plymouth Arg	Sch	07/07	07	0	2	0
Morecambe	L	09/08	08	0	2	0
SMITH David						
Born: Stonehouse, Gloucestershire, England, 29 March, 1968						LW
England: U21-10						
Coventry C	App	07/86	87-92	144	10	19
Bournemouth	L	01/93	92	1	0	0
Birmingham C	Tr	03/93	92-93	35	3	3
West Bromwich A	Tr	01/94	93-97	82	20	2
Grimsby T	Tr	01/98	97-01	101	11	9
Swansea C	Tr	06/02	02	3	1	1
SMITH David						
Born: Frome, Somerset, England, 13 October, 1964						FB
Bristol Rov	App	-	81	0	1	0
SMITH David (Dave)						
Born: South Shields, Tyne and Wear, England, 12 October, 1915						IF
Died: Derby, England, November, 1997						
Newcastle U	Reyrolles	10/35	35	1	-	0
Northampton T	South Shields	09/43	46-50	128	-	31
SMITH David (Dave)						
Born: Thornaby, Cleveland, England, 8 December, 1947						LW/M
England: Schools						
Middlesbrough	App	12/64	67	1	1	0
Lincoln C	Tr	07/68	68-77	358	13	52
Rotherham U	Tr	07/78	78-79	32	1	3
SMITH David Alan						
Born: Sidcup, SE London, England, 25 June, 1961						LW
Gillingham	Welling U	08/86	86-88	90	14	10
Bristol C	Tr	08/89	89-91	94	3	10
Plymouth Arg	Tr	12/91	91	14	4	2
Notts Co	Tr	07/92	92	37	0	8
SMITH David Alan						
Born: Stockport, Greater Manchester, England, 2 May, 1973						G
Doncaster Rov	Bramhall	10/97	97	1	0	0
SMITH David Bowman (Dave)						
Born: Dundee, Scotland, 22 September, 1933						FB
Burnley	East Craigie	09/50	54-60	99	-	1
Brighton & HA	Tr	07/61	61	15	-	0
Bristol C	Tr	07/62	62	3	-	0
SMITH David Bryan (Dave)						
Born: Sheffield, England, 11 December, 1950						F
Huddersfield T	Jnr	04/69	71-73	27	7	7
Stockport Co	L	12/73	73	7	1	0
Halifax T	L	03/74	73	12	1	4
Cambridge U	Tr	07/74	74	15	2	3
Hartlepool U	Tr	02/75	74-75	42	0	13
SMITH David Christopher (Dave)						
Born: Liverpool, England, 26 December, 1970						M
Norwich C	YT	07/89	89-93	13	5	0
Oxford U	Tr	07/94	94-98	193	5	2
Stockport Co	Tr	02/99	98-01	64	7	3
Macclesfield T	L	02/02	01	8	0	0
Macclesfield T	Drogheda (ROI)	01/03	02-03	10	3	0
SMITH David Frederick (Dave)						
Born: Nottingham, England, 11 March, 1956						M
Notts Co	App	03/74	75-77	45	5	0
Torquay U	Tr	06/79	79	20	3	1
SMITH David Robert						
Born: Bristol, England, 5 October, 1934						LW
Died: Bristol, England, 17 December, 2003						
England: Youth						
Bristol C	Jnr	04/53	55-58	21	-	1
Millwall	Tr	09/59	59	13	-	1
SMITH Dean						
Born: Leicester, England, 28 November, 1958						F
Died: Leicester, England, April, 2009						
Leicester C	App	12/76	77	8	2	1
Brentford	Tr	10/78	78-80	48	6	16
SMITH Dean						
Born: West Bromwich, West Midlands, England, 19 March, 1971						CD
Walsall	YT	07/89	88-93	137	5	2
Hereford U	Tr	06/94	94-96	116	1	19
Leyton Orient	Tr	06/97	97-02	239	0	32
Sheffield Wed	Tr	02/03	02-03	55	0	1
Port Vale	Tr	08/04	04	12	1	0

League Club	Source	Date Signed	Seasons Played	Apps	Subs	Gls

SMITH Denis
Born: Meir, Potteries, England, 19 November, 1947 — CD
England: FLge-1

League Club	Source	Date Signed	Seasons Played	Apps	Subs	Gls
Stoke C	Jnr	09/66	68-81	406	1	29
York C	L	03/82	81	7	0	1
York C	Tr	08/82	82	30	0	4

SMITH Denis Noel
Born: Grimsby, North Lincolnshire, England, 23 December, 1932 — LB

League Club	Source	Date Signed	Seasons Played	Apps	Subs	Gls
Grimsby T	Jnr	07/50	52-53	4	-	0

SMITH Dennis
Born: Nelson, Lancashire, England, 22 August, 1925 — WH

League Club	Source	Date Signed	Seasons Played	Apps	Subs	Gls
Hull C	Frickley Colliery	07/46	46	15	-	0
Accrington Stan	Tr	10/47	47-53	155	-	15

SMITH Derek Leonard
Born: Liverpool, England, 5 July, 1946 — CD/F

League Club	Source	Date Signed	Seasons Played	Apps	Subs	Gls
Everton	App	11/63	65-66	3	1	0
Tranmere Rov	Tr	03/68	67-69	77	5	21

SMITH Dominic Rooney
Born: Crewe, Cheshire, England, 22 September, 1995 — F

League Club	Source	Date Signed	Seasons Played	Apps	Subs	Gls
Colchester U	Crewe Alex (Sch)	07/14	14	0	1	0

SMITH Edmund William Alfred (Eddie)
Born: Marylebone, Central London, England, 23 March, 1929 — IF
Died: Westminster, Central London, England, April, 1993

League Club	Source	Date Signed	Seasons Played	Apps	Subs	Gls
Chelsea	Wealdstone	05/50				
Bournemouth	Tr	08/52				
Watford	Tr	07/53	53-54	38	-	12
Northampton T	Tr	01/55	54-55	53	-	12
Colchester U	Tr	06/56	56	36	-	13
Queens Park Rgrs	Tr	07/57	57	17	-	1

SMITH Edward Ferriday (Ted)
Born: Stoke-on-Trent, England, 19 October, 1920 — CF
Died: Hackney, E London, England, 1982

League Club	Source	Date Signed	Seasons Played	Apps	Subs	Gls
Arsenal		05/38				
Aldershot	Tr	06/47	47	7	-	2

SMITH Edward James (Ted)
Born: Benfleet, Essex, England, 18 January, 1996 — G
England: Youth

League Club	Source	Date Signed	Seasons Played	Apps	Subs	Gls
Southend U	Sch	12/13	14	4	0	0

SMITH Edward John William (Ted)
Born: Grays, Essex, England, 3 September, 1914 — FB
Died: Algarve, Portugal, 18 January, 1989

League Club	Source	Date Signed	Seasons Played	Apps	Subs	Gls
Millwall	Tilbury	05/35	35-47	143	-	1

SMITH Edwin Colin (Colin)
Born: Doncaster, South Yorkshire, England, 3 March, 1936 — CF

League Club	Source	Date Signed	Seasons Played	Apps	Subs	Gls
Hull C	Army Police	01/57	56-59	65	-	39
Rotherham U	Tr	06/60	60	9	-	3

SMITH Emmanuele Gabriel (Manny)
Born: Birmingham, England, 8 November, 1988 — CD

League Club	Source	Date Signed	Seasons Played	Apps	Subs	Gls
Walsall	Jnr	09/05	06-11	111	13	7
Notts Co	Tr	07/12	12-13	24	5	0

SMITH Eric Victor
Born: Reading, England, 20 March, 1928 — LB
Died: Burghfield, Berkshire, England, 13 April, 1992

League Club	Source	Date Signed	Seasons Played	Apps	Subs	Gls
Reading		04/49	52-55	61	-	1

SMITH Frank Anthony
Born: Colchester, Essex, England, 30 April, 1936 — G

League Club	Source	Date Signed	Seasons Played	Apps	Subs	Gls
Tottenham H	Colchester Casuals	02/54				
Queens Park Rgrs	Tr	05/62	62-65	66	0	0

SMITH Frank David (Dave)
Born: Holymoorside, Derbyshire, England, 27 July, 1936 — RW

League Club	Source	Date Signed	Seasons Played	Apps	Subs	Gls
Chesterfield	Jnr	09/53	53	7	-	0
Mansfield T	Boston U	08/55	55-56	31	-	4
Derby Co	Tr	07/57				
Coventry C	Tr	11/57	57-58	28	-	2

SMITH Frederick Adamson (Fred)
Born: Aberdeen, Scotland, 14 February, 1926 — IF
Died: Aberdeen, Scotland, 30 December, 2005

League Club	Source	Date Signed	Seasons Played	Apps	Subs	Gls
Hull C	Aberdeen	10/49	49-50	17	-	1
Sheffield U	Tr	04/51	50-52	40	-	11
Millwall	Tr	01/53	52-55	92	-	20
Chesterfield	Tr	07/56	56	7	-	1

SMITH Frederick Edward (Fred)
Born: Draycott, Derbyshire, England, 7 May, 1926 — CF

League Club	Source	Date Signed	Seasons Played	Apps	Subs	Gls
Derby Co	Draycott	06/47	47	1	-	0
Sheffield U	Tr	03/48	47-51	53	-	18
Manchester C	Tr	05/52	52	2	-	1
Grimsby T	Tr	09/52	52-53	50	-	24
Bradford C	Tr	07/54	54	9	-	3

SMITH Frederick Gregg (Fred)
Born: West Sleekburn, Northumberland, England, 25 December, 1942 — RB

League Club	Source	Date Signed	Seasons Played	Apps	Subs	Gls
Burnley	Jnr	12/59	63-69	84	0	1
Portsmouth	Tr	07/70	70-72	82	0	1
Halifax T	Dallas Tornado (USA)	09/74	74	3	0	0

SMITH Gareth Shaun (Shaun)
Born: Leeds, England, 9 April, 1971 — LB

League Club	Source	Date Signed	Seasons Played	Apps	Subs	Gls
Halifax T	YT	07/89	88-89	6	1	0
Crewe Alex	Emley	12/91	91-01	380	22	41
Hull C	Tr	07/02	02	17	5	1
Stockport Co	L	09/03	03	3	3	0
Carlisle U	L	10/03	03	4	0	0
Rochdale	Tr	03/04	03	13	0	0

SMITH Gary
Born: Chasetown, Staffordshire, England, 30 December, 1968 — M

League Club	Source	Date Signed	Seasons Played	Apps	Subs	Gls
Walsall	App	01/87				
Gillingham	Chasetown	07/89	89	0	1	0

SMITH Gary Anthony
Born: Trowbridge, Wiltshire, England, 12 November, 1962 — W

League Club	Source	Date Signed	Seasons Played	Apps	Subs	Gls
Bristol C	App	11/79	80	7	7	0

SMITH Gary Michael
Born: Greenford, W London, England, 4 November, 1955 — CD

League Club	Source	Date Signed	Seasons Played	Apps	Subs	Gls
Brentford		01/74	74	3	0	0

SMITH Gary Neil
Born: Harlow, Essex, England, 3 December, 1968 — M

League Club	Source	Date Signed	Seasons Played	Apps	Subs	Gls
Fulham	App	08/86	85	0	1	0
Colchester U	Tr	09/87	87	11	0	0
Barnet	Welling U	08/93	93-94	11	2	0

SMITH Gary Stephen
Born: Middlesbrough, England, 30 January, 1984 — M

League Club	Source	Date Signed	Seasons Played	Apps	Subs	Gls
Middlesbrough	Sch	07/02				
Wimbledon	L	03/04	03	10	1	3
MK Dons	Tr	08/04	04-06	47	24	5
Brentford	Tr	08/07	07-08	28	5	1
Darlington	Tr	08/09	09	32	2	1

SMITH Gavin
Born: Cambuslang, Lanarkshire, Scotland, 25 September, 1917 — RW
Died: Barnsley, South Yorkshire, England, October, 1992

League Club	Source	Date Signed	Seasons Played	Apps	Subs	Gls
Barnsley	Dumbarton	02/39	46-53	257	-	35

SMITH Geoffrey (Geoff)
Born: Bingley, West Yorkshire, England, 14 March, 1928 — G
Died: Keighley, West Yorkshire, England, 19 October, 2013

League Club	Source	Date Signed	Seasons Played	Apps	Subs	Gls
Bradford C	Rossendale U	12/52	52-58	253	-	0

SMITH George
Born: United Kingdom — CF

League Club	Source	Date Signed	Seasons Played	Apps	Subs	Gls
Walsall (Am)		09/53	53	1	-	0

SMITH George
Born: Newcastle-upon-Tyne, England, 7 October, 1945 — M

League Club	Source	Date Signed	Seasons Played	Apps	Subs	Gls
Newcastle U	App	09/63				
Barrow	Tr	03/65	64-66	91	1	11
Portsmouth	Tr	05/67	67-68	64	0	3
Middlesbrough	Tr	01/69	68-70	74	0	0
Birmingham C	Tr	03/71	70-72	36	3	0
Cardiff C	Tr	06/73	73-74	43	2	1
Swansea C	Tr	05/75	75-77	86	2	8
Hartlepool U	Tr	10/77	77-79	81	4	2

SMITH George Beacher
Born: Fleetwood, Lancashire, England, 7 February, 1921 — IF
Died: Bury, Greater Manchester, England, 14 July, 2013

League Club	Source	Date Signed	Seasons Played	Apps	Subs	Gls
Manchester C	Adelphi LC	05/38	46-51	166	-	75
Chesterfield	Tr	10/51	51-57	250	-	98

SMITH George Casper
Born: Bow, E London, England, 23 April, 1915 — CH
Died: Bodmin, Cornwall, England, 31 October, 1993
England: War-1

League Club	Source	Date Signed	Seasons Played	Apps	Subs	Gls
Charlton Ath	Bexleyheath & Welling	08/38	38	1	-	0
Brentford	Tr	11/45	46	41	-	1
Queens Park Rgrs	Tr	06/47	47-48	75	-	1
Ipswich T	Tr	09/49	49	8	-	0

SMITH George Clarence Bassett
Born: Portsmouth, England, 24 March, 1919 — RH
Died: New South Wales, Australia, 21 December, 2001

League Club	Source	Date Signed	Seasons Played	Apps	Subs	Gls
Southampton	Guernsey Rov	07/38	38-48	95	-	1
Crystal Palace	Tr	05/50	50	7	-	0

SMITH George Henry
Born: Nottingham, England, 13 April, 1936 — G

League Club	Source	Date Signed	Seasons Played	Apps	Subs	Gls
Notts Co	Dale Rov	07/53	55-66	323	0	0
Hartlepool U	Tr	07/67	67-69	112	0	0

SMITH George Thomas
Born: Barnsley, South Yorkshire, England, 14 August, 1996 — LB

League Club	Source	Date Signed	Seasons Played	Apps	Subs	Gls
Barnsley	Sch	06/14	14	16	2	0

SMITH Gerald (Gerry)
Born: Huddersfield, West Yorkshire, England, 18 November, 1939 — LW

League Club	Source	Date Signed	Seasons Played	Apps	Subs	Gls
Huddersfield T	Jnr	05/58				
Bradford C	Tr	07/60	60	7	-	0

SMITH Gordon Duffield
Born: Kilwinning, Ayrshire, Scotland, 29 December, 1954 — W/M
Scotland: U21-1

League Club	Source	Date Signed	Seasons Played	Apps	Subs	Gls
Brighton & HA	Glasgow Rangers	06/80	80-83	97	12	22
Manchester C	Tr	03/84	83-85	40	2	13
Oldham Ath	Tr	01/86	85	14	1	0

SMITH Gordon Melville
Born: Partick, Glasgow, Scotland, 3 July, 1954 — FB/M
Died: Glasgow, Scotland, 5 April, 2014
Scotland: U23-4

League Club	Source	Date Signed	Seasons Played	Apps	Subs	Gls
Aston Villa	St Johnstone	08/76	76-78	76	3	0
Tottenham H	Tr	02/79	78-81	34	4	1
Wolverhampton W	Tr	08/82	82-83	35	3	3

SMITH Graeme Meldrum
Born: Edinburgh, Scotland, 8 June, 1983 — G
Scotland: B-1/U21-8

League Club	Source	Date Signed	Seasons Played	Apps	Subs	Gls
Brighton & HA	Motherwell	07/09	09	5	1	0

SMITH Graham
Born: Wimbledon, SW London, England, 7 August, 1951 — CD

League Club	Source	Date Signed	Seasons Played	Apps	Subs	Gls
Brentford	Wimbledon	08/74	74	7	0	0

SMITH Graham Leslie
Born: Pudsey, West Yorkshire, England, 20 June, 1946 — D

League Club	Source	Date Signed	Seasons Played	Apps	Subs	Gls
Leeds U	Jnr	02/64				
Rochdale	Tr	06/66	66-73	316	1	3
Stockport Co	Tr	07/74	74-78	147	4	2

SMITH Graham William Charles
Born: Liverpool, England, 2 November, 1947 — G

League Club	Source	Date Signed	Seasons Played	Apps	Subs	Gls
Notts Co	Loughborough College	08/68	68	10	0	0
Colchester U	Tr	06/69	69-71	95	0	0
West Bromwich A	Tr	12/71	71-72	10	0	0
Cambridge U	Tr	01/73	72-75	85	0	0

SMITH Grant Gordon
Born: Irvine, Ayrshire, Scotland, 5 May, 1980 — M

League Club	Source	Date Signed	Seasons Played	Apps	Subs	Gls
Reading	Wycombe W (YT)	08/98				
Sheffield U	Clydebank	07/01	01-02	2	8	0
Halifax T	L	09/01	01	11	0	0
Plymouth Arg	L	03/03	02	4	1	1
Swindon T	Tr	07/03	03-04	23	14	10
Bristol C	Tr	07/05	05	4	7	0
Walsall	L	01/06	05	13	0	3
Carlisle U	HJK Helsinki (FIN)	01/08	07-08	16	1	1

SMITH Granville
Born: Penrhiwceiber, Rhondda Cynon Taff, Wales, 4 February, 1937 — W

League Club	Source	Date Signed	Seasons Played	Apps	Subs	Gls
Bristol Rov	Jnr	05/57	58-59	21	-	2
Newport Co	Tr	06/60	60-67	240	0	37

SMITH Harold Raymond (Ray)
Born: Hull, England, 13 September, 1934 — IF

League Club	Source	Date Signed	Seasons Played	Apps	Subs	Gls
Hull C	Jnr	08/52	54-55	23	-	2
Peterborough U	Tr	07/56	60-62	92	-	33
Northampton T	Tr	10/62	62-63	23	-	7
Luton T	Tr	10/63	63	10	-	1

SMITH Harry Arthur
Born: Wolverhampton, England, 10 October, 1932 — LB

League Club	Source	Date Signed	Seasons Played	Apps	Subs	Gls
Torquay U	West Bromwich A (Am)	01/54	53-60	188	-	1
Bristol C	Tr	07/61	61	1	-	0

SMITH Henry Stanley (Harry)
Born: Throckley, Tyne and Wear, England, 11 October, 1908 — CH
Died: Newcastle-upon-Tyne, England, 13 June, 1993

League Club	Source	Date Signed	Seasons Played	Apps	Subs	Gls
Nottingham F	Throckley Welfare	01/29	29-36	156	-	1
Darlington	Tr	08/37	37-38	65	-	0
Bristol Rov	Tr	08/39	46	3	-	0

SMITH Henry Stuart (Harry)
Born: Chester, England, 27 August, 1930 — IF/WH

League Club	Source	Date Signed	Seasons Played	Apps	Subs	Gls
Chester C	Connah's Quay Nomads	01/53	52-57	73	-	7

SMITH Herbert Henry (Herbie)
Born: Birmingham, England, 17 December, 1922 — RW
Died: Birmingham, England, 11 January, 1996

League Club	Source	Date Signed	Seasons Played	Apps	Subs	Gls
Aston Villa	Moor Green	05/47	49-53	51	-	8
Southend U	Tr	06/54	54	5	-	0

SMITH Ian Lennox Taylor
Born: Edinburgh, Scotland, 2 April, 1952 — F

League Club	Source	Date Signed	Seasons Played	Apps	Subs	Gls
Birmingham C	Queen's Park	03/75	74	0	2	0

SMITH Ian Paul (Paul)
Born: Peterlee, County Durham, England, 22 January, 1976 — LB/M

League Club	Source	Date Signed	Seasons Played	Apps	Subs	Gls
Burnley	YT	07/94	93-00	79	33	5
Oldham Ath	L	09/00	00	3	1	0
Hartlepool U	Tr	11/01	01-02	45	10	4
Sheffield Wed	Tr	07/03	03-04	19	8	2

SMITH Ian Ralph
Born: Rotherham, South Yorkshire, England, 15 February, 1957 — D
England: Youth/Schools

League Club	Source	Date Signed	Seasons Played	Apps	Subs	Gls
Tottenham H	App	04/74	75	2	0	0
Rotherham U	Tr	06/76	77	3	1	0

SMITH Jack
Born: Batley, West Yorkshire, England, 17 February, 1915 — CF
Died: Urmston, Greater Manchester, England, 21 April, 1975

League Club	Source	Date Signed	Seasons Played	Apps	Subs	Gls
Huddersfield T	Dewsbury Moor Welfare	06/32	32-34	45	-	24
Newcastle U	Tr	09/34	34-37	104	-	69
Manchester U	Tr	02/38	37-38	36	-	14
Blackburn Rov	Tr	03/46	46	30	-	12
Port Vale	Tr	05/47	46-47	29	-	10

SMITH Jack David
Born: Hemel Hempstead, Hertfordshire, England, 14 October, 1983 — RB

League Club	Source	Date Signed	Seasons Played	Apps	Subs	Gls
Watford	Sch	04/02	02-04	23	2	2
Swindon T	Tr	07/05	05-08	134	4	9
Millwall	Tr	08/09	09-13	86	11	1
AFC Wimbledon	Tr	07/14	14	21	0	3

SMITH James
Born: Liverpool, England, 17 October, 1985 — RB

League Club	Source	Date Signed	Seasons Played	Apps	Subs	Gls
Liverpool	Sch	10/04				
Stockport Co	L	08/07	07	11	0	0
Stockport Co	Tr	01/08	07	13	2	0

SMITH James (Jim)
Born: Bolton, Greater Manchester, England, 1 January, 1920 — RW

League Club	Source	Date Signed	Seasons Played	Apps	Subs	Gls
Burnley		03/43				
Leyton Orient	Tr	04/46	46-47	22	-	3

SMITH James (Jimmy)
Born: Glasgow, Scotland, 20 January, 1947 — M
Scotland: 4/SLge-1/U23-1

League Club	Source	Date Signed	Seasons Played	Apps	Subs	Gls
Newcastle U	Aberdeen	08/69	69-74	124	5	13

SMITH James Alan (Alan)
Born: Birkenhead, Wirral, England, 8 June, 1939 — D

League Club	Source	Date Signed	Seasons Played	Apps	Subs	Gls
Torquay U	Port Sunlight	08/56	57-68	277	1	2

SMITH James Alexander Grant (Jim)
Born: Arbroath, Angus, Scotland, 16 October, 1937 — D
Died: Preston, Lancashire, England, April, 2002
Scotland: Schools

League Club	Source	Date Signed	Seasons Played	Apps	Subs	Gls
Preston NE	Arbroath Lads	10/55	58-68	314	0	13
Stockport Co	Tr	10/69	69-70	78	0	2

SMITH James Aloysius
Born: Coatbridge, Lanarkshire, Scotland, 9 September, 1925 — LW
Died: Airdrie, Lanarkshire, Scotland, 20 October, 2006

League Club	Source	Date Signed	Seasons Played	Apps	Subs	Gls
Walsall	Coatdyke Jnrs	06/48	48	2	-	0

SMITH James Dean (Jimmy)
Born: Newham, E London, England, 7 January, 1987 — M
England: Youth

League Club	Source	Date Signed	Seasons Played	Apps	Subs	Gls
Chelsea	Sch	03/05	05	0	1	0
Queens Park Rgrs	L	09/06	06	22	7	6
Norwich C	L	07/07	07	6	3	0
Sheffield Wed	L	07/08	08	3	9	0
Leyton Orient	Tr	02/09	08-12	130	30	18
Stevenage	Tr	06/13	13	40	2	3
Crawley T	Tr	05/14	14	28	8	1

SMITH James Harold (Jimmy)
Born: Sheffield, England, 6 December, 1930 — W

League Club	Source	Date Signed	Seasons Played	Apps	Subs	Gls
Chelsea	Shildon	04/51	51-53	19	-	3
Leyton Orient	Tr	07/55	55-57	37	-	3

SMITH James Hay (Jimmy)
Born: Johnstone, Renfrewshire, Scotland, 22 November, 1969 — F

League Club	Source	Date Signed	Seasons Played	Apps	Subs	Gls
Torquay U	YT	07/88	87-89	27	17	5

League Club	Source	Date Signed	Seasons Played	Career Record Apps	Subs	Gls
SMITH James Jade Anthony (Jamie)						
Born: Birmingham, England, 17 September, 1974						RB
Wolverhampton W	YT	06/93	94-97	81	6	0
Crystal Palace	Tr	10/97	97-03	136	13	4
Fulham	L	03/99	98	9	0	1
Bristol C	Tr	08/04	04-05	39	6	2
Brentford	L	03/06	05	7	0	0
MK Dons	Tr	07/06	06	16	1	0
SMITH James Michael (Jim)						
Born: Sheffield, England, 17 October, 1940						RH
Sheffield U	Oaksfield	01/59				
Aldershot	Tr	07/61	61-64	74	-	1
Halifax T	Tr	07/65	65-67	113	1	7
Lincoln C	Tr	03/68	67-68	54	0	0
Colchester U	Boston U	11/72	72	7	1	0
SMITH James Peter (Jamie)						
Born: Woodford, NE London, England, 16 September, 1989						M
Crystal Palace	Sch	07/08				
Brighton & HA	Tr	08/09	09-10	4	6	0
Leyton Orient	Tr	03/12	11	0	1	0
SMITH Jason Leslie						
Born: Bromsgrove, Worcestershire, England, 6 September, 1974						CD
England: Schools						
Coventry C	Tiverton T	07/93				
Swansea C	Tiverton T	07/98	98-02	141	1	8
SMITH Jay Alexander						
Born: Lambeth, S London, England, 24 September, 1981						M
Aston Villa	YT	07/00				
Southend U	Tr	08/02	02-05	49	13	7
Oxford U	L	03/06	05	5	1	0
Notts Co	Tr	11/06	06-08	47	13	4
SMITH Jay Mark						
Born: Hammersmith, W London, England, 29 December, 1981						M
Brentford	YT	07/00	00-04	37	11	0
SMITH Jeffrey (Jeff)						
Born: Middlesbrough, England, 28 June, 1980						LW
Hartlepool U	YT	07/98	98	2	1	0
Bolton W	Bishop Auckland	03/01	00-01	1	1	0
Macclesfield T	L	11/01	01	7	1	2
Scunthorpe U	L	01/04	03	1	0	0
Rochdale	L	02/04	03	1	0	0
Preston NE	Tr	03/04	03	0	5	0
Port Vale	Tr	07/04	04-06	65	23	5
Carlisle U	Tr	01/07	06-08	41	14	2
Darlington	Tr	08/09	09	22	2	0
SMITH Jeffrey Edward (Jeff)						
Born: Macclesfield, Cheshire, England, 8 December, 1935						LB
Sheffield U	Jnr	06/53	56	1	-	0
Lincoln C	Tr	02/58	57-66	315	0	2
SMITH Jeremy						
Born: Leeds, England, 20 July, 1971						F
Wigan Ath	Goole T	08/91	91	0	6	0
SMITH Johann Anwar Ryan						
Born: Hartford, Connecticut, USA, 25 April, 1987						LW
Bolton W	Sch	10/06	06	0	1	0
Carlisle U	L	01/07	06	9	5	1
Darlington	L	10/07	07	3	0	0
Stockport Co	L	03/08	07	0	2	0
SMITH John						
Born: Johnstown, Wrexham, Wales, 13 September, 1944						D
Wrexham	Burnley (Jnr)	05/63	64-65	23	1	0
SMITH John						
Born: Liverpool, England, 14 March, 1953						M
England: Schools						
Everton	App	09/70	73	2	0	0
Carlisle U	Tr	06/76	76	4	1	0
Southport	L	02/77	76	17	1	2
SMITH John						
Born: Coatbridge, Lanarkshire, Scotland, 27 November, 1956						F
Preston NE	App	11/74	73-78	80	11	14
Halifax T	Los Angeles Sk's (USA)	11/79	79	26	2	6
SMITH John						
Born: Shoreditch, Central London, England, 4 January, 1939						M
Died: Brent, NW London, England, February, 1988						
England: U23-1/Youth						
West Ham U	Jnr	01/56	56-59	125	-	20
Tottenham H	Tr	03/60	59-63	21	-	1
Coventry C	Tr	03/64	63-65	34	1	1
Leyton Orient	Tr	10/65	65-66	38	1	3
Torquay U	Tr	10/66	66-67	67	1	8
Swindon T	Tr	06/68	68-70	79	5	9
Walsall	Tr	06/71	71	13	0	1
SMITH John (Jackie)						
Born: Hartlepool, Cleveland, England, 24 April, 1936						CF
Hartlepool U	Jnr	05/53	53-59	119	-	49
Watford	Tr	07/60	60	20	-	8
Swindon T	Tr	06/61	61-63	97	-	37
Brighton & HA	Tr	01/64	63-66	88	0	33
Notts Co	Tr	09/66	66-68	74	4	12
SMITH John (Jack)						
Born: Liverpool, England						IF
Ipswich T	Army	12/45	46	2	-	0
SMITH John						
Born: Liverpool, England, 23 July, 1970						LB
Tranmere Rov	Jnr	11/87	88	1	1	0
SMITH John Clayton (Jack)						
Born: Stocksbridge, South Yorkshire, England, 15 September, 1910						G
Died: Sheffield, England, 7 April, 1986						
Sheffield U	Worksop T	10/30	30-49	347	-	0
SMITH John Edward						
Born: Canning Town, E London, England, 9 November, 1930						LB
England: Youth						
Millwall	Barking	04/56	55-57	64	-	1
SMITH John Eric (Eric)						
Born: Glasgow, Scotland, 29 July, 1934						WH
Died: Dubai, United Arab Emirates, 12 June, 1991						
Scotland: 2						
Leeds U	Glasgow Celtic	06/60	60-62	65	-	3
SMITH John Owen						
Born: Enderby, Leicestershire, England, 4 September, 1928						WH
Died: Northampton, England, April, 2013						
Northampton T	Leicester C (Am)	09/49	50-59	186	-	9
SMITH John Thomas (Jack)						
Born: Birkenhead, Wirral, England, 21 December, 1927						CF/W
Died: Birkenhead, Wirral, England, August, 2000						
Liverpool	Bromborough Pool	03/51	51-53	57	-	14
Torquay U	Tr	05/54	54-57	65	-	16
SMITH John Trevor (Trevor)						
Born: Stanley, County Durham, England, 8 September, 1910						IF
Died: Bracknell, Berkshire, England, 23 October, 1997						
Charlton Ath	Annfield Plain	05/33	33-34	23	-	6
Fulham	Tr	03/35	34-37	93	-	19
Crystal Palace	Tr	02/38	37-38	57	-	14
Watford	Colchester U	06/47	47	10	-	0
SMITH John Vivian Thomas						
Born: Plymouth, England, 12 November, 1927						RB
Died: Paignton, Devon, England, 11 December, 2013						
Plymouth Arg	Plymouth U	07/50	50-52	3	-	0
Torquay U	Tr	07/54	54-59	164	-	0
SMITH John William (Jackie)						
Born: Camden, N London, England, 27 May, 1920						W
Died: Bradford, England, November, 1991						
Bradford Park Ave	Avro Works	10/43	46-52	204	-	26
SMITH Jonathan Peter						
Born: Preston, Lancashire, England, 17 October, 1986						M
Swindon T	York C	06/11	11	28	10	3
York C	Tr	07/12	12	8	4	0
Luton T	Tr	11/12	14	35	0	2
SMITH Jonte Jahki						
Born: Hamilton, Bermuda, 10 July, 1994						F
Crawley T	Jnr	04/12	12	0	4	0
SMITH Joseph Barry (Barry)						
Born: South Kirkby, West Yorkshire, England, 15 March, 1934						CF
Died: New Zealand, February, 2007						
Leeds U	Farsley Celtic	10/51	52	2	-	1
Bradford Park Ave	Tr	05/55	55-56	64	-	38
Wrexham	Tr	06/57	57	18	-	10
Stockport Co	Tr	07/58	58	17	-	4
Oldham Ath	Headington U	08/60	60	1	-	0
Southport	Bangor C	08/61				
Accrington Stan	Tr	10/61				

SMITH Joseph Leslie (Les)
Born: Halesowen, West Midlands, England, 24 December, 1927 RW
Died: Stourbridge, West Midlands, England, 8 March, 2008

League Club	Source	Date Signed	Seasons Played	Apps	Subs	Gls
Wolverhampton W	Jnr	04/46	47-55	88	-	22
Aston Villa	Tr	02/56	55-58	115	-	24

SMITH Keith
Born: Sheffield, England, 17 October, 1963 F

League Club	Source	Date Signed	Seasons Played	Apps	Subs	Gls
Exeter C	Alfreton T	01/89	88	2	13	2

SMITH Keith Wilson
Born: Swadlincote, Derbyshire, England, 15 September, 1940 CF

League Club	Source	Date Signed	Seasons Played	Apps	Subs	Gls
West Bromwich A	Jnr	01/58	59-62	63	-	30
Peterborough U	Tr	06/63	63-64	55	-	28
Crystal Palace	Tr	11/64	64-65	47	3	14
Darlington	Tr	11/66	66	17	0	2
Leyton Orient	Tr	05/67	66	3	0	0
Notts Co	Tr	07/67	67-69	85	4	7

SMITH Kenneth (Ken)
Born: Consett, County Durham, England, 7 December, 1927 IF

League Club	Source	Date Signed	Seasons Played	Apps	Subs	Gls
Blackpool	Annfield Plain	04/49				
Gateshead	Tr	08/52	52-58	256	-	75

SMITH Kenneth (Ken)
Born: South Shields, Tyne and Wear, England, 21 May, 1932 CF
Died: Hertfordshire, England, June, 2011

League Club	Source	Date Signed	Seasons Played	Apps	Subs	Gls
Sunderland	Jnr	08/49	50-52	5	-	2
Blackpool	Headington U	12/54	54-57	6	-	4
Shrewsbury T	Tr	10/57	57-58	44	-	20
Gateshead	Tr	11/58	58-59	45	-	18
Darlington	Tr	12/59	59	24	-	7
Carlisle U	Tr	07/60	60	14	-	12
Halifax T	Toronto Italia (CAN)	10/61	61	27	-	6

SMITH Kenneth George (Ken)
Born: Norwich, England, 22 April, 1936 D

League Club	Source	Date Signed	Seasons Played	Apps	Subs	Gls
Norwich C	Gothic FC	09/55	55-56	10	-	0

SMITH Kevan
Born: Eaglescliffe, Cleveland, England, 13 December, 1959 CD

League Club	Source	Date Signed	Seasons Played	Apps	Subs	Gls
Darlington	Stockton	09/79	79-84	242	3	11
Rotherham U	Tr	07/85	85-86	59	0	4
Coventry C	Tr	12/86	87	5	1	0
York C	Tr	05/88	88	30	1	5
Darlington	Tr	06/89	90-92	98	0	5
Hereford U	L	10/92	92	6	0	0
Hereford U		09/93	93	17	1	0

SMITH Kevin James
Born: Edinburgh, Scotland, 20 March, 1987 F

League Club	Source	Date Signed	Seasons Played	Apps	Subs	Gls
Leeds U	Sch	03/05				
Sunderland	Tr	01/06				
Wrexham	L	11/06	06	5	3	1
Notts Co	Dundee U	08/10	10	6	7	1

SMITH Kevin John
Born: Wallsend, Tyne and Wear, England, 20 April, 1965 M

League Club	Source	Date Signed	Seasons Played	Apps	Subs	Gls
Cambridge U	App	11/82	82-84	30	8	4
Exeter C	Tr	10/84	84	21	4	2
Torquay U	Tr	07/85	85	20	3	1

SMITH Kevin Paul
Born: St Pauls Cray, SE London, England, 5 December, 1962 M

League Club	Source	Date Signed	Seasons Played	Apps	Subs	Gls
Charlton Ath	App	08/80	79-83	79	25	14

SMITH Khano
Born: Paget, Bermuda, 10 January, 1981 W
Bermuda: 24

League Club	Source	Date Signed	Seasons Played	Apps	Subs	Gls
Lincoln C	New York R Bulls (USA)	10/09	09	4	1	0

SMITH Korey Alexander
Born: Hatfield, Hertfordshire, England, 31 January, 1991 DM

League Club	Source	Date Signed	Seasons Played	Apps	Subs	Gls
Norwich C	Sch	07/08	08-10	56	11	4
Barnsley	L	01/12	11	10	2	0
Yeovil T	L	09/12	12	16	1	0
Oldham Ath	Tr	03/13	12-13	51	1	1
Bristol C	Tr	06/14	14	44	0	0

SMITH Leslie (Les)
Born: Tamworth, Staffordshire, England, 16 November, 1921 RH
Died: Newark, Nottinghamshire, England, January, 1993

League Club	Source	Date Signed	Seasons Played	Apps	Subs	Gls
Mansfield T	Nottingham F (Am)	08/45	46-47	38	-	0

SMITH Leslie (Les)
Born: Manchester, England, 2 October, 1920 RH
Died: Hazel Grove, Greater Manchester, England, 6 December, 2001

League Club	Source	Date Signed	Seasons Played	Apps	Subs	Gls
Huddersfield T	Stockport Co (Am)	03/46	46-47	37	-	0
Oldham Ath	Tr	07/49	49-55	178	-	3

SMITH Leslie George Frederick
Born: Ealing, W London, England, 13 March, 1918 LW
Died: Lichfield, Staffordshire, England, 24 May, 1995
England: 1/War-13

League Club	Source	Date Signed	Seasons Played	Apps	Subs	Gls
Brentford	Hayes	03/36	36-38	62	-	6
Aston Villa	Tr	10/45	46-51	181	-	31
Brentford	Tr	06/52	52	14	-	1

SMITH Lindsay James
Born: Enfield, N London, England, 18 September, 1954 CD/M

League Club	Source	Date Signed	Seasons Played	Apps	Subs	Gls
Colchester U	App	03/72	70-76	185	27	16
Charlton Ath	L	08/77	77	1	0	0
Millwall	L	09/77	77	4	1	0
Cambridge U	Tr	10/77	77-82	173	1	7
Lincoln C	L	09/81	81	5	0	0
Plymouth Arg	Tr	07/84	82-83	76	0	5
Millwall	Tr	07/84	84-85	54	1	5
Cambridge U	Tr	07/86	86-88	102	0	16

SMITH Lionel
Born: Mexborough, South Yorkshire, England, 23 August, 1920 LB
Died: Stoke Newington, N London, England, 8 November, 1980
England: 6/FLge-3

League Club	Source	Date Signed	Seasons Played	Apps	Subs	Gls
Arsenal	Denaby U	08/39	47-53	162	-	0
Watford	Tr	06/54	54	7	-	0

SMITH Malcolm
Born: Stockton-on-Tees, Cleveland, England, 21 September, 1953 F

League Club	Source	Date Signed	Seasons Played	Apps	Subs	Gls
Middlesbrough	App	10/70	71-75	32	24	11
Bury	L	10/75	75	5	0	1
Blackpool	L	01/76	75	8	0	5
Burnley	Tr	09/76	76-79	82	3	17
York C	Tr	08/80	80-81	28	7	6

SMITH Malcolm Alan
Born: Maidstone, Kent, England, 3 August, 1970 M

League Club	Source	Date Signed	Seasons Played	Apps	Subs	Gls
Gillingham	YT	06/88	87	1	1	0

SMITH Mark
Born: Redruth, Cornwall, England, 21 September, 1963 LB

League Club	Source	Date Signed	Seasons Played	Apps	Subs	Gls
Bristol C	App	09/81	81	1	4	0
Plymouth Arg	Exmouth T	03/84	83	3	0	0

SMITH Mark
Born: Torquay, Devon, England, 9 October, 1961 FB

League Club	Source	Date Signed	Seasons Played	Apps	Subs	Gls
Torquay U		09/81	81-83	28	2	0

SMITH Mark Alexander
Born: Bellshill, Lanarkshire, Scotland, 16 December, 1964 W

League Club	Source	Date Signed	Seasons Played	Apps	Subs	Gls
Stoke C (L)	Dunfermline Ath	02/90	89	2	0	0
Nottingham F	Dunfermline Ath	03/90				
Reading	L	12/90	90	3	0	0
Mansfield T	L	03/91	90	6	1	0
Shrewsbury T	Tr	08/91	91-94	64	14	4

SMITH Mark Allen
Born: Birmingham, England, 2 January, 1973 G

League Club	Source	Date Signed	Seasons Played	Apps	Subs	Gls
Nottingham F	YT	02/91				
Crewe Alex	Tr	02/93	92-94	61	2	0

SMITH Mark Craig
Born: Sheffield, England, 21 March, 1960 CD
England: U21-5

League Club	Source	Date Signed	Seasons Played	Apps	Subs	Gls
Sheffield Wed	App	03/78	77-86	281	1	16
Plymouth Arg	Tr	07/87	87-89	82	0	6
Barnsley	Tr	11/89	89-92	101	3	10
Notts Co	Tr	10/92	92	4	1	0
Port Vale	L	01/93	92	6	0	0
Huddersfield T	L	02/93	92	5	0	0
Chesterfield	L	03/93	92	6	0	1
Lincoln C	Tr	08/93	93	20	0	1

SMITH Mark Cyril
Born: Sheffield, England, 19 December, 1961 LW

League Club	Source	Date Signed	Seasons Played	Apps	Subs	Gls
Sheffield U	Jnr	08/80				
Scunthorpe U	Gainsborough Trinity	09/85	85	0	1	0
Rochdale	Kettering T	07/88	88	26	1	7
Huddersfield T	Tr	02/89	88-90	85	11	11
Grimsby T	Tr	03/91	90-92	37	40	4
Scunthorpe U	Tr	08/93	93-94	50	12	8

SMITH Mark Jonathan
Born: Bristol, England, 13 September, 1979 CD

League Club	Source	Date Signed	Seasons Played	Apps	Subs	Gls
Bristol Rov	YT	07/98	98-01	28	5	0

SMITH Mark Leslie
Born: Canning Town, E London, England, 10 October, 1961 LB

League Club	Source	Date Signed	Seasons Played	Apps	Subs	Gls
West Ham U	App	10/79	79	1	0	0

League Club	Source	Date Signed	Seasons Played	Career Record Apps	Subs	Gls
SMITH Mark Stuart						
Born: Carlisle, Cumbria, England, 4 April, 1962						FB
England: Youth						
Leyton Orient	App	12/79	78-79	3	0	0
SMITH Martin Geoffrey						
Born: Sunderland, England, 13 November, 1974						F
England: U21-1/Youth/Schools						
Sunderland	YT	09/92	93-98	90	29	25
Sheffield U	Tr	08/99	99	24	2	10
Huddersfield T	Tr	02/00	99-02	72	8	29
Northampton T	Tr	08/03	03-05	96	8	24
Darlington	Tr	07/06	06-07	30	8	5
SMITH Martyn Christopher						
Born: Stoke-on-Trent, England, 16 September, 1961						LW
Port Vale	Leek T	07/84	84	12	1	1
SMITH Mathieu James (Matt)						
Born: Birmingham, England, 7 June, 1989						F
Oldham Ath	Solihull Moors	07/11	11-12	17	45	9
Macclesfield T	L	03/12	11	6	2	1
Leeds U	Tr	06/13	13-14	21	21	12
Fulham	Tr	09/14	14	8	7	5
Bristol C	L	11/14	14	11	3	7
SMITH Michael (Mick)						
Born: Sunderland, England, 28 October, 1958						CD
Lincoln C	Lambton Street BC	07/77	77-78	20	5	0
Wimbledon	Tr	12/79	79-86	203	2	14
Aldershot	L	10/84	84	7	0	0
Hartlepool U	Seaham Red Star	10/89	89-91	53	2	6
SMITH Michael						
Born: Ballyclare, Antrim, Northern Ireland, 4 September, 1988						RB
Northern Ireland: U23-1						
Bristol Rov	Ballymena U	07/11	11-13	84	17	1
Peterborough U	Tr	07/14	14	40	3	1
SMITH Michael (Mike)						
Born: Haddington, East Lothian, Scotland, 15 October, 1923						CF
Died: Conwy, Wales, January, 2010						
Plymouth Arg	Preston Ath	02/48	47	1	-	0
Chelsea	Tr	06/48				
SMITH Michael John						
Born: Wallsend, Tyne and Wear, England, 17 October, 1991						F
Darlington	Sch	07/10	09	3	4	1
Charlton Ath	Tr	08/11				
Accrington Stan	L	01/12	11	4	2	3
Colchester U	L	03/13	12	3	5	1
AFC Wimbledon	L	07/13	13	23	0	9
Swindon T	Tr	01/14	13-14	52	8	21
SMITH Michael John (Mike)						
Born: Quarndon, Derbyshire, England, 22 September, 1935						CH
Died: 22 April, 2013						
England: Schools						
Derby Co	Jnr	10/52	57-60	22	-	0
Bradford C	Tr	06/61	61-65	134	0	0
SMITH Michael Kenneth (Mike)						
Born: Hull, England, 19 December, 1968						W
Hull C	App	05/87	88-90	14	5	1
SMITH Michael Robert (Mike)						
Born: Liverpool, England, 28 September, 1973						LB/M
Tranmere Rov	YT	05/92				
Doncaster Rov	Runcorn	01/96	95-97	33	17	5
SMITH Nathan Adam (Adam)						
Born: Huddersfield, West Yorkshire, England, 20 February, 1985						RW
Chesterfield	Sch	08/04	03-07	23	43	3
Lincoln C	L	01/08	07	0	4	0
Aldershot T (L)	Mansfield T	10/11	11	7	5	0
SMITH Nathan Colin Leslie						
Born: Enfield, N London, England, 11 January, 1987						LB
Yeovil T	Potters Bar T	03/08	07-10	100	14	1
Chesterfield	Tr	07/11	11-13	61	6	0
Yeovil T	Tr	07/14	14	36	5	0
SMITH Neil						
Born: Warley, West Midlands, England, 10 February, 1970						M
Shrewsbury T	YT	07/88	87	0	1	0
Lincoln C	Redditch U	03/90	89-91	13	4	0
SMITH Neil James						
Born: Lambeth, S London, England, 30 September, 1971						M
Tottenham H	YT	07/90				

League Club	Source	Date Signed	Seasons Played	Career Record Apps	Subs	Gls
Gillingham	Tr	10/91	91-96	204	8	10
Fulham	Tr	07/97	97-98	62	11	1
Reading	Tr	08/99	99-01	33	32	3
SMITH Nicholas Leslie (Nicky)						
Born: Berkeley, Gloucestershire, England, 28 January, 1969						LW
Southend U	YT	07/87	86-89	49	11	6
Colchester U	Tr	08/90	92-93	71	10	4
Northampton T	Sudbury T	01/95	94	6	0	1
SMITH Nigel Godfrey						
Born: Manchester, England, 22 April, 1959						CD
Stockport Co	Blackburn Rov (Am)	08/79	79-85	119	5	1
SMITH Nigel Keith						
Born: Bath, England, 12 January, 1966						M
Bristol C	App	01/84	82	2	0	0
Exeter C	L	11/84	84	1	0	0
SMITH Nigel Paul						
Born: Banstead, Surrey, England, 3 January, 1958						CD
Brentford	Queens Park Rgrs (Jnr)	03/75	74-78	81	4	0
Cambridge U	Tr	11/78	78	0	1	0
SMITH Nigel Peter						
Born: Leeds, England, 21 December, 1969						RW
Leeds U	YT	07/88				
Burnley	Tr	07/89	89-90	6	7	0
Bury	Tr	08/91	91	30	4	3
Shrewsbury T	Guiseley	09/92	92	2	0	0
SMITH Norman						
Born: Boldon, Tyne and Wear, England, 23 November, 1919						CF
Died: Coventry, England, 18 November, 2010						
Coventry C	Standard Apprentices	05/38	38-47	13	-	0
Millwall	Tr	12/47	47	10	-	0
SMITH Norman						
Born: Darwen, Lancashire, England, 2 January, 1925						RH/IF
Died: Barnsley, South Yorkshire, England, 26 July, 1990						
Arsenal	Darwen	07/47				
Barnsley	Tr	10/52	52-58	156	-	14
Shrewsbury T	Tr	07/59				
SMITH Norman Henry						
Born: Burton-on-Trent, Staffordshire, England, 27 January, 1924						IF
Died: Burton-on-Trent, Staffordshire, England, 10 January, 2000						
Accrington Stan	Army	02/46	46-47	39	-	6
Oldham Ath	Tr	06/48	48	1	-	0
SMITH Norman Leonard						
Born: Carshalton, S London, England, 2 July, 1928						RH
Died: Surrey, England, January, 2003						
England: Amateur-1						
Fulham	Bishop Auckland	07/48	52-56	60	-	0
SMITH Paul Andrew						
Born: Bath, England, 12 September, 1953						W
Manchester C	Jnr	09/70				
Portsmouth	Tr	06/73	73	0	1	0
SMITH Paul Antony						
Born: Hastings, East Sussex, England, 25 January, 1976						RW
Nottingham F	Hastings T	01/95				
Lincoln C	Tr	10/97	97-02	122	35	19
SMITH Paul Daniel						
Born: Epsom, Surrey, England, 17 December, 1979						G
Charlton Ath	Walton & Hersham	07/98				
Brentford	Carshalton Ath	07/00	00-03	86	1	0
Southampton	Tr	01/04	04-05	14	1	0
Nottingham F	Tr	07/06	06-09	120	0	0
Middlesbrough	L	03/11	10	10	0	0
Southend U	Tr	08/12	12	34	0	0
SMITH Paul Elton						
Born: Lewisham, SE London, England, 2 November, 1971						M
Barnet	Horsham	05/95	95	0	1	0
SMITH Paul John						
Born: Liverpool, England, 17 November, 1990						RB/M
Chester C	Sch	-	08	0	5	0
SMITH Paul Michael						
Born: Rotherham, South Yorkshire, England, 9 November, 1964						RB/M
Sheffield U	App	11/82	82-85	29	7	1
Stockport Co	L	08/85	85	7	0	5
Port Vale	Tr	07/86	86-87	42	2	7
Lincoln C	Tr	08/87	88-94	219	13	27

SMITH Paul Stepney
Born: Wembley, NW London, England, 5 October, 1967 — RW

League Club	Source	Date Signed	Seasons Played	Apps	Subs	Gls
Arsenal	App	07/85				
Brentford	Tr	08/87	87	10	7	1
Bristol Rov	Tr	07/88	88	14	2	1
Torquay U	Tr	03/89	88-91	66	9	12

SMITH Paul William
Born: East Ham, E London, England, 18 September, 1971 — M

League Club	Source	Date Signed	Seasons Played	Apps	Subs	Gls
Southend U	YT	03/90	89-92	18	2	1
Brentford	Tr	08/93	93-96	159	0	11
Gillingham	Tr	07/97	97-04	338	4	21
Walsall	Tr	08/05	05	8	0	1
Gillingham	L	10/05	05	3	0	0
Swindon T	Tr	01/06	05	5	4	0
Torquay U	AFC Sudbury	01/07	06	5	3	0

SMITH Paul William
Born: Doncaster, South Yorkshire, England, 15 October, 1954 — M

League Club	Source	Date Signed	Seasons Played	Apps	Subs	Gls
Huddersfield T	App	12/71	72-73	1	1	0
Cambridge U	Tr	09/74	74-75	35	3	3

SMITH Peter Alec
Born: Islington, N London, England, 10 November, 1964 — CD

League Club	Source	Date Signed	Seasons Played	Apps	Subs	Gls
Leyton Orient	App	11/82	82	8	6	0

SMITH Peter Edward
Born: Skelmersdale, Lancashire, England, 30 October, 1980 — M

League Club	Source	Date Signed	Seasons Played	Apps	Subs	Gls
Exeter C	YT	07/99	98-99	3	5	0

SMITH Peter John
Born: Balham, S London, England, 27 May, 1935 — RH

League Club	Source	Date Signed	Seasons Played	Apps	Subs	Gls
Gillingham	Tunbridge Wells	06/58	58-59	39	-	2

SMITH Peter John
Born: Cannock, Staffordshire, England, 12 July, 1969 — RB

League Club	Source	Date Signed	Seasons Played	Apps	Subs	Gls
Brighton & HA	Alma Swanley	08/94	94-98	122	18	5

SMITH Peter John
Born: Gosport, Hampshire, England, 6 May, 1932 — FB

League Club	Source	Date Signed	Seasons Played	Apps	Subs	Gls
Gillingham	Fleetland	11/54	54-56	6	-	0

SMITH Peter Lee
Born: Rhyl, Denbighshire, Wales, 18 September, 1978 — F
England: Youth/Schools

League Club	Source	Date Signed	Seasons Played	Apps	Subs	Gls
Crewe Alex	YT	07/96	96-00	3	19	0
Macclesfield T	L	09/98	98	12	0	3

SMITH Philip (Phil)
Born: Fleetwood, Lancashire, England, 20 November, 1961 — F

League Club	Source	Date Signed	Seasons Played	Apps	Subs	Gls
Blackpool	App	11/79	79	1	0	0

SMITH Philip Anthony (Phil)
Born: Harrow, NW London, England, 14 December, 1979 — G
England: Semi Pro-1

League Club	Source	Date Signed	Seasons Played	Apps	Subs	Gls
Millwall	YT	01/98	98	5	0	0
Swindon T	Crawley T	06/06	06-11	110	2	0
Portsmouth		12/12	13	4	0	0

SMITH Raymond (Ray)
Born: Portadown, Armagh, Northern Ireland, 20 November, 1950 — W

League Club	Source	Date Signed	Seasons Played	Apps	Subs	Gls
Oldham Ath	Glenavon	01/68	67	0	2	0

SMITH Raymond James (Ray)
Born: Islington, N London, England, 18 April, 1943 — CF

League Club	Source	Date Signed	Seasons Played	Apps	Subs	Gls
Southend U	Basildon Minors	12/61	61-66	150	0	55
Wrexham	Tr	07/67	67-71	161	14	60
Peterborough U	Tr	07/72	72	22	0	8

SMITH Raymond Scorer (Ray)
Born: Evenwood, County Durham, England, 14 April, 1929 — WH

League Club	Source	Date Signed	Seasons Played	Apps	Subs	Gls
Luton T	Evenwood T	02/50	51-56	12	-	0
Southend U	Tr	08/57	57-59	46	-	1

SMITH Richard Francis
Born: Reading, England, 22 October, 1967 — W

League Club	Source	Date Signed	Seasons Played	Apps	Subs	Gls
Wolverhampton W	App	07/85	85	0	1	0
Mansfield T	Moor Green	03/87	86	1	1	0

SMITH Richard Geoffrey
Born: Lutterworth, Leicestershire, England, 3 October, 1970 — CD

League Club	Source	Date Signed	Seasons Played	Apps	Subs	Gls
Leicester C	YT	12/88	89-95	82	14	1
Cambridge U	L	09/89	89	4	0	0
Grimsby T	L	09/95	95	8	0	0
Grimsby T	Tr	03/96	95-00	72	7	1

SMITH Robert (Bobby)
Born: Barnsley, South Yorkshire, England, 20 June, 1941 — W

League Club	Source	Date Signed	Seasons Played	Apps	Subs	Gls
Barnsley	Jnr	06/60	62	3	-	0

SMITH Robert (Rob)
Born: Hull, England, 25 April, 1950 — RB/M

League Club	Source	Date Signed	Seasons Played	Apps	Subs	Gls
Hull C	App	11/67				
Grimsby T	Tr	09/71	71	10	1	0
Hartlepool U	Tr	07/72	72-75	141	11	4

SMITH Robert Alexander (Alex)
Born: Billingham, Cleveland, England, 6 February, 1944 — RB

League Club	Source	Date Signed	Seasons Played	Apps	Subs	Gls
Middlesbrough	Haverton Hill	12/61	65-71	119	2	1
Darlington	Bangor C	07/74	74-75	43	0	0

SMITH Robert Alfred (Bobby)
Born: Lingdale, Cleveland, England, 22 February, 1933 — CF
Died: Enfield, N London, England, 18 September, 2010
England: 15

League Club	Source	Date Signed	Seasons Played	Apps	Subs	Gls
Chelsea	Jnr	05/50	50-55	74	-	23
Tottenham H	Tr	12/55	55-63	271	-	176
Brighton & HA	Tr	05/64	64	31	-	19

SMITH Robert Gordon John (Bobby)
Born: Bournemouth, England, 15 December, 1941 — WH

League Club	Source	Date Signed	Seasons Played	Apps	Subs	Gls
Portsmouth	Jnr	05/59				
Gillingham	Tr	07/62	62	7	-	0

SMITH Robert Nisbet (Bobby)
Born: Dalkeith, Midlothian, Scotland, 21 December, 1953 — M/LB
Died: Edinburgh, Scotland, 22 February, 2010

League Club	Source	Date Signed	Seasons Played	Apps	Subs	Gls
Leicester C	Hibernian	12/78	78-85	175	6	21
Peterborough U	L	02/82	81	5	0	0

SMITH Robert William (Bobby)
Born: Prestbury, Cheshire, England, 14 March, 1944 — M
England: Youth/Schools

League Club	Source	Date Signed	Seasons Played	Apps	Subs	Gls
Manchester U	App	04/61				
Scunthorpe U	Tr	03/65	64-66	82	0	12
Grimsby T	Tr	01/67	66-67	48	4	1
Brighton & HA	Tr	06/68	68-70	72	3	2
Chester C	Tr	06/71	71	2	0	0
Hartlepool U	Tr	10/71	71-72	67	2	7

SMITH Roger Anthony
Born: Welwyn Garden City, Hertfordshire, England, 3 November, 1944 — LW

League Club	Source	Date Signed	Seasons Played	Apps	Subs	Gls
Tottenham H	App	06/62				
Exeter C	Tr	06/66	66	6	0	3

SMITH Roger William
Born: Tamworth, Staffordshire, England, 19 February, 1945 — RW

League Club	Source	Date Signed	Seasons Played	Apps	Subs	Gls
Walsall	App	09/62	62-64	43	-	2
Port Vale	Tr	08/65	65	29	1	6
Walsall	Tr	05/66	66	8	1	0

SMITH Ronald (Ron)
Born: Liverpool, England, 7 June, 1936 — LW

League Club	Source	Date Signed	Seasons Played	Apps	Subs	Gls
Liverpool	Stoke C (Am)	12/57				
Bournemouth	Tr	05/59	59-60	36	-	6
Crewe Alex	Tr	07/61	61-63	91	-	11
Port Vale	Tr	10/63	63-64	59	-	6
Southport	Tr	07/65	65-66	77	2	14

SMITH Ronald (Ron)
Born: Aberystwyth, Ceredigion, Wales, 9 April, 1934 — RB

League Club	Source	Date Signed	Seasons Played	Apps	Subs	Gls
Arsenal	Maidenhead U	07/54				
Watford	Tr	08/55	55	2	-	0

SMITH Ronald Herbert (Ron)
Born: York, England, 25 November, 1929 — CH
Died: East Riding of Yorkshire, England, September, 2010

League Club	Source	Date Signed	Seasons Played	Apps	Subs	Gls
York C	Harrogate RI	05/54	54	1	-	0

SMITH Ross Graham
Born: Guelph, Ontario, Canada, 4 November, 1980 — CD

League Club	Source	Date Signed	Seasons Played	Apps	Subs	Gls
Dagenham & Red	Gravesend & Northfleet	07/07	07	23	0	1

SMITH Roy Harold
Born: Rawalpindi, India, 19 March, 1936 — IF

League Club	Source	Date Signed	Seasons Played	Apps	Subs	Gls
West Ham U	Woodford YC	06/55	55-56	6	-	1
Portsmouth	Hereford U	01/62	61-62	8	-	3

SMITH Roy Peter
Born: Haydock, Merseyside, England, 18 June, 1936 — CF
Died: Haydock, Merseyside, England, 3 June, 1959

League Club	Source	Date Signed	Seasons Played	Apps	Subs	Gls
Southport	Wigan Ath	09/58	58	23	-	4

SMITH Royston Leonard (Roy)
Born: Shirebrook, Derbyshire, England, 22 September, 1916 — G
Died: Nottingham, England, October, 1971

League Club	Source	Date Signed	Seasons Played	Apps	Subs	Gls
Sheffield Wed	Selby T	02/36	36-47	84	-	0
Notts Co	Tr	12/48	48-52	110	-	0

League Club	Source	Date Signed	Seasons Played	Apps	Subs	Gls

SMITH Ryan Craig Matthew
Born: Islington, N London, England, 10 November, 1986 — W
England: Youth

League Club	Source	Date Signed	Seasons Played	Apps	Subs	Gls
Arsenal	Sch	11/04				
Leicester C	L	09/05	05	10	7	1
Derby Co	Tr	08/06	06	5	10	0
Millwall	Tr	03/07	06-08	14	9	0
Southampton	Tr	10/08	08	7	6	0
Crystal Palace	Tr	08/09	09	0	5	0

SMITH Scott David
Born: Christchurch, New Zealand, 6 March, 1975 — RB
New Zealand: 28

League Club	Source	Date Signed	Seasons Played	Apps	Subs	Gls
Rotherham U	YT	10/93	93-96	30	6	0

SMITH Septimus Charles (Sep)
Born: Whitburn, Tyne and Wear, England, 15 March, 1912 — RH/IF
Died: York, England, 28 July, 2006
England: 1/FLge-1/Schools

League Club	Source	Date Signed	Seasons Played	Apps	Subs	Gls
Leicester C	Whitburn	03/29	29-48	350	-	35

SMITH Stanley James (Stan)
Born: Kidsgrove, Potteries, England, 24 February, 1931 — IF
Died: Kidsgrove, Staffordshire, England, 8 April, 2010

League Club	Source	Date Signed	Seasons Played	Apps	Subs	Gls
Port Vale	Chesterton PSA	05/50	54-56	60	-	19
Crewe Alex	Tr	07/57	57	28	-	6
Oldham Ath	Tr	03/58	57	4	-	0

SMITH Stanley Walter (Stan)
Born: Coventry, England, 24 February, 1925 — WH
Died: Coventry, England, 6 October, 2012

League Club	Source	Date Signed	Seasons Played	Apps	Subs	Gls
Coventry C	Nuffield Mechanics	08/46	47-48	29	-	0
Swansea C	Tr	08/50				

SMITH Stephen (Steve)
Born: Huddersfield, West Yorkshire, England, 28 April, 1946 — M

League Club	Source	Date Signed	Seasons Played	Apps	Subs	Gls
Huddersfield T	Jnr	10/63	64-76	330	12	30
Bolton W	L	12/74	74	3	0	0
Halifax T	Tr	08/77	77-78	78	3	4

SMITH Stephen James (Steve)
Born: Lydney, Gloucestershire, England, 12 June, 1957 — G

League Club	Source	Date Signed	Seasons Played	Apps	Subs	Gls
Birmingham C	App	07/75	75	2	0	0
Bradford C	Tr	03/78	78-81	105	0	0
Crewe Alex	Tr	08/82	82-83	54	0	0

SMITH Stephen Martin
Born: Harlow, Essex, England, 19 September, 1986 — RB

League Club	Source	Date Signed	Seasons Played	Apps	Subs	Gls
Cambridge U	Sch	-	03	1	1	0

SMITH Steven
Born: Airdrie, Lanarkshire, Scotland, 30 August, 1985 — LB
Scotland: B-1/U21-1

League Club	Source	Date Signed	Seasons Played	Apps	Subs	Gls
Norwich C	Glasgow Rangers	07/10	10	5	2	0
Preston NE	Tr	08/11	11	9	4	0

SMITH Terence (Terry)
Born: Runcorn, Cheshire, England, 16 September, 1987 — G

League Club	Source	Date Signed	Seasons Played	Apps	Subs	Gls
Oldham Ath	Sch	07/06	06	0	1	0

SMITH Terence Peter (Terry)
Born: Cheltenham, Gloucestershire, England, 10 September, 1951 — F

League Club	Source	Date Signed	Seasons Played	Apps	Subs	Gls
Stoke C	App	12/68	70-71	3	1	1
Shrewsbury T	L	02/73	72	2	0	0

SMITH Terence Victor (Terry)
Born: Rainworth, Nottinghamshire, England, 10 July, 1942 — RH

League Club	Source	Date Signed	Seasons Played	Apps	Subs	Gls
Mansfield T	Jnr	04/60	60	8	-	0

SMITH Thomas (Tot)
Born: Horden, County Durham, England, 2 February, 1923 — CH
Died: County Durham, England, April, 1993

League Club	Source	Date Signed	Seasons Played	Apps	Subs	Gls
Newcastle U	Horden CW	03/41	46-49	8	-	0

SMITH Thomas (Tommy)
Born: Liverpool, England, 5 April, 1945 — D/M
England: 1/FLge-1/U23-10/Youth

League Club	Source	Date Signed	Seasons Played	Apps	Subs	Gls
Liverpool	App	04/62	62-77	467	0	36
Swansea C	Tr	08/78	78	34	2	2

SMITH Thomas Edgar (Tommy)
Born: Wolverhampton, England, 30 July, 1959 — F

League Club	Source	Date Signed	Seasons Played	Apps	Subs	Gls
Sheffield U	Bromsgrove Rov	04/78	78	2	1	1
Huddersfield T	Tr	03/79	78	0	1	0

SMITH Thomas Edward (Tommy)
Born: Northampton, England, 25 November, 1977 — CD

League Club	Source	Date Signed	Seasons Played	Apps	Subs	Gls
Manchester U	YT	05/95				
Cambridge U	Tr	04/98	97	0	1	0

SMITH Thomas George (Tommy)
Born: Helsby, Cheshire, England, 14 April, 1992 — D

League Club	Source	Date Signed	Seasons Played	Apps	Subs	Gls
Manchester C	Sch	07/10				
Huddersfield T	Oxford U (NC)	08/12	13-14	63	2	0

SMITH Thomas Henry Eric (Eric)
Born: Tamworth, Staffordshire, England, 3 November, 1921 — CH
Died: Lichfield, Staffordshire, England, 13 May, 2006

League Club	Source	Date Signed	Seasons Played	Apps	Subs	Gls
Leicester C	Castle Bromwich	04/43	46	5	-	0

SMITH Thomas Jefferson (Tommy)
Born: Macclesfield, Cheshire, England, 31 March, 1990 — CD
England: Youth//New Zealand: 29

League Club	Source	Date Signed	Seasons Played	Apps	Subs	Gls
Ipswich T	Sch	08/07	08-14	180	9	19
Brentford	L	01/10	09	8	0	0
Colchester U	L	03/11	10	6	0	0

SMITH Thomas Spencer (Tom)
Born: Swindon, England, 25 February, 1998 — M

League Club	Source	Date Signed	Seasons Played	Apps	Subs	Gls
Swindon T	Sch	-	14	0	1	0

SMITH Thomas William (Tommy)
Born: Hemel Hempstead, Hertfordshire, England, 22 May, 1980 — W/F
England: U21-1/Youth

League Club	Source	Date Signed	Seasons Played	Apps	Subs	Gls
Watford	YT	10/97	97-02	114	35	33
Sunderland	Tr	09/03	03	22	13	4
Derby Co	Tr	07/04	04-06	88	2	20
Watford	Tr	08/06	06-09	123	1	27
Portsmouth	Tr	08/09	09-10	15	4	1
Queens Park Rgrs	Tr	09/10	10-11	27	23	8
Cardiff C	Tr	08/12	12	19	5	1
Brentford	Tr	08/14	14	1	27	1

SMITH Timothy Carl (Tim)
Born: Gloucester, England, 19 April, 1959 — M

League Club	Source	Date Signed	Seasons Played	Apps	Subs	Gls
Luton T	App	05/76	76-77	1	1	0

SMITH Trevor
Born: Brierley Hill, West Midlands, England, 13 April, 1936 — CH
Died: Colchester, Essex, England, 20 August, 2003
England: 2/B-2/FLge-2/U23-15

League Club	Source	Date Signed	Seasons Played	Apps	Subs	Gls
Birmingham C	Jnr	05/53	53-64	365	-	3
Walsall	Tr	10/64	64-65	12	0	0

SMITH Trevor John
Born: Birmingham, England, 7 May, 1954 — W
England: Schools

League Club	Source	Date Signed	Seasons Played	Apps	Subs	Gls
Coventry C	App	05/71				
Walsall	Tr	08/72	72	2	1	0

SMITH Trevor Martin
Born: Middlesbrough, England, 4 April, 1959 — D/M

League Club	Source	Date Signed	Seasons Played	Apps	Subs	Gls
Hartlepool U	Whitby T	11/76	76-78	27	6	1
Hartlepool U	Whitby T	08/82	82	30	2	3

SMITH Trevor Richard
Born: Lowestoft, Suffolk, England, 12 August, 1946 — FB

League Club	Source	Date Signed	Seasons Played	Apps	Subs	Gls
Ipswich T	App	08/64	64-65	22	1	0

SMITH Wilfred
Born: Stoke-on-Trent, England, 18 April, 1917 — WH/FB
Died: Hanley, Potteries, England, 4 May, 1995

League Club	Source	Date Signed	Seasons Played	Apps	Subs	Gls
Port Vale	Sneyd Colliery	10/36	36-48	87	-	0

SMITH Wilfred (Wilf)
Born: Manchester, England, 20 January, 1935 — IF
Died: Manchester, England, 1977

League Club	Source	Date Signed	Seasons Played	Apps	Subs	Gls
Stockport Co		02/57	57-59	6	-	1

SMITH Wilfred Samuel (Wilf)
Born: Neumunster, Germany, 3 September, 1946 — RB
England: FLge-3/U23-6/Youth

League Club	Source	Date Signed	Seasons Played	Apps	Subs	Gls
Sheffield Wed	App	09/63	64-70	206	0	4
Coventry C	Tr	08/70	70-74	132	3	1
Brighton & HA	L	10/74	74	5	0	0
Millwall	L	01/75	74	5	0	0
Bristol Rov	Tr	03/75	74-76	54	0	2
Chesterfield	Tr	11/76	76	26	1	2

SMITH Wilfred Victor (Wilf)
Born: Pucklechurch, Avon, England, 7 April, 1918 — FB
Died: Pucklechurch, Avon, England, 14 April, 1968

League Club	Source	Date Signed	Seasons Played	Apps	Subs	Gls
Bristol Rov	Clevedon T	05/36	37-46	26	-	0
Newport Co	Tr	12/46	46-47	9	-	0

SMITH William (Willie)
Born: Glasgow, Scotland, 6 December, 1943 — WH

League Club	Source	Date Signed	Seasons Played	Apps	Subs	Gls
Brentford	Glasgow Celtic	06/63	63-65	25	0	0

League Club	Source	Date Signed	Seasons Played	Career Record Apps	Subs	Gls

SMITH William
Born: Aberdeen, Scotland, 23 December, 1938 — IF

Darlington	Raith Rov	07/63	63	26	-	7

SMITH William
Born: Cumnock, Ayrshire, Scotland, 12 October, 1942 — IF

Sheffield U	Cumnock Jnrs	07/65	66	2	0	1

SMITH William (Willie)
Born: Tooting, SW London, England, 29 September, 1948 — FB
England: Amateur-14

Wimbledon	Leatherhead	08/77	77	2	0	0

SMITH William Arthur (Bill)
Born: Lambeth, S London, England, 2 November, 1938 — G

Crystal Palace	Jnr	12/56				
Watford	Tr	08/57	58	10	-	0

SMITH William Conway (Conway)
Born: Huddersfield, West Yorkshire, England, 13 July, 1926 — IF
Died: Dewsbury, West Yorkshire, England, 23 March, 1989

Huddersfield T	Jnr	05/45	47-50	37	-	5
Queens Park Rgrs	Tr	03/51	50-55	174	-	81
Halifax T	Tr	06/56	56-61	179	-	73

SMITH William Henry (Bill)
Born: Plymouth, England, 7 September, 1926 — WH/IF
Died: Lancashire, England, December, 2014

Plymouth Arg	Plymouth U	08/45				
Reading	Tr	08/47	47	3	-	0
Northampton T	Tr	07/48	48	26	-	6
Birmingham C	Tr	02/50	50-52	55	-	21
Blackburn Rov	Tr	12/52	52-59	119	-	10
Accrington Stan	Tr	07/60	60	34	-	3

SMITH William Roy (Billy)
Born: Stafford, England, 20 December, 1930 — LB
Died: Stafford, England, February, 2012

Crewe Alex		12/55	55-56	43	-	0

SMITHARD Matthew Philip
Born: Leeds, England, 13 June, 1976 — M

Leeds U	YT	03/93				
Bradford C	Tr	08/96	96	0	1	0

SMITHERS Timothy (Tim)
Born: Ramsgate, Kent, England, 22 January, 1956 — LB
England: Semi Pro-3

Oxford U	Nuneaton Bor	05/80	80-82	95	4	6

SMITHIES Alexander (Alex)
Born: Huddersfield, West Yorkshire, England, 25 March, 1990 — G
England: Youth

Huddersfield T	Sch	03/07	07-14	245	1	0

SMITHIES Michael Howard (Mike)
Born: Hartlepool, Cleveland, England, 18 September, 1962 — RB

Hartlepool U		12/82	82-86	32	3	0

SMITHSON Rodney George
Born: Leicester, England, 9 October, 1943 — CD
England: Youth/Schools

Arsenal	App	10/60	62	2	-	0
Oxford U	Tr	07/64	65-74	150	6	6

SMOLAREK Euzebiusz (Ebi)
Born: Lodz, Poland, 9 January, 1981 — W
Poland: 47

Bolton W (L)	RC Santander (SPN)	09/08	08	1	11	0

SMOUT John Richard
Born: Newtown, Powys, Wales, 30 October, 1941 — G

Crystal Palace	Newtown	08/65	65	1	0	0
Exeter C	Tr	06/66	66-67	75	0	0

SMYLIE Daryl
Born: Portadown, Armagh, Northern Ireland, 10 September, 1985 — M
Northern Ireland: U21-6/Youth

Newcastle U	Sch	07/05				
Stockport Co	L	02/06	05	1	2	0

SMYTH Cecil (Cec)
Born: Belfast, Northern Ireland, 4 May, 1941 — RB
Died: Exeter, England, 7 November, 2008

Exeter C	Distillery	08/62	62-68	270	3	1
Torquay U	Tr	08/69	69-70	22	1	0

SMYTH Gerry
Born: Belfast, Northern Ireland, 5 November, 1931 — RW

Cardiff C	Jnr	08/50				
Chester C	Tr	07/51	51	2	-	0

SMYTH Herbert Robert (Bob)
Born: Manchester, England, 28 February, 1921 — LH
Died: Leeds, England, August, 1998

Ipswich T	HMS Ganges	12/45	46-47	2	-	0
Halifax T	Tr	08/50	50	2	-	0
Rochdale	Tr	09/50	50	3	-	1
Accrington Stan	Tr	01/51	50	7	-	0

SMYTH John Michael
Born: Dundalk, Republic of Ireland, 28 April, 1970 — RB

Liverpool	Dundalk (ROI)	05/87				
Burnley	Tr	08/90				
Wigan Ath	Tr	09/91	91	2	6	0

SMYTH Michael (Mike)
Born: Dublin, Republic of Ireland, 13 May, 1940 — G
Republic of Ireland: 1/LoI-1

Barrow	Drumcondra (ROI)	08/62	62-63	8	-	0

SMYTH Peter Rufus Adair
Born: Derry, Northern Ireland, 3 December, 1924 — IF
Died: Southport, Merseyside, England, 4 September, 2001

Exeter C	Albion Rov	06/50	50	5	-	0
Southport	Tr	07/51	51	5	-	0

SMYTH Samuel (Sammy)
Born: Belfast, Northern Ireland, 25 February, 1925 — IF
Northern Ireland: 9/NILge-1

Wolverhampton W	Linfield	07/47	47-51	102	-	34
Stoke C	Tr	09/51	51-52	40	-	17
Liverpool	Tr	01/53	52-53	45	-	20

SMYTH Thomas Joseph (Tom)
Born: Southport, Merseyside, England, 18 March, 1991 — CD

Preston NE	Sch	05/09				
Accrington Stan	Tr	06/10	10	3	1	0

SNAPE Jack
Born: Birmingham, England, 2 July, 1917 — RH
Died: Coventry, England, 16 February, 2000

Coventry C	Solihull T	05/36	37-49	106	-	2

SNEDDEN John Duncan
Born: Bonnybridge, Falkirk, Scotland, 3 February, 1942 — CH
Scotland: Schools

Arsenal	Bonnyvale Star Jnrs	02/59	59-64	83	-	0
Charlton Ath	Tr	03/65	64-65	18	2	0
Leyton Orient	Tr	07/66	66-67	26	1	3
Halifax T	L	11/67	67	5	0	0

SNEDDON Charles (Charlie)
Born: Bo'ness, Falkirk, Scotland, 10 June, 1930 — LH
Died: Accrington, Lancashire, England, 6 September, 1992

Accrington Stan	Stenhousemuir	10/53	53-60	213	-	3

SNEDDON David (Dave)
Born: Kilwinning, Ayrshire, Scotland, 24 April, 1936 — IF
Scotland: U23-1

Preston NE	Dundee	04/59	58-61	91	-	17

SNEDDON Thomas (Tom)
Born: Livingston, West Lothian, Scotland, 22 August, 1912 — LB
Died: Chadwell Heath, E London, England, 11 December, 1983

Rochdale	Queen of the South	07/37	37-46	67	-	0

SNEDDON William Cleland (Billy)
Born: Wishaw, Lanarkshire, Scotland, 1 April, 1914 — WH
Died: Bangor, Gwynedd, Wales, April, 1995

Brentford	Falkirk	06/37	37-38	66	-	2
Swansea C	Tr	07/39	46	2	-	0
Newport Co	Tr	10/46	46	18	-	0

SNEEKES Richard
Born: Amsterdam, Netherlands, 30 October, 1968 — M
Netherlands: U21-2/Schools

Bolton W	Fortuna Sittard (NED)	08/94	94-95	51	4	7
West Bromwich A	Tr	03/96	95-00	208	19	30
Stockport Co	Tr	09/01	01	8	1	0
Hull C	Tr	11/01	01	17	5	0

SNELL Albert Edward
Born: Dunscroft, South Yorkshire, England, 7 February, 1931 — WH
Died: Sunderland, England, 31 March, 2007

Sunderland	Doncaster Rov (Am)	08/49	52-54	9	-	1
Halifax T	Tr	11/55	55-56	25	-	0

SNELL Victor Derek Robert (Vic)
Born: Ipswich, England, 29 October, 1927 — D
Died: Hounslow, SW London, England, 20 August, 2009

Ipswich T	Jnr	11/45	49-58	64	-	2

SNIJDERS Mark Werner
Born: Alkmaar, Netherlands, 12 March, 1972 — CD

League Club	Source	Date Signed	Seasons Played	Apps	Subs	Gls
Port Vale	AZ67 Alkmaar (NED)	09/97	97-99	46	9	2

SNO Evander
Born: Dordrecht, Netherlands, 9 April, 1987 — DM
Netherlands: U21-15

League Club	Source	Date Signed	Seasons Played	Apps	Subs	Gls
Bristol C (L)	Ajax (NED)	09/09	09	16	8	3

SNODGRASS Robert (Rob)
Born: Glasgow, Scotland, 7 September, 1987 — RW
Scotland: 15/U21-2/Youth

League Club	Source	Date Signed	Seasons Played	Apps	Subs	Gls
Leeds U	Livingston	07/08	08-11	141	25	35
Norwich C	Tr	07/12	12-13	64	3	12
Hull C	Tr	06/14	14	1	0	0

SNODIN Glynn
Born: Rotherham, South Yorkshire, England, 14 February, 1960 — LB/M

League Club	Source	Date Signed	Seasons Played	Apps	Subs	Gls
Doncaster Rov	App	10/77	76-84	288	21	59
Sheffield Wed	Tr	06/85	85-86	51	8	1
Leeds U	Tr	07/87	87-90	83	11	10
Oldham Ath	L	08/91	91	8	0	1
Rotherham U	L	02/92	91	3	0	0
Barnsley	Heart of Midlothian	07/93	93-94	18	7	0

SNODIN Ian
Born: Rotherham, South Yorkshire, England, 15 August, 1963 — M
England: B-2/U21-4/Youth

League Club	Source	Date Signed	Seasons Played	Apps	Subs	Gls
Doncaster Rov	App	08/80	79-84	181	7	27
Leeds U	Tr	05/85	85-86	51	0	6
Everton	Tr	01/87	86-94	142	6	3
Sunderland	L	10/94	94	6	0	0
Oldham Ath	Tr	01/95	94-96	55	2	0
Scarborough	Tr	08/97	97	33	2	0

SNOOKES Eric
Born: Birmingham, England, 6 March, 1955 — LB

League Club	Source	Date Signed	Seasons Played	Apps	Subs	Gls
Preston NE	App	03/73	72-73	20	0	0
Crewe Alex	Tr	07/74	74	33	1	0
Southport	Tr	07/75	75-77	106	4	2
Rochdale	Tr	07/78	78-82	183	0	1
Bolton W	Tr	07/83	83	6	0	0

SNOW Simon Gordon
Born: Sheffield, England, 3 April, 1966 — F

League Club	Source	Date Signed	Seasons Played	Apps	Subs	Gls
Scunthorpe U	App	08/83	82-83	1	1	0
Preston NE	Sutton T	08/89	89	1	0	0

SNOWBALL Raymond (Ray)
Born: Sunderland, England, 10 March, 1932 — G

League Club	Source	Date Signed	Seasons Played	Apps	Subs	Gls
Darlington (Am)	Crook T	10/64	64-66	13	0	0

SNOWDEN Trevor
Born: Sunderland, England, 4 October, 1973 — LW

League Club	Source	Date Signed	Seasons Played	Apps	Subs	Gls
Rochdale	Seaham Red Star	02/93	92-93	8	6	0

SNOWDON Brian Victor
Born: Bishop Auckland, County Durham, England, 1 January, 1935 — CH

League Club	Source	Date Signed	Seasons Played	Apps	Subs	Gls
Blackpool		09/52	55-59	18	-	1
Portsmouth	Tr	10/59	59-63	114	-	0
Millwall	Tr	10/63	63-66	128	0	0
Crystal Palace	Margate	02/69	68	1	4	0

SOAMES David Michael
Born: Grimsby, North Lincolnshire, England, 10 December, 1984 — F

League Club	Source	Date Signed	Seasons Played	Apps	Subs	Gls
Grimsby T	Sch	07/04	02-04	0	24	1

SOARES Louie Pierre
Born: Reading, England, 8 January, 1985 — RW
Barbados: 2

League Club	Source	Date Signed	Seasons Played	Apps	Subs	Gls
Reading	Sch	07/04				
Bristol Rov	L	05/05	04	0	1	0
Barnet	Tr	08/05	05	14	6	1
Aldershot T	Tr	07/06	08-09	58	13	10
Southend U	Tr	08/10	10	17	14	0

SOARES Thomas James (Tom)
Born: Reading, England, 10 July, 1986 — M
England: U21-4/Youth

League Club	Source	Date Signed	Seasons Played	Apps	Subs	Gls
Crystal Palace	Sch	09/04	03-08	128	21	11
Stoke C	Tr	08/08	08	5	2	0
Charlton Ath	L	01/09	08	10	1	1
Sheffield Wed	L	11/09	09	17	8	2
Bury	Portsmouth (NC)	11/12	12-14	87	9	16

SOBERS Jerrome Roxin
Born: Whitechapel, Central London, England, 18 April, 1986 — CD

League Club	Source	Date Signed	Seasons Played	Apps	Subs	Gls
Ipswich T	Ford U	05/04				
Brentford	L	03/05	04	1	0	1

SOBIECH Jorg
Born: Gelsenkirchen, Germany, 15 January, 1969 — LB

League Club	Source	Date Signed	Seasons Played	Apps	Subs	Gls
Stoke C (L)	NEC Nijmegen (NED)	03/98	97	3	0	0

SODEN Walter James William
Born: Birmingham, England, 22 January, 1921 — CF
Died: Hednesford, Staffordshire, England, 16 November, 1977

League Club	Source	Date Signed	Seasons Played	Apps	Subs	Gls
Coventry C	Boldmere St Michael's	03/48	47-48	2	-	0

SODERBERG Ole Petter
Born: Norrkoping, Sweden, 20 July, 1990 — G
Sweden: U21-1/Youth

League Club	Source	Date Signed	Seasons Played	Apps	Subs	Gls
Newcastle U	BK Hacken (SWE)	02/08				
Chesterfield	L	11/11	11	2	0	0

SODJE Efetobore Peter (Efe)
Born: Greenwich, SE London, England, 5 October, 1972 — CD
Nigeria: 12

League Club	Source	Date Signed	Seasons Played	Apps	Subs	Gls
Macclesfield T	Stevenage Bor	07/97	97-98	83	0	6
Luton T	Tr	08/99	99	5	4	0
Colchester U	Tr	03/00	99	3	0	0
Crewe Alex	Tr	07/00	00-02	86	12	3
Huddersfield T	Tr	08/03	03-04	61	6	5
Yeovil T	Tr	03/05	04-05	23	2	3
Southend U	Tr	01/06	05-06	35	2	2
Gillingham	Tr	07/07	07	12	1	0
Bury	Tr	02/08	07-12	192	4	16

SODJE Idoro Akpoeyere Ujoma (Akpo)
Born: Greenwich, SE London, England, 31 January, 1981 — F

League Club	Source	Date Signed	Seasons Played	Apps	Subs	Gls
Queens Park Rgrs	Jnr	10/00				
Huddersfield T	Erith & Belvedere	09/04	04	1	6	0
Darlington	Tr	03/05	04-05	18	25	9
Port Vale	Tr	07/06	06-07	41	5	14
Sheffield Wed	Tr	08/07	07-09	18	23	9
Charlton Ath	L	11/09	09	2	7	2
Charlton Ath	Tr	02/10	09-10	9	22	4
Preston NE	Tianjin Teda (CHN)	08/12	12	5	9	4
Scunthorpe U	Tr	01/13	12	13	3	6
Tranmere Rov	Tr	07/13	13	3	6	0

SODJE Onome Sympson
Born: Warri, Nigeria, 17 July, 1988 — F

League Club	Source	Date Signed	Seasons Played	Apps	Subs	Gls
Barnsley	York C	06/09	09	0	1	0

SODJE Samuel Okeremute (Sam)
Born: Greenwich, SE London, England, 29 May, 1979 — CD
Nigeria: 4

League Club	Source	Date Signed	Seasons Played	Apps	Subs	Gls
Brentford	Margate	07/04	04-05	83	0	12
Reading	Tr	07/06	06	2	1	0
West Bromwich A	L	03/07	06	7	0	1
Charlton Ath	L	08/07	07	20	7	2
Watford	L	09/08	08	1	0	0
Leeds U	L	03/09	08	5	0	0
Charlton Ath	Tr	09/09	09	24	3	4
Notts Co	Skoda Xanthi (GRE)	11/10	10-11	12	15	2
Portsmouth		01/13	12	9	0	0

SOFIANE Youssef
Born: Lyon, France, 8 July, 1984 — F
France: Youth

League Club	Source	Date Signed	Seasons Played	Apps	Subs	Gls
West Ham U	AJ Auxerre (FRA)	06/02	03	0	1	0
Notts Co	L	09/04	04	2	2	0
Coventry C	Tr	10/05	05	0	1	0

SOKOLIK Jakub
Born: Ostrava, Czech Republic, 28 August, 1993 — CD
Czech Republic: Youth

League Club	Source	Date Signed	Seasons Played	Apps	Subs	Gls
Liverpool	Sch	10/10				
Southend U	L	03/14	13	10	0	0
Yeovil T	Tr	06/14	14	11	0	0
Southend U	L	10/14	14	1	0	0

SOLAN Kenneth (Ken)
Born: Middlesbrough, England, 13 October, 1948 — M
Died: Middlesbrough, England, 23 April, 1971

League Club	Source	Date Signed	Seasons Played	Apps	Subs	Gls
Middlesbrough		11/66				
Hartlepool U	L	10/68	68	6	0	1
Darlington	L	03/69	68	6	0	1

SOLANO Nolberto Albino (Nobby)
Born: Lima, Peru, 12 December, 1974 — RW
Peru: 88/Youth

League Club	Source	Date Signed	Seasons Played	Apps	Subs	Gls
Newcastle U	Boca Juniors (ARG)	08/98	98-03	158	14	29
Aston Villa	Tr	01/04	03-05	44	5	8
Newcastle U	Tr	08/05	05-07	52	6	8
West Ham U	Tr	08/07	07	14	9	4
Leicester C	Universitario (PER)	01/10	09	6	5	0
Hull C	Tr	07/10	10	6	5	0
Hartlepool U	Tr	07/11	11	11	3	2

SOLBAKKEN Stale
Born: Kongsvinger, Norway, 27 February, 1968 M
Norway: 58/U21-2

League Club	Source	Date Signed	Seasons Played	Apps	Subs	Gls
Wimbledon	Lillestrom (NOR)	10/97	97	4	2	1

SOLDADO Roberto
Born: Valencia, Spain, 27 May, 1985 F
Spain: 12/U21-9/Youth

League Club	Source	Date Signed	Seasons Played	Apps	Subs	Gls
Tottenham H	Valencia (SPN)	08/13	13-14	29	23	7

SOLEY Seyfo
Born: Lamin, Gambia, 16 February, 1980 DM
Gambia: 37

League Club	Source	Date Signed	Seasons Played	Apps	Subs	Gls
Preston NE	KRC Genk (BEL)	01/07	06	6	0	0

SOLEY Stephen (Steve)
Born: Widnes, Cheshire, England, 22 April, 1971 M

League Club	Source	Date Signed	Seasons Played	Apps	Subs	Gls
Portsmouth	Leek T	07/98	98	1	7	0
Macclesfield T	L	03/99	98	5	5	0
Carlisle U	Tr	08/99	99-01	75	8	16

SOLIS Mauricio Mora
Born: Heredia, Costa Rica, 13 December, 1972 DM
Costa Rica: 110

League Club	Source	Date Signed	Seasons Played	Apps	Subs	Gls
Derby Co	CS Heridiano (CRC)	03/97	96-97	3	8	0

SOLKHON Brett Michael
Born: Canvey Island, Essex, England, 12 September, 1982 M

League Club	Source	Date Signed	Seasons Played	Apps	Subs	Gls
Rushden & D	Arsenal (Jnr)	07/00	01-02	1	1	0

SOLLITT Adam James
Born: Sheffield, England, 22 June, 1977 G
England: Semi Pro-3

League Club	Source	Date Signed	Seasons Played	Apps	Subs	Gls
Barnsley	YT	07/95				
Northampton T	Kettering T	07/00	00-01	14	2	0
Rushden & D	Tr	08/02	02	3	0	0

SOLLY Christopher James (Chris)
Born: Rochester, Kent, England, 20 January, 1991 RB
England: Youth

League Club	Source	Date Signed	Seasons Played	Apps	Subs	Gls
Charlton Ath	Sch	07/08	08-14	148	15	2

SOLOMAN Jason Rafael
Born: Welwyn Garden City, Hertfordshire, England, 6 October, 1970 D/M
England: Youth

League Club	Source	Date Signed	Seasons Played	Apps	Subs	Gls
Watford	YT	12/88	90-94	79	21	5
Peterborough U	L	01/95	94	4	0	0
Wycombe W	Tr	03/95	94-95	11	2	1
Wrexham	Tr	08/96	96	2	0	0
Fulham	Tr	11/96	96	1	3	0

SOLSKJAER Ole Gunnar
Born: Kristiansund, Norway, 26 February, 1973 F
Norway: 67/U21-19

League Club	Source	Date Signed	Seasons Played	Apps	Subs	Gls
Manchester U	Molde FK (NOR)	07/96	96-06	151	84	91

SOLTVEDT Trond Egil
Born: Voss, Norway, 15 February, 1967 M
Norway: 4

League Club	Source	Date Signed	Seasons Played	Apps	Subs	Gls
Coventry C	Rosenborg (NOR)	07/97	97-98	47	10	3
Southampton	Tr	08/99	99-00	20	10	2
Sheffield Wed	Tr	02/01	00-02	74	0	2

SOMA Ragnvald
Born: Bryne, Norway, 10 November, 1979 D
Norway: 5/U21-22/Youth

League Club	Source	Date Signed	Seasons Played	Apps	Subs	Gls
West Ham U	Bryne (NOR)	01/01	00-01	3	4	0

SOMERFIELD Alfred George (Alf)
Born: South Kirkby, West Yorkshire, England, 22 March, 1918 CF
Died: Mansfield, Nottinghamshire, England, April, 1985

League Club	Source	Date Signed	Seasons Played	Apps	Subs	Gls
Mansfield T	Frickley Colliery	05/38	38	14	-	6
Wolverhampton W	Tr	03/39				
Wrexham	Chelmsford C	06/47	46	2	-	1
Crystal Palace	Tr	09/47	47	10	-	3

SOMERS Michael Robert (Micky)
Born: Nottingham, England, 27 February, 1945 LW

League Club	Source	Date Signed	Seasons Played	Apps	Subs	Gls
Chelsea	Nottingham F (Am)	11/62				
Torquay U	Tr	05/64	64-65	39	1	3
Hartlepool U	Tr	07/66	66-68	63	3	3

SOMMA Davide Enrico
Born: Johannesburg, South Africa, 26 March, 1985 F
South Africa: 3

League Club	Source	Date Signed	Seasons Played	Apps	Subs	Gls
Leeds U	San Jose E'quake (USA)	09/09	10-12	13	20	12
Chesterfield	L	11/09	09	1	2	0
Lincoln C	L	02/10	09	14	0	9

SOMMEIL David
Born: Point-a-Pitre, Guadeloupe, 10 August, 1974 CD
France: B-1//Guadeloupe: 8

League Club	Source	Date Signed	Seasons Played	Apps	Subs	Gls
Manchester C	Bordeaux (FRA)	01/03	02-05	47	2	4
Sheffield U	Tr	07/06	06	4	1	0

SOMMER Juergen Peterson
Born: New York, USA, 27 February, 1969 G
USA: 10

League Club	Source	Date Signed	Seasons Played	Apps	Subs	Gls
Luton T	Indiana Univ (USA)	09/91	93-95	82	0	0
Brighton & HA	L	11/91	91	1	0	0
Torquay U	L	10/92	92	10	0	0
Queens Park Rgrs	Tr	08/95	95-96	66	0	0

SOMNER Matthew James (Matt)
Born: Isleworth, W London, England, 8 December, 1982 DM
Wales: U21-2

League Club	Source	Date Signed	Seasons Played	Apps	Subs	Gls
Brentford	YT	07/01	00-04	72	12	1
Cambridge U	Tr	12/04	04	24	0	0
Bristol Rov	Tr	08/05	05	1	0	0
Notts Co	Aldershot T	06/06	06-07	47	7	1

SONG Alexandre Dimitri (Alex)
Born: Douala, Cameroon, 9 April, 1987 DM
Cameroon: 48

League Club	Source	Date Signed	Seasons Played	Apps	Subs	Gls
Arsenal	SC Bastia (FRA)	08/05	05-11	121	17	7
Charlton Ath	L	01/07	06	12	0	0
West Ham U (L)	Barcelona (SPN)	08/14	14	25	3	0

SONG Bahanag Rigobert (Rigobert)
Born: Eseka, Cameroon, 1 July, 1976 CD
Cameroon: 137

League Club	Source	Date Signed	Seasons Played	Apps	Subs	Gls
Liverpool	Salernitana (ITA)	01/99	98-00	27	7	0
West Ham U	Tr	11/00	00-01	23	1	0

SONGO'O Franck Steven
Born: Yaounde, Cameroon, 14 May, 1987 W
Cameroon: 1//France: Youth

League Club	Source	Date Signed	Seasons Played	Apps	Subs	Gls
Portsmouth	Barcelona Jnrs (SPN)	08/05	05-07	0	3	0
Bournemouth	L	10/06	06	3	1	0
Preston NE	L	03/07	06	4	2	0
Crystal Palace	L	10/07	07	9	0	0
Sheffield Wed	L	03/08	07	12	0	1

SONKO Edrissa (Eddy)
Born: Essau, Gambia, 23 March, 1980 RW
Gambia: 14

League Club	Source	Date Signed	Seasons Played	Apps	Subs	Gls
Walsall	Xanthi (GRE)	07/07	07	30	7	5
Tranmere Rov	Tr	07/08	08	29	9	5
Hereford U	Tr	09/09	09	5	5	0

SONKO Ibrahima (Ibu)
Born: Bignona, Senegal, 22 January, 1981 CD
Senegal: 4

League Club	Source	Date Signed	Seasons Played	Apps	Subs	Gls
Brentford	Grenoble (FRA)	08/02	02-03	79	1	8
Reading	Tr	07/04	04-08	122	5	8
Stoke C	Tr	08/08	08	7	7	0
Hull C	L	09/09	09	9	0	0
Portsmouth	L	07/10	10	16	7	1
Ipswich T	Tr	08/11	11	20	2	1

SONNER Daniel James (Danny)
Born: Wigan, Greater Manchester, England, 9 January, 1972 M
Northern Ireland: 13/B-4

League Club	Source	Date Signed	Seasons Played	Apps	Subs	Gls
Burnley	Wigan Ath (YT)	08/90	90-92	1	5	0
Bury	L	11/92	92	5	0	3
Ipswich T	Erzgebirge Aue (GER)	06/96	96-98	28	28	3
Sheffield Wed	Tr	10/98	98-99	42	11	3
Birmingham C	Tr	08/00	00-01	32	9	2
Walsall	Tr	08/02	02	20	4	4
Nottingham F	Tr	08/03	03	19	9	0
Peterborough U	Tr	08/04	04	11	4	0
Port Vale	L	02/05	04-06	71	4	2
Walsall	Tr	07/07	07	6	0	0
Wrexham	Port Vale (NC)	01/08	07	9	0	1

SOO Hong Ying (Frank)
Born: Buxton, Derbyshire, England, 12 March, 1914 RH
Died: Cheadle, Staffordshire, England, 25 January, 1991
England: War-9

League Club	Source	Date Signed	Seasons Played	Apps	Subs	Gls
Stoke C	Prescot Cables	01/33	33-38	173	-	5
Leicester C	Tr	09/45				
Luton T	Tr	07/46	46-47	71	-	4

SORDELL Marvin Anthony
Born: Pinner, NW London, England, 17 February, 1991 F
England: U21-14

League Club	Source	Date Signed	Seasons Played	Apps	Subs	Gls
Watford	Sch	07/09	09-11	51	24	21
Tranmere Rov	L	01/10	09	6	2	1

League Club	Source	Date Signed	Seasons Played	Apps	Subs	Gls
Bolton W	Tr	01/12	11-12	13	12	4
Charlton Ath	L	08/13	13	20	11	7
Burnley	Tr	06/14	14	2	12	0

SORENSEN Thomas Lovendal
Born: Fredericia, Denmark, 12 June, 1976 — G
Denmark: 101/B-1/U21-25

League Club	Source	Date Signed	Seasons Played	Apps	Subs	Gls
Sunderland	OB Odense (DEN)	08/98	98-02	171	0	0
Aston Villa	Tr	08/03	03-06	139	0	0
Stoke C	Tr	08/08	08-13	98	1	0

SORONDO Amaro Gonzalo (Gonzalo)
Born: Montevideo, Uruguay, 9 October, 1979 — CD
Uruguay: 27/Youth

League Club	Source	Date Signed	Seasons Played	Apps	Subs	Gls
Crystal Palace (L)	Inter Milan (ITA)	09/04	04	16	4	0
Charlton Ath	Inter Milan (ITA)	07/05	05-06	7	1	0

SORRELL Anthony Charles (Tony)
Born: Hornchurch, E London, England, 17 October, 1966 — M

League Club	Source	Date Signed	Seasons Played	Apps	Subs	Gls
Maidstone U	Bishops Stortford	08/88	89-90	46	9	8
Colchester U	Boston U	11/92	92	4	1	1
Barnet	Tr	02/93	92	8	0	2

SORRELL Dennis James
Born: Lambeth, S London, England, 7 October, 1940 — LH

League Club	Source	Date Signed	Seasons Played	Apps	Subs	Gls
Leyton Orient	Woodford T	10/57	58-60	37	-	1
Chelsea	Tr	02/62	61-63	3	-	0
Leyton Orient	Tr	09/64	64-66	74	0	3

SORVEL Neil Simon
Born: Widnes, Cheshire, England, 2 March, 1973 — M

League Club	Source	Date Signed	Seasons Played	Apps	Subs	Gls
Crewe Alex	YT	07/91	91	5	4	0
Macclesfield T	Tr	08/92	97-98	79	7	7
Crewe Alex	Tr	06/99	99-04	229	21	13
Shrewsbury T	Tr	07/05	05-06	59	4	5
Morecambe	Tr	01/07	07	14	8	0

SOUARE Pape N'Diaye
Born: Mbour, Senegal, 6 June, 1990 — LB
Senegal: 13/U23-4

League Club	Source	Date Signed	Seasons Played	Apps	Subs	Gls
Crystal Palace	Lille OSC (FRA)	01/15	14	7	2	0

SOUKOUNA Ladjie
Born: Paris, France, 15 December, 1990 — CD

League Club	Source	Date Signed	Seasons Played	Apps	Subs	Gls
Plymouth Arg	Creteil (FRA)	08/11	11	15	5	1

SOUNESS Graeme James
Born: Edinburgh, Scotland, 6 May, 1953 — M
Scotland: 54/U23-2/Schools

League Club	Source	Date Signed	Seasons Played	Apps	Subs	Gls
Tottenham H	App	05/70				
Middlesbrough	Tr	01/73	72-77	174	2	22
Liverpool	Tr	01/78	77-83	246	1	38

SOUTAR Timothy John (Tim)
Born: Oxford, England, 25 February, 1946 — IF

League Club	Source	Date Signed	Seasons Played	Apps	Subs	Gls
Brentford	Jnr	07/63	63	1	-	0

SOUTER Donald Davidson (Don)
Born: Hammersmith, W London, England, 1 December, 1961 — CD

League Club	Source	Date Signed	Seasons Played	Apps	Subs	Gls
Ipswich T	App	01/79				
Barnsley	Tr	08/82	82	19	2	0
Aldershot	Tr	08/83	83-84	45	0	0

SOUTER Ryan John
Born: Bedford, England, 5 February, 1978 — CD

League Club	Source	Date Signed	Seasons Played	Apps	Subs	Gls
Bury	Weston-super-Mare	01/99	98-99	2	3	0

SOUTER William (Bill)
Born: Dundee, Scotland, 3 May, 1931 — LB
Died: Chester, England, 24 August, 2012

League Club	Source	Date Signed	Seasons Played	Apps	Subs	Gls
Burnley	Broughty Ath	12/53				
Chester C	Tr	06/57	57-59	51	-	1

SOUTH Alexander William (Alex)
Born: Brighton, England, 7 July, 1931 — CH

League Club	Source	Date Signed	Seasons Played	Apps	Subs	Gls
Brighton & HA	Whitehawk BC	03/49	49-54	81	-	4
Liverpool	Tr	12/54	54	6	-	1
Halifax T	Tr	10/56	56-64	301	-	12

SOUTH John Alan
Born: Bow, E London, England, 30 November, 1952 — CD

League Club	Source	Date Signed	Seasons Played	Apps	Subs	Gls
Colchester U	Leyton Orient (Am)	07/72	72	4	0	0

SOUTH John Edward
Born: Lambeth, S London, England, 8 April, 1948 — CF

League Club	Source	Date Signed	Seasons Played	Apps	Subs	Gls
Brentford	Fulham (App)	11/66	66	1	0	0

SOUTHALL Leslie Nicholas (Nicky)
Born: Stockton-on-Tees, Cleveland, England, 28 January, 1972 — RW

League Club	Source	Date Signed	Seasons Played	Apps	Subs	Gls
Hartlepool U	Darlington (Jnr)	02/91	91-94	118	20	24
Grimsby T	Tr	07/95	95-97	55	17	6
Gillingham	Tr	12/97	97-00	141	13	17
Bolton W	Tr	07/01	01	10	8	1
Norwich C	L	09/02	02	4	5	0
Gillingham	Tr	12/02	02-04	86	6	2
Nottingham F	Tr	06/05	05-06	63	4	13
Gillingham	Tr	01/07	06-08	74	10	4

SOUTHALL Neville
Born: Llandudno, Conwy, Wales, 16 September, 1958 — G
Wales: 92

League Club	Source	Date Signed	Seasons Played	Apps	Subs	Gls
Bury	Winsford U	06/80	80	39	0	0
Everton	Tr	07/81	81-97	578	0	0
Port Vale	L	01/83	82	9	0	0
Southend U	L	12/97	97	9	0	0
Stoke C	Tr	02/98	97	12	0	0
Torquay U	Doncaster Rov	12/98	98-99	53	0	0
Bradford C	Tr	02/00	99	1	0	0

SOUTHALL Robert
Born: Rotherham, South Yorkshire, England, 10 May, 1922 — RH/IF
Died: Sheffield, England, 1979

League Club	Source	Date Signed	Seasons Played	Apps	Subs	Gls
Chesterfield	Rother Works	12/43	47-52	127	-	11

SOUTHAM Glen Andrew James
Born: Enfield, N London, England, 27 August, 1980 — M
England: Semi Pro-12

League Club	Source	Date Signed	Seasons Played	Apps	Subs	Gls
Dagenham & Red	Bishops Stortford	05/04	07-08	61	14	3
Hereford U	Tr	07/09	09	5	1	0
Barnet	Histon	06/10	10	31	2	1

SOUTHAM James Henry (Jack)
Born: Willenhall, West Midlands, England, 19 August, 1917 — FB
Died: Willenhall, West Midlands, England, 25 September, 1996

League Club	Source	Date Signed	Seasons Played	Apps	Subs	Gls
West Bromwich A	Shornhill Rec	12/42				
Newport Co	Tr	05/46	46	8	-	0
Birmingham C	Tr	11/46	47	1	-	0
Northampton T	Tr	06/49	49-54	145	-	1

SOUTHERN Keith William
Born: Gateshead, Tyne and Wear, England, 24 April, 1981 — M

League Club	Source	Date Signed	Seasons Played	Apps	Subs	Gls
Everton	YT	05/99				
Blackpool	Tr	08/02	02-11	292	38	25
Huddersfield T	Tr	07/12	12-13	32	7	2
Fleetwood T	Tr	06/14	14	1	1	0
Shrewsbury T	L	01/15	14	3	3	0

SOUTHEY Peter Charles
Born: Fulham, W London, England, 4 January, 1962 — FB
Died: Ham, SW London, England, 28 December, 1983

League Club	Source	Date Signed	Seasons Played	Apps	Subs	Gls
Tottenham H	App	10/79	79	1	0	0

SOUTHGATE Gareth
Born: Watford, Hertfordshire, England, 3 September, 1970 — CD
England: 57

League Club	Source	Date Signed	Seasons Played	Apps	Subs	Gls
Crystal Palace	YT	01/89	90-94	148	4	15
Aston Villa	Tr	07/95	95-00	191	0	7
Middlesbrough	Tr	07/01	01-05	160	0	4

SOUTHON Jamie Peter
Born: Dagenham, E London, England, 13 October, 1974 — M

League Club	Source	Date Signed	Seasons Played	Apps	Subs	Gls
Southend U	YT	07/93	92	0	1	0

SOUTHREN Thomas Cansfield (Tommy)
Born: Sunderland, England, 1 August, 1927 — RW
Died: Welwyn Garden City, Hertfordshire, England, 10 May, 2004

League Club	Source	Date Signed	Seasons Played	Apps	Subs	Gls
West Ham U	Peartree OB, Welwyn GC	12/49	50-53	64	-	3
Aston Villa	Tr	12/54	54-58	63	-	6
Bournemouth	Tr	10/58	58-59	64	-	11

SOUTHWELL Aubrey Allen
Born: Grantham, Lincolnshire, England, 21 August, 1921 — RB
Died: West Bridgford, Nottinghamshire, England, 9 February, 2005

League Club	Source	Date Signed	Seasons Played	Apps	Subs	Gls
Notts Co	Nottingham F (Am)	12/44	46-56	328	-	2

SOUZA Dennis
Born: Sao Paulo, Brazil, 9 January, 1980 — RB

League Club	Source	Date Signed	Seasons Played	Apps	Subs	Gls
Barnsley	RSC Charleroi (BEL)	08/07	07-08	77	1	2
Doncaster Rov	Al-Saliya (QAT)	11/10	10	3	5	0

SOW Mamadou
Born: Paris, France, 22 August, 1981 — LW

League Club	Source	Date Signed	Seasons Played	Apps	Subs	Gls
Torquay U	Villemomble (FRA)	08/05	05	9	2	0

SOWAH Lennard Adjetey
Born: Hamburg, Germany, 23 August, 1992 — LB
Germany: Youth

League Club	Source	Date Signed	Seasons Played	Apps	Subs	Gls
Portsmouth	Sch	-	09	3	2	0

SOWDEN Maurice
Born: Doncaster, South Yorkshire, England, 21 October, 1954 — M

League Club	Source	Date Signed	Seasons Played	Apps	Subs	Gls
Scunthorpe U	App	10/72	72	3	0	0

SOWDEN Peter Tasker (Paddy)
Born: Bradford, England, 1 May, 1929 — IF
Died: Cambridge, England, 12 November, 2010

League Club	Source	Date Signed	Seasons Played	Apps	Subs	Gls
Blackpool	Jnr	06/47				
Hull C	Bacup Bor	09/48				
Aldershot	Elgin C	10/50	50	4	-	0
Hull C	Tr	08/51				
Gillingham	Tr	08/52	52-55	134	-	27
Accrington Stan	Tr	09/56	56-57	54	-	13
Wrexham	Tr	06/58	58-59	38	-	4

SOWDEN William (Billy)
Born: Manchester, England, 8 December, 1930 — CF
Died: Stockport, Greater Manchester, England, 13 November, 2010

League Club	Source	Date Signed	Seasons Played	Apps	Subs	Gls
Manchester C	Greenwood Victoria	04/49	52-53	11	-	2
Chesterfield	Tr	11/54	54-56	97	-	59
Stockport Co	Tr	06/57	57	15	-	7

SOWERBY William Henry Roy
Born: Hull, England, 31 August, 1932 — IF
Died: Leeds, England, June, 2014

League Club	Source	Date Signed	Seasons Played	Apps	Subs	Gls
Wolverhampton W	Pilkington Rec	05/50				
Grimsby T	Tr	01/54	53-54	12	-	1

SPACKMAN Nigel James
Born: Romsey, Hampshire, England, 2 December, 1960 — DM

League Club	Source	Date Signed	Seasons Played	Apps	Subs	Gls
Bournemouth	Andover	05/80	80-82	118	1	10
Chelsea	Tr	06/83	83-86	139	2	12
Liverpool	Tr	02/87	86-88	39	12	0
Queens Park Rgrs	Tr	02/89	88-89	27	2	1
Chelsea	Glasgow Rangers	09/92	92-95	60	7	0
Sheffield U	Tr	06/96	96	19	4	0

SPALDING William (Bill)
Born: Glasgow, Scotland, 24 November, 1926 — RW
Died: Bristol, England, 18 December, 1999

League Club	Source	Date Signed	Seasons Played	Apps	Subs	Gls
Bristol C	Ballymena U	01/50	49-50	10	-	0

SPANN Silvio Reinaldo
Born: Couva, Trinidad, 21 August, 1981 — M
Trinidad & Tobago: 41

League Club	Source	Date Signed	Seasons Played	Apps	Subs	Gls
Wrexham	West Connection (TRD)	08/07	07	7	2	1

SPARHAM Sean Ricky
Born: Bexley, SE London, England, 4 December, 1968 — LB

League Club	Source	Date Signed	Seasons Played	Apps	Subs	Gls
Millwall	Jnr	05/87	87-89	22	6	0
Brentford	L	03/90	89	5	0	1

SPARK Alexander McAlpine (Alex)
Born: Stenhousemuir, Falkirk, Scotland, 16 October, 1949 — CD

League Club	Source	Date Signed	Seasons Played	Apps	Subs	Gls
Preston NE	Jnr	11/66	67-75	207	18	6
Bradford C	Motherwell	12/76	76-77	32	2	0

SPARKS Christopher James (Chris)
Born: Islington, N London, England, 22 May, 1960 — RB

League Club	Source	Date Signed	Seasons Played	Apps	Subs	Gls
Crystal Palace	App	11/77				
Reading	L	08/79	79	3	0	0

SPARROW Brian Edward
Born: Bethnal Green, E London, England, 24 June, 1962 — LB

League Club	Source	Date Signed	Seasons Played	Apps	Subs	Gls
Arsenal	App	02/80	83	2	0	0
Wimbledon	L	01/83	82	17	0	1
Millwall	L	12/83	83	5	0	2
Gillingham	L	01/84	83	5	0	1
Crystal Palace	Tr	07/84	84-86	62	1	2

SPARROW John Paul
Born: Bethnal Green, E London, England, 3 June, 1957 — LB
England: Youth/Schools

League Club	Source	Date Signed	Seasons Played	Apps	Subs	Gls
Chelsea	App	08/74	73-79	63	6	2
Millwall	L	03/79	78	7	0	0
Exeter C	Tr	01/81	80-82	62	1	3

SPARROW Matthew Ronald (Matt)
Born: Wembley, NW London, England, 3 October, 1981 — M

League Club	Source	Date Signed	Seasons Played	Apps	Subs	Gls
Scunthorpe U	YT	07/01	99-09	275	61	37
Brighton & HA	Tr	07/10	10-11	36	11	6
Crawley T	Tr	01/13	12	13	4	3
Scunthorpe U	Tr	07/13	13-14	26	9	4
Cheltenham T	L	02/15	14	11	0	1

SPARROW Paul
Born: Wandsworth, SW London, England, 24 March, 1975 — RB

League Club	Source	Date Signed	Seasons Played	Apps	Subs	Gls
Crystal Palace	YT	07/93	95	1	0	0
Preston NE	Tr	03/96	95-97	20	0	0
Rochdale	Tr	07/98	98	21	4	2

SPAVIN Alan
Born: Lancaster, England, 20 February, 1942 — M

League Club	Source	Date Signed	Seasons Played	Apps	Subs	Gls
Preston NE	Jnr	08/59	60-73	411	6	26
Preston NE	Washington Dip's (USA)	11/77	77-78	3	4	0

SPEAK Christopher (Chris)
Born: Preston, Lancashire, England, 20 August, 1973 — FB

League Club	Source	Date Signed	Seasons Played	Apps	Subs	Gls
Blackpool	Jnr	07/92	92	0	1	0

SPEAKMAN Robert (Rob)
Born: Swansea, Wales, 5 December, 1980 — F

League Club	Source	Date Signed	Seasons Played	Apps	Subs	Gls
Exeter C	YT	07/99	98-00	4	15	3

SPEAKMAN Samuel (Sammy)
Born: Huyton, Merseyside, England, 27 January, 1934 — LW

League Club	Source	Date Signed	Seasons Played	Apps	Subs	Gls
Bolton W		09/51				
Middlesbrough	Tr	07/53				
Tranmere Rov	Tr	09/54	54-55	68	-	9

SPEARE James Peter Vincent (Jamie)
Born: Liverpool, England, 5 November, 1976 — G

League Club	Source	Date Signed	Seasons Played	Apps	Subs	Gls
Everton	YT	07/95				
Darlington	Tr	03/97	96	3	0	0

SPEARING Anthony (Tony)
Born: Romford, E London, England, 7 October, 1964 — LB
England: Youth

League Club	Source	Date Signed	Seasons Played	Apps	Subs	Gls
Norwich C	App	08/82	83-87	67	2	0
Stoke C	L	11/84	84	9	0	0
Oxford U	L	02/85	84	5	0	0
Leicester C	Tr	07/88	88-90	71	2	1
Plymouth Arg	Tr	07/91	91-92	35	0	0
Peterborough U	Tr	01/93	92-96	105	6	2

SPEARING Jay Francis
Born: Wallasey, Wirral, England, 25 November, 1988 — M

League Club	Source	Date Signed	Seasons Played	Apps	Subs	Gls
Liverpool	Sch	08/06	09-11	26	4	0
Leicester C	L	03/10	09	6	1	1
Bolton W	L	08/12	12	36	1	2
Bolton W	Tr	08/13	13-14	60	6	3
Blackburn Rov	L	01/15	14	12	3	1

SPEARRITT Edward Alfred (Eddie)
Born: Lowestoft, Suffolk, England, 31 January, 1947 — LB/M

League Club	Source	Date Signed	Seasons Played	Apps	Subs	Gls
Ipswich T	App	02/65	65-68	62	10	13
Brighton & HA	Tr	01/69	68-73	203	7	22
Carlisle U	Tr	06/74	74-75	29	2	1
Gillingham	Tr	08/76	76	19	0	1

SPEARS Alan Frederick
Born: Amble, Northumberland, England, 27 December, 1938 — LW
England: Schools

League Club	Source	Date Signed	Seasons Played	Apps	Subs	Gls
Newcastle U	Jnr	02/56				
Millwall	Tr	06/60	60-62	31	-	6
Lincoln C	Tr	07/63	63	2	-	0

SPECTOR Jonathan Michael Paul
Born: Chicago, Illinois, USA, 1 March, 1986 — D/M
USA: 34/Youth

League Club	Source	Date Signed	Seasons Played	Apps	Subs	Gls
Manchester U	Chicago Fire (USA)	11/03	04	2	1	0
Charlton Ath	L	07/05	05	13	7	0
West Ham U	Tr	06/06	06-10	66	35	1
Birmingham C	Tr	08/11	11-14	98	8	0

SPECTOR Miles David
Born: Hendon, N London, England, 4 August, 1934 — LW
England: Amateur-1/Youth

League Club	Source	Date Signed	Seasons Played	Apps	Subs	Gls
Chelsea (Am)	Jnr	05/52	52-53	3	-	0
Millwall (Am)	Hendon	05/56	56	1	-	0

SPEDDING Duncan
Born: Camberley, Surrey, England, 7 September, 1977 — LB/M

League Club	Source	Date Signed	Seasons Played	Apps	Subs	Gls
Southampton	YT	05/96	97	4	3	0
Northampton T	Tr	07/98	98-02	107	16	2

SPEDDING Thomas William (Billy)
Born: Tynemouth, Tyne and Wear, England, 8 December, 1925 — CH
Died: Northumberland, England, October, 2014

League Club	Source	Date Signed	Seasons Played	Apps	Subs	Gls
Doncaster Rov	Alnwick T	03/49	48	1	-	0

SPEED Gary Andrew
Born: Hawarden, Flintshire, Wales, 8 September, 1969 — M
Died: Chester, England, 27 November, 2011
Wales: 85/U21-3/Youth

League Club	Source	Date Signed	Seasons Played	Apps	Subs	Gls
Leeds U	YT	06/88	88-95	231	17	39
Everton	Tr	07/96	96-97	58	0	16
Newcastle U	Tr	02/98	97-03	206	7	29
Bolton W	Tr	07/04	04-07	115	6	14
Sheffield U	Tr	01/08	07-08	37	0	6

SPEED Leslie (Les)
Born: Caergwrle, Flintshire, Wales, 3 October, 1923 — FB/WH
Died: Ruabon, Wrexham, Wales, 5 June, 2012

League Club	Source	Date Signed	Seasons Played	Apps	Subs	Gls
Wrexham	Llandudno	04/45	46-54	211	-	0

SPEEDIE David Robert
Born: Glenrothes, Fife, Scotland, 20 February, 1960 — F
Scotland: 10/U21-1

League Club	Source	Date Signed	Seasons Played	Apps	Subs	Gls
Barnsley	Jnr	10/78	78-79	10	13	0
Darlington	Tr	06/80	80-81	88	0	21
Chelsea	Tr	06/82	82-86	155	7	47
Coventry C	Tr	07/87	87-90	121	1	31
Liverpool	Tr	02/91	90	8	4	6
Blackburn Rov	Tr	08/91	91	34	2	23
Southampton	Tr	07/92	92	11	0	0
Birmingham C	L	10/92	92	10	0	2
West Bromwich A	L	01/93	92	7	0	2
West Ham U	L	03/93	92	11	0	4
Leicester C	Tr	07/93	93	37	0	12

SPEIGHT Jake Carl
Born: Sheffield, England, 28 September, 1983 — F

League Club	Source	Date Signed	Seasons Played	Apps	Subs	Gls
Bury	Scarborough	11/05	05-06	7	23	2
Bradford C	Mansfield T	07/10	10	13	15	4
Port Vale	L	11/10	10	1	3	1
Mansfield T	Wrexham	07/12	13	1	7	1

SPEIGHT Martyn Stephen ●
Born: Stockton-on-Tees, Cleveland, England, 26 July, 1978 — CD

League Club	Source	Date Signed	Seasons Played	Apps	Subs	Gls
Doncaster Rov	YT	07/96	95	1	0	0

SPEIGHT Michael (Mick)
Born: Upton, West Yorkshire, England, 1 November, 1951 — M
England: B-4

League Club	Source	Date Signed	Seasons Played	Apps	Subs	Gls
Sheffield U	App	05/69	71-79	184	15	14
Blackburn Rov	Tr	07/80	80-81	50	1	4
Grimsby T	Tr	08/82	82-83	35	3	2
Chester C	Tr	08/84	84-85	40	0	1

SPEIRS Walter Gardner (Gardner)
Born: Airdrie, Lanarkshire, Scotland, 14 April, 1963 — M
Scotland: Youth

League Club	Source	Date Signed	Seasons Played	Apps	Subs	Gls
Hartlepool U	St Mirren	08/89	89	0	1	0

SPELMAN Isaac
Born: Newcastle-upon-Tyne, England, 9 March, 1914 — RH
Died: Newcastle-upon-Tyne, England, April, 2003

League Club	Source	Date Signed	Seasons Played	Apps	Subs	Gls
Leeds U	Usworth Colliery	03/33				
Southend U	Tr	05/35	35-36	43	-	3
Tottenham H	Tr	05/37	37-38	28	-	2
Hartlepool U	Tr	05/46	46	25	-	0

SPELMAN Michael Thomas (Mike)
Born: Newcastle-upon-Tyne, England, 8 December, 1950 — M
England: Schools

League Club	Source	Date Signed	Seasons Played	Apps	Subs	Gls
Wolverhampton W	Whitley Bay	11/69				
Watford	Tr	08/71				
Hartlepool U	Tr	10/71	71-76	115	6	4
Darlington	L	12/72	72	4	0	0

SPELMAN Ronald Edward (Ron)
Born: Blofield, Norfolk, England, 22 May, 1938 — RW
Died: Norwich, England, June, 2006

League Club	Source	Date Signed	Seasons Played	Apps	Subs	Gls
Norwich C	City of Norwich SOBU	08/56	57-60	2	-	0
Northampton T	Tr	11/60	60-61	33	-	3
Bournemouth	Tr	03/62	61-63	28	-	4
Watford	Tr	09/63	63-64	40	-	3
Oxford U	Tr	05/65	65	15	1	1

SPENCE Alan Nicholson
Born: Seaham, County Durham, England, 7 February, 1940 — IF
England: Youth

League Club	Source	Date Signed	Seasons Played	Apps	Subs	Gls
Sunderland	Murton Colliery Jnrs	05/57	57	5	-	1
Darlington	Tr	06/60	60-61	24	-	11
Southport	Tr	07/62	62-68	225	5	98
Oldham Ath	Tr	12/68	68-69	26	1	12
Chester C	Tr	12/69	69	5	4	2

SPENCE Colin
Born: Glasgow, Scotland, 7 January, 1960 — F

League Club	Source	Date Signed	Seasons Played	Apps	Subs	Gls
Crewe Alex	App	02/78	76-78	10	8	1

SPENCE Derek William
Born: Belfast, Northern Ireland, 18 January, 1952 — F
Northern Ireland: 29

League Club	Source	Date Signed	Seasons Played	Apps	Subs	Gls
Oldham Ath	Crusaders	09/70	71-72	5	1	0
Bury	Tr	02/73	72-76	140	0	44
Blackpool	Tr	10/76	76	24	3	3
Blackpool	Olympiakos (GRE)	08/78	78-79	58	0	18
Southend U	Tr	12/79	79-81	100	4	32
Bury	Hong Kong Rgrs (HKG)	08/83	83	9	4	1

SPENCE Jordan James
Born: Woodford, NE London, England, 24 May, 1990 — RB
England: U21-1/Youth

League Club	Source	Date Signed	Seasons Played	Apps	Subs	Gls
West Ham U	Sch	07/07	09-12	2	5	0
Leyton Orient	L	11/08	08	20	0	0
Scunthorpe U	L	08/09	09	9	0	0
Bristol C	L	03/11	10	11	0	0
Bristol C	L	08/11	11	9	1	0
Sheffield Wed	L	08/13	13	4	0	0
MK Dons	Tr	10/13	13-14	62	5	2

SPENCE Joseph Lown (Joe)
Born: Salford, England, 13 October, 1925 — CH
Died: Chesterfield, Derbyshire, England, December, 2009

League Club	Source	Date Signed	Seasons Played	Apps	Subs	Gls
Chesterfield	Buxton	01/48				
York C	Tr	07/50	50-53	110	-	0

SPENCE Joseph William (Bill)
Born: Hartlepool, Cleveland, England, 10 January, 1926 — CH

League Club	Source	Date Signed	Seasons Played	Apps	Subs	Gls
Portsmouth	Fleet Air Arm	03/47	49-50	19	-	0
Queens Park Rgrs	Tr	12/51	51-53	56	-	0

SPENCE Lewwis Gavin
Born: Kennington, S London, England, 29 October, 1987 — M

League Club	Source	Date Signed	Seasons Played	Apps	Subs	Gls
Crystal Palace	Sch	07/06	06	1	1	0
Wycombe W	Tr	07/08	08	21	9	2

SPENCE Mason Kendle
Born: Milton Keynes, England, 20 November, 1994 — FB
Wales: Youth

League Club	Source	Date Signed	Seasons Played	Apps	Subs	Gls
Colchester U	MK Dons (Sch)	07/13	13	0	1	0

SPENCE Richard (Dickie)
Born: Hoyland, South Yorkshire, England, 18 July, 1908 — W
Died: Ealing, W London, England, March, 1983
England: 2

League Club	Source	Date Signed	Seasons Played	Apps	Subs	Gls
Barnsley	Thorpe Colliery	02/33	32-34	64	-	25
Chelsea	Tr	10/34	34-47	221	-	62

SPENCE Ronald (Ron)
Born: Spennymoor, County Durham, England, 7 January, 1927 — LH
Died: Doncaster, South Yorkshire, England, 24 April, 1996

League Club	Source	Date Signed	Seasons Played	Apps	Subs	Gls
York C	Rossington Main	03/48	47-58	280	-	25

SPENCER Anthony Raymond (Tony)
Born: Chiswick, W London, England, 23 April, 1965 — LB

League Club	Source	Date Signed	Seasons Played	Apps	Subs	Gls
Brentford	App	04/83	81-83	17	1	0
Aldershot	L	12/84	84	10	0	0

SPENCER Damian Michael
Born: Windsor, Berkshire, England, 19 September, 1981 — F

League Club	Source	Date Signed	Seasons Played	Apps	Subs	Gls
Bristol C	YT	06/00	99-00	8	5	1
Exeter C	L	03/01	00	2	4	0
Cheltenham T	Tr	08/02	02-08	120	104	35
Brentford	L	03/09	08	3	2	1
Aldershot T	Kettering T	03/10	09-10	12	18	4

SPENCER Derek
Born: Coventry, England, 10 January, 1931 — G
Died: Coventry, England, February, 1989

League Club	Source	Date Signed	Seasons Played	Apps	Subs	Gls
Coventry C	Lockheed Leamington	12/51	51-52	20	-	0

SPENCER Harold John
Born: Burnley, Lancashire, England, 30 April, 1919 — D
Died: Burnley, Lancashire, England, 19 May, 2003

League Club	Source	Date Signed	Seasons Played	Apps	Subs	Gls
Burnley	Jnr	09/37	46	4	-	1
Wrexham	Tr	07/50	50	11	-	0

SPENCER James Christopher
Born: Leeds, England, 13 December, 1991 — F

League Club	Source	Date Signed	Seasons Played	Apps	Subs	Gls
Huddersfield T	Sch	01/09	12	0	1	0
Morecambe	L	07/10	10	20	12	8
Cheltenham T	L	07/11	11	27	14	10
Brentford	L	10/12	12	0	2	0
Scunthorpe U	L	08/13	13	5	8	1
Notts Co	Tr	02/14	13-14	21	1	6

SPENCER James Matthew
Born: Stockport, Greater Manchester, England, 11 April, 1985 — G

League Club	Source	Date Signed	Seasons Played	Apps	Subs	Gls
Stockport Co	Sch	04/02	01-06	90	1	0
Rochdale	Tr	06/07	07	20	0	0
Chester C	L	04/09	08	5	0	0

SPENCER John
Born: Glasgow, Scotland, 11 September, 1970 — F
Scotland: 14/U21-3/Youth/Schools

League Club	Source	Date Signed	Seasons Played	Apps	Subs	Gls
Chelsea	Glasgow Rangers	08/92	92-96	75	28	36
Queens Park Rgrs	Tr	11/96	96-97	47	1	22
Everton	Tr	03/98	97-98	5	4	0

SPENCER John Raymond
Born: Bradfield, South Yorkshire, England, 20 November, 1934 — IF

Died: Sheffield, England, 22 August, 2007
England: Youth

League Club	Source	Date Signed	Seasons Played	Apps	Subs	Gls
Sheffield U	Jnr	06/54	54-56	24	-	10

SPENCER John Shepherd (Jack)
Born: Bacup, Lancashire, England, 24 August, 1920 IF
Died: Burnley, Lancashire, England, 1 August, 1966

League Club	Source	Date Signed	Seasons Played	Apps	Subs	Gls
Burnley	Bacup U	06/48	48-50	37	-	8
Accrington Stan	Tr	06/51	51	29	-	7

SPENCER Leslie (Les)
Born: Manchester, England, 16 September, 1936 IF
Died: Sale, Greater Manchester, England, 4 April, 2012

League Club	Source	Date Signed	Seasons Played	Apps	Subs	Gls
Rochdale		01/58	57-59	74	-	17
Luton T	Tr	07/60	60	7	-	1

SPENCER Raymond (Ray)
Born: Birmingham, England, 25 March, 1933 WH
England: Schools

League Club	Source	Date Signed	Seasons Played	Apps	Subs	Gls
Aston Villa	Jnr	06/50				
Darlington	Tr	03/58	57-60	97	-	5
Torquay U	Tr	06/61	61-63	59	-	1

SPENCER Scott Kernaghan
Born: Oldham, Greater Manchester, England, 1 January, 1989 F

League Club	Source	Date Signed	Seasons Played	Apps	Subs	Gls
Everton	Oldham Ath (Sch)	06/06				
Macclesfield T	L	03/08	07	0	3	0
Rochdale	Tr	08/09	09	0	4	0
Southend U	Tr	01/10	09-10	6	11	4
Lincoln C	Tr	01/11	10	2	8	0

SPENCER Simon Dean
Born: Islington, N London, England, 10 September, 1976 M

League Club	Source	Date Signed	Seasons Played	Apps	Subs	Gls
Tottenham H	YT	07/95				
Brentford	Tr	07/97	97	1	0	0

SPENCER Thomas Hannah (Tommy)
Born: Glasgow, Scotland, 28 November, 1945 CH/CF

League Club	Source	Date Signed	Seasons Played	Apps	Subs	Gls
Southampton	Glasgow Celtic	07/65	65	3	0	0
York C	Tr	06/66	66-67	54	3	21
Workington	Tr	03/68	67-71	167	0	10
Lincoln C	Tr	01/72	71-73	67	7	10
Rotherham U	Tr	07/74	74-77	137	1	10

SPENDER Simon
Born: Mold, Flintshire, Wales, 15 November, 1985 RB
Wales: U21-6/Youth

League Club	Source	Date Signed	Seasons Played	Apps	Subs	Gls
Wrexham	Sch	08/05	03-07	82	15	5

SPERONI Julian Maria
Born: Buenos Aires, Argentina, 18 May, 1979 G
Argentina: Youth

League Club	Source	Date Signed	Seasons Played	Apps	Subs	Gls
Crystal Palace	Dundee	07/04	04-14	356	1	0

SPERREVIK Tim
Born: Bergen, Norway, 1 January, 1976 F

League Club	Source	Date Signed	Seasons Played	Apps	Subs	Gls
Hartlepool U	Fana IL (NOR)	08/00	00	4	11	1

SPERRIN Martyn Robin
Born: Edmonton, N London, England, 6 December, 1956 F

League Club	Source	Date Signed	Seasons Played	Apps	Subs	Gls
Luton T	Edgware T	10/77	77	0	1	0

SPERRIN William Thomas (Billy)
Born: Wood Green, N London, England, 9 April, 1922 IF
Died: Sawbridgeworth, Hertfordshire, England, 21 June, 2000

League Club	Source	Date Signed	Seasons Played	Apps	Subs	Gls
Brentford	Guildford C	09/49	49-55	90	-	27

SPERRING George Burgess
Born: Epsom, Surrey, England, 30 April, 1935 CF

League Club	Source	Date Signed	Seasons Played	Apps	Subs	Gls
Gillingham (Am)	RAF Halton	07/55	55	1	-	0

SPERTI Francesco (Franco)
Born: Rome, Italy, 28 January, 1955 FB

League Club	Source	Date Signed	Seasons Played	Apps	Subs	Gls
Swindon T	App	01/73	73	1	0	0

SPICER Edwin Warren (Eddie)
Born: Liverpool, England, 20 September, 1922 FB
Died: Rhyl, Denbighshire, Wales, 25 December, 2004
England: Schools

League Club	Source	Date Signed	Seasons Played	Apps	Subs	Gls
Liverpool	Jnr	10/39	46-53	158	-	2

SPICER John William
Born: Romford, E London, England, 13 September, 1983 M
England: Youth

League Club	Source	Date Signed	Seasons Played	Apps	Subs	Gls
Arsenal	YT	07/01				
Bournemouth	Tr	09/04	04-05	43	0	6
Burnley	Tr	08/05	05-07	31	38	4
Doncaster Rov	Tr	07/08	08-09	35	15	1
Leyton Orient	L	03/10	09	9	0	1
Notts Co	Tr	07/10	10-11	15	9	2
Southend U	Tr	08/12	12	10	3	0

SPIEGEL Raphael Simon
Born: Solothurn, Switzerland, 19 December, 1992 G
Switzerland: U21-3/Youth

League Club	Source	Date Signed	Seasons Played	Apps	Subs	Gls
West Ham U	G'hopper Zurich (SUI)	07/12				
Carlisle U	L	02/15	14	2	0	0

SPIERS George Smyth
Born: Belfast, Northern Ireland, 3 September, 1941 LW

League Club	Source	Date Signed	Seasons Played	Apps	Subs	Gls
Exeter C	Crusaders	08/63	63	5	-	0

SPIERS Richard Alan Jesse (Dick)
Born: Benson, Oxfordshire, England, 27 November, 1937 CH
Died: Bullingdon, Oxfordshire, England, 22 October, 2000

League Club	Source	Date Signed	Seasons Played	Apps	Subs	Gls
Reading	Cholsey U	10/55	55-69	451	2	3

SPIESS Fabian
Born: Wesel, Germany, 30 November, 1993 G

League Club	Source	Date Signed	Seasons Played	Apps	Subs	Gls
Notts Co	Sch	06/12	11-13	7	2	0

SPILLANE Michael Edward
Born: Jersey, Channel Islands, 23 March, 1989 D/M
Republic of Ireland: U21-7/Youth

League Club	Source	Date Signed	Seasons Played	Apps	Subs	Gls
Norwich C	Sch	07/06	05-09	20	6	1
Luton T	L	08/08	08	35	4	3
Brentford	Tr	07/10	10-11	18	7	1
Dagenham & Red	Tr	11/11	11-12	53	0	8
Southend U	Tr	01/13	12	9	0	0

SPILLER Daniel (Danny)
Born: Maidstone, Kent, England, 10 October, 1981 M

League Club	Source	Date Signed	Seasons Played	Apps	Subs	Gls
Gillingham	YT	07/00	01-06	88	41	6
Millwall	Tr	07/07	07-08	6	2	1
Wycombe W	Tr	08/09				
Dagenham & Red	Tr	09/09	09	7	3	0
Gillingham	Tr	08/10	10-11	29	16	4

SPINK Anthony Arthur (Tony)
Born: Doncaster, South Yorkshire, England, 16 November, 1929 CF
Died: Eastbourne, East Sussex, England, 7 February, 2011

League Club	Source	Date Signed	Seasons Played	Apps	Subs	Gls
Sheffield Wed		12/49				
Chester C	Tr	06/50	51-52	13	-	3
Workington	Weymouth	07/55				
Sunderland	Tr	12/55				
Tranmere Rov	Tr	06/56	56	7	-	3

SPINK Dean Peter
Born: Birmingham, England, 22 January, 1967 F

League Club	Source	Date Signed	Seasons Played	Apps	Subs	Gls
Aston Villa	Halesowen T	07/89				
Scarborough	L	11/89	89	3	0	2
Bury	L	02/90	89	6	0	1
Shrewsbury T	Tr	03/90	89-96	244	29	52
Wrexham	Tr	07/97	97-99	72	13	9
Shrewsbury T	L	11/99	99	1	3	0

SPINK Nigel Philip
Born: Chelmsford, England, 8 August, 1958 G
England: 1/B-2/FLge

League Club	Source	Date Signed	Seasons Played	Apps	Subs	Gls
Aston Villa	Chelmsford C	01/77	79-95	357	4	0
West Bromwich A	Tr	01/96	95-96	19	0	0
Millwall	Tr	09/97	97-99	44	0	0

SPINKS Henry Charles
Born: Great Yarmouth, Norfolk, England, 1 February, 1920 CF
Died: Norwich, England, 5 February, 2005

League Club	Source	Date Signed	Seasons Played	Apps	Subs	Gls
Norwich C (Am)	Norwich CEYMS	12/46	46	2	-	1

SPINNER Terence James (Terry)
Born: Woking, Surrey, England, 6 November, 1953 F
England: Schools

League Club	Source	Date Signed	Seasons Played	Apps	Subs	Gls
Southampton	App	07/71	72-73	1	1	0
Walsall	Tr	07/74	74-75	10	6	5

SPIRING Peter John
Born: Glastonbury, Somerset, England, 13 December, 1950 M/F
England: Youth

League Club	Source	Date Signed	Seasons Played	Apps	Subs	Gls
Bristol C	Jnr	06/68	69-72	58	5	16
Liverpool	Tr	03/73				
Luton T	Tr	11/74	74-75	12	3	2
Hereford U	Tr	02/76	75-82	205	22	20

SPITTLE Paul David
Born: Wolverhampton, England, 16 December, 1964 M

League Club	Source	Date Signed	Seasons Played	Apps	Subs	Gls
Oxford U	App	10/82				
Crewe Alex	Tr	08/83	83	4	2	1

SPOFFORTH David John
Born: York, England, 21 March, 1969 D

League Club	Source	Date Signed	Seasons Played	Apps	Subs	Gls
York C	Jnr	07/87	87	3	0	0

SPOONER Nicholas Michael (Nicky)
Born: Manchester, England, 5 June, 1971 — RB

League Club	Source	Date Signed	Seasons Played	Apps	Subs	Gls
Bolton W	YT	07/89	91-94	22	1	2
Oldham Ath	L	10/98	98	2	0	0
Chester C	Charleston Bat'y (USA)	11/99	99	9	0	0

SPOONER Stephen Alan (Steve)
Born: Sutton, S London, England, 25 January, 1961 — M

League Club	Source	Date Signed	Seasons Played	Apps	Subs	Gls
Derby Co	App	12/78	78-81	7	1	0
Halifax T	Tr	12/81	81-82	71	1	13
Chesterfield	Tr	07/83	83-85	89	4	14
Hereford U	Tr	07/86	86-87	84	0	19
York C	Tr	07/88	88-89	72	0	11
Rotherham U	Tr	07/90	90	15	4	1
Mansfield T	Tr	03/91	90-92	55	3	3
Blackpool	Tr	02/93	92	2	0	0
Chesterfield	Tr	10/93	93-94	11	1	0

SPRAGGON Frank
Born: Marley Hill, Tyne and Wear, England, 27 October, 1945 — D

League Club	Source	Date Signed	Seasons Played	Apps	Subs	Gls
Middlesbrough	App	11/62	63-75	277	3	3
Hartlepool U	Minnesota Kicks (USA)	11/76	76	1	0	0

SPRAGUE Martyn Leslie
Born: Risca, Caerphilly, Wales, 10 April, 1949 — LB

League Club	Source	Date Signed	Seasons Played	Apps	Subs	Gls
Newport Co	Lovells Ath	08/68	69-73	155	1	1

SPRAKE Gareth (Gary)
Born: Swansea, Wales, 3 April, 1945 — G
Wales: 37/U23-5

League Club	Source	Date Signed	Seasons Played	Apps	Subs	Gls
Leeds U	App	05/62	61-72	380	0	0
Birmingham C	Tr	10/73	73-74	16	0	0

SPRATLEY Alan Sidney
Born: Maidenhead, Berkshire, England, 5 June, 1949 — G

League Club	Source	Date Signed	Seasons Played	Apps	Subs	Gls
Queens Park Rgrs	App	05/67	68-72	29	0	0
Swindon T	Tr	07/73	73	7	0	0

SPRATT Graham William
Born: Leicester, England, 17 July, 1939 — G

League Club	Source	Date Signed	Seasons Played	Apps	Subs	Gls
Coventry C	Oadby T	12/56	57-58	28	-	0

SPRATT Thomas (Tommy)
Born: Cambois, Northumberland, England, 20 December, 1941 — IF
England: Youth/Schools

League Club	Source	Date Signed	Seasons Played	Apps	Subs	Gls
Manchester U	Jnr	12/59				
Bradford Park Ave	Tr	02/61	60-63	118	-	45
Torquay U	Weymouth	07/65	65-66	60	1	19
Workington	Tr	01/67	66-67	51	1	14
York C	Tr	03/68	67-68	26	3	1
Workington	Tr	03/69	68-71	141	2	26
Stockport Co	Tr	06/72	72-73	65	0	6

SPRAY James Kenneth Michael Tony
Born: Halesowen, West Midlands, England, 2 December, 1992 — F

League Club	Source	Date Signed	Seasons Played	Apps	Subs	Gls
Wolverhampton W	Sch	12/09				
Accrington Stan	L	10/11	11	3	0	0

SPRIDGEON Frederick Arthur (Fred)
Born: Swansea, Wales, 13 July, 1935 — RB

League Club	Source	Date Signed	Seasons Played	Apps	Subs	Gls
Leeds U	Jnr	08/52				
Crewe Alex	Tr	07/56	56	7	-	0

SPRIGGS Stephen (Steve)
Born: Armthorpe, South Yorkshire, England, 16 February, 1956 — M

League Club	Source	Date Signed	Seasons Played	Apps	Subs	Gls
Huddersfield T	App	02/73	74	2	2	0
Cambridge U	Tr	07/75	75-86	411	5	58
Middlesbrough	L	03/87	86	3	0	0

SPRING Andrew John (Andy)
Born: Gateshead, Tyne and Wear, England, 17 November, 1965 — D

League Club	Source	Date Signed	Seasons Played	Apps	Subs	Gls
Coventry C	App	11/83	83-84	3	2	0
Bristol Rov	Tr	07/85	85	18	1	0
Cardiff C	L	10/85	85	1	0	0

SPRING Matthew John
Born: Harlow, Essex, England, 17 November, 1979 — M

League Club	Source	Date Signed	Seasons Played	Apps	Subs	Gls
Luton T	YT	07/97	97-03	243	7	25
Leeds U	Tr	07/04	04	4	9	1
Watford	Tr	08/05	05-06	38	7	8
Luton T	Tr	01/07	06-07	58	0	10
Sheffield U	L	08/08	08	8	3	1
Charlton Ath	Tr	01/09	08-09	19	6	2
Leyton Orient	Tr	07/10	10-11	80	0	6
Wycombe W	Tr	07/12	12-13	21	9	0

SPRINGETT Peter John
Born: Fulham, W London, England, 8 May, 1946 — G
Died: Sheffield, England, 30 September, 1997
England: U23-6/Youth

League Club	Source	Date Signed	Seasons Played	Apps	Subs	Gls
Queens Park Rgrs	App	05/63	62-66	137	0	0
Sheffield Wed	Tr	05/67	67-74	180	0	0
Barnsley	Tr	07/75	75-79	191	0	0

SPRINGETT Ronald Derrick (Ron)
Born: Fulham, W London, England, 22 July, 1935 — G
Died: London, England, 12 September, 2015
England: 33/FLge-9

League Club	Source	Date Signed	Seasons Played	Apps	Subs	Gls
Queens Park Rgrs	Victoria U	02/53	55-57	88	-	0
Sheffield Wed	Tr	03/58	57-66	345	0	0
Queens Park Rgrs	Tr	06/67	67-68	45	0	0

SPRINGTHORPE Terence Alfred (Terry)
Born: Draycott, Derbyshire, England, 4 December, 1923 — LB
Died: Ottery St Mary, Devon, England, 19 July, 2006
USA: 2

League Club	Source	Date Signed	Seasons Played	Apps	Subs	Gls
Wolverhampton W	Jnr	12/40	47-49	35	-	0
Coventry C	Tr	12/50	50	12	-	0

SPROATES Alan
Born: Houghton-le-Spring, Tyne and Wear, England, 30 June, 1944 — M
Died: California, USA, 5 February, 2015

League Club	Source	Date Signed	Seasons Played	Apps	Subs	Gls
Sunderland	Jnr	07/61				
Swindon T	Tr	08/63	63-64	3	-	0
Darlington	Tr	09/65	65-73	304	11	17
Scunthorpe U	Tr	08/74	74	19	5	0

SPROATES John
Born: Houghton-le-Spring, Tyne and Wear, England, 11 April, 1943 — WH
Died: County Durham, England, 7 February, 2006

League Club	Source	Date Signed	Seasons Played	Apps	Subs	Gls
Barnsley	West Auckland T	12/63	63	2	-	0

SPROSON Philip Jesse (Phil)
Born: Stoke-on-Trent, England, 13 October, 1959 — CD

League Club	Source	Date Signed	Seasons Played	Apps	Subs	Gls
Port Vale	Jnr	12/77	77-88	422	4	33
Birmingham C	Tr	07/89	89	12	0	0

SPROSON Roy
Born: Stoke-on-Trent, England, 23 September, 1930 — CH
Died: Stoke-on-Trent, England, January, 1997

League Club	Source	Date Signed	Seasons Played	Apps	Subs	Gls
Port Vale	Stoke C (Am)	07/49	50-71	755	5	30

SPROSTON Bert
Born: Elworth, Cheshire, England, 22 June, 1915 — RB
Died: Bolton, Greater Manchester, England, 27 January, 2000
England: 11/FLge-4/War-2

League Club	Source	Date Signed	Seasons Played	Apps	Subs	Gls
Leeds U	Sandbach Ramblers	06/33	33-37	130	-	1
Tottenham H	Tr	06/38	38	9	-	0
Manchester C	Tr	11/38	38-49	125	-	5

SPROSTON Neil Robert
Born: Dudley, West Midlands, England, 20 November, 1970 — CD

League Club	Source	Date Signed	Seasons Played	Apps	Subs	Gls
Birmingham C	YT	07/89	87	0	1	0

SPROULE Ivan
Born: Omagh, Tyrone, Northern Ireland, 18 February, 1981 — LW
Northern Ireland: 11

League Club	Source	Date Signed	Seasons Played	Apps	Subs	Gls
Bristol C	Hibernian	07/07	07-10	61	58	6
Yeovil T	L	11/10	10	2	0	0
Notts Co	L	03/11	10	4	1	0

SPRUCE David George (George)
Born: Chester, England, 3 April, 1923 — CD
Died: Chester, England, October, 1998

League Club	Source	Date Signed	Seasons Played	Apps	Subs	Gls
Wrexham	Heath Rgrs	10/48	48-51	135	-	3
Barnsley	Tr	05/52	52-56	149	-	0
Chester C	Tr	07/58	58-60	63	-	0

SPRUCE Philip Thomas (Phil)
Born: Chester, England, 16 November, 1929 — D
Died: Chesterfield, Derbyshire, England, August, 2010

League Club	Source	Date Signed	Seasons Played	Apps	Subs	Gls
Wrexham	Heath Rgrs	11/50	51-55	23	-	0

SPUHLER John Oswald (Johnny)
Born: Sunderland, England, 18 September, 1917 — RW/CF
Died: Middlesbrough, England, 7 January, 2007
England: Schools

League Club	Source	Date Signed	Seasons Played	Apps	Subs	Gls
Sunderland	Jnr	09/34	36-38	35	-	5
Middlesbrough	Tr	10/45	46-53	216	-	69
Darlington	Tr	06/54	54-55	67	-	19

SPURDLE William (Bill)
Born: St Peter Port, Guernsey, Channel Islands, 28 January, 1926 — WH/IF
Died: Guernsey, Channel Islands, 16 June, 2011

League Club	Source	Date Signed	Seasons Played	Apps	Subs	Gls
Oldham Ath	Jnr	03/48	47-49	56	-	5
Manchester C	Tr	01/50	49-56	160	-	32
Port Vale	Tr	11/56	56	21	-	7
Oldham Ath	Tr	06/57	57-62	144	-	19

SPURR Thomas (Tommy)
Born: Leeds, England, 13 September, 1987 — LB

League Club	Source	Date Signed	Seasons Played	Apps	Subs	Gls
Sheffield Wed	Sch	07/06	05-10	186	6	5
Doncaster Rov	Tr	06/11	11-12	65	0	1
Blackburn Rov	Tr	08/13	13-14	53	2	3

SQUILLACI Sebastien
Born: Toulon, France, 11 August, 1980 — CD
France: 21

League Club	Source	Date Signed	Seasons Played	Apps	Subs	Gls
Arsenal	Sevilla (SPN)	08/10	10-11	20	3	1

SQUIRE Michael Richard (Mike)
Born: Poole, Dorset, England, 18 October, 1963 — F
England: Schools

League Club	Source	Date Signed	Seasons Played	Apps	Subs	Gls
Fulham	Jnr	07/82				
Torquay U	Dorchester T	02/84	83	12	1	3

SQUIRES Alan
Born: Fleetwood, Lancashire, England, 26 February, 1923 — LB
Died: Morecambe, Lancashire, England, 3 January, 2007

League Club	Source	Date Signed	Seasons Played	Apps	Subs	Gls
Preston NE		12/44				
Carlisle U	Tr	12/46	46-47	24	-	0

SQUIRES Barry
Born: Birmingham, England, 29 July, 1931 — LW

League Club	Source	Date Signed	Seasons Played	Apps	Subs	Gls
Birmingham C	Lye T	05/53	53	1	-	0
Bradford C	Tr	06/54	54	7	-	0

SQUIRES Frank
Born: Swansea, Wales, 8 March, 1921 — IF
Died: Swansea, Wales, 1 March, 1988
Wales: War-2

League Club	Source	Date Signed	Seasons Played	Apps	Subs	Gls
Swansea C	Jnr	05/38	46-47	36	-	5
Plymouth Arg	Tr	10/47	47-49	86	-	13
Grimsby T	Tr	07/50	50	36	-	2

SQUIRES James Alexander (Jamie)
Born: Preston, Lancashire, England, 15 November, 1975 — CD

League Club	Source	Date Signed	Seasons Played	Apps	Subs	Gls
Preston NE	YT	04/94	93-96	24	7	0
Mansfield T	L	08/97	97	1	0	0
Carlisle U	Dunfermline Ath	08/00	00	2	3	0

SQUIRES Robert
Born: Selby, North Yorkshire, England, 6 April, 1919 — LH
Died: Salisbury, Wiltshire, England, 21 March, 2011

League Club	Source	Date Signed	Seasons Played	Apps	Subs	Gls
Doncaster Rov	Selby T	09/37	47	21	-	0
Exeter C	Tr	07/49	49	1	-	0

SRNICEK Pavel
Born: Ostrava, Czech Republic, 10 March, 1968 — G
Czech Republic: 49

League Club	Source	Date Signed	Seasons Played	Apps	Subs	Gls
Newcastle U	Banik Ostrava (CZE)	02/91	90-97	148	1	0
Sheffield Wed	Banik Ostrava (CZE)	11/98	98-99	44	0	0
Portsmouth	Brescia (ITA)	09/03	03	3	0	0
West Ham U	L	02/04	03	2	1	0
Newcastle U	Beira Mar (POR)	10/06	06	1	1	0

STABB Christopher John (Chris)
Born: Bradford, England, 12 October, 1976 — CD

League Club	Source	Date Signed	Seasons Played	Apps	Subs	Gls
Bradford C	YT	07/95	94	1	0	0

STABB George Herbert
Born: Paignton, Devon, England, 26 September, 1912 — CF
Died: Bradford, England, 11 December, 1994

League Club	Source	Date Signed	Seasons Played	Apps	Subs	Gls
Torquay U	Dartmouth U	09/31	31-34	93	-	44
Notts Co	Tr	10/34	34	24	-	5
Port Vale	Tr	07/35	35-36	32	-	9
Bradford Park Ave	Tr	09/36	36-46	94	-	4

STACEY Jack William
Born: Windsor, Berkshire, England, 6 April, 1996 — M/RB

League Club	Source	Date Signed	Seasons Played	Apps	Subs	Gls
Reading	Sch	12/13	14	2	4	0

STACEY Stephen Darrow (Steve)
Born: Bristol, England, 27 August, 1944 — FB

League Club	Source	Date Signed	Seasons Played	Apps	Subs	Gls
Bristol C	App	11/61				
Wrexham	Tr	02/66	65-68	101	4	6
Ipswich T	Tr	09/68	68	3	0	0
Chester C	L	12/69	69	1	0	0
Charlton Ath	L	01/70	69	1	0	1
Bristol C	Tr	09/70	70	9	0	0
Exeter C	Tr	09/71	71-72	57	2	0

STACEY Steven John Anthony (Steve)
Born: Bristol, England, 9 June, 1975 — FB

League Club	Source	Date Signed	Seasons Played	Apps	Subs	Gls
Torquay U	YT	10/93	93	1	0	0

STACEY Terence John (Terry)
Born: Mitcham, S London, England, 28 September, 1936 — RB
England: Amateur-6

League Club	Source	Date Signed	Seasons Played	Apps	Subs	Gls
Plymouth Arg	Carshalton Ath	05/59	59-61	22	-	0
Watford	Tr	07/62				
Gillingham	Tr	08/63	63-64	17	-	0

STACK Graham Christopher
Born: Hampstead, NW London, England, 26 September, 1981 — G
Republic of Ireland: U21-7/Youth

League Club	Source	Date Signed	Seasons Played	Apps	Subs	Gls
Arsenal	YT	07/00				
Millwall	L	07/04	04	25	1	0
Reading	Tr	07/05	05	1	0	0
Leeds U	L	10/06	06	12	0	0
Wolverhampton W	L	08/07	07	0	2	0
Plymouth Arg	Tr	07/08	08	5	0	0
Barnet	Hibernian	08/12	12	42	0	0

STACK William John
Born: Liverpool, England, 17 January, 1948 — LW

League Club	Source	Date Signed	Seasons Played	Apps	Subs	Gls
Crystal Palace	Jnr	01/65	65	2	0	0

STACKMAN Harry Scott (Scott)
Born: Arizona, USA, 16 November, 1975 — CD

League Club	Source	Date Signed	Seasons Played	Apps	Subs	Gls
Northampton T	YT	08/94	93	0	1	0

STAFF David Steven
Born: Market Harborough, Leicestershire, England, 8 November, 1979 — F

League Club	Source	Date Signed	Seasons Played	Apps	Subs	Gls
Boston U	King's Lynn	08/04	04	0	5	0

STAFF Paul
Born: Brancepeth, County Durham, England, 30 August, 1962 — W

League Club	Source	Date Signed	Seasons Played	Apps	Subs	Gls
Hartlepool U	App	08/80	79-83	88	10	14
Aldershot	Tr	08/84	84-85	25	12	11

STAFFORD Andrew Grant (Andy)
Born: Stretford, Greater Manchester, England, 28 October, 1960 — LW

League Club	Source	Date Signed	Seasons Played	Apps	Subs	Gls
Halifax T	Blackburn Rov (NC)	01/79	78-80	33	8	1
Stockport Co	Tr	08/81	81	21	4	1
Rochdale	Tr	08/82	82	1	0	1

STAFFORD Clive Andrew
Born: Ipswich, England, 4 April, 1963 — LB

League Club	Source	Date Signed	Seasons Played	Apps	Subs	Gls
Colchester U	Diss T	02/89	88-89	31	2	0
Exeter C	L	02/90	89	2	0	0

STAFFORD Ellis
Born: Sheffield, England, 17 August, 1929 — RB
Died: Peterborough, England, 29 October, 2007

League Club	Source	Date Signed	Seasons Played	Apps	Subs	Gls
Peterborough U	Scarborough	07/54	60-62	17	-	0

STAFYLIDIS Konstantinos (Kostas)
Born: Thessalonika, Greece, 2 December, 1993 — LB
Greece: 5/U21-10/Youth

League Club	Source	Date Signed	Seasons Played	Apps	Subs	Gls
Fulham (L)	Bayer Leverkusen (GER)	07/14	14	34	4	0

STAGG William (Billy)
Born: Ealing, W London, England, 17 October, 1957 — W

League Club	Source	Date Signed	Seasons Played	Apps	Subs	Gls
Brentford	App	-	74	4	0	0

STAINROD Simon Allan
Born: Sheffield, England, 1 February, 1959 — F
England: Youth

League Club	Source	Date Signed	Seasons Played	Apps	Subs	Gls
Sheffield U	App	07/76	75-78	59	8	14
Oldham Ath	Tr	03/79	78-80	69	0	21
Queens Park Rgrs	Tr	11/80	80-84	143	2	48
Sheffield Wed	Tr	02/85	84-85	8	7	2
Aston Villa	Tr	09/85	85-87	58	5	16
Stoke C	Tr	12/87	87-88	27	1	6

STAINSBY John
Born: Barnsley, South Yorkshire, England, 25 September, 1937 — CF
Died: Barnsley, South Yorkshire, England, September, 2000

League Club	Source	Date Signed	Seasons Played	Apps	Subs	Gls
Barnsley	Wath W	12/55	59-60	34	-	12
York C	Tr	07/61	61-62	69	-	21
Stockport Co	Tr	07/63	63	5	-	0

STAINTON Bryan Edward
Born: Scampton, Lincolnshire, England, 8 January, 1942 — D

League Club	Source	Date Signed	Seasons Played	Apps	Subs	Gls
Lincoln C	Ingham FC	03/62	61-65	25	1	0

STAINTON James Kenneth (Jim)
Born: Sheffield, England, 14 December, 1931 — RB
Died: Haywards Heath, West Sussex, England, December, 2009

League Club	Source	Date Signed	Seasons Played	Apps	Subs	Gls
Bradford Park Ave		04/53				
Mansfield T	Tr	08/54	55-56	9	-	0

STAINWRIGHT David Peter (Dave)
Born: Nottingham, England, 13 June, 1948 — F

League Club	Source	Date Signed	Seasons Played	Apps	Subs	Gls
Nottingham F	App	08/65	65-66	4	3	1
Doncaster Rov	Tr	07/68	68	1	1	0
York C	Tr	07/69	69	6	2	1

STALKER Alan
Born: Ponteland, Northumberland, England, 18 March, 1939 — G

League Club	Source	Date Signed	Seasons Played	Apps	Subs	Gls
Gateshead (Am)	Bishop Auckland	05/58	58	4	-	0

STALKER John Alexander Hastie Inglis
Born: Musselburgh, East Lothian, Scotland, 12 March, 1959 — F

League Club	Source	Date Signed	Seasons Played	Apps	Subs	Gls
Leicester C		07/79				
Darlington	Tr	10/79	79-82	107	9	36
Hartlepool U	Tr	01/83	82	3	1	0

STALLARD Mark
Born: Derby, England, 24 October, 1974 — F

League Club	Source	Date Signed	Seasons Played	Apps	Subs	Gls
Derby Co	YT	11/91	91-95	19	8	2
Fulham	L	09/94	94	4	0	3
Bradford C	Tr	01/96	95-96	33	10	10
Preston NE	L	02/97	96	4	0	1
Wycombe W	Tr	03/97	96-98	67	3	23
Notts Co	Tr	03/99	98-03	168	17	67
Barnsley	Tr	01/04	03-04	10	5	1
Chesterfield	L	10/04	04	7	2	2
Notts Co	L	02/05	04	16	0	3
Shrewsbury T	Tr	07/05	05	25	12	6
Lincoln C	Tr	07/06	06-07	55	11	17

STALTERI Paul Andrew
Born: Toronto, Canada, 18 October, 1977 — RB
Canada: 84

League Club	Source	Date Signed	Seasons Played	Apps	Subs	Gls
Tottenham H	Werder Bremen (GER)	07/05	05-07	37	5	2
Fulham	L	01/08	07	13	0	0

STAM Jakob (Jaap)
Born: Kampen, Netherlands, 17 July, 1972 — CD
Netherlands: 67

League Club	Source	Date Signed	Seasons Played	Apps	Subs	Gls
Manchester U	PSV Eindhoven (NED)	07/98	98-01	79	0	1

STAM Ronald Teodorus (Ronnie)
Born: Breda, Netherlands, 18 June, 1984 — RB

League Club	Source	Date Signed	Seasons Played	Apps	Subs	Gls
Wigan Ath	FC Twente (NED)	08/10	10-12	41	21	1

STAM Stefan
Born: Amersfoort, Netherlands, 14 September, 1979 — CD

League Club	Source	Date Signed	Seasons Played	Apps	Subs	Gls
Oldham Ath	Huizen (NED)	02/05	04-08	84	13	1
Yeovil T	Tr	07/09	09-10	21	0	1
Hereford U	Tr	03/11	10-11	31	3	0

STAMBOULI Benjamin
Born: Marseille, France, 13 August, 1990 — DM
France: U21-14

League Club	Source	Date Signed	Seasons Played	Apps	Subs	Gls
Tottenham H	Montpellier (FRA)	09/14	14	4	8	0

STAMP Darryn Michael
Born: Hessle, East Riding of Yorkshire, England, 21 September, 1978 — F

League Club	Source	Date Signed	Seasons Played	Apps	Subs	Gls
Scunthorpe U	Pontefract Collieries	07/97	97-00	18	39	6
Halifax T	L	02/00	99	5	0	0
Northampton T	Scarborough	05/02	02	12	10	4
Chester C	Tr	08/03	04	2	2	0
Kidderminster Hrs	L	11/04	04	4	0	1

STAMP Neville
Born: Reading, England, 7 July, 1981 — M/D

League Club	Source	Date Signed	Seasons Played	Apps	Subs	Gls
Reading	YT	06/99	98	0	1	0
York C	Tr	10/00	00-01	17	3	0

STAMP Philip Lawrence (Phil)
Born: Middlesbrough, England, 12 December, 1975 — M
England: Youth

League Club	Source	Date Signed	Seasons Played	Apps	Subs	Gls
Middlesbrough	YT	02/93	93-01	75	41	6
Millwall	L	09/01	01	0	1	0
Darlington	Heart of Midlothian	10/05	05	5	3	1

STAMPER Frank Fielden Thorpe
Born: Hartlepool, Cleveland, England, 22 February, 1926 — LH/IF
Died: Hartlepool, Cleveland, England, July, 1999

League Club	Source	Date Signed	Seasons Played	Apps	Subs	Gls
Hartlepool U	Colchester U	08/49	49-57	301	-	26

STAMPS John David (Jackie)
Born: Rotherham, South Yorkshire, England, 2 December, 1918 — CF
Died: Burton-on-Trent, Staffordshire, England, 19 November, 1991

League Club	Source	Date Signed	Seasons Played	Apps	Subs	Gls
Mansfield T	Silverwood Colliery	10/37	37	1	-	0
New Brighton	Tr	08/38	38	12	-	5
Derby Co	Tr	01/39	38-53	233	-	100
Shrewsbury T	Tr	12/53	53	22	-	4

STAMPS Scott
Born: Birmingham, England, 20 March, 1975 — LB

League Club	Source	Date Signed	Seasons Played	Apps	Subs	Gls
Torquay U	YT	07/93	92-96	80	6	5
Colchester U	Tr	03/97	96-98	52	4	1
Kidderminster Hrs	Tr	09/99	00-03	123	6	0

STANBRIDGE George
Born: Campsall, South Yorkshire, England, 28 March, 1920 — FB
Died: Doncaster, South Yorkshire, England, 27 June, 1973

League Club	Source	Date Signed	Seasons Played	Apps	Subs	Gls
Rotherham U		11/38	46-48	36	-	1
Aldershot	Tr	06/49	49	15	-	0

STANCLIFFE Paul Ian
Born: Sheffield, England, 5 May, 1958 — CD

League Club	Source	Date Signed	Seasons Played	Apps	Subs	Gls
Rotherham U	App	03/76	75-82	285	0	7
Sheffield U	Tr	08/83	83-90	278	0	12
Rotherham U	L	09/90	90	5	0	0
Wolverhampton W	Tr	11/90	90	17	0	0
York C	Tr	07/91	91-94	89	2	3

STANDEN James Alfred (Jim)
Born: Edmonton, N London, England, 30 May, 1935 — G

League Club	Source	Date Signed	Seasons Played	Apps	Subs	Gls
Arsenal	Rickmansworth T	04/53	57-60	35	-	0
Luton T	Tr	10/60	60-62	36	-	0
West Ham U	Tr	11/62	62-67	178	0	0
Millwall	Detroit Cougars (USA)	10/68	68-69	8	0	0
Portsmouth	Tr	07/70	70-71	13	0	0

STANDING John Robert
Born: Walberton, West Sussex, England, 3 September, 1943 — RB

League Club	Source	Date Signed	Seasons Played	Apps	Subs	Gls
Brighton & HA	Bognor Regis T	12/61	61-62	10	-	0

STANDING Michael John
Born: Shoreham-by-Sea, West Sussex, England, 20 March, 1981 — M
England: Youth/Schools

League Club	Source	Date Signed	Seasons Played	Apps	Subs	Gls
Aston Villa	YT	03/98				
Bradford C	Tr	03/02	02-03	16	14	2
Walsall	Tr	05/04	04-05	37	15	4
Chesterfield	Tr	09/06				
Bournemouth	Queens Park Rgrs (NC)	03/07	06	0	1	0

STANDLEY Thomas Leslie (Tommy)
Born: Poplar, E London, England, 23 December, 1932 — WH

League Club	Source	Date Signed	Seasons Played	Apps	Subs	Gls
Queens Park Rgrs	Basildon U	05/57	57	15	-	2
Bournemouth	Tr	11/58	58-64	159	-	5

STANFORD Edward John (Eddie)
Born: Blackburn, Greater Manchester, England, 4 February, 1985 — M/LB

League Club	Source	Date Signed	Seasons Played	Apps	Subs	Gls
Coventry C	Sch	-	02	0	1	0

STANIC Mario
Born: Sarajevo, Bosnia & Herzegovina, 10 April, 1972 — M
Croatia: 49/U21-2//Yugoslavia: 2

League Club	Source	Date Signed	Seasons Played	Apps	Subs	Gls
Chelsea	Parma (ITA)	07/00	00-03	39	20	7

STANIFORTH David Albry (Dave)
Born: Chesterfield, Derbyshire, England, 6 October, 1950 — F

League Club	Source	Date Signed	Seasons Played	Apps	Subs	Gls
Sheffield U	App	05/68	68-73	22	4	3
Bristol Rov	Tr	03/74	73-78	135	18	31
Bradford C	Tr	06/79	79-81	107	8	25
Halifax T	Tr	07/82	82-83	66	3	21

STANIFORTH Gordon
Born: Hull, England, 23 March, 1957 — F
England: Schools

League Club	Source	Date Signed	Seasons Played	Apps	Subs	Gls
Hull C	App	04/74	73-76	7	5	2
York C	Tr	12/76	76-79	128	0	33
Carlisle U	Tr	10/79	79-82	118	8	33
Plymouth Arg	Tr	03/83	82-84	87	4	19
Newport Co	Tr	08/85	85-86	84	3	13
York C	Tr	10/87	87	15	4	1

STANIFORTH Ronald (Ron)
Born: Manchester, England, 13 April, 1924 — RB
Died: Barrow, Cumbria, England, 5 October, 1988
England: 8/B-3

League Club	Source	Date Signed	Seasons Played	Apps	Subs	Gls
Stockport Co	Newton A	10/46	46-51	223	-	1
Huddersfield T	Tr	05/52	52-54	110	-	0
Sheffield Wed	Tr	07/55	55-58	102	-	2
Barrow	Tr	10/59	59-60	38	-	0

STANISLAS Felix Junior (Junior)
Born: Eltham, SE London, England, 26 November, 1989 — W
England: U21-2/Youth

League Club	Source	Date Signed	Seasons Played	Apps	Subs	Gls
West Ham U	Sch	07/07	08-11	22	20	6
Southend U	L	11/08	08	6	0	1
Burnley	Tr	08/11	11-13	59	34	7
Bournemouth	Tr	06/14	14	6	7	1

STANISLAUS Roger Edmund Philbert
Born: Hammersmith, W London, England, 2 November, 1968 — LB

League Club	Source	Date Signed	Seasons Played	Apps	Subs	Gls
Arsenal	App	07/86				
Brentford	Tr	09/87	87-89	109	2	4
Bury	Tr	07/90	90-94	167	9	5
Leyton Orient	Tr	07/95	95	20	1	0

STANLEY Craig
Born: Bedworth, Warwickshire, England, 3 March, 1983 M
England: Semi Pro-4

League Club	Source	Date Signed	Seasons Played	Apps	Subs	Gls
Walsall	Sch	07/02				
Morecambe	Hereford U	07/06	07-10	115	12	13
Torquay U	L	01/11	10	19	0	1
Bristol Rov	Tr	07/11	11	30	4	1
Aldershot T	Tr	07/12	12	5	0	1

STANLEY Garry Ernest
Born: Burton-on-Trent, Staffordshire, England, 4 March, 1954 M

League Club	Source	Date Signed	Seasons Played	Apps	Subs	Gls
Chelsea	App	03/71	75-78	105	4	15
Everton	Tr	08/79	79-80	52	0	1
Swansea C	Tr	10/81	81-83	60	12	4
Portsmouth	Tr	01/84	83-85	43	4	1
Bristol C	Wichita Wings (USA)	08/88	88	8	2	0

STANLEY Graham
Born: Sheffield, England, 27 January, 1938 RH
Died: Bolton, Greater Manchester, England, 14 January, 1997

League Club	Source	Date Signed	Seasons Played	Apps	Subs	Gls
Bolton W	Jnr	10/55	56-63	141	-	3
Tranmere Rov	Tr	07/65	65	0	1	1

STANLEY Patrick Joseph (Pat)
Born: Dublin, Republic of Ireland, 9 March, 1938 RB

League Club	Source	Date Signed	Seasons Played	Apps	Subs	Gls
Leeds U	Jnr	03/55				
Halifax T	Tr	05/58	58-62	118	-	1

STANLEY Terence James (Terry)
Born: Brighton, England, 2 January, 1951 M/FB

League Club	Source	Date Signed	Seasons Played	Apps	Subs	Gls
Brighton & HA	Lewes	11/69	69-70	16	6	0

STANLEY Thomas (Tommy)
Born: Hemsworth, West Yorkshire, England, 7 December, 1962 M

League Club	Source	Date Signed	Seasons Played	Apps	Subs	Gls
York C	App	12/80	80-82	14	4	0

STANNARD James David (Jim)
Born: Harold Hill, E London, England, 16 October, 1962 G

League Club	Source	Date Signed	Seasons Played	Apps	Subs	Gls
Fulham	Ford U	06/80	80-84	41	0	0
Southend U	L	09/84	84	6	0	0
Charlton Ath	L	02/85	84	1	0	0
Southend U	Tr	03/85	84-86	103	0	0
Fulham	Tr	08/87	87-94	348	0	1
Gillingham	Tr	08/95	95-98	106	0	0

STANNERS Walter (Wally)
Born: Bo'ness, Falkirk, Scotland, 2 January, 1921 G
Died: Rochdale, Greater Manchester, England, April, 2010

League Club	Source	Date Signed	Seasons Played	Apps	Subs	Gls
Bournemouth	Bo'ness U	07/47	47	3	-	0
Rochdale	Tr	08/49	49	5	-	0

STANSBRIDGE Leonard Edward Charles (Len)
Born: Southampton, England, 19 February, 1919 G
Died: Southampton, England, 19 May, 1986

League Club	Source	Date Signed	Seasons Played	Apps	Subs	Gls
Southampton	Jnr	08/36	37-51	48	-	0

STANSFIELD Adam
Born: Tiverton, Devon, England, 10 September, 1978 F
Died: Exeter, England, 10 August, 2010
England: Semi Pro-5

League Club	Source	Date Signed	Seasons Played	Apps	Subs	Gls
Yeovil T	Elmore	11/01	03	7	25	6
Exeter C	Hereford U	06/06	08-09	51	13	17

STANSFIELD Frederick (Fred)
Born: Cardiff, Wales, 12 December, 1917 CH
Died: Cardiff, Wales, 30 March, 2014
Wales: 1

League Club	Source	Date Signed	Seasons Played	Apps	Subs	Gls
Cardiff C	Grange Ath	08/43	46-48	106	-	1
Newport Co	Tr	09/49	49	21	-	0

STANSFIELD James Edward
Born: Dewsbury, West Yorkshire, England, 18 September, 1978 CD

League Club	Source	Date Signed	Seasons Played	Apps	Subs	Gls
Huddersfield T	YT	07/97				
Halifax T	Tr	07/98	98-00	24	2	1

STANT Philip Richard (Phil)
Born: Bolton, Greater Manchester, England, 13 October, 1962 F

League Club	Source	Date Signed	Seasons Played	Apps	Subs	Gls
Reading	Camberley T	08/82	82	3	1	2
Hereford U	Army	11/86	86-88	83	6	38
Notts Co	Tr	07/89	89	14	8	6
Blackpool	L	09/90	90	12	0	5
Lincoln C	L	11/90	90	4	0	0
Huddersfield T	L	01/91	90	5	0	1
Fulham	Tr	02/91	90	19	0	5
Mansfield T	Tr	08/91	91-92	56	1	32
Cardiff C	Tr	12/92	92-94	77	2	34
Mansfield T	L	08/93	93	4	0	1
Bury	Tr	01/95	94-96	49	13	23
Northampton T	L	11/96	96	4	1	2
Lincoln C	Tr	12/96	96-99	42	22	20
Brighton & HA	Tr	03/01	00	0	7	1

STANTON Brian
Born: Liverpool, England, 7 February, 1956 M

League Club	Source	Date Signed	Seasons Played	Apps	Subs	Gls
Bury	New Brighton	10/75	76-78	72	11	13
Huddersfield T	Tr	09/79	79-85	199	10	45
Wrexham	L	03/86	85	8	0	0
Rochdale	Morecambe	12/86	86-87	42	7	4

STANTON Nathan
Born: Nottingham, England, 6 May, 1981 CD
England: Youth

League Club	Source	Date Signed	Seasons Played	Apps	Subs	Gls
Scunthorpe U	YT	03/99	97-05	215	22	0
Rochdale	Tr	07/06	06-09	138	1	0
Burton A	Tr	08/10	10-12	60	3	1

STANTON Sidney Horley (Sid)
Born: Dudley, West Midlands, England, 16 June, 1923 WH
Died: Dudley, West Midlands, England, 30 February, 2005

League Club	Source	Date Signed	Seasons Played	Apps	Subs	Gls
Birmingham C		03/46				
Northampton T	Tr	07/46	47-48	7	-	0

STANTON Thomas (Tom)
Born: Glasgow, Scotland, 3 May, 1948 M/FB
Scotland: Schools

League Club	Source	Date Signed	Seasons Played	Apps	Subs	Gls
Liverpool	Jnr	05/65				
Arsenal	Tr	09/66				
Mansfield T	Tr	09/67	67	37	0	1
Bristol Rov	Tr	07/68	68-75	160	12	7

STAPLES Leonard Eric (Len)
Born: Leicester, England, 23 January, 1926 RB
Died: Barrow, Cumbria, England, 2 September, 2008
England: Schools

League Club	Source	Date Signed	Seasons Played	Apps	Subs	Gls
Leicester C	Jnr	07/47				
Newport Co	Tr	08/49	49-56	164	-	2

STAPLETON Francis Anthony (Frank)
Born: Dublin, Republic of Ireland, 10 July, 1956 F
Republic of Ireland: 71/Youth

League Club	Source	Date Signed	Seasons Played	Apps	Subs	Gls
Arsenal	App	09/73	74-80	223	2	75
Manchester U	Tr	08/81	81-86	204	19	60
Derby Co	Ajax (NED)	03/88	87	10	0	1
Blackburn Rov	Le Havre (FRA)	07/89	89-90	80	1	13
Huddersfield T	Aldershot (NC)	10/91	91	5	0	0
Bradford C	Tr	12/91	91-93	49	19	2
Brighton & HA	Tr	11/94	94	1	1	0

STAPLETON John Robert
Born: Manchester, England, 30 September, 1969 LB

League Club	Source	Date Signed	Seasons Played	Apps	Subs	Gls
Stockport Co	West Bromwich A (YT)	08/88	88	1	0	0

STAPLETON Joseph Edward (Joe)
Born: Marylebone, Central London, England, 27 June, 1928 CH
Died: Twickenham, W London, England, 14 July, 2005

League Club	Source	Date Signed	Seasons Played	Apps	Subs	Gls
Fulham	Uxbridge T	08/52	54-59	97	-	2

STAPLETON Simon John
Born: Oxford, England, 10 December, 1968 M/FB
England: Semi Pro-1

League Club	Source	Date Signed	Seasons Played	Apps	Subs	Gls
Portsmouth	App	12/86				
Bristol Rov	Tr	07/88	88	4	1	0
Wycombe W	Tr	08/89	93-95	46	3	3

STARBUCK Philip Michael (Phil)
Born: Nottingham, England, 24 November, 1968 F

League Club	Source	Date Signed	Seasons Played	Apps	Subs	Gls
Nottingham F	App	08/86	86-90	9	27	2
Birmingham C	L	03/88	87	3	0	0
Hereford U	L	02/90	89	6	0	0
Blackburn Rov	L	09/90	90	5	1	1
Huddersfield T	Tr	08/91	91-94	120	17	36
Sheffield U	Tr	10/94	94-96	26	10	2
Bristol C	L	09/95	95	5	0	1
Oldham Ath	Tr	08/97	97	7	2	1
Plymouth Arg	Tr	03/98	97	6	1	0

STARK Roy Howard
Born: Nottingham, England, 28 November, 1953 CD

League Club	Source	Date Signed	Seasons Played	Apps	Subs	Gls
Aston Villa	App	06/69	73	2	0	0

STARK Wayne
Born: Derby, England, 14 October, 1976 M

League Club	Source	Date Signed	Seasons Played	Apps	Subs	Gls
Mansfield T	YT	-	93	0	1	0

STARK William Reid (Billy)
Born: Glasgow, Scotland, 27 May, 1937 IF

League Club	Source	Date Signed	Seasons Played	Apps	Subs	Gls
Crewe Alex	Glasgow Rangers	08/60	60-61	38	-	13
Carlisle U	Tr	12/61	61-62	35	-	17
Colchester U	Tr	11/62	62-65	95	0	31

League Club	Source	Date Signed	Seasons Played	Apps	Subs	Gls
Luton T	Tr	09/65	65	8	2	4
Chesterfield	Corby T	07/66	66	30	1	15
Newport Co	Tr	07/67	67	11	0	2

STARKEY Malcolm John
Born: Bulwell, Nottinghamshire, England, 25 January, 1936 — IF/LB

League Club	Source	Date Signed	Seasons Played	Apps	Subs	Gls
Blackpool		08/54	56-58	3	-	0
Shrewsbury T	Tr	06/59	59-62	121	-	33
Chester C	Tr	04/63	62-66	109	0	1

STARLING Alan William
Born: Dagenham, E London, England, 2 April, 1951 — G

League Club	Source	Date Signed	Seasons Played	Apps	Subs	Gls
Luton T	App	04/69	69-70	7	0	0
Torquay U	L	02/71	70	1	0	0
Northampton T	Tr	06/71	71-76	238	0	1
Huddersfield T	Tr	03/77	76-79	112	0	0

STARLING Ronald William (Ronnie)
Born: Pelaw, Tyne and Wear, England, 11 October, 1909 — IF
Died: Sheffield, England, 4 December, 1991
England: 2

League Club	Source	Date Signed	Seasons Played	Apps	Subs	Gls
Hull C	Washington Colliery	10/26	27-29	78	-	13
Newcastle U	Tr	05/30	30-31	51	-	8
Sheffield Wed	Tr	06/32	32-36	176	-	31
Aston Villa	Tr	01/37	36-46	88	-	11

STAROCSIK Felix Bernhard
Born: Silesia, Poland, 20 May, 1920 — W
Died: Bedford, England, 7 August, 2009

League Club	Source	Date Signed	Seasons Played	Apps	Subs	Gls
Northampton T	Third Lanark	07/51	51-54	49	-	19

STAROSTA Ben Mark
Born: Sheffield, England, 7 January, 1987 — RB
England: Youth//Poland: U21-5

League Club	Source	Date Signed	Seasons Played	Apps	Subs	Gls
Sheffield U	Sch	07/06				
Brentford	L	08/07	07	20	1	0
Bradford C	L	01/08	07	12	3	0
Aldershot T	L	07/08	08	3	0	0

STATHAM Brian
Born: Harare, Zimbabwe, 21 May, 1969 — RB
England: U21-3

League Club	Source	Date Signed	Seasons Played	Apps	Subs	Gls
Tottenham H	YT	08/87	87-88	20	4	0
Reading	L	03/91	90	8	0	0
Bournemouth	L	11/91	91	2	0	0
Brentford	Tr	01/92	91-96	148	18	1
Gillingham	Tr	08/97	97	16	4	0

STATHAM Derek James
Born: Wolverhampton, England, 24 March, 1959 — FB
England: 3/B-2/U21-6/Youth

League Club	Source	Date Signed	Seasons Played	Apps	Subs	Gls
West Bromwich A	App	01/77	76-87	298	1	8
Southampton	Tr	08/87	87-88	64	0	2
Stoke C	Tr	08/89	89-90	41	0	1
Walsall	Tr	08/91	91-92	47	3	0

STATHAM Mark Andrew
Born: Urmston, Greater Manchester, England, 11 November, 1975 — G

League Club	Source	Date Signed	Seasons Played	Apps	Subs	Gls
Nottingham F	Jnr	03/93				
Wigan Ath	Tr	07/94	94	1	1	0

STATHAM Terence (Terry)
Born: Shirebrook, Derbyshire, England, 11 March, 1940 — G

League Club	Source	Date Signed	Seasons Played	Apps	Subs	Gls
Mansfield T	Jnr	03/57	56-59	26	-	0

STATON Barry
Born: Doncaster, South Yorkshire, England, 9 September, 1938 — LB
England: Youth/Schools

League Club	Source	Date Signed	Seasons Played	Apps	Subs	Gls
Doncaster Rov	Jnr	05/56	55-61	85	-	0
Norwich C	Tr	07/62	62	23	-	1

STAUNTON Stephen (Steve)
Born: Drogheda, Republic of Ireland, 19 January, 1969 — LB
Republic of Ireland: 102/U21-4/Youth

League Club	Source	Date Signed	Seasons Played	Apps	Subs	Gls
Liverpool	Dundalk (ROI)	09/86	88-90	55	10	0
Bradford C	L	11/87	87	7	1	0
Aston Villa	Tr	08/91	91-97	205	3	16
Liverpool	Tr	07/98	98-00	38	6	0
Crystal Palace	L	10/00	00	6	0	1
Aston Villa	Tr	12/00	00-02	65	8	0
Coventry C	Tr	08/03	03-04	66	4	4
Walsall	Tr	08/05	05	5	2	0

STEAD Jonathan Graeme (Jon)
Born: Huddersfield, West Yorkshire, England, 7 April, 1983 — F
England: U21-11

League Club	Source	Date Signed	Seasons Played	Apps	Subs	Gls
Huddersfield T	YT	11/01	02-03	54	14	22
Blackburn Rov	Tr	02/04	03-04	32	10	8
Sunderland	Tr	06/05	05-06	22	13	2
Derby Co	L	10/06	06	15	2	3
Sheffield U	Tr	01/07	06-08	24	15	8
Ipswich T	Tr	09/08	08-10	41	23	19
Coventry C	L	02/10	09	9	1	2
Bristol C	Tr	08/10	10-12	61	18	20
Huddersfield T	Tr	06/13	13-14	8	11	2
Oldham Ath	L	01/14	13	4	1	0
Bradford C	L	03/14	13	8	0	1
Bradford C	L	10/14	14	27	5	6

STEAD Kevin
Born: West Ham, E London, England, 2 October, 1958 — FB

League Club	Source	Date Signed	Seasons Played	Apps	Subs	Gls
Tottenham H	App	04/76				
Arsenal	Tr	07/77	78	1	1	0

STEAD Michael John (Micky)
Born: West Ham, E London, England, 28 February, 1957 — RB/M

League Club	Source	Date Signed	Seasons Played	Apps	Subs	Gls
Tottenham H	App	11/74	75-77	14	1	0
Swansea C	L	02/77	76	5	0	0
Southend U	Tr	09/78	78-85	297	1	4
Doncaster Rov	Tr	11/85	85-87	83	2	0

STEANE Nigel Brian
Born: Nottingham, England, 18 January, 1963 — F

League Club	Source	Date Signed	Seasons Played	Apps	Subs	Gls
Sheffield U	App	01/81	79	0	1	0

STEARMAN Richard James
Born: Wolverhampton, England, 19 August, 1987 — CD
England: U21-4/Youth

League Club	Source	Date Signed	Seasons Played	Apps	Subs	Gls
Leicester C	Sch	11/04	04-07	94	22	7
Wolverhampton W	Tr	07/08	08-14	184	24	5
Ipswich T	L	01/13	12	15	0	0

STEBBING Gary Stanley
Born: Croydon, S London, England, 11 August, 1965 — M
England: Youth

League Club	Source	Date Signed	Seasons Played	Apps	Subs	Gls
Crystal Palace	App	08/83	83-87	95	7	3
Southend U	L	01/86	85	5	0	0
Maidstone U	KV Ostend (BEL)	07/89	89-91	69	7	4

STECH Marek
Born: Prague, Czech Republic, 28 January, 1990 — G
Czech Republic: U21-12/Youth

League Club	Source	Date Signed	Seasons Played	Apps	Subs	Gls
West Ham U	Sch	07/08				
Wycombe W	L	03/09	08	2	0	0
Bournemouth	L	12/09	09	1	0	0
Yeovil T	L	10/11	11	5	0	0
Leyton Orient	L	02/12	11	2	0	0
Yeovil T	Tr	07/12	12-13	72	0	0

STEEDMAN Alexander (Alex)
Born: Edinburgh, Scotland, 13 May, 1938 — LW

League Club	Source	Date Signed	Seasons Played	Apps	Subs	Gls
Barrow	Eyemouth U	09/64	64	9	-	1

STEEDS Cecil
Born: Bristol, England, 11 January, 1929 — IF

League Club	Source	Date Signed	Seasons Played	Apps	Subs	Gls
Bristol C	Jnr	03/47	49-51	9	-	0
Bristol Rov	Tr	05/52	56	1	-	0

STEEL Alfred (Alf)
Born: Glasgow, Scotland, 15 August, 1925 — G
Died: York, England, August, 1997

League Club	Source	Date Signed	Seasons Played	Apps	Subs	Gls
Walsall	Petershill	10/47	48-49	2	-	0
Cardiff C	Tr	01/50	49	10	-	0

STEEL Gregory (Greg)
Born: Clevedon, Somerset, England, 11 March, 1959 — FB

League Club	Source	Date Signed	Seasons Played	Apps	Subs	Gls
Newport Co	Clevedon T	01/78	77	3	0	0

STEEL Richard (Dick)
Born: Sedgefield, County Durham, England, 13 March, 1930 — FB

League Club	Source	Date Signed	Seasons Played	Apps	Subs	Gls
Bristol C	Ferryhill Ath	06/53	53-55	3	-	0
York C	Tr	07/56	56-57	3	-	0

STEEL Ronald (Ron)
Born: Newburn, Tyne and Wear, England, 3 June, 1929 — WH/RW

League Club	Source	Date Signed	Seasons Played	Apps	Subs	Gls
Darlington	Bishop Auckland	01/50	49-51	66	-	5

STEEL William (Billy)
Born: Denny, Falkirk, Scotland, 1 May, 1923 — IF
Died: Los Angeles, California, USA, 13 May, 1982
Scotland: 30/SLge-4

League Club	Source	Date Signed	Seasons Played	Apps	Subs	Gls
Derby Co	Greenock Morton	06/47	47-49	109	-	27

STEEL William James (Jim)
Born: Dalbeattie, Dumfries & Galloway, Scotland, 4 December, 1959 — F

League Club	Source	Date Signed	Seasons Played	Apps	Subs	Gls
Oldham Ath	App	12/77	78-82	101	7	24
Wigan Ath	L	11/82	82	2	0	2
Wrexham	L	01/83	82	9	0	6
Port Vale	Tr	03/83	82-83	27	1	6
Wrexham	Tr	01/84	83-87	164	0	51
Tranmere Rov	Tr	11/87	87-91	161	13	29

STEELE Bennett John Stanley
Born: Cramlington, Northumberland, England, 5 August, 1939 — W

League Club	Source	Date Signed	Seasons Played	Apps	Subs	Gls
Everton	Seaton Delaval	05/57				
Chesterfield	Tr	05/58	58	18	-	1
Gateshead	Tr	08/59	59	25	-	5

STEELE Daniel (Danny)
Born: Southwark, S London, England, 11 October, 1982 — CD

League Club	Source	Date Signed	Seasons Played	Apps	Subs	Gls
Millwall	Jnr	02/00				
Colchester U	Tr	07/02	02	6	2	0

STEELE Eric Graham
Born: Wallsend, Tyne and Wear, England, 14 May, 1954 — G
England: Schools

League Club	Source	Date Signed	Seasons Played	Apps	Subs	Gls
Newcastle U	Jnr	07/72				
Peterborough U	Tr	12/73	73-76	124	0	0
Brighton & HA	Tr	02/77	76-79	87	0	0
Watford	Tr	10/79	79-83	51	0	0
Cardiff C	L	03/83	82	7	0	0
Derby Co	Tr	07/84	84-86	47	0	0
Southend U	Tr	07/87	87	27	0	0
Mansfield T	L	03/88	87	5	0	0

STEELE Frederick Charles (Freddie)
Born: Hanley, Potteries, England, 6 May, 1916 — CF
Died: Newcastle-under-Lyme, Potteries, England, 23 April, 1976
England: 6/FLge-2

League Club	Source	Date Signed	Seasons Played	Apps	Subs	Gls
Stoke C	Downings Tileries	08/33	34-48	224	-	140
Mansfield T	Tr	06/49	49-51	53	-	39
Port Vale	Tr	12/51	51-52	25	-	12

STEELE Hedley Verity
Born: Barnsley, South Yorkshire, England, 3 February, 1954 — CD

League Club	Source	Date Signed	Seasons Played	Apps	Subs	Gls
Exeter C	Tiverton T	07/74	74	6	1	1

STEELE James (Jim)
Born: Edinburgh, Scotland, 11 March, 1950 — CD

League Club	Source	Date Signed	Seasons Played	Apps	Subs	Gls
Southampton	Dundee	01/72	71-76	160	1	2

STEELE Jason Sean
Born: Newton Aycliffe, County Durham, England, 18 August, 1990 — G
England: U21-7/Youth

League Club	Source	Date Signed	Seasons Played	Apps	Subs	Gls
Middlesbrough	Sch	05/08	10-13	131	0	0
Northampton T	L	02/10	09	13	0	0
Blackburn Rov	Tr	09/14	14	31	0	0

STEELE John (Johnny)
Born: Glasgow, Scotland, 24 November, 1916 — IF
Died: Barnsley, South Yorkshire, England, 14 January, 2008

League Club	Source	Date Signed	Seasons Played	Apps	Subs	Gls
Barnsley	Ayr U	06/38	38-48	49	-	21

STEELE Joseph McGuire (Joe)
Born: Blackridge, West Lothian, Scotland, 4 October, 1928 — W
Died: Newcastle-upon-Tyne, England, November, 1993

League Club	Source	Date Signed	Seasons Played	Apps	Subs	Gls
Newcastle U	Bellshill Ath	12/48				
Bury	Tr	05/50	50	18	-	1
Leyton Orient	Tr	08/51				

STEELE Lee Anthony James
Born: Liverpool, England, 2 December, 1973 — F

League Club	Source	Date Signed	Seasons Played	Apps	Subs	Gls
Shrewsbury T	Northwich Victoria	07/97	97-99	104	9	37
Brighton & HA	Tr	07/00	00-01	24	36	11
Oxford U	Tr	07/02	02-03	6	20	4
Leyton Orient	Tr	07/04	04-06	60	17	24
Chester C	Tr	10/06	06	11	9	1

STEELE Luke David
Born: Peterborough, England, 24 September, 1984 — G
England: Youth

League Club	Source	Date Signed	Seasons Played	Apps	Subs	Gls
Peterborough U	YT	09/01	01	2	0	0
Manchester U	Tr	03/02				
Coventry C	L	09/04	04	32	0	0
West Bromwich A	Tr	08/06	07	2	0	0
Coventry C	L	12/06	06	5	0	0
Barnsley	Tr	02/08	07-13	209	0	0

STEELE Percival Edmund (Percy)
Born: Liverpool, England, 26 December, 1923 — FB
Died: Liverpool, England, 21 October, 2009

League Club	Source	Date Signed	Seasons Played	Apps	Subs	Gls
Tranmere Rov	Carlton	01/44	46-56	311	-	0

STEELE Simon Paul
Born: Liverpool, England, 29 February, 1964 — G

League Club	Source	Date Signed	Seasons Played	Apps	Subs	Gls
Everton	App	03/82				
Brighton & HA	Tr	06/83	83	1	0	0
Blackpool	L	09/83	83	3	0	0
Scunthorpe U	Tr	03/84	83	5	0	0

STEELE Stanley Frederick (Stan)
Born: Fenton, Potteries, England, 5 January, 1937 — IF
Died: Fenton, Potteries, England, 15 July, 2005

League Club	Source	Date Signed	Seasons Played	Apps	Subs	Gls
Port Vale	Jnr	05/55	56-60	185	-	66
West Bromwich A	Tr	03/61	60	1	-	0
Port Vale	Tr	08/61	61-64	148	-	22
Port Vale	Port Elizabeth C (RSA)	01/68	67	2	0	0

STEELE Timothy Wesley (Tim)
Born: Coventry, England, 1 December, 1967 — LM

League Club	Source	Date Signed	Seasons Played	Apps	Subs	Gls
Shrewsbury T	App	12/85	85-88	41	20	5
Wolverhampton W	Tr	02/89	88-92	53	22	7
Stoke C	L	02/92	91	7	0	1
Bradford C	Tr	07/93	93	8	3	0
Hereford U	Tr	01/94	93-95	24	8	2
Exeter C	Tr	08/96	96	14	14	3

STEELE William McCallum (Billy)
Born: Kirkmuirhill, Lanarkshire, Scotland, 16 June, 1955 — M

League Club	Source	Date Signed	Seasons Played	Apps	Subs	Gls
Norwich C	App	06/73	73-76	56	12	3
Bournemouth	L	01/76	75	7	0	2

STEEN Alan William
Born: Crewe, Cheshire, England, 26 June, 1922 — W
Died: Wirral, England, 26 August, 2012

League Club	Source	Date Signed	Seasons Played	Apps	Subs	Gls
Wolverhampton W	Jnr	03/39	38	1	-	1
Luton T	Tr	05/46	46	10	-	0
Aldershot	Northwich Victoria	06/49	49	9	-	0
Rochdale	Tr	06/50	50-51	45	-	8
Carlisle U	Tr	12/51	51	19	-	2

STEEPLES John
Born: Doncaster, South Yorkshire, England, 28 April, 1959 — F

League Club	Source	Date Signed	Seasons Played	Apps	Subs	Gls
Grimsby T	Pilkington Rec	05/80	80-81	4	3	0
Torquay U	L	09/82	82	4	1	0

STEER Jed John
Born: Norwich, England, 23 September, 1992 — G
England: Youth

League Club	Source	Date Signed	Seasons Played	Apps	Subs	Gls
Norwich C	Sch	10/09				
Yeovil T	L	07/11	11	12	0	0
Aston Villa	Tr	06/13	14	1	0	0
Doncaster Rov	L	08/14	14	13	0	0
Yeovil T	L	10/14	14	12	0	0

STEER Rene Alexander
Born: Luton, England, 31 January, 1990 — LB

League Club	Source	Date Signed	Seasons Played	Apps	Subs	Gls
Arsenal	Sch	09/07				
Gillingham	L	01/09	08	3	2	0
Oldham Ath	Tr	07/09				

STEFANOVIC Dejan
Born: Vranje, Yugoslavia, 28 October, 1974 — CD
Serbia: 4//Yugoslavia: 19

League Club	Source	Date Signed	Seasons Played	Apps	Subs	Gls
Sheffield Wed	R Star Belgrade (YUG)	12/95	95-98	59	7	4
Portsmouth	Vitesse Arnhem (NED)	07/03	03-06	111	1	3
Fulham	Tr	08/07	07	13	0	0
Norwich C	Tr	07/08	08	12	0	0

STEFFEN Willi
Born: Bern, Switzerland, 17 March, 1925 — LB
Died: Bern, Switzerland, 3 May, 2005
Switzerland: 28/War-2

League Club	Source	Date Signed	Seasons Played	Apps	Subs	Gls
Chelsea	Cant. Neuchatel (SUI)	11/46	46	15	-	0

STEGGLES Kevin Peter
Born: Ditchingham, Norfolk, England, 19 March, 1961 — D

League Club	Source	Date Signed	Seasons Played	Apps	Subs	Gls
Ipswich T	App	12/78	80-85	49	1	1
Southend U	L	02/84	83	3	0	1
Fulham	L	08/86	86	3	0	0
West Bromwich A	Tr	02/87	86-87	14	0	0
Port Vale	Tr	11/87	87	20	0	0

STEIN Brian
Born: Cape Town, South Africa, 19 October, 1957 — F
England: 1/U21-3

League Club	Source	Date Signed	Seasons Played	Apps	Subs	Gls
Luton T	Edgware T	10/77	77-87	378	10	126
Luton T	Annecy (FRA)	07/91	91	32	7	3
Barnet	Tr	08/92	92	17	23	8

STEIN Colin Anderson
Born: Linlithgow, West Lothian, Scotland, 10 May, 1947 — F
Scotland: 21/SLge-4/U23-1

League Club	Source	Date Signed	Seasons Played	Apps	Subs	Gls
Coventry C	Glasgow Rangers	10/72	72-74	83	0	22

STEIN Earl Mark Sean (Mark)
Born: Cape Town, South Africa, 28 January, 1966 — F
England: Youth

League Club	Source	Date Signed	Seasons Played	Apps	Subs	Gls
Luton T	Jnr	01/84	83-87	41	13	19
Aldershot	L	01/86	85	2	0	1
Queens Park Rgrs	Tr	06/88	88-89	20	13	4
Oxford U	Tr	09/89	89-91	72	10	18

League Club	Source	Date Signed	Seasons Played	Apps	Subs	Gls
Stoke C	L	09/91	91	5	0	0
Stoke C	Tr	11/91	91-93	89	0	50
Chelsea	Tr	10/93	93-95	46	4	21
Stoke C	L	11/96	96	11	0	4
Ipswich T	L	08/97	97	6	1	2
Bournemouth	Tr	03/98	97-99	90	0	30
Luton T	Tr	07/00	00	19	11	3

STEIN Edwin
Born: Cape Town, South Africa, 28 September, 1955 — M

League Club	Source	Date Signed	Seasons Played	Apps	Subs	Gls
Barnet	Dagenham	07/82	91	0	1	0

STEINER Geoffrey Gordon (Geoff)
Born: Hackney, E London, England, 8 June, 1928 — FB

League Club	Source	Date Signed	Seasons Played	Apps	Subs	Gls
Watford	Barnet	11/50	51	3	-	0

STEINER Robert Herman (Rob)
Born: Finspang, Sweden, 20 June, 1973 — F
Sweden: 3

League Club	Source	Date Signed	Seasons Played	Apps	Subs	Gls
Bradford C	IFK Norrkoping (SWE)	10/96	96-97	40	12	14
Queens Park Rgrs	L	11/98	98	5	7	3
Walsall	L	03/99	98	10	0	3
Queens Park Rgrs	Tr	07/99	99	24	0	6

STEINSSON Gretar Rafn
Born: Siglufjordur, Iceland, 9 January, 1982 — RB
Iceland: 46

League Club	Source	Date Signed	Seasons Played	Apps	Subs	Gls
Bolton W	AZ Alkmaar (NED)	01/08	07-11	121	5	5

STEJSKAL Jan
Born: Brno, Czechoslovakia, 15 January, 1962 — G
Czechoslovakia: 29//Czech Republic: 2

League Club	Source	Date Signed	Seasons Played	Apps	Subs	Gls
Queens Park Rgrs	Sparta Prague (CZE)	10/90	90-93	107	1	0

STEKELENBURG Maarten
Born: Haarlem, Netherlands, 22 September, 1982 — G
Netherlands: 54/U21-4

League Club	Source	Date Signed	Seasons Played	Apps	Subs	Gls
Fulham	AS Roma (ITA)	06/13	13	19	0	0

STELL Barry
Born: Felling, Tyne and Wear, England, 3 September, 1961 — M

League Club	Source	Date Signed	Seasons Played	Apps	Subs	Gls
Sheffield Wed	App	09/79				
Darlington	Tr	10/79	80	7	2	0

STELLING John Graham Surtees (Jack)
Born: Washington, Tyne and Wear, England, 23 May, 1924 — RB
Died: Sunderland, England, 29 March, 1993

League Club	Source	Date Signed	Seasons Played	Apps	Subs	Gls
Sunderland	Usworth High Grange	11/44	46-55	259	-	8

STEMP Wayne Darren
Born: Plymouth, England, 9 September, 1970 — FB

League Club	Source	Date Signed	Seasons Played	Apps	Subs	Gls
Brighton & HA		10/88	89-90	4	0	0

STENHOUSE Alexander (Alec)
Born: Stirling, Scotland, 1 January, 1933 — RW

League Club	Source	Date Signed	Seasons Played	Apps	Subs	Gls
Portsmouth	Dundee	02/57	56-57	4	-	1
Southend U	Tr	11/58	58-60	84	-	7

STENNER Arthur William John
Born: Yeovil, Somerset, England, 7 January, 1934 — LW
Died: Yeovil, Somerset, England, 11 March, 2010

League Club	Source	Date Signed	Seasons Played	Apps	Subs	Gls
Bristol C	Yeovil	08/54				
Plymouth Arg	Tr	08/55	55	9	-	1
Norwich C	Tr	08/56	56	6	-	0
Exeter C	Tr	12/56				
Oldham Ath	Tr	04/57	56	3	-	0

STENSAAS Stale
Born: Trondheim, Norway, 7 July, 1971 — LB
Norway: 9

League Club	Source	Date Signed	Seasons Played	Apps	Subs	Gls
Nottingham F (L)	Glasgow Rangers	01/99	98	6	1	0

STENSON Gerard Patrick (Ged)
Born: Bootle, Merseyside, England, 30 December, 1959 — M

League Club	Source	Date Signed	Seasons Played	Apps	Subs	Gls
Port Vale	Everton (App)	08/78	78-79	11	1	0

STENSON John Andrew
Born: Catford, SE London, England, 16 December, 1949 — M
England: Youth/Schools

League Club	Source	Date Signed	Seasons Played	Apps	Subs	Gls
Charlton Ath	Jnr	12/66	67-68	3	8	0
Mansfield T	Tr	06/69	69-71	103	4	21
Peterborough U	L	01/72	71	2	0	0
Aldershot	Tr	07/72	72-73	34	11	4

STEPANOV Andrei
Born: Tallinn, Estonia, 16 March, 1979 — CD
Estonia: 79

League Club	Source	Date Signed	Seasons Played	Apps	Subs	Gls
Watford (L)	FC Khimki (RUS)	03/09	08	0	1	0

STEPANOVIC Dragoslav
Born: Rekovac, Yugoslavia, 30 August, 1948 — CD
Yugoslavia: 54

League Club	Source	Date Signed	Seasons Played	Apps	Subs	Gls
Manchester C	Wormatia Worms (GER)	08/79	79-80	14	1	0

STEPANOVS Igors Nauris
Born: Ogre, Latvia, 21 January, 1976 — CD
Latvia: 100

League Club	Source	Date Signed	Seasons Played	Apps	Subs	Gls
Arsenal	Skonto Riga (LAT)	09/00	00-02	17	0	0

STEPHAN Harold William (Harry)
Born: Farnworth, Greater Manchester, England, 24 February, 1924 — WH
Died: Leeds, England, June, 2010
Died: June, 2010

League Club	Source	Date Signed	Seasons Played	Apps	Subs	Gls
Blackburn Rov		09/44	46-47	13	-	1
Accrington Stan	Tr	09/48				

STEPHEN George Allan
Born: Ellon, Aberdeenshire, Scotland, 21 September, 1927 — FB
Died: Peterhead, Aberdeenshire, Scotland, 14 April, 2000

League Club	Source	Date Signed	Seasons Played	Apps	Subs	Gls
Aldershot	Aldershot Garrison	08/48	48	2	-	0

STEPHEN James Findlay (Jimmy)
Born: Fettercairn, Aberdeenshire, Scotland, 23 August, 1922 — RB
Died: Southsea, Hampshire, England, 5 November, 2012
Scotland: 2/War-5

League Club	Source	Date Signed	Seasons Played	Apps	Subs	Gls
Bradford Park Ave	Johnshaven Dauntless	08/39	46-48	94	-	1
Portsmouth	Tr	11/49	49-53	100	-	0

STEPHENS Alan
Born: Liverpool, England, 13 October, 1952 — LB

League Club	Source	Date Signed	Seasons Played	Apps	Subs	Gls
Wolverhampton W	App	10/70				
Crewe Alex	Tr	07/72	72-73	30	3	0

STEPHENS Alfred (Alf)
Born: Cramlington, Northumberland, England, 13 June, 1919 — IF
Died: North Tyneside, Tyne and Wear, England, February, 1993

League Club	Source	Date Signed	Seasons Played	Apps	Subs	Gls
Leeds U	Cramlington BW	09/38				
Swindon T	Tr	08/46	46-47	16	-	2

STEPHENS Arnold Edwin
Born: Ross-on-Wye, Herefordshire, England, 31 January, 1928 — RW
Died: Bournemouth, England, 1955

League Club	Source	Date Signed	Seasons Played	Apps	Subs	Gls
Wolverhampton W	Jnr	04/45				
Bournemouth	Tr	12/48	48-53	70	-	12

STEPHENS Arthur (Archie)
Born: Liverpool, England, 19 May, 1954 — F

League Club	Source	Date Signed	Seasons Played	Apps	Subs	Gls
Bristol Rov	Melksham T	08/81	81-84	100	27	40
Middlesbrough	Tr	03/85	84-87	87	5	24
Carlisle U	Tr	12/87	87-88	20	4	3
Darlington	Tr	03/89	88	10	0	4

STEPHENS Dale Christopher
Born: Bolton, Greater Manchester, England, 12 June, 1989 — M

League Club	Source	Date Signed	Seasons Played	Apps	Subs	Gls
Bury	Sch	07/07	06-07	6	3	1
Oldham Ath	Tr	07/08	09-10	58	2	11
Rochdale	L	08/09	09	3	3	1
Southampton	L	03/11	10	5	1	0
Charlton Ath	Tr	06/11	11-13	78	6	10
Brighton & HA	Tr	01/14	13-14	22	8	4

STEPHENS David Rhys Remington
Born: Welwyn Garden City, Hertfordshire, England, 8 October, 1991 — CD
Wales: U21-7/Youth

League Club	Source	Date Signed	Seasons Played	Apps	Subs	Gls
Norwich C	Sch	07/09				
Lincoln C	L	03/10	09	3	0	0
Barnet	Hibernian	08/12	12	42	0	1

STEPHENS Herbert James (Bert)
Born: Chatham, Kent, England, 13 May, 1909 — LW
Died: Thanet, Kent, England, August, 1987

League Club	Source	Date Signed	Seasons Played	Apps	Subs	Gls
Brentford	Ealing Association	02/31	31-32	6	-	1
Brighton & HA	Tr	06/35	35-47	180	-	86

STEPHENS Jack
Born: Torpoint, Cornwall, England, 27 January, 1994 — CD/M
England: Youth

League Club	Source	Date Signed	Seasons Played	Apps	Subs	Gls
Plymouth Arg	Sch	-	10	2	3	0
Southampton	Tr	04/11				
Swindon T	L	03/14	13	10	0	0
Swindon T	L	09/14	14	36	1	1

STEPHENS James Edward (Jamie)
Born: Wotton-under-Edge, Gloucestershire, England, 25 August, 1993 — G

League Club	Source	Date Signed	Seasons Played	Apps	Subs	Gls
Liverpool	Swindon T (Sch)	08/10				
Newport Co	Tr	07/13	13-14	8	1	0

STEPHENS Kenneth John (Kenny)
Born: Bristol, England, 14 November, 1946 — RW

League Club	Source	Date Signed	Seasons Played	Apps	Subs	Gls
West Bromwich A	App	11/64	66-67	21	1	2
Walsall	Tr	12/68	68-69	6	1	0

League Club	Source	Date Signed	Seasons Played	Apps	Subs	Gls
Bristol Rov	Tr	10/70	70-77	215	10	13
Hereford U	Tr	10/77	77-79	56	4	2

STEPHENS Kevin Alexander
Born: Enfield, N London, England, 28 July, 1984 — FB

League Club	Source	Date Signed	Seasons Played	Apps	Subs	Gls
Leyton Orient	Sch	08/03	02-03	2	2	0

STEPHENS Kirk William
Born: Coventry, England, 27 February, 1955 — RB

League Club	Source	Date Signed	Seasons Played	Apps	Subs	Gls
Luton T	Nuneaton Bor	06/78	78-83	226	1	2
Coventry C	Tr	08/84	84-85	33	1	2

STEPHENS Lee Michael
Born: Cardiff, Wales, 30 September, 1971 — F

League Club	Source	Date Signed	Seasons Played	Apps	Subs	Gls
Cardiff C	YT	07/90	90	1	2	0

STEPHENS Malcolm Keith
Born: Doncaster, South Yorkshire, England, 17 February, 1930 — IF
Died: Plymouth, England, 6 February, 2005

League Club	Source	Date Signed	Seasons Played	Apps	Subs	Gls
Brighton & HA	Royal Navy	07/54	54-56	29	-	14
Rotherham U	Tr	07/57	57	12	-	3
Doncaster Rov	Tr	07/58	58	10	-	2

STEPHENS Ross
Born: Llanidloes, Powys, Wales, 28 May, 1985 — LW

League Club	Source	Date Signed	Seasons Played	Apps	Subs	Gls
Shrewsbury T	Sch	-	02-04	0	3	0

STEPHENS Terence Guy (Terry)
Born: Neath, Wales, 5 November, 1935 — IF

League Club	Source	Date Signed	Seasons Played	Apps	Subs	Gls
Tranmere Rov	Everton (Am)	08/55	55-56	15	-	5

STEPHENS William John (Johnny)
Born: Cardiff, Wales, 26 June, 1935 — RW
Died: Barry, Vale of Glamorgan, Wales, February, 1992
Wales: U23-1

League Club	Source	Date Signed	Seasons Played	Apps	Subs	Gls
Hull C	Jnr	08/53	52-57	94	-	20
Swindon T	Tr	06/58	58-59	18	-	2
Coventry C	Tr	02/60	59	14	-	0

STEPHENS William John (Bill)
Born: Cramlington, Northumberland, England, 13 June, 1919 — CF
Died: Slough, Berkshire, England, 1974

League Club	Source	Date Signed	Seasons Played	Apps	Subs	Gls
Leeds U	Cramlington BW	09/38				
Swindon T	Tr	07/46	46-47	47	-	25
West Ham U	Tr	12/47	47-48	22	-	6
Cardiff C	Tr	12/50				

STEPHENSON Alan Charles
Born: Chesham, Buckinghamshire, England, 26 September, 1944 — CD
England: U23-7

League Club	Source	Date Signed	Seasons Played	Apps	Subs	Gls
Crystal Palace	Jnr	02/62	61-67	170	0	13
West Ham U	Tr	03/68	67-71	106	2	0
Fulham	L	10/71	71	10	0	0
Portsmouth	Tr	05/72	72-74	98	0	1

STEPHENSON Ashlyn
Born: South Africa, 6 July, 1974 — G
England: Youth

League Club	Source	Date Signed	Seasons Played	Apps	Subs	Gls
Darlington	Waterford (ROI)	09/95	95	1	0	0

STEPHENSON Darren Coil Anthony
Born: Spanish Town, Jamaica, 6 March, 1993 — F

League Club	Source	Date Signed	Seasons Played	Apps	Subs	Gls
Bradford C	Sch	10/11	10	0	1	0

STEPHENSON Geoffrey (Geoff)
Born: Tynemouth, Tyne and Wear, England, 28 April, 1970 — LB

League Club	Source	Date Signed	Seasons Played	Apps	Subs	Gls
Grimsby T	YT	07/88	88-89	19	2	0

STEPHENSON George Robert (Bob)
Born: Derby, England, 19 November, 1942 — IF

League Club	Source	Date Signed	Seasons Played	Apps	Subs	Gls
Derby Co	Derwent Sports	09/60	61-62	11	-	1
Shrewsbury T	Tr	06/64	64	3	-	0
Rochdale	Tr	07/65	65-66	50	1	16

STEPHENSON Paul
Born: Wallsend, Tyne and Wear, England, 2 January, 1968 — RW
England: Youth

League Club	Source	Date Signed	Seasons Played	Apps	Subs	Gls
Newcastle U	App	01/86	85-88	58	3	1
Millwall	Tr	11/88	88-92	81	17	6
Gillingham	L	11/92	92	12	0	2
Brentford	Tr	03/93	92-94	70	0	2
York C	Tr	08/95	95-97	91	6	8
Hartlepool U	Tr	03/98	97-01	136	9	9

STEPHENSON Peter
Born: Ashington, Northumberland, England, 2 May, 1936 — RW
Died: Newcastle-upon-Tyne, England, February, 2003

League Club	Source	Date Signed	Seasons Played	Apps	Subs	Gls
Middlesbrough	Sunderland (Am)	08/55				
Gateshead	Ashington	09/59	59	35	-	6

STEPHENSON Robert Leonard (Len)
Born: Blackpool, Lancashire, England, 14 July, 1930 — CF
Died: Blackpool, Lancashire, England, 29 September, 2014

League Club	Source	Date Signed	Seasons Played	Apps	Subs	Gls
Blackpool	Highfield YC	11/48	50-54	24	-	10
Port Vale	Tr	03/55	54-56	61	-	16
Oldham Ath	Tr	06/57	57	8	-	0

STEPHENSON Ronald (Ron)
Born: Barrow, Cumbria, England, 13 April, 1948 — M

League Club	Source	Date Signed	Seasons Played	Apps	Subs	Gls
Barrow	App	05/66	66-67	2	0	1

STEPHENSON Roy
Born: Crook, County Durham, England, 27 May, 1932 — RW
Died: Ipswich, England, 4 February, 2000

League Club	Source	Date Signed	Seasons Played	Apps	Subs	Gls
Burnley	Crook T	06/49	49-55	78	-	27
Rotherham U	Tr	09/56	56-57	43	-	14
Blackburn Rov	Tr	11/57	57-58	21	-	5
Leicester C	Tr	03/59	58-59	12	-	0
Ipswich T	Tr	07/60	60-64	144	-	21

STEPNEY Alexander Cyril (Alex)
Born: Mitcham, S London, England, 18 September, 1942 — G
England: 1/FLge-2/U23-3

League Club	Source	Date Signed	Seasons Played	Apps	Subs	Gls
Millwall	Tooting & Mitcham U	05/63	63-65	137	0	0
Chelsea	Tr	05/66	66	1	0	0
Manchester U	Tr	09/66	66-77	433	0	2

STEPNEY Robin Edward (Robbie)
Born: Horsham, West Sussex, England, 26 February, 1936 — IF/WH

League Club	Source	Date Signed	Seasons Played	Apps	Subs	Gls
Aldershot	Redhill	09/58	58-64	213	-	36

STERGIOPOULOS Marcus
Born: Melbourne, Australia, 12 June, 1973 — M

League Club	Source	Date Signed	Seasons Played	Apps	Subs	Gls
Lincoln C	Auckland Kingz (NZL)	08/00	00	2	5	0

STERJOWSKI Mile
Born: Wollongong, NSW, Australia, 27 May, 1979 — RW
Australia: 40

League Club	Source	Date Signed	Seasons Played	Apps	Subs	Gls
Derby Co	Genclerbirligi (TKY)	01/08	07-08	15	12	2

STERLAND Melvyn (Mel)
Born: Sheffield, England, 1 October, 1961 — RB
England: 1/B-3/FLge/U21-7

League Club	Source	Date Signed	Seasons Played	Apps	Subs	Gls
Sheffield Wed	App	10/79	78-88	271	8	37
Leeds U	Glasgow Rangers	07/89	89-92	111	3	16

STERLING Raheem Shaquliie
Born: Kingston, Jamaica, 8 December, 1994 — W/F
England: 16/U21-8/Youth

League Club	Source	Date Signed	Seasons Played	Apps	Subs	Gls
Liverpool	Sch	12/11	11-14	77	18	18

STERLING Worrell Ricardo
Born: Bethnal Green, E London, England, 8 June, 1965 — RW

League Club	Source	Date Signed	Seasons Played	Apps	Subs	Gls
Watford	YT	06/83	82-88	82	12	14
Peterborough U	Tr	03/89	88-92	190	3	28
Bristol Rov	Tr	07/93	93-95	117	2	6
Lincoln C	Tr	07/96	96	15	6	0

STERLING-JAMES Omari Shaquil
Born: Birmingham, England, 15 September, 1993 — M

League Club	Source	Date Signed	Seasons Played	Apps	Subs	Gls
Cheltenham T	Redditch U	07/14	14	9	13	1

STEVEN Trevor McGregor
Born: Berwick-on-Tweed, Northumberland, England, 21 September, 1963 — RW
England: 36/U21-2/Youth/Schools

League Club	Source	Date Signed	Seasons Played	Apps	Subs	Gls
Burnley	App	09/81	80-82	74	2	11
Everton	Tr	07/83	83-88	210	4	48

STEVENS Arthur Harold
Born: Battersea, SW London, England, 13 January, 1921 — RW
Died: Surrey, England, 15 January, 2007

League Club	Source	Date Signed	Seasons Played	Apps	Subs	Gls
Fulham	Sutton U	12/43	46-58	386	-	110

STEVENS Brian Edward
Born: Andover, Hampshire, England, 13 November, 1933 — G
Died: Hursley, Hampshire, England, 10 May, 1980

League Club	Source	Date Signed	Seasons Played	Apps	Subs	Gls
Southampton	Andover OB	09/56	56-57	12	-	0

STEVENS Danny Robert
Born: Enfield, N London, England, 26 November, 1986 — RW

League Club	Source	Date Signed	Seasons Played	Apps	Subs	Gls
Luton T	Tottenham H (Sch)	03/05	05	0	1	0
Torquay U	Tr	08/07	09-13	90	44	15

STEVENS Dean William
Born: Torquay, Devon, England, 7 February, 1986 — W

League Club	Source	Date Signed	Seasons Played	Apps	Subs	Gls
Torquay U	Sch	-	02	0	3	0

STEVENS Dennis
Born: Dudley, West Midlands, England, 30 November, 1933 — IF
Died: Bolton, Greater Manchester, England, 20 December, 2012

England: FLge-1/U23-2

League Club	Source	Date Signed	Seasons Played	Apps	Subs	Gls
Bolton W	Jnr	12/50	53-61	273	-	90
Everton	Tr	03/62	61-65	120	0	20
Oldham Ath	Tr	12/65	65-66	33	0	0
Tranmere Rov	Tr	03/67	66-67	28	4	3

STEVENS Enda John
Born: Dublin, Republic of Ireland, 9 July, 1990 — LB
Republic of Ireland: U21-3

League Club	Source	Date Signed	Seasons Played	Apps	Subs	Gls
Aston Villa	Shamrock Rov (ROI)	01/12	12	6	1	0
Notts Co	L	08/13	13	2	0	0
Doncaster Rov	L	11/13	13	11	2	0
Northampton T	L	10/14	14	4	0	1
Doncaster Rov	L	11/14	14	27	1	1

STEVENS Gary Andrew
Born: Hillingdon, W London, England, 30 March, 1962 — RB/M
England: 7/U21-8

League Club	Source	Date Signed	Seasons Played	Apps	Subs	Gls
Brighton & HA	App	10/79	79-82	120	13	2
Tottenham H	Tr	06/83	83-89	140	7	6
Portsmouth	Tr	01/90	89-90	52	0	3

STEVENS Gary Martin
Born: Birmingham, England, 30 August, 1954 — F/CD

League Club	Source	Date Signed	Seasons Played	Apps	Subs	Gls
Cardiff C	Evesham U	09/78	78-81	138	12	44
Shrewsbury T	Tr	09/82	82-85	144	6	30
Brentford	Tr	07/86	86	29	3	10
Hereford U	Tr	03/87	86-89	85	9	10

STEVENS Gregor MacKenzie
Born: Glasgow, Scotland, 13 January, 1955 — CD
Scotland: SLge-2/U21-1

League Club	Source	Date Signed	Seasons Played	Apps	Subs	Gls
Leicester C	Motherwell	05/79	79	4	0	0

STEVENS Ian David
Born: Valletta, Malta, 21 October, 1966 — F

League Club	Source	Date Signed	Seasons Played	Apps	Subs	Gls
Preston NE	App	11/84	84-85	9	2	2
Stockport Co	Morecambe	10/86	86	1	1	0
Bolton W	Lancaster C	03/87	86-90	26	21	7
Bury	Tr	07/91	91-93	100	10	38
Shrewsbury T	Tr	08/94	94-96	94	17	37
Carlisle U	Tr	05/97	97-98	64	14	26
Wrexham	Tr	07/99	99	14	2	4
Cheltenham T	L	03/00	99	1	0	0
Carlisle U	Tr	08/00	00-01	64	3	20
Shrewsbury T	Tr	07/02	02	4	14	2

STEVENS James Daniel (Jamie)
Born: Grays, Essex, England, 10 October, 1992 — M
Northern Ireland: Youth

League Club	Source	Date Signed	Seasons Played	Apps	Subs	Gls
Southend U	Sch	07/11	10	1	0	0

STEVENS Jamie Andrew
Born: Holbeach, Lincolnshire, England, 25 February, 1989 — CD

League Club	Source	Date Signed	Seasons Played	Apps	Subs	Gls
Boston U	Sch	-	06	11	1	2

STEVENS John Miles Northmore
Born: Hertford, England, 21 August, 1941 — CF
Died: Mansfield, Nottinghamshire, England, 13 April, 2010

League Club	Source	Date Signed	Seasons Played	Apps	Subs	Gls
Swindon T	RAF Kings Lynn	06/62	62-63	22	-	10

STEVENS Keith Henry
Born: Merton, SW London, England, 21 June, 1964 — D

League Club	Source	Date Signed	Seasons Played	Apps	Subs	Gls
Millwall	App	03/81	80-98	452	10	9

STEVENS Leslie William George (Les)
Born: Croydon, S London, England, 15 August, 1920 — LW
Died: Romford, E London, England, 14 February, 1991

League Club	Source	Date Signed	Seasons Played	Apps	Subs	Gls
Tottenham H	Jnr	01/40	46-48	54	-	5
Bradford Park Ave	Tr	02/49	48-49	44	-	4
Crystal Palace	Tr	08/50	50	20	-	3

STEVENS Mark Anthony
Born: Bristol, England, 31 January, 1963 — G
England: Schools

League Club	Source	Date Signed	Seasons Played	Apps	Subs	Gls
Bristol C	App	02/81				
Swindon T	Tr	06/81	82	1	0	0

STEVENS Mark Richard
Born: Swindon, England, 3 December, 1977 — F
England: Schools

League Club	Source	Date Signed	Seasons Played	Apps	Subs	Gls
Oxford U	Jnr	07/96	97	0	1	0

STEVENS Michael Gary (Gary)
Born: Barrow, Cumbria, England, 27 March, 1963 — FB
England: 46/B-1

League Club	Source	Date Signed	Seasons Played	Apps	Subs	Gls
Everton	App	04/81	81-87	207	1	9
Tranmere Rov	Glasgow Rangers	09/94	94-97	126	1	2

STEVENS Norman John
Born: Shoreham-by-Sea, West Sussex, England, 13 May, 1938 — FB

League Club	Source	Date Signed	Seasons Played	Apps	Subs	Gls
Brighton & HA	Jnr	10/55	58	1	-	0

STEVENS Paul David
Born: Bristol, England, 4 April, 1960 — RB

League Club	Source	Date Signed	Seasons Played	Apps	Subs	Gls
Bristol C	App	04/78	77-84	146	1	3

STEVENS Samuel Batson (Sam)
Born: Rutherglen, Glasgow, Scotland, 2 December, 1935 — LH

League Club	Source	Date Signed	Seasons Played	Apps	Subs	Gls
Southampton	Airdrieonians	06/57	58	14	-	0

STEVENSON Alan
Born: Staveley, Derbyshire, England, 6 November, 1950 — G

League Club	Source	Date Signed	Seasons Played	Apps	Subs	Gls
Chesterfield	Jnr	10/69	69-71	104	0	0
Burnley	Tr	01/72	71-82	438	0	0
Rotherham U	Tr	08/83	83	24	0	0
Hartlepool U	Tr	09/84	84	35	0	0

STEVENSON Alexander Ernest (Alex)
Born: Dublin, Republic of Ireland, 9 August, 1912 — IF
Died: Liverpool, England, September, 1985
Republic of Ireland: 7//Northern Ireland: 17/War-1

League Club	Source	Date Signed	Seasons Played	Apps	Subs	Gls
Everton	Glasgow Rangers	01/34	33-48	255	-	82

STEVENSON Andrew John (Andy)
Born: Scunthorpe, North Lincolnshire, England, 29 September, 1967 — D/M

League Club	Source	Date Signed	Seasons Played	Apps	Subs	Gls
Scunthorpe U	Jnr	01/86	85-92	78	25	4
Doncaster Rov	L	01/92	91	1	0	0

STEVENSON Arthur
Born: Lanchester, County Durham, England, 2 March, 1924 — RB
Died: Bristol, England, December, 1989

League Club	Source	Date Signed	Seasons Played	Apps	Subs	Gls
Doncaster Rov	Denaby U	11/44	47-48	14	-	0

STEVENSON Ernest (Ernie)
Born: Rotherham, South Yorkshire, England, 28 December, 1923 — IF
Died: St Helens, Merseyside, England, 15 October, 1970

League Club	Source	Date Signed	Seasons Played	Apps	Subs	Gls
Wolverhampton W	Jnr	12/40	47-48	8	-	0
Cardiff C	Tr	10/48	48-49	50	-	15
Southampton	Tr	02/50	49-50	23	-	8
Leeds U	Tr	02/51	50-51	16	-	5

STEVENSON James (Jimmy)
Born: Bellshill, Lanarkshire, Scotland, 4 August, 1946 — LH
Scotland: Schools

League Club	Source	Date Signed	Seasons Played	Apps	Subs	Gls
Southend U	Hibernian	07/67	67	33	1	0

STEVENSON James Adam (Jim)
Born: Luton, England, 17 May, 1992 — M

League Club	Source	Date Signed	Seasons Played	Apps	Subs	Gls
Luton T	Histon	07/13	14	2	9	1

STEVENSON Jonathan Ashlee (Jon)
Born: Leicester, England, 13 October, 1982 — F

League Club	Source	Date Signed	Seasons Played	Apps	Subs	Gls
Leicester C	YT	03/01	01-02	0	12	2
Swindon T	Tr	07/03	03	1	4	0

STEVENSON Lee Cameron
Born: Sheffield, England, 1 June, 1984 — M

League Club	Source	Date Signed	Seasons Played	Apps	Subs	Gls
Mansfield T	Eastwood T	05/11	13	19	2	5

STEVENSON Morris John
Born: Tranent, East Lothian, Scotland, 16 April, 1943 — IF
Died: Tranent, East Lothian, Scotland, 22 July, 2014

League Club	Source	Date Signed	Seasons Played	Apps	Subs	Gls
Luton T	Greenock Morton	11/68	68	1	0	0

STEVENSON Nigel Charles Ashley
Born: Swansea, Wales, 2 November, 1958 — CD
Wales: 4/U21-2

League Club	Source	Date Signed	Seasons Played	Apps	Subs	Gls
Swansea C	App	11/76	75-86	247	12	15
Cardiff C	L	10/85	85	14	0	0
Reading	L	03/86	85	3	0	0
Cardiff C	Tr	08/87	87-88	66	2	2

STEVENSON Ryan Cairns
Born: Ayr, Scotland, 24 August, 1984 — M

League Club	Source	Date Signed	Seasons Played	Apps	Subs	Gls
Ipswich T	Heart of Midlothian	01/12	11	3	8	1

STEVENSON Walter Harry Horace (Horace)
Born: Derby, England, 26 June, 1923 — RW
Died: Derby, England, 30 December, 1989

League Club	Source	Date Signed	Seasons Played	Apps	Subs	Gls
Nottingham F	Holbrook MW	11/44				
Ipswich T	Tr	02/48	47	3	-	0

STEVENSON William (Willie)
Born: Leith, Edinburgh, Scotland, 26 October, 1939 — M
Scotland: SLge-1

League Club	Source	Date Signed	Seasons Played	Apps	Subs	Gls
Liverpool	Glasgow Rangers	10/62	62-67	188	0	15
Stoke C	Tr	12/67	67-72	82	12	5
Tranmere Rov	Tr	07/73	73	20	0	0

League Club	Source	Date Signed	Seasons Played	Career Record Apps	Subs	Gls

STEVENSON William Byron (Byron)
Born: Llanelli, Carmarthenshire, Wales, 7 September, 1956 — M/D
Died: Llanelli, Carmarthenshire, Wales, 6 September, 2007
Wales: 15/U21-3

Leeds U	App	09/73	74-81	88	7	4
Birmingham C	Tr	03/82	81-84	69	5	3
Bristol Rov	Tr	07/85	85	30	1	3

STEWART Alan Victor
Born: Newcastle-upon-Tyne, England, 24 July, 1922 — CH
Died: York, England, 13 July, 2004

Huddersfield T		04/40	46-48	14	-	0
York C	Tr	08/49	49-56	208	-	1

STEWART Andrew Couper (Andy)
Born: Methil, Fife, Scotland, 29 October, 1956 — F

Portsmouth	App	07/74	73-75	14	5	3

STEWART Anthony Kelvin
Born: Brixton, S London, England, 18 September, 1992 — CD

Wycombe W	Sch	07/11	11-13	45	11	4
Crewe Alex	Tr	11/14	14	2	8	0

STEWART Arthur
Born: Ballymena, Antrim, Northern Ireland, 13 January, 1942 — M
Northern Ireland: 7/NILge-5

Derby Co	Glentoran	12/67	67-69	29	1	1

STEWART Bryan William
Born: Stockton-on-Tees, Cleveland, England, 13 September, 1985 — LW

York C	Sch	-	03	2	8	0

STEWART Cameron Reece
Born: Manchester, England, 8 April, 1991 — LW
England: Youth

Manchester U	Sch	07/09				
Yeovil T	L	07/10	10	1	4	0
Hull C	Tr	11/10	10-12	41	6	1
Burnley	L	08/12	12	2	7	0
Blackburn Rov	L	03/13	12	3	4	0
Charlton Ath	L	09/13	13	15	3	3
Leeds U	L	01/14	13	9	2	0
Ipswich T	Tr	07/14				
Barnsley	L	03/15	14	3	1	0

STEWART Charles David (Dave)
Born: Belfast, Northern Ireland, 20 May, 1958 — LW
Northern Ireland: 1

Hull C	App	08/75	74-78	46	5	7
Chelsea	Tr	05/79				
Scunthorpe U	Tr	11/79	79-81	88	9	19
Hartlepool U	Goole T	03/83	82	6	2	0

STEWART Damion Delano
Born: Kingston, Jamaica, 18 August, 1980 — CD
Jamaica: 57

Bradford C	Harbour View (JAM)	08/05	05	20	3	1
Queens Park Rgrs	Tr	07/06	06-09	147	4	9
Bristol C	Tr	08/10	10-11	21	3	1
Notts Co	L	01/12	11	16	1	2
Notts Co	Tr	11/12	12	2	1	0

STEWART David Steel
Born: Glasgow, Scotland, 11 March, 1947 — G
Scotland: 1/U23-7

Leeds U	Ayr U	10/73	73-78	55	0	0
West Bromwich A	Tr	11/78				
Swansea C	Tr	02/80	79-80	57	0	0

STEWART Edward McDonald (Eddie)
Born: Dundee, Scotland, 15 November, 1934 — LH

Norwich C	Dundee U	07/57	57	13	-	0

STEWART Gareth John
Born: Preston, Lancashire, England, 3 February, 1980 — G
England: Youth/Schools

Blackburn Rov	YT	02/97				
Bournemouth	Tr	07/99	99-07	163	1	0
Yeovil T	Welling U	01/11	11-14	1	2	0

STEWART George Gartshone
Born: Chirnside, Borders, Scotland, 18 October, 1920 — IF

Brentford	Hamilton Academical	08/46	46-47	24	-	3
Queens Park Rgrs	Tr	03/48	47-52	38	-	5
Shrewsbury T	Tr	01/53	52	10	-	2

STEWART George Scott
Born: Larkhall, Lanarkshire, Scotland, 16 November, 1932 — G
Died: Glasgow, Scotland, 28 May, 1998

Bradford C	Stirling A	05/59	59-60	22	-	0

STEWART George Thompson Scott
Born: Buckie, Moray, Scotland, 17 February, 1927 — CF
Died: Buckie, Moray, Scotland, 4 June, 2011

Accrington Stan	Worcester C	09/54	54-58	182	-	136
Coventry C	Tr	11/58	58-59	40	-	23
Carlisle U	Tr	06/60	60	7	-	2

STEWART Gerald (Gerry)
Born: Dundee, Scotland, 2 September, 1946 — G

Preston NE	Jnr	09/63	66-69	4	0	0
Barnsley	Tr	09/71	71-74	138	0	0

STEWART Graham
Born: Birkenhead, Wirral, England, 8 March, 1938 — CF

Sheffield U	Everton (Am)	08/58				
Chesterfield	Tr	05/59	59	5	-	2

STEWART Henry
Born: Wigan, Greater Manchester, England, 28 April, 1925 — LB
Died: Doncaster, South Yorkshire, England, April, 1996

Huddersfield T	Thorne Colliery	08/48	48-50	49	-	0

STEWART Ian Edwin
Born: Belfast, Northern Ireland, 10 September, 1961 — LW
Northern Ireland: 31/Schools

Queens Park Rgrs	Jnr	05/80	80-84	55	12	2
Millwall	L	03/83	82	10	1	3
Newcastle U	Tr	08/85	85-86	34	8	3
Portsmouth	Tr	07/87	87	0	1	0
Brentford	L	02/88	87	4	3	0
Aldershot	Tr	01/89	88-90	94	6	0

STEWART James Garvin (Jim)
Born: Kilwinning, Ayrshire, Scotland, 9 March, 1954 — RW
Scotland: 2/SLge-2/U23-5/U21-3

Middlesbrough	Kilmarnock	06/78	78-80	34	0	0

STEWART James Gordon (Gordon)
Born: Durban, South Africa, 7 August, 1927 — IF
Died: Natal, South Africa, December, 1980

Leeds U	Parkhill (RSA)	10/51	51-52	9	-	2

STEWART John (Jackie)
Born: Armadale, West Lothian, Scotland, 23 January, 1929 — W
Died: Edinburgh, Scotland, 10 January, 2004
Scotland: SLge-2

Walsall	East Fife	06/57	57	28	-	4

STEWART John Barry
Born: Middlesbrough, England, 28 March, 1937 — RW

York C	Whitby T	09/56	56	1	-	0
Darlington	Tr	12/57				

STEWART John Gebbie (Jackie)
Born: Lochgelly, Fife, Scotland, 4 September, 1921 — W
Died: Kirkcaldy, Fife, Scotland, 17 May, 1990

Birmingham C	Raith Rov	01/48	47-54	203	-	52

STEWART Jonathan Harris (Jon)
Born: Hayes, W London, England, 13 March, 1989 — G

Portsmouth	Weymouth	09/08				
Bournemouth	Tr	09/10	10	3	1	0
Burnley	Tr	08/11				

STEWART Jordan Barrington
Born: Birmingham, England, 3 March, 1982 — LB
England: U21-1/Youth

Leicester C	YT	03/00	99-04	86	24	6
Bristol Rov	L	03/00	99	1	3	0
Watford	Tr	07/05	05-07	92	13	2
Derby Co	Tr	07/08	08	26	0	2
Sheffield U	Tr	09/09	09	15	8	0
Millwall	Skoda Xanthi (GRE)	07/11	11	3	1	0
Notts Co		11/12	12	7	0	0
Coventry C	Tr	02/13	12	6	0	0

STEWART Kevin Linford
Born: Enfield, N London, England, 7 September, 1993 — M

Tottenham H	Sch	07/12				
Crewe Alex	L	03/13	12	4	0	0
Liverpool	Tr	07/14				
Cheltenham T	L	01/15	14	4	0	1
Burton A	L	03/15	14	4	3	2

STEWART Mark Gordon
Born: Glasgow, Scotland, 22 June, 1988 — F

Bradford C	Falkirk	07/11	11	5	7	0

STEWART Michael James (Mickey)
Born: Herne Hill, S London, England, 16 September, 1932 — IF

England: Amateur-1

League Club	Source	Date Signed	Seasons Played	Apps	Subs	Gls
Charlton Ath	Corinthian Casuals	10/56	56-58	9	-	3

STEWART Michael James
Born: Edinburgh, Scotland, 26 February, 1981 — M
Scotland: 4/U21-17/Schools

League Club	Source	Date Signed	Seasons Played	Apps	Subs	Gls
Manchester U	YT	03/98	00-02	5	2	0
Nottingham F	L	07/03	03	11	2	0
Charlton Ath	Genclerbirligi (TKY)	03/11	10	6	3	0

STEWART Paul Andrew
Born: Manchester, England, 7 October, 1964 — M/F
England: 3/B-5/U21-1/Youth

League Club	Source	Date Signed	Seasons Played	Apps	Subs	Gls
Blackpool	App	10/81	81-86	188	13	55
Manchester C	Tr	03/87	86-87	51	0	26
Tottenham H	Tr	06/88	88-91	126	5	28
Liverpool	Tr	07/92	92-93	28	4	1
Crystal Palace	L	01/94	93	18	0	3
Wolverhampton W	L	09/94	94	5	3	2
Burnley	L	02/95	94	6	0	0
Sunderland	Tr	08/95	95-96	31	5	5
Stoke C	Tr	07/97	97	22	0	3

STEWART Raymond Strean McDonald (Ray)
Born: Perth, Scotland, 7 September, 1959 — RB
Scotland: 10/U21-12/Schools

League Club	Source	Date Signed	Seasons Played	Apps	Subs	Gls
West Ham U	Dundee U	09/79	79-90	344	1	62

STEWART Reginald (Reg)
Born: Sheffield, England, 30 October, 1925 — CH
Died: Colchester, Essex, England, 6 March, 2011

League Club	Source	Date Signed	Seasons Played	Apps	Subs	Gls
Sheffield Wed	Sheffield YMCA	09/44	46	6	-	0
Colchester U	Tr	07/49	50-56	256	-	2

STEWART Robert (Bobby)
Born: Kirkcaldy, Fife, Scotland, 4 December, 1933 — IF
Died: Dunfermline, Fife, Scotland, 17 July, 2005
Scotland: Schools

League Club	Source	Date Signed	Seasons Played	Apps	Subs	Gls
Crewe Alex	Cowdenbeath	08/55	55	22	-	3

STEWART Robert Ashcroft (Robbie)
Born: Broxburn, West Lothian, Scotland, 14 June, 1971 — M

League Club	Source	Date Signed	Seasons Played	Apps	Subs	Gls
Doncaster Rov	YT	-	88	1	0	0

STEWART Simon Andrew
Born: Leeds, England, 1 November, 1973 — CD

League Club	Source	Date Signed	Seasons Played	Apps	Subs	Gls
Sheffield Wed	YT	07/92	92	6	0	0
Shrewsbury T	L	08/95	95	4	0	0
Fulham	Tr	06/96	96	2	1	0

STEWART Thomas James (Tom)
Born: Bradford, England, 17 April, 1996 — G

League Club	Source	Date Signed	Seasons Played	Apps	Subs	Gls
Morecambe	Guiseley	08/13	14	0	1	0

STEWART William (Willie)
Born: Clydebank, Dunbartonshire, Scotland, 10 March, 1922 — IF
Died: Aldershot, Hampshire, England, June, 1987

League Club	Source	Date Signed	Seasons Played	Apps	Subs	Gls
Aldershot	St Mirren	06/51	51-53	27	-	4

STEWART William Ian (Billy)
Born: Liverpool, England, 1 January, 1965 — G

League Club	Source	Date Signed	Seasons Played	Apps	Subs	Gls
Liverpool	App	01/83				
Wigan Ath	Tr	07/84	84-85	14	0	0
Chester C	Tr	08/86	86-93	272	0	0
Northampton T	Tr	07/94	94	26	1	0
Chesterfield	L	03/95	94	1	0	0
Chester C	Tr	07/95	95	45	0	0

STEWART William Marcus Paul (Marcus)
Born: Bristol, England, 7 November, 1972 — F
England: FLge/Schools

League Club	Source	Date Signed	Seasons Played	Apps	Subs	Gls
Bristol Rov	YT	07/91	91-95	137	34	57
Huddersfield T	Tr	07/96	96-99	129	4	58
Ipswich T	Tr	02/00	99-02	65	10	27
Sunderland	Tr	08/02	02-04	77	25	31
Bristol C	Tr	07/05	05	16	11	5
Preston NE	L	03/06	05	4	0	0
Yeovil T	L	08/06	06	11	0	5
Yeovil T	Tr	01/07	06-07	55	1	7
Exeter C	Tr	07/08	08-10	73	12	9

STIEBER Zoltan
Born: Sarvar, Hungary, 16 October, 1988 — LW
Hungary: 9/U21-1/Youth

League Club	Source	Date Signed	Seasons Played	Apps	Subs	Gls
Aston Villa	Sch	01/07				
Yeovil T	L	11/07	07	14	1	1

STIENS Craig
Born: Swansea, Wales, 31 July, 1984 — F
Wales: Youth

League Club	Source	Date Signed	Seasons Played	Apps	Subs	Gls
Leeds U	YT	08/01				
Swansea C	L	12/02	02	0	3	0

STIFFLE Nelson Everard
Born: India, 30 July, 1928 — W
Died: Brisbane, Australia, 8 April, 2005

League Club	Source	Date Signed	Seasons Played	Apps	Subs	Gls
Chester C	Ashton U	12/51	51	7	-	2
Chesterfield	Altrincham	03/54	54	38	-	9
Bournemouth	Tr	05/55	55-57	35	-	7
Exeter C	Tr	03/58	57-59	94	-	17
Coventry C	Tr	07/60	60	15	-	2

STILES John Charles
Born: Manchester, England, 6 May, 1964 — M

League Club	Source	Date Signed	Seasons Played	Apps	Subs	Gls
Leeds U	Vancouver W'caps (CAN)	05/84	84-88	49	16	2
Doncaster Rov	Tr	08/89	89-91	88	1	2
Rochdale	L	03/92	91	2	2	0

STILES Norbert Peter (Nobby)
Born: Manchester, England, 18 May, 1942 — DM
England: 28/FLge-3/U23-3/Youth/Schools

League Club	Source	Date Signed	Seasons Played	Apps	Subs	Gls
Manchester U	Jnr	06/59	60-70	311	0	17
Middlesbrough	Tr	05/71	71-72	57	0	2
Preston NE	Tr	08/73	73-74	44	2	1

STILL John Leonard
Born: West Ham, E London, England, 24 April, 1950 — CD

League Club	Source	Date Signed	Seasons Played	Apps	Subs	Gls
Leyton Orient (Am)	Jnr	05/67	67	1	0	0

STILL Robert Arthur (Bob)
Born: Brinscall, Lancashire, England, 15 December, 1912 — WH
Died: Crewe, Cheshire, England, 23 August, 1983

League Club	Source	Date Signed	Seasons Played	Apps	Subs	Gls
Stockport Co	Chorley	06/34	34-38	155	-	2
Crewe Alex	Tr	08/39	46	1	-	0

STILL Ronald George (Ron)
Born: Aberdeen, Scotland, 10 June, 1943 — CF/LH

League Club	Source	Date Signed	Seasons Played	Apps	Subs	Gls
Arsenal	Woodside BC	08/61				
Notts Co	Tr	07/65	65-66	46	0	15
Brentford	Tr	07/67	67	1	0	0

STILLE Giles Kevin
Born: Westminster, Central London, England, 10 November, 1958 — M

League Club	Source	Date Signed	Seasons Played	Apps	Subs	Gls
Brighton & HA	Kingstonian	05/79	79-83	20	7	4

STILLIE Derek Daniel
Born: Cumnock, Ayrshire, Scotland, 3 December, 1973 — G
Scotland: U21-14

League Club	Source	Date Signed	Seasons Played	Apps	Subs	Gls
Wigan Ath	Aberdeen	08/99	99-01	42	2	0
Gillingham	Dundee U	07/07	07	13	1	0

STILLYARDS George Edward William
Born: Whisby, Lincolnshire, England, 29 December, 1918 — RB
Died: Lincoln, England, 19 January, 2010

League Club	Source	Date Signed	Seasons Played	Apps	Subs	Gls
Lincoln C	Botolph U	11/42	46-49	100	-	2

STIMAC Igor
Born: Metkovic, Croatia, 6 September, 1967 — CD
Croatia: 53

League Club	Source	Date Signed	Seasons Played	Apps	Subs	Gls
Derby Co	Hajduk Split (CRO)	10/95	95-98	84	0	3
West Ham U	Tr	09/99	99-00	43	0	1

STIMPSON Barrie George
Born: Billingham, Cleveland, England, 8 February, 1964 — LB

League Club	Source	Date Signed	Seasons Played	Apps	Subs	Gls
Hartlepool U	App	02/82	80-83	66	2	2
Chesterfield	Tr	11/83	83	27	0	0
Hartlepool U	Tr	11/84	84	18	0	0

STIMSON Charlie Thomas Frederick
Born: Newcastle-upon-Tyne, England, 1 March, 1992 — F

League Club	Source	Date Signed	Seasons Played	Apps	Subs	Gls
Barnet	Gillingham (Sch)	07/10	10	0	6	0

STIMSON Mark Nicholas
Born: Plaistow, E London, England, 27 December, 1967 — LB

League Club	Source	Date Signed	Seasons Played	Apps	Subs	Gls
Tottenham H	App	07/85	86-88	1	1	0
Leyton Orient	L	03/88	87	10	0	0
Gillingham	L	01/89	88	18	0	0
Newcastle U	Tr	06/89	89-92	82	4	2
Portsmouth	L	12/92	92	3	1	0
Portsmouth	Tr	07/93	93-95	57	1	2
Barnet	L	09/93	95	5	0	0
Southend U	Tr	03/96	95-98	51	5	0
Leyton Orient	Tr	03/99	98	2	0	0

STINSON Hugh Michael John
Born: Rossendale, Lancashire, England, 18 May, 1937 — WH
Died: July, 2015

League Club	Source	Date Signed	Seasons Played	Apps	Subs	Gls
Accrington Stan	Whitewell Bottom	05/55	58	3	-	0
Gillingham	Tr	07/59	59	1	-	0

STIRK John
Born: Consett, County Durham, England, 5 September, 1955 RB
England: Youth

League Club	Source	Date Signed	Seasons Played	Apps	Subs	Gls
Ipswich T	App	06/73	77	6	0	0
Watford	Tr	06/78	78	46	0	0
Chesterfield	Tr	03/80	79-82	54	2	0

STIRLAND John Cecil (Cec)
Born: Adwick-le-Street, South Yorkshire, England, 15 July, 1921 WH
Died: Collingham, Nottinghamshire, England, 27 January, 2004

League Club	Source	Date Signed	Seasons Played	Apps	Subs	Gls
Doncaster Rov	Jnr	07/38	46-48	68	-	0
New Brighton	Tr	01/50	49-50	51	-	0
Scunthorpe U	Tr	08/51	51	17	-	0

STIRLING James Russell (Jimmy)
Born: Airdrie, Lanarkshire, Scotland, 23 July, 1925 CH
Died: Brockenhurst, Hampshire, England, November, 2006

League Club	Source	Date Signed	Seasons Played	Apps	Subs	Gls
Bournemouth	Coltness U	07/47	47-49	73	-	1
Birmingham C	Tr	06/50				
Southend U	Tr	12/50	50-59	218	-	2

STIRLING Jude Barrington
Born: Enfield, N London, England, 29 June, 1982 D/M

League Club	Source	Date Signed	Seasons Played	Apps	Subs	Gls
Luton T	YT	07/99	00-01	6	4	0
Oxford U	Grays Ath	08/05	05	6	4	0
Lincoln C	Tr	01/06	05	0	6	0
Peterborough U	Tr	07/06	06	14	8	0
MK Dons	Tr	01/07	06-10	48	47	5
Grimsby T	L	03/10	09	2	2	0
Barnet	L	03/11	10	5	1	0
Notts Co	Tr	07/11	11	0	8	0

STITFALL Albert Edward
Born: Cardiff, Wales, 7 July, 1924 LB/W
Died: Cardiff, Wales, 26 September, 1998

League Club	Source	Date Signed	Seasons Played	Apps	Subs	Gls
Cardiff C	Jnr	11/48	48-50	7	-	1
Torquay U	Tr	03/52	51-52	22	-	1

STITFALL Ronald Frederick (Ron)
Born: Cardiff, Wales, 14 December, 1925 FB
Died: Cardiff, Wales, 22 June, 2008
Wales: 2/WLge-1

League Club	Source	Date Signed	Seasons Played	Apps	Subs	Gls
Cardiff C	Jnr	09/47	47-63	398	-	8

STOBART Barry Henry
Born: Doncaster, South Yorkshire, England, 6 June, 1938 CF
Died: Sedgley, West Midlands, England, 28 August, 2013

League Club	Source	Date Signed	Seasons Played	Apps	Subs	Gls
Wolverhampton W	Jnr	12/55	59-63	49	-	20
Manchester C	Tr	08/64	64	14	-	1
Aston Villa	Tr	11/64	64-67	45	0	18
Shrewsbury T	Tr	10/67	67-68	34	2	9

STOBART Sean Anthony
Born: Wolverhampton, England, 31 July, 1966 F

League Club	Source	Date Signed	Seasons Played	Apps	Subs	Gls
Scunthorpe U	Jnr	07/84	84	0	2	1

STOBBART George Campbell
Born: Pegswood, Northumberland, England, 9 January, 1921 CF
Died: North Tyneside, Tyne and Wear, England, January, 1995

League Club	Source	Date Signed	Seasons Played	Apps	Subs	Gls
Middlesbrough	Netherton	11/45				
Newcastle U	Tr	09/46	46-48	66	-	21
Luton T	Tr	10/49	49-51	107	-	30
Millwall	Tr	08/52	52-53	68	-	27
Brentford	Tr	05/54	54-55	57	-	17

STOBBS Jack Thomas
Born: Leeds, England, 27 February, 1997 M

League Club	Source	Date Signed	Seasons Played	Apps	Subs	Gls
Sheffield Wed	Sch	03/14	13	0	1	0

STOCCO Thomas Luca (Tom)
Born: Westminster, Central London, England, 4 January, 1983 F

League Club	Source	Date Signed	Seasons Played	Apps	Subs	Gls
Torquay U	YT	07/01	99-00	2	8	2

STOCH Miroslav
Born: Nitra, Slovakia, 19 October, 1989 LW
Slovakia: 50/U21-7/Youth

League Club	Source	Date Signed	Seasons Played	Apps	Subs	Gls
Chelsea	Sch	07/07	08	0	4	0

STOCK Brian Benjamin
Born: Winchester, Hampshire, England, 24 December, 1981 M
Wales: 3/U21-4

League Club	Source	Date Signed	Seasons Played	Apps	Subs	Gls
Bournemouth	YT	01/00	99-05	113	32	16
Preston NE	Tr	01/06	05-06	5	3	1
Doncaster Rov	Tr	09/06	06-11	181	9	17
Burnley	Tr	08/12	12-13	20	14	0

STOCK Harold (Harry)
Born: Stockport, Greater Manchester, England, 31 July, 1918 IF
Died: Stockport, Greater Manchester, England, June, 1977

League Club	Source	Date Signed	Seasons Played	Apps	Subs	Gls
Stockport Co	Cheadle	07/38	38-47	19	-	5
Oldham Ath	Tr	07/48	48-50	35	-	10

STOCK Russell John
Born: Great Yarmouth, Norfolk, England, 25 June, 1977 M

League Club	Source	Date Signed	Seasons Played	Apps	Subs	Gls
Cambridge U	YT	07/95	95	15	2	1

STOCKDALE David Adam
Born: Leeds, England, 20 September, 1985 G
England: Semi Pro-1

League Club	Source	Date Signed	Seasons Played	Apps	Subs	Gls
York C	Sch	07/04	02	0	1	0
Darlington	Tr	08/06	06-07	46	1	0
Fulham	Tr	06/08	09-13	37	2	0
Rotherham U	L	11/08	08	8	0	0
Leicester C	L	03/09	08	8	0	0
Plymouth Arg	L	01/10	09	21	0	0
Ipswich T	L	07/11	11	18	0	0
Hull C	L	11/12	12	5	0	0
Hull C	L	01/13	12	19	0	0
Brighton & HA	Tr	07/14	14	42	0	0

STOCKDALE Robert Keith (Robbie)
Born: Redcar, Cleveland, England, 30 November, 1979 RB
England: U21-1//Scotland: 5/B-2

League Club	Source	Date Signed	Seasons Played	Apps	Subs	Gls
Middlesbrough	YT	07/98	97-03	62	13	2
Sheffield Wed	L	09/00	00	6	0	0
West Ham U	L	10/03	03	5	2	0
Rotherham U	Tr	02/04	03-04	43	0	1
Hull C	Tr	01/05	04	12	2	0
Darlington	L	02/06	05	3	0	0
Tranmere Rov	Tr	07/06	06-07	78	2	0
Grimsby T	Tr	07/08	08-09	27	1	0

STOCKIN Ronald (Ron)
Born: Birmingham, England, 27 June, 1931 IF

League Club	Source	Date Signed	Seasons Played	Apps	Subs	Gls
Walsall	West Bromwich A (Am)	01/52	51	6	-	3
Wolverhampton W	Tr	02/52	52-53	21	-	7
Cardiff C	Tr	06/54	54-56	57	-	16
Grimsby T	Tr	06/57	57-59	49	-	14

STOCKLEY Jayden Connor
Born: Poole, Dorset, England, 10 October, 1993 F

League Club	Source	Date Signed	Seasons Played	Apps	Subs	Gls
Bournemouth	Jnr	11/10	09-11	1	15	0
Accrington Stan	L	11/11	11	5	4	3
Leyton Orient	L	09/13	13	0	8	1
Torquay U	L	01/14	13	7	12	1
Cambridge U	L	08/14	14	1	2	2
Luton T	L	01/15	14	11	2	3

STOCKLEY Kenneth Sidney (Ken)
Born: Watford, Hertfordshire, England, 24 November, 1926 LH
Died: Watford, Hertfordshire, England, 5 August, 2006

League Club	Source	Date Signed	Seasons Played	Apps	Subs	Gls
Luton T	Jnr	02/44				
Watford	Tr	07/48	49	1	-	0

STOCKLEY Samuel Joshua (Sam)
Born: Tiverton, Devon, England, 5 September, 1977 RB

League Club	Source	Date Signed	Seasons Played	Apps	Subs	Gls
Southampton	YT	07/96				
Barnet	Tr	12/96	96-00	177	5	2
Oxford U	Tr	07/01	01	39	2	0
Colchester U	Tr	08/02	02-05	129	12	3
Blackpool	L	03/06	05	3	4	0
Wycombe W	Tr	07/06	06-07	51	5	1
Port Vale	Tr	07/08	08-09	29	2	0

STOCKS David Henry
Born: Dulwich, S London, England, 20 April, 1943 D

League Club	Source	Date Signed	Seasons Played	Apps	Subs	Gls
Charlton Ath	Jnr	01/62	61-64	26	-	0
Gillingham	Tr	05/65	65	45	0	0
Bournemouth	Tr	06/66	66-71	220	0	2
Torquay U	Tr	01/72	71-76	150	0	3

STOCKS Joseph Ronald (Joe)
Born: Hull, England, 27 November, 1941 LH

League Club	Source	Date Signed	Seasons Played	Apps	Subs	Gls
Hull C	Jnr	12/58	59-60	9	-	1
Millwall	Tr	08/61	61-63	30	-	1

STOCKTON Cole John
Born: Huyton, Merseyside, England, 13 March, 1994 F

League Club	Source	Date Signed	Seasons Played	Apps	Subs	Gls
Tranmere Rov	Sch	04/12	11-14	22	53	9

STOCKWELL Michael Thomas (Mick)
Born: Chelmsford, England, 14 February, 1965 M

League Club	Source	Date Signed	Seasons Played	Apps	Subs	Gls
Ipswich T	App	12/82	85-99	464	42	35
Colchester U	Tr	07/00	00-02	121	11	22

STODDART Terence (Terry)
Born: Newcastle-upon-Tyne, England, 28 November, 1931 LH
Died: Newcastle-on-Tyne, England, October, 2014

League Club	Source	Date Signed	Seasons Played	Apps	Subs	Gls
Newcastle U	Jnr	01/49				
Darlington	Tr	05/54	54-55	9	-	0
York C	Tr	07/56	56	3	-	0

STOJKOVIC Vladimir
Born: Loznica, Serbia, 29 July, 1983 — G
Serbia: 61

League Club	Source	Date Signed	Seasons Played	Apps	Subs	Gls
Wigan Ath (L)	Sporting Lisbon (POR)	01/10	09	4	0	0

STOKER Gareth
Born: Bishop Auckland, County Durham, England, 22 February, 1973 — M

League Club	Source	Date Signed	Seasons Played	Apps	Subs	Gls
Hull C	Leeds U (YT)	09/91	91-92	24	6	2
Hereford U	Bishop Auckland	03/95	94-96	65	5	6
Cardiff C	Tr	01/97	96-97	29	8	4
Rochdale	Tr	02/99	98	11	1	1

STOKES Albert William
Born: Sheffield, England, 26 January, 1933 — CF
Died: Grimsby, North Lincolnshire, England, 1 May, 2014

League Club	Source	Date Signed	Seasons Played	Apps	Subs	Gls
Grimsby T	Hampton Sports	02/54	54-56	16	-	3
Scunthorpe U	Tr	07/57	57	5	-	2
Southport	Tr	02/59	58	6	-	2

STOKES Alfred Frederick (Alfie)
Born: Hackney, E London, England, 3 October, 1932 — IF
Died: Worthing, West Sussex, England, 30 March, 2002
England: B-1/FLge-1/U23-1

League Club	Source	Date Signed	Seasons Played	Apps	Subs	Gls
Tottenham H	Clapton	02/53	52-58	65	-	40
Fulham	Tr	07/59	59	15	-	6
Watford	Cambridge C	04/61	61	14	-	2

STOKES Anthony
Born: Dublin, Republic of Ireland, 25 July, 1988 — F
Republic of Ireland: 9/B-1/U21-10/Youth

League Club	Source	Date Signed	Seasons Played	Apps	Subs	Gls
Arsenal	Sch	07/06				
Sunderland	Tr	01/07	06-08	15	21	3
Sheffield U	L	10/08	08	5	7	0
Crystal Palace	L	03/09	08	11	2	1

STOKES Christopher Martin Thomas (Chris)
Born: Frome, Somerset, England, 8 March, 1991 — LB
England: Semi Pro-1/Youth

League Club	Source	Date Signed	Seasons Played	Apps	Subs	Gls
Crewe Alex	Bolton W (Sch)	03/10	09	2	0	0
Coventry C (L)	Forest Green Rov	02/15	14	16	0	1

STOKES Dean Anthony
Born: Birmingham, England, 23 May, 1970 — LB

League Club	Source	Date Signed	Seasons Played	Apps	Subs	Gls
Port Vale	Halesowen T	01/93	93-97	53	7	0
Rochdale	Tr	07/98	98-99	28	2	0

STOKES Derek
Born: Normanton, West Yorkshire, England, 13 September, 1939 — CF
England: U23-4

League Club	Source	Date Signed	Seasons Played	Apps	Subs	Gls
Bradford C	Snydale Ath, Cudworth	04/57	57-59	94	-	44
Huddersfield T	Tr	06/60	60-64	153	-	65
Bradford C	Tr	01/66	65-66	31	1	11

STOKES Robert William Thomas (Bobby)
Born: Portsmouth, England, 30 January, 1951 — F
Died: Portsmouth, England, 30 May, 1995
England: Youth

League Club	Source	Date Signed	Seasons Played	Apps	Subs	Gls
Southampton	Jnr	02/68	68-76	194	22	40
Portsmouth	Tr	08/77	77	23	1	2

STOKES Tony Ronald
Born: Bethnal Green, E London, England, 7 January, 1987 — W

League Club	Source	Date Signed	Seasons Played	Apps	Subs	Gls
West Ham U	Sch	07/05				
Rushden & D	L	01/06	05	18	1	0
Brighton & HA	L	08/06	06	5	1	0

STOKES Wayne Darren
Born: Wolverhampton, England, 16 February, 1965 — CD

League Club	Source	Date Signed	Seasons Played	Apps	Subs	Gls
Gillingham	Coventry C (App)	07/82	82-83	2	1	0
Stockport Co	Gloucester C	10/86	86	17	1	1
Hartlepool U	Tr	07/87	87-89	62	0	1

STOKLE David
Born: Hartlepool, Cleveland, England, 1 December, 1969 — CD

League Club	Source	Date Signed	Seasons Played	Apps	Subs	Gls
Hartlepool U	YT	07/88	86-89	9	0	0

STOKOE Dennis
Born: Blyth, Northumberland, England, 6 June, 1925 — WH
Died: Chester-le-Street, County Durham, England, 22 July, 2005

League Club	Source	Date Signed	Seasons Played	Apps	Subs	Gls
Chesterfield	North Shields	01/47				
Carlisle U	Tr	07/48	48-53	151	-	2
Workington	Tr	10/53	53-55	107	-	2
Gateshead	Tr	08/56	56	13	-	0

STOKOE Graham Lloyd
Born: Newcastle-upon-Tyne, England, 17 December, 1975 — M

League Club	Source	Date Signed	Seasons Played	Apps	Subs	Gls
Stoke C	Newcastle U (YT)	07/94	96	0	2	0
Hartlepool U	L	02/96	95	8	0	0
Hartlepool U	Tr	08/98	98	15	5	0

STOKOE Robert (Bob)
Born: Prudhoe, Northumberland, England, 21 September, 1930 — CH
Died: Hartlepool, Cleveland, England, 1 February, 2004

League Club	Source	Date Signed	Seasons Played	Apps	Subs	Gls
Newcastle U	Jnr	09/47	50-60	261	-	4
Bury	Tr	02/61	60-63	82	-	0

STOLCERS Andrejs
Born: Riga, Latvia, 8 July, 1974 — M
Latvia: 81

League Club	Source	Date Signed	Seasons Played	Apps	Subs	Gls
Fulham	Shakhtar Donetsk (UKR)	12/00	00-02	8	17	2
Yeovil T	Tr	09/04	04	23	13	5

STONE Craig Brian Raymond
Born: Strood, Kent, England, 29 December, 1988 — RB

League Club	Source	Date Signed	Seasons Played	Apps	Subs	Gls
Gillingham	Sch	07/07	05-07	6	9	0
Brentford	L	01/08	07	5	1	0

STONE Daniel John Cooper (Danny)
Born: Liverpool, England, 14 September, 1982 — RB/M

League Club	Source	Date Signed	Seasons Played	Apps	Subs	Gls
Notts Co	Blackburn Rov (YT)	08/01	01-02	16	5	0

STONE David Kenneth (Dave)
Born: Bristol, England, 29 December, 1942 — D

League Club	Source	Date Signed	Seasons Played	Apps	Subs	Gls
Bristol Rov	Jnr	03/60	62-67	145	3	6
Southend U	Tr	07/68	68	6	0	0

STONE Edward Leonard
Born: Gorleston, Norfolk, England, 5 January, 1942 — LH

League Club	Source	Date Signed	Seasons Played	Apps	Subs	Gls
Charlton Ath	Jnr	08/59				
Crystal Palace	Tr	05/61	61	1	-	0

STONE Frederick William (Fred)
Born: Bristol, England, 5 July, 1925 — FB
Died: Bristol, England, 24 January, 2002

League Club	Source	Date Signed	Seasons Played	Apps	Subs	Gls
Bristol C	Oldland Common	06/47	47-52	64	-	3

STONE Geoffrey (Geoff)
Born: Mansfield, Nottinghamshire, England, 10 April, 1924 — CH
Died: Nottingham, England, August, 1993

League Club	Source	Date Signed	Seasons Played	Apps	Subs	Gls
Notts Co	Beeston BC	09/48	48-49	4	-	0
Darlington	Tr	08/50	50-51	31	-	0

STONE John George
Born: Carlin How, Cleveland, England, 3 March, 1953 — D/M

League Club	Source	Date Signed	Seasons Played	Apps	Subs	Gls
Middlesbrough	South Bank	07/70	71	2	0	0
York C	Tr	07/72	72-75	86	0	5
Darlington	Tr	07/76	76-78	120	0	14
Grimsby T	Tr	07/79	79-82	89	5	2
Rotherham U	Tr	09/83	83	10	0	1

STONE Michael (Mick)
Born: Hucknall, Nottinghamshire, England, 23 May, 1938 — G

League Club	Source	Date Signed	Seasons Played	Apps	Subs	Gls
Notts Co	Linby Colliery	07/58	58	7	-	0

STONE Peter James
Born: Oxford, England, 8 October, 1922 — CH

League Club	Source	Date Signed	Seasons Played	Apps	Subs	Gls
Luton T (Am)	Oxford C	12/51	51	1	-	0

STONE Steven Brian (Steve)
Born: Gateshead, Tyne and Wear, England, 20 August, 1971 — RM
England: 9

League Club	Source	Date Signed	Seasons Played	Apps	Subs	Gls
Nottingham F	YT	05/89	91-98	189	4	23
Aston Villa	Tr	03/99	98-01	66	24	4
Portsmouth	L	10/02	02	5	0	1
Portsmouth	Tr	12/02	02-04	64	4	8
Leeds U	Tr	07/05	05-06	6	6	1

STONEBRIDGE Ian Robert
Born: Lewisham, SE London, England, 30 August, 1981 — F
England: Youth

League Club	Source	Date Signed	Seasons Played	Apps	Subs	Gls
Plymouth Arg	Tottenham H (YT)	07/99	99-03	124	47	38
Wycombe W	Tr	08/04	04-06	40	34	6
Torquay U	L	11/05	05	3	0	0

STONEHOUSE Basil Henry
Born: Guisborough, Cleveland, England, 27 October, 1952 — FB

League Club	Source	Date Signed	Seasons Played	Apps	Subs	Gls
Middlesbrough	App	12/69				
Halifax T	L	10/72	72	1	1	0

STONEHOUSE Bernard
Born: Manchester, England, 23 December, 1934 — LW

League Club	Source	Date Signed	Seasons Played	Apps	Subs	Gls
Rochdale	Crewe Alex (Am)	08/55	55-56	19	-	1

STONEHOUSE Derek
Born: Lingdale, Cleveland, England, 18 November, 1932 — FB
Died: Middlesbrough, England, 9 April, 2004
England: Youth

League Club	Source	Date Signed	Seasons Played	Apps	Subs	Gls
Middlesbrough	Lingdale	05/51	53-61	174	-	0
Hartlepool U	Tr	09/63	63-64	34	-	0

League Club	Source	Date Signed	Seasons Played	Career Record Apps	Subs	Gls

STONEHOUSE Kevin
Born: Bishop Auckland, County Durham, England, 20 September, 1959 — F

League Club	Source	Date Signed	Seasons Played	Apps	Subs	Gls
Blackburn Rov	Shildon	07/79	79-82	77	8	27
Huddersfield T	Tr	03/83	82-83	20	2	4
Blackpool	Tr	03/84	83-85	53	3	19
Darlington	Tr	07/87	87-88	59	13	20
Carlisle U	L	03/89	88	0	3	0
Rochdale	Tr	07/89	89	13	1	2

STONEMAN Paul
Born: Whitley Bay, Tyne and Wear, England, 26 February, 1973 — CD

League Club	Source	Date Signed	Seasons Played	Apps	Subs	Gls
Blackpool	YT	07/91	91-94	38	5	0
Colchester U	L	12/94	94	3	0	1
Halifax T	Tr	07/95	98-01	137	2	11

STONES Craig
Born: Scunthorpe, North Lincolnshire, England, 31 May, 1980 — M

League Club	Source	Date Signed	Seasons Played	Apps	Subs	Gls
Lincoln C	YT	07/97	96-99	10	11	0

STONES Gordon
Born: Kearsley, Greater Manchester, England, 18 November, 1934 — CH

League Club	Source	Date Signed	Seasons Played	Apps	Subs	Gls
Accrington Stan	Bury (Am)	09/54	55-60	109	-	1

STONES John
Born: Barnsley, South Yorkshire, England, 28 May, 1994 — CD
England: 4/U21-10/Youth

League Club	Source	Date Signed	Seasons Played	Apps	Subs	Gls
Barnsley	Sch	12/11	11-12	19	5	0
Everton	Tr	01/13	13-14	38	6	1

STOOR Fredrik Olof Esaias
Born: Stockholm, Sweden, 28 February, 1984 — RB
Sweden: 11/U21-9

League Club	Source	Date Signed	Seasons Played	Apps	Subs	Gls
Fulham	Rosenborg (NOR)	08/08	08-09	0	4	0
Derby Co	L	09/09	09	10	1	0

STOPFORD Alan
Born: Sheffield, England, 20 November, 1946 — RW

League Club	Source	Date Signed	Seasons Played	Apps	Subs	Gls
Chesterfield	Sheffield U (Am)	01/67	66	2	0	0

STOPFORD Leslie (Les)
Born: Manchester, England, 9 May, 1942 — IF

League Club	Source	Date Signed	Seasons Played	Apps	Subs	Gls
Chester C	Jnr	03/60	59-61	6	-	1

STORER Peter Russell
Born: Shoreditch, Central London, England, 14 February, 1935 — G

League Club	Source	Date Signed	Seasons Played	Apps	Subs	Gls
Watford (Am)	Berkhamsted T	03/59	58	9	-	0

STORER Stuart John
Born: Rugby, Warwickshire, England, 16 January, 1967 — RW

League Club	Source	Date Signed	Seasons Played	Apps	Subs	Gls
Mansfield T	Jnr	-	83	0	1	0
Birmingham C	VS Rugby	07/84	85-86	5	3	0
Everton	Tr	03/87				
Wigan Ath	L	07/87	87	9	3	0
Bolton W	Tr	12/87	87-92	95	28	12
Exeter C	Tr	03/93	92-94	75	2	8
Brighton & HA	Tr	03/95	94-98	114	28	11

STOREY Brett Barry
Born: Sheffield, England, 7 July, 1977 — M

League Club	Source	Date Signed	Seasons Played	Apps	Subs	Gls
Sheffield U	YT	07/95				
Lincoln C	Tr	03/96	95	0	1	1

STOREY James (Jim)
Born: Rowlands Gill, Tyne and Wear, England, 30 December, 1929 — FB

League Club	Source	Date Signed	Seasons Played	Apps	Subs	Gls
Newcastle U	Spen Black & White	05/48				
Exeter C	Tr	06/53	53	9	-	0
Bournemouth	Tr	07/54				
Rochdale	Tr	06/55	55-56	24	-	1
Darlington	Tr	06/57	57	6	-	0

STOREY Luke Dawson
Born: Seaham, County Durham, England, 17 December, 1920 — RW
Died: Sunderland, England, 20 August, 1987

League Club	Source	Date Signed	Seasons Played	Apps	Subs	Gls
Lincoln C	Blackhall CW	09/47	47-48	11	-	2

STOREY Miles James
Born: West Bromwich, West Midlands, England, 4 January, 1994 — F
England: Youth

League Club	Source	Date Signed	Seasons Played	Apps	Subs	Gls
Swindon T	Sch	07/12	10-13	9	23	4
Shrewsbury T	L	02/14	13	4	2	0
Portsmouth	L	07/14	14	10	7	2
Newport Co	L	01/15	14	14	4	2

STOREY Peter Edwin
Born: Farnham, Surrey, England, 7 September, 1945 — RB/DM
England: 19/FLge-2/Schools

League Club	Source	Date Signed	Seasons Played	Apps	Subs	Gls
Arsenal	App	10/62	65-76	387	4	9
Fulham	Tr	03/77	76-77	17	0	0

STOREY Sidney (Sid)
Born: Darfield, South Yorkshire, England, 25 December, 1919 — IF
Died: York, England, 6 April, 2010

League Club	Source	Date Signed	Seasons Played	Apps	Subs	Gls
Huddersfield T	Grimethorpe Ath	09/43				
York C	Wombwell Ath	05/47	46-55	330	-	40
Barnsley	Tr	05/56	56	29	-	4
Accrington Stan	Tr	10/57	57-58	30	-	2
Bradford Park Ave	Tr	07/59	59	2	-	0

STOREY-MOORE Ian
Born: Ipswich, England, 17 January, 1945 — W/F
England: 1/FLge-2/U23-2

League Club	Source	Date Signed	Seasons Played	Apps	Subs	Gls
Nottingham F	Jnr	05/62	62-71	235	1	105
Manchester U	Tr	03/72	71-73	39	0	11

STORF David Alan
Born: Sheffield, England, 4 December, 1943 — LW

League Club	Source	Date Signed	Seasons Played	Apps	Subs	Gls
Sheffield Wed	Jnr	12/60				
Rochdale	Tr	06/63	63-66	138	0	19
Barrow	Tr	07/67	67-71	154	4	26

STORRAR David McKinnon
Born: Lochgelly, Fife, Scotland, 16 January, 1933 — LW

League Club	Source	Date Signed	Seasons Played	Apps	Subs	Gls
Sheffield Wed	Wanderers, Sheffield	02/51	52	4	-	0

STORRIE James (Jim)
Born: Kirkintilloch, Dunbartonshire, Scotland, 31 March, 1940 — F
Died: Cumbernauld, Lanarkshire, Scotland, 11 November, 2014

League Club	Source	Date Signed	Seasons Played	Apps	Subs	Gls
Leeds U	Airdrieonians	06/62	62-66	123	3	58
Rotherham U	Aberdeen	12/67	67-69	70	1	19
Portsmouth	Tr	12/69	69-71	43	0	12
Aldershot	L	03/72	71	5	0	1

STORTON Stanley Eugene (Stan)
Born: Keighley, West Yorkshire, England, 5 January, 1939 — FB

League Club	Source	Date Signed	Seasons Played	Apps	Subs	Gls
Bradford C	Huddersfield T (Am)	07/57	59-63	111	-	5
Darlington	Tr	01/64	63	15	-	0
Hartlepool U	Tr	07/64	64-65	72	0	0
Tranmere Rov	Tr	07/66	66-69	114	9	2

STORTON Trevor George
Born: Keighley, West Yorkshire, England, 26 November, 1949 — CD
Died: Bradford, England, 23 March, 2011

League Club	Source	Date Signed	Seasons Played	Apps	Subs	Gls
Tranmere Rov	Jnr	10/67	67-71	112	6	8
Liverpool	Tr	08/72	72-73	5	0	0
Chester C	Tr	07/74	74-83	396	0	17

STORY Owen Grant
Born: Burton-on-Trent, Staffordshire, England, 3 August, 1984 — W

League Club	Source	Date Signed	Seasons Played	Apps	Subs	Gls
Rushden & D	Sch	-	03	0	5	0
Torquay U	Team Bath	12/04	04	0	2	0

STOTT Ian
Born: Wallingford, Oxfordshire, England, 17 October, 1955 — CD
England: Schools

League Club	Source	Date Signed	Seasons Played	Apps	Subs	Gls
Oxford U	West Ham U (NC)	01/76	77-79	27	0	3

STOTT Keith
Born: Atherton, Greater Manchester, England, 12 March, 1944 — CD
Died: Chesterfield, Derbyshire, England, 5 March, 2012

League Club	Source	Date Signed	Seasons Played	Apps	Subs	Gls
Crewe Alex	Atherton Laburnum Rov	10/64	64-69	188	0	11
Chesterfield	Tr	07/70	70-74	141	1	4

STOUTT Stephen Paul (Steve)
Born: Halifax, West Yorkshire, England, 5 April, 1964 — FB

League Club	Source	Date Signed	Seasons Played	Apps	Subs	Gls
Huddersfield T	Bradley Rgrs	01/84	83-84	6	0	0
Wolverhampton W	Tr	04/85	85-87	91	3	5
Grimsby T	Tr	07/88	88-89	3	0	1
Lincoln C	Tr	12/89	89-90	36	10	1

STOWE Dean Desmond
Born: Burnley, Lancashire, England, 27 March, 1975 — M

League Club	Source	Date Signed	Seasons Played	Apps	Subs	Gls
Hull C	YT	10/93	92	0	1	0

STOWELL Bruce
Born: Bradford, England, 20 September, 1941 — WH/IF

League Club	Source	Date Signed	Seasons Played	Apps	Subs	Gls
Bradford C	Leeds U (Am)	12/58	59-71	401	0	16
Rotherham U	Tr	07/72	72	14	2	0

STOWELL Michael (Mike)
Born: Preston, Lancashire, England, 19 April, 1965 — G

League Club	Source	Date Signed	Seasons Played	Apps	Subs	Gls
Preston NE	Leyland Motors	02/85				
Everton	Tr	12/85				
Chester C	L	09/87	87	14	0	0
York C	L	12/87	87	6	0	0
Manchester C	L	02/88	87	14	0	0
Port Vale	L	10/88	88	7	0	0
Wolverhampton W	L	03/89	88	7	0	0
Preston NE	L	02/90	89	2	0	0
Wolverhampton W	Tr	06/90	90-00	377	1	0
Bristol C	Tr	07/01	01	25	0	0

League Club	Source	Date Signed	Seasons Played	Career Record Apps	Subs	Gls

STRACHAN Craig Scott
Born: Aberdeen, Scotland, 19 May, 1982 — M

League Club	Source	Date Signed	Seasons Played	Apps	Subs	Gls
Coventry C	YT	12/99				
Rochdale	Tr	08/03	03	0	1	0

STRACHAN Gavin David
Born: Aberdeen, Scotland, 23 December, 1978 — M
Scotland: U21-8/Youth

League Club	Source	Date Signed	Seasons Played	Apps	Subs	Gls
Coventry C	YT	11/96	97-02	5	11	0
Peterborough U	Tr	02/03	02	1	1	0
Southend U	Tr	03/03	02	6	1	0
Hartlepool U	Tr	08/03	03-06	63	15	7
Stockport Co	L	10/05	05	4	0	0
Peterborough U	Tr	01/07	06-07	13	6	3
Notts Co	Tr	01/08	07-08	20	5	1

STRACHAN Gordon David
Born: Edinburgh, Scotland, 9 February, 1957 — RM
Scotland: 50/U21-1/Youth/Schools

League Club	Source	Date Signed	Seasons Played	Apps	Subs	Gls
Manchester U	Aberdeen	08/84	84-88	155	5	33
Leeds U	Tr	03/89	88-94	188	9	37
Coventry C	Tr	03/95	94-96	13	13	0

STRACQUALARSI Denis
Born: Rafaela, Argentina, 20 October, 1987 — F

League Club	Source	Date Signed	Seasons Played	Apps	Subs	Gls
Everton (L)	CA Tigre (ARG)	08/11	11	7	14	1

STRAIN James Henry (Jimmy)
Born: Chesham, Buckinghamshire, England, 28 November, 1937 — CH

League Club	Source	Date Signed	Seasons Played	Apps	Subs	Gls
Watford	Chesham U	11/55	56	3	-	0
Millwall	Tr	09/58	58	5	-	0

STRAKER Anthony Othneal
Born: Ealing, W London, England, 23 September, 1988 — LB
England: Youth//Grenada: 8

League Club	Source	Date Signed	Seasons Played	Apps	Subs	Gls
Aldershot T	Crystal Palace (Sch)	08/07	08-11	143	8	6
Wycombe W	L	01/11	10	2	2	0
Southend U	Tr	07/12	12-13	48	19	2
York C	Tr	06/14	14	7	5	1

STRANDLI Frank
Born: Kristiansand, Norway, 16 May, 1972 — F
Norway: 24

League Club	Source	Date Signed	Seasons Played	Apps	Subs	Gls
Leeds U	IK Start (NOR)	01/93	92-93	5	9	2

STRATFORD Daniel James (Dan)
Born: Sutton, S London, England, 29 May, 1985 — M

League Club	Source	Date Signed	Seasons Played	Apps	Subs	Gls
Hereford U	Inverness CT	08/10	10	2	5	0

STRATFORD Paul
Born: Northampton, England, 4 September, 1955 — F

League Club	Source	Date Signed	Seasons Played	Apps	Subs	Gls
Northampton T	App	10/72	72-77	169	3	58

STRATHIE William James (James)
Born: Falkirk, Scotland, 12 February, 1913 — CH
Died: Hatfield, Hertfordshire, England, 23 June, 1976

League Club	Source	Date Signed	Seasons Played	Apps	Subs	Gls
Luton T	St Bernard's	05/37	37-38	2	-	0
Northampton T	Tr	07/39	46	6	-	0

STRATTON Reginald Malcolm (Reg)
Born: Kingsley, Hampshire, England, 10 July, 1939 — CF
England: Amateur-2/Youth

League Club	Source	Date Signed	Seasons Played	Apps	Subs	Gls
Fulham	Woking	05/59	59-64	21	-	1
Colchester U	Tr	06/65	65-67	112	0	51

STRAUSS William Henry (Bill)
Born: Benoni, Transvaal, South Africa, 6 January, 1916 — W
Died: Plymouth, England, 16 November, 1987

League Club	Source	Date Signed	Seasons Played	Apps	Subs	Gls
Plymouth Arg	Aberdeen	07/46	46-53	158	-	40

STRAW Ian Ernest
Born: Sheffield, England, 27 May, 1967 — M

League Club	Source	Date Signed	Seasons Played	Apps	Subs	Gls
Grimsby T	Southampton (App)	08/86	86	7	3	0

STRAW Raymond (Ray)
Born: Ilkeston, Derbyshire, England, 22 May, 1933 — CF
Died: Ilkeston, Derbyshire, England, 13 May, 2001

League Club	Source	Date Signed	Seasons Played	Apps	Subs	Gls
Derby Co	Ilkeston T	10/51	51-57	94	-	57
Coventry C	Tr	11/57	57-60	143	-	79
Mansfield T	Tr	08/61	61-62	44	-	12

STREET Jeffrey Leslie (Jeff)
Born: Manchester, England, 20 April, 1948 — CD

League Club	Source	Date Signed	Seasons Played	Apps	Subs	Gls
Manchester C	Jnr	08/65				
Southport	Tr	08/67	67	9	0	0
Plymouth Arg	Tr	07/68				
Barrow	Altrincham	07/69	69	11	1	1

STREET John (Jack)
Born: Sheffield, England, 27 July, 1934 — W

League Club	Source	Date Signed	Seasons Played	Apps	Subs	Gls
Bradford C	Jnr	11/51	51	1	-	0

STREET John (Jack)
Born: Liverpool, England, 30 May, 1928 — WH

League Club	Source	Date Signed	Seasons Played	Apps	Subs	Gls
Southport	Tranmere Rov (Am)	01/49	48-49	7	-	1
Reading	Bootle	05/51				
Barrow	Tr	07/53	53-54	30	-	5

STREET John
Born: Rotherham, South Yorkshire, England, 19 November, 1926 — G
Died: Sheffield, England, July, 1988

League Club	Source	Date Signed	Seasons Played	Apps	Subs	Gls
Sheffield Wed	Liverpool (Am)	05/45				
Rotherham U		06/47	47	2	-	0

STREET Kevin
Born: Crewe, Cheshire, England, 25 November, 1977 — M

League Club	Source	Date Signed	Seasons Played	Apps	Subs	Gls
Crewe Alex	YT	07/96	97-01	57	58	9
Luton T	L	11/01	01	1	1	0
Bristol Rov	Northwich Victoria	11/02	02-03	21	12	2
Shrewsbury T	Tr	10/03	04	15	6	1

STREET Terence Edward (Terry)
Born: Poplar, E London, England, 9 December, 1948 — CD

League Club	Source	Date Signed	Seasons Played	Apps	Subs	Gls
Leyton Orient	Jnr	12/66	66	1	0	0

STREETE Floyd Anthony
Born: Kingston, Jamaica, 5 May, 1959 — CD

League Club	Source	Date Signed	Seasons Played	Apps	Subs	Gls
Cambridge U	Rivet Spts, Aylesbury	07/76	76-82	111	14	19
Derby Co	SC Cambuur (NED)	10/84	84-85	35	0	0
Wolverhampton W	Tr	10/85	85-89	157	2	6
Reading	Tr	07/90	90-91	38	0	0

STREETE Remie
Born: Aylesbury, Buckinghamshire, England, 2 November, 1994 — CD

League Club	Source	Date Signed	Seasons Played	Apps	Subs	Gls
Newcastle U	Sch	11/11				
Port Vale	L	10/14	14	1	1	0

STREETE Theo
Born: Birmingham, England, 23 November, 1987 — CD

League Club	Source	Date Signed	Seasons Played	Apps	Subs	Gls
Derby Co	Solihull College	06/06				
Doncaster Rov	L	09/06	06	2	4	1
Rotherham U	Tr	01/07	06	4	0	0

STREETER Terence Stephen (Terry)
Born: Brighton, England, 26 October, 1979 — F

League Club	Source	Date Signed	Seasons Played	Apps	Subs	Gls
Brighton & HA	YT	06/98	97	0	2	0

STRETEN Bernard Reginald
Born: Beccles, Suffolk, England, 14 January, 1921 — G
Died: Norwich, England, 10 May, 1994
England: 1/Amateur-4

League Club	Source	Date Signed	Seasons Played	Apps	Subs	Gls
Luton T	Shrewsbury T	01/47	46-56	276	-	0

STRETTON Donald (Don)
Born: Clowne, Derbyshire, England, 4 September, 1920 — CF
Died: Doncaster, South Yorkshire, England, 1978

League Club	Source	Date Signed	Seasons Played	Apps	Subs	Gls
Halifax T	Thorne Colliery	07/47	47	10	-	5

STREVENS Benjamin John (Ben)
Born: Edgware, NW London, England, 24 May, 1980 — F

League Club	Source	Date Signed	Seasons Played	Apps	Subs	Gls
Barnet	Wingate & Finchley	01/99	99-05	44	25	9
Dagenham & Red	Crawley T	01/07	07-08	85	7	29
Brentford	Tr	07/09	09	20	5	6
Wycombe W	Tr	07/10	10-11	65	11	11
Gillingham	Tr	07/12	12	4	8	1
Dagenham & Red	Tr	01/13	12	10	4	1

STRICKLAND Derek
Born: Stoneyburn, West Lothian, Scotland, 7 November, 1959 — F
Scotland: Schools

League Club	Source	Date Signed	Seasons Played	Apps	Subs	Gls
Leicester C	Glasgow Rangers	09/79	79	4	3	2

STRIDE Darren Neil
Born: Burton-on-Trent, Staffordshire, England, 28 September, 1975 — M
England: Semi Pro-1

League Club	Source	Date Signed	Seasons Played	Apps	Subs	Gls
Burton A	Jnr	08/93	09	5	4	0

STRIDE David Roy
Born: Lymington, Hampshire, England, 14 March, 1958 — LB

League Club	Source	Date Signed	Seasons Played	Apps	Subs	Gls
Chelsea	App	01/76	78-79	35	0	0
Millwall	Jacksonville TM (USA)	01/83	82-83	55	0	3
Leyton Orient	Tr	07/84	84	29	0	0

STRIHAVKA David
Born: Prague, Czech Republic, 4 March, 1983 — F
Czech Republic: Youth

League Club	Source	Date Signed	Seasons Played	Apps	Subs	Gls
Norwich C (L)	Banik Ostrava (CZE)	07/07	07	3	7	1

STRINGER Christopher (Chris)
Born: Grimsby, North Lincolnshire, England, 16 June, 1983 — G

League Club	Source	Date Signed	Seasons Played	Apps	Subs	Gls
Sheffield Wed	YT	06/00	00-02	6	3	0

STRINGER David Ronald (Dave)
Born: Great Yarmouth, Norfolk, England, 15 October, 1944 — D
England: Youth

League Club	Source	Date Signed	Seasons Played	Apps	Subs	Gls
Norwich C	Gorleston	05/63	64-76	417	2	18
Cambridge U	Tr	09/76	76-80	153	4	1

STRINGER Edmund
Born: Sheffield, England, 6 February, 1925 — IF
Died: Derbyshire, England, July, 2014

League Club	Source	Date Signed	Seasons Played	Apps	Subs	Gls
Oldham Ath	Norton Woodseats	07/49	49	1	-	0

STRINGFELLOW Ian Robert
Born: Nottingham, England, 8 May, 1969 — F

League Club	Source	Date Signed	Seasons Played	Apps	Subs	Gls
Mansfield T	App	04/86	85-93	109	58	28
Blackpool	L	09/92	92	3	0	1
Chesterfield	L	12/93	93	0	1	0

STRINGFELLOW Michael David (Mike)
Born: Kirkby-in-Ashfield, Nottinghamshire, England, 27 January, 1943 — LW

League Club	Source	Date Signed	Seasons Played	Apps	Subs	Gls
Mansfield T	Jnr	02/60	60-61	57	-	10
Leicester C	Tr	01/62	61-74	292	23	82

STRINGFELLOW Peter
Born: Walkden, Greater Manchester, England, 21 February, 1939 — IF

League Club	Source	Date Signed	Seasons Played	Apps	Subs	Gls
Oldham Ath	Walkden T	12/58	58-60	54	-	16
Gillingham	Sankey's	12/62	62-63	35	-	2
Oldham Ath	Tr	01/64				
Chesterfield	Tr	08/64	64	28	-	7

STRODDER Colin John
Born: Hessle, East Riding of Yorkshire, England, 23 December, 1941 — FB

League Club	Source	Date Signed	Seasons Played	Apps	Subs	Gls
Huddersfield T		04/60				
Halifax T	Tr	07/61	61-62	20	-	0

STRODDER Gary John
Born: Cleckheaton, West Yorkshire, England, 1 April, 1965 — CD

League Club	Source	Date Signed	Seasons Played	Apps	Subs	Gls
Lincoln C	App	04/83	82-86	122	10	6
West Ham U	Tr	03/87	86-89	59	6	2
West Bromwich A	Tr	08/90	90-94	123	17	8
Notts Co	Tr	07/95	95-98	116	5	10
Rotherham U	L	01/99	98	3	0	0
Hartlepool U	Tr	02/99	98-00	58	3	0

STRONACH Peter
Born: Seaham, County Durham, England, 1 September, 1956 — M
England: Schools

League Club	Source	Date Signed	Seasons Played	Apps	Subs	Gls
Sunderland	App	09/73	77	2	1	0
York C	Tr	06/78	78-79	30	4	2

STRONG Andrew Forster
Born: Hartlepool, Cleveland, England, 17 September, 1966 — LB

League Club	Source	Date Signed	Seasons Played	Apps	Subs	Gls
Middlesbrough	App	09/84	84	6	0	0

STRONG Geoffrey Hugh (Geoff)
Born: Throckley, Tyne and Wear, England, 19 September, 1937 — IF/LB
Died: Southport, Merseyside, England, 17 June, 2013

League Club	Source	Date Signed	Seasons Played	Apps	Subs	Gls
Arsenal	Stanley U	04/58	60-64	125	-	69
Liverpool	Tr	11/64	64-69	150	5	29
Coventry C	Tr	07/70	70-71	33	0	0

STRONG George James (Jimmy)
Born: Morpeth, Northumberland, England, 7 June, 1916 — G
Died: Burnley, Lancashire, England, 11 October, 1989

League Club	Source	Date Signed	Seasons Played	Apps	Subs	Gls
Hartlepool U	Pegswood U	02/34	33	1	-	0
Chesterfield	Tr	08/34	34	18	-	0
Portsmouth	Tr	03/35	34-37	59	-	0
Walsall	Gillingham	07/39				
Burnley	Tr	01/46	46-52	264	-	0

STRONG Gregory (Greg)
Born: Bolton, Greater Manchester, England, 5 September, 1975 — CD
England: Youth/Schools

League Club	Source	Date Signed	Seasons Played	Apps	Subs	Gls
Wigan Ath	YT	10/92	93-94	28	7	3
Bolton W	Tr	09/95	95-99	10	2	1
Blackpool	L	11/97	97	11	0	1
Stoke C	L	03/99	98	5	0	1
Hull C	Motherwell	06/02	02	3	0	0
Cheltenham T	L	02/03	02	3	1	0
Scunthorpe U	L	03/03	02	7	0	0
Bury	L	08/03	03	10	0	0
Boston U	Tr	03/04	04	8	1	0
Macclesfield T	L	12/04	04	4	0	0

STRONG Leslie (Les)
Born: Streatham, S London, England, 3 July, 1953 — LB

League Club	Source	Date Signed	Seasons Played	Apps	Subs	Gls
Fulham	App	06/71	72-82	369	3	5
Brentford	L	12/82	82	5	0	0
Crystal Palace	Tr	08/83	83	7	0	0
Rochdale	USA	10/84	84	1	0	0

STRONG Steven (Steve)
Born: Bristol, England, 17 April, 1962 — CD

League Club	Source	Date Signed	Seasons Played	Apps	Subs	Gls
Hereford U	App	02/80	78-80	16	0	0

STRONG Steven George (Steve)
Born: Watford, Hertfordshire, England, 15 March, 1978 — CD

League Club	Source	Date Signed	Seasons Played	Apps	Subs	Gls
Bournemouth	YT	07/96	94-95	0	2	0

STROUD David Alexander
Born: Swindon, England, 10 November, 1987 — LW

League Club	Source	Date Signed	Seasons Played	Apps	Subs	Gls
Swindon T	Sch	07/06	05	1	1	0

STROUD Derek Neville Lester
Born: Wimborne, Dorset, England, 11 February, 1930 — RW

League Club	Source	Date Signed	Seasons Played	Apps	Subs	Gls
Bournemouth	Poole T	08/50	50-52	79	-	17
Grimsby T	Tr	06/53	53-54	71	-	12

STROUD Kenneth Allan (Ken)
Born: Fulham, W London, England, 1 December, 1953 — M
England: Schools

League Club	Source	Date Signed	Seasons Played	Apps	Subs	Gls
Swindon T	App	03/71	71-81	302	9	16
Newport Co	Tr	08/82	82-83	47	1	0
Bristol C	Tr	10/83	83-84	68	1	4

STROUD Roy William
Born: Silvertown, E London, England, 16 March, 1925 — CF
England: Amateur-9/Schools

League Club	Source	Date Signed	Seasons Played	Apps	Subs	Gls
West Ham U	Hendon	04/52	51-56	13	-	4

STROUD William James Alfred (Billy)
Born: Hammersmith, W London, England, 7 July, 1919 — WH
Died: Southampton, England, 5 October, 2006

League Club	Source	Date Signed	Seasons Played	Apps	Subs	Gls
Southampton	Jnr	02/40	46	29	-	4
Leyton Orient	Tr	06/47	47-49	65	-	1
Newport Co	Tr	06/50	50-52	63	-	1
Newport Co	Hastings U	11/53	54	1	-	0

STRUGNELL Daniel Stephen (Dan)
Born: Christchurch, Dorset, England, 30 June, 1992 — RB

League Club	Source	Date Signed	Seasons Played	Apps	Subs	Gls
Bournemouth	Jnr	07/11	11	0	1	0

STRUPAR Branko
Born: Zagreb, Croatia, 9 February, 1970 — F
Belgium: 17

League Club	Source	Date Signed	Seasons Played	Apps	Subs	Gls
Derby Co	KRC Genk (BEL)	12/99	99-02	32	9	16

STRUTT Brian John
Born: Valletta, Malta, 21 September, 1959 — F

League Club	Source	Date Signed	Seasons Played	Apps	Subs	Gls
Sheffield Wed	App	09/77	79	2	0	0

STRUTTON Charles George (Charlie)
Born: Brent, NW London, England, 17 April, 1989 — F

League Club	Source	Date Signed	Seasons Played	Apps	Subs	Gls
AFC Wimbledon	Chalfont St Peter	03/12	12-13	3	14	0

STUART Edward Albert (Eddie)
Born: Middelburg, South Africa, 12 May, 1931 — D
Died: Wrexham, Wales, 4 November, 2014

League Club	Source	Date Signed	Seasons Played	Apps	Subs	Gls
Wolverhampton W	Jo'burg Rgrs (RSA)	01/51	51-61	287	-	5
Stoke C	Tr	07/62	62-63	63	-	2
Tranmere Rov	Tr	08/64	64-65	83	0	2
Stockport Co	Tr	07/66	66-67	77	0	1

STUART Graham Charles
Born: Tooting, SW London, England, 24 October, 1970 — W
England: U21-5/Youth

League Club	Source	Date Signed	Seasons Played	Apps	Subs	Gls
Chelsea	YT	06/89	89-92	70	17	14
Everton	Tr	08/93	93-97	116	20	22
Sheffield U	Tr	11/97	97-98	52	1	11
Charlton Ath	Tr	03/99	98-04	136	12	22
Norwich C	Tr	01/05	04	7	1	0

STUART Jamie Christopher
Born: Southwark, S London, England, 15 October, 1976 — CD
England: U21-4/Youth

League Club	Source	Date Signed	Seasons Played	Apps	Subs	Gls
Charlton Ath	YT	01/95	94-97	49	1	3
Millwall	Tr	09/98	98-00	42	3	0
Bury	Cambridge U (NC)	10/01	01-02	56	5	1
Southend U	Tr	06/03	03	23	3	0
AFC Wimbledon	Rushden & D	01/11	11	33	1	1

STUART Mark Richard
Born: Chiswick, W London, England, 15 December, 1966 — LW
England: Schools

League Club	Source	Date Signed	Seasons Played	Apps	Subs	Gls
Charlton Ath	Jnr	07/84	84-88	89	17	28
Plymouth Arg	Tr	11/88	88-89	55	2	11
Ipswich T	L	03/90	89	5	0	2
Bradford C	Tr	08/90	90-91	22	7	5
Huddersfield T	Tr	10/92	92	9	6	3
Rochdale	Tr	07/93	93-98	166	36	41

League Club	Source	Date Signed	Seasons Played	Career Record Apps	Subs	Gls

STUART Robert William (Bobby)
Born: Middlesbrough, England, 9 October, 1913 RB
Died: Middlesbrough, England, 25 August, 1987
England: Schools

League Club	Source	Date Signed	Seasons Played	Apps	Subs	Gls
Middlesbrough	South Bank	01/31	31-47	247	-	2
Plymouth Arg	Tr	10/47	47	20	-	0

STUBBINS Albert
Born: Wallsend, Tyne and Wear, England, 13 July, 1919 CF
Died: Whitley Bay, Tyne and Wear, England, 26 December, 2002
England: FLge-4/War-1

League Club	Source	Date Signed	Seasons Played	Apps	Subs	Gls
Newcastle U	Whitley & Monkseaton	04/37	37-46	27	-	5
Liverpool	Tr	09/46	46-52	161	-	75

STUBBS Alan
Born: Kirkby, Merseyside, England, 6 October, 1971 CD
England: B-1

League Club	Source	Date Signed	Seasons Played	Apps	Subs	Gls
Bolton W	YT	07/90	90-95	181	21	9
Everton	Glasgow Celtic	07/01	01-04	117	7	3
Sunderland	Tr	08/05	05	8	2	1
Everton	Tr	01/06	05-07	43	2	3
Derby Co	Tr	01/08	07-08	9	0	0

STUBBS Alfred Thomas (Alf)
Born: West Ham, E London, England, 18 April, 1922 RH
Died: Hillingdon, W London, England, January, 1986

League Club	Source	Date Signed	Seasons Played	Apps	Subs	Gls
Crystal Palace		12/46	47-48	3	-	0

STUBBS Brian Henry
Born: Keyworth, Nottinghamshire, England, 8 February, 1950 CD

League Club	Source	Date Signed	Seasons Played	Apps	Subs	Gls
Notts Co	Loughborough Univ	09/68	68-79	423	3	21

STUBBS Charles Frederick (Charlie)
Born: West Ham, E London, England, 22 January, 1920 IF
Died: Bath, England, 12 May, 1984

League Club	Source	Date Signed	Seasons Played	Apps	Subs	Gls
Darlington	Bamforths	01/44	46-47	41	-	17

STUBBS Leslie Levi (Les)
Born: Great Wakering, Essex, England, 18 February, 1929 IF
Died: Great Wakering, Essex, England, 1 February, 2011

League Club	Source	Date Signed	Seasons Played	Apps	Subs	Gls
Southend U	Great Wakering Rov	05/48	49-52	83	-	40
Chelsea	Tr	11/52	52-58	112	-	34
Southend U	Tr	11/58	58-59	22	-	3

STUBBS Robin Gregory
Born: Warley, West Midlands, England, 22 April, 1941 CF

League Club	Source	Date Signed	Seasons Played	Apps	Subs	Gls
Birmingham C	Jnr	04/58	58-62	61	-	17
Torquay U	Tr	08/63	63-68	214	3	120
Bristol Rov	Tr	07/69	69-71	90	3	32
Torquay U	Tr	02/72	71-72	19	2	1

STUBBS William (Billy)
Born: Hartlepool, Cleveland, England, 1 August, 1966 F

League Club	Source	Date Signed	Seasons Played	Apps	Subs	Gls
Nottingham F	Seaham Red Star	04/87				
Doncaster Rov	L	09/87	87	8	1	1
Grimsby T	L	03/88	87	2	5	2

STUCKEY Bruce George
Born: Torquay, Devon, England, 19 February, 1947 W

League Club	Source	Date Signed	Seasons Played	Apps	Subs	Gls
Exeter C	App	02/65	65-67	37	2	6
Sunderland	Tr	11/67	67-69	24	2	2
Torquay U	Tr	02/71	70-73	70	18	6
Reading	Tr	11/73	73-76	92	5	7
Torquay U	L	01/75	74	4	0	0
Bournemouth	L	03/77	76	5	0	0

STUCKMANN Thorsten
Born: Gutersloh, Germany, 17 March, 1981 G

League Club	Source	Date Signed	Seasons Played	Apps	Subs	Gls
Preston NE	Alem'ia Aachen (GER)	11/11	11-14	57	0	0

STUDER Sascha
Born: Olten, Switzerland, 3 September, 1991 G
Switzerland: Youth

League Club	Source	Date Signed	Seasons Played	Apps	Subs	Gls
Mansfield T	FC Winterthur (SUI)	08/14	14	17	0	0

STURGESS Paul Christopher
Born: Dartford, Kent, England, 4 August, 1975 LB

League Club	Source	Date Signed	Seasons Played	Apps	Subs	Gls
Charlton Ath	YT	07/93	92-96	43	8	0
Millwall	Tr	07/97	97	12	2	0
Brighton & HA	Tr	09/98	98	28	2	0

STURM Florian
Born: Worgl, Austria, 6 May, 1982 LW
Austria: U21-7

League Club	Source	Date Signed	Seasons Played	Apps	Subs	Gls
MK Dons	FC Vaduz (SUI)	07/08	08	2	3	0

STURRIDGE Daniel Andre
Born: Birmingham, England, 1 September, 1989 F
England: 14/U21-16/Youth

League Club	Source	Date Signed	Seasons Played	Apps	Subs	Gls
Manchester C	Sch	09/06	06-08	5	16	5
Chelsea	Tr	07/09	09-12	31	32	13
Bolton W	L	01/11	10	11	1	8
Liverpool	Tr	01/13	12-14	44	11	35

STURRIDGE Dean Constantine
Born: Birmingham, England, 27 July, 1973 F

League Club	Source	Date Signed	Seasons Played	Apps	Subs	Gls
Derby Co	YT	07/91	91-00	142	48	53
Torquay U	L	12/94	94	10	0	5
Leicester C	Tr	01/01	00-01	20	2	6
Wolverhampton W	Tr	11/01	01-04	51	31	31
Sheffield U	L	01/04	03	2	2	0
Queens Park Rgrs	Tr	03/05	04-05	6	5	0

STURRIDGE Michael Alexander (Mike)
Born: Birmingham, England, 18 September, 1962 F

League Club	Source	Date Signed	Seasons Played	Apps	Subs	Gls
Birmingham C	App	06/80				
Wrexham	L	12/83	83	3	1	0

STURRIDGE Simon Andrew
Born: Birmingham, England, 9 December, 1969 F

League Club	Source	Date Signed	Seasons Played	Apps	Subs	Gls
Birmingham C	YT	07/88	88-92	129	21	30
Stoke C	Tr	09/93	93-98	43	28	14
Blackpool	L	03/99	98	5	0	1
Northampton T	Tr	08/99	99	10	8	1
Shrewsbury T	L	03/00	99	10	1	1

STURROCK Blair David
Born: Dundee, Scotland, 25 August, 1981 F

League Club	Source	Date Signed	Seasons Played	Apps	Subs	Gls
Plymouth Arg	Dundee U	10/01	01-03	9	54	2
Kidderminster Hrs	Tr	12/04	04	17	5	5
Rochdale	Tr	08/05	05	15	16	6
Swindon T		12/06	06-08	22	28	6
Bournemouth	L	09/08	08	1	3	0
Southend U	Mansfield T	08/10	10-11	39	13	6

STURROCK David
Born: Dundee, Scotland, 22 February, 1938 IF

League Club	Source	Date Signed	Seasons Played	Apps	Subs	Gls
Accrington Stan	Dundee U	07/60	60	17	-	5

STUTTARD John Ellis (Ellis)
Born: Padiham, Lancashire, England, 24 April, 1920 D
Died: Burnley, Lancashire, England, 16 December, 1983

League Club	Source	Date Signed	Seasons Played	Apps	Subs	Gls
Plymouth Arg	Burnley (Am)	09/38	38-46	29	-	1
Torquay U	Tr	09/47	47-50	82	-	0

STYCHE Reece
Born: Birmingham, England, 3 May, 1989 F
England: Semi Pro-1

League Club	Source	Date Signed	Seasons Played	Apps	Subs	Gls
Wycombe W (L)	Forest Green Rov	01/14	13	8	6	0

STYLES Arthur (Archie)
Born: Liverpool, England, 3 September, 1949 LB
England: Youth/Schools

League Club	Source	Date Signed	Seasons Played	Apps	Subs	Gls
Everton	App	08/67	72-73	22	1	0
Birmingham C	Tr	02/74	73-77	71	3	4
Peterborough U	Tr	07/78	78	32	0	1
Portsmouth	Tr	07/79	79	28	0	0

STYLES Arthur John
Born: Smethwick, West Midlands, England, 29 October, 1939 WH/IF

League Club	Source	Date Signed	Seasons Played	Apps	Subs	Gls
West Bromwich A	Jnr	11/56	59	1	-	0
Wrexham	Tr	03/60	59-60	16	-	0

STYVAR Peter
Born: Roznava, Slovakia, 13 August, 1980 F
Slovakia: 2

League Club	Source	Date Signed	Seasons Played	Apps	Subs	Gls
Bristol C	MSK Zilina (SVK)	01/09	08	2	8	0

SUAREZ Luis Alberto
Born: Salto, Uruguay, 24 January, 1987 F
Uruguay: 82/U23-3/Youth

League Club	Source	Date Signed	Seasons Played	Apps	Subs	Gls
Liverpool	Ajax (NED)	01/11	10-13	107	3	69

SUART Ronald (Ron)
Born: Kendal, Cumbria, England, 18 November, 1920 FB
Died: 25 March, 2015

League Club	Source	Date Signed	Seasons Played	Apps	Subs	Gls
Blackpool	Netherfield	01/39	46-49	103	-	0
Blackburn Rov	Tr	09/49	49-54	176	-	0

SUCKLING Perry John
Born: Leyton, NE London, England, 12 October, 1965 G
England: U21-10/Youth

League Club	Source	Date Signed	Seasons Played	Apps	Subs	Gls
Coventry C	App	10/83	82-83	27	0	0
Manchester C	Tr	06/86	86-87	39	0	0
Crystal Palace	Tr	01/88	87-91	59	0	0
West Ham U	L	12/89	89	6	0	0
Brentford	L	10/91	91	8	0	0
Watford	Tr	07/92	92-93	39	0	0
Doncaster Rov	Tr	07/94	94-95	30	0	0

SUDDABY Peter
Born: Stockport, Greater Manchester, England, 23 December, 1947 CD
England: Amateur-3

League Club	Source	Date Signed	Seasons Played	Apps	Subs	Gls
Blackpool	Skelmersdale U	05/70	70-79	330	1	10
Brighton & HA	Tr	11/79	79	21	2	0
Wimbledon	Tr	11/81	81	6	0	0

SUDDARDS Jeffrey (Jeff)
Born: Bradford, England, 17 January, 1929 RB
Died: Fakenham, Norfolk, England, 28 August, 2012

League Club	Source	Date Signed	Seasons Played	Apps	Subs	Gls
Bradford Park Ave	Hull C (Am)	03/49	49-58	327	-	0

SUDDICK Alan
Born: Chester-le-Street, County Durham, England, 2 May, 1944 M/F
Died: Manchester, England, 16 March, 2009
England: U23-2/Youth

League Club	Source	Date Signed	Seasons Played	Apps	Subs	Gls
Newcastle U	App	10/61	61-66	144	0	41
Blackpool	Tr	12/66	66-76	305	5	65
Stoke C	Tr	12/76	76	9	0	1
Southport	L	08/77	77	6	0	0
Bury	Tr	09/77	77	30	4	2

SUFFO Kengne Herve Patrick (Patrick)
Born: Ebolowa, Cameroon, 17 January, 1978 F
Cameroon: 29

League Club	Source	Date Signed	Seasons Played	Apps	Subs	Gls
Sheffield U	FC Nantes (FRA)	11/00	00-01	16	20	5
Coventry C	Numancia (SPN)	07/03	03-04	22	26	10

SUGDEN Ryan Stephen
Born: Bradford, England, 26 December, 1980 F

League Club	Source	Date Signed	Seasons Played	Apps	Subs	Gls
Oldham Ath	YT	11/98	98-00	4	17	1

SUGGETT Colin
Born: Chester-le-Street, County Durham, England, 30 December, 1948 M
England: Youth/Schools

League Club	Source	Date Signed	Seasons Played	Apps	Subs	Gls
Sunderland	App	01/66	66-68	83	3	24
West Bromwich A	Tr	07/69	69-72	123	5	20
Norwich C	Tr	02/73	72-77	200	3	21
Newcastle U	Tr	08/78	78	20	3	0

SUGRUE Paul Anthony
Born: Coventry, England, 6 November, 1960 M

League Club	Source	Date Signed	Seasons Played	Apps	Subs	Gls
Manchester C	Nuneaton Bor	02/80	79-80	5	1	0
Cardiff C	Tr	08/81	81	2	3	0
Middlesbrough	Tr	12/82	82-84	66	3	6
Portsmouth	Tr	12/84	84-85	2	2	0
Northampton T	Tr	03/86	85	2	6	2
Newport Co	Tr	08/86	86	1	1	0

SUHAJ Pavel
Born: Lipany, Slovakia, 16 April, 1981 F

League Club	Source	Date Signed	Seasons Played	Apps	Subs	Gls
Crewe Alex	AS Trencin (SVK)	08/05	05-06	1	7	0

SUKER Davor
Born: Osijek, Croatia, 1 January, 1968 F
Croatia: 69//Yugoslavia: 2/Youth

League Club	Source	Date Signed	Seasons Played	Apps	Subs	Gls
Arsenal	Real Madrid (SPN)	08/99	99	8	14	8
West Ham U	Tr	07/00	00	7	4	2

SUKUR Hakan
Born: Adapazan, Turkey, 1 September, 1971 F
Turkey: 112/U21-16/Youth

League Club	Source	Date Signed	Seasons Played	Apps	Subs	Gls
Blackburn Rov	Parma (ITA)	12/02	02	7	2	2

SULLEY Christopher Stephen (Chris)
Born: Camberwell, S London, England, 3 December, 1959 LB

League Club	Source	Date Signed	Seasons Played	Apps	Subs	Gls
Chelsea	App	12/77				
Bournemouth	Tr	03/81	80-85	205	1	3
Blackburn Rov	Dundee U	03/87	86-91	134	0	3
Port Vale	Tr	07/92	92	40	0	1
Preston NE	Tr	07/93	93	21	0	1

SULLIVAN Alan
Born: Aberdare, Rhondda Cynon Taff, Wales, 12 November, 1953 W
Wales: Schools

League Club	Source	Date Signed	Seasons Played	Apps	Subs	Gls
Swansea C	App	08/71	70-71	7	0	1

SULLIVAN Brian Anthony John
Born: Edmonton, N London, England, 30 December, 1941 IF
Died: Enfield, N London, England, October, 1985
England: Youth/Schools

League Club	Source	Date Signed	Seasons Played	Apps	Subs	Gls
Fulham	Jnr	05/59	59	2	-	1

SULLIVAN Colin John
Born: Saltash, Cornwall, England, 24 June, 1951 LB
England: U23-2/Youth

League Club	Source	Date Signed	Seasons Played	Apps	Subs	Gls
Plymouth Arg	App	07/68	67-73	225	4	7
Norwich C	Tr	06/74	74-78	154	3	3
Cardiff C	Tr	02/79	78-81	61	2	1
Hereford U	Tr	12/81	81	8	0	0
Portsmouth	Tr	03/82	81-83	94	0	0
Swansea C	Tr	03/85	84-85	53	0	0

SULLIVAN Cornelius Henry (Con)
Born: Bristol, England, 22 August, 1928 G

League Club	Source	Date Signed	Seasons Played	Apps	Subs	Gls
Bristol C	Horfield OB	05/49	50-52	73	-	0
Arsenal	Tr	02/54	53-57	28	-	0

SULLIVAN Danny Michael
Born: Plymouth, England, 1 September, 1994 LW

League Club	Source	Date Signed	Seasons Played	Apps	Subs	Gls
Torquay U	Sch	07/13	13	0	4	0

SULLIVAN Derrick
Born: Newport, Wales, 10 August, 1930 D/IF
Died: Newport, Wales, 16 September, 1983
Wales: 17

League Club	Source	Date Signed	Seasons Played	Apps	Subs	Gls
Cardiff C	Jnr	09/47	47-60	275	-	19
Exeter C	Tr	06/61	61	44	-	0
Newport Co	Tr	07/62	62	23	-	0

SULLIVAN John Denis
Born: Worthing, West Sussex, England, 8 March, 1988 G

League Club	Source	Date Signed	Seasons Played	Apps	Subs	Gls
Brighton & HA	Sch	06/06	08	13	0	0
Millwall	Tr	07/09				
Yeovil T	L	07/10	10	13	0	0
Charlton Ath	Tr	03/11	10-11	5	2	0
Colchester U	L	11/12	12	4	0	0
AFC Wimbledon	L	03/13	12	11	0	0
Portsmouth	Tr	05/13	13	6	0	0

SULLIVAN Neil
Born: Sutton, S London, England, 24 February, 1970 G
Scotland: 28

League Club	Source	Date Signed	Seasons Played	Apps	Subs	Gls
Wimbledon	YT	07/88	90-99	180	1	0
Crystal Palace	L	05/92	91	1	0	0
Tottenham H	Tr	06/00	00-01	64	0	0
Chelsea	Tr	08/03	03	4	0	0
Leeds U	Tr	08/04	04-06	95	0	0
Doncaster Rov	L	11/06	06	3	0	0
Doncaster Rov	Tr	02/07	06-12	193	1	0
AFC Wimbledon	L	11/12	12	18	0	0

SUMMERBEE George Michael
Born: Winchester, Hampshire, England, 22 October, 1914 D
Died: Cirencester, Gloucestershire, England, 19 April, 1955

League Club	Source	Date Signed	Seasons Played	Apps	Subs	Gls
Aldershot	Basingstoke T	05/34	33-34	19	-	0
Preston NE	Tr	01/35	37-38	3	-	0
Chester C	Tr	05/46	46	9	-	0
Barrow	Tr	06/47	47-49	122	-	0

SUMMERBEE Michael George (Mike)
Born: Cheltenham, Gloucestershire, England, 15 December, 1942 RW/F
England: 8/FLge-1/U23-1

League Club	Source	Date Signed	Seasons Played	Apps	Subs	Gls
Swindon T	Cheltenham T	03/60	59-64	218	-	39
Manchester C	Tr	08/65	65-74	355	2	47
Burnley	Tr	06/75	75-76	51	0	0
Blackpool	Tr	12/76	76	3	0	0
Stockport Co	Tr	08/77	77-79	86	1	6

SUMMERBEE Nicholas John (Nicky)
Born: Altrincham, Greater Manchester, England, 26 August, 1971 RB/M
England: B-1/U21-3

League Club	Source	Date Signed	Seasons Played	Apps	Subs	Gls
Swindon T	YT	07/89	89-93	89	23	6
Manchester C	Tr	06/94	94-97	119	12	6
Sunderland	Tr	11/97	97-99	87	6	7
Bolton W	Tr	01/01	00	9	3	1
Nottingham F	Tr	11/01	01	17	0	2
Leicester C	Tr	08/02	02	7	22	0
Bradford C	Tr	09/03	03-04	64	4	4
Swindon T	Tr	08/05	05	1	0	0
Tranmere Rov	Tr	09/05	05	4	2	0

SUMMERBELL Mark
Born: Chester-le-Street, County Durham, England, 30 October, 1976 M

League Club	Source	Date Signed	Seasons Played	Apps	Subs	Gls
Middlesbrough	YT	07/95	95-00	35	16	1
Bristol C	L	09/01	01	5	0	0
Portsmouth	L	03/02	01	5	0	0
Carlisle U	Tr	08/02	02-03	43	2	1

SUMMERFIELD Kevin
Born: Walsall, West Midlands, England, 7 January, 1959 M
England: Youth

League Club	Source	Date Signed	Seasons Played	Apps	Subs	Gls
West Bromwich A	App	01/77	78-81	5	4	3
Birmingham C	Tr	05/82	82	2	3	1
Walsall	L	12/82	82	4	0	2
Walsall	Tr	02/83	82-83	38	12	15
Cardiff C	Tr	07/84	84	10	0	1
Plymouth Arg	Tr	12/84	84-90	118	21	26
Exeter C	L	03/90	89	4	0	0
Shrewsbury T	Tr	10/90	90-95	140	23	22

SUMMERFIELD Luke John
Born: Ivybridge, Devon, England, 6 December, 1987 — M

League Club	Source	Date Signed	Seasons Played	Apps	Subs	Gls
Plymouth Arg	Sch	08/05	04-10	57	22	4
Bournemouth	L	03/07	06	5	3	1
Leyton Orient	L	09/09	09	14	0	0
Cheltenham T	Tr	08/11	11	37	4	4
Shrewsbury T	Tr	07/12	12-13	54	10	3
York C	Tr	06/14	14	26	5	4

SUMMERHAYES David Michael
Born: Cardiff, Wales, 21 March, 1947 — WH
Wales: U23-1

League Club	Source	Date Signed	Seasons Played	Apps	Subs	Gls
Cardiff C	App	03/65	65-67	7	6	0

SUMMERHAYES Robert Edward (Bob)
Born: Cardiff, Wales, 8 January, 1951 — M
Wales: Schools

League Club	Source	Date Signed	Seasons Played	Apps	Subs	Gls
Cardiff C	App	01/69				
Newport Co	Tr	08/72	72-74	74	6	4

SUMMERHILL Alan
Born: Liss, Hampshire, England, 25 November, 1950 — D

League Club	Source	Date Signed	Seasons Played	Apps	Subs	Gls
Bournemouth	Jnr	07/68	69	28	0	0
Crewe Alex	Tr	09/70	70-71	46	4	1

SUMMERILL Philip Ernest (Phil)
Born: Birmingham, England, 20 November, 1947 — F/W
England: Youth

League Club	Source	Date Signed	Seasons Played	Apps	Subs	Gls
Birmingham C	App	12/64	66-72	108	10	46
Huddersfield T	Tr	01/73	72-74	48	6	11
Millwall	Tr	11/74	74-77	83	4	20
Wimbledon	Tr	09/77	77-78	27	4	4

SUMMERS Christopher (Chris)
Born: Cardiff, Wales, 6 January, 1972 — F
Wales: Youth

League Club	Source	Date Signed	Seasons Played	Apps	Subs	Gls
Cardiff C	YT	07/90	90	0	3	0

SUMMERS George
Born: Glasgow, Scotland, 30 July, 1941 — CF/RW

League Club	Source	Date Signed	Seasons Played	Apps	Subs	Gls
Brentford	Shawfield Jnrs	01/59	60-64	71	-	24

SUMMERS Gerald Thomas Francis (Gerry)
Born: Birmingham, England, 4 October, 1933 — LH

League Club	Source	Date Signed	Seasons Played	Apps	Subs	Gls
West Bromwich A	Erdington A	08/51	55-56	22	-	0
Sheffield U	Tr	05/57	57-63	260	-	4
Hull C	Tr	04/64	63-65	59	0	1
Walsall	Tr	10/65	65-66	41	3	1

SUMMERS John Henry (Johnny)
Born: Hammersmith, W London, England, 10 September, 1927 — CF/LW
Died: Bloomsbury, London, England, 2 June, 1962

League Club	Source	Date Signed	Seasons Played	Apps	Subs	Gls
Fulham	Jnr	02/47	49	4	-	0
Norwich C	Tr	06/50	50-53	71	-	33
Millwall	Tr	05/54	54-56	91	-	41
Charlton Ath	Tr	11/56	56-60	171	-	100

SUMMERSBY Roy Donald
Born: Lambeth, S London, England, 19 March, 1935 — IF/WH

League Club	Source	Date Signed	Seasons Played	Apps	Subs	Gls
Millwall	Jnr	03/52	51-58	87	-	13
Crystal Palace	Tr	12/58	58-62	176	-	59
Portsmouth	Tr	06/63	63-64	12	-	1

SUMMERSCALES William Charles (Bill)
Born: Willesden, NW London, England, 4 January, 1949 — CD

League Club	Source	Date Signed	Seasons Played	Apps	Subs	Gls
Port Vale	Leek T	02/70	69-74	126	3	4
Rochdale	Tr	07/75	75-76	87	0	4

SUMNER Alan
Born: Wrexham, Wales, 18 April, 1949 — M

League Club	Source	Date Signed	Seasons Played	Apps	Subs	Gls
Stockport Co		06/78	78	3	2	0

SUMNER Justin Thomas
Born: Harrogate, North Yorkshire, England, 19 October, 1970 — LW

League Club	Source	Date Signed	Seasons Played	Apps	Subs	Gls
Doncaster Rov	Leeds U (YT)	08/89	89	2	0	0

SUMPNER Richard Anthony
Born: Leeds, England, 12 April, 1947 — CF

League Club	Source	Date Signed	Seasons Played	Apps	Subs	Gls
Bradford Park Ave	Leeds U (Am)	01/67	66	2	0	1

SUMULIKOSKI Velice
Born: Struga, Macedonia, 24 April, 1981 — DM
Macedonia: 84/U21-9

League Club	Source	Date Signed	Seasons Played	Apps	Subs	Gls
Ipswich T	Bursaspor (TKY)	01/08	07-08	32	10	1
Preston NE	Tr	08/09	09	9	6	0

SUNDERLAND Alan
Born: Conisbrough, South Yorkshire, England, 1 July, 1953 — F/M
England: 1/B-7/U23-1/U21-1

League Club	Source	Date Signed	Seasons Played	Apps	Subs	Gls
Wolverhampton W	App	06/71	71-77	139	19	30
Arsenal	Tr	11/77	77-83	204	2	55
Ipswich T	Tr	02/84	83-85	51	7	11

SUNDERLAND Jonathan Paul (Jon)
Born: Newcastle-upon-Tyne, England, 2 November, 1975 — M

League Club	Source	Date Signed	Seasons Played	Apps	Subs	Gls
Blackpool	YT	07/94	94	0	2	0
Scarborough	Tr	03/96	95-96	3	5	0
Hartlepool U	Tr	12/96	96	6	7	1

SUNDGOT Ole Bjorn
Born: Ulsteinvik, Norway, 21 March, 1972 — F

League Club	Source	Date Signed	Seasons Played	Apps	Subs	Gls
Bradford C	Molde FK (NOR)	11/96	96-97	11	14	6

SUN JIHAI (Sunji)
Born: Dalian, China, 30 September, 1977 — RB
China: 80

League Club	Source	Date Signed	Seasons Played	Apps	Subs	Gls
Crystal Palace	Dalian Wanda (CHN)	09/98	98	22	1	0
Manchester C	Dalian Wanda (CHN)	02/02	01-07	93	37	3
Sheffield U	Tr	07/08	08	11	1	0

SUNLEY David
Born: Skelton, Cleveland, England, 6 February, 1952 — F

League Club	Source	Date Signed	Seasons Played	Apps	Subs	Gls
Sheffield Wed	App	01/70	70-75	121	9	21
Nottingham F	L	10/75	75	1	0	0
Hull C	Tr	01/76	75-77	58	11	11
Lincoln C	Tr	07/78	78-79	36	5	6
Stockport Co	Tr	03/80	79-81	79	4	6

SUNLEY Mark
Born: Guisborough, Cleveland, England, 13 October, 1971 — CD

League Club	Source	Date Signed	Seasons Played	Apps	Subs	Gls
Middlesbrough	YT	10/89				
Millwall	Tr	02/91				
Darlington	Tr	07/91	91-93	34	1	0
Hartlepool U	Stalybridge Celtic	02/95	94	1	1	0

SUNU Gilles
Born: Chateauroux, France, 30 March, 1991 — F
France: U21-6/Youth

League Club	Source	Date Signed	Seasons Played	Apps	Subs	Gls
Arsenal	Sch	04/08				
Derby Co	L	02/10	09	6	3	1

SUPPLE Shane
Born: Dublin, Republic of Ireland, 4 May, 1987 — G
Republic of Ireland: U21-1/Youth

League Club	Source	Date Signed	Seasons Played	Apps	Subs	Gls
Ipswich T	Sch	06/04	05-06	32	2	0
Oldham Ath	L	03/09	08	5	0	0

SURMAN Andrew Ronald Edward
Born: Johannesburg, South Africa, 20 August, 1986 — M
England: U21-4

League Club	Source	Date Signed	Seasons Played	Apps	Subs	Gls
Southampton	Sch	08/03	05-08	116	17	15
Walsall	L	01/05	04	10	4	2
Bournemouth	L	08/05	05	24	0	6
Wolverhampton W	Tr	07/09	09	3	4	0
Norwich C	Tr	06/10	10-14	45	7	7
Bournemouth	L	07/13	13	30	5	0
Bournemouth	Tr	09/14	14	40	1	3

SURMAN Leslie (Les)
Born: Tamworth, Staffordshire, England, 23 November, 1947 — G
Died: Congleton, Cheshire, England, 1978

League Club	Source	Date Signed	Seasons Played	Apps	Subs	Gls
Charlton Ath	App	11/65	65	1	0	0
Rotherham U	Tr	06/66	66	1	0	0

SURTEES George Harrison Hall (Harry)
Born: Ryhope, Tyne and Wear, England, 20 December, 1926 — G

League Club	Source	Date Signed	Seasons Played	Apps	Subs	Gls
Southport	Murton CW	08/46	46	3	-	0

SURTEES Hubert (Hugh)
Born: Durham, England, 16 July, 1921 — W
Died: Surrey, England, 1979

League Club	Source	Date Signed	Seasons Played	Apps	Subs	Gls
Watford	Bushey U	07/46	47-48	13	-	1
Crystal Palace	Tr	08/49	49	5	-	0

[SUSO] FERNANDEZ SAEZ DE LA TOR Jesus Joaquin
Born: Cadiz, Spain, 19 November, 1993 — M
Spain: U21-5/Youth

League Club	Source	Date Signed	Seasons Played	Apps	Subs	Gls
Liverpool	Sch	11/10	12	8	6	0

SUSSEX Andrew Robert (Andy)
Born: Islington, N London, England, 23 November, 1964 — M/F

League Club	Source	Date Signed	Seasons Played	Apps	Subs	Gls
Leyton Orient	App	11/82	81-87	126	18	17
Crewe Alex	Tr	06/88	88-90	86	16	24
Southend U	Tr	07/91	91-95	63	13	14
Brentford	L	12/95	95	3	0	0

SUTCH Daryl
Born: Beccles, Suffolk, England, 11 September, 1971 — RB/M
England: U21-4/Youth

League Club	Source	Date Signed	Seasons Played	Apps	Subs	Gls
Norwich C	YT	07/90	90-01	255	50	9

League Club	Source	Date Signed	Seasons Played	Apps	Subs	Gls
Southend U	Tr	01/03	02	16	0	1
Boston U	Tr	07/03	03	6	0	0

SUTCLIFFE Frederick (Fred)
Born: Brotherton, West Yorkshire, England, 29 May, 1931 LH/IF

League Club	Source	Date Signed	Seasons Played	Apps	Subs	Gls
Birmingham C		09/51				
Chester C	Tr	06/52	52-54	50	-	2

SUTCLIFFE Frederick William Joseph (Fred)
Born: Fulham, W London, England, 29 July, 1923 CF
Died: Kensington, Central London, England, 3 March, 2006

League Club	Source	Date Signed	Seasons Played	Apps	Subs	Gls
Millwall		02/47	47-48	12	-	3
Walsall	Tr	07/50	50	4	-	0

SUTCLIFFE Peter David
Born: Manchester, England, 25 January, 1957 RW
England: Youth

League Club	Source	Date Signed	Seasons Played	Apps	Subs	Gls
Manchester U	App	07/74				
Stockport Co	Tr	12/75	75-76	19	8	2
Port Vale	Tr	03/77	76-78	44	6	6
Chester C	Tr	12/78	78-81	103	6	7
Chester C	Bangor C	11/83	83	11	0	0
Stockport Co	Tr	03/84	83	0	1	0

SUTHERLAND Christopher Paul (Chris)
Born: Middleton, Greater Manchester, England, 4 August, 1995 W

League Club	Source	Date Signed	Seasons Played	Apps	Subs	Gls
Oldham Ath	Sch	07/13	12	1	9	0

SUTHERLAND Colin Craig
Born: Glasgow, Scotland, 15 March, 1975 LB

League Club	Source	Date Signed	Seasons Played	Apps	Subs	Gls
Scarborough	Clydebank	12/96	96-97	35	8	0

SUTHERLAND Craig Stephen
Born: Edinburgh, Scotland, 17 December, 1988 F

League Club	Source	Date Signed	Seasons Played	Apps	Subs	Gls
Blackpool	N Carolina Univ (USA)	07/11	11	2	5	0
Plymouth Arg	L	11/11	11	5	4	1

SUTHERLAND Frankie Jay
Born: Hillingdon, W London, England, 6 December, 1993 M
Republic of Ireland: U21-6/Youth

League Club	Source	Date Signed	Seasons Played	Apps	Subs	Gls
Queens Park Rgrs	Sch	12/10				
Portsmouth	L	01/13	12	0	1	0
AFC Wimbledon	L	10/14	14	4	3	1

SUTHERLAND George Burns
Born: Bathgate, West Lothian, Scotland, 11 September, 1923 CF
Died: Poplar, E London, England, 24 February, 1969

League Club	Source	Date Signed	Seasons Played	Apps	Subs	Gls
Leyton Orient	Partick Thistle	08/49	49-50	42	-	22

SUTHERLAND Harry Ross
Born: Salford, England, 30 July, 1915 CF

League Club	Source	Date Signed	Seasons Played	Apps	Subs	Gls
Leeds U	Mossley	07/38	38	3	-	1
Exeter C	Tr	05/47	46-47	14	-	3
Bournemouth	Tr	07/48				

SUTHERLAND James Sinclair (Jimmy)
Born: Armadale, West Lothian, Scotland, 6 August, 1918 LB
Died: Bathgate, West Lothian, Scotland, 16 September, 1987

League Club	Source	Date Signed	Seasons Played	Apps	Subs	Gls
Newport Co	Forth W	07/47	47-48	32	-	0

SUTHERLAND John Francis
Born: Cork, Republic of Ireland, 10 February, 1932 RB

League Club	Source	Date Signed	Seasons Played	Apps	Subs	Gls
Everton	Evergreen U (ROI)	05/50	56	6	-	0
Chesterfield	Tr	06/57	57-58	47	-	0
Crewe Alex	Tr	11/58	58-59	46	-	1

SUTTLE Kenneth George (Ken)
Born: Hammersmith, W London, England, 25 August, 1928 LW
Died: Mauritius, 25 March, 2005

League Club	Source	Date Signed	Seasons Played	Apps	Subs	Gls
Chelsea	Worthing	08/48				
Brighton & HA	Tr	07/49	49	3	-	0

SUTTON Brian
Born: Rochdale, Greater Manchester, England, 8 December, 1934 G

League Club	Source	Date Signed	Seasons Played	Apps	Subs	Gls
Rochdale	Norden YC	10/52	52-55	13	-	0

SUTTON Christopher Roy (Chris)
Born: Nottingham, England, 10 March, 1973 F
England: 1/B-2/U21-13

League Club	Source	Date Signed	Seasons Played	Apps	Subs	Gls
Norwich C	YT	07/91	90-93	89	13	35
Blackburn Rov	Tr	07/94	94-98	125	5	47
Chelsea	Tr	07/99	99	21	7	1
Birmingham C	Glasgow Celtic	01/06	05	10	0	1
Aston Villa	Tr	10/06	06	6	2	1

SUTTON David William
Born: Tarleton, Lancashire, England, 21 January, 1957 CD

League Club	Source	Date Signed	Seasons Played	Apps	Subs	Gls
Plymouth Arg	App	07/74	73-77	60	1	0
Reading	L	11/77	77	9	0	0
Huddersfield T	Tr	03/78	77-83	242	0	11
Bolton W	Tr	06/85	85-87	98	0	4
Rochdale	Tr	08/88	88	28	0	2

SUTTON David William (Dave)
Born: Leek, Staffordshire, England, 15 December, 1966 F

League Club	Source	Date Signed	Seasons Played	Apps	Subs	Gls
Crewe Alex	Stoke C (App)	07/86	86	0	1	1

SUTTON Gary
Born: Folkestone, Kent, England, 2 February, 1962 G

League Club	Source	Date Signed	Seasons Played	Apps	Subs	Gls
Gillingham	App	02/80	80-81	11	0	0

SUTTON James Peter
Born: Glasgow, Scotland, 6 September, 1949 M

League Club	Source	Date Signed	Seasons Played	Apps	Subs	Gls
Newcastle U	St Roch's	06/69				
Mansfield T	Tr	07/70	70	11	2	0

SUTTON John William Michael
Born: Norwich, England, 26 December, 1983 F
England: Youth

League Club	Source	Date Signed	Seasons Played	Apps	Subs	Gls
Tottenham H	YT	07/01				
Carlisle U	L	10/02	02	7	0	1
Swindon T	Tr	12/02	02	0	1	0
Millwall	Raith Rov	01/04	03	2	2	0
Wycombe W	St Mirren	07/07	07	23	20	6

SUTTON Melvyn Charles (Mel)
Born: Birmingham, England, 13 February, 1946 M

League Club	Source	Date Signed	Seasons Played	Apps	Subs	Gls
Cardiff C	Aston Villa (Am)	12/67	68-71	135	3	5
Wrexham	Tr	07/72	72-80	355	5	21
Crewe Alex	Tr	08/82	82	13	0	1

SUTTON Michael John (Mike)
Born: Norwich, England, 5 October, 1944 M/CD

League Club	Source	Date Signed	Seasons Played	Apps	Subs	Gls
Norwich C	Jnr	09/62	62-66	46	5	3
Chester C	Tr	05/67	67-69	137	1	9
Carlisle U	Tr	06/70	70-71	51	2	1

SUTTON Richard Melvyn
Born: Gravesend, Kent, England, 21 August, 1965 CD
England: Youth

League Club	Source	Date Signed	Seasons Played	Apps	Subs	Gls
Peterborough U	App	-	82	1	0	0

SUTTON Ritchie Aidan
Born: Stoke-on-Trent, England, 29 April, 1986 D

League Club	Source	Date Signed	Seasons Played	Apps	Subs	Gls
Crewe Alex	Sch	08/05				
Port Vale	Nantwich T	07/10	10	5	6	0
Mansfield T	Tr	06/11	13-14	69	1	0

SUTTON Stephen John (Steve)
Born: Hartington, Derbyshire, England, 16 April, 1961 G

League Club	Source	Date Signed	Seasons Played	Apps	Subs	Gls
Nottingham F	App	04/79	80-89	199	0	0
Mansfield T	L	03/81	80	8	0	0
Derby Co	L	01/85	84	14	0	0
Coventry C	L	02/91	90	1	0	0
Luton T	L	11/91	91	14	0	0
Derby Co	Tr	03/92	91-95	60	1	0
Reading	L	01/96	95	2	0	0
Birmingham C	Tr	08/96	96	6	0	0

SUTTON Wayne Frank
Born: Derby, England, 1 October, 1975 D/M

League Club	Source	Date Signed	Seasons Played	Apps	Subs	Gls
Derby Co	YT	10/92	94-95	4	3	0
Hereford U	L	09/96	96	4	0	0

SVARC Robert Louis (Bobby)
Born: Leicester, England, 8 February, 1946 F

League Club	Source	Date Signed	Seasons Played	Apps	Subs	Gls
Leicester C	App	03/63	64-68	13	0	2
Lincoln C	Tr	12/68	68-71	40	5	16
Barrow	L	09/70	70	15	0	4
Colchester U	Boston U	12/72	72-75	116	0	59
Blackburn Rov	Tr	10/75	75-76	42	8	16
Watford	L	09/77	77	1	0	0

SVARD Sebastian Steve Qvacoe
Born: Copenhagen, Denmark, 15 January, 1983 DM
Denmark: U21-9/Youth

League Club	Source	Date Signed	Seasons Played	Apps	Subs	Gls
Arsenal	FC Copenhagen (DEN)	11/00				
Stoke C	L	01/04	03	9	4	1

SVENSSON Anders
Born: Gothenburg, Sweden, 17 July, 1976 M
Sweden: 148/U21-16

League Club	Source	Date Signed	Seasons Played	Apps	Subs	Gls
Southampton	Elfsborg (SWE)	07/01	01-04	97	30	9

SVENSSON Mathias
Born: Boras, Sweden, 24 September, 1974 F
Sweden: 3

League Club	Source	Date Signed	Seasons Played	Apps	Subs	Gls
Portsmouth	Elfsborg (SWE)	12/96	96-97	34	11	10
Crystal Palace	Tirol Innsbruck (AUT)	09/98	98-99	26	6	10
Charlton Ath	Tr	01/00	99-03	42	28	7

League Club	Source	Date Signed	Seasons Played	Apps	Subs	Gls
Derby Co	L	08/03	03	9	1	3
Norwich C	Tr	12/03	03-04	26	16	11

SVENSSON Michael Lennart
Born: Varnamo, Sweden, 25 November, 1975 CD
Sweden: 25

League Club	Source	Date Signed	Seasons Played	Apps	Subs	Gls
Southampton	Troyes AC (FRA)	07/02	02-05	66	1	4
Southampton	Rtd	08/08	08	4	0	0

SWAIBU Moses
Born: Southwark, S London, England, 9 May, 1989 CD

League Club	Source	Date Signed	Seasons Played	Apps	Subs	Gls
Crystal Palace	Sch	07/07				
Lincoln C	Bromley	01/09	08-10	51	5	3

SWAILES Christopher William (Chris)
Born: Gateshead, Tyne and Wear, England, 19 October, 1970 CD

League Club	Source	Date Signed	Seasons Played	Apps	Subs	Gls
Ipswich T	YT	05/89				
Peterborough U	Tr	03/91				
Doncaster Rov	Bridlington T	10/93	93-94	49	0	0
Ipswich T	Tr	03/95	94-97	34	3	1
Bury	Tr	11/97	97-00	125	1	10
Rotherham U	Tr	07/01	01-04	167	0	14
Oldham Ath	Tr	07/05	05-06	18	1	0

SWAILES Daniel (Danny)
Born: Bolton, Greater Manchester, England, 1 April, 1979 CD

League Club	Source	Date Signed	Seasons Played	Apps	Subs	Gls
Bury	YT	07/97	99-04	154	10	13
Macclesfield T	Tr	01/05	04-06	94	0	5
MK Dons	Tr	08/07	07-09	43	0	4
Northampton T	L	11/09	09	3	0	0
Stockport Co	Tr	01/10	09-10	33	0	0

SWAIN Kenneth (Kenny)
Born: Birkenhead, Wirral, England, 28 January, 1952 RB/F

League Club	Source	Date Signed	Seasons Played	Apps	Subs	Gls
Chelsea	Wycombe W	08/73	73-78	114	5	26
Aston Villa	Tr	12/78	78-82	148	0	4
Nottingham F	Tr	10/82	82-84	112	0	2
Portsmouth	Tr	07/85	85-87	113	0	0
West Bromwich A	L	02/88	87	7	0	1
Crewe Alex	Tr	08/88	88-91	123	3	1

SWAIN Kenneth John (Kenny)
Born: Cardiff, Wales, 31 December, 1954 LB
Wales: Schools

League Club	Source	Date Signed	Seasons Played	Apps	Subs	Gls
Newport Co	App	12/72	71-73	7	1	0

SWAIN Malcolm
Born: Hornsey, N London, England, 2 February, 1952 M

League Club	Source	Date Signed	Seasons Played	Apps	Subs	Gls
Reading	App	02/70	70-71	37	4	2

SWAIN Robert
Born: Ripon, North Yorkshire, England, 26 March, 1944 W

League Club	Source	Date Signed	Seasons Played	Apps	Subs	Gls
Bradford C	Jnr	09/61	62	7	-	0

SWAIN Sidney (Sid)
Born: Liverpool, England, 14 October, 1927 W
Died: Liverpool, England, 16 January, 1978

League Club	Source	Date Signed	Seasons Played	Apps	Subs	Gls
Halifax T	Bangor C	07/51	51	8	-	1

SWAINE Mark
Born: Hammersmith, W London, England, 13 February, 1958 W

League Club	Source	Date Signed	Seasons Played	Apps	Subs	Gls
Gillingham	App	-	74	1	0	0

SWALES Stephen Colin (Steve)
Born: Whitby, North Yorkshire, England, 26 December, 1973 LB

League Club	Source	Date Signed	Seasons Played	Apps	Subs	Gls
Scarborough	YT	08/92	91-94	51	3	1
Reading	Tr	07/95	95-97	33	10	1
Hull C	Tr	12/98	98-00	57	11	0
Halifax T	Tr	08/01	01	20	4	1

SWALLOW Benjamin Owen (Ben)
Born: Barry, Vale of Glamorgan, Wales, 20 October, 1989 LM

League Club	Source	Date Signed	Seasons Played	Apps	Subs	Gls
Bristol Rov	Jnr	07/08	09-10	17	23	0

SWALLOW Ernest (Ernie)
Born: Wheatley Hill, County Durham, England, 9 July, 1919 RB
Died: Doncaster, South Yorkshire, England, 18 January, 1962

League Club	Source	Date Signed	Seasons Played	Apps	Subs	Gls
Doncaster Rov	Bentley Colliery	11/41	46-47	50	-	0
Barnsley	Tr	01/48	47-49	36	-	0
Oldham Ath	Tr	08/50	50	6	-	0

SWALLOW Ernest Barry (Barry)
Born: Arksey, South Yorkshire, England, 2 July, 1942 CH

League Club	Source	Date Signed	Seasons Played	Apps	Subs	Gls
Doncaster Rov	Jnr	07/59	60-61	51	-	10
Crewe Alex	Tr	08/62	62-63	14	-	0
Barnsley	Tr	07/64	64-66	96	0	1
Bradford C	Tr	02/67	66-69	79	6	7
York C	Tr	10/69	69-75	268	1	21

SWALLOW Raymond (Ray)
Born: Southwark, S London, England, 15 June, 1935 W/IF

League Club	Source	Date Signed	Seasons Played	Apps	Subs	Gls
Arsenal	Tooting & Mitcham U	12/52	54-57	13	-	4
Derby Co	Tr	09/58	58-63	118	-	21

SWAN Carl
Born: Sheffield, England, 12 December, 1957 CD

League Club	Source	Date Signed	Seasons Played	Apps	Subs	Gls
Doncaster Rov	Burton A	12/80	80-82	14	1	1
Rochdale	L	10/82	82	3	0	0

SWAN Iain
Born: Glasgow, Scotland, 16 October, 1979 CD

League Club	Source	Date Signed	Seasons Played	Apps	Subs	Gls
Oldham Ath	YT	11/96	98	1	0	0

SWAN Maurice Michael George
Born: Dublin, Republic of Ireland, 27 September, 1938 G
Republic of Ireland: 1

League Club	Source	Date Signed	Seasons Played	Apps	Subs	Gls
Cardiff C	Drumcondra (ROI)	07/60	60-62	15	-	0
Hull C	Tr	06/63	63-67	103	0	0

SWAN Peter
Born: South Elmsall, West Yorkshire, England, 8 October, 1936 CD
England: 19/FLge-6/U23-3/Youth

League Club	Source	Date Signed	Seasons Played	Apps	Subs	Gls
Sheffield Wed	Jnr	11/53	55-63	260	-	0
Sheffield Wed	Rtd	07/72	72	13	2	0
Bury	Tr	08/73	73	35	0	2

SWAN Peter Harold
Born: Leeds, England, 28 September, 1966 CD/F

League Club	Source	Date Signed	Seasons Played	Apps	Subs	Gls
Leeds U	App	08/84	85-88	43	6	11
Hull C	Tr	03/89	88-90	76	4	24
Port Vale	Tr	08/91	91-93	105	6	5
Plymouth Arg	Tr	07/94	94	24	3	2
Burnley	Tr	08/95	95-96	47	2	7
Bury	Tr	08/97	97	26	11	6
Burnley	Tr	08/98	98-99	11	8	0
York C	Tr	03/00	99-00	11	0	0

SWAN Ronald McDonald (Ron)
Born: Plean, Stirlingshire, Scotland, 8 January, 1941 G

League Club	Source	Date Signed	Seasons Played	Apps	Subs	Gls
Oldham Ath	East Stirlingshire	05/64	64-66	64	0	0
Luton T	Tr	01/67	66	14	0	0

SWANKIE Robert Beattie (Bob)
Born: Arbroath, Angus, Scotland, 25 February, 1932 WH
Died: Gloucester, England, 28 June, 2011

League Club	Source	Date Signed	Seasons Played	Apps	Subs	Gls
Burnley	Arbroath YC	07/50				
Darlington	Gloucester C	01/54	53	1	-	0

SWANN Gary
Born: York, England, 11 April, 1962 FB/M

League Club	Source	Date Signed	Seasons Played	Apps	Subs	Gls
Hull C	App	04/80	80-86	176	10	9
Preston NE	Tr	11/86	86-91	194	5	37
York C	Tr	06/92	92-93	82	0	4
Scarborough	Tr	08/94	94	24	3	3

SWANN Gordon
Born: Maltby, South Yorkshire, England, 7 December, 1937 LW

League Club	Source	Date Signed	Seasons Played	Apps	Subs	Gls
Rotherham U		07/57	58-60	11	-	1
Barnsley	Tr	07/61	61	2	-	0

SWANNELL John
Born: Walton-on-Thames, Surrey, England, 26 January, 1939 G
England: Amateur-61

League Club	Source	Date Signed	Seasons Played	Apps	Subs	Gls
Stockport Co (Am)	Corinthian Casuals	06/59	59	1	-	0

SWANSON Daniel Joseph (Danny)
Born: Leith, Edinburgh, Scotland, 28 December, 1986 M

League Club	Source	Date Signed	Seasons Played	Apps	Subs	Gls
Peterborough U	Dundee U	06/12	12-13	35	27	4
Coventry C	Tr	07/14	14	8	7	0

SWEENEY Alan
Born: Paisley, Renfrewshire, Scotland, 31 October, 1956 RB

League Club	Source	Date Signed	Seasons Played	Apps	Subs	Gls
Huddersfield T	App	11/73	74-77	65	1	0
Hartlepool U	Emley	09/79	79-81	97	0	2

SWEENEY Andrew (Andy)
Born: Chadderton, Greater Manchester, England, 15 October, 1951 RW

League Club	Source	Date Signed	Seasons Played	Apps	Subs	Gls
Oldham Ath	Jnr	02/71	70-74	37	5	2
Bury	L	03/73	72	2	0	0
Rochdale	Tr	07/75	75	12	5	0

SWEENEY Antony Thomas
Born: Stockton-on-Tees, Cleveland, England, 5 September, 1983 M

League Club	Source	Date Signed	Seasons Played	Apps	Subs	Gls
Hartlepool U	YT	01/02	01-13	332	53	52
Carlisle U	Tr	06/14	14	26	3	1

SWEENEY Gerald (Gerry)
Born: Renfrew, Renfrewshire, Scotland, 10 July, 1945 RB/M

League Club	Source	Date Signed	Seasons Played	Apps	Subs	Gls
Bristol C	Greenock Morton	08/71	71-81	396	10	22
York C	Tr	02/82	81	12	0	0

SWEENEY Paul Martin

Born: Glasgow, Scotland, 10 January, 1965 LB

League Club	Source	Date Signed	Seasons Played	Apps	Subs	Gls
Newcastle U	Raith Rov	03/89	88-90	28	8	0
Hartlepool U	Gateshead	08/94	94	1	0	0

SWEENEY Peter Henry

Born: Glasgow, Scotland, 25 September, 1984 M
Scotland: B-1/U21-8/Youth

League Club	Source	Date Signed	Seasons Played	Apps	Subs	Gls
Millwall	Jnr	12/00	01-04	45	14	5
Stoke C	Tr	07/05	05-07	18	17	2
Yeovil T	L	01/07	06	5	3	0
Walsall	L	11/07	07	7	0	0
Leeds U	Tr	01/08	07	6	3	0
Grimsby T	Tr	03/09	08-09	44	4	4
Bury	Tr	07/10	10-12	72	10	5
AFC Wimbledon	Tr	01/13	12-13	25	4	0

SWEENEY Ryan Joseph

Born: Kingston-on-Thames, SW London, England, 15 April, 1997 D

League Club	Source	Date Signed	Seasons Played	Apps	Subs	Gls
AFC Wimbledon	Sch	02/15	14	2	1	0

SWEENEY Terry Neil

Born: Paisley, Renfrewshire, Scotland, 26 January, 1979 M

League Club	Source	Date Signed	Seasons Played	Apps	Subs	Gls
Luton T	YT	03/97				
Plymouth Arg	Tr	10/98	98	6	7	1

SWEENEY William Clerihew

Born: St Andrews, Fife, Scotland, 23 October, 1918 G
Died: Glasgow, Scotland, 4 June, 1971

League Club	Source	Date Signed	Seasons Played	Apps	Subs	Gls
Carlisle U	Clyde	01/48	47-48	37	-	0

SWEENIE Thomas Thornton (Tom)

Born: Paisley, Renfrewshire, Scotland, 15 July, 1945 IF

League Club	Source	Date Signed	Seasons Played	Apps	Subs	Gls
Leicester C	Johnstone Burgh	06/63	63-66	50	1	11
Arsenal	Tr	07/68				
Huddersfield T	Tr	08/68				
York C	Tr	10/68	68	6	0	1

SWEETZER Gordon Eric Peter

Born: Toronto, Canada, 27 January, 1957 F
Canada: 3

League Club	Source	Date Signed	Seasons Played	Apps	Subs	Gls
Brentford	Queens Park Rgrs (NC)	07/75	75-77	68	4	40
Cambridge U	Tr	04/78	77-79	9	0	3
Brentford	Toronto Blizzard (CAN)	01/82	81	8	1	1

SWEETZER James Edward (Jimmy)

Born: Woking, Surrey, England, 8 January, 1960 F

League Club	Source	Date Signed	Seasons Played	Apps	Subs	Gls
Oxford U	App	02/77	78	0	8	1
Millwall	Tr	11/79	79	2	1	1

SWIERCZEWSKI Piotr

Born: Nowy Sacz, Poland, 8 April, 1972 M
Poland: 70

League Club	Source	Date Signed	Seasons Played	Apps	Subs	Gls
Birmingham C	Olymp Marseille (FRA)	01/03	02	0	1	0

SWIFT Colin

Born: Barnsley, South Yorkshire, England, 23 December, 1933 RB
Died: Barnsley, South Yorkshire, England, April, 2011

League Club	Source	Date Signed	Seasons Played	Apps	Subs	Gls
Barnsley	Jnr	08/51	55-61	241	-	0

SWIFT Frank Victor

Born: Blackpool, Lancashire, England, 26 December, 1913 G
Died: Munich, Germany, 6 February, 1958
England: 19/FLge-3/War-14

League Club	Source	Date Signed	Seasons Played	Apps	Subs	Gls
Manchester C	Fleetwood	10/32	33-49	338	-	0

SWIFT Humphrey Mills (Hugh)

Born: Sheffield, England, 22 January, 1921 LB
Died: Sheffield, England, 1979
England: B-1

League Club	Source	Date Signed	Seasons Played	Apps	Subs	Gls
Sheffield Wed	Lopham Street Meth's	09/42	46-50	181	-	0

SWIFT John David

Born: Portsmouth, England, 23 June, 1995 M
England: Youth

League Club	Source	Date Signed	Seasons Played	Apps	Subs	Gls
Chelsea	Sch	07/12	13	0	1	0
Rotherham U	L	08/14	14	1	2	0
Swindon T	L	01/15	14	12	6	2

SWIFT John Kenneth (Kenny)

Born: Fazakerley, Merseyside, England, 26 July, 1928 RW

League Club	Source	Date Signed	Seasons Played	Apps	Subs	Gls
Liverpool	Jnr	08/45				
Southport	Tr	07/51	51	5	-	0

SWIFT John Maxwell

Born: Leeds, England, 20 September, 1984 RB

League Club	Source	Date Signed	Seasons Played	Apps	Subs	Gls
Bradford C	Sch	08/04	04-06	7	5	0

SWIFT Trevor

Born: Rotherham, South Yorkshire, England, 14 September, 1948 CD

League Club	Source	Date Signed	Seasons Played	Apps	Subs	Gls
Rotherham U	Jnr	09/65	67-74	283	4	21

SWIGGS Bradley

Born: Plymouth, England, 12 October, 1959 F

League Club	Source	Date Signed	Seasons Played	Apps	Subs	Gls
Plymouth Arg	Liskeard Ath	03/84	83	1	1	0

SWIGGS Robert (Bob)

Born: Plymouth, England, 30 March, 1930 CF
Died: Plymouth, England, December, 2010

League Club	Source	Date Signed	Seasons Played	Apps	Subs	Gls
Plymouth Arg	St Blazey	01/56	55-56	3	-	0

SWINBOURNE Royston Harry (Roy)

Born: Denaby Main, South Yorkshire, England, 25 August, 1929 CF
England: B-1

League Club	Source	Date Signed	Seasons Played	Apps	Subs	Gls
Wolverhampton W	Jnr	09/46	49-55	211	-	107

SWINBURNE Alan Thomas Anderson

Born: Houghton-le-Spring, Tyne and Wear, England, 18 May, 1946 G

League Club	Source	Date Signed	Seasons Played	Apps	Subs	Gls
Oldham Ath	App	09/63	63	4	-	0
Newcastle U	Tr	06/64				

SWINBURNE Thomas Anderson (Tom)

Born: Houghton-le-Spring, Tyne and Wear, England, 9 August, 1915 G
Died: County Durham, England, 1969
England: War-1

League Club	Source	Date Signed	Seasons Played	Apps	Subs	Gls
Newcastle U	Herrington CW	04/34	34-46	77	-	0

SWINBURNE Trevor

Born: Houghton-le-Spring, Tyne and Wear, England, 20 June, 1953 G

League Club	Source	Date Signed	Seasons Played	Apps	Subs	Gls
Sunderland	App	06/70	72-76	10	0	0
Carlisle U	Tr	05/77	77-82	248	0	0
Brentford	Tr	08/83	83-84	45	0	0
Leeds U	Tr	06/85	85	2	0	0
Doncaster Rov	L	09/85	85	4	0	0
Lincoln C	Tr	02/86	85-86	34	0	0

SWINDELLS Jack (Jackie)

Born: Manchester, England, 12 April, 1937 IF
Died: St Kew, Cornwall, England, 23 June, 2009
England: Youth

League Club	Source	Date Signed	Seasons Played	Apps	Subs	Gls
Blackburn Rov	Manchester C (Am)	11/57	57-59	9	-	1
Accrington Stan	Tr	12/59	59-60	65	-	28
Barnsley	Tr	06/61	61	14	-	8
Workington	Tr	02/62	61-62	62	-	19
Torquay U	Tr	07/63	63	18	-	6
Newport Co	Tr	07/64	64	23	-	3

SWINDIN George Hedley

Born: Campsall, South Yorkshire, England, 4 December, 1914 G
Died: Kettering, Northamptonshire, England, 26 October, 2005

League Club	Source	Date Signed	Seasons Played	Apps	Subs	Gls
Bradford C	Rotherham YMCA	02/33	34-35	26	-	0
Arsenal	Tr	04/36	36-53	271	-	0

SWINDLEHURST David (Dave)

Born: Edgware, NW London, England, 6 January, 1956 F
England: B-1/U21-1/Youth

League Club	Source	Date Signed	Seasons Played	Apps	Subs	Gls
Crystal Palace	App	01/73	73-79	221	16	73
Derby Co	Tr	02/80	79-82	110	0	29
West Ham U	Tr	03/83	82-84	52	9	16
Sunderland	Tr	08/85	85-86	59	0	11
Wimbledon	Anorthosis (CYP)	03/88	87	2	0	0
Colchester U	Tr	06/88	88	12	0	6
Peterborough U	L	12/88	88	4	0	1

SWINFEN Reginald (Reg)

Born: Battersea, SW London, England, 4 May, 1915 RW
Died: Crawley, West Sussex, England, October, 1996

League Club	Source	Date Signed	Seasons Played	Apps	Subs	Gls
Queens Park Rgrs	Civil Service	03/36	36-46	26	-	5

SWINSCOE Terence (Terry)

Born: Shirebrook, Derbyshire, England, 31 August, 1934 D

League Club	Source	Date Signed	Seasons Played	Apps	Subs	Gls
Stockport Co	Spalding U	02/56				
Mansfield T	Tr	11/56	56-58	14	-	0

SWINSCOE Thomas William (Tom)

Born: Mansfield, Nottinghamshire, England, 16 October, 1919 CF
Died: Sutton-in-Ashfield, Nottinghamshire, England, February, 1993

League Club	Source	Date Signed	Seasons Played	Apps	Subs	Gls
Chesterfield	Shirebrook Supporters	03/46	46-47	43	-	12
Stockport Co	Tr	02/48	47-49	72	-	31

SWITZER George

Born: Salford, England, 13 October, 1973 LB

League Club	Source	Date Signed	Seasons Played	Apps	Subs	Gls
Manchester U	YT	07/92				
Darlington	Tr	08/93	93	12	2	0

SWONNELL Samuel Alfred (Sam)

Born: Brentwood, Essex, England, 13 September, 1982 M

League Club	Source	Date Signed	Seasons Played	Apps	Subs	Gls
Watford	YT	03/01	02	1	1	0

SWORD Alan

Born: Newcastle-upon-Tyne, England, 5 July, 1934 CF

League Club	Source	Date Signed	Seasons Played	Apps	Subs	Gls
Newcastle U	Jnr	08/51				
Exeter C	Tr	09/53	55	9	-	4

SWORD Thomas William (Tommy)
Born: Newcastle-upon-Tyne, England, 12 November, 1957 CD/F

League Club	Source	Date Signed	Seasons Played	Apps	Subs	Gls
Stockport Co	Bishop Auckland	11/79	79-85	236	2	51
Hartlepool U	Tr	07/86	86	18	0	0
Halifax T	L	02/87	86	8	0	2
Stockport Co	Tr	03/87	86-87	6	1	1

SYDENHAM John
Born: Eastleigh, Hampshire, England, 15 September, 1939 W
England: U23-2/Youth

League Club	Source	Date Signed	Seasons Played	Apps	Subs	Gls
Southampton	Jnr	04/57	56-69	341	2	36
Aldershot	Tr	03/70	69-71	54	5	4

SYERS David Thomas (Dave)
Born: Leeds, England, 30 November, 1987 M

League Club	Source	Date Signed	Seasons Played	Apps	Subs	Gls
Bradford C	Guiseley	08/10	10-11	38	17	10
Doncaster Rov	Tr	06/12	12-13	20	14	3
Scunthorpe U	L	10/13	13	15	0	5
Scunthorpe U	Tr	01/14	13-14	23	5	5

SYKES Alexander Barrett (Alex)
Born: Newcastle-under-Lyme, Potteries, England, 2 April, 1974 W

League Club	Source	Date Signed	Seasons Played	Apps	Subs	Gls
Mansfield T	Westfields	06/92	93	1	1	1

SYKES George Robert James
Born: Buckhurst Hill, Essex, England, 14 September, 1994 F

League Club	Source	Date Signed	Seasons Played	Apps	Subs	Gls
Barnet	Sch	07/13	12	0	3	0

SYKES John
Born: Huddersfield, West Yorkshire, England, 2 November, 1950 IF

League Club	Source	Date Signed	Seasons Played	Apps	Subs	Gls
Bradford Park Ave	App	11/68	68	1	0	0
Wrexham	Tr	01/69	68	1	0	0

SYKES Kenneth (Ken)
Born: Darlington, County Durham, England, 29 January, 1926 CF
Died: Darlington, County Durham, England, 27 April, 2008

League Club	Source	Date Signed	Seasons Played	Apps	Subs	Gls
Darlington	Darlington ATC	05/46	46	6	-	2
Middlesbrough	Tr	06/47				
Hartlepool U	Tr	09/49	49	1	-	0

SYKES Norman Albert John
Born: Bristol, England, 16 October, 1936 WH
Died: Hillingdon, W London, England, 9 December, 2009
England: Youth/Schools

League Club	Source	Date Signed	Seasons Played	Apps	Subs	Gls
Bristol Rov	Jnr	10/53	56-63	214	-	5
Plymouth Arg	Tr	09/64	64	3	-	0
Stockport Co	Tr	09/65	65-66	52	0	7
Doncaster Rov	Tr	02/67	66	15	0	0

SYLLA Mohammed (Momo)
Born: Bouake, Ivory Coast, 13 March, 1977 DM
Guinea: 2

League Club	Source	Date Signed	Seasons Played	Apps	Subs	Gls
Leicester C	Glasgow Celtic	06/05	05-06	27	7	0

SYLLA Yacouba
Born: Etampes, France, 29 November, 1990 DM
France: U21-1//Mali: 12

League Club	Source	Date Signed	Seasons Played	Apps	Subs	Gls
Aston Villa	Clermont Foot (FRA)	01/13	12-13	12	10	0

SYLVESTRE Ludovic
Born: Paris, France, 5 February, 1984 M

League Club	Source	Date Signed	Seasons Played	Apps	Subs	Gls
Blackpool	Mlada Boleslav (CZE)	08/10	10-12	47	18	6

SYME Colin
Born: Rosyth, Fife, Scotland, 23 January, 1924 RW
Died: Leicester, England, 2 October, 2001

League Club	Source	Date Signed	Seasons Played	Apps	Subs	Gls
Torquay U	Dunfermline Ath	12/46	46	1	-	0

SYMES Michael
Born: Great Yarmouth, Norfolk, England, 31 October, 1983 F

League Club	Source	Date Signed	Seasons Played	Apps	Subs	Gls
Everton	Sch	02/02				
Crewe Alex	L	03/04	03	1	3	1
Bradford C	Tr	08/04	04-05	6	9	3
Stockport Co	L	01/06	05	0	1	0
Shrewsbury T	Tr	08/06	06-08	33	29	14
Macclesfield T	L	01/08	07	10	4	1
Bournemouth	L	11/08	08	3	2	0
Accrington Stan	Tr	03/09	08-09	46	2	14
Bournemouth	Tr	07/10	10-11	23	14	11
Rochdale	L	01/12	11	14	1	4
Leyton Orient	Tr	06/12	12	5	8	1
Burton A	Tr	01/13	12-13	21	7	6

SYMINGTON David Alexander
Born: Whitehaven, Cumbria, England, 28 January, 1994 RW

League Club	Source	Date Signed	Seasons Played	Apps	Subs	Gls
Carlisle U	Sch	07/12	12-14	26	48	4

SYMM Colin
Born: Dunston-on-Tyne, Tyne and Wear, England, 26 November, 1946 M

League Club	Source	Date Signed	Seasons Played	Apps	Subs	Gls
Sheffield Wed	Gateshead	05/65	66-68	16	3	1
Sunderland	Tr	06/69	69-71	9	5	0
Lincoln C	Tr	06/72	72-74	60	9	7

SYMMONS Iorwerth
Born: Swansea, Wales, 3 February, 1930 RB
Died: Swansea, Wales, 20 March, 2004

League Club	Source	Date Signed	Seasons Played	Apps	Subs	Gls
Swansea C	Hafod	05/48	50-51	16	-	0

SYMONDS Anthony (Tony)
Born: Wakefield, England, 10 November, 1944 CD
Died: Leeds, England, July, 2002

League Club	Source	Date Signed	Seasons Played	Apps	Subs	Gls
Bradford Park Ave	Great Preston Jnrs	07/62	64-66	28	1	2

SYMONDS Richard
Born: Langham, Norfolk, England, 21 November, 1959 FB

League Club	Source	Date Signed	Seasons Played	Apps	Subs	Gls
Norwich C	App	08/78	78-82	55	4	0

SYMONDS Roderick Calvin Hilgrove (Calvin)
Born: Pembroke, Bermuda, 29 March, 1932 CF

League Club	Source	Date Signed	Seasons Played	Apps	Subs	Gls
Rochdale	Pemb'ke Hamilton (BER)	10/54	55	1	-	0

SYMONS Christopher Jeremiah (Kit)
Born: Basingstoke, Hampshire, England, 8 March, 1971 CD
Wales: 37/B-1/U21-2/Youth

League Club	Source	Date Signed	Seasons Played	Apps	Subs	Gls
Portsmouth	YT	12/88	88-95	161	0	10
Manchester C	Tr	08/95	95-97	124	0	4
Fulham	Tr	07/98	98-01	96	6	13
Crystal Palace	Tr	12/01	01-03	42	7	0

SYMONS Paul
Born: North Shields, Tyne and Wear, England, 20 April, 1976 F

League Club	Source	Date Signed	Seasons Played	Apps	Subs	Gls
Blackpool	YT	07/94	93	0	1	0

SYRETT David Kenneth (Dave)
Born: Salisbury, Wiltshire, England, 20 January, 1956 F
England: Youth

League Club	Source	Date Signed	Seasons Played	Apps	Subs	Gls
Swindon T	App	11/73	73-76	110	12	30
Mansfield T	Tr	08/77	77-78	65	0	20
Walsall	Tr	03/79	78	11	0	3
Peterborough U	Tr	08/79	79-81	75	4	23
Northampton T	Tr	06/82	82-83	42	2	13

SYROS George
Born: Athens, Greece, 8 February, 1976 CD

League Club	Source	Date Signed	Seasons Played	Apps	Subs	Gls
Bury	Akratitos (GRE)	08/01	01	9	0	1

SZABO Tibor Lewis
Born: Bradford, England, 28 October, 1959 F

League Club	Source	Date Signed	Seasons Played	Apps	Subs	Gls
Bradford C	App	10/77	78	8	5	1

SZCZESNY Wojciech Tomasz
Born: Warsaw, Poland, 18 April, 1990 G
Poland: 23/U21-7

League Club	Source	Date Signed	Seasons Played	Apps	Subs	Gls
Arsenal	Sch	07/07	10-14	132	0	0
Brentford	L	11/09	09	28	0	0

SZMID Marek Andrezj
Born: Nuneaton, Warwickshire, England, 2 March, 1982 M
England: Youth/Schools

League Club	Source	Date Signed	Seasons Played	Apps	Subs	Gls
Manchester U	YT	09/99				
Southend U	Tr	11/01	01	1	1	0

SZMODICS Sammie Joseph
Born: Colchester, Essex, England, 24 September, 1995 M

League Club	Source	Date Signed	Seasons Played	Apps	Subs	Gls
Colchester U	Sch	10/13	13-14	17	21	4

SZTYBEL Jay
Born: Redditch, Worcestershire, England, 1 October, 1987 RB

League Club	Source	Date Signed	Seasons Played	Apps	Subs	Gls
Walsall	Sch	-	05	1	0	0

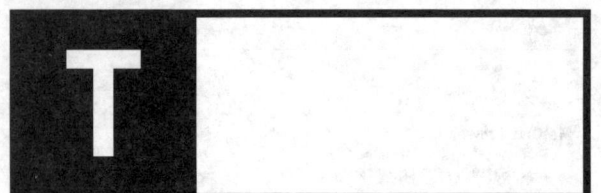

TAAFFE Steven Lee
Born: Stoke-on-Trent, England, 10 September, 1979 — F

League Club	Source	Date Signed	Seasons Played	Apps	Subs	Gls
Stoke C	YT	08/96	97-99	3	5	0

TAARABT Adel
Born: Fez, Morocco, 24 May, 1989 — M/F
France: Youth//Morocco: 18

League Club	Source	Date Signed	Seasons Played	Apps	Subs	Gls
Tottenham H	RC Lens (FRA)	01/07	06-08	0	9	0
Queens Park Rgrs	L	03/09	08	5	2	1
Queens Park Rgrs	Tr	07/09	09-14	127	23	33
Fulham	L	08/13	13	7	5	0

TABB Jay Anthony
Born: Tooting, SW London, England, 21 February, 1984 — M
Republic of Ireland: U21-10

League Club	Source	Date Signed	Seasons Played	Apps	Subs	Gls
Brentford	YT	07/01	00-05	95	33	20
Coventry C	Tr	07/06	06-08	83	12	11
Reading	Tr	01/09	08-12	70	19	0
Ipswich T	Tr	03/13	12-14	54	22	4

TABIRI Joseph Owusu (Joe)
Born: Kingsbury, NW London, England, 16 October, 1989 — M

League Club	Source	Date Signed	Seasons Played	Apps	Subs	Gls
Barnet	Jnr	07/08	08-09	6	6	0

TADIC Dusan
Born: Subotica, Serbia, 20 November, 1988 — W
Serbia: 30/U21-11/Youth

League Club	Source	Date Signed	Seasons Played	Apps	Subs	Gls
Southampton	FC Twente (NED)	07/14	14	24	7	4

TADMAN Maurice Roy
Born: Rainham, Kent, England, 28 June, 1921 — CF
Died: Basildon, England, 27 January, 1994

League Club	Source	Date Signed	Seasons Played	Apps	Subs	Gls
Charlton Ath	Bexleyheath & Welling	06/38	46	3	-	0
Plymouth Arg	Tr	08/47	47-54	240	-	108

TAFAZOLLI Ryan Sirous
Born: Sutton, S London, England, 28 September, 1991 — CD

League Club	Source	Date Signed	Seasons Played	Apps	Subs	Gls
Southampton	Sch	07/10				
Mansfield T	Cambridge C	08/12	13-14	59	1	3

TAFT Douglas (Doug)
Born: Leicester, England, 9 March, 1926 — CF
Died: Derby, England, 29 September, 1987

League Club	Source	Date Signed	Seasons Played	Apps	Subs	Gls
Derby Co	Gresley Rov	11/47	48	6	-	1
Wolverhampton W	Tr	07/49				

TAFT George William
Born: Leicester, England, 29 July, 1993 — LB
England: Youth

League Club	Source	Date Signed	Seasons Played	Apps	Subs	Gls
Leicester C	Sch	04/11				
York C	L	08/13	13	2	1	0
Burton A	Tr	05/14	14	22	8	1

TAGG Anthony Peter (Tony)
Born: Epsom, Surrey, England, 10 April, 1957 — CD

League Club	Source	Date Signed	Seasons Played	Apps	Subs	Gls
Queens Park Rgrs	App	03/75	75	4	0	0
Millwall	Tr	07/77	77-81	130	3	9
Wimbledon	Tr	07/82	82	14	0	0

TAGG Ernest (Ernie)
Born: Crewe, Cheshire, England, 15 September, 1917 — RH/IF
Died: Crewe, Cheshire, England, 29 November, 2006

League Club	Source	Date Signed	Seasons Played	Apps	Subs	Gls
Crewe Alex		10/37	37	19	-	7
Wolverhampton W	Tr	05/38	38	1	-	0
Bournemouth	Tr	05/39	46-48	80	-	8
Carlisle U	Tr	11/48	48	5	-	1

TAGGART Gerald Paul (Gerry)
Born: Belfast, Northern Ireland, 18 October, 1970 — CD
Northern Ireland: 51/U23-2/Youth/Schools

League Club	Source	Date Signed	Seasons Played	Apps	Subs	Gls
Manchester C	YT	07/89	88-89	10	2	1
Barnsley	Tr	01/90	89-94	209	3	16
Bolton W	Tr	08/95	95-97	68	1	4
Leicester C	Tr	07/98	98-03	105	12	9
Stoke C	L	12/03	03	8	0	2
Stoke C	Tr	02/04	03-05	47	0	3

TAGGART Robert (Bobby)
Born: Newmains, Lanarkshire, Scotland, 10 March, 1927 — IF
Died: Newmains, Lanarkshire, Scotland, 30 November, 1979

League Club	Source	Date Signed	Seasons Played	Apps	Subs	Gls
Cardiff C	Coltness U	05/49	49	2	-	0
Torquay U	Tr	06/50	50	14	-	2
Aldershot	Tr	08/51	51	16	-	2

TAIBI Massimo
Born: Palermo, Italy, 18 February, 1970 — G

League Club	Source	Date Signed	Seasons Played	Apps	Subs	Gls
Manchester U	Venezia (ITA)	09/99	99	4	0	0

TAINIO Teemu
Born: Tornio, Finland, 27 November, 1979 — DM
Finland: 63/U21-20

League Club	Source	Date Signed	Seasons Played	Apps	Subs	Gls
Tottenham H	AJ Auxerre (FRA)	06/05	05-07	48	13	3
Sunderland	Tr	07/08	08	18	3	0
Birmingham C	L	09/09	09	5	1	0

TAINTON Trevor Keith
Born: Bristol, England, 8 June, 1948 — M
England: Schools

League Club	Source	Date Signed	Seasons Played	Apps	Subs	Gls
Bristol C	App	09/65	67-81	456	30	24
Torquay U	Tr	02/82	81	19	0	1

TAIT Alexander (Alex)
Born: West Sleekburn, Northumberland, England, 28 November, 1933 — CF
England: Youth

League Club	Source	Date Signed	Seasons Played	Apps	Subs	Gls
Newcastle U	Jnr	09/52	54-59	32	-	8
Bristol C	Tr	06/60	60-63	117	-	38
Doncaster Rov	Tr	06/64	64	19	-	7

TAIT Barry Stuart
Born: York, England, 17 June, 1938 — IF

League Club	Source	Date Signed	Seasons Played	Apps	Subs	Gls
York C	Doncaster Rov (Am)	09/58	58-60	15	-	5
Peterborough U	Tr	06/61				
Bradford C	Tr	11/61	61	20	-	10
Halifax T	Tr	07/62	62-63	36	-	23
Crewe Alex	Tr	09/63	63	9	-	2
Notts Co	Tr	07/64	64	3	-	0

TAIT Jordan Alexander
Born: Berwick-on-Tweed, Northumberland, England, 27 September, 1979 — RB

League Club	Source	Date Signed	Seasons Played	Apps	Subs	Gls
Newcastle U	YT	07/98				
Oldham Ath	Tr	08/99	99	0	1	0
Darlington	Tr	10/00	00	2	1	0

TAIT Michael Paul (Mick)
Born: Wallsend, Tyne and Wear, England, 30 September, 1956 — M/D

League Club	Source	Date Signed	Seasons Played	Apps	Subs	Gls
Oxford U	App	10/74	74-76	61	3	23
Carlisle U	Tr	02/77	76-79	101	5	20
Hull C	Tr	09/79	79	29	4	3
Portsmouth	Tr	06/80	80-86	228	12	31
Reading	Tr	09/87	87-89	98	1	9
Darlington	Tr	08/90	90-91	79	0	2
Hartlepool U	Tr	07/92	92-93	60	1	1
Hartlepool U	Gretna	09/94	94-96	74	4	2

TAIT Paul
Born: Newcastle-upon-Tyne, England, 24 October, 1974 — F

League Club	Source	Date Signed	Seasons Played	Apps	Subs	Gls
Everton	YT	07/93				
Wigan Ath	Tr	07/94	94	1	4	0
Crewe Alex	Northwich Victoria	06/99	99-01	31	32	6
Hull C	L	11/01	01	0	2	0
Bristol Rov	Tr	07/02	02-03	61	13	19
Rochdale	Tr	07/04	04-05	31	16	3
Chester C	Tr	02/06	05	3	6	0
Boston U	Tr	07/06	06	9	5	2

TAIT Paul Ronald
Born: Sutton Coldfield, West Midlands, England, 31 July, 1971 — M

League Club	Source	Date Signed	Seasons Played	Apps	Subs	Gls
Birmingham C	YT	08/88	87-96	135	35	14
Northampton T	L	12/97	97	2	1	0
Oxford U	Tr	01/99	98-01	86	5	3

TAIT Peter
Born: York, England, 17 October, 1936 — CF

League Club	Source	Date Signed	Seasons Played	Apps	Subs	Gls
York C (Am)	Jnr	08/55	55	3	-	1

TAIT Richard Neil Peter
Born: Galashiels, Borders, Scotland, 2 December, 1989 — RB

League Club	Source	Date Signed	Seasons Played	Apps	Subs	Gls
Nottingham F	Curzon Ashton	12/07				
Cambridge U	Tamworth	05/13	14	34	3	0

TAIT Robert James (Bobby)
Born: Edinburgh, Scotland, 4 October, 1938 — IF

League Club	Source	Date Signed	Seasons Played	Apps	Subs	Gls
Notts Co	Aberdeen	07/62	62-63	60	-	11
Barrow	Tr	07/64	64-65	78	1	29
Chesterfield	Tr	07/66	66	27	1	2

TAIWO Solomon Oladiran (Sol)
Born: Lagos, Nigeria, 29 April, 1985 — M

League Club	Source	Date Signed	Seasons Played	Apps	Subs	Gls
Dagenham & Red	Sutton U	10/07	07-09	47	7	4
Cardiff C	Tr	08/09	09-11	2	7	0
Dagenham & Red	L	10/10	10	16	2	0
Leyton Orient	L	01/12	11	2	3	0

TAIWO Taye Ismaila
Born: Lagos, Nigeria, 16 April, 1985 — LB
Nigeria: 53

League Club	Source	Date Signed	Seasons Played	Apps	Subs	Gls
Queens Park Rgrs (L)	AC Milan (ITA)	01/12	11	13	2	1

TAIWO Thomas James William (Tom)
Born: Pudsey, West Yorkshire, England, 27 February, 1990 — M
England: Youth

League Club	Source	Date Signed	Seasons Played	Apps	Subs	Gls
Chelsea	Sch	07/07				
Port Vale	L	08/08	08	2	2	0
Carlisle U	Tr	07/09	09-11	106	12	6

TAL Idan
Born: Petah Tikva, Israel, 13 September, 1975 — M
Israel: 69/U21-13

League Club	Source	Date Signed	Seasons Played	Apps	Subs	Gls
Everton	M Petah Tikva (ISR)	10/00	00-01	13	16	2
Bolton W	Maccabi Haifa (ISR)	07/06	06	4	12	0

TALBOT Andrew (Drew)
Born: Barnsley, South Yorkshire, England, 19 July, 1986 — M/RB

League Club	Source	Date Signed	Seasons Played	Apps	Subs	Gls
Sheffield Wed	Dodworth MW	02/04	04-06	5	24	4
Scunthorpe U	L	01/07	06	2	1	1
Luton T	Tr	01/07	06-08	33	16	3
Chesterfield	Tr	01/09	08-14	203	7	15
Plymouth Arg	L	01/15	14	9	0	0

TALBOT Brian Ernest
Born: Ipswich, England, 21 July, 1953 — M
England: 6/B-8/U21-1

League Club	Source	Date Signed	Seasons Played	Apps	Subs	Gls
Ipswich T	App	07/70	73-78	177	0	25
Arsenal	Tr	01/79	78-84	245	9	40
Watford	Tr	06/85	85-86	46	2	8
Stoke C	Tr	10/86	86-87	51	3	5
West Bromwich A	Tr	01/88	87-89	66	8	5
Fulham	Tr	03/91	90	5	0	1
Aldershot	Tr	03/91	90	10	0	0

TALBOT Daniel Brian (Danny)
Born: Enfield, N London, England, 30 January, 1984 — M

League Club	Source	Date Signed	Seasons Played	Apps	Subs	Gls
Rushden & D	Jnr	02/01	01-03	10	13	1

TALBOT Ernest (Ernie)
Born: Workington, Cumbria, England, 13 November, 1932 — IF
Died: Cockermouth, Cumbria, England, April, 2009

League Club	Source	Date Signed	Seasons Played	Apps	Subs	Gls
Workington		08/51	52-57	18	-	7

TALBOT Frank Leslie (Les)
Born: Hednesford, Staffordshire, England, 3 August, 1910 — IF
Died: Alkmaar, Netherlands, 5 December, 1983

League Club	Source	Date Signed	Seasons Played	Apps	Subs	Gls
Blackburn Rov	Hednesford T	10/30	30-35	90	-	20
Cardiff C	Tr	06/36	36-38	94	-	21
Walsall	Tr	06/39	46	18	-	5

TALBOT Gary
Born: Blackburn, Greater Manchester, England, 15 December, 1937 — CF

League Club	Source	Date Signed	Seasons Played	Apps	Subs	Gls
Chester C		09/63	63-66	110	1	61
Crewe Alex	Tr	07/67	67	37	0	20
Chester C	Tr	06/68	68	43	0	22

TALBOT Jason Christopher
Born: Irlam, Greater Manchester, England, 30 September, 1985 — LB

League Club	Source	Date Signed	Seasons Played	Apps	Subs	Gls
Bolton W	Sch	09/04				
Derby Co	L	09/04	04	2	0	0
Mansfield T	L	11/04	04	2	0	0
Mansfield T	Tr	08/05	05	6	0	0
Port Vale	L	02/06	05	4	1	0
Port Vale	Tr	07/06	06-07	39	8	0

TALBOT Paul Michael
Born: Gateshead, Tyne and Wear, England, 11 August, 1979 — RB/M

League Club	Source	Date Signed	Seasons Played	Apps	Subs	Gls
Newcastle U	YT	07/97				
York C	Tr	03/00	99	5	1	0

TALBOT Stewart Dean
Born: Birmingham, England, 14 June, 1973 — M

League Club	Source	Date Signed	Seasons Played	Apps	Subs	Gls
Port Vale	Moor Green	08/94	94-99	112	25	10
Rotherham U	Tr	07/00	00-03	100	14	8
Shrewsbury T	L	02/03	02	5	0	0
Brentford	Tr	02/04	03-04	50	2	3
Boston U	Tr	07/05	05-06	44	4	3

TALBOTT Nathan Anthony
Born: Wolverhampton, England, 21 October, 1984 — LB

League Club	Source	Date Signed	Seasons Played	Apps	Subs	Gls
Yeovil T	Wolverhampton W (Sch)	03/04	03	0	1	0

TALBOYS Steven John (Steve)
Born: Bristol, England, 18 September, 1966 — LW

League Club	Source	Date Signed	Seasons Played	Apps	Subs	Gls
Wimbledon	Gloucester C	01/92	92-95	19	7	1
Watford	Tr	06/96	96-97	2	3	0

TALBUT John
Born: Oxford, England, 20 October, 1940 — CH
England: U23-7/Schools

League Club	Source	Date Signed	Seasons Played	Apps	Subs	Gls
Burnley	Jnr	10/57	58-66	138	0	0
West Bromwich A	Tr	12/66	66-70	143	1	0

TALIA Francesco (Frank)
Born: Melbourne, Australia, 20 July, 1972 — G
Australia: Schools

League Club	Source	Date Signed	Seasons Played	Apps	Subs	Gls
Blackburn Rov	Sunshine GC (AUS)	08/92				
Hartlepool U	L	12/92	92	14	0	0
Swindon T	Tr	09/95	95-99	107	0	0
Sheffield U	Tr	09/00	00	6	0	0
Reading	Royal Antwerp (BEL)	03/02				
Wycombe W	Tr	08/02	02-05	132	0	0

TALKES Wayne Anthony Norman
Born: Ealing, W London, England, 2 June, 1952 — M

League Club	Source	Date Signed	Seasons Played	Apps	Subs	Gls
Southampton	App	07/69	71-73	7	2	0
Doncaster Rov	L	12/73	73	3	1	0
Bournemouth	Tr	07/74	74	5	0	0

TALLON Darren John Bernard
Born: Plymouth, England, 1 June, 1972 — CD

League Club	Source	Date Signed	Seasons Played	Apps	Subs	Gls
Plymouth Arg	YT	10/90	90	1	0	0

TALLON Gerrit Thomas (Gary)
Born: Drogheda, Republic of Ireland, 5 September, 1973 — LW

League Club	Source	Date Signed	Seasons Played	Apps	Subs	Gls
Blackburn Rov	Drogheda (ROI)	11/91				
Chester C (L)	Kilmarnock	03/97	96	1	0	0
Mansfield T	Kilmarnock	12/97	97-99	68	7	2

TAMAS Gabriel Sebastian
Born: Brasov, Romania, 9 November, 1983 — CD
Romania: 63/U21-7/Youth

League Club	Source	Date Signed	Seasons Played	Apps	Subs	Gls
West Bromwich A	AJ Auxerre (FRA)	01/10	09-12	59	9	2
Doncaster Rov	CFR Cluj (ROM)	01/14	13	13	1	0
Watford	Tr	07/14	14	6	1	0

TAMBLING Robert Victor (Bobby)
Born: Storrington, West Sussex, England, 18 September, 1941 — F
England: 3/FLge-1/U23-13/Schools

League Club	Source	Date Signed	Seasons Played	Apps	Subs	Gls
Chelsea	Jnr	09/58	58-69	298	4	164
Crystal Palace	Tr	01/70	69-73	67	1	12

TANCOCK Scott Russell
Born: Swansea, Wales, 29 December, 1993 — CD
Wales: U21-6

League Club	Source	Date Signed	Seasons Played	Apps	Subs	Gls
Swansea C	Sch	07/12				
Newport Co	L	09/14	14	4	0	0

TANKARD Allen John
Born: Islington, N London, England, 21 May, 1969 — LB
England: Youth

League Club	Source	Date Signed	Seasons Played	Apps	Subs	Gls
Southampton	App	05/87	85-86	5	0	0
Wigan Ath	Tr	07/88	88-92	205	4	4
Port Vale	Tr	07/93	93-00	261	14	11
Mansfield T	Tr	08/01	01	22	8	2

TANKOVIC Muamer
Born: Norrkoping, Sweden, 22 February, 1995 — W
Sweden: 1/U21-2/Youth

League Club	Source	Date Signed	Seasons Played	Apps	Subs	Gls
Fulham	Sch	02/12	13	1	2	0

TANN Adam John
Born: Fakenham, Norfolk, England, 12 May, 1982 — CD
England: Youth

League Club	Source	Date Signed	Seasons Played	Apps	Subs	Gls
Cambridge U	YT	09/99	00-04	111	10	4
Notts Co	Gravesend & Northfleet	11/05	05	4	1	0
Leyton Orient	Tr	01/06	05-06	21	10	2
Notts Co	Ipswich T (NC)	07/07	07-08	49	6	1

TANNER Adam David
Born: Maldon, Essex, England, 25 October, 1973 — M/D

League Club	Source	Date Signed	Seasons Played	Apps	Subs	Gls
Ipswich T	YT	07/92	94-98	49	24	7
Peterborough U	Tr	03/00				
Colchester U	Tr	08/00	00	1	3	0

TANNER Craig David
Born: Reading, England, 27 October, 1994 — F

League Club	Source	Date Signed	Seasons Played	Apps	Subs	Gls
Reading	Sch	10/11	14	0	3	0
AFC Wimbledon	L	01/15	14	16	3	0

TANNER Graham George
Born: Bridgwater, Somerset, England, 4 September, 1947 — CH

League Club	Source	Date Signed	Seasons Played	Apps	Subs	Gls
Bristol C	App	09/64				
Bradford Park Ave	Tr	10/67	67-68	44	0	2
TANNER John Denys Parkin						
Born: Harrogate, North Yorkshire, England, 2 July, 1921						W
Died: Bradford, England, 25 October, 1987						
England: Amateur-3						
Huddersfield T (Am)	Yorkshire Amats	08/48	48	1	-	1
TANNER Michael William (Micky)						
Born: Bristol, England, 28 October, 1964						M
Bristol C		07/85	85-87	16	3	1
TANNER Nicholas (Nick)						
Born: Kingswood, Avon, England, 24 May, 1965						CD
Bristol Rov	Mangotsfield U	06/85	85-87	104	3	3
Liverpool	Tr	07/88	89-92	36	4	1
Norwich C	L	03/90	89	6	0	0
Swindon T	L	09/90	90	7	0	0
TANNER Thomas (Tom)						
Born: Devonport, Devon, England, 24 June, 1922						LW
Torquay U (Am)	Plymouth U	09/46	46	1	-	0
TANSER Scott						
Born: Blackpool, Lancashire, England, 23 October, 1994						LB
Rochdale	Sch	07/13	12-14	27	4	1
TANSEY Gerard						
Born: Liverpool, England, 15 October, 1933						LW
Everton	Jnr	10/51				
Tranmere Rov	Tr	07/55	55	3	-	1
TANSEY Gregory James (Greg)						
Born: Huyton, Merseyside, England, 21 November, 1988						M
Stockport Co	Sch	07/06	06-10	71	27	13
Stevenage	Inverness CT	05/12	12-13	40	16	9
TANSEY James (Jimmy)						
Born: Liverpool, England, 29 January, 1929						LB
Died: Liverpool, England, 7 July, 2012						
Everton		05/48	52-59	133	-	0
Crewe Alex	Tr	06/60	60	9	-	0
TAPKEN Norman						
Born: Wallsend, Tyne and Wear, England, 21 February, 1913						G
Died: Stoke-on-Trent, England, June, 1996						
Republic of Ireland: LoI-2						
Newcastle U	Wallsend Thermal Welf.	05/33	34-37	106	-	0
Manchester U	Tr	12/38	38	14	-	0
Darlington	Tr	04/47	46-47	31	-	0
TAPLEY Reginald (Reg)						
Born: Nantwich, Cheshire, England, 2 November, 1932						LW
Crewe Alex		09/53				
Rochdale	Bangor C	10/56	56	1	-	0
TAPLEY Steven (Steve)						
Born: Camberwell, S London, England, 3 October, 1963						CD
Fulham	App	10/81	83-84	2	0	1
Rochdale	L	02/85	84	1	0	0
TAPP Alexander Nicholas (Alex)						
Born: Redhill, Surrey, England, 7 June, 1982						LM
England: Schools						
Wimbledon	YT	01/00	02-03	35	3	3
MK Dons	Wimbledon relocation	07/04	04	5	7	1
TAPPING Frederick Harold (Fred)						
Born: Derby, England, 29 July, 1921						WH
Died: Bretby, Derbyshire, England, 22 February, 2007						
Blackpool	Rolls Royce	10/43				
Chesterfield	Tr	11/47	47	1	-	0
TAPSCOTT Derek Robert						
Born: Barry, Vale of Glamorgan, Wales, 30 June, 1932						IF
Died: Cardiff, Wales, 12 June, 2008						
Wales: 14						
Arsenal	Barry T	10/53	53-57	119	-	62
Cardiff C	Tr	09/58	58-64	193	-	79
Newport Co	Tr	07/65	65	12	1	1
TAPSCOTT Eli John (Johnnie)						
Born: Falmouth, Cornwall, England, 29 April, 1928						LH
Died: Plymouth, England, 1981						
Leeds U	Oak Villa	03/50				
Wrexham	Tr	05/50	50-55	172	-	4
TARACHULSKI Bartosz						
Born: Gliwice, Poland, 14 May, 1975						F
Yeovil T	Polonia Warsaw (POL)	07/04	04	27	15	10
TARANTINI Alberto Cesar						
Born: Buenos Aires, Argentina, 3 December, 1955						LB
Argentina: 61						
Birmingham C	Boca Juniors (ARG)	10/78	78	23	0	1
TARBUCK Alan David						
Born: Liverpool, England, 10 October, 1948						W/F
Everton	App	08/66				
Crewe Alex	Tr	06/67	67-69	79	6	18
Chester C	Tr	10/69	69-71	69	0	24
Preston NE	Tr	09/71	71-72	42	6	17
Shrewsbury T	Tr	03/73	72-75	107	17	17
Rochdale	Tr	07/76	76-77	48	0	1
TARBUCK Bradley Mark						
Born: Emsworth, Hampshire, England, 6 November, 1995						RW
Portsmouth	Sch	07/14	14	0	2	0
TARDIF Christopher Luke (Chris)						
Born: Guernsey, Channel Islands, 19 September, 1979						G
Portsmouth	YT	07/98	00-01	3	2	0
Bournemouth	L	08/02	02	9	0	0
Oxford U	Tr	07/04	04-05	50	1	0
TARGETT Haydn Roy (Roy)						
Born: Shepton Mallet, Somerset, England, 1 July, 1928						FB
Died: Hampshire, England, November, 2014						
Torquay U	Shepton Mallet	10/49	50	1	-	0
TARGETT Matthew Robert (Matt)						
Born: Eastleigh, Hampshire, England, 18 September, 1995						LB
England: U21-1/Youth//Scotland: Youth						
Southampton	Sch	08/13	14	3	3	0
TARICCO Mauricio Ricardo						
Born: Buenos Aires, Argentina, 10 March, 1973						LB
Ipswich T	Argentinos Jnrs (ARG)	09/94	95-98	134	3	4
Tottenham H	Tr	12/98	98-03	125	5	2
West Ham U	Tr	11/04	04	1	0	0
Brighton & HA	Rtd	08/10	10-11	11	4	0
TARKOWSKI James Alan						
Born: Manchester, England, 19 November, 1992						CD
Oldham Ath	Sch	07/11	10-13	63	9	5
Brentford	Tr	01/14	13-14	47	0	3
TARNAT Michael						
Born: Hilden, Germany, 27 October, 1969						LB
Germany: 19						
Manchester C	Bayern Munich (GER)	07/03	03	32	0	3
TARRANT Brian Leslie						
Born: Stainforth, South Yorkshire, England, 22 July, 1938						IF
Leeds U	Jnr	08/55				
Mansfield T	Tr	07/60	60	3	-	0
TARRANT John Edward (Ted)						
Born: Stainforth, South Yorkshire, England, 12 February, 1932						LH/IF
Died: Peterborough, England, November, 2005						
Hull C	Jnr	02/49	50-53	30	-	2
Walsall	Tr	12/53	53-57	102	-	10
TARRANT Neil Kenneth						
Born: Darlington, County Durham, England, 24 June, 1979						F
Scotland: U21-5						
Darlington	YT	07/97				
Aston Villa	Ross Co	04/99				
York C	L	10/00	00	6	1	1
TARTT Colin						
Born: Liverpool, England, 23 November, 1950						D/M
Port Vale	Alsager College	07/72	72-76	171	4	7
Chesterfield	Tr	03/77	76-81	185	1	7
Port Vale	Tr	10/81	81-84	111	6	9
TATE Alan						
Born: Easington, County Durham, England, 2 September, 1982						CD
Manchester U	YT	07/00				
Swansea C	L	11/02	02	27	0	0
Swansea C	L	10/03	03	9	0	0
Swansea C	Tr	02/04	03-12	231	23	5
Leeds U	L	11/12	12	10	0	0
Yeovil T	L	07/13	13	4	0	0
Crewe Alex	L	09/14	14	26	0	0
TATE Christopher Douglas (Chris)						
Born: York, England, 27 December, 1977						F
Sunderland	York C (YT)	07/96				
Scarborough	Tr	08/97	97-98	21	28	13
Halifax T	Tr	07/99	99	18	0	4

League Club	Source	Date Signed	Seasons Played	Career Record Apps	Subs	Gls
Leyton Orient	Scarborough	11/00	00-03	34	41	10
Mansfield T	Tr	07/04	04	0	4	0
TATE Craig David						
Born: South Shields, Tyne and Wear, England, 16 October, 1979						F
Shrewsbury T	YT	-	96	0	1	0
TATE Geoffrey Michael (Geoff)						
Born: Leicester, England, 16 December, 1937						W
Died: Leicester, England, 18 April, 2005						
England: Youth/Schools						
Derby Co	Jnr	08/55	55	1	-	1
TATE Jeffrey (Jeff)						
Born: Blyth, Northumberland, England, 11 May, 1959						M
England: Schools						
Burnley	Jnr	08/78	79	5	0	1
TAUNDRY Richard Daniel						
Born: Walsall, West Midlands, England, 15 February, 1989						RB/M
Walsall	Sch	07/07	07-12	130	39	3
TAVARES Mickael Zidro						
Born: Paris, France, 25 October, 1982						M
Senegal: 25						
Middlesbrough (L)	Hamburger SV (GER)	08/10	10	10	3	0
TAVENER Colin Raymond						
Born: Bath, England, 26 June, 1945						M
Hereford U	Trowbridge T	06/72	72-73	50	1	3
TAVERNIER James Henry						
Born: Bradford, England, 31 October, 1991						RB
Newcastle U	Sch	07/09	12	0	2	0
Carlisle U	L	08/11	11	16	0	0
Sheffield Wed	L	11/11	11	6	0	0
MK Dons	L	01/12	11	7	0	0
Shrewsbury T	L	07/13	13	1	0	0
Rotherham U	L	11/13	13	27	0	5
Wigan Ath	Tr	06/14	14	7	4	0
Bristol C	L	01/15	14	9	3	3
TAVLARIDIS Eustathis (Stathis)						
Born: Serres, Greece, 25 January, 1980						CD
Greece: U21						
Arsenal	Iraklis Salonika (GRE)	09/01	02	0	1	0
Portsmouth	L	01/03	02	3	1	0
TAWSE Brian						
Born: Ellon, Aberdeenshire, Scotland, 30 July, 1945						W
Arsenal	King Street, Aberdeen	04/63	64	5	-	0
Brighton & HA	Tr	12/65	65-69	97	5	14
Brentford	Tr	02/70	69-70	19	2	1
TAYLFORTH Sean James						
Born: Middlewich, Cheshire, England, 10 March, 1989						LW
Bradford C	Sch	06/07	07	1	0	0
TAYLOR Aaron Mark						
Born: Morecambe, Lancashire, England, 9 March, 1990						F
Morecambe	Jnr	07/08	08-09	7	13	2
TAYLOR Alan						
Born: Thornton-Cleveleys, Lancashire, England, 17 May, 1943						LW
Blackpool	Blackpool Rgrs	10/63	65-70	94	0	0
Oldham Ath	L	12/69	69	2	0	0
Stockport Co	L	08/70	70	5	0	0
Southport	Tr	07/71	71-73	102	0	0
TAYLOR Alan David						
Born: Hinckley, Leicestershire, England, 14 November, 1953						F
Rochdale	Morecambe	05/73	73-74	55	0	7
West Ham U	Tr	11/74	74-78	88	10	25
Norwich C	Tr	08/79	79	20	4	5
Cambridge U	Vancouver W'caps (CAN)	10/80	80-81	17	1	4
Hull C	Vancouver W'caps (CAN)	01/84	83	13	1	3
Burnley	Tr	08/84	84-85	60	4	23
Bury	Tr	06/86	86-87	55	7	10
Norwich C	Tr	09/88	88	1	3	1
TAYLOR Alastair William						
Born: Sheffield, England, 13 September, 1991						RW
Barnsley	Sch	07/10	09-11	0	4	0
TAYLOR Albert Herbert (Bert)						
Born: Worksop, Nottinghamshire, England, 2 May, 1924						G
Died: Kiveton Park, South Yorkshire, England, 3 June, 2011						
Bury	Worksop T	10/45	46-47	4	-	0
Sheffield U	Tr	05/48				
Halifax T	Tr	07/51	51	8	-	0

League Club	Source	Date Signed	Seasons Played	Career Record Apps	Subs	Gls
TAYLOR Alexander (Alex)						
Born: Menstrie, Stirlingshire, Scotland, 25 December, 1916						CH
Died: 1982						
Carlisle U	King's Park	06/38	38-46	24	-	0
TAYLOR Alexander (Alex)						
Born: Baillieston, Glasgow, Scotland, 13 June, 1962						M
Walsall	Hamilton Academical	08/88	88-89	43	2	6
TAYLOR Andrew (Andy)						
Born: Chesterfield, Derbyshire, England, 30 December, 1967						F
Chesterfield	App	07/86	86-87	7	5	1
TAYLOR Andrew (Andy)						
Born: Rawmarsh, South Yorkshire, England, 19 January, 1973						LB
Rotherham U	YT	06/91	90-92	17	1	0
TAYLOR Andrew (Andy)						
Born: Blackburn, Greater Manchester, England, 14 March, 1986						LB
England: Youth						
Blackburn Rov	Sch	07/04				
Queens Park Rgrs	L	01/06	05	1	2	0
Blackpool	L	02/06	05	3	0	0
Crewe Alex	L	10/06	06	4	0	0
Huddersfield T	L	01/07	06	7	1	0
Tranmere Rov	Tr	11/07	07-08	67	2	3
Sheffield U	Tr	07/09	09-11	33	6	0
Walsall	Tr	08/12	12-14	103	3	2
TAYLOR Andrew Derek (Andy)						
Born: Hartlepool, Cleveland, England, 1 August, 1986						LB
England: U21-13/Youth						
Middlesbrough	Sch	08/03	05-10	107	18	3
Bradford C	L	08/05	05	24	0	0
Watford	L	08/10	10	19	0	1
Cardiff C	Tr	07/11	11-13	103	0	1
Wigan Ath	Tr	06/14	14	26	0	1
TAYLOR Andrew Ian (Andy)						
Born: Stratford-on-Avon, Warwickshire, England, 4 April, 1963						RB
Northampton T	Aston Villa (App)	06/81	81	17	0	0
TAYLOR Andrew John (Andy)						
Born: Caistor, Lincolnshire, England, 30 October, 1988						F
Grimsby T	Sch	12/06	06-08	6	37	7
TAYLOR Anthony (Tony)						
Born: Glasgow, Scotland, 6 September, 1946						LB/M
Crystal Palace	Greenock Morton	11/68	68-73	192	3	8
Southend U	Tr	08/74	74-75	56	0	1
Swindon T	Tr	08/76	76	20	6	0
Bristol Rov	Athlone T (ROI)	09/77	77	12	0	0
Portsmouth	Tr	02/78	77	17	0	0
Northampton T	Tr	07/79	79	4	0	0
TAYLOR Archibald (Archie)						
Born: Glasgow, Scotland, 4 October, 1918						RH/IF
Died: Cheltenham, Gloucestershire, England, 1976						
Burnley	Cambuslang	05/37	38	3	-	1
Reading	Tr	06/39	46-47	15	-	2
Leyton Orient	Tr	08/48	48-50	46	-	1
TAYLOR Arthur Alexander						
Born: Lisburn, Belfast, Northern Ireland, 5 April, 1931						W
Luton T	Glentoran	07/50	52-55	8	-	0
TAYLOR Arthur Matson (Archie)						
Born: Dunscroft, South Yorkshire, England, 7 November, 1939						RW
Bristol C	Doncaster Rov (Am)	05/58	59-60	12	-	2
Barnsley	Tr	07/61	61	2	-	0
Mansfield T	Tr	11/61				
Hull C	Goole T	05/62	62	1	-	0
Halifax T	Tr	07/63	63-67	174	0	16
Bradford C	Tr	12/67	67	10	1	0
York C	Tr	10/68	68-70	93	3	8
TAYLOR Arthur Sidney						
Born: Birmingham, England, 14 March, 1925						CF
Died: Birmingham, England, 8 December, 2012						
West Bromwich A	Handsworth Wood	03/42	47	4	-	5
TAYLOR Ashley						
Born: Conisbrough, South Yorkshire, England, 11 December, 1959						LB
Rotherham U	App	12/77	79-81	21	1	0
TAYLOR Ashton John (Ash)						
Born: Bromborough, Wirral, England, 2 September, 1990						CD
Wales: U21-3/Youth						
Tranmere Rov	Sch	12/08	08-13	171	12	8

TAYLOR Bobby-Joe
Born: Ashford, Kent, England, 4 February, 1995 — W

League Club	Source	Date Signed	Seasons Played	Apps	Subs	Gls
Cambridge U	Jnr	05/13	14	1	6	0

TAYLOR Brian
Born: Hammersmith, W London, England, 2 July, 1944 — FB
Died: Ealing, W London, England, 7 December, 2013

League Club	Source	Date Signed	Seasons Played	Apps	Subs	Gls
Queens Park Rgrs	Jnr	03/62	62-65	50	0	0

TAYLOR Brian
Born: Manchester, England, 29 June, 1942 — WH

League Club	Source	Date Signed	Seasons Played	Apps	Subs	Gls
Rochdale	Jnr	03/62	63-67	131	1	7

TAYLOR Brian
Born: Whitwell, Derbyshire, England, 12 February, 1954 — CD

League Club	Source	Date Signed	Seasons Played	Apps	Subs	Gls
Middlesbrough	App	07/71	72-75	14	4	1
Doncaster Rov	Tr	12/75	75-78	118	1	12
Rochdale	Tr	12/78	78-82	152	2	10

TAYLOR Brian John
Born: Gateshead, Tyne and Wear, England, 2 July, 1949 — RB/M
Died: Preston, Lancashire, England, 10 December, 1993

League Club	Source	Date Signed	Seasons Played	Apps	Subs	Gls
Coventry C	Durham C	02/68				
Walsall	Tr	05/71	71-77	204	12	25
Plymouth Arg	Tr	10/77	77-78	34	1	5
Preston NE	Tr	10/78	78-81	93	6	1
Wigan Ath	L	03/82	81	7	1	0

TAYLOR Brian Joseph
Born: Walsall, West Midlands, England, 24 March, 1937 — LW
Died: Menorca, Spain, 10 June, 2015

League Club	Source	Date Signed	Seasons Played	Apps	Subs	Gls
Walsall	Jnr	09/54	54-57	77	-	17
Birmingham C	Tr	06/58	58-61	54	-	7
Rotherham U	Tr	10/61	61-62	42	-	5
Shrewsbury T	Tr	08/63	63-64	73	-	8
Port Vale	Tr	08/65	65-66	44	2	2
Barnsley	Tr	06/67	67	23	1	2

TAYLOR Carl
Born: Gateshead, Tyne and Wear, England, 12 January, 1998 — M

League Club	Source	Date Signed	Seasons Played	Apps	Subs	Gls
Carlisle U	Sch	-	14	0	1	0

TAYLOR Carl Wilson
Born: Kirkby Stephen, Cumbria, England, 20 January, 1937 — W

League Club	Source	Date Signed	Seasons Played	Apps	Subs	Gls
Middlesbrough	Penrith	01/56	57-59	11	-	1
Aldershot	Tr	06/60	60-62	78	-	13
Darlington	Tr	09/62	62	19	-	1

TAYLOR Charles James (Charlie)
Born: York, England, 18 September, 1993 — LB
England: Youth

League Club	Source	Date Signed	Seasons Played	Apps	Subs	Gls
Leeds U	Sch	07/11	11-14	24	1	2
Bradford C	L	01/12	11	1	2	0
York C	L	08/12	12	3	1	0
Fleetwood T	L	10/13	13	31	1	0

TAYLOR Charlie James
Born: Lewisham, SE London, England, 28 December, 1985 — F

League Club	Source	Date Signed	Seasons Played	Apps	Subs	Gls
Crystal Palace	Charlton Ath (Sch)	02/03				
Nottingham F	Tr	08/03				
Barnet	Sutton U	08/10	10-11	4	32	2

TAYLOR Christopher David (Chris)
Born: Oldham, Greater Manchester, England, 20 December, 1986 — LW

League Club	Source	Date Signed	Seasons Played	Apps	Subs	Gls
Oldham Ath	Jnr	02/06	05-11	239	15	33
Millwall	Tr	05/12	12	17	5	3
Blackburn Rov	Tr	07/13	13-14	21	29	1

TAYLOR Christopher James (Chris)
Born: Swindon, England, 30 October, 1985 — M

League Club	Source	Date Signed	Seasons Played	Apps	Subs	Gls
Swindon T	Sch	06/05	02	0	4	0

TAYLOR Cleveland Ken Wayne
Born: Leicester, England, 9 September, 1983 — RW

League Club	Source	Date Signed	Seasons Played	Apps	Subs	Gls
Bolton W	Sch	08/02				
Exeter C	L	08/02	02	1	2	0
Scunthorpe U	Tr	01/04	03-07	121	53	15
Carlisle U	Tr	01/08	07-09	52	9	3
Brentford	Tr	08/09	09	8	4	1
Burton A	L	01/10	09	23	1	4
Burton A	St Johnstone	07/11	11-12	34	15	3

TAYLOR Colin
Born: Stourbridge, West Midlands, England, 24 August, 1940 — W
Died: Dudley, West Midlands, England, 29 June, 2005

League Club	Source	Date Signed	Seasons Played	Apps	Subs	Gls
Walsall	Stourbridge	02/58	58-62	213	-	94
Newcastle U	Tr	06/63	63-64	33	-	7
Walsall	Tr	10/64	64-67	148	0	52
Crystal Palace	Tr	05/68	68	32	2	8
Walsall	Tr	09/69	69-72	85	11	24

TAYLOR Colin David
Born: Liverpool, England, 25 December, 1971 — F
England: Youth

League Club	Source	Date Signed	Seasons Played	Apps	Subs	Gls
Wolverhampton W	YT	03/90	90-92	7	12	2
Wigan Ath	L	01/92	91	7	0	2
Preston NE	L	11/92	92	4	0	0
Doncaster Rov	L	02/93	92	2	0	0

TAYLOR Craig
Born: Plymouth, England, 24 January, 1974 — CD

League Club	Source	Date Signed	Seasons Played	Apps	Subs	Gls
Exeter C	YT	06/92	92	2	3	0
Swindon T	Dorchester T	04/97	97-99	47	8	2
Plymouth Arg	L	10/98	98	6	0	1
Plymouth Arg	Tr	08/99	99-02	80	2	6
Torquay U	L	02/03	02	5	0	0
Torquay U	Tr	07/03	03-06	116	7	5

TAYLOR Daniel George (Danny)
Born: Chester, England, 1 September, 1991 — RB

League Club	Source	Date Signed	Seasons Played	Apps	Subs	Gls
Shrewsbury T	Jnr	09/09	09	2	1	0

TAYLOR Daniel John (Danny)
Born: Oldham, Greater Manchester, England, 28 July, 1982 — FB

League Club	Source	Date Signed	Seasons Played	Apps	Subs	Gls
Rochdale	YT	-	99	0	1	0

TAYLOR Daniel Scott (Dan)
Born: North Shields, Tyne and Wear, England, 17 March, 1993 — F

League Club	Source	Date Signed	Seasons Played	Apps	Subs	Gls
Oldham Ath	Newcastle U (Sch)	07/12	12	1	7	1

TAYLOR Daryl Shea
Born: Birmingham, England, 14 November, 1984 — M

League Club	Source	Date Signed	Seasons Played	Apps	Subs	Gls
Walsall	Sch	07/04	04-05	14	16	3
Bournemouth	Tr	07/06				
Bury	Tr	08/06	06	1	3	0

TAYLOR David (Dave)
Born: Rochester, Kent, England, 17 September, 1940 — IF

League Club	Source	Date Signed	Seasons Played	Apps	Subs	Gls
Gillingham	Jnr	09/57	57-58	21	-	3
Portsmouth	Tr	06/59	59	2	-	0

TAYLOR Derek Milton
Born: Bradford, England, 6 June, 1927 — RW
Died: Bradford, England, January, 1984

League Club	Source	Date Signed	Seasons Played	Apps	Subs	Gls
Halifax T (Am)	Bradford Park Ave (Am)	08/48	48	2	-	0

TAYLOR Douglas (Doug)
Born: Wolverhampton, England, 20 April, 1931 — F

League Club	Source	Date Signed	Seasons Played	Apps	Subs	Gls
Wolverhampton W	West Bromwich A (Am)	10/49	54	3	-	0
Walsall	Tr	11/55	55-56	36	-	8

TAYLOR Edward Kenneth (Ken)
Born: Irvine, Ayrshire, Scotland, 17 May, 1956 — M

League Club	Source	Date Signed	Seasons Played	Apps	Subs	Gls
Scunthorpe U	Ipswich T (App)	08/74	74	7	0	0

TAYLOR Ernest (Ernie)
Born: Sunderland, England, 2 September, 1925 — IF
Died: Birkenhead, Wirral, England, 9 April, 1985
England: 1/B-1

League Club	Source	Date Signed	Seasons Played	Apps	Subs	Gls
Newcastle U	Hylton CW	09/42	47-51	107	-	19
Blackpool	Tr	10/51	51-57	217	-	53
Manchester U	Tr	02/58	57-58	22	-	2
Sunderland	Tr	12/58	58-60	68	-	11

TAYLOR Francis Gerald (Frank)
Born: Bangor, Down, Northern Ireland, 2 January, 1923 — W

League Club	Source	Date Signed	Seasons Played	Apps	Subs	Gls
Leeds U	Bangor	07/49	49	3	-	0

TAYLOR Frederick (Fred)
Born: Burnley, Lancashire, England, 24 February, 1920 — RW
Died: Wallasey, Wirral, England, April, 1983

League Club	Source	Date Signed	Seasons Played	Apps	Subs	Gls
Burnley	Briercliffe St James	03/37	37-46	49	-	7
New Brighton	Tr	07/48	48-49	55	-	10

TAYLOR Frederick Alan (Alan)
Born: Derby, England, 7 March, 1954 — W

League Club	Source	Date Signed	Seasons Played	Apps	Subs	Gls
Chelsea	Alfreton T	10/72				
Reading	Tr	05/74	74	13	8	4

TAYLOR Frederick Robert (Freddie)
Born: Doncaster, South Yorkshire, England, 28 October, 1943 — LW

League Club	Source	Date Signed	Seasons Played	Apps	Subs	Gls
Doncaster Rov	Jnr	07/61	61-64	34	-	2

TAYLOR Gareth Keith
Born: Weston-super-Mare, Somerset, England, 25 February, 1973 — F
Wales: 15/U21-7

League Club	Source	Date Signed	Seasons Played	Apps	Subs	Gls
Bristol Rov	Southampton (YT)	07/91	91-95	31	16	16
Crystal Palace	Tr	09/95	95	18	2	1
Sheffield U	Tr	03/96	95-98	56	28	25
Manchester C	Tr	11/98	98-99	28	15	9
Port Vale	L	01/00	99	4	0	0

League Club	Source	Date Signed	Seasons Played	Apps	Subs	Gls
Queens Park Rgrs	L	03/00	99	2	4	1
Burnley	Tr	02/01	00-02	88	7	36
Nottingham F	Tr	08/03	03-05	78	12	19
Crewe Alex	L	01/06	05	15	0	4
Tranmere Rov	Tr	07/06	06-07	55	5	10
Doncaster Rov	Tr	01/08	07-08	15	14	1
Carlisle U	L	03/09	08	5	0	1

TAYLOR Geoffrey Arthur (Geoff)
Born: Kessingland, Suffolk, England, 22 January, 1923 — W
Died: Germany, 20 July, 2007

League Club	Source	Date Signed	Seasons Played	Apps	Subs	Gls
Norwich C	City of Norwich SOBU	08/46	46	1	-	0
Reading	Tr	03/47	46	1	-	0
Lincoln C	Tr	08/47	47	1	-	0
Brighton & HA	Stade Rennais (FRA)	08/48	48	2	-	0
Bristol Rov	Stade Rennais (FRA)	09/51	51	3	-	0
Queens Park Rgrs	SC Bruhl (SUI)	11/53	53	2	-	0

TAYLOR George Alexander
Born: Turriff, Aberdeenshire, Scotland, 9 June, 1915 — LH
Died: Plymouth, England, June, 1982

League Club	Source	Date Signed	Seasons Played	Apps	Subs	Gls
Plymouth Arg	Aberdeen	08/48	48-49	48	-	2

TAYLOR George Barry (Barry)
Born: Sheffield, England, 3 December, 1939 — FB
Died: Dronfield, Derbyshire, England, 15 March, 1996

League Club	Source	Date Signed	Seasons Played	Apps	Subs	Gls
Sheffield U	Jnr	04/59				
Oldham Ath	Tr	06/63	63	40	-	0
Chesterfield	Tr	08/64	64-65	35	0	2

TAYLOR George Edward
Born: Wigan, Greater Manchester, England, 21 March, 1920 — G
Died: Newham, E London, England, October, 1983

League Club	Source	Date Signed	Seasons Played	Apps	Subs	Gls
West Ham U	Gainsborough Trinity	12/38	46-55	115	-	0

TAYLOR George Jack
Born: Dundee, Scotland, 23 October, 1948 — W

League Club	Source	Date Signed	Seasons Played	Apps	Subs	Gls
Grimsby T	Jnr	11/65	65	0	1	0

TAYLOR George Leslie
Born: Edinburgh, Scotland, 11 May, 1925 — G
Died: Edinburgh, Scotland, 26 July, 1997

League Club	Source	Date Signed	Seasons Played	Apps	Subs	Gls
Aldershot	Dunfermline Ath	06/53				
Hartlepool U	Tr	11/53	53-54	34	-	0

TAYLOR George McGregor
Born: Edinburgh, Scotland, 12 December, 1927 — RW

League Club	Source	Date Signed	Seasons Played	Apps	Subs	Gls
Aldershot	Hamilton Academical	07/52	52	8	-	2

TAYLOR Gerald William (Gerry)
Born: Hull, England, 15 August, 1947 — RB

League Club	Source	Date Signed	Seasons Played	Apps	Subs	Gls
Wolverhampton W	Jnr	11/64	66-75	151	3	1
Swindon T	L	10/75	75	19	0	0

TAYLOR Gordon
Born: Ashton-under-Lyne, Greater Manchester, England, 28 December, 1944 — LW

League Club	Source	Date Signed	Seasons Played	Apps	Subs	Gls
Bolton W	Curzon Ashton	01/62	62-70	253	5	41
Birmingham C	Tr	12/70	70-75	156	10	9
Blackburn Rov	Tr	03/76	75-77	62	2	3
Bury	Tr	06/78	78-79	58	2	2

TAYLOR Gordon Stanley
Born: Stanley, County Durham, England, 10 June, 1936 — G
Died: Sunderland, England, 1976

League Club	Source	Date Signed	Seasons Played	Apps	Subs	Gls
Gateshead	West Stanley	02/57	57	3	-	0

TAYLOR Graham
Born: Worksop, Nottinghamshire, England, 15 September, 1944 — LB

League Club	Source	Date Signed	Seasons Played	Apps	Subs	Gls
Grimsby T	Jnr	07/62	63-67	189	0	2
Lincoln C	Tr	07/68	68-72	150	1	1

TAYLOR Gregory Vaughan (Greg)
Born: Bedford, England, 15 January, 1990 — LB
England: Semi Pro-2

League Club	Source	Date Signed	Seasons Played	Apps	Subs	Gls
Northampton T	Sch	07/08				
Cambridge U	Luton T	06/13	14	41	2	0

TAYLOR Ian
Born: Doncaster, South Yorkshire, England, 25 November, 1967 — G

League Club	Source	Date Signed	Seasons Played	Apps	Subs	Gls
Carlisle U	Bridlington T	08/90				
Scarborough	Tr	02/92	91	1	0	0

TAYLOR Ian Kenneth
Born: Birmingham, England, 4 June, 1968 — M

League Club	Source	Date Signed	Seasons Played	Apps	Subs	Gls
Port Vale	Moor Green	07/92	92-93	83	0	28
Sheffield Wed	Tr	07/94	94	9	5	1
Aston Villa	Tr	12/94	94-02	202	31	28
Derby Co	Tr	07/03	03-04	67	14	14
Northampton T	Tr	07/05	05-06	59	7	8

TAYLOR Jake William Trevor
Born: Bracknell, Berkshire, England, 1 December, 1991 — F
Wales: 1/U21-12/Youth

League Club	Source	Date Signed	Seasons Played	Apps	Subs	Gls
Reading	Sch	07/10	10-14	14	17	2
Aldershot T	L	07/11	11	0	3	0
Exeter C	L	09/11	11	26	4	3
Cheltenham T	L	11/12	12	7	1	1
Crawley T	L	03/13	12	4	0	0
Leyton Orient	L	03/15	14	3	0	0

TAYLOR James
Born: Ashton-in-Makerfield, Greater Manchester, England, 7 April, 1925 — LW

League Club	Source	Date Signed	Seasons Played	Apps	Subs	Gls
Manchester C		10/44				
Crewe Alex	Tr	06/47	47-48	49	-	8

TAYLOR James (Jim)
Born: Strood, Kent, England, 13 May, 1934 — IF

League Club	Source	Date Signed	Seasons Played	Apps	Subs	Gls
Charlton Ath	Tonbridge	08/54				
Gillingham	Tr	08/56	56-57	30	-	16
Watford	Tr	07/58				

TAYLOR James (Jimmy)
Born: Salford, England, 2 November, 1936 — W

League Club	Source	Date Signed	Seasons Played	Apps	Subs	Gls
Bolton W	Jnr	12/54				
Southport	Tr	07/59	59	29	-	0

TAYLOR James Guy (Jim)
Born: Uxbridge, W London, England, 5 November, 1917 — CH
Died: Reading, England, 6 March, 2001
England: 2/FLge-3

League Club	Source	Date Signed	Seasons Played	Apps	Subs	Gls
Fulham	Hillingdon BL	03/38	46-52	261	-	5
Queens Park Rgrs	Tr	04/53	53	41	-	0

TAYLOR Jamie
Born: Crawley, West Sussex, England, 16 December, 1982 — F

League Club	Source	Date Signed	Seasons Played	Apps	Subs	Gls
Dagenham & Red	Woking	03/07	07	2	10	1

TAYLOR Jamie Lee
Born: Bury, Greater Manchester, England, 11 January, 1977 — F/M

League Club	Source	Date Signed	Seasons Played	Apps	Subs	Gls
Rochdale	YT	01/94	93-96	10	26	4

TAYLOR Jason James Francis
Born: Droylsden, Greater Manchester, England, 28 January, 1987 — M

League Club	Source	Date Signed	Seasons Played	Apps	Subs	Gls
Oldham Ath	Sch	02/06				
Stockport Co	Tr	03/06	05-06	98	6	6
Rotherham U	Tr	01/09	08-12	103	15	10
Rochdale	L	11/09	09	23	0	1
Cheltenham T	Tr	01/13	12-14	55	10	2
Northampton T	L	01/15	14	21	0	0

TAYLOR Jason Lee
Born: Kettering, Northamptonshire, England, 12 October, 1985 — F

League Club	Source	Date Signed	Seasons Played	Apps	Subs	Gls
Rushden & D	Sch	07/05	04-05	8	24	3

TAYLOR Jason Scott
Born: Wrexham, Wales, 29 August, 1970 — F

League Club	Source	Date Signed	Seasons Played	Apps	Subs	Gls
Wrexham	YT	-	88	0	1	0

TAYLOR Jeffrey Neilson (Jeff)
Born: Huddersfield, West Yorkshire, England, 20 September, 1930 — CF
Died: Holmfirth, West Yorkshire, England, 28 December, 2010

League Club	Source	Date Signed	Seasons Played	Apps	Subs	Gls
Huddersfield T	Huddersfield YMCA	09/49	49-51	68	-	27
Fulham	Tr	11/51	51-53	33	-	14
Brentford	Tr	08/54	54-56	94	-	34

TAYLOR John (Jack)
Born: Barnsley, South Yorkshire, England, 15 February, 1914 — FB
Died: Barnsley, South Yorkshire, England, 22 February, 1978

League Club	Source	Date Signed	Seasons Played	Apps	Subs	Gls
Wolverhampton W	Worsbrough Bridge	01/34	35-37	79	-	0
Norwich C	Tr	06/38	38-46	50	-	0
Hull C	Tr	07/47	47-49	72	-	0

TAYLOR John
Born: Durham, England, 10 July, 1926 — IF

League Club	Source	Date Signed	Seasons Played	Apps	Subs	Gls
Crystal Palace (Am)	Leytonstone	05/48	48	1	-	0

TAYLOR John
Born: Creswell, Derbyshire, England, 11 January, 1939 — CF

League Club	Source	Date Signed	Seasons Played	Apps	Subs	Gls
Mansfield T	Chesterfield (Am)	05/57	59	5	-	2
Peterborough U	Tr	07/60	60	1	-	0

TAYLOR John
Born: Bradford, England, 24 June, 1924 — IF

League Club	Source	Date Signed	Seasons Played	Apps	Subs	Gls
Bradford C	Kilmarnock	09/46	46	2	-	2

TAYLOR John Brian (Brian)
Born: Rossington, South Yorkshire, England, 7 October, 1931 — G

League Club	Source	Date Signed	Seasons Played	Apps	Subs	Gls
Doncaster Rov	Sheffield Wed (Am)	03/49				
Leeds U	Worksop T	05/51	51	11	-	0
Bradford Park Ave	King's Lynn	06/54	54-55	66	-	0

TAYLOR John Ephraim (Jack)
Born: Chilton, County Durham, England, 11 September, 1924 — IF
Died: Luton, England, 9 August, 1970
England: B-1

League Club	Source	Date Signed	Seasons Played	Apps	Subs	Gls
Luton T	Stockton	02/49	48-51	85	-	29
Wolverhampton W	Tr	06/52	52	10	-	1
Notts Co	Tr	02/54	53-56	53	-	19
Bradford Park Ave	Tr	07/57	57	12	-	6

TAYLOR John Henry (Harry)
Born: Crawcrook, Tyne and Wear, England, 5 October, 1935 — RW
Died: Sunderland, England, February, 2002

League Club	Source	Date Signed	Seasons Played	Apps	Subs	Gls
Newcastle U	Jnr	11/52	54-59	28	-	5
Fulham	L	02/57	57	4	-	0

TAYLOR John James
Born: Manchester, England, 12 October, 1928 — RW

League Club	Source	Date Signed	Seasons Played	Apps	Subs	Gls
Blackpool		09/49				
Accrington Stan	Tr	07/52	52	16	-	0

TAYLOR John Keith
Born: Bradford, England, 7 September, 1935 — CF

League Club	Source	Date Signed	Seasons Played	Apps	Subs	Gls
Bradford C (Am)		02/56	55	1	-	0

TAYLOR John Leslie
Born: Birmingham, England, 25 June, 1949 — G

League Club	Source	Date Signed	Seasons Played	Apps	Subs	Gls
Chester C	Pwllheli	07/70	70-73	70	0	0
Rochdale	L	10/74	74	3	0	0
Stockport Co	Bangor C	11/75	75	1	0	0

TAYLOR John Patrick
Born: Norwich, England, 24 October, 1964 — F

League Club	Source	Date Signed	Seasons Played	Apps	Subs	Gls
Colchester U	Jnr	12/82				
Cambridge U	Sudbury T	08/88	88-91	139	21	46
Bristol Rov	Tr	03/92	91-93	91	4	44
Bradford C	Tr	07/94	94	35	1	11
Luton T	Tr	03/95	94-95	27	10	3
Lincoln C	L	09/96	96	5	0	2
Colchester U	L	11/96	96	8	0	5
Cambridge U	Tr	01/97	96-03	103	72	40
Northampton T	Tr	03/04	03	3	5	1

TAYLOR Jonathan Peter (Jon)
Born: Liverpool, England, 23 December, 1989 — W

League Club	Source	Date Signed	Seasons Played	Apps	Subs	Gls
Shrewsbury T	Jnr	09/09	09-13	100	33	21
Peterborough U	Tr	06/14	14	22	2	3

TAYLOR Kenneth (Ken)
Born: Porthmadog, Gwynedd, Wales, 5 June, 1952 — FB

League Club	Source	Date Signed	Seasons Played	Apps	Subs	Gls
Wrexham	Jnr	05/70	70	1	0	0

TAYLOR Kenneth (Ken)
Born: Huddersfield, West Yorkshire, England, 21 August, 1935 — CH

League Club	Source	Date Signed	Seasons Played	Apps	Subs	Gls
Huddersfield T	Yorkshire Amats	09/52	53-64	250	-	14
Bradford Park Ave	Tr	02/65	64-66	51	0	1

TAYLOR Kenneth Gordon (Ken)
Born: South Shields, Tyne and Wear, England, 15 March, 1931 — RB

League Club	Source	Date Signed	Seasons Played	Apps	Subs	Gls
Blackburn Rov	North Shields	01/50	54-63	200	-	0

TAYLOR Kenneth Victor (Ken)
Born: Manchester, England, 18 June, 1936 — CH

League Club	Source	Date Signed	Seasons Played	Apps	Subs	Gls
Manchester C	Manchester Corp T'port	08/54	57	1	-	0

TAYLOR Kevin
Born: Wakefield, England, 22 January, 1961 — M

League Club	Source	Date Signed	Seasons Played	Apps	Subs	Gls
Sheffield Wed	App	10/78	78-83	118	7	21
Derby Co	Tr	07/84	84	22	0	2
Crystal Palace	Tr	03/85	84-87	85	2	14
Scunthorpe U	Tr	10/87	87-90	149	8	25

TAYLOR Kris
Born: Stafford, England, 12 January, 1984 — M/LB
England: Youth

League Club	Source	Date Signed	Seasons Played	Apps	Subs	Gls
Manchester U	YT	02/01				
Walsall	Tr	02/03	03-06	58	22	6
Hereford U	Tr	07/07	07-08	60	10	2
Port Vale	Tr	08/09	09-10	53	8	3

TAYLOR Lawrence Desmond (Larry)
Born: Exeter, England, 23 November, 1947 — G

League Club	Source	Date Signed	Seasons Played	Apps	Subs	Gls
Bristol Rov	App	12/65	66-69	90	0	0

TAYLOR Lee Vincent
Born: Hammersmith, W London, England, 24 February, 1976 — D

League Club	Source	Date Signed	Seasons Played	Apps	Subs	Gls
Shrewsbury T	Faweh FC, Southwark	08/96	96-97	14	3	0

TAYLOR Leslie (Les)
Born: North Shields, Tyne and Wear, England, 4 December, 1956 — M

League Club	Source	Date Signed	Seasons Played	Apps	Subs	Gls
Oxford U	App	12/74	74-80	219	0	15
Watford	Tr	11/80	80-85	167	5	13
Reading	Tr	10/86	86-88	69	6	3
Colchester U	Tr	01/89	88-89	44	8	1

TAYLOR Lyle James Alfred
Born: Greenwich, SE London, England, 29 March, 1990 — F

League Club	Source	Date Signed	Seasons Played	Apps	Subs	Gls
Millwall	Staines T	05/08				
Bournemouth	Concord Rgrs	08/10	10-11	9	20	0
Hereford U	L	02/12	11	6	2	2
Sheffield U	Falkirk	07/13	13	9	11	2
Scunthorpe U	Tr	06/14	14	11	7	3

TAYLOR Maik Stefan
Born: Hildesheim, Germany, 4 September, 1971 — G
Northern Ireland: 88/B-1/U21-1

League Club	Source	Date Signed	Seasons Played	Apps	Subs	Gls
Barnet	Farnborough T	06/95	95-96	70	0	0
Southampton	Tr	01/97	96	18	0	0
Fulham	Tr	11/97	97-02	183	1	0
Birmingham C	Tr	08/03	03-09	214	0	0
Leeds U		11/11				
Millwall	Tr	03/12	11-12	16	0	0

TAYLOR Mark
Born: Hartlepool, Cleveland, England, 5 December, 1962 — FB

League Club	Source	Date Signed	Seasons Played	Apps	Subs	Gls
Hartlepool U	Henry Smith's BC	08/82	82	1	0	0

TAYLOR Mark Simon
Born: Cleveland, England, 8 November, 1974 — LB

League Club	Source	Date Signed	Seasons Played	Apps	Subs	Gls
Middlesbrough	YT	03/93				
Darlington	L	10/94	94	8	0	0
Fulham	Tr	09/95	95	7	0	0
Northampton T	Tr	02/96	95	1	0	0

TAYLOR Martin
Born: Ashington, Northumberland, England, 9 November, 1979 — CD
England: U21-1/Youth

League Club	Source	Date Signed	Seasons Played	Apps	Subs	Gls
Blackburn Rov	YT	08/97	98-03	68	20	5
Darlington	L	01/00	99	4	0	0
Stockport Co	L	03/00	99	7	0	0
Birmingham C	Tr	02/04	03-09	91	8	2
Norwich C	L	11/07	07	8	0	1
Watford	Tr	01/10	09-12	86	4	10
Sheffield Wed	Tr	08/12	12	10	1	0
Brentford	L	09/13	13	5	0	2

TAYLOR Martin James
Born: Tamworth, Staffordshire, England, 9 December, 1966 — G

League Club	Source	Date Signed	Seasons Played	Apps	Subs	Gls
Derby Co	Mile Oak Rov	04/85	89-96	97	0	0
Carlisle U	L	09/87	87	10	0	0
Scunthorpe U	L	12/87	87	8	0	0
Crewe Alex	L	09/96	96	6	0	0
Wycombe W	L	03/97	96	4	0	0
Wycombe W	Tr	06/97	97-02	234	0	0
Barnsley	L	03/03	02	3	0	0

TAYLOR Matthew James (Matt)
Born: Chorley, Lancashire, England, 30 January, 1982 — CD

League Club	Source	Date Signed	Seasons Played	Apps	Subs	Gls
Exeter C	Team Bath	07/07	08-10	101	4	9
Charlton Ath	Tr	07/11	11-12	44	9	0
Bradford C	Tr	08/13	13	1	1	0
Colchester U	L	09/13	13	5	0	1
Cheltenham T	Tr	07/14	14	31	2	1

TAYLOR Matthew Simon
Born: Oxford, England, 27 November, 1981 — LM
England: B-1/U21-3

League Club	Source	Date Signed	Seasons Played	Apps	Subs	Gls
Luton T	YT	02/99	99-01	127	2	16
Portsmouth	Tr	07/02	02-07	139	40	23
Bolton W	Tr	01/08	07-10	100	23	23
West Ham U	Tr	07/11	11-13	56	20	2
Burnley	Tr	07/14	14	7	3	0

TAYLOR Michael John
Born: Liverpool, England, 21 November, 1982 — CD

League Club	Source	Date Signed	Seasons Played	Apps	Subs	Gls
Blackburn Rov	YT	11/99				
Carlisle U	L	09/02	02	10	0	0
Rochdale	L	03/03	02	2	0	0
Cheltenham T	Tr	07/04	04-05	19	4	0

TAYLOR Nathaniel David (Nat)
Born: Manchester, England, 3 September, 1992 — F

League Club	Source	Date Signed	Seasons Played	Apps	Subs	Gls
Accrington Stan	Rossendale College	08/11	11	1	1	0

TAYLOR Neil John
Born: Ruthin, Denbighshire, Wales, 7 February, 1989 — LB
Wales: 22/U21-13/Youth

League Club	Source	Date Signed	Seasons Played	Apps	Subs	Gls
Wrexham	Sch	07/07	07	21	5	0
Swansea C	Tr	07/10	10-14	104	11	0

TAYLOR Oliver Scott (Olly)
Born: Oxford, England, 13 December, 1993 — F

League Club	Source	Date Signed	Seasons Played	Apps	Subs	Gls
Wycombe W	Sch	05/12	12	1	5	0

TAYLOR Paul
Born: Leith, Edinburgh, Scotland, 20 December, 1966 — LB

League Club	Source	Date Signed	Seasons Played	Apps	Subs	Gls
Mansfield T	App	-	83	3	0	0

TAYLOR Paul Anthony
Born: Sheffield, England, 3 December, 1949 — M

League Club	Source	Date Signed	Seasons Played	Apps	Subs	Gls
Sheffield Wed	Loughborough College	06/71	71-72	5	1	0
York C	Tr	07/73	73	4	0	0
Hereford U	L	01/74	73	0	1	0
Colchester U	Tr	03/74	73	6	3	0
Southport	Tr	07/74	74-76	95	0	16

TAYLOR Paul Thomas
Born: Liverpool, England, 4 November, 1987 — F

League Club	Source	Date Signed	Seasons Played	Apps	Subs	Gls
Chester C (L)	Vauxhall Motors	07/08	08	2	7	0
Peterborough U	Anderlecht (BEL)	03/11	10-12	38	10	12
Ipswich T	Tr	08/12	12-13	7	14	1
Peterborough U	L	09/13	13	6	0	0
Rotherham U	L	08/14	14	13	4	0
Blackburn Rov	L	03/15	14	2	3	0

TAYLOR Peter John
Born: Canvey Island, Essex, England, 3 January, 1953 — LW
England: 4/U23-4/Semi Pro

League Club	Source	Date Signed	Seasons Played	Apps	Subs	Gls
Southend U	App	01/71	70-73	57	18	12
Crystal Palace	Tr	10/73	73-76	122	0	33
Tottenham H	Tr	09/76	76-80	116	7	31
Leyton Orient	Tr	11/80	80-82	49	7	11
Oldham Ath	L	01/83	82	4	0	0
Exeter C	Maidstone U	10/83	83	8	0	0

TAYLOR Peter Mark Richard (Mark)
Born: Hartlepool, Cleveland, England, 20 November, 1964 — LW

League Club	Source	Date Signed	Seasons Played	Apps	Subs	Gls
Hartlepool U	Brinkburn Jnrs	08/82	83-85	42	5	4
Crewe Alex	L	12/85	85	3	0	0
Blackpool	Tr	08/86	86-91	104	15	43
Cardiff C	L	12/90	90	6	0	3
Wrexham	Tr	03/92	91-94	50	11	9

TAYLOR Peter Thomas
Born: Nottingham, England, 2 July, 1928 — G
Died: Mallorca, Spain, 4 October, 1990

League Club	Source	Date Signed	Seasons Played	Apps	Subs	Gls
Coventry C	Nottingham F (Am)	05/46	50-54	86	-	0
Middlesbrough	Tr	08/55	55-59	140	-	0
Port Vale	Tr	06/61	61	1	-	0

TAYLOR Philip Anthony (Phil)
Born: Sheffield, England, 11 July, 1958 — M

League Club	Source	Date Signed	Seasons Played	Apps	Subs	Gls
York C	App	07/76	74-77	14	7	1
Darlington	Tr	07/78	78-79	18	8	2

TAYLOR Philip Henry (Phil)
Born: Bristol, England, 18 September, 1917 — RH/IF
Died: Cambridgeshire, England, 1 December, 2012
England: 3/B-2/FLge-4/Schools

League Club	Source	Date Signed	Seasons Played	Apps	Subs	Gls
Bristol Rov	Bristol St George	05/35	35	21	-	2
Liverpool	Tr	03/36	35-53	312	-	32

TAYLOR Quade Gerald
Born: Tooting, SW London, England, 11 December, 1993 — CD/M

League Club	Source	Date Signed	Seasons Played	Apps	Subs	Gls
Crystal Palace	Dulwich Hamlet	03/11				
Bolton W	Tr	07/14	14	1	0	0

TAYLOR Raymond Jeffrey (Ray)
Born: Jump, South Yorkshire, England, 1 March, 1930 — LW
Died: Barnsley, South Yorkshire, England, August, 2012

League Club	Source	Date Signed	Seasons Played	Apps	Subs	Gls
Huddersfield T	Wath W	09/49	49	2	-	0
Southport	Tr	08/53	53-54	51	-	7

TAYLOR Rhys Francis
Born: Port Talbot, Wales, 7 April, 1990 — G
Wales: U21-5/Youth

League Club	Source	Date Signed	Seasons Played	Apps	Subs	Gls
Chelsea	Sch	07/07				
Crewe Alex	L	07/10	10	44	0	0
Rotherham U	L	01/12	11	20	0	0

TAYLOR Richard Eric (Dick)
Born: Wolverhampton, England, 9 April, 1918 — CH
Died: Birmingham, England, 28 January, 1995

League Club	Source	Date Signed	Seasons Played	Apps	Subs	Gls
Grimsby T	Wolverhampton W (Am)	05/35	38-47	36	-	0
Scunthorpe U	Tr	05/48	50-53	131	-	2

TAYLOR Richard Herbert
Born: Huddersfield, West Yorkshire, England, 24 January, 1957 — G
England: Youth

League Club	Source	Date Signed	Seasons Played	Apps	Subs	Gls
Huddersfield T	App	01/74	73-81	105	0	0
York C	L	03/80	79	2	0	0

TAYLOR Richard Marshall (Dick)
Born: Oldham, Greater Manchester, England, 21 August, 1928 — G

League Club	Source	Date Signed	Seasons Played	Apps	Subs	Gls
Everton	Marine	06/51				
Southport	Formby	08/54	54	1	-	0

TAYLOR Richard William (Richie)
Born: Silksworth, Tyne and Wear, England, 20 June, 1951 — LW

League Club	Source	Date Signed	Seasons Played	Apps	Subs	Gls
Sunderland	App	10/68	71	0	1	0
York C	Tr	07/72	72	26	2	2

TAYLOR Robert (Bob)
Born: Horden, County Durham, England, 3 February, 1967 — F

League Club	Source	Date Signed	Seasons Played	Apps	Subs	Gls
Leeds U	Horden CW	03/86	85-88	33	9	9
Bristol C	Tr	03/89	88-91	96	10	50
West Bromwich A	Tr	01/92	91-97	211	27	96
Bolton W	L	01/98	97	4	0	1
Bolton W	Tr	03/98	97-99	53	20	20
West Bromwich A	Tr	03/00	99-02	45	41	17
Cheltenham T	Tr	08/03	03	19	9	7

TAYLOR Robert Anthony
Born: Norwich, England, 30 April, 1971 — F

League Club	Source	Date Signed	Seasons Played	Apps	Subs	Gls
Norwich C	YT	03/90				
Leyton Orient	L	03/91	90	0	3	1
Birmingham C	Tr	08/91				
Leyton Orient	Tr	10/91	91-93	54	19	20
Brentford	Tr	03/94	93-97	172	1	56
Gillingham	Tr	08/98	98-99	56	2	31
Manchester C	Tr	11/99	99	14	2	5
Wolverhampton W	Tr	08/00	00	5	4	0
Queens Park Rgrs	L	08/01	01	3	1	0
Gillingham	L	10/01	01	3	8	0
Grimsby T	Tr	01/02	01-02	5	0	1
Scunthorpe U	Tr	02/03	02	4	4	0

TAYLOR Robert James (Rob)
Born: Shrewsbury, Shropshire, England, 16 January, 1985 — LB/M

League Club	Source	Date Signed	Seasons Played	Apps	Subs	Gls
Port Vale	Nuneaton Bor	06/08	08-13	100	60	15
Mansfield T	Tr	08/14	14	10	6	0
Tranmere Rov	Tr	01/15	14	15	0	0

TAYLOR Robert John (Bob)
Born: Croydon, S London, England, 16 March, 1936 — RH/RW

League Club	Source	Date Signed	Seasons Played	Apps	Subs	Gls
Crystal Palace	Fulham (Am)	08/54	54	2	-	0
Gillingham	Tr	09/56	56-58	31	-	5
Millwall	Tr	08/59	59	2	-	1

TAYLOR Robert Mark (Mark)
Born: Walsall, West Midlands, England, 22 February, 1966 — M

League Club	Source	Date Signed	Seasons Played	Apps	Subs	Gls
Walsall	YT	07/84	84-88	101	13	4
Sheffield Wed	Tr	06/89	89	8	1	0
Shrewsbury T	L	02/91	90	19	0	2
Shrewsbury T	Tr	09/91	91-97	244	5	13

TAYLOR Robert Shaun (Robbie)
Born: Plymouth, England, 3 December, 1967 — F

League Club	Source	Date Signed	Seasons Played	Apps	Subs	Gls
Portsmouth	YT	08/86				
Newport Co	Tr	03/87	86-87	38	6	7
Torquay U	Weymouth	09/89	89	11	7	1

TAYLOR Robin Graham
Born: Rinteln, Germany, 14 January, 1971 — M

League Club	Source	Date Signed	Seasons Played	Apps	Subs	Gls
Wigan Ath	Leicester C (NC)	10/89	89	0	1	0

TAYLOR Rodney Victor (Rod)
Born: Corfe Castle, Dorset, England, 9 September, 1943 — CD/M

League Club	Source	Date Signed	Seasons Played	Apps	Subs	Gls
Portsmouth	Jnr	05/61				
Gillingham	Tr	07/63	63-65	9	2	0
Bournemouth	Tr	02/66	65-66	29	1	0

TAYLOR Roy
Born: Hoyland, South Yorkshire, England, 2 April, 1933 — G
Died: Barnsley, South Yorkshire, England, 18 November, 2013

League Club	Source	Date Signed	Seasons Played	Apps	Subs	Gls
Scunthorpe U	Denaby U	01/53	52	2	-	0

TAYLOR Royston (Roy)
Born: Blackpool, Lancashire, England, 28 September, 1956 — M

League Club	Source	Date Signed	Seasons Played	Apps	Subs	Gls
Preston NE	App	10/74	75	3	0	0
Blackburn Rov	Sunderland (NC)	11/76	78	3	0	1

TAYLOR Ryan Anthony
Born: Liverpool, England, 19 August, 1984 — M/RB
England: U21-4/Youth

League Club	Source	Date Signed	Seasons Played	Apps	Subs	Gls
Tranmere Rov	Sch	04/02	02-04	82	16	14
Wigan Ath	Tr	07/05	05-08	38	18	6
Newcastle U	Tr	02/09	09-14	64	28	6

TAYLOR Ryan Paul
Born: Rotherham, South Yorkshire, England, 4 May, 1988 — F

League Club	Source	Date Signed	Seasons Played	Apps	Subs	Gls
Rotherham U	Sch	07/06	05-10	72	60	21

League Club	Source	Date Signed	Seasons Played	Apps	Subs	Gls
Exeter C	L	03/10	09	3	4	0
Bristol C	Tr	07/11	11-13	18	21	2
Portsmouth	Tr	01/14	13-14	46	9	14

TAYLOR Samuel McGregor (Sammy)
Born: Gorbals, Glasgow, Scotland, 23 September, 1933 — LW
Died: Preston, Lancashire, England, 6 November, 2013

League Club	Source	Date Signed	Seasons Played	Apps	Subs	Gls
Preston NE	Falkirk	06/55	55-60	149	-	41
Carlisle U	Tr	06/61	61-63	93	-	12
Southport	Tr	07/64	64	36	-	3

TAYLOR Scott Dean
Born: Portsmouth, England, 23 November, 1970 — M

League Club	Source	Date Signed	Seasons Played	Apps	Subs	Gls
Reading	YT	06/89	88-94	164	43	24
Leicester C	Tr	07/95	95-96	59	5	6
Wolverhampton W	Tr	09/99	99-00	21	11	3
Cambridge U	Tr	11/01	01	0	3	0

TAYLOR Scott James
Born: Chertsey, Surrey, England, 5 May, 1976 — F

League Club	Source	Date Signed	Seasons Played	Apps	Subs	Gls
Millwall	Staines T	02/95	94-95	13	15	0
Bolton W	Tr	03/96	95-96	2	10	1
Rotherham U	L	12/97	97	10	0	3
Blackpool	L	03/98	97	3	2	1
Tranmere Rov	Tr	10/98	98-00	78	30	17
Stockport Co	Tr	08/01	01	19	9	4
Blackpool	Tr	01/02	01-04	97	19	43
Plymouth Arg	Tr	12/04	04-05	17	17	4
MK Dons	Tr	01/06	05-06	16	29	5
Brentford	L	03/07	06	3	3	0
Rochdale	L	10/07	07	2	2	0

TAYLOR Sean
Born: Amble, Northumberland, England, 9 December, 1985 — RB

League Club	Source	Date Signed	Seasons Played	Apps	Subs	Gls
Sunderland	Sch	01/03				
Blackpool	L	01/06	05	3	1	0

TAYLOR Shaun
Born: Plymouth, England, 26 March, 1963 — CD

League Club	Source	Date Signed	Seasons Played	Apps	Subs	Gls
Exeter C	Bideford T	12/86	86-90	200	0	16
Swindon T	Tr	07/91	91-96	212	0	30
Bristol C	Tr	09/96	96-99	105	0	7

TAYLOR Stanley (Stan)
Born: Southport, Merseyside, England, 17 November, 1932 — LW

League Club	Source	Date Signed	Seasons Played	Apps	Subs	Gls
Southport	Liverpool (Am)	02/56	55	2	-	0

TAYLOR Stephen Christopher Edward (Steve)
Born: Cannock, Staffordshire, England, 7 January, 1970 — F
England: Semi Pro-1

League Club	Source	Date Signed	Seasons Played	Apps	Subs	Gls
Crystal Palace	Bromsgrove Rov	06/95				
Northampton T	L	10/95	95	1	1	0

TAYLOR Steven (Steve)
Born: Chesterfield, Derbyshire, England, 18 December, 1973 — F

League Club	Source	Date Signed	Seasons Played	Apps	Subs	Gls
Chesterfield	Brampton Rov	08/93	93	1	0	0

TAYLOR Steven John (Steve)
Born: Royton, Greater Manchester, England, 18 October, 1955 — F

League Club	Source	Date Signed	Seasons Played	Apps	Subs	Gls
Bolton W	App	10/73	74-77	34	6	16
Port Vale	L	10/75	75	4	0	2
Oldham Ath	Tr	10/77	77-78	45	2	25
Luton T	Tr	01/79	78	15	5	1
Mansfield T	Tr	07/79	79	30	7	7
Burnley	Tr	07/80	80-82	80	6	37
Wigan Ath	Tr	08/83	83	29	1	7
Stockport Co	Tr	03/84	83-84	26	0	8
Rochdale	Tr	11/84	84-86	84	0	42
Preston NE	Tr	10/86	86	5	0	2
Burnley	Tr	08/87	87-88	38	7	6
Rochdale	Tr	03/89	88	16	1	4

TAYLOR Steven Vincent
Born: Greenwich, SE London, England, 23 January, 1986 — CD
England: B-1/U21-29/Youth

League Club	Source	Date Signed	Seasons Played	Apps	Subs	Gls
Newcastle U	Sch	01/03	03-14	191	14	13
Wycombe W	L	12/03	03	6	0	0

TAYLOR Stewart Raymond
Born: Owston Ferry, North Lincolnshire, England, 6 April, 1946 — LB

League Club	Source	Date Signed	Seasons Played	Apps	Subs	Gls
Scunthorpe U		08/65	65-68	64	3	0

TAYLOR Stuart
Born: Bristol, England, 18 April, 1947 — CD

League Club	Source	Date Signed	Seasons Played	Apps	Subs	Gls
Bristol Rov	Jnr	01/66	65-79	546	0	28

TAYLOR Stuart James
Born: Romford, E London, England, 28 November, 1980 — G
England: U21-3/Youth

League Club	Source	Date Signed	Seasons Played	Apps	Subs	Gls
Arsenal	YT	07/98	01-02	16	2	0
Bristol Rov	L	09/99	99	4	0	0
Crystal Palace	L	08/00	00	10	0	0
Peterborough U	L	02/01	00	6	0	0
Leicester C	L	11/04	04	10	0	0
Aston Villa	Tr	07/05	05-07	9	3	0
Cardiff C	L	03/09	08	8	0	0
Manchester C	Tr	07/09				
Reading	Tr	08/12	12	4	0	0
Leeds U	Tr	07/14	14	3	0	0

TAYLOR Thomas (Tommy)
Born: Barnsley, South Yorkshire, England, 29 January, 1932 — CF
Died: Munich, Germany, 6 February, 1958
England: 19/B-2/FLge-2

League Club	Source	Date Signed	Seasons Played	Apps	Subs	Gls
Barnsley	Smithies U	07/49	50-52	44	-	26
Manchester U	Tr	03/53	52-57	166	-	112

TAYLOR Thomas Frederick (Tommy)
Born: Hornchurch, E London, England, 26 September, 1951 — CD
England: U23-11/Youth/Schools

League Club	Source	Date Signed	Seasons Played	Apps	Subs	Gls
Leyton Orient	App	10/68	67-70	112	2	4
West Ham U	Tr	10/70	70-78	340	0	8
Leyton Orient	Tr	05/79	79-81	116	0	5

TAYLOR Thomas William James (Tommy)
Born: Wandsworth, SW London, England, 10 September, 1946 — M

League Club	Source	Date Signed	Seasons Played	Apps	Subs	Gls
Portsmouth	Tottenham H (Jnr)	04/64				
Gillingham	Tr	05/65	65	19	1	0
Bournemouth	Tr	06/66	66-67	26	0	8

TAYLOR Walter Bingley (Wally)
Born: Kirton-in-Lindsey, North Lincolnshire, England, 30 October, 1926 — D
Died: Scunthorpe, North Lincolnshire, England, 18 August, 2005

League Club	Source	Date Signed	Seasons Played	Apps	Subs	Gls
Grimsby T	Hibaldstow	08/44	49-50	21	-	0
Southport	Tr	07/51	51-57	269	-	1
Oldham Ath	Tr	07/58	58-59	51	-	0

TAYLOR William (Billy)
Born: Edinburgh, Scotland, 31 July, 1939 — M
Died: Manchester, England, 30 November, 1981

League Club	Source	Date Signed	Seasons Played	Apps	Subs	Gls
Leyton Orient	Bonnyrigg Rose	08/59	60-62	23	-	0
Nottingham F	Tr	10/63	63-68	10	10	1
Lincoln C	Tr	05/69	69-70	74	5	7

TAYLOR William Donnachie (Billy)
Born: Kirkconnel, Dumfries & Galloway, Scotland, 3 June, 1938 — G

League Club	Source	Date Signed	Seasons Played	Apps	Subs	Gls
Luton T	Partick Thistle	12/67	67-68	6	0	0

TAYLOR-FLETCHER Gary
Born: Widnes, Cheshire, England, 4 June, 1981 — F/W
England: Schools

League Club	Source	Date Signed	Seasons Played	Apps	Subs	Gls
Hull C (L)	Northwich Victoria	03/01	00	1	4	0
Leyton Orient	Northwich Victoria	07/01	01-02	10	11	1
Lincoln C	Tr	08/03	03-04	77	3	27
Huddersfield T	Tr	07/05	05-06	69	13	21
Blackpool	Tr	07/07	07-12	191	24	36
Leicester C	Tr	09/13	13-14	2	20	3
Sheffield Wed	L	10/14	14	2	2	0
Millwall	L	02/15	14	6	4	0

TCHOYI Somen Alfred
Born: Douala, Cameroon, 29 March, 1983 — M
Cameroon: 15

League Club	Source	Date Signed	Seasons Played	Apps	Subs	Gls
West Bromwich A	RB Salzburg (AUT)	08/10	10-11	13	28	7

TEAGUE Andrew Harry
Born: Preston, Lancashire, England, 5 February, 1986 — CD

League Club	Source	Date Signed	Seasons Played	Apps	Subs	Gls
Macclesfield T	Sch	07/05	04-07	39	5	2

TEAGUE William Edward (Bill)
Born: Lydney, Gloucestershire, England, 26 September, 1937 — G
Died: Gloucester, England, 12 August, 1998

League Club	Source	Date Signed	Seasons Played	Apps	Subs	Gls
Swindon T	Gloucester C	03/61	60-61	3	-	0

TEALE Gary Stewart
Born: Glasgow, Scotland, 21 July, 1978 — RW
Scotland: 13/B-1/U21-6

League Club	Source	Date Signed	Seasons Played	Apps	Subs	Gls
Wigan Ath	Ayr U	12/01	01-06	121	41	8
Derby Co	Tr	01/07	06-09	65	22	4
Plymouth Arg	L	02/08	07	8	4	0
Barnsley	L	08/08	08	2	1	0
Sheffield Wed	Tr	07/10	10	37	4	2

TEALE Richard Grant
Born: Staines, Surrey, England, 27 February, 1952 — G

League Club	Source	Date Signed	Seasons Played	Apps	Subs	Gls
Queens Park Rgrs	Slough T	07/73	74	1	0	0
Fulham	Tr	06/76	76	5	0	0
Wimbledon	Tr	08/77	77	15	0	0

TEALE Shaun
Born: Southport, Merseyside, England, 10 March, 1964 — CD

England: Semi Pro-1

League Club	Source	Date Signed	Seasons Played	Apps	Subs	Gls
Bournemouth	Weymouth	01/89	88-90	99	1	4
Aston Villa	Tr	07/91	91-94	146	1	2
Tranmere Rov	Tr	08/95	95-96	54	0	0
Preston NE	L	02/97	96	5	0	0
Carlisle U	Motherwell	02/00	99	18	0	0

TEARSE David James (Dave)
Born: Newcastle-upon-Tyne, England, 7 August, 1951 — F

League Club	Source	Date Signed	Seasons Played	Apps	Subs	Gls
Leicester C	North Kenton BC	10/69	69-70	7	1	1
Torquay U	Tr	11/71	71-74	77	0	23
Reading	L	01/75	74	2	0	0

TEASDALE John George (Jack)
Born: Rossington, South Yorkshire, England, 15 March, 1929 — WH

League Club	Source	Date Signed	Seasons Played	Apps	Subs	Gls
Doncaster Rov	Rossington Main	10/49	50-55	113	-	0

TEASDALE John Stewart
Born: Glasgow, Scotland, 15 October, 1962 — F

League Club	Source	Date Signed	Seasons Played	Apps	Subs	Gls
Wolverhampton W	Nairn Co	12/80	80-81	6	2	0
Walsall	Tr	03/82	81-82	13	0	3
Hereford U	Tr	01/83	82	5	0	1
Blackpool	Wiener Sportklub (AUT)	11/84	84	1	6	1

TEASDALE Thomas (Tommy)
Born: England — W

League Club	Source	Date Signed	Seasons Played	Apps	Subs	Gls
Hull C (Am)		05/47	46	1	-	0

TEATHER Paul
Born: Rotherham, South Yorkshire, England, 26 December, 1977 — M
England: Youth/Schools

League Club	Source	Date Signed	Seasons Played	Apps	Subs	Gls
Manchester U	YT	08/94				
Bournemouth	L	12/97	97	5	5	0

TEBAR Marcos
Born: Madrid, Spain, 7 February, 1986 — DM
Spain: Youth

League Club	Source	Date Signed	Seasons Played	Apps	Subs	Gls
Brentford	UD Almeria (SPN)	06/14	14	1	3	0

TEBBUTT Robert Stanley (Bobby)
Born: Irchester, Northamptonshire, England, 10 November, 1934 — IF

League Club	Source	Date Signed	Seasons Played	Apps	Subs	Gls
Northampton T	Rushden T	10/56	56-59	57	-	21

TEBILY Olivier
Born: Abidjan, Ivory Coast, 19 December, 1975 — CD
Ivory Coast: 18//France: U21-4

League Club	Source	Date Signed	Seasons Played	Apps	Subs	Gls
Sheffield U	Chateauroux (FRA)	03/99	98	7	1	0
Birmingham C	Glasgow Celtic	03/02	01-06	62	21	0

TEDALDI Domenico Arch (Dino)
Born: Aberystwyth, Ceredigion, Wales, 12 August, 1980 — F
Wales: Youth

League Club	Source	Date Signed	Seasons Played	Apps	Subs	Gls
Doncaster Rov	YT	04/97	97	0	2	1

TEDDS William Henry (Bill)
Born: Bedworth, Warwickshire, England, 27 July, 1943 — RB

League Club	Source	Date Signed	Seasons Played	Apps	Subs	Gls
Coventry C	Jnr	09/60	61-64	8	-	0

TEDESCO John Joseph
Born: Modbury, Devon, England, 7 March, 1949 — F

League Club	Source	Date Signed	Seasons Played	Apps	Subs	Gls
Plymouth Arg	App	05/66	66-69	34	8	4
Bristol Rov	Tr	07/70				

TEECE David Alfred
Born: Middleton, Greater Manchester, England, 1 September, 1927 — G
Died: Rochdale, Greater Manchester, England, March, 2007

League Club	Source	Date Signed	Seasons Played	Apps	Subs	Gls
Hull C	Hyde U	02/52	53-55	25	-	0
Oldham Ath	Tr	06/56	56-58	91	-	0

TEER Kevin Paul
Born: Wood Green, N London, England, 7 December, 1963 — FB

League Club	Source	Date Signed	Seasons Played	Apps	Subs	Gls
Brentford	App	12/81	80	0	1	0

TEES Matthew (Matt)
Born: Johnstone, Renfrewshire, Scotland, 13 October, 1939 — IF

League Club	Source	Date Signed	Seasons Played	Apps	Subs	Gls
Grimsby T	Airdrieonians	07/63	63-66	113	0	51
Charlton Ath	Tr	02/67	66-69	88	1	32
Luton T	Tr	08/69	69-70	33	2	13
Grimsby T	Tr	11/70	70-72	83	0	42

TEGGART Neil
Born: Downpatrick, Northern Ireland, 16 September, 1984 — F
Northern Ireland: U21-2/Youth

League Club	Source	Date Signed	Seasons Played	Apps	Subs	Gls
Sunderland	Sch	04/02				
Darlington	L	02/04	03	9	6	0
Scunthorpe U	L	12/04	04	1	0	0

TEHOUE Jonathan Kahne
Born: Paris, France, 3 May, 1984 — F

League Club	Source	Date Signed	Seasons Played	Apps	Subs	Gls
Leyton Orient	Alfortville (FRA)	01/10	09-11	18	44	12
Swindon T	L	03/12	11	1	2	0

TEIXEIRA Dionatan
Born: Londrina, Brazil, 24 July, 1992 — D
Brazil: Youth//Slovenia: U21-3

League Club	Source	Date Signed	Seasons Played	Apps	Subs	Gls
Stoke C	Banska Bystrica (SVN)	06/14	14	0	1	0

TEIXEIRA Felipe Andrade
Born: Paris, France, 2 October, 1980 — M
Portugal: U21-9

League Club	Source	Date Signed	Seasons Played	Apps	Subs	Gls
West Bromwich A	Acad Coimbra (POR)	07/07	07-09	26	23	5
Barnsley	L	02/10	09	14	0	0

TEIXEIRA Joao Carlos
Born: Braga, Portugal, 18 January, 1993 — M
Portugal: U21-2/Youth

League Club	Source	Date Signed	Seasons Played	Apps	Subs	Gls
Liverpool	Sporting Lisbon (POR)	01/12	13	0	1	0
Brentford	L	09/13	13	0	2	0
Brighton & HA	L	08/14	14	27	5	6

TEIXEIRA Valdemar Lereno Goncal (Val)
Born: Lisbon, Portugal, 16 March, 1977 — M

League Club	Source	Date Signed	Seasons Played	Apps	Subs	Gls
Chesterfield (L)	CP Baltimore (USA)	09/08	08	0	5	0

TEJAN-SIE Thomas Malcolm (Tommy)
Born: Camden, N London, England, 23 November, 1988 — M

League Club	Source	Date Signed	Seasons Played	Apps	Subs	Gls
Dagenham & Red	Leicester C (Sch)	10/07	08-09	1	3	0

TELFER George Andrew
Born: Liverpool, England, 6 July, 1955 — LW/F

League Club	Source	Date Signed	Seasons Played	Apps	Subs	Gls
Everton	App	08/72	73-80	81	16	20
Scunthorpe U	San Diego Sock's (USA)	12/81	81-82	34	2	11
Preston NE	Altrincham	08/83	83	0	2	0

TELFER Paul Norman
Born: Edinburgh, Scotland, 21 October, 1971 — M/RB
Scotland: 1/B-2/U21-3

League Club	Source	Date Signed	Seasons Played	Apps	Subs	Gls
Luton T	YT	11/88	90-94	136	8	19
Coventry C	Tr	07/95	95-00	178	13	6
Southampton	Tr	11/01	01-04	112	16	1
Bournemouth	Glasgow Celtic	07/07	07	17	1	0
Leeds U	Rtd	08/08	08	14	0	0

TELFORD Dominic David
Born: Burnley, Lancashire, England, 5 December, 1996 — F

League Club	Source	Date Signed	Seasons Played	Apps	Subs	Gls
Blackpool	Sch	-	14	9	5	1

TELFORD William Albert (Billy)
Born: Carlisle, Cumbria, England, 5 March, 1956 — F

League Club	Source	Date Signed	Seasons Played	Apps	Subs	Gls
Manchester C	Tranmere Rov (App)	08/75	75	0	1	0
Peterborough U	Tr	09/75	75	3	1	2
Colchester U	L	01/76	75	1	1	1

TELLING Maurice William
Born: Southwark, S London, England, 5 August, 1919 — IF
Died: Hemel Hempstead, Hertfordshire, England, 1973

League Club	Source	Date Signed	Seasons Played	Apps	Subs	Gls
Millwall	Berkhamsted T	10/46	46	1	-	0

TEMBY William (Bill)
Born: Dover, Kent, England, 16 September, 1934 — IF

League Club	Source	Date Signed	Seasons Played	Apps	Subs	Gls
Queens Park Rgrs	Dover	02/55	55-56	7	-	3

TEMPEST Dale Michael
Born: Leeds, England, 30 December, 1963 — F
Hong Kong: 6

League Club	Source	Date Signed	Seasons Played	Apps	Subs	Gls
Fulham	App	12/81	80-83	25	9	6
Huddersfield T	Tr	08/84	84-85	63	2	27
Gillingham	L	03/86	85	9	0	4
Colchester U	Lokeren (BEL)	08/87	87-88	69	8	17

TEMPEST Gregory (Greg)
Born: Nottingham, England, 28 December, 1993 — M/LB
Northern Ireland: U21-6

League Club	Source	Date Signed	Seasons Played	Apps	Subs	Gls
Notts Co	Sch	07/12	12-13	9	8	0

TEMPLE Derek William
Born: Liverpool, England, 13 November, 1938 — LW
England: 1/FLge-2/Youth/Schools

League Club	Source	Date Signed	Seasons Played	Apps	Subs	Gls
Everton	Jnr	08/56	56-67	231	1	72
Preston NE	Tr	09/67	67-69	75	1	14

TEMPLE William (Bill)
Born: Winlaton, Tyne and Wear, England, 12 December, 1914 — IF
Died: Newcastle-upon-Tyne, England, April, 2006

League Club	Source	Date Signed	Seasons Played	Apps	Subs	Gls
Aldershot	Newbiggin West End	11/34	34-36	14	-	2
Carlisle U	Tr	05/37	37	11	-	4
Grimsby T	Tr	09/38	38	2	-	0
Gateshead	Tr	05/46	46	10	-	1

TEMPLEMAN John Henry
Born: Yapton, West Sussex, England, 21 September, 1947 — RB/M

League Club	Source	Date Signed	Seasons Played	Apps	Subs	Gls
Brighton & HA	Arundel T	07/66	66-73	219	7	16

League Club	Source	Date Signed	Seasons Played	Apps	Subs	Gls
Exeter C	Tr	05/74	74-78	205	1	7
Swindon T	Tr	07/79	79-80	20	1	0

TEN HEUVEL Laurens
Born: Amsterdam, Netherlands, 6 June, 1976 — F

League Club	Source	Date Signed	Seasons Played	Apps	Subs	Gls
Barnsley	FC Den Bosch (NED)	03/96	95-97	1	7	0
Sheffield U	Stormv's Telstar (NED)	07/02	02	0	5	0
Bradford C	L	03/03	02	4	1	0
Grimsby T	L	08/03	03	3	1	0

TENNANT Albert
Born: Ilkeston, Derbyshire, England, 29 October, 1917 — FB
Died: South Africa, 1986

League Club	Source	Date Signed	Seasons Played	Apps	Subs	Gls
Chelsea	Stanton Ironworks	11/34	46-48	2	-	0

TENNANT David
Born: Prestwick, Ayrshire, Scotland, 13 June, 1945 — G

League Club	Source	Date Signed	Seasons Played	Apps	Subs	Gls
Walsall	Jnr	08/63	63-64	19	-	0
Grimsby T	Worcester C	08/66				
Lincoln C	Tr	09/66	66-68	39	0	0
Rochdale	Tr	08/69	70	16	0	0

TENNANT Desmond Warren (Des)
Born: Cardiff, Wales, 17 October, 1925 — RB/RW
Died: Neath, Wales, 12 January, 2009

League Club	Source	Date Signed	Seasons Played	Apps	Subs	Gls
Cardiff C	Jnr	08/45				
Brighton & HA	Barry T	07/48	48-58	400	-	40

TENNANT Frederick Roy (Roy)
Born: Durban, South Africa, 12 September, 1936 — CH

League Club	Source	Date Signed	Seasons Played	Apps	Subs	Gls
Brighton & HA		08/57				
Workington	Tr	07/58	58-61	151	-	1

TENNANT John Graham
Born: Darlington, County Durham, England, 1 August, 1939 — G
Died: County Durham, England, December, 1985

League Club	Source	Date Signed	Seasons Played	Apps	Subs	Gls
Darlington		05/57	56-57	8	-	0
Chelsea	Tr	08/59				
Southend U	Tr	10/59	60-62	2	-	0

TENNANT Sydney David Keith (Keith)
Born: Newport, Wales, 6 June, 1934 — RH

League Club	Source	Date Signed	Seasons Played	Apps	Subs	Gls
Newport Co	Jnr	01/55	55-57	39	-	1

TENNEBO Thomas
Born: Bergen, Norway, 19 March, 1975 — M

League Club	Source	Date Signed	Seasons Played	Apps	Subs	Gls
Hartlepool U	Fana IL (NOR)	08/99	99-00	6	7	0

TENNENT David Millar
Born: Prestwick, Ayrshire, Scotland, 22 January, 1930 — LW
Died: Prestwick, Ayrshire, Scotland, 10 May, 2007

League Club	Source	Date Signed	Seasons Played	Apps	Subs	Gls
Ipswich T	Annbank Jnrs	07/52	52	4	-	0

TERESKINAS Andrejus
Born: Telsiai, Lithuania, 10 July, 1970 — LB
Lithuania: 56

League Club	Source	Date Signed	Seasons Played	Apps	Subs	Gls
Macclesfield T (L)	Skonto Riga (LAT)	11/00	00	0	1	0

TERNENT Francis Stanley (Stan)
Born: Gateshead, Tyne and Wear, England, 16 June, 1946 — DM

League Club	Source	Date Signed	Seasons Played	Apps	Subs	Gls
Burnley	App	06/63	66-67	5	0	0
Carlisle U	Tr	05/68	68-73	187	2	5
Sunderland	Tr	05/74				

TERNENT Raymond (Ray)
Born: Blyth, Northumberland, England, 9 September, 1948 — FB/M

League Club	Source	Date Signed	Seasons Played	Apps	Subs	Gls
Burnley	App	09/65	66-70	13	0	0
Southend U	Tr	06/71	71-72	82	0	1
Doncaster Rov	Tr	08/73	73-76	78	6	3

TERRIER David
Born: Verdun, France, 4 August, 1973 — FB

League Club	Source	Date Signed	Seasons Played	Apps	Subs	Gls
West Ham U (L)	FC Metz (FRA)	06/97	97	0	1	0

TERRIS James
Born: Dunfermline, Fife, Scotland, 25 July, 1933 — LB

League Club	Source	Date Signed	Seasons Played	Apps	Subs	Gls
Bristol C	Chippenham T	10/55	56-57	4	-	0
Carlisle U	Tr	04/59	59-60	28	-	1

TERRY John George
Born: Barking, E London, England, 7 December, 1980 — CD
England: 78/U21-9

League Club	Source	Date Signed	Seasons Played	Apps	Subs	Gls
Chelsea	YT	03/98	98-14	443	16	39
Nottingham F	L	03/00	99	5	1	0

TERRY Patrick Alfred (Pat)
Born: Lambeth, S London, England, 2 October, 1933 — CF
Died: Bromley, SE London, England, 23 February, 2007

League Club	Source	Date Signed	Seasons Played	Apps	Subs	Gls
Charlton Ath	Eastbourne U	03/54	53-54	4	-	1
Newport Co	Tr	05/56	56-57	55	-	30
Swansea C	Tr	02/58	57-58	17	-	9
Gillingham	Tr	10/58	58-60	108	-	60
Northampton T	Tr	07/61	61	24	-	10
Millwall	Tr	02/62	61-63	97	-	41
Reading	Tr	08/64	64-66	99	0	42
Swindon T	Tr	02/67	66-67	60	1	23
Brentford	Tr	06/68	68	29	0	12

TERRY Paul Edward
Born: Barking, E London, England, 3 April, 1979 — M
England: Semi Pro-3

League Club	Source	Date Signed	Seasons Played	Apps	Subs	Gls
Yeovil T	Dagenham & Red	08/03	03-06	111	24	10
Leyton Orient	Tr	07/07	07-08	65	6	1

TERRY Peter Edward
Born: Edmonton, N London, England, 11 September, 1972 — M

League Club	Source	Date Signed	Seasons Played	Apps	Subs	Gls
Aldershot	YT	07/91	90	1	0	0

TERRY Steven Graham (Steve)
Born: Clapton, NE London, England, 14 June, 1962 — CD

League Club	Source	Date Signed	Seasons Played	Apps	Subs	Gls
Watford	App	01/80	79-87	160	0	14
Hull C	Tr	06/88	88-89	62	0	4
Northampton T	Tr	03/90	89-93	181	0	17

TESCHE Robert
Born: Wismar, Germany, 27 May, 1987 — M

League Club	Source	Date Signed	Seasons Played	Apps	Subs	Gls
Nottingham F	Hamburger SV (GER)	08/14	14	18	4	2
Birmingham C	L	03/15	14	12	0	2

TESSEM Jo
Born: Brekstad, Norway, 28 February, 1972 — M
Norway: 9/B-1

League Club	Source	Date Signed	Seasons Played	Apps	Subs	Gls
Southampton	Molde FK (NOR)	11/99	99-03	67	43	12
Millwall	L	10/04	04	11	1	1
Bournemouth	Lyn Oslo (NOR)	01/08	07	5	6	0

TESTEMITANU Ivan
Born: Chisinau, Moldova, 27 April, 1974 — M
Moldova: 56

League Club	Source	Date Signed	Seasons Played	Apps	Subs	Gls
Bristol C	Zimbru Chisinau (MDA)	12/98	98-00	23	12	2

TESTER Paul Leonard
Born: Stroud, Gloucestershire, England, 10 March, 1959 — LW

League Club	Source	Date Signed	Seasons Played	Apps	Subs	Gls
Shrewsbury T	Cheltenham T	07/83	83-87	86	12	12
Hereford U	L	11/84	84	4	0	0
Hereford U	Tr	08/88	88-90	105	9	14

TETHER Colin
Born: Halesowen, West Midlands, England, 11 August, 1939 — RB
England: Youth

League Club	Source	Date Signed	Seasons Played	Apps	Subs	Gls
Wolverhampton W	Jnr	08/55	56	1	-	0
Oxford U	Tr	07/60				

TETTEY Alexander Banor
Born: Accra, Ghana, 4 April, 1986 — DM
Norway: 24/U21-14/Youth

League Club	Source	Date Signed	Seasons Played	Apps	Subs	Gls
Norwich C	Stade Rennais (FRA)	08/12	12-14	72	12	3

TEVEZ Carlos Alberto
Born: Buenos Aires, Argentina, 5 February, 1984 — F
Argentina: 72/U23-6/Youth

League Club	Source	Date Signed	Seasons Played	Apps	Subs	Gls
West Ham U (L)	Corinthians (BRA)	08/06	06	19	7	7
Manchester U (L)	Corinthians (BRA)	08/07	07-08	49	14	19
Manchester C	Tr	07/09	09-12	97	16	58

TEWLEY Alan Bernard
Born: Leicester, England, 22 January, 1945 — RW

League Club	Source	Date Signed	Seasons Played	Apps	Subs	Gls
Leicester C	App	03/62	66-68	15	3	5
Bradford Park Ave	Tr	11/69	69	28	0	4
Crewe Alex	Tr	10/70	70-72	57	11	12

[TEYMOURIAN] TIMOTIAN-SAMARANI Adranik
Born: Tehran, Iran, 6 March, 1983 — M
Iran: 60

League Club	Source	Date Signed	Seasons Played	Apps	Subs	Gls
Bolton W	Abu Moslem (IRA)	08/06	06-07	7	13	2
Fulham	Tr	07/08	08	0	1	0
Barnsley	L	02/09	08	10	1	0

THACKERAY Andrew John (Andy)
Born: Huddersfield, West Yorkshire, England, 13 February, 1968 — RB/M

League Club	Source	Date Signed	Seasons Played	Apps	Subs	Gls
Manchester C	Jnr	02/86				
Huddersfield T	Tr	08/86	86	2	0	0
Newport Co	Tr	03/87	86-87	53	1	4
Wrexham	Tr	07/88	88-91	139	13	14
Rochdale	Tr	07/92	92-96	161	4	13
Halifax T	Tr	08/97	98	37	1	5

THALASSITIS Michael
Born: Edmonton, N London, England, 19 January, 1993 — F
Cyprus: U21-4/Youth

League Club	Source	Date Signed	Seasons Played	Apps	Subs	Gls
Stevenage	Jnr	05/11	11-12	0	5	0

League Club	Source	Date Signed	Seasons Played	Apps	Subs	Gls
THARME Derek						
Born: Brighton, England, 19 August, 1938						RB
Tottenham H	Brighton & HA (Jnr)	10/56				
Southend U	Tr	05/62	62	7	-	0
THATCHER Benjamin David (Ben)						
Born: Swindon, England, 30 November, 1975						LB
England: U21-4/Youth//Wales: 7						
Millwall	FA School, Lilleshall	12/92	93-95	87	3	1
Wimbledon	Tr	07/96	96-99	82	4	0
Tottenham H	Tr	07/00	00-02	29	7	0
Leicester C	Tr	07/03	03	28	1	1
Manchester C	Tr	06/04	04-06	46	1	0
Charlton Ath	Tr	01/07	06-07	21	1	0
Ipswich T	Tr	08/08	08	20	0	0
THEAKER Clarence Alfred (Cam)						
Born: Spalding, Lincolnshire, England, 8 December, 1912						G
Died: Hartlepool, Cleveland, England, 7 February, 1992						
Grimsby T	Spalding T	05/34	35-38	5	-	0
Newcastle U	Tr	11/38	38-46	13	-	0
Hartlepool U	Tr	06/47	47	14	-	0
THEAR Anthony Charles (Tony)						
Born: Edmonton, N London, England, 4 February, 1948						CF
Arsenal	Jnr	02/65				
Luton T	Tr	07/66	66	12	1	5
Gillingham	Tr	02/67	66-68	7	0	1
THELWELL Alton Anthony						
Born: Holloway, N London, England, 5 September, 1980						CD
England: U21-1						
Tottenham H	YT	01/99	00-01	13	5	0
Hull C	Tr	07/03	03-06	33	7	1
Leyton Orient	Tr	10/06	06-08	70	8	1
THEOBALD David John						
Born: Cambridge, England, 15 December, 1978						CD
Ipswich T	YT	06/97				
Brentford	Tr	07/99	99-01	26	5	0
Swansea C	Tr	07/02	02	9	1	0
Cambridge U	Tr	02/03	02	1	3	0
THEODOSIOU Andrew (Andy)						
Born: Stoke Newington, N London, England, 30 October, 1970						CD
Norwich C	Tottenham H (YT)	07/89				
Hereford U	Tr	07/91	91-92	41	1	2
THEOKLITOS Michael						
Born: Melbourne, Australia, 11 February, 1981						G
Blackpool	Auckland Kingz (NZL)	08/02	02	2	0	0
Norwich C	Melbourne Vic (AUS)	07/09	09	1	0	0
THEOPHILE-CATHERINE Kevin						
Born: Saint Brieuc, France, 28 October, 1989						CD
France: U21-1/Youth						
Cardiff C	Stade Rennais (FRA)	08/13	13	26	2	0
THETIS Jean-Manuel						
Born: Paris, France, 5 November, 1971						LB/M
Ipswich T	Sevilla (SPN)	09/98	98-99	44	3	2
Wolverhampton W	L	08/00	00	3	0	0
Sheffield U	Tr	03/01	00	0	1	0
THEW Lee						
Born: Sunderland, England, 23 October, 1974						M
Doncaster Rov	YT	08/93	93-94	21	11	2
Scarborough	Tr	08/95	95	9	5	0
[THIEVY] BIFOUMA Thievy Guivane						
Born: Paris, France, 13 May, 1992						F
France: U21-3/Youth						
West Bromwich A (L)	RCD Espanyol (SPN)	01/14	13	3	3	2
THIJSSEN Franciscus Johannes (Frans)						
Born: Nijmegen, Netherlands, 23 January, 1952						M
Netherlands: 14						
Ipswich T	Twente Enschede (NED)	02/79	78-82	123	2	10
Nottingham F	Vancouver W'caps (CAN)	10/83	83	17	0	3
THIRLBY Anthony Dennis						
Born: Berlin, Germany, 4 March, 1976						M
Northern Ireland: Youth						
Exeter C	YT	07/94	93-95	27	12	2
Torquay U	Dorchester T	02/97	96	1	2	0
THIRLWELL Paul						
Born: Washington, Tyne and Wear, England, 13 February, 1979						M
England: U21-1						
Sunderland	YT	04/97	98-03	55	22	0
Swindon T	L	09/99	99	12	0	0
Sheffield U	Tr	07/04	04	24	6	1
Derby Co	Tr	08/05	05	15	6	0
Carlisle U	Tr	09/06	06-14	212	19	7
THOGERSEN Thomas						
Born: Copenhagen, Denmark, 2 April, 1968						M/RB
Portsmouth	Brondby (DEN)	08/98	98-01	95	13	8
Walsall	L	10/01	01	7	0	2
THOLOT Didier						
Born: Feurs, Loire, France, 2 April, 1964						F
Walsall (L)	FC Sion (SUI)	03/98	97	13	1	4
THOM Lewis McDonald						
Born: Stornoway, Lewis, Western Isles, Scotland, 10 April, 1944						LW
Shrewsbury T	Dundee U	09/65	65-66	48	1	5
Lincoln C	Tr	05/67	66-68	45	2	4
Bradford Park Ave	Tr	06/69	69	31	0	1
THOM Stuart Paul						
Born: Dewsbury, West Yorkshire, England, 27 December, 1976						CD
Nottingham F	YT	01/94				
Mansfield T	L	12/97	97	5	0	0
Oldham Ath	Tr	10/98	98-99	28	6	3
Scunthorpe U	Tr	08/00	00-01	34	7	2
THOMAS Andrew Mark (Andy)						
Born: Keynsham, Avon, England, 16 December, 1962						M/F
Oxford U	App	12/80	80-85	89	27	32
Fulham	L	12/82	82	3	1	2
Derby Co	L	03/83	82	0	1	0
Newcastle U	Tr	09/86	86-87	24	7	6
Bradford C	Tr	06/88	88	15	8	5
Plymouth Arg	Tr	07/89	89-90	47	3	18
THOMAS Andrew Richard (Andy)						
Born: Stockport, Greater Manchester, England, 2 December, 1982						D
Stockport Co	YT	07/01	01-02	8	4	0
THOMAS Anthony (Tony)						
Born: Liverpool, England, 12 July, 1971						LB/M
Tranmere Rov	YT	02/89	88-96	254	3	12
Everton	Tr	08/97	97-98	6	2	0
THOMAS Anthony Christopher						
Born: Hammersmith, W London, England, 30 August, 1982						F
Barnet	Hemel Hempstead T	07/07	07	14	12	4
THOMAS Aswad Kwame						
Born: Westminster, Central London, England, 9 August, 1989						LB
Charlton Ath	Sch	07/07				
Accrington Stan	L	01/08	07	13	0	2
Barnet	L	08/08	08	2	0	0
THOMAS Barrie						
Born: Merthyr Tydfil, Wales, 27 August, 1954						M
Swansea C (Am)	Jnr	08/71	71	2	0	0
Bournemouth	Merthyr Tydfil	08/79	79	3	0	0
THOMAS Bradley Mark (Brad)						
Born: Forest Gate, E London, England, 29 March, 1984						CD
Peterborough U	Sch	07/03				
Yeovil T	Eastleigh	01/06				
Boston U	L	01/07	06	11	0	2
THOMAS Brian						
Born: Neath, Wales, 7 June, 1976						G
Hereford U	YT	-	93	3	0	0
THOMAS Brian Hugh						
Born: Carmarthen, Wales, 28 June, 1944						WH
Swansea C	Jnr	06/62	64	4	-	0
THOMAS Brynley (Bryn)						
Born: Coventry, England, 13 December, 1932						CF
Died: Kent, England, March, 2005						
Coventry C	Longford Rov, Coventry	09/50	52-53	12	-	1
THOMAS Casey Elliot						
Born: Port Talbot, Wales, 14 November, 1990						W
Wales: U21-3/Youth						
Swansea C	Sch	07/09	09	0	1	0
Colchester U	L	11/11	11	0	2	0
THOMAS Cedric David						
Born: Hebden Bridge, West Yorkshire, England, 19 September, 1936						RW
Halifax T	Heptonstall	07/57	57-59	20	-	5
Southport	Tr	07/60				

THOMAS Conor
Born: Coventry, England, 29 October, 1993 — DM
England: Youth

League Club	Source	Date Signed	Seasons Played	Apps	Subs	Gls
Coventry C	Sch	10/10	11-14	79	18	1

THOMAS Daniel Anthony (Dan)
Born: Poole, Dorset, England, 1 September, 1991 — G

League Club	Source	Date Signed	Seasons Played	Apps	Subs	Gls
Bournemouth	Jnr	07/10	09	1	1	0

THOMAS Daniel Joseph (Danny)
Born: Worksop, Nottinghamshire, England, 12 November, 1961 — RB
England: 2/U21-7/Schools

League Club	Source	Date Signed	Seasons Played	Apps	Subs	Gls
Coventry C	App	12/78	79-82	103	5	5
Tottenham H	Tr	06/83	83-86	80	7	1

THOMAS Daniel Justin (Danny)
Born: Leamington Spa, Warwickshire, England, 1 May, 1981 — LW

League Club	Source	Date Signed	Seasons Played	Apps	Subs	Gls
Leicester C	Nottingham F (YT)	05/98	99	0	3	0
Bournemouth	Tr	02/02	01-03	35	24	2
Boston U	Tr	03/04	03-05	55	27	8
Shrewsbury T	Cheltenham T (NC)	11/06	06	3	3	0
Hereford U	Tr	01/07	06	15	0	2
Macclesfield T	Tr	07/07	07-08	67	16	6

THOMAS Daniel Wayne (Danny)
Born: Blackwood, Caerphilly, Wales, 13 May, 1985 — F
Wales: Youth

League Club	Source	Date Signed	Seasons Played	Apps	Subs	Gls
Cardiff C	Sch	05/02	04	0	1	0

THOMAS David (Dave)
Born: Kirkby-in-Ashfield, Nottinghamshire, England, 5 October, 1950 — RW
England: 8/U23-11/Youth

League Club	Source	Date Signed	Seasons Played	Apps	Subs	Gls
Burnley	App	10/67	66-72	153	4	19
Queens Park Rgrs	Tr	10/72	72-76	181	1	27
Everton	Tr	08/77	77-78	71	0	4
Wolverhampton W	Tr	10/79	79	10	0	0
Middlesbrough	Vancouver W'caps (CAN)	03/82	81	13	0	1
Portsmouth	Tr	07/82	82-84	24	6	0

THOMAS David Anthony (Dai)
Born: Cymmer, Neath Port Talbot, Wales, 1 August, 1926 — FB/IF
Died: November, 2014
Wales: 2

League Club	Source	Date Signed	Seasons Played	Apps	Subs	Gls
Swansea C	Abercregan Jnrs	08/48	49-59	296	-	15
Newport Co	Tr	07/61	61-62	58	-	1

THOMAS David Gwyn (Gwyn)
Born: Swansea, Wales, 26 September, 1957 — M
Wales: U21-3/Youth/Schools

League Club	Source	Date Signed	Seasons Played	Apps	Subs	Gls
Leeds U	App	07/75	74-83	79	10	3
Barnsley	Tr	03/84	83-89	197	4	17
Hull C	Tr	03/90	89-90	21	1	0
Carlisle U	Tr	08/91	91	35	2	1

THOMAS David John (Dai)
Born: Caerphilly, Wales, 26 September, 1975 — F
Wales: U21-2

League Club	Source	Date Signed	Seasons Played	Apps	Subs	Gls
Swansea C	YT	07/94	94-96	36	20	10
Watford	Tr	07/97	97	8	8	3
Cardiff C	Tr	08/98	98-99	21	10	5

THOMAS David Sidney (Sidney)
Born: Machynlleth, Powys, Wales, 12 November, 1919 — W
Died: Machynlleth, Powys, Wales, 19 January, 2012
Wales: 4

League Club	Source	Date Signed	Seasons Played	Apps	Subs	Gls
Fulham	Treharris	08/38	46-49	57	-	4
Bristol C	Tr	06/50	50	13	-	1

THOMAS David Stuart Lynne (Lyn)
Born: Swansea, Wales, 19 September, 1920 — CF
Died: Waltham Forest, NE London, England, 21 April, 1993
Wales: Schools

League Club	Source	Date Signed	Seasons Played	Apps	Subs	Gls
Swansea C	Abercregan Jnrs	10/42				
Brighton & HA	Tr	06/47	47	13	-	4

THOMAS David Watkin John (Dave)
Born: Stepney, E London, England, 6 July, 1917 — CF
Died: Dovercourt, Essex, England, 30 March, 1991

League Club	Source	Date Signed	Seasons Played	Apps	Subs	Gls
Plymouth Arg	Romford	06/38	38-47	74	-	29
Watford	Tr	02/48	47-50	105	-	41
Gillingham	Tr	10/50	50-52	80	-	42

THOMAS Dean Ronald
Born: Bedworth, Warwickshire, England, 19 December, 1961 — LB/M

League Club	Source	Date Signed	Seasons Played	Apps	Subs	Gls
Wimbledon	Nuneaton Bor	07/81	81-83	57	0	8
Northampton T	Fort Dusseldorf (GER)	08/88	88-89	74	0	11
Notts Co	Tr	03/90	89-93	129	5	8

THOMAS Dennis
Born: Hebburn, Tyne and Wear, England, 2 February, 1926 — LW

League Club	Source	Date Signed	Seasons Played	Apps	Subs	Gls
Bury	Wardley CW	01/49	49	3	-	0
Accrington Stan	Tr	07/50	50	34	-	5

THOMAS Edward (Eddie)
Born: Newton-le-Willows, Merseyside, England, 23 October, 1933 — IF
Died: Derby, England, 12 November, 2003

League Club	Source	Date Signed	Seasons Played	Apps	Subs	Gls
Everton	Jnr	10/51	56-59	86	-	39
Blackburn Rov	Tr	02/60	59-61	37	-	9
Swansea C	Tr	07/62	62-64	68	-	21
Derby Co	Tr	08/64	64-67	102	3	43
Leyton Orient	Tr	09/67	67	11	0	2

THOMAS Edwin Henry Charles
Born: Swindon, England, 9 November, 1932 — G

League Club	Source	Date Signed	Seasons Played	Apps	Subs	Gls
Southampton	Swindon British Rail	05/51	50-51	8	-	0

THOMAS Ernest Barrie (Barrie)
Born: Measham, Leicestershire, England, 19 May, 1937 — CF
England: Youth

League Club	Source	Date Signed	Seasons Played	Apps	Subs	Gls
Leicester C	Measham Imperial	07/54	54-55	7	-	3
Mansfield T	Tr	06/57	57-59	72	-	48
Scunthorpe U	Tr	09/59	59-61	91	-	67
Newcastle U	Tr	01/62	61-64	73	-	48
Scunthorpe U	Tr	11/64	64-66	52	0	26
Barnsley	Tr	11/66	66-67	43	0	19

THOMAS Geoffrey (Geoff)
Born: Swansea, Wales, 18 February, 1948 — M
Died: Mumbles, Swansea, Wales, 13 January, 2013
Wales: U23-3

League Club	Source	Date Signed	Seasons Played	Apps	Subs	Gls
Swansea C	App	02/66	65-75	345	12	52

THOMAS Geoffrey Paul (Geoff)
Born: Bradford, England, 12 March, 1946 — RB

League Club	Source	Date Signed	Seasons Played	Apps	Subs	Gls
Bradford Park Ave	App	03/63	63-65	53	0	0

THOMAS Geoffrey Robert (Geoff)
Born: Manchester, England, 5 August, 1964 — M
England: 9/B-3

League Club	Source	Date Signed	Seasons Played	Apps	Subs	Gls
Rochdale	Littleborough	08/82	82-83	10	1	1
Crewe Alex	Tr	03/84	83-86	120	5	21
Crystal Palace	Tr	06/87	87-92	192	3	26
Wolverhampton W	Tr	06/93	93-96	36	10	8
Nottingham F	Tr	07/97	97-98	18	7	4
Barnsley	Tr	07/99	99-00	14	24	4
Notts Co	Tr	03/01	00	8	0	1
Crewe Alex	Tr	08/01	01	8	6	2

THOMAS George Stanley
Born: Oadby, Leicestershire, England, 24 March, 1997 — M

League Club	Source	Date Signed	Seasons Played	Apps	Subs	Gls
Coventry C	Sch	05/15	13-14	1	6	0

THOMAS George Vincent
Born: Cardiff, Wales, 25 June, 1930 — WH
Died: Rhondda, Wales, February, 2014

League Club	Source	Date Signed	Seasons Played	Apps	Subs	Gls
Cardiff C	Cardiff Nomads	05/49				
Newport Co	Tr	07/53	53-58	137	-	0

THOMAS Gerald Shannon (Geoff)
Born: Derby, England, 21 February, 1926 — FB
Died: Nottingham, England, 18 July, 2006

League Club	Source	Date Signed	Seasons Played	Apps	Subs	Gls
Nottingham F	Jnr	09/43	46-59	404	-	1

THOMAS Glen Andrew
Born: Hackney, E London, England, 6 October, 1967 — D

League Club	Source	Date Signed	Seasons Played	Apps	Subs	Gls
Fulham	App	10/85	86-94	246	5	6
Peterborough U	Tr	11/94	94	6	2	0
Barnet	Tr	03/95	94-95	22	1	0
Gillingham	Tr	01/96	95-97	20	8	0
Brighton & HA	Tr	07/98	98	2	1	0

THOMAS Hendry Bernardo
Born: La Ceiba, Honduras, 23 February, 1985 — DM
Honduras: 52

League Club	Source	Date Signed	Seasons Played	Apps	Subs	Gls
Wigan Ath	Olimpia (HON)	07/09	09-10	49	6	0

THOMAS Jack
Born: Sutton-in-Ashfield, Nottinghamshire, England, 3 June, 1996 — M

League Club	Source	Date Signed	Seasons Played	Apps	Subs	Gls
Mansfield T	Jnr	07/13	13-14	11	2	1

THOMAS James Alan
Born: Swansea, Wales, 16 January, 1979 — F
Wales: U21-21/Youth

League Club	Source	Date Signed	Seasons Played	Apps	Subs	Gls
Blackburn Rov	YT	07/96	00	1	3	1
West Bromwich A	L	08/97	97	1	2	0
Blackpool	L	03/00	99	9	0	2
Sheffield U	L	11/00	00	3	7	1
Bristol Rov	L	03/02	01	7	0	1
Swansea C	Tr	07/02	02-04	42	15	16

League Club	Source	Date Signed	Seasons Played	Career Record Apps	Subs	Gls
THOMAS Jeffrey (Jeff)						
Born: Newport, Wales, 18 May, 1949						RW
Wales: U23-1/Youth/Schools						
Newport Co	Jnr	05/66	65-72	207	3	31
THOMAS Jerome William						
Born: Wembley, NW London, England, 23 March, 1983						LW
England: U21-2/Youth						
Arsenal	YT	07/01				
Queens Park Rgrs	L	03/02	01	4	0	1
Queens Park Rgrs	L	08/02	02	5	1	2
Charlton Ath	Tr	02/04	03-08	74	29	7
Portsmouth	Tr	08/08	08	0	3	0
West Bromwich A	Tr	08/09	09-12	84	15	11
Leeds U	L	11/12	12	6	0	1
Crystal Palace	Tr	07/13	13-14	3	7	0
THOMAS Joel Fabrice Goho Bah						
Born: Caen, France, 30 June, 1987						F
Colchester U	Hamilton Academical	07/09	09	0	4	0
THOMAS John (Jack)						
Born: Poole, Dorset, England, 28 May, 1936						G
Bournemouth	Poole T	05/58	58	4	-	0
THOMAS John Charles (Joe)						
Born: Great Houghton, South Yorkshire, England, 22 September, 1932						RB
Wolverhampton W	Wath W	08/51				
Barnsley	Tr	06/52	52-57	134	-	0
Mansfield T	Tr	03/58	57-58	41	-	0
Chesterfield	Tr	07/59	59	6	-	0
THOMAS John Ernest						
Born: Walsall, West Midlands, England, 15 July, 1922						CF
Died: Smethwick, West Midlands, England, 28 November, 1999						
Bournemouth		05/46				
West Bromwich A	Tr	07/46				
Crystal Palace	Tr	10/48	48-51	53	-	17
THOMAS John Wilfred (Johnny)						
Born: Liverpool, England, 23 December, 1926						RW
Died: Melksham, Wiltshire, England, 5 February, 2006						
Everton		12/48				
Swindon T	Tr	02/49	50-51	17	-	3
Chester C	Headington U	07/53	53	29	-	5
Stockport Co	Tr	07/54	54	6	-	0
THOMAS John William						
Born: Wednesbury, West Midlands, England, 5 August, 1958						F
Everton	Jnr	07/77				
Tranmere Rov	L	03/79	78	10	1	2
Halifax T	L	10/79	79	5	0	0
Bolton W	Tr	06/80	80-81	18	4	6
Chester C	Tr	08/82	82	44	0	20
Lincoln C	Tr	08/83	83-84	56	11	17
Preston NE	Tr	06/85	85-86	69	9	38
Bolton W	Tr	07/87	87-88	71	2	31
West Bromwich A	Tr	07/89	89	8	10	1
Preston NE	Tr	02/90	89-91	24	3	6
Hartlepool U	Tr	03/92	91	5	2	1
Halifax T	Tr	07/92	92	10	2	0
THOMAS Kevin Anthony						
Born: Prescot, Merseyside, England, 13 August, 1945						G
Blackpool	Prescot T	06/66	66-68	12	0	0
Tranmere Rov	Tr	09/69	69-70	18	0	0
Oxford U	Tr	07/71	72	5	0	0
Southport	Tr	07/74	74-75	67	0	0
THOMAS Kwame Blair						
Born: Nottingham, England, 28 September, 1995						F
England: Youth						
Derby Co	Sch	07/13	14	0	4	0
Notts Co	L	01/15	14	2	3	0
THOMAS Lee						
Born: Tredegar, Blaenau Gwent, Wales, 1 November, 1970						FB
Hereford U	Newport Co (YT)	07/89	89	0	1	0
THOMAS Martin Richard						
Born: Senghenydd, Caerphilly, Wales, 28 November, 1959						G
Wales: 1/U21-2/Youth						
Bristol Rov	App	09/77	76-81	162	0	0
Cardiff C	L	07/82	82	15	0	0
Southend U	L	02/83	82	6	0	0
Newcastle U	Tr	03/83	82-87	118	0	0
Middlesbrough	L	10/84	84	4	0	0
Birmingham C	Tr	10/88	88-92	144	0	0
THOMAS Martin Russell						
Born: Lyndhurst, Hampshire, England, 12 September, 1973						M
Southampton	YT	06/92				
Leyton Orient	Tr	03/94	93	5	0	2
Fulham	Tr	07/94	94-97	59	31	8
Swansea C	Tr	07/98	98-00	70	21	8
Brighton & HA	Tr	03/01	00	1	7	0
Oxford U	Tr	07/01	01	13	1	2
Exeter C	Tr	08/02	02	22	4	3
THOMAS Michael David						
Born: Manchester, England, 12 August, 1992						M
Macclesfield T	Sch	06/10	09-11	2	8	0
THOMAS Michael Lauriston						
Born: Lambeth, S London, England, 24 August, 1967						M
England: 2/B-5/U21-12/Youth/Schools						
Arsenal	App	12/84	86-91	149	14	24
Portsmouth	L	12/86	86	3	0	0
Liverpool	Tr	12/91	91-97	96	28	9
Middlesbrough	L	02/98	97	10	0	0
Wimbledon	Benfica (POR)	08/00	00	5	3	0
THOMAS Michael Reginald (Mickey)						
Born: Colwyn Bay, Conwy, Wales, 7 July, 1954						M
Wales: 51/U23-1/U21-2						
Wrexham	Jnr	05/72	71-78	217	13	33
Manchester U	Tr	11/78	78-80	90	0	11
Everton	Tr	08/81	81	10	0	0
Brighton & HA	Tr	11/81	81	18	2	0
Stoke C	Tr	08/82	82-83	57	0	14
Chelsea	Tr	01/84	83-84	43	1	9
West Bromwich A	Tr	09/85	85	20	0	0
Derby Co	L	03/86	85	9	0	0
Shrewsbury T	Wichita Wings (USA)	08/88	88	40	0	1
Leeds U	Tr	06/89	89	3	0	0
Stoke C	L	03/90	89	8	0	0
Stoke C	Tr	08/90	90	32	6	7
Wrexham	Tr	07/91	91-92	34	0	2
THOMAS Mitchell Anthony						
Born: Luton, England, 2 October, 1964						LB
England: B-1/U21-3/Youth						
Luton T	App	08/82	82-85	106	1	1
Tottenham H	Tr	07/86	86-90	136	21	6
West Ham U	Tr	08/91	91-92	37	1	3
Luton T	Tr	11/93	93-98	170	15	5
Burnley	Tr	07/99	99-01	95	4	0
THOMAS Nathan						
Born: Thornaby, Cleveland, England, 27 September, 1994						W
Plymouth Arg	Darlington 1883	12/13	13-14	3	16	1
THOMAS Patrick (Pat)						
Born: Sidmouth, Devon, England, 7 March, 1965						M
Exeter C	Sidmouth T	06/82	82	0	1	0
THOMAS Peter John						
Born: Treforest, Rhondda Cynon Taff, Wales, 18 October, 1932						RW
Cardiff C	Jnr	03/53	53	4	-	1
Exeter C	Tr	12/54	54-55	29	-	4
Newport Co	Tr	07/56	56-57	6	-	1
THOMAS Peter John						
Born: Coventry, England, 20 November, 1944						G
Republic of Ireland: 2						
Coventry C	GEC, Coventry	06/66	66	1	0	0
THOMAS Philip Leslie (Phil)						
Born: Sherborne, Dorset, England, 14 December, 1952						M/RB
Died: Poole, Dorset, England, August, 1998						
Bournemouth	App	12/70				
Colchester U	Tr	05/72	72-75	103	5	8
THOMAS Rees						
Born: Aberdare, Rhondda Cynon Taff, Wales, 3 January, 1934						RB
Cardiff C	Jnr	01/51				
Torquay U	L	08/53	53	1	-	0
Brighton & HA	Tr	09/56	56-57	31	-	1
Bournemouth	Tr	01/58	57-58	48	-	0
Portsmouth	Tr	07/59	59-60	30	-	0
Aldershot	Tr	07/61	61-63	103	-	2
THOMAS Robert Albert (Bob)						
Born: Stepney, E London, England, 2 August, 1919						IF
Died: Sutton, S London, England, March, 1990						
Brentford	Hendon	05/39				
Plymouth Arg	Tr	04/46	46	41	-	17
Fulham	Tr	06/47	47-51	167	-	55
Crystal Palace	Tr	09/52	52-54	96	-	31

League Club	Source	Date Signed	Seasons Played	Apps	Subs	Gls

THOMAS Robert Owen
Born: Redditch, Worcestershire, England, 27 August, 1950 — M

Blackpool		06/69	69	0	1	0

THOMAS Roderick Clive (Rod)
Born: Harlesden, NW London, England, 10 October, 1970 — RW
England: U21-1/Youth/Schools

Watford	YT	05/88	87-92	63	21	9
Gillingham	L	03/92	91	8	0	1
Carlisle U	Tr	07/93	93-96	124	22	16
Chester C	Tr	07/97	97-98	28	16	7
Brighton & HA	Tr	10/98	98-00	25	23	4

THOMAS Roderick John (Rod)
Born: Glyncorrwg, Neath Port Talbot, Wales, 11 January, 1947 — RB
Wales: 50/U23-6

Swindon T	Gloucester C	07/64	65-73	296	0	4
Derby Co	Tr	11/73	73-77	89	0	2
Cardiff C	Tr	11/77	77-81	89	7	0
Newport Co	Gloucester C	03/82	81	3	0	0

THOMAS Scott Lee
Born: Bury, Greater Manchester, England, 30 October, 1974 — M

Manchester C	YT	03/92	94	0	2	0
Brighton & HA	L	03/98	97	7	0	0

THOMAS Simon Vaughn
Born: Stratford, E London, England, 21 July, 1984 — F

Crystal Palace	Boreham Wood	07/08	08	0	1	0
Rotherham U	L	02/09	08	2	0	0
Darlington	L	10/09	09	7	0	1

THOMAS Stanley Herbert (Stan)
Born: Birkenhead, Wirral, England, 5 September, 1919 — IF
Died: Taunton, Somerset, England, October, 1985

Tranmere Rov (Am)	Oxford Univ	12/48	48	1	-	0

THOMAS Stephen (Steve)
Born: Hartlepool, Cleveland, England, 23 June, 1979 — M
Wales: U21-5/Youth

Wrexham	YT	07/97	98-03	85	31	7
Darlington	Tr	08/04	04-05	11	7	0

THOMAS Steven
Born: Batley, West Yorkshire, England, 29 January, 1957 — FB

Swansea C (Am)	Jnr	08/73	73-74	10	0	0

THOMAS Valmore Neville
Born: Worksop, Nottinghamshire, England, 30 April, 1958 — LB

Coventry C	App	03/76				
Hereford U	Tr	03/79	78-80	31	1	1

THOMAS Walter Keith (Keith)
Born: Oswestry, Shropshire, England, 28 July, 1929 — RW

Sheffield Wed	Oswestry T	09/50	50-51	10	-	1
Cardiff C	Tr	07/52	52-53	9	-	4
Plymouth Arg	Tr	11/53	53-55	35	-	8
Exeter C	Tr	03/56	55-56	43	-	6

THOMAS Wayne
Born: Walsall, West Midlands, England, 28 August, 1978 — M

Walsall	YT	07/96	96-99	18	20	0
Mansfield T	L	08/99	99	4	1	0
Shrewsbury T	Tr	01/00	99-00	15	2	1

THOMAS Wayne Junior Robert
Born: Gloucester, England, 17 May, 1979 — CD

Torquay U	YT	07/97	95-99	89	34	5
Stoke C	Tr	06/00	00-04	188	1	7
Burnley	Tr	07/05	05-07	46	4	1
Southampton	Tr	08/07	07-09	39	6	0
Doncaster Rov	Tr	08/10	10	17	4	0
Rochdale (L)	Luton T	03/13	12	2	0	0

THOMAS Wesley Alexander Nevada (Wes)
Born: Barking, E London, England, 23 January, 1987 — F

Dagenham & Red	Fisher Ath	09/08	08-09	4	24	3
Cheltenham T	Tr	07/10	10	40	1	18
Crawley T	Tr	07/11	11	2	4	1
Bournemouth	Tr	09/11	11-13	40	12	11
Portsmouth	L	09/12	12	6	0	3
Blackpool	L	11/12	12	7	2	3
Birmingham C	L	01/13	12	5	6	3
Rotherham U	Tr	01/14	13	8	5	5
Birmingham C	Tr	06/14	14	9	24	4

THOMAS William Pryce (Billy)
Born: Glyn Neath, Neath Port Talbot, Wales, 28 October, 1923 — LW
Died: Torbay, Devon, England, August, 2014

Torquay U	Merthyr Tydfil	09/47	47-54	90	-	17

THOMAS Wilson George (Bill)
Born: Derby, England, 18 November, 1918 — IF
Died: Long Ashton, Avon, England, 24 November, 2001

Bristol C	Matlock T	10/44	46-49	77	-	18

THOMAS-MOORE Ian Ronald
Born: Birkenhead, Wirral, England, 26 August, 1976 — F
England: U21-7/Youth

Tranmere Rov	YT	07/94	94-96	41	17	12
Bradford C	L	09/96	96	6	0	0
Nottingham F	Tr	03/97	96-97	3	12	1
West Ham U	L	09/97	97	0	1	0
Stockport Co	Tr	07/98	98-00	83	10	20
Burnley	Tr	11/00	00-04	170	22	37
Leeds U	Tr	03/05	04-06	20	39	2
Hartlepool U	Tr	07/07	07	22	2	6
Tranmere Rov	Tr	01/08	07-10	113	8	33
Rotherham U	Tr	01/11	10	11	1	3

THOME Emerson Augusto
Born: Porto Alegre, Brazil, 30 March, 1972 — CD

Sheffield Wed	Benfica (POR)	03/98	97-99	60	1	1
Chelsea	Tr	12/99	99-00	19	2	0
Sunderland	Tr	09/00	00-02	43	1	2
Bolton W	Tr	08/03	03	25	1	0
Wigan Ath	Tr	08/04	04	11	4	0
Derby Co	L	10/05	05	3	1	0

THOMPSON Adam Lee
Born: Harlow, Essex, England, 28 September, 1992 — D
Northern Ireland: 2/U21-11

Watford	Sch	11/10	10-12	7	7	1
Brentford	L	08/11	11	8	0	0
Brentford	L	02/12	11	8	4	0
Wycombe W	L	08/12	12	2	0	0
Barnet	L	01/13	12	0	1	0
Southend U	L	08/13	13	7	2	0
Southend U	Tr	01/14	13-14	33	2	0

THOMPSON Alan
Born: Goole, East Riding of Yorkshire, England, 2 September, 1931 — FB

Luton T	Westpark Jnrs	12/49	56	1	-	0

THOMPSON Alan
Born: Newcastle-upon-Tyne, England, 22 December, 1973 — LW
England: U21-2/Youth

Newcastle U	YT	03/91	91-92	13	3	0
Bolton W	Tr	07/93	93-97	143	14	33
Aston Villa	Tr	06/98	98-99	36	10	4
Leeds U	Glasgow Celtic	01/07	06-07	18	6	5
Hartlepool U	L	01/08	07	7	0	1

THOMPSON Alexander (Alex)
Born: Sheffield, England, 8 December, 1917 — RB
Died: Sheffield, England, August, 2002

Sheffield Wed	Woodhouse Alliance	06/37				
Lincoln C	Tr	03/39	46-47	34	-	1
Tranmere Rov	Tr	06/48	48	1	-	0

THOMPSON Andrew Richard (Andy)
Born: Cannock, Staffordshire, England, 9 November, 1967 — LB/M

West Bromwich A	App	11/85	85-86	18	6	1
Wolverhampton W	Tr	11/86	86-96	356	20	43
Tranmere Rov	Tr	07/97	97-99	91	5	4
Cardiff C	Tr	08/00	00	5	2	0
Shrewsbury T	Tr	01/02	01-02	29	1	0

THOMPSON Arthur
Born: Dewsbury, West Yorkshire, England, 15 June, 1922 — IF
Died: Mirfield, West Yorkshire, England, 6 July, 1996

Huddersfield T	Thornhill Edge	09/41	46-48	25	-	5

THOMPSON Brian
Born: Kingswinford, West Midlands, England, 9 February, 1950 — M

Wolverhampton W	App	02/67				
Oxford U	Tr	10/69	69-72	52	5	4
Torquay U	L	03/73	72	9	0	1

THOMPSON Charles Maskery (Charlie)
Born: Chesterfield, Derbyshire, England, 19 July, 1920 — CH/CF
Died: Hereford, England, August, 1997

Sheffield U	Bolsover Colliery	07/37	46	17	-	3

THOMPSON Christopher David (Chris)
Born: Walsall, West Midlands, England, 24 January, 1960 — M
Died: Sandwell, West Midlands, England, 5 June, 2012
England: Youth

Bolton W	App	07/77	79-82	66	7	18
Lincoln C	L	03/83	82	5	1	0

League Club	Source	Date Signed	Seasons Played	Apps	Subs	Gls
Blackburn Rov	Tr	08/83	83-85	81	4	24
Wigan Ath	Tr	07/86	86-87	67	7	12
Blackpool	Tr	07/88	88-89	27	12	8
Cardiff C	Tr	03/90	89	1	1	0
Walsall		02/91	90	3	0	0

THOMPSON Christopher Michael (Chris)
Born: Warrington, Cheshire, England, 7 February, 1982 — F

League Club	Source	Date Signed	Seasons Played	Apps	Subs	Gls
Grimsby T	Liverpool (YT)	07/01	01-02	7	7	1

THOMPSON Curtis Liam
Born: Nottingham, England, 2 September, 1993 — M/RB

League Club	Source	Date Signed	Seasons Played	Apps	Subs	Gls
Notts Co	Sch	10/11	12-14	29	15	0

THOMPSON Cyril Alfred
Born: Southend-on-Sea, England, 18 December, 1918 — CF
Died: Folkestone, Kent, England, 5 April, 1972

League Club	Source	Date Signed	Seasons Played	Apps	Subs	Gls
Southend U		07/45	46-47	66	-	36
Derby Co	Tr	07/48	48-49	16	-	3
Brighton & HA	Tr	03/50	49-50	41	-	15
Watford	Tr	03/51	50-52	78	-	36

THOMPSON David
Born: Middlesbrough, England, 26 February, 1945 — IF

League Club	Source	Date Signed	Seasons Played	Apps	Subs	Gls
Lincoln C	Whitby T	06/64	64	3	-	1

THOMPSON David Anthony
Born: Birkenhead, Wirral, England, 12 September, 1977 — M
England: U21-7/Youth

League Club	Source	Date Signed	Seasons Played	Apps	Subs	Gls
Liverpool	YT	11/94	96-99	24	24	5
Swindon T	L	11/97	97	10	0	0
Coventry C	Tr	08/00	00-02	61	5	15
Blackburn Rov	Tr	08/02	02-05	46	18	5
Wigan Ath	Tr	01/06	05	7	3	2
Portsmouth	Tr	07/06	06	5	7	0
Bolton W	Tr	01/07	06	3	5	0

THOMPSON David George (Dave)
Born: Ashington, Northumberland, England, 20 November, 1968 — CD

League Club	Source	Date Signed	Seasons Played	Apps	Subs	Gls
Millwall	App	11/86	87-91	88	9	6
Bristol C	Tr	06/92	92	17	0	0
Brentford	Tr	02/94	93	9	1	1
Blackpool	Tr	09/94	94	17	0	0
Cambridge U	Tr	03/95	94-96	36	8	2

THOMPSON David Stanley (Dave)
Born: Catterick Camp, North Yorkshire, England, 12 March, 1945 — RW

League Club	Source	Date Signed	Seasons Played	Apps	Subs	Gls
Wolverhampton W	Jnr	04/62	64	8	-	1
Southampton	Tr	08/66	66-70	21	2	0
Mansfield T	Tr	10/70	70-73	129	2	21
Chesterfield	Tr	12/73	73	14	0	3

THOMPSON David Stephen (Dave)
Born: Manchester, England, 27 May, 1962 — W

League Club	Source	Date Signed	Seasons Played	Apps	Subs	Gls
Rochdale	Withington	09/81	81-85	147	8	13
Notts Co	Tr	08/86	86-87	52	3	8
Wigan Ath	Tr	10/87	87-89	107	1	16
Preston NE	Tr	08/90	90-91	39	7	4
Chester C	Tr	08/92	92-93	70	10	9
Rochdale	Tr	08/94	94-96	90	21	11

THOMPSON Dennis
Born: Whitburn, Tyne and Wear, England, 10 April, 1924 — CF
Died: South Tyneside, Tyne and Wear, England, September, 2001

League Club	Source	Date Signed	Seasons Played	Apps	Subs	Gls
Hull C	Whitburn Colliery	04/47	46-47	9	-	8

THOMPSON Dennis
Born: Bolsover, Derbyshire, England, 19 July, 1934 — IF/RW

League Club	Source	Date Signed	Seasons Played	Apps	Subs	Gls
Chesterfield	Jnr	07/51	50-52	24	-	0
Scunthorpe U	Tr	07/55	55	3	-	0

THOMPSON Dennis
Born: Sheffield, England, 2 June, 1925 — W/IF
Died: Bournemouth, England, June, 1986
England: Schools

League Club	Source	Date Signed	Seasons Played	Apps	Subs	Gls
Sheffield U	Jnr	08/42	46-50	96	-	20
Southend U	Tr	07/51	51-53	51	-	11

THOMPSON Desmond (Des)
Born: Southampton, England, 4 December, 1928 — G
Died: Rotherham, South Yorkshire, England, July, 2010

League Club	Source	Date Signed	Seasons Played	Apps	Subs	Gls
York C	Dinnington	01/51	50-52	80	-	0
Burnley	Tr	11/52	52-54	62	-	0
Sheffield U	Tr	05/55	55-63	25	-	0

THOMPSON Edward Peter (Ed)
Born: Enfield, N London, England, 8 January, 1983 — G

League Club	Source	Date Signed	Seasons Played	Apps	Subs	Gls
Dagenham & Red	Wingate & Finchley	08/07	07-08	3	1	0

THOMPSON Frederick Norman (Freddie)
Born: Swindon, England, 24 November, 1937 — LH/FB
Died: Swindon, England, 22 May, 1998

League Club	Source	Date Signed	Seasons Played	Apps	Subs	Gls
Swindon T	Jnr	04/55	54-60	21	-	1

THOMPSON Garry Lindsey
Born: Birmingham, England, 7 October, 1959 — F
England: U21-6

League Club	Source	Date Signed	Seasons Played	Apps	Subs	Gls
Coventry C	App	06/77	77-82	127	7	38
West Bromwich A	Tr	02/83	82-84	91	0	39
Sheffield Wed	Tr	08/85	85	35	1	7
Aston Villa	Tr	06/86	86-88	56	4	17
Watford	Tr	12/88	88-89	24	10	8
Crystal Palace	Tr	03/90	89-90	17	3	3
Queens Park Rgrs	Tr	08/91	91-92	10	9	1
Cardiff C	Tr	07/93	93-94	39	4	5
Northampton T	Tr	02/95	94-96	36	14	6

THOMPSON Gary Kevin Langrish
Born: Kendal, Cumbria, England, 24 November, 1980 — RW
England: Semi Pro-5

League Club	Source	Date Signed	Seasons Played	Apps	Subs	Gls
Morecambe	Jnr	06/99	07	36	4	7
Scunthorpe U	Tr	07/08	08-11	60	51	20
Bradford C	Tr	07/12	12-13	55	30	8
Notts Co	Tr	07/14	14	36	5	12

THOMPSON George
Born: Lisburn, Belfast, Northern Ireland, 5 November, 1913 — RB
Republic of Ireland: LoI-1

League Club	Source	Date Signed	Seasons Played	Apps	Subs	Gls
Huddersfield T	Sligo Rov (ROI)	12/38				
Exeter C	Tr	06/46	46-47	63	-	4
Rochdale	Tr	07/48				

THOMPSON George Brian (Brian)
Born: Ashington, Northumberland, England, 7 August, 1952 — RB
England: Semi Pro-15

League Club	Source	Date Signed	Seasons Played	Apps	Subs	Gls
Sunderland		06/71				
York C	L	03/73	72	4	2	0
Mansfield T	Yeovil T	11/79	79	9	0	0

THOMPSON George Herbert
Born: Maltby, South Yorkshire, England, 15 September, 1926 — G
Died: Blackburn, Greater Manchester, England, 7 March, 2004
England: B-1

League Club	Source	Date Signed	Seasons Played	Apps	Subs	Gls
Huddersfield T	Dinnington	04/45				
Chesterfield	Tr	06/47				
Scunthorpe U	Tr	06/50	50-52	92	-	0
Preston NE	Tr	10/52	52-55	140	-	0
Manchester C	Tr	06/56	56	2	-	0
Carlisle U	Tr	06/57	57-61	204	-	0

THOMPSON Glyn William
Born: Telford, England, 24 February, 1981 — G

League Club	Source	Date Signed	Seasons Played	Apps	Subs	Gls
Shrewsbury T	YT	12/98	98	1	0	0
Fulham	Tr	11/99				
Mansfield T	L	01/00	99	16	0	0
Northampton T	Tr	11/02	02-03	18	1	0
Walsall	Tr	08/04				
Chesterfield	Stafford Rgrs	03/05	04	1	0	0
Shrewsbury T	Tr	07/05				
Hereford U	Tr	07/06				

THOMPSON Harold (Harry)
Born: Mansfield, Nottinghamshire, England, 29 April, 1915 — IF/WH
Died: Oxford, England, 29 January, 2000

League Club	Source	Date Signed	Seasons Played	Apps	Subs	Gls
Mansfield T	Mansfield Invicta	06/32				
Wolverhampton W	Tr	06/33	35-38	69	-	16
Sunderland	Tr	12/38	38	13	-	1
York C	Tr	12/45				
Northampton T	Tr	11/46	46-48	38	-	2

THOMPSON Henry
Born: South Shields, Tyne and Wear, England, 21 February, 1932 — CF
Died: South Shields, Tyne and Wear, England, 1981

League Club	Source	Date Signed	Seasons Played	Apps	Subs	Gls
Gateshead		08/51	51-55	24	-	5

THOMPSON Ian Peter
Born: Dartford, Kent, England, 8 June, 1958 — F

League Club	Source	Date Signed	Seasons Played	Apps	Subs	Gls
Bournemouth	Salisbury	07/83	83-85	119	2	30

THOMPSON James (Jimmy)
Born: Oldham, Greater Manchester, England, 26 November, 1935 — LH

League Club	Source	Date Signed	Seasons Played	Apps	Subs	Gls
Oldham Ath	Chadderton	01/54	53-58	110	-	19
Exeter C	Tr	12/58	58-60	105	-	10
Rochdale	Tr	03/61	60-65	199	0	15
Bradford C	Tr	12/65	65	23	1	1

THOMPSON James Butters (Jimmy)
Born: Felling, Tyne and Wear, England, 7 January, 1943 — RB

League Club	Source	Date Signed	Seasons Played	Apps	Subs	Gls
Grimsby T	St Mary's BC	09/61	62-66	156	0	2
Cambridge U	Port Elizabeth C (RSA)	01/69	70-72	117	1	0

THOMPSON John (Jack)
Born: Cramlington, Northumberland, England, 21 March, 1915 — IF
Died: Sheffield, England, November, 1996

League Club	Source	Date Signed	Seasons Played	Apps	Subs	Gls
Sheffield Wed	Blyth Spartans	06/33	33-38	36	-	9
Doncaster Rov	Tr	05/46	46-47	59	-	17
Chesterfield	Tr	07/48	48-52	82	-	8

THOMPSON John Henry
Born: Newcastle-upon-Tyne, England, 4 July, 1932 — G
Died: Beadnell, Northumberland, England, 29 December, 2006

League Club	Source	Date Signed	Seasons Played	Apps	Subs	Gls
Newcastle U	Jnr	09/50	54-55	8	-	0
Lincoln C	Tr	05/57	57-59	42	-	0

THOMPSON John Paul
Born: Dublin, Republic of Ireland, 12 October, 1981 — D/M
Republic of Ireland: 1/U21-11/Youth

League Club	Source	Date Signed	Seasons Played	Apps	Subs	Gls
Nottingham F	Home Farm (ROI)	07/99	01-06	100	29	7
Tranmere Rov	L	10/06	06	5	0	0
Tranmere Rov	L	01/07	06	7	0	0
Oldham Ath	Tr	07/07	07	6	1	0
Notts Co	Tr	10/08	08-10	96	4	2

THOMPSON John Trevor (Trevor)
Born: North Shields, Tyne and Wear, England, 21 May, 1955 — FB

League Club	Source	Date Signed	Seasons Played	Apps	Subs	Gls
West Bromwich A	App	05/73	73-75	20	0	0
Newport Co	Washington Dip's (USA)	08/78	78-79	32	3	2
Lincoln C	Tr	12/79	79-81	80	0	1

THOMPSON Joseph (Joe)
Born: Rochdale, Greater Manchester, England, 5 March, 1989 — W

League Club	Source	Date Signed	Seasons Played	Apps	Subs	Gls
Rochdale	Sch	07/07	05-11	84	56	15
Tranmere Rov	Tr	08/12	12-13	13	12	3
Rochdale	L	03/13	12	5	2	0
Bury	Tr	08/14	14	0	1	0

THOMPSON Joseph Prudhoe (Joe)
Born: Seaham, County Durham, England, 15 November, 1927 — RB
Died: Pontypridd, Rhondda Cynon Taff, Wales, October, 1996

League Club	Source	Date Signed	Seasons Played	Apps	Subs	Gls
Luton T	Electrolux	05/46				
Shrewsbury T	Tr	07/51	51	7	-	0

THOMPSON Joshua William (Josh)
Born: Bolton, Greater Manchester, England, 25 February, 1991 — CD
England: Youth

League Club	Source	Date Signed	Seasons Played	Apps	Subs	Gls
Stockport Co	Sch	05/09	08	6	3	0
Rochdale (L)	Glasgow Celtic	08/10	10	11	1	1
Chesterfield (L)	Glasgow Celtic	01/12	11	20	0	1
Portsmouth	Glasgow Celtic	08/12	12	2	0	0
Colchester U	Tr	11/12	12	16	6	1
Tranmere Rov	Tr	10/14	14	15	0	0

THOMPSON Justin
Born: Prince Rupert, British Columbia, Canada, 9 January, 1981 — CD
Canada: U23-7/Youth

League Club	Source	Date Signed	Seasons Played	Apps	Subs	Gls
Bury	Fairfield Univ (CAN)	10/03	03	1	0	0

THOMPSON Keith Anthony
Born: Birmingham, England, 24 April, 1965 — W
England: Youth

League Club	Source	Date Signed	Seasons Played	Apps	Subs	Gls
Coventry C	App	01/83	82-84	9	3	0
Wimbledon	L	10/83	83	0	3	0
Northampton T	L	03/85	84	10	0	1
Coventry C	Real Oviedo (SPN)	09/88	88-90	2	9	1

THOMPSON Kenneth Hurst (Ken)
Born: Sunderland, England, 24 April, 1926 — RB
Died: Shipston-on-Stour, Warwickshire, England, February, 2008

League Club	Source	Date Signed	Seasons Played	Apps	Subs	Gls
Middlesbrough	Jnr	11/44				
Gateshead	L	11/46	46	9	-	0
York C	Tr	07/50	50-51	22	-	0

THOMPSON Kenneth John (Ken)
Born: Ipswich, England, 1 March, 1945 — LH

League Club	Source	Date Signed	Seasons Played	Apps	Subs	Gls
Ipswich T	Jnr	03/62	64-65	11	1	0
Exeter C	Tr	06/66	66	38	1	1

THOMPSON Kevin John
Born: Middlesbrough, England, 8 September, 1948 — F

League Club	Source	Date Signed	Seasons Played	Apps	Subs	Gls
Hartlepool U (Am)	Threadhalls	09/69	69-70	6	0	1

THOMPSON Lee Jonathan
Born: Sheffield, England, 25 March, 1983 — RW
England: Schools

League Club	Source	Date Signed	Seasons Played	Apps	Subs	Gls
Sheffield U	Jnr	07/00				
Boston U	Tr	10/02	02-04	40	55	12

THOMPSON Leslie Allen (Les)
Born: Cleethorpes, North Lincolnshire, England, 23 September, 1968 — LB

League Club	Source	Date Signed	Seasons Played	Apps	Subs	Gls
Hull C	App	03/87	87-90	31	4	4
Scarborough	L	12/88	88	2	1	1
Maidstone U	Tr	07/91	91	38	0	0
Burnley	Tr	07/92	92-93	38	1	0

THOMPSON Leslie Allotey
Born: Newham, E London, England, 3 October, 1988 — W

League Club	Source	Date Signed	Seasons Played	Apps	Subs	Gls
Bolton W	Sch	08/07				
Stockport Co	L	10/07	07	3	0	0

THOMPSON Louis Clyde William
Born: Bristol, England, 19 December, 1994 — DM
Wales: Youth

League Club	Source	Date Signed	Seasons Played	Apps	Subs	Gls
Swindon T	Sch	06/13	12-14	23	13	2
Norwich C	Tr	08/14				
Swindon T	L	09/14	14	26	2	2

THOMPSON Malcolm George
Born: Hessle, East Riding of Yorkshire, England, 19 October, 1946 — F
Died: Anlaby, Hull, East Riding of Yorkshire, England, 24 October, 2014

League Club	Source	Date Signed	Seasons Played	Apps	Subs	Gls
Hartlepool U	Goole T	11/68	68-69	43	3	9
Gillingham	Tr	06/70				

THOMPSON Marc
Born: York, England, 15 January, 1982 — FB/M

League Club	Source	Date Signed	Seasons Played	Apps	Subs	Gls
York C	YT	06/00	99-00	18	4	0

THOMPSON Maxwell Stewart (Max)
Born: Liverpool, England, 31 December, 1956 — CD

League Club	Source	Date Signed	Seasons Played	Apps	Subs	Gls
Liverpool	App	01/74	73	1	0	0
Blackpool	Tr	12/77	77-80	92	7	7
Swansea C	Tr	09/81	81-82	25	1	2
Bournemouth	Tr	08/83	83	9	0	0
Port Vale	L	11/83	83	2	0	0

THOMPSON Nathan Michael
Born: Chester, England, 9 November, 1990 — RB

League Club	Source	Date Signed	Seasons Played	Apps	Subs	Gls
Swindon T	Sch	07/09	10-14	103	7	1

THOMPSON Neil
Born: Beverley, East Riding of Yorkshire, England, 2 October, 1963 — LB
England: Semi Pro-4

League Club	Source	Date Signed	Seasons Played	Apps	Subs	Gls
Hull C	Nottingham F (App)	11/81	81-82	29	2	0
Scarborough	Tr	08/83	87-88	87	0	15
Ipswich T	Tr	06/89	89-95	199	7	19
Barnsley	Tr	06/96	96-97	27	0	5
Oldham Ath	L	12/97	97	8	0	0
York C	Tr	03/98	97-99	42	0	8
Boston U	Scarborough	06/01	02	3	0	0

THOMPSON Neil Philip
Born: Hackney, E London, England, 30 April, 1978 — LB

League Club	Source	Date Signed	Seasons Played	Apps	Subs	Gls
Barnet	YT	07/96	95-96	2	1	0

THOMPSON Niall Joseph
Born: Birmingham, England, 16 April, 1974 — F
Canada: 9

League Club	Source	Date Signed	Seasons Played	Apps	Subs	Gls
Crystal Palace	Jnr	07/92				
Colchester U	Hong Kong	11/94	94	5	8	5
Brentford	Zultse VV (BEL)	02/98	97	6	2	0
Wycombe W	Bay Area Seals (USA)	10/00	00	6	2	0

THOMPSON Niall Joseph Israel
Born: Derby, England, 3 September, 1993 — RW

League Club	Source	Date Signed	Seasons Played	Apps	Subs	Gls
Torquay U	Sch	05/12	12-13	4	17	0

THOMPSON Nigel David
Born: Leeds, England, 1 March, 1967 — M

League Club	Source	Date Signed	Seasons Played	Apps	Subs	Gls
Leeds U	App	12/84	83-86	6	1	0
Rochdale	L	08/87	87	3	2	0
Chesterfield	Tr	03/88	87-89	18	2	1

THOMPSON O'Neil Anthony Michael Tyrone
Born: Kingston, Jamaica, 11 August, 1983 — DM
Jamaica: 21

League Club	Source	Date Signed	Seasons Played	Apps	Subs	Gls
Barnsley	Notodden FK (NOR)	08/09	09	1	0	0
Burton A	L	01/10	09	1	1	0
Hereford U	L	07/10	10	5	1	0

THOMPSON Patrick Alfred (Pat)
Born: Exeter, England, 11 February, 1932 — IF

League Club	Source	Date Signed	Seasons Played	Apps	Subs	Gls
Brighton & HA	Topsham	01/51	50	1	-	0

THOMPSON Paul Derek Zetland
Born: Newcastle-upon-Tyne, England, 17 April, 1973 — F

League Club	Source	Date Signed	Seasons Played	Apps	Subs	Gls
Hartlepool U	Redheugh BC, Gateshead	11/91	92-94	44	12	9

THOMPSON Peter
Born: Belfast, Northern Ireland, 2 May, 1984 — F
Northern Ireland: 8/U21-4

League Club	Source	Date Signed	Seasons Played	Apps	Subs	Gls
Stockport Co	Linfield	07/08	08-09	26	15	5

THOMPSON Peter
Born: Blackhall, County Durham, England, 16 February, 1936 — CF
England: Amateur-4

League Club	Source	Date Signed	Seasons Played	Apps	Subs	Gls
Wrexham (Am)	Blackhall CW	11/55	55-56	42	-	21
Hartlepool U	Tr	07/57	57-58	47	-	22
Derby Co	Tr	11/58	58-61	52	-	19
Bournemouth	Tr	01/62	61-62	39	-	14
Hartlepool U	Tr	09/63	63-65	91	0	34

THOMPSON Peter
Born: Carlisle, Cumbria, England, 27 November, 1942 — LW
England: 16/FLge-5/U23-4/Schools

League Club	Source	Date Signed	Seasons Played	Apps	Subs	Gls
Preston NE	Jnr	11/59	60-62	122	-	20
Liverpool	Tr	08/63	63-71	318	4	41
Bolton W	Tr	11/73	73-77	111	6	2

THOMPSON Peter Colin
Born: Mombasa, Kenya, 25 July, 1942 — W/FB

League Club	Source	Date Signed	Seasons Played	Apps	Subs	Gls
Peterborough U	Grantham	03/64	63-68	79	6	15

THOMPSON Philip Bernard (Phil)
Born: Liverpool, England, 21 January, 1954 — CD
England: 42/B-1/FLge/U23-1/Youth

League Club	Source	Date Signed	Seasons Played	Apps	Subs	Gls
Liverpool	App	02/71	71-82	337	3	7
Sheffield U	Tr	12/84	84-85	36	1	0

THOMPSON Philip Paul (Phil)
Born: Blackpool, Lancashire, England, 1 April, 1981 — CD

League Club	Source	Date Signed	Seasons Played	Apps	Subs	Gls
Blackpool	YT	09/98	97-01	37	10	3

THOMPSON Raymond (Ray)
Born: Coundon, County Durham, England, 21 October, 1925 — LB
Died: Bishop Auckland, County Durham, England, December, 1996

League Club	Source	Date Signed	Seasons Played	Apps	Subs	Gls
Sunderland	Ferryhill Jnrs	11/45				
Hartlepool U	Tr	01/47	46-57	396	-	2

THOMPSON Richard John
Born: Hawkesbury Upton, Gloucestershire, England, 11 April, 1969 — F

League Club	Source	Date Signed	Seasons Played	Apps	Subs	Gls
Newport Co	Yate T	01/87	87	10	3	2
Torquay U	Tr	06/88	88	11	4	4

THOMPSON Richard Omar
Born: Balham, S London, England, 2 May, 1974 — F

League Club	Source	Date Signed	Seasons Played	Apps	Subs	Gls
Wycombe W	Crawley T	03/99	99	1	5	0

THOMPSON Robert Eric (Eric)
Born: Mexborough, South Yorkshire, England, 3 December, 1944 — CH

League Club	Source	Date Signed	Seasons Played	Apps	Subs	Gls
Doncaster Rov	Leeds U (App)	07/62	62	9	-	0

THOMPSON Ronald (Ron)
Born: Carlisle, Cumbria, England, 20 January, 1932 — WH

League Club	Source	Date Signed	Seasons Played	Apps	Subs	Gls
Carlisle U	Raffles Rov	07/51	51-63	373	-	12

THOMPSON Ronald (Ron)
Born: Sheffield, England, 24 December, 1921 — IF
Died: Sheffield, England, 10 February, 1988

League Club	Source	Date Signed	Seasons Played	Apps	Subs	Gls
Sheffield Wed	Wadsley Common	04/45				
Rotherham U	Tr	05/47	47-48	30	-	11
York C	Tr	06/49	49	8	-	0

THOMPSON Ryan James Daley
Born: Lambeth, S London, England, 24 June, 1982 — F

League Club	Source	Date Signed	Seasons Played	Apps	Subs	Gls
Northampton T	YT	07/00	00	0	2	0

THOMPSON Sidney (Sid)
Born: Bedlington, Northumberland, England, 14 July, 1928 — IF
Died: Northumberland, England, July, 2012

League Club	Source	Date Signed	Seasons Played	Apps	Subs	Gls
Nottingham F	West Sleekburn	09/47	52-54	22	-	8
Scunthorpe U	Tr	08/55				

THOMPSON Simon Lee
Born: Sheffield, England, 27 February, 1970 — M/RB

League Club	Source	Date Signed	Seasons Played	Apps	Subs	Gls
Rotherham U	YT	06/88	88-90	12	16	0
Scarborough	Tr	12/91	91-94	99	9	6

THOMPSON Stephen (Steve)
Born: Peterlee, County Durham, England, 15 April, 1989 — F

League Club	Source	Date Signed	Seasons Played	Apps	Subs	Gls
Port Vale	Middlesbrough (Sch)	07/08	08	5	12	2

THOMPSON Steven Anthony (Steve)
Born: Manchester, England, 17 February, 1972 — CD

League Club	Source	Date Signed	Seasons Played	Apps	Subs	Gls
Gillingham	YT	-	89	1	1	0

THOMPSON Steven Howard (Steve)
Born: Paisley, Renfrewshire, Scotland, 14 October, 1978 — F
Scotland: 16/U21-12

League Club	Source	Date Signed	Seasons Played	Apps	Subs	Gls
Cardiff C	Glasgow Rangers	01/06	05-08	71	26	16
Burnley	Tr	09/08	08-10	26	57	13

THOMPSON Steven James (Steve)
Born: Oldham, Greater Manchester, England, 2 November, 1964 — M

League Club	Source	Date Signed	Seasons Played	Apps	Subs	Gls
Bolton W	App	11/82	82-91	329	6	50
Luton T	Tr	08/91	91	5	0	0
Leicester C	Tr	10/91	91-94	121	6	18
Burnley	Tr	02/95	94-96	44	5	1
Rotherham U	Tr	07/97	97-99	87	16	14
Halifax T	Tr	07/00	00	35	1	2

THOMPSON Steven John (Steve)
Born: Plymouth, England, 12 January, 1963 — M
England: Semi Pro-1

League Club	Source	Date Signed	Seasons Played	Apps	Subs	Gls
Bristol C	Jnr	07/81	81-82	10	2	1
Torquay U	Tr	02/83	82	0	1	0
Wycombe W	Slough T	02/92	93-94	41	21	3

THOMPSON Steven Paul (Steve)
Born: Sheffield, England, 28 July, 1955 — CD

League Club	Source	Date Signed	Seasons Played	Apps	Subs	Gls
Lincoln C	Boston U	04/80	80-84	153	1	8
Charlton Ath	Tr	08/85	85-87	95	0	0
Leicester C	Tr	07/88				
Sheffield U	Tr	11/88	88	20	0	1
Lincoln C	Tr	07/89	89	27	0	0

THOMPSON Stewart Christopher
Born: Littleborough, Greater Manchester, England, 2 September, 1964 — F
England: Schools

League Club	Source	Date Signed	Seasons Played	Apps	Subs	Gls
Rochdale	Blackburn Rov (App)	09/82	82-83	23	8	8

THOMPSON Terence William (Terry)
Born: Barlestone, Leicestershire, England, 25 December, 1946 — LB/M

League Club	Source	Date Signed	Seasons Played	Apps	Subs	Gls
Wolverhampton W	App	01/64				
Notts Co	Tr	03/66	65-67	66	0	3

THOMPSON Thomas (Tommy)
Born: Fencehouses, County Durham, England, 10 November, 1928 — IF
Died: 15 September, 2015
England: 2/B/FLge-2

League Club	Source	Date Signed	Seasons Played	Apps	Subs	Gls
Newcastle U	Lumley YMCA	08/46	47-49	20	-	6
Aston Villa	Tr	08/50	50-54	149	-	67
Preston NE	Tr	07/55	55-60	189	-	116
Stoke C	Tr	06/61	61-62	42	-	17
Barrow	Tr	03/63	62-63	44	-	16

THOMPSON Thomas William (Tommy)
Born: Stockton-on-Tees, Cleveland, England, 9 March, 1938 — FB
England: Amateur-4

League Club	Source	Date Signed	Seasons Played	Apps	Subs	Gls
Blackpool	Stockton	08/61	61-68	155	1	1
York C	Tr	07/70	70	4	0	0

THOMPSON Tyrone I'Yungo
Born: Sheffield, England, 8 May, 1982 — M

League Club	Source	Date Signed	Seasons Played	Apps	Subs	Gls
Sheffield U	YT	07/00				
Lincoln C	L	10/02	02	0	1	0
Huddersfield T	Tr	08/03	03	1	1	0
Torquay U	Crawley T	05/08	09	17	7	0

THOMPSON William (Billy)
Born: Bedlington, Northumberland, England, 5 January, 1940 — CH
Died: Bedlington, Northumberland, England, 30 September, 2011

League Club	Source	Date Signed	Seasons Played	Apps	Subs	Gls
Newcastle U	Jnr	01/57	60-66	79	1	1
Rotherham U	Tr	06/67	67	8	0	0
Darlington	Tr	01/68	67-69	30	0	5

THOMPSON William (Bill)
Born: Berwick-on-Tweed, Northumberland, England, 31 August, 1916 — G
Died: Sunderland, England, February, 1989

League Club	Source	Date Signed	Seasons Played	Apps	Subs	Gls
Leeds U	Ashington	08/35				
Watford		08/46	46	9	-	0

THOMPSON William
Born: Ashington, Northumberland, England, 23 December, 1921 — LW
Died: Ashington, Northumberland, England, 23 February, 1986

League Club	Source	Date Signed	Seasons Played	Apps	Subs	Gls
Gateshead		09/45	46-47	3	-	0

THOMPSON William Alan (Alan)
Born: Liverpool, England, 20 January, 1952 — CD

League Club	Source	Date Signed	Seasons Played	Apps	Subs	Gls
Sheffield Wed	App	01/69	70-75	150	6	3
Stockport Co	Tr	08/76	76-78	93	1	17
Bradford C	Portland Timbers (USA)	01/80	79-81	31	0	0
Scunthorpe U	Tr	03/82	81	11	0	0

THOMPSON William Gordon (Bill)
Born: Glasgow, Scotland, 10 August, 1921 — D
Died: Portsmouth, England, 26 December, 1986

League Club	Source	Date Signed	Seasons Played	Apps	Subs	Gls
Portsmouth	Carnoustie	03/46	48-52	40	-	2
Bournemouth	Tr	01/53	52-53	46	-	0

THOMPSON Zac Joseph
Born: Ashton-in-Makerfield, Greater Manchester, England, 5 January, 1993 RB/M

League Club	Source	Date Signed	Seasons Played	Apps	Subs	Gls
Leeds U	Everton (Sch)	04/11	11	7	2	0
Bury	L	10/12	12	29	0	1

THOMPSTONE Ian Philip
Born: Bury, Greater Manchester, England, 17 January, 1971 M

League Club	Source	Date Signed	Seasons Played	Apps	Subs	Gls
Manchester C	YT	09/89	87	0	1	1
Oldham Ath	Tr	05/90				
Exeter C	Tr	01/92	91	15	0	3
Halifax T	Tr	07/92	92	31	0	9
Scunthorpe U	Tr	03/93	92-94	47	13	8
Rochdale	Tr	07/95	95	11	14	1
Scarborough	Tr	08/96	96	12	7	2

THOMSEN Claus
Born: Aarhus, Denmark, 31 May, 1970 M
Denmark: 20/U21-18/Youth

League Club	Source	Date Signed	Seasons Played	Apps	Subs	Gls
Ipswich T	Aarhus GF (DEN)	06/94	94-96	77	4	7
Everton	Tr	01/97	96-97	17	7	1

THOMSON Andrew (Andy)
Born: Motherwell, Lanarkshire, Scotland, 1 April, 1971 F

League Club	Source	Date Signed	Seasons Played	Apps	Subs	Gls
Southend U	Queen of the South	07/94	94-97	87	35	28
Oxford U	Tr	07/98	98	25	13	7
Gillingham	Tr	08/99	99-00	32	20	14
Queens Park Rgrs	Tr	03/01	00-02	43	24	28

THOMSON Andrew John (Andy)
Born: Swindon, England, 28 March, 1974 CD

League Club	Source	Date Signed	Seasons Played	Apps	Subs	Gls
Swindon T	YT	05/93	93-94	21	1	0
Portsmouth	Tr	12/95	95-98	85	8	3
Bristol Rov	Tr	01/99	98-01	124	3	6
Wycombe W	Tr	03/02	01-03	48	2	2

THOMSON Arthur Campbell
Born: Edinburgh, Scotland, 2 September, 1948 CD
Died: Edinburgh, Scotland, 7 March, 2002
Scotland: U23-3

League Club	Source	Date Signed	Seasons Played	Apps	Subs	Gls
Oldham Ath	Heart of Midlothian	01/70	69-70	27	1	0

THOMSON Bertram (Bert)
Born: Glasgow, Scotland, 18 February, 1929 RH

League Club	Source	Date Signed	Seasons Played	Apps	Subs	Gls
Rochdale	Yeovil T	06/58	58-59	55	-	1

THOMSON Brian Lamont
Born: Paisley, Renfrewshire, Scotland, 1 March, 1959 W

League Club	Source	Date Signed	Seasons Played	Apps	Subs	Gls
West Ham U	Morecambe	01/77				
Mansfield T	Tr	08/79	79-81	54	9	1

THOMSON Charles Richard (Chick)
Born: Perth, Scotland, 2 March, 1930 G
Died: Nottingham, England, 6 January, 2009

League Club	Source	Date Signed	Seasons Played	Apps	Subs	Gls
Chelsea	Clyde	10/52	52-55	46	-	0
Nottingham F	Tr	08/57	57-60	121	-	0

THOMSON David Laing
Born: Carronshore, Falkirk, Scotland, 2 February, 1938 IF

League Club	Source	Date Signed	Seasons Played	Apps	Subs	Gls
Leicester C	Dunfermline Ath	08/61	61	1	-	1

THOMSON George Matthewson
Born: Edinburgh, Scotland, 19 October, 1936 LB
Died: Lancashire, England, July, 2007
Scotland: SLge-2

League Club	Source	Date Signed	Seasons Played	Apps	Subs	Gls
Everton	Heart of Midlothian	11/60	60-62	73	-	1
Brentford	Tr	11/63	63-67	160	2	5

THOMSON Henry Watson (Harry)
Born: Edinburgh, Scotland, 25 August, 1940 G
Died: Barrow, Cumbria, England, 14 March, 2013

League Club	Source	Date Signed	Seasons Played	Apps	Subs	Gls
Burnley	Bo'ness U	08/59	64-68	117	0	0
Blackpool	Tr	07/69	69-70	60	0	0
Barrow	Tr	08/71	71	40	0	0

THOMSON Jake Samuel
Born: Portsmouth, England, 12 May, 1989 M
England: Youth//Trinidad & Tobago: 2

League Club	Source	Date Signed	Seasons Played	Apps	Subs	Gls
Southampton	Sch	05/06	08-09	6	8	0
Bournemouth	L	01/09	08	6	0	1
Torquay U	L	10/09	09	13	2	1
Exeter C	Tr	07/10	10	1	15	0
Cheltenham T	L	02/11	10	3	2	1

THOMSON James Arnott (Jimmy)
Born: Glasgow, Scotland, 28 June, 1948 M

League Club	Source	Date Signed	Seasons Played	Apps	Subs	Gls
Newcastle U	Petershill	06/68	69	4	1	0
Barrow	L	12/70	70	2	0	0
Grimsby T	Tr	07/71	71	23	3	4

THOMSON James Donaldson (Jimmy)
Born: Govan, Glasgow, Scotland, 17 March, 1931 IF

League Club	Source	Date Signed	Seasons Played	Apps	Subs	Gls
Southend U	Raith Rov	05/56	56-58	40	-	10

THOMSON James Shaw (Jim)
Born: Glasgow, Scotland, 1 October, 1946 CD

League Club	Source	Date Signed	Seasons Played	Apps	Subs	Gls
Chelsea	Provanside Hibernian	01/65	65-67	33	6	1
Burnley	Tr	09/68	68-80	294	3	3

THOMSON John
Born: Newcastle-upon-Tyne, England, 3 December, 1954 CD

League Club	Source	Date Signed	Seasons Played	Apps	Subs	Gls
Newcastle U	App	12/72				
Bury	Tr	11/73	73-77	92	11	8

THOMSON John Ballantyne
Born: Muirhead, Lanarkshire, Scotland, 22 October, 1934 LB

League Club	Source	Date Signed	Seasons Played	Apps	Subs	Gls
Workington	Heart of Midlothian	05/58	58	11	-	1

THOMSON Kenneth Gordon (Kenny)
Born: Aberdeen, Scotland, 25 February, 1930 CH
Died: Middlesbrough, England, 15 June, 1969

League Club	Source	Date Signed	Seasons Played	Apps	Subs	Gls
Stoke C	Aberdeen	09/52	52-59	278	-	6
Middlesbrough	Tr	12/59	59-62	84	-	1
Hartlepool U	Tr	10/62	62	28	-	2

THOMSON Kevin
Born: Peebles, Borders, Scotland, 14 October, 1984 DM
Scotland: 3/B-2/U21-6

League Club	Source	Date Signed	Seasons Played	Apps	Subs	Gls
Middlesbrough	Glasgow Rangers	07/10	10-12	33	17	0

THOMSON Lawrence James (Lawrie)
Born: Menstrie, Stirlingshire, Scotland, 26 August, 1936 IF

League Club	Source	Date Signed	Seasons Played	Apps	Subs	Gls
Carlisle U	Partick Thistle	01/60	59	13	-	1

THOMSON Peter David
Born: Crumpsall, Greater Manchester, England, 30 June, 1977 F

League Club	Source	Date Signed	Seasons Played	Apps	Subs	Gls
Bury	Stand Ath	11/95				
Luton T	NAC Breda (NED)	09/00	00	4	7	2
Rushden & D	L	11/01	01	1	1	1

THOMSON Richard Blair (Ricky)
Born: Edinburgh, Scotland, 26 June, 1957 F

League Club	Source	Date Signed	Seasons Played	Apps	Subs	Gls
Preston NE	App	06/75	74-79	60	11	20

THOMSON Robert (Bobby)
Born: Glasgow, Scotland, 21 March, 1955 M
Scotland: SLge-2

League Club	Source	Date Signed	Seasons Played	Apps	Subs	Gls
Middlesbrough	Greenock Morton	09/81	81	18	2	2
Blackpool	Hibernian	09/85	85-86	50	2	6
Hartlepool U	Tr	08/87	87	2	1	0

THOMSON Robert (Bobby)
Born: Menstrie, Stirlingshire, Scotland, 21 November, 1939 RB

League Club	Source	Date Signed	Seasons Played	Apps	Subs	Gls
Liverpool	Partick Thistle	12/62	62-63	6	-	0
Luton T	Tr	08/65	65-66	74	0	0

THOMSON Robert Anthony (Bobby)
Born: Smethwick, West Midlands, England, 5 December, 1943 LB
Died: Dudley, West Midlands, England, 19 August, 2009
England: 8/FLge-4/U23-15

League Club	Source	Date Signed	Seasons Played	Apps	Subs	Gls
Wolverhampton W	App	07/61	61-68	277	1	2
Birmingham C	Tr	03/69	68-70	63	0	0
Walsall	L	11/71	71	9	0	1
Luton T	Tr	07/72	72-75	110	0	1
Port Vale	Hartford B'ls (USA)	10/76	76	18	0	0

THOMSON Robert Gillies McKenzie (Bobby)
Born: Dundee, Scotland, 21 March, 1937 IF/RH

League Club	Source	Date Signed	Seasons Played	Apps	Subs	Gls
Wolverhampton W	Airdrieonians	08/54	56	1	-	1
Aston Villa	Tr	06/59	59-63	140	-	56
Birmingham C	Tr	09/63	63-67	109	3	23
Stockport Co	Tr	12/67	67	16	1	0

THOMSON Robert Scott (Robbie)
Born: Falkirk, Scotland, 7 March, 1993 G
Scotland: Youth

League Club	Source	Date Signed	Seasons Played	Apps	Subs	Gls
Rochdale	Glasgow Celtic	07/13	13	1	0	0

THOMSON Scott Yuill
Born: Edinburgh, Scotland, 8 November, 1966 G

League Club	Source	Date Signed	Seasons Played	Apps	Subs	Gls
Hull C	St Johnstone	08/97	97	9	0	0

THOMSON Steven John (Steve)
Born: Glasgow, Scotland, 23 January, 1978 DM
Scotland: Youth

League Club	Source	Date Signed	Seasons Played	Apps	Subs	Gls
Crystal Palace	YT	12/95	98-02	68	37	1
Peterborough U	Tr	09/03	03-04	58	8	3
Brighton & HA	Falkirk	01/08	07-08	37	0	0

THORBURN James Hope Forrest (Jim)
Born: Douglas, Lanarkshire, Scotland, 10 March, 1938 — G

League Club	Source	Date Signed	Seasons Played	Apps	Subs	Gls
Ipswich T	Raith Rov	06/63	63-64	24	-	0

THORDARSON Stefan Thor
Born: Reykjavik, Iceland, 27 March, 1975 — F
Iceland: 6/U21-8/Youth

League Club	Source	Date Signed	Seasons Played	Apps	Subs	Gls
Stoke C	Bayer Uerdingen (GER)	06/00	00-01	18	33	8

THORLEY Dennis
Born: Stoke-on-Trent, England, 7 November, 1956 — D/M

League Club	Source	Date Signed	Seasons Played	Apps	Subs	Gls
Stoke C	Jnr	07/76	76-80	9	4	0
Blackburn Rov	L	03/80	79	2	2	0

THORN Andrew Charles (Andy)
Born: Carshalton, S London, England, 12 November, 1966 — CD
England: U21-5

League Club	Source	Date Signed	Seasons Played	Apps	Subs	Gls
Wimbledon	App	11/84	84-87	106	1	2
Newcastle U	Tr	08/88	88-89	36	0	2
Crystal Palace	Tr	12/89	89-93	128	0	3
Wimbledon	Tr	10/94	94-95	33	4	1
Tranmere Rov	Heart of Midlothian	09/96	96-97	36	0	1

THORNBER Stephen John (Steve)
Born: Dewsbury, West Yorkshire, England, 11 October, 1965 — M

League Club	Source	Date Signed	Seasons Played	Apps	Subs	Gls
Halifax T	Jnr	01/83	83-87	94	10	4
Swansea C	Tr	08/88	88-91	98	19	5
Blackpool	Tr	08/92	92	21	3	0
Scunthorpe U	Tr	07/93	93-95	71	6	7

THORNE Adrian Ernest
Born: Brighton, England, 2 August, 1937 — LW

League Club	Source	Date Signed	Seasons Played	Apps	Subs	Gls
Brighton & HA	Jnr	08/54	57-60	76	-	38
Plymouth Arg	Tr	06/61	61-63	11	-	2
Exeter C	Tr	12/63	63-64	41	-	8
Leyton Orient	Tr	07/65	65	2	0	0

THORNE George Louis Elliot
Born: Chatham, Kent, England, 4 January, 1993 — RM

League Club	Source	Date Signed	Seasons Played	Apps	Subs	Gls
West Bromwich A	Sch	01/10	09-12	4	6	0
Portsmouth	L	11/11	11	4	0	0
Portsmouth	L	02/12	11	10	0	0
Peterborough U	L	11/12	12	7	0	1
Watford	L	11/13	13	8	0	0
Derby Co	Tr	01/14	13-14	12	0	1

THORNE Peter Lee
Born: Manchester, England, 21 June, 1973 — F

League Club	Source	Date Signed	Seasons Played	Apps	Subs	Gls
Blackburn Rov	YT	06/91				
Wigan Ath	L	03/94	93	10	1	0
Swindon T	Tr	01/95	94-96	66	11	27
Stoke C	Tr	07/97	97-01	147	11	65
Cardiff C	Tr	09/01	01-04	116	10	46
Norwich C	Tr	07/05	05-06	15	21	1
Bradford C	Tr	07/07	07-09	67	10	31

THORNE Steven Terence (Steve)
Born: Hampstead, NW London, England, 15 September, 1968 — M

League Club	Source	Date Signed	Seasons Played	Apps	Subs	Gls
Watford	App	07/86				
Brentford	Tr	09/87	87	1	0	1

THORNE Terry
Born: Kirton-in-Lindsey, North Lincolnshire, England, 2 February, 1947 — M
Died: Boston, Lincolnshire, England, 7 September, 2006

League Club	Source	Date Signed	Seasons Played	Apps	Subs	Gls
Ipswich T	Lincoln C (Am)	08/64				
Notts Co	Tr	06/66	66	2	0	0

THORNHILL Dennis
Born: Draycott, Derbyshire, England, 5 July, 1923 — CH
Died: Southend-on-Sea, England, August, 1992

League Club	Source	Date Signed	Seasons Played	Apps	Subs	Gls
Wolverhampton W	Jnr	07/40				
Southend U	Tr	03/48	48-49	11	-	0

THORNHILL Keith Eric
Born: Crewe, Cheshire, England, 20 December, 1963 — F

League Club	Source	Date Signed	Seasons Played	Apps	Subs	Gls
Crewe Alex	Nantwich T	07/83	83	1	0	0

THORNHILL Matthew Mark (Matt)
Born: Nottingham, England, 11 October, 1988 — M

League Club	Source	Date Signed	Seasons Played	Apps	Subs	Gls
Nottingham F	Sch	12/07	07-08	18	20	5
Brighton & HA	L	07/09	09	3	4	0
Cheltenham T	L	01/10	09	16	1	3

THORNHILL Rodney Derek (Rod)
Born: Reading, England, 24 January, 1942 — D/M

League Club	Source	Date Signed	Seasons Played	Apps	Subs	Gls
Reading		05/63	63-69	188	4	19

THORNLEY Barry Edward
Born: Gravesend, Kent, England, 11 February, 1948 — LW

League Club	Source	Date Signed	Seasons Played	Apps	Subs	Gls
Brentford	Gravesend & Northfleet	09/65	65	7	0	0
Oxford U	Tr	07/67	67-68	22	1	4

THORNLEY Benjamin Lindsay (Ben)
Born: Bury, Greater Manchester, England, 21 April, 1975 — W
England: U21-3/Schools

League Club	Source	Date Signed	Seasons Played	Apps	Subs	Gls
Manchester U	YT	01/93	93-97	1	8	0
Stockport Co	L	11/95	95	8	2	1
Huddersfield T	L	02/96	95	12	0	2
Huddersfield T	Tr	07/98	98-00	77	22	5
Blackpool	Aberdeen	12/02	02	7	5	0
Bury	Tr	09/03	03	5	0	0

THORNLEY Roderick Neil (Rod)
Born: Bury, Greater Manchester, England, 2 August, 1977 — F

League Club	Source	Date Signed	Seasons Played	Apps	Subs	Gls
Doncaster Rov	Warrington T	09/97	97	1	0	0

THORNLEY Timothy James (Tim)
Born: Leicester, England, 3 March, 1977 — G

League Club	Source	Date Signed	Seasons Played	Apps	Subs	Gls
Torquay U	YT	-	94	0	1	0

THORNS John William
Born: Newcastle-upon-Tyne, England, 10 July, 1928 — RW
Died: Middlesbrough, England, 1975

League Club	Source	Date Signed	Seasons Played	Apps	Subs	Gls
Darlington (Am)		08/49	49	1	-	0

THORNTON Kevin Anthony
Born: Drogheda, Republic of Ireland, 9 July, 1986 — M
Republic of Ireland: Youth

League Club	Source	Date Signed	Seasons Played	Apps	Subs	Gls
Coventry C	Sch	07/03	05-08	19	31	2
Brighton & HA	L	09/08	08	4	8	0
Northampton T	Nuneaton T	01/10	09-11	20	18	7

THORNTON Sean
Born: Drogheda, Republic of Ireland, 18 May, 1983 — M
Republic of Ireland: U21-12/Youth

League Club	Source	Date Signed	Seasons Played	Apps	Subs	Gls
Tranmere Rov	YT	-	01	9	2	1
Sunderland	Tr	07/02	02-04	28	21	9
Blackpool	L	11/02	02	1	2	0
Doncaster Rov	Tr	07/05	05-06	38	21	2
Leyton Orient	Tr	07/07	07-09	76	15	11
Shrewsbury T	L	09/08	08	5	0	1

THORP Hamilton
Born: Darwin, Australia, 21 August, 1973 — F

League Club	Source	Date Signed	Seasons Played	Apps	Subs	Gls
Portsmouth	W Adelaide Sh'ks (AUS)	08/97	97	0	7	0

THORP Michael Stephen
Born: Wallingford, Oxfordshire, England, 5 December, 1975 — CD

League Club	Source	Date Signed	Seasons Played	Apps	Subs	Gls
Reading	YT	01/95	95-97	2	3	0

THORPE Adrian
Born: Chesterfield, Derbyshire, England, 25 November, 1963 — LW

League Club	Source	Date Signed	Seasons Played	Apps	Subs	Gls
Mansfield T	YT	08/82	82	0	2	1
Bradford C	Heanor T	08/85	85-87	9	8	1
Tranmere Rov	L	11/86	86	4	1	3
Notts Co	Tr	11/87	87-88	48	11	9
Walsall	Tr	08/89	89	24	3	1
Northampton T	Tr	03/90	89-91	36	16	6

THORPE Andrew (Andy)
Born: Stockport, Greater Manchester, England, 15 September, 1960 — CD

League Club	Source	Date Signed	Seasons Played	Apps	Subs	Gls
Stockport Co	Jnr	08/78	77-85	312	2	3
Tranmere Rov	Tr	07/86	86-87	51	2	0
Stockport Co	Tr	01/88	87-91	172	3	0
Doncaster Rov	Chorley	09/97	97	2	0	0

THORPE Anthony Lee (Tony)
Born: Leicester, England, 10 April, 1974 — F

League Club	Source	Date Signed	Seasons Played	Apps	Subs	Gls
Luton T	Leicester C (YT)	08/92	93-97	93	27	50
Fulham	Tr	02/98	97	5	8	3
Bristol C	Tr	06/98	98-01	102	26	50
Reading	L	02/99	98	6	0	1
Luton T	L	03/99	98	7	1	4
Luton T	L	11/99	99	3	1	1
Luton T	Tr	07/02	02-03	30	2	15
Queens Park Rgrs	Tr	08/03	03-04	26	15	10
Rotherham U	L	03/05	04	5	0	1
Swindon T	Tr	07/05	05	6	1	1
Colchester U	Tr	01/06	05	5	9	0
Grimsby T (L)	Stevenage Bor	09/06	06	5	0	0
Grimsby T (L)	Stevenage Bor	01/07	06	0	1	0

THORPE Arthur William
Born: Lucknow, India, 31 July, 1939 — LW

League Club	Source	Date Signed	Seasons Played	Apps	Subs	Gls
Scunthorpe U	Ossett T	09/60	60-62	27	-	5
Bradford C	Tr	07/63	63-65	81	0	17

THORPE Ian Richard
Born: Blackheath, SE London, England, 3 September, 1953 — G
England: Amateur

League Club	Source	Date Signed	Seasons Played	Apps	Subs	Gls
Gillingham	Charlton Ath (Am)	08/72	73	5	0	0

THORPE Jeffrey Roger (Jeff)
Born: Whitehaven, Cumbria, England, 17 November, 1972 M/LB

League Club	Source	Date Signed	Seasons Played	Apps	Subs	Gls
Carlisle U	YT	07/91	90-99	104	72	6

THORPE Lee Anthony
Born: Wolverhampton, England, 14 December, 1975 F

League Club	Source	Date Signed	Seasons Played	Apps	Subs	Gls
Blackpool	YT	07/94	93-96	2	10	0
Lincoln C	Tr	08/97	97-01	183	9	58
Leyton Orient	Tr	05/02	02-03	42	13	12
Grimsby T	L	02/04	03	5	1	0
Bristol Rov	Tr	03/04	03-04	25	10	4
Swansea C	L	02/05	04-05	9	9	3
Peterborough U	L	09/05	05	6	0	0
Torquay U	Tr	02/06	05-06	49	2	11
Brentford	Tr	07/07	07	17	2	4
Rochdale	Tr	01/08	07-08	23	13	6
Darlington	Tr	08/09	09	7	1	0

THORPE Leonard (Len)
Born: Warsop, Nottinghamshire, England, 7 June, 1924 WH
Died: Nottingham, England, April, 2012

League Club	Source	Date Signed	Seasons Played	Apps	Subs	Gls
Mansfield T	Nottingham F (Am)	08/45	46	5	-	0

THORPE Samuel (Sam)
Born: Sheffield, England, 2 December, 1920 RH
Died: Sheffield, England, 6 August, 2002

League Club	Source	Date Signed	Seasons Played	Apps	Subs	Gls
Sheffield U	Norton Woodseats	04/45	47-48	2	-	0

THORPE Thomas Joseph (Tom)
Born: Manchester, England, 13 January, 1993 CD
England: U21-1/Youth

League Club	Source	Date Signed	Seasons Played	Apps	Subs	Gls
Manchester U	Sch	07/10	14	0	1	0
Birmingham C	L	01/14	13	6	0	0

THORRINGTON John Gerard
Born: Johannesburg, South Africa, 17 October, 1979 RM
USA: 4/Youth

League Club	Source	Date Signed	Seasons Played	Apps	Subs	Gls
Manchester U	Mission Viejo (USA)	10/97				
Huddersfield T	Bayer Leverkusen (GER)	03/01	01-03	48	19	7
Grimsby T	Tr	03/04	03	2	1	0

THORSTVEDT Erik
Born: Stavanger, Norway, 28 October, 1962 G
Norway: 97/U21-5

League Club	Source	Date Signed	Seasons Played	Apps	Subs	Gls
Tottenham H	IFK Goteberg (SWE)	12/88	88-94	171	2	0

THORUP Borge
Born: Copenhagen, Denmark, 4 October, 1943 FB
Denmark: 1

League Club	Source	Date Signed	Seasons Played	Apps	Subs	Gls
Crystal Palace	Greenock Morton	03/69	69	0	1	0

THORVALDSSON Gunnar Heidar
Born: Vestmannaeyjar, Iceland, 1 April, 1982 F
Iceland: 24/U21-7

League Club	Source	Date Signed	Seasons Played	Apps	Subs	Gls
Reading (L)	Esbjerg (DEN)	01/10	09	2	2	0

THREADGOLD Joseph Henry (Harry)
Born: Tattenhall, Cheshire, England, 6 November, 1924 G
Died: Southend-on-Sea, England, December, 1996

League Club	Source	Date Signed	Seasons Played	Apps	Subs	Gls
Chester C	Tarvin U	10/47	50-51	83	-	0
Sunderland	Tr	07/52	52	35	-	0
Southend U	Tr	07/53	53-62	320	-	0

THRELFALL Jack
Born: Little Lever, Greater Manchester, England, 22 March, 1935 FB/RH
Died: Germany, 29 March, 1989

League Club	Source	Date Signed	Seasons Played	Apps	Subs	Gls
Bolton W		12/54	55-62	47	-	1
Bury	Tr	11/62	62-64	37	-	1

THRELFALL Joseph Richard (Dick)
Born: Ashton-under-Lyne, Greater Manchester, England, 5 March, 1916 RB
Died: Birmingham, England, April, 1994

League Club	Source	Date Signed	Seasons Played	Apps	Subs	Gls
Bolton W	Ashton National	07/45	46	3	-	0
Halifax T	Mossley	10/47	47	30	-	0

THRELFALL Robert Richard (Robbie)
Born: Liverpool, England, 25 November, 1988 LB
England: Youth

League Club	Source	Date Signed	Seasons Played	Apps	Subs	Gls
Liverpool	Sch	07/06				
Hereford U	L	11/07	07	6	3	0
Hereford U	L	07/08	08	3	0	0
Stockport Co	L	01/09	08	1	1	0
Northampton T	L	08/09	09	1	3	0
Bradford C	Tr	02/10	09-11	49	5	2
Morecambe	Tr	05/12	12-13	51	8	3

THRELKELD Oscar George
Born: Bolton, Greater Manchester, England, 15 February, 1994 CD

League Club	Source	Date Signed	Seasons Played	Apps	Subs	Gls
Bolton W	Sch	07/13	13-14	5	1	0

THRESHER Theodore Michael (Mike)
Born: Cullompton, Devon, England, 9 March, 1931 LB
Died: Bristol, England, 28 December, 1999

League Club	Source	Date Signed	Seasons Played	Apps	Subs	Gls
Bristol C	Chard T	01/54	54-64	379	-	1

THRIPPLETON Allen
Born: Huddersfield, West Yorkshire, England, 16 June, 1928 LH/CF
Died: Southwark, S London, England, May, 2005

League Club	Source	Date Signed	Seasons Played	Apps	Subs	Gls
Millwall	Rainham T	11/50	50-54	26	-	4

THROWER Dennis Alan
Born: Ipswich, England, 1 August, 1938 LH

League Club	Source	Date Signed	Seasons Played	Apps	Subs	Gls
Ipswich T	Landseer OB	08/55	56-64	27	-	2

THROWER Nigel John
Born: Nottingham, England, 12 March, 1962 LB

League Club	Source	Date Signed	Seasons Played	Apps	Subs	Gls
Nottingham F	App	03/80				
Chesterfield	L	02/83	82	4	0	0

THURAM-ULIEN Yohann
Born: Evry, France, 31 October, 1988 G
France: U21-2/Youth

League Club	Source	Date Signed	Seasons Played	Apps	Subs	Gls
Charlton Ath (L)	Standard Liege (BEL)	01/14	13	4	0	0

THURGOOD Stuart Anthony
Born: Enfield, N London, England, 4 November, 1981 M
England: Semi Pro-5

League Club	Source	Date Signed	Seasons Played	Apps	Subs	Gls
Southend U	Shimuzu S Pulse (JPN)	01/01	00-02	49	30	1
Gillingham	Grays Ath	11/07	07	11	1	0
Dagenham & Red	Grays Ath	07/09	09	17	0	0

THURLOW Alec Charles Edward
Born: Diss, Norfolk, England, 24 February, 1922 G
Died: Kettering, Northamptonshire, England, 5 March, 1956

League Club	Source	Date Signed	Seasons Played	Apps	Subs	Gls
Huddersfield T	RAF	09/44				
Manchester C	Tr	09/46	46-48	21	-	0

THURLOW Bryan Alfred
Born: Loddon, Norfolk, England, 6 June, 1936 RB
Died: Norwich, England, January, 2002

League Club	Source	Date Signed	Seasons Played	Apps	Subs	Gls
Norwich C	Loddon	07/54	55-63	193	-	1
Bristol C	Tr	07/64				

THURNHAM Roy Thomas
Born: Macclesfield, Cheshire, England, 17 December, 1942 CH

League Club	Source	Date Signed	Seasons Played	Apps	Subs	Gls
Manchester C	Jnr	06/60				
Wrexham	Tr	06/61	62	2	-	0

THURSTAN Mark Richard
Born: Cockermouth, Cumbria, England, 10 February, 1980 M

League Club	Source	Date Signed	Seasons Played	Apps	Subs	Gls
Carlisle U	Jnr	07/98	00-01	4	2	0

THWAITES Adam Martin
Born: Kendal, Cumbria, England, 8 December, 1981 LB

League Club	Source	Date Signed	Seasons Played	Apps	Subs	Gls
Carlisle U	YT	06/00	01	0	1	0

THWAITES Denis
Born: Stockton-on-Tees, Cleveland, England, 14 December, 1944 LW
Died: Sousse, Tunisia, 26 June, 2015
England: Youth/Schools

League Club	Source	Date Signed	Seasons Played	Apps	Subs	Gls
Birmingham C	App	05/62	62-70	83	3	18

THWAITES Peter
Born: Batley, West Yorkshire, England, 21 August, 1936 CF
Died: Leeds, England, February, 2010

League Club	Source	Date Signed	Seasons Played	Apps	Subs	Gls
Halifax T (Am)	Swillington	02/61	60	2	-	0

THYNE Robert Brown (Bob)
Born: Glasgow, Scotland, 9 January, 1920 CH
Died: Newton Mearns, Renfrewshire, Scotland, 16 September, 1986
Scotland: War-2

League Club	Source	Date Signed	Seasons Played	Apps	Subs	Gls
Darlington	Clydebank Jnrs	10/43	46	7	-	0

[TIAGO] MENDES TIAGO Cardoso
Born: Viana do Castelo, Portugal, 2 May, 1981 M
Portugal: 63/U21-21

League Club	Source	Date Signed	Seasons Played	Apps	Subs	Gls
Chelsea	Benfica (POR)	08/04	04	21	13	4

TIATTO Daniele Amadio (Danny)
Born: Melbourne, Australia, 22 May, 1973 LB/M
Australia: 23/U23

League Club	Source	Date Signed	Seasons Played	Apps	Subs	Gls
Stoke C (L)	FC Baden (SUI)	11/97	97	11	4	1
Manchester C	FC Baden (SUI)	07/98	98-03	112	28	3
Leicester C	Tr	08/04	04-06	60	13	3

TIBBOTT Leslie (Les)
Born: Oswestry, Shropshire, England, 25 August, 1955 LB
Wales: U21-2

League Club	Source	Date Signed	Seasons Played	Apps	Subs	Gls
Ipswich T	App	03/73	75-78	52	2	0
Sheffield U	Tr	03/79	78-81	78	0	2

TICKELL Brian Gerard
Born: Carlisle, Cumbria, England, 15 November, 1939 CF

League Club	Source	Date Signed	Seasons Played	Apps	Subs	Gls
Huddersfield T	Raffles U, Carlisle	11/56	58	1	-	0
Carlisle U	Tr	05/59	59	3	-	1

TICKELL Enoch Roy (Roy)
Born: Bootle, Merseyside, England, 25 April, 1924 RW
Died: Southport, Merseyside, England, 8 February, 2006

League Club	Source	Date Signed	Seasons Played	Apps	Subs	Gls
Exeter C	Tranmere Rov (Am)	12/45				
Southport	Tr	05/47	47	6	-	1

TICKRIDGE Sidney (Sid)
Born: Stepney, E London, England, 10 April, 1923 FB
Died: Canterbury, England, 6 January, 1997
England: Schools

League Club	Source	Date Signed	Seasons Played	Apps	Subs	Gls
Tottenham H	Jnr	04/46	46-50	95	-	0
Chelsea	Tr	03/51	50-52	61	-	0
Brentford	Tr	07/55	55-56	62	-	0

TIDDY Michael Douglas (Mike)
Born: Helston, Cornwall, England, 4 April, 1929 RW
Died: Truro, Cornwall, England, 25 November, 2009

League Club	Source	Date Signed	Seasons Played	Apps	Subs	Gls
Torquay U	Helston	11/46	46-50	5	-	0
Cardiff C	Tr	11/50	50-54	146	-	20
Arsenal	Tr	09/55	55-57	48	-	8
Brighton & HA	Tr	10/58	58-61	133	-	11

TIDMAN Ola
Born: Malmo, Sweden, 11 May, 1979 G
Sweden: U21-2/Youth

League Club	Source	Date Signed	Seasons Played	Apps	Subs	Gls
Stockport Co	La Louviere (BEL)	01/03	02	18	0	0
Sheffield Wed	Tr	07/03	03-04	12	1	0

TIDSER Michael
Born: Glasgow, Scotland, 15 January, 1990 M
Scotland: Youth

League Club	Source	Date Signed	Seasons Played	Apps	Subs	Gls
Rotherham U	Greenock Morton	07/13	13-14	2	9	0
Oldham Ath	L	09/14	14	1	4	0

TIENDALLI Dwight Marciano
Born: Paramaribo, Suriname, 21 October, 1985 FB
Netherlands: 2/U21-16

League Club	Source	Date Signed	Seasons Played	Apps	Subs	Gls
Swansea C	FC Twente (NED)	09/12	12-14	21	6	1
Middlesbrough	L	03/15	14	2	0	0

TIERLING Lee
Born: Wegburg, Germany, 25 October, 1972 M

League Club	Source	Date Signed	Seasons Played	Apps	Subs	Gls
Portsmouth	YT	07/91				
Fulham	Tr	05/92	92-93	7	12	0

TIERNEY Francis
Born: Liverpool, England, 10 September, 1975 M
England: Youth

League Club	Source	Date Signed	Seasons Played	Apps	Subs	Gls
Crewe Alex	YT	03/93	92-97	57	30	10
Notts Co	Tr	07/98	98-99	19	14	4
Exeter C	Witton A	11/00	00	4	3	1
Doncaster Rov	Witton A	03/01	03	10	3	3

TIERNEY James McMahon (Jim)
Born: Ayr, Scotland, 2 May, 1940 RW

League Club	Source	Date Signed	Seasons Played	Apps	Subs	Gls
Bradford C	Saltcoats Victoria	01/60	60	2	-	0

TIERNEY Lawrence James William (Lawrie)
Born: Leith, Edinburgh, Scotland, 4 April, 1959 M
Died: Phoenix, Arizona, USA, 6 December, 2011

League Club	Source	Date Signed	Seasons Played	Apps	Subs	Gls
Wigan Ath	Hibernian	07/80	80	4	3	0

TIERNEY Marc Peter
Born: Prestwich, Greater Manchester, England, 23 August, 1985 LB

League Club	Source	Date Signed	Seasons Played	Apps	Subs	Gls
Oldham Ath	Jnr	08/03	03-06	21	16	0
Shrewsbury T	Tr	01/07	06-08	78	1	1
Colchester U	Tr	11/08	08-10	79	1	1
Norwich C	Tr	01/11	10-12	32	2	0
Bolton W	Tr	06/13	13	8	0	0

TIERNEY Paul Thomas
Born: Salford, England, 15 September, 1982 LB
Republic of Ireland: U21-7

League Club	Source	Date Signed	Seasons Played	Apps	Subs	Gls
Manchester U	YT	07/00				
Crewe Alex	L	11/02	02	14	3	1
Colchester U	L	01/04	03	2	0	0
Bradford C	L	12/04	04	14	2	0
Blackpool	Livingston	06/06	06	8	2	0
Stockport Co	L	08/07	07	15	1	0

TIGHE John
Born: Aghamore, Republic of Ireland, 13 March, 1923 G

League Club	Source	Date Signed	Seasons Played	Apps	Subs	Gls
West Bromwich A	Larkhall Thistle	11/45	46	1	-	0

TIGHE Terence William (Terry)
Born: Edinburgh, Scotland, 12 August, 1934 WH/IF
Died: Oswaldtwistle, Lancashire, England, 23 March, 2000

League Club	Source	Date Signed	Seasons Played	Apps	Subs	Gls
Accrington Stan	Dunfermline Ath	06/57	57-60	117	-	20
Crewe Alex	Tr	12/60	60-62	81	-	5
Southport	Tr	08/63	63	36	-	3

TIHINEN Hannu
Born: Kemi, Finland, 1 July, 1976 CD
Finland: 76

League Club	Source	Date Signed	Seasons Played	Apps	Subs	Gls
West Ham U (L)	Viking Stavanger (NOR)	12/00	00	5	3	0

TILER Brian
Born: Rotherham, South Yorkshire, England, 15 March, 1943 CD
Died: Latina, Italy, 30 June, 1990

League Club	Source	Date Signed	Seasons Played	Apps	Subs	Gls
Rotherham U	Jnr	07/62	62-68	213	0	27
Aston Villa	Tr	12/68	68-72	106	1	3
Carlisle U	Tr	10/72	72-73	51	1	1

TILER Carl
Born: Sheffield, England, 11 February, 1970 CD
England: U21-13

League Club	Source	Date Signed	Seasons Played	Apps	Subs	Gls
Barnsley	YT	08/88	87-90	67	4	3
Nottingham F	Tr	05/91	91-94	67	2	1
Swindon T	L	11/94	94	2	0	0
Aston Villa	Tr	10/95	95-96	10	2	1
Sheffield U	Tr	03/97	96-97	23	0	2
Everton	Tr	11/97	97-98	21	0	1
Charlton Ath	Tr	09/98	98-00	38	7	2
Birmingham C	L	02/01	00	1	0	0
Portsmouth	Tr	03/01	00-02	16	3	1

TILER Kenneth David (Ken)
Born: Sheffield, England, 23 May, 1950 FB

League Club	Source	Date Signed	Seasons Played	Apps	Subs	Gls
Chesterfield	Swallownest	09/70	70-74	139	1	1
Brighton & HA	Tr	11/74	74-78	130	0	0
Rotherham U	Tr	07/79	79-80	45	1	1

TILL Peter
Born: Walsall, West Midlands, England, 7 September, 1985 RW

League Club	Source	Date Signed	Seasons Played	Apps	Subs	Gls
Birmingham C	Sch	07/05				
Scunthorpe U	L	10/05	05	6	2	0
Boston U	L	01/06	05	10	6	1
Leyton Orient	L	10/06	06	4	0	0
Grimsby T	Tr	11/06	06-08	63	9	4
Chesterfield	L	01/09	08	14	2	0
Walsall	Tr	07/09	09	18	10	0

TILLEN Joseph Edward (Joe)
Born: Newbury, Berkshire, England, 15 December, 1986 W

League Club	Source	Date Signed	Seasons Played	Apps	Subs	Gls
Chelsea	Sch	03/05				
MK Dons	Tr	07/06	06	0	1	0

TILLEN Samuel Lee (Sam)
Born: Newbury, Berkshire, England, 16 April, 1985 LB/M
England: Youth

League Club	Source	Date Signed	Seasons Played	Apps	Subs	Gls
Chelsea	Sch	07/02				
Brentford	Tr	07/05	05-07	48	20	1

TILLEY Darren John
Born: Keynsham, Avon, England, 15 March, 1967 F

League Club	Source	Date Signed	Seasons Played	Apps	Subs	Gls
York C	Yate T	01/92	91-92	17	4	0

TILLEY Herbert Rex (Rex)
Born: Swindon, England, 16 February, 1929 WH

League Club	Source	Date Signed	Seasons Played	Apps	Subs	Gls
Plymouth Arg	Chippenham T	03/51	52-57	123	-	0
Swindon T	Tr	08/58	58-59	31	-	0

TILLEY James Alex David
Born: Billingshurst, West Sussex, England, 13 June, 1998 F

League Club	Source	Date Signed	Seasons Played	Apps	Subs	Gls
Brighton & HA	Sch	-	14	0	1	0

TILLEY Kevin
Born: Feltham, SW London, England, 6 September, 1957 RB

League Club	Source	Date Signed	Seasons Played	Apps	Subs	Gls
Wimbledon	Queens Park Rgrs (App)	09/75	77	11	2	0

TILLEY Peter
Born: Lurgan, Armagh, Northern Ireland, 13 January, 1930 WH/IF
Died: Manchester, England, 11 August, 2008

League Club	Source	Date Signed	Seasons Played	Apps	Subs	Gls
Arsenal	Witton A	05/52	53	1	-	0
Bury	Tr	11/53	53-57	86	-	12
Halifax T	Tr	07/58	58-62	183	-	17

TILLING Harold Kynaston (Harry)
Born: Warrington, Cheshire, England, 6 January, 1918 LW
Died: Warrington, Cheshire, England, November, 1998

League Club	Source	Date Signed	Seasons Played	Apps	Subs	Gls
Oldham Ath	Whitecross, Warrington	09/42	47	3	-	0

TILLOTSON Maurice
Born: Silsden, West Yorkshire, England, 20 January, 1944 FB

New Zealand: 15

League Club	Source	Date Signed	Seasons Played	Apps	Subs	Gls
Huddersfield T	Jnr	07/62				
Stockport Co	Toronto Italia (CAN)	10/64	64-65	35	0	0

TILLSON Andrew (Andy)
Born: Huntingdon, Cambridgeshire, England, 30 June, 1966 — CD

League Club	Source	Date Signed	Seasons Played	Apps	Subs	Gls
Grimsby T	Kettering T	07/88	88-90	104	1	5
Queens Park Rgrs	Tr	12/90	90-91	27	2	2
Grimsby T	L	09/92	92	4	0	0
Bristol Rov	Tr	11/92	92-99	250	3	11
Walsall	Tr	08/00	00-01	50	1	2
Rushden & D	Tr	02/02	01-02	19	0	0

TILLSON Jordan Roy
Born: Bath, England, 21 February, 1993 — CD

League Club	Source	Date Signed	Seasons Played	Apps	Subs	Gls
Exeter C	Bristol Rov (Sch)	07/12	13-14	4	0	0

TILSED Ronald William (Ron)
Born: Weymouth, Dorset, England, 6 August, 1952 — G
England: Youth

League Club	Source	Date Signed	Seasons Played	Apps	Subs	Gls
Bournemouth	App	01/70	69	2	0	0
Chesterfield	Tr	02/72	71	16	0	0
Arsenal	Tr	09/72				
Portsmouth	Tr	03/73	72-73	14	0	0
Hereford U	Tr	06/74				

TILSON Stephen Brian (Steve)
Born: Wickford, Essex, England, 27 July, 1966 — M

League Club	Source	Date Signed	Seasons Played	Apps	Subs	Gls
Southend U	Witham T	02/89	88-96	199	40	26
Brentford	L	09/93	93	2	0	0
Southend U	Canvey Island	10/02	02-03	2	2	0

TILSTON Thomas Arthur Anthony (Tommy)
Born: Chester, England, 19 February, 1926 — IF

League Club	Source	Date Signed	Seasons Played	Apps	Subs	Gls
Chester C	Jnr	09/43	49-50	22	-	7
Tranmere Rov	Tr	06/51	51	25	-	15
Wrexham	Tr	03/52	51-53	78	-	29
Crystal Palace	Tr	02/54	53-55	58	-	13

TILT Luke Graham
Born: Dudley, West Midlands, England, 18 June, 1988 — G

League Club	Source	Date Signed	Seasons Played	Apps	Subs	Gls
Walsall	Sch	-	05	0	1	0

TILTMAN Richard George
Born: Shoreham-by-Sea, West Sussex, England, 14 December, 1960 — F

League Club	Source	Date Signed	Seasons Played	Apps	Subs	Gls
Brighton & HA	Maidstone U	11/86	86-87	10	3	1

TIMAR Krisztian
Born: Budapest, Hungary, 4 October, 1979 — CD
Hungary: 4/Youth

League Club	Source	Date Signed	Seasons Played	Apps	Subs	Gls
Plymouth Arg	Ferencvaros (HUN)	01/07	06-10	70	14	5
Oldham Ath	L	01/10	09	2	0	0

TIMLIN Michael Anthony
Born: New Cross, SE London, England, 19 March, 1985 — M
Republic of Ireland: U21-8/Youth

League Club	Source	Date Signed	Seasons Played	Apps	Subs	Gls
Fulham	Sch	07/02				
Scunthorpe U	L	02/06	05	0	1	0
Doncaster Rov	L	03/06	05	3	0	0
Swindon T	L	11/06	06	18	6	1
Swindon T	Tr	03/08	07-11	72	23	5
Southend U	L	09/10	10	8	0	1
Southend U	Tr	08/11	11-14	125	8	9

TIMM Mads
Born: Odense, Denmark, 31 October, 1984 — F
Denmark: Youth

League Club	Source	Date Signed	Seasons Played	Apps	Subs	Gls
Manchester U	Jnr	12/01				
Walsall	L	01/06	05	6	3	1

TIMMINS Arnold
Born: Whitehaven, Cumbria, England, 29 January, 1940 — IF
Died: Chorley, Lancashire, England, 14 May, 1994

League Club	Source	Date Signed	Seasons Played	Apps	Subs	Gls
Workington	Lowca	09/60	60-63	44	-	10

TIMMINS Charles (Charlie)
Born: Birmingham, England, 29 May, 1922 — LB
Died: Birmingham, England, 12 April, 2010

League Club	Source	Date Signed	Seasons Played	Apps	Subs	Gls
Coventry C	Jack Moulds Ath	09/46	49-57	161	-	5

TIMMINS John
Born: Brierley Hill, West Midlands, England, 30 May, 1936 — LB
Died: Telford, England, 13 July, 2006

League Club	Source	Date Signed	Seasons Played	Apps	Subs	Gls
Wolverhampton W	Jnr	06/53				
Plymouth Arg	Tr	01/58	57	5	-	0
Bristol Rov	Tr	09/58	58	3	-	0

TIMONS Christopher Bryan (Chris)
Born: Langwith, Derbyshire, England, 8 December, 1974 — CD

League Club	Source	Date Signed	Seasons Played	Apps	Subs	Gls
Mansfield T	Clipstone Welfare	02/94	93-95	35	4	2
Leyton Orient	Gainsborough Trinity	03/97	96	6	0	2

TIMOSKA Sampsa
Born: Kokemaki, Finland, 12 February, 1979 — LB
Finland: 2

League Club	Source	Date Signed	Seasons Played	Apps	Subs	Gls
Queens Park Rgrs	MyPa 47 (FIN)	01/07	06-07	14	7	0

TIMSON David Youles
Born: Syston, Leicestershire, England, 24 August, 1947 — G

League Club	Source	Date Signed	Seasons Played	Apps	Subs	Gls
Leicester C	App	09/64	63-66	3	0	0
Newport Co	Tr	08/67	67	22	0	0

TINDALL Jason
Born: Mile End, E London, England, 15 November, 1977 — CD

League Club	Source	Date Signed	Seasons Played	Apps	Subs	Gls
Charlton Ath	YT	07/96				
Bournemouth	Tr	07/98	98-05	129	42	6
Bournemouth	Weymouth	02/09	08	0	2	0

TINDALL Michael Chadwick (Mike)
Born: Birmingham, England, 5 April, 1941 — RH/IF
England: Youth

League Club	Source	Date Signed	Seasons Played	Apps	Subs	Gls
Aston Villa	Jnr	04/58	59-67	118	2	8
Walsall	Tr	06/68	68	7	0	0

TINDALL Ronald Albert Ernest (Ron)
Born: Streatham, S London, England, 23 September, 1935 — CF/D
Died: Perth, Australia, 9 September, 2012
England: FLge-1

League Club	Source	Date Signed	Seasons Played	Apps	Subs	Gls
Chelsea	Jnr	04/53	55-61	160	-	67
West Ham U	Tr	11/61	61	13	-	3
Reading	Tr	10/62	62-63	36	-	12
Portsmouth	Tr	09/64	64-69	160	2	7

TINDILL Herbert (Bert)
Born: South Hiendley, West Yorkshire, England, 31 December, 1926 — W/IF
Died: Hemsworth, West Yorkshire, England, 10 July, 1973

League Club	Source	Date Signed	Seasons Played	Apps	Subs	Gls
Doncaster Rov	South Hiendley	04/44	46-57	401	-	125
Bristol C	Tr	02/58	57-58	56	-	29
Barnsley	Tr	03/59	59-61	98	-	29

TINGAY Philip (Phil)
Born: Chesterfield, Derbyshire, England, 2 May, 1950 — G

League Club	Source	Date Signed	Seasons Played	Apps	Subs	Gls
Chesterfield	Chesterfield Tube W'ks	07/72	71-80	181	0	0
Barnsley	L	03/73	72	8	0	0

[TININHO] FAZENDA Miguel Angelo Karim
Born: Beira, Mozambique, 13 October, 1980 — LB

League Club	Source	Date Signed	Seasons Played	Apps	Subs	Gls
West Bromwich A	Beira Mar (POR)	07/07	07	1	0	0
Barnsley	L	01/08	07	3	0	0

TINKLER Eric
Born: Johannesburg, South Africa, 30 July, 1970 — M
South Africa: 48

League Club	Source	Date Signed	Seasons Played	Apps	Subs	Gls
Barnsley	Cagliari (ITA)	07/97	97-01	78	21	9

TINKLER John
Born: Trimdon, County Durham, England, 24 August, 1968 — M

League Club	Source	Date Signed	Seasons Played	Apps	Subs	Gls
Hartlepool U		12/86	86-91	153	17	7
Preston NE	Tr	07/92	92	22	2	2
Walsall	Tr	08/93	93	6	0	0

TINKLER Luke (Lou)
Born: Chester-le-Street, County Durham, England, 4 December, 1923 — LW
Died: Kidderminster, Worcestershire, England, April, 1995

League Club	Source	Date Signed	Seasons Played	Apps	Subs	Gls
Plymouth Arg	West Bromwich A (Am)	10/45	46-47	24	-	4
Walsall	Tr	06/48	48	18	-	0

TINKLER Mark Roland
Born: Bishop Auckland, County Durham, England, 24 October, 1974 — M
England: Youth/Schools

League Club	Source	Date Signed	Seasons Played	Apps	Subs	Gls
Leeds U	YT	11/91	92-96	14	11	0
York C	Tr	03/97	96-98	88	2	8
Southend U	Tr	08/99	99-00	55	1	1
Hartlepool U	Tr	11/00	00-06	200	11	34

TINNEY Hugh Joseph
Born: Glasgow, Scotland, 14 May, 1944 — RB
Scotland: U23-2

League Club	Source	Date Signed	Seasons Played	Apps	Subs	Gls
Bury	Partick Thistle	03/67	66-72	235	3	3

TINNION Brian
Born: Workington, Cumbria, England, 11 June, 1948 — F
England: Youth

League Club	Source	Date Signed	Seasons Played	Apps	Subs	Gls
Workington	Jnr	03/66	65-68	93	5	25
Wrexham	Tr	01/69	68-75	265	14	54
Chester C	L	12/71	71	3	0	0

TINNION Brian
Born: Stanley, County Durham, England, 23 February, 1968 — M/LB

League Club	Source	Date Signed	Seasons Played	Apps	Subs	Gls
Newcastle U	App	02/86	86-88	30	2	2
Bradford C	Tr	03/89	88-92	137	8	22
Bristol C	Tr	03/93	92-04	415	43	36

TINSLEY Alan
Born: Fleetwood, Lancashire, England, 1 January, 1951 — M

League Club	Source	Date Signed	Seasons Played	Apps	Subs	Gls
Preston NE	App	01/69	69	8	1	1
Bury	Tr	08/70	70-74	82	12	15

TINSLEY Colin
Born: Redcar, Cleveland, England, 24 October, 1935 — G

League Club	Source	Date Signed	Seasons Played	Apps	Subs	Gls
Grimsby T	Redcar BC	09/54	54-57	24	-	0
Darlington	Tr	08/58	58-60	79	-	0
Exeter C	Tr	07/61	61-62	56	-	1
Luton T	Tr	08/63	63-67	55	0	0

TINSON Darren Lee
Born: Birmingham, England, 15 November, 1969 — CD

League Club	Source	Date Signed	Seasons Played	Apps	Subs	Gls
Macclesfield T	Northwich Victoria	02/96	97-02	263	0	5
Shrewsbury T	Tr	07/03	04	42	1	0

TIOTE Cheick Ismael
Born: Yamoussoukro, Ivory Coast, 21 June, 1986 — DM
Ivory Coast: 48

League Club	Source	Date Signed	Seasons Played	Apps	Subs	Gls
Newcastle U	FC Twente (NED)	08/10	10-14	113	5	1

TIPPETT Michael Frederick
Born: Cadbury Heath, Avon, England, 11 June, 1930 — RW
Died: Frome, Somerset, England, 5 April, 2003

League Club	Source	Date Signed	Seasons Played	Apps	Subs	Gls
Bristol Rov	Cadbury Heath	04/48	49-51	8	-	2

TIPPETT Thomas Johan (Tommy)
Born: Gateshead, Tyne and Wear, England, 4 August, 1924 — LW
Died: Romford, E London, England, 8 March, 2005

League Club	Source	Date Signed	Seasons Played	Apps	Subs	Gls
Southend U	Ilford Youth Ass	05/46	46-51	92	-	20
Bournemouth	Tr	09/51	51-52	37	-	10

TIPTON Matthew John
Born: Bangor, Gwynedd, Wales, 29 June, 1980 — F
Wales: U21-6/Youth

League Club	Source	Date Signed	Seasons Played	Apps	Subs	Gls
Oldham Ath	YT	07/97	97-01	51	61	15
Macclesfield T	Tr	02/02	01-04	114	17	41
Mansfield T	Tr	07/05	05	4	0	0
Bury	Tr	08/05	05	15	9	3
Macclesfield T	L	08/06	06	15	17	4
Macclesfield T	Droylsden	07/09	09	11	20	5

TIRYAKI Mustafa
Born: Hackney, E London, England, 2 March, 1987 — F

League Club	Source	Date Signed	Seasons Played	Apps	Subs	Gls
Tranmere Rov	Havant & Waterlooville	08/11	11	16	14	3

TISDALE Paul Robert
Born: Valletta, Malta, 14 January, 1973 — M
England: Schools

League Club	Source	Date Signed	Seasons Played	Apps	Subs	Gls
Southampton	Jnr	06/91	94-95	5	11	1
Northampton T	L	03/92	92	5	0	0
Huddersfield T	L	11/96	96	1	1	0
Bristol C	Tr	06/97	97	2	3	0
Exeter C	L	12/97	97	10	0	1
Exeter C	Rtd	08/10	10	0	1	0

TITCHENER Alexander Mark (Alex)
Born: Abergele, Conwy, Wales, 13 June, 1991 — F

League Club	Source	Date Signed	Seasons Played	Apps	Subs	Gls
Crewe Alex	Sch	07/09				
Fleetwood T	Witton A	07/12	12	3	6	0

TITTERTON David Stewart John
Born: Hatton, Warwickshire, England, 25 September, 1971 — LB

League Club	Source	Date Signed	Seasons Played	Apps	Subs	Gls
Coventry C	YT	05/90	89-90	0	2	0
Hereford U	Tr	09/91	91-92	39	12	1
Wycombe W	Tr	08/93	93-94	15	4	1

TIVEY Mark Ronald
Born: Brentwood, Essex, England, 10 February, 1971 — W

League Club	Source	Date Signed	Seasons Played	Apps	Subs	Gls
Charlton Ath	YT	05/89	91	0	1	0

TOALE Ian
Born: Liverpool, England, 28 August, 1967 — RB

League Club	Source	Date Signed	Seasons Played	Apps	Subs	Gls
Liverpool	App	05/85				
Grimsby T	Tr	07/87	87	16	4	0

TOASE Donald Vickers (Don)
Born: Darlington, County Durham, England, 31 December, 1929 — RB
Died: Darlington, County Durham, England, 18 June, 1992
England: Youth

League Club	Source	Date Signed	Seasons Played	Apps	Subs	Gls
Newcastle U	Portsmouth (Am)	06/48				
Darlington	Tr	08/51	51	7	-	0

TOBIN Donald Joseph (Don)
Born: Prescot, Merseyside, England, 1 November, 1955 — M

League Club	Source	Date Signed	Seasons Played	Apps	Subs	Gls
Rochdale	Everton (App)	08/73	73-75	46	2	5

TOBIN Maurice
Born: Longriggend, Lanarkshire, Scotland, 30 July, 1920 — LB
Died: Norwich, England, 19 August, 2005

League Club	Source	Date Signed	Seasons Played	Apps	Subs	Gls
Norwich C	Longriggend BC	09/38	46-50	102	-	0

TOBIN Robert (Bobby)
Born: Cardiff, Wales, 29 March, 1921 — IF
Died: Cardiff, Wales, July, 2013

League Club	Source	Date Signed	Seasons Played	Apps	Subs	Gls
Cardiff C	Cardiff Corinthians	08/40	47	2	-	0

TOCKNELL Brian Thomas
Born: Pretoria, South Africa, 21 May, 1937 — WH/CH

League Club	Source	Date Signed	Seasons Played	Apps	Subs	Gls
Charlton Ath	Berea Park (RSA)	07/59	60-65	199	0	14

TOD Andrew (Andy)
Born: Dunfermline, Fife, Scotland, 4 November, 1971 — CD

League Club	Source	Date Signed	Seasons Played	Apps	Subs	Gls
Stockport Co (L)	Dunfermline Ath	10/00	00	11	0	3
Bradford C	Dunfermline Ath	08/01	01-02	29	6	5

TODA Kazuyuki
Born: Tokyo, Japan, 30 December, 1977 — DM
Japan: 20

League Club	Source	Date Signed	Seasons Played	Apps	Subs	Gls
Tottenham H (L)	Shimizu S-Pulse (JPN)	01/03	02	2	2	0

TODD Alexander (Alex)
Born: South Shields, Tyne and Wear, England, 7 November, 1929 — LH
Died: South Shields, Tyne and Wear, England, 8 March, 2012

League Club	Source	Date Signed	Seasons Played	Apps	Subs	Gls
Hartlepool U	South Shields Butchers	04/50	52-53	4	-	0

TODD Andrew John James (Andy)
Born: Derby, England, 21 September, 1974 — CD

League Club	Source	Date Signed	Seasons Played	Apps	Subs	Gls
Middlesbrough	YT	03/92	93-94	7	1	0
Swindon T	L	02/95	94	13	0	0
Bolton W	Tr	08/95	95-99	66	18	2
Charlton Ath	Tr	11/99	99-01	27	13	1
Grimsby T	L	02/02	01	12	0	3
Blackburn Rov	Tr	05/02	02-06	78	10	4
Burnley	L	09/03	03	7	0	0
Derby Co	Tr	07/07	07-08	21	9	1
Northampton T	L	11/08	08	7	0	0
Oldham Ath	Perth Glory (AUS)	01/11	10	5	1	0

TODD Andrew Jonathan (Andy)
Born: Nottingham, England, 22 February, 1979 — W

League Club	Source	Date Signed	Seasons Played	Apps	Subs	Gls
Nottingham F	Eastwood T	02/96				
Scarborough	Tr	02/99	98	0	1	0
Accrington Stan	Burton A	01/06	06	44	2	10
Rotherham U	Tr	07/07	07	11	2	0
Accrington Stan	L	01/08	07	14	7	0

TODD Christopher Richard (Chris)
Born: Swansea, Wales, 22 August, 1981 — CD

League Club	Source	Date Signed	Seasons Played	Apps	Subs	Gls
Swansea C	YT	07/00	00-01	39	4	4
Exeter C	Drogheda (ROI)	01/03	02	12	0	0
Torquay U	Tr	07/07	09	9	0	1

TODD Colin
Born: Chester-le-Street, County Durham, England, 12 December, 1948 — CD
England: 27/FLge-3/U23-14/Youth

League Club	Source	Date Signed	Seasons Played	Apps	Subs	Gls
Sunderland	App	02/66	66-70	170	3	3
Derby Co	Tr	02/71	70-78	293	0	6
Everton	Tr	09/78	78-79	32	0	1
Birmingham C	Tr	09/79	79-81	92	1	0
Nottingham F	Tr	08/82	82-83	36	0	0
Oxford U	Tr	02/84	83	12	0	0
Luton T	Vancouver W'caps (CAN)	10/84	84	2	0	0

TODD James (Jimmy)
Born: Belfast, Northern Ireland, 19 March, 1921 — WH
Died: Stoke-on-Trent, England, 19 December, 2007
Northern Ireland: War-2

League Club	Source	Date Signed	Seasons Played	Apps	Subs	Gls
Blackpool	Ards	02/45				
Port Vale	Tr	10/46	46-52	145	-	0

TODD Josh
Born: Carlisle, Cumbria, England, 11 June, 1994 — M

League Club	Source	Date Signed	Seasons Played	Apps	Subs	Gls
Carlisle U	Sch	06/12	12	0	1	0

TODD Keith Harris
Born: Clydach, Swansea, Wales, 2 March, 1941 — CF
Wales: U23-1

League Club	Source	Date Signed	Seasons Played	Apps	Subs	Gls
Swansea C	Clydach	09/59	60-67	196	2	78

TODD Kenneth (Kenny)
Born: Butterknowle, County Durham, England, 24 August, 1957 — M

League Club	Source	Date Signed	Seasons Played	Apps	Subs	Gls
Wolverhampton W	App	08/75	76-77	4	1	1
Port Vale	Tr	08/78	78-79	42	2	9
Portsmouth	Tr	10/79	79	1	2	1

TODD Kevin
Born: Sunderland, England, 28 February, 1958 — F/M

League Club	Source	Date Signed	Seasons Played	Apps	Subs	Gls
Newcastle U	Ryehope CW	08/81	81-82	5	2	3
Darlington	Tr	02/83	82-84	99	3	23

TODD Lee
Born: Hartlepool, Cleveland, England, 7 March, 1972 — LB

League Club	Source	Date Signed	Seasons Played	Apps	Subs	Gls
Stockport Co	Hartlepool U (YT)	07/90	90-96	214	11	2
Southampton	Tr	07/97	97	9	1	0
Bradford C	Tr	08/98	98	14	1	0
Walsall	L	09/99	99	1	0	0
Rochdale	Tr	08/00	00-01	48	2	3

TODD Mark Kenneth
Born: Belfast, Northern Ireland, 4 December, 1967 — M
Northern Ireland: U23-1/Youth/Schools

League Club	Source	Date Signed	Seasons Played	Apps	Subs	Gls
Manchester U	App	08/85				
Sheffield U	Tr	07/87	87-90	62	8	5
Wolverhampton W	L	03/91	90	6	1	0
Rotherham U	Tr	09/91	91-94	60	4	7
Scarborough	Tr	08/95	95	23	0	1
Mansfield T	Tr	02/96	95	10	2	0

TODD Paul Raymond
Born: Middlesbrough, England, 8 May, 1920 — IF
Died: Boston, Lincolnshire, England, October, 2000

League Club	Source	Date Signed	Seasons Played	Apps	Subs	Gls
Doncaster Rov	RAF Ceylon	09/45	46-49	160	-	49
Blackburn Rov	Tr	07/50	50-51	46	-	12
Hull C	Tr	10/51	51-52	27	-	3

TODD Robert Charles (Bob)
Born: Goole, East Riding of Yorkshire, England, 11 September, 1949 — RW

League Club	Source	Date Signed	Seasons Played	Apps	Subs	Gls
Liverpool	Scunthorpe U (App)	05/67				
Rotherham U	Tr	03/68	68	2	4	0
Mansfield T	Tr	11/68	68	3	1	0
Workington	Tr	07/69	69	10	6	0

TODD Ronald (Ronnie)
Born: Bellshill, Lanarkshire, Scotland, 4 October, 1935 — RH

League Club	Source	Date Signed	Seasons Played	Apps	Subs	Gls
Accrington Stan	Lesmahagow	02/56	59	5	-	0

TODD Samuel John (Sammy)
Born: Belfast, Northern Ireland, 22 September, 1945 — D/M
Northern Ireland: 11/U23-4

League Club	Source	Date Signed	Seasons Played	Apps	Subs	Gls
Burnley	Glentoran	09/62	63-69	108	8	1
Sheffield Wed	Tr	05/70	70-72	22	2	1
Mansfield T	L	02/74	73	6	0	0

TODD Thomas Bell (Tommy)
Born: Stonehouse, Lanarkshire, Scotland, 1 June, 1926 — CF
Died: 2014

League Club	Source	Date Signed	Seasons Played	Apps	Subs	Gls
Crewe Alex	Hamilton Academical	08/55	55	13	-	3
Derby Co	Tr	11/55	55	4	-	3
Rochdale	Tr	05/56	56	5	-	1

TODOROV Svetoslav
Born: Dobrich, Bulgaria, 30 August, 1978 — F
Bulgaria: 41/Youth

League Club	Source	Date Signed	Seasons Played	Apps	Subs	Gls
West Ham U	Liteks Lovech (BUL)	01/01	00-01	4	10	1
Portsmouth	Tr	03/02	01-06	54	23	33
Wigan Ath	L	08/06	06	2	3	0
Charlton Ath	Tr	07/07	07-08	5	15	3

TOFAS Georgios
Born: Larnaca, Cyprus, 17 June, 1989 — M
Cyprus: U21-5

League Club	Source	Date Signed	Seasons Played	Apps	Subs	Gls
Queens Park Rgrs	Anorthosis (CYP)	11/10	10	0	1	0

TOFFOLO Harry Stefane
Born: Welwyn Garden City, Hertfordshire, England, 19 August, 1995 — LB
England: Youth

League Club	Source	Date Signed	Seasons Played	Apps	Subs	Gls
Norwich C	Sch	07/13				
Swindon T	L	10/14	14	22	6	1

TOFTING Stig
Born: Aarhus, Denmark, 14 August, 1969 — M
Denmark: 41/U21-5

League Club	Source	Date Signed	Seasons Played	Apps	Subs	Gls
Bolton W	SV Hamburg (GER)	02/02	01-02	8	6	0

TOGWELL Samuel James (Sam)
Born: Beaconsfield, Buckinghamshire, England, 14 October, 1984 — DM

League Club	Source	Date Signed	Seasons Played	Apps	Subs	Gls
Crystal Palace	Sch	08/04	02	0	1	0
Oxford U	L	10/04	04	3	1	0
Northampton T	L	03/05	04	7	1	0
Port Vale	L	11/05	05	26	1	2
Barnsley	Tr	07/06	06-07	54	12	2
Scunthorpe U	Tr	08/08	08-11	136	20	5
Chesterfield	Tr	07/12	12-13	50	5	3
Wycombe W	L	03/14	13	3	1	0

TOLCHARD Jeffrey Graham (Jeff)
Born: Torquay, Devon, England, 17 March, 1944 — W

League Club	Source	Date Signed	Seasons Played	Apps	Subs	Gls
Torquay U	Newton Abbot Spurs	03/64	63-64	11	-	4
Exeter C	Tr	07/65	65	1	0	0

TOLLEY Glenn Anthony
Born: Knighton, Powys, Wales, 24 September, 1984 — M

League Club	Source	Date Signed	Seasons Played	Apps	Subs	Gls
Shrewsbury T	Sch	-	02	0	1	0

TOLLEY Jamie Christopher
Born: Ludlow, Shropshire, England, 12 May, 1983 — RW
Wales: U21-12

League Club	Source	Date Signed	Seasons Played	Apps	Subs	Gls
Shrewsbury T	YT	01/01	99-05	142	18	14
Macclesfield T	Tr	08/06	06-08	56	7	3
Hereford U	Tr	07/09	09	6	4	0

TOLLIDAY Stanley Albert (Stan)
Born: Hackney, E London, England, 6 August, 1922 — G
Died: Northampton, England, 26 June, 1951

League Club	Source	Date Signed	Seasons Played	Apps	Subs	Gls
Leyton Orient	Army	12/46	46-48	64	-	0
Walsall	Tr	06/50				

TOLMIE James (Jim)
Born: Glasgow, Scotland, 20 November, 1960 — LW
Scotland: SLge-1/U21-1

League Club	Source	Date Signed	Seasons Played	Apps	Subs	Gls
Manchester C	Lokeren (BEL)	08/83	83-85	46	15	15
Carlisle U	L	03/86	85	7	1	1

TOLSON Maxwell Norman (Max)
Born: Wollongong, NSW, Australia, 18 July, 1945 — CF
Australia: 16

League Club	Source	Date Signed	Seasons Played	Apps	Subs	Gls
Workington	South Coast U (AUS)	02/66	65-66	29	1	6

TOLSON Neil
Born: Stourbridge, West Midlands, England, 25 October, 1973 — F

League Club	Source	Date Signed	Seasons Played	Apps	Subs	Gls
Walsall	YT	12/91	91	3	6	1
Oldham Ath	Tr	03/92	92	0	3	0
Bradford C	Tr	12/93	93-95	32	31	12
Chester C	L	01/95	94	3	1	0
York C	Tr	07/96	96-98	66	18	18
Southend U	Tr	07/99	99-00	34	2	11

TOLSON William (Bill)
Born: Rochdale, Greater Manchester, England, 29 March, 1931 — IF

League Club	Source	Date Signed	Seasons Played	Apps	Subs	Gls
Rochdale	St Albans BC, Rochdale	10/53	53-54	10	-	0

TOM Steven (Steve)
Born: Ware, Hertfordshire, England, 5 February, 1951 — D/M

League Club	Source	Date Signed	Seasons Played	Apps	Subs	Gls
Queens Park Rgrs	App	02/69				
Brentford	Tr	06/71	71	13	5	1

TOMAN James Andrew (Andy)
Born: Northallerton, North Yorkshire, England, 7 March, 1962 — M

League Club	Source	Date Signed	Seasons Played	Apps	Subs	Gls
Lincoln C	Bishop Auckland	08/85	85	21	3	4
Hartlepool U	Bishop Auckland	01/87	86-88	112	0	28
Darlington	Tr	08/89	90-92	108	7	10
Scarborough	L	02/93	92	6	0	0
Scunthorpe U	Tr	08/93	93	15	0	5
Scarborough	Tr	12/93	93-95	33	12	3

TOMASSON Jon Dahl
Born: Roskilde, Denmark, 29 August, 1976 — F
Denmark: 112/U21-10/Youth

League Club	Source	Date Signed	Seasons Played	Apps	Subs	Gls
Newcastle U	Heerenveen (NED)	06/97	97	17	6	3

TOMKIN Cyril John
Born: Barrow, Cumbria, England, 18 November, 1918 — RW

League Club	Source	Date Signed	Seasons Played	Apps	Subs	Gls
Barrow	Dumbarton	03/48	46-47	3	-	0

TOMKINS James Oliver Charles
Born: Basildon, England, 29 March, 1989 — CD
England: U21-10/Youth

League Club	Source	Date Signed	Seasons Played	Apps	Subs	Gls
West Ham U	Sch	05/06	07-14	167	16	8
Derby Co	L	11/08	08	5	2	0

TOMKINS Leonard Anthony (Len)
Born: Isleworth, W London, England, 16 January, 1949 — LW
England: Youth

League Club	Source	Date Signed	Seasons Played	Apps	Subs	Gls
Crystal Palace	Jnr	04/67	67-69	18	2	2

TOMKINSON Derek
Born: Stoke-on-Trent, England, 6 April, 1931 — IF/LH

League Club	Source	Date Signed	Seasons Played	Apps	Subs	Gls
Port Vale	Burton A	12/52	52-54	29	-	5
Crewe Alex		08/56	56	17	-	1

TOMKYS Michael George (Mike)
Born: Kensington, Central London, England, 14 December, 1932 — RW
England: Youth

League Club	Source	Date Signed	Seasons Played	Apps	Subs	Gls
Queens Park Rgrs	Fulham (Am)	11/51	51-58	86	-	16

TOMLEY Frederick William (Fred)
Born: Liverpool, England, 11 July, 1931 — CH
Died: Liverpool, England, 13 February, 1981

League Club	Source	Date Signed	Seasons Played	Apps	Subs	Gls
Liverpool	Litherland	09/53	54	2	-	0
Chester C	Tr	07/55	55	1	-	0

TOMLIN David (Dave)
Born: Nuneaton, Warwickshire, England, 9 February, 1953 — W

League Club	Source	Date Signed	Seasons Played	Apps	Subs	Gls
Leicester C	App	02/71	71-75	20	7	2
Torquay U	Tr	04/77	76-77	37	1	2
Aldershot	Tr	08/78	78-80	24	6	2

TOMLIN Gavin Glenrick
Born: Gillingham, Kent, England, 13 January, 1983 — F/W

League Club	Source	Date Signed	Seasons Played	Apps	Subs	Gls
Brentford	Windsor & Eton	08/06	06	6	6	0
Yeovil T	Fisher Ath	07/08	08-09	58	19	14
Dagenham & Red	Tr	07/10	10-11	31	5	2
Torquay U	L	03/11	10	12	0	4
Gillingham	L	01/12	11	9	1	6
Southend U	Tr	07/12	12	28	5	13
Port Vale	Tr	06/13	13	17	7	5
Crawley T	Tr	06/14	14	29	6	3

TOMLIN Lee Marc
Born: Leicester, England, 12 January, 1989 — F/W
England: Semi Pro-2

League Club	Source	Date Signed	Seasons Played	Apps	Subs	Gls
Rushden & D	Sch	01/06	05	4	17	0
Peterborough U	Tr	08/10	10-13	120	15	32
Middlesbrough	Tr	01/14	13-14	41	15	11

TOMLINSON Ashley Darrell
Born: Doncaster, South Yorkshire, England, 28 September, 1966 — W

League Club	Source	Date Signed	Seasons Played	Apps	Subs	Gls
Doncaster Rov	App	-	83	2	2	0

TOMLINSON Ben
Born: Dinnington, South Yorkshire, England, 31 October, 1989 — F

League Club	Source	Date Signed	Seasons Played	Apps	Subs	Gls
Macclesfield T	Worksop T	07/11	11	15	10	6

TOMLINSON Charles Conway (Charlie)
Born: Sheffield, England, 2 December, 1919 — LW
Died: Sheffield, England, 1971

League Club	Source	Date Signed	Seasons Played	Apps	Subs	Gls
Bradford Park Ave	Sheffield Wed (Am)	04/39				
Sheffield Wed	Tr	07/44	46-50	68	-	7
Rotherham U	Tr	03/51	50-51	32	-	12

TOMLINSON David Ian
Born: Rotherham, South Yorkshire, England, 13 December, 1968 — RW

League Club	Source	Date Signed	Seasons Played	Apps	Subs	Gls
Sheffield Wed	App	12/86	86	0	1	0
Rotherham U	Tr	08/87	87	6	3	0
Barnet	Boston U	12/90	91	0	3	0

TOMLINSON Ezekiel Jeremiah
Born: Birmingham, England, 9 November, 1985 — M

League Club	Source	Date Signed	Seasons Played	Apps	Subs	Gls
Stockport Co	West Bromwich A (Sch)	03/05	04	2	3	0

TOMLINSON Francis (Frank)
Born: Manchester, England, 5 April, 1926 — RW
Died: Oldham, Greater Manchester, England, April, 1999

League Club	Source	Date Signed	Seasons Played	Apps	Subs	Gls
Oldham Ath	Goslings	11/46	46-50	115	-	28
Rochdale	Tr	11/51	51	20	-	2
Chester C	Tr	08/52	52	11	-	0

TOMLINSON Francis Anthony (Frank)
Born: Manchester, England, 23 October, 1925 — RW

League Club	Source	Date Signed	Seasons Played	Apps	Subs	Gls
Halifax T	Stalybridge Celtic	11/50	50	14	-	4

TOMLINSON Graeme Murdoch
Born: Watford, Hertfordshire, England, 10 December, 1975 — F

League Club	Source	Date Signed	Seasons Played	Apps	Subs	Gls
Bradford C	YT	-	93	12	5	6
Manchester U	Tr	07/94				
Luton T	L	03/96	95	1	6	0
Bournemouth	L	08/97	97	6	1	1
Millwall	L	03/98	97	2	1	1
Macclesfield T	Tr	07/98	98-99	22	24	6
Exeter C	Tr	07/00	00-01	38	18	6

TOMLINSON Harry
Born: Plymouth, England, 26 October, 1922 — RB
Died: Ingleton, North Yorkshire, England, January, 1988

League Club	Source	Date Signed	Seasons Played	Apps	Subs	Gls
Doncaster Rov	Army	10/44	46-48	58	-	0

TOMLINSON John
Born: Bebington, Wirral, England, 26 June, 1934 — RW
Died: Corby, Northamptonshire, England, 4 February, 2014
England: Youth

League Club	Source	Date Signed	Seasons Played	Apps	Subs	Gls
Everton	Jnr	06/52	56	2	-	0
Chesterfield	Tr	06/57	57-58	47	-	5

TOMLINSON Michael Lloyd (Micky)
Born: Lambeth, S London, England, 15 September, 1972 — RW

League Club	Source	Date Signed	Seasons Played	Apps	Subs	Gls
Leyton Orient	YT	07/91	90-93	7	7	1
Barnet	Tr	03/94	93-96	67	26	4

TOMLINSON Paul
Born: Rotherham, South Yorkshire, England, 4 February, 1965 — G

League Club	Source	Date Signed	Seasons Played	Apps	Subs	Gls
Sheffield U	Middlewood Rov	06/83	83-86	37	0	0
Birmingham C	L	03/87	86	11	0	0
Bradford C	Tr	06/87	87-94	293	0	0

TOMLINSON Robert Windle (Bob)
Born: Blackburn, Greater Manchester, England, 4 June, 1924 — FB
Died: Blackburn, Greater Manchester, England, 30 December, 1996

League Club	Source	Date Signed	Seasons Played	Apps	Subs	Gls
Blackburn Rov	Feniscowles	01/43	46-47	25	-	0
Halifax T	Mossley	06/51	51	8	-	0

TOMLINSON Stuart Charles
Born: Ellesmere Port, Cheshire, England, 10 May, 1985 — G

League Club	Source	Date Signed	Seasons Played	Apps	Subs	Gls
Crewe Alex	Sch	07/03	02-08	17	3	0
Port Vale	Barrow	07/10	10-11	72	2	0
Burton A	Tr	09/12	12	25	0	0

TOMMASI Damiano
Born: Verona, Italy, 17 May, 1974 — M
Italy: 25/U21-4

League Club	Source	Date Signed	Seasons Played	Apps	Subs	Gls
Queens Park Rgrs	Levante (SPN)	09/08	08	5	2	0

TOMPKIN Maurice
Born: Countesthorpe, Leicestershire, England, 17 February, 1919 — IF
Died: Leicester, England, 27 September, 1956

League Club	Source	Date Signed	Seasons Played	Apps	Subs	Gls
Leicester C	Countesthorpe U	03/38	37	1	-	0
Bury	Tr	12/45				
Huddersfield T	Tr	09/46	46	10	-	1

TOMS Frazer Peter
Born: Ealing, W London, England, 13 September, 1979 — LW

League Club	Source	Date Signed	Seasons Played	Apps	Subs	Gls
Charlton Ath	YT	07/98				
Barnet	Tr	07/99	99-00	46	19	1

TONER Ciaran
Born: Craigavon, Armagh, Northern Ireland, 30 June, 1981 — M
Northern Ireland: 2/U21-17/Youth/Schools

League Club	Source	Date Signed	Seasons Played	Apps	Subs	Gls
Tottenham H	YT	07/99				
Peterborough U	L	12/01	01	6	0	0
Bristol Rov	Tr	03/02	01	6	0	0
Leyton Orient	Tr	05/02	02-03	41	11	2
Lincoln C	Tr	08/04	04	10	5	2
Cambridge U	L	03/05	04	6	2	0
Grimsby T	Tr	07/05	05-07	80	14	14
Rochdale	Tr	07/08	08-09	39	11	1

TONER James (Jimmy)
Born: Shettleston, Glasgow, Scotland, 23 August, 1924 — RW

League Club	Source	Date Signed	Seasons Played	Apps	Subs	Gls
Leeds U	Dundee	06/54	54	7	-	1

TONER William (Willie)
Born: Glasgow, Scotland, 18 December, 1929 — D
Died: Glasgow, Scotland, 16 March, 1999
Scotland: SLge-5

League Club	Source	Date Signed	Seasons Played	Apps	Subs	Gls
Sheffield U	Glasgow Celtic	05/51	51-53	55	-	2

TONES John David
Born: Silksworth, Tyne and Wear, England, 3 December, 1950 — CD

League Club	Source	Date Signed	Seasons Played	Apps	Subs	Gls
Sunderland	App	05/68	72	2	4	0
Arsenal	Tr	07/73				
Swansea C	L	09/74	74	7	0	0
Mansfield T	L	10/74	74	3	0	0

TONEV Aleksander Antonov
Born: Sofia, Bulgaria, 3 February, 1990 — LW
Bulgaria: 17/U21-15/Youth

League Club	Source	Date Signed	Seasons Played	Apps	Subs	Gls
Aston Villa	Lech Poznan (POL)	06/13	13	6	11	0

TONEY Ivan Benjamin Elijah
Born: Northampton, England, 16 March, 1996 — F

League Club	Source	Date Signed	Seasons Played	Apps	Subs	Gls
Northampton T	Sch	09/13	13-14	26	27	11

TONG David Joseph
Born: Blackpool, Lancashire, England, 21 September, 1955 — M

League Club	Source	Date Signed	Seasons Played	Apps	Subs	Gls
Blackpool	App	09/73	74-78	71	8	7
Shrewsbury T	Tr	09/78	78-81	156	4	8
Cardiff C	Tr	08/82	82-85	119	1	3
Rochdale	L	09/85	85	0	2	0
Bristol C	Tr	10/85	85	19	0	0
Gillingham	Tr	03/86	85	5	0	0
Cambridge U	Tr	08/86	86	4	2	0

TONG Raymond (Ray)
Born: Bolton, Greater Manchester, England, 3 February, 1942 — LW

League Club	Source	Date Signed	Seasons Played	Apps	Subs	Gls
Blackburn Rov		07/62				
Bradford C	Tr	06/63	63-64	20	-	2

TONGE Alan John
Born: Bury, Greater Manchester, England, 25 February, 1972 — M/FB

League Club	Source	Date Signed	Seasons Played	Apps	Subs	Gls
Manchester U	YT	07/90				
Exeter C	Horwich RMI	12/91	91-93	14	5	1

League Club	Source	Date Signed	Seasons Played	Career Record Apps	Subs	Gls
TONGE Dale						
Born: Doncaster, South Yorkshire, England, 7 May, 1985						RB
Barnsley	Sch	07/04	03-06	30	15	0
Gillingham	L	03/07	06	3	0	0
Rotherham U	Tr	07/07	07-12	146	17	1
Torquay U	Tr	07/13	13	36	0	0
TONGE Jeffrey Alan (Jeff)						
Born: Manchester, England, 5 May, 1942						RW
Died: Manchester, England, 29 October, 1996						
Bury	Droylsden	03/60	59	1	-	0
TONGE Keith Andrew						
Born: Edmonton, N London, England, 6 November, 1964						F
Brentford	App	11/82	81	0	1	0
TONGE Michael William Eric						
Born: Manchester, England, 7 April, 1983						M
England: U21-2/Youth						
Sheffield U	YT	03/01	00-08	234	28	21
Stoke C	Tr	09/08	08-10	1	11	0
Preston NE	L	11/09	09	7	0	0
Derby Co	L	02/10	09	18	0	2
Preston NE	L	11/10	10	5	0	1
Barnsley	L	01/12	11	7	3	0
Leeds U	Tr	09/12	12-14	52	16	4
Millwall	L	02/15	14	5	1	0
TONKIN Anthony Richard						
Born: Penzance, Cornwall, England, 17 January, 1980						LB
England: Semi Pro-1						
Stockport Co	Yeovil T	09/02	02	23	1	0
Crewe Alex	Tr	08/03	03-05	80	8	0
Yeovil T	Tr	08/06	06	1	4	0
Oxford U	Cambridge U	01/10	10-11	43	10	0
Aldershot T	Tr	05/12	12	36	1	0
TONNE Erik						
Born: Trondheim, Norway, 7 May, 1991						W
Sheffield U	Strindheim (NOR)	01/11	10-11	0	4	1
TOON Colin						
Born: New Houghton, Derbyshire, England, 26 April, 1940						RB
Mansfield T	Jnr	07/57	57-65	213	0	1
TOOTILL George Albert (Alf)						
Born: Walkden, Greater Manchester, England, 29 October, 1913						CH
Died: Sheffield, England, 29 July, 1984						
Plymouth Arg	Chorley	05/36	36-37	9	-	0
Sheffield U	Tr	01/38	38	12	-	0
Hartlepool U	Tr	07/47	47	18	-	0
TOOTLE Matthew James Anthony (Matt)						
Born: Widnes, Cheshire, England, 11 October, 1990						RB
Crewe Alex	Sch	07/09	09-14	186	13	2
TOOZE Dennis George						
Born: Swansea, Wales, 12 October, 1917						FB
Died: Rugby, Warwickshire, England, March, 1994						
Coventry C	Redditch	05/37	46-48	36	-	0
TOOZE Robert William (Bob)						
Born: Bristol, England, 19 December, 1946						G
Bristol C	Jnr	07/65				
Shrewsbury T	Tr	03/69	68-72	73	0	0
Gillingham	L	03/72	71	7	0	0
TOPP Willy Adolfo						
Born: Temuco, Chile, 4 March, 1986						F
Bradford C	Catolica Univ (CHL)	12/07	07-08	6	7	0
TOPPING Christopher (Chris)						
Born: Bubwith, East Riding of Yorkshire, England, 6 March, 1951						CD
York C	App	03/69	68-77	410	2	11
Huddersfield T	Tr	05/78	78-80	43	0	1
TOPPING David (Dave)						
Born: Shotts, Lanarkshire, Scotland, 9 March, 1926						RB
Died: Yeovil, Somerset, England, 20 May, 2013						
Torquay U	Clyde	05/48	48-52	151	-	3
TOPPING Henry Westby (Harry)						
Born: St Helens, Merseyside, England, 28 September, 1915						RB
Died: St Helens, Merseyside, England, July, 2004						
Stockport Co	Rossendale U	03/39	38	3	-	0
New Brighton	Tr	08/46	46-47	67	-	0
TORAL Jon-Miquel (Jon)						
Born: Reus, Spain, 5 February, 1995						W
Arsenal	Sch	02/12				
Brentford	L	08/14	14	8	26	6

League Club	Source	Date Signed	Seasons Played	Career Record Apps	Subs	Gls
TORFASON Gudmundur (Gunni)						
Born: Vestmannaeyjar, Iceland, 13 December, 1961						F
Iceland: 26						
Doncaster Rov	St Johnstone	07/94	94	1	3	0
TORGHELLE Sandor						
Born: Budapest, Hungary, 5 May, 1982						F
Hungary: 42/U21-7/Youth						
Crystal Palace	MTK Budapest (HUN)	08/04	04	3	9	0
TORPEY Stephen David James (Steve)						
Born: Islington, N London, England, 8 December, 1970						F
Millwall	YT	02/89	89	3	4	0
Bradford C	Tr	11/90	90-92	86	10	22
Swansea C	Tr	08/93	93-96	151	11	44
Bristol C	Tr	08/97	97-99	53	17	13
Notts Co	L	08/98	98	4	2	1
Scunthorpe U	Tr	02/00	99-06	214	25	59
Lincoln C	Tr	07/07	07	7	6	0
TORPEY Stephen Robert (Steve)						
Born: Kirkby, Merseyside, England, 16 September, 1981						F
England: Youth						
Liverpool	YT	05/99				
Port Vale	Tr	08/01	01	0	1	0
TORRANCE Andrew (Andy)						
Born: Glasgow, Scotland, 8 April, 1934						RW/CF
Died: Glasgow, Scotland, 23 October, 2004						
Barrow	Yeovil T	05/58	58	29	-	2
TORRANCE George Clark						
Born: Rothesay, Isle of Bute, Scotland, 17 September, 1957						M
Brentford	Wokingham T	12/84	84-85	29	5	1
TORRANCE George Syme						
Born: Glasgow, Scotland, 27 November, 1935						G
Leicester C	Thorniewood U	07/54				
Oldham Ath	Tr	08/56	56	4	-	0
Rochdale	Tr	09/57	57	2	-	0
TORRES Fernando Jose						
Born: Madrid, Spain, 20 March, 1984						F
Spain: 110/U21-10/Youth						
Liverpool	Atletico Madrid (SPN)	07/07	07-10	91	11	65
Chelsea	Tr	01/11	10-13	72	38	20
TORRES Sergio Raul						
Born: Mar del Plata, Argentina, 8 November, 1983						M
Wycombe W	Basingstoke T	08/05	05-07	57	29	6
Peterborough U	Tr	07/08	08-09	17	7	1
Lincoln C	L	09/09	09	7	1	1
Crawley T	Tr	07/10	11-13	50	33	3
TOSELAND Geoffrey (Geoff)						
Born: Kettering, Northamptonshire, England, 31 January, 1931						LW
Sunderland	Kettering T	12/48	52	6	-	1
TOSER Ernest William (Ernie)						
Born: London, England, 30 November, 1912						CH
Died: Hastings, East Sussex, England, 25 March, 2002						
England: Schools						
Millwall	Dulwich Hamlet	05/37	37	2	-	0
Notts Co	Tr	09/46	46	2	-	0
TOSH Paul James						
Born: Arbroath, Angus, Scotland, 18 October, 1973						F
Exeter C (L)	Hibernian	02/99	98	8	2	2
TOSHACK John Benjamin						
Born: Cardiff, Wales, 22 March, 1949						F
Wales: 40/U23-3/Schools						
Cardiff C	Jnr	03/66	65-70	158	4	74
Liverpool	Tr	11/70	70-77	169	3	74
Swansea C	Tr	03/78	77-83	58	5	25
TOSHACK Jonathan Cameron (Cameron)						
Born: Cardiff, Wales, 7 March, 1970						F
Swansea C	Jnr	09/88				
Bristol C	Tr	11/89				
Cardiff C	Tr	02/91	90-91	1	4	0
TOSIC Dusko						
Born: Zrenjanin, Serbia, 19 January, 1985						LB
Serbia: 14						
Portsmouth	Werder Bremen (GER)	02/10				
Queens Park Rgrs	L	03/10	09	5	0	0
TOSIC Zoran						
Born: Zrenjanin, Serbia, 28 April, 1987						LW

League Club	Source	Date Signed	Seasons Played	Career Record Apps	Subs	Gls
Serbia: 65/U21-17						
Manchester U	Part'n Belgrade (SRB)	01/09	08	0	2	0
TOTTEN Alexander Reginald (Alex)						
Born: Southampton, England, 1 October, 1976						M
Portsmouth	YT	11/94	94	3	1	0
TOTTOH Melvyn (Mel)						
Born: Manchester, England, 26 July, 1956						W
Preston NE	Lytham	05/85	85	0	1	0
TOULOUSE Cyril Harvey						
Born: Acton, W London, England, 24 December, 1923						CH
Died: Pembroke, Wales, 22 January, 1980						
Brentford	St Cuthman's	05/46	46-47	13	-	0
Tottenham H	Tr	12/47	48	2	-	0
TOUNKARA Oumare						
Born: Paris, France, 25 May, 1990						F
Sunderland	CS Sedan (FRA)	11/09				
Oldham Ath	L	08/10	10	40	4	7
Oldham Ath	L	03/12	11	3	5	1
Bristol Rov	Red Star Paris (FRA)	02/13	12	4	5	2
Stevenage	Tr	05/13	13	6	9	0
TOURE Alioune Kissima						
Born: St Brieuc, France, 9 September, 1978						F
France: Youth						
Manchester C	FC Nantes (FRA)	09/01	01	0	1	0
TOURE Gnegneri Yaya (Yaya)						
Born: Bouake, Ivory Coast, 13 May, 1983						M
Ivory Coast: 95						
Manchester C	Barcelona (SPN)	07/10	10-14	160	3	51
TOURE Kolo Habib						
Born: Bouake, Ivory Coast, 19 March, 1981						CD
Ivory Coast: 118						
Arsenal	ASEC Mimosa (IVC)	02/02	02-08	203	22	9
Manchester C	Tr	07/09	09-12	70	12	2
Liverpool	Tr	07/13	13-14	22	10	0
TOVEY Paul William						
Born: Wokingham, Berkshire, England, 5 December, 1973						M
Bristol Rov	YT	07/92	93-95	8	1	0
TOVEY Ronald Arthur (Ron)						
Born: Bristol, England, 24 September, 1930						CF
Bristol C	Southmead Sports	01/53	52-53	12	-	3
TOVEY William James						
Born: Bristol, England, 18 October, 1931						LH
Died: Bristol, England, 8 January, 2000						
Bristol C	Jnr	12/48	48-52	57	-	2
TOWERS Edwin James (Jim)						
Born: Shepherds Bush, W London, England, 15 April, 1933						IF
Died: Ealing, W London, England, 16 September, 2010						
Brentford	Jnr	05/51	54-60	262	-	153
Queens Park Rgrs	Tr	05/61	61	28	-	15
Millwall	Tr	08/62	62	19	-	7
Gillingham	Tr	01/63	62	8	-	6
Aldershot	Tr	07/63	63	28	-	13
TOWERS Ian Joseph						
Born: Consett, County Durham, England, 11 October, 1940						F/W
Died: Cape Town, South Africa, 25 January, 2015						
Burnley	Jnr	10/57	60-65	43	1	12
Oldham Ath	Tr	01/66	65-67	94	1	45
Bury	Tr	07/68	68-70	43	5	7
TOWERS John						
Born: Willington, County Durham, England, 21 December, 1913						IF/WH
Died: Middlesbrough, England, 3 January, 1979						
Darlington (Am)	Willington	09/34	34-38	94	-	22
Darlington	Willington	05/46	46	13	-	0
TOWERS Mark Anthony (Tony)						
Born: Manchester, England, 13 April, 1952						M
England: 3/U23-8/Youth/Schools						
Manchester C	App	04/69	68-73	117	5	10
Sunderland	Tr	03/74	73-76	108	0	19
Birmingham C	Tr	07/77	77-79	90	2	4
Rochdale	Vancouver W'caps (CAN)	02/85	84	1	1	0
TOWERS William Henry (Bill)						
Born: Leicester, England, 13 July, 1920						WH
Died: Newport, Isle of Wight, England, 15 April, 2000						
Leicester C	Bentley Engineering	01/45	46	4	-	0
Torquay U	Tr	10/46	46-55	274	-	0

League Club	Source	Date Signed	Seasons Played	Career Record Apps	Subs	Gls
TOWN David Edward						
Born: Bournemouth, England, 9 December, 1976						F
Bournemouth	YT	04/95	93-98	18	38	2
Boston U	Hayes	03/01	02	0	8	0
TOWNEND Gary Alfred						
Born: Kilburn, NW London, England, 1 April, 1940						IF
Millwall	Redhill	08/60	60-63	50	-	20
TOWNER Antony James (Tony)						
Born: Brighton, England, 2 May, 1955						RW
Brighton & HA	App	01/73	72-78	153	9	24
Millwall	Tr	10/78	78-79	68	0	13
Rotherham U	Tr	08/80	80-82	108	0	12
Sheffield U	L	03/83	82	9	1	1
Wolverhampton W	Tr	08/83	83	25	6	2
Charlton Ath	Tr	09/84	84-85	22	5	2
Rochdale	Tr	11/85	85	4	1	0
Cambridge U	Tr	03/86	85-86	8	0	0
TOWNLEY Leon						
Born: Loughton, Essex, England, 16 February, 1976						M/D
Tottenham H	YT	07/94				
Brentford	Tr	09/97	97	15	1	2
TOWNSEND Andrew David (Andy)						
Born: Maidstone, Kent, England, 27 July, 1963						M
Republic of Ireland: 70/B-1						
Southampton	Weymouth	01/85	84-87	77	6	5
Norwich C	Tr	08/88	88-89	66	5	8
Chelsea	Tr	07/90	90-92	110	0	12
Aston Villa	Tr	07/93	93-97	133	1	8
Middlesbrough	Tr	08/97	97-99	73	4	3
West Bromwich A	Tr	09/99	99	15	3	0
TOWNSEND Andros Darryl						
Born: Chingford, NE London, England, 16 July, 1991						RW
England: 9/U21-3/Youth						
Tottenham H	Sch	12/08	12-14	22	25	3
Yeovil T	L	03/09	08	10	0	1
Leyton Orient	L	08/09	09	17	5	2
MK Dons	L	01/10	09	8	1	2
Ipswich T	L	08/10	10	11	2	1
Watford	L	01/11	10	2	1	0
Millwall	L	03/11	10	11	0	2
Leeds U	L	01/12	11	5	1	1
Birmingham C	L	02/12	11	11	4	0
Queens Park Rgrs	L	01/13	12	12	0	2
TOWNSEND Benjamin (Ben)						
Born: Reading, England, 8 October, 1981						RB
Wycombe W	YT	01/01	99-01	12	1	0
TOWNSEND Christopher Gordon (Chris)						
Born: Caerleon, Monmouthshire, Wales, 30 March, 1966						F
Wales: Youth/Schools						
Cardiff C	Jnr	07/83	83	2	3	0
TOWNSEND Conor Stephen						
Born: Hessle, East Riding of Yorkshire, England, 4 March, 1993						LB
Hull C	Sch	05/11				
Chesterfield	L	11/12	12	16	4	1
Carlisle U	L	09/13	13	10	2	0
Scunthorpe U	L	02/15	14	5	1	0
TOWNSEND Donald Edward (Don)						
Born: Swindon, England, 17 September, 1930						LB
Charlton Ath	Trowbridge T	07/50	54-61	249	-	1
Crystal Palace	Tr	07/62	62-64	77	-	0
TOWNSEND George Ernest						
Born: Ashton-under-Lyne, Greater Manchester, England, 29 July, 1957						LB
Rochdale	App	07/75	74-75	31	1	0
TOWNSEND James Clabby (Jim)						
Born: Greenock, Inverclyde, Scotland, 2 February, 1945						WH/IF
Middlesbrough	St Johnstone	02/64	63-65	65	2	6
TOWNSEND Leonard Francis (Len)						
Born: Brentford, W London, England, 31 August, 1917						IF
Died: Sleaford, Lincolnshire, England, August, 1997						
Northern Ireland: NILge-1						
Brentford	Hayes	05/37	38-46	33	-	12
Bristol C	Tr	06/47	47-48	74	-	45
Millwall	Tr	07/49	49	5	-	1
TOWNSEND Luke Allen						
Born: Guildford, Surrey, England, 28 September, 1986						F
Queens Park Rgrs	Sch	-	04	0	2	0

TOWNSEND Martin Vincent
Born: Romford, E London, England, 15 June, 1946 — G

League Club	Source	Date Signed	Seasons Played	Apps	Subs	Gls
Fulham	App	-	63	2	-	0

TOWNSEND Michael John
Born: Walsall, West Midlands, England, 17 May, 1986 — CD

League Club	Source	Date Signed	Seasons Played	Apps	Subs	Gls
Cheltenham T	Wolverhampton W (Sch)	01/05	05-09	127	7	6
Barnet	L	10/08	08	13	0	0
Hereford U	Tr	07/10	10-11	78	4	1

TOWNSEND Neil Royston
Born: Long Buckby, Northamptonshire, England, 1 February, 1950 — CD
England: Youth

League Club	Source	Date Signed	Seasons Played	Apps	Subs	Gls
Northampton T	Jnr	09/68	68-71	65	2	1
Southend U	Bedford T	07/73	73-78	156	1	7
Bournemouth	Weymouth	07/79	79-80	34	0	2

TOWNSEND Quentin Lee
Born: Worcester, England, 13 February, 1977 — CD

League Club	Source	Date Signed	Seasons Played	Apps	Subs	Gls
Wolverhampton W	YT	07/95				
Hereford U	Tr	07/96	96	6	1	0

TOWNSEND Russell Nelson (Russ)
Born: Reading, England, 17 January, 1960 — M

League Club	Source	Date Signed	Seasons Played	Apps	Subs	Gls
Northampton T	Barnet	09/79	79	12	1	0

TOWNSEND Ryan Matthew George
Born: Ashton-under-Lyne, Greater Manchester, England, 2 September, 1985 — FB

League Club	Source	Date Signed	Seasons Played	Apps	Subs	Gls
Burnley	Sch	-	03	0	1	0

TOWNSEND William (Billy)
Born: Bedworth, Warwickshire, England, 27 December, 1922 — G
Died: Blackpool, Lancashire, England, 21 December, 1988

League Club	Source	Date Signed	Seasons Played	Apps	Subs	Gls
Derby Co	Nuneaton Bor	09/42	46-52	79	-	0

TOWNSLEY Derek Johnstone
Born: Carlisle, Cumbria, England, 21 March, 1973 — M

League Club	Source	Date Signed	Seasons Played	Apps	Subs	Gls
Oxford U	Hibernian	07/03	03	9	2	0

TOWNSON Kevin
Born: Liverpool, England, 19 April, 1983 — F
England: Youth

League Club	Source	Date Signed	Seasons Played	Apps	Subs	Gls
Rochdale	Everton (Jnr)	07/00	00-04	41	61	25
Macclesfield T	Tr	03/05	04-05	5	19	2

TOWSE Gary Thomas
Born: Dover, Kent, England, 14 May, 1952 — G

League Club	Source	Date Signed	Seasons Played	Apps	Subs	Gls
Crystal Palace	Folkestone	01/72				
Brentford	Tr	06/73	73	5	0	0

TOZE Edward
Born: Manchester, England, 6 March, 1923 — G
Died: Salford, England, November, 1987

League Club	Source	Date Signed	Seasons Played	Apps	Subs	Gls
Halifax T	Jnr	08/50	50	5	-	0

TOZER Ben Peter Anthony
Born: Plymouth, England, 1 March, 1990 — CD

League Club	Source	Date Signed	Seasons Played	Apps	Subs	Gls
Swindon T	Sch	-	07	1	1	0
Newcastle U	Tr	01/08	09	0	1	0
Northampton T	L	09/10	10	28	3	3
Northampton T	Tr	07/11	11-14	123	19	3
Colchester U	L	11/13	13	1	0	0

TOZSER Daniel
Born: Szolnok, Hungary, 12 May, 1985 — M
Hungary: 27/U21-2

League Club	Source	Date Signed	Seasons Played	Apps	Subs	Gls
Watford (L)	Genoa (ITA)	01/14	13-14	54	11	5

TRABELSI Hatem
Born: Ariana, Tunisia, 25 January, 1977 — RB
Tunisia: 61

League Club	Source	Date Signed	Seasons Played	Apps	Subs	Gls
Manchester C	Ajax (NED)	08/06	06	16	4	1

TRACEY Michael George (Mike)
Born: Blackburn, Greater Manchester, England, 14 February, 1935 — W
Died: Roshin, County Donegal , Republic of Ireland, 30 May, 2014
England: Amateur-3

League Club	Source	Date Signed	Seasons Played	Apps	Subs	Gls
Luton T	Crook T	11/59	59-60	23	-	3
Lincoln C	Tr	07/61	61	21	-	5

TRACEY Richard Shaun
Born: Dewsbury, West Yorkshire, England, 9 July, 1979 — F

League Club	Source	Date Signed	Seasons Played	Apps	Subs	Gls
Sheffield U	YT	06/97				
Rotherham U	Tr	02/98	98	0	3	0
Carlisle U	Tr	03/99	98-00	39	14	11
Macclesfield T	Tr	01/01	00-01	21	12	5

TRACEY Simon Peter
Born: Woolwich, SE London, England, 9 December, 1967 — G

League Club	Source	Date Signed	Seasons Played	Apps	Subs	Gls
Wimbledon	App	02/86	88	1	0	0

TRAORE Lacina
Born: Abidjan, Ivory Coast, 20 August, 1990 — F
Ivory Coast: 8

League Club	Source	Date Signed	Seasons Played	Apps	Subs	Gls
Everton (L)	AS Monaco (FRA)	01/14	13	0	1	0

TRAUTMANN Bernhard Carl (Bert)
Born: Bremen, Germany, 22 October, 1923 — G
Died: Valencia, Spain, 19 July, 2013
England: FLge-2

League Club	Source	Date Signed	Seasons Played	Apps	Subs	Gls
Manchester C	St Helens T	11/49	49-63	508	-	0

TRAVERS Michael Joseph Patrick (Mike)
Born: Camberley, Surrey, England, 23 June, 1942 — FB/LW

League Club	Source	Date Signed	Seasons Played	Apps	Subs	Gls
Reading	Jnr	10/60	60-66	156	2	34
Portsmouth	Tr	07/67	67-71	74	10	6
Aldershot	Tr	07/72	72	29	1	2

TRAVIS David Alan
Born: Doncaster, South Yorkshire, England, 4 July, 1964 — M

League Club	Source	Date Signed	Seasons Played	Apps	Subs	Gls
Doncaster Rov	Hatfield Main	08/84	84-85	10	2	0
Scunthorpe U	Tr	02/86	85-86	13	0	1
Chesterfield	Gainsborough Trinity	08/87	87	6	5	0

TRAVIS Donald (Don)
Born: Manchester, England, 21 January, 1924 — CF
Died: Yeovil, Somerset, England, February, 2002

League Club	Source	Date Signed	Seasons Played	Apps	Subs	Gls
West Ham U	Blackpool (Am)	09/45	46-47	5	-	0
Southend U	Tr	05/48	48	1	-	0
Accrington Stan	Tr	12/48	48-50	71	-	36
Crewe Alex	Tr	11/50	50-51	36	-	12
Oldham Ath	Tr	10/51	51	5	-	1
Chester C	Tr	02/52	51-53	99	-	45
Oldham Ath	Tr	08/54	54-56	109	-	61

TRAVIS Nicolas Vaughan (Nicky)
Born: Sheffield, England, 12 March, 1987 — M

League Club	Source	Date Signed	Seasons Played	Apps	Subs	Gls
Sheffield U	Sch	07/04				
Chesterfield	L	08/07	07	0	2	0

TRAVIS Simon Christopher
Born: Preston, Lancashire, England, 22 March, 1977 — RB

League Club	Source	Date Signed	Seasons Played	Apps	Subs	Gls
Torquay U	YT	-	95	4	4	0
Stockport Co	Holywell T	08/97	97-98	4	18	2
Hereford U	Stevenage Bor	02/04	06	34	2	0

TRAVNER Jure
Born: Celje, Yugoslavia, 28 September, 1985 — LB
Slovenia: U21

League Club	Source	Date Signed	Seasons Played	Apps	Subs	Gls
Watford	NK Celje (SVN)	07/09				
Reading	FC Baku (AZE)	12/14	14	1	0	0

TRAYNOR Gregory (Greg)
Born: Salford, England, 17 October, 1984 — W

League Club	Source	Date Signed	Seasons Played	Apps	Subs	Gls
Wigan Ath	Sch	07/04	01	0	1	0

TRAYNOR Robert Terence (Bobby)
Born: Burnham, Buckinghamshire, England, 1 November, 1983 — F

League Club	Source	Date Signed	Seasons Played	Apps	Subs	Gls
Brentford	Sch	07/02	02	0	2	0

TRAYNOR Thomas Joseph (Tommy)
Born: Dundalk, Republic of Ireland, 22 July, 1933 — LB
Died: Southampton, England, 20 September, 2006
Republic of Ireland: 8

League Club	Source	Date Signed	Seasons Played	Apps	Subs	Gls
Southampton	Dundalk (ROI)	06/52	52-65	433	0	7

TREACY Darren Paul
Born: Lambeth, S London, England, 6 September, 1970 — M

League Club	Source	Date Signed	Seasons Played	Apps	Subs	Gls
Millwall	YT	02/89	88-89	7	0	0
Bradford C	Tr	11/90	90	16	0	2

TREACY Francis (Frank)
Born: Glasgow, Scotland, 14 July, 1939 — IF

League Club	Source	Date Signed	Seasons Played	Apps	Subs	Gls
Ipswich T	Johnstone Burgh	03/61	63-65	17	1	5

TREACY Keith Patrick
Born: Dublin, Republic of Ireland, 13 September, 1988 — LW
Republic of Ireland: 6/U21-5/Youth

League Club	Source	Date Signed	Seasons Played	Apps	Subs	Gls
Blackburn Rov	Sch	10/05	08	2	10	0
Stockport Co	L	11/06	06	2	2	0
Sheffield U	L	07/09	09	12	4	1
Preston NE	Tr	02/10	09-10	41	14	9
Burnley	Tr	08/11	11-13	29	37	5
Sheffield Wed	L	03/12	11	2	5	1
Barnsley	Tr	08/14	14	6	6	1

TREACY Raymond Christopher Patrick (Ray)
Born: Dublin, Republic of Ireland, 18 June, 1946 — F
Died: Dublin, Republic of Ireland, 10 April, 2015
Republic of Ireland: 42/U23-1

League Club	Source	Date Signed	Seasons Played	Apps	Subs	Gls
West Bromwich A	App	06/64	66-67	2	3	1

League Club	Source	Date Signed	Seasons Played	Apps	Subs	Gls
Charlton Ath	Tr	02/68	67-71	144	5	44
Swindon T	Tr	06/72	72-73	55	0	16
Preston NE	Tr	12/73	73-75	54	4	11
Oldham Ath	L	03/75	74	3	0	1
West Bromwich A	Tr	08/76	76	20	1	6

TREBBLE David Neil (Neil)
Born: Hitchin, Hertfordshire, England, 16 February, 1969 F

League Club	Source	Date Signed	Seasons Played	Apps	Subs	Gls
Scunthorpe U	Stevenage Bor	07/93	93	8	6	2
Preston NE	Tr	07/94	94	8	11	4
Scarborough	Tr	02/95	94-95	40	7	8

TREBILCOCK Michael (Mike)
Born: Gunnislake, Cornwall, England, 29 November, 1944 F

League Club	Source	Date Signed	Seasons Played	Apps	Subs	Gls
Plymouth Arg	Tavistock	12/62	62-65	71	0	27
Everton	Tr	12/65	65-67	11	0	3
Portsmouth	Tr	01/68	67-71	100	8	33
Torquay U	Tr	07/72	72	23	1	10

TREES Robert Victor
Born: Manchester, England, 18 December, 1977 M/RB

League Club	Source	Date Signed	Seasons Played	Apps	Subs	Gls
Manchester U	YT	07/96				
Bristol Rov	Witton A	06/98	98-99	38	8	1

TREHARNE Colin
Born: Bridgend, Wales, 30 July, 1937 G

League Club	Source	Date Signed	Seasons Played	Apps	Subs	Gls
Mansfield T	Methley, Castleford	12/60	61-65	191	0	0
Lincoln C	Tr	07/66	66	20	0	0

TREHERNE Cyril Albert
Born: Wellington, Telford & Wrekin, England, 12 March, 1928 CF

League Club	Source	Date Signed	Seasons Played	Apps	Subs	Gls
Shrewsbury T	R Artillery, Oswestry	01/49	50	4	-	1

TREMARCO Carl Philip
Born: Liverpool, England, 11 October, 1985 LB
England: Semi Pro-1

League Club	Source	Date Signed	Seasons Played	Apps	Subs	Gls
Tranmere Rov	Sch	04/04	04-07	34	18	1
Wrexham	Tr	01/08	07	10	0	0
Darlington (L)	Wrexham	01/09	08	2	0	0
Macclesfield T	Wrexham	07/09	09-11	82	7	0

TREMMEL Gerhard Martin
Born: Munich, Germany, 16 November, 1978 G

League Club	Source	Date Signed	Seasons Played	Apps	Subs	Gls
Swansea C	RB Salzburg (AUT)	08/11	11-14	26	3	0

TRENTER Ronald Herbert (Ron)
Born: Ipswich, England, 13 December, 1928 RW

League Club	Source	Date Signed	Seasons Played	Apps	Subs	Gls
Ipswich T	Jnr	12/45				
Ipswich T	Clacton T	06/51	51	2	-	0

TRETTON Andrew David (Andy)
Born: Derby, England, 9 October, 1976 CD

League Club	Source	Date Signed	Seasons Played	Apps	Subs	Gls
Derby Co	YT	10/93				
Shrewsbury T	Chesterfield (NC)	12/97	97-01	105	6	6

TREVIS Derek Alan
Born: Birmingham, England, 9 September, 1942 M/D
Died: Sacramento, California, USA, 20 November, 2000

League Club	Source	Date Signed	Seasons Played	Apps	Subs	Gls
Aston Villa		06/62				
Colchester U	Tr	03/64	63-68	196	0	13
Walsall	Tr	09/68	68-69	63	2	6
Lincoln C	Tr	07/70	70-72	100	8	18
Stockport Co	Tr	09/73	73	33	2	2

TREVITT Simon
Born: Dewsbury, West Yorkshire, England, 20 December, 1967 RB

League Club	Source	Date Signed	Seasons Played	Apps	Subs	Gls
Huddersfield T	App	06/86	86-95	216	13	3
Hull C	Tr	11/95	95-97	50	1	1
Swansea C	L	12/97	97	1	0	0

TREWICK Alan
Born: Blyth, Northumberland, England, 27 April, 1941 CF
Died: Newcastle-upon-Tyne, England, June, 1993

League Club	Source	Date Signed	Seasons Played	Apps	Subs	Gls
Gateshead		06/59	59	10	-	1

TREWICK George
Born: Stakeford, Northumberland, England, 15 November, 1933 CH
Died: Northumberland, England, March, 2003

League Club	Source	Date Signed	Seasons Played	Apps	Subs	Gls
Gateshead	West Sleekburn	04/53	56-59	110	-	0

TREWICK John
Born: Bedlington, Northumberland, England, 3 June, 1957 M/FB
England: Youth/Schools

League Club	Source	Date Signed	Seasons Played	Apps	Subs	Gls
West Bromwich A	App	07/74	74-80	83	13	11
Newcastle U	Tr	12/80	80-83	76	2	8
Oxford U	L	01/84	83	3	0	0
Oxford U	Tr	08/84	84-87	109	2	4
Birmingham C	Tr	09/87	87-88	35	2	0
Hartlepool U	Bromsgrove Rov	10/89	89	8	0	0

TRICK Desmond (Des)
Born: Swansea, Wales, 7 November, 1969 CD

League Club	Source	Date Signed	Seasons Played	Apps	Subs	Gls
Swansea C	YT	07/88	89-90	25	4	0

TRIGG Cyril
Born: Measham, Leicestershire, England, 8 April, 1917 CF
Died: Birmingham, England, 9 April, 1993

League Club	Source	Date Signed	Seasons Played	Apps	Subs	Gls
Birmingham C	Bedworth T	08/35	35-53	268	-	67

TRIM Reginald Frederick (Reg)
Born: Portsmouth, England, 1 October, 1913 LB
Died: Bournemouth, England, 1 June, 1997
England: Schools

League Club	Source	Date Signed	Seasons Played	Apps	Subs	Gls
Bournemouth	Winton & Moordown	04/31	30-32	22	-	0
Arsenal	Tr	04/33	34	1	-	0
Nottingham F	Tr	07/37	37-38	70	-	0
Derby Co	Tr	12/43				
Swindon T	Tr	07/46	46	15	-	0

TRIMMER Lewis
Born: Norwich, England, 30 October, 1989 F

League Club	Source	Date Signed	Seasons Played	Apps	Subs	Gls
Mansfield T	Jnr	12/06	06-07	0	3	0

TRINDER Jason Lee
Born: Leicester, England, 3 March, 1970 G

League Club	Source	Date Signed	Seasons Played	Apps	Subs	Gls
Grimsby T	Oadby T	12/92				
Mansfield T	Oadby T	11/94	94-95	5	3	0

TRINER Donald Arthur (Don)
Born: Longton, Potteries, England, 21 August, 1919 RW
Died: Stoke-on-Trent, England, July, 2002

League Club	Source	Date Signed	Seasons Played	Apps	Subs	Gls
Port Vale	Downings Tileries	12/38	38-47	25	-	7

TRIPPIER Kieran John
Born: Bury, Greater Manchester, England, 19 September, 1990 RB
England: U21-2/Youth

League Club	Source	Date Signed	Seasons Played	Apps	Subs	Gls
Manchester C	Sch	10/07				
Barnsley	L	02/10	09	3	0	0
Barnsley	L	08/10	10	37	2	2
Burnley	Tr	07/11	11-14	170	0	4

TRISE Guy Gavin
Born: Portsmouth, England, 22 November, 1933 IF

League Club	Source	Date Signed	Seasons Played	Apps	Subs	Gls
Portsmouth	Jnr	05/53				
Aldershot	Tr	08/54	54	1	-	0

TRISTAN Diego
Born: Seville, Spain, 1 May, 1976 F
Spain: 15

League Club	Source	Date Signed	Seasons Played	Apps	Subs	Gls
West Ham U	Livorno (ITA)	10/08	08	8	6	3

TROLLOPE Norman John (John)
Born: Wroughton, Wiltshire, England, 14 June, 1943 LB

League Club	Source	Date Signed	Seasons Played	Apps	Subs	Gls
Swindon T	Jnr	07/60	60-80	767	3	22

TROLLOPE Paul Jonathan
Born: Swindon, England, 3 June, 1972 M
Wales: 9/B-1

League Club	Source	Date Signed	Seasons Played	Apps	Subs	Gls
Swindon T	YT	12/89				
Torquay U	Tr	03/92	91-94	103	3	16
Derby Co	Tr	12/94	94-97	47	18	5
Grimsby T	L	08/96	96	6	1	1
Crystal Palace	L	10/96	96	0	9	0
Fulham	Tr	11/97	97-00	54	22	5
Coventry C	Tr	03/02	01	5	1	0
Northampton T	Tr	07/02	02-03	84	0	8
Bristol Rov	Tr	07/04	04	26	4	2

TROOPS Harold (Harry)
Born: Sheffield, England, 10 February, 1926 LB/RW
Died: Sheffield, England, 5 March, 1963

League Club	Source	Date Signed	Seasons Played	Apps	Subs	Gls
Barnsley	Hadfield Works	12/46	48	3	-	1
Lincoln C	Tr	08/49	49-57	295	-	32
Carlisle U	Tr	06/58	58-59	60	-	1

TROTMAN Neal Anthony
Born: Manchester, England, 11 March, 1987 CD

League Club	Source	Date Signed	Seasons Played	Apps	Subs	Gls
Oldham Ath	Burnley (Sch)	07/06	06-07	16	2	1
Preston NE	Tr	01/08	07	2	1	0
Colchester U	L	03/09	08	5	1	0
Southampton	L	08/09	09	17	1	2
Huddersfield T	L	01/10	09	21	0	2
Oldham Ath	L	11/10	10	15	3	0
Rochdale	Tr	07/11	11	12	0	0
Chesterfield	Tr	11/11	11-12	54	0	1
Plymouth Arg	Tr	08/13	13	41	0	2

TROTT Dean
Born: Barnsley, South Yorkshire, England, 13 May, 1967 F

League Club	Source	Date Signed	Seasons Played	Apps	Subs	Gls
Northampton T	Boston U	06/94	94	20	2	4

League Club	Source	Date Signed	Seasons Played	Apps	Subs	Gls
TROTT Robin Francis						
Born: Orpington, SE London, England, 17 August, 1974						CD
Gillingham	YT	05/93	93-94	8	2	0
TROTTA Marcello						
Born: Caserta, Italy, 29 September, 1992						F
Italy: Youth						
Fulham	Sch	08/10	11	0	1	0
Wycombe W	L	11/11	11	8	0	8
Watford	L	02/12	11	1	0	0
Brentford	L	11/12	12	16	6	6
Brentford	L	09/13	13	28	9	12
Barnsley	L	11/14	14	3	2	1
TROTTER Liam Antony						
Born: Ipswich, England, 24 August, 1988						M
Ipswich T	Sch	08/06	05-09	15	8	2
Millwall	L	08/06	06	1	1	0
Grimsby T	L	09/08	08	15	0	2
Scunthorpe U	L	02/09	08	4	8	1
Millwall	Tr	01/10	09-13	137	8	24
Bolton W	Tr	01/14	13-14	17	13	2
TROTTER Michael (Mike)						
Born: Hartlepool, Cleveland, England, 27 October, 1969						M/D
Middlesbrough	YT	11/87				
Doncaster Rov	L	11/88	88	3	0	0
Darlington	Tr	06/90	90-91	16	13	2
Leicester C	Tr	12/91	91-92	1	2	0
Chesterfield	Tr	11/93	93	14	1	1
TROUGHT Michael John (Mike)						
Born: Bristol, England, 19 October, 1980						CD
Bristol Rov	YT	03/99	98-01	25	8	0
TROUGHTON Samuel Edward (Sammy)						
Born: Lisburn, Belfast, Northern Ireland, 27 March, 1964						F
Northern Ireland: Youth/Schools						
Wolverhampton W	Glentoran	12/83	83	17	0	2
TRUDGIAN Ryan						
Born: St Austell, Cornwall, England, 15 September, 1983						F
Plymouth Arg	YT	-	00	0	1	0
TRUELOVE Jack Christopher						
Born: Burnley, Lancashire, England, 27 December, 1995						D
Oldham Ath	Sch	07/14	12	0	1	0
TRUETT Geoffrey Frederick (Geoff)						
Born: West Ham, E London, England, 23 May, 1935						WH
Died: 5 January, 2015						
Crystal Palace	Wycombe W	06/57	57-61	38	-	5
TRUNDLE Lee Christopher						
Born: Liverpool, England, 10 October, 1976						F
Wrexham	Rhyl	02/01	00-02	73	21	27
Swansea C	Tr	07/03	03-06	135	8	77
Bristol C	Tr	07/07	07-08	25	29	7
Leeds U	L	01/09	08	7	3	1
Swansea C	L	08/09	09	2	17	5
Preston NE	Neath	08/12	12	0	1	0
TRUSLER John William (Johnny)						
Born: Shoreham-by-Sea, West Sussex, England, 7 June, 1934						CF
Brighton & HA	Shoreham	08/54	54	1	-	0
TRUSSON Michael Sydney (Mike)						
Born: Northolt, W London, England, 26 May, 1959						M
Plymouth Arg	App	01/77	76-79	65	8	15
Sheffield U	Tr	07/80	80-83	125	1	31
Rotherham U	Tr	12/83	83-86	124	0	19
Brighton & HA	Tr	07/87	87-88	34	3	2
Gillingham	Tr	09/89	89-91	69	5	7
TRUSTFULL Orlando						
Born: Amsterdam, Netherlands, 4 August, 1970						M
Netherlands: 2						
Sheffield Wed	Feyenoord (NED)	08/96	96	9	10	3
TSHIBOLA Aaron						
Born: Newham, E London, England, 2 January, 1995						M
England: Youth						
Reading	Sch	01/12	14	0	1	0
Hartlepool U	L	01/15	14	23	0	0
TSKHADADZE Kakhaber						
Born: Rustavi, Georgia, 7 September, 1968						CD
Georgia: 25//Commonwealth of Independent States: 6						
Manchester C	FCA Vladikavkaz (RUS)	02/98	97-98	12	0	2
TSOUMOU Juvhel Fred						
Born: Brazzaville, Congo, 27 December, 1990						F
Germany: Youth						
Preston NE	Alem'ia Aachen (GER)	08/11	11	5	11	3
Plymouth Arg	L	01/12	11	4	7	2
TUBBS Matthew Stephen (Matt)						
Born: Salisbury, Wiltshire, England, 15 July, 1984						F
England: Semi Pro-2						
Bournemouth (L)	Salisbury C	11/08	08	6	2	1
Crawley T	Salisbury C	06/10	11	23	1	12
Bournemouth	Tr	01/12	11-12	11	27	7
Rotherham U	L	07/13	13	7	10	1
Crawley T	L	01/14	13	18	0	8
AFC Wimbledon	L	06/14	14	22	0	12
Portsmouth	Tr	01/15	14	23	0	9
TUCK Peter George						
Born: Plaistow, E London, England, 14 May, 1932						IF
Died: Chelmsford, England, 5 April, 2009						
Chelsea	Jnr	06/51	51	3	-	1
TUCK Stuart Gary						
Born: Brighton, England, 1 October, 1974						LB
Brighton & HA	YT	07/93	93-98	78	15	1
TUCKER Dexter Calbert						
Born: Pontefract, West Yorkshire, England, 22 September, 1979						F
Hull C	YT	07/98	97	1	6	0
TUCKER Gordon						
Born: Manchester, England, 5 January, 1968						CD
Derby Co	YT	08/86				
Huddersfield T	Shepshed Charterhouse	07/87	87-88	30	5	0
Scunthorpe U	Tr	07/89	89	14	1	1
TUCKER Jason James						
Born: Isleworth, W London, England, 3 February, 1973						CD
Aldershot	YT	07/91	90	0	1	0
TUCKER Keith						
Born: Deal, Kent, England, 25 November, 1936						LB
Charlton Ath	Betteshanger CW	02/54	54-60	3	-	0
TUCKER Kenneth (Ken)						
Born: Poplar, E London, England, 2 October, 1925						W
Died: Southend-on-Sea, England, May, 2008						
West Ham U	Finchley	08/46	47-56	83	-	31
Notts Co	Tr	03/57	56-57	28	-	5
TUCKER Kenneth John (Ken)						
Born: Merthyr Tydfil, Wales, 15 July, 1935						W
Cardiff C	Aston Villa (Am)	10/55	56-57	13	-	0
Shrewsbury T	Tr	02/58	57-59	46	-	8
Northampton T	Tr	03/60	59-60	10	-	3
TUCKER Lee Antony						
Born: Plymouth, England, 10 August, 1978						M
Torquay U	YT	-	96	0	1	0
TUCKER Lee Derek						
Born: Middlesbrough, England, 14 September, 1971						W
Middlesbrough	YT	10/89				
Darlington	Tr	07/91	91	0	5	0
TUCKER Malcolm						
Born: Cramlington, Northumberland, England, 12 April, 1933						CH
Grimsby T	Newcastle U (Am)	11/50	53-57	40	-	0
TUCKER Mark James						
Born: Woking, Surrey, England, 27 April, 1972						RB
Fulham	YT	07/90	91-92	3	1	0
TUCKER William Barrington (Barry)						
Born: Swansea, Wales, 28 August, 1952						FB
Northampton T	App	08/70	71-77	209	5	3
Brentford	Tr	02/78	77-82	168	1	5
Northampton T	Tr	10/82	82-83	62	1	5
TUCKER William John (Billy)						
Born: Kidderminster, Worcestershire, England, 17 May, 1948						CD
Hereford U	Kidderminster Hrs	07/72	72-76	135	2	12
Bury	Tr	12/76	76-78	96	0	8
Swindon T	Tr	06/79	79	35	0	4
TUCUDEAN Marius George (George)						
Born: Arad, Romania, 30 April, 1991						F
Romania: U21-5/Youth						
Charlton Ath	Standard Liege (BEL)	07/14	14	14	6	2

TUDDENHAM Anthony Richard (Tony)
Born: Reepham, Norfolk, England, 28 September, 1956 — RB

League Club	Source	Date Signed	Seasons Played	Apps	Subs	Gls
West Ham U	App	09/74				
Cambridge U	Tr	02/76	75-76	11	1	0

TUDGAY Marcus
Born: Shoreham-by-Sea, West Sussex, England, 3 February, 1983 — F

League Club	Source	Date Signed	Seasons Played	Apps	Subs	Gls
Derby Co	Sch	07/02	02-05	53	39	17
Sheffield Wed	Tr	01/06	05-10	178	17	49
Nottingham F	Tr	11/10	10-13	44	17	13
Barnsley	L	11/12	12	8	1	3
Barnsley	L	11/13	13	5	0	1
Charlton Ath	L	02/14	13	0	2	0
Coventry C	Tr	07/14	14	18	4	4

TUDOR John Arthur
Born: Ilkeston, Derbyshire, England, 25 June, 1946 — F

League Club	Source	Date Signed	Seasons Played	Apps	Subs	Gls
Coventry C	Ilkeston T	01/66	66-68	63	6	13
Sheffield U	Tr	11/68	68-70	64	7	30
Newcastle U	Tr	01/71	70-76	161	3	53
Stoke C	Tr	06/76	76	28	2	3

TUDOR Shane Anthony
Born: Wolverhampton, England, 10 February, 1982 — RW

League Club	Source	Date Signed	Seasons Played	Apps	Subs	Gls
Wolverhampton W	YT	08/99	00	0	1	0
Cambridge U	Tr	11/01	01-04	109	12	21
Leyton Orient	Tr	07/05	05-06	57	9	6
Port Vale	Tr	07/07	07-08	11	8	0

TUDOR Thomas Edward (Ed)
Born: Neston, Wirral, England, 15 March, 1935 — IF

League Club	Source	Date Signed	Seasons Played	Apps	Subs	Gls
Gillingham	Bolton W (Am)	04/58	58	1	-	0

TUDOR William Henry (Billy)
Born: Deeside, Flintshire, Wales, 14 February, 1918 — CH
Died: Hawarden, Flintshire, Wales, 1965
Wales: Schools

League Club	Source	Date Signed	Seasons Played	Apps	Subs	Gls
West Bromwich A	Lavender	05/35	38	31	-	0
Wrexham	Tr	05/46	46-48	56	-	2

TUDUR-JONES Owain
Born: Bangor, Gwynedd, Wales, 15 October, 1984 — M
Wales: 7/U21-3

League Club	Source	Date Signed	Seasons Played	Apps	Subs	Gls
Swansea C	Bangor C	08/05	05-08	26	16	3
Swindon T	L	03/09	08	11	0	1
Norwich C	Tr	06/09	09-10	3	2	1
Yeovil T	L	01/10	09	6	0	1
Yeovil T	L	08/10	10	12	2	0
Brentford	L	01/11	10	4	2	0

TUEART Dennis
Born: Newcastle-upon-Tyne, England, 27 November, 1949 — LW
England: 6/FLge-2/U23-1

League Club	Source	Date Signed	Seasons Played	Apps	Subs	Gls
Sunderland	Jnr	08/67	68-73	173	5	46
Manchester C	Tr	03/74	73-82	216	8	86
Stoke C	Tr	08/83	83	2	1	0
Burnley	Tr	12/83	83	8	7	5

[TUGAY] KERIMOGLU Tugay
Born: Istanbul, Turkey, 24 August, 1970 — M
Turkey: 92

League Club	Source	Date Signed	Seasons Played	Apps	Subs	Gls
Blackburn Rov	Glasgow Rangers	07/01	01-08	183	50	10

TUGMAN James Robert (Jimmy)
Born: Workington, Cumbria, England, 14 March, 1945 — D

League Club	Source	Date Signed	Seasons Played	Apps	Subs	Gls
Workington		07/64	65-67	31	12	0

TULIP William Edward (Bill)
Born: Gateshead, Tyne and Wear, England, 3 May, 1933 — CF
Died: Gateshead, Tyne and Wear, England, December, 2013

League Club	Source	Date Signed	Seasons Played	Apps	Subs	Gls
Newcastle U		06/51				
Darlington	Tr	05/56	56-57	44	-	34

TULLOCH Roland (Ron)
Born: Pretoria, South Africa, 15 July, 1932 — WH

League Club	Source	Date Signed	Seasons Played	Apps	Subs	Gls
Hull C	South Africa	12/53	54	3	-	0

TULLOCH Ronald Thomas (Ron)
Born: Haddington, East Lothian, Scotland, 5 June, 1933 — IF
Died: Carlisle, Cumbria, England, 1981

League Club	Source	Date Signed	Seasons Played	Apps	Subs	Gls
Southend U	Heart of Midlothian	05/56	56	11	-	3
Carlisle U	Tr	07/57	57-59	73	-	23

TULLY Kevin Francis
Born: Manchester, England, 18 December, 1952 — LW

League Club	Source	Date Signed	Seasons Played	Apps	Subs	Gls
Blackpool	Prestwich Heys	11/72	72-73	10	1	0
Cambridge U	Tr	07/74	74-75	40	4	8
Crewe Alex	Tr	01/76	75-78	81	5	4
Port Vale	Tr	10/78	78-79	7	6	2
Bury	Chorley	08/80	80	7	3	1

TULLY Stephen Richard (Steve)
Born: Paignton, Devon, England, 10 February, 1980 — RB

League Club	Source	Date Signed	Seasons Played	Apps	Subs	Gls
Torquay U	YT	05/98	97-01	90	16	3
Exeter C	Weymouth	01/07	08-12	179	9	2

TUMBRIDGE Raymond Alan (Ray)
Born: Hampstead, NW London, England, 6 March, 1955 — LB
Died: Chatham, Kent, England, 4 June, 2009

League Club	Source	Date Signed	Seasons Played	Apps	Subs	Gls
Charlton Ath	App	03/73	72-74	43	3	0
Northampton T	L	02/75	74	11	0	0

TUNA Tamer Hakan
Born: Bexley, SE London, England, 19 October, 1991 — F

League Club	Source	Date Signed	Seasons Played	Apps	Subs	Gls
Charlton Ath	Sch	07/10	08-09	0	3	0

[TUNCAY] SANLI Tuncay
Born: Sakarya, Turkey, 16 January, 1982 — M/F
Turkey: 80/U21-14/Youth

League Club	Source	Date Signed	Seasons Played	Apps	Subs	Gls
Middlesbrough	Fenerbahce (TKY)	07/07	07-09	57	13	17
Stoke C	Tr	08/09	09-10	18	26	5
Bolton W (L)	VfL Wolfsburg (GER)	08/11	11	3	13	0

TUNCHEV Aleksandar Blagov
Born: Pazardzhik, Bulgaria, 10 July, 1981 — CD
Bulgaria: 26

League Club	Source	Date Signed	Seasons Played	Apps	Subs	Gls
Leicester C	CSKA Sofia (BUL)	07/08	08-11	22	4	1
Crystal Palace	L	08/11	11	9	0	0

TUNE David Barrie
Born: Reading, England, 1 November, 1938 — WH

League Club	Source	Date Signed	Seasons Played	Apps	Subs	Gls
Reading	Jnr	11/55	57	1	-	0

TUNE Michael Gerard (Mike)
Born: Stoke-on-Trent, England, 28 February, 1962 — M

League Club	Source	Date Signed	Seasons Played	Apps	Subs	Gls
Crewe Alex	Stoke C (App)	06/79	79	0	1	0

TUNKS Roy William
Born: Wuppertal, Germany, 21 January, 1951 — G

League Club	Source	Date Signed	Seasons Played	Apps	Subs	Gls
Rotherham U	App	03/68	67-73	138	0	0
York C	L	01/69	68	4	0	0
Preston NE	Tr	11/74	74-80	277	0	0
Wigan Ath	Tr	11/81	81-87	245	0	0
Hartlepool U	Tr	07/88	88	5	0	0
Preston NE	Tr	11/88	88-89	25	0	0

TUNNEY Edward Luton (Eddie)
Born: Liverpool, England, 23 September, 1915 — RB
Died: Wirral, England, September, 2011

League Club	Source	Date Signed	Seasons Played	Apps	Subs	Gls
Everton		08/36				
Wrexham	Tr	09/37	37-51	222	-	0

TUNNICLIFFE James Mark
Born: Denton, Greater Manchester, England, 17 January, 1989 — CD

League Club	Source	Date Signed	Seasons Played	Apps	Subs	Gls
Stockport Co	Sch	07/06	05-08	32	9	0
Brighton & HA	Tr	07/09	09	17	0	2
MK Dons	L	02/10	09	9	0	1
Bristol Rov	L	07/10	10	21	4	0
Wycombe W	Tr	07/11	11	16	1	1
Crewe Alex	L	02/12	11	2	0	0

TUNNICLIFFE Ryan
Born: Heywood, Greater Manchester, England, 30 December, 1992 — M
England: Youth

League Club	Source	Date Signed	Seasons Played	Apps	Subs	Gls
Manchester U	Sch	01/10				
Peterborough U	L	07/11	11	10	17	0
Barnsley	L	02/13	12	2	0	0
Ipswich T	L	07/13	13	23	4	0
Fulham	Tr	01/14	13-14	24	1	0
Wigan Ath	L	02/14	13	3	2	0
Blackburn Rov	L	09/14	14	10	7	1

TUNNICLIFFE William Francis (Billy)
Born: Stoke-on-Trent, England, 5 January, 1920 — LW
Died: Newcastle-under-Lyme, Potteries, England, 24 March, 1997

League Club	Source	Date Signed	Seasons Played	Apps	Subs	Gls
Port Vale	Jnr	01/37	36-37	3	-	0
Bournemouth	Tr	05/38	38-46	50	-	7
Wrexham	Tr	06/47	47-52	236	-	74
Bradford C	Tr	01/53	52-54	89	-	20

TUNSTALL Eric Walter
Born: Hartlepool, Cleveland, England, 21 November, 1950 — M

League Club	Source	Date Signed	Seasons Played	Apps	Subs	Gls
Hartlepool U	App	11/68	68	0	1	0
Newcastle U	Tr	01/69				

TUOHY Jack Samuel
Born: Oldham, Greater Manchester, England, 6 September, 1996 — M

League Club	Source	Date Signed	Seasons Played	Apps	Subs	Gls
Oldham Ath	Sch	03/15	14	0	1	0

TUOHY Michael Patrick Francis (Mickey)
Born: West Bromwich, West Midlands, England, 28 March, 1956 — F

League Club	Source	Date Signed	Seasons Played	Apps	Subs	Gls
Southend U	Redditch U	06/79	79	20	1	4

TUOHY William (Liam)
Born: Dublin, Republic of Ireland, 27 April, 1933 — LW
Republic of Ireland: 8/B-3/LoI-24

League Club	Source	Date Signed	Seasons Played	Apps	Subs	Gls
Newcastle U	Shamrock Rov (ROI)	05/60	60-62	38	-	9

TUOMELA Marko
Born: Stockholm, Sweden, 3 March, 1972 — CD
Finland: 24/U21-3

League Club	Source	Date Signed	Seasons Played	Apps	Subs	Gls
Swindon T (L)	Tromso (NOR)	09/00	00	1	1	0

TUPLING Stephen (Steve)
Born: Wensleydale, North Yorkshire, England, 11 July, 1964 — M

League Club	Source	Date Signed	Seasons Played	Apps	Subs	Gls
Middlesbrough	App	07/82				
Carlisle U	Tr	07/84	84	1	0	0
Darlington	Tr	10/84	84-86	105	6	8
Newport Co	Tr	08/87	87	30	3	2
Cardiff C	Tr	08/88	88-89	3	2	0
Torquay U	L	09/88	88	1	2	0
Exeter C	L	01/89	88	8	1	1
Hartlepool U	Tr	12/89	89-91	83	6	3
Darlington	Tr	08/92	92	8	3	0

TURBITT Peter
Born: Keighley, West Yorkshire, England, 1 July, 1951 — RW
England: Youth

League Club	Source	Date Signed	Seasons Played	Apps	Subs	Gls
Bradford C	Keighley Central YC	08/69	69-70	5	3	0

TURGOTT Blair Sebastian
Born: Bromley, SE London, England, 22 May, 1994 — W
England: Youth

League Club	Source	Date Signed	Seasons Played	Apps	Subs	Gls
West Ham U	Sch	07/11				
Bradford C	L	11/12	12	0	4	0
Colchester U	L	11/13	13	3	1	1
Rotherham U	L	01/14	13	0	1	0
Dagenham & Red	L	03/14	13	3	2	0
Coventry C	Tr	02/15	14	0	3	1

TURIENZO Federico Ezequiel
Born: La Plata, Argentina, 2 June, 1983 — F

League Club	Source	Date Signed	Seasons Played	Apps	Subs	Gls
Brighton & HA	Gimnastica (ARG)	08/05	05	1	3	0

TURLEY James
Born: Manchester, England, 24 June, 1981 — RW

League Club	Source	Date Signed	Seasons Played	Apps	Subs	Gls
York C	YT	06/99	99-00	14	7	2

TURLEY John William
Born: Bebington, Wirral, England, 26 January, 1939 — CF

League Club	Source	Date Signed	Seasons Played	Apps	Subs	Gls
Sheffield U	Ellesmere Port	05/56	57	5	-	3
Peterborough U	Tr	07/61	61-63	32	-	14
Rochdale	Tr	05/64	64	22	-	5

TURLEY Michael Douglas (Mike)
Born: Rotherham, South Yorkshire, England, 14 February, 1936 — WH
Died: Lancaster, England, 1982

League Club	Source	Date Signed	Seasons Played	Apps	Subs	Gls
Sheffield Wed	Jnr	03/53	54	3	-	0
Burnley	Tr	10/56				

TURLEY William Lee (Billy)
Born: Wolverhampton, England, 15 July, 1973 — G

League Club	Source	Date Signed	Seasons Played	Apps	Subs	Gls
Northampton T	Evesham U	07/95	95-98	28	0	0
Leyton Orient	L	02/98	97	14	0	0
Rushden & D	Tr	06/99	01-04	133	1	0
Oxford U	Tr	07/05	05	32	1	0

TURNBULL Frederick (Fred)
Born: Wallsend, Tyne and Wear, England, 28 August, 1946 — CD

League Club	Source	Date Signed	Seasons Played	Apps	Subs	Gls
Aston Villa	Centre '64, Blyth	09/66	67-73	160	1	3
Halifax T	L	10/69	69	7	0	0

TURNBULL George Frederick
Born: Gateshead, Tyne and Wear, England, 4 February, 1927 — G
Died: Gateshead, Tyne and Wear, England, February, 2002

League Club	Source	Date Signed	Seasons Played	Apps	Subs	Gls
Grimsby T	Alnwick T	08/50	50	2	-	0
Accrington Stan	Tr	09/51	51	33	-	0
Gateshead	Tr	07/52	52	3	-	0

TURNBULL Jordan Robert
Born: Trowbridge, Wiltshire, England, 30 October, 1994 — CD
England: Youth

League Club	Source	Date Signed	Seasons Played	Apps	Subs	Gls
Southampton	Sch	10/11				
Swindon T	L	08/14	14	44	0	1

TURNBULL Lee Mark
Born: Stockton-on-Tees, Cleveland, England, 27 September, 1967 — M/F

League Club	Source	Date Signed	Seasons Played	Apps	Subs	Gls
Middlesbrough	App	09/85	85-86	8	8	4
Aston Villa	Tr	08/87				
Doncaster Rov	Tr	11/87	87-90	108	15	21
Chesterfield	Tr	02/91	90-93	80	7	26
Doncaster Rov	Tr	10/93	93	10	1	1
Wycombe W	Tr	01/94	93-94	8	3	1
Scunthorpe U	Tr	03/95	94-96	37	10	7
Darlington	Tr	07/97	97	4	5	0

TURNBULL Paul Daniel
Born: Handforth, Cheshire, England, 23 January, 1989 — M

League Club	Source	Date Signed	Seasons Played	Apps	Subs	Gls
Stockport Co	Jnr	05/06	04-10	90	35	6
Northampton T	Tr	07/11	11	9	5	0

TURNBULL Ronald William (Ron)
Born: Newbiggin, Northumberland, England, 18 July, 1922 — CF
Died: Sunderland, England, 17 November, 1966
Wales: WLge-1

League Club	Source	Date Signed	Seasons Played	Apps	Subs	Gls
Sunderland	Dundee	11/47	47-48	40	-	16
Manchester C	Tr	09/49	49-50	30	-	5
Swansea C	Tr	01/51	50-52	67	-	37

TURNBULL Ross
Born: Bishop Auckland, County Durham, England, 4 January, 1985 — G
England: Youth

League Club	Source	Date Signed	Seasons Played	Apps	Subs	Gls
Middlesbrough	Sch	07/02	05-08	27	0	0
Darlington	L	11/03	03	1	0	0
Barnsley	L	04/04	03	3	0	0
Bradford C	L	08/04	04	2	0	0
Barnsley	L	10/04	04	23	0	0
Crewe Alex	L	08/05	05	29	0	0
Cardiff C	L	07/07	07	6	0	0
Chelsea	Tr	07/09	09-12	6	1	0
Doncaster Rov	Tr	07/13	13	28	0	0
Barnsley	Tr	07/14	14	22	0	0

TURNBULL Roy
Born: Edinburgh, Scotland, 22 October, 1948 — M
Scotland: Youth/Schools

League Club	Source	Date Signed	Seasons Played	Apps	Subs	Gls
Lincoln C	Heart of Midlothian	09/69	69	0	2	0

TURNBULL Stephen
Born: South Shields, Tyne and Wear, England, 7 January, 1987 — M

League Club	Source	Date Signed	Seasons Played	Apps	Subs	Gls
Hartlepool U	Sch	07/06	04-07	16	8	0
Bury	L	11/06	06	4	1	0
Rochdale	L	03/07	06	2	2	0

TURNBULL Terence Michael (Terry)
Born: Stockton-on-Tees, Cleveland, England, 18 October, 1945 — F

League Club	Source	Date Signed	Seasons Played	Apps	Subs	Gls
Hartlepool U	Crook T	08/76	76	13	0	3

TURNER Adam Ernest
Born: Glasgow, Scotland, 13 March, 1934 — RH

League Club	Source	Date Signed	Seasons Played	Apps	Subs	Gls
Gateshead	Dunfermline Ath	10/58	58	6	-	0

TURNER Alan
Born: Sheffield, England, 22 September, 1935 — IF

League Club	Source	Date Signed	Seasons Played	Apps	Subs	Gls
Sheffield U		09/57				
Halifax T	Tr	07/58	58	7	-	0

TURNER Alan
Born: Hull, England, 5 July, 1943 — M

League Club	Source	Date Signed	Seasons Played	Apps	Subs	Gls
Coventry C	Scunthorpe U (Am)	03/62	61-65	4	0	0
Shrewsbury T	Tr	07/66	66	14	2	3
Bradford Park Ave	Tr	05/67	67	30	2	4

TURNER Alfred Thomas (Alf)
Born: USA, 26 December, 1929 — CF
Died: Birkenhead, Wirral, England, December, 1987

League Club	Source	Date Signed	Seasons Played	Apps	Subs	Gls
New Brighton (Am)	Port Sunlight	02/51	50	4	-	0

TURNER Andrew Peter (Andy)
Born: Woolwich, SE London, England, 23 March, 1975 — LW
England: Youth/Schools//Republic of Ireland: U21-7

League Club	Source	Date Signed	Seasons Played	Apps	Subs	Gls
Tottenham H	YT	04/92	92-94	8	12	3
Wycombe W	L	08/94	94	3	1	0
Doncaster Rov	L	10/94	94	4	0	1
Huddersfield T	L	11/95	95	2	3	1
Southend U	L	03/96	95	4	2	0
Portsmouth	Tr	09/96	96-97	34	6	3
Crystal Palace	Tr	10/98	98	0	2	0
Rotherham U	Tr	07/99	99-00	29	7	1
Rochdale	L	03/01	00	2	2	0
Northampton T	Tamworth	01/03	02	0	3	0

TURNER Arthur Alexander
Born: Poplar, E London, England, 22 January, 1922 — CF

League Club	Source	Date Signed	Seasons Played	Apps	Subs	Gls
Colchester U	Charlton Ath (Am)	07/47	50-51	45	-	14

TURNER Arthur Owen
Born: Chesterton, Potteries, England, 1 April, 1909 — CH
Died: Sheffield, England, 12 January, 1994

League Club	Source	Date Signed	Seasons Played	Apps	Subs	Gls
Stoke C	Woolstanton PSA	11/30	30-38	290	-	17
Birmingham C	Tr	11/39	38-46	39	-	0
Southport	Tr	02/48	47-48	28	-	0

TURNER Benjamin Howard (Ben)
Born: Birmingham, England, 21 January, 1988 — CD
England: Youth

League Club	Source	Date Signed	Seasons Played	Apps	Subs	Gls
Coventry C	Sch	07/06	05-10	69	3	4
Peterborough U	L	09/06	06	7	1	0
Oldham Ath	L	02/07	06	1	0	0
Cardiff C	Tr	08/11	11-14	107	3	3

TURNER Brian
Born: Whittlesey, Cambridgeshire, England, 27 August, 1925 — CF

League Club	Source	Date Signed	Seasons Played	Apps	Subs	Gls
Lincoln C (Am)	March T	11/47	47	5	-	0

TURNER Brian
Born: Salford, England, 23 July, 1936 — RH/CH
Died: Southport, Merseyside, England, January, 1999

League Club	Source	Date Signed	Seasons Played	Apps	Subs	Gls
Bury	Bury Amats	02/57	57-69	452	3	23
Oldham Ath	Tr	08/70	70	10	1	0

TURNER Brian Alfred
Born: East Ham, E London, England, 31 July, 1949 — M
New Zealand: 59

League Club	Source	Date Signed	Seasons Played	Apps	Subs	Gls
Chelsea	Eden AFC (NZL)	05/68				
Portsmouth	Tr	06/69	69	3	1	0
Brentford	Tr	01/70	69-71	88	5	7

TURNER Charles John (Charlie)
Born: Newport, Wales, 1 July, 1919 — G
Died: Pontypool, Torfaen, Wales, April, 1999

League Club	Source	Date Signed	Seasons Played	Apps	Subs	Gls
Newport Co	Ebbw Junction	05/38	38-47	37	-	0
Swansea C	Tr	08/48	48	2	-	0

TURNER Christopher Jack Michael (Chris)
Born: Burnley, Lancashire, England, 26 August, 1990 — LW

League Club	Source	Date Signed	Seasons Played	Apps	Subs	Gls
Accrington Stan	Sch	08/08	07-10	25	35	2

TURNER Christopher James (Chris)
Born: St Neots, Cambridgeshire, England, 3 April, 1951 — CD
Died: Wisbech, Cambridgeshire, England, 27 April, 2015

League Club	Source	Date Signed	Seasons Played	Apps	Subs	Gls
Peterborough U	Jnr	11/69	69-77	308	6	37
Luton T	Tr	07/78	78	30	0	5
Cambridge U	New England TM (USA)	09/79	79	15	4	0
Swindon T	New England TM (USA)	09/80	80	0	3	0
Cambridge U	Tr	10/80	80-83	68	3	3
Southend U	Tr	10/83	83	22	2	2

TURNER Christopher Robert (Chris)
Born: Sheffield, England, 15 September, 1958 — G
England: Youth

League Club	Source	Date Signed	Seasons Played	Apps	Subs	Gls
Sheffield Wed	App	08/76	76-78	91	0	0
Lincoln C	L	10/78	78	5	0	0
Sunderland	Tr	07/79	79-84	195	0	0
Manchester U	Tr	08/85	85-87	64	0	0
Sheffield Wed	Tr	09/88	88-90	75	0	0
Leeds U	L	11/89	89	2	0	0
Leyton Orient	Tr	10/91	91-94	58	0	0

TURNER David (Dave)
Born: Derby, England, 26 December, 1948 — RB

League Club	Source	Date Signed	Seasons Played	Apps	Subs	Gls
Everton	App	10/66	67	1	0	0
Southport	Tr	05/70	70-72	69	2	0

TURNER David John (Dave)
Born: Stretford, Greater Manchester, England, 7 September, 1943 — M

League Club	Source	Date Signed	Seasons Played	Apps	Subs	Gls
Newcastle U	App	10/60	61-62	2	-	0
Brighton & HA	Tr	12/63	63-71	292	8	30
Blackburn Rov	Tr	08/72	72-73	23	2	0

TURNER Eric
Born: Huddersfield, West Yorkshire, England, 13 January, 1921 — RH
Died: Barnsley, South Yorkshire, England, 18 November, 1993

League Club	Source	Date Signed	Seasons Played	Apps	Subs	Gls
Halifax T	Wooldale W	04/46	46	7	-	0

TURNER Frederick Arthur (Fred)
Born: Southampton, England, 28 February, 1930 — RB
Died: Southampton, England, 9 July, 1955

League Club	Source	Date Signed	Seasons Played	Apps	Subs	Gls
Southampton	Jnr	02/50				
Torquay U	Tr	08/51	51	1	-	0
Southampton	Tr	03/53	53-54	19	-	0

TURNER Gordon Reginald
Born: Hull, England, 7 June, 1930 — IF
Died: Luton, England, 23 December, 1976
England: FLge-1

League Club	Source	Date Signed	Seasons Played	Apps	Subs	Gls
Luton T	Royal Navy	03/50	50-63	406	-	243

TURNER Graham John
Born: Ellesmere Port, Cheshire, England, 5 October, 1947 — CD/M
England: Youth

League Club	Source	Date Signed	Seasons Played	Apps	Subs	Gls
Wrexham	Jnr	07/65	64-67	77	0	0
Chester C	Tr	01/68	67-72	215	3	5
Shrewsbury T	Tr	01/73	72-83	342	13	22

TURNER Graham Mark (Mark)
Born: Bebington, Wirral, England, 4 October, 1972 — M

League Club	Source	Date Signed	Seasons Played	Apps	Subs	Gls
Wolverhampton W	Paget Rgrs	07/91	92	1	0	0
Northampton T	Tr	07/94	94	2	2	0
Hereford U (L)	Telford U	03/97	96	6	0	0

TURNER Herbert Gwyn (Bert)
Born: Rhymney, Caerphilly, Wales, 19 June, 1909 — RB
Died: Birchington, Kent, England, 8 June, 1981
Wales: 8/War-8

League Club	Source	Date Signed	Seasons Played	Apps	Subs	Gls
Charlton Ath	Brithdir	08/33	33-46	176	-	2

TURNER Hugh Peter
Born: Middlesbrough, England, 12 May, 1917 — RB
Died: Middlesbrough, England, March, 1992

League Club	Source	Date Signed	Seasons Played	Apps	Subs	Gls
Middlesbrough		08/35				
Darlington	Tr	08/39	46	6	-	0

TURNER Iain Ross
Born: Stirling, Scotland, 26 January, 1984 — G
Scotland: B-1/U21-6

League Club	Source	Date Signed	Seasons Played	Apps	Subs	Gls
Everton	Stirling A	01/03	05-06	3	1	0
Doncaster Rov	L	03/05	04	8	0	0
Wycombe W	L	11/05	05	3	0	0
Crystal Palace	L	11/06	06	5	0	0
Sheffield Wed	L	02/07	06	11	0	0
Nottingham F	L	03/09	08	3	0	0
Coventry C	L	08/10	10	2	0	0
Preston NE	Tr	02/11	10-11	28	0	1
Barnsley	Rtd	01/14				
Sheffield U	Tr	08/14	14	11	0	0

TURNER Ian
Born: Middlesbrough, England, 17 January, 1953 — G

League Club	Source	Date Signed	Seasons Played	Apps	Subs	Gls
Huddersfield T	South Bank	10/70				
Grimsby T	Tr	01/72	71-73	26	0	0
Walsall	L	02/73	72	3	0	0
Southampton	Tr	03/74	73-77	77	0	0
Newport Co	L	03/78	77	7	0	0
Lincoln C	L	10/78	78	7	0	0
Walsall	Tr	01/79	78-80	39	0	0
Halifax T	L	01/81	80	5	0	0

TURNER Jack Anthony
Born: Ashford, Surrey, England, 17 September, 1992 — G

League Club	Source	Date Signed	Seasons Played	Apps	Subs	Gls
AFC Wimbledon	Jnr	04/10	11	2	0	0

TURNER John Andrew James
Born: Harrow, NW London, England, 12 February, 1986 — F

League Club	Source	Date Signed	Seasons Played	Apps	Subs	Gls
Cambridge U	Sch	12/03	02-04	33	42	10
Rushden & D	Tr	01/06	05	4	7	1

TURNER John Graham Anthony
Born: Gateshead, Tyne and Wear, England, 23 December, 1954 — G

League Club	Source	Date Signed	Seasons Played	Apps	Subs	Gls
Derby Co	App	12/72				
Doncaster Rov	L	02/74	73	4	0	0
Huddersfield T	L	03/75	74	1	0	0
Reading	Tr	05/75	75-77	31	0	0
Torquay U	Tr	08/78	78-79	76	0	0
Chesterfield	Tr	02/80	79-82	132	0	0
Torquay U	Tr	08/83	83	34	0	0
Burnley	Weymouth	08/84				
Peterborough U	Tr	10/84	84-85	60	0	0

TURNER John Samuel (Sam)
Born: Pontypool, Torfaen, Wales, 9 September, 1980 — G

League Club	Source	Date Signed	Seasons Played	Apps	Subs	Gls
Charlton Ath	YT	05/99				
Stockport Co	Tr	07/00	01	4	2	0

TURNER Joseph (Joe)
Born: Barnsley, South Yorkshire, England, 21 March, 1931 — G
Died: Barnsley, South Yorkshire, England, 6 February, 2008

League Club	Source	Date Signed	Seasons Played	Apps	Subs	Gls
Stockport Co	Denaby U	07/54	54-56	79	-	0
Darlington	Tr	12/57	57-59	68	-	0
Scunthorpe U	Tr	06/60	60-61	22	-	0
Barnsley	Tr	11/61	61	7	-	0

TURNER Keith John
Born: Coventry, England, 9 April, 1934 — IF

League Club	Source	Date Signed	Seasons Played	Apps	Subs	Gls
Nottingham F		06/54	54	1	-	0

TURNER Kenneth (Ken)
Born: Great Houghton, South Yorkshire, England, 22 April, 1941 — LB

League Club	Source	Date Signed	Seasons Played	Apps	Subs	Gls
Huddersfield T	Jnr	10/58	61	5	-	0
Shrewsbury T	Tr	07/63	63-65	64	0	1
York C	Tr	06/66	66-67	88	0	2

TURNER Mark Brendan
Born: Stockport, Greater Manchester, England, 19 September, 1956 — RB/M

League Club	Source	Date Signed	Seasons Played	Apps	Subs	Gls
Stockport Co	Everton (Am)	08/75	75	8	0	0

League Club	Source	Date Signed	Seasons Played	Career Record Apps	Subs	Gls
TURNER Michael Christopher (Mike)						
Born: Stafford, England, 2 April, 1976						F
Barnsley	Bilston T	12/98	98	2	11	1
TURNER Michael George Elliott (Mike)						
Born: Bridport, Dorset, England, 20 September, 1938						G
England: Youth						
Swindon T	Dorchester T	12/61	61-63	75	-	0
Torquay U	Tr	07/64	64-65	14	0	0
TURNER Michael Thomas						
Born: Lewisham, SE London, England, 9 November, 1983						CD
Charlton Ath	YT	03/01				
Leyton Orient	L	03/03	02	7	0	1
Brentford	Tr	08/04	04-05	91	0	3
Hull C	Tr	07/06	06-09	128	1	12
Sunderland	Tr	08/09	09-11	67	1	2
Norwich C	Tr	07/12	12-14	69	2	4
Fulham	L	03/15	14	9	0	1
TURNER Neil Stuart Thomson						
Born: Blackpool, Lancashire, England, 15 March, 1942						M
Died: Kuala Lumpur, Malaysia, 29 May, 2001						
Blackpool	Jnr	12/59	63-66	10	1	1
Crewe Alex	Tr	07/68	68-71	80	5	4
TURNER Paul						
Born: Barnsley, South Yorkshire, England, 8 July, 1953						RB
Barnsley	App	07/71	70-74	27	8	1
TURNER Paul Edward						
Born: Cheshunt, Hertfordshire, England, 13 November, 1968						M
Arsenal	App	07/86				
Cambridge U	Tr	09/87	87-88	28	9	0
TURNER Peter Ambrose						
Born: Leicester, England, 14 August, 1931						IF
Crewe Alex	Brush Sports	03/54	54-55	23	-	4
TURNER Philip (Phil)						
Born: Frodsham, Cheshire, England, 20 February, 1927						IF
Chester C	Jnr	07/46	46-47	27	-	6
Carlisle U	Tr	09/48	48-50	78	-	24
Bradford Park Ave	Tr	06/51	51-53	55	-	24
Scunthorpe U	Tr	06/54	54	5	-	2
Accrington Stan	Tr	10/55	55-56	14	-	5
Chester C	Tr	11/56	56	16	-	3
TURNER Philip (Phil)						
Born: Sheffield, England, 12 February, 1962						M
Lincoln C	App	02/80	79-85	237	2	18
Grimsby T	Tr	08/86	86-87	62	0	7
Leicester C	Tr	02/88	87-88	18	6	2
Notts Co	Tr	03/89	88-95	223	14	16
TURNER Rhys James						
Born: Preston, Lancashire, England, 22 July, 1995						F
Oldham Ath	Stockport Co	01/14	13-14	10	6	3
TURNER Robert Peter (Robbie)						
Born: Liversedge, West Yorkshire, England, 18 September, 1966						F
Huddersfield T	App	09/84	84	0	1	0
Cardiff C	Tr	07/85	85-86	34	5	8
Hartlepool U	L	10/86	86	7	0	1
Bristol Rov	Tr	12/86	86-87	19	7	2
Wimbledon	Tr	12/87	87-88	2	8	0
Bristol C	Tr	01/89	88-89	45	7	12
Plymouth Arg	Tr	07/90	90-92	66	0	17
Notts Co	Tr	11/92	92	7	1	1
Shrewsbury T	L	03/93	92	9	0	0
Exeter C	Tr	02/94	93-95	38	7	7
Cambridge U	Tr	12/95	95-96	12	5	4
Hull C	L	10/96	96	5	0	2
TURNER Robin David						
Born: Carlisle, Cumbria, England, 10 September, 1955						F
England: Youth						
Ipswich T	App	04/73	75-83	22	26	2
Swansea C	Tr	03/85	84-85	20	0	8
Colchester U	Tr	11/85	85	6	5	0
TURNER Ross Keith						
Born: Sheffield, England, 17 June, 1979						G
Scunthorpe U	Worsbrough Bridge	03/00	99	1	0	0
TURNER Samuel James (Sam)						
Born: Lincoln, England, 30 August, 1993						RW
Lincoln C	Sch	-	10	0	2	0
TURNER Stanley Frederick (Stan)						
Born: Wokingham, Berkshire, England, 31 May, 1941						RW
Reading	Jnr	12/58	60	3	-	0
TURNER Stanley Simpson (Stan)						
Born: Hanley, Potteries, England, 21 October, 1926						RB
Died: Stoke-on-Trent, England, 28 April, 1991						
Port Vale		03/49	50-56	227	-	0
TURNER Wayne Leslie						
Born: Luton, England, 9 March, 1961						M
Luton T	App	04/78	78-84	81	3	2
Lincoln C	L	10/81	81	18	0	0
Coventry C	Tr	07/85	85	14	1	1
Brentford	Tr	09/86	86-87	56	0	2
TURNEY James Allan (Jim)						
Born: Cramlington, Northumberland, England, 8 July, 1922						RW
Died: North Tyneside, Tyne and Wear, England, 18 July, 1995						
Darlington	Blackhall CW	08/48	48-49	40	-	3
TURPIE Robert Paul (Bob)						
Born: Hampstead, NW London, England, 13 November, 1949						M
Queens Park Rgrs	App	11/67	69	1	1	0
Peterborough U	Tr	07/70	70-71	31	6	3
TURTON Cyril						
Born: South Kirkby, West Yorkshire, England, 20 September, 1921						CH
Died: North Yorkshire, England, January, 2000						
Sheffield Wed	Frickley Colliery	11/44	46-53	146	-	0
TURTON Oliver Anthony						
Born: Manchester, England, 6 December, 1992						M
Crewe Alex	Sch	07/11	10-14	54	25	2
TUTILL Stephen Alan (Steve)						
Born: York, England, 1 October, 1969						CD
England: Schools						
York C	YT	01/88	87-97	293	8	6
Darlington	Tr	02/98	97-99	65	5	0
Chesterfield	Tr	07/00	00	17	2	1
TUTIN Harry						
Born: Sunderland, England, 6 June, 1919						RW
Died: Grangetown, Cleveland, England, 21 September, 1994						
Southport (Am)	Houghton SC	09/46	46	2	-	0
TUTONDA David						
Born: Kinshasa, DR Congo, 11 October, 1995						LB
Cardiff C	Sch	07/14				
Newport Co	L	02/15	14	10	2	2
TUTT Graham Charles						
Born: Deptford, SE London, England, 27 August, 1956						G
Charlton Ath	Jnr	03/74	73-75	65	0	0
Workington	L	09/74	74	4	0	0
TUTTE Andrew William						
Born: Huyton, Merseyside, England, 21 September, 1990						M
England: Youth						
Manchester C	Sch	10/07				
Rochdale	L	08/10	10	5	2	0
Shrewsbury T	L	11/10	10	2	0	0
Yeovil T	L	01/11	10	12	3	2
Rochdale	Tr	07/11	11-13	72	16	10
Bury	Tr	01/14	13-14	56	5	4
TUTTLE David Philip						
Born: Mortimer, Berkshire, England, 6 February, 1972						CD
England: Youth						
Tottenham H	YT	02/90	90-92	10	3	0
Peterborough U	L	01/93	92	7	0	0
Sheffield U	Tr	08/93	93-95	63	0	1
Crystal Palace	Tr	03/96	95-99	73	8	5
Barnsley	Tr	08/99	99	11	1	0
Millwall	Tr	03/00	99-02	19	4	0
Wycombe W	L	02/02	01	4	0	0
TUTTON Alan						
Born: Bexley, SE London, England, 23 February, 1973						M
Maidstone U	Alma Swanley	07/91	91	0	4	0
TUTTY Paul						
Born: Manchester, England, 22 February, 1952						CD
Stockport Co	Manchester U (Am)	07/70	70	1	0	0
TUTTY Wayne Keith						
Born: Oxford, England, 18 June, 1963						M/RB
Reading	Banbury U	08/82	82-83	11	2	4

League Club	Source	Date Signed	Seasons Played	Apps	Subs	Gls
TWADDLE Marc Ian						
Born: Glasgow, Scotland, 27 August, 1986						D
Rochdale	Falkirk	07/11	11	1	1	0
TWAMLEY Bruce Richardson						
Born: Victoria, British Columbia, Canada, 23 May, 1952						FB
Canada: 8						
Ipswich T	Jnr	10/69	73-74	2	0	0
TWARDZIK Filip						
Born: Trinec, Czech Republic, 10 February, 1993						M
Czech Republic: Youth						
Bolton W	Glasgow Celtic	02/15	14	1	2	1
TWEED Steven						
Born: Edinburgh, Scotland, 8 August, 1972						CD
Scotland: B-2/U21-3						
Stoke C	Ionikos (GRE)	08/97	97-98	35	4	0
TWEEDY George Jacob						
Born: Bedlington, Northumberland, England, 8 January, 1913						G
Died: Grimsby, North Lincolnshire, England, 23 April, 1987						
England: 1						
Grimsby T	Willington	08/31	32-52	347	-	0
TWELL Terence Keith (Terry)						
Born: Doncaster, South Yorkshire, England, 21 February, 1947						G
Died: Doncaster, South Yorkshire, England, March, 2013						
Birmingham C	Bourne T	10/64	67	2	0	0
TWENTYMAN Geoffrey (Geoff)						
Born: Liverpool, England, 10 March, 1959						CD
Preston NE	Chorley	08/83	83-85	95	3	4
Bristol Rov	Tr	08/86	86-92	248	4	6
TWENTYMAN Geoffrey (Geoff)						
Born: Brampton, Cumbria, England, 19 January, 1930						LH/CH
Died: Southport, Merseyside, England, 16 February, 2004						
Northern Ireland: NILge-9						
Carlisle U	Swifts Rov	02/47	46-53	149	-	2
Liverpool	Tr	12/53	53-59	170	-	18
Carlisle U	Ballymena U	06/63	63	10	-	0
TWIDDY Christopher (Chris)						
Born: Pontypridd, Rhondda Cynon Taff, Wales, 19 January, 1976						LW
Wales: U21-3/Youth						
Plymouth Arg	YT	06/94	94-95	14	3	1
TWIDLE Kenneth George (Ken)						
Born: Brigg, North Lincolnshire, England, 10 October, 1931						CF
Rotherham U	Retford T	12/57	57-58	24	-	6
TWIGG Gary						
Born: Glasgow, Scotland, 19 March, 1984						F
Derby Co	YT	03/01	01-02	1	8	0
Bristol Rov	L	03/04	03	7	1	0
TWIGG Richard Lance (Dick)						
Born: Barry, Vale of Glamorgan, Wales, 10 September, 1939						G
Died: Cardiff, Wales, January, 2012						
Notts Co	Barry T	11/57	58	2	-	0
TWISS Michael John						
Born: Salford, England, 26 December, 1977						LW
Manchester U	YT	07/96				
Sheffield U	L	08/98	98	2	10	1
Port Vale	Tr	07/00	00	15	3	3
Morecambe	Chester C	05/04	07-09	71	19	10
TWISSELL Charles Herbert (Charlie)						
Born: Singapore, 16 December, 1932						LW
England: Amateur-5						
Plymouth Arg	Royal Navy	04/55	55-57	41	-	9
York C	Tr	11/58	58-60	53	-	8
TWIST Franklin (Frank)						
Born: Liverpool, England, 2 November, 1940						RW/IF
England: Youth						
Liverpool	Jnr	08/58				
Bury	Prescot Cables	10/61	61-62	8	-	0
Halifax T	Tr	07/63	63-64	64	-	10
Tranmere Rov	Tr	07/65	65	7	0	3
TWITCHIN Ian Robert						
Born: Teignmouth, Devon, England, 22 January, 1952						RB/M
England: Youth						
Torquay U	Jnr	01/70	69-80	374	27	14
TWOMEY James Francis (Jim)						
Born: Newry, Armagh, Northern Ireland, 13 April, 1914						G

League Club	Source	Date Signed	Seasons Played	Apps	Subs	Gls
Died: Leeds, England, 9 November, 1984						
Northern Ireland: 2/NILge-2						
Leeds U	Newry T	12/37	37-48	108	-	0
TWYNHAM Gary Steven						
Born: Manchester, England, 8 February, 1976						M
Manchester U	YT	07/94				
Darlington	Tr	03/96	95-96	23	8	3
Macclesfield T	Hednesford T	08/00	00	5	4	0
TYDEMAN Richard (Dick)						
Born: Chatham, Kent, England, 26 May, 1951						M
Gillingham	App	05/69	69-76	293	2	13
Charlton Ath	Tr	12/76	76-80	158	0	7
Gillingham	Tr	08/81	81-83	75	1	2
Peterborough U	Tr	10/83	83	29	0	0
TYLER Dudley Hugh John						
Born: Salisbury, Wiltshire, England, 21 September, 1944						RM
West Ham U	Hereford U	06/72	72-73	29	0	1
Hereford U	Tr	11/73	73-76	97	5	10
TYLER Leonard Victor (Len)						
Born: Rotherhithe, SE London, England, 7 January, 1919						LB
Died: Lewisham, SE London, England, 6 January, 1988						
Millwall	Redhill	03/43	46-49	90	-	0
Ipswich T	Tr	07/50	50-51	73	-	0
TYLER Mark Richard						
Born: Norwich, England, 2 April, 1977						G
England: Youth						
Peterborough U	YT	12/94	94-07	412	1	0
Bury	L	01/09	08	11	0	0
Luton T	Tr	07/09	14	31	0	0
TYLER Simon						
Born: Pontypool, Torfaen, Wales, 1 May, 1962						F
Newport Co	Abergavenny Thursday	10/84	84-85	0	4	0
TYNAN Paul						
Born: Whitehaven, Cumbria, England, 15 July, 1969						M
Carlisle U	Ipswich T (App)	08/87	87	2	3	0
TYNAN Robert (Bobby)						
Born: Liverpool, England, 7 December, 1955						M
England: Youth						
Tranmere Rov	App	07/73	72-77	193	2	26
Blackpool	Tr	07/78				
TYNAN Scott John						
Born: Kirkby, Merseyside, England, 27 November, 1983						G
England: Semi Pro-4						
Nottingham F	Wigan Ath (YT)	04/02				
Barnet	Tr	09/04	05	7	0	0
Rushden & D	Tr	01/06	05	13	1	0
Hereford U	L	08/06	06	7	0	0
TYNAN Thomas Edward (Tommy)						
Born: Liverpool, England, 17 November, 1955						F
Liverpool	App	11/72				
Swansea C	L	10/75	75	6	0	2
Sheffield Wed	Tr	09/76	76-78	89	2	31
Lincoln C	Tr	10/78	78	9	0	1
Newport Co	Tr	02/79	78-82	168	15	66
Plymouth Arg	Tr	08/83	83-84	80	0	43
Rotherham U	Tr	07/85	85-86	32	0	13
Plymouth Arg	L	03/86	85	9	0	9
Plymouth Arg	Tr	09/86	86-89	172	1	73
Torquay U	Tr	05/90	90	34	1	13
Doncaster Rov	Tr	07/91	91	5	6	1
TYNE Thomas Richard (Tommy)						
Born: Lambeth, S London, England, 2 March, 1981						F
Millwall	Slade Green	02/99	00	0	3	0
TYRELL Joseph James (Joe)						
Born: Stepney, E London, England, 21 January, 1932						IF
Aston Villa	Bretforton OB, Evesham	05/50	53-55	7	-	3
Millwall	Tr	03/56	55-56	37	-	18
Bournemouth	Tr	06/57	57-58	3	-	1
TYRER Alan						
Born: Liverpool, England, 8 December, 1942						M
Died: Middlesbrough, England, January, 2008						
Everton	Jnr	12/59	59-61	9	-	2
Mansfield T	Tr	07/63	63-64	41	-	5
Arsenal	Tr	08/65				
Bury	Tr	08/67	67	2	1	0
Workington	Tr	07/68	68-75	228	16	18

League Club	Source	Date Signed	Seasons Played	Apps	Subs	Gls

TYRER Arthur
Born: Liverpool, England, 14 October, 1934 — CF

Crewe Alex	St Helens	03/58	57	6	-	3

TYRER Arthur Spencer
Born: Manchester, England, 25 February, 1931 — LH/LW

Leeds U	Mossley	09/50	51-53	39	-	4
Shrewsbury T	Peterborough U	06/55	55	24	-	3
Aldershot	Tr	06/56	56-63	234	-	9

TYSON John (Jack)
Born: Barrow, Cumbria, England, 19 November, 1935 — RW

Barrow		04/54	53-56	8	-	0

TYSON Nathan
Born: Reading, England, 4 May, 1982 — F
England: Youth

Reading	YT	03/00	99-03	9	24	1
Swansea C	L	08/01	01	7	4	1
Cheltenham T	L	03/02	01	1	7	1
Wycombe W	Tr	01/04	03-05	76	2	42
Nottingham F	Tr	11/05	05-10	122	62	35
Derby Co	Tr	07/11	11-12	17	22	4
Millwall	L	01/13	12	1	3	0
Blackpool	Tr	09/13	13	0	10	0
Fleetwood T	L	11/13	13	4	0	0
Notts Co	L	03/14	13	4	6	0
Doncaster Rov	Tr	07/14	14	31	8	12

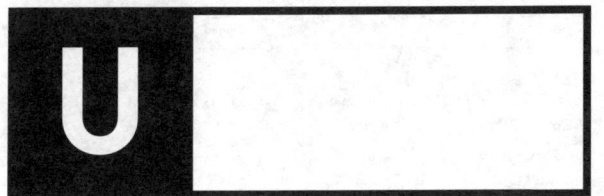

League Club	Source	Date Signed	Seasons Played	Career Record Apps	Subs	Gls
UCHECHI Chima Daniel (Danny)						
Born: Abia State, Nigeria, 14 September, 1989						F
Nigeria: U23-5/Youth						
Sheffield Wed (L)	FC Dender (NIG)	08/11	11	0	1	0
UDDIN Anwar						
Born: Stepney, E London, England, 1 November, 1981						CD
West Ham U	YT	07/01				
Sheffield Wed	Tr	02/02				
Bristol Rov	Tr	07/02	02-03	18	1	1
Dagenham & Red	Tr	07/04	07-09	53	11	1
Barnet	Tr	07/10	10-11	37	2	1
UDEZE Ifeanyi (Iffy)						
Born: Lagos, Nigeria, 21 July, 1980						LB
Nigeria: 35						
West Bromwich A (L)	PAOK Salonika (GRE)	01/03	02	7	4	0
UFTON Derek Gilbert						
Born: Crayford, SE London, England, 31 May, 1928						CH
England: 1						
Charlton Ath	Bexleyheath & Welling	09/48	49-59	263	-	0
UGARTE Juan						
Born: San Sebastian, Spain, 7 November, 1980						F
Wrexham	Dorchester T	11/04	04	23	7	17
Crewe Alex	Tr	07/05	05	0	2	0
Wrexham	L	10/05	05	2	0	0
Wrexham		11/06	06-07	0	3	0
UGOLINI Rolando						
Born: Lucca, Italy, 4 June, 1924						G
Died: Edinburgh, Scotland, 10 April, 2014						
Middlesbrough	Glasgow Celtic	05/48	48-55	320	-	0
Wrexham	Tr	06/57	57-59	83	-	0
UGWU Chigozie Eze (Gozie)						
Born: Oxford, England, 22 April, 1993						F
Reading	Sch	07/11				
Yeovil T	L	07/12	12	4	11	3
Plymouth Arg	L	01/13	12	2	4	0
Shrewsbury T	L	11/13	13	7	0	1
Yeovil T	Dunfermline Ath	01/15	14	21	1	5
UHLENBEEK Gustav Reinier (Gus)						
Born: Paramaribo, Suriname, 20 August, 1970						RB
Ipswich T	Tops SV (NED)	08/95	95-97	77	12	4
Fulham	Tr	07/98	98-99	22	17	1
Sheffield U	Tr	08/00	00-01	47	4	0
Walsall	L	03/02	01	5	0	0
Bradford C	Tr	08/02	02	42	0	1
Chesterfield	Tr	08/03	03	36	1	0
Wycombe W	Tr	07/04	04	36	6	4
Mansfield T	Tr	08/05	05	28	12	2
UKAH Ugochuchwu (Ugo)						
Born: Parma, Italy, 18 January, 1984						D
Queens Park Rgrs	Pro Vasta (ITA)	08/05	05	0	1	0
ULLATHORNE Robert (Rob)						
Born: Wakefield, England, 11 October, 1971						LB
England: Youth						
Norwich C	YT	07/90	90-95	86	8	7
Leicester C	CA Osasuna (SPN)	02/97	97-98	28	3	1
Sheffield U	Tr	12/00	00-02	39	1	0
Northampton T	Tr	02/04	03	13	0	1
Notts Co	Tr	07/04	04-05	65	4	0
ULLOA Jose Leonardo (Leonardo)						
Born: Rio Negro, Argentina, 26 July, 1986						F
Brighton & HA	UD Almeria (SPN)	01/13	12-13	47	3	23
Leicester C	Tr	08/14	14	29	8	11
ULVESTAD Fredrik Stensoe						
Born: Aalesund, Norway, 17 June, 1992						M
Norway: 1/U23-2/U21-14/Youth						
Burnley	Aalesunds FK (NOR)	03/15	14	1	1	0

League Club	Source	Date Signed	Seasons Played	Career Record Apps	Subs	Gls
UNDERHILL Graham Stuart						
Born: Bristol, England, 10 April, 1968						CD
Bristol C	App	04/86	85	1	0	0
UNDERWOOD Edmund David (Dave)						
Born: Camden, N London, England, 15 March, 1928						G
Died: Durban, South Africa, 25 January, 1989						
Queens Park Rgrs	Edgware T	12/49	51	2	-	0
Watford	Tr	02/52	51-53	52	-	0
Liverpool	Tr	12/53	53-55	45	-	0
Watford	Tr	06/56	56	16	-	0
Watford	Dartford	04/60	60-62	108	-	0
Fulham	Tr	07/63	63-64	18	-	0
UNDERWOOD George Ronald						
Born: Sheffield, England, 6 September, 1925						RB
Sheffield U		09/46	49-50	17	-	0
Sheffield Wed	Tr	10/51				
Scunthorpe U	Tr	06/53	53	8	-	0
Rochdale	Tr	06/54	54	19	-	0
UNDERWOOD Paul Victor						
Born: Wimbledon, SW London, England, 16 August, 1973						LB
England: Semi Pro-4						
Rushden & D	Enfield	06/97	01-03	110	0	1
Luton T	Tr	03/04	03-05	66	1	5
UNDERWOOD William Kenneth (Bill)						
Born: Brigg, North Lincolnshire, England, 28 December, 1921						W
Died: Middlesbrough, England, November, 1993						
Hartlepool U (Am)	South Bank	01/48	47	1	-	0
UNGER Lars						
Born: Eutin, Germany, 30 September, 1972						M
Germany: U21-11						
Southend U (L)	Fort Dusseldorf (GER)	02/99	98	14	0	0
UNSAL Hakan						
Born: Sinop, Turkey, 14 May, 1973						LB
Turkey: 33/U21-12						
Blackburn Rov	Galatasaray (TKY)	03/02	01	7	1	0
UNSWORTH David Gerald						
Born: Chorley, Lancashire, England, 16 October, 1973						CD
England: 1/U21-6/Youth						
Everton	YT	06/92	91-96	108	8	11
West Ham U	Tr	08/97	97	32	0	2
Aston Villa	Tr	07/98				
Everton	Tr	08/98	98-03	164	24	23
Portsmouth	Tr	07/04	04	15	0	2
Ipswich T	L	01/05	04	16	0	1
Sheffield U	Tr	08/05	05-06	38	1	4
Wigan Ath	Tr	01/07	06	6	4	1
Burnley	Tr	08/07	07	26	3	1
Huddersfield T	Tr	08/08	08	4	0	0
UNSWORTH Jamie Jonathan						
Born: Bury, Greater Manchester, England, 1 May, 1973						RB
Cardiff C	YT	07/91	90-91	1	3	0
UNSWORTH Lee Peter						
Born: Eccles, Greater Manchester, England, 25 February, 1973						RB
Crewe Alex	Ashton U	02/95	95-99	93	33	0
Bury	Tr	08/00	00-05	141	10	6
UPHILL Edward Dennis Herbert (Dennis)						
Born: Bath, England, 11 August, 1931						IF
Died: Watford, Hertfordshire, England, 7 February, 2007						
Tottenham H	Peasedown MW	09/49	50-52	6	-	2
Reading	Tr	02/53	52-55	92	-	42
Coventry C	Tr	10/55	55-56	49	-	16
Mansfield T	Tr	03/57	56-58	83	-	38
Watford	Tr	06/59	59-60	51	-	30
Crystal Palace	Tr	10/60	60-62	63	-	17
UPRICHARD William Norman McCourt (Norman)						
Born: Lurgan, Armagh, Northern Ireland, 20 February, 1928						G
Died: Hastings, East Sussex, England, 31 January, 2011						
Northern Ireland: 18						
Arsenal	Distillery	06/48				
Swindon T	Tr	11/49	49-52	73	-	0
Portsmouth	Tr	11/52	52-58	182	-	0
Southend U	Tr	07/59	59	12	-	0
UPSON Edward James (Ed)						
Born: Bury St Edmunds, Suffolk, England, 21 November, 1989						M
Ipswich T	Sch	11/06				
Barnet	L	03/10	09	5	4	1
Yeovil T	Tr	07/10	10-13	117	12	9
Millwall	Tr	01/14	13-14	25	11	2

League Club	Source	Date Signed	Seasons Played	Career Record Apps	Subs	Gls

UPSON Matthew James

Born: Eye, Suffolk, England, 18 April, 1979 CD
England: 21/U21-11/Youth

League Club	Source	Date Signed	Seasons Played	Apps	Subs	Gls
Luton T	YT	04/96	96	0	1	0
Arsenal	Tr	05/97	97-01	20	14	0
Nottingham F	L	12/00	00	1	0	0
Crystal Palace	L	03/01	00	7	0	0
Reading	L	09/02	02	13	1	0
Birmingham C	Tr	01/03	02-06	112	1	5
West Ham U	Tr	01/07	06-10	131	0	4
Stoke C	Tr	08/11	11-12	11	4	2
Brighton & HA	Tr	01/13	12-13	61	0	3
Leicester C	Tr	05/14	14	5	0	0

UPTON Colin Clive

Born: Reading, England, 2 October, 1960 F

League Club	Source	Date Signed	Seasons Played	Apps	Subs	Gls
Plymouth Arg	App	10/78	78	2	1	0

UPTON Frank

Born: Atherstone, Warwickshire, England, 18 October, 1934 LH
Died: Derby, England, 18 May, 2011

League Club	Source	Date Signed	Seasons Played	Apps	Subs	Gls
Northampton T	Nuneaton Bor	03/53	52-53	17	-	1
Derby Co	Tr	06/54	54-60	224	-	12
Chelsea	Tr	08/61	61-64	74	-	3
Derby Co	Tr	09/65	65-66	35	0	5
Notts Co	Tr	09/66	66	33	1	3
Workington	Worcester C	01/68	67	6	1	0

UPTON James Edwin Glen (Jim)

Born: Coatbridge, Lanarkshire, Scotland, 3 June, 1940 LB

League Club	Source	Date Signed	Seasons Played	Apps	Subs	Gls
Cardiff C	Glasgow Celtic	08/63	63	5	-	0

UPTON Robin Patrick (Nobby)

Born: Lincoln, England, 9 November, 1942 WH/CH

League Club	Source	Date Signed	Seasons Played	Apps	Subs	Gls
Brighton & HA	Jnr	11/59	62-66	40	0	0

URE John Francombe (Ian)

Born: Ayr, Scotland, 7 December, 1939 CD
Scotland: 11/SLge-4/U23-1

League Club	Source	Date Signed	Seasons Played	Apps	Subs	Gls
Arsenal	Dundee	08/63	63-69	168	0	2
Manchester U	Tr	08/69	69-70	47	0	1

URQUHART George Stuart McWilliam

Born: Glasgow, Scotland, 22 April, 1950 M

League Club	Source	Date Signed	Seasons Played	Apps	Subs	Gls
Wigan Ath	Ross Co	07/79	79-80	63	5	6

URQUHART William Murray (Billy)

Born: Inverness, Scotland, 22 November, 1956 F

League Club	Source	Date Signed	Seasons Played	Apps	Subs	Gls
Wigan Ath	Glasgow Rangers	11/80	80	5	5	2

URSEM Loek Aloysius Jacobus Maria

Born: Amsterdam, Netherlands, 7 January, 1958 W
Netherlands: U23

League Club	Source	Date Signed	Seasons Played	Apps	Subs	Gls
Stoke C	AZ67 Alkmaar (NED)	07/79	79-82	32	8	7
Sunderland	L	03/82	81	0	4	0

URWIN Graham Edward

Born: South Shields, Tyne and Wear, England, 15 February, 1949 RW

League Club	Source	Date Signed	Seasons Played	Apps	Subs	Gls
Darlington		08/67	67	1	0	0

USHER Brian

Born: Durham, England, 11 March, 1944 W
England: U23-1

League Club	Source	Date Signed	Seasons Played	Apps	Subs	Gls
Sunderland	Jnr	03/61	63-64	61	-	5
Sheffield Wed	Tr	06/65	65-67	55	1	2
Doncaster Rov	Tr	06/68	68-72	164	6	6

USHER John Allison Grey (Johnny)

Born: Hexham, Northumberland, England, 6 September, 1918 WH
Died: Fulham, W London, England, 5 January, 1989

League Club	Source	Date Signed	Seasons Played	Apps	Subs	Gls
Watford		05/46	46-47	23	-	3

UTAKA John Chukwudi

Born: Enugu, Nigeria, 8 January, 1982 W
Nigeria: 43

League Club	Source	Date Signed	Seasons Played	Apps	Subs	Gls
Portsmouth	Stade Rennais (FRA)	07/07	07-10	62	28	10

UTLEY Darren

Born: Barnsley, South Yorkshire, England, 28 September, 1977 CD

League Club	Source	Date Signed	Seasons Played	Apps	Subs	Gls
Doncaster Rov	YT	12/95	95-97	22	6	1

UWEZU Michael

Born: Owerri, Nigeria, 12 December, 1990 F

League Club	Source	Date Signed	Seasons Played	Apps	Subs	Gls
Fulham	Sch	05/09				
Lincoln C	L	01/10	09	0	2	0
Northampton T	Dulwich Hamlet	03/11	10	2	2	1

UYTENBOGAARDT Albert George

Born: Cape Town, South Africa, 5 March, 1930 G
South Africa:

League Club	Source	Date Signed	Seasons Played	Apps	Subs	Gls
Charlton Ath	Cape Town Trams (RSA)	10/48	48-52	6	-	0

UZELAC Steven (Steve)

Born: Doncaster, South Yorkshire, England, 12 March, 1953 CD

League Club	Source	Date Signed	Seasons Played	Apps	Subs	Gls
Doncaster Rov	Jnr	06/71	71-76	182	3	9
Mansfield T	L	02/76	75	2	0	0
Preston NE	Tr	05/77	77-78	9	0	0
Stockport Co	Tr	03/80	79-81	31	0	2

UZZELL John Edward

Born: Plymouth, England, 31 March, 1959 D

League Club	Source	Date Signed	Seasons Played	Apps	Subs	Gls
Plymouth Arg	App	03/77	77-88	292	10	6
Torquay U	Tr	08/89	89-91	91	1	2

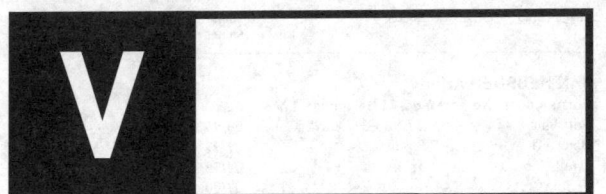

VAESEN Nico Jos-Theodor
Born: Hasselt, Belgium, 28 September, 1969 — G

League Club	Source	Date Signed	Seasons Played	Apps	Subs	Gls
Huddersfield T	Eendracht Aalst (BEL)	07/98	98-00	134	0	0
Birmingham C	Tr	06/01	01-05	53	1	0
Gillingham	L	12/03	03	5	0	0
Bradford C	L	02/04	03	6	0	0
Crystal Palace	L	03/04	03	10	0	0

VAESSEN Leon Henry
Born: Market Bosworth, Leicestershire, England, 8 November, 1940 — LH
England: Schools

League Club	Source	Date Signed	Seasons Played	Apps	Subs	Gls
Millwall	Chelsea (Am)	01/58	57-60	26	-	2
Gillingham	Tr	08/61	61-62	29	-	0

VAESSEN Paul Leon
Born: Gillingham, Kent, England, 16 October, 1961 — F
Died: Bristol, England, 8 August, 2001

League Club	Source	Date Signed	Seasons Played	Apps	Subs	Gls
Arsenal	App	07/79	78-81	23	9	6

VAFIADIS Odysseus Yickanis (Seth)
Born: Hammersmith, W London, England, 8 September, 1945 — W

League Club	Source	Date Signed	Seasons Played	Apps	Subs	Gls
Queens Park Rgrs	Chelsea (App)	11/62	63	15	-	4
Millwall	Tr	09/64	64	4	-	0

VAIREY Roy Henry
Born: South Elmsall, West Yorkshire, England, 10 June, 1932 — G

League Club	Source	Date Signed	Seasons Played	Apps	Subs	Gls
Stockport Co	Frickley Colliery	09/51	56	5	-	0

VAISANEN Ville Tapio
Born: Oulu, Finland, 19 April, 1977 — CD
Finland: 5

League Club	Source	Date Signed	Seasons Played	Apps	Subs	Gls
Darlington	FF Jaro (FIN)	09/06	06	5	0	0

VALAKARI Simo Johannes
Born: Helsinki, Finland, 28 April, 1973 — M
Finland: 32/U21-1

League Club	Source	Date Signed	Seasons Played	Apps	Subs	Gls
Derby Co	Motherwell	07/00	00-03	34	12	3

VALDES Victor
Born: Barcelona, Spain, 14 January, 1982 — G
Spain: 20/U21-11/Youth

League Club	Source	Date Signed	Seasons Played	Apps	Subs	Gls
Manchester U	Barcelona (SPN)	01/15	14	1	1	0

VALENCIA Enner Remberto
Born: Esmeraldas, Ecuador, 4 November, 1989 — F
Ecuador: 22

League Club	Source	Date Signed	Seasons Played	Apps	Subs	Gls
West Ham U	Pachuca (MEX)	08/14	14	25	7	4

VALENCIA Luis Antonio (Antonio)
Born: Nueva Loja, Ecuador, 4 August, 1985 — RW
Ecuador: 75/Youth

League Club	Source	Date Signed	Seasons Played	Apps	Subs	Gls
Wigan Ath	Villarreal (SPN)	08/06	06-08	78	6	7
Manchester U	Tr	07/09	09-14	132	30	13

VALENTE Nuno Jorge
Born: Lisbon, Portugal, 12 September, 1974 — LB
Portugal: 33

League Club	Source	Date Signed	Seasons Played	Apps	Subs	Gls
Everton	FC Porto (POR)	08/05	05-08	39	6	0

VALENTINE Carl Howard
Born: Droylsden, Greater Manchester, England, 4 July, 1958 — W
Canada: 31

League Club	Source	Date Signed	Seasons Played	Apps	Subs	Gls
Oldham Ath	Jnr	01/76	76-79	75	7	8
West Bromwich A	Vancouver W'caps (CAN)	10/84	84-85	44	0	6

VALENTINE Peter
Born: Huddersfield, West Yorkshire, England, 16 April, 1963 — CD

League Club	Source	Date Signed	Seasons Played	Apps	Subs	Gls
Huddersfield T	App	04/81	81-82	19	0	1
Bolton W	Tr	07/83	83-84	66	2	1
Bury	Tr	07/85	85-92	314	5	16
Carlisle U	Tr	08/93	93-94	27	2	2
Rochdale	Tr	11/94	94-95	49	1	2

VALENTINE Ryan David
Born: Wrexham, Wales, 19 August, 1982 — RB
Wales: U21-8/Youth

League Club	Source	Date Signed	Seasons Played	Apps	Subs	Gls
Everton	YT	09/99				
Darlington	Tr	08/02	02-05	151	11	4
Wrexham	Tr	08/06	06-07	46	2	2
Darlington	Tr	01/08	07-08	43	5	0
Hereford U	Tr	07/09	09-10	56	0	4

VALERO Borja
Born: Madrid, Spain, 12 January, 1985 — M
Spain: 1/Youth

League Club	Source	Date Signed	Seasons Played	Apps	Subs	Gls
West Bromwich A	RCD Mallorca (SPN)	08/08	08-09	27	4	0

VALERO Vincente Xavier
Born: Castellon, Spain, 28 February, 1973 — G

League Club	Source	Date Signed	Seasons Played	Apps	Subs	Gls
Wrexham	Ciudad de Murcia (SPN)	01/05	04	3	0	0

VALERY Patrick Jean-Claude
Born: Brignoles, Provence, France, 3 July, 1969 — RB

League Club	Source	Date Signed	Seasons Played	Apps	Subs	Gls
Blackburn Rov	SC Bastia (FRA)	06/97	97	14	1	0

VALLANCE Thomas Henshall Wilson (Tom)
Born: Stoke-on-Trent, England, 28 March, 1924 — LW
Died: Sutton, S London, England, 7 July, 1980

League Club	Source	Date Signed	Seasons Played	Apps	Subs	Gls
Arsenal	Torquay U (Am)	07/47	48-49	15	-	2

VALLARD Leonard Gerald Harold (Len)
Born: Sherborne, Dorset, England, 6 July, 1940 — LB

League Club	Source	Date Signed	Seasons Played	Apps	Subs	Gls
Reading	Yeovil T	05/58	59-61	37	-	2

VALOIS Jean-Louis
Born: Lyon, France, 15 October, 1973 — LW

League Club	Source	Date Signed	Seasons Played	Apps	Subs	Gls
Luton T	OSC Lille (FRA)	09/01	01	32	2	6
Burnley	Clyde	09/04	04	18	12	3

VAN AANHOLT Patrick John Miguel
Born: Den Bosch, Netherlands, 29 August, 1990 — LB
Netherlands: 2/U21-16/Youth

League Club	Source	Date Signed	Seasons Played	Apps	Subs	Gls
Chelsea	Sch	08/07	09	0	2	0
Coventry C	L	07/09	09	19	1	0
Newcastle U	L	01/10	09	7	0	0
Leicester C	L	01/11	10	12	0	1
Wigan Ath	L	08/11	11	3	0	0
Sunderland	Tr	07/14	14	26	2	0

VAN BLERK Jason
Born: Sydney, Australia, 16 March, 1968 — LB
Australia: 33/Youth

League Club	Source	Date Signed	Seasons Played	Apps	Subs	Gls
Millwall	GAE Deventer (NED)	09/94	94-96	68	5	2
Manchester C	Tr	08/97	97	10	9	0
West Bromwich A	Tr	03/98	97-00	106	3	3
Stockport Co	Tr	08/01	01	13	0	0
Hull C	Tr	01/02	01	10	0	1
Shrewsbury T	Tr	08/02	02	17	6	1

VAN BREUKELEN Johannes Franciscus (Hans)
Born: Utrecht, Netherlands, 4 October, 1956 — G
Netherlands: 73

League Club	Source	Date Signed	Seasons Played	Apps	Subs	Gls
Nottingham F	FC Utrecht (NED)	09/82	82-83	61	0	0

VAN BRONCKHORST Giovanni Christiaan
Born: Rotterdam, Netherlands, 5 February, 1975 — LB
Netherlands: 106

League Club	Source	Date Signed	Seasons Played	Apps	Subs	Gls
Arsenal	Glasgow Rangers	06/01	01-02	22	19	2

VAN BUYTEN Daniel
Born: Chimay, Belgium, 7 February, 1978 — CD
Belgium: 85

League Club	Source	Date Signed	Seasons Played	Apps	Subs	Gls
Manchester C (L)	Olymp Marseille (FRA)	01/04	03	5	0	0

VAN DAMME Jelle Francois Maria
Born: Lokeren, Belgium, 10 October, 1983 — LB
Belgium: 31/U21-4/Youth

League Club	Source	Date Signed	Seasons Played	Apps	Subs	Gls
Southampton	Ajax (NED)	05/04	04	4	2	0
Wolverhampton W	Anderlecht (BEL)	07/10	10	4	2	1

VANDEN BORRE Anthony Henri
Born: Likasi, DR Congo, 24 October, 1987 — RB/M
Belgium: 28/U21-11/Youth

League Club	Source	Date Signed	Seasons Played	Apps	Subs	Gls
Portsmouth (L)	Genoa (ITA)	08/09	09	15	4	0

VAN DEN BROEK Benjamin
Born: Geleen, Netherlands, 21 September, 1987 — M

League Club	Source	Date Signed	Seasons Played	Apps	Subs	Gls
Shrewsbury T	Haarlem (NED)	02/10	09-10	5	17	1

VAN DEN HAUWE Patrick William Roger (Pat)
Born: Dendermonde, Belgium, 16 December, 1960 — D
Wales: 13

League Club	Source	Date Signed	Seasons Played	Apps	Subs	Gls
Birmingham C	App	08/78	78-84	119	4	1
Everton	Tr	09/84	84-88	134	1	2
Tottenham H	Tr	08/89	89-92	110	6	0
Millwall	Tr	09/93	93-94	27	0	0

VAN DER ELST Francois Jean Cecile
Born: Opwijk, Belgium, 1 December, 1954 — RW
Belgium: 44

League Club	Source	Date Signed	Seasons Played	Apps	Subs	Gls
West Ham U	New York Cosmos (USA)	12/81	81-82	61	1	14

VAN DER GEEST Francisus Wilhelmus (Frank)
Born: Beverwijk, Netherlands, 30 April, 1973 — G

League Club	Source	Date Signed	Seasons Played	Apps	Subs	Gls
Darlington	Heracles (NED)	08/00	00	2	0	0

VAN DER GOUW Raimond
Born: Oldenzaal, Netherlands, 24 March, 1963 — G

League Club	Source	Date Signed	Seasons Played	Apps	Subs	Gls
Manchester U	Vitesse Arnhem (NED)	07/96	96-01	26	11	0
West Ham U	Tr	07/02				

VAN DER GUN Cedric
Born: Den Haag, Netherlands, 5 May, 1979 — LW
Netherlands: U21-3

League Club	Source	Date Signed	Seasons Played	Apps	Subs	Gls
Swansea C	FC Utrecht (NED)	09/09	09-10	21	14	3

VAN DER KWAAK Peter
Born: Haarlem, Netherlands, 12 October, 1968 — G

League Club	Source	Date Signed	Seasons Played	Apps	Subs	Gls
Reading	SVV Dordrecht (NED)	08/98	98-99	3	1	0
Carlisle U	L	02/00	99	2	0	0

VAN DER LAAN Robertus Petrus (Robin)
Born: Schiedam, Netherlands, 5 September, 1968 — M

League Club	Source	Date Signed	Seasons Played	Apps	Subs	Gls
Port Vale	FC Wageningen (NED)	02/91	90-94	154	22	24
Derby Co	Tr	08/95	95-97	61	4	8
Wolverhampton W	L	10/96	96	7	0	0
Barnsley	Tr	07/98	98-00	52	15	5

VAN DER LINDEN Antoine
Born: Rotterdam, Netherlands, 17 March, 1976 — CD

League Club	Source	Date Signed	Seasons Played	Apps	Subs	Gls
Swindon T	Sparta Rotterdam (NED)	08/00	00	17	16	1

VAN DER MEYDE Andy
Born: Arnhem, Netherlands, 30 September, 1979 — W
Netherlands: 18

League Club	Source	Date Signed	Seasons Played	Apps	Subs	Gls
Everton	Inter Milan (ITA)	08/05	05-08	12	8	0

VANDERMOTTEN William (Willie)
Born: Glasgow, Scotland, 26 August, 1930 — IF
Died: Hatfield, Hertfordshire, England, 30 June, 1979

League Club	Source	Date Signed	Seasons Played	Apps	Subs	Gls
Bradford Park Ave	Cowdenbeath	03/53	52	1	-	0

VAN DER SAR Edwin
Born: Leiden, Netherlands, 29 October, 1970 — G
Netherlands: 130

League Club	Source	Date Signed	Seasons Played	Apps	Subs	Gls
Fulham	Juventus (ITA)	08/01	01-04	126	1	0
Manchester U	Tr	06/05	05-10	186	0	0

VAN DER SCHAAF Remco Jelmer
Born: Groningen, Netherlands, 28 February, 1979 — M
Netherlands: U21-1

League Club	Source	Date Signed	Seasons Played	Apps	Subs	Gls
Burnley	Vitesse Arnhem (NED)	07/08	08	1	0	0

VAN DER VAART Rafael Ferdinand
Born: Heemskerk, Netherlands, 11 February, 1983 — M/F
Netherlands: 109/U21-4/Youth

League Club	Source	Date Signed	Seasons Played	Apps	Subs	Gls
Tottenham H	Real Madrid (SPN)	08/10	10-12	57	6	24

VAN DER VELDEN Carel
Born: Arnhem, Netherlands, 3 August, 1972 — M

League Club	Source	Date Signed	Seasons Played	Apps	Subs	Gls
Barnsley	FC Den Bosch (NED)	03/96	95-96	7	2	0
Scarborough	Tr	08/97	97	5	3	1

VAN DEURZEN Jurgen
Born: Genk, Belgium, 26 January, 1974 — M/LB
Belgium: U21/Youth

League Club	Source	Date Signed	Seasons Played	Apps	Subs	Gls
Stoke C	KFC Turnhout (BEL)	08/01	01-02	44	8	5

VAN DULLEMEN Raymond Robert (Ray)
Born: Den Haag, Netherlands, 6 May, 1973 — F

League Club	Source	Date Signed	Seasons Played	Apps	Subs	Gls
Northampton T	VIOS Beltrum (NED)	08/97	97	0	1	0

VAN GINKEL Wulfert Cornelius (Marco)
Born: Amersfoort, Netherlands, 1 December, 1992 — M
Netherlands: 2/U21-19/Youth

League Club	Source	Date Signed	Seasons Played	Apps	Subs	Gls
Chelsea	Vitesse Arnhem (NED)	07/13	13	0	2	0

VAN GOBBEL Ulrich
Born: Paramaribo, Suriname, 16 January, 1971 — D
Netherlands: 8

League Club	Source	Date Signed	Seasons Played	Apps	Subs	Gls
Southampton	Galatasaray (TKY)	10/96	96-97	25	2	1

VAN GOOL Roger
Born: Essen, Belgium, 1 June, 1950 — RW
Belgium: 7

League Club	Source	Date Signed	Seasons Played	Apps	Subs	Gls
Coventry C	FC Cologne (GER)	03/80	79-80	17	0	0

VANHALA Jari
Born: Helsinki, Finland, 29 August, 1965 — F
Finland: 23

League Club	Source	Date Signed	Seasons Played	Apps	Subs	Gls
Bradford C	FF Jaro (FIN)	12/96	96	0	1	0

VAN HEUSDEN Arjan
Born: Alphen, Netherlands, 11 December, 1972 — G

League Club	Source	Date Signed	Seasons Played	Apps	Subs	Gls
Port Vale	VV Noordwijk (NED)	08/94	94-97	27	0	0
Oxford U	L	09/97	97	11	0	0
Cambridge U	Tr	08/98	98-99	41	1	0
Exeter C	Tr	07/00	00-01	74	0	0
Mansfield T	Tr	09/02	02	5	0	0
Torquay U	Tr	11/02	02-04	47	0	0

VAN HOMOET Marcelo Bruma
Born: Rotterdam, Netherlands, 7 March, 1984 — D

League Club	Source	Date Signed	Seasons Played	Apps	Subs	Gls
Barnsley	Sparta Rotterdam (NED)	07/07	07-08	31	5	0

VAN HOOIJDONK Pierre
Born: Steenbergen, Netherlands, 29 November, 1969 — F
Netherlands: 46

League Club	Source	Date Signed	Seasons Played	Apps	Subs	Gls
Nottingham F	Glasgow Celtic	03/97	96-98	68	3	36

VAN LA PARRA Rajiv Ramon
Born: Rotterdam, Netherlands, 4 June, 1991 — RW
Netherlands: U21-6/Youth

League Club	Source	Date Signed	Seasons Played	Apps	Subs	Gls
Wolverhampton W	Heerenveen (NED)	07/14	14	29	11	1

VAN MIERLO Antonius Wilhelmus Matthis (Toine)
Born: Soerendonk, Netherlands, 24 August, 1957 — W
Netherlands: 3

League Club	Source	Date Signed	Seasons Played	Apps	Subs	Gls
Birmingham C	Willem II (NED)	08/81	81-82	44	0	4

VAN NIEUWSTADT Jos
Born: Waalwijk, Netherlands, 19 November, 1979 — CD

League Club	Source	Date Signed	Seasons Played	Apps	Subs	Gls
Doncaster Rov	Excelsior (NED)	08/08	08	9	7	1

VANNINEN Jukka
Born: Riihimaki, Finland, 31 January, 1977 — M

League Club	Source	Date Signed	Seasons Played	Apps	Subs	Gls
Exeter C	RoPs Rovaniemi (FIN)	12/99	99	3	2	0

VAN NISTELROOY Rutgerus Johannes Martinus (Ruud)
Born: Oss, Netherlands, 1 July, 1976 — F
Netherlands: 70

League Club	Source	Date Signed	Seasons Played	Apps	Subs	Gls
Manchester U	PSV Eindhoven (NED)	07/01	01-05	137	13	95

VAN PERSIE Robin
Born: Rotterdam, Netherlands, 6 August, 1983 — F
Netherlands: 98/U21-6

League Club	Source	Date Signed	Seasons Played	Apps	Subs	Gls
Arsenal	Feyenoord (NED)	04/04	04-11	149	45	96
Manchester U	Tr	08/12	12-14	78	8	48

VAN ROSSUM Johannes Christison (Erik)
Born: Nijmegen, Netherlands, 27 March, 1963 — CD

League Club	Source	Date Signed	Seasons Played	Apps	Subs	Gls
Plymouth Arg	Germinal Ekeren (BEL)	01/92	91	9	0	0

VANSITTART Thomas (Tom)
Born: Merton, SW London, England, 23 January, 1950 — D

League Club	Source	Date Signed	Seasons Played	Apps	Subs	Gls
Crystal Palace	App	04/67	67-69	10	1	2
Wrexham	Tr	02/70	69-74	86	2	1

VAN VEEN Kevin
Born: Eindhoven, Netherlands, 1 June, 1991 — F

League Club	Source	Date Signed	Seasons Played	Apps	Subs	Gls
Scunthorpe U	FC Oss (NED)	01/15	14	11	9	2

VAN WIJK Dennis Johannes
Born: Zaandam, Netherlands, 16 December, 1962 — LB/M

League Club	Source	Date Signed	Seasons Played	Apps	Subs	Gls
Norwich C	Ajax (NED)	10/82	82-85	109	9	3

VAN WOLFSWINKEL Ricky
Born: Woudenberg, Netherlands, 27 January, 1989 — F
Netherlands: 2/U21-7/Youth

League Club	Source	Date Signed	Seasons Played	Apps	Subs	Gls
Norwich C	Sporting Lisbon (POR)	07/13	13	16	9	1

VARADI Imre
Born: Paddington, Central London, England, 8 July, 1959 — F

League Club	Source	Date Signed	Seasons Played	Apps	Subs	Gls
Sheffield U	Letchworth Garden C	04/78	78	6	4	4
Everton	Tr	03/79	79-80	22	4	6
Newcastle U	Tr	08/81	81-82	81	0	39
Sheffield Wed	Tr	08/83	83-84	72	4	33
West Bromwich A	Tr	07/85	85	30	2	9
Manchester C	Tr	10/86	86-88	56	9	26
Sheffield Wed	Tr	09/88	88-89	14	8	3
Leeds U	Tr	02/90	89-92	21	5	5
Luton T	L	03/92	91	5	1	1
Oxford U	L	01/93	92	3	2	0
Rotherham U	Tr	03/93	92-94	55	12	25
Mansfield T	Tr	08/95	95	1	0	0
Scunthorpe U	Boston U	09/95	95	0	2	0

VARDY Jamie Richard
Born: Sheffield, England, 11 January, 1987 — F
England: 1

League Club	Source	Date Signed	Seasons Played	Apps	Subs	Gls
Leicester C	Fleetwood T	05/12	12-14	79	18	25

VARELA Silvestre Manuel
Born: Almada, Portugal, 2 February, 1985 — W
Portugal: 26/U21-28

League Club	Source	Date Signed	Seasons Played	Apps	Subs	Gls
West Bromwich A (L)	FC Porto (POR)	08/14	14	3	4	1

VARGA Jozsef
Born: Debrecen, Hungary, 6 June, 1988 — DM
Hungary: 31/U21-7

League Club	Source	Date Signed	Seasons Played	Apps	Subs	Gls
Middlesbrough (L)	Debrecen (HUN)	06/13	13	29	5	0

VARGA Stanislav
Born: Lipany, Slovakia, 8 October, 1972 — CD
Slovakia: 54

League Club	Source	Date Signed	Seasons Played	Apps	Subs	Gls
Sunderland	Slov Bratislava (SVK)	08/00	00-01	18	3	1
West Bromwich A	L	03/02	01	3	1	0
Sunderland	Glasgow Celtic	08/06	06	20	0	1
Burnley	L	01/08	07	10	0	0

VARGAS Eduardo Jesus
Born: Santiago, Chile, 20 November, 1989 — RW
Chile: 48/Youth

League Club	Source	Date Signed	Seasons Played	Apps	Subs	Gls
Queens Park Rgrs (L)	Napoli (ITA)	08/14	14	16	5	3

VARNEY Alexander (Alex)
Born: Bromley, SE London, England, 27 December, 1984 — F

League Club	Source	Date Signed	Seasons Played	Apps	Subs	Gls
Charlton Ath	Sch	12/03				
Barnet	L	01/06	05	0	1	0

VARNEY John Francis (Frank)
Born: Oxford, England, 27 November, 1929 — LB

League Club	Source	Date Signed	Seasons Played	Apps	Subs	Gls
Hull C	Oxford C	12/49	50	9	-	0
Lincoln C	Tr	05/51	51-52	20	-	4

VARNEY Luke Ivan
Born: Leicester, England, 28 September, 1982 — F

League Club	Source	Date Signed	Seasons Played	Apps	Subs	Gls
Crewe Alex	Quorn	03/03	03-06	68	27	27
Charlton Ath	Tr	05/07	07-08	39	18	10
Derby Co	Tr	11/08	08-10	10	2	1
Sheffield Wed	L	03/09	08	3	1	2
Sheffield Wed	L	08/09	09	32	7	9
Blackpool	L	08/10	10	24	6	5
Portsmouth	Tr	07/11	11	28	2	6
Leeds U	Tr	07/12	12-13	37	8	6
Blackburn Rov	Tr	02/14	13-14	3	20	0
Ipswich T	L	02/15	14	5	5	1

VARTY John William (Will)
Born: Workington, Cumbria, England, 1 October, 1976 — CD

League Club	Source	Date Signed	Seasons Played	Apps	Subs	Gls
Carlisle U	YT	07/95	96-98	79	3	1
Rotherham U	Tr	03/99	98-00	45	2	0
Carlisle U	Tr	08/01				

VARTY Thomas Heppell (Tommy)
Born: Hetton-le-Hole, Tyne and Wear, England, 2 December, 1921 — IF
Died: Enfield, N London, England, April, 2004

League Club	Source	Date Signed	Seasons Played	Apps	Subs	Gls
Darlington	South Shields	08/45	46-49	162	-	33
Watford	Tr	09/50	50	34	-	5

VASKO Tamas
Born: Budapest, Hungary, 20 February, 1984 — CD
Hungary: 12

League Club	Source	Date Signed	Seasons Played	Apps	Subs	Gls
Bristol C (L)	Ujpest (HUN)	08/07	07	8	11	1

VASPER Peter John
Born: Bromley, SE London, England, 3 September, 1945 — G

League Club	Source	Date Signed	Seasons Played	Apps	Subs	Gls
Leyton Orient	Queens Park Rgrs (Jnr)	11/63				
Norwich C	Guildford C	02/68	67-69	31	0	0
Cambridge U	Tr	09/70	70-73	136	0	0

VASS Stephen (Steve)
Born: Leicester, England, 10 January, 1954 — FB

League Club	Source	Date Signed	Seasons Played	Apps	Subs	Gls
Hartlepool U	Wycombe W	10/79	79	4	0	0
Huddersfield T	Tr	01/81				

VASSALLO Barrie Emmanuel
Born: Newport, Wales, 3 March, 1956 — M
Wales: Schools

League Club	Source	Date Signed	Seasons Played	Apps	Subs	Gls
Arsenal	App	05/73				
Plymouth Arg	Tr	11/74	74-75	6	7	2
Torquay U	Barnstaple T	03/77	76-78	44	2	4

VASSELL Darius Martin Clarke
Born: Birmingham, England, 13 June, 1980 — F
England: 22/U21-11/Youth

League Club	Source	Date Signed	Seasons Played	Apps	Subs	Gls
Aston Villa	YT	04/98	98-04	107	55	35
Manchester C	Tr	07/05	05-08	91	12	17
Leicester C	Ankaragucu (TKY)	10/10	10-11	36	8	6

VASSELL Isaac Cleveland
Born: Newquay, Cornwall, England, 9 September, 1993 — W

League Club	Source	Date Signed	Seasons Played	Apps	Subs	Gls
Plymouth Arg	Sch	07/12	11	0	6	0

VASSELL Kyle Thomas
Born: Milton Keynes, England, 7 February, 1993 — F

League Club	Source	Date Signed	Seasons Played	Apps	Subs	Gls
Peterborough U	Bishops Stortford	11/13	13-14	15	8	5
Oxford U	L	03/15	14	2	4	1

VASSEUR Emmanuel
Born: Calais, France, 3 September, 1976 — M

League Club	Source	Date Signed	Seasons Played	Apps	Subs	Gls
Leyton Orient	Calais (FRA)	01/01	00	0	2	0

VAUGHAN Anthony John (Tony)
Born: Manchester, England, 11 October, 1975 — D
England: Youth/Schools

League Club	Source	Date Signed	Seasons Played	Apps	Subs	Gls
Ipswich T	YT	07/94	94-96	56	11	3
Manchester C	Tr	07/97	97-99	54	4	2
Cardiff C	L	09/99	99	14	0	0
Nottingham F	Tr	02/00	99-01	38	5	1
Scunthorpe U	L	03/02	01	5	0	0
Mansfield T	L	10/02	02	4	0	0
Mansfield T	Tr	08/03	03	32	0	2
Barnsley	Tr	07/04	04-05	25	2	4
Stockport Co	L	08/05	05	10	0	1

VAUGHAN Charles John (Charlie)
Born: Bermondsey, SE London, England, 23 April, 1921 — CF
Died: Sutton, S London, England, 16 March, 1989
England: B-1/Amateur-1

League Club	Source	Date Signed	Seasons Played	Apps	Subs	Gls
Charlton Ath	Sutton U	01/47	46-52	227	-	91
Portsmouth	Tr	03/53	52-53	26	-	14

VAUGHAN David Owen
Born: Abergele, Conwy, Wales, 18 February, 1983 — LM
Wales: 39/U21-8/Youth

League Club	Source	Date Signed	Seasons Played	Apps	Subs	Gls
Crewe Alex	YT	02/01	00-07	166	19	18
Blackpool	Real Sociedad (SPN)	08/08	08-10	98	11	4
Sunderland	Tr	07/11	11-13	25	24	3
Nottingham F	Tr	10/13	13-14	19	3	0

VAUGHAN Ian
Born: Sheffield, England, 3 July, 1961 — CD

League Club	Source	Date Signed	Seasons Played	Apps	Subs	Gls
Rotherham U	App	07/79	78-80	4	0	0
Stockport Co	L	12/81	81	2	0	1

VAUGHAN James
Born: Liverpool, England, 6 December, 1986 — RB

League Club	Source	Date Signed	Seasons Played	Apps	Subs	Gls
Tranmere Rov	Sch	07/04				
Chester C	Tr	01/06	06-08	76	2	0

VAUGHAN James Oliver
Born: Birmingham, England, 14 July, 1988 — F
England: U21-4/Youth

League Club	Source	Date Signed	Seasons Played	Apps	Subs	Gls
Everton	Sch	09/05	04-10	8	39	7
Derby Co	L	09/09	09	2	0	0
Leicester C	L	03/10	09	2	6	1
Crystal Palace	L	09/10	10	14	0	5
Crystal Palace	L	01/11	10	14	2	4
Norwich C	Tr	05/11	11	1	4	0
Huddersfield T	Tr	08/12	12-14	72	10	31

VAUGHAN John
Born: Isleworth, W London, England, 26 June, 1964 — G

League Club	Source	Date Signed	Seasons Played	Apps	Subs	Gls
West Ham U	App	06/82				
Charlton Ath	L	03/85	84	6	0	0
Bristol Rov	L	09/85	85	6	0	0
Wrexham	L	10/85	85	4	0	0
Bristol C	L	03/86	85	2	0	0
Fulham	Tr	08/86	86	44	0	0
Bristol C	L	01/88	87	3	0	0
Cambridge U	Tr	06/88	88-92	178	0	0
Charlton Ath	Tr	08/93	93	5	1	0
Preston NE	Tr	07/94	94-95	65	1	0
Lincoln C	Tr	08/96	96-99	66	0	0
Colchester U	L	02/97	96	5	0	0
Colchester U	L	11/99	99	6	0	0
Chesterfield	L	01/00	99	3	0	0

VAUGHAN John Daniel (Danny)
Born: Liverpool, England, 18 February, 1972 — LB/M

League Club	Source	Date Signed	Seasons Played	Apps	Subs	Gls
Crewe Alex		09/92	92	3	4	0
Wigan Ath	Tr	07/93	93	2	2	0

VAUGHAN Lee
Born: Birmingham, England, 15 July, 1986 — RB
England: Semi Pro-2

League Club	Source	Date Signed	Seasons Played	Apps	Subs	Gls
Cheltenham T	Kidderminster Hrs	05/14	14	31	1	0

VAUGHAN Nigel Mark
Born: Caerleon, Monmouthshire, Wales, 20 May, 1959 — M
Wales: 10/U21-2/Youth

League Club	Source	Date Signed	Seasons Played	Apps	Subs	Gls
Newport Co	App	05/77	76-83	215	9	32

League Club	Source	Date Signed	Seasons Played	Apps	Subs	Gls
Cardiff C	Tr	09/83	83-86	144	5	41
Reading	L	02/87	86	5	0	1
Wolverhampton W	Tr	08/87	87-89	86	7	10
Hereford U	Tr	08/90	90-91	9	4	1

VAUGHAN Norman Glyndwr (Glyn)
Born: Llanidloes, Powys, Wales, 25 August, 1921 — IF
Died: Llanidloes, Powys, Wales, April, 2004

League Club	Source	Date Signed	Seasons Played	Apps	Subs	Gls
Exeter C	Oldham Ath (Am)	05/46	46-47	6	-	0

VAUGHAN Stephen James
Born: Liverpool, England, 22 January, 1985 — RB/M

League Club	Source	Date Signed	Seasons Played	Apps	Subs	Gls
Liverpool	Sch	04/02				
Chester C	Tr	06/04	04-06	41	17	0
Boston U	Tr	01/07	06	6	1	0
Chester C	Tr	01/08	08	7	1	0

VAUGHAN Terence Ronald (Terry)
Born: Ebbw Vale, Blaenau Gwent, Wales, 22 April, 1938 — IF

League Club	Source	Date Signed	Seasons Played	Apps	Subs	Gls
Mansfield T	Ollerton Colliery	06/57	58	6	-	2

VAYRYNEN Mika
Born: Eskilstuna, Sweden, 28 December, 1981 — M
Finland: 64

League Club	Source	Date Signed	Seasons Played	Apps	Subs	Gls
Leeds U	Heerenveen (NED)	09/11	11	2	8	0

VAZQUEZ Alvaro
Born: Barcelona, Spain, 27 April, 1991 — F
Spain: U21-14/Youth

League Club	Source	Date Signed	Seasons Played	Apps	Subs	Gls
Swansea C (L)	Getafe (SPN)	09/13	13	5	7	0

VAZ TE Ricardo Jorge
Born: Lisbon, Portugal, 1 October, 1986 — F
Portugal: U21-19/Youth

League Club	Source	Date Signed	Seasons Played	Apps	Subs	Gls
Bolton W	Sch	10/04	03-08	10	48	3
Hull C	L	03/07	06	1	5	0
Barnsley	Hibernian	08/11	11	12	10	10
West Ham U	Tr	01/12	11-14	37	14	15

VEACOCK James (Jimmy)
Born: Liverpool, England, 5 September, 1919 — CF/RW

League Club	Source	Date Signed	Seasons Played	Apps	Subs	Gls
Liverpool	Prescot Cables	11/36				
Southport	Marine	11/47	47	10	-	0

VEALL Raymond Joseph (Ray)
Born: Skegness, Lincolnshire, England, 16 March, 1943 — LW

League Club	Source	Date Signed	Seasons Played	Apps	Subs	Gls
Doncaster Rov	Skegness T	03/61	60-61	19	-	6
Everton	Tr	09/61	62	11	-	1
Preston NE	Tr	05/65	65	10	0	0
Huddersfield T	Tr	12/65	65-66	12	0	1

VEARNCOMBE Graham
Born: Cardiff, Wales, 28 March, 1934 — G
Died: Cardiff, Wales, 5 March, 1993
Wales: 2

League Club	Source	Date Signed	Seasons Played	Apps	Subs	Gls
Cardiff C	Jnr	02/52	52-63	207	-	0

VEART Robert (Bobby)
Born: Hartlepool, Cleveland, England, 11 August, 1944 — F/W
England: Amateur-1

League Club	Source	Date Signed	Seasons Played	Apps	Subs	Gls
Hartlepool U	Whitby T	07/70	70-72	59	12	12

VEART Thomas Carl (Carl)
Born: Whyalla, Australia, 21 May, 1970 — F/W
Australia: 18/U23

League Club	Source	Date Signed	Seasons Played	Apps	Subs	Gls
Sheffield U	Adelaide C (AUS)	07/94	94-95	47	19	15
Crystal Palace	Tr	03/96	95-97	41	16	6
Millwall	Tr	12/97	97	7	1	1

VECK Robert (Bobby)
Born: Titchfield, Hampshire, England, 1 April, 1920 — LW
Died: Canterbury, England, 14 May, 1999

League Club	Source	Date Signed	Seasons Played	Apps	Subs	Gls
Southampton	Jnr	09/45	46-49	23	-	2
Gillingham	Tr	07/50	50	36	-	12

VEGA Ramon
Born: Olten, Switzerland, 14 June, 1971 — CD
Switzerland: 24/B-1

League Club	Source	Date Signed	Seasons Played	Apps	Subs	Gls
Tottenham H	Cagliari (ITA)	01/97	96-00	53	11	7
Watford	Tr	07/01	01	23	4	1

[VEIGA] DA VEIGA Jose Manuel Monteiro
Born: Lisbon, Portugal, 18 December, 1976 — G
Cape Verde Islands: 13

League Club	Source	Date Signed	Seasons Played	Apps	Subs	Gls
Hereford U	Atherstone T	12/08	08	1	0	0
Macclesfield T	Tr	08/09	09-11	86	0	0

VEITCH George Hardy
Born: Sunderland, England, 18 January, 1931 — RH
Died: North Yorkshire, England, February, 2000

League Club	Source	Date Signed	Seasons Played	Apps	Subs	Gls
Hull C	Silksworth CW	08/51				
Millwall	Tr	06/52	52-57	93	-	0

VEITCH Thomas (Tommy)
Born: Edinburgh, Scotland, 16 October, 1949 — M
Died: Clydebank, Dunbartonshire, Scotland, 16 October, 1987

League Club	Source	Date Signed	Seasons Played	Apps	Subs	Gls
Tranmere Rov	Heart of Midlothian	07/72	72-74	76	3	5
Halifax T	Denver Dynamos (USA)	08/75	75	20	2	0
Hartlepool U	Tr	08/76	76	10	0	0

VELA Carlos Alberto
Born: Cancun, Mexico, 1 March, 1989 — F
Mexico: 44/Youth

League Club	Source	Date Signed	Seasons Played	Apps	Subs	Gls
Arsenal	Guadalajara (MEX)	08/06	08-10	3	26	3
West Bromwich A	L	01/11	10	3	5	2

VELA Joshua James (Josh)
Born: Salford, England, 14 December, 1993 — M/RB

League Club	Source	Date Signed	Seasons Played	Apps	Subs	Gls
Bolton W	Sch	03/11	11-14	28	8	0
Notts Co	L	03/14	13	7	0	0

VELASCO Juan
Born: Seville, Spain, 15 May, 1977 — RB
Spain: 5

League Club	Source	Date Signed	Seasons Played	Apps	Subs	Gls
Norwich C (L)	RCD Espanyol (SPN)	02/08	07	2	1	0

VELDWIJK Lars
Born: Uithoorn, Netherlands, 21 August, 1991 — F

League Club	Source	Date Signed	Seasons Played	Apps	Subs	Gls
Nottingham F	Excelsior (NED)	06/14	14	0	11	0

VELICKA Andrius
Born: Kaunas, Lithuania, 5 April, 1979 — F
Lithuania: 26

League Club	Source	Date Signed	Seasons Played	Apps	Subs	Gls
Bristol C (L)	Glasgow Rangers	08/09	09	0	1	0

VELIKONJA Etien
Born: Nova Gorica, Slovenia, 26 December, 1988 — F
Slovenia: 3/U21-14/Youth

League Club	Source	Date Signed	Seasons Played	Apps	Subs	Gls
Cardiff C	NK Maribor (SVN)	07/12	12	1	2	0

VELJKOVIC Milos
Born: Belgrade, Serbia, 26 September, 1995 — CD
Serbia: U21-4/Youth

League Club	Source	Date Signed	Seasons Played	Apps	Subs	Gls
Tottenham H	Sch	09/12	13	0	2	0
Middlesbrough	L	10/14	14	1	2	0
Charlton Ath	L	01/15	14	3	0	0

VELLIOS Apostolos
Born: Thessalonika, Greece, 8 January, 1992 — F
Greece: U21-24/Youth

League Club	Source	Date Signed	Seasons Played	Apps	Subs	Gls
Everton	Iraklis (GRE)	01/11	10-12	2	20	3
Blackpool	L	03/14	13	2	0	0

VENABLES Terence Frederick (Terry)
Born: Dagenham, E London, England, 6 January, 1943 — M
England: 2/FLge-1/U21-4/Amateur-1/Youth/Schools

League Club	Source	Date Signed	Seasons Played	Apps	Subs	Gls
Chelsea	Jnr	08/60	59-65	202	0	26
Tottenham H	Tr	05/66	65-68	114	1	5
Queens Park Rgrs	Tr	06/69	69-74	176	1	19
Crystal Palace	Tr	09/74	74	14	0	0

VENISON Barry
Born: Consett, County Durham, England, 16 August, 1964 — RB
England: 2/U21-10/Youth

League Club	Source	Date Signed	Seasons Played	Apps	Subs	Gls
Sunderland	App	01/82	81-85	169	4	2
Liverpool	Tr	07/86	86-91	103	7	1
Newcastle U	Tr	07/92	92-94	108	1	1
Southampton	Galatasaray (TKY)	10/95	95-96	23	1	0

VENNARD Walter
Born: Belfast, Northern Ireland, 17 October, 1919 — LH
Died: Stockport, Greater Manchester, England, 1993

League Club	Source	Date Signed	Seasons Played	Apps	Subs	Gls
Stockport Co	Crusaders	09/47	47	5	-	0

VENNEGOR OF HESSELINK Johannes (Jan)
Born: Oldenzaal, Netherlands, 7 November, 1978 — F
Netherlands: 19

League Club	Source	Date Signed	Seasons Played	Apps	Subs	Gls
Hull C	Glasgow Celtic	09/09	09	17	14	3

VENTA Javier Rodriguez (Javi)
Born: Asturias, Spain, 13 December, 1975 — RB

League Club	Source	Date Signed	Seasons Played	Apps	Subs	Gls
Brentford	Villarreal (SPN)	07/13	13	0	1	0

VENTERS Alexander (Alec)
Born: Cowdenbeath, Fife, Scotland, 9 June, 1913 — IF
Died: Cowdenbeath, Fife, Scotland, 30 April, 1959
Scotland: 3/SLge-5/War-3

League Club	Source	Date Signed	Seasons Played	Apps	Subs	Gls
Blackburn Rov	Third Lanark	02/47	46-47	25	-	7

VENTOLA Nicola
Born: Bari, Italy, 24 May, 1978 — F

Italy: 1/U21-21

League Club	Source	Date Signed	Seasons Played	Apps	Subs	Gls
Crystal Palace (L)	Inter Milan (ITA)	09/04	04	0	3	1

VENTOM Eric George
Born: Hemsworth, West Yorkshire, England, 15 February, 1920 — LB
Died: Wakefield, England, June, 1998

League Club	Source	Date Signed	Seasons Played	Apps	Subs	Gls
Brentford	Gailes Army Camp	02/46	47	1	-	0

VENTRE Daniel James (Danny)
Born: Chester, England, 23 January, 1986 — RB

League Club	Source	Date Signed	Seasons Played	Apps	Subs	Gls
Chester C	Sch	12/04				
Accrington Stan	Tr	08/05	06	4	2	0

VENUS Mark
Born: Hartlepool, Cleveland, England, 6 April, 1967 — LB

League Club	Source	Date Signed	Seasons Played	Apps	Subs	Gls
Hartlepool U	Jnr	03/85	84	4	0	0
Leicester C	Tr	09/85	85-87	58	3	1
Wolverhampton W	Tr	03/88	87-96	271	16	7
Ipswich T	Tr	07/97	97-02	144	4	16
Cambridge U	Tr	08/03	03	21	0	0

VERDE Pedro Andres
Born: Buenos Aires, Argentina, 12 March, 1952 — F

League Club	Source	Date Signed	Seasons Played	Apps	Subs	Gls
Sheffield U	Hercul Alicante (SPN)	08/79	79	9	1	3

VERGINI Santiago
Born: Rosario, Argentina, 3 August, 1988 — D
Argentina: 3

League Club	Source	Date Signed	Seasons Played	Apps	Subs	Gls
Sunderland (L)	Estudiantes (ARG)	01/14	13	10	1	0
Sunderland (L)	Estudiantes (ARG)	08/14	14	28	3	0

VERHOENE Kenny
Born: Ghent, Belgium, 15 April, 1973 — CD

League Club	Source	Date Signed	Seasons Played	Apps	Subs	Gls
Crystal Palace (L)	KRC Harelbeke (BEL)	03/01	00	0	1	0

VERITY Daniel Richard
Born: Bradford, England, 19 April, 1980 — CD

League Club	Source	Date Signed	Seasons Played	Apps	Subs	Gls
Bradford C	YT	03/98	97	0	1	0

VERITY David Anthony (Dave)
Born: Halifax, West Yorkshire, England, 21 September, 1949 — M

League Club	Source	Date Signed	Seasons Played	Apps	Subs	Gls
Scunthorpe U	App	09/67	66-67	3	2	0
Halifax T	Tr	09/68	69-72	64	14	5

VERITY Kevin Patrick
Born: Halifax, West Yorkshire, England, 16 March, 1940 — RW

League Club	Source	Date Signed	Seasons Played	Apps	Subs	Gls
Halifax T	Jnr	10/58	58-59	13	-	6

VERMA Aman Kumar
Born: Leicester, England, 3 January, 1987 — W

League Club	Source	Date Signed	Seasons Played	Apps	Subs	Gls
Leicester C	Redditch U	12/08				
Crewe Alex	L	08/09	09	5	2	0

VERMAELEN Thomas
Born: Antwerp, Belgium, 14 November, 1985 — CD
Belgium: 49/U21-5

League Club	Source	Date Signed	Seasons Played	Apps	Subs	Gls
Arsenal	Ajax (NED)	06/09	09-13	98	12	13

VERMIJL Marnick Danny
Born: Overpelt, Belgium, 13 January, 1992 — RB
Belgium: U21-7/Youth

League Club	Source	Date Signed	Seasons Played	Apps	Subs	Gls
Manchester U	Standard Liege (BEL)	07/10				
Sheffield Wed	Tr	02/15	14	8	3	0

VERNAZZA Paolo Andrea Pietro
Born: Islington, N London, England, 1 November, 1979 — M
England: U21-2/Youth

League Club	Source	Date Signed	Seasons Played	Apps	Subs	Gls
Arsenal	YT	11/97	97-00	2	3	1
Ipswich T	L	10/98	98	2	0	0
Portsmouth	L	01/00	99	7	0	0
Watford	Tr	12/00	00-03	71	25	2
Rotherham U	Tr	07/04	04	14	13	0
Barnet	L	11/05	05	11	6	0

VERNON John Eric
Born: Cape Town, South Africa, 2 March, 1956 — LW

League Club	Source	Date Signed	Seasons Played	Apps	Subs	Gls
Stockport Co	Jnr	04/75	74-75	4	2	0

VERNON John Joseph (Jack)
Born: Belfast, Northern Ireland, 26 September, 1918 — CH
Died: Belfast, Northern Ireland, August, 1981
Republic of Ireland: 2//Northern Ireland: 17/NILge-12/War-3

League Club	Source	Date Signed	Seasons Played	Apps	Subs	Gls
West Bromwich A	Belfast Celtic	02/47	46-51	190	-	1

VERNON Scott Malcolm
Born: Manchester, England, 13 December, 1983 — F

League Club	Source	Date Signed	Seasons Played	Apps	Subs	Gls
Oldham Ath	Sch	07/02	02-04	43	32	20
Blackpool	L	09/04	04	4	0	3
Blackpool	Tr	06/05	05-07	37	33	16
Colchester U	L	03/06	05	4	3	1
Colchester U	Tr	01/08	07-09	27	30	12
Northampton T	L	03/09	08	4	2	1
Gillingham	L	10/09	09	1	0	0
Southend U	L	01/10	09	17	0	4
Shrewsbury T	Aberdeen	04/14	14	12	10	1

VERNON Thomas Royston (Roy)
Born: Prestatyn, Denbighshire, Wales, 14 April, 1937 — IF
Died: Blackburn, Greater Manchester, England, 4 December, 1993
Wales: 32/U23-2

League Club	Source	Date Signed	Seasons Played	Apps	Subs	Gls
Blackburn Rov	Mostyn YMCA	03/55	55-59	131	-	49
Everton	Tr	02/60	59-64	176	-	101
Stoke C	Tr	03/65	64-68	85	3	22
Halifax T	L	01/70	69	4	0	0

VERON Juan Sebastian
Born: La Plata, Argentina, 9 March, 1975 — M
Argentina: 73

League Club	Source	Date Signed	Seasons Played	Apps	Subs	Gls
Manchester U	SS Lazio (ITA)	07/01	01-02	45	6	7
Chelsea	Tr	08/03	03	5	2	1

VERSCHAVE Matthias
Born: Lille, France, 24 December, 1977 — F

League Club	Source	Date Signed	Seasons Played	Apps	Subs	Gls
Swansea C (L)	Paris St-Germain (FRA)	02/01	00	12	0	3

VERTANNES Desmond Mark Stephen (Des)
Born: Chiswick, W London, England, 25 April, 1972 — CD

League Club	Source	Date Signed	Seasons Played	Apps	Subs	Gls
Fulham	YT	01/89	89	0	2	0

VERTONGHEN Jan Bert Lieve
Born: Sint Niklaas, Belgium, 24 April, 1987 — CD
Belgium: 69/U21-3/Youth

League Club	Source	Date Signed	Seasons Played	Apps	Subs	Gls
Tottenham H	Ajax (NED)	08/12	12-14	88	1	4

VERVEER Etienne Evert
Born: Paramaribo, Suriname, 22 September, 1967 — M

League Club	Source	Date Signed	Seasons Played	Apps	Subs	Gls
Millwall	FC Chur (SUI)	12/91	91-93	46	10	7
Bradford C	L	02/95	94	9	0	1

VESELI Frederic
Born: Renens, Switzerland, 20 November, 1992 — D
Switzerland: U21-1/Youth

League Club	Source	Date Signed	Seasons Played	Apps	Subs	Gls
Manchester C	Sch	12/09				
Manchester U	Tr	01/12				
Ipswich T	Tr	07/13				
Bury	L	01/14	13	18	0	0
Port Vale	Tr	07/14	14	37	0	1

VESEY Kieron Gerard
Born: Manchester, England, 24 November, 1965 — G

League Club	Source	Date Signed	Seasons Played	Apps	Subs	Gls
Halifax T	Jnr	02/83	83	2	0	0

VESSEY Anthony William (Tony)
Born: Derby, England, 28 November, 1961 — FB

League Club	Source	Date Signed	Seasons Played	Apps	Subs	Gls
Brighton & HA	App	11/79	80	1	0	0

VETOKELE Igor
Born: Ostend, Belgium, 23 March, 1992 — F
Angola: 3//Belgium: U21-14

League Club	Source	Date Signed	Seasons Played	Apps	Subs	Gls
Charlton Ath	FC Copenhagen (DEN)	06/14	14	37	4	11

VEYSEY Kenneth John (Ken)
Born: Hackney, E London, England, 8 June, 1967 — G

League Club	Source	Date Signed	Seasons Played	Apps	Subs	Gls
Torquay U	Dawlish T	11/87	88-90	72	0	0
Oxford U	Tr	10/90	90-91	57	0	0
Exeter C	Reading (NC)	10/93	93	11	1	0
Torquay U	Dorchester T	08/97	97-98	37	0	0
Plymouth Arg	Tr	08/99	99	5	1	0

VIAFARA Jhon Eduis
Born: Robles, Colombia, 27 October, 1978 — M
Colombia: 32

League Club	Source	Date Signed	Seasons Played	Apps	Subs	Gls
Portsmouth	Once Caldas (COL)	07/05	05	10	4	1
Southampton	Tr	08/06	06-07	59	17	5

VIALLI Gianluca
Born: Cremona, Italy, 9 July, 1964 — F
Italy: 59/U21-20

League Club	Source	Date Signed	Seasons Played	Apps	Subs	Gls
Chelsea	Juventus (ITA)	07/96	96-98	46	12	21

VIANA Hugo Miguel Ferreira
Born: Barcelos, Portugal, 15 January, 1983 — LW
Portugal: 29/B-1/U21-22/Youth

League Club	Source	Date Signed	Seasons Played	Apps	Subs	Gls
Newcastle U	Sporting Lisbon (POR)	07/02	02-03	16	23	2

VICK Leigh
Born: Cardiff, Wales, 8 January, 1978 — M

League Club	Source	Date Signed	Seasons Played	Apps	Subs	Gls
Cardiff C	YT	07/96	94-95	2	2	0

VICKERS Ashley James Ward
Born: Sheffield, England, 14 June, 1972 — CD

League Club	Source	Date Signed	Seasons Played	Apps	Subs	Gls
Peterborough U	Heybridge Swifts	12/97	97	1	0	0

VICKERS Peter
Born: Kilnhurst, South Yorkshire, England, 6 March, 1934 — IF
Died: Leeds, England, 1982
England: Schools

League Club	Source	Date Signed	Seasons Played	Apps	Subs	Gls
Leeds U	Jnr	03/51	50-55	20	-	4
Northampton T	Wisbech T	02/60	59	2	-	0

VICKERS Stephen (Steve)
Born: Bishop Auckland, County Durham, England, 13 October, 1967 — CD

League Club	Source	Date Signed	Seasons Played	Apps	Subs	Gls
Tranmere Rov	Spennymoor U	09/85	85-93	310	1	11
Middlesbrough	Tr	12/93	93-01	248	11	8
Crystal Palace	L	09/01	01	6	0	0
Birmingham C	Tr	11/01	01-02	18	1	1

VICKERS Wilfred (Wilf)
Born: Wakefield, England, 3 August, 1924 — CF

League Club	Source	Date Signed	Seasons Played	Apps	Subs	Gls
Brighton & HA		09/47	47	5	-	1
West Bromwich A	Tr	05/48				
Aldershot	Tr	06/49	49-51	15	-	1

VICKERTON Martin David
Born: Ilkeston, Derbyshire, England, 24 June, 1987 — LB

League Club	Source	Date Signed	Seasons Played	Apps	Subs	Gls
Nottingham F	Sch	-	05	0	1	0

VICKERY Paul
Born: Chelmsford, England, 20 May, 1953 — M

League Club	Source	Date Signed	Seasons Played	Apps	Subs	Gls
Southend U	App	-	69	0	1	0

VICTORY Jamie Charles
Born: Hackney, E London, England, 14 November, 1975 — LB
England: Semi Pro-1

League Club	Source	Date Signed	Seasons Played	Apps	Subs	Gls
West Ham U	YT	07/94				
Bournemouth	Tr	07/95	95	5	11	1
Cheltenham T	Tr	07/96	99-06	249	9	22

VIDAL Javan Noel
Born: Manchester, England, 10 May, 1989 — RB/M
England: Youth

League Club	Source	Date Signed	Seasons Played	Apps	Subs	Gls
Manchester C	Sch	07/07				
Grimsby T	L	09/08	08	2	1	0
Derby Co	L	02/10	09	0	1	0
Chesterfield	L	01/11	10	5	1	0
Rochdale	Stockport Co	07/13	13	2	0	0

VIDARSSON Bjarni Thor
Born: Reykjavik, Iceland, 5 March, 1988 — M
Iceland: 1/U21-26

League Club	Source	Date Signed	Seasons Played	Apps	Subs	Gls
Everton	Sch	03/06				
Bournemouth	L	02/07	06	4	2	1

VIDIC Nemanja
Born: Uzice, Serbia, 9 October, 1975 — F
Serbia: 56

League Club	Source	Date Signed	Seasons Played	Apps	Subs	Gls
Manchester U	Spartak Moscow (RUS)	01/06	05-13	205	6	15

VIDMAR Antony (Tony)
Born: Adelaide, Australia, 15 April, 1969 — CD
Australia: 76/U23-18/Youth

League Club	Source	Date Signed	Seasons Played	Apps	Subs	Gls
Middlesbrough	Glasgow Rangers	09/02	02	9	3	0
Cardiff C	Tr	07/03	03-04	68	5	2

VIDUKA Mark Anthony
Born: Melbourne, Australia, 9 October, 1975 — F
Australia: 43/U23-18/Youth

League Club	Source	Date Signed	Seasons Played	Apps	Subs	Gls
Leeds U	Glasgow Celtic	07/00	00-03	126	4	59
Middlesbrough	Tr	07/04	04-06	56	16	26
Newcastle U	Tr	07/07	07-08	25	13	7

VIEIRA Magno Silva
Born: Bahia, Brazil, 13 February, 1985 — F

League Club	Source	Date Signed	Seasons Played	Apps	Subs	Gls
Wigan Ath	Jnr	08/03				
Northampton T	L	01/04	03	7	3	2
Barnet	PAOK Salonika (GRE)	07/06	06	8	13	3
Wycombe W	Crawley T	07/08	08	2	12	2

VIEIRA Patrick
Born: Dakar, Senegal, 23 June, 1976 — DM
France: 107/U21-7

League Club	Source	Date Signed	Seasons Played	Apps	Subs	Gls
Arsenal	AC Milan (ITA)	08/96	96-04	272	7	28
Manchester C	Inter Milan (ITA)	01/10	09-10	12	16	3

VIGNAL Gregory
Born: Montpellier, France, 19 July, 1981 — LB
France: U21-4/Youth

League Club	Source	Date Signed	Seasons Played	Apps	Subs	Gls
Liverpool	Montpellier (FRA)	09/00	00-02	7	4	0
Portsmouth	Glasgow Rangers	07/05	05	13	1	0
Southampton (L)	RC Lens (FRA)	08/07	07	20	0	3
Birmingham C	RC Lens (FRA)	08/09	09	6	2	0

VILHETE Mauro Alexandre de Silva
Born: Sintra, Portugal, 10 May, 1993 — W

League Club	Source	Date Signed	Seasons Played	Apps	Subs	Gls
Barnet	Sch	05/10	09-12	11	19	0

VILHJALMSSON Matthias (Matt)
Born: Isafjordur, Iceland, 30 January, 1987 — M
Iceland: 11/U21

League Club	Source	Date Signed	Seasons Played	Apps	Subs	Gls
Colchester U (L)	Hafnar Fjordur (ICE)	01/11	10	0	3	0

VILJANEN Ville
Born: Helsinki, Finland, 2 February, 1971 — F
Finland: 1

League Club	Source	Date Signed	Seasons Played	Apps	Subs	Gls
Port Vale	Vastra Frolunda (SWE)	02/99	99-00	26	8	6

VILJOEN Colin
Born: Johannesburg, South Africa, 20 June, 1948 — M
England: 2

League Club	Source	Date Signed	Seasons Played	Apps	Subs	Gls
Ipswich T	Jo'burg Rgrs (RSA)	03/67	66-77	303	2	45
Manchester C	Tr	08/78	78-79	25	2	0
Chelsea	Tr	03/80	79-81	19	1	0

VILJOEN Nicholas Luke (Nik)
Born: Auckland, New Zealand, 3 December, 1976 — F

League Club	Source	Date Signed	Seasons Played	Apps	Subs	Gls
Rotherham U	YT	06/95	95	5	3	2

VILLA Emanuel Alejandro
Born: Casilda, Argentina, 24 February, 1982 — F

League Club	Source	Date Signed	Seasons Played	Apps	Subs	Gls
Derby Co	UAG Tecos (MEX)	01/08	07-08	21	25	5

VILLA Julio Ricardo (Ricky)
Born: Buenos Aires, Argentina, 18 August, 1952 — M
Argentina: 25

League Club	Source	Date Signed	Seasons Played	Apps	Subs	Gls
Tottenham H	Racing Club (ARG)	07/78	78-82	124	9	18

VILLANUEVA Carlos Andres
Born: La Serena, Chile, 5 February, 1986 — M
Chile: 12

League Club	Source	Date Signed	Seasons Played	Apps	Subs	Gls
Blackburn Rov	Audax Italiano (CHL)	08/08	08	6	7	0

VILLARS Anthony Keith (Tony)
Born: Cwmbran, Torfaen, Wales, 24 January, 1952 — RW
Wales: 3/U23-2

League Club	Source	Date Signed	Seasons Played	Apps	Subs	Gls
Cardiff C	Cwmbran T	06/71	71-75	66	7	4
Newport Co	Tr	07/76	76	23	6	1

VILLAZAN Rafael
Born: Montevideo, Uruguay, 19 July, 1956 — D
Uruguay:

League Club	Source	Date Signed	Seasons Played	Apps	Subs	Gls
Wolverhampton W	Rec'tivo Huelva (SPN)	05/80	80-81	20	3	0

VILLIS Matthew (Matt)
Born: Bridgwater, Somerset, England, 13 April, 1984 — CD

League Club	Source	Date Signed	Seasons Played	Apps	Subs	Gls
Plymouth Arg	Bridgwater T	09/02				
Torquay U	Tr	07/04	04-06	26	14	0

VILSTRUP Johnny Pederson
Born: Copenhagen, Denmark, 27 February, 1969 — M

League Club	Source	Date Signed	Seasons Played	Apps	Subs	Gls
Luton T	Lyngby (DEN)	09/95	95	6	1	0

VINALL Albert
Born: Birmingham, England, 6 March, 1922 — LB
Died: Birmingham, England, September, 1999

League Club	Source	Date Signed	Seasons Played	Apps	Subs	Gls
Aston Villa	Southampton (Am)	07/46	47-53	11	-	1
Walsall	Tr	08/54	54-55	78	-	0

VINALL Edward John (Jack)
Born: Birmingham, England, 16 December, 1910 — CF
Died: Worcester, England, 26 May, 1997

League Club	Source	Date Signed	Seasons Played	Apps	Subs	Gls
Sunderland	Folkestone	10/31	31-32	16	-	3
Norwich C	Tr	06/33	33-37	168	-	72
Luton T	Tr	10/37	37-38	44	-	18
Walsall	Tr	07/46	46	2	-	0

VINCELOT Romain Marcel Georges
Born: Poitiers, France, 29 October, 1985 — M

League Club	Source	Date Signed	Seasons Played	Apps	Subs	Gls
Dagenham & Red	Gueugnon (FRA)	01/10	09-10	53	2	13
Brighton & HA	Tr	07/11	11	10	5	1
Gillingham	L	10/12	12	8	1	1
Leyton Orient	Tr	02/13	12-14	78	3	3

VINCENT Ashley Derek
Born: Oldbury, West Midlands, England, 26 May, 1985 — LW

League Club	Source	Date Signed	Seasons Played	Apps	Subs	Gls
Cheltenham T	Wolverhampton W (Sch)	07/04	04-08	50	60	8
Colchester U	Tr	03/09	08-11	53	18	10
Port Vale	Tr	07/12	12	32	2	7
Cheltenham T	Tr	07/13	13	7	11	2
Shrewsbury T	Tr	07/14	14	4	4	0

VINCENT James Michael
Born: Glossop, Derbyshire, England, 27 September, 1989 — M

League Club	Source	Date Signed	Seasons Played	Apps	Subs	Gls
Stockport Co	Sch	07/08	07-10	51	19	2

VINCENT Jamie Roy
Born: Wimbledon, SW London, England, 18 June, 1975 — LB

League Club	Source	Date Signed	Seasons Played	Apps	Subs	Gls
Crystal Palace	YT	07/93	95	19	6	0
Bournemouth	L	11/94	94	8	0	0
Bournemouth	Tr	08/96	96-98	102	3	5
Huddersfield T	Tr	03/99	98-00	54	5	2
Portsmouth	Tr	02/01	00-01	43	5	1
Walsall	L	10/03	03	12	0	0
Derby Co	Tr	01/04	03-04	22	0	2
Millwall	L	08/05	05	15	0	0
Yeovil T	Tr	01/06				
Millwall	L	03/06	05	3	1	0
Swindon T	Tr	07/06	06-08	84	0	0
Walsall	Tr	07/09	09	37	1	0
Aldershot T	Tr	07/10	10	22	1	0

VINCENT John Victor (Johnny)
Born: West Bromwich, West Midlands, England, 8 February, 1947 — M
Died: Kidderminster, Worcestershire, England, 23 December, 2006
England: Youth

League Club	Source	Date Signed	Seasons Played	Apps	Subs	Gls
Birmingham C	App	02/64	63-70	168	3	41
Middlesbrough	Tr	03/71	70-72	37	3	7
Cardiff C	Tr	10/72	72-74	58	8	11

VINCENT Norman Edwin (Ned)
Born: Prudhoe, Northumberland, England, 3 March, 1909 — RB
Died: Oldham, Greater Manchester, England, 1980

League Club	Source	Date Signed	Seasons Played	Apps	Subs	Gls
Stockport Co	Spennymoor U	03/28	28-33	132	-	20
Grimsby T	Tr	06/34	34-46	144	-	2

VINCENT Robert (Bobby)
Born: Leicester, England, 29 May, 1949 — CF

League Club	Source	Date Signed	Seasons Played	Apps	Subs	Gls
Notts Co (Am)	Jnr	01/66	65	1	0	0

VINCENT Robert George
Born: Newcastle-upon-Tyne, England, 23 November, 1962 — F
England: Schools

League Club	Source	Date Signed	Seasons Played	Apps	Subs	Gls
Sunderland	App	11/79	80	1	1	0
Leyton Orient	Tr	05/82	81-82	8	1	0

VINCENTI Peter Ian
Born: Jersey, Channel Islands, 7 July, 1986 — M

League Club	Source	Date Signed	Seasons Played	Apps	Subs	Gls
Millwall	St Paul's, Jersey	08/07				
Stevenage	Tr	01/08	10	1	4	0
Aldershot T	Tr	01/11	10-12	90	14	14
Rochdale	Tr	07/13	13-14	67	12	18

VINDHEIM Rune
Born: Hoyanger, Norway, 18 May, 1972 — CD

League Club	Source	Date Signed	Seasons Played	Apps	Subs	Gls
Burnley	Fana IL (NOR)	10/98	98	8	0	2
Hartlepool U	Tr	09/99	99	7	0	0

VINE Peter William
Born: Abingdon, Oxfordshire, England, 11 December, 1940 — IF
England: Youth

League Club	Source	Date Signed	Seasons Played	Apps	Subs	Gls
Southampton	Jnr	12/57	58	1	-	0

VINE Rowan Lewis
Born: Basingstoke, Hampshire, England, 21 September, 1982 — F

League Club	Source	Date Signed	Seasons Played	Apps	Subs	Gls
Portsmouth	YT	04/01	00-01	3	10	0
Brentford	L	08/02	02	37	5	10
Colchester U	L	08/03	03	30	5	6
Luton T	Tr	08/04	04-06	90	12	31
Birmingham C	Tr	01/07	06	10	7	1
Queens Park Rgrs	Tr	10/07	07-09	42	27	8
Hull C	L	10/10	10	4	1	0
MK Dons	L	01/11	10	12	5	1
Exeter C	L	08/11	11	4	1	0
Gillingham	L	03/12	11	3	6	1

VINEY Keith Brian
Born: Portsmouth, England, 26 October, 1957 — LB

League Club	Source	Date Signed	Seasons Played	Apps	Subs	Gls
Portsmouth	App	10/75	75-81	160	6	3
Exeter C	Tr	08/82	82-88	270	0	8
Bristol Rov	L	09/88	88	2	1	0

VINNICOMBE Christopher (Chris)
Born: Exeter, England, 20 October, 1970 — LB
England: U21-12

League Club	Source	Date Signed	Seasons Played	Apps	Subs	Gls
Exeter C	YT	07/89	88-89	35	4	1
Burnley	Glasgow Rangers	06/94	94-97	90	5	3
Wycombe W	Tr	08/98	98-03	217	4	2

VINTER Michael (Mick)
Born: Boston, Lincolnshire, England, 23 May, 1954 — F

League Club	Source	Date Signed	Seasons Played	Apps	Subs	Gls
Notts Co	Boston U	08/71	72-78	135	31	53
Wrexham	Tr	06/79	79-81	89	12	25
Oxford U	Tr	08/82	82-83	67	2	21
Mansfield T	Tr	08/84	84-85	52	2	7
Newport Co	Tr	08/86	86	30	2	7

VIOLLET Dennis Sydney
Born: Manchester, England, 20 September, 1933 — IF
Died: Jacksonville, USA, 6 March, 1999
England: 2/FLge-3/Schools

League Club	Source	Date Signed	Seasons Played	Apps	Subs	Gls
Manchester U	Jnr	09/50	52-61	259	-	159
Stoke C	Tr	01/62	61-66	181	1	59

VIPHAM Peter
Born: Rawtenstall, Lancashire, England, 9 September, 1942 — G

League Club	Source	Date Signed	Seasons Played	Apps	Subs	Gls
Accrington Stan	Jnr	06/61	60	6	-	0

VIPOND Shaun David
Born: Hexham, Northumberland, England, 25 December, 1988 — M

League Club	Source	Date Signed	Seasons Played	Apps	Subs	Gls
Carlisle U	Sch	07/07	06	1	3	0

VIRGIN Derek Edward
Born: South Petherton, Somerset, England, 10 February, 1934 — W

League Club	Source	Date Signed	Seasons Played	Apps	Subs	Gls
Bristol C	South Petherton	09/55	55-60	21	-	4

VIRGO Adam John
Born: Brighton, England, 25 January, 1983 — M/D
Scotland: B-2

League Club	Source	Date Signed	Seasons Played	Apps	Subs	Gls
Brighton & HA	Ardingly College	07/00	00-04	65	8	10
Exeter C (L)	L	11/02	02	8	1	0
Coventry C (L)	Glasgow Celtic	08/06	06	10	5	1
Colchester U (L)	Glasgow Celtic	08/07	07	30	6	1
Brighton & HA	Glasgow Celtic	07/08	08-09	56	5	4
Yeovil T	Tr	08/10	10	28	5	5
Bristol Rov	Tr	07/11	11-12	18	1	1

VITTY John (Jack)
Born: Chilton, County Durham, England, 19 January, 1923 — LB

League Club	Source	Date Signed	Seasons Played	Apps	Subs	Gls
Charlton Ath	Boldon Villa	11/46	48	2	-	0
Brighton & HA	Tr	10/49	49-51	47	-	1
Workington	Tr	07/52	52-56	196	-	3

VITTY Ronald (Ron)
Born: Sedgefield, County Durham, England, 18 April, 1927 — RB
Died: Birmingham, England, April, 2013

League Club	Source	Date Signed	Seasons Played	Apps	Subs	Gls
Charlton Ath	Boldon Villa	09/47				
Hartlepool U	Tr	08/49	49	7	-	0
Bradford C	Tr	07/50				

VIVAS Nelson David
Born: Rosario, Argentina, 18 October, 1969 — RB
Argentina: 39

League Club	Source	Date Signed	Seasons Played	Apps	Subs	Gls
Arsenal	Lugano (SUI)	08/98	98-00	14	26	0

VIVEASH Adrian Lee
Born: Swindon, England, 30 September, 1969 — CD

League Club	Source	Date Signed	Seasons Played	Apps	Subs	Gls
Swindon T	YT	07/88	90-94	51	3	2
Reading	L	01/93	92	5	0	0
Reading	L	01/95	94	6	0	0
Barnsley	L	08/95	95	2	0	1
Walsall	Tr	10/95	95-99	200	2	13
Reading	Tr	07/00	00-02	62	1	3
Oxford U	L	09/02	02	11	0	0
Swindon T	Tr	07/03	03	14	1	0
Kidderminster Hrs	L	03/04	03	7	0	0
Kidderminster Hrs	L	08/04	04	7	0	0

VIZARD Colin John
Born: Newton-le-Willows, Merseyside, England, 18 June, 1933 — LW

League Club	Source	Date Signed	Seasons Played	Apps	Subs	Gls
Everton	Jnr	09/51				
Rochdale	Tr	05/57	57-58	41	-	7

VLAAR Ron Peter
Born: Alkmaar, Netherlands, 16 February, 1985 — CD
Netherlands: 32/U21-15

League Club	Source	Date Signed	Seasons Played	Apps	Subs	Gls
Aston Villa	Feyenoord (NED)	08/12	12-14	78	1	2

VLACHOS Michalis
Born: Athens, Greece, 20 September, 1967 — DM
Greece: 10

League Club	Source	Date Signed	Seasons Played	Apps	Subs	Gls
Portsmouth	AEK Athens (GRE)	01/98	97-99	55	2	0
Walsall	Tr	02/00	99	11	0	1

VOGEL Johann Louis Francois
Born: Geneva, Switzerland, 8 March, 1977 — CD
Switzerland: 94

League Club	Source	Date Signed	Seasons Played	Apps	Subs	Gls
Blackburn Rov	Real Betis (SPN)	03/08	07-08	6	1	0

VOKES Samuel Michael (Sam)
Born: Lymington, Hampshire, England, 21 October, 1989 — F

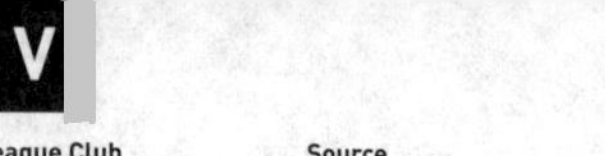

League Club	Source	Date Signed	Seasons Played	Career Record Apps	Subs	Gls
Wales: 33/U21-14						
Bournemouth	Brockenhurst College	12/06	06-07	38	16	6
Wolverhampton W	Tr	06/08	08-11	4	43	6
Leeds U	L	10/09	09	8	0	1
Bristol C	L	08/10	10	0	1	0
Sheffield U	L	02/11	10	4	2	1
Norwich C	L	03/11	10	1	3	1
Burnley	L	11/11	11	3	6	2
Brighton & HA	L	01/12	11	7	7	3
Burnley	Tr	07/12	12-14	57	43	24

VOLMER Joost Gerard Bernard
Born: Enschede, Netherlands, 7 March, 1974 — CD

League Club	Source	Date Signed	Seasons Played	Apps	Subs	Gls
West Bromwich A	AZ67 Alkmaar (NED)	08/03	03	10	5	0

VOLZ Moritz
Born: Siegen, Germany, 21 January, 1983 — RB
Germany: U21-20/Youth

League Club	Source	Date Signed	Seasons Played	Apps	Subs	Gls
Arsenal	Schalke 04 (GER)	01/00				
Wimbledon	L	02/03	02	10	0	1
Fulham	Tr	08/03	03-07	115	10	2
Ipswich T	L	08/08	08	20	2	0

VONK Michel Christian
Born: Alkmaar, Netherlands, 28 October, 1968 — CD

League Club	Source	Date Signed	Seasons Played	Apps	Subs	Gls
Manchester C	SVV Dordrecht (NED)	03/92	91-94	97	4	4
Oldham Ath	L	11/95	95	5	0	1
Sheffield U	Tr	12/95	95-97	37	0	2

VORM Michel Armand
Born: Ijsselstein, Netherlands, 20 October, 1983 — G
Netherlands: 15

League Club	Source	Date Signed	Seasons Played	Apps	Subs	Gls
Swansea C	FC Utrecht (NED)	08/11	11-13	89	0	0
Tottenham H	Tr	07/14	14	3	1	0

VORONIN Andriy Viktorovych
Born: Odessa, Ukraine, 21 July, 1979 — F
Ukraine: 74

League Club	Source	Date Signed	Seasons Played	Apps	Subs	Gls
Liverpool	Bayer Leverkusen (GER)	07/07	07-09	14	13	5

VOSE Dominic Jack Spencer
Born: Lambeth, S London, England, 23 November, 1993 — M

League Club	Source	Date Signed	Seasons Played	Apps	Subs	Gls
West Ham U	Sch	11/10				
Barnet	Tooting & Mitcham U	01/13	12	0	2	0
Colchester U	Tr	11/13	13-14	21	13	0

VOSER Kay Fabian
Born: Baden, Switzerland, 4 January, 1987 — RB
Switzerland: U21-6/Youth

League Club	Source	Date Signed	Seasons Played	Apps	Subs	Gls
Fulham	FC Basel (SUI)	07/14	14	2	1	0

VOSSEN Jelle
Born: Bilzen, Belgium, 22 March, 1989 — F
Belgium: 12/U21-8/Youth

League Club	Source	Date Signed	Seasons Played	Apps	Subs	Gls
Middlesbrough (L)	KRC Genk (BEL)	09/14	14	20	13	7

VOWDEN Colin Dean
Born: Newmarket, Suffolk, England, 13 September, 1971 — CD

League Club	Source	Date Signed	Seasons Played	Apps	Subs	Gls
Cambridge U	Cambridge C	05/95	95-96	27	3	0

VOWDEN Geoffrey Alan (Geoff)
Born: Barnsley, South Yorkshire, England, 27 April, 1941 — IF

League Club	Source	Date Signed	Seasons Played	Apps	Subs	Gls
Nottingham F	Jersey DM	01/60	59-64	90	-	40
Birmingham C	Tr	10/64	64-70	213	8	79
Aston Villa	Tr	03/71	70-73	93	4	22

VUCKIC Haris
Born: Ljubljana, Slovenia, 21 August, 1992 — M
Slovenia: 1/U21-12/Youth

League Club	Source	Date Signed	Seasons Played	Apps	Subs	Gls
Newcastle U	Sch	08/09	09-14	2	5	0
Cardiff C	L	02/12	11	2	3	1
Rotherham U	L	11/13	13	9	13	4

VUKCEVIC Simon
Born: Titograd, Yugoslavia, 29 January, 1986 — M
Montenegro: 45/U21-2//Serbia: 5

League Club	Source	Date Signed	Seasons Played	Apps	Subs	Gls
Blackburn Rov	Sporting Lisbon (POR)	08/11	11-12	8	8	1

VUKIC Zvonimir
Born: Zrenjanin, Serbia, 17 September, 1979 — M
Serbia: 26

League Club	Source	Date Signed	Seasons Played	Apps	Subs	Gls
Portsmouth (L)	Shakhtar Donetsk (UKR)	08/05	05	6	3	1

VYDRA Matej
Born: Chotebor, Czech Republic, 1 May, 1992 — F
Czech Republic: 15/U21-2/Youth

League Club	Source	Date Signed	Seasons Played	Apps	Subs	Gls
Watford (L)	Udinese (ITA)	08/12	12	27	14	20
West Bromwich A (L)	Udinese (ITA)	08/13	13	7	16	3
Watford (L)	Udinese (ITA)	06/14	14	31	11	16

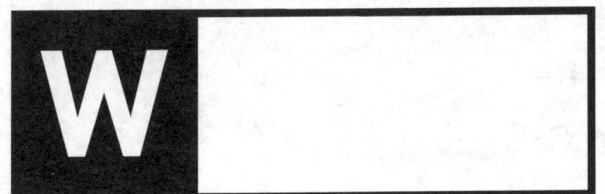

WABARA Reece
Born: Birmingham, England, 28 December, 1991 — RB
England: Youth

League Club	Source	Date Signed	Seasons Played	Apps	Subs	Gls
Manchester C	Sch	01/09	10	0	1	0
Ipswich T	L	09/11	11	1	5	0
Oldham Ath	L	09/12	12	25	0	0
Blackpool	L	01/13	12	0	1	0
Doncaster Rov	L	08/13	13	13	0	0
Doncaster Rov	Tr	08/14	14	42	1	1

WADDELL Robert (Bobby)
Born: Kirkcaldy, Fife, Scotland, 5 September, 1939 — CF

League Club	Source	Date Signed	Seasons Played	Apps	Subs	Gls
Blackpool	Dundee	03/65	64-66	28	0	5
Bradford Park Ave	Tr	11/66	66	20	0	3

WADDELL William (Willie)
Born: Denny, Falkirk, Scotland, 16 April, 1950 — F
Scotland: Schools

League Club	Source	Date Signed	Seasons Played	Apps	Subs	Gls
Leeds U	Jnr	04/67				
Barnsley	Kilmarnock	05/71	71	17	1	4
Hartlepool U	Tr	03/72	71-73	43	5	9
Workington	L	02/73	72	1	2	0

WADDINGTON Anthony (Tony)
Born: Manchester, England, 9 November, 1924 — RH
Died: Crewe, Cheshire, England, 29 January, 1994

League Club	Source	Date Signed	Seasons Played	Apps	Subs	Gls
Crewe Alex	Manchester U (Am)	01/46	46-52	178	-	8

WADDINGTON David Paul (Paul)
Born: Oldbury, West Midlands, England, 14 February, 1961 — M
England: Schools

League Club	Source	Date Signed	Seasons Played	Apps	Subs	Gls
Walsall	App	11/78	78-81	14	5	0

WADDINGTON John
Born: Darwen, Lancashire, England, 16 February, 1952 — CD/F

League Club	Source	Date Signed	Seasons Played	Apps	Subs	Gls
Liverpool	Darwen	05/70				
Blackburn Rov	Tr	08/73	73-78	139	9	18
Bury	Tr	08/79	79-80	46	1	0

WADDINGTON Mark Thomas
Born: Standish, Lancashire, England, 11 October, 1996 — M

League Club	Source	Date Signed	Seasons Played	Apps	Subs	Gls
Blackpool	Sch	07/14	14	1	2	0

WADDINGTON Steven (Steve)
Born: Nantwich, Cheshire, England, 5 February, 1956 — M/RW

League Club	Source	Date Signed	Seasons Played	Apps	Subs	Gls
Stoke C	App	06/73	76-78	49	3	5
Walsall	Tr	09/78	78-81	122	8	13
Port Vale	Tr	08/82	82	0	1	0
Chesterfield	Tr	07/83	83	14	4	1

WADDLE Alan Robert
Born: Wallsend, Tyne and Wear, England, 9 June, 1954 — F

League Club	Source	Date Signed	Seasons Played	Apps	Subs	Gls
Halifax T	Wallsend BC	11/71	71-72	33	6	4
Liverpool	Tr	06/73	73-74	11	5	1
Leicester C	Tr	09/77	77	11	0	1
Swansea C	Tr	05/78	78-80	83	7	34
Newport Co	Tr	12/80	80-81	19	8	8
Mansfield T	Happy Valley (HKG)	08/82	82	14	0	4
Hartlepool U	Happy Valley (HKG)	08/83	83	12	0	2
Peterborough U	Tr	10/83	83-84	35	1	12
Hartlepool U	Tr	01/85	84	4	0	0
Swansea C	Tr	03/85	84-85	39	1	10

WADDLE Christopher Roland (Chris)
Born: Felling, Tyne and Wear, England, 14 December, 1960 — W
England: 62/U21-1

League Club	Source	Date Signed	Seasons Played	Apps	Subs	Gls
Newcastle U	Tow Law T	07/80	80-84	169	1	46
Tottenham H	Tr	07/85	85-88	137	1	33
Sheffield Wed	Olymp Marseille (FRA)	07/92	92-95	94	15	10
Bradford C	Falkirk	10/96	96	25	0	5
Sunderland	Tr	03/97	96	7	0	1
Burnley	Tr	07/97	97	26	5	1
Torquay U	Tr	09/98	98	7	0	0

WADDOCK Gary Patrick
Born: Kingsbury, NW London, England, 17 March, 1962 — M
Republic of Ireland: 21/B/U23-1/U21-1

League Club	Source	Date Signed	Seasons Played	Apps	Subs	Gls
Queens Park Rgrs	App	07/79	79-86	191	12	8
Millwall	RSC Charleroi (BEL)	08/89	89-90	51	7	2
Queens Park Rgrs	Tr	12/91				
Swindon T	L	03/92	91	5	1	0
Bristol Rov	Tr	11/92	92-94	71	0	1
Luton T	Tr	09/94	94-97	146	7	3

WADE Allen
Born: Scunthorpe, North Lincolnshire, England, 19 July, 1926 — CH
Died: Ruislip, W London, England, 6 November, 2008

League Club	Source	Date Signed	Seasons Played	Apps	Subs	Gls
Notts Co	British Universities	07/52	52-55	9	-	0

WADE Bryan Alexander
Born: Bath, England, 25 June, 1963 — F

League Club	Source	Date Signed	Seasons Played	Apps	Subs	Gls
Swindon T	Trowbridge T	05/85	85-87	48	12	18
Swansea C	Tr	08/88	88-89	19	17	5
Brighton & HA	Tr	09/90	90-91	12	6	9

WADE Donald Geoffrey (Don)
Born: Tottenham, N London, England, 5 June, 1926 — IF
Died: Ceredigion, Wales, April, 2013

League Club	Source	Date Signed	Seasons Played	Apps	Subs	Gls
West Ham U	Edgware T	12/47	47-49	36	-	5

WADE Psalms Meshach (Meshach)
Born: Hamilton, Bermuda, 23 January, 1973 — M

League Club	Source	Date Signed	Seasons Played	Apps	Subs	Gls
Hereford U	Pemb'ke Hamilton (BER)	08/91	91-92	13	4	0

WADE Samuel Joseph (Joe)
Born: Shoreditch, Central London, England, 7 July, 1921 — FB
Died: Hereford, England, 12 November, 2005
England: FLge-1

League Club	Source	Date Signed	Seasons Played	Apps	Subs	Gls
Arsenal	Hoxton BC	09/45	46-54	86	-	0

WADE Shaun Peter
Born: Stoke-on-Trent, England, 22 September, 1969 — F

League Club	Source	Date Signed	Seasons Played	Apps	Subs	Gls
Stoke C	Newcastle T	10/94	94	0	1	0

WADSWORTH Albert William
Born: Heywood, Greater Manchester, England, 22 March, 1925 — IF
Died: Bury, Greater Manchester, England, 26 March, 1982

League Club	Source	Date Signed	Seasons Played	Apps	Subs	Gls
Oldham Ath	Stalybridge Celtic	08/49	49-51	33	-	8

WADSWORTH Ian Jack
Born: Huddersfield, West Yorkshire, England, 24 September, 1966 — F

League Club	Source	Date Signed	Seasons Played	Apps	Subs	Gls
Huddersfield T	App	09/84	84	0	1	0
Doncaster Rov	Tr	02/86	85	1	1	0

WADSWORTH Michael (Mick)
Born: Barnsley, South Yorkshire, England, 3 November, 1950 — W

League Club	Source	Date Signed	Seasons Played	Apps	Subs	Gls
Scunthorpe U	Gainsborough Trinity	08/76	76	19	9	3

WAFULA Jonathan Walukana
Born: Alfreton, Derbyshire, England, 17 June, 1994 — F

League Club	Source	Date Signed	Seasons Played	Apps	Subs	Gls
Chesterfield	Chesterfield College	07/12	12	0	1	0

WAGENAAR Joshua Frederick (Josh)
Born: Hamilton, Ontario, Canada, 26 January, 1985 — G
Canada: 4

League Club	Source	Date Signed	Seasons Played	Apps	Subs	Gls
Yeovil T	Lyngby (DEN)	08/08	08	22	1	0

WAGHORN Martyn Thomas
Born: South Shields, Tyne and Wear, England, 23 January, 1990 — F
England: U21-5/Youth

League Club	Source	Date Signed	Seasons Played	Apps	Subs	Gls
Sunderland	Sch	02/08	07-10	2	4	0
Charlton Ath	L	11/08	08	4	3	1
Leicester C	L	08/09	09	27	16	12
Leicester C	Tr	08/10	10-13	21	39	8
Hull C	L	08/11	11	5	0	1
Millwall	L	09/13	13	13	1	3
Wigan Ath	Tr	01/14	13-14	21	17	8

WAGSTAFF Anthony (Tony)
Born: Wombwell, South Yorkshire, England, 19 February, 1944 — M

League Club	Source	Date Signed	Seasons Played	Apps	Subs	Gls
Sheffield U	App	03/61	60-68	138	3	19
Reading	Tr	07/69	69-73	166	7	6

WAGSTAFF Barry
Born: Wombwell, South Yorkshire, England, 28 November, 1945 — M/CD

League Club	Source	Date Signed	Seasons Played	Apps	Subs	Gls
Sheffield U	App	06/63	64-68	107	10	5
Reading	Tr	07/69	69-74	197	6	23
Rotherham U	Tr	03/75	74-76	42	3	1

WAGSTAFF Kenneth (Ken)
Born: Langwith, Derbyshire, England, 24 November, 1942 — F

League Club	Source	Date Signed	Seasons Played	Apps	Subs	Gls
Mansfield T	Woodland Imperial	05/60	60-64	181	-	93
Hull C	Tr	11/64	64-75	374	4	17

WAGSTAFF Scott Andrew
Born: Maidstone, Kent, England, 31 March, 1990 — W

League Club	Source	Date Signed	Seasons Played	Apps	Subs	Gls
Charlton Ath	Sch	12/07	07-12	70	47	17
Bournemouth	L	08/08	08	3	2	0
Leyton Orient	L	10/12	12	6	1	0
Bristol C	Tr	07/13	13-14	37	26	7

WAGSTAFFE David (Dave)
Born: Manchester, England, 5 April, 1943 — LW
Died: Wolverhampton, England, 5 August, 2013
England: FLge-1/Youth

League Club	Source	Date Signed	Seasons Played	Apps	Subs	Gls
Manchester C	Jnr	05/60	60-64	144	-	8
Wolverhampton W	Tr	12/64	64-75	324	0	27
Blackburn Rov	Tr	01/76	75-77	72	3	7
Blackpool	Tr	08/78	78	17	2	1
Blackburn Rov	Tr	03/79	78	2	0	0

WAIN Leslie John (Les)
Born: Crewe, Cheshire, England, 2 August, 1954 — M
England: Schools

League Club	Source	Date Signed	Seasons Played	Apps	Subs	Gls
Crewe Alex	App	08/72	70-74	48	5	1
Southport	Tr	07/75	75	3	2	0

WAINE Andrew Paul (Andy)
Born: Manchester, England, 24 February, 1983 — M

League Club	Source	Date Signed	Seasons Played	Apps	Subs	Gls
Burnley	Sch	07/02	02	0	2	0

WAINMAN William Henry (Harry)
Born: Hull, England, 22 March, 1947 — G
England: Youth

League Club	Source	Date Signed	Seasons Played	Apps	Subs	Gls
Grimsby T	Hull C (Am)	07/64	64-77	420	0	0
Rochdale	L	10/72	72	9	0	0

WAINWRIGHT Edward Francis (Eddie)
Born: Southport, Merseyside, England, 22 June, 1924 — IF
Died: Birkenhead, Wirral, England, 30 September, 2005
England: FLge-1

League Club	Source	Date Signed	Seasons Played	Apps	Subs	Gls
Everton	High Park, Southport	03/44	46-55	207	-	68
Rochdale	Tr	06/56	56-58	100	-	27

WAINWRIGHT Lewis
Born: Kirton-in-Lindsey, North Lincolnshire, England, 15 December, 1930 — RB

League Club	Source	Date Signed	Seasons Played	Apps	Subs	Gls
Scunthorpe U	Brigg T	05/51	55	2	-	0

WAINWRIGHT Neil
Born: Warrington, Cheshire, England, 4 November, 1977 — RW

League Club	Source	Date Signed	Seasons Played	Apps	Subs	Gls
Wrexham	YT	07/96	97	7	4	3
Sunderland	Tr	07/98	98	0	2	0
Darlington	L	02/00	99	16	1	4
Halifax T	L	10/00	00	13	0	0
Darlington	Tr	08/01	01-07	167	68	24
Shrewsbury T	L	10/07	07	2	1	0
Mansfield T	L	03/08	07	1	4	0
Morecambe	Tr	07/08	08-10	38	22	1

WAINWRIGHT Robin Keith
Born: Luton, England, 9 March, 1951 — M

League Club	Source	Date Signed	Seasons Played	Apps	Subs	Gls
Luton T	App	12/68	71	15	1	3
Cambridge U	L	03/71	70	1	0	0
Millwall	Tr	11/72	73	2	2	0
Northampton T	Tr	02/74	73-74	23	9	5

WAITE Gareth
Born: Thornaby, Cleveland, England, 16 February, 1986 — M

League Club	Source	Date Signed	Seasons Played	Apps	Subs	Gls
Darlington	Spennymoor T	01/10	09	14	0	1

WAITE John Aidan
Born: Grimsby, North Lincolnshire, England, 16 January, 1942 — W
England: Youth

League Club	Source	Date Signed	Seasons Played	Apps	Subs	Gls
Grimsby T	Jnr	11/60	61-62	8	-	1

WAITE Thomas John Aldwyn (Aldwyn)
Born: Pontllanfraith, Caerphilly, Wales, 3 August, 1928 — WH/IF
Died: Caerphilly, Wales, February, 2012

League Club	Source	Date Signed	Seasons Played	Apps	Subs	Gls
Newport Co		12/51	51-53	56	-	1

WAITE Tyrell Michael Nathaniel
Born: Derby, England, 1 July, 1994 — F

League Club	Source	Date Signed	Seasons Played	Apps	Subs	Gls
Notts Co	Ilkeston	03/12	12-13	3	6	1

WAITE William John (Bill)
Born: Newport, Wales, 29 November, 1917 — CF
Died: Weston-super-Mare, Somerset, England, 23 June, 1980

League Club	Source	Date Signed	Seasons Played	Apps	Subs	Gls
Oldham Ath		11/42	46	4	-	4

WAITERS Anthony Keith (Tony)
Born: Southport, Merseyside, England, 1 February, 1937 — G
England: 5/FLge-5/Amateur-1

League Club	Source	Date Signed	Seasons Played	Apps	Subs	Gls
Blackpool	Bishop Auckland	10/59	59-66	257	0	0
Burnley	Tr	07/70	70-71	38	0	0

WAITES George Edward
Born: Stepney, E London, England, 12 March, 1938 — RW/IF
Died: Watford, Hertfordshire, England, 24 August, 2000

League Club	Source	Date Signed	Seasons Played	Apps	Subs	Gls
Leyton Orient	Harwich & Parkeston	12/58	58-60	43	-	9
Norwich C	Tr	01/61	60-61	36	-	11
Leyton Orient	Tr	07/62	62	2	-	0
Brighton & HA	Tr	12/62	62-63	23	-	1
Millwall	Tr	04/65				

WAITES Paul
Born: Hull, England, 24 January, 1971 — M

League Club	Source	Date Signed	Seasons Played	Apps	Subs	Gls
Hull C	YT	07/89	89-90	11	0	0

WAITT Michael Hugh (Mick)
Born: Hexham, Northumberland, England, 25 June, 1960 — F

League Club	Source	Date Signed	Seasons Played	Apps	Subs	Gls
Notts Co	Keyworth U	12/84	84-86	71	11	27
Lincoln C	Tr	06/87	89	7	1	1

WAKE Brian Christopher
Born: Stockton-on-Tees, Cleveland, England, 13 August, 1982 — F

League Club	Source	Date Signed	Seasons Played	Apps	Subs	Gls
Carlisle U	Tow Law T	05/02	02-03	12	31	9

WAKE Geoffrey Graham (Geoff)
Born: Bristol, England, 25 February, 1954 — G

League Club	Source	Date Signed	Seasons Played	Apps	Subs	Gls
Torquay U	Barnstaple T	12/77	77	9	0	0

WAKEFIELD Albert Joseph
Born: Pudsey, West Yorkshire, England, 19 November, 1921 — CF
Died: Southend-on-Sea, England, November, 2006

League Club	Source	Date Signed	Seasons Played	Apps	Subs	Gls
Leeds U	Stanningley Works	01/42	47-48	49	-	24
Southend U	Tr	08/49	49-52	109	-	58

WAKEFIELD David (Dave)
Born: South Shields, Tyne and Wear, England, 15 January, 1965 — M

League Club	Source	Date Signed	Seasons Played	Apps	Subs	Gls
Darlington	App	01/83	82-83	7	15	0
Torquay U	Tr	03/84	83	10	0	1

WAKEFIELD Joshua John Christopher (Josh)
Born: Frimley, Surrey, England, 6 November, 1993 — M

League Club	Source	Date Signed	Seasons Played	Apps	Subs	Gls
Bournemouth	Jnr	04/12	11-12	0	3	0

WAKEFIELD Liam
Born: Doncaster, South Yorkshire, England, 9 April, 1994 — RB

League Club	Source	Date Signed	Seasons Played	Apps	Subs	Gls
Doncaster Rov	Sch	07/12	13-14	6	4	0

WAKEHAM Peter Francis
Born: Kingsbridge, Devon, England, 14 March, 1936 — G
Died: Bridgend, Wales, 4 March, 2013

League Club	Source	Date Signed	Seasons Played	Apps	Subs	Gls
Torquay U	Kingsbridge	10/53	53-58	58	-	0
Sunderland	Tr	09/58	58-61	134	-	0
Charlton Ath	Tr	07/62	62-64	55	-	0
Lincoln C	Tr	05/65	65	44	0	0

WAKEMAN Alan
Born: Walsall, West Midlands, England, 20 November, 1920 — G
Died: Stafford, England, 15 December, 2002
England: Schools

League Club	Source	Date Signed	Seasons Played	Apps	Subs	Gls
Aston Villa	Bloxwich Strollers	12/38	38-49	12	-	0
Doncaster Rov	Tr	07/50	50-51	5	-	0
Shrewsbury T	Bloxwich Strollers	02/53	52-53	6	-	0

WAKENSHAW Robert Andrew (Robbie)
Born: Hazlerigg, Tyne and Wear, England, 22 December, 1965 — F
England: Youth

League Club	Source	Date Signed	Seasons Played	Apps	Subs	Gls
Everton	App	12/83	83-84	2	1	1
Carlisle U	Tr	09/85	85	6	2	2
Doncaster Rov	L	03/86	85	8	0	3
Rochdale	Tr	09/86	86	28	1	5
Crewe Alex	Tr	06/87	87-88	18	4	1

WALCOTT Theo James
Born: Stanmore, NW London, England, 16 March, 1989 — RW/F
England: 40/B-1/U21-21/Youth

League Club	Source	Date Signed	Seasons Played	Apps	Subs	Gls
Southampton	Sch	07/05	05	13	8	4
Arsenal	Tr	01/06	06-14	132	76	50

WALDEN Harold Bertram (Harry)
Born: Walgrave, Northamptonshire, England, 22 December, 1940 — RW

League Club	Source	Date Signed	Seasons Played	Apps	Subs	Gls
Luton T	Kettering T	01/61	60-63	96	-	11
Northampton T	Tr	06/64	64-66	76	0	3

WALDEN Richard Frank
Born: Hereford, England, 4 May, 1948 — RB
Died: Frimley, Surrey, England, 19 November, 2009

League Club	Source	Date Signed	Seasons Played	Apps	Subs	Gls
Aldershot	App	05/65	64-75	400	4	16
Sheffield Wed	Tr	01/76	75-77	100	0	1
Newport Co	Tr	08/78	78-81	151	0	2

WALDOCK Desmond Haigh (Des)
Born: Northampton, England, 4 December, 1961 — CD

League Club	Source	Date Signed	Seasons Played	Apps	Subs	Gls
Northampton T	App	11/79	78-80	52	2	4

WALDOCK Ronald (Ronnie)
Born: Heanor, Derbyshire, England, 6 December, 1932 — IF

League Club	Source	Date Signed	Seasons Played	Apps	Subs	Gls
Coventry C	Loscoe YC	02/50	52-53	27	-	9
Sheffield U	Tr	05/54	54-56	52	-	10
Scunthorpe U	Tr	02/57	56-59	97	-	45

League Club	Source	Date Signed	Seasons Played	Apps	Subs	Gls
Plymouth Arg	Tr	09/59	59	18	-	6
Middlesbrough	Tr	01/60	59-61	34	-	7
Gillingham	Tr	10/61	61-63	66	-	14

WALDON Connor Mark
Born: Swindon, England, 13 February, 1995 — F

League Club	Source	Date Signed	Seasons Played	Apps	Subs	Gls
Swindon T	Sch	07/13	12-14	2	3	0

WALDRON Alan
Born: Royton, Greater Manchester, England, 6 September, 1951 — M

League Club	Source	Date Signed	Seasons Played	Apps	Subs	Gls
Bolton W	App	09/69	70-77	127	14	6
Blackpool	Tr	12/77	77-78	22	1	1
Bury	Tr	06/79	79-80	34	0	0
York C	Tr	09/81	81	3	0	1

WALDRON Colin
Born: Bristol, England, 22 June, 1948 — CD

League Club	Source	Date Signed	Seasons Played	Apps	Subs	Gls
Bury	App	05/66	66	20	0	0
Chelsea	Tr	07/67	67	9	0	0
Burnley	Tr	10/67	67-75	308	0	16
Manchester U	Tr	05/76	76	3	0	0
Sunderland	Tr	02/77	76-77	20	0	1
Rochdale	Atlanta Chiefs (USA)	10/79	79	19	0	1

WALDRON Ernest (Ernie)
Born: Birmingham, England, 3 June, 1913 — IF
Died: Droxford, Hampshire, England, April, 1994

League Club	Source	Date Signed	Seasons Played	Apps	Subs	Gls
Crystal Palace	Bromsgrove Rov	11/34	34-46	80	-	30

WALDRON Malcolm
Born: Hemsworth, West Yorkshire, England, 6 September, 1956 — D
England: B-1

League Club	Source	Date Signed	Seasons Played	Apps	Subs	Gls
Southampton	App	09/74	74-82	177	1	10
Burnley	Tr	09/83	83	16	0	0
Portsmouth	Tr	03/84	83-84	23	0	1

WALES Anthony (Tony)
Born: Dunscroft, South Yorkshire, England, 12 May, 1943 — RB
England: Youth

League Club	Source	Date Signed	Seasons Played	Apps	Subs	Gls
Doncaster Rov	Jnr	05/60	60-62	25	-	0

WALES Gary
Born: East Calder, West Lothian, Scotland, 4 January, 1979 — F
Scotland: U21-1

League Club	Source	Date Signed	Seasons Played	Apps	Subs	Gls
Walsall (L)	Heart of Midlothian	01/04	03	5	2	1
Gillingham	Heart of Midlothian	03/04	03	3	3	1

WALFORD Stephen James (Steve)
Born: Highgate, N London, England, 5 January, 1958 — D
England: Youth

League Club	Source	Date Signed	Seasons Played	Apps	Subs	Gls
Tottenham H	App	04/75	75	1	1	0
Arsenal	Tr	08/77	77-80	64	13	3
Norwich C	Tr	03/81	80-82	93	0	2
West Ham U	Tr	08/83	83-86	114	1	2
Huddersfield T	L	10/87	87	12	0	0
Gillingham	L	12/88	88	4	0	0
West Bromwich A	L	03/89	88	3	1	0

WALKDEN Francis (Frank)
Born: Aberdeen, Scotland, 21 June, 1921 — LW
Died: Bolton, Greater Manchester, England, 23 December, 1992

League Club	Source	Date Signed	Seasons Played	Apps	Subs	Gls
Rochdale	Bolton W (Am)	11/46	46	1	-	0

WALKER Adam Richard
Born: Coventry, England, 22 January, 1991 — M

League Club	Source	Date Signed	Seasons Played	Apps	Subs	Gls
Coventry C	Sch	06/09	08	0	2	0

WALKER Alan
Born: Mossley, Greater Manchester, England, 17 December, 1959 — CD

League Club	Source	Date Signed	Seasons Played	Apps	Subs	Gls
Stockport Co	Mossley	08/78				
Lincoln C	Telford U	10/83	83-84	74	1	4
Millwall	Tr	07/85	85-87	92	0	8
Gillingham	Tr	03/88	87-91	150	1	7
Plymouth Arg	Tr	09/92	92	2	0	1
Mansfield T	Tr	09/92	92	22	0	1
Barnet	Tr	08/93	93-94	59	0	2

WALKER Andrew Francis (Andy)
Born: Glasgow, Scotland, 6 April, 1965 — F
Scotland: 3/U21-1

League Club	Source	Date Signed	Seasons Played	Apps	Subs	Gls
Newcastle U (L)	Glasgow Celtic	09/91	91	2	0	0
Bolton W	Glasgow Celtic	01/92	91-93	61	6	44
Sheffield U	Glasgow Celtic	02/96	95-97	32	20	20
Carlisle U	Ayr U	08/99	99	3	0	0

WALKER Andrew William (Andy)
Born: Bexleyheath, SE London, England, 30 September, 1981 — G

League Club	Source	Date Signed	Seasons Played	Apps	Subs	Gls
Colchester U	YT	-	98-99	3	0	0
Exeter C	St Albans C	08/01	01	1	0	0

WALKER Arnold
Born: Haltwhistle, Northumberland, England, 23 December, 1932 — LH

League Club	Source	Date Signed	Seasons Played	Apps	Subs	Gls
Grimsby T	Appleby Frodingham	05/50	50-57	65	-	0
Walsall	Tr	05/58	58-59	7	-	0

WALKER Bradley Paul (Brad)
Born: Billingham, Cleveland, England, 25 April, 1996 — M

League Club	Source	Date Signed	Seasons Played	Apps	Subs	Gls
Hartlepool U	Sch	07/13	13-14	56	8	8

WALKER Bruce Alan
Born: Hungerford, Berkshire, England, 27 August, 1946 — LW

League Club	Source	Date Signed	Seasons Played	Apps	Subs	Gls
Swindon T	Jnr	12/63	65-67	26	3	5
Bradford C	Tr	03/68	67-68	27	1	1
Exeter C	Tr	06/69	69	21	2	2

WALKER Charles (Charlie)
Born: Brighton, England, 8 March, 1990 — F

League Club	Source	Date Signed	Seasons Played	Apps	Subs	Gls
Luton T	Peacehaven & Telscombe	07/14	14	0	3	0

WALKER Clive
Born: Oxford, England, 26 May, 1957 — LW
England: Schools

League Club	Source	Date Signed	Seasons Played	Apps	Subs	Gls
Chelsea	App	04/75	76-83	168	30	60
Sunderland	Tr	07/84	84-85	48	2	10
Queens Park Rgrs	Tr	12/85	85-86	16	4	1
Fulham	Tr	10/87	87-89	102	7	29
Brighton & HA	Tr	08/90	90-92	104	2	8

WALKER Colin
Born: Rotherham, South Yorkshire, England, 1 May, 1958 — F
New Zealand: 15

League Club	Source	Date Signed	Seasons Played	Apps	Subs	Gls
Barnsley	Gisborne C (NZL)	11/80	80-82	21	3	12
Doncaster Rov	L	02/83	82	12	0	5
Doncaster Rov	Gisborne C (NZL)	11/85	85	3	2	0
Cambridge U	Tr	01/86	85	3	0	1
Sheffield Wed	Harworth CI	08/86	86	2	0	0
Darlington	L	12/86	86	6	1	0
Torquay U	L	10/87	87	3	0	0

WALKER Colin
Born: Stapleford, Nottinghamshire, England, 7 July, 1929 — LH

League Club	Source	Date Signed	Seasons Played	Apps	Subs	Gls
Derby Co	Jnr	10/46	48-54	25	-	0

WALKER Cyril John
Born: Newport Pagnell, Buckinghamshire, England, 24 February, 1914 — IF
Died: Chatham, Kent, England, July, 2002

League Club	Source	Date Signed	Seasons Played	Apps	Subs	Gls
Watford	Leavesdon MH	11/35				
Gillingham	Tr	06/37	37	10	-	3
Sheffield Wed	Tr	10/37	37	4	-	0
Norwich C	Shorts Sports	08/46	46	3	-	2

WALKER David (Dave)
Born: Colne, Lancashire, England, 15 October, 1941 — CD
Died: Hythe, Hampshire, England, 21 January, 2015

League Club	Source	Date Signed	Seasons Played	Apps	Subs	Gls
Burnley	Jnr	05/59	60-64	38	-	1
Southampton	Tr	05/65	65-73	189	8	1

WALKER David Clive Allan (Clive)
Born: Watford, Hertfordshire, England, 24 October, 1945 — LB
England: Schools

League Club	Source	Date Signed	Seasons Played	Apps	Subs	Gls
Leicester C	App	10/62	63-65	17	0	0
Northampton T	Tr	10/66	66-68	72	0	1
Mansfield T	Tr	07/69	69-74	223	6	8

WALKER Dean
Born: Newcastle-upon-Tyne, England, 18 May, 1962 — CD

League Club	Source	Date Signed	Seasons Played	Apps	Subs	Gls
Burnley	App	05/80				
Scunthorpe U		03/82	81	1	0	0

WALKER Dennis Allen
Born: Northwich, Cheshire, England, 26 October, 1944 — M
Died: Stockport, Greater Manchester, England, September, 2003
England: Schools

League Club	Source	Date Signed	Seasons Played	Apps	Subs	Gls
Manchester U	App	11/61	62	1	-	0
York C	Tr	04/64	64-67	149	5	19
Cambridge U	Tr	07/68	70-72	48	8	4

WALKER Dennis George
Born: Spennymoor, County Durham, England, 5 July, 1948 — F

League Club	Source	Date Signed	Seasons Played	Apps	Subs	Gls
West Ham U	App	05/66				
Luton T	Tr	08/67	67	0	1	0

WALKER Derek William
Born: Perth, Scotland, 24 November, 1964 — F

League Club	Source	Date Signed	Seasons Played	Apps	Subs	Gls
Chesterfield	Kinnoull Jnrs, Perth	08/86	86-87	19	4	3

WALKER Desmond Sinclair (Des)
Born: Hackney, E London, England, 26 November, 1965 — CD
England: 59/U21-7

League Club	Source	Date Signed	Seasons Played	Apps	Subs	Gls
Nottingham F	App	12/83	83-91	259	5	1

League Club	Source	Date Signed	Seasons Played	Career Record Apps	Subs	Gls
Sheffield Wed	Sampdoria (ITA)	07/93	93-00	307	0	0
Nottingham F	Rtd	07/02	02-04	52	5	0

WALKER Donald Hunter (Don)
Born: Edinburgh, Scotland, 10 September, 1935 — LH
Died: Isle of Man, England, 21 December, 2011

League Club	Source	Date Signed	Seasons Played	Apps	Subs	Gls
Leicester C	Tranent Jnrs	11/55	57-58	32	-	1
Middlesbrough	Tr	10/59	59-61	23	-	1
Grimsby T	Tr	09/63	63	15	-	1

WALKER Edward Richard Walter (Dick)
Born: Hackney, E London, England, 22 July, 1913 — CH
Died: Brentwood, Essex, England, 4 October, 1988

League Club	Source	Date Signed	Seasons Played	Apps	Subs	Gls
West Ham U	Park Royal	05/34	34-52	292	-	2

WALKER Frederick (Fred)
Born: Stirling, Scotland, 7 April, 1929 — LB
Died: Burnley, Lancashire, England, 6 October, 1966

League Club	Source	Date Signed	Seasons Played	Apps	Subs	Gls
Southport	Queen's Park	10/51	51-52	5	-	0

WALKER Gary
Born: Manchester, England, 11 October, 1963 — G

League Club	Source	Date Signed	Seasons Played	Apps	Subs	Gls
Stockport Co	Oldham T	09/85	85-86	29	0	0

WALKER George Henry (Harry)
Born: Aysgarth, North Yorkshire, England, 20 May, 1916 — G
Died: Beeston, Nottinghamshire, England, 9 January, 1976

League Club	Source	Date Signed	Seasons Played	Apps	Subs	Gls
Darlington	Leyburn	12/34	35-37	50	-	0
Portsmouth	Tr	03/38	37-46	49	-	0
Nottingham F	Tr	04/47	46-54	293	-	0

WALKER George William
Born: Sunderland, England, 30 May, 1934 — IF
Died: Carlisle, Cumbria, England, 8 August, 2012

League Club	Source	Date Signed	Seasons Played	Apps	Subs	Gls
Bristol C	Chippenham T	05/56	56-58	15	-	5
Carlisle U	Tr	03/59	58-62	164	-	53

WALKER Glenn Philip
Born: Warrington, Cheshire, England, 15 March, 1967 — M

League Club	Source	Date Signed	Seasons Played	Apps	Subs	Gls
Crewe Alex	Burnley (App)	03/85	84	1	1	0

WALKER Greig George
Born: Dundee, Scotland, 11 October, 1963 — F

League Club	Source	Date Signed	Seasons Played	Apps	Subs	Gls
Chesterfield	Broughty Ath	10/83	83	6	0	0

WALKER Ian Michael
Born: Watford, Hertfordshire, England, 31 October, 1971 — G
England: 4/B-1/U21-9/Youth

League Club	Source	Date Signed	Seasons Played	Apps	Subs	Gls
Tottenham H	YT	12/89	90-00	257	2	0
Oxford U	L	08/90	90	2	0	0
Leicester C	Tr	07/01	01-04	140	0	0

WALKER James (Jimmy)
Born: Aberdeen, Scotland, 25 August, 1933 — RB
Died: Taverham, Norfolk, England, 10 January, 2006

League Club	Source	Date Signed	Seasons Played	Apps	Subs	Gls
Bradford Park Ave	Aberdeen	05/59	59-63	144	-	2

WALKER James (Jimmy)
Born: Belfast, Northern Ireland, 29 March, 1932 — CF
Northern Ireland: 1/NILge-3

League Club	Source	Date Signed	Seasons Played	Apps	Subs	Gls
Doncaster Rov	Linfield	05/54	54-56	47	-	19

WALKER James Barry (Jimmy)
Born: Sutton-in-Ashfield, Nottinghamshire, England, 9 July, 1973 — G

League Club	Source	Date Signed	Seasons Played	Apps	Subs	Gls
Notts Co	YT	07/91				
Walsall	Tr	08/93	93-03	401	2	0
West Ham U	Tr	07/04	04-05	13	0	0
Colchester U	L	11/08	08	16	0	0
Walsall	Rtd	10/10	10-11	50	0	0

WALKER James Frederick (Jim)
Born: Sheffield, England, 1 July, 1931 — LB

League Club	Source	Date Signed	Seasons Played	Apps	Subs	Gls
Sheffield U	Jnr	11/48	49-53	4	-	0
Huddersfield T	Tr	08/55				
Peterborough U	Tr	06/57	60-64	125	-	0

WALKER James Luke Newton (Jimmy)
Born: Hackney, E London, England, 25 November, 1987 — F
England: Youth

League Club	Source	Date Signed	Seasons Played	Apps	Subs	Gls
Charlton Ath	Sch	12/04				
Hartlepool U	L	01/06	05	1	3	0
Bristol Rov	L	09/06	06	3	1	1
Leyton Orient	L	11/06	06	9	5	2
Notts Co	L	03/07	06	2	6	0
Yeovil T	L	10/07	07	11	2	3
Southend U	Tr	02/08	07-09	25	20	6
Hereford U	L	09/09	09	6	0	1
Gillingham	Tr	02/10	09	2	3	0
Leyton Orient	Tr	09/10	10	0	11	0

WALKER James McIntyre (Jim)
Born: Northwich, Cheshire, England, 10 June, 1947 — LB/M

League Club	Source	Date Signed	Seasons Played	Apps	Subs	Gls
Derby Co	Northwich Victoria	02/68	67-73	35	7	3
Hartlepool U	L	03/70	69	10	0	0
Brighton & HA	Tr	09/74	74-75	24	4	4
Peterborough U	Tr	10/75	75-76	20	11	1
Chester C	Tr	11/76	76-80	171	1	4

WALKER Jason
Born: Barrow, Cumbria, England, 21 March, 1984 — F
England: Semi Pro-1

League Club	Source	Date Signed	Seasons Played	Apps	Subs	Gls
York C	Luton T	06/11	12	36	7	9

WALKER John (Johnny)
Born: Glasgow, Scotland, 12 December, 1973 — M
Scotland: Youth

League Club	Source	Date Signed	Seasons Played	Apps	Subs	Gls
Grimsby T	Clydebank	09/95	95-96	1	2	1
Mansfield T	Tr	09/96	96-98	51	23	4

WALKER John
Born: Leigh-on-Sea, Essex, England, 10 December, 1958 — D

League Club	Source	Date Signed	Seasons Played	Apps	Subs	Gls
Southend U	App	12/76	77-82	38	13	0

WALKER John Gordon (Gordon)
Born: Sheffield, England, 26 November, 1949 — F

League Club	Source	Date Signed	Seasons Played	Apps	Subs	Gls
Grimsby T	Stocksbridge Works	11/68	68-69	25	2	5

WALKER John Young Hilley (Johnny)
Born: Glasgow, Scotland, 17 December, 1928 — WH

League Club	Source	Date Signed	Seasons Played	Apps	Subs	Gls
Wolverhampton W	Campsie Black Watch	07/47	49-51	37	-	21
Southampton	Tr	10/52	52-57	172	-	48
Reading	Tr	12/57	57-64	287	-	24

WALKER Joseph Nicol (Nicky)
Born: Aberdeen, Scotland, 29 September, 1962 — G
Scotland: 2/Youth

League Club	Source	Date Signed	Seasons Played	Apps	Subs	Gls
Leicester C	Elgin C	08/80	81	6	0	0
Burnley (L)	Heart of Midlothian	02/92	91	6	0	0

WALKER Joshua (Josh)
Born: Newcastle-upon-Tyne, England, 21 February, 1989 — M
England: Youth

League Club	Source	Date Signed	Seasons Played	Apps	Subs	Gls
Middlesbrough	Sch	03/06	05-09	3	5	0
Bournemouth	L	03/07	06	5	1	0
Northampton T	L	11/09	09	3	0	0
Rotherham U	L	02/10	09	15	0	3
Watford	Tr	08/10	10-11	0	6	0
Stevenage	L	11/10	10	1	0	0
Northampton T	L	01/11	10	19	0	0
Stevenage	L	08/11	11	0	5	1
Scunthorpe U	Tr	01/12	11-12	38	3	3

WALKER Joshua George (Josh)
Born: Solihull, West Midlands, England, 20 December, 1981 — M

League Club	Source	Date Signed	Seasons Played	Apps	Subs	Gls
Manchester U	YT	09/99				
Shrewsbury T	Tr	07/01	01	0	3	0

WALKER Justin Matthew
Born: Nottingham, England, 6 September, 1975 — M
England: Youth/Schools

League Club	Source	Date Signed	Seasons Played	Apps	Subs	Gls
Nottingham F	Jnr	09/92				
Scunthorpe U	Tr	03/97	96-99	126	6	2
Lincoln C	Tr	07/00	00-01	68	8	4
Exeter C	Tr	08/02	02	35	4	5
Cambridge U	Tr	06/03	03-04	59	0	2
York C	L	01/04	03	7	2	0
Chester C	Tr	07/05	05	13	8	0

WALKER Keith Cameron
Born: Edinburgh, Scotland, 17 April, 1966 — CD

League Club	Source	Date Signed	Seasons Played	Apps	Subs	Gls
Swansea C	St Mirren	11/89	89-98	262	8	9

WALKER Kyle Andrew
Born: Sheffield, England, 28 May, 1990 — RB
England: 11/U21-7/Youth

League Club	Source	Date Signed	Seasons Played	Apps	Subs	Gls
Sheffield U	Sch	07/08	08	2	0	0
Northampton T	L	11/08	08	9	0	0
Tottenham H	Tr	07/09	09-14	116	1	3
Sheffield U	L	08/09	09	26	0	0
Queens Park Rgrs	L	09/10	10	20	0	0
Aston Villa	L	01/11	11	15	0	1

WALKER Lee
Born: Pontypool, Torfaen, Wales, 27 June, 1976 — M

League Club	Source	Date Signed	Seasons Played	Apps	Subs	Gls
Cardiff C	YT	07/94	93	1	0	0

WALKER Leonard (Len)
Born: Darlington, County Durham, England, 4 March, 1944 — D

League Club	Source	Date Signed	Seasons Played	Apps	Subs	Gls
Newcastle U	Spennymoor U	05/63	63	1	-	0
Aldershot	Tr	07/64	64-75	439	10	23
Darlington	Tr	08/76	76-77	10	0	0

League Club	Source	Date Signed	Seasons Played	Career Record Apps	Subs	Gls
WALKER Liam						
Born: Gibraltar, 13 April, 1988						W
Gibraltar: 4						
Portsmouth	CD San Roque (SPN)	08/12	12	16	10	2
WALKER Michael (Mick)						
Born: Mexborough, South Yorkshire, England, 8 March, 1952						D
Bradford Park Ave	App	03/70	68-69	2	2	0
WALKER Michael John (Mickey)						
Born: Harrogate, North Yorkshire, England, 10 April, 1945						M
Doncaster Rov	Sheffield Wed (App)	08/63				
Bradford C	Bourne T	10/64	64-65	19	1	1
Rotherham U	Tr	03/66				
Mansfield T	Los Angeles Wolv (USA)	03/69	68	2	0	0
Stockport Co	Altrincham	08/70	70	1	1	0
Chesterfield	Tr	09/70	70	1	0	0
WALKER Michael Stewart Gordon (Mike)						
Born: Colwyn Bay, Conwy, Wales, 28 November, 1945						G
Wales: U23-4						
Reading	Jnr	01/63				
Shrewsbury T	Tr	06/64	64-65	7	0	0
York C	Tr	06/66	66-68	60	0	0
Watford	Tr	09/68	68-72	137	0	0
Charlton Ath	L	03/73	72	1	0	0
Colchester U	Tr	06/73	73-82	451	0	0
WALKER Mitchell Charles Alan (Mitch)						
Born: St Albans, Hertfordshire, England, 24 September, 1991						G
Brighton & HA	Sch	09/09	09	1	0	0
WALKER Nicholas Thomas (Nicky)						
Born: Rotherham, South Yorkshire, England, 8 September, 1994						W
Rotherham U	Sch	06/13	12	0	2	0
WALKER Nigel Stephen						
Born: Gateshead, Tyne and Wear, England, 7 April, 1959						M
Died: Newcastle-upon-Tyne, England, 2 February, 2014						
Newcastle U	Whickham	07/77	77-81	65	5	3
Crewe Alex	San Diego Sock's (USA)	01/83	82	20	0	5
Sunderland	Tr	07/83	83	0	1	0
Blackpool	L	03/84	83	8	2	3
Chester C	Tr	07/84	84	41	0	9
Hartlepool U	Tr	07/85	85-86	77	5	8
WALKER Patrick Joseph (Pat)						
Born: Carlow, Republic of Ireland, 20 December, 1959						RB/M
Republic of Ireland: U21-2						
Gillingham	App	10/77	77-80	34	17	3
WALKER Paul Ernest						
Born: Hetton-le-Hole, Tyne and Wear, England, 26 February, 1958						M
England: Semi Pro-4						
Hull C	Sunderland (App)	05/76				
Doncaster Rov	L	12/76	76	4	0	0
WALKER Paul Graham						
Born: Bradford, England, 3 April, 1949						M
Wolverhampton W	Bradford Park Ave (Am)	11/66	68-71	17	9	0
Watford	L	12/71	71	2	1	0
Swindon T	L	03/73	72	2	3	0
Peterborough U	Tr	07/73	73-74	75	3	3
Barnsley	Tr	07/75	75	11	2	0
Huddersfield T	Ottawa Tigers (CAN)	11/76	76	1	0	0
WALKER Paul Henry						
Born: Haverhill, Suffolk, England, 18 April, 1992						G
Northampton T	Sch	07/10	10	0	1	0
WALKER Paul James						
Born: Wood Green, N London, England, 17 December, 1960						M
England: Schools						
Brentford	App	01/78	76-82	53	18	5
WALKER Peter Martin						
Born: Watford, Hertfordshire, England, 31 March, 1933						IF
Watford	Bushey U	07/54	54-61	172	-	37
WALKER Philip (Phil)						
Born: Sheffield, England, 27 November, 1956						G
Cambridge U	Sheffield U (App)	02/75	74-75	19	0	0
Rotherham U	Tr	09/77				
WALKER Philip Albert (Phil)						
Born: Kirkby-in-Ashfield, Nottinghamshire, England, 27 January, 1957						F/W
Chesterfield	Old Newark Road BC	12/77	77-82	151	15	38
Rotherham U	Tr	12/82	82-83	20	5	3
Cardiff C	L	09/83	83	2	0	0
Chesterfield	Tr	10/84	84-85	30	8	9
Scarborough	Tr	08/86	87	0	1	0
WALKER Philip Leonardus (Phil)						
Born: Fulham, W London, England, 24 August, 1954						M
Millwall	Epsom & Ewell	10/75	75-78	143	3	17
Charlton Ath	Tr	07/79	79-82	80	9	15
Gillingham	L	11/82	82	1	1	0
WALKER Raymond (Ray)						
Born: North Shields, Tyne and Wear, England, 28 September, 1963						M
England: Youth						
Aston Villa	App	09/81	82-85	15	8	0
Port Vale	L	09/84	84	15	0	1
Port Vale	Tr	08/86	86-96	322	29	33
Cambridge U	L	09/94	94	5	0	0
WALKER Regan Craig						
Born: Manchester, England, 4 June, 1996						F
Bury	Sch	11/13	13	0	3	0
WALKER Richard Martin						
Born: Sutton Coldfield, West Midlands, England, 8 November, 1977						F
Aston Villa	YT	12/95	97-99	2	4	2
Cambridge U	L	12/98	98	7	14	3
Blackpool	L	02/01	00	6	12	3
Wycombe W	L	09/01	01	10	2	3
Blackpool	Tr	12/01	01-03	38	24	12
Northampton T	L	10/03	03	11	1	4
Oxford U	Tr	03/04	03	3	1	0
Bristol Rov	Tr	08/04	04-07	115	28	46
Shrewsbury T	L	07/08	08	16	11	5
Burton A	Tr	07/09	09-10	19	16	4
WALKER Richard Neil						
Born: Derby, England, 9 November, 1971						CD
Notts Co	YT	07/90	92-96	63	4	4
Mansfield T	L	03/95	94	4	0	0
Cheltenham T	Hereford U	10/98	99-02	67	3	1
WALKER Richard Patrick (Ricky)						
Born: Northampton, England, 4 April, 1959						RB
Coventry C	App	03/77				
Northampton T	Tr	08/78	78-80	50	3	0
WALKER Richard Stuart						
Born: Stafford, England, 17 September, 1980						CD
Crewe Alex	YT	07/99	00-05	82	18	6
Port Vale	Tr	07/06	06	12	4	0
Wrexham	L	03/07	06	3	0	0
Macclesfield T	Tr	02/08	07-08	24	1	0
WALKER Robert (Bob)						
Born: Wallsend, Tyne and Wear, England, 23 July, 1942						D
Brighton & HA	Gateshead	05/62	62	12	-	1
Hartlepool U	Ashford T, Kent	08/64				
Bournemouth	Margate	01/65	65-66	10	0	0
Colchester U	Tr	07/67	67	13	4	0
WALKER Robert Geoffrey (Geoff)						
Born: Bradford, England, 29 September, 1926						LW
Died: Chelmsford, England, 13 March, 1997						
Bradford Park Ave	Jnr	12/43				
Middlesbrough	Tr	06/46	46-54	240	-	50
Doncaster Rov	Tr	12/54	54-56	77	-	10
Bradford C	Tr	06/57	57	2	-	0
WALKER Robert Malcolm (Bob)						
Born: Glasgow, Scotland, 15 January, 1935						LW
Middlesbrough	Redcar	08/52				
Barrow	Tr	08/55	55	10	-	1
WALKER Robert Stephen (Rob)						
Born: Bolton, Greater Manchester, England, 20 September, 1985						CD
Oldham Ath	Sch	-	03	1	0	0
WALKER Robert Wilson						
Born: Aberdeen, Scotland, 21 May, 1922						RH/CF
Died: Aberdeen, Scotland, 13 September, 1991						
Bournemouth	Aberdeen	11/46	46	2	-	2
Wrexham	Tr	06/47	47	2	-	0
WALKER Roger						
Born: Shrewsbury, Shropshire, England, 17 February, 1944						W
Shrewsbury T (Am)	Jnr	05/60	60	1	-	0
WALKER Roger Anthony						
Born: Bolton, Greater Manchester, England, 15 November, 1966						RW
Bolton W	App	07/85	84-85	7	5	1
WALKER Ronald (Ron)						
Born: Swansea, Wales, 24 March, 1933						CF
Died: Swansea, Wales, July, 1989						
Shrewsbury T		11/55	55	1	-	0

League Club	Source	Date Signed	Seasons Played	Career Record Apps	Subs	Gls
WALKER Ronald (Ronnie)						
Born: Sheffield, England, 4 February, 1932						LW
Doncaster Rov	Sunderland (Am)	05/50	52-60	240	-	46
WALKER Ronald Leslie (Ronnie)						
Born: Kingsbury, NW London, England, 2 September, 1952						CD
Watford	App	08/70				
Workington	Tr	08/71	71-75	143	10	3
Newport Co	Tr	08/76	76-78	88	1	5
WALKER Ronald William (Ron)						
Born: Westminster, Central London, England, 10 April, 1930						IF
Died: Devizes, Wiltshire, England, June, 1988						
Watford	Walthamstow Ave	04/54	54	3	-	0
WALKER Samuel (Sam)						
Born: Eccles, Greater Manchester, England, 22 April, 1922						CH
Oldham Ath	Darwen	08/47	47	1	-	0
WALKER Samuel Colin (Sam)						
Born: Gravesend, Kent, England, 2 October, 1991						G
Chelsea	Sch	07/09				
Barnet	L	03/11	10	7	0	0
Northampton T	L	07/11	11	21	0	0
Yeovil T	L	01/12	11	20	0	0
Bristol Rov	L	08/12	12	11	0	0
Colchester U	Tr	01/13	12-14	110	0	0
WALKER Scott Edward						
Born: Glasgow, Scotland, 5 March, 1975						CD
Hartlepool U	Alloa Ath	01/04	03	5	1	0
WALKER Shane						
Born: Pontypool, Torfaen, Wales, 25 November, 1957						M
Hereford U	Arsenal (App)	03/75	74-76	15	2	2
Newport Co	Sligo Rov (ROI)	08/77	77	27	1	2
WALKER Stephen (Steve)						
Born: Sheffield, England, 16 October, 1914						LH/CH
Died: Warminster, Wiltshire, England, November, 1987						
Sheffield U	Gainsborough Trinity	05/37				
Exeter C	Tr	05/38	38-49	141	-	3
WALKER Steven						
Born: Ashington, Northumberland, England, 2 November, 1973						M
England: Schools						
Doncaster Rov	Blyth Spartans	07/96	96	1	0	0
WALKER Steven (Steve)						
Born: Ilkeston, Derbyshire, England, 25 December, 1963						M
Halifax T	Ilkeston T	01/82	81	0	1	0
WALKER Stuart						
Born: Garforth, West Yorkshire, England, 9 January, 1951						G
York C	Tadcaster A	08/75	76	2	0	0
WALKER Terence (Terry)						
Born: Poppleton, North Yorkshire, England, 29 November, 1921						IF
York C	Selby T	05/49	49	16	-	9
WALKER Thomas (Tommy)						
Born: Livingston, West Lothian, Scotland, 26 May, 1915						IF
Died: Edinburgh, Scotland, 11 January, 1993						
Scotland: 20/SLge-5/Schools/War-11						
Chelsea	Heart of Midlothian	09/46	46-48	98	-	23
WALKER Thomas Jackson (Tom)						
Born: Newcastle-upon-Tyne, England, 20 February, 1952						M
Stoke C	App	07/69	71	2	0	0
WALKER Thomas Jackson (Tommy)						
Born: Cramlington, Northumberland, England, 14 November, 1923						W
Died: Middleton, Greater Manchester, England, 13 June, 2005						
Newcastle U	Netherton	10/41	46-53	184	-	35
Oldham Ath	Tr	02/54	53-56	120	-	19
Chesterfield	Tr	02/57	56	14	-	1
Oldham Ath	Tr	07/57	57-58	38	-	4
WALKER Thomas James (Tom)						
Born: Salford, England, 12 December, 1995						M
Bolton W	Sch	07/14	14	9	2	1
WALKER Tyler						
Born: Nottingham, England, 7 October, 1996						F
Nottingham F	Sch	01/15	14	0	7	1
WALKER Victor (Vic)						
Born: Kirkby-in-Ashfield, Nottinghamshire, England, 14 April, 1922						RH
Died: Mansfield, Nottinghamshire, England, June, 1992						
Nottingham F	Basford Villa	08/43				
Stockport Co	Tr	06/46	46-49	94	-	10
WALKLATE Steven (Steve)						
Born: Chester-le-Street, County Durham, England, 27 September, 1979						M
Middlesbrough	YT	07/98				
Darlington	Tr	02/00	00	2	4	0
WALL Adrian Arthur						
Born: Clowne, Derbyshire, England, 25 November, 1949						RW
Sheffield Wed	App	05/67	67	3	0	0
Workington	Tr	08/69	69	21	3	2
WALL Alexander David (Alex)						
Born: Thatcham, Berkshire, England, 22 September, 1990						F
Luton T	Maidenhead U	03/13	14	1	6	1
WALL Thomas Peter (Peter)						
Born: Westbury, Shropshire, England, 13 September, 1944						LB
Shrewsbury T	Jnr	09/62	63-64	18	-	0
Wrexham	Tr	11/65	65-66	15	7	1
Liverpool	Tr	10/66	67-69	31	0	0
Crystal Palace	Tr	06/70	70-77	167	10	4
Leyton Orient	L	12/72	72	10	0	0
WALL William John (Billy)						
Born: Taunton, Somerset, England, 28 October, 1939						RW
Chelsea	Jnr	01/57				
Southend U	Tr	03/60	59-62	56	-	5
WALLACE Adam John						
Born: Ashford, Surrey, England, 5 October, 1981						F
Southampton	YT	08/01				
Southend U	Tr	03/02	01	0	2	0
WALLACE Barry Danny						
Born: Plaistow, E London, England, 17 April, 1959						M
Died: Kansas, USA, 17 October, 2006						
Queens Park Rgrs	Jnr	08/77	77-79	17	8	0
WALLACE Clive Low						
Born: Kirriemuir, Angus, Scotland, 6 January, 1939						IF/W
Died: Lambeth, S London, England, July, 2008						
Bury	Montrose	03/59				
Stockport Co	Tr	08/59	59	13	-	4
WALLACE David Lloyd (Danny)						
Born: Greenwich, SE London, England, 21 January, 1964						F/W
England: 1/B-1/U21-14/Youth						
Southampton	App	01/82	80-89	238	15	64
Manchester U	Tr	09/89	89-92	36	11	6
Millwall	L	03/93	92	3	0	0
Birmingham C	Tr	10/93	93-94	12	4	2
Wycombe W	L	03/95	94	0	1	0
WALLACE George						
Born: Aberdeen, Scotland, 18 April, 1920						IF
Scunthorpe U	Army	03/46	51-52	33	-	8
WALLACE Gordon Henry						
Born: Glasgow, Scotland, 13 June, 1944						F/M
Liverpool	App	07/61	62-64	19	-	3
Crewe Alex	Tr	10/67	67-71	90	3	21
WALLACE Ian Andrew						
Born: Glasgow, Scotland, 23 May, 1956						F
Scotland: 3/U21-1						
Coventry C	Dumbarton	08/76	76-79	128	2	58
Nottingham F	Tr	07/80	80-83	128	6	36
Sunderland	Brest (FRA)	01/85	84-85	28	6	6
WALLACE Ian Robert						
Born: Wellington, Telford & Wrekin, England, 12 September, 1948						WH
Wolverhampton W	App	09/66	66	0	1	0
WALLACE James (Jim)						
Born: Bridge of Allan, Stirlingshire, Scotland, 9 June, 1954						LB
Scotland: SLge-1/U23-1						
Aldershot	Dunfermline Ath	07/75	75-76	53	3	0
WALLACE James (Jimmy)						
Born: Bebington, Wirral, England, 13 December, 1937						LW
Died: Stoke-on-Trent, England, 22 March, 2007						
Stoke C		10/55	58-59	8	-	1
Doncaster Rov	Northwich Victoria	03/63	62	14	-	1
WALLACE James						
Born: Kirkintilloch, Dunbartonshire, Scotland, 17 February, 1933						CH
Died: Bristol, England, November, 1998						
Northampton T	Aberdeen	05/55	55	1	-	0
WALLACE James Robert						
Born: Kirkby, Merseyside, England, 19 December, 1991						M

England: Youth

League Club	Source	Date Signed	Seasons Played	Apps	Subs	Gls
Everton	Sch	12/08				
Stockport Co	L	02/11	10	14	0	1
Shrewsbury T	L	11/11	11	1	2	0
Tranmere Rov	Tr	01/12	11-13	53	2	6
Sheffield U	Tr	06/14	14	7	3	0

WALLACE Jed Fernley
Born: Reading, England, 15 December, 1993 — W
England: Youth

League Club	Source	Date Signed	Seasons Played	Apps	Subs	Gls
Portsmouth	Lewes	08/11	12-14	100	10	27

WALLACE John Collins (Jock)
Born: Glasgow, Scotland, 11 January, 1936 — LB
Died: Glasgow, Scotland, 12 October, 1993

League Club	Source	Date Signed	Seasons Played	Apps	Subs	Gls
Rochdale	St Roch's	03/58	57-58	7	-	0

WALLACE John Martin (Jock)
Born: Wallyford, East Lothian, Scotland, 13 April, 1911 — G
Died: Inveresk, East Lothian, Scotland, 5 September, 1978

League Club	Source	Date Signed	Seasons Played	Apps	Subs	Gls
Blackpool	Raith Rov	02/34	33-47	240	-	0
Derby Co	Tr	02/48	47	16	-	0

WALLACE John Martin Bokas (Jock)
Born: Wallyford, East Lothian, Scotland, 6 September, 1935 — G
Died: Basingstoke, Hampshire, England, July, 1996

League Club	Source	Date Signed	Seasons Played	Apps	Subs	Gls
Workington	Blackpool (Am)	09/52	52	6	-	0
West Bromwich A	Airdrieonians	10/59	59-61	69	-	0

WALLACE Joseph Burt (Joe)
Born: Glasgow, Scotland, 28 December, 1933 — RH/CH
Died: Shrewsbury, Shropshire, England, 19 April, 1993

League Club	Source	Date Signed	Seasons Played	Apps	Subs	Gls
Shrewsbury T	RAOC Donnington	03/54	54-62	337	-	3
Southport	Tr	10/62	62-64	78	-	0

WALLACE Kenneth (Ken)
Born: Frizington, Cumbria, England, 14 January, 1932 — RB
Died: Workington, Cumbria, England, 24 January, 2005

League Club	Source	Date Signed	Seasons Played	Apps	Subs	Gls
Workington	Keekle	07/49	51-52	47	-	1

WALLACE Kenneth (Ken)
Born: Workington, Cumbria, England, 5 January, 1953 — LB

League Club	Source	Date Signed	Seasons Played	Apps	Subs	Gls
Workington		02/74	73-76	6	1	0

WALLACE Kenneth Robert (Kenny)
Born: Islington, N London, England, 8 June, 1952 — W

League Club	Source	Date Signed	Seasons Played	Apps	Subs	Gls
West Ham U	Jnr	07/69				
Brentford	L	02/72	71	3	0	0
Hereford U	Tr	07/72	72	26	6	4
Exeter C	Tr	09/73	73	8	2	1

WALLACE Kieran Neil
Born: Bingham, Nottinghamshire, England, 26 January, 1995 — LW
England: Youth

League Club	Source	Date Signed	Seasons Played	Apps	Subs	Gls
Nottingham F	Sch	05/12				
Sheffield U	Ilkeston	11/14	14	2	2	0

WALLACE Michael (Mick)
Born: Farnworth, Greater Manchester, England, 5 October, 1970 — LB/M
England: Youth

League Club	Source	Date Signed	Seasons Played	Apps	Subs	Gls
Manchester C	YT	07/89				
Stockport Co	Tr	10/92	92-94	65	5	5

WALLACE Murray
Born: Glasgow, Scotland, 10 January, 1993 — CD
Scotland: U21-4/Youth

League Club	Source	Date Signed	Seasons Played	Apps	Subs	Gls
Huddersfield T	Falkirk	01/12	12-14	33	16	3

WALLACE Raymond George (Ray)
Born: Greenwich, SE London, England, 2 October, 1969 — M/RB
England: U21-4

League Club	Source	Date Signed	Seasons Played	Apps	Subs	Gls
Southampton	YT	04/88	88-89	33	2	0
Leeds U	Tr	07/91	92-93	5	2	0
Swansea C	L	03/92	91	2	0	0
Reading	L	03/94	93	3	0	0
Stoke C	Tr	08/94	94-98	152	27	15
Hull C	L	12/94	94	7	0	0

WALLACE Robert (Bob)
Born: Huddersfield, West Yorkshire, England, 14 February, 1948 — M

League Club	Source	Date Signed	Seasons Played	Apps	Subs	Gls
Huddersfield T	App	05/65	66	4	0	0
Halifax T	Tr	03/67	66-71	190	11	16
Chester C	Tr	06/72	72	41	0	9
Aldershot	Tr	07/73	73-76	70	6	1

WALLACE Rodney Seymour (Rod)
Born: Greenwich, SE London, England, 2 October, 1969 — F
England: B-1/U21-11

League Club	Source	Date Signed	Seasons Played	Apps	Subs	Gls
Southampton	YT	04/88	87-90	111	17	45
Leeds U	Tr	06/91	91-97	187	25	53
Bolton W	Glasgow Rangers	09/01	01	14	5	3
Gillingham	Tr	08/02	02-03	27	9	12

WALLACE Ross
Born: Dundee, Scotland, 23 May, 1985 — LW
Scotland: 1/B-1/U21-4

League Club	Source	Date Signed	Seasons Played	Apps	Subs	Gls
Sunderland	Glasgow Celtic	08/06	06-07	38	15	8
Preston NE	Tr	08/08	08-09	74	6	12
Burnley	Tr	07/10	10-14	104	45	12

WALLACE William Semple Brown (Willie)
Born: Kirkintilloch, Dunbartonshire, Scotland, 23 June, 1941 — F
Scotland: 7/SLge-4

League Club	Source	Date Signed	Seasons Played	Apps	Subs	Gls
Crystal Palace	Glasgow Celtic	10/71	71-72	36	3	4

WALLBANK Bernard Frederick
Born: Preston, Lancashire, England, 11 November, 1943 — CF

League Club	Source	Date Signed	Seasons Played	Apps	Subs	Gls
Southport	St Andrew's, Preston	08/61	61	1	-	0

WALLBANKS Harold (Harry)
Born: Chopwell, Tyne and Wear, England, 27 July, 1921 — RH
Died: Whitehaven, Cumbria, England, April, 1993

League Club	Source	Date Signed	Seasons Played	Apps	Subs	Gls
Fulham	West Stanley	10/38	46-47	33	-	1
Southend U	Tr	10/49	49-50	39	-	2
Workington	Tr	08/52	52	26	-	9

WALLBANKS James (Jimmy)
Born: Wigan, Greater Manchester, England, 12 September, 1909 — CD
Died: Reading, England, 28 October, 1979

League Club	Source	Date Signed	Seasons Played	Apps	Subs	Gls
Barnsley	Annfield Plain	03/29	30	9	-	0
Norwich C	Tr	05/31	31	3	-	0
Northampton T	Tr	08/32	32	2	-	0
Millwall	Wigan Ath	06/34	34-38	88	-	0
Reading	Tr	10/38	38-46	48	-	1

WALLBANKS William Horace (Horace)
Born: Chopwell, Tyne and Wear, England, 4 September, 1918 — RW
Died: Kettering, Northamptonshire, England, 17 October, 2004

League Club	Source	Date Signed	Seasons Played	Apps	Subs	Gls
Grimsby T	Aberdeen	11/46	46	9	-	1
Luton T	Tr	05/47	46-47	4	-	1

WALLBRIDGE Trevor
Born: Southampton, England, 8 February, 1959 — F

League Club	Source	Date Signed	Seasons Played	Apps	Subs	Gls
Bournemouth	AFC Totton	01/78	77	0	1	0

WALLEMME Jean-Guy
Born: Maubeuge, France, 10 August, 1967 — CD

League Club	Source	Date Signed	Seasons Played	Apps	Subs	Gls
Coventry C	RC Lens (FRA)	07/98	98	4	2	0

WALLER David Harold
Born: Urmston, Greater Manchester, England, 20 December, 1963 — F

League Club	Source	Date Signed	Seasons Played	Apps	Subs	Gls
Crewe Alex		01/82	81-85	165	3	55
Shrewsbury T	Tr	07/86	86	11	0	3
Chesterfield	Tr	03/87	87-89	117	2	53

WALLER Henry Harold (Harry)
Born: Ashington, Northumberland, England, 20 August, 1917 — RH
Died: Ashington, Northumberland, England, April, 1984

League Club	Source	Date Signed	Seasons Played	Apps	Subs	Gls
Arsenal	Ashington	10/37	46	8	-	0
Leyton Orient	Tr	07/47	47	17	-	0

WALLER Philip (Phil)
Born: Leeds, England, 12 April, 1943 — CD

League Club	Source	Date Signed	Seasons Played	Apps	Subs	Gls
Derby Co	Jnr	05/61	61-67	102	2	5
Mansfield T	Tr	03/68	67-71	153	6	1

WALLEY Ernest (Ernie)
Born: Caernarfon, Gwynedd, Wales, 19 April, 1933 — WH

League Club	Source	Date Signed	Seasons Played	Apps	Subs	Gls
Tottenham H	Jnr	05/51	55-57	5	-	0
Middlesbrough	Tr	05/58	58	8	-	0

WALLEY John Thomas (Tom)
Born: Caernarfon, Gwynedd, Wales, 27 February, 1945 — CD/M
Wales: 1/U23-4

League Club	Source	Date Signed	Seasons Played	Apps	Subs	Gls
Arsenal	Caernarvon T	12/64	65-66	10	4	1
Watford	Tr	03/67	66-71	202	2	17
Leyton Orient	Tr	12/71	71-75	155	2	6
Watford	Tr	06/76	76	12	1	0

WALLEY Keith John
Born: Weymouth, Dorset, England, 19 October, 1954 — M

League Club	Source	Date Signed	Seasons Played	Apps	Subs	Gls
Crystal Palace	App	03/72	73	6	1	1

WALLING Dean Anthony
Born: Leeds, England, 17 April, 1969 — CD/F
St Kitts & Nevis: 2

League Club	Source	Date Signed	Seasons Played	Apps	Subs	Gls
Rochdale	Leeds U (App)	07/87	87-89	43	22	8
Carlisle U	Guiseley	07/91	91-97	230	6	22
Lincoln C	Tr	09/97	97-98	35	3	5
Cambridge U	Northwich Victoria	08/01	01	20	0	0

League Club	Source	Date Signed	Seasons Played	Career Record Apps	Subs	Gls

WALLINGTON Francis Mark (Mark)
Born: Sleaford, Lincolnshire, England, 17 September, 1952 — G
England: U23-2/Youth/Schools

League Club	Source	Date Signed	Seasons Played	Apps	Subs	Gls
Walsall	Heckington U	10/71	71	11	0	0
Leicester C	Tr	03/72	71-84	412	0	0
Derby Co	Tr	07/85	85-86	67	0	0
Lincoln C	Tr	08/88	88-90	87	0	0

WALLIS Derek
Born: Hartlepool, Cleveland, England, 6 October, 1937 — CF

League Club	Source	Date Signed	Seasons Played	Apps	Subs	Gls
Hartlepool U (Am)	Durham C	05/63	63	2	-	0

WALLIS Jonathan Kevin (Jon)
Born: Gravesend, Kent, England, 4 April, 1986 — RB

League Club	Source	Date Signed	Seasons Played	Apps	Subs	Gls
Gillingham	Sch	08/05	05	16	1	0
Hereford U	Tr	07/06	06	0	2	0

WALLIS Scott Edward
Born: Enfield, N London, England, 28 June, 1988 — RW

League Club	Source	Date Signed	Seasons Played	Apps	Subs	Gls
Leyton Orient	Sch	-	04	0	3	0

WALLS Arthur Joseph
Born: Glasgow, Scotland, 15 January, 1931 — IF
Died: Haddington, East Lothian, Scotland, 27 July, 2006

League Club	Source	Date Signed	Seasons Played	Apps	Subs	Gls
Tranmere Rov	Airdrieonians	06/54	54-55	22	-	6

WALLS David (Dave)
Born: Leeds, England, 16 June, 1953 — W

League Club	Source	Date Signed	Seasons Played	Apps	Subs	Gls
Lincoln C	Leeds U (App)	07/71	71-72	9	0	0

WALLS James Parker (Jimmy)
Born: Dunfermline, Fife, Scotland, 11 March, 1928 — CH
Died: Dover, Kent, England, July, 1995

League Club	Source	Date Signed	Seasons Played	Apps	Subs	Gls
Charlton Ath	Crossgates	09/45	49-52	10	-	0
Ipswich T	Tr	05/54	54	1	-	0

WALLS John (Jack)
Born: Seaham, County Durham, England, 8 May, 1932 — G
Died: Barnsley, South Yorkshire, England, 2 February, 2013

League Club	Source	Date Signed	Seasons Played	Apps	Subs	Gls
Barnsley	Dawdon Jnrs	05/49	52	7	-	0
Peterborough U	Tr	05/56	60-61	78	-	0

WALLWORK Ronald (Ronnie)
Born: Manchester, England, 10 September, 1977 — M
England: Youth

League Club	Source	Date Signed	Seasons Played	Apps	Subs	Gls
Manchester U	YT	03/95	97-01	4	15	0
Carlisle U	L	12/97	97	10	0	1
Stockport Co	L	03/98	97	7	0	0
West Bromwich A	Tr	07/02	02-06	86	7	2
Bradford C	L	01/04	03	7	0	4
Barnsley	L	11/06	06	2	0	0
Huddersfield T	L	09/07	07	16	0	3
Sheffield Wed	Tr	01/08	07	4	3	0

WALMSLEY David Geoffrey
Born: Hull, England, 23 November, 1972 — F

League Club	Source	Date Signed	Seasons Played	Apps	Subs	Gls
Hull C	YT	07/91	90-91	5	5	4

WALMSLEY Dennis
Born: Birkdale, Merseyside, England, 1 May, 1935 — RW

League Club	Source	Date Signed	Seasons Played	Apps	Subs	Gls
Southport (Am)	Crossens	05/54	54	4	-	1

WALSCHAERTS Wim
Born: Antwerp, Belgium, 5 November, 1972 — M/RB

League Club	Source	Date Signed	Seasons Played	Apps	Subs	Gls
Leyton Orient	KFC Tielen (BEL)	07/98	98-00	120	5	9

WALSH Alan
Born: Hartlepool, Cleveland, England, 9 December, 1956 — F/M

League Club	Source	Date Signed	Seasons Played	Apps	Subs	Gls
Middlesbrough	Horden CW	12/76	77	0	3	0
Darlington	Tr	10/78	78-83	245	6	87
Bristol C	Tr	08/84	84-88	215	3	77
Walsall	Besiktas (TKY)	10/91	91	4	0	0
Huddersfield T	Glenavon	12/91	91	0	4	0
Shrewsbury T	Tr	01/92	91	2	0	0
Cardiff C	Southampton (NC)	03/92	91	1	0	0
Hartlepool U	Backwell U	09/94	94	4	0	1

WALSH Andrew (Andy)
Born: Blackburn, Greater Manchester, England, 15 February, 1970 — CD

League Club	Source	Date Signed	Seasons Played	Apps	Subs	Gls
Bury	Preston NE (NC)	11/87	87	0	1	0

WALSH Colin David
Born: Hamilton, Lanarkshire, Scotland, 22 July, 1962 — LW
Scotland: U21-5/Youth/Schools

League Club	Source	Date Signed	Seasons Played	Apps	Subs	Gls
Nottingham F	App	08/79	80-85	115	24	32
Charlton Ath	Tr	09/86	86-95	223	19	21
Peterborough U	L	02/89	88	5	0	1
Middlesbrough	L	01/91	90	10	3	1

WALSH Daniel Gareth (Danny)
Born: Manchester, England, 23 September, 1979 — M

League Club	Source	Date Signed	Seasons Played	Apps	Subs	Gls
Oldham Ath	YT	07/98	98-99	0	2	0
Chesterfield	Emley	12/01	01	0	1	0

WALSH David (Dave)
Born: Wrexham, Wales, 29 April, 1979 — G
Wales: U21-8

League Club	Source	Date Signed	Seasons Played	Apps	Subs	Gls
Wrexham	YT	07/97	00-01	12	2	0

WALSH David John (Dave)
Born: Waterford, Republic of Ireland, 28 April, 1923 — CF
Republic of Ireland: 20//Northern Ireland: 9/NILge-3/War-2

League Club	Source	Date Signed	Seasons Played	Apps	Subs	Gls
West Bromwich A	Linfield	07/46	46-50	165	-	94
Aston Villa	Tr	12/50	50-54	108	-	37
Walsall	Tr	07/55	55	20	-	6

WALSH Derek
Born: Hamilton, Lanarkshire, Scotland, 24 October, 1967 — M/D

League Club	Source	Date Signed	Seasons Played	Apps	Subs	Gls
Everton	App	10/84	84	1	0	0
Carlisle U	Hamilton Academical	08/88	88-92	108	13	7

WALSH Francis (Frank)
Born: Wishaw, Lanarkshire, Scotland, 15 September, 1923 — CF
Died: Wishaw, Lanarkshire, Scotland, 5 February, 2006

League Club	Source	Date Signed	Seasons Played	Apps	Subs	Gls
Southport	Glasgow Celtic	10/49	49	5	-	3

WALSH Gary
Born: Wigan, Greater Manchester, England, 21 March, 1968 — G
England: U21-2

League Club	Source	Date Signed	Seasons Played	Apps	Subs	Gls
Manchester U	Jnr	04/85	86-94	49	1	0
Oldham Ath	L	11/93	93	6	0	0
Middlesbrough	Tr	08/95	95-96	44	0	0
Bradford C	Tr	09/97	97-02	131	1	0
Middlesbrough	L	09/00	00	3	0	0
Wigan Ath	Tr	07/03	03	1	2	0

WALSH Ian Patrick
Born: St Davids, Pembrokeshire, Wales, 4 September, 1958 — F
Wales: 18/U21-2/Youth/Schools

League Club	Source	Date Signed	Seasons Played	Apps	Subs	Gls
Crystal Palace	App	10/75	76-81	101	16	23
Swansea C	Tr	02/82	81-83	32	5	11
Barnsley	Tr	07/84	84-85	45	4	15
Grimsby T	Tr	08/86	86-87	36	5	14
Cardiff C	Tr	01/88	87-88	5	12	4

WALSH James (Jimmy)
Born: Bellshill, Lanarkshire, Scotland, 3 December, 1930 — IF
Died: Leicester, England, 6 August, 2014
Scotland: U23-1

League Club	Source	Date Signed	Seasons Played	Apps	Subs	Gls
Leicester C	Glasgow Celtic	11/56	56-62	176	-	79

WALSH James Thomas Patrick (Jimmy)
Born: Paddington, Central London, England, 20 November, 1954 — FB/M

League Club	Source	Date Signed	Seasons Played	Apps	Subs	Gls
Watford	App	11/72	73-77	60	5	0
York C	Tr	06/78	78-80	91	8	2

WALSH John Brian (Brian)
Born: Aldershot, Hampshire, England, 26 March, 1932 — RW
Died: Epsom, Surrey, England, January, 2001

League Club	Source	Date Signed	Seasons Played	Apps	Subs	Gls
Arsenal	Jnr	08/49	53-55	17	-	0
Cardiff C	Tr	09/55	55-61	206	-	33
Newport Co	Tr	11/61	61-62	27	-	4

WALSH Joseph Kevin (Joe)
Born: Cardiff, Wales, 13 May, 1992 — CD
Wales: U21-11/Youth

League Club	Source	Date Signed	Seasons Played	Apps	Subs	Gls
Swansea C	Sch	07/10				
Crawley T	Tr	08/12	12-14	94	3	8
MK Dons	Tr	03/15	14	2	0	0

WALSH Kevin William
Born: Rochdale, Greater Manchester, England, 11 February, 1928 — LH

League Club	Source	Date Signed	Seasons Played	Apps	Subs	Gls
Oldham Ath	St Patrick's OB	10/49	49-50	3	-	0
Southport	Tr	07/52	52-53	67	-	1
Bradford C	Tr	07/54	54-55	24	-	3
Southport	Tr	08/56	56	3	-	0

WALSH Mario Markus
Born: Paddington, Central London, England, 19 January, 1966 — F

League Club	Source	Date Signed	Seasons Played	Apps	Subs	Gls
Portsmouth	App	01/84				
Torquay U	Tr	01/85	84-86	89	11	18
Colchester U	Tr	08/87	87-88	29	9	12
Southend U	Tr	07/89	89	10	1	2

WALSH Mark
Born: Preston, Lancashire, England, 7 October, 1962 — M

League Club	Source	Date Signed	Seasons Played	Apps	Subs	Gls
Preston NE	App	10/80	81-83	56	6	2
Exeter C	New Zealand	08/85	85	0	1	0

League Club	Source	Date Signed	Seasons Played	Career Record Apps	Subs	Gls
WALSH Michael Anthony (Mickey)						
Born: Chorley, Lancashire, England, 13 August, 1954						F
Republic of Ireland: 21						
Blackpool	Chorley	11/71	73-77	172	8	72
Everton	Tr	08/78	78	18	3	1
Queens Park Rgrs	Tr	03/79	78-80	13	5	3
WALSH Michael George						
Born: Liverpool, England, 30 May, 1986						F
Chester C	Rhyl	01/05	04	2	3	1
WALSH Michael Shane						
Born: Rotherham, South Yorkshire, England, 5 August, 1977						CD
Scunthorpe U	YT	07/95	94-97	94	9	1
Port Vale	Tr	07/98	98-06	164	9	4
WALSH Michael Thomas (Mike)						
Born: Blackley, Greater Manchester, England, 20 June, 1956						CD
Republic of Ireland: 4						
Bolton W	Jnr	07/74	74-80	169	8	4
Everton	Tr	08/81	81-82	20	0	0
Norwich C	L	10/82	82	5	0	0
Burnley	L	12/82	82	3	0	0
Manchester C	Ft Laud'ale St's (USA)	10/83	83	3	1	0
Blackpool	Tr	02/84	83-88	146	7	6
Bury	Tr	07/89				
WALSH Paul Anthony						
Born: Plumstead, SE London, England, 1 October, 1962						F
England: 5/U21-4/Youth						
Charlton Ath	App	10/77	79-81	85	2	24
Luton T	Tr	07/82	82-83	80	0	25
Liverpool	Tr	05/84	84-87	63	14	25
Tottenham H	Tr	02/88	87-91	84	44	19
Queens Park Rgrs	L	09/91	91	2	0	0
Portsmouth	Tr	06/92	92-93	67	6	14
Manchester C	Tr	03/94	93-95	53	0	16
Portsmouth	Tr	09/95	95	21	0	5
WALSH Peter						
Born: Dublin, Republic of Ireland, 18 October, 1922						CF
Died: Dublin, Republic of Ireland, 13 October, 2007						
Republic of Ireland: LoI-2						
Luton T	Dundalk (ROI)	08/49	49	8	-	2
Brighton & HA	Tr	08/50				
WALSH Philip Andrew (Phil)						
Born: Hartlepool, Cleveland, England, 4 February, 1984						F/CD
Dagenham & Red	Dorchester T	01/10	09-11	4	16	0
Barnet	L	08/10	10	6	3	3
Cheltenham T	L	01/11	10	0	4	0
WALSH Roy						
Born: Belfast, Northern Ireland, 25 November, 1955						D
Northern Ireland: NILge-1						
Swindon T	Glentoran	03/80	80	7	0	0
WALSH Roy William						
Born: Dedham, Essex, England, 15 January, 1947						IF
Ipswich T	App	01/65	65	6	1	0
Southend U	Tr	07/67				
WALSH Steven (Steve)						
Born: Preston, Lancashire, England, 3 November, 1964						CD
Wigan Ath	Jnr	09/82	82-85	123	3	4
Leicester C	Tr	06/86	86-00	352	17	53
Norwich C	Tr	09/00	00	1	3	0
Coventry C	Tamworth	08/02	02	1	1	0
WALSH Wilfred (Wilf)						
Born: Pontlottyn, Caerphilly, Wales, 29 July, 1917						IF
Died: Hednesford, Staffordshire, England, 23 December, 1977						
Arsenal	Jnr	05/36	38	3	-	0
Derby Co	Tr	06/39	46	1	-	0
Walsall	Tr	03/47	46-47	33	-	4
WALSH William (Billy)						
Born: Dublin, Republic of Ireland, 31 May, 1921						WH
Died: Queensland, Australia, 28 July, 2006						
Republic of Ireland: 9//Northern Ireland: 5						
Manchester C	Manchester U (Am)	06/38	46-49	109	-	1
WALSH William (Billy)						
Born: Horden, County Durham, England, 4 December, 1923						CH
Died: Queensland, Australia, 28 July, 2014						
Sunderland	Horden CW	09/46	46-52	98	-	1
Northampton T	Tr	07/53	53	19	-	0
Darlington	Tr	06/54	54	28	-	4
WALSHAW Kenneth (Ken)						
Born: Tynemouth, Tyne and Wear, England, 28 August, 1918						IF
Died: Blyth, Northumberland, England, 16 May, 1979						
Sunderland	North Shields	08/44				
Lincoln C	Tr	08/47	47	17	-	6
Carlisle U	Tr	12/47	47-49	50	-	15
Bradford C	Tr	08/50	50	9	-	3
WALSHAW Lee						
Born: Sheffield, England, 20 January, 1967						M
Sheffield U	App	01/85	84-86	8	1	1
WALSHAW Philip Desmond						
Born: Leeds, England, 16 April, 1929						RW
Halifax T (Am)	Jnr	09/46	46	6	-	1
WALSHE Benjamin Matthew (Ben)						
Born: Hammersmith, W London, England, 24 May, 1983						M
Queens Park Rgrs	YT	07/00	00-02	1	1	0
WALTER William David (David)						
Born: Holsworthy, Devon, England, 3 September, 1964						G
Exeter C	Bideford	11/88	88-89	44	0	0
Plymouth Arg	Tr	07/90	90-91	15	0	0
Torquay U	Tr	06/92	92	1	0	0
WALTERS George						
Born: Wolverhampton, England, 21 June, 1935						FB/LH
Shrewsbury T	Jenks & Cattell	02/57	56-62	246	-	3
Newport Co	Tr	09/63	63-65	80	0	2
WALTERS George Archibald						
Born: Glasgow, Scotland, 30 March, 1939						LW
Oldham Ath	Clyde	08/59	59	13	-	2
WALTERS Henry						
Born: Wath-on-Dearne, South Yorkshire, England, 15 March, 1925						WH/FB
Died: Barnsley, South Yorkshire, England, May, 1994						
Wolverhampton W	Jnr	06/42				
Walsall	Tr	05/46	46-52	254	-	2
Barnsley	Tr	07/53	53-59	160	-	4
WALTERS Jonathan Ronald (Jon)						
Born: Moreton, Wirral, England, 20 September, 1983						F
Republic of Ireland: 33/B-1/U21-1/Youth						
Blackburn Rov	YT	08/01				
Bolton W	Tr	04/02	02	0	4	0
Hull C	L	02/03	02	11	0	5
Barnsley	L	11/03	03	7	1	0
Hull C	Tr	02/04	03-04	9	28	2
Scunthorpe U	L	02/05	04	3	0	0
Wrexham	Tr	08/05	05	33	5	5
Chester C	Tr	07/06	06	24	2	9
Ipswich T	Tr	01/07	06-10	124	12	30
Stoke C	Tr	08/10	10-14	158	18	34
WALTERS Mark Everton						
Born: Birmingham, England, 2 June, 1964						LW
England: 1/B-1/U21-9/Youth/Schools						
Aston Villa	App	05/82	81-87	168	13	39
Liverpool	Glasgow Rangers	08/91	91-94	58	36	14
Stoke C	L	03/94	93	9	0	2
Wolverhampton W	L	09/94	94	11	0	3
Southampton	Tr	01/96	95	4	1	0
Swindon T	Tr	07/96	96-99	91	21	25
Bristol Rov	Tr	11/99	99-01	46	36	13
WALTERS Michael (Mick)						
Born: Banbury, Oxfordshire, England, 17 November, 1939						WH
Coventry C	Jnr	12/56	57	3	-	0
Bradford C	Rugby T	01/62	61-62	19	-	0
WALTERS Peter Louis						
Born: Whickham, Tyne and Wear, England, 8 June, 1952						G
Hull C	Middlesbrough (Jnr)	08/70	70-71	2	0	0
Darlington	L	03/72	71	16	0	0
WALTERS Robert James (Bobby)						
Born: Glasgow, Scotland, 9 March, 1944						CH
Shrewsbury T	Winsford U	12/62	62	1	-	0
WALTERS Steven Paul (Steve)						
Born: Plymouth, England, 9 January, 1972						M
England: Semi Pro-1/Youth/Schools						
Crewe Alex	YT	03/89	87-94	135	11	10
WALTERS Trevor Bowen						
Born: Aberdare, Rhondda Cynon Taff, Wales, 13 January, 1916						CH
Died: Chester, England, 1 June, 1989						
Chester C	Aberaman Ath	05/37	37-48	151	-	1

WALTERS William Edward (Sonny)
Born: Edmonton, N London, England, 5 September, 1924 — RW
Died: Enfield, N London, England, 25 November, 1970
England: B-1

League Club	Source	Date Signed	Seasons Played	Apps	Subs	Gls
Tottenham H	Jnr	08/44	46-55	210	-	66
Aldershot	Tr	07/57	57-58	66	-	11

WALTON Christian Timothy
Born: Wadebridge, Cornwall, England, 9 November, 1995 — G
England: Youth

League Club	Source	Date Signed	Seasons Played	Apps	Subs	Gls
Brighton & HA	Plymouth Arg (Sch)	07/13	14	3	0	0

WALTON David Lee (Dave)
Born: Bedlington, Northumberland, England, 10 April, 1973 — CD

League Club	Source	Date Signed	Seasons Played	Apps	Subs	Gls
Sheffield U	Ashington	03/92				
Shrewsbury T	Tr	11/93	93-97	127	1	10
Crewe Alex	Tr	10/97	97-02	146	9	3
Derby Co	Tr	07/03	03	3	2	0
Stockport Co	L	02/04	03	7	0	0
Shrewsbury T	Tr	08/04	04-05	35	3	4

WALTON Frank Hillard
Born: Southend-on-Sea, England, 9 April, 1918 — LB
Died: Southend-on-Sea, England, 2 December, 1986

League Club	Source	Date Signed	Seasons Played	Apps	Subs	Gls
Southend U	Jnr	12/37	37-50	144	-	0

WALTON Harold (Harry)
Born: Manchester, England, 1 April, 1924 — WH
Died: Leicester, England, October, 1992

League Club	Source	Date Signed	Seasons Played	Apps	Subs	Gls
Southend U	Leicester C (Am)	05/46	46	1	-	0

WALTON Ian Jeffrey
Born: Goole, East Riding of Yorkshire, England, 17 April, 1958 — M

League Club	Source	Date Signed	Seasons Played	Apps	Subs	Gls
Grimsby T	App	-	75	2	0	1
Scunthorpe U	Tr	03/76	76	1	0	0

WALTON John Andrew (Johnny)
Born: Horwich, Greater Manchester, England, 21 March, 1928 — IF
Died: Horwich, Greater Manchester, England, 17 July, 1979
England: Amateur-18

League Club	Source	Date Signed	Seasons Played	Apps	Subs	Gls
Bury (Am)	Saltash	05/49	49-50	26	-	4
Manchester U (Am)	Tr	07/51	51	2	-	0
Bury (Am)	Tr	07/52	52-53	29	-	2
Burnley	Tr	02/54	54-55	18	-	2
Coventry C	Tr	10/56	56-57	13	-	0
Chester C	Kettering T	07/59	59	1	-	0

WALTON Joseph (Joe)
Born: Manchester, England, 5 June, 1925 — LB
Died: Preston, Lancashire, England, 31 December, 2006
England: FLge-1

League Club	Source	Date Signed	Seasons Played	Apps	Subs	Gls
Manchester U	Jnr	10/43	46-47	21	-	0
Preston NE	Tr	03/48	47-60	401	-	4
Accrington Stan	Tr	02/61	60	18	-	0

WALTON Mark Andrew
Born: Merthyr Tydfil, Wales, 1 June, 1969 — G
Wales: U21-1

League Club	Source	Date Signed	Seasons Played	Apps	Subs	Gls
Luton T	Swansea C (Jnr)	02/87				
Colchester U	Tr	11/87	87-88	40	0	0
Norwich C	Tr	08/89	89-91	22	0	0
Wrexham	L	08/93	93	6	0	0
Bolton W	Tr	03/94	93	3	0	0
Fulham	Fakenham T	08/96	96-97	40	0	0
Gillingham	L	02/98	97	1	0	0
Brighton & HA	Tr	07/98	98-99	58	0	0
Cardiff C	Tr	08/00	00	40	0	0

WALTON Paul Anthony
Born: Sunderland, England, 2 July, 1979 — W

League Club	Source	Date Signed	Seasons Played	Apps	Subs	Gls
Hartlepool U	YT	07/97	95-96	3	7	0

WALTON Richard (Dick)
Born: Hull, England, 12 September, 1924 — RB
Died: Deal, Kent, England, 23 June, 2012

League Club	Source	Date Signed	Seasons Played	Apps	Subs	Gls
Leicester C		01/43				
Leyton Orient	Tr	07/48	48-51	63	-	4
Exeter C	Tr	12/51	51-55	135	-	6

WALTON Ronald Pattern (Ronnie)
Born: Plymouth, England, 12 October, 1945 — RW

League Club	Source	Date Signed	Seasons Played	Apps	Subs	Gls
Northampton T	Rotherham U (Am)	09/63	64	1	-	0
Crewe Alex	Tr	10/65	65	2	0	0
Carlisle U	Tr	01/66	65	1	0	0
Aldershot	Tr	08/66	66-71	190	4	41
Cambridge U	Tr	11/71	71-72	62	0	9
Aldershot	Tr	07/73	73-76	108	5	14

WALTON Roy
Born: Crewe, Cheshire, England, 19 July, 1928 — RH
Died: Crewe, Cheshire, England, 9 April, 2003

League Club	Source	Date Signed	Seasons Played	Apps	Subs	Gls
Crewe Alex		06/50	50-51	11	-	0

WALTON Simon William
Born: Sherburn-in-Elmet, North Yorkshire, England, 13 September, 1987 — M

League Club	Source	Date Signed	Seasons Played	Apps	Subs	Gls
Leeds U	Sch	09/04	04-05	26	8	3
Charlton Ath	Tr	07/06				
Ipswich T	L	08/06	06	13	6	3
Cardiff C	L	01/07	06	5	1	0
Queens Park Rgrs	Tr	08/07	07	1	4	0
Hull C	L	01/08	07	5	5	0
Plymouth Arg	Tr	08/08	08-11	54	7	9
Blackpool	L	03/09	08	0	1	0
Crewe Alex	L	08/09	09	26	5	1
Hartlepool U	Tr	07/12	12-13	69	4	4
Stevenage	Tr	06/14	14	25	4	5

WALWYN Kenford Keith Ian (Keith)
Born: Nevis, 17 February, 1956 — F
Died: Liverpool, England, 15 April, 2003

League Club	Source	Date Signed	Seasons Played	Apps	Subs	Gls
Chesterfield	Winterton Rgrs	11/79	80	3	0	2
York C	Tr	07/81	81-86	245	0	117
Blackpool	Tr	06/87	87-88	51	18	16
Carlisle U	Tr	07/89	89-90	59	3	15

WANCHOPE Watson Pablo Cesar (Paulo)
Born: Heredia, Costa Rica, 31 July, 1976 — F
Costa Rica: 73

League Club	Source	Date Signed	Seasons Played	Apps	Subs	Gls
Derby Co	CS Heridiano (CRC)	03/97	96-98	65	7	23
West Ham U	Tr	07/99	99	33	2	12
Manchester C	Tr	08/00	00-03	51	13	27

WANDS Alexander Mitchell Doig (Alex)
Born: Cowdenbeath, Fife, Scotland, 5 December, 1922 — LH
Died: North Tyneside, Tyne and Wear, England, February, 2007

League Club	Source	Date Signed	Seasons Played	Apps	Subs	Gls
Sheffield Wed	Gateshead (Am)	05/45	46	11	-	1
Doncaster Rov	Tr	05/47	47	22	-	0

WANKLYN Edward Wayne (Wayne)
Born: Hull, England, 21 January, 1960 — M

League Club	Source	Date Signed	Seasons Played	Apps	Subs	Gls
Reading	App	01/78	77-80	47	7	3
Aldershot	Tr	08/81	81	15	3	2

WANLESS Paul Steven
Born: Banbury, Oxfordshire, England, 14 December, 1973 — M

League Club	Source	Date Signed	Seasons Played	Apps	Subs	Gls
Oxford U	YT	12/91	91-94	12	20	0
Lincoln C	Tr	07/95	95	7	1	0
Cambridge U	Tr	03/96	95-02	264	20	44
Oxford U	Tr	08/03	03-04	56	9	6

WANN Alexander Halley (Sandy)
Born: Perth, Scotland, 20 December, 1940 — RH

League Club	Source	Date Signed	Seasons Played	Apps	Subs	Gls
Manchester C	Luncarty Jnrs	07/58				
Oldham Ath	St Mirren	12/60	60	19	-	0

WANN John Dennis (Dennis)
Born: Blackpool, Lancashire, England, 17 November, 1950 — W

League Club	Source	Date Signed	Seasons Played	Apps	Subs	Gls
Blackpool	App	07/67	69-71	11	6	0
York C	Tr	01/72	71-75	65	1	7
Chesterfield	L	11/75	75	3	0	0
Hartlepool U	L	01/76	75	2	0	0
Darlington	Tr	07/76	76-78	119	2	13
Rochdale	Tr	06/79	79-80	66	1	7
Blackpool	Tr	10/81	81	13	6	0
Chester C	Workington	10/83	83	2	1	0

WANT Anthony George (Tony)
Born: Hackney, E London, England, 13 December, 1948 — D
England: Youth

League Club	Source	Date Signed	Seasons Played	Apps	Subs	Gls
Tottenham H	App	12/65	67-71	46	4	0
Birmingham C	Tr	06/72	72-77	98	3	1

WANYAMA Victor Mugubi
Born: Nairobi, Kenya, 25 June, 1991 — DM
Kenya: 31

League Club	Source	Date Signed	Seasons Played	Apps	Subs	Gls
Southampton	Glasgow Celtic	07/13	13-14	45	10	3

WAPENAAR Harald Paul
Born: Vlaardingen, Netherlands, 10 April, 1970 — G

League Club	Source	Date Signed	Seasons Played	Apps	Subs	Gls
Portsmouth	FC Utrecht (NED)	07/03	03	5	0	0

WARBOYS Alan
Born: Goldthorpe, South Yorkshire, England, 18 April, 1949 — F

League Club	Source	Date Signed	Seasons Played	Apps	Subs	Gls
Doncaster Rov	App	04/67	66-67	39	0	11
Sheffield Wed	Tr	06/68	68-70	66	5	13
Cardiff C	Tr	12/70	70-72	57	4	27
Sheffield U	Tr	09/72	72	7	0	0

League Club	Source	Date Signed	Seasons Played	Apps	Subs	Gls
Bristol Rov	Tr	03/73	72-76	141	3	53
Fulham	Tr	02/77	76-77	19	0	2
Hull C	Tr	09/77	77-78	44	5	9
Doncaster Rov	Tr	07/79	79-81	89	0	21

WARBURTON Callum Scott
Born: Stockport, Greater Manchester, England, 25 February, 1989 — M

League Club	Source	Date Signed	Seasons Played	Apps	Subs	Gls
Rochdale	Sch	07/07	06	4	0	0

WARBURTON George
Born: Brymbo, Wrexham, Wales, 13 September, 1934 — RB

League Club	Source	Date Signed	Seasons Played	Apps	Subs	Gls
Wrexham	Brymbo Steel Works	11/57	58-59	22	-	0
Barrow	Tr	06/60	60	14	-	0

WARBURTON Ian Thomas
Born: Haslingden, Lancashire, England, 22 March, 1952 — F

League Club	Source	Date Signed	Seasons Played	Apps	Subs	Gls
Bury	Haslingden	11/72	72	6	0	2
Southport	Tr	07/74	74	5	2	1

WARBURTON Raymond (Ray)
Born: Rotherham, South Yorkshire, England, 7 October, 1967 — CD

League Club	Source	Date Signed	Seasons Played	Apps	Subs	Gls
Rotherham U	App	10/85	84-86	3	1	0
York C	Tr	08/89	89-93	86	4	9
Northampton T	Tr	02/94	93-98	186	0	12
Rushden & D	Tr	10/98	01	1	0	0
Boston U	Tr	03/02	02	16	0	0

WARD Anthony (Tony)
Born: Warrington, Cheshire, England, 4 April, 1970 — M

League Club	Source	Date Signed	Seasons Played	Apps	Subs	Gls
Everton	YT	06/88				
Doncaster Rov	L	12/88	88	4	0	0
Wigan Ath	Tr	06/89	89	8	3	2

WARD Ashley Stuart
Born: Manchester, England, 24 November, 1970 — F

League Club	Source	Date Signed	Seasons Played	Apps	Subs	Gls
Manchester C	YT	08/89	89	0	1	0
Wrexham	L	01/91	90	4	0	2
Leicester C	Tr	07/91	91	2	8	0
Blackpool	L	11/92	92	2	0	1
Crewe Alex	Tr	12/92	92-94	58	3	25
Norwich C	Tr	12/94	94-95	53	0	18
Derby Co	Tr	03/96	95-97	32	8	9
Barnsley	Tr	09/97	97-98	45	1	20
Blackburn Rov	Tr	12/98	98-99	52	2	13
Bradford C	Tr	08/00	00-02	75	9	17
Sheffield U	Tr	08/03	03-04	25	8	5

WARD Christopher (Chris)
Born: Preston, Lancashire, England, 28 April, 1981 — F

League Club	Source	Date Signed	Seasons Played	Apps	Subs	Gls
Birmingham C	Lancaster C	04/01				
Lincoln C	Leigh RMI	10/02	02	5	1	2

WARD Daniel (Danny)
Born: Wrexham, Wales, 22 June, 1993 — G
Wales: U21-4/Youth

League Club	Source	Date Signed	Seasons Played	Apps	Subs	Gls
Liverpool	Wrexham	01/12				
Morecambe	L	03/15	14	5	0	0

WARD Daniel Carl (Danny)
Born: Bradford, England, 11 December, 1990 — LW/F

League Club	Source	Date Signed	Seasons Played	Apps	Subs	Gls
Bolton W	Sch	12/08	09	0	2	0
Swindon T	L	11/09	09	24	4	7
Coventry C	L	09/10	10	4	1	0
Huddersfield T	Tr	03/11	10-14	82	42	19
Rotherham U	Tr	01/15	14	10	6	3

WARD Darren
Born: Worksop, Nottinghamshire, England, 11 May, 1974 — G
Wales: 5/B-1/U21-2

League Club	Source	Date Signed	Seasons Played	Apps	Subs	Gls
Mansfield T	YT	07/92	92-94	81	0	0
Notts Co	Tr	07/95	95-00	251	0	0
Nottingham F	Tr	05/01	01-03	123	0	0
Norwich C	Tr	08/04	04	0	1	0
Sunderland	Tr	08/06	06-07	33	0	0

WARD Darren Philip
Born: Harrow, NW London, England, 13 September, 1978 — CD

League Club	Source	Date Signed	Seasons Played	Apps	Subs	Gls
Watford	YT	02/97	95-01	56	3	2
Queens Park Rgrs	L	12/99	99	14	0	0
Millwall	Tr	10/01	01-04	135	7	4
Crystal Palace	Tr	05/05	05-06	62	1	5
Wolverhampton W	Tr	07/07	07-08	30	1	0
Watford	L	09/08	08	9	0	1
Charlton Ath	L	01/09	08	16	0	0
Millwall	Tr	09/09	09-12	86	7	2
Swindon T	Tr	08/12	12-13	75	0	2
Crawley T	L	01/15	14	17	1	1

WARD David (Dai)
Born: Barry, Vale of Glamorgan, Wales, 16 July, 1934 — IF
Died: Cambridge, England, 12 January, 1996
Wales: 2

League Club	Source	Date Signed	Seasons Played	Apps	Subs	Gls
Bristol Rov	Barry T	11/54	54-60	175	-	90
Cardiff C	Tr	02/61	60-61	34	-	18
Watford	Tr	06/62	62-63	59	-	31
Brentford	Tr	10/63	63-64	47	-	21

WARD David Alan
Born: Crewe, Cheshire, England, 8 March, 1941 — LB

League Club	Source	Date Signed	Seasons Played	Apps	Subs	Gls
Swansea C	Taunton T	01/59	60-65	44	0	0

WARD Denis
Born: Burton Joyce, Nottinghamshire, England, 25 October, 1924 — G
Died: Basford, Nottinghamshire, England, April, 2006

League Club	Source	Date Signed	Seasons Played	Apps	Subs	Gls
Nottingham F	Jnr	08/47	47	1	-	0
Stockport Co	Tr	08/49	49-52	52	-	0
Bradford Park Ave	Hastings U	08/55	55-57	50	-	0

WARD Derek
Born: Birkenhead, Wirral, England, 17 May, 1972 — RB

League Club	Source	Date Signed	Seasons Played	Apps	Subs	Gls
Bury	Heswall	08/92	92-93	27	1	0

WARD Derrick
Born: Stoke-on-Trent, England, 23 December, 1934 — W/IF
Died: Stoke-on-Trent, England, 6 October, 2011

League Club	Source	Date Signed	Seasons Played	Apps	Subs	Gls
Stoke C	Jnr	08/52	52-60	54	-	9
Stockport Co	Tr	07/61	61-63	81	-	21

WARD Elliott Leslie
Born: Harrow, NW London, England, 19 January, 1985 — CD

League Club	Source	Date Signed	Seasons Played	Apps	Subs	Gls
West Ham U	Sch	01/02	04-05	13	2	0
Bristol Rov	L	12/04	04	0	3	0
Plymouth Arg	L	11/05	05	15	1	1
Coventry C	Tr	07/06	06-09	111	6	14
Doncaster Rov	L	02/10	09	6	0	1
Preston NE	L	03/10	09	4	0	0
Norwich C	Tr	07/10	10-11	51	0	1
Nottingham F	L	10/12	12	29	2	3
Bournemouth	Tr	06/13	13-14	22	3	0

WARD Gavin John
Born: Sutton Coldfield, West Midlands, England, 30 June, 1970 — G

League Club	Source	Date Signed	Seasons Played	Apps	Subs	Gls
Shrewsbury T	Aston Villa (YT)	09/88				
West Bromwich A	Tr	09/89				
Cardiff C	Tr	10/89	89-92	58	1	0
Leicester C	Tr	07/93	93-94	38	0	0
Bradford C	Tr	07/95	95	36	0	0
Bolton W	Tr	03/96	95-97	19	3	0
Burnley	L	08/98	98	17	0	0
Stoke C	Tr	02/99	98-01	79	0	0
Walsall	Tr	08/02	02	5	2	0
Coventry C	Tr	08/03	03	12	0	0
Barnsley	L	04/04	03	1	0	0
Preston NE	Tr	08/04	04	6	1	0
Tranmere Rov	Tr	07/06	06	36	2	1
Chester C	Tr	07/07				
Wrexham	Tr	01/08	07	22	0	0

WARD Gerald (Gerry)
Born: Stepney, E London, England, 5 October, 1936 — RH
Died: Sheffield, England, 7 January, 1994
England: Amateur-1/Youth/Schools

League Club	Source	Date Signed	Seasons Played	Apps	Subs	Gls
Arsenal	Jnr	10/53	53-62	81	-	10
Leyton Orient	Tr	07/63	63-64	44	-	2

WARD Graham William
Born: Dublin, Republic of Ireland, 25 February, 1983 — M
Republic of Ireland: U21-3/Youth

League Club	Source	Date Signed	Seasons Played	Apps	Subs	Gls
Wolverhampton W	YT	07/00				
Kidderminster Hrs	Tr	08/03	03	17	4	0
Cheltenham T	Tr	08/04	04	0	2	0

WARD Grant Anthony
Born: Lewisham, SE London, England, 5 December, 1994 — DM

League Club	Source	Date Signed	Seasons Played	Apps	Subs	Gls
Tottenham H	Sch	07/13				
Coventry C	L	03/15	14	11	0	0

WARD Henry Ronald (Ron)
Born: Walthamstow, NE London, England, 29 March, 1932 — G

League Club	Source	Date Signed	Seasons Played	Apps	Subs	Gls
Tottenham H		05/50				
Darlington	Headington U	08/56	56	26	-	0

WARD Iain Campbell
Born: Cleethorpes, North Lincolnshire, England, 13 May, 1983 — FB

League Club	Source	Date Signed	Seasons Played	Apps	Subs	Gls
Grimsby T	Jnr	11/00	01-02	10	2	0

WARD James (Jim)
Born: Glasgow, Scotland, 26 July, 1929 — CF
Died: Bournemouth, England, October, 1985

League Club	Source	Date Signed	Seasons Played	Apps	Subs	Gls
Crewe Alex (Am)	Queen's Park	08/56	56	6	-	0

W

WARD Jamie John
Born: Birmingham, England, 12 May, 1986 — F/W
Northern Ireland: 13/U21-7/Youth

League Club	Source	Date Signed	Seasons Played	Apps	Subs	Gls
Aston Villa	Sch	05/04				
Stockport Co	L	03/06	05	7	2	1
Torquay U	Tr	07/06	06	21	4	9
Chesterfield	Tr	01/07	06-08	58	9	29
Sheffield U	Tr	01/09	08-10	45	18	9
Derby Co	Tr	02/11	10-14	123	15	34

WARD Joel Edward Philip
Born: Emsworth, Hampshire, England, 29 October, 1989 — D

League Club	Source	Date Signed	Seasons Played	Apps	Subs	Gls
Portsmouth	Sch	07/08	09-11	72	17	6
Bournemouth	L	08/08	08	16	5	1
Crystal Palace	Tr	05/12	12-14	95	3	1

WARD John
Born: Mansfield, Nottinghamshire, England, 18 January, 1948 — RB

League Club	Source	Date Signed	Seasons Played	Apps	Subs	Gls
Notts Co	App	07/65	65	5	0	0

WARD John Patrick
Born: Lincoln, England, 7 April, 1951 — F

League Club	Source	Date Signed	Seasons Played	Apps	Subs	Gls
Lincoln C	Adelaide Park	03/71	70-78	223	17	91
Workington	L	09/72	72	9	2	3
Watford	Tr	07/79	79-80	22	5	6
Grimsby T	Tr	06/81	81	2	1	0
Lincoln C	Tr	03/82	81	1	0	0

WARD John Richard (Richie)
Born: Scunthorpe, North Lincolnshire, England, 16 September, 1940 — IF
England: Amateur-3

League Club	Source	Date Signed	Seasons Played	Apps	Subs	Gls
Scunthorpe U (Am)	Jnr	05/58	58	1	-	0
Northampton T (Am)	Tr	06/59	59-61	7	-	0
Millwall	Tooting & Mitcham U	07/62	62-63	13	-	3

WARD John Stuart (Stuart)
Born: Frodsham, Cheshire, England, 15 June, 1933 — W
Died: Carlisle, Cumbria, England, April, 2007

League Club	Source	Date Signed	Seasons Played	Apps	Subs	Gls
Crewe Alex (Am)		12/56	56	5	-	1

WARD Joseph (Joe)
Born: Glasgow, Scotland, 25 November, 1954 — F

League Club	Source	Date Signed	Seasons Played	Apps	Subs	Gls
Aston Villa	Clyde	12/78	78-79	2	1	0

WARD Lawrence Whelan (Polly)
Born: Halifax, West Yorkshire, England, 15 June, 1929 — IF

League Club	Source	Date Signed	Seasons Played	Apps	Subs	Gls
Bradford C	Ovenden	10/48	48-53	149	-	37
Bradford Park Ave	King's Lynn	07/55	55-58	108	-	31

WARD Mark Steven
Born: Sheffield, England, 27 January, 1982 — F
England: Schools

League Club	Source	Date Signed	Seasons Played	Apps	Subs	Gls
Sheffield U	Sheffield Colleges	07/00	00-01	0	2	0

WARD Mark William
Born: Huyton, Merseyside, England, 10 October, 1962 — W
England: Semi Pro-1

League Club	Source	Date Signed	Seasons Played	Apps	Subs	Gls
Everton	App	09/80				
Oldham Ath	Northwich Victoria	07/83	83-84	84	0	12
West Ham U	Tr	08/85	85-89	163	2	12
Manchester C	Tr	12/89	89-90	55	0	14
Everton	Tr	08/91	91-93	82	1	6
Birmingham C	Tr	03/94	93-95	63	0	7
Huddersfield T	Tr	03/96	95	7	1	0
Wigan Ath	Tr	09/96	96	5	0	0

WARD Michael Henry (Mike)
Born: Nottingham, England, 30 August, 1920 — IF
Died: Nottingham, England, October, 2004

League Club	Source	Date Signed	Seasons Played	Apps	Subs	Gls
Stockport Co		10/48	48	1	-	0

WARD Mitchum David (Mitch)
Born: Sheffield, England, 19 June, 1971 — M/RB

League Club	Source	Date Signed	Seasons Played	Apps	Subs	Gls
Sheffield U	YT	07/89	90-97	135	19	11
Crewe Alex	L	11/90	90	4	0	1
Everton	Tr	11/97	97-99	18	6	0
Barnsley	Tr	07/00	00-02	68	9	0
York C	Tr	08/03	03	27	4	0

WARD Nicholas (Nick)
Born: Perth, Australia, 24 March, 1985 — M
Australia: U23-16/Youth

League Club	Source	Date Signed	Seasons Played	Apps	Subs	Gls
Queens Park Rgrs	Perth Glory (AUS)	07/06	06-07	11	9	1
Brighton & HA	L	01/07	06	6	2	1

WARD Nicholas John (Nick)
Born: Wrexham, Wales, 30 November, 1977 — F

League Club	Source	Date Signed	Seasons Played	Apps	Subs	Gls
Shrewsbury T	YT	07/96	96-97	8	12	1

WARD Noel Gerard
Born: Strabane, Tyrone, Northern Ireland, 8 December, 1952 — CD

League Club	Source	Date Signed	Seasons Played	Apps	Subs	Gls
Wigan Ath	Aberdeen	07/76	78-79	47	1	4

WARD Patrick (Pat)
Born: Dumbarton, Dunbartonshire, Scotland, 28 December, 1926 — LH
Died: Dumbarton, Dunbartonshire, Scotland, 15 March, 2003

League Club	Source	Date Signed	Seasons Played	Apps	Subs	Gls
Leicester C	Hibernian	09/55	55-57	57	-	0
Crewe Alex	Tr	06/58	58	31	-	1

WARD Paul Terence
Born: Fishburn, County Durham, England, 15 September, 1963 — M/FB

League Club	Source	Date Signed	Seasons Played	Apps	Subs	Gls
Chelsea	App	08/81				
Middlesbrough	Tr	09/82	82-85	69	7	1
Darlington	Tr	09/85	85-87	124	0	9
Leyton Orient	Tr	07/88	88-89	30	1	1
Scunthorpe U	Tr	10/89	89-90	53	2	6
Lincoln C	Tr	03/91	90-92	38	1	0

WARD Peter
Born: Rotherham, South Yorkshire, England, 20 October, 1954 — LB/M

League Club	Source	Date Signed	Seasons Played	Apps	Subs	Gls
Sheffield U	App	10/72				
Workington	Tr	07/74	74-75	39	4	2

WARD Peter
Born: Chester-le-Street, County Durham, England, 15 October, 1964 — M

League Club	Source	Date Signed	Seasons Played	Apps	Subs	Gls
Huddersfield T	Chester-le-Street T	01/87	86-88	24	13	2
Rochdale	Tr	07/89	89-90	83	1	10
Stockport Co	Tr	06/91	91-94	140	2	10
Wrexham	Tr	07/95	95-98	117	3	14

WARD Peter David
Born: Derby, England, 27 July, 1955 — F
England: 1/B-2/U21-2

League Club	Source	Date Signed	Seasons Played	Apps	Subs	Gls
Brighton & HA	Burton A	05/75	75-80	172	6	79
Nottingham F	Tr	10/80	80-82	28	5	7
Brighton & HA	L	10/82	82	16	0	2

WARD Ralph Arthur
Born: Oadby, Leicestershire, England, 5 February, 1911 — RB
Died: Oadby, Leicestershire, England, March, 1983
England: Schools

League Club	Source	Date Signed	Seasons Played	Apps	Subs	Gls
Bradford Park Ave	Hinckley U	11/29	30-35	129	-	0
Tottenham H	Tr	03/36	35-38	115	-	10
Crewe Alex	Tr	08/46	46-48	91	-	7

WARD Robert (Bobby)
Born: Glasgow, Scotland, 21 October, 1958 — M

League Club	Source	Date Signed	Seasons Played	Apps	Subs	Gls
Newport Co	Glasgow Celtic	01/80	79-80	2	1	0

WARD Robert Andrew (Bob)
Born: West Bromwich, West Midlands, England, 4 August, 1953 — G

League Club	Source	Date Signed	Seasons Played	Apps	Subs	Gls
West Bromwich A	Imperial Star	03/73	74-76	9	0	0
Northampton T	L	02/77	76	8	0	0
Blackpool	Tr	09/77	77-78	41	0	0
Wigan Ath	Tr	07/79	80-81	46	0	0

WARD Ronald (Ron)
Born: Altrincham, Greater Manchester, England, 17 October, 1932 — IF
Died: Manchester, England, 9 February, 1998

League Club	Source	Date Signed	Seasons Played	Apps	Subs	Gls
Stockport Co		03/54	53-55	17	-	3

WARD Ronald (Ron)
Born: Killamarsh, Derbyshire, England, 10 February, 1935 — G
Died: Chesterfield, Derbyshire, England, December, 2010
England: Schools

League Club	Source	Date Signed	Seasons Played	Apps	Subs	Gls
Chesterfield	Jnr	02/52	51-52	8	-	0

WARD Scott James
Born: Harrow, NW London, England, 5 October, 1981 — G

League Club	Source	Date Signed	Seasons Played	Apps	Subs	Gls
Luton T	YT	10/98	00	0	1	0

WARD Stephen (Steve)
Born: Chapeltown, South Yorkshire, England, 27 December, 1960 — RB

League Club	Source	Date Signed	Seasons Played	Apps	Subs	Gls
Lincoln C	App	12/78	79	2	0	0

WARD Stephen Charles (Steve)
Born: Derby, England, 21 July, 1959 — W/LB

League Club	Source	Date Signed	Seasons Played	Apps	Subs	Gls
Brighton & HA	App	10/76				
Northampton T	Tr	08/79	79	13	2	2
Halifax T	Tr	06/80	80-85	233	13	17

WARD Stephen Robert
Born: Dublin, Republic of Ireland, 20 August, 1985 — LB
Republic of Ireland: 29/B-1/U21-14/Youth

League Club	Source	Date Signed	Seasons Played	Apps	Subs	Gls
Wolverhampton W	Bohemians (ROI)	01/07	06-12	192	30	9
Brighton & HA	L	08/13	13	44	0	4
Burnley	Tr	08/14	14	7	2	0

League Club	Source	Date Signed	Seasons Played	Career Record Apps	Subs	Gls
WARD Sydney (Syd)						
Born: Dewsbury, West Yorkshire, England, 26 November, 1923						G
Bradford C	Upton Colliery	09/47	47	2	-	0
WARD Terence (Terry)						
Born: Stoke-on-Trent, England, 10 December, 1939						RB
Died: Stoke-on-Trent, England, 30 December, 1968						
Stoke C	Jnr	03/58	59-62	43	-	0
WARD Thomas Alfred (Tommy)						
Born: Wolsingham, County Durham, England, 6 August, 1917						F/RH
Died: Scunthorpe, North Lincolnshire, England, November, 1992						
Sheffield Wed	Crook T	03/37	46-47	35	-	19
Darlington	Tr	08/48	48-53	119	-	32
WARD Timothy Victor (Tim)						
Born: Cheltenham, Gloucestershire, England, 17 October, 1918						RH
Died: 28 January, 1993						
England: 2						
Derby Co	Cheltenham T	04/37	37-50	238	-	4
Barnsley	Tr	03/51	50-52	33	-	0
WARD Warren						
Born: Plympton, Devon, England, 25 May, 1962						F
York C	Guiseley	03/85	84	4	0	3
Lincoln C	Tr	07/85	85	15	6	8
Exeter C	L	02/86	85	14	0	3
WARD Wayne Walter						
Born: Colchester, Essex, England, 28 April, 1964						LB
Colchester U	App	05/82	81-82	17	2	0
WARD William (Billy)						
Born: Chester-le-Street, County Durham, England, 30 June, 1949						W
Hartlepool U (Am)	Spennymoor U	01/72	71-72	8	0	1
Hartlepool U	Shildon	01/73	72-74	79	8	9
WARD-PROWSE James Michael Edward						
Born: Portsmouth, England, 1 November, 1994						DM
England: U21-15/Youth						
Southampton	Sch	11/11	12-14	36	38	1
WARDEN Daniel (Danny)						
Born: Stepney, E London, England, 11 April, 1973						M
Charlton Ath	Arsenal (YT)	07/92	92	1	2	0
WARDLE Ernest (Ernie)						
Born: Stockton-on-Tees, Cleveland, England, 13 June, 1930						RB
Died: Stockton-on-Tees, Cleveland, England, March, 2003						
Middlesbrough	Billingham Synthonia	05/48				
York C	Tr	01/55	54-58	60	-	2
WARDLE Geoffrey (Geoff)						
Born: Trimdon, County Durham, England, 7 January, 1940						WH
Sunderland	Houghton Jnrs	01/58				
Lincoln C	Tr	06/61	61	1	-	0
WARDLE George						
Born: Kibblesworth, County Durham, England, 24 September, 1919						RH/W
Died: Kimblesworth, County Durham, England, November, 1991						
Middlesbrough	Durham BC	05/37	37	1	-	0
Exeter C	Tr	06/39	46	38	-	6
Cardiff C	Tr	05/47	46-48	40	-	11
Queens Park Rgrs	Tr	01/49	48-50	53	-	4
Darlington	Tr	08/51	51-53	95	-	6
WARDLE Ian Spencer						
Born: Doncaster, South Yorkshire, England, 27 March, 1970						G
England: Schools						
Barnsley	Jnr	05/88	89	9	0	0
WARDLE Robert Ian (Bob)						
Born: Halifax, West Yorkshire, England, 5 March, 1955						G
Bristol C	App	11/72				
Shrewsbury T	Tr	07/74	77-81	131	0	0
Liverpool	Tr	08/82				
Wrexham	L	09/83	83	13	0	0
WARDLE William (Billy)						
Born: Houghton-le-Spring, Tyne and Wear, England, 20 January, 1918						LW
Died: Caterham, Surrey, England, 4 March, 1989						
Southport	Houghton Main	12/36	36-37	14	-	0
Manchester C	Tr	10/37	37	6	-	0
Grimsby T	Tr	07/39	46-47	73	-	11
Blackpool	Tr	05/48	48-50	60	-	1
Birmingham C	Tr	09/51	51-52	60	-	5
Barnsley	Tr	11/53	53-54	28	-	1
WARDLEY Shane David						
Born: Ipswich, England, 26 February, 1980						M
Southend U	Cambridge C	12/00	00	0	2	0

League Club	Source	Date Signed	Seasons Played	Career Record Apps	Subs	Gls
WARDLEY Stuart James						
Born: Cambridge, England, 10 September, 1975						LM
Queens Park Rgrs	Saffron Walden T	07/99	99-01	72	15	14
Rushden & D	Tr	01/02	01-02	54	3	10
Torquay U	Tr	08/04	04	5	2	2
Leyton Orient	Tr	10/04	04	4	2	0
Cambridge U	Tr	01/05	04	1	2	0
WARDROBE Michael (Micky)						
Born: Newcastle-upon-Tyne, England, 24 March, 1962						F
Burnley	App	03/80	80	0	1	0
Stockport Co	Tr	08/81	81-82	19	8	2
WARDROBE Thomas Barrie (Barrie)						
Born: Newcastle-upon-Tyne, England, 3 July, 1963						F
Sunderland	App	04/81				
Hartlepool U	Tr	07/84	84	23	4	2
WARE Charles (Charlie)						
Born: York, England, 9 March, 1931						LW
York C	Jnr	12/48	53	9	-	0
WARE Paul David						
Born: Congleton, Cheshire, England, 7 November, 1970						M
Died: Sandbach, Cheshire, England, 17 April, 2013						
Stoke C	YT	11/88	87-93	92	23	10
Stockport Co	Tr	09/94	94-96	42	12	4
Cardiff C	L	01/97	96	5	0	0
Macclesfield T	Hednesford T	07/99	99	9	9	2
Rochdale	Tr	07/00	00-01	21	17	2
WARHURST Paul						
Born: Stockport, Greater Manchester, England, 26 September, 1969						M/D
England: U21-8						
Manchester C	YT	07/88				
Oldham Ath	Tr	10/88	88-90	60	7	2
Sheffield Wed	Tr	07/91	91-93	60	6	6
Blackburn Rov	Tr	08/93	93-96	30	27	4
Crystal Palace	Tr	07/97	97-98	27	0	4
Bolton W	Tr	11/98	98-02	81	10	0
Stoke C	L	03/03	02	4	1	1
Chesterfield	Tr	10/03	03	3	1	0
Barnsley	Tr	12/03	03	3	1	0
Carlisle U	Tr	02/04	03	0	1	0
Grimsby T	Tr	03/04	03	5	2	0
Blackpool	Tr	11/04	04	2	2	0
Wrexham	Forest Green Rov	08/05	05	6	5	1
Barnet	Tr	03/06	05-06	18	10	0
WARHURST Roy						
Born: Sheffield, England, 18 September, 1926						LH
Died: Birmingham, England, 7 January, 2014						
Sheffield U	Huddersfield T (Am)	09/44	46-49	17	-	2
Birmingham C	Tr	03/50	49-56	213	-	10
Manchester C	Tr	06/57	57-58	40	-	2
Crewe Alex	Tr	03/59	58-59	52	-	1
Oldham Ath	Tr	08/60	60	8	-	0
WARING George Philip						
Born: Kingsley, Cheshire, England, 2 December, 1994						F
Stoke C	Everton (Sch)	07/13				
Barnsley	L	01/15	14	17	2	6
WARING Thomas Allan (Allan)						
Born: Preston, Lancashire, England, 3 August, 1929						CD
Died: Crosby, Merseyside, England, 1972						
Burnley		08/48				
Halifax T	Tr	07/54	54	12	-	0
WARK John						
Born: Glasgow, Scotland, 4 August, 1957						M
Scotland: 29/U21-8/Youth						
Ipswich T	App	08/74	74-83	295	1	94
Liverpool	Tr	03/84	83-87	64	6	28
Ipswich T	Tr	01/88	87-89	87	2	23
Middlesbrough	Tr	08/90	90	31	1	2
Ipswich T	Tr	09/91	91-96	151	3	18
WARK Scott Andrew						
Born: Glasgow, Scotland, 9 June, 1987						M
Rushden & D	Sch	-	04	0	1	0
WARLOW Owain James						
Born: Pontypridd, Rhondda Cynon Taff, Wales, 3 July, 1988						LW
Wales: U21-2						
Lincoln C	Sch	07/06	06-07	6	16	0
WARMAN Philip Roy (Phil)						
Born: Bromley, SE London, England, 18 December, 1950						LB

England: Youth

League Club	Source	Date Signed	Seasons Played	Apps	Subs	Gls
Charlton Ath	Jnr	03/68	69-80	313	3	19
Millwall	Tr	08/81	81	27	0	1

WARMINGTON Peter John
Born: Wythall, Worcestershire, England, 8 April, 1934 CF

League Club	Source	Date Signed	Seasons Played	Apps	Subs	Gls
Birmingham C	Redditch Jnrs	12/51	54-56	8	-	3

WARN Keith Donald
Born: Watford, Hertfordshire, England, 20 March, 1941 G
Died: Market Rasen, Lincolnshire, England, 6 March, 2012

League Club	Source	Date Signed	Seasons Played	Apps	Subs	Gls
Watford	Croxley BC	04/59	59	3	-	0

WARNE Paul
Born: Norwich, England, 8 May, 1973 M

League Club	Source	Date Signed	Seasons Played	Apps	Subs	Gls
Wigan Ath	Wroxham	07/97	97-98	11	25	3
Rotherham U	Tr	01/99	98-04	173	57	28
Mansfield T	L	11/04	04	7	0	1
Oldham Ath	Tr	07/05	05-06	80	6	18
Yeovil T	Tr	07/07	07-08	64	13	5
Rotherham U	Tr	08/09	09-11	11	17	3

WARNE Raymond John (Ray)
Born: Ipswich, England, 16 June, 1929 CF
Died: Ipswich, England, 21 May, 2009

League Club	Source	Date Signed	Seasons Played	Apps	Subs	Gls
Ipswich T	Leiston	10/50	50-51	30	-	11

WARNE Stephen James
Born: Sutton-in-Ashfield, Nottinghamshire, England, 27 February, 1984 M

League Club	Source	Date Signed	Seasons Played	Apps	Subs	Gls
Chesterfield	Sch	07/03	02	2	1	0

WARNER Anthony Randolph (Tony)
Born: Liverpool, England, 11 May, 1974 G
Trinidad & Tobago: 2

League Club	Source	Date Signed	Seasons Played	Apps	Subs	Gls
Liverpool	Jnr	01/94				
Swindon T	L	11/97	97	2	0	0
Millwall	Tr	07/99	99-03	200	0	0
Cardiff C	Tr	07/04	04	26	0	0
Fulham	Tr	08/05	05-07	19	2	0
Leeds U	L	08/06	06	13	0	0
Norwich C	L	03/07	06	13	0	0
Barnsley	L	01/08	07	3	0	0
Hull C	Tr	07/08				
Leicester C	L	03/09	08	4	0	0
Charlton Ath	Tr	03/10				
Scunthorpe U	Leeds U (NC)	10/10	10	2	0	0
Tranmere Rov	Tr	01/11	10	25	0	0

WARNER Dennis Peter Alfred
Born: Rotherham, South Yorkshire, England, 6 December, 1930 LB

League Club	Source	Date Signed	Seasons Played	Apps	Subs	Gls
Rotherham U	Spurley Hey OB	03/50	52-56	64	-	0
Chesterfield	Tr	05/57	57	8	-	0

WARNER John (Jack)
Born: Tonyrefail, Rhondda Cynon Taff, Wales, 21 September, 1911 RH
Died: Tonypandy, Rhondda Cynon Taff, Wales, 4 November, 1980
Wales: 2/War-1

League Club	Source	Date Signed	Seasons Played	Apps	Subs	Gls
Swansea C	Aberaman Ath	01/34	33-37	135	-	9
Manchester U	Tr	06/38	38-49	102	-	1
Oldham Ath	Tr	06/51	51	34	-	2
Rochdale	Tr	07/52	52	21	-	0

WARNER John
Born: Ashington, Northumberland, England, 6 May, 1940 W

League Club	Source	Date Signed	Seasons Played	Apps	Subs	Gls
Luton T		10/59	59	1	-	0

WARNER John
Born: Paddington, Central London, England, 20 November, 1961 F

League Club	Source	Date Signed	Seasons Played	Apps	Subs	Gls
Colchester U	Burnham Ramblers	02/89	88	7	8	3
Colchester U	Heybridge Swifts	12/89	89	1	1	0

WARNER Leslie Horace (Les)
Born: Birmingham, England, 19 December, 1918 RW
Died: Warwick, England, 12 January, 1982

League Club	Source	Date Signed	Seasons Played	Apps	Subs	Gls
Coventry C	Jack Moulds Ath	07/37	37-53	199	-	19

WARNER Michael James
Born: Harrogate, North Yorkshire, England, 17 January, 1974 M/RB

League Club	Source	Date Signed	Seasons Played	Apps	Subs	Gls
Northampton T	Tamworth	07/95	96-98	9	19	0

WARNER Philip (Phil)
Born: Southampton, England, 2 February, 1979 LB

League Club	Source	Date Signed	Seasons Played	Apps	Subs	Gls
Southampton	YT	05/97	97-98	5	1	0
Brentford	L	07/99	99	1	13	0
Cambridge U	Tr	06/01	01-02	18	2	0

WARNER Reginald Owen (Reg)
Born: Anstey, Leicestershire, England, 1 March, 1931 LH/CH
Died: Leicester, England, September, 1996
England: Youth

League Club	Source	Date Signed	Seasons Played	Apps	Subs	Gls
Leicester C	Anstey Nomads	04/49	52-53	7	-	0
Mansfield T	Tr	03/55	54-56	33	-	0

WARNER Robert Mark (Rob)
Born: Stratford-on-Avon, Warwickshire, England, 20 April, 1977 RB/M

League Club	Source	Date Signed	Seasons Played	Apps	Subs	Gls
Hereford U	YT	01/95	94-96	31	6	0

WARNER Scott John
Born: Rochdale, Greater Manchester, England, 3 December, 1983 RM

League Club	Source	Date Signed	Seasons Played	Apps	Subs	Gls
Rochdale	Sch	07/03	02-05	57	16	2

WARNER Vance
Born: Leeds, England, 3 September, 1974 CD
England: Youth

League Club	Source	Date Signed	Seasons Played	Apps	Subs	Gls
Nottingham F	YT	09/91	93-96	4	1	0
Grimsby T	L	02/96	95	3	0	0
Rotherham U	Tr	08/97	97-99	60	2	1

WARNES George
Born: Worksop, Nottinghamshire, England, 4 December, 1925 G
Died: Rotherham, South Yorkshire, England, April, 2004

League Club	Source	Date Signed	Seasons Played	Apps	Subs	Gls
Rotherham U	Dinnington Colliery	12/44	46-49	98	-	0
Aldershot	Tr	06/50	50-51	32	-	0

WARNOCK Neil
Born: Sheffield, England, 1 December, 1948 W

League Club	Source	Date Signed	Seasons Played	Apps	Subs	Gls
Chesterfield	Sheffield FC	03/68	67-68	20	4	2
Rotherham U	Tr	06/69	69-70	46	6	5
Hartlepool U	Tr	07/71	71-72	58	2	5
Scunthorpe U	Tr	02/72	72-74	63	9	7
Aldershot	Tr	03/75	74-76	35	2	6
Barnsley	Tr	10/76	76-77	53	4	10
York C	Tr	05/78	78	1	3	0
Crewe Alex	Tr	12/78	78	20	1	1

WARNOCK Stephen
Born: Ormskirk, Lancashire, England, 12 December, 1981 LB
England: 2/Youth/Schools

League Club	Source	Date Signed	Seasons Played	Apps	Subs	Gls
Liverpool	YT	04/99	04-06	27	13	1
Bradford C	L	09/02	02	12	0	1
Coventry C	L	07/03	03	42	2	3
Blackburn Rov	Tr	01/07	06-09	88	0	5
Aston Villa	Tr	08/09	09-11	83	1	2
Bolton W	L	09/12	12	15	0	0
Leeds U	Tr	01/13	12-14	64	0	3
Derby Co	Tr	01/15	14	6	1	0

WARREN Christer Simon
Born: Weymouth, Dorset, England, 10 October, 1974 LB/M

League Club	Source	Date Signed	Seasons Played	Apps	Subs	Gls
Southampton	Cheltenham T	03/95	95-96	1	7	0
Brighton & HA	L	10/96	96	3	0	0
Fulham	L	03/97	96	8	3	1
Bournemouth	Tr	10/97	97-99	94	9	13
Queens Park Rgrs	Tr	06/00	00-01	24	12	0
Bristol Rov	Tr	09/02	02	0	2	0

WARREN David John Paul
Born: Cork, Republic of Ireland, 28 February, 1981 RM
Republic of Ireland: Youth

League Club	Source	Date Signed	Seasons Played	Apps	Subs	Gls
Wrexham	Mayfield U (ROI)	08/99	99-01	6	0	0

WARREN Derek Bernard
Born: Colyton, Devon, England, 23 May, 1923 RB
Died: Seaton, Devon, England, 3 October, 2010

League Club	Source	Date Signed	Seasons Played	Apps	Subs	Gls
Exeter C	Axminster	01/48	48-51	55	-	0

WARREN Freddie Robert
Born: Barking, E London, England, 2 November, 1992 M

League Club	Source	Date Signed	Seasons Played	Apps	Subs	Gls
Charlton Ath	Sch	07/11				
Barnet	Tr	07/12	12	1	1	0

WARREN Lee Anthony
Born: Manchester, England, 28 February, 1969 D/M

League Club	Source	Date Signed	Seasons Played	Apps	Subs	Gls
Leeds U	YT	08/87				
Rochdale	Tr	10/87	87	31	0	1
Hull C	Tr	08/88	88-93	141	12	1
Lincoln C	L	09/90	90	2	1	1
Doncaster Rov	Tr	07/94	94-97	115	10	3

WARREN Mark Wayne
Born: Clapton, NE London, England, 12 November, 1974 D/M
England: Youth

League Club	Source	Date Signed	Seasons Played	Apps	Subs	Gls
Leyton Orient	YT	07/92	91-98	134	18	5
Oxford U	L	12/98	98	4	0	0
Notts Co	Tr	01/99	98-01	76	8	1
Colchester U	Tr	08/02	02	20	0	0
Southend U	Tr	06/03	03	27	5	2

WARREN Raymond Richard (Ray)
Born: Bristol, England, 23 June, 1918 CD

League Club	Source	Date Signed	Seasons Played	Career Record Apps	Subs	Gls
Died: Bristol, England, 13 March, 1988						
Bristol Rov	Parson Street OB	11/35	35-55	450	-	28

WARREN Robert Edward (Bob)
Born: Devonport, Devon, England, 8 January, 1927 — CD
Died: Plymouth, England, November, 2002

League Club	Source	Date Signed	Seasons Played	Apps	Subs	Gls
Plymouth Arg	Plymouth U	02/46	46	3	-	0
Chelsea	Tr	07/48	48	1	-	0
Torquay U	Tr	08/51	51	5	-	1

WARRENDER Daniel John (Danny)
Born: Manchester, England, 28 April, 1986 — RB

League Club	Source	Date Signed	Seasons Played	Apps	Subs	Gls
Manchester C	Sch	07/04				
Blackpool	Tr	10/05	05	13	2	0

WARRENDER Robert (Bobby)
Born: Leven, Fife, Scotland, 13 February, 1929 — CH
Died: Leven, Fife, Scotland, 19 September, 2003

League Club	Source	Date Signed	Seasons Played	Apps	Subs	Gls
York C	East Fife	05/52	52-53	24	-	5

WARRILOW Thomas (Tommy)
Born: Plumstead, SE London, England, 26 July, 1964 — CD

League Club	Source	Date Signed	Seasons Played	Apps	Subs	Gls
Torquay U	Gravesend & Northfleet	03/87	86	2	0	0

WARRINER Stephen William (Steve)
Born: Liverpool, England, 18 December, 1958 — FB/M

League Club	Source	Date Signed	Seasons Played	Apps	Subs	Gls
Liverpool	App	12/76				
Newport Co	Tr	07/78	78-80	28	8	2
Rochdale	Tr	08/81	81-82	11	1	1
Tranmere Rov	Tr	02/83	82	5	4	0

WARRINGTON Andrew Clifford (Andy)
Born: Sheffield, England, 10 June, 1976 — G

League Club	Source	Date Signed	Seasons Played	Apps	Subs	Gls
York C	YT	06/94	95-98	61	0	0
Doncaster Rov	Tr	06/99	03-05	89	0	0
Bury	Tr	11/06	06	20	0	0
Rotherham U	Tr	06/07	07-12	202	0	0

WARRINGTON Tony
Born: Ecclesfield, South Yorkshire, England, 12 February, 1934 — G

League Club	Source	Date Signed	Seasons Played	Apps	Subs	Gls
Lincoln C	Thorncliffe Jnrs	03/54	53-55	2	-	0

WARSAP William John Benjamin (Johnny)
Born: Leytonstone, NE London, England, 18 May, 1921 — W
Died: Maidstone, Kent, England, May, 1992

League Club	Source	Date Signed	Seasons Played	Apps	Subs	Gls
Gillingham	Royal Berkshire Reg't	11/45	50-52	9	-	1

WARZYCHA Robert
Born: Siemkowice, Poland, 20 June, 1963 — RW
Poland: 47

League Club	Source	Date Signed	Seasons Played	Apps	Subs	Gls
Everton	Gornik Zabrze (POL)	03/91	90-93	51	21	6

WASHINGTON Conor James
Born: Chatham, Kent, England, 18 May, 1992 — F

League Club	Source	Date Signed	Seasons Played	Apps	Subs	Gls
Newport Co	St Ives T	10/12	13	16	8	4
Peterborough U	Tr	01/14	13-14	43	14	17

WASILEWSKI Marcin
Born: Krakow, Poland, 9 June, 1980 — RB
Poland: 60

League Club	Source	Date Signed	Seasons Played	Apps	Subs	Gls
Leicester C	Anderlecht (BEL)	09/13	13-14	48	8	1

WASILEWSKI Zdzislaw (Adam)
Born: Poland, 8 April, 1925 — CF
Died: Salford, England, 22 July, 1956

League Club	Source	Date Signed	Seasons Played	Apps	Subs	Gls
Rochdale	Altrincham	07/53	53	4	-	1

WASIU Akanni Sunday (Sunday)
Born: Nigeria, 18 March, 1984 — F

League Club	Source	Date Signed	Seasons Played	Apps	Subs	Gls
Colchester U	St Albans C	08/08	08	3	12	2
Luton T	L	01/09	08	2	3	1

WASS William
Born: Ryhope, Tyne and Wear, England, 16 November, 1922 — RW
Died: Sunderland, England, October, 2009

League Club	Source	Date Signed	Seasons Played	Apps	Subs	Gls
Middlesbrough	Murton CW	02/45				
Bradford C	Tr	07/46	46	7	-	1

WASSALL Darren Paul James
Born: Birmingham, England, 27 June, 1968 — CD

League Club	Source	Date Signed	Seasons Played	Apps	Subs	Gls
Nottingham F	App	06/86	87-91	17	10	0
Hereford U	L	10/87	87	5	0	0
Bury	L	03/89	88	7	0	1
Derby Co	Tr	06/92	92-95	90	8	0
Manchester C	L	09/96	96	14	1	0
Birmingham C	Tr	03/97	96-98	22	3	0

WASSALL John Charles
Born: Birmingham, England, 9 June, 1933 — D
Died: Rowington, Warwickshire, England, 23 December, 1987

League Club	Source	Date Signed	Seasons Played	Apps	Subs	Gls
Coventry C	Jnr	05/51	55-56	17	-	0
Southport	Tr	08/57	57	4	-	0

WASSALL John Victor (Jackie)
Born: Shrewsbury, Shropshire, England, 11 February, 1917 — IF
Died: Shrewsbury, Shropshire, England, April, 1994

League Club	Source	Date Signed	Seasons Played	Apps	Subs	Gls
Manchester U	Wellington T	02/35	35-38	45	-	6
Stockport Co	Tr	10/46	46-47	19	-	2

WASSELL Kim
Born: Wolverhampton, England, 9 June, 1957 — LW

League Club	Source	Date Signed	Seasons Played	Apps	Subs	Gls
West Bromwich A	App	06/75				
Northampton T	Tr	09/77	77-78	13	7	0
Hull C	Doveton SC (AUS)	08/83	83	1	0	0
Swansea C	Tr	09/84	84	1	1	0
Wolverhampton W	VPS Vaasa (FIN)	10/85	85	2	0	0
Shrewsbury T	Gresley Rov	11/89	89	0	2	0

WASSMER Charlie
Born: Hammersmith, W London, England, 21 March, 1991 — CD

League Club	Source	Date Signed	Seasons Played	Apps	Subs	Gls
Crawley T	Hayes & Yeading U	03/11	11	12	1	2
Dagenham & Red	L	03/12	11	0	1	0

WATERFALL Luke Matthew
Born: Sheffield, England, 30 July, 1990 — CD

League Club	Source	Date Signed	Seasons Played	Apps	Subs	Gls
Tranmere Rov	Barnsley (Sch)	07/08				
Scunthorpe U	Gainsborough Trinity	07/13	13	2	7	1
Mansfield T	L	11/14	14	5	0	0

WATERHOUSE Kenneth (Ken)
Born: Ormskirk, Lancashire, England, 23 January, 1930 — LH

League Club	Source	Date Signed	Seasons Played	Apps	Subs	Gls
Preston NE	Burscough	12/48	53-56	20	-	5
Rotherham U	Tr	05/58	58-62	123	-	12
Bristol C	Tr	04/63	62-63	16	-	1
Darlington	Tr	08/64	64	1	-	0

WATERMAN David Graham (Dave)
Born: Guernsey, Channel Islands, 16 May, 1977 — D
Northern Ireland: U21-14

League Club	Source	Date Signed	Seasons Played	Apps	Subs	Gls
Portsmouth	YT	07/95	96-01	60	20	0
Oxford U	Tr	03/02	01-03	37	10	1

WATERMAN Derek James
Born: Guildford, Surrey, England, 12 April, 1939 — LH

League Club	Source	Date Signed	Seasons Played	Apps	Subs	Gls
Exeter C	Guildford C	06/57	57	4	-	0

WATERS Billy Henry Penna
Born: Epsom, Surrey, England, 15 October, 1994 — M

League Club	Source	Date Signed	Seasons Played	Apps	Subs	Gls
Crewe Alex	Sch	07/13	13-14	12	13	2

WATERS Graham John
Born: St Austell, Cornwall, England, 5 November, 1971 — FB

League Club	Source	Date Signed	Seasons Played	Apps	Subs	Gls
Oxford U	YT	05/90				
Exeter C	Tr	07/91	91	1	1	0

WATERS Joseph John Wary (Joe)
Born: Limerick, Republic of Ireland, 20 September, 1953 — M
Republic of Ireland: 2

League Club	Source	Date Signed	Seasons Played	Apps	Subs	Gls
Leicester C	App	10/70	73-74	11	2	1
Grimsby T	Tr	01/76	75-83	356	1	65

WATERS Patrick Mary (Paddy)
Born: Dublin, Republic of Ireland, 31 January, 1922 — CH
Died: Carlisle, Cumbria, England, 2 March, 2004
Northern Ireland: War-1

League Club	Source	Date Signed	Seasons Played	Apps	Subs	Gls
Preston NE	Glentoran	06/47	47-49	64	-	0
Carlisle U	Tr	12/50	50-57	252	-	0

WATERS Richard
Born: Gateshead, Tyne and Wear, England, 18 May, 1945 — G

League Club	Source	Date Signed	Seasons Played	Apps	Subs	Gls
Darlington (Am)	Blyth Spartans	03/65	64	2	-	0

WATERS Samuel (Sam)
Born: Croydon, S London, England, 30 May, 1917 — LW
Died: Cumbernauld, Lanarkshire, Scotland, 4 May, 1975

League Club	Source	Date Signed	Seasons Played	Apps	Subs	Gls
Halifax T	Third Lanark	07/46	46	25	-	9

WATERS William Anthony (Billy)
Born: Swansea, Wales, 19 September, 1931 — G

League Club	Source	Date Signed	Seasons Played	Apps	Subs	Gls
Blackpool	Hillsbro U	11/50				
Stoke C	Tr	09/52				
Southend U	Army	11/53				
Swansea C	Tr	08/54				
Wrexham	Tr	06/55	55-59	99	-	0
Millwall	Tr	07/60	60	5	-	0

WATFORD Albert
Born: Chesterfield, Derbyshire, England, 12 February, 1917 — RB
Died: Chesterfield, Derbyshire, England, December, 1982

League Club	Source	Date Signed	Seasons Played	Apps	Subs	Gls
Chester C (Am)	Mosborough	08/38	38	1	-	0
Chesterfield	Eckington Colliery	02/44				
Lincoln C	Tr	09/46	46	14	-	0

League Club	Source	Date Signed	Seasons Played	Career Record Apps	Subs	Gls

WATKIN Alan James
Born: Felling, Tyne and Wear, England, 16 May, 1940 — W

League Club	Source	Date Signed	Seasons Played	Apps	Subs	Gls
Gateshead (Am)		08/59	59	3	-	0

WATKIN Cyril
Born: Stoke-on-Trent, England, 21 July, 1926 — RB
Died: Stoke-on-Trent, England, 3 July, 2007

League Club	Source	Date Signed	Seasons Played	Apps	Subs	Gls
Stoke C	Port Vale (Am)	09/44	48-51	86	-	0
Bristol C	Tr	07/52	52	3	-	0

WATKIN George
Born: Chopwell, Tyne and Wear, England, 14 April, 1944 — CF

League Club	Source	Date Signed	Seasons Played	Apps	Subs	Gls
Newcastle U	App	04/62	62	1	-	0
Chesterfield	King's Lynn	07/64	64	7	-	1

WATKIN Stephen (Steve)
Born: Wrexham, Wales, 16 June, 1971 — F
Wales: B-2/Schools

League Club	Source	Date Signed	Seasons Played	Apps	Subs	Gls
Wrexham	Jnr	07/89	90-97	167	33	55
Swansea C	Tr	09/97	97-02	167	39	44

WATKIN Thomas William Steel (William)
Born: Grimsby, North Lincolnshire, England, 21 September, 1932 — LW/IF
Died: Grimsby, North Lincolnshire, England, 15 February, 2001
England: Schools

League Club	Source	Date Signed	Seasons Played	Apps	Subs	Gls
Grimsby T	Jnr	10/49				
Gateshead	Tr	12/52	52-53	39	-	14
Middlesbrough	Tr	03/54	53-54	11	-	2
Mansfield T	Tr	06/55	55	25	-	4

WATKINS Albert John (Alan)
Born: Usk, Monmouthshire, Wales, 21 April, 1922 — WH
Died: Kidderminster, Worcestershire, England, 3 August, 2011

League Club	Source	Date Signed	Seasons Played	Apps	Subs	Gls
Plymouth Arg	Royal Navy	12/45	46	4	-	1
Cardiff C	Tr	07/48				

WATKINS Charles (Charlie)
Born: Glasgow, Scotland, 14 January, 1921 — WH/IF
Died: Hitchin, Hertfordshire, England, 22 February, 1998

League Club	Source	Date Signed	Seasons Played	Apps	Subs	Gls
Luton T	Glasgow Rangers	09/48	48-54	218	-	16

WATKINS Dale Allan
Born: Peterborough, England, 4 November, 1971 — F
England: Semi Pro-5

League Club	Source	Date Signed	Seasons Played	Apps	Subs	Gls
Peterborough U	Sheffield U (YT)	08/90	89-90	5	5	0
Cheltenham T	Gloucester C	07/97	99	4	5	0

WATKINS John Vincent (Johnny)
Born: Bristol, England, 9 April, 1933 — LW
England: Youth

League Club	Source	Date Signed	Seasons Played	Apps	Subs	Gls
Bristol C	Clifton St Vincent's	06/51	53-58	95	-	19
Cardiff C	Tr	06/59	59-60	65	-	17
Bristol Rov	Tr	02/61	60-61	23	-	0

WATKINS Marley Joseph
Born: Lewisham, SE London, England, 17 October, 1990 — M

League Club	Source	Date Signed	Seasons Played	Apps	Subs	Gls
Cheltenham T	Sch	03/09	08-10	8	18	1

WATKINS Oliver George Arthur (Ollie)
Born: Newton Abbot, Devon, England, 30 December, 1995 — F

League Club	Source	Date Signed	Seasons Played	Apps	Subs	Gls
Exeter C	Sch	07/14	13-14	0	3	0

WATKINS Philip John (Phil)
Born: Caerphilly, Wales, 2 January, 1945 — WH

League Club	Source	Date Signed	Seasons Played	Apps	Subs	Gls
Cardiff C	Jnr	09/62	63	1	-	0

WATKINS Randall Burnell (Barry)
Born: Bedlinog, Merthyr Tydfil, Wales, 30 November, 1921 — FB
Died: Bristol, England, 20 June, 2004

League Club	Source	Date Signed	Seasons Played	Apps	Subs	Gls
Bristol Rov	BAC, Filton	10/45	46-54	116	-	7

WATKINS Robert Stephen (Wally)
Born: Bristol, England, 20 December, 1946 — LW

League Club	Source	Date Signed	Seasons Played	Apps	Subs	Gls
Bristol Rov	Bristol C (Am)	07/65	65	1	0	0

WATKINSON Russell (Russ)
Born: Epsom, Surrey, England, 3 December, 1977 — W

League Club	Source	Date Signed	Seasons Played	Apps	Subs	Gls
Southampton	Woking	09/96	96	0	2	0

WATKINSON William Wainwright (Billy)
Born: Prescot, Merseyside, England, 16 March, 1922 — CF
Died: Knowsley, Merseyside, England, February, 2001

League Club	Source	Date Signed	Seasons Played	Apps	Subs	Gls
Liverpool	Prescot Cables	02/46	46-49	24	-	2
Accrington Stan	Tr	01/51	50-54	105	-	45
Halifax T	Tr	09/54	54-55	60	-	24

WATKISS Stuart Paul
Born: Wolverhampton, England, 8 May, 1966 — CD

League Club	Source	Date Signed	Seasons Played	Apps	Subs	Gls
Wolverhampton W	App	07/84	83	2	0	0
Crewe Alex	Gresley Rov	02/86	85	3	0	0
Walsall	Rushall Olympic	08/93	93-95	60	2	2
Hereford U	Tr	02/96	95	19	0	0
Mansfield T	Tr	07/96	96-97	40	1	1

WATLING Barry John
Born: Walthamstow, NE London, England, 16 July, 1946 — G

League Club	Source	Date Signed	Seasons Played	Apps	Subs	Gls
Leyton Orient	App	07/64				
Bristol C	Tr	07/65	67-68	2	0	0
Notts Co	Tr	07/69	69-71	65	1	0
Hartlepool U	Tr	07/72	72-75	139	0	0
Chester C	L	09/75	75	5	0	0
Rotherham U	L	12/75	75	5	0	0
Sheffield Wed	Tr	01/76	75	1	0	0

WATLING John Daniel
Born: Bristol, England, 11 May, 1925 — LW

League Club	Source	Date Signed	Seasons Played	Apps	Subs	Gls
Bristol Rov	St Andrew's BC	01/47	47-61	323	-	19

WATSON Albert
Born: Bolton-on-Dearne, South Yorkshire, England, 1 June, 1918 — LH
Died: Sunderland, England, October, 2009

League Club	Source	Date Signed	Seasons Played	Apps	Subs	Gls
Huddersfield T	Jnr	12/35	37-47	17	-	0
Oldham Ath	Tr	07/48	48-49	42	-	0

WATSON Alexander Francis (Alex)
Born: Liverpool, England, 5 April, 1968 — CD
England: Youth

League Club	Source	Date Signed	Seasons Played	Apps	Subs	Gls
Liverpool	App	05/85	87-88	3	1	0
Derby Co	L	08/90	90	5	0	0
Bournemouth	Tr	01/91	90-94	145	6	5
Gillingham	L	09/95	95	10	0	1
Torquay U	Tr	11/95	95-00	201	1	8
Exeter C	Tr	07/01	01-02	45	1	1

WATSON Andrew (Andy)
Born: Aberdeen, Scotland, 3 September, 1959 — M
Scotland: U21-4

League Club	Source	Date Signed	Seasons Played	Apps	Subs	Gls
Leeds U	Aberdeen	06/83	83-84	37	1	7

WATSON Andrew Anthony (Andy)
Born: Leeds, England, 1 April, 1967 — F

League Club	Source	Date Signed	Seasons Played	Apps	Subs	Gls
Halifax T	Harrogate T	08/88	88-89	75	8	15
Swansea C	Tr	07/90	90	9	5	1
Carlisle U	Tr	09/91	91-92	55	1	22
Blackpool	Tr	02/93	92-95	88	27	43
Walsall	Tr	09/96	96-98	57	27	15

WATSON Andrew Lyon (Andy)
Born: Huddersfield, West Yorkshire, England, 3 April, 1967 — CD

League Club	Source	Date Signed	Seasons Played	Apps	Subs	Gls
Huddersfield T	App	04/85				
Exeter C	Tr	07/86	86-87	41	1	1

WATSON Arthur
Born: South Hiendley, West Yorkshire, England, 12 July, 1913 — RB
Died: Hull, England, November, 1995

League Club	Source	Date Signed	Seasons Played	Apps	Subs	Gls
Lincoln C	Monckton CW	05/34	34-35	37	-	0
Chesterfield	Tr	06/36	36-38	10	-	0
Hull C	Tr	06/39	46	35	-	2

WATSON Benjamin (Ben)
Born: Camberwell, S London, England, 9 July, 1985 — M
England: U21-1

League Club	Source	Date Signed	Seasons Played	Apps	Subs	Gls
Crystal Palace	Sch	08/04	02-08	145	24	18
Wigan Ath	Tr	01/09	08-14	86	25	13
Queens Park Rgrs	L	09/09	09	16	0	2
West Bromwich A	L	02/10	09	6	1	1
Watford	Tr	01/15	14	19	1	0

WATSON Benjamin Charles (Ben)
Born: Shoreham-by-Sea, West Sussex, England, 6 December, 1985 — F

League Club	Source	Date Signed	Seasons Played	Apps	Subs	Gls
Exeter C	Grays Ath	03/08	08-09	4	9	2

WATSON Charles Richard (Charlie)
Born: Newark, Nottinghamshire, England, 10 March, 1949 — G

League Club	Source	Date Signed	Seasons Played	Apps	Subs	Gls
Notts Co	Southwell	02/67	67	1	0	0

WATSON David (Dave)
Born: Liverpool, England, 20 November, 1961 — CD
England: 12/U21-7

League Club	Source	Date Signed	Seasons Played	Apps	Subs	Gls
Liverpool	Jnr	05/79				
Norwich C	Tr	11/80	80-85	212	0	11
Everton	Tr	08/86	86-99	419	4	22

WATSON David Neil
Born: Barnsley, South Yorkshire, England, 10 November, 1973 — G
England: U21-5/Youth

League Club	Source	Date Signed	Seasons Played	Apps	Subs	Gls
Barnsley	YT	07/92	92-98	178	0	0

WATSON David Vernon (Dave)
Born: Stapleford, Nottinghamshire, England, 5 October, 1946 — CD

England: 65

League Club	Source	Date Signed	Seasons Played	Apps	Subs	Gls
Notts Co	Stapleford OB	01/67	66-67	24	1	1
Rotherham U	Tr	01/68	67-70	121	0	19
Sunderland	Tr	12/70	70-74	177	0	27
Manchester C	Tr	06/75	75-78	146	0	4
Southampton	Werder Bremen (GER)	10/79	79-81	73	0	7
Stoke C	Tr	01/82	81-82	59	0	5
Derby Co	Vancouver W'caps (CAN)	09/83	83	34	0	1
Notts Co	Ft Laud'ale Suns (USA)	09/84	84	23	2	1

WATSON Donald (Don)
Born: Barnsley, South Yorkshire, England, 27 August, 1932 IF

League Club	Source	Date Signed	Seasons Played	Apps	Subs	Gls
Sheffield Wed	Worsbrough Bridge	09/54	54-56	8	-	3
Lincoln C	Tr	12/56	56-57	14	-	2
Bury	Tr	11/57	57-61	172	-	65
Barnsley	Tr	01/62	61	8	-	1
Rochdale	Tr	07/62	62-63	58	-	15
Barrow	Tr	07/64	64	17	-	1

WATSON Garry
Born: Bradford, England, 7 October, 1955 LB

League Club	Source	Date Signed	Seasons Played	Apps	Subs	Gls
Bradford C	App	10/73	72-83	246	17	28
Doncaster Rov	L	10/82	82	13	0	0
Halifax T	Tr	07/84	84	21	0	0

WATSON Gary
Born: Easington, County Durham, England, 2 March, 1961 LB

League Club	Source	Date Signed	Seasons Played	Apps	Subs	Gls
Oxford U	App	11/78	78-79	24	0	0
Carlisle U	Tr	05/80	80	17	1	0

WATSON Gordon William George
Born: Sidcup, SE London, England, 20 March, 1971 F
England: U21-2

League Club	Source	Date Signed	Seasons Played	Apps	Subs	Gls
Charlton Ath	YT	04/89	89-90	20	11	7
Sheffield Wed	Tr	02/91	90-94	29	37	15
Southampton	Tr	03/95	94-96	37	15	8
Bradford C	Tr	01/97	96-98	8	13	5
Bournemouth	Tr	08/99	99	2	4	0
Hartlepool U	Portsmouth (NC)	09/01	01-02	43	6	23

WATSON Graham Sidney
Born: Doncaster, South Yorkshire, England, 3 August, 1949 M

League Club	Source	Date Signed	Seasons Played	Apps	Subs	Gls
Doncaster Rov	App	11/66	66-67	47	1	11
Rotherham U	Tr	02/68	67-68	13	0	1
Doncaster Rov	Tr	01/69	68-72	105	4	23
Cambridge U	Tr	09/72	72-78	206	3	24
Lincoln C	Tr	09/78	78-79	43	0	2
Cambridge U	Tr	03/80	79	0	1	0

WATSON Ian
Born: North Shields, Tyne and Wear, England, 5 February, 1960 G

League Club	Source	Date Signed	Seasons Played	Apps	Subs	Gls
Sunderland	App	02/78	78	1	0	0
Rochdale	L	08/79	79	33	0	0
Newport Co	Tr	10/81				

WATSON Ian Lionel
Born: Hammersmith, W London, England, 7 January, 1944 FB

League Club	Source	Date Signed	Seasons Played	Apps	Subs	Gls
Chelsea	Jnr	02/62	62-64	5	-	1
Queens Park Rgrs	Tr	07/65	65-73	196	6	1

WATSON James (Jimmy)
Born: Cowie, Stirlingshire, Scotland, 16 January, 1924 IF
Died: Dunfermline, Fife, Scotland, 11 April, 1996
Scotland: 2/SLge-1

League Club	Source	Date Signed	Seasons Played	Apps	Subs	Gls
Huddersfield T	Motherwell	06/52	52-56	140	-	29

WATSON James
Born: Birmingham, England, 3 March, 1937 LB

League Club	Source	Date Signed	Seasons Played	Apps	Subs	Gls
Walsall		05/55	55	1	-	0
Birmingham C	Tr	08/57				

WATSON John
Born: Ruabon, Wrexham, Wales, 2 May, 1942 LB
Wales: Schools

League Club	Source	Date Signed	Seasons Played	Apps	Subs	Gls
Everton	Jnr	05/59				
Chester C	Tr	08/60	60-61	25	-	0

WATSON John
Born: Dewsbury, West Yorkshire, England, 10 April, 1959 G

League Club	Source	Date Signed	Seasons Played	Apps	Subs	Gls
Huddersfield T	Jnr	03/77				
Hartlepool U	Tr	03/79	78-82	44	0	0

WATSON John Fox (Jack)
Born: Hamilton, Lanarkshire, Scotland, 31 December, 1917 CD
Died: Southend-on-Sea, England, 15 April, 1976

League Club	Source	Date Signed	Seasons Played	Apps	Subs	Gls
Bury	Douglas Water Thistle	06/36	38	6	-	0
Fulham	Tr	08/46	46-47	71	-	2
Crystal Palace	Real Madrid (SPN)	07/49	49-50	61	-	1

WATSON John Ian
Born: South Shields, Tyne and Wear, England, 14 April, 1974 W

League Club	Source	Date Signed	Seasons Played	Apps	Subs	Gls
Newcastle U	YT	04/92	90	0	1	0
Scunthorpe U	Tr	07/93	93	1	4	0

WATSON John Martin
Born: Edinburgh, Scotland, 13 February, 1959 F

League Club	Source	Date Signed	Seasons Played	Apps	Subs	Gls
Fulham	Dunfermline Ath	08/89	89	12	2	0

WATSON Kenneth (Ken)
Born: Whickham, Tyne and Wear, England, 8 September, 1934 RH

League Club	Source	Date Signed	Seasons Played	Apps	Subs	Gls
Lincoln C		05/52				
Aldershot	Tr	07/55	57-59	29	-	1

WATSON Kevin Edward
Born: Hackney, E London, England, 3 January, 1974 M

League Club	Source	Date Signed	Seasons Played	Apps	Subs	Gls
Tottenham H	YT	05/92	92	4	1	0
Brentford	L	03/94	93	2	1	0
Bristol C	L	12/94	94	1	1	0
Barnet	L	02/95	94	13	0	0
Swindon T	Tr	07/96	96-98	39	24	1
Rotherham U	Tr	07/99	99-01	109	0	7
Reading	L	11/01	01	6	0	0
Reading	Tr	03/02	01-03	40	20	2
Colchester U	Tr	07/04	04-07	132	3	3
Luton T	Tr	08/08	08	2	4	0

WATSON Liam
Born: Liverpool, England, 21 May, 1970 F
England: Semi Pro-2

League Club	Source	Date Signed	Seasons Played	Apps	Subs	Gls
Preston NE	Warrington T	03/93	92-93	7	2	3

WATSON Mark Leon
Born: Birmingham, England, 28 December, 1973 F

League Club	Source	Date Signed	Seasons Played	Apps	Subs	Gls
West Ham U	Sutton U	05/95	95	0	1	0
Leyton Orient	L	09/95	95	0	1	1
Cambridge U	L	10/95	95	1	3	1
Shrewsbury T	L	02/96	95	1	0	0
Bournemouth	Tr	05/96	96	6	9	2

WATSON Mark Stewart
Born: Vancouver, Canada, 8 September, 1970 CD
Canada: 78/U23-13

League Club	Source	Date Signed	Seasons Played	Apps	Subs	Gls
Watford	Vancouver 86ers (CAN)	11/93	93-94	18	0	0
Oxford U	Osters IF (SWE)	12/98	98-99	57	1	0
Oldham Ath	Tr	09/00	00	1	1	0

WATSON Paul Douglas
Born: Hastings, East Sussex, England, 4 January, 1975 FB

League Club	Source	Date Signed	Seasons Played	Apps	Subs	Gls
Gillingham	YT	12/92	92-95	57	5	2
Fulham	Tr	07/96	96-97	48	2	4
Brentford	Tr	12/97	97-98	37	0	0
Brighton & HA	Tr	07/99	99-04	191	6	14
Coventry C	Tr	09/05	05	1	2	0

WATSON Peter
Born: Newcastle-upon-Tyne, England, 18 March, 1935 CF

League Club	Source	Date Signed	Seasons Played	Apps	Subs	Gls
Workington	North Shields	11/62	62-64	45	-	10

WATSON Peter Frederick
Born: Stapleford, Nottinghamshire, England, 15 April, 1934 CH
Died: Brighton, England, 17 August, 2013

League Club	Source	Date Signed	Seasons Played	Apps	Subs	Gls
Nottingham F	Jnr	05/55	55-58	13	-	0
Southend U	Tr	07/59	59-65	247	0	3

WATSON Ryan James
Born: Crewe, Cheshire, England, 7 July, 1993 M

League Club	Source	Date Signed	Seasons Played	Apps	Subs	Gls
Wigan Ath	Sch	07/11				
Leicester C	Tr	08/13				
Northampton T	L	08/14	14	5	0	0

WATSON Stanley (Stan)
Born: Darlington, County Durham, England, 17 March, 1937 CH
Died: Darlington, County Durham, England, 16 January, 2014

League Club	Source	Date Signed	Seasons Played	Apps	Subs	Gls
Darlington		11/57	57-58	27	-	0

WATSON Stephen Craig (Steve)
Born: North Shields, Tyne and Wear, England, 1 April, 1974 RB/M
England: B-1/U21-12/Youth

League Club	Source	Date Signed	Seasons Played	Apps	Subs	Gls
Newcastle U	YT	04/91	90-98	179	29	12
Aston Villa	Tr	10/98	98-99	39	2	0
Everton	Tr	07/00	00-04	106	20	14
West Bromwich A	Tr	07/05	05-06	38	4	1
Sheffield Wed	Tr	02/07	06-08	46	10	5

WATSON Thomas (Tommy)
Born: Lesmahagow, Lanarkshire, Scotland, 23 August, 1943 RW

League Club	Source	Date Signed	Seasons Played	Apps	Subs	Gls
Peterborough U	Stevenage T	05/65	65-67	75	0	20
Walsall	Tr	09/67	67-69	84	2	17
Gillingham	Tr	06/70	70-71	42	7	7

WATSON Thomas Duncan
Born: Boldon, Tyne and Wear, England, 3 February, 1936 — LW
Died: South Tyneside, Tyne and Wear, England, June, 2011

League Club	Source	Date Signed	Seasons Played	Apps	Subs	Gls
West Bromwich A	Boldon CW	11/53				
Gateshead	Tr	06/57	57	21	-	5

WATSON Thomas Gordon (Gordon)
Born: Wolsingham, County Durham, England, 1 March, 1914 — LH
Died: Liverpool, England, April, 2001

League Club	Source	Date Signed	Seasons Played	Apps	Subs	Gls
Everton	Blyth Spartans	01/33	36-48	61	-	1

WATSON Thomas Robert (Tommy)
Born: Liverpool, England, 29 September, 1969 — RW

League Club	Source	Date Signed	Seasons Played	Apps	Subs	Gls
Grimsby T	YT	07/88	87-95	134	38	24
Hull C	L	10/95	95	4	0	0

WATSON Thomas Sidney (Sid)
Born: Mansfield, Nottinghamshire, England, 12 December, 1927 — LH

League Club	Source	Date Signed	Seasons Played	Apps	Subs	Gls
Mansfield T	Palterton MW	01/49	51-60	292	-	9

WATSON Trevor Peter
Born: Great Yarmouth, Norfolk, England, 26 September, 1938 — RW

League Club	Source	Date Signed	Seasons Played	Apps	Subs	Gls
Fulham	Jnr	07/56	56-63	17	-	1

WATSON Vaughan
Born: Mansfield, Nottinghamshire, England, 5 November, 1931 — CF
Died: Mansfield, Nottinghamshire, England, 10 December, 1984

League Club	Source	Date Signed	Seasons Played	Apps	Subs	Gls
Mansfield T	Mansfield West End	04/52	52-53	14	-	9
Chesterfield	Tr	05/54	54	13	-	5

WATSON William (Willie)
Born: Stevenston, Ayrshire, Scotland, 4 December, 1949 — RB

League Club	Source	Date Signed	Seasons Played	Apps	Subs	Gls
Manchester U	Jnr	12/66	70-72	11	0	0

WATSON William (Willie)
Born: Bolton-on-Dearne, South Yorkshire, England, 7 March, 1920 — RH/LW
Died: Johannesburg, South Africa, 24 April, 2004
England: 4/B-3/War-1

League Club	Source	Date Signed	Seasons Played	Apps	Subs	Gls
Huddersfield T	Jnr	10/37	38	11	-	0
Sunderland	Tr	04/46	46-53	211	-	15
Halifax T	Tr	11/54	54-55	33	-	1

WATSON William (Bill)
Born: South Hiendley, West Yorkshire, England, 29 May, 1916 — RB
Died: Northampton, England, 26 February, 1986

League Club	Source	Date Signed	Seasons Played	Apps	Subs	Gls
Lincoln C	Monckton CW	02/35	34-35	9	-	0
Chesterfield	Tr	06/36	46-47	36	-	0
Rochdale	Tr	06/48	48-53	200	-	0

WATSON William Thomas (Willie)
Born: Swansea, Wales, 11 June, 1918 — FB
Died: Swansea, Wales, 1978

League Club	Source	Date Signed	Seasons Played	Apps	Subs	Gls
Preston NE		02/46	46	15	-	0
Cardiff C	Tr	10/47	47	1	-	0

WATT Anthony Paul (Tony)
Born: Coatbridge, Lanarkshire, Scotland, 29 December, 1993 — F
Scotland: U21-9/Youth

League Club	Source	Date Signed	Seasons Played	Apps	Subs	Gls
Charlton Ath	Standard Liege (BEL)	01/15	14	16	6	5

WATT Hershel Oulio Sanchez (Sanchez)
Born: Hackney, E London, England, 14 February, 1991 — LW
England: Youth

League Club	Source	Date Signed	Seasons Played	Apps	Subs	Gls
Arsenal	Sch	07/08				
Southend U	L	02/10	09	4	0	0
Leeds U	L	03/10	09	1	5	0
Leeds U	L	08/10	10	9	13	1
Sheffield Wed	L	11/11	11	2	2	0
Crawley T	L	01/12	11	6	8	2
Colchester U	L	09/12	12	5	1	2
Colchester U	Tr	06/13	13-14	36	7	6

WATT Jerome Anthony
Born: Preston, Lancashire, England, 20 October, 1984 — W

League Club	Source	Date Signed	Seasons Played	Apps	Subs	Gls
Blackburn Rov	Sch	10/01				
Northampton T	Tr	08/06	06	2	8	0

WATT John (Johnny)
Born: Hurlford, Ayrshire, Scotland, 17 June, 1943 — RW

League Club	Source	Date Signed	Seasons Played	Apps	Subs	Gls
Blackpool	Saxone Jnrs	08/60	62	5	-	0
Stockport Co	Tr	07/63	63-64	55	-	4
Southport	Tr	03/65	64-65	17	1	2

WATT John Gibson
Born: Airdrie, Lanarkshire, Scotland, 23 November, 1954 — FB

League Club	Source	Date Signed	Seasons Played	Apps	Subs	Gls
Watford	App	11/72	71	0	1	0

WATT Michael George
Born: Aberdeen, Scotland, 27 November, 1970 — G
Scotland: B-1/U21-12/Schools

League Club	Source	Date Signed	Seasons Played	Apps	Subs	Gls
Norwich C	Aberdeen	08/98	98	7	1	0

WATT Philip Alexander (Phil)
Born: Rotherham, South Yorkshire, England, 10 January, 1988 — D

League Club	Source	Date Signed	Seasons Played	Apps	Subs	Gls
Lincoln C	Sch	07/06	07	1	0	0

WATT Steven Mair (Steve)
Born: Banff, Aberdeenshire, Scotland, 1 May, 1985 — CD
Scotland: B-1/U21-5

League Club	Source	Date Signed	Seasons Played	Apps	Subs	Gls
Chelsea	Sch	07/02	04	0	1	0
Barnsley	L	10/05	05	3	0	1
Swansea C	Tr	01/06	05-06	2	1	0

WATT William Douglas (Willie)
Born: Aberdeen, Scotland, 6 June, 1946 — LW

League Club	Source	Date Signed	Seasons Played	Apps	Subs	Gls
Preston NE	Jnr	06/63	64-65	7	1	0

WATTERS John
Born: Glasgow, Scotland, 24 September, 1913 — IF
Died: Glasgow, Scotland, 12 April, 1989

League Club	Source	Date Signed	Seasons Played	Apps	Subs	Gls
New Brighton	Ayr U	07/36	36	19	-	2
Stockport Co	Cowdenbeath	08/47	47	5	-	1

WATTLEY David Anthony
Born: Enfield, N London, England, 5 September, 1983 — RB

League Club	Source	Date Signed	Seasons Played	Apps	Subs	Gls
Queens Park Rgrs	YT	09/00				
Lincoln C	Tr	07/03	03	1	2	0

WATTON James (Jim)
Born: Wolverhampton, England, 1 November, 1936 — LB

League Club	Source	Date Signed	Seasons Played	Apps	Subs	Gls
Port Vale	De Graafschap (NED)	09/62	62	5	-	0
Doncaster Rov	Tr	07/64	64-67	121	2	0

WATTS Adam James
Born: Hackney, E London, England, 4 March, 1988 — CD
England: Youth

League Club	Source	Date Signed	Seasons Played	Apps	Subs	Gls
Fulham	Sch	02/07				
MK Dons	L	03/07	06	1	1	0
Northampton T	L	03/09	08	3	2	0
Lincoln C	Tr	10/09	09-10	58	0	1

WATTS Derek
Born: Leicester, England, 30 October, 1952 — F
England: Schools

League Club	Source	Date Signed	Seasons Played	Apps	Subs	Gls
Leicester C	App	05/70				
Northampton T	L	10/73	73	0	1	0

WATTS Grant Steven
Born: Croydon, S London, England, 5 November, 1973 — F

League Club	Source	Date Signed	Seasons Played	Apps	Subs	Gls
Crystal Palace	YT	06/92	92	2	2	0
Colchester U	L	01/94	93	8	4	2
Gillingham	Sheffield U (NC)	09/94	94	2	1	0

WATTS James Alan
Born: Cowes, Isle of Wight, England, 25 October, 1933 — CF
Died: Chatham, Kent, England, October, 2000

League Club	Source	Date Signed	Seasons Played	Apps	Subs	Gls
Gillingham (Am)	119th AA Battery	12/56	56	12	-	1

WATTS John William (Johnny)
Born: Birmingham, England, 13 April, 1931 — RH
Died: Walsall, West Midlands, England, March, 2006

League Club	Source	Date Signed	Seasons Played	Apps	Subs	Gls
Birmingham C	Saltley OB	08/51	51-62	206	-	3

WATTS Julian
Born: Sheffield, England, 17 March, 1971 — CD

League Club	Source	Date Signed	Seasons Played	Apps	Subs	Gls
Rotherham U	Frecheville CA	07/90	90-91	17	3	1
Sheffield Wed	Tr	03/92	92-95	12	4	1
Shrewsbury T	L	12/92	92	9	0	0
Leicester C	Tr	03/96	95-97	31	7	1
Crewe Alex	L	08/97	97	5	0	0
Huddersfield T	L	02/98	97	8	0	0
Bristol C	Tr	07/98	98	16	1	1
Lincoln C	L	12/98	98	2	0	0
Blackpool	L	03/99	98	9	0	0
Luton T	Tr	08/99	99-00	71	2	8

WATTS Mark Robert
Born: Welham Green, Hertfordshire, England, 24 September, 1965 — F

League Club	Source	Date Signed	Seasons Played	Apps	Subs	Gls
Luton T	App	01/83	82	1	0	0

WATTS Ryan Dale
Born: Greenford, W London, England, 18 May, 1988 — LB/M

League Club	Source	Date Signed	Seasons Played	Apps	Subs	Gls
Brentford	Sch	-	04	0	1	0

WATTS Steven (Steve)
Born: Peckham, SE London, England, 11 July, 1976 — F

League Club	Source	Date Signed	Seasons Played	Apps	Subs	Gls
Leyton Orient	Fisher Ath	10/98	98-02	69	63	29
Lincoln C	L	12/02	02	5	0	1
Shrewsbury T	Tr	03/03	02	3	4	0

WAUGH Keith
Born: Sunderland, England, 27 October, 1956 — G

League Club	Source	Date Signed	Seasons Played	Apps	Subs	Gls
Sunderland	App	07/74				
Peterborough U	Tr	07/76	76-80	195	0	0
Sheffield U	Tr	08/81	81-84	99	0	0
Cambridge U	L	11/84	84	4	0	0
Bristol C	L	12/84	84	3	0	0
Bristol C	Tr	07/85	85-88	167	0	0
Coventry C	Tr	08/89	89	1	0	0
Watford	Tr	01/91	91-92	7	0	0
WAUGH Kenneth (Ken)						
Born: Newcastle-upon-Tyne, England, 6 August, 1933						FB
Newcastle U	Film Renters	08/52	55	7	-	0
Hartlepool U	Tr	12/56	56-61	195	-	0
WAUGH Warren Anthony						
Born: Harlesden, NW London, England, 9 October, 1980						F
Exeter C	YT	07/99	98-99	0	10	0
WAUGH William Lindsay (Billy)						
Born: Edinburgh, Scotland, 27 November, 1921						LW
Died: Felixstowe, Suffolk, England, 26 March, 2009						
Luton T	Bathgate Thistle	09/44	46-49	135	-	9
Queens Park Rgrs	Tr	07/50	50-52	77	-	6
Bournemouth	Tr	07/53	53	18	-	3
WAY Darren						
Born: Plymouth, England, 21 November, 1979						M
England: Semi Pro-3						
Norwich C	YT	09/98				
Yeovil T	Tr	08/00	03-05	98	1	13
Swansea C	Tr	01/06	05-07	6	10	0
Yeovil T	L	11/07	07	7	0	1
Yeovil T	Tr	07/08	08	15	0	2
WAY Michael Andrew (Mike)						
Born: Salisbury, Wiltshire, England, 18 May, 1950						RB/M
Oxford U	Thame U	08/69	69-71	14	2	0
WAYMAN Charles (Charlie)						
Born: Bishop Auckland, County Durham, England, 16 May, 1921						CF
Died: Bishop Auckland, County Durham, England, 26 February, 2006						
Newcastle U	Spennymoor U	09/41	46-47	47	-	32
Southampton	Tr	10/47	47-49	100	-	73
Preston NE	Tr	09/50	50-54	157	-	105
Middlesbrough	Tr	09/54	54-55	55	-	31
Darlington	Tr	12/56	56-57	23	-	14
WAYMAN Franklyn (Frank)						
Born: Bishop Auckland, County Durham, England, 30 December, 1931						RW
Died: Ferryhill, County Durham, England, 7 February, 2008						
Preston NE	West Auckland T	09/53				
Chester C	Tr	08/55	55	30	-	2
Darlington	Easington CW	06/57	57	1	-	0
WDOWCZYK Dariusz						
Born: Warsaw, Poland, 25 September, 1962						CD
Poland: 53						
Reading	Glasgow Celtic	08/94	94-97	77	5	0
WEAH George						
Born: Monrovia, Liberia, 1 October, 1966						F
Liberia: 60						
Chelsea (L)	AC Milan (ITA)	01/00	99	9	2	3
Manchester C	AC Milan (ITA)	08/00	00	5	2	1
WEAKLEY Bernard						
Born: Rotherham, South Yorkshire, England, 20 December, 1932						W
Rotherham U		08/55	55	2	-	1
WEALANDS Jeffrey Andrew (Jeff)						
Born: Darlington, County Durham, England, 26 August, 1951						G
Wolverhampton W	App	10/68				
Darlington	Tr	07/70	71	28	0	0
Hull C	Tr	03/72	71-78	240	0	0
Birmingham C	Tr	07/79	79-81	102	0	0
Manchester U	Tr	02/83	82-83	7	0	0
Oldham Ath	L	03/84	83	10	0	0
Preston NE	L	12/84	84	4	0	0
WEALE Christopher (Chris)						
Born: Chard, Somerset, England, 9 February, 1982						G
England: Semi Pro-4						
Yeovil T	Jnr	06/00	03-05	97	1	0
Bristol C	Tr	07/06	06-08	5	4	0
Hereford U	L	08/07	07	1	0	0
Hereford U	L	11/08	08	1	0	0
Yeovil T	L	03/09	08	10	0	1
Leicester C	Tr	07/09	09-11	73	2	0
Northampton T	L	01/12	11	3	0	0
Shrewsbury T	Tr	07/12	12-13	81	0	0
Yeovil T	Tr	06/14	14	8	0	0

League Club	Source	Date Signed	Seasons Played	Apps	Subs	Gls
WEALTHALL Barry Arthur						
Born: Nottingham, England, 1 May, 1942						RB
England: Youth						
Nottingham F	Jnr	06/59	60	2	-	0
Grimsby T	Tr	05/62	61-62	9	-	0
York C	Tr	06/63	63-66	75	0	0
WEARE Arthur John (Jack)						
Born: Newport, Wales, 21 September, 1912						G
Wolverhampton W	Lovells Ath	05/33	33-36	42	-	0
West Ham U	Tr	09/36	36-37	57	-	0
Bristol Rov	St Mirren	11/45	46-49	141	-	0
WEARE Leonard Nicholas (Len)						
Born: Newport, Wales, 23 July, 1934						G
Died: Newport, Wales, 21 September, 2012						
Newport Co	Temple Street YMCA	08/55	55-69	528	0	0
WEARE Ross Michael						
Born: Perivale, W London, England, 19 March, 1977						F
Queens Park Rgrs	East Ham U	03/99	99	0	4	0
Bristol Rov	Tr	07/01	01	9	1	1
WEAREN Eoin Patrick						
Born: Dublin, Republic of Ireland, 2 October, 1992						CD
Republic of Ireland: Youth						
West Ham U	Sch	07/11				
Dagenham & Red	L	01/12	11	0	2	0
WEARMOUTH Michael (Mike)						
Born: Barrow, Cumbria, England, 16 May, 1944						CH
Barrow	Jnr	06/62	61-63	33	-	0
Preston NE	Tr	03/64	64-66	11	0	0
WEATHERALL Leonard (Len)						
Born: Middlesbrough, England, 21 May, 1936						IF
Grimsby T	Redcar BC	04/55	54-55	10	-	1
WEATHERHEAD Shaun						
Born: Halifax, West Yorkshire, England, 3 September, 1970						CD
Huddersfield T	YT	07/89				
York C	Tr	09/90	90	6	2	0
WEATHERLY Colin Mark (Mark)						
Born: Ramsgate, Kent, England, 18 January, 1958						CD/F
Gillingham	App	12/75	74-88	408	49	47
WEATHERSPOON Charles William (Charlie)						
Born: Newcastle-on-Tyne, England, 3 October, 1929						CF
Died: North Tyneside, Tyne and Wear, England, April, 1986						
Sunderland	Jnr	08/47				
Sheffield U	Annfield Plain	01/51	50	1	-	0
Hartlepool U	Tr	08/52	52	3	-	2
WEATHERSTONE Ross						
Born: Reading, England, 16 May, 1981						CD
Oxford U	YT	10/99	99-00	4	0	0
Boston U	Tr	02/01	02	2	6	0
WEATHERSTONE Simon						
Born: Reading, England, 26 January, 1980						M
England: Semi Pro-3						
Oxford U	YT	03/97	96-00	25	27	3
Boston U	Tr	02/01	02-03	57	5	10
Yeovil T	Tr	01/04	03-04	11	10	1
WEAVER Eric						
Born: Rhymney, Caerphilly, Wales, 1 July, 1943						W
Swindon T	Box Rov	12/61	61-66	55	0	6
Notts Co	Tr	08/67	67	16	1	4
Northampton T	Tr	12/67	67-69	61	2	9
WEAVER John Noel						
Born: Wrexham, Wales, 26 November, 1924						RB
Wrexham	Jnr	05/46	46	2	-	0
WEAVER Luke Dennis Spencer						
Born: Woolwich, SE London, England, 26 June, 1979						G
England: Youth/Schools						
Leyton Orient	YT	06/96	96	9	0	0
Sunderland	Tr	01/98				
Scarborough	L	12/98	98	6	0	0
Carlisle U	Tr	08/99	99-01	53	0	0
Northampton T	Tr	07/03				
WEAVER Nicholas James (Nicky)						
Born: Sheffield, England, 2 March, 1979						G
England: U21-10						
Mansfield T	YT	-	95	1	0	0
Manchester C	Tr	05/97	98-06	170	2	0

League Club	Source	Date Signed	Seasons Played	Apps	Subs	Gls
Sheffield Wed	L	11/05	05	14	0	0
Charlton Ath	Tr	07/07	07-08	67	0	0
Burnley	Dundee U	01/10				
Sheffield Wed	Tr	08/10	10-11	44	0	0

WEAVER Samuel (Sam)
Born: Pilsley, Derbyshire, England, 8 February, 1909 WH/IF
Died: Basford, Nottinghamshire, England, 15 April, 1985
England: 3/FLge-2

League Club	Source	Date Signed	Seasons Played	Apps	Subs	Gls
Hull C	Sutton T	03/28	28-29	48	-	5
Newcastle U	Tr	11/29	29-35	204	-	41
Chelsea	Tr	08/36	36-38	116	-	4
Stockport Co	Tr	12/45	46	2	-	0

WEAVER Simon Daniel
Born: Doncaster, South Yorkshire, England, 20 December, 1977 CD

League Club	Source	Date Signed	Seasons Played	Apps	Subs	Gls
Sheffield Wed	YT	05/96				
Doncaster Rov	L	02/97	96	2	0	0
Lincoln C	Nuneaton Bor	08/02	02-04	88	0	3
Macclesfield T	L	10/04	04	7	0	0
Kidderminster Hrs	Tr	12/04	04	22	1	0

WEBB Alan Richard
Born: Oakengates, Telford & Wrekin, England, 1 January, 1963 D

League Club	Source	Date Signed	Seasons Played	Apps	Subs	Gls
West Bromwich A	App	01/80	81-83	23	1	0
Lincoln C	L	03/84	83	11	0	0
Port Vale	Tr	08/84	84-91	187	3	2

WEBB Daniel John (Danny)
Born: Poole, Dorset, England, 2 July, 1983 F/CD

League Club	Source	Date Signed	Seasons Played	Apps	Subs	Gls
Southend U	Southampton (YT)	12/00	00-01	16	15	3
Brighton & HA	L	12/01	01	7	5	1
Brighton & HA	L	11/02	02	0	3	0
Hull C	Tr	12/02	02-03	4	12	0
Lincoln C	L	03/03	02	4	1	1
Cambridge U	Tr	12/03	03-04	34	9	4
Yeovil T	Weymouth	01/06	05-06	0	8	0

WEBB David James (Dave)
Born: Stratford, E London, England, 9 April, 1946 D

League Club	Source	Date Signed	Seasons Played	Apps	Subs	Gls
Leyton Orient	West Ham U (Am)	05/63	64-65	62	0	3
Southampton	Tr	03/66	65-67	75	0	2
Chelsea	Tr	02/68	67-73	230	0	21
Queens Park Rgrs	Tr	07/74	74-77	116	0	7
Leicester C	Tr	09/77	77-78	32	1	0
Derby Co	Tr	12/78	78-79	25	1	1
Bournemouth	Tr	05/80	80-82	11	0	0
Torquay U	Rtd	10/84	84	2	0	1

WEBB Douglas John (Doug)
Born: Stokenchurch, Buckinghamshire, England, 10 March, 1939 IF/LW

League Club	Source	Date Signed	Seasons Played	Apps	Subs	Gls
Reading	Jnr	11/56	56-66	178	2	81

WEBB George Andrew
Born: Poole, Dorset, England, 1 May, 1991 M

League Club	Source	Date Signed	Seasons Played	Apps	Subs	Gls
Bournemouth	Jnr	08/09	08-09	0	2	0

WEBB James Keith
Born: Warrington, Cheshire, England, 6 July, 1938 CF

League Club	Source	Date Signed	Seasons Played	Apps	Subs	Gls
Shrewsbury T	Lymm Rgrs	04/56	55-56	2	-	1

WEBB John
Born: Liverpool, England, 10 February, 1952 RB

League Club	Source	Date Signed	Seasons Played	Apps	Subs	Gls
Liverpool	App	02/69				
Plymouth Arg	L	09/73	73	4	0	0
Tranmere Rov	Tr	07/74	74	17	3	0

WEBB Luke Alexander
Born: Nottingham, England, 12 September, 1986 M

League Club	Source	Date Signed	Seasons Played	Apps	Subs	Gls
Coventry C	Arsenal (Sch)	07/05				
Hereford U	Tr	08/06	06-07	16	19	3

WEBB Matthew Leslie
Born: Bristol, England, 24 September, 1976 M

League Club	Source	Date Signed	Seasons Played	Apps	Subs	Gls
Birmingham C	YT	07/95	94	0	1	0

WEBB Neil John
Born: Reading, England, 30 July, 1963 M
England: 26/B-4/FLge/U21-3/Youth

League Club	Source	Date Signed	Seasons Played	Apps	Subs	Gls
Reading	App	11/80	79-81	65	7	22
Portsmouth	Tr	07/82	82-84	123	0	34
Nottingham F	Tr	06/85	85-88	146	0	47
Manchester U	Tr	06/89	89-92	70	5	8
Nottingham F	Tr	11/92	92-93	26	4	3
Swindon T	L	10/94	94	5	1	0
Grimsby T	Tr	08/96	96	3	1	0

WEBB Paul Andrew
Born: Wolverhampton, England, 30 November, 1967 M
England: Semi Pro-11

League Club	Source	Date Signed	Seasons Played	Apps	Subs	Gls
Shrewsbury T	App	11/85				
Kidderminster Hrs	Bromsgrove Rov	07/94	00	23	9	1

WEBB Robert (Bobby)
Born: Altofts, West Yorkshire, England, 29 November, 1933 RW

League Club	Source	Date Signed	Seasons Played	Apps	Subs	Gls
Leeds U	Whitwood Tech College	04/51	53-54	3	-	0
Walsall	Tr	03/55	54	9	-	3
Bradford C	Tr	07/55	55-61	208	-	59
Torquay U	Tr	07/62	62-63	49	-	12

WEBB Ronald Charles Thomas (Ron)
Born: Brentford, W London, England, 13 March, 1925 WH
Died: Derby, England, May, 1999

League Club	Source	Date Signed	Seasons Played	Apps	Subs	Gls
Queens Park Rgrs	Jnr	10/44				
Crystal Palace	Tr	09/46	46	3	-	0

WEBB Sean Michael
Born: Dungannon, Tyrone, Northern Ireland, 4 January, 1983 CD
Northern Ireland: 4/U21-6/Youth

League Club	Source	Date Signed	Seasons Played	Apps	Subs	Gls
Accrington Stan	Ross Co	08/07	07	18	0	0

WEBB Simon
Born: Castlebar, Co. Mayo, Republic of Ireland, 19 January, 1978 M
Republic of Ireland: Youth/Schools

League Club	Source	Date Signed	Seasons Played	Apps	Subs	Gls
Tottenham H	YT	01/94				
Leyton Orient	Tr	10/99	99	3	1	0

WEBB Stanley John (Stan)
Born: Middlesbrough, England, 6 December, 1947 F

League Club	Source	Date Signed	Seasons Played	Apps	Subs	Gls
Middlesbrough	Thorntree	07/67	67-70	20	8	6
Carlisle U	Tr	02/71	70-72	16	10	5
Brentford	Tr	10/72	72-73	37	2	8
Darlington	Tr	07/74	74-75	69	5	21

WEBB William (Billy)
Born: Mexborough, South Yorkshire, England, 7 March, 1932 LB

League Club	Source	Date Signed	Seasons Played	Apps	Subs	Gls
Leicester C	Wath W	06/51	51-56	47	-	0
Stockport Co	Tr	06/57	57-62	243	-	0

WEBB-FOSTER Reece Patrick
Born: Keighley, West Yorkshire, England, 7 March, 1998 F

League Club	Source	Date Signed	Seasons Played	Apps	Subs	Gls
Bradford C	Sch	-	14	0	1	0

WEBBER Andrew
Born: Port Talbot, Wales, 15 March, 1963 F

League Club	Source	Date Signed	Seasons Played	Apps	Subs	Gls
Swansea C	Afan Lido	11/84	84	0	1	0
Exeter C	Tr	09/85	85	1	0	0

WEBBER Damien John
Born: Littlehampton, West Sussex, England, 8 October, 1968 CD

League Club	Source	Date Signed	Seasons Played	Apps	Subs	Gls
Brighton & HA	YT	07/87				
Millwall	Bognor Regis T	10/94	94-97	52	13	4

WEBBER Daniel Vaughn (Danny)
Born: Manchester, England, 28 December, 1981 CD
England: Youth

League Club	Source	Date Signed	Seasons Played	Apps	Subs	Gls
Manchester U	YT	01/99				
Port Vale	L	11/01	01	2	2	0
Watford	L	03/02	01	4	1	2
Watford	L	08/02	02	11	1	2
Watford	Tr	07/03	03-04	48	7	17
Sheffield U	Tr	03/05	04-08	72	42	23
Portsmouth	Tr	09/09	09-10	5	20	1
Leeds U		02/12	11	2	11	1
Accrington Stan	Doncaster Rov (NC)	07/13	13	14	8	3

WEBBER Eric Victor
Born: Steyning, West Sussex, England, 22 December, 1919 CH
Died: Southampton, England, 10 December, 1996

League Club	Source	Date Signed	Seasons Played	Apps	Subs	Gls
Southampton	Gosport Ath	03/46	38-50	182	-	0
Torquay U	Tr	10/51	51-54	149	-	2

WEBBER George Marshall
Born: Abercynon, Rhondda Cynon Taff, Wales, 28 June, 1925 G
Died: Torbay, Devon, England, 7 October, 2009

League Club	Source	Date Signed	Seasons Played	Apps	Subs	Gls
Torquay U	Cardiff C (Am)	06/50	50-53	118	-	0
Northampton T	Tr	06/54	54	13	-	0

WEBBER John Vincent
Born: Blackpool, Lancashire, England, 2 July, 1918 IF
Died: Blackpool, Lancashire, England, September, 1989

League Club	Source	Date Signed	Seasons Played	Apps	Subs	Gls
Blackburn Rov	Hyde U	02/47	46-47	8	-	1

WEBBER Keith James
Born: Cardiff, Wales, 5 January, 1943 CF
Died: Wrexham, Wales, 1983

League Club	Source	Date Signed	Seasons Played	Apps	Subs	Gls
Everton	Barry T	02/60	60-61	4	-	0
Brighton & HA	Tr	04/63	62-64	35	-	14
Wrexham	Tr	09/64	64-65	73	0	33
Doncaster Rov	Tr	07/66	66-68	63	2	18

League Club	Source	Date Signed	Seasons Played	Apps	Subs	Gls
Chester C	Tr	06/69	69-70	66	8	14
Stockport Co	Tr	07/71	71	36	4	7

WEBBER Trevor
Born: Bovey Tracey, Devon, England, 5 September, 1968 W

League Club	Source	Date Signed	Seasons Played	Apps	Subs	Gls
Torquay U	YT	-	85	5	0	0

WEBER Nicolas
Born: Metz, France, 28 October, 1970 CD

League Club	Source	Date Signed	Seasons Played	Apps	Subs	Gls
Sheffield U (L)	Le Havre (FRA)	08/00	00	3	1	0

WEBSTER Aaron Denton
Born: Burton-on-Trent, Staffordshire, England, 19 December, 1980 LB/M
England: Semi Pro-3

League Club	Source	Date Signed	Seasons Played	Apps	Subs	Gls
Burton A	Jnr	01/98	09-12	94	16	18

WEBSTER Adam
Born: Leicester, England, 3 July, 1980 F

League Club	Source	Date Signed	Seasons Played	Apps	Subs	Gls
Notts Co	Thurmaston	02/99	99	0	1	0

WEBSTER Adam Harry
Born: West Wittering, West Sussex, England, 4 January, 1995 D
England: Youth

League Club	Source	Date Signed	Seasons Played	Apps	Subs	Gls
Portsmouth	Sch	01/12	11-14	25	15	3

WEBSTER Adrian
Born: Hawkes Bay, New Zealand, 11 October, 1980 M
New Zealand: 5

League Club	Source	Date Signed	Seasons Played	Apps	Subs	Gls
Darlington	St George-B'pest (AUS)	10/04	04-05	22	13	1

WEBSTER Alan John
Born: Melton Mowbray, Leicestershire, England, 3 July, 1948 M

League Club	Source	Date Signed	Seasons Played	Apps	Subs	Gls
Scunthorpe U	Jnr	07/66	66-67	4	2	0

WEBSTER Andrew
Born: Colne, Lancashire, England, 18 March, 1947 CF

League Club	Source	Date Signed	Seasons Played	Apps	Subs	Gls
Bradford C	Clitheroe	07/65	65-66	10	2	1

WEBSTER Andrew Neil (Andy)
Born: Dundee, Scotland, 23 April, 1982 CD
Scotland: 28/B-1/U21-2

League Club	Source	Date Signed	Seasons Played	Apps	Subs	Gls
Wigan Ath	Heart of Midlothian	08/06	06	3	1	0
Bristol C (L)	Glasgow Rangers	08/08	08	2	3	0
Coventry C	Heart of Midlothian	08/13	13-14	65	6	2

WEBSTER Byron Clark
Born: Sherburn-in-Elmet, North Yorkshire, England, 31 March, 1987 CD

League Club	Source	Date Signed	Seasons Played	Apps	Subs	Gls
Doncaster Rov	Banik Most (CZE)	08/09	09-10	2	10	0
Hereford U	L	11/10	10	2	0	0
Northampton T	Tr	03/11	10-11	16	5	0
Yeovil T	Tr	07/12	12-13	83	2	8
Millwall	Tr	06/14	14	9	2	0
Yeovil T	L	02/15	14	14	0	0

WEBSTER Colin
Born: Halifax, West Yorkshire, England, 5 March, 1930 RH

League Club	Source	Date Signed	Seasons Played	Apps	Subs	Gls
Halifax T		09/50	50	16	-	1
Rochdale	Tr	09/51				

WEBSTER Colin
Born: Cardiff, Wales, 17 July, 1932 F
Died: Cardiff, Wales, 1 March, 2001
Wales: 4

League Club	Source	Date Signed	Seasons Played	Apps	Subs	Gls
Cardiff C	Cardiff Nomads	05/50				
Manchester U	Tr	05/52	53-58	65	-	26
Swansea C	Tr	09/58	58-62	157	-	66
Newport Co	Tr	03/63	62-63	31	-	4

WEBSTER Eric
Born: Manchester, England, 24 June, 1931 WH

League Club	Source	Date Signed	Seasons Played	Apps	Subs	Gls
Manchester C	Ardwick LC	02/52	52	1	-	0

WEBSTER Harry
Born: Sheffield, England, 22 August, 1930 IF
Died: Bolton, Greater Manchester, England, 2 April, 2008

League Club	Source	Date Signed	Seasons Played	Apps	Subs	Gls
Bolton W	Woodburn	10/48	49-56	98	-	38
Chester C	Tr	06/58	58-59	34	-	11

WEBSTER Ian Adrian
Born: Askern, South Yorkshire, England, 30 December, 1965 CD

League Club	Source	Date Signed	Seasons Played	Apps	Subs	Gls
Scunthorpe U	App	07/83	82-85	15	3	0

WEBSTER John Barry (Barry)
Born: Sheffield, England, 3 March, 1935 RW

League Club	Source	Date Signed	Seasons Played	Apps	Subs	Gls
Rotherham U	Gainsborough Trinity	05/56	56-61	179	-	37
Bradford C	Tr	06/62	62-63	53	-	9

WEBSTER Keith
Born: Newcastle-upon-Tyne, England, 6 November, 1945 M

League Club	Source	Date Signed	Seasons Played	Apps	Subs	Gls
Newcastle U	Stockton	12/62				
Darlington	Tr	11/66	66	7	1	0

WEBSTER Malcolm Walter
Born: Rossington, South Yorkshire, England, 12 November, 1950 G
England: Youth/Schools

League Club	Source	Date Signed	Seasons Played	Apps	Subs	Gls
Arsenal	App	01/68	69	3	0	0
Fulham	Tr	12/69	69-73	94	0	0
Southend U	Tr	01/74	73-75	96	0	0
Cambridge U	Tr	09/76	76-83	256	0	0

WEBSTER Richard (Dick)
Born: Accrington, Lancashire, England, 6 August, 1919 LB/LH
Died: Blackburn, Greater Manchester, England, 11 October, 1979

League Club	Source	Date Signed	Seasons Played	Apps	Subs	Gls
Accrington Stan	Woodnook Amats	11/37	37-38	41	-	0
Sheffield U	Tr	01/39				
Accrington Stan	Tr	08/45	46-50	186	-	3

WEBSTER Ronald (Ron)
Born: Belper, Derbyshire, England, 21 June, 1943 RB/WH

League Club	Source	Date Signed	Seasons Played	Apps	Subs	Gls
Derby Co	Jnr	06/60	61-77	451	4	7

WEBSTER Simon Paul
Born: Earl Shilton, Leicestershire, England, 20 January, 1964 CD

League Club	Source	Date Signed	Seasons Played	Apps	Subs	Gls
Tottenham H	App	12/81	82-83	2	1	0
Exeter C	L	11/83	83	6	0	0
Exeter C	L	01/84	83	20	0	0
Huddersfield T	Tr	02/85	84-87	118	0	4
Sheffield U	Tr	03/88	87-89	26	11	3
Charlton Ath	Tr	08/90	90-92	127	0	7
West Ham U	Tr	06/93	94	0	5	0
Oldham Ath	L	03/95	94	7	0	0
Derby Co	L	08/95	95	3	0	0

WEBSTER Terence (Terry)
Born: Stretford, Greater Manchester, England, 27 September, 1941 WH

League Club	Source	Date Signed	Seasons Played	Apps	Subs	Gls
Sheffield U	Jnr	10/58				
Accrington Stan	Tr	11/59				
Barrow	Tr	07/60	60	4	-	0

WEBSTER Terence Charles (Terry)
Born: Doncaster, South Yorkshire, England, 9 July, 1930 G

League Club	Source	Date Signed	Seasons Played	Apps	Subs	Gls
Doncaster Rov	Intake YC	06/48				
Derby Co	Tr	10/48	48-57	172	-	0

WEDDERBURN Nathaniel Carl (Nathan)
Born: Wolverhampton, England, 30 June, 1991 M
England: Youth

League Club	Source	Date Signed	Seasons Played	Apps	Subs	Gls
Stoke C	Sch	10/08				
Notts Co	L	11/08	08	3	6	0
Hereford U	L	11/09	09	3	0	0
Northampton T	Tr	07/10	10-11	22	11	0

WEDDLE Derek Keith
Born: Newcastle-upon-Tyne, England, 27 December, 1935 F

League Club	Source	Date Signed	Seasons Played	Apps	Subs	Gls
Sunderland	Jnr	05/53	55-56	2	-	0
Portsmouth	Tr	12/56	56-58	24	-	8
Middlesbrough	Cambridge C	08/61	61	3	-	1
Darlington	Tr	06/62	62-63	37	-	10
York C	Tr	07/64	64-65	44	0	13

WEDDLE George Davison
Born: Ashington, Northumberland, England, 24 February, 1919 IF/W

League Club	Source	Date Signed	Seasons Played	Apps	Subs	Gls
Gateshead		06/46	46-48	46	-	10

WEDGBURY Samuel (Sam)
Born: Oldbury, West Midlands, England, 26 February, 1989 M

League Club	Source	Date Signed	Seasons Played	Apps	Subs	Gls
Sheffield U	Sch	02/07				
Macclesfield T	Tr	07/10	10-11	50	12	2
Stevenage	Tr	05/13	13	6	8	0

WEEDON Benjamin David (Ben)
Born: Kidlington, Oxfordshire, England, 30 March, 1989 LB

League Club	Source	Date Signed	Seasons Played	Apps	Subs	Gls
Oxford U	Sch	-	05	1	1	0

WEEKS Graham
Born: Exeter, England, 3 March, 1958 M

League Club	Source	Date Signed	Seasons Played	Apps	Subs	Gls
Exeter C	App	03/76	76-77	49	4	1
Bournemouth	Tr	05/78	78	3	0	0

WEETMAN Darren Graham
Born: Oswestry, Shropshire, England, 7 June, 1968 W

League Club	Source	Date Signed	Seasons Played	Apps	Subs	Gls
Wrexham	Jnr	06/85	85	1	0	0

WEGERLE Roy Connon
Born: Pretoria, South Africa, 19 March, 1964 F/W
USA: 41

League Club	Source	Date Signed	Seasons Played	Apps	Subs	Gls
Chelsea	Tacoma Stars (USA)	06/86	86-87	15	8	3
Swindon T	L	03/88	87	7	0	1
Luton T	Tr	07/88	88-89	39	6	10
Queens Park Rgrs	Tr	12/89	89-91	71	4	29
Blackburn Rov	Tr	03/92	91-92	20	14	6
Coventry C	Tr	03/93	92-94	46	7	9

WEI FENG (Li)
Born: Changchun, China, 26 January, 1978 — CD
China: 112

League Club	Source	Date Signed	Seasons Played	Apps	Subs	Gls
Everton (L)	Shenzen Ping'an (CHN)	07/02	02	1	0	0

WEIGH Raymond Edward (Ray)
Born: Flint, Wales, 23 June, 1928 — CF/LW

League Club	Source	Date Signed	Seasons Played	Apps	Subs	Gls
Bournemouth	Royal Engineers	03/49	49-50	28	-	8
Stockport Co	Tr	07/51	51-53	75	-	29
Shrewsbury T	Tr	06/54	54-56	107	-	43
Aldershot	Tr	07/57	57	11	-	1

WEIMANN Andreas
Born: Vienna, Austria, 5 August, 1991 — F
Austria: 14/U21-10/Youth

League Club	Source	Date Signed	Seasons Played	Apps	Subs	Gls
Aston Villa	Sch	08/08	10-14	82	31	17
Watford	L	01/11	10	10	8	4
Watford	L	08/11	11	3	0	0

WEIR Alan
Born: South Shields, Tyne and Wear, England, 1 September, 1959 — D
England: Youth

League Club	Source	Date Signed	Seasons Played	Apps	Subs	Gls
Sunderland	App	05/77	77	1	0	0
Rochdale	Tr	06/79	79-82	96	10	3
Hartlepool U	Tr	08/83	83	9	1	0

WEIR Alexander (Alex)
Born: Longridge, West Lothian, Scotland, 20 October, 1916 — W
Died: Margate, Kent, England, 10 January, 2003

League Club	Source	Date Signed	Seasons Played	Apps	Subs	Gls
Preston NE	Stoneyburn Jnrs	02/36				
Watford	Glentoran	12/45	46	1	-	0
Northampton T	Tr	09/47				

WEIR David Gillespie
Born: Falkirk, Scotland, 10 May, 1970 — CD
Scotland: 69/Schools

League Club	Source	Date Signed	Seasons Played	Apps	Subs	Gls
Everton	Heart of Midlothian	02/99	98-06	223	12	9

WEIR James (Jimmy)
Born: Glasgow, Scotland, 12 April, 1939 — LW

League Club	Source	Date Signed	Seasons Played	Apps	Subs	Gls
Fulham	Clydebank Jnrs	07/57	57	3	-	0
York C	Tr	06/60	60-62	82	-	38
Mansfield T	Tr	09/62	62	18	-	3
Luton T	Tr	08/63	63	12	-	1
Tranmere Rov	Tr	07/64	64	13	-	3

WEIR John Britton (Jock)
Born: Fauldhouse, West Lothian, Scotland, 20 October, 1923 — CF
Died: Bellshill, Lanarkshire, Scotland, 7 January, 2003

League Club	Source	Date Signed	Seasons Played	Apps	Subs	Gls
Blackburn Rov	Hibernian	01/47	46-47	23	-	7

WEIR Michael Graham (Micky)
Born: Edinburgh, Scotland, 16 January, 1966 — W

League Club	Source	Date Signed	Seasons Played	Apps	Subs	Gls
Luton T	Hibernian	09/87	87	7	1	0
Millwall (L)	Hibernian	03/96	95	8	0	0

WEIR Peter Russell
Born: Johnstone, Renfrewshire, Scotland, 18 January, 1958 — W
Scotland: 6

League Club	Source	Date Signed	Seasons Played	Apps	Subs	Gls
Leicester C	Aberdeen	01/88	87-88	26	2	2

WEIR Robert James (Robbie)
Born: Belfast, Northern Ireland, 9 December, 1988 — M
Northern Ireland: B-1/U21-8

League Club	Source	Date Signed	Seasons Played	Apps	Subs	Gls
Sunderland	Sch	07/07				
Tranmere Rov	Tr	02/11	10-11	45	12	3
Burton A	Tr	05/12	12-14	121	3	7

WEIR Tyler Carlton
Born: Hereford, England, 21 December, 1990 — LB

League Club	Source	Date Signed	Seasons Played	Apps	Subs	Gls
Hereford U	Jnr	05/09	09-10	5	2	0

WEIR William Houston (Willie)
Born: Baillieston, Glasgow, Scotland, 11 April, 1968 — RW

League Club	Source	Date Signed	Seasons Played	Apps	Subs	Gls
Shrewsbury T	Baillieston Jnrs	03/90	89-90	4	13	1

WEIR-DALEY Spencer James Andrew
Born: Leicester, England, 5 September, 1988 — F

League Club	Source	Date Signed	Seasons Played	Apps	Subs	Gls
Nottingham F	Sch	01/04	05-06	0	7	1
Macclesfield T	L	08/06	06	5	2	2
Lincoln C	L	01/07	06	4	7	5
Bradford C	L	03/07	06	2	3	1
Notts Co	Tr	06/07	07-08	12	28	3

WEISS Vladimir
Born: Bratislava, Slovakia, 30 November, 1989 — RW
Slovakia: 43/U21-8/Youth

League Club	Source	Date Signed	Seasons Played	Apps	Subs	Gls
Manchester C	Sch	09/07	08	0	1	0
Bolton W	L	01/10	09	3	10	0

WELBECK Daniel Nii Takie Mensah (Danny)
Born: Manchester, England, 26 November, 1990 — F
England: 33/U21-14/Youth

League Club	Source	Date Signed	Seasons Played	Apps	Subs	Gls
Manchester U	Sch	07/08	08-14	53	39	20
Preston NE	L	01/10	09	8	0	2
Sunderland	L	08/10	10	21	5	6
Arsenal	Tr	09/14	14	18	7	4

WELBOURNE Donald (Don)
Born: Scunthorpe, North Lincolnshire, England, 12 March, 1949 — CD

League Club	Source	Date Signed	Seasons Played	Apps	Subs	Gls
Scunthorpe U	App	03/67	66-75	251	3	5

WELBOURNE Duncan
Born: Scunthorpe, North Lincolnshire, England, 28 July, 1940 — FB/WH

League Club	Source	Date Signed	Seasons Played	Apps	Subs	Gls
Grimsby T	Scunthorpe U (Am)	08/57	57-63	130	-	3
Watford	Tr	11/63	63-73	404	7	22
Southport	Tr	07/74	74-75	52	1	2

WELCH Keith James
Born: Bolton, Greater Manchester, England, 3 October, 1968 — G

League Club	Source	Date Signed	Seasons Played	Apps	Subs	Gls
Rochdale	Bolton W (Jnr)	03/87	86-90	205	0	0
Bristol C	Tr	07/91	91-98	271	0	0
Northampton T	Tr	07/99	99-01	117	0	0
Tranmere Rov	Tr	08/02	02	2	0	0
Torquay U	Tr	11/02	02	3	0	0
Mansfield T	Tr	02/03	02	9	0	0

WELCH Michael (Micky)
Born: Bridgetown, Barbados, 21 May, 1958 — F

League Club	Source	Date Signed	Seasons Played	Apps	Subs	Gls
Wimbledon	Grays Ath	11/84	84	2	2	0
Southend U	Grays Ath	02/85	84	4	0	0

WELCH Michael Francis
Born: Winsford, Cheshire, England, 11 January, 1982 — CD
Republic of Ireland: Youth

League Club	Source	Date Signed	Seasons Played	Apps	Subs	Gls
Macclesfield T	Barnsley (YT)	08/01	01-04	108	6	5
Accrington Stan	Tr	08/05	06	25	6	3

WELCH Ronald (Ronnie)
Born: Chesterfield, Derbyshire, England, 26 September, 1952 — M

League Club	Source	Date Signed	Seasons Played	Apps	Subs	Gls
Burnley	App	10/69	70	1	0	0
Brighton & HA	Tr	12/73	73-74	35	1	4
Chesterfield	Tr	11/74	74-76	17	7	1

WELFORD William Frederick (Bill)
Born: Newcastle-upon-Tyne, England, 14 April, 1934 — RH
Died: Northumberland, England, December, 1999

League Club	Source	Date Signed	Seasons Played	Apps	Subs	Gls
Hartlepool U	Crook T	11/58	58	8	-	0

WELLARD Ricky Ben
Born: Hammersmith, W London, England, 9 May, 1988 — M

League Club	Source	Date Signed	Seasons Played	Apps	Subs	Gls
AFC Wimbledon	Ashford T, Surrey	07/09	11	16	6	1

WELLENS Richard Paul (Richie)
Born: Manchester, England, 26 March, 1980 — M
England: Youth

League Club	Source	Date Signed	Seasons Played	Apps	Subs	Gls
Manchester U	YT	05/97				
Blackpool	Tr	03/00	99-04	173	15	16
Oldham Ath	Tr	06/05	05-06	87	0	8
Doncaster Rov	Tr	07/07	07-08	84	0	9
Leicester C	Tr	07/09	09-12	126	3	4
Ipswich T	L	10/12	12	7	0	0
Doncaster Rov	Tr	07/13	13-14	73	3	3

WELLER Christopher William (Chris)
Born: Reading, England, 25 December, 1939 — IF

League Club	Source	Date Signed	Seasons Played	Apps	Subs	Gls
Bournemouth	Reading (Am)	09/59	60-64	74	-	17
Bristol Rov	Tr	07/65	65	2	1	0
Bournemouth	Tr	01/66	65-66	39	2	8

WELLER Keith
Born: Islington, N London, England, 11 June, 1946 — W/F
Died: Seattle, Washington, USA, 12 November, 2004
England: 4/FLge-1

League Club	Source	Date Signed	Seasons Played	Apps	Subs	Gls
Tottenham H	App	01/64	64-66	19	2	1
Millwall	Tr	06/67	67-69	121	0	40
Chelsea	Tr	05/70	70-71	34	4	14
Leicester C	Tr	09/71	71-78	260	2	37

WELLER Paul Anthony
Born: Brighton, England, 6 March, 1975 — M/RB

League Club	Source	Date Signed	Seasons Played	Apps	Subs	Gls
Burnley	YT	11/93	95-03	199	53	11
Rochdale	Tr	09/04	04	5	0	0

WELLINGS Barry
Born: Liverpool, England, 10 June, 1958 — F

League Club	Source	Date Signed	Seasons Played	Apps	Subs	Gls
Everton	App	06/76				
York C	Tr	06/78	78-79	40	7	9
Rochdale	Tr	07/80	80-82	111	5	30
Tranmere Rov	Tr	02/83	82	16	0	3

League Club	Source	Date Signed	Seasons Played	Apps	Subs	Gls
Tranmere Rov	Northwich Victoria	12/83	83	9	0	0
Swansea C	Oswestry T	09/84	84	5	0	3

WELLS Archibald (Archie)
Born: Clydebank, Dunbartonshire, Scotland, 4 October, 1920 — IF
Died: Birkenhead, Wirral, England, July, 2008

League Club	Source	Date Signed	Seasons Played	Apps	Subs	Gls
New Brighton	Alloa Ath	07/46	46-48	37	-	4

WELLS Benjamin (Ben)
Born: Basingstoke, Hampshire, England, 26 March, 1988 — M

League Club	Source	Date Signed	Seasons Played	Apps	Subs	Gls
Swindon T	Sch	07/06	04-06	0	6	0

WELLS David Peter
Born: Portsmouth, England, 29 December, 1977 — G
Northern Ireland: Youth

League Club	Source	Date Signed	Seasons Played	Apps	Subs	Gls
Bournemouth	YT	07/96	94	0	1	0

WELLS Dean Thomas
Born: Twickenham, W London, England, 25 March, 1985 — CD

League Club	Source	Date Signed	Seasons Played	Apps	Subs	Gls
Brentford	Sch	-	03	0	1	0
Stevenage	Braintree T	06/14	14	43	0	4

WELLS Ian Michael
Born: Wolverhampton, England, 27 October, 1964 — F
Died: Zakynthos, Greece, 19 January, 2013

League Club	Source	Date Signed	Seasons Played	Apps	Subs	Gls
Hereford U	Harrisons, Gt Wyrley	06/85	85-86	47	4	12

WELLS Mark Anthony
Born: Leicester, England, 15 October, 1971 — LB/M

League Club	Source	Date Signed	Seasons Played	Apps	Subs	Gls
Notts Co	YT	07/90	91-92	0	2	0
Huddersfield T	Tr	08/93	93	21	1	4
Scarborough	Tr	07/94	94-96	48	14	3

WELLS Nahki
Born: Pembroke, Bermuda, 1 June, 1990 — F
Bermuda: 9

League Club	Source	Date Signed	Seasons Played	Apps	Subs	Gls
Carlisle U	Eccleshill U	01/11	10	0	3	0
Bradford C	Tr	07/11	11-13	65	26	42
Huddersfield T	Tr	01/14	13-14	50	7	18

WELLS Peter Alan
Born: Nottingham, England, 13 August, 1956 — G

League Club	Source	Date Signed	Seasons Played	Apps	Subs	Gls
Nottingham F	App	10/74	75-76	27	0	0
Southampton	Tr	12/76	76-82	141	0	0
Millwall	Tr	02/83	82-83	33	0	0
Leyton Orient	Tr	07/85	85-88	148	0	0

WELLS William David (David)
Born: Eccleston, Lancashire, England, 16 December, 1940 — RB

League Club	Source	Date Signed	Seasons Played	Apps	Subs	Gls
Blackburn Rov	Jnr	05/58				
Rochdale	Tr	07/63	63	8	-	0

WELSH Alan
Born: Edinburgh, Scotland, 9 July, 1947 — M/F

League Club	Source	Date Signed	Seasons Played	Apps	Subs	Gls
Millwall	Bonnyrigg Rose	07/65	65-67	3	2	0
Torquay U	Tr	11/67	67-71	140	6	45
Plymouth Arg	Tr	07/72	72-73	64	2	14
Bournemouth	Tr	02/74	73-74	33	2	3
Millwall	Tr	08/75	75	5	4	1

WELSH Andrew John (Andy)
Born: Fleetwood, Lancashire, England, 20 January, 1962 — F

League Club	Source	Date Signed	Seasons Played	Apps	Subs	Gls
Blackpool	App	08/80	80	1	0	0
Bury		07/84	85	0	1	0

WELSH Andrew Peter David (Andy)
Born: Manchester, England, 24 January, 1983 — LW
Scotland: Youth

League Club	Source	Date Signed	Seasons Played	Apps	Subs	Gls
Stockport Co	YT	07/01	01-04	44	31	3
Macclesfield T	L	08/02	02	4	2	2
Sunderland	Tr	11/04	04-05	15	6	1
Leicester C	L	03/06	05	4	6	1
Leicester C	L	10/06	06	4	3	0
Blackpool	Toronto FC (CAN)	08/07	07	3	18	0
Yeovil T	Tr	09/08	08-10	82	31	6
Carlisle U	Tr	07/11	11-12	12	21	0
Scunthorpe U	Tr	07/13	13	2	2	0

WELSH Colin
Born: Liverpool, England, 9 June, 1945 — RW
Died: Liverpool, England, 16 March, 1993

League Club	Source	Date Signed	Seasons Played	Apps	Subs	Gls
Southport	Everton (Am)	10/63	64	1	-	0

WELSH Donald (Don)
Born: Manchester, England, 25 February, 1911 — IF/CH
Died: Stevenage, Hertfordshire, England, 2 February, 1990
England: 3/FLge-1/War-9

League Club	Source	Date Signed	Seasons Played	Apps	Subs	Gls
Torquay U	RN Devonport	02/33	32-34	79	-	4
Charlton Ath	Tr	02/35	34-47	199	-	43

WELSH Eric
Born: Belfast, Northern Ireland, 1 May, 1942 — RW
Northern Ireland: 4/U23-1

League Club	Source	Date Signed	Seasons Played	Apps	Subs	Gls
Exeter C	Distillery	09/59	59-65	105	0	19
Carlisle U	Tr	10/65	65-68	72	5	20
Torquay U	Tr	06/69	69-70	38	1	12
Hartlepool U	Tr	07/71	71	13	2	2

WELSH James Patrick (Jimmy)
Born: Edinburgh, Scotland, 21 December, 1923 — IF
Died: Mostyn, Flintshire, Wales, 19 May, 2001

League Club	Source	Date Signed	Seasons Played	Apps	Subs	Gls
Luton T	Tranent Jnrs	09/46				
Aldershot	Tr	06/48	48	5	-	0

WELSH John Joseph
Born: Liverpool, England, 10 January, 1984 — M
England: U21-8/Youth

League Club	Source	Date Signed	Seasons Played	Apps	Subs	Gls
Liverpool	YT	01/01	03-04	2	2	0
Hull C	Tr	08/05	05-06	38	12	3
Chester C	L	01/08	07	6	0	0
Carlisle U	L	10/08	08	2	2	0
Bury	L	03/09	08	3	2	0
Tranmere Rov	Tr	07/09	09-11	128	2	11
Preston NE	Tr	05/12	12-14	92	12	3

WELSH Paul William
Born: Liverpool, England, 10 May, 1966 — CD

League Club	Source	Date Signed	Seasons Played	Apps	Subs	Gls
Preston NE	Formby	05/84	84-85	13	7	1

WELSH Peter Martin
Born: Coatbridge, Lanarkshire, Scotland, 19 July, 1959 — D
England: Schools

League Club	Source	Date Signed	Seasons Played	Apps	Subs	Gls
Leicester C	App	08/76	76-81	24	17	4

WELSH Stephen George (Steve)
Born: Glasgow, Scotland, 19 April, 1968 — CD

League Club	Source	Date Signed	Seasons Played	Apps	Subs	Gls
Cambridge U	Wimborne T	02/90	90	0	1	0
Peterborough U	Tr	08/91	91-94	146	0	2
Peterborough U (L)	Partick Thistle	07/96	96	6	0	0
Lincoln C	Ayr U	08/99	99-00	42	1	0

WELSH-ELLIOTT Ishmael
Born: Deptford, SE London, England, 4 September, 1987 — W

League Club	Source	Date Signed	Seasons Played	Apps	Subs	Gls
Yeovil T	West Ham U (Sch)	07/06	06-07	4	17	1

WELTON Roy Patrick (Pat)
Born: Eltham, SE London, England, 3 May, 1928 — G
Died: Romford, E London, England, 28 June, 2010

League Club	Source	Date Signed	Seasons Played	Apps	Subs	Gls
Leyton Orient	Chislehurst	05/49	49-57	263	-	0
Queens Park Rgrs	Tr	03/58	58	3	-	0

WENT Paul Frank
Born: Bow, E London, England, 12 October, 1949 — CD
England: Youth/Schools

League Club	Source	Date Signed	Seasons Played	Apps	Subs	Gls
Leyton Orient	App	10/66	65-66	48	2	5
Charlton Ath	Tr	06/67	67-71	160	3	15
Fulham	Tr	07/72	72-73	58	0	3
Portsmouth	Tr	12/73	73-76	92	0	5
Cardiff C	Tr	10/76	76-78	71	1	11
Leyton Orient	Tr	09/78	78-79	45	0	3

WERGE Edwin (Eddie)
Born: Sidcup, SE London, England, 9 September, 1936 — W
Died: Emsworth, Hampshire, England, 2 May, 2007

League Club	Source	Date Signed	Seasons Played	Apps	Subs	Gls
Charlton Ath	Jnr	05/55	57-60	44	-	19
Crystal Palace	Tr	05/61	61-64	82	-	6
Leyton Orient	Arcadia Shep's (RSA)	11/66	66-67	30	3	0

WERLING Dominik Patrick
Born: Ludwigshafen, Germany, 13 December, 1982 — LB

League Club	Source	Date Signed	Seasons Played	Apps	Subs	Gls
Barnsley (L)	Sakaryaspor (TKY)	07/07	07	16	1	1
Huddersfield T	Erzebirge Aue (GER)	01/09	08	0	3	0
Darlington		04/10				
Hereford U	Tr	08/10	10	4	2	0

WESOLOWSKI James Peter
Born: Sydney, Australia, 25 August, 1987 — M
Australia: Youth

League Club	Source	Date Signed	Seasons Played	Apps	Subs	Gls
Leicester C	Sch	09/04	05-07	29	17	0
Cheltenham T	L	10/08	08	4	0	0
Peterborough U	Tr	06/10	10	23	9	2
Oldham Ath	Tr	08/11	11-13	90	3	7
Shrewsbury T	Tr	06/14	14	18	3	1

WESSELS Stefan
Born: Rahden, Germany, 28 February, 1979 — G
Germany: U21-2

League Club	Source	Date Signed	Seasons Played	Apps	Subs	Gls
Everton	FC Koln (GER)	08/07	07	2	0	0

WESSON Robert William (Bob)
Born: Thornaby, Cleveland, England, 15 October, 1940 — G

League Club	Source	Date Signed	Seasons Played	Apps	Subs	Gls
Coventry C	Thornaby Boys Brigade	11/58	60-65	133	0	0
Walsall	Tr	09/66	66-72	192	0	0
Doncaster Rov	L	02/70	69	5	0	0

WEST Alan
Born: Hyde, Greater Manchester, England, 18 December, 1951 — M
England: U23-1

League Club	Source	Date Signed	Seasons Played	Apps	Subs	Gls
Burnley	App	12/68	69-72	41	4	3
Luton T	Tr	10/73	73-80	272	13	16
Millwall	Tr	07/81	81-82	58	0	4

WEST Colin
Born: Wallsend, Tyne and Wear, England, 13 November, 1962 — F

League Club	Source	Date Signed	Seasons Played	Apps	Subs	Gls
Sunderland	App	07/80	81-84	88	14	21
Watford	Tr	03/85	84-85	45	0	20
Sheffield Wed	Glasgow Rangers	09/87	87-88	40	5	8
West Bromwich A	Tr	02/89	88-91	64	9	22
Port Vale	L	11/91	91	5	0	1
Swansea C	Tr	08/92	92	29	4	12
Leyton Orient	Tr	07/93	93-97	132	10	42
Northampton T	L	09/97	97	1	1	0
Hartlepool U	Northwich Victoria	11/99	99	0	1	0

WEST Colin William
Born: Middlesbrough, England, 19 September, 1967 — F
England: Youth

League Club	Source	Date Signed	Seasons Played	Apps	Subs	Gls
Chelsea	App	09/85	86-87	8	8	4
Swansea C	L	03/89	88	14	0	3
Hartlepool U	Dundee	08/93	93	29	7	5

WEST David Christopher (Dave)
Born: Dorchester, Dorset, England, 16 November, 1964 — LW

League Club	Source	Date Signed	Seasons Played	Apps	Subs	Gls
Liverpool	Dorchester T	03/83				
Torquay U	Bristol C (NC)	09/85	85	19	2	2

WEST Dean
Born: Morley, West Yorkshire, England, 5 December, 1972 — RB/M

League Club	Source	Date Signed	Seasons Played	Apps	Subs	Gls
Lincoln C	YT	08/91	90-95	93	26	20
Bury	Tr	09/95	95-98	100	10	8
Burnley	Tr	07/99	99-03	145	13	5
Lincoln C	Tr	07/04	04	4	0	0
Boston U	Tr	09/04	04	22	2	0

WEST Edward (Ted)
Born: Parbold, Lancashire, England, 4 November, 1930 — LB
Died: Mansfield, Nottinghamshire, England, April, 2002

League Club	Source	Date Signed	Seasons Played	Apps	Subs	Gls
Doncaster Rov	Eastbourne U	02/53				
Gillingham	Tr	07/54	54-56	98	-	0
Oldham Ath	Tr	07/57	57-60	117	-	0

WEST Gary
Born: Scunthorpe, North Lincolnshire, England, 25 August, 1964 — CD
England: Youth

League Club	Source	Date Signed	Seasons Played	Apps	Subs	Gls
Sheffield U	App	08/82	82-84	75	0	1
Lincoln C	Tr	08/85	85-86	83	0	4
Gillingham	Tr	07/87	87-88	51	1	3
Port Vale	Tr	02/89	88-89	14	3	1
Gillingham	L	11/90	90	1	0	0
Lincoln C	L	01/91	90	3	0	0
Lincoln C	Tr	08/91	91	14	4	1
Walsall	L	09/92	92	9	0	1

WEST Gordon
Born: Darfield, South Yorkshire, England, 24 April, 1943 — G
Died: Crosby, Merseyside, England, 10 June, 2012
England: 3/FLge-1/U23-3

League Club	Source	Date Signed	Seasons Played	Apps	Subs	Gls
Blackpool	Jnr	05/61	60-61	31	-	0
Everton	Tr	03/62	61-72	335	0	0
Tranmere Rov	Tr	10/75	76-78	17	0	0

WEST Michael
Born: Maidstone, Kent, England, 9 February, 1991 — RW

League Club	Source	Date Signed	Seasons Played	Apps	Subs	Gls
Crewe Alex	Ebbsfleet U	07/12	12-13	5	5	0

WEST Paul Darrell
Born: Stafford, England, 22 June, 1970 — D

League Club	Source	Date Signed	Seasons Played	Apps	Subs	Gls
Port Vale	Alcester T	12/91				
Bradford C	Tr	07/92				
Wigan Ath	Tr	08/93	93-94	2	1	0

WEST Taribo
Born: Port Harcourt, Nigeria, 26 March, 1974 — CD
Nigeria: 41

League Club	Source	Date Signed	Seasons Played	Apps	Subs	Gls
Derby Co (L)	AC Milan (ITA)	11/00	00	18	0	0
Plymouth Arg	Al Arabi (QAT)	07/05	05	4	0	0

WEST Thomas Norton (Tom)
Born: Salford, England, 8 December, 1916 — CF
Died: Salford, England, May, 1987

League Club	Source	Date Signed	Seasons Played	Apps	Subs	Gls
Stockport Co		03/38	37-38	3	-	1
Oldham Ath		10/45				
Rochdale	Tr	06/46	46	4	-	2

WEST Trefor John
Born: Coventry, England, 14 December, 1944 — RB

League Club	Source	Date Signed	Seasons Played	Apps	Subs	Gls
West Bromwich A	App	05/62				
Walsall	Tr	05/64	64	12	-	0

WESTAWAY Kevin David
Born: Bristol, England, 24 November, 1962 — FB

League Club	Source	Date Signed	Seasons Played	Apps	Subs	Gls
Bristol Rov	App	11/80	80-81	2	0	0

WESTBY Jack Leslie
Born: Braintree, Essex, England, 20 May, 1917 — RB
Died: Liverpool, England, 17 November, 2006

League Club	Source	Date Signed	Seasons Played	Apps	Subs	Gls
Blackburn Rov	Burscough	01/37	37	2	-	0
Liverpool	Tr	05/44				
Southport	Tr	08/47	47	13	-	0

WESTCARR Craig Naptali
Born: Nottingham, England, 29 January, 1985 — F/W
England: Youth/Schools

League Club	Source	Date Signed	Seasons Played	Apps	Subs	Gls
Nottingham F	Sch	01/02	01-04	2	21	1
Lincoln C	L	12/04	04	5	1	1
MK Dons	L	03/05	04	0	4	0
Notts Co	Kettering T	05/09	09-11	71	16	21
Chesterfield	Tr	08/11	11-12	42	11	10
Walsall	Tr	11/12	12-13	58	9	19
Portsmouth	Tr	06/14	14	21	12	6

WESTCOTT Dennis
Born: Wallasey, Wirral, England, 2 July, 1917 — CF
Died: Stafford, England, 13 July, 1960
England: FLge-1/War-4

League Club	Source	Date Signed	Seasons Played	Apps	Subs	Gls
New Brighton	Leasowe Rd Brickworks	01/36	35	18	-	10
Wolverhampton W	Tr	07/36	36-47	128	-	105
Blackburn Rov	Tr	04/48	48-49	63	-	37
Manchester C	Tr	02/50	49-51	72	-	37
Chesterfield	Tr	06/52	52	40	-	21

WESTCOTT John Peter James
Born: Eastbourne, East Sussex, England, 31 May, 1979 — RW

League Club	Source	Date Signed	Seasons Played	Apps	Subs	Gls
Brighton & HA	YT	07/97	97-98	19	19	0

WESTERVELD Sander
Born: Enschede, Netherlands, 23 October, 1974 — G
Netherlands: 6/Youth

League Club	Source	Date Signed	Seasons Played	Apps	Subs	Gls
Liverpool	Vitesse Arnhem (NED)	06/99	99-01	75	0	0
Portsmouth	Real Sociedad (SPN)	07/05	05	6	0	0
Everton	L	02/06	05	2	0	0

WESTHEAD Mark Lee
Born: Blackpool, Lancashire, England, 19 July, 1975 — G

League Club	Source	Date Signed	Seasons Played	Apps	Subs	Gls
Bolton W	Blackpool Mechanics	11/94				
Wycombe W	Telford U	08/98	98-99	3	1	0

WESTLAKE Brian
Born: Newcastle-under-Lyme, Potteries, England, 19 September, 1943 — CF/M

League Club	Source	Date Signed	Seasons Played	Apps	Subs	Gls
Stoke C		09/61				
Doncaster Rov	Tr	06/63	63	5	-	1
Halifax T	Tr	01/64	63-66	100	0	28
Tranmere Rov	Tr	09/66	66	13	1	3
Colchester U	Tr	02/67	66	14	1	5

WESTLAKE Darryl James
Born: Sutton Coldfield, West Midlands, England, 1 March, 1991 — RB

League Club	Source	Date Signed	Seasons Played	Apps	Subs	Gls
Walsall	Sch	07/09	09-11	60	7	1
Sheffield U	Tr	07/12	12-13	12	6	0
Mansfield T	L	11/13	13	23	0	0

WESTLAKE Francis Arthur (Frank)
Born: Bolton-on-Dearne, South Yorkshire, England, 11 August, 1915 — RB
Died: Doncaster, South Yorkshire, England, 13 February, 1999

League Club	Source	Date Signed	Seasons Played	Apps	Subs	Gls
Sheffield Wed	Thurnscoe Victoria	05/37	37-49	110	-	0
Halifax T	Tr	06/50	50	2	-	0

WESTLAKE Ian John
Born: Clacton, Essex, England, 10 July, 1983 — M

League Club	Source	Date Signed	Seasons Played	Apps	Subs	Gls
Ipswich T	Sch	08/02	02-05	90	24	15
Leeds U	Tr	08/06	06-07	29	18	1
Brighton & HA	L	03/08	07	11	0	2
Cheltenham T	Tr	10/08	08	22	0	2
Oldham Ath	L	03/09	08	5	0	0
Wycombe W	Tr	07/09	09	7	2	0

WESTLAND James (Jim)
Born: Aberdeen, Scotland, 21 July, 1916 — IF
Died: Newcastle-under-Lyme, Potteries, England, 21 April, 1972

League Club	Source	Date Signed	Seasons Played	Apps	Subs	Gls
Stoke C	Aberdeen	09/35	35-38	60	-	16
Mansfield T	Tr	11/46	46	10	-	0

WESTLEY Graham Neil
Born: Hounslow, SW London, England, 4 March, 1968 — F
England: Youth

League Club	Source	Date Signed	Seasons Played	Apps	Subs	Gls
Gillingham	Queens Park Rgrs (App)	03/86	85-86	1	1	0

WESTLEY Shane Lee Mark
Born: Canterbury, England, 16 June, 1965 — CD

League Club	Source	Date Signed	Seasons Played	Apps	Subs	Gls
Charlton Ath	App	06/83	83	8	0	0
Southend U	Tr	03/85	84-88	142	2	10
Wolverhampton W	Tr	06/89	89-92	48	2	1
Brentford	Tr	10/92	92-94	61	3	1
Southend U	L	02/95	94	4	1	0
Cambridge U	Tr	08/95	95	3	0	0
Lincoln C	Tr	10/95	95	9	0	1

WESTMORLAND Joseph Edward (Joe)
Born: Dalston, Cumbria, England, 30 June, 1937 — LB

League Club	Source	Date Signed	Seasons Played	Apps	Subs	Gls
Carlisle U		02/59	58	3	-	0

WESTON Anthony Douglas (Tony)
Born: Yalding, Kent, England, 3 April, 1945 — RB

League Club	Source	Date Signed	Seasons Played	Apps	Subs	Gls
Gillingham	Bromley	11/63	64-69	162	0	3

WESTON Curtis James
Born: Greenwich, SE London, England, 24 January, 1987 — M

League Club	Source	Date Signed	Seasons Played	Apps	Subs	Gls
Millwall	Sch	03/04	03-04	2	2	0
Swindon T	Tr	07/06	06	21	6	1
Leeds U	Tr	08/07	07	1	6	1
Scunthorpe U	L	03/08	07	2	5	0
Gillingham	Tr	08/08	08-11	129	18	15
Barnet	Tr	08/12	12	19	10	0

WESTON Donald Patrick (Don)
Born: Mansfield, Nottinghamshire, England, 6 March, 1936 — IF
Died: Mansfield, Nottinghamshire, England, 19 January, 2007

League Club	Source	Date Signed	Seasons Played	Apps	Subs	Gls
Wrexham	Kinnell Park Barracks	06/59	58-59	42	-	21
Birmingham C	Tr	01/60	59-60	23	-	3
Rotherham U	Tr	12/60	60-62	74	-	23
Leeds U	Tr	12/62	62-65	68	0	24
Huddersfield T	Tr	10/65	65-66	20	2	7
Wrexham	Tr	12/66	66-67	42	0	19
Chester C	Tr	06/68	68	1	2	0

WESTON Ian Paul
Born: Bristol, England, 6 May, 1968 — M

League Club	Source	Date Signed	Seasons Played	Apps	Subs	Gls
Bristol Rov	App	05/86	86-87	13	3	0
Torquay U	Tr	09/88	88-89	57	5	2

WESTON James John (Jimmy)
Born: Prescot, Merseyside, England, 16 November, 1955 — W/LB

League Club	Source	Date Signed	Seasons Played	Apps	Subs	Gls
Blackpool	Skelmersdale U	01/74	75-79	97	8	8
Torquay U	Tr	06/80	80-81	38	0	1
Wigan Ath	Tr	09/81	81-82	63	3	2

WESTON Myles Arthur Eugene Wesley
Born: Lewisham, SE London, England, 12 March, 1988 — LW
Antigua & Barbuda: 1//England: Youth

League Club	Source	Date Signed	Seasons Played	Apps	Subs	Gls
Charlton Ath	Sch	06/06				
Notts Co	Tr	03/07	06-08	59	14	3
Brentford	Tr	07/09	09-11	76	32	12
Gillingham	Tr	08/12	12-13	42	34	10
Southend U	Tr	06/14	14	17	17	2

WESTON Reginald Harold (Reg)
Born: Greenhithe, Kent, England, 16 January, 1918 — CH
Died: Burton-on-Trent, Staffordshire, England, 17 February, 1998
Wales: WLge-1

League Club	Source	Date Signed	Seasons Played	Apps	Subs	Gls
Swansea C	Northfleet	03/45	46-51	229	-	1
Derby Co	Tr	10/52				

WESTON Rhys David
Born: Kingston-on-Thames, SW London, England, 27 October, 1980 — CD
England: Youth/Schools//Wales: 7/U21-4

League Club	Source	Date Signed	Seasons Played	Apps	Subs	Gls
Arsenal	YT	07/99	99	1	0	0
Cardiff C	Tr	11/00	00-05	170	12	2
Port Vale	Viking Stavanger (NOR)	02/07	06	15	0	0
Walsall	Tr	07/07	07-09	96	6	1
AFC Wimbledon	Sabah (MLY)	08/13	13	6	1	0

WESTWELL Simon
Born: Clitheroe, Lancashire, England, 12 November, 1961 — D

League Club	Source	Date Signed	Seasons Played	Apps	Subs	Gls
Preston NE	App	10/79	80-82	63	0	1

WESTWOOD Ashley Michael
Born: Bridgnorth, Shropshire, England, 31 August, 1976 — CD
England: Youth

League Club	Source	Date Signed	Seasons Played	Apps	Subs	Gls
Manchester U	YT	07/94				
Crewe Alex	Tr	07/95	95-97	93	5	9
Bradford C	Tr	07/98	98-99	18	6	2
Sheffield Wed	Tr	08/00	00-02	79	3	5
Northampton T	Tr	07/03	03-05	27	4	2
Chester C	Tr	08/06	06	21	0	3
Swindon T	L	03/07	06	8	1	0
Port Vale	L	08/07	07	11	1	0
Crewe Alex	Kettering T	01/11	10	7	1	0
Northampton T	Tr	08/11	11	14	3	1

WESTWOOD Ashley Roy
Born: Nantwich, Cheshire, England, 1 April, 1990 — M

League Club	Source	Date Signed	Seasons Played	Apps	Subs	Gls
Crewe Alex	Sch	05/08	08-12	121	7	14
Aston Villa	Tr	08/12	12-14	88	4	3

WESTWOOD Christopher John (Chris)
Born: Dudley, West Midlands, England, 13 February, 1977 — CD

League Club	Source	Date Signed	Seasons Played	Apps	Subs	Gls
Wolverhampton W	YT	07/95	97	3	1	1
Hartlepool U	Reading (NC)	03/99	98-04	244	6	7
Walsall	Tr	07/05	05-06	64	5	5
Peterborough U	Tr	07/07	07-08	45	8	0
Cheltenham T	L	01/09	08	9	0	2
Wycombe W	Tr	07/09	09-10	52	3	3

WESTWOOD Daniel Robert (Danny)
Born: Dagenham, E London, England, 25 July, 1953 — F

League Club	Source	Date Signed	Seasons Played	Apps	Subs	Gls
Queens Park Rgrs	Billericay T	07/74	74	0	1	1
Gillingham	Tr	11/75	75-81	201	10	74

WESTWOOD Eric
Born: Manchester, England, 25 September, 1917 — LB
Died: Manchester, England, July, 2001
England: B-2/FLge-2

League Club	Source	Date Signed	Seasons Played	Apps	Subs	Gls
Manchester C	Manchester U (Am)	11/37	38-52	248	-	3

WESTWOOD Gary Michael
Born: Barrow, Cumbria, England, 3 April, 1963 — G
England: Youth

League Club	Source	Date Signed	Seasons Played	Apps	Subs	Gls
Ipswich T	App	04/81				
Reading	L	09/83	83	5	0	0
Reading	Tr	07/84	84-87	123	0	0

WESTWOOD Keiren
Born: Manchester, England, 23 October, 1984 — G
Republic of Ireland: 17

League Club	Source	Date Signed	Seasons Played	Apps	Subs	Gls
Manchester C	Sch	10/01				
Carlisle U	Tr	08/04	05-07	127	0	0
Coventry C	Tr	06/08	08-10	131	0	0
Sunderland	Tr	07/11	11-13	18	1	0
Sheffield Wed	Tr	07/14	14	43	0	0

WESTWOOD William Raymond (Ray)
Born: Kingswinford, West Midlands, England, 14 April, 1912 — IF
Died: Brierley Hill, West Midlands, England, January, 1982
England: 6/FLge-5

League Club	Source	Date Signed	Seasons Played	Apps	Subs	Gls
Bolton W	Brierley Hill Alliance	03/30	30-47	301	-	127
Chester C	Tr	12/47	47-48	38	-	13

WETHERALL David
Born: Sheffield, England, 14 March, 1971 — CD
England: Schools

League Club	Source	Date Signed	Seasons Played	Apps	Subs	Gls
Sheffield Wed	YT	07/89				
Leeds U	Tr	07/91	91-98	188	14	12
Bradford C	Tr	07/99	99-07	301	3	18

WETTON Albert Smailes (Bert)
Born: Winlaton, Tyne and Wear, England, 23 October, 1928 — CH
Died: Enfield, N London, England, 17 December, 1996

League Club	Source	Date Signed	Seasons Played	Apps	Subs	Gls
Tottenham H	Cheshunt	10/49				
Brighton & HA	Tr	06/51	51-52	3	-	0
Crewe Alex	Tr	10/53	53	2	-	0

WETTON Ralph
Born: Winlaton, Tyne and Wear, England, 6 June, 1927 — LH

League Club	Source	Date Signed	Seasons Played	Apps	Subs	Gls
Tottenham H	Cheshunt	08/50	51-54	45	-	0
Plymouth Arg	Tr	06/55	55	36	-	1
Aldershot	Tr	11/56	56-57	50	-	1

WHALE Raymond (Ray)
Born: West Bromwich, West Midlands, England, 23 February, 1937 — LH/LB
Died: Walsall, West Midlands, England, November, 2002

League Club	Source	Date Signed	Seasons Played	Apps	Subs	Gls
West Bromwich A	West Bromwich CA	12/54				
Southend U	Tr	04/59	59-60	29	-	0

WHALEY Kenneth (Ken)
Born: Leeds, England, 22 June, 1935 — CF

League Club	Source	Date Signed	Seasons Played	Apps	Subs	Gls
Bradford Park Ave		06/57	58	1	-	0

WHALEY Simon
Born: Bolton, Greater Manchester, England, 7 June, 1985 — W

League Club	Source	Date Signed	Seasons Played	Apps	Subs	Gls
Bury	Sch	10/02	02-05	48	25	11
Preston NE	Tr	01/06	05-08	74	46	14
Barnsley	L	11/08	08	4	0	1
Norwich C	Tr	07/09	09	3	0	0
Rochdale	L	09/09	09	8	1	2
Bradford C	L	11/09	09	5	1	1
Chesterfield	Tr	02/10	09	5	1	1
Doncaster Rov		11/10				
Burton A	Tr	03/11	10	1	2	0

WHALLEY David Neil (Neil)
Born: Liverpool, England, 29 October, 1965 — M

League Club	Source	Date Signed	Seasons Played	Apps	Subs	Gls
Preston NE	Warrington T	03/93	92-94	45	5	1

WHALLEY Gareth
Born: Manchester, England, 19 December, 1973 — M

League Club	Source	Date Signed	Seasons Played	Apps	Subs	Gls
Crewe Alex	YT	07/92	92-97	174	6	9
Bradford C	Tr	07/98	98-01	99	4	3
Crewe Alex	L	03/02	01	7	0	0
Cardiff C	Tr	07/02	02-03	33	8	2
Wigan Ath	Tr	09/04	04	7	1	0
Swindon T	Tr	07/05	05	23	1	0

WHALLEY George Douglas
Born: Darlington, County Durham, England, 30 July, 1920 — LW
Died: Darlington, County Durham, England, 25 September, 2006

League Club	Source	Date Signed	Seasons Played	Apps	Subs	Gls
Gateshead	Heart of Midlothian	09/46	46	5	-	0

WHALLEY Harold
Born: Nelson, Lancashire, England, 4 April, 1923 — LW
Died: Nelson, Lancashire, England, October, 1997

League Club	Source	Date Signed	Seasons Played	Apps	Subs	Gls
Accrington Stan	Barnoldswick T	12/46	46	3	-	0

WHALLEY Herbert (Bert)
Born: Ashton-under-Lyne, Greater Manchester, England, 6 August, 1913 — LH
Died: Munich, Germany, 6 February, 1958

League Club	Source	Date Signed	Seasons Played	Apps	Subs	Gls
Manchester U	Stalybridge Celtic	05/34	35-46	32	-	0

WHALLEY Jeffrey Hugh (Jeff)
Born: Rossendale, Lancashire, England, 8 February, 1952 — W

League Club	Source	Date Signed	Seasons Played	Apps	Subs	Gls
Blackburn Rov	App	02/70	69-70	2	0	0

WHALLEY Selwyn Davies
Born: Stoke-on-Trent, England, 24 February, 1934 — RB/WH
Died: Stafford, England, 8 August, 2008

League Club	Source	Date Signed	Seasons Played	Apps	Subs	Gls
Port Vale		08/53	56-65	178	0	7

WHALLEY Shaun James
Born: Prescot, Merseyside, England, 7 August, 1987 — LW

League Club	Source	Date Signed	Seasons Played	Apps	Subs	Gls
Chester C	Southport (Jnr)	09/04	04	0	3	0
Accrington Stan	Witton A	11/06	06-07	27	24	5
Luton T	Southport	05/13	14	14	4	3

WHARE William Frederick (Bill)
Born: Guernsey, Channel Islands, 14 May, 1924 — RB
Died: Nottingham, England, 28 May, 1995

League Club	Source	Date Signed	Seasons Played	Apps	Subs	Gls
Nottingham F	St Martin's, Guernsey	05/47	48-59	298	-	2

WHARTON Andrew (Andy)
Born: Bacup, Lancashire, England, 21 December, 1961 — LB

League Club	Source	Date Signed	Seasons Played	Apps	Subs	Gls
Burnley	App	12/79	80-83	63	2	6
Torquay U	L	11/83	83	10	0	0
Chester C	Tr	02/84	83-84	19	4	2

WHARTON Benjamin Francis (Ben)
Born: Stockport, Greater Manchester, England, 17 June, 1990 — F

League Club	Source	Date Signed	Seasons Played	Apps	Subs	Gls
Rochdale	Sch	07/06	07	0	1	0

WHARTON Guy
Born: Darfield, South Yorkshire, England, 5 December, 1916 — LH
Died: Chelmsford, England, April, 1990

League Club	Source	Date Signed	Seasons Played	Apps	Subs	Gls
Chester C	Broomhill	05/34	35	12	-	5
Wolverhampton W	Tr	05/36	36-37	29	-	2
Portsmouth	Tr	11/37	37-47	93	-	4
Darlington	Wellington T	07/48	48-49	39	-	2

WHARTON John Edwin (Jackie)
Born: Bolton, Greater Manchester, England, 18 June, 1920 — W
Died: Worcester, England, May, 1997

League Club	Source	Date Signed	Seasons Played	Apps	Subs	Gls
Plymouth Arg	Bolton W (Am)	06/37	38	11	-	2
Preston NE	Tr	07/39	46	25	-	7
Manchester C	Tr	03/47	46-47	23	-	2
Blackburn Rov	Tr	06/48	48-52	129	-	14
Newport Co	Tr	02/53	52-54	72	-	10

WHARTON Kenneth (Ken)
Born: Newcastle-upon-Tyne, England, 28 November, 1960 — LB/M

League Club	Source	Date Signed	Seasons Played	Apps	Subs	Gls
Newcastle U	Grainger Park BC	01/79	78-88	268	22	26
Carlisle U	Tr	08/89	89	1	0	0
Bradford C	Tr	08/89	89	5	0	0

WHARTON Paul William
Born: Newcastle-upon-Tyne, England, 26 June, 1977 — M
England: Youth

League Club	Source	Date Signed	Seasons Played	Apps	Subs	Gls
Leeds U	YT	06/94				
Hull C	Tr	02/96	95-97	8	3	0

WHARTON Sean Robert
Born: Newport, Wales, 31 October, 1968 — F

League Club	Source	Date Signed	Seasons Played	Apps	Subs	Gls
Sunderland	YT	07/87	88	1	0	0

WHARTON Terence John (Terry)
Born: Bolton, Greater Manchester, England, 1 July, 1942 — RW

League Club	Source	Date Signed	Seasons Played	Apps	Subs	Gls
Wolverhampton W	Jnr	01/59	61-67	223	1	69
Bolton W	Tr	11/67	67-70	101	1	28
Crystal Palace	Tr	01/71	70-71	19	1	1
Walsall	Durban C (RSA)	11/73	73	1	0	0

WHATLING Keith Richard
Born: Worlingworth, Suffolk, England, 1 November, 1947 — LW

League Club	Source	Date Signed	Seasons Played	Apps	Subs	Gls
Ipswich T	Jnr	03/66				
Exeter C	Tr	07/67	67-68	19	3	3

WHATMORE Neil
Born: Ellesmere Port, Cheshire, England, 17 May, 1955 — F

League Club	Source	Date Signed	Seasons Played	Apps	Subs	Gls
Bolton W	App	05/73	72-80	262	15	102
Birmingham C	Tr	08/81	81-82	24	2	6
Oxford U	L	10/82	82	7	0	5
Bolton W	L	12/82	82	10	0	3
Oxford U	Tr	02/83	82-83	26	3	10
Bolton W	L	03/84	83	7	0	2
Burnley	Tr	08/84	84	8	0	1
Mansfield T	Tr	11/84	84-86	71	1	20
Bolton W	Tr	08/87				
Mansfield T	Tr	11/87	87	0	6	0

WHATMOUGH Jack David Vincent
Born: Gosport, Hampshire, England, 24 June, 1996 — CD

League Club	Source	Date Signed	Seasons Played	Apps	Subs	Gls
Portsmouth	Sch	08/13	13-14	32	2	0

WHEAT Arthur Bradley
Born: Selston, Nottinghamshire, England, 26 October, 1921 — LH/IF

League Club	Source	Date Signed	Seasons Played	Apps	Subs	Gls
Bradford Park Ave	Montrose	12/49	50-51	22	-	3
York C	Tr	08/52	52	4	-	0

WHEATCROFT Paul Michael
Born: Manchester, England, 22 November, 1980 — F
England: Youth/Schools

League Club	Source	Date Signed	Seasons Played	Apps	Subs	Gls
Manchester U	YT	07/98				
Bolton W	Tr	07/00				
Rochdale	L	09/01	01	6	0	3
Mansfield T	L	02/02	01	1	1	0
Scunthorpe U	Tr	08/02	02	2	2	0

WHEATER David James
Born: Redcar, Cleveland, England, 14 February, 1987 — CD
England: U21-11/Youth

League Club	Source	Date Signed	Seasons Played	Apps	Subs	Gls
Middlesbrough	Sch	02/05	05-10	136	4	9
Doncaster Rov	L	02/06	05	7	0	1
Wolverhampton W	L	09/06	06	1	0	0
Darlington	L	01/07	06	15	0	2
Bolton W	Tr	01/11	10-14	63	12	4

WHEATLEY Barrie
Born: Sandbach, Cheshire, England, 21 February, 1938 — IF

League Club	Source	Date Signed	Seasons Played	Apps	Subs	Gls
Liverpool	Rode Heath	03/56				
Crewe Alex	Tr	07/57	57-65	235	0	49
Rochdale	Tr	07/66	66	13	0	4

WHEATLEY Harold Joseph (Joe)
Born: Bromborough, Wirral, England, 8 May, 1920 — RH
Died: Wrexham, Wales, November, 2014

League Club	Source	Date Signed	Seasons Played	Apps	Subs	Gls
Port Vale	Ellesmere Port T	03/38	38	2	-	0
Shrewsbury T	Tr	07/46	50	7	-	0

WHEATLEY Roland (Ron)
Born: Nottingham, England, 20 June, 1924 — LH/IF
Died: Nottingham, England, 21 July, 2003

League Club	Source	Date Signed	Seasons Played	Apps	Subs	Gls
Nottingham F	Beeston BC	06/46	47-48	6	-	0
Southampton	Tr	01/49	48-50	10	-	1
Grimsby T	Tr	06/51	51	5	-	0

WHEATLEY Stephen John (Steve)
Born: Bishop Auckland, County Durham, England, 12 April, 1959 — G

League Club	Source	Date Signed	Seasons Played	Apps	Subs	Gls
Gillingham	App	04/77	76-77	4	0	0

WHEATLEY Stephen Peter (Steve)
Born: Hinckley, Leicestershire, England, 26 December, 1929 — RW
Died: Hinckley, Leicestershire, England, 23 September, 2008

League Club	Source	Date Signed	Seasons Played	Apps	Subs	Gls
Derby Co	Hinckley U	12/50	51-52	4	-	0
Chesterfield	Boston U	07/55	55	3	-	0

WHEATLEY Thomas (Tom)
Born: Hebburn, Tyne and Wear, England, 1 June, 1929 — G
Died: Chesterfield, Derbyshire, England, April, 2009

League Club	Source	Date Signed	Seasons Played	Apps	Subs	Gls
Leeds U	Amble	04/53	53	6	-	0

WHEATLEY William
Born: Mansfield, Nottinghamshire, England, 5 November, 1920 — W
Died: Mansfield, Nottinghamshire, England, 20 May, 1965

League Club	Source	Date Signed	Seasons Played	Apps	Subs	Gls
Mansfield T	Mansfield Colliery	08/48	48-49	38	-	3

WHEATON Gilbert John (Gil)
Born: Mickley, Northumberland, England, 1 November, 1941 — CH

League Club	Source	Date Signed	Seasons Played	Apps	Subs	Gls
Grimsby T	Mickley Colliery	09/60	62	7	-	0
Chester C	Tr	06/63	63	1	-	0

WHEELDON Thomas Edward (Tommy)
Born: Prescot, Merseyside, England, 28 December, 1957 — M
England: Schools

League Club	Source	Date Signed	Seasons Played	Apps	Subs	Gls
Everton	YT	12/76				
Torquay U	Runcorn	09/81	81	5	3	0
Torquay U	Falmouth	08/85	85	6	2	0

WHEELER Adam Lawrence
Born: Sheffield, England, 29 November, 1977 — G

League Club	Source	Date Signed	Seasons Played	Apps	Subs	Gls
Doncaster Rov	Newcastle U (YT)	04/96	96	1	0	0

WHEELER Alfred John (Alf)
Born: Fareham, Hampshire, England, 6 April, 1922 — RW
Died: Lancashire, England, January, 2013

League Club	Source	Date Signed	Seasons Played	Apps	Subs	Gls
Blackburn Rov	Portsmouth (Am)	04/47	47-48	21	-	5
Swindon T	Tr	07/49	49-50	23	-	4

WHEELER Arthur James (Jimmy)
Born: Reading, England, 21 December, 1933 — W/IF

League Club	Source	Date Signed	Seasons Played	Apps	Subs	Gls
Reading	Huntley & Palmers	08/52	52-66	404	1	143

WHEELER David John
Born: Brighton, England, 4 October, 1990 — RW
England: Schools

League Club	Source	Date Signed	Seasons Played	Apps	Subs	Gls
Exeter C	Staines T	08/13	13-14	34	46	10

WHEELER John Edward (Johnny)
Born: Crosby, Merseyside, England, 26 July, 1928 — WH/IF
England: 1/B-4/FLge-2

League Club	Source	Date Signed	Seasons Played	Apps	Subs	Gls
Tranmere Rov	Carlton	04/46	48-50	101	-	9
Bolton W	Tr	02/51	50-55	189	-	18
Liverpool	Tr	09/56	56-61	164	-	21

WHEELER Paul
Born: Caerphilly, Wales, 3 January, 1965 — M/F

League Club	Source	Date Signed	Seasons Played	Apps	Subs	Gls
Bristol Rov	App	01/83				
Cardiff C	Aberaman	08/85	85-88	72	29	10
Hull C	Tr	10/89	89	0	5	0
Hereford U	Tr	02/90	89-90	34	20	12
Stockport Co	Tr	08/91	91-92	13	10	5
Scarborough	L	10/92	92	2	5	1
Chester C	Tr	01/93	92-93	34	5	7

WHEELER William Hunter
Born: Carlisle, Cumbria, England, 27 September, 1920 — WH

League Club	Source	Date Signed	Seasons Played	Apps	Subs	Gls
Carlisle U		10/46	46	4	-	0

WHEELER William John (Jack)
Born: Evesham, Worcestershire, England, 13 July, 1919 — G
Died: Nottingham, England, 10 January, 2009

League Club	Source	Date Signed	Seasons Played	Apps	Subs	Gls
Birmingham C	Cheltenham T	03/38	38-47	12	-	0
Huddersfield T	Tr	08/48	48-55	166	-	0

WHELAN Anthony Gerard (Tony)
Born: Dublin, Republic of Ireland, 23 November, 1959 — FB
Republic of Ireland: U21-1

League Club	Source	Date Signed	Seasons Played	Apps	Subs	Gls
Manchester U	Bohemians (ROI)	08/80	80	0	1	0

WHELAN Anthony Michael (Tony)
Born: Salford, England, 20 November, 1952 — F/M

League Club	Source	Date Signed	Seasons Played	Apps	Subs	Gls
Manchester U	App	12/69				
Manchester C	Tr	03/73	72-73	3	3	0
Rochdale	Tr	07/74	74-76	124	0	20

WHELAN David (Dave)
Born: Bradford, England, 24 November, 1936 — FB

League Club	Source	Date Signed	Seasons Played	Apps	Subs	Gls
Blackburn Rov	Wigan BC	12/53	56-59	78	-	3
Crewe Alex	Tr	01/63	62-65	115	0	0

WHELAN Glenn David
Born: Dublin, Republic of Ireland, 13 January, 1984 — DM
Republic of Ireland: 61/U21-14/Youth

League Club	Source	Date Signed	Seasons Played	Apps	Subs	Gls
Manchester C	YT	01/01				
Bury	L	09/03	03	13	0	0
Sheffield Wed	Tr	07/04	04-07	136	6	12
Stoke C	Tr	01/08	07-14	185	39	5

WHELAN Noel David
Born: Leeds, England, 30 December, 1974 — F
England: U21-2/Youth

League Club	Source	Date Signed	Seasons Played	Apps	Subs	Gls
Leeds U	YT	03/93	92-95	28	20	7
Coventry C	Tr	12/95	95-99	127	7	31
Middlesbrough	Tr	08/00	00-02	33	28	6
Crystal Palace	L	03/03	02	7	1	3
Millwall	Tr	08/03	03	8	7	4
Derby Co	Tr	01/04	03	3	5	0
Boston U	Aberdeen	07/05	05	8	7	4
Darlington	Harrogate T	10/09	09	2	1	0

WHELAN Philip James (Phil)
Born: Reddish, Greater Manchester, England, 7 August, 1972 — CD
England: U21-3

League Club	Source	Date Signed	Seasons Played	Apps	Subs	Gls
Ipswich T	Jnr	07/90	91-94	76	6	2
Middlesbrough	Tr	04/95	95-96	18	4	1
Oxford U	Tr	07/97	97-99	51	3	2
Rotherham U	L	03/99	98	13	0	4
Southend U	Tr	07/00	00-02	96	4	6

WHELAN Robert (Bob)
Born: Salford, England, 9 November, 1930 — RH

League Club	Source	Date Signed	Seasons Played	Apps	Subs	Gls
Manchester C	Salford LC	04/50				
Oldham Ath	Tr	07/52	52	1	-	0

WHELAN Ronald Andrew (Ronnie)
Born: Dublin, Republic of Ireland, 25 September, 1961 — M
Republic of Ireland: 53/B/U21-1/Youth/Schools

League Club	Source	Date Signed	Seasons Played	Apps	Subs	Gls
Liverpool	Home Farm (ROI)	10/79	80-93	351	11	45
Southend U	Tr	09/94	94-95	34	0	1

WHELAN Spencer Randall
Born: Liverpool, England, 17 September, 1971 — D

League Club	Source	Date Signed	Seasons Played	Apps	Subs	Gls
Chester C	Liverpool (YT)	04/90	90-97	196	19	8
Shrewsbury T	Tr	11/98	98-99	24	1	0

WHELAN William Augustine (Liam)
Born: Dublin, Republic of Ireland, 1 April, 1935 — IF
Died: Munich, Germany, 6 February, 1958
Republic of Ireland: 4

League Club	Source	Date Signed	Seasons Played	Apps	Subs	Gls
Manchester U	Home Farm (ROI)	05/53	54-57	79	-	43

WHELLANS Robert (Robbie)
Born: Harrogate, North Yorkshire, England, 14 February, 1969 — F

League Club	Source	Date Signed	Seasons Played	Apps	Subs	Gls
Bradford C	App	06/87				
Hartlepool U	L	12/87	87	8	3	1
Rochdale	Tr	07/89	89	5	6	1

WHELPDALE Christopher Mark (Chris)
Born: Harold Wood, E London, England, 27 January, 1987 — RW

League Club	Source	Date Signed	Seasons Played	Apps	Subs	Gls
Peterborough U	Billericay T	05/07	07-10	101	24	12
Gillingham	L	11/10	10	4	0	3
Gillingham	Tr	07/11	11-13	92	12	20
Stevenage	Tr	06/14	14	35	4	7

WHENT John Richard (Jackie)
Born: Darlington, County Durham, England, 3 May, 1920 — CH/WH

League Club	Source	Date Signed	Seasons Played	Apps	Subs	Gls
Brighton & HA	Canadian Army	08/47	47-49	101	-	4
Luton T	Tr	08/50	50	11	-	3

WHETTER Gary
Born: Middlesbrough, England, 6 September, 1963 — M

League Club	Source	Date Signed	Seasons Played	Apps	Subs	Gls
Darlington	Crook T	09/86	86	3	2	1

WHICHELOW Matthew Robert (Matt)
Born: Islington, N London, England, 28 September, 1991 — LW

League Club	Source	Date Signed	Seasons Played	Apps	Subs	Gls
Watford	Sch	07/10	10-11	4	17	3
Exeter C	L	09/11	11	2	0	0
Wycombe W	L	01/12	11	4	0	1
Accrington Stan	L	09/12	12	2	2	0

WHIFFEN Stuart Kingsley Gears (Kingsley)
Born: Welshpool, Powys, Wales, 3 December, 1950 — G
Died: Dorchester, Dorset, England, 15 December, 2006

League Club	Source	Date Signed	Seasons Played	Apps	Subs	Gls
Chelsea	App	-	66	1	0	0

WHIGHAM William Murdoch Morrison (Willie)
Born: Airdrie, Lanarkshire, Scotland, 9 October, 1939 — G

League Club	Source	Date Signed	Seasons Played	Apps	Subs	Gls
Middlesbrough	Falkirk	10/66	66-71	187	0	0
Darlington	Dumbarton	08/74	74	4	0	0

WHING Andrew John (Andy)
Born: Birmingham, England, 20 September, 1984 — RB

League Club	Source	Date Signed	Seasons Played	Apps	Subs	Gls
Coventry C	Sch	04/03	02-06	87	19	2
Brighton & HA	L	10/06	06	12	0	0
Brighton & HA	Tr	07/07	07-09	91	0	0
Chesterfield	L	03/10	09	9	2	0
Leyton Orient	Tr	10/10	10	23	1	2
Oxford U	Tr	07/11	11-14	90	12	2

WHISTON Donald (Don)
Born: Chesterton, Potteries, England, 4 April, 1930 — RB/CF

League Club	Source	Date Signed	Seasons Played	Apps	Subs	Gls
Stoke C	Jnr	12/49	49-56	30	-	4
Crewe Alex	Tr	02/57	56-57	52	-	8
Rochdale	Tr	05/58	58	14	-	0

WHISTON Joseph Rowland (Joe)
Born: Stoke-on-Trent, England, 5 October, 1928 — CF

League Club	Source	Date Signed	Seasons Played	Apps	Subs	Gls
Crewe Alex	Johnson Matthey	09/51	51-52	9	-	2

WHISTON Peter Michael
Born: Widnes, Cheshire, England, 4 January, 1968 — CD

League Club	Source	Date Signed	Seasons Played	Apps	Subs	Gls
Plymouth Arg		12/87	88-89	4	6	0
Torquay U	Tr	03/90	89-91	39	1	1
Exeter C	Tr	09/91	91-93	85	0	7
Southampton	Tr	08/94	94	0	1	0
Shrewsbury T	Tr	09/95	95-96	54	1	3

WHITAKER Colin
Born: Leeds, England, 14 June, 1932 — LW
Died: Oldham, Greater Manchester, England, 12 May, 2015

League Club	Source	Date Signed	Seasons Played	Apps	Subs	Gls
Sheffield Wed	Leeds U (Jnr)	11/51	51	1	-	0
Bradford Park Ave	Tr	06/53	53-55	49	-	10
Shrewsbury T	Tr	06/56	56-60	152	-	59
Queens Park Rgrs	Tr	02/61	60	8	-	0
Rochdale	Tr	05/61	61-62	54	-	11
Oldham Ath	Tr	10/62	62-63	72	-	29
Barrow	Tr	08/64	64	12	-	0

WHITAKER Daniel Philip (Danny)
Born: Wilmslow, Cheshire, England, 14 November, 1980 — M

League Club	Source	Date Signed	Seasons Played	Apps	Subs	Gls
Macclesfield T	Wilmslow A	07/00	01-05	156	15	23
Port Vale	Tr	07/06	06-07	80	6	14
Oldham Ath	Tr	07/08	08-09	61	19	8
Chesterfield	Tr	07/10	10-12	85	21	21

WHITAKER William (Billy)
Born: Chesterfield, Derbyshire, England, 7 October, 1923 — CH
Died: Chesterfield, Derbyshire, England, 29 August, 1995
England: FLge-1

League Club	Source	Date Signed	Seasons Played	Apps	Subs	Gls
Chesterfield	Tapton School OB	08/42	46	13	-	0
Middlesbrough	Tr	06/47	47-54	177	-	1

WHITBREAD Adrian Richard
Born: Epping, Essex, England, 22 October, 1971 — CD

League Club	Source	Date Signed	Seasons Played	Apps	Subs	Gls
Leyton Orient	YT	11/89	89-92	125	0	2
Swindon T	Tr	07/93	93-94	35	1	1
West Ham U	Tr	08/94	94-95	3	7	0
Portsmouth	L	11/95	95	13	0	0
Portsmouth	Tr	10/96	96-99	133	1	2
Luton T	L	11/00	00	9	0	0
Reading	Tr	02/01	00-01	33	0	0
Exeter C	L	01/03	02	7	0	0

WHITBREAD Zak Benjamin
Born: Houston, Texas, USA, 4 March, 1984 — CD
USA: Youth

League Club	Source	Date Signed	Seasons Played	Apps	Subs	Gls
Liverpool	Sch	05/03				
Millwall	Tr	11/05	05-08	93	7	3
Norwich C	Tr	01/10	09-11	39	5	1
Leicester C	Tr	07/12	12-13	17	2	1
Derby Co	L	09/13	13	4	0	1
Derby Co	Tr	06/14	14	8	1	0

WHITBY Brian Kenneth
Born: Luton, England, 21 February, 1939 — W

League Club	Source	Date Signed	Seasons Played	Apps	Subs	Gls
Luton T	Vauxhall Motors	05/57	57-58	7	-	1

WHITCHURCH Charles Henry (Charlie)
Born: Grays, Essex, England, 29 October, 1920 — LW
Died: Michigan, USA, July, 1977
England: Schools

League Club	Source	Date Signed	Seasons Played	Apps	Subs	Gls
West Ham U	Portsmouth (Am)	05/45				
Tottenham H	Tr	01/46	46	8	-	2
Southend U	Tr	07/47	47	17	-	5

WHITE Aidan Peter
Born: Otley, West Yorkshire, England, 10 October, 1991 — LB/M
England: Youth//Republic of Ireland: U21-10

League Club	Source	Date Signed	Seasons Played	Apps	Subs	Gls
Leeds U	Sch	12/08	08-14	61	24	1
Oldham Ath	L	11/10	10	19	5	4
Sheffield U	L	10/13	13	8	0	0

WHITE Alan
Born: Darlington, County Durham, England, 22 March, 1976 — CD

League Club	Source	Date Signed	Seasons Played	Apps	Subs	Gls
Middlesbrough	YT	07/94				
Luton T	Tr	09/97	97-99	60	20	3
Colchester U	L	11/99	99	4	0	0
Colchester U	Tr	07/00	00-03	128	11	4
Leyton Orient	Tr	07/04	04	26	0	0
Boston U	Tr	03/05	04-05	48	0	4
Notts Co	Tr	07/06	06	32	3	0
Peterborough U	L	03/07	06	7	0	3
Darlington	Tr	07/07	07-08	75	0	3
Darlington (L)	Luton T	01/10	09	23	1	1

WHITE Alexander (Alex)
Born: Lasswade, Midlothian, Scotland, 28 January, 1916 — RB
Died: Armadale, West Lothian, Scotland, 4 November, 1995

League Club	Source	Date Signed	Seasons Played	Apps	Subs	Gls
Chelsea	Bonnyrigg Rose	02/37	46-47	17	-	0
Swindon T	Tr	07/48	48-49	35	-	0
Southport	Tr	07/50	50	3	-	0

WHITE Andrew Charles John (Andy)
Born: Newport, Wales, 6 November, 1948 — LW

League Club	Source	Date Signed	Seasons Played	Apps	Subs	Gls
Newport Co	Caerleon	08/69	69-76	226	28	26

WHITE Andrew David (Andy)
Born: Alfreton, Derbyshire, England, 6 November, 1981 — F

League Club	Source	Date Signed	Seasons Played	Apps	Subs	Gls
Mansfield T	Hucknall T	07/00	00-03	37	31	10
Crewe Alex	L	10/02	02	0	2	0
Boston U	L	09/03	03	3	3	0
Kidderminster Hrs	L	10/03	03	6	1	1
Crewe Alex	Tr	06/04	04	11	11	4
Notts Co	Tr	07/05	05	10	16	2

WHITE Andrew Jordon (Andy)
Born: Reading, England, 1 September, 1991 — F

League Club	Source	Date Signed	Seasons Played	Apps	Subs	Gls
Gillingham	Reading (Sch)	07/10	10	0	1	0

WHITE Antony John (Tony)
Born: Clacton, Essex, England, 3 November, 1966 — FB

League Club	Source	Date Signed	Seasons Played	Apps	Subs	Gls
Bournemouth	Dorchester T	07/85	85	1	0	0

WHITE Archibald (Archie)
Born: Dumbarton, Dunbartonshire, Scotland, 16 January, 1959 — M

League Club	Source	Date Signed	Seasons Played	Apps	Subs	Gls
Oxford U	App	01/76	76-79	10	14	1

WHITE Arnie
Born: Bristol, England, 25 July, 1924 — IF
Died: Chesterfield, Derbyshire, England, 29 June, 2010

League Club	Source	Date Signed	Seasons Played	Apps	Subs	Gls
Bristol C	Soundwell	03/47	46-50	82	-	12
Millwall	Tr	08/51	51-52	14	-	0

WHITE Barry James
Born: Beverley, East Riding of Yorkshire, England, 30 July, 1950 — G

League Club	Source	Date Signed	Seasons Played	Apps	Subs	Gls
Hull C	App	08/68				
Halifax T	Tr	08/70	71-74	23	0	0

WHITE Christopher Jason (Chris)
Born: Chatham, Kent, England, 11 December, 1970 — RB

League Club	Source	Date Signed	Seasons Played	Apps	Subs	Gls
Portsmouth	YT	07/89				
Peterborough U	Tr	05/91	91-92	10	3	0
Doncaster Rov	L	01/93	92	6	0	0
Exeter C	Tr	03/93	92-93	18	1	0

WHITE Dale
Born: Sunderland, England, 17 March, 1968 — F
England: Schools

League Club	Source	Date Signed	Seasons Played	Apps	Subs	Gls
Sunderland	App	03/86	85	2	2	0
Peterborough U	L	12/87	87	14	0	4

WHITE David
Born: Urmston, Greater Manchester, England, 30 October, 1967 — RW/F
England: 1/B-2/U21-6/Youth

League Club	Source	Date Signed	Seasons Played	Apps	Subs	Gls
Manchester C	App	11/85	86-93	273	12	79
Leeds U	Tr	12/93	93-95	28	14	9
Sheffield U	Tr	11/95	95-97	55	11	13

WHITE Dean
Born: Hastings, East Sussex, England, 4 December, 1958 — M

League Club	Source	Date Signed	Seasons Played	Apps	Subs	Gls
Chelsea	App	12/76				
Gillingham	Tr	07/78	78-82	108	8	26
Millwall	Tr	03/83	82-83	41	0	4

WHITE Dennis
Born: Hartlepool, Cleveland, England, 10 November, 1948 — FB

League Club	Source	Date Signed	Seasons Played	Apps	Subs	Gls
Hartlepool U		11/67	67-72	55	3	0

WHITE Devon Winston
Born: Nottingham, England, 2 March, 1964 — F

League Club	Source	Date Signed	Seasons Played	Apps	Subs	Gls
Lincoln C	Arnold T	12/84	84-85	21	8	4
Bristol Rov	Shepshed Charterhouse	08/87	87-91	190	12	53
Cambridge U	Tr	03/92	91-92	15	7	4
Queens Park Rgrs	Tr	01/93	92-94	16	10	9
Notts Co	Tr	12/94	94-95	34	6	15
Watford	Tr	02/96	95-96	28	10	7
Notts Co	Tr	03/97	96-97	11	4	2
Shrewsbury T	Tr	09/97	97-98	37	6	10

WHITE Edward (Ted)
Born: Crewe, Cheshire, England, 22 November, 1956 — F

League Club	Source	Date Signed	Seasons Played	Apps	Subs	Gls
Crewe Alex		11/78	78	1	0	0

WHITE Edward Ritchie (Eddie)
Born: Musselburgh, East Lothian, Scotland, 13 April, 1935 — CF

League Club	Source	Date Signed	Seasons Played	Apps	Subs	Gls
Bradford C	Falkirk	10/59	59	4	-	1

WHITE Eric Winston (Winston)
Born: Leicester, England, 26 October, 1958 — RW

League Club	Source	Date Signed	Seasons Played	Apps	Subs	Gls
Leicester C	App	10/76	76-78	10	2	1
Hereford U	Tr	03/79	78-82	169	6	21
Chesterfield	Hong Kong Rgrs (HKG)	09/83	83	0	1	0
Port Vale	Tr	10/83	83	0	1	0
Stockport Co	Tr	11/83	83	4	0	0
Bury	Tr	12/83	83-86	125	0	12
Rochdale	L	10/86	86	4	0	0
Colchester U	Tr	02/87	86-88	64	1	8
Burnley	Tr	10/88	88-90	93	11	14
West Bromwich A	Tr	03/91	90-91	13	3	1
Bury	Tr	10/92	92	1	1	0
Doncaster Rov	Tr	01/93	92	4	0	2
Carlisle U	Tr	02/93	92	6	0	0
Wigan Ath	Tr	03/93	92	10	0	2

WHITE Frederick (Fred)
Born: Wolverhampton, England, 5 December, 1916 — G
Died: Sheffield, England, 13 January, 2007

League Club	Source	Date Signed	Seasons Played	Apps	Subs	Gls
Everton		05/35				
Sheffield U	Tr	05/37	47-49	44	-	0
Lincoln C	Tr	06/50	50	42	-	0

WHITE Gwilym David (George)
Born: Doncaster, South Yorkshire, England, 23 February, 1936 — FB

League Club	Source	Date Signed	Seasons Played	Apps	Subs	Gls
Oldham Ath	Plymouth Arg (Am)	08/60	60	1	-	0

WHITE Hayden Anthony Roy
Born: Greenwich, SE London, England, 15 April, 1995 — RB

League Club	Source	Date Signed	Seasons Played	Apps	Subs	Gls
Bolton W	Sheffield Wed (Sch)	07/13	13-14	3	2	0
Carlisle U	L	09/14	14	8	0	0
Bury	L	11/14	14	2	0	0
Notts Co	L	01/15	14	2	1	0

WHITE Howard Kenneth
Born: Timperley, Greater Manchester, England, 2 March, 1954 — CD

League Club	Source	Date Signed	Seasons Played	Apps	Subs	Gls
Manchester C	App	05/71	70	1	0	0

WHITE Ian Samuel
Born: Glasgow, Scotland, 20 December, 1935 — RH

League Club	Source	Date Signed	Seasons Played	Apps	Subs	Gls
Leicester C	Glasgow Celtic	05/58	59-61	47	-	1
Southampton	Tr	06/62	62-66	60	1	5

WHITE James (Jimmy)
Born: Poole, Dorset, England, 13 June, 1942 — CH/CF
England: Youth

League Club	Source	Date Signed	Seasons Played	Apps	Subs	Gls
Bournemouth (Am)	Jnr	04/58	57	1	-	0
Portsmouth	Tr	06/59	58-61	34	-	6
Gillingham	Bath C	06/63	63-65	65	0	1
Bournemouth	Tr	07/66	66-69	175	0	5
Cambridge U	Tr	12/70	70-71	28	2	2

WHITE Jamie Andrew
Born: Southampton, England, 17 November, 1989 — F

League Club	Source	Date Signed	Seasons Played	Apps	Subs	Gls
Southampton	Sch	11/06	08	2	1	0
Shrewsbury T	L	11/08	08	3	6	1

WHITE Jason Gregory
Born: Coleshill, Warwickshire, England, 19 October, 1971 — F

League Club	Source	Date Signed	Seasons Played	Apps	Subs	Gls
Derby Co	YT	07/90				
Scunthorpe U	Tr	09/91	91-93	44	24	16
Darlington	L	08/93	93	4	0	1
Scarborough	Tr	12/93	93-94	60	3	20
Northampton T	Tr	06/95	95-96	55	22	18
Rotherham U	Tr	09/97	97-99	52	21	22
Cheltenham T	Tr	07/00	00-01	8	23	1
Mansfield T	L	09/01	01	6	1	0

WHITE Jason Lee
Born: Sutton-in-Ashfield, Nottinghamshire, England, 28 January, 1984 — G

League Club	Source	Date Signed	Seasons Played	Apps	Subs	Gls
Mansfield T	Sch	08/02	02-07	49	4	0

WHITE John (Jack)
Born: Doncaster, South Yorkshire, England, 17 March, 1924 — D/F
Died: Tunbridge Wells, Kent, England, July, 2011

League Club	Source	Date Signed	Seasons Played	Apps	Subs	Gls
Aldershot	Sheffield FC	07/44	46-52	209	-	25
Bristol C	Tr	10/52	52-57	216	-	11

WHITE John Alan
Born: Maldon, Essex, England, 26 July, 1986 — CD

League Club	Source	Date Signed	Seasons Played	Apps	Subs	Gls
Colchester U	Sch	02/05	04-12	186	41	0
Southend U	L	07/09	09	5	0	0
Southend U	Tr	06/13	13-14	81	2	1

WHITE John Anderson
Born: Musselburgh, East Lothian, Scotland, 28 April, 1937 — IF
Died: Enfield, N London, England, 21 July, 1964
England: FLge-1//Scotland: 22/SLge-2/U23-1

League Club	Source	Date Signed	Seasons Played	Apps	Subs	Gls
Tottenham H	Falkirk	10/59	59-63	183	-	40

WHITE Kenneth (Ken)
Born: Selby, North Yorkshire, England, 15 March, 1922 — RH

League Club	Source	Date Signed	Seasons Played	Apps	Subs	Gls
Hull C	Selby T	12/47	48	1	-	0

WHITE Kevin Nicholas
Born: Poole, Dorset, England, 26 June, 1948 — RW

League Club	Source	Date Signed	Seasons Played	Apps	Subs	Gls
Bournemouth	App	08/66	66-68	46	3	6

WHITE Leonard Roy (Len)
Born: Skellow, South Yorkshire, England, 23 March, 1930 — CF/W
Died: Huddersfield, West Yorkshire, England, 3 June, 1994
England: FLge-2

League Club	Source	Date Signed	Seasons Played	Apps	Subs	Gls
Rotherham U	Upton Colliery	05/48	50-52	43	-	15
Newcastle U	Tr	02/53	52-61	244	-	142
Huddersfield T	Tr	02/62	61-64	102	-	37
Stockport Co	Tr	01/65	64-65	53	0	24

WHITE Lewis
Born: Stoke-on-Trent, England, 2 August, 1927 — W
Died: Stafford, England, 1982

League Club	Source	Date Signed	Seasons Played	Apps	Subs	Gls
Port Vale		10/48	48	1	-	0

WHITE Malcolm
Born: Wolverhampton, England, 24 April, 1941 — G

League Club	Source	Date Signed	Seasons Played	Apps	Subs	Gls
Grimsby T	Wolverhampton W (Am)	08/58	58-62	65	-	0
Walsall	Tr	08/63	63	28	-	0
Lincoln C	Tr	07/64	64	25	-	0
Bradford C	Tr	07/65	65	9	0	0
Halifax T	Tr	11/65	65-67	100	0	0

WHITE Mark Ivan
Born: Sheffield, England, 26 October, 1958 — LB/M

League Club	Source	Date Signed	Seasons Played	Apps	Subs	Gls
Reading	Sheffield U (App)	03/77	77-87	265	13	11

WHITE Maurice Henry
Born: Keadby, North Lincolnshire, England, 29 January, 1938 — FB

League Club	Source	Date Signed	Seasons Played	Apps	Subs	Gls
Doncaster Rov		04/56	57-60	55	-	0

WHITE Philip George John (Phil)
Born: Fulham, W London, England, 29 December, 1930 — RW
Died: Kingston-on-Thames, SW London, England, June, 2000

League Club	Source	Date Signed	Seasons Played	Apps	Subs	Gls
Leyton Orient	Wealdstone	07/53	53-63	217	-	28

WHITE Raymond (Ray)
Born: Ely, Cambridgeshire, England, 5 February, 1941 — RH

League Club	Source	Date Signed	Seasons Played	Apps	Subs	Gls
Millwall	Jnr	08/58	58	2	-	0
Stoke C	Tr	07/60				

WHITE Raymond Bernard William (Ray)
Born: Bootle, Merseyside, England, 13 August, 1918 — RH
Died: Bradford, England, December, 1988

League Club	Source	Date Signed	Seasons Played	Apps	Subs	Gls
Bradford Park Ave	Tottenham H (Am)	05/46	46-50	151	-	3

WHITE Raymond Sidney (Ray)
Born: Southend-on-Sea, England, 14 January, 1948 — G

League Club	Source	Date Signed	Seasons Played	Apps	Subs	Gls
Southend U	App	01/66	63-67	10	0	0
Bristol Rov	Tr	07/68	68	3	0	0

WHITE Richard (Dick)
Born: Scunthorpe, North Lincolnshire, England, 18 August, 1931 — CH
Died: Nottingham, England, 15 June, 2002

League Club	Source	Date Signed	Seasons Played	Apps	Subs	Gls
Scunthorpe U	Brumby Amats	07/50	50-55	133	-	7
Liverpool	Tr	11/55	55-61	203	-	0
Doncaster Rov	Tr	07/62	62-63	83	-	0

WHITE Ronald Thomas (Ron)
Born: Bethnal Green, E London, England, 9 November, 1931 — IF
Died: London, England, 12 August, 1994

League Club	Source	Date Signed	Seasons Played	Apps	Subs	Gls
Charlton Ath	Maccabi Sports	03/54	53-61	165	-	8

WHITE Stephen James (Steve)
Born: Chipping Sodbury, Avon, England, 2 January, 1959 — F
England: Schools

League Club	Source	Date Signed	Seasons Played	Apps	Subs	Gls
Bristol Rov	Mangotsfield U	07/77	77-79	46	4	20
Luton T	Tr	12/79	79-81	63	9	25
Charlton Ath	Tr	07/82	82	29	0	12
Lincoln C	L	01/83	82	2	1	0
Luton T	L	02/83	82	4	0	0
Bristol Rov	Tr	08/83	83-85	89	12	24
Swindon T	Tr	07/86	86-93	200	44	83
Hereford U	Tr	08/94	94-95	70	6	44
Cardiff C	Tr	06/96	96-97	44	23	15

WHITE Thomas (Tom)
Born: Pelton, County Durham, England, 10 November, 1924 — IF
Died: Newcastle-upon-Tyne, England, 19 June, 1998

League Club	Source	Date Signed	Seasons Played	Apps	Subs	Gls
Sunderland	Chester Moor Amats	04/45	46	2	-	1

WHITE Thomas (Tom)
Born: Musselburgh, East Lothian, Scotland, 12 August, 1939 — CF

League Club	Source	Date Signed	Seasons Played	Apps	Subs	Gls
Crystal Palace	Aberdeen	06/66	66-67	37	2	13
Blackpool	Tr	03/68	67-69	34	0	9
Bury	Tr	06/70	70-71	46	2	13
Crewe Alex	Tr	12/71	71	4	0	0

WHITE Thomas Matthew (Tom)
Born: Bristol, England, 26 January, 1976 — CD

League Club	Source	Date Signed	Seasons Played	Apps	Subs	Gls
Bristol Rov	YT	07/94	94-99	47	7	1

WHITE William (Willie)
Born: Clackmannan, Stirlingshire, Scotland, 25 September, 1932 — G

League Club	Source	Date Signed	Seasons Played	Apps	Subs	Gls
Accrington Stan	Motherwell	08/53	53	18	-	0
Mansfield T	Tr	05/54	54	3	-	0
Derby Co	L	08/55	55	3	-	0
Mansfield T	Tr	09/55				

WHITE William Henry (Billy)
Born: Liverpool, England, 13 October, 1936 — IF
Died: Ormskirk, Lancashire, England, 7 December, 2000

League Club	Source	Date Signed	Seasons Played	Apps	Subs	Gls
Burnley	Clubmoor BC, Liverpool	01/54	57-59	9	-	4
Wrexham	Tr	03/61	60	8	-	0
Chester C	Tr	07/61	61	13	-	3

WHITEAR John Michael
Born: Isleworth, W London, England, 31 May, 1935 — IF
England: Youth

League Club	Source	Date Signed	Seasons Played	Apps	Subs	Gls
Aston Villa	Walton & Hersham	04/53				
Crystal Palace	Tr	05/56	56	5	-	1

WHITEFOOT Jeffrey (Jeff)
Born: Cheadle, Greater Manchester, England, 31 December, 1933 — WH
England: U23-1/Schools

League Club	Source	Date Signed	Seasons Played	Apps	Subs	Gls
Manchester U	Jnr	12/51	49-55	93	-	0
Grimsby T	Tr	11/57	57	26	-	5
Nottingham F	Tr	07/58	58-67	255	0	5

WHITEHALL Steven Christopher (Steve)
Born: Bromborough, Wirral, England, 8 December, 1966 — F

League Club	Source	Date Signed	Seasons Played	Apps	Subs	Gls
Rochdale	Southport	07/91	91-96	212	26	75
Mansfield T	Tr	08/97	97	42	1	24
Oldham Ath	Tr	07/98	98-00	55	21	13

WHITEHEAD Alan
Born: Bury, Greater Manchester, England, 20 November, 1956 — CD

League Club	Source	Date Signed	Seasons Played	Apps	Subs	Gls
Bury	Darwen	12/77	77-80	98	1	13
Brentford	Tr	08/81	81-83	101	1	4
Scunthorpe U	Tr	01/84	83-86	106	2	8
York C	Tr	10/86	86-87	40	1	1
Wigan Ath	L	03/87	86	2	0	0
Halifax T	Tr	08/88	88	10	1	1

WHITEHEAD Alan John
Born: Birmingham, England, 3 September, 1951 — CD

League Club	Source	Date Signed	Seasons Played	Apps	Subs	Gls
Birmingham C	App	07/69	71-72	4	0	0

WHITEHEAD Barry
Born: Sheffield, England, 3 December, 1946 — IF

League Club	Source	Date Signed	Seasons Played	Apps	Subs	Gls
Chesterfield	Lindsey Road YC	07/65	65	5	1	1

WHITEHEAD Clive Robert
Born: Birmingham, England, 24 November, 1955 — W/FB
England: Youth

League Club	Source	Date Signed	Seasons Played	Apps	Subs	Gls
Bristol C	Northfield Jnrs	08/73	73-81	209	20	10
West Bromwich A	Tr	11/81	81-86	157	11	6
Wolverhampton W	L	01/86	85	2	0	0
Portsmouth	Tr	06/87	87-88	57	8	2
Exeter C	Tr	07/89	89-90	44	2	5

WHITEHEAD Damien Stephen
Born: St Helens, Merseyside, England, 24 April, 1979 — F

League Club	Source	Date Signed	Seasons Played	Apps	Subs	Gls
Macclesfield T	Warrington T	08/99	99-01	20	38	14

WHITEHEAD Danny
Born: Stretford, Greater Manchester, England, 23 October, 1993 — M

League Club	Source	Date Signed	Seasons Played	Apps	Subs	Gls
West Ham U	Stockport Co	06/13				
Accrington Stan	Tr	03/15	14	1	1	0

WHITEHEAD Dean
Born: Abingdon, Oxfordshire, England, 12 January, 1982 — M

League Club	Source	Date Signed	Seasons Played	Apps	Subs	Gls
Oxford U	YT	04/00	00-03	92	30	9
Sunderland	Tr	08/04	04-08	176	9	13
Stoke C	Tr	07/09	09-12	100	32	3
Middlesbrough	Tr	07/13	13-14	45	10	1

WHITEHEAD Norman John
Born: Fazakerley, Merseyside, England, 22 April, 1948 — RW

League Club	Source	Date Signed	Seasons Played	Apps	Subs	Gls
Southport	Skelmersdale U	12/67	67	7	1	0
Rochdale	Tr	07/68	68-71	153	2	11
Rotherham U	Tr	03/72	71-72	29	4	2
Chester C	Tr	08/73	73-75	66	8	5
Grimsby T	Tr	08/76	76	3	1	0

WHITEHEAD Philip Matthew (Phil)
Born: Halifax, West Yorkshire, England, 17 December, 1969 — G

League Club	Source	Date Signed	Seasons Played	Apps	Subs	Gls
Halifax T	YT	07/88	86-89	42	0	0
Barnsley	Tr	03/90	91-92	16	0	0
Halifax T	L	03/91	90	9	0	0
Scunthorpe U	L	11/91	91	8	0	0
Scunthorpe U	L	09/92	92	8	0	0
Bradford C	L	11/92	92	6	0	0
Oxford U	Tr	11/93	93-98	207	0	0
West Bromwich A	Tr	12/98	98	26	0	0
Reading	Tr	10/99	99-02	94	0	0
Tranmere Rov	L	09/02	02	2	0	0
York C	L	04/03	02	2	0	0

WHITEHEAD Robert (Bob)
Born: Ashington, Northumberland, England, 22 September, 1936 — RB

League Club	Source	Date Signed	Seasons Played	Apps	Subs	Gls
Newcastle U	Fatfield Ath	12/54	57-59	20	-	0
Darlington	Tr	08/62	62-63	53	-	0

WHITEHEAD Scott Anthony
Born: Doncaster, South Yorkshire, England, 20 April, 1974 — W

League Club	Source	Date Signed	Seasons Played	Apps	Subs	Gls
Chesterfield	YT	07/92	91-92	4	5	0

WHITEHEAD Stuart David
Born: Bromsgrove, Worcestershire, England, 17 July, 1976 — CD

League Club	Source	Date Signed	Seasons Played	Apps	Subs	Gls
Bolton W	Bromsgrove Rov	09/95				
Carlisle U	Tr	07/98	98-02	148	4	2
Darlington	Tr	10/02	02	23	0	0
Shrewsbury T	Telford U	07/04	04-05	57	6	0

WHITEHEAD William George (Billy)
Born: Maltby, South Yorkshire, England, 6 February, 1920 — LW
Died: Rotherham, South Yorkshire, England, August, 2012

League Club	Source	Date Signed	Seasons Played	Apps	Subs	Gls
Queens Park Rgrs	Maltby Main	08/39				
Aldershot	Tr	08/47	47	6	-	1

WHITEHOUSE Billy Haywood
Born: Rotherham, South Yorkshire, England, 13 June, 1996 — W

League Club	Source	Date Signed	Seasons Played	Apps	Subs	Gls
Doncaster Rov	Sch	08/14	14	0	4	0

WHITEHOUSE Brian
Born: West Bromwich, West Midlands, England, 8 September, 1935 — IF/WH

League Club	Source	Date Signed	Seasons Played	Apps	Subs	Gls
West Bromwich A	Vono Sports	10/52	55-59	37	-	13
Norwich C	Tr	03/60	59-61	41	-	14
Wrexham	Tr	03/62	61-63	45	-	19
Crystal Palace	Tr	11/63	63-65	82	0	17
Charlton Ath	Tr	03/66	65	13	0	1
Leyton Orient	Tr	07/66	66-67	52	0	6

WHITEHOUSE Dane Lee
Born: Sheffield, England, 14 October, 1970 — LW

League Club	Source	Date Signed	Seasons Played	Apps	Subs	Gls
Sheffield U	YT	07/89	88-97	204	27	39

WHITEHOUSE Dean
Born: Mexborough, South Yorkshire, England, 30 October, 1963 — M

League Club	Source	Date Signed	Seasons Played	Apps	Subs	Gls
Barnsley	App	10/81	83	1	1	0
Torquay U	Tr	08/84	84	7	2	0

WHITEHOUSE Elliott Mark
Born: Worksop, Nottinghamshire, England, 27 October, 1993 — M

League Club	Source	Date Signed	Seasons Played	Apps	Subs	Gls
Sheffield U	Sch	07/13	12	1	2	0
York C	L	09/13	13	15	0	0
Notts Co	Tr	08/14	14	3	4	1

WHITEHOUSE James (Jimmy)
Born: West Bromwich, West Midlands, England, 19 September, 1934 — IF

League Club	Source	Date Signed	Seasons Played	Apps	Subs	Gls
West Bromwich A	Jnr	11/54				
Reading	Tr	06/56	56-61	203	-	61
Coventry C	Tr	08/62	62-63	46	-	12
Millwall	Tr	03/64	63-64	38	-	13

League Club	Source	Date Signed	Seasons Played	Career Record Apps	Subs	Gls

WHITEHOUSE James Edward (Jimmy)
Born: West Bromwich, West Midlands, England, 19 September, 1924 — IF
Died: Carlisle, Cumbria, England, 20 September, 2005

West Bromwich A	Hawthorns	05/48				
Walsall	Tr	06/49	49	20	-	8
Rochdale	Tr	07/50	50-51	46	-	13
Carlisle U	Tr	10/51	51-56	198	-	100

WHITEHOUSE Philip (Phil)
Born: Wolverhampton, England, 23 March, 1971 — LB

West Bromwich A	YT	07/89				
Walsall	Tr	12/89	89-90	10	2	0

WHITEHURST Walter
Born: Manchester, England, 7 June, 1934 — RH
Died: Blackpool, Lancashire, England, 20 January, 2012

Manchester U	Jnr	05/52	55	1	-	0
Chesterfield	Tr	11/56	56-59	91	-	2
Crewe Alex	Tr	07/60	60	3	-	1

WHITEHURST William (Billy)
Born: Thurnscoe, South Yorkshire, England, 10 June, 1959 — F

Hull C	Mexborough T	10/80	80-85	176	17	47
Newcastle U	Tr	12/85	85-86	28	0	7
Oxford U	Tr	10/86	86-87	36	4	4
Reading	Tr	02/88	87-88	17	0	8
Sunderland	Tr	09/88	88	17	0	3
Hull C	Tr	12/88	88-89	36	0	5
Sheffield U	Tr	02/90	89-90	12	10	2
Stoke C	L	11/90	90	3	0	0
Doncaster Rov	Tr	02/91	90-91	22	0	1
Crewe Alex	L	01/92	91	4	6	0

WHITELAW George
Born: Paisley, Renfrewshire, Scotland, 1 January, 1937 — CF
Died: Paisley, Renfrewshire, Scotland, 8 August, 2004
Scotland: Amateur

Sunderland	St Johnstone	02/58	57-58	5	-	0
Queens Park Rgrs	Tr	03/59	58-59	26	-	10
Halifax T	Tr	10/59	59-60	52	-	22
Carlisle U	Tr	02/61	60-61	34	-	9
Stockport Co	Tr	01/62	61-62	52	-	18
Barrow	Tr	08/63	63	7	-	0

WHITELEY Albert
Born: Sheffield, England, 13 July, 1932 — LW
Died: Waltham Forest, NE London, England, November, 2002

Leyton Orient	Sheffield Wed (Am)	11/52	52-53	23	-	3

WHITELEY Andrew Mark (Andy)
Born: Sowerby Bridge, West Yorkshire, England, 1 August, 1961 — M/LB

Halifax T		08/79	79-81	20	16	1

WHITELOCK Arthur
Born: Stockton-on-Tees, Cleveland, England, 31 July, 1931 — RB

Hartlepool U	South Bank	12/50	50	6	-	0

WHITELUM Clifford (Cliff)
Born: Farnworth, Greater Manchester, England, 2 December, 1919 — CF
Died: Kings Lynn, Norfolk, England, August, 2000

Sunderland	Bentley Colliery	12/38	38-47	43	-	18
Sheffield U	Tr	10/47	47-48	41	-	14

WHITESIDE Arnold
Born: Garstang, Lancashire, England, 6 November, 1911 — WH
Died: Chorley, Lancashire, England, September, 1994

Blackburn Rov	Woodplumpton Jnrs	01/33	32-48	218	-	3

WHITESIDE Charles William Parker
Born: Liverpool, England, 16 August, 1927 — IF
Died: Southport, Merseyside, England, 17 August, 1988

Swindon T		12/48	49	1	-	0

WHITESIDE Edward Kenneth (Ken)
Born: Liverpool, England, 11 December, 1929 — IF

Preston NE	British Eckna Works	05/52				
Chesterfield	British Eckna Works	05/53	53	9	-	3
York C	Tr	05/54	54	8	-	0
Bournemouth	Tr	07/55	55	1	-	0

WHITESIDE Norman
Born: Belfast, Northern Ireland, 7 May, 1965 — M/F
Northern Ireland: 38/Schools

Manchester U	App	07/82	81-88	193	13	47
Everton	Tr	07/89	89-90	27	2	9

WHITESIDE William Richard (Billy)
Born: Belfast, Northern Ireland, 24 September, 1935 — RW

Exeter C	Portadown	11/55	55	3	-	1
Scunthorpe U	Portadown	08/56	56	2	-	0
Rotherham U	Tr	12/56				

WHITFIELD George Allan
Born: Penrith, Cumbria, England, 10 February, 1934 — FB

Carlisle U		11/55	56	1	-	0

WHITFIELD James (Jimmy)
Born: Hull, England, 18 May, 1919 — IF
Died: Cleethorpes, North Lincolnshire, England, 22 April, 1984

Grimsby T	Humber U	05/46	46-48	29	-	7
Scunthorpe U	Tr	04/49	50	16	-	6
Southport	Tr	08/51	51	12	-	0
Scunthorpe U	Tr	02/52	51-54	104	-	25

WHITFIELD John Spoor
Born: Gateshead, Tyne and Wear, England, 10 June, 1938 — LW

Gateshead		07/59	59	1	-	1

WHITFIELD Kenneth (Ken)
Born: Spennymoor, County Durham, England, 24 March, 1930 — CH
Died: Barry, Vale of Glamorgan, Wales, November, 1995

Wolverhampton W	Shildon	12/47	51-52	9	-	3
Manchester C	Tr	03/53	52-53	13	-	3
Brighton & HA	Tr	07/54	54-58	175	-	4
Queens Park Rgrs	Tr	07/59	59-60	19	-	3

WHITFIELD Michael (Mick)
Born: Sunderland, England, 17 October, 1962 — M

Sunderland	App	10/80	82	3	0	0
Hartlepool U	Tr	08/83	83	15	1	0

WHITFIELD Paul Michael
Born: Flint, Wales, 6 May, 1982 — G
Wales: U21-1/Youth

Wrexham	YT	07/01	02-03	7	3	0

WHITFIELD Robert (Bob)
Born: Prudhoe, Northumberland, England, 30 June, 1920 — D
Died: Hull, England, 20 January, 2004

Charlton Ath	Prudhoe	05/39				
Torquay U	Tr	02/47	46-49	11	-	1

WHITFIELD Wilfred (Wilf)
Born: Chesterfield, Derbyshire, England, 17 November, 1916 — LH
Died: Hamilton, Lanarkshire, Scotland, 1995

Bristol Rov	Worksop T	07/38	38-46	26	-	1
Torquay U	Bangor C	08/49	49-50	47	-	1

WHITHAM Jack
Born: Burnley, Lancashire, England, 8 December, 1946 — F
England: U23-1

Sheffield Wed	Holy Trinity BC	11/64	66-69	54	9	27
Liverpool	Tr	05/70	70-71	15	0	7
Cardiff C	Tr	01/74	73-74	12	2	3
Reading	Tr	07/75	75	13	6	3

WHITHAM Terence (Terry)
Born: Sheffield, England, 14 August, 1935 — WH

Sheffield Wed	Jnr	09/52	56-58	4	-	0
Chesterfield	Tr	06/61	61-63	66	-	3

WHITINGTON Craig
Born: Brighton, England, 3 September, 1970 — F

Scarborough	Crawley T	11/93	93	26	1	10
Huddersfield T	Tr	08/94	94	1	0	0
Rochdale	L	11/94	94	1	0	0

WHITINGTON Eric Richard
Born: Brighton, England, 18 September, 1946 — M/F
England: Youth

Brighton & HA	Chelsea (Am)	10/64	65-67	26	6	8

WHITLEY James (Jim)
Born: Ndola, Zambia, 14 April, 1975 — M/RB
Northern Ireland: 3/B-1

Manchester C	Jnr	08/94	97-99	27	11	0
Blackpool	L	08/99	99	7	1	0
Norwich C	L	08/00	00	7	1	1
Swindon T	L	12/00	00	2	0	0
Northampton T	L	02/01	00	13	0	0
Wrexham	Tr	10/01	01-05	135	5	1

WHITLEY Jeffrey (Jeff)
Born: Ndola, Zambia, 28 January, 1979 — M
Northern Ireland: 20/B-2/U21-17

Manchester C	YT	02/96	96-01	96	27	8
Wrexham	L	01/99	98	9	0	2
Notts Co	L	03/02	01	6	0	0
Notts Co	L	10/02	02	12	0	0
Sunderland	Tr	08/03	03-04	65	3	2
Cardiff C	Tr	08/05	05	32	2	1
Stoke C	L	08/06	06	0	3	0

League Club	Source	Date Signed	Seasons Played	Apps	Subs	Gls
Wrexham	L	02/07	06	11	0	1
Wrexham		01/08	07	5	6	0

WHITLOCK Mark
Born: Portsmouth, England, 14 March, 1961 CD

League Club	Source	Date Signed	Seasons Played	Apps	Subs	Gls
Southampton	App	03/79	81-85	55	6	1
Grimsby T	L	10/82	82	7	1	0
Aldershot	L	03/83	82	14	0	0
Bournemouth	Tr	07/86	86-88	98	1	1
Reading	Tr	12/88	88-89	26	1	0
Aldershot	Tr	08/90	90	28	1	2

WHITLOCK Philip John (Phil)
Born: Llanhilleth, Blaenau Gwent, Wales, 1 May, 1930 LH
Died: Chester, England, December, 2009

League Club	Source	Date Signed	Seasons Played	Apps	Subs	Gls
Cardiff C		02/49				
Chester C	Tr	08/50	50-58	142	-	3

WHITLOW Michael William (Mike)
Born: Northwich, Cheshire, England, 13 January, 1968 LB/M

League Club	Source	Date Signed	Seasons Played	Apps	Subs	Gls
Leeds U	Witton A	11/88	88-91	62	15	4
Leicester C	Tr	03/92	91-96	141	6	8
Bolton W	Tr	09/97	97-02	124	8	2
Sheffield U	Tr	07/03	03	13	4	1
Notts Co	Tr	07/04	04	22	2	0

WHITMARSH Paul
Born: Beckenham, SE London, England, 18 September, 1973 F
England: Schools

League Club	Source	Date Signed	Seasons Played	Apps	Subs	Gls
West Ham U	YT	07/92				
Doncaster Rov	Tr	09/93	93	2	4	1

WHITMORE Theodore Eccleston (Theo)
Born: Montego Bay, Jamaica, 5 August, 1972 M
Jamaica: 105

League Club	Source	Date Signed	Seasons Played	Apps	Subs	Gls
Hull C	Seba U (JAM)	10/99	99-01	63	14	9
Tranmere Rov	Livingston	07/04	04-05	17	20	5

WHITNALL Brian
Born: Adwick-le-Street, South Yorkshire, England, 25 May, 1933 FB

League Club	Source	Date Signed	Seasons Played	Apps	Subs	Gls
Hull C	Jnr	06/50	54	2	-	0
Scunthorpe U	Tr	05/56	56-57	2	-	0
Exeter C	Tr	07/58	58-61	36	-	0

WHITNEY Jonathan David (Jon)
Born: Nantwich, Cheshire, England, 23 December, 1970 LB

League Club	Source	Date Signed	Seasons Played	Apps	Subs	Gls
Huddersfield T	Winsford U	10/93	93-95	17	1	0
Wigan Ath	L	03/95	94	12	0	0
Lincoln C	Tr	10/95	95-98	98	3	8
Hull C	Tr	12/98	98-00	54	3	3

WHITTAKER Frederick (Fred)
Born: Vancouver, Canada, 12 October, 1923 CF

League Club	Source	Date Signed	Seasons Played	Apps	Subs	Gls
Notts Co	Vancouver NS (CAN)	08/46	46	10	-	2

WHITTAKER Raymond Henry (Ray)
Born: Bow, E London, England, 15 January, 1945 LW
England: Youth/Schools

League Club	Source	Date Signed	Seasons Played	Apps	Subs	Gls
Arsenal	Jnr	05/62				
Luton T	Tr	03/64	63-68	169	1	40
Colchester U	Tr	07/69	69-70	41	2	7

WHITTAKER Richard (Dick)
Born: Dublin, Republic of Ireland, 10 October, 1934 RB
Died: Stamford, Lincolnshire, England, 18 September, 1998
Republic of Ireland: 1/B

League Club	Source	Date Signed	Seasons Played	Apps	Subs	Gls
Chelsea	St Mary's BC (ROI)	05/52	55-59	48	-	0
Peterborough U	Tr	09/60	60-62	82	-	0
Queens Park Rgrs	Tr	07/63	63	17	-	0

WHITTAKER Steven Gordon
Born: Edinburgh, Scotland, 16 June, 1984 RB
Scotland: 29/B-2/U21-18

League Club	Source	Date Signed	Seasons Played	Apps	Subs	Gls
Norwich C	Glasgow Rangers	07/12	12-14	65	5	4

WHITTAKER Stuart
Born: Liverpool, England, 2 January, 1975 LW

League Club	Source	Date Signed	Seasons Played	Apps	Subs	Gls
Bolton W	Liverpool (YT)	05/93	93-94	2	1	0
Wigan Ath	L	08/96	96	2	1	0
Macclesfield T	Tr	08/97	97-99	49	18	5

WHITTAKER William Paul (Bill)
Born: Charlton, SE London, England, 20 December, 1922 WH
Died: Greenwich, SE London, England, 30 August, 1977
England: Schools

League Club	Source	Date Signed	Seasons Played	Apps	Subs	Gls
Charlton Ath	Arsenal (Am)	02/40	46-48	28	-	0
Huddersfield T	Tr	11/48	48-49	43	-	0
Crystal Palace	Tr	06/50	50	35	-	1

WHITTALL Samuel (Sam)
Born: Wolverhampton, England, 5 October, 1993 M

League Club	Source	Date Signed	Seasons Played	Apps	Subs	Gls
Wolverhampton W	Sch	07/12				
Cambridge U	Tr	08/14	14	0	2	0

WHITTAM Ernest (Ernie)
Born: Thurcroft, South Yorkshire, England, 29 October, 1924 FB

League Club	Source	Date Signed	Seasons Played	Apps	Subs	Gls
Rotherham U	Dinnington Ath	04/45	46	1	-	0
Leeds U	Wombwell Ath	12/47				

WHITTINGHAM Alfred (Alf)
Born: Altofts, West Yorkshire, England, 19 June, 1914 CF
Died: Altofts, West Yorkshire, England, October, 1993

League Club	Source	Date Signed	Seasons Played	Apps	Subs	Gls
Bradford C	Altofts WRC	10/36	36-46	87	-	24
Huddersfield T	Tr	02/47	46-48	67	-	17
Halifax T	Tr	03/49	48-49	39	-	9

WHITTINGHAM Guy
Born: Evesham, Worcestershire, England, 10 November, 1964 F

League Club	Source	Date Signed	Seasons Played	Apps	Subs	Gls
Portsmouth	Yeovil T	06/89	89-92	149	11	88
Aston Villa	Tr	08/93	93-94	17	8	5
Wolverhampton W	L	02/94	93	13	0	8
Sheffield Wed	Tr	12/94	94-98	90	23	22
Wolverhampton W	L	11/98	98	9	1	1
Portsmouth	L	01/99	98	9	0	7
Watford	L	03/99	98	4	1	0
Portsmouth	Tr	07/99	99-00	15	11	4
Peterborough U	L	08/00	00	1	4	1
Oxford U	L	10/00	00	1	0	1
Wycombe W	Tr	03/01	00	9	3	1

WHITTINGHAM Peter Michael
Born: Nuneaton, Warwickshire, England, 8 September, 1984 M/F
England: U21-17/Youth

League Club	Source	Date Signed	Seasons Played	Apps	Subs	Gls
Aston Villa	Sch	11/02	02-06	32	24	1
Burnley	L	02/05	04	7	0	0
Derby Co	L	09/05	05	11	0	0
Cardiff C	Tr	01/07	06-14	308	32	72

WHITTINGHAM Stephen Paul (Steve)
Born: Wallasey, Wirral, England, 4 February, 1962 F

League Club	Source	Date Signed	Seasons Played	Apps	Subs	Gls
Tranmere Rov	App	02/80	78-80	0	2	0

WHITTLE Alan
Born: Liverpool, England, 10 March, 1950 F/M
England: U23-1/Youth/Schools

League Club	Source	Date Signed	Seasons Played	Apps	Subs	Gls
Everton	App	07/65	67-72	72	2	21
Crystal Palace	Tr	12/72	72-75	103	5	19
Leyton Orient	Tr	09/76	76	31	2	5
Leyton Orient	Persepolis (IRA)	02/78	78-79	16	1	1
Bournemouth	Tr	01/81	80	8	1	0

WHITTLE Ernest (Ernie)
Born: Lanchester, County Durham, England, 25 November, 1925 IF
Died: Lincoln, England, 8 May, 1998

League Club	Source	Date Signed	Seasons Played	Apps	Subs	Gls
Newcastle U	South Moor Jnrs	11/44				
Lincoln C	Seaham CW	01/50	49-53	145	-	62
Workington	Tr	03/54	53-56	110	-	44
Chesterfield	Tr	11/56	56	15	-	4
Bradford Park Ave	Tr	08/57	57	18	-	6

WHITTLE Graham
Born: Liverpool, England, 30 May, 1953 F/M

League Club	Source	Date Signed	Seasons Played	Apps	Subs	Gls
Wrexham	Hartshill BC	04/71	70-80	288	18	91

WHITTLE James Archibald
Born: Hamilton, Lanarkshire, Scotland, 5 September, 1929 CF
Died: Rutherglen, Glasgow, Scotland, 23 July, 2001

League Club	Source	Date Signed	Seasons Played	Apps	Subs	Gls
Southampton (L)	Heart of Midlothian	01/54	53	2	-	0

WHITTLE Justin Philip
Born: Derby, England, 18 March, 1971 CD

League Club	Source	Date Signed	Seasons Played	Apps	Subs	Gls
Stoke C	Glasgow Celtic	10/94	95-98	66	13	1
Hull C	Tr	11/98	98-03	184	9	2
Grimsby T	Tr	08/04	04-07	118	9	3

WHITTLE Maurice
Born: Wigan, Greater Manchester, England, 5 July, 1948 LB

League Club	Source	Date Signed	Seasons Played	Apps	Subs	Gls
Blackburn Rov	App	07/66	68	5	2	0
Oldham Ath	Tr	05/69	69-76	307	5	39
Wigan Ath	Barrow	03/80	79-80	21	0	1

WHITTON Stephen Paul (Steve)
Born: East Ham, E London, England, 4 December, 1960 M/F

League Club	Source	Date Signed	Seasons Played	Apps	Subs	Gls
Coventry C	App	09/78	79-82	64	10	21
West Ham U	Tr	07/83	83-84	35	4	6
Birmingham C	L	01/86	85	8	0	3
Birmingham C	Tr	08/86	86-88	94	1	28
Sheffield Wed	Tr	03/89	88-90	22	10	4
Ipswich T	Tr	01/91	90-93	80	8	15
Colchester U	Tr	03/94	93-97	105	11	21

WHITWORTH George Geoffrey
Born: Eckington, Derbyshire, England, 22 September, 1927 — RH
Died: Basford, Nottinghamshire, England, March, 2006

League Club	Source	Date Signed	Seasons Played	Apps	Subs	Gls
Liverpool	Stanton Ironworks	03/50	51	9	-	0

WHITWORTH Harry
Born: Manchester, England, 1 December, 1920 — RH/RW
Died: Blackpool, Lancashire, England, 4 April, 2002

League Club	Source	Date Signed	Seasons Played	Apps	Subs	Gls
Bury	Prestwich Central	11/45	46-50	112	-	14
Rochdale	Tr	07/51	51-52	70	-	9
Southport	Northwich Victoria	09/53	53	33	-	6
Crewe Alex	Tr	07/54	54	13	-	1

WHITWORTH Neil Anthony
Born: Wigan, Greater Manchester, England, 12 April, 1972 — CD
England: Youth

League Club	Source	Date Signed	Seasons Played	Apps	Subs	Gls
Wigan Ath	YT	-	89	1	1	0
Manchester U	Tr	07/90	90	1	0	0
Preston NE	L	01/92	91	6	0	0
Barnsley	L	02/92	91	11	0	0
Rotherham U	L	10/93	93	8	0	1
Blackpool	L	12/93	93	3	0	0
Wigan Ath	Kilmarnock	03/98	97	1	3	0
Hull C	Tr	07/98	98-99	18	1	2
Exeter C	Tr	08/00	00-02	53	4	1

WHITWORTH Stephen (Steve)
Born: Coalville, Leicestershire, England, 20 March, 1952 — RB
England: 7/U23-6/Youth/Schools

League Club	Source	Date Signed	Seasons Played	Apps	Subs	Gls
Leicester C	App	11/69	70-78	352	1	0
Sunderland	Tr	03/79	78-81	83	0	0
Bolton W	Tr	10/81	81-82	67	0	0
Mansfield T	Tr	08/83	83-84	80	0	2

WHOLEY Jake Anthony
Born: Nottingham, England, 1 December, 1993 — LB

League Club	Source	Date Signed	Seasons Played	Apps	Subs	Gls
Notts Co	Sch	07/12	12	0	2	0
Nottingham F	Ange IF (SWE)	01/14				

WHYKE Peter
Born: Barnsley, South Yorkshire, England, 7 September, 1939 — W

League Club	Source	Date Signed	Seasons Played	Apps	Subs	Gls
Barnsley	Smithies U	01/58	57-60	26	-	1
Rochdale	Tr	07/61	61	5	-	0

WHYMARK Trevor John
Born: Burston, Norfolk, England, 4 May, 1950 — F
England: 1/U23-6

League Club	Source	Date Signed	Seasons Played	Apps	Subs	Gls
Ipswich T	Diss T	05/69	69-78	249	12	75
Derby Co	Sparta Rotterdam (NED)	12/79	79	2	0	0
Grimsby T	Vancouver W'caps (CAN)	12/80	80-83	83	10	16
Southend U	Tr	01/84	83-84	37	2	6
Peterborough U	Tr	08/85	85	3	0	0
Colchester U	Diss T	10/85	85	2	0	0

WHYTE Christopher Anderson (Chris)
Born: Islington, N London, England, 2 September, 1961 — D
England: U21-4

League Club	Source	Date Signed	Seasons Played	Apps	Subs	Gls
Arsenal	App	12/79	81-85	86	4	8
Crystal Palace	L	08/84	84	13	0	0
West Bromwich A	Los Angeles Laz (USA)	08/88	88-89	83	1	7
Leeds U	Tr	06/90	90-92	113	0	5
Birmingham C	Tr	08/93	93-95	68	0	1
Coventry C	L	12/95	95	1	0	0
Charlton Ath	Tr	03/96	95	10	1	0
Leyton Orient	Detroit Safari (USA)	01/97	96	1	0	0
Oxford U	Tr	02/97	96	10	0	0

WHYTE David
Born: Dunfermline, Fife, Scotland, 2 March, 1959 — CD

League Club	Source	Date Signed	Seasons Played	Apps	Subs	Gls
Leeds U	App	03/77	76	1	1	0

WHYTE David Antony
Born: Greenwich, SE London, England, 20 April, 1971 — F
Died: London, England, 9 September, 2014

League Club	Source	Date Signed	Seasons Played	Apps	Subs	Gls
Crystal Palace	Greenwich Bor	02/89	91-93	17	10	4
Charlton Ath	L	03/92	91	7	1	2
Charlton Ath	Tr	07/94	94-96	65	20	28
Ipswich T	Tr	10/97	97	2	0	0
Bristol Rov	Tr	01/98	97	0	4	0
Southend U	Tr	03/98	97-98	17	9	3

WHYTE Derek
Born: Glasgow, Scotland, 31 August, 1968 — CD
Scotland: 12/B-4/U21-9/Youth/Schools

League Club	Source	Date Signed	Seasons Played	Apps	Subs	Gls
Middlesbrough	Glasgow Celtic	08/92	92-97	160	7	2

WHYTE Francis O'Hare (Frank)
Born: Govanhill, Glasgow, Scotland, 6 October, 1934 — CH
Died: Bournemouth, England, September, 1984

League Club	Source	Date Signed	Seasons Played	Apps	Subs	Gls
Swindon T	Glasgow Celtic	06/56	56	7	-	0

WHYTE James McCreadie (Jimmy)
Born: Glasgow, Scotland, 19 January, 1930 — IF
Died: Medway, Kent, England, November, 2013

League Club	Source	Date Signed	Seasons Played	Apps	Subs	Gls
Southend U	Third Lanark	05/54	54-56	33	-	8

WHYTE John Archibald (Archie)
Born: Falkirk, Scotland, 17 July, 1919 — CH
Died: Middleton, Greater Manchester, England, 1 October, 1973

League Club	Source	Date Signed	Seasons Played	Apps	Subs	Gls
Barnsley	Armadale Thistle	05/38	46-49	91	-	2
Oldham Ath	Tr	08/50	50-55	234	-	0

WHYTE John Nimmo (Jock)
Born: West Calder, West Lothian, Scotland, 7 May, 1921 — RB
Died: Bradford, England, 17 October, 1998

League Club	Source	Date Signed	Seasons Played	Apps	Subs	Gls
Bradford C	Falkirk	08/50	50-56	236	-	2

WICKHAM Connor Neil Ralph
Born: Hereford, England, 31 March, 1993 — F
England: U21-17/Youth

League Club	Source	Date Signed	Seasons Played	Apps	Subs	Gls
Ipswich T	Sch	04/10	08-10	33	32	13
Sunderland	Tr	06/11	11-14	49	30	11
Sheffield Wed	L	02/13	12	4	2	1
Sheffield Wed	L	11/13	13	11	0	8
Leeds U	L	02/14	13	5	0	0

WICKS Alan Hayward
Born: Henley-on-Thames, Oxfordshire, England, 8 February, 1933 — WH

League Club	Source	Date Signed	Seasons Played	Apps	Subs	Gls
Reading		05/52	55	1	-	0

WICKS Matthew Jonathan
Born: Reading, England, 8 September, 1978 — CD
England: Youth

League Club	Source	Date Signed	Seasons Played	Apps	Subs	Gls
Arsenal	Manchester U (YT)	01/96				
Crewe Alex	Tr	06/98	98	4	2	0
Peterborough U	Tr	03/99	98-99	28	3	0
Brighton & HA	Tr	09/00	00-01	25	1	3
Hull C	Tr	01/02	01	14	0	0

WICKS Peter
Born: Hemsworth, West Yorkshire, England, 14 May, 1948 — G
England: Youth

League Club	Source	Date Signed	Seasons Played	Apps	Subs	Gls
Sheffield Wed	App	05/65	64-69	13	0	0

WICKS Roger Charles
Born: Warrington, Cheshire, England, 19 April, 1957 — M

League Club	Source	Date Signed	Seasons Played	Apps	Subs	Gls
Darlington	Netherfield	02/81	80-82	31	10	4

WICKS Stanley Maurice (Stan)
Born: Reading, England, 11 July, 1928 — CH
Died: Henley-on-Thames, Oxfordshire, England, 20 February, 1983
England: B-1/FLge-1

League Club	Source	Date Signed	Seasons Played	Apps	Subs	Gls
Reading	Castle Street Inst	08/48	49-53	170	-	1
Chelsea	Tr	01/54	54-56	71	-	1

WICKS Stephen John (Steve)
Born: Reading, England, 3 October, 1956 — CD
England: U21-1/Youth

League Club	Source	Date Signed	Seasons Played	Apps	Subs	Gls
Chelsea	App	06/74	74-78	117	1	5
Derby Co	Tr	01/79	78-79	24	0	0
Queens Park Rgrs	Tr	09/79	79-80	73	0	0
Crystal Palace	Tr	06/81	81	14	0	1
Queens Park Rgrs	Tr	03/82	81-85	116	0	6
Chelsea	Tr	07/86	86-87	32	0	1

WIDDOP Dennis
Born: Keighley, West Yorkshire, England, 14 March, 1931 — W

League Club	Source	Date Signed	Seasons Played	Apps	Subs	Gls
Bradford C	Portadown	08/54	54	1	-	0

WIDDOWSON John Robert (Bob)
Born: Loughborough, Leicestershire, England, 12 September, 1941 — G

League Club	Source	Date Signed	Seasons Played	Apps	Subs	Gls
Sheffield U	British Ropes	07/59	61-67	7	0	0
York C	Tr	06/68	68-69	30	0	0
Portsmouth	L	11/69	69	4	0	0

WIDDOWSON Joseph (Joe)
Born: Forest Gate, E London, England, 28 March, 1989 — LB

League Club	Source	Date Signed	Seasons Played	Apps	Subs	Gls
West Ham U	Sch	07/07				
Rotherham U	L	02/08	07	3	0	0
Grimsby T	Tr	01/09	08-09	55	3	1
Rochdale	Tr	06/10	10-11	60	6	0
Northampton T	Tr	07/12	12-13	63	1	0
Bury	Tr	07/14	14	0	1	0
Morecambe	L	08/14	14	8	0	0
Dagenham & Red	Tr	11/14	14	20	1	0

WIDDRINGTON Thomas (Tommy)
Born: Newcastle-upon-Tyne, England, 1 October, 1971 — M

League Club	Source	Date Signed	Seasons Played	Apps	Subs	Gls
Southampton	YT	05/90	91-95	67	8	3
Wigan Ath	L	09/91	91	5	1	0
Grimsby T	Tr	07/96	96-98	72	17	8

League Club	Source	Date Signed	Seasons Played	Career Record Apps	Subs	Gls
Port Vale	Tr	03/99	98-00	77	5	8
Hartlepool U	Tr	07/01	01-02	50	6	5
Macclesfield T	Tr	08/03	03-04	55	3	0
Port Vale	Tr	01/05	04	2	4	0
WIEKENS Gerard						
Born: Winschoten, Netherlands, 25 February, 1973						CD/M
Manchester C	SC Veendam (NED)	07/97	97-02	167	15	10
WIFFILL David Phillip (Dave)						
Born: Bristol, England, 19 April, 1961						M
Manchester C	Bath C	04/80				
Bristol Rov	Bath C	08/87	87	2	0	0
WIGG Nathan Marlow						
Born: Cardiff, Wales, 27 September, 1974						M
Cardiff C	Jnr	08/93	93-95	40	18	1
WIGG Ronald George (Ron)						
Born: Great Dunmow, Essex, England, 18 May, 1949						F
Died: Ohio, USA, July, 1997						
Ipswich T	Leyton Orient (App)	04/67	67-69	35	2	14
Watford	Tr	06/70	70-72	91	6	20
Rotherham U	Tr	03/73	72-74	65	0	22
Grimsby T	Tr	01/75	74-76	51	12	12
Barnsley	Tr	03/77	76-77	14	4	5
Scunthorpe U	Tr	10/77	77-78	48	2	7
WIGGAN Trenton Ashton						
Born: Kingston, Jamaica, 20 September, 1962						RW
England: Schools						
Sheffield U	App	08/80	79-81	20	4	3
WIGGETT David Jonathan (Dave)						
Born: Chapeltown, South Yorkshire, England, 25 May, 1957						LB
Died: Hartlepool, Cleveland, England, 23 March, 1978						
Lincoln C	App	06/75	73-75	4	2	0
Hartlepool U	Tr	10/76	76-77	54	0	1
WIGGIN Raymond (Ray)						
Born: Rushall, West Midlands, England, 13 September, 1942						CF
Walsall	Rushall Olympic	09/62	62-63	19	-	6
WIGGINS Rhoys Barrie						
Born: Uxbridge, W London, England, 4 November, 1987						LB
Wales: U21-9/Youth						
Crystal Palace	Sch	07/06	08	1	0	0
Bournemouth	L	01/09	08	12	1	0
Norwich C	Tr	07/09				
Bournemouth	Tr	01/10	09-10	53	1	2
Charlton Ath	Tr	06/11	11-14	123	1	1
WIGGINTON Clive Anthony						
Born: Sheffield, England, 18 October, 1950						CD
Grimsby T	App	10/68	68-74	164	9	6
Scunthorpe U	Tr	07/75	75-76	88	0	7
Lincoln C	Tr	09/77	77-78	60	0	6
Grimsby T	Tr	03/79	78-81	122	0	2
Doncaster Rov	L	03/82	81	13	0	1
Torquay U	Tr	07/82	82	9	0	0
Doncaster Rov	Tr	10/82	82	18	0	0
WIGHTMAN John Renton (Jock)						
Born: Dunscroft, South Yorkshire, England, 2 November, 1912						WH
Died: Blackburn, Greater Manchester, England, 20 April, 1964						
York C	Scarborough	08/33	33	5	-	0
Bradford Park Ave	Tr	09/34	34	17	-	0
Huddersfield T	Tr	01/35	34-36	64	-	0
Blackburn Rov	Tr	01/37	36-46	66	-	2
Carlisle U	Tr	08/47	47	36	-	0
WIGLEY Steven (Steve)						
Born: Ashton-under-Lyne, Greater Manchester, England, 15 October, 1961						W
Nottingham F	Curzon Ashton	03/81	82-85	69	13	2
Sheffield U	Tr	10/85	85-86	21	7	1
Birmingham C	Tr	03/87	86-88	87	0	4
Portsmouth	Tr	03/89	88-91	103	17	12
Exeter C	Tr	08/93	93	22	1	1
WIGNALL David Arthur						
Born: Wallasey, Wirral, England, 3 April, 1959						M
Doncaster Rov	App	07/76	75-77	35	6	1
WIGNALL Frank						
Born: Blackrod, Greater Manchester, England, 21 August, 1939						CF
England: 2/FLge-2						
Everton	Horwich RMI	05/58	59-62	33	-	15
Nottingham F	Tr	06/63	63-67	156	1	47
Wolverhampton W	Tr	03/68	67-68	32	0	15
Derby Co	Tr	02/69	68-71	29	16	15
Mansfield T	Tr	11/71	71-72	50	6	15
WIGNALL Jack David						
Born: Liverpool, England, 26 September, 1981						CD
Colchester U	YT	-	99	0	1	0
WIGNALL Mark						
Born: Preston, Lancashire, England, 6 December, 1952						M
Wigan Ath	App	12/80	80-81	34	0	0
WIGNALL Steven Leslie (Steve)						
Born: Liverpool, England, 17 September, 1954						CD
Doncaster Rov	Liverpool (Jnr)	03/72	72-76	127	3	1
Colchester U	Tr	09/77	77-83	279	2	21
Brentford	Tr	08/84	84-86	67	0	2
Aldershot	Tr	09/86	86-90	158	3	4
WIJNHARD Clyde						
Born: Paramaribo, Suriname, 9 November, 1973						F
Leeds U	Willem II (NED)	07/98	98	11	7	3
Huddersfield T	Tr	07/99	99-01	51	11	16
Preston NE	Tr	03/02	01	6	0	3
Oldham Ath	Tr	08/02	02	24	1	10
Darlington	Beira Mar (POR)	10/04	04-05	36	3	15
Macclesfield T	Tr	10/05	05	19	1	8
Brentford	Tr	09/06	06	7	2	0
WILBERT George Norman						
Born: Dunston-on-Tyne, Tyne and Wear, England, 11 July, 1924						CF
Died: Alnwick, Northumberland, England, 10 September, 1993						
Gateshead	Tottenham H (Am)	08/42	47-54	269	-	95
WILBRAHAM Aaron Thomas						
Born: Knutsford, Cheshire, England, 21 October, 1979						F
Stockport Co	YT	08/97	97-03	118	54	35
Hull C	Tr	07/04	04	10	9	2
Oldham Ath	L	10/04	04	4	0	2
MK Dons	Tr	07/05	05-10	140	36	49
Bradford C	L	03/06	05	5	0	1
Norwich C	Tr	01/11	10-11	7	16	2
Crystal Palace	Tr	07/12	12-13	5	20	0
Bristol C	Tr	07/14	14	33	4	18
WILBY Edward						
Born: Rotherham, South Yorkshire, England, 18 May, 1922						FB
Died: Halifax, West Yorkshire, England, February, 1998						
Wolverhampton W		05/46				
Bradford C	Tr	09/46	46	3	-	0
WILCOCK Roderick William (Rod)						
Born: Middlesbrough, England, 28 February, 1956						M
Crewe Alex	Southampton (Am)	08/74	74	2	2	0
WILCOCKSON Harold						
Born: Sheffield, England, 23 July, 1943						RB
Rotherham U	Hillsborough BC	07/63	64-67	109	0	2
Doncaster Rov	Tr	02/68	67-69	75	0	3
Sheffield Wed	Tr	12/69	69-70	40	0	1
Doncaster Rov	Tr	05/71	71-72	36	0	1
WILCOX Anthony (Tony)						
Born: Rotherham, South Yorkshire, England, 13 June, 1944						G
Rotherham U		10/62				
Barnsley	Tr	08/64	64	6	-	0
WILCOX Caradoc (Crad)						
Born: Treharris, Merthyr Tydfil, Wales, 8 November, 1923						D
Died: Rhondda, Rhondda Cynon Taff, Wales, August, 2003						
Cardiff C	Treharris	05/49				
Newport Co	Tr	07/52	52-53	32	-	0
WILCOX Edward Evan						
Born: Blaengarw, Bridgend, Wales, 24 March, 1927						IF
Died: 11 January, 2015						
West Bromwich A	Oxford C	05/48	48-50	12	-	3
WILCOX Frederick (Fred)						
Born: St Helens, Merseyside, England, 23 October, 1922						RB
Died: Liverpool, England, 22 January, 2015						
Chester C	Everton (Am)	07/47	47	16	-	0
WILCOX George Edwin						
Born: Treeton, South Yorkshire, England, 23 August, 1917						FB
Died: Rotherham, South Yorkshire, England, October, 1991						
Derby Co	Denaby U	10/36	37-46	12	-	0
Rotherham U	Tr	08/48	48	1	-	0
WILCOX Jason Malcolm						
Born: Farnworth, Greater Manchester, England, 15 July, 1971						LW
England: 3/B-2						

League Club	Source	Date Signed	Seasons Played	Apps	Subs	Gls
Blackburn Rov	YT	06/89	89-99	242	27	31
Leeds U	Tr	12/99	99-03	52	29	4
Leicester C	Tr	08/04	04-05	14	6	1
Blackpool	Tr	11/05	05	26	0	0

WILCOX Raymond (Ray)
Born: Treharris, Merthyr Tydfil, Wales, 12 April, 1921 — CH
Died: Newport, Wales, 26 January, 2003
Wales: WLge-2

League Club	Source	Date Signed	Seasons Played	Apps	Subs	Gls
Newport Co	Treharris	05/39	46-59	487	-	0

WILCOX Russell (Russ)
Born: Hemsworth, West Yorkshire, England, 25 March, 1964 — CD
England: Semi Pro-3

League Club	Source	Date Signed	Seasons Played	Apps	Subs	Gls
Doncaster Rov	App	-	80	1	0	0
Northampton T	Frickley Ath	06/86	86-89	137	1	9
Hull C	Tr	08/90	90-92	92	8	7
Doncaster Rov	Tr	07/93	93-95	81	0	6
Preston NE	Tr	09/95	95-96	62	0	1
Scunthorpe U	Tr	07/97	97-01	106	12	4

WILD Peter
Born: Bramhall, Greater Manchester, England, 12 October, 1982 — F

League Club	Source	Date Signed	Seasons Played	Apps	Subs	Gls
Stockport Co	YT	07/01	01-02	1	3	1

WILDE Adam Matthew
Born: Southampton, England, 22 May, 1979 — LW

League Club	Source	Date Signed	Seasons Played	Apps	Subs	Gls
Cambridge U	YT	02/97	96-98	1	3	0

WILDER Christopher John (Chris)
Born: Stocksbridge, South Yorkshire, England, 23 September, 1967 — RB

League Club	Source	Date Signed	Seasons Played	Apps	Subs	Gls
Southampton	App	09/85				
Sheffield U	Tr	08/86	86-91	89	4	1
Walsall	L	11/89	89	4	0	0
Charlton Ath	L	10/90	90	1	0	0
Charlton Ath	L	11/91	91	2	0	0
Leyton Orient	L	02/92	91	16	0	1
Rotherham U	Tr	07/92	92-95	129	3	11
Notts Co	Tr	01/96	95-96	46	0	0
Bradford C	Tr	03/97	96-97	35	7	0
Sheffield U	Tr	03/98	97-98	11	1	0
Northampton T	L	11/98	98	1	0	0
Lincoln C	L	03/99	98	2	1	0
Brighton & HA	Tr	07/99	99	11	0	0
Halifax T	Tr	10/99	99-00	51	0	1

WILDIG Aaron Keith
Born: Hereford, England, 15 April, 1992 — M
Wales: Youth

League Club	Source	Date Signed	Seasons Played	Apps	Subs	Gls
Cardiff C	Sch	04/09	09-10	4	9	1
Shrewsbury T	L	11/11	11	10	2	2
Shrewsbury T	Tr	06/12	11-14	43	9	2
Morecambe	L	03/15	14	9	0	1

WILDING Craig Anthony
Born: Birmingham, England, 30 October, 1981 — F

League Club	Source	Date Signed	Seasons Played	Apps	Subs	Gls
Chesterfield	YT	07/01				
York C	Tr	07/02	02	1	6	0

WILDING Peter John
Born: Shrewsbury, Shropshire, England, 28 November, 1968 — CD/M

League Club	Source	Date Signed	Seasons Played	Apps	Subs	Gls
Shrewsbury T	Telford U	06/97	97-02	170	23	7

WILDON Leslie Eric (Eric)
Born: Middlesbrough, England, 5 April, 1924 — CF
Died: Middlesbrough, England, 9 September, 1998

League Club	Source	Date Signed	Seasons Played	Apps	Subs	Gls
Hartlepool U	Price's Taylors	12/47	47-54	200	-	87

WILDSCHUT Yanic Sonny
Born: Amsterdam, Netherlands, 1 November, 1991 — LW
Netherlands: U21-10

League Club	Source	Date Signed	Seasons Played	Apps	Subs	Gls
Middlesbrough	Heerenveen (NED)	09/14	14	3	8	2

WILDSMITH Joseph Charles (Joe)
Born: Sheffield, England, 28 December, 1995 — G

League Club	Source	Date Signed	Seasons Played	Apps	Subs	Gls
Sheffield Wed	Sch	11/13				
Barnsley	L	03/15	14	2	0	0

WILE John David
Born: Sherburn, County Durham, England, 9 March, 1947 — CD

League Club	Source	Date Signed	Seasons Played	Apps	Subs	Gls
Sunderland	Durham C	06/66				
Peterborough U	Tr	07/67	67-70	116	2	7
West Bromwich A	Tr	12/70	70-82	499	1	24
Peterborough U	Tr	08/83	83-85	86	1	3

WILEMAN Richard Anthony
Born: Breedon, Leicestershire, England, 4 October, 1947 — LW

League Club	Source	Date Signed	Seasons Played	Apps	Subs	Gls
Notts Co		07/66	66	2	0	0

WILES Ian Robert
Born: Woodford, NE London, England, 28 April, 1980 — CD

League Club	Source	Date Signed	Seasons Played	Apps	Subs	Gls
Colchester U	YT	07/98	98	0	1	0

WILES Simon Peter
Born: Preston, Lancashire, England, 22 April, 1985 — W

League Club	Source	Date Signed	Seasons Played	Apps	Subs	Gls
Blackpool	Sch	05/04	03-05	14	17	3
Macclesfield T	L	10/06	06	2	0	0
Macclesfield T	L	01/07	06	0	5	0
Macclesfield T	L	07/07	07	1	16	0

WILFORD Aron Leslie
Born: Scarborough, North Yorkshire, England, 14 January, 1982 — F

League Club	Source	Date Signed	Seasons Played	Apps	Subs	Gls
Middlesbrough	Harrogate College	07/99				
York C	Whitby T	07/03	03	4	2	2
Lincoln C	Tr	03/04	03	0	5	1

WILHELMSSON Christian Ulf
Born: Malmo, Sweden, 8 December, 1979 — RW
Sweden: 77/U21-16

League Club	Source	Date Signed	Seasons Played	Apps	Subs	Gls
Bolton W (L)	FC Nantes (FRA)	08/07	07	0	8	0

WILKES David Allan
Born: Barnsley, South Yorkshire, England, 10 March, 1964 — M

League Club	Source	Date Signed	Seasons Played	Apps	Subs	Gls
Barnsley	App	03/82	81-83	14	3	2
Halifax T	L	03/83	82	4	0	0
Stockport Co	Harps (HKG)	08/86	86	8	0	0
Carlisle U	Bridlington T	11/90	90-91	1	4	0

WILKES Stephen Brian (Steve)
Born: Preston, Lancashire, England, 30 June, 1967 — M

League Club	Source	Date Signed	Seasons Played	Apps	Subs	Gls
Wigan Ath	App	06/85				
Preston NE	Tr	08/86	87	1	2	0

WILKES Timothy Craig (Tim)
Born: Nottingham, England, 7 November, 1977 — F

League Club	Source	Date Signed	Seasons Played	Apps	Subs	Gls
Notts Co	YT	07/96	96	3	0	0

WILKIE Arthur William
Born: Woolwich, SE London, England, 7 October, 1942 — G

League Club	Source	Date Signed	Seasons Played	Apps	Subs	Gls
Reading	Jnr	10/59	61-67	169	0	2

WILKIE Derrick
Born: Brandon, County Durham, England, 27 July, 1939 — CH
Died: Durham, England, 3 March, 2012

League Club	Source	Date Signed	Seasons Played	Apps	Subs	Gls
Middlesbrough	Browney Jnrs	03/57	59-60	4	-	0
Hartlepool U	Tr	09/61	61-63	74	-	0

WILKIE Glen Alan
Born: Stepney, E London, England, 11 January, 1977 — RB

League Club	Source	Date Signed	Seasons Played	Apps	Subs	Gls
Leyton Orient	YT	03/95	94	10	1	0

WILKIE John Carlin
Born: Dundee, Scotland, 1 July, 1947 — F

League Club	Source	Date Signed	Seasons Played	Apps	Subs	Gls
Halifax T	Ross Co	02/73	72-73	29	8	8
Wigan Ath	Elgin C	08/76	78	3	1	0

WILKIE Lee
Born: Dundee, Scotland, 20 April, 1980 — CD
Scotland: 11/B-1/U21-8

League Club	Source	Date Signed	Seasons Played	Apps	Subs	Gls
Plymouth Arg (L)	Dundee	01/01	00	2	0	0
Notts Co (L)	Dundee	08/01	01	2	0	0

WILKIE Robert Mackintosh (Bob)
Born: Dundee, Scotland, 7 October, 1935 — LW

League Club	Source	Date Signed	Seasons Played	Apps	Subs	Gls
Tottenham H	Lochee Harp	12/56	56	1	-	0

WILKIN Kevin
Born: Cambridge, England, 1 October, 1967 — F

League Club	Source	Date Signed	Seasons Played	Apps	Subs	Gls
Northampton T	Cambridge C	08/90	90-94	67	11	11

WILKINS Alan James
Born: Treherbert, Rhondda Cynon Taff, Wales, 3 October, 1944 — IF

League Club	Source	Date Signed	Seasons Played	Apps	Subs	Gls
Swansea C	Treorchy BC	05/63	63-64	5	-	0

WILKINS Dean Mark
Born: Hillingdon, W London, England, 12 July, 1962 — M

League Club	Source	Date Signed	Seasons Played	Apps	Subs	Gls
Queens Park Rgrs	App	05/80	80-82	1	5	0
Brighton & HA	Tr	08/83	83	2	0	0
Leyton Orient	L	03/84	83	10	0	0
Brighton & HA	PEC Zwolle (NED)	07/87	87-95	295	15	25

WILKINS Ernest George (George)
Born: Hackney, E London, England, 27 October, 1919 — IF
Died: Bournemouth, England, 19 January, 1999

League Club	Source	Date Signed	Seasons Played	Apps	Subs	Gls
Brentford	Hayes	02/38	38-46	29	-	7
Bradford Park Ave	Tr	02/47	46-47	27	-	6
Nottingham F	Tr	12/47	47-48	24	-	6
Leeds U	Tr	09/49	49	3	-	0

League Club	Source	Date Signed	Seasons Played	Career Record Apps	Subs	Gls

WILKINS Graham George
Born: Hillingdon, W London, England, 28 June, 1955 — FB

League Club	Source	Date Signed	Seasons Played	Apps	Subs	Gls
Chelsea	App	07/72	72-81	136	1	1
Brentford	Tr	07/82	82-83	36	2	0
Southend U	L	03/84	83	3	0	0

WILKINS Ian John
Born: Lincoln, England, 3 April, 1980 — CD

League Club	Source	Date Signed	Seasons Played	Apps	Subs	Gls
Lincoln C	YT	03/98	97-99	4	2	0

WILKINS Kenneth (Ken)
Born: Salford, England, 24 October, 1928 — IF
Died: Cape Town, South Africa, August, 1995

League Club	Source	Date Signed	Seasons Played	Apps	Subs	Gls
Southampton		10/49	50	2	-	1
Exeter C	Tr	10/51	51	3	-	0
Southampton	Tr	07/52	52	1	-	0
Fulham	Tr	07/53				

WILKINS Leonard (Len)
Born: Southampton, England, 20 September, 1925 — D
Died: British Columbia, Canada, 13 August, 2003

League Club	Source	Date Signed	Seasons Played	Apps	Subs	Gls
Southampton	Cunliffe-Owen	10/45	48-57	260	-	2

WILKINS Leonard Henry Jack (Jack)
Born: Dublin, Republic of Ireland, 12 August, 1920 — D
Died: Cornwall, England, March, 2009

League Club	Source	Date Signed	Seasons Played	Apps	Subs	Gls
Brighton & HA	Guildford C	10/48	48-50	44	-	2

WILKINS Michael John (Mike)
Born: Leeds, England, 6 May, 1942 — CF

League Club	Source	Date Signed	Seasons Played	Apps	Subs	Gls
Bradford C	Ashley Road Meth's	09/59	59	1	-	0

WILKINS Paul
Born: Hackney, E London, England, 20 March, 1964 — F

League Club	Source	Date Signed	Seasons Played	Apps	Subs	Gls
Crystal Palace	Tottenham H (App)	02/82	81-83	9	4	3
Preston NE	Tr	06/84	84	3	3	2

WILKINS Raymond Colin (Ray)
Born: Hillingdon, W London, England, 14 September, 1956 — M
England: 84/FLge-1/U23-2/U21-1/Youth/Schools

League Club	Source	Date Signed	Seasons Played	Apps	Subs	Gls
Chelsea	App	10/73	73-78	176	3	30
Manchester U	Tr	08/79	79-83	158	2	7
Queens Park Rgrs	Glasgow Rangers	11/89	89-93	153	1	7
Crystal Palace	Tr	05/94	94	1	0	0
Queens Park Rgrs	Tr	11/94	94-96	16	5	0
Wycombe W	Tr	09/96	96	1	0	0
Millwall	Hibernian	01/97	96	3	0	0
Leyton Orient	Tr	02/97	96	3	0	0

WILKINS Raymond John Hamilton (Ray)
Born: Church Gresley, Derbyshire, England, 16 August, 1928 — CF

League Club	Source	Date Signed	Seasons Played	Apps	Subs	Gls
Derby Co	Moira U	01/50	49-53	30	-	11
Wrexham	Boston U	05/57	57	3	-	1

WILKINS Richard John
Born: Lambeth, S London, England, 28 May, 1965 — M

League Club	Source	Date Signed	Seasons Played	Apps	Subs	Gls
Colchester U	Haverhill Rov	11/86	86-89	150	2	22
Cambridge U	Tr	07/90	90-93	79	2	7
Hereford U	Tr	07/94	94-95	76	1	5
Colchester U	Tr	07/96	96-99	125	2	11

WILKINS Ronald (Ron)
Born: Treherbert, Rhondda Cynon Taff, Wales, 21 December, 1923 — IF
Died: Neath, Wales, 21 November, 1983

League Club	Source	Date Signed	Seasons Played	Apps	Subs	Gls
Newport Co	Gwynfi BC	01/46	46	1	-	0

WILKINSON Alan
Born: Middlewich, Cheshire, England, 5 June, 1935 — IF

League Club	Source	Date Signed	Seasons Played	Apps	Subs	Gls
Crewe Alex (Am)	Middlewich	10/55	55	1	-	0

WILKINSON Albert
Born: Barnsley, South Yorkshire, England, 3 November, 1928 — W
Died: Barnsley, South Yorkshire, England, 26 June, 2011

League Club	Source	Date Signed	Seasons Played	Apps	Subs	Gls
Bradford C (Am)		03/51	50	2	-	0
Halifax T	Denaby U	07/52	52	14	-	2
Rotherham U	Tr	07/53				
Chesterfield	Tr	06/54				

WILKINSON Andrew Gordon (Andy)
Born: Stone, Staffordshire, England, 6 August, 1984 — RB

League Club	Source	Date Signed	Seasons Played	Apps	Subs	Gls
Stoke C	Sch	07/02	03-13	126	34	0
Shrewsbury T	L	03/05	04	9	0	0
Blackpool	L	11/06	06	5	2	0
Millwall	L	10/14	14	9	0	0

WILKINSON Barry John
Born: Lincoln, England, 19 July, 1942 — CF
Died: Lincoln, England, 9 May, 2007

League Club	Source	Date Signed	Seasons Played	Apps	Subs	Gls
Lincoln C	Bracebridge CC	08/61	62-63	6	-	3

WILKINSON Conor Dominic Geoffrey
Born: Croydon, S London, England, 23 January, 1995 — F
Republic of Ireland: U21-1/Youth

League Club	Source	Date Signed	Seasons Played	Apps	Subs	Gls
Bolton W	Millwall (Sch)	07/13	14	2	2	0
Torquay U	L	02/14	13	2	1	0
Oldham Ath	L	09/14	14	4	2	1
Oldham Ath	L	02/15	14	6	5	2

WILKINSON Darron Bromley
Born: Reading, England, 24 November, 1969 — M

League Club	Source	Date Signed	Seasons Played	Apps	Subs	Gls
Brighton & HA	Wokingham T	08/92	92-93	34	4	3

WILKINSON David
Born: Sunderland, England, 28 May, 1928 — IF

League Club	Source	Date Signed	Seasons Played	Apps	Subs	Gls
Blackburn Rov	North Shields	07/48	48	1	-	0
Bournemouth	Tr	06/50	50-51	8	-	3

WILKINSON Derek
Born: Stalybridge, Greater Manchester, England, 4 June, 1935 — RW
England: FLge-2

League Club	Source	Date Signed	Seasons Played	Apps	Subs	Gls
Sheffield Wed	Dukinfield	11/53	54-64	212	-	53

WILKINSON Eric
Born: Sheffield, England, 6 March, 1931 — IF
Died: Winlaton, Tyne and Wear, England, 11 October, 2002

League Club	Source	Date Signed	Seasons Played	Apps	Subs	Gls
Bradford C		01/51				
Sheffield U	Tr	08/53				
Bournemouth	Tr	07/55	55	4	-	0

WILKINSON Eric
Born: Stalybridge, Greater Manchester, England, 4 June, 1935 — W

League Club	Source	Date Signed	Seasons Played	Apps	Subs	Gls
Sheffield Wed	Dukinfield	03/58	58	1	-	0

WILKINSON Ernest Stanley (Ernie)
Born: Chesterfield, Derbyshire, England, 13 February, 1947 — CH

League Club	Source	Date Signed	Seasons Played	Apps	Subs	Gls
Arsenal	App	02/64				
Exeter C	Tr	06/66	66-67	59	1	0
Rochdale	L	03/68	67	9	0	0

WILKINSON George Barry (Barry)
Born: Bishop Auckland, County Durham, England, 16 June, 1935 — WH
Died: Liverpool, England, May, 2004
England: Youth

League Club	Source	Date Signed	Seasons Played	Apps	Subs	Gls
Liverpool	West Auckland T	06/54	53-59	78	-	0
Tranmere Rov	Bangor C	08/63	63	3	-	0

WILKINSON Graham James
Born: Hull, England, 21 October, 1934 — FB

League Club	Source	Date Signed	Seasons Played	Apps	Subs	Gls
Hull C	Jnr	09/52	58-59	3	-	0

WILKINSON Harry Sanderson
Born: Sunderland, England, 20 March, 1926 — WH

League Club	Source	Date Signed	Seasons Played	Apps	Subs	Gls
Chelsea		06/46				
Exeter C	Tr	05/50	50	1	-	0
Colchester U	Tr	08/51	52	1	-	0

WILKINSON Herbert (Bert)
Born: Sunderland, England, 2 August, 1922 — FB
Died: Lincoln, England, 9 July, 2011

League Club	Source	Date Signed	Seasons Played	Apps	Subs	Gls
Lincoln C	Murton CW	08/45	46-50	39	-	0

WILKINSON Howard
Born: Sheffield, England, 13 November, 1943 — RW

League Club	Source	Date Signed	Seasons Played	Apps	Subs	Gls
Sheffield Wed	Sheffield U (Am)	06/62	64-65	22	0	3
Brighton & HA	Tr	07/66	66-70	116	13	18

WILKINSON Ian James
Born: North Ferriby, East Riding of Yorkshire, England, 19 September, 1977 — CD

League Club	Source	Date Signed	Seasons Played	Apps	Subs	Gls
Hull C	YT	07/96	95	8	0	1

WILKINSON Ian Matthew
Born: Warrington, Cheshire, England, 2 July, 1973 — G

League Club	Source	Date Signed	Seasons Played	Apps	Subs	Gls
Manchester U	YT	06/91				
Crewe Alex	Stockport Co (NC)	10/93	93	2	1	0

WILKINSON Jack
Born: Middlewich, Cheshire, England, 17 September, 1931 — CF
Died: Middlesbrough, England, 10 April, 1996

League Club	Source	Date Signed	Seasons Played	Apps	Subs	Gls
Arsenal	Witton A	10/53	54	1	-	0
Sheffield U	Tr	03/56	55-56	29	-	16
Port Vale	Tr	06/57	57-59	80	-	39
Exeter C	Poole T	10/59	59-60	48	-	26

WILKINSON Jack Lloyd
Born: Bridlington, East Riding of Yorkshire, England, 12 September, 1985 — F

League Club	Source	Date Signed	Seasons Played	Apps	Subs	Gls
Hartlepool U	Sch	09/05	03-04	3	4	2

WILKINSON John
Born: Worksop, Nottinghamshire, England, 1 April, 1949 — LB
Died: Mansfield, Nottinghamshire, England, 22 September, 2007

League Club	Source	Date Signed	Seasons Played	Apps	Subs	Gls
Grimsby T	App	04/66	65-67	8	1	0

League Club	Source	Date Signed	Seasons Played	Career Record Apps	Subs	Gls
WILKINSON John Colbridge						
Born: Exeter, England, 24 August, 1979						LW
Exeter C	YT	07/98	97-00	6	14	2
WILKINSON Joseph (Joe)						
Born: Seaham, County Durham, England, 8 December, 1934						G
Died: Seaham, County Durham, England, 11 February, 2007						
Burnley	West Auckland T	12/55				
Bradford C	Tr	03/59	58-59	17	-	0
Hartlepool U	Tr	02/60	59-61	74	-	0
WILKINSON Joseph Francis (Joe)						
Born: Dewsbury, West Yorkshire, England, 2 November, 1995						CD
Huddersfield T	Sch	07/14	14	1	0	0
WILKINSON Kenneth (Ken)						
Born: Gateshead, Tyne and Wear, England, 9 May, 1924						LH/CF
Died: Stockton-on-Tees, Cleveland, England, February, 2002						
Huddersfield T	Jnr	05/42				
Hartlepool U	Tr	04/47	46-48	53	-	5
WILKINSON Luke Alexander						
Born: Wells, Somerset, England, 2 December, 1991						D
Portsmouth	Bristol C (Sch)	07/09				
Dagenham & Red	Tr	07/10	12-13	60	5	6
Luton T	Tr	07/14	14	42	0	4
WILKINSON Neil						
Born: Blackburn, Greater Manchester, England, 16 February, 1955						RB
Blackburn Rov	App	02/73	72-76	27	3	0
Port Vale	Great Harwood T	07/78	78	7	0	0
Crewe Alex	Tr	10/78	78-80	68	7	0
WILKINSON Norman						
Born: Tantobie, County Durham, England, 9 June, 1910						G
Died: Stoke-on-Trent, England, 18 May, 1975						
Huddersfield T	Tanfield Lea	05/32				
Stoke C	Tr	07/35	35-51	186	-	0
WILKINSON Norman Francis						
Born: Alnwick, Northumberland, England, 16 February, 1931						CF
Died: Sunderland, England, 11 January, 2011						
Hull C (Am)	Crook T	11/52	53	8	-	3
York C	Tr	05/54	54-65	354	0	127
WILKINSON Paul						
Born: Grimoldby, Lincolnshire, England, 30 October, 1964						F
England: U21-4						
Grimsby T	App	11/82	82-84	69	2	27
Everton	Tr	03/85	84-86	19	12	6
Nottingham F	Tr	03/87	86-87	32	2	5
Watford	Tr	08/88	88-90	133	1	53
Middlesbrough	Tr	08/91	91-95	161	5	50
Oldham Ath	L	10/95	95	4	0	1
Watford	L	12/95	95	4	0	0
Luton T	L	03/96	95	3	0	0
Barnsley	Tr	07/96	96-97	48	1	9
Millwall	Tr	09/97	97	22	8	3
Northampton T	Tr	07/98	98	12	3	1
WILKINSON Paul Ian						
Born: Themelthorpe, Norfolk, England, 19 April, 1952						M
Norwich C	App	04/70				
Plymouth Arg	L	01/71	70	2	0	0
WILKINSON Roy Joseph						
Born: Hindley, Greater Manchester, England, 17 September, 1941						LH
Bolton W	Jnr	02/60	60-61	3	-	0
WILKINSON Shaun Frederick						
Born: Portsmouth, England, 12 September, 1981						M
Brighton & HA	YT	08/01	99-03	4	13	0
Chesterfield	L	11/02	02	0	1	0
WILKINSON Stephen (Steve)						
Born: Halifax, West Yorkshire, England, 6 August, 1946						G
Halifax T (Am)	Jnr	08/63	63	2	-	0
WILKINSON Stephen John (Steve)						
Born: Lincoln, England, 1 September, 1968						F
Leicester C	App	09/86	86-89	5	4	1
Crewe Alex	L	09/88	88	3	2	2
Mansfield T	Tr	10/89	89-94	214	18	83
Preston NE	Tr	06/95	95-96	44	8	13
Chesterfield	Tr	07/97	97-99	57	18	13
WILKINSON Thomas (Tommy)						
Born: Wingate, County Durham, England, 8 May, 1931						WH
Hartlepool U	Blackhall CW	09/52	53-57	22	-	0
WILKINSON Thomas (Tom)						
Born: Lincoln, England, 26 September, 1985						M
Lincoln C	Sch	07/05	05	0	1	0
WILKINSON Wesley Michael (Wes)						
Born: Wythenshawe, Greater Manchester, England, 1 May, 1984						F
Oldham Ath	Nantwich T	03/04	03-04	2	4	0
WILKINSON William (Billy)						
Born: Stockton-on-Tees, Cleveland, England, 24 March, 1943						M
Died: Melbourne, Australia, 18 July, 1996						
Hull C	Thornaby Jnrs	05/62	62-72	208	15	34
Rotherham U	Tr	11/72	72-73	25	1	0
Southport	Tacoma Tides (USA)	10/76	76	10	0	0
WILKS Alan						
Born: Slough, Berkshire, England, 5 October, 1946						F
Chelsea	App	08/64				
Queens Park Rgrs	Tr	05/65	66-70	44	6	14
Gillingham	Tr	07/71	71-75	138	13	29
WILKSHIRE Luke						
Born: Wollongong, NSW, Australia, 2 October, 1981						M/RB
Australia: 80/U23-17/Youth						
Middlesbrough	Australian IOS (AUS)	05/99	01-02	13	8	0
Bristol C	Tr	08/03	03-05	90	20	17
WILLARD Cecil Thomas Frederick (Jess)						
Born: Chichester, West Sussex, England, 16 January, 1924						RH/F
Died: Chichester, West Sussex, England, 6 May, 2005						
Brighton & HA	Chichester C	11/46	46-52	190	-	22
Crystal Palace	Tr	07/53	53-54	46	-	5
WILLDER Frederick (Fred)						
Born: Lytham St Annes, Lancashire, England, 20 March, 1944						IF
England: Youth						
Blackpool	Jnr	05/62				
Chester C	Tr	09/63	64-65	1	1	0
WILLDIG Patrick Gerald (Pat)						
Born: Stoke-on-Trent, England, 5 June, 1932						IF
Port Vale	Stoke C (Am)	05/50	55	2	-	0
WILLEMS Menno						
Born: Amsterdam, Netherlands, 3 October, 1977						DM
Grimsby T	Vitesse Arnhem (NED)	11/00	00-01	44	10	2
WILLEMS Ron						
Born: Vaassen, Netherlands, 20 September, 1966						F
Derby Co	G'hopper Zurich (SUI)	07/95	95-97	41	18	13
WILLEMSE Stanley Bernard (Stan)						
Born: Brighton, England, 23 August, 1924						LB
Died: Brighton, England, 5 August, 2011						
England: B-1/FLge-1/Schools						
Brighton & HA	Jnr	06/46	46-48	91	-	3
Chelsea	Tr	07/49	49-55	198	-	2
Leyton Orient	Tr	06/56	56-57	59	-	2
WILLER-JENSEN Thomas						
Born: Copenhagen, Denmark, 19 September, 1968						CD
Swansea C	HIK Copenhagen (DEN)	03/97	96	7	0	0
WILLETT Ernest (Ernie)						
Born: Burslem, Potteries, England, 27 July, 1919						WH
Died: Stoke-on-Trent, England, 13 February, 1985						
Port Vale	Stoke C (Am)	01/46	46	1	-	0
WILLETT Leonard William (Len)						
Born: Ruabon, Wrexham, Wales, 17 September, 1940						WH
Wales: Schools						
Wrexham	Rhosddu	05/58	59	1	-	0
WILLETTS Joseph (Joe)						
Born: Shotton Colliery, County Durham, England, 12 July, 1924						FB
Died: Hartlepool, Cleveland, England, 1980						
Hartlepool U	Newcastle U (Am)	09/43	46-55	239	-	20
WILLEY Alan						
Born: Exeter, England, 16 September, 1941						IF
Oxford U	Bridgwater T	12/60	62-65	85	1	23
Millwall	Tr	03/66	65-66	9	1	0
WILLEY Alan Steven						
Born: Houghton-le-Spring, Tyne and Wear, England, 18 October, 1956						F
Middlesbrough	App	09/74	74-77	27	22	7
WILLGRASS Alexandre Paul (Alex)						
Born: Scarborough, North Yorkshire, England, 8 April, 1976						M
Scarborough	Jnr	07/94	95	2	5	0

WILLIAMS Aaron John
Born: West Bromwich, West Midlands, England, 21 October, 1993 — F

League Club	Source	Date Signed	Seasons Played	Apps	Subs	Gls
Walsall	Sch	07/12	12	0	6	0

WILLIAMS Adrian
Born: Bristol, England, 4 August, 1943 — IF
England: Youth/Schools

League Club	Source	Date Signed	Seasons Played	Apps	Subs	Gls
Bristol C	Jnr	08/60	60	4	-	0
Exeter C	Tr	07/63				

WILLIAMS Adrian
Born: Reading, England, 16 August, 1971 — CD
Wales: 13

League Club	Source	Date Signed	Seasons Played	Apps	Subs	Gls
Reading	YT	03/89	88-95	191	5	14
Wolverhampton W	Tr	07/96	96-99	26	1	0
Reading	L	02/00	99	5	0	1
Reading	Tr	03/00	99-04	130	2	3
Coventry C	Tr	11/04	04-05	33	2	2
Millwall	L	09/05	05	12	0	1
Swindon T	Tr	07/06	06-07	27	1	0

WILLIAMS Alan
Born: Bristol, England, 3 June, 1938 — CH

League Club	Source	Date Signed	Seasons Played	Apps	Subs	Gls
Bristol C	Jnr	09/55	56-60	134	-	2
Oldham Ath	Tr	06/61	61-64	172	-	9
Watford	Tr	07/65	65-66	43	0	4
Newport Co	Tr	11/66	66-68	63	0	2
Swansea C	Tr	10/68	68-71	141	2	7

WILLIAMS Aled Albert
Born: Holywell, Flintshire, Wales, 14 June, 1933 — RH
Died: Rhyl, Denbighshire, Wales, 8 December, 2005

League Club	Source	Date Signed	Seasons Played	Apps	Subs	Gls
Burnley	Rhyl	10/52				
Chester C	Tr	07/57	57	33	-	1

WILLIAMS Alexander (Alex)
Born: Manchester, England, 13 November, 1961 — G
England: Youth

League Club	Source	Date Signed	Seasons Played	Apps	Subs	Gls
Manchester C	App	11/79	80-85	114	0	0
Port Vale	Tr	11/86	86-87	35	0	0

WILLIAMS Alfred Stanley (Stan)
Born: Cape Town, South Africa, 1 May, 1919 — LW
Scotland: War-1

League Club	Source	Date Signed	Seasons Played	Apps	Subs	Gls
Plymouth Arg	Aberdeen	08/49	49	35	-	4

WILLIAMS Allen Clifford
Born: Aberdare, Rhondda Cynon Taff, Wales, 4 December, 1923 — RH
Died: Barry, Vale of Glamorgan, Wales, December, 1992

League Club	Source	Date Signed	Seasons Played	Apps	Subs	Gls
Norwich C	Fulham (Am)	01/47	46	1	-	0

WILLIAMS Alvan
Born: Beaumaris, Anglesey, Wales, 21 November, 1932 — CF/CH
Died: Llandderfel, Gwynedd, Wales, 22 December, 2003

League Club	Source	Date Signed	Seasons Played	Apps	Subs	Gls
Bury	Stalybridge Celtic	12/54	55	2	-	1
Wrexham	Tr	06/56	56	13	-	7
Bradford Park Ave	Tr	06/57	57-59	92	-	21
Exeter C	Tr	08/60	60	19	-	1

WILLIAMS Andrew (Andy)
Born: Birmingham, England, 29 July, 1962 — M

League Club	Source	Date Signed	Seasons Played	Apps	Subs	Gls
Coventry C	Solihull Bor	07/85	85-86	3	6	0
Rotherham U	Tr	10/86	86-88	87	0	13
Leeds U	Tr	11/88	88-90	25	21	3
Port Vale	L	12/91	91	5	0	0
Notts Co	Tr	02/92	91-93	32	7	2
Huddersfield T	L	09/93	93	4	2	0
Rotherham U	Tr	10/93	93-94	51	0	2
Hull C	Tr	07/95	95	33	1	0
Scarborough	Tr	08/96	96	1	0	0

WILLIAMS Andrew David (Andy)
Born: Hereford, England, 14 August, 1986 — F/W

League Club	Source	Date Signed	Seasons Played	Apps	Subs	Gls
Hereford U	Pershore College	05/04	06	30	11	8
Bristol Rov	Tr	07/07	07-09	37	51	8
Hereford U	L	09/08	08	19	7	2
Yeovil T	Tr	07/10	10-11	58	14	22
Swindon T	Tr	06/12	12-14	69	20	32
Yeovil T	L	08/13	13	7	2	0

WILLIAMS Andrew Phillip (Andy)
Born: Bristol, England, 8 October, 1977 — LW
Wales: 2/U21-9

League Club	Source	Date Signed	Seasons Played	Apps	Subs	Gls
Southampton	YT	05/96	97-98	3	18	0
Swindon T	Tr	09/99	99-00	38	6	1

WILLIAMS Anthony Simon (Tony)
Born: Maesteg, Bridgend, Wales, 20 September, 1977 — G
Wales: U21-16/Youth

League Club	Source	Date Signed	Seasons Played	Apps	Subs	Gls
Blackburn Rov	YT	07/96				
Macclesfield T	L	10/98	98	4	0	0
Bristol Rov	L	03/99	98	9	0	0
Gillingham	L	08/99	99	2	0	0
Macclesfield T	L	01/00	99	11	0	0
Hartlepool U	Tr	07/00	00-03	131	0	0
Stockport Co	L	01/04	03	15	0	0
Grimsby T	Tr	07/04	04	46	0	0
Carlisle U	Tr	07/05	05	11	0	0
Bury	L	01/06	05	3	0	0
Wrexham	Tr	03/07	06-07	31	0	0

WILLIAMS Ashley Errol
Born: Wolverhampton, England, 23 March, 1984 — CD
Wales: 51

League Club	Source	Date Signed	Seasons Played	Apps	Subs	Gls
Stockport Co	Hednesford T	12/03	03-07	159	3	3
Swansea C	Tr	03/08	07-14	285	1	12

WILLIAMS Benjamin (Benny)
Born: Lincoln, England, 14 April, 1951 — W

League Club	Source	Date Signed	Seasons Played	Apps	Subs	Gls
Grimsby T	Lincoln U	07/69	69	2	0	0

WILLIAMS Benjamin Philip (Ben)
Born: Manchester, England, 27 August, 1982 — G
England: Schools

League Club	Source	Date Signed	Seasons Played	Apps	Subs	Gls
Manchester U	Jnr	07/01				
Chesterfield	L	12/02	02	14	0	0
Crewe Alex	Tr	03/04	03-07	134	1	0
Carlisle U	Tr	07/08	08	31	0	0
Colchester U	Tr	07/09	09-11	115	0	0
Bradford C	Hibernian	08/14	14	12	2	0

WILLIAMS Bert Frederick
Born: Bilston, West Midlands, England, 31 January, 1920 — G
Died: Wolverhampton, England, 19 January, 2014
England: 24/B-1/FLge-5/War-4

League Club	Source	Date Signed	Seasons Played	Apps	Subs	Gls
Walsall	Thompson's	05/37	37-38	25	-	0
Wolverhampton W	Tr	09/45	46-56	381	-	0

WILLIAMS Brett
Born: Dudley, West Midlands, England, 19 March, 1968 — LB

League Club	Source	Date Signed	Seasons Played	Apps	Subs	Gls
Nottingham F	App	12/85	85-92	43	0	0
Stockport Co	L	03/87	86	2	0	0
Northampton T	L	01/88	87	3	1	0
Hereford U	L	09/89	89	14	0	0
Oxford U	L	02/92	91	7	0	0
Stoke C	L	08/93	93	2	0	0

WILLIAMS Brett Anthony
Born: Southampton, England, 1 December, 1987 — F

League Club	Source	Date Signed	Seasons Played	Apps	Subs	Gls
Reading	Eastleigh	01/11				
Rotherham U	L	08/11	11	4	7	2
Northampton T	L	02/12	11	8	10	3

WILLIAMS Brian
Born: Salford, England, 5 November, 1955 — LB/M

League Club	Source	Date Signed	Seasons Played	Apps	Subs	Gls
Bury	App	04/73	71-76	149	12	18
Queens Park Rgrs	Tr	07/77	77	9	10	0
Swindon T	Tr	06/78	78-80	89	10	8
Bristol Rov	Tr	07/81	81-84	172	0	21
Bristol C	Tr	07/85	85-86	77	0	3
Shrewsbury T	Tr	07/87	87-88	62	3	1

WILLIAMS Carl Junior
Born: Letchworth, Hertfordshire, England, 14 January, 1977 — LW

League Club	Source	Date Signed	Seasons Played	Apps	Subs	Gls
Fulham	YT	07/95	95	2	11	0

WILLIAMS Ceri
Born: Tonyrefail, Rhondda Cynon Taff, Wales, 16 October, 1965 — LW
Wales: Youth

League Club	Source	Date Signed	Seasons Played	Apps	Subs	Gls
Newport Co	Jnr	06/83	82-84	19	8	2

WILLIAMS Charles Adolphus (Charlie)
Born: Barnsley, South Yorkshire, England, 23 December, 1927 — CH
Died: Barnsley, South Yorkshire, England, 2 September, 2006

League Club	Source	Date Signed	Seasons Played	Apps	Subs	Gls
Doncaster Rov	Upton Colliery	10/48	49-58	157	-	1

WILLIAMS Christopher John (Chris)
Born: Neath, Wales, 21 September, 1976 — F

League Club	Source	Date Signed	Seasons Played	Apps	Subs	Gls
Hereford U	YT	09/94	93-94	1	3	0

WILLIAMS Christopher Jonathan (Chris)
Born: Manchester, England, 26 February, 1985 — W

League Club	Source	Date Signed	Seasons Played	Apps	Subs	Gls
Stockport Co	Sch	03/02	01-05	12	22	3
Grimsby T	L	09/04	04	1	2	0

WILLIAMS Christopher Robert (Chris)
Born: Brecon, Powys, Wales, 25 December, 1955 — F

League Club	Source	Date Signed	Seasons Played	Apps	Subs	Gls
Cardiff C	Talgarth	12/77	77	3	0	0

WILLIAMS Clarence (Clarrie)
Born: Felling, Tyne and Wear, England, 13 January, 1933 — G

League Club	Source	Date Signed	Seasons Played	Apps	Subs	Gls
Grimsby T	Doncaster Rov (Am)	03/53	52-59	188	-	0
Barnsley	Tr	03/60	60-61	24	-	0

WILLIAMS Corey Dean
Born: Sheffield, England, 22 February, 1972 — F

League Club	Source	Date Signed	Seasons Played	Apps	Subs	Gls
Rotherham U	Denaby U	08/94	94	0	2	0

WILLIAMS Curtley Benjamin
Born: Ipswich, England, 19 March, 1990 — RB

League Club	Source	Date Signed	Seasons Played	Apps	Subs	Gls
Luton T	Lowestoft T	05/14	14	3	0	0

WILLIAMS Cyril Edward
Born: Bristol, England, 17 November, 1921 — IF
Died: Weston-super-Mare, Somerset, England, 5 February, 1980

League Club	Source	Date Signed	Seasons Played	Apps	Subs	Gls
Bristol C	Jnr	05/39	46-47	78	-	27
West Bromwich A	Tr	06/48	48-50	71	-	19
Bristol C	Tr	08/51	51-57	218	-	42

WILLIAMS Dale Thomas
Born: Neath, Wales, 26 March, 1987 — M
Wales: U21-1

League Club	Source	Date Signed	Seasons Played	Apps	Subs	Gls
Yeovil T	Jnr	05/04	05	0	1	0
Shrewsbury T	Tr	07/06	06	0	2	0

WILLIAMS Daniel (Danny)
Born: Maltby, South Yorkshire, England, 20 November, 1924 — LH/IF

League Club	Source	Date Signed	Seasons Played	Apps	Subs	Gls
Rotherham U	Silverwood Colliery	10/43	46-59	461	-	22

WILLIAMS Daniel Charles (Danny)
Born: Karlsruhe, Germany, 8 March, 1989 — DM
USA: 16

League Club	Source	Date Signed	Seasons Played	Apps	Subs	Gls
Reading	TSG Hoffenheim (GER)	07/13	13-14	45	10	4

WILLIAMS Daniel Ivor Llewellyn (Danny)
Born: Wrexham, Wales, 12 July, 1979 — M
Wales: U21-9

League Club	Source	Date Signed	Seasons Played	Apps	Subs	Gls
Liverpool	YT	05/97				
Wrexham	Tr	03/99	99-00	38	1	3
Kidderminster Hrs	Tr	07/01	01-03	108	3	8
Bristol Rov	Tr	03/04	03	6	0	1
Wrexham	Tr	08/04	04-07	117	4	7

WILLIAMS Daniel Josef (Danny)
Born: Sheffield, England, 2 March, 1981 — M

League Club	Source	Date Signed	Seasons Played	Apps	Subs	Gls
Chesterfield	YT	07/99	99-01	23	8	0
Hereford U	AFC Telford U	08/11	11	3	2	0

WILLIAMS Darren
Born: Birmingham, England, 15 December, 1968 — M

League Club	Source	Date Signed	Seasons Played	Apps	Subs	Gls
Leicester C	App	12/86	88-89	7	3	2
Lincoln C	L	11/89	89	2	0	0
Lincoln C	L	03/90	89	5	2	0
Chesterfield	L	09/90	90	4	1	1

WILLIAMS Darren
Born: Middlesbrough, England, 28 April, 1977 — CD
England: B-1/U21-2

League Club	Source	Date Signed	Seasons Played	Apps	Subs	Gls
York C	YT	06/95	94-96	16	4	0
Sunderland	Tr	10/96	96-04	155	44	4
Cardiff C	Tr	09/04	04	17	3	0
Hartlepool U	Tr	07/05	05-06	52	13	0
Bradford C	Tr	08/07	07	28	0	0

WILLIAMS Darwell
Born: Llanelli, Carmarthenshire, Wales, 4 November, 1926 — WH
Died: Swansea, Wales, 13 October, 2001

League Club	Source	Date Signed	Seasons Played	Apps	Subs	Gls
Swansea C	Loughor	05/46	50-54	130	-	4

WILLIAMS David
Born: Sheffield, England, 7 October, 1931 — LH

League Club	Source	Date Signed	Seasons Played	Apps	Subs	Gls
Grimsby T	Beighton MW	03/53	53	5	-	0

WILLIAMS David
Born: Shafton, South Yorkshire, England, 25 February, 1946 — CH

League Club	Source	Date Signed	Seasons Played	Apps	Subs	Gls
Doncaster Rov		07/64	64	1	-	0

WILLIAMS David Geraint (Geraint)
Born: Treorchy, Rhondda Cynon Taff, Wales, 5 January, 1962 — M
Wales: 13/U21-2/Youth

League Club	Source	Date Signed	Seasons Played	Apps	Subs	Gls
Bristol Rov	App	01/80	80-84	138	3	8
Derby Co	Tr	03/85	84-91	276	1	9
Ipswich T	Tr	07/92	92-97	217	0	3
Colchester U	Tr	07/98	98	38	1	0

WILLIAMS David Michael
Born: Cardiff, Wales, 11 March, 1955 — M
Wales: 5/U21-1/Youth

League Club	Source	Date Signed	Seasons Played	Apps	Subs	Gls
Bristol Rov	Clifton Ath	08/75	75-84	342	10	65
Norwich C	Tr	07/85	85-87	56	4	11
Bournemouth	Rtd	08/92	92	0	1	0

WILLIAMS David Peter
Born: Liverpool, England, 18 September, 1968 — G

League Club	Source	Date Signed	Seasons Played	Apps	Subs	Gls
Oldham Ath	YT	08/87				
Burnley	Tr	03/88	88-92	24	0	0
Rochdale	L	09/91	91	6	0	0
Cardiff C	Tr	08/94	94-95	82	0	0

WILLIAMS David Samuel
Born: Newport, Wales, 1 March, 1942 — RB
Died: 23 February, 2015

League Club	Source	Date Signed	Seasons Played	Apps	Subs	Gls
Newport Co	Nash U	10/60	60-72	302	4	2

WILLIAMS Dean Anton
Born: Hemel Hempstead, Hertfordshire, England, 14 November, 1970 — F

League Club	Source	Date Signed	Seasons Played	Apps	Subs	Gls
Cambridge U	YT	-	87	1	0	0
Brentford	St Albans C	07/93	93	2	1	1
Doncaster Rov	Stevenage Bor	09/94	94	1	0	0

WILLIAMS Dean Paul
Born: Lichfield, Staffordshire, England, 5 January, 1972 — G

League Club	Source	Date Signed	Seasons Played	Apps	Subs	Gls
Birmingham C	YT	07/90	89-90	4	0	0
Brentford	Tamworth	08/93	93	6	1	0
Doncaster Rov	Tr	08/94	94-97	83	2	0

WILLIAMS Derek
Born: Wardley, Tyne and Wear, England, 28 January, 1937 — IF

League Club	Source	Date Signed	Seasons Played	Apps	Subs	Gls
Grimsby T	Doncaster YMCA	01/57	56-61	44	-	19
Bradford Park Ave	Tr	08/62	62	19	-	8

WILLIAMS Derek
Born: Mold, Flintshire, Wales, 15 June, 1934 — G
Died: Chester, England, May, 2014
Wales: Amateur

League Club	Source	Date Signed	Seasons Played	Apps	Subs	Gls
Manchester C (Am)	Pwllheli	05/51	51	1	-	0
Wrexham (Am)	Bangor Univ	08/54	54	12	-	0
Oldham Ath (Am)	Mold Alex	09/56	56	28	-	0

WILLIAMS Derek Owen
Born: Chirk, Wrexham, Wales, 3 September, 1949 — G

League Club	Source	Date Signed	Seasons Played	Apps	Subs	Gls
Shrewsbury T	Oswestry T	10/69	69	1	0	0

WILLIAMS Derrick Shaun
Born: Waterford, Republic of Ireland, 17 January, 1993 — LB
Republic of Ireland: U21-6/Youth

League Club	Source	Date Signed	Seasons Played	Apps	Subs	Gls
Aston Villa	Sch	01/10	12	0	1	0
Bristol C	Tr	06/13	13-14	84	3	3

WILLIAMS Donald Rowland (Roley)
Born: Swansea, Wales, 10 July, 1927 — IF/RW
Died: Newport, Wales, 30 June, 1999
Wales: WLge-1

League Club	Source	Date Signed	Seasons Played	Apps	Subs	Gls
Cardiff C	Milford U	02/49	48-55	138	-	19
Northampton T	Tr	03/56	55-56	15	-	0

WILLIAMS Edgar
Born: Sheffield, England, 20 May, 1919 — G
Died: Sunderland, England, August, 2001

League Club	Source	Date Signed	Seasons Played	Apps	Subs	Gls
Rotherham U		05/46				
Nottingham F	Tr	05/47				
Northampton T	Tr	06/48	48	3	-	0

WILLIAMS Edward Mailor Lloyd
Born: Chester, England, 28 November, 1935 — RW

League Club	Source	Date Signed	Seasons Played	Apps	Subs	Gls
Aston Villa	Everton (Am)	08/53				
Wrexham	Tr	08/54	54	1	-	0

WILLIAMS Eifion Wyn
Born: Llangoed, Anglesey, Wales, 15 November, 1975 — F
Wales: B-1/U21-2

League Club	Source	Date Signed	Seasons Played	Apps	Subs	Gls
Torquay U	Barry T	03/99	98-01	84	27	24
Hartlepool U	Tr	03/02	01-06	175	33	50
Wrexham	Tr	07/07	07	7	6	1

WILLIAMS Elfyn
Born: Barmouth, Gwynedd, Wales, 25 September, 1939 — W
Died: Westminster, Central London, England, February, 1995

League Club	Source	Date Signed	Seasons Played	Apps	Subs	Gls
Wrexham	Portmadoc	03/58	58	1	-	0
Crystal Palace	Tr	07/59				

WILLIAMS Emlyn
Born: Maesteg, Bridgend, Wales, 15 January, 1912 — D
Died: Pontypridd, Rhondda Cynon Taff, Wales, November, 1989

League Club	Source	Date Signed	Seasons Played	Apps	Subs	Gls
Barnsley	Buxton	10/36	36-38	88	-	0
Preston NE	Tr	06/39	46-47	62	-	0
Barnsley	Tr	04/48	47-48	17	-	0
Accrington Stan	Tr	12/48	48	15	-	0

WILLIAMS Eric
Born: Salford, England, 10 July, 1921 — RB

League Club	Source	Date Signed	Seasons Played	Apps	Subs	Gls
Manchester C	Brindle Heath LC	03/45	46-49	38	-	0
Halifax T	Mossley	10/51	51-53	111	-	0

WILLIAMS Evan Maerdy
Born: Swansea, Wales, 12 October, 1932 — LB

League Club	Source	Date Signed	Seasons Played	Apps	Subs	Gls
Cardiff C	Penllegaer	03/50				
Exeter C	Tr	05/54	54	1	-	0
Aldershot	Tr	07/55				

WILLIAMS Evan Samuel
Born: Dumbarton, Dunbartonshire, Scotland, 15 July, 1943 — G

League Club	Source	Date Signed	Seasons Played	Apps	Subs	Gls
Wolverhampton W	Third Lanark	03/66	67	13	0	0
Aston Villa	L	08/69	69	12	0	0

WILLIAMS Everton Anthony
Born: Jamaica, 1 February, 1957 — F

League Club	Source	Date Signed	Seasons Played	Apps	Subs	Gls
Wrexham	Jnr	07/75	75	1	1	0

WILLIAMS Frank
Born: Halifax, West Yorkshire, England, 23 May, 1921 — LW
Died: Halifax, West Yorkshire, England, March, 1999

League Club	Source	Date Signed	Seasons Played	Apps	Subs	Gls
Halifax T (Am)	Boothstown	09/47	47	4	-	0

WILLIAMS Gareth Ashley
Born: Cardiff, Wales, 10 September, 1982 — F
Wales: U21-5/Youth

League Club	Source	Date Signed	Seasons Played	Apps	Subs	Gls
Crystal Palace	Sch	07/02	02	0	5	0
Colchester U	L	01/03	02	6	2	6
Cambridge U	L	10/03	03	4	0	1
Bournemouth	L	02/04	03	0	1	0
Colchester U	L	03/04	03	5	2	2
Colchester U	Tr	09/04	04-05	18	29	4
Blackpool	L	03/06	05	6	3	3

WILLIAMS Gareth Cyril
Born: Hendon, N London, England, 30 October, 1941 — M

League Club	Source	Date Signed	Seasons Played	Apps	Subs	Gls
Cardiff C	Jnr	04/59	62-67	161	0	13
Bolton W	Tr	10/67	67-70	108	1	11
Bury	Tr	10/71	71-72	37	2	4

WILLIAMS Gareth James
Born: Cowes, Isle of Wight, England, 12 March, 1967 — W

League Club	Source	Date Signed	Seasons Played	Apps	Subs	Gls
Aston Villa	Gosport Bor	01/88	87-89	6	6	0
Barnsley	Tr	08/91	91-93	23	11	6
Hull C	L	09/92	92	4	0	0
Hull C	L	01/94	93	16	0	2
Bournemouth	Tr	09/94	94	0	1	0
Northampton T	Tr	09/94	94-95	38	12	1
Scarborough	Tr	08/96	96-98	102	3	27
Hull C	Tr	11/98	98-99	36	2	2

WILLIAMS Gareth John Glyn
Born: Glasgow, Scotland, 16 December, 1981 — M
Scotland: 5/B-1/U21-9/Youth

League Club	Source	Date Signed	Seasons Played	Apps	Subs	Gls
Nottingham F	YT	12/98	99-03	132	10	9
Leicester C	Tr	08/04	04-06	63	15	3
Watford	Tr	01/07	06	2	1	0

WILLIAMS Gary
Born: Birkenhead, Wirral, England, 14 May, 1959 — D/M

League Club	Source	Date Signed	Seasons Played	Apps	Subs	Gls
Tranmere Rov	Jnr	09/76	76	1	0	0
Blackpool	Djurgaardens (SWE)	08/80	80	30	1	2
Swindon T	Tr	08/81	81	37	1	3
Tranmere Rov	Tr	02/83	82-88	163	11	16

WILLIAMS Gary
Born: Wolverhampton, England, 17 June, 1960 — FB

League Club	Source	Date Signed	Seasons Played	Apps	Subs	Gls
Aston Villa	App	06/78	78-86	235	5	0
Walsall	L	03/80	79	9	0	0
Leeds U	Tr	07/87	87-88	39	0	3
Watford	Tr	01/90	89-90	39	3	0
Bradford C	Tr	12/91	91-93	84	1	5

WILLIAMS Gary Alan
Born: Bristol, England, 8 June, 1963 — FB/M

League Club	Source	Date Signed	Seasons Played	Apps	Subs	Gls
Bristol C	App	08/80	80-83	98	2	1
Swansea C	Portsmouth (NC)	01/85	84	6	0	0
Oldham Ath	Bristol Rov (NC)	08/85	85-90	45	16	12

WILLIAMS Gary Peter
Born: Liverpool, England, 8 March, 1954 — LB

League Club	Source	Date Signed	Seasons Played	Apps	Subs	Gls
Preston NE	Marine	04/72	71-76	107	5	2
Brighton & HA	Tr	07/77	77-81	158	0	7
Crystal Palace	Tr	07/82	82	10	0	0

WILLIAMS Gavin John
Born: Pontypridd, Rhondda Cynon Taff, Wales, 20 June, 1980 — RW
Wales: 2

League Club	Source	Date Signed	Seasons Played	Apps	Subs	Gls
Yeovil T	Hereford U	05/02	03-04	54	1	11
West Ham U	Tr	12/04	04	7	3	1
Ipswich T	Tr	11/05	05-07	47	7	3
Bristol C	Tr	07/08	08-10	26	26	3
Yeovil T	L	03/10	09	7	1	5
Yeovil T	L	09/10	10	11	1	1
Bristol Rov	Tr	02/11	10	17	2	2
Yeovil T	Tr	07/11	11-12	32	20	7

WILLIAMS George
Born: Ynysddu, Caerphilly, Wales, 19 May, 1914 — LB
Died: Whitburn, Tyne and Wear, England, May, 1993
Wales: War-2

League Club	Source	Date Signed	Seasons Played	Apps	Subs	Gls
Charlton Ath		11/34				
Aldershot	Tr	05/36	36-38	68	-	0
Millwall	Tr	11/38	38-46	25	-	0

WILLIAMS George Benjamin
Born: Hillingdon, W London, England, 14 April, 1993 — RB

League Club	Source	Date Signed	Seasons Played	Apps	Subs	Gls
Barnsley	Worcester C	12/14	14	1	3	0

WILLIAMS George Christopher
Born: Milton Keynes, England, 7 September, 1995 — LW
Wales: 5/U21-2/Youth

League Club	Source	Date Signed	Seasons Played	Apps	Subs	Gls
MK Dons	Sch	-	11	0	2	0
Fulham	Sch	09/12	14	7	7	0
MK Dons	L	02/15	14	2	2	0

WILLIAMS George Graham (Graham)
Born: Wrexham, Wales, 31 December, 1936 — LW
Wales: 5/U23-1/Schools

League Club	Source	Date Signed	Seasons Played	Apps	Subs	Gls
Bradford C	Oswestry T	08/55	55	8	-	2
Everton	Tr	03/56	55-58	31	-	6
Swansea C	Tr	02/59	58-61	90	-	18
Wrexham	Tr	07/64	64	24	-	6
Tranmere Rov	Wellington T	08/66	66-67	73	1	12
Port Vale	Tr	07/68	68	21	2	1

WILLIAMS George Robert (Robert)
Born: Felling, Tyne and Wear, England, 18 November, 1932 — RH
Died: Rotherham, South Yorkshire, England, March, 2003

League Club	Source	Date Signed	Seasons Played	Apps	Subs	Gls
Rotherham U	Jnr	07/50	53	4	-	2
Sheffield U	Tr	05/54				
Bradford C	Wisbech T	05/56	56	6	-	0
Mansfield T	Tr	07/57	57-61	154	-	5

WILLIAMS Gilbert
Born: West Bromwich, West Midlands, England, 12 January, 1925 — RH
Died: Sandwell, West Midlands, England, April, 1993

League Club	Source	Date Signed	Seasons Played	Apps	Subs	Gls
West Bromwich A	Harvills Hawthorn	02/44	47	7	-	0

WILLIAMS Glyndwr James John (Glyn)
Born: Maesteg, Bridgend, Wales, 3 November, 1918 — WH/FB
Died: Bridgend, Wales, 6 June, 2011
Wales: 1/WLge-3

League Club	Source	Date Signed	Seasons Played	Apps	Subs	Gls
Cardiff C	Caerau	08/46	46-52	144	-	0

WILLIAMS Gordon
Born: Newcastle-upon-Tyne, England, 22 February, 1929 — CF

League Club	Source	Date Signed	Seasons Played	Apps	Subs	Gls
Sheffield U		09/49	49	5	-	0
Darlington	Tr	06/50	50	5	-	1

WILLIAMS Gordon George
Born: Swindon, England, 19 June, 1925 — LH/LW
Died: Swindon, England, 23 June, 1996

League Club	Source	Date Signed	Seasons Played	Apps	Subs	Gls
Swindon T	Pinehurst YC	05/45	46-56	129	-	15

WILLIAMS Graham Evan
Born: Denbigh, Wales, 2 April, 1938 — LB
Wales: 26/U23-2

League Club	Source	Date Signed	Seasons Played	Apps	Subs	Gls
West Bromwich A	Rhyl Ath	04/55	55-69	308	6	10

WILLIAMS Grenville Rees
Born: Swansea, Wales, 30 June, 1921 — LH/CH
Died: Norwich, England, 8 February, 2009

League Club	Source	Date Signed	Seasons Played	Apps	Subs	Gls
Arsenal	Jnr	07/42				
Norwich C	Tr	06/46	46-47	40	-	0
Newport Co	Tr	04/49	49	5	-	0

WILLIAMS Harold
Born: Briton Ferry, Neath Port Talbot, Wales, 17 June, 1924 — RW
Died: Leeds, England, 14 September, 2015
Wales: 4

League Club	Source	Date Signed	Seasons Played	Apps	Subs	Gls
Newport Co	Briton Ferry Ath	11/46	46-48	75	-	17
Leeds U	Tr	06/49	49-55	211	-	32
Newport Co	Tr	03/57	56	10	-	0
Bradford Park Ave	Tr	07/57	57	15	-	0

WILLIAMS Harry John Robert
Born: Cheltenham, Gloucestershire, England, 17 January, 1996 — LW

League Club	Source	Date Signed	Seasons Played	Apps	Subs	Gls
Cheltenham T	Sch	07/14	13-14	6	7	0

WILLIAMS Henry George (Harry)
Born: Salford, England, 24 February, 1929 — IF

League Club	Source	Date Signed	Seasons Played	Apps	Subs	Gls
Manchester U		05/49				
West Ham U	Witton A	04/51	51	5	-	1

League Club	Source	Date Signed	Seasons Played	Apps	Subs	Gls
Bury	Tr	06/53	53	2	-	0
Swindon T	Tr	06/54	54	14	-	7

WILLIAMS Herbert (Bert)
Born: Cwmbran, Torfaen, Wales, 19 June, 1925 IF
Wales: Amateur

League Club	Source	Date Signed	Seasons Played	Apps	Subs	Gls
Newport Co (Am)	Weston's	09/48	48	2	-	1

WILLIAMS Herbert Derek (Derek)
Born: Ellesmere Port, Cheshire, England, 9 December, 1922 WH

League Club	Source	Date Signed	Seasons Played	Apps	Subs	Gls
Chester C	Little Sutton	09/41	46	2	-	0

WILLIAMS Herbert John (Herbie)
Born: Swansea, Wales, 6 October, 1940 IF
Wales: 3/U23-5/Schools

League Club	Source	Date Signed	Seasons Played	Apps	Subs	Gls
Swansea C	Jnr	05/58	58-74	491	19	102

WILLIAMS Horace Oswald
Born: Laughton, South Yorkshire, England, 4 October, 1921 CH
Died: Rotherham, South Yorkshire, England, 1978

League Club	Source	Date Signed	Seasons Played	Apps	Subs	Gls
Rotherham U	Thurcroft Main	01/43	46-52	206	-	11

WILLIAMS Ivor
Born: Scunthorpe, North Lincolnshire, England, 29 May, 1935 G

League Club	Source	Date Signed	Seasons Played	Apps	Subs	Gls
Scunthorpe U		08/59	59	8	-	0

WILLIAMS Jacques
Born: Wallasey, Wirral, England, 25 April, 1981 M

League Club	Source	Date Signed	Seasons Played	Apps	Subs	Gls
Birmingham C	Bordeaux (FRA)	07/99	00	1	2	0

WILLIAMS James (Jimmy)
Born: Liverpool, England, 15 July, 1982 D/M

League Club	Source	Date Signed	Seasons Played	Apps	Subs	Gls
Swindon T	YT	12/99	98-01	21	16	1

WILLIAMS James Leslie (Jimmy)
Born: Wolverhampton, England, 8 May, 1953 F

League Club	Source	Date Signed	Seasons Played	Apps	Subs	Gls
Walsall	Worcester C	03/79	78-79	29	9	2

WILLIAMS Jason Norell
Born: Islington, N London, England, 1 November, 1995 F

League Club	Source	Date Signed	Seasons Played	Apps	Subs	Gls
Southend U	Sch	07/14	13-14	0	4	0

WILLIAMS Jeffrey Bell (Jeff)
Born: Salford, England, 1 January, 1933 IF

League Club	Source	Date Signed	Seasons Played	Apps	Subs	Gls
Oldham Ath	North Salford BC	06/51	51	1	-	0

WILLIAMS Jeremy Simon (Jerry)
Born: Didcot, Oxfordshire, England, 24 March, 1960 M/RB

League Club	Source	Date Signed	Seasons Played	Apps	Subs	Gls
Reading	App	03/78	76-87	283	26	17
Gillingham	Tr	08/88	88	7	6	0
Aldershot	Tr	07/89	89-90	64	3	7

WILLIAMS John
Born: Doncaster, South Yorkshire, England, 14 April, 1920 RB
Died: Doncaster, South Yorkshire, England, 1979

League Club	Source	Date Signed	Seasons Played	Apps	Subs	Gls
Leeds U	Denaby U	12/48	48	1	-	0

WILLIAMS John
Born: Pwllheli, Gwynedd, Wales, 22 August, 1965 CD

League Club	Source	Date Signed	Seasons Played	Apps	Subs	Gls
Wrexham	Jnr	08/82	82	0	1	0

WILLIAMS John (Johnny)
Born: Greenock, Inverclyde, Scotland, 21 November, 1925 RH

League Club	Source	Date Signed	Seasons Played	Apps	Subs	Gls
Blackburn Rov	Port Glasgow Rgrs	06/47				
Southport	Tr	07/48	48	2	-	0

WILLIAMS John Derek
Born: Trelewis, Caerphilly, Wales, 15 May, 1935 LW

League Club	Source	Date Signed	Seasons Played	Apps	Subs	Gls
Everton		05/56				
Crewe Alex	Tr	06/57	57	5	-	0

WILLIAMS John Lloyd
Born: Rhymney, Caerphilly, Wales, 27 January, 1936 WH/RB

League Club	Source	Date Signed	Seasons Played	Apps	Subs	Gls
Cardiff C	Jnr	05/53				
Plymouth Arg	Tr	07/58	58-61	34	-	0
Torquay U	Tr	06/62	62-64	42	-	0

WILLIAMS John Nelson
Born: Birmingham, England, 11 May, 1968 W

League Club	Source	Date Signed	Seasons Played	Apps	Subs	Gls
Swansea C	Cradley T	08/91	91	36	3	11
Coventry C	Tr	07/92	92-94	66	14	11
Notts Co	L	10/94	94	3	2	2
Stoke C	L	12/94	94	1	3	0
Swansea C	L	02/95	94	6	1	2
Wycombe W	Tr	09/95	95-96	34	14	9
Hereford U	Tr	02/97	96	8	3	3
Walsall	Tr	07/97	97	0	1	0
Exeter C	Tr	08/97	97	16	20	4
Cardiff C	Tr	08/98	98	25	18	12
York C	Tr	08/99	99-00	29	13	3
Darlington	Tr	12/00	00	23	1	5
Swansea C	Tr	07/01	01-02	37	31	5
Kidderminster Hrs	Tr	08/03	03	28	16	4

WILLIAMS John Robert (Johnny)
Born: Tottenham, N London, England, 26 March, 1947 LB

League Club	Source	Date Signed	Seasons Played	Apps	Subs	Gls
Watford	App	10/64	64-74	371	3	2
Colchester U	Tr	07/75	75-77	107	1	1

WILLIAMS John Stanley James (Johnny)
Born: Bristol, England, 16 August, 1935 WH/IF
Died: Plymouth, England, 24 November, 2011

League Club	Source	Date Signed	Seasons Played	Apps	Subs	Gls
Plymouth Arg	Dockland Elect Eng	10/55	55-65	411	1	48
Bristol Rov	Tr	12/66	66-68	66	2	10
Plymouth Arg	Tr	07/69				

WILLIAMS John William (Jackie)
Born: Garston, Merseyside, England, 1 August, 1929 LW

League Club	Source	Date Signed	Seasons Played	Apps	Subs	Gls
Tranmere Rov (Am)	Jnr	08/46	46	1	-	0

WILLIAMS Jonathan Peter
Born: Tunbridge Wells, Kent, England, 9 October, 1993 M
Wales: 7/U21-8/Youth

League Club	Source	Date Signed	Seasons Played	Apps	Subs	Gls
Crystal Palace	Sch	11/10	11-14	16	38	0
Ipswich T	L	02/14	13	11	2	1
Ipswich T	L	09/14	14	4	1	1
Ipswich T	L	03/15	14	0	2	0

WILLIAMS Keith David
Born: Burntwood, Staffordshire, England, 12 April, 1957 M

League Club	Source	Date Signed	Seasons Played	Apps	Subs	Gls
Aston Villa	App	04/75				
Northampton T	Tr	02/77	76-80	128	3	6
Bournemouth	Tr	08/81	81-86	99	3	1
Colchester U	Bath C	12/87	87	9	1	0

WILLIAMS Kenneth (Ken)
Born: United Kingdom IF

League Club	Source	Date Signed	Seasons Played	Apps	Subs	Gls
Watford		01/47	46	2	-	0

WILLIAMS Kenneth (Ken)
Born: Doncaster, South Yorkshire, England, 7 January, 1927 WH

League Club	Source	Date Signed	Seasons Played	Apps	Subs	Gls
Rotherham U		09/48	49	3	-	0
York C	Tr	07/51	53	1	-	0

WILLIAMS Lee
Born: Birmingham, England, 3 February, 1973 M
England: Youth

League Club	Source	Date Signed	Seasons Played	Apps	Subs	Gls
Aston Villa	YT	01/91				
Shrewsbury T	L	11/92	92	2	1	0
Peterborough U	Tr	03/94	93-95	83	8	1
Mansfield T	Shamrock Rov (ROI)	03/97	96-01	149	28	9
Cheltenham T	Tr	09/01	01-02	42	9	3

WILLIAMS Lee Charles
Born: Harold Wood, E London, England, 13 March, 1977 M

League Club	Source	Date Signed	Seasons Played	Apps	Subs	Gls
Leyton Orient	Purfleet	07/95	95	1	2	0

WILLIAMS Leroy Daniel
Born: Birmingham, England, 22 October, 1986 F

League Club	Source	Date Signed	Seasons Played	Apps	Subs	Gls
Walsall	Sch	08/04	04	2	5	1

WILLIAMS Leslie (Les)
Born: Thurcroft, South Yorkshire, England, 27 March, 1935 G
Died: 2006

League Club	Source	Date Signed	Seasons Played	Apps	Subs	Gls
Sheffield Wed	Rotherham U (Jnr)	07/53	55-56	11	-	0
Swindon T	Tr	01/57				
Rotherham U	Tr	01/58				

WILLIAMS Luke Anthony
Born: Middlesbrough, England, 11 June, 1993 F
England: Youth

League Club	Source	Date Signed	Seasons Played	Apps	Subs	Gls
Middlesbrough	Sch	07/10	09-14	14	20	2
Hartlepool U	L	01/14	13	7	0	2
Scunthorpe U	L	10/14	14	6	0	2
Coventry C	L	02/15	14	4	1	0
Peterborough U	L	03/15	14	1	1	0

WILLIAMS Marc Lloyd
Born: Llanberis, Gwynedd, Wales, 8 February, 1973 F
Wales: B-1/Semi Pro-1

League Club	Source	Date Signed	Seasons Played	Apps	Subs	Gls
Stockport Co	Bangor C	03/95	94-95	12	6	1
Halifax T	Bangor C	09/98	98	18	6	6
York C	Tr	03/99	98-99	22	11	9

WILLIAMS Marc Richard
Born: Colwyn Bay, Conwy, Wales, 27 July, 1988 F
Wales: U21-6/Youth

League Club	Source	Date Signed	Seasons Played	Apps	Subs	Gls
Wrexham	Sch	08/06	05-07	24	15	4

WILLIAMS Marcus Vincent
Born: Doncaster, South Yorkshire, England, 8 April, 1986 LB

League Club	Source	Date Signed	Seasons Played	Apps	Subs	Gls
Scunthorpe U	Sch	07/05	03-09	152	14	0
Reading	Tr	05/10	10	3	0	0
Peterborough U	L	11/10	10	3	0	0
Scunthorpe U	L	03/11	10	5	0	0
Sheffield U	Tr	09/11	11-13	30	9	0
Scunthorpe U	Tr	11/13	13-14	65	1	0
WILLIAMS Mark						
Born: Hereford, England, 17 September, 1957						M
Newport Co	Bromsgrove Rov	08/76	76-78	59	9	9
WILLIAMS Mark						
Born: Holyhead, Anglesey, Wales, 10 December, 1973						F
Shrewsbury T	YT	07/92	91-92	0	3	0
Shrewsbury T	Telford U	07/97	97	0	5	0
WILLIAMS Mark Frank						
Born: Cape Town, South Africa, 11 August, 1966						F
South Africa: 23						
Wolverhampton W	RWD Molenbeek (BEL)	09/95	95	5	7	0
WILLIAMS Mark Ross						
Born: Chatham, Kent, England, 19 October, 1981						M
Brentford	YT	11/00	00-02	10	62	4
WILLIAMS Mark Stuart						
Born: Stalybridge, Greater Manchester, England, 28 September, 1970						CD
Northern Ireland: 36/B-1						
Shrewsbury T	Newtown	03/92	91-94	96	6	3
Chesterfield	Tr	08/95	95-98	168	0	12
Watford	Tr	07/99	99	20	2	1
Wimbledon	Tr	07/00	00-02	69	1	7
Stoke C	Tr	03/03	02	5	1	0
Wimbledon	Columbus Crew (USA)	02/04	03	11	0	1
MK Dons	Wimbledon relocation	07/04	04	11	2	0
Rushden & D	L	03/05	04	7	0	0
WILLIAMS Mark Thomas						
Born: Liverpool, England, 10 November, 1978						RB
Rochdale	Barrow	09/98	98	11	3	1
Rotherham U	Tr	03/99	98	10	1	0
WILLIAMS Martin Keith						
Born: Luton, England, 12 July, 1973						M/F
Luton T	Leicester C (YT)	09/91	91-94	12	28	2
Colchester U	L	03/95	94	3	0	0
Reading	Tr	07/95	95-99	99	29	26
Swindon T	Tr	08/00	00	17	2	2
Peterborough U	Tr	01/01	00	13	2	2
WILLIAMS Marvin Travis						
Born: Sydenham, S London, England, 12 August, 1987						RW
Millwall	Sch	01/06	05-06	27	24	7
Torquay U	L	03/07	06	2	0	1
Yeovil T	Tr	08/07	07	8	15	0
Brentford	Tr	07/08	08	21	13	0
Torquay U	Tr	09/09	09	1	3	0
Stevenage	Ostersunds (SWE)	09/10	10	0	1	0
WILLIAMS Matthew (Matt)						
Born: Denbigh, Wales, 5 November, 1982						F
Wales: U21-10/Youth						
Manchester U	YT	02/00				
Notts Co	Tr	03/04	03-05	13	13	1
WILLIAMS Matthew (Matt)						
Born: Bury, Greater Manchester, England, 21 June, 1988						CD
Rochdale	Sch	-	04	0	1	0
WILLIAMS Michael (Mike)						
Born: Buckley, Flintshire, Wales, 6 February, 1965						CD
Wales: Youth						
Chester C	App	02/83	81-83	30	4	4
Wrexham	Tr	07/84	84-89	172	6	3
WILLIAMS Michael (Mike)						
Born: Bangor, Gwynedd, Wales, 1 December, 1956						W
Wrexham	Jnr	06/75	74-77	9	0	0
WILLIAMS Michael Anthony (Mike)						
Born: Bradford, England, 21 November, 1969						RM
Sheffield Wed	Maltby MW	02/91	92-96	16	7	1
Halifax T	L	12/92	92	9	0	1
Huddersfield T	L	10/96	96	2	0	0
Peterborough U	L	03/97	96	6	0	0
Burnley	Tr	07/97	97-98	15	1	1
Oxford U	Tr	03/99	98	0	2	0
Halifax T	Tr	11/99	99	2	1	0

League Club	Source	Date Signed	Seasons Played	Apps	Subs	Gls
WILLIAMS Michael John (Mike)						
Born: Hull, England, 23 October, 1944						G
Hull C	App	10/62	62-65	88	0	0
Aldershot	Tr	07/66				
Workington	Tr	07/68	68-69	15	0	0
Scunthorpe U	Tr	07/70	70-73	28	0	0
WILLIAMS Michael John (Mike)						
Born: Mansfield, Nottinghamshire, England, 3 November, 1976						F
Mansfield T	YT	-	94	0	1	0
WILLIAMS Michael John						
Born: Stepney, E London, England, 9 October, 1978						CD
Leyton Orient	YT	07/97	97	0	1	0
WILLIAMS Michael Jordan (Jordan)						
Born: Bangor, Gwynedd, Wales, 6 November, 1995						CD/M
Wales: U21-1/Youth						
Liverpool	Sch	07/14				
Notts Co	L	03/15	14	8	0	0
WILLIAMS Michael Paul John (Mike)						
Born: Colwyn Bay, Conwy, Wales, 27 October, 1986						CD
Wales: U21-14						
Wrexham	Sch	08/06	05-07	42	19	0
WILLIAMS Mostyn Thomas Webb						
Born: Cwmfelinfach, Caerphilly, Wales, 2 October, 1928						RB
Died: Newport, Wales, 4 May, 1990						
Newport Co	Ynysddu Welfare	12/49	49-51	28	-	0
WILLIAMS Neil John Frederick						
Born: Waltham Abbey, Essex, England, 23 October, 1964						M/RB
Watford	App	08/82				
Hull C	Tr	07/84	84-87	75	16	9
Preston NE	Tr	07/88	88-91	109	12	6
Carlisle U	Tr	08/92	92	19	0	1
WILLIAMS Nigel John						
Born: Canterbury, England, 29 July, 1954						RB/M
Wolverhampton W	App	08/72	74-75	11	0	0
Gillingham	Tr	07/76	76-78	51	2	1
WILLIAMS Oshor Joseph						
Born: Stockton-on-Tees, Cleveland, England, 21 April, 1958						RW
Manchester U	Middlesbrough (App)	08/76				
Southampton	Gateshead	03/78	78-79	5	2	0
Exeter C	L	08/78	78	2	1	0
Stockport Co	Tr	08/79	79-84	192	1	26
Port Vale	Tr	11/84	84-85	47	2	6
Preston NE	Tr	08/86	86-87	38	1	12
WILLIAMS Owain Fon						
Born: Caernarfon, Gwynedd, Wales, 17 March, 1987						G
Wales: U21-10						
Crewe Alex	Sch	07/06				
Stockport Co	Tr	07/08	08-10	82	0	0
Bury	L	10/10	10	6	0	0
Rochdale	Tr	01/11	10	22	0	0
Tranmere Rov	Tr	07/11	11-14	161	0	0
WILLIAMS Paul Andrew						
Born: Sheffield, England, 8 September, 1963						F/CD
Northern Ireland: 1/Youth						
Preston NE	Nuneaton Bor	12/86	86	1	0	0
Carlisle U	Tr	07/87				
Newport Co	Tr	08/87	87	26	0	3
Sheffield U	Tr	03/88	87-88	6	2	0
Hartlepool U	Tr	10/89	89	7	1	0
Stockport Co	Tr	08/90	90	24	0	14
West Bromwich A	Tr	03/91	90-91	26	18	5
Coventry C	L	10/92	92	1	1	0
Stockport Co	Tr	01/93	92	6	10	3
Rochdale	Tr	11/93	93-95	22	15	7
Doncaster Rov	L	03/96	95	2	1	1
WILLIAMS Paul Anthony						
Born: Stratford, E London, England, 16 August, 1965						F
England: B-3/U21-4						
Charlton Ath	Woodford T	02/87	87-89	74	8	23
Brentford	L	10/87	87	7	0	3
Sheffield Wed	Tr	08/90	90-92	78	15	25
Crystal Palace	Tr	09/92	92-94	38	8	7
Sunderland	L	01/95	94	3	0	0
Birmingham C	L	03/95	94	8	3	0
Charlton Ath	Tr	09/95	95	2	7	0
Torquay U	L	03/96	95	9	0	0
Southend U	Tr	08/96	96-97	30	9	7

League Club	Source	Date Signed	Seasons Played	Apps	Subs	Gls
WILLIAMS Paul Darren						
Born: Burton-on-Trent, Staffordshire, England, 26 March, 1971						CD/M
England: U21-6						
Derby Co	YT	07/89	89-94	153	7	26
Lincoln C	L	11/89	89	3	0	0
Coventry C	Tr	08/95	95-01	153	16	5
Southampton	Tr	10/01	01-02	37	2	0
Stoke C	Tr	08/03	03	16	3	0
WILLIAMS Paul John						
Born: Lambeth, S London, England, 16 November, 1962						CD
Chelsea	App	07/80	82	1	0	0
WILLIAMS Paul Leslie						
Born: Liverpool, England, 25 September, 1970						RB/M
Sunderland	YT	07/89	88-91	6	4	0
Swansea C	L	03/91	90	12	0	0
Doncaster Rov	Tr	07/93	93-94	6	2	0
WILLIAMS Paul Richard Curtis						
Born: Leicester, England, 11 September, 1969						LB
Leicester C	YT	07/88				
Stockport Co	Tr	07/89	89-92	61	9	4
Coventry C	Tr	08/93	93-94	8	6	0
West Bromwich A	L	11/93	93	5	0	0
Huddersfield T	L	11/94	94	2	0	0
Huddersfield T	L	03/95	94	7	0	0
Plymouth Arg	Tr	08/95	95-97	131	0	4
Gillingham	Tr	08/98	98	9	1	1
Bury	Tr	11/98	98-99	36	5	1
WILLIAMS Paul Sylvester						
Born: Newton Abbot, Devon, England, 20 February, 1964						F
Bristol C	Ottery St Mary	03/83	82-83	16	3	1
Exeter C	Saltash U	08/85	85-87	8	10	1
WILLIAMS Peter John						
Born: Nottingham, England, 21 October, 1931						RW
Derby Co	South Normanton MW	08/52	52	2	-	0
Chesterfield	Boston U	07/55	55	13	-	4
WILLIAMS Peter Sidney Herbert						
Born: Plymouth, England, 18 December, 1938						WH
Died: Plymouth, England, May, 2013						
Exeter C	Plymouth Arg (Am)	04/60	60	1	-	0
WILLIAMS Peter Wesley						
Born: Hawarden, Flintshire, Wales, 17 May, 1960						F
Wrexham	Jnr	07/78	78-80	4	6	1
WILLIAMS Philip Dean (Phil)						
Born: Morriston, Swansea, Wales, 24 November, 1966						M
Swansea C	App	10/84	83-87	42	16	5
WILLIAMS Philip James (Phil)						
Born: Swansea, Wales, 7 February, 1963						LW
Wales: Schools						
Blackpool	Arsenal (App)	11/80				
Crewe Alex	Tr	08/81	81	39	0	3
Wigan Ath	Tr	08/82	82-83	1	2	0
Chester C	L	09/83	83	6	1	0
Crewe Alex	Tr	12/83	83	14	6	3
WILLIAMS Philip Leslie (Phil)						
Born: Birkenhead, Wirral, England, 5 April, 1958						F
Chester C	Jnr	07/76	76	1	0	0
WILLIAMS Raymond (Ray)						
Born: Wrexham, Wales, 1 May, 1931						RB
Wrexham	Holyhead T	05/51	51	12	-	0
WILLIAMS Raymond (Ray)						
Born: Stoke-on-Trent, England, 30 August, 1946						F
Port Vale	Stafford Rgrs	08/72	72-76	165	8	39
WILLIAMS Raymond Robert (Robert)						
Born: Liverpool, England, 25 October, 1927						IF
Liverpool	Jnr	11/45				
Wrexham	Tr	06/51	51	7	-	0
Shrewsbury T	Tr	10/51	51	5	-	0
WILLIAMS Reginald Frank (Frank)						
Born: Overton, Wrexham, Wales, 12 March, 1917						G
Died: Wrexham, Wales, 24 November, 1978						
Wrexham	Whitchurch	08/46	46-47	36	-	0
WILLIAMS Reginald Frederick (Reg)						
Born: Watford, Hertfordshire, England, 28 January, 1922						IF
Died: Hertfordshire, England, October, 2011						
Chelsea	Watford (Am)	10/45	46-51	58	-	13

League Club	Source	Date Signed	Seasons Played	Apps	Subs	Gls
WILLIAMS Rhys						
Born: Perth, Australia, 14 July, 1988						M
Australia: 14//Wales: U21-10						
Middlesbrough	Sch	04/07	09-14	118	7	5
Burnley	L	01/09	08	17	0	0
WILLIAMS Robert (Robbie)						
Born: Liverpool, England, 12 April, 1979						CD
Accrington Stan	St Dominic's	08/99	06-08	84	8	4
WILLIAMS Robert Bryan (Bryan)						
Born: Liverpool, England, 4 October, 1927						LH/FB
Liverpool	South Liverpool	08/45	48-52	31	-	5
Crewe Alex	South Liverpool	05/54	54-57	140	-	5
WILLIAMS Robert Francis (Bobby)						
Born: Chester, England, 24 November, 1932						RW
New Brighton (Am)	Jnr	08/49	49	1	-	0
Chester C (Am)	Saltney Jnrs	10/51	51-53	4	-	0
Chester C	Runcorn	05/56	56-59	33	-	3
WILLIAMS Robert Gordon (Bobby)						
Born: Bristol, England, 17 February, 1940						IF
Bristol C	Jnr	05/58	58-64	187	-	76
Rotherham U	Tr	02/65	64-66	47	0	13
Bristol Rov	Tr	03/67	66-68	28	1	5
Reading	Tr	08/69	69-70	60	5	21
WILLIAMS Robert Ian (Robbie)						
Born: Pontefract, West Yorkshire, England, 2 October, 1984						LB
Barnsley	Sch	07/04	02-06	44	22	4
Blackpool	L	03/07	06	9	0	4
Huddersfield T	Tr	08/07	07-09	68	9	4
Stockport Co	Tr	08/10	10	19	3	1
Rochdale	Tr	01/11	10	9	0	0
Plymouth Arg	Tr	07/11	11-12	40	2	4
WILLIAMS Robert James (Bobby)						
Born: Bridgend, Wales, 9 October, 1968						RB
Oxford U	YT	08/87				
Hereford U	Tr	08/88	88	5	0	0
WILLIAMS Ronald Albert Keith (Keith)						
Born: Bromborough, Wirral, England, 14 January, 1937						IF
Everton	Jnr	03/54				
Tranmere Rov	Tr	05/57	57-60	161	-	88
Plymouth Arg	Tr	06/61	61	10	-	4
Bristol Rov	Tr	01/62	61-62	49	-	18
WILLIAMS Ronald Arthur (Ron)						
Born: Swansea, Wales, 12 September, 1949						W
Wales: Youth						
Swansea C	Jnr	09/68	67-68	8	1	1
WILLIAMS Royston Brian (Roy)						
Born: Hereford, England, 3 March, 1932						IF
Died: Hereford, England, 25 October, 2011						
Southampton	Hereford U	11/52	52-54	41	-	7
WILLIAMS Ryan Anthony						
Born: Birkenhead, Wirral, England, 8 April, 1991						M
Morecambe	Rhyl	11/12	12-14	40	13	5
WILLIAMS Ryan Dale						
Born: Perth, Australia, 28 October, 1993						W
Australia: U23-3/Youth						
Portsmouth	Sch	07/11	11	0	4	0
Fulham	Tr	01/12	14	1	1	0
Oxford U	L	08/13	13	27	9	7
Barnsley	L	10/14	14	5	0	0
WILLIAMS Ryan Neil						
Born: Sutton-in-Ashfield, Nottinghamshire, England, 31 August, 1978						W
England: Youth						
Mansfield T	YT	-	95-96	9	17	3
Tranmere Rov	Tr	08/97	98	2	3	0
Chesterfield	Tr	11/99	99-00	69	6	13
Hull C	Tr	07/01	01-02	40	12	2
Bristol Rov	Tr	10/03	03-05	26	17	4
WILLIAMS Samuel (Sam)						
Born: Greenwich, SE London, England, 9 June, 1987						F
Aston Villa	Sch	06/05				
Wrexham	L	01/06	05	14	1	2
Brighton & HA	L	09/06	06	3	0	1
Colchester U	L	11/08	08	1	0	0
Walsall	L	01/09	08	0	5	1
Brentford	L	03/09	08	5	6	2
Yeovil T	Tr	07/09	09-10	51	19	6
Dagenham & Red	Tr	08/11	11-12	39	4	10

League Club	Source	Date Signed	Seasons Played	Career Record Apps	Subs	Gls

WILLIAMS Scott John
Born: Bangor, Gwynedd, Wales, 7 August, 1974 — LB
Wales: U21-5/Youth

Wrexham	YT	07/93	92-97	26	6	0

WILLIAMS Shaun
Born: Dublin, Republic of Ireland, 19 October, 1986 — M
Republic of Ireland: U23-1

MK Dons	Sporting Fingal (ROI)	03/11	11-13	101	7	19
Millwall	Tr	01/14	13-14	53	2	3

WILLIAMS Sidney Frederick (Sid)
Born: Bristol, England, 21 December, 1919 — W
Died: Patchway, Avon, England, 9 June, 2003

Bristol C	Eastville U	07/46	46-51	100	-	11

WILLIAMS Stephen Michael (Steve)
Born: Swansea, Wales, 5 November, 1954 — W
Wales: Schools

Swansea C	Barry T	03/76	75	7	3	1

WILLIAMS Steven (Steve)
Born: Oxford, England, 21 April, 1983 — G

Wycombe W	Sch	04/02	03-05	20	1	0

WILLIAMS Steven Antony
Born: Preston, Lancashire, England, 25 April, 1987 — CD

Bradford C	Bamber Bridge	08/09	09-11	63	5	7

WILLIAMS Steven Brian
Born: Mansfield, Nottinghamshire, England, 8 July, 1970 — M/LB

Mansfield T	YT	07/88	86-88	4	5	0
Chesterfield	Eastwood T	10/89	89-92	76	22	12

WILLIAMS Steven Charles (Steve)
Born: Hammersmith, W London, England, 12 July, 1958 — M
England: 6/B-4/U21-14

Southampton	App	07/76	75-84	276	1	18
Arsenal	Tr	12/84	84-87	93	2	4
Luton T	Tr	08/88	88-90	39	1	1
Exeter C	Tr	08/91	91-92	44	4	0

WILLIAMS Steven David (Steve)
Born: Aberystwyth, Ceredigion, Wales, 16 October, 1974 — G
Wales: Youth

Cardiff C	Coventry C (YT)	08/93	93-96	33	0	0

WILLIAMS Steven John (Steve)
Born: Barry, Vale of Glamorgan, Wales, 27 April, 1963 — W
Wales: Youth

Bristol Rov	App	04/81	80	8	0	1

WILLIAMS Steven Robert (Steve)
Born: Sheffield, England, 3 November, 1975 — F

Lincoln C	YT	06/94	93-95	8	9	2
Peterborough U	Tr	02/96	95	0	3	0

WILLIAMS Stuart Grenville
Born: Wrexham, Wales, 9 July, 1930 — FB
Died: Southampton, England, 5 November, 2013
Wales: 43

Wrexham (Am)	Victoria YC	06/47	48-49	5	-	0
West Bromwich A	Tr	02/51	51-62	226	-	6
Southampton	Tr	09/62	62-65	148	2	3

WILLIAMS Terence John (Terry)
Born: Stoke-on-Trent, England, 23 October, 1966 — M

Stoke C	App	10/84	84-86	6	5	0

WILLIAMS Thomas Alan (Tommy)
Born: Liverpool, England, 1 August, 1929 — WH
Died: Chester, England, 29 October, 1979

Tranmere Rov	Jnr	03/47	46-56	53	-	2
Southport	Tr	08/58	58	17	-	0

WILLIAMS Thomas Andrew (Tommy)
Born: Carshalton, S London, England, 8 July, 1980 — LB
Cyprus: 1

West Ham U	Walton & Hersham	04/00				
Peterborough U	Tr	03/01	00-01	32	4	2
Birmingham C	Tr	03/02	01	4	0	0
Queens Park Rgrs	L	08/02	02	22	4	1
Queens Park Rgrs	L	08/03	03	4	1	0
Peterborough U	Tr	02/04	03	20	1	1
Barnsley	Tr	06/04	04	38	1	0
Gillingham	Tr	08/05	05	13	0	0
Swansea C	Tr	01/06	05-06	30	16	0
Wycombe W	Tr	07/07	07	6	4	0
Peterborough U	Tr	01/08	07-09	39	8	0
Queens Park Rgrs	L	11/09	09	5	0	0
Preston NE	L	02/10	09	8	2	0
Bristol C	Tr	08/10	10	0	1	0
Colchester U	L	10/10	10	7	0	1
Walsall	Tr	02/11	10	14	0	1
Notts Co		08/12	12	1	0	0

WILLIAMS Thomas Edward (Tommy)
Born: Winchburgh, West Lothian, Scotland, 18 December, 1957 — D

Leicester C	App	12/75	77-85	236	5	10
Birmingham C	Tr	08/86	86-87	62	0	1
Grimsby T	Tr	07/88	88-89	19	1	0

WILLIAMS Thomas John (Tommy)
Born: Battersea, SW London, England, 10 February, 1935 — RW
Died: Westminster, Central London, England, August, 1987

Colchester U	Carshalton Ath	09/56	56-60	150	-	31
Watford	Tr	06/61	61	12	-	6

WILLIAMS Wayne
Born: Telford, England, 17 November, 1963 — RB

Shrewsbury T	App	11/81	82-88	212	9	7
Northampton T	L	11/88	88	3	0	1
Northampton T	Tr	01/89	88-90	47	5	0
Walsall	Tr	08/91	91-92	56	0	1

WILLIAMS Wayne
Born: Swansea, Wales, 2 July, 1945 — W

Swansea C (Am)	Ammanford T	10/68	69	0	1	0

WILLIAMS William Hubert (Bert)
Born: Manchester, England, 24 September, 1925 — IF
Died: Salford, England, 1973

Bury		01/47	46	1	-	0
Rochdale	Tr	08/49	49	8	-	3
Aldershot	Tr	06/50	50	8	-	4

WILLIAMS William John (John)
Born: Liverpool, England, 3 October, 1960 — CD

Tranmere Rov	Jnr	10/79	78-84	167	6	13
Port Vale	Tr	07/85	85-86	50	0	3
Bournemouth	Tr	12/86	86-89	115	2	9
Wigan Ath	L	10/91	91	4	0	0
Cardiff C	Tr	12/91	91-92	5	1	0

WILLIAMS William Raymond (Bill)
Born: Littleborough, Greater Manchester, England, 7 October, 1960 — CD

Rochdale	Ashe Laboratories	08/81	81-84	89	6	2
Stockport Co	Tr	07/85	85-88	104	0	1
Manchester C	Tr	10/88	88	0	1	0
Stockport Co	Tr	12/88	88-93	153	3	7

WILLIAMS William Raymond (Ray)
Born: Bebington, Wirral, England, 30 December, 1930 — WH/IF

Tranmere Rov		02/49	51-58	197	-	12

WILLIAMS William Thomas (Bill)
Born: Esher, Surrey, England, 23 August, 1942 — CH
England: Youth/Schools

Portsmouth	Jnr	06/60	60	3	-	0
Queens Park Rgrs	Tr	07/61	61-62	45	-	0
West Bromwich A	Tr	06/63	64	1	-	0
Mansfield T	Tr	01/66	65-67	47	2	0
Gillingham	Tr	09/67	67-71	169	2	8

WILLIAMSON Arthur Hamilton
Born: Bankfoot, Perthshire, Scotland, 26 July, 1930 — RB

Southend U	Clyde	05/55	55-61	269	-	2

WILLIAMSON Benjamin Marc (Ben)
Born: Lambeth, S London, England, 25 December, 1988 — F

Bournemouth	Jerez Industrial (SPN)	01/11	10	0	4	0
Port Vale	Hyde FC	08/11	11-14	71	78	21

WILLIAMSON Brian William
Born: Blyth, Northumberland, England, 6 October, 1939 — G
Died: Sydney, Australia, 13 May, 2013

Gateshead	Seaton Delaval	10/58	58-59	55	-	0
Crewe Alex	Tr	07/60	60-62	54	-	0
Leeds U	Tr	12/62	62-64	5	-	0
Nottingham F	Tr	02/66	67-68	19	0	0
Leicester C	L	08/67	67	6	0	0
Fulham	Tr	11/68	68-69	12	0	0

WILLIAMSON Charles (Charlie)
Born: Falkirk, Scotland, 12 April, 1956 — LB

Bristol C	Jnr	07/74				
Torquay U	L	03/77	76	5	0	0

WILLIAMSON Charles Harold (Charlie)
Born: Sheffield, England, 16 March, 1962 — LB

League Club	Source	Date Signed	Seasons Played	Apps	Subs	Gls
Sheffield Wed	App	02/80	79-83	61	1	1
Lincoln C	L	01/84	83	5	0	0
Southend U	L	03/85	84	10	0	0
Chesterfield	Tr	07/85	85-86	47	8	2

WILLIAMSON Colin James
Born: Gretna, Dumfries & Galloway, Scotland, 25 October, 1957 — LW

League Club	Source	Date Signed	Seasons Played	Apps	Subs	Gls
Workington	Liverpool (NC)	08/76	76	11	4	2

WILLIAMSON Daniel Alan (Danny)
Born: West Ham, E London, England, 5 December, 1973 — M

League Club	Source	Date Signed	Seasons Played	Apps	Subs	Gls
West Ham U	YT	07/92	93-96	47	4	5
Doncaster Rov	L	10/93	93	10	3	1
Everton	Tr	08/97	97	15	0	0

WILLIAMSON David Francis (Davey)
Born: Hong Kong, 15 December, 1975 — M

League Club	Source	Date Signed	Seasons Played	Apps	Subs	Gls
Cambridge U	Motherwell	08/96	97	2	4	0

WILLIAMSON Garry Barnes
Born: Darlington, County Durham, England, 24 January, 1982 — F

League Club	Source	Date Signed	Seasons Played	Apps	Subs	Gls
Darlington	YT	-	00	1	5	0

WILLIAMSON George
Born: Newcastle-upon-Tyne, England, 13 September, 1925 — CH/IF
Died: Chester, England, April, 1994

League Club	Source	Date Signed	Seasons Played	Apps	Subs	Gls
Middlesbrough		12/45				
Chester C	Tr	07/47	47-49	75	-	4
Bradford C	Tr	06/50	50-56	223	-	31

WILLIAMSON James (Jim)
Born: Birkenhead, Wirral, England, 16 June, 1926 — IF

League Club	Source	Date Signed	Seasons Played	Apps	Subs	Gls
Tranmere Rov	Jnr	08/46	46	4	-	3

WILLIAMSON John
Born: Manchester, England, 8 May, 1929 — CF

League Club	Source	Date Signed	Seasons Played	Apps	Subs	Gls
Manchester C	Newton Heath	08/49	49-54	59	-	18
Blackburn Rov	Tr	03/56	55-56	9	-	3

WILLIAMSON John Barry
Born: Derby, England, 3 March, 1981 — FB

League Club	Source	Date Signed	Seasons Played	Apps	Subs	Gls
Burnley	YT	07/99	98	0	1	0

WILLIAMSON John Ian (Ian)
Born: Larbert, Falkirk, Scotland, 14 March, 1939 — LH/LW

League Club	Source	Date Signed	Seasons Played	Apps	Subs	Gls
Norwich C	Falkirk	05/58	58	10	-	1
Bradford Park Ave	Wisbech T	06/62	62	17	-	0

WILLIAMSON Kenneth (Ken)
Born: Stockton-on-Tees, Cleveland, England, 7 August, 1928 — IF
Died: Stockton-on-Tees, Cleveland, England, 9 May, 2000

League Club	Source	Date Signed	Seasons Played	Apps	Subs	Gls
Darlington (Am)	Bishop Auckland	08/52	52	13	-	3

WILLIAMSON Lee Trevor
Born: Derby, England, 7 June, 1982 — M

League Club	Source	Date Signed	Seasons Played	Apps	Subs	Gls
Mansfield T	YT	07/00	99-04	114	30	3
Northampton T	Tr	09/04	04	31	6	0
Rotherham U	Tr	07/05	05-06	54	2	9
Watford	Tr	01/07	06-08	57	14	4
Preston NE	L	03/09	08	5	0	1
Sheffield U	Tr	06/09	09-11	59	17	19
Portsmouth	Tr	08/12	12	19	3	0
Blackburn Rov	Tr	01/13	12-14	54	15	0

WILLIAMSON Michael (Micky)
Born: Ashbourne, Derbyshire, England, 30 May, 1942 — LW

League Club	Source	Date Signed	Seasons Played	Apps	Subs	Gls
Derby Co	Ashbourne T	08/61	61-63	12	-	0
Gillingham	Tr	07/64	65	1	0	0

WILLIAMSON Michael James (Mike)
Born: Stoke-on-Trent, England, 8 November, 1983 — CD

League Club	Source	Date Signed	Seasons Played	Apps	Subs	Gls
Torquay U	YT	-	01	3	0	0
Southampton	Tr	11/01				
Torquay U	L	09/03	03	9	2	0
Wycombe W	L	07/04	04	32	5	2
Wycombe W	Tr	07/05	05-08	100	6	9
Watford	Tr	01/09	08-09	21	0	2
Portsmouth	Tr	09/09				
Newcastle U	Tr	01/10	09-14	143	7	1

WILLIAMSON Philip James (Phil)
Born: Macclesfield, Cheshire, England, 19 September, 1962 — FB

League Club	Source	Date Signed	Seasons Played	Apps	Subs	Gls
Blackburn Rov	App	09/80	81	0	1	0

WILLIAMSON Robert (Bobby)
Born: Glasgow, Scotland, 13 August, 1961 — F

League Club	Source	Date Signed	Seasons Played	Apps	Subs	Gls
West Bromwich A	Glasgow Rangers	08/86	86-87	40	13	11
Rotherham U	Tr	07/88	88-90	91	2	49

WILLIAMSON Robert (Bobby)
Born: Edinburgh, Scotland, 6 December, 1933 — G
Died: Old Kilpatrick, Dunbartonshire, Scotland, 22 August, 1990

League Club	Source	Date Signed	Seasons Played	Apps	Subs	Gls
Barnsley	St Mirren	08/63	63-64	46	-	0
Leeds U	Tr	06/65				
Rochdale	Tr	07/66	66-67	36	0	0

WILLIAMSON Russell Ian
Born: Loughton, Essex, England, 17 March, 1980 — M

League Club	Source	Date Signed	Seasons Played	Apps	Subs	Gls
Wimbledon	YT	06/98				
Southend U		11/00	00	9	3	0

WILLIAMSON Sam James
Born: Macclesfield, Cheshire, England, 13 October, 1987 — LB

League Club	Source	Date Signed	Seasons Played	Apps	Subs	Gls
Manchester C	Sch	07/06	07	0	1	0

WILLIAMSON Stewart (Stewie)
Born: Wallasey, Wirral, England, 7 April, 1926 — W

League Club	Source	Date Signed	Seasons Played	Apps	Subs	Gls
Tranmere Rov	Harrogate, Rock Ferry	03/44	46-52	92	-	21
Swindon T	Tr	06/53	53-54	17	-	0

WILLIAMSON Thomas (Tommy)
Born: Salford, England, 16 March, 1913 — CH
Died: Lowestoft, Suffolk, England, 28 June, 1992

League Club	Source	Date Signed	Seasons Played	Apps	Subs	Gls
Leeds U	Pendleton FC	09/32				
Oldham Ath	Northwich Victoria	05/35	35-46	157	-	4

WILLIAMSON Thomas (Tom)
Born: Coalville, Leicestershire, England, 24 December, 1984 — M

League Club	Source	Date Signed	Seasons Played	Apps	Subs	Gls
Leicester C	Sch	09/02	01	0	1	0

[WILLIAN] BORGES DA SILVA Willian
Born: Sao Paulo, Brazil, 9 August, 1988 — RW
Brazil: 26/Youth

League Club	Source	Date Signed	Seasons Played	Apps	Subs	Gls
Chelsea	Anzhi Makhachk'a (RUS)	08/13	13-14	46	15	6

WILLINGHAM Charles Kenneth (Ken)
Born: Sheffield, England, 1 December, 1912 — RH
Died: Dewsbury, West Yorkshire, England, May, 1975
England: 12/FLge-7/War-6

League Club	Source	Date Signed	Seasons Played	Apps	Subs	Gls
Huddersfield T	Worksop T	11/30	32-38	247	-	4
Sunderland	Tr	12/45	46	14	-	0
Leeds U	Tr	03/47	46-47	35	-	0

WILLIS Adam Peter
Born: Nuneaton, Warwickshire, England, 21 September, 1976 — CD

League Club	Source	Date Signed	Seasons Played	Apps	Subs	Gls
Coventry C	YT	07/95				
Swindon T	Tr	04/98	98-02	76	16	1
Mansfield T	L	03/99	98	10	0	0
Kidderminster Hrs	Tr	08/03	03	12	0	1

WILLIS Arthur
Born: Denaby, South Yorkshire, England, 2 February, 1920 — FB
Died: Haverfordwest, Pembrokeshire, Wales, 7 November, 1987
England: 1

League Club	Source	Date Signed	Seasons Played	Apps	Subs	Gls
Tottenham H	Finchley	01/44	46-53	144	-	1
Swansea C	Tr	09/54	54-57	98	-	0

WILLIS George
Born: Burnopfield, County Durham, England, 9 November, 1926 — IF
Died: Exeter, England, 23 May, 2011

League Club	Source	Date Signed	Seasons Played	Apps	Subs	Gls
Wolverhampton W		01/45				
Brighton & HA	Tr	02/48	47-48	28	-	13
Plymouth Arg	Tr	05/49	49-55	56	-	14
Exeter C	Tr	03/56	55-56	26	-	3

WILLIS Graham
Born: Gorleston, Norfolk, England, 20 October, 1946 — RB

League Club	Source	Date Signed	Seasons Played	Apps	Subs	Gls
Norwich C	App	10/64	64	1	-	0

WILLIS James Anthony (Jimmy)
Born: Liverpool, England, 12 July, 1968 — CD

League Club	Source	Date Signed	Seasons Played	Apps	Subs	Gls
Halifax T	Blackburn Rov (App)	08/86				
Stockport Co	Tr	12/87	87	10	0	0
Darlington	Tr	03/88	87-91	90	0	6
Leicester C	Tr	12/91	91-95	58	2	3
Bradford C	L	03/92	91	9	0	1

WILLIS John George (George)
Born: Shotton Colliery, County Durham, England, 25 July, 1933 — RW
Died: Sunderland, England, March, 2002

League Club	Source	Date Signed	Seasons Played	Apps	Subs	Gls
Leeds U	Evenwood T	03/53	53	3	-	0
Hartlepool U	Tr	11/54	54-58	25	-	7

WILLIS John Johnson
Born: Boldon, Tyne and Wear, England, 28 May, 1934 — CF

League Club	Source	Date Signed	Seasons Played	Apps	Subs	Gls
Blackburn Rov	Boldon CW	08/54	55	1	-	0
Accrington Stan	Tr	07/57				
Aston Villa	Mossley	08/58	58	1	-	0

WILLIS Jordan Kenneth
Born: Coventry, England, 24 August, 1994 — FB

League Club	Source	Date Signed	Seasons Played	Apps	Subs	Gls

England: Youth

League Club	Source	Date Signed	Seasons Played	Apps	Subs	Gls
Coventry C	Sch	06/12	11-14	55	11	0

WILLIS Liam James
Born: Liverpool, England, 21 May, 1993 — LB

League Club	Source	Date Signed	Seasons Played	Apps	Subs	Gls
Wigan Ath	Southport	07/11				
Accrington Stan	Tr	01/12	11	1	1	0

WILLIS Paul Edward
Born: Liverpool, England, 24 January, 1970 — M

League Club	Source	Date Signed	Seasons Played	Apps	Subs	Gls
Halifax T	YT	05/88	87-88	1	4	0
Darlington	Tr	03/89	88	1	1	1

WILLIS Roger Christopher
Born: Sheffield, England, 17 June, 1967 — M/F
England: Semi Pro-1

League Club	Source	Date Signed	Seasons Played	Apps	Subs	Gls
Grimsby T	Dunkirk, Nottingham	07/89	89	1	8	0
Barnet	Tr	08/90	91-92	39	5	13
Watford	Tr	10/92	92-93	30	6	2
Birmingham C	Tr	12/93	93-94	12	7	5
Southend U	Tr	09/94	94-95	30	1	7
Peterborough U	Tr	08/96	96	34	6	6
Chesterfield	Tr	07/97	97-01	68	67	21
Peterborough U	Tr	08/02	02	1	3	0

WILLIS Ronald Ian (Ron)
Born: Romford, E London, England, 27 December, 1947 — G
England: Youth

League Club	Source	Date Signed	Seasons Played	Apps	Subs	Gls
Leyton Orient	Coventry C (Am)	01/66	66-67	45	0	0
Charlton Ath	Tr	10/67	67	1	0	0
Brentford	L	09/68	68	1	0	0
Colchester U	Tr	10/68	68-69	6	0	0

WILLIS Scott Leon
Born: Liverpool, England, 20 February, 1982 — M

League Club	Source	Date Signed	Seasons Played	Apps	Subs	Gls
Mansfield T	Wigan Ath (YT)	03/00				
Carlisle U	Doncaster Rov	08/01	01	0	1	0
Lincoln C	Droylsden	08/02	02-03	23	10	3

WILLMOTT Christopher Alan (Chris)
Born: Bedford, England, 30 September, 1977 — CD

League Club	Source	Date Signed	Seasons Played	Apps	Subs	Gls
Luton T	YT	05/96	98	13	1	0
Wimbledon	Tr	07/99	99-02	50	3	2
Luton T	L	02/03	02	7	1	0
Luton T	L	04/03	02	5	0	0
Northampton T	Tr	07/03	03-04	80	1	1
Oxford U	Tr	07/05	05	38	3	2

WILLMOTT Ian Michael
Born: Bristol, England, 10 July, 1968 — LM

League Club	Source	Date Signed	Seasons Played	Apps	Subs	Gls
Bristol Rov	Weston-super-Mare	11/88	89-91	18	4	0

WILLMOTT Robert James (Robbie)
Born: Buntingford, Hertfordshire, England, 16 May, 1990 — LW
England: Semi Pro-1

League Club	Source	Date Signed	Seasons Played	Apps	Subs	Gls
Newport Co	Cambridge U	01/13	13-14	54	8	4

WILLOCK Calum Daniel
Born: Lambeth, S London, England, 29 October, 1981 — F
England: Schools//St Kitts & Nevis: 3

League Club	Source	Date Signed	Seasons Played	Apps	Subs	Gls
Fulham	ADT College	07/00	00-02	0	5	0
Queens Park Rgrs	L	11/02	02	3	0	0
Bristol Rov	L	08/03	03	0	5	0
Peterborough U	Tr	10/03	03-05	60	19	23
Brentford	Tr	01/06	05-06	23	18	4
Port Vale	Tr	08/07	07	8	7	3

WILLOX Alexander (Sandy)
Born: Lossiemouth, Moray, Scotland, 5 November, 1923 — CF
Died: Dingwall, Highlands, Scotland, 14 April, 1981

League Club	Source	Date Signed	Seasons Played	Apps	Subs	Gls
Hartlepool U	Alloa Ath	07/51	51	6	-	0

WILLS Gordon Francis
Born: West Bromwich, West Midlands, England, 24 April, 1934 — LW

League Club	Source	Date Signed	Seasons Played	Apps	Subs	Gls
Wolverhampton W	West Bromwich A (Am)	12/51				
Notts Co	Tr	08/53	53-57	154	-	45
Leicester C	Tr	05/58	58-61	111	-	30
Walsall	Tr	06/62	62-63	35	-	1

WILLS Kevin Michael
Born: Torquay, Devon, England, 15 October, 1980 — M

League Club	Source	Date Signed	Seasons Played	Apps	Subs	Gls
Plymouth Arg	YT	07/99	98-01	17	15	1
Torquay U	Tr	11/02	02-03	12	31	4

WILLS Leonard Edward (Len)
Born: Hackney, E London, England, 8 November, 1927 — RB
Died: Essex, England, September, 2010

League Club	Source	Date Signed	Seasons Played	Apps	Subs	Gls
Arsenal	Eton Manor	10/49	53-60	195	-	4

WILLSHAW George James
Born: Hackney, E London, England, 18 October, 1912 — LW
Died: Bournemouth, England, September, 1993

League Club	Source	Date Signed	Seasons Played	Apps	Subs	Gls
Southend U	Walthamstow Ave	02/36	35-37	28	-	6
Bristol C	Tr	06/38	38	34	-	9
Leyton Orient	Tr	07/39	46	12	-	2

WILMOT Rhys James
Born: Newport, Wales, 21 February, 1962 — G
Wales: U21-6/Youth/Schools

League Club	Source	Date Signed	Seasons Played	Apps	Subs	Gls
Arsenal	App	02/80	85-86	8	0	0
Hereford U	L	03/83	82	9	0	0
Leyton Orient	L	05/84	84	46	0	0
Swansea C	L	08/88	88	16	0	0
Plymouth Arg	L	03/89	88	17	0	0
Plymouth Arg	Tr	07/89	89-91	116	0	0
Grimsby T	Tr	07/92	92	33	0	0
Crystal Palace	Tr	08/94	94	5	1	0
Torquay U	Tr	06/96	96	34	0	0

WILMOT Richard Garry
Born: Matlock, Derbyshire, England, 29 August, 1969 — G

League Club	Source	Date Signed	Seasons Played	Apps	Subs	Gls
Scunthorpe U	Stevenage Bor	03/93	92	3	0	0

WILMOTT Gordon Alfred
Born: Brinsley, Nottinghamshire, England, 26 May, 1929 — CH
Died: Stockport, Greater Manchester, England, 27 April, 1998

League Club	Source	Date Signed	Seasons Played	Apps	Subs	Gls
Birmingham C		05/47				
Stockport Co	Tr	06/48	48-58	205	-	1
Crewe Alex	Tr	03/59	58-60	52	-	0

WILNIS Fabian
Born: Paramaribo, Suriname, 23 August, 1970 — RB

League Club	Source	Date Signed	Seasons Played	Apps	Subs	Gls
Ipswich T	De Graafschap (NED)	01/99	98-07	255	27	6

WILSHAW Dennis James
Born: Stoke-on-Trent, England, 11 March, 1926 — IF
Died: Newcastle-under-Lyme, Potteries, England, 10 May, 2004
England: 12/B-2

League Club	Source	Date Signed	Seasons Played	Apps	Subs	Gls
Wolverhampton W	Packmoor BC	09/43	48-57	211	-	105
Walsall	L	05/46	46	35	-	18
Walsall	L	08/47	47	36	-	8
Walsall	L	08/48	48	3	-	1
Stoke C	Tr	12/57	57-60	95	-	41

WILSHAW Steven Edward (Steve)
Born: Stoke-on-Trent, England, 11 January, 1959 — M

League Club	Source	Date Signed	Seasons Played	Apps	Subs	Gls
Stoke C	App	01/77				
Crewe Alex	Tr	08/78	78	20	2	1

WILSHERE Jack Andrew Garry
Born: Stevenage, Hertfordshire, England, 1 January, 1992 — M
England: 28/U21-7/Youth

League Club	Source	Date Signed	Seasons Played	Apps	Subs	Gls
Arsenal	Sch	01/09	08-14	79	21	6
Bolton W	L	01/10	09	13	1	1

WILSHIRE Peter John
Born: Bristol, England, 15 October, 1934 — CF

League Club	Source	Date Signed	Seasons Played	Apps	Subs	Gls
Bristol Rov	Jnr	01/54	53	1	-	0
Bristol C	Tr	06/55				

WILSON Alan
Born: Liverpool, England, 17 November, 1952 — M

League Club	Source	Date Signed	Seasons Played	Apps	Subs	Gls
Everton	App	07/70	71-72	2	0	0
Southport	Tr	07/75	75-77	134	0	13
Torquay U	Tr	06/78	78	38	4	2

WILSON Albert
Born: Rotherham, South Yorkshire, England, 28 January, 1915 — RW
Died: Rotherham, South Yorkshire, England, July, 1998

League Club	Source	Date Signed	Seasons Played	Apps	Subs	Gls
Derby Co	Stafford Rgrs	05/36	36	1	-	0
Mansfield T	Tr	07/38	38	20	-	2
Crystal Palace	Tr	01/39	38	20	-	6
Rotherham U	Tr	06/46	46	38	-	19
Grimsby T	Tr	07/47	47	17	-	1

WILSON Alexander (Alex)
Born: Stenhousemuir, Falkirk, Scotland, 13 July, 1938 — RW

League Club	Source	Date Signed	Seasons Played	Apps	Subs	Gls
Rotherham U	Clyde	07/61	61	5	-	0

WILSON Alexander (Alex)
Born: Buckie, Moray, Scotland, 29 October, 1933 — FB
Died: Forres, Moray, Scotland, 28 July, 2010
Scotland: 1

League Club	Source	Date Signed	Seasons Played	Apps	Subs	Gls
Portsmouth	Buckie Rov	11/50	51-66	348	2	4

WILSON Alexander Adams (Alex)
Born: Wishaw, Lanarkshire, Scotland, 29 October, 1908 — G
Died: Boston, Lincolnshire, England, 16 March, 1971

League Club	Source	Date Signed	Seasons Played	Apps	Subs	Gls
Arsenal	Greenock Morton	05/33	33-38	82	-	0
Brighton & HA	St Mirren	09/47	47	1	-	0

WILSON Allan Armstrong
Born: Bathgate, West Lothian, Scotland, 10 January, 1945 — G

League Club	Source	Date Signed	Seasons Played	Apps	Subs	Gls
Scunthorpe U	Partick Thistle	07/64				
Mansfield T	Tr	08/66	66	5	0	0

WILSON Ambrose Maxwell
Born: Lurgan, Armagh, Northern Ireland, 10 October, 1924 — WH

League Club	Source	Date Signed	Seasons Played	Apps	Subs	Gls
Swansea C	Glenavon	09/50	50	1	-	0

WILSON Andrew (Andy)
Born: Rotherham, South Yorkshire, England, 27 September, 1940 — W

League Club	Source	Date Signed	Seasons Played	Apps	Subs	Gls
Sheffield U		01/60	59-60	4	-	0
Scunthorpe U	Tr	06/61	61-64	112	-	14
Doncaster Rov	Tr	07/65	65	20	1	0
Chesterfield	Tr	07/66	66-67	70	2	13
Aldershot	Tr	07/68	68	19	1	1

WILSON Andrew Philip (Andy)
Born: Maltby, South Yorkshire, England, 13 October, 1947 — RW

League Club	Source	Date Signed	Seasons Played	Apps	Subs	Gls
Rotherham U	Robert Jenkins	06/67	67	12	2	3
Notts Co	L	08/68	68	1	0	0
Scunthorpe U	Tr	09/68	68	23	0	4

WILSON Andrew William (Andy)
Born: Wigan, Greater Manchester, England, 7 January, 1965 — M

League Club	Source	Date Signed	Seasons Played	Apps	Subs	Gls
Wigan Ath	Skelmersdale U	08/87	87-88	1	1	0

WILSON Archibald (Archie)
Born: South Shields, Tyne and Wear, England, 4 December, 1924 — G
Died: South Shields, Tyne and Wear, England, 1979

League Club	Source	Date Signed	Seasons Played	Apps	Subs	Gls
Gateshead	Tyne Dock Engineers	08/45	46	5	-	0
Lincoln C	South Shields	04/51	50-51	4	-	0

WILSON Beverley (Bev)
Born: Stockport, Greater Manchester, England, 11 April, 1953 — CD

League Club	Source	Date Signed	Seasons Played	Apps	Subs	Gls
Stockport Co	App	07/70	69-73	59	2	1

WILSON Bevis Alan McLean (Bev)
Born: Eccles, Greater Manchester, England, 14 May, 1924 — CH
Died: Barrow, Cumbria, England, 27 August, 1987

League Club	Source	Date Signed	Seasons Played	Apps	Subs	Gls
Wrexham	Army	06/47	47-50	98	-	0
Barrow	Tr	03/51	50-58	307	-	1

WILSON Brian
Born: Newcastle-upon-Tyne, England, 14 April, 1957 — D/M

League Club	Source	Date Signed	Seasons Played	Apps	Subs	Gls
Blackpool	App	05/74	76-79	21	10	6
Torquay U	Tr	11/79	79-82	129	2	6

WILSON Brian Jason
Born: Manchester, England, 9 May, 1983 — RB/M

League Club	Source	Date Signed	Seasons Played	Apps	Subs	Gls
Stoke C	YT	07/01	01-03	1	5	0
Cheltenham T	L	12/03	03	7	0	0
Cheltenham T	Tr	03/04	03-06	105	13	14
Bristol C	Tr	01/07	06-09	53	7	1
Colchester U	Tr	07/10	10-13	150	1	1
Oldham Ath	Tr	06/14	14	33	0	0

WILSON Callum Eddie Graham
Born: Coventry, England, 27 February, 1992 — F
England: U21-1

League Club	Source	Date Signed	Seasons Played	Apps	Subs	Gls
Coventry C	Sch	06/10	10-13	40	9	22
Bournemouth	Tr	07/14	14	45	0	20

WILSON Carl Alan
Born: Consett, County Durham, England, 8 May, 1940 — CF

League Club	Source	Date Signed	Seasons Played	Apps	Subs	Gls
Newcastle U	Delves Lane Jnrs	02/58	58	1	-	0
Gateshead	Tr	01/60	59	17	-	4
Doncaster Rov	Tr	07/60	60	15	-	2
Millwall	Tr	07/61	61	5	-	1

WILSON Che Christian Aaron Clay
Born: Ely, Cambridgeshire, England, 17 January, 1979 — LB

League Club	Source	Date Signed	Seasons Played	Apps	Subs	Gls
Norwich C	YT	07/97	98-99	16	6	0
Bristol Rov	Tr	07/00	00-01	74	1	0
Southend U	Cambridge C	07/03	03-07	98	8	2
Brentford	L	01/07	06	3	0	0
Rotherham U	L	03/07	06	5	1	0

WILSON Clive Euclid Aklana
Born: Manchester, England, 13 November, 1961 — LB/M

League Club	Source	Date Signed	Seasons Played	Apps	Subs	Gls
Manchester C	Moss Side Amats	12/79	81-86	96	2	9
Chester C	L	09/82	82	21	0	2
Chelsea	Tr	03/87	87-89	68	13	5
Manchester C	L	03/87	86	11	0	0
Queens Park Rgrs	Tr	07/90	90-94	170	2	12
Tottenham H	Tr	06/95	95-97	67	3	1
Cambridge U	Tr	08/99	99	27	0	0

WILSON Daniel John (Danny)
Born: Livingston, West Lothian, Scotland, 27 December, 1991 — CD
Scotland: 5/U21-13/Youth

League Club	Source	Date Signed	Seasons Played	Apps	Subs	Gls
Liverpool	Glasgow Rangers	07/10	10	1	1	0
Blackpool	L	01/12	11	6	0	0
Bristol C	L	11/12	12	0	1	0

WILSON Daniel Joseph (Danny)
Born: Wigan, Greater Manchester, England, 1 January, 1960 — M
Northern Ireland: 24

League Club	Source	Date Signed	Seasons Played	Apps	Subs	Gls
Bury	Wigan Ath	09/77	77-79	87	3	9
Chesterfield	Tr	07/80	80-82	100	0	13
Nottingham F	Tr	01/83	82	9	1	1
Scunthorpe U	L	10/83	83	6	0	3
Brighton & HA	Tr	11/83	83-86	132	3	33
Luton T	Tr	07/87	87-89	110	0	24
Sheffield Wed	Tr	08/90	90-92	91	7	11
Barnsley	Tr	06/93	93-94	77	0	2

WILSON Darren Anthony
Born: Manchester, England, 30 September, 1971 — FB

League Club	Source	Date Signed	Seasons Played	Apps	Subs	Gls
Manchester C	YT	07/90				
Bury	Tr	06/91	91	30	3	1

WILSON David
Born: Glasgow, Scotland, 21 November, 1923 — LW

League Club	Source	Date Signed	Seasons Played	Apps	Subs	Gls
Manchester C		07/47				
Bury	Tr	07/48	48	2	-	1
Torquay U	Tr	08/49				

WILSON David Charles (Dave)
Born: Nelson, Lancashire, England, 24 December, 1942 — RW
England: U23-7/Schools

League Club	Source	Date Signed	Seasons Played	Apps	Subs	Gls
Preston NE	Jnr	04/60	60-66	169	1	29
Liverpool	Tr	02/67	66	0	1	0
Preston NE	Tr	06/68	68-73	99	11	10
Bradford C	L	03/72	71	5	0	0
Southport	L	10/73	73	2	0	0

WILSON David Edward Joseph (Dave)
Born: Wednesfield, West Midlands, England, 4 October, 1944 — F

League Club	Source	Date Signed	Seasons Played	Apps	Subs	Gls
Nottingham F	Jnr	10/61	62-65	8	1	1
Carlisle U	Tr	10/65	65-66	55	1	22
Grimsby T	Tr	03/67	66-68	63	0	22
Walsall	Tr	09/68	68-69	33	2	5
Burnley	Tr	09/69	69-70	10	3	0
Chesterfield	Tr	06/71	71-74	125	3	22

WILSON David Graham
Born: Todmorden, West Yorkshire, England, 20 March, 1969 — M
England: Schools

League Club	Source	Date Signed	Seasons Played	Apps	Subs	Gls
Manchester U	App	03/87	88	0	4	0
Lincoln C	L	11/90	90	3	0	0
Charlton Ath	L	03/91	90	6	1	2
Bristol Rov	Tr	07/91	91-92	11	0	0

WILSON Denis
Born: Bebington, Wirral, England, 30 April, 1936 — FB

League Club	Source	Date Signed	Seasons Played	Apps	Subs	Gls
Wrexham	Jnr	07/54				
Stoke C	Rhyl	08/59	59-60	15	-	0

WILSON Denis Fletcher
Born: Farnham, Surrey, England, 6 September, 1929 — FB
Died: Norwich, England, September, 2006

League Club	Source	Date Signed	Seasons Played	Apps	Subs	Gls
Norwich C	Jnr	09/46				
Aldershot	Tr	06/50	50-51	5	-	0
Crewe Alex		10/55	55	23	-	0

WILSON Donald (Don)
Born: Heywood, Greater Manchester, England, 4 June, 1930 — RB
Died: Bury, Greater Manchester, England, 12 October, 2003

League Club	Source	Date Signed	Seasons Played	Apps	Subs	Gls
Bury	Manchester U (Am)	05/51	52-58	63	-	1

WILSON Eugene (Gene)
Born: Sheffield, England, 11 September, 1932 — RW
Died: Sheffield, England, March, 2006

League Club	Source	Date Signed	Seasons Played	Apps	Subs	Gls
Rotherham U	Sheffield Wed (Am)	05/53				
Stockport Co	Tr	05/54	54-61	223	-	42

WILSON Eugene Anthony (Gus)
Born: Manchester, England, 11 April, 1963 — D

League Club	Source	Date Signed	Seasons Played	Apps	Subs	Gls
Crewe Alex	Runcorn	07/91	91-94	112	3	0

WILSON Frederick Charles (Fred)
Born: Nottingham, England, 10 November, 1918 — CH
Died: Poole, Dorset, England, December, 1993

League Club	Source	Date Signed	Seasons Played	Apps	Subs	Gls
Wolverhampton W	Mansfield Baptists	05/36				
Bournemouth	Tr	05/37	38-50	98	-	0

WILSON Frederick Peter (Peter)
Born: Newcastle-upon-Tyne, England, 15 September, 1947 — FB

League Club	Source	Date Signed	Seasons Played	Apps	Subs	Gls
Middlesbrough	St Mary's BC	04/66	67	1	0	0

League Club	Source	Date Signed	Seasons Played	Career Record Apps	Subs	Gls

WILSON Glenn Michael
Born: Lewisham, SE London, England, 16 March, 1986 RB/M

League Club	Source	Date Signed	Seasons Played	Apps	Subs	Gls
Crystal Palace	Sch	07/05				
Crawley T	Rushden & D	07/07	11	2	2	0

WILSON Glenton Edward (Glen)
Born: Winlaton, Tyne and Wear, England, 2 July, 1929 LH
Died: Brighton, England, 8 November, 2005

League Club	Source	Date Signed	Seasons Played	Apps	Subs	Gls
Brighton & HA	Newcastle U (Am)	09/49	49-59	409	-	25
Exeter C	Tr	06/60	60-61	36	-	2

WILSON Harry
Born: Hetton-le-Hole, Tyne and Wear, England, 29 November, 1953 LB
England: Youth/Schools

League Club	Source	Date Signed	Seasons Played	Apps	Subs	Gls
Burnley	App	12/70	70-71	12	0	0
Brighton & HA	Tr	12/73	73-76	130	0	4
Preston NE	Tr	07/77	77-79	38	4	0
Darlington	Tr	09/80	80-82	82	3	0
Hartlepool U	Tr	08/83	83	16	0	0

WILSON Ian William
Born: Aberdeen, Scotland, 27 March, 1958 M
Scotland: 5

League Club	Source	Date Signed	Seasons Played	Apps	Subs	Gls
Leicester C	Elgin C	04/79	79-87	276	9	17
Everton	Tr	09/87	87-88	24	10	1
Derby Co	Besiktas (TKY)	02/91	90	11	0	0
Bury	Tr	08/91	91	21	2	1
Wigan Ath	Tr	08/92	92	5	0	0

WILSON James (Jimmy)
Born: Glasgow, Scotland, 19 December, 1929 RW

League Club	Source	Date Signed	Seasons Played	Apps	Subs	Gls
Leicester C	Alloa Ath	07/54				
Mansfield T	Tr	03/55	54-55	19	-	1

WILSON James (Jimmy)
Born: Newmains, Lanarkshire, Scotland, 20 April, 1942 LW
Scotland: SLge-1

League Club	Source	Date Signed	Seasons Played	Apps	Subs	Gls
Newcastle U	Shotts Bon Accord	09/59	60-61	12	-	2

WILSON James Allan (Jim)
Born: Musselburgh, East Lothian, Scotland, 28 June, 1922 RB
Died: Edinburgh, Scotland, 2 April, 1997

League Club	Source	Date Signed	Seasons Played	Apps	Subs	Gls
Luton T	Peterborough U	07/47	47-50	39	-	1
Northampton T	Tr	07/51	51	23	-	0

WILSON James Anthony
Born: Biddulph, Staffordshire, England, 1 December, 1995 F
England: Youth

League Club	Source	Date Signed	Seasons Played	Apps	Subs	Gls
Manchester U	Sch	12/12	13-14	3	11	3

WILSON James Murray (Jim)
Born: Saltcoats, Ayrshire, Scotland, 19 March, 1923 IF
Died: Largs, Ayrshire, Scotland, 5 August, 1989
Republic of Ireland: LoI-1

League Club	Source	Date Signed	Seasons Played	Apps	Subs	Gls
Accrington Stan	Dundalk (ROI)	07/49	49	4	-	0

WILSON James Steven
Born: Chepstow, Monmouthshire, Wales, 26 February, 1989 CD
Wales: 1/U21-3/Youth

League Club	Source	Date Signed	Seasons Played	Apps	Subs	Gls
Bristol C	Sch	04/06	08-12	21	10	0
Brentford	L	08/08	08	14	0	0
Brentford	L	08/09	09	13	0	0
Cheltenham T	L	09/13	13	4	0	0
Oldham Ath	Tr	01/14	13-14	56	1	2

WILSON James Thompson (Jimmy)
Born: Middlesbrough, England, 15 March, 1924 IF/LH
Died: Fulham, W London, England, 16 January, 1987

League Club	Source	Date Signed	Seasons Played	Apps	Subs	Gls
Chelsea	Gravesend & Northfleet	06/47				
Leeds U	Tr	08/50				
Watford	Tr	11/50	50-56	49	-	12
Southend U	Tr	07/57				

WILSON Jared Andrew
Born: Cheltenham, Gloucestershire, England, 24 January, 1989 RB

League Club	Source	Date Signed	Seasons Played	Apps	Subs	Gls
Birmingham C	Sch	07/07	08	0	1	0
Chesterfield	L	02/09	08	15	1	0

WILSON Jeffrey Hansel (Jeff)
Born: South Shields, Tyne and Wear, England, 7 December, 1964 D/M

League Club	Source	Date Signed	Seasons Played	Apps	Subs	Gls
Darlington	App	12/82	82-83	10	1	0

WILSON John (Jock)
Born: Airdrie, Lanarkshire, Scotland, 29 October, 1916 IF
Died: Dunfermline, Fife, Scotland, 2 November, 2010

League Club	Source	Date Signed	Seasons Played	Apps	Subs	Gls
Chesterfield	Glasgow Celtic	05/39	46	16	-	3
Oldham Ath	Tr	07/47	47-48	29	-	2
Accrington Stan	Tr	10/48	48-49	27	-	1

WILSON John Allan
Born: Jarrow, Tyne and Wear, England, 11 April, 1952 M

League Club	Source	Date Signed	Seasons Played	Apps	Subs	Gls
Darlington	Consett	09/71	71-72	15	5	1

WILSON John Christopher
Born: Norwich, England, 28 October, 1934 FB

League Club	Source	Date Signed	Seasons Played	Apps	Subs	Gls
Norwich C	Jnr	08/53	53-58	47	-	0
Chesterfield	Tr	07/59	59	16	-	0

WILSON John Grieve (Ian)
Born: Kennoway, Fife, Scotland, 11 February, 1923 LW

League Club	Source	Date Signed	Seasons Played	Apps	Subs	Gls
Preston NE	Forfar Ath	11/46	46-47	16	-	6
Burnley	Tr	06/48	48-49	19	-	1
Leicester C	Tr	03/50	49-50	12	-	2
Chesterfield	Tr	10/51	51-52	77	-	18
Rotherham U	Tr	05/53	53-55	108	-	45

WILSON John Robert (Bob)
Born: Liverpool, England, 8 September, 1928 RB
Died: Upton, Wirral, England, 17 August, 2006

League Club	Source	Date Signed	Seasons Played	Apps	Subs	Gls
Preston NE	Burscough	04/50	52-62	92	-	0
Tranmere Rov	Tr	09/62	62-63	54	-	0

WILSON Joseph (Joe)
Born: Workington, Cumbria, England, 6 July, 1937 RB

League Club	Source	Date Signed	Seasons Played	Apps	Subs	Gls
Workington	Jnr	01/56	55-61	152	-	5
Nottingham F	Tr	03/62	61-64	84	-	1
Wolverhampton W	Tr	03/65	64-66	58	0	0
Newport Co	Tr	05/67	67	43	1	0
Workington	Tr	09/68	68-72	168	1	4

WILSON Joseph Alexander (Joe)
Born: High Spen, Tyne and Wear, England, 23 March, 1911 IF
Died: Hove, East Sussex, England, 3 April, 1984

League Club	Source	Date Signed	Seasons Played	Apps	Subs	Gls
Newcastle U	Tanfield Lea Inst	09/33	34-35	28	-	5
Brighton & HA	Tr	05/36	36-46	156	-	15

WILSON Joseph Henry (Joe)
Born: Manchester, England, 17 May, 1925 LB
Died: Manchester, England, November, 2004

League Club	Source	Date Signed	Seasons Played	Apps	Subs	Gls
Manchester U	Jnr	09/44				
Accrington Stan	Tr	10/46	46-50	109	-	4

WILSON Joseph William (Joe)
Born: Lanchester, County Durham, England, 29 September, 1911 CH
Died: Consett, County Durham, England, 3 April, 1996

League Club	Source	Date Signed	Seasons Played	Apps	Subs	Gls
Newcastle U	Stanley U	09/27	29	1	-	0
Southend U	Tr	08/30	30-34	164	-	4
Brentford	Tr	07/35	35-38	60	-	2
Reading	Tr	08/39				
Barnsley	Tr	05/46	46	20	-	0

WILSON Keith
Born: Beverley, East Riding of Yorkshire, England, 14 December, 1935 IF
Died: Braishfield, Hampshire, England, 21 December, 2006

League Club	Source	Date Signed	Seasons Played	Apps	Subs	Gls
Southampton	Andover	07/59				
Gillingham	Tr	07/61	61	5	-	2

WILSON Kelvin James
Born: Nottingham, England, 3 September, 1985 CD

League Club	Source	Date Signed	Seasons Played	Apps	Subs	Gls
Notts Co	Sch	07/04	03-05	71	7	3
Preston NE	Tr	03/06	05-06	16	11	1
Nottingham F	Tr	07/07	07-10	118	5	0
Nottingham F	Glasgow Celtic	08/13	13-14	29	3	0

WILSON Kenneth Malcolm (Kenny)
Born: Dumbarton, Dunbartonshire, Scotland, 15 September, 1946 F

League Club	Source	Date Signed	Seasons Played	Apps	Subs	Gls
Carlisle U	Dumbarton	09/72	72	14	6	1
York C	L	09/73	73	2	0	0
Workington	L	10/73	73	4	1	0

WILSON Kevin James
Born: Banbury, Oxfordshire, England, 18 April, 1961 F
Northern Ireland: 42

League Club	Source	Date Signed	Seasons Played	Apps	Subs	Gls
Derby Co	Banbury U	12/79	79-84	106	16	30
Ipswich T	Tr	01/85	84-86	94	4	34
Chelsea	Tr	06/87	87-91	124	28	42
Notts Co	Tr	03/92	91-93	58	11	3
Bradford C	L	01/94	93	5	0	0
Walsall	Tr	08/94	94-96	124	1	38
Northampton T	Tr	07/97	97-00	13	18	2

WILSON Kyle Philip
Born: Bebington, Wirral, England, 14 November, 1985 F

League Club	Source	Date Signed	Seasons Played	Apps	Subs	Gls
Crewe Alex	Sch	07/03				
Macclesfield T	FC United, Manchester	07/09	09	0	4	0

WILSON Laurence Thomas (Laurie)
Born: Huyton, Merseyside, England, 10 October, 1986 LB/M
England: Youth

League Club	Source	Date Signed	Seasons Played	Apps	Subs	Gls
Everton	Sch	11/04				
Mansfield T	L	02/06	05	14	1	1
Chester C	Tr	07/06	06-08	108	7	4
Morecambe	Tr	07/09	09-11	108	1	11
Rotherham U	Tr	06/12	12	5	0	0
Accrington Stan	Tr	01/13	12-13	32	2	0
Morecambe	Tr	07/14	14	34	0	1

WILSON Lawrie Robert
Born: Romford, E London, England, 11 September, 1987 RB/M

League Club	Source	Date Signed	Seasons Played	Apps	Subs	Gls
Colchester U	Charlton Ath (Sch)	08/06				
Stevenage	Tr	08/07	10-11	83	5	10
Charlton Ath	Tr	07/12	12-14	74	22	4
Rotherham U	L	03/15	14	3	0	0

WILSON Lee
Born: Mansfield, Nottinghamshire, England, 23 May, 1972 F

League Club	Source	Date Signed	Seasons Played	Apps	Subs	Gls
Mansfield T	Clipstone Welfare	02/93	92-93	9	9	1

WILSON Leslie John (Les)
Born: Manchester, England, 10 July, 1947 RB

League Club	Source	Date Signed	Seasons Played	Apps	Subs	Gls
Wolverhampton W	Jnr	09/64	65-71	90	11	7
Bristol C	L	03/71	70	10	0	0
Bristol C	Tr	11/71	71-72	32	1	1
Norwich C	Tr	09/73	73	6	0	0

WILSON Lewis Anthony
Born: Milton Keynes, England, 19 February, 1993 F

League Club	Source	Date Signed	Seasons Played	Apps	Subs	Gls
Northampton T	Newport Pagnell T	01/12	11-12	4	4	1

WILSON Marc David
Born: Lurgan, Armagh, Northern Ireland, 17 August, 1987 LB
Republic of Ireland: 22/U21-1/Youth//Northern Ireland: Youth

League Club	Source	Date Signed	Seasons Played	Apps	Subs	Gls
Portsmouth	Sch	07/05	08-10	34	1	0
Yeovil T	L	03/06	05	1	1	0
Bournemouth	L	01/07	06	19	0	3
Bournemouth	L	08/07	07	7	0	0
Luton T	L	11/07	07	4	0	0
Stoke C	Tr	09/10	10-14	130	12	1

WILSON Mark
Born: Glasgow, Scotland, 5 June, 1984 RB
Scotland: 1/U21-19

League Club	Source	Date Signed	Seasons Played	Apps	Subs	Gls
Bristol C	Glasgow Celtic	08/12	12	7	1	0

WILSON Mark Antony
Born: Scunthorpe, North Lincolnshire, England, 9 February, 1979 M
England: U21-2/Youth/Schools

League Club	Source	Date Signed	Seasons Played	Apps	Subs	Gls
Manchester U	YT	02/96	99	1	2	0
Wrexham	L	02/98	97	12	1	4
Middlesbrough	Tr	08/01	01-02	6	10	0
Stoke C	L	03/03	02	4	0	0
Swansea C	L	09/03	03	12	0	2
Sheffield Wed	L	01/04	03	3	0	0
Doncaster Rov	L	09/04	04	1	2	0
Doncaster Rov	Dallas Burn (USA)	11/06	06-11	99	42	3
Tranmere Rov	L	11/08	08	4	1	0
Walsall	L	10/11	11	4	0	0
Oxford U	Tr	01/12	11	3	3	0

WILSON Patrick (Padi)
Born: Manchester, England, 9 November, 1971 F

League Club	Source	Date Signed	Seasons Played	Apps	Subs	Gls
Plymouth Arg	Ashton U	08/97	97	7	4	1
Doncaster Rov	Tr	01/98	97	10	0	1

WILSON Paul Adam
Born: Maidstone, Kent, England, 22 February, 1977 F

League Club	Source	Date Signed	Seasons Played	Apps	Subs	Gls
Gillingham	YT	04/95	94	0	2	0

WILSON Paul Andrew
Born: Norwich, England, 19 June, 1956 M

League Club	Source	Date Signed	Seasons Played	Apps	Subs	Gls
Norwich C	App	07/74	75	0	1	0

WILSON Paul Anthony
Born: Bradford, England, 2 August, 1968 LB

League Club	Source	Date Signed	Seasons Played	Apps	Subs	Gls
Huddersfield T	App	06/86	85-86	15	0	0
Norwich C	Tr	07/87				
Northampton T	Tr	02/88	87-91	132	9	6
Halifax T	Tr	12/91	91-92	45	0	7
Burnley	Tr	02/93	92-93	31	0	0
York C	Tr	10/94	94	21	1	0
Scunthorpe U	Tr	08/95	95-96	77	0	2
Cambridge U	Tr	03/97	96-97	38	0	5

WILSON Paul Derek
Born: Doncaster, South Yorkshire, England, 16 November, 1960 F
England: Semi Pro-1

League Club	Source	Date Signed	Seasons Played	Apps	Subs	Gls
Scunthorpe U	Yeovil T	02/96	96	0	1	0

WILSON Paul Robert
Born: Forest Gate, E London, England, 26 September, 1964 M

League Club	Source	Date Signed	Seasons Played	Apps	Subs	Gls
Barnet	Barking	03/88	91-99	240	23	24

WILSON Philip (Phil)
Born: Hemsworth, West Yorkshire, England, 16 October, 1960 M

League Club	Source	Date Signed	Seasons Played	Apps	Subs	Gls
Bolton W	App	10/78	79-80	35	4	4
Huddersfield T	Tr	08/81	81-86	229	4	16
York C	Tr	08/87	87-88	38	8	2
Scarborough	Macclesfield T	12/89	89-90	39	4	2

WILSON Philip John (Phil)
Born: Oxford, England, 17 October, 1982 G

League Club	Source	Date Signed	Seasons Played	Apps	Subs	Gls
Oxford U	YT	-	00	1	1	0

WILSON Philip Michael (Phil)
Born: Billingham, Cleveland, England, 5 February, 1972 CD

League Club	Source	Date Signed	Seasons Played	Apps	Subs	Gls
Hartlepool U	YT	-	89	0	1	0

WILSON Ramon (Ray)
Born: Shirebrook, Derbyshire, England, 17 December, 1934 LB
England: 63/FLge-10

League Club	Source	Date Signed	Seasons Played	Apps	Subs	Gls
Huddersfield T	Langwith Imperial	08/52	55-63	266	-	6
Everton	Tr	07/64	64-68	114	2	0
Oldham Ath	Tr	07/69	69	25	0	0
Bradford C	Tr	07/70	70	2	0	0

WILSON Raymond Thomson (Ray)
Born: Grangemouth, Falkirk, Scotland, 8 April, 1947 LB
Scotland: U23-1

League Club	Source	Date Signed	Seasons Played	Apps	Subs	Gls
West Bromwich A	Woodburn Ath	05/64	65-75	230	2	3

WILSON Richard
Born: Orpington, SE London, England, 8 May, 1960 F

League Club	Source	Date Signed	Seasons Played	Apps	Subs	Gls
Chelsea	App	08/78				
Charlton Ath	Tr	08/79	79	16	1	1

WILSON Robert
Born: Motherwell, Lanarkshire, Scotland RW

League Club	Source	Date Signed	Seasons Played	Apps	Subs	Gls
Workington	Stirling A	12/52	52	2	-	0

WILSON Robert
Born: Oxford, England, 29 May, 1944 IF

League Club	Source	Date Signed	Seasons Played	Apps	Subs	Gls
Brentford (Am)	Feltham	04/67	66	1	0	1

WILSON Robert James
Born: Kensington, Central London, England, 5 June, 1961 M
Republic of Ireland: U21-2

League Club	Source	Date Signed	Seasons Played	Apps	Subs	Gls
Fulham	App	06/79	79-84	168	7	33
Millwall	Tr	08/85	85	28	0	12
Luton T	Tr	08/86	86-87	19	5	1
Fulham	Tr	09/87	87-88	43	4	4
Huddersfield T	Tr	07/89	89-90	52	5	8
Rotherham U	Tr	09/91	91	11	3	3

WILSON Robert John (Bob)
Born: Birmingham, England, 23 May, 1943 G

League Club	Source	Date Signed	Seasons Played	Apps	Subs	Gls
Aston Villa	Jnr	09/61	63	9	-	0
Cardiff C	Tr	08/64	64-67	115	0	0
Bristol C	L	10/69	69	1	0	0
Exeter C	Tr	01/70	69-75	205	0	0

WILSON Robert Primrose (Bob)
Born: Chesterfield, Derbyshire, England, 30 October, 1941 G
England: Schools//Scotland: 2

League Club	Source	Date Signed	Seasons Played	Apps	Subs	Gls
Arsenal	Wolverhampton W (Am)	03/64	63-73	234	0	0

WILSON Robert Smail Whitelaw (Bobby)
Born: Musselburgh, East Lothian, Scotland, 29 June, 1934 RH

League Club	Source	Date Signed	Seasons Played	Apps	Subs	Gls
Norwich C	Aberdeen	05/57	57-58	62	-	0
Gillingham	Tr	06/60	60	35	-	0
Accrington Stan	Tr	07/61				
Chester C	Tr	04/62	62	15	-	0

WILSON Ronald (Ron)
Born: Ellesmere Port, Cheshire, England, 7 August, 1933 RW

League Club	Source	Date Signed	Seasons Played	Apps	Subs	Gls
Crewe Alex		11/57	57	1	-	0

WILSON Ronald (Ron)
Born: Edinburgh, Scotland, 6 September, 1941 LB

League Club	Source	Date Signed	Seasons Played	Apps	Subs	Gls
Stoke C	Musselburgh Ath	08/59	59-63	11	-	0
Port Vale	Tr	11/63	63-70	261	3	5

WILSON Ronald Gerard (Ron)
Born: Sale, Greater Manchester, England, 10 September, 1924 CF

League Club	Source	Date Signed	Seasons Played	Apps	Subs	Gls
West Ham U	Ford Sports	10/44	46-47	3	-	0

WILSON Samuel (Sammy)
Born: Glasgow, Scotland, 16 December, 1931 IF
Died: Uddingston, Lanarkshire, Scotland, 20 August, 2014

League Club	Source	Date Signed	Seasons Played	Apps	Subs	Gls
Millwall	Glasgow Celtic	07/59	59	23	-	11

League Club	Source	Date Signed	Seasons Played	Career Record Apps	Subs	Gls
WILSON Scott Andrew						
Born: Farnworth, Greater Manchester, England, 25 October, 1980						M
Rochdale	YT	07/99	99	0	1	0
WILSON Scott Peter						
Born: Edinburgh, Scotland, 19 March, 1977						CD
Scotland: U21-7						
Portsmouth (L)	Glasgow Rangers	03/02	01	5	0	0
WILSON Stephen Lee (Steve)						
Born: Hull, England, 24 April, 1974						G
Hull C	YT	07/92	90-99	180	1	0
Macclesfield T	Tr	03/01	00-04	132	2	0
Tranmere Rov	Tr	07/05	05	12	0	0
WILSON Stuart Kevin						
Born: Leicester, England, 16 September, 1977						W
Leicester C	YT	07/96	96-98	1	21	3
Sheffield U	L	03/00	99	4	2	0
Cambridge U	Tr	12/00	00	3	3	0
WILSON Terence (Terry)						
Born: Broxburn, West Lothian, Scotland, 8 February, 1969						CD/M
Scotland: U21-4						
Nottingham F	App	04/86	87-92	94	11	9
Newcastle U	L	01/92	91	2	0	0
WILSON Thomas (Tommy)						
Born: Bedlington, Northumberland, England, 15 September, 1930						CF
Died: Brentwood, Essex, England, 21 April, 1992						
Nottingham F	Cinderhill Colliery	04/51	51-60	191	-	75
Walsall	Tr	11/60	60-61	53	-	18
WILSON Thomas (Tom)						
Born: Rosewell, Midlothian, Scotland, 29 November, 1940						CH
Millwall	Falkirk	07/61	61-67	200	1	15
Hull C	Tr	11/67	67-69	60	0	1
WILSON Thomas Bastin (Tom)						
Born: Windygates, Fife, Scotland, 25 July, 1933						RW
Died: Bridgwater, Somerset, England, 4 April, 2006						
Reading	Thornton Hibs	03/56	56	8	-	1
Exeter C	Tr	07/57	57	22	-	2
WILSON Thomas Frederick (Tommy)						
Born: Southampton, England, 3 July, 1930						RB
Died: Wandsworth, SW London, England, 30 March, 2010						
Fulham	Southampton (Am)	08/50	52-56	45	-	0
Brentford	Tr	07/57	57-61	148	-	0
WILSON Ulrich Johan						
Born: Nieuw Nickerie, Suriname, 5 May, 1964						LB
Ipswich T (L)	Twente Enschede (NED)	12/87	87	5	1	0
WILSON William (Billy)						
Born: Seaton Delaval, Northumberland, England, 10 July, 1946						FB/M
Blackburn Rov	Jnr	09/63	64-71	246	1	0
Portsmouth	Tr	01/72	71-78	188	6	5
WILSON William James Randolph						
Born: Portadown, Armagh, Northern Ireland, 23 September, 1936						WH
Northern Ireland: B						
Burnley	Portadown	09/55	56-57	2	-	0
WILSTERMAN Brian Hank						
Born: Paramaribo, Suriname, 19 November, 1966						CD
Oxford U	Germ'l Beerschot (BEL)	02/97	96-98	28	14	2
Rotherham U	Tr	07/99	99-00	47	5	4
WILTON Graham Ernest						
Born: Chesterfield, Derbyshire, England, 19 October, 1942						W
Chesterfield (Am)	Chesterfield Tube W'ks	06/61	61	1	-	0
WILTORD Sylvain						
Born: Paris, France, 10 May, 1974						F
France: 92						
Arsenal	Bordeaux (FRA)	08/00	00-03	78	28	31
WILTSHIRE David (Dave)						
Born: Folkestone, Kent, England, 8 July, 1954						RB
Gillingham	Canterbury C	01/74	73-75	54	8	2
Aldershot	Tr	07/76	76	5	0	0
WIMBLETON Paul Philip						
Born: Havant, Hampshire, England, 13 November, 1964						M
England: Schools						
Portsmouth	App	02/82	81-83	5	5	0
Cardiff C	Tr	08/86	86-88	118	1	17
Bristol C	Tr	05/89	89	10	6	2
Shrewsbury T	Tr	01/90	89-90	25	10	1

League Club	Source	Date Signed	Seasons Played	Career Record Apps	Subs	Gls
Maidstone U	L	01/91	90	2	0	1
Exeter C	Tr	09/91	91	35	1	4
Swansea C	Tr	08/92	92	10	5	1
WIMSHURST Kenneth Pinkney (Ken)						
Born: South Shields, Tyne and Wear, England, 23 March, 1938						RH
Newcastle U	South Shields	07/57				
Gateshead	Tr	11/58	58-59	7	-	0
Wolverhampton W	Tr	11/60				
Southampton	Tr	07/61	61-67	148	4	9
Bristol C	Tr	10/67	67-71	146	3	9
WINCHESTER Carl						
Born: Belfast, Northern Ireland, 12 April, 1993						RB/M
Northern Ireland: 1/U21-14/Youth						
Oldham Ath	Linfield	07/11	10-14	63	17	6
WINDASS Dean						
Born: Hull, England, 1 April, 1969						F
Hull C	North Ferriby U	10/91	91-95	173	3	57
Oxford U	Aberdeen	08/98	98	33	0	15
Bradford C	Tr	03/99	98-00	64	10	16
Middlesbrough	Tr	03/01	00-02	16	21	3
Sheffield Wed	L	12/01	01	2	0	0
Sheffield U	L	11/02	02	4	0	3
Sheffield U	Tr	01/03	02	16	0	3
Bradford C	Tr	07/03	03-06	138	4	60
Hull C	Tr	01/07	06-08	45	15	20
Oldham Ath	L	01/09	08	9	2	1
Darlington	Tr	08/09	09	3	3	0
WINDASS Joshua Dean (Josh)						
Born: Hull, England, 9 January, 1994						M
Accrington Stan	Harrogate Railway Ath	07/13	13-14	27	18	6
WINDER Nathan James						
Born: Barnsley, South Yorkshire, England, 17 February, 1983						CD
Halifax T	YT	-	01	0	1	0
Chesterfield	Tr	10/02				
WINDLE Charles						
Born: Barnsley, South Yorkshire, England, 8 January, 1917						RW
Died: Bury, Greater Manchester, England, 1975						
Bury		09/38				
Exeter C	Tr	07/39				
Bristol Rov	Tr	12/46	46	7	-	1
WINDLE William Henry (Billy)						
Born: Maltby, South Yorkshire, England, 9 July, 1920						LW
Died: Chester, England, 4 November, 2011						
Leeds U	Kilnhurst Colliery	10/47	47	2	-	0
Lincoln C	Tr	02/48	47-51	91	-	22
Chester C	Tr	10/51	51-54	127	-	20
WINDRIDGE David Howard (Dave)						
Born: Atherstone, Warwickshire, England, 7 December, 1961						W/M
Sheffield U	Jnr	01/79				
Chesterfield	Tr	03/80	80-82	66	12	14
Blackpool	Tr	08/83	83-86	87	14	18
Bury	Cork C (ROI)	11/88	88	1	0	0
Rochdale	Tr	01/89	88	5	0	0
WINDROSS Dennis						
Born: Guisborough, Cleveland, England, 12 March, 1938						RH/CF
Died: Cleveland, England, October, 1989						
Middlesbrough	Blackett Hutton	05/56	59-60	4	-	1
Brighton & HA	Tr	11/60	60	18	-	2
Darlington	Tr	06/61	61	25	-	4
Doncaster Rov	Tr	06/62	62-63	51	-	4
WINDSOR Robert (Bobby)						
Born: Stoke-on-Trent, England, 31 January, 1926						RW
Died: Stoke-on-Trent, England, May, 2000						
Stoke C	Jnr	12/43				
Lincoln C	Tr	02/49	48-49	11	-	1
WINFIELD Bernard John (John)						
Born: Draycott, Derbyshire, England, 28 February, 1943						LB/WH
Nottingham F	Jnr	05/60	61-73	353	2	4
Peterborough U	Tr	07/74	74	11	0	0
WINFIELD David Thomas (Dave)						
Born: Aldershot, Hampshire, England, 24 March, 1988						CD
Aldershot T	Jnr	07/06	08-09	28	7	2
Wycombe W	Tr	07/10	10-12	87	4	6
Shrewsbury T	Tr	06/13	13	15	2	0
York C	Tr	06/14	14	9	1	2
AFC Wimbledon	L	02/15	14	7	0	0
WINFIELD Philip (Phil)						
Born: Mexborough, South Yorkshire, England, 16 February, 1937						WH
Lincoln C	Denaby U	10/57	57	1	-	0

League Club	Source	Date Signed	Seasons Played	Apps	Subs	Gls

WINGATE John Anthony
Born: Budleigh Salterton, Devon, England, 19 December, 1948 — M/CF

League Club	Source	Date Signed	Seasons Played	Apps	Subs	Gls
Plymouth Arg (Am)	Dawlish T	12/68	68	1	0	0
Exeter C	Dawlish T	02/69	68-73	187	16	32
Bournemouth	Tr	07/74	74	30	3	3
Exeter C	Tr	07/75	75	44	1	2

WINGATE Tony
Born: Islington, N London, England, 21 March, 1955 — FB

League Club	Source	Date Signed	Seasons Played	Apps	Subs	Gls
Colchester U	App	03/73	71	0	1	0

WINN Ashley
Born: Stockton-on-Tees, Cleveland, England, 1 December, 1985 — M

League Club	Source	Date Signed	Seasons Played	Apps	Subs	Gls
Oldham Ath	Sch	-	04	0	2	0

WINN Peter Henry
Born: Cleethorpes, North Lincolnshire, England, 19 December, 1988 — LW

League Club	Source	Date Signed	Seasons Played	Apps	Subs	Gls
Scunthorpe U	Sch	07/07	07	0	4	0
Stevenage	Tr	07/10	10	13	15	2

WINN Stephen (Steve)
Born: Thornaby, Cleveland, England, 16 September, 1959 — F

League Club	Source	Date Signed	Seasons Played	Apps	Subs	Gls
Rotherham U		03/78	78-80	17	7	3
Torquay U	Tr	01/82	81	12	2	2
Hartlepool U	Scunthorpe U (NC)	03/83	82	1	0	0

WINNALL Samuel Thomas (Sam)
Born: Wolverhampton, England, 19 January, 1991 — F

League Club	Source	Date Signed	Seasons Played	Apps	Subs	Gls
Wolverhampton W	Sch	07/09				
Burton A	L	02/11	10	12	7	7
Hereford U	L	08/11	11	5	3	2
Shrewsbury T	L	09/12	12	3	1	0
Scunthorpe U	Tr	07/13	13	43	2	23
Barnsley	Tr	07/14	14	23	9	9

WINNARD Dean
Born: Wigan, Greater Manchester, England, 20 August, 1989 — D

League Club	Source	Date Signed	Seasons Played	Apps	Subs	Gls
Blackburn Rov	Sch	03/07				
Accrington Stan	Tr	07/09	09-14	230	5	5

WINNIE David Peter
Born: Glasgow, Scotland, 26 October, 1966 — LB
Scotland: U21-1/Youth/Schools

League Club	Source	Date Signed	Seasons Played	Apps	Subs	Gls
Middlesbrough (L)	Aberdeen	03/94	93	1	0	0

WINSPEAR John (Jack)
Born: Leeds, England, 24 December, 1946 — RW

League Club	Source	Date Signed	Seasons Played	Apps	Subs	Gls
Leeds U	Jnr	10/64				
Cardiff C	Tr	06/66	66	1	0	0
Rochdale	Tr	07/67	67	15	1	3

WINSTANLEY Craig Jason
Born: Hartlepool, Cleveland, England, 23 August, 1978 — M

League Club	Source	Date Signed	Seasons Played	Apps	Subs	Gls
Hartlepool U	YT	12/96	96	0	1	0

WINSTANLEY Eric
Born: Barnsley, South Yorkshire, England, 15 November, 1944 — CD
England: Youth

League Club	Source	Date Signed	Seasons Played	Apps	Subs	Gls
Barnsley	Jnr	05/62	61-72	410	0	35
Chesterfield	Tr	08/73	73-76	100	1	7

WINSTANLEY Graham
Born: Croxdale, County Durham, England, 20 January, 1948 — CD

League Club	Source	Date Signed	Seasons Played	Apps	Subs	Gls
Newcastle U	App	12/68	66-68	5	2	0
Carlisle U	Tr	08/69	69-74	165	1	8
Brighton & HA	Tr	10/74	74-78	63	1	4
Carlisle U	Tr	07/79	79	32	1	1

WINSTANLEY Mark Andrew
Born: St Helens, Merseyside, England, 22 January, 1968 — CD

League Club	Source	Date Signed	Seasons Played	Apps	Subs	Gls
Bolton W	App	07/86	85-93	215	5	3
Burnley	Tr	08/94	94-98	151	1	5
Shrewsbury T	L	09/98	98	8	0	0
Preston NE	Tr	03/99				
Shrewsbury T	Tr	07/99	99	32	1	1
Carlisle U	Tr	08/00	00-01	70	2	1

WINSTON Samuel Anthony (Sammy)
Born: Islington, N London, England, 6 August, 1978 — F

League Club	Source	Date Signed	Seasons Played	Apps	Subs	Gls
Leyton Orient	Norwich C (YT)	08/96	96	3	8	1

WINSTONE Simon John
Born: Bristol, England, 4 October, 1974 — M

League Club	Source	Date Signed	Seasons Played	Apps	Subs	Gls
Stoke C	YT	07/93				
Torquay U	Tr	09/94	94	1	1	0

WINTER Daniel Thomas (Danny)
Born: Tonypandy, Rhondda Cynon Taff, Wales, 14 June, 1918 — RB
Died: Trealaw, Rhondda Cynon Taff, Wales, 22 March, 2004
Wales: War-2

League Club	Source	Date Signed	Seasons Played	Apps	Subs	Gls
Bolton W	Maes-y-Hof	06/35	36-38	34	-	0
Chelsea	Tr	12/45	46-50	131	-	0

WINTER Jamie
Born: Dundee, Scotland, 4 August, 1985 — M

League Club	Source	Date Signed	Seasons Played	Apps	Subs	Gls
Leeds U	Sch	10/02				
Chesterfield	Aberdeen	08/07	07-08	38	11	2

WINTER John George Adrian (Jack)
Born: Stoke Newington, N London, England, 6 March, 1928 — CF
Died: Sheffield, England, February, 2009

League Club	Source	Date Signed	Seasons Played	Apps	Subs	Gls
Sheffield U	Gleadless Tel Exch	11/48				
Walsall	Tr	01/51	50-51	41	-	12

WINTER Julian
Born: Huddersfield, West Yorkshire, England, 6 September, 1965 — M

League Club	Source	Date Signed	Seasons Played	Apps	Subs	Gls
Huddersfield T	App	09/83	84-88	89	4	5
Scunthorpe U	L	08/88	88	4	0	0
Sheffield U	Tr	07/89				

WINTER Steven David (Steve)
Born: Bristol, England, 26 October, 1973 — RB/M

League Club	Source	Date Signed	Seasons Played	Apps	Subs	Gls
Walsall	YT	03/92	91-92	14	4	0
Torquay U	Taunton T	08/95	95-96	72	1	6

WINTERBOTTOM Dennis Trevor Wilson
Born: Glossop, Derbyshire, England, 23 October, 1928 — CH

League Club	Source	Date Signed	Seasons Played	Apps	Subs	Gls
Accrington Stan	Stalybridge Celtic	06/51	51	12	-	0

WINTERBURN Nigel
Born: Nuneaton, Warwickshire, England, 11 December, 1963 — LB
England: 2/B-3/FLge/U21-1/Youth

League Club	Source	Date Signed	Seasons Played	Apps	Subs	Gls
Birmingham C	App	08/81				
Wimbledon	Tr	09/83	83-86	164	1	8
Arsenal	Tr	05/87	87-99	429	11	8
West Ham U	Tr	07/00	00-02	78	4	1

WINTERS Francis (Frank)
Born: Johnstone, Renfrewshire, Scotland, 30 October, 1923 — CH

League Club	Source	Date Signed	Seasons Played	Apps	Subs	Gls
Torquay U	Clyde	05/49	49-51	14	-	0

WINTERS Herbert Richard (Bert)
Born: Coalpit Heath, Avon, England, 14 April, 1920 — CH

League Club	Source	Date Signed	Seasons Played	Apps	Subs	Gls
Bristol Rov	Westerleigh Sports	09/46	46-47	13	-	0

WINTERS Ian Anderson
Born: Renfrew, Renfrewshire, Scotland, 8 February, 1921 — IF
Died: Hull, England, 3 May, 1994

League Club	Source	Date Signed	Seasons Played	Apps	Subs	Gls
York C	Earswick	08/45	46-47	27	-	10
Gateshead	Boston U	12/48	48-52	152	-	49
Workington	Tr	07/53	53	30	-	3

WINTERS John Mark
Born: Wisbech, Cambridgeshire, England, 24 October, 1960 — RB

League Club	Source	Date Signed	Seasons Played	Apps	Subs	Gls
Peterborough U	App	10/78	80-82	60	0	3

WINTERS Robert (Robbie)
Born: East Kilbride, Lanarkshire, Scotland, 4 November, 1974 — LW
Scotland: 1

League Club	Source	Date Signed	Seasons Played	Apps	Subs	Gls
Luton T	Aberdeen	08/02	02	1	0	0

WINTERS Thomas Richard (Tom)
Born: Banbury, Oxfordshire, England, 11 December, 1985 — LW

League Club	Source	Date Signed	Seasons Played	Apps	Subs	Gls
Oxford U	Sch	07/05	03-04	0	5	0

WINTERSGILL David
Born: Northallerton, North Yorkshire, England, 19 September, 1965 — M/LB

League Club	Source	Date Signed	Seasons Played	Apps	Subs	Gls
Wolverhampton W	App	06/83	82-83	3	1	0
Chester C	L	03/84	83	5	0	0
Darlington	TP Seinajoki (FIN)	11/86	86	15	2	1

WINTLE Frank James
Born: Stoke-on-Trent, England, 20 December, 1929 — FB
Died: Birmingham, England, 4 January, 2005

League Club	Source	Date Signed	Seasons Played	Apps	Subs	Gls
Port Vale		05/49	56	1	-	0
Crewe Alex	Tr	06/57				

WINTON George Douglas (Doug)
Born: Perth, Scotland, 6 October, 1929 — LB
Died: Burnley, Lancashire, England, 29 October, 2006
Scotland: B-1

League Club	Source	Date Signed	Seasons Played	Apps	Subs	Gls
Burnley	Jeanfield Swifts	09/47	52-58	183	-	1
Aston Villa	Tr	01/59	58-60	37	-	0
Rochdale	Tr	06/61	61-63	119	-	0

WIPFLER Charles John (Charlie)
Born: Trowbridge, Wiltshire, England, 15 July, 1915 — W
Died: Petts Wood, SE London, England, 1 June, 1983

League Club	Source	Date Signed	Seasons Played	Apps	Subs	Gls
Bristol Rov	Trowbridge T	09/34	34	18	-	5
Watford	Heart of Midlothian	06/37	37-38	22	-	7
Watford	Canterbury C	09/46	46	13	-	1

WIRMOLA Jonas
Born: Vaxjo, Sweden, 17 July, 1969 CD

League Club	Source	Date Signed	Seasons Played	Apps	Subs	Gls
Sheffield U	Sparvagens (SWE)	08/93	93	8	0	0

WISDOM Andre Alexander Shaquille
Born: Leeds, England, 9 May, 1993 RB
England: U21-10/Youth

League Club	Source	Date Signed	Seasons Played	Apps	Subs	Gls
Liverpool	Sch	05/10	12-13	13	1	0
Derby Co	L	10/13	13	34	0	0
West Bromwich A	L	07/14	14	22	2	0

WISE Dennis Frank
Born: Kensington, Central London, England, 16 December, 1966 M
England: 21/B-3/U21-1

League Club	Source	Date Signed	Seasons Played	Apps	Subs	Gls
Wimbledon	Southampton (App)	03/85	84-89	127	8	27
Chelsea	Tr	07/90	90-00	322	10	53
Leicester C	Tr	06/01	01	15	2	1
Millwall	Tr	09/02	02-04	70	15	7
Southampton	Tr	06/05	05	8	3	1
Coventry C	Tr	01/06	05	11	2	6

WISE Stuart Graeme
Born: Middlesbrough, England, 4 April, 1984 D/M

League Club	Source	Date Signed	Seasons Played	Apps	Subs	Gls
York C	Sch	07/03	01-03	24	9	1

WISEMAN George
Born: East Dereham, Norfolk, England, 23 May, 1921 G
Died: Exeter, England, 5 October, 2008

League Club	Source	Date Signed	Seasons Played	Apps	Subs	Gls
Notts Co	Bottesford T	05/45				
Norwich C	Tr	09/46	46	8	-	0

WISEMAN Scott Nigel Kenneth
Born: Hull, England, 9 October, 1985 RB
England: Youth

League Club	Source	Date Signed	Seasons Played	Apps	Subs	Gls
Hull C	Sch	04/04	03-05	10	6	0
Boston U	L	02/05	04	1	1	0
Rotherham U	L	07/06	06	9	9	1
Darlington	Tr	03/07	06-07	12	5	0
Rochdale	Tr	07/08	08-10	100	5	1
Barnsley	Tr	06/11	11-13	91	11	1
Preston NE	Tr	01/14	13-14	30	7	2

WISS Jarkko
Born: Tampere, Finland, 17 April, 1972 M
Finland: 45

League Club	Source	Date Signed	Seasons Played	Apps	Subs	Gls
Stockport Co	Moss FK (NOR)	08/00	00-01	34	7	6

WITCOMB Douglas Frank (Doug)
Born: Ebbw Vale, Blaenau Gwent, Wales, 18 April, 1918 WH
Died: Newport, Wales, 6 August, 1999
Wales: 3/War-7

League Club	Source	Date Signed	Seasons Played	Apps	Subs	Gls
West Bromwich A	Enfield	10/37	38-46	55	-	3
Sheffield Wed	Tr	03/47	46-52	224	-	12
Newport Co	Tr	11/53	53	25	-	0

WITHAM Richard (Dick)
Born: Bowburn, County Durham, England, 4 May, 1913 LB
Died: Blackpool, Lancashire, England, 29 October, 1999

League Club	Source	Date Signed	Seasons Played	Apps	Subs	Gls
Huddersfield T	Durham C	01/34	33	4	-	0
Blackpool	Tr	02/34	33-37	149	-	0
Oldham Ath	Tr	06/46	46	5	-	0

WITHE Christopher (Chris)
Born: Speke, Merseyside, England, 25 September, 1962 LB

League Club	Source	Date Signed	Seasons Played	Apps	Subs	Gls
Newcastle U	App	10/80	80	2	0	0
Bradford C	Tr	06/83	83-87	141	2	2
Notts Co	Tr	10/87	87-88	80	0	3
Bury	Tr	07/89	89	22	9	1
Chester C	L	10/90	90	2	0	0
Mansfield T	Tr	01/91	90-92	75	1	5
Shrewsbury T	Tr	08/93	93-95	80	9	2

WITHE Peter
Born: Liverpool, England, 30 August, 1951 F
England: 11

League Club	Source	Date Signed	Seasons Played	Apps	Subs	Gls
Southport	Smiths Coggins	11/70	70-71	3	0	0
Barrow	Tr	12/71	71	1	0	0
Wolverhampton W	Arcadia Shep's (RSA)	11/73	73-74	12	5	3
Birmingham C	Tr	08/75	75-76	35	0	9
Nottingham F	Tr	09/76	76-78	74	1	28
Newcastle U	Tr	08/78	78-79	76	0	25
Aston Villa	Tr	05/80	80-84	182	0	74
Sheffield U	Tr	07/85	85-87	70	4	18
Birmingham C	L	09/87	87	8	0	2
Huddersfield T	Tr	07/88	88-89	22	16	1

WITHEFORD James Douglas (Jim)
Born: Sheffield, England, 16 April, 1930 RW

League Club	Source	Date Signed	Seasons Played	Apps	Subs	Gls
Chesterfield (Am)	Norton Woodseats	12/53	53	9	-	0

WITHERS Alan
Born: Nottingham, England, 20 October, 1930 LW

League Club	Source	Date Signed	Seasons Played	Apps	Subs	Gls
Blackpool	Aspley BC	07/49	50-54	17	-	6
Lincoln C	Tr	02/55	54-58	97	-	18
Notts Co	Tr	01/59	58-62	121	-	22

WITHERS Charles Francis (Charlie)
Born: Edmonton, N London, England, 6 September, 1922 LB
Died: Torquay, Devon, England, 7 June, 2005
England: B-1

League Club	Source	Date Signed	Seasons Played	Apps	Subs	Gls
Tottenham H	Jnr	10/47	47-55	153	-	0

WITHERS Colin Charles
Born: Birmingham, England, 21 March, 1940 G
England: Schools

League Club	Source	Date Signed	Seasons Played	Apps	Subs	Gls
Birmingham C	West Bromwich A (Am)	05/57	60-64	98	-	0
Aston Villa	Tr	11/64	64-68	146	0	0
Lincoln C	Tr	06/69	69	1	0	0

WITHERS David Russell (Dai)
Born: Llwynypia, Rhondda Cynon Taff, Wales, 28 April, 1967 F

League Club	Source	Date Signed	Seasons Played	Apps	Subs	Gls
Newport Co	Bristol Rov (YT)	10/86	86-87	5	4	1
Newport Co	Ton Pentre	04/88	87	2	0	0

WITHEY Graham Alfred
Born: Bristol, England, 11 June, 1960 F

League Club	Source	Date Signed	Seasons Played	Apps	Subs	Gls
Bristol Rov	Bath C	08/82	82	19	3	10
Coventry C	Tr	08/83	83-84	11	11	4
Cardiff C	Tr	12/84	84-85	27	0	7
Bristol C	Bath C	09/86	86	1	1	0
Exeter C	Cheltenham T	07/88	88	5	2	2

WITHINGTON Richard Stanley (Dick)
Born: South Shields, Tyne and Wear, England, 8 April, 1921 IF
Died: Sheffield, England, 1981

League Club	Source	Date Signed	Seasons Played	Apps	Subs	Gls
Blackpool	Jnr	05/38				
Rochdale	Tr	06/47	47	32	-	6
Chesterfield	Tr	06/48	48	6	-	0

WITSCHGE Richard
Born: Amsterdam, Netherlands, 20 September, 1969 M
Netherlands: 31

League Club	Source	Date Signed	Seasons Played	Apps	Subs	Gls
Blackburn Rov (L)	Bordeaux (FRA)	03/95	94	1	0	0

WITTER Anthony Junior (Tony)
Born: Kingston, Jamaica, 12 August, 1965 CD

League Club	Source	Date Signed	Seasons Played	Apps	Subs	Gls
Crystal Palace	Grays Ath	10/90				
Queens Park Rgrs	Tr	08/91	93	1	0	0
Plymouth Arg	L	01/92	91	3	0	1
Reading	L	02/94	93	4	0	0
Millwall	Tr	10/94	94-97	99	3	2
Northampton T	Tr	08/98	98	1	3	0
Torquay U	Tr	11/98	98	4	0	0
Scunthorpe U	Welling U	02/99	98	14	0	0

WOAN Alan Esplin
Born: Liverpool, England, 8 February, 1931 IF

League Club	Source	Date Signed	Seasons Played	Apps	Subs	Gls
Norwich C	New Brighton	12/53	53-55	21	-	7
Northampton T	Tr	07/56	56-59	119	-	68
Crystal Palace	Tr	10/59	59-60	41	-	21
Aldershot	Tr	02/61	60-63	108	-	44

WOAN Donald (Don)
Born: Bootle, Merseyside, England, 7 November, 1927 RW

League Club	Source	Date Signed	Seasons Played	Apps	Subs	Gls
Liverpool	Bootle	10/50	50	2	-	0
Leyton Orient	Tr	11/51	51-52	25	-	5
Bradford C	Tr	10/52	52-53	21	-	4
Tranmere Rov	Tr	02/54	53-54	27	-	2

WOAN Ian Simon
Born: Heswall, Wirral, England, 14 December, 1967 LW

League Club	Source	Date Signed	Seasons Played	Apps	Subs	Gls
Nottingham F	Runcorn	03/90	90-99	189	32	31
Barnsley	Tr	08/00	00	2	1	0
Swindon T	Tr	10/00	00	21	1	3
Shrewsbury T	Miami Fusion (USA)	01/02	01-02	47	3	7

WOFFINDEN Colin
Born: Hove, East Sussex, England, 6 August, 1947 F

League Club	Source	Date Signed	Seasons Played	Apps	Subs	Gls
Brighton & HA (Am)	Lewes	11/70	70	0	3	0

WOJTCZAK Edouard Andrew
Born: Syzran, Russia, 29 April, 1921 G
Died: Cheam, S London, England, 11 March, 1995

League Club	Source	Date Signed	Seasons Played	Apps	Subs	Gls
York C (Am)	Polish Army (POL)	10/46	46	8	-	0

WOLFENDEN Matthew (Matty)
Born: Oldham, Greater Manchester, England, 23 July, 1987 F

League Club	Source	Date Signed	Seasons Played	Apps	Subs	Gls
Oldham Ath	Jnr	07/06	03-08	8	31	2

WOLLEASTON Robert Ainsley
Born: Perivale, W London, England, 21 December, 1979 M

League Club	Source	Date Signed	Seasons Played	Career Record Apps	Subs	Gls
Chelsea	YT	06/98	99	0	1	0
Bristol Rov	L	03/00	99	0	4	0
Portsmouth	L	03/01	00	5	1	0
Northampton T	L	07/01	01	2	5	0
Bradford C	Tr	07/03	03	6	8	1
Oxford U	Tr	07/04	04	14	6	0

WOLLEN Terence Leslie (Terry)
Born: Swindon, England, 30 July, 1943 — RB

League Club	Source	Date Signed	Seasons Played	Apps	Subs	Gls
Swindon T	Jnr	08/60	60-64	84	-	0

WOLLSCHEID Philipp Johannes
Born: Wadern, Germany, 6 March, 1989 — CD
Germany: 2/Youth

League Club	Source	Date Signed	Seasons Played	Apps	Subs	Gls
Stoke C	Bayer Leverkusen (GER)	01/15	14	12	0	0

WOLSKI Mickael
Born: Moulins, France, 5 March, 1979 — M

League Club	Source	Date Signed	Seasons Played	Apps	Subs	Gls
Stockport Co	Shamrock Rov (ROI)	08/05	05	14	6	1

WOLSTENHOLME Ian Arthur
Born: Bradford, England, 12 January, 1943 — G
England: Amateur-1

League Club	Source	Date Signed	Seasons Played	Apps	Subs	Gls
York C (Am)	St John's College	10/63	63	2	-	0

WOLSTENHOLME John Trevor (Trevor)
Born: Prestbury, Cheshire, England, 18 June, 1943 — LH

League Club	Source	Date Signed	Seasons Played	Apps	Subs	Gls
Birmingham C	Chloride	09/60				
Torquay U	Tr	08/63	63-65	82	0	2
York C	Tr	07/66	66	11	0	0

WOMACK Albert Roy (Kim)
Born: Denaby, South Yorkshire, England, 20 September, 1934 — RW
Died: Doncaster, South Yorkshire, England, 2 November, 2010

League Club	Source	Date Signed	Seasons Played	Apps	Subs	Gls
Derby Co	Denaby U	10/57	57	2	-	0
Southampton	Tr	05/59				
Workington	Tr	07/60	60	9	-	1

WOMBLE Trevor
Born: South Shields, Tyne and Wear, England, 7 June, 1951 — M/F

League Club	Source	Date Signed	Seasons Played	Apps	Subs	Gls
Rotherham U	App	10/68	68-77	185	30	39
Crewe Alex	L	11/71	71	4	0	1
Halifax T	L	03/73	72	9	1	2

WOME Pierre Nlend
Born: Douala, Cameroon, 26 March, 1979 — LB/M
Cameroon: 69

League Club	Source	Date Signed	Seasons Played	Apps	Subs	Gls
Fulham (L)	Bologna (ITA)	08/02	02	13	1	1

WOMERSLEY Ernest
Born: Liversedge, West Yorkshire, England, 28 August, 1932 — RW

League Club	Source	Date Signed	Seasons Played	Apps	Subs	Gls
Huddersfield T	Jnr	09/49	50	2	-	0
Bradford C	Tr	05/57				

WOOD Alan Ernest
Born: Gravesend, Kent, England, 1 December, 1954 — CD

League Club	Source	Date Signed	Seasons Played	Apps	Subs	Gls
Charlton Ath	App	12/72	72	1	0	0

WOOD Alan Herbert
Born: Newport, Wales, 13 January, 1941 — CD
Wales: Amateur

League Club	Source	Date Signed	Seasons Played	Apps	Subs	Gls
Bristol Rov	Lovells Ath	10/62	62	1	-	0
Newport Co	Merthyr Tydfil	05/65	65-72	149	5	5

WOOD Alfred Edward Howson (Alf)
Born: Macclesfield, Cheshire, England, 25 October, 1945 — F/CH
England: Youth

League Club	Source	Date Signed	Seasons Played	Apps	Subs	Gls
Manchester C	App	06/63	62-65	24	1	0
Shrewsbury T	Tr	06/66	66-71	257	1	65
Millwall	Tr	06/72	72-74	99	1	38
Hull C	Tr	11/74	74-76	51	2	10
Middlesbrough	Tr	10/76	76	22	1	2
Walsall	Tr	07/77	77	26	3	2

WOOD Alfred Robert (Alf)
Born: Aldridge, West Midlands, England, 14 May, 1915 — G
Died: Coventry, England, 17 December, 2001

League Club	Source	Date Signed	Seasons Played	Apps	Subs	Gls
Coventry C	Nuneaton T	12/35	37-51	221	-	0
Northampton T	Tr	12/51	51-54	139	-	0
Coventry C	Tr	07/55	55-58	13	-	0

WOOD Archibald (Archie)
Born: Leven, Fife, Scotland, 18 March, 1926 — LW
Died: Leven, Fife, Scotland, 17 June, 1986

League Club	Source	Date Signed	Seasons Played	Apps	Subs	Gls
Tranmere Rov	Bowhill	08/49	49	31	-	5

WOOD Barrie Wilmot
Born: Doncaster, South Yorkshire, England, 5 December, 1936 — IF

League Club	Source	Date Signed	Seasons Played	Apps	Subs	Gls
Doncaster Rov	Wolverhampton W (Am)	08/54	55	2	-	0
Scunthorpe U	Tr	07/58	58	3	-	1
Barnsley	South Shields	03/61	60-61	4	-	2

WOOD Bradley Alan
Born: Leicester, England, 2 September, 1991 — RB/M
England: Semi Pro-1

League Club	Source	Date Signed	Seasons Played	Apps	Subs	Gls
Grimsby T	Sch	10/09	09	7	1	0

WOOD Brian Thomas
Born: Poole, Dorset, England, 8 December, 1940 — CD
Died: Saxtead, Suffolk, England, 5 July, 2014

League Club	Source	Date Signed	Seasons Played	Apps	Subs	Gls
West Bromwich A	Hamworthy Ath	01/58				
Crystal Palace	Tr	05/61	61-66	142	1	1
Leyton Orient	Tr	12/66	66-67	58	0	3
Colchester U	Tr	08/68	68-69	71	0	2
Workington	Tr	07/70	70-75	202	2	9

WOOD Charles William (Charlie)
Born: Poplar, E London, England, 7 June, 1919 — CH
Died: Lambeth, S London, England, July, 2000

League Club	Source	Date Signed	Seasons Played	Apps	Subs	Gls
Millwall (Am)		05/46	46	3	-	0

WOOD Christopher Charles (Chris)
Born: Penistone, South Yorkshire, England, 18 May, 1955 — G

League Club	Source	Date Signed	Seasons Played	Apps	Subs	Gls
Huddersfield T	App	05/72	72	7	0	0
Barnsley	L	02/73	72	1	0	0
Doncaster Rov	L	07/74	74	4	0	0

WOOD Christopher Grant (Chris)
Born: Auckland, New Zealand, 7 December, 1991 — F
New Zealand: 39

League Club	Source	Date Signed	Seasons Played	Apps	Subs	Gls
West Bromwich A	Sch	05/09	08-11	6	15	1
Barnsley	L	09/10	10	4	3	0
Brighton & HA	L	11/10	10	22	7	8
Birmingham C	L	08/11	11	13	10	9
Bristol C	L	01/12	11	12	7	3
Millwall	L	09/12	12	18	1	11
Leicester C	Tr	01/13	12-14	26	27	14
Ipswich T	L	02/15	14	3	5	0

WOOD Christopher Hayden (Chris)
Born: Worksop, Nottinghamshire, England, 24 January, 1987 — D

League Club	Source	Date Signed	Seasons Played	Apps	Subs	Gls
Mansfield T	Sch	07/06	04-07	9	6	0

WOOD Darren
Born: Alfreton, Derbyshire, England, 22 October, 1968 — D/M

League Club	Source	Date Signed	Seasons Played	Apps	Subs	Gls
Chesterfield	App	06/87	86-88	61	6	3
Reading	Tr	07/89	89	31	1	2
Northampton T	Tr	08/90	90-93	4	0	1

WOOD Darren Terence
Born: Scarborough, North Yorkshire, England, 9 June, 1964 — RB/M
England: Schools

League Club	Source	Date Signed	Seasons Played	Apps	Subs	Gls
Middlesbrough	App	07/81	81-84	101	0	6
Chelsea	Tr	09/84	84-88	134	10	3
Sheffield Wed	Tr	01/89	88-89	10	1	0

WOOD Edward John (Jackie)
Born: Canning Town, E London, England, 23 October, 1919 — IF/LW
Died: Exeter, England, October, 1993
England: Amateur

League Club	Source	Date Signed	Seasons Played	Apps	Subs	Gls
West Ham U	Leytonstone	03/38	37-48	58	-	13
Leyton Orient	Tr	10/49	49	9	-	1

WOOD Eric
Born: Bolton, Greater Manchester, England, 13 March, 1920 — WH/IF
Died: Bolton, Greater Manchester, England, November, 2000

League Club	Source	Date Signed	Seasons Played	Apps	Subs	Gls
Rochdale	Bolton W (Am)	08/43	46-50	148	-	15

WOOD Frank
Born: Manchester, England, 17 August, 1924 — CD

League Club	Source	Date Signed	Seasons Played	Apps	Subs	Gls
Bury	Hulme	10/48	50	1	-	0
Shrewsbury T	Tr	10/52				
Exeter C		01/53	52	8	-	0

WOOD Gary Terence
Born: Corby, Northamptonshire, England, 2 December, 1955 — LB

League Club	Source	Date Signed	Seasons Played	Apps	Subs	Gls
Notts Co	Kettering T	12/77	77-80	7	4	0

WOOD George
Born: Douglas, Lanarkshire, Scotland, 26 September, 1952 — G
Scotland: 4

League Club	Source	Date Signed	Seasons Played	Apps	Subs	Gls
Blackpool	East Stirlingshire	01/72	71-76	117	0	0
Everton	Tr	08/77	77-79	103	0	0
Arsenal	Tr	08/80	80-82	60	0	0
Crystal Palace	Tr	08/83	83-87	192	0	0
Cardiff C	Tr	01/88	87-89	67	0	0
Blackpool	Tr	03/90	89	15	0	0
Hereford U	Tr	08/90	90	41	0	0

WOOD Graham
Born: Doncaster, South Yorkshire, England, 10 February, 1933 — CF

League Club	Source	Date Signed	Seasons Played	Apps	Subs	Gls
Wolverhampton W		09/50				
Halifax T	Tr	06/53	53-54	19	-	3

League Club	Source	Date Signed	Seasons Played	Career Record Apps	Subs	Gls
WOOD Harry						
Born: Barrow, Cumbria, England, 31 December, 1911						IF
Died: Barrow, Cumbria, England, October, 1994						
Barrow	Vickers Ath	02/33	32-36	10	-	2
Barrow	Netherfield	08/47	47-48	11	-	1
WOOD Henry						
Born: Liverpool, England, 8 April, 1927						RW
Chesterfield	South Liverpool	07/53	53	9	-	1
WOOD Hugh Sutherland						
Born: Bellshill, Lanarkshire, Scotland, 16 November, 1960						FB
Scunthorpe U	Grantham	09/80	80	0	1	0
WOOD Ian Nigel						
Born: Kirkby-in-Ashfield, Nottinghamshire, England, 24 May, 1958						D
Mansfield T	App	06/76	75-81	135	14	9
Aldershot	Tr	08/82	82	14	0	1
WOOD Ian Thomas						
Born: Radcliffe, Greater Manchester, England, 15 January, 1948						RB
Oldham Ath	Park Lane Olympic	11/65	65-79	517	7	22
Burnley	Tr	05/80	80	14	3	0
WOOD Jack						
Born: Royton, Greater Manchester, England, 12 February, 1931						LB/LH
Aldershot	Aldershot Garrison	09/52	52-54	38	-	1
WOOD James Henry (Jimmy)						
Born: Liverpool, England, 25 October, 1938						G
Southport	Burscough	04/58	57	1	-	0
WOOD Jamie						
Born: Salford, England, 21 September, 1978						F
Cayman Islands: 2						
Manchester U	YT	07/97				
Hull C	Tr	07/99	99-00	15	32	6
Halifax T	Tr	08/01	01	10	6	0
Swansea C	Tr	07/02	02	13	4	2
WOOD Jeffrey Reginald (Jeff)						
Born: Islington, N London, England, 4 February, 1954						G
Charlton Ath	Harlow T	11/75	75-80	147	0	0
Colchester U	Denmark	09/81				
Exeter C	HJK Helsinki (FIN)	08/84	84	33	0	0
WOOD John Michael						
Born: Walsall Wood, West Midlands, England, 9 September, 1948						FB
Wrexham	Jnr	07/66	65-67	4	3	0
WOOD Kevin						
Born: Armthorpe, South Yorkshire, England, 3 November, 1929						IF
Died: Doncaster, South Yorkshire, England, 19 September, 2012						
Doncaster Rov		10/49				
Grimsby T	Worksop T	03/51	50-51	3	-	2
WOOD Leigh James						
Born: Selby, North Yorkshire, England, 21 May, 1983						D/M
York C	Sch	03/02	00-03	44	20	0
WOOD Mark						
Born: Scarborough, North Yorkshire, England, 27 June, 1972						M
York C	YT	07/90	90	0	1	0
WOOD Michael (Mick)						
Born: Halifax, West Yorkshire, England, 9 March, 1962						F
Rochdale	Guiseley	08/86	86	5	1	3
WOOD Michael James (Mick)						
Born: Bury, Greater Manchester, England, 3 July, 1952						LB/M
Blackburn Rov	App	02/70	69-77	140	8	2
Bradford C	Tr	02/78	77-81	143	3	9
Halifax T	Tr	08/82	82-83	80	1	2
WOOD Neil Anthony						
Born: Manchester, England, 4 January, 1983						LM
England: Youth						
Manchester U	YT	01/00				
Peterborough U	L	09/03	03	2	1	1
Burnley	L	01/04	03	8	2	1
Coventry C	Tr	07/04	04-05	6	11	0
Blackpool	Tr	01/06	05	7	0	0
Oldham Ath	Tr	07/06	06	3	2	0
WOOD Nicholas Anthony (Nick)						
Born: Oldham, Greater Manchester, England, 6 January, 1966						F
England: Youth						
Manchester U	App	06/83	85-86	2	1	0
WOOD Nicholas Jack (Nick)						
Born: Ossett, West Yorkshire, England, 9 November, 1990						CD
Sheffield Wed	Sch	07/09				
Tranmere Rov	Tr	07/10	10	5	6	0
WOOD Norman						
Born: Sunderland, England, 10 August, 1932						WH
Sunderland	Silksworth Jnrs	05/54	54	1	-	0
WOOD Norman						
Born: Chadderton, Greater Manchester, England, 20 October, 1921						RW
Died: Bridgnorth, Shropshire, England, May, 2005						
Oldham Ath (Am)	Royton Amats	09/46	46	1	-	0
WOOD Paul						
Born: Uppermill, Greater Manchester, England, 20 March, 1970						M
Sheffield U	YT	09/88	87	0	1	0
Rochdale	L	11/88	88	2	3	0
WOOD Paul Anthony						
Born: Cleveland, England, 1 November, 1964						RW
Portsmouth	App	11/82	83-86	25	22	6
Brighton & HA	Tr	08/87	87-89	77	15	8
Sheffield U	Tr	02/90	89-91	19	9	3
Bournemouth	L	01/91	90	20	1	0
Bournemouth	Tr	10/91	91-93	73	5	18
Portsmouth	Tr	02/94	93-95	25	7	3
WOOD Raymond Ernest (Ray)						
Born: Hebburn, Tyne and Wear, England, 11 June, 1931						G
Died: Bexhill, East Sussex, England, 7 July, 2002						
England: 3/B-1/FLge-3/U23-1						
Darlington	Newcastle U (Am)	09/49	49	12	-	0
Manchester U	Tr	12/49	49-58	178	-	0
Huddersfield T	Tr	12/58	58-64	207	-	0
Bradford C	Inter Roma (CAN)	10/65	65	32	0	0
Barnsley	Tr	08/66	66-67	30	0	0
WOOD Richard Mark						
Born: Ossett, West Yorkshire, England, 5 July, 1985						CD
Sheffield Wed	Sch	04/03	02-09	162	9	7
Coventry C	Tr	11/09	09-12	105	12	8
Charlton Ath	Tr	07/13	13	18	3	0
Rotherham U	Tr	06/14	14	3	3	0
Crawley T	L	02/15	14	10	0	3
WOOD Robert (Bobby)						
Born: Elphinstone, East Lothian, Scotland, 15 February, 1930						WH/IF
Died: Barnsley, South Yorkshire, England, September, 1997						
Barnsley	Hibernian	07/51	51-64	338	-	41
WOOD Royden (Roy)						
Born: Wallasey, Wirral, England, 16 October, 1930						G
Leeds U	Clitheroe	05/52	53-59	196	-	0
WOOD Samuel James (Sam)						
Born: Sidcup, SE London, England, 9 August, 1986						LB/M
Brentford	Bromley	06/08	08-11	90	18	4
Rotherham U	L	11/11	11	24	2	1
Wycombe W	Tr	07/12	12-14	118	4	10
WOOD Simon Onward						
Born: Hull, England, 24 September, 1976						M
Coventry C	YT	11/93				
Mansfield T	Tr	03/96	95-96	32	9	4
WOOD Stephen Alan (Steve)						
Born: Bracknell, Berkshire, England, 2 February, 1963						CD
Reading	App	02/81	79-86	216	3	9
Millwall	Tr	06/87	87-91	108	2	0
Southampton	Tr	10/91	91-93	46	0	0
Oxford U	Tr	07/94	94-95	12	1	0
WOOD Steven Ronald (Steve)						
Born: Oldham, Greater Manchester, England, 23 June, 1963						M
Macclesfield T	Ashton U	07/93	97-00	129	22	19
WOOD Terence Laurence (Terry)						
Born: Newport, Wales, 3 September, 1920						WH
Cardiff C (Am)	Newport Docks	09/46	46	4	-	0
WOOD Thomas Leslie (Les)						
Born: Haslingden, Lancashire, England, 20 December, 1932						G
Died: Manchester, England, 24 January, 2005						
Wales: Schools						
Huddersfield T	Bolton W (Am)	04/52				
Barrow	Tr	08/55	55	31	-	0
Port Vale	Tr	06/56	56	2	-	0
Southport	Tr	01/58	57	1	-	0
WOOD Trevor John						
Born: Jersey, Channel Islands, 3 November, 1968						G

League Club	Source	Date Signed	Seasons Played	Apps	Subs	Gls

Northern Ireland: 1/B

League Club	Source	Date Signed	Seasons Played	Apps	Subs	Gls
Brighton & HA	App	11/86				
Port Vale	Tr	07/88	88-92	42	0	0
Walsall	Tr	07/94	94-96	69	0	0
Hereford U	Tr	01/97	96	19	0	0

WOOD William (Bill)
Born: Barnsley, South Yorkshire, England, 28 December, 1927 — LB

League Club	Source	Date Signed	Seasons Played	Apps	Subs	Gls
Sunderland	Spen Jnrs	10/48	49	1	-	0
Hull C	Tr	07/51				
Sheffield U	Tr	06/52	52	5	-	0

WOOD William Ronald (Ron)
Born: Manchester, England, 11 November, 1925 — IF
Died: Manchester, England, April, 2012

League Club	Source	Date Signed	Seasons Played	Apps	Subs	Gls
Wrexham	Droylsden	11/49	49	16	-	5

WOODALL Arthur John
Born: Stoke-on-Trent, England, 4 June, 1930 — LW
Died: Winsford, Cheshire, England, 14 May, 2005

League Club	Source	Date Signed	Seasons Played	Apps	Subs	Gls
Stoke C	Jnr	05/50	53	1	-	0

WOODALL Bertram John (John)
Born: Goole, East Riding of Yorkshire, England, 16 January, 1949 — F

League Club	Source	Date Signed	Seasons Played	Apps	Subs	Gls
York C	Goole T	02/67	67	2	0	0
Rotherham U	Gainsborough Trinity	03/74	73-74	25	1	6

WOODALL Brian
Born: Bielefeld, Germany, 28 December, 1987 — F

League Club	Source	Date Signed	Seasons Played	Apps	Subs	Gls
Dagenham & Red	Gresley FC	07/11	11-13	39	36	13

WOODALL Brian Harold
Born: Chester, England, 6 June, 1948 — LW
Died: Chester, England, 4 May, 2007

League Club	Source	Date Signed	Seasons Played	Apps	Subs	Gls
Sheffield Wed	App	06/65	67-69	19	3	4
Oldham Ath	L	02/70	69	3	1	1
Chester C	Tr	06/70	70	11	2	2
Crewe Alex	L	03/71	70	10	1	3

WOODARDS Daniel Mark (Danny)
Born: Forest Gate, E London, England, 7 October, 1983 — RB

League Club	Source	Date Signed	Seasons Played	Apps	Subs	Gls
Chelsea	Sch	07/03				
Crewe Alex	Exeter C	01/07	06-08	80	4	0
MK Dons	Tr	07/09	09-10	59	7	1
Bristol Rov	Tr	08/11	11-13	65	5	4
Tranmere Rov	Tr	07/14	14	4	1	0

WOODBURN James (Jimmy)
Born: Rutherglen, Glasgow, Scotland, 29 January, 1917 — LH
Died: Leeds, England, 2 January, 1978

League Club	Source	Date Signed	Seasons Played	Apps	Subs	Gls
Newcastle U	Coltness U	02/38	38-47	44	-	4
Gateshead	Tr	09/48	48-51	131	-	10

WOODCOCK Anthony Stewart (Tony)
Born: Eastwood, Nottinghamshire, England, 6 December, 1955 — F
England: 42/B-1/U21-2

League Club	Source	Date Signed	Seasons Played	Apps	Subs	Gls
Nottingham F	App	01/74	73-79	125	4	36
Lincoln C	L	02/76	75	2	2	1
Doncaster Rov	L	09/76	76	6	0	2
Arsenal	FC Cologne (GER)	07/82	82-85	129	2	56

WOODCOCK David Keith
Born: Long Eaton, Derbyshire, England, 13 October, 1966 — M

League Club	Source	Date Signed	Seasons Played	Apps	Subs	Gls
Sunderland	App	10/84				
Darlington	Tr	08/85	85-86	14	13	2

WOODCOCK Ernest (Ernie)
Born: Salford, England, 14 May, 1925 — W

League Club	Source	Date Signed	Seasons Played	Apps	Subs	Gls
Bury	Blackburn Rov (Am)	01/47	46-47	18	-	3
Oldham Ath	Tr	06/48	48-49	28	-	4

WOODCOCK Harold (Harry)
Born: Darlington, County Durham, England, 18 September, 1928 — IF
Died: Darlington, County Durham, England, 31 March, 2003

League Club	Source	Date Signed	Seasons Played	Apps	Subs	Gls
Darlington		08/52	52-53	5	-	0

WOODCOCK Thomas (Tommy)
Born: Chorley, Lancashire, England, 19 March, 1926 — IF
Died: Lancashire, England, September, 2007

League Club	Source	Date Signed	Seasons Played	Apps	Subs	Gls
Southport	Preston NE (Am)	07/46	46	1	-	0

WOODDIN Stephen (Steve)
Born: Birkenhead, Wirral, England, 6 January, 1955 — F
New Zealand: 24

League Club	Source	Date Signed	Seasons Played	Apps	Subs	Gls
Tranmere Rov	Cammell Laird	02/75	74	1	2	0

WOODFIELD David
Born: Leamington Spa, Warwickshire, England, 11 October, 1943 — CD

League Club	Source	Date Signed	Seasons Played	Apps	Subs	Gls
Wolverhampton W	Jnr	10/60	61-69	247	3	13
Watford	Tr	09/71	71-73	14	1	0

WOODFIELD Terry
Born: Nottingham, England, 21 January, 1946 — RH

League Club	Source	Date Signed	Seasons Played	Apps	Subs	Gls
Notts Co	Jnr	07/63	63	5	-	0

WOODFORD Robert Michael
Born: Keyworth, Nottinghamshire, England, 6 December, 1943 — RH

League Club	Source	Date Signed	Seasons Played	Apps	Subs	Gls
Notts Co	Jnr	03/61	61	3	-	0

WOODGATE John Terence (Terry)
Born: East Ham, E London, England, 11 December, 1919 — LW
Died: March, Cambridgeshire, England, 26 April, 1985

League Club	Source	Date Signed	Seasons Played	Apps	Subs	Gls
West Ham U	Beckton	09/38	38-52	259	-	48

WOODGATE Jonathan Simon
Born: Middlesbrough, England, 22 January, 1980 — CD
England: 8/U21-1/Youth

League Club	Source	Date Signed	Seasons Played	Apps	Subs	Gls
Leeds U	YT	05/97	98-02	100	4	4
Newcastle U	Tr	01/03	02-03	28	0	0
Middlesbrough	Real Madrid (SPN)	08/06	06-07	46	0	0
Tottenham H	Tr	01/08	07-09	49	0	2
Stoke C	Tr	07/11	11	16	1	0
Middlesbrough	Tr	07/12	12-14	53	3	2

WOODHEAD Andrew
Born: Wallsend, Tyne and Wear, England, 12 July, 1966 — M

League Club	Source	Date Signed	Seasons Played	Apps	Subs	Gls
Gillingham	App	-	83	1	1	0

WOODHEAD Dennis
Born: Huddersfield, West Yorkshire, England, 2 September, 1924 — LW
Died: Huddersfield, West Yorkshire, England, January, 2001

League Club	Source	Date Signed	Seasons Played	Apps	Subs	Gls
Bradford C		01/48				
Accrington Stan	Tr	05/48	48	6	-	0

WOODHEAD Dennis
Born: Hillsborough, South Yorkshire, England, 12 June, 1925 — LW
Died: Sheffield, England, 26 July, 1995

League Club	Source	Date Signed	Seasons Played	Apps	Subs	Gls
Sheffield Wed	Hillsborough BC	04/45	46-54	213	-	73
Chesterfield	Tr	09/55	55	15	-	6
Derby Co	Tr	01/56	55-58	94	-	24
Southport	L	02/59	58	4	-	1

WOODHEAD Simon Christopher
Born: Dewsbury, West Yorkshire, England, 26 December, 1962 — FB/F

League Club	Source	Date Signed	Seasons Played	Apps	Subs	Gls
Mansfield T	Jnr	09/80	80-84	108	14	6
Crewe Alex	Tr	08/85				

WOODHOUSE Curtis
Born: Driffield, East Riding of Yorkshire, England, 17 April, 1980 — M
England: U21-4/Youth

League Club	Source	Date Signed	Seasons Played	Apps	Subs	Gls
Sheffield U	YT	12/97	97-00	92	12	6
Birmingham C	Tr	02/01	00-02	35	13	2
Rotherham U	L	02/03	02	11	0	0
Peterborough U	Tr	10/03	03-04	58	3	11
Hull C	Tr	05/05	05	14	4	0
Grimsby T	Tr	01/06	05	16	0	1

WOODHOUSE John
Born: Middlesbrough, England, 5 April, 1937 — RW

League Club	Source	Date Signed	Seasons Played	Apps	Subs	Gls
Leeds U	South Bank	06/55				
Gateshead	Tr	07/57	57	2	-	0

WOODLAND Luke
Born: Abu Dhabi, United Arab Emirates, 21 July, 1995 — M
England: Youth

League Club	Source	Date Signed	Seasons Played	Apps	Subs	Gls
Bolton W	Sch	07/13				
Oldham Ath	L	03/15	14	6	0	0

WOODLEY Derek George
Born: Isleworth, W London, England, 2 March, 1942 — RW
Died: Southend-on-Sea, England, 29 September, 2002
England: Youth/Schools

League Club	Source	Date Signed	Seasons Played	Apps	Subs	Gls
West Ham U	Jnr	04/59	59-61	12	-	3
Southend U	Tr	08/62	62-66	160	2	23
Charlton Ath	Tr	06/67	67	2	1	0
Southend U	Tr	10/67	67	7	2	0
Gillingham	Tr	01/68	67-70	99	1	9

WOODLEY Victor Robert (Vic)
Born: Slough, Berkshire, England, 26 February, 1910 — G
Died: Bradford-on-Avon, Wiltshire, England, 23 October, 1978
England: 19/FLge-4/War-2

League Club	Source	Date Signed	Seasons Played	Apps	Subs	Gls
Chelsea	Windsor & Eton	05/31	31-38	252	-	0
Derby Co	Bath C	03/46	46	30	-	0

WOODMAN Andrew John (Andy)
Born: Camberwell, S London, England, 11 August, 1971 — G

League Club	Source	Date Signed	Seasons Played	Apps	Subs	Gls
Crystal Palace	YT	07/89				
Exeter C	Tr	07/94	94	6	0	0
Northampton T	Tr	03/95	94-98	163	0	0
Brentford	Tr	01/99	98-99	61	0	0

League Club	Source	Date Signed	Seasons Played	Apps	Subs	Gls
Southend U	L	08/00	00	17	0	0
Colchester U	Tr	11/00	00-01	54	0	0
Oxford U	Tr	01/02	01-03	101	0	0
Rushden & D	Thurrock	07/05	05	3	0	0

WOODMAN Craig Alan
Born: Tiverton, Devon, England, 22 December, 1982 — LB

League Club	Source	Date Signed	Seasons Played	Apps	Subs	Gls
Bristol C	YT	02/00	00-06	71	19	1
Mansfield T	L	09/04	04	8	0	1
Torquay U	L	12/04	04	20	2	1
Torquay U	L	11/05	05	2	0	0
Wycombe W	Tr	07/07	07-09	117	2	2
Brentford	Tr	07/10	10-11	58	1	1
Exeter C	Tr	07/12	12-14	116	1	1

WOODROFFE Lewis Christopher (Lew)
Born: Portsmouth, England, 29 October, 1921 — RW

League Club	Source	Date Signed	Seasons Played	Apps	Subs	Gls
Manchester C		10/45	46	9	-	1
Watford	Tr	08/47	47-50	64	-	6

WOODROW Cauley Martin
Born: Hemel Hempstead, Hertfordshire, England, 2 December, 1994 — F
England: U21-1/Youth

League Club	Source	Date Signed	Seasons Played	Apps	Subs	Gls
Fulham	Sch	12/11	13-14	15	20	4
Southend U	L	09/13	13	10	9	2

WOODRUFF Arthur
Born: Barnsley, South Yorkshire, England, 12 April, 1913 — RB
Died: Burnley, Lancashire, England, 5 January, 1983
England: FLge-2

League Club	Source	Date Signed	Seasons Played	Apps	Subs	Gls
Bradford C	Huddersfield T (Am)	08/34				
Burnley	Tr	07/36	36-51	271	-	0
Workington	Tr	07/52	52	11	-	0

WOODRUFF Robert James (Bobby)
Born: Wolverhampton, England, 11 March, 1965 — F
Wales: Youth/Schools

League Club	Source	Date Signed	Seasons Played	Apps	Subs	Gls
Newport Co	Cardiff C (Jnr)	08/83	83	9	1	0
Swindon T	L	05/84	83	1	1	0

WOODRUFF Robert William (Bobby)
Born: Highworth, Wiltshire, England, 9 November, 1940 — M/F

League Club	Source	Date Signed	Seasons Played	Apps	Subs	Gls
Swindon T	Jnr	05/58	58-63	180	-	20
Wolverhampton W	Tr	03/64	63-65	63	0	18
Crystal Palace	Tr	06/66	66-69	123	2	48
Cardiff C	Tr	11/69	69-73	141	9	22
Newport Co	Tr	08/74	74-75	52	0	7

WOODS Alan Edward
Born: Dinnington, South Yorkshire, England, 15 February, 1937 — RH
England: Youth/Schools

League Club	Source	Date Signed	Seasons Played	Apps	Subs	Gls
Tottenham H	Jnr	02/54	54	6	-	0
Swansea C	Tr	12/56	57-58	30	-	0
York C	Tr	07/60	60-65	227	1	4

WOODS Calum Jack
Born: Liverpool, England, 5 February, 1987 — FB

League Club	Source	Date Signed	Seasons Played	Apps	Subs	Gls
Huddersfield T	Dunfermline Ath	06/11	11-13	54	18	1
Preston NE	Tr	06/14	14	12	6	0

WOODS Charles Morgan Parkinson (Charlie)
Born: Whitehaven, Cumbria, England, 18 March, 1941 — IF/W

League Club	Source	Date Signed	Seasons Played	Apps	Subs	Gls
Newcastle U	Cleator Moor Celtic	05/59	60-61	26	-	7
Bournemouth	Tr	11/62	62-64	70	-	26
Crystal Palace	Tr	11/64	64-65	49	0	5
Ipswich T	Tr	07/66	66-69	65	17	5
Watford	Tr	06/70	70-71	40	2	3
Colchester U	L	11/71	71	3	0	0
Blackburn Rov	Tr	07/72				

WOODS Christopher Charles Eric (Chris)
Born: Swineshead, Lincolnshire, England, 14 November, 1959 — G
England: 43/B-2/U21-6/Youth

League Club	Source	Date Signed	Seasons Played	Apps	Subs	Gls
Nottingham F	App	12/76				
Queens Park Rgrs	Tr	07/79	79-80	63	0	0
Norwich C	Tr	03/81	80-85	216	0	0
Sheffield Wed	Glasgow Rangers	08/91	91-95	106	1	0
Reading	L	10/95	95	5	0	0
Southampton	Colorado Rapids (USA)	11/96	96	4	0	0
Burnley	Tr	06/97	97	12	0	0

WOODS Clive Richard
Born: Norwich, England, 18 December, 1947 — LW

League Club	Source	Date Signed	Seasons Played	Apps	Subs	Gls
Ipswich T	Wisbech T	06/69	69-79	217	50	24
Norwich C	Tr	03/80	79-81	29	3	4

WOODS Darragh William (Billy)
Born: Cork, Republic of Ireland, 24 October, 1973 — W
Republic of Ireland: U21-6/Youth

League Club	Source	Date Signed	Seasons Played	Apps	Subs	Gls
Coventry C	YT	07/92				
Tranmere Rov	Cork C (ROI)	07/95	96	1	0	0
Blackpool	L	10/96	96	3	0	0

WOODS Dennis James
Born: Norwich, England, 12 December, 1936 — RW

League Club	Source	Date Signed	Seasons Played	Apps	Subs	Gls
Watford	Cambridge U	10/62	62	13	-	2

WOODS Derek Edward
Born: Northampton, England, 23 March, 1941 — RW
England: Amateur-2

League Club	Source	Date Signed	Seasons Played	Apps	Subs	Gls
Northampton T (Am)	Jnr	06/59	61	6	-	2

WOODS Edward (Eddie)
Born: Ton Pentre, Rhondda Cynon Taff, Wales, 29 July, 1951 — F

League Club	Source	Date Signed	Seasons Played	Apps	Subs	Gls
Bristol C	Ton Pentre	09/71	72	1	1	0
Scunthorpe U	L	10/73	73	4	0	2
Newport Co	Tr	09/74	74-78	149	2	54

WOODS Gary
Born: Kettering, Northamptonshire, England, 1 October, 1990 — G

League Club	Source	Date Signed	Seasons Played	Apps	Subs	Gls
Doncaster Rov	Manchester U (Sch)	03/09	08-12	72	1	0
Watford	Tr	09/13				
Leyton Orient	Tr	07/14	14	16	1	0

WOODS Jonathan Paul
Born: Blackwood, Caerphilly, Wales, 5 October, 1966 — F

League Club	Source	Date Signed	Seasons Played	Apps	Subs	Gls
Cardiff C	Jnr	08/84	84	0	1	0

WOODS Kenneth Stephen (Kenny)
Born: Liverpool, England, 15 April, 1974 — M

League Club	Source	Date Signed	Seasons Played	Apps	Subs	Gls
Everton	YT	06/92				
Bury	Tr	07/93	93	0	2	0

WOODS Martin Paul
Born: Airdrie, Lanarkshire, Scotland, 1 January, 1986 — M
Scotland: U21-2/Youth

League Club	Source	Date Signed	Seasons Played	Apps	Subs	Gls
Leeds U	Sch	01/03	04	0	1	0
Hartlepool U	L	09/04	04	3	3	0
Sunderland	Tr	07/05	05	1	6	0
Rotherham U	Tr	08/06	06	31	5	4
Doncaster Rov	Tr	07/07	07-13	97	22	7
Yeovil T	L	02/08	07	3	0	0
Barnsley	Tr	01/14	13	6	2	0

WOODS Matthew James (Matt)
Born: Gosport, Hampshire, England, 9 September, 1976 — CD

League Club	Source	Date Signed	Seasons Played	Apps	Subs	Gls
Everton	YT	07/95				
Chester C	Tr	08/96	96-99	114	21	4

WOODS Maurice (Matt)
Born: Skelmersdale, Lancashire, England, 1 November, 1931 — CH
Died: Stockport, Greater Manchester, England, 26 September, 2014
England: FLge-1

League Club	Source	Date Signed	Seasons Played	Apps	Subs	Gls
Everton	Burscough	11/49	52-56	8	-	1
Blackburn Rov	Tr	11/56	56-62	260	-	2
Luton T	Sydney Hakoah (AUS)	07/65	65	34	0	0
Stockport Co	Tr	07/66	66-67	85	0	2

WOODS Michael James
Born: Pocklington, East Riding of Yorkshire, England, 6 April, 1990 — M
England: Youth

League Club	Source	Date Signed	Seasons Played	Apps	Subs	Gls
Chelsea	Sch	07/07				
Yeovil T		02/12	11	2	3	1
Doncaster Rov	Tr	10/12				
Hartlepool U	Harrogate T	08/14	14	16	7	1

WOODS Neil Stephen
Born: Goole, East Riding of Yorkshire, England, 30 July, 1966 — F

League Club	Source	Date Signed	Seasons Played	Apps	Subs	Gls
Doncaster Rov	App	01/83	82-86	55	10	16
Ipswich T	Glasgow Rangers	08/87	87-89	15	12	5
Bradford C	Tr	03/90	89	13	1	2
Grimsby T	Tr	08/90	90-97	175	51	42
Wigan Ath	L	11/97	97	1	0	0
Scunthorpe U	L	01/98	97	2	0	0
Mansfield T	L	02/98	97	5	1	0
York C	Tr	07/98	98	5	3	0

WOODS Patrick James (Pat)
Born: Islington, N London, England, 29 April, 1933 — RB
Died: Nambucca Heads, NSW, Australia, 14 August, 2012

League Club	Source	Date Signed	Seasons Played	Apps	Subs	Gls
Queens Park Rgrs	Jnr	06/50	52-60	304	-	15
Colchester U	Hellenic Ath (AUS)	08/63	63	36	-	0

WOODS Peter Anthony
Born: Sale, Greater Manchester, England, 21 January, 1950 — M/LB

League Club	Source	Date Signed	Seasons Played	Apps	Subs	Gls
Manchester U	App	04/67				
Luton T	Tr	04/70				
Southend U	Tr	02/72	71-72	25	0	0
Doncaster Rov	Tr	07/73	73-74	41	8	1

League Club	Source	Date Signed	Seasons Played	Career Record Apps	Subs	Gls
WOODS Raymond (Ray)						
Born: Peterborough, England, 27 April, 1930						RH
Southend U	Peterborough U	05/48	50-51	3	-	1
Crystal Palace	Tr	06/53	53-54	18	-	0
WOODS Raymond Guy (Ray)						
Born: Birkenhead, Wirral, England, 7 June, 1965						RW
Tranmere Rov	App	06/83	82-84	9	5	2
Wigan Ath	Colne Dynamoes	03/89	88-90	25	3	3
Coventry C	Tr	01/91	90-91	21	0	1
Wigan Ath	L	01/93	92	12	1	0
Shrewsbury T	Tr	03/94	93-95	40	11	1
WOODS Ryan Michael						
Born: Cannock, Staffordshire, England, 13 December, 1993						M/RB
Shrewsbury T	Sch	07/12	12-14	78	8	1
WOODS Stephen Gerard (Steve)						
Born: Glasgow, Scotland, 23 February, 1970						G
Preston NE	Clydebank	10/93	93	19	1	0
WOODS Stephen John (Steve)						
Born: Northwich, Cheshire, England, 15 December, 1976						CD
Stoke C	YT	08/95	97-98	33	1	0
Plymouth Arg	L	03/98	97	4	1	0
Chesterfield	Tr	07/99	99	22	3	0
Torquay U	Tr	08/01	01-06	192	7	10
WOODS William (Billy)						
Born: Farnworth, Greater Manchester, England, 12 March, 1926						IF
Died: Rugby, Warwickshire, England, 1980						
Rochdale	Moss Grove	04/45	46	15	-	1
Bradford Park Ave	Tr	01/47	46	5	-	0
Rochdale	Tr	01/49	48-49	13	-	1
Barrow	Tr	11/49	49	16	-	3
Crewe Alex	Tr	07/50				
Accrington Stan	Tr	11/50	50	3	-	0
WOODSFORD Jamie Marcus						
Born: Ipswich, England, 9 November, 1976						F
England: Youth						
Luton T	YT	03/95	94-95	2	8	0
WOODTHORPE Colin John						
Born: Ellesmere Port, Cheshire, England, 13 January, 1969						LB
Chester C	App	08/86	86-89	154	1	6
Norwich C	Tr	07/90	90-93	36	7	1
Stockport Co	Aberdeen	07/97	97-01	114	39	4
Bury	Tr	08/02	02-07	171	10	1
WOODWARD Alan						
Born: Chapeltown, South Yorkshire, England, 7 September, 1946						RW
Died: Tulsa, Oklahoma, USA, 21 May, 2015						
England: FLge-2/Youth						
Sheffield U	App	09/63	64-78	536	2	158
WOODWARD Alan						
Born: Sutton-in-Ashfield, Nottinghamshire, England, 19 June, 1947						W
Grimsby T	Alfreton T	07/70	70-71	54	0	13
WOODWARD Andrew Stephen (Andy)						
Born: Stockport, Greater Manchester, England, 23 September, 1973						RB/M
Crewe Alex	YT	07/92	92-94	9	11	0
Bury	Tr	03/95	94-99	95	20	1
Sheffield U	Tr	03/00	99	2	1	0
Scunthorpe U	L	09/00	00	12	0	0
Halifax T	Tr	07/01	01	29	1	1
WOODWARD Brian						
Born: Leeds, England, 12 July, 1929						CF
Leeds U	Jnr	07/47				
York C	Hereford U	08/50	50	5	-	0
WOODWARD Harry George						
Born: Bromley, SE London, England, 29 August, 1919						CH
Died: Barking, E London, England, September, 1984						
Southend U	Chelmsford C	05/46	50-51	14	-	0
WOODWARD Horace John (Johnny)						
Born: Islington, N London, England, 16 January, 1924						CH
Died: Cricklewood, NW London, England, 3 August, 2002						
Tottenham H	Jnr	05/46	46-48	63	-	1
Queens Park Rgrs	Tr	06/49	49-50	57	-	0
Walsall	Snowdown CW	07/53	53	5	-	0
WOODWARD John						
Born: Stoke-on-Trent, England, 16 January, 1947						F
Stoke C	App	03/64	64-66	10	1	1
Aston Villa	Tr	10/66	66-68	22	4	7
Walsall	Tr	05/69	69-72	116	9	23
Port Vale	Tr	02/73	72-74	88	11	30
Scunthorpe U	Tr	07/75	75	16	3	5
WOODWARD John						
Born: Glasgow, Scotland, 10 January, 1949						M/D
Scotland: Youth						
Arsenal	Possilpark YMCA	01/66	66	2	1	0
York C	Tr	07/71	71-77	152	15	6
WOODWARD Kenneth Robert (Ken)						
Born: Battersea, SW London, England, 16 November, 1947						W
Crystal Palace	App	12/65				
Leyton Orient	Tr	08/66	66	1	0	0
WOODWARD Laurence (Dai)						
Born: Troedyrhiw, Merthyr Tydfil, Wales, 5 July, 1918						WH
Died: Bournemouth, England, December, 1997						
Wolverhampton W	Folkestone	05/38				
Walsall	L	11/38	38	29	-	0
Bournemouth	Tr	05/39	46-53	272	-	7
WOODWARD Thomas (Tom)						
Born: Westhoughton, Greater Manchester, England, 8 December, 1917						RW
Died: Bolton, Greater Manchester, England, November, 1994						
Bolton W	White Horse Temperance	01/35	35-49	152	-	18
Middlesbrough	Tr	10/49	49-50	19	-	6
WOODWARD Thomas Peter (Peter)						
Born: Birmingham, England, 6 July, 1934						G
Died: St Neots, Cambridgeshire, England, 6 January, 2012						
West Bromwich A	Moor Green	09/54				
Walsall	Tr	08/58	58	13	-	0
WOODWARD Vivian						
Born: Troedyrhiw, Merthyr Tydfil, Wales, 20 May, 1914						IF/WH
Wales: War-1						
Fulham	Folkestone	01/36	35-46	92	-	25
Millwall	Tr	02/47	46-47	42	-	13
Brentford	Tr	07/48	48-49	20	-	4
Aldershot	Tr	02/50	49-50	53	-	5
WOODWORTH Anthony David (Tony)						
Born: Manchester, England, 5 March, 1968						G
Burnley	App	03/86	86	1	0	0
WOODYARD Alexander James (Alex)						
Born: Gravesend, Kent, England, 16 November, 1992						M
Southend U	Sch	07/11	10-12	7	1	0
WOOF Clifford Eric (Cliff)						
Born: Liverpool, England, 20 September, 1956						F
Liverpool	Jnr	05/76				
Southport	Jacob's, Aintree	12/77	77	1	0	0
WOOF William (Billy)						
Born: Gateshead, Tyne and Wear, England, 16 August, 1956						F
Middlesbrough	App	08/74	74-81	30	16	5
Peterborough U	L	03/77	76	2	1	0
Cardiff C	Blyth Spartans	09/82	82	1	0	1
Hull C	Gateshead	02/83	82	9	2	3
WOOKEY Kenneth George (Ken)						
Born: Newport, Wales, 30 December, 1946						RW/F
Died: Taunton, Somerset, England, 16 December, 1992						
Newport Co	Jnr	01/64	64-68	57	6	6
Port Vale	Tr	07/69	69	23	1	4
Workington	Tr	07/70	70	11	6	4
WOOKEY Kenneth William (Ken)						
Born: Newport, Wales, 23 February, 1922						RW
Died: Newport, Wales, 11 January, 2003						
Wales: Schools						
Newport Co	Jnr	02/39	46	14	-	2
Bristol Rov	Tr	12/46	46-48	54	-	9
Swansea C	Tr	11/48	48-49	12	-	0
Ipswich T	Hereford U	10/50	50	15	-	1
WOOLCOTT Roy Alfred						
Born: Leyton, NE London, England, 29 July, 1946						F
Tottenham H	Eton Manor	02/68	69	1	0	0
Gillingham	L	02/72	71	13	0	5
WOOLDRIDGE James (Jim)						
Born: Rossington, South Yorkshire, England, 28 September, 1918						LB
Died: North Yorkshire, England, 10 November, 2008						
Doncaster Rov	Benburb Jnrs	12/40	46-47	30	-	0
WOOLDRIDGE Stephen Joseph (Steve)						
Born: Chiswick, W London, England, 18 July, 1950						RB
Crystal Palace	App	07/67				

League Club	Source	Date Signed	Seasons Played	Apps	Subs	Gls
Plymouth Arg	L	08/70	70	20	0	0
Colchester U	Tr	06/72	72	3	0	0

WOOLER Alan Thomas
Born: Poole, Dorset, England, 17 August, 1953 — LB

League Club	Source	Date Signed	Seasons Played	Apps	Subs	Gls
Reading	Weymouth	11/71	71-72	38	0	0
West Ham U	Tr	08/73	73-75	3	1	0
Aldershot	Tr	04/76	76-83	264	2	3

WOOLER Michael Graham (Graham)
Born: Huddersfield, West Yorkshire, England, 23 October, 1944 — F

League Club	Source	Date Signed	Seasons Played	Apps	Subs	Gls
Huddersfield T		08/64				
Halifax T	Tr	12/64	64-67	50	7	7

WOOLERY Kaiyne River
Born: Hackney, E London, England, 11 January, 1995 — W

League Club	Source	Date Signed	Seasons Played	Apps	Subs	Gls
Bolton W	Tamworth	08/14	14	0	1	0
Notts Co	L	01/15	14	3	2	0

WOOLFALL Alan Francis
Born: Liverpool, England, 30 November, 1956 — RW

League Club	Source	Date Signed	Seasons Played	Apps	Subs	Gls
Bury	Skelmersdale U	10/74	74-78	46	11	11
Port Vale	Tr	08/79	79-80	13	5	3

WOOLFORD Martyn Paul
Born: Castleford, West Yorkshire, England, 13 October, 1985 — LW
England: Semi Pro-2

League Club	Source	Date Signed	Seasons Played	Apps	Subs	Gls
Scunthorpe U	York C	08/08	08-10	79	24	15
Bristol C	Tr	01/11	10-12	31	24	4
Millwall	Tr	01/13	12-14	79	14	11

WOOLFORD Michael Elijah George (Mike)
Born: Swindon, England, 29 September, 1939 — IF

League Club	Source	Date Signed	Seasons Played	Apps	Subs	Gls
Swindon T	Swindon British Rail	12/59	59	3	-	0

WOOLGAR James Stewart (Stewart)
Born: Chesterfield, Derbyshire, England, 21 September, 1952 — M

League Club	Source	Date Signed	Seasons Played	Apps	Subs	Gls
West Bromwich A	App	10/69	72	2	2	0
Doncaster Rov	Tr	07/74	74	2	5	1

WOOLGAR Philip Robert John (Phil)
Born: Worthing, West Sussex, England, 24 September, 1948 — G

League Club	Source	Date Signed	Seasons Played	Apps	Subs	Gls
Brighton & HA (Am)	Wigmore Ath	06/66	66	1	0	0

WOOLISCROFT Ashley David
Born: Stoke-on-Trent, England, 28 December, 1979 — RB

League Club	Source	Date Signed	Seasons Played	Apps	Subs	Gls
Stoke C	YT	02/97	98	0	1	0

WOOLLARD Arnold James
Born: Pembroke, Bermuda, 24 August, 1930 — FB

League Club	Source	Date Signed	Seasons Played	Apps	Subs	Gls
Northampton T	Bermuda AA (BER)	06/49	50	3	-	0
Newcastle U	Peterborough U	12/52	52-55	8	-	0
Bournemouth	Tr	06/56	56-61	159	-	0
Northampton T	Tr	03/62	61-62	28	-	0

WOOLLETT Alan Howard
Born: Wigston, Leicestershire, England, 4 March, 1947 — D

League Club	Source	Date Signed	Seasons Played	Apps	Subs	Gls
Leicester C	App	08/64	66-77	212	15	0
Northampton T	Tr	07/78	78	23	0	0

WOOLLETT Charles (Charlie)
Born: Seaham, County Durham, England, 25 November, 1920 — LW
Died: Peterlee, County Durham, England, 16 July, 2011

League Club	Source	Date Signed	Seasons Played	Apps	Subs	Gls
Newcastle U	Eppleton CW	11/42				
Bradford C	Tr	08/46	46-48	43	-	5
York C	Murton CW	02/49	48	4	-	0

WOOLLEY Matthew David (Matt)
Born: Manchester, England, 22 February, 1982 — M

League Club	Source	Date Signed	Seasons Played	Apps	Subs	Gls
Macclesfield T	Stockport Co (YT)	07/99	00-01	1	4	0

WOOLLEY Robert Alan
Born: Nottingham, England, 29 December, 1947 — CF
Died: Arnold, Nottinghamshire, England, 2 October, 1971

League Club	Source	Date Signed	Seasons Played	Apps	Subs	Gls
Notts Co	App	07/65	63-65	9	0	2

WOOLMER Anthony John (Tony)
Born: Swardeston, Norfolk, England, 25 March, 1946 — F

League Club	Source	Date Signed	Seasons Played	Apps	Subs	Gls
Norwich C	Jnr	12/65	66-67	4	1	1
Bradford Park Ave	Tr	10/69	69	30	0	7
Scunthorpe U	Tr	11/70	70-71	35	5	2

WOOLSEY Jeffrey Alexander (Jeff)
Born: Upminster, E London, England, 8 November, 1977 — CD

League Club	Source	Date Signed	Seasons Played	Apps	Subs	Gls
Arsenal	YT	07/96				
Queens Park Rgrs	Tr	08/97				
Brighton & HA	Tr	03/98	97	1	2	0

WOON Andrew Geoffrey (Andy)
Born: Bognor Regis, West Sussex, England, 26 June, 1952 — F

League Club	Source	Date Signed	Seasons Played	Apps	Subs	Gls
Brentford	Bognor Regis T	10/72	72-74	42	8	12

WOOSNAM Philip Abraham (Phil)
Born: Caersws, Powys, Wales, 22 December, 1932 — IF
Died: Atlanta, USA, 19 July, 2013
England: FLge-1//Wales: 17/Amateur/Schools

League Club	Source	Date Signed	Seasons Played	Apps	Subs	Gls
Manchester C (Am)	Bangor C	06/52	52	1	-	0
Leyton Orient	Sutton U	03/55	54-58	108	-	19
West Ham U	Tr	11/58	58-62	138	-	26
Aston Villa	Tr	11/62	62-65	106	0	24

WOOTER Nordin
Born: Breda, Netherlands, 24 August, 1976 — RW
Netherlands: U21-15

League Club	Source	Date Signed	Seasons Played	Apps	Subs	Gls
Watford	Real Zaragoza (SPN)	09/99	99-01	37	26	3

WOOTTON Jamie
Born: Rotherham, South Yorkshire, England, 2 October, 1994 — F

League Club	Source	Date Signed	Seasons Played	Apps	Subs	Gls
Scunthorpe U	Sch	07/13	12-13	0	2	0

WOOTTON Kyle Leon
Born: Epworth, North Lincolnshire, England, 11 October, 1996 — F

League Club	Source	Date Signed	Seasons Played	Apps	Subs	Gls
Scunthorpe U	Sch	01/15	14	1	11	1

WOOTTON Leonard (Len)
Born: Stoke-on-Trent, England, 13 June, 1925 — IF
Died: Stoke-on-Trent, England, 9 September, 1990

League Club	Source	Date Signed	Seasons Played	Apps	Subs	Gls
Port Vale	Everton (Am)	08/45	46	10	-	1
Wrexham	Queen of the South	08/51	51	20	-	2

WOOTTON Scott James
Born: Birkenhead, Wirral, England, 12 September, 1991 — CD
England: Youth

League Club	Source	Date Signed	Seasons Played	Apps	Subs	Gls
Manchester U	Sch	07/09				
Tranmere Rov	L	09/10	10	7	0	1
Peterborough U	L	08/11	11	7	4	0
Nottingham F	L	01/12	11	7	6	0
Peterborough U	L	01/13	12	2	0	1
Leeds U	Tr	08/13	13-14	42	1	0
Rotherham U	L	11/14	14	7	0	0

WOOZLEY David James
Born: Windsor, Berkshire, England, 6 December, 1979 — CD

League Club	Source	Date Signed	Seasons Played	Apps	Subs	Gls
Crystal Palace	YT	11/97	98-99	21	9	0
Bournemouth	L	09/00	00	6	0	0
Torquay U	L	08/01	01	12	0	0
Torquay U	Tr	03/02	01-03	52	8	3
Oxford U	Tr	07/04	04	11	2	1
Yeovil T	L	03/05	04	0	1	0

WORBOYS Gavin Anthony
Born: Doncaster, South Yorkshire, England, 14 July, 1974 — F

League Club	Source	Date Signed	Seasons Played	Apps	Subs	Gls
Doncaster Rov	YT	04/92	91	6	1	2
Notts Co	Tr	05/92				
Exeter C	L	12/93	93	4	0	1
Darlington	Tr	11/94	94-95	30	11	8
Northampton T	Tr	01/96	95	4	9	1

WORDLEY Edward Henry (Ted)
Born: Stoke-on-Trent, England, 17 October, 1923 — LH
Died: Stoke-on-Trent, England, April, 1989

League Club	Source	Date Signed	Seasons Played	Apps	Subs	Gls
Stoke C	Jnr	10/41	46-49	10	-	0
Bury	Tr	06/50				

WORDSWORTH Anthony Daniel
Born: Camden, N London, England, 3 January, 1989 — M

League Club	Source	Date Signed	Seasons Played	Apps	Subs	Gls
Colchester U	Sch	07/07	07-12	139	38	35
Ipswich T	Tr	01/13	12-14	8	10	2
Rotherham U	L	08/14	14	3	3	1
Crawley T	L	01/15	14	18	0	4

WORGAN Lee John
Born: Eastbourne, East Sussex, England, 1 December, 1983 — G
Wales: U21-5/Youth

League Club	Source	Date Signed	Seasons Played	Apps	Subs	Gls
Wimbledon	Sch	04/03	03	0	3	0
Wycombe W	L	04/04	03	2	0	0
Rushden & D	Tr	08/04	04	7	0	0

WORKMAN Peter Ian (Ian)
Born: Liverpool, England, 13 November, 1962 — M

League Club	Source	Date Signed	Seasons Played	Apps	Subs	Gls
Chester C	Southport	01/83	82	3	0	0

WORLEY Harry Jonathan
Born: Lymm, Cheshire, England, 25 November, 1988 — CD

League Club	Source	Date Signed	Seasons Played	Apps	Subs	Gls
Chelsea	Stockport Co (Jnr)	12/05				
Doncaster Rov	L	03/07	06	10	0	0
Carlisle U	L	08/07	07	1	0	0
Leicester C	Tr	03/08	07	1	1	0
Luton T	L	09/08	08	6	2	0
Crewe Alex	L	08/09	09	21	2	1
Oxford U	Tr	07/10	10-12	49	13	2

League Club	Source	Date Signed	Seasons Played	Apps	Subs	Gls
Newport Co	Tr	06/13	13	26	0	4
Stevenage	Tr	06/14	14	3	0	0

WORLEY Leonard Francis (Len)
Born: Amersham, Buckinghamshire, England, 27 June, 1937 — LW
England: Amateur-7/Youth

League Club	Source	Date Signed	Seasons Played	Apps	Subs	Gls
Charlton Ath (Am)	Wycombe W	10/56	56	1	-	0
Tottenham H (Am)	Wycombe W	05/59	59	1	-	0

WORMLEY Paul
Born: Leeds, England, 16 September, 1961 — F

League Club	Source	Date Signed	Seasons Played	Apps	Subs	Gls
Barnsley	Yorkshire Amats	10/79	79	1	0	0

WORMULL Simon James
Born: Crawley, West Sussex, England, 1 December, 1976 — M
England: Semi Pro-5

League Club	Source	Date Signed	Seasons Played	Apps	Subs	Gls
Tottenham H	YT	07/95				
Brentford	Tr	07/97	97	3	2	0
Brighton & HA	Tr	03/98				
Rushden & D	Dover Ath	03/00	01	4	1	0

WORNER Ross Nicholas
Born: Hindhead, Surrey, England, 3 October, 1989 — G

League Club	Source	Date Signed	Seasons Played	Apps	Subs	Gls
Charlton Ath	Woking	08/10	10	7	1	0
Aldershot T	Tr	07/11	11-12	23	0	0
AFC Wimbledon	Tr	06/13	13-14	50	0	0

WORRALL Benjamin Joseph (Ben)
Born: Swindon, England, 7 December, 1975 — M
England: Youth

League Club	Source	Date Signed	Seasons Played	Apps	Subs	Gls
Swindon T	YT	07/94	94	1	2	0
Scarborough	Tr	08/96	96-98	45	22	3
Exeter C	Tr	08/99	99	1	3	0

WORRALL David Richard
Born: Manchester, England, 12 June, 1990 — RM

League Club	Source	Date Signed	Seasons Played	Apps	Subs	Gls
Bury	Sch	06/06	06	0	1	0
West Bromwich A	Tr	07/07				
Accrington Stan	L	08/08	08	1	3	0
Shrewsbury T	L	03/09	08	7	2	0
Bury	Tr	08/09	09-12	127	35	11
Rotherham U	Tr	06/13	13	1	2	1
Oldham Ath	L	01/14	13	17	1	1
Southend U	Tr	07/14	14	23	15	6

WORRALL Frederick (Fred)
Born: Warrington, Cheshire, England, 8 September, 1910 — W
Died: Warrington, Cheshire, England, 13 April, 1979
England: 2/FLge-2

League Club	Source	Date Signed	Seasons Played	Apps	Subs	Gls
Oldham Ath	Nantwich	12/28	28-31	105	-	21
Portsmouth	Tr	10/31	31-38	313	-	68
Crewe Alex	Tr	04/46	46	6	-	1
Stockport Co	Tr	09/46				

WORRALL Gary George
Born: Salford, England, 4 November, 1961 — LW

League Club	Source	Date Signed	Seasons Played	Apps	Subs	Gls
Manchester U	App	11/78				
Peterborough U	Tr	03/84	83-85	93	2	16
Carlisle U	Tr	07/86	86	32	0	0

WORRALL Harold (Harry)
Born: Northwich, Cheshire, England, 19 November, 1918 — LB
Died: North Tyneside, Tyne and Wear, England, 5 December, 1979

League Club	Source	Date Signed	Seasons Played	Apps	Subs	Gls
Manchester U	Winsford U	10/37	46-47	6	-	0
Swindon T	Tr	06/48				

WORRELL Colin Harvey
Born: Great Yarmouth, Norfolk, England, 29 August, 1943 — LB
Died: Essex, England, 15 December, 2013

League Club	Source	Date Signed	Seasons Played	Apps	Subs	Gls
Norwich C	Jnr	11/61	62-64	9	-	0
Leyton Orient	Tr	09/64	64-65	51	0	0

WORRELL David
Born: Dublin, Republic of Ireland, 12 January, 1978 — RB
Republic of Ireland: U21-17/Youth

League Club	Source	Date Signed	Seasons Played	Apps	Subs	Gls
Blackburn Rov	Shelbourne (ROI)	01/95				
Plymouth Arg	Dundee U	11/00	00-04	147	0	0
Rotherham U	Tr	07/05	05-06	78	4	0

WORSDALE Michael John (John)
Born: Stoke-on-Trent, England, 29 October, 1948 — RW

League Club	Source	Date Signed	Seasons Played	Apps	Subs	Gls
Stoke C	App	11/65	68	4	0	0
Lincoln C	Tr	05/71	71-73	55	12	9

WORSLEY Graeme
Born: Liverpool, England, 4 January, 1969 — RB

League Club	Source	Date Signed	Seasons Played	Apps	Subs	Gls
Shrewsbury T	Bootle	03/89	88-92	83	22	4
Bury	Doncaster Rov (NC)	12/93	93	0	1	0

WORSMAN Reginald Herbert (Reg)
Born: Bradford, England, 19 March, 1933 — IF

League Club	Source	Date Signed	Seasons Played	Apps	Subs	Gls
Bradford Park Ave	Jnr	10/53	54-55	22	-	5
Bradford C	Tr	06/56	56	1	-	0
Darlington	Nelson	06/60	60	4	-	1

WORSWICK Michael Anthony (Micky)
Born: Preston, Lancashire, England, 14 March, 1945 — W
England: Amateur-1

League Club	Source	Date Signed	Seasons Played	Apps	Subs	Gls
Wigan Ath	Chorley	08/72	78	0	1	0

WORTHINGTON David (Dave)
Born: Halifax, West Yorkshire, England, 28 March, 1945 — RB

League Club	Source	Date Signed	Seasons Played	Apps	Subs	Gls
Halifax T	Jnr	04/62	61-63	37	-	9
Barrow	Tr	07/64	64-65	60	1	7
Grimsby T	Tr	06/66	66-72	292	1	14
Halifax T	L	10/73	73	5	0	0
Southend U	Tr	12/73	73-75	92	3	0

WORTHINGTON Eric Senior
Born: Sheffield, England, 29 December, 1925 — IF
Died: Sydney, Australia, 16 November, 2006

League Club	Source	Date Signed	Seasons Played	Apps	Subs	Gls
Queens Park Rgrs	Willesden T	09/47				
Watford	Tr	08/49	49-50	24	-	4
Bradford C	Dover	09/53	53	2	-	1

WORTHINGTON Frank Stewart
Born: Halifax, West Yorkshire, England, 23 November, 1948 — F
England: 8/FLge-1/U23-2

League Club	Source	Date Signed	Seasons Played	Apps	Subs	Gls
Huddersfield T	App	11/66	66-71	166	5	41
Leicester C	Tr	08/72	72-77	209	1	72
Bolton W	Tr	09/77	77-79	81	3	35
Birmingham C	Tr	11/79	79-81	71	4	29
Leeds U	Tr	03/82	81-82	32	0	14
Sunderland	Tr	12/82	82	18	1	2
Southampton	Tr	06/83	83	34	0	4
Brighton & HA	Tr	05/84	84	27	4	7
Tranmere Rov	Tr	06/85	85-86	51	8	21
Preston NE	Tr	02/87	86-87	10	13	3
Stockport Co	Tr	11/87	87	18	1	6

WORTHINGTON Frederick (Fred)
Born: Manchester, England, 6 January, 1924 — IF
Died: Tameside, Greater Manchester, England, 4 December, 1995

League Club	Source	Date Signed	Seasons Played	Apps	Subs	Gls
Bury		07/47	47-50	69	-	14
Leicester C	Tr	03/51	50-54	55	-	9
Exeter C	Tr	07/55	55	16	-	1
Oldham Ath	Tr	06/56	56	10	-	1

WORTHINGTON Gary Lee
Born: Cleethorpes, North Lincolnshire, England, 10 November, 1966 — F
England: Youth

League Club	Source	Date Signed	Seasons Played	Apps	Subs	Gls
Manchester U	App	11/84				
Huddersfield T	Tr	07/86				
Darlington	Tr	07/87	87-88	31	9	15
Wrexham	Tr	06/89	89-90	68	4	18
Wigan Ath	Tr	03/91	90-92	51	12	20
Exeter C	Tr	07/93	93	8	7	1
Doncaster Rov	L	03/94	93	8	0	2

WORTHINGTON Jonathan Alan (Jon)
Born: Dewsbury, West Yorkshire, England, 16 April, 1983 — M

League Club	Source	Date Signed	Seasons Played	Apps	Subs	Gls
Huddersfield T	YT	09/01	02-08	184	29	12
Yeovil T	L	01/09	08	9	0	0
Oldham Ath	Tr	07/09	09	11	5	0
Bradford C	Tr	01/11	10	16	0	0

WORTHINGTON Martin Paul
Born: Torquay, Devon, England, 25 January, 1981 — F

League Club	Source	Date Signed	Seasons Played	Apps	Subs	Gls
Torquay U	YT	07/99	98	0	1	0

WORTHINGTON Nigel
Born: Ballymena, Antrim, Northern Ireland, 4 November, 1961 — LB/M
Northern Ireland: 66/NILge-1/Youth

League Club	Source	Date Signed	Seasons Played	Apps	Subs	Gls
Notts Co	Ballymena U	07/81	81-83	67	0	4
Sheffield Wed	Tr	02/84	83-93	334	4	12
Leeds U	Tr	07/94	94-95	33	10	1
Stoke C	Tr	07/96	96	12	0	0
Blackpool	Tr	07/97	97	4	5	0

WORTHINGTON Peter Robert (Bob)
Born: Halifax, West Yorkshire, England, 22 April, 1947 — LB

League Club	Source	Date Signed	Seasons Played	Apps	Subs	Gls
Halifax T	App	05/65	64	12	-	0
Middlesbrough	Tr	08/66	67	2	0	0
Notts Co	Tr	09/68	68-73	230	2	1
Southend U	Tr	08/74	74	20	0	1
Hartlepool U	L	03/75	74	6	0	0

WOSAHLO Bradley Edward
Born: Ipswich, England, 14 February, 1975 W

League Club	Source	Date Signed	Seasons Played	Apps	Subs	Gls
Brighton & HA	YT	07/93	93	1	0	0
Cambridge U	Sudbury T	12/95	95	0	4	0

WOSAHLO Roger Frank
Born: Cambridge, England, 11 September, 1947 W
Died: Ipswich, England, 10 January, 2015
England: Schools

League Club	Source	Date Signed	Seasons Played	Apps	Subs	Gls
Chelsea	App	12/64	66	0	1	0
Ipswich T	Tr	07/67	67	1	0	0
Peterborough U	Tr	07/68	68	13	2	1
Ipswich T	Tr	07/69	69	0	1	0

WOTTON Paul Anthony
Born: Plymouth, England, 17 August, 1977 CD

League Club	Source	Date Signed	Seasons Played	Apps	Subs	Gls
Plymouth Arg	YT	07/95	94-07	359	35	54
Southampton	Tr	07/08	08-10	30	27	0
Oxford U	L	11/10	10	4	0	0
Yeovil T	Tr	01/11	10-11	45	0	4
Plymouth Arg	Tr	01/12	11-13	47	5	3

WRACK Darren
Born: Cleethorpes, North Lincolnshire, England, 5 May, 1976 RW

League Club	Source	Date Signed	Seasons Played	Apps	Subs	Gls
Derby Co	YT	07/94	94-95	4	22	1
Grimsby T	Tr	07/96	96-97	5	8	1
Shrewsbury T	L	02/97	96	3	1	0
Walsall	Tr	08/98	98-07	289	47	46

WRAGG Douglas (Doug)
Born: Nottingham, England, 12 September, 1934 RW
England: Schools

League Club	Source	Date Signed	Seasons Played	Apps	Subs	Gls
West Ham U	Hyson Green BC	06/53	56-59	16	-	0
Mansfield T	Tr	03/60	59-60	46	-	13
Rochdale	Tr	07/61	61-63	103	-	15
Chesterfield	Tr	07/64	64	17	-	4

WRAGG Peter
Born: Rotherham, South Yorkshire, England, 12 January, 1931 IF/WH
Died: Torbay, Devon, England, 24 June, 2004
England: Schools

League Club	Source	Date Signed	Seasons Played	Apps	Subs	Gls
Rotherham U	Jnr	05/48	48-52	31	-	6
Sheffield U	Tr	01/53	52-55	56	-	17
York C	Tr	08/56	56-62	264	-	78
Bradford C	Tr	07/63	63-64	73	-	5

WRAIGHT Gary Paul
Born: Epping, Essex, England, 5 March, 1979 RB

League Club	Source	Date Signed	Seasons Played	Apps	Subs	Gls
Wycombe W	YT	07/97	97-98	7	0	0

WRAITH Robert (Bobby)
Born: Largs, Ayrshire, Scotland, 26 April, 1948 G

League Club	Source	Date Signed	Seasons Played	Apps	Subs	Gls
Southport	Glasgow Celtic	07/69	69-70	28	0	0

WRATTEN Paul
Born: Middlesbrough, England, 29 November, 1970 M
England: Youth/Schools

League Club	Source	Date Signed	Seasons Played	Apps	Subs	Gls
Manchester U	YT	12/88	90	0	2	0
Hartlepool U	Tr	09/92	92-93	52	5	1

WRAY John Gordon
Born: Mytholmroyd, West Yorkshire, England, 7 July, 1941 G

League Club	Source	Date Signed	Seasons Played	Apps	Subs	Gls
Halifax T	Stainland Ath	11/64	64	7	-	0

WRAY Shaun Warren
Born: Birmingham, England, 14 March, 1978 W

League Club	Source	Date Signed	Seasons Played	Apps	Subs	Gls
Shrewsbury T	YT	07/95	95-96	1	3	0

WREH Christopher
Born: Monrovia, Liberia, 14 May, 1975 F
Liberia: 36

League Club	Source	Date Signed	Seasons Played	Apps	Subs	Gls
Arsenal	AS Monaco (FRA)	08/97	97-98	10	18	3
Birmingham C	L	10/99	99	6	1	1

WREN John Mackie (Jackie)
Born: Bonnybridge, Falkirk, Scotland, 26 April, 1936 G

League Club	Source	Date Signed	Seasons Played	Apps	Subs	Gls
Southend U	Hibernian	05/60				
Rotherham U	Tr	08/60	60	1	-	0

WRENCH Mark Nicholas
Born: Warrington, Cheshire, England, 27 September, 1969 LB

League Club	Source	Date Signed	Seasons Played	Apps	Subs	Gls
Wrexham	YT	09/88	88-89	5	1	0

WRIGGLESWORTH John Lancelot (Lance)
Born: Halifax, West Yorkshire, England, 4 July, 1924 IF
Died: Hampshire, England, March, 2010

League Club	Source	Date Signed	Seasons Played	Apps	Subs	Gls
Halifax T	Watford (Am)	07/46	46	10	-	1

WRIGGLESWORTH William Herbert (Billy)
Born: South Elmsall, West Yorkshire, England, 12 November, 1912 LW
Died: Blackpool, Lancashire, England, 8 August, 1980

League Club	Source	Date Signed	Seasons Played	Apps	Subs	Gls
Chesterfield	Frickley Colliery	05/32	32-34	34	-	6
Wolverhampton W	Tr	12/34	34-36	50	-	21
Manchester U	Tr	02/37	36-46	27	-	7
Bolton W	Tr	01/47	46-47	13	-	1
Southampton	Tr	10/47	47	12	-	4
Reading	Tr	06/48	48	5	-	0

WRIGHT Alan Geoffrey
Born: Ashton-under-Lyne, Greater Manchester, England, 28 September, 1971 LB
England: U21-2/Youth/Schools

League Club	Source	Date Signed	Seasons Played	Apps	Subs	Gls
Blackpool	YT	04/89	87-91	91	7	0
Blackburn Rov	Tr	10/91	91-94	67	7	1
Aston Villa	Tr	03/95	94-02	255	5	5
Middlesbrough	Tr	08/03	03	2	0	0
Sheffield U	Tr	10/03	03-06	36	6	1
Derby Co	L	02/06	05	7	0	0
Leeds U	L	10/06	06	1	0	0
Cardiff C	L	11/06	06	6	1	0
Doncaster Rov	L	02/07	06	3	0	0
Nottingham F	L	03/07	06	9	0	0
Cheltenham T	Tr	10/07	07-08	55	1	1

WRIGHT Alan George
Born: Birmingham, England, 20 March, 1938 IF

League Club	Source	Date Signed	Seasons Played	Apps	Subs	Gls
Walsall		05/58	58	1	-	1

WRIGHT Albert
Born: Clowne, Derbyshire, England, 21 July, 1925 G

League Club	Source	Date Signed	Seasons Played	Apps	Subs	Gls
Lincoln C	Ollerton Colliery	10/46	46	1	-	0

WRIGHT Alexander Mason (Alex)
Born: Kirkcaldy, Fife, Scotland, 18 October, 1925 IF
Died: Kirkcaldy, Fife, Scotland, 15 March, 1999

League Club	Source	Date Signed	Seasons Played	Apps	Subs	Gls
Barnsley	Hibernian	08/47	47-50	84	-	31
Tottenham H	Tr	09/50	50	2	-	1
Bradford Park Ave	Tr	08/51	51-54	131	-	25

WRIGHT Andrew David
Born: Formby, Merseyside, England, 15 January, 1985 RB/M

League Club	Source	Date Signed	Seasons Played	Apps	Subs	Gls
Scunthorpe U	Cape Cod Crus'rs (USA)	01/08	07-11	60	27	0
Morecambe	Tr	05/12	12-14	79	13	0

WRIGHT Andrew James (Andy)
Born: Leeds, England, 21 October, 1978 W

League Club	Source	Date Signed	Seasons Played	Apps	Subs	Gls
Leeds U	YT	10/95				
Reading	L	12/98	98	0	2	0

WRIGHT Anthony Allan (Tony)
Born: Swansea, Wales, 1 September, 1979 M
Wales: B-1/U21-3/Youth

League Club	Source	Date Signed	Seasons Played	Apps	Subs	Gls
Oxford U	YT	12/97	97-98	4	3	0

WRIGHT Archibald Watson (Archie)
Born: Glasgow, Scotland, 23 November, 1924 IF
Died: Airdrie, Lanarkshire, Scotland, 30 April, 1990

League Club	Source	Date Signed	Seasons Played	Apps	Subs	Gls
Blackburn Rov	Falkirk	05/51	51-52	22	-	10
Grimsby T	Tr	07/53	53	39	-	9
Accrington Stan	Tr	06/54	54-56	80	-	27

WRIGHT Arthur William Tempest
Born: Burradon, Tyne and Wear, England, 23 September, 1919 LH
Died: Burradon, Tyne and Wear, England, 27 May, 1985
England: FLge-2/Schools

League Club	Source	Date Signed	Seasons Played	Apps	Subs	Gls
Sunderland	Hylton CW	09/36	37-54	270	-	13

WRIGHT Bailey Colin
Born: Melbourne, Australia, 28 July, 1992 CD
Australia: 3/Youth

League Club	Source	Date Signed	Seasons Played	Apps	Subs	Gls
Preston NE	Victoria IoS (AUS)	12/10	10-14	118	5	8

WRIGHT Barrie
Born: Bradford, England, 6 November, 1945 LB
England: Youth/Schools

League Club	Source	Date Signed	Seasons Played	Apps	Subs	Gls
Leeds U	App	11/62	62-63	5	-	0
Brighton & HA	New York Gen'ls (USA)	01/69	68-69	8	2	0

WRIGHT Barry Albert
Born: Wrexham, Wales, 23 July, 1939 LB

League Club	Source	Date Signed	Seasons Played	Apps	Subs	Gls
Wrexham	Jnr	05/59	59-61	11	-	0
Chester C	Tr	08/62	62	1	-	0

WRIGHT Benjamin (Ben)
Born: Munster, Germany, 1 July, 1980 F

League Club	Source	Date Signed	Seasons Played	Apps	Subs	Gls
Bristol C	Kettering T	03/99	99	0	2	0
Lincoln C	IK Start (NOR)	08/07	07-08	41	26	17
Macclesfield T	Tr	07/09	09	25	14	6

WRIGHT Benjamin Matthew (Ben)
Born: Basingstoke, Hampshire, England, 20 August, 1988 F

League Club	Source	Date Signed	Seasons Played	Apps	Subs	Gls
Peterborough U	Hampton & Richmond Bor	01/09	08-09	0	5	0
Grimsby T	L	11/09	09	1	1	0
Barnet	L	03/10	09	0	3	0

WRIGHT Bernard
Born: Walthamstow, NE London, England, 19 September, 1923 — G

League Club	Source	Date Signed	Seasons Played	Apps	Subs	Gls
Notts Co	Walthamstow Ave	02/46	46	2	-	0

WRIGHT Bernard Anthony
Born: Derry, Northern Ireland, 8 June, 1940 — RW

League Club	Source	Date Signed	Seasons Played	Apps	Subs	Gls
Port Vale	Sligo Rov (ROI)	09/62	62	14	-	2

WRIGHT Bernard Peter (Bernie)
Born: Birmingham, England, 17 September, 1952 — F

League Club	Source	Date Signed	Seasons Played	Apps	Subs	Gls
Walsall	Birmingham C (Am)	09/71	71	15	0	2
Everton	Tr	02/72	71-72	10	1	2
Walsall	Tr	01/73	72-76	145	7	38
Bradford C	Tr	02/77	76-77	65	1	13
Port Vale	Tr	06/78	78-79	76	0	23

WRIGHT Brian Raymond
Born: Leicester, England, 9 January, 1937 — IF
England: Youth

League Club	Source	Date Signed	Seasons Played	Apps	Subs	Gls
Leicester C	Jnr	02/54				
Lincoln C	Tr	01/59	58-60	22	-	3

WRIGHT Charles George (Charlie)
Born: Glasgow, Scotland, 11 December, 1938 — G

League Club	Source	Date Signed	Seasons Played	Apps	Subs	Gls
Workington	Glasgow Rangers	06/58	58-62	123	-	0
Grimsby T	Tr	02/63	62-65	129	0	0
Charlton Ath	Tr	03/66	65-70	195	0	0
Bolton W	Tr	06/71	71-72	88	0	0

WRIGHT Christopher William (Chris)
Born: Clacton, Essex, England, 27 September, 1986 — G

League Club	Source	Date Signed	Seasons Played	Apps	Subs	Gls
Boston U	Arsenal (Sch)	08/05	05	1	0	0

WRIGHT Darren
Born: Warrington, Cheshire, England, 7 September, 1979 — F

League Club	Source	Date Signed	Seasons Played	Apps	Subs	Gls
Chester C	YT	07/98	97-99	24	24	2

WRIGHT Darren James
Born: West Bromwich, West Midlands, England, 14 March, 1968 — LB

League Club	Source	Date Signed	Seasons Played	Apps	Subs	Gls
Wolverhampton W	App	07/85	85	1	0	0
Wrexham	Tr	08/86	86-89	105	5	4

WRIGHT David
Born: Warrington, Cheshire, England, 1 May, 1980 — D/M
England: Youth

League Club	Source	Date Signed	Seasons Played	Apps	Subs	Gls
Crewe Alex	YT	06/97	97-03	206	5	3
Wigan Ath	Tr	06/04	04-06	26	19	0
Norwich C	L	11/05	05	5	0	0
Ipswich T	Tr	01/07	06-09	117	3	5
Crystal Palace	Tr	07/10	10-12	49	2	0
Gillingham	L	09/12	12	7	0	0
Colchester U	Tr	01/13	12-14	45	4	1

WRIGHT Dennis
Born: Royton, Greater Manchester, England, 9 January, 1930 — LW
Died: Rochdale, Greater Manchester, England, 7 April, 2003

League Club	Source	Date Signed	Seasons Played	Apps	Subs	Gls
Oldham Ath (Am)	Jnr	05/46	46	3	-	0
Oldham Ath	Glasgow Rangers	08/51	51	6	-	0

WRIGHT Dennis
Born: Chesterfield, Derbyshire, England, 19 December, 1919 — G
Died: Chesterfield, Derbyshire, England, July, 1993

League Club	Source	Date Signed	Seasons Played	Apps	Subs	Gls
Mansfield T	Clay Lane Rgrs	03/39	46-56	379	-	0

WRIGHT Drey Jermaine
Born: Greenwich, SE London, England, 30 April, 1995 — W

League Club	Source	Date Signed	Seasons Played	Apps	Subs	Gls
Colchester U	Sch	07/12	12-14	12	26	3

WRIGHT Evran
Born: Wolverhampton, England, 17 January, 1965 — F

League Club	Source	Date Signed	Seasons Played	Apps	Subs	Gls
Walsall	Halesowen T	08/93	93	16	13	5

WRIGHT Gary
Born: Torquay, Devon, England, 21 May, 1966 — RB

League Club	Source	Date Signed	Seasons Played	Apps	Subs	Gls
Torquay U	Jnr	08/84	84	2	0	0
Torquay U	Chard T	08/87	87	1	1	0

WRIGHT Gary
Born: Sunderland, England, 15 September, 1964 — G

League Club	Source	Date Signed	Seasons Played	Apps	Subs	Gls
Hartlepool U	App	10/82	82	12	0	0

WRIGHT Geoffrey Derrick (Geoff)
Born: Countesthorpe, Leicestershire, England, 1 March, 1930 — IF

League Club	Source	Date Signed	Seasons Played	Apps	Subs	Gls
Aston Villa		05/49				
Bournemouth	Tr	06/51				
Walsall	Rugby T	03/52	52	16	-	1

WRIGHT George Albert (Bert)
Born: Sheffield, England, 4 February, 1920 — IF

League Club	Source	Date Signed	Seasons Played	Apps	Subs	Gls
Cardiff C		03/42				
Hull C	Tr	06/46	46	4	-	1

WRIGHT George Brian (Brian)
Born: Sunderland, England, 16 September, 1939 — RH

League Club	Source	Date Signed	Seasons Played	Apps	Subs	Gls
Newcastle U	Jnr	09/56	59-62	45	-	1
Peterborough U	Tr	05/63	63-71	291	2	9

WRIGHT George Clifford (Cliff)
Born: Lingdale, Cleveland, England, 18 October, 1944 — IF

League Club	Source	Date Signed	Seasons Played	Apps	Subs	Gls
Middlesbrough	App	10/62				
Hartlepool U	Tr	06/64	64-69	179	5	31
Darlington	Tr	02/70	69-70	16	0	4

WRIGHT George William
Born: Ramsgate, Kent, England, 19 March, 1930 — RB
Died: Dover, Kent, England, July, 2000

League Club	Source	Date Signed	Seasons Played	Apps	Subs	Gls
West Ham U	Margate	02/51	51-57	161	-	0
Leyton Orient	Tr	05/58	58-61	87	-	1
Gillingham	Tr	07/62	62	4	-	0

WRIGHT George William
Born: Plymouth, England, 10 October, 1919 — G
Died: Tarleton, Lancashire, England, 23 April, 2008

League Club	Source	Date Signed	Seasons Played	Apps	Subs	Gls
Plymouth Arg	Kitto Inst	10/38	38-46	12	-	0
Colchester U	Tr	07/49	50-54	151	-	0

WRIGHT Glenn
Born: Liverpool, England, 27 May, 1956 — M

League Club	Source	Date Signed	Seasons Played	Apps	Subs	Gls
Blackburn Rov	App	-	73	1	0	0

WRIGHT Herbert Montague (Monty)
Born: Shirebrook, Derbyshire, England, 29 May, 1931 — IF
Died: Sutton-in-Ashfield, Nottinghamshire, England, 6 April, 2012

League Club	Source	Date Signed	Seasons Played	Apps	Subs	Gls
Leeds U	Bolsover Colliery	10/51				
Stockport Co	Tr	06/53	53	1	-	0
Chester C	Tr	07/54	54	21	-	4

WRIGHT Horace Raymond (Ray)
Born: Pontefract, West Yorkshire, England, 6 September, 1918 — IF
Died: Luton, England, August, 1987

League Club	Source	Date Signed	Seasons Played	Apps	Subs	Gls
Wolverhampton W	Woodbourne Ath	05/36	37-38	8	-	1
Exeter C	Tr	03/46	46-47	56	-	11

WRIGHT Ian Edward
Born: Woolwich, SE London, England, 3 November, 1963 — F
England: 33/B-3

League Club	Source	Date Signed	Seasons Played	Apps	Subs	Gls
Crystal Palace	Greenwich Bor	08/85	85-91	206	19	90
Arsenal	Tr	09/91	91-97	212	9	128
West Ham U	Tr	08/98	98	20	2	9
Nottingham F	L	08/99	99	10	0	5
Burnley	Glasgow Celtic	02/00	99	4	11	4

WRIGHT Ian Matthew
Born: Lichfield, Staffordshire, England, 10 March, 1972 — CD

League Club	Source	Date Signed	Seasons Played	Apps	Subs	Gls
Stoke C	YT	07/90	89-92	6	0	0
Bristol Rov	Tr	09/93	93-95	50	4	1
Hull C	Tr	07/96	96-97	65	8	2

WRIGHT Jake Maxwell
Born: Keighley, West Yorkshire, England, 11 March, 1986 — CD

League Club	Source	Date Signed	Seasons Played	Apps	Subs	Gls
Bradford C	Sch	07/05	05	0	1	0
Brighton & HA	Crawley T	07/09	09	4	2	0
Oxford U	Tr	07/10	10-14	191	2	0

WRIGHT James Frank (Jim)
Born: Manchester, England, 19 February, 1924 — G
Died: Bury, Greater Manchester, England, March, 1994

League Club	Source	Date Signed	Seasons Played	Apps	Subs	Gls
Accrington Stan (Am)	Bury Amats	09/47	47	1	-	0

WRIGHT Jeffrey Kenneth (Jeff)
Born: Galston, Ayrshire, Scotland, 23 June, 1952 — M

League Club	Source	Date Signed	Seasons Played	Apps	Subs	Gls
Wigan Ath	Netherfield	03/74	78-81	139	4	19

WRIGHT Jermaine Malaki
Born: Greenwich, SE London, England, 21 October, 1975 — RB/M
England: Youth

League Club	Source	Date Signed	Seasons Played	Apps	Subs	Gls
Millwall	YT	11/92				
Wolverhampton W	Tr	12/94	94-97	4	16	0
Doncaster Rov	L	03/96	95	13	0	0
Crewe Alex	Tr	02/98	97-98	47	2	5
Ipswich T	Tr	07/99	99-03	147	37	10
Leeds U	Tr	07/04	04-05	36	2	3
Millwall	L	09/05	05	15	0	2
Southampton	Tr	02/06	05-07	87	4	1
Blackpool	Tr	07/08	08	3	0	0

League Club	Source	Date Signed	Seasons Played	Career Record Apps	Subs	Gls
WRIGHT John (Jackie)						
Born: Tyldesley, Greater Manchester, England, 11 August, 1926						LB
Died: Lancashire, England, 22 June, 2005						
England: B-1						
Blackpool	Mossley	06/46	48-58	159	-	1
WRIGHT John Bryant						
Born: South Shields, Tyne and Wear, England, 16 November, 1922						CH
Died: South Tyneside, Tyne and Wear, England, August, 2009						
Hull C	Tyne Dock U	09/47	47	1	-	0
WRIGHT John Douglas (Doug)						
Born: Southend-on-Sea, England, 29 April, 1917						WH
Died: Blyth, Northumberland, England, December, 1992						
England: 1						
Southend U	Chelmsford C	08/36	36-37	31	-	2
Newcastle U	Tr	05/38	38-46	72	-	1
Lincoln C	Tr	12/48	48-54	233	-	2
WRIGHT John Francis Dominic						
Born: Aldershot, Hampshire, England, 13 August, 1933						G
Colchester U	Colchester Casuals	11/54	54-55	4	-	0
Colchester U	Great Bentley	01/61	60	1	-	0
WRIGHT John Michael (Mick)						
Born: Ellesmere Port, Cheshire, England, 25 September, 1946						RB
England: Youth						
Aston Villa	App	09/63	63-72	280	2	1
WRIGHT John William (Billy)						
Born: Blackpool, Lancashire, England, 4 March, 1931						W
Blackpool		05/50	51-54	15	-	2
Leicester C	Tr	08/55	55-57	27	-	10
Newcastle U	Tr	08/58	58	5	-	3
Plymouth Arg	Tr	08/59	59-60	42	-	9
Millwall	Tr	08/61	61	15	-	0
WRIGHT Jonathan (Johnny)						
Born: Belfast, Northern Ireland, 24 November, 1975						FB
Northern Ireland: B/Youth						
Norwich C	YT	07/94	94-96	5	2	0
WRIGHT Jonathan (John)						
Born: Newburn, Tyne and Wear, England, 30 January, 1925						IF
Darlington		01/47	46-48	17	-	0
WRIGHT Joshua Harris (Josh)						
Born: Hartlepool, Cleveland, England, 18 August, 1988						F
Darlington	Barnsley (Sch)	-	06	0	1	0
WRIGHT Joshua William (Josh)						
Born: Bethnal Green, E London, England, 6 November, 1989						M
England: Youth						
Charlton Ath	Sch	07/07	08	2	0	0
Barnet	L	08/07	07	12	1	1
Barnet	L	01/08	07	19	0	0
Brentford	L	09/08	08	5	0	0
Gillingham	L	03/09	08	5	0	0
Scunthorpe U	Tr	07/09	09-10	55	16	0
Millwall		11/11	11-14	38	8	1
Leyton Orient	L	11/13	13	0	2	0
Crawley T	L	09/14	14	2	2	0
Leyton Orient	Tr	11/14	14	26	3	2
WRIGHT Kenneth Laurence (Ken)						
Born: Newmarket, Suffolk, England, 16 May, 1922						IF
Died: Stratford-on-Avon, Warwickshire, England, 6 June, 1994						
West Ham U	Cambridge T	05/46	46-49	51	-	20
WRIGHT Mark						
Born: Dorchester-on-Thames, Oxfordshire, England, 1 August, 1963						CD
England: 45/U21-4						
Oxford U	Jnr	08/80	81	8	2	0
Southampton	Tr	03/82	81-86	170	0	7
Derby Co	Tr	08/87	87-90	144	0	10
Liverpool	Tr	07/91	91-97	156	2	5
WRIGHT Mark Andrew						
Born: Manchester, England, 29 January, 1970						D
Everton	YT	06/88	89	1	0	0
Blackpool	L	08/90	90	3	0	0
Huddersfield T	Tr	03/91	90-92	25	7	1
Wigan Ath	Accrington Stan	11/93	93-94	27	3	1
WRIGHT Mark Anthony						
Born: Wolverhampton, England, 24 February, 1982						RW
Walsall	YT	01/01	00-06	94	30	9
MK Dons	Tr	07/07	07-08	58	8	18
Brighton & HA	Tr	07/09	09	2	2	0
Bristol Rov	Tr	09/09	09	19	5	0
Shrewsbury T	Tr	07/10	10-12	100	8	25
WRIGHT Mark Stephen						
Born: Chorley, Lancashire, England, 4 September, 1981						F
Preston NE	YT	04/99	98-99	1	2	0
WRIGHT Martin Harold						
Born: Chesterfield, Derbyshire, England, 1 April, 1950						F
Chesterfield	Alfreton T	10/68	68-71	40	3	12
Torquay U	Tr	07/72	72	8	5	3
WRIGHT Matthew Paul						
Born: Norwich, England, 6 January, 1978						CD
Torquay U	YT	01/97	96	7	2	0
WRIGHT Michael (Mike)						
Born: Darlington, County Durham, England, 17 February, 1950						D/M
Darlington	Jnr	06/68	68-72	82	7	0
WRIGHT Michael Eric (Mick)						
Born: Newmarket, Suffolk, England, 16 January, 1942						IF
Northampton T	Newmarket T	11/59	59-61	26	-	7
WRIGHT Michael Howard (Howard)						
Born: Winsford, Cheshire, England, 22 October, 1948						IF
Shrewsbury T	App	-	65	1	0	1
Crewe Alex	Tr	09/66				
WRIGHT Myles Harvey						
Born: Matlock, Derbyshire, England, 14 September, 1996						G
Chesterfield	Matlock T	07/14	14	0	1	0
WRIGHT Nicholas (Nick)						
Born: Birmingham, England, 25 November, 1987						W/F
England: Semi Pro-1						
Birmingham C	Sch	07/06				
Bristol C	L	10/06	06	1	3	0
Northampton T	L	11/06	06	2	2	0
WRIGHT Nicholas John (Nick)						
Born: Ilkeston, Derbyshire, England, 15 October, 1975						LW
Derby Co	YT	07/94				
Carlisle U	Tr	11/97	97	25	0	5
Watford	Tr	07/98	98-99	32	5	6
WRIGHT Patrick Daniel Joseph (Pat)						
Born: Oldbury, West Midlands, England, 17 November, 1940						RB
Birmingham C	Brookfield	11/59	59-61	3	-	0
Shrewsbury T	Tr	09/62	62-67	201	1	3
Derby Co	Tr	10/67	67	12	1	0
Southend U	L	03/70	69	11	0	0
Rotherham U	Tr	09/70	70	2	0	0
WRIGHT Paul Antony						
Born: Barking, E London, England, 29 July, 1969						F
Halifax T	USA	10/92	92	1	0	0
WRIGHT Paul Hamilton						
Born: East Kilbride, Lanarkshire, Scotland, 17 August, 1967						F
Scotland: U21-3/Youth						
Queens Park Rgrs	Aberdeen	07/89	89	9	6	5
WRIGHT Peter Brooke						
Born: Colchester, Essex, England, 26 January, 1934						LW
Died: Colchester, Essex, England, 24 October, 2012						
Colchester U	Jnr	11/51	51-63	427	-	90
WRIGHT Peter David						
Born: Preston, Lancashire, England, 15 August, 1982						F
Halifax T	Newcastle U (YT)	08/01	01	3	11	0
WRIGHT Ralph Lawrence						
Born: Newcastle-upon-Tyne, England, 3 August, 1947						M/CD
Norwich C	Spennymoor U	07/68				
Bradford Park Ave	Tr	10/69	69	13	1	1
Hartlepool U	Tr	06/70	70	23	1	3
Stockport Co	Tr	07/71	71	19	2	0
Bolton W	Tr	02/72	71-72	25	7	5
Southport	L	12/72	72	6	0	1
Southport	New York Cosmos (USA)	08/73	73	34	3	2
WRIGHT Richard (Dick)						
Born: Mexborough, South Yorkshire, England, 5 December, 1931						G
Died: Chester, England, October, 2003						
Leeds U	Hickleton Main	05/49				
Chester C	Tr	08/51	52-54	52	-	0
Bradford C	Tr	03/55				
WRIGHT Richard Ian						
Born: Ipswich, England, 5 November, 1977						G

England: 2/U21-15/Youth/Schools

League Club	Source	Date Signed	Seasons Played	Apps	Subs	Gls
Ipswich T	YT	01/95	94-00	240	0	0
Arsenal	Tr	07/01	01	12	0	0
Everton	Tr	07/02	02-06	58	2	0
West Ham U	Tr	07/07				
Southampton	L	03/08	07	7	0	0
Ipswich T	Tr	07/08	08-09	58	0	0
Sheffield U	Tr	09/10	10	2	0	0
Ipswich T	Tr	11/11	11	1	0	0
Manchester C	Tr	08/12				

WRIGHT Robert Cooper Allen (Bob)
Born: Glasgow, Scotland, 20 February, 1913 — LH
Died: Great Missenden, Buckinghamshire, England, 27 May, 1998

League Club	Source	Date Signed	Seasons Played	Apps	Subs	Gls
Hartlepool U	Jnr	10/31				
Charlton Ath	Horden CW	05/37	38-46	28	-	0

WRIGHT Ronald William (Ronnie)
Born: Glasgow, Scotland, 6 December, 1940 — IF

League Club	Source	Date Signed	Seasons Played	Apps	Subs	Gls
Leeds U	Shettleston Jnrs	06/59	60	1	-	0

WRIGHT Stephen
Born: Bellshill, Lanarkshire, Scotland, 27 August, 1971 — RB
Scotland: 2/B-2/U21-14

League Club	Source	Date Signed	Seasons Played	Apps	Subs	Gls
Wolverhampton W (L)	Glasgow Rangers	03/98	97	3	0	0
Bradford C	Glasgow Rangers	07/98	98	21	1	0
Scunthorpe U	Dundee U	09/02	02	2	0	0

WRIGHT Stephen John
Born: Bootle, Merseyside, England, 8 February, 1980 — RB
England: U21-10/Youth

League Club	Source	Date Signed	Seasons Played	Apps	Subs	Gls
Liverpool	YT	10/97	00-01	10	4	0
Crewe Alex	L	08/99	99	17	6	0
Sunderland	Tr	08/02	02-06	88	4	2
Stoke C	L	08/07	07	14	2	0
Coventry C	Tr	08/08	08-09	55	0	0
Brentford	Tr	10/10	10	9	2	0
Hartlepool U	Tr	09/11	11	10	0	0

WRIGHT Stephen Peter (Steve)
Born: Clacton, Essex, England, 16 June, 1959 — D

League Club	Source	Date Signed	Seasons Played	Apps	Subs	Gls
Colchester U	Jnr	06/77	77-81	112	5	3
Wrexham	HJK Helsinki (FIN)	09/83	83-84	76	0	0
Torquay U	Tr	07/85	85	33	0	0
Crewe Alex	Tr	07/86	86-87	67	5	3

WRIGHT Terence Ian (Terry)
Born: Newcastle-upon-Tyne, England, 22 June, 1939 — LW

League Club	Source	Date Signed	Seasons Played	Apps	Subs	Gls
Barrow	Nuneaton Bor	11/62	62-64	10	-	0

WRIGHT Thomas (Tommy)
Born: Clackmannan, Stirlingshire, Scotland, 20 January, 1928 — RW
Died: Sunderland, England, 5 May, 2011
Scotland: 3

League Club	Source	Date Signed	Seasons Played	Apps	Subs	Gls
Sunderland	Partick Thistle	03/49	48-54	170	-	51
Oldham Ath	East Fife	03/57	56	7	-	2

WRIGHT Thomas Andrew (Tommy)
Born: Kirby Muxloe, Leicestershire, England, 28 September, 1984 — F
England: Youth

League Club	Source	Date Signed	Seasons Played	Apps	Subs	Gls
Leicester C	Sch	06/03	01-05	3	18	2
Brentford	L	09/03	03	18	7	3
Blackpool	L	08/05	05	10	3	6
Barnsley	Tr	01/06	05-06	11	23	2
Walsall	L	11/06	06	5	1	2
Darlington	Tr	01/07	06-07	46	7	17
Grimsby T	Aberdeen	01/10	09	13	1	1

WRIGHT Thomas Birtles (Tom)
Born: Glossop, Derbyshire, England, 11 January, 1917 — LW
Died: Blackpool, Lancashire, England, December, 1995

League Club	Source	Date Signed	Seasons Played	Apps	Subs	Gls
Manchester C	Droylsden	06/37				
Hull C	Altrincham	07/47				
Accrington Stan	Tr	10/47	47-48	20	-	4

WRIGHT Thomas Elliott (Tommy)
Born: Dunfermline, Fife, Scotland, 10 January, 1966 — LW
Scotland: U21-1/Youth

League Club	Source	Date Signed	Seasons Played	Apps	Subs	Gls
Leeds U	App	01/83	82-85	73	8	24
Oldham Ath	Tr	10/86	86-88	110	2	23
Leicester C	Tr	08/89	89-91	122	7	22
Middlesbrough	Tr	07/92	92-94	44	9	5
Bradford C	Tr	07/95	95-96	30	15	5
Oldham Ath	Tr	08/97	97	10	2	2

WRIGHT Thomas James (Tommy)
Born: Maghull, Merseyside, England, 21 October, 1944 — RB
England: 11/U23-7

League Club	Source	Date Signed	Seasons Played	Apps	Subs	Gls
Everton	Jnr	03/63	64-72	307	1	4

WRIGHT Thomas James (Tommy)
Born: Ballyclare, Antrim, Northern Ireland, 29 August, 1963 — G
England: FLge//Northern Ireland: 31/U23-1

League Club	Source	Date Signed	Seasons Played	Apps	Subs	Gls
Newcastle U	Linfield	01/88	88-93	72	1	0
Hull C	L	02/91	90	6	0	0
Nottingham F	Tr	09/93	93-96	11	0	0
Reading	L	10/96	96	17	0	0
Manchester C	L	01/97	96	5	0	0
Manchester C	Tr	03/97	96-00	29	0	0
Wrexham	L	02/99	98	16	0	0
Newcastle U	L	08/99	99	3	0	0
Bolton W	L	01/01	00	3	1	0

WRIGHT Thomas Kentigern (Tommy)
Born: Stepps, Glasgow, Scotland, 11 January, 1925 — RW
Died: Glasgow, Scotland, 30 June, 2003

League Club	Source	Date Signed	Seasons Played	Apps	Subs	Gls
Aldershot	Dunfermline Ath	07/52	52	14	-	1

WRIGHT Vincent (Vince)
Born: Bradford, England, 12 April, 1931 — W
Died: Kent, England, June, 2004
England: Youth

League Club	Source	Date Signed	Seasons Played	Apps	Subs	Gls
Derby Co	Blackpool (Am)	09/51				
Mansfield T	Tr	07/52	52	2	-	0

WRIGHT William (Billy)
Born: Liverpool, England, 28 April, 1958 — CD
England: B-2/U21-6

League Club	Source	Date Signed	Seasons Played	Apps	Subs	Gls
Everton	Jnr	01/77	77-82	164	2	10
Birmingham C	Tr	07/83	83-85	111	0	9
Chester C	L	02/86	85	6	0	1
Carlisle U	Tr	08/86	86-87	87	0	3

WRIGHT William Ambrose (Billy)
Born: Ironbridge, Telford & Wrekin, England, 6 February, 1924 — LH/CH
Died: Barnet, N London, England, 3 September, 1994
England: 105/FLge-21/War-4

League Club	Source	Date Signed	Seasons Played	Apps	Subs	Gls
Wolverhampton W	Jnr	02/41	46-58	490	-	13

WRIGHT William Hardy Rogers (Billy)
Born: Corbridge, Northumberland, England, 4 November, 1962 — F
New Zealand: 15

League Club	Source	Date Signed	Seasons Played	Apps	Subs	Gls
Burnley	Jnr	01/81				
Crewe Alex	L	11/82	82	3	0	1

WRIGHT William Stephen (Billy)
Born: Dudley, West Midlands, England, 26 April, 1959 — RB

League Club	Source	Date Signed	Seasons Played	Apps	Subs	Gls
Birmingham C	App	04/77				
Lincoln C	Tr	07/78	78	3	0	0

WRIGHT-PHILLIPS Bradley Edward
Born: Lewisham, SE London, England, 12 March, 1985 — F
England: Youth

League Club	Source	Date Signed	Seasons Played	Apps	Subs	Gls
Manchester C	Sch	07/02	04-05	1	31	2
Southampton	Tr	07/06	06-08	58	53	22
Plymouth Arg	Tr	07/09	09-10	29	3	17
Charlton Ath	Tr	01/11	10-12	71	11	32
Brentford	L	02/13	12	10	5	5

WRIGHT-PHILLIPS Shaun Cameron
Born: Greenwich, SE London, England, 25 October, 1981 — RW
England: 36/U21-6

League Club	Source	Date Signed	Seasons Played	Apps	Subs	Gls
Manchester C	YT	10/98	99-04	130	23	26
Chelsea	Tr	07/05	05-08	43	39	4
Manchester C	Tr	08/08	08-10	48	16	9
Queens Park Rgrs	Tr	08/11	11-14	43	24	1

WRIGHTSON Jeffrey George (Jeff)
Born: Newcastle-upon-Tyne, England, 18 May, 1968 — CD

League Club	Source	Date Signed	Seasons Played	Apps	Subs	Gls
Newcastle U	App	05/86	86	3	1	0
Preston NE	Tr	07/87	87-91	161	5	4

WRIGLEY Wilfred (Wilf)
Born: Clitheroe, Lancashire, England, 4 October, 1949 — CD

League Club	Source	Date Signed	Seasons Played	Apps	Subs	Gls
Burnley	Jnr	07/68	68-69	6	0	1

WRING Daniel Ronald (Danny)
Born: Portishead, Avon, England, 26 October, 1986 — M

League Club	Source	Date Signed	Seasons Played	Apps	Subs	Gls
Bristol C	Sch	-	04	0	1	0

WROE Mark
Born: Manchester, England, 1 June, 1966 — W

League Club	Source	Date Signed	Seasons Played	Apps	Subs	Gls
Stockport Co	Jnr	01/84	84-85	26	4	4

WROE Nicholas (Nicky)
Born: Sheffield, England, 28 September, 1985 — M
England: Semi Pro-2

League Club	Source	Date Signed	Seasons Played	Apps	Subs	Gls
Barnsley	Sch	08/04	02-06	34	15	1
Bury	L	02/07	06	4	1	0
Torquay U	York C	06/08	09-10	65	0	12
Shrewsbury T	Tr	01/11	10-11	50	6	7

League Club	Source	Date Signed	Seasons Played	Career Record Apps	Subs	Gls
Preston NE	Tr	05/12	12-13	37	6	8
Shrewsbury T	L	10/13	13	7	3	0
Oxford U	L	01/14	13	16	2	2
Notts Co	Tr	06/14	14	6	6	0

WYATT George Albert
Born: Whitechapel, Central London, England, 28 March, 1924 LB
Died: York, England, 16 July, 1957

League Club	Source	Date Signed	Seasons Played	Apps	Subs	Gls
Crystal Palace		11/47	48	7	-	0

WYATT Michael James (Mike)
Born: Bristol, England, 12 September, 1974 M

League Club	Source	Date Signed	Seasons Played	Apps	Subs	Gls
Bristol C	YT	07/93	93-94	9	4	0
Bristol Rov	Tr	07/95	95	3	1	0

WYATT Reginald Gordon (Reg)
Born: Plymouth, England, 18 September, 1932 CH
Died: Plymouth, England, 16 November, 2007

League Club	Source	Date Signed	Seasons Played	Apps	Subs	Gls
Plymouth Arg	Oak Villa	08/50	55-64	202	-	2
Torquay U	Tr	10/64	64-66	80	0	6

WYER Peter William
Born: Coventry, England, 10 February, 1937 IF

League Club	Source	Date Signed	Seasons Played	Apps	Subs	Gls
Coventry C		10/55	55	1	-	0
Derby Co	Tr	06/56	56	2	-	1
Coventry C	Tr	07/58	58	4	-	0

WYKE Charles Thomas (Charlie)
Born: Middlesbrough, England, 6 December, 1992 F

League Club	Source	Date Signed	Seasons Played	Apps	Subs	Gls
Middlesbrough	Sch	07/11				
Hartlepool U	L	10/12	12	21	4	2
AFC Wimbledon	L	01/14	13	11	6	2
Hartlepool U	L	08/14	14	13	0	4
Carlisle U	Tr	01/15	14	16	1	6

WYLDE Gregory (Greg)
Born: Kirkintilloch, Dunbartonshire, Scotland, 23 March, 1991 W
Scotland: U21-7/Youth

League Club	Source	Date Signed	Seasons Played	Apps	Subs	Gls
Bolton W	Glasgow Rangers	06/12				
Bury	L	11/12	12	4	0	0

WYLDE Michael Joseph
Born: Birmingham, England, 6 January, 1987 CD
England: Semi Pro-1

League Club	Source	Date Signed	Seasons Played	Apps	Subs	Gls
Cheltenham T	Sch	07/06	05-06	4	4	0

WYLDE Rodger James
Born: Sheffield, England, 8 March, 1954 F

League Club	Source	Date Signed	Seasons Played	Apps	Subs	Gls
Sheffield Wed	App	07/71	72-79	157	11	54
Oldham Ath	Tr	02/80	79-82	109	4	51
Sunderland	Sporting Lisbon (POR)	07/84	84	8	3	3
Barnsley	Tr	12/84	84-87	50	2	19
Rotherham U	L	03/88	87	6	0	1
Stockport Co	Tr	07/88	88	24	2	12

WYLDES Robert Jack (Bobby)
Born: Southport, Merseyside, England, 6 October, 1928 LW
Died: Northampton, England, November, 2011

League Club	Source	Date Signed	Seasons Played	Apps	Subs	Gls
Luton T	Desborough	10/49	49-51	26	-	8
Southend U	Tr	09/52				

WYLES Harold
Born: Melton Mowbray, Leicestershire, England, 28 October, 1922 FB
Died: Wavertree, Merseyside, England, 1982

League Club	Source	Date Signed	Seasons Played	Apps	Subs	Gls
Leicester C	Midland Woodworkers	04/42				
Gateshead	Tr	03/48	47-53	234	-	7

WYLES Thomas Cecil (Cec)
Born: Gosberton, Lincolnshire, England, 1 November, 1919 CF
Died: Liverpool, England, 10 October, 1990

League Club	Source	Date Signed	Seasons Played	Apps	Subs	Gls
Everton	Peterborough U	02/38				
Blackburn Rov	Tr	10/45				
Bury	Tr	05/46	46	2	-	0
Southport	Tr	11/46	46-49	143	-	53

WYLIE John Edward
Born: Newcastle-upon-Tyne, England, 25 September, 1936 RH
Died: Doncaster, South Yorkshire, England, 18 September, 2013

League Club	Source	Date Signed	Seasons Played	Apps	Subs	Gls
Huddersfield T	Jnr	09/54				
Preston NE	Tr	05/57	58-62	91	-	1
Stockport Co	Tr	11/62	62-63	69	-	2
Doncaster Rov	Tr	08/64	64-67	123	1	2

WYLIE Ronald Maurice (Ron)
Born: Glasgow, Scotland, 6 August, 1933 IF/RH
Scotland: Schools

League Club	Source	Date Signed	Seasons Played	Apps	Subs	Gls
Notts Co	Clydesdale Jnrs	09/50	51-58	227	-	36
Aston Villa	Tr	11/58	58-64	196	-	16
Birmingham C	Tr	06/65	65-69	125	3	2

WYLLIE James (Jimmy)
Born: Saltcoats, Ayrshire, Scotland, 15 October, 1927 IF
Died: Southport, Merseyside, England, 27 June, 1992

League Club	Source	Date Signed	Seasons Played	Apps	Subs	Gls
Southport	Kilmarnock	07/50	50	15	-	1
Wrexham	Tr	12/50	50	20	-	4

WYLLIE Robinson Gourlay Nicholl (Bob)
Born: Dundee, Scotland, 4 April, 1929 G
Died: Belper, Derbyshire, England, 1981

League Club	Source	Date Signed	Seasons Played	Apps	Subs	Gls
Blackpool	Dundee U	05/53	53-54	13	-	0
West Ham U	Tr	05/56	56	13	-	0
Plymouth Arg	Tr	07/58	58	5	-	0
Mansfield T	Tr	10/59	59-61	92	-	0

WYNN Walter Ronald (Ron)
Born: Wrexham, Wales, 2 November, 1923 CH/CF
Died: Liverpool, England, 8 October, 1983

League Club	Source	Date Signed	Seasons Played	Apps	Subs	Gls
Wrexham	Chester C (Am)	04/48	47-55	182	-	12

WYNNE Darren Lee
Born: Deeside, Flintshire, Wales, 12 October, 1970 M

League Club	Source	Date Signed	Seasons Played	Apps	Subs	Gls
Chester C	YT	07/89	88-89	0	12	0

WYNTER Alex James
Born: Camberwell, S London, England, 15 September, 1993 FB/M

League Club	Source	Date Signed	Seasons Played	Apps	Subs	Gls
Crystal Palace	Sch	09/10				
Colchester U	L	03/14	13	5	1	1
Portsmouth	L	07/14	14	10	0	0
Colchester U	Tr	01/15	14	16	2	0

WYNTER Curtis Gian
Born: Birmingham, England, 24 June, 1991 RB

League Club	Source	Date Signed	Seasons Played	Apps	Subs	Gls
Coventry C	Sch	06/09	08	1	0	0

WYNTER Jordan James Cecil
Born: Ilford, E London, England, 24 November, 1993 M

League Club	Source	Date Signed	Seasons Played	Apps	Subs	Gls
Arsenal	Sch	07/12				
Bristol C	Tr	05/13	13	2	1	0
Cheltenham T	L	08/14	14	6	0	1
Cheltenham T	Tr	02/15	14	6	4	0

WYNTER Thomas Lenworth (Tom)
Born: Lewisham, SE London, England, 20 June, 1990 LB

League Club	Source	Date Signed	Seasons Played	Apps	Subs	Gls
Gillingham	Sch	07/08	09	4	4	0

XAUSA Davide Antonio
Born: Vancouver, Canada, 10 March, 1976 — F
Canada: 32

League Club	Source	Date Signed	Seasons Played	Apps	Subs	Gls
Port Vale	St Cath's Wolv (CAN)	01/98				
Stoke C	Tr	02/98	97	1	0	0

XAVIER Faisal Abel (Abel)
Born: Nampula, Mozambique, 30 November, 1972 — RB
Portugal: 20/U21/Youth

League Club	Source	Date Signed	Seasons Played	Apps	Subs	Gls
Everton	PSV Eindhoven (NED)	09/99	99-01	39	4	0
Liverpool	Tr	01/02	01-02	13	1	1
Middlesbrough	AS Roma (ITA)	08/05	05-06	18	0	1

[XISCO] TEJADA JIMENEZ Francisco
Born: Palma de Mallorca, Spain, 26 June, 1986 — F
Spain: U21-11

League Club	Source	Date Signed	Seasons Played	Apps	Subs	Gls
Newcastle U	Depo la Coruna (SPN)	09/08	08-10	3	6	1

YACOB Claudio Ariel
Born: Santa Fe, Argentina, 18 July, 1987 — DM
Argentina: 3/Youth

League Club	Source	Date Signed	Seasons Played	Apps	Subs	Gls
West Bromwich A	Racing Club (ARG)	07/12	12-14	67	10	1

YAKUBU Aiyegbini
Born: Benin City, Nigeria, 22 November, 1982 — F
Nigeria: 57

League Club	Source	Date Signed	Seasons Played	Apps	Subs	Gls
Reading	Al-Rayyan (QAT)	-				
Portsmouth	Maccabi Haifa (ISR)	01/03	02-04	76	5	35
Middlesbrough	Tr	07/05	05-07	67	6	25
Everton	Tr	08/07	07-10	56	26	25
Leicester C	L	01/11	10	19	1	11
Blackburn Rov	Tr	08/11	11	29	1	17
Reading	Al-Rayyan (QAT)	02/15	14	3	4	0

YAKUBU Ismail Salami
Born: Kano, Nigeria, 8 April, 1985 — CD
England: Semi Pro-6

League Club	Source	Date Signed	Seasons Played	Apps	Subs	Gls
Barnet	Sch	05/02	05-09	144	2	9
Newport Co	AFC Wimbledon	06/11	13-14	54	4	5

YALCIN Levent (Lev)
Born: Middlesbrough, England, 25 March, 1985 — M
Turkey: Youth

League Club	Source	Date Signed	Seasons Played	Apps	Subs	Gls
York C	YT	07/04	02-03	5	15	0

YALLOP Frank Walter
Born: Watford, Hertfordshire, England, 4 April, 1964 — FB
Canada: 52//England: Youth

League Club	Source	Date Signed	Seasons Played	Apps	Subs	Gls
Ipswich T	App	01/82	83-95	289	27	7
Blackpool	L	11/95	95	3	0	0

YANGA-MBIWA Mapou
Born: Bangui, Central African Republic, 15 May, 1989 — CD
France: 4/U21-8

League Club	Source	Date Signed	Seasons Played	Apps	Subs	Gls
Newcastle U	Montpellier (FRA)	01/13	12-13	28	9	0

YANTORNO Fabian Rodrigo
Born: Montevideo, Uruguay, 4 September, 1982 — M

League Club	Source	Date Signed	Seasons Played	Apps	Subs	Gls
Hartlepool U	San Carlos (UGY)	08/10	10	9	8	0

YANUSHEVSKI Victor Frantsevich
Born: Minsk, Belarus, 23 January, 1960 — CD
Died: Berlin, Germany, 23 June, 1992
Soviet Union: 2

League Club	Source	Date Signed	Seasons Played	Apps	Subs	Gls
Aldershot	CSKA Moscow (RUS)	03/91	90	6	0	1

YAO Sosthene Aubin
Born: Guiglo, Ivory Coast, 7 August, 1987 — F

League Club	Source	Date Signed	Seasons Played	Apps	Subs	Gls
Cheltenham T	West Ham U (Sch)	04/06	05-07	2	21	0

YARD Ernest John (Ernie)
Born: Stranraer, Dumfries & Galloway, Scotland, 3 May, 1941 — M/CF
Died: Cape Town, South Africa, November, 2004

League Club	Source	Date Signed	Seasons Played	Apps	Subs	Gls
Bury	Partick Thistle	12/63	63-64	45	-	13
Crystal Palace	Tr	05/65	65-66	35	2	3
Reading	Tr	11/66	66-68	101	3	6

YARDLEY George McArthur
Born: Kirkcaldy, Fife, Scotland, 8 October, 1942 — F

League Club	Source	Date Signed	Seasons Played	Apps	Subs	Gls
Luton T	St George-B'pest (AUS)	10/66	66	1	0	0
Tranmere Rov	Tr	11/66	66-70	123	0	68

YATES Adam Paul
Born: Stoke-on-Trent, England, 28 May, 1983 — RB
England: Semi Pro-3

League Club	Source	Date Signed	Seasons Played	Apps	Subs	Gls
Crewe Alex	YT	02/01				
Morecambe	Leek T	08/06	07-08	74	2	0
Port Vale	Tr	07/09	09-14	182	19	4

YATES David (Sammy)
Born: Barnsley, South Yorkshire, England, 18 March, 1953 — RB

League Club	Source	Date Signed	Seasons Played	Apps	Subs	Gls
Barnsley	App	03/71	72-77	104	0	2
Grimsby T	L	03/77	76	10	0	0

YATES Dean Richard
Born: Leicester, England, 26 October, 1967 — CD
England: U21-5

League Club	Source	Date Signed	Seasons Played	Apps	Subs	Gls
Notts Co	App	06/85	84-94	312	2	33
Derby Co	Tr	01/95	94-97	65	3	3
Watford	Tr	07/98	98	9	0	1

YATES Harry
Born: Huddersfield, West Yorkshire, England, 28 September, 1925 — IF
Died: Liverpool, England, 26 November, 1987

League Club	Source	Date Signed	Seasons Played	Apps	Subs	Gls
Huddersfield T	Jnr	10/43	49	1	-	0
Darlington	Tr	05/50	50-51	91	-	29

YATES Jamie
Born: Sheffield, England, 24 December, 1988 — W

League Club	Source	Date Signed	Seasons Played	Apps	Subs	Gls
Rotherham U	Sch	06/07	06-08	5	21	3

YATES Jerry Arron
Born: Doncaster, South Yorkshire, England, 10 November, 1996 — F

League Club	Source	Date Signed	Seasons Played	Apps	Subs	Gls
Rotherham U	Sch	04/15	14	0	1	0

YATES John
Born: Rotherham, South Yorkshire, England, 18 November, 1929 — RW

League Club	Source	Date Signed	Seasons Played	Apps	Subs	Gls
Sheffield U		06/50				
Chester C	Tr	08/51	51	2	-	0

YATES Mark Jason
Born: Birmingham, England, 24 January, 1970 — M
England: Semi Pro-2

League Club	Source	Date Signed	Seasons Played	Apps	Subs	Gls
Birmingham C	YT	07/88	87-91	38	16	6
Burnley	Tr	08/91	91-92	9	9	1
Lincoln C	L	02/93	92	10	4	0
Doncaster Rov	Tr	07/93	93	33	1	4
Cheltenham T	Kidderminster Hrs	01/99	99-03	190	4	19
Kidderminster Hrs	Tr	02/04	03	14	0	2

YATES Richard (Dick)
Born: Queensferry, Flintshire, Wales, 6 June, 1921 — CF
Died: Queensferry, Flintshire, Wales, 1976

League Club	Source	Date Signed	Seasons Played	Apps	Subs	Gls
Chester C	Wolverhampton W (Am)	08/39	46-47	52	-	37
Wrexham	Tr	12/47	47-48	31	-	18
Carlisle U	Tr	11/48	48	16	-	9
New Brighton	Tr	08/49	49-50	43	-	14

YATES Stephen (Steve)
Born: Measham, Leicestershire, England, 8 December, 1953 — LB

League Club	Source	Date Signed	Seasons Played	Apps	Subs	Gls
Leicester C	App	12/71	73-76	12	7	0
Southend U	Tr	11/77	77-83	223	2	8
Doncaster Rov	Tr	12/83	83-84	44	0	1
Darlington	L	01/85	84	4	0	0
Chesterfield	L	03/85	84	1	0	0
Stockport Co	Tr	08/85	85	2	0	0

YATES Stephen (Steve)
Born: Bristol, England, 29 January, 1970 — CD

League Club	Source	Date Signed	Seasons Played	Apps	Subs	Gls
Bristol Rov	YT	07/88	86-93	196	1	0
Queens Park Rgrs	Tr	08/93	93-98	122	12	2
Tranmere Rov	Tr	08/99	99-01	109	4	7
Sheffield U	Tr	07/02	02	11	1	0
Huddersfield T	Tr	08/03	03-04	50	2	1

YEATES Mark Stephen Anthony
Born: Dublin, Republic of Ireland, 11 January, 1985 — RW
Republic of Ireland: B-1/U21-4/Youth

League Club	Source	Date Signed	Seasons Played	Apps	Subs	Gls
Tottenham H	Sch	07/02	03-04	1	2	0
Brighton & HA	L	11/03	03	9	0	0
Swindon T	L	08/04	04	3	1	0
Colchester U	L	08/05	05	42	2	5
Hull C	L	08/06	06	2	3	0
Leicester C	L	01/07	06	5	4	1
Colchester U	Tr	07/07	07-08	71	1	20
Middlesbrough	Tr	07/09	09	11	8	1
Sheffield U	Tr	01/10	09-10	29	26	7
Watford	Tr	07/11	11-12	46	16	7
Bradford C	Tr	07/13	13-14	36	34	5

League Club	Source	Date Signed	Seasons Played	Career Record Apps	Subs	Gls
YEATS Ronald (Ron)						
Born: Aberdeen, Scotland, 15 November, 1937						CH
Scotland: 2/Schools						
Liverpool	Dundee U	07/61	61-70	357	1	13
Tranmere Rov	Tr	12/71	71-73	96	1	5
YEATS Thomas Brandon (Tom)						
Born: Newcastle-upon-Tyne, England, 30 May, 1935						RW
Sunderland	Jnr	02/53				
Gateshead	Tr	08/54	54	1	-	0
YEATS William (Billy)						
Born: Hebburn, Tyne and Wear, England, 4 February, 1951						F
Died: South Tyneside, Tyne and Wear, England, December, 2013						
Newcastle U	North Shields	06/71				
York C	Tr	03/72	71-72	8	1	0
Darlington	Tr	08/73	73-74	22	3	7
YEBDA Hassan						
Born: Paris, France, 14 May, 1984						DM
Algeria: 25//France: Youth						
Portsmouth (L)	Benfica (POR)	08/09	09	15	3	2
YEBOAH Anthony (Tony)						
Born: Kumasi, Ghana, 6 June, 1966						F
Ghana: 59						
Leeds U	Eintracht F'furt (GER)	01/95	94-96	44	3	24
YEDLIN DeAndre Roselle						
Born: Seattle, Washington, USA, 9 July, 1993						RB
USA: 23/Youth						
Tottenham H	Seattle Sounders (USA)	01/15	14	0	1	0
YELLDELL David Raymond						
Born: Stuttgart, Germany, 1 October, 1981						G
USA: 1						
Blackburn Rov	Stuttgart Kick's (GER)	07/03				
Brighton & HA	L	01/05	04	3	0	0
YENNARIS Nicholas Harry (Nico)						
Born: Leytonstone, NE London, England, 23 May, 1993						RB/M
England: Youth						
Arsenal	Sch	07/10	11	0	1	0
Notts Co	L	03/12	11	2	0	0
Brentford	Tr	01/14	13-14	6	3	0
Wycombe W	L	02/15	14	14	0	1
YEO Brian Geoffrey						
Born: Worthing, West Sussex, England, 12 April, 1944						F/M
Portsmouth	Jnr	05/61				
Gillingham	Tr	07/63	63-74	345	11	137
YEO Simon John						
Born: Stockport, Greater Manchester, England, 20 October, 1973						F
Lincoln C	Hyde U	08/02	02-04	73	49	37
Lincoln C	NZ Knights (NZL)	01/06	05	11	1	5
Peterborough U	Tr	08/06	06	8	5	2
Chester C	Tr	01/07	06-07	21	15	8
Bury	L	01/08	07	0	8	0
Macclesfield T	Tr	07/08	08	22	11	7
YEOMAN Ashley Scott						
Born: Kingsbridge, Devon, England, 25 February, 1992						F
Torquay U	Sch	07/10	11-13	6	17	5
YEOMAN Ramon Irvine (Ray)						
Born: Perth, Scotland, 13 May, 1934						WH
Died: Middlesbrough, England, 15 March, 2004						
Northampton T	St Johnstone	09/53	53-58	169	-	4
Middlesbrough	Tr	11/58	58-63	210	-	3
Darlington	Tr	06/64	64-66	104	0	2
YEOMANS Kelvin						
Born: Nottingham, England, 25 August, 1947						FB
Notts Co	Beeston	06/67	67	1	0	0
YEOMANSON John William (Jack)						
Born: Margate, Kent, England, 3 March, 1920						RB
Died: Margate, Kent, England, October, 1997						
West Ham U	Margate	02/47	47-50	106	-	1
YETTON Stewart David						
Born: Plymouth, England, 27 July, 1985						F
Plymouth Arg	Sch	08/04	02-04	0	3	0
YEUELL Jasper Herbert						
Born: Bilston, West Midlands, England, 23 March, 1925						RB
Died: Hastings, East Sussex, England, 1 July, 2003						
Portsmouth	West Bromwich A (Am)	08/46	46-51	30	-	0
Barnsley	Tr	08/52	52	19	-	0

League Club	Source	Date Signed	Seasons Played	Career Record Apps	Subs	Gls
YIADOM Andrew Kyere (Andy)						
Born: Holloway, N London, England, 2 December, 1991						RB/M
Barnet	Braintree T	01/12	11-12	32	14	4
YOBO Joseph Phillip						
Born: Kano, Nigeria, 6 September, 1980						CD
Nigeria: 101						
Everton	Olymp Marseille (FRA)	08/02	02-09	204	16	8
Norwich C (L)	Fenerbahce (TKY)	01/14	13	8	0	0
YORATH Terence Charles (Terry)						
Born: Cardiff, Wales, 27 March, 1950						M
Wales: 59/U23-7/Schools						
Leeds U	App	04/67	67-76	121	20	10
Coventry C	Tr	08/76	76-78	99	0	3
Tottenham H	Tr	08/79	79-80	44	4	1
Bradford C	Vancouver W'caps (CAN)	12/82	82-84	22	5	0
Swansea C	Tr	10/86	86	1	0	0
[YORDI] GONZALEZ DIAZ Jorge						
Born: San Fernando, Cadiz, Spain, 14 September, 1974						F
Blackburn Rov (L)	Real Zaragoza (SPN)	02/02	01	5	3	2
YORK Allan						
Born: Newcastle-upon-Tyne, England, 13 July, 1941						LB
Bradford C	Gateshead	02/65	64-66	42	3	2
Lincoln C	Tr	07/67				
YORKE Dwight Eversley						
Born: Canaan, Tobago, 3 November, 1971						F
Trinidad & Tobago: 58						
Aston Villa	Signal Hill (TRD)	12/89	89-98	195	36	73
Manchester U	Tr	08/98	98-01	80	16	48
Blackburn Rov	Tr	07/02	02-04	42	18	12
Birmingham C	Tr	08/04	04	4	9	2
Sunderland	Sydney U (AUS)	08/06	06-08	49	10	6
YOSHIDA Maya						
Born: Nagasaki, Japan, 24 August, 1988						CD
Japan: 53/U23-12						
Southampton	VVV Venlo (NED)	08/12	12-14	56	6	2
YOUDS Edward Paul (Eddie)						
Born: Liverpool, England, 3 May, 1970						CD
Everton	YT	06/88	90	5	3	0
Cardiff C	L	12/89	89	0	1	0
Wrexham	L	02/90	89	20	0	2
Ipswich T	Tr	11/91	91-94	38	12	1
Bradford C	L	01/95	94	7	0	2
Bradford C	Tr	03/95	94-97	78	0	6
Charlton Ath	Tr	03/98	97-99	52	1	2
Huddersfield T	Tr	07/02	02	25	0	0
YOUGA Kelly Alexandre						
Born: Bangui, Central African Republic, 22 September, 1985						LB
Central African Republic: 6						
Charlton Ath	Olymp Lyonnais (FRA)	06/05	07-09	61	1	1
Bristol C	L	10/05	05	4	0	0
Bradford C	L	01/07	06	11	0	0
Scunthorpe U	L	07/07	07	18	1	1
Yeovil T		01/12	11	0	1	0
AFC Wimbledon	Ipswich T (NC)	03/13	12	3	0	0
Crawley T	Qingdao Hainiu (CHN)	03/15	14	5	0	1
YOULDEN Thomas Frederick (Tommy)						
Born: Islington, N London, England, 8 July, 1949						CD
England: Schools						
Arsenal	App	07/66				
Portsmouth	Tr	04/68	68-71	82	7	1
Reading	Tr	07/72	72-76	161	2	3
Aldershot	Tr	04/77	76-80	118	5	1
YOUNG Alan James						
Born: Swindon, England, 12 August, 1983						F
England: Youth						
Swindon T	YT	10/00	00-02	7	22	1
YOUNG Albert Edward						
Born: Caerleon, Monmouthshire, Wales, 11 September, 1917						FB
Died: Chelmsford, England, January, 2013						
Arsenal	Ponthir Star Brickw'ks	09/38				
Swindon T	Tr	06/46	46-49	123	-	1
YOUNG Alexander (Alex)						
Born: Loanhead, Midlothian, Scotland, 3 February, 1937						F
Scotland: 8/SLge-2/U23-6						
Everton	Heart of Midlothian	11/60	60-67	227	1	77
Stockport Co	Glentoran	11/68	68	23	0	5

YOUNG Alexander Forbes (Alan)
Born: Kirkcaldy, Fife, Scotland, 26 October, 1955 — CF
Scotland: Schools

League Club	Source	Date Signed	Seasons Played	Apps	Subs	Gls
Oldham Ath	Kirkcaldy YMCA	07/74	74-78	107	15	30
Leicester C	Tr	07/79	79-81	102	2	26
Sheffield U	Tr	08/82	82	23	3	7
Brighton & HA	Tr	08/83	83	25	1	12
Notts Co	Tr	09/84	84-85	39	4	13
Rochdale	Tr	08/86	86	19	9	2

YOUNG Allan Robert
Born: Hornsey, N London, England, 20 January, 1941 — CH

League Club	Source	Date Signed	Seasons Played	Apps	Subs	Gls
Arsenal	Jnr	04/59	60	4	-	0
Chelsea	Tr	11/61	61-66	20	0	0
Torquay U	Tr	01/69	68-71	59	0	1

YOUNG Ashley Simon
Born: Stevenage, Hertfordshire, England, 9 July, 1985 — LW
England: 30/U21-10

League Club	Source	Date Signed	Seasons Played	Apps	Subs	Gls
Watford	Jnr	07/02	03-06	73	25	19
Aston Villa	Tr	01/07	06-10	155	2	30
Manchester U	Tr	07/11	11-14	72	18	10

YOUNG Cecil Rodney (Ron)
Born: Bournemouth, England, 22 July, 1925 — RH
Died: Barton-on-Sea, Hampshire, England, 18 March, 1991

League Club	Source	Date Signed	Seasons Played	Apps	Subs	Gls
Bournemouth	Southampton (Am)	06/48	48-49	18	-	0

YOUNG Charles Frederick (Charlie)
Born: Nicosia, Cyprus, 14 February, 1958 — D

League Club	Source	Date Signed	Seasons Played	Apps	Subs	Gls
Aston Villa	App	11/75	76	9	1	0
Gillingham	Tr	03/78	77-81	27	1	1

YOUNG Charles Stuart Robertson (Stuart)
Born: Falkirk, Scotland, 23 August, 1929 — G
Died: Oldham, Greater Manchester, England, March, 2005

League Club	Source	Date Signed	Seasons Played	Apps	Subs	Gls
Sheffield U	Stalybridge Celtic	06/51	51	3	-	0

YOUNG Christopher William (Chris)
Born: Manchester, England, 11 August, 1979 — F

League Club	Source	Date Signed	Seasons Played	Apps	Subs	Gls
Mansfield T	YT	-	96	0	1	0

YOUNG Clarence William (Clarrie)
Born: Bow, E London, England, 23 February, 1920 — LW
Died: Chelmsford, England, 5 May, 2009

League Club	Source	Date Signed	Seasons Played	Apps	Subs	Gls
Coventry C	Margate	09/38	46	1	-	0

YOUNG David
Born: Newcastle-upon-Tyne, England, 12 November, 1945 — CD

League Club	Source	Date Signed	Seasons Played	Apps	Subs	Gls
Newcastle U	Jnr	09/64	69-72	41	2	2
Sunderland	Tr	01/73	72-73	24	6	1
Charlton Ath	Tr	08/74	74-76	76	1	0
Southend U	Tr	09/76	76-77	56	4	0

YOUNG David
Born: Birkenhead, Wirral, England, 27 April, 1962 — M

League Club	Source	Date Signed	Seasons Played	Apps	Subs	Gls
Wigan Ath	Mossley	03/83	82	3	0	0

YOUNG David Alan
Born: Trimdon, County Durham, England, 31 January, 1965 — LB

League Club	Source	Date Signed	Seasons Played	Apps	Subs	Gls
Darlington	App	01/83	82-83	13	5	0

YOUNG Douglas (Doug)
Born: Islington, N London, England, 2 February, 1927 — RB
Died: St Neots, Cambridgeshire, England, 23 December, 2001
England: Amateur-4

League Club	Source	Date Signed	Seasons Played	Apps	Subs	Gls
Southend U	Walthamstow Ave	06/53	53-55	38	-	0

YOUNG Eric
Born: Singapore, 25 March, 1960 — CD
Wales: 21

League Club	Source	Date Signed	Seasons Played	Apps	Subs	Gls
Brighton & HA	Slough T	11/82	83-86	126	0	10
Wimbledon	Tr	07/87	87-89	96	3	9
Crystal Palace	Tr	08/90	90-94	161	0	15
Wolverhampton W	Tr	09/95	95-96	31	0	2

YOUNG Eric Royston
Born: Stockton-on-Tees, Cleveland, England, 26 November, 1952 — M
England: Youth/Schools

League Club	Source	Date Signed	Seasons Played	Apps	Subs	Gls
Manchester U	App	12/69				
Peterborough U	L	11/72	72	24	1	2
Walsall	L	10/73	73	8	0	0
Stockport Co	L	01/74	73	16	0	0
Darlington	Tr	07/74	74-77	123	7	15

YOUNG George
Born: Dundee, Scotland, 2 November, 1919 — IF
Died: Ealing, W London, England, 1982

League Club	Source	Date Signed	Seasons Played	Apps	Subs	Gls
Watford	Hibernian	07/46	46-48	43	-	5

YOUNG George Raymond (Ray)
Born: Derby, England, 14 March, 1934 — CH
England: Schools

League Club	Source	Date Signed	Seasons Played	Apps	Subs	Gls
Derby Co	Jnr	03/51	53-65	253	1	5

YOUNG Gerald Morton (Gerry)
Born: Jarrow, Tyne and Wear, England, 1 October, 1936 — LH
England: 1

League Club	Source	Date Signed	Seasons Played	Apps	Subs	Gls
Sheffield Wed	Hawthorn Leslie	05/55	56-70	308	2	13

YOUNG Gregory James (Greg)
Born: Doncaster, South Yorkshire, England, 25 April, 1983 — CD

League Club	Source	Date Signed	Seasons Played	Apps	Subs	Gls
Grimsby T	Sheffield Wed (YT)	07/02	02-04	13	11	0

YOUNG Jamie Iain
Born: Brisbane, Australia, 25 August, 1985 — G
England: Youth

League Club	Source	Date Signed	Seasons Played	Apps	Subs	Gls
Reading	Sch	10/03	03	0	1	0
Rushden & D	L	07/05	05	19	1	0
Wycombe W	Tr	08/06	06-09	36	3	0
Aldershot T	Tr	03/10	09-12	122	2	0

YOUNG John
Born: Hartlepool, Cleveland, England, 9 November, 1951 — W

League Club	Source	Date Signed	Seasons Played	Apps	Subs	Gls
Hartlepool U (Am)	Newcastle U (Am)	08/68	68	3	0	0

YOUNG John Robert
Born: Gateshead, Tyne and Wear, England, 19 October, 1925 — G
Died: Gateshead, Tyne and Wear, England, 16 April, 1988

League Club	Source	Date Signed	Seasons Played	Apps	Subs	Gls
Gateshead (Am)		08/49	49	4	-	0

YOUNG Kenneth (Ken)
Born: Halifax, West Yorkshire, England, 11 June, 1930 — IF

League Club	Source	Date Signed	Seasons Played	Apps	Subs	Gls
Halifax T	Jnr	11/49	49	1	-	0

YOUNG Kevin
Born: Sunderland, England, 12 August, 1961 — M

League Club	Source	Date Signed	Seasons Played	Apps	Subs	Gls
Burnley	App	05/79	78-83	114	6	11
Torquay U	L	11/83	83	3	0	1
Port Vale	L	12/83	83	28	0	4
Bury	Tr	07/84	84-86	85	3	10

YOUNG Leonard Archibald (Len)
Born: West Ham, E London, England, 23 February, 1912 — CH

League Club	Source	Date Signed	Seasons Played	Apps	Subs	Gls
West Ham U	Ilford	04/34	33-37	12	-	0
Reading	Tr	11/37	37-47	84	-	0
Brighton & HA	Tr	02/48	47-48	8	-	0

YOUNG Lewis Jack
Born: Stevenage, Hertfordshire, England, 27 September, 1989 — M/RB

League Club	Source	Date Signed	Seasons Played	Apps	Subs	Gls
Watford	Sch	07/08	08	0	1	0
Hereford U	L	03/10	09	5	1	0
Burton A	Tr	07/10	10	9	10	0
Northampton T	Tr	07/11	11	20	10	0
Yeovil T	Tr	07/12	12	2	13	0
Bury	Aldershot T	02/14	13	0	4	0
Crawley T	Tr	07/14	14	29	9	0

YOUNG Luke
Born: Ivybridge, Devon, England, 22 February, 1993 — RW

League Club	Source	Date Signed	Seasons Played	Apps	Subs	Gls
Plymouth Arg	Sch	07/11	10-13	69	30	8

YOUNG Luke Paul
Born: Harlow, Essex, England, 19 July, 1979 — RB
England: 7/U21-12/Youth

League Club	Source	Date Signed	Seasons Played	Apps	Subs	Gls
Tottenham H	YT	07/97	98-00	44	14	0
Charlton Ath	Tr	07/01	01-06	181	6	4
Middlesbrough	Tr	08/07	07	35	0	1
Aston Villa	Tr	08/08	08-11	72	3	2
Queens Park Rgrs	Tr	08/11	11-13	24	0	2

YOUNG Martin
Born: Grimsby, North Lincolnshire, England, 9 April, 1955 — CD

League Club	Source	Date Signed	Seasons Played	Apps	Subs	Gls
Grimsby T	Jnr	03/74	74-78	87	7	4

YOUNG Matthew Geoffrey
Born: Woodlesford, West Yorkshire, England, 25 October, 1985 — M

League Club	Source	Date Signed	Seasons Played	Apps	Subs	Gls
Huddersfield T	Sch	07/05	05-07	20	19	2

YOUNG Matthew Robert (Matt)
Born: Isle of Wight, England, 26 January, 1994 — RB

League Club	Source	Date Signed	Seasons Played	Apps	Subs	Gls
Southampton	Sch	07/12				
Sheffield Wed	Tr	06/14				
Carlisle U	L	01/15	14	20	0	0

YOUNG Michael Samuel
Born: Chester-le-Street, County Durham, England, 15 March, 1973 — W

League Club	Source	Date Signed	Seasons Played	Apps	Subs	Gls
Middlesbrough	Newcastle U (YT)	07/91	91	0	1	0

YOUNG Neil Anthony
Born: Harlow, Essex, England, 31 August, 1973 — RB

League Club	Source	Date Signed	Seasons Played	Apps	Subs	Gls
Tottenham H	YT	08/91				
Bournemouth	Tr	10/94	94-07	408	21	4

YOUNG Neil James
Born: Manchester, England, 17 February, 1944 — IF/W
Died: Manchester, England, 3 February, 2011
England: Youth

League Club	Source	Date Signed	Seasons Played	Apps	Subs	Gls
Manchester C	App	02/61	61-71	332	2	86
Preston NE	Tr	01/72	71-73	67	3	16
Rochdale	Tr	07/74	74	8	5	4

YOUNG Noel Johnston
Born: Derry, Northern Ireland, 22 December, 1932 — LH
Northern Ireland: NILge-3

League Club	Source	Date Signed	Seasons Played	Apps	Subs	Gls
Middlesbrough	Jnr	04/50				
Doncaster Rov		01/55	54	3		0

YOUNG Quintin
Born: Drongan, Ayrshire, Scotland, 19 September, 1947 — RW
Scotland: U23-1

League Club	Source	Date Signed	Seasons Played	Apps	Subs	Gls
Coventry C	Ayr U	07/71	71-72	25	1	2

YOUNG Richard (Dick)
Born: Felling, Tyne and Wear, England, 13 July, 1939 — CF
Died: Stockport, Greater Manchester, England, July, 1988

League Club	Source	Date Signed	Seasons Played	Apps	Subs	Gls
Newcastle U	Usworth Jnrs	07/57				
Grimsby T	South Shields	03/62	62-64	33	-	13
Stockport Co	Tr	05/65	65	27	0	5

YOUNG Richard Anthony
Born: Nottingham, England, 18 October, 1968 — F

League Club	Source	Date Signed	Seasons Played	Apps	Subs	Gls
Notts Co	App	08/86	86	18	17	5
Southend U	Tr	08/87	87-88	5	4	0
Exeter C	Tr	03/89	88-90	32	17	10

YOUNG Richard Harter (Dick)
Born: Gateshead, Tyne and Wear, England, 17 April, 1918 — LB
Died: Carlisle, Cumbria, England, 31 January, 1989

League Club	Source	Date Signed	Seasons Played	Apps	Subs	Gls
Sheffield U	Hebburn St Cuthbert's	11/35	36-48	71	-	0
Lincoln C	Tr	03/49	48-53	100	-	2

YOUNG Robert George (George)
Born: Newport, Wales, 5 January, 1950 — M
Wales: U23-1

League Club	Source	Date Signed	Seasons Played	Apps	Subs	Gls
Newport Co	Cromwell Jnrs	07/67	67-71	90	15	6

YOUNG Robert Gerald (Bob)
Born: Bournemouth, England, 24 December, 1923 — LB
Died: Liverpool, NSW, Australia, 25 May, 2005

League Club	Source	Date Signed	Seasons Played	Apps	Subs	Gls
Bournemouth	Jnr	01/46	47	1	-	0
Crewe Alex	Tr	06/48	48-51	144	-	2

YOUNG Ronald (Ron)
Born: Dunston-on-Tyne, Tyne and Wear, England, 31 August, 1945 — W

League Club	Source	Date Signed	Seasons Played	Apps	Subs	Gls
Hull C		08/63	64-67	24	2	5
Hartlepool U	Tr	09/68	68-72	176	10	40

YOUNG Roy
Born: Sheffield, England, 2 October, 1950 — RB/M

League Club	Source	Date Signed	Seasons Played	Apps	Subs	Gls
Doncaster Rov	Sheffield U (Am)	07/70	70	6	1	0

YOUNG Scott
Born: Tonypandy, Rhondda Cynon Taff, Wales, 14 January, 1976 — CD
Wales: B-1/U21-5

League Club	Source	Date Signed	Seasons Played	Apps	Subs	Gls
Cardiff C	YT	07/94	93-02	257	20	22

YOUNG Stuart Rodney
Born: Hull, England, 16 December, 1972 — F

League Club	Source	Date Signed	Seasons Played	Apps	Subs	Gls
Hull C	Arsenal (YT)	07/91	91-92	11	8	2
Northampton T	Tr	02/93	92	7	1	2
Scarborough	Tr	08/93	93-94	28	13	10
Scunthorpe U	Tr	12/94	94-95	19	9	3

YOUNG Thomas Anthony (Tony)
Born: Urmston, Greater Manchester, England, 24 December, 1952 — FB/M

League Club	Source	Date Signed	Seasons Played	Apps	Subs	Gls
Manchester U	App	12/69	70-75	69	14	1
Charlton Ath	Tr	01/76	75-76	20	0	1
York C	Tr	09/76	76-78	76	2	2

YOUNG Thomas McIlwaine (Tommy)
Born: Glasgow, Scotland, 24 December, 1947 — M/F

League Club	Source	Date Signed	Seasons Played	Apps	Subs	Gls
Tranmere Rov	Falkirk	06/72	72-76	170	2	27
Rotherham U	Tr	07/77	77-78	11	4	1

YOUNG William David (Willie)
Born: Edinburgh, Scotland, 25 November, 1951 — CD
Scotland: U23-5

League Club	Source	Date Signed	Seasons Played	Apps	Subs	Gls
Tottenham H	Aberdeen	09/75	75-76	54	0	3
Arsenal	Tr	03/77	76-81	170	0	11
Nottingham F	Tr	12/81	81-82	59	0	5
Norwich C	Tr	08/83	83	5	1	0
Brighton & HA	L	03/84	83	4	0	0
Darlington	Tr	09/84	84	4	0	0

YOUNG William John (Willie)
Born: Glasgow, Scotland, 24 February, 1956 — LW

League Club	Source	Date Signed	Seasons Played	Apps	Subs	Gls
Aston Villa	Arthurlie	07/78	78	3	0	0
Torquay U	Tr	10/81	81-82	35	3	0

YOUNGER Thomas (Tommy)
Born: Edinburgh, Scotland, 10 April, 1930 — G
Died: Edinburgh, Scotland, 13 January, 1984
Scotland: 24/SLge-4

League Club	Source	Date Signed	Seasons Played	Apps	Subs	Gls
Liverpool	Hibernian	06/56	56-58	120	-	0
Stoke C	Falkirk	03/60	59	10	-	0
Leeds U	Toronto C (CAN)	09/61	61-62	37	-	0

YOUNGER William (Billy)
Born: Seaton Delaval, Northumberland, England, 22 March, 1940 — IF
Died: Northumberland, England, January, 2006

League Club	Source	Date Signed	Seasons Played	Apps	Subs	Gls
Nottingham F	Whitley Bay	05/57	58-60	12	-	2
Lincoln C	L	02/61	60	4	-	0
Walsall	Tr	06/61	61	8	-	5
Doncaster Rov	Tr	12/61	61	18	-	1
Hartlepool U	Tr	08/62	62	37	-	4

YOUNGMAN Stuart Trevor
Born: Beccles, Suffolk, England, 15 October, 1965 — M

League Club	Source	Date Signed	Seasons Played	Apps	Subs	Gls
Colchester U	App	07/84	84	0	1	0

YOUNGS Thomas Anthony John (Tom)
Born: Bury St Edmunds, Suffolk, England, 31 August, 1979 — F

League Club	Source	Date Signed	Seasons Played	Apps	Subs	Gls
Cambridge U	Jnr	07/97	97-02	118	32	43
Northampton T	Tr	03/03	02-04	11	15	0
Leyton Orient	Tr	01/05	04	6	4	1
Bury	Tr	07/05	05-06	25	24	7

YOUNGS Thomas Ronald (Tom)
Born: Greenwich, SE London, England, 6 September, 1994 — F

League Club	Source	Date Signed	Seasons Played	Apps	Subs	Gls
Bolton W	Sch	10/13	13	0	1	0

YOUSSOUF Sammy
Born: Copenhagen, Denmark, 7 September, 1976 — W

League Club	Source	Date Signed	Seasons Played	Apps	Subs	Gls
Queens Park Rgrs	CS Maritimo (POR)	01/06	05	2	4	0

YULU Christian
Born: Luanda, Angola, 2 February, 1982 — F

League Club	Source	Date Signed	Seasons Played	Apps	Subs	Gls
Coventry C	Stade Rennais (FRA)	02/03	02	1	2	0

YUN Suk-Young
Born: Suwon, South Korea, 13 February, 1990 — LB
South Korea: 10/U23-27

League Club	Source	Date Signed	Seasons Played	Apps	Subs	Gls
Queens Park Rgrs	Chunnam Dragons (KOR)	02/13	13-14	23	7	1
Doncaster Rov	L	10/13	13	2	1	0

YURAN Sergei Nikolayevich
Born: Ukraine, 11 June, 1969 — F
Russia: 25//Soviet Union: 15

League Club	Source	Date Signed	Seasons Played	Apps	Subs	Gls
Millwall (L)	Spartak Moscow (RUS)	01/96	95	13	0	1

YUSSUF Abdillahie (Adi)
Born: Zanzibar, Tanzania, 3 October, 1992 — F

League Club	Source	Date Signed	Seasons Played	Apps	Subs	Gls
Leicester C	Sch	07/10				
Burton A	Tr	08/11	11-12	3	22	1

YUSSUFF Rashid Olatokunbo Oladobe Alao
Born: Poplar, E London, England, 23 September, 1989 — W
England: Youth

League Club	Source	Date Signed	Seasons Played	Apps	Subs	Gls
Charlton Ath	Sch	03/08				
Gillingham	Tr	08/09	09	2	6	0
AFC Wimbledon	Tr	07/10	11-12	45	18	6

YUSUFF Adam Adeoye (Adeoye)
Born: Lewisham, SE London, England, 25 May, 1994 — F

League Club	Source	Date Signed	Seasons Played	Apps	Subs	Gls
Dagenham & Red	Chatham T	09/14	14	9	9	2

ZAABOUB Sofiane
Born: Melun, France, 23 January, 1983 — LB/M

League Club	Source	Date Signed	Seasons Played	Apps	Subs	Gls
Swindon T	FCM Brussels (BEL)	11/06	06-07	41	15	1
Walsall	Tr	07/08	08	24	5	0
Southend U		08/10	10	2	1	0

ZABALETA Pablo Javier
Born: Buenos Aires, Argentina, 16 January, 1985 — RB
Argentina: 53/U23-9/Youth

League Club	Source	Date Signed	Seasons Played	Apps	Subs	Gls
Manchester C	RCD Espanyol (SPN)	09/08	08-14	180	17	8

ZABEK Lee Kevin
Born: Bristol, England, 13 October, 1978 — M

League Club	Source	Date Signed	Seasons Played	Apps	Subs	Gls
Bristol Rov	YT	07/97	96-99	21	8	1
Exeter C	Tr	08/00	00-01	28	5	0

ZABICA Robert
Born: Perth, Australia, 9 April, 1964 — G
Australia: 28

League Club	Source	Date Signed	Seasons Played	Apps	Subs	Gls
Bradford C	Perth Glory (AUS)	08/97	97	3	0	0

ZADKOVICH Ruben Anton
Born: Sydney, Australia, 23 May, 1986 — M/RB
Australia: 3/U23-25/Youth

League Club	Source	Date Signed	Seasons Played	Apps	Subs	Gls
Queens Park Rgrs	Wollongong Rgrs (AUS)	09/04				
Notts Co	Wollongong Wolv (AUS)	03/05	04	6	3	1
Derby Co	Sydney U (AUS)	07/08	08	2	3	0

ZAGORAKIS Theodoros (Theo)
Born: Kavala, Greece, 17 October, 1971 — DM
Greece: 120

League Club	Source	Date Signed	Seasons Played	Apps	Subs	Gls
Leicester C	PAOK Salonika (GRE)	02/98	97-99	34	16	3

ZAHA Dazet Wilfried Armel (Wilfried)
Born: Abidjan, Ivory Coast, 10 November, 1992 — RW
England: 2/U21-13/Youth

League Club	Source	Date Signed	Seasons Played	Apps	Subs	Gls
Crystal Palace	Sch	07/10	09-12	87	23	12
Manchester U	Tr	01/13	13	0	2	0
Crystal Palace	L	02/13	12	16	0	1
Cardiff C	L	01/14	13	5	7	0
Crystal Palace	Tr	08/14	14	23	8	4

ZAHANA-ONI Landry
Born: Abidjan, Ivory Coast, 8 August, 1976 — F
France: Youth

League Club	Source	Date Signed	Seasons Played	Apps	Subs	Gls
Luton T	Bromley	01/99	98-99	4	5	0

ZAKI Amr Hassan
Born: Mansoura, Egypt, 1 April, 1983 — F
Egypt: 63

League Club	Source	Date Signed	Seasons Played	Apps	Subs	Gls
Wigan Ath (L)	El Zamalek (EGY)	07/08	08	22	7	10
Hull C (L)	El Zamalek (EGY)	01/10	09	2	4	0

ZAKUANI Gabriel Abdala (Gaby)
Born: Kinshasa, DR Congo, 31 May, 1986 — CD
DR Congo: 10

League Club	Source	Date Signed	Seasons Played	Apps	Subs	Gls
Leyton Orient	Sch	06/05	02-04	84	3	3
Fulham	Tr	07/06				
Stoke C	L	01/07	06	9	0	0
Stoke C	L	08/07	07	11	8	0
Peterborough U	Tr	09/08	08-13	174	6	5
Peterborough U	AEL Kalloni (GRE)	06/14	14	20	2	1

ZALIUKAS Marius
Born: Kaunas, Lithuania, 10 November, 1983 — CD
Lithuania: 25/U21-9

League Club	Source	Date Signed	Seasons Played	Apps	Subs	Gls
Leeds U	Heart of Midlothian	10/13	13	13	2	0

ZAMORA Robert Lester (Bobby)
Born: Barking, E London, England, 16 January, 1981 — F
England: 2/U21-6

League Club	Source	Date Signed	Seasons Played	Apps	Subs	Gls
Bristol Rov	YT	07/99	99	0	4	0
Brighton & HA	L	02/00	99	6	0	6
Brighton & HA	Tr	08/00	00-02	117	2	70
Tottenham H	Tr	07/03	03	6	10	0
West Ham U	Tr	02/04	03-07	85	45	30
Fulham	Tr	07/08	08-11	82	9	20
Queens Park Rgrs	Tr	01/12	11-14	56	27	12

ZAMPERINI Alessandro
Born: Rome, Italy, 15 August, 1982 — CD

League Club	Source	Date Signed	Seasons Played	Apps	Subs	Gls
Portsmouth	AS Roma (ITA)	07/01	01	16	0	2

ZARATE Mauro Matias
Born: Buenos Aires, Argentina, 18 March, 1987 — F
Argentina: Youth

League Club	Source	Date Signed	Seasons Played	Apps	Subs	Gls
Birmingham C (L)	Al-Sadd (QAT)	01/08	07	6	8	4
West Ham U	Velez Sarsfield (ARG)	06/14	14	5	2	2
Queens Park Rgrs	L	01/15	14	0	4	0

ZAVAGNO Luciano
Born: Rosario, Argentina, 6 August, 1977 — LB

League Club	Source	Date Signed	Seasons Played	Apps	Subs	Gls
Derby Co	Troyes AC (FRA)	10/01	01-03	48	4	3

ZAYATTE Kamil
Born: Conakry, Guinea, 7 March, 1985 — CD
Guinea: 46

League Club	Source	Date Signed	Seasons Played	Apps	Subs	Gls
Hull C	Young Boys Bern (SUI)	09/08	08-10	68	3	3
Sheffield Wed	Istanbul BB (TKY)	08/13	13-14	22	0	2

ZDRILIC David Allen
Born: Sydney, Australia, 14 April, 1974 — F
Australia: 30

League Club	Source	Date Signed	Seasons Played	Apps	Subs	Gls
Walsall	Unterhaching (GER)	08/02	02	9	15	3

ZEBROSKI Christopher Matthew (Chris)
Born: Swindon, England, 29 October, 1986 — F

League Club	Source	Date Signed	Seasons Played	Apps	Subs	Gls
Plymouth Arg	Sch	07/06	05	0	4	0
Millwall	Tr	09/06	06	10	15	3
Wycombe W	Tr	07/08	08-09	43	5	9
Torquay U	Tr	11/09	09-10	74	0	20
Bristol Rov	Tr	07/11	11	28	11	3
Cheltenham T	Tr	07/12	12	20	1	5
Newport Co	Eastleigh	06/13	13-14	60	11	19

ZEEGELAAR Marvin Romeo Kwasie
Born: Amsterdam, Netherlands, 12 August, 1990 — LB/M

League Club	Source	Date Signed	Seasons Played	Apps	Subs	Gls
Blackpool (L)	Elazigspor (TKY)	09/13	13	0	2	0

ZEGHDANE Lehit
Born: Sedan, France, 3 October, 1977 — M

League Club	Source	Date Signed	Seasons Played	Apps	Subs	Gls
Darlington	Sedan (FRA)	09/00	00	1	2	0

ZELEM Peter Richard
Born: Manchester, England, 13 February, 1962 — CD

League Club	Source	Date Signed	Seasons Played	Apps	Subs	Gls
Chester C	App	02/80	80-84	124	5	15
Wolverhampton W	Tr	01/85	84-86	45	0	1
Preston NE	Tr	03/87	86	6	0	1
Burnley	Tr	08/87	87-88	17	2	2

ZELIC Nedijeljko (Ned)
Born: Sydney, Australia, 4 July, 1971 — DM
Australia: 34/U23-16/Youth

League Club	Source	Date Signed	Seasons Played	Apps	Subs	Gls
Queens Park Rgrs	Bor Dortmund (GER)	08/95	95	3	1	0

ZEMMAMA Merouane
Born: Sale, Morocco, 7 October, 1983 — M
Morocco: 7

League Club	Source	Date Signed	Seasons Played	Apps	Subs	Gls
Middlesbrough	Hibernian	01/11	10-12	13	28	3

ZENCHUK Steven John
Born: Peterborough, England, 20 November, 1966 — G

League Club	Source	Date Signed	Seasons Played	Apps	Subs	Gls
Peterborough U	App	08/83	83	1	0	0

ZENDEN Boudewijn (Bolo)
Born: Maastricht, Netherlands, 15 August, 1976 — LM
Netherlands: 54

League Club	Source	Date Signed	Seasons Played	Apps	Subs	Gls
Chelsea	Barcelona (SPN)	08/01	01-02	24	19	4
Middlesbrough	Tr	08/03	03-04	67	0	9
Liverpool	Tr	07/05	05-06	14	9	2
Sunderland	Olymp Marseille (FRA)	10/09	09-10	11	36	4

ZENYOV Sergei
Born: Parnu, Estonia, 20 April, 1989 — F
Estonia: 45/U21-2

League Club	Source	Date Signed	Seasons Played	Apps	Subs	Gls
Blackpool	Karpaty Lviv (UKR)	07/14	14	2	6	0

ZHANG ENHUA (Zhang)
Born: Dalian, China, 28 April, 1973 — CD
China: 62

League Club	Source	Date Signed	Seasons Played	Apps	Subs	Gls
Grimsby T (L)	Dalian Shide (CHN)	12/00	00	16	1	3

ZHENG ZHI (Zheng)
Born: Shenyang, China, 20 August, 1980 — M
China: 50

League Club	Source	Date Signed	Seasons Played	Apps	Subs	Gls
Charlton Ath	Shandong Luneng (CHN)	01/07	06-08	57	10	9

ZHIRKOV Yuri Valentinovich
Born: Tambov, Russia, 20 August, 1983 — LB/M
Russia: 65

League Club	Source	Date Signed	Seasons Played	Apps	Subs	Gls
Chelsea	CSKA Moscow (RUS)	07/09	09-10	16	13	0

ZIEGE Christian
Born: Berlin, Germany, 1 February, 1972 — LB
Germany: 72/U21-12

League Club	Source	Date Signed	Seasons Played	Apps	Subs	Gls
Middlesbrough	AC Milan (ITA)	08/99	99	29	0	6
Liverpool	Tr	08/00	00	11	5	1
Tottenham H	Tr	08/01	01-03	44	3	7

ZIEGLER Reto Pirmin
Born: Nyon, Switzerland, 16 January, 1986 — M/LB
Switzerland: 35/U21-30/Youth

League Club	Source	Date Signed	Seasons Played	Apps	Subs	Gls
Tottenham H	G'hopper Zurich (SUI)	08/04	04-06	12	12	1
Wigan Ath	L	01/06	05	5	5	0

ZIELER Ron-Robert
Born: Cologne, Germany, 12 February, 1989 — G
Germany: 6/Youth

League Club	Source	Date Signed	Seasons Played	Apps	Subs	Gls
Manchester U	Sch	07/06				
Northampton T	L	11/08	08	2	0	0

ZIGIC Nikola
Born: Vojvodina, Serbia, 25 September, 1980 — F
Serbia: 57

League Club	Source	Date Signed	Seasons Played	Apps	Subs	Gls
Birmingham C	Valencia (SPN)	06/10	10-14	77	60	33

League Club	Source	Date Signed	Seasons Played	Career Record Apps	Subs	Gls

ZIVKOVIC Boris
Born: Zivinice, Yugoslavia, 15 November, 1975 — FB
Croatia: 39

League Club	Source	Date Signed	Seasons Played	Apps	Subs	Gls
Portsmouth	Bayer Leverkusen (GER)	07/03	03	17	1	0

ZOHAR Itzhak (Itzik)
Born: Tel Aviv, Israel, 31 October, 1970 — M
Israel: 31/U21-2

League Club	Source	Date Signed	Seasons Played	Apps	Subs	Gls
Crystal Palace	Beitar Jerusalem (ISR)	08/97	97	2	4	0

ZOIS Peter
Born: Melbourne, Australia, 21 April, 1978 — G

League Club	Source	Date Signed	Seasons Played	Apps	Subs	Gls
Cardiff C	Purfleet	02/98	97	1	0	0

ZOKO Bernard Francois Dassise (Francois)
Born: Daloa, Ivory Coast, 13 September, 1983 — F
Ivory Coast: Youth

League Club	Source	Date Signed	Seasons Played	Apps	Subs	Gls
Carlisle U	KV Oostende (BEL)	08/10	10-11	74	15	19
Notts Co	Tr	08/12	12-13	25	14	7
Stevenage	Tr	10/13	13	33	0	10
Blackpool	Tr	08/14	14	7	7	1
Bradford C	L	11/14	14	3	13	1

ZOKORA Deguy Alain Didier (Didier)
Born: Abidjan, Ivory Coast, 14 December, 1980 — DM
Ivory Coast: 123

League Club	Source	Date Signed	Seasons Played	Apps	Subs	Gls
Tottenham H	Saint-Etienne (FRA)	07/06	06-08	75	13	0

ZOLA Gianfranco
Born: Oliena, Sardinia, Italy, 5 July, 1966 — F
Italy: 35

League Club	Source	Date Signed	Seasons Played	Apps	Subs	Gls
Chelsea	Parma (ITA)	11/96	96-02	185	44	59

ZOLA-MAKONGO Calvin
Born: Kinshasa, DR Congo, 31 December, 1984 — F

League Club	Source	Date Signed	Seasons Played	Apps	Subs	Gls
Newcastle U	Sch	01/02				
Oldham Ath	L	08/03	03	21	4	5
Tranmere Rov	Tr	07/04	04-07	55	41	16
Crewe Alex	Tr	06/08	08-10	52	15	21
Burton A	Tr	01/11	10-12	74	11	26
Stevenage	Aberdeen	06/14	14	1	6	0

ZONDERVAN Romeo
Born: Paramaribo, Suriname, 4 March, 1959 — M
Netherlands: 1

League Club	Source	Date Signed	Seasons Played	Apps	Subs	Gls
West Bromwich A	Twente Enschede (NED)	03/82	81-83	82	2	5
Ipswich T	Tr	03/84	83-91	270	4	13

ZORICICH Christopher Vincent (Chris)
Born: Auckland, New Zealand, 3 May, 1969 — D/M
New Zealand: 57

League Club	Source	Date Signed	Seasons Played	Apps	Subs	Gls
Leyton Orient	Papatoetoe (NZL)	02/90	90-92	53	9	1

ZOUMA Kurt Happy
Born: Lyon, France, 27 October, 1994 — CD
France: 1/U21-7/Youth

League Club	Source	Date Signed	Seasons Played	Apps	Subs	Gls
Chelsea	Saint-Etienne (FRA)	01/14	14	7	8	0

ZUBAR Ronald
Born: Les Abymes, Guadeloupe, 20 September, 1985 — RB
France: U21-15/Youth//Guadeloupe: 1

League Club	Source	Date Signed	Seasons Played	Apps	Subs	Gls
Wolverhampton W	Olymp Marseille (FRA)	07/09	09-12	58	3	3

ZUBAR Stephane
Born: Les Abymes, Guadeloupe, 9 October, 1986 — D
Guadeloupe: 2

League Club	Source	Date Signed	Seasons Played	Apps	Subs	Gls
Plymouth Arg	FC Vaslui (ROM)	08/10	10-11	33	0	2
Bournemouth	Tr	09/11	11-12	19	5	0
Bury	L	01/13	12	6	0	0
Port Vale	L	09/14	14	2	0	0
York C	L	11/14	14	22	1	2

ZUBERBUHLER Pascal
Born: Frauenfeld, Switzerland, 8 January, 1971 — G
Switzerland: 51

League Club	Source	Date Signed	Seasons Played	Apps	Subs	Gls
West Bromwich A	FC Basel (SUI)	07/06	06	15	0	0
Fulham	Neuchatel Xamax (SUI)	08/08				

ZUIVERLOON Gianni Michel Eugene
Born: Rotterdam, Netherlands, 30 December, 1986 — RB
Netherlands: U21-22

League Club	Source	Date Signed	Seasons Played	Apps	Subs	Gls
West Bromwich A	Heerenveen (NED)	07/08	08-10	60	5	4
Ipswich T	L	11/10	10	4	0	0

ZUNIGA Yanez Herlin Ysrael (Ysrael)
Born: Lima, Peru, 27 August, 1976 — F
Peru: 22

League Club	Source	Date Signed	Seasons Played	Apps	Subs	Gls
Coventry C	FCB Melgar (PER)	03/00	99-01	11	18	3

ZVEROTIC Elsad
Born: Berane, Montenegro, 31 October, 1988 — RB/M
Switzerland: Youth//Montenegro: 52/U21-6

League Club	Source	Date Signed	Seasons Played	Apps	Subs	Gls
Fulham	Young Boys Bern (SUI)	09/13	13-14	10	6	0

ZWIJNENBERG Clemens
Born: Enschede, Netherlands, 18 May, 1970 — CD

League Club	Source	Date Signed	Seasons Played	Apps	Subs	Gls
Bristol C (L)	Aalborg BK (DEN)	09/98	98	1	2	0

AWARD WINNERS 2006-2015

MENS' PLAYERS' PLAYER OF THE YEAR

2006 Steven Gerrard
2007 Cristiano Ronaldo
2008 Cristiano Ronaldo
2009 Ryan Giggs
2010 Wayne Rooney
2011 Gareth Bale
2012 Robin Van Persie
2013 Gareth Bale
2014 Luis Suarez
2015 Eden Hazard

PFA WOMEN'S PLAYERS' PLAYER OF THE YEAR

2013 Kim Little (Arsenal Ladies FC)
2014 Lucy Bronze (Liverpool Ladies FC)
2015 Ji So-Yun (Chelsea Ladies FC)

PFA YOUNG PLAYER OF THE YEAR

2006 Wayne Rooney
2007 Cristiano Ronaldo
2008 Cesc Fabregas
2009 Ashley Young
2010 James Milner
2011 Jack Wilshere
2012 Kyle Walker
2013 Gareth Bale
2014 Eden Hazard
2015 Harry Kane

PFA WOMEN'S YOUNG PLAYER OF THE YEAR

2014 Martha Harris (Lincoln Ladies FC)
2015 Leah Williamson (Arsenal Ladies FC)

MERIT AWARD

2006 George Best
2007 Sir Alex Ferguson CBE
2008 Jimmy Armfield OBE
2009 John McDermott
2010 Lucas Radebe
2011 Howard Webb
2012 Graham Alexander
2013 Manchester United Class of 92'
2014 Donald Bell
2015 Steven Gerrard and Frank Lampard

PREMIER LEAGUE TEAM OF THE YEAR 2015

David de Gea
(Goalkeeper, Manchester United)
John Terry
(Centre back, Chelsea)
Gary Cahill
(Centre back, Chelsea)
Ryan Bertrand
(Left back, Southampton)
Branislav Ivanovic
(Right back, Chelsea)
Nemanja Matic
(Midfield, Chelsea)
Philippe Coutinho
(Midfield, Liverpool)
Eden Hazard
(Midfield, Chelsea)
Alexis Sanchez
(Midfield, Arsenal)
Diego Costa
(Forward, Chelsea)
Harry Kane
(Forward, Tottenham)

PROFESSIONAL FOOTBALLERS' ASSOCIATION

Organised professional football began in 1888 with the formation of the Football League. Early attempts were made to form a Players' Union but it was not until 2nd December, 1907, that the first meeting of the current Association took place at the Imperial Hotel, Manchester. It was chaired by the famous Welsh international, Billy Meredith of Manchester United. From that early beginning of players joining together to improve their working conditions, the Professional Footballers' Association (PFA) grew to become the highly respected professional body it is today, and is now the world's longest established professional sportspersons' union.

The aims of the PFA are to protect and improve the conditions, rights and status of all current and former members through negotiation and collective bargaining agreements. The experience and expertise the PFA has gained since its formation ensures that it is able to provide the best advice, representation and assistance in all areas of players' careers and their lives beyond.

This involves many different aspects including enforcement of contracts, advising players in contract negotiations, representing players at disciplinary hearings with the Premier League, the Football League or The Football Association, assisting members in dispute with their clubs over fines or other disciplinary problems, providing insurance against death-in-service and premature retirement through injury and acting as Trustees of the Professional Footballers' Pension Scheme. Above all, there are collective bargaining agreements in place with The FA, the Premier League and the Football League under which no changes can be made to the rules and regulations affecting players without the agreement of the PFA.

Throughout its history the PFA has been successful meeting the challenges it has faced due to the strength of support from its members. Milestone disputes include the removal of the maximum wage in 1961 and the court ruling that football's retain and transfer system was illegal in 1963. In the 1970s, a commission on industrial relations eventually brought in all the present-day procedures that footballers enjoy today. The most important decision was the establishment in 1978 of the rights of players to change clubs at the end of their contracts. Since the Bosman judgement in the European Court in December 1995, our system has been refined so that all players are free at the end of their contracts to join another club. However, domestically, if an out-of-contract player is under 24 years of age a compensation fee will still be payable. This is in order to encourage clubs to develop youth systems.

In more recent times, the role of the PFA has been fully appreciated by its members who supported it in disputes with the Premier League, the Football League and The Football Association with regard to the PFA's negotiated entitlement to a percentage of television revenue in return for members' co-operation with televised interviews before and after matches. In particular, in 2001, members were balloted with regard to strike action with a union record return of 92%, 99% of whom supported the union taking industrial action if necessary. This overwhelming show of support and strength for the Association enabled a satisfactory agreement to be reached and strike action was averted.

The union is involved in all aspects of the game which affect its members but has also maintained a core focus of caring for the interests of the game as a whole. Here is a brief overview of the union's remit:

PFA Coaching: The role of the PFA Coaching department is to prepare its members for a secondary career within the professional game. In fact, over 70% of PFA members express a desire to stay within football when their playing days are over and the Coaching department therefore has a big role to play in their development as prospective coaches. It delivers and offers support with FA/UEFA qualifications at club sites and regional venues across the country, including delivery of the Level 2 award, UEFA B License, FA Youth Modules 1, 2 and 3, regionalised 'Safeguarding Children' and 'Emergency Aid' workshops, tailored UEFA A Licence assistance and support for members on the UEFA Pro Licence. The PFA's Coach Educators are former players who understand the needs of the professional game and the courses are exclusive to PFA members.

PFA Education: The main aim of the department is to encourage as many current and former PFA members as possible to undertake suitable academic/vocational qualifications to develop their career prospects, both within and outside the game. PFA Education supports all members in terms of offering information and advice while the PFA Charity provides grants for educational and vocational training.

PFA Community: The PFA is committed to raising the profile and awareness of the extensive work and participation of players in support of Community and Charitable activities. PFA Community involvement extends across many areas such as: health, education, social inclusion and Equalities, underlining the union's commitment to making a positive difference in society. As a department, there is a proactive approach to improve standards of support with players, and an encouragement for greater support from football clubs to adapt their philosophy toward corporate social responsibility.

PFA Equalities: Equality and Diversity is at the centre of all our work as the players union. Our dedicated Equalities team work with the various PFA departments, current and former players, clubs and the football community to promote inclusion and work towards equality across the game. The department is responsible for providing Equality and Diversity training programmes to first team players to ensure everyone is aware of the procedures to tackle discriminatory language, attitudes and conduct on or off the field of play. We are working to redress the under-representation of Black and Minority Ethnic (BAME) groups across the game and challenging the comparatively low numbers of BAME coaches and managers. Since 2003, the PFA have been pivotal in promoting the Rooney Rule to ensure transparency and equality of opportunity for all our members interested in a career in coaching and/or management. We are delighted with the progress of the women's game and have worked to ensure that contractual negotiations and advice is available for our female members who have been part of the union since 2000, when Fulham Ladies became the first professional women's team.

Equalities is an on-going, ever-evolving issue and we remain committed and focused in supporting our members regardless of age, race, religion or belief, gender, sexuality or disability. We also offer support for members experiencing pregnancy and maternity, gender reassignment and marriage/civil partnership.

PFA Wellbeing: The union has been addressing issues of emotional well-being and addiction for over 14 years, and now has a 24/7/365 counselling telephone helpline service available to members. In addition to the helpline, players past and present can access a national network of 62 fully-trained counsellors, all of whom understand the emotional roller-coaster that involvement in professional sport can entail. The PFA continues to offer support and funding to the Sporting Chance Clinic, allowing PFA members to receive residential treatment there. The combination of these services offers current and former PFA members a dedicated team of people and a safe and confidential environment to receive support and counselling.

PFA Accident Fund: The PFA's Accident Fund provides monies to ensure that all Premier League and Football League contracted players are covered for up to £25,000 each under the PFA's Accident and Sickness Insurance Scheme in the event that they suffer a specific injury or illness which results in their permanent total disability to play professional football. In addition, the fund provides financial assistance to current and former members towards private medical expenses and access to the Residential Rehabilitation scheme at St George's Park.

Player Management: The PFA communicates with football clubs on a daily basis to protect and serve the interests of all professional players and the Player Management department is an extension of that premise. The department provides hands-on representation for players at every stage of their careers as well as offering ethical 'best advice' at all times. It is important that a player seeks advice and representation in contractual negotiations with a club. The quality of that advice and representation is crucial. The sole aim of all our representatives will always be the best interests of the player. The combination of having experienced first-hand the demands of being a professional footballer as well as having strong business acumen means the representatives can relate to players, using their commercial experience to benefit the client.

PFA Commercial: The commercial arm of the PFA generates revenue opportunities for members and has developed close relationships with a number of companies who have become official PFA Business Partners. The department is responsible for providing members playing in the Football League with over half a million pounds worth of boot vouchers each season. PFA Commercial operates 'Legends Tours' which showcase former members in games and tournaments across the globe. The Football Live Service, run in partnership with Opta and the Press Association, provides employment for over 125 former members through radio, television and digital broadcasts. The agreement covers approximately 3,800 live matches each season. That's 5,700 hours of football before time added on!

FIFPro: The PFA is a leading member of FIFPro, the International Players' Association, which was instrumental in the changes to the international transfer system following the Bosman ruling. Senior PFA staff play key roles in FIFPro negotiations with FIFA and the European Commission.